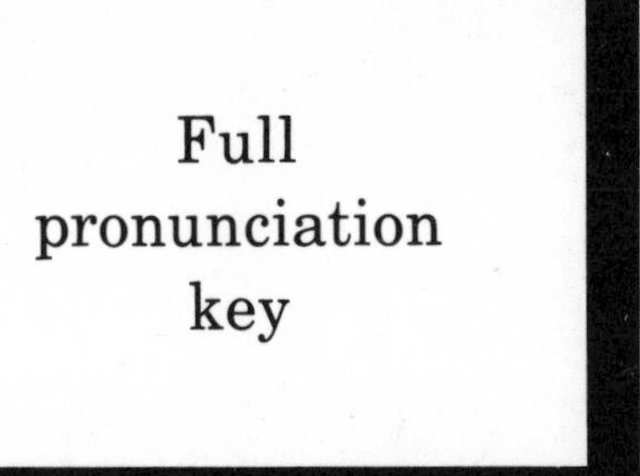

Full pronunciation key

The pronunciation of each word is shown just after the word, in this way: **ab bre vi ate** (ə brē′vē āt). The letters and signs used are pronounced as in the words below. The mark ′ is placed after a syllable with primary or heavy accent, as in the example above. The mark ′ after a syllable shows a secondary or lighter accent, as in **ab bre vi a tion** (ə brē′vē ā′shən).

Some words, taken from foreign languages, are spoken with sounds that do not otherwise occur in English. Symbols for these sounds are given in the key as "foreign sounds."

a	hat, cap
ā	age, face
ä	father, far
b	bad, rob
ch	child, much
d	did, red
e	let, best
ē	equal, be
ėr	term, learn
f	fat, if
g	go, bag
h	he, how
i	it, pin
ī	ice, five
j	jam, enjoy
k	kind, seek
l	land, coal
m	me, am
n	no, in
ng	long, bring
o	hot, rock
ō	open, go
ô	order, all
oi	oil, voice
ou	house, out
p	paper, cup
r	run, try
s	say, yes
sh	she, rush
t	tell, it
th	thin, both
ᴛʜ	then, smooth
u	cup, butter
u̇	full, put
ü	rule, move
v	very, save
w	will, woman
y	young, yet
z	zero, breeze
zh	measure, seizure
ə	represents: a in about, e in taken, i in pencil, o in lemon, u in circus

foreign sounds

ʏ as in French *du.* Pronounce (ē) with the lips rounded as for (ü).

à as in French *ami.* Pronounce (ä) with the lips spread and held tense.

œ as in French *peu.* Pronounce (ā) with the lips rounded as for (ō).

ɴ as in French *bon.* The ɴ is not pronounced, but shows that the vowel before it is nasal.

ʜ as in German *ach.* Pronounce (k) without closing the breath passage.

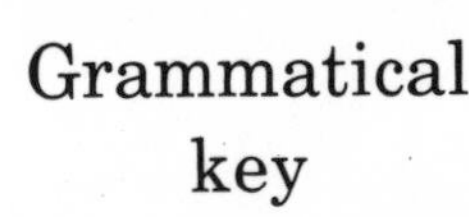

Grammatical key

adj.	adjective	*prep.*	preposition
adv.	adverb	*pron.*	pronoun
conj.	conjunction	*v.*	verb
interj.	interjection	*v.i.*	intransitive verb
n.	noun	*v.t.*	transitive verb
sing.	singular	*pl.*	plural

A B C D E F G H I J K L M N O P Q R S T U V W X Y Z

Thorndike Barnhart advanced dictionary

Thorndike Barnhart advanced dictionary

SECOND EDITION

by E.L. THORNDIKE / CLARENCE L. BARNHART

DOUBLEDAY & COMPANY, INC.
GARDEN CITY, NEW YORK

ISBN: 0-385 07543-X

Copyright © 1974 Scott, Foresman and Company, Glenview, Illinois.
This dictionary is a revision of the THORNDIKE-BARNHART ADVANCED DICTIONARY
Copyright © 1973 Scott, Foresman and Company.
This dictionary is a major revision of the THORNDIKE-BARNHART HIGH SCHOOL DICTIONARY
Copyright © 1968, 1965, 1962, 1957, 1952, 1941 Scott, Foresman and Company.
Philippines Copyright 1974, 1973 Scott, Foresman and Company.
All Rights Reserved.
Printed in the United States of America.

CONTENTS

Cover symbols for Thorndike Barnhart Dictionaries

for the ADVANCED DICTIONARY
is the letter **A** from
the Hebrew alphabet.

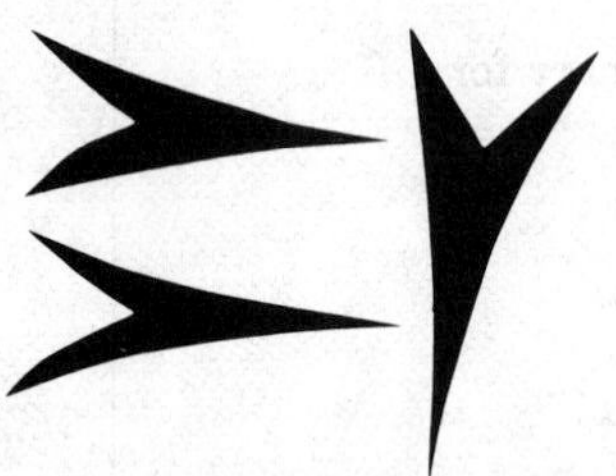

for the BEGINNING DICTIONARY
is the letter **B** from the Persian cuneiform
alphabet used between the
sixth and fourth centuries B.C.

for the INTERMEDIATE DICTIONARY
is the letter **I** from an alphabet
designed by Albrecht Dürer in 1525.

USING THIS DICTIONARY

A dictionary is a book of words. In it you will find a lot of helpful information about a great many words, provided you know how to find it and how to interpret what you find. Dictionaries do not have enough space available to explain everything at each entry. This section of 23 pages, "Using This Dictionary," explains some shortcuts this dictionary takes. Reading these explanations before you start using this book will help alert you to how different kinds of information will be listed.

Here is an entry from page 187:

> **clar i on** (klar′ē ən), *adj.* clear and shrill: *a clarion sound or call.* —*n.* 1 a trumpet with clear, shrill tones. 2 sound made by this trumpet. 3 a clear, shrill sound like it. [< Medieval Latin *clarionem* < Latin *clarus* clear]

For example, someone who knows how to read and interpret dictionary entries could restate what is given there in a much more understandable way:

> **clarion** is a word spelled *c-l-a-r-i-o-n.* When writing *clarion* at the end of a crowded line it may be divided either *clar-ion* or *clari-on.*
>
> *Clarion* is pronounced in three syllables. Its syllable breaks in pronunciation are the same as those in writing. The first syllable receives an accent. Four of the letters used in spelling *clarion* — *l, a, r,* and *n* — are pronounced in the most usual way. The *c* is pronounced like the *c* in *cat*—with a *k-* sound rather than an *s-* sound. The *i* is pronounced like the *e* in *equal.* The *o* is pronounced lightly and indistinctly, so that it sounds like the *o* in *lemon.*
>
> When *clarion* is an adjective, it means "clear and shrill." An illustration of its use is in the phrase *a clarion sound.*
>
> *Clarion* can also be used as a noun meaning "a trumpet with clear, shrill tones," "sound made by this trumpet," or "a clear, shrill sound like it."
>
> English borrowed *clarion* from a Medieval Latin word, *clarionem,* which means "trumpet." That was derived from a Latin word, *clarus,* which means "clear."

Different dictionaries present information in different ways. Perhaps you used a different dictionary in the lower grades. It probably was smaller and contained less information than this one does, but gave it in an easier form to understand. Larger dictionaries usually give even more information in an even more compact form. The more concentrated the information in a dictionary is, the more careful you need to be. Try to use the same dictionary frequently. Then you can become acquainted with its ways and understand its entries more readily.

There is no one *right* way for a dictionary to report any fact about language. Pronunciations, particularly, differ from dictionary to dictionary. Some early dictionaries showed how vowels were pronounced by putting numbers above them. This dictionary respells every word for pronunciation. (Some dictionaries don't.) It puts special marks above some vowels in the pronunciations to indicate special sounds. Some dictionaries which appear to treat pronunciations just as this one does use different pronunciation symbols or have the same symbols mean different things. Be sure when you use a dictionary that you understand how the entry was intended to be understood.

If you study the following pages carefully, using this dictionary effectively will become easier for you. After each section, browse in the dictionary. Look at some unfamiliar words to see how well you can interpret what you have just read. Then you will find it easier later on to understand an entry without referring to the instructions.

Refer to these lessons whenever you need help. You won't remember all of the information here. The important thing is to remember where to find it. The lessons are divided into sections to help you quickly locate the one you need:

How to Find Words
How to Use and Understand the Pronunciations
How to Find and Understand Meanings
How to Use This Dictionary for Spelling
How to Use This Dictionary for Writing

How to Find Words

One alphabetical list

To find a word in this dictionary, you need only to know the order of the letters of the alphabet. All main entries—words in the common vocabulary, technical terms, proper names, abbreviations—are in one alphabetical list.

Look at page 1. You will find *a* and *aardvark, abandon* and *abase.* You will also find *Aachen,* a geographical name; *Aaron,* the name of a person in the Bible; the symbol *A;* and the abbreviations *A.A.* and *A.B.* In this dictionary, you have only one place to look for a word.

Guide words

Printed at the top of the outside column of every page in the dictionary is a guide word to help you narrow your search for a word to the right page. On pages 648 and 649, for example, the guide words are *metabolite* and *metropolis.* All the main entries that fall alphabetically between these two words can be found on those pages.

EXERCISES:

1. Write the following words on a sheet of paper: *metabolic, metric system, mettle, metronome, metallic, Mexico,* and *meteor.* Put a check mark after the ones you would find on pages 648 and 649, and then turn to these pages and check yourself. Did you put a check mark after any words that are not on pages 648 and 649?
2. By using the guide words, see how long it takes you to find *pt., consumerism, Thirty Years' War, Es, graduate, -ry, Martinez.*

Homographs

Sometimes there are two or more words which have the same spelling but different origins and meanings. These words are called homographs:

> **boon**[1] (bün), *n.* 1 great benefit; blessing: *Those warm boots were a boon to me in the cold weather.* 2 ARCHAIC. something asked for or granted as a favor. [< Scandinavian (Old Icelandic) *bōn* petition]
> **boon**[2] (bün), *adj.* 1 full of cheer; jolly; merry: *a boon companion.* 2 kindly; pleasant. [< Old French *bon* good < Latin *bonus*]

In this dictionary, each homograph is entered separately. A small raised number called a *superscript* follows each entry which is a homograph. It will remind you to look at the other entry or entries spelled the same way if you do not find the information you need under the first one.

Homographs usually are pronounced alike, but sometimes they are pronounced differently:

> **slough**[1] (slou *for 1 and 3;* slü *for 2*), *n.* . . .
> **slough**[2] (sluf), *n.* . . .

EXERCISES:

1. How many different words are spelled *bass, bay, hatch, mow, prop, sound?*
2. Find the entries for *bark.* Which entry (*bark*[1], *bark*[2], or *bark*[3]) is referred to in the following sentences?
   The bark sailed out to sea.
   He stripped off the bark of the tree.
   Many dogs bark at strangers.

When looking up cross-references, be sure to refer to the right homograph. For example:

> **scarves** (skärvz), *n.* a pl. of **scarf**[1].

tells you to look at

> **scarf**[1] (skärf), *n.* . . . 1 a long, broad strip of silk, lace, etc., worn about the neck . . . .

not

> **scarf**[2] (skärf), *n.* . . . 1 joint in which the ends of beams are cut so that they lap over and join firmly . . . .

EXERCISE:

Look at the entry *rung*[1]. Is *rung* a past tense and past participle for all entries spelled *ring?*

Foreign words and phrases

Some foreign words and phrases are used often enough for them to appear in a dictionary of English. These entries are in boldface italic type:

> ***in me mo ri am*** (in mə môr′ē əm; in mə mōr′ē əm), LATIN. in memory (of); to the memory (of).

Inflected forms

At one time or another, you have undoubtedly had your speaking or writing corrected by your parents or teachers, though there was no question about the meaning of the words you were using. Very often, such slips in speech or writing have to do with inflected forms of words. This dictionary provides a great deal of help with inflected forms, both those that are irregular and those that are difficult to spell or pronounce.

How to find inflected forms. The first three kinds of information you will find in a dictionary entry are the entry word, the pronunciation, and the part-of-speech label. Inflected forms are given immediately after the part of speech:

> **come** (kum), *v.i.,* **came, come, com ing** . . . .
> **ox** (oks), *n., pl.* **ox en** . . . .
> **safe** (sāf), *adj.,* **saf er, saf est** . . . .
> **well**[1] (wel), *adv.,* **bet ter, best** . . . .

Inflected forms of verbs. In the sentences below think where you would look for the meaning of the words in italics:

The horse *headed* for the barn.
The stock *advanced* three points.
The hot coffee was *steaming.*
The canoe glided past a rock *jutting* into the stream.
The wind *blew* the curtains.

Headed is a form of the verb *head* which shows that the action took place in past time. To find the meaning of *headed* you have to look under *head.* Such a verb formed by adding *-ed* to the root word to show past time is called a past tense.

In the sentence "The hot coffee was *steaming,*" *steaming* is a verb form (a present participle) that describes the coffee. *Steaming* is formed by adding *-ing* to the root word *steam.* Such verb forms as *headed* and *steaming* are called inflected forms of the verb. If these inflected forms are made by adding *-ed* and *-ing* to the verb without any change in the verb or the ending, the inflected forms are not given in the dictionary.

However, if the verb changes in any way when it is put into the past tense, past participle, or present participle, this dictionary shows the different forms. In the sentences above, *advanced* and *jutting* are inflected forms given after the parts of speech of *advance* and *jut* because they may cause you difficulty in spelling. The *-e* is dropped from the root word *advance* when *-ed* and *-ing* are added. In *jutting* the final consonant *-t* is doubled when the suffixes *-ed* and *-ing* are added.

> **ad vance** (ad vans′), *v.,* **-vanced, -vanc ing** . . . .
> **jut** (jut), *v.,* **jut ted, jut ting** . . . .

Blow is an irregular verb. Its past tense *blew* is not formed by adding *-ed* to the root word. Such irregular forms are entered in this book.

> **blow**[2] (blō), *v.,* **blew, blown, blow ing** . . . .

EXERCISE:
To see how your dictionary helps you write past forms of verbs, look up the following:

arise	send	reach
sag	fly	grab
argue	renew	seek

Inflected forms of nouns. One thing that may bother you in writing is the plural forms of some nouns. You may know how to spell *calf,* or *city,* but be uncertain about the plural forms. How can you find out? The answer is very simple. Just find the singular form in your dictionary; then look after the part-of-speech label. If the plural form is different from the regular plural spelling, the dictionary will show you how to spell it. Of course the dictionary will not need to spell the plural for you if it is made just by adding *-s,* as *hound, hounds.* And you probably already know that nouns ending in *ch, sh, s, x,* and *z* form their plurals by adding *-es* (for example, *batch, batches; dish, dishes; glass, glasses; box, boxes; buzz, buzzes*). Your dictionary does not spell out for you the plural forms of these easy words, but it does spell out all irregular plural forms.

EXERCISE:
Write the plural form of the following nouns:

piano	armful
ally	potato
humerus	mongoose
galley	brother-in-law
moose	life

Inflected forms of adjectives and adverbs. Probably you often need to change a word like *rich* into the form *richer* (the comparative) or *richest* (the superlative). Such a change is simple, because you just add *-er* or *-est* to the word. But if the word is changed in another way, the dictionary will show you the right spelling. Suppose you want to say that your dinner was a more hearty meal than your lunch. Should you take *hearty* and add *-er?* Look the word up in the dictionary, and you will find after the part-of-speech label for *hearty* the different forms, *heartier, heartiest.* The first of these answers your question.

EXERCISE:
Write the comparative and superlative forms of the following adjectives and adverbs:

able	flighty
well	fast
good	thin

Forms entered separately. All commonly used irregular inflected forms are also entered separately, as main entries, to help you locate them easily:

> **came** (kām), *v.* pt. of **come.**
> **nu cle i** (nü′klē ī, nyü′klē ī), *n.* a pl. of **nucleus.**
> **ox en** (ok′sən), *n.* pl. of **ox.**
> **slid** (slid), *v.* pt. and pp. of **slide.**
> **taught** (tôt), *v.* pt. and pp. of **teach.**

Variant inflected forms. Sometimes, the plural form of a noun may be spelled in two different ways; or, the inflected forms of verbs may be spelled differently. The dictionary entry for the root word will include both spellings, either of which is acceptable in speech or writing:

> **a moe ba** (ə mē′bə), *n., pl.* **-bas, -bae** (-bē) . . . .
> **ap pen dix** (ə pen′diks), *n., pl.* **-dix es** or **-di ces** . . . .
> **kill deer** (kil′dir′), *n., pl.* **-deers** or **-deer** . . . .
> **na ta to ri um** (nā′tə tôr′ē əm, nā′tə tōr′ē-əm), *n., pl.* **-to ri ums, -to ri a** (-tôr′ē ə, -tōr′ē ə) . . . .
> **ser aph** (ser′əf), *n., pl.* **-aphs** or **-a phim** . . . .
> **crow**[1] (krō), *n., v.,* **crowed** (or **crew** for 1), **crowed, crow ing** . . . .
> **heave** (hēv), *v.,* **heaved** or **hove, heav ing** . . . .

10 > **kid nap** (kid′nap), *v.t.,* **-naped, -nap ing** or **-napped, -nap ping** . . . .

EXERCISE:
Write the plural forms of the following nouns:
hippopotamus swordfish

Derivatives

Derivatives are words formed by adding prefixes or suffixes to other words, either to the complete word or to the root. For example, the derivative verb *remake* is formed by adding the prefix *re-,* meaning "again," to the verb *make.* The derivative adjective *achievable* is formed by adding the suffix *-able,* meaning "able to be ____ed," to the root of the verb *achieve.*

Main entries. When a derivative has difficult or specialized meanings, it is entered in this dictionary as a main entry. For example, *hardness* is an obvious derivative of *hard,* but because it has a specialized meaning, it is entered separately:

> **hard ness** (härd′nis), *n.* 1 condition of being hard. 2 the comparative capacity of one mineral to scratch or be scratched by another mineral, as measured on Mohs' scale.

Also entered separately are derivatives that are in any way hard to pronounce, derivatives that fall alphabetically far away from the root word, and derivatives formed with all but the most common suffixes.

Run-on entries. Many derivatives present no problems of meaning or pronunciation, and would fall alphabetically very close to their root words if they were entered separately.

A derivative of this kind, when formed with a suffix, is given in small boldface type at the end of the entry for the root word. You will find several examples of run-on entries on page 442 (for example, *graphically, grappler, graspable, grassless, grassiness, gratelike, gratifyingly*).

Lists of derivatives. Words formed by adding the prefixes *non-, over-, re-, ultra-,* or *un-* are listed under the prefix without a definition if they can be understood by combining the meaning of the prefix with that of the word to which it is added. *Nonabsorbent,* for example, can be found under *non-.* The meaning of the word is merely "not absorbent." If you want any further information, look up *absorbent,* and add "not" to the beginning of each of its definitions.

If a word beginning with *non-, over-, re-, ultra-,* or *un-* is not in the list of words under that prefix, look for it in the proper place in the main entry list. *Noncombatant* and *nonconductor,* for example, have specialized meanings and will therefore be found in the main alphabetical list.

EXERCISE:
Look up the following derivative words to see the different ways in which your dictionary presents information about them:
goodness (main entry)
badness (run-on to *bad)*
unappetizing (listed in *un-* list)
unreasonable (main entry)

Idioms

Often words occur in phrases or expressions that have a special meaning which cannot be fully understood from the ordinary meanings of the words that form them. Such special phrases are called idioms, and there are many of them in our language. Examples are *parcel out, make reference to, go to bat for, let slide,* and *acquit oneself.* You can find an idiom by looking under its most important word. For example, the idioms *chip off the old block, chip on one's shoulder,* and *when the chips are down* are placed in the entry *chip.* Since *chip* is used as a noun in these idioms, they are placed with the other noun definitions. *Chip* in the idiom *chip in* is used as a verb, and so it is placed with the verb definitions.

chip (chip), *n., v.,* **chipped, chip ping.** —*n.* 1 a small, thin piece cut or broken off. 2 place where a small, thin piece has been cut or broken off. . . . **7 chip off the old block,** boy who is much like his father. 8 **chip on one's shoulder,** INFORMAL. readiness to quarrel or fight. 9 **when the chips are down,** when the moment of decision or definite action arrives; in a crisis. —*v.i.* cut or break off in small, thin pieces . . . . —*v.t.* 1 separate (small pieces) by cutting or breaking . . . . 2 shape by cutting . . . . 3 **chip in,** INFORMAL. **a** join with others in giving (money or help). **b** put in (a remark) when others are talking . . . .

EXERCISES:

1. Under what entry will you find the following idioms?

foot the bill	by hook or by crook
over and above	world without end
bell the cat	pull in one's horns
break even	horse of a different color

2. Find the idiom *near at hand.* Notice that it has two meanings. Which of these fits in the following sentence? *Mother stayed near at hand while I was sick.* Is another meaning used in this sentence? *Examination time is near at hand.* Test yourself to see whether you chose the right meaning for each of these sentences by substituting the meaning itself for the idiom in each one. Do they make sense with the meanings you have chosen?

How to Use and Understand the Pronunciations

The letters of the alphabet are directions to produce sounds: the letters used in *bet* direct us to make different sounds from those called for by the letters in *sad.*

The directions, however, may be misleading. In English we have only 26 letters to represent around 40 sounds. The letters are used in over 200 spelling combinations directing us to use these sounds.

Since a word's spelling is not always a sure guide to its pronunciation, the dictionary provides respellings to direct you to produce the proper sounds. The respelling, or pronunciation, is given in parentheses right after the main entry:

an them (an′thəm)
buy (bī)
ban dan na or **ban dan a** (ban dan′ə)

The pronunciation key

Each symbol used in the respellings directs you to say one particular sound. The 41 symbols used in this dictionary to represent the speech sounds of English are given in the full pronunciation key which appears in both the front and the back of the book. The words following each symbol in the key contain the sound represented by that symbol.

More than half of the symbols for English sounds are letters of the alphabet, printed in regular type, without diacritical marks of any kind.

The five unmarked vowel letters (a, e, i, o, u) are used to represent the short vowel sounds.

The unmarked consonant letters (all except the letters *c, q,* and *x*) are used to represent the single consonant sounds.

Six of the two-letter symbols (oi, ou, ch, ng, sh, th) are used to represent the sounds with which they are commonly associated:

moist	(moist)	**sing**	(sing)
pout	(pout)	**hush**	(hush)
chin	(chin)	**bath**	(bath)

Another two-letter symbol (ėr) includes a diacritical mark. It combines a vowel sound and a consonant sound, and is spelled many different ways, but its spelling almost always includes an *r:*

germ (jėrm) **myrrh** (mėr)
word (wėrd) **girl** (gėrl)

There are nine special symbols for vowel sounds (ā, ē, ī, ō, ä, ü, u̇, ô, ə). There are just two special symbols for consonant sounds (ᴛʜ, zh).

EXERCISE:

1. Turn to the full pronunciation key at either the front or back of your dictionary. Look at each of the symbols for English sounds and pronounce the key words following them.
2. Write on a sheet of paper the pronunciations given below. Pronounce each word by using the pronunciation key, and write the spelling of the word before the pronunciation.

(bet)	(ᴛʜōz)	(ᴛʜīn)
(nāl)	(thingk)	(fül)
(yung)	(sēt)	(noiz)
(lach)	(chär)	(chôr)
(bėrd)	(hou)	(lu̇k)

Now check your work by looking each word up in your dictionary.

3. Open your dictionary to any page. Look at the top of the third column of the right-hand page. There you will see a short pronunciation key. It contains key words for all the vowel sounds and all the two-letter symbols. Pronounce each key word.

   On a sheet of paper, make a list of all the symbols in the short pronunciation key followed by their key words. After each key word, write another word which has in it the same sound.

   Check your work by looking up each word you have written.

4. Turn again to the full pronunciation key. Look at the column headed "foreign sounds." The five symbols given here represent sounds which appear in the respellings of foreign words. Read the directions for pronouncing these sounds, and pronounce the key words which are given with each symbol.

Syllables and accent

Sounds produced together as a unit make up a syllable. Many words in English, such as *I, send,* and *could,* have only one syllable. Many others, such as *chemist* and *somebody,* have more than one syllable. A space is used in the respellings to show how words are divided into syllables.

When a word has two or more syllables, we usually pronounce one syllable more strongly, or with more stress, than we do the others. In the pronunciations, syllables which receive the strongest stress are followed by a primary accent (**ʹ**):

chem ist (kemʹist)
heart i ness (härʹtē nis)

Some words also have one or more syllables which are pronounced with medium stress. In the pronunciations, these syllables are followed by a secondary accent (ˊ):

nee dle work (nēʹdl wėrkˊ)
cur i os i ty (kyu̇rˊē osʹə tē)
book case (bu̇kʹkāsˊ)

EXERCISE:

Find the following words in your dictionary and look at the pronunciations. Pronounce each word and tell which syllables are accented. Which have the strongest, or primary, accent? Which have the secondary accent?

computerize	handwriting
enthusiastic	streamline

On page 10 you learned that some derived words, which are formed by adding a suffix to a root word, are listed at the end of the entry for the root word. These are called run-on entries. The pronunciation of a run-on entry is the pronunciation of the root word plus that of the suffix. Sometimes, however, the syllables in a run-on entry will be accented differently than they are in the root word. All run-on entries in this dictionary are divided into syllables. Primary and secondary accents are shown on the syllables which are stressed.

EXERCISE:

Look up each of the words in the list below and pronounce them. How are the syllables accented? Now look at the end of each entry and find the run-on entries. Pronounce them. How are the syllables in the run-on entries accented? Are they accented in the same way as those in the root word? If not, how have the accents changed?

astronautic	liberalize
decentralize	materialize
figurative	perambulate

The schwa. One symbol in our key occurs only in unaccented syllables. This symbol (ə), called *schwa,* is used to represent a soft, neutral, unaccented vowel sound. It is the sound of *a* in *about, e* in *taken, i* in *pencil, o* in *lemon,* and *u* in *circus.* It is also the sound spelled by some combinations of these vowels. It represents the most common sound in English.

EXERCISE:

Copy the words below on a sheet of paper. Find them in your dictionary and look at their pronunciations. Now pronounce each word. Circle the vowels or combinations of vowels in each word which have the sound represented by (ə).

among	effect
bargain	interpretation
daffodil	nebula
delicious	necessity
dungeon	stencil

The symbol (ėr). One pronunciation symbol, (ėr), is used only in accented syllables. Note its use in the pronunciations of the words below:

per fect (*adj., n.* pėr′fikt; *v.* pər fekt′)
bur nish (bėr′nish)
black bird (blak′bėrd′)

In the first example, *perfect,* you can see that when the accent changes from the first to the second syllable, the respelling of *-er* changes from (ėr) to (ər).

The syllabic consonants (l) and (n). In some unaccented syllables, we do not usually pronounce a vowel sound at all. Instead, (l) or (n) will serve as the central part of the syllable. When (l) or (n) occurs in a syllable without a vowel, it is called a syllabic consonant.

EXERCISE:

Pronounce the words below. Tell in which syllables we do not pronounce a vowel sound. What is the syllabic consonant in each of these syllables?

bot tle (bot′l)	**jour nal ist** (jėr′nl ist)
car ton (kärt′n)	**maid en** (mād′n)
cur dle (kėr′dl)	**or di nance** (ôrd′n əns)
dan de li on (dan′dl ī′ən)	**sea son** (sē′zn)
fas ci nate (fas′n āt)	**ven ti late** (ven′tl āt)

Interpreting dictionary pronunciations

No two speakers pronounce a sound in exactly the same way, although the human ear is not sensitive enough to catch the subtler distinctions in sound. From a scientific point of view, the same speaker never produces a word in exactly the same way twice. A dictionary cannot give all the possible varying pronunciations used by the same speaker.

Furthermore, a dictionary must present its material one word at a time, but we do not speak one word at a time. Even such a simple question as "How do you pronounce *the?*" can never have a single answer. One's pronunciation of this word and of other words depends on neighboring sounds, on accent, and on the speed at which one speaks.

The pronunciations in this dictionary are, so far as is practicable and possible when words must be treated in isolation, those of educated informal speech.

Variant pronunciations. Pronunciation is constantly changing. New pronunciations coming into the language often force older ones out. But the process generally takes a long time, during which two or more pronunciations may be in common use.

For example, the pronunciation (ad vėr′tiz-mənt) for *advertisement* has been the common British one since Shakespeare's time. In America the pronunciation (ad′vər tīz′mənt) was for many years more common, but the variants (ad vėr′tiz mənt) and (ad vėr′tis mənt) may now be equally common.

This dictionary gives the most widely established American pronunciation and the commonest acceptable variants for each word. In general, the more common pronunciations are given first, although it is sometimes impossible to determine which pronunciations are used more than others, and usage may sometimes be evenly divided.

It should not be assumed that the first pronunciation given is preferable to the second or third. For example, there are two pronunciations given for *rodeo* (rō′dē ō, rō dā′ō); the fact that the pronunciation (rō′dē ō) is given first simply means that, in the opinion of many scholars, (rō′dē ō) is more commonly used in English.

EXERCISE:

Find the entries given below in your dictionary. Notice that two pronunciations are given for each one. Which way do you pronounce each word? Find out if anyone in your class pronounces any of them the other way.

amateur	Eustachian tube
catchup	juvenile

Regional variations in pronunciation. Although speakers in different parts of the United States sound more alike than speakers in any other area of comparable size and population in the world, there are, nevertheless, certain rather noticeable differences in the speech of different parts of the country. Educated people do not pronounce English in exactly the same way in Chicago and New York, Atlanta and Boston, Dallas and Seattle.

A dictionary of this size cannot record these regional differences of pronunciation in minute detail, but it should include the more important regional pronunciations. The pronunciation system in this book has been designed to achieve this end.

The symbols and key words taken together will sometimes make it unnecessary to enter certain regional differences separately. For example, speakers from New England and from the north central states will not pronounce the key word *father* with the same vowel. But if each speaker pronounces every word respelled with (ä) with the same vowel he uses in the key word, he will be using an acceptable pronunciation which fits the pattern of his natural speech.

In the more important cases where this advice is not sufficient, as many pronunciations are included as are necessary to record the regional differences.

Foreign pronunciations. Some entries in this dictionary give both an English and a foreign pronunciation. The foreign pronunciation shows that a word or phrase often receives the pronunciation it had in the language where it originated:

dan seur (dan sėr′; *French* däɴ sœr′)

Words and phrases still regarded as foreign—those given in boldface italic type—have been given foreign pronunciations:

bon ap pé tit (bôɴ nȧp pā tē′). FRENCH. good appetite.

In the pronunciations of entries like the two above, you may find one or more of the symbols for foreign sounds. Refer to the full pronunciation key if you have a question about the sound represented by any of these symbols.

Pronunciations for different parts of speech and different meanings. Some words are pronounced differently as different parts of speech or when they have different meanings. These pronunciations are labeled in accordance with the parts of speech and definition numbers shown in the entry:

af fix (*v.* ə fiks′; *n.* af′iks)
ab stract (*adj.* ab′strakt, ab strakt′; *v.* ab strakt′ *for 1,3-5,* ab′strakt *for 2;* *n.* ab′strakt)

EXERCISE:

The word *record* is used as a different part of speech in each of the following sentences. Copy the sentences on a sheet of paper. Look in your dictionary at the pronunciations for *record.* Write the correct pronunciation after each sentence.

She kept a careful record of what she spent.
The group will soon record another song.
The city had a record snowfall this year.

Pronunciations of inflected forms. Any inflected form in this dictionary that is entered separately is, of course, followed by a pronunciation. Pronunciations are given, too, for those inflected forms which are difficult to pronounce, but which are not entered separately:

hyp no sis (hip nō′sis), *n.,* *pl.* **-ses** (-sēz′) . . . .
coc cyx (kok′siks), *n.,* *pl.* **coc cy ges** (kok sī′jēz′) . . . .

Notice in the example *hypnosis* that only the last syllable of the plural form is given a pronunciation. This means that the first two syllables are pronounced just as they are in the singular form.

In the example *coccyx,* however, the full pronunciation of the plural form *coccyges* is given to show that it is changed throughout from the pronunciation of the singular form.

Entries not pronounced. If you look up the entry *cellulose acetate,* you will find that no pronunciation is given. Since both *cellulose* and *acetate* are pronounced where they are entered as separate words, the pronunciations are not duplicated at *cellulose acetate.*

How to Find and Understand Meanings

Many times when you meet an unfamiliar word in reading, you will not have to look it up. The words used with it (its context) influence it and make its meaning clear. Suppose you were reading a magazine article and came across the following sentence:

Although his knowledge of pugilism was great, he was kept from actually boxing by his weak heart.

You would probably continue reading even if you had never met the word *pugilism* before. Several things in the sentence—the clause introduced by *although* and the use of the word *actually*—tell you that boxing is being discussed. If you looked up *pugilism* to make sure your understanding was correct, here is what you would find:

pu gi lism (pyü′jə liz′əm), *n.* art or sport of boxing. [< Latin *pugil* boxer]

Checking the dictionary helped reinforce your knowledge of the word's meaning, even though the sentence was already clear to you. It probably also helped to imprint the new word in your memory, so that you will recognize it if you see it again.

Many times the context does not explain an unfamiliar word. Then you need the dictionary to look up the entry and provide the appropriate definition. The meaning given can often serve as a substitute in context for the word you had to look up. Read the sentence below:

Scrooge was a penurious old man.

Can you tell what *penurious* means? Nothing in the context gives a clue, so look up the entry on page 757. Many definitions, including this one, consist of a phrase followed by one or several synonyms. Roughly equivalent parts of the definition are separated by semicolons. In the entry *penurious,* the synonym *stingy* is obviously the best word to substitute in the sentence. It describes Scrooge perfectly.

EXERCISES:

1. Look up the italicized words in the following sentences. Then copy each sentence, substituting the definition for the italicized word.
   Everyone enjoyed her *jocular* remarks.
   His *indolence* annoyed his parents.
   The astronauts' *indomitable* courage impressed everyone.
2. Read the sentence below. Then in your own words, using context clues, write the meaning of the italicized word.
   To decrease pollution, *biodegradable* products more palatable to bacteria and more easily broken down were developed.
   Now look up *biodegradable* to check your understanding. Remember, not all words listed are main entries.

Finding meanings

The meaning is one of the most important parts of a dictionary entry. Whether you're looking up a word because it is brand-new to you or because it is used in a new way, you need to have a clear idea of how meanings are organized and explained.

Meanings are grouped according to part of speech—all transitive verb meanings, all intransitive verb meanings, all noun meanings, etc., are grouped together (see *present*[1] below). Within each group, meanings are arranged according to the frequency of their use. Meanings that are used more often are put first; technical meanings or meanings which have disappeared from current usage are put last.

pres ent[1] (prez′nt), *adj.* 1 being in the place or thing in question; at hand, not absent: *Every member of the class was present. Oxygen is present in the air.* 2 at this time; being or occurring now: *present prices.* See **current** for synonym study. 3 (in grammar) of or expressing the present tense: *The present forms of "ate" and "smiled" are "eat" and "smile."* —*n.* 1 **the present,** the time being; this time; now: *That is enough for the present.* 2 the present tense or a verb form in that tense. 3 **at present,** at the present time; now. 4 **by these presents,** by these words; by this document . . . .

Closely related meanings are usually grouped together. For example, look at the entry *club.* Noun definitions 1 and 2 deal with the heavy stick. Definitions 3 and 4 deal with the group of people. Definition 5 deals with the figure ♣, and definitions 6 and 7 deal with the playing cards on which this figure appears.

Sometimes you have to read a number of definitions before you come to the meaning you are looking for. When a word is used as more than one part of speech and has many meanings, the entry can be very long. In such a case, each part of speech after the first begins a new paragraph, so you can find the meaning you want easily. Look, for example, at the entry *advance.* How many parts of speech do you see there? How many definitions?

EXERCISE:

Each group of sentences below illustrates different meanings of the same word. First, check the entries in your dictionary. Then copy each sentence and write after it the part of speech and definition number used.

1. My uncle works at the watchmaker's *trade.*
   The company does a lot of foreign *trade.*
   If you don't like that game, let's make a *trade.*
2. My sister gave me a chocolate *bar.*
   He was admitted to the *bar* last month.
   I ate lunch at the snack *bar.*
3. The exciting story *fired* his enthusiasm.
   She was sorry when her friend was *fired.*
   The janitor *fired* the furnace.

Special grammatical labels

Some nouns in English appear only in their plural form. Many of these nouns, such as *bitters* and *trousers,* cause no problem, because they are plural in use, too; they are always followed by the plural form of a verb. In this dictionary, the entries for these words have the label "*n.pl.*"

bit ters (bit′ərz), *n.pl.* 1 a liquid . . . . 2 a bitter, dark beer.
trou sers (trou′zərz), *n.pl.* a two-legged outer garment . . . .

Some other nouns, although they are plural in form, are always singular in use. They should cause no problem, either, because they follow the same pattern as nouns which are singular in both form and use—they are labeled "*n.*" and are followed by the singular form of a verb.

e lec tron ics (i lek′tron′iks, ē′lek-tron′iks), *n.* branch of physics . . . .
lin guis tics (ling gwis′tiks), *n.* the science of language . . . .

With some nouns which appear only in the plural form, verb usage is divided. Some people will use the plural form of a verb, while others will use the singular form. The grammatical labels for these words will vary, depending upon which usage is considered to be more common. If more people use the plural form of a verb, *pl.* will appear before *sing.* in the grammatical label. If more use the singular form, *sing.* will appear first.

bel lows (bel′ōz, bel′əs), *n. sing. or pl.* 1 device for producing a strong current . . . . 2 the folding part of certain cameras . . . .
pin cers (pin′sərz), *n. pl. or sing.* 1 tool for gripping . . . .

Still other nouns which are plural in form are followed by a singular verb when they have one meaning and a plural verb when they have another. The entries for these words are labeled as in the following examples:

a cous tics (ə kü′stiks), *n.* 1 *pl. in form and use.* the structural features of a room . . . . 2 *pl. in form, sing. in use.* the science of sound.
sta tis tics (stə tis′tiks), *n.* 1 *pl. in form and use.* numerical facts about people . . . . 2 *pl. in form, sing. in use.* science of collecting, classifying, and using such facts . . . .

Ways in which meanings are given

A basic explanation appears for each meaning of every word. This explanation may be accompanied by an illustrative sentence or phrase or by a picture, chart, or table. The meaning is explained as briefly as possible, usually in a phrase, sometimes by a single word.

dow er (dou′ər), *n.* 1 a widow's share for life of her dead husband's property. 2 dowry. —*v.t.* provide with a dower; endow . . . .

Dower has two noun meanings and a transitive verb meaning. The definition for the second noun meaning is not as full as that for the first meaning. If you want more help with the second meaning, turn to the entry for *dowry.* Notice that the definition for the verb meaning has two parts, separated by a semicolon. *Endow* is another way to say "provide with a dower."

Special constructions. A number of words are followed by particular prepositions (see *adhere*) and some have different meanings when followed by different prepositions (see *answer*). In this dictionary these prepositions are printed in italic type and enclosed in parentheses in the definitions:

ad here (ad hir′), *v.i.,* **-hered, -her ing.** 1 stick fast; remain firmly attached; cling *(to).* See **stick**[2] for synonym study. 2 hold closely or firmly; cleave *(to): In spite of objections the manager adhered to the plan.* 3 be a follower or upholder; give allegiance (*to* a party, leader, belief, etc.) . . . .
an swer (an′sər) . . . . —*v.i.* . . . 4 be responsible *(for): The bus driver must answer for the safety of the children in his bus.* 5 be similar *(to);* correspond: *This dog answers to the description of the one we lost . . . .*

EXERCISES:

1. Look up the entry *accessible.* Which definition tells you something about prepositional use? Now write your own sentence using this meaning of *accessible.*

2. Read the following sentences and pick out the preposition you think is correct. Then check your answer in the dictionary.
   When a friend asks (for) (about) help, I try to give it.
   Most of her tastes accord (to) (with) mine.
   Although both pears and apples are fruit, they differ (with) (from) each other.

Illustrative sentences and phrases. Many definitions also include a sentence or phrase, printed in italic type, that illustrates the use of the word in the particular sense being defined:

> **ob li gate** . . . . —*v.t.* bind morally or legally; pledge: *A witness in court is obligated to tell the truth . . . .*
> **o bliv i on** . . . *n.* 1 condition of being entirely forgotten: *Many ancient cities have long since passed into oblivion . . . .*

Notice how the illustrative sentences above give you a feeling for the kind of contexts in which these somewhat formal words might be used.

Illustrative sentences and phrases are often helpful in showing prepositional use in context (as in *adhere* and *answer* above), and in distinguishing closely related meanings:

> **ob scure** (əb skyůr′), *adj.*, **-scur er, -scur est,** *v.*, **-scured, -scur ing.** —*adj.* 1 not clearly expressed; hard to understand: *an obscure passage in a book . . . .* 2 not expressing meaning clearly: *an obscure style of writing . . . .* 5 not distinct; not clear: *an obscure form, obscure sounds, an obscure view.* 6 dark; dim: *an obscure corner.* 7 indefinite: *an obscure brown, an obscure vowel . . . .*

Illustrations, charts, and tables. Many pictures, diagrams, maps, charts, and tables are included in this dictionary. Each one makes a specific definition of a word more meaningful to you.

A picture, such as the one for *iguana,* can help you identify something:

iguana
about 5 ft. long

Read the entry *esophagus:*

> **e soph a gus** (ē sof′ə gəs), *n., pl.* **-gi** (-jī). passage for food from the pharynx to the stomach; gullet. See **alimentary canal** for diagram . . . .

At the end of the definition, you are referred to a diagram at *alimentary canal:*

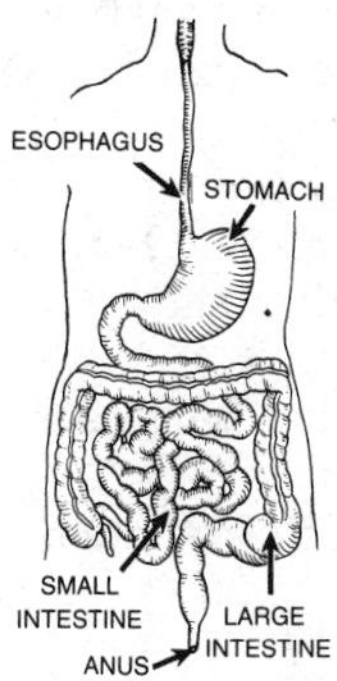

alimentary canal of a person—a 30 ft. tube beginning at the mouth, where food enters, and ending at the anus, where undigested solids leave the body.

You learn from the diagram where the esophagus is, and that it is part of the alimentary canal. You learn even more from the caption.

Maps, labeled with the names of countries, rivers, oceans, other bodies of water, and sometimes cities, help you locate places with which you may not be familiar.

Historical maps in this dictionary are often shaded and superimposed on maps showing present-day boundaries. These maps locate areas which may only be names in a history book to you. Often, a caption gives additional information. Turn to the entry *Provence.* After reading the definition, look carefully at the map and read its caption. You should now be able to answer the following questions:

1. On what body of water is Provence located?
2. Was Provence an independent country in 50 B.C.?
3. What important French city is located there?

EXERCISES:

1. Where did the Oregon Trail start and through which states did it pass? What other pioneer trail is shown on the same map?
2. What present-day countries were included in Austria-Hungary? Did Austria-Hungary have a seacoast?

Each of the seven charts and tables included in this dictionary has to do with a subject in which you may have a special interest.

Maybe you are interested in geology, for example, and look up the entry *Jurassic,* a geological period. Perhaps you want to know more about this period and about the other periods, eras, and epochs of geological time. Turn to page 424 for the chart referred to in the entry *Jurassic.* Here you will find a great deal of the information you want.

Helpful and interesting information is included in each of the charts and tables listed below. Refer to the Contents for page numbers:

Regions of the Atmosphere
Classification of Animals and Plants
Periodic Table of the Elements
Geological Time
Indo-European and Other Language Families
Measures and Weights
Types of Electromagnetic Radiation

EXERCISE:

Use the appropriate chart or table to answer each of the following questions. Copy the number of the question. Then write down the answer and the name of the chart or table in which you found it.

1. How many years ago did dinosaurs first appear?
2. Which element has the highest atomic number?
3. What are gamma rays used for?
4. What category in the vegetable kingdom is equivalent to a phylum?
5. How many people speak North American Indian languages?
6. How far from the earth's surface does the troposphere reach?
7. How many kilometers are in a mile?

Restrictive labels and phrases

Many English words are shared by all users of the language, but not all words or meanings are used by every speaker or writer of English for all occasions. Some words and some meanings are used chiefly by members of certain trades and professions. Others are common only in certain geographical areas. Still others are used only on certain occasions—in speaking and in informal writing, but not in formal writing. Others are the words of former generations, which are now seldom used in speech or writing.

Restrictive labels. Many of these specialized words and meanings have labels to show how, when, or where they are used. The commonest labels used in this dictionary are explained below.

INFORMAL. The word or meaning is used in everyday speech or writing, but not in formal speech or writing.

> **choos y** or **choos ey** (chü′zē), *adj.,* **choos i er, choos i est.** INFORMAL. particular or fussy . . . .
> **ne go ti ate** (ni gō′shē āt), *v.,* **-at ed, -at ing** . . . . —*v.t.* . . . . 2 INFORMAL. get past or over: *The car negotiated the sharp curve by slowing down.* . . .

SLANG. The word or meaning is used in very informal speaking, or, rarely, for an unusual effect in writing.

> **paste** (pāst), *n., v.,* **past ed, past ing** . . . . —*v.t.* 1 stick with paste . . . . 3 SLANG. hit with a hard, sharp blow . . . .

DIALECT. The word or meaning is used only in the folk speech of a certain geographical area.

> **poke**[2] (pōk), *n.* DIALECT. bag; sack . . . .
> **swang** (swang), *v.* DIALECT. pt. of **swing.**

ARCHAIC. The word or meaning is very rare except in old books or in books written in the style of an earlier period.

> **a vaunt** (ə vônt′, ə vänt′), *interj.* ARCHAIC. begone! get out! go away! . . .

LANGUAGE LABELS. The labels FRENCH, LATIN, GERMAN, etc., are used to distinguish words or phrases that are not thought of as English.

> ***gar çon*** (gàr sôN′), *n., pl.* ***-çons*** (-sôN′). FRENCH. 1 a young man; boy. 2 servant. 3 waiter.

> ***ad in fi ni tum*** (ad in′fə nī′təm), LATIN. without limit; endlessly.

Restrictive phrases. Other specialized meanings are shown by a phrase rather than by a capitalized label. Sometimes the restrictive phrase applies to the entire entry. In such cases, the phrase appears before the definitions and is followed by a colon.

> **ar roy o** (ə roi′ō), *n., pl.* **-roy os.** in the southwestern United States: 1 the dry bed of a stream; gully. 2 a small river . . . .

More often it applies to one particular meaning and appears in parentheses following the definition number for that meaning.

> **field** (fēld), *n.* . . . . 10 (in physics) the space throughout which a force operates. A magnet has a magnetic field around it . . . . 12 (in television) the entire screen area occupied by an image . . . .

Compare these examples with those in the preceding section. You see that the phrases do not restrict usage in the same way as the capitalized labels. These phrases—*in the southwestern United States, in physics, in television*—aid in your understanding of the definitions. A word or meaning with such a phrase may be used in both formal and informal English.

Synonym studies

Many entries in this dictionary have synonym studies to help you distinguish between words of closely related meanings. These discussions all follow the same pattern. First the meaning shared by the group of synonyms is explained. Then the way these words differ in implication is discussed. Illustrative sentences show each word in use. See, for example, the discussion of *advice* and *counsel* at the end of the entry for *advice:*

> **ad vice** (ad vīs′), *n.* 1 opinion, suggestion, or recommendation as to what should be done; counsel: *My advice is that you study more.* See synonym study below. 2 Often, **advices,** *pl.* news, especially from a distance; information: *advices from the battlefront.* [< Old French *avis* < Latin *ad-* + *visum* thing seen]
> **Syn.** 1 **Advice, counsel** mean an opinion given by a person for the guidance of another. **Advice** is the general word: *I asked her advice about which paint to buy.* **Counsel** is more formal, suggesting the giving of a professional or more carefully considered opinion: *I asked the bank president for counsel about a career in banking.*

Synonym studies are placed under the least specialized word of the group, the one which is most likely to be appropriate. For example, the synonym study for *frighten, scare, alarm* is placed under *frighten.* Cross-references to this study will be found at the end of the specific definitions of *scare* and *alarm* that are discussed there:

> **a larm** (ə lärm′) . . . . —*v.t.* 1 fill with sudden fear; frighten: *I was alarmed because my friends were so long in returning.* See **frighten** for synonym study . . . .

> **scare** (sker, skar) . . . . —*v.t.* 1 make afraid; frighten. See **frighten** for synonym study . . . .

EXERCISES:

1. Turn to the entry *deft* and read the synonym study, which discusses *deft, adroit,* and *dexterous.* Now write the following sentences on a sheet of paper, inserting the most appropriate of the three words in each blank.

   Franklin D. Roosevelt was known for his ______ political leadership.

   With ______ fingers she quickly mended the torn shirt.

   His ______ acrobatics on the trapeze were exciting to watch.
2. Read the synonym study contained in the entry *late.* Now write sentences of your own using *late* and *tardy.*

Usage notes

Usage notes, marked with the symbol ➤, are found at the end of many entries:

> **com prise** (kəm prīz′), *v.t.,* **-prised, -pris ing.** 1 consist of; include: *The United States comprises 50 states.* See **include** for synonym study. 2 make up; compose; constitute: *Fifty states comprise the United States. The committee is comprised of five members.* [< Old French *compris,* past participle of *comprendre* < Latin *comprehendere.* See COMPREHEND.]
> ➤ **Comprise** has recently developed a meaning that is the reverse of its original one, perhaps by being confused with *compose.* Although some people insist that it can mean only "include," more people now use it to mean "be included in."

These notes deal with questions of conflicting or changing usage. Many of them give specific answers to questions you may have ("What preposition should I use after the verb *center?*" "Do I want *disinterested* or *uninterested* in this sentence?"). Others give you a basis for making a choice (whether to write *everyday* or *every day,* whether to hyphenate a word beginning with the prefix *re-*). You will also find explanations of grammatical and rhetorical terms like *gerund* and *metaphor* in the usage notes.

Words frequently confused. Many words, such as *council* and *counsel, eminent* and *imminent,* are frequently confused because they are nearly alike in spelling or pronunciation. Usage notes for many such words are given in this dictionary to help you learn how to distinguish between them:

> **af fect**[1] (ə fekt′), *v.t.* 1 have an effect on; act on; influence or change: *Nothing you say will affect my decision. The disease affected her eyesight.* 2 stir the feelings of; move: *a tale of woe that deeply affected us . . . .*
> ➤ **Affect** and **effect** are often confused in writing, partly because they are pronounced very similarly or identically, and partly because *to affect* is synonymous with *to have an effect on.* But in the general vocabulary *affect* is used only as a verb, whereas *effect* is most commonly used as a noun: *Overwork has had a serious effect on (has seriously affected) his health.*

That note should help you decide which of the two words should be used in the blanks of the following sentences. If you are unsure, read it again, noting the illustrative sentence.

How did that book ______ you?

What do you think the ______ of this new ruling will be?

Turn to the entry *disinterested* and study the usage note carefully. Then see if you can write sentences of your own making the distinction between *disinterested* and *uninterested* clear.

Now look up the entry *uninterested.* You will find a cross-reference to *disinterested* for the usage note. Whenever you see such a cross-reference as you're looking up a word, check it. Quite possibly the information you specially want will be given in the usage note.

Pronunciation. Usage notes sometimes contain additional information on the pronunciations of words. For example, in the usage note under the prefix *anti-* you are shown how a following consonant or vowel affects the pronunciation of the prefix:

> ➤ **Anti-** is usually pronounced (an′ti) before consonants and (an′tē) before vowels, although (an′tī) is often used for emphasis.

Spelling. Usage notes such as those in the entries for *anyway, re-,* and *alright* help you with spelling problems:

> **an y way** (en′ē wā), *adv.* 1 in any case; at least . . . . 2 in any way whatever. 3 carelessly.
> ➤ **Anyway** is one word when the *any* is stressed: *I can't do it anyway.* It is two words when the stress is about equal: *Any way I try, it comes out wrong.*

> **re-,** *prefix.* 1 again; anew; once more: *Reappear = appear again.* 2 back: *Repay = pay back* . . . .
> ➤ **re-.** Words formed with the prefix *re-* are sometimes hyphenated (1) when the word to which it is joined begins with *e: re-echo,* (2) when the form with hyphen can have a different meaning from the form without: *reform,* to make better—*re-form,* to shape again, and (3) (rarely) for emphasis, as in "now *re-seated* in fair comfort," or in informal or humorous compounds: *re-re-married.*

> **al right** (ôl rīt′), *adv., adj.* INFORMAL. all right.
> ➤ The spelling **alright** is not yet generally acceptable in formal and in most informal writing. **All right** is the correct spelling of both the adjective phrase *(I am all right)* and the sentence adverb meaning yes, certainly *(All right, I'll come).*

Prepositional usage. The problem of which preposition to use after certain words is also solved in many of the usage notes. For example:

> **be gin** (bi gin′), *v.,* **be gan, be gun, be gin ning.** —*v.i.* 1 do the first part; make a start . . . .
> ➤ **Begin** is followed by *at* when the meaning is start from a definite place: *Let us begin at the third chapter.* It is followed by *on* or *upon* when the meaning is set to work at: *We must begin on the government survey tomorrow.* When the meaning is take first in an order of succession, the idiom is *begin with: We always begin with the hardest problems.*

> **cen ter** (sen′tər), *n.* . . . . —*v.t.* . . . . 2 concentrate; focus; rest: *All his hopes are centered on being promoted* . . . . —*v.i.* . . . . 2 rest on; be concentrated; rest: *All his hopes centered on being promoted* . . . .
> ➤ **Center around** or **center about** is used informally to mean "focus upon": *The story centers around* (or *about*) *a robbery.* The formal expression is *center on* or *center upon.*

Grammatical and rhetorical terms. Special grammatical information about terms such as *copula, gerund,* and *infinitive* is given in detail:

> **in fin i tive** (in fin′ə tiv), *n.* (in grammar) a form of a verb not limited by person and number. EXAMPLES: Let him *go.* We want *to go* now. —*adj.* of the infinitive.
> ➤ **infinitive.** The present infinitive is the simple form of the verb, with or without *to: I want* to buy *a hat. Let them* leave *if they want* to leave. Infinitives are used as: **a** nouns: To swim *across the English Channel is her ambition.* **b** adjectives: *They had money* to burn. **c** adverbs: *I went home* to rest. **d** part of verb phrases: *He will* do *most of the work.*

You will find similar notes on such rhetorical terms as *irony* and *metaphor.* For example:

> **met a phor** (met′ə fôr, met′ə fər), *n.* . . . .
> ➤ **Metaphors** and **similes** both make comparisons, but in a *metaphor* the comparison is implied and in a *simile* it is indicated by *like* or *as.* "The sea of life" is a metaphor. "Life is like a sea" is a simile.

Formal and informal use of words. Some usage notes tell which word to use in informal speech or writing and which to use in formal speech or writing:

> **aw ful** (ô′fəl), *adj.* 1 causing fear; dreadful; terrible: *an awful storm.* 2 deserving great respect and reverence: *the awful power of God.* 3 filling with awe; impressive; imposing: *The mountains rose to awful heights.* 4 INFORMAL. very bad, great, ugly, etc.: *an awful mess.* —*adv.* INFORMAL. very: *I was awful mad.* —**aw′ful ness,** *n.*
> ➤ The widespread informal use of **awful** as a word of disapproval has made the more literal meanings difficult to understand. It is usually wise to substitute *awe-inspiring* or *awesome* when those meanings are intended.

> **hence** (hens), *adv.* 1 as a result of this; therefore . . . .
> ➤ **Hence** is a more formal word than *consequently, therefore,* and *so that: They performed a series of experiments, all successful; hence their theory is well supported.*

> **of** (ov, uv; *unstressed* əv), *prep.* . . .
> ➤ **of, off.** A reduntant *of* (as in *off of, inside of,* etc.) is sometimes used in informal English, but the usage is not regarded as standard: *step off* (not *off of*) *a sidewalk.*

> **bade** (bad, bād), *v.* a pt. of **bid** (defs. 3-10).
> ➤ **Bade** is used chiefly in formal and literary English: *The king bade her remain.*

EXERCISES:

1. Read the usage notes dealing with the words in parentheses in the following sentences. Then copy the sentences, inserting the appropriate word.

   She wants to (emigrate) (immigrate) to Canada.
   Many people who live in poor countries would like to (emigrate) (immigrate).

   The gangster's (elicit) (illicit) activities were known to the police.
   The attorney tried to (elicit) (illicit) incriminating evidence from the witness.

   The (impracticable) (impractical) composer ended his life in poverty despite the popularity of his music.
   The invention seemed to be a breakthrough, but tests proved it (impracticable) (impractical).

2. Look up the entry *just*[1]. What does the usage note tell you? Now arrange the following words in a sentence illustrating what you learned.

   have to just we pages two study

3. Look up the entry *already* and read the usage note. When you understand the difference in usage, write your own sentences using *already* and *all ready.*

Etymologies

Finding the etymologies. In this dictionary the etymology, or word origin, is placed at the end of the definition, and is enclosed in square brackets, as in the six entries below:

> **dor mi to ry** (dôr′mə tôr′ē, dôr′mə tōr′ē), *n., pl.* **-ries.** 1 a building with many sleeping rooms. Colleges often provide dormitories where students live and study. 2 a sleeping room containing several beds. [< Latin *dormitorium* < *dormire* to sleep]
>
> **dor sal** (dôr′səl), *adj.* of, on, or near the back or upper surface of an organ, part, etc.: *a dorsal nerve.* [< Latin *dorsum* the back] **—dor′sal ly,** *adv.*
>
> **drake** (drāk), *n.* a male duck. [Middle English]
>
> **drear y** (drir′ē), *adj.,* **drear i er, drear i est.** 1 without cheer; dull; gloomy: *a cold, dreary day.* 2 ARCHAIC. sad; sorrowful. [Old English *drēorig*] **—drear′i ly,** *adv.* **—drear′i ness,** *n.*
>
> **drought** (drout), *n.* 1 a long period of dry weather; continued lack of rain. 2 lack of moisture; dryness. Also, **drouth.** [Old English *drūgath.* Related to DRY.]
> ➤ **drought, drouth.** Both forms are in good use, though *drought* is more usual in formal English.
>
> **duc at** (duk′ət), *n.* any of various gold or silver coins of different values, formerly used in Europe. [< Middle French < Italian *ducato,* ultimately < Latin *ducem* leader (because it bore the title of the ruler issuing it)]

Etymologies usually come at the end of entries, although they may be followed by run-on entries (as in *dorsal* and *dreary*), synonym studies, or usage notes (as in *drought*).

Some entries do not include etymologies:

> **hes i ta tion** (hez′ə tā′shən), *n.* 1 a hesitating; doubt; indecision. 2 a speaking with short stops or pauses; stammering.
>
> **hf.,** half.
>
> **he li ot ro pism** (hē′lē ot′rə piz′əm), *n.* phototropism in which a plant turns or bends in response to sunlight.
>
> **high fidelity,** reproduction of sound by a radio or phonograph with as little distortion of the original sound as possible. **—high′-fi del′i ty,** *adj.*

If you are curious about the origin of these words, you should look up the entries for *hesitate, half, helio-, tropism, high,* and *fidelity.* Etymologies are not given for derived words or abbreviations, for compounds or phrases whose elements are entered separately, or for proper names.

EXERCISE:

Look up the etymologies for the following words in your dictionary:

school	pupil[1]	pupil[2]
salary	plastic	pecan
squash[1]	squash[2]	karate
kibitzer	pajamas	potato

Reading the etymologies. For ease in reading the etymologies in this book, no abbreviations have been used. You should note that the symbol (<) means "from," "derived from," or "taken from."

WORD ORIGINS. The simplest type of etymology is represented by the following:

> **book** . . . . [Old English *bōc*]
> **fa ther** . . . . [Old English *fæder*]

This means that the words *book* and *father,* though then spelled differently, were already in the English language in Old English times (before

1100), and that, since no other languages are shown in the etymology, they are native words.

The word *church* is an example of a word that appears in Old English but is nevertheless a borrowed word:

> **church** . . . . [Old English *cirice* < Greek *kyriakon (dōma)* (house) of the Lord < *kyrios* lord < *kyros* power]

This means that the word *cirice,* from which *church* developed, was used during the Old English period, and that it came from the Greek word *kyriakon* (appearing in the phrase *kyriakon dōma* meaning "house of the Lord") which was derived from the word *kyrios* meaning "lord," which came from another Greek word, *kyros,* meaning "power."

Now you might like to try reading the etymologies below:

> **cof fee** . . . . [< Italian *caffè* < Turkish *kahveh* < Arabic *qahwa*]

Coffee came into English from Italian *caffè,* which came from Turkish *kahveh,* which, in turn, came from Arabic *qahwa.*

> **cous in** . . . . [< Old French < Latin *consobrinus* mother's sister's child < *com-* together + *soror* sister]

Cousin was taken into English from an Old French word with the same spelling and meaning, which was derived from a Latin noun *consobrinus* meaning "mother's sister's child." *Consobrinus,* in turn, came from the two Latin elements, *com-* meaning "together," and *soror* meaning "sister."

> **al low** . . . . [< Old French *alouer* < Latin *allaudare* approve < *ad-* to + *laudare* to praise]

Allow was taken into English from an Old French word *alouer,* which came from the Latin verb *allaudare* meaning "to approve." *Allaudare* was formed from the two Latin elements *ad-* meaning "to," and *laudare* meaning "to praise."

> **con trast** . . . . [< French *contraste* < Italian *contrasto* < *contrastare* to contrast < Latin *contra-* against + *stare* stand]

Contrast was taken from French *contraste,* which came from Italian *contrasto,* which was derived from the Italian verb *contrastare* meaning "to contrast." *Contrastare* came from the two Latin elements, *contra-* meaning "against," and *stare* meaning "to stand."

Humbug and *scrimp* are examples of words whose origin is unknown or uncertain.

> **hum bug** . . . . [origin unknown]
> **scrimp** . . . . [origin uncertain]

Clop and *cluck* are examples of words of "imitative" origin.

> **clop** . . . . [imitative]
> **cluck** . . . . [imitative]

For the etymology of a word that is a "variant of" another word entered in this dictionary, you should see the entry for the other word. For example, if you would like to know the etymology of *cocoa*[1], you should see the etymology given for *cacao.* If a word is a variant of a word *not* entered in this dictionary, the etymology may be treated as at *cog*[2].

> **co coa**[1] . . . . [variant of *cacao*]
> **ca ca o** . . . . [< Spanish < Nahuatl *cacauatl*]
> **cog**[2] . . . . [variant of earlier *cock* to secure]

The word *ultimately* is used in an etymology to indicate that intermediate steps have been omitted, mostly in order to shorten the etymology. At *embrace,* for example, intermediate steps in Old French or Popular Latin have been omitted. Similar steps have been omitted at *encounter,* where the intermediate steps are uncertain between Old French *encontrer* and the Latin elements *in-* and *contra.* Middle French and other Latin forms have been omitted at *equitation.* (For another example, see *ducat* above under "Finding the etymologies.")

> **em brace** . . . . [< Old French *embracer,* ultimately < Latin *in-* in + *brachium* arm]
> **en coun ter** . . . . [< Old French *encontrer,* ultimately < Latin *in-* in + *contra* against]
> **eq ui ta tion** . . . . [ultimately < Latin *equus* horse]

In the etymology for *accident,* the Latin form *accidentem* helps explain the *t* found at the end of the English word; in *ambition,* the Latin form *ambitionem* explains the English final *n;* and in *branchiopod,* the Greek form *podos* explains our spelling with a final *d.*

> **ac ci dent** . . . . [< Latin *accidentem* happening, befalling < *ad-* to + *cadere* to fall]
> **am bi tion** . . . . [< Latin *ambitionem* a canvassing for votes < *ambire* go around < *ambi-* around + *ire* go]
> **bran chi o pod** . . . . [< Greek *branchia* gills + *podos* foot]

The Latin past participle (usually the masculine singular accusative) has been used in order to account for the complete stem of the English word. For example, Latin *erasum* has been cited in the etymology of *erase;* Latin *moderatum,* in that of *moderate.*

> **e rase** . . . . [< Latin *erasum* scraped out < *ex-* out + *radere* scrape]
> **mod er ate** . . . . [< Latin *moderatum* regulated < *modus* measure]

WORD RELATIVES. English words show many different types of relationship, some of which have their source far back in the words' histories. Several devices are used in the etymologies to indicate some of the relationships which will prove especially interesting or helpful to you.

Doublets are words which can be traced directly back to a single recorded word which they share as a common source. The fact that they often differ greatly in form in modern English is due to the different routes which they have taken in passing from their common source down to English.

> **chef** . . . . [< French < Old French. Doublet of CHIEF.]
> **chief** . . . . [< Old French *chief, chef* < Latin *caput* head. Doublet of CHEF.]
> **frag ile** . . . . [< Latin *fragilis,* related to *frangere* to break. Doublet of FRAIL.]
> **frail** . . . . [< Old French *fraile* < Latin *fragilis* fragile. Doublet of FRAGILE.]

For other doublets, see *griddle* and *grill*^{1}, *corona* and *crown.* For four words that are doublets of each other, see *genteel, gentile, gentle,* and *jaunty.*

EXERCISE:
What are the doublets of the following words?
potion police hotel

Two modern English words may show a relationship that goes back to the Middle English or Old English period or to another language. This kind of relationship is indicated by the phrase "related to":

> **bier** . . . . [Old English *bēr.* Related to *beran* BEAR^1.]
> **bear**^{1} . . . . [Old English *beran*]
> **bar ra try** . . . . [< Old French *baraterie* < *barater* to exchange, cheat. Related to BARTER.]
> **bar ter** . . . . [< Old French *barater* to exchange]

You can see from the etymologies that *bier* and *bear*^{1} go back to related Old English words, and that *barratry* and *barter* go back to related Old French forms.

"Related to" is also used occasionally with two forms from a foreign language when it seems helpful to carry the etymology further by citing a related form:

> **cer tain** . . . . [< Old French < Latin *certus* sure, related to *cernere* decide]
> **im i tate** . . . . [< Latin *imitatum* imitated, related to *imago* image]

Another example of "related to" occurs in the etymology of *fragile,* in the section above on doublets.

Cross-references saying "See . . . . " are used when related words are close together in the alphabet and the last part of the etymologies would be the same if both were given in full. The cross-reference is made in such a way that you can obtain the full etymology of the second word by referring to the first; at the same time, you can see the exact relationship between the two.

> **ac cess** . . . . [< Latin *accessum* < *accedere.* See ACCEDE.]
> **ac cede** . . . . [< Latin *accedere* < *ad-* to + *cedere* move, go]
> **cit a del** . . . . [< Middle French *citadelle* < Italian *cittadella,* diminutive of *città* city < Latin *civitatem.* See CITY.]
> **cit y** . . . . [< Old French *cite* < Latin *civitatem* citizenship, state, city < *civis* citizen]

Notice that *access* and *accede* have the Latin form *accedere* in common. Additional information about *accedere* is given in the etymology for *accede.* Similarly, *citadel* and *city* both go back to Latin *civis.* At least one of the words in this type of cross-reference has been modified by one or more affixes, as Latin *cedere* by the prefix *ad-*.

How to Use This Dictionary for Spelling

Spelling tables

Sometimes you will want to use your dictionary to find the spelling of a word that you have heard but have never seen. The 26 letters of the alphabet occur in over 200 spelling combinations directing us to use some 40 sounds, and a dictionary lists words in strict alphabetical order. How, then, can you find a word you can't spell?

The first problem is finding the initial letter by using the initial sound of the word as a guide. Often, just knowing the first letter will enable you to find the word.

Initial consonant sounds. The spellings of consonant sounds are much more limited than those of vowel sounds. A word starting with a consonant sound is more likely to be spelled with the letter you expect than one starting with an initial vowel sound. You will have no problem, for example, finding a word starting with the sound (m), because words starting with this sound always begin with the letter *m.* But you may want to find the spelling of a word beginning with the sound (f). If you look for the word in the letter *f* and don't find it, you will have to know that the sound (f) can also be spelled *ph* to know where you should look next. On page 26 you will find a table of the common spellings of initial consonant sounds and instructions on how to use the table effectively to find words in the dictionary.

Vowel sounds. The spellings of vowel sounds are more difficult. The five vowel letters—*a, e, i, o,* and *u*—are used in a wide variety of combinations to spell 16 different sounds. These sounds are symbolized by the vowel letters—sometimes with diacritical marks and sometimes in combination—and the special symbols, schwa (ə) and (ėr).

The table for the spellings of vowel sounds on page 27 may be used either for spelling the initial vowel sounds in words or for spelling the vowels of first syllables. Even when you know how to spell the initial consonant, a vowel spelling might be unexpected.

EXERCISES:

1. Turn to the spelling tables on pages 26 and 27. Read the instructions on how to use them. Study the tables. Now, using the tables, tell under which letter in the dictionary you will find the following.

   (fez′nt) (yůr′əp)
   (i nam′əl) (ves′əl)
   (kem′ə strē) (kwī′ət)
   (ə grē′) (ôl ᴛʜō′)
   (sī kol′ə jē) (sit′ə zən)

2. In the table on page 26, there are two words that have the same pronunciation as the word *sent.* What are they?
3. On a sheet of paper, write the pronunciations given below. After each pronunciation, write all the words which have that pronunciation. Use the spelling tables. Look each word you think of up in your dictionary to check yourself.

   (nīt) (sēn)
   (sō) (sīt)
   (nü, nyü) (rīt)
   (sēm) (sir′ē əl)

Additional spelling hints

If you can spell the first syllable of a word, it is much easier to find the complete spelling by checking dictionary entries than by using spelling charts. English spelling has enough irregularities, though, that some additional reminders might be helpful.

1. A consonant sound not in the initial position may be spelled in the different ways indicated in the chart. When a word starts with two consonant sounds together, the second sound sometimes has one of its less common spellings: *school* (skül), *sphere* (sfir), *suede* (swād), *Guinevere* (gwin′ə vir), *view* (vyü), *queue* (kyü).
2. A doubled consonant often occurs after the first vowel: *account, addition, illustrate, immature.* You may need to check entries at two places to find words like *agree* and *aggregate, coral* and *correct, inoculate* and *innocence.*
3. Some words have a cluster of two different consonants pronounced as one: *acknowledge, acquire.*
4. Double *c* before *e* or *i* often has two different sounds: *accident* (ak′sə dənt), *success* (sək-ses′).
5. Except initially, the letter *x* is usually pro-

nounced (ks), as in *mix,* or (gz), as in *exact.* The spelling *-xc-* is pronounced (ks): *except.*

6. Initial *h* is sometimes not pronounced, especially before *e* or *o: heir, herb, honor, hour.*
7. The spelling *ng* does not occur initially in English. It is usually pronounced (ng): *long.* When another syllable follows in the same word, (g) is often pronounced at the beginning of the next syllable: *longer* (lông′gər). Sometimes *nk* is pronounced (ngk): *ink.*
8. The sound of (zh) does not often occur at the beginnings of words. Additional spellings for it are *si, su,* and *zu: division, measure, azure.*
9. The charts do not include pronunciations for abbreviations and symbols. Many of them are pronounced as words by saying the names of each of the letters composing them: *SOS* (es′ō′es′).
10. Silent letters occur frequently at the ends of words, as in *solemn* (sol′əm) and *apropos* (ap′rə pō′), but these present no problem in finding the word in the dictionary.
11. The abbreviations *Mr.* (mis′tər) and *Mrs.* (mis′iz) are almost never written as words.
12. A few words start with consonants which are called by their letter names, such as *nth* (enth). The chart does not cover them.
13. Some words you will not find by using the charts. The spellings of their vowel or initial consonant sounds occur rarely or only in one word in English. Many of them are proper nouns. Others are words whose pronunciations approximate those of the language from which they originated. Here are some examples:

Bhu tan (bü tän′)
cel lo (chel′ō)
Chou En-lai (jō′ en′lī′)
czar (zär)
Czech (chek)
gen re (zhän′rə)
Gi la monster (hē′lə)
Lha sa (lä′sə)
lla ma (lä′mə)
Mc Kin ley (mə kin′lē)
Phnom Penh (pə nôm′ pen′)
Rwan da (rü än′də)
Seoul (sōl)
Tchai kov sky (chī kôf′skē)
vo ya geur (vwä yä zhėr′)

Variant spellings

Often there are two or more accepted ways of spelling the same word in English. In this book you will find all of the common variants of each word.

When the variant spellings are pronounced alike, have the same inflected forms, and fall together alphabetically, they are combined into one entry:

adz or **adze** (adz), *n., pl.* **adz es.** a cutting tool for shaping heavy timbers . . . .

Variants entered separately. If the spellings occur together alphabetically, but the pronunciations or inflected forms differ, the variants are entered separately and the commoner spelling is used to define the other:

i o din (ī′ə dən), *n.* iodine.
i o dine (ī′ə dīn, ī′ə dən, ī′ə dēn′), *n.* 1 a nonmetallic element . . . .

cat a log (kat′l ôg, kat′l og), *n., v.* —*n.* 1 list of items . . . .
cat a logue (kat′l ôg, kat′l og), *n., v.,* **-logued, -logu ing.** catalog . . . .

When variants like *enclose* and *inclose* must be entered in different parts of the dictionary, the more common spelling is used to define the other. In addition, the less common spelling is given in boldface type at the end of the entry for the more common spelling:

en close (en klōz′), *v.t.,* **-closed, -clos ing.** 1 shut in on all sides; surround . . . . Also, **inclose.**
in close (in klōz′), *v.t.,* **-closed, -clos ing.** enclose.

Choosing between variant spellings. The simplest rule to follow, when you have a choice to make between variant spellings, is to use the commoner one. The most important thing is to be consistent. If you write *enroll* in one paragraph, don't shift to *enrol* in another. If you start with *catalogue,* don't write *catalog* a bit farther on.

Choosing between variant inflected forms. You have learned that some words, such as *appendix* and *kidnap,* have variant spellings for their inflected forms:

ap pen dix (ə pen′diks), *n., pl.* **-dix es** or **-di ces** . . . .
kid nap (kid′nap), *v.t.,* **-naped, -nap ing** or **-napped, -nap ping** . . . .

When you have to choose between these variant spellings, you will probably want to use the regularly formed one. Again, the rule is to be consistent. If you write *appendixes* once, don't later write *appendices.* If you ordinarily write *kidnaped,* don't absent-mindedly double the *p* later on.

Common Spellings of Initial Consonant Sounds

Each common initial consonant sound of English appears in this table followed by a list of words showing the spellings of the sound. The spellings are arranged according to frequency, beginning with the most frequent. Use this table to determine under which letter in the dictionary to find a word. Your chance of finding it under the first spelling is usually far greater than your chance of finding it under the last.

The part of each word that spells the sound is in boldface type.

Remember that some words start with consonant sounds but vowel letters, like *use* (yüz) and *eureka* (yu̇ rē′kə).

The table includes five combinations of sounds: (hw), (kw), (wu), (yü), and (yu̇).

Sound	Spellings and examples
(b)	**b**ad
(ch)	**ch**ild
(d)	**d**o
(f)	**f**at, **ph**rase
(g)	**g**o, **gu**est, **gh**ost
(h)	**h**e, **wh**o
(hw)	**wh**eat
(j)	**j**am, **g**em
(k)	**c**oat, **k**ind, **ch**emist
(kw)	**qu**ick
(l)	**l**and
(m)	**m**e
(n)	**n**o, **kn**ife, **gn**aw, **pn**eumonia
(p)	**p**ay
(r)	**r**un, **wr**ong, **rh**ythm
(s)	**s**ay, **c**ent, **ps**alm, **sc**ent, **sch**ism
(sh)	**sh**e, **ch**ef, **s**ugar, **sch**wa
(t)	**t**ell, **t**wo, **pt**omaine, **Th**omas
(th)	**th**in
(ŦH)	**th**en
(v)	**v**ery
(w)	**w**ill, **wh**eat [a variant of (hw)]
(wu)	**o**ne
(y)	**y**es
(yü)	**u**se, **eu**logy
(yu̇)	**u**ranium, **eu**reka
(z)	**z**ero, **x**ylophone

Spellings of Vowel Sounds

In this chart each vowel sound is followed by a list of words showing the range of spelling of the sound. The part of each word that spells the sound is in boldface type. Common spellings appear before rare spellings. The first word in the list gives a much more likely spelling of the sound than the last. *E,* as in *eve,* is a spelling for (ē) hundreds of times more common than *eo,* as in *people.*

Some of the words used as examples appear in more than one list because they have variant pronunciations. For example, *aerial* (er/ē-əl, ar/ē əl) is in the lists for both the sound (e) and the sound (a).

This chart includes only pronunciations given in this dictionary. Be sure to check key words given in the pronunciation key as a guide in determining the vowel symbols listed in the chart.

Sound	Spellings and examples
(a)	**a**nd, pl**ai**d, h**a**lf, l**au**gh, **ae**rial, **ey**rie, **A**aron, **e**re, pr**ay**er, th**ei**r, p**ea**r
(ā)	**a**ge, **ai**d, s**ay**, **eigh**t, th**ey**, br**ea**k, str**aigh**t, bouqu**et**, **é**lite, v**ei**n, **eh**, g**ao**l, g**au**ge
(ä)	**a**rt, **ah**, c**al**m, serg**ea**nt, h**ea**rt
(e)	**e**nd, s**ai**d, **ae**rial, **a**ny, br**ea**d, s**ay**s, h**ei**fer, l**eo**pard, fr**ie**nd, b**u**ry, **ey**rie, **e'**er, **Oe**dipus, **A**aron
(ē)	**e**ve, **ea**ch, b**ee**, **ei**ther, k**ey**, l**ie**ge, C**ae**sar, qu**ay**, p**i**ano, ph**oe**nix, p**eo**ple
(ėr)	st**er**n, **ear**l, t**ur**n, f**ir**st, w**or**d, j**our**ney, m**yr**tle, **err**, wh**irr**, p**urr**
(i)	**i**n, **e**nough, **ea**r, h**y**mn, b**ee**n, s**ie**ve, w**o**men, b**u**sy, b**ui**ld, w**ei**rd, **Ae**gean, **ey**rie
(ī)	**i**ce, l**ie**, sk**y**, r**ye**, **eye**, **is**land, h**igh**, **Ei**senhower, **Ai**nu, **ais**le, b**ay**ou, **aye**, h**eigh**t, b**uy**, g**ey**ser
(o)	**o**dd, w**a**tch, y**ach**t
(ō)	**o**ld, **oa**k, t**oe**, **ow**n, **oh**, **owe**, f**o**lk, th**ough**, b**eau**, y**eo**man, s**ew**, br**oo**ch, s**ou**l, m**au**ve
(ô)	**o**ff, **a**ll, **au**tomobile, **aw**ful, **awe**, **oa**r, **ough**t, w**a**lk, **o'**er, t**augh**t, c**ou**gh, Ut**ah**
(oi)	**oi**l, b**oy**
(ou)	**ou**t, **ow**l, b**ough**, **aou**dad
(u)	**u**nder, **o**ther, tr**ou**ble, d**oe**s, fl**oo**d
(u̇)	f**u**ll, g**oo**d, w**o**lf, sh**ou**ld
(ü)	f**oo**d, r**u**le, bl**ue**, m**o**ve, thr**ew**, s**ou**p, thr**ough**, sh**oe**, tw**o**, fr**ui**t, man**eu**ver, l**ieu**tenant
(ə)	**a**bout, **o**ccur, **e**ffect, **au**thority, barg**ai**n, penc**i**l, cauti**ou**s, circ**u**s, raj**ah**, pag**ea**nt, dung**eo**n, tort**oi**se

How to Use This Dictionary for Writing

Syllable division

In this dictionary, entries having more than one syllable are printed with thin spaces between the syllables:

> **de cel e rate** (dē sel′ə rāt′), *v.t., v.i.,* **-rat ed, -rat ing.** decrease the velocity (of); slow down. **—de cel′e ra′tion,** *n.* **—de cel′e ra′tor,** *n.*
>
> **dink y** (ding′kē), *adj.,* **dink i er, dink i est.** INFORMAL. small and insignificant. [origin uncertain]

Notice that not only the main entries, but the inflected forms (shown in the entries as *-rated, -rating* and *dinkier, dinkiest*) and the derivatives (*deceleration* and *decelerator*) are syllabicated. These syllable spaces show you where a word can be divided if it falls at the end of a line in writing.

No syllabication is given for entries made up of two or more words, each of which is entered and syllabicated separately:

> **decimal system,** system of numeration which is based on units of 10.

Here are some additional hints for syllable division:

1. Never divide one-syllable words, even if they are fairly long like *straight,* or are formed with an ending like *plunged.*
2. Divide hyphenated compound words only at the hyphen. Although *right-handed* has three syllables, it should only be divided at the hyphen, never between *hand-* and *-ed.*
3. Don't break a word in such a way that only one letter is left at the end of a line or carried over to the next line. You save very little space by dividing *a-bout.* You save no space by dividing *leaf-y,* since the space required for the hyphen could have been used for the final letter.

Other writing aids

Think back over what you have read in this section, "Using This Dictionary." It has told you how to find information about each word which can help you to write effectively. Review especially the sections on synonym studies and usage notes. They can be particularly helpful to you in your writing.

If you are in doubt about which word to choose among those of closely related meanings, the synonym studies can help you to choose the appropriate one for the context.

The usage notes can help you to avoid in formal writing those words and phrases which are appropriate only in informal writing. They can help you with spelling problems and prepositional usage, and they can help you to choose between words which may be confusing to you.

Five sample entries from this dictionary appear on page 29, labeled with the parts of an entry. Study these entries carefully so that you will learn where, in an entry in the dictionary, to find the information you need.

The Parts of a Dictionary Entry

On the right are five complete entries from this dictionary.
The parts of these entries are keyed to the numbered paragraphs on the left.

[1] **The entry word,** in boldface type, shows you how the word is spelled and how it may be divided in writing.
[2] **The homograph number** appears when successive entries are spelled the same way. See page 8 for a detailed discussion of homographs.
[3] **The pronunciation** is enclosed in parentheses. Letter symbols used in the pronunciation are explained in the pronunciation key. See pages 11 through 14 for a detailed discussion of pronunciations.
[4] **The part-of-speech label** is an abbreviation in italic type naming the function of the entry word. Many words function as more than one part of speech. When this is the case, a part-of-speech label appears before the definition or group of definitions for each part of speech.
[5] **Inflected forms,** in small boldface type, are given whenever their spelling or form might give you trouble. See pages 8 through 10 for a detailed discussion of inflected forms.
[6] **A restrictive label** shows that use of a word or meaning is limited to a particular region or level of usage. See page 18 for a detailed discussion of restrictive labels.
[7] **The definition** of a word tells its meaning. A word with several different meanings has numbered definitions, one for each meaning. See pages 15 through 17 for a detailed discussion of definitions.
[8] **An illustrative sentence** is printed in italic type following the definition. It shows how the entry word may be used with that particular meaning in a sentence. See page 17 for a detailed discussion of illustrative sentences.
[9] **An idiom,** in small boldface type, can be found under its most important word. Idioms have special meanings which cannot be understood from their word combinations. See pages 10 and 11 for a detailed discussion of idioms.
[10] **The etymology,** in square brackets, tells the origin of the entry word. See pages 21 through 23 for a detailed discussion of etymologies.
[11] **A run-on entry,** in small boldface type, is an undefined word. Its meaning combines the meaning of the entry word with that of its suffix. Each run-on entry has a part-of-speech label. See page 10 for a detailed discussion of run-on entries.
[12] **A synonym study** discusses words of closely related meanings. It appears under the most commonly used word and is keyed to the definition to which it applies. See page 19 for a detailed discussion of synonym studies.
[13] **A usage note,** indicated by an arrow, discusses words frequently confused, formal and informal usage, and similar problems. See pages 19 through 21 for a detailed discussion of usage notes.

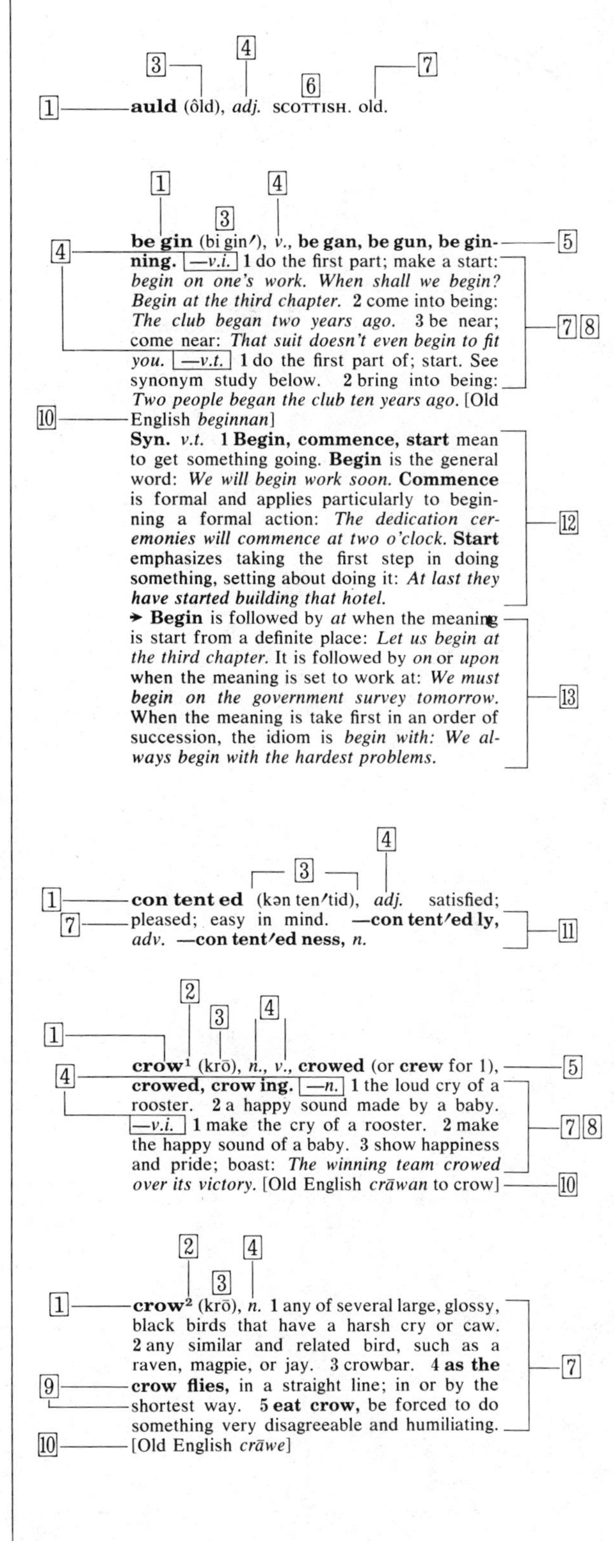

auld (ôld), *adj.* SCOTTISH. old.

be gin (bi gin′), *v.,* **be gan, be gun, be gin ning.** —*v.i.* 1 do the first part; make a start: *begin on one's work. When shall we begin? Begin at the third chapter.* 2 come into being: *The club began two years ago.* 3 be near; come near: *That suit doesn't even begin to fit you.* —*v.t.* 1 do the first part of; start. See synonym study below. 2 bring into being: *Two people began the club ten years ago.* [Old English *beginnan*]

Syn. *v.t.* 1 **Begin, commence, start** mean to get something going. **Begin** is the general word: *We will begin work soon.* **Commence** is formal and applies particularly to beginning a formal action: *The dedication ceremonies will commence at two o'clock.* **Start** emphasizes taking the first step in doing something, setting about doing it: *At last they have started building that hotel.*

➤ **Begin** is followed by *at* when the meaning is start from a definite place: *Let us begin at the third chapter.* It is followed by *on* or *upon* when the meaning is set to work at: *We must begin on the government survey tomorrow.* When the meaning is take first in an order of succession, the idiom is *begin with: We always begin with the hardest problems.*

con tent ed (kən ten′tid), *adj.* satisfied; pleased; easy in mind. —**con tent′ed ly,** *adv.* —**con tent′ed ness,** *n.*

crow[1] (krō), *n., v.,* **crowed** (or **crew** for 1), **crowed, crow ing.** —*n.* 1 the loud cry of a rooster. 2 a happy sound made by a baby. —*v.i.* 1 make the cry of a rooster. 2 make the happy sound of a baby. 3 show happiness and pride; boast: *The winning team crowed over its victory.* [Old English *crāwan* to crow]

crow[2] (krō), *n.* 1 any of several large, glossy, black birds that have a harsh cry or caw. 2 any similar and related bird, such as a raven, magpie, or jay. 3 crowbar. 4 **as the crow flies,** in a straight line; in or by the shortest way. 5 **eat crow,** be forced to do something very disagreeable and humiliating. [Old English *crāwe*]

A a

A[1] or **a**[1] (ā), *n., pl.* **A's** or **a's.** the first letter of the English alphabet.

a[2] (ə; *stressed* ā), *adj.* or *indefinite article.* 1 some single; any: *Call a doctor.* 2 one: *a million dollars.* 3 each; every: *once a year.* 4 the same: *two at a time.* 5 one kind of: *Chemistry is a science.* 6 to or for each: *ten dollars a day.* [Old English *ān* one]
➔ **A** is used before words pronounced with an initial consonant sound, as in *a* man, *a* year, *a* union, *a* hospital. Before *h* in an unaccented syllable we usually use *a*, as in *a* hotel or *a* historian, but some people use *an* in such cases.

A[2] (ā), *n., pl.* **A's.** the sixth tone of the musical scale of C major.

a-[1], *prefix.* 1 in; on; to: *Abed = in bed.* 2 in the act of ___ing: *Aflutter = in the act of fluttering.* 3 in a ___ condition: *Aweary = in a weary condition.* [Old English *an, on* on]

a-[2], *prefix.* form of **ab-**[1] before *m, p, v,* as in *avert.*

a-[3], *prefix.* form of **ad-** before *sc, sp, st,* as in *ascribe, aspire, astringent.*

a-[4], *prefix.* form of **an-**[1] before consonants except *h,* as in *atonal.*

A, 1 argon. 2 one of the four main blood groups.

Å, angstrom or angstroms.

a., 1 acre or acres. 2 ampere or amperes. 3 are (100 square meters).

A1, *adj.* INFORMAL. A one.

AA, antiaircraft.

A.A., Associate in Arts.

Aa chen (ä′kən), *n.* city in W West Germany. 178,000. Also, FRENCH **Aix-la-Chapelle.**

aard vark (ärd′värk), *n.* a burrowing African mammal with a piglike snout, a long, sticky tongue, and very strong claws; ant bear. It feeds on ants and termites. [< Afrikaans < *aarde* earth + *varken* pig]

aardvark 6 ft. long including tail

Aar on (er′ən, ar′ən), *n.* (in the Bible) the brother of Moses and first high priest of the Hebrews.

ab-[1], *prefix.* from; away; away from; off: *Abnormal = away from normal.* See also **a-** and **abs-.** [< Latin < *ab* off, away from]

ab-[2], *prefix.* form of **ad-** before *b,* as in *abbreviate.*

AB, one of the four main blood groups.

A.B., 1 Bachelor of Arts. Also, **B.A.** 2 able-bodied seaman.

ab a ca (ab′ə kä′), *n.* 1 a strong fiber made from the leaves of a Philippine banana plant, used for making ropes and fabrics; Manila hemp. 2 the plant itself. [< Spanish *abacá* < Tagalog *abaká*]

a back (ə bak′), *adv.* **taken aback,** upset or confused by something unexpected; disconcerted.

ab a cus (ab′ə kəs), *n., pl.* **-cus es, -ci** (-sī). 1 device for making arithmetical calculations, consisting of a frame with rows of counters or beads that slide back and forth, used especially in Asian countries. 2 slab forming the top of the capital of a column. See **column** for picture. [< Latin < Greek *abax, abakos*]

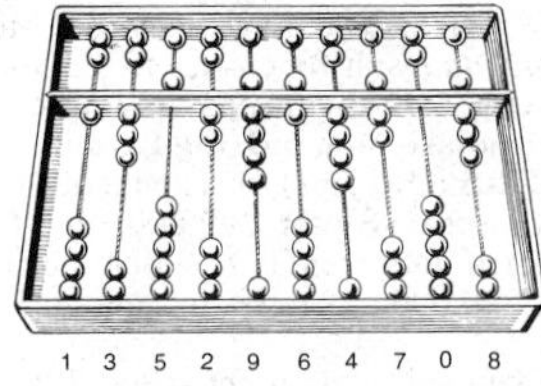

abacus (def. 1)—beads above middle bar, 5 each when lowered toward bar; beads below middle bar, 1 each when raised toward bar. Beads above and below the middle bar are totaled in each row. Numbers are shown below each wire for the setting of 1,352,964,708.

a baft (ə baft′), *adv.* at or toward the stern; aft. —*prep.* back of; behind. [< *a-*[1] on + Middle English *baft* behind]

ab a lo ne (ab′ə lō′nē), *n.* an edible saltwater mollusk with a large, rather flat shell lined with mother-of-pearl, found along the Pacific coast of North America. [< Mexican Spanish]

a ban don (ə ban′dən), *v.t.* 1 give up entirely; renounce or relinquish: *abandon a career.* 2 leave without intending to return to: *Abandon ship!* See **desert**[2] for synonym study. 3 give (oneself) up completely (to a feeling, impulse, etc.); surrender: *abandon oneself to despair.* —*n.* a yielding to natural impulses; freedom from restraint: *cheer with abandon.* [< Old French *abandoner* < *a bandon* in the power (of)] **—a ban′don er,** *n.* **—a ban′don ment,** *n.*

a ban doned (ə ban′dənd), *adj.* 1 deserted. 2 shamelessly wicked; immoral. 3 unrestrained. **—a ban′doned ly,** *adv.*

a base (ə bās′), *v.t.,* **a based, a bas ing.** make lower in rank, condition, or character; degrade: *A traitor abases himself.* [< Old French *abaissier* < *a-* to + *baissier* lower] **—a base′ment,** *n.*

a bash (ə bash′), *v.t.* embarrass and confuse; make uneasy and somewhat ashamed; disconcert: *I was not abashed by the laughter of my classmates.* [< Old French *esbaïss-,* a form of *esbaïr* astonish] **—a bash′ment,** *n.*

a bate (ə bāt′), *v.,* **a bat ed, a bat ing.** —*v.t.* 1 lessen in force or intensity; reduce or decrease: *Soft words did not abate her fury.* 2 put an end to; stop: *abate a nuisance.* —*v.i.* become less in force or intensity; diminish: *The storm has abated.* [< Old French *abatre* beat down < *a-* to + *batre* to beat] **—a bat′a ble,** *adj.* **—a bat′er,** *n.*

a bate ment (ə bāt′mənt), *n.* 1 a decrease; lessening. 2 amount abated; reduction. 3 a putting an end to.

ab a tis (ab′ə tis), *n., pl.* **-tis** (-tēz′). barricade of trees cut down and placed with their sharpened branches directed toward the enemy. [< French]

ab at toir (ab′ə twär), *n.* slaughterhouse. [< French]

ab ba cy (ab′ə sē), *n., pl.* **-cies.** position, term of office, or district of an abbot.

hat, āge, fär; let, ēqual, tėrm;
it, īce; hot, ōpen, ôrder;
oil, out; cup, pu̇t, rüle;
ch, child; ng, long; sh, she;
th, thin; ᴛʜ, then; zh, measure;

ə represents *a* in about, *e* in taken, *i* in pencil, *o* in lemon, *u* in circus.

< = from, derived from, taken from.

ab ba tial (ə bā′shəl), *adj.* of an abbot, abbess, abbey, or abbacy.

ab bé (ab′ā, a bā′), *n.* 1 (in France) a title of respect for anyone entitled to wear clerical dress. 2 (in Quebec) a priest or abbot. [< French]

ab bess (ab′is), *n.* woman who is the head of an abbey of nuns.

ab bey (ab′ē), *n., pl.* **-beys.** 1 a monastery ruled by an abbot or a convent ruled by an abbess. 2 the monks or nuns living there. 3 church or building that was once an abbey or part of an abbey: *Westminster Abbey.*

ab bot (ab′ət), *n.* man who is the head of an abbey of monks. [Old English *abbad* < Late Latin *abbatem* < Late Greek *abbas* < Aramaic *abbā* father]

abbrev. or **abbr.,** abbreviation.

ab bre vi ate (ə brē′vē āt), *v.t.,* **-at ed, -at ing.** 1 shorten (a word or phrase) so that a part stands for the whole: *"Hour" is abbreviated to "hr."* 2 make briefer; reduce; condense: *abbreviate a long speech.* See **shorten** for synonym study. [< Late Latin *abbreviatum* shortened < Latin *ad-* to + *brevis* short. Doublet of ABRIDGE.] **—ab bre′vi a′tor,** *n.*

ab bre vi a tion (ə brē′vē ā′shən), *n.* 1 part of a word or phrase standing for the whole; shortened form: *"Dr." is an abbreviation of "Doctor."* 2 a making shorter; abridgment.

ABC, American Broadcasting Company.

A B C (ā′bē′sē′), *n.* 1 *pl.* **ABC's** or **ABCs.** elementary principles; rudiments: *the ABC of chemistry.* 2 **ABC's,** *pl.* the alphabet.

ab di cate (ab′də kāt), *v.,* **-cat ed, -cat ing.** —*v.t.* give up or relinquish (office, power, or authority) formally; renounce; resign. —*v.i.* renounce office, power, or authority; resign. [< Latin *abdicatum* renounced < *ab-* away + *dicare* proclaim] **—ab′di ca′tion,** *n.* **—ab′di ca′tor,** *n.*

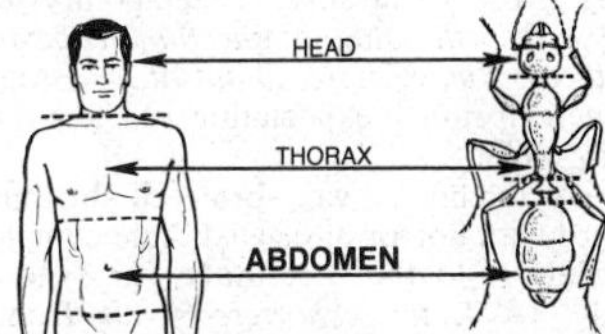

ab do men (ab′də mən, ab dō′mən), *n.* 1 the lower part of the body of mammals between the thorax and the pelvis, containing the major digestive organs. 2 the posterior of the three parts of the body of an insect or a crustacean. [< Latin]

ab dom i nal (ab dom′ə nəl), *adj.* of, in, or for the abdomen. **—ab dom′i nal ly,** *adv.*

ab duct (ab dukt′), *v.t.* 1 carry off (a person) by force or by trickery; kidnap. 2 pull (a part of the body) away from its normal position, as to raise an arm upward and outward. [< Latin *abductum* led away < *ab-* away + *ducere* to lead] **—ab duc′tion,** *n.*

ab duc tor (ab duk′tər), *n.* 1 person who abducts someone; kidnaper. 2 muscle that abducts.

a beam (ə bēm′), *adv.* in or into a direction at right angles to the keel of a ship; directly opposite the middle of a ship's side.

a bed (ə bed′), *adv.* in bed.

A bel (ā′bəl), *n.* (in the Bible) the second son of Adam and Eve, killed by his older brother Cain.

Ab é lard (ab′ə lärd; *French* à bā làr′), *n.* **Pierre,** 1079-1142, French philosopher, teacher, and theologian. See **Héloïse.**

Ab er deen (ab′ər dēn′), *n.* city in E Scotland. 182,000.

Ab er deen An gus (ab′ər dēn′ ang′gəs), any of a breed of small, entirely black, hornless cattle raised for beef and originally bred in Scotland.

Ab er do ni an (ab′ər dō′nē ən), *adj.* of Aberdeen or its people. *—n.* native or inhabitant of Aberdeen.

Ab er nath y (ab′ər nath′ē), *n.* **Ralph David,** born 1926, American civil rights leader.

ab er rance (ab er′əns), *n.* deviation from what is regular, normal, or right.

ab er ran cy (ab er′ən sē), *n., pl.* **-cies.** aberrance.

ab er rant (ab er′ənt), *adj.* deviating from what is regular, normal, or right. *—n.* person who deviates from normal behavior. **—ab er′rant ly,** *adv.*

ab er ra tion (ab′ə rā′shən), *n.* 1 a deviating from the right path or usual course of action. 2 an abnormal structure or development. 3 a temporary mental disorder. 4 failure of a lens or mirror to bring to a single focus the rays of light coming from one point. Aberration causes a blurred image or an image with a colored rim. 5 a slight periodic variation in the apparent position of a heavenly body, caused by the movement of the earth while the light from the heavenly body travels through the telescope. [< Latin *aberrationem* < *ab-* away + *errare* wander]

a bet (ə bet′), *v.t.,* **a bet ted, a bet ting.** 1 encourage by aid or approval in doing something wrong. 2 urge on or assist in any way. [< Old French *abeter* arouse < *a-* to + *beter* to bait] **—a bet′ment,** *n.* **—a bet′tor, a bet′ter,** *n.*

a bey ance (ə bā′əns), *n.* temporary inactivity: *We will hold that question in abeyance until we know more about it.* [< Anglo-French *abeiance* expectation < Old French *abeër* covet]

ab hor (ab hôr′), *v.t.,* **-horred, -hor ring.** regard with horror or disgust; hate completely; detest; loathe. See **hate** for synonym study. [< Latin *abhorrere* < *ab-* from + *horrere* to shudder, shrink] **—ab hor′rer,** *n.*

ab hor rence (ab hôr′əns, ab hor′əns), *n.* 1 a feeling of very great hatred. 2 something detested.

ab hor rent (ab hôr′ənt, ab hor′ənt), *adj.* 1 causing horror and disgust; detestable. 2 contrary or repugnant *(to): Lying is abhorrent to his nature.* 3 having or showing dislike *(of): be abhorrent of excess.* **—ab hor′rent ly,** *adv.*

a bid ance (ə bīd′ns), *n.* 1 an abiding. 2 **abidance by,** conformity to: *The coach demanded abidance by the rules of the game.*

a bide (ə bīd′), *v.,* **a bode** or **a bid ed, a bid ing.** *—v.t.* 1 put up with; endure; tolerate: *She can't abide him.* 2 submit to. 3 await or withstand defiantly. 4 ARCHAIC. wait for. *—v.i.* 1 stay; remain. 2 **abide by, a** accept and follow out: *abide by the judge's decision.* **b** remain true to; fulfill: *Abide by your promise.* 3 continue to live (in a place); dwell; reside. [Old English *ābīdan* stay on, and *onbīdan* wait for] **—a bid′er,** *n.*

a bid ing (ə bī′ding), *adj.* permanent; lasting; steadfast. **—a bid′ing ly,** *adv.*

Ab i djan (ab′i jän′), *n.* capital of the Ivory Coast, in the SE part. 282,000.

Ab i lene (ab′ə lēn′), *n.* 1 city in central Texas. 90,000. 2 town in central Kansas. 7000.

a bil i ty (ə bil′ə tē), *n., pl.* **-ties.** 1 quality or condition of being able; power to perform or accomplish; capacity: *the ability to work.* 2 competence in any occupation or field of action; skill. 3 special aptitude; talent: *musical ability.* See synonym study below.

Syn. 3 **Ability, talent** mean special power to do or for doing something. **Ability** applies to a demonstrated physical or mental power to do a certain thing well: *She has unusual ability as a dancer.* **Talent** applies to an inborn capacity for doing a special thing: *a remarkable talent for painting.*

ab i o gen e sis (ab′ē ō jen′ə sis), *n.* spontaneous generation.

ab ject (ab′jekt, ab jekt′), *adj.* 1 so low or degraded as to be hopeless; wretched; miserable: *to live in abject poverty.* 2 deserving contempt; despicable: *the most abject flattery.* 3 slavish: *abject submission.* [< Latin *abjectum* cast down < *ab-* down + *jacere* to throw] **—ab ject′ly,** *adv.* **—ab ject′ness,** *n.*

ab jure (ab jür′), *v.t.,* **-jured, -jur ing.** 1 swear to give up; renounce: *abjure power or allegiance.* 2 retract formally or solemnly; repudiate: *abjure a belief formerly held.* 3 refrain from; avoid: *abjure humor.* [< Latin *abjurare* < *ab-* away + *jurare* swear] **—ab′ju ra′tion,** *n.* **—ab jur′er,** *n.*

abl., ablative.

ab late (ab lāt′), *v.,* **-lat ed, -lat ing.** *—v.t.* 1 remove by burning away, wearing down, or cutting off. 2 remove by ablation. *—v.i.* be removed by ablation. [< Latin *ablatum* taken away]

ab la tion (ab lā′shən), *n.* 1 the melting, vaporizing, or otherwise disintegrating of part of the nose cone of a missile or spacecraft when it reenters the atmosphere. Ablation protects the rest of the structure from excessive heat. 2 removal.

ab la tive (*n., adj. 1* ab′lə tiv; *adj. 2* ab-lā′tiv), *n.* in grammar: 1 the case that in Latin expresses place from or in which, source, agent, cause, association, or instrument. 2 a case with similar uses in some other inflected languages. 3 word or construction in this case. *—adj.* 1 of or showing the ablative: *ablative case.* 2 removed by ablation: *an ablative nose cone.*

a blaze (ə blāz′), *adj.* 1 on fire; blazing. 2 flashing or brilliant. 3 violently excited: *ablaze with anger.*

a ble (ā′bəl), *adj.,* **a bler, a blest.** 1 having enough power, skill, or means to do something (followed by *to* plus an infinitive); capable: *A cat is able to see in the dark.* 2 having more power or skill than usual; skillful: *an able teacher.* See synonym study below. 3 expertly done; effective: *an able speech.* 4 legally authorized or qualified. [< Old French *hable, able* < Latin *habilis* apt, easily handled < *habere* to hold]

Syn. Able, capable, competent mean having the skill or means of doing something: *able to swim, capable of going ninety miles an hour, competent to handle one's own affairs.* Placed immediately before the modified word, **competent** gains the idea of satisfactory accomplishment *(A competent typist is not necessarily a competent secretary.),* while both **able** and **capable** gain the idea of superior accomplishment: *an able teacher, a capable doctor.*

-able, *suffix forming adjectives from verbs and nouns.* 1 that can be ___ed: *Enjoyable = that can be enjoyed.* 2 giving ___; suitable for ___: *Comfortable = giving comfort.* 3 inclined to ___: *Peaceable = inclined to peace.* 4 deserving to be ___ed: *Lovable = deserving to be loved.* 5 liable to be ___: *Breakable = liable to be broken.* [< Old French < Latin *-abilem*]

a ble-bod ied (ā′bəl bod′ēd), *adj.* strong and healthy; physically fit.

able-bodied seaman or **able seaman,** a trained deckhand on a merchant vessel.

a bloom (ə blüm′), *adj.* in bloom.

ab lu tion (ab lü′shən), *n.* Often, **ablutions,** *pl.* 1 a washing of one's person. 2 a washing or cleansing as a religious ceremony of purification. [< Latin *ablutionem* < *ab-* away + *lavere* to wash]

a bly (ā′blē), *adv.* in an able manner; with skill; capably.

ABM, antiballistic missile.

ab ne gate (ab′nə gāt), *v.t.,* **-gat ed, -gat ing.** deny (anything) to oneself; renounce or give up (a privilege or luxury). [< Latin *abnegatum* refused < *ab-* off, away + *negare* deny] **—ab′ne ga′tion,** *n.* **—ab′ne ga′tor,** *n.*

ab nor mal (ab nôr′məl), *adj.* away from the normal; deviating from the ordinary conditions, the standard, or a type; markedly irregular; exceptional. See **irregular** for synonym study. **—ab nor′mal ly,** *adv.*

ab nor mal i ty (ab′nôr mal′ə tē), *n., pl.* **-ties.** 1 an abnormal feature, act, or happening. 2 an abnormal condition.

ABO, of or having to do with four blood groups, A, B, AB, and O, that must be matched in transfusions.

a board (ə bôrd′, ə bōrd′), *adv.* 1 on board; in or on a ship, train, bus, airplane, etc.: *All aboard!* 2 alongside (a ship or shore). *—prep.* on board of; on, in, or into (a ship, train, bus, airplane, etc.): *Get aboard the train.*

a bode (ə bōd′), *n.* place of residence; dwelling; house or home. *—v.* a pt. and a pp. of **abide.**

a bol ish (ə bol′ish), *v.t.* do away with (a law, institution, or custom) completely; put an end to: *Slavery was abolished in the United States in 1865.* [< Middle French *aboliss-,* a form of *abolir* < Latin *abolere* destroy] **—a bol′ish a ble,** *adj.* **—a bol′ish er,** *n.* **—a bol′ish ment,** *n.*

ab o li tion (ab′ə lish′ən), *n.* 1 an abolishing. 2 a being abolished; abrogation. 3 the abolishing of slavery.

ab o li tion ist (ab′ə lish′ə nist), *n.* 1 person who advocates abolition of any institution or custom. 2 **Abolitionist,** person in the 1830's to 1860's who favored the compulsory abolition of slavery in the United States.

ab o ma sum (ab′ə mā′səm), *n., pl.* **-sa** (-sə). the fourth and true stomach of cows, sheep, and other ruminants, in which the food is digested.

A-bomb (ā′bom′), *n.* atomic bomb. *—v.t.* bomb with an atomic bomb or bombs.

a bom i na ble (ə bom′ə nə bəl), *adj.* 1 arousing disgust and hatred; detestable; loathsome: *Kidnaping is an abominable crime.* 2 very unpleasant; disagreeable: *abominable manners.* **—a bom′i na bly,** *adv.*

Abominable Snowman, an apelike creature supposed to inhabit the higher parts of the Himalayas; Yeti.

a bom i nate (ə bom′ə nāt), *v.t.,* **-nat ed, -nat ing.** 1 feel extreme disgust for; detest; loathe. 2 dislike: *abominate hot weather.* [< Latin *abominatum* deplored as an ill omen < *ab-* off + *ominari* prophesy < *omen* omen]

a bom i na tion (ə bom′ə nā′shən), *n.* 1 something that arouses strong disgust. 2 a feeling of disgust; loathing.

ab o ral (ab ôr′əl, ab ōr′əl), *adj.* (in zoology) situated at the opposite end from the mouth. **—ab o′ral ly,** *adv.*

ab o rig i nal (ab′ə rij′ə nəl), *adj.* 1 first or earliest so far as science or history gives record; original; native: *aboriginal inhabitants.* 2 of or belonging to the earliest known inhabitants: *an aboriginal custom.* *—n.* aborigine. **—ab′o rig′i nal ly,** *adv.*

ab o rig i ne (ab′ə rij′ə nē), *n.* an original inhabitant of a country or area, especially as distinguished from European or other colonists. [< Latin < *ab origine* from the beginning]

a born ing (ə bôr′ning), *adv., adj.* while being produced.

a bort (ə bôrt′), *v.i.* 1 fail to develop or come to completion; end prematurely: *The rocket flight aborted.* 2 give birth before the fetus can live; give birth prematurely. *—v.t.* 1 end or abandon before completion: *abort a mission.* 2 cause to give birth prematurely. [< Latin *abortum* miscarried < *ab-* amiss + *oriri* be born]

a bor tion (ə bôr′shən), *n.* 1 birth that occurs before the fetus has developed enough to live, usually during the first twelve weeks of pregnancy. 2 the inducing of premature delivery to destroy offspring. 3 failure to develop properly; imperfect development. 4 plan, project, or idea that fails to develop properly.

a bor tion ist (ə bôr′shə nist), *n.* person who induces illegal abortions.

a bor tive (ə bôr′tiv), *adj.* 1 coming to nothing; unsuccessful: *an abortive rebellion.* 2 born prematurely. 3 imperfectly formed or developed; rudimentary. **—a bor′tive ly,** *adv.* **—a bor′tive ness,** *n.*

a bound (ə bound′), *v.i.* 1 be plentiful or numerous: *Fish abound in the ocean.* 2 be well supplied or filled; be rich: *The ocean abounds with fish. America abounds in oil.* [< Old French *abonder* < Latin *abundare* abound, overflow < *ab-* off + *undare* rise in waves]

a bout (ə bout′), *prep.* 1 of; having to do with: *a book about bridges.* 2 in connection with: *something strange about him.* 3 somewhere near; in or not far from: *My father is about the house.* 4 approximately at: *About 1850 the westward movement was in full swing.* 5 on every side of; all around; around: *A collar goes about the neck.* 6 on (one's person); with: *She has no money about her.* 7 in many parts of; everywhere in: *scatter papers about the room.* 8 doing; working at: *An expert knows what he is about.* 9 **about to,** going to; ready to: *The plane is about to take off.*
—adv. 1 approximately; roughly: *He weighs about 100 pounds.* 2 somewhere near: *A stray dog has been lurking about.* 3 all around; in every direction: *I looked about.* 4 nearly; almost: *I have about finished my work.* 5 in many places; here and there: *The rumor went about that you were ill.* 6 in the opposite direction: *You are going the wrong way. Face about!* 7 one after another; by turns: *Turn about is fair play.* 8 moving around; active: *He is able to be up and about.*
[Old English *onbūtan* on the outside of]

a bout-face (*n.* ə bout′fās′; *v.* ə bout′fās′), *n., v.,* **-faced, -fac ing.** *—n.* 1 a turning or going in the opposite direction. 2 a shift to the opposite attitude or opinion. *—v.i.* make an about-face.

a bove (ə buv′), *adv.* 1 in or at a higher place; overhead: *The sky is above.* 2 on the upper side or on top: *leaves dark above and light below.* 3 higher in rank or power: *the courts above.* 4 in or from a direction thought of as higher: *There's good fishing above.* 5 earlier in a book or article: *See what is written above.* 6 above zero: *The temperature is five above.* *—prep.* 1 to or in a higher place than: *Birds fly above the trees.* 2 higher than; over: *She kept her head above water.* 3 more than: *The weight is above a ton.* 4 beyond: *Turn at the first corner above the school.* 5 too great in importance for; superior to: *be above petty gossip.* *—adj.* made or mentioned earlier in a book or article: *the above statement.* *—n.* **the above,** something that is written above. [Old English *abufan*]

a bove board (ə buv′bôrd′, ə buv′bōrd′), *adj., adv.* in open sight; without tricks or concealment.

a bove ground (ə buv′ground′), *adv., adj.* 1 above the surface of the ground. 2 in the open; not secret or underground.

ab ra ca dab ra (ab′rə kə dab′rə), *n.* 1 a mystical word used in incantations or as a charm to ward off disease. 2 meaningless talk; gibberish. [< Latin]

a brad ant (ə brād′nt), *adj.* wearing down; abrading. *—n.* an abrasive.

a brade (ə brād′), *v.t., v.i.,* **a brad ed, a brad ing.** wear down or away by friction; rub away; scrape off: *Glaciers abrade rocks.* [< Latin *abradere* < *ab-* off + *radere* scrape] **—a brad′er,** *n.*

A bra ham (ā′brə ham), *n.* (in the Bible) the ancestor of the Hebrews.

a bra sion (ə brā′zhən), *n.* 1 place scraped or worn by friction: *She had an abrasion on her knee from falling on gravel.* 2 a wearing down or away by friction; scraping off: *abrasion of rocks by flowing water laden with sand.* [< Latin *abrasionem* < *abradere.* See ABRADE.]

a bra sive (ə brā′siv, ə brā′ziv), *n.* substance used for grinding, smoothing, or polishing. Sandpaper, pumice, and emery are abrasives. *—adj.* causing abrasion. **—a bra′sive ly,** *adv.* **—a bra′sive ness,** *n.*

a breast (ə brest′), *adv., adj.* 1 side by side. 2 up with; alongside of: *Keep abreast of what is going on. Keep abreast with the flow of events.*

a bridge (ə brij′), *v.t.,* **a bridged, a bridg ing.** 1 make shorter by using fewer words but retaining the sense and substance; condense: *abridge a novel.* 2 make less; diminish; curtail: *abridge the rights of citizens.* 3 deprive (someone *of*); divest: *abridge citizens of their rights.* 4 shorten in length of time. [< Old French *abregier* < Late Latin *abbreviare* < *ad-* to + *brevis* short. Doublet of ABBREVIATE.] **—a bridg′a ble, a bridge′a ble,** *adj.* **—a bridg′er,** *n.*

hat, āge, fär; let, ēqual, tėrm;
it, īce; hot, ōpen, ôrder;
oil, out; cup, pu̇t, rüle;
ch, child; ng, long; sh, she;
th, thin; ᴛʜ, then; zh, measure;

ə represents *a* in about, *e* in taken, *i* in pencil, *o* in lemon, *u* in circus.

< = from, derived from, taken from.

a bridg ment or **a bridge ment** (ə brij′mənt), *n.* 1 a shortened form of a book, long article, etc., that retains the sense and substance of the original; condensation. 2 an abridging. 3 a being abridged.

a broad (ə brôd′), *adv.* 1 outside one's country; in or to a foreign land or lands: *The diplomat lived abroad much of his life.* 2 out in the open air; outdoors: *My grandfather walks abroad only on warm days.* 3 far and wide; widely: *The news of the victory quickly spread abroad.* 4 going around; in motion; current: *A false rumor is abroad.*

ab ro gate (ab′rə gāt), *v.t.,* **-gat ed, -gat ing.** 1 abolish or annul by an authoritative act; repeal; cancel: *abrogate a trade agreement.* 2 do away with. [< Latin *abrogatum* repealed < *ab-* away + *rogare* propose (a law)] **—ab′ro ga′tion,** *n.* **—ab′ro ga′tor,** *n.*

a brupt (ə brupt′), *adj.* 1 characterized by sudden change; unexpected: *an abrupt turn.* 2 very steep. See **steep**[1] for synonym study. 3 short or sudden in speech or manner; blunt. 4 disconnected: *an abrupt style of writing.* 5 (in botany) suddenly tapering off; truncate. [< Latin *abruptum* broken off < *ab-* off + *rumpere* to break] **—a brupt′ly,** *adv.* **—a brupt′ness,** *n.*

abs-, *prefix.* form of **ab-**[1] before *c* and *t,* as in *abscond, abstain.*

ABS, 1 acrylonitrile butadiene styrene (a plastic). 2 alkyl benzene sulfonate (a detergent).

Ab sa lom (ab′sə ləm), *n.* (in the Bible) David's favorite son, who led a rebellion against his father and was later killed in battle.

ab scess (ab′ses), *n.* collection of pus in the tissues of some part of the body, resulting from an infection and often accompanied by inflammation. [< Latin *abscessus* a going away < *abs-* away + *cedere* go]

ab scessed (ab′sest), *adj.* having an abscess: *an abscessed tooth.*

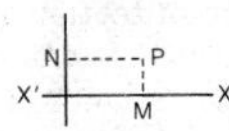

abscissa
The abscissa of point P is the distance NP measured on the axis X′X.

ab scis sa (ab sis′ə), *n., pl.* **-scis sas, -scis sae** (-sis′ē). the distance of a point on a graph to the left or right of the vertical axis, measured on a line parallel to the horizontal axis. The abscissa and the ordinate together are coordinates of the point. [< Latin *(linea) abscissa* (line) cut off]

ab scis sion (ab sizh′ən), *n.* the normal separation of a mature fruit, leaf, or stem from a twig by the formation of a corky layer of young cells at the base.

ab scond (ab skond′), *v.i.* go away hurriedly and secretly, especially to avoid punishment; go off and hide. [< Latin *abscondere* < *abs-* away + *condere* store up] **—ab scond′er,** *n.*

ab sence (ab′səns), *n.* 1 condition of being away: *absence from work.* 2 period of being away: *an absence of two weeks.* 3 a being without; lack: *Darkness is the absence of light.* 4 absent-mindedness.

ab sent (*adj.* ab′sənt; *v.* ab sent′), *adj.* 1 away; not present: *I will be absent tomorrow.* 2 lacking; not existing: *In certain fishes the ribs are entirely absent.* 3 absent-minded: *an absent look.* —*v.t.* keep or take (oneself) away: *absent oneself from class.* [< Latin *absentem* being away < *ab-* away + *esse* be]

ab sen tee (ab′sən tē′), *n.* person who is absent or remains absent.

absentee ballot, ballot of or for a voter who is permitted to vote by mail.

ab sen tee ism (ab′sən tē′iz′əm), *n.* 1 practice or habit of being an absentee. 2 an economic system under which a landowner controls the use of land in a country or place where he does not live.

ab sent ly (ab′sənt lē), *adv.* in an absent-minded manner; inattentively.

ab sent-mind ed (ab′sənt min′did), *adj.* not aware of what is going on around one; forgetful or inattentive; abstracted; preoccupied. **—ab′sent-mind′ed ly,** *adv.* **—ab′sent-mind′ed ness,** *n.*

ab sinthe or **ab sinth** (ab′sinth), *n.* a bitter, green alcoholic drink flavored with wormwood, anise, or other herbs. [< French *absinthe*]

ab so lute (ab′sə lüt), *adj.* 1 free from imperfection or lack; complete; whole; entire: *the absolute truth.* 2 with no limits or restrictions: *absolute power.* 3 not modified, limited, or restricted in any way; unqualified: *an absolute statement.* 4 certain; positive; infallible: *absolute proof.* 5 not compared with anything else: *absolute velocity.* 6 in grammar: **a** forming a part of a sentence, but not connected with it grammatically. In "The train being late, we missed the boat," *the train being late* is an absolute construction. **b** used without an expressed object. In "I will not ask again," *ask* is an absolute verb. **c** having its noun understood, but not expressed. In "The older pupils may help the younger," *younger* is an absolute adjective. 7 of or having to do with absolute temperature. 273° absolute is the same as 0° centigrade. 8 based on some primary units (especially those of length, mass, and time) of invariable value which are taken as fundamental: *the centimeter-gram-second system of absolute units.* —*n.* **the absolute,** fundamental reality thought of as apart from all special relations or conditions. [< Latin *absolutum* loosened or freed from < *ab-* from + *solvere* loosen] **—ab′so lute′ness,** *n.*

absolute alcohol, ethyl alcohol that is theoretically pure and in practice contains not more than 1 per cent of water by weight.

ab so lute ly (ab′sə lüt′lē, ab′sə lüt′lē), *adv.* 1 completely; entirely. 2 without doubt; certainly.

absolute majority, more than half the total number voting or qualified to vote.

absolute pitch, 1 pitch of a tone determined solely by the frequency of its vibrations. 2 perfect pitch.

absolute temperature, temperature measured from or expressed in degrees above absolute zero.

absolute value, value of a real number regardless of any accompanying sign: *The absolute value of +5, or −5, is 5.*

absolute zero, the theoretical temperature at which substances would have no heat whatever and all molecules would stop moving. It is −273.16 degrees centigrade, −459.69 degrees Fahrenheit, and 0 degrees Kelvin.

ab so lu tion (ab′sə lü′shən), *n.* 1 a freeing from sin, guilt, or blame. 2 declaration that frees a person from guilt or punishment for sin. 3 release from a duty or promise; discharge.

ab so lut ism (ab′sə lü′tiz′əm), *n.* system or form of government in which the ruler has unrestricted power; despotism.

ab so lut ist (ab′sə lü′tist), *n.* person who favors or supports absolutism. —*adj.* despotic.

ab so lut is tic (ab′sə lü tis′tik), *adj.* of absolutists or absolutism.

ab solve (ab solv′, ab zolv′), *v.t.,* **-solved, -solv ing.** 1 pronounce or set (a person) free from sin, guilt, blame, or their penalties or consequences. 2 set free (*from* a promise, obligation, or duty); release. [< Latin *absolvere* < *ab-* from + *solvere* loosen] **—ab solv′er,** *n.*

ab sorb (ab sôrb′, ab zôrb′), *v.t.* 1 take in or suck up (a liquid or gas): *The sponge absorbed the spilled milk.* 2 take in and make a part of itself; assimilate: *The United States has absorbed millions of immigrants.* 3 take in without reflecting: *Rugs absorb sounds and make a house quieter.* 4 take up all the attention of; interest very much: *Building a dam in the brook absorbed the girl.* 5 grasp with the mind; understand: *absorb the full meaning of a remark.* 6 take in and endure; sustain: *absorb punishment.* 7 pay (a cost, tax, etc.) without adding it to the price of an article, etc.: *The manufacturer absorbed the new tax.* 8 take (digested food, oxygen, etc.) into the bloodstream by osmosis. [< Latin *absorbere* < *ab-* from + *sorbere* suck in] **—ab sorb′a ble,** *adj.* **—ab sorb′er,** *n.*

ab sorb a bil i ty (ab sôr′bə bil′ə tē, ab zôr′bə bil′ə tē), *n.* absorbable quality or condition.

ab sorbed (ab sôrbd′, ab zôrbd′), *adj.* very much interested; engrossed. **—ab sorb′ed ly,** *adv.* **—ab sorb′ed ness,** *n.*

ab sorb en cy (ab sôr′bən sē, ab zôr′bən sē), *n.* absorbent quality or condition.

ab sorb ent (ab sôr′bənt, ab zôr′bənt), *adj.* able to absorb: *an absorbent paper towel.* —*n.* any substance or thing that absorbs moisture, light, or heat.

ab sorb ing (ab sôr′bing, ab zôr′bing), *adj.* extremely interesting; engrossing. **—ab sorb′ing ly,** *adv.*

ab sorp tion (ab sôrp′shən, ab zôrp′shən), *n.* 1 act or process of absorbing: *the absorption of ink by a blotter, the absorption of light rays by black objects.* 2 great interest (*in* something): *the children's absorption in their game.* 3 the process of taking (digested food, oxygen, etc.) into the bloodstream by osmosis.

absorption spectrum, a continuous spectrum broken by dark lines or bands, formed by passing white light or other electromagnetic radiation through a gas or liquid. The lines or bands indicate the presence of a particular chemical element or compound by the absorption of certain frequencies.

ab sorp tive (ab sôrp′tiv, ab zôrp′tiv), *adj.* able to absorb. **—ab sorp′tive ness,** *n.*

ab stain (ab stān′), *v.i.* 1 hold oneself back voluntarily, especially because of one's principles; refrain: *When the cigars were passed, he abstained. He abstained from smoking.* 2 refrain from voting. [< Old French *abstenir* < Latin *abstinere* < *abs-* off + *tenere* to hold] **—ab stain′er,** *n.*

ab ste mi ous (ab stē′mē əs), *adj.* 1 sparing in eating, drinking, etc.; moderate; temperate. 2 very plain; restricted: *an abstemious diet.* [< Latin *abstemius*] **—ab ste′mi ous ly,** *adv.* **—ab ste′mi ous ness,** *n.*

ab sten tion (ab sten′shən), *n.* 1 an abstaining; abstinence. 2 fact of not voting: *There were five votes in favor, four against, and three abstentions.*

ab sten tious (ab sten′shəs), *adj.* abstemious.

ab sti nence (ab′stə nəns), *n.* 1 an abstaining; partly or entirely giving up certain pleasures, food, drink, etc. 2 Also, **total abstinence.** a refraining from drinking any alcoholic liquor.

ab sti nent (ab′stə nənt), *adj.* abstemious. **—ab′sti nent ly,** *adv.*

ab stract (*adj.* ab′strakt, ab strakt′; *v.* ab strakt′ *for 1,3-5,* ab′strakt *for 2; n.* ab′strakt), *adj.* 1 thought of apart from any particular object or actual instance; not concrete: *Sweetness is an abstract quality. Truth is an abstract concept.* 2 expressing or naming a quality, idea, etc., rather than a particular object or concrete thing: *"Honesty" is an abstract noun.* 3 hard to understand; difficult; abstruse: *abstract arguments.* 4 concerned with ideas or concepts rather than actual particulars or instances; not practical or applied; ideal or theoretical: *abstract reasoning, abstract mathematics.* 5 not representing any actual object or concrete thing; having little or no resemblance to real or material things: *abstract paintings.* —*v.t.* 1 think of (a quality) apart from any particular object or actual instance. 2 make an abstract of; summarize. 3 take away; remove; extract: *Iron is abstracted from ore.* 4 take away secretly, slyly, or dishonestly. 5 withdraw (the attention of); divert. —*n.* 1 a brief statement of the main ideas in an article, book, case in court, etc.; summary. 2 **in the abstract,** in theory rather than in practice. [< Latin *abstractum* drawn away < *abs-* away + *trahere* draw] **—ab stract′er, ab strac′tor,** *n.* **—ab′stract ly,** *adv.* **—ab′stract ness,** *n.*

ab stract ed (ab strak′tid), *adj.* absent-minded; preoccupied. **—ab stract′ed ly,** *adv.* **—ab stract′ed ness,** *n.*

ab strac tion (ab strak′shən), *n.* 1 an abstract idea, concept, or term: *Whiteness, bravery, and length are abstractions. A line that has no width is only an abstraction.* 2 formation of an abstract idea or concept. 3 a taking away; removal: *the abstraction of iron from ore.* 4 a being lost in thought; absentmindedness. 5 work of abstract art.

ab strac tion ism (ab strak′shə niz′əm), *n.* 1 theory or principles of abstract art. 2 art or practice of making abstractions, especially in art.

ab strac tion ist (ab strak′shə nist), *n.* artist who produces works of abstract art.

ab struse (ab strüs′), *adj.* hard to understand; difficult; recondite. [< Latin *abstrusum* concealed < *abs-* away + *trudere* to thrust] **—ab struse′ly,** *adv.* **—ab struse′ness,** *n.*

ab surd (ab sėrd′, ab zėrd′), *adj.* plainly not true, logical, or sensible; ridiculous. See **ridiculous** for synonym study. [< Latin *absurdus* out of tune, senseless] **—ab surd′ly,** *adv.* **—ab surd′ness,** *n.*

ab surd ist (ab sėr′dist, ab zėr′dist), *n.* playwright who stresses the absurd or irrational aspects of life in his plays. *—adj.* of such a playwright or his plays.

ab surd i ty (ab sėr′də tē, ab zėr′də tē), *n., pl.* **-ties.** 1 absurd quality or condition; folly; nonsense. 2 something absurd.

a bun dance (ə bun′dəns), *n.* 1 an overflowing quantity or amount; great plenty; profusion. 2 plentiful supply of money and possessions; affluence; wealth.

a bun dant (ə bun′dənt), *adj.* 1 existing in great or overflowing quantity; very plentiful; profuse: *an abundant supply of food.* 2 well supplied or rich *(in);* abounding: *a river abundant in salmon.* [< Latin *abundantem* overflowing < *ab-* off + *undare* rise in waves] **—a bun′dant ly,** *adv.*

abundant number, a whole number whose divisors have a sum greater than twice this number. The number 18 is an abundant number because the sum of its divisors (18, 9, 6, 3, 2, 1) is greater than 2 × 18.

a buse (*v.* ə byüz′; *n.* ə byüs′), *v.,* **a bused, a bus ing,** *n.* *—v.t.* 1 use wrongly; make improper use of; misuse: *to abuse a privilege.* 2 treat roughly or cruelly; mistreat: *to abuse a dog by beating it.* 3 use harsh and insulting language about or to; revile: *The candidates abused each other.* *—n.* 1 a wrong or improper use; misuse: *an abuse of civil rights.* 2 rough or cruel treatment: *abuse of a helpless prisoner.* 3 a bad practice or custom: *Slavery is an abuse.* 4 harsh and insulting language. [< Old French *abuser* < Latin *abusum* misused < *ab-* away + *uti* to use] **—a bus′er,** *n.*

a bu sive (ə byü′siv, ə byü′ziv), *adj.* 1 using harsh and insulting language; containing abuse; reviling. 2 treating roughly or cruelly. **—a bu′sive ly,** *adv.* **—a bu′sive ness,** *n.*

a but (ə but′), *v.,* **a but ted, a but ting.** *—v.i.* touch at one end or edge; border: *Our property abuts on the street. The shed abuts against the stone wall.* *—v.t.* border on; adjoin: *A shed abuts the barn.* [< Old French *abouter* join end to end < *a-* to + *bout* end] **—a but′ter,** *n.*

abutment (def. 1) These abutments support the arches and turn aside strong currents that might weaken the structure.

a but ment (ə but′mənt), *n.* 1 a support for an arch or bridge. 2 an abutting.

a bysm (ə biz′əm), *n.* abyss.

a bys mal (ə biz′məl), *adj.* 1 too deep or great to be measured; bottomless: *abysmal ignorance.* 2 of the lowest depths of the ocean. 3 INFORMAL. extremely bad; of very low quality. **—a bys′mal ly,** *adv.*

a byss (ə bis′), *n.* 1 a bottomless or very great depth; chasm. 2 anything too deep or great to be measured; lowest depth. 3 the chaos before the Creation. [< Greek *abyssos* < *a-* without + *byssos* bottom]

a byss al (ə bis′əl), *adj.* 1 of or inhabiting the depths of the ocean to which light does not penetrate. 2 unfathomable.

Ab ys sin i a (ab′ə sin′ē ə), *n.* Ethiopia. **—Ab′ys sin′i an,** *adj., n.*

Abyssinian cat, any of a breed of medium-sized cats having a long, tapering tail and short, silky hair with dark-colored tips.

ac-, *prefix.* form of **ad-** before *c, k,* and *q,* as in *accede, acknowledge, acquaint.*

Ac, 1 actinium. 2 alto-cumulus.

a.c., A.C., or **a-c,** alternating current.

a ca cia (ə kā′shə), *n.* 1 any of a genus of trees or shrubs of the pea family, having finely divided leaves and growing in tropical or warm regions. Acacias are sometimes called mimosas. Certain species yield gum arabic. 2 a locust tree of North America. [< Latin < Greek *akakia*]

acad., 1 academic. 2 academy.

ac a deme (ak′ə dēm′, ak′ə dēm′), *n.* 1 academy. 2 the world of scholars; academic life.

ac a de mi a (ak′ə dē′mē ə), *n.* academe.

ac a dem ic (ak′ə dem′ik), *adj.* 1 of or having to do with schools, colleges, universities, and their studies; scholastic: *the academic year.* 2 concerned with general education, especially classical and literary studies, rather than commercial, technical, or professional education: *History and French are academic subjects.* 3 theoretical; not practical; speculative: *"Which came first, the chicken or the egg?" is an academic question.* 4 following fixed rules and traditions; formal; conventional: *academic verse.* *—n.* 1 a college student or teacher. 2 academician. **—ac′a dem′i cal ly,** *adv.*

ac a dem i cal (ak′ə dem′ə kəl), *adj.* academic.

academic freedom, 1 freedom of a teacher or student to investigate and discuss controversial issues and problems without fear of interference or loss of standing. 2 freedom of an educational institution to decide the subjects it will teach and how it will teach them.

a cad e mi cian (ə kad′ə mish′ən, ak′ə də mish′ən), *n.* member of a society for encouraging literature, science, or art.

ac a dem i cism (ak′ə dem′ə siz′əm), *n.* conformity to convention in art, literature, or music; formalism.

a cad e mism (ə kad′ə miz′əm), *n.* academicism.

a cad e my (ə kad′ə mē), *n., pl.* **-mies.** 1 place for instruction. 2 a private high school. 3 school for instruction in some special subject: *a military academy.* 4 group of authors, scholars, scientists, or artists, organized to encourage literature, science, or art. [< Latin *academia* < Greek *Akademeia,* the grove near ancient Athens where Plato taught]

A ca di a (ə kā′dē ə), *n.* region in SE Canada. It was a French colony from 1604 until 1713, when it was ceded to Great Britain. Acadia included what is now Nova Scotia and New Brunswick.

A ca di an (ə kā′dē ən), *n.* 1 native or inhabitant of Acadia. 2 descendant of the Acadians who moved to Louisiana; Cajun. *—adj.* of Acadia or the Acadians.

hat, āge, fär; let, ēqual, tėrm;
it, īce; hot, ōpen, ôrder;
oil, out; cup, pu̇t, rüle;
ch, child; ng, long; sh, she;
th, thin; ᴛʜ, then; zh, measure;

ə represents *a* in about, *e* in taken, *i* in pencil, *o* in lemon, *u* in circus.

< = from, derived from, taken from.

acanthus (def. 1) leaf of a plant — acanthus (def. 2) architectural ornament

a can thus (ə kan′thəs), *n., pl.* **-thus es, -thi** (-thī). 1 any of a family of prickly plants with large, toothed leaves, native to Mediterranean regions. 2 an architectural ornament imitating these leaves. [< Latin < Greek *akanthos*]

a cap pel la or **a ca pel la** (ä′ kə pel′ə), (in music) without instrumental accompaniment. [< Italian *a cappella* in chapel style]

A ca pul co (ä′kə pu̇l′kō), *n.* resort and port in SW Mexico, on the Pacific Ocean. 235,000.

acc., 1 account. 2 accusative.

ac cede (ak sēd′), *v.i.,* **-ced ed, -ced ing.** 1 give in; agree; consent *(to): Please accede to my request.* 2 become a party *(to): Our government acceded to the treaty.* 3 come, attain, or succeed (*to* an office or dignity): *When the king died, his eldest son acceded to the throne.* [< Latin *accedere* < *ad-* to + *cedere* move, go]

accel., accelerando.

ac cel e ran do (ak sel′ə rän′dō), *adv., adj.* (in music) gradually increasing in speed. [< Italian]

ac cel e rate (ak sel′ə rāt′), *v.,* **-rat ed, -rat ing.** *—v.t.* 1 cause (anything in motion or process) to go or move faster; speed up: *accelerate a train.* 2 cause to happen sooner; hasten: *Rest often accelerates a person's recovery from sickness.* 3 change the speed or velocity of (a moving object). *—v.i.* 1 become or go faster: *accelerate in one's studies.* 2 change in velocity. [< Latin *acceleratum* hastened < *ad-* to + *celer* swift]

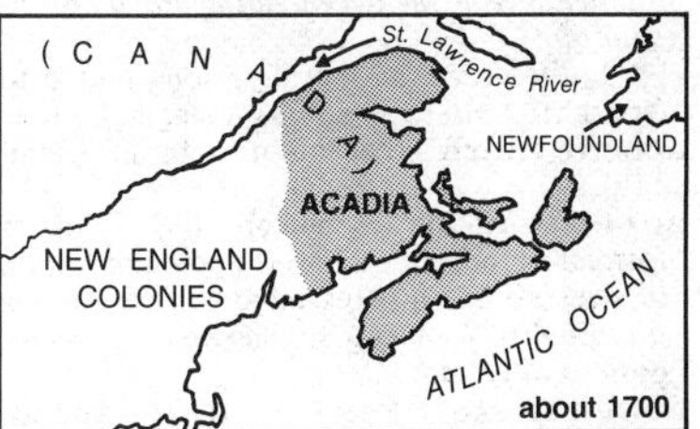

ac cel e ra tion (ak sel′ə rā′shən), *n.* 1 act or process of accelerating. 2 condition of being accelerated; increased speed. 3 change in velocity, either a gradual increase (**positive acceleration**) or a gradual decrease

(negative acceleration). 4 rate of change in the velocity of a moving body.

acceleration of gravity, the rate of change in velocity of a freely falling body, caused by the force of gravity. The rate varies slightly with changes in latitude and altitude. At sea level it is approximately 32 feet per second in each second of the fall of the body.

ac cel e ra tive (ak sel′ə rā′tiv), *adj.* tending to accelerate; quickening.

ac cel e ra tor (ak sel′ə rā′tər), *n.* 1 means of increasing speed. 2 pedal or lever that controls the speed of the engine of a motor vehicle by regulating the flow of fuel to it. 3 particle accelerator. 4 catalyst (def. 1).

ac cel e rom e ter (ak sel′ə rom′ə tər), *n.* instrument for measuring the acceleration of an aircraft, a rocket, etc.

ac cent (*n.* ak′sent; *v.* ak′sent, ak sent′), *n.* 1 special force or emphasis given to a syllable or word in pronouncing it, as by a change of pitch or by stress: *In "letter," the accent is on the first syllable.* 2 mark (′) used to indicate stress in pronunciation, as in *to day* (tə dā′). In this dictionary we use (′) to show a primary or stronger accent and (′) to show a secondary or weaker accent, as in *ac cel e ra tor* (ak sel′ə rā′tər). 3 a characteristic manner of pronunciation heard in a particular section or locality of a country, or in the speech of a person speaking a language not his own: *a Southern accent, a foreign accent.* 4 **accents,** *pl.* tone of voice: *speak in tender accents.* 5 a distinguishing mark or quality: *The accent of humor characterizes his writings.* 6 stress; emphasis: *The manager of the store placed considerable accent on good service to her customers.* 7 mark used to indicate syllabic pitch, quality of vowel sound, etc. The acute (´), grave (`), and circumflex (ˆ) accents are used in Greek, and in French words such as *blasé, à la carte,* and *tête-à-tête.* 8 emphasis on certain words or syllables in a line of poetry to give them rhythm. In "The stag at eve had drunk his fill," the accents are on *stag, eve, drunk,* and *fill.* 9 mark at the right of a number indicating minutes of a degree, two such marks indicating seconds. 20° 10′ 30″ is read 20 degrees, 10 minutes, 30 seconds. 10 mark at the right of a number to indicate feet, two such marks indicating inches. 3′6″ is read three feet six inches. 11 in music: **a** emphasis on certain notes or chords. **b** symbol indicating this. —*v.t.* 1 pronounce or mark with an accent: *Is "acceptable" accented on the first or second syllable?* 2 emphasize; accentuate: *Throughout her speech she accented the gravity of the situation.*
[< Latin *accentus,* literally, song added to (speech) < *ad-* to + *cantus* a singing]

accent mark, accent (n. defs. 2, 7, and 11b).

ac cen tu al (ak sen′chü əl), *adj.* 1 of or formed by accent. 2 based upon alternation of stressed and unstressed syllables: *Almost all English poetry is accentual.* **—ac cen′tu al ly,** *adv.*

ac cen tu ate (ak sen′chü āt), *v.t.,* **-at ed, -at ing.** 1 call special attention to; emphasize: *Her white dress accentuated her sunburn.* 2 pronounce with an accent. 3 mark with an accent. **—ac cen′tu a′tion,** *n.*

ac cept (ak sept′), *v.t.* 1 willingly take or receive (something offered or given); consent to take: *She accepted my gift gratefully.* See **receive** for synonym study. 2 agree to; consent to: *accept a proposal.* 3 take as true and satisfactory; believe; acknowledge: *accept an excuse.* 4 receive with favor; approve: *The design for the new car was not accepted by the public.* 5 undertake as a responsibility; assume: *accept a position as a cashier.* 6 sign and agree to pay: *accept a promissory note.* 7 receive (a committee report) as satisfactory. —*v.i.* say yes to an invitation, offer, etc.: *She asked me to go with her and I accepted.* [< Latin *acceptare* < *ad-* to + *capere* take] **—ac cept′er, ac cep′tor,** *n.*

➤ **Accept** and **except** are often confused because they are similar in sound. *Accept,* always a verb, means "receive": *He accepted the gift.* As a verb, *except* means either "omit" or "exclude": *We can call his career brilliant if we except that one serious blunder.* As a preposition, *except* means "but": *Everyone except John went home.*

ac cept a bil i ty (ak sep′tə bil′ə tē), *n.* acceptable quality.

ac cept a ble (ak sep′tə bəl), *adj.* 1 likely to be well received; agreeable; welcome. 2 good enough but not outstanding; satisfactory; passable: *an acceptable performance.* **—ac cept′a ble ness,** *n.* **—ac cept′a bly,** *adv.*

ac cept ance (ak sep′təns), *n.* 1 act or fact of taking something offered or given. 2 favorable reception; approval. 3 belief; assent. 4 a promise or signed agreement to pay a draft or bill of exchange when it is due. 5 the draft or bill of exchange itself.

ac cep ta tion (ak′sep tā′shən), *n.* 1 the usual or generally accepted meaning of a word, phrase, etc. 2 acceptance.

ac cess (ak′ses), *n.* 1 right to approach, enter, or use; admittance: *All students have access to the library during the afternoon.* 2 approach to places, persons, or things; accessibility: *Access to mountain towns is often difficult because of poor roads. Have you access to people who can help you get work?* 3 way or means of approach; entrance: *A ladder provided the only access to the attic.* 4 an attack (of disease). 5 outburst (of anger, grief, etc.). 6 increase; accession. [< Latin *accessum* < *accedere.* See ACCEDE.]

ac ces sar y (ak ses′ər ē), *n., pl.* **-sar ies,** *adj.* (in law) accessory.

ac ces si bil i ty (ak ses′ə bil′ə tē), *n.* condition of being accessible.

ac ces si ble (ak ses′ə bəl), *adj.* 1 easy to reach, enter, or use; convenient or attainable: *A telephone should be put where it will be accessible.* 2 that can be entered or reached; approachable: *This rocky island is accessible only by helicopter.* 3 capable of being influenced; susceptible *(to): An open-minded person is accessible to reason.* 4 that can be obtained; available: *Not many facts about the case were accessible.* **—ac ces′si ble ness,** *n.* **—ac ces′si bly,** *adv.*

ac ces sion (ak sesh′ən), *n.* 1 act of attaining to a right, office, etc.; attainment: *the prince's accession to the throne.* 2 increase; addition: *The accession of forty new pupils overcrowded the school.* 3 thing added: *accessions to the library.* 4 agreement; assent: *We got her accession to the plan.* 5 approach; access. —*v.t.* record (additions to a library) by entering the titles and authors in a file, list, or register.

ac ces sion al (ak sesh′ə nəl), *adj.* of or due to accession; additional.

ac ces sor y (ak ses′ər ē), *n., pl.* **-sor ies,** *adj.* —*n.* 1 subordinate part or detail; adjunct. 2 Often, **accessories,** *pl.* nonessential but usually desirable additional clothing, equipment, etc. 3 (in law) a person who knowingly helps an offender against the law and thus shares his guilt, although not present at the time or place of violation. An **accessory before the fact** encourages an offender to break the law. An **accessory after the fact** hides the offender, helps him to escape, or fails to report the offense. —*adj.* 1 added; extra; additional. 2 helping in an offense against the law. Also, (in law) **accessary. —ac ces′sor i ly,** *adv.*

accessory fruit, any fruit having conspicuous fleshy parts surrounding an ovary or ovaries, as an apple or strawberry.

ac ci dence (ak′sə dəns), *n.* the part of grammar dealing with those changes in words that show case, number, tense, etc.

ac ci dent (ak′sə dənt), *n.* 1 an undesirable or unfortunate occurrence; something that happens by chance and results in some loss, damage, or death; mishap: *an automobile accident.* 2 any unexpected or unintentional happening: *Their meeting was an accident.* 3 **by accident,** by chance; not on purpose: *We met by accident.* 4 a nonessential quality. [< Latin *accidentem* happening, befalling < *ad-* to + *cadere* to fall]

ac ci den tal (ak′sə den′tl), *adj.* 1 happening by accident; not intended or expected: *an accidental meeting, an accidental death by drowning.* 2 nonessential; incidental: *Songs are essential to musical comedy, but accidental to Shakespeare's plays.* 3 (in music) of or having to do with an accidental. —*n.* (in music) sign used to show a change of pitch; a flat (♭), a sharp (♯), or a natural (♮) after the key signature and before the note to be changed. **—ac′ci den′tal ly,** *adv.* **—ac′ci den′tal ness,** *n.*

ac ci dent-prone (ak′sə dənt prōn′), *adj.* tending to have accidents. **—ac′ci dent-prone′ness,** *n.*

ac claim (ə klām′), *v.t.* 1 welcome with shouts or other signs of approval; praise highly; applaud: *The crowd acclaimed the winning team.* 2 proclaim or announce with approval: *The newspapers acclaimed the results of the election.* —*n.* a shout or show of approval; approval; applause. [< Latin *acclamare* < *ad-* to + *clamare* cry out] **—ac claim′er,** *n.*

ac cla ma tion (ak′lə mā′shən), *n.* 1 shout of welcome or show of approval by a crowd; applause. 2 **by acclamation,** with an overwhelming oral vote of approval in which the votes are not counted: *elected by acclamation.*

ac cli mate (ə klī′mit, ak′lə māt), *v.t., v.i.,* **-mat ed, -mat ing.** accustom or become accustomed to a new climate, surroundings, or conditions. **—ac cli ma tion** (ak′lə mā′shən), *n.*

ac cli ma tize (ə klī′mə tīz), *v.t., v.i.,* **-tized, -tiz ing.** acclimate. **—ac cli′ma ti za′tion,** *n.*

ac cliv i ty (ə kliv′ə tē), *n., pl.* **-ties.** an upward slope of ground; ascent. [< Latin *acclivitatem* < *acclivis* ascending < *ad-* toward + *clivus* a slope]

ac co lade (ak′ə lād), *n.* 1 recognition of merit; praise in recognition of an accomplishment; award. 2 a tap on the shoulder with the flat side of a sword given in making a person

hat, āge, fär; let, ēqual, tėrm;
it, īce; hot, ōpen, ôrder;
oil, out; cup, pu̇t, rüle;
ch, child; ng, long; sh, she;
th, thin; ᴛʜ, then; zh, measure;

ə represents *a* in about, *e* in taken, *i* in pencil, *o* in lemon, *u* in circus.

< = from, derived from, taken from.

a knight. Formerly an embrace or kiss was given instead. [< French, literally, an embrace (about the neck) < Latin *ad-* to + *collum* neck]

ac com mo date (ə kom′ə dāt), *v.*, **-dat ed, -dat ing.** —*v.t.* 1 have room for; hold comfortably: *This airplane is large enough to accommodate 220 passengers.* See **contain** for synonym study. 2 help out; oblige: *I could not accommodate them with a loan.* 3 supply with a place to sleep or live for a time, and sometimes with food as well: *Tourists are accommodated here.* 4 provide with a loan of money. 5 make fit; make suitable; adjust: *accommodate oneself to changed circumstances.* See **adjust** for synonym study. 6 bring to harmony or agreement; reconcile: *accommodate different points of view.* —*v.i.* 1 become adjusted; be adapted. 2 settle differences; agree. [< Latin *accommodatum* made fit < *ad-* to + *commodus* fit, suitable]

ac com mo dat ing (ə kom′ə dā′ting), *adj.* willing to help; obliging. **—ac com′mo dat′ing ly,** *adv.*

ac com mo da tion (ə kom′ə dā′shən), *n.* 1 anything that supplies a want or gives aid; help, favor, or convenience: *It will be an accommodation to me if you will meet me tomorrow instead of today.* 2 **accommodations,** *pl.* **a** lodging and sometimes food as well. **b** a reserved seat, berth, or room on a train, airplane, bus, or ship. 3 willingness to help out. 4 loan. 5 a fitting or being fitted to a purpose or situation; adjustment; adaptation. 6 the automatic adjustment of the focal length of the lens of the eye to see objects at varying distances. 7 settlement of differences; reconciliation; compromise.

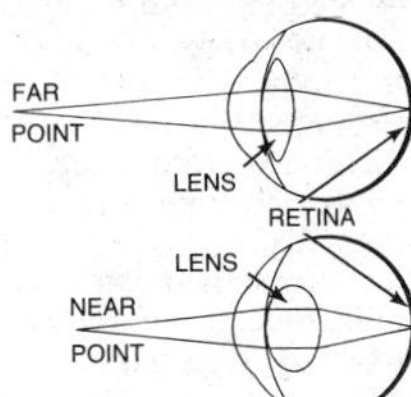

accommodation (def. 6) in a human eye. The eye muscles change the thickness of the eye lens to adjust the focus of near or far points in an image on the retina.

ac com pa ni ment (ə kum′pə nē mənt), *n.* 1 anything that accompanies something else. 2 (in music) a subsidiary instrumental or vocal part to support or enrich a voice or voices or a solo instrument.

ac com pa nist (ə kum′pə nist), *n.* person who plays a musical accompaniment.

ac com pa ny (ə kum′pə nē), *v.t.,* **-nied, -ny ing.** 1 go in company with: *May we accompany you on your walk?* See synonym study below. 2 be or happen in connection with: *A high wind accompanied the rainstorm.* 3 cause to be attended by; supplement *(with): He accompanied his speech with gestures.* 4 play or sing a musical accompaniment for: *She accompanied the singer on the piano.* [< Middle French *accompagner* take as a companion < *a-* to + *compain* companion] **—ac com′pa ni er,** *n.*

Syn. 1 **Accompany, attend, escort** mean to go with someone or something. To **accompany** is to go with as a companion: *He accompanied the other boys to the game.* To **attend** is to go with as a subordinate: *The lady-in-waiting attended the queen at court.* To **escort** is to go with as a sign of special attention or protection: *He escorted a girl to the dance.*

ac com pa ny ist (ə kum′pə nē ist), *n.* accompanist.

ac com plice (ə kom′plis), *n.* person who knowingly aids another in committing a crime or other wrong act: *Without an accomplice to open the door the thief could not have got into the house so easily.* [< earlier *a complice* a confederate < Middle French *complice* < Late Latin *complicem* < Latin *complicare* fold together]

ac com plish (ə kom′plish), *v.t.* 1 succeed in completing; fulfill, perform, or carry out (a promise, plan, etc.): *Did you accomplish your purpose?* See **do**[1] for synonym study. 2 actually do; finish: *accomplish nothing.* 3 complete (a distance): *accomplish a journey.* 4 perfect; polish. [< Old French *acompliss-*, a form of *acomplir* < Latin *ad-* to + *complere* fill up] **—ac com′plish a ble,** *adj.* **—ac com′plish er,** *n.*

ac com plished (ə kom′plisht), *adj.* 1 carried out; completed; done. 2 expert; skilled: *an accomplished surgeon.* 3 skilled in social arts and graces: *an accomplished host.*

ac com plish ment (ə kom′plish mənt), *n.* 1 something accomplished; completed undertaking; achievement. 2 skill in some social art or grace; acquirement. 3 an accomplishing; fulfillment; completion.

ac cord (ə kôrd′), *v.i.* be in harmony; agree; correspond; harmonize *(with): Her report accords with yours.* —*v.t.* 1 give wholeheartedly; grant freely or readily; award: *Accord her praise for her good work.* 2 reconcile. —*n.* 1 agreement; harmony: *All of us are now in accord on the matter.* 2 an informal agreement between nations: *an accord with France.* 3 harmony of colors or of pitch and tone. 4 **of one's own accord,** without being asked; without suggestion from another: *leave of one's own accord.* 5 **with one accord,** with complete agreement; unanimously: *The club members voted with one accord to raise the dues.* [< Old French *acorder* < Latin *ad-* to + *cor, cordis* heart]

ac cord ance (ə kôrd′ns), *n.* agreement; harmony: *in accordance with the rules.*

ac cord ant (ə kôrd′nt), *adj.* in harmony; agreeing. **—ac cord′ant ly,** *adv.*

ac cord ing (ə kôr′ding), *adv.* 1 **according to, a** in agreement with: *She came according to her promise.* **b** in proportion to; on the basis of: *You will be ranked according to the work you do.* **c** on the authority of: *According to this book, cats and tigers are related.* 2 **according as,** to the extent that; in proportion as: *According as you have informed yourself, you will be able to answer the questions.*

ac cord ing ly (ə kôr′ding lē), *adv.* 1 in agreement with what is expected or stated; correspondingly: *These are the rules; you can act accordingly or leave the club.* 2 for this reason; therefore; consequently.

➤ **Accordingly** is most appropriately used in formal writing. A semicolon should be put before a coordinate clause introduced by *accordingly: I was told to speak briefly; accordingly I cut short my remarks.*

ac cor di on (ə kôr′dē ən), *n.* a portable musical wind instrument with a bellows, metallic reeds, and keys, played by pressing the keys and the bellows to force air through the reeds. —*adj.* having folds like the bellows of an accordion: *a skirt with accordion pleats.* [< German *Akkordion*]

ac cor di on ist (ə kôr′dē ə nist), *n.* person who plays an accordion.

ac cost (ə kôst′, ə kost′), *v.t.* approach and speak to first; address: *The stranger accosted me and asked for directions.* [< Middle French *accoster* < Latin *ad-* to + *costa* side, rib]

ac count (ə kount′), *n.* 1 statement telling in detail about an event or thing; description or report: *Give me an account of everything that happened.* 2 statement explaining one's conduct, especially to a superior. 3 statement of reasons, causes, etc., explaining some event: *No satisfactory account has yet been given of these phenomena.* 4 importance or value; worth: *books of little account.* 5 statement of money received and spent. 6 record of business dealings: *Businesses and factories keep accounts.* 7 statement of money due: *settle one's accounts before the end of the year.* 8 charge account. 9 bank account.
call to account, a demand an explanation of (someone). **b** scold; rebuke; reprimand.
give a good account of oneself, conduct oneself well.
on account, as part payment.
on account of, because of.
on any account, under any conditions; for any reason.
on no account, under no conditions; for no reason.
on one's account, for one's sake.
on one's own account, for one's own purposes and at one's own risk.
take account of, a make allowance for; consider. **b** make a note of; note.
take into account, make allowance for; consider.
turn to account, get advantage or profit from.
—*v.i.* 1 give a statement of money received or spent: *The treasurer of our club has to account to the faculty advisor.* 2 **account for, a** tell what has been done with; answer for. **b** explain. **c** cause the death or capture of. —*v.t.* hold to be; consider: *In law, an accused person is accounted innocent until he is proved guilty.*
[< Old French *aconter* count up < *a-* to + *conter* to count]

ac count a bil i ty (ə koun′tə bil′ə tē), *n.* a being accountable; responsibility.

ac count a ble (ə koun′tə bəl), *adj.* 1 liable to be called to account; responsible: *accountable for one's work.* 2 explainable. **—ac count′a ble ness,** *n.* **—ac count′a bly,** *adv.*

ac count an cy (ə koun′tən sē), *n.* work of an accountant; accounting.

ac count ant (ə koun′tənt), *n.* person whose profession is examining or interpreting business accounts and financial records.

ac count ing (ə koun′ting), *n.* 1 system or practice of keeping, analyzing, and interpreting business accounts and financial records. 2 statement of accounts.

ac cou ter (ə kü′tər), *v.t.* furnish with clothing or equipment; equip; outfit. [< Middle French *accoutrer*]

ac cou ter ment (ə kü′tər mənt), *n.* 1 an accoutering. 2 a being accoutered. 3 **accouterments,** *pl.* **a** a soldier's equipment with the exception of his weapons and clothing. **b** clothes; outfit.

ac cou tre (ə kü′tər), *v.t.,* **-tred, -tring.** accouter.

ac cou tre ment (ə kü′tər mənt, ə kü′trə-mənt), *n.* accouterment.

Ac cra (ə krä′), *n.* seaport and capital of Ghana. 634,000. Also, **Akkra.**

ac cred it (ə kred′it), *v.t.* 1 give authority to; authorize: *The president will accredit you as her representative.* 2 send or provide with credentials: *An ambassador is accredited to a foreign country to represent his government there.* 3 recognize as coming up to an official standard: *an accredited high school.* 4 accept as true; believe; trust: *an accredited authority.* 5 **accredit with,** give (a person) credit for (something); regard (a person) as having: *Accredit her with kindness.* 6 consider (a thing) as belonging or due (*to* a person); attribute: *We accredit the invention of the telephone to Bell.* See **credit** for synonym study. **—ac cred′i ta′tion,** *n.*

ac cre tion (ə krē′shən), *n.* 1 a growing together of separate things. 2 an increase in size by natural growth or gradual external addition. 3 something formed or resulting from such growth or additions. 4 thing added; addition. [< Latin *accretionem* < *ad-* to + *crescere* grow]

ac cre tive (ə krē′tiv), *adj.* of or by accretion: *accretive growth.*

ac cru al (ə krü′əl), *n.* 1 an accruing: *Money left in a savings bank increases by the accrual of interest.* 2 amount accrued or accruing.

ac crue (ə krü′), *v.i.,* **-crued, -cru ing.** 1 come as a natural product or result: *Ability to think clearly will accrue to you from good habits of study.* 2 grow or arise as the product of money invested: *accrued interest.* [< Old French *acreüe* an increase < *acreistre* to increase < Latin *accrescere* < *ad-* to + *crescere* grow] **—ac crue′ment,** *n.*

acct., 1 account. 2 accountant.

ac cul tu rate (ə kul′chə rāt′), *v.,* **-rat ed, -rat ing.** —*v.t.* cause (an individual or a group) to adopt the culture or cultural elements of another group: *Schools help to acculturate the children of immigrants.* —*v.i.* become acculturated. **—ac cul′tu ra′tion,** *n.*

ac cu mu late (ə kyü′myə lāt), *v.,* **-lat ed, -lat ing.** —*v.t.* collect little by little; heap up by degrees; amass. See synonym study below. —*v.i.* grow into a heap by degrees; pile up; gather: *Dust had accumulated in the empty house.* [< Latin *accumulatum* heaped up < *ad-* in addition + *cumulus* a heap]

Syn. *v.t.* **Accumulate, amass** mean to collect a large amount. **Accumulate** emphasizes the idea of heaping up, little by little, over a period of time: *Through the years he had accumulated sufficient money to buy a farm when he retired.* **Amass** suggests the idea of gathering a large amount to oneself within a relatively short time: *Before he was forty he had amassed a fortune.*

ac cu mu la tion (ə kyü′myə lā′shən), *n.* 1 material collected; mass. 2 a collecting together; amassing: *the accumulation of knowledge.* 3 growth by continuous addition.

ac cu mu la tive (ə kyü′myə lā′tiv), *adj.* 1 cumulative. 2 acquisitive. **—ac cu′mu la′tive ly,** *adv.* **—ac cu′mu la′tive ness,** *n.*

ac cu mu la tor (ə kyü′myə lā′tər), *n.* 1 person or thing that accumulates. 2 any of various devices that collect, store, or absorb energy. 3 BRITISH. storage battery.

ac cur a cy (ak′yər ə sē), *n.* condition of being without errors or mistakes; precise correctness; exactness.

ac cur ate (ak′yər it), *adj.* 1 without errors or mistakes because of care taken to avoid them; precisely correct; exact: *an accurate report.* See **correct** for synonym study. 2 functioning exactly and without defect: *an accurate watch.* 3 making few or no errors: *an accurate observer.* [< Latin *accuratum* done with care < *ad-* to + *cura* care] **—ac′cur ate ly,** *adv.* **—ac′cur ate ness,** *n.*

ac curs ed (ə kėr′sid, ə kėrst′), *adj.* 1 annoying and troublesome; hateful. 2 under a curse; doomed. **—ac curs ed ly** (ə kėr′sid lē), *adv.* **—ac curs ed ness** (ə kėr′sid nis), *n.*

ac curst (ə kėrst′), *adj.* accursed.

accus., accusative.

ac cu sa tion (ak′yə zā′shən), *n.* 1 charge of wrongdoing. 2 the offense charged. 3 an accusing. 4 a being accused.

ac cu sa tive (ə kyü′zə tiv), *adj.* showing the direct object of a verb or the object of a preposition. —*n.* 1 the accusative case. 2 word in this case. **—ac cu′sa tive ly,** *adv.* ➤ See **dative** for usage note.

ac cu sa to ry (ə kyü′zə tôr′ē, ə kyü′zə-tōr′ē), *adj.* containing an accusation.

ac cuse (ə kyüz′), *v.t.,* **-cused, -cus ing.** 1 charge with an offense or crime; bring a charge of wrongdoing against: *They accused him of stealing.* See **charge** for synonym study. 2 find fault with; blame; censure. [< Latin *accusare* < *ad-* to + *causa* cause, case] **—ac cus′er,** *n.* **—ac cus′ing ly,** *adv.*

ac cused (ə kyüzd′), *n.* **the accused,** the person or persons formally charged with an offense or a crime in a court of law.

ac cus tom (ə kus′təm), *v.t.* make familiar by use or habit; get used; habituate.

ac cus tomed (ə kus′təmd), *adj.* 1 usual; customary. 2 **accustomed to,** used to; in the habit of: *The farmer was accustomed to hard work. She is accustomed to jogging daily.*

ace (ās), *n., adj., v.,* **aced, ac ing.** —*n.* 1 a playing card, domino, or side of a die having one spot. 2 (in tennis, handball, etc.) a point won by a single stroke, especially a serve which the opponent fails to return. 3 an expert. 4 a combat pilot who has shot down five or more enemy planes. 5 **ace in the hole,** INFORMAL. any decisive advantage held in reserve until needed. 6 **within an ace of,** on the very point of. —*adj.* very skilled; expert. —*v.t.* (in tennis, etc.) to score an ace against (an opponent). [< Old French *as* < Latin, smallest unit (of coinage, measure, etc.)]

a cel lu lar (ā sel′yə lər), *adj.* lacking cells; not cellular.

a cerb (ə sėrb′), *adj.* 1 sharp in taste; sour or bitter. 2 harsh in manner; severe: *acerb wit.* [< Latin *acerbus*] **—a cerb′ly,** *adv.*

a cer bi ty (ə sėr′bə tē), *n.* 1 sharpness of taste; sourness or bitterness. 2 harshness of manner; severity.

ac e tab u lum (as′ə tab′yə ləm), *n., pl.* **-lums, -la** (-lə). a cup-shaped socket in the hipbone into which the top part of the thighbone fits. [< Latin]

ac et al de hyde (as′ə tal′də hīd), *n.* a colorless, highly volatile, fragrant substance, used as a source of acetic acid and in the synthesis of many other compounds; aldehyde. *Formula:* CH_3CHO

ac et an i lid (as′ə tan′l id), *n.* acetanilide.

ac et an i lide (as′ə tan′l īd, as′ə tan′l id), *n.* a white, crystalline drug, used to relieve pain and fever. *Formula:* C_8H_9NO

ac e tate (as′ə tāt), *n.* 1 salt or ester of acetic acid. 2 any of a group of synthetic resins or fibers made from cellulose acetate.

a ce tic (ə sē′tik), *adj.* of, producing, or derived from vinegar or acetic acid. [< Latin *acetum* vinegar]

acetic acid, an acrid, pungent, colorless liquid responsible for the characteristic taste and odor of vinegar. It is used as a solvent and in making acetates, in pharmaceuticals, etc. *Formula:* CH_3COOH

a cet i fy (ə set′ə fī, ə sē′tə fī), *v.t., v.i.,* **-fied, -fy ing.** turn into vinegar or acetic acid. **—a cet′i fi ca′tion,** *n.*

ac e tone (as′ə tōn), *n.* a colorless, volatile, flammable liquid, used as a solvent and in making varnishes, pharmaceuticals, etc. *Formula:* CH_3COCH_3

a ce tyl (ə sē′tl), *n.* the univalent radical of acetic acid and its derivatives. *Formula:* CH_3CO-

a ce tyl cho line (ə sē′tl kō′lēn′), *n.* substance produced in nerve tissue, closely associated with the transmission of nerve impulses in the body. *Formula:* $C_7H_{17}O_3N$

a cet y lene (ə set′l ēn′, ə set′l ən), *n.* a colorless gas that burns with a luminous, smoky flame, used for lighting and for preparing other compounds to make synthetic fibers and plastics. Combined with oxygen, it is used in welding metals. *Formula:* C_2H_2

a ce tyl sal i cyl ic acid (ə sē′tl sal′ə-sil′ik), aspirin.

A chae a (ə kē′ə), *n.* region in ancient Greece, in the S part. See **Peloponnesus** for map. Also, **Achaia.**

A chae an (ə kē′ən), *n.* native or inhabitant of Achaea. In Homer, the term *Achaean* is used for any Greek. —*adj.* 1 of Achaea or the Achaeans. 2 having to do with a league of cities formed in southern Greece in 280 B.C. Also, **Achaian.**

A cha ia (ə kā′ə, ə kī′ə), *n.* Achaea.

A cha ian (ə kā′ən, ə kī′ən), *n., adj.* Achaean.

ache (āk), *n., v.,* **ached, ach ing.** —*n.* a continuous pain, usually dull rather than acute: *Muscular aches follow hard exercise.* See **pain** for synonym study. —*v.i.* 1 suffer a dull, continuous pain; be in pain; hurt: *My broken arm aches.* 2 INFORMAL. be eager; wish very much; long; yearn: *During the hot days we ached to go swimming.* [Old English *æce*] **—ach′ing ly,** *adv.*

a chene (ā kēn′), *n.* any small, dry, hard fruit consisting of one seed with a thin outer covering that does not burst open when ripe, such as the sunflower seed. Also, **akene.**

Ach e ron (ak′ə ron′), *n.* in Greek and Roman myths: 1 a river in Hades. 2 the lower world; Hades.

a chieve (ə chēv′), *v.t.,* **a chieved, a chiev ing.** 1 carry out successfully; accomplish; perform: *Did you achieve your purpose?* 2 reach by one's own efforts; get by effort; gain; attain: *achieve high grades in mathematics.* [< Old French *achever* < Latin *ad-* to + *caput* head] **—a chiev′a ble,** *adj.* **—a chiev′er,** *n.*

a chieve ment (ə chēv′mənt), *n.* 1 something achieved or won by exertion; accomplishment; feat: *Martin Luther King, Jr., won the Nobel Prize for his achievements in behalf of civil rights.* 2 act of achieving: *the achievement of victory.*

A chil les (ə kil′ēz), *n.* (in Greek legends) a great Greek warrior of the Trojan War; the hero of Homer's *Iliad.* He was slain by Paris, who pierced his heel, his only vulnerable spot, with an arrow.

Achilles' heel, a weak point.

Achilles' tendon, tendon at the back of the leg that connects the muscles in the calf to the bone of the heel.

a chon dro pla sia (ā′kon′drə plā′zhə), *n.* dwarfism characterized by extreme shortness of limbs.

ach ro mat ic (ak′rə mat′ik), *adj.* 1 refracting white light without breaking it up into the colors of the spectrum: *an achromatic lens.* 2 colorless.

ach y (ā′kē), *adj.* full of aches.

ac id (as′id), *n.* 1 in chemistry: **a** any compound yielding hydrated hydrogen ions when dissolved in water. Such substances turn blue litmus paper red, have a pH value of less than 7, and usually react with a base to form a salt. Hydrochloric acid and sulfuric acid are common acids. **b** any ionic or molecular substance which can give up a proton. **c** any molecule or ion that can attach itself to a pair of electrons from a base, forming a covalent bond. 2 substance with a sour taste like that of vinegar. 3 SLANG. LSD. *—adj.* 1 of acids; having the properties of an acid: *an acid solution.* 2 sharp or biting to the taste; sour. 3 sharp in manner or temper; caustic: *an acid comment.* See **sour** for synonym study. 4 containing a large proportion of silica: *Granite is an acid rock.* [< Latin *acidus* sour] **—ac′id ly,** *adv.* **—ac′id ness,** *n.*

ac id-fast (as′id fast′), *adj.* tenaciously retaining dyes when treated by an acid to remove the dye.

a cid ic (ə sid′ik), *adj.* 1 forming acid. 2 having the properties of an acid: *an acidic solution.* 3 sharp and biting in manner or temper; caustic.

a cid i fy (ə sid′ə fī), *v.t., v.i.,* **-fied, -fy ing.** 1 make or become sour. 2 change into an acid. **—a cid′i fi ca′tion,** *n.* **—a cid′i fi′er,** *n.*

a cid i ty (ə sid′ə tē), *n.* 1 acid quality or condition: *the acidity of vinegar.* 2 degree of acid quality: *the acidity of a soil.* 3 hyperacidity.

ac i do sis (as′ə dō′sis), *n.* a harmful condition in which the blood and tissues are less alkaline than is normal.

acid test, a decisive test.

a cid u late (ə sij′ə lāt), *v.t.,* **-lat ed, -lat ing.** make slightly acid or sour. **—a cid′u la′tion,** *n.*

a cid u lous (ə sij′ə ləs), *adj.* 1 slightly acid or sour. 2 caustic; harsh: *acidulous satire.* **—a cid′u lous ly,** *adv.* **—a cid′u lous ness,** *n.*

ac i nus (as′n əs), *n., pl.* **ac i ni** (as′n ī). one of the small, fleshy berries that make up such compound fruits as the blackberry. [< Latin, berry, grape]

ack-ack (ak′ak′), *n.* INFORMAL. antiaircraft fire. [British radio operator's code word for AA (antiaircraft)]

ac knowl edge (ak nol′ij), *v.t.,* **-edged, -edg ing.** 1 admit to be true; recognize the fact of; concede: *I acknowledged my mistake.* See **admit** for synonym study. 2 recognize the authority or claims of; accept: *We acknowledge the pitcher to be the best player on the baseball team.* 3 make known that one has received or noted (a service, favor, gift, message, etc.): *I acknowledged her letter at once.* 4 recognize or certify as genuine: *acknowledge a deed before a notary public.* [blend of obsolete *acknow* admit and obsolete verb *knowledge* admit] **—ac knowl′edge a ble,** *adj.* **—ac knowl′edged ly,** *adv.* **—ac knowl′edg er,** *n.*

ac knowl edg ment or **ac knowl edge ment** (ak nol′ij mənt), *n.* 1 something given or done to show that one has received a service, favor, gift, message, etc.: *A receipt is an acknowledgment that a bill has been paid.* 2 act of admitting the existence or truth of anything; admission: *acknowledgment of a mistake.* 3 a making known that one has received or noted a service, favor, gift, message, etc.: *acknowledgment of a friend's letter.* 4 recognition of authority, claims, or merit; acceptance. 5 an official certificate in legal form.

ac me (ak′mē), *n.* the highest point; culmination. [< Greek *akmē* point]

ac ne (ak′nē), *n.* a chronic skin disease in which the oil glands in the skin become clogged and inflamed, often causing pimples, especially on the face. [< Late Greek *aknē*]

ac o lyte (ak′ə līt), *n.* 1 person who helps a priest, deacon, etc., during certain religious services: *The acolyte lit the candles on the altar.* 2 attendant or assistant. [< Medieval Latin *acolytus*]

A con ca gua (ä′kông kä′gwə), *n.* mountain in the Andes, in W Argentina near Chile, the highest mountain in the Western Hemisphere. 22,834 ft.

ac o nite (ak′ə nīt), *n.* 1 any of a genus of poisonous plants with blue, purple, or yellow hood-shaped flowers. Monkshood and wolf's-bane are two species. 2 a poisonous drug used as a sedative, prepared from the roots of monkshood. [< Latin *aconitum*]

a corn (ā′kôrn, ā′kərn), *n.* the nut of the oak tree. [Old English *æcern*]

a cous tic (ə kü′stik), *adj.* 1 having to do with the sense or the organs of hearing. 2 having to do with the science of sound. 3 directed, controlled, or actuated by sound waves: *an acoustic mine.* 4 designed to absorb or reduce noise: *a ceiling of acoustic tile.* [< Greek *akoustikos* < *akouein* hear] **—a cous′ti cal ly,** *adv.*

a cous ti cal (ə kü′stə kəl), *adj.* having to do with the science of sound.

ac ous ti cian (ak′ü stish′ən), *n.* an expert in acoustics.

a cous tics (ə kü′stiks), *n.* 1 *pl. in form and use.* the structural features of a room, hall, auditorium, etc., that determine how well sounds can be heard in it; acoustic qualities. 2 *pl. in form, sing. in use.* the science of sound.

ac quaint (ə kwānt′), *v.t.* 1 make aware; inform: *Let me acquaint you with your new duties.* See **inform** for synonym study. 2 **be acquainted with,** have personal knowledge of; know: *I am not acquainted with them.* 3 **become acquainted with,** get to know: *We became acquainted with our new neighbors.* [< Old French *acointer,* ultimately < Latin *ad-* to + *cognoscere* know]

hat, āge, fär; let, ēqual, tėrm;
it, īce; hot, ōpen, ôrder;
oil, out; cup, pu̇t, rüle;
ch, child; ng, long; sh, she;
th, thin; ᴛʜ, then; zh, measure;

ə represents *a* in about, *e* in taken, *i* in pencil, *o* in lemon, *u* in circus.

< = from, derived from, taken from.

ac quaint ance (ə kwān′təns), *n.* 1 person whom one knows slightly; person known to one, but not a close friend. 2 knowledge of persons or things gained from experience with them: *I have some acquaintance with French, but I do not know it well.* 3 **make the acquaintance of,** get to know: *My parents soon made the acquaintance of my new teacher.*

ac quaint ance ship (ə kwān′təns ship), *n.* 1 relation between acquaintances. 2 personal knowledge; acquaintance.

ac qui esce (ak′wē es′), *v.i.,* **-esced, -esc ing.** give consent by keeping silent or by not making objections; accept (the conclusions or arrangements of others); accede: *acquiesce in a decision.* [< Latin *acquiescere* < *ad-* to + *quies* rest, quiet]

ac qui es cence (ak′wē es′ns), *n.* consent given without making objections; assent.

ac qui es cent (ak′wē es′nt), *adj.* inclined to consent or agree quietly; acquiescing. **—ac′qui es′cent ly,** *adv.*

ac quire (ə kwīr′), *v.t.,* **-quired, -quir ing.** 1 get by one's own efforts or actions: *acquire an education.* See **get** for synonym study. 2 come into the possession of: *acquire land.* [< Latin *acquirere* < *ad-* to + *quaerere* seek] **—ac quir′a ble,** *adj.* **—ac quir′er,** *n.*

acquired character or **acquired characteristic,** change of structure or function in a plant or animal as a result of use or disuse or in response to the environment. An acquired character can not be inherited.

ac quire ment (ə kwīr′mənt), *n.* 1 act of acquiring. 2 something acquired; attainment; accomplishment: *She has remarkable musical acquirements for a girl of her age.*

ac qui si tion (ak′wə zish′ən), *n.* 1 act of acquiring: *the acquisition of skill by practicing.* 2 something acquired or gained; addition to an existing group. [< Latin *acquisitionem* < *acquirere.* See ACQUIRE.]

ac quis i tive (ə kwiz′ə tiv), *adj.* fond of acquiring (money, ideas, etc.); likely to get and keep. **—ac quis′i tive ly,** *adv.* **—ac quis′i tive ness,** *n.*

ac quit (ə kwit′), *v.t.,* **-quit ted, -quit ting.** 1 declare not guilty; set free after considering evidence; exonerate: *The jury acquitted the accused man.* 2 release from (a duty, obligation, etc.). 3 **acquit oneself,** do one's part; behave: *You acquitted yourself well in the debate.* [< Old French *aquiter* < *a-* to + *quite* free] **—ac quit′ter,** *n.*

ac quit tal (ə kwit′l), *n.* an acquitting; discharge; release.

ac quit tance (ə kwit′ns), *n.* a written release from a debt or obligation.

a cre (ā′kər), *n.* 1 unit of area equal to 160 square rods or 43,560 square feet. See **measure** for table. 2 **acres,** *pl.* **a** lands; property. **b** large quantities. [Old English *æcer* field]

a cre age (ā′kər ij), *n.* 1 number of acres. 2 piece of land sold by the acre.

a cre-foot (ā′kər fu̇t′), *n., pl.* **-feet.** a measure of the volume of water in irrigation, equal to an acre of water 1 foot deep; 43,560 cubic feet.

ac rid (ak′rid), *adj.* 1 sharp, bitter, or stinging to the mouth, eyes, skin, or nose. 2 irritating in manner; acrimonious. [< Latin *acer, acris* sharp] **—ac′rid ly,** *adv.* **—ac′rid ness,** *n.*

a crid i ty (ə krid′ə tē), *n., pl.* **-ties.** 1 acrid quality. 2 a caustic comment.

Ac ri lan (ak′rə lan), *n.* trademark for an acrylic fiber that resembles wool and resists wrinkling.

ac ri mo ni ous (ak′rə mō′nē əs), *adj.* bitter and irritating in disposition or manner; caustic. **—ac′ri mo′ni ous ly,** *adv.* **—ac′ri mo′ni ous ness,** *n.*

ac ri mo ny (ak′rə mō′nē), *n.* biting sharpness of temper; bitterness of language or manner; acerbity. [< Latin *acrimonia* < *acer, acris* sharp]

ac ro bat (ak′rə bat), *n.* 1 person highly skilled in gymnastic feats, such as swinging on a trapeze, walking a tightrope, etc. 2 a daring performer. [< French *acrobate* < Greek *akrobatos* walking on tiptoe < *akros* tip + *-batos* going]

ac ro bat ic (ak′rə bat′ik), *adj.* 1 of an acrobat. 2 like an acrobat's. **—ac′ro bat′i cal ly,** *adv.*

ac ro bat ics (ak′rə bat′iks), *n. pl. in form, sometimes sing. in use.* 1 tricks or performances of an acrobat; gymnastic feats. 2 feats like those of an acrobat: *a monkey's acrobatics, the acrobatics of stunt flying.*

ac ro gen (ak′rə jən), *n.* plant growing only at the apex, such as ferns and mosses.

ac ro me gal ic (ak′rō mə gal′ik), *adj.* 1 of acromegaly. 2 having acromegaly.

ac ro meg a ly (ak′rō meg′ə lē), *n.* a chronic condition in which the bones of the face, hands, and feet become progressively and permanently enlarged, caused by abnormal activity of the pituitary gland.

ac ro nym (ak′rə nim), *n.* word formed from the first letters or syllables of other words, such as UNESCO (United Nations Educational, Scientific, and Cultural Organization). [< Greek *akros* tip + *onyma* name]

ac ro pho bi a (ak′rə fō′bē ə), *n.* an abnormal fear of being in high places.

a crop o lis (ə krop′ə lis), *n.* 1 the high, fortified part or citadel of an ancient Greek city. 2 **the Acropolis,** the citadel of Athens on which the Parthenon was built. [< Greek *akropolis* < *akros* highest part + *polis* city]

a cross (ə krôs′, ə kros′), *prep.* 1 from one side to the other of; over: *a bridge laid across a river.* 2 on the other side of; beyond: *across the sea.* 3 **come across** or **run across,** meet or fall in with; find: *We come across hard words in many books.* —*adv.* 1 from one side to the other: *The pool is twenty feet across.* 2 on or to the other side: *When are you going across? Let me know when you are across.* 3 crossed; crosswise: *with arms across.*

a cross-the-board (ə krôs′ᴛʜə bôrd′, ə krôs′ᴛʜə bōrd′; ə kros′ᴛʜə bôrd′, ə kros′ᴛʜə bōrd′), *adj.* U.S. applying to all members of a group, industry, etc.; general.

North
East
West
South

acrostic (def. 1) with first letters forming the word "news" in a column

a cros tic (ə krô′stik, ə kros′tik), *n.* 1 composition in verse or arrangement of words in which the first, last, or certain other letters in each line, taken in order, spell a word or phrase. 2 acronym. 3 puzzle to be solved by discovering acrostics from clues. —*adj.* of or like an acrostic. [< Greek *akrostichis* < *akros* tip + *stichos* line] **—a cros′ti cal ly,** *adv.*

ac ryl ate resin (ak′rə lāt), acrylic resin.

a cryl ic fiber (ə kril′ik), any of various synthetic textile fibers produced from acrylonitrile. Acrilan and Orlon are acrylic fibers.

acrylic resin, any of various tough, glass-like plastics used to make instrument panels, dental plates, etc.; acrylate resin.

a cry lo ni trile (ak′rə lō nī′trəl), *n.* a colorless, flammable liquid, used in making synthetic rubber, plastics, and acrylic fibers. *Formula:* C_3H_3N

act (akt), *n.* 1 something done; deed: *an act of kindness.* See synonym study below. 2 process of doing: *in the act of stealing.* 3 a main division of a play or opera: *a play with three acts.* 4 one of several performances on a program: *the comedian's act.* 5 decision of a legislature; law; statute: *the Social Security Act.* 6 INFORMAL. a display of affected or pretended behavior: *She's not really angry; she's just putting on an act.*
—*v.i.* 1 do something: *act at once.* 2 have effect: *The medicine failed to act.* 3 behave: *She acted bad in school. He acts older than he is.* 4 perform on the stage, in motion pictures, on television, or over the radio; play a part. 5 **act for** or **act as,** take the place of; do the work of. 6 **act on** or **act upon, a** follow; obey: *I will act on your suggestion.* **b** have an effect or influence on: *Yeast acted on the dough and made it rise.* 7 **act up,** INFORMAL. **a** behave badly. **b** play tricks; make mischief: *act up on Halloween.* —*v.t.* 1 behave like: *Most people act the fool now and then.* 2 play (a role); play the part of: *She is acting Lady Macbeth.*
[< Latin *actus* a doing, and *actum* (thing) done; both < *agere* do] **—act′a ble,** *adj.*

Syn. *n.* 1 **Act, action** mean a thing done. **Act** applies especially to a single thing done by a single effort in an instant: *Slapping his face was a childish act.* **Action** may apply to more than one act and therefore often suggests continued or repeated effort over a period of time: *Covering the retreat of his platoon was the action for which he was decorated.*

act a bil i ty (ak′tə bil′ə tē), *n.* actable quality or condition.

ACTH, 1 hormone of the pituitary gland which stimulates the cortex of the adrenal gland to produce other hormones. 2 this hormone obtained from animals, used in treating arthritis, rheumatic fever, etc.; corticotropin. [< *a(dreno)-c(ortico)-t(ropic) h(ormone)*]

ac tin (ak′tən), *n.* a protein component of muscle cells that acts with another protein, myosin, in muscle contraction.

act ing (ak′ting), *adj.* temporarily taking another's place and doing his duties; substitute: *an acting principal.* —*n.* art of playing a part or performing on the stage, in motion pictures, on television, or over the radio.

ac tin ic (ak tin′ik), *adj.* producing chemical changes by radiation. [< Greek *aktis, aktinos* ray]

actinic rays, the visible and invisible rays of radiant energy, as from the sun, that produce chemical changes. Actinic rays include green, blue, violet, and ultraviolet rays, X rays, gamma rays, and infrared radiation.

ac ti nide (ak′tə nīd), *n.* any of the series of heavy, radioactive metallic elements belonging to the series with atomic numbers 89 through 103.

ac tin ism (ak′tə niz′əm), *n.* property in radiant energy that produces chemical changes.

ac tin i um (ak tin′ē əm), *n.* a radioactive chemical element somewhat like radium, found in pitchblende after uranium has been extracted. *Symbol:* Ac; *atomic number* 89. See pages 326 and 327 for table.

ac ti nom e ter (ak′tə nom′ə tər), *n.* 1 instrument for measuring the degree of actinic action in radiant energy. 2 instrument for measuring photographic exposure.

ac ti no mor phic (ak′tə nə môr′fik), *adj.* having radial symmetry.

ac ti no my cete (ak′tə nō mī′sēt′), *n.* any of a group of bacteria found in soil that are structurally similar to certain fungi. Antibiotics such as streptomycin are derived from some actinomycetes. [< Greek *aktinos* ray + *mykēs* fungus]

ac ti no my cin (ak′tə nō mī′sn), *n.* an antibiotic related to streptomycin, derived from actinomycetes.

ac ti no my co sis (ak′tə nō mī kō′sis), *n.* an infectious disease caused by a parasitic actinomycete. It is characterized by lumpy abscesses about the jaw.

ac tin on (ak′tə non), *n.* a gaseous, radioactive isotope of radon, formed by the decay of actinium. *Symbol:* An; *atomic number* 86; *mass number* 219.

ac tion (ak′shən), *n.* 1 process of acting; doing something: *quick action by the firemen.* 2 initiative shown by physical activity: *a man of action.* 3 something done; act: *a kind action.* See **act** for synonym study. 4 **actions,** *pl.* conduct; behavior: *rude actions.* 5 effect or influence of one thing on another: *the action of wind on a ship's sails.* 6 way of moving or working; movement: *a pulley with an easy action.* 7 the working parts of a machine, instrument, etc. The keys of a piano are part of its action. 8 battle or part of a battle; combat. See **battle** for synonym study. 9 series of events in a story or play. 10 lawsuit. 11 **in action, a** active; taking part. **b** working. 12 **take action, a** begin to do something. **b** start working. **c** start a lawsuit; sue. **—ac′tion less,** *adj.*

ac tion a ble (ak′shə nə bəl), *adj.* giving cause for a lawsuit; justifying a lawsuit. **—ac′tion a bly,** *adv.*

Ac ti um (ak′tē əm, ak′shē əm), *n.* cape in the NW part of ancient Greece. The fleet of Octavian defeated the combined navies of Antony and Cleopatra near Actium in 31 B.C.

ac ti vate (ak′tə vāt), *v.t.,* **-vat ed, -vat ing.** 1 make active; cause to act. 2 make radioactive. 3 make capable of reacting or of speeding up a chemical reaction. 4 purify (sewage) by treating it with air and bacteria. 5 make (charcoal, carbon, etc.) capable of absorbing

hat, āge, fär; let, ēqual, tėrm;
it, īce; hot, ōpen, ôrder;
oil, out; cup, pu̇t, rüle;
ch, child; ng, long; sh, she;
th, thin; ᴛʜ, then; zh, measure;

ə represents *a* in about, *e* in taken, *i* in pencil, *o* in lemon, *u* in circus.

< = from, derived from, taken from.

impurities, especially in the form of gases. **—ac′ti va′tion,** *n.* **—ac′ti va′tor,** *n.*

activation analysis, method of identifying the elements in a substance by analyzing the radiation given off when the substance is bombarded with neutrons.

ac tive (ak′tiv), *adj.* 1 moving or capable of moving rather quickly much of the time; nimble: *as active as a kitten.* 2 showing much or constant action; brisk: *an active market, active trade.* 3 acting; working: *an active volcano, an active poison.* 4 working hard or with energy; busy and energetic: *still active in public affairs at the age of 70.* 5 in action, operation, use, etc.: *an active account.* 6 causing action or change. 7 radioactive. 8 (in grammar) of or having to do with the active voice. *—n.* in grammar: 1 the active voice. 2 a verb form in the active voice. **—ac′tive ly,** *adv.* **—ac′tive ness,** *n.*

active duty, 1 military service with full pay and regular duties. 2 service in the armed forces in time of war.

active immunity, immunity from a disease due to the production of antibodies by the organism.

active satellite, a communications satellite that receives, amplifies, and retransmits microwave signals of television, radio, telephone, etc., sent to a distant part of the world.

active service, active duty.

active voice, (in grammar) the form of the verb that shows that its subject is performing the action which the verb expresses. In "I wrote a letter," *wrote* is in the active voice (the subject is acting).

ac ti vism (ak′tə viz′əm), *n.* policy or practice of furthering one's political or national interests by every available means, including violence, warfare, etc.

ac ti vist (ak′tə vist), *n.* person who practices or supports a policy of activism. *—adj.* of activism.

ac tiv i ty (ak tiv′ə tē), *n., pl.* **-ties.** 1 condition of being active; use of power; movement: *physical activity, mental activity.* 2 action; doing: *the activities of enemy spies.* 3 vigorous action; liveliness: *the activity of children playing.* 4 thing to do; pursuit: *a student's outside activities.* 5 active force: *The study of the activities of a living being is called its physiology.* 6 radioactivity.

act of God, a sudden, unforeseeable, and uncontrollable, natural event. Floods, storms, and earthquakes are called acts of God.

ac to my o sin (ak′tō mī′ə sən), *n.* substance consisting of the proteins actin and myosin, found in muscle cells, thought to be the means by which muscles are enabled to contract.

ac tor (ak′tər), *n.* 1 person who acts on the stage, in motion pictures, on television, or over the radio. 2 person who does something; doer.

ac tress (ak′tris), *n.* girl or woman actor.

Acts (akts), *n.* the fifth book of the New Testament, telling about the beginnings of the Christian church.

Acts of the Apostles, Acts.

ac tu al (ak′chü əl), *adj.* 1 existing as a fact; real: *What I told you was not a dream but an actual happening.* See **real**[1] for synonym study. 2 now existing; in action at the time; present; current: *the actual state of affairs.* **—ac′tu al ness,** *n.*

ac tu al i ty (ak′chü al′ə tē), *n., pl.* **-ties.** 1 an actual thing; fact: *A trip to the moon has become an actuality.* 2 actual existence; reality.

ac tu al ize (ak′chü ə līz), *v.t.,* **-ized, -iz ing.** make (a plan or idea) actual; realize in action or as a fact. **—ac′tu al i za′tion,** *n.*

ac tu al ly (ak′chü ə lē), *adv.* really; in fact: *Are you actually going to Europe?*

ac tu ar i al (ak′chü er′ē əl), *adj.* 1 of actuaries or their work. 2 determined by actuaries. **—ac′tu ar′i al ly,** *adv.*

ac tu ar y (ak′chü er′ē), *n., pl.* **-ar ies.** person who figures risks, rates, premiums, etc., for insurance companies. [< Latin *actuarius* account keeper < *actus* public business < *agere* do]

ac tu ate (ak′chü āt), *v.t.,* **-at ed, -at ing.** 1 put into action; activate: *a pump actuated by a belt.* 2 influence to act; impel: *Kindness actuated him to help.* See **move** for synonym study. **—ac′tu a′tion,** *n.* **—ac′tu a′tor,** *n.*

a cu i ty (ə kyü′ə tē), *n.* sharpness; keenness: *acuity of vision, acuity of wit.* [< Medieval Latin *acuitatem,* ultimately < Latin *acutum.* See ACUTE.]

a cu men (ə kyü′mən), *n.* sharpness and quickness in seeing and understanding; keen insight; discernment. [< Latin < *acuere* sharpen]

a cu mi nate (ə kyü′mə nit), *adj.* (of leaves) tapering to a point.

acuminate leaf

a cute (ə kyüt′), *adj.* 1 acting keenly on the senses; sharp; intense: *acute pain.* 2 coming quickly to a crisis; brief and severe: *an acute disease.* 3 crucial; critical: *an acute shortage of water.* 4 quick in perceiving and responding to impressions; keen: *Dogs have an acute sense of smell.* 5 quick in discernment; sharp-witted; clever: *an acute thinker.* See **sharp** for synonym study. 6 high in pitch; shrill: *A siren makes an acute sound.* 7 having or ending in a sharp point. 8 (of a vowel) having an acute accent over it. 9 having one or more acute angles. *—n.* an acute accent. [< Latin *acutum* sharpened < *acuere* sharpen] **—a cute′ly,** *adv.* **—a cute′ness,** *n.*

acute accent, mark (′) placed over a vowel letter in the spellings of some languages, usually to show a feature of pronunciation, as in French *attaché* (showing quality of the vowel), or place of accent, as in Spanish *Asunción* (showing stress).

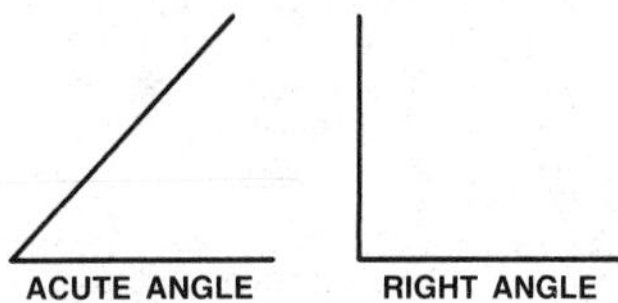
ACUTE ANGLE RIGHT ANGLE

acute angle, angle less than a right angle; any angle less than 90 degrees.

ad (ad), *n.* INFORMAL. advertisement.

ad-, *prefix.* 1 to; toward, as in *admit, administer, adverb, advert.* See also **a-, ab-, ac-, af-, ag-, al-, an-, ap-, ar-, as-,** and **at-.** 2 at; near, as in *adjacent, adrenal.* [< Latin]

A.D., in the year of our Lord; after the birth of Christ. From 63 B.C. to A.D. 14 is 77 years. [for Latin *Anno Domini* in the year of the Lord].

ad age (ad′ij), *n.* a well-known proverb. EXAMPLE: Haste makes waste. [< Middle French < Latin *adagium*]

a da gio (ə dä′jō, ə dä′zhō), *adv., adj., n., pl.* **-gios.** *—adv.* (in music) slowly. *—adj.* (in music) slow. *—n.* 1 a musical passage, movement, or piece in adagio time. 2 a slow ballet dance in which the female partner is supported or lifted while she holds various poses. [< Italian]

Ad am (ad′əm), *n.* 1 (in the Bible) the first man; father of the human race. 2 **the old Adam,** the human tendency to sin.

ad a mant (ad′ə mənt, ad′ə mant), *adj.* 1 not giving in readily; firm and unyielding; immovable. 2 too hard to be cut or broken. [< Latin *adamantem* < Greek *adamantos* the hardest metal < *a-* not + *damnanai* to tame, conquer. Doublet of DIAMOND.] **—ad′a mant ly,** *adv.*

ad a man tine (ad′ə man′tēn′, ad′ə man′tīn), *adj.* unyielding; firm; immovable.

Ad ams (ad′əmz), *n.* 1 **Henry (Brooks),** 1838-1918, American historian, grandson of John Quincy Adams. 2 **John,** 1735-1826, the second president of the United States, from 1797 to 1801, and one of the leaders of the American Revolution. 3 **John Quincy,** 1767-1848, the sixth president of the United States, from 1825 to 1829, son of John Adams. 4 **Samuel,** 1722-1803, one of the leaders of the American Revolution.

Adam's apple, the slight lump in the front of a person's throat formed by the thyroid cartilage of the larynx.

a dapt (ə dapt′), *v.t.* 1 make fit or suitable; adjust: *adapt one's way of working to the needs of the job.* See **adjust** for synonym study. 2 modify or alter so as to make fit or suitable for a different use or a particular place or purpose: *The story was adapted for the movies from a novel by Pearl Buck.* *—v.i.* be adjusted. [< Latin *adaptare* < *ad-* to + *aptus* fitted, suitable]

a dapt a bil i ty (ə dap′tə bil′ə tē), *n.* adaptable quality.

a dapt a ble (ə dap′tə bəl), *adj.* easily changed or changing easily to fit different conditions; pliant; flexible. **—a dapt′a ble ness,** *n.*

ad ap ta tion (ad′ap tā′shən), *n.* 1 act of adapting; adjustment (to different circumstances or conditions). 2 a being adapted; suitableness. 3 something made by adapting: *This motion picture is an adaptation of that novel.* 4 change in structure, form, or habits to fit different conditions: *Wings are adaptations of the upper limbs for flight.* 5 adjustment of a sense organ to a changed situation or condition.

ad ap ta tion al (ad′ap tā′shə nəl), *adj.* of

or involving adaptation. **—ad′ap ta′tion al ly,** *adv.*

a dapt ed (ə dap′tid), *adj.* fitted; suitable. **—a dapt′ed ness,** *n.*

a dapt er or **a dap tor** (ə dap′tər), *n.* 1 person who adapts. 2 device that adapts different-sized parts to each other or a machine to a different use.

a dap tive (ə dap′tiv), *adj.* of, characterized by, or showing adaptation. **—a dap′tive ly,** *adv.* **—a dap′tive ness,** *n.*

ADC, aide-de-camp.

add (ad), *v.t.* 1 find the sum of (two or more numbers or quantities). 2 say further; go on to say or write: *She said good-by and added that she had had a pleasant visit.* 3 join (one thing to another) so as to increase the number, quantity, or importance: *She added a new wing to the house.* 4 **add in,** include: *These figures are not complete; the cost of transportation must be added in.* *—v.i.* 1 perform arithmetical addition: *The first-graders are learning to add and subtract.* 2 **add to,** make greater; increase: *The fine day added to our pleasure.* 3 **add up,** **a** make the correct total. **b** INFORMAL. make sense; fit together: *The facts just don't add up.* 4 **add up to,** amount to. [< Latin *addere* < *ad-* to + *dare* put] **—add′er,** *n.*

add a ble (ad′ə bəl), *adj.* addible.

Ad dams (ad′əmz), *n.* **Jane,** 1860-1935, American social worker.

ad dax (ad′aks), *n.* a large antelope with a heavy body, short legs, and long, loosely spiraled horns, living in the deserts of northern Africa. [< Latin]

ad dend (ad′end, ə dend′), *n.* number or quantity to be added to another number or quantity: *In the problem "421 + 365 = ?" 365 is the addend.*

ad den dum (ə den′dəm), *n., pl.* **-da** (-də). 1 appendix to a book or document. 2 thing added or to be added. [< Latin < *addere.* See ADD.]

ad der (ad′ər), *n.* 1 a small, poisonous snake of Europe and the only poisonous snake in England. 2 hognose snake. 3 puff adder. [Old English *nædre;* in Middle English *a nadder* came to be understood and written as *an adder*]

ad der's-tongue (ad′ərz tung′), *n.* 1 a small fern with a spike springing from the base of a frond so as to suggest the mouth and tongue of a snake. 2 dogtooth violet.

add i ble (ad′ə bəl), *adj.* that can be added. Also, **addable.**

ad dict (*n.* ad′ikt; *v.* ə dikt′), *n.* 1 person who is a slave to a habit, especially to the habitual and excessive use of a drug. 2 devotee or enthusiast: *a baseball addict.* *—v.t.* devote or give (oneself) up slavishly to a habit or practice. [< Latin *addictum* given over to < *ad-* to + *dicere* say, declare]

ad dict ed (ə dik′tid), *adj.* slavishly following or unable to give up (a habit or practice).

ad dic tion (ə dik′shən), *n.* condition of being addicted.

ad dict ive (ə dik′tiv), *adj.* causing or tending to cause addiction.

Ad dis Ab a ba (ad′is ab′ə bə), capital of Ethiopia, in the central part. 644,000.

Ad di son (ad′ə sən), *n.* **Joseph,** 1672-1719, English essayist, poet, and statesman.

Addison's disease, a chronic, wasting disease of the cortex of the adrenal glands, characterized by low blood pressure, weakened muscles, intestinal disturbances, and a brownish discoloration of the skin. [< Thomas *Addison,* 1793-1860, English doctor who described it]

ad di tion (ə dish′ən), *n.* 1 act or process of adding. 2 process, indicated by the sign +, of collecting separate numbers or quantities into one number or quantity known as the sum. 3 result of adding; thing added. 4 part added to a building. 5 **in addition** or **in addition to,** besides; as well as.

ad di tion al (ə dish′ə nəl), *adj.* added; extra. **—ad di′tion al ly,** *adv.*

ad di tive (ad′ə tiv), *n.* substance added as an ingredient to another substance to preserve it, increase its effectiveness, etc.: *Vitamins and preservatives are some of the additives in this bread.* *—adj.* involving addition. **—ad′di tive ly,** *adv.*

additive inverse, either of two numbers whose sum is zero. The additive inverse of +5 is −5; the additive inverse of −5 is +5.

ad dle (ad′l), *v.,* **-dled, -dling,** *adj.* *—v.t., v.i.* 1 make or become muddled. 2 make or become rotten. *—adj.* 1 muddled; confused. 2 rotten: *addle eggs.* [Old English *adela* muck]

ad dle pat ed (ad′l pā′tid), *adj.* muddled; confused.

ad dress (ə dres′; *n. 2 and 3 also* ad′res), *n., v.,* **-dressed** or **-drest, -dress ing.** *—n.* 1 a speech, especially a formal one: *the President's inaugural address.* See **speech** for synonym study. 2 the place at which a person, business, etc., receives mail. 3 the writing on an envelope, package, etc., that shows where and to whom it is to be sent. 4 symbol identifying the place where a bit of information is stored in the core of an electronic computer. 5 manner of speaking to another: *A salesman should be a man of pleasant address.* 6 skillful management; adroitness: *A good manager solves problems with speed and address.* 7 a formal request to those in authority to do a particular thing: *an address from the colonists to the king, listing grievances.* 8 **addresses,** *pl.* attentions paid in courtship.

—v.t. 1 make an address to: *The President addressed the nation.* 2 direct speech or writing to: *He addressed me as though we were old friends.* 3 use titles or other set forms in speaking or writing to: *How do you address the mayor?* 4 write on (a letter, package, etc.) to whom and where it is to be sent: *Address this letter to Alaska.* 5 direct to the attention: *Let us address a petition to the Governor.* 6 apply (oneself) in speech (to a person): *She addressed herself to the chairman.* 7 speak directly to: *Address the chair!* 8 apply or devote (oneself); direct one's energies: *I addressed myself to the task of learning French.* 9 (in golf) prepare for a stroke by placing the head of a club behind (the ball). [< Old French *adresser* < Popular Latin *addirectiare* make straight < Latin *ad-* to + *directus* straight] **—ad dress′er, ad dres′sor,** *n.*

ad dress ee (ə dre sē′, ad′re sē′), *n.* person or persons to whom a letter, package, etc., is addressed.

ad duce (ə düs′, ə dyüs′), *v.t.,* **-duced, -duc ing.** offer as a reason in support of an argument; give as proof or evidence for consideration; cite as pertinent or conclusive. [< Latin *adducere* < *ad-* to + *ducere* bring, lead] **—ad duc′er,** *n.*

ad duct (ə dukt′), *v.t.* pull (a part of the body) inward toward the main axis.

ad duc tion (ə duk′shən), *n.* 1 an adducing; the bringing forward of arguments. 2 an adducting; pulling a part of the body inward.

ad duc tive (ə duk′tiv), *adj.* tending to lead toward.

ad duc tor (ə duk′tər), *n.* muscle that adducts.

Ad e laide (ad′l ād), *n.* city in S Australia. 75,000; with suburbs, 809,000.

A den (äd′n, ād′n), *n.* 1 former British protectorate in SW Arabia. It became the country of Southern Yemen in 1967. 2 former British colony in this protectorate, now a part of Southern Yemen. 3 seaport and capital of this former colony. 250,000. 4 **Gulf of,** part of the Arabian Sea between S Arabia and E Africa.

A de nau er (ad′n ou′ər), *n.* **Konrad,** 1876-1967, German statesman, first chancellor of West Germany, from 1949 to 1963.

A de nese (äd′n ēz′, ād′n ēz′), *adj., n., pl.* **-nese.** *—adj.* of Aden or its people. *—n.* native or inhabitant of Aden.

A de ni (äd′n ē), *adj., n., pl.* **-nis.** Adenese.

ad e nine (ad′n ēn′, ad′n ən), *n.* substance present in nucleic acid in cells. It is one of the purine bases of DNA and RNA. *Formula:* $C_5H_5N_5$

ad e noid (ad′n oid), *adj.* 1 of the lymphatic glands or lymphoid tissue. 2 like a gland; glandular. [< Greek *adenoeides* < *adēn* gland + *eidos* form]

ad e noi dal (ad′n oi′dl), *adj.* 1 adenoid. 2 having adenoids. 3 characteristic of a person having adenoids.

ad e noids (ad′n oidz), *n.pl.* enlarged growths of lymphoid tissue in the upper part of the throat, just back of the nose, often hindering natural breathing and speaking.

a den o sine (ə den′ə sēn′), *n.* substance in ribonucleic acid important in muscle contraction and the metabolism of sugars. *Formula:* $C_{10}H_{13}N_5O_4$

adenosine di phos phate (dī fos′fāt), ADP.

adenosine tri phos phate (trī fos′fāt), ATP.

a de no vi rus (ə dē′nō vī′rəs), *n.* one of a group of viruses that attacks mucous tissues, especially of the respiratory tract.

a dept (*adj.* ə dept′; *n.* ad′ept), *adj.* thoroughly skilled; expert. *—n.* person thoroughly skilled in some art, science, occupation, etc. [< Medieval Latin *adeptum* skilled (in alchemy) < Latin < *ad-* to + *apisci* reach] **—a dept′ly,** *adv.* **—a dept′ness,** *n.*

ad e qua cy (ad′ə kwə sē), *n.* a being adequate; sufficiency.

ad e quate (ad′ə kwit), *adj.* 1 as much as is needed for a particular purpose; fully sufficient. See **enough** for synonym study. 2 suitable or competent: *He is barely adequate for the job.* [< Latin *adaequatum* made equal < *ad-* to + *aequus* equal] **—ad′e quate ly,** *adv.* **—ad′e quate ness,** *n.*

ad here (ad hir′), *v.i.,* **-hered, -her ing.** 1 stick fast; remain firmly attached; cling *(to).* See **stick**[2] for synonym study. 2 hold closely or firmly; cleave *(to): In spite of objections the manager adhered to the plan.* 3 be a follower or upholder; give allegiance (*to* a party, leader, belief, etc.). [< Latin *adhaerere* < *ad-* to + *haerere* to stick] **—ad her′er,** *n.*

ad her ence (ad hir′əns), *n.* 1 a holding to and following closely; adhering: *the judge's rigid adherence to rules.* 2 attachment or devotion to a person, group, belief, etc.; faithfulness.

ad her ent (ad hir′ənt), *n.* a faithful supporter or follower: *an adherent of the conservative party. Our church has many adherents.* See **follower** for synonym study. *—adj.* sticking fast; attached. **—ad her′ent ly,** *adv.*

ad he sion (ad hē′zhən), *n.* 1 act or condition of adhering; sticking fast. 2 faithfulness; adherence. 3 the molecular attraction exerted between the surfaces of unlike bodies in contact, as a solid and a liquid. 4 a growing together of body tissues that are normally separate, especially after surgery. [< Latin *adhaesionem* < *adhaerere.* See ADHERE.]

ad he sive (ad hē′siv, ad hē′ziv), *n.* 1 gummed tape used to hold bandages in place; adhesive tape. 2 glue, paste, or other substance for sticking things together. *—adj.* 1 holding fast; adhering easily; sticky. 2 coated with a sticky substance; gummed: *an adhesive label.* **—ad he′sive ly,** *adv.* **—ad he′sive ness,** *n.*

adhesive tape, strip of cloth coated on one surface with a sticky substance, used especially for holding bandages in place.

ad hoc (ad hok′), for a specific purpose; special: *an ad hoc committee.* [Latin, for this (matter)]

ad ho mi nem (ad hom′ə nem), appealing to a person's personal prejudices, interests, etc., rather than to his power to reason: *an argument ad hominem.* [Latin, to the man]

ad i a bat ic (ad′ē ə bat′ik, ā′dī ə bat′ik), *adj.* (in physics) occurring without loss or gain of heat. [< Greek *adiabatos* impassable] **—ad′i a bat′i cal ly,** *adv.*

a dieu (ə dü′, ə dyü′), *interj., n., pl.* **a dieus** or **a dieux** (ə düz′, ə dyüz′). good-by. [< Middle French < *à Dieu* to God]

ad in fi ni tum (ad in′fə nī′təm), LATIN. without limit; endlessly.

ad in ter im (ad in′tər əm), LATIN. 1 in the meantime: *serve ad interim.* 2 temporary: *an ad interim report.*

a di os (ä′dē ōs′, ad′ē ōs′), *interj., n.* good-by. [< Spanish *adiós* < *a Dios* to God]

ad i pose (ad′ə pōs), *adj.* consisting of or resembling fat; fatty: *adipose tissue.* [< Medieval Latin *adiposus* < Latin *adeps, adipis* fat] **—ad′i pose′ness,** *n.*

ad i pos i ty (ad′ə pos′ə tē), *n.* adipose condition; fatness.

Ad i ron dack Mountains (ad′ə ron′dak), mountain system of a large area in NE New York State. Highest peak, 5344 ft.

Ad i ron dacks (ad′ə ron′daks), *n.pl.* Adirondack Mountains.

adj., 1 adjective. 2 adjustment.

Adj., Adjutant.

ad ja cen cy (ə jā′sn sē), *n.* a being adjacent; nearness.

ad ja cent (ə jā′snt), *adj.* lying near or close; adjoining; next: *The house adjacent to ours has been sold.* [< Latin *adjacentem* < *ad-* near + *jacere* to lie] **—ad ja′cent ly,** *adv.*

adjacent angles, two angles that have the same vertex and one side in common.

ad jec ti val (aj′ik tī′vəl), *adj.* 1 of, forming, or having to do with an adjective: *-able is an adjectival suffix.* 2 used as an adjective. *—n.* a word or group of words used as an adjective. **—ad′jec ti′val ly,** *adv.*

ad jec tive (aj′ik tiv), *n.* one of a class of words that qualify, limit, or add to the meaning of a noun or pronoun. A **descriptive adjective** shows a quality or condition of the thing named by the noun or pronoun, as in *great* happiness, a *tiny* brook, the day is *warm.* A **limiting adjective** points out the thing named, or indicates quantity or number, as in *this* pencil, *his* book, *any* person, *twenty-five* cents. *—adj.* 1 of or used as an adjective; adjectival. 2 not standing by itself; dependent. [< Latin *adjectivum* added < *ad-* to + *jacere* throw, put] **—ad′jec tive ly,** *adv.*

ad join (ə join′), *v.t.* be next to; be in contact with: *Canada adjoins the United States.* *—v.i.* be next to or close to each other; be in contact: *Canada and the United States adjoin.*

ad join ing (ə joi′ning), *adj.* being next to or in contact with; bordering.

ad journ (ə jėrn′), *v.t.* put off until a later time; postpone: *The members of the club voted to adjourn the meeting until two o'clock tomorrow.* *—v.i.* 1 stop business or proceedings for a time; recess: *The court adjourned from Friday until Monday.* 2 transfer the place of meeting. 3 INFORMAL. go (*to* another place), especially for conversation. [< Old French *ajorner* < *a* to + *jorn* day]

ad journ ment (ə jėrn′mənt), *n.* 1 an adjourning. 2 a being adjourned. 3 time during which a court, legislature, etc., is adjourned; recess.

Adjt., Adjutant.

ad judge (ə juj′), *v.t.,* **-judged, -judg ing.** 1 decree or decide by law. 2 award by law; allot. 3 condemn or sentence by law. 4 deem; consider. [< Old French *ajugier* < Latin *adjudicare* < *ad-* to + *judicare* to judge. Doublet of ADJUDICATE.]

ad ju di cate (ə jü′də kāt), *v.,* **-cat ed, -cat ing.** *—v.t.* decide or settle by law or as an authority. *—v.i.* act as judge; pass judgment. [< Latin *adjudicatum* awarded < *ad-* to + *judicare* to judge. Doublet of ADJUDGE.] **—ad ju′di ca′tor,** *n.*

ad ju di ca tion (ə jü′də kā′shən), *n.* 1 an adjudicating. 2 decision of a judge or court of law.

ad ju di ca to ry (ə jü′də kə tôr′ē, ə jü′də kə tōr′ē), *adj.* judicial.

ad junct (aj′ungkt), *n.* 1 something connected with and subordinate in position, function, or character to a more important thing; accessory. 2 an assistant to, or associate of, a more important person. 3 word or phrase that qualifies or modifies one of the essential elements of a sentence. Adjectives and adverbs are adjuncts. *—adj.* 1 subordinate. 2 accompanying. [< Latin *adjunctum* joined to < *ad-* to + *jungere* join] **—ad′junct ly,** *adv.*

ad junc tive (ə jungk′tiv), *adj.* forming an adjunct. **—ad junc′tive ly,** *adv.*

ad ju ra tion (aj′ə rā′shən), *n.* an earnest or solemn appeal.

ad jur a to ry (ə jur′ə tôr′ē, ə jur′ə tōr′ē), *adj.* containing an adjuration; adjuring.

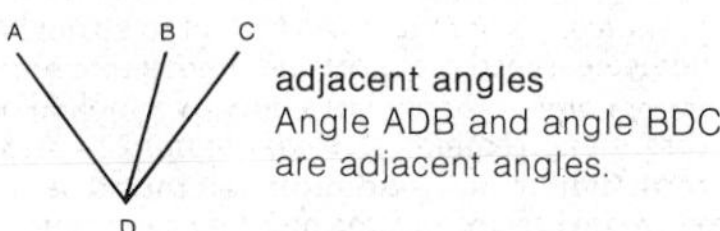

adjacent angles
Angle ADB and angle BDC are adjacent angles.

ad jure (ə jur′), *v.t.,* **-jured, -jur ing.** 1 request earnestly or solemnly; entreat. 2 command or charge (a person) on oath or the penalty of a curse (*to* do something). [< Latin *adjurare* < *ad-* to + *jurare* swear]

ad just (ə just′), *v.t.* 1 change (something) to make fit; adapt. See synonym study below. 2 put in proper order, position, or relation; arrange: *Please adjust the radio so that it is not so loud.* 3 arrange (differences, discrepancies, etc.) satisfactorily; set right; settle. 4 decide the amount to be paid in settling (a bill, insurance claim, etc.). *—v.i.* 1 adapt oneself; get used *(to): Some wild animals never adjust to captivity.* 2 have its angle, focus, height, etc., changed so as to fit different users: *The new camera has a lens that adjusts automatically.* [< Old French *ajuster* < *a-* for + *just* straight] **—ad just′a ble,** *adj.* **—ad just′a bly,** *adv.* **—ad just′er, ad jus′tor,** *n.*

Syn. *v.t.* 1 **Adjust, adapt, accommodate** have in common the idea of fitting one thing or person to another. **Adjust** emphasizes the idea of matching one thing to another: *The teacher adjusted the seat to the height of the child.* **Adapt** emphasizes the idea of making minor changes in a thing (or person) to make it fit, suit, or fit into something: *I adapted the pattern to the material.* **Accommodate** emphasizes that the things to be fitted together are so different that one must be subordinated to the other: *I have to accommodate my desires to my income.*

ad just ment (ə just′mənt), *n.* 1 act or process of adjusting. 2 process by which a person adapts himself to the natural or social conditions around him. 3 means of adjusting one thing to another. 4 settlement of a dispute, claim, etc.

ad just ment al (ə just men′tl), *adj.* of or having to do with adjustment.

ad ju tan cy (aj′ə tən sē), *n., pl.* **-cies.** rank or position of an adjutant in the army.

ad ju tant (aj′ə tənt), *n.* 1 an army officer who assists a commanding officer by sending out orders, writing letters, and doing other administrative work. 2 assistant. 3 adjutant bird. *—adj.* helping. [< Latin *adjutantem,* ultimately < *ad-* to + *juvare* to help]

adjutant bird, a very large species of stork of India, southeastern Asia, and Africa, so called from its stiff gait when walking.

adjutant general, *pl.* **adjutants general.** adjutant of a division or a larger military unit.

adjutant stork, adjutant bird.

ad lib (ad lib′), *v.,* **-libbed, -lib bing,** *adv., adj., n.* *—v.t., v.i.* make up words or music as one goes along; improvise; extemporize. *—adv.* on the spur of the moment; freely. *—adj.* made up on the spot; improvised. *—n.* music or words made up as one goes along. [short for *ad libitum*]

ad lib i tum (ad lib′ə təm), (in music) as one wishes; free to change, omit, or expand a passage at will. [< Latin, at pleasure]

Adm., 1 Admiral. 2 Admiralty.

ad man (ad′man′), *n., pl.* **-men.** man who prepares advertisements and places them in suitable media; an advertising man.

ad min is ter (ad min′ə stər), *v.t.* 1 manage the affairs of (a business, a city, etc.); control in behalf of others; supervise or direct: *ad-*

hat, āge, fär; let, ēqual, tėrm;
it, īce; hot, ōpen, ôrder;
oil, out; cup, put, rüle;
ch, child; ng, long; sh, she;
th, thin; ᴛʜ, then; zh, measure;

ə represents *a* in about, *e* in taken, *i* in pencil, *o* in lemon, *u* in circus.

< = from, derived from, taken from.

minister a department of the government, administer a household. 2 give out, apply, or dispense: *administer first aid, administer justice.* 3 deliver or bestow (a blow, rebuke, advice, etc., to a person, animal, etc.). 4 tender (an oath): *The witness could not testify until the judge administered an oath to him to tell the truth.* 5 settle or take charge of (an estate). *—v.i.* give aid; contribute beneficially; minister *(to): administer to the needs of flood victims.* [< Latin *administrare* < *ad-* to + *minister* servant]

ad min is tra ble (ad min′ə strə bəl), *adj.* that can be administered.

ad min is tra tion (ad min′ə strā′shən), *n.* 1 the managing of the affairs of a business, an office, etc.; management. 2 group of persons in charge: *the school administration.* 3 management of public affairs by government officials. 4 the officials as a group; the government. 5 **the Administration,** the executive branch of the United States government, consisting of the President, his cabinet, and the departments of the government managed by persons appointed by the President. 6 the period of time during which a government holds office. 7 act or process of administering something: *the administration of justice.*

ad min is tra tive (ad min′ə strā′tiv), *adj.* having to do with the management or conduct of affairs; executive. **—ad min′is tra′tive-ly,** *adv.*

ad min is tra tor (ad min′ə strā′tər), *n.* 1 manager. 2 person appointed by law to settle or take charge of an estate.

ad min is tra trix (ad min′ə strā′triks), *n.* a woman administrator.

ad mir a ble (ad′mər ə bəl), *adj.* 1 worth admiring. 2 very good; excellent. **—ad′mir-a ble ness,** *n.* **—ad′mir a bly,** *adv.*

ad mir al (ad′mər əl), *n.* 1 a naval officer of the highest rank. 2 officer in the United States Navy ranking next below a fleet admiral and next above a vice-admiral. 3 commander of a fleet of fishing or merchant ships. 4 either of two species of large, colorful European butterflies. [earlier *amiral* < Old French < Arabic *amīr al* chief of the]

Admiral of the Fleet, officer having the highest rank in the British Navy.

ad mir al ty (ad′mər əl tē), *n., pl.* **-ties.** 1 branch of law dealing with maritime affairs. 2 court of law dealing with maritime affairs. 3 **the Admiralty,** (in Great Britain until 1963) the government department in charge of naval affairs.

ad mi ra tion (ad′mə rā′shən), *n.* 1 a feeling of wonder mingled with approval. 2 a regarding with delight (something fine, great, or beautiful). 3 person or thing that is admired: *My new bike was the admiration of all my friends.*

ad mire (ad mīr′), *v.t.,* **-mired, -mir ing.** 1 regard with wonder, mingled with approval; look on with pleasure: *admire a beautiful painting.* 2 feel or express admiration for: *admire someone's new car.* 3 wonder or marvel at: *I admire your nerve.* [< Latin *admirari* < *ad-* at + *mirari* to wonder] **—ad mir′er,** *n.* **—ad mir′ing ly,** *adv.*

ad mis si bil i ty (ad mis′ə bil′ə tē), *n.* admissible quality or condition.

ad mis si ble (ad mis′ə bəl), *adj.* 1 capable or worthy of being admitted. 2 permitted by authority or by the rules; allowable. **—ad-mis′si ble ness,** *n.* **—ad mis′si bly,** *adv.*

ad mis sion (ad mish′ən), *n.* 1 act of allowing to enter: *the admission of aliens into a country.* 2 power or right of entering; permission to enter: *apply for admission into a college.* See synonym study below. 3 price paid for the right to enter. 4 acceptance into an office or position. 5 an admitting (of anything) as proper, valid, or true; confession: *an admission of guilt.* 6 an acknowledgment; concession. [< Latin *admissionem* < *admittere.* See ADMIT.]

Syn. 2 Admission, admittance mean right to enter. **Admission,** the more frequent term, emphasizes the privileges, rights, etc., of being admitted: *He is eligible for admission to the honor society.* **Admittance,** the rarer term, stresses the literal action of letting into a place: *With the ticket I gained admittance to the arena.*

ad mis sive (ad mis′iv), *adj.* admitting or tending to admit.

ad mit (ad mit′), *v.,* **-mit ted, -mit ting.** *—v.t.* 1 say (something) is real or true; acknowledge: *admit a mistake.* See synonym study below. 2 accept as true or valid: *admit evidence.* 3 allow (a person or thing) to enter or use; let in: *Windows admit light and air to the room.* 4 give the right to enter to: *This ticket admits one person to the game.* 5 allow, concede, or grant: *admit a possibility.* 6 have room for; be large enough for: *The harbor admits many ships.* *—v.i.* 1 be a means of entrance *(to): This door admits to the dining room.* 2 **admit of,** leave room for: *Your answer admits of no reply.* [< Latin *admittere* < *ad-* to + *mittere* let go]

Syn. *v.t.* **1 Admit, acknowledge, confess** mean to grant or disclose that something is true. **Admit** means to own or grant the existence or truth of something, usually after hesitating and then giving in to outside forces, one's own conscience, or one's judgment: *I admit that you are right.* **Acknowledge** means to declare openly one's knowledge of the existence or truth of something, sometimes reluctantly: *They now have acknowledged defeat.* **Confess** means to admit something about oneself that is unfavorable or criminal: *I confess I am a coward.*

ad mit tance (ad mit′ns), *n.* 1 right to enter; permission to enter. See **admission** for synonym study. 2 act of admitting.

ad mit ted ly (ad mit′id lē), *adv.* without denial; by general consent.

ad mix (ad miks′), *v.t., v.i.* add as an ingredient; mix in; mingle.

ad mix ture (ad miks′chər), *n.* 1 act of mixing. 2 mixture. 3 anything added in mixing; ingredient.

ad mon ish (ad mon′ish), *v.t.* 1 advise against something; warn: *admonish a person of danger.* 2 scold gently; reprove: *admonish a student for careless work.* 3 urge strongly; advise earnestly; exhort: *admonish one to be more careful.* 4 recall to a duty overlooked or forgotten; remind. [< *admonition*] **—ad-mon′ish er,** *n.* **—ad mon′ish ment,** *n.*

ad mo ni tion (ad′mə nish′ən), *n.* act of admonishing; gentle reproof or warning. [< Latin *admonitionem* < *ad-* to + *monere* warn]

ad mon i to ry (ad mon′ə tôr′ē, ad mon′ə-tōr′ē), *adj.* admonishing; warning.

ad nate (ad′nāt), *adj.* (of unlike parts of plants or animals) growing together or adhering throughout their length. [< Latin *adnatum* grown onto]

ad nau se am (ad nô′shē əm; ad nô′-sē əm; ad nô′zē əm), LATIN. to a disgusting extent.

a do (ə dü′), *n.* 1 noisy activity; bustle. See **stir**[1] for synonym study. 2 trouble; difficulty. [Middle English *at do* to do]

a do be (ə dō′bē), *n.* 1 brick made of sun-dried clay. 2 building made of such bricks or of sun-dried clay. *—adj.* built or made of adobe. [< Spanish < Arabic *aṭ-ṭūb* the brick]

ad o les cence (ad′l es′ns), *n.* 1 growth from childhood to adulthood. 2 period or time of this growth; youth.

ad o les cent (ad′l es′nt), *n.* person growing up from childhood to adulthood, especially a person from about 12 to about 20 years of age. *—adj.* 1 growing up from childhood to adulthood; youthful. 2 of or characteristic of adolescents. [< Latin *adolescentem* < *ad-* to + *alescere* grow up] **—ad′o les′cent ly,** *adv.*

A don is (ə don′is, ə dō′nis), *n.* 1 (in Greek and Roman myths) a handsome young man who was loved by Aphrodite (Venus). 2 any handsome young man.

a dopt (ə dopt′), *v.t.* 1 take or use as one's own choice: *adopt an idea, adopt a new custom.* 2 accept, endorse, or approve formally or officially: *The committee adopted the resolution by a vote of 20 to 5.* 3 take (a child of other parents), as approved by law, and bring up as one's own child. 4 take (a word) from a foreign language into regular use without intentionally changing its form: *In English we have adopted the German words "Gneiss" and "Hamburger."* [< Latin *adoptare* < *ad-* to + *optare* choose] **—a dopt′a-ble,** *adj.* **—a dopt′er,** *n.*

a dop tion (ə dop′shən), *n.* 1 act of adopting: *the adoption of a new name.* 2 fact or condition of being adopted: *offer a child for adoption.*

a dop tive (ə dop′tiv), *adj.* adopted: *an adoptive son.*

a dor a ble (ə dôr′ə bəl, ə dōr′ə bəl), *adj.* 1 worthy of being adored. 2 INFORMAL. attractive or delightful: *What an adorable hat!* **—a dor′a ble ness,** *n.* **—a dor′a bly,** *adv.*

ad o ra tion (ad′ə rā′shən), *n.* 1 devoted love and admiration. 2 worship.

a dore (ə dôr′, ə dōr′), *v.t.,* **a dored, a dor-ing.** 1 love and admire very greatly. 2 INFORMAL. like very much: *I just adore that dress.* 3 worship. [< Latin *adorare* < *ad-* to + *orare* pray] **—a dor′ing ly,** *adv.* **—a dor′er,** *n.*

a dorn (ə dôrn′), *v.t.* 1 add beauty to; enhance: *Wild flowers adorned the river bank.* 2 put ornaments on; decorate. See **decorate** for synonym study. [< Latin *adornare* < *ad-* to + *ornare* fit out] **—a dorn′er,** *n.*

a dorn ment (ə dôrn′mənt), *n.* 1 something that adorns; ornament; decoration. 2 act of adorning; ornamentation.

ADP, 1 adenosine diphosphate, a compound formed from ATP in the muscles. *Formula:* $C_{10}H_{15}N_5O_{10}P_2$ 2 automatic data processing.

ad rem (ad rem′), LATIN. to the point.

ad re nal (ə drē′nl), *adj.* 1 near or on the kidney; suprarenal. 2 of or derived from the adrenal glands. *—n.* an adrenal gland. [< Latin *ad-* near + *renes* kidneys]

adrenal gland, either of two ductless glands, on or near the upper part of the kidneys of vertebrates, whose outer wall or cortex secretes cortisone and other important hormones and whose inner part or medulla secretes adrenaline; suprarenal gland.

Ad ren al in (ə dren′l ən), *n.* trademark for a drug prepared from adrenaline.

hat, āge, fär; let, ēqual, tėrm;
it, īce; hot, ōpen, ôrder;
oil, out; cup, pu̇t, rüle;
ch, child; ng, long; sh, she;
th, thin; ᴛʜ, then; zh, measure;

ə represents *a* in about, *e* in taken, *i* in pencil, *o* in lemon, *u* in circus.

< = from, derived from, taken from.

ad ren al ine (ə dren′l ən), *n.* hormone secreted by the medulla of the adrenal glands, which speeds up the heartbeat and thereby increases bodily energy and resistance to fatigue; epinephrine.

ad ren er gic (ad′re nėr′jik), *adj.* producing or activated by adrenaline: *an adrenergic nerve fiber.*

ad re no cor ti cal (ə drē′nō kôr′tə kəl), *adj.* having to do with or derived from the outer wall or cortex of an adrenal gland: *adrenocortical steroids.*

A dri an (ā′drē ən), name of six popes, including **Adrian IV,** 1100?-1159, pope from 1154 to 1159, the only English-born pope, and **Adrian VI,** 1459-1523, pope from 1522 to 1523, the only Dutch-born pope.

A dri a no ple (ā′drē ə nō′pəl), *n.* Edirne.

A dri at ic Sea (ā′drē at′ik), arm of the Mediterranean between Italy and Yugoslavia. 500 mi. long.

a drift (ə drift′), *adj.* 1 floating without being guided; drifting. 2 without guidance or direction: *The basketball team was adrift while the coach was sick.*

a droit (ə droit′), *adj.* 1 resourceful in reaching one's objective; ingenious; clever. 2 skillful in the use of the hands or body; dexterous. See **deft** for synonym study. [< French < *à droit* rightly] **—a droit′ly,** *adv.* **—a droit′ness,** *n.*

ad sorb (ad sôrb′, ad zôrb′), *v.t.* take up and hold (a gas, liquid, or dissolved substance) in a thin layer of molecules on the surface of a solid substance. [< Latin *ad-* to + *sorbere* suck in]

ad sorb ent (ad sôr′bənt, ad zôr′bənt), *adj.* adsorbing readily. *—n.* substance that adsorbs readily.

ad sorp tion (ad sôrp′shən, ad zôrp′shən), *n.* 1 process of adsorbing. 2 condition of being adsorbed.

ad sorp tive (ad sôrp′tiv, ad zôrp′tiv), *adj.* of or having to do with adsorption.

ad u late (aj′ə lāt), *v.t.,* **-lat ed, -lat ing.** praise excessively; flatter slavishly. [< Latin *adulatum* fawned upon] **—ad′u la′tor,** *n.*

ad u la tion (aj′ə lā′shən), *n.* excessive praise; slavish flattery.

ad u la to ry (aj′ə lə tôr′ē, aj′ə lə tōr′ē), *adj.* characterized by adulation.

a dult (ə dult′, ad′ult), *adj.* 1 that has reached full size and strength; fully developed; grown-up; mature. 2 of or for adults: *adult books, adult behavior.* *—n.* 1 a grown-up person. 2 person who has reached an age of maturity as defined by law, usually the age of 21. 3 a full-grown plant or animal. [< Latin *adultum.* Related to ADOLESCENT.] **—a dult′ness,** *n.*

a dul ter ant (ə dul′tər ənt), *n.* substance used to adulterate something, especially something that destroys purity or quality without greatly altering appearance.

a dul te rate (ə dul′tə rāt′), *v.t.,* **-rat ed, -rat ing.** make lower the purity or quality of (food, drugs, etc.) without greatly altering appearance by adding or mixing in inferior, impure, or improper materials of little cost, especially so as to increase in bulk or quantity; debase: *adulterate milk with water.* [< Latin *adulteratum* made different, debased < *ad-* to + *alter* other, different] **—a dul′te ra′tor,** *n.*

a dul te ra tion (ə dul′tə rā′shən), *n.* 1 act or process of adulterating. 2 an adulterated product or substance.

a dul ter er (ə dul′tər ər), *n.* person, especially a man, guilty of adultery.

a dul ter ess (ə dul′tər is, ə dul′tris), *n.* woman guilty of adultery.

a dul ter ous (ə dul′tər əs, ə dul′trəs), *adj.* 1 guilty of adultery. 2 having to do with adultery. **—a dul′ter ous ly,** *adv.*

a dul ter y (ə dul′tər ē, ə dul′trē), *n., pl.* **-ter ies.** voluntary sexual intercourse by a married man with a woman not his wife, or by a married woman with a man not her husband.

a dult hood (ə dult′hu̇d), *n.* condition or time of being an adult.

ad um brate (ad um′brāt, ad′əm brāt), *v.t.,* **-brat ed, -brat ing.** 1 give a faint indication of; outline. 2 foreshadow. 3 overshadow; obscure. [< Latin *adumbratum* overshadowed < *ad-* + *umbra* shade] **—ad′um bra′tion,** *n.*

ad um bra tive (ad um′brə tiv), *adj.* faintly indicating. **—ad um′bra tive ly,** *adv.*

adv., 1 adverb. 2 adverbial. 3 advertisement.

ad val., ad valorem.

ad va lo rem (ad və lôr′əm; ad və lōr′əm), (of taxes, import duties, etc.) levied in proportion to the certified value of the merchandise or goods. [< Medieval Latin, according to the value]

ad vance (ad vans′), *v.,* **-vanced, -vanc ing,** *n., adj.* *—v.t.* 1 put, move, or push forward: *advance troops.* 2 help forward; further: *advance the cause of peace.* 3 bring forward; offer; suggest: *advance an opinion.* 4 raise to a higher rank or position; promote: *The teacher was advanced to principal.* 5 raise (prices); increase: *advance the price of milk.* 6 make earlier; hasten: *advance the time of the meeting.* 7 supply beforehand: *advance a salesman funds for expenses.* 8 lend (money), especially on security: *advance a loan.* *—v.i.* 1 move or go forward: *The troops advanced.* See synonym study below. 2 make progress; improve: *advance in skill.* 3 rise in rank or position; be promoted: *advance in one's profession.* 4 rise in price or value; increase: *The stock advanced three points.*

—n. 1 a moving forward or onward: *The army's advance was very slow.* 2 the distance covered: *an advance of nine miles.* 3 onward movement in any process or course of action; progress: *the advance of knowledge.* 4 a step forward; a degree of progress: *advances in aircraft design.* 5 a rise in amount, value, or price; increase. 6 payment beforehand. 7 money or goods furnished before they are due or as a loan. 8 **advances,** *pl.* attempts or offers toward another or others to settle a difference, to make an acquaintance, etc. 9 **in advance, a** in front; ahead: *The leader of the band marched in advance.* **b** ahead of time: *I paid for my ticket in advance.*

—adj. 1 going before: *the advance guard.* 2 ahead of time: *advance notice.* 3 made available before the date of general publication or release: *an advance copy of a book.* [< Old French *avancier* < Latin *abante* from before < *ab* from + *ante* before] **—ad vanc′er,** *n.*

Syn. *v.i.* 1 **Advance, proceed** mean to move forward. **Advance** emphasizes moving forward toward a definite end or destination: *In two plays the team advanced to the one-yard line.* **Proceed** emphasizes continuing to move forward from a definite point, such as a temporary stop or an intermediate goal: *From New York the Presidential party proceeded to Philadelphia. If we get the money to finish the hospital, we can proceed with construction.*

ad vanced (ad vanst′), *adj.* 1 in front of others; forward: *an advanced position.* 2 ahead of most others in progress, knowledge, skill, etc.: *an advanced class, an advanced design.* 3 far along in time, development, etc.: *an advanced age, the advanced stage of a disease.* 4 increased: *greatly advanced prices.* 5 carried far or too far toward an extreme: *advanced political ideas.*

ad vance ment (ad vans′mənt), *n.* 1 movement forward; advance. 2 helping forward; progress; improvement. 3 promotion.

ad van tage (ad van′tij), *n., v.,* **-taged, -tag ing.** *—n.* 1 a favorable circumstance or condition; any gain resulting from a better or superior position; benefit: *the advantages of good health and a sound education.* See synonym study below. 2 a better or superior position; superiority: *maintain a scientific advantage by pioneering in research.* 3 the first point scored in a tennis game after deuce. 4 **take advantage of, a** use to help or benefit oneself. **b** impose upon. 5 **to advantage,** to a good effect; favorably: *The frame sets off the painting to advantage.* 6 **to one's advantage,** to one's benefit or help. *—v.t.* give an advantage to; help; benefit. [< Old French *advantage* < *avant* before < Latin *abante.* See ADVANCE.]

Syn. *n.* 1 **Advantage, benefit, profit** mean gains of different kinds. **Advantage** applies to a gain resulting from a position of superiority over others: *A person who can think for himself has an advantage when he begins to work.* **Benefit** applies to gain in personal or social improvement: *The general relaxation of the body is one of the chief benefits of swimming.* While **profit** applies especially to material gain it is also applied to gain in anything valuable: *There is profit even in mistakes.*

ad van ta geous (ad′vən tā′jəs), *adj.* giving an advantage or advantages; favorable; beneficial. **—ad′van ta′geous ly,** *adv.* **—ad′van ta′geous ness,** *n.*

ad vec tion (ad vek′shən), *n.* the transference of heat, cold, or other properties of air by the horizontal motion of a mass of air. [< Latin *advectionem* a conveying]

ad vent (ad′vent), *n.* 1 a coming; arrival: *the advent of the new year, the advent of industrialism.* 2 **Advent, a** the season of devotion including the four Sundays before Christmas. **b** the birth of Christ. **c** Second Advent. [< Latin *adventum* < *ad-* to + *venire* come]

Ad vent ist (ad′ven tist), *n.* 1 member of a Christian denomination that believes that the second coming of Christ is near at hand. 2 Seventh-Day Adventist. —*adj.* of or having to do with the Adventists.

ad ven ti tious (ad′ven tish′əs), *adj.* 1 coming from outside; extraneously added; accidental. 2 (in botany and zoology) appearing out of the normal or usual place, as roots on stems, buds on leaves, etc. —**ad′ven ti′tious ly,** *adv.* —**ad′ven ti′tious ness,** *n.*

Advent Sunday, first of the four Sundays in Advent.

ad ven ture (ad ven′chər), *n., v.,* **-tured, -tur ing.** —*n.* 1 an exciting or unusual experience: *The trip to Alaska was an adventure for her.* 2 a bold and difficult undertaking of uncertain outcome, usually exciting and somewhat dangerous: *Sailing across the Pacific on a raft was a daring adventure.* 3 the seeking of excitement or danger: *spirit of adventure.* 4 a business undertaking; commercial speculation; venture. —*v.t., v.i.* dare; risk; venture. [< Old French *aventure* < Latin *adventura (res)* (thing) about to happen]

ad ven tur er (ad ven′chər ər), *n.* 1 person who seeks or has adventures. 2 soldier of fortune. 3 person who schemes to get money or social position. 4 speculator. 5 person who financed early trading ventures.

ad ven ture some (ad ven′chər səm), *adj.* bold and daring; adventurous.

ad ven tur ess (ad ven′chər is), *n.* woman who schemes to get money or social position.

ad ven tur ous (ad ven′chər əs), *adj.* 1 fond of adventures; ready to take risks; rashly daring; venturesome. 2 enterprising; daring: *an adventurous people.* 3 involving risk; hazardous; dangerous. —**ad ven′tur ous ly,** *adv.* —**ad ven′tur ous ness,** *n.*

ad verb (ad′vėrb′), *n.* one of a class of words that modify or qualify verbs (She sings *well*), adjectives (She is *very* pretty), other adverbs (She sings *quite* well), and phrases, clauses, or even sentences (*almost* through the wall; *just* what I wanted; *Finally,* I went home), usually to express time, place, manner, degree, or circumstance. Many adverbs are freely formed from adjectives or participles by adding *-ly (badly, cheaply, admiringly).* [< Latin *adverbium* < *ad-* to + *verbum* verb, word]

ad ver bi al (ad vėr′bē əl), *adj.* 1 used as an adverb. In the sentence "He worked as quickly as possible," *as quickly as possible* is an adverbial phrase. 2 of an adverb; forming adverbs: *"-ly" is an adverbial suffix.* —**ad ver′bi al ly,** *adv.*

ad ver sar y (ad′vər ser′ē), *n., pl.* **-sar ies.** 1 person or group opposing or resisting another or others; antagonist; enemy. 2 person or group on the other side in a contest; opponent. See **opponent** for synonym study.

ad ver sa tive (ad vėr′sə tiv), *adj.* (of words, etc.) expressing contrast or opposition. *But* and *yet* are adversative conjunctions. —**ad ver′sa tive ly,** *adv.*

ad verse (ad′vėrs′, ad vėrs′), *adj.* 1 unfriendly in purpose or effect; antagonistic; hostile: *adverse criticism.* 2 acting against one's interests; unfavorable; harmful: *Dirt and disease are adverse to the best growth of children.* 3 coming from or acting in a contrary direction; opposing: *Adverse winds delayed the voyage.* [< Latin *adversum* turned against < *ad-* to + *vertere* to turn] —**ad verse′ly,** *adv.* —**ad verse′ness,** *n.*

ad ver si ty (ad vėr′sə tē), *n., pl.* **-ties.** 1 condition of being in unfavorable circumstances, especially unfavorable financial circumstances; misfortune; distress. See **misfortune** for synonym study. 2 a particular misfortune; calamity.

ad vert (ad vėrt′), *v.i.* direct attention in speaking or writing; refer or allude *(to): The speaker adverted to the need for more parks.* [< Latin *advertere* < *ad-* to + *vertere* to turn]

ad ver tise (ad′vər tīz), *v.,* **-tised, -tis ing.** —*v.t.* 1 give public notice of in a newspaper or magazine, on the radio or television, etc.; announce: *advertise the opening of a new store.* 2 make known or recommend publicly (a product, service, etc.) by praising its good quality in order to create a demand or promote sales: *advertise automobiles.* —*v.i.* 1 ask by public notice *(for): advertise for a job.* 2 seek to sell products, etc., by advertising; issue advertising: *It pays to advertise.* [< Middle French *advertiss-*, a form of *advertir* make known < Latin *advertere.* See ADVERT.] —**ad′ver tis′er,** *n.*

ad ver tise ment (ad′vər tīz′mənt, ad vėr′tis mənt, ad vėr′tiz mənt), *n.* a public notice or announcement, now always paid for, recommending some product or service or informing of some need, usually published in a newspaper or magazine, displayed by poster, distributed by circulars, or broadcast over radio or television.

ad ver tis ing (ad′vər tī′zing), *n.* 1 business of preparing, publishing, or circulating advertisements. 2 advertisements. 3 a bringing to public notice by advertisements.

ad vice (ad vīs′), *n.* 1 opinion, suggestion, or recommendation as to what should be done; counsel: *My advice is that you study more.* See synonym study below. 2 Often, **advices,** *pl.* news, especially from a distance; information: *advices from the battlefront.* [< Old French *avis* < Latin *ad-* + *visum* thing seen]

Syn. 1 **Advice, counsel** mean an opinion given by a person for the guidance of another. **Advice** is the general word: *I asked her advice about which paint to buy.* **Counsel** is more formal, suggesting the giving of a professional or more carefully considered opinion: *I asked the bank president for counsel about a career in banking.*

ad vis a bil i ty (ad vī′zə bil′ə tē), *n.* quality of being advisable; fitness.

ad vis a ble (ad vī′zə bəl), *adj.* to be advised or recommended; wise; sensible; suitable. —**ad vis′a bly,** *adv.*

ad vise (ad vīz′), *v.,* **-vised, -vis ing.** —*v.t.* 1 give advice to; counsel: *I advise you to be cautious.* 2 recommend as a remedy, policy, etc.: *My doctor advised complete rest.* 3 give information to; inform; tell: *Please advise me of the date of delivery.* —*v.i.* 1 give advice; recommend: *I shall do as you advise.* 2 talk over plans; consult; confer *(with): Before deciding, I advised with several friends.* [< Old French *aviser* < *avis.* See ADVICE.]

ad vised (ad vīzd′), *adj.* 1 considered: *well advised.* 2 informed.

ad vis ed ly (ad vī′zid lē), *adv.* after careful consideration; deliberately.

ad vise ment (ad vīz′mənt), *n.* careful consideration; consultation: *The lawyer took our case under advisement.*

ad vis er or **ad vi sor** (ad vī′zər), *n.* 1 person who gives advice. 2 teacher or other person appointed to advise students.

ad vi sor y (ad vī′zər ē), *adj., n., pl.* **-sor ies.** —*adj.* 1 having the power only to advise, not to determine or direct policy. 2 of, concerned with, or containing advice. —*n.* bulletin or report to advise of developments. —**ad vi′sor i ly,** *adv.*

ad vo ca cy (ad′və kə sē), *n.* a speaking or writing in favor of something; public recommendation; support.

ad vo cate (*v.* ad′və kāt; *n.* ad′və kit, ad′və kāt), *v.,* **-cat ed, -cat ing,** *n.* —*v.t.* speak or write in favor of; recommend publicly (a measure, policy, etc.); support. —*n.* 1 person who defends, maintains, or publicly recommends a proposal, belief, theory, etc.; supporter. 2 lawyer who pleads the cause of anyone in certain courts of law. [< Latin *advocatum* summoned < *ad-* to + *vocare* to call] —**ad′vo ca′tion,** *n.* —**ad′vo ca′tor,** *n.*

advt., advertisement.

adz or **adze** (adz), *n., pl.* **adz es.** a cutting tool for shaping heavy timbers, similar to an ax but with a blade set across the end of the handle and curving inward. [Old English *adesa*]

adz
man using an adz to shape and smooth a log

AEC or **A.E.C.,** Atomic Energy Commission.

a ë des (ā ē′dēz), *n.* 1 any mosquito of the species that transmits yellow fever and dengue. 2 any other mosquito of the same genus. [< Greek *aēdēs* unpleasant < *a-* without + *ēdos* pleasure]

ae dile (ē′dīl), *n.* (in ancient Rome) an official in charge of public buildings, games and circuses, the police, etc. Also, **edile.** [< Latin *aedilis* < *aedes* temple]

A.E.F., American Expeditionary Forces (soldiers sent to Europe by the United States during World War I).

Ae ge an (i jē′ən), *adj.* 1 of or in the Aegean Sea. 2 of or relating to the first great European civilization, 3500-1400 B.C., that flourished on Crete and nearby islands during the Bronze Age, and spread to Greece before 1400 B.C.

Aegean Islands, group of islands in the Aegean Sea that includes the Cyclades.

Aegean Sea, sea between Greece and Turkey. It is an arm of the Mediterranean. 400 mi. long; 200 mi. wide. See **Adriatic Sea** for map.

Ae gi na (i jī′nə), *n.* Greek island near the SE coast of Greece, near Athens. 9000 pop.; 32 sq. mi.

ae gis (ē′jis), *n.* 1 (in Greek myths) a shield or breastplate used by the Greek god Zeus or by his daughter Athena. 2 an effective protection. 3 auspices; sponsorship. Also, **egis.** [< Latin < Greek *aigis*]

Ae ne as (i nē′əs), *n.* (in Greek and Roman

legends) a Trojan hero who after the fall of Troy and years of wandering reached Italy, where his descendants supposedly founded Rome.

Ae ne id (i nē′id), *n.* a Latin epic poem by Vergil, describing the wanderings of Aeneas.

Ae o li an (ē ō′lē ən), *adj.* 1 of Aeolus. 2 **aeolian,** of, produced by, or carried by the winds. 3 belonging to a certain branch of the Greek people that lived in Boeotia, Thessaly, and Asia Minor. Also, **Eolian.**

aeolian harp, box with six or more tuned strings, fitted across openings in its top, that gives out musical sounds when currents of air vibrate the strings.

Ae o lis (ē′ə lis), *n.* a coastal region in NW Asia Minor, colonized by the ancient Greeks.

Ae o lus (ē′ə ləs), *n.* (in Greek myths) the god of the winds.

ae on (ē′ən, ē′on), *n.* eon.

aer ate (er′āt, ar′āt), *v.t.,* **-at ed, -at ing.** 1 expose to and mix with air: *Water in some reservoirs is aerated and purified by being sprayed high into the air.* 2 charge or mix with a gas, often under pressure. 3 expose to chemical action with oxygen: *Blood is aerated in the lungs.* [< Latin *aer* air < Greek *aēr*] **—aer′a′tion,** *n.* **—aer′a tor,** *n.*

aer i al (er′ē əl, ar′ē əl; *adj. also* ā ir′ē əl), *n.* 1 a long wire or set of wires or rods used in television or radio for sending out or receiving electromagnetic waves; antenna. 2 (in football) a forward pass. *—adj.* 1 of, for, between, or used by aircraft: *aerial navigation.* 2 carried out from or done by aircraft: *an aerial photograph.* 3 growing in the air instead of in soil: *The banyan tree has aerial roots.* 4 of the air; atmospheric: *aerial currents.* 5 extending high in the air; lofty: *aerial mountains.* 6 as light as air; ethereal: *The dancer moved with aerial grace.* 7 as thin as air; unsubstantial; imaginary: *aerial beings.* [< Latin *aer* air] **—aer′i al ly,** *adv.*

aer i al ist (er′ē ə list, ar′ē ə list, ā ir′ē ə list), *n.* acrobat who performs feats on a trapeze, tightrope, etc.

aer ie or **aer y** (er′ē, ar′ē, ir′ē), *n., pl.* **aer ies.** 1 the nest of an eagle, hawk, or other bird of prey, usually built in a lofty place. 2 house, castle, etc., placed high on a rock or mountainside. Also, **eyrie, eyry.** [< Medieval Latin *aeria* < Old French *aire* < Latin *area* area]

aer o (er′ō, ar′ō), *adj.* 1 of or having to do with aviation or flying. 2 of or for aircraft.

aero-, *combining form.* 1 air; of the air: *Aeroplane = airplane.* 2 atmosphere; atmospheric: *Aerospace = space in the atmosphere.* 3 gas; of gas or gases: *Aerodynamics = dynamics of gases.* 4 of or for aircraft: *Aerobatics = aircraft acrobatics.* [< Greek *aēr* air]

aer o bat ics (er′ə bat′iks, ar′ə bat′iks), *n.* the performance of tricks, stunts, etc., with an aircraft in flight. [< *aero-* + *(acro)batics*]

aer obe (er′ōb, ar′ōb), *n.* an aerobic bacterium or other microorganism.

aer o bic (er′ō′bik, ar′ō′bik, ā′ə rō′bik), *adj.* 1 living and growing only where there is atmospheric oxygen: *aerobic bacteria.* 2 of or caused by aerobic bacteria. [ultimately < Greek *aēr* air + *bios* life] **—aer′o′bi cal ly,** *adv.*

aer o drome (er′ə drōm, ar′ə drōm), *n.* BRITISH. airdrome.

aer o dy nam ic (er′ō dī nam′ik, ar′ō dī nam′ik), *adj.* of aerodynamics. **—aer′o dy nam′i cal ly,** *adv.*

aer o dy nam ics (er′ō dī nam′iks, ar′ō dī nam′iks), *n.* branch of physics that deals with forces such as pressure or resistance exerted by air or other gases in motion on both flying and wind-blown bodies.

aer o log ic (er′ə loj′ik, ar′ə loj′ik), *adj.* of aerology. **—aer′o log′i cal ly,** *adv.*

aer o log i cal (er′ə loj′ə kəl, ar′ə loj′ə kəl), *adj.* aerologic.

aer ol o gist (er′ol′ə jist, ar′ol′ə jist), *n.* an expert in aerology.

aer ol o gy (er′ol′ə jē, ar′ol′ə jē), *n.* branch of meteorology in which the properties and phenomena of the upper atmosphere are studied.

aer o naut (er′ə nôt, ar′ə nôt), *n.* 1 pilot of an airship or balloon; balloonist. 2 person who travels in an airship or balloon. [< *aero-* + Greek *nautēs* sailor]

aer o nau tic (er′ə nô′tik, ar′ə nô′tik), *adj.* aeronautical.

aer o nau ti cal (er′ə nô′tə kəl, ar′ə nô′tə kəl), *adj.* of or having to do with aeronautics or aeronauts. **—aer′o nau′ti cal ly,** *adv.*

aer o nau tics (er′ə nô′tiks, ar′ə nô′tiks), *n.* science or art having to do with the design, manufacture, and operation of aircraft.

aer on o my (er′on′ə mē, ar′on′ə mē), *n.* study of the physical and chemical conditions of the upper atmosphere. [< *aero-* + Greek *nomos* distribution]

aer o pause (er′ə pôz, ar′ə pôz), *n.* 1 the limit of man's penetration in the upper atmosphere at any particular time. 2 the upper limit of manned airborne flight.

aer o plane (er′ə plān, ar′ə plān), *n.* BRITISH. airplane.

aer o sol (er′ə sol, er′ə sôl; ar′ə sol, ar′ə sôl), *n.* 1 a dispersion of very fine colloidal particles of a solid or liquid suspended in the air or in some other gas. Smoke and fog are common aerosols. 2 aerosol bomb. [< *aero-* + *sol*[3]]

aerosol bomb, container in which an insecticide, cosmetic, paint, or other product is contained under pressure and from which it may be released as a spray or mist.

aer o space (er′ō spās, ar′ō spās), *n.* 1 the earth's atmosphere and the space beyond it, especially the space in which rockets and other spacecraft operate. 2 field of science, technology, and industry dealing with the flight of rockets and other spacecraft through the atmosphere or the space beyond it.

aer o stat ics (er′ə stat′iks, ar′ə stat′iks), *n.* branch of physics dealing with the static equilibrium of the air and other gases and of solid objects suspended or moving in them.

aer y (er′ē, ar′ē), *adj.,* **aer i er, aer i est.** 1 aerial; lofty. 2 ethereal.

Aes chy lus (es′kə ləs), *n.* 525-456 B.C., Greek tragic poet and dramatist.

Aes cu la pi us (es′kyə lā′pē əs), *n.* (in Roman myths) the god of medicine and healing.

Ae sir (ā′sir, ē′sir), *n.pl.* the chief Scandinavian gods and goddesses.

Ae sop (ē′səp, ē′sop), *n.* 620?-560? B.C., Greek writer of fables.

Ae so pi an (ē sō′pē ən), *adj.* 1 of Aesop. 2 composed by Aesop or in his manner.

aes thete (es′thēt′), *n.* 1 person who pretends to appreciate or be specially sensitive to the beautiful in nature or art. 2 person who appreciates beauty in nature and art. Also, **esthete.**

aes thet ic (es thet′ik), *adj.* 1 based on or determined by beauty rather than by practically useful, scientific, or moral considerations. 2 having or showing an appreciation of beauty in nature or art. 3 showing good taste; artistic. Also, **esthetic.** [< Greek *aisthētikos* sensitive, perceptive < *aisthanesthai* perceive] **—aes thet′i cal ly,** *adv.*

hat, āge, fär; let, ēqual, tėrm;
it, īce; hot, ōpen, ôrder;
oil, out; cup, pu̇t, rüle;
ch, child; ng, long; sh, she;
th, thin; ᴛʜ, then; zh, measure;

ə represents *a* in about, *e* in taken,
i in pencil, *o* in lemon, *u* in circus.

< = from, derived from, taken from.

aes thet i cism (es thet′ə siz′əm), *n.* 1 the belief in beauty as the basic standard of value in human life, underlying all moral and other considerations. 2 great love for and sensitivity to beauty and the arts.

aes thet ics (es thet′iks), *n.* study of beauty in art and nature; philosophy of beauty or taste; theory of the fine arts. Also, **esthetics.**

aes ti val (es′tə vəl, e stī′vəl), *adj.* estival.

aes ti vate (es′tə vāt), *v.,* **-vat ed, -vat ing.** estivate. **—aes′ti va′tion,** *n.*

aet. or **aetat.,** at the age of: *John Richards, aet. 71.* [for Latin *aetatis*].

ae ther (ē′thər), *n.* ether (defs. 2 and 3).

ae ther e al (i thir′ē əl), *adj.* ethereal.

Aet na (et′nə), *n.* **Mount.** See **Etna.**

Ae to li a (i tō′lē ə), *n.* ancient region in central Greece, north of the Gulf of Corinth. **—Ae to′li an,** *adj., n.*

af-, *prefix.* form of **ad-** before *f,* as in *affix.*

AF, Air Force.

A.F. or **a.f.,** audio frequency.

a far (ə fär′), *adv.* 1 at a great distance; far away. 2 **from afar,** from a distance: *I saw her from afar.*

A fars and Is sas (ä′färz and is′äz), French territory in E Africa. It was formerly known as **French Somaliland.** 125,000 pop.; 8500 sq. mi. *Capital:* Djibouti.

AFB or **A.F.B.,** Air Force Base.

a feard or **a feared** (ə fird′), *adj.* ARCHAIC or DIALECT. frightened; afraid.

af fa bil i ty (af′ə bil′ə tē), *n.* condition or quality of being affable.

af fa ble (af′ə bəl), *adj.* 1 courteous and pleasant in receiving and responding to the conversation or approaches of others. 2 gracious: *an affable smile.* [< Latin *affabilis* easy to speak to < *affari* speak to < *ad-* to + *fari* speak] **—af′fa ble ness,** *n.* **—af′fa bly,** *adv.*

af fair (ə fer′, ə far′), *n.* 1 anything done or to be done; job; task: *The project was an important but time-consuming affair.* 2 **affairs,** *pl.* matters of interest, especially public or business matters: *affairs of state, men of affairs.* 3 a particular action, event, or happening: *a brilliant social affair.* 4 a private concern: *That's my own affair.* 5 thing; matter: *This machine is a complicated affair.* 6 an amorous or romantic experience, especially a temporary one: *a love affair.* 7 an important or notorious case: *the Dreyfus affair.* [< Old French *afaire* < *a faire* to do]

af faire (ə fer′, ə far′), *n.* affair (defs. 6 and 7). [< French]

af fect[1] (ə fekt′), *v.t.* 1 have an effect on; act on; influence or change: *Nothing you say will affect my decision. The disease affected her eyesight.* 2 stir the feelings of; move: *a tale of* *woe that deeply affected us.* [< Latin *affectum* done to, acted on < *ad-* to + *facere* do]

➔ **Affect** and **effect** are often confused in writing, partly because they are pronounced very similarly or identically, and partly because *to affect* is synonymous with *to have an effect on.* But in the general vocabulary *affect* is used only as a verb, whereas *effect* is most commonly used as a noun: *Overwork has had a serious effect on (has seriously affected) his health.*

af fect[2] (ə fekt′), *v.t.* 1 pretend to have or feel; feign; simulate: *They affected ignorance of the fight, but we knew that they had seen it.* See **pretend** for synonym study. 2 choose to use, wear, own, etc.; fancy: *affect carelessness in dress.* 3 make a show of liking; adopt falsely or ostentatiously: *affect a taste for abstract art.* [< Middle French *affecter* < Latin *affectare* strive for < *ad-* to + *facere* do]

➔ See **affect**[1] for usage note concerning the confusion of *affect* and *effect.*

af fec ta tion (af′ek tā′shən), *n.* 1 behavior that is not natural, but assumed to impress others; pretense. 2 mannerism, choice of language, etc., that indicates a tendency toward this: *Your little affectations are annoying.*

af fect ed[1] (ə fek′tid), *adj.* 1 acted on; influenced. 2 influenced injuriously. 3 moved in feeling; stirred up.

af fect ed[2] (ə fek′tid), *adj.* 1 put on for effect; unnatural; artificial. 2 behaving, speaking, writing, etc., unnaturally for effect. **—af fect′ed ly,** *adv.* **—af fect′ed ness,** *n.*

af fect ing (ə fek′ting), *adj.* having an effect on the feelings; touching; moving. **—af fect′ing ly,** *adv.*

af fec tion (ə fek′shən), *n.* 1 feeling of warm liking and tender attachment; fondness; love: *His constant nagging destroyed her affection for him.* See **love** for synonym study. 2 unhealthy condition; disease. 3 tendency; inclination.

af fec tion ate (ə fek′shə nit), *adj.* having or showing affection; loving; tender. **—af fec′tion ate ly,** *adv.*

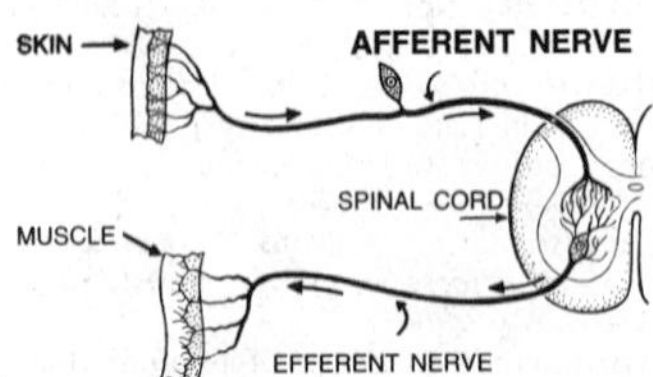

af fer ent (af′ər ənt), *adj.* carrying inward to a central organ or point. Afferent nerves carry stimuli from nerve endings to the spinal cord. [< Latin *afferentem* carrying to < *ad-* to + *ferre* bring]

af fi ance (ə fī′əns), *v.t.,* **-anced, -anc ing.** promise solemnly (oneself or another) in marriage; engage; betroth. [< Old French *afiancer* < *afiance* a trust < *afier* to trust]

af fi da vit (af′ə dā′vit), *n.* statement written down and sworn to be true, usually before a notary public or other authorized official. [< Medieval Latin, he has stated on oath]

af fil i ate (*v.* ə fil′ē āt; *n.* ə fil′ē it, ə fil′ē āt), *v.,* **-at ed, -at ing,** *n.* —*v.t.* join in close association; connect or associate: *The two clubs were affiliated with each other.* —*v.i.* connect or associate oneself *(with): affiliate with a political party.* —*n.* organization or group associated with another or larger organization or group. [< Medieval Latin *affiliatum* adopted < Latin *ad-* to + *filius* son] **—af fil′i a′tion,** *n.*

af fin i ty (ə fin′ə tē), *n., pl.* **-ties.** 1 a natural attraction to a person or liking for a thing: *If you have an affinity for mathematics, you will probably enjoy physics.* 2 relation; connection. 3 relationship by marriage. 4 resemblance between species, genera, etc., that makes a common ancestry probable. 5 force that attracts certain chemical elements to others and keeps them combined. [< Latin *affinitatem* relation < *affinis* related, bordering on < *ad-* on + *finis* border]

af firm (ə fėrm′), *v.t.* 1 declare positively to be true; maintain firmly; assert: *I affirmed the report to be true.* 2 confirm or ratify: *The higher court affirmed the lower court's decision.* —*v.i.* declare solemnly, but without taking an oath. [< Latin *affirmare* < *ad-* to + *firmus* strong]

af fir ma tion (af′ər mā′shən), *n.* 1 a positive statement; assertion. 2 a solemn declaration having the legal force of an oath, and made by persons whose religion or conscience forbids the taking of an oath. 3 confirmation or ratification.

af firm a tive (ə fėr′mə tiv), *adj.* 1 stating that a fact is so; answering yes to a question put or implied. 2 arguing in favor of a question being formally debated: *the affirmative side.* 3 positive in manner. —*n.* 1 word or statement that says yes or agrees: *"I will" is an affirmative.* 2 **in the affirmative,** expressing agreement by saying yes. 3 **the affirmative,** the side arguing in favor of a question being formally debated. **—af firm′a tive ly,** *adv.*

af fix (*v.* ə fiks′; *n.* af′iks), *v.t.* 1 make firm or fix (one thing to or on another); fasten: *affix a stamp on a letter.* See **attach** for synonym study. 2 add at the end: *affix a signature to a letter.* 3 make an impression of (a seal, etc.). 4 connect with; attach: *affix blame.* —*n.* 1 thing affixed; addition. 2 prefix or suffix. *Un-* and *-ly* are affixes. **—af′fix a′tion,** *n.* **—af fix′er,** *n.*

af fix al (ə fik′səl), *adj.* of, having to do with, or of the nature of an affix.

af fla tus (ə flā′təs), *n.* inspiration, especially divine inspiration. [< Latin]

af flict (ə flikt′), *v.t.* cause to suffer severely; trouble greatly; distress: *be afflicted with arthritis. The pangs of conscience afflicted me.* [< Latin *afflictum* dashed down, damaged < *ad-* + *fligere* to dash]

af flic tion (ə flik′shən), *n.* 1 condition of continued pain or distress; misery. 2 cause of continued pain or distress; misfortune.

af flic tive (ə flik′tiv), *adj.* causing misery or pain; distressing. **—af flic′tive ly,** *adv.*

af flu ence (af′lü əns), *n.* 1 great abundance of material goods; wealth; riches. 2 a plentiful flow or abundant supply of tears, words, etc.; profusion.

af flu ent (af′lü ənt), *adj.* 1 having an abundance of money, property, etc.; wealthy; rich. 2 abundant; plentiful. 3 flowing freely. —*n.* stream flowing into a larger stream or body of water; tributary. [< Latin *affluentem* flowing out < *ad-* + *fluere* to flow] **—af′flu ent ly,** *adv.*

af ford (ə fôrd′, ə fōrd′), *v.t.* 1 have or spare the money for: *We can't afford a new car.* 2 manage to give, spare, or have: *Can you afford the time?* 3 be able without difficulty or harm; have the means: *I can't afford to take the chance.* 4 give as an effect or a result; provide; yield: *Reading affords pleasure.* 5 furnish from natural resources; yield: *Some trees afford resin.* [Old English *geforthian* to further, accomplish]

af fo rest (ə fôr′ist, ə for′ist), *v.t.* change (open land) into forest.

af fo rest a tion (ə fôr′ə stā′shən, ə for′ə stā′shən), *n.* the changing of open land into forest.

af fray (ə frā′), *n.* 1 a noisy quarrel; fight in public; brawl. 2 (in law) a fighting in a public place so as to frighten others. [< Old French *effrei*]

af fri cate (af′rə kit), *n.* (in phonetics) a sound which begins as a stop and ends as a fricative. The *ch* in *chin* is an affricate because it starts with *t* and ends almost as *sh.* [< Latin *affricatum* rubbed against < *ad-* against + *fricare* rub]

af fright (ə frīt′), ARCHAIC. —*v.t.* excite with sudden fear; frighten. —*n.* sudden fear; fright; terror.

af front (ə frunt′), *n.* 1 word or act that openly and purposely expresses disrespect; open insult: *To be called a coward is an affront.* See **insult** for synonym study. 2 a slight or injury to one's dignity. —*v.t.* 1 insult openly; offend purposely and to one's face. 2 face courageously and defiantly; confront. [< Old French *afronter* strike on the forehead, defy, face < *a front* against the forehead]

Af ghan (af′gən, af′gan), *n.* 1 native or inhabitant of Afghanistan. 2 the principal language of Afghanistan; Pashto. 3 **afghan,** blanket or shawl made of knitted or crocheted wool, nylon, etc. —*adj.* of Afghanistan, its people, or their language.

Afghan hound, any of a breed of large, swift, hunting dogs, having a narrow head and silky hair.

af ghan i (af gan′ē), *n.* unit of money of Afghanistan, worth about 2 cents.

Af ghan i stan (af gan′ə stan), *n.* country in SW Asia, between Pakistan and Iran. 13,600,000 pop.; 250,000 sq. mi. *Capital:* Kabul.

a fi cio na do (ə fis′yə nä′dō, ə fish′ē ə nä′dō), *n., pl.* **-dos.** person who is a devotee of some sport, hobby, or special field; enthusiast. [< Spanish]

a field (ə fēld′), *adv.* 1 away from home; away. 2 out of the right way; astray. 3 on or in the field; to the field.

a fire (ə fīr′), *adv., adj.* 1 on fire; burning. 2 enthusiastic.

AFL or **A.F.L.,** American Football League.

a flame (ə flām′), *adv., adj.* 1 in flames; on fire. 2 in a glow; glowing. 3 eager; enthusiastic; excited.

af la tox in (af′lə tok′sən), *n.* a poisonous substance produced in certain plants, es-

hat, āge, fär; let, ēqual, tėrm;
it, ice; hot, ōpen, ôrder;
oil, out; cup, pu̇t, rüle;
ch, child; ng, long; sh, she;
th, thin; ᴛʜ, then; zh, measure;

ə represents *a* in about, *e* in taken, *i* in pencil, *o* in lemon, *u* in circus.

< = from, derived from, taken from.

pecially peanuts, by a common mold. [< *A(spergillus) fla(vus),* the mold + *toxin*]

AFL-CIO, a labor organization formed by the merger in 1955 of the craft unions of the American Federation of Labor **(AFL)** and the industrial unions of the Congress of Industrial Organizations **(CIO).**

a float (ə flōt′), *adv., adj.* 1 floating on the water or in the air. 2 on shipboard; at sea. 3 adrift. 4 flooded with water. 5 being spread; going around: *Rumors of a revolt were afloat.*

a flut ter (ə flut′ər), *adv., adj.* 1 fluttering or waving. 2 in a flutter; excited.

a foot (ə fu̇t′), *adv., adj.* 1 on foot; by walking: *He came all the way afoot.* 2 going on; in progress: *There is mischief afoot.* 3 on the move; astir.

a fore (ə fôr′, ə fōr′), *adv., prep., conj.* ARCHAIC or DIALECT. before.

a fore men tioned (ə fôr′men′shənd, ə fōr′men′shənd), *adj.* aforesaid.

a fore said (ə fôr′sed′, ə fōr′sed′), *adj.* spoken of before; mentioned earlier.

a fore thought (ə fôr′thôt′, ə fōr′thôt′), *adj.* thought out beforehand; deliberately planned: *with malice aforethought.*

a fore time (ə fôr′tīm′, ə fōr′tīm′), *adv.* ARCHAIC. in time past; formerly.

a for ti o ri (ā fôr′shē ôr′ī, ā fôr′shē ôr′ē; ā fôr′shē ōr′ī, ā fôr′shē ōr′ē), LATIN. for a still stronger reason. Thus if *A* exceeds *B,* and *B* is proved greater than *X, a fortiori* is *A* greater than *X.*

a foul (ə foul′), *adv., adj.* 1 in a tangle; in a collision; entangled. 2 **run afoul of,** get into difficulties with: *run afoul of the law.*

Afr., 1 Africa. 2 African.

a fraid (ə frād′), *adj.* 1 feeling fear; frightened: *afraid of the dark.* See synonym study below. 2 unwilling because of fear: *afraid to speak up.* 3 sorry to have to say: *I'm afraid you are wrong about that.* [originally past participle of archaic verb *afray* frighten < Old French *effreer.* Related to AFFRAY.]

Syn. 1 Afraid, frightened, terrified mean feeling fear. **Afraid,** which is never used before the noun, means being in a mental state of fear which may have either a real or an imagined cause and may be brief or last long: *He is afraid of snakes.* **Frightened,** commonly used instead of *afraid* before the noun, particularly means suddenly made afraid, often only momentarily, by a real and present cause: *The frightened child ran home.* **Terrified** means suddenly filled with a very great and paralyzing fear: *Terrified by heights, I couldn't bring myself to look at the bottom of the canyon.*

a fresh (ə fresh′), *adv.* once more; again.

Af ri ca (af′rə kə), *n.* the continent south of Europe. It is the second largest continent. 344,484,000 pop.; 11,700,000 sq. mi.

Af ri can (af′rə kən), *adj.* 1 of or having to do with Africa, its peoples, their languages, or their customs. 2 Negro. *—n.* 1 native of Africa, especially a person belonging to one of the native tribes of Africa. 2 Negro.

African violet, a tropical, perennial, African plant with violet, white, or pink flowers, often grown as a house plant.

Af ri kaans (af′rə käns′, af′rə känz′), *n.* language spoken in South Africa, which developed from the Dutch of the colonists who came in the 1600's; South African Dutch.

Af ri ka ner (af′rə kä′nər), *n.* person born in South Africa of European, especially Dutch, descent; Boer.

Af ro (af′rō), *n.* a bushy hairdo like that worn in parts of Africa. [< *Afro-*]

Afro-, *combining form.* 1 African: *Afro-Socialism = African Socialism.* 2 African and: *Afro-European trade = African and European trade.* [< Latin *Afer, Afri* African]

Af ro-A mer i can (af′rō ə mer′ə kən), *adj.* of or having to do with American Negroes. *—n.* an American Negro.

aft (aft), *adv.* at, or toward the stern; abaft. *—adj.* in or near the stern. [Old English *æftan* from behind]

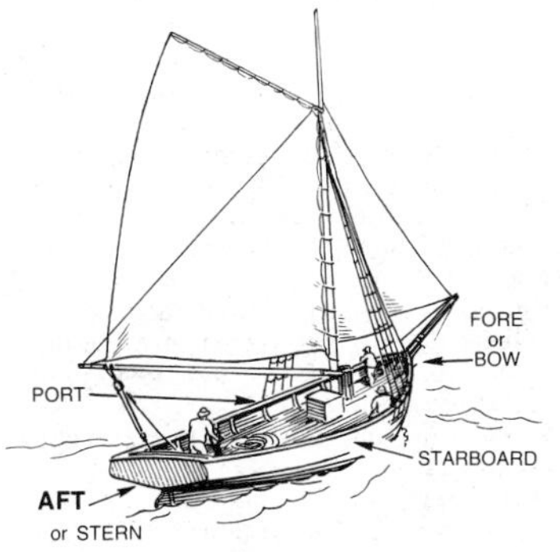

AFT or **A.F.T.,** American Federation of Teachers.

af ter (af′tər), *prep.* 1 coming or going in the rear of; behind in place: *marching in line one after another.* See **behind** for synonym study. 2 next to; following: *day after day.* 3 in pursuit of; in search of: *Run after them.* 4 about; concerning: *Your aunt asked after you.* 5 later in time than: *after supper.* See synonym study below. 6 considering; because of: *After the big dinner, I couldn't finish my dessert.* 7 in spite of: *After all her suffering, she is still cheerful.* 8 in imitation of; imitating: *I wrote a fable after the manner of Aesop.* 9 lower in rank or importance than: *A major comes after a colonel.* 10 according to: *act after one's own ideas.* 11 in honor of; for: *I am named after my grandmother.*
—adv. 1 in the rear; behind: *follow after.* 2 later; afterwards: *three hours after.*
—adj. 1 later; subsequent: *In after years he regretted the mistakes of his boyhood.* 2 nearer or toward the stern: *after sails.*
—conj. later than the time that: *After they go, we shall eat.*
[Old English *æfter* more to the rear, later]

Syn. *prep.* 5 **After, behind** express a relationship between occurrences in time. **After** merely notes their sequence: *I played football after school.* **Behind** suggests that an event occurred after it was expected to: *The builder is so far behind schedule that he is unlikely to finish our home this year.*

af ter birth (af′tər bėrth′), *n.* the placenta and membranes expelled from the uterus shortly after birth.

af ter brain (af′tər brān′), *n.* portion of the hindbrain containing the medulla oblongata; myelencephalon.

af ter burn er (af′tər bėr′nər), *n.* device in the engine of a jet plane which supplies additional fuel to the exhaust and reignites it, thus increasing the thrust of the plane so that bursts of very high speed can be obtained.

af ter care (af′tər ker′, af′tər kar′), *n.* care or nursing of convalescent patients after treatment.

af ter deck (af′tər dek′), *n.* part of a deck toward or at the stern of a ship.

af ter ef fect (af′tər i fekt′), *n.* 1 result or effect that follows after the cause has disappeared; a delayed effect. 2 a secondary effect of a drug or disease; side effect.

af ter glow (af′tər glō′), *n.* 1 glow remaining after something bright has gone. 2 glow in the sky after sunset. 3 a pleasurable feeling following something greatly enjoyed.

af ter im age (af′tər im′ij), *n.* visual sensation that persists or recurs after the stimulus causing it has ceased to act.

af ter life (af′tər līf′), *n.* life after death.

af ter math (af′tər math), *n.* 1 result or consequence, especially of something destructive. 2 a second crop of grass from land in the same season. [< *after* + dialectal *math* a mowing (Old English *mæth*)]

af ter most (af′tər mōst), *adj.* 1 nearest the stern of a ship. 2 last in order of time; hindmost.

af ter noon (*n.* af′tər nün′; *adj.* af′tər-nün′), *n.* the part of the day between noon and evening. *—adj.* of, in, or suitable for the afternoon: *an afternoon dress.*

af ter taste (af′tər tāst′), *n.* 1 taste that is noticed in the mouth after eating or drinking. 2 retrospective feeling.

af ter thought (af′tər thôt′), *n.* 1 thought that comes too late to be used. 2 a second or later thought or explanation.

af ter ward (af′tər wərd), *adv.* afterwards; later.

af ter wards (af′tər wərdz), *adv.* later.

ag-, *prefix.* form of **ad-** before *g,* as in *aggrandize.*

Ag, silver. [for Latin *argentum*]

a gain (ə gen′, ə gān′), *adv.* 1 once more; another time: *try again.* 2 in return; in reply: *answer again.* 3 to the same place or person; back: *Bring us word again.* 4 moreover; besides: *Again, I must say that you are wrong.* 5 on the other hand; yet: *It might rain, and again it might not.* 6 **again and again,** many times over; often; frequently. 7 **as much again,** twice as much; twice as many. [Old English *ongegn* toward, opposite < *on-* on + *gegn* direct]

a gainst (ə genst′, ə gānst′), *prep.* 1 in opposition to; contrary to: *This is against the rules of the game.* 2 actively opposed; hostile to: *Why are you against me?* 3 in an opposite direction to, so as to meet; upon or toward: *sail against the wind.* 4 directly opposite to; facing: *over against the wall.* 5 in contact with: *lean against a wall.* 6 in contrast to or with: *The ship appeared against the sky.* 7 in preparation for: *Squirrels store up nuts against the winter.* 8 in defense from: *protection against cold.* 9 in return for: *trade one thing against another.* [Middle English *agenes* < *agen,* Old English *ongegn.* See AGAIN.]

Ag a mem non (ag′ə mem′non), *n.* (in Greek legends) the leader of the Greeks in the Trojan War. He was the husband of Clytemnestra, the brother of Menelaus, and the father of Orestes, Electra, and Iphigenia.

a gam ic (ə gam′ik), *adj.* 1 asexual. 2 (of ova) not requiring fertilization by the male. [< Greek *agamos* not married] **—a gam′i cal ly,** *adv.*

A ga ña (ä gä′nyə), *n.* capital of Guam. 2000.

a gape[1] (ə gāp′, ə gap′), *adj.* open-mouthed with wonder or surprise; gaping.

ag a pe[2] (ag′ə pē′, ä′gə pā′), *n., pl.* **-pae** (-pē′, -pī′). 1 love (def. 8). 2 love feast (def. 1). [< Greek *agapē*]

a gar (ä′gər, ag′ər), *n.* 1 a gelatinlike extract obtained from certain species of seaweeds, used in making culture media for bacteria and fungi, and in food processing. 2 a culture medium containing agar. [< Malay]

a gar-a gar (ä′gər ä′gər, ag′ər ag′ər), *n.* agar.

ag ar ic (ag′ər ik, ə gar′ik), *n.* type of fungus having blade-shaped gills on the under surface of an umbrellalike structure on which naked spores are produced. The group includes toadstools and edible mushrooms. [< Latin *agaricum* < Greek *agarikon* < *Agaria,* place name]

Ag as siz (ag′ə sē), *n.* **(Jean) Louis (Rodolphe),** 1807-1873, American zoologist and geologist, born in Switzerland.

agate (def. 1) polished, showing stripes

ag ate (ag′it), *n.* 1 a variety of quartz with variously colored stripes, clouded colors, or mosslike formations. 2 a playing marble that looks like this. 3 a size of printing type (5½ point). **This sentence is set in agate.** [< Old French *agathe* < Latin *achates* < Greek *achatēs*] **—ag′ate like′,** *adj.*

ag ate ware (ag′it wer′, ag′it war′), *n.* 1 cooking dishes, cups, or other household utensils made of iron or steel covered with variegated enamel. 2 type of pottery colored to look like agate.

a ga ve (ə gä′vē), *n.* any of a large genus of American desert plants, chiefly found in Mexico, having a dense cluster of rigid, fleshy leaves with spines along the edges and at the tips. The century plant and sisal are agaves. [< New Latin < Greek *Agauē,* proper name < *agauos* noble]

age (āj), *n., v.,* **aged, ag ing** or **age ing.** *—n.* 1 time of life: *She died at the age of eighty.* 2 length of life; time anything has existed: *Turtles live to a great age.* 3 a particular period or stage in life: *middle age.* 4 latter part of life; old age: *the wisdom of age.* 5 **of age,** at the time of life when a person is ready for adult rights and responsibilities, 18 or 21 years old. 6 the full or average term of life: *The age of a horse is from 25 to 30 years.* 7 a period in history; era; epoch: *the golden age, the atomic age.* 8 generation: *ages yet unborn.* 9 **ages, a** INFORMAL. a long, or apparently long, time: *I haven't seen you for ages.* **b** hundreds of years: *the work of ages.* 10 (in psychology) the level of a person's attainment, mental, educational, emotional, etc., determined by tests. *—v.i.* 1 grow old: *He is aging fast.* 2 become mature: *a cheese that ages slowly.* *—v.t.* 1 make old; produce the effects of age in: *Worry ages a person.* 2 mature by keeping in storage, etc.: *age wine.* [< Old French *aage* < Latin *aetas, aetatis*]

-age, *suffix forming nouns from other nouns or from verbs.* 1 act of ____ing: *Breakage = act of breaking.* 2 group of ____s: *Baggage = a group of bags.* 3 condition or rank of ____s: *Peerage = rank of peers.* 4 cost of or fee for ____ing: *Postage = cost of posting (mailing).* 5 home for ____s: *Orphanage = home for orphans.* [< Old French < Latin *-aticum*]

a ged (ā′jid *for 1 and 3;* ājd *for 2 and 4*), *adj.* 1 having lived a long time; old: *an aged woman.* See **old** for synonym study. 2 having the age of: *a child aged six.* 3 characteristic of old age. 4 improved by aging: *aged meat, aged cheese.* **—a ged ly** (ā′jid lē), *adv.* **—a ged ness** (ā′jid nis), *n.*

age less (āj′lis), *adj.* never growing old or coming to an end. **—age′less ly,** *adv.* **—age′less ness,** *n.*

age long (āj′lông′, āj′long′), *adj.* lasting a long time; everlasting.

a gen cy (ā′jən sē), *n., pl.* **-cies.** 1 person or company that has the authority to act for or in place of another: *an employment agency, a real estate agency.* 2 office of such a person or company. 3 a special department of the government concerned with the administration of affairs within a specific field: *the Central Intelligence Agency.* 4 means of producing effects; action or operation; instrumentality: *obtain a position through the agency of friends. Snow is drifted by the agency of the wind.*

a gen da (ə jen′də), *n.* 1 list of items of business to be brought before a meeting of a committee, council, board, etc., as things to be dealt with or done: *The agenda has already been settled.* 2 routine of things to be done. 3 a pl. of **agendum.** [< Latin, things to be done < *agere* do]

a gen dum (ə jen′dəm), *n., pl.* **-da** or **-dums.** agenda.

a gent (ā′jənt), *n.* 1 person or company that has the authority to act for or in place of another; representative: *a business agent, an insurance agent.* 2 any power or cause that produces an effect by its action: *Yeast is an important agent in causing bread to rise.* 3 means; instrument. 4 a law enforcement officer. 5 member of the government secret service. [< Latin *agentem* doing < *agere* do]

a gent pro vo ca teur (ä zhäɴ′ prô vô kȧ tœr′), *pl.* ***a gents pro vo ca teurs*** (ä zhäɴ′ prô vô kȧ tœr′). FRENCH. person hired to join secretly a group of persons in order to induce or incite the members of the group to do something unlawful which will make them liable to punishment.

age-old (āj′ōld′), *adj.* very old; ancient.

ag e ra tum (aj′ə rā′təm), *n.* any of a genus of tropical American plants of the composite family with small, dense flower heads of blue, or sometimes white, flowers, planted in gardens. [< Greek *ageratōn*]

Ag ge us (ə gē′əs), *n.* (in the Douay Bible) Haggai.

ag gior na men to (äd jôr′nä men′tō), *n.* ITALIAN. 1 (in the Roman Catholic Church) the modernization of old customs and practices. 2 (literally) an updating.

ag glom e rate (*v.* ə glom′ə rāt′; *n.* ə glom′ər it, ə glom′ə rāt′), *v.,* **-rat ed, -rat ing,** *n.* *—v.t., v.i.* gather together in a rounded mass; cluster or heap together. *—n.* 1 a loose or rough mass or collection of things; cluster. 2 rock composed of volcanic fragments fused by heat. [< Latin *agglomeratum* wound onto a ball < *ad-* to + *glomus* ball]

ag glom e ra tion (ə glom′ə rā′shən), *n.* 1 mass of things gathered or clustered together. 2 act of agglomerating. 3 agglomerated condition.

ag glom e ra tive (ə glom′ə rā′tiv), *adj.* tending to agglomerate.

ag glu ti nate (*v.* ə glüt′n āt; *adj.* ə glüt′n it, ə glüt′n āt), *v.,* **-nat ed, -nat ing,** *adj.* *—v.t.* 1 unite or fasten as with glue; stick together; join together. 2 form (words) by agglutination. 3 cause (cells, etc.) to mass together. *—v.i.* become agglutinated; join or clump together. *—adj.* stuck or joined together: *"Never-to-be-forgotten" is an agglutinate word.* [< Latin *agglutinatum* glued together < *ad-* to + *gluten* glue]

ag glu ti na tion (ə glüt′n ā′shən), *n.* 1 process of agglutinating. 2 an agglutinated condition. 3 mass or group formed by the sticking together of separate things. 4 the clumping together of bacteria or blood cells, usually by the introduction of antibodies. 5 the forming of words by joining together words that retain their individual form and meaning.

ag glu ti na tive (ə glüt′n ā′tiv), *adj.* 1 tending to stick together; adhesive. 2 forming words by agglutination.

ag glu ti nin (ə glüt′n ən), *n.* antibody that causes bacteria or blood cells to agglutinate.

ag glu tin o gen (ag′lü tin′ə jən), *n.* any of a group of antigens which stimulate the production of agglutinins.

ag gran dize (ə gran′dīz, ag′rən dīz), *v.t.,* **-dized, -diz ing.** make greater or larger in power; increase the rank or wealth of: *The ruler sought to aggrandize himself by new conquests.* **—ag gran′dize ment,** *n.* **—ag gran′diz er,** *n.*

ag gra vate (ag′rə vāt), *v.t.,* **-vat ed, -vat ing.** 1 make more burdensome; make worse; exacerbate: *The danger from foreign enemies was aggravated by rebellion at home.* 2 make more serious or offensive: *A lie will only aggravate your guilt.* 3 INFORMAL. annoy; irritate; exasperate. [< Latin *aggravatum* made heavy < *ad-* on, to + *gravis* heavy] **—ag′gra vat′ing ly,** *adv.*

ag gra va tion (ag′rə vā′shən), *n.* 1 a making worse or more severe. 2 a being made worse or more severe. 3 something that aggravates. 4 INFORMAL. annoyance.

ag gre gate (*n., adj.* ag′rə git, ag′rə gāt; *v.* ag′rə gāt), *n., adj., v.,* **-gat ed, -gat ing.** *—n.* 1 total amount; sum: *The aggregate of all the gifts was $100.* 2 **in the aggregate,** taken together; considered as a whole. 3 mass of separate things joined together; collection. 4 sand, gravel, etc., that is mixed with water and cement to form concrete. *—adj.* 1 total. 2 gathered together in one mass or group. 3 (of a flower) consisting of many florets arranged in a dense mass. *—v.t.* 1 amount to; come to; total: *The money collected will aggregate $1000.* 2 gather together in a mass or group; collect; unite. [< Latin *aggregatum* added to < *ad-* to + *grex* flock] **—ag′gre gate ly,** *adv.* **—ag′gre gate ness,** *n.*

aggregate fruit, a fruit composed of a cluster of several ripened ovaries that were separate in the flower, as the blackberry and raspberry.

ag gre ga tion (ag′rə gā′shən), *n.* 1 the collecting of separate things into one mass or whole. 2 the group or mass collected.

ag gres sion (ə gresh′ən), *n.* 1 the first step in a quarrel or war; an unprovoked attack. 2 practice of making assaults or attacks on the rights or territory of others as a method or policy. 3 (in psychology) an act or attitude of hostility, usually arising from feelings of inferiority or frustration. [< Latin *aggressionem* < *ad-* up to + *gradi* to step]

ag gres sive (ə gres′iv), *adj.* 1 taking the first step in a quarrel or war; attacking; quarrelsome: *an aggressive country.* 2 characterized by aggression; offensive: *an aggressive war.* 3 very active; energetic: *an aggressive campaign against crime.* 4 too confident and certain; assertive: *an insultingly aggressive manner.* **—ag gres′sive ly,** *adv.* **—ag gres′sive ness,** *n.*

ag gres sor (ə gres′ər), *n.* one that begins an attack or quarrel, especially a country that starts a war by committing aggression.

ag grieved (ə grēvd′), *adj.* 1 injured or wronged in one's rights, relations, or positions, especially one's legal rights. 2 feeling troubled or distressed.

a ghast (ə gast′), *adj.* struck with surprise or horror; filled with shocked amazement. [past participle of obsolete *agast* terrify < Old English *on-* on + *gæstan* frighten. Related to GHOST.]

ag ile (aj′əl), *adj.* 1 moving with speed, ease, and elegance; lively; nimble: *as agile as a kitten.* 2 mentally alert; quick-witted. [< Latin *agilis* < *agere* to move] **—ag′ile ly,** *adv.* **—ag′ile ness,** *n.*

a gil i ty (ə jil′ə tē), *n.* 1 liveliness; nimbleness. 2 alertness.

Ag in court (aj′in kôrt, aj′in kōrt), *n.* village in N France, near Calais, scene of an English victory under Henry V in 1415.

ag i tate (aj′ə tāt), *v.,* **-tat ed, -tat ing.** *—v.t.* 1 move or shake violently: *A sudden wind agitated the surface of the river.* 2 disturb or excite very much: *She was much agitated by the news of her brother's death.* 3 argue about; discuss vigorously and publicly. *—v.i.* keep urging a matter vigorously by public discussion, argument, demonstration, etc., to arouse public interest and feeling: *agitate for a shorter working day.* [< Latin *agitatum* moved to and fro < *agere* to move] **—ag′i tat′ed ly,** *adv.*

ag i ta tion (aj′ə tā′shən), *n.* 1 a violent moving or shaking. 2 a disturbed, upset, or troubled state. 3 vigorous argument, discussion, etc., to arouse public interest and feeling.

a gi ta to (ä′jē tä′tō), *adj., adv.* (in music) in an agitated manner; hurried and restless in style. [< Italian]

ag i ta tor (aj′ə tā′tər), *n.* 1 person who stirs up public feeling for or against something. 2 device or machine for shaking or stirring.

A gla ia (ə glā′ə), *n.* (in Greek myths) one of the three Graces.

a gleam (ə glēm′), *adj.* gleaming.

a gley (ə glē′, ə glī′), *adv.* SCOTTISH. out of the right way; wrong.

a glit ter (ə glit′ər), *adj.* glittering.

a glow (ə glō′), *adj.* glowing.

Ag new (ag′nü, ag′nyü), *n.* **Spiro T(heodore),** born 1918, vice-president of the United States from 1969 to 1973.

ag nos tic (ag nos′tik), *n.* person who believes that nothing is known or can be known about the existence of God or about things outside of human experience. *—adj.* of agnostics or their beliefs. [(coined by Thomas H. Huxley) < Greek *agnōstos* not knowing < *a-* not + *gnōstos* (to be) known] **—ag nos′ti cal ly,** *adv.*

ag nos ti cism (ag nos′tə siz′əm), *n.* the belief or intellectual attitude of agnostics.

Ag nus De i (ag′nəs dē′ī; ag′nəs dā′ē), 1 image of a lamb as a symbol of Christ. 2 the part of the Mass beginning "Agnus Dei." 3 music for it. [< Latin, Lamb of God]

a go (ə gō′), *adj.* gone by; past (always placed after the noun): *I met her a year ago.* *—adv.* in the past: *He went long ago.* [Old English *āgān* gone by]

a gog (ə gog′), *adj.* full of expectation or excitement; eager. [< French *en gogues* in happy mood]

a gon ic line (ə gon′ik, ā gon′ik), the irregular north-south line of places where a compass does not vary from true north. [< *a-*[4] + Greek *gōnia* angle]

ag o nist (ag′ə nist), *n.* muscle which is resisted or counteracted by another muscle.

ag o nize (ag′ə nīz), *v.,* **-nized, -niz ing.** *—v.i.* 1 feel great anguish; suffer agony. 2 strive painfully; struggle. *—v.t.* cause to suffer extreme pain; torture. **—ag′o niz′ing ly,** *adv.*

ag o ny (ag′ə nē), *n., pl.* **-nies.** 1 extreme pain or distress; great anguish; torment. 2 a sudden powerful emotion: *agonies of delight.* 3 the struggle often preceding death. [< Late Latin *agonia* < Greek *agōnia* a struggle < *agōn* a contest]

ag or a[1] (ag′ər ə), *n., pl.* **-or ae** (-ə rē′), **-or as.** 1 the marketplace in an ancient Greek city. 2 **the Agora,** the assembly place of ancient Athens. [< Greek]

a go ra[2] (ä gō rä′), *n., pl.* **-rot** (-rot′). unit of money in Israel, a coin worth $^1/_{100}$ of an Israeli pound. [< Hebrew]

ag or a pho bi a (ag′ər ə fō′bē ə), *n.* an abnormal fear of open spaces.

a gou ti (ə gü′tē), *n., pl.* **-tis** or **-ties.** 1 rodent of tropical America about the size of a rabbit, usually grizzled in color. 2 an alternation of light and dark bands in the hair of various rodents. [< French < Spanish *agutí* < Tupi-Guarani]

A gra (ä′grə), *n.* city in N India, site of the Taj Mahal. 610,000.

a grar i an (ə grer′ē ən), *adj.* 1 having to do with farming land, its use, or its ownership: *agrarian laws.* 2 for the support and advancement of farmers and farming: *an agrarian movement.* 3 agricultural. *—n.* person who favors a new or more equitable division of rural land. [< Latin *agrarius* < *ager* field]

a grar i an ism (ə grer′ē ə niz′əm), *n.* 1 political agitation or civil dissension arising from dissatisfaction with the existing tenure of the land. 2 principle of a more equitable division of agricultural land. 3 promotion of the farmer's interests, especially by political means.

a gree (ə grē′), *v.,* **a greed, a gree ing.** *—v.i.* 1 have the same feeling or opinion; concur: *He and I agree on this matter.* 2 be in harmony; correspond *(with): Your account of the accident agrees with mine.* See synonym study below. 3 get along well together: *Brothers and sisters don't always agree.* 4 say that one is willing; consent *(to): I agreed to accompany them.* 5 come to terms or to an understanding; settle: *They agreed on $5 as the price.* 6 **agree with,** have a good effect on; suit: *Lobster doesn't agree with me.* 7 (in grammar) have the same number, case, gender, person, etc. In the sentences "The man is going," "The men are going" the subjects and the verbs agree in person and number. *—v.t.* admit; grant; concede: *I agreed that I had been thoughtless.* [< Old French *agreer* < *a gre* to (one's) liking]

Syn. *v.i.* 2 **Agree, correspond, coincide** mean to be consistent. **Agree** means to be consistent or harmonious in all essentials, without differences or contradictions: *All the reports agree about the magnitude of the disaster.* **Correspond** means to agree or to equal in essentials or as a whole, in spite of superficial differences: *The Canadian Dominion Day corresponds to the American Independence Day.* **Coincide** means to agree so closely as to be identical: *His tastes coincide with mine.*

hat, āge, fär; let, ēqual, tėrm;
it, īce; hot, ōpen, ôrder;
oil, out; cup, pu̇t, rüle;
ch, child; ng, long; sh, she;
th, thin; ᴛʜ, then; zh, measure;

ə represents *a* in about, *e* in taken, *i* in pencil, *o* in lemon, *u* in circus.

< = from, derived from, taken from.

a gree a ble (ə grē′ə bəl), *adj.* 1 giving pleasure; pleasing: *agreeable manners.* See **pleasant** for synonym study. 2 ready to agree; willing: *agreeable to a suggestion.* 3 in agreement; suitable *(to): music agreeable to the occasion.* **—a gree′a ble ness,** *n.* **—a gree′a bly,** *adv.*

a greed (ə grēd′), *adj.* fixed by common consent: *pay the agreed price.*

a gree ment (ə grē′mənt), *n.* 1 a mutual understanding or arrangement reached by two or more nations, persons, or groups of persons among themselves. 2 document in which such an understanding or arrangement is set forth; contract, treaty, or covenant. 3 a coming to terms or to an understanding; settlement: *remove every obstacle to agreement.* 4 sameness of feeling or opinion. 5 harmony; correspondence. 6 (in grammar) correspondence of words with respect to number, case, gender, person, etc.

ag ri busi ness (ag′rə biz′nis), *n.* the business of producing, processing, and distributing agricultural products.

agric., agriculture.

ag ri cul tur al (ag′rə kul′chər əl), *adj.* 1 of or having to do with farming; connected with agriculture. 2 promoting the interests or the study of agriculture: *an agricultural college.* **—ag′ri cul′tur al ly,** *adv.*

ag ri cul tur al ist (ag′rə kul′chər ə list), *n.* U.S. agriculturist.

ag ri cul ture (ag′rə kul′chər), *n.* science, art, or occupation of cultivating the soil, including the production of crops and the raising of livestock; farming. [< Late Latin *agricultura* < Latin *ager* field + *cultura* cultivation]

ag ri cul tur ist (ag′rə kul′chər ist), *n.* 1 farmer. 2 an expert in farming.

ag ri mo ny (ag′rə mō′nē), *n., pl.* **-nies.** plant of the rose family with slender stalks of feathery leaves and small yellow flowers, whose roots are used as an astringent. [< Latin *agrimonia*]

A grip pa (ə grip′ə), *n.* **Marcus,** 63-12 B.C., Roman general and son-in-law of the emperor Augustus, victor over Antony and Cleopatra at Actium in 31 B.C.

ag ro bi o log ic (ag′rō bī′ə loj′ik), *adj.* agrobiological.

ag ro bi o log i cal (ag′rō bī′ə loj′ə kəl), *adj.* of or having to do with agrobiology. **—ag′ro bi′o log′i cal ly,** *adv.*

ag ro bi ol o gy (ag′rō bī ol′ə jē), *n.* the study of plant nutrition and growth in relation to the condition and constituents of the soil, especially to increase crops.

ag ro log ic (ag′rə loj′ik), *adj.* agrological.

ag ro log i cal (ag′rə loj′ə kəl), *adj.* of or having to do with agrology.

a grol o gy (ə grol′ə jē), *n.* branch of agriculture that deals with soils.

ag ro nom ic (ag′rə nom′ik), *adj.* of or having to do with agronomy.

a gron o mist (ə gron′ə mist), *n.* an expert in agronomy.

a gron o my (ə gron′ə mē), *n.* science of managing farm land; branch of agriculture dealing with crop production. [< Greek *agronomos* land overseer < *agros* land + *nemein* manage]

a ground (ə ground′), *adv., adj.* 1 stranded on the shore or on the bottom in shallow water. 2 in or into difficulties.

agt., agent.

a gue (ā′gyü), *n.* 1 a malarial fever with chills and sweating that alternate at regular intervals. 2 any fit of shaking or shivering; chill. [< Middle French *aguë* < Latin *(febris) acuta* severe (fever)]

A gui nal do (ä′gē näl′dō), *n.* **Emilio,** 1870?-1964, Philippine leader against Spain and later, after the Spanish-American War, against the United States.

a gu ish (ā′gyü ish), *adj.* 1 of or like ague. 2 liable to have ague.

A gul has (ə gul′əs), *n.* **Cape,** cape at the southernmost point of Africa.

ah (ä), *interj.* exclamation of pain, sorrow, regret, pity, admiration, surprise, joy, dislike, contempt, etc.

a ha (ä hä′), *interj.* exclamation of triumph, satisfaction, surprise, joy, etc.

A hab (ā′hab), *n.* king of Israel from about 873 to 853 B.C., who was led to the worship of idols by his wife Jezebel.

a head (ə hed′), *adv.* 1 in front; before: *Walk ahead of me.* 2 forward; onward: *Go ahead with this work.* 3 in advance: *Columbus was ahead of his time in his belief that the world was round.* 4 **be ahead, a** be winning: *Our team is ahead by six points.* **b** have more than is needed: *We are ahead $10 on the budget.* 5 **get ahead,** succeed. 6 **get ahead of,** surpass; excel.

a hem (ə hem′), *interj.* sound made by coughing or clearing the throat, sometimes used to attract attention, express doubt, or gain time.

Ah med a bad or **Ah mad a bad** (ä′mə dä bäd′), *n.* city in W India. 1,508,000.

a hoy (ə hoi′), *interj.* call used by sailors to attract the attention of persons at a distance: *Ship ahoy!*

Ah ri man (är′i mən), *n.* (in the Zoroastrian religion) the spirit of evil.

a hun gered (ə hung′gərd), *adj.* ARCHAIC. hungry.

A hu ra Maz da (ä′hür ə maz′də), Ormazd.

aid (ād), *v.t.* 1 give needed support to; help; assist: *The Red Cross aids flood victims.* See **help** for synonym study. 2 help in bringing about; further; facilitate: *The doctor did all in her power to aid my recovery.* —*v.i.* give assistance; help. —*n.* 1 help; support: *I did this without aid.* 2 helper; assistant. 3 tool, instrument, etc., that facilitates an operation. 4 U.S. aide-de-camp. [< Middle French *aider* < Latin *adjutare,* frequentative of *adjuvare* help out < *ad-* + *juvare* to help] **—aid′er,** *n.*

AID, Agency for International Development.

aid-de-camp (ād′də kamp′), *n., pl.* **aids-de-camp.** U.S. aide-de-camp.

aide (ād), *n.* 1 helper; assistant. 2 aide-de-camp.

aide-de-camp (ād′də kamp′), *n., pl.* **aides-de-camp.** a military officer who assists a superior officer by taking and sending messages and acting as a secretary. [< French, literally, camp helper]

ai grette (ā′gret, ā gret′), *n.* 1 tuft of feathers worn as an ornament on the head, on a helmet, etc. 2 anything shaped or used like this. 3 egret. [< French]

ail (āl), *v.t.* be the matter with; trouble: *What ails the child?* —*v.i.* be ill; feel sick: *He is ailing.* [Old English *eglan*]

ai lan thus (ā lan′thəs), *n.* tree native to Asia with many leaves and clusters of small, greenish flowers having a somewhat disagreeable odor, often used as a shade tree; tree of heaven. [< New Latin]

ai le ron (ā′lə ron′), *n.* a hinged, movable part on the rear edge of an airplane wing, used for banking, rolling, or balancing the airplane. See **airplane** for picture. [< French, diminutive of *aile* wing < Latin *ala*]

ail ment (āl′mənt), *n.* disorder of the body or mind, especially as distinguished from an acute or specific disease; illness; sickness.

aim (ām), *v.t.* 1 point or direct (a gun, blow, etc.) in order to hit a target: *aim a gun.* 2 direct (words or acts) at someone or something: *The President's speech was aimed at the press.* —*v.i.* 1 point or direct a gun, blow, etc., at or toward an object: *The hunter aimed at the lion.* 2 direct one's intention, purpose, or action in order to accomplish something: *aim at perfection.* 3 U.S. intend: *I aim to go.* 4 U.S. try: *I aim to please.* —*n.* 1 act of aiming: *Take steady aim.* 2 ability to point or direct a gun, blow, etc.: *The hunter's aim was poor.* 3 object of efforts; purpose; intention. [< Old French *esmer, aesmer,* ultimately < Latin *aestimare* appraise]

aim less (ām′lis), *adj.* without purpose; pointless: *engage in friendly but aimless talk.* **—aim′less ly,** *adv.* **—aim′less ness,** *n.*

ain't (ānt), 1 am not; is not; are not. 2 have not; has not.

➤ **Ain't** is not now acceptable in formal English. Even in informal English its use is subject to sharp criticism. However, it is often heard, especially in substandard speech.

Ai nu (ī′nü), *n., pl.* **-nu** or **-nus.** 1 member of an aboriginal, light-skinned people in northern Japan, now becoming extinct. 2 their language.

air (er, ar), *n.* 1 the odorless, tasteless, and invisible mixture of gases that surrounds the earth and directly or indirectly supports every form of life on earth; atmosphere. Air consists chiefly of nitrogen and oxygen, along with argon, carbon dioxide, hydrogen, and small quantities of neon, helium, and other inert gases. 2 space overhead; sky: *Birds fly in the air.* 3 a light wind; breeze. 4 fresh air: *Open the window to let some air in.* 5 a simple melody or tune. 6 public mention; publicity: *She gave air to her opinions.* 7 general character or outward appearance of a person or thing: *The secret was told with an air of mystery.* 8 **airs,** *pl.* unnatural or affected manners. 9 medium through which radio waves travel.

in the air, a being spread; going around. **b** uncertain or unsettled.

off the air, a not engaged in broadcasting. **b** not being broadcast.

on the air, a engaged in broadcasting. **b** being broadcast.

take the air, 1 go outdoors; take a walk or ride. 2 start broadcasting.

up in the air, a uncertain or unsettled. **b** INFORMAL. very angry or excited.

walk on air, be very gay or pleased.

—*v.t.* 1 put out in the air: *air clothes.* 2 let fresh air in: *air a room.* 3 make known; express publicly: *Do not air your troubles.* 4 take on a stroll: *air the dog.* 5 INFORMAL. broadcast by radio or television, or both.

—*adj.* 1 relating to aviation; done by means of aircraft: *air photography.* 2 of or having to do with aircraft: *an air armada.*

[< Old French < Latin *aer* < Greek *aēr*]

air base, headquarters and airport for military aircraft.

air bladder, sac in most fishes and various animals and plants that is filled with air. The air bladder of a fish adjusts the specific gravity of the fish to the water pressure at varying depths.

air boat (er′bōt′, ar′bōt′), *n.* a small flat-bottomed boat driven by an airplane propeller, used for travel in large swamps and flooded areas.

air borne (er′bôrn′, er′bōrn′; ar′bôrn′, ar′bōrn′), *adj.* 1 supported by the air; off the ground: *The kite was finally airborne.* 2 carried in aircraft: *airborne troops.* 3 carried by air: *airborne dust.*

air brake, brake or system of brakes operated by a piston or pistons worked by compressed air.

air brush (er′brush′, ar′brush′), *n.* device like an atomizer, operated by compressed air, that is used to spray paint on a surface. —*v.t.* paint, touch up, etc., with an airbrush.

air castle, a daydream; castle in the air.

air cell, a tiny cavity for air in an organism, as the air sac of a bird.

air cleaner, air filter.

air coach, U.S. 1 class of air travel with lower fares than first class. 2 a commercial aircraft with comparatively low fares.

air-con di tion (er′kən dish′ən, ar′kən dish′ən), *v.t.* 1 supply (a building, room, car, etc.) with the equipment for air conditioning. 2 treat (air) by means of air conditioning.

air-con di tioned (er′kən dish′ənd, ar′kən dish′ənd), *adj.* having air conditioning.

air conditioner, equipment used to air-condition a building, room, car, etc.

air conditioning, means of treating and circulating air in a building, room, car, etc., to regulate its temperature or humidity and to free it from dust.

air-cool (er′kül′, ar′kül′), *v.t.* 1 remove heat from (an internal-combustion engine) by forcing air on or around the cylinders. 2 remove heat in (a room) by blowing cool air in.

air craft (er′kraft′, ar′kraft′), *n., pl.* **-craft.** machine for air navigation that is supported in air by its own buoyancy (such as a balloon) or by dynamic reaction of air particles to its surface (such as an airplane), or by reaction

hat, āge, fär; let, ēqual, tėrm;
it, īce; hot, ōpen, ôrder;
oil, out; cup, pu̇t, rüle;
ch, child; ng, long; sh, she;
th, thin; ᴛʜ, then; zh, measure;

ə represents *a* in about, *e* in taken, *i* in pencil, *o* in lemon, *u* in circus.

< = from, derived from, taken from.

to a jet stream. Airplanes, airships, gliders, helicopters, and balloons are aircraft.

aircraft carrier, warship designed as a base for aircraft, with a large, flat deck on which to land or take off.

air crew (er′krü′, ar′krü′), *n.* the crew that flies an aircraft but does not service it.

air cushion vehicle, Hovercraft.

air drome (er′drōm′, ar′drōm′), *n.* airport. Also, BRITISH **aerodrome.** [< *air* + Greek *dromos* racecourse]

air drop (er′drop′, ar′drop′), *n., v.,* **-dropped, -drop ping.** *—n.* a delivering of food, supplies, cargo, or persons by parachute from aircraft in flight. *—v.t.* deliver (food, supplies, cargo, or persons) by parachute from aircraft in flight.

Aire dale (er′dāl, ar′dāl), *n.* any of a breed of large terriers having a wiry brown or tan coat with dark markings. [< *Airedale,* valley in Yorkshire, England]

air express, the shipment of packages by aircraft.

air field (er′fēld′, ar′fēld′), *n.* the landing area of an airport or air base.

air filter, a mechanical or electronic device that filters dust, pollen, etc., from the air, as in air conditioning.

air flow (er′flō′, ar′flō′), *n.* 1 a natural movement of air. 2 the flow of air around and relative to an object moving in air. *—adj.* 1 streamlined. 2 that is produced by air currents.

air foil (er′foil′, ar′foil′), *n.* a wing, rudder, or other surface designed to help lift or control an aircraft.

air force, 1 branch of the military forces that uses aircraft. 2 **Air Force,** a separate branch of the armed forces of the United States that includes aviation personnel, equipment, etc.

Air Force Academy, the officer-training service school of the United States Air Force at Colorado Springs, Colorado.

air frame (er′frām′, ar′frām′), *n.* framework, excluding engines, of an airplane, a ballistic missile, or a dirigible.

air glow (er′glō′, ar′glō′), *n.* a faint glow in the sky, not visible to the naked eye, believed due to chemical reactions in the upper atmosphere.

air gun, 1 air rifle. 2 device utilizing compressed air to force grease, putty, etc., into or onto something.

air hole, 1 a hole that air can pass through. 2 U.S. an open space in the ice on a river, pond, etc. 3 air pocket.

air i ly (er′ə lē, ar′ə lē), *adv.* in an airy manner.

air i ness (er′ē nis, ar′ē nis), *n.* airy quality.

air ing (er′ing, ar′ing), *n.* 1 exposure to air for drying, warming, etc. 2 a walk, ride, or drive in the open air. 3 exposure to public notice, discussion, criticism, etc.

air lane, a regular route used by aircraft; airway; skyway.

air less (er′lis, ar′lis), *adj.* 1 without fresh air; stuffy. 2 without a breeze; still.

air letter, 1 a lightweight sheet of paper designed to fold and seal as an envelope, with a message on its inner surfaces. 2 letter sent by air mail.

air lift (er′lift′, ar′lift′), *n.* 1 transportation by air of personnel, passengers, and freight in an emergency. 2 the aircraft used. 3 the cargo transported. *—v.t.* transport by airlift.

air line (er′līn′, ar′līn′), *n.* 1 an established system of transportation of people and freight by aircraft. 2 company owning or operating such a system. 3 route for aircraft; airway. 4 a straight line through the air.

air lin er (er′lī′nər, ar′lī′nər), *n.* a large passenger airplane.

air lock (er′lok′, ar′lok′), *n.* an airtight compartment between places where there is a difference in air pressure. The pressure in an airlock can be raised or lowered.

air mail (er′māl′, ar′māl′), *v.t.* send by air mail: *Please airmail this letter. —adj.* sent or to be sent by aircraft.

air mail, 1 mail sent by aircraft. 2 system of sending mail by aircraft.

air man (er′mən, ar′mən), *n., pl.* **-men.** 1 pilot of an aircraft; aviator. 2 one of the crew of an aircraft. 3 an enlisted man or woman in the Air Force, comparable in grade to a private.

airman first class, (in the U.S. Air Force) an airman of the highest rank, ranking next below a staff sergeant.

air mass, a large body of air within the atmosphere that has nearly uniform temperature and humidity at any given level and moves horizontally over great distances without changing.

air mattress, pad that can be inflated to serve as a mattress.

air mile, a nautical mile, 6076.11549 feet, used as a measure of distance in the flight of aircraft.

air-mind ed (er′mīn′did, ar′mīn′did), *adj.* 1 interested in aviation. 2 fond of air travel. **—air′-mind′ed ness,** *n.*

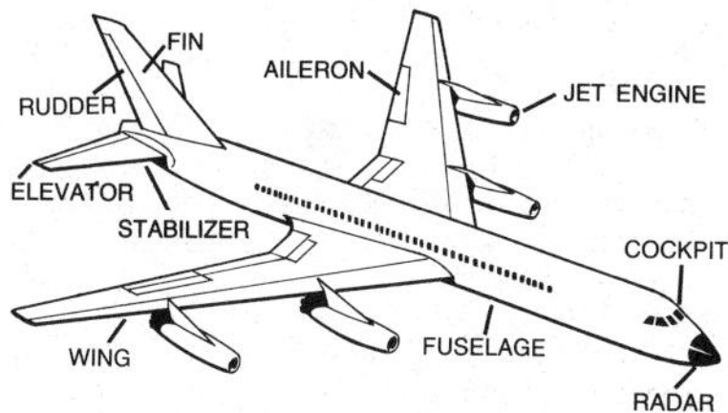

airplane with jet engines

air plane (er′plān′, ar′plān′), *n.* any of various aircraft heavier than air, supported in flight by its fixed wings and driven by propeller, jet propulsion, etc. Also, BRITISH **aeroplane.**

air plant, epiphyte.

air pocket, a downward current of air formed by the sudden sinking of cooled air, that causes an aircraft to lose altitude suddenly.

air pollution, the contamination of the air by industrial waste gases, fuel exhaust, and atomic fallout.

air port (er′pôrt′, er′pōrt′; ar′pôrt′, ar′pōrt′), *n.* area, especially on land, used regularly by aircraft to land or take off, usually having several runways, buildings for passenger facilities, and hangars for storing, repairing, and servicing aircraft.

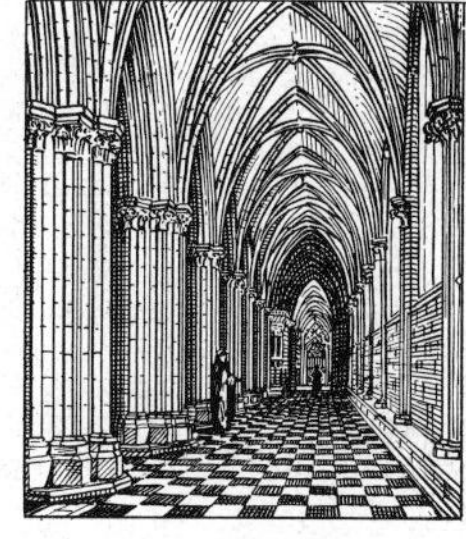
aisle (def. 2) of a church

air post, BRITISH. air mail.

air pressure, atmospheric pressure.

air pump, apparatus for forcing, compressing, or removing air.

air raid, attack by enemy aircraft, especially by bombers.

air rifle, gun that uses compressed air to shoot a single pellet or dart; air gun.

air sac, any of various air-filled spaces in different parts of the body of a bird, connected with the lungs. It aids in breathing and in regulating body temperature.

air ship (er′ship′, ar′ship′), *n.* a lighter-than-air propeller-driven aircraft that can be steered; dirigible.

air sick (er′sik′, ar′sik′), *adj.* sick as a result of the motion of aircraft. **—air′sick′ness,** *n.*

air space (er′spās′, ar′spās′), *n.* space in the air, especially that belonging to a particular country.

air speed (er′spēd′, ar′spēd′), *n.* speed of an aircraft in relation to the speed of the air through which it moves, as distinguished from ground speed.

air stream (er′strēm′, ar′strēm′), *n.* the relative flow of air around or against an object in flight, usually in a direction opposite to that of the object's flight.

air strip (er′strip′, ar′strip′), *n.* a paved or cleared runway on which aircraft land and take off, especially one made hastily for temporary use; landing strip.

air tight (er′tīt′, ar′tīt′), *adj.* 1 so tight that no air or gas can get in or out. 2 having no weak points open to an opponent's attack: *an airtight alibi.*

air-to-air (er′tə er′, ar′tə ar′), *adj.* passing between two flying aircraft, as a rocket launched by one to destroy another: *air-to-air missiles.*

air waves (er′wāvz′, ar′wāvz′), *n. pl.* radio or television broadcasting.

air way (er′wā′, ar′wā′), *n.* 1 route for aircraft; air lane; airline. 2 a passage for air. 3 a specified radio frequency for broadcasting. 4 **airways,** *pl.* channels for radio or television broadcasting.

air wor thy (er′wėr′ᴛʜē, ar′wėr′ᴛʜē), *adj.* fit or safe for service in the air. **—air′wor′thi ness,** *n.*

air y (er′ē, ar′ē), *adj.,* **air i er, air i est.** 1 light as air; graceful; delicate: *an airy step.* 2 light-hearted and gay: *airy music.* 3 breezy: *a high, airy knoll.* 4 well supplied with fresh air: *a large, airy room.* 5 of or in the air; aerial: *birds and other airy creatures.* 6 reaching high into the air; lofty: *airy pinnacles.* 7 like air; not solid or substantial: *airy plans.* 8 unnatural; affected: *an airy tone of voice.* 9 flippant: *airy criticism.*

aisle (īl), *n.* 1 passage between rows of seats in a hall, theater, school, etc. 2 passage on either side of a church parallel to the nave, often set off by pillars. See **apse** for diagram. 3 any long or narrow passageway. [< Middle French *ele* < Latin *ala* wing]

Aisne River (ān), river in N France. 175 mi.

Aix-la-Cha pelle (äks′lä shä pel′), *n.* French name of **Aachen.**

A jac cio (ä yät′chō), *n.* capital of Corsica. Napoleon I was born there. 41,000.

a jar[1] (ə jär′), *adj.* slightly open: *Please leave the door ajar.* [Middle English *on char* on the turn; Old English *cerr* turn]

a jar[2] (ə jär′), *adv., adj.* not in harmony. [< *a-*[1] + *jar*[2] discord]

A jax (ā′jaks), *n.* in Greek legends: 1 a Greek hero at the siege of Troy, second to Achilles in strength and courage. 2 **Ajax the Lesser,** another Greek hero of Troy, second to Achilles in swiftness.

a kene (ā kēn′), *n.* achene.

a kim bo (ə kim′bō), *adj.* with the hands on the hips and the elbows bent outward. [Middle English *in kenebowe,* apparently, in keen bow, at a sharp angle]

akimbo
boy with arms akimbo

a kin (ə kin′), *adj.* 1 of the same kind; alike; similar: *Your opinions are akin to mine.* 2 of the same family; related: *Your cousins are akin to you.* [for *of kin*]

Ak kad (ak′ad), *n.* 1 ancient country in Mesopotamia, constituting most of N Babylonia. 2 its capital. Also, **Accad.**

Ak ka di an (ə kā′dē ən), *n.* 1 the eastern division of the Semitic languages, spoken in ancient times in Mesopotamia. 2 any language of this division. 3 one of the ancient inhabitants of Akkad. —*adj.* 1 of Akkad. 2 of or in the language of Akkadians.

Ak kra (ə krä′), *n.* Accra.

Ak ron (ak′rən), *n.* city in NE Ohio. 275,000.

al-, *prefix.* form of **ad-** before *l,* as in *allure.*

-al[1], *suffix forming adjectives from nouns.* of; like; having the nature of: *Ornamental = having the nature of ornament.* Also, **-ial.** [< Latin *-alem*]

-al[2], *suffix forming nouns from verbs.* act of ____ing: *Refusal = act of refusing.* [< Latin *-alia,* neuter plural of *-alem*]

Al, aluminum.

a la (ā′lə), *n., pl.* **a lae** (ā′lē′). wing or winglike structure. [< Latin]

a la or **à la** (ä′ lə; *French* ä lä), in the manner of; in the style of. [< French *à la*]

➜ **a la, à la.** Although originally French, *a la* is now regarded as an English preposition: *a la Hollywood, a la Winston Churchill.* In formal writing and some advertising (for cosmetics and fashionable clothes), the French spelling is usually used: *à la.*

Ala., Alabama.

A.L.A., American Library Association.

Al a bam a (al′ə bam′ə), *n.* one of the south central states of the United States. 3,444,000 pop.; 51,600 sq. mi. *Capital:* Montgomery. *Abbrev.:* Ala. **—Al′a bam′an, Al′a-bam′i an,** *adj., n.*

al a bas ter (al′ə bas′tər), *n.* 1 a smooth, white, delicately shaded, translucent variety of gypsum, often carved into ornaments and vases. 2 a variety of calcite that is somewhat translucent and often banded like marble. —*adj.* 1 of alabaster. 2 smooth, white, and delicately shaded like alabaster. [< Latin < Greek *alabastros* an alabaster box]

à la carte (ä′ lə kärt′, al′ə kärt′), with a stated price for each dish (instead of one price for the whole meal). [< French, according to the bill of fare]

a lack (ə lak′), *interj.* ARCHAIC. exclamation of sorrow or regret; alas.

a lac ri tous (ə lak′rə təs), *adj.* full of alacrity; brisk.

a lac ri ty (ə lak′rə tē), *n.* 1 brisk and eager action; liveliness: *move with alacrity.* 2 cheerful willingness. [< Latin *alacritatem* < *alacer* brisk]

A lad din (ə lad′n), *n.* youth in *The Arabian Nights,* who found a magic lamp and a magic ring. By rubbing either one of them he could call either of two powerful spirits to do whatever he commanded.

à la king (ä′ lə king′, al′ə king′), creamed with pimento, green pepper, and mushrooms: *chicken à la king.*

Al a mo (al′ə mō), *n.* mission building in San Antonio, Texas, used as a fort by a band of Texas rebels fighting for independence from Mexico. Besieged by an army of Mexicans, the Texans were overwhelmed and killed on March 6, 1836.

à la mode or **a la mode** (ä′ lə mōd′, al′ə mōd′), 1 in style; fashionable. 2 served with ice cream: *pie à la mode.* 3 cooked with vegetables: *beef à la mode.* [< French *à la mode* in the fashion]

Å land Islands (ō′lənd), group of Finnish islands in the Baltic Sea between Finland and Sweden. 22,000 pop.; 572 sq. mi.

al a nine (al′ə nēn′, al′ə nin), *n.* a crystalline amino acid occurring in several proteins. *Formula:* $C_3H_7NO_2$

Al ar ic (al′ər ik), *n.* A.D. 370?-410, king of the Visigoths whose army captured and pillaged Rome in A.D. 410.

a larm (ə lärm′), *n.* 1 sudden fear; fright; excitement caused by fear of danger: *The deer darted off in alarm.* See **fear** for synonym study. 2 a warning of approaching danger. 3 signal that gives such a warning; signal: *a fire alarm.* 4 a call to arms or action. 5 a device that makes noise to warn or awaken people. —*v.t.* 1 fill with sudden fear; frighten: *I was alarmed because my friends were so long in returning.* See **frighten** for synonym study. 2 warn (anyone) of approaching danger. [< Old French *alarme* < Italian *all'arme!* to arms!]

alarm clock, clock that can be set to ring or sound at any desired time.

a larm ing (ə lär′ming), *adj.* causing alarm; frightening. **—a larm′ing ly,** *adv.*

a larm ism (ə lär′miz′əm), *n.* the attitude and habits of alarmists.

a larm ist (ə lär′mist), *n.* person who is easily alarmed or who alarms others needlessly or on very slight grounds.

a lar um (ə lar′əm, ə lär′əm), *n.* ARCHAIC. alarm.

a las (ə las′, ə läs′), *interj.* exclamation of sorrow, grief, regret, pity, or dread. [< Old French *a* ah + *las* miserable < Latin *lassus* weary]

Alas., Alaska.

A las ka (ə las′kə), *n.* 1 one of the Pacific states of the United States, in the NW part of North America. 302,000 pop.; 586,400 sq. mi. *Capital:* Juneau. *Abbrev.:* Alas. 2 **Gulf of,** arm of the Pacific, off S Alaska. **—A las′kan,** *adj., n.*

Alaska Highway, highway that extends from Dawson Creek, in British Columbia, Canada, to Fairbanks, Alaska. 1523 mi.

Alaskan malamute, any of an Alaskan breed of large, strong dogs having a gray or black and white coat and commonly used for pulling sleds. Also, **malamute, malemute.** [*malamute* < Eskimo *Mahle,* name of a tribe + *mut* village]

Alaska Standard Time, the standard time in central Alaska and all of Hawaii, two hours behind Pacific Standard Time; Hawaii Standard Time.

a late (ā′lāt), *adj.* having wings or winglike parts.

a lat ed (ā′lā tid), *adj.* alate.

alb (alb), *n.* a white linen robe worn by Roman Catholic and some Anglican priests at the Eucharist. [< Latin *(vestis) alba* white (robe)]

Alb., 1 Albanian. 2 Albany.

al ba core (al′bə kôr, al′bə kōr), *n., pl.* **-cores** or **-core.** a large tuna of all tropical seas, having long pectoral fins and light-colored flesh valued for canning. [ultimately < Arabic *al-bakūra*]

Al ba ni a (al bā′nē ə), *n.* country in SE Europe, between Yugoslavia and Greece. 2,100,000 pop.; 10,600 sq. mi. *Capital:* Tirana. See **Adriatic Sea** for map. **—Al-ba′ni an,** *adj., n.*

Al ba ny (ôl′bə nē), *n.* capital of New York State, on the Hudson River. 116,000.

al ba tross (al′bə trôs, al′bə tros), *n., pl.* **-tross es** or **-tross.** any of various web-footed sea birds related to the petrel, noted as the largest sea birds and for their ability to fly long distances. [ultimately < Arabic *al-ghaṭṭās,* a sea eagle]

albatross
30 in. long, wingspread up to 11½ ft.

al be do (al bē′dō), *n., pl.* **-dos** or **-does.** reflecting power, especially of a planet or other heavenly body. [< Latin, whiteness < *albus* white]

Al bee (ôl′bē), *n.* **Edward,** born 1928, American playwright.

al be it (ôl bē′it), *conj.* even though; even if; although. [Middle English *al be it* although it be]

Al be marle Sound (al′bə märl), inlet of the Atlantic Ocean, on the coast of North Carolina. 60 mi.

Al bert (al′bərt), *n.* 1 **Lake,** lake in central Africa, between Zaïre and Uganda. 100 mi. long; 1640 sq. mi. 2 1819-1861, German prince who was the husband of Queen Victoria of Great Britain.

Albert I, 1875-1934, king of the Belgians from 1909 to 1934.

Al ber ta (al bėr′tə), *n.* province in W Canada. 1,628,000 pop.; 255,300 sq. mi. *Capital:* Edmonton. *Abbrev.:* Alta. **—Al ber′tan,** *adj., n.*

al bi nism (al′bə niz′əm), *n.* absence of color; condition of being an albino.

al bi nis tic (al′bə nis′tik), *adj.* 1 of albinism. 2 having albinism.

al bi no (al bī′nō), *n., pl.* **-nos.** 1 person distinguished by the absence from birth of coloring pigment in the skin, hair, and eyes so that the skin and hair are abnormally white or milky and the eyes have a pink color with a deep-red pupil and are unable to bear ordinary light. 2 any animal or plant that has pale, defective coloring. [< Portuguese < *albo* white < Latin *albus*]

Al bi on (al′bē ən), *n.* ancient Latin name for England.

al bum (al′bəm), *n.* 1 book with blank pages for holding photographs, stamps, autographs, etc. 2 holder designed like a book for a phonograph record or records. 3 a single, long-playing phonograph record. 4 set of phonograph records or tape recordings. [< Latin, tablet, neuter of *albus* white]

al bu men (al byü′mən), *n.* 1 white of an egg, consisting mostly of albumin dissolved in water. 2 albumin. [< Latin < *albus* white]

al bu min (al byü′mən), *n.* any of a class of proteins that are soluble in water and can be coagulated by heat, found in the white of an egg, milk, blood serum, and in many other animal and plant tissues and juices.

al bu mi nous (al byü′mə nəs), *adj.* of, like, or containing albumin.

Al bu quer que (al′bə kėr′kē), *n.* city in central New Mexico. 244,000.

al bur num (al bėr′nəm), *n.* sapwood. [< Latin < *albus* white]

Al ca traz (al′kə traz), *n.* 1 small island in San Francisco Bay. 2 former penitentiary there used by the United States government for dangerous criminals.

al ca zar (al′kə zär, al kaz′ər), *n.* palace, castle, or fortress in Spain, originally of the Spanish Moors. [< Spanish < Arabic *al-qaṣr* the castle < Latin *castrum* fort]

al chem i cal (al kem′ə kəl), *adj.* of alchemy or alchemists. **—al chem′i cal ly,** *adv.*

al che mist (al′kə mist), *n.* person who studied or practiced alchemy.

al che my (al′kə mē), *n.* 1 the chemistry of the Middle Ages, which combined science, magic, and philosophy. Alchemy tried to find a means of transmuting cheaper metals into gold and silver and to discover a universal solvent, a universal remedy for disease, and an elixir for prolonging life. 2 any miraculous power of transformation. [< Old French *alkemie* < Medieval Latin *alchimia* < Arabic *al-kīmiyā'* the art of alloying metals]

Al ci bi a des (al′sə bī′ə dēz′), *n.* 450?-404 B.C., Athenian politician and general.

al co hol (al′kə hôl, al′kə hol), *n.* 1 the colorless, flammable, volatile liquid in wine, beer, whiskey, gin, and other fermented and distilled liquids that makes them intoxicating, commercially prepared from grain; grain alcohol; ethyl alcohol. Alcohol is used in medicine, in manufacturing, and as a fuel. *Formula:* C_2H_5OH 2 any intoxicating liquor containing this liquid. 3 any of a group of similar organic compounds. Alcohols contain a hydroxyl group and react with organic acids to form esters. Wood alcohol or methyl alcohol, CH_3OH, is very poisonous. [< Medieval Latin, originally, "fine powder," then "essence" < Arabic *al-kuḥl* the powdered antimony]

al co hol ic (al′kə hô′lik, al′kə hol′ik), *adj.* 1 of alcohol: *alcoholic fumes.* 2 containing alcohol: *alcoholic drinks.* 3 caused by alcohol. 4 having alcoholism. —*n.* person having alcoholism. **—al′co hol′i cal ly,** *adv.*

al co hol ism (al′kə hô liz′əm, al′kə-ho liz′əm), *n.* 1 disease which has as its chief symptom the inability to stop drinking alcoholic liquors to excess. 2 a diseased condition caused by drinking too much alcoholic liquor.

al com e ter (al kom′ə tər), *n.* U.S. a device, used by law-enforcement agents, to determine whether a driver is intoxicated.

Al co ran (al′kō rän′, al′kō ran′), *n.* the Koran.

Al cott (ôl′kət, ôl′kot), *n.* **Louisa May,** 1832-1888, American author.

al cove (al′kōv), *n.* 1 a small room opening out of a larger room. 2 recess or large, hollow space in a wall. 3 summerhouse. [< Spanish *alcoba* < Arabic *al-qubba* the vaulted chamber]

Al cy o ne (al sī′ə nē), *n.* the brightest star in the Pleiades.

Ald., Alderman. Also, **Aldm.**

Al deb ar an (al deb′ər ən), *n.* the brightest star in the constellation Taurus.

al de hyde (al′də hīd), *n.* 1 any of a group of organic chemical compounds having the radical CHO, derived from various alcohols by oxidation. Formaldehyde is an aldehyde produced by the oxidation of methyl alcohol. 2 acetaldehyde. [< New Latin *al(cohol) dehyd(rogenatum)* alcohol dehydrogenated]

Al den (ôl′dən), *n.* **John,** 1599?-1687, one of the Pilgrims who settled at Plymouth, Massachusetts.

al der (ôl′dər), *n.* any of a genus of trees and shrubs that usually grow in wet land and have clusters of catkins which develop into small, woody cones. [Old English *alor*]

al der man (ôl′dər mən), *n., pl.* **-men.** 1 member of a governing council of certain cities in the United States, usually elected by the voters of a ward or district. 2 one of the senior elected councilors of an English or Irish borough or county council, who ranks next to the mayor in importance. [Old English *ealdormann* < *ealdor* elder, chief + *mann* man]

al der man ic (ôl′dər man′ik), *adj.* of, like, or suitable for an alderman.

Al der ney (ôl′dər nē), *n.* one of the Channel Islands. 1500 pop.; 3 sq. mi.

Al der shot (ôl′dər shot), *n.* 1 city in S England. 36,000. 2 famous military camp near there.

Aldm., Alderman. Also, **Ald.**

Al drich (ôl′drich), *n.* **Thomas Bailey,** 1836-1907, American author.

al drin (al′drən), *n.* a very powerful insecticide derived from naphthalene. *Formula:* $C_{12}H_8Cl_6$ [< Kurt *Alder,* 1902-1958, German chemist]

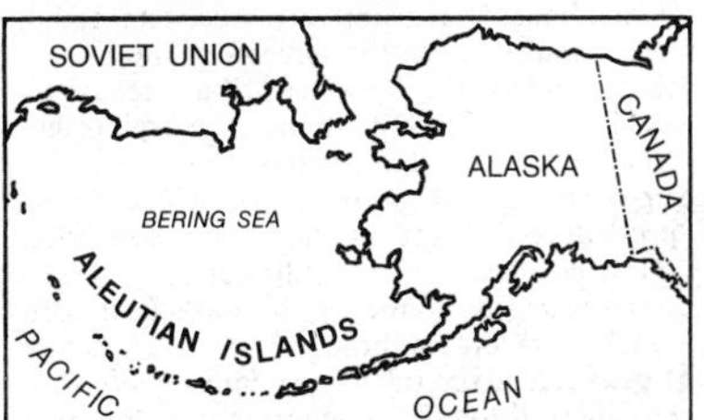

hat, āge, fär; let, ēqual, tėrm;
it, īce; hot, ōpen, ôrder;
oil, out; cup, pu̇t, rüle;
ch, child; ng, long; sh, she;
th, thin; ᴛʜ, then; zh, measure;

ə represents *a* in about, *e* in taken, *i* in pencil, *o* in lemon, *u* in circus.

< = from, derived from, taken from.

ale (āl), *n.* a heavy, bitter alcoholic beverage, fermented from malt and flavored with hops. Ale is similar to beer but contains more alcohol. [Old English *alu*]

a le a to ric (ā′lē ə tôr′ik, ā′lē ə tōr′ik), *adj.* consisting of random or chance elements: *aleatoric music.*

a le a to ry (ā′lē ə tôr′ē, ā′lē ə tōr′ē), *adj.* 1 dependent on an uncertain event; contingent. 2 aleatoric. [< Latin *aleatorius* < *aleator* dice player]

a lee (ə lē′), *adv.* on or to the lee side; leeward.

ale house (āl′hous′), *n., pl.* **-hous es** (-hou′ziz). place where ale or beer is sold to be drunk on the premises.

a lem bic (ə lem′bik), *n.* a glass or metal container, formerly used in chemistry for distilling. [< Medieval Latin *alambicus* < Arabic *al-anbīq* the still]

A len çon (à läɴ sôɴ′ *for 1;* ə len′sen, ə len′son *for 2*), *n.* 1 city in NW France. 26,000. 2 kind of fine lace made there.

A lep po (ə lep′ō), *n.* city in NW Syria. 639,000.

a lert (ə lėrt′), *adj.* 1 keen and watchful; wide-awake; vigilant: *A good hunting dog is alert to every sound and movement in the field.* See **watchful** for synonym study. 2 quick in action; brisk; nimble: *A sparrow is very alert in its movements.* 3 ready to speak, think, or act. —*n.* 1 a signal warning of an attack by approaching enemy aircraft, a hurricane, or other threatening danger. 2 period of time after this warning until the attack is over or the danger has passed: *The hurricane alert is over.* 3 **on the alert,** on the lookout; watchful; wide-awake: *A driver must be on the alert.* —*v.t.* 1 warn against and prepare for an approaching attack by aircraft, a hurricane, or other threatening danger. 2 notify (troops) to get ready for action. 3 make alert; warn. [< French *alerte* < Italian *all'erta* on the watch] **—a lert′ly,** *adv.* **—a lert′ness,** *n.*

a leur one (ə lür′ōn, al′yə rōn′), *n.* minute protein granules found in seeds and grains. [< Greek *aleuron* flour]

Al e ut (al′ē üt), *n.* 1 native or inhabitant of the Aleutian Islands. 2 the language spoken there, distantly related to Eskimo.

A leu tian (ə lü′shən), *adj.* of the Aleuts or the Aleutian Islands.

Aleutian Islands, chain of about 150

small islands in the N Pacific, part of Alaska, and extending southwest from the mainland for 1200 miles. 8000 pop.; 6800 sq. mi.

ale wife[1] (āl′wīf′), *n., pl.* **-wives.** woman who keeps an alehouse.

ale wife[2] (āl′wīf′), *n., pl.* **-wives.** fish found in great numbers along the United States Atlantic coast, related to the herring and the shad. [origin uncertain]

Al ex an der Archipelago (al′ig-zan′dər), group of over 1000 islands in SE Alaska.

Alexander I, 1777-1825, czar of Russia from 1801 to 1825.

Alexander II, 1818-1881, czar of Russia from 1855 to 1881. He abolished serfdom.

Alexander III, 1845-1894, czar of Russia from 1881 to 1894, son of Alexander II.

Alexander VI, 1431-1503, pope from 1492 to 1503.

Alexander the Great, 356-323 B.C., king of Macedonia from 336 to 323 B.C. He conquered the Greek city-states and the whole Persian empire, from the coasts of Asia Minor and Egypt to India.

Al ex an dri a (al′ig zan′drē ə), *n.* 1 seaport in N Egypt, on the Mediterranean, at the NW end of the Nile delta. Founded by Alexander the Great in 332 B.C.; capital of Egypt under the Ptolemies; ancient center of Greek culture and later of Christianity. 1,804,000. See **Byzantine Empire** for map. 2 city in NE Virginia, near Washington, D.C. 111,000.

Al ex an dri an (al′ig zan′drē ən), *adj.* 1 of Alexandria, Egypt. 2 of Alexander the Great. 3 of an alexandrine or alexandrines.

al ex an drine or **Al ex an drine** (al′ig-zan′drən), *n.* line of verse having six iambic feet, with a caesura (pause) after the third foot. EXAMPLE: He seeks′ out might′y charms′, to trou′ble sleep′y minds′. [< French *alexandrin;* because this meter was used in Old French poems on *Alexander the Great*]

al fal fa (al fal′fə), *n.* a plant of the pea family with deep roots, cloverlike leaves, and bluish-purple flowers; lucerne. Alfalfa is grown as food for livestock and can be cut several times a season and then dried as hay. [< Spanish < Arabic *al-fasfaṣ* the best kind of fodder]

Al fon so XIII (al fon′sō, al fon′zō), 1886-1941, king of Spain from 1902 until he was deposed in 1931.

Al fred the Great (al′frid), A.D. 849-899, king of the West Saxons from A.D. 871 to 899, who united southern England after defeating the invading Danes.

al fres co (al fres′kō), *adv., adj.* in the open air; outdoors. [< Italian *al fresco* in the cool]

alg., algebra.

al ga (al′gə), *n., pl.* **-gae.** one of the algae.

al gae (al′jē), *n.pl.* group of related plants, mostly aquatic, containing chlorophyll but lacking true stems, roots, or leaves. Some algae are single-celled and form scum on rocks; others, such as the seaweeds, are multicellular and may be very large. [< Latin, plural of *alga* seaweed]

al gal (al′gəl), *adj.* of, having to do with, or like algae.

al ge bra (al′jə brə), *n.* branch of mathematics dealing with the relations and properties of quantities by the use of symbols and letters, negative numbers as well as ordinary numbers, and equations to solve problems involving a finite number of operations. $x + y = x^2$ is a way of stating, by algebra, the arithmetical fact that the sum of two numbers equals the square of one of them. [< Medieval Latin < Arabic *al-jabr* the bone setting; hence, reduction (i.e., of parts to a whole)]

al ge bra ic (al′jə brā′ik), *adj.* of or having to do with algebra; used in algebra: $(a + b)(a - b) = a^2 - b^2$ *is an algebraic statement.* **—al′ge bra′i cal ly,** *adv.*

al ge bra i cal (al′jə brā′ə kəl), *adj.* algebraic.

Al ge cir as (al′jə sir′əs), *n.* seaport in S Spain, on the Strait of Gibraltar. 77,000.

Al ger (al′jər), *n.* **Horatio,** 1834-1899, American author of a series of inspirational books for boys.

Al ger i a (al jir′ē ə), *n.* country in N Africa, on the Mediterranean, which became independent of France in 1962. 13,200,000 pop.; 919,600 sq. mi. *Capital:* Algiers.

Al ger i an (al jir′ē ən), *adj.* 1 of Algeria or Algiers. *—n.* native or inhabitant of Algeria or Algiers.

Al ge rine (al′jə rēn′), *adj., n.* Algerian.

Al giers (al jirz′), *n.* 1 capital of Algeria, on the Mediterranean. 943,000. 2 one of the Barbary States, now Algeria.

al gin (al′jən), *n.* a gelatinous compound found in certain algae, used in plastics, and as a food emulsifier and thickener.

Al gol (al′gol), *n.* a binary star in the constellation Perseus, that varies in apparent brightness periodically because its brighter component is eclipsed by the fainter.

AL GOL (al′gol), *n.* an algebraic system for programing a computer to solve scientific problems. [< *Algo(rithmic) L(anguage)*]

Al gon ki an (al gong′kē ən), *n., adj.* Algonquian.

Al gon qui an (al gong′kē ən, al gong′-kwē ən), *n.* 1 the most widespread family of North American Indian languages. 2 Indian belonging to an Algonquian tribe. *—adj.* of or belonging to this family of languages. The languages of the Arapaho, Blackfoot, Cheyenne, Ojibwa, Delaware, Sauk, Fox, and Shawnee Indian tribes belong to the Algonquian languages.

Al gon quin (al gong′kən, al gong′kwən), *n.* 1 member of a group of American Indian tribes that lived in the valleys of the Ottawa River and of the northern tributaries of the St. Lawrence River. 2 the Algonquian language of any of these tribes.

al go rithm (al′gə riᴛʜ′əm), *n.* a formal procedure for any mathematical operation: *the division algorithm.* [ultimately < Arabic *al-khuwārizmī,* name of the author of a famous work on algebra]

al go rith mic (al′gə riᴛʜ′mik), *adj.* of, having to do with, or according to algorithm.

Al ham bra (al ham′brə), *n.* palace of the Moorish kings at Granada, Spain. It was the last stronghold of the Moors in Europe and was conquered in 1492.

a li as (ā′lē əs), *n.* name used by a person instead of his real name to hide who he is; assumed name; other name. *—adv.* otherwise called; with the assumed name of: *The spy's name was Harrison, alias Johnson.* [< Latin, otherwise < *alius* other]

A li Ba ba (ä′lē bä′bə; al′ē bab′ə), a poor woodcutter in *The Arabian Nights* who discovers a treasure hidden in a cave by forty thieves.

al i bi (al′ə bī), *n., v.,* **-bied, -bi ing.** *—n.* 1 the plea or fact that a person accused of an offense was somewhere else when the offense was committed. 2 U.S. INFORMAL. an excuse. *—v.i.* U.S. INFORMAL. make an excuse. *—v.t.* U.S. INFORMAL. make an excuse for. [< Latin, elsewhere]

al i dade (al′ə dād), *n.* a measuring instrument consisting of a sighting device attached to a straightedge, used in surveying, etc., to make a map or a scale drawing of a given area. [< Medieval Latin *alhidada* < Arabic *al-'iḍāda*]

al ien (ā′lyən, ā′lē ən), *n.* 1 person who is not a citizen of the country in which he lives; a resident foreigner whose allegiance is owed to a foreign state. 2 person belonging to a different ethnic or social group; stranger; foreigner. *—adj.* 1 of or by another country; foreign: *an alien language, alien domination.* 2 having the legal status of an alien: *an alien resident.* 3 entirely different from one's own; strange: *alien customs.* 4 not in agreement; opposed, adverse, or repugnant: *Unkindness is alien to her nature.* [< Latin *alienus* < *alius* other]

al ien a bil i ty (ā′lyə nə bil′ə tē, ā′lē-ə nə bil′ə tē), *n.* quality or state of being transferable.

al ien a ble (ā′lyə nə bəl, ā′lē ə nə bəl), *adj.* that can be transferred to another owner: *alienable property.*

al ien ate (ā′lyə nāt, ā′lē ə nāt), *v.t.,* **-at ed, -at ing.** 1 turn away the normal feelings, fondness, or devotion of anyone; make unfriendly; estrange: *The colonies were alienated from England by disputes over trade and taxation.* 2 transfer (property, a property right, etc.) to the ownership of another: *Enemy property was alienated during the war.* 3 turn away; transfer. **—al′ien a′tor,** *n.*

al ien a tion (ā′lyə nā′shən, ā′lē ə nā′shən), *n.* 1 an alienating; estrangement. 2 a being alienated. 3 transfer of the ownership of property, etc., to another.

al ien ist (ā′lyə nist, ā′lē ə nist), *n.* psychiatrist, especially one who testifies in a court of law. [< French *aliéniste* < Latin *alienus* insane, strange]

a light[1] (ə līt′), *v.i.,* **a light ed** or **a lit, a light ing.** 1 get out of, off, or down from. 2 descend and lightly settle, as a bird, a snowflake, etc. 3 come by chance; happen: *His eyes alighted on the ring lost in the grass.* [Old English *ālīhtan*]

a light[2] (ə līt′), *adj.* 1 on fire; lighted. 2 lighted up; aglow. [Old English *ālīht*]

a lign (ə līn′), *v.t.* 1 bring (anything) into line; adjust to a line: *align the sights of a gun.* 2 join with others for or against a cause: *Germany was aligned with Japan in World War II.* *—v.i.* form a line: *The troops aligned.* Also, **aline.** [< French *aligner* < *a-* to + *ligne* line]

a lign ment (ə līn′mənt), *n.* 1 arrangement

or formation in a line or pattern of lines. 2 a bringing into line. 3 the line or lines so formed. 4 a joining of persons or groups having similar interests, ideals, etc., for a common purpose. 5 (in electronics) the adjustment or synchronization of circuits, components, etc., so that they perform properly. Also, **alinement.**

a like (ə līk′), *adv.* in the same way; similarly; equally. *—adj.* like one another; similar. [Old English *onlīc*] **—a like′ness,** *n.*

al i ment (al′ə mənt), *n.* 1 food; nourishment. 2 means of support; sustenance. [< Latin *alimentum* < *alere* nourish]

al i men tal (al′ə men′tl), *adj.* of food; nourishing. **—al′i men′tal ly,** *adv.*

al i men tar y (al′ə men′tər ē), *adj.* having to do with food and nutrition.

alimentary canal, tube or passage of the body of any animal through which food passes and in or by means of which food is digested and wastes are eliminated, including, in mammals, the mouth, esophagus, stomach, intestines, and anus.

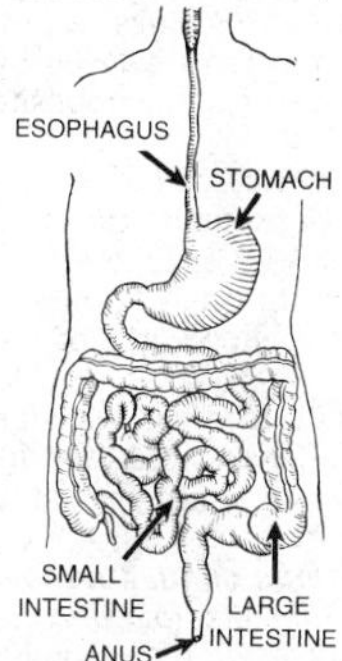

alimentary canal of a person—a 30 ft. tube beginning at the mouth, where food enters, and ending at the anus, where undigested solids leave the body.

al i mo ny (al′ə mō′nē), *n.* a fixed sum of money paid regularly to a woman for her support by her husband or former husband, under orders from a court. [< Latin *alimonia* sustenance < *alere* nourish]

a line (ə līn′), *v.t., v.i.,* **a lined, a lin ing.** align.

a line ment (ə līn′mənt), *n.* alignment.

Al i oth (al′ē oth), *n.* a bright star, of the second magnitude, in the handle of the Big Dipper.

al i phat ic (al′ə fat′ik), *adj.* of or belonging to a class of organic compounds in which the carbon atoms form chains with open ends rather than rings, including the fats, the paraffins, etc. [< Greek *aleiphatos* fat, oil]

al i quant (al′ə kwənt), *adj.* not dividing a number or quantity without a remainder: *5 is an aliquant part of 14.* [< Latin *aliquantus* somewhat < *alius* some + *quantus* how much]

al i quot (al′ə kwət), *adj.* dividing a number or quantity without a remainder: *3 is an aliquot part of 12.* [< Latin, several < *alius* some + *quot* how many]

a lit (ə lit′), *v.* a pt. and a pp. of **alight**[1]. *The bird alit upon a branch.*

a live (ə līv′), *adj.* 1 having life; living: *Was the snake alive or dead?* 2 in continued activity; in full force; active: *We celebrate Memorial Day to keep alive the memory of soldiers and sailors who have died for their country.* 3 of all living: *the happiest man alive.* 4 active; lively. 5 connected to a source of electricity. 6 (of a microphone) connected for broadcasting or recording. 7 **alive to,** awake to; sensitive to; noticing: *alive to the needs of the people.* 8 **alive with,** full of; swarming with. 9 **look alive!** hurry up! be quick! [Old English *on līfe* in life]

a liz ar in (ə liz′ər ən), *n.* a red crystalline dye prepared from coal tar, formerly obtained from madder. *Formula:* $C_{14}H_8O_4$ [< French < *alizari* madder]

al ka li (al′kə lī), *n., pl.* **-lis** or **-lies.** 1 any base or hydroxide that is soluble in water, neutralizes acids and forms salts with them, and turns red litmus blue. Lye and ammonia are alkalis. 2 any salt or mixture of salts that neutralizes acids, found in some desert soils. [< Arabic *al-qalī* the soda ash]

alkali metal, any of the group of univalent metals that includes lithium, sodium, potassium, rubidium, cesium, and francium.

al ka line (al′kə līn, al′kə lən), *adj.* 1 of or like an alkali. 2 containing an alkali. 3 containing more alkali than is normal.

alkaline earth, any oxide of the alkaline-earth metals.

al ka line-earth metals (al′kə līn ėrth′, al′kə lən ėrth′), calcium, strontium, and barium. Some authorities include beryllium, magnesium, and radium.

al ka lin i ty (al′kə lin′ə tē), *n.* alkaline quality or condition.

al ka lize (al′kə līz), *v.t., v.i.,* **-lized, -liz ing.** make or become alkaline. **—al′ka li za′tion,** *n.*

al ka loid (al′kə loid), *n.* any of a group of complex organic compounds of nitrogen with alkaline properties, found in or obtained from many plants. Most alkaloids are drugs, such as cocaine, strychnine, morphine, and quinine. Most alkaloids are colorless, crystalline, have a bitter taste, and some are very poisonous.

al ka loid al (al′kə loi′dl), *adj.* of or having to do with an alkaloid.

Al ko ran (al′kō rän′, al′kō ran′), *n.* the Koran.

al kyd (al′kid), *n.* alkyd resin.

alkyd resin, any of a group of sticky resins that become plastic when heated, used in paints, lacquers, etc.

al kyl (al′kəl), *n.* a univalent radical occurring in aliphatic hydrocarbon derivatives from which a hydrogen atom has been removed. *Formula:* $C_nH_{2n+1}-$

all (ôl), *adj.* 1 the whole of: *We ate all the food. All America rejoiced.* 2 every one of: *All the children are here.* 3 the greatest possible: *She made all haste to reach home in time.* 4 every (kind or manner of something): *all sorts of arguments.* 5 any; any whatever: *The prisoner denied all connection with the crime.* 6 nothing but; only: *all words and no thought.*
—pron. 1 the whole number; everyone: *All of us are going.* 2 everything: *All that glitters is not gold.* 3 the whole amount or extent: *All of the bread has been eaten.*
—n. everything one has: *They lost all in the fire.*
above all, before everything else: *Above all, he loves his work.*
after all, when everything has been considered; nevertheless.
all but, almost; nearly.
all in all, **a** everything. **b** when everything has been taken into account. **c** completely.
at all, **a** under any conditions. **b** in any way.
for all (that), in spite of; notwithstanding.
in all, counting every person or thing; altogether: *There were 100 people in all.*
—adv. 1 wholly; entirely: *The cake is all gone.* 2 only; exclusively: *money spent all on pleasure.* 3 each; apiece: *The score was even at forty all.* 4 **all in,** INFORMAL. worn out; weary. 5 **all of,** as much as; no less than. 6 **all over,** **a** everywhere. **b** done with; finished.
[Old English *eall*]

hat, āge, fär; let, ēqual, tėrm;
it, īce; hot, ōpen, ôrder;
oil, out; cup, pu̇t, rüle;
ch, child; ng, long; sh, she;
th, thin; ᴛʜ, then; zh, measure;

ə represents *a* in about, *e* in taken, *i* in pencil, *o* in lemon, *u* in circus.

< = from, derived from, taken from.

al la bre ve (ä′lə brā′vā), in music: 1 a measure having two or four beats in which a half note represents one beat, played or sung twice as fast as the common measure. 2 using or having this measure. 3 the symbol (¢) indicating this measure. [< Italian, in breve style]

Al lah (al′ə, ä′lə), *n.* the Moslem name of the one Supreme Being, or God.

Al la ha bad (al′ə hə bad′, ä′lə hä bäd′), *n.* city in E India, on the Ganges River. 522,000.

all-A mer i can (ôl′ə mer′ə kən), *adj.* 1 selected as the best of its class in the United States. 2 made up entirely of Americans or American elements. 3 representing the whole United States. *—n.* (in sports) a player selected as one of the best in the United States at his position.

al lan to ic (al′ən tō′ik), *adj.* of or relating to the allantois.

al lan to is (ə lan′tō is), *n.* appendage on the embryos of reptiles, birds, and mammals, developing as a membranous sac from the posterior part of the intestinal cavity. It is important in the formation of the umbilical cord and the placenta in mammals. [< New Latin < Greek *allantoeidēs* sausage-shaped]

al lar gan do (ä′lär gän′dō), *adv., adj.* (in music) gradually becoming slower and louder. [< Italian]

all-a round (ôl′ə round′), *adj.* U.S. not limited or specialized; useful in many ways.

al lay (ə lā′), *v.t.,* **-layed, -lay ing.** 1 put at rest; quiet: *My fears were allayed by the news that my family was safe.* 2 relieve (pain, trouble, thirst, etc.); alleviate. [Old English *ālecgan* < *ā-* away, off + *lecgan* to lay] **—al lay′er,** *n.*

all clear, signal indicating the end of an air raid or other danger.

al le ga tion (al′ə gā′shən), *n.* 1 an assertion without proof. 2 act of asserting what one is prepared to prove; an assertion. 3 act of making a charge before a legal tribunal. 4 the charge undertaken to be proved. 5 act of alleging.

al lege (ə lej′), *v.t.,* **-leged, -leg ing.** 1 state positively; assert; declare. 2 assert without proof; claim. 3 give or bring forward as a reason, argument, or excuse. [< Latin *allegare* to cite < *ad-* to + *legare* to commission] **—al lege′a ble,** *adj.* **—al leg′er,** *n.*

al leg ed ly (ə lej′id lē), *adv.* according to what is or has been alleged.

Al le ghe nies (al′ə gā′nēz), *n.pl.* Allegheny Mountains.

Al le ghe ny Mountains (al′ə gā′nē), range of the Appalachian Mountains, in Pennsylvania, Maryland, Virginia, and West Virginia.

Allegheny River, river in NW New York State and W Pennsylvania. It joins the Monongahela at Pittsburgh to form the Ohio River. 325 mi.

al le giance (ə lē′jəns), *n.* 1 the loyalty owed by a citizen to his country; obligation of a subject to his ruler or government. 2 faithfulness to a person, cause, etc.; loyalty; fidelity. [Middle English *alegeaunce* < Old French *ligeance* < *lige* liege]

al le go ri cal (al′ə gôr′ə kəl, al′ə gor′ə-kəl), *adj.* explaining or teaching something by a story; using allegory. **—al′le-go′ri cal ly,** *adv.*

al le go rist (al′ə gôr′ist, al′ə gōr′ist), *n.* writer of allegories.

al le go rize (al′ə gə rīz′), *v.,* **-rized, -riz-ing.** *—v.t.* 1 make into allegory. 2 treat or explain as an allegory. *—v.i.* use allegory. **—al′le go′ri za′tion,** *n.* **—al′le go-riz′er,** *n.*

al le go ry (al′ə gôr′ē, al′ə gōr′ē), *n., pl.* **-ries.** a long and complicated story with an underlying meaning different from the surface meaning of the story itself, told to explain or teach something: *Bunyan's "The Pilgrim's Progress" is an allegory.* [< Latin *allegoria* < Greek < *allēgorein* speak figuratively < *allos* other + *agoreuein* speak publicly < *agora* public place or assembly]

al le gret to (al′ə gret′ō), *adj., adv., n., pl.* **-tos.** in music: *—adj.* quick, but not so quick as allegro. *—adv.* in allegretto tempo. *—n.* an allegretto part in a piece of music. [< Italian]

al leg ro (ə leg′rō, ə lā′grō), *adj., adv., n., pl.* **-ros.** in music: *—adj.* quick; lively. *—adv.* in quick time. *—n.* a quick, lively part in a piece of music. [< Italian]

al lele (ə lēl′), *n.* 1 either of a pair of alternative characters, such as tallness and dwarfness, potentially present in the germ cell. 2 a gene, especially one of a pair that bear alternative characters. [< Greek *allēlōn* of each other]

al le lic (ə lē′lik, ə lel′ik), *adj.* of or having to do with an allele or alleles.

al le lu ia (al′ə lü′yə), *interj., n.* the Latin and liturgical form of **hallelujah.**

al le mande (al′ə mand′; *French* äl mäɴd′), *n.* 1 a German dance popular in France in the 1700's, in which the participants hold hands. 2 music for such a dance. [< French *(danse) allemande* German (dance)]

Al len (al′ən), *n.* **Ethan,** 1737-1789, American officer in the Revolutionary War.

Al len town (al′ən toun), *n.* city in E Pennsylvania. 110,000.

al ler gen (al′ər jən), *n.* any substance that causes or reveals an allergy in a particular individual or individuals.

al ler gen ic (al′ər jen′ik), *adj.* of or having to do with allergens.

al ler gic (ə lėr′jik), *adj.* 1 having an allergy: *allergic to eggs.* 2 of or caused by allergy: *Hay fever is an allergic reaction.* 3 SLANG. having a strong dislike: *She is allergic to camping.* **—al ler′gi cal ly,** *adv.*

al ler gist (al′ər jist), *n.* doctor who specializes in treating allergies.

al ler gy (al′ər jē), *n., pl.* **-gies.** 1 an unusual sensitiveness to a particular substance, differing in symptoms according to the substance, which may be a food, pollen, hair, or cloth. Hay fever, asthma, headaches, and hives are common signs of allergy. 2 anaphylaxis. 3 SLANG. a strong dislike: *an allergy for work.* [< New Latin *allergia* < Greek *allos* different, other + *ergon* action, work]

al le vi ate (ə lē′vē āt), *v.t.,* **-at ed, -at ing.** 1 make easier to endure (suffering of the body or mind); relieve; mitigate: *Heat often alleviates pain.* 2 lessen or lighten; diminish: *Something must be done to alleviate the traffic congestion.* [< Late Latin *alleviatum* lightened < Latin *ad-* up + *levis* light] **—al le′vi a′tor,** *n.*

al le vi a tion (ə lē′vē ā′shən), *n.* 1 an alleviating. 2 a being alleviated. 3 thing that alleviates.

al ley[1] (al′ē), *n., pl.* **-leys.** 1 a narrow back street in a city or town, especially one running between rows of buildings. 2 BRITISH. a narrow street. 3 path in a park or garden, bordered by trees, shrubbery, or bushes. 4 a long, narrow lane along which the ball is rolled in bowling; bowling alley. 5 Often, **alleys,** *pl.* building having a number of alleys for bowling. [< Old French *alee* a going < *aler* go]

al ley[2] (al′ē), *n., pl.* **-leys.** a large marble used to shoot at the other marbles in the game of marbles. [short for *alabaster*]

al ley way (al′ē wā′), *n.* 1 U.S. alley in a city or town. 2 a narrow passageway.

All Fools' Day, April Fools' Day.

all fours, 1 all four legs of an animal. 2 arms and legs of a person; hands and knees: *The baby crawled on all fours.*

All hal lows (ôl′hal′ōz), *n.* All Saints' Day.

al li ance (ə lī′əns), *n.* 1 union formed by mutual agreement, especially to protect or further mutual interests. 2 a joining of independent nations by treaty. 3 a joining of family interests through marriage. 4 the nations, persons, etc., who are allied. 5 any joining of efforts or interests by persons, families, states, or organizations: *an alliance between church and state.* 6 similarity in structure or descent; relationship. [< Old French *aliance* < *alier* unite. See ALLY.]

al lied (ə līd′, al′īd), *adj.* 1 united by agreement or treaty; combined for some special purpose: *allied nations.* 2 associated; connected: *allied banks.* 3 related: *The dog and the wolf are allied animals.* 4 **Allied,** of or by the Allies.

Al lies (al′īz, ə līz′), *n.pl.* 1 the countries that fought against Germany, Austria-Hungary, Turkey, and Bulgaria in World War I. 2 the countries that fought against Germany, Italy, and Japan in World War II.

al li ga tor (al′ə gā′tər), *n.* 1 a large reptile with a rather thick skin, similar to the crocodile, but having a shorter and flatter head. There are two species of alligators, one of them living in the rivers and marshes of the southeastern United States, the other in and near the Yangtze River in China. 2 leather prepared from an alligator's skin. [< Spanish *el lagarto* the lizard]

alligator pear, avocado.

al lit e rate (ə lit′ə rāt′), *v.,* **-rat ed, -rat-ing.** *—v.i.* 1 have the same first sound or letter. 2 use alliteration. *—v.t.* write or speak (anything) with alliteration. [< Latin *ad-* to + *litera* letter] **—al lit′e ra′tor,** *n.*

al lit e ra tion (ə lit′ə rā′shən), *n.* repetition of the same first sound or letter in a group of words or a line of poetry. EXAMPLE: "The sun sank slowly" contains alliteration of *s.*

al lit e ra tive (ə lit′ə rā′tiv), *adj.* having words beginning with the same sound or letter. **—al lit′e ra′tive ly,** *adv.*

allo-, *combining form.* other; different: *Allophone = other sound.* [< Greek *allos*]

al lo cate (al′ə kāt), *v.t.,* **-cat ed, -cat ing.** 1 set or lay aside for a special purpose; assign, allot, or apportion: *The Ford Foundation allocated millions of dollars among colleges and hospitals.* 2 locate. [< Medieval Latin *allocatum* located < Latin *ad-* to, at + *locus* place]

al lo ca tion (al′ə kā′shən), *n.* 1 an allocating; allotment; apportionment. 2 share, portion, or thing allocated.

al log a mous (ə log′ə məs), *adj.* of or caused by allogamy.

al log a my (ə log′ə mē), *n.* cross-fertilization.

al lo met ric (al′ə met′rik), *adj.* of or characterized by allometry.

al lom e try (ə lom′ə trē), *n.* the relative growth rate of one part of an organism with reference to the rest.

al lop a thy (ə lop′ə thē), *n.* method of treating a disease by using remedies to produce effects different from those caused by the disease treated. Allopathy is the opposite of homeopathy.

al lo phone (al′ə fōn), *n.* any one of several slightly different speech sounds that are heard as the same sound by speakers of a given language or dialect. In English, the *t* in *top* and the *t* in *stop* are allophones of the phoneme *t.*

al lot (ə lot′), *v.t.,* **-lot ted, -lot ting.** 1 divide and distribute in parts or shares: *The profits have all been allotted.* See synonym study below. 2 give as a share, task, duty, etc.; assign: *The dance chairman allotted responsibility for tickets, refreshments, and decorations.* See **assign** for synonym study. 3 appropriate (anything) to a special purpose; allocate. [< Middle French *allotir* < *a-* to + *lot* lot] **—al lot′ter,** *n.*

Syn. 1 **Allot, apportion** mean to give out in shares. **Allot** emphasizes giving set amounts for a definite purpose or to particular persons, and does not suggest the way in which the shares are set or distributed: *The Government is ready to allot homesteads in that area.* **Apportion** emphasizes division and distribution according to a fair plan, usually in proportions settled by some rule: *The reward money was apportioned among those who had helped in the rescue.*

alligator (def. 1) to 12 ft. long

al lot ment (ə lot′mənt), *n.* 1 division and distribution in parts or shares. 2 a share, part, or portion.

al lo trope (al′ə trōp), *n.* an allotropic form.

al lo trop ic (al′ə trop′ik), *adj.* occurring in two or more forms that differ in physical and chemical properties but not in the kind of atoms of which they are composed. Oxygen gas and ozone are allotropic forms of the element oxygen. [< *allo-* + Greek *tropos* way]

al lot ro pism (ə lot′rə piz′əm), *n.* allotropy.

al lot ro py (ə lot′rə pē), *n.* property or fact of being allotropic.

all-out (ôl′out′), *adj.* greatest possible; complete: *an all-out effort.* —*adv.* to the utmost extent: *go all-out to win.*

all o ver (ôl′ō′vər), *adj.* 1 covering the whole surface. 2 having a pattern that is repeated over the whole surface of a fabric, especially an embroidered or lace fabric. —*n.* fabric with such a pattern.

al low (ə lou′), *v.t.* 1 let (someone) do something; permit: *The class was not allowed to leave until the bell rang.* See **permit** for synonym study. 2 let (anyone) have as a share; give as allowance: *I am allowed $2 a week as spending money.* 3 accept as true; admit; acknowledge; recognize: *The judge allowed the claim of the person whose property was damaged.* 4 add or subtract to make up for something: *allow an extra hour for traveling time.* 5 let happen, especially through carelessness or neglect: *allow a cake to burn.* 6 U.S. DIALECT. say; think: *He allowed that he was going to the dance.* 7 **allow for,** take into consideration; provide for: *Don't forget to allow for changes in the weather.* [< Old French *alouer* < Latin *allaudare* approve < *ad-* to + *laudare* to praise] —**al low′er,** *n.*

al low a ble (ə lou′ə bəl), *adj.* allowed by law or by a person in authority; permitted by custom or usage; not forbidden. —**al low′a ble ness,** *n.* —**al low′a bly,** *adv.*

al low ance (ə lou′əns), *n.* 1 a definite portion, sum, or amount granted to meet expenses or requirements; allotment: *My weekly allowance is $2.* 2 amount granted as a deduction; discount: *We got an allowance of $500 on our old car against the price of a new one.* 3 **make allowance** or **make allowance for,** take into consideration; allow for: *You should make allowance for the wishes of others.* 4 an allowing; conceding: *allowance of a claim.* 5 tolerance: *allowance of slavery.* 6 (in machinery) permissible variation in the dimension of connecting parts. 7 (in certain sports) a handicap.

al loy (*n.* al′oi, ə loi′; *v.* ə loi′), *n.* 1 metal made by mixing and fusing two or more metals, or a metal and a nonmetal, to secure some desirable quality or qualities, as toughness, resistance to wear, etc. Brass is an alloy of copper and zinc. 2 an inferior metal mixed with a more valuable one: *This gold is not pure; there is some alloy in it.* 3 any injurious addition; impurity. —*v.t.* 1 make into an alloy. 2 make less valuable by mixing with a cheaper metal. 3 make worse by mixing with something bad; debase. [< Middle French *aloi* < *alier* unite, combine < Latin *alligare* bind to. Doublet of ALLY.]

all-pur pose (ôl′pėr′pəs), *adj.* that can be used for any purpose: *All-purpose flour is as suitable for pastry and cakes as it is for bread.*

all right, 1 without error; correct. 2 satisfactory. 3 in a satisfactory way. 4 in good health. 5 yes. 6 without doubt; certainly.

all-right (ôl′rīt′), *adj.* U.S. SLANG. very good or excellent of its kind; very dependable.

all-round (ôl′round′), *adj.* all-around.

All Saints' Day, November 1, a church festival honoring all the saints; Allhallows; Hallowmas.

All Souls' Day, November 2, a day when services are held in the Roman Catholic Church and prayers said for all the souls in purgatory.

all spice (ôl′spīs′), *n.* 1 a spice having a flavor suggesting a mixture of cloves with cinnamon and nutmeg; pimento. 2 the berry of the pimento tree from which this spice is made.

all-star (ôl′stär′), *adj.* made up of the best players or performers.

al lude (ə lüd′), *v.i.,* **-lud ed, -lud ing.** refer indirectly *(to);* mention slightly in passing: *I didn't tell him of your decision; I didn't even allude to it.* See **refer** for synonym study. [< Latin *alludere* < *ad-* + *ludere* to play]

all-up weight (ôl′up′), the gross weight of an aircraft.

al lure (ə lůr′), *v.,* **-lured, -lur ing,** *n.* —*v.t.* tempt or attract very strongly; fascinate; charm: *City life allured her with its action and excitement.* See **charm** and **lure** for synonym studies. —*n.* great charm; fascination. [< Middle French *alurer* < *a-* to + *leurre* lure] —**al lur′er,** *n.*

al lure ment (ə lůr′mənt), *n.* 1 charm; fascination. 2 thing that allures; temptation; attraction.

al lur ing (ə lůr′ing), *adj.* 1 strongly attracting; tempting. 2 charming; fascinating. —**al lur′ing ly,** *adv.* —**al lur′ing ness,** *n.*

al lu sion (ə lü′zhən), *n.* act of alluding; slight or incidental mention of something. [< Latin *allusionem* < *alludere.* See ALLUDE.]

➔ **Allusion, illusion** are sometimes confused. An *allusion* is an indirect reference or slight mention: *She made allusions to several recent novels.* An *illusion* is a misleading appearance: *an illusion of wealth.*

al lu sive (ə lü′siv), *adj.* containing an allusion; full of allusions. —**al lu′sive ly,** *adv.* —**al lu′sive ness,** *n.*

al lu vi al (ə lü′vē əl), *adj.* having to do with, consisting of, or formed by sand, silt, mud, etc., left by flowing water. A delta is an alluvial deposit at the mouth of a river.

al lu vi um (ə lü′vē əm), *n., pl.* **-vi ums, -vi a** (-vē ə). deposit of sand, silt, mud, etc., left by flowing water. [< Late Latin < Latin *alluere* wash against < *ad-* against + *lavere* to wash]

al ly (*n.* al′ī, ə lī′; *v.* ə lī′), *n., pl.* **-lies,** *v.,* **-lied, -ly ing.** —*n.* 1 person, group, or nation united with another for some special purpose. See also **Allies.** 2 a related animal, plant, form, or thing. 3 helper; supporter. —*v.t.* 1 combine for some special purpose; unite by formal agreement: *Our nation allies itself with Great Britain to protect our interests in Europe. The premier allied his country to France.* 2 associate; connect: *This newspaper is allied with three others.* 3 be similar in nature, structure, descent, etc.; relate: *Dogs are allied to wolves.* —*v.i.* join or unite; enter into alliance. [< Old French *alier* to ally < Latin *alligare* bind to < *ad-* to + *ligare* to bind. Doublet of ALLOY.]

-ally, *suffix forming adverbs.* in a ___ic manner: *Basically = in a basic manner.* [< *-al*[1] + *-ly*[1]]

Al ma-A ta (äl′mə ä′tə), *n.* city in SE Soviet Union, capital of the Kazakh S.S.R. 730,000.

al ma ma ter or **Al ma Ma ter** (al′mə mä′tər; äl′mə mā′tər), school, college, or university at which one is or has been a student. [< Latin *alma mater* fostering mother]

al ma nac (ôl′mə nak), *n.* 1 an annual table or book of tables containing a calendar of days, weeks, and months and often including astronomical data, weather predictions, church days, dates of holidays, changes of the moon, hours of sunrise and sunset, and other miscellaneous information. 2 an annual reference book containing summaries of information on particular subjects. [< Medieval Latin *almanachus* < Arabic *almanākh*]

hat, āge, fär; let, ēqual, tėrm;
it, īce; hot, ōpen, ôrder;
oil, out; cup, pu̇t, rüle;
ch, child; ng, long; sh, she;
th, thin; ᴛʜ, then; zh, measure;

ə represents *a* in about, *e* in taken, *i* in pencil, *o* in lemon, *u* in circus.

< = from, derived from, taken from.

al might y (ôl mī′tē), *adj.* 1 having supreme power; omnipotent. 2 having overwhelming power. 3 INFORMAL. great. —*adv.* INFORMAL. exceedingly. —*n.* **the Almighty,** God. —**al might′i ly,** *adv.* —**al might′i ness,** *n.*

al mond (ä′mənd, am′ənd; äl′mənd, al′mənd), *n.* 1 the flattish, oval-shaped nut of a peachlike fruit growing in warm regions. 2 tree that the fruit grows on. It belongs to the rose family. 3 something shaped like an almond. [< Old French *almande,* ultimately < Greek *amygdalē*] —**al′mond like′,** *adj.*

al mond-eyed (ä′mənd īd′, am′ənd īd′; äl′mənd īd′, al′mənd īd′), *adj.* having eyes that appear to be oval-shaped and to have pointed ends.

al mon er (al′mə nər, ä′mə nər), *n.* person who distributes alms for a king, a monastery, or a person of rank.

al most (ôl′mōst, ôl mōst′), *adv.* 1 nearly: *I almost missed the train.* 2 **almost never,** scarcely ever. 3 **almost no,** scarcely any. [for *all most*]

alms (ämz, älmz), *n. sing. or pl.* money or gifts given freely to help the poor; charity. [Old English *ælmysse* < Latin *eleemosyna* < Greek *eleēmosynē* pity, alms < *eleos* pity]

alms giv er (ämz′giv′ər, älmz′giv′ər), *n.* person who gives alms.

alms giv ing (ämz′giv′ing, älmz′giv′ing), *n.* the giving of help to the poor.

alms house (ämz′hous′, älmz′hous′), *n., pl.* **-hous es** (-hou′ziz). home for very poor persons supported at public expense or, in Great Britain, by private charity.

al ni co (al′nə kō), *n.* any of several powerful magnetic alloys, made mostly of iron in combination with aluminum, nickel, and cobalt, with very small amounts of other metals. [< *al(uminum)* + *ni(ckel)* + *co(balt)*]

al oe (al′ō), *n.* 1 plant of the lily family growing chiefly in the warm, dry parts of southern Africa, having a long spike of flowers and thick, narrow leaves. 2 **aloes,** *pl. in form, sing. in use.* a bitter drug made from the dried juice of this plant's leaves, used as a laxative or tonic. 3 century plant. [< Latin < Greek]

a loft (ə lôft′, ə loft′), *adv.* 1 far above the earth; high up. 2 in or into the air; off from the ground. 3 high up among the sails, rigging, or masts of a ship. [< Scandinavian (Old Icelandic) *ā lopti* in the air]

a lo ha (ə lō′ə, ä lō′hä), *interj.* 1 greetings; hello. 2 good-by; farewell. —*n.* (in Hawaii) love. [< Hawaiian]

a lone (ə lōn′), *adj.* 1 quite by oneself; apart from other persons or things; solitary: *I was alone.* 2 without anyone else; only: *I alone remained.* 3 without anything more: *A diet of meat alone is not adequate for most people.* 4 **leave alone,** not bother; not meddle with. 5 **let alone, a** not bother; not meddle with. **b** not to mention: *It would have been a hot day for summer, let alone early spring.* 6 **let well enough alone,** be satisfied with conditions and not try to change them. *—adv.* 1 apart from other persons or things: *One tree stood alone on the hill.* 2 and nothing more; only: *I did the job for money alone.* [Middle English *al one* all (completely) one] **—a lone′ness,** *n.*

a long (ə lông′, ə long′), *prep.* 1 on or by the whole length of; from one end to or toward the other of; lengthwise of: *walk along a river.* 2 on or during: *We met along the way.* *—adv.* 1 lengthwise: *cars parked along by the stadium.* 2 onward; forward: *Let us walk along.* 3 U.S. together with someone or something: *You should take a tent along if you are going camping. I took my dog along.* 4 U.S. INFORMAL. (of time) somewhere: *along about four o'clock.* 5 **all along,** all the time: *I knew the answer all along.* 6 **along with,** in company with; together with: *I'll go along with you.* 7 **get along, a** manage with at least some success. **b** agree. **c** go away. **d** move forward; advance. **e** succeed; prosper. [Old English *andlang* the length of < *and-* opposite + *lang* long]

a long shore (ə lông′shôr′, ə lông′shōr′; ə long′shôr′, ə long′shōr′), *adv.* near or along the shore.

a long side (ə lông′sīd′, ə long′sīd′), *adv.* 1 at the side; side by side. 2 **alongside of,** beside; next to. *—prep.* by the side of; side by side with: *The boat was alongside the wharf.*

a loof (ə lüf′), *adv.* 1 away at some distance but within view; apart. 2 without community of feeling: *stand aloof from family joys and sorrows.* *—adj.* unsympathetic; not interested; reserved: *an aloof manner.* [< *a-* on + obsolete *loof* windward, probably < Dutch *loef*] **—a loof′ly,** *adv.* **—a loof′ness,** *n.*

a loud (ə loud′), *adv.* 1 loud enough to be heard; not in a whisper. 2 loudly.

alp (alp), *n.* 1 a high mountain. 2 mountain grassland, occurring especially above the timber line. [< Latin *Alpes* the Alps]

alpaca (def. 1) $4\frac{1}{2}$ ft. long; 5 ft. high to top of head

al pac a (al pak′ə), *n., pl.* **-pac as** or **-pac a.** 1 a sheeplike mammal of South America with long, soft, silky hair or wool. It is closely related to but somewhat smaller than the llama. 2 its wool. 3 cloth made from this wool. 4 a glossy, wiry cloth made of wool and cotton, usually black. 5 imitation of this made of rayon or cotton. [< Spanish]

al pen horn (al′pən hôrn′), *n.* a long, powerful, wooden horn used in Switzerland for signals and for calling cattle. Also, **alphorn.** [< German *Alpenhorn*]

al pen stock (al′pən stok′), *n.* a strong staff with an iron point, used in climbing mountains. [< German *Alpenstock*]

al pha (al′fə), *n.* 1 the first letter of the Greek alphabet (A, α). 2 the first of a series. 3 **Alpha,** the principal and usually brightest star in a constellation.

alpha and omega, the first and the last; the beginning and the end.

al pha bet (al′fə bet), *n.* 1 the letters of a language, arranged in their usual order, not as they are in words. 2 set of letters or characters representing sounds, used in writing a language. The English alphabet has only 26 letters to represent more than 40 sounds. [< Greek *alphabētos* < *alpha* A + *bēta* B]

al pha bet ic (al′fə bet′ik), *adj.* alphabetical.

al pha bet i cal (al′fə bet′ə kəl), *adj.* 1 arranged by letters in the order of the alphabet. 2 of the alphabet. 3 using or expressed by an alphabet. **—al′pha bet′i cal ly,** *adv.*

al pha bet ize (al′fə bə tīz), *v.t.,* **-ized, -iz ing.** arrange in alphabetical order. **—al′pha bet′i za′tion,** *n.* **—al′pha bet iz′er,** *n.*

al pha nu mer ic (al′fə nü mer′ik, al′fə nyü mer′ik), *adj.* using both letters and numbers: *an alphanumeric computer.*

alpha particle, (in physics) a positively charged particle consisting of two protons and two neutrons, released at a very high speed in the disintegration of radium and other radioactive substances. By the acquisition of two electrons it becomes an atom of helium.

alpha ray, 1 a stream of alpha particles. 2 alpha particle accelerated to a high speed, as in nuclear reactions.

Al phe us (al fē′əs), *n.* (in Greek myths) a river god who fell in love with the nymph Arethusa.

alp horn (alp′hôrn′), *n.* alpenhorn.

Al pine (al′pīn), *adj.* 1 of or like the Alps. 2 **alpine, a** of or like high mountains: *alpine terrain.* **b** very high. **c** growing at high places, especially on mountains above the timber line: *alpine plants.* *—n.* 1 one of the generally recognized types of the Caucasian racial stock, characterized by a broad, round head, medium height, and brunette complexion, and including many of the peoples of central Europe. 2 **alpine,** an alpine plant.

Alps (alps), *n.pl.* mountain system in S Europe, chiefly in Switzerland and W Austria, with ranges extending also into SE France, S West Germany, N Italy, and N and W Yugoslavia. The highest peak is Mont Blanc, 15,781 ft.

al read y (ôl red′ē), *adv.* 1 before this time: *We arrived at noon but you had already left.* 2 by this time; even now: *Are you finished already with all your work?* [for *all ready*]

➔ The adverb **already** is distinguished from **all ready,** an adjective phrase meaning "quite ready" or "completely ready": *They were all ready to start their next job.*

al right (ôl rīt′), *adv., adj.* INFORMAL. all right.

➔ The spelling **alright** is not yet generally acceptable in formal and in most informal writing. **All right** is the correct spelling of both the adjective phrase *(I am all right)* and the sentence adverb meaning yes, certainly *(All right, I'll come).*

Al sace (al sās′, al sas′; al′sās, al′sas), *n.* region in NE France, between the Vosges Mountains and the Rhine.

Al sace-Lor raine (al sās′lə rān′, al sas′lə rān′), *n.* region in NE France, consisting of Alsace and Lorraine. It formed a German province from 1871 to 1919 and from 1940 to 1945.

Al sa tian (al sā′shən), *adj.* of or having to do with Alsace or its people. *—n.* 1 native or inhabitant of Alsace. 2 German shepherd.

al so (ôl′sō), *adv.* 1 in addition; besides; too: *That dress is pretty and cheap also.* 2 OBSOLETE. likewise. [Old English *ealswā* all so, quite so]

al so-ran (ôl′sō ran′), *n.* 1 an unsuccessful contestant; loser. 2 any horse that finishes behind the first three in a race, and thus wins nothing.

alt., 1 alternate. 2 altitude.

Alta., Alberta, a province in Canada.

Al ta ic (al tā′ik), *adj.* 1 of or having to do with a family of languages that includes Turkish, Mongolian, and Manchu. 2 of or having to do with the Altai Mountains. *—n.* the Altaic family of languages.

Al tai Mountains (al′tī, äl′tī), mountain system in central Asia, between the Soviet Union and China. Highest peak, 15,157 ft.

Al ta ir (al tä′ir), *n.* star of the first magnitude in the constellation Aquila. It is about ten times as bright as the sun.

al tar (ôl′tər), *n.* 1 table, stand, or similar raised structure in the most sacred part of a church, synagogue, or temple, always thought of as the central point of worship. In Christian churches the altar is used in the Communion service or in celebrating Mass. 2 block of stone, mound of turf, etc., on which to place sacrifices or burn offerings to a god. 3 **lead to the altar,** marry. [Old English < Latin *altare,* related to *adolere* burn up]

altar boy, man or boy who helps a priest during certain religious services; acolyte.

al tar piece (ôl′tər pēs′), *n.* a decorated panel or wall behind and above an altar in a church; reredos.

al ter (ôl′tər), *v.t.* 1 make different; change the appearance of; modify. See **change** for synonym study. 2 adjust the measurements of (a garment) to obtain a better fit. 3 U.S. **a** castrate (a male animal). **b** spay (a female animal). *—v.i.* become different. See **change** for synonym study. [< Late Latin *alterare* < Latin *alter* other] **—al′ter a ble,** *adj.* **—al′ter a ble ness,** *n.* **—al′ter a bly,** *adv.*

al ter a bil i ty (ôl′tər ə bil′ə tē), *n.* quality of being alterable.

al ter a tion (ôl′tə rā′shən), *n.* 1 a change in the appearance or form of anything; altered or changed condition. 2 act of altering: *The alteration of our house took three months.*

al ter cate (ôl′tər kāt, al′tər kāt), *v.i.,* **-cat ed, -cat ing.** dispute angrily; quarrel; wrangle. [< Latin *altercatum* engaged in dispute with another < *alter* other]

al ter ca tion (ôl′tər kā′shən, al′tər kā′shən), *n.* an angry dispute; noisy quarrel; wrangle.

al ter e go (ôl′tər ē′gō; ôl′tər eg′ō), a very intimate or trusted friend or associate. [< Latin, other I]

al ter nate (*v.* ôl′tər nāt, al′tər nāt; *adj., n.* ôl′tər nit, al′tər nit), *v.,* **-nat ed, -nat ing,** *adj., n.* *—v.i.* 1 (of two or more things) succeed each other by turns, in time or space: *Night and day alternate.* 2 (of a whole) vary shape, type, direction, etc., by turns: *a land which alternates between hills and valleys.* 3 (of one thing or class of things) come or appear with another, in time or space: *Good times seem to alternate with bad.* 4 take turns: *I will alternate with you on that job.* 5 in electricity: **a** reverse direction at regular intervals. **b** produce or be operated by such a current. —*v.t.* 1 arrange, do, or perform (two things) each after the other continuously: *alternate work and pleasure.* 2 interchange regularly: *alternate two hours of work with one hour of rest.* —*adj.* 1 placed or occurring by turns; first one and then the other: *a flag with alternate red and white stripes.* 2 every other: *The milkman comes on alternate days.* 3 reciprocal. 4 (in botany) placed singly at different heights along the sides of a stem; not opposite: *alternate leaves.* —*n.* 1 person or thing that alternates. 2 U.S. person appointed to take the place of another if it should be necessary; substitute. [< Latin *alternatum* placed by turns < *alternus* every other < *alter* other]

alternate angles, two angles, both interior or both exterior but not adjacent, formed on either side of a line that crosses two other lines.

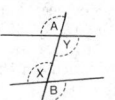

alternate angle
A and B, exterior alternate angles.
X and Y, interior alternate angles.

al ter nate ly (ôl′tər nit lē, al′tər nit lē), *adv.* 1 one after the other by turns. 2 on each side in turn.

alternating current, an electric current in which the electricity flows regularly in one direction and then the other, usually reversing 120 times per second.

al ter na tion (ôl′tər nā′shən, al′tər nā′shən), *n.* act of alternating; succession by turns, first one and then the other.

alternation of generations, (in genetics) the regular alternation of forms or of mode of reproduction in successive generations of an animal or plant, especially the alternation between sexual and asexual propagation in certain invertebrates and some lower plants; heterogenesis.

al ter na tive (ôl tėr′nə tiv, al tėr′nə tiv), *n.* 1 choice from among two or more things: *She had the alternative of staying in college or going to work.* 2 one of the things to be chosen: *She chose the former alternative and stayed in college.* See **choice** for synonym study. —*adj.* giving or requiring a choice between two or more things: *alternative suggestions, alternative routes.* —**al ter′na tive ly,** *adv.* —**al ter′na tive ness,** *n.*

➤ **Alternative** derives from the Latin word *alter,* meaning "other" or the second of two. Some formal writers, in deference to the word's origin, confine its meaning to one of two possibilities, but it is commonly used to mean one of several possibilities.

al ter na tor (ôl′tər nā′tər, al′tər nā′tər), *n.* dynamo or generator for producing an alternating electric current.

al the a or **al thae a** (al thē′ə), *n.* rose of Sharon. [< Greek *althaia* wild mallow]

Al thing (äl′thing, ôl′thing), *n.* the parliament of Iceland. It is the oldest parliament in the world. [< Old Icelandic *althing* whole assembly]

al tho (ôl ŦHō′), *conj.* INFORMAL. although.

alt horn (alt′hôrn′), *n.* a musical instrument related to the saxhorn, usually pitched in E flat or B flat, used especially in military bands in place of the French horn. Also, **alto horn.**

al though (ôl ŦHō′), *conj.* in spite of the fact that; though. [Middle English *al thogh* even though]

➤ Either **although** or **though** may be used to connect an adverbial clause with the main clause of a sentence but *although* is more likely to introduce a clause that precedes a main clause: *Although it rained all morning, they went on the hike. Though* often connects an adverbial clause that follows a main clause: *They went on the hike, though it rained all morning.*

al tim e ter (al tim′ə tər, al′tə mē′tər), *n.* any instrument for measuring altitude, especially an aneroid barometer that shows the atmospheric pressure at any given altitude. Altimeters are used in aircraft.

al ti pla no (äl′ti plä′nō), *n.* the high upland plains of Bolivia, Peru, and other countries in or adjoining the Andes, reaching altitudes of more than 15,000 feet above sea level. [< American Spanish]

al ti tude (al′tə tüd, al′tə tyüd), *n.* 1 height above the earth's surface: *The airplane was flying at an altitude of 10,000 feet.* 2 height above sea level: *The altitude of Denver is 5300 feet.* See **height** for synonym study. 3 a high place; height. 4 **altitudes,** *pl.* elevated regions; great heights. 5 the vertical distance from the base of a geometrical figure to its highest point. 6 the angular distance of a star, planet, etc., above the horizon. 7 position of high rank or great power. [< Latin *altitudo* < *altus* high]

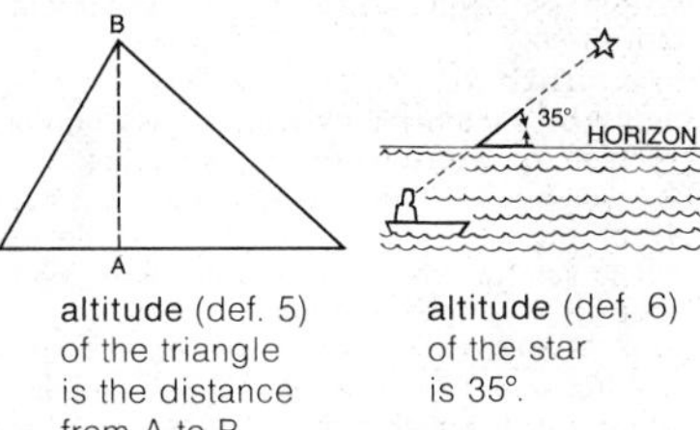

altitude (def. 5) of the triangle is the distance from A to B.

altitude (def. 6) of the star is 35°.

al ti tu di nal (al′tə tüd′n əl, al′tə-tyüd′n əl), *adj.* of or having to do with altitude.

al to (al′tō), *n., pl.* **-tos,** *adj.* in music: —*n.* 1 the lowest female voice; contralto. 2 the highest male voice; countertenor. 3 singer with such a voice. 4 part in music for such a voice or for an instrument of similar range. 5 instrument playing such a part, as a viola or althorn. —*adj.* of or for an alto. [< Italian < Latin *altus* high]

alto clef, the C clef when the clef symbol is placed on the third line of the staff. See **clef** for diagram.

al to cu mu lus (al′tō kyü′myə ləs), *n., pl.* **-li** (-lī). a fleecy cloud formation consisting of rounded heaps of white or grayish clouds, often partly shaded, occurring at heights of between 8000 and 20,000 feet.

al to geth er (ôl′tə geŦH′ər, ôl′tə geŦH′ər), *adv.* 1 to the whole extent; completely; entirely: *The house was altogether destroyed by fire.* 2 on the whole; considering everything: *Altogether, I'm sorry it happened.* 3 in all; all included: *Altogether there were 14 books.* [for *all together*]

hat, āge, fär; let, ēqual, tėrm;
it, īce; hot, ōpen, ôrder;
oil, out; cup, pu̇t, rüle;
ch, child; ng, long; sh, she;
th, thin; ŦH, then; zh, measure;

ə represents *a* in about, *e* in taken, *i* in pencil, *o* in lemon, *u* in circus.

< = from, derived from, taken from.

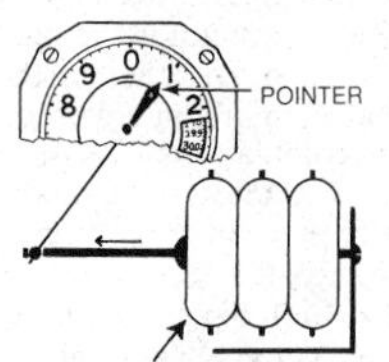

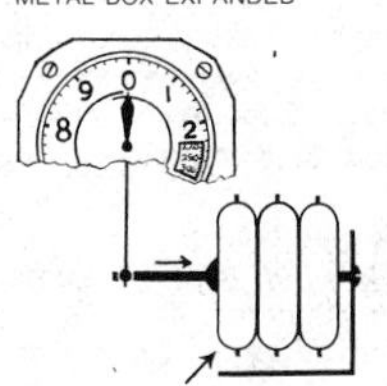

altimeter—As an airplane climbs, air pressure on the flexible, airtight metal box decreases and its sides expand, forcing the pointer to move up from zero. With a loss in altitude, air pressure on the box increases and its sides contract, forcing the pointer to move back toward zero.

➤ The adverb **altogether** is distinguished from the adjective phrase **all together** meaning "everyone in a group": *We found the boys all together in the kitchen.*

alto horn, althorn.

Al too na (al tü′nə), *n.* city in S Pennsylvania. 63,000.

al to stra tus (al′tō strā′təs, al′tō strat′əs), *n., pl.* **-ti** (-tī). a bluish-gray sheetlike cloud formation, ill-defined at the base, occurring at heights between 6500 and 20,000 feet.

al tri cial (al trish′əl), *adj.* (of certain birds) born blind, usually without feathers, and thus helpless for some time after hatching. [< Latin *altricem* a nurse]

al tru ism (al′trü iz′əm), *n.* unselfish devotion to the interests and welfare of others; disinterested regard for others as a principle of action. [< French *altruisme* < Italian *altrui* of or for others < Latin *alter* other]

al tru ist (al′trü ist), *n.* person who works for the welfare of others.

al tru is tic (al′trü is′tik), *adj.* thoughtful of the welfare of others. —**al′tru is′ti cal ly,** *adv.*

al um (al′əm), *n.* 1 a white mineral salt used in medicine and in dyeing. Alum is sometimes used to stop the bleeding of a small cut. *Formula:* $KAl(SO_4)_2 \cdot 12H_2O$ 2 a colorless, crystalline salt containing ammonia, used in foam fire extinguishers, water purification, medicine, etc. *Formula:* $NH_4Al(SO_4)_2 \cdot 12H_2O$ 3 a white salt made by treating bauxite with sulfuric acid, used in dyeing, medicine, water purification, and in paper and leather manufacture. *Formula:* $Al_2(SO_4)_3 \cdot 18H_2O$ [< Old French < Latin *alumen*]

a lu mi na (ə lü′mə nə), *n.* mineral occurring in nature as corundum, found mainly in bauxite and in clay or loam; aluminum oxide. Emery, rubies, and sapphires are crystalline forms of alumina colored by various impurities. Alumina is used in making aluminum, porcelain, abrasives, etc. *Formula:* Al_2O_3 [< New Latin < Latin *aluminis* alum]

al u min i um (al′yü min′ē əm), *n.* BRITISH. aluminum.

a lu mi nize (ə lü′mə nīz), *v.t.,* **-nized, -niz ing.** treat, coat, or impregnate with aluminum.

a lu mi num (ə lü′mə nəm), *n.* a very lightweight, silver-white, ductile, and malleable metallic element which is an excellent conductor of electricity and highly resistant to tarnish and oxidation. Aluminum is the most abundant metallic element in the earth's crust, of which it makes up about seven per cent. It occurs only in combination with other elements. Aluminum is widely used in alloys and to make utensils, instruments, aircraft parts, etc. *Symbol:* Al; *atomic number* 13. See pages 326 and 327 for table. [< *alumina*]

aluminum foil, a very thin sheet of aluminum used especially as a wrapper for foods or as a protective liner in baking or broiling.

aluminum hydroxide, a white, tasteless, odorless powder used in medicine and for dyeing, waterproofing, and ceramic glazing. *Formula:* $Al(OH_3)$

aluminum oxide, alumina.

a lum na (ə lum′nə), *n., pl.* **-nae.** a woman graduate or former student of a certain school, college, or university. [< Latin, feminine of *alumnus*]

a lum nae (ə lum′nē), *n.* pl. of **alumna.**
➛ See **alumni** for usage note.

a lum ni (ə lum′nī), *n.* pl. of **alumnus.**
➛ **Alumnae** and **alumni** are sometimes confused in writing because in Latin the *ae* of *alumnae* is pronounced (ī) and the *i* of *alumni* is pronounced (ē), while in English these pronunciations are reversed.

a lum nus (ə lum′nəs), *n., pl.* **-ni,** a graduate or former student of a certain school, college, or university. [< Latin, foster son < *alere* nourish]

Al va (al′və), *n.* **Duke of,** 1508-1582, **Fernando Álvarez de Toledo,** Spanish general who suppressed the Dutch in 1567.

al ve o lar (al vē′ə lər), *adj.* 1 of the part of the jaws where the sockets of the teeth are. 2 of, containing, or like an alveolus or alveoli. 3 formed by placing the tip or blade of the tongue near or against the alveoli. English *t* and *d* are alveolar consonants.

al ve o li (al vē′ə lī), *n.pl. of* **alveolus.** the ridge behind and above the upper front teeth.

al ve o lus (al vē′ə ləs), *n., pl.* **-li.** in anatomy and zoology: 1 a small cavity, pit, or cell. The air cells in the lung are alveoli. 2 socket of a tooth. 3 one of the cells of a honeycomb. [< Latin, diminutive of *alveus* cavity]

al way (ôl′wā), *adv.* ARCHAIC. always.

al ways (ôl′wiz, ôl′wāz), *adv.* 1 every time; at all times: *Night always follows day.* 2 all the time; continually: *I am always available for advice.* [for *all ways*]

a lys sum (ə lis′əm), *n.* 1 plant of the mustard family, having small yellow or white flowers. 2 sweet alyssum. [< New Latin < Greek *alysson*]

am (am; *unstressed* əm), *v.* first person singular, present indicative of **be.** *I am.* [Old English *eom*]

Am, americium.

a.m. or **A.M.,** the time from midnight to noon. [for Latin *ante meridiem*]
➛ **A.m.** and **p.m.** are usually written in small letters except in headlines and tables. In ordinary text they are used only with figures for specific hours: *from 2 to 4 a.m.*

Am., 1 America. 2 American.

AM or **A.M.,** amplitude modulation.

A.M., Master of Arts. Also, M.A.

A.M.A., American Medical Association.

a mah (ä′mə, am′ə), *n.* in India, China, etc.: 1 a baby's nurse. 2 maid. [< Portuguese *ama*]

a main (ə mān′), *adv.* 1 at full speed. 2 with full force; violently. 3 in haste; at once. [< *a-*[1] in + *main* force]

a mal gam (ə mal′gəm), *n.* 1 an alloy of mercury with some other metal or metals. Tin amalgam is used in silvering mirrors. Silver amalgam is used as fillings for teeth. 2 mixture or blend of different things. [< Medieval Latin *amalgama*]

a mal gam ate (ə mal′gə māt), *v.,* **-at ed, -at ing.** —*v.t.* 1 unite (distinct elements, ideas, etc.) so as to form a whole; blend; merge: *amalgamate two competing companies.* 2 combine mercury with (another metal). —*v.i.* 1 become united; be combined. 2 enter into combination with mercury. **—a mal′gam a ble,** *adj.* **—a mal′ga ma′tor,** *n.*

a mal gam a tion (ə mal′gə mā′shən), *n.* 1 act or process of amalgamating. 2 condition of being amalgamated. 3 result of amalgamating; combination; blend; union: *Our nation is an amalgamation of many different peoples.*

am a ni ta (am′ə nī′tə, am′ə nē′tə), *n.* any of a group of fungi composed chiefly of very poisonous mushrooms, as the death cup. [< Greek *amanitai*]

a man u en sis (ə man′yü en′sis), *n., pl.* **-ses** (-sēz). person who writes down what another says, or who copies what another has written. [< Latin < *(servus) a manu* (servant) with the hand]

am a ranth (am′ə ranth′), *n.* 1 any of a family of annual plants with showy purple, greenish, or crimson flowers, including love-lies-bleeding and various pigweeds. 2 a purple or purplish red. 3 an imaginary flower that never fades. [< Greek *amarantos* everlasting < *a-* not + *marainein* wither]

am a ran thine (am′ə ran′thin, am′ə ran′thīn), *adj.* 1 never-fading; undying. 2 purple or purplish-red.

Am a ril lo (am′ə ril′ō), *n.* city in NW Texas. 127,000.

am a ryl lis (am′ə ril′is), *n.* a bulbous plant with clusters of large and lilylike red, white, purple, or pink flowers. [< Latin < Greek]

amaryllis family, group of perennial herbs resembling those of the lily family, including the narcissus, amaryllis, snowdrop, and onion.

a mass (ə mas′), *v.t.* heap together; pile up, especially for oneself; accumulate: *amass a fortune.* See **accumulate** for synonym study. [< Old French *amasser* < *a-* to + *masse* mass] **—a mass′a ble,** *adj.* **—a mass′er,** *n.*

am a teur (am′ə chər, am′ə tər), *n.* 1 person who does something for pleasure, not for money or as a profession. 2 athlete who is not a professional. 3 person who does something rather poorly. 4 a superficial student or worker; dabbler. —*adj.* 1 of amateurs; made or done by amateurs: *an amateur orchestra.* 2 being an amateur: *an amateur pianist.* [< French < Latin *amator* lover < *amare* to love]

am a teur ish (am′ə chủr′ish, am′ə tyủr′ish, am′ə tėr′ish), *adj.* not expert; not very skillful. **—am′a teur′ish ly,** *adv.* **—am′a teur′ish ness,** *n.*

am a teur ism (am′ə chə riz′əm, am′ə tə riz′əm), *n.* 1 amateurish way of doing things. 2 position or rank of an amateur.

A ma ti (ä mä′tē), *n.* **Nicolò,** 1596-1684, Italian violin maker.

am a to ry (am′ə tôr′ē, am′ə tōr′ē), *adj.* of love, lovers, or lovemaking; expressing love: *amatory verses.* [< Latin *amatorius* < *amare* to love]

a maze (ə māz′), *v.,* **a mazed, a maz ing,** *n.* —*v.t.* overwhelm with wonder; greatly astonish; astound. See **surprise** for synonym study. —*n.* ARCHAIC. amazement. [Old English *āmasian*] **—a maz′ed ly,** *adv.*

a maze ment (ə māz′mənt), *n.* sudden and overwhelming wonder; great surprise; astonishment.

a maz ing (ə mā′zing), *adj.* causing amazement; astounding; astonishing. **—a maz′ing ly,** *adv.*

Am a zon (am′ə zon, am′ə zən), *n.* 1 **Amazon River,** largest river in the world, in N South America, flowing from the Andes Mountains of Peru across Brazil into the Atlantic. 3900 mi. 2 (in Greek legends) one of a race of women warriors supposed to have lived near the Black Sea. 3 Also, **amazon.** a tall, strong, aggressive woman.

Am a zo ni an (am′ə zō′nē ən), *adj.* 1 of the Amazon River or the region it drains. 2 of the Amazons. 3 Also, **amazonian.** (of a woman) like an Amazon; warlike or aggressive.

am a zon ite (am′ə zə nīt), *n.* a semiprecious stone, a bright, bluish-green variety of feldspar. [< the *Amazon* River]

Amazon stone, amazonite.

Amb., ambassador.

am bas sa dor (am bas′ə dər, am bas′ə dôr), *n.* 1 a diplomatic representative of the highest rank sent by one government or ruler to another. An ambassador lives in the capital of the foreign country to which he is assigned and speaks and acts in behalf of his government or his ruler. 2 any official messenger, agent, or representative with a special assignment: *Miles Standish chose John Alden to be his ambassador.* Also, **embassador.** [< Old French *ambassadeur* < Italian *ambasciatore.* Related to EMBASSY.]

am bas sa do ri al (am bas′ə dôr′ē əl, am bas′ə dōr′ē əl), *adj.* of an ambassador or ambassadors.

am bas sa dor ship (am bas′ə dər ship), *n.* 1 position or rank of an ambassador. 2 term of office of an ambassador.

am bas sa dress (am bas′ə dris), *n.* a woman ambassador.

am ber (am′bər), *n.* 1 a hard, translucent, yellow or yellowish-brown fossil resin, easily polished and used for jewelry, in making pipe stems, etc. 2 the color of amber; yellow or yellowish brown. —*adj.* 1 made of amber. 2 yellow or yellowish-brown. [< Old French *ambre* < Arabic *'anbar* ambergris]

am ber gris (am′bər grēs′, am′bər gris), *n.* a waxlike, grayish substance found floating in tropical seas, originating as a secretion in the intestines of the sperm whale. It is used as a fixative in perfumery. [< Middle French *ambre gris* gray amber]

ambi-, *combining form.* both: *Ambidextrous = dextrous with both hands.* [< Latin < *ambi-* around, in two ways]

am bi ance (am′bē əns; *French* äɴ byäɴs′), *n.* surroundings; atmosphere. [< French]

hat, āge, fär; let, ēqual, tėrm;
it, īce; hot, ōpen, ôrder;
oil, out; cup, pu̇t, rüle;
ch, child; ng, long; sh, she;
th, thin; ᴛʜ, then; zh, measure;

ə represents *a* in about, *e* in taken, *i* in pencil, *o* in lemon, *u* in circus.

< = from, derived from, taken from.

am bi dex ter i ty (am′bə dek ster′ə tē), *n.* 1 ability to use both hands equally well. 2 unusual skillfulness. 3 deceitfulness.

am bi dex trous (am′bə dek′strəs), *adj.* 1 able to use both hands equally well. 2 unusually skillful. 3 deceitful. **—am′bi-dex′trous ly,** *adv.* **—am′bi dex′-trous ness,** *n.*

am bi ence (am′bē əns), *n.* ambiance.

am bi ent (am′bē ənt), *adj.* all around; surrounding; encompassing. [< Latin *ambientem* < *ambi-* around + *ire* go]

am bi gu i ty (am′bə gyü′ə tē), *n., pl.* **-ties.** 1 possibility of being understood in two or more ways. 2 word or expression capable of having more than one meaning. 3 lack of clarity; vagueness; uncertainty.

am big u ous (am big′yü əs), *adj.* 1 having or permitting more than one interpretation or explanation; equivocal: *an ambiguous remark.* See **obscure** for synonym study. 2 of doubtful position or classification: *an ambiguous character.* 3 not clearly defined; doubtful; uncertain. [< Latin *ambiguus* < *ambigere* be uncertain, wander < *ambi-* + *agere* to drive] **—am big′u ous ly,** *adv.* **—am-big′u ous ness,** *n.*

am bi tion (am bish′ən), *n.* 1 the desire to distinguish oneself from other people; a strong desire to rise to high position or to attain rank, influence, or distinction. 2 thing strongly desired or sought after: *Her ambition is to be an oceanographer.* [< Latin *ambitionem* a canvassing for votes < *ambire* go around < *ambi-* around + *ire* go] **—am-bi′tion less,** *adj.*

am bi tious (am bish′əs), *adj.* 1 full of or guided by ambition. 2 strongly desirous; eager: *ambitious for money, ambitious of power, ambitious to succeed.* 3 arising from or showing ambition: *an ambitious plan.* 4 too greatly aspiring; showy; pretentious. **—am bi′tious ly,** *adv.* **—am bi′tious-ness,** *n.*

am biv a lence (am biv′ə ləns), *n.* condition of having conflicting attitudes or feelings, as love and hate, about the same person or thing at the same time.

am biv a lent (am biv′ə lənt), *adj.* acting in opposite ways; having or showing conflicting feelings. **—am biv′a lent ly,** *adv.*

am ble (am′bəl), *n., v.,* **-bled, -bling.** *—n.* 1 gait of a horse or mule when it lifts first the two legs on one side and then the two on the other. 2 an easy, slow pace in walking. *—v.i.* 1 (of a horse or mule) go with such a gait. 2 walk at an easy, slow pace. [< Old French *ambler* to amble < Latin *ambulare* to walk] **—am′bler,** *n.*

Am boi na (am boi′nə), *n.* 1 principal island of the Moluccas in Indonesia. 100,000 pop.; 314 sq. mi. 2 seaport and principal city of the Moluccas. 56,000.

Am brose (am′brōz), *n.* **Saint,** A.D. 340?-397, bishop of Milan who opposed the Arian doctrine.

am bro sia (am brō′zhə), *n.* 1 (in Greek and Roman myths) the food of the gods. 2 anything especially delightful to taste or smell. [< Greek < *ambrotos* of the gods, immortal < *a-* not + *brotos* mortal]

am bro sial (am brō′zhəl), *adj.* like ambrosia; very fragrant or delicious. **—am-bro′sial ly,** *adv.*

am bu lance (am′byə ləns), *n.* an automobile, boat, or aircraft equipped to carry sick, injured, or wounded persons.

am bu lant (am′byə lənt), *adj.* moving about; walking; ambulatory.

am bu la to ry (am′byə lə tôr′ē, am′byə-lə tōr′ē), *adj., n., pl.* **-ries.** *—adj.* 1 having to do with walking; fitted for walking. 2 capable of walking; not bedridden: *an ambulatory patient.* *—n.* a covered place for walking; cloister. [ultimately < Latin *ambulare* to walk]

am bus cade (am′bə skād′), *n., v.,* **-cad ed, -cad ing.** *—n.* an ambush. *—v.t., v.i.* to ambush. **—am′bus cad′er,** *n.*

am bush (am′bu̇sh), *n.* 1 soldiers or other persons hidden so that they can make a surprise attack on an approaching enemy. 2 a secret or concealed place where soldiers or others lie in wait to make such an attack. 3 act of attacking unexpectedly from a concealed position. 4 a lying in wait for the purpose of attacking by surprise. *—v.t.* 1 attack unexpectedly and from a hidden position. 2 ARCHAIC. put (soldiers or others) in hiding for a surprise attack. *—v.i.* wait in hiding to make a surprise attack. [< Old French *embusche* < *en-* in + *busche* wood, bush] **—am′bush er,** *n.*

a me ba (ə mē′bə), *n., pl.* **-bas, -bae** (-bē). amoeba.

a me ban (ə mē′bən), *adj.* amoeban.

am e bi a sis (am′ə bī′ə sis), *n.* infection or disease caused by amoebas, as amoebic dysentery.

a me bic (ə mē′bik), *adj.* amoebic.

a me boid (ə mē′boid), *adj.* amoeboid.

a mel io rate (ə mē′lyə rāt′, ə mē′lē ə rāt′), *v.,* **-rat ed, -rat ing.** *—v.t.* make better or more tolerable, satisfactory, prosperous, etc.; improve. *—v.i.* become better. [< French *améliorer* + English *-ate*[1]] **—a mel′io ra′tor,** *n.*

a mel io ra tion (ə mē′lyə rā′shən, ə mē′-lē ə rā′shən), *n.* 1 process of making better. 2 condition of being made better; improvement.

a mel io ra tive (ə mē′lyə rā′tiv, ə mē′-lē ə rā′tiv), *adj.* improving.

a men (ā′men′, ä′men′), *interj.* so be it; may it become true. *Amen* is said after a prayer, a wish, or a statement with which one agrees. *—n.* the word *amen.* [< Latin < Greek *amēn* < Hebrew *āmēn*]

A men (ä′mən), *n.* a local fertility god of ancient Egypt, later combined with the sun god Ra as the chief deity of Egypt. His center of worship was in Thebes. Also, **Amon.**

a me na bil i ty (ə mē′nə bil′ə tē, ə men′-ə bil′ə tē), *n.* a being amenable.

a me na ble (ə mē′nə bəl, ə men′ə bəl), *adj.* 1 open to influence, suggestion, advice, etc.; responsive; submissive: *amenable to persuasion.* 2 accountable or answerable to some jurisdiction or authority: *People living in a country are amenable to its laws.* [< Middle French *amener* lead to < *a-* to + *mener* to lead] **—a me′na ble ness,** *n.* **—a me′-na bly,** *adv.*

a men corner (ā′men′), U.S. that part of a church occupied by the worshipers who assist the preacher with occasional and irregular responses.

a mend (ə mend′), *v.t.* 1 make a change or changes in the form of (a law, bill, or motion) by addition, omission, or alteration of language. 2 change for the better; improve. 3 free from faults; make right; correct; emend. *—v.i.* reform oneself: *After he criticized me, I took pains to amend.* [< Old French *amender* < Latin *emendare* < *ex-* out of + *menda* fault. Doublet of EMEND.] **—a mend′a ble,** *adj.* **—a mend′er,** *n.*

a mend a to ry (ə men′də tôr′ē, ə men′-də tōr′ē), *adj.* that amends; corrective.

a mend ment (ə mend′mənt), *n.* 1 change made or offered in a law, bill, or motion by addition, omission, or alteration of language. The Constitution of the United States has over twenty amendments. 2 act of making such a change. 3 improvement. 4 correction.

a mends (ə mendz′), *n. sing. or pl.* something given or paid to make up for a wrong or an injury done; payment for loss; compensation: *make amends to a person who was imprisoned unjustly.*

a men i ty (ə men′ə tē, ə mē′nə tē), *n., pl.* **-ties.** 1 **amenities,** *pl.* pleasant ways; polite acts. Saying "Thank you" and holding the door open for a person to pass through are amenities. 2 something which makes life easier and more pleasant; pleasant feature. 3 quality of being pleasant; agreeableness: *the amenity of a warm climate.* [< Latin *amoenitatem* < *amoenus* pleasant]

am ent (am′ənt, ā′mənt), *n.* a long, slender, scaly flower spike that grows on willows, birches, etc.; catkin. [< Latin *amentum* thong]

Amer., 1 America. 2 American.

a merce (ə mėrs′), *v.t.,* **a merced, a merc ing.** punish by an arbitrary fine; fine (a person) that amount which seems proper to a court. [< Anglo-French *amercier* < *a merci* at the mercy (of)] **—a merce′ment,** *n.* **—a merc′er,** *n.*

A mer i ca (ə mer′ə kə), *n.* 1 the United States of America. 2 North America. 3 Also, **the Americas.** North America and South America; the Western Hemisphere. 4 South America.

A mer i can (ə mer′ə kən), *adj.* 1 of, having to do with, or in the United States: *an American citizen.* 2 native only to America: *Tomatoes, corn, chocolate, and tobacco are American plants.* 3 of or in the Western Hemisphere: *the Amazon and other American rivers.* *—n.* 1 citizen or inhabitant of the United States. 2 native or inhabitant of the Western Hemisphere. 3 American English.

A mer i ca na (ə mer′ə kä′nə, ə mer′ə-kan′ə, ə mer′ə kā′nə), *n.pl.* 1 collection of documents, books, facts, etc., about America, especially its history. 2 collection of early American furniture, textiles, etc. 3 anecdotes, folklore, etc., about America.

American eagle, bald eagle. The coat of arms of the United States has a design of the American eagle on it.

American English, the form of English spoken and written in the United States.

American Indian, one of the aboriginal peoples of North or South America or the West Indies, often excepting the Eskimos; Indian.

A mer i can ism (ə mer′ə kə niz′əm), *n.* 1 devotion or loyalty to the United States and to its customs and traditions. 2 word, phrase, or meaning originating in the United States or more widely used in American English than in other varieties of English. 3 custom or trait peculiar to the United States.

A mer i can ize (ə mer′ə kə nīz), *v.t., v.i.,* **-ized, -iz ing.** make or become American in habits, customs, or character. **—A mer′i can i za′tion,** *n.*

American Legion, organization founded in 1919, composed of veterans of the United States army, air force, and navy.

American plan, system used in hotels where one price covers room, board, and service.

American Revised Version, revision of the Bible published in the United States in 1901, differing from the Authorized Version more than does the Revised Version.

American Revolution, 1 the series of protests and acts of American colonists from 1763 to 1783 against England's attempts to increase her power over them. 2 Revolutionary War.

American Samoa, group of islands in E Samoa belonging to the United States; Eastern Samoa. 28,000 pop.; 76 sq. mi. *Capital:* Pago Pago.

American Spanish, the dialect of Spanish spoken in South America, Central America, and the West Indies.

American Standard Version, American Revised Version.

am e ri ci um (am′ə rish′ē əm), *n.* an artificial, radioactive metallic element produced by bombarding plutonium with high-energy alpha particles. *Symbol:* Am; *atomic number* 95. See pages 326 and 327 for table. [< New Latin < *America*]

Amerigo Vespucci. See **Vespucci.**

Am er in di an (am′ə rin′dē ən), *n.* 1 an American Indian. 2 an Eskimo. *—adj.* of or having to do with Amerindians.

am e thyst (am′ə thist), *n.* 1 a purple or violet variety of quartz, used for jewelry. 2 a violet-colored corundum, used for jewelry. 3 a purple or violet color. *—adj.* purple; violet. [< Greek *amethystos* < *a-* not + *methy* wine; thought to prevent intoxication].

Am ex (am′eks′), *n.* U.S. American Stock Exchange.

Am har ic (am har′ik, äm här′ik), *n.* a Semitic language related to Ethiopic. It is the official language of Ethiopia.

a mi a bil i ty (ā′mē ə bil′ə tē), *n.* a being amiable; good nature.

a mi a ble (ā′mē ə bəl), *adj.* having a good-natured and friendly disposition; pleasant and agreeable. [< Old French < Late Latin *amicabilis* < Latin *amicus* friend. Doublet of AMICABLE.] **—a′mi a ble ness,** *n.* **—a′mi a bly,** *adv.*

am i ca bil i ty (am′ə kə bil′ə tē), *n.* a being amicable; friendliness.

am i ca ble (am′ə kə bəl), *adj.* having or showing a friendly attitude; peaceable: *settle a quarrel in an amicable way.* [< Late Latin *amicabilis* < Latin *amicus* friend < *amare* to love. Doublet of AMIABLE.] **—am′i ca ble ness,** *n.* **—am′i ca bly,** *adv.*

am ice (am′is), *n.* an oblong piece of white linen worn under the alb by priests at Mass. It is placed around the neck and shoulders. [< Old French *amis* < Latin *amictus* cloak]

a mi cus cu ri ae (ə mē′kəs kyůr′ē ī; ə mī′kəs kyůr′ē ē), (in law) a person with no interest in a case who is called in to advise the judge; friend of the court. [< New Latin]

a mid (ə mid′), *prep.* in the middle of; surrounded by; among.

am ide (am′īd, am′id), *n.* 1 any of a group of organic compounds having the univalent radical $—CONH_2$. 2 compound in which a metal is substituted for one of the hydrogen atoms of ammonia. [< *am(monia)* + *-ide*]

a mid ship (ə mid′ship), *adv.* amidships.

a mid ships (ə mid′ships), *adv.* in or toward the middle of a ship; halfway between the bow and stern.

a midst (ə midst′), *prep.* amid.

a mi go (ə mē′gō), *n., pl.* **-gos.** friend. [< Spanish]

a mine (ə mēn′, am′ən), *n.* any of a group of organic compounds formed from ammonia by replacement of one or more of its three hydrogen atoms by univalent hydrocarbon radicals. [< *am(monia)* + *-ine*[2]]

a mi no (ə mē′nō, am′ə nō), *adj.* of or containing the $—NH_2$ group combined with a nonacid radical.

amino acid, any of a number of complex organic compounds containing the $—NH_2$ and $—COOH$ groups that combine in various ways to form the proteins that make up living matter.

a mir (ə mir′), *n.* emir.

a mir ate (ə mir′āt), *n.* emirate.

Am ish (ä′mish, am′ish), *n.* a very strict Mennonite sect, founded in the 1600's. *—adj.* of this sect or its members. [< Jacob *Amman,* a Swiss Mennonite preacher of the 1600's]

Am ish man (ä′mish mən, am′ish mən), *n., pl.* **-men.** one of the Amish.

a miss (ə mis′), *adv.* 1 in a wrong way; wrongly. 2 **take amiss,** be offended at (something not intended to offend). *—adj.* improper; wrong. [Middle English *a mis* by mistake]

am i to sis (am′ə tō′sis), *n.* method of cell division in which the cell separates into two new cells without the formation of chromosomes.

am i ty (am′ə tē), *n., pl.* **-ties.** peace and friendship, especially between nations; friendly relations; friendliness: *a treaty of amity and commerce.* [< Middle French *amitié,* ultimately < Latin *amicus* friend. See AMICABLE.]

Am man (ä′mən, ä män′), *n.* capital of Jordan, in the NW part. 330,000.

am me ter (am′ē′tər), *n.* instrument for measuring in amperes the strength of an electric current.

am mo (am′ō), *n., pl.* **-mos.** INFORMAL. ammunition.

Am mon (am′ən), *n.* 1 the Greek and Roman name for Amen. 2 ancient country of the Ammonites. 3 the Ammonites.

am mo nia (ə mō′nyə, ə mō′nē ə), *n.* 1 a colorless soluble gas, consisting of nitrogen and hydrogen, that has a pungent smell and a strong alkaline reaction. Ammonia can be condensed to a colorless liquid under pressure and cold. *Formula:* NH_3 2 this gas dissolved in water; ammonia water. Ammonia is used for cleaning and for making fertilizers, explosives, and plastics. *Formula:* NH_4OH [< New Latin < Latin *(sal) ammoniacus* ammonium chloride < Greek *Ammōniakos* of Ammon; applied to a salt obtained near the shrine of Ammon in Libya]

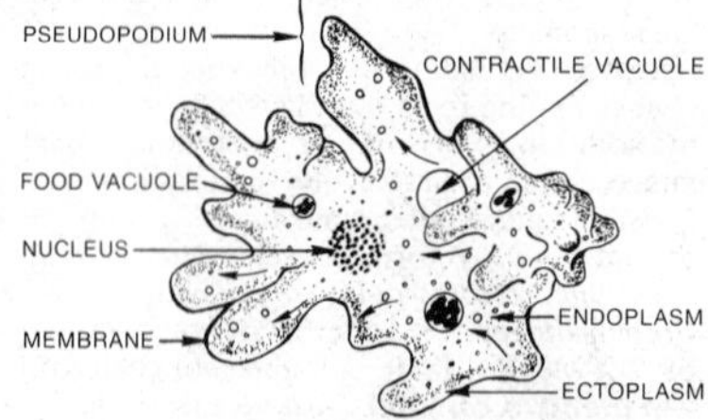

amoeba—Arrows indicate movement.

am mo ni a cal (am′ə nī′ə kəl), *adj.* of, containing, or like ammonia.

ammonia water, ammonia (def. 2).

am mon i fi ca tion (ə mon′ə fə kā′shən), *n.* 1 an ammonifying. 2 a being ammonified. 3 the production of ammonia in the decomposition of organic matter, especially through the action of bacteria.

am mon i fy (ə mon′ə fī), *v.t., v.i.,* **-fied, -fy ing.** combine or be combined with ammonia or ammonium compounds.

am mo nite (am′ə nīt), *n.* the fossil shell of a mollusk extinct in the Cretaceous period, coiled in a flat spiral and up to 6 feet in diameter. [< New Latin *ammonites* < Medieval Latin *cornu Ammonis* horn of Ammon]

Am mon ite (am′ə nīt), *n.* member of an ancient Semitic tribe that inhabited the region of Palestine east of the Jordan river.

am mo ni um (ə mō′nē əm), *n.* a univalent basic radical whose compounds or salts are similar to those of the alkali metals. It never appears in a free state. *Formula:* $—NH_4$

ammonium chloride, compound in the form of colorless crystals or white powder, used in dry cells, medicines, printing on cloth, etc.; sal ammoniac. *Formula:* NH_4Cl

ammonium hydroxide, ammonia (def. 2).

am mu ni tion (am′yə nish′ən), *n.* 1 bullets, shells, gunpowder, bombs, etc., that can be exploded or fired from guns or other weapons; military explosives and missiles to be used against an enemy. 2 thing or things that can be shot, hurled, or thrown. 3 error, mistake, etc., that can be used against someone. [< obsolete French *amunition,* used for *munition*]

am ne sia (am nē′zhə), *n.* partial or entire loss of memory caused by injury to the brain, or by disease, shock, etc. [< Greek *amnēsia* forgetfulness < *a-* not + *mimnēskesthai* remember]

am ne si ac (am nē′zhē ak, am nē′zē ak), *adj., n.* amnesic.

am ne sic (am nē′sik, am nē′zik), *adj.* of, causing, or characterized by amnesia. *—n.* person who has amnesia.

am nes ty (am′nə stē), *n., pl.* **-ties,** *v.,* **-tied, -ty ing.** *—n.* a general pardon or conditional offer of pardon for past offenses against a government: *After order was restored, the king granted amnesty to those who had plotted against him.* *—v.t.* give amnesty to; pardon. [< Greek *amnēstia* a forgetting < *a-* not + *mimnēskesthai* remember]

am ni on (am′nē ən), *n., pl.* **-ni ons, -ni a** (-nē ə). membrane forming the inner sac which encloses the embryos of reptiles, birds, and mammals. The amnion is filled with a serous fluid that protects the embryo and keeps it moist. [< Greek, diminutive of *amnos* lamb]

am ni ote (am′nē ōt), *n.* any of the group of vertebrates that develop amnions in their embryonic stages.

am ni ot ic (am′nē ot′ik), *adj.* 1 of or inside the amnion. 2 having an amnion.

a moe ba (ə mē′bə), *n., pl.* **-bas, -bae** (-bē). any of a group of protozoans classified as

hat, āge, fär; let, ēqual, tėrm;
it, īce; hot, ōpen, ôrder;
oil, out; cup, pu̇t, rüle;
ch, child; ng, long; sh, she;
th, thin; ᴛʜ, then; zh, measure;

ə represents *a* in about, *e* in taken, *i* in pencil, *o* in lemon, *u* in circus.

< = from, derived from, taken from.

rhizopods, found in fresh and salt water, in the soil, and in animal bodies. An amoeba is essentially a shapeless mass of protoplasm enclosed by a flexible membrane and containing one or more nuclei. Amoebas move and ingest food with fingerlike projections (pseudopodia) formed by protruding portions of the body. Also, **ameba.** [< Greek *amoibē* change] **—a moe′ba like′,** *adj.*

a moe ban (ə mē′bən), *adj.* 1 of or having to do with an amoeba or amoebas. 2 like an amoeba. Also, **ameban.**

a moe bic (ə mē′bik), *adj.* 1 of or like an amoeba or amoebas. 2 caused by amoebas. Also, **amebic.**

amoebic dysentery, type of dysentery caused by a species of amoeba and usually accompanied by intestinal ulcers.

a moe boid (ə mē′boid), *adj.* 1 of or like an amoeba; like that of an amoeba. 2 related to amoebas. Also, **ameboid.**

a mok (ə muk′, ə mok′), *adv., adj.* 1 in a murderous frenzy; made with a desire to attack. 2 **run amok** or **go amok, a** run about in a murderous frenzy. **b** behave wildly; disregard rules, instructions, etc. Also, **amuck.** [< Malay]

A mon (ä′mən), *n.* Amen.

a mong (ə mung′), *prep.* 1 in the number or class of: *That book is the best among modern novels.* 2 in the company of; in with: *spend one's time among musicians.* 3 surrounded by: *a house among the trees.* 4 in comparison with: *one among many.* 5 with a portion for each of: *Divide the money among them.* 6 by the combined action of: *You have among you spoiled the child.* 7 **among ourselves, among yourselves,** or **among themselves,** each with all the others; as a group: *They fought among themselves.* 8 by, with, or through the whole of: *political unrest among the people.* [Old English *amang* < *on (ge)mang* in a crowd]

➤ **among, between.** *Among* implies more than two objects: *They distributed the provisions among the survivors. Between* is always used when only two are concerned: *They divided the prize between the two boys.* When *between* is used of several it tends to suggest the individuals more than the situation: *The family of seven hadn't a pair of shoes between them.*

a mongst (ə mungst′), *prep.* among.

a mon til la do (ə mon′tə lä′dō), *n., pl.* **-dos.** a pale, moderately dry sherry. [< Spanish]

a mo ral (ā môr′əl, ā mor′əl; a môr′əl, a-mor′əl), *adj.* 1 not classifiable as good or bad because not involving any question of morality; nonmoral. 2 unable to distinguish between right and wrong. **—a mo′ral ly,** *adv.*

a mo ral i ty (ā′mə ral′ə tē, am′ə ral′ə tē), *n.* quality of being amoral.

Am o rite (am′ə rīt′), *n.* member of an ancient Semitic people that inhabited the highlands of Palestine and Syria before their conquest by the Israelites. In the 1900's B.C. the Amorites built a state in Babylonia, with its capital at Babylon.

am or ous (am′ər əs), *adj.* 1 inclined to love; fond of making love: *an amorous disposition.* 2 in love; enamored. 3 showing love; loving: *an amorous letter.* 4 having to do with love or courtship. [< Old French < *amour* love < Latin *amor*] **—am′or ous ly,** *adv.* **—am′or ous ness,** *n.*

a mor pa tri ae (ā′môr pā′trē ē; ä′môr pä′trē ī), LATIN. love of one's own country; patriotism.

a mor phous (ə môr′fəs), *adj.* 1 having no definite form; shapeless; formless. 2 of no particular type or pattern; not classifiable; anomalous. 3 not consisting of crystals; uncrystallized. 4 without the definite shape or organization found in most higher animals and plants. [< Greek *amorphos* < *a-* without + *morphē* shape] **—a mor′phous ly,** *adv.* **—a mor′phous ness,** *n.*

am or ti za tion (am′ər tə zā′shən, ə môr′-tə zā′zhən), *n.* 1 an amortizing of a debt. 2 money regularly set aside for this.

am or tize (am′ər tīz, ə môr′tīz), *v.t.,* **-tized, -tiz ing.** extinguish or wipe out (a debt or other liability), usually by setting aside regularly in a special fund certain amounts of money to accumulate at interest. [< Old French *amortiss-*, a form of *amortir* deaden < *a-* to + *mort* death]

A mos (ā′məs), *n.* 1 Hebrew prophet and social reformer who lived about 750 B.C. 2 book of the Old Testament containing his prophecies.

a mount (ə mount′), *n.* 1 the sum total to which anything mounts up or reaches; quantity: *a great amount of snow.* 2 the arithmetical total; sum: *the amount of the day's sale.* 3 the full effect, value, or extent: *the amount of evidence against him.* 4 quantity viewed as a whole: *a great amount of intelligence.* 5 the sum of the principal and interest due on a loan. *—v.i.* 1 add up *(to): Losses amount to ten million dollars.* 2 be equal *(to): Her unfriendly comment amounted to an insult.* [< Old French *amonter* to reach up to < *a mont* up to, literally, to the mountain]

➤ **amount, number.** *Amount* is used of things viewed in the bulk, weight, or sum; *number* is used of persons or things that can be counted: *an amount of milk, a number of cans of milk.*

a mour (ə mu̇r′), *n.* a love affair, especially a secret love affair. [< Old French < Latin *amor* love]

a mour-pro pre (à mür′prô′prə), *n.* FRENCH. conceit; self-esteem.

A moy (ä moi′, ə moi′), *n.* 1 seaport on an island near the SE coast of China. 224,000. 2 the island.

amp., 1 amperage. 2 ampere or amperes.

am per age (am′pər ij), *n.* strength of an electric current measured in amperes.

am pere (am′pir), *n.* unit for measuring the strength of an electric current. It is the amount of current one volt can send through a resistance of one ohm. Ordinary light bulbs take from 1/4 to 1/2 ampere. [< André-Marie *Ampère,* 1775-1836, French physicist]

am per sand (am′pər sand), *n.* the sign (&) meaning "and." [alteration of the phrase *and per se and,* which meant "the sign & by itself (stands for) *and*"]

am phet a mine (am fet′ə mēn′, am-fet′ə mən), *n.* 1 drug used as an inhalant or, in solution, as a spray for the relief of colds, hay fever, etc. *Formula:* $C_9H_{13}N$ 2 phosphate or sulfate of amphetamine used in tablet form as a stimulant to combat fatigue or reduce appetite.

amphi-, *combining form.* 1 around; on both sides: *Amphitheater = a theater (with seats) all around.* 2 in two ways; of two kinds: *Amphibious = living in two ways.* [< Greek < *amphi* around, on both sides]

amphora

Am phib i a (am fib′ē ə), *n.pl.* class of vertebrates comprising the amphibians. [< New Latin]

am phib i an (am fib′ē ən), *n.* 1 any of a class of cold-blooded vertebrates with moist, scaleless skin that, typically, lay eggs in water where the young hatch and go through a larval or tadpole stage, breathing by means of gills; the larval forms lose their gills and develop lungs for breathing and limbs. Frogs, toads, newts, and salamanders belong to this class. 2 animal living both on land and in water but unable to breathe under water. Crocodiles, seals, and beavers are amphibians. 3 plant that grows on land or in water. 4 aircraft that can take off from and land on either land or water. 5 a tank, truck, or other vehicle able to travel across land or water. *—adj.* 1 able to live both on land and in water. 2 able to start from and land on either land or water.

am phib i ous (am fib′ē əs), *adj.* 1 able to live both on land and in water: *Frogs are amphibious animals.* 2 able to travel across land or water: *an amphibious tank.* 3 carried out by the combined action of land, sea, and air forces: *an amphibious attack.* 4 trained for amphibious attack or assault: *amphibious troops.* [< Greek *amphibios* living in two ways < *amphi-* + *bios* life] **—am phib′i ous ly,** *adv.* **—am phib′i ous ness,** *n.*

am phi bole (am′fə bōl), *n.* any of a group of silicate minerals, including hornblende and asbestos. Amphiboles usually consist of a silicate of calcium, magnesium, and one or more other metals, as iron. [< Greek *amphibolos* ambiguous < *amphi-* + *-bolos* struck]

am phi mix is (am′fə mik′sis), *n., pl.* **-mix es** (-mik′sēz′). the uniting of the gametes of two organisms; fertilization. [< *amphi-* + Greek *mixis* a mingling]

am phi neu ran (am′fə nu̇r′ən, am′fə-nyu̇r′ən), *n.* any of a class of marine mollusks that adhere to rocks; chiton. They have bilateral symmetry and a shell of eight overlapping plates. [< *amphi-* + Greek *neuron* nerve]

am phi ox us (am′fē ok′səs), *n., pl.* **-ox i** (-ok′sī), **-us es.** 1 any of a genus of lancelets. 2 species of lancelet. [< Greek *amphi-* + *oxys* sharp]

am phi the a ter or **am phi the a tre** (am′fə thē′ə tər), *n.* 1 a circular or oval building with tiers of seats around a central open space. 2 place of public contest; arena. 3 something resembling an amphitheater in shape.

am phor a (am′fər ə), *n., pl.* **-phor ae** (-fə rē′), **-phor as.** a tall, two-handled jar, used by the ancient Greeks and Romans for storing grain, oil, etc. [< Latin < Greek *amphoreus* < *amphi-* + *phoreus* bearer]

am pho ter ic (am′fə ter′ik), *adj.* reacting

as an acid or as a base. [< Greek *amphoteros* both]

am ple (am′pəl), *adj.*, **-pler, -plest.** 1 more than enough to satisfy all demands; abundant: *an ample supply of food.* 2 as much as is needed; enough: *an allowance ample for carfare and lunches.* 3 large in capacity or volume; roomy: *a house with ample closets.* 4 large in extent or amount; extensive: *ample praise.* [< Latin *amplus*] **—am′ple ness,** *n.*

am pli fi ca tion (am′plə fə kā′shən), *n.* 1 act of amplifying. 2 detail or example that amplifies a statement, narrative, etc. 3 an expanded statement, narrative, etc. 4 an increase in the strength of an electric current.

am pli fi er (am′plə fī′ər), *n.* 1 person or thing that amplifies. 2 transistor, vacuum tube, or other device in a radio, phonograph, etc., for strengthening electrical impulses. 3 loudspeaker.

am pli fy (am′plə fī), *v.*, **-fied, -fy ing.** *—v.t.* 1 make greater; make stronger or larger: *amplify sounds, amplify the demand for a product.* 2 make fuller and more extensive; expand: *Please amplify your description.* 3 make too much of; exaggerate. 4 increase the strength of (electric current, power, or voltage). *—v.i.* write or talk more at length.

am pli tude (am′plə tüd, am′plə tyüd), *n.* 1 a being ample in size; largeness. 2 a being ample in amount; abundance: *an amplitude of money.* 3 intellectual scope; breadth of mind. 4 one half width of the swing of an oscillation. 5 the peak strength of an alternating current in a given cycle. 6 (of a heavenly body) the arc along the horizon measured between either true east or west and a point where a line drawn from the zenith through the body would intersect the horizon.

amplitude modulation, deliberate change of the amplitude of radio waves in order to transmit sound or visual images. Amplitude modulation is used for ordinary radio broadcasting and for the transmission of the picture portion of television.

am ply (am′plē), *adv.* in an ample manner; to an ample degree; abundantly.

am poule (am′pül, am pül′), *n.* a small, sealed glass container, usually holding one dose of a drug, medicine, etc., for a hypodermic injection, etc. [< French]

am pul (am′pul), *n.* ampoule.

am pule (am′pyül), *n.* ampoule.

am pul la (am pul′ə), *n.*, *pl.* **-pul lae** (-pul′ē). 1 a two-handled jar or bottle used in ancient Rome to hold oil, perfume, wine, etc. 2 a vessel used in churches to hold consecrated oil. 3 (in anatomy and zoology) the dilated portion of a canal or duct. 4 (in botany) a flask-shaped organ or bladder on an aquatic plant. [< Latin]

am pu tate (am′pyə tāt), *v.t.*, **-tat ed, -tat ing.** 1 cut off (all or part of a leg, arm, hand, etc.) from the body by surgery. 2 lop off (anything); prune. [< Latin *amputatum* cut around, pruned < *ambi-* around + *putare* to cut, prune] **—am′pu ta′tor,** *n.*

am pu ta tion (am′pyə tā′shən), *n.* 1 a cutting off all or a part of a leg, arm, hand, etc., by surgery. 2 a lopping off.

am pu tee (am′pyə tē′), *n.* person who has had all or part of a leg or arm amputated.

Am rit sar (əm rit′sər), *n.* city in the N part of India near Lahore, Pakistan. 425,000.

Am ster dam (am′stər dam), *n.* the largest city and official capital of the Netherlands, a North Sea port. The unofficial capital is The Hague. 831,000.

amt., amount.

Am trak (am′trak), *n.* a public corporation that since 1970 has operated rail passenger service on selected routes in the United States, using existing railroad equipment and tracks.

amu, atomic mass unit.

a muck (ə muk′), *adv., adj.* amok.

am u let (am′yə lit), *n.* locket, carved image, or some other small object worn as a magic charm against evil, disease, etc. [< Latin *amuletum*]

A mund sen (ä′mən sən), *n.* **Roald,** 1872-1928, Norwegian explorer who discovered the South Pole in 1911.

A mur River (ä mür′), river in E Asia flowing into the Sea of Okhotsk. 2900 mi.

a muse (ə myüz′), *v.t.*, **a mused, a mus ing.** 1 cause to laugh or smile: *That joke amused everyone.* 2 keep pleasantly interested; cause to feel cheerful or happy; entertain. See synonym study below. 3 cause (time) to pass pleasantly. [< Old French *amuser* divert < *a-* to + *muser* to gape] **—a mus′a ble,** *adj.* **—a mus′er,** *n.* **—a mus′ing ly,** *adv.*

Syn. 2 **Amuse, entertain** mean to keep pleasantly interested. **Amuse** emphasizes the idea of passing time by keeping one's attention occupied with something interesting and pleasing and at the same time often light and trivial: *The new toys amused the children.* **Entertain** emphasizes greater effort or more elaborate means to hold attention: *He entertained them by playing the piano.*

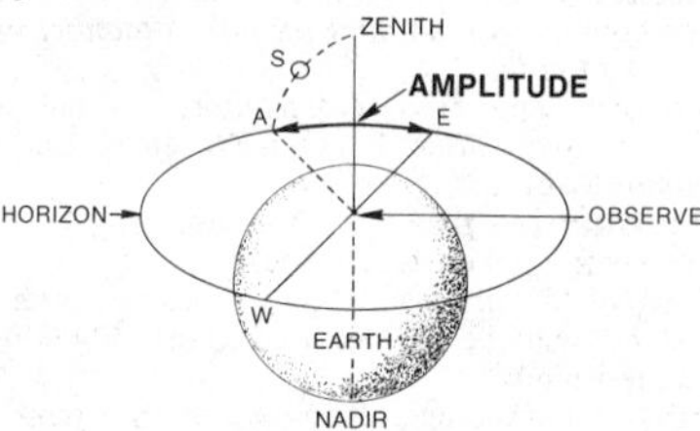

amplitude (def. 6)—The vertical circle through the star, S, intersects the horizon at A. E is the true east point. Arc AE is the amplitude.

a mus ed ly (ə myü′zid lē), *adv.* in an amused manner.

a muse ment (ə myüz′mənt), *n.* 1 condition of being amused. 2 anything which pleasantly whiles away the time; means of recreation.

amusement park, an outdoor place of entertainment with booths for games, rides on roller coasters, and other amusements.

Am vets (am′vets′), *n.* American Veterans of World War II and Korea, an organization founded in 1944.

am yl (am′əl), *n.* any of various forms of a univalent radical derived from pentane. *Formula:* —C_5H_{11} [< Greek *amylon* starch]

amyl alcohol, an acrid, oily liquid, the chief constituent of fusel oil. *Formula:* $C_5H_{11}OH$

am yl ase (am′ə lās), *n.* enzyme in saliva, pancreatic juice, etc., or in parts of plants, that helps to change starch into sugar.

am y lop sin (am′ə lop′sən), *n.* the amylase in the pancreatic juice.

an[1] (an; *unstressed* ən), *adj.* or *indefinite article.* used in place of *a* before a vowel or silent *h: an apple, an heir.* 1 some single; any: *Please give me an answer.* 2 one: *I need an ounce of butter.* 3 each; every: *twice an hour.* 4 one kind of: *Painting is an art.* 5 to or for each: *ten dollars an hour.* [Old English *ān* one] ➤ See **a**[2] for usage note.

an[2] or **an'** (an; *unstressed* ən), *conj.* 1 DIALECT or INFORMAL. and. 2 ARCHAIC. if.

an-[1], *prefix.* 1 not: *Anastigmatic = not astigmatic.* 2 without: *Anhydrous = without water.* Also, **a-**, before consonants except *h.* [< Greek]

an-[2], *prefix.* form of **ad-** before *n,* as in *annex.*

-an, *suffix forming adjectives and nouns, especially from proper nouns.* 1 of or having to do with ____: *Mohammedan = of or having to do with Mohammed.* 2 of or having to do with ____ or its people: *Asian = of or having to do with Asia or its people.* 3 native or inhabitant of ____: *American = native or inhabitant of America.* 4 person who knows much about or is skilled in ____: *Magician = person skilled in magic. Historian = person who knows much about history.* Also, **-ian, -ean.** [< Latin *-anus*]

An, actinon.

ana-, *prefix.* 1 back, as in *anachronism.* 2 up, as in *analysis, anatomy.* [< Greek]

-ana, *suffix forming nouns, especially from proper nouns.* sayings, writings, or articles belonging to or associated with ____: *Shakespeariana = things written by or about Shakespeare.* [< Latin, neuter plural of *-anus* -an]

An a bap tist (an′ə bap′tist), *n.* member of a former Protestant sect opposing infant baptism. The Anabaptists originated in Switzerland in the 1520's.

an a bol ic (an′ə bol′ik), *adj.* of, involving, or exhibiting anabolism.

a nab o lism (ə nab′ə liz′əm), *n.* process by which food substances are changed into the tissues of a living animal or plant. [< *ana-* back + *(meta)bolism*]

a nach ro nism (ə nak′rə niz′əm), *n.* 1 error in fixing a date or dates; erroneous reference of an event, circumstance, or custom to a wrong, especially an earlier date. 2 anything out of keeping with a specified time, especially something proper to a former age but not to the present. [< Greek *anachronismos* < *ana-* back + *chronos* time]

a nach ro nis tic (ə nak′rə nis′tik), *adj.* having or involving an anachronism. **—a nach′ro nis′ti cal ly,** *adv.*

an a co lu thon (an′ə kə lü′thon), *n.*, *pl.* **-tha** (-thə). a change from one grammatical construction to another in the same sentence, especially one made deliberately for greater force. EXAMPLE: "If thou beest he—but O, how fall'n! how changed." [< Greek *anakolouthon* < *an-* not + *akolouthos* following]

an a con da (an′ə kon′də), *n.* 1 a very large, tropical South American snake related to the boa that crushes its prey in its coils. 2 any large snake that crushes its prey in its coils. [probably < Singhalese *henakandayā,* a python]

An a con da (an′ə kon′də), *n.* city in SW Montana, important for its copper mines and zinc smelting. 10,000.

a nad ro mous (ə nad′rə məs), *adj.* going up rivers from the sea to spawn. Salmon are anadromous. [< Late Greek *anadromos* < Greek *ana-* up + *dromos* a running]

a nae mi a (ə nē′mē ə), *n.* anemia.

a nae mic (ə nē′mik), *adj.* anemic.

hat, āge, fär; let, ēqual, tėrm; it, īce; hot, ōpen, ôrder; oil, out; cup, pu̇t, rüle; ch, child; ng, long; sh, she; th, thin; ᴛʜ, then; zh, measure;

ə represents *a* in about, *e* in taken, *i* in pencil, *o* in lemon, *u* in circus.

< = from, derived from, taken from.

an aer obe (a ner′ōb, a nar′ōb), *n.* an anaerobic bacterium or other microorganism. [< Greek *an-* without + *aēr* air + *bios* life]

an ae ro bic (an′ə rō′bik), *adj.* 1 living, growing, or taking place where there is no free oxygen. Anaerobic bacteria get their oxygen by decomposing compounds containing oxygen. 2 having to do with or caused by anaerobic bacteria: *anaerobic infection.* **—an′ae ro′bi cal ly,** *adv.*

an aes the sia (an′əs thē′zhə), *n.* anesthesia.

an aes the si ol o gist (an′əs thē′zē ol′ə jist), *n.* anesthesiologist.

an aes the si ol o gy (an′əs thē′zē ol′ə jē), *n.* anesthesiology.

an aes thet ic (an′əs thet′ik), *n., adj.* anesthetic.

an aes the tist (ə nes′thə tist), *n.* anesthetist.

an aes the tize (ə nes′thə tīz), *v.t.,* **-tized, -tiz ing.** anesthetize. **—an aes′the ti za′tion,** *n.*

an a gram (an′ə gram), *n.* 1 word or phrase formed from another by rearranging the letters. EXAMPLE: lived—devil. 2 **anagrams,** *pl.* game in which the players make words by changing and adding letters. [< Greek *anagrammatizein* transpose letters < *ana-* back + *gramma* letter]

An a heim (an′ə hīm), *n.* city in SW California. 167,000.

a nal (ā′nl), *adj.* 1 of the anus. 2 at or near the anus. **—a′nal ly,** *adv.*

anal., 1 analogous. 2 analogy. 3 analysis. 4 analytic.

anal fin, a fin located near the anus on the underside of fishes. See **fin** for picture.

an al ge sia (an′l jē′zhə), *n.* a deadening or absence of the sense of pain without loss of consciousness. [< Greek *analgēsia* < *an-* not + *algein* feel pain]

an al ge sic (an′l jē′zik, an′l jē′sik), *adj.* of or causing analgesia. *—n.* drug that relieves or lessens pain.

an a log (an′l ôg, an′l og), *n.* analogue.

analog computer, an electronic calculating machine or automatic control which deals directly with physical quantities (weights, voltages, lengths, etc.) rather than with a numerical code.

an a log i cal (an′l oj′ə kəl), *adj.* 1 based on analogy; using analogy. 2 expressing an analogy, as the *heart* of an apple, the *mouth* of a cave. **—an′a log′i cal ly,** *adv.*

a nal o gous (ə nal′ə gəs), *adj.* 1 similar in certain qualities, circumstances, or uses; comparable: *The heart is analogous to a pump.* 2 (in biology) corresponding in function, but not in structure and origin: *The wing of a fly is analogous to the wing of a bird.* [< Greek *analogos* proportionate < *ana logon* according to due ratio] **—a nal′o gous ly,** *adv.* **—a nal′o gous ness,** *n.*

an a logue (an′l ôg, an′l og), *n.* an analogous thing, organ, or part. Also, **analog.**

analogue computer, analog computer.

a nal o gy (ə nal′ə jē), *n., pl.* **-gies.** 1 a partial or limited similarity or correspondence in some special qualities, circumstances, etc., of two or more things in other respects essentially different: *the analogy between music and poetry.* 2 likeness of one thing to another or others; similarity. 3 (in biology) correspondence of organs or other parts in function but not in structure and origin. 4 the inference that things alike in some respects will be alike in others: *a prediction based on the analogy of history.* 5 tendency in linguistic change of irregular or less frequent forms to conform to the pattern of regular or more frequent ones. The past tense *crowed* replaced *crew* by analogy.

an a lyse (an′l īz), *v.t.,* **-lysed, -lys ing.** BRITISH. analyze. **—an′a lys′er,** *n.*

a nal y sis (ə nal′ə sis), *n., pl.* **-ses** (-sēz′). 1 a breaking up of anything complex into its various simple elements. 2 this process as a method of studying the nature of a thing or of determining its essential features. An analysis can be made of a book, a person's character, a situation, etc. 3 **in the last analysis** or **in the final analysis,** fundamentally; ultimately. 4 a brief presentation of essential features; outline or summary. 5 in chemistry: **a** the determination of the nature or amount of one or more components of a substance. **b** the intentional separation of a compound into its parts or elements. 6 in mathematics: **a** algebraic reasoning, especially as applied to geometry. **b** treatment by the calculus. 7 psychoanalysis. [< Greek < *analyein* loosen up < *ana-* up + *lyein* loosen]

an a lyst (an′l ist), *n.* 1 person who analyzes or is skilled in analysis. 2 psychoanalyst.

an a lyt ic (an′l it′ik), *adj.* 1 analytical. 2 (in linguistics) characterized by the use of separate words, such as auxiliary verbs and prepositions, rather than by the use of inflectional endings. English is an analytic language, whereas Latin is synthetic.

an a lyt i cal (an′l it′ə kəl), *adj.* 1 of analysis; using analysis as a method or process. 2 concerned with or based on analysis. **—an′a lyt′i cal ly,** *adv.*

analytic geometry, the use of algebra and coordinates to solve problems in geometry; coordinate geometry.

an a lyze (an′l īz), *v.t.,* **-lyzed, -lyz ing.** 1 separate or distinguish the elements of (anything complex). 2 examine carefully in order to determine why something has happened or may be expected to happen: *analyze the results of an election.* 3 examine critically so as to bring out the essential elements of (a piece of writing or any part of it). 4 in chemistry: **a** determine the nature or amount of the components of (a substance). **b** separate intentionally (a compound) into its elements. 5 (in mathematics) submit (a problem) to treatment by algebra, and especially by the calculus. **—an′a lyz′a ble,** *adj.* **—an′a ly za′tion,** *n.* **—an′a lyz′er,** *n.*

An a ni as (an′ə nī′əs), *n.* 1 (in the New Testament) a famous liar, struck dead for lying. 2 any liar.

an a pest or **an a paest** (an′ə pest), *n.* a metrical foot of three syllables, two unaccented followed by one accented, or two short followed by one long. EXAMPLE:

From the cen′ | tre all round′ | to the sea′ |
I am lord′ | of the fowl′ | and the brute′. |

[< Greek *anapaistos (daktylos)* (dactyl) reversed < *ana-* back + *paiein* to strike]

an a pes tic or **an a paes tic** (an′ə pes′tik), *adj.* of or consisting of anapests.

an a phase (an′ə fāz), *n.* (in biology) the third stage in mitosis, characterized by the movement of the two sets of daughter chromosomes to opposite ends of the spindle.

an a phy lax is (an′ə fə lak′sis), *n.* increased sensitivity to the action of a normally nontoxic drug upon injection with it for the second time, sometimes causing severe or even fatal shock. [< Greek *ana-* back + *phylaxis* protection]

an ar chic (a när′kik), *adj.* producing anarchy; favoring anarchy; lawless. **—an ar′chi cal ly,** *adv.*

an ar chi cal (a när′kə kəl), *adj.* anarchic.

an ar chism (an′ər kiz′əm), *n.* 1 a political and social movement advocating the overthrow of all government and the abolition of all institutions requiring governmental protection. 2 practice or support of this belief. 3 disorder and confusion; lawlessness.

an ar chist (an′ər kist), *n.* 1 person who seeks to bring about the destruction of government and law; advocate of anarchism. 2 person who promotes disorder and stirs up revolt. *—adj.* anarchistic.

an ar chis tic (an′ər kis′tik), *adj.* of anarchism; like that of anarchists.

an ar chy (an′ər kē), *n.* 1 absence of a system of government and law. 2 disorder and confusion; lawlessness. 3 anarchism (def. 1). [< Greek *anarchia* < *an-* without + *archos* ruler]

an as tig mat ic (an′ə stig mat′ik, an′as′tig mat′ik), *adj.* free from astigmatism.

a nas to mose (ə nas′tə mōz), *v.t., v.i.* **-mosed, -mos ing.** communicate, unite, or connect by anastomosis.

a nas to mo sis (ə nas′tə mō′sis), *n., pl.* **-ses** (-sēz′). a cross connection between separate parts of any branching system, as the veins of leaves, the veins in the wings of insects, or rivers and their branches. [< Greek *anastomōsis* < *ana-* back + *stoma* mouth]

anat., 1 anatomical. 2 anatomy.

a nath e ma (ə nath′ə mə), *n., pl.* **-mas.** 1 a solemn curse by church authorities excommunicating some person from the church. 2 denunciation of some person or thing as evil; curse. 3 person or thing that has been cursed or is utterly detested. [< Latin < Greek]

a nath e ma tize (ə nath′ə mə tīz), *v.,* **-tized, -tiz ing.** *—v.t.* pronounce an anathema against; denounce; curse. *—v.i.* utter anathemas; curse. **—a nath′e ma ti za′tion,** *n.* **—a nath′e ma tiz′er,** *n.*

An a to li a (an′ə tō′lē ə), *n.* region between the Black and Mediterranean seas, nearly equivalent to the peninsula of Asia Minor. **—An′a to′li an,** *adj., n.*

an a tom ic (an′ə tom′ik), *adj.* anatomical.

an a tom i cal (an′ə tom′ə kəl), *adj.* 1 connected with the study or practice of anatomy or dissection. 2 of anatomy; structural. **—an′a tom′i cal ly,** *adv.*

a nat o mist (ə nat′ə mist), *n.* 1 an expert in anatomy. 2 person who analyzes.

a nat o mize (ə nat′ə mīz), *v.t.,* **-mized, -miz ing.** 1 dissect (an animal, plant, etc.) to study the structure and relation of the parts. 2 examine the parts of; analyze. **—a nat′o mi za′tion,** *n.*

a nat o my (ə nat′ə mē), *n., pl.* **-mies.** 1 science of the structure of animals and plants based upon dissection, microscopic observation, etc. 2 the dissecting of animals or plants to study the position and structure of their parts. 3 the bodily structure of an animal or plant: *the anatomy of an earthworm.* 4 detailed examination; analysis. [< Late Latin *anatomia* dissection < Greek *anatomē* < *ana-* up + *tomos* a cutting]

anc., ancient.

-ance, *suffix forming nouns chiefly from verbs.* 1 act or fact of ___ing: *Avoidance = act or fact of avoiding.* 2 quality or state of being ___ed: *Annoyance = quality or state of being annoyed.* 3 thing that ___s: *Conveyance = thing that conveys.* 4 what is ___ed: *Contrivance = what is contrived.* 5 quality or state of being ___ant: *Importance = quality or state of being important.* [< Old French < Latin *-antia, -entia*]

an ces tor (an′ses′tər), *n.* 1 person from whom one is descended, usually one more remote than a grandparent; forefather. 2 a forerunner; precursor. 3 the early form from which a species or group is descended. [< Old French *ancestre* < Latin *antecessor* < *antecedere* go before]

an ces tral (an ses′trəl), *adj.* of, having to do with, or inherited from ancestors: *an ancestral home, an ancestral trait.* **—an ces′tral ly,** *adv.*

an ces tress (an′ses′tris), *n.* woman from whom one is descended.

an ces try (an′ses′trē), *n., pl.* **-tries.** 1 ancestors: *Many of the early settlers in America had English ancestry.* 2 line of descent from ancestors; lineage.

An chi ses (an kī′sēz), *n.* (in Greek and Roman legends) a prince of Troy and the father of Aeneas.

an chor (ang′kər), *n.* 1 a heavy, shaped piece of iron or steel lowered into the water to hold a ship or boat fixed in a particular place. When lowered on a chain, rope, or cable the anchor grips the bottom of the sea, river, etc., by means of flat, pointed flukes. 2 something that makes a person feel safe and secure. 3 thing for holding something else in place. 4 anchor man (def. 1).

at anchor, held by an anchor; anchored.

cast anchor, let down or drop the anchor.

ride at anchor, be kept at some place by being anchored.

weigh anchor, take up the anchor.

—v.t. 1 hold in place with an anchor: *anchor a ship.* 2 hold in place; fix firmly: *anchor a tent to the ground.* *—v.i.* drop anchor; stop or stay in place by using an anchor. [Old English *ancor* < Latin *ancora* < Greek *ankyra*]

an chor age (ang′kər ij), *n.* 1 place where a ship anchors or can anchor. 2 money paid for the right to anchor. 3 an anchoring. 4 a being anchored. 5 position affording support; a hold. 6 something on which to depend.

An chor age (ang′kər ij), *n.* seaport in S Alaska. 48,000.

an chor et (ang′kər it, ang′kə ret′), *n.* anchorite.

an cho rite (ang′kə rīt′), *n.* person who has withdrawn or secluded himself from the world, usually for religious reasons. [< Medieval Latin *anachorita* < Greek *anachōrētēs* < *anachōrein* withdraw]

anchor man, 1 the last man to run or swim on a relay team. 2 person on a television or radio program who coordinates reports from correspondents in several different cities, countries, etc.

an cho vy (an′chō vē, an chō′vē), *n., pl.* **-vies.** any of several small fishes that look somewhat like herrings, especially one abundant in the Mediterranean, much used pickled and in the form of a salt paste. [< Spanish and Portuguese *anchova*]

an cien ré gime (äɴ syaɴ′ rā zhēm′), FRENCH. 1 the social and political structure of France before the Revolution of 1789. 2 the old order of things.

an cient (ān′shənt), *adj.* 1 of or belonging to times long past: *ancient records.* 2 of the time before the fall of the Western Roman Empire (A.D. 476). 3 of great age; very old: *the ancient hills, an ancient city, an ancient custom.* 4 old-fashioned; antique: *an ancient turn of phrase.* 5 INFORMAL. no longer news; out of fashion. 6 ARCHAIC. having the experience and wisdom of age. *—n.* 1 **the ancients,** the ancient Greeks, Romans, etc., and other civilized nations of antiquity. 2 a very old person; patriarch. [< Old French *ancien* < Late Latin *anteanus* former < Latin *ante* before] **—an′cient ness,** *n.*

ancient history, 1 history from the earliest known civilizations to the fall of the Western Roman Empire in A.D. 476. 2 INFORMAL. a well-known fact or event of the recent past.

an cient ly (ān′shənt lē), *adv.* in ancient times.

an cil lar y (an′sə ler′ē, an sil′ər ē), *adj.* 1 subordinate; dependent; subservient. 2 assisting; auxiliary: *an ancillary engine in a boat.* [< Latin *ancilla* handmaid]

-ancy, *suffix.* variant of **-ance,** as in *ascendancy, buoyancy.*

and (and; *unstressed* ənd, ən), *conj.* 1 as well as: *nice and cold. You can come and go in the car.* 2 added to; with: *4 and 2 make 6. I like ham and eggs.* 3 as a result: *The sun came out and the grass dried.* 4 INFORMAL. to: *Try and do better.* [Old English]

➤ **And** is a coordinating conjunction; that is, it connects words, phrases, or clauses of grammatically equivalent constructions.

An da lu sia (an′də lü′zhə, an′də lü′shə), *n.* region in S Spain, the last stronghold of the Moors. **—An′da lu′sian,** *adj., n.*

An da man Islands (an′də mən), group of small islands in the Bay of Bengal. Together with the Nicobar Islands it forms a territory of India. 42,000 pop.; 2600 sq. mi.

an dan te (än dän′tā, an dan′tē), *adv., adj., n.* in music: *—adv., adj.* moderately slow. *—n.* a moderately slow movement in a piece of music. [< Italian, literally, walking]

an dan ti no (än′dän tē′nō, an′dan tē′nō), *adv., adj., n., pl.* **-nos.** in music: *—adv., adj.* slightly faster than andante. *—n.* a composition or part of one that is played andantino. [< Italian]

An de an (an′dē ən, an dē′ən), *adj.* of or having to do with the Andes Mountains.

An der sen (an′dər sən), *n.* **Hans Christian,** 1805-1875, Danish writer of fairy tales.

An der son (an′dər sən), *n.* 1 **Maxwell,** 1888-1959, American dramatist. 2 **Sherwood,** 1876-1941, American writer of short stories and novels.

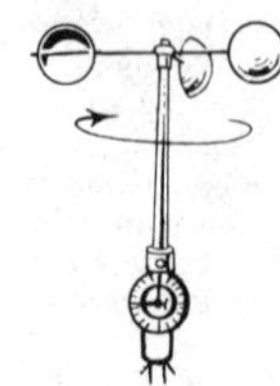

anemometer
Wind catches the cups and moves them around, causing the shaft below to turn. The speed of the turning is shown on the dial.

An des Mountains (an′dēz), mountain system in W South America, roughly paralleling the W coast of the continent. The highest peak is Aconcagua, 22,834 ft.

and i ron (and′ī′ərn), *n.* one of a pair of metal supports for wood in a fireplace; firedog. [< Old French *andier; -iron* by association with *iron*]

and/or, both or either: *income from stocks and/or bonds.*

➤ **And/or** is used primarily in business and legal writing. It is useful when three choices exist (both items mentioned or either one of the two).

An dor ra (an dôr′ə, an dor′ə), *n.* 1 small country between France and Spain, in the Pyrenees. 21,000 pop.; 191 sq. mi. 2 its capital. 8000. **—An dor′ran,** *adj., n.*

An dré (an′drā, an′drē, än′drā), *n.* **John,** 1751-1780, British major hanged as a spy during the Revolutionary War.

An dre a del Sar to (än drā′ə del sär′tō), 1486-1531, Italian painter.

An drew (an′drü), *n.* (in the Bible) one of Christ's twelve Apostles, the patron saint of Greece, Russia, and Scotland.

an droe ci um (an drē′shē əm, an drē′sē əm), *n., pl.* **-ci a** (-shē ə, -sē ə), the male organs of a flower; the stamens. [< Greek *andros* man + *oikos* house]

an dro gen (an′drə jən), *n.* any hormone that induces or strengthens masculine characteristics.

an dro gen ic (an′drə jen′ik), *adj.* of or having to do with an androgen.

an drog y nous (an droj′ə nəs), *adj.* 1 having flowers with stamens and flowers with pistils in the same cluster. 2 being both male and female; hermaphroditic. [< Greek *andros* man + *gynē* woman]

An drom a che (an drom′ə kē′), *n.* (in Greek legends) wife of Hector.

An drom e da (an drom′ə də), *n.* 1 (in Greek legends) the wife of Perseus, who rescued her from a sea monster. 2 a northern constellation, between Perseus and Pegasus, having the only spiral nebula in the Northern Hemisphere visible to the unaided eye.

An dros (an′drəs), *n.* Sir **Edmund,** 1637-1714, British colonial governor in America.

-ane, *suffix forming nouns.* (in chemistry) saturated carbon of the methane series, as in *butane, propane.* [patterned on *-ine*[2]]

an ec dot al (an′ik dō′tl, an′ik dō′tl), *adj.* of, characterized by, or consisting of anecdotes. **—an′ec dot′al ly,** *adv.*

an ec dote (an′ik dōt), *n.* a short account of some interesting incident or single event, especially one in the life of a person. See **story**[1] for synonym study. [< Greek *anekdota* (things) unpublished < *an-*not + *ek-*out + *didonai* give]

an e cho ic (an′ē kō′ik), *adj.* having or admitting no echoes: *an anechoic chamber.*

a ne mi a (ə nē′mē ə), *n.* 1 condition resulting from an insufficiency of hemoglobin or red blood cells or by a loss of blood, characterized by weakness, pallor, palpitation of the heart, and a tendency to fatigue. 2 lack of vigor or strength; weakness. Also, **anaemia.** [< Greek *anaimia* < *an-* not + *haima* blood]

a ne mic (ə nē′mik), *adj.* 1 of or having anemia. 2 lacking in vigor or strength; weak. Also, **anaemic.** **—a ne′mi cal ly,** *adv.*

an e mom e ter (an′ə mom′ə tər), *n.* instrument for measuring the velocity of wind. [< Greek *anemos* wind]

hat, āge, fär; let, ēqual, tėrm;
it, īce; hot, ōpen, ôrder;
oil, out; cup, pu̇t, rüle;
ch, child; ng, long; sh, she;
th, thin; ᴛʜ, then; zh, measure;

ə represents *a* in about, *e* in taken, *i* in pencil, *o* in lemon, *u* in circus.

< = from, derived from, taken from.

a nem o ne (ə nem′ə nē), *n.* 1 any of a genus of perennial plants of the same family as the buttercup, having slender stems and small white or colored cup-shaped flowers; windflower. 2 sea anemone. [< Greek *anemōnē* windflower < *anemos* wind]

a nent (ə nent′), *prep.* concerning; about. [Old English *on emn, on efn* on even (ground with)]

an e roid barometer (an′ə roid′), barometer worked by the pressure of air on the elastic lid of an airtight metal box from which the air has been pumped out. A change of pressure causes a pointer attached to the lid to move along a scale. [< French *anéroïde* < Greek *a-* without + Late Greek *nēron* water]

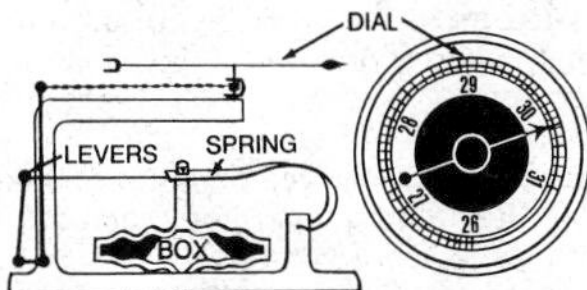

aneroid barometer—Rising air pressure forces down the elastic lid of the airtight box. This action lowers the spring and, by means of levers, moves the pointer on the dial. Falling air pressure reverses the movements.

an es the sia (an′əs thē′zhə), *n.* entire (**general anesthesia**) or partial (**local anesthesia**) loss of the feeling of pain, touch, cold, etc., produced by ether, chloroform, Novocaine, etc., by hypnotism, or as the result of hysteria, paralysis, or disease. Also, **anaesthesia.** [< Greek *anaisthēsia* insensibility < *an-* without + *aisthēsis* sensation]

an es the si ol o gist (an′əs thē′zē ol′ə jist), *n.* an expert in anesthesiology. Also, **anaesthesiologist.**

an es the si ol o gy (an′əs thē′zē ol′ə jē), *n.* science of administering general and local anesthetics. Also, **anaesthesiology.**

an es thet ic (an′əs thet′ik), *n.* substance that causes anesthesia, as chloroform, ether, procaine, etc. —*adj.* 1 causing anesthesia. 2 of or with anesthesia. Also, **anaesthetic.** **—an′es thet′i cal ly,** *adv.*

an es the tist (ə nes′thə tist), *n.* person specially trained to give anesthetics. Also, **anaesthetist.**

an es the tize (ə nes′thə tīz), *v.t.,* **-tized, -tiz ing.** 1 make (a person, animal, area of the body, etc.) unable to feel pain, touch, cold, etc.; make insensible. 2 lessen or deaden (the emotional or critical response of a person). Also, **anaesthetize. —an es′the ti za′tion,** *n.* **—an es′the tiz′er,** *n.*

an eu rysm or **an eu rism** (an′yə riz′əm), *n.* a permanent swelling of an artery or vein, caused by pressure of the blood on a part weakened by disease or injury. [< Greek *aneurysma* dilation < *an-* up + *eurys* wide]

a new (ə nü′, ə nyü′), *adv.* 1 once more; again: *I made so many mistakes I had to begin my work anew.* 2 in a new form or different way: *plan a building anew.* [Old English *of niowe*]

an gel (ān′jəl), *n.* 1 (in some religious beliefs) one of an order of spiritual beings that are the attendants and messengers of God. 2 a conventional representation of such a being, usually as a winged human figure clothed in white. 3 person as good or lovely as an angel. 4 any supernatural (but not divine) spirit, either good or bad. 5 SLANG. person who pays for producing a play. 6 an old English gold coin in use between 1465 and 1634. 7 unexplained, invisible physical phenomenon that causes a radar echo. [< Old French *angele* < Latin *angelus* < Greek *angelos,* originally, messenger]

Angel Falls, waterfall in SE Venezuela, the highest in the world. 3212 ft.

an gel fish (ān′jəl fish′), *n., pl.* **-fish es** or **-fish.** 1 shark with large fins which spread out like wings. 2 any of several colorful tropical marine fishes with spiny fins.

an gel ic (an jel′ik), *adj.* 1 of angels; heavenly. 2 like an angel; innocent, good, and lovely. **—an gel′i cal ly,** *adv.*

an gel i ca (an jel′ə kə), *n.* a perennial plant of the same family as the parsley, used in cooking, in medicine, and in making perfume. Candied angelica is cut into shapes to decorate cakes, etc.

an gel i cal (an jel′ə kəl), *adj.* angelic.

An gel i co (an jel′ə kō), *n.* **Fra,** 1387-1455, Italian painter.

An ge lus or **an ge lus** (an′jə ləs), *n.* 1 prayer said by Roman Catholics in memory of Christ's assuming human form. 2 the bell, **Angelus bell,** rung at morning, noon, and night to signal the times this prayer is said. [< Latin, angel (the first word in the prayer)]

an ger (ang′gər), *n.* the feeling one has toward something that hurts, opposes, offends, or annoys; strong displeasure; wrath. See synonym study below. —*v.t.* make angry; arouse anger in. —*v.i.* become angry. [< Scandinavian (Old Icelandic) *angr* grief]

Syn. *n.* **Anger, indignation, wrath** mean the feeling of strong displeasure turned against anyone or anything that has hurt or wronged us or others. **Anger** is the general word for the emotion: *He never speaks in anger.* **Indignation,** more formal, means intense anger with scorn, caused by something mean, base, or unjust and therefore often justified: *The atrocity caused widespread indignation.* **Wrath,** a formal word, means great anger or indignation accompanied by a desire to punish: *Their sins provoked the wrath of God.*

An ge vin (an′jə vin), *adj.* 1 of or from Anjou. The Plantagenet family of the kings of England was Angevin. 2 of or belonging to the Plantagenet family. —*n.* 1 member of the Plantagenet family. 2 native or inhabitant of Anjou.

an gi na (an jī′nə), *n.* 1 any inflammation of the throat, such as quinsy, croup, or mumps. 2 angina pectoris. 3 a sudden, acute pain. [< Latin, quinsy < *angere* to choke]

angina pec tor is (pek′tər is), a serious condition of the heart marked by sharp chest pains and a feeling of being suffocated. [< New Latin, angina of the chest]

an gi o sperm (an′jē ə spėrm′), *n.* any of a subdivision of plants of the spermatophyte division, having its seeds enclosed in an ovary or fruit; a flowering plant. Grasses, beans, strawberries, and oaks are angiosperms. [< Greek *angeion* vessel + *sperma* seed]

an gi o sper mous (an′jē ə spėr′məs), *adj.* having the seeds enclosed in an ovary.

an gle[1] (ang′gəl), *n., v.,* **-gled, -gling.** —*n.* 1 the space between two lines or surfaces that meet. 2 the figure formed by two such lines or surfaces. 3 the difference in direction between two such lines or surfaces, measured especially in degrees or parts of degrees. 4 corner of a building, room, etc. 5 a special approach to or way of regarding a task, problem, etc., selected so as to achieve a particular result. 6 one aspect or phase of a problem or situation. —*v.i.* move, turn, or bend at an angle. —*v.t.* present (a report, narrative, item of news, etc.) with bias or prejudice; slant. [< Old French < Latin *angulus*]

an gle[2] (ang′gəl), *v.,* **-gled, -gling,** *n.* —*v.i.* 1 fish with a hook and line. 2 try to get something by using tricks or schemes. —*n.* SLANG. a special, often underhanded way of profiting. [Old English *angel* fishhook]

An gle (ang′gəl), *n.* member of a Germanic tribe that, with the Jutes and Saxons, invaded and settled in England in the A.D. 400's and 500's.

angle of incidence, the angle that a line or ray of light falling upon a surface makes with a line perpendicular to that surface.

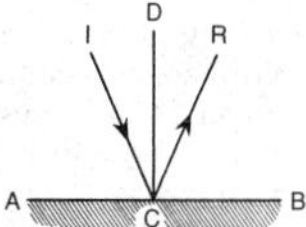

angle of incidence, angle of reflection—Ray IC meets surface AB at point C, CD being the perpendicular and angle ICD the angle of incidence. The angle DCR is the angle of reflection. Angle ICD equals angle DCR.

angle of reflection, the angle that a line or ray of light reflected from a surface makes with a line perpendicular to that surface.

an gler (ang′glər), *n.* 1 fisherman who uses a hook and line, especially one who fishes for sport. 2 kind of saltwater fish, found on the coasts of Europe and North America, that preys upon small fish which it attracts by the movements of filaments attached to its head.

an gle worm (ang′gəl wėrm′), *n.* earthworm.

An gli can (ang′glə kən), *adj.* of or having to do with the Church of England or other churches of the same faith or in communion with it elsewhere. —*n.* member of an Anglican church.

An gli can ism (ang′glə kə niz′əm), *n.* the principles and beliefs of the Anglican church or communion of churches.

An gli cism (ang′glə siz′əm), *n.* 1 custom or trait peculiar to the English. 2 Briticism.

An gli cize or **an gli cize** (ang′glə sīz),

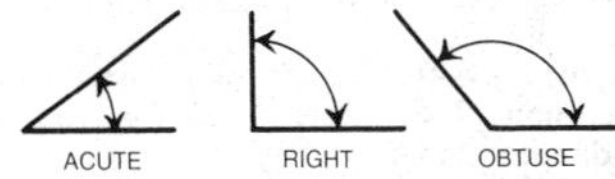

angle[1] (def. 2)—three kinds of angles

v.t., v.i., **-cized, -ciz ing.** make or become English in form, pronunciation, habits, customs, or character. *Cajole, lace,* and *cousin* are French words that have been Anglicized. **—An′gli ci za′tion, an′gli ci za′tion,** *n.*

an gling (ang′gling), *n.* act, art, or sport of fishing with a hook and line.

Anglo-, *combining form.* 1 English: *Anglo-Catholic = English Catholic.* 2 English and: *Anglo-Egyptian Sudan = English and Egyptian Sudan.* [< Late Latin *Angli* the English < Latin, the Angles]

An glo-Cath o lic (ang′glō kath′ə lik), *n.* member of the Church of England who maintains the Catholic character of the Anglican Church. *—adj.* emphasizing the Catholic character of the Anglican Church.

An glo-Ca thol i cism (ang′glō kə thol′ə siz′əm), *n.* the beliefs and practices of Anglo-Catholics.

An glo-E gyp tian Sudan (ang′glō-i jip′shən), former country in NE Africa jointly ruled by Great Britain and Egypt until 1956, now called **Sudan.**

An glo-French (ang′glō french′), *n.* the dialect of French introduced into England mainly by the Norman conquerors after 1066, and used through the 1300's; Anglo-Norman; Norman-French.

An glo-In di an (ang′glō in′dē ən), *n.* 1 person of British birth or descent living in India. 2 dialect of English spoken by Anglo-Indians.

An glo-Nor man (ang′glō nôr′mən), *n.* 1 one of the Normans who settled in England between 1066 and 1154. 2 descendant of an English Norman. 3 Anglo-French. *—adj.* English and Norman.

An glo phile (ang′glə fīl), *n.* person who greatly admires England, its people, and its culture.

An glo phobe (ang′glə fōb), *n.* person who hates or fears England and its people.

An glo pho bi a (ang′glə fō′bē ə), *n.* hatred or fear of England and the English.

An glo-Sax on (ang′glō sak′sən), *n.* 1 member of the Germanic tribes that invaded England in the A.D. 400's and 500's and ruled most of England until the Norman Conquest in 1066. 2 the language of these tribes; Old English. 3 person who in any period of history has spoken English. 4 person of English descent. 5 plain English, without Latin or other foreign words. 6 the English language as spoken or written in any part of the world at any date; English. *—adj.* 1 having to do with the Anglo-Saxons or their language. 2 having to do with any English-speaking people.

An go la (ang gō′lə), *n.* Portuguese colony in SW Africa; Portuguese West Africa. *Capital:* Luanda. 5,000,000 pop.; 481,300 sq. mi. See **Zaïre** for map. **—An go′lan,** *adj., n.*

An go ra (ang gôr′ə, ang gōr′ə), *n.* 1 Angora cat. 2 Angora goat. 3 Angora rabbit. 4 Ankara. 5 **angora,** a mohair. b a very fluffy yarn made partly or entirely from the hair of Angora goats or Angora rabbits.

Angora cat, variety of the domestic cat with long, silky hair.

Angora goat, variety of goat with long, silky hair. This hair is used for wool and made into mohair.

Angora rabbit, any of a domestic breed of rabbits with long, soft hair, usually white. This hair is used in making a very fluffy yarn or fabric.

an gry (ang′grē), *adj.,* **-gri er, -gri est.** 1 feeling or showing anger; roused by anger; enraged: *He gets angry about nothing. I was angry at their slipshod work. I am angry with you.* 2 characterized by or suggestive of anger; raging or stormy: *an angry sky.* 3 expressing, moved, or caused by anger: *angry words.* 4 inflamed and congested: *an angry sore.* **—an′gri ly,** *adv.* **—an′gri ness,** *n.*

Angst (ängst), *n.* GERMAN. anxiety.

ang strom (ang′strəm), *n.* unit of measurement of the wavelength of light, equal to one ten-millionth of a millimeter. *Abbrev.:* Å [< Anders J. *Ångström,* 1814-1874, Swedish physicist]

angstrom unit, angstrom.

an guish (ang′gwish), *n.* 1 severe physical pain; great suffering: *the anguish of unrelieved toothache.* 2 extreme mental pain or suffering: *the anguish of despair.* [< Old French *anguisse* < Latin *angustia* tightness < *angustus* narrow]

an guished (ang′gwisht), *adj.* full of anguish; distressed with severe pain; tormented.

an gu lar (ang′gyə lər), *adj.* 1 having an angle or angles; having corners; pointed. 2 consisting of an angle: *an angular point.* 3 measured by an angle: *angular distance.* 4 somewhat thin and bony; not plump. 5 stiff and awkward: *angular movements.* **—an′gu lar ly,** *adv.*

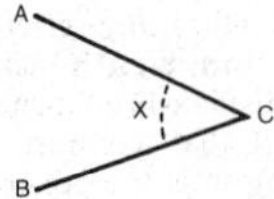

angular (def. 3) The angular distance of A from B, when measured from C, is the angle X.

an gu lar i ty (ang′gyə lar′ə tē), *n., pl.* **-ties.** 1 condition of being angular. 2 **angularities,** *pl.* sharp corners.

An gus (ang′gəs), *n.* 1 county in E Scotland. 2 Aberdeen Angus.

an hy dride (an hī′drīd, an hī′drid), *n.* 1 any oxide that unites with water to form an acid or base. 2 any compound formed by the removal of water.

an hy drite (an hī′drīt), *n.* a white or grayish mineral consisting of anhydrous sulfate of calcium. *Formula:* $CaSO_4$

an hy drous (an hī′drəs), *adj.* 1 without water. 2 containing no water of crystallization; not hydrated.

an i lin (an′l ən), *n.* aniline.

an i line (an′l ən, an′l īn), *n.* a colorless, poisonous, oily liquid, obtained from coal tar and especially from nitrobenzene, used in making dyes, medicines, plastics, etc. *Formula:* $C_6H_5NH_2$ [< German *Anilin* < *Anil* indigo < Arabic *al-nīl*]

aniline dye, 1 dye made from aniline. 2 any artificial dye.

an i mad ver sion (an′ə mad vėr′zhən), *n.* 1 comment, criticism, or remark expressing censure. 2 censure; blame.

an i mad vert (an′ə mad vėrt′), *v.i.* comment critically or adversely; censure. [< Latin *animadvertere* < *animus* mind + *ad-* to + *vertere* to turn]

an i mal (an′ə məl), *n.* 1 any living organism that is not a plant and is distinguished from plants by a capacity for voluntary motion and more advanced types of sensation and response to stimuli; any member of the animal kingdom. 2 animal other than man; brute; beast. See synonym study below. 3 any mammal, as distinguished from a bird, reptile, etc. 4 a brutish or degenerate person. *—adj.* 1 of, relating to, or connected with animals. 2 like that of animals: *animal cunning.* 3 sensual: *animal appetites.* [< Latin, living being < *anima* life, breath]

Syn. *n.* 2 **Animal, beast, brute** mean a living creature of a lower order than man. **Animal,** the general word, usually suggests nothing more: *I like animals.* **Beast** usually applies to four-legged animals, as distinct from birds, insects, etc.: *The horse is a noble beast.* **Brute** emphasizes lack of the ability to reason, the ability which sets man above animals: *The poor brutes, maddened by fear, dashed back into the center of the fire.*

an i mal cule (an′ə mal′kyül), *n.* a minute animal, nearly or wholly invisible to the naked eye. [< New Latin *animalculum,* diminutive of Latin *animal*]

animal heat, the temperature maintained during life in an animal body, and requisite for physiological functions.

an i mal ism (an′ə mə liz′əm), *n.* 1 doctrine that men are mere animals without spirit or soul. 2 physical activity. 3 mere physical enjoyment; sensuality.

an i mal ist (an′ə mə list), *n.* 1 believer in animalism. 2 sensualist.

an i mal is tic (an′ə mə lis′tik), *adj.* 1 of animalism or animalists. 2 sensual.

an i mal i ty (an′ə mal′ə tē), *n.* 1 animal side of human nature. 2 animal life.

animal kingdom, division of the natural world that includes all animals. See **classification** for chart.

animal spirits, natural liveliness.

an i mate (*v.* an′ə māt; *adj.* an′ə mit), *v.,* **-mat ed, -mat ing,** *adj.* *—v.t.* 1 make lively, gay, or vigorous: *His arrival animated the whole party.* 2 inspire; encourage: *The ideals which animate great reformers.* 3 put into action; cause to act or work: *Windmills are animated by the wind.* 4 give life to; make alive or as if alive. *—adj.* 1 living; having life. Animate nature means all living plants and animals. 2 lively; vigorous; animated. [< Latin *animatum* filled with breath < *anima* life, breath] **—an′i mate ly,** *adv.* **—an′i ma′tor,** *n.*

an i mat ed (an′ə mā′tid), *adj.* 1 lively; vigorous: *an animated discussion.* 2 gay; joyful: *an animated smile.* 3 seeming to be alive: *animated dolls.* 4 living; alive; animate. **—an′i mat′ed ly,** *adv.*

animated cartoon, series of drawings arranged to be photographed and shown as a motion picture. Each drawing shows a slight change from the one before it so that when projected in rapid sequence the figures appear to move.

an i ma tion (an′ə mā′shən), *n.* 1 liveliness of manner; spirit; vivacity: *She talks with great animation.* 2 an animating. 3 a being animated: *a case of suspended animation.* 4 the production of an animated cartoon.

a ni ma to (ä′ni mä′tō), *adj.* (in music) with spirit; lively. [< Italian]

an i mism (an′ə miz′əm), *n.* belief that there are living souls in trees, stones, stars, etc.

an i mist (an′ə mist), *n.* believer in some form of animism.

an i mis tic (an′ə mis′tik), *adj.* of or having to do with animism.

an i mos i ty (an′ə mos′ə tē), *n., pl.* **-ties.** keen hostile feelings; active dislike or enmity; ill will.

hat, āge, fär; let, ēqual, tėrm;
it, īce; hot, ōpen, ôrder;
oil, out; cup, pu̇t, rüle;
ch, child; ng, long; sh, she;
th, thin; ᴛʜ, then; zh, measure;

ə represents *a* in about, *e* in taken, *i* in pencil, *o* in lemon, *u* in circus.

< = from, derived from, taken from.

an i mus (an′ə məs), *n.* 1 animosity. 2 moving spirit; intention. [< Latin, spirit, feeling]

an i on (an′ī′ən), *n.* 1 a negatively charged ion that moves toward the positive pole in electrolysis. 2 atom or group of atoms having a negative charge. [< Greek, (thing) going up < *anienai* go up < *ana-* up + *ienai* go]

an i on ic (an′ī on′ik), *adj.* of or having to do with an anion or anions.

an ise (an′is), *n.* 1 plant of the same family as the parsley, grown especially for its fragrant seeds. 2 the seed. [ultimately < Greek *anison*]

an i seed (an′ə sēd′, an′is sēd′), *n.* seed of the anise, used as a flavoring in liqueurs, etc., or in medicine.

An jou (an′jü; *French* äɴ zhü′), *n.* region in W France, a former province.

An kar a (ang′kər ə), *n.* capital since 1923 of Turkey, in the central part. 2,209,000. Also, **Angora.**

an kle (ang′kəl), *n.* 1 joint that connects the foot with the leg; tarsus. 2 the slender part of the leg between this joint and the calf. [< Scandinavian (Danish) *ankel*]

an kle bone (ang′kəl bōn′), *n.* the principal bone of the ankle; talus.

an klet (ang′klit), *n.* 1 a short sock reaching just above the ankle. 2 band or chain worn around the ankle, especially as an ornament.

an ky lo sis (ang′kə lō′sis), *n.* 1 a growing together of bones as a result of disease or injury. 2 stiffness of a joint caused by this. [< Greek *ankylōsis* < *ankylos* crooked]

ann., 1 annals. 2 annual. 3 annuity. 4 years [for Latin *anni*].

an na (an′ə), *n.* in India and Pakistan: 1 a former unit of money equal to one-sixteenth of a rupee. 2 a coin equal to one anna. [< Hindustani *ānā*]

an nal ist (an′l ist), *n.* 1 writer of annals. 2 historian. 3 any keeper of records.

an nal is tic (an′l is′tik), *adj.* of an annalist or annals.

an nals (an′lz), *n.pl.* 1 historical events; history. 2 a written account of events year by year. 3 record of any proceedings. [< Latin *annales (libri)* annual (books) < *annus* year]

An nam (ə nam′, an′am), *n.* former French protectorate in Indochina, now divided between North Vietnam and South Vietnam.

An na mese (an′ə mēz′), *adj., n., pl.* **-mese.** —*adj.* of or having to do with Annam, its people, or their language. —*n.* 1 native or inhabitant of Annam. 2 language spoken by the Annamese; Vietnamese.

An na mite (an′ə mīt), *adj., n.* Annamese.

An nap o lis (ə nap′ə lis), *n.* seaport and capital of Maryland. The U.S. Naval Academy is located there. 30,000.

Ann Ar bor (an′ är′bər), city in SE Michigan. 100,000.

Anne (an), *n.* 1665-1714, queen of Great Britain and Ireland from 1702 to 1714, daughter of James II. During her reign England and Scotland were formally united under one crown.

an neal (ə nēl′), *v.t.* 1 make (glass, metals, etc.) less brittle by heating and then gradually cooling. 2 toughen or harden. [Old English *anǣlan* < *an-* on + *ǣlan* to burn] **—an neal′er,** *n.*

an ne lid (an′l id), *n.* any of a phylum of worms or wormlike animals characterized by a soft, elongated body composed of a series of similar ringlike segments. Earthworms, leeches, and various sea worms belong to this phylum. —*adj.* of or belonging to this phylum. [< Latin *annellus,* diminutive of *annulus* ring]

An nel i da (ə nel′ə də), *n.pl.* phylum of invertebrates comprising the annelids.

an nel i dan (ə nel′ə dən), *adj., n.* annelid.

an nex (*v.* ə neks′, an′eks; *n.* an′eks), *v.t.* 1 join or add to a larger or more important thing: *The United States annexed Texas in 1845.* 2 attach as a qualification, etc.: *annex a clause to a contract.* 3 add to a book or other writing; append: *a reader with a glossary annexed.* 4 INFORMAL. take as one's own; appropriate. —*n.* 1 an addition to an existing building; extension; wing. 2 appendage to a document, book, etc. 3 anything annexed; an added part. [< Latin *annexum* bound to < *ad-* to + *nectere* to bind] **—an nex′a ble,** *adj.* **—an nex′ment,** *n.*

an nex a tion (an′ek sā′shən), *n.* 1 an annexing. 2 a being annexed. 3 something annexed.

an nex a tion ist (an′ek sā′shə nist), *n.* person who favors or advocates annexation, especially of a territory.

an ni hi late (ə nī′ə lāt), *v.t.,* **-lat ed, -lat ing.** destroy completely; wipe out of existence: *The flood annihilated over thirty towns and villages.* [< Late Latin *annihilatum* brought to nothing < Latin *ad-* to + *nihil* nothing] **—an ni′hi la′tor,** *n.*

an ni hi la tion (ə nī′ə lā′shən), *n.* complete destruction.

an ni ver sar y (an′ə vėr′sər ē), *n., pl.* **-sar ies,** *adj.* —*n.* 1 the yearly return of a special date: *Your birthday is an anniversary.* 2 celebration of the yearly return of a special date. —*adj.* 1 celebrated each year at the same date. 2 having to do with an anniversary: *an anniversary dinner.* [< Latin *anniversarius* returning annually < *annus* year + *versus* turned]

an no Dom i ni (an′ō dom′ə nī; an′ō dom′ə nē), LATIN. 1 in the (specified) year since the birth of Christ. 2 (literally) in the year of the Lord. *Abbrev.:* A.D.

an no tate (an′ə tāt), *v.,* **-tat ed, -tat ing.** —*v.t.* provide with explanatory or critical notes or comments: *Shakespeare's plays are often annotated.* —*v.i.* write or insert explanatory or critical notes or comments. **—an′no ta′tor,** *n.*

an no ta tion (an′ə tā′shən), *n.* 1 an annotating. 2 a being annotated. 3 note added to a text, document, etc., to explain or criticize.

an nounce (ə nouns′), *v.,* **-nounced, -nounc ing.** —*v.t.* 1 give formal or public notice of: *announce a wedding in the papers.* See synonym study below. 2 make known the presence or arrival of: *The butler announced each guest in a loud voice.* 3 make known the readiness of: *Dinner will soon be announced.* 4 give or be evidence of: *Black clouds announced the coming thunderstorm.* 5 be an announcer for. —*v.i.* introduce programs, read news, etc., on the radio or television. [< Old French *anoncier* < Latin *annuntiare* < *ad-* to + *nuntius* messenger]

Syn. *v.t.* 1 **Announce, proclaim, declare** mean to make known formally or publicly. **Announce** means to give formal notice of something of interest to the public or a particular group: *They announced the birth of their first baby.* **Proclaim** means to announce publicly and with authority something of importance to the general public: *The President proclaimed an emergency.* **Declare** means to make known clearly and plainly, usually formally or officially: *An armistice was declared.*

an nounce ment (ə nouns′mənt), *n.* 1 act of announcing: *the announcement of a meeting.* 2 a public or formal notice: *Announcements of marriages often appear in the newspapers.*

an nounc er (ə noun′sər), *n.* 1 person or thing that announces. 2 person who makes announcements, introduces programs, reads news, etc., on a radio or television program.

an noy (ə noi′), *v.t.* cause uneasiness to, especially by repeated acts; make somewhat angry; trouble; vex: *I was annoyed at the interruption. I was annoyed with you for interrupting.* See **worry** for synonym study. [< Old French *enoier* < Late Latin *inodiare* make loathsome < Latin *in odio* in hatred] **—an noy′er,** *n.*

an noy ance (ə noi′əns), *n.* 1 a being annoyed; feeling of dislike or trouble; vexation. 2 act of annoying. 3 something that causes uneasiness or discomfort; nuisance.

an noy ing (ə noi′ing), *adj.* disturbing; troublesome. **—an noy′ing ly,** *adv.* **—an noy′ing ness,** *n.*

an nu al (an′yü əl), *adj.* 1 coming once a year: *A birthday is an annual event.* 2 in a year; for a year: *an annual salary of $8000.* 3 lasting for a whole year: *the earth's annual course around the sun.* 4 living but one year or season: *Corn and beans are annual plants.* —*n.* 1 plant that lives but one year or growing season. 2 book, journal, etc., published once a year. [< Late Latin *annualis* < Latin *annus* year] **—an′nu al ly,** *adv.*

annual ring, any of the concentric rings of wood seen when the stem of a tree or shrub is cut across; growth ring. Each ring shows one year's growth.

an nu i tant (ə nü′ə tənt, ə nyü′ə tənt), *n.* person who receives an annuity.

an nu i ty (ə nü′ə tē, ə nyü′ə tē), *n., pl.* **-ties.** 1 sum of money paid every year or at certain regular times. 2 right to receive or duty to pay such a sum of money. 3 investment that provides a fixed yearly income during one's lifetime or for a specified time. [< Medieval Latin *annuitatem* < Latin *annuus* yearly < *annus* year]

an nul (ə nul′), *v.t.,* **-nulled, -nul ling.** 1 destroy the force of; make void; nullify: *The judge annulled the contract because one of the signers was too young.* 2 do away with; cancel: *annul a plan.* 3 reduce to nothing; annihilate. [< Late Latin *annullare* < Latin *ad-* to + *nullus* none]

an nu lar (an′yə lər), *adj.* of or like a ring; ring-shaped; ringed. **—an′nu lar ly,** *adv.*

annular eclipse, eclipse of the sun in which the moon covers the sun incompletely, leaving a narrow uneclipsed ring which surrounds the dark moon.

an nu la tion (an′yə lā′shən), *n.* 1 formation of rings. 2 a ringlike structure.

an nul ment (ə nul′mənt), *n.* 1 act of annulling. 2 condition or fact of being annulled. 3 judgment declaring that a marriage was void from the beginning.

an nu lus (an′yə ləs), *n., pl.* **-li** (-lī), **-lus es.** a ringlike part, band, or space. [< Latin, ring]

an nun ci ate (ə nun′sē āt, ə nun′shē āt), *v.t.*, **-at ed, -at ing.** make known; announce. [< Latin *annuntiatum* announced]

an nun ci a tion (ə nun′sē ā′shən, ə nun′shē ā′shən), *n.* 1 announcement. 2 **the Annunciation, a** (in the Bible) the announcement by the angel Gabriel to the Virgin Mary that she was to be the mother of Christ. **b** Annunciation Day.

Annunciation Day, March 25, a church holiday in commemoration of the Annunciation; Lady Day.

an nun ci a tor (ə nun′sē ā′tər, ə nun′shē ā′tər), *n.* 1 an indicator for showing where a signal comes from. 2 person or thing that announces.

A No. 1, INFORMAL. A one.

an ode (an′ōd), *n.* 1 a positive electrode. Electrons flow from the cathode to the anode, producing an electric current. The carbon of a dry cell and the plate of a vacuum tube are anodes. 2 the positive pole of any source of current. [< Greek *anodos* a way up]

an od ize (an′ə dīz), *v.t.*, **-ized, -iz ing.** coat the surface of (a metal) with a protective film by making it the anode of a cell and subjecting it to the action of an electrolyte.

an o dyne (an′ə dīn), *n.* 1 medicine or drug that lessens pain. 2 anything that soothes. *—adj.* 1 lessening pain. 2 soothing. [< Greek *anōdynos* painless]

a noint (ə noint′), *v.t.* 1 apply an ointment, oil, or similar substance to; cover or smear with oil, etc.: *Anoint sunburned arms with cold cream.* 2 consecrate by applying oil. 3 rub or smear with any other substance or liquid. [< Old French *enoint* smeared on < Latin *inunctum* < *in-* on + *unguere* to smear] **—a noint′er,** *n.* **—a noint′ment,** *n.*

anointing of the sick, extreme unction.

a nom a lous (ə nom′ə ləs), *adj.* 1 deviating from the rule or recognized standards; irregular; abnormal. 2 (in biology) differing from the type. [< Greek *anōmalos* < *an-* not + *homalos* even] **—a nom′a lous ly,** *adv.* **—a nom′a lous ness,** *n.*

a nom a ly (ə nom′ə lē), *n., pl.* **-lies.** 1 something anomalous: *A bird that cannot fly is an anomaly.* 2 deviation from the rule; irregularity.

a non (ə non′), *adv.* ARCHAIC. 1 in a little while; soon. 2 at another time; again. 3 **ever and anon,** now and then. [Old English *on ān* into one]

anon., anonymous.

an o nym i ty (an′ə nim′ə tē), *n.* condition or quality of being anonymous.

a non y mous (ə non′ə məs), *adj.* 1 by or from a person whose name is not known or given: *an anonymous letter.* 2 having no name; whose name is not known; nameless: *This book was written by an anonymous author.* [< Greek *anōnymos* < *an-* without + *onyma* name] **—a non′y mous ly,** *adv.* **—a non′y mous ness,** *n.*

a noph e les (ə nof′ə lēz′), *n., pl.* **-les.** any of a genus of mosquitoes that transmit the protozoans causing malaria to human beings. [< Greek *anōphelēs* useless, harmful]

a no rak (ä′nə räk′), *n.* a heavy jacket with a fur hood, worn in arctic regions. [< Eskimo (Greenland) *ánorâq* clothing]

an oth er (ə nuᴛʜ′ər), *adj.* 1 one more: *Have another glass of milk.* 2 not the same; different: *That is another matter entirely.* 3 similar in some respect but not actually the same: *That singer is another Caruso.* *—pron.* 1 one more: *I ate a bar of candy and then asked for another.* 2 a different one: *I don't like this book; give me another.* 3 the other: *They walked out, one after another.* [for *an other*]

a nox i a (a nok′sē ə), *n.* insufficiency of oxygen in the body tissues. [< New Latin]

ans., 1 answer. 2 answered.

An schluss (än′shlůs), *n.* GERMAN. a union, especially that of Germany and Austria in 1938 under Hitler.

an swer (an′sər), *v.t.* 1 speak or write in response to; reply to: *He finally answered my question.* 2 act or move in response to: *She answered the doorbell.* 3 satisfy the needs, requirements, wishes, etc., of; serve: *This will answer your purpose.* 4 make a defense against (a charge). 5 find the solution to: *answer a problem.* *—v.i.* 1 speak or write in response to a question; make answer; reply: *I asked him a question, but he would not answer.* See synonym study below. 2 reply or respond by act or motion; respond: *She knocked on the door, but no one answered.* 3 meet one's needs, requirements, wishes, etc.; serve: *On the picnic, a newspaper answered for a tablecloth.* 4 be responsible *(for): The bus driver must answer for the safety of the children in his bus.* 5 be similar *(to);* correspond: *This dog answers to the description of the one we lost.* 6 **answer back,** INFORMAL. reply in a rude, saucy way. *—n.* 1 words spoken or written in return to a question: *She gave a quick answer.* 2 gesture or act done in return: *A nod was her only answer.* 3 solution to a problem: *What is the correct answer to this algebra problem?* 4 a reply to a charge or accusation; defense. [Old English *andswaru* < *and-* against + *swerian* swear] **—an′swer er,** *n.*

Syn. *v.i.* 1 **Answer, reply, respond** mean to say something in return to something said, asked, or demanded. **Answer** is the general word meaning to speak or write in return: *I called, but no one answered.* **Reply** is used in more formal style or to suggest more formal answering, as with thought and care: *I sent in my application, and the university replied immediately.* **Respond,** formal in this sense, suggests giving the answer hoped for or counted on: *When we requested information and instructions, the chairman responded.*

an swer a ble (an′sər ə bəl), *adj.* 1 responsible or accountable (*to* someone *for* something): *The club treasurer is held answerable to the club for the money given to her.* 2 that can be answered: *an answerable question.* **—an′swer a ble ness,** *n.* **—an′swer a bly,** *adv.*

ant (ant), *n.* any of a family of small insects that live together in tunnels burrowed in the ground or in wood in highly organized colonies of from dozens of individuals to half a million or more. Ants are black, brown, reddish, or yellowish, and belong to the same order as the bees and wasps. [Old English *ǣmete*] **—ant′like′,** *adj.*

ant-, *prefix.* form of **anti-** before vowels and *h,* as in *antacid.*

-ant, *suffix forming adjectives and nouns from verbs.* 1 that ___s; ___ing: *Compliant = that complies* or *complying.* 2 one that ___s: *Assistant = one that assists.* [< Old French < Latin *-antem*]

ant., antonym.

ant ac id (ant′as′id), *n.* substance that neutralizes acids, as baking soda and magnesia. *—adj.* counteracting acidity.

an tag o nism (an tag′ə niz′əm), *n.* activity or relation of contending parties or conflicting forces; active opposition; hostility: *the antagonism between good and evil.*

an tag o nist (an tag′ə nist), *n.* 1 person who fights, struggles, or contends against another; adversary; opponent. See **opponent** for synonym study. 2 a muscle which resists or counteracts another muscle, relaxing while the opposite one contracts, or conversely.

an tag o nis tic (an tag′ə nis′tik), *adj.* actively opposed to each other; opposing; hostile. **—an tag′o nis′ti cal ly,** *adv.*

an tag o nize (an tag′ə nīz), *v.t.*, **-nized, -niz ing.** 1 make an enemy of; arouse dislike in: *Your unkind remarks antagonized people who had been your friends.* 2 oppose actively. 3 counteract or neutralize. [< Greek *antagōnizesthai* < *anti-* against + *agōn* contest] **—an tag′o niz′er,** *n.*

ant arc tic (ant′ärk′tik, ant′är′tik), *adj.* at or near the South Pole; of the south polar region. *—n.* **the Antarctic,** the south polar region. [< Greek *antarktikos* opposite the arctic < *anti-* opposite + *arktikos* arctic]

Ant arc ti ca (ant′ärk′tə kə, ant′är′tə kə), *n.* continent around or near the South Pole, comprising principally a centrally located high plateau covered by an ice sheet. 5,000,000 sq. mi.

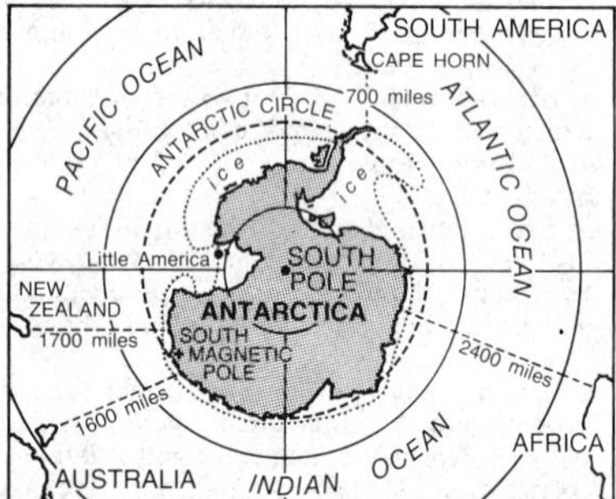

antarctic circle or **Antarctic Circle,** the imaginary boundary of the south polar region, running parallel to the equator at 23 degrees 28 minutes (23°28′) north of the South Pole.

Antarctic Continent, Antarctica.

Antarctic Ocean, the ocean of the south polar region.

Antarctic Zone, region between the antarctic circle and the South Pole, including the Antarctic Ocean and Antarctica.

An tar es (an ter′ēz, an tar′ēz), *n.* a red star of the first magnitude, the brightest in the constellation Scorpio.

ant bear, 1 a large South American anteater having long front claws, a very slender head, and a shaggy, gray coat with a black band on the breast. 2 aardvark.

an te (an′tē), *n., v.,* **-ted** or **-teed, -te ing.** *—n.* stake in the game of poker that every player must put up before receiving a hand or drawing new cards. *—v.i.* **ante up, a** (in poker) put in one's stake. **b** INFORMAL. pay one's share. *—v.t.* INFORMAL. 1 put (one's stake) into the pool. 2 pay (one's share). [< *ante-*]

ante-, *prefix.* 1 before: *Antedate* = *to date before.* 2 in front of: *Anteroom* = *a room in front of (another).* [< Latin]

ant eat er (ant′ē′tər), *n.* any of various mammals with long, slender heads and snouts, that eat ants and termites which they catch with their long, sticky tongues. Aardvarks, sloths, armadillos, and echidnas are also anteaters.

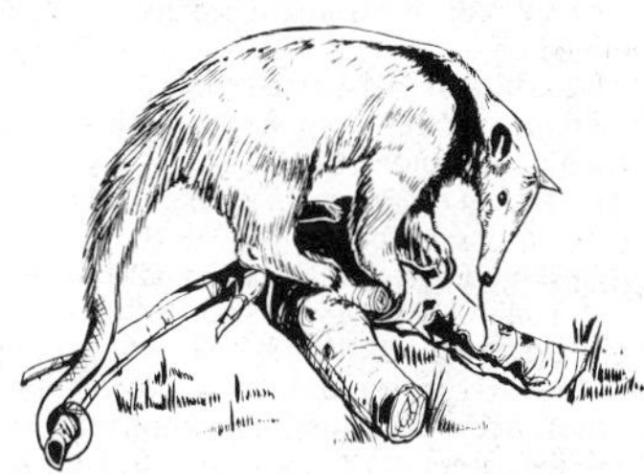

anteater—This species is about 3½ ft. long, including the tail.

an te-bel lum (an′ti bel′əm), *adj.* 1 before the war. 2 before the American Civil War. [< Latin *ante bellum* before the war]

an te ced ence (an′tə sēd′ns), *n.* 1 a going before; precedence. 2 the seeming motion of a planet from east to west.

an te ced ent (an′tə sēd′nt), *n.* 1 the noun, noun phrase, or clause that is referred to by a pronoun or relative adverb. In "This is the house that Jack built," *house* is the antecedent of *that.* 2 a previous thing or event; something happening before and leading up to another. 3 in mathematics: **a** the first term of a ratio. **b** the first or third term in a proportion. 4 **antecedents,** *pl.* **a** past life or history: *No one knew the antecedents of the mysterious stranger.* **b** ancestors. —*adj.* 1 coming or happening before; preceding; previous. 2 functioning as an antecedent: *an antecedent clause.* [< Latin *antecedentem* going before < *ante-* before + *cedere* go] **—an′te ced′ent ly,** *adv.*

an te cham ber (an′ti chām′bər), *n.* anteroom.

an te date (an′ti dāt), *v.t.,* **-dat ed, -dat ing.** 1 be or happen before; precede in time: *Radio antedated television.* 2 give an earlier date to (a document, event, etc.).

an te di lu vi an (an′ti də lü′vē ən), *adj.* 1 very old or old-fashioned; antiquated. 2 belonging to times before the Flood. —*n.* 1 a very old or old-fashioned person. 2 person who lived before the Flood. [< *ante-* + Latin *diluvium* deluge]

an te lope (an′tl ōp), *n., pl.* **-lope** or **-lopes.** 1 any of certain cud-chewing hoofed mammals of Africa and Asia related to the goat and cow but resembling the deer in appearance, grace, and speed. Antelopes usually have a single pair of hollow horns that curve backward and do not fork or branch. 2 pronghorn. 3 leather made from the hide of any of these animals. [< Medieval Latin *antilopus* < Late Greek *antholops*]

an te me rid i em (an′ti mə rid′ē əm), LATIN. before noon. *Abbrev.:* a.m., A.M.

an te na tal (an′ti nā′tl), *adj.* happening or existing before birth; prenatal: *antenatal care.*

an ten na (an ten′ə), *n., pl.* **-ten nae, -ten nas.** 1 one of the long, slender, segmented feelers on the heads of insects and certain other arthropods, such as centipedes and lobsters. Insects have one pair of antennae; crustaceans have two pairs. Most antennae function primarily as organs of touch, but some are sensitive to odors and other stimuli. 2 the aerial of a radio or television set. [< Latin, sail yard]

an ten nae (an ten′ē), *n.* pl. of **antenna.**

an ten nule (an ten′yül), *n.* a small antenna or similar organ.

an te pe nult (an′ti pē′nult), *n.* the third from the last syllable in a word. In *an ter i or, ter* is the antepenult.

an te pe nul ti mate (an′ti pi nul′tə mit), *adj.* third from the end; last but two. —*n.* antepenult.

an ter i or (an tir′ē ər), *adj.* 1 more to the front; fore: *The anterior part of a fish contains the head and gills.* 2 going before; earlier; previous. [< Latin < comparative of *ante* before, on analogy of *posterior*] **—an ter′i or ly,** *adv.*

an te room (an′ti rüm′, an′ti rům′), *n.* a small room leading to a larger or more important one; waiting room; antechamber.

an them (an′thəm), *n.* 1 song of praise, devotion, or patriotism. 2 piece of sacred music, usually with words from some passage in the Bible. 3 hymn sung in alternate parts; antiphon. [Old English *antefn* < Late Latin *antiphona* antiphon. Doublet of ANTIPHON.]

an ther (an′thər), *n.* the part of the stamen of a flower that bears the pollen. It is usually a double-celled sac situated at the end of the filament. See **stamen** for diagram. [< Greek *antherós* flowery < *anthos* flower]

an ther id i al (an′thə rid′ē əl), *adj.* of an antheridium.

an ther id i um (an′thə rid′ē əm), *n., pl.* **-ther id i a** (-thə rid′ē ə). the part of a fern, moss, etc., that produces male reproductive cells.

ant hill, the part of an ant's nest above ground.

an tho cy a nin (an′thə sī′ə nən), *n.* any of a group of pigments in the cell sap of plants, which produce the deep red, blue, lavender, and purple colors of petals, fruits, etc. [< Greek *anthos* flower + *kyanos* blue]

an thol o gist (an thol′ə jist), *n.* person who makes an anthology.

an thol o gy (an thol′ə jē), *n., pl.* **-gies.** collection of poems or prose selections, usually from various authors. [< Greek *anthologia* collection of flowers < *anthos* flower + *legein* gather]

An tho ny (an′thə nē, an′tə nē *for 1 and 2;* an′thə nē *for 3*), *n.* 1 **Saint,** A.D. 251-356?, hermit in Egypt who founded Christian monasticism. 2 **Saint,** 1195-1231, Franciscan monk of Padua. 3 **Susan B.,** 1820-1906, American leader in work for women's suffrage.

an tho zo an (an′thə zō′ən), *n.* any of a class of marine coelenterates with radial segments, including the sea anemone, coral, and other polyps. —*adj.* of or belonging to this class. [< Greek *anthos* flower + *zōia* animals]

an thra cene (an′thrə sēn′), *n.* a colorless, crystalline compound used in making alizarin dyes. It is a complex hydrocarbon obtained in distilling coal tar. *Formula:* $C_{14}H_{10}$

an thra cite (an′thrə sīt), *n.* coal that burns with very little smoke and flame; hard coal. It consists almost entirely of carbon. [< Greek *anthrakitis,* name of a gem < *anthrax* live coal, charcoal]

hat, āge, fär; let, ēqual, tėrm;
it, īce; hot, ōpen, ôrder;
oil, out; cup, pu̇t, rüle;
ch, child; ng, long; sh, she;
th, thin; ᴛʜ, then; zh, measure;

ə represents *a* in about, *e* in taken, *i* in pencil, *o* in lemon, *u* in circus.

< = from, derived from, taken from.

an thra cit ic (an′thrə sit′ik), *adj.* of or like anthracite.

an thrax (an′thraks), *n.* an infectious, often fatal, disease of cattle, sheep, etc., that may be transmitted to human beings. [< Greek, carbuncle, live coal]

anthropo-, *combining form.* man; human being; human: *Anthropology* = *the study of man.* [< Greek *anthrōpos*]

an thro po cen tric (an′thrə pə sen′trik), *adj.* 1 regarding man as the central fact, and his existence, welfare, etc., as the ultimate aim, of the universe. 2 interpreting all things in the universe in terms of man and his values.

an thro poid (an′thrə poid), *adj.* 1 (of certain apes) manlike; resembling man. Anthropoid apes have no tail and lack cheek pouches. 2 (of human beings) apelike. —*n.* a manlike ape. Chimpanzees, gorillas, orangutans, and gibbons are anthropoids.

an thro poid al (an′thrə poi′dl), *adj.* of anthropoid nature or structure.

an thro po log i cal (an′thrə pə loj′ə kəl), *adj.* of anthropology. **—an′thro po log′i cal ly,** *adv.*

an thro pol o gist (an′thrə pol′ə jist), *n.* an expert in anthropology.

an thro pol o gy (an′thrə pol′ə jē), *n.* science of man, dealing with his physical characteristics, with the origin and development of races, and with the cultures, customs, and beliefs of mankind.

an thro po met ric (an′thrə pə met′rik), *adj.* of or having to do with anthropometry. **—an′thro po met′ri cal ly,** *adv.*

an thro po met ri cal (an′thrə pə met′rə kəl), *adj.* anthropometric.

an thro pom e try (an′thrə pom′ə trē), *n.* branch of anthropology that deals with measurement of the human body.

an thro po mor phic (an′thrə pə môr′fik), *adj.* attributing human form or qualities to gods, animals, or things. **—an′thro po mor′phi cal ly,** *adv.*

an thro po mor phism (an′thrə pə môr′fiz′əm), *n.* the attribution of human form or qualities to gods, animals, or things.

an thro po mor phize (an′thrə pə môr′fīz), *v.t., v.i.,* **-phized, -phiz ing.** attribute human form or qualities to animals, objects, etc.

an ti (an′tī, an′tē), *n., pl.* **-tis,** *prep.* INFORMAL. —*n.* person opposed to some plan, idea, political party, etc. —*prep.* opposed to; against: *anti everything new.* [< *anti-*]

anti-, *prefix.* 1 against ___; opposed to ___: *Antiaircraft* = *against aircraft.* 2 not ___; the opposite of ___: *Antisocial* = *the opposite of social.* 3 rival ___: *Antipope* = *rival pope.* 4 reducing or counteracting ___: *Antifriction* = *reducing or counteracting friction.* 5 preventing, curing, or alleviating ___: *Antiscorbutic* = *preventing or curing* *scurvy.* Also, **ant-** before vowels and *h.* [< Greek]

➔ **Anti-** is usually pronounced (an′ti) before consonants and (an′tē) before vowels, although (an′tī) is often used for emphasis.

an ti air craft (an′tē er′kraft′, an′tē ar′kraft′), *adj.* used in defense against enemy aircraft.

an ti-A mer i can (an′tē ə mer′ə kən), *adj.* opposed to the interests or the people of the United States.

an ti bac ter i al (an′ti bak tir′ē əl), *adj.* counteracting or destroying bacteria.

an ti bi o sis (an′ti bī ō′sis), *n.* an association between organisms which is detrimental to one of them.

an ti bi ot ic (an′ti bī ot′ik), *n.* substance produced by a living organism, especially a bacterium or a fungus, that destroys or weakens harmful microorganisms. Penicillin, tetracycline, and streptomycin are antibiotics. *—adj.* of or being an antibiotic.

an ti bod y (an′ti bod′ē), *n., pl.* **-bod ies.** a protein substance produced in the blood or tissues that destroys or weakens bacteria or neutralizes poisons of organic origin. Antibodies are formed in response to specific antigens.

an tic (an′tik), *n.* 1 Usually, **antics,** *pl.* a funny gesture or action; silly trick; caper: *the antics of a clown.* 2 ARCHAIC. clown. *—adj.* grotesque; odd. [< Italian *antico* old < Latin *antiquus.* Doublet of ANTIQUE.]

An ti christ (an′ti krīst′), *n.* 1 (in the Bible) the last great enemy or opponent of Christ and Christianity, who will spread destruction through the world but will be crushed for eternity at the second coming of Christ. 2 **antichrist, a** person who denies or opposes Christ. **b** a false Christ.

an tic i pate (an tis′ə pāt), *v.t.,* **-pat ed, -pat ing.** 1 look forward to; expect: *We anticipated a good vacation in the mountains.* See **expect** for synonym study. 2 do before others do; be ahead of in doing: *The Chinese anticipated the European discovery of gunpowder.* 3 take care of ahead of time; consider in advance: *The host anticipated all his guest's wishes.* 4 be before (another) in thinking, acting, etc. 5 consider or mention before the proper time. 6 cause to happen sooner; hasten. [< Latin *anticipatum* taken beforehand < *ante-* before + *capere* take] **—an tic′i pa′tor,** *n.*

an tic i pa tion (an tis′ə pā′shən), *n.* 1 act of anticipating; looking forward to; expectation. 2 enjoyment or celebration of an event, experience, etc., in advance.

an tic i pa to ry (an tis′ə pə tôr′ē, an tis′ə pə tōr′ē), *adj.* anticipating. **—an tic′i pa to′ri ly,** *adv.*

an ti cler i cal (an′ti kler′ə kəl), *adj.* opposed to the influence of the church and clergy, especially in public affairs. *—n.* person who is anticlerical.

an ti cler i cal ism (an′ti kler′ə kə liz′əm), *n.* opposition to the influence of the church and clergy, especially in public affairs.

an ti cli mac tic (an′ti klī mak′tik), *adj.* of or like an anticlimax.

an ti cli max (an′ti klī′maks), *n.* 1 an abrupt descent from the important to the trivial or unimportant. EXAMPLE: "Alas! Alas! what shall I do? I've lost my wife and best hat, too!" 2 descent (in importance, interest, etc.) contrasting sharply with a previous rise or high point.

an ti cli nal (an′ti klī′nl), *adj.* of or like an anticline.

an ti cline (an′ti klīn), *n.* (in geology) a fold of rock strata that bends downward on both sides from its center. [< *anti-* + Greek *klinein* to lean]

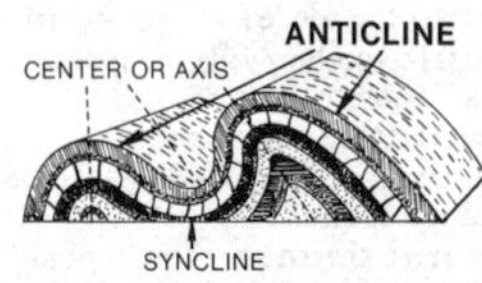

an ti clock wise (an′ti klok′wīz′), *adv., adj.* counterclockwise.

an ti co ag u lant (an′ti kō ag′yə lənt), *n.* substance that prevents or slows up the clotting of blood. *—adj.* preventing or delaying coagulation.

an ti co lo ni al (an′ti kə lō′nē əl), *adj.* opposed to colonialism.

an ti co lo ni al ism (an′ti kə lō′nē ə liz′əm), *n.* opposition to colonialism.

an ti cy clone (an′ti sī′klōn), *n.* storm or winds moving spirally outward from a center of high pressure, which also moves. The motion of an anticyclone is clockwise in the Northern Hemisphere and counterclockwise in the Southern.

an ti cy clon ic (an′ti sī klon′ik), *adj.* of or like an anticyclone.

an ti dot al (an′ti dō′tl), *adj.* like an antidote; serving as an antidote. **—an′ti dot′al ly,** *adv.*

an ti dote (an′ti dōt), *n.* 1 medicine or remedy that counteracts the effects of a poison: *Milk is an antidote for some poisons.* 2 remedy for any evil: *Prosperity is a good antidote for political unrest.* [< Greek *antidoton* < *anti-* against + *didonai* give]

An tie tam (an tē′təm), *n.* creek in NW Maryland near which a major battle of the Civil War was fought in 1862 between Lee and McClellan, resulting in Lee's retreat.

An ti fed er al ist (an′ti fed′ər ə list), *n.* U.S. member of a political party that opposed the adoption of the Constitution before 1789.

an ti freeze (an′ti frēz′), *n.* liquid with a low freezing point added to the cooling medium in the radiator of an internal-combustion engine to prevent the cooling system from freezing.

an ti fric tion (an′ti frik′shən), *adj.* preventing or reducing friction.

an ti gen (an′tə jən), *n.* any protein substance that causes the body to produce antibodies to counteract this substance. Antigens include toxins, bacterial cells, foreign blood cells, etc.

an ti gen ic (an′tə jen′ik), *adj.* of or like an antigen. **—an′ti gen′i cal ly,** *adv.*

An tig o ne (an tig′ə nē), *n.* (in Greek legends) the daughter of Oedipus who gave her dead brother a proper burial, though doing so meant her own death.

an ti grav i ty (an′ti grav′ə tē), *n.* any force that opposes or neutralizes gravity.

An ti gua (an tē′gwə, an tē′gə), *n.* island in the West Indies, southeast of Puerto Rico. 62,000 pop.; 108 sq. mi.

an ti her o (an′ti hir′ō), *n., pl.* **-her oes.** a main character in a novel, play, etc., who has none of the qualities normally expected of a hero.

an ti his ta mine (an′ti his′tə mēn′, an′ti his′tə mən), *n.* any of various drugs that inhibit or relieve the effects of histamine in the body, used in the treatment of colds and allergies.

an ti-in tel lec tu al (an′tē in′tə lek′chü əl), *adj.* opposed to intellectuals or to intellectualism. *—n.* an anti-intellectual person.

an ti-in tel lec tu al ism (an′tē in′tə lek′chü ə liz′əm), *n.* opposition to intellectualism or to intellectuals.

an ti knock (an′ti nok′), *n.* substance added to the fuel of an internal-combustion engine to reduce noise caused by too rapid combustion.

An ti-Leb a non Mountains (an′ti leb′ə nən), mountain range on the border of Syria and Lebanon.

An til les (an til′ēz), *n. pl.* chain of islands in the West Indies consisting of the Greater Antilles and Lesser Antilles. See **Caribbean Sea** for map.

an ti lo ga rithm (an′ti lô′gə riᴛʜ′əm, an′ti log′ə riᴛʜ′əm), *n.* number corresponding to a given logarithm. The antilogarithms of the logarithms 1, 2, and 3 are 10, 100, and 1000.

an ti ma cas sar (an′ti mə kas′ər), *n.* a small covering to protect the back or arms of a chair, sofa, etc., against soiling. [< *anti-* against + *Macassar,* a hair oil]

an ti mag net ic (an′ti mag net′ik), *adj.* (of a watch, etc.) made with materials that resist magnetization so as to prevent a magnetic field from affecting the speed of the moving parts.

an ti mat ter (an′ti mat′ər), *n.* matter composed of antiparticles.

an ti mi cro bi al (an′ti mī krō′bē əl), *adj.* destroying or inhibiting the growth of microbes. *—n.* an antimicrobial drug or agent.

an ti mis sile (an′ti mis′əl), *adj.* designed or used to intercept and destroy enemy missiles: *an antimissile missile.*

an ti mo ni al (an′tə mō′nē əl), *adj.* containing antimony in combination.

an ti mo ny (an′tə mō′nē), *n.* a brittle, silver-white, metallic element with a crystalline texture, that occurs chiefly in combination with other elements. Antimony is used to make alloys harder, and its compounds are used to make medicines, pigments, and glass. *Symbol:* Sb; *atomic number* 51. See pages 326 and 327 for table. [< Medieval Latin *antimonium*]

an ti neu tron (an′ti nü′tron, an′ti nyü′tron), *n.* antiparticle of the neutron.

An ti och (an′tē ok), *n.* city in S Turkey, the capital of ancient Syria from 300 to 64 B.C. 58,000.

An ti o chus III (an tī′ə kəs), 241?-187 B.C., king of Syria from 223 to 187 B.C. who fought many battles with the Romans.

an ti par ti cle (an′ti pär′tə kəl), *n.* unit of matter such as a positron, antiproton, or antineutron, corresponding in mass and properties to an elementary particle but with an opposite electrical charge or opposite magnetic properties. When an antiparticle collides with a corresponding particle, they destroy each other, thereby releasing great energy.

an ti pas to (an′ti pas′tō; *Italian* än′tē päs′tō), *n., pl.* **-tos.** appetizer or hors d'oeuvre consisting of fish, meats, peppers, olives, etc. [< Italian]

an tip a thet ic (an tip′ə thet′ik, an′ti pə thet′ik), *adj.* having antipathy; contrary or opposed in nature or disposition. **—an tip′a thet′i cal ly,** *adv.*

an tip a thy (an tip′ə thē), *n., pl.* **-thies.** 1 a strong or fixed dislike; feeling against; aversion: *an antipathy to snakes.* 2 object of aversion or dislike. [< Greek *antipatheia* < *anti-* against + *pathos* feeling]

an ti per son nel (an′ti pėr′sə nel′), *adj.* directed against enemy troops rather than mechanized equipment, supplies, etc.: *antipersonnel weapons.*

an ti phon (an′tə fon), *n.* 1 psalm, hymn, or prayer sung or chanted in alternate parts. 2 verses sung or chanted in response in a church service. [< Late Latin *antiphona* < Greek *antiphōnos* sounding in response < *anti-* opposed to + *phōnē* sound. Doublet of ANTHEM.]

an tiph o nal (an tif′ə nəl), *adj.* like an antiphon; sung or chanted alternately. *—n.* book of antiphons. **—an tiph′o nal ly,** *adv.*

an tip o dal (an tip′ə dəl), *adj.* 1 on the opposite side of the earth. 2 directly opposite; exactly contrary.

an ti pode (an′tə pōd), *n. sing. of* **antipodes.** anything exactly opposite; direct opposite.

an tip o de an (an tip′ə dē′ən), *adj.* antipodal.

an tip o des (an tip′ə dēz′), *n.pl.* 1 two places on directly opposite sides of the earth: *The North Pole and the South Pole are antipodes.* 2 *pl. or sing. in use.* a place on the opposite side of the earth. 3 two opposites or contraries: *Forgiveness and revenge are antipodes.* 4 *pl. or sing. in use.* the direct opposite. [< Greek, with feet opposite < *anti-* + *pous, podos* foot]

an ti pope (an′ti pōp′), *n.* a person claiming the papacy in opposition to a canonically chosen pope.

an ti pov er ty (an′ti pov′ər tē), *adj.* U.S. designed to combat poverty on a large scale: *an antipoverty program.*

an ti pro ton (an′ti prō′ton), *n.* antiparticle of the proton. Antiprotons are created when a proton hits a neutron.

an ti py ret ic (an′ti pī ret′ik), *adj.* checking or preventing fever. *—n.* any medicine or remedy for checking or reducing fever.

an ti quar i an (an′tə kwer′ē ən), *adj.* of or having to do with antiquities or antiquaries: *the antiquarian section of a museum.* *—n.* antiquary.

an ti quar y (an′tə kwer′ē), *n., pl.* **-quar ies.** student or collector of relics from ancient times.

an ti quate (an′tə kwāt), *v.t.,* **-quat ed, -quat ing.** make old-fashioned or out-of-date. **—an′ti qua′tion,** *n.*

an ti quat ed (an′tə kwā′tid), *adj.* 1 old-fashioned; out-of-date. 2 too old for work or service.

an tique (an tēk′), *adj.* 1 old-fashioned; out-of-date: *She wore an antique gown to the costume party.* 2 of or belonging to ancient Greece or Rome. 3 of times long ago; old; ancient: *antique heroes.* 4 of or belonging to a distinctly earlier age than the present: *This antique chair was made in 1750.* 5 in the style of times long ago: *An antique gold finish is dull and slightly greenish.* *—n.* 1 something belonging to an earlier age; a piece of china, silver, furniture, etc., made long ago. 2 antique style, usually of Greek or Roman art: *a statue imitating the antique.* 3 style of type. **This sentence is set in antique.** [< Latin *antiquus* old, ancient < *ante* before. Doublet of ANTIC.] **—an tique′ly,** *adv.* **—an tique′ness,** *n.*

an tiq ui ty (an tik′wə tē), *n., pl.* **-ties.** 1 great age; oldness. 2 times long ago, especially the period from 5000 B.C. to A.D. 476. 3 the people of ancient times. 4 **antiquities,** *pl.* **a** relics, monuments, or records of ancient times. **b** customs and life of ancient times.

an ti scor bu tic (an′ti skôr byü′tik), *adj.* preventing or curing scurvy. *—n.* remedy for scurvy.

an ti-Sem ite (an′ti sem′īt), *n.* person who shows dislike or hatred of Jews.

an ti-Se mit ic (an′ti sə mit′ik), *adj.* prejudiced against Jews.

an ti-Sem i tism (an′ti sem′ə tiz′əm), *n.* prejudice against Jews.

an ti sep sis (an′tə sep′sis), *n.* 1 prevention of infection. 2 method or medicine that prevents infection.

an ti sep tic (an′tə sep′tik), *n.* substance that prevents the growth of germs that cause infection. Iodine, peroxide, Mercurochrome, alcohol, and boric acid are antiseptics. *—adj.* 1 preventing infection by stopping the growth of disease germs. 2 of, having to do with, or using antiseptics. 3 having a sterilized or sterile quality; cold, barren, lifeless, etc.: *an antiseptic nursery.* **—an′ti sep′ti cal ly,** *adv.*

an ti ser um (an′ti sir′əm), *n., pl.* **-ser ums, -ser a** (-sir′ə). serum containing antibodies that are specific for certain antigens.

an ti slav er y (an′ti slā′vər ē), *adj.* opposed to slavery.

an ti so cial (an′ti sō′shəl), *adj.* 1 opposed to the principles upon which society is based: *Murder and stealing are antisocial acts.* 2 against the general welfare: *antisocial behavior.* 3 opposed to friendly relationship and normal companionship with others; not sociable.

an ti spas mod ic (an′ti spaz mod′ik), *adj.* preventing or relieving spasms.

an ti tank (an′ti tangk′), *adj.* designed for use against armored vehicles, especially tanks: *antitank mines.*

an tith e sis (an tith′ə sis), *n., pl.* **-ses** (-sēz′). 1 the direct opposite: *Hate is the antithesis of love.* 2 the expression in balanced constructions of opposed ideas. EXAMPLE: "To err is human; to forgive, divine." 3 either of the two ideas contrasted. 4 opposition; contrast *(of* or *between): antithesis of theory and fact.* 5 anything opposed, or forming a contrast. [< Greek < *anti-* against + *tithenai* to set]

an ti thet ic (an′tə thet′ik), *adj.* 1 of or using antithesis. 2 contrasted; opposite. **—an′ti thet′i cal ly,** *adv.*

an ti thet i cal (an′tə thet′ə kəl), *adj.* antithetic.

an ti tox ic (an′ti tok′sik), *adj.* 1 counteracting toxins or diseases caused by toxins. 2 having to do with or like an antitoxin.

an ti tox in (an′ti tok′sən), *n.* 1 antibody formed in response to the presence of a toxin to prevent or reduce the effects of that toxin. 2 serum containing antitoxin, injected into a person to make him immune to a specific disease or to treat him if already infected.

an ti trades (an′ti trādz′), *n.pl.* 1 (at tropical latitudes) winds that blow in a direction opposite to the trade winds on a level above them. 2 (at temperate latitudes) the prevailing westerlies.

an ti trust (an′ti trust′), *adj.* opposed to trusts or other business monopolies: *antitrust legislation.*

an ti ven in (an′ti ven′ən), *n.* serum containing an antitoxin to snake venom.

hat, āge, fär; let, ēqual, tėrm;
it, īce; hot, ōpen, ôrder;
oil, out; cup, pu̇t, rüle;
ch, child; ng, long; sh, she;
th, thin; ᴛʜ, then; zh, measure;

ə represents *a* in about, *e* in taken, *i* in pencil, *o* in lemon, *u* in circus.

< = from, derived from, taken from.

antler (def. 1)
antlers of a deer

ant ler (ant′lər), *n.* 1 a bony, hornlike growth on the head of a deer, elk, or moose, usually having one or more branches. 2 branch of such a horn. [< Old French *antoillier* < Latin *ante* before + *oculus* eye]

ant lered (ant′lərd), *adj.* having antlers.

ant lion, 1 any of a family of insects whose larva digs a pit, where it lies in wait to catch ants and other insects as they fall and are trapped. 2 the larva itself; doodlebug.

An toi nette (an′twə net′), *n.* **Marie.** See **Marie Antoinette.**

An to ni nus (an′tə nī′nəs), *n.* **Marcus Aurelius.** See **Marcus Aurelius.**

An to ni nus Pi us (an′tə nī′nəs pī′əs), A.D. 86-161, Roman emperor from A.D. 138 to 161.

An to ni us (an tō′nē əs), *n.* **Marcus.** See **Antony, Mark.**

An to ny (an′tə nē), *n.* **Mark,** 83?-30 B.C. Anglicized name of **Marcus Antonius,** Roman general and statesman, friend of Julius Caesar, and rival of Augustus.

an to nym (an′tə nim), *n.* word that means the opposite of another word: *"Hot" is the antonym of "cold."* [< Greek *anti-* + *onyma* name]

an ton y mous (an ton′ə məs), *adj.* of or like an antonym or antonyms.

an trum (an′trəm), *n., pl.* **-tra** (-trə). cavity, especially one in a bone, often applied to the sinus in the maxilla. [< Latin < Greek *antron* cave]

Ant werp (ant′wərp), *n.* seaport in NW Belgium. 230,000.

A number 1, INFORMAL. A one.

a nus (ā′nəs), *n.* the opening at the lower end of the alimentary canal, through which solid waste material is excreted from the body. [< Latin]

an vil (an′vəl), *n.* 1 an iron or steel block on which metals are hammered and shaped. 2 incus. [Old English *anfilt*]

anx i e ty (ang zī′ə tē), *n., pl.* **-ties.** 1 uneasy thoughts or fears over the possibility of coming misfortune; troubled, worried, or uneasy feeling: *We all felt anxiety when the airplane was caught in the thunderstorm.* 2 eager desire: *anxiety to succeed.*

anx ious (angk′shəs, ang′shəs), *adj.* 1 uneasy because of thoughts or fears over the possibility of coming misfortune;

troubled; worried: *I was anxious about you. I was anxious at your delay.* 2 causing uneasy feelings or troubled thoughts: *The week of the flood was an anxious time for all of us.* 3 eagerly desiring; wishing very much: *I was anxious for a new bicycle.* See **eager** for synonym study. [< Latin *anxius* < *angere* to choke, cause distress] **—anx′ious ly,** *adv.* **—anx′ious ness,** *n.*

an y (en′ē), *adj.* 1 one (no matter which) out of many: *Any book will do.* 2 some (no matter which) out of many or much: *Have you any fresh fruit?* 3 every: *Any child knows that.* 4 even a little; even one or two: *There has never been any doubt about that.* 5 in no matter what quantity or number: *Have you any sugar?* 6 enough to be noticed: *I had hardly any money.* *—pron.* 1 any person or thing; any part: *Keep the cake; I don't want any.* 2 some: *I need more ink; have you any?* *—adv.* 1 to some extent or degree; at all: *Has the sick child improved any?* 2 even a little: *Do not go any closer.* [Old English *ǣnig*]

➤ **any.** In comparisons of things of the same class, idiomatic English calls for *any other: This book is better than any other on the subject.* But: *I think a movie is more entertaining than any book* (not the same class of things).

an y bod y (en′ē bod′ē), *pron., n., pl.* **-bod ies.** 1 any person; anyone: *Has anybody been here?* 2 an important person: *Is he anybody?*

an y how (en′ē hou), *adv.* 1 in any case; at least: *I can see as well as you, anyhow.* 2 in any way whatever: *The answer is wrong anyhow you look at it.* 3 carelessly.

an y more (en′ē môr′, en′ē mōr′), *adv.* at present; now; currently.

➤ In standard usage **anymore** appears only with a negative, either expressed directly *(He doesn't smoke anymore)* or by implication *(I seldom see her anymore).* Its use in positive statements is dialectal: *He is always tired anymore.*

an y one (en′ē wun, en′ē wən), *pron.* any person; anybody.

➤ **Anyone** is written as one word when the stress is on the *any: Anyone* (en′ē wun) *would know that.* It is two words when the stress is on the *one: I'd like any one* (en′ē wun′) *of them.*

an y place (en′ē plās), *adv.* INFORMAL. anywhere.

an y thing (en′ē thing), *pron.* any thing. *—n.* a thing of any kind whatever. *—adv.* 1 in any way; at all. 2 **anything but,** not at all.

an y time (en′ē tīm), *adv.* at any time; no matter when.

an y way (en′ē wā), *adv.* 1 in any case; at least: *I am coming anyway, no matter what you say.* 2 in any way whatever. 3 carelessly.

➤ **Anyway** is one word when the *any* is stressed: *I can't do it anyway.* It is two words when the stress is about equal: *Any way I try, it comes out wrong.*

an y ways (en′ē wāz), *adv.* INFORMAL. anyway.

an y where (en′ē hwer), *adv.* in, at, or to any place.

an y wise (en′ē wīz), *adv.* in any way; to any degree; at all.

An zac (an′zak), *n.* soldier from Australia or New Zealand. [< *A(ustralia and) N(ew) Z(ealand) A(rmy) C(orps)*]

AN ZUS (an′zus), *n.* Australia, New Zealand, and the United States as partners in an alliance for mutual defense in the Pacific formed in 1951.

a.o. or **a/o,** account of.

a o dai (ä′ō dī′), dress worn by Vietnamese women, consisting of wide pantaloons under a long tunic split to the waist on each side. [< Vietnamese]

A-OK (ā′ō′kā′), *adj., adv., interj.* INFORMAL. OK.

A one (ā′ wun′), INFORMAL. first-rate; first-class; excellent. Also, **A 1, A No. 1,** or **A number 1.**

A o ran gi (ä′ō räng′gē), *n.* Mount Cook.

a or ist (ā′ər ist), *n.* tense of Greek verbs showing that an action took place at some time in the past without indicating whether the act was completed, repeated, or continued. *—adj.* of or in the aorist. [< Greek *aoristos* indefinite < *a-* not + *horos* boundary]

a or ta (ā ôr′tə), *n., pl.* **-tas, -tae** (-tē′). the main artery that carries the blood from the left side of the heart and, with its branches, distributes it to all parts of the body except the lungs. See **heart** for diagram. [< New Latin < Greek *aortē*]

a or tic (ā ôr′tik), *adj.* of or having to do with the aorta.

aou dad (ou′dad), *n.* a wild sheep of northern Africa. [< French < Berber *audad*]

ap-[1], *prefix.* form of **ad-** before *p,* as in *apprehend.*

ap-[2], *prefix.* form of **apo-** before vowels and *h,* as in *aphelion.*

Ap., April.

AP or **A.P.,** Associated Press.

a pace (ə pās′), *adv.* very soon; swiftly; quickly; fast.

a pache (ə päsh′, ə pash′), *n.* one of a band of gangsters of Paris, Brussels, etc. [< French, special use of *Apache*]

A pach e (ə pach′ē), *n., pl.* **A pach es** or **A pach e** for 1. 1 member of a tribe of Indians living in the southwestern United States. They were formerly warlike and nomadic. 2 their language.

ap a nage (ap′ə nij), *n.* appanage.

a part (ə pärt′), *adv.* 1 to pieces; in pieces; in separate parts: *Take the watch apart.* 2 away from each other: *Keep the dogs apart.* 3 to one side; aside: *I set some money apart for a vacation.* 4 away from others; separately; independently: *View each idea apart.* 5 **apart from,** besides. *—adj.* separate: *He became a man apart.* **—a part′ness,** *n.*

a part heid (ə pärt′hāt, ə pärt′hīt), *n.* racial segregation, especially as practiced by law in the Republic of South Africa. [< Afrikaans, separateness]

a part ment (ə pärt′mənt), *n.* 1 room or group of rooms to live in; flat[2]. 2 U.S. a single room. 3 apartment house.

apartment house, building with a number of apartments in it.

ap a thet ic (ap′ə thet′ik), *adj.* 1 lacking interest or desire for action; indifferent. 2 lacking in feeling; unemotional. **—ap′a thet′i cal ly,** *adv.*

ap a thy (ap′ə thē), *n., pl.* **-thies.** 1 lack of interest in or desire for activity; indifference. See **indifference** for synonym study. 2 lack of feeling. [< Greek *apatheia* < *a-* without + *pathos* feeling]

ape (āp), *n., v.,* **aped, ap ing.** *—n.* 1 any large, tailless monkey with long arms, able to stand almost erect and walk on two feet. Chimpanzees, gorillas, orangutans, and gibbons are apes. 2 any monkey. 3 person who imitates or mimics. 4 a rough, clumsy person. *—v.t.* imitate; mimic. [Old English *apa*] **—ape′like′,** *adj.*

Ap en nines (ap′ə nīnz), *n.pl.* chief mountain range in Italy, extending north and south throughout the central part, about 840 mi. long. Highest peak, 9560 ft.

a per i ent (ə pir′ē ənt), *adj.* mildly laxative. *—n.* a mild laxative. [< Latin *aperientem* opening]

a per i tif (ə per′ə tēf′; *French* à pā rē tēf′), *n.* an alcoholic drink taken before a meal to stimulate the appetite. [< French *apéritif*]

ap er ture (ap′ər chůr, ap′ər chər), *n.* an opening; hole. A shutter regulates the size of the aperture through which light passes into a camera. [< Latin *apertura* < *aperire* to open. Doublet of OVERTURE.]

a pet a lous (ā pet′l əs), *adj.* having no petals.

a pex (ā′peks), *n., pl.* **a pex es** or **ap i ces.** 1 the highest point; tip: *the apex of a triangle.* 2 climax; peak: *the apex of her career.* [< Latin]

a phaer e sis (ə fer′ə sis), *n.* apheresis.

a pha sia (ə fā′zhə, ə fā′zhē ə), *n.* a total or partial loss of the ability to use or understand words. [< Greek < *a-* not + *phanai* speak]

a pha si ac (ə fā′zē ak), *adj., n.* aphasic.

a pha sic (ə fā′zik, ə fā′sik), *adj.* of, having to do with, or suffering from aphasia. *—n.* person who has aphasia.

a phe li on (ə fē′lē ən), *n., pl.* **-li a** (-lē ə). the point farthest from the sun in the orbit of a planet or comet. [< Greek *apo-* + *hēlios* sun]

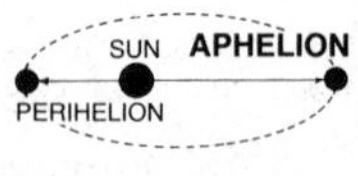

aphelion—a planet in orbit around the sun shown at aphelion and perihelion

a pher e sis (ə fer′ə sis), *n.* omission of a sound, syllable, or letter at the beginning of a word. Also, **aphaeresis.** [< Greek *aphairesis* a taking away]

aph e sis (af′ə sis), *n.* apheresis with omission of an initial unaccented vowel, as *possum* for *opossum.* [< Greek, a letting go]

a phid (ā′fid, af′id), *n.* any of various very small insects that live by sucking juices from plants; plant louse. [< *aphides,* plural of *aphis*]

a phis (ā′fis, af′is), *n., pl.* **aph i des** (af′ə dēz′, af′ə dēz′). aphid. [< New Latin, coined by Linnaeus]

aph o rism (af′ə riz′əm), *n.* 1 a short sentence expressing a general truth or some practical wisdom; maxim. EXAMPLE: "A living dog is better than a dead lion." See **epigram** for synonym study. 2 a concise statement of a principle in any science. [< Greek *aphorismos* definition < *apo-* off + *horos* boundary]

aph o ris tic (af′ə ris′tik), *adj.* of, containing, or like aphorisms. **—aph′o ris′ti cal ly,** *adv.*

aph ro dis i ac (af′rə diz′ē ak), *adj.* arousing or increasing sexual desire. *—n.* any drug, food, etc., that arouses or increases sexual desire. [< Greek *aphrodisiakos* < *Aphrodisios* of Aphrodite]

Aph ro di te (af′rə dī′tē), *n.* 1 (in Greek myths) the goddess of love and beauty, identified with the Roman goddess Venus. 2 a brown butterfly of North America, with black spots.

hat, āge, fär; let, ēqual, tėrm;
it, īce; hot, ōpen, ôrder;
oil, out; cup, pu̇t, rüle;
ch, child; ng, long; sh, she;
th, thin; ᴛʜ, then; zh, measure;

ə represents *a* in about, *e* in taken, *i* in pencil, *o* in lemon, *u* in circus.

< = from, derived from, taken from.

A pi a (ä pē′ə, ä′pē ə), *n.* capital of Western Samoa. 25,000.

a pi ar ist (ā′pē ər ist), *n.* beekeeper.

a pi ar y (ā′pē er′ē), *n., pl.* **-ar ies.** place where bees are kept; group of beehives. [< Latin *apiarium* < *apis* bee]

ap i cal (ap′ə kəl, ā′pə kəl), *adj.* of, at, or forming the apex. **—ap′i cal ly,** *adv.*

ap i ces (ap′ə sēz′, ā′pə sēz′), *n.* a pl. of **apex.**

a pi cul tur al (ā′pə kul′chər əl), *adj.* of or having to do with apiculture.

a pi cul ture (ā′pə kul′chər), *n.* the raising and care of bees; beekeeping.

a pi cul tur ist (ā′pə kul′chər ist), *n.* person who engages in apiculture.

a piece (ə pēs′), *adv.* for each one; each: *These apples cost ten cents apiece.*

ap ish (ā′pish), *adj.* 1 foolish; silly. 2 like an ape. 3 senselessly imitative. **—ap′ish ly,** *adv.* **—ap′ish ness,** *n.*

a plen ty (ə plen′tē), *adv.* INFORMAL. in plenty.

a plomb (ə plom′), *n.* self-possession springing from perfect confidence in oneself; assurance; poise. [< French < *à plomb* according to the plummet]

APO or **A.P.O.,** Army Post Office.

apo-, *prefix.* from; away from; detached; separate, as in *apostrophe, apothem.* See also **ap-**[2]. [< Greek]

a poc a lypse (ə pok′ə lips), *n.* 1 revelation, especially a revelation or vision of a great world upheaval. 2 a great upheaval or cataclysm. 3 **the Apocalypse,** the last book of the New Testament; book of Revelation. 4 any of the apocalyptic writings. [< Greek *apokalypsis* < *apo-* + *kalyptein* to cover]

a poc a lyp tic (ə pok′ə lip′tik), *adj.* 1 like a revelation; giving a revelation. 2 envisaging or portending violent upheaval; cataclysmic. 3 Also, **Apocalyptic,** of the Apocalypse. 4 having to do with a class of Jewish and Christian visionary literature written between 200 B.C. and A.D. 200, describing the ultimate triumph of God over evil. **—a poc′a lyp′ti cal ly,** *adv.*

a poc o pe (ə pok′ə pē), *n.* omission of a sound, syllable, or letter at the end of a word. *Th'* for *the* and *i'* for *in* are examples of apocope. [< Greek *apokopē* < *apo-* off + *koptein* to cut]

A poc ry pha (ə pok′rə fə), *n.pl.* 1 fourteen books of the Old Testament appearing in the Septuagint and the Vulgate, but not included in Jewish or Protestant Bibles. 2 **apocrypha,** certain early Christian writings excluded from the New Testament. 3 **apocrypha,** writings or statements of doubtful authorship or authority. [< Greek *apokryphos* hidden < *apo-* + *kryptein* to hide]

a poc ry phal (ə pok′rə fəl), *adj.* 1 of doubtful authorship, authenticity, or inspiration. 2 spurious; counterfeit. 3 **Apocryphal,** of or from the Apocrypha. **—a poc′ry phal ly,** *adv.* **—a poc′ry phal ness,** *n.*

ap o gee (ap′ə jē), *n.* 1 the point farthest from the earth in the orbit of the moon or any other earth satellite. 2 furthermost point; highest point; peak; apex. [< Greek *apogaion* < *apo-* + *gē* or *gaia* earth]

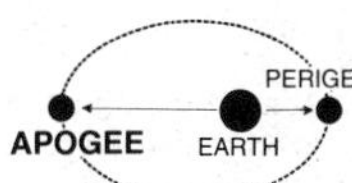

apogee (def. 1) the moon in orbit around the earth shown at apogee and perigee

a po lit i cal (ā′pə lit′ə kəl), *adj.* not concerned with politics or political issues.

A pol lo (ə pol′ō), *n., pl.* **-los** for 2. 1 (in Greek and Roman myths) the god of the sun, poetry, music, prophecy, healing, and archery. Apollo was the highest type of youthful, manly beauty to the Greeks and Romans. 2 an extremely handsome young man.

A pol lyon (ə pol′yən), *n.* (in the Bible) the Devil.

a pol o get ic (ə pol′ə jet′ik), *adj.* 1 making an apology; expressing regret or offering an excuse for a fault or failure: *an apologetic reply.* 2 defending by speech or writing. **—a pol′o get′i cal ly,** *adv.*

a pol o get ics (ə pol′ə jet′iks), *n.* branch of theology that deals with the rational defense of a religious faith.

ap o lo gi a (ap′ə lō′jē ə), *n.* statement in defense or justification of an idea, belief, religion, etc.; apology.

a pol o gist (ə pol′ə jist), *n.* person who defends an idea, belief, religion, etc., in speech or writing.

a pol o gize (ə pol′ə jīz), *v.i.,* **-gized, -giz ing.** 1 make an apology; express regret; acknowledge a fault; offer an excuse: *She apologized for hurting my feelings.* 2 defend an idea, belief, religion, etc., in speech or writing. **—a pol′o giz′er,** *n.*

ap o logue (ap′ə lôg, ap′ə log), *n.* fable with a moral.

a pol o gy (ə pol′ə jē), *n., pl.* **-gies.** 1 words of regret for an offense or accident; acknowledgment of a fault or failure, expressing regret and asking pardon. 2 defense in speech or writing; explanation of the truth or justice of something: *an apology for the Christian religion.* 3 a poor substitute; makeshift: *a skimpy apology for a breakfast.* [< Late Latin *apologia* a speech in defense < Greek < *apo-* + *legein* speak]

ap o phthegm (ap′ə them), *n.* apothegm.

a poph y sis (ə pof′ə sis), *n., pl.* **-ses** (-sēz′). a natural outgrowth, projection, or swelling, especially any process of a vertebra. [< Greek < *apo-* + *phyein* grow]

ap o plec tic (ap′ə plek′tik), *adj.* 1 of or causing apoplexy. 2 suffering from apoplexy. 3 showing symptoms of a tendency to apoplexy. *—n.* person who has or is likely to have apoplexy. **—ap′o plec′ti cal ly,** *adv.*

ap o plex y (ap′ə plek′sē), *n., pl.* **-plex ies.** a sudden loss of the power to feel or think or move, caused by injury to the brain when a blood vessel breaks or the blood supply becomes obstructed; stroke. [< Greek *apoplēxia* < *apo-* off, from + *plēssein* to strike]

a port (ə pôrt′, ə pōrt′), *adv.* to the port side; to the left of a ship.

a pos ta sy (ə pos′tə sē), *n., pl.* **-sies.** 1 abandonment of one's principles; desertion of one's party or cause. 2 renunciation of one's religious faith or moral principles. [< Greek *apostasia* < *apo-* + *stēnai* to stand]

a pos tate (ə pos′tāt, ə pos′tit), *n.* 1 person who forsakes his allegiance, party, or cause; renegade. 2 person who renounces or forsakes his religious faith or moral principles. *—adj.* unfaithful to one's religion or moral or political allegiance.

a pos ta tize (ə pos′tə tīz), *v.i.,* **-tized, -tiz ing.** 1 desert principles or party. 2 renounce one's religious faith.

a pos ter i o ri (ā pos tir′ē ôr′ī; ä pos tir′ē ōr′ī), 1 from effect to cause; from particular cases to a general rule. 2 based on actual observation or experience. [< Medieval Latin, from what comes after]

a pos tle or **A pos tle** (ə pos′əl), *n.* 1 one of the twelve disciples, **the Apostles,** chosen by Christ to preach the gospel to all the world. 2 an early Christian leader or missionary, such as Paul. 3 the first Christian missionary to any country or region. 4 leader of any reform movement or new belief who displays great vigor in seeking to popularize it. 5 one of the council of twelve officials of the Mormon Church who help administer the affairs of the church. [< Greek *apostolos* messenger < *apo-* + *stellein* send]

Apostles' Creed, statement of belief that contains the fundamental doctrines of Christianity, beginning "I believe in God, the Father. . . ." In its present form it dates back to about A.D. 600 and was formerly supposed to have been composed by the Apostles.

a pos tle ship (ə pos′əl ship), *n.* apostolate.

a pos to late (ə pos′tl it, ə pos′tl āt), *n.* rank or office of an apostle.

ap os tol ic or **Ap os tol ic** (ap′ə stol′ik), *adj.* 1 of or having to do with an apostle or apostles. 2 of the Apostles, their beliefs, teachings, time, or nature. 3 coming from or originating with the Apostles. 4 of or having to do with the Pope; papal.

a pos to lic i ty (ə pos′tl is′ə tē), *n.* quality of being apostolic.

a pos tro phe[1] (ə pos′trə fē), *n.* sign (') used: 1 to show the omission of one or more letters in contractions, as in *o'er* for *over, thro'* for *through.* 2 to show the possessive forms of nouns or indefinite pronouns, as in *John's book, the lions' den, everybody's business.* 3 to form plurals of letters and numbers: *There are two o's in apology and four 9's in 9999.* 4 to show that certain sounds represented in the usual spelling have not been spoken: *'lectric.* [< Greek *apostrophos* omission]

a pos tro phe[2] (ə pos′trə fē), *n.* words addressed to an absent person as if he were present or to a thing or idea as if it could hear or reply. [< Greek *apostrophē* < *apo-* + *strephein* to turn]

a pos tro phize (ə pos′trə fīz), *v.,* **-phized, -phiz ing.** *—v.i.* stop in a speech, poem, etc., and address some absent person as if he were present or a thing or idea as if it could appreciate what is said. *—v.t.* address an apostrophe to.

apothecaries' measure, system of units used in the United States to measure volume in compounding and dispensing liquid drugs. See **measure** for table.

apothecaries' weight, system of weights used in mixing drugs and filling prescriptions. See **measure** for table.

a poth e car y (ə poth′ə ker′ē), *n., pl.* **-car ies.** druggist; pharmacist. [< Late Latin *apothecarius* shopkeeper < Latin *apotheca* storehouse < Greek *apothēkē* < *apo-* + *tithenai* put]

ap o thegm (ap′ə them), *n.* a short, forceful saying; maxim. EXAMPLE: "Beauty is only skin deep." Also, **apophthegm.** [< Greek *apophthegma* < *apo-* + *phthengesthai* to utter]

ap o them (ap′ə them), *n.* the radius of the inscribed circle of a regular polygon; the perpendicular from the center to any one of its sides. [< *apo-* + Greek *thema* thing placed]

a poth e o sis (ə poth′ē ō′sis, ap′ə thē′ə-sis), *n., pl.* **-ses** (-sēz′). 1 a glorified ideal. 2 the raising of a human being to the rank of a god; deification. [< Greek *apotheōsis* < *apo-* + *theos* god]

a poth e o size (ə poth′ē ə sīz, ap′ə thē′ə-sīz), *v.t.,* **-sized, -siz ing.** 1 glorify; exalt. 2 deify.

app., 1 apparent. 2 appendix.

Ap pa la chia (ap′ə lā′chə), *n.* region in the E United States covering parts of 11 states from N Pennsylvania to N Alabama, with a population of about 15 million, regarded as an area of widespread poverty and unemployment.

Ap pa la chian Mountains (ap′ə lā′-chən, ap′ə lach′ən), chief mountain system in E North America, extending from Quebec Province in Canada to central Alabama, about 1600 miles long. The highest peak is Mount Mitchell, 6684 ft.

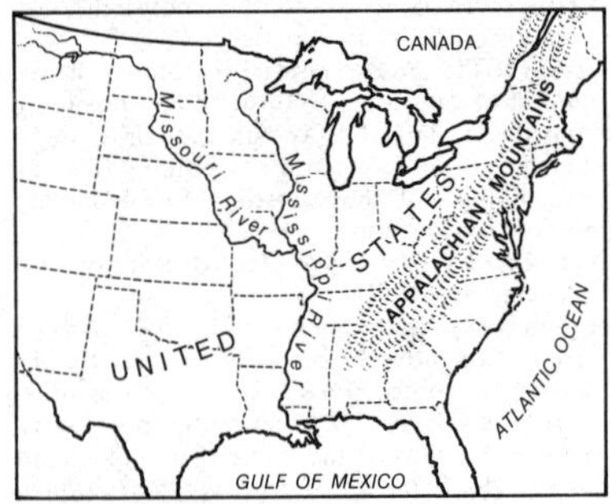

Ap pa la chians (ap′ə lā′chənz, ap′ə-lach′ənz), *n.pl.* Appalachian Mountains.

ap pall or **ap pal** (ə pôl′), *v.t.,* **-palled, -pall ing.** fill with consternation and horror; dismay; terrify: *The thought of another war appalled us.* [< Old French *apallir* make pale < *a-* to + *pale* pale]

ap pall ing (ə pô′ling), *adj.* causing consternation and horror; dismaying; terrifying. **—ap pall′ing ly,** *adv.*

ap pa nage (ap′ə nij), *n.* 1 land, property, or money set aside to support the younger children of kings, princes, etc. 2 person's assigned portion; rightful property. 3 something that accompanies; adjunct: *The millionaire had three houses, a yacht, and all the other appanages of wealth.* 4 territory controlled by another country. Also, **apa-nage.** [< Old French *apanage* < *apaner* give bread to, ultimately < Latin *ad-* to + *panis* bread]

ap pa ra tus (ap′ə rā′təs, ap′ə rat′əs), *n., pl.* **-tus,** or **-tus es.** 1 the tools, machines, or other equipment necessary to carry out a purpose or for a particular use: *apparatus for an experiment in chemistry, gardening apparatus.* 2 a mechanism or piece of machinery: *An automobile is a complicated apparatus.* 3 the group of organs of the body by which a specific natural process is carried on: *the digestive apparatus.* 4 a political or party organization; an administrative machine. [< Latin < *ad-* + *parare* make ready]

ap par el (ə par′əl), *n., v.,* **-eled, -el ing** or **-elled, -el ling.** *—n.* clothing; dress. See **clothes** for synonym study. *—v.t.* clothe; dress up. [< Old French *apareil* < *apareiller* fit out, clothe]

ap par ent (ə par′ənt), *adj.* 1 plain to see; so plain that one cannot help seeing it: *The stain is apparent from across the room.* 2 easily understood; evident: *It is apparent that you dislike your job.* 3 appearing to be; seeming: *The apparent truth was really a lie.* [< Latin *apparentem*] **—ap par′ent ly,** *adv.* **—ap par′ent ness,** *n.*

ap pa ri tion (ap′ə rish′ən), *n.* 1 a supernatural sight or thing; ghost or phantom. 2 the appearance of something strange, remarkable, or unexpected. [< Late Latin *apparitionem*]

ap peal (ə pēl′), *v.i.* 1 make an earnest request (*to* or *for*); ask for help, sympathy, etc.: *I appeal to you to support the hospital drive.* 2 call on some person to decide a matter in one's favor. 3 (in law) ask that a case be taken to a higher court or judge to be heard again. 4 be attractive, interesting, or enjoyable: *Blue and red appeal to me, but I don't like gray or yellow.* *—v.t.* (in law) apply for a retrial of (a case) before a higher court. *—n.* 1 an earnest request; call for help, sympathy, etc. 2 in law: **a** a request to have a case heard again before a higher court or judge. **b** the right to have a case heard again. 3 a call on some person to decide a matter in one's favor. 4 attraction or interest: *Television has a great appeal for most young people.* [< Old French *apeler* < Latin *appellare* accost < *ad-* up to + *pellere* to drive]

ap peal ing (ə pē′ling), *adj.* that appeals; attractive or interesting. **—ap peal′ing-ly,** *adv.*

ap pear (ə pir′), *v.i.* 1 be seen; come in sight: *One by one the stars appear.* 2 look as if; seem: *The apple appeared sound on the outside, but it was rotten inside.* 3 be published: *The book appeared in the autumn.* 4 come before the public as a performer or author: *appear on the stage.* 5 become known to the mind; be plain: *It appears that we must go.* 6 present oneself formally before an authority: *A person accused of a crime must appear in court.* [< Latin *apparere* < *ad-* + *parere* come in sight]

ap pear ance (ə pir′əns), *n.* 1 act of coming in sight. 2 a coming before the public as a performer or author: *a singer's first appearance.* 3 outward look; aspect. See synonym study below. 4 outward show or seeming: *keep up appearances.* 5 thing that appears in sight; object seen. 6 the coming into court of a party to a lawsuit. 7 apparition. 8 **put in an appearance,** be present and noticed, at least briefly, at a meeting, party, etc.

Syn. 3 **Appearance, aspect** mean the look or looks of a person or thing. **Appearance** is the general word applying to what one sees when he looks at someone or something: *His pleasing appearance wins him many friends.* **Aspect** applies to the appearance at certain times or under certain conditions: *I love the bay in all its aspects, even its stormy, frightening aspect in winter.*

ap pease (ə pēz′), *v.t.,* **-peased, -peas ing.** 1 put an end to by satisfying (an appetite or desire): *A good dinner will appease your hunger.* 2 make calm or quiet; pacify. See synonym study below. 3 give in to the demands of (especially those of a potential enemy): *Chamberlain appeased Hitler at Munich.* [< Old French *apaisier* < *a-* to + *pais* peace] **—ap peas′er,** *n.* **—ap-peas′ing ly,** *adv.*

Syn. 2 **Appease, pacify** mean to make calm. **Appease** means to calm or quiet a person who is excited, upset, and demanding by making concessions to him: *To appease my angry neighbor, I offered to make good the damage.* **Pacify** means to quiet people or things that are quarreling or fighting among themselves or against some condition, by making peace though not necessarily by eliminating the cause of the disturbance: *She pacified the angry crowd.*

ap pease ment (ə pēz′mənt), *n.* an appeasing or a being appeased; pacification; satisfaction.

ap pel lant (ə pel′ənt), *n.* person who appeals. *—adj.* appealing; having to do with appeals.

ap pel late (ə pel′it), *adj.* having to do with appeals.

appellate court, court having the power to reexamine and reverse the decisions of a lower court.

ap pel la tion (ap′ə lā′shən), *n.* 1 name or title describing or identifying someone. In "John the Baptist," the appellation of *John* is *the Baptist.* 2 act of calling by a name.

ap pend (ə pend′), *v.t.* add to a larger thing; attach as a supplement: *append notes to a book.* [< Latin *appendere* < *ad-* on + *pendere* hang]

ap pend age (ə pen′dij), *n.* 1 thing attached to something larger or more important; addition. 2 (in biology) any of various external or subordinate parts. Arms, tails, fins, legs, etc., are appendages.

ap pend ant (ə pen′dənt), *adj.* added; attached. *—n.* appendage.

ap pen dec to my (ap′ən dek′tə mē), *n., pl.* **-mies.** removal of the vermiform appendix by a surgical operation.

ap pen di ces (ə pen′də sēz′), *n.* a pl. of **appendix.**

ap pen di ci tis (ə pen′də sī′tis), *n.* inflammation of the vermiform appendix.

ap pen dix (ə pen′diks), *n., pl.* **-dix es** or **-di ces.** 1 addition at the end of a book or document. See **supplement** for synonym study. 2 vermiform appendix. [< Latin]

ap per ceive (ap′ər sēv′), *v.t.,* **-ceived, -ceiv ing.** perceive clearly.

ap per cep tion (ap′ər sep′shən), *n.* 1 clear perception; full understanding. 2 (in psychology) assimilation of a new perception by means of a mass of ideas already in the mind.

ap per cep tive (ap′ər sep′tiv), *adj.* of or having to do with apperception.

ap per tain (ap′ər tān′), *v.i.* belong as a part; be connected; pertain; relate: *Forestry appertains to geography, botany, and agriculture.* [< Old French *apartenir* < Late Latin *appertinere* < Latin *ad-* to + *pertinere* pertain]

ap pe tite (ap′ə tīt), *n.* 1 desire or craving for food. 2 desire or craving: *an appetite for amusement.* 3 taste; liking. [< Latin *appetitus* < *appetere* to long for < *ad-* + *petere* seek]

ap pe tiz er (ap′ə tī′zər), *n.* something that arouses the appetite or gives relish to food. Pickles and olives are appetizers.

ap pe tiz ing (ap′ə tī′zing), *adj.* arousing or exciting the appetite: *appetizing food.* **—ap′pe tiz′ing ly,** *adv.*

Ap pi an Way (ap′ē ən), a famous ancient Roman road extending about 366 miles southeast from Rome to Brundisium.

ap plaud (ə plôd′), *v.i.* express approval by clapping hands, shouting, etc. *—v.t.* 1 express approval of in this way. 2 be pleased with; approve; praise: *applaud a decision.* [< Latin *applaudere* < *ad-* to + *plaudere* to clap] **—ap plaud′a ble,** *adj.* **—ap plaud′er,** *n.*

ap plause (ə plôz′), *n.* 1 approval expressed by clapping the hands, shouting, etc. 2 approval; praise.

ap ple (ap′əl), *n.* 1 the firm, fleshy, somewhat round fruit of a tree widely grown in temperate regions. Apples have red, yellow, or green skin, and are eaten either raw or cooked. 2 the tree it grows on, belonging to the rose family. 3 any of various other fruits or fruitlike products, such as the oak apple and love apple. [Old English *æppel*] **—ap′ple like′,** *adj.*

ap ple jack (ap′əl jak′), *n.* a brandy distilled from hard cider.

apple of one's eye, person or thing that is cherished or valued.

ap ple sauce (ap′əl sôs′), *n.* 1 apples cut in pieces and cooked with sugar, spices, and water until soft. 2 SLANG. nonsense.

ap pli ance (ə plī′əns), *n.* 1 instrument, device, contrivance, or machine designed for a particular use, such as a can opener, a vacuum cleaner, a washing machine, etc. 2 an applying; act of putting into use.

ap pli ca bil i ty (ap′lə kə bil′ə tē), *n.* quality of being applicable.

ap pli ca ble (ap′lə kə bəl, ə plik′ə bəl), *adj.* capable of being applied; appropriate.

ap pli cant (ap′lə kənt), *n.* person who applies (for a job, money, position, etc.).

ap pli ca tion (ap′lə kā′shən), *n.* 1 action of putting anything to use; use: *the application of atomic energy to the production of electricity.* 2 way of using: *Freedom is a word of many applications.* 3 an applying; putting on: *the application of paint to a house.* 4 thing applied: *This application is made of cold cream and ointment.* 5 a spoken or written request (for employment, an award, tickets, etc.): *I filled out an application for the position of clerk.* 6 process of giving continued effort or close attention to a task or study: *By application to my work I got a better job.* See **effort** for synonym study. [< Latin *applicationem* < *applicare.* See APPLY.]

ap pli ca tor (ap′lə kā′tər), *n.* instrument or device for applying a medicine, cosmetic, paint, etc.

ap plied (ə plīd′), *adj.* put to practical use; used to solve actual problems: *Engineering is applied mathematics.*

ap pli qué (ap′lə kā′), *n., v.,* **-quéd, -qué ing,** *adj.* *—n.* ornaments made of one material sewed or otherwise fastened to another. *—v.t.* trim or ornament with appliqué. *—adj.* trimmed in this way: *an appliqué quilt.* [< French]

ap ply (ə plī′), *v.,* **-plied, -ply ing.** *—v.t.* 1 bring a thing into contact with something else; put on; lay on: *apply the foot to the control pedal, apply paint to a house, apply the salve to the cut.* 2 put into use or operation; use: *The same rule should be applied to all.* 3 use for a special purpose; appropriate: *The surplus in our club treasury was applied to paying for the party.* 4 attach or associate (a word or expression) to or with a person or object: *apply a nickname.* 5 turn or keep (oneself or one's attention) on a task or study: *She applied herself to learning French.* *—v.i.* 1 be useful or suitable; fit: *When does this rule apply?* 2 make a request; ask: *I am applying for a job as a clerk.* 3 have a bearing on; refer: *This applies to us as much as to them.* [< Old French *aplier* < Latin *applicare* < *ad-* on + *plicare* to fold, lay] **—ap pli′er,** *n.*

ap pog gia tur a (ə poj′ə tůr′ə, ə poj′ə-tyůr′ə), *n.,* grace note. [< Italian, literally, a leaning]

ap point (ə point′), *v.t.* 1 name for an office or position; choose; designate: *She was appointed postmaster.* 2 decide on; set: *appoint a time for the meeting.* 3 fix; prescribe: *appoint death as punishment for a crime.* 4 furnish; equip: *a fully appointed workshop.* [< Old French *apointer* < *a-* to + *point* point] **—ap point′er,** *n.*

ap point ee (ə poin′tē′, a′poin tē′), *n.* person appointed to an office or position.

ap poin tive (ə poin′tiv), *adj.* subject to or filled by appointment: *Positions in the President's cabinet are appointive.*

ap point ment (ə point′mənt), *n.* 1 act of naming for or placing in an office or position: *The President announced his cabinet appointments.* 2 office or position of or to which the holder is appointed: *She had a government appointment.* 3 a meeting with someone at a certain time and place; engagement: *I have an appointment to see the doctor at four o'clock.* 4 **appointments,** *pl.* furniture; equipment: *The old hotel has rather shabby appointments.*

Ap po mat tox (ap′ə mat′əks), *n.* town in central Virginia where Lee surrendered to Grant on April 9, 1865.

ap por tion (ə pôr′shən, ə pōr′shən), *v.t.* divide and give out in fair shares; distribute according to some rule: *Grandmother's property was apportioned among her children after her death.* See **allot** for synonym study.

ap por tion ment (ə pôr′shən mənt, ə pōr′shən mənt), *n.* 1 a dividing and giving out in fair shares; distribution according to some rule. 2 the determination and assignment of representation in a legislative body.

ap pose (a pōz′), *v.t.,* **-posed, -pos ing.** 1 put next; place side by side. 2 put (one thing to another); apply: *An official seal was apposed to the document.*

ap po site (ap′ə zit), *adj.* fittingly applied; appropriate; suitable. [< Latin *appositum* placed near < *ad-* near + *ponere* to place] **—ap′po site ly,** *adv.* **—ap′po site ness,** *n.*

ap po si tion (ap′ə zish′ən), *n.* 1 act of placing one thing beside another; apposing. 2 position side by side; juxtaposition. 3 relation between two expressions, usually nouns or noun phrases, equivalent in meaning and having the same grammatical function in the sentence. 4 the placing of words or phrases in this relation. In "Mr. Brown, our neighbor, has a new car," *Mr. Brown* and *our neighbor* are in apposition.

ap pos i tive (ə poz′ə tiv), *n.* word, phrase, or clause in apposition. *—adj.* placed in apposition. **—ap pos′i tive ly,** *adv.*

ap prais al (ə prā′zəl), *n.* 1 estimate of the value, amount, quality, etc.: *Their appraisal of the stock was too low.* 2 an appraising; evaluating.

ap praise (ə prāz′), *v.t.,* **-praised, -prais ing.** 1 estimate the quality or merit of; judge: *Few can properly appraise the work of a new artist.* 2 estimate the value of; fix a price for; value: *The paintings were appraised at $100,000.* See **estimate** for synonym study. [< Middle French *aprisier* < Latin *appretiare* < *ad-* to + *pretium* price] **—ap prais′ing ly,** *adv.*

hat, āge, fär; let, ēqual, tėrm;
it, īce; hot, ōpen, ôrder;
oil, out; cup, půt, rüle;
ch, child; ng, long; sh, she;
th, thin; ᴛʜ, then; zh, measure;

ə represents *a* in about, *e* in taken,
i in pencil, *o* in lemon, *u* in circus.

< = from, derived from, taken from.

ap praise ment (ə prāz′mənt), *n.* appraisal.

ap prais er (ə prā′zər), *n.* 1 person authorized to fix the value of property, imported goods, etc. 2 person who appraises.

ap pre ci a ble (ə prē′shē ə bəl, ə prē′shə-bəl), *adj.* enough to be felt or estimated; noticeable; perceptible: *A slight hill makes an appreciable difference in the ease of walking.* **—ap pre′ci a bly,** *adv.*

ap pre ci ate (ə prē′shē āt), *v.,* **-at ed, -at ing.** *—v.t.* 1 think highly of; recognize the worth or quality of; value: *Her merits are appreciated.* See **value** for synonym study. 2 be thankful for: *We appreciate your help.* 3 have an opinion of the value, worth, or quality of; estimate: *A scholar appreciates knowledge.* 4 be aware of; be sensitive to; discern: *I appreciate the risk I am taking.* 5 raise in value: *New buildings appreciate the price of land.* *—v.i.* rise in value. [< Latin *appretiatum* appraised < *ad-* + *pretium* price] **—ap pre′ci a′tor,** *n.*

ap pre ci a tion (ə prē′shē ā′shən), *n.* 1 a valuing highly; sympathetic understanding: *an appreciation of art and music.* 2 an appreciating; valuing: *He showed his appreciation of her help by sending flowers.* 3 favorable criticism. 4 a rise in value.

ap pre ci a tive (ə prē′shē ā′tiv, ə prē′-shə tiv), *adj.* feeling or showing appreciation: *appreciative of the smallest kindness.* **—ap-pre′ci a′tive ly,** *adv.* **—ap pre′ci a′tive-ness,** *n.*

ap pre hend (ap′ri hend′), *v.t.* 1 look forward to with fear; expect anxiously; fear: *I apprehend no worsening of the situation.* 2 formally arrest or seize (a person): *No one can be apprehended on suspicion alone.* 3 become or be conscious of; notice or perceive. 4 grasp with the mind; understand: *I apprehended his meaning from his gestures.* See **comprehend** for synonym study. 5 regard; view: *These are the rights and wrongs of the case, as I apprehend them.* [< Latin *apprehendere* < *ad-* upon + *prehendere* seize]

ap pre hen si ble (ap′ri hen′sə bəl), *adj.* that can be apprehended; understandable. **—ap′pre hen′si bly,** *adv.*

ap pre hen sion (ap′ri hen′shən), *n.* 1 expectation of misfortune; dread of impending danger; fear. 2 arrest. 3 understanding.

ap pre hen sive (ap′ri hen′siv), *adj.* afraid that some misfortune is about to occur; anxious about the future; fearful. **—ap′pre-**

hen′sive ly, *adv.* **—ap′pre hen′sive-ness,** *n.*

ap pren tice (ə pren′tis), *n., v.,* **-ticed, -tic ing.** *—n.* 1 person learning a trade or art, especially one bound by a legal agreement to work for an employer for a certain length of time in return for instruction and, formerly, maintenance, but little or no pay. 2 beginner; learner. *—v.t.* bind or take as an apprentice. [< Old French *aprentis* < *aprendre* learn < Latin *apprehendere.* See APPREHEND.]

ap pren tice ship (ə pren′tis ship), *n.* 1 condition of being an apprentice. 2 time during which one is an apprentice.

ap prise (ə prīz′), *v.t.,* **-prised, -pris ing.** give notice to; let know; inform; notify; advise. [< French *appris,* past participle of *apprendre* learn < Latin *apprehendere*]

ap prize (ə prīz′), *v.t.,* **-prized, -priz ing.** apprise.

ap proach (ə prōch′), *v.t.* 1 come near or nearer to: *We are approaching the town.* 2 come near to in quality, character, time, or condition: *The wind was approaching a gale.* 3 bring near (to something). 4 make advances or overtures to: *I approached my boss with the idea of asking for a promotion.* 5 start work on: *approach a difficult task.* *—v.i.* 1 come near or nearer: *Winter approaches.* 2 be nearly equal *(to).* *—n.* 1 act of coming near or nearer: *the approach of night.* 2 way by which a place or a person can be reached; access. 3 method of starting work on a task or problem: *a good approach to the problem.* 4 nearness in quality, likeness, or character: *In mathematics there must be more than an approach to accuracy.* 5 Also, **approaches,** *pl.* advances; overtures. 6 (in golf) a stroke by which a player tries to get his ball onto the putting green. [< Old French *aprochier* < Late Latin *appropiare* < Latin *ad-* to + *prope* near]

ap proach a bil i ty (ə prō′chə bil′ə tē), *n.* approachable quality or condition.

ap proach a ble (ə prō′chə bəl), *adj.* 1 that can be approached; accessible. 2 friendly and sociable.

ap pro ba tion (ap′rə bā′shən), *n.* 1 favorable opinion; approval. 2 act of formally and authoritatively approving; sanction. [< Latin *approbationem*]

ap pro pri ate (*adj.* ə prō′prē it; *v.* ə prō′prē āt), *adj., v.,* **-at ed, -at ing.** *—adj.* especially right or proper for the occasion; suitable; fitting: *Plain, simple clothes are appropriate for school wear.* See **fit**[1] for synonym study. *—v.t.* 1 set apart for a special purpose: *The legislature appropriated a billion dollars for foreign aid.* 2 take for oneself; use as one's own: *You should not appropriate other people's belongings without their permission.* [< Late Latin *appropriatum* made one's own < Latin *ad-* to + *proprius* one's own] **—ap pro′pri ate ly,** *adv.* **—ap pro′pri ate ness,** *n.* **—ap pro′pri-a′tor,** *n.*

ap pro pri a tion (ə prō′prē ā′shən), *n.* 1 sum of money or other thing appropriated. 2 act of appropriating. 3 a being appropriated.

ap prov al (ə prü′vəl), *n.* 1 favorable opinion; approving; praise: *My work earned the teacher's approval.* 2 permission; consent; sanction: *The principal gave her approval to plans for the holiday.* 3 **on approval,** so that the customer can inspect the item and decide whether to buy or return it: *Postage stamps are often mailed to collectors on approval.* 4 **approvals,** *pl.* items sent to a customer on approval.

ap prove (ə prüv′), *v.,* **-proved, -prov ing.** *—v.t.* 1 express one's agreement with or admiration of; be pleased with: *The teacher found my work correct and approved it.* See **praise** for synonym study. 2 authorize or make legal; sanction; consent to: *Congress approved the bill.* See synonym study below. 3 provide proof of; demonstrate. *—v.i.* give a favorable opinion *(of): I'm not sure I can approve of what you propose to do.* [< Old French *aprover* < Latin *approbare* < *ad-* to + *probus* good] **—ap prov′er,** *n.* **—ap-prov′ing ly,** *adv.*

Syn. *v.t.* 2 **Approve, sanction, ratify** mean to give consent or support through formal action or through the force of public opinion. **Approve,** the general word, means to consent formally or officially to something one thinks favorably of: *The school board approved the budget.* **Sanction** means to give official authorization or support: *Society does not sanction child labor.* **Ratify** means to give formal approval or confirmation of something of importance, as by a vote: *The club council ratified the by-laws.*

approx., 1 approximate. 2 approximately.

ap prox i mate (*adj.* ə prok′sə mit; *v.* ə prok′sə māt), *adj., v.,* **-mat ed, -mat ing.** *—adj.* nearly correct: *The approximate length of a meter is 40 inches; the exact length is 39.37 inches.* *—v.t.* 1 come near to; approach: *The crowd approximated a thousand people.* 2 bring near. *—v.i.* come near or close *(to).* [< Latin *approximatum* approached < *ad-* to + *proximus* nearest] **—ap prox′i mate ly,** *adv.*

ap prox i ma tion (ə prok′sə mā′shən), *n.* 1 a nearly correct amount; close estimate: *25,000 miles is an approximation of the circumference of the earth.* 2 an approximating; approach: *a close approximation to the truth.* 3 condition of being near.

ap pur te nance (ə pėrt′n əns), *n.* addition to something more important; added thing; accessory. [< Anglo-French *apurtenance.* Related to APPERTAIN.]

ap pur te nant (ə pėrt′n ənt), *adj.* pertaining; belonging; appertaining *(to).*

Apr., April.

a pri cot (ā′prə kot, ap′rə kot), *n.* 1 a roundish, pale, orange-colored fruit, about the size of a plum, with a downy skin somewhat like that of a peach. 2 the tree it grows on, belonging to the rose family. 3 a pale orange yellow. *—adj.* pale orange-yellow. [< Portuguese *albricoque* < Arabic *al-barqūq*]

A pril (ā′prəl), *n.* the fourth month of the year. It has 30 days. [< Latin *Aprilis*]

April fool, person who gets fooled on April Fools' Day.

April Fools' Day, April 1, a day observed by fooling people with tricks and jokes; All Fools' Day.

a pri o ri (ā prī ôr′ī, ā prī ōr′ī), 1 from cause to effect; from a general rule to particular cases. 2 based on opinion or theory rather than on actual observation or experience. [< Medieval Latin, from what comes before]

a pron (ā′prən, ā′pərn), *n.* 1 garment worn over the front part of the body to cover or protect clothes: *a kitchen apron, a carpenter's apron.* 2 area in front of an airport terminal or hangar on which to park aircraft. 3 area of a stage in front of the curtain. 4 a protective structure, layer of material, etc., to prevent the washing away of a surface, as a river bank, by water. [< Old French *naperon,* diminutive of *nape* < Latin *mappa* napkin; Middle English *a napron* taken as *an apron*] **—a′pron like′,** *adj.*

ap ro pos (ap′rə pō′), *adv.* 1 fittingly; opportunely. 2 **apropos of,** with regard to. *—adj.* to the point; fitting; suitable: *an apropos remark.* [< French *à propos* to the purpose]

apse (aps), *n.* a vaulted or arched semicircular or many-sided recess in a church, usually at the east end. [< Latin *apsis* arch, vault < Greek *hapsis* loop, arch]

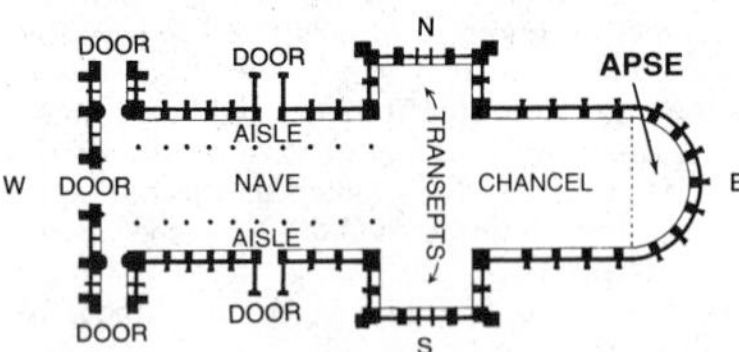

apt (apt), *adj.* 1 fitted by nature; likely; prone: *A careless person is apt to make mistakes.* See **likely** for synonym study. 2 right for the occasion; suitable; fitting: *an apt reply.* 3 quick to learn; intelligent: *an apt pupil.* [< Latin *aptum* joined, fitted] **—apt′ly,** *adv.* **—apt′ness,** *n.*

apt., *pl.* **apts.** apartment.

ap ter ous (ap′tər əs), *adj.* wingless. Lice are apterous insects. [< Greek *apteros* < *a-* without + *pteron* wing]

ap ter yx (ap′tər iks), *n., pl.* **-yx es** (-ik siz). kiwi. [< New Latin < *Greek a-* without + *pteryx* wing]

ap ti tude (ap′tə tüd, ap′tə tyüd), *n.* 1 natural capacity; talent: *an aptitude for business.* 2 natural disposition; propensity; tendency. 3 readiness in learning; quickness to understand; intelligence. 4 special fitness; appropriateness. [< Late Latin *aptitudo* < Latin *aptum* joined, fitted. Doublet of ATTITUDE.]

aptitude test, test given to a person to find out the sort of work, studies, etc., for which he is specially suited.

A pu li a (ə pyü′lē ə, ə pyü′lyə), *n.* district in SE Italy, between the Adriatic and the Gulf of Taranto.

aq., 1 aqua. 2 aqueous.

Aq a ba (ak′ə bə, ä′kä bä), *n.* 1 **Gulf of,** arm of the Red Sea, between NW Arabia and the Sinai Peninsula. 2 seaport in SW Jordan, on the Gulf of Aqaba. 9000.

aq ua (ak′wə), *n.* water. [< Latin]

aq ua cade (ak′wə kād), *n.* display of swimming, diving, and other aquatic skills before an audience. [< *aqua* + *(caval)cade*]

aq ua for tis (ak′wə fôr′tis), nitric acid. [< Latin, strong water]

Aq ua-Lung (ak′wə lung′), *n.* trademark for an underwater breathing device used in skin diving, consisting of one or more cylinders of compressed air strapped to the diver's back, a hose and mouthpiece through which the diver breathes, and sometimes a glass mask placed over the eyes and nose. The supply of air to the diver is regulated automatically by a valve.

aq ua ma rine (ak′wə mə rēn′), *n.* 1 a transparent, bluish-green semiprecious stone that is a variety of beryl. 2 a light bluish

hat, āge, fär; let, ēqual, tėrm;
it, īce; hot, ōpen, ôrder;
oil, out; cup, pu̇t, rüle;
ch, child; ng, long; sh, she;
th, thin; ᴛʜ, then; zh, measure;

ə represents *a* in about, *e* in taken, *i* in pencil, *o* in lemon, *u* in circus.

< = from, derived from, taken from.

green. —*adj.* light bluish-green. [< Latin *aqua marina* sea water]

aq ua naut (ak′wə nôt), *n.* an underwater explorer. [< *aqua* + *-naut,* as in *astronaut*]

aq ua plane (ak′wə plān′), *n., v.,* **-planed, -plan ing.** —*n.* a wide board on which a person rides for sport as it is towed by a speeding motorboat. —*v.t.* ride on an aquaplane for sport.

aq ua re gi a (ak′wə rē′jē ə), mixture of nitric acid and hydrochloric acid that will dissolve gold and platinum. [< New Latin, royal water]

aq ua relle (ak′wə rel′), *n.* a painting done with ink and very thin transparent water colors. [< French]

a quar i um (ə kwer′ē əm), *n., pl.* **a quar i ums, a quar i a** (ə kwer′ē ə). 1 pond, tank, or glass bowl in which living fish, other water animals, and water plants are kept alive for observation and study. 2 building used for showing collections of living fish, water animals, and water plants. [< Latin, a watering place]

A quar i us (ə kwer′ē əs), *n.* 1 a northern constellation supposed to represent a water carrier. 2 the 11th sign of the zodiac; Water Carrier. The sun enters Aquarius about January 21.

a quat ic (ə kwat′ik, ə kwot′ik), *adj.* 1 growing or living in water: *Water lilies are aquatic plants.* 2 taking place in or on water: *Swimming and sailing are aquatic sports.* —*n.* 1 plant or animal that lives in water. 2 **aquatics,** *pl.* sports that take place in or on water. **—a quat′i cal ly,** *adv.*

aq ua tint (ak′wə tint′), *n.* 1 method of etching on copper by the use of a resinous solution and nitric acid, which produces finely granular shaded effects as well as lines resembling those of ink or water-color drawing. 2 etching made by this process. —*v.t., v.i.* etch in aquatint.

aq ue duct (ak′wə dukt), *n.* 1 an artificial channel or large pipe for bringing water from a distance. 2 structure that supports such a channel or pipe. 3 canal or passage in the body. [< Latin *aquaeductus* channel for water]

aqueduct (def. 2)

a que ous (ā′kwē əs, ak′wē əs), *adj.* 1 of or made with water: *The medicine came in an aqueous solution.* 2 like water; watery: *Aqueous matter ran from the sore.* 3 produced by the action of water. Aqueous rocks are formed of the sediment carried and deposited by water.

aqueous humor, watery liquid which fills the space in the eye between the cornea and the lens. See **eye** for diagram.

aq ui fer (ak′wə fər), *n.* (in geology) a stratum of earth or porous rock that contains water. [< Latin *aqua* water + *ferre* to carry]

Aq ui la (ak′wə lə), *n.* a northern constellation in the Milky Way, between Cygnus and Sagittarius; Eagle. It contains the star Altair.

aq ui line (ak′wə līn, ak′wə lən), *adj.* 1 of or like an eagle. 2 curved like an eagle's beak; hooked: *an aquiline nose.* [< Latin *aquilinus* < *aquila* eagle]

A qui nas (ə kwī′nəs), *n.* **Saint Thomas,** 1225?-1274, Italian philosopher and theologian of the Roman Catholic Church.

Aq ui taine (ak′wə tān), *n.* region in SW France. In ancient times the SW part of Gaul, it later became a duchy and finally in 1453 became part of France.

ar-, *prefix.* form of **ad-** before *r,* as in *arrive.*

-ar, *suffix forming adjectives from nouns.* of or having to do with ____: *Polar = of the pole(s). Nuclear = having to do with a nucleus or nuclei.* [< Latin *-aris*]

Ar, argon. Also, **A.**

Ar ab (ar′əb), *n.* 1 native or inhabitant of Arabia. 2 member of a Semitic people now widely scattered over southwestern and southern Asia and northern Africa. 3 Arabian horse. 4 street Arab. —*adj.* of or having to do with the Arabs, their culture, or Arabia.

ar a besque (ar′ə besk′), *n.* 1 an elaborate and fanciful design of flowers, leaves, geometrical figures, etc. 2 a ballet pose in which the dancer stands on one leg, with the other leg extended horizontally behind him. —*adj.* 1 carved or painted in arabesque. 2 elaborate; fanciful. [< French < Italian *arabesco* < *Arabo* Arab]

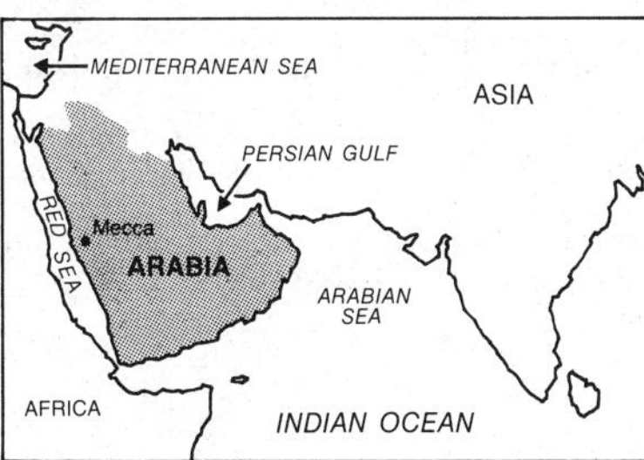

A ra bi a (ə rā′bē ə), *n.* large peninsula in SW Asia. It now includes Saudi Arabia, Yemen, Southern Yemen, Kuwait, Oman, Qatar, and the Union of Arab Emirates. 15,612,000 pop.; 1,000,000 sq. mi.

A ra bi an (ə rā′bē ən), *adj.* of Arabia or the Arabs. —*n.* native or inhabitant of Arabia; Arab.

Arabian camel, dromedary.

Arabian horse, any of a breed of swift, graceful horses originally developed by the Arabs for use in the deserts of Arabia, now used as saddle horses.

Arabian Nights, The, collection of old tales from Arabia, Persia, and India, dating from the A.D. 900's. It contains tales of Ali Baba, Aladdin, and many others.

Arabian Sea, part of the Indian Ocean between Arabia and India.

Ar a bic (ar′ə bik), *n.* the Semitic language of the Arabs, related to Hebrew. Arabic is now spoken chiefly in Arabia, Iraq, Syria, Jordan, Lebanon, and North Africa. —*adj.* of or having to do with the Arabs or their language.

Arabic numerals or **Arabic figures,** the figures 1, 2, 3, 4, 5, 6, 7, 8, 9, 0. They are called Arabic because they were introduced into western Europe by Arabian scholars.

ar a bil i ty (ar′ə bil′ə tē), *n.* quality or condition of being arable.

ar a ble (ar′ə bəl), *adj.* (of land) suitable for producing crops which require plowing and tillage. —*n.* arable land. [< Latin *arabilis* able to be plowed < *arare* to plow]

Arab League, a group of Arab nations organized in 1945 to promote closer relations among its members. The Arab League includes Algeria, Egypt, Iraq, Jordan, Kuwait, Lebanon, Libya, Morocco, Saudi Arabia, Southern Yemen, Sudan, Syria, Tunisia, and Yemen.

Ar a by (ar′ə bē), *n.* ARCHAIC. Arabia.

A rach ne (ə rak′nē), *n.* (in Greek myths) a maiden who dared to challenge Athena to a contest in weaving, and was changed by her into a spider.

a rach nid (ə rak′nid), *n.* any of a class of arthropods closely allied to the insects and crustaceans, but distinguished by the possession of eight legs, the absence of wings and antennae, having the body divided into two regions, and breathing by means of tracheal tubes or pulmonary sacs. Spiders, scorpions, mites, ticks, and daddy-longlegs belong to this class. —*adj.* arachnidan. [< Greek *arachnē* spider, web]

A rach ni da (ə rak′nə də), *n.pl.* class of invertebrates comprising the arachnids.

a rach ni dan (ə rak′nə dən), *adj.* of or having to do with arachnids. —*n.* arachnid.

a rach noid (ə rak′noid), *adj.* 1 of or resembling an arachnid. 2 of or designating the delicate serous membrane enveloping the brain and spinal cord.

Ar a gon (ar′ə gon), *n.* region in NE Spain, adjoining France. In the Middle Ages it was a kingdom; it was united to Castile by the marriage of Ferdinand V and Isabella I in 1469. See **Castile** for map.

a rag o nite (ə rag′ə nīt, ar′ə gə nīt), *n.* one of the two crystalline forms of calcium carbonate, the other being calcite. [< *Aragon,* where it was found]

Ar al (ar′əl), *n.* **Lake,** Aral Sea.

Aral Sea, inland sea in the SW Soviet Union, east of the Caspian Sea. 26,200 sq. mi. See **Assyria** for map.

Ar a ma ic (ar′ə mā′ik), *n.* a Semitic language or group of dialects, including Syriac and the language spoken in Palestine at the time of Jesus. Much Jewish and early Christian literature was written in Aramaic. —*adj.* of or in Aramaic.

A rap a ho (ə rap′ə hō), *n., pl.* **-ho** or **-hos.** member of an Algonquian Indian tribe of originally nomadic and warlike Indians that once lived in Colorado and are now settled on reservations in Wyoming and Oklahoma.

A rap a hoe (ə rap′ə hō), *n., pl.* **-hoes.** Arapaho.

Ar a rat (ar′ə rat′), *n.* mountain in E Turkey. Noah's Ark is said to have grounded there after the Flood. 16,900 ft.

Ar au ca ni an (ar′ô kā′nē ən), *n.* member

of a group of South American Indian tribes in Chile and Argentina.

A ra wak (ä′rä wäk), *n.* 1 member of a South American Indian tribe now living mostly in Brazil. 2 language of this tribe.

A ra wak an (ä′rä wä′kən), *adj.* 1 of or denoting a large family of South American Indian languages now found chiefly in northern South America, but formerly spoken also in the West Indies. 2 of or having to do with the Arawaks. —*n.* 1 an Arawak. 2 the Arawakan language family.

ar ba lest or **ar ba list** (är′bə list), *n.* a powerful medieval crossbow with a steel bow. See **crossbow** for picture. [< Old French *arbaleste* < Late Latin *arcuballista* < Latin *arcus* bow + *ballista* machine for throwing heavy missiles]

ar bi ter (är′bə tər), *n.* 1 person considered to have full power to decide; judge: *an arbiter of good taste.* 2 person chosen to decide a dispute; arbitrator. [< Latin]

ar bi tra ble (är′bə trə bəl), *adj.* that can be decided by arbitration.

ar bit ra ment (är bit′rə mənt), *n.* 1 decision by an arbitrator or arbiter. 2 act of deciding a dispute as an arbiter or arbitrator.

ar bi trar y (är′bə trer′ē), *adj.* 1 based on one's own wishes, notions, or will; not going by rule or law: *The judge tried to be fair and did not make arbitrary decisions.* 2 fixed or determined by chance: *an arbitrary serial number.* 3 using or abusing unlimited power; tyrannical; despotic: *an arbitrary king.* **—ar′bi trar′i ly,** *adv.* **—ar′bi trar′i ness,** *n.*

ar bi trate (är′bə trāt), *v.*, **-trat ed, -trat ing.** —*v.i.* give a decision in a dispute; act as arbiter; mediate: *arbitrate between two persons in a quarrel.* —*v.t.* settle by arbitration: *arbitrate a dispute.* [< Latin *arbitratum* decided, judged < *arbiter*]

ar bi tra tion (är′bə trā′shən), *n.* act of arbitrating; settlement of a dispute by a person or persons to whom the conflicting parties agree to refer it for a decision.

ar bi tra tion al (är′bə trā′shə nəl), *adj.* of or involving arbitration.

ar bi tra tive (är′bə trā′tiv), *adj.* having power to arbitrate; done by arbitration.

ar bi tra tor (är′bə trā′tər), *n.* 1 person chosen to decide or settle a dispute. 2 person with full power to judge or decide; arbiter.

ar bor[1] (är′bər), *n.* a shady place formed by trees, shrubs, or by vines growing on a lattice. [< Anglo-French *erber* < Late Latin *herbarium* < Latin *herba* herb. Doublet of HERBARIUM.]

ar bor[2] (är′bər), *n.* the main shaft or axle of a machine by means of which mechanical force is transmitted. [< Latin, tree]

Arbor Day, day set aside in many states of the United States for planting trees. The date varies in different states.

ar bo re al (är bôr′ē əl, är bōr′ē əl), *adj.* 1 living in or among trees. A squirrel is an arboreal animal. 2 of or like trees. **—ar bo′re al ly,** *adv.*

ar bo res cent (är′bə res′nt), *adj.* like a tree in structure, growth, or appearance; branching.

ar bo re tum (är′bə rē′təm), *n., pl.* **-tums, -ta** (-tə). place where trees and shrubs are grown and exhibited for scientific and educational purposes.

ar bo rize (är′bə rīz′), *v.i.*, **-rized, -riz ing.** have or produce branching formations.

ar bor vi rus (är′bər vī′rəs), *n.* virus transmitted by arthropods. Yellow fever, dengue, and equine encephalitis are caused by arborviruses. [< *ar(thropod-)bor(ne) virus*]

ar bor vi tae (är′bər vī′tē), *n.* any of several evergreen trees of the pine family, often planted for ornament and for hedges. [< Latin *arbor vitae* tree of life]

ar bu tus (är byü′təs), *n.* 1 a trailing plant of eastern North America, belonging to the heath family, having clusters of fragrant, pink or white flowers blooming very early in the spring; mayflower; trailing arbutus. 2 shrub or tree of the heath family that has clusters of large white or pinkish flowers and scarlet berries. [< Latin]

arc (ärk), *n., v.,* **arced** (ärkt), **arc ing** (är′king), or **arcked, arck ing.** —*n.* 1 a continuous part of the circumference of a circle or any curve. 2 a curved stream of brilliant light or sparks formed as a strong electric current jumps from one conductor to another. —*v.i.* 1 form an electric arc. 2 take or follow a curved path. [< Latin *arcus* bow] **—arc′like′,** *adj.*

Arc (ärk), *n.* See **Joan of Arc.**

ar cade (är kād′), *n.* 1 passageway with an arched roof, often lined with small stores. 2 building having such a passageway. 3 row of arches supported by columns. [< French]

Ar ca di a (är kā′dē ə), *n.* 1 mountain district in the S part of ancient Greece, famous for the simple, contented life of its people. See **Peloponnesus** for map. 2 any region of simple, quiet contentment. **—Ar ca′di an,** *adj., n.*

ar cane (är kān′), *adj.* understood only by a few; secret. [< Latin *arcanus* hidden < *arca* chest, box]

ar ca num (är kā′nəm), *n., pl.* **-nums, -na** (-nə). a secret. [< Latin]

arch[1] (def. 1)

arch[1] (ärch), *n.* 1 a curved structure capable of bearing the weight of the material above it and usually spanning an opening such as a door, window, or gateway. 2 monument forming an arch or arches. 3 archway. 4 instep. Fallen arches cause flat feet. 5 something like an arch: *the great blue arch of the sky.* —*v.t.* 1 bend into an arch; curve. 2 furnish with an arch. 3 form an arch over; span. —*v.i.* bend into an arch; curve. [< Old French *arche* < Medieval Latin *arca* < Latin *arcus* arch; bow]

arch[2] (ärch), *adj.* 1 playfully mischievous; saucy; sly; roguish: *an arch look.* 2 chief; principal; leading: *an arch rebel.* 3 ARCHAIC. cunning; crafty. [< *arch-*] **—arch′ly,** *adv.* **—arch′ness,** *n.*

arch-, *prefix.* 1 chief or principal ____: *Archbishop = chief bishop.* 2 extreme; ultra-: *Archconservative = extreme conservative.* [< Greek < *archein* be first, lead]

arch., 1 archipelago. 2 architecture.

archaeo-, *combining form.* ancient; primitive: *Archaeology = study of ancient (things).* [< Greek *archaios* < *archē* beginning]

ar chae o log i cal (är′kē ə loj′ə kəl), *adj.* of or having to do with archaeology. Also, **archeological. —ar′chae o log′i cal ly,** *adv.*

ar chae ol o gist (är′kē ol′ə jist), *n.* an expert in archaeology. Also, **archeologist.**

ar chae ol o gy (är′kē ol′ə jē), *n.* the scientific study of the people, customs, and life of ancient times, antedating the keeping of historic records. Through excavation, identification, and study of the remains of ancient cities and of tools, pottery, monuments, or any other remains archaeology is able to reconstruct a picture of life in the past. Also, **archeology.**

archaeopteryx
1½ ft. long,
wingspread
up to 2 ft.

ar chae op ter yx (är′kē op′tər iks), *n.* the oldest known fossil bird, belonging to the European Jurassic period and having such reptilian characteristics as teeth and a bony tail. [< *archaeo-* + Greek *pteryx* wing]

ar cha ic (är kā′ik), *adj.* 1 no longer used in ordinary language, but surviving in certain special contexts, as that of law or older translations of the Bible. The words *forsooth* and *methinks* are archaic. 2 of earlier times; out-of-date; antiquated. [< Greek *archaikos* < *archē* beginning]

ar cha ism (är′kē iz′əm, är′kā iz′əm), *n.* 1 word or expression no longer in general use. 2 the use in literature, art, etc., of what is characteristic of an earlier period. 3 law, custom, etc., that is archaic or is thought of as archaic.

arch an gel (ärk′ān′jəl), *n.* angel of the highest order; one of the seven chief angels.

Arch an gel (ärk′ān′jəl), *n.* seaport in the NW Soviet Union, on the White Sea. 343,000.

arch an gel ic (ärk′an jel′ik), *adj.* of or like an archangel.

arch bish op (ärch′bish′əp), *n.* a bishop of the highest rank, especially one presiding over an archdiocese.

arch bish op ric (ärch′bish′əp rik), *n.* 1 archdiocese. 2 position, rank, or dignity of an archbishop.

arch con serv a tive (ärch′kən sėr′və tiv), *adj.* ultraconservative. —*n.* an extreme conservative; reactionary.

arch dea con (ärch′dē′kən), *n.* 1 assistant to a bishop in the Church of England, who superintends the work of other members of the clergy. 2 (formerly, in the Roman Catholic Church) member of a cathedral chapter possessing great temporal and ecclesiastical powers.

arch dea con ate (ärch′dē′kə nit), *n.* office of an archdeacon.

arch dea con ry (ärch′dē′kən rē), *n., pl.* **-ries.** district, position, rank, or residence of an archdeacon.

arch di oc e san (ärch′dī os′ə sən), *adj.* of an archdiocese.

hat, āge, fär; let, ēqual, tėrm;
it, īce; hot, ōpen, ôrder;
oil, out; cup, pu̇t, rüle;
ch, child; ng, long; sh, she;
th, thin; ᴛʜ, then; zh, measure;

ə represents *a* in about, *e* in taken, *i* in pencil, *o* in lemon, *u* in circus.

< = from, derived from, taken from.

arch di o cese (ärch′dī′ə sis, ärch′dī′ə-sēs′), *n.* a church district governed by an archbishop.

arch du cal (ärch′dü′kəl, ärch′dyü′kəl), *adj.* of an archduke or archduchy.

arch duch ess (ärch′duch′is), *n.* 1 wife or widow of an archduke. 2 princess of the former ruling house of Austria-Hungary.

arch duch y (ärch′duch′ē), *n., pl.* **-duch-ies.** territory under the rule of an archduke or archduchess.

arch duke (ärch′dük′, ärch′dyük′), *n.* prince of the former ruling house of Austria-Hungary.

arched (ärcht), *adj.* having an arch or arches.

ar che go ni al (är′kə gō′nē əl), *adj.* of or having to do with an archegonium.

ar che go ni um (är′kə gō′nē əm), *n., pl.* **-ni a** (-nē ə). the female reproductive organ in ferns, mosses, etc. [< Greek *archē* beginning + *gonos* race]

arch en e my (ärch′en′ə mē), *n., pl.* **-mies.** a principal enemy.

ar chen te ron (är ken′tə ron′), *n.* the primitive intestinal or alimentary cavity of a gastrula.

ar che o log i cal (är′kē ə loj′ə kəl), *adj.* archaeological. **—ar′che o log′i cal ly,** *adv.*

ar che ol o gist (är′kē ol′ə jist), *n.* archaeologist.

ar che ol o gy (är′kē ol′ə jē), *n.* archaeology.

Ar che o zo ic (är′kē ə zō′ik), *n.* 1 the oldest geological era, during which the first forms of life appeared. See chart under **geology.** 2 rocks formed during this era. *—adj.* of or having to do with this era or its rocks.

arch er (är′chər), *n.* 1 person who shoots with a bow and arrow; bowman. 2 **Archer,** Sagittarius. [< Anglo-French, ultimately < Latin *arcus* bow]

arch er y (är′chər ē), *n.* 1 practice or sport of shooting with a bow and arrow. 2 archers.

ar che typ al (är′kə tī′pəl), *adj.* of or constituting an archetype.

ar che type (är′kə tīp), *n.* an original model or pattern from which copies are made, or out of which later forms develop; prototype. [< Greek *archetypon* < *archein* begin + *typos* type]

arch fiend (ärch′fēnd′), *n.* 1 chief fiend. 2 Satan.

ar chi e pis co pal (är′kē i pis′kə pəl), *adj.* of or having to do with an archbishop or an archbishopric.

Ar chi me de an (är′kə mē′dē ən), *adj.* of or invented by Archimedes.

Ar chi me des (är′kə mē′dēz), *n.* 287?-212 B.C., Greek mathematician, physicist, and inventor, who first stated the principles underlying specific gravity and the use of the lever.

ar chi pel a gic (är′kə pə laj′ik, är′chə-pə laj′ik), *adj.* of or having to do with an archipelago.

ar chi pel a go (är′kə pel′ə gō, är′chə-pel′ə gō), *n., pl.* **-gos** or **-goes.** 1 group of many islands. 2 sea having many islands in it. [< Italian *arcipelago* < *arci-* chief + *pelago* sea]

ar chi tect (är′kə tekt), *n.* 1 person whose profession it is to design, lay out plans for, and thereafter to supervise generally the construction of buildings. 2 designer; maker; creator. [< Greek *architektōn* < *archi-* chief + *tektōn* builder]

ar chi tec ton ic (är′kə tek ton′ik), *adj.* having to do with architecture, construction, or design, especially as an organized set of principles. **—ar′chi tec ton′i cal ly,** *adv.*

ar chi tec ton ics (är′kə tek ton′iks), *n.* 1 *pl. in form, sing. in use.* science of architecture. 2 *pl. in form, sometimes sing. in use.* the design or structure of a work of art.

ar chi tec tur al (är′kə tek′chər əl), *adj.* of or having to do with architecture; according to the principles of architecture. **—ar′chi-tec′tur al ly,** *adv.*

ar chi tec ture (är′kə tek′chər), *n.* 1 science or art of planning and designing buildings. 2 style or qualities that distinguish the buildings of one time, region, or group from those of another: *Greek architecture made much use of columns.* 3 architectural work; construction. 4 structure.

ar chi trave (är′kə trāv), *n.* the main beam resting on the top of a column or row of columns. See **entablature** for diagram. [< Italian < *archi-* chief + *trave* beam]

ar chiv al (är kī′vəl), *adj.* of or having to do with an archive or archives.

ar chive (är′kīv), *n.* Usually, **archives,** *pl.* 1 place where public records or historical documents are kept. 2 the public records or historical documents kept in such a place. [< Latin *archivum* < Greek *archeia* < *archē* government]

ar chiv ist (är′kə vist, är′kī vist), *n.* keeper of archives.

ar chon (är′kon), *n.* 1 (in ancient Athens) a chief magistrate. 2 ruler. [< Greek *archōn* < *archein* to rule]

arch way (ärch′wā′), *n.* 1 entrance or passageway with an arch above it. 2 an arch covering a passageway.

arc lamp or **arc light,** lamp in which the light comes from an electric arc.

arc tic (ärk′tik, är′tik), *adj.* 1 at or near the North Pole; of the north polar region: *the arctic fox.* 2 extremely cold; frigid. *—n.* 1 **the Arctic,** the north polar region. 2 **arctics,** *pl.* warm, waterproof overshoes. [< Greek *arktikos* of the Bear (constellation) < *arktos* bear]

arctic circle or **Arctic Circle,** the imaginary boundary of the north polar region, running parallel to the equator at 66 degrees 30 minutes (66°30′) north latitude.

Arctic Ocean, ocean of the north polar region. 5,400,000 sq. mi.

Arctic Sea, Arctic Ocean.

Arctic Zone, region between the arctic circle and the North Pole.

Arc tur us (ärk tu̇r′əs, ärk tyu̇r′əs), *n.* the brightest star in the constellation Boötes, in the northern sky.

ar den cy (ärd′n sē), *n.* condition of being ardent.

Ar dennes (är den′), *n.* mountain and forest region in NE France, SE Belgium, and Luxembourg.

ar dent (ärd′nt), *adj.* 1 glowing with passion; passionate; impassioned: *ardent love.* 2 eager; keen. 3 burning; fiery; hot: *an ardent fever.* 4 glowing. [< Latin *ardentem* burning] **—ar′dent ly,** *adv.*

ar dor (är′dər), *n.* 1 warmth of emotion; passion. 2 great enthusiasm; eagerness; zeal: *patriotic ardor.* [< Latin < *ardere* to burn]

ar du ous (är′jü əs), *adj.* 1 hard to do; requiring much effort; difficult: *an arduous lesson.* 2 using up much energy; strenuous: *an arduous climb.* [< Latin *arduus* steep] **—ar′du ous ly,** *adv.* **—ar′du ous ness,** *n.*

are[1] (är; *unstressed* ər), *v.* the plural and second person singular, present indicative of **be.** [Old English *aron*]

are[2] (er, ar, är), *n.* unit of surface measure in the metric system, equal to 100 square meters, or 119.6 square yards. See **measure** for table. [< French < Latin *area* area]

ar e a (er′ē ə, ar′ē ə), *n.* 1 amount of surface; extent of surface: *The area of this floor is 600 square feet.* 2 range of knowledge or interest; sphere of activity; field: *the area of the exact sciences.* 3 region or district: *the Rocky Mountain area.* 4 a level, open space. 5 yard or court of a building. [< Latin, piece of level ground]

area code, combination of three numerals used to dial directly by telephone from one region of the United States and Canada to another.

ar e al (er′ē əl, ar′ē əl), *adj.* of or having to do with an area.

ar e a way (er′ē ə wā′, ar′ē ə wā′), *n.* 1 a sunken area or court at the entrance to a cellar or basement. 2 area used as a passageway between buildings.

a re na (ə rē′nə), *n.* 1 space in an ancient Roman amphitheater in which contests or shows took place. 2 a similar space, surrounded by seats, used today for contests or shows: *a boxing arena.* 3 building in which indoor sports are played. 4 any place of conflict and trial. 5 field of endeavor: *the political arena.* [< Latin, variant of *harena* sand]

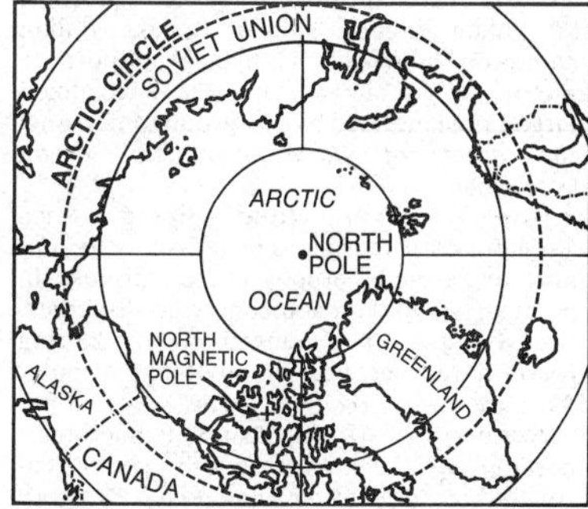

arena theater, theater-in-the-round.

aren't (ärnt, är′ənt), 1 are not. 2 am not: *Why aren't I allowed to stay?*

a re o la (ə rē′ə lə), *n., pl.* **-lae** (-lē′), **-las.** a ring of color: *the areola about a pustule.* [< Latin, diminutive of *area* area]

Ar e op a gus (ar′ē op′ə gəs), *n.* 1 a hill in Athens, west of the Acropolis. 2 the highest judicial court of ancient Athens, which met there.

Ar es (er′ēz, ar′ēz), *n.* (in Greek myths) the god of war, identified with the Roman god Mars.

Ar e thu sa (ar′ə thü′zə), *n.* (in Greek legends) a nymph who was changed into a stream by Artemis to save her from the pursuing river god Alpheus.

ar gent (är′jənt), *n.* silver. *—adj.* silvery. [< Latin *argentum*]

Ar gen ti na (är′jən tē′nə), *n.* country in S South America. 24,352,000 pop.; 1,084,000 sq. mi. *Capital:* Buenos Aires. **—Ar gen tin e an** or **Ar gen tin i an** (är′jən-tin′ē ən), *adj., n.*

Ar gen tine (är′jən tēn′, är′jən tīn), *adj.* of Argentina or its people. *—n.* 1 native or inhabitant of Argentina. 2 **the Argentine,** Argentina.

ar gi nine (är′jə nīn), *n.* one of the amino acids in plant and animal proteins. *Formula:* $C_6H_{14}O_2N_4$

Ar give (är′jīv, är′gīv), *adj.* 1 of Argos. 2 Greek. *—n.* 1 native or inhabitant of Argos. 2 a Greek.

Ar go (är′gō), *n.* 1 (in Greek legends) the ship in which Jason and the Argonauts sailed. 2 a large southern constellation between Canis Major and the Southern Cross.

ar gon (är′gon), *n.* a colorless, odorless, inert gaseous element that forms a very small part of the air. Argon is used in electric light bulbs and radio tubes. *Symbol:* A or Ar; *atomic number* 18. See pages 326 and 327 for table. [< Greek, neuter of *argos* idle < *a-* without + *ergon* work]

Ar go naut (är′gə nôt), *n.* 1 **the Argonauts,** (in Greek legends) a group of men who sailed with Jason in search of the Golden Fleece. 2 person who went to California in 1849 in search of gold.

Ar gonne (är′gon), *n.* forest in NE France. Battles of World War I and World War II were fought there.

Ar gos (är′gos, är′gəs), *n.* town in S Greece. In ancient times it was one of the principal city-states of the Peloponnesus. 17,000. See **Peloponnesus** for map.

ar go sy (är′gə sē), *n., pl.* **-sies.** ARCHAIC. 1 a large merchant ship. 2 fleet of such ships. [< Italian *Ragusea* ship of Ragusa, Italian name for Dubrovnik, a Yugoslavian port]

ar got (är′gō, är′gət), *n.* the specialized jargon or slang used by any group of persons: *the argot of thieves, soldiers' argot.* [< French]

ar gue (är′gyü), *v.,* **-gued, -gu ing.** *—v.i.* 1 put forward reasons selected so as to support or refute a proposal, etc.; discuss (a point of view) with someone who disagrees. See **discuss** for synonym study. 2 bring forward reasons against anything; dispute: *You are always ready to argue.* *—v.t.* 1 put forward reasons for or against (something): *argue a question.* 2 persuade by giving reasons: *They argued me into going.* 3 try to prove by reasoning; maintain: *Columbus argued that the world was round.* 4 indicate; show; prove: *Her rich clothes argue her to be wealthy.* [< Old French *arguer* < Latin *argutare* to chatter < *arguere* make clear] **—ar′gu a ble,** *adj.* **—ar′gu a bly,** *adv.* **—ar′gu er,** *n.*

ar gu ment (är′gyə mənt), *n.* 1 discussion by persons who disagree. See synonym study below. 2 a giving reasons for or against something. 3 reason or reasons offered for or against something. 4 summary or synopsis of what is in a book, poem, etc.

Syn. 1 Argument, controversy, dispute mean presentation of varying opinions by persons who disagree on some question. **Argument** suggests an intellectual encounter in which each side uses facts and reasons to try to convince the other: *I won the argument by producing figures to prove my point.* **Controversy** tends to suggest a more or less formal argument between groups, often carried on in writing or speeches: *The controversy over American schools still continues.* **Dispute** suggests contradicting rather than reasoning, and applies to an argument marked by feeling: *The dispute over the property was settled in court.*

ar gu men ta tion (är′gyə men tā′shən), *n.* 1 discussion of reasons for and against anything. 2 methodical presentation of arguments. 3 series of arguments.

ar gu men ta tive (är′gyə men′tə tiv), *adj.* 1 fond of arguing; quarrelsome. 2 containing argument; controversial. **—ar′gu men′ta tive ly,** *adv.* **—ar′gu men′ta tive ness,** *n.*

Ar gus (är′gəs), *n.* 1 (in Greek myths) a giant with a hundred eyes. 2 a watchful guardian.

Ar gus-eyed (är′gəs īd′), *adj.* keenly watchful; observant.

ar gyle (är′gīl), *adj.* of or designating a pattern of diamond-shaped areas and lines in various colors resembling a plaid, used for knitted articles such as socks or neckties. *—n.* sock or other article having such a pattern. [< variant of *Argyll*]

Ar gyll (är gīl′), *n.* county in W Scotland.

a ri a (är′ē ə, er′ē ə, ar′ē ə), *n.* 1 song for a voice or instrument; air; melody. 2 (in operas, oratorios, and cantatas) a vocal solo, often consisting of two or three parts. [< Italian < Latin *aer* air < Greek *aēr*]

Ar i ad ne (ar′ē ad′nē), *n.* (in Greek legends) the daughter of Minos, king of Crete, who gave Theseus a ball of thread to help him find his way out of the Labyrinth after he killed the Minotaur.

Ar i an (er′ē ən, ar′ē ən), *adj.* of or having to do with the doctrine, denounced as heretical, that Christ the Son is subordinate to God the Father because Christ was begotten of, created by, and therefore came into being after God. *—n.* believer in this doctrine. [< *Arius*]

ar id (ar′id), *adj.* 1 having very little rainfall; dry: *an arid climate.* 2 unfruitful because of lack of moisture; barren: *arid soil.* 3 uninteresting and empty; dull: *an arid, tiresome speech.* [< Latin *aridus* < *arere* be dry] **—ar′id ly,** *adv.* **—ar′id ness,** *n.*

a rid i ty (ə rid′ə tē), *n.* 1 arid condition. 2 dullness.

Ar i el (er′ē əl, ar′ē əl), *n.* an airy spirit who helped Prospero in Shakespeare's play *The Tempest.*

Ar ies (er′ēz, er′ē ēz′; ar′ēz, ar′ē ēz′), *n.* 1 a northern constellation between Pisces and Taurus, thought to be shaped like a ram. 2 the first sign of the zodiac; Ram. The sun enters Aries about March 21.

a right (ə rīt′), *adv.* correctly; rightly.

ar il (ar′il), *n.* an outside covering of certain seeds. The pulpy inner pod of the bittersweet is an aril. [< Medieval Latin *arilli* raisins]

ar il late (ar′ə lāt), *adj.* having an aril or arils.

A ri os to (ä′rē os′tō), *n.* **Ludovico,** 1474-1533, Italian poet.

a rise (ə rīz′), *v.i.,* **a rose, a ris en, a ris ing.** 1 rise up; get up: *arise from one's seat, arise from bed.* 2 move upward; ascend: *Smoke arose from the chimney.* 3 come into being or action; come about; appear; begin: *A great wind arose. Accidents arise from carelessness.* [Old English *ārīsan*]

a ris en (ə riz′n), *v.* pp. of **arise.**

Ar is ti des (ar′ə stī′dēz), *n.* 530?-468? B.C., Athenian statesman and general. He was often called "the Just."

ar is toc ra cy (ar′ə stok′rə sē), *n., pl.* **-cies.** 1 class of people having a high position in society because of birth, rank, or title; nobility. Earls, dukes, and princes belong to the aristocracy. 2 class of people considered superior because of intelligence, culture, or wealth; upper class. 3 government in which the nobility or any privileged upper class rules. 4 country or state having such a government. 5 government by the best citizens. [< Late Latin *aristocratia* < Greek *aristokratia* < *aristos* best + *kratos* rule]

a ris to crat (ə ris′tə krat), *n.* 1 person who belongs to the aristocracy; noble. 2 person like an aristocrat in tastes, opinions, and manners. 3 person who favors government by an aristocracy.

a ris to crat ic (ə ris′tə krat′ik), *adj.* 1 of or connected with aristocrats: *the aristocratic class.* 2 in keeping with the character of an aristocrat; stylish or grand: *an aristocratic air.* 3 snobbish; exclusive. 4 favoring aristocrats or government by aristocrats. **—a ris′to crat′i cal ly,** *adv.*

Ar is toph a nes (ar′ə stof′ə nēz′), *n.* 448?-385 B.C., Greek writer of comedies.

Ar is to te li an (ar′ə stə tē′lē ən, ə ris′tə-tē′lyən), *adj.* of Aristotle or his philosophy. *—n.* 1 follower or student of Aristotle or his philosophy. 2 person whose reasoning is characterized by an emphasis on the empirical and the particular as opposed to the hypothetical and the general.

Ar is to te li an ism (ar′ə stə tē′lē ə niz′-əm, ə ris′tə tē′lyə niz′əm), *n.* the philosophic system or principles of Aristotle.

Ar is tot le (ar′ə stot′l), *n.* 384-322 B.C., Greek philosopher and scientist, student of Plato and the tutor of Alexander the Great.

arith., 1 arithmetic. 2 arithmetical.

a rith me tic (*n.* ə rith′mə tik; *adj.* ar′ith-met′ik), *n.* 1 art or practice of computing with numbers, especially positive, real numbers by addition, subtraction, multiplication, division, involution, and extraction of roots. 2 the study of numbers and their relationship. 3 textbook or treatise on arithmetic. *—adj.* arithmetical. [< Greek *arithmētikē* < *arithmos* number]

ar ith met i cal (ar′ith met′ə kəl), *adj.* of arithmetic; according to the rules of arithmetic. **—ar′ith met′i cal ly,** *adv.*

arithmetical mean, arithmetic mean.

arithmetical progression, sequence of numbers, each of which is obtained from the preceding number of the sequence by adding or subtracting the same number. 2, 4, 6, 8, 10 form an arithmetical progression.

a rith me ti cian (ə rith′mə tish′ən), *n.* an expert in arithmetic.

ar ith met ic mean (ar′ith met′ik), average (def. 1).

ar ith met ic unit (ar′ith met′ik), part of a digital computer in which arithmetical operations are performed.

Ar i us (er′ē əs, ar′ē əs, ə rī′əs), *n.* died A.D. 336, Greek priest of Alexandria who asserted that Christ the Son was subordinate to God the Father.

Ariz., Arizona.

Ar i zo na (ar′ə zō′nə), *n.* one of the southwestern states of the United States. 1,773,000 pop.; 113,900 sq. mi. *Capital:*

Phoenix. *Abbrev.:* Ariz. **—Ar′i zo′nan, Ar′i zo′ni an,** *adj., n.*

ark (ärk), *n.* 1 (in the Bible) the large boat in which Noah saved himself, his family, and a pair of each kind of animal from the Flood. 2 INFORMAL. any large, clumsy boat. 3 Ark of the Covenant. 4 cabinet in a synagogue for housing scrolls of the Pentateuch. [Old English *earc* < Latin *arca* chest]

Ark., Arkansas.

Ar kan sas (är′kən sô *for 1;* är′kən sô, är-kan′zəs *for 2*), *n.* 1 one of the south central states of the United States. 1,923,000 pop.; 53,100 sq. mi. *Capital:* Little Rock. *Abbrev.:* Ark. 2 **Arkansas River,** river flowing from central Colorado southeast into the Mississippi. 1450 mi. **—Ar kan san** (är kan′zən), *adj., n.*

Ark of the Covenant, (in the Bible) the wooden chest or box in which the Hebrews kept the two tablets of stone containing the Ten Commandments.

Ark wright (ärk′rīt), *n.* Sir **Richard,** 1732-1792, English inventor of the spinning jenny.

Ar ling ton (är′ling tən), *n.* 1 the largest national cemetery in the United States, in NE Virginia, across the Potomac from Washington, D.C. 2 the county in which it is located. 174,000. 3 city in NE Texas. 90,000.

arm[1] (ärm), *n.* 1 the part of the human body between the shoulder and the hand, sometimes including the latter. 2 forelimb of any vertebrate, especially of a bear, ape, or other animal that stands on its hind legs. 3 a support for an arm: *the arm of a chair.* 4 a main branch or limb of any tree. 5 part of an instrument or machine projecting from a trunk, axis, etc. 6 a narrow bay or inlet: *an arm of the sea.* 7 the part of a garment covering the arm; sleeve. 8 power; authority: *the strong arm of the law.* 9 **arm in arm,** with arms linked: *She walked arm in arm with her sister.* 10 **with open arms,** in a warm, friendly way; cordially. [Old English *earm*] **—arm′like′,** *adj.*

arm[2] (ärm), *n.* 1 weapon, or anything used as a weapon. See **arms.** 2 a combat branch of one of the armed forces, such as the infantry, or artillery. 3 one of the armed forces viewed as an organized unit, such as the army, navy, or air force. *—v.t.* 1 supply with weapons. 2 install guns in or on: *arm a vessel.* 3 supply with any means of defense or attack: *Each lawyer entered court armed with the evidence.* 4 make ready for use in war: *arm a torpedo with a warhead.* 5 provide with a protective covering. *—v.i.* 1 take up weapons; prepare for war: *The soldiers armed for battle.* 2 prepare to take action *(against): Let us arm against injustice.* [singular of *arms* < Old French *armes* < Latin *arma,* plural] **—arm′er,** *n.*

ar ma da (är mä′də), *n.* 1 a large fleet of warships. 2 **the Armada,** the Spanish fleet that was sent to attack England in 1588 but was defeated in the English Channel. 3 any large group of military vehicles. [< Spanish < Medieval Latin *armata* armed force. Doublet of ARMY.]

ar ma dil lo (är′mə dil′ō), *n., pl.* **-los.** any of several small, burrowing, chiefly nocturnal mammals ranging from Texas to tropical America. Armadillos are covered with an armorlike shell of small, bony plates and some species can roll themselves, when attacked, into a ball sheltered by this armor. [< Spanish, diminutive of *armado* armed (one) < Latin *armatum* armed]

Ar ma ged don (är′mə ged′n), *n.* 1 (in the Bible) the great and final conflict between the forces of good and evil at the end of the world. 2 any great and final conflict.

ar ma ment (är′mə mənt), *n.* 1 the weapons, ammunition, and equipment of a military force, vehicle, or installation; war equipment and supplies. 2 the army, navy, and other military forces of a country, including both men and equipment. 3 act or process of arming; preparation for war.

ar ma ture (är′mə chər), *n.* 1 a revolving part of an electric motor or dynamo, consisting of wire wound around an iron core placed between opposite poles of a magnet. 2 piece of soft iron placed in contact with the poles of a magnet. 3 a movable part of an electric relay or buzzer. 4 armor. 5 the protective or defensive covering of an animal or plant. A turtle's shell is an armature. 6 (in sculpture) a framework over which clay is applied in modeling. [< Latin *armatura* armor < *armare* to arm. Doublet of ARMOR.]

arm band (ärm′band′), *n.* band of cloth worn around the upper arm as a symbol or badge: *She wore a mourning armband of black.*

arm chair (ärm′cher′, ärm′char′), *n.* chair with sidepieces to support a person's arms or elbows. *—adj.* 1 expressing opinions or theorizing about a subject without being directly involved or having practical experience in it: *an armchair politician.* 2 sharing by reading, etc., in another's experiences: *an armchair explorer.*

armed forces, all the military, naval, and air forces of a country.

Ar me ni a (är mē′nē ə), *n.* 1 former country of SW Asia, now divided among Turkey, Iran, and the Soviet Union. See **Persia** for map. 2 Armenian S.S.R. **—Ar me′ni an,** *adj., n.*

Armenian S.S.R., one of the constituent republics of the U.S.S.R., in the SW part, on the Black Sea. 2,500,000 pop.; 11,500 sq. mi. *Capital:* Yerevan.

arm ful (ärm′fu̇l), *n., pl.* **-fuls.** as much as one arm or both arms can hold.

arm hole (ärm′hōl′), *n.* hole for the arm or sleeve in a garment.

Ar min i us (är min′ē əs), *n.* **Jacobus,** 1560-1609, Dutch Protestant theologian who criticized Calvin's doctrines and believed that there was a chance of salvation for all men through God's grace.

ar mi stice (är′mə stis), *n.* a stop in fighting, by agreement on all sides; temporary peace; truce. [< New Latin *armistitium* < Latin *arma* arms + *sistere* to stop, stand]

Armistice Day, U.S. November 11, the anniversary of the end of World War I in 1918. As an official holiday it is now called Veterans Day, and is celebrated on the fourth Monday in October.

arm less (ärm′lis), *adj.* without either arm.

arm let (ärm′lit), *n.* an ornamental band or bracelet for the upper arm.

armadillo—total length $2\frac{1}{2}$ ft.

hat, āge, fär; let, ēqual, tėrm;
it, īce; hot, ōpen, ôrder;
oil, out; cup, pu̇t, rüle;
ch, child; ng, long; sh, she;
th, thin; TH, then; zh, measure;

ə represents *a* in about, *e* in taken, *i* in pencil, *o* in lemon, *u* in circus.

< = from, derived from, taken from.

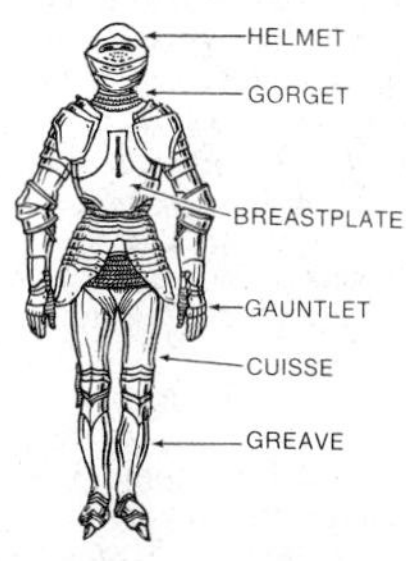

armor (def. 1) of the 1400's, weighing about 65 pounds

ar mor (är′mər), *n.* 1 a covering, usually of metal or leather, worn to protect the body in fighting. 2 any similar type of protective covering, such as a diver's suit or the scales of a fish. 3 armor plate. 4 the armored forces and equipment, such as the tanks, of a military unit. *—v.t., v.i.* cover or protect with armor. Also, BRITISH **armour.** [< Old French *armeüre* < Latin *armatura* < *armare* to arm. Doublet of ARMATURE.] **—ar′mor-like′,** *adj.*

ar mored (är′mərd), *adj.* 1 covered or protected with armor: *an armored car.* 2 using or equipped with armored vehicles: *an armored division.*

ar mor er (är′mər ər), *n.* 1 (in former times) person who made or repaired armor. 2 manufacturer of firearms. 3 member of the armed forces who takes care of the firearms aboard a warship or in a military unit, or who loads and services weapons aboard a combat airplane.

ar mo ri al (är môr′ē əl, är mōr′ē əl), *adj.* having to do with coats of arms or heraldry: *armorial bearings.*

armor plate, metal plating to protect warships, tanks, aircraft, etc., now usually a specially toughened alloy of steel.

ar mor y (är′mər ē), *n., pl.* **-mor ies.** 1 place where weapons are kept; arsenal. 2 place where weapons are manufactured. 3 a building with a drill hall, offices, etc., for militia. 4 ARCHAIC. armor; arms.

ar mour (är′mər), *n., v.* BRITISH. armor.

arm pit (ärm′pit′), *n.* the hollow place under the arm at the shoulder; axilla.

arm rest (ärm′rest′), *n.* support for the arm on an armchair, couch, etc.

arms (ärmz), *n.pl.* 1 weapons. 2 the use of arms; fighting; war: *A soldier is a man of arms.* 3 coat of arms.
bear arms, serve as a soldier; fight.
carry arms or **shoulder arms,** hold a rifle vertically against the right shoulder.
take up arms, arm for attack or defense.
to arms! prepare for battle!
under arms, having weapons; equipped for fighting.
up in arms, very angry; in rebellion.

ar my (är′mē), *n., pl.* **-mies.** 1 a large, organized group of soldiers trained and armed for war. 2 Often, **Army.** all the land forces of the military organization of a nation, in some countries including also the air forces. 3 field army. 4 any group of people organized for a purpose: *the Salvation Army.* 5 a very large number; multitude: *an army of ants.* [< Old French *armee* < Medieval Latin *armata* armed force < Latin *armare* to arm. Doublet of ARMADA.]

army worm, the larva of any of various night-flying moths that often travel in large numbers, destroying grain and garden crops.

Arn hem (ärn′hem, är′nəm), *n.* city in E Netherlands, on the Rhine. 133,000.

ar ni ca (är′nə kə), *n.* 1 a healing liquid applied to bruises, sprains, etc., prepared from the dried flowers, leaves, or roots of a plant of the composite family. 2 the plant itself, which has showy yellow flowers. [< New Latin]

Ar no (är′nō), *n.* river in central Italy. 140 mi.

Ar nold (är′nld), *n.* 1 **Benedict,** 1741-1801, American general in the Revolutionary War who became a traitor. 2 **Matthew,** 1822-1888, English poet and essayist. 3 **Thomas,** 1795-1842, English clergyman and headmaster of Rugby, father of Matthew Arnold.

a ro ma (ə rō′mə), *n.* 1 a pleasantly spicy odor; fragrance: *the aroma of cake baking in the oven.* 2 a distinctive fragrance or flavor; subtle quality. [< Latin, spice < Greek *arōma*]

ar o mat ic (ar′ə mat′ik), *adj.* 1 sweet-smelling; fragrant; spicy. 2 of or designating a group of chemical compounds containing a closed chain of carbon atoms that includes benzene and its derivatives. *—n.* a fragrant plant or substance. **—ar′o mat′i cal ly,** *adv.*

a rose (ə rōz′), *v.* pt. of **arise.**

a round (ə round′), *prep.* 1 in a circle about: *travel around the world.* 2 closely surrounding: *a coat around her shoulders.* 3 on all sides of: *Woods lay around the house.* 4 here and there in; about: *She leaves her books around the house.* 5 INFORMAL. somewhere about; near: *Play around the house.* 6 INFORMAL. near in amount, number, or time to; approximately; about: *around six o'clock, around five dollars.* 7 on the far side of: *just around the corner.*

—adv. 1 in a circle: *She spun around like a top.* 2 in circumference: *The tree measures four feet around.* 3 on all sides; in every direction: *A dense fog lay around.* 4 here and there; about: *We walked around to see the town.* 5 INFORMAL. somewhere near: *Wait around awhile.* 6 in the opposite direction: *Turn around! You are going the wrong way.* 7 going about; out of bed; astir: *He is now able to get around, but is not yet fully well.* 8 from one to another: *If you pass the class roll around, everyone can sign his name.* ➔ See **round** for usage note.

a round-the-clock (ə round′ᴛʜə klok′), *adj.* never stopping; constant. Also, **round-the-clock.**

a rous al (ə rou′zəl), *n.* 1 an arousing. 2 a being aroused.

a rouse (ə rouz′), *v.,* **a roused, a rous ing.** *—v.t.* 1 stir to action; excite. 2 wake up (a person); stir from sleep; awaken. *—v.i.* awaken; bestir oneself.

ar peg gi o (är pej′ē ō, är pej′ō), *n., pl.* **-gi os.** in music: 1 the sounding of the notes of a chord in rapid succession instead of simultaneously. 2 chord sounded in this way. [< Italian < *arpeggiare* play the harp < *arpa* harp]

ar que bus (är′kwə bəs), *n.* harquebus.

arr., 1 arranged. 2 arrival.

ar raign (ə rān′), *v.t.* 1 bring before a court of law to answer an indictment. 2 call to account; find fault with; accuse. [< Anglo-French *arainer* < Old French *a-* to + *raisnier* speak] **—ar raign′er,** *n.* **—ar raign′ment,** *n.*

ar range (ə rānj′), *v.,* **-ranged, -rang ing.** *—v.t.* 1 place (objects) in the proper, or any desired, order: *Please arrange the books on the library shelf.* 2 plan for; prepare beforehand: *arrange a dinner, arrange a conference.* 3 reach an understanding about; settle (a dispute): *The two neighbors have now arranged their differences.* 4 adapt (a piece of music) to voices or instruments for which it was not written or to the style of a particular performer or group. *—v.i.* prepare beforehand; plan: *Can you arrange to meet me this evening?* [< Old French *arangier* < *a-* to + *rangier* assemble < *rang* rank] **—ar rang′er,** *n.*

ar range ment (ə rānj′mənt), *n.* 1 a putting or a being put in proper order. 2 way or order in which things or persons are put: *You can make six arrangements of the letters A, B, and C.* 3 something arranged in a particular way: *Make an arrangement of the chairs to form a circle.* 4 settlement of disputed matters; agreement. 5 Usually, **arrangements,** *pl.* plans or preparations for an occasion, function, or act. 6 adaptation of a piece of music to voices or instruments for which it was not written. 7 piece so adapted.

ar rant (ar′ənt), *adj.* thoroughgoing; downright: *Nobody believes an arrant liar.* [variant of *errant*] **—ar′rant ly,** *adv.*

ar ras (ar′əs), *n.* 1 a rich tapestry fabric, with figures and scenes in color. 2 curtain, screen, or hangings of tapestry. [< *Arras,* city in northern France]

ar ray (ə rā′), *n.* 1 proper order; regular arrangement; formation: *The troops marched in battle array.* 2 display of persons or things; imposing group: *The array of good players on the other team made our side look weak.* 3 military force; soldiers. 4 clothes, especially for some special or festive occasion; dress; attire: *bridal array.* 5 (in mathematics) an orderly arrangement of objects or symbols in rows and columns. *—v.t.* 1 put in order for some purpose; marshal: *The general arrayed his troops for the battle.* 2 dress in fine clothes; adorn. [< Anglo-French *arayer* < Old French *a-* to + *rei* order] **—ar ray′er,** *n.*

ar rears (ə rirz′), *n.pl.* 1 money due but not paid; unpaid debts. 2 unfinished work; things not done on time. 3 **in arrears,** behind in payments, work, etc. [< Old French *arere* < Popular Latin *ad retro* to the rear]

ar rest (ə rest′), *v.t.* 1 seize (a person) and keep in custody by legal authority; apprehend: *A policeman arrested the thief.* 2 cause to stop (in a course of action); halt: *A fallen tree arrested traffic on the road.* See **stop** for synonym study. 3 attract and hold (the attention of a person): *They were arrested by an unusual sound.* 4 stop the growth or development of; inactivate: *Filling a tooth arrests decay.* *—n.* 1 the seizing and taking into custody of a person by legal authority. 2 **under arrest,** held by the police. 3 act of seizing; seizure. 4 act of stopping anything in motion or progress; check. [< Old French *arester* < Latin *ad-* + *restare* remain] **—ar rest′er,** *n.*

ar rest ing (ə res′ting), *adj.* catching and holding attention; striking.

ar riv al (ə rī′vəl), *n.* 1 act of arriving; coming: *the arrival of the train.* 2 person or thing that arrives: *a new arrival.*

ar rive (ə rīv′), *v.i.* **-rived, -riv ing.** 1 reach the end of a journey; come to a place: *We arrived in Boston a week ago.* 2 **arrive at,** come to; reach: *You should arrive at school before nine o'clock. You must arrive at a decision soon.* 3 come; occur: *The time has arrived for us to go.* 4 be successful: *It took years for Beethoven to arrive as a composer.* [< Old French *arriver* come to shore < Latin *ad ripam* to the shore]

ar ri viste (à rē vēst′), *n.* FRENCH. an upstart or parvenu.

ar ro gance (ar′ə gəns), *n.* excessive pride with contempt of others; haughtiness.

ar ro gant (ar′ə gənt), *adj.* excessively proud and contemptuous of others. See **haughty** for synonym study. [< Latin *arrogantem* < *ad-* to + *rogare* ask] **—ar′ro gant ly,** *adv.*

ar ro gate (ar′ə gāt), *v.t.,* **-gat ed, -gat ing.** 1 claim or take without right: *The king arrogated to himself the power that belonged to the nobles.* 2 claim for another or assign without good reasons: *He suspiciously arrogated bad motives to other people.* [< Latin *arrogatum* asked for oneself < *ad-* to + *rogare* ask] **—ar′ro ga′tion,** *n.* **—ar′ro ga′tor,** *n.*

ar ron disse ment (à rôɴ dēs mäɴ′), *n., pl.* **-ments** (-mäɴ′). FRENCH. 1 the largest administrative subdivision of a department in France. 2 an administrative district of Paris.

ar row (ar′ō), *n.* 1 a slender, pointed shaft or stick fitted with feathers at the end, which is shot from a bow. 2 anything resembling an arrow in shape or speed. 3 sign (➔) used to show direction or position in maps, on road signs, and in writing. [Old English *arwe*] **—ar′row like′,** *adj.*

ar row head (ar′ō hed′), *n.* the pointed tip of an arrow, usually a wedge-shaped piece made of harder material than the shaft.

ar row root (ar′ō rüt′, ar′ō rủt′), *n.* 1 an easily digested starch made from the roots of a tropical American plant. 2 the plant itself.

ar roy o (ə roi′ō), *n., pl.* **-roy os.** in the southwestern United States: 1 the dry bed of a stream; gully. 2 a small river. [< Spanish]

ar se nal (är′sə nəl), *n.* 1 place for storing or manufacturing military weapons and ammunition. 2 source of supply; storehouse. [< Italian *arsenale* < Arabic *(dār) aṣṣ-ināʻa* (house) of the manufacturing]

ar se nate (är′sə nāt, är′sə nit), *n.* salt or ester of arsenic acid.

arsenate of lead, lead arsenate.

ar se nic (är′sə nik; *adj. also* är sen′ik), *n.* 1 a very brittle metalloid element which occurs chiefly in combination with other elements. It forms poisonous compounds with oxygen and is used to make insecticides, weed killers, certain medicines, etc. *Symbol:* As; *atomic number* 33. See pages 326 and 327 for table. 2 arsenic trioxide. *—adj.* of or containing arsenic. [< Latin *arsenicum* < Greek *arsenikon*]

ar sen ic acid (är sen′ik), a crystalline compound used in preparing arsenates. *Formula:* H_3AsO_4

hat, āge, fär; let, ēqual, tėrm;
it, īce; hot, ōpen, ôrder;
oil, out; cup, pu̇t, rüle;
ch, child; ng, long; sh, she;
th, thin; ᴛʜ, then; zh, measure;

ə represents *a* in about, *e* in taken, *i* in pencil, *o* in lemon, *u* in circus.

< = from, derived from, taken from.

ar sen i cal (är sen′ə kəl), *adj.* of, of the nature of, or containing arsenic.

ar sen i cals (är sen′ə kəlz), *n. pl.* group of preparations containing arsenic, used as fungicides, drugs, etc.

ar sen ic trioxide (är′sə nik), a white, tasteless, violently poisonous powder used in industry and in medicine. *Formula:* As_2O_3 or As_4O_6

ar se no py rite (är′sə nō pī′rīt), *n.* a silvery gray mineral, important as an ore of arsenic. *Formula:* FeAsS

ar son (är′sən), *n.* the crime of intentionally and maliciously setting fire to a building or other property. [< Old French < Late Latin *arsionem* a burning < Latin *ardere* to burn]

ar son ist (är′sə nist), *n.* person who commits arson.

art[1] (ärt), *n.* 1 Usually, **arts,** *pl.* a branch or division of learning. History, literature, and philosophy are included among the arts; biology, chemistry, and physics are among the sciences. 2 branch of learning that depends more on special practice than on general principles. Writing compositions is an art; grammar is a science. 3 ARCHAIC. learning in general. 4 any form of human activity that is the product of and appeals primarily to the imagination, especially drawing, painting, and sculpture, but also including architecture, poetry, music, and dancing. 5 these types of activity taken together: *"Art is long and time is fleeting."* 6 painting, drawing, and sculpture: *She is studying art and music.* 7 paintings, sculptures, and other works of art: *a museum of art.* 8 working principles; methods: *the art of making friends, the art of war.* 9 special skill; knack: *the art of saying things well.* 10 some kind of skill or practical application of skill. Cooking, sewing, and housekeeping are household arts. 11 human skill or effort: *This well-kept garden owes more to art than to nature.* 12 a skillful act; cunning; trick. [< Old French < Latin *artem*]

art[2] (ärt), *v.* ARCHAIC. are. "Thou art" means "You are." [Old English *eart*]

art., 1 article. 2 artist.

Ar ta xerx es II (är′tə zėrk′sēz′), died 359? B.C., king of Persia from 404? to 359? B.C.

ar te fact (är′tə fakt), *n.* artifact.

Ar te mis (är′tə mis), *n.* (in Greek myths) the goddess of the hunt, of the forests, of wild animals, and of the moon. She was the twin sister of Apollo and was identified by the Romans with Diana.

ar ter i al (är tir′ē əl), *adj.* 1 of an artery or the arteries. 2 of or indicating blood in the arteries which is bright red because it has been purified by passing through the lungs. 3 serving as a major route of transportation, supply, or access: *an arterial highway.* **—ar ter′i al ly,** *adv.*

ar ter i ole (är tir′ē ōl), *n.* a small artery, especially one leading into capillaries.

ar ter i o scle ro sis (är tir′ē ō sklə rō′sis), *n.* abnormal thickening and hardening of the walls of the arteries, which makes circulation of the blood difficult, occurring chiefly in old age.

ar ter i o scle rot ic (är tir′ē ō sklə rot′ik), *adj.* of or having arteriosclerosis. *—n.* person having arteriosclerosis.

ar ter y (är′tər ē), *n., pl.* **-ter ies.** 1 any of the membranous, elastic, muscular tubes forming part of the system of vessels that carry blood from the heart to all parts of the body. 2 a main road; important channel: *Main Street and Broadway are the two chief arteries of traffic in our city.* [< Greek *artēria*]

ar te sian well (är tē′zhən), a deep-drilled well, especially one from which water gushes up without pumping. [< French *artésien* of Artois, French province where such wells first existed]

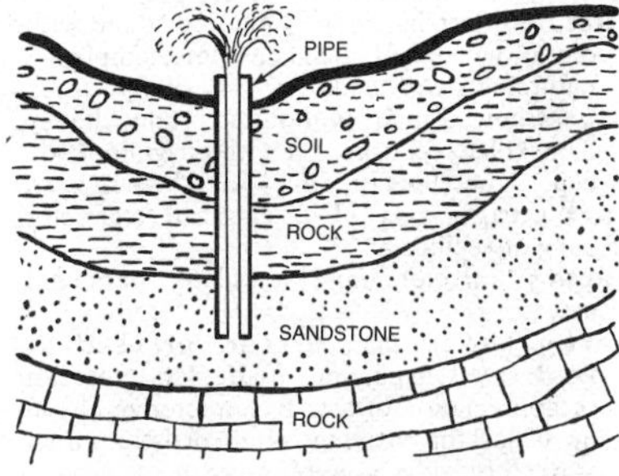

artesian well—Water, under pressure in the sandstone layer, rises in a pipe drilled through the seal of the rock layer above it.

art ful (ärt′fəl), *adj.* 1 slyly clever; crafty; deceitful: *a swindler's artful tricks.* 2 skillful; clever. 3 artificial. **—art′ful ly,** *adv.* **—art′ful ness,** *n.*

ar thrit ic (är thrit′ik), *adj.* 1 of arthritis. 2 caused by arthritis. *—n.* person having arthritis.

ar thri tis (är thrī′tis), *n.* inflammation of a joint or joints of the body. Gout is one kind of arthritis. [< Latin < Greek < *arthron* joint]

ar thro pod (är′thrə pod), *n.* any of a phylum of invertebrate animals having segmented bodies to which jointed antennae, wings, or legs are articulated in pairs. Insects, arachnids, and crustaceans belong to this phylum. [< Greek *arthron* joint + *pous, podos* foot]

Ar throp o da (är throp′ə də), *n.pl.* phylum of invertebrates comprising the arthropods.

ar throp o dal (är throp′ə dəl), *adj.* arthropodous.

ar throp o dous (är throp′ə dəs), *adj.* of or belonging to the arthropods.

Ar thur (är′thər), *n.* 1 (in medieval legends) a king of ancient Britain said to have lived about A.D. 500, who gathered about him the knights of the Round Table. 2 **Chester A.,** 1830-1886, the 21st president of the United States, from 1881 to 1885.

Ar thur i an (är thu̇r′ē ən), *adj.* of or having to do with King Arthur, his court, and his knights.

ar ti choke (är′tə chōk), *n.* 1 a thistlelike plant of the composite family with large prickly leaves. 2 its immature flowering head, which is cooked and eaten as a vegetable. 3 Jerusalem artichoke. [< Italian *articiocco* < Arabic *al-kharshūf*]

ar ti cle (är′tə kəl), *n., v.,* **-cled, -cling** (-kling). *—n.* 1 a written composition on a special subject forming part of the contents of a magazine, newspaper, or book: *an article on gardening in today's paper.* 2 clause in a contract, treaty, statute, etc.: *the third article of the Constitution.* 3 **article of,** a particular thing or item (of the class indicated): *Bread is a main article of food.* 4 piece of goods or property; commodity. 5 a distinct part or aspect of any subject or business; detail. 6 one of the words *a, an,* or *the* or the corresponding words in certain other languages. *A* and *an* are indefinite articles; *the* is the definite article. *—v.t.* bind by a contract: *The apprentice was articled to serve the master workman for seven years.* [< Old French < Latin *articulus,* diminutive of *artus* joint]

Articles of Confederation, constitution adopted by the thirteen original states of the United States in 1781 and replaced by the present Constitution in 1789.

ar tic u lar (är tik′yə lər), *adj.* of, belonging to, or having to do with the joints.

ar tic u late (*adj.* är tik′yə lit; *v.* är tik′yə lāt), *adj., v.,* **-lat ed, -lat ing.** *—adj.* 1 uttered in distinct syllables of words: *A baby cries and gurgles, but does not use articulate sounds.* 2 able to put one's thoughts into words easily and clearly: *She is the most articulate of the sisters.* 3 consisting of sections united by joints; jointed. The backbone is an articulate structure. *—v.t.* 1 speak distinctly; express in clear sounds and words: *Be careful to articulate your words so that everyone in the room can understand you.* 2 unite by joints: *The two bones are articulated like a hinge.* *—v.i.* 1 express oneself in words: *I was so excited I could hardly articulate.* 2 fit together in a joint: *After his knee was injured, he was lame because the bones did not articulate well.* **—ar tic u late ly** (är tik′yə lit lē), *adv.* **—ar tic u late ness** (är tik′yə lit nis), *n.* **—ar tic′u la′tor,** *n.*

ar tic u la tion (är tik′yə lā′shən), *n.* 1 way of pronouncing words and syllables; enunciation. 2 joint between parts of an animal or plant. 3 act or manner of connecting by a joint or joints.

ar tic u la to ry (är tik′yə lə tôr′ē, är tik′yə lə tōr′ē), *adj.* of or having to do with articulation.

ar ti fact (är′tə fakt), *n.* anything made by human skill or work, especially a tool or weapon. Also, **artefact.** [< Latin *artem* art + *factum* made]

ar ti fice (är′tə fis), *n.* 1 a clever device or trick: *He will use any artifice to get his own way.* See **stratagem** for synonym study. 2 trickery; craft: *His conduct is free from artifice.* 3 skill or ingenuity. [< Latin *artificium* < *artem* art + *facere* make]

ar tif i cer (är tif′ə sər), *n.* a skilled workman; craftsman.

ar ti fi cial (är′tə fish′əl), *adj.* 1 produced by human skill or labor; not natural: *artificial light.* See synonym study below. 2 made to imitate and compete with or as a substitute for something natural: *artificial flowers.* 3 put on for effect; assumed; affected: *an artificial laugh.* [< Latin *artificialis* < *artificium* artifice] **—ar′ti fi′cial ly,** *adv.* **—ar′ti fi′cial ness,** *n.*

Syn. 1 **Artificial, synthetic** mean man-made, not natural. **Artificial** describes that which is produced by human skill and labor, in contrast to that produced in nature, but which often corresponds to natural things or processes: *an artificial leg. Artificial respiration has saved the lives of many people who would have otherwise drowned.* **Synthetic** describes substances put together in a laboratory by chemical combination or treatment of natural materials, often to serve as substitutes for natural products: *When Teflon, a synthetic substance, is used to coat a pan, food can be fried without grease.*

ar ti fi ci al i ty (är′tə fish′ē al′ə tē), *n., pl.* **-ties.** 1 artificial quality or condition. 2 something unnatural or unreal.

artificial respiration, act or means of restoring normal breathing to a person who has stopped breathing by forcing air alternately into and out of his lungs.

artificial satellite, satellite of any heavenly body, manufactured and placed in orbit by man.

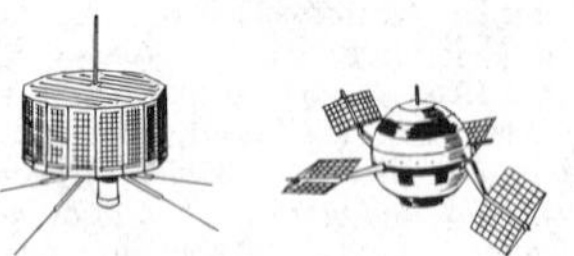

artificial satellite
left, Tiros I, used to photograph storm centers;
right, Explorer IV, used to obtain radiation and temperature data in space

ar til ler y (är til′ər ē), *n.* 1 mounted guns or rocket launchers manned by a crew; guns of larger caliber than machine guns; cannon; ordnance. 2 the part of an army that uses and manages such guns. 3 science or practice of firing and coordinating the firing of guns of larger caliber than machine guns. [< Old French *artillerie* < *artiller* equip]

ar til ler y man (är til′ər ē mən), *n., pl.* **-men.** soldier who belongs to the artillery; gunner.

ar ti o dac tyl (är′tē ō dak′tl), *n.* any of an order of hoofed mammals, usually with two toes on each foot. Antelope, hippopotamuses, pigs, and giraffes belong to this order. [< Greek *artios* even-numbered + *dactylos* finger, toe]

ar ti san (är′tə zən), *n.* a skilled worker in some industry or trade; craftsman. Carpenters, masons, plumbers, and electricians are artisans. See **artist** for synonym study. [< Middle French < Italian *artigiano* < *arte* art < Latin *artem*]

art ist (är′tist), *n.* 1 person who paints pictures; painter. 2 person skilled in any of the fine arts, such as sculpture, music, or literature. 3 a public performer, especially an actor or singer; artiste. 4 person who does work with skill and good taste. See synonym study below.

Syn. 4 **Artist, artisan** mean a person who does work with skill. **Artist** usually applies to a person working in the fine arts who uses taste, imagination, and creative ability in addition to skill: *Her creative interpretation makes that dancer an artist.* **Artisan** applies to a skillful craftsman working in the manual arts: *This furniture factory needs artisans to make cabinets.*

ar tiste (är tēst′), *n.* a skillful dancer, singer, or other performer. [< French]

ar tis tic (är tis′tik), *adj.* 1 of art or artists. 2 done with skill and good taste. 3 having good color and design; pleasing to the senses. 4 having or showing appreciation of beauty. **—ar tis′ti cal ly,** *adv.*

art ist ry (är′tə strē), *n., pl.* **-ries.** 1 artistic qualities or workmanship. 2 profession or occupation of an artist.

art less (ärt′lis), *adj.* 1 made or done without knowledge of social customs; simple and natural: *Small children ask many artless questions.* 2 made without art; rude; clumsy. 3 unskilled; ignorant. 4 without guile or deceit. **—art′less ly,** *adv.* **—art′less ness,** *n.*

art song, song of a classical character, sung at recitals.

arts y (ärt′sē), *adj.,* **arts i er, arts i est.** arty.

art y (är′tē), *adj.,* **art i er, art i est.** INFORMAL. 1 displaying an affected interest in or appreciation of art. 2 characterized by an unsuccessful striving after artistic effect. **—art′i ly,** *adv.* **—art′i ness,** *n.*

A ru ba (ä rü′bä), *n.* island of the Netherlands Antilles, off the NW coast of Venezuela. 59,000 pop.; 68 sq. mi.

ar um (er′əm, ar′əm), *n.* any of a family of plants having a club-shaped spike of small flowers partly surrounded by a hooded sheath, such as the jack-in-the-pulpit. [< Latin]

Ar vin (är′vən), *n.* member of the ARVN.

ARVN, Army of the Republic of (South) Vietnam.

-ary, *suffix forming nouns and adjectives.* 1 place for ___: *Infirmary = place for the infirm.* 2 collection of ___: *Statuary = collection of statues.* 3 person or thing that ___s: *Boundary = thing that bounds.* 4 of or having to do with ___: *Legendary = of legend.* 5 being; having the nature of ___: *Secondary = being second.* 6 characterized by ___: *Customary = characterized by custom.* [< Latin *-arium*]

Ar yan (er′ē ən, ar′ē ən), *adj.* Indo-European. *—n.* 1 person belonging to a prehistoric group of people who spoke the language from which the Indo-European languages are derived. 2 person supposed to be descended from this prehistoric group of people. 3 the assumed prehistoric language of this people. 4 (in Nazi use) a Caucasian non-Jew, especially of the Nordic type. [< Sanskrit *ārya* noble]

as[1] (az; *unstressed* əz), *adv.* 1 to the same degree or extent; equally: *as black as coal.* 2 for example: *Some animals, as dogs and cats, eat meat.*

—prep. 1 in the character of; doing the work of: *Who will act as teacher?* 2 like: *They treat him as an equal.*

—conj. 1 to the same degree or extent that: *They worked just as much as they were told to.* 2 during the time that; when; while: *She sang as she worked.* 3 in the same way that: *run as I do.* 4 because: *We paid them generously, as they had done the work well.* 5 though: *Brave as they were, the danger made them afraid.* 6 that the result was: *The child so marked the picture as to spoil it.*

as for, about; concerning: *As for me, I prefer to stay home.*

as if, similar to what it would be if: *You sound as if you were angry.*

as is, in the present condition: *If you buy the car as is, it will cost you very little.*

as of, beginning on or at (a certain date or time): *The new contract becomes effective as of January 1st.*

as though, similar to what it would be if.

as to, about; concerning: *I'd like a cat, but I have no preference as to its color.*

as yet, up to this time; so far.

—pron. 1 a condition or fact that: *She is very careful, as her work shows.* 2 that: *Do the same thing as I do.*

[Old English (unstressed) *ealswā* quite so. Related to ALSO.] ➤ See **like**[1] for usage note.

as[2] (as), *n., pl.* **as ses** (as′iz). 1 an ancient Roman pound, equal to twelve ounces. 2 an ancient Roman coin, worth a few cents. [< Latin]

as-, *prefix.* form of **ad-** before *s,* as in *assist.*

As, arsenic.

AS or **A.S.,** Anglo-Saxon.

as a fet i da or **as a foet i da** (as′ə-fet′ə də), *n.* gum resin that smells like garlic, formerly used in medicine to prevent spasms. Also, **assafetida, assafoetida.** [< Medieval Latin < Persian *azā* mastic + Latin *fetidus, foetidus* stinking]

as bes tos or **as bes tus** (as bes′təs, az-bes′təs), *n.* 1 a mineral, a silicate of calcium and magnesium, that does not burn or conduct heat, usually occurring in fibers. 2 fabric made of these fibers, resistant to both heat and chemical reaction, used to make insulating materials, fire-resistant clothing, etc. [< Greek *asbestos* quicklime; originally, unquenchable]

ASCAP or **A.S.C.A.P.,** American Society of Composers, Authors, and Publishers.

as car id (as′kər id), *n.* roundworm or similar nematode worm living as a parasite in the intestines of vertebrates. [< Greek *askaris*]

as cend (ə send′), *v.i.* go up; rise; move upward: *He watched the airplane ascend.* *—v.t.* go to or toward the top of: *A small party is planning to ascend Mount Everest.* See **climb** for synonym study. [< Latin *ascendere* < *ad-* up + *scandere* climb] **—as-cend′a ble, as cend′i ble,** *adj.*

as cend ance (ə sen′dəns), *n.* ascendancy.

as cend an cy (ə sen′dən sē), *n.* controlling influence; domination; rule.

as cend ant (ə sen′dənt), *adj.* 1 moving upward; rising. 2 superior; paramount; controlling. 3 near the eastern horizon; rising toward the zenith: *ascendant Venus.* *—n.* 1 position of power; controlling influence. 2 **in the ascendant, a** in control; supreme; dominant. **b** increasing in influence, popularity, etc. 3 (in astrology) horoscope.

as cend en cy (ə sen′dən sē), *n.* ascendancy.

as cend ent (ə sen′dənt), *adj.* ascendant.

as cen sion (ə sen′shən), *n.* 1 act of ascending; ascent. 2 **the Ascension, a** (in the New Testament) the ascent of Christ from earth to heaven after the Resurrection. **b** Ascension Day.

As cen sion (ə sen′shən), *n.* British island in the S Atlantic. 1400 pop.; 34 sq. mi.

Ascension Day, a church festival in honor of the Ascension of Christ, observed on the fortieth day after Easter.

as cent (ə sent′), *n.* 1 act of going up; upward movement; rising: *early balloon ascents.* 2 improvement in position, rank, etc.; advancement; promotion. 3 act of climbing a ladder, mountain, etc. 4 way of ascending; upward route: *a very steep ascent.* 5 degree of upward slope: *an ascent of ten degrees.*

as cer tain (as′ər tān′), *v.t.* find out for certain by trial and research; make sure of; determine: *ascertain the facts about a robbery.* [< Old French *ascertener* < *a-* to + *certain* certain] **—as′cer tain′a ble,** *adj.* **—as′cer tain′ment,** *n.*

hat, āge, fär; let, ēqual, tėrm;
it, īce; hot, ōpen, ôrder;
oil, out; cup, pu̇t, rüle;
ch, child; ng, long; sh, she;
th, thin; ᴛʜ, then; zh, measure;

ə represents *a* in about, *e* in taken, *i* in pencil, *o* in lemon, *u* in circus.

< = from, derived from, taken from.

as cet ic (ə set′ik), *n.* 1 person who practices unusual self-denial or severe discipline over himself, especially for religious reasons. Fasting is a common practice of ascetics. 2 person who refrains from pleasures and comforts. *—adj.* refraining from pleasures and comforts; practicing unusual self-denial. [< Greek *askētikos* exercised < *askein* to exercise, discipline] **—as cet′i cal ly,** *adv.*

as cet i cism (ə set′ə siz′əm), *n.* life or habits of an ascetic; unusual or extreme self-denial.

as cid i an (ə sid′ē ən), *n.* any of a genus of tunicates with a tough, saclike covering.

as cid i um (ə sid′ē əm), *n., pl.* **-cid i a** (-sid′ē ə). (in botany) a baglike or pitcherlike part of a plant. [< Greek *askidion* small bag]

As cle pi us (as klē′pē əs), *n.* (in Greek myths) the god of medicine and healing, adopted by the Romans under the spelling Aesculapius.

as co my cete (as′kō mī sēt′), *n.* any of a large class of fungi, including yeasts, molds, mildews, etc., characterized by the formation of spores in elongated sacs; sac fungus. [< Greek *askos* skin bag + *mykēs, mykētos* fungus]

as co my ce tous (as′kō mī sē′təs), *adj.* of or belonging to the ascomycetes.

a scor bic acid (ə skôr′bik, ā skôr′bik), vitamin C.

as co spore (as′kə spôr, as′kə spōr), *n.* one of the cluster of spores formed within an ascus.

as cot (as′kət, as′kot), *n.* necktie with broad ends, resembling a scarf, tied so that the ends may be laid flat, one across the other. [< *Ascot,* English race track]

as cribe (ə skrīb′), *v.t.,* **-cribed, -crib ing.** 1 think of as caused by or coming from; assign; attribute *(to): The police ascribed the automobile accident to fast driving.* See **attribute** for synonym study. 2 consider as belonging *(to): Men have ascribed their own characteristics to their gods.* [< Latin *ascribere* < *ad-* to + *scribere* write] **—as crib′a ble,** *adj.*

as crip tion (ə skrip′shən), *n.* 1 act of ascribing. 2 statement or words ascribing something.

as cus (as′kəs), *n., pl.* **as ci** (as′kī, as′ī). the elongated sac or cell in which the spores of ascomycetes are formed. [< Greek *askos* skin bag]

-ase, suffix used to form the names of enzymes, as in *amylase, catalase, lipase.* [< *(diast)ase*]

a sep sis (ə sep′sis, ā sep′sis), *n.* 1 aseptic condition. 2 aseptic methods or treatment.

a sep tic (ə sep′tik, ā sep′tik), *adj.* free from the living germs causing infection. **—a sep′ti cal ly,** *adv.*

a sex u al (ā sek′shü əl), *adj.* in biology: 1 having no sex. 2 independent of sexual processes. Budding and fission are forms of asexual reproduction. **—a sex′u al ly,** *adv.*

As gard (as′gärd, az′gärd), *n.* (in Scandinavian myths) the home of the gods and of heroes slain in battle.

ash[1] (ash), *n.* 1 what remains of a thing after it has been thoroughly burned; the incombustible residue of organic substances remaining after combustion. 2 fine material thrown out of a volcano in eruption. See also **ashes.** [Old English *æsce*]

ash[2] (ash), *n.* 1 a timber or shade tree of the olive family that has a silver-gray bark, grayish twigs, and straight-grained wood. 2 its tough, springy wood. [Old English *æsc*]

a shamed (ə shāmd′), *adj.* 1 feeling shame; disturbed or uncomfortable because one has done something wrong, improper, or foolish. See synonym study below. 2 unwilling or held back by the belief shame would be felt: *He was ashamed to tell his mother he had failed.* **—a sham ed ly** (ə shā′mid lē), *adv.*

Syn. 1 **Ashamed, humiliated, mortified** mean feeling embarrassed and disgraced. **Ashamed** emphasizes a feeling of having disgraced oneself by doing something wrong, improper, or foolish: *I was ashamed when I cried at the movies.* **Humiliated** emphasizes a painful feeling of being lowered and shamed in the eyes of others: *Parents are humiliated if their children behave badly when guests are present.* **Mortified** means feeling greatly embarrassed and humiliated, sometimes ashamed: *I was mortified when I forgot my speech.*

A shan ti (ə shän′tē, ə shan′tē), *n.* region in central Ghana.

ash en[1] (ash′ən), *adj.* 1 like ashes; pale as ashes. 2 of ashes.

ash en[2] (ash′ən), *adj.* 1 of the ash tree or its timber. 2 made from the wood of the ash tree.

ash es (ash′iz), *n.pl.* 1 what remains of any combustible thing after it has been thoroughly burned. 2 what remains of a dead body when burned. 3 a dead body; corpse.

Ash ke naz im (ash′kə naz′im), *n.pl.* the Jews of eastern and central Europe and their descendants.

Ash kha bad (äsh kä bäd′), *n.* city in S central Soviet Union, capital of Turkmen S.S.R. 253,000.

ash lar or **ash ler** (ash′lər), *n.* 1 a square stone used in building. 2 masonry made of ashlars. [< Old French *aisselier*]

a shore (ə shôr′, ə shōr′), *adv.* 1 to the shore; to land. 2 on the shore; on land.

ash tray (ash′trā′), *n.* a small dish to put tobacco ashes in.

A shur (ä′shu̇r), *n.* the chief god of the Assyrians.

Ash Wednesday, the first day of Lent; the seventh Wednesday before Easter.

ash y (ash′ē), *adj.,* **ash i er, ash i est.** 1 like ashes; pale as ashes; ashen. 2 of ashes. 3 covered with ashes.

A sia (ā′zhə, ā′shə), *n.* the largest continent, extending eastward from Europe and Africa and bounded on the north by the Arctic Ocean and on the south by the Indian Ocean. 2,055,775,000 pop.; 16,000,000 sq. mi.

Asia Minor, peninsula of SW Asia, between the Black Sea and the Mediterranean Sea; Anatolia. It includes most of Asian Turkey.

A sian (ā′zhən, ā′shən), *n.* native or inhabitant of Asia. *—adj.* of or having to do with Asia or its people.

Asian flu, kind of influenza caused by a new strain of virus, first identified in Hong Kong in early 1957.

A si at ic (ā′zhē at′ik, ā′shē at′ik), *adj., n.* Asian.

Asiatic cholera, cholera (def. 1).

a side (ə sīd′), *adv.* 1 on one side; to one side: *Move the table aside.* 2 away from oneself; off: *I laid aside my overcoat.* 3 out of one's thoughts, consideration, etc.: *Put your fears aside.* 4 **aside from, a** away or apart from: *Your remark is aside from the question.* **b** except for: *Aside from some reading, I have finished my homework.* 5 **aside of,** alongside of; compared with. 6 **set aside,** quash (a judgment, conviction, etc.). *—n.* 1 remark made in an undertone. 2 words spoken by an actor and heard by the audience which the other persons on the stage are not supposed to hear. 3 digression.

as i nine (as′n īn), *adj.* 1 of asses. 2 like an ass. 3 obviously silly; foolish and stupid. [< Latin *asininus* < *asinus* ass] **—as′i nine ly,** *adv.*

as i nin i ty (as′n in′ə tē), *n., pl.* **-ties.** silliness; stupidity.

ask (ask), *v.t.* 1 try to find out by words; inquire: *Ask the way.* See synonym study below. 2 seek the answer to: *Ask any questions you wish.* 3 put a question to; inquire of: *Ask him how old he is.* See **question** for synonym study. 4 try to get by words; request: *Ask her to sing.* See synonym study below. 5 claim; demand: *ask too high a price for a house.* 6 invite: *She asked ten guests to the party.* 7 call for; need; require: *This job asks hard work.* *—v.i.* 1 try to get something by words; make a request *(for): Ask for help if you need it.* 2 try to find out; inquire: *She asked about our health. Did anyone ask after me while I was ill?* See synonym study below. 3 **ask for it,** INFORMAL. invite danger or unpleasant consequences. [Old English *āscian*] **—ask′er,** *n.*

Syn. *v.t.* 1, *v.i.* 2 **Ask, inquire** mean to try to find out by a question. **Ask** is the general word meaning to seek information from someone: *I asked about you. Ask someone where that street is.* **Inquire** is more formal, but suggests more strongly going into a subject, asking in an effort to get definite information: *I inquired about you; I wanted to know when you are leaving. You had better inquire how to get there.*
v.t. 4 **Ask, request, solicit** mean to try to get by words. **Ask** is the general word: *I asked permission to do it.* **Request,** a more formal word, means to ask in a polite and more formal way: *We request contributions to the library.* **Solicit,** a formal word, means to request respectfully or earnestly: *They are soliciting funds for a new hospital.*

a skance (ə skans′), *adv.* 1 with suspicion or disapproval: *The students looked askance at the suggestion for having classes on Saturday.* 2 to one side; sideways. [origin uncertain]

a skant (ə skant′), *adv.* askance.

a skew (ə skyü′), *adv., adj.* out of the proper position; turned or twisted the wrong way; awry.

a slant (ə slant′), *adv.* in a slanting direction. *—prep.* slantingly across. *—adj.* slanting.

a sleep (ə slēp′), *adj.* 1 not awake; sleeping: *The cat is asleep.* 2 oblivious: *They were asleep to the danger.* 3 dull; inactive: *His mind is asleep.* 4 having lost the power of feeling; numb: *My foot is asleep.* 5 dead. *—adv.* into a condition of sleep: *The tired children fell asleep.*

A sma ra (ä smär′ə, äz mär′ə), *n.* city in N

Ethiopia, the capital of Eritrea. 179,000.

a so cial (ā sō′shəl), *adj.* 1 indifferent to social customs or laws; not social. 2 reluctant to associate with other people; not sociable.

asp (asp), *n.* any of several small, poisonous snakes of Africa, especially the Egyptian cobra. [< Latin *aspis* < Greek]

as par a gus (ə spar′ə gəs), *n.* 1 a perennial plant of the lily family, with a red berry and no bulb. The stems have many branches covered with threadlike branchlets, the true leaves being reduced to scales. 2 its green, tender shoots, which are used as a vegetable. [< Latin < Greek *asparagos*]

as par tic acid (a spär′tik), a crystalline amino acid derived from the juice of asparagus, beets, and young sugar cane. *Formula:* $C_4H_7O_4N$

A.S.P.C.A., American Society for the Prevention of Cruelty to Animals.

as pect (as′pekt), *n.* 1 way in which a subject or situation appears to the mind: *The whole aspect of the situation is changing.* 2 way in which an object appears to the eye; appearance: *the general aspect of the countryside.* See **appearance** for synonym study. 3 facial expression; countenance: *the solemn aspect of the judge.* 4 the facing of a house, window, etc., in a particular direction; exposure: *This house has a western aspect.* 5 (in astrology) the relative position of the heavenly bodies, especially planets, as determining their supposed influence upon human affairs. [< Latin *aspectus* < *ad-* at + *specere* look]

as pen (as′pən), *n.* any of several poplar trees of North America and Europe whose leaves tremble and rustle in the slightest breeze. —*adj.* of this tree. [Old English *æspe*]

as per i ty (a sper′ə tē), *n., pl.* **-ties.** 1 harshness or sharpness of temper, especially as shown in tone or manner. 2 severity; rigor: *The settlers suffered the asperities of a very cold winter.* 3 unevenness or roughness of surface. [< Latin *asperitatem* < *asper* rough]

as perse (ə spėrs′), *v.t.,* **-persed, -pers ing.** spread damaging or false reports about; slander. [< Latin *aspersum* sprinkled on < *ad-* on + *spargere* to sprinkle] **—as pers′er,** *n.*

as per sion (ə spėr′zhən), *n.* a damaging or false statement; slander.

as phalt (as′fôlt), *n.* 1 a dark, waterproof substance much like tar, found in natural beds in various parts of the world or obtained by refining petroleum. 2 mixture of this substance with crushed rock or sand, used to pave streets, etc. —*v.t.* cover, permeate, or lay with asphalt. [< Greek *asphaltos*]

as phal tic (a sfôl′tik), *adj.* of or containing asphalt.

as phal tum (a sfôl′təm), *n.* asphalt.

as pho del (as′fə del), *n.* 1 plant of the lily family, with spikes of white, pink, or yellow flowers. 2 flower of the Greek paradise. 3 daffodil. [< Greek *asphodelos*]

a sphyx i a (a sfik′sē ə), *n.* suffocation or unconscious condition caused by lack of oxygen and excess of carbon dioxide in the blood, as in choking or drowning. [< Greek, a stopping of the pulse < *a-* without + *sphyxis* pulse < *sphyzein* to throb]

a sphyx i ate (a sfik′sē āt), *v.t., v.i.,* **-at ed, -at ing.** produce asphyxia in; suffocate. **—a sphyx′i a′tion,** *n.* **—a sphyx′i a′tor,** *n.*

as pic (as′pik), *n.* kind of jelly made from meat or fish stock, tomato juice, etc., used as a garnish or in salads. [< French]

as pi dis tra (as′pə dis′trə), *n.* an Asian plant of the lily family, with large, green leaves and very small flowers, much used as a house plant. [< New Latin < Greek *aspis* shield + *astron* star]

as pir ant (ə spī′rənt, as′pər ənt), *n.* person who aspires; person who seeks a position of honor. —*adj.* aspiring.

as pi rate (*v.* as′pə rāt′; *adj., n.* as′pər it), *v.,* **-rat ed, -rat ing,** *adj., n.* —*v.t.* 1 begin (a word or syllable) with a breathing or *h*-sound. *Hot* is aspirated; *honor* is not. 2 pronounce with such a sound. The *h* in *forehead* is usually not aspirated. 3 pronounce (a stop) with a following or accompanying puff of air. *P* is aspirated in *pin* but not in *tip.* 4 to draw by suction. —*adj.* pronounced with a breathing or *h*-sound. The *h* in *here* is aspirate. —*n.* an aspirated sound. English *p* is an aspirate in *pat,* but not in *tap.* [< Latin *aspiratum* breathed toward < *ad-* + *spirare* breathe]

as pi ra tion (as′pə rā′shən), *n.* 1 earnest desire; longing; ambition: *She had aspirations to be a doctor.* 2 an aspirating (of sounds). 3 an aspirated sound. 4 act of drawing air into the lungs; breathing.

as pi ra tor (as′pə rā′tər), *n.* apparatus or device employing suction.

as pire (ə spīr′), *v.i.,* **-pired, -pir ing.** 1 have an ambition for something; desire earnestly; seek: *Scholars aspire after knowledge. I aspired to be captain of the team.* 2 rise high. [< Latin *aspirare* breathe toward, aspire < *ad-* toward + *spirare* breathe] **—as pir′er,** *n.* **—as pir′ing ly,** *adv.*

as pir in (as′pər ən), *n.* a white crystalline drug used to relieve the pain of headaches, arthritis, etc., and the fever of colds, etc.; acetylsalicylic acid. *Formula:* $C_9H_8O_4$ [< German *Aspirin* (originally a trademark)]

As quith (as′kwith), *n.* **Herbert Henry,** 1852-1928, British statesman, prime minister from 1908 to 1916.

ass (def. 1)
3 ft. high
at the shoulder

ass (as), *n.* 1 any of various hoofed mammals related to the horse, but smaller, with longer ears and a shorter mane, shorter hair on the tail, and a dark stripe along the back; donkey. An ass is a patient, relatively slow, but very sure-footed beast of burden when domesticated. 2 a stupid, silly, or stubborn person; fool. [Old English *assa* < Latin *asinus*]

as sa fet i da or **as sa foet i da** (as′ə-fet′ə də), *n.* asafetida.

as sa gai (as′ə gī), *n., pl.* **-gais.** a slender spear or javelin of hard wood, once used by the Zulus and other African tribes. Also, **assegai.** [< Portuguese *azagaya*]

as sail (ə sāl′), *v.t.* 1 attack repeatedly with violent blows. 2 attack with hostile words, arguments, or abuse. See **attack** for synonym study. 3 (of a feeling) come over (a person) strongly; beset; trouble: *No doubts ever assail them.* [< Old French *asalir* < Latin *ad-* at + *salire* to leap] **—as sail′a ble,** *adj.* **—as sail′er,** *n.*

as sail ant (ə sā′lənt), *n.* person who attacks.

As sam (a sam′), *n.* state in NE India, bordered by Bhutan, China, Burma, and Bangladesh.

As sa mese (as′ə mēz′), *adj., n., pl.* **-mese.** —*adj.* of Assam or its people. —*n.* 1 native or inhabitant of Assam. 2 the Indic language of Assam.

as sas sin (ə sas′n), *n.* murderer, especially one hired or chosen to murder by a sudden or secret attack. [< Italian *assassino* < Arabic *hashshāshīn* hashish eaters]

as sas si nate (ə sas′n āt), *v.t.,* **-nat ed, -nat ing.** murder (someone, especially a public personage) by a sudden or secret attack. **—as sas′si na′tion,** *n.* **—as sas′si na′tor,** *n.*

as sault (ə sôlt′), *n.* 1 a sudden, vigorous attack made with blows or weapons; onslaught; charge. 2 a sudden and violent attack made on institutions, opinions, etc., with hostile words or actions. 3 the final phase of a military attack; closing with the enemy in hand-to-hand fighting. 4 (in law) a threat or attempt to strike or otherwise harm a person but without actually touching the person. —*v.t.* make an assault on by means of blows, hand-to-hand fighting, or hostile words. See **attack** for synonym study. —*v.i.* make an assault. [< Old French *asaut* < Latin *ad-* at + *saltare* to leap] **—as sault′er,** *n.*

as say (ə sā′; *also especially for n.* as′ā), *v.t.* 1 analyze (an ore or alloy) to find out the quantity of gold, silver, or other metal in it. 2 examine by testing or trial; test. 3 ARCHAIC. attempt. —*v.i.* U.S. (of ore) be found by analysis to contain a certain proportion of metal. —*n.* 1 determination of the proportion of gold or other metal in an ore or alloy or of an ingredient in a drug. 2 the substance or sample analyzed or tested. 3 a list of the results of assaying an ore, drug, etc. 4 ARCHAIC. attempt; trial. [< Old French *assayer,* ultimately < Latin *exigere* weigh, prove] **—as say′er,** *n.*

as se gai (as′ə gī), *n.* assagai.

as sem blage (ə sem′blij), *n.* 1 group of persons gathered together; assembly. 2 collection; group. 3 a bringing together; coming together; meeting. 4 process of putting together; fitting together. 5 work of art made by putting together pieces of metal, wood, and other odds and ends.

as sem bla gist (ə sem′blə jist), *n.* artist who makes assemblages.

as sem ble (ə sem′bəl), *v.,* **-bled, -bling.** —*v.t.* 1 gather together; bring together: *The principal assembled all the students in the auditorium.* See **gather** for synonym study. 2 put together; fit together: *assemble a model airplane.* —*v.i.* come together; meet; congregate: *Congress assembles in January.* [< Old French *assembler,* ultimately < Latin *ad-* to + *simul* together] **—as sem′bler,** *n.*

as sem bly (ə sem′blē), *n., pl.* **-blies.** 1 group of people gathered together for some purpose; gathering; meeting: *The principal addressed the school assembly.* See **meeting** for synonym study. 2 a meeting of lawmakers. 3 **Assembly,** the lower branch of the state legislature of some states of the United States. 4 a coming together; assembling: *unlawful assembly.* 5 a putting together; fitting together: *the assembly of parts to make an automobile.* 6 the complete group of parts required to put something together: *the tail assembly of an airplane.* 7 signal on a bugle or drum for troops to form in ranks.

assembly line, row of workers and machines along which work is passed until the final product is made: *Automobiles are produced on an assembly line.*

as sem bly man (ə sem′blē mən), *n., pl.* **-men.** U.S. 1 member of a lawmaking group. 2 **Assemblyman,** member of an Assembly.

as sent (ə sent′), *v.i.* express agreement; agree; consent: *Everyone assented to the plans for the dance.* See **consent** for synonym study. —*n.* acceptance of a proposal, statement, etc.; agreement. [< Latin *assentire* < *ad-* along with + *sentire* feel, think]

as sert (ə sėrt′), *v.t.* 1 state positively; declare firmly; affirm: *She asserts that she will go whether we do or not.* See **declare** for synonym study. 2 maintain (a right, a claim, etc.); insist upon: *Assert your independence.* 3 **assert oneself,** put oneself forward; make demands: *A leader must assert himself sometimes in order to be followed.* [< Latin *assertum* asserted < *ad-* to + *serere* join] —**as sert′er, as ser′tor,** *n.*

as ser tion (ə sėr′shən), *n.* 1 a positive statement; firm declaration. 2 an insisting on a right, a claim, etc.

as ser tive (ə sėr′tiv), *adj.* too confident and certain; positive; forward. —**as ser′tive ly,** *adv.* —**as ser′tive ness,** *n.*

as sess (ə ses′), *v.t.* 1 estimate the value of (property or income) for taxation; value: *The town clerk has assessed our house at $20,000.* 2 fix the amount of (a tax, fine, damages, etc.). 3 put a tax on (a person, property, etc.). 4 determine the shares to be contributed by each of several persons toward a common object. 5 examine critically and estimate the merit, significance, value, etc., of: *The committee met to assess the idea of establishing a new university.* [< Medieval Latin *assessare* fix a tax < Latin *assidere* sit by, attend < *ad-* by + *sedere* sit] —**as sess′a ble,** *adj.*

as sess ment (ə ses′mənt), *n.* 1 act of assessing. 2 amount of tax which is decided to be payable. 3 an official valuation of property, etc., for purposes of taxation. 4 valuation in general; appraisal.

as ses sor (ə ses′ər), *n.* person who estimates the value of property or income for taxation.

as set (as′et), *n.* 1 something having value; advantage: *Ability to get along with people is an asset in business.* 2 **assets,** *pl.* **a** all items of value owned by a person or business and constituting the resources of the person or business. Real estate, cash, securities, inventories, patents, and good will are assets. **b** property that can be used to pay debts. [< Old French *asez* enough < Latin *ad satis*]

as sev e rate (ə sev′ə rāt′), *v.t.* **-rat ed, -rat ing.** declare solemnly; state positively. [< Latin *asseveratum* declared solemnly < *ad-* + *severus* serious] —**as sev′e ra′tion,** *n.*

as si du i ty (as′ə dü′ə tē, as′ə dyü′ə tē), *n., pl.* **-ties.** careful and steady attention; diligence.

as sid u ous (ə sij′ü əs), *adj.* careful and attentive; diligent. [< Latin *assiduus* < *assidere* sit by. See ASSESS.] —**as sid′u ous ly,** *adv.* —**as sid′u ous ness,** *n.*

as sign (ə sīn′), *v.t.* 1 give as a share, task, duty, etc.; allot: *The teacher has assigned the next ten problems for today.* See synonym study below. 2 designate or appoint (to a post or duty): *We were assigned to collect tickets at the door.* 3 name definitely; fix; set: *The judge assigned a day for the trial.* 4 ascribe as belonging to; attribute: *A student should be able to assign events to their places in history.* 5 transfer or hand over (some property, right, etc.) legally: *He assigned his home and farm to his creditors.* —*n.* person to whom property, a right, etc., is legally transferred. [< Latin *assignare* < *ad-* to, for + *signare* to mark < *signum* mark] —**as sign′a ble,** *adj.* —**as sign′er,** *n.*

Syn. *v.t.* 1 **Assign, allot** mean to give something to a particular person, group, or institution as a share. **Assign** emphasizes giving something that has been established as a share by some plan or principle: *The teacher assigned two acts so that we would finish the play before the holidays.* **Allot** emphasizes giving an amount or part which is set more or less by chance: *Mother allots our household tasks so that I do more than my fair share of the work.*

as sig nat (as′ig nat; *French* à sē nyà′), *n.* piece of paper money issued between 1789 and 1796 in France by the revolutionary government, based on the value of confiscated lands. [< French]

as sig na tion (as′ig nā′shən), *n.* 1 a secret meeting of lovers. 2 the appointment of a time and place for such a meeting. 3 an allotting; apportionment.

as sign ee (ə sī nē′, as′ə nē′), *n.* person to whom some property, right, etc., is legally transferred.

as sign ment (ə sīn′mənt), *n.* 1 something assigned, especially a task or responsibility allotted to a particular person, group, etc. 2 an assigning; appointment: *assignment to a different classroom.* 3 the legal transfer of some property, right, etc.

as sign or (ə sī nôr′, as′ə nôr′), *n.* person who legally transfers to another some property, right, etc.

as sim i la bil i ty (ə sim′ə lə bil′ə tē), *n.* capability of being assimilated.

as sim i la ble (ə sim′ə lə bəl), *adj.* that can be assimilated.

as sim i late (ə sim′ə lāt), *v.,* **-lat ed, -lat ing.** —*v.t.* 1 take in and make part of oneself; absorb; digest: *assimilate what one reads. The human body will not assimilate sawdust.* 2 cause to be like the people of a nation in customs, viewpoint, character, etc.: *We have assimilated immigrants from many lands.* 3 make (a speech sound, usually a consonant) more like the sound which follows or precedes. —*v.i.* 1 become absorbed; be digested. 2 become like the people of a nation in customs, viewpoint, character, etc. 3 become like. [< Latin *assimilatum* made similar < *ad-* to + *similis* like] —**as sim′i la′tor,** *n.*

as sim i la tion (ə sim′ə lā′shən), *n.* 1 act or process of assimilating. 2 condition of being assimilated.

as sim i la tive (ə sim′ə lā′tiv), *adj.* assimilating.

As si si (ə sē′zē), *n.* commune in Umbria, central Italy, birthplace of Saint Francis. 25,000.

as sist (ə sist′), *v.t.* 1 help (a person) either in doing something or when in need; aid: *They assisted the committee by addressing envelopes.* See **help** for synonym study. 2 further or promote (an action or process): *These tablets assist digestion.* 3 be the assistant of (a person). —*v.i.* 1 give aid; help: *When all assist, the job can be done quickly.*

hat, āge, fär; let, ēqual, tėrm;
it, īce; hot, ōpen, ôrder;
oil, out; cup, pu̇t, rüle;
ch, child; ng, long; sh, she;
th, thin; ᴛʜ, then; zh, measure;

ə represents *a* in about, *e* in taken,
i in pencil, *o* in lemon, *u* in circus.

< = from, derived from, taken from.

2 be present either as a spectator or as one taking part in a ceremony, observance, etc. 3 (in sports) make an assist. —*n.* 1 INFORMAL. act of assistance; aid. 2 (in sports) a play directly helping a teammate to score, as in basketball or hockey, or to put a runner out, as in baseball. [< Latin *assistere* stand by < *ad-* by + *sistere* stand]

as sist ance (ə sis′təns), *n.* an assisting; help; aid.

as sist ant (ə sis′tənt), *n.* person who assists another, especially as a subordinate in some office or work; helper; aid. —*adj.* helping; assisting: *an assistant teacher.*

as size (ə sīz′), *n.* 1 session of a court of law. 2 **assizes,** *pl.* the periodic sessions of a court of law held in each county of England. [< Old French *assise,* ultimately < Latin *assidere.* See ASSESS.]

assn., ass'n, or **Assn.,** association.

assoc., 1 associate. 2 association.

as so ci ate (*v.* ə sō′shē āt, ə sō′sē āt; *n., adj.* ə sō′shē it, ə sō′shē āt; ə sō′sē it, ə sō′sē āt), *v.,* **-at ed, -at ing,** *n., adj.* —*v.t.* 1 connect in thought *(with): We associate turkey with Thanksgiving.* 2 join as a companion, partner, or friend: *He is associated with his sons in business. They were associated in several clothing companies.* 3 join; combine in action; unite. —*v.i.* 1 be friendly or keep company *(with): Do not associate with bad companions.* 2 combine for a common purpose. —*n.* 1 thing usually connected with another. 2 companion, partner, or friend. 3 member of an association or institution without the rights and privileges of full membership. —*adj.* 1 joined with another or others: *an associate editor of a paper.* 2 admitted to some, but not all, rights and privileges: *an associate member of a club.* [< Latin *associatum* joined in companionship < *ad-* to + *socius* companion]

Associate in Arts, 1 degree given by a junior, or two-year college to a person who has completed a course of study. 2 person who has this degree.

as so ci a tion (ə sō′sē ā′shən, ə sō′shē ā′shən), *n.* 1 group of people organized or joined together for some common purpose; society. 2 an associating: *association of ideas.* 3 a being associated: *I look forward to my association with the other counselors at camp.* 4 companionship, partnership, or friendship. 5 mental connection or union between an object and ideas that have some relation to it: *What association do you make with the color red?*

association football, BRITISH. soccer.

as so ci a tive (ə sō′shē ā′tiv, ə sō′sē ā′tiv), *adj.* 1 tending to associate. 2 having to do with association. 3 (in mathematics) of or having to do with a rule that the combinations by which numbers are added or multiplied will not change their sum or product. EXAMPLE: (2×3)×5 will give the same product as 2×(3×5). **—as so′ci a′tive ly,** *adv.*

as soil (ə soil′), *v.t.* ARCHAIC. 1 absolve. 2 atone for. [< Old French *assoill-*, a form of *assoldre* < Latin *absolvere.* Doublet of ABSOLVE.]

as so nance (as′n əns), *n.* 1 resemblance in sound of words or syllables. EXAMPLE: "So all day long the noise of battle rolled." 2 a substitute for rhyme in which the vowels are alike but the consonants are different. EXAMPLES: *brave—vain, lone—show.* [< French < Latin *assonantem* sounding back < *ad-* to + *sonare* sound]

as so nant (as′n ənt), *adj.* characterized by assonance. *—n.* an assonant word or syllable.

as sort (ə sôrt′), *v.t.* 1 distribute into groups by sorts; arrange by kinds; classify. 2 furnish with a variety of goods. *—v.i.* 1 agree in sort or kind; match; suit: *This article assorted well with the rest.* 2 associate *(with): He assorted with men of his own age.* [< Middle French *assortir* < *a-* to + *sorte* sort] **—as sort′er,** *n.*

as sort ed (ə sôr′tid), *adj.* 1 selected so as to be of different kinds; various: *assorted cakes.* 2 arranged by kinds; classified: *socks assorted by size.* 3 suited to one another; matched: *a poorly assorted couple.*

as sort ment (ə sôrt′mənt), *n.* 1 a sorting out or classifying. 2 collection of various kinds. 3 group; class.

asst. or **Asst.,** assistant.

as suage (ə swāj′), *v.t.,* **-suaged, -suag ing.** 1 make (angry or excited feelings, etc.) less intense; calm or soothe: *Her words assuaged the child's fears.* 2 make (physical or mental pain) easier or milder; relieve or lessen. 3 satisfy or appease (appetites or desires): *assuage thirst.* [< Old French *assuagier,* ultimately < Latin *ad-* + *suavis* sweet] **—as suag′er,** *n.* **—as suage′ment,** *n.*

as sume (ə süm′), *v.t.* **-sumed, -sum ing.** 1 take for granted without actual proof; presume; suppose: *She assumed that the train would be on time.* 2 take upon oneself formally; undertake (an office or responsibility): *assume leadership.* 3 take on; put on: *The problem had assumed a new form.* 4 pretend; feign; simulate: *You are more likely to make a good impression if you assume an air of confidence.* See **pretend** for synonym study. 5 take for oneself; appropriate; usurp. [< Latin *assumere* < *ad-* to + *sumere* take]

as sum ing (ə sü′ming), *adj.* taking too much upon oneself; presumptuous.

as sump tion (ə sump′shən), *n.* 1 act of assuming: *She bustled about with an assumption of authority.* 2 thing assumed: *His assumption that he would win the prize proved incorrect.* 3 unpleasant boldness; presumption; arrogance. 4 **the Assumption, a** (in Roman Catholic doctrine) the bodily taking of the Virgin Mary from earth to heaven after her death. **b** a church festival in honor of this on August 15.

as sur ance (ə shůr′əns), *n.* 1 a making sure or certain. 2 statement intended to make a person more sure or certain. 3 security, certainty, or confidence. 4 self-confidence. 5 too much boldness; impudence; audacity: *He has the assurance to deny all knowledge of the affair.* 6 BRITISH. insurance.

as sure (ə shůr′), *v.t.,* **-sured, -sur ing.** 1 tell confidently or positively: *They assured us that the plane would be on time.* 2 make (a person) sure or certain; convince: *I assured myself that the bridge was safe before crossing it.* 3 make safe; secure: *The company's profits were assured by the popularity of its new product.* 4 insure against loss. 5 give or restore confidence to; reassure. [< Old French *aseürer* < Latin *ad-* + *securus* safe] **—as sur′er,** *n.*

as sured (ə shůrd′), *adj.* 1 sure; certain. 2 confident; bold. 3 insured against loss. *—n.* person whose life or property is insured. **—as sur ed ly** (ə shůr′id lē), *adv.* **—as sur ed ness** (ə shůr′id nis), *n.*

As syr i a (ə sir′ē ə), *n.* ancient country in SW Asia, once a great empire extending from the Nile to the Caspian Sea. The capital was Nineveh. **—As syr′i an,** *adj., n.*

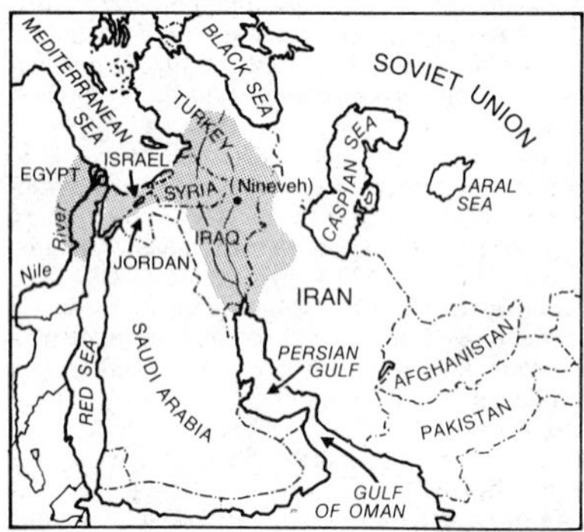

Assyria, 670 B.C.
shown by shaded area on a modern map

As tar te (a stär′tē), *n.* (in Phoenician myths) the goddess of fertility and love.

as ta tine (as′tə tēn′), *n.* a rare, highly unstable, radioactive nonmetallic element belonging to the halogen series. Astatine can be produced by bombarding bismuth with alpha particles. *Symbol:* At; *atomic number* 85. See pages 326 and 327 for table. [< Greek *astatos* unstable]

as ter (as′tər), *n.* 1 any of a genus of plants of the composite family, having white, pink, red, blue, or purple daisylike petals around a yellow center. 2 any plant like this of other genera of the composite family. 3 the flower of any of these plants. 4 (in biology) one of two star-shaped structures found in a cell during mitosis. [< Greek *astēr* star]

as ter isk (as′tə risk′), *n.* a star-shaped mark (*) used in printing and writing to call attention to a footnote, indicate the omission of words or letters, etc. *—v.t.* mark with an asterisk. [< Greek *asteriskos,* diminutive of *astēr* star]

as ter ism (as′tə riz′əm), *n.* group of stars smaller than a constellation.

a stern (ə stėrn′), *adv.* 1 at or toward the rear; aft. 2 backward. 3 behind.

as ter oid (as′tə roid′), *n.* 1 any of numerous minor planets which revolve about the sun, chiefly between the orbits of Mars and Jupiter; planetoid. See **solar system** for diagram. 2 any of a class of echinoderms, usually having five arms or rays radiating from a central disc, a mouth under this disc, and rows of tubular walking feet; starfish. [< Greek *asteroeidēs* starlike < *astēr* star]

as the ni a (as thē′nē ə), *n.* lack or loss of strength; weakness; debility. [< Greek *astheneia*]

as then ic (as then′ik), *adj.* 1 of or showing asthenia; weak; debilitated. 2 characterized by a tall, spare body build.

asth ma (az′mə), *n.* a chronic disease of respiration, characterized by intermittent paroxysms of breathing with a wheezing sound, a sense of constriction in the chest, and coughing. [< Greek]

asth mat ic (az mat′ik), *adj.* 1 of or having to do with asthma. 2 having asthma. *—n.* person who has asthma. **—asth mat′i cal ly,** *adv.*

as tig mat ic (as′tig mat′ik), *adj.* 1 having astigmatism. 2 having to do with astigmatism. 3 correcting astigmatism. **—as′tig mat′i cal ly,** *adv.*

a stig ma tism (ə stig′mə tiz′əm), *n.* a structural defect of an eye or of a lens which prevents rays of light that enter through the cornea from converging at a single point in the retina, thus producing indistinct or imperfect images. [< *a-*[4] without + Greek *stigmatos* mark]

a stir (ə stėr′), *adj.* in motion; up and about.

as ton ish (ə ston′ish), *v.t.* surprise greatly; amaze; astound. See **surprise** for synonym study. [< Old French *estoner* < Popular Latin *extonare* < Latin *ex-* + *tonare* to thunder]

as ton ish ing (ə ston′i shing), *adj.* very surprising; amazing. **—as ton′ish ing ly,** *adv.*

as ton ish ment (ə ston′ish mənt), *n.* 1 great surprise; sudden wonder; amazement. 2 anything that causes great surprise.

As tor (as′tər), *n.* **John Jacob,** 1763-1848, American fur merchant and capitalist, born in Germany.

as tound (ə stound′), *v.t.* shock with alarm or surprise; surprise greatly; amaze. [earlier *astoun* < Old French *estoner.* See ASTONISH.]

as tound ing (ə stoun′ding), *adj.* shocking with alarm or surprise; amazing. **—as tound′ing ly,** *adv.*

as tra chan (as′trə kən), *n.* astrakhan.

a strad dle (ə strad′l), *adv., prep.* astride.

as trag a lus (a strag′ə ləs), *n., pl.* **-li** (-lī). the uppermost bone of the tarsus; anklebone; talus. [< Greek *astragalos*]

as tra khan (as′trə kən), *n.* 1 the curly furlike wool on the skin of young caracul lambs from Astrakhan. 2 a rough woolen cloth that looks like this. Also, **astrachan.**

As tra khan (as′trə kan), *n.* 1 district in SW Soviet Union. 2 capital of this district. 411,000.

as tral (as′trəl), *adj.* 1 of the stars; starry. 2 (in biology) of or like an aster. 3 (in theosophy) of or having to do with a substance beyond the capability of the human senses to discover, supposed to pervade the universe and enter all bodies. [< Latin *astrum* star < Greek *astron*] **—as′tral ly,** *adv.*

astral body, (in theosophy) a ghostlike double of the human body supposed to be able to leave it at will.

a stray (ə strā′), *adj., adv.* 1 out of the right way; off. 2 in or into error.

a stride (ə strīd′), *prep.* with one leg on each side of: *She sits astride her horse.* *—adj., adv.* 1 with one leg on each side: *The knight sat astride on his horse.* 2 with legs far apart.

as trin gen cy (ə strin′jən sē), *n.* quality of being astringent.

as trin gent (ə strin′jənt), *n.* substance, such as alum, that draws together or contracts body tissues and thus checks the flow of blood or other secretions. *—adj.* 1 having the property of drawing together or contracting tissues. 2 severe; austere; stern. [< Latin *astringentem* drawing tight < *ad-* to + *stringere* bind] **—as trin′gent ly,** *adv.*

as tro gate (as′trə gāt), *v.i.,* **-gat ed, -gat ing.** navigate in a spacecraft. [< *astro-(naut)* + *(navi)gate*] **—as′tro ga′tion,** *n.* **—as′tro ga′tor,** *n.*

as tro ge ol o gist (as′trō jē ol′ə jist), *n.* an expert in astrogeology.

as tro ge ol o gy (as′trō jē ol′ə jē), *n.* study of the rocks and other physical features of the moon or other heavenly body.

astrol., astrology.

as tro labe (as′trə lāb), *n.* an astronomical instrument formerly used for measuring the altitude of the sun or stars, later replaced by the sextant. [< Greek *astrolabos*]

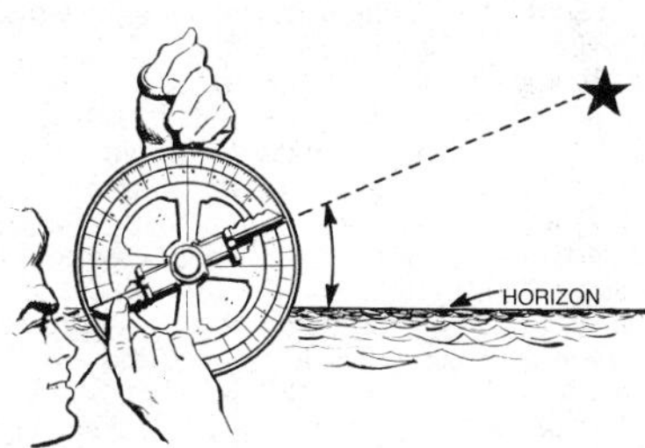

astrolabe—A star is sighted along the length of the movable notched piece. The angle between the horizon and the star is read at the spot where the man's finger rests.

as trol o ger (ə strol′ə jər), *n.* person who professes to determine the influence of the stars and planets on persons or events.

as tro log i cal (as′trə loj′ə kəl), *adj.* of or having to do with astrology. **—as′tro log′i cal ly,** *adv.*

as trol o gy (ə strol′ə jē), *n.* study of the stars to foretell what will happen; pseudoscience which assumes that the stars and planets exert a direct influence on persons, events, etc., and which proposes to determine in any given case what this influence is. [< Greek *astrologia* < *astron* star + *-logos* treating of]

astron., 1 astronomer. 2 astronomy.

as tro naut (as′trə nôt), *n.* pilot or member of the crew of a spacecraft. [< Greek *astron* star + *nautēs* sailor]

as tro naut ic (as′trə nô′tik), *adj.* of or having to do with astronauts or astronautics. **—as′tro naut′i cal ly,** *adv.*

as tro naut i cal (as′trə nô′tə kəl), *adj.* astronautic.

as tro naut ics (as′trə nô′tiks), *n.* 1 science or art having to do with the design, manufacture, and operation of spacecraft. 2 space travel.

as tron o mer (ə stron′ə mər), *n.* an expert in astronomy.

as tro nom ic (as′trə nom′ik), *adj.* astronomical.

as tro nom i cal (as′trə nom′ə kəl), *adj.* 1 of or having to do with astronomy. 2 so large as to be beyond comprehension; enormous: *The government has astronomical expenses.* **—as′tro nom′i cal ly,** *adv.*

astronomical unit, the mean distance of the earth from the sun (about 93 million miles), used as a unit of measurement in expressing distances between planets and stars.

astronomical year, period of the earth's revolution around the sun; solar year. It lasts 365 days, 5 hours, 48 minutes, and 45.51 seconds.

as tron o my (ə stron′ə mē), *n.* science that deals with the constitution, motions, relative positions, sizes, etc., of the sun, moon, planets, stars, and all other heavenly bodies, as well as with the earth in its relation to them. [< Greek *astronomia* < *astron* star + *nomos* distribution]

as tro phys i cal (as′trō fiz′ə kəl), *adj.* of or having to do with astrophysics.

as tro phys i cist (as′trō fiz′ə sist), *n.* an expert in astrophysics.

as tro phys ics (as′trō fiz′iks), *n.* branch of astronomy that deals with the physical characteristics of heavenly bodies, such as luminosity, temperature, size, mass, and density, and also their chemical composition.

as tute (ə stüt′, ə styüt′), *adj.* shrewd, especially with regard to one's own interests; crafty; sagacious. See **shrewd** for synonym study. [< Latin *astutus* < *astus* sagacity] **—as tute′ly,** *adv.* **—as tute′ness,** *n.*

A sun ci ón (ä sün′syôn′), *n.* capital and major port of Paraguay, on the Paraguay River. 437,000.

a sun der (ə sun′dər), *adv.* in pieces; into separate parts: *Lightning split the tree asunder.* —*adj.* apart or separate from each other: *miles asunder.* [Old English *on sundran*]

As wan Dam (ä swän′), large dam in SE Egypt, built on the Nile for irrigation and flood control.

a sy lum (ə sī′ləm), *n.* 1 institution for the support and care of the mentally ill, blind, orphans, or other people who are unable to care for themselves. 2 refuge; shelter. 3 (in former times) sanctuary or inviolable place of refuge and protection for debtors or criminals, from which they could not be forcibly removed without sacrilege. 4 shelter given by one nation to persons of another nation who are accused of political or other crimes. [< Latin < Greek *asylon* refuge]

a sym met ric (ā′sə met′rik), *adj.* not symmetrical; lacking symmetry. **—a′sym met′ri cal ly,** *adv.*

a sym met ri cal (ā′sə met′rə kəl), *adj.* asymmetric.

a sym me try (ā sim′ə trē), *n.* lack of symmetry.

as ymp tote (as′im tōt), *n.* a straight line that continually approaches a curve but does not meet it within a finite distance. [< Greek *asymptōtos*]

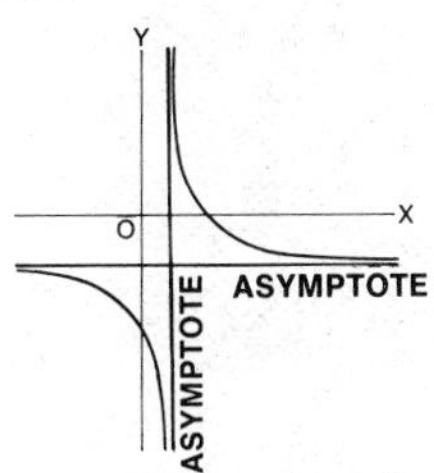

at (at; *unstressed* ət, it), *prep.* 1 in; on; by; near: *at school, at the front door.* 2 in the direction of; to; toward: *aim at the mark. Look at me.* 3 on or near the time of: *at midnight.* 4 in a place or condition of: *at right angles, at war.* 5 by way of; through: *Smoke came out at the chimney.* 6 doing; trying to do; engaged in: *at work.* 7 for: *two books at a dollar each.* 8 because of; by reason of; with: *The shipwrecked sailors were happy at the arrival of the rescue ship.* 9 according to: *at will.* 10 from: *I got good treatment at the hospital.* [Old English *æt*]

➤ **At, in** are used to connect to a sentence a word stating a place or a time. *At* is used when the place or time is thought of as a point, as on a map or a clock. *In* is used when the place or time is thought of as having boundaries and the idea to be expressed is that of being *inside* or *within* the boundaries: *On our trip we stopped at Chicago and stayed two days in New York.*

at-, *prefix.* form of **ad-** before *t,* as in *attain.*

At, astatine.

at., 1 atmosphere. 2 atomic.

At a brine (at′ə brən, at′ə brēn′), *n.* trademark for a yellow, crystalline, synthetic compound used in treating malaria.

A ta ca ma Desert (ä′tä kä′mä), arid region in N Chile, rich in copper and other minerals. 600 mi. long.

A ta hual pa (ä′tä wäl′pä), *n.* 1500?-1533, the last ruler of the Inca empire in Peru, murdered by the Spaniards under Pizarro.

At a lan ta (at′l an′tə), *n.* (in Greek legends) a maiden famous for her beauty and her speed in running. She promised to marry any suitor who could outrun her, but those who failed were put to death.

at a rac tic (at′ə rak′tik), *adj.* that acts as a tranquilizer; *an ataractic drug.* —*n.* tranquilizer. [< Greek *ataraktos* not disturbed]

A ta türk (ä′tä tyrk′, at′ə tėrk′), *n.* **Kemal.** See **Kemal Atatürk.**

at a vism (at′ə viz′əm), *n.* 1 (in biology) the reappearance in an animal or plant of characteristics of a remote ancestor not found in its immediate ancestors, generally as a result of a recombination of genes. 2 reversion to a primitive type. [< Latin *atavus* ancestor]

at a vis tic (at′ə vis′tik), *adj.* 1 having to do with atavism. 2 having a tendency to atavism. **—at′a vis′ti cal ly,** *adv.*

a tax i a (ə tak′sē ə), *n.* inability to coordinate voluntary movements of the muscles. [< Greek, disorder]

ate (āt), *v.* pt. of **eat.** *The boy ate his dinner.*

A te (ā′tē), *n.* (in Greek myths) the goddess of recklessness and mischief, later regarded as the goddess of revenge.

-ate¹, *suffix forming adjectives, verbs, and nouns.* 1 of or having to do with ____: *Collegiate = having to do with college.* 2 having or containing ____: *Compassionate = having compassion.* 3 having the form of ____; like ____: *Stellate = having the form of a star.* 4 become ____: *Maturate = become mature.* 5 cause to be ____: *Alienate = cause to be alien.* 6 produce ____: *Ulcerate = produce ulcers.* 7 supply or treat with ____: *Aerate = treat with air.* 8 combine with ____: *Oxygenate = combine with oxygen.* [< Latin *-atus, -atum,* past participle endings]

-ate², *suffix forming nouns.* office, rule, or condition of ____: *Caliphate = rule of a caliph.* [< Latin *-atus*]

hat, āge, fär; let, ēqual, tėrm;
it, īce; hot, ōpen, ôrder;
oil, out; cup, pu̇t, rüle;
ch, child; ng, long; sh, she;
th, thin; ᴛʜ, then; zh, measure;

ə represents *a* in about, *e* in taken, *i* in pencil, *o* in lemon, *u* in circus.

< = from, derived from, taken from.

-ate[3], *suffix forming nouns.* salt or ester of ___ic acid: *Sulfate = salt or ester of sulfuric acid.* [special use of *-ate*[1]]

at el ier (at′l yā), *n.* workshop, especially an artist's studio. [< French]

a tem po (ä tem′pō), (in music) in time; returning to the former speed. [< Italian]

Ath a bas ca (ath′ə bas′kə), *n.* 1 **Lake,** lake in N Saskatchewan and Alberta. 3085 sq. mi. 2 **Athabasca River,** river in Alberta that empties into this lake. 765 mi.

Ath a na sian Creed (ath′ə nā′zhən, ath′ə nā′shən), one of the three main Christian creeds or professions of faith, the other two being the Apostles' Creed and the Nicene Creed. Its authorship is unknown, but it was probably composed around A.D. 430. [< St. *Athanasius,* A.D. 296?-373, bishop of Alexandria, who opposed the Arian doctrine]

a the ism (ā′thē iz′əm), *n.* 1 disbelief in the existence of God. 2 neglect of the service of God; godlessness. [< French *athéisme* < Greek *atheos* denying the gods]

a the ist (ā′thē ist), *n.* 1 person who does not believe in the existence of God. 2 a godless person.

a the is tic (ā′thē is′tik), *adj.* 1 of atheism or atheists. 2 godless; impious. **—a′the-is′ti cal ly,** *adv.*

a the is ti cal (ā′thē is′tə kəl), *adj.* atheistic.

ath el ing (ath′ə ling), *n.* an Anglo-Saxon noble or prince. [Old English *æthelinɡ*]

Ath el stan (ath′əl stan), *n.* A.D. 895?-940, king of the English from A.D. 925 to 940.

A the na (ə thē′nə), *n.* (in Greek myths) the goddess of wisdom and prudent warfare, patroness of arts and industries, identified with the Roman goddess Minerva; Pallas. Also, **Pallas Athena.**

ath e nae um (ath′ə nē′əm), *n.* 1 a scientific or literary club. 2 a reading room; library. Also, **atheneum.** [< Greek *Athēnaion* temple of Athena]

A the ne (ə thē′nē), *n.* Athena.

ath e ne um (ath′ə nē′əm), *n.* athenaeum.

A the ni an (ə thē′nē ən, ə thē′nyən), *adj.* of Athens (especially ancient Athens) or its people. *—n.* 1 person having the right of citizenship in ancient Athens. 2 native or inhabitant of Athens.

Ath ens (ath′ənz), *n.* capital of Greece, in the SE part. Athens was famous in ancient times for its art and literature. 628,000; with suburbs, 1,853,000. See **Peloponnesus** for map.

ath er o scle ro sis (ath′ər ō sklə rō′sis), *n.* form of arteriosclerosis in which a deposit of fatty material narrows the interior of the arteries. [< Greek *athērē* mush + English *sclerosis*]

a thirst (ə thėrst′), *adj.* 1 thirsty. 2 keenly desirous; eager.

ath lete (ath′lēt′), *n.* person trained to do physical exercises of agility and strength, especially one who participates or competes in games requiring physical skill and stamina. [< Greek *athlētēs* < *athlein* compete for a prize < *athlon* prize]

athlete's foot, a highly contagious skin disease of the feet, which may be caused by any of various related fungi; ringworm of the feet.

ath let ic (ath let′ik), *adj.* 1 of, like, or suited to an athlete. 2 having to do with active games and sports: *an athletic association.* 3 strong and active: *an athletic person.* 4 for athletes or athletics: *an athletic field.* 5 characterized by a robust physique. **—ath let′i cal ly,** *adv.*

ath let ics (ath let′iks), *n.* 1 *pl. in form and use.* exercises of physical strength, speed, and skill; active games and sports. 2 *pl. in form, sing. in use.* the practice and principles of physical training.

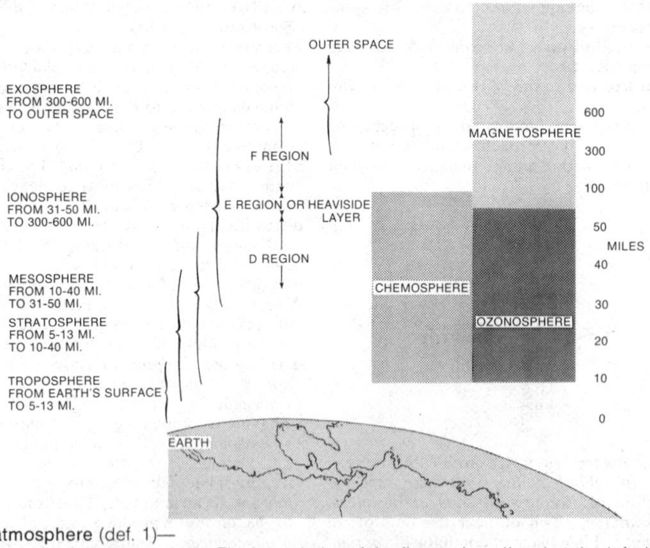

at-home (ət hōm′), *n.* an informal reception, usually in the afternoon.

Ath os (ath′os), *n.* **Mount,** mountain in NE Greece. 6350 ft.

a thwart (ə thwôrt′), *adv.* across from side to side; crosswise. *—prep.* 1 across. 2 across the line or course of. 3 in opposition to; against.

a tilt (ə tilt′), *adj.* 1 at a tilt; tilted. 2 in a tilting encounter.

a tin gle (ə ting′gəl), *adj.* tingling.

-ation, *suffix forming nouns chiefly from verbs.* 1 act or process of ___ing: *Admiration = act or process of admiring.* 2 condition or state of being ___ed: *Cancellation = condition or state of being canceled.* 3 result of ___ing: *Civilization = result of civilizing.* [< Latin *-ationem*]

-ative, *suffix forming adjectives from verbs and nouns.* 1 tending to ___: *Talkative = tending to talk.* 2 having to do with ___: *Qualitative = having to do with quality.* [< Latin *-ativus*]

At lan ta (at lan′tə), *n.* capital of Georgia, in the NW part. 497,000.

At lan tic (at lan′tik), *n.* **Atlantic Ocean,** ocean east of North and South America, west of Europe and Africa. 31,814,640 sq. mi.; with connecting seas, 41,081,040 sq. mi. *—adj.* 1 of the Atlantic Ocean. 2 on, in, over, or near the Atlantic Ocean: *Atlantic air routes.* 3 of or on the Atlantic coast of the United States: *an Atlantic state.* 4 of or having to do with NATO: *the Atlantic alliance.*

Atlantic City, seaside resort in SE New Jersey. 48,000.

At lan ti cist (at lan′tə sist), *n.* supporter or advocate of NATO.

Atlantic Standard Time, the standard time in the zone of the 60th meridian, one hour ahead of Eastern Standard Time, used in the easternmost part of Canada.

At lan tis (at lan′tis), *n.* legendary island somewhere west of Gibraltar, said to have sunk beneath the Atlantic.

at las (at′ləs), *n.* 1 book of maps. 2 book of plates or tables illustrating any subject. 3 **Atlas,** (in Greek myths) a Titan whose punishment for revolt against Zeus was to support the heavens on his shoulders. 4 the first cervical vertebra, which supports the skull. [< Latin < Greek]

Atlas Mountains, mountain range in NW Africa, extending northeast from Morocco to Tunisia. Highest peak, 13,665 ft.

atm., 1 atmosphere. 2 atmospheric.

at mo sphere (at′mə sfir), *n.* 1 the mass of gases that surrounds the earth and is held to it by the force of gravity; the air. 2 mass of gases that surrounds, or may surround, any heavenly body: *the cloudy atmosphere of Venus.* 3 air in any given place: *the damp atmosphere of a cellar.* 4 mental and moral environment; surrounding influence. 5 coloring or feeling that pervades a work of art. 6 (in physics) a unit of pressure equal to 14.69 pounds per square inch. [< New Latin *atmosphaera* < Greek *atmos* vapor + *sphaira* sphere]

at mo spher ic (at′mə sfir′ik, at′mə-sfer′ik), *adj.* 1 of or having to do with the atmosphere. 2 in the atmosphere: *Atmospheric conditions may prevent observations of the stars.* **—at′mo spher′i cal ly,** *adv.*

atmospheric pressure, pressure caused by the weight of the air. The normal atmospheric pressure on the earth's surface at sea

atmosphere (def. 1)—
regions of the atmosphere. The boundaries of the five regions listed at the left do not overlap. Instead they vary with the time of day and year, solar and weather conditions, latitude, etc. The brackets indicate the limits within which each of the five atmospheric regions might be located. The ionosphere is divided into three regions, D, E or Heaviside layer, and F. For certain purposes, different divisions are convenient, such as those indicated on the right.

hat, āge, fär; let, ēqual, tėrm;
it, īce; hot, ōpen, ôrder;
oil, out; cup, pu̇t, rüle;
ch, child; ng, long; sh, she;
th, thin; ᴛʜ, then; zh, measure;

ə represents *a* in about, *e* in taken, *i* in pencil, *o* in lemon, *u* in circus.

< = from, derived from, taken from.

level is 14.69 pounds to the square inch.

at mo spher ics (at′mə sfir′iks, at′mə-sfer′iks), *n.pl.* static (def. 2).

at. no., atomic number.

at oll (at′ol, at′ôl; ə tol′, ə tôl′), *n.* a ring-shaped coral island or group of islands enclosing or partly enclosing a lagoon. [< language of the Maldive Islands]

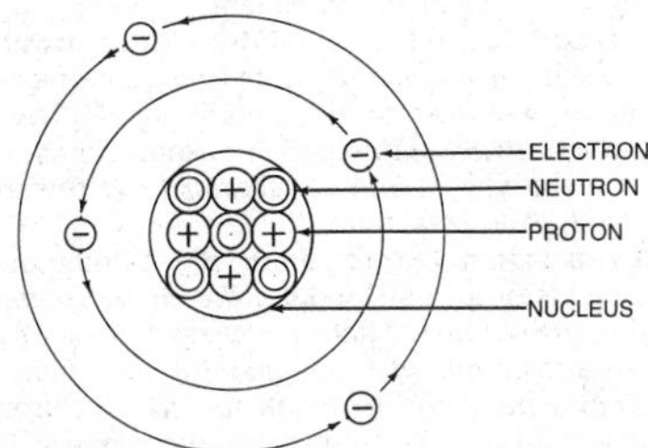

atom (def. 1) of beryllium.
The electrons orbit the nucleus.
In all elements the number of electrons equals the number of protons.

at om (at′əm), *n.* 1 the smallest particle of a chemical element that can take part in a chemical reaction without being permanently changed. An atom is made up of protons and neutrons in a central nucleus surrounded by electrons. A molecule of water consists of two atoms of hydrogen and one atom of oxygen. 2 a very small particle; tiny bit. [< Latin *atomus* < Greek *atomos* indivisible < *a-* not + *tomos* a cutting]

atom bomb, atomic bomb.

at om-bomb (at′əm bom′), *v.t.* destroy or lay waste with atomic bombs.

a tom ic (ə tom′ik), *adj.* 1 of or having to do with atoms: *atomic research.* 2 using or produced by atomic energy: *an atomic submarine.* 3 of or with atomic bombs: *atomic fallout.* 4 (in chemistry) separated into atoms. 5 extremely small; minute. **—a tom′-i cal ly,** *adv.*

atomic age, the present era, as that marked by the first use of atomic energy.

atomic bomb, bomb in which the splitting of atomic nuclei results in an explosion of tremendous force and heat, accompanied by a blinding light; A-bomb; fission bomb.

atomic clock, a highly accurate instrument for measuring time using atomic vibrations as its standard of accuracy rather than the revolution of the earth.

atomic energy, energy that exists in atoms; nuclear energy. Some atoms can be made to release some of their energy, either slowly (in a reactor) or very suddenly (in a bomb), by the splitting or the fusion of their nuclei.

atomic mass, the mass of an atom, as expressed on a scale in which the mass of the most abundant isotope of carbon is placed at 12.

atomic mass unit, unit for expressing atomic mass, equal to approximately 1.66×10^{-24} grams.

atomic number, the number of protons in the nucleus of an atom of an element, used in describing the element and giving its relation to other elements in a series ranging from 1 (hydrogen) to 103 or more.

atomic pile, reactor.

atomic theory, theory that all matter is composed of atoms, especially the modern theory that an atom is made up of a nucleus around which electrons revolve in planetlike orbits.

atomic weight, the relative weight of an atom of a chemical element, based on the weight of an atom of carbon, which is taken as 12. Formerly, atomic weights were based on the weight of an atom of oxygen, which was taken as 16.

at om ize (at′ə mīz), *v.t.,* **-ized, -iz ing.** 1 change (a liquid) into a spray of very small drops. 2 reduce to small particles or units; fragmentize. 3 separate into atoms. 4 obliterate by an atomic explosion. **—at′om i za′tion,** *n.*

at om iz er (at′ə mī′zər); *n.* apparatus used to blow a liquid in a spray of very small drops.

atom smasher, INFORMAL. particle accelerator.

a ton al (ā tō′nl), *adj.* (in music) having no key. **—a ton′al ly,** *adv.*

a ton al i ty (ā′tō nal′ə tē), *n.* lack of tonality in music.

a tone (ə tōn′), *v.i.,* **a toned, a ton ing.** make amends *(for): Nothing can atone for a murder.* [< *atonement*]

a tone ment (ə tōn′mənt), *n.* 1 a giving of satisfaction for a wrong, loss, or injury; amends. 2 **the Atonement** or **the atonement,** the reconciliation of God with sinners through the sufferings and death of Christ. [< earlier *at onement* a being at one, that is, in accord]

a top (ə top′), *prep.* on the top of. *—adv.* on or at the top.

ATP, adenosine triphosphate, a compound found in cells that can release large amounts of energy in sugar metabolism which is used in muscle contraction and other physiological functions. *Formula:* $C_{10}H_{16}N_5O_{13}P_3$

a tri um (ā′trē əm), *n., pl.* **a tri a** (ā′trē ə), **a tri ums.** 1 the main room of an ancient Roman house. 2 hall or court. 3 auricle (def. 1). 4 any of various cavities or sacs, especially in certain marine animals. [< Latin]

a tro cious (ə trō′shəs), *adj.* 1 monstrously wicked or cruel; very savage or brutal; heinous: *an atrocious crime.* 2 INFORMAL. shockingly bad or unpleasant; abominable: *atrocious weather.* **—a tro′cious ly,** *adv.* **—a tro′cious ness,** *n.*

a troc i ty (ə tros′ə tē), *n., pl.* **-ties.** 1 monstrous wickedness or cruelty. 2 a very cruel or brutal act. 3 INFORMAL. anything that violates or is thought of as violating good taste, ordinary convention, etc.: *Her dress is an atrocity.* [< Latin *atrocitatem* < *atrox* fierce]

a troph ic (ə trof′ik), *adj.* of or characterized by atrophy.

at ro phy (at′rə fē), *n., v.,* **-phied, -phy ing.** *—n.* 1 a wasting away of the body or a part of it, especially through imperfect nourishment or disuse. 2 arrested development of an organ of an animal or plant. 3 a halting in growth or withering of anything. *—v.i., v.t.* undergo atrophy; waste away. [< Greek *atrophia* < *a-* without + *trophē* nourishment]

at ro pine (at′rə pēn′, at′rə pən), *n.* a poisonous drug obtained from belladonna and similar plants, used in medicine to relax muscles and dilate the pupil of the eye. *Formula:* $C_{17}H_{23}NO_3$ [< New Latin *Atropa* belladonna < Greek *Atropos*]

At ro pos (at′rə pos), *n.* (in Greek and Roman myths) one of the three Fates. Atropos cuts the thread of life.

at tach (ə tach′), *v.t.* 1 fix in place; fasten *(to).* See synonym study below. 2 join to a person, group, etc.: *He has attached himself to us.* 3 add at the end; affix: *The signers attached their names to the Constitution.* 4 assign, connect, or allocate (a military unit, soldiers, or equipment) temporarily to an organization or commander. 5 bind by sympathy or affection: *I am very attached to my cousin.* 6 regard as belonging; attribute: *The world at first attached little importance to rockets.* 7 seize and hold (property, etc.) by order of a court of law: *If you owe money to a person, he can attach a part of your salary unless you pay him.* *—v.i.* 1 fasten itself; belong: *No responsibility attaches to us for the accident.* 2 be associated as a circumstance or incident: *the advantages which attach to wealth.* [< Old French *atachier, estachier* fasten < Germanic *stakōn*] **—at-tach′a ble,** *adj.*

Syn. *v.t.* 1 **Attach, affix** mean to add one thing to another. **Attach** is the general word and suggests only joining or fastening one thing to another by some means: *I attached a trailer to the car.* **Affix** is a more formal word and often suggests putting something smaller or less important on another firmly and permanently: *With each new state, a star is affixed to the flag.*

at ta ché (at′ə shā′), *n., pl.* **-chés.** a subordinate official on the diplomatic staff of an ambassador or minister to a foreign country: *a naval attaché.* [< French, literally, attached]

attaché case, a flat, rectangular, leather or plastic case for carrying documents, books, etc.

at tach ment (ə tach′mənt), *n.* 1 an attaching or a being attached; connection. 2 thing attached, such as an additional device. Some sewing machines have attachments for making buttonholes. 3 means of attaching; fastening. 4 a being bound to another by sympathy or affection; loyalty or devotion. 5 the legal taking of a person or property.

at tack (ə tak′), *v.t.* 1 fall upon with force or weapons; go against as an enemy; begin fighting against: *The dog attacked the cat.* 2 set upon with hostile actions or words so as to injure or discredit. See synonym study below. 3 work vigorously on: *attack a hard job.* 4 act harmfully on: *Locusts attacked the crops.* *—v.i.* make an attack: *The enemy attacked at dawn.* *—n.* 1 an attacking; assault: *The attack of the enemy took us by surprise.* 2 a sudden occurrence of illness, discomfort, etc.: *an attack of flu.* 3 the offensive part in any active proceeding or contest. 4 the beginning of vigorous work or action on some task, problem, etc. [< French *attaquer* < Italian *attaccare (battaglia)* join (battle) < Germanic *stakōn* fasten. Related to ATTACH.] **—at tack′er,** *n.*

Syn. *v.t.* 1, 2 **Attack, assail, assault** mean to set upon either with physical force or with words. **Attack,** the general word, emphasizes the idea of falling upon a person or enemy without warning, sometimes without cause, or of starting the fighting: *Germany attacked Belgium in 1914. The candidate attacked his opponent's voting record on environmental problems.* **Assail** means to attack with violence and repeated blows or continuous criticism: *The enemy assailed our defense positions. Rip Van Winkle's wife assailed his drinking.* **Assault** means to attack suddenly with furious or brutal force, and always suggests actual contact as in hand-to-hand fighting: *In a rage he assaulted his neighbor with a stick. The mayor assaulted the chief of police and forced him to resign.*

at tain (ə tān′), *v.t.* 1 reach (a state or condition) by living, growing, or developing: *attain the age of 80.* 2 win, gain, or acquire by effort; accomplish: *attain freedom, attain a goal.* 3 reach (a place); arrive at; gain: *attain the top of a hill.* —*v.i.* 1 succeed in coming or getting *(to): attain to a position of great influence.* 2 reach by living, growing, or developing *(to): This tree attains to a great height.* [< Old French *ataindre* < Latin *attingere* < *ad-* to + *tangere* to touch]

at tain a bil i ty (ə tā′nə bil′ə tē), *n.* quality of being attainable.

at tain a ble (ə tā′nə bəl), *adj.* capable of being attained. —**at tain′a ble ness,** *n.*

at tain der (ə tān′dər), *n.* loss of property and civil rights as the result of being sentenced to death or being outlawed.

at tain ment (ə tān′mənt), *n.* 1 act or process of attaining. 2 something attained, especially a personal accomplishment; acquirement.

at taint (ə tānt′), *v.t.* 1 condemn by attainder. 2 taint; stain; disgrace.

at tar (at′ər), *n.* perfume made from the petals of roses or other flowers. [< Persian *'atar* < Arabic *'itr*]

at tempt (ə tempt′), *v.t.* 1 make an effort; try hard: *I will attempt to reply to your question.* See **try** for synonym study. 2 try to accomplish; endeavor to make or perform: *attempt a reply.* 3 make an effort against; attack; assail. —*n.* 1 a putting forth of effort to accomplish something, especially something difficult; endeavor: *an attempt to climb Mount Everest.* 2 an attack: *an attempt upon one's life.* [< Latin *attemptare* < *ad-* to + *temptare* to try]

at tend (ə tend′), *v.t.* 1 be present at: *attend school.* 2 go with as a subordinate: *Noble ladies attend the queen.* See **accompany** for synonym study. 3 go with as a result: *Success often attends hard work.* 4 wait on; care for; tend; serve: *attend the sick.* —*v.i.* 1 apply oneself: *Attend to your work.* 2 be present: *attend at such a church.* 3 give attention: *Attend to my story.* 4 direct one's care; give thought *(to): attend to the baggage.* [< Latin *attendere* < *ad-* toward + *tendere* to stretch]

at tend ance (ə ten′dəns), *n.* 1 act of attending. 2 number of people present; persons attending. 3 **dance attendance on,** be too polite and obedient to. 4 **take attendance,** call the roll.

at tend ant (ə ten′dənt), *n.* 1 person who waits on another, such as a servant or follower. 2 employee who waits on customers. 3 person who is present. —*adj.* 1 waiting on another to help or serve: *an attendant nurse.* 2 going with as a result; accompanying: *Coughing and sneezing are some of the attendant discomforts of a cold.* 3 present.

at ten tion (ə ten′shən), *n.* 1 act or fact of attending; heed: *give attention to the teacher.* 2 power of attending; notice: *call one's attention to a problem.* 3 care and thought; consideration: *Your letter will receive early attention.* 4 **attentions,** *pl.* acts of courtesy or devotion, especially of a suitor. 5 a military attitude of readiness: *come to attention, stand at attention.* —*interj.* command to soldiers to come to attention. [< Latin *attentionem* < *attendere.* See ATTEND.]

at ten tive (ə ten′tiv), *adj.* 1 paying attention; observant. 2 courteous; polite: *an attentive host.* —**at ten′tive ly,** *adv.* —**at ten′tive ness,** *n.*

at ten u ate (*v.* ə ten′yü āt; *adj.* ə ten′yü it), *v.,* **-at ed, -at ing,** *adj.* —*v.t.* 1 make thin or slender: *attenuated by hunger.* 2 weaken; reduce: *attenuated power.* 3 make less dense; dilute. 4 (in bacteriology) make (microorganisms or viruses) less virulent. —*v.i.* become thin or slender. —*adj.* (in botany) gradually tapering. [< Latin *attenuatum* made thin < *ad-* + *tenuis* thin] —**at ten′u a′tion,** *n.*

at test (ə test′), *v.t.* 1 give proof or evidence of; certify: *The high quality of your performance attests your ability.* 2 bear witness to; testify to. —*v.i.* bear witness; testify: *The handwriting expert attested to the genuineness of the signature.* [< Latin *attestari* < *ad-* to + *testis* witness] —**at test′er,** *n.*

at tes ta tion (at′ə stā′shən), *n.* 1 act of attesting. 2 proof or evidence. 3 testimony.

at tic (at′ik), *n.* 1 space in a house just below the roof and above the other rooms; garret. 2 (in architecture) a low story above an entablature or the main cornice of a building. [ultimately < *Attica,* where this architectural feature was common]

At tic (at′ik), *adj.* 1 of Attica or Athens; Athenian. 2 characterized by simple and refined elegance; classical. —*n.* 1 native of Attica. 2 the ancient Greek dialect of Attica.

At ti ca (at′ə kə), *n.* district in SE Greece. Its chief city is Athens. Attica was famous in ancient times for its literature and art.

At ti la (at′l ə, ə til′ə), *n.* A.D. 406?-453, leader of the Huns in their invasions of Europe. He was defeated by the Romans and Goths in A.D. 451.

at tire (ə tīr′), *n., v.,* **-tired, -tir ing.** —*n.* clothing or dress; array: *wear rich attire.* See **clothes** for synonym study. —*v.t.* clothe or dress; array: *attired in purple.* [< Old French *atirer* arrange < *a-* to + *tire* row, order]

at ti tude (at′ə tüd, at′ə tyüd), *n.* 1 the feeling, manner, and behavior of a person toward a situation or cause: *My attitude toward school has changed.* 2 position of the body appropriate to an action, purpose, emotion, etc.; posture; pose. 3 the position of an aircraft, spacecraft, etc., in relation to some line or plane, such as the horizon or the horizontal. 4 **strike an attitude,** pose for effect. [< French < Italian *attitudine* < Late Latin *aptitudo.* Doublet of APTITUDE.]

at ti tu di nize (at′ə tüd′n īz, at′ə tyüd′n īz), *v.i.,* **-nized, -niz ing.** assume attitudes; pose for effect.

Att lee (at′lē), *n.* **Clement Richard,** 1883-1967, British prime minister from 1945 to 1951.

attn., attention.

at tor ney (ə tėr′nē), *n., pl.* **-neys.** 1 person who has power to act for another in business or legal matters. 2 lawyer. [< Old French *atourné* assigned < *a-* to + *tourner* to turn]

attorney at law, lawyer.

attorney general, *n., pl.* **attorneys general** or **attorney generals.** 1 the chief law officer of a country, state, or province. 2 **Attorney General,** the head of the United States Department of Justice and the chief legal adviser of the President.

at tract (ə trakt′), *v.t.* 1 draw to or toward oneself: *A magnet attracts iron.* 2 be pleasing to; win the attention and liking of: *Bright colors attract children.* See **charm** for synonym study. [< Latin *attractum* drawn toward < *ad-* to + *trahere* to draw]

at trac tion (ə trak′shən), *n.* 1 thing that delights or attracts people: *the theater's coming attractions.* 2 act or power of attracting: *the attraction of a magnet for iron filings. Sports have no attraction for me.* 3 charm; fascination. 4 (in physics) the electric or magnetic force exerted by oppositely charged particles on one another, tending to draw or hold them together, or the gravitational force exerted by one body on another.

at trac tive (ə trak′tiv), *adj.* 1 winning attention and liking; pleasing: *an attractive hat.* 2 attracting: *the attractive power of a magnet.* —**at trac′tive ly,** *adv.* —**at trac′tive ness,** *n.*

attrib., 1 attribute. 2 attributive.

at trib ute (*v.* ə trib′yüt; *n.* at′rə byüt), *v.,* **-ut ed, -ut ing,** *n.* —*v.t.* 1 regard as an effect or product of; think of as caused by: *She attributes her great age to a carefully planned diet.* 2 think of as belonging to or appropriate to: *We attribute courage to the lion and cunning to the fox.* See synonym study below. —*n.* 1 an object considered appropriate to a person, rank, or office; symbol: *The eagle was the attribute of Jupiter.* 2 a quality considered as belonging to a person or thing; characteristic: *Patience is an attribute of a good teacher.* 3 adjective, or any word or phrase used as an adjective. [< Latin *attributum* assigned < *ad-* to + *tribuere* divide] —**at trib′ut a ble,** *adj.* —**at trib′ut er,** *n.*

Syn. *v.t.* 2 **Attribute, ascribe** mean to consider something as belonging or due to someone or something, and are often interchangeable. But **attribute** suggests believing something appropriate to a person or thing or belonging to it by nature or right: *We attribute importance to the words of great men.* **Ascribe** suggests guessing or basing a conclusion on evidence and reasoning: *I ascribe your failure to your lack of interest.*

at tri bu tion (at′rə byü′shən), *n.* 1 act of attributing. 2 thing or quality attributed; attribute.

at trib u tive (ə trib′yə tiv), *adj.* 1 expressing a quality or attribute. An adjective used before or immediately after a noun is an attributive adjective as in "a *white* shirt," "the ocean *blue.*" A noun placed immediately before another noun and serving as a modifier is an attributive noun, as in "*highway* patrol." 2 that attributes. 3 of or like an attribute. —*n.* an attributive word. In the phrase "big brown dog," *big* and *brown* are attributives. —**at trib′u tive ly,** *adv.*

at tri tion (ə trish′ən), *n.* 1 a rubbing away, or wearing or grinding down, by friction. 2 any gradual process of wearing down, especially so as to exhaust an opponent's energy or resources: *a war of attrition.* [< Latin *attritionem* < *atterere* rub away < *ad-* away + *terere* rub]

at tune (ə tün′, ə tyün′), *v.t.*, **-tuned, -tun ing.** put in tune or accord; tune. **—at tune′ment,** *n.*

atty., attorney.

at. wt., atomic weight.

a typ i cal (ā tip′ə kəl), *adj.* not typical; irregular; abnormal. **—a typ′i cal ly,** *adv.*

Au, gold. [for Latin *aurum*]

A.U., astronomical unit.

au burn (ô′bərn), *n.* a reddish brown. *—adj.* reddish-brown. [< Old French *auborne*]

Auck land (ôk′lənd), *n.* important seaport in N New Zealand. 604,000.

au cou rant (ō kü räɴ′), FRENCH. in the current of events; well-informed on the topics of the day.

auc tion (ôk′shən), *n.* a public sale in which each thing is sold to the person who offers the most money for it. *—v.t.* sell at an auction. [< Latin *auctionem* < *augere* to increase]

auction bridge, variety of bridge in which the partnerships bid to win a stated minimum of tricks at a given trump suit or at no trumps, and are credited with as many tricks as they win.

auc tion eer (ôk′shə nir′), *n.* person whose business is conducting auctions. *—v.t.* sell at an auction.

au da cious (ô dā′shəs), *adj.* 1 having the courage to take risks; recklessly daring; bold: *an audacious pilot.* 2 rudely bold; impudent. **—au da′cious ly,** *adv.* **—au da′cious ness,** *n.*

au dac i ty (ô das′ə tē), *n.* 1 reckless daring; boldness. 2 rude boldness; impudence; presumption. [< Latin *audacia* < *audax* bold < *audere* to dare]

au di bil i ty (ô′də bil′ə tē), *n.* quality of being audible.

au di ble (ô′də bəl), *adj.* that can be heard; loud enough to be heard. [< Latin *audire* hear] **—au′di bly,** *adv.*

au di ence (ô′dē əns), *n.* 1 people gathered in a place to hear or see: *a theater audience.* 2 any persons within hearing: *a radio audience.* 3 the readers of a book, newspaper, or magazine. 4 a chance to be heard; hearing: *The committee will give you an audience to hear your plan.* 5 a formal interview with a person of high rank: *The king granted an audience to the noble.* 6 act or fact of hearing. [< Latin *audientia* < *audire* hear]

au di o (ô′dē ō), *adj.* 1 using, involving, or having to do with audio frequencies. 2 of, having to do with, or used in transmitting or receiving sound in television. An audio problem is a sound problem; a video problem involves the image that is supposed to appear on the screen. *—n.* sound reproduction: *the audio for a film.* [< Latin *audire* hear]

audio frequency, frequency corresponding to audible sound vibrations, from about 15 to about 20,000 cycles per second for human beings.

au di om e ter (ô′dē om′ə tər), *n.* instrument for measuring the keenness and range of hearing.

au di o phile (ô′dē ə fil), *n.* devotee of high-fidelity sound reproduction.

au di o-vis u al (ô′dē ō vizh′ü əl), *adj.* of or having to do with both hearing and sight. Schools use motion pictures, slides, and recordings as audio-visual aids in teaching.

au dit (ô′dit), *v.t.* 1 examine and check (business accounts) systematically and officially. 2 attend (a college class) as a listener without getting academic credit for the course. *—n.* 1 a systematic and official examination and check of business accounts. 2 statement of an account that has been examined and checked officially. [< Latin *auditus* a hearing < *audire* hear]

au di tion (ô dish′ən), *n.* 1 a hearing to test the ability, quality, or performance of a singer, actor, or other performer. 2 act of hearing. 3 power or sense of hearing. *—v.t.* give (a singer, actor, or other performer) an audition. *—v.i.* sing, act, or perform at an audition.

au di tor (ô′də tər), *n.* 1 person who audits business accounts. 2 hearer; listener.

au di to ri um (ô′də tôr′ē əm, ô′də tōr′ē əm), *n., pl.* **-to ri ums, -to ri a** (-tôr′ē ə, -tōr′ē ə). 1 a large room for an audience in a church, theater, school, etc. 2 building especially designed for public meetings, lectures, concerts, etc.

au di to ry (ô′də tôr′ē, ô′də tōr′ē), *adj.* of or having to do with hearing, the sense of hearing, or the organs of hearing: *The auditory nerve transmits impulses from the ear to the brain.*

Au du bon (ô′də bon), *n.* **John James,** 1785-1851, American painter and ornithologist.

auf Wie der seh en (ouf vē′dər zā′ən), GERMAN. good-by; till we see each other again.

Aug., August.

Au ge an stables (ô jē′ən), (in Greek myths) the stables, sheltering 3000 oxen, that remained uncleaned for 30 years until Hercules turned two rivers through them.

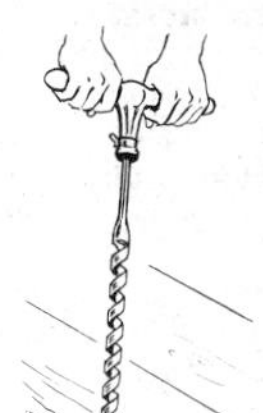

auger (def. 1) Each turn of the handle makes the spiral cutting edge at the end of the bit bite deeper into the wood.

au ger (ô′gər), *n.* 1 tool for boring holes in wood. 2 a large tool for boring holes in the earth. [Old English *nafugār,* originally, a nave borer; Middle English *a nauger* taken as *an auger*]

aught[1] (ôt), *n.* anything: *Has he done aught to help you?* *—adv.* in any way; to any degree; at all: *Help came too late to avail aught.* Also, **ought.** [Old English *āwiht* < *ā-* ever + *wiht* thing]

aught[2] (ôt), *n.* zero; cipher; nothing. Also, **ought.** [< *naught; a naught* taken as *an aught*]

aug ment (ôg ment′), *v.t., v.i.* make or become greater in size, number, amount, or degree; increase or enlarge. See **increase** for synonym study. [< Late Latin *augmentare* < *augmentum* an increase < Latin *augere* to increase] **—aug ment′a ble,** *adj.* **—aug ment′er,** *n.*

aug men ta tion (ôg′men tā′shən), *n.* 1 an augmenting; increase or enlargement. 2 thing that augments; addition.

au gra tin (ō grat′n, ō grät′n; *French* ō grä taɴ′), cooked with a layer of bread crumbs or grated cheese, to make a browned crust. [< French]

Augs burg (ôgz′bėrg′), *n.* city in S West Germany. 214,000.

au gur (ô′gər), *n.* 1 priest in ancient Rome who made predictions and gave advice from

hat, āge, fär; let, ēqual, tėrm;
it, īce; hot, ōpen, ôrder;
oil, out; cup, pu̇t, rüle;
ch, child; ng, long; sh, she;
th, thin; ᴛʜ, then; zh, measure;

ə represents *a* in about, *e* in taken, *i* in pencil, *o* in lemon, *u* in circus.

< = from, derived from, taken from.

signs and omens. 2 soothsayer; fortuneteller. *—v.t.* 1 guess from signs or omens; predict; foretell. 2 be a sign or promise of. *—v.i.* 1 **augur ill,** be a bad sign. 2 **augur well,** be a good sign. [< Latin]

au gur y (ô′gyər ē), *n., pl.* **-gur ies.** 1 prediction; sign; omen. 2 art or practice of foretelling events by interpreting such signs and omens as the flight of birds, thunder and lightning, etc.

au gust (ô gust′), *adj.* inspiring reverence and admiration; majestic; venerable. [< Latin *augustus* < *augere* to increase] **—au gust′ly,** *adv.* **—au gust′ness,** *n.*

Au gust (ô′gəst), *n.* the eighth month of the year. It has 31 days. [< *Augustus*]

Au gus ta (ô gus′tə), *n.* capital of Maine, in the SW part. 22,000.

Au gus tan (ô gus′tən), *adj.* of the Roman emperor Augustus or his reign. *—n.* any writer of the Augustan age.

Augustan age, 1 period of Latin literature from 27 B.C. to A.D. 14. 2 period of English literature from about 1700 to 1750.

Au gus tine (ô′gə stēn′, ô gus′tən), *n.* 1 **Saint,** A.D. 354-430, bishop of northern Africa and one of the leaders in the early Christian church. 2 **Saint,** died A.D. 604, Roman monk sent in A.D. 597 to preach Christianity in England, and first archbishop of Canterbury. Also, **Saint Austin.**

Au gus tin i an (ô′gə stin′ē ən), *adj.* of or having to do with Saint Augustine, A.D. 354-430, his teachings, or the religious orders named for him. *—n.* 1 person who follows the teachings of Saint Augustine. 2 member of any of the religious orders named for Saint Augustine.

Au gus tus (ô gus′təs), *n.* 63 B.C.-A.D. 14, title of Octavian, grandnephew and heir of Julius Caesar, after he became first emperor of Rome, from 27 B.C. to A.D. 14.

au jus (ō zhʏ′), FRENCH. (of meat) served in its own gravy or juice.

auk (ôk), *n.* any of several diving sea birds found in arctic regions, with short wings used chiefly as paddles in swimming and legs set so far back that it stands like a penguin. [< Scandinavian (Old Icelandic) *ālka*]

auk let (ôk′lit), *n.* any of various small northern Pacific auks.

auld (ôld), *adj.* SCOTTISH. old.

auld lang syne (ôld′ lang sīn′; ôld′ lang zīn′), SCOTTISH. old times; long ago in one's life.

aunt (ant), *n.* 1 sister of one's father or mother. 2 wife of one's uncle. [< Old French *ante* < Latin *amita*]

aunt ie (an′tē), *n.* INFORMAL. aunt.

au ra (ôr′ə), *n., pl.* **au ras, au rae** (ôr′ē). 1 something supposed to come from a person or thing and surround him or it as an atmosphere: *An aura of holiness enveloped the saint.* 2 a subtle emanation or exhalation from any substance, as the odor of flowers. [< Latin, breeze, breath < Greek]

au ral (ôr′əl), *adj.* of, having to do with, or perceived by the ear. [< Latin *auris* ear] **—au′ral ly,** *adv.*

au re ate (ôr′ē it, ôr′ē āt), *adj.* 1 golden; gilded. 2 brilliant; splendid. [< Latin *aureus* golden < *aurum* gold]

au re o la (ô rē′ə lə), *n.* aureole.

au re ole (ôr′ē ōl), *n.* 1 ring of light surrounding a figure or object, especially in religious paintings. 2 ring of light surrounding the sun. [< Late Latin *aureola* golden < Latin *aurum* gold]

Au re o my cin (ôr′ē ō mī′sn), *n.* trademark for an antibiotic derived from a microorganism found in the soil, used to check or kill certain bacterial infections and viruses; chlortetracycline.

au re voir (ō rə vwär′), FRENCH. good-by; till we see each other again.

au ric (ôr′ik), *adj.* of or containing gold, especially with a valence of three.

au ri cle (ôr′ə kəl), *n.* 1 chamber of the heart that receives the blood from the veins and forces it into a ventricle; atrium. See **heart** for diagram. 2 the outer projecting portion of the ear; pinna. 3 an earlike part. [< Latin *auricula,* diminutive of *auris* ear]

au ric u lar (ô rik′yə lər), *adj.* 1 having to do with an auricle of the heart. 2 of or near the ear; aural. 3 heard by or addressed to the ear. 4 shaped like an ear.

au rif er ous (ô rif′ər əs), *adj.* containing or yielding gold. [< Latin *aurifer* < *aurum* gold + *ferre* carry]

Au ri ga (ô rī′gə), *n.* a northern constellation between Perseus and Gemini, supposed to represent a charioteer kneeling in his chariot.

Au rig na cian (ôr′ig nā′shən), *adj.* of or having to do with Upper Paleolithic culture, especially that of the Cro-Magnon man. [< *Aurignac,* village in southern France]

au rochs (ôr′oks), *n., pl.* **-rochs.** 1 bison of Europe, now almost extinct; wisent. 2 an extinct wild ox of Europe; urus. [< German *Auerochs*]

Au ro ra (ô rôr′ə, ô rōr′ə), *n., pl.* **-ras** or **-rae** (-rē) for 3. 1 (in Roman myths) the goddess of the dawn, identified with the Greek goddess Eos. 2 city in NE Colorado. 75,000. 3 **aurora, a** dawn. **b** streamers or bands of light appearing in the sky at night, especially in polar regions, probably due to the impact of streams of particles from the sun on the upper regions of the earth's atmosphere.

au ro ra aus tra lis (ô rôr′ə ô strā′lis; ô rōr′ə ô strā′lis), the aurora of the southern sky; southern lights. [< New Latin]

au ro ra bo re al is (ô rôr′ə bôr′ē al′is; ô rōr′ə bōr′ē al′is), the aurora of the northern sky; northern lights. [< New Latin]

au ro ral (ô rôr′əl, ô rōr′əl), *adj.* 1 of or like the aurora. 2 shining; bright.

au rous (ôr′əs), *adj.* of or containing gold, especially with a valence of one.

aus cul tate (ôs′kəl tāt), *v.t., v.i.,* **-tat ed, -tat ing.** examine by auscultation.

aus cul ta tion (ôs′kəl tā′shən), *n.* a listening to sounds within the human body, especially with a stethoscope, to determine the condition of the heart, lungs, or abdominal organs. [< Latin *auscultationem* a listening < *auscultare* listen]

aus pic es (ô′spə siz, ô′spə sēz′), *n.pl.* 1 helpful influence; approval or support; patronage: *The school fair was held under the auspices of the Parents' Association.* 2 observations of birds, especially their flight, as a sign or token of the future. 3 omens; signs. [< Latin *auspicium* < *avis* bird + *specere* look at]

aus pi cious (ô spish′əs), *adj.* 1 with signs of success; favorable. See **favorable** for synonym study. 2 prosperous; fortunate. **—aus pi′cious ly,** *adv.* **—aus pi′cious ness,** *n.*

Aus ten (ô′stən), *n.* **Jane,** 1775-1817, English novelist.

aus tere (ô stir′), *adj.* 1 stern in manner or appearance; harsh: *a silent, austere man.* 2 severe in self-discipline; strict in morals: *The Puritans were austere.* 3 severely simple: *The tall, plain columns stood against the sky in austere beauty.* 4 grave; somber; serious. [< Greek *austēros* < *auos* dry] **—aus tere′ly,** *adv.* **—aus tere′ness,** *n.*

aus ter i ty (ô ster′ə tē), *n., pl.* **-ties.** 1 sternness in manner or appearance; harshness; severity. 2 severe simplicity. 3 a strict limiting or rationing of food, clothing, etc., in order to conserve national resources. 4 **austerities,** *pl.* severe practices, such as going without food or praying all night.

Aus tin (ô′stən), *n.* 1 capital of Texas, in the central part. 252,000. 2 **Saint,** Saint Augustine (def. 2).

aus tral (ô′strəl), *adj.* southern. [< Latin *auster* the south wind]

Aus tral a sia (ô′strə lā′zhə, ô′strə lā′shə), *n.* Australia, Tasmania, New Guinea, New Zealand, and other nearby islands. **—Aus′tral a′sian,** *adj., n.*

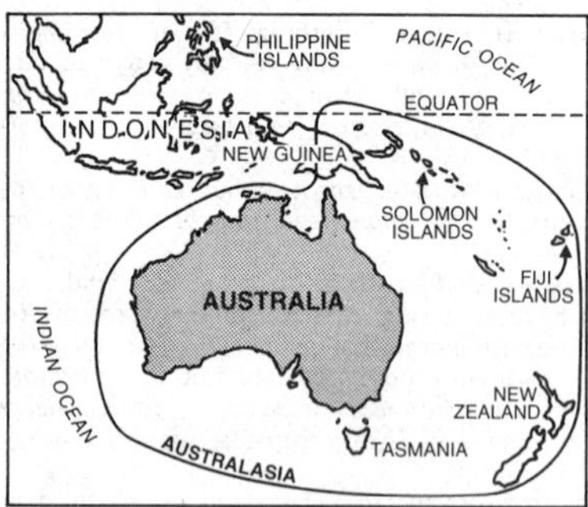

Aus tral ia (ô strā′lyə), *n.* 1 island continent in the E hemisphere, SE of Asia, between the Indian Ocean and the South Pacific. 12,159,000 pop.; 2,948,400 sq. mi. 2 **Commonwealth of,** country that includes this continent and Tasmania, a member of the Commonwealth of Nations. 12,552,000 pop.; 2,974,600 sq. mi. *Capital:* Canberra. **—Aus tral′ian,** *adj., n.*

Australian ballot, ballot with the names of all candidates for election to public office on it, marked by the voter in a private booth to guarantee secrecy.

Aus tra loid (ô′strə loid), *adj.* of the racial type characterized by the Australian aborigines and related peoples. *—n.* member of an Australoid people.

Aus tra lo pi the cine (ô′strə lō pith′ə sēn′), *n.* any of a group of extinct primates of the early Pleistocene, whose fossil remains have been found in various parts of the world and especially in South Africa. *—adj.* of or belonging to this group. [< Latin *australis* southern + Greek *pithēkos* ape]

Aus tri a (ô′strē ə), *n.* country in central Europe. 7,373,000 pop.; 32,400 sq. mi. *Capital:* Vienna. **—Aus′tri an,** *adj., n.*

Aus tri a-Hun gar y (ô′strē ə hung′gər ē), *n.* monarchy in central Europe from 1867 to 1918, composed of the Austrian empire and the kingdom of Hungary and their territories. 260,200 sq. mi.

Austria-Hungary
Shaded area shows its extent in 1914.

Aus tro ne sia (ô′strō nē′zhə, ô′strō nē′shə), *n.* islands of the south and mid-Pacific.

Aus tro ne sian (ô′strō nē′zhən, ô′strō nē′shən), *adj.* of Austronesia, its people, or its languages. *—n.* 1 native or inhabitant of Austronesia. 2 a linguistic family of the Pacific, comprising the Indonesian, Polynesian, and Melanesian languages.

au tar ky (ô′tär kē), *n., pl.* **-kies.** economic self-sufficiency; a being independent of imports from other nations. [< Greek *autarkeia*]

auth., 1 author. 2 authorized.

au then tic (ô then′tik), *adj.* 1 worthy of acceptance, trust, or belief; reliable: *an authentic account of the incident.* 2 coming from the source stated; not copied; real: *A comparison of signatures showed that the letter was authentic.* See **genuine** for synonym study. [< Greek *authentikos* < *auto-* by oneself + *-hentēs* one who acts] **—au then′ti cal ly,** *adv.*

au then ti cate (ô then′tə kāt), *v.t.,* **-cat ed, -cat ing.** 1 establish the truth or genuineness of; prove authentic. See **confirm** for synonym study. 2 make valid or authoritative; establish the validity of. **—au then′ti ca′tion,** *n.* **—au then′ti ca′tor,** *n.*

au then tic i ty (ô′then tis′ə tē), *n.* 1 reliability: *question the authenticity of a report.* 2 genuineness: *doubt the authenticity of a signature.*

au thor (ô′thər), *n.* 1 writer of a book, poem, article, or other literary work. 2 the works of an author: *Have you read this author?* 3 originator, inventor, or creator. 4 person responsible for anything. [< Old French *autor* < Latin *auctor* one who creates or builds < *augere* to increase]

au tho ri al (ô thôr′ē əl, ô thōr′ē əl), *adj.* of or having to do with an author.

au thor i tar i an (ə thôr′ə ter′ē ən, ə thor′ə ter′ē ən), *adj.* based on or supporting the principle of subjection to authority instead of individual freedom: *an authoritarian government.* —*n.* person who supports the principle of subjection to authority instead of individual freedom.

au thor i tar i an ism (ə thôr′ə ter′ē ə niz′əm, ə thor′ə ter′ē ə niz′əm), *n.* body of principles underlying authoritarian belief or practice.

au thor i ta tive (ə thôr′ə tā′tiv, ə thor′ə tā′tiv), *adj.* 1 proceeding from a recognized authority; official: *The president issued an authoritative declaration of policy.* 2 of or characterized by authority; commanding: *In authoritative tones the policeman shouted, "Keep back."* 3 entitled to obedience and respect; having the authority of expert knowledge: *We have long desired an authoritative edition of this author's works.* **—au thor′i ta′tive ly,** *adv.* **—au thor′i ta′tive ness,** *n.*

au thor i ty (ə thôr′ə tē, ə thor′ə tē), *n., pl.* **-ties.** 1 the right to control, command, or make decisions; power to enforce obedience; jurisdiction: *parents' authority over their children.* See synonym study below. 2 person, body, board, or the like having such power, right, or jurisdiction: *the Transit Authority.* 3 **the authorities,** the government of a country, state, etc.; officials in control. 4 book or passage regarded as settling disputed points in a particular subject: *A good dictionary is an authority on the meaning of words.* 5 person whose advice or opinion is generally accepted in a particular field or subject; expert. 6 power over the action of others; practical influence in affairs. 7 power over the opinions of others. 8 delegated power; authorization: *An appointed official derives his authority from the President.* 9 a judicial opinion that may be cited as a precedent.

Syn. 1 **Authority, control, influence** mean power to direct or act on others. **Authority** often implies legal power, given by a person's position or office, to give commands and enforce obedience: *A policeman has the authority to arrest speeding drivers.* **Control** applies to power, given by a person's position, to direct people and things: *Parents should have control over their children.* **Influence** applies to personal power, coming from a person's character, personality, or position, to shape the actions of others: *Some teachers have great influence over young people.*

au thor i za tion (ô′thər ə zā′shən), *n.* 1 act or process of authorizing. 2 legal right; official permission; sanction; warrant.

au thor ize (ô′thə rīz′), *v.t.,* **-ized, -iz ing.** 1 give power or right to; empower: *She was authorized to speak for the school board.* 2 make legal; sanction: *Congress authorized the spending of money for rearmament.* 3 give authority for; justify: *The dictionary authorizes the two spellings "acknowledgment" and "acknowledgement."* **—au′thor iz′er,** *n.*

Authorized Version, the English translation of the Bible published in 1611; King James Version.

au thor ship (ô′thər ship), *n.* 1 occupation of an author; writing. 2 origin as to author: *What is the authorship of that novel?* 3 the source or cause of anything.

au tism (ô′tiz′əm), *n.* an escaping from reality by daydreaming and fantasy. [< Greek *autos* self]

au tis tic (ô tis′tik), *adj.* indulging in daydreaming and fantasy.

au to (ô′tō), *n., pl.* **-tos.** automobile.

auto-, *combining form.* 1 self: *Autointoxication = self-intoxication.* 2 of or by oneself: *Autobiography = biography of oneself.* [< Greek *autos* self]

au to an ti bod y (ô′tō an′ti bod′ē), *n., pl.* **-bod ies.** antibody that attacks the body's own cells and tissues.

au to bahn (ô′tō bän; *German* ou′tō bän′), *n.* (in Germany) a four-lane express highway. [< German *Autobahn*]

au to bi og ra pher (ô′tə bī og′rə fər, ô′tə bē og′rə fər), *n.* person who writes the story of his own life.

au to bi o graph ic (ô′tə bī′ə graf′ik), *adj.* autobiographical.

au to bi o graph i cal (ô′tə bī′ə graf′ə kəl), *adj.* 1 having to do with the story of one's own life. 2 telling or writing the story of one's own life. **—au′to bi′o graph′i cal ly,** *adv.*

au to bi og ra phy (ô′tə bī og′rə fē, ô′tə bē og′rə fē), *n., pl.* **-phies.** account of a person's life written by himself.

au toch tho nous (ô tok′thə nəs), *adj.* originating where found; aboriginal; indigenous. [< Greek *autochthōn*] **—au toch′tho nous ly,** *adv.*

au to clave (ô′tə klāv), *n.* a strong, closed vessel which develops superheated steam under pressure, used for sterilizing, cooking, etc. [< French]

au toc ra cy (ô tok′rə sē), *n., pl.* **-cies.** 1 supreme power of government exerted by one person. 2 country or state characterized by such a centralization of power. 3 supreme control; paramount influence in any sphere or group of persons.

au to crat (ô′tə krat), *n.* 1 ruler who claims or exerts unrestricted power and uncontrolled authority over his subjects. 2 person who rules with undisputed sway or supremacy in any group or sphere. [< Greek *autokratēs* ruling by oneself < *auto-* + *kratos* strength]

au to crat ic (ô′tə krat′ik), *adj.* of or like an autocrat; absolute in power or authority; despotic; dictatorial. **—au′to crat′i cal ly,** *adv.*

au to-da-fé (ô′tō də fā′, ou′tō də fā′), *n., pl.* **au tos-da-fé** (ô′tōz də fā′, ou′tōz də fā′). 1 a public ceremony accompanying the passing of sentence by the Inquisition. 2 the burning of a heretic. [< Portuguese *auto da fé* act of the faith]

au tog a my (ô tog′ə mē), *n.* self-fertilization.

au tog e nous (ô toj′ə nəs), *adj.* produced by or within oneself.

Au to gi ro (ô′tō jī′rō), *n., pl.* **-ros.** trademark for a propeller-driven wingless aircraft supported in flight by a large rotor above the fuselage that spins from the air pressure against its blades.

au to graft (ô′tə graft), *n.* tissue or organ grafted from one part of a person's body onto another.

au to graph (ô′tə graf), *n.* 1 a person's signature. 2 something written in a person's own handwriting, especially the original copy of a manuscript, letter, etc. —*v.t.* 1 write one's signature in or on. 2 write with one's own hand.

au to im mune (ô′tō i myün′), *adj.* caused by autoantibodies: *an autoimmune disease.*

hat, āge, fär; let, ēqual, tėrm;
it, īce; hot, ōpen, ôrder;
oil, out; cup, pu̇t, rüle;
ch, child; ng, long; sh, she;
th, thin; ᴛʜ, then; zh, measure;

ə represents *a* in about, *e* in taken, *i* in pencil, *o* in lemon, *u* in circus.

< = from, derived from, taken from.

au to in tox i ca tion (ô′tō in tok′sə kā′shən), *n.* a poisoning by or resulting from toxin formed within the body.

au to mat (ô′tə mat), *n.* restaurant in which food is obtained from compartments that can be opened after coins are inserted in slots.

au to mate (ô′tə māt), *v.t.,* **-mat ed, -mat ing.** convert to automation; operate by automation: *automate a production line.*

au to mat ic (ô′tə mat′ik), *adj.* 1 (of machinery, etc.) moving or acting by itself; regulating itself: *an automatic pump, an automatic elevator.* 2 done normally without thought or attention; not voluntary: *Breathing and swallowing are usually automatic.* See synonym study below. 3 (of a firearm) reloading by itself: *an automatic pistol.* —*n.* firearm that throws out the empty shell, reloads by itself, and continues to fire until the pressure on the trigger is released. [< Greek *automatos* self-acting] **—au′to mat′i cal ly,** *adv.*

Syn. *adj.* 2 **Automatic, involuntary** mean not controlled by the will. **Automatic** means done unconsciously due to a natural or habitual reaction to a situation or stimulus: *My automatic response when I see a red light while driving is to brake.* **Involuntary** means done without conscious intention: *I gave an involuntary jump because I had been startled.*

automatic pilot, a gyroscopic mechanism designed to keep an aircraft, missile, etc., on a given course and at a given altitude without human assistance; autopilot.

automatic transmission, any of various mechanisms in an automobile for automatically altering the ratio of engine speed to the speed of rotation of the driving wheels.

Autogiro

au to ma tion (ô′tə mā′shən), *n.* 1 the use of automatic controls in the operation of a machine or group of machines. In automation, electronic or mechanical devices do many of the tasks formerly performed by people. 2 method of making a manufacturing process, a production line, etc., operate more automatically by the use of built-in or supplementary controls in a machine or number of machines.

au tom a tism (ô tom′ə tiz′əm), *n.* 1 action not controlled by the will; involuntary action;

automatic action. 2 quality or condition of being automatic or of acting mechanically only.

au tom a tize (ô tom′ə tīz), *v.t.*, **-tized, -tiz ing.** 1 make automatic. 2 automate. **—au tom′a ti za′tion,** *n.*

au tom a ton (ô tom′ə ton, ô tom′ə tən), *n., pl.* **-tons, -ta** (-tə). 1 person or animal whose actions are entirely mechanical. 2 machine or toy with its motive power concealed so that it appears to move spontaneously.

au to mo bile (ô′tə mə bēl′, ô′tə mə bēl′, ô′tə mō′bēl′), *n.* a four-wheeled passenger vehicle, for use on roads and streets, that is self-propelled by an internal-combustion engine. *—adj.* 1 of or for automobiles: *an automobile mechanic.* 2 self-propelled: *an automobile torpedo.*

au to mo bil ist (ô′tə mə bē′list), *n.* person who uses an automobile; motorist.

au to mo tive (ô′tə mō′tiv), *adj.* 1 of or having to do with cars, trucks, and other self-moving vehicles. Automotive engineering deals with the design and construction of motor vehicles. 2 furnishing its own power; self-propelled.

au to nom ic (ô′tə nom′ik), *adj.* 1 having to do with the autonomic nervous system. 2 autonomous. **—au′to nom′i cal ly,** *adv.*

autonomic nervous system, the ganglia and nerves of the nervous system of vertebrates, which control involuntary reactions, such as digestive processes and breathing.

au ton o mous (ô ton′ə məs), *adj.* self-governing; independent. **—au ton′o mous ly,** *adv.*

au ton o my (ô ton′ə mē), *n., pl.* **-mies.** 1 self-government; independence. 2 a self-governing state, community, etc. [< Greek *autonomia* < *auto-* + *nomos* law]

au to pi lot (ô′tə pī′lət), *n.* automatic pilot.

au top sy (ô′top sē, ô′təp sē), *n., pl.* **-sies.** medical examination of a dead body to find either the cause of death or the character and site of the disease of which the person died; post-mortem; necropsy. [< Greek *autopsia* a seeing for oneself < *auto-* + *opsis* a seeing]

au to some (ô′tə sōm), *n.* any chromosome other than a sex chromosome. [< *auto-* + Greek *sōma* body]

au to sug ges tion (ô′tō səg jes′chən, ô′tō sə jes′chən), *n.* suggestion to oneself of ideas that produce mental or physiological effects.

au to troph (ô′tə trof), *n.* organism that can manufacture its own food from inorganic substances, getting its energy either from photosynthesis or from chemosynthesis. All green plants and certain bacteria are autotrophs.

au to troph ic (ô′tə trof′ik), *adj.* of or having to do with an autotroph.

au tumn (ô′təm), *n.* 1 season of the year between summer and winter; fall. 2 a time of maturity and the beginning of decay. *—adj.* of or coming in autumn: *autumn flowers, autumn rains.* [< Latin *autumnus*]

au tum nal (ô tum′nəl), *adj.* of or coming in autumn.

aux il iar y (ôg zil′yər ē, ôg zil′ər ē), *adj., n., pl.* **-iar ies.** *—adj.* 1 giving help or support; assisting: *The army was sent auxiliary troops.* 2 additional; subsidiary: *The main library has several auxiliary branches.* 3 kept in reserve or as a substitute; supplementary: *Some sailboats have auxiliary engines.* *—n.* 1 person or thing that helps; aid. 2 a subsidiary group: *a men's club with a women's auxiliary.* 3 auxiliary verb. 4 **auxiliaries,** *pl.* foreign or allied troops that help the army of a nation at war; mercenaries. [< Latin *auxilium* aid]

auxiliary verb, verb used to form the tenses, moods, or voices of other verbs; helping verb. *Be, can, do, have, may, must, shall,* and *will* are auxiliary verbs. EXAMPLES: I *am* going; he *will* go; they *are* lost; they *were* lost.

aux in (ôk′sən), *n.* any of a group of hormones synthesized in the protoplasm of the young, active parts of plants, which regulate plant growth and development. [< Greek *auxein* to increase]

av., 1 avenue. 2 average. 3 avoirdupois.

A.V., Authorized Version.

a vail (ə vāl′), *v.t.* 1 be of use or value to; help: *Money will not avail you after you are dead.* 2 **avail oneself of,** take advantage of; profit by; make use of. *—v.i.* be of use or value; help: *Talk will not avail without work.* *—n.* **of no avail** or **to no avail,** of no use or value. [< Old French *a-* to + *vail-*, a form of *valoir* be worth < Latin *valere* be worth]

a vail a bil i ty (ə vā′lə bil′ə tē), *n., pl.* **-ties.** 1 a being available; capability of being used. 2 person, object, or facility that is available.

a vail a ble (ə vā′lə bəl), *adj.* 1 that can be used or secured: *She is not available for the job; she has other work.* 2 that can be had: *All available tickets were sold.* **—a vail′a ble ness,** *n.* **—a vail′a bly,** *adv.*

av a lanche (av′ə lanch), *n., v.,* **-lanched, -lanch ing.** *—n.* 1 a large mass of snow and ice, or of dirt and rocks, loosened from a mountainside and descending swiftly into the valley below. 2 anything like an avalanche: *an avalanche of questions.* *—v.i.* move like an avalanche. [< French]

Av a lon (av′ə lon), *n.* (in Arthurian legends) an earthly paradise in the western seas, to which King Arthur and other heroes were carried at death.

a vant-garde (ä′vänt gärd′; *French* à′väɴ-gärd′), *n.* group of people, especially in the arts, who are ahead of all others in using or creating new ideas, methods, designs, etc. *—adj.* of or having to do with an avant-garde: *avant-garde poetry.* [< French, literally, advance guard]

a vant-gard ism (ä′vänt gär′diz′əm), *n.* the beliefs and practices of the avant-garde.

a vant-gard ist (ä′vänt gär′dist), *n.* member of the avant-garde.

av ar ice (av′ər is), *n.* too great a desire for money or property; greed for wealth. [< Old French < Latin *avaritia* < *avarus* greedy]

av a ri cious (av′ə rish′əs), *adj.* greatly desiring money or property; greedy for wealth. **—av′a ri′cious ly,** *adv.* **—av′a ri′cious ness,** *n.*

a vast (ə vast′), *interj.* (in nautical use) stop! stay! [probably < Dutch *houd vast* hold fast!]

av a tar (av′ə tär′), *n.* 1 (in Hindu myths) the descent of a god to earth in bodily form; incarnation. 2 any manifestation in bodily form. [< Sanskrit *avatāra* descent]

a vaunt (ə vônt′, ə vänt′), *interj.* ARCHAIC. begone! get out! go away! [Middle French *avant* forward < Latin *abante* < *ab* from + *ante* before]

a ve (ā′vē, ä′vā), *interj.* LATIN. hail! farewell!

Ave. or **ave.,** Avenue; avenue.

A ve Ma ri a (ä′vā mə rē′ə; ä′vē mə rē′ə), 1 "Hail Mary!", the first words of the Latin form of a prayer of the Roman Catholic Church. 2 this prayer.

a venge (ə venj′), *v.,* **a venged, a veng ing.** *—v.t.* take revenge for or on behalf of: *avenge an insult. Hamlet avenged his father's murder.* See **revenge** for synonym study. *—v.i.* get revenge. [< Old French *avengier* < *a-* to + *vengier* avenge < Latin *vindicare*] **—a veng′er,** *n.*

av e nue (av′ə nü, av′ə nyü), *n.* 1 a wide or main street; thoroughfare; boulevard. 2 a wide road or walk bordered by trees. 3 way of approach or departure; passage: *There are various avenues to fame.* [< Middle French < *avenir* arrive < Latin *advenire* < *ad-* to + *venire* come]

a ver (ə vėr′), *v.t.,* **a verred, a ver ring.** state positively to be true; assert; affirm. [< Old French *averer,* ultimately < Latin *ad-* + *verus* true]

av er age (av′ər ij), *n., adj., v.,* **-aged, ag ing.** *—n.* 1 quantity found by dividing the sum of all the quantities by the number of quantities; arithmetic mean: *The average of 3, 5, and 10 is 6.* 2 ratio or percentage indicating a record of achievement: *a batting average, an A average.* 3 the usual sort or amount; the generally prevailing, normal, or typical quantity, degree, rate, quality, kind, etc.: *The amount of rain this year has been below average. His mind is about like the average.* 4 **on the average** or **on an average,** considered on the basis of the average: *I work six hours a day on the average.* *—adj.* 1 obtained by averaging; being an average: *an average price, the average temperature.* 2 usual; ordinary: *average intelligence.* *—v.t.* 1 find the average of. 2 have as an average; amount on the average to: *The cost of our lunches at school averaged two dollars a week.* 3 do, get, yield, etc., on an average: *I average six hours of work a day. The farmer averaged forty bushels to the acre.* 4 divide among several proportionately: *We averaged our gains according to what each had put in.* [< Middle French *avarie* damage to ship or cargo < Italian *avaria* < Arabic *'awārīya* damage from sea water. In English the original sense extended to "equal distribution (of loss from damage)."] **—av′er age ly,** *adv.* **—av′er age ness,** *n.*

a ver ment (ə vėr′mənt), *n.* positive declaration; assertion.

A ver nus (ə vėr′nəs), *n.* (in Roman myths) the lower world; Hades.

a verse (ə vėrs′), *adj.* having a strong or fixed dislike; opposed or unwilling: *I am averse to fighting.* [< Latin *aversum* turned away < *ab-* from + *vertere* to turn] **—a verse′ly,** *adv.* **—a verse′ness,** *n.*

a ver sion (ə vėr′zhən, ə vėr′shən), *n.* 1 a strong or fixed dislike; antipathy: *an aversion to working hard. We'll eat alone; they have an aversion for fried shrimp.* 2 thing or person disliked. 3 unwillingness.

a vert (ə vėrt′), *v.t.* 1 keep (a disaster, misfortune, etc.) from happening; prevent; avoid: *She averted the accident by a quick turn of her car.* 2 turn away or turn aside (the face, eyes, mind, etc.). [< Latin *avertere* < *ab-* from + *vertere* to turn]

A ves (ā′vēz), *n.pl.* class of warm-blooded vertebrates with wings and feathers. All birds belong to this class. [< Latin]

A ves ta (ə ves′tə), *n.* the sacred writings of the ancient Zoroastrian religion, still in use by the Parsees.

A ves tan (ə ves′tən), *n.* the Iranian language in which the Avesta is written.

hat, āge, fär; let, ēqual, tėrm;
it, īce; hot, ōpen, ôrder;
oil, out; cup, pu̇t, rüle;
ch, child; ng, long; sh, she;
th, thin; ᴛʜ, then; zh, measure;

ə represents *a* in about, *e* in taken, *i* in pencil, *o* in lemon, *u* in circus.

< = from, derived from, taken from.

avg., average.

a vi an (ā′vē ən), *adj.* of or having to do with birds.

a vi ar ist (ā′vē ər ist), *n.* keeper of an aviary.

a vi ar y (ā′vē er′ē), *n., pl.* **-ar ies.** house, enclosure, or large cage in which many birds, especially wild birds, are kept; birdhouse. [< Latin *aviarium* < *avis* bird]

a vi a tion (ā′vē ā′shən, av′ē ā′shən), *n.* 1 art or science of operating and navigating aircraft. 2 the designing and manufacturing of aircraft, especially airplanes. 3 aircraft collectively, together with personnel and equipment. [< French < Latin *avis* bird]

a vi a tor (ā′vē ā′tər, av′ē ā′tər), *n.* person who flies an aircraft; pilot.

a vi a trix (ā′vē ā′triks, av′ē ā′triks), *n.* a woman aviator.

av id (av′id), *adj.* extremely eager; greatly desirous: *an avid desire for power. The miser was avid for gold.* [< Latin *avidus* < *avere* desire eagerly] **—av′id ly,** *adv.*

a vid i ty (ə vid′ə tē), *n.* 1 great eagerness: *The hungry children looked at the food with avidity.* 2 greed for wealth; avarice.

A vi gnon (à vē nyôɴ′), *n.* city in SE France, the residence of the popes from 1309 to 1377. 86,000.

a vi on ics (ā′vē on′iks), *n.* the development, production, and application of electronic devices to aviation, rocketry, and astronautics.

a vi ta min o sis (ā vī′tə mə nō′sis), *n.* any disease caused by a lack of one or more vitamins.

av o ca do (av′ə kä′dō), *n., pl.* **-dos.** 1 a usually pear-shaped tropical fruit with a dark-green to purplish-black skin and a very large seed; alligator pear. Its yellow-green pulp has a nutty flavor and is used in salads. 2 tree that it grows on, of the same family as the laurel. [< Spanish *aguacate* < Nahuatl *ahuacatl*]

av o ca tion (av′ə kā′shən), *n.* something that a person does besides his regular business; minor occupation; hobby: *He is a lawyer by vocation, but writing stories is his avocation.* [< Latin *avocationem* < *avocare* call away < *ab-* away + *vocare* to call] ➤ See **vocation** for usage note.

av o cet (av′ə set), *n.* a web-footed wading bird with long legs and a long, slender beak that curves upward. Also, **avoset.** [< French *avocette*]

avocet
2 ft. tall

A vo ga dro's law (ä′vō gä′drōz), (in chemistry and physics) a law stating that equal volumes of different gases, under like conditions of pressure and temperature, contain the same number of molecules. [< Count Amedeo *Avogadro,* 1776-1856, Italian physicist, who stated it]

a void (ə void′), *v.t.* 1 keep away from: *We avoided large cities on our trip.* 2 have nothing to do with. See synonym study below. 3 (in law) make void; annul. [< Anglo-French *avoider* < Old French *esvuidier* empty out, quit < *es-* out + *vuidier* to void, empty] **—a void′a ble,** *adj.* **—a void′a bly,** *adv.*

Syn. 1, 2 Avoid, shun mean to keep out of the way of. **Avoid** suggests trying not to meet someone or something that might be unpleasant or keeping away from danger: *I have to avoid the butcher until I pay the bill.* **Shun** suggests feeling strong dislike or disgust for the person or thing avoided: *We are likely to shun people with contagious diseases.*

a void ance (ə void′ns), *n.* 1 an avoiding; keeping away from. 2 act of making void; invalidating; annulment.

av oir du pois (av′ər də poiz′), *n.* 1 avoirdupois weight. 2 INFORMAL. a person's weight. [< Middle French *avoir de pois* goods of weight]

avoirdupois weight, system of weights in which a pound containing 16 ounces is used. The avoirdupois weight system is used to weigh everything except gems, precious metals, and drugs. See **measure** for table.

A von River (ā′vən), 1 river in S central England, on which Stratford-on-Avon is located. 96 mi. 2 river in S England. 65 mi. 3 river in SW England. 62 mi.

av o set (av′ə set), *n.* avocet.

a vouch (ə vouch′), *v.t.* 1 declare positively to be true; affirm. 2 vouch for; guarantee: *I can avouch her honesty.* 3 acknowledge; avow. [< Old French *avochier* < *a-* to + *vochier* to call] **—a vouch′ment,** *n.*

a vow (ə vou′), *v.t.* declare frankly or openly; admit; acknowledge. [< Old French *avouer* < *a-* to + *vouer* vow]

a vow al (ə vou′əl), *n.* a frank or open declaration; admission; acknowledgment.

a vowed (ə voud′), *adj.* frankly or openly declared; admitted.

a vow ed ly (ə vou′id lē), *adv.* admittedly; openly.

a vun cu lar (ə vung′kyə lər), *adj.* 1 of an uncle. 2 like an uncle. [< Latin *avunculus* mother's brother, uncle]

a wait (ə wāt′), *v.t.* 1 wait for (a person or event); look forward to; expect: *I have awaited your coming for a week.* 2 be ready for; be in store for: *Many pleasures await you on your trip.*

a wake (ə wāk′), *v.,* **a woke** or **a waked, a wak ing,** *adj.* *—v.i.* 1 come out of sleep; wake up; arouse. 2 bestir oneself; become vigilant. *—v.t.* 1 arouse from sleep; waken: *The alarm clock awoke me at dawn.* 2 stir up: *These words awoke his anger.* 3 **awake to,** become aware of; realize. *—adj.* 1 roused from sleep; not asleep. 2 on the alert; watchful.

a wak en (ə wā′kən), *v.i.* 1 wake up; arouse. 2 **awaken to,** come to realize. *—v.t.* 1 arouse from sleep; wake up. 2 rouse to activity or awareness; stir. **—a wak′en er,** *n.*

a wak en ing (ə wā′kə ning), *n.* a waking up; arousing. *—adj.* arousing.

a ward (ə wôrd′), *v.t.* 1 give after careful consideration; grant: *A medal was awarded to the best speller in the class.* 2 decide or settle by law; adjudge: *The court awarded damages of $500.* *—n.* 1 something given after careful consideration; prize: *My dog won the highest award.* 2 decision by a judge. [< Anglo-French *awarder* < Old French *esguarder* observe, decide < *es-* out + *guarder* to guard] **—a ward′a ble,** *adj.* **—a ward′er,** *n.*

a ward ee (ə wôr dē′, ə wôr′dē), *n.* the receiver of an award.

a ware (ə wer′, ə war′), *adj.* having knowledge; realizing; conscious: *I was aware how dangerous it would be to fall asleep in that bitter cold. She was not aware of our presence.* See **conscious** for synonym study. [Old English *gewær*] **—a ware′ness,** *n.*

a wash (ə wosh′, ə wôsh′), *adj.* 1 level with the surface of the water; just covered with water. 2 carried about by water; floating.

a way (ə wā′), *adv.* 1 from a place; to a distance: *Stay away from the fire.* 2 at a distance; a way off: *The traveler was far away from home.* 3 out of one's possession, notice, or use: *He gave his boat away.* 4 out of existence: *The sounds died away.* 5 in another direction; aside: *turn away.* 6 without stopping; continuously: *She worked away at her job.* 7 without delay; at once: *Fire away!*

away with, take (someone or something) away.

away with you, go away.

do away with, a put an end to; get rid of. **b** kill.

—adj. 1 at a distance; far: *Her home is miles away.* 2 absent; gone: *My mother is away today.*

[Old English *onweg*]

awe (ô), *n., v.,* **awed, aw ing.** *—n.* 1 a feeling of wonder and reverence inspired by anything of great beauty, sublimity, majesty, or power: *The sight of the great waterfall filled us with awe. The young girl stood in awe before the queen.* 2 dread mingled with reverence. *—v.t.* 1 cause to feel awe; fill with awe: *The majesty of the mountains awed us.* 2 influence or restrain by awe. [< Scandinavian (Old Icelandic) *agi*]

a wear y (ə wir′ē), *adj.* weary; tired.

a weigh (ə wā′), *adj.* (of an anchor) just clear of the bottom and hanging straight down, leaving a ship free to move.

awe-in spir ing (ô′in spīr′ing), *adj.* causing awe; awesome.

awe some (ô′səm), *adj.* 1 causing awe. 2 showing awe; awed. **—awe′some ly,** *adv.* **—awe′some ness,** *n.*

awe-strick en (ô′strik′ən), *adj.* awestruck.

awe-struck (ô′struk′), *adj.* filled with awe.

aw ful (ô′fəl), *adj.* 1 causing fear; dreadful; terrible: *an awful storm.* 2 deserving great respect and reverence: *the awful power of God.* 3 filling with awe; impressive; imposing: *The mountains rose to awful heights.* 4 INFORMAL. very bad, great, ugly, etc.: *an awful mess.* *—adv.* INFORMAL. very: *I was awful mad.* **—aw′ful ness,** *n.*

➤ The widespread informal use of **awful** as a word of disapproval has made the more literal meanings difficult to understand. It is usually wise to substitute *awe-inspiring* or *awesome* when those meanings are intended.

aw ful ly (ô′flē, ô′fə lē), *adv.* 1 dreadfully; terribly: *The broken leg hurt awfully.* 2 INFORMAL. very: *I'm awfully sorry that I hurt your feelings.*

a while (ə hwīl′), *adv.* for a short time: *She stayed awhile after dinner.*

awk ward (ôk′wərd), *adj.* 1 not graceful or skillful in movement; clumsy; ungainly: *The seal is very awkward on land, but graceful in the water.* See synonym study below. 2 not well suited to use; unhandy: *The handle of this pitcher has an awkward shape.* 3 not easily managed: *an awkward bend in the road.* 4 inconvenient: *an awkward moment.* 5 unpleasant to deal with. 6 ill at ease; embarrassed. [< obsolete *awk* perversely, in the wrong way < Scandinavian (Old Icelandic) *öfugr* + *-ward*] **—awk′ward ly,** *adv.* **—awk′ward ness,** *n.*

Syn. 1 **Awkward, clumsy** mean not graceful. **Awkward** means lacking grace, ease, quickness, and skill: *An awkward girl is no help in the kitchen.* **Clumsy** suggests moving heavily and stiffly: *The clumsy boy bumped into all the furniture.*

awl (ôl), *n.* a sharp-pointed tool used for making small holes in leather or wood. [Old English *æl*]

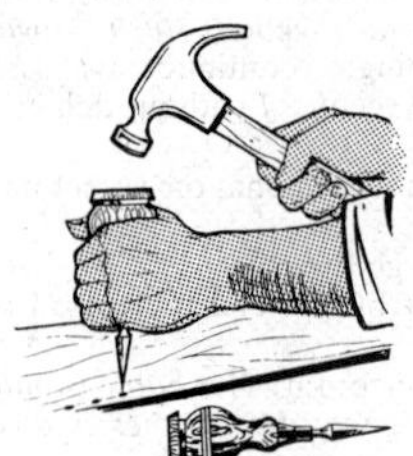

awl being used to mark places for screws on a piece of wood

awn (ôn), *n.* one of the bristly hairs forming the beard on a head of barley, oats, etc. [< Scandinavian (Old Icelandic) *ögn* chaff] **—awn′less,** *adj.*

awn ing (ô′ning), *n.* piece of canvas, metal, wood, or plastic spread over or before a door, window, porch, deck, or patio for protection from the sun or rain. [origin uncertain]

a woke (ə wōk′), *v.* a pt. and pp. of **awake.** *He awoke at seven. My sister has not yet awoke.*

AWOL, A.W.O.L., or **a.w.o.l.** (ā′wôl, *or pronounced as initials*), *adj., adv.* absent without leave. —*n.* SLANG. person who is absent without leave. [< A(bsent) W(ith)o(ut) L(eave), military designation for someone missing from his place of duty]

a wry (ə rī′), *adv.* 1 with a twist or turn to one side: *Her hat was blown awry by the wind.* 2 wrong; out of order: *Our plans have gone awry.*

ax or **axe** (aks), *n., pl.* **ax es.** 1 tool with a flat, sharp blade fastened on a handle, used for chopping, splitting, and shaping wood. 2 **have an ax to grind,** have a special purpose or reason for taking action or being interested. [Old English *æx*] **—ax′ like′, axe′like′,** *adj.*

ax es[1] (ak′siz), *n.* pl. of **ax.**

ax es[2] (ak′sēz′), *n.* pl. of **axis.**

ax i al (ak′sē əl), *adj.* 1 of or forming an axis: *The wheels turn on an axial rod.* 2 on or around an axis. **—ax′i al ly,** *adv.*

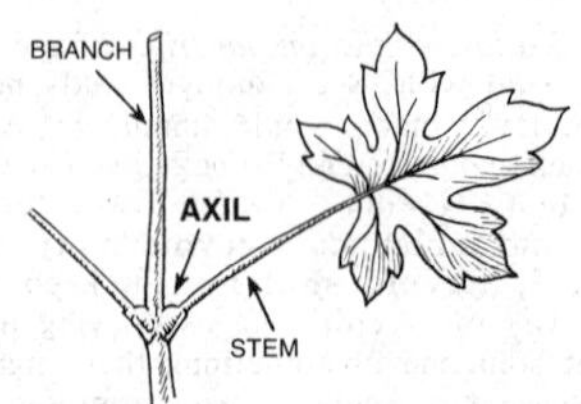

ax il (ak′səl), *n.* angle between the upper side of a leaf or stem and the supporting stem or branch. A bud is usually found in the axil. [< Latin *axilla* armpit]

ax il la (ak sil′ə), *n., pl.* **ax il lae** (ak sil′ē). 1 armpit. 2 axil.

ax il lar (ak′sə lər), *adj.* axillary.

ax il lar y (ak′sə ler′ē), *adj.* 1 of or near the armpit. 2 in or growing from an axil.

ax i om (ak′sē əm), *n.* 1 statement taken to be true without proof; self-evident truth: *It is an axiom that if equals are added to equals the results will be equal.* 2 a well-established principle; rule or law. [< Latin *axioma* < Greek *axiōma* < *axios* worthy]

ax i o mat ic (ak′sē ə mat′ik), *adj.* accepted without proof; self-evident: *It is axiomatic that a whole is greater than any of its parts.* **—ax′i o mat′i cal ly,** *adv.*

ax is (ak′sis), *n., pl.* **ax es.** 1 an imaginary or real line that passes through an object and about which an object turns or seems to turn. The earth's axis passes through the North and the South Poles. 2 a central or principal line around which parts are arranged symmetrically. The axis of a cone is the straight line joining its apex and the center of its base. 3 any line used for reference. 4 in anatomy: **a** a central or principal structure extending lengthwise and having the parts of the body arranged around it: *The axis of the skeleton is the spinal column.* **b** the second cervical vertebra. 5 in botany: **a** the central part or support on which parts are arranged. **b** the main stem and root. 6 any of three lines, one parallel to the axis of the propeller, and the other two perpendicular to this and to each other, about which an aircraft or spacecraft revolves. 7 (in art, design, etc.) an imaginary central line in a composition, referred to for balance of parts or the like. 8 one of the three or four imaginary lines assumed in defining the position of the plane faces of a crystal and classifying the crystal. 9 an important line of relation: *the Rome-Berlin axis.* 10 **the Axis,** Germany, Italy, Japan, and their allies, during World War II. [< Latin]

ax le (ak′səl), *n.* 1 bar or shaft on which or with which a wheel turns. 2 axletree. [shortened from Middle English *axeltre* axletree < Scandinavian (Old Icelandic) *öxul-trē* < *öxul* axle + *trē* tree]

ax le tree (ak′səl trē′), *n.* crossbar that connects two opposite wheels of a vehicle on the ends of which the wheels turn.

Ax min ster (aks′min stər), *n.* kind of carpet with a finely tufted, velvetlike pile. [< *Axminster,* town in England where it was formerly made]

ax o lotl (ak′sə lot′l), *n.* any of several salamanders, common in lakes and lagoons in Mexico and the southwestern United States, that usually retain their gills and tadpole form through life. [< Nahuatl]

ax on (ak′son), *n.* the long extension of a nerve cell that carries impulses away from the body of the cell. [< Greek *axōn* axis]

ax one (ak′sōn), *n.* axon.

ay[1] (ā), *adv.* always; ever. Also, **aye.** [< Scandinavian (Old Icelandic) *ei*]

ay[2] (ī), *adv., n.* aye[2].

a yah (ä′yə), *n.* a native maid or nurse in India. [< Hindustani *āya* < Portuguese *aia* governess < Latin *avia* grandmother]

aye[1] (ā), *adv.* ay[1].

aye[2] (ī), *adv.* yes: *Aye, aye, sir.* —*n.* an affirmative answer, vote, or voter: *The ayes were in the majority when the vote was taken.* Also, **ay.** [apparently Old English *gī*]

aye-aye (ī′ī′), *n.* a squirrellike lemur of Madagascar. [< Malagasy *aiay*]

Ayr (er, ar), *n.* county in SW Scotland.

Ayr shire (er′shər, er′shir; ar′shər, ar′shir), *n.* any of a breed of dairy cattle that are red and white or brown and white, originating in Ayr. —*adj.* of or having to do with this breed.

a zal ea (ə zā′lyə), *n.* 1 any of several species of rhododendron. Azaleas are shrubs growing mainly in northeastern North America and in China. 2 its showy flower. [< Greek]

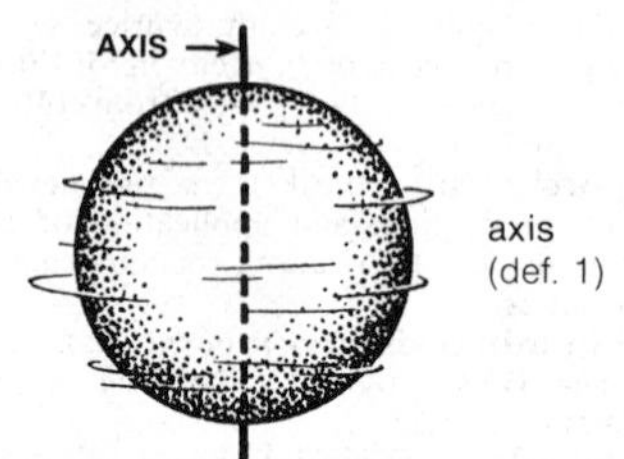

axis (def. 1)

A zer bai jan S.S.R. (ä′zər bī jän′), one of the constituent republics of the U.S.S.R., in the SW part, on the Caspian Sea. 5,100,000 pop.; 33,100 sq. mi. *Capital:* Baku.

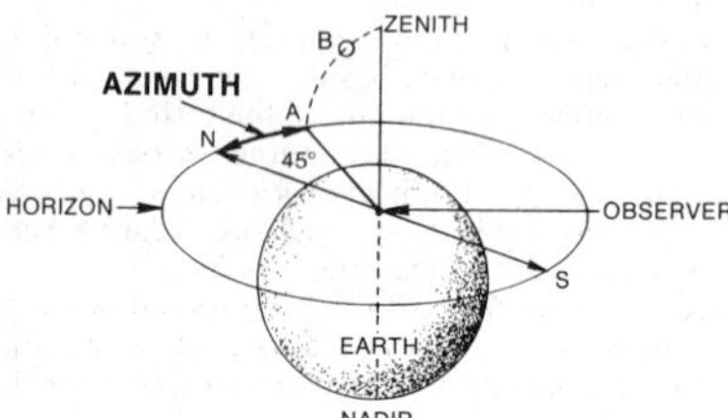

azimuth (def. 1)—The vertical circle through the star, B, intersects the horizon at A. S is the south point. Arc NA is the azimuth.

az i muth (az′ə məth), *n.* 1 an arc measured clockwise from the north point of the horizon (in navigation), or the south point (in astronomy), to the intersection of a vertical circle passing through a heavenly body with the horizon. 2 (in surveying and gunnery) horizontal distance expressed as an angle between a fixed point of reference and an object. [< Middle French *azimut* < Arabic *as-sumūt* the ways < *samt* way]

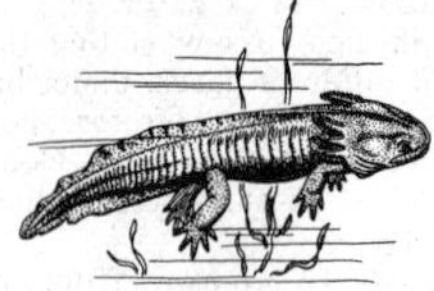

axolotl 6 to 9 in. long

az o (az′ō, ā′zō), *adj.* (in chemistry) containing nitrogen. [< French *azote* nitrogen < Greek *a-* not + *zōē* life]

A zores (ə zôrz′, ə zōrz′; ā′zôrz, ā′zōrz), *n.pl.* group of islands in the Atlantic west of and belonging to Portugal. 328,000 pop.; 922 sq. mi.

A zov (ā′zov, ä zôf′), *n.* **Sea of,** shallow sea in S Soviet Union in Europe, connected with the Black Sea by a narrow channel. 14,500 sq. mi.

Az tec (az′tek), *n.* 1 member of a highly civilized American Indian people who ruled a large empire in central Mexico before its conquest by the Spaniards in 1521. 2 their language; Nahuatl. —*adj.* of the Aztecs or their language.

Az tec an (az′tek′ən), *adj.* Aztec.

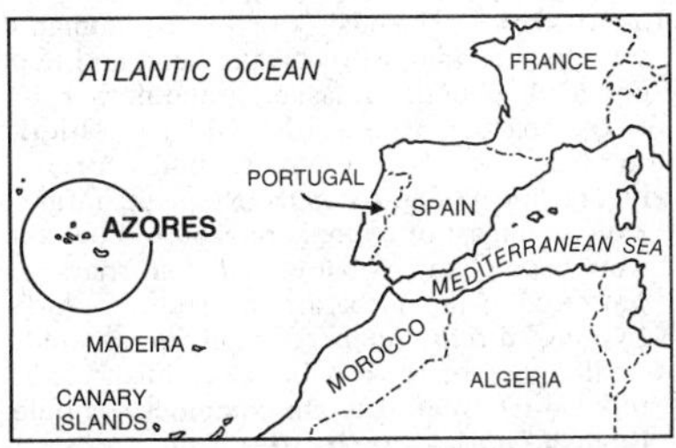

az ure (azh′ər), *n.* the clear blue color of the unclouded sky; sky blue. —*adj.* *sky-blue.* [< Old French *l'azur* the azure < Arabic *lāzuward* < Persian *lajward* lapis lazuli]

hat, āge, fär; let, ēqual, tėrm;
it, īce; hot, ōpen, ôrder;
oil, out; cup, pu̇t, rüle;
ch, child; ng, long; sh, she;
th, thin; ᴛʜ, then; zh, measure;

ə represents *a* in about, *e* in taken, *i* in pencil, *o* in lemon, *u* in circus.

< = from, derived from, taken from.

az ur ite (azh′ə rīt′), *n.* 1 a blue copper ore, a basic carbonate of copper. *Formula:* $2CuCO_3 \cdot Cu(OH)_2$ 2 form of this mineral used as a semiprecious stone.

B b

B[1] or **b** (bē), *n., pl.* **B's** or **b's.** the second letter of the English alphabet.
B[2] (bē), *n., pl.* **B's.** the seventh tone of the musical scale of C major.
B, 1 (in chess) bishop. 2 boron. 3 one of the four main blood groups.
b., 1 bachelor. 2 base. 3 baseman. 4 bass. 5 bay. 6 book. 7 born.
B., 1 Bay. 2 Bible. 3 British.
Ba, barium.
B.A., Bachelor of Arts. Also, **A.B.**
baa (bä, ba), *n.* the sound a sheep makes; bleat. —*v.i.* make this sound; bleat. [imitative]
Ba al (bā′əl, bāl), *n., pl.* **Ba al im** (bā′ə lim), **Ba als.** 1 the chief god of the Canaanites and Phoenicians. In some places he was the god of fertility; in others, he was the sun god. 2 a false god. [< Hebrew *ba'al* lord]
Baal bek (bäl′bək), *n.* town in E Lebanon, site of an ancient center of the worship of Baal; called by the ancient Greeks **Heliopolis.** 16,000.
bab bitt (bab′it), *n.* alloy of tin, antimony, and copper, or a similar alloy, used in bearings to lessen friction. [< Isaac *Babbitt,* 1799-1862, American inventor]
Bab bitt (bab′it), *n.* a self-satisfied businessman who conforms to middle-class ideas of respectability and business success. [< George F. *Babbitt,* main character of the novel *Babbitt* (1922) by Sinclair Lewis]
Babbitt metal, babbitt.
bab bitt ry or **Bab bitt ry** (bab′ə trē), *n.* smug conformity to middle-class ideals.
bab ble (bab′əl), *v.,* **-bled, -bling,** *n.* —*v.i.* 1 make indistinct or meaningless sounds like a baby. 2 talk foolishly; prattle. 3 talk too much; chatter. 4 tell secrets. 5 murmur. —*v.t.* reveal foolishly: *babble a secret.* —*n.* 1 indistinct sounds that cannot be understood. 2 idle or foolish talk. 3 a murmuring sound: *the babble of the brook.* [Middle English *babelen*] —**bab′bler,** *n.*
babe (bāb), *n.* baby.
Ba bel (bā′bəl, bab′əl), *n.* 1 **Tower of Babel,** (in the Bible) a high tower whose builders hoped to reach heaven. God punished them by changing their language into several new and different languages so that they could not understand one another and had to leave the tower unfinished. 2 **babel, a** noise; confusion. **b** place of noise and confusion.
Bab el Man deb (bab el man′deb), strait that connects the Red Sea and the Gulf of Aden. 20 mi. wide.
ba bies'-breath (bā′bēz breth′), *n.* a tall plant, of the same family as the pink, bearing clusters of small, fragrant, white or pink flowers. Also, **baby's-breath.**
bab ka (bäb′kə), *n.* a round yeast cake made with raisins, spice, etc., and often flavored with rum or vanilla. [< Polish]
ba boon (ba bün′), *n.* any of various large, fierce monkeys of Africa and Arabia, with a doglike face, such as the drill and the mandrill. [< Old French *babouin* stupid person]
ba boon ish (ba bü′nish), *adj.* 1 like a baboon. 2 characteristic of baboons.
ba bush ka (bə būsh′kə), *n.* a woman's scarf or kerchief worn on the head and tied under the chin. [< Russian, grandmother]
ba by (bā′bē), *n., pl.* **-bies,** *adj., v.,* **-bied, -by ing.** —*n.* 1 a very young child, especially one too young to walk or speak; infant. 2 the youngest of a family or group. 3 person who acts like a baby; childish person. 4 SLANG. plan, idea, or project. —*adj.* 1 young: *a baby lamb.* 2 small for its kind; small. 3 of or for a baby. 4 childish: *baby talk.* —*v.t.* treat as a baby; pamper. [Middle English *babi*] —**ba′by like′,** *adj.*
ba by hood (bā′bē hūd), *n.* condition or time of being a baby.
ba by ish (bā′bē ish), *adj.* like a baby; childish. —**ba′by ish ly,** *adv.* —**ba′by ish ness,** *n.*
Bab y lon (bab′ə lən, bab′ə lon), *n.* 1 capital of ancient Babylonia, in SW Asia, on the Euphrates. It was noted for its wealth, power, and magnificence, and for the wickedness of its people. 2 any great, rich, or wicked city.
Bab y lo ni a (bab′ə lō′nē ə), *n.* ancient empire in SW Asia which reached its peak about 1800 B.C. The capital was Babylon. —**Bab′y lo′ni an,** *adj., n.*

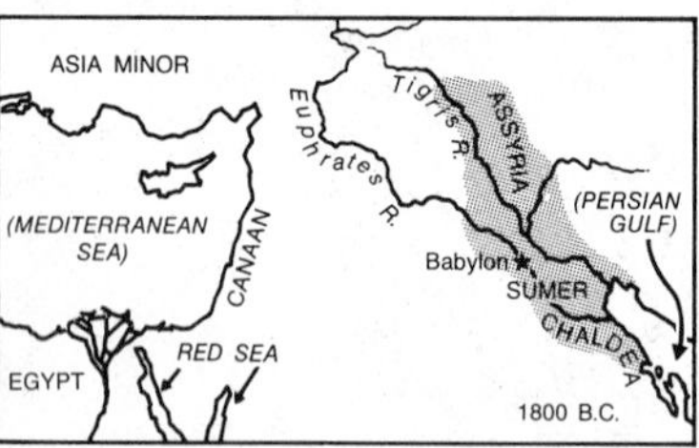

Babylonia—The shaded area shows the Babylonian Empire at its greatest extent.

ba by's-breath (bā′bēz breth′), *n.* babies'-breath.
ba by-sit (bā′bē sit′), *v.i.,* **-sat** (-sat′), **-sit ting.** take care of a child or children while the parents are away for a while.
ba by-sit ter (bā′bē sit′ər), *n.* person who baby-sits.
baby teeth, the first set of teeth.
bac ca lau re ate (bak′ə lôr′ē it), *n.* 1 degree of bachelor given by a college or university. 2 sermon or other address delivered to a graduating class at commencement. [< Medieval Latin *baccalaureatus* < *baccalaureus,* variant of *baccalarius* bachelor]
bac ca rat (bak′ə rä′, bak′ər ä), *n.* a card game in which the rest of the players bet against one who is the banker. [< French *baccara*]
Bac chae (bak′ē), *n.pl.* 1 women companions of Bacchus. 2 priestesses or women worshipers of Bacchus; bacchantes.
bac cha nal (bak′ə nəl, bak′ə nal), *adj.* having to do with Bacchus or his worship. —*n.* 1 worshiper of Bacchus. 2 a drunken reveler. 3 a drunken revelry; orgy. 4 **Bacchanals,** *pl.* the Bacchanalia.
Bac cha na li a (bak′ə nā′lē ə, bak′ə-nā′lyə), *n.* 1 *pl. in form and use.* (in ancient Rome) a wild, noisy festival in honor of Bacchus. 2 **bacchanalia,** *pl. in form, sing. in use.* a drunken revelry; orgy.
bac cha na li an (bak′ə nā′lē ən, bak′ə-nā′lyən), *adj.* 1 having to do with the Bacchanalia. 2 drunken and wildly merry; bacchantic; bacchic. —*n.* a drunken reveler; bacchant.
bac chant (bak′ənt), *n., pl.* **bac chants, bac chan tes** (bə kan′tēz), *adj.* —*n.* 1 priest or worshiper of Bacchus. 2 a drunken reveler. —*adj.* 1 worshiping Bacchus. 2 given to drunken carousing.
bac chan te (bə kan′tē), *n.* priestess or woman worshiper of Bacchus.
bac chan tic (bə kan′tik), *adj.* bacchanalian (def. 2).
Bac chic (bak′ik), *adj.* 1 of Bacchus or his worship. 2 **bacchic,** bacchanalian (def. 2).
Bac chus (bak′əs), *n.* (in Roman and Greek myths) the god of wine. The Greeks also called him Dionysus.
Bach (bäk; *German* bäн), *n.* **Johann Sebastian,** 1685-1750, German composer and organist.
bach e lor (bach′ə lər), *n.* 1 man who has not married. 2 Bachelor of Arts (def. 2) or Bachelor of Science (def. 2). 3 (formerly) a young knight who served under the banner of another. 4 the male of any animal unmated during breeding season, especially a male seal. [< Old French *bacheler* < Medieval Latin *baccalarius,* originally, small landowner]
bach e lor-at-arms (bach′ə lər ət ärmz′), *n., pl.* **bach e lors-at-arms.** bachelor (def. 3).
bach e lor hood (bach′ə lər hūd), *n.* condition of being a bachelor.
Bachelor of Arts, 1 degree given by a four-year college or by a university to a person who has completed an undergraduate course of study in the liberal arts. 2 person who has this degree.
Bachelor of Science, 1 degree given by a four-year college or by a university to a person who has completed an undergraduate course of study in the sciences. 2 person who has this degree.
bach e lor's-but ton (bach′ə lərz but′n), *n.* 1 plant of the composite family having a single, small, button-shaped flower of a blue, purple, pink, or white color; cornflower. 2 its flower.
ba cil lar (bə sil′ər, bas′ə lər), *adj.* bacillary.
ba cil lar y (bas′ə ler′ē), *adj.* 1 of, like, or caused by bacilli. 2 rod-shaped.
ba cil lus (bə sil′əs), *n., pl.* **-cil li** (-sil′ī). 1 any of the rod-shaped aerobic bacteria, especially one that forms spores. 2 any bacterium. [< New Latin, diminutive of Latin *baculus* rod]
bac i tra cin (bas′ə trā′sən), *n.* antibiotic obtained from a soil bacillus, effective against Gram-positive bacteria and used especially to treat skin infections.
back (bak), *n.* 1 the part of a person's body opposite to the front part of his body. 2 the upper part of an animal's body from the neck to the end of the backbone. 3 the backbone. 4 power to act or continue to act: *The back of the opposition was broken last week.* 5 the side of anything away from one; rear, upper, or farther part: *the back of the head, the back of the hand, the back of the room.* 6 the reverse, under, or wrong side: *the back of a rug, the back of a medal.* 7 the rear part of an object serving to support or protect: *the back of a chair, the back of a book.* 8 (in football) a player whose position is behind the line of scrimmage.
behind one's back, without one's knowing it; secretly.
get one's back up, 1 make one angry. 2 become angry. 3 be stubborn.

hat, āge, fär; let, ēqual, tėrm;
it, īce; hot, ōpen, ôrder;
oil, out; cup, pu̇t, rüle;
ch, child; ng, long; sh, she;
th, thin; ᴛʜ, then; zh, measure;

ə represents *a* in about, *e* in taken, *i* in pencil, *o* in lemon, *u* in circus.

< = from, derived from, taken from.

on one's back, 1 helpless. 2 sick.
put one's back up, 1 make one angry. 2 be stubborn.
turn one's back on, abandon; forsake.
with one's back to the wall, hard pressed; unable to escape without fighting.
—*v.t.* 1 support or help; uphold: *Many of his friends backed his plan.* 2 cause to move backward or in the opposite direction: *She backed her car slowly.* 3 endorse: *back a check.* 4 bet on: *back a baseball team in the World Series.* 5 make or be a back for: *Our little farm was backed by woods.* 6 provide with a back: *back satin with crepe.*
—*v.i.* 1 move backward: *I backed away from the dog.* 2 change direction counterclockwise: *The wind backed from west to southwest.*
back and fill, 1 trim sails so as to keep a boat in a channel and floating with the current. 2 INFORMAL. be undecided; keep changing one's mind.
back down, give up an attempt or claim; withdraw.
back out or **back out of,** 1 break a promise. 2 withdraw from an undertaking.
back up, 1 move backward. 2 support or help.
—*adj.* 1 opposite the front; away from one; rear: *the back seat of a car.* 2 belonging to the past: *back files, the back issues of a newspaper.* 3 due but not yet paid; overdue: *back bills.* 4 (in phonetics) pronounced at the back of the mouth. The *o* in *go* is a back vowel. 5 in distant or frontier regions: *back country.* 6 in a backward direction; coming back; returning: *a back swing.*
—*adv.* 1 to or toward the rear; backward; behind: *Please step back.* 2 in or toward the past: *some years back.* 3 in return: *Pay back what you borrow.* 4 in the place from which someone or something came: *Put the books back.* 5 in check: *Hold back your temper.*
back and forth, first one way and then the other.
back of, 1 in the rear of; behind. 2 supporting or helping.
go back on, 1 withdraw from (a plan, etc.). 2 INFORMAL. break a promise to.
in back of, back of; behind.
[Old English *bæc*]

back ache (bak′āk′), *n.* a continuous pain in the back.

back bench er (bak′ben′chər), *n.* an ordinary member of Parliament or of a legislative assembly in Great Britain, Canada, etc.

back bite (bak′bīt′), *v.t.,v.i.,* **-bit** (-bit′), **-bit ten** (-bit′n) or **-bit, -bit ing.** say malicious things about; slander (an absent person). **—back′bit′er,** *n.*

back board (bak′bôrd′, bak′bōrd′), *n.* (in basketball) the flat, elevated surface of wood, metal, or glass, on which the basket is mounted.

back bone (bak′bōn′), *n.* 1 the main bone along the middle of the back in man and other vertebrates; spine; spinal column. The backbone consists of many separate bones, called vertebrae, held together by muscles and tendons. 2 the most important part; chief support; basis. 3 strength of character; firmness.

back boned (bak′bōnd′), *adj.* having a backbone.

back break ing (bak′brā′king), *adj.* very exhausting.

back door (bak′dôr′, bak′dōr′), *adj.* unofficial or underhand; secret; sly.

back drop (bak′drop′), *n.* 1 curtain at the back of a stage, often painted and used as part of the scenery. 2 background.

back er (bak′ər), *n.* person who supports another person, a plan, or an idea.

back field (bak′fēld′), *n.* (in football) the players whose position is behind the line of scrimmage.

back fire (bak′fīr′), *n., v.,* **-fired, -fir ing.** —*n.* 1 explosion of gas occurring at the wrong time or in the wrong place in an internal-combustion engine. 2 fire set to check a forest or prairie fire by controlled burning off of the space in front of it. —*v.i.* 1 (of gas) explode at the wrong time or in the wrong place. 2 have a result opposite to the expected result. 3 use a backfire in fire-fighting.

back-for ma tion (bak′fôr mā′shən), *n.* word formed by dropping an ending from another word that appears to be derived from the shorter word. EXAMPLES: *burgle* from *burglar; enthuse* from *enthusiasm; pea* from *pease* taken as plural.

back gam mon (bak′gam′ən), *n.* game for two played on a divided board with 12 spaces on each side. Each player has 15 pieces, which are moved according to the throw of the dice.

back ground (bak′ground′), *n.* 1 the part of a picture or scene toward the back: *The cottage stands in the foreground with the mountains in the background.* 2 surface upon which things are made or placed: *Her dress had pink flowers on a white background.* 3 earlier conditions or events that help to explain some later condition or event: *This book gives the background of the Revolutionary War.* 4 past experience, knowledge, and training. 5 the accompanying music or sound effects in a play, motion picture, television show, etc. 6 **in the background,** out of sight; not in clear view.

back hand (bak′hand′), *n.* 1 stroke in tennis and other games made with the back of the hand turned outward. 2 handwriting in which the letters slant to the left. —*adj.* backhanded. —*adv.* with a backhanded stroke or motion. —*v.t.* hit or catch backhand.

backhand (def. 1)→
backhand (def. 2)

back hand ed (bak′han′did), *adj.* 1 done or made with the back of the hand turned outward. 2 indirect: *He means to help, even though he does so in a backhanded way.* 3 sounding like praise but actually an insult; insincere: *a backhanded compliment.* 4 slanting to the left: *backhanded writing.* —*adv.* backhand.

back ing (bak′ing), *n.* 1 support or help. 2 supporters or helpers. 3 something placed at the back of anything to support or strengthen it.

back lash (bak′lash′), *n.* 1 the jarring reaction of a machine or mechanical device. 2 movement or play between worn or loosely fitting parts. 3 a sudden, adverse reaction caused by fear, anger, etc.

back log (bak′lôg′, bak′log′), *n.* 1 a reserve of orders, duties, or commitments that have not been filled or carried out. 2 a large log at the back of a wood fire in a fireplace.

back number, 1 an old issue of a magazine or newspaper. 2 INFORMAL. an old-fashioned person; out-of-date thing.

back rest (bak′rest′), *n.* 1 anything that supports the back. 2 a support at the back.

back seat, INFORMAL. place of inferiority or insignificance.

back side (bak′sīd′), *n.* 1 back. 2 INFORMAL. rump; buttocks.

back slap per (bak′slap′ər), *n.* INFORMAL. person whose friendly manner is so hearty and effusive as to seem insincere.

back slap ping (bak′slap′ing), *n.* a too hearty and friendly manner.

back slide (bak′slīd′), *v.i.,* **-slid** (-slid′), **-slid** or **-slid den** (-slid′n), **-slid ing.** slide back into wrongdoing, especially to practices forbidden by the church; relapse. **—back′slid′er,** *n.*

back spin (bak′spin′), *n.* spin given to a ball to check or reverse its forward motion when it strikes the ground or an object; underspin.

back stage (bak′stāj′), *adv.* 1 in or to the part of a theater not seen by the audience; off-stage. 2 in or at the back part of the stage; upstage. —*adj.* 1 happening, located, etc., backstage. 2 secret or confidential.

back stay (bak′stā′), *n.* 1 rope or wire extending aft from the top of the mast to the ship's side and helping to support the mast. See **shroud** for picture. 2 spring, rod, strap, etc., used for support at the back of various mechanisms or other objects.

back stitch (bak′stich′), *n.* a stitching or stitch in which the thread doubles back each time on the preceding stitch. —*v.t., v.i.* sew with such stitches.

back stop (bak′stop′), *n.* 1 wall, fence, or screen used in baseball, tennis, etc., to keep the ball in the area of play. 2 INFORMAL. catcher in baseball and cricket. 3 anything that supports or reinforces.

back stretch (bak′strech′), *n.* the portion of a racetrack opposite and parallel to the homestretch, usually farthest from those watching a race.

back stroke (bak′strōk′), *n.* 1 a swimming stroke made by a swimmer lying on his back. 2 a backhanded stroke.

back talk, INFORMAL. an impertinent or impudent reply, especially by a younger person or a subordinate.

back track (bak′trak′), *v.i.* 1 go back over a course or path. 2 withdraw from an undertaking, position, etc.

back up (bak′up′), *n.* 1 reserve: *a backup of troops.* 2 accumulation: *a backup of traffic.* —*adj.* kept in readiness or reserve: *a backup pilot.*

back ward (bak′wərd), *adv.* 1 toward the back: *walk backward.* 2 with the back first: *tumble over backward.* 3 toward the starting point: *look backward.* 4 opposite to the usual way; in the reverse order or way: *read backward.* 5 from better to worse; *Educational conditions in the town went backward.* 6 toward the past: *He looked backward forty years and talked about his childhood.*

—adj. 1 directed toward the back: *a backward look.* 2 with the back first: *a backward fall.* 3 directed to or toward the starting point; returning: *a backward movement.* 4 done in the reverse way or order: *a backward process.* 5 reaching back into the past. 6 slow in development: *a backward place. Backward children need special help in school.* 7 behind time; late: *a backward season.* 8 lacking in self-confidence; shy; bashful. **—back′ward ly,** *adv.* **—back′ward ness,** *n.*

back wards (bak′wərdz), *adv.* backward.

back wash (bak′wosh′, bak′wôsh′), *n.* 1 water thrown back by oars, a passing ship, etc. 2 stream of air sent backwards by a jet engine or propeller. 3 a disturbed condition caused by and remaining after any act or event: *the backwash of war.*

back wa ter (bak′wô′tər, bak′wot′ər), *n.* 1 stretch of water held, thrown, or pushed back. 2 a backward place. 3 a sluggish, stagnant condition or situation.

back woods (bak′wu̇dz′), *n.pl.* 1 uncleared forests or wild regions far away from towns. 2 a remote area; backward place. *—adj.* crude; rough.

back woods man (bak′wu̇dz′mən), *n., pl.* **-men.** man who lives in the backwoods.

back yard (bak′yärd′), *n.* yard behind a house or building.

ba con (bā′kən), *n.* salted and smoked meat from the back and sides of a hog. [< Middle French < Germanic]

Ba con (bā′kən), *n.* 1 **Francis,** 1561-1626, English essayist, statesman, and philosopher. 2 **Roger,** 1214?-1294, English philosopher and pioneer of modern science.

Ba co ni an (bā kō′nē ən), *adj.* of or having to do with Francis Bacon, his writings, or his doctrines and methods.

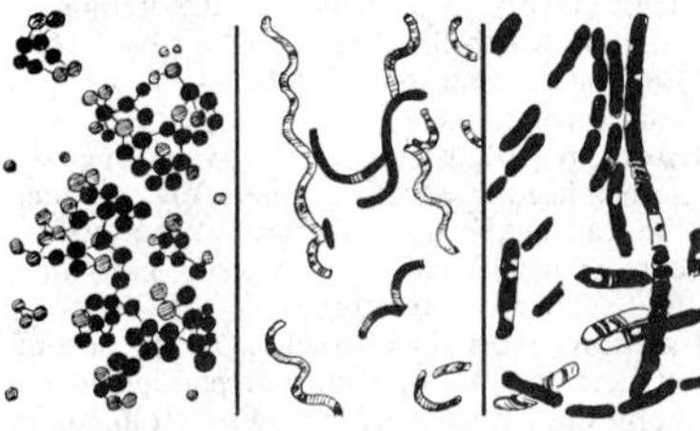

bacteria—the three main types: spherical, spiral, and rod-shaped

bac ter i a (bak tir′ē ə), *n.pl.* of **bacterium.** a large group of one-celled microscopic plants that multiply by fission or by forming spores. Bacteria are spherical, spiral, or rod-shaped, and most kinds have no chlorophyll. Certain species cause diseases such as pneumonia, typhoid fever, etc.; others are concerned in such processes as fermentation, nitrogen fixation, etc. [< New Latin, plural of *bacterium* < Greek *baktērion,* diminutive of *baktron* rod]

bac ter i al (bak tir′ē əl), *adj.* 1 of or like bacteria. 2 caused by bacteria. **—bac ter′i al ly,** *adv.*

bac ter i cid al (bak tir′ə sī′dl), *adj.* destructive to bacteria.

bac ter i cide (bak tir′ə sīd), *n.* substance that destroys bacteria.

bac ter i o log i cal (bak tir′ē ə loj′ə kəl), *adj.* 1 of or having to do with bacteriology. 2 using bacteria: *bacteriological warfare.* **—bac ter′i o log′i cal ly,** *adv.*

bac ter i ol o gist (bak tir′ē ol′ə jist), *n.* an expert in bacteriology.

bac ter i ol o gy (bak tir′ē ol′ə jē), *n.* branch of biology that deals with bacteria.

bac ter i o phage (bak tir′ē ə fāj), *n.* a virus that destroys various bacteria, normally present in the intestines, blood, etc.; phage.

bac ter i um (bak tir′ē əm), *n.* sing. of **bacteria.**

Bac tri an camel (bak′trē ən), camel having two humps and long hair, found in central Asia. [< *Bactria,* ancient country in central Asia]

bad[1] (bad), *adj.,* **worse, worst,** *n., adv.* *—adj.* 1 not good; not as it ought to be; inferior; poor: *bad soil, reading in a bad light.* 2 evil; wicked. See synonym study below. 3 not friendly; cross; unpleasant: *a bad temper.* 4 unfavorable: *You came at a bad time.* 5 severe: *a bad thunderstorm, a bad case of pneumonia.* 6 rotten; spoiled: *a bad egg.* 7 sorry; regretful: *I feel bad about losing your baseball.* 8 sick; ill: *Her cold made her feel bad.* 9 incorrect; faulty: *a bad guess.* 10 worthless: *a bad check.* 11 (in law) not valid: *a bad debt.* **12 not bad,** fairly good. **13 not half bad,** rather good. **14 not so bad,** rather good.

—n. 1 something that is bad; bad condition, quality, etc. **2 be in bad,** INFORMAL. be in disfavor (with a person over a thing). **3 to the bad, a** toward ruin. **b** in debt; in deficit: *I am now $100 to the bad.*

—adv. INFORMAL. badly.

[perhaps originally past participle of Old English *ge-bǣdan* oppress] **—bad′ness,** *n.*

Syn. *adj.* 2 **Bad, evil, wicked** mean morally wrong. **Bad,** the common word, is very general, ranging in application from naughtiness to being very corrupt, immoral, vile, etc.: *Lying is a bad habit.* **Evil** means very bad and sometimes suggests threatening great harm: *It is evil for judges to accept bribes.* **Wicked** emphasizes willfully defying and breaking moral laws: *Deliberately leading an evil life is wicked.*

➤ **bad, badly.** Following a linking verb, formal English prefers the predicate adjective *bad,* not the adverb *badly: I feel bad about the news.* Informal speech sometimes uses *badly: I feel badly about the news.* In formal English and informal writing, the adverb *badly* is used to modify verbs: *She sings badly.*

bad[2] (bad), *v.* ARCHAIC. a pt. of **bid** (defs. 1, 2).

bad blood, unfriendly feeling; hate.

bade (bad, bād), *v.* a pt. of **bid** (defs. 3-10).

➤ **Bade** is used chiefly in formal and literary English: *The king bade her remain.*

Ba den (bäd′n), *n.* 1 region in S West Germany. 2 Baden-Baden.

Ba den-Ba den (bäd′n bäd′n), *n.* health resort in S West Germany. 40,000.

Ba den-Pow ell (bād′n pō′əl), *n.* Sir **Robert,** 1857-1941, British general who founded the Boy Scouts in 1908.

badge (baj), *n.* 1 something worn to show that a person belongs to a certain occupation, school, class, club, society, etc. 2 emblem showing achievement or proficiency: *the badge of an expert marksman.* 3 symbol or sign; emblem: *Chains are a badge of slavery.* [Middle English *bage*]

badg er (baj′ər), *n.* 1 a hairy, gray, nocturnal and burrowing carnivorous mammal of Europe, Asia, and North America, related to the weasel, but larger and more heavily built. 2 its fur. *—v.t.* torment by nagging or bullying; tease; bait. [perhaps < *badge;* referring to the white spot on the badger's head]

bad i nage (bad′n äzh′), *n.* good-natured joking; banter. [< French]

Bad lands (bad′landz′), *n.pl.* 1 rugged, barren region in SW South Dakota and NW Nebraska in which erosion has produced unusual land formations. **2 badlands,** any similar region.

bad ly (bad′lē), *adv.* 1 in a bad manner. 2 INFORMAL. very much; greatly. **3 badly off,** INFORMAL. in a state of poverty, need, or distress. ➤ See **bad**[1] for usage note.

bad man (bad′man′), *n., pl.* **-men.** INFORMAL. 1 an outlaw. 2 the villain in a motion picture, play, etc.

bad min ton (bad′mint′n), *n.* game somewhat like tennis but played with a shuttlecock instead of a ball, lighter rackets, and a higher net. [< *Badminton,* the Duke of Beaufort's estate in England, where the game was first played]

bad-tem pered (bad′tem′pərd), *adj.* cross; irritable.

Baf fin Bay (baf′ən) large, deep bay west of Greenland.

Baffin Island, large island between Greenland and Hudson Bay, belonging to Canada. 211,000 sq. mi.

baf fle (baf′əl), *v.,* **-fled, -fling,** *n.* *—v.t.* 1 hinder (a person) by being too hard to understand or solve; perplex: *This puzzle baffles me.* See **frustrate** for synonym study. 2 control or regulate by a baffle. *—n.* wall, screen, or other device for controlling the flow of air, water, or sound waves by hindering its movement or changing its course. [origin uncertain] **—baf′fle ment,** *n.* **—baf′fler,** *n.*

baf fling (baf′ling), *adj.* 1 puzzling. 2 hindering; thwarting.

bag (bag), *n., v.,* **bagged, bag ging.** *—n.* 1 container made of paper, cloth, leather, etc., that can be pulled together to close at the top. See synonym study below. 2 amount that a bag holds. 3 sac in an animal's body: *the honey bag of a bee.* 4 an udder. 5 something suggesting a bag in its use or shape: handbag, purse, suitcase, etc. 6 the game or fish killed or caught at one time by a hunter. 7 base in baseball. 8 SLANG. an ugly or old woman. **9 bag and baggage,** with all one's belongings; entirely. **10 hold the bag,** U.S. INFORMAL. **a** be left to take the blame, responsibility, etc. **b** be left empty-handed. **11 in the bag.** INFORMAL. certain of success; sure.

—v.t. 1 put into a bag or bags. 2 kill, trap, or catch in hunting. 3 INFORMAL. take possession of; catch, take, or steal. *—v.i.* 1 bulge; swell. 2 hang loosely: *The boy's trousers bag at the knees.*

[< Scandinavian (Old Icelandic) *baggi* pack] **—bag′like′,** *n.*

Syn. *n.* 1 **Bag, sack** mean a container made of paper, cloth, etc., that can be closed at the top. **Bag** is the general word, applying to any such container of suitable size and material: *Fresh vegetables sometimes are sold in cellophane bags.* **Sack** applies particularly to a large bag made of coarse cloth: *Mail is*

hat, āge, fär; let, ēqual, tėrm;
it, īce; hot, ōpen, ôrder;
oil, out; cup, pu̇t, rüle;
ch, child; ng, long; sh, she;
th, thin; ᴛʜ, then; zh, measure;

ə represents *a* in about, *e* in taken, *i* in pencil, *o* in lemon, *u* in circus.

< = from, derived from, taken from.

carried in sacks, and grain and potatoes are shipped in sacks. But *sack* is now often used of a heavy paper bag, and in some places of any paper or similar bag: *Put my groceries in a sack.*

ba gasse (bə gas′), *n.* pulp of sugar cane after the juice has been extracted, used in the manufacture of wallboard, paper, etc. [< French]

bag a telle (bag′ə tel′), *n.* 1 a mere trifle; thing of no importance. 2 game somewhat like billiards played on a table having a semicircular end at which are nine holes. [< French < Italian *bagatella*]

Bag dad (bag′dad), *n.* Baghdad.

ba gel (bā′gəl), *n.* a hard roll made of raised dough shaped into a ring, simmered in water, and then baked. [< Yiddish *beigel*]

bag gage (bag′ij), *n.* 1 the trunks, bags, suitcases, etc., that a person takes with him when he travels; luggage. 2 equipment that an army takes with it, such as tents, blankets, ammunition, and cooking utensils. 3 burden of beliefs, ideas, practices, etc., especially when excessive or superfluous. 4 a sly, pert, or saucy young woman. [< Old French *baggage* < *bague* bundle]

bag ging (bag′ing), *n.* cloth for making bags, covering bales of cotton, etc.

bag gy (bag′ē), *adj.,* **-gi er, -gi est.** 1 hanging loosely; baglike: *baggy trousers.* 2 swelling; bulging. **—bag′gi ly,** *adv.* **—bag′gi ness,** *n.*

Bagh dad (bag′dad), *n.* capital of Iraq, in the central part, on the Tigris. 1,745,000. Also, **Bagdad.**

bagn io (ban′yō, bä′nyō), *n., pl.* **bagn ios.** 1 brothel. 2 prison. [< Italian *bagno* < Latin *balneum* bath]

bag pipe (bag′pīp′), *n.* Often, **bagpipes,** *pl.* a shrill-toned musical instrument consisting of a leather bag and five wooden pipes. Air is blown into the bag through one pipe and forced out of the bag through four sounding pipes by pressure from the player's arm. Bagpipes are now used chiefly in Scotland and Ireland.

bagpipe

bag pip er (bag′pī′pər), *n.* person who plays the bagpipe.

ba guette (ba get′), *n.* gem cut in a narrow, rectangular shape. [< French]

Bag ui o (bag′ē ō), *n.* mountain city in the N Philippines. It is the summer capital of the Philippines. 50,000.

bag worm (bag′wėrm), *n.* the larva, of any of a family of moths, which spin a bag of silk, leaves, etc., for their protection, and move around with the bag hanging downward while feeding on leaves of trees and shrubs.

bah (bä), *interj.* exclamation of scorn, contempt, or impatience.

Ba ha ma Islands (bə hä′mə, bə hā′mə), group of over 700 islands in the West Indies, southeast of Florida, belonging to the British Commonwealth. 160,000 pop.; 4400 sq. mi. *Capital:* Nassau. See **Caribbean Sea** for map.

Ba ha mas (bə hä′məz, bə hā′məz), *n.pl.* Bahama Islands.

Ba ha mi an (bə hä′mē ən, bə hā′mē ən), *n.* native or inhabitant of the Bahamas. *—adj.* of, having to do with, or in the Bahamas.

Ba hi a (bə ē′ə, bä ē′ə), *n.* Salvador. Also, **Baía.**

Bah rein or **Bah rain** (bä rān′), *n.* island country in the Persian Gulf. 200,000 pop.; 231 sq. mi. *Capital:* Manama.

baht (bät), *n., pl.* **bahts** or **baht,** the monetary unit of Thailand, a coin or note worth about five cents. [< Thai *bāt*]

Ba í a (bə ē′ə, bä ē′ə), *n.* Bahia.

Bai kal (bī käl′), *n.* **Lake,** lake in S Siberia. It is the deepest freshwater lake in the world. 12,741 sq. mi.

bail[1] (bāl), *n.* 1 guarantee of money necessary to release a person under arrest from jail or prison until he is to appear for trial. 2 amount of money guaranteed. 3 person or persons who stand ready to pay the money guaranteed. 4 **go bail for,** supply bail for. *—v.t.* 1 obtain the release of (a person under arrest) by supplying bail. 2 **bail out, a** supply bail for. **b** help or assist (a person in trouble). [< Old French, custody < *baillier* deliver < Latin *bajulare* carry for pay < *bajulus* carrier] **—bail′a ble,** *adj.*

bail[2] (bāl), *n.* 1 the curved handle of a kettle or pail. 2 a hooplike support. The bails of a covered wagon hold up the canvas. [probably < Scandinavian (Old Icelandic) *beygla*]

bail[3] (bāl), *n.* scoop or pail used to throw water out of a boat. *—v.t.* 1 throw (water) out of a boat with a pail, a dipper, or any other container. 2 dip water from. *—v.i.* 1 remove water from a boat with a bail or other container. 2 **bail out,** jump from an airplane by parachute. [< Middle French *baille* bucket, ultimately < Latin *bajulus* carrier]

bail[4] (bāl), *n.* either of two small bars that form the top of a wicket used in the game of cricket. [< Old French, barrier < Latin *baculum* stick]

bail ey (bā′lē), *n., pl.* **-eys.** the external wall enclosing the outer court of a feudal castle, or the outer court itself. [Middle English variant of *bail*[4]]

bail iff (bā′lif), *n.* 1 officer of a court of law who has charge of jurors and guards prisoners while they are in the courtroom. 2 assistant to a sheriff, who executes writs and processes, makes arrests, etc. 3 (in England) an overseer or steward of an estate. The bailiff collects rents, directs the work of employees, etc., for the owner. 4 the chief magistrate in certain towns in England. [< Old French *baillif* < *baillir* govern < *bail* guardian, manager < Latin *bajulus* carrier]

bail i wick (bā′lə wik), *n.* 1 district over which a bailiff has authority. 2 a person's field of knowledge, work, or authority. [Middle English *bailie* bailiff + *wick* office]

bails man (bālz′mən), *n., pl.* **-men.** person who gives bail.

bairn (bern, barn), *n.* SCOTTISH. child. [Old English *bearn*]

bait (bāt), *n.* 1 anything, especially food, used to attract fish or other animals so that they may be caught. 2 thing used to tempt or attract; temptation. *—v.t.* 1 put bait on (a hook) or in (a trap). 2 tempt; attract. 3 set dogs to attack: *Men used to bait bulls and bears for sport.* 4 attack; torment: *The dogs baited the bear.* 5 torment or worry by unkind or annoying remarks. 6 ARCHAIC. give food and water to (a horse or other animal), especially on a journey. [< Scandinavian (Old Icelandic) *beita* cause to bite] **—bait′er,** *n.*

baize (bāz), *n.* a thick woolen or cotton cloth resembling felt, used for curtains, table covers, etc. [< French *baies*]

Ba ja California (bä′hä), Lower California.

bake (bāk), *v.,* **baked, bak ing,** *n.* *—v.t.* 1 cook (food) by dry heat without exposing it directly to the fire: *The cook bakes bread and cake in the oven.* 2 dry or harden by heat: *bake bricks or china.* *—v.i.* 1 cook foods by dry heat; do the work of baking: *I bake every Saturday.* 2 become baked: *Cookies bake quickly.* *—n.* 1 act of baking. 2 U.S. a social gathering at which a meal is served. [Old English *bacan*]

Ba ke lite (bā′kə līt), *n.* trademark for any of various plastics made by condensing phenols with formaldehyde.

bak er (bā′kər), *n.* 1 person who makes or sells bread, pies, cakes, etc. 2 a small portable oven.

Bak er (bā′kər), *n.* **Mount,** mountain in NW Washington. 10,750 ft.

baker's dozen, thirteen.

bak er y (bā′kər ē), *n., pl.* **-er ies.** store where bread, pies, cakes, etc., are made or sold; bakeshop.

bake shop (bāk′shop′), *n.* bakery.

bak ing (bā′king), *n.* 1 a cooking in dry heat without exposing directly to the fire. 2 a drying or hardening by heat. 3 amount baked at one time; batch.

baking powder, mixture of sodium bicarbonate and an acid-forming ingredient such as cream of tartar in a starch base, which, when moistened, produces carbon dioxide and thus causes dough to expand. It is used instead of yeast to raise biscuits, cakes, etc.

baking soda, sodium bicarbonate.

bak sheesh or **bak shish** (bak′shēsh′), *n.* money given as a tip in Egypt, Turkey, India, etc. [< Persian *bakhshīsh* gift < *bakhshīdan* give]

Ba ku (bä kü′), *n.* seaport in S Soviet Union, on the Caspian Sea, the capital of the Azerbaijan S.S.R. 1,261,000.

bal., balance.

Ba laam (bā′ləm), *n.* (in the Bible) a heathen prophet who blessed the Israelites instead of cursing them after he was rebuked by the donkey he rode.

bal a lai ka (bal′ə lī′kə), *n.* a Russian musical instrument somewhat like a guitar, with a triangular body and usually with three strings. [< Russian]

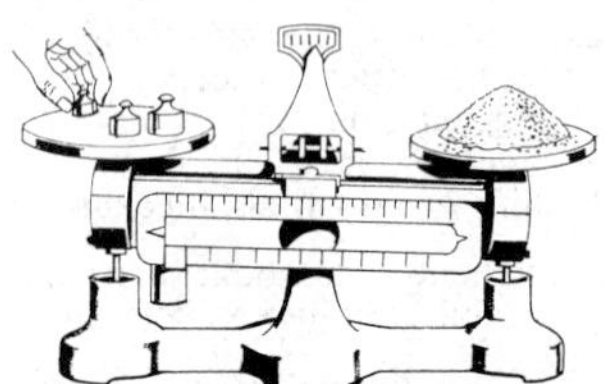
balance (def. 1)—Material on the right platform is weighed by adding weights of known value to the left platform. When the two platforms balance, the value of the weights is added up.

bal ance (bal′əns), *n. v.*, **-anced, -anc ing.** —*n.* 1 instrument for weighing, especially a horizontal beam or lever poised so as to move freely on a central support, with a scale or pan suspended at each end. 2 equality in weight, amount, force, effect, etc. 3 comparison of weight, value, importance, etc.; estimate. 4 proportion in design; harmony. 5 steady condition or position; steadiness: *lose one's balance and fall.* 6 equilibrium of mind, character, etc.; poise: *Her balance is never disturbed by the tantrums of others.* 7 anything that counteracts the effect, weight, force, etc., of something else. 8 equality between the totals of the two sides of an account. 9 difference between the amount one owes or has withdrawn from an account and the amount one is owed or deposits in an account: *I have a balance of $20 in the bank.* 10 INFORMAL. part that is left over; rest; remainder: *I will be away for the balance of the week.* 11 an oscillating wheel in a clock or watch which by the regularity of its motion determines the beat or stroke; balance wheel. 12 greatest weight, amount, or power. 13 a balancing movement in dancing. 14 **in the balance,** with its outcome undecided; uncertain: *The outcome of the baseball game was in the balance until the last inning.*
—*v.t.* 1 weigh in a balance. 2 make or be equal to in weight, amount, force, effect, etc.: *Balance your exercise with rest.* 3 compare the value, importance, etc., of: *I balanced a camping trip against the chance of a summer job.* 4 make or be proportionate to. 5 put or keep in a steady condition or position: *Can you balance a coin on its edge?* 6 make up for the effect, influence, etc., of; counteract; offset. 7 in accounting: **a** add up the debit and credit sides of (an account) to find the difference between their amounts. **b** make the debit and credit sides of (an account) equal. **c** settle (an account) by paying an amount due. —*v.i.* 1 be equal or equivalent in weight, amount, force, effect, etc.: *These scales balance.* 2 keep a steady condition or position: *to balance on one foot.* 3 be equal in the debit and credit sides of an account. 4 hesitate; waver.
[< Old French < Late Latin *bilancem* two-scaled < Latin *bi-* two + *lanx* scale[2]] —**bal′anc er,** *n.*

balanced diet, diet having the correct amounts of all kinds of foods necessary for health.

balance of nature, the balanced condition existing in the animal and plant population due to factors such as disease, natural enmity, food supply, etc., which keep the number of animals and plants relatively constant.

balance of payments, the net surplus or deficiency of money when all transactions for a given period between one country and another are balanced, including imports, exports, investments, tourist expenditures, etc.

balance of power, 1 distribution of strength by alliances among independent nations so that no one nation or group of nations becomes strong enough to dominate or conquer the others. 2 the ability of a small nation, group of people, etc., to give a dominant position to either one of two opposing larger nations or groups by allying itself with one of them.

balance of trade, the difference within a given period between the value of all the imports and exports of a country.

balance sheet, a written statement showing the profits and losses, the assets and liabilities, and the net worth of a business.

balance wheel, 1 balance (*n.*, def. 11). 2 any wheel that regulates motion. 3 anything that is a source of regularity or stability.

Bal an chine (bal′ən chēn′), *n.* **George,** born 1904, American choreographer, born in Russia.

bal a ta (bal′ə tə), *n.* 1 the dried gumlike juice of an American tropical tree related to the sapodilla, used in making gaskets, golf-ball covers, insulation for wires, etc. 2 the tree itself. [< Spanish]

bal bo a (bal bō′ə), *n.* the monetary unit of Panama, a silver coin equal to 100 centesimi and worth about $1. [< Vasco de *Balboa*]

Bal bo a (bal bō′ə), *n.* **Vasco de,** 1475?-1517, Spanish explorer who discovered the Pacific in 1513.

bal brig gan (bal brig′ən), *n.* 1 a knitted cotton cloth, used for stockings and underwear. 2 **balbriggans,** *pl.* stockings, pajamas, and underwear made of this fabric. [< *Balbriggan,* town in Ireland, where originally made]

bal co ny (bal′kə nē), *n., pl.* **-nies.** 1 an outside projecting platform, usually enclosed by a balustrade or railing, with an entrance from an upper floor of a building. 2 a projecting upper floor in a theater, hall, or church with seats for part of the audience; gallery. [< Italian *balcone* < *balco* scaffold]

bald (bôld), *adj.* 1 wholly or partly without hair on the head. 2 without its usual or natural covering. 3 unadorned: *bald prose.* 4 plainly evident: *the bald truth, a bald lie.* 5 (of a horse) having a white spot or blaze on the head. [Middle English *balled*] —**bald′ly,** *adv.* —**bald′ness,** *n.*

bal da chin (bal′də kən, bôl′də kən), *n.* structure in the form of a canopy, placed above an altar, throne, etc. [< Italian *baldacchino* < *Baldacco* Baghdad]

Balkan States

bald eagle, a large, powerful, North American eagle with white feathers on its head, neck, and tail when adult; American eagle. It is the national emblem of the United States.

Bal der (bôl′dər), *n.* (in Scandinavian myths) the god of light, beauty, goodness, wisdom, and peace.

bal der dash (bôl′dər dash), *n.* nonsense.

bald pate (bôld′pāt′), *n.* 1 person who has a bald head. 2 a wild duck of North America, a kind of widgeon. The male has a white crown and forehead.

bal dric (bôl′drik), *n.* belt, usually of leather and richly ornamented, hung from one shoulder to the opposite side of the body to support the wearer's sword, bugle, etc. [Middle English]

Bald win (bôld′wən), *n.* **Stanley,** 1867-1947, British statesman, prime minister from 1923 to 1924, from 1924 to 1929, and from 1935 to 1937.

bale[1] (bāl), *n., v.,* **baled, bal ing.** —*n.* a large bundle of merchandise or material closely pressed, tightly corded or hooped, and (sometimes) wrapped or bound for shipping or storage: *a bale of cotton, a bale of hay.* —*v.t.* make into bales; tie in large bundles. [< Flemish < Old French *balle* round package] —**bal′er,** *n.*

bale[2] (bāl), *n.* ARCHAIC. 1 evil; harm. 2 sorrow; pain. [Old English *bealu*]

Bal e ar ic Islands (bal′ē ar′ik), group of Spanish islands in the W Mediterranean, including Majorca and Minorca. 443,000 pop.; 1900 sq. mi. *Capital:* Palma.

ba leen (bə lēn′), *n.* whalebone. [< Latin *ballena, ballaena* whale]

bale ful (bāl′fəl), *adj.* 1 full of hurtful or deadly influence; destructive. 2 full of misfortune; disastrous. —**bale′ful ly,** *adv.* —**bale′ful ness,** *n.*

Bal four (bal′fůr), *n.* **Arthur James,** 1848-1930, Earl of Balfour, British statesman and writer, prime minister from 1902 to 1905.

Ba li (bä′lē), *n.* island in Indonesia, south of Borneo and east of Java. 1,783,000 pop.; 2200 sq. mi.

Ba li nese (bä′lə nēz′), *n., pl.* **-nese,** *adj.* —*n.* 1 native or inhabitant of Bali. 2 language of Bali. —*adj.* of Bali, its people, or their language.

balk (bôk), *v.i.* 1 stop short and stubbornly refuse to go on: *My horse balked at the fence.* 2 (in baseball) make a balk. —*v.t.* 1 check, hinder, or thwart (a person or his actions); frustrate: *The police balked the robber's plans.* 2 fail to use; let slip; miss. —*n.* 1 a hindrance, check, or defeat. 2 a blunder or mistake. 3 a ridge between furrows; strip left unplowed. 4 a large beam or timber. 5 (in baseball) an illegal motion made by a pitcher, especially one in which he fails to complete a throw he has started. Also, **baulk.** [Old English *balca* ridge] —**balk′er,** *n.*

Bal kan (bôl′kən), *n.* **Balkans,** *pl.* the Balkan States. —*adj.* 1 of the people living in the Balkan States. 2 of the Balkan Peninsula or the countries on it. 3 of the Balkan Mountains.

Balkan Mountains, mountain range in the Balkan Peninsula, extending between W Bulgaria and the Black Sea. Highest peak, about 7800 ft.

Balkan Peninsula, peninsula in SE Europe, extending south into the Mediterranean.

Balkan States, countries on the Balkan Peninsula; Yugoslavia, Romania, Bulgaria,

Albania, Greece, and European Turkey; Balkans.

balk y (bô′kē), *adj.,* **balk i er, balk i est.** stopping short and stubbornly refusing to go on; likely to balk.

ball[1] (bôl), *n.* 1 a round or oval body thrown, hit, or kicked in various games. Different sizes and types of balls are used in tennis, golf, baseball, football, and soccer. 2 game in which some kind of ball is thrown, hit, or kicked, especially baseball. 3 anything round or roundish: *a ball of string. I had a blister on the ball of my thumb.* See synonym study below. 4 a particular throw or play of a ball in certain games: *a fast ball.* 5 pitched baseball that the batter does not strike at because it does not pass over home plate between his shoulders and knees. 6 a round, solid object to be shot from a gun. 7 globe; the earth: *this terrestrial ball.* 8 **keep the ball rolling,** do one's part. 9 **on the ball,** SLANG. aware of what is going on or needs to be done; alert. 10 **play ball,** INFORMAL. **a** begin a game or start it again after stopping. **b** get busy; get active. **c** work together; join in partnership. —*v.i.* 1 form or gather into a ball. 2 **ball up,** SLANG. confuse. —*v.t.* make into a ball. [< Scandinavian (Old Icelandic) *böllr*]

Syn. *n.* 3 **Ball, globe** mean something round. **Ball** is the general word for any round or roundish object: *I put melon balls in the salad.* **Globe** applies to anything shaped like a ball, but is used especially of objects which are perfectly round or thought of as being perfectly round: *The principal uses a glass globe for a paperweight.*

ball[2] (bôl), *n.* 1 a large, formal party with dancing. 2 SLANG. a very good time. [< French *bal* < *baler* to dance < Late Latin *ballare* < Greek *ballizein*]

bal lad (bal′əd), *n.* 1 poem that tells a story in a simple verse form, especially one that tells a popular legend and is passed from one generation to another orally. Ballads are often sung. 2 a simple song. 3 a sentimental or romantic popular song. 4 a folk song. [< Old French *balade* < Provençal *balada,* originally, poem for dancing < Late Latin *ballare* to dance]

bal lad ry (bal′ə drē), *n.* poetry in the ballad style.

ball-and-sock et joint (bôl′ən sok′it), a flexible joint formed by a ball or knob fitting in a socket, such as the shoulder and hip joints, permitting motion in a rotary direction.

bal last (bal′əst), *n.* 1 something heavy placed in the hold of a ship to steady it. 2 bags of sand or other heavy material carried in a balloon or dirigible to steady it or regulate its ascent. 3 anything which steadies a person or thing. 4 gravel or crushed rock used in making the bed for a road or railroad track. —*v.t.* 1 furnish or steady with ballast. 2 put gravel or crushed rock on. [apparently < Scandinavian (Old Danish) *barlast*]

ball bearing, 1 bearing in which the shaft revolves upon a number of freely moving, very smooth metal balls which are contained in a channel or groove around the shaft. Ball bearings are used to lessen friction. 2 one of the metal balls.

bal le ri na (bal′ə rē′nə), *n.* a woman ballet dancer. [< Italian]

bal let (bal′ā, ba lā′), *n.* 1 an elaborate dance by a group on a stage. A ballet tells a story or expresses a theme by means of graceful, intricate steps, movements, and poses accompanied by music often written especially for it. 2 the art of creating or performing ballets. 3 the dancers in a ballet. 4 the music for a ballet. [< French < Italian *balletto,* diminutive of *ballo* dance]

bal let o mane (ba let′ə mān), *n.* a ballet enthusiast. [< French]

bal lis tic (bə lis′tik), *adj.* 1 having to do with the motion or throwing of projectiles. 2 having to do with the science of ballistics. [< Latin *ballista* machine for throwing stones < Greek *ballein* to throw] —**bal lis′ti cal ly,** *adv.*

ballistic missile, missile that is propelled through the upward part of a curved trajectory and becomes a free-falling body after the thrust has ended. A ballistic missile reaches its target as a result of aim at or before the time of launching, unlike a guided missile, which can be aimed during flight.

bal lis tics (bə lis′tiks), *n.* 1 *pl. in form, sing. in use.* science that deals with the motion of projectiles, such as bullets, shells, or bombs, and also rockets and missiles after thrust has ended. 2 *pl. in form and use.* the qualities of a projectile or missile that determine its flight; ballistic properties.

bal loon (bə lün′), *n.* 1 an airtight bag filled with some gas lighter than air so that it will rise and float, used to carry persons or instruments up in the air. 2 a child's toy made of rubber that may be blown up by mouth or filled with gas. 3 a circled space in a cartoon in which the words of a speaker are written. —*v.i.* 1 ride in a balloon. 2 swell out like a balloon. 3 grow or increase rapidly and greatly. [< Middle French *ballon* < Italian *ballone* < *balla* ball] —**bal loon′like′,** *adj.*

bal loon ist (bə lü′nist), *n.* 1 person who goes up in balloons. 2 pilot of a dirigible balloon.

bal lot (bal′ət), *n.* 1 piece of paper, ticket, or other object used in secret voting. 2 the total number of votes cast. 3 method of secret voting that uses paper slips, voting machines, etc. 4 right to vote: *gain the ballot.* —*v.i.* vote or decide by using ballots. [< Italian *ballotta,* diminutive of *balla* ball]

ball park (bôl′pärk′), *n.* a baseball field together with grandstands, bleachers, etc., for spectators.

ball play er (bôl′plā′ər), *n.* person who plays ball, especially baseball.

ball-point pen (bôl′point′), pen whose point is a small metal ball which rotates against a reservoir of ink in semisolid form, transferring the ink to the paper against which it is pressed.

ball room (bôl′rüm′, bôl′rům′), *n.* a large room designed or used for dancing.

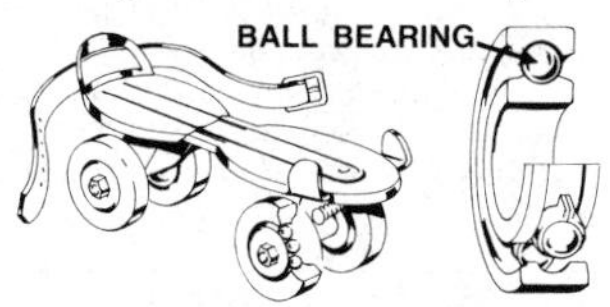

ball bearing
left, wheel cut away to show
ball bearing (def. 1); right, (def. 2)

bal lute (bə lüt′), *n.* parachute in the form of a balloon, used by a spacecraft when descending through very thin atmosphere, especially during reentry. [< *ball(oon)* + *(parach)ute*]

bal ly hoo (bal′ē hü), *n., pl.* **-hoos,** *v.* —*n.* 1 noisy advertising; sensational way of attracting attention. 2 uproar; outcry. —*v.t., v.i.* advertise noisily; make exaggerated or false statements. [origin uncertain] —**bal′ly hoo′er,** *n.*

hat, āge, fär; let, ēqual, tėrm;
it, īce; hot, ōpen, ôrder;
oil, out; cup, půt, rüle;
ch, child; ng, long; sh, she;
th, thin; ᴛʜ, then; zh, measure;

ə represents *a* in about, *e* in taken, *i* in pencil, *o* in lemon, *u* in circus.

< = from, derived from, taken from.

balm (bäm, bälm), *n.* 1 a fragrant, oily, sticky substance obtained from certain kinds of trees, used to heal or to relieve pain; balsam. 2 an ointment or similar preparation that heals or soothes. 3 a healing or soothing influence. 4 a fragrant ointment or oil used in anointing. 5 sweet odor; fragrance. 6 a fragrant plant of the mint family. [< Old French *basme* < Latin *balsamum* < Greek *balsamon.* Doublet of BALSAM.]

balm of Gilead, 1 a fragrant ointment prepared from the resin of a small evergreen tree of Arabia and Ethiopia. 2 the tree itself. 3 kind of poplar with large, fragrant, resinous buds. 4 balsam fir.

balm y[1] (bä′mē, bäl′mē), *adj.,* **balm i er, balm i est.** 1 mild, gentle, and soothing: *a balmy breeze.* 2 fragrant. [< *balm*] —**balm′i ly,** *adv.* —**balm′i ness,** *n.*

balm y[2] (bä′mē, bäl′mē), *adj.,* **balm i er, balm i est.** BRITISH SLANG. silly; crazy. [variant of *barmy*]

ba lo ney (bə lō′nē), *n.* 1 SLANG. nonsense. 2 INFORMAL. bologna. [< *bologna*]

bal sa (bôl′sə), *n.* 1 a tropical American tree with very lightweight, strong wood. 2 its wood, used in making rafts, airplane models, etc. 3 raft, especially one made up of two or more floats fastened to a framework. [< Spanish]

bal sam (bôl′səm), *n.* 1 any of several fragrant, oily, sticky resins which contain benzoic acid. 2 balm (def. 1). 3 a balsam-yielding tree, such as the balsam fir. 4 something that heals or soothes; balm. 5 a garden plant with seed vessels that burst open violently when ripe. [< Latin *balsamum* < Greek *balsamon.* Doublet of BALM.]

balsam fir, 1 a North American evergreen tree of the pine family whose resin is used in making varnish and turpentine; balm of Gilead. Balsam firs are much used as Christmas trees. 2 its wood.

bal sam ic (bôl sam′ik), *adj.* 1 of or containing balsam. 2 yielding balsam.

Bal tic (bôl′tik), *adj.* 1 of or having to do with the Baltic Sea. 2 of or having to do with the Baltic States. 3 of or belonging to the Indo-European languages of the eastern Baltic region, including Lithuanian and Lettish.

Baltic Sea, sea in N Europe, north of Germany and Poland and south and southeast of Sweden. 160,000 sq. mi.

Baltic States, Estonia, Latvia, Lithuania (before their absorption into the U.S.S.R.), and sometimes Finland.

Bal ti more (bôl′tə môr, bôl′tə mōr), *n.* 1 city in N Maryland, near Chesapeake Bay. 906,000. 2 **Lord.** See **Calvert.**

Ba lu chi stan (bə lü′chə stan), *n.* former country on the Arabian Sea, now a part of Pakistan.

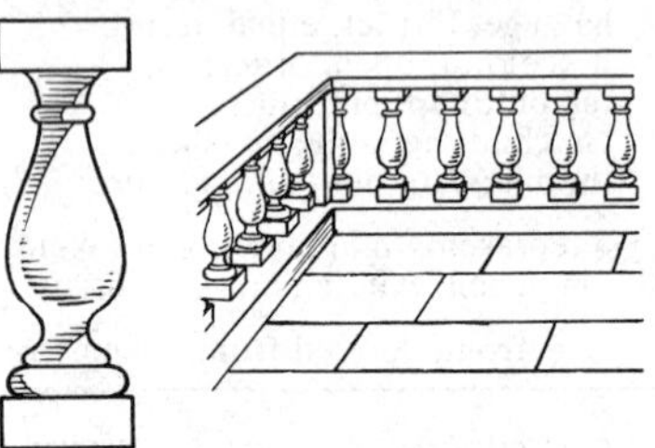
baluster (left)
and balusters in a balustrade (right)

bal us ter (bal′ə stər), *n.* one of a row of short posts or columns supporting the railing of a staircase, balcony, etc. [< French *balustre* < Italian *balaustro* < *balaustra* wild pomegranate flower; from the shape]

bal us trade (bal′ə strād), *n.* row of balusters and the railing on them.

Bal zac (bôl′zak, bal′zak), *n.* **Honoré de,** 1799-1850, French novelist.

Ba ma ko (bam′ə kō), *n.* capital of Mali, a river port on the Niger. 170,000.

bam bi no (bam bē′nō), *n., pl.* **-ni** (-nē), **-nos.** 1 baby. 2 a little child. 3 image or picture of the infant Jesus. [< Italian, diminutive of *bambo* simple, childish]

bam boo (bam bü′), *n., pl.* **-boos,** *adj.* —*n.* any of various species of woody or treelike tropical or semitropical grasses having stiff, hollow, jointed stems, which are used for making canes, fishing poles, furniture, etc. —*adj.* of bamboo; made of the stems of bamboo. [< Dutch *bamboe* < Malay *bambu*]

Bamboo Curtain, an imaginary wall or dividing line separating Communist China from the non-Communist nations, behind which strict censorship and secrecy are enforced.

bam boo zle (bam bü′zəl), *v.,* **-zled, -zling.** INFORMAL. —*v.t.* 1 impose upon; cheat; trick. 2 puzzle; perplex. —*v.i.* use trickery. [origin uncertain] **—bam boo′zle ment,** *n.* **—bam boo′zler,** *n.*

ban (ban), *v.,* **banned, ban ning,** *n.* —*v.t.* 1 forbid by law or authority; prohibit: *Swimming is banned in this lake.* 2 place a ban on; pronounce a curse on; curse. —*n.* 1 the forbidding of an act or speech by authority of the law, the church, or public opinion; prohibition. 2 ARCHAIC. a solemn curse by the church; anathema; decree of excommunication. [< Scandinavian (Old Icelandic) *banna* forbid]

ba nal (bā′nl, bə nal′, ban′l), *adj.* not new or interesting; commonplace; trite. [< French] **—ba′nal ly,** *adv.*

ba nal i ty (bə nal′ə tē), *n., pl.* **-ties.** 1 commonplaceness; triteness; triviality. 2 a banal remark, idea, etc.

ba nan a (bə nan′ə), *n.* 1 an oblong, slightly curved, yellow or red fruit growing in dense clusters two or three feet long and having firm, creamy flesh. 2 any of a family of treelike, tropical plants, with great, long leaves, on which bananas grow. [< Portuguese or Spanish, of West African origin]

banana oil, a colorless liquid having a smell somewhat like that of bananas, used in flavorings and as a solvent.

Ba na ras (bə när′əs), *n.* Benares.

band[1] (band), *n.* 1 number of persons or animals joined or acting together: *a band of robbers, a band of wild dogs.* See **company** for synonym study. 2 group of musicians performing together, especially on wind and percussion instruments. —*v.i., v.t.* unite or cause to unite in a group. [< Middle French *bande* troop]

band[2] (band), *n.* 1 a thin, flat strip of material for binding, trimming, or some other purpose. 2 stripe: *a white cup with a gold band.* 3 collar with two strips hanging in front, worn by certain clergymen. 4 anything having the shape or appearance of a flat strip, especially a section considered separately from its surroundings because of some feature. A separate section of grooves on a phonograph record is a band. 5 a particular range of wavelengths or frequencies in radio broadcasting. —*v.t.* 1 put a band on. 2 mark with stripes. [< Old French *bande* flat strip] **—band′er,** *n.*

band[3] (band), *n.* 1 ARCHAIC. anything with which one's body or limbs are bound; shackle; fetter; chain. 2 a moral, spiritual, or legal restraint. [< Scandinavian (Old Icelandic) *band*]

band age (ban′dij), *n., v.,* **-aged, -ag ing.** —*n.* strip of cloth or other material used in binding up and dressing a wound or injury. —*v.t.* bind, cover, or dress with a bandage. **—band′ag er,** *n.*

ban dan na or **ban dan a** (ban dan′ə), *n.* a large, gaily colored kerchief or handkerchief, often worn on the head or neck. [< Hindustani *bāndhnū* way of tying cloth so as to produce designs when dyed]

band box (band′boks′), *n.* a light cardboard box to put hats, collars, etc., in.

ban deau (ban dō′), *n., pl.* **-deaux** or **-deaus** (-dōz′). 1 a narrow band worn about the head. 2 any narrow band. 3 a narrow brassiere. [< French]

ban de role or **ban de rol** (ban′də rōl′), *n.* 1 a long, narrow flag with a cleft end, flying from the masthead of ships. 2 a small ornamental streamer. [< Middle French < Italian *banderuola* < *bandiera* banner]

ban di coot (ban′də küt), *n.* 1 either of two very large, destructive rats of southern Asia and the Near East. 2 a burrowing, ratlike marsupial of Australia and New Guinea. [< Telugu (a Dravidian language) *pandikokku* pig-rat]

ban di do (ban dē′dō), *n., pl.* **-dos.** bandit, especially in the southwestern United States and in Central and South America. [< Spanish]

ban dit (ban′dit), *n., pl.* **ban dits, ban dit ti** (ban dit′ē). 1 person who robs, especially one of a gang of highwaymen or robbers; brigand. 2 any outlaw. [< Italian *bandito* < *bandire* banish, proscribe]

ban dit ry (ban′də trē), *n.* 1 robbery. 2 bandits.

band lead er (band′lē′dər), *n.* leader of a dance band.

band mas ter (band′mas′tər), *n.* leader or conductor of a band of musicians.

ban do leer or **ban do lier** (ban′dl ir′), *n.* a broad belt worn over the shoulder and across the breast, often with loops for carrying cartridges or with small cases for bullets, gunpowder, etc. [< French *bandoulière* < Spanish *bandolera*]

band saw, saw in the form of an endless steel belt running over two pulleys.

band shell, an outdoor platform with a shell-shaped, resonant covering open on one side, for musical concerts.

bands man (bandz′mən), *n., pl.* **-men.** member of a band of musicians.

band stand (band′stand′), *n.* an outdoor platform, usually roofed, for band concerts.

Ban dung (bän′düng), *n.* city in W Java, Indonesia, where the first conference of Asian and African nations was held in 1955. 973,000.

band wag on (band′wag′ən), *n.* 1 wagon that carries a musical band in a parade. 2 **climb on the bandwagon,** INFORMAL. join what appears to be a winning or successful group, movement, fashion, etc.

band width (band′width′, band′witth′), *n.* the range of radio frequencies within a band.

ban dy (ban′dē), *v.,* **-died, -dy ing,** *adj.* —*v.t.* 1 hit or throw back and forth; toss about: *bandy a tennis ball.* 2 give and take; exchange: *bandy blows, bandy words, bandy reproaches.* 3 pass from one to another in a circle or group: *bandy stories, bandy gossip.* —*adj.* having a bend or curve outward: *bandy legs.*

ban dy-leg ged (ban′dē leg′id, ban′dē-legd′), *adj.* having legs that curve outward like a bow; bowlegged.

bane (bān), *n.* 1 cause of death, ruin, or harm. 2 destruction of any kind; ruin; harm. [Old English *bana* murderer]

bane ful (bān′fəl), *adj.* 1 causing harm or destruction; pernicious; injurious. 2 poisonous. **—bane′ful ly,** *adv.* **—bane′ful ness,** *n.*

Banff (bamf), *n.* 1 summer resort in SW Canada, in the Rocky Mountains. 3000. 2 county in NE Scotland.

bang[1] (bang), *n.* 1 a sudden, loud noise: *the bang of a gun.* 2 a violent, noisy blow. 3 INFORMAL. a striking result or success. 4 INFORMAL. vigor; impetus. 5 U.S. INFORMAL. thrill.
—*v.i.* make a sudden, loud noise: *The door banged as it blew shut.* —*v.t.* 1 cause to make a sudden, loud noise: *She banged the door.* 2 hit with violent, noisy blows; strike noisily. 3 handle roughly: *My trunk was banged in the accident.* 4 **bang up,** damage: *My car was banged up in the accident.*
—*adv.* 1 violently and noisily. 2 suddenly and loudly. 3 suddenly and abruptly; all at once.
—*interj.* imitation of gunfire: *"Bang! Bang!" shouted the children.*
[probably < Scandinavian (Old Icelandic) *banga* to strike]

bang[2] (bang), *n.* **bangs,** *pl.* fringe of hair cut short and worn over the forehead. —*v.t.* cut (hair) squarely across. [origin uncertain]

Ban ga lore (bang′gə lôr′, bang′gə lōr′), *n.* city in S India. 1,027,000.

Bang kok (bang′kok), *n.* capital and chief port of Thailand. 2,040,000.

Ban gla desh (bäng′glə desh′), *n.* country in S Asia, on the Bay of Bengal, a member of the Commonwealth of Nations. It was formerly the Pakistani province of **East**

Pakistan. 75,000,000 pop.; 54,500 sq. mi. *Capital:* Dacca.

Bangla Desh, Bangladesh.

ban gle (bang′gəl), *n.* 1 a small ornament suspended from a bracelet. 2 a bracelet or anklet without a clasp. [< Hindustani *bangrī* glass bracelet]

Ban gor (bang′gôr, bang′gər), *n.* city in S Maine. 33,000.

Ban gui (bäng′gē), *n.* capital of the Central African Republic, in the SW part. 150,000.

bang-up (bang′up′), *adj.* INFORMAL. strikingly good or effective; first-rate.

ban ian (ban′yən), *n.* banyan.

ban ish (ban′ish), *v.t.* 1 compel (a person) to leave a country by order of political or judicial authority; exile. See synonym study below. 2 force to go away; drive away; dismiss; expel: *banish all cares.* [< Old French *baniss-*, a form of *banir* < Germanic. Related to BAN.] **—ban′ish er,** *n.* **—ban′ish ment,** *n.*

Syn. 1 **Banish, exile, deport** mean cause to leave a country. **Banish** means to force a person, by order of authority, to leave his own or a foreign country, permanently or for a stated time: *Napoleon was banished to Elba.* **Exile** means either to compel another to leave his own country or home or voluntarily to remove oneself from either for a protracted period: *Napoleon was exiled to Elba. The man exiled himself abroad because of his dissatisfaction with the government.* **Deport** usually means to banish a person from a country of which he is not a citizen: *Aliens who have entered the United States illegally may be deported.*

ban is ter (ban′ə stər), *n.* 1 Often, **banisters,** *pl.* balustrade of a staircase. 2 baluster. [variant of *baluster*]

ban jo (ban′jō), *n., pl.* **-jos** or **-joes.** a musical instrument having four or five strings, played by plucking the strings with the fingers or with a plectrum. It has a head and neck like a guitar and a body like a tambourine. [apparently < a Bantu word]

banjo—Tightly stretched skin over the round body amplifies the sound made by plucking the strings.

ban jo ist (ban′jō ist), *n.* person who plays a banjo.

bank[1] (bangk), *n.* 1 a long pile or heap: *a bank of snow, a bank of clouds.* 2 the rising ground bordering a river, lake, etc.; shore: *She fished from the bank.* 3 a shallow place in a body of water; shoal: *the fishing banks of Newfoundland.* 4 any steep slope, especially one forming the side of a ravine or hill. 5 the sloping of an airplane to one side, especially when making a turn. *—v.t.* 1 form into a bank; pile up; heap up: *bank snow.* 2 cause to slope. 3 make (an airplane) slope to one side, especially when making a turn. 4 cover (a fire) with ashes or add fresh fuel and lessen the draft so that it will burn slowly: *bank a fire for the night.* 5 raise a ridge or mound about; border with a bank or ridge. *—v.i.* 1 form banks: *Clouds are banking along the horizon.* 2 (of an airplane) slope to one side, especially when turning. [probably < Scandinavian (Old Icelandic) *bakki* ridge]

bank[2] (bangk), *n.* 1 institution whose business is the custody, lending, transmitting, and paying orders for money: *A bank pays interest on money deposited in a savings account.* 2 fund of money out of which the dealer or manager in some gambling games pays his losses. 3 (in dominoes, etc.) stock of pieces from which players draw. 4 a small metal or plastic container with a slot through which coins can be dropped to save money. 5 any place where reserve supplies are kept: *a bank for blood plasma.* *—v.i.* 1 keep a bank; act as a banker. 2 deposit money in or keep an account with a bank. *—v.t.* 1 deposit (money) in a bank. 2 **bank on,** depend on; be sure of. [< Middle French *banque* < Italian *banca,* originally, counter or bench] **—bank′a ble,** *adj.*

bank[3] (bangk), *n.* 1 row or close arrangement of things: *a bank of switches, a bank of machines.* 2 row of keys on an organ, typewriter, etc. 3 row or tier of oars. 4 bench occupied by the rowers of each oar in a galley. *—v.t.* arrange in rows. [< Old French *banc* bench]

bank account, money in a bank that can be withdrawn by a depositor.

bank book (bangk′bu̇k′), *n.* book in which a record of a person's account at a bank is kept; passbook.

bank er (bang′kər), *n.* 1 person or company that manages a bank. 2 dealer or manager in a gambling game.

bank holiday, any day except Saturday or Sunday on which banks are legally closed; legal holiday.

bank ing (bang′king), *n.* business of a bank or banker.

bank note, a promissory note issued by a bank and payable on demand. Bank notes, in use until 1935, were intended to circulate as money.

bank roll (bangk′rōl′), *n.* INFORMAL. amount of money a person has in his possession or readily available.

bank rupt (bang′krupt), *n.* 1 person who is declared by a court of law to be unable to pay his debts, and whose property is distributed as far as it will go among his creditors. 2 person who is unable to pay his debts. *—adj.* 1 unable to pay one's debts; declared legally unable to pay debts. 2 at the end of one's resources; destitute. 3 completely lacking in something: *The story was entirely bankrupt of any new ideas.* *—v.t.* make bankrupt. [< Middle French *banqueroute* < Italian *bancarotta* bankruptcy < *banca* bank + *rotta* broken]

bank rupt cy (bang′krupt sē, bang′krəp-sē), *n., pl.* **-cies.** bankrupt condition.

ban ner (ban′ər), *n.* 1 flag. 2 piece of cloth with some design or words on it, attached by its upper edge to a pole or staff. 3 a newspaper headline extending across the top of a page. *—adj.* leading or outstanding; foremost. [< Old French *baniere* < Germanic]

ban nock (ban′ək), *n.* SCOTTISH. a flat cake made of oatmeal or barley flour. [Old English *bannuc* small piece]

Ban nock burn (ban′ək bėrn′), *n.* town in central Scotland, near which in a battle fought in 1314 the Scottish under Robert the Bruce defeated the English.

banns (banz), *n.pl.* public notice, given on three separate occasions in church, that a certain man and woman are to be married. [plural of *bann* proclamation, Old English *gebann*]

hat, āge, fär; let, ēqual, tėrm;
it, ice; hot, ōpen, ôrder;
oil, out; cup, pu̇t, rüle;
ch, child; ng, long; sh, she;
th, thin; ᴛʜ, then; zh, measure;

ə represents *a* in about, *e* in taken, *i* in pencil, *o* in lemon, *u* in circus.

< = from, derived from, taken from.

ban quet (bang′kwit), *n.* 1 an elaborate meal prepared for a special occasion or for many people; feast. See **feast** for synonym study. 2 a formal dinner with speeches. *—v.t.* give a banquet to. *—v.i.* take part in a banquet. [< Middle French < Italian *banchetto,* diminutive of *banco* bench] **—ban′quet er,** *n.*

ban quette (bang ket′), *n.* 1 platform along the inside of a parapet or trench for soldiers to stand on when firing. 2 an upholstered bench, especially one along a wall in restaurants, etc.

ban shee or **ban shie** (ban′shē, ban shē′), *n.* (in Irish and Scottish folklore) a female spirit whose wail means that there will soon be a death in the family. [< Irish *bean sidhe* woman of the fairies]

ban tam (ban′təm), *n.* 1 Often, **Bantam.** a small variety of domestic fowl. The roosters are often spirited fighters. 2 a small person who is fond of fighting. *—adj.* 1 light in weight; small. 2 laughably aggressive. [< *Bantam,* town in Java, where the fowl are imported from]

ban tam weight (ban′təm wāt′), *n.* boxer who weighs more than 112 and less than 118 pounds.

ban ter (ban′tər), *n.* playful teasing; joking. *—v.t.* tease playfully; make fun of. *—v.i.* talk in a joking way. [origin uncertain] **—ban′ter er,** *n.* **—ban′ter ing ly,** *adv.*

bant ling (bant′ling), *n.* a young child; brat. [origin uncertain]

Ban tu (ban′tü), *n., pl.* **-tu** or **-tus,** *adj.* *—n.* 1 member of a large group of Negro tribes living in central and southern Africa. 2 any of the languages of these tribes. *—adj.* of these tribes or their languages.

Ban tu stan (ban′tü stan), *n.* any of several regions in the Republic of South Africa designated as separate states to be inhabited and governed by the Bantu.

ban yan (ban′yən), *n.* an East Indian fig tree whose branches have hanging roots that grow down to the ground and start new trunks. One tree may cover several acres. Also, **banian.** [< Portuguese *banian* < Hindi *baniyā*]

ban zai (bän′zī′), *interj.* a Japanese greeting, patriotic cheer, or battle cry. It means "May you live ten thousand years!"

ba o bab (bā′ō bab), *n.* a tall, tropical tree of Africa, India, and Australia, with a very thick trunk and an edible, gourdlike, woolly fruit. The fibers of its bark are used for making rope, cloth, and paper. [probably < an African word]

Bap. or **Bapt.,** Baptist.

bap tism (bap′tiz′əm), *n.* 1 rite or sacrament of dipping a person into water or sprinkling water on him, as a sign of washing away sin and admission into the Christian church. 2 experience or trial that tests a person or initiates him into a new kind of life. 3 a baptizing or a being baptized.

bap tis mal (bap tiz′məl), *adj.* of or having to do with baptism; used in baptism: *baptismal vows.* **—bap tis′mal ly,** *adv.*

Bap tist (bap′tist), *n.* 1 member of a Protestant church believing in baptism by immersion, restricted to believers old enough to make their own declaration of faith. 2 Often, **baptist.** person who baptizes. 3 **the Baptist,** (in the Bible) John the Baptist. *—adj.* of or having to do with the Baptists.

bap tis ter y (bap′tə stər ē), *n., pl.* **-ter ies.** building or part of a church where baptism is performed.

bap tis try (bap′tə strē), *n., pl.* **-tries.** baptistery.

bap tize (bap tīz′, bap′tīz), *v.t.,* **-tized, -tiz ing.** 1 dip (a person) into water or sprinkle with water as a sign of washing away sin and admission into the Christian church. 2 give a first name to (a person) at baptism; christen. 3 give a name to; name. 4 purify; cleanse. 5 introduce; initiate. [< Greek *baptizein* < *baptein* to dip] **—bap tiz′er,** *n.*

bar[1] (def. 6a)

bar[1] (defs. 6b, 6c)

bar[1] (bär), *n., v.,* **barred, bar ring,** *prep.* *—n.* 1 an evenly shaped piece of some solid, longer than it is wide or thick: *a bar of iron, bar of soap, a bar of chocolate.* 2 pole or rod put across a door, gate, window, or across any opening, to fasten or shut off something. 3 anything that blocks the way or prevents progress; barrier; obstacle; obstruction: *A bad temper is a bar to making friends.* 4 sandbar. 5 band of color; stripe. 6 in music: **a** unit of rhythm. The regular accent falls on the first note of each bar. **b** the vertical line between two such units on a musical staff, dividing a composition into measures. **c** a double bar. 7 counter where drinks, usually alcoholic, and sometimes food are served to customers. 8 place with such a counter; barroom; tavern. 9 place where a prisoner stands in a court of law. 10 the railing around the place where lawyers sit in a court of law. 11 profession of a lawyer: *After passing his law examinations, the young man was admitted to the bar.* 12 lawyers as a group: *Judges are chosen from the bar.* 13 court of law. 14 anything like a court of law; any place of judgment: *the bar of public opinion.*
—v.t. 1 put bars across; fasten or shut off with a bar: *Bar the doors and windows.* 2 block; obstruct: *The exits were barred by chairs.* 3 exclude or forbid: *All talking is barred during a study period.* 4 mark with stripes.
—prep. except; excluding: *He is the best student, bar none.*
[< Old French *barre* < Popular Latin *barra* thick ends of bushes]

bar[2] (bär), *n.* unit of pressure equal to one million dynes per square centimeter. [< Greek *baros* weight]

bar., 1 barometer. 2 barometric. 3 barrel.

Ba rab bas (bə rab′əs), *n.* (in the Bible) a robber whose release the people demanded when Pilate offered to free Jesus.

barb[1] (bärb), *n.* 1 point sticking out and curving backward from the main point of an arrow, fishhook, etc. 2 one of the hairlike branches on the shaft of a feather. 3 barbel (def. 1). 4 something that wounds or stings: *the barb of sarcasm.* *—v.t.* furnish with barbs. [< Old French *barbe* < Latin *barba* beard]

barb[2] (bärb), *n.* a breed of horse brought to Spain by the Moors, noted for its great speed, endurance, and gentleness. [< French *barbe* < Italian *barbero* of Barbary]

Bar ba di an (bär bā′dē ən), *adj.* of or having to do with Barbados. *—n.* native or inhabitant of Barbados.

Bar ba dos (bär bā′dōz), *n.* island country in the West Indies, a member of the Commonwealth of Nations. 238,000 pop.; 166 sq. mi. *Capital:* Bridgetown.

bar bar i an (bär ber′ē ən, bär bar′ē ən), *n.* 1 person belonging to a people or to a tribe that is not civilized. 2 person who rejects or lacks interest in literature, the arts, etc. 3 foreigner differing from the speaker or writer in language and customs. In ancient times, a barbarian was successively a person who was not a Greek, a person outside of the Roman Empire, or a person who was not a Christian. *—adj.* 1 not civilized; coarse. See synonym study below. 2 of barbarians: *barbarian customs.* 3 differing from the speaker or writer in language and customs; foreign. [< Latin *barbaria* foreign country < *barbarus* foreigner < Greek *barbaros* foreign; originally, stammering]
Syn. *adj.* 1 **Barbarian, barbaric, barbarous** mean not civilized. **Barbarian** suggests the full range of lack of civilization: *The Roman Empire was conquered by barbarian peoples.* **Barbaric** emphasizes the love of show and the lack of refinement and gentleness, that distinguish less highly civilized peoples: *The dress of gypsies is barbaric.* **Barbarous,** more than the others, emphasizes the harshness and cruelty of uncivilized peoples: *Torture of prisoners is a barbarous custom.*

bar bar ic (bär bar′ik), *adj.* 1 like barbarians; suited to an uncivilized people; rough and rude. 2 crudely rich or splendid; flamboyant. See **barbarian** for synonym study. **—bar bar′i cal ly,** *adv.*

bar ba rism (bär′bə riz′əm), *n.* 1 condition of uncivilized people: *People who have no form of writing live in barbarism.* 2 a barbarous act, custom, or trait. 3 use of a word or expression not in accepted use. 4 a nonstandard word or expression. EXAMPLE: *his'n* for *his.*

bar bar i ty (bär bar′ə tē), *n., pl.* **-ties.** 1 brutal cruelty; inhumanity. 2 act of cruelty. 3 barbaric manner or style; gaudy taste.

bar ba rize (bär′bə rīz′), *v.t., v.i.,* **-rized, -riz ing.** make or become barbarous. **—bar′ba ri za′tion,** *n.*

Bar ba ros sa (bär′bə ros′ə), *n.* See **Frederick Barbarossa.**

bar bar ous (bär′bər əs), *adj.* 1 not civilized; savage. 2 savagely cruel; brutal. See **barbarian** for synonym study. 3 rough and rude; coarse; unrefined. 4 (of a word or expression) not in accepted use. **—bar′bar ous ly,** *adv.* **—bar′bar ous ness,** *n.*

Bar bar y (bär′bər ē), *n.* Moslem countries west of Egypt on the N coast of Africa.

Barbary ape, a tailless monkey that lives in northern Africa and on the Rock of Gibraltar.

Barbary States, former name for Morocco, Algeria, Tunisia, and Tripoli, once noted as pirate strongholds. The United States went to war against them in the early 1800's because they had been demanding tribute from ships passing through the Mediterranean.

bar be cue (bär′bə kyü), *n., v.,* **-cued, -cu ing.** *—n.* 1 an outdoor meal in which meat is roasted over an open fire. 2 grill or open fireplace for cooking meat, usually over charcoal. 3 meat roasted over an open fire. 4 an outdoor feast at which animals are roasted whole. 5 food at such a feast or meal. 6 animal roasted whole. *—v.t.* 1 roast (meat) over an open fire. 2 cook (meat or fish) in a highly flavored sauce. 3 roast (an animal) whole. [< American Spanish *barbacoa*]

barbed (bärbd), *adj.* 1 having a barb or barbs: *A fishhook is barbed.* 2 sharply critical; cutting: *a barbed remark.*

barbed wire, wire with sharp points on it every few inches, used for fences.

bar bel (bär′bəl), *n.* 1 a long, thin, fleshy growth on the mouths or nostrils of some fishes; barb. 2 a large, freshwater fish of Europe having such growths. It is related to the carp. [< Middle French < Latin *barbus* kind of fish < *barba* beard]

bar bell (bär′bel′), *n.* device like a dumbbell but with a much longer bar, to the ends of which weights may be added, used for exercising.

bar ber (bär′bər), *n.* person whose business is cutting hair and shaving or trimming beards. *—v.t.* cut the hair of; shave; trim the beard of. [< Anglo-French *barbour* < *barbe* beard < Latin *barba*]

Bar ber (bär′bər), *n.* **Samuel,** born 1910, American composer.

bar ber ry (bär′ber′ē, bär′bər ē), *n., pl.* **-ries.** 1 any of a genus of low, thorny shrubs with small, yellow flowers and sour red or purple berries. Some species are used for hedges. 2 the berry of any of these shrubs. [< Medieval Latin *barberis* < Arabic *barbaris*]

bar ber shop (bär′bər shop′), *n.* the place where a barber works.

bar bette (bär bet′), *n.* 1 platform or mound in a fort from which guns may be fired over the wall, rather than through an opening. 2 an armored cylinder protecting a gun turret on a warship. [< French]

barbican

bar bi can (bär′bə kən), *n.* an outer fortification of a castle or city, especially a tower built over a gate or bridge. [< Old French *barbacane*]

bar bi tal (bär′bə tôl), *n.* a white, crystalline powder containing barbituric acid, used as a

hat, āge, fär; let, ēqual, tėrm;
it, īce; hot, ōpen, ôrder;
oil, out; cup, pu̇t, rüle;
ch, child; ng, long; sh, she;
th, thin; ᴛʜ, then; zh, measure;

ə represents *a* in about, *e* in taken, *i* in pencil, *o* in lemon, *u* in circus.

< = from, derived from, taken from.

sedative or hypnotic. *Formula:* $C_8H_{12}N_2O_3$

bar bit ur ate (bär bich′ər it, bär bich′ə rāt′), *n.* 1 salt or ester of barbituric acid. 2 any of a group of drugs derived from barbituric acid used in medicine as hypnotics and sedatives.

bar bi tu ric acid (bär′bə tu̇r′ik, bär′bə tyu̇r′ik), a crystalline acid much used as the basis of sedatives and hypnotics. *Formula:* $CO(NHCO)_2CH_2$ [*barbituric* < New Latin *(Usnea) barbata* bearded (lichen) + English *uric*]

bar bule (bär′byül), *n.* 1 a little barb. 2 one of a series of small, pointed processes fringing the barbs of a feather.

bar ca role or **bar ca rolle** (bär′kə rōl′), *n.* 1 a Venetian boat song, sung by gondoliers. 2 music imitating such a song, typically with a lilting rhythm. [< French *barcarolle* < Italian *barcarola* < *barca* bark³]

Bar ce lo na (bär′sə lō′nə), *n.* seaport in NE Spain, on the Mediterranean. 1,759,000.

bar chart, bar graph.

bard (bärd), *n.* 1 a Celtic minstrel and poet who from earliest times to the Middle Ages sang his own poems, usually to harp accompaniment, celebrating martial exploits, etc. 2 any poet. [< Irish and Scottish Gaelic]

bard ic (bär′dik), *adj.* of or characterizing a bard or bards.

Bard of Avon, William Shakespeare.

bare¹ (ber, bar), *adj.,* **bar er, bar est,** *v.,* **bared, bar ing.** —*adj.* 1 without covering; not clothed; naked: *bare hands. The top of the hill was bare.* See synonym study below. 2 with the head uncovered; bareheaded. 3 not concealed; not disguised; open: *the bare truth of the matter.* 4 not furnished; empty: *The room was bare of furniture.* 5 plain; unadorned: *They lived in a bare little cabin.* 6 much worn; threadbare. 7 just enough and no more; mere: *They earn only a bare living by their work.* 8 **lay bare,** uncover; expose: *lay bare a plot.* —*v.t.* make bare; uncover; reveal: *bare one's feelings. The dog bared his teeth.* [Old English *bær*] —**bare′ness,** *n.*

Syn. *adj.* 1 **Bare, nude, naked,** when applied to the human body, mean without clothing. **Bare** suggests that a specified part of the body is unclothed: *The sun burned her bare shoulders.* **Nude** and **naked** usually suggest the absence of all clothing from the body. **Nude** is the more neutral, objective term: *Many famous artists have painted nude models.* **Naked** often suggests an unprotected or a shameless condition: *We were shocked at the poverty of naked children in the cities of India. A group of naked boys were swimming in the river.*

bare² (ber, bar), *v.* ARCHAIC. a pt. of **bear¹**.

bare back (ber′bak′, bar′bak′), *adj., adv.* without a saddle; on the bare back of a horse, etc.

bare backed (ber′bakt′, bar′bakt′), *adj., adv.* bareback.

bare faced (ber′fāst′, bar′fāst′), *adj.* 1 with the face bare. 2 shameless; impudent: *a barefaced lie.* 3 ARCHAIC. not disguised. —**bare′fac′ed ly,** *adv.* —**bare′fac′ed ness,** *n.*

bare foot (ber′fu̇t′, bar′fu̇t′), *adj., adv.* without shoes and stockings on.

bare foot ed (ber′fu̇t′id, bar′fu̇t′id), *adj., adv.* barefoot.

bare hand ed (ber′han′did, bar′han′did), *adj., adv.* 1 without any covering on the hands. 2 with empty hands. 3 with no aid but one's own hands.

bare head ed (ber′hed′id, bar′hed′id), *adj., adv.* wearing nothing on the head. —**bare′head′ed ness,** *n.*

bare leg ged (ber′leg′id, ber′legd′; bar′leg′id, bar′legd′), *adj., adv.* without stockings on.

bare ly (ber′lē, bar′lē), *adv.* 1 with nothing to spare; only just; scarcely: *They have barely enough money to live on.* 2 poorly; scantily.

Bar ents Sea (bar′ents), arm of the Arctic Ocean, north of European Russia.

bar gain (bär′gən), *n.* 1 an agreement to trade or exchange; deal. 2 something offered for sale cheap, or bought cheap. 3 a good trade or exchange; price below the real value. 4 any arrangement or deal considered advantageous or the reverse: *That investment was a bad bargain.* 5 **into the bargain** or **in the bargain,** besides; also: *My new dress shrank and it faded into the bargain.* 6 **strike a bargain,** make a bargain; reach an agreement. —*v.i.* 1 try to get good terms; try to make a good deal. 2 make a bargain; come to terms. 3 trade. —*v.t.* **bargain for,** be ready for; expect: *He hadn't bargained for rain and had left his umbrella at home.* [< Old French *bargaigne*] —**bar′gain er,** *n.*

barge (bärj), *n., v.,* **barged, barg ing.** —*n.* 1 a large, strongly built, flat-bottomed boat for carrying freight on rivers, canals, etc., now usually towed or pushed by tugboats. 2 a large boat used for excursions, pageants, and special occasions. 3 a large motorboat or rowboat used by the commanding officer of a flagship. —*v.t.* carry by barge. —*v.i.* 1 move clumsily like a barge: *I barged into the table and knocked the lamp over.* 2 INFORMAL. push oneself rudely; intrude: *Don't barge in where you're not wanted.* [< Old French < Medieval Latin *barga,* variant of Late Latin *barca* bark³]

barge man (bärj′mən), *n., pl.* **-men.** man who works on a barge.

bar graph, graph representing different quantities by rectangles of different lengths; bar chart.

bar ite (ber′īt, bar′īt), *n.* barium sulfate in its natural form, as a mineral found in many parts of the world; barytes.

bar i tone (bar′ə tōn), *n.* 1 the male voice between tenor and bass. 2 singer with such a voice. 3 part in music for such a voice or for an instrument of similar range. 4 a brass wind musical instrument that has the quality or range of this voice. —*adj.* of or for a baritone. Also, BRITISH **barytone.** [< Greek *barytonos* deep-sounding < *barys* deep + *tonos* pitch]

bar i um (ber′ē əm, bar′ē əm), *n.* a soft, silvery-white metallic element, which occurs only in combination with other elements, especially in barite. Barium compounds are used in making pigments, safety matches, vacuum tubes, etc. *Symbol:* Ba; *atomic number* 56. See pages 326 and 327 for table. [< New Latin < Greek *barytēs* weight]

barium sulfate, compound occurring as a mineral, barite, or prepared synthetically. It is used in taking X rays of the stomach and intestines, as a filler in making linoleum, etc., and as a pigment. *Formula:* $BaSO_4$

bark¹ (bärk), *n.* the tough outside covering of the trunk, branches, and roots of trees and certain other plants. —*v.t.* 1 strip the bark from (a tree or other plant). 2 cut out a ring of bark from (a tree) in order to kill it. 3 cover with bark. 4 tan (hides, skins, etc.). 5 scrape the skin from (shins, knuckles, etc.). [< Scandinavian (Old Icelandic) *börkr*]

bark² (bärk), *n.* 1 the short, sharp sound that a dog makes. 2 a sound like this: *the bark of a fox, the bark of a gun, the bark of a cough.* —*v.i.* 1 make this sound or one like it. 2 INFORMAL. cough. 3 INFORMAL. call or shout to attract people into a circus tent, sideshow at a fair, store, etc. —*v.t.* speak gruffly or sharply: *bark out orders.* [Old English *beorcan*]

bark³ (bärk), *n.* 1 a three-masted ship, square-rigged on the first two masts and fore-and-aft-rigged on the other. 2 ARCHAIC. boat; ship. Also, **barque.** [< Middle French *barque* < Italian *barca* < Late Latin]

bar keep (bär′kēp′), *n.* U.S. barkeeper.

bar keep er (bär′kē′pər), *n.* 1 person who owns or manages a bar where alcoholic drinks are sold. 2 bartender.

bar ken tine (bär′kən tēn′), *n.* a three-masted ship with the foremast square-rigged and the other masts fore-and-aft-rigged. Also, **barquentine.** [< *bark³;* patterned on *brigantine*]

bark er (bär′kər), *n.* 1 person or thing that barks. 2 person who stands in front of a circus tent, sideshow at a fair, store, etc., urging people to go in.

bar ley (bär′lē), *n.* 1 the seed or grain of an annual, widely cultivated cereal grass, bearing compact spikes of flowers, each spike having from one to three spikelets at each of its joints. 2 its seeds or grain, used for food, fodder, and for making malt. [Old English *bærlīc*]

bar ley corn (bär′lē kôrn′), *n.* a grain of barley.

barm (bärm), *n.* a foamy yeast that forms on malt liquors while they are fermenting. [Old English *beorma*]

bar magnet, a permanent magnet in the shape of a bar or rod: *A bar magnet suspended from a string will serve as a simple compass.*

bar maid (bär′mād′), *n.* a woman bartender.

bar man (bär′mən), *n., pl.* **-men.** bartender.

Bar me cide feast (bär′mə sīd), 1 a pretended feast with empty dishes. 2 an empty pretense of hospitality, generosity, etc. [< *Barmecide,* a wealthy man in *The Arabian Nights* who gave a beggar a pretended feast on empty dishes]

bar mitz vah (bär mits′və), 1 ceremony or celebration held when a Jewish boy becomes thirteen years old, to affirm that he has reached the age of religious responsibility. 2 the boy himself. [< Hebrew *bar miṣwah,* literally, son of the commandment]

barm y (bär′mē), *adj.,* **barm i er, barm i est.** 1 full of barm; fermenting. 2 BRITISH SLANG. silly; crazy.

barn (bärn), *n.* building for storing hay, grain, or other farm produce, and for sheltering cows, horses, and farm machinery. [Old

English *bærn* < *bere* barley + *ærn* place] **—barn′like′**, *adj.*

Bar na bas (bär′nə bəs), *n.* (in the Bible) a Christian apostle who was a companion of Paul.

bar na cle (bär′nə kəl), *n.* a small, salt-water crustacean that attaches itself to rocks, the bottoms of ships, the timbers of wharves, etc. [Middle English *bernacle* < Old French]

bar na cled (bär′nə kəld), *adj.* covered with barnacles.

barn dance, 1 an informal party for square-dancing, formerly often held in a barn. 2 a lively square dance resembling a polka.

barn storm (bärn′stôrm′), *v.i.* travel from one small town or country district to another, acting in plays, making political speeches, giving short airplane rides or exhibitions of stunt flying, etc. *—v.t.* act in plays, make speeches, etc., in (small towns and country districts). **—barn′storm′er,** *n.*

barn swallow, swallow with a reddish breast and a long, forked tail, that usually nests in barns.

Bar num (bär′nəm), *n.* **P(hineas) T(aylor),** 1810-1891, American showman.

barn yard (bärn′yärd′), *n.* yard adjoining a barn for livestock, often fenced.

Ba ro da (bə rō′də), *n.* city in W India. 295,000.

bar o gram (bar′ə gram), *n.* a record made by a barograph or similar instrument.

bar o graph (bar′ə graf), *n.* instrument that automatically records changes in air pressure. [< Greek *baros* weight + English *-graph*]

ba rom e ter (bə rom′ə tər), *n.* 1 instrument for measuring the pressure of air, used in determining height above sea level and in predicting probable changes in the weather. 2 something that indicates changes: *His newspaper column is a barometer of public opinion.* [< Greek *baros* weight + English *-meter*]

bar o met ric (bar′ə met′rik), *adj.* 1 of a barometer. 2 indicated by a barometer: *barometric pressure.* **—bar′o met′ri cal ly,** *adv.*

bar o met ri cal (bar′ə met′rə kəl), *adj.* barometric.

bar on (bar′ən), *n.* 1 nobleman of the lowest hereditary rank. In British peerage, a baron ranks next below a viscount and has "Lord" before his name instead of "Baron." In other European countries "Baron" is used before his name. 2 an English nobleman during the Middle Ages who held his lands directly from the king. 3 a powerful industrialist, merchant, or financier: *a beef baron, a coal baron.* [< Old French < *ber* military leader < Germanic]

bar on age (bar′ə nij), *n.* 1 all the barons. 2 rank or title of a baron. 3 the nobility.

bar on ess (bar′ə nis), *n.* 1 wife or widow of a baron. 2 woman whose rank is equal to that of a baron.

bar on et (bar′ə nit), *n.* man in Great Britain ranking next below a baron and next above a knight. He has "Sir" before his name and "Bart." after it. EXAMPLE: Sir John Brown, Bart.

bar on et cy (bar′ə nit sē), *n., pl.* **-cies.** rank or position of a baronet.

ba ro ni al (bə rō′nē əl), *adj.* 1 of a baron or barons. 2 suitable for a baron; splendid, stately, and grand.

bar on y (bar′ə nē), *n., pl.* **-on ies.** 1 lands of a baron. 2 rank or title of a baron.

ba roque (bə rōk′, bə rok′), *adj.* 1 having to do with a style of art and architecture that prevailed in Europe from about 1550 to the late 1700's, characterized by the use of curved forms and lavish ornamentation. 2 having to do with a style of music characterized by complex rhythms and melodic ornamentation. 3 tastelessly odd; fantastic; grotesque. 4 irregular in shape: *baroque pearls.* *—n.* a baroque style. [< French < Portuguese *barroco* irregular]

ba rouche (bə rüsh′), *n.* a four-wheeled carriage with a driver's seat in front, two double passenger seats inside facing each other, and a folding top. [< German *Barutsche*]

barque (bärk), *n.* bark[3].

bar quen tine (bär′kən tēn′), *n.* barkentine.

Bar qui si me to (bär′kə sə mā′tō), *n.* city in NW Venezuela. 235,000.

bar rack (bar′ək), *n.* barracks. [< French *baraque* < Catalan *baracca*]

bar racks (bar′əks), *n. pl. or sing.* 1 building or group of buildings for soldiers to live in, usually in a fort or camp. 2 a large, plain building in which many people live.

bar ra cu da (bar′ə kü′də), *n., pl.* **-da** or **-das.** a large, fierce fish of tropical and subtropical seas, that looks somewhat like a pike. It sometimes attacks swimmers. [< American Spanish]

bar rage (bə räzh′), *n., v.,* **-raged, -rag ing.** *—n.* 1 barrier of artillery fire to check the enemy or to protect one's own soldiers when advancing or retreating. 2 a large number of words, blows, etc., coming quickly one after the other: *The reporters kept up a barrage of questions for an hour.* *—v.t., v.i.* fire at with artillery; subject to a barrage. [< French < *barrer* to bar]

Bar ran quil la (bar′ən kē′yə), *n.* city in N Colombia. 641,000.

bar ra try (bar′ə trē), *n., pl.* **-tries.** 1 fraud or gross negligence of a ship's officer or seaman against owners, insurers, etc. 2 act or practice of stirring up lawsuits or quarrels. [< Old French *baraterie* < *barater* to exchange, cheat. Related to BARTER.]

barred (bärd), *adj.* 1 having bars: *a barred window.* 2 marked with stripes: *a chicken with barred feathers.*

bar rel (bar′əl), *n., v.,* **-reled, -rel ing** or **-relled, -rel ling.** *—n.* 1 container with a round, flat top and bottom and sides that curve out slightly. Barrels are usually made of thick boards held together by hoops. 2 amount that a barrel can hold; barrelful. 3 any container, case, or part shaped somewhat like a barrel: *the barrel of a drum.* 4 a varying unit of liquid and dry measure, often fixed by law for different commodities. 5 the metal tube of a gun through which the bullet is discharged. 6 the central portion of the body of a horse, mule, cow, etc. 7 INFORMAL. a great deal; much: *a barrel of fun.* *—v.t.* put in barrels. *—v.i.* U.S. SLANG. move with great speed. [< Old French *baril*]

bar rel ful (bar′əl fu̇l′), *n., pl.* **-fuls.** amount that a barrel can hold.

barrel organ, hand organ.

bar ren (bar′ən), *adj.* 1 not producing anything; unproductive: *A sandy desert is barren.* 2 not able to produce offspring or yield fruit; not fertile; sterile. 3 without interest; unattractive; dull. 4 of no advantage; fruitless; unprofitable. *—n.* 1 stretch of barren land. 2 Usually, **barrens,** *pl.* area of level land, mostly unproductive, poorly forested, and generally having sandy soil. [< Old French *baraine*] **—bar′ren ly,** *adv.* **—bar′ren ness,** *n.*

bar rette (bə ret′), *n.* pin with a clasp, used by women and girls for holding their hair in place. [< French, diminutive of *barre* bar]

bar ri cade (bar′ə kād′, bar′ə kād), *n., v.,* **-cad ed, -cad ing.** *—n.* 1 a rough, hastily made barrier for defense. 2 any barrier or obstruction. *—v.t.* block or obstruct with a barricade: *Our street was barricaded for a week so that it could be resurfaced.* [< French]

Bar rie (bar′ē), *n.* Sir **James Matthew,** 1860-1937, Scottish novelist and playwright.

bar ri er (bar′ē ər), *n.* 1 something that stands in the way; something stopping progress or preventing approach; obstacle: *A moat around a castle is a barrier. Lack of water was a barrier to settling much of New Mexico. Different languages are a barrier to communication between people of different nationalities.* 2 something that separates or keeps apart: *The Isthmus of Panama forms a barrier between the Atlantic and Pacific oceans.* [< Anglo-French *barrere* < *barre* bar]

barrier reef, ridge of coral deposits parallel to the mainland and separated from it by a deep lagoon.

bar ring (bär′ing), *prep.* leaving out of consideration; excepting: *Barring poor weather, the plane will leave Chicago at noon.*

bar ri o (bär′ē ō), *n., pl.* **-ri os.** 1 (in Spanish-speaking countries) a district of a city or town. 2 U.S. section of a city inhabited chiefly by Spanish-speaking people. [< Spanish < Arabic *barri* outside]

bar ris ter (bar′ə stər), *n.* lawyer in England who can plead in any court. [< *bar*[1] + *-ster*]

bar room (bär′rüm′, bär′ru̇m′), *n.* room with a bar for the sale of alcoholic drinks; taproom.

bar row[1] (bar′ō), *n.* 1 frame with two short handles at each end, as a stretcher has, used for carrying a load. 2 wheelbarrow. 3 handcart. [Old English *bearwe.* Related to BEAR[1].]

bar row[2] (bar′ō), *n.* mound of earth or stones over an ancient grave. [Old English *beorg*]

bar row[3] (bar′ō), *n.* a castrated male pig. [Old English *bearg*]

Bar row (bar′ō), *n.* **Point,** the N tip of Alaska, the northernmost point of land in the United States.

Bar ry (bar′ē), *n.* **John,** 1745-1803, naval officer in the Revolutionary War.

bar sinister, a diagonal bar on a coat of arms, wrongly supposed to indicate illegitimate descent.

Bart., Baronet.

bar tend er (bär′ten′dər), *n.* person who serves alcoholic drinks to customers at a bar.

bar ter (bär′tər), *v.i.* trade by exchanging one kind of goods or services for other goods or services without using money. *—v.t.* 1 exchange (goods or services of equivalent or supposed equivalent value): *The Indians bartered furs for beads and guns.* 2 **barter away,** give away without an equal return: *barter away one's soul for wealth.* *—n.* 1 act of bartering; trading by exchanging goods. 2 something bartered. [< Old French *barater* to exchange] **—bar′ter er,** *n.*

Bar thol di (bär thol′dē; *French* bär tôl-dē′), *n.* **Frédéric Auguste,** 1834-1904, French sculptor.

Bar thol o mew (bär thol′ə myü), *n.* (in the Bible) one of Christ's twelve Apostles. Saint Bartholomew's Day is August 24.

bar ti zan (bär′tə zən, bär′tə zan′), *n.* a small, overhanging turret on a wall or tower. [alteration of *bratticing* < *brattice* parapet < Old French *bretesche*]

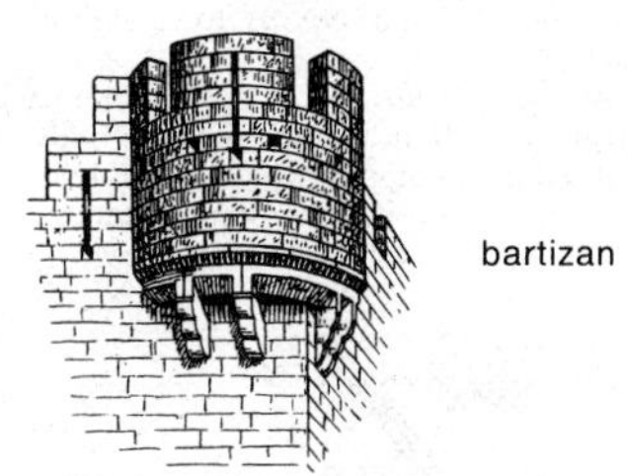
bartizan

Bar tók (bär′tok), *n.* **Béla,** 1881-1945, Hungarian composer and pianist.

Bar ton (bärt′n), *n.* **Clara,** 1821-1912, American nurse who organized the American Red Cross in 1881.

Bar uch (ber′ək, bar′ək *for 1 and 2;* bə rük′ *for 3*), *n.* 1 (in the Bible) the secretary and friend of Jeremiah. 2 book of the Old Testament Apocrypha supposed to have been written by him. 3 **Bernard M.,** 1870-1965, American financier and statesman.

bar y on (bar′ē on), *n.* any of a class of heavy elementary particles that includes the proton, neutron, and hyperon. [< Greek *barys* heavy]

ba ry tes (bə rī′tēz), *n.* barite.

bar y tone (bar′ə tōn), *n., adj.* BRITISH. baritone.

bas al (bā′səl), *adj.* 1 of the base; at the base; forming the base. 2 fundamental; basic. **—bas′al ly,** *adv.*

basal metabolic rate, the rate at which an animal or plant at complete rest uses up food and produces heat and other forms of energy, measured by the amount of oxygen it takes in.

basal metabolism, amount of energy used by an animal or plant at complete rest, measured by the basal metabolic rate and used as a standard for comparing metabolism under varying conditions.

ba salt (bə sôlt′, bā′sôlt), *n.* a hard, dark-colored rock of volcanic origin. It often occurs in a form resembling a group of columns. [< Late Latin *basaltes*]

ba sal tic (bə sôl′tik), *adj.* of or like basalt.

bas cule (bas′kyül), *n.* device that works like a seesaw. In a **bascule bridge** the rising part is counterbalanced by a weight. [< French, seesaw]

bascule bridge

base[1] (bās), *n., v.,* **based, bas ing,** *adj.* —*n.* 1 the bottom of anything, on which it stands or rests; underlying support: *The machine rests on a wide base of steel.* 2 starting place. 3 place from which an army, air force, or navy operates and from which supplies are obtained; headquarters. 4 main or supporting part; basis; groundwork. See synonym study below. 5 **off base,** INFORMAL. incorrect; wrong. 6 the most important element of anything; essential part: *This paint has an oil base.* 7 place that is a station or goal in certain games, such as baseball. 8 part of a column on which the shaft rests. See **column** for picture. 9 part at the bottom of a wall or monument. 10 the part of an organ of an animal or plant nearest its point of attachment. 11 the point of attachment. 12 in chemistry: **a** any compound yielding hydroxyl ions when dissolved in water. Such substances turn red litmus paper blue, have a pH value of more than 7, and usually react with an acid to form a salt. Sodium hydroxide and calcium hydroxide are common bases. **b** any ionic or molecular substance which can take on a proton. **c** any molecule or ion that has available an unshared pair of electrons. 13 line or surface forming that part of a geometrical figure on which it is supposed to rest. Any side of a triangle can be its base. 14 line used as the starting point in surveying. 15 number that is a definite starting point for a system of numeration or logarithms. 10 is the base of the decimal system. 16 (in grammar) the form of a word to which prefixes and suffixes are attached; root.
—*v.t.* make or form a base or foundation for.
—*v.i.* establish; found: *Their large business was based on good service.*
—*adj.* 1 that forms a base. 2 that serves as a base: *a base camp.*
[< Old French < Latin *basis* < Greek. Doublet of BASIS.]

Syn. *n.* 4 **Base, basis, foundation** mean the part on which anything stands for support. **Base,** though chiefly used literally, is also used figuratively to emphasize the support it gives to larger things: *The new charter was welcomed as a base on which to build needed reforms.* **Basis,** chiefly used figuratively, emphasizes how essential the support is: *The basis of her opinion is something she read in the paper.* **Foundation,** used literally and figuratively, emphasizes the firmness and solidness of the base or basis: *His honesty and willingness to work are the foundation of his success.*

base[2] (bās), *adj.,* **bas er, bas est.** 1 morally low or mean; selfish and cowardly: *Betraying a friend is a base action.* See synonym study below. 2 fit for an inferior person or thing; menial; unworthy. 3 ARCHAIC. of humble birth or origin. 4 having little comparative value; inferior: *Iron and lead are base metals; gold and silver are precious metals.* 5 debased; counterfeit: *base coin.* [< Old French *bas* < Medieval Latin *bassus* low. Doublet of BASSO.] **—base′ly,** *adv.* **—base′ness,** *n.*

Syn. *adj.* 1 **Base, vile, low** mean morally inferior and comtemptible. **Base** means reduced to a low moral state, without honor or without moral standards, usually by selfishness or cowardliness: *Betraying a friend for a reward is base.* **Vile** means evil and without moral standards or decency: *In the slums of some cities even small children learn vile language.* **Low** means without a sense of decency or of what is honorable: *To steal from the collection plate in church is low.*

base ball (bās′bôl′). *n.* 1 game played with bat and ball between two teams of nine players each, alternately fielding and batting in each of the usually nine innings, on a field with four bases. The team scoring the greater number of runs wins. 2 ball used in this game.

hat, āge, fär; let, ēqual, tėrm;
it, īce; hot, ōpen, ôrder;
oil, out; cup, pu̇t, rüle;
ch, child; ng, long; sh, she;
th, thin; ᴛʜ, then; zh, measure;

ə represents *a* in about, *e* in taken, *i* in pencil, *o* in lemon, *u* in circus.

< = from, derived from, taken from.

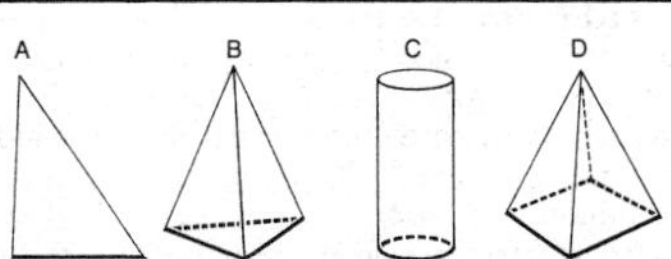

base[1] (def. 13)—The base of figure A is a line; figure B, a triangle; figure C, a circle; figure D, a square.

base board (bās′bôrd′, bās′bōrd′), *n.* 1 line of boards around the interior walls of a room, next to the floor. 2 board forming the base of anything.

base born (bās′bôrn′), *adj.* 1 born of slaves, peasants, or other humble parents. 2 born of a mother who was not married; illegitimate. 3 of base origin or nature.

base hit, a hitting of the baseball by a batter so that he gets at least to first base without the help of a defensive error and without forcing out one of his teammates.

Ba sel (bä′zəl), *n.* city in NW Switzerland, on the Rhine River. 213,000. Also, **Basle.**

base less (bās′lis), *adj.* without foundation; groundless: *a baseless rumor.* **—base′less ly,** *adv.* **—base′less ness,** *n.*

base line, 1 line used as a base. 2 (in baseball) the path connecting one base with the next.

base man (bās′mən), *n., pl.* **-men.** a baseball fielder stationed at or near first, second, or third base.

base ment (bās′mənt), *n.* the lowest story of a building, partly or wholly below ground.

ba sen ji (bə sen′jē), *n.* a small, reddish, terrierlike hunting dog native to Africa, distinguished by its inability to bark. [< Afrikaans]

base runner, (in baseball) player on the team at bat who is on a base or trying to reach a base.

bas es[1] (bā′siz), *n.* pl. of **base[1]**.

ba ses[2] (bā′sēz′), *n.* pl. of **basis.**

bash (bash), *v.t., v.i.* INFORMAL. strike with a smashing blow. —*n.* 1 INFORMAL. a smashing blow. 2 SLANG. a big party or meal. [perhaps < Danish *baske* to beat]

bash ful (bash′fəl), *adj.* 1 uneasy in unaccustomed situations or in the presence of others; easily embarrassed; shy. See **shy** for synonym study. 2 of or like that of a bashful person: *a bashful smile.* [< *bash* (short for *abash*) + *-ful*] **—bash′ful ly,** *adv.* **—bash′ful ness,** *n.*

ba sic (bā′sik), *adj.* 1 of, at, or forming a base; fundamental: *Addition, subtraction, multiplication, and division are the basic processes of arithmetic.* 2 being a basis or starting point: *a basic scale of pay.* 3 (in chemistry) being, having the properties of, or containing a base; alkaline. 4 (of rocks) containing less than about 52 per cent of silica. —*n.* an essential part; fundamental, rule, etc. —**ba′si cal ly,** *adv.*

ba sic i ty (bā sis′ə tē), *n.* quality or condition of being a base.

ba sid i o my cete (bə sid′ē ō mī′sēt′), *n.* any of a large class of fungi that includes smuts, rusts, mushrooms, and puffballs, characterized by the formation of spores on a basidium. [< *basidium* + Greek *mykēs, mykētos* fungus]

ba sid i o my ce tous (bə sid′ē ō mī-sē′təs), *adj.* of or belonging to the basidiomycetes.

ba sid i o spore (bə sid′ē ō spôr, bə sid′-ē ō spōr), *n.* one of the spores produced on a basidium.

ba sid i um (bə sid′ē əm), *n., pl.* **-sid i a** (-sid′ē ə). a small, club-shaped structure on basidiomycetes that produces spores, usually four, at the tips of minute stalks. [< New Latin < Greek *basis* basis]

bas il (baz′əl), *n.* a sweet-smelling plant of the mint family, used in cooking. [< Old French *basile,* ultimately < Greek *basilikon (phyton)* royal (plant)]

bas i lar (bas′ə lər), *adj.* of or at the base, especially of the skull.

bas i lar y (bas′ə ler′ē), *adj.* basilar.

ba sil i ca (bə sil′ə kə), *n.* 1 (in ancient Rome) an oblong hall used as a court of law, consisting of a high main portion separated by columns from side aisles. 2 an early Christian church having an oblong plan, a high central nave separated by columns from aisles on each side, and an apse at the east end. 3 (in the Roman Catholic Church) a title given to some churches, conferring certain rights and privileges. [< Latin < Greek *(stoa) basilikē* royal (portico)]

bas i lisk (bas′ə lisk, baz′ə lisk), *n.* 1 (in ancient and medieval legends) a lizardlike reptile whose breath and look were thought to be fatal. 2 any of several tropical American lizards related to the iguanas, having a crest along its head and back which it can raise or lower. [< Greek *basiliskos* kind of serpent < *basileus* king]

ba sin (bā′sn), *n.* 1 a wide, shallow bowl for holding liquids. 2 amount that a basin can hold. 3 a shallow area containing water: *Part of the harbor is a basin for yachts.* 4 all the land drained by a river and its tributaries: *the Mississippi basin.* [< Old French *bacin* < Popular Latin *baccinum*] —**ba′sin like′,** *adj.*

ba sis (bā′sis), *n., pl.* **-ses.** 1 a fundamental principle or set of principles; foundation. 2 the main or supporting part; base. See **base**[1] for synonym study. 3 the essential part: *The basis of this medicine is an oil.* 4 a starting point. [< Latin < Greek. Doublet of BASE[1].]

bask (bask), *v.i.* 1 expose oneself to the warmth of sunshine, the heat of a fire, etc.; warm oneself pleasantly. 2 feel great pleasure: *bask in the love of one's family.* —*v.t.* warm pleasantly. [Middle English]

bas ket (bas′kit), *n.* 1 container made of twigs, grasses, fibers, strips of wood, etc., woven together. 2 amount that a basket holds. 3 anything like a basket in appearance, shape, or use. 4 structure beneath a balloon for carrying passengers or ballast. 5 net hung from a metal ring, shaped like a basket but open at the bottom, used as a goal in basketball. 6 score made in basketball by tossing the ball through this net. [Middle English] —**bas′ket like′,** *adj.*

bas ket ball (bas′kit bôl′), *n.* 1 game played between two teams of five players each with an inflated leather or rubber ball, which is dribbled, or thrown from player to player. The object of the game is to toss the ball through a basket (def. 5). 2 ball used in this game.

bas ket ful (bas′kit fůl), *n., pl.* **-fuls.** as much as a basket can hold.

Basket Makers, any of several North American Indian cultures of the southwestern United States that preceded the Pueblo.

bas ket ry (bas′kə trē), *n.* 1 art of making baskets. 2 basketwork; baskets.

basket weave, a weave in cloth that looks like the interlaced weave used in making most baskets.

bas ket work (bas′kit wėrk′), *n.* work woven like a basket; wickerwork.

Basle (bäl), *n.* Basel.

bas mitz vah (bäs mits′və), 1 a ceremony held in a Reform or Conservative synagogue when a Jewish girl becomes thirteen years old, corresponding to the bar mitzvah for boys. 2 the girl herself. Also, **bat mitzvah.** [< Hebrew *bath miṣwah,* literally, daughter of the commandment]

ba so phil (bā′sə fil), *n.* cell, especially a white blood cell, that stains readily with a basic dye.

Basque (bask), *n.* 1 member of a people living in the Pyrenees region of northern Spain and southern France, differing in language and origin from other Europeans. 2 the language of this people. —*adj.* of the Basques or their language.

Bas ra (bus′rə, baz′rə), *n.* seaport in SE Iraq, near the Persian Gulf. 313,000.

bas-re lief (bä′ri lēf′, bas′ri lēf′), *n.* carving or sculpture in which the figures stand out only slightly from the background. See **relief** for picture. [< French, literally, low relief]

bass[1] (bās), *n.* 1 the lowest male voice in music. 2 singer with such a voice. 3 part in music for such a voice or for a corresponding instrument. 4 instrument playing such a part. 5 the low tones of an instrument. —*adj.* 1 having a deep, low sound. 2 for the lowest part in music; that can sing such a part. [variant of *base*[2]; influenced by Italian *basso*]

bass[2] (bas), *n., pl.* **bass es** or **bass.** any of various North American freshwater or saltwater fishes with spiny fins, used for food. [Old English *bærs* perch]

bass clef (bās), (in music) a symbol showing that the pitch of the notes on a staff is below middle C; F clef. See **clef** for diagram.

bass drum (bās), a large drum that makes a deep, low tone of no fixed pitch when struck on one or both of its heads.

bas set (bas′it), *n.* a hunting dog with short legs and a long body, like a dachshund, but larger and heavier. [< Middle French, diminutive of *bas* low]

Basse-Terre (bäs′ter′), *n.* capital of Guadeloupe. 16,000.

bass horn (bās), tuba.

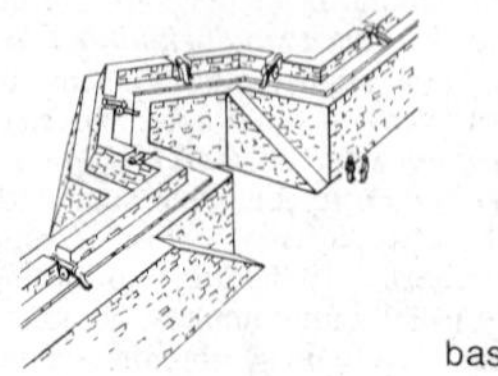

bastion (def. 1)

bas si net (bas′n et′, bas′n et), *n.* a baby's basketlike cradle, usually with a hood over one end. [< French, diminutive of *bassin* basin]

bass ist (bā′sist), *n.* person who plays a bass instrument.

bas so (bas′ō; *Italian* bäs′sō), *n., pl.* **bas-sos;** ITALIAN **bas si** (bäs′sē). 1 singer with a bass voice. 2 the bass part. [< Italian < Medieval Latin *bassus* low. Doublet of BASE[2].]

bas soon (bə sün′), *n.* a deep-toned wind instrument with a doubled wooden body and a curved metal pipe to which a double reed is attached. [< French *basson* < Italian *bassone* < *basso* basso]

bassoon

bas soon ist (bə sü′nist), *n.* person who plays a bassoon.

bass viol (bās), double bass.

bass wood (bas′wůd′), *n.* 1 the American linden tree. 2 its wood.

bast (bast), *n.* 1 the inner layer of the bark of trees that contains cells for carrying sap; phloem. 2 the tough fiber in this inner layer used in making rope, matting, etc. [Old English *bæst*]

bas tard (bas′tərd), *n.* 1 child whose parents are not legally married to each other; illegitimate child. 2 anything inferior or not genuine, especially anything of bad or spurious origin. 3 SLANG. an especially unpleasant, disliked person. —*adj.* 1 illegitimate. 2 inferior; not genuine. 3 irregular or unusual in form, style, etc. [< Old French]

bas tard ly (bas′tərd lē), *adj.* like a bastard; base; debased.

bas tard y (bas′tər dē), *n.* illegitimacy.

baste[1] (bāst) *v.t.,* **bast ed, bast ing.** moisten (meat, fowl, etc.) while roasting by dripping or pouring melted fat, butter, etc., on it. [origin unknown] —**bast′er,** *n.*

baste[2] (bāst), *v.t.,* **bast ed, bast ing.** sew with long, loose stitches to hold the cloth until the final sewing. [< Middle French *bastir*] —**bast′er,** *n.*

baste[3] (bāst), *v.t.,* **bast ed, bast ing.** beat soundly; thrash. [< Scandinavian (Old Icelandic) *beysta*]

Bas tille (ba stēl′), *n.* an old fort in Paris used as a prison, especially for political offenders. A mob captured it on July 14, 1789, at the beginning of the French Revolution, and later destroyed it.

Bastille Day, July 14, a French national holiday commemorating the capture of the Bastille.

bas ti na do (bas′tə nā′dō), *n., pl.* **-does,** *v.* —*n.* 1 a beating with a stick, especially on the soles of the feet. 2 stick; cudgel. —*v.t.* beat or flog with a stick, especially on the soles of the feet. [< Spanish *bastonada* < *bastón* stick < Late Latin *bastum*]

bast ings (bā′stingz), *n.pl.* 1 long, loose stitches to hold cloth in place until the final sewing. 2 the threads used for these.

bas tion (bas′chən, bas′tē ən), *n.* 1 a projecting part of a fortification made so that the defenders can fire at attackers from several angles. 2 any strongly fortified or defended place. [< Middle French < *bastille* fort, building < *bastir* to build]

Ba su to land (bə sü′tō land′), *n.* former name of **Lesotho.**

bat[1] (bat), *n., v.,* **bat ted, bat ting.** *—n.* 1 a stout wooden stick or club, used to hit the ball in baseball, cricket, etc. 2 act of batting. 3 a turn at batting: *Who goes to bat first?* 4 a stroke; blow. 5 SLANG. a wild, gay time; spree. 6 a batting. 7 **at bat,** in position to bat; having a turn at batting. 8 **go to bat for,** INFORMAL. support the cause of. 9 **right off the bat,** INFORMAL. without hesitation; immediately. *—v.i.* 1 strike, or strike at, the ball with a bat. 2 be at bat; take one's turn as a batter. *—v.t.* hit with a bat; hit. [Old English *batt* cudgel]

bat[2] (bat), *n.* 1 any of a large order of nocturnal flying mammals having a mouselike body and membranous wings supported by the long, slim bones of the forelimbs; chiropter. Most bats are insect-eating but some live on fruit and a few suck the blood of other mammals. 2 **blind as a bat,** completely blind. [alteration of Middle English *bakke,* perhaps < Scandinavian] **—bat′like′,** *adj.*

bat[3] (bat), *v.t.,* **bat ted, bat ting.** INFORMAL. wink, especially from surprise or emotion: *The ball nearly hit her, but she didn't bat an eye.* [< Old French *batre* to beat < Latin *battuere*]

Ba taan (bə tan′, bə tän′), *n.* peninsula near Manila in the Philippines, where United States and Philippine troops surrendered to the Japanese in 1942.

Ba ta vi a (bə tā′vē ə), *n.* former name of **Djakarta.**

batch (bach), *n.* 1 quantity of bread, cookies, etc., made at one baking. 2 quantity of anything made as one lot or set: *a batch of candy.* 3 number of persons or things put or treated together: *a batch of fish.* [Middle English *bacche* < Old English *bacan* bake]

bate (bāt), *v.t.,* **bat ed, bat ing.** 1 **with bated breath,** holding the breath in great fear, wonder, interest, etc.: *They listened with bated breath to the story.* 2 deduct; lessen. short for *abate*]

ba teau (ba tō′), *n., pl.* **-teaux** (-tōz′). a light river boat with a flat bottom and tapering ends, used in Canada and Louisiana. [< French]

bath (bath), *n., pl.* **baths** (baᴛʜz, baths). 1 a washing of the body or exposure of it to the action of water for cleansing, etc. 2 water for a bath: *Your bath is ready.* 3 tub for bathing; bathtub. 4 room for bathing; bathroom. 5 a building containing facilities for bathing: *a public bath.* 6 Often, **baths,** *pl.* **a** (in ancient times, especially in Rome) an elaborate establishment used for bathing and for various forms of exercise and recreation. **b** place or resort with baths for medical treatment. 7 liquid in which something is washed or dipped, as the solution in which photographic film or prints are immersed. 8 container holding the liquid. [Old English *bæth*] **—bath′less,** *adj.*

Bath (bath), *n.* city in SW England, once famous as a health resort. 85,000.

bathe (bāᴛʜ), *v.,* **bathed, bath ing.** *—v.i.* 1 take a bath. 2 go swimming; go into a river, lake, ocean, etc., for pleasure or to get cool. *—v.t.* 1 give a bath to. 2 apply water to; wash or moisten with any liquid; wet. 3 cover or surround; suffuse: *The valley was bathed in sunlight.* [Old English *bathian*] **—bath′er,** *n.*

ba thet ic (bə thet′ik), *adj.* characterized by bathos. **—ba thet′i cal ly,** *adv.*

bath house (bath′hous′), *n., pl.* **-hous es** (-hou′ziz). 1 house or building fitted out for bathing. 2 building containing one or more dressing rooms for swimmers.

bathing suit, garment worn for swimming.

bath o lith (bath′ə lith), *n.* a great mass of granite or other igneous rock intruded below the surface, commonly along the axis of a mountain range, and sometimes exposed by erosion. See **volcano** for diagram.

ba thos (bā′thos), *n.* 1 ludicrous descent from the elevated to the commonplace in speech or writing; anticlimax. EXAMPLE: The exile came back to his home, crippled, unfriended, and hatless. 2 strained or insincere pathos. [< Greek, depth]

bath robe (bath′rōb′), *n.* a long, loose garment worn to and from a bath or when resting or lounging.

bath room (bath′rüm′, bath′ru̇m′), *n.* 1 room fitted out for taking baths. 2 toilet.

bath tub (bath′tub′), *n.* tub to bathe in, especially one permanently fixed in a bathroom.

Bath urst (bath′ėrst′), *n.* capital of the Gambia, in the W part. 37,000.

bath y scaph or **bath y scaphe** (bath′ə skaf), *n.* apparatus for deep-sea exploration consisting of a spherical steel chamber suspended from a large, cigar-shaped float. [< Greek *bathys* deep + *skaphē* bowl, tub]

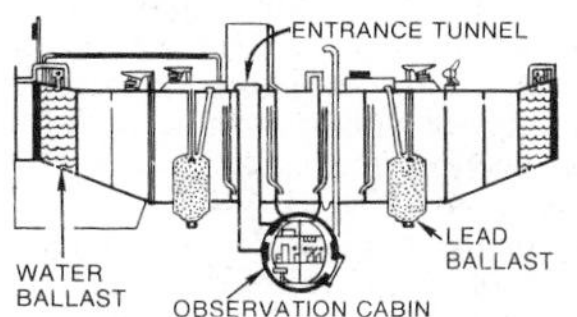

bathyscaph

bath y sphere (bath′ə sfir), *n.* a spherical watertight diving chamber with observation windows, lowered by cables from a ship, formerly used to study deep-sea life.

ba tik (bə tēk′, bat′ik), *n.* 1 method of executing designs on textiles by covering the material with wax in a pattern, dyeing the parts left exposed, and then removing the wax. 2 fabric dyed in this way. 3 design formed in this way. *—adj.* 1 made by or of batik. 2 like batik; brightly or gaily colored. [< Javanese *mbatik*]

ba tiste (bə tēst′), *n.* a fine, thin cloth made of cotton, rayon, or wool. [< French]

bat man (bat′mən), *n., pl.* **-men.** BRITISH. an enlisted man assigned to act as an officer's orderly.

bat mitz vah (bät mits va′), bas mitzvah.

ba ton (ba ton′), *n.* 1 a light stick or wand used by the leader of an orchestra, chorus, or band to indicate the beat and direct the performance. 2 staff or stick carried as a symbol of office or authority. 3 stick passed from runner to runner in a relay race. 4 a light, hollow, metal rod twirled by a drum major or majorette as a showy display. [< Middle French, ultimately from Late Latin *bastum* stick]

Bat on Rouge (bat′n rüzh′), capital of Louisiana, in the SE part, on the Mississippi. 166,000.

ba tra chi an (bə trā′kē ən), *adj.* 1 of or having to do with frogs, toads, and other tailless amphibians. 2 like frogs and toads.

hat, āge, fär; let, ēqual, tėrm;
it, īce; hot, ōpen, ôrder;
oil, out; cup, pu̇t, rüle;
ch, child; ng, long; sh, she;
th, thin; ᴛʜ, then; zh, measure;

ə represents *a* in about, *e* in taken, *i* in pencil, *o* in lemon, *u* in circus.

< = from, derived from, taken from.

—n. a tailless amphibian. [< Greek *batrachos* frog]

bats man (bats′mən), *n., pl.* **-men.** batter (in cricket, baseball, etc.).

bat tal ion (bə tal′yən), *n.* 1 a military unit of infantry, etc., consisting of at least two companies, batteries, etc., and a headquarters company, usually forming part of a regiment, and commanded by a major or a lieutenant colonel. 2 a large division of an army in battle array. 3 **battalions,** *pl.* armies; military forces. 4 any large group of people thought of as having a common purpose. [< Middle French *bataillon,* ultimately < Late Latin *batallia.* See BATTLE.]

bat ten[1] (bat′n), *n.* 1 strip of wood nailed across parallel boards to strengthen them. 2 board used for flooring. 3 a narrow strip of wood used on shipboard to fasten tarpaulins over hatchways, keep a sail flat, etc. *—v.t.* fasten down or strengthen with battens. [< Middle French *batant,* from *batre* to beat]

bat ten[2] (bat′n), *v.i.* 1 grow fat; thrive. 2 feed greedily. *—v.t.* fatten up; fatten. [< Scandinavian (Old Icelandic) *batna* improve]

bat ter[1] (bat′ər), *v.t.* strike with repeated blows; beat so as to bruise, break, or get out of shape; pound: *Violent storms battered the coast for days.* *—v.i.* inflict repeated blows; pound. [< Old French *batre* to beat. See BAT[3].]

bat ter[2] (bat′ər), *n.* a semiliquid mixture of flour, milk, eggs, etc., beaten together, that thickens when cooked. A batter may always be poured. [< Old French *bature* a beating < *batre* to beat]

bat ter[3] (bat′ər), *n.* player whose turn it is to bat in baseball, cricket, etc.

bat tered (bat′ərd), *adj.* beaten out of shape, worn, or damaged by hard use: *a battered old bookcase.*

battering ram, 1 a heavy beam of wood with a mass of metal at the striking end, used in ancient and medieval warfare for battering down walls, gates, etc. 2 anything resembling this in purpose or effect.

bat ter y (bat′ər ē), *n., pl.* **-ter ies.** 1 a single electric cell: *a flashlight battery.* 2 set of two or more electric cells connected together for the production of electric current: *a car battery.* 3 set of similar pieces of equipment, such as mounted guns, searchlights, mortars, etc., used as a unit. 4 any set of similar or connected things: *a battery of tests.* 5 a military unit of artillery, usually commanded by a captain. A battery corresponds to a company or troop in other branches of the army. 6 the armament, or one part of it, of a warship. 7 (in baseball) the pitcher and catcher together. 8 (in law) the unlawful beating of another person or any threatening touch to his clothes or body.

bat ting (bat′ing), *n.* 1 action or manner of using or striking with a bat. 2 cotton or wool pressed into thin layers, used to line comforters, quilts, etc.

bat tle (bat′l), *n., v.,* **-tled, -tling.** —*n.* 1 a hostile engagement or encounter between opposing armies, air forces, or navies; combat; fight. See synonym study below. 2 a fight between two persons; single combat; duel. 3 actual hostilities between nations; fighting or warfare. 4 any struggle for victory; conflict; contest: *a battle of words.* 5 **join battle,** begin to fight. —*v.i.* 1 take part in battle; fight. 2 strive for victory; struggle contend. [< Old French *bataille* < Late Latin *battalia* < Latin *battuere* to beat] **—bat′tler,** *n.*

Syn. *n.* 1 **Battle, action, engagement** mean a fight between armed forces. **Battle** applies to a fight between large forces, such as armies or navies, lasting some time: *The battle for Guadalcanal lasted six months.* **Action** applies to a lively offensive or defensive part of a battle or campaign: *The Normandy landing was a daring action.* **Engagement** emphasizes the meeting of forces, large or small, in combat: *The engagement in Leyte Gulf weakened the Japanese Navy.*

bat tle-ax or **bat tle-axe** (bat′l aks′), *n.* 1 ax with a broad blade, used in medieval times as a weapon in battle. 2 SLANG. a disagreeable and obstinate woman.

battle cruiser, a large, fast warship, with relatively light armor for its size, intended to combine the speed of a cruiser with the firepower of a battleship.

battle cry, 1 the shout of soldiers in battle. 2 motto or slogan in any contest.

bat tle dore (bat′l dôr, bat′l dōr), *n.* a small racket used to hit a shuttlecock back and forth. [Middle English *batyldoure,* ultimately from Latin *battuere* to beat]

bat tle field (bat′l fēld′), *n.* place where a battle is fought or has been fought.

bat tle front (bat′l frunt′), *n.* place where the fighting between armies takes place; front.

bat tle ground (bat′l ground′), *n.* battlefield.

battle group, U.S. unit of an army division, somewhat smaller than a regiment.

bat tle ment (bat′l mənt), *n.* 1 a low wall for defense at the top of a tower or wall, with indentations and and loopholes through which soldiers could shoot. 2 wall built like this for ornament.

battlement (def. 1)

bat tle ment ed (bat′l men′tid), *adj.* having battlements.

battle royal, *pl.* **battles royal.** 1 fight in which several take part; riot. 2 a long, hard fight.

bat tle ship (bat′l ship′), *n.* a large warship having the heaviest armor and the greatest conventional firepower. The last battleships were built during World War II.

bat ty (bat′ē), *adj.,* **-ti er, -ti est.** U.S. SLANG. crazy. [< *bat*^{2}]

bat wing (bat′wing′), *adj.* resembling the wing or wings of a bat: *batwing sleeves.*

bau ble (bô′bəl), *n.* 1 a showy trifle of little value; trinket. 2 a jester's staff. [< Old French *babel, baubel* toy]

Bau de laire (bōd ler′, bōd lar′), *n.* **Pierre Charles,** 1821-1867, French poet and critic.

Bau douin I (bō dwaN′), born 1930, king of Belgium since 1951.

baulk (bôk), *v.i., v.t., n.* balk.

Bau mé (bō mā′), *adj.* of or according to a scale used with a hydrometer to measure the specific gravity of liquids. [< Antoine *Baumé,* 1728-1804, French chemist]

baux ite (bôk′sīt, bō′zīt), *n.* a claylike mineral from which aluminum is obtained, consisting chiefly of hydrated aluminum oxide and some iron and silica. [< French < Les *Baux,* commune in southern France]

Ba var i a (bə ver′ē ə, bə var′ē ə), *n.* state in S West Germany. Its capital is Munich. **—Ba var′i an,** *adj., n.*

bawd (bôd), *n.* 1 person who keeps a brothel. 2 prostitute. [< Old French *baud* lively]

bawd ry (bô′drē), *n.* obscenity; lewdness.

bawd y (bô′dē), *adj.,* **bawd i er, bawd i est.** not decent; lewd; obscene. **—bawd′i ly,** *adv.* **—bawd′i ness,** *n.*

bawl (bôl), *v.i.* 1 shout at the top of one's voice; cry loudly and roughly; bellow: *a lost calf bawling for its mother.* 2 weep loudly. —*v.t.* 1 utter with bawling; shout at the top of one's voice: *The peddler bawled his wares in the street.* 2 **bawl out,** U.S. INFORMAL. scold loudly; reprimand. —*n.* 1 a shout at the top of one's voice. 2 a loud crying. [probably < Medieval Latin *baulare* to bark] **—bawl′er,** *n.*

bay^{1} (bā), *n.* part of a sea or lake extending into the land, having a wide opening. A bay is usually smaller than a gulf and larger than a cove. [< Old French *baie* < Late Latin *baia*]

bay^{2} (bā), *n.* 1 a deep, prolonged barking of a dog when pursuing or attacking. 2 position of a hunted animal that turns to face its pursuers when further flight is impossible: *The stag stood at bay on the edge of the cliff.* 3 a stand by a person forced to face a foe, difficulty, persecution, etc. 4 position of an enemy or pursuers thus faced or kept off: *The stag held the hounds at bay.* 5 **bring to bay,** put in a position from which escape is impossible. —*v.i.* bark with long, deep sounds. —*v.t.* 1 bark at; assail with barking. 2 utter or express by baying. 3 bring to bay. [< Old French *abai* a barking]

bay^{3} (bā), *n.* 1 the laurel of southern Europe, the leaves of which are used in cooking. 2 **bays,** *pl.* **a** laurel wreath worn by poets or victors. **b** honor; renown; fame. [< Old French *baie* berry, seed < Latin *baca*]

bay^{4} (bā), *adj.* reddish-brown: *a bay horse.* —*n.* 1 a reddish-brown horse with black mane and tail. 2 a reddish brown. [< Old French *bai* < Latin *badius*]

bay^{5} (bā), *n.* 1 a main space or division of a wall or building between columns, pillars, buttresses, etc. 2 bay window. 3 place in a barn for storing hay or grain. 4 compartment in an airplane, especially one for carrying bombs. 5 sick bay. [< Old French *baée* opening < *baer* to gape]

bay ber ry (bā′ber′ē, bā′bər ē), *n., pl.* **-ries.** 1 a North American shrub of the same genus as the wax myrtle, with clusters of grayish-white berries coated with wax. Candles made from the wax of the berries burn with a pleasant fragrance. 2 one of the berries. 3 a West Indian tree whose leaves contain an oil used in bay rum.

bay leaf, leaf of the laurel or bay of southern Europe, used after drying for flavoring soups, stews, etc.

bay o net (bā′ə nit, bā′ə net′), *n., v.,* **net ed, -net ing** or **-net ted, -net ting.** —*n.* a heavy, daggerlike blade for piercing or stabbing, made to be attached to the muzzle of a rifle, etc. —*v.t.* pierce or stab with a bayonet. —*v.i.* use a bayonet. [< French *baïonnette,* probably < *Bayonne,* city in southwestern France]

bay ou (bī′ü), *n.* U.S. a sluggish, marshy inlet or outlet of a lake, river, or gulf in the south central United States. [< Louisiana French < Choctaw *bayuk* creek]

Bay reuth (bī roit′), *n.* city in S West Germany, noted for its Wagnerian music festivals. 63,000.

bay rum, a fragrant liquid used as a soothing lotion for the skin, made of oil from leaves of the West Indian bayberry.

bay window, window or set of windows projecting from the exterior wall of a building to form an alcove or small space in a room.

bay window

ba zaar or **ba zar** (bə zär′), *n.* 1 (in various countries of Asia) a marketplace consisting of a street or streets full of small shops and booths. 2 place for the sale of many kinds of goods. 3 sale of articles contributed by various people, held for some charity or other special purpose. [< Persian *bāzār*]

ba zoo ka (bə zü′kə), *n.,* a portable rocket launcher used against tanks. [< name of a trombonelike instrument invented and named by Bob Burns, 1896-1956, American comedian]

BB (bē′bē′), *n.* 1 a standard size of shot, approximately .18 of an inch in diameter. 2 shot of this size, used especially in an air rifle.

BBC, British Broadcasting Corporation.

BB gun, air rifle.

bbl., *pl.* **bbls.** barrel.

B.C., 1 before Christ; before the birth of Christ. 350 B.C. is 100 years earlier than 250 B.C. 2 British Columbia.

B complex, vitamin B complex.

bd., 1 board. 2 bond. 3 bound.

B.D., Bachelor of Divinity.

bd. ft., board foot or board feet.

bdl., *pl.* **bdls.** bundle.

be (bē), *v.i., present indicative sing.* **am, are, is,** *pl.* **are;** *past indicative sing.* **was, were, was,** *pl.* **were;** *pp.* **been;** *ppr.* **be ing.** 1 have reality; exist; live: *Veterans of the Revolutionary War are no more.* 2 take place; happen: *The circus was last month.* 3 remain; continue: *She will be here all year.* 4 to equal; represent: *Let "x" be the unknown quantity.* 5 *Be* is used as a linking verb between a subject and a predicate. *He was the secretary* (predicate noun). *She is sick* (predicate adjective). 6 *Be* is used as an

hat, āge, fär; let, ēqual, tėrm;
it, īce; hot, ōpen, ôrder;
oil, out; cup, pu̇t, rüle;
ch, child; ng, long; sh, she;
th, thin; ᴛʜ, then; zh, measure;

ə represents *a* in about, *e* in taken, *i* in pencil, *o* in lemon, *u* in circus.

< = from, derived from, taken from.

auxiliary verb with: **a** the present participle of another verb to form the progressive tense. *I am asking. He was asking. You will be asking.* **b** the past participle of another verb to form the passive voice. *I am asked. You will be asked. He was asked.* 7 *Be* is used to express future time, duty, intention, and possibility. *She is to arrive there at nine. No shelter was to be seen.* 8 *Be* is used with the past participles of some verbs to form the perfect tense. *The sun is set.* [Old English *bēon*]

be-, *prefix.* 1 thoroughly; all around: *Bespatter = spatter thoroughly.* 2 make; cause to seem: *Belittle = cause to seem little.* 3 provide with: *Bespangle = provide with spangles.* 4 at; on; to; for; about; against: *Bewail = wail about.* [Old English *be-*, unstressed form of *bī* by]

Be, beryllium.

beach (bēch), *n.,* 1 an almost flat, sandy or stony part of the seashore, over which water washes when high; strand. 2 the shore of a lake or large river. *—v.t., v.i.* run or haul (a boat) up on the beach. [origin uncertain] **—beach′less,** *adj.*

beach buggy, dune buggy.

beach comb er (bēch′kō′mər), *n.* 1 a white man living as a vagrant or loafer on the islands of the Pacific, supporting himself by various, often disreputable, means. 2 any vagrant or loafer living on a waterfront, coast, etc. 3 U.S. a long wave rolling in from the ocean upon the beach; breaker; comber.

beach flea, a small crustacean found on saltwater beaches that leaps like a flea; sand flea.

beach head (bēch′hed′), *n.* 1 the first position capable of military use established by an amphibious force on an enemy shore. 2 any preliminary foothold.

beach wagon, U.S. station wagon.

bea con (bē′kən), *n.* 1 fire or light used as a signal to guide or warn. 2 an apparatus that sends out radio beams or light to guide aircraft, ships, etc., through fogs, storms, etc. 3 a tall tower for a signal; lighthouse. 4 any thing or person that is a guiding or warning signal. *—v.t.* 1 give light to; guide; warn. 2 supply with beacons. *—v.i.* 1 shine brightly. 2 serve as a beacon. [Old English *bēacen*]

Bea cons field (bē′kənz fēld′), *n.* **Earl of.** See **Disraeli.**

bead (bēd), *n.* 1 a small ball or bit of glass, metal, etc., with a hole through it, so that it can be strung on a thread with others like it to form a necklace, bracelet, etc., or sewn upon various fabrics as ornaments. 2 **beads,** *pl.* **a** string of beads for the neck. **b** rosary. 3 a beadlike drop of liquid. 4 a bubble in sparkling wines or the foam on beer, ale, etc. 5 piece of metal that forms the front sight of a gun. 6 a narrow, semicircular molding; beading. 7 **draw a bead on,** aim; take aim at. 8 **say one's beads, tell one's beads,** or **count one's beads,** say prayers, using a rosary. *—v.t.* put beads on; ornament with beads. *—v.i.* form a bead or beads. [Old English *bed* prayer, rosary bead] **—bead′like′,** *adj.*

bead ed (bē′did), *adj.* 1 trimmed with beads. 2 formed into beads.

bead ing (bē′ding), *n.* 1 dress fabric, trimming, etc., ornamented with or consisting of beads; beadwork. 2 a narrow lace or openwork trimming. 3 pattern or edge on woodwork, silver, etc., made of small beads. 4 a narrow, semicircular molding.

bea dle (bē′dl), *n.* a minor parish officer in the Church of England whose duties include keeping order and waiting on the clergy. [< Old French *bedel*]

beads man (bēdz′mən), *n., pl.* **-men.** ARCHAIC. person who says prayers for others, especially one hired to do so.

bead work (bēd′wėrk′), *n.* beading.

bead y (bē′dē), *adj.,* **bead i er, bead i est.** 1 small, round, and glittering: *beady eyes.* 2 trimmed with beads. 3 full of bubbles; frothy.

bea gle (bē′gəl), *n.* a small, smooth-haired dog with short legs and drooping ears, bred for hunting. [Middle English *begle*]

beak (bēk), *n.* 1 a bird's bill, especially one that is strong and hooked and useful in striking or tearing. Eagles, hawks, and parrots have beaks. 2 a similar, often horny, part in other animals. Turtles and octopuses have beaks. 3 SLANG. the human nose, especially when somewhat pointed or hooked. 4 a beak-shaped point or projection; a peak, point, spout, etc. 5 a pointed metal or metal-sheathed projection at the prow of an ancient warship for piercing the sides of an enemy's ship. [< Old French *bec* < Latin *beccum*] **—beak′like′,** *adj.*

beaked (bēkt), *adj.* 1 having a beak. 2 shaped like a beak; hooked.

beak er (bē′kər), *n.* 1 a large cup or drinking glass with a wide mouth. 2 contents of a beaker. 3 a thin, flat-bottomed glass or metal cup with no handle and a small lip for pouring, used in laboratories. [< Scandinavian (Old Icelandic) *bikarr*]

beam (bēm), *n.* 1 a large, long piece of timber, ready for use in building. 2 a similar piece of metal, stone, reinforced concrete, etc. 3 any of the main horizontal supports of a building or ship. 4 part of a plow by which it is pulled. 5 the crosswise bar of a balance, from the ends of which the scales or pans are suspended. 6 the balance itself. 7 ray or rays of light. See synonym study below. 8 a bright look or smile. 9 a radio signal directed in a straight line, used to guide aircraft, ships, etc. 10 side of a ship, or the sideward direction at right angles to the keel, with reference to wind, sea, etc. The weather beam is the side toward the wind. 11 the widest part of a ship. 12 **on the beam, a** (of a ship) at right angles to the keel. **b** (of an aircraft) on the right course, as indicated by the directing radio signals. **c** SLANG. just right.
—v.t. 1 throw out or radiate (beams or rays of light); emit in rays. 2 direct (a broadcast): *beam programs at Russia.* *—v.i.* 1 shine radiantly. 2 look or smile brightly.
[Old English *bēam* tree, piece of wood, ray of light]

Syn. *n.* 7 **Beam, ray** mean a line of light. **Beam** applies to a shaft, long and with some width, coming from something that gives out light: *The beam from the flashlight showed a kitten.* **Ray** applies to a thin line of light, usually thought of as radiating, or coming out like the spokes of a wheel, from something bright: *There was not a ray of moonlight in the forest.*

beam ing (bē′ming), *adj.* 1 shining; bright. 2 cheerful. **—beam′ing ly,** *adv.*

bean (bēn), *n.* 1 a smooth, somewhat flat seed used as a vegetable. Lima beans, kidney beans, and navy beans are three kinds of beans. 2 the long pod containing such seeds. In an immature stage, the green or yellow pods of some varieties, together with the seeds, are also used as a vegetable. 3 any of several plants of the pea family that beans grow on. 4 any of various seeds of other plants, shaped somewhat like a bean: *coffee beans.* 5 SLANG. head. 6 **beans,** *pl.* INFORMAL. **a** the smallest amount. **b** something of little value. 7 **spill the beans,** INFORMAL. reveal a secret; confess. *—v.t.* SLANG. hit (someone) on the head, especially with a thrown object. [Old English *bēan*] **—bean′like′,** *adj.*

bean bag (bēn′bag′), *n.* a small bag partly filled with dried beans, used to toss back and forth in certain games.

bean ie (bē′nē), *n.* a small skullcap, worn especially by schoolboys.

bean pole (bēn′pōl′), *n.* 1 pole stuck in the ground for bean vines to climb on as they grow. 2 SLANG. a tall, thin person.

bean stalk (bēn′stôk′), *n.* stem of a bean plant.

bear[1] (ber, bar), *v.,* **bore** or (ARCHAIC) **bare, borne** or **born, bear ing.** *—v.t.* 1 take from one place to another; carry: *A voice was borne upon the wind.* 2 hold up; support: *That board is too thin to bear your weight.* 3 put up with; abide: *She can't bear the noise.* 4 undergo; experience: *He cannot bear any more pain.* See synonym study below. 5 bring forth; produce; yield: *This tree bears fine apples.* 6 give birth to; have (offspring): *bear a child. She was born on June 4.* 7 behave; conduct: *He bore himself with great dignity.* 8 bring forward; give: *A person who saw an accident can bear witness to what happened.* 9 hold in mind; hold: *bear a grudge, bear affection.* 10 have as an identification or characteristic: *He bears the name of John, the title of earl, and a reputation for learning.* 11 ARCHAIC. have as a duty, right, privilege, etc.: *The king bears sway over the empire.* 12 take on oneself as a duty: *bear the cost, bear the responsibility.* 13 allow; permit: *The accident bears two explanations.* *—v.i.* 1 bring forth fruit, etc.: *The tree is too young to bear.* 2 press; push: *Don't bear so hard on the lever.* 3 move; go: *The ship bore north.* 4 lie; be situated: *The land bore due north of the ship.*

bear down or **bear down on, a** put pressure on; press down: *Don't bear down so hard on your pencil.* **b** put all one's efforts on; try hard: *I bore down on my homework and got it done on time.* **c** move toward; approach.

bear on, have an effect on; have something to do with: *Your story does not bear on the question.*

bear out, confirm; prove.

bear up, keep one's courage; not lose hope or faith.

bear with, put up with; be patient with.

[Old English *beran*]

Syn. *v.t.* 4 **Bear, endure, stand** mean to undergo something hard to take. **Bear,** the general word, suggests only being able to hold up: *He is bearing his grief very well.*

Endure means to bear hardship or misfortune for a long time without giving in: *The pioneers endured many hardships in settling the West.* **Stand** is the informal word used interchangeably with *bear,* but it suggests bearing stubbornly and bravely: *He can stand more pain than anyone else I know.* ➔ See **borne** for usage note.

bear[2] (ber, bar), *n.* 1 any of a family of large, heavy, carnivorous or omnivorous mammals with thick, coarse fur, flat feet, and a very short tail, as the brown bear, grizzly bear, black bear, and polar bear; bruin. 2 a gruff or surly person. 3 speculator who sells short, hoping to lower prices in the stock market, etc., in order to buy cheap. [Old English *bera*] **—bear′ like′,** *adj.*

bear a ble (ber′ə bəl, bar′ə bəl), *adj.* that can be borne; endurable. **—bear′ a ble ness,** *n.* **—bear′a bly,** *adv.*

bear bait ing (ber′bā′ting, bar′bā′ting), *n.* sport of setting dogs to fight a chained bear, now illegal.

bear ber ry (ber′ber′ē, ber′bər ē; bar′ber′ē, bar′bər ē), *n., pl.* **-ries.** 1 a trailing evergreen shrub of the heath family, having small bright-red berries and astringent leaves. 2 a similar shrub having black berries. 3 kind of holly growing in the southern United States.

beard (bird), *n.* 1 hair growing on a man's face, now usually excluding the upper lip. 2 something resembling or suggesting this, as the chin tuft of a goat, the stiff hairs around the beak of a bird, and the hairs on the heads of plants like oats, barley, and wheat. *—v.t.* oppose openly and boldly; defy. [Old English] **—beard′like′,** *adj.*

Beard (bird), *n.* **Daniel Carter,** 1850-1941, American naturalist who founded the Boy Scouts of America in 1910.

beard ed (bir′did), *adj.* having a beard.

beard less (bird′lis), *adj.* 1 having no beard. 2 young or immature; youthful. **—beard′less ness,** *n.*

bear er (ber′ər, bar′ər), *n.* 1 person or thing that carries or brings. 2 person who holds or presents a check, draft, or note for payment. 3 tree or plant that produces fruit or flowers.

bear ing (ber′ing, bar′ing), *n.* 1 way of standing, sitting, walking, or behaving; manner. See synonym study below. 2 connection in thought or meaning; reference; relation: *Your question has no bearing on the problem.* 3 **bearings,** *pl.* position in relation to other things; direction: *Having no compass, we got our bearings from the stars.* 4 part of a machine on or in which a shaft, journal, pivot, pin, etc., turns or slides. A bearing serves to support the moving part and to reduce friction by turning with the motion. See **ball bearing** for diagram. 5 act, power, or time of producing or bringing forth: *a tree past bearing.* 6 that which is produced; fruit; crop. 7 power of abiding; endurance. 8 a single device in a coat of arms.

Syn. 1 **Bearing, carriage** mean manner of carrying oneself. **Bearing** applies to a person's manner of managing his whole body, including his gestures, mannerisms, posture, the way he holds his head, and the way he walks and sits: *the regal bearing of the king.* **Carriage** applies only to a person's way of holding his head and body when he stands and walks: *He was thin and tall, with an awkward, slouching carriage.*

bear ish (ber′ish, bar′ish), *adj.* 1 like a bear in manner or temper; rough or surly. 2 aiming at or tending to lower prices in the stock market, etc. **—bear′ish ly,** *adv.* **—bear′ish ness,** *n.*

bear skin (ber′skin′, bar′skin′), *n.* 1 the skin of a bear. 2 rug, blanket, or the like made from this. 3 a tall, black fur cap worn by some soldiers and drum majors, especially in the British army.

beast (bēst), *n.* 1 any four-footed animal, as distinguished from birds, reptiles, fishes, etc., as well as from man. See **animal** for synonym study. 2 any animal except man. 3 a domesticated animal, as a horse or cow. 4 a coarse, dirty, or brutal person. [< Old French < Latin *bestiam*] **—beast′like′,** *adj.*

beast ly (bēst′lē), *adj.,* **-li er, -li est,** *adv.* *—adj.* 1 like a beast. 2 coarse, dirty, or brutal; vile. 3 INFORMAL. unpleasant: *a beastly headache.* *—adv.* INFORMAL. very; unpleasantly. **—beast′li ness,** *n.*

beast of burden, animal used for carrying or pulling heavy loads.

beast of prey, animal that kills other animals for food.

beat (bēt), *v.,* **beat, beat en** or **beat, beat ing,** *n., adj.* *—v.t.* 1 strike again and again; whip; thrash: *The rider beat his horse.* See synonym study below. 2 dash or strike against, as water or wind. 3 get the better of; defeat; overcome: *Their team beat ours by a huge score.* 4 INFORMAL. baffle: *This problem beats me.* 5 INFORMAL. cheat; swindle. 6 make flat; shape with a hammer; forge: *beat gold into gold leaf.* 7 make flat by much walking; tread (a path). 8 mix by stirring or striking with a fork, spoon, or other utensil: *beat eggs.* 9 move up and down; flap: *The bird beat its wings.* 10 mark (time) with drumsticks or by tapping with hands or feet. 11 sound (a signal) on a drum: *beat a tattoo.* 12 show (a unit of time or accent in music) by a stroke of the hand, etc. 13 go through in a hunt or search: *They beat the woods in search of the lost child.* 14 outdo; surpass: *Nothing can beat sailing as a sport.* *—v.i.* 1 strike repeatedly; pound. 2 pulsate; throb: *Her heart beats fast with joy.* 3 make a sound by being struck: *The drums beat loudly.* 4 move against the wind by a zigzag course: *The sailboat beat along the coast.* 5 INFORMAL. win: *I hope you'll beat.*

beat about, search around; try to discover something.

beat back, force to retreat; push back.

beat down, INFORMAL. force to set a lower price.

beat it, U.S. SLANG. go away.

beat off, drive away by blows: *He beat off the savage dog.*

beat up, SLANG. thrash soundly.

—n. 1 stroke or blow made again and again: *the beat of waves on a beach.* 2 pulsation; throb: *the beat of the heart.* 3 unit of time or accent in music: *three beats to a measure.* 4 stroke of the hand, baton, etc., showing a musical beat. 5 a regular round or route taken by a policeman or watchman. 6 **off one's beat,** **a** not at one's regular work. **b** not in one's sphere of knowledge. 7 INFORMAL. person, thing, or event that wins. 8 U.S. (in journalism) the securing and publishing of news ahead of one's competitors. 9 (in physics) the regular pulsation arising from the interference of simultaneous sound waves, radio waves, or electric currents which have slightly different frequencies. 10 SLANG. beatnik.

—adj. U.S. INFORMAL. 1 worn out; exhausted. 2 overcome by astonishment. 3 of or characteristic of beatniks.

[Old English *bēatan*]

Syn. *v.t.* 1 **Beat, hit, pound** mean to strike. **Beat** means to strike again and again, but does not suggest how hard nor with what: *He beat a complicated rhythm on the drums.* **Hit** means to strike a single blow with force and aim: *The batter hit the ball.* **Pound** means to hit hard again and again with the fist or something heavy: *The child pounded the floor with a hammer.*

beat en (bēt′n), *adj.* 1 struck repeatedly; whipped: *a beaten dog.* 2 much walked on or traveled: *a beaten path.* 3 defeated; overcome: *a beaten army.* 4 exhausted. 5 shaped by blows of a hammer: *beaten silver.* *—v.* a pp. of **beat.**

beat er (bē′tər), *n.* 1 person or thing that beats. 2 man hired to rouse game during a hunt. 3 device or utensil for beating eggs, cream, etc.

be a tif ic (bē′ə tif′ik), *adj.* 1 showing very great happiness; blissful: *a beatific smile.* 2 making blessed; blessing or making happy: *a beatific vision.*

be at i fi ca tion (bē at′ə fə kā′shən), *n.* 1 act of making blessed. 2 condition of being made blessed. 3 a formal declaration by the pope that a dead person is among the blessed in heaven and deserves religious honor. Beatification is often the immediate prelude to canonization.

be at i fy (bē at′ə fī), *v.t.,* **-fied, -fy ing.** 1 make supremely happy; bless. 2 declare (a dead person) by a decree of the pope to be among the blessed in heaven and to deserve religious honor. The person beatified is thereafter entitled "Blessed." [< Late Latin *beatificare* < Latin *beatus* happy + *facere* to make]

beat ing (bē′ting), *n.* 1 act of one that beats; striking. 2 a whipping; thrashing. 3 a defeat. 4 a throbbing.

be at i tude (bē at′ə tüd, bē at′ə tyüd), *n.* 1 supreme happiness; bliss. 2 a blessing. 3 **the Beatitudes,** (in the Bible) the eight verses in the Sermon on the Mount which begin with "Blessed," as "Blessed are the poor in spirit."

beat nik (bēt′nik), *n.* a person who rejects conventions and accepted standards by adopting unusual dress, speech, etc. [< *beat,* adjective + *-nik,* a Slavic personal suffix]

beat-up (bēt′up′), *adj.* INFORMAL. battered or worn out from long use or from abuse: *a beat-up car.*

beau (bō), *n., pl.* **beaus** or **beaux.** 1 a young man courting a young woman; suitor or lover. 2 man who pays much attention to the way he dresses and to the fashion of his clothes; dandy. [< French < Latin *bellus* fine]

Beau Brum mell (bō′ brum′əl), 1 the nickname of George Bryan Brummel, 1778-1840, English leader in men's fashions. 2 a dandy.

Beau fort scale (bō′fərt), an internationally used scale of wind velocities, ranging from 0 (calm) to 17 (hurricane), used in weather maps. [< Sir Francis *Beaufort,* 1774-1857, British admiral who devised it]

beau geste (bō zhest′), *pl.* ***beaux gestes*** (bō zhest′). FRENCH. 1 a graceful or kindly act. 2 pretense of kindness or unselfishness merely for effect.

Beau har nais (bō är nā′), *n.* **Josephine de.** See **Josephine.**

beau i de al (bō′ ī dē′əl), *pl.* **beau**

i de als. the perfect type of excellence or beauty; highest ideal; model. [< French *beau idéal*]

Beau mar chais (bō mär shā′), *n.* **Pierre Augustin Caron de,** 1732-1799, French dramatist.

beau monde (bō mond′; *French* bō môNd′), *pl.* **beaux mondes** (bō mond′; *French* bō môNd′). fashionable society. [< French]

Beau mont (bō′mont), *n.* 1 city in SE Texas. 116,000. 2 **Francis,** 1584-1616, English dramatist who wrote many plays with John Fletcher.

Beau re gard (bō′rə gärd), *n.* **Pierre G. T.,** 1818-1893, Confederate general in the Civil War.

beau te ous (byü′tē əs), *adj.* beautiful. **—beau′te ous ly,** *adv.* **—beau′te ous ness,** *n.*

beau ti cian (byü tish′ən), *n.* specialist in the use of cosmetics, especially a person who works in a beauty shop.

beau ti fi ca tion (byü′tə fə kā′shən), *n.* a making beautiful or more beautiful; beautifying.

beau ti ful (byü′tə fəl), *adj.* very pleasing to see or hear; delighting the mind or senses. **—beau′ti ful ly,** *adv.* **—beau′ti ful ness,** *n.*

Syn. Beautiful, lovely, handsome mean pleasing the senses or mind. **Beautiful** suggests delighting the senses by excellence and harmony, and often also giving great pleasure to the mind by an inner goodness: *Looking at a beautiful painting always gives one satisfaction.* **Lovely** suggests appealing to the emotions and giving delight to the heart as well as to the senses and mind: *Her lovely smile shows a sweet disposition.* **Handsome** means pleasing to look at because well formed, well proportioned, etc.: *That is a handsome phonograph. Beautiful* and *lovely* are usually not applied to men.

beau ti fy (byü′tə fī), *v.*, **-fied, fy ing.** *—v.t.* make beautiful; make more beautiful; ornament; adorn. *—v.i.* become or grow beautiful or more beautiful. **—beau′ti fi′er,** *n.*

beau ty (byü′tē), *n., pl.* **-ties.** 1 good looks. 2 quality that pleases in flowers, pictures, music, etc.; loveliness. 3 something beautiful. 4 a beautiful woman. 5 INFORMAL. act, achievement, or the like, of superior or excellent quality. [< Old French *beaute,* ultimately < Latin *bellus* fine]

beauty shop or **beauty parlor,** U.S. place where women have their hair, skin, and nails cared for.

beaux (bōz), *n.* a pl. of **beau.**

beaux-arts (bō zär′), *n.pl.* FRENCH. fine arts; painting, sculpture, music, etc.

beaver[1] (def. 1)
3½ ft. long

bea ver[1] (bē′vər), *n.* 1 a large, amphibious rodent with soft fur, a broad, flat tail, webbed hind feet for swimming, and hard incisor teeth for cutting down trees, noted for its skill in constructing mud and wood lodges and dams. 2 its soft brown fur. 3 a man's high silk hat, formerly made of beaver fur. [Old English *beofor*] **—bea′ver like′,** *adj.*

beaver[2]
(def. 1)

bea ver[2] (bē′vər), *n.* 1 the movable lower part of a helmet, protecting the chin and mouth. 2 the movable front part of a helmet; visor. [Old French *baviere* bib < *bave* saliva]

be bop (bē′bop′), *n.* form of jazz characterized by much improvisation, unusual rhythms, dissonance, and, frequently, by the singing of meaningless syllables. Also, **bop.** [imitative]

be calmed (bi kämd′, bi kälmd′), *adj.* 1 kept from moving because there is no wind. 2 made calm; calm.

be came (bi kām′), *v.* pt. of **become.** *The seed became a plant.*

be cause (bi kôz′), *conj.* for the reason that; since: *Children play ball because it's fun.* *—adv.* **because of,** by reason of; on account of: *We did not go because of the rain.* [Middle English *bi cause* by (the) cause]

be chance (bi chans′), *v.,* **-chanced, -chanc ing.** ARCHAIC. *—v.i.* happen. —v.t. happen to; befall.

Bech u a na land (bech′ü ä′nə land′), *n.* former name of **Botswana.**

beck (bek), *n.* 1 motion of the head or hand meant as a call or command. 2 **at one's beck and call, a** ready whenever wanted. **b** under one's complete control. [< *beck,* verb, short for *beckon*]

Beck et (bek′it), *n.* **Saint Thomas à,** 1118?-1170, archbishop of Canterbury. He was murdered in the cathedral there for resisting the policies of Henry II of England.

Beck ett (bek′it), *n.* **Samuel,** born 1906, Irish playwright and novelist, now living in France.

beck on (bek′ən), *v.i., v.t.* to signal by a motion of the head or hand: *He beckoned me to follow him. The tall man beckoned to her.* [Old English *bēcnan* < *bēacen* sign, beacon]

be cloud (bi kloud′), *v.t.* 1 hide or darken by a cloud or clouds. 2 make obscure; hide.

be come (bi kum′), *v.,* **be came, be com ing,** *—v.i.* come to be; grow to be: *become wiser as one grows older.* *—v.t.* 1 seem proper or fitting for; befit; *It does not become you to question the teacher's decision.* 2 look well on; suit: *A white dress becomes her.* 3 **become of,** happen to: *What has become of the box of candy?* [Old English *becuman*]

be com ing (bi kum′ing), *adj.* 1 fitting or suitable; appropriate: *becoming conduct for a gentleman.* See **fitting** for synonym study. 2 that looks well on the person wearing it; attractive: *a becoming dress.* **—be com ing ly,** *adv.*

Becque rel rays (bek rel′), the invisible rays given off by radium, uranium, and other radioactive substances. This term has been replaced by the more specific terms, *alpha rays, beta rays,* and *gamma rays.* [<Antoine H. *Becquerel,* 1852-1908, French physicist who first reported these rays]

bed (bed), *n., v.,* **bed ded, bed ding.** *—n.* 1 something to sleep or rest on, usually consisting of a mattress raised upon a support and covered with sheets and blankets. 2 any place where people or animals rest or sleep. 3 a flat base on which anything rests; foundation: *They set the lathe on a bed of concrete.* 4 the ground under a body of water: *the bed of a river.* 5 piece of ground in a garden in which plants are grown. 6 layer; stratum: *a bed of coal.* 7 **bed and board,** sleeping accommodation and meals. 8 **get up on the wrong side of the bed,** be irritable or bad-tempered. 9 **take to one's bed,** stay in bed because of sickness or weakness. *—v.t.* 1 provide with a bed; put to bed: *I bedded the horse in the barn.* 2 fix or set in a permanent position; embed. 3 plant in a garden bed: *These tulips should be bedded in rich soil.* 4 lay flat or in order. *—v.i.* 1 go to bed; retire for the night. 2 **bed down, a** make or arrange a bed or sleeping place for. **b** go to bed; lie down to sleep. 3 form a compact layer. [Old English *bedd*]

hat, āge, fär; let, ēqual, tėrm;
it, īce; hot, ōpen, ôrder;
oil, out; cup, pu̇t, rüle;
ch, child; ng, long; sh, she;
th, thin; ᴛʜ, then; zh, measure;

ə represents *a* in about, *e* in taken, *i* in pencil, *o* in lemon, *u* in circus.

< = from, derived from, taken from.

be daub (bi dôb′), *v.t.* 1 smear with something dirty or sticky. 2 ornament in a gaudy or showy way.

be daz zle (bi daz′əl), *v.t.,* **-zled, -zling.** dazzle completely; confuse by dazzling.

bed bug (bed′bug′), *n.* a small, wingless, reddish-brown, bloodsucking insect found in houses and especially in beds. Its bite is painful.

bed cham ber (bed′chām′bər), *n.* bedroom.

bed clothes (bed′klōz′, bed′klōᴛʜz′), *n.pl.* sheets, blankets, quilts, etc.

bed ding (bed′ing), *n.* 1 bedclothes. 2 material for beds: *Straw is used as bedding for cows and horses.* 3 foundation; bottom layer. 4 stratification.

Bede (bēd), *n.* A.D. 673?-735, English monk who was the first great English prose writer. He wrote an ecclesiastical history of England and was called "the Venerable Bede."

be deck (bi dek′), *v.t.* deck out; adorn.

be dev il (bi dev′əl), *v.t.,* **-iled, -il ing** or **-illed, -il ling.** 1 drive frantic; trouble greatly; torment. 2 confuse completely; muddle. **—be dev′il ment,** *n.*

be dew (bi dü′, bi dyü′), *v.t.* make wet with dew or with drops like dew.

bed fast (bed′fast′), *adj.* confined to bed; bedridden.

bed fel low (bed′fel′ō), *n.* 1 sharer of one's bed. 2 associate.

Bed ford (bed′fərd), *n.* county in S England.

Bed ford shire (bed′fərd shər, bed′fərdshir), *n.* Bedford.

be dight (bi dīt′), *v.,* **-dight, -dight** or **-dight ed, -dight ing,** *adj.* ARCHAIC. *—v.t.* adorn; array. *—adj.* adorned; arrayed. [< *be-* + *dight*]

be dim (bi dim′), *v.t.,* **-dimmed, -dim ming.** make dim; darken; obscure.

Bed i vere (bed′ə vir), *n.* **Sir,** (in Arthurian legends) the faithful knight of the Round Table who brought the dying King Arthur to the barge that carried him to Avalon.

be di zen (bi dī′zn, bi diz′n), *v.t.* dress or ornament with showy finery. [< *be-* + *dizen*] **—be di′zen ment,** *n.*

bed lam (bed′ləm), *n.* 1 noisy confusion; uproar. 2 ARCHAIC. insane asylum; madhouse. [< *Bedlam,* old name for the Hospital of St. Mary of *Bethlehem,* an insane asylum in London]

bed lam ite (bed′lə mīt), *n.* lunatic.

Bed ling ton terrier (bed′ling tən), one of a breed of medium-sized terriers with rough, woolly fur. [< *Bedlington,* town in England]

Bed loe's Island (bed′lōz), former name of **Liberty Island.**

Bed ou in (bed′ü ən), *n.* 1 member of certain tribes of wandering Arabs who live in the deserts of Arabia, Syria, and northern Africa. 2 wanderer; nomad. [< Old French < Arabic *badawīy* desert dweller]

bed pan (bed′pan′), *n.* pan used as a toilet by sick people in bed.

be drag gled (bi drag′əld), *adj.* 1 wet and hanging limp. 2 soiled by being dragged in the dirt.

bed rid (bed′rid′), *adj.* bedridden.

bed rid den (bed′rid′n), *adj.* confined to bed for a long time because of sickness or weakness.

bed rock (bed′rok′), *n.* 1 the solid rock beneath the soil and under looser rocks. 2 a firm foundation. 3 the lowest level; bottom.

bed roll (bed′rōl′), *n.* blankets or a sleeping bag that can be rolled up and tied for carrying.

bed room (bed′rüm′, bed′rům′), *n.* a room with a bed or beds, used to sleep in.

bed side (bed′sīd′), *n.* side of a bed. *—adj.* with the sick; attending the sick.

bed-sit ter (bed′sit′ər), *n.* BRITISH. a room combining a bedroom and sitting room.

bed sore (bed′sôr′, bed′sōr′), *n.* sore caused by lying too long in the same position.

bed spread (bed′spred′), *n.* the uppermost covering, usually ornamental, for a bed.

bed spring (bed′spring′), *n.* set of springs forming part of a bed and supporting a mattress.

bed stead (bed′sted′), *n.* the wooden or metal framework of a bed that supports the springs and mattress.

bed straw (bed′strô′), *n.* a small plant of the same family as the madder, with clusters of white flowers, formerly dried and used as straw for beds.

bed time (bed′tīm′), *n.* the usual time for going to bed.

bee (bē), *n.* 1 insect with four wings that produces wax to make honeycombs and gathers nectar and pollen to make honey; honeybee. Honeybees live in highly organized communities, each including a queen, many workers, and drones. Only the queen and the workers have stings. 2 any of a large number of various related insects typically having hairy bodies and thus distinguished from wasps to which they are related, and showing gradations from elaborately organized colonies to solitary nests, as bumblebees, carpenter bees, etc. 3 **have a bee in one's bonnet,** be preoccupied with or overenthusiastic about one thing. 4 U.S. a gathering for work or amusement: *a sewing bee.* [Old English *bēo*]

bee bread (bē′bred′), *n.* a brownish, bitter substance consisting of pollen, or pollen mixed with honey, used by bees as food for their larvae or young.

beech (bēch), *n.* 1 any of a genus of trees of the Northern Hemisphere with smooth, gray bark and glossy leaves, bearing a small sweet, edible nut. 2 the wood of any of these trees. *—adj.* made of beech. [Old English *bēce*]

beech en (bē′chən), *adj.* made of beechwood.

Bee cher (bē′chər), *n.* **Henry Ward,** 1813-1887, American clergyman and reformer.

beech nut (bēch′nut′), *n.* the small, triangular nut of the beech tree.

beech wood (bēch′wůd′), *n.* wood of a beech tree.

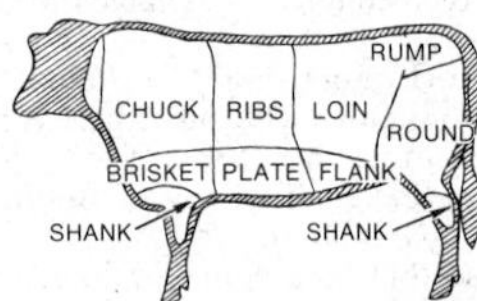

beef (def. 1)—various cuts

beef (bēf), *n., pl.* **beeves** for 2, **beefs** for 5; *v.* *—n.* 1 meat from a steer, cow, or bull. 2 steer, cow, or bull when full-grown and fattened for food. 3 INFORMAL. strength; muscle; brawn. 4 INFORMAL. weight; heaviness. 5 U.S. SLANG. complaint; grievance. *—v.i.* U.S. SLANG. complain. *—v.t.* **beef up,** SLANG. enlarge; strengthen: *beef up benefits to retired workers.* [< Old French *boef* < Latin *bovem* ox]

beef cattle, cattle raised for meat.

beef eat er (bēf′ē′tər), *n.* 1 yeoman of the guard. 2 warder of the Tower of London.

beef steak (bēf′stāk′), *n.* slice of beef for broiling or frying.

beef y (bē′fē), *adj.,* **beef i er, beef i est.** 1 like beef: *a beefy taste.* 2 strong, solid, and heavy. **—beef′i ness,** *n.*

bee hive (bē′hīv′), *n.* 1 hive or house for bees. 2 a busy, swarming place. *—adj.* having the top dome-shaped like certain beehives: *a beehive oven.*

bee keep er (bē′kē′pər), *n.* person who raises bees for their honey.

bee keep ing (bē′kē′ping), *n.* apiculture.

bee line (bē′līn′), *n.* the straightest way or line between two places, such as a bee usually takes in returning to its hive.

Be el ze bub (bē el′zə bub), *n.* 1 (in the Bible) the Devil; Satan. 2 a devil.

been (bin; *esp. in British use* bēn), *v.* pp. of **be.** *I have been ill.*

beep (bēp), *n.* 1 a sharp, short sound issued as a signal in broadcasting. 2 any sharp, short sound. *—v.t.* cause to make sharp, short sounds. [imitative]

beer (bir), *n.* 1 an alcoholic drink made usually from malted barley flavored with hops. 2 a soft drink made from roots or plants, such as root beer or ginger beer. [Old English *bēor*]

beer and skittles, material comforts and pleasures; enjoyment.

Beer bohm (bir′bōm), *n.* Sir **Max,** 1872-1956, English writer and caricaturist.

beer y (bir′ē), *adj.,* **beer i er, beer i est.** 1 of or like beer. 2 caused by or influenced by beer.

bees wax (bēz′waks′), *n.* wax secreted by bees, from which they make their honeycomb.

beet (bēt), *n.* 1 any of a genus of biennial plants of the same family as the goosefoot, including the common red beet whose fleshy root is eaten as a vegetable, and the sugar beet, whose white root is a source of sugar. The young leaves of the red beet are eaten as greens. 2 the root of any of these plants. [Old English *bēte* < Latin *beta*] **—beet′like′,** *adj.*

Bee tho ven (bā′tō vən), *n.* **Ludwig van,** 1770-1827, German composer.

bee tle[1] (bē′tl), *n.* 1 any of an order of insects that have the forward pair of wings modified as hard, shiny sheaths which, when at rest, cover and protect the hinder membranous pair. 2 any of several insects somewhat resembling beetles, as the cockroach. [Old English *bitula* < *bītan* to bite]

bee tle[2] (bē′tl), *n., v.,* **-tled, -tling.** *—n.* 1 a heavy wooden mallet for ramming, crushing, or smoothing. 2 a wooden household utensil for beating or mashing. *—v.t.* pound with a beetle. [Old English *bietel* < *bēatan* to beat]

bee tle[3] (bē′tl), *v.,* **-tled, -tling,** *adj.* *—v.i.* to project or overhang. *—adj.* projecting or overhanging. [< *beetle-browed*]

bee tle-browed (bē′tl broud′), *adj.* 1 having projecting or overhanging eyebrows. 2 scowling; sullen. [Middle English *bitel* biting + *brow.* Related to BEETLE[1].]

beet ling (bēt′ling), *adj.* projecting or overhanging.

beeves (bēvz), *n.* pl. of **beef** (def. 2).

be fall (bi fôl′), *v.,* **-fell, -fall en, -fall ing.** *—v.t.* happen to: *Be careful that no harm befalls you.* *—v.i.* happen.

be fall en (bi fô′lən), *v.* pp. of **befall.**

be fell (bi fel′), *v.* pt. of **befall.**

be fit (bi fit′), *v.t.,* **-fit ted, -fit ting.** be suitable for; be proper for; suit: *clothes that befit the occasion.* **—be fit′ting ly,** *adv.*

be fog (bi fog′, bi fôg′), *v.t.,* **-fogged, -fogging.** 1 surround with fog; make foggy. 2 make obscure; confuse.

be fool (bi fül′), *v.t.* deceive; fool.

be fore (bi fôr′, bi fōr′), *prep.* 1 earlier than: *Come before five o'clock.* 2 in front of; in advance of; ahead of: *Walk before me. A happy future lies before you.* 3 rather than; sooner than: *I will die before giving in.* 4 in the presence of or sight of: *perform before an audience.* *—adv.* 1 earlier; sooner: *Come at five o'clock, not before.* 2 in front; in advance; ahead: *I went before to see if the road was safe.* 3 until now; in the past: *I didn't know that before.* *—conj.* 1 previously to the time when: *I would like to talk to her before she goes.* 2 rather than; sooner than: *I will die before I give in.* [Old English *beforan*]

be fore hand (bi fôr′hand′, bi fōr′hand′), *adv., adj.* ahead of time; in advance: *Get everything ready beforehand. Aren't you a little beforehand with your request for your allowance?*

be foul (bi foul′), *v.t.* make dirty; cover with filth.

be friend (bi frend′), *v.t.* act as a friend to; help.

be fud dle (bi fud′l), *v.t.,* **-dled, -dling.** 1 stupefy; confuse. 2 make stupid with alcoholic drink. **—be fud′dle ment,** *n.*

beg (beg), *v.,* **begged, beg ging.** *—v.t.* 1 ask for (food, money, clothes, etc.) as a charity: *The tramp begged his meals.* 2 ask as a favor; ask earnestly or humbly: *I begged them to forgive me.* See synonym study below. 3 ask formally and courteously: *I beg your pardon.* *—v.i.* 1 ask help or charity. 2 ask a favor. 3 **beg off,** make an excuse for

hat, āge, fär; let, ēqual, tėrm;
it, īce; hot, ōpen, ôrder;
oil, out; cup, pu̇t, rüle;
ch, child; ng, long; sh, she;
th, thin; ᴛʜ, then; zh, measure;

ə represents *a* in about, *e* in taken, *i* in pencil, *o* in lemon, *u* in circus.

< = from, derived from, taken from.

not being able to keep a promise. 4 **go begging,** find no one who will accept. [Middle English *beggen*]

Syn. *v.t.* 2 **Beg, implore, beseech** mean to ask earnestly. **Beg,** the commonest word, means to ask earnestly or humbly and can be used in all contexts: *The children were begging a ride on the pony.* **Implore,** a more formal word, adds to *beg* the idea of pleading with warm feeling and great humility: *We implored him not to ruin his life by doing anything so foolish.* **Beseech,** still more formal, suggests greater earnestness or humility than *beg: She besought the governor to pardon her son.*

be gan (bi gan′), *v.* pt. of **begin.**

be gat (bi gat′), *v.* ARCHAIC. a pt. of **beget.**

be get (bi get′), *v.t.,* **be got** or (ARCHAIC) **be gat, be got ten** or **be got, be get ting.** 1 become the father of. 2 cause to be; produce. [Old English *begitan*] **—be get′ter,** *n.*

beg gar (beg′ər), *n.* 1 person who lives by begging. 2 a very poor person; pauper. 3 fellow: *a friendly little beggar.* —*v.t.* 1 bring to poverty: *Your reckless spending will beggar you.* 2 make seem poor or impossible; outdo: *The grandeur of Niagara Falls beggars description.*

beg gar-lice (beg′ər līs′), *n. sing. or pl.* beggar's-lice.

beg gar ly (beg′ər lē), *adj.* 1 fit for a beggar; poor; shabby. 2 mean; sordid. **—beg′gar li ness,** *n.*

beg gar's-lice (beg′ərz līs′), *n. pl. or sing.* 1 the prickly burs or seeds of various plants, that stick to clothes. 2 weed on which such burs or seeds grow.

beg gar's-ticks (beg′ərz tiks′), *n. pl. or sing.* beggar's-lice.

beg gar-ticks (beg′ər tiks′), *n. pl. or sing.* beggar's-lice.

beg gar y (beg′ər ē), *n.* very great poverty.

be gin (bi gin′), v., **be gan, be gun, be gin ning.** —*v.i.* 1 do the first part; make a start: *begin on one's work. When shall we begin? Begin at the third chapter.* 2 come into being: *The club began two years ago.* 3 be near; come near: *That suit doesn't even begin to fit you.* —*v.t.* 1 do the first part of; start. See synonym study below. 2 bring into being: *Two people began the club ten years ago.* [Old English *beginnan*]

Syn. *v.t.* 1 **Begin, commence, start** mean to get something going. **Begin** is the general word: *We will begin work soon.* **Commence** is formal and applies particularly to beginning a formal action: *The dedication ceremonies will commence at two o'clock.* **Start** emphasizes taking the first step in doing something, setting about doing it: *At last they have started building that hotel.*

➔ **Begin** is followed by *at* when the meaning is start from a definite place: *Let us begin at the third chapter.* It is followed by *on* or *upon* when the meaning is set to work at: *We must begin on the government survey tomorrow.* When the meaning is take first in an order of succession, the idiom is *begin with: We always begin with the hardest problems.*

be gin ner (bi gin′ər), *n.* 1 person who is doing something for the first time; person who lacks skill and experience. 2 person who begins anything.

be gin ning (bi gin′ing), *n.* 1 a start: *make a good beginning.* 2 time when anything begins: *"In the beginning God created the heaven and the earth."* 3 first part. 4 source; origin. —*adj.* that begins.

be gone (bi gôn′, bi gon′), *v.i.* go away; depart: *Begone, and do not come back!*

be go nia (bi gō′nyə, bi gō′nē ə), *n.* any of a family of tropical plants often grown as house plants for their large, fleshy, richly colored leaves and waxy flowers. [< Michel *Bégon,* 1638-1710, French patron of botany]

be got (bi got′), *v.* a pt. and a pp. of **beget.**

be got ten (bi got′n), *v.* a pp. of **beget.**

be grimed (bi grīmd′), *adj.* made grimy; soiled and dirty.

be grudge (bi gruj′), *v.t.,* **-grudged, -grudg ing.** 1 be reluctant to give or allow (something); grudge: *They are so stingy that they begrudge their dog a bone.* 2 envy (somebody) the possession of: *They begrudge us our new house.* **—be grudg′ing ly,** *adv.*

be guile (bi gīl′), *v.t.,* **-guiled, -guil ing.** 1 trick or mislead (a person); deceive; delude: *Your flattery beguiled me into thinking that you were my friend.* 2 take away from deceitfully or cunningly. 3 win the attention of; entertain; amuse. 4 while away (time) pleasantly. See **while** for synonym study. **—be guile′ment,** *n.* **—be guil′er,** *n.*

be guine (bə gēn′), *n.* 1 dance resembling the rumba, originally from Martinique. 2 the music for it. [< French *béguin* flirtation]

be gum (bē′gəm), *n.* queen, princess, or lady of high rank in Moslem countries. [< Hindustani *begam*]

be gun (bi gun′), *v.* pp. of **begin.** *It has begun to rain.*

be half (bi haf′), *n.* 1 side, interest, or favor: *My friends will act in my behalf.* 2 **in behalf of** or **on behalf of,** in the interest of; for: *I am speaking in behalf of my friend.* [Old English *be healfe* by (his) side]

be have (bi hāv′), *v.,* **-haved, -hav ing.** —*v.i.* 1 manage, handle, or conduct oneself: *The little girl behaves badly in school. The ship behaves well.* 2 act properly; do what is right: *Did you behave today?* 3 act or react to a stimulus, environment, etc.: *Water behaves in different ways when it is heated and when it is frozen.* —*v.t.* 1 manage, handle, or conduct (oneself). 2 conduct (oneself) well or properly. [Middle English *behaven* < *be-* by + *haven* have]

be hav ior (bi hā′vyər), *n.* 1 manner of conducting oneself; bearing; manners. See **conduct** for synonym study. 2 course of action; conduct. 3 manner in which a living organism or a physical substance acts under specified conditions or circumstances, or in relation to other things. Also, BRITISH **behaviour.**

be hav ior al (bi hā′vyər əl), *adj.* of or having to do with behavior: *Sociology and psychology are behavioral sciences.* **—be hav′ior al ly,** *adv.*

be hav ior ism (bi hā′vyə riz′əm), *n.* doctrine that the objective acts of persons and animals are the chief or only subject matter of scientific psychology.

be hav ior ist (bi hā′vyər ist), *n.* person who believes in behaviorism.

be hav iour (bi hā′vyər), *n.* BRITISH. behavior.

be head (bi hed′), *v.t.* cut off the head of; decapitate.

be held (bi held′), *v.* pt. and pp. of **behold.**

be he moth (bi hē′məth, bē′ə məth), *n.* 1 a huge and powerful animal mentioned in the Bible and thought to be the hippopotamus. 2 anything very large and powerful. [< Hebrew *b'hēmoth,* plural, beasts]

be hest (bi hest′), *n.* command; order. [Old English *behǣs* promise]

be hind (bi hīnd′), *prep.* 1 at the back of; in the rear of: *The child hid behind the door.* See synonym study below. 2 at or on the far side of: *A beautiful valley lies behind the hill.* 3 in support of; supporting: *Her friends are behind her.* 4 concealed by: *Treachery lurked behind the spy's smooth manners.* 5 later than; after: *The milkman is behind his usual time today.* See **after** for synonym study. 6 remaining after: *The dead man left a family behind him.* 7 inferior to; less advanced than: *be behind others in one's class in school.* —*adv.* 1 at or toward the back; in the rear: *The dog's tail hung down behind.* 2 farther back in place or time: *The rest of the hikers are still far behind.* 3 in reserve: *More supplies are behind.* 4 not on time; slow; late: *The train is behind today.* —*adj.* 1 coming after; following: *You must watch the cars behind.* 2 late in payments, work, etc. —*n.* INFORMAL. the rump. [Old English *behindan*]

Syn. *prep.* 1 **Behind, after** express a relation in which one thing is thought of as to the rear of another. **Behind** refers chiefly to position in space and usually implies a definite and usually close interval: *The broom is behind the door. We walked behind the others.* **After** suggests moving in succession or being in a definite order: *We followed after them. They entered the hall one after the other.*

be hind hand (bi hīnd′hand′), *adv., adj.* 1 behind time; late. 2 behind others in progress; backward; slow. 3 in debt; in arrears.

be hind-the-scenes (bi hīnd′ᴛʜə sēnz′), *adj.* not public; private; secret.

be hold (bi hōld′), *v.,* **be held, be hold ing,** *interj.* —*v.t.* look at; see; observe. —*interj.* look; take notice. [Old English *behealdan*] **—be hold′er,** *n.*

be hold en (bi hōl′dən), *adj.* under personal obligation for favors or services.

be hoof (bi hüf′), *n.* advantage; benefit. [Old English *behōf* need]

be hoove (bi hüv′), *v.,* **-hooved, -hoov ing.** —*v.t.* 1 be necessary for: *It behooves you to work hard if you want to keep this job.* 2 be proper for: *It behooves a child to obey his parents.* —*v.i.* be proper or due. [Old English *behōfian*]

be hove (bi hōv′), *v.t., v.i.,* **-hoved, -hov ing.** BRITISH. behoove.

beige (bāzh), *adj.* pale-brown; brownish-gray. —*n.* 1 a pale brown. 2 a lightweight woolen dress fabric, originally beige in color. [< French]

be ing (bē′ing), *v.* ppr. of **be.** —*n.* 1 person; living creature: *a human being.* 2 life; existence: *A new era came into being.* 3 nature; constitution: *She threw her whole being into her work.*

Bei rut (bā rüt′, bā′rüt), *n.* capital and chief seaport of Lebanon, on the Mediterranean. 600,000. Also, **Beyrouth.**

be jew el (bi jü′əl), *v.t.,* **-eled, -el ing** or **-elled, -el ling.** adorn with jewels, or as if with jewels.

bel (bel), *n.* (in physics) a unit for measuring

the difference in intensity level of sounds, equal to ten decibels. [< Alexander Graham *Bell*]

be la bor (bi lā′bər), *v.t.* 1 beat vigorously; thrash. 2 set upon with too much talk, advice, etc.

be lat ed (bi lā′tid), *adj.* 1 happening or coming late or too late; delayed: *The belated letter arrived at last.* 2 overtaken by darkness: *The belated travelers lost their way in the mountains.* **—be lat′ed ly,** *adv.* **—be lat′ed ness,** *n.*

be lay (bi lā′), *v.t., v.i.* 1 coil (a rope) by winding around a pin, cleat, etc., so as to fasten or secure it. 2 fasten in this way. 3 INFORMAL. stop. [Old English *belecgan* to cover]

belaying pin, a sturdy metal or wooden pin in a rail of a ship around which ropes can be wound and fastened.

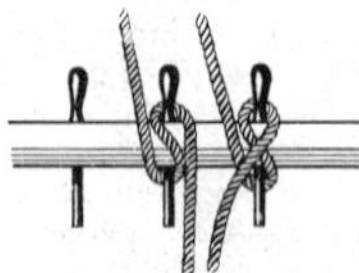
belaying pin
belaying pins with ropes on them

belch (belch), *v.i.* 1 throw out gas noisily from the stomach through the mouth. 2 throw out or shoot forth contents violently: *cannon belching at the enemy.* —*v.t.* throw out or shoot forth violently: *The volcano belched fire and smoke.* —*n.* act of belching. [Old English *bealcian*]

bel dam (bel′dəm), *n.* 1 an old woman. 2 an ugly old woman; hag; witch. [< *bel-* grand (< Old French *belle* fair) + *dam* dame < Old French *dame*]

bel dame (bel′dəm, bel′dām′), *n.* beldam.

be lea guer (bi lē′gər), *v.t.* 1 surround with troops; besiege. 2 surround; beset. [< Dutch *belegeren*]

Be lém (bə lem′), *n.* seaport in NE Brazil. 643,000. Also, **Pará.**

Bel fast (bel′fast), *n.* seaport and capital of Northern Ireland, on the E coast. 399,000.

bel fry (bel′frē), *n., pl.* **-fries.** 1 tower for a bell or bells, usually attached to a church or other building. 2 room, cupola, or turret in which a bell or bells may be hung. [Old French *berfrei*]

belfry (defs. 1 and 2)

Belg., 1 Belgian. 2 Belgium.

Bel gian (bel′jən), *n.* 1 native or inhabitant of Belgium. 2 any of a breed of large, heavy draft horses. —*adj.* of or having to do with Belgium or its people.

Belgian Congo, former Belgian colony in central Africa, now called Zaïre.

Belgian hare, a large, reddish-brown, domestic rabbit.

Bel gium (bel′jəm), *n.* country in W Europe, on the North Sea. 9,676,000 pop.; 11,800 sq. mi. *Capital:* Brussels.

Bel grade (bel′grād, bel grād′), *n.* capital of Yugoslavia, a port on the Danube. 598,000.

Be li al (bē′lē əl, bē′lyəl), *n.* the Devil.

be lie (bi lī′), *v.t.,* **-lied, -ly ing.** 1 give a false idea of; misrepresent: *Her frown belied her usual good nature.* 2 show to be false; prove to be mistaken. 3 fail to come up to; disappoint: *He stole again, and so belied our hopes.* [Old English *belēogan*] **—be li′er,** *n.*

be lief (bi lēf′), *n.* 1 thing believed; what is held to be true or real; opinion. See synonym study below. 2 acceptance of a statement, etc., as true or real: *belief in ghosts.* 3 confidence in any person or thing; faith; trust: *express belief in a person's honesty.* 4 religious faith; creed: *What is your belief?* [Middle English *bileafe*]

Syn. 1 **Belief, conviction** mean what is held true. **Belief** is the general word, implying acceptance with or without certainty: *It was once a common belief that the earth is flat.* **Conviction** implies that the belief is unshakable and undoubting: *It is my conviction that they are innocent.*

be lieve (bi lēv′), *v.,* **-lieved, -liev ing.** —*v.t.* 1 accept as true or real: *We all believe that the earth is round.* 2 think (somebody) tells the truth: *My friends believe me.* 3 think; suppose. —*v.i.* 1 have faith (in a person or thing); trust: *We believe in our friends.* 2 accept something as true or existing: *believe in ghosts.* 3 have religious belief. 4 think; suppose. [Old English *belēfan*] **—be liev′a ble,** *adj.* **—be liev′a bly,** *adv.*

be liev er (bi lē′vər), *n.* 1 person who believes (in anything). 2 person who has faith in the doctrines of religion, especially a Christian.

be like (bi līk′), *adv.* ARCHAIC. very likely; probably; perhaps.

be lit tle (bi lit′l), *v.t.,* **-tled, -tling.** 1 cause to seem little, unimportant or less important; speak slightingly of; depreciate; disparage: *Jealous people belittled the explorer's great discoveries.* 2 ARCHAIC. cause to appear small; dwarf. **—be lit′tle ment,** *n.* **—be lit′tler,** *n.*

Be lize (be lēz′), *n.* seaport and former capital of British Honduras. 39,000.

bell (bel), *n.* 1 a hollow metal cup that makes a musical sound when struck by a clapper or hammer. 2 anything that makes a ringing sound as a signal: *Did I hear the bell at the front door?* 3 **ring a bell,** INFORMAL. call forth response, as of memory or enthusiasm. 4 stroke or sound of a bell. 5 stroke of a bell used on shipboard to indicate a half hour of time. 1 bell = 12:30, 4:30, or 8:30; 2 bells = 1:00, 5:00, or 9:00; and so on up to 8 bells = 4:00, 8:00, or 12:00. 6 anything shaped like a bell. The wide, outward curving or spreading end of a funnel or of a musical wind instrument is a bell. —*v.t.* 1 put a bell on. 2 cause to swell or bulge out. —*v.i.* 1 swell out like a bell; flare. 2 make the sound of a bell; toll. [Old English *belle*] **—bell′-like′,** *adj.*

Bell (bel), *n.* **Alexander Graham,** 1847-1922, American physicist, born in Scotland, inventor of the telephone.

bel la don na (bel′ə don′ə), *n.* 1 a poisonous plant of the nightshade family of Europe and Asia with black berries and red, bell-shaped flowers; deadly nightshade. 2 drug made from the leaves and root of this plant; atropine. [< Italian *bella donna,* literally, fair lady]

bell bird (bel′bėrd′), *n.* any of several birds with a clear, bell-like call.

bell-bot tom (bel′bot′əm), *adj.* with the bottom of the legs flared.

bell-bot toms (bel′bot′əmz), *n.pl.* bell-bottom trousers.

bell boy (bel′boi′), *n.* man or boy whose work is carrying baggage and doing errands for the guests of a hotel or club; bellhop.

bell buoy, a warning buoy with a bell hung so as to ring when the buoy is rocked by the waves.

belle (bel), *n.* 1 a beautiful woman or girl. 2 the prettiest or most admired woman or girl: *the belle of the ball.* [< French, feminine of *beau.* See BEAU.]

Bel leau Wood (bel′ō), forest in N France, the site of a battle of World War I in 1918.

belles-let tres (bel′let′rə), *n.pl.* 1 the finer forms of literature, especially poetry or essays. 2 novels, plays, or any type of literature that is not explicitly educational, informational, etc. 3 literature as an art. [< French]

bel le tris tic (bel′le tris′tik), *adj.* of or having to do with belles-lettres.

bell flow er (bel′flou′ər), *n.* campanula.

bell hop (bel′hop′), *n.* U.S. bellboy.

bel li cose (bel′ə kōs), *adj.* fond of fighting and quarreling; inclined to war; warlike; pugnacious. [< Latin *bellicosus* < *bellum* war] **—bel′li cose ly,** *adv.*

bel li cos i ty (bel′ə kos′ə tē), *n.* bellicose quality or attitude.

bel lig er ence (bə lij′ər əns), *n.* 1 a belligerent attitude; fondness for fighting and war. 2 act of fighting; being at war.

bel lig er en cy (bə lij′ər ən sē), *n.* 1 position or status of a belligerent. 2 pugnacious and stubborn hostility. 3 warfare.

bel lig er ent (bə lij′ər ənt), *adj.* 1 waging or carrying on regular recognized war; actually engaged in hostilities; at war; fighting. 2 having to do with nations or persons at war. 3 fond of fighting; tending or inclined to war; warlike; pugnacious. —*n.* 1 nation or state engaged in war. 2 person engaged in fighting with another person. [< Latin *belligerantem* < *bellum* war + *gerere* to wage] **—bel lig′er ent ly,** *adv.*

Bel li ni (be lē′nē), *n.* 1 **Gentile,** 1427?-1507, Venetian painter of portraits and contemporary Venetian life. 2 **Giovanni,** 1430?-1516, Venetian painter. 3 **Jacopo,** 1400?-1470?, Venetian painter of religious subjects. He was the father of Gentile and Giovanni. 4 **Vincenzo,** 1801-1835, Italian composer of operas.

bell jar, a bell-shaped container or cover made of glass, used to cover objects that require protection from variations of the atmosphere or, in laboratories, to hold gases in chemical operations.

bell man (bel′mən), *n., pl.* **-men.** man who rings a bell, especially a town crier.

Bel loc (bel′ək, bel′ok), *n.* **Hilaire,** 1870-1953, English writer, born in France.

bel low (bel′ō), *v.i.* 1 (of an animal, especially of a bull) make a loud, roaring noise, as when excited or enraged. 2 shout loudly, angrily, or with pain. See **cry** for synonym study. 3 make a loud, deep noise; roar. —*v.t.* shout in a loud and deep voice; roar. —*n.* 1 the roar of a bull. 2 any noise made by bellowing; loud, deep noise; roar. [Old English *bylgian*] **—bel′low er,** *n.*

hat, āge, fär; let, ēqual, tėrm;
it, īce; hot, ōpen, ôrder;
oil, out; cup, pu̇t, rüle;
ch, child; ng, long; sh, she;
th, thin; ᴛʜ, then; zh, measure;

ə represents *a* in about, *e* in taken, *i* in pencil, *o* in lemon, *u* in circus.

< = from, derived from, taken from.

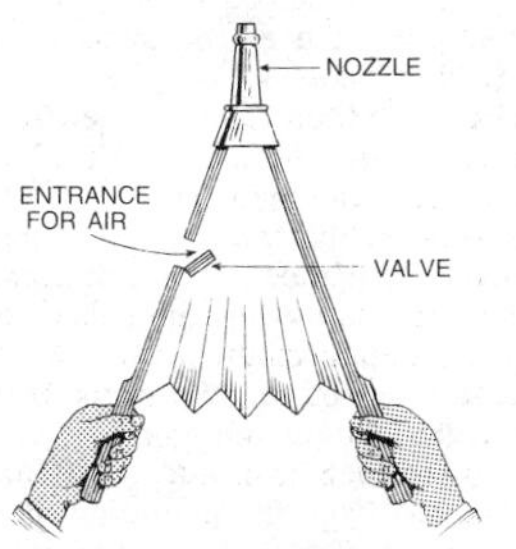

bellows (def. 1)
Air is sucked into the bellows as the sides are pulled apart. When the sides are pushed together, the valve closes and air is forced out the nozzle.

bel lows (bel′ōz, bel′əs), *n. sing. or pl.* 1 device for producing a strong current of air, used for blowing fires or sounding an organ, accordion, etc. A bellows consists of an air chamber which expands when air enters through a valve and a nozzle through which the air is forced out in a stream when the air chamber is compressed. 2 the folding part of certain cameras, behind the lens. [Old English *belgas,* plural of *belg* bag, belly]

bell weth er (bel′weᴛʜ′ər), *n.* 1 a male sheep that leads the flock, usually with a bell on its neck. 2 a chief or leader. 3 person or thing that sets a standard or pattern for a group.

bel ly (bel′ē), *n., pl.* **-lies,** *v.,* **-lied, -ly ing.** —*n.* 1 the lower part of the human body, between the breast and the thighs, which contains the stomach and intestines; abdomen. 2 the underpart of an animal's body. 3 stomach. 4 the appetite for food. 5 the bulging part of anything: *the belly of a pot.* 6 a hollow in a surface: *the belly of a sail.* 7 the thick portion of a muscle. —*v.i.* swell out; bulge: *The ship's sails bellied in the wind.* —*v.t.* cause to swell out. [Old English *belg*]

bel ly ache (bel′ē āk′), *n., v.,* **-ached, -ach ing.** INFORMAL. —*n.* 1 pain in the abdomen; stomach ache. 2 reason for complaining; grievance. —*v.i.* complain or grumble, especially over trifles.

bel ly band (bel′ē band′), *n.* strap around an animal's body to keep a saddle, harness, etc., in place.

bel ly but ton (bel′ē but′n), *n.* INFORMAL. navel.

bel ly land (bel′ē land), *v.i., v.t.* land an airplane with the landing gear retracted.

belly laugh, INFORMAL. a hearty, unrestrained fit of laughter.

Bel mo pan (bel′mō pän′), *n.* capital of British Honduras, in the central part. 3000.

be long (bi lông′, bi long′), *v.i.* 1 have one's or its proper place: *That book belongs on the top shelf.* 2 **belong to, a** be the property of: *That coat belongs to me.* **b** be a part of; be connected with: *That top belongs to this box.* **c** be a member of: *She belongs to a large family.* [Middle English *belongen* < *be-* by + *longen* belong]

be long ings (bi lông′ingz, bi long′ingz), *n.pl.* things that belong to a person; possessions; goods.

Be lo rus sia (bel′ə rush′ə), *n.* Byelorussia. —**Be′lo rus′sian,** *adj., n.*

be lov ed (bi luv′id, bi luvd′), *adj.* dearly loved; dear. —*n.* person who is loved; darling.

be low (bi lō′), *adv.* 1 in a lower place; to a lower place: *From the airplane we could see the fields below.* 2 on or to a lower floor or deck; downstairs: *The sailor went below.* 3 on earth. 4 in hell. 5 after or later on a page or in a book or article: *See the note below.* 6 below zero: *The temperature was five below last night.* —*prep.* 1 lower than; under: *below the third floor.* See **under** for synonym study. 2 less than; lower in rank or degree than: *four degrees below freezing.* 3 too low to be worthy of: *below contempt.* [< *be-* + *low*]

be low decks (bi lō′deks), *adj., adv.* under the deck; in or into the cabin or hold of a ship.

belt (belt), *n.* 1 strip of leather, cloth, etc., fastened around the waist to hold in or support clothes or weapons. 2 any broad strip or band: *a belt of trees.* 3 region having distinctive characteristics; zone: *The cotton belt is the region where cotton is grown.* 4 an endless band that transfers motion from one wheel or pulley to another. 5 SLANG. a blow. 6 **below the belt, a** foul; unfair. **b** foully; unfairly. 7 **tighten one's belt,** be or become more thrifty. —*v.t.* 1 put a belt around. 2 fasten on with a belt. 3 surround or mark with a circle or zone of any kind. 4 beat with a belt. 5 SLANG. hit suddenly and hard. 6 **belt out,** SLANG. sing or play forcefully. [Old English < Latin *balteus* girdle; belt]

belt ed (bel′tid), *adj.* 1 having a belt. 2 wearing a special belt as a sign of honor. 3 marked by a belt of color.

belt ing (bel′ting), *n.* 1 material for making belts. 2 belts. 3 SLANG. a beating.

belt way (belt′wā′), *n.* highway that makes a circuit around a city or special area.

be lu ga (bə lü′gə), *n.* 1 a large, white sturgeon of the Black Sea and the Caspian Sea, valued as a source of caviar. 2 a small, white whale of arctic seas; white whale. [< Russian *beluga, belukha* < *belyj* white]

bel ve dere (bel′və dir), *n.* structure from which a fine view may be had, often a top story on a building, open on several sides. [< Italian, literally, fine view]

be mire (bi mīr′), *v.t.,* **-mired, -mir ing.** 1 make dirty with mud. 2 sink or stick in mud.

be moan (bi mōn′), *v.t.* moan or weep for; lament. —*v.i.* lament; grieve.

be muse (bi myüz′), *v.t.,* **-mused, -mus ing.** make utterly confused; bewilder; stupefy.

be mused (bi myüzd′), *adj.* 1 confused; bewildered; stupefied. 2 absorbed in reverie or thought.

Be na res (bə när′ēz), *n.* former name of **Varanasi.**

bench (bench), *n.* 1 a long seat, with or without a back, usually of wood or stone. 2 seat where judges sit in a court of law. 3 judge or group of judges sitting in a court of law. 4 position of a judge. 5 court of law. 6 seat where persons sit side by side in some official capacity. 7 place where players sit while not actually taking part in a game. 8 **on the bench, a** sitting in a court of law as a judge. **b** held out of the game. 9 worktable used by a carpenter or by any worker with tools and materials; workbench. 10 platform on which dogs stand for exhibition at a dog show. 11 a narrow stretch of high, flat land. —*v.t.* 1 furnish with benches. 2 assign a seat on a bench. 3 take (a player) out of a game. 4 exhibit (a dog) at a show. [Old English *benc*]

bench mark, mark made on a rock, post, etc., in surveying, used as a starting point or guide in a line of levels to determine altitudes.

bench warrant, a written order from a judge or court of law to arrest a person.

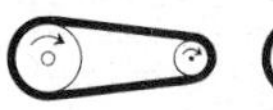  

belt (def. 4)
belts used to transmit power in different directions

bend[1] (bend), *n., v.,* **bent** or (ARCHAIC) **bend ed, bend ing.** —*n.* 1 part that is not straight; curve; turn: *There is a sharp bend in the road here.* 2 a stoop; bow. 3 knot for tying two ropes together or tying a rope to something else. 4 **the bends,** U.S. INFORMAL. cramps caused by changing too suddenly from an environment of high air pressure to ordinary air pressure. —*v.i.* 1 be or become curved or crooked: *The branch began to bend as I climbed along it.* 2 stoop; bow: *She bent down and picked up a stone.* 3 submit: *I bend to God's will.* —*v.t.* 1 make curved or crooked: *The chromium rod had been bent to form the frame of a chair.* 2 force to submit. 3 turn or move in a certain direction; direct (mind or effort); apply: *She bent her mind to the new work.* 4 fasten (a sail, rope, etc.). [Old English *bendan* tighten (a bow)]

bend[2] (bend), *n.* a diagonal band on a coat of arms. [Old English]

bend ed (ben′did), *adj.* bent: *on bended knee.* —*v.* ARCHAIC. a pt. and a pp. of **bend**[1].

bend er (ben′dər), *n.* 1 person or thing that bends. 2 U.S. SLANG. a drinking spree.

be neath (bi nēth′), *adv.* 1 in a lower place, position, or state; below. 2 directly below; underneath: *Whatever you drop will fall upon the spot beneath.* —*prep.* 1 under: *The dog sat beneath the tree.* See **under** for synonym study. 2 immediately under: *No wise man kicks the ladder from beneath himself.* 3 at the foot of: *a house built beneath a tall cliff.* 4 unworthy of; worthy not even of: *Traitors are so low that they are beneath contempt.* 5 lower than in rank, dignity, etc.; below. [Old English *beneothan*]

ben e dict (ben′ə dikt), *n.* 1 a recently married man, especially one who was a bachelor for a long time. 2 a married man. [< *Benedick,* character in Shakespeare's *Much Ado About Nothing*]

Ben e dict (ben′ə dikt), *n.* **Saint,** A.D. 480?-543?, Italian monk who founded the Benedictine order.

Benedict XIV, 1675-1758, pope from 1740 to 1758.

Benedict XV, 1854-1922, pope from 1914 to 1922.

Ben e dic tine (ben′ə dik′tən, ben′ə-dik′tēn′, ben′ə dik′tīn *for n. 1 and adj.;*

ben′ə dik′tēn′, ben′ə dik′tēn *for n. 2*), *n.* 1 monk or nun following the rules of Saint Benedict or the order founded by him about A.D. 530, known for its scholarly efforts in literature and the arts. 2 **benedictine,** a kind of liqueur. *—adj.* of Saint Benedict or his order.

ben e dic tion (ben′ə dik′shən), *n.* 1 the asking of God's blessing, as at the end of a church service or a marriage ceremony. 2 the form or ritual of this invocation. 3 blessing. [< Latin *benedictionem* < *benedicere* bless < *bene* well + *dicaere* say. Doublet of BENISON.]

Ben e dic tus (ben′ə dik′təs), *n.* 1 a short hymn or canticle beginning in English "Blessed is He that cometh in the name of the Lord." 2 canticle or hymn beginning in English "Blessed be the Lord God of Israel." [< Latin *benedictus* blessed]

ben e fac tion (ben′ə fak′shən), *n.* 1 a kindly or generous action; beneficence. 2 benefit conferred; gift for charity; help given for any good purpose.

ben e fac tor (ben′ə fak′tər, ben′ə fak′tər), *n.* person who has helped others, either by gifts of money or by some kind act. [< Late Latin < Latin *benefactum* befitted < *bene* well + *facere* do]

ben e fac tress (ben′ə fak′tris, ben′ə-fak′tris), *n.* a woman benefactor.

ben e fice (ben′ə fis), *n.* a permanent office or position in the church created by proper ecclesiastical authority and consisting of a sacred duty and the income that goes with it.

be nef i cence (bə nef′ə səns), *n.* 1 a doing of good; kindness. 2 a kindly act; gift.

be nef i cent (bə nef′ə sənt), *adj.* 1 doing good; kind. 2 having good results. **—be-nef′i cent ly,** *adv.*

ben e fi cial (ben′ə fish′əl), *adj.* producing good; favorable; helpful: *Sunshine and moisture are beneficial to plants.* **—ben′e-fi′cial ly,** *adv.* **—ben′e fi′cial ness,** *n.*

ben e fi ci ar y (ben′ə fish′ē er′ē, ben′ə-fish′ər ē), *n., pl.* **-ar ies.** 1 person who receives benefit: *All the children are beneficiaries of the new playground.* 2 person who receives or is to receive money or property from an insurance policy, a will, etc.

ben e fit (ben′ə fit), *n.* 1 anything which is for the good of a person or thing; advantage; help: *Universal peace would be of great benefit to the world.* See **advantage** for synonym study. 2 ARCHAIC. act of kindness; favor. 3 performance at the theater, a game, etc., to raise money which goes to a special person or persons or to a worthy cause. 4 money paid to a sick or disabled person by an insurance company, government agency, or the like. *—v.t.* give benefit to; be good for: *Rest will benefit a sick person.* *—v.i.* receive good; profit: *I benefited from the medicine.* [Anglo-French *benfet* < Latin *benefactum* good deed < *bene* well + *facere* do]

benefit of clergy, 1 (formerly) the privilege of being tried in church courts instead of secular courts. 2 services and rites or approval of the church.

Ben e lux (ben′ə luks), *n.* an economic union of Belgium, the Netherlands, and Luxembourg organized in 1948 and now part of the European Common Market.

Be neš (be′nesh), *n.* **Eduard,** 1884-1948, Czech statesman, president of Czechoslovakia from 1935 to 1938 and from 1946 to 1948.

Be nét (bə nā′), *n.* **Stephen Vincent,** 1898-1943, American poet, novelist, and short-story writer.

be nev o lence (bə nev′ə ləns), *n.* 1 desire to promote the happiness of others; good will; kindly feeling. 2 act of kindness; something good that is done; generous gift. 3 (formerly) a forced loan to an English king, now illegal. [< Latin *benevolentia* < *bene* well + *velle* to wish]

be nev o lent (bə nev′ə lənt), *adj.* wishing or intended to promote the happiness of others; kindly; charitable. **—be-nev′o lent ly,** *adv.*

Ben gal (ben gôl′, beng gôl′), *n.* 1 former province of India, in the NE part, now divided into **West Bengal,** a part of India, and **East Bengal,** formerly a part of Pakistan and, since 1972, the country of Bangladesh. 2 **Bay of,** bay between India and Burma, the NE part of the Indian Ocean. *—adj.* of or from Bengal: *a Bengal tiger.*

Ben ga lese (ben′gə lēz′, beng′gə lēz′), *n., pl.* **-lese,** *adj.* *—n.* native or inhabitant of Bengal. *—adj.* of Bengal or its people.

Ben ga li (ben gô′lē, beng gô′lē), *adj.* of Bengal, its people, or their language. *—n.* 1 native or inhabitant of Bengal. 2 language of Bengal, a modern Indo-European language.

ben ga line (beng′gə lēn′, beng′gə lēn′), *n.* a corded cloth of silk, rayon, or cotton mixed with worsted, similar to poplin. [< French]

Ben gha zi or **Ben ga si** (ben gä′zē), *n.* one of the two capitals of Libya, on the Mediterranean. The other is Tripoli. 140,000.

Ben-Gur i on (ben gůr′ē ən), *n.* **David,** 1886-1973, prime minister of Israel from 1948 to 1953 and from 1955 to 1963.

be night ed (bi nī′tid), *adj.* 1 not knowing right from wrong; ignorant. 2 ARCHAIC. overtaken by darkness. [< obsolete verb *benight* < *be-* + *night*]

be nign (bi nīn′), *adj.* 1 kindly in feeling; benevolent; gracious: *a benign old woman.* 2 showing a kindly feeling; gentle: *a benign countenance.* 3 favorable; propitious. 4 mild: *a benign climate.* 5 not dangerous to health; not malignant: *a benign tumor.* [< Latin *benignus* < *bene* well + *-gnus* born] **—be nign′ly,** *adv.*

be nig nant (bi nig′nənt), *adj.* 1 having or showing a kindly feeling toward inferiors and dependents; benevolent: *a benignant ruler.* 2 having a good effect; beneficial. 3 (of tumors, etc.) benign. **—be nig′nant ly,** *adv.*

be nig ni ty (bi nig′nə tē), *n., pl.* **-ties.** 1 kindly feeling; graciousness. 2 a kindly act; favor.

ben i son (ben′ə zən, ben′ə sən), *n.* a blessing; benediction. [< Old French *beneison* < Latin *benedictionem.* Doublet of BENEDICTION.]

Ben ja min (ben′jə mən), *n.* 1 (in the Bible) the youngest son of Jacob. 2 one of the twelve tribes of Israel.

Ben nett (ben′it), *n.* **(Enoch) Arnold,** 1867-1931, English novelist.

Ben Ne vis (ben nē′vis; ben nev′is), mountain in W Scotland, the highest in Great Britain. 4406 ft.

bent[1] (bent), *v.* pt. and pp. of **bend.** *—adj.* 1 not straight; curved or crooked. 2 strongly inclined; determined: *I was bent on going home.* *—n.* 1 a natural inclination; tendency. 2 capacity for endurance.

bent[2] (bent), *n.* any of several fine, very resistant grasses used for lawns and pasture. [Old English *beonet-*]

Ben tham (ben′thəm, ben′təm), *n.* **Jeremy,** 1748-1832, English philosopher and political scientist.

ben thic (ben′thik), *adj.* of the benthos.

ben thos (ben′thos), *n.* 1 bottom of the ocean. 2 the plants and animals living there. [< Greek, depth (of the sea)]

Ben ton (bent′n), *n.* **Thomas Hart,** born 1889, American painter.

ben ton ite (ben′tə nīt), *n.* a soft, absorbent clay formed from the alteration of volcanic ash. [< Fort *Benton,* Montana, where it is found]

be numb (bi num′), *v.t.* 1 make numb, especially with cold. 2 stupefy; deaden. **—be-numb′ing ly,** *adv.*

Ben ze drine (ben′zə drēn′, ben′zə drin), *n.* trademark for an amphetamine.

ben zene (ben′zēn′, ben zēn′), *n.* a colorless, volatile, flammable liquid obtained chiefly from coal tar; benzol. It is used for removing grease stains and in making dyes and synthetic rubber. *Formula:* C_6H_6 [< *benzoin*]

benzene ring, a hexagonal arrangement of six carbon atoms bonded to each other by identical bonds with each carbon atom also bonded to a hydrogen atom. This structure is found in benzene and many other compounds derived from benzene.

ben zine (ben′zēn′, ben zēn′), *n.* 1 a colorless, flammable, liquid mixture of hydrocarbons obtained in distilling petroleum, used in cleaning and dyeing and as a motor fuel. 2 benzene.

ben zo ate (ben′zō āt, ben′zō it), *n.* salt or ester of benzoic acid.

benzoate of soda, a white, crystalline or powdery salt of benzoic acid, used in medicine and as a food preservative; sodium benzoate. *Formula:* C_6H_5COONa

ben zo ic acid (ben zō′ik), acid occurring in benzoin, cranberries, etc., used in medicine and as a food preservative. *Formula:* C_6H_5COOH

ben zo in (ben′zō ən, ben′zoin), *n.* a dry, brittle, fragrant resin obtained from certain species of trees of southeastern Asia, used in perfumes and in medicine. [< French *benjoin,* ultimately < Arabic *lubān jāwī* incense of Java]

ben zol (ben′zōl, ben′zol), *n.* 1 (in industrial use) benzene. 2 a mixture containing benzene and various impurities, obtained from coal tar.

Be o wulf (bā′ə wůlf), *n.* 1 an Old English epic poem in alliterative verse, composed about A.D. 700. 2 hero of this poem.

be queath (bi kwēᴛʜ′, bi kwēth′), *v.t.* 1 give or leave (especially money or other personal property) by a will. 2 hand down or leave to posterity; pass along. [Old English *becwethan* < *be-* to, for + *cwethan* say] **—be queath′er,** *n.*

be queath al (bi kwē′ᴛʜəl), *n.* act of bequeathing; bequest.

be quest (bi kwest′), *n.* 1 something bequeathed; legacy: *When she died, she left a bequest of ten thousand dollars to the university.* 2 act of bequeathing.

be rate (bi rāt′), *v.t.,* **-rat ed, -rat ing.** scold sharply; upbraid.

Ber ber (bėr′bər), *n.* 1 member of a group of Moslem tribes living in northern Africa, west of Egypt. 2 the Hamitic language of these tribes.

ber ceuse (ber sœz′), *n.* FRENCH. 1 lullaby.

2 (in music) a vocal or instrumental composition having the tender, soothing qualities of a lullaby.

be reave (bi rēv′), *v.t.*, **-reaved** or **-reft, -reav ing.** 1 leave desolate and alone: *The family was bereaved by the death of the father.* 2 deprive ruthlessly; rob: *bereaved of hope.* [Old English *berēafian* < *be-* away + *rēafian* rob]

be reave ment (bi rēv′mənt), *n.* 1 loss of a relative or friend by death. 2 bereaved condition; great loss. 3 act of bereaving.

be reft (bi reft′), *adj.* bereaved: *Bereft of hope and friends, the old man led a lonely life.* —*v.* a pt. and a pp. of **bereave.**

be ret (bə rā′, ber′ā), *n.* a soft, flat, round cap of wool, felt, etc., with no visor. [< French *béret* < Popular Latin *birrittum* < Late Latin *birrus* cloak]

berg (bėrg), *n.* iceberg.

ber ga mot (bėr′gə mot), *n.* 1 a pear-shaped variety of orange grown in southern Europe, California, and the Gulf States. 2 tree on which it grows. 3 an oil obtained from its rind, used in perfumes. 4 any of various plants of the mint family. [< French *bergamote*]

Ber gen (bėr′gən), *n.* seaport in SW Norway. 117,000.

Ber ge rac (ber′zhə räk′), *n.* **Cyrano de,** 1619-1655, French dramatist and poet, hero of a play by Rostand.

Berg son (berg′sən), *n.* **Henri,** 1859-1941, French philosopher.

be rib boned (bi rib′ənd), *adj.* trimmed or decorated with many ribbons or medals.

ber i ber i (ber′ē ber′ē), *n.* disease of the peripheral nerves characterized by muscular paralysis, weakness, and extreme loss of weight, caused by lack of vitamin B_1 in the diet. [< Singhalese, reduplication of *beri* weakness]

Ber ing Sea (bir′ing, ber′ing), sea in the N Pacific, between Alaska and Siberia. 878,000 sq. mi. See **Aleutian Islands** for map.

Bering Standard Time, the standard time in the extreme western portion of Alaska, three hours behind Pacific Standard Time.

Bering Strait, strait between the Bering Sea and the Arctic Ocean. About 50 mi. wide.

Ber keley (bėr′klē), *n.* city in W California, near San Francisco. 117,000.

ber keli um (bėr′klē əm, bėr′kē′lē əm), *n.* a radioactive metallic element produced artificially from americium, curium, or plutonium. *Symbol:* Bk; *atomic number* 97. See pages 326 and 327 for table. [< *Berkeley,* California, where it was first produced]

Berk shire (bėrk′shər, bėrk′shir; *British* bärk′shir), *n.* county in S England.

Berk shire Hills (bėrk′shər, bėrk′shir), Berkshires.

Berk shires (bėrk′shərz, bėrk′shirz), *n.pl.* range of hills in W Massachusetts. Highest peak, 3505 ft.

Ber lin (bər lin′), *n.* former capital of Germany, in the E part, now divided into West Berlin and East Berlin. 3,218,000.

Ber li oz (ber′lē ōz), *n.* **(Louis) Hector,** 1803-1869, French composer.

Ber mu da (bər myü′də), *n.* group of British islands in the N Atlantic, 580 miles east of North Carolina. 53,000 pop.; 19 sq. mi. *Capital:* Hamilton. **—Ber mu′dan, Ber mu′di an,** *adj., n.*

Ber mu das (bər myü′dəz), *n.pl.* Bermuda.

Bermuda shorts, shorts that end an inch or two above the knee.

Bern or **Berne** (bėrn, bern), *n.* capital of Switzerland, in the W part. 166,000.

Ber nard (bėr′nərd, bər närd′), *n.* **Saint,** 1090-1153, French abbot, one of the most influential churchmen in the Middle Ages.

Ber nese Alps (bėr′nēz), mountain range in SW Switzerland. Highest peak, 14,026 ft.

Bern hardt (bėrn′härt), *n.* **Sarah,** 1844-1923, French actress.

ber ry (ber′ē), *n., pl.* **-ries,** *v.,* **-ried, -ry ing.** —*n.* 1 any small, juicy fruit having many seeds instead of a stone, as the strawberry, raspberry, and gooseberry. 2 a simple fruit having a skin or rind surrounding the seeds in the pulp. Botanists classify grapes, tomatoes, currants, and bananas as berries. 3 the dry seed or kernel of certain kinds of grain or other plants: *Coffee is made from the berries of the coffee plant.* 4 a single egg of a lobster or fish. —*v.i.* 1 gather or pick berries. 2 produce berries. [Old English *berie*] **—ber′ry like′,** *adj.*

ber serk (bėr′sėrk′, bər sėrk′), *adv.* **go berserk** or **run berserk,** be carried away by madness or wild fury; become violently angry. —*adj.* 1 of unsound mind; mad; insane. 2 violently angry. [< *berserker*]

ber serk er (bėr′sėr′kər), *n.* (in Scandinavian legends) a Norse warrior who fought on the battlefield with wild fury. [< Scandinavian (Old Icelandic) *berserkr*]

berth (bėrth), *n.* 1 place to sleep on a ship, train, or airplane. 2 a ship's place at anchor or at a wharf. 3 the space necessary for safety or convenience between a ship and other ships or the shore, rocks, etc. 4 **give a wide berth to,** keep well away from. 5 appointment or position; job. —*v.t.* provide with a berth. —*v.i.* have or occupy a berth. [perhaps < *bear*[1]]

ber tha (bėr′thə), *n.* a woman's wide collar, usually of lace, that often extends over the shoulders. [< French *berthe* < *Berthe,* mother of Charlemagne]

Ber til lon system (bėr′tə lon; *French* ber tē yôN′), system of identifying criminals by recording of individual measurements, replaced by fingerprinting. [< Alphonse *Bertillon,* 1853-1914, French criminologist, who devised it]

ber yl (ber′əl), *n.* a very hard translucent or opaque mineral, usually green or blue-green, a silicate of beryllium and aluminum, used as a gem. Emeralds and aquamarines are transparent varieties of beryl. [< Latin *beryllus* < Greek *bēryllos*]

be ryl li um (bə ril′ē əm), *n.* a hard, light, metallic element found in various minerals, used in alloys and in controlling the speed of neutrons in atomic reactors. *Symbol:* Be; *atomic number* 4. See pages 326 and 327 for table. [< New Latin < *beryllus* beryl]

Ber ze li us (bər zē′lē əs; *Swedish* ber sā′lē us), *n.* **Jöns Jakob,** 1779-1848, Swedish chemist who invented the modern system of chemical symbols and writing of formulas.

be seech (bi sēch′), *v.t.,* **-sought** or **-seeched, -seech ing.** ask earnestly; beg; implore. See **beg** for synonym study. [Middle English *bisechen* < *be-* thoroughly + *sechen* seek] **—be seech′er,** *n.* **—be seech′ing ly,** *adv.*

be seem (bi sēm′), ARCHAIC. —*v.t.* seem proper for; befit; suit. —*v.i.* seem proper or fitting.

be set (bi set′), *v.t.,* **-set, -set ting.** 1 attack from all sides; set upon in attack: *We were beset by mosquitoes in the swamp.* 2 surround; hem in: *beset by a crowd.* 3 set with decorative objects; stud: *Her bracelet was beset with pearls.* [Old English *besettan* < *be-* around + *settan* set]

hat, āge, fär; let, ēqual, tėrm;
it, īce; hot, ōpen, ôrder;
oil, out; cup, pu̇t, rüle;
ch, child; ng, long; sh, she;
th, thin; ᴛʜ, then; zh, measure;

ə represents *a* in about, *e* in taken,
i in pencil, *o* in lemon, *u* in circus.

< = from, derived from, taken from.

be set ting (bi set′ing), *adj.* habitually attacking: *a besetting sin.*

be shrew (bi shrü′), *v.t.* ARCHAIC. curse (used as a mild exclamation).

be side (bi sīd′), *prep.* 1 by the side of; close to; near: *Grass grows beside the fence.* 2 in addition to: *Other men beside ourselves were helping.* 3 compared with: *The wolf seems tame beside the tiger.* 4 away from; aside from; not related to: *That question is beside the point.* 5 besides. 6 **beside oneself,** out of one's mind; crazy or upset. —*adv.* besides. [Old English *bi sīdan* by side]

be sides (bi sīdz′), *adv.* 1 more than that; also; moreover: *I didn't want to fight; besides, I had come to see the game.* 2 in addition: *We tried two other ways besides.* —*prep.* 1 in addition to; over and above: *The picnic was attended by others besides our own club members.* 2 other than; except: *We spoke of no one besides you.*

be siege (bi sēj′), *v.t.,* **-sieged, -sieg ing.** 1 surround by armed forces in order to compel surrender; lay siege to: *For ten years the Greeks besieged the city of Troy.* 2 crowd around: *Hundreds of admirers besieged the famous astronaut.* 3 overwhelm with requests, questions, etc. **—be sieg′er,** *n.*

be smear (bi smir′), *v.t.* 1 smear over. 2 sully.

be smirch (bi smėrch′), *v.t.* 1 make dirty. 2 sully. **—be smirch′er,** *n.*

be som (bē′zəm), *n.* broom made of twigs. [Old English *besema*]

be sot (bi sot′), *v.t.,* **-sot ted, -sot ting.** 1 make foolish. 2 stupefy. 3 intoxicate.

be sought (bi sôt′), *v.* a pt. and a pp. of **beseech.**

be spake (bi spāk′), *v.* ARCHAIC. a pt. of **bespeak.**

be span gle (bi spang′gəl), *v.t.,* **-gled, -gling.** adorn with spangles or anything like them.

be spat ter (bi spat′ər), *v.t.* 1 spatter all over. 2 soil by spattering. 3 to slander. **—be spat′ter er,** *n.*

be speak (bi spēk′), *v.t.,* **-spoke, -spo ken** or **-spoke, -speak ing.** 1 ask for in advance; order; reserve: *We want to bespeak two tickets for the new play.* 2 be a sign of; show; indicate: *The neat house bespeaks care.* 3 show in advance; point toward (some future event). 4 ARCHAIC. speak to; address.

be spec ta cled (bi spek′tə kəld), *adj.* wearing glasses.

be spoke (bi spōk′), *v.* a pt. and a pp. of **bespeak.** —*adj.* BRITISH. made-to-order: *a bespoke overcoat.*

be spo ken (bi spō′kən), *v.* a pp. of **bespeak.**

be sprent (bi sprent′), *adj.* ARCHAIC. sprinkled all over; besprinkled. [Middle English, past participle of *besprengen* sprinkle on]

be sprin kle (bi spring′kəl), *v.t.,* **-kled, -kling.** sprinkle all over.

Bes sa ra bi a (bes′ə rā′bē ə), *n.* region in SW Soviet Union, on the Black Sea. **—Bes′sa ra′bi an,** *adj., n.*

Bes se mer (bes′ə mər), *n.* Sir **Henry,** 1813-1898, English engineer who invented the Bessemer process.

Bessemer converter, a large container for making molten iron into steel by the Bessemer process.

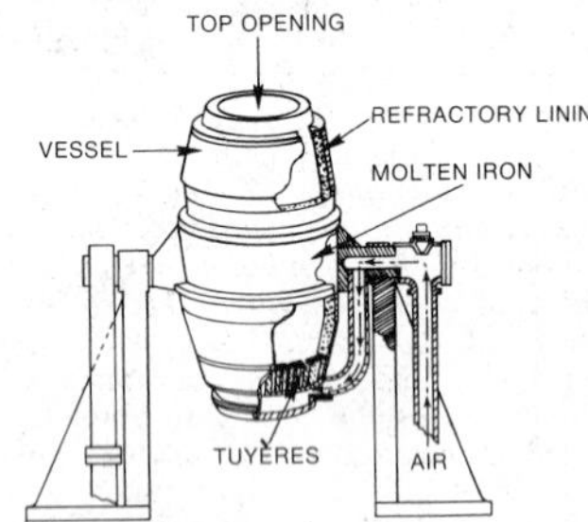

Bessemer converter
The vessel is tilted, to prevent blockage of the tuyères, while being filled through the top opening with molten iron. As the vessel is righted, air is blasted through the tuyères, bubbling through the iron and refining it into steel, which is then poured out through the top opening.

Bessemer process, method of making steel by forcing a blast of air through molten iron in order to burn out carbon and other impurities.

best (best), *adj., superlative of* **good;** *adv., superlative of* **well**[1]**;** *n., v.* *—adj.* 1 of the most desirable, valuable or superior quality: *the best food to eat.* 2 of the greatest advantage, usefulness, or suitability: *the best thing to do.* 3 largest: *the best part of the day.* 4 chief: *our best hope.*
—adv. 1 in the most excellent way; most thoroughly: *Who reads best?* 2 in or to the highest degree: *I like this book best.* 3 **had best,** ought to; will be wise to; should.
—n. 1 person, thing, part, or state that is best: *We want the best. The ending was the best of all.* 2 the most that is possible; utmost: *I did my best to finish the work on time.* 3 best clothes: *dressed in their Sunday best.* 4 the greatest part: *the best of three games.*
all for the best, not so bad as it seems.
at best, under the most favorable circumstances.
get the best of, defeat.
have the best of, defeat.
make the best of, do as well as possible with.
with the best, as well as anyone.
—v.t. INFORMAL. get the better of; outdo; defeat.
[Old English *betst*]

be stead (bi sted′), *v.,* **-stead ed, -stead ed** or **-stead, -stead ing,** *adj.* ARCHAIC. *—v.t.* be of help to; assist. *—adj.* beset (by dangers, fears, etc.).

bes tial (bes′chəl), *adj.* 1 like a beast; beastly. 2 sensual; obscene. 3 of beasts. [< Latin *bestialis* < *bestia* beast] **—bes′tial ly,** *adv.*

bes ti al i ty (bes′chē al′ə tē), *n., pl.* **-ties.** 1 bestial qualities; brutality. 2 unrestricted indulgence; lust; sensuality. 3 a bestial act.

be stir (bi stėr′), *v.t.,* **-stirred, -stir ring.** rouse to action; stir up.

best man, the chief attendant of the bridegroom at a wedding.

be stow (bi stō′), *v.t.* 1 give (something) as a gift; give; confer. 2 make use of; apply. 3 ARCHAIC. put safely; store. 4 ARCHAIC. find quarters for; lodge.

be stow al (bi stō′əl), *n.* act of bestowing.

be strew (bi strü′), *v.t.,* **-strewed, -strewed** or **-strewn, -strew ing.** 1 strew (a surface) with things. 2 strew or scatter (things) about. 3 lie scattered over (a surface).

be strewn (bi strün′), *adj.* scattered about. *—v.* a pp. of **bestrew.**

be strid den (bi strid′n), *v.* pp. of **bestride.**

be stride (bi strīd′), *v.t.,* **-strode, -stridden, -strid ing.** 1 get on, sit on, or stand over (something) with one leg on each side. 2 straddle over. 3 stride across; step over.

be strode (bi strōd′), *v.* pt. of **bestride.** *He bestrode his horse.*

best seller, 1 anything, especially a book, that has a very large sale. 2 author of a book with a very large sale.

bet (bet), *v.,* **bet** or **bet ted, bet ting,** *n.* *—v.t.* 1 promise (some money or a certain thing) to another if he is right and you are wrong; wager. 2 be very sure: *I bet you are wrong about that.* *—v.i.* make a bet; lay a wager: *Which horse did he bet on?* *—n.* 1 a promise or pledge to give some money or a certain thing to another if he is right and you are wrong. 2 the money or thing promised. 3 thing to bet on: *That horse is a good bet.* [origin uncertain]

be ta (bā′tə), *n.* 1 the second letter of the Greek alphabet (Β, β). 2 the second of a series. 3 the second brightest star of a constellation.

be take (bi tāk′), *v.t.,* **-took, -tak en, -tak ing. betake oneself, a** make one's way; go: *They betake themselves to the mountains every summer.* **b** apply oneself: *I betook myself to hard study.*

beta particle, electron or positron released by the nucleus of a radioactive substance in the process of disintegration.

beta ray, stream of beta particles.

be ta tron (bā′tə tron), *n.* particle accelerator in which electrons are accelerated to high speeds by a changing magnetic field.

be tel (bē′tl), *n.* a climbing pepper plant of the East Indies, whose leaves are wrapped around betel nuts with a little lime and chewed. [< Portuguese < Malayalam *vettila*]

Be tel geuse (bē′tl jüz, bet′l jüz), *n.* a red giant star of the first magnitude in the constellation Orion.

betel nut, the orange-colored nut of a tropical Asiatic palm tree.

bête noire (bāt′ nwär′), thing or person especially dreaded or detested; bugbear. [< French, black beast]

Beth a ny (beth′ə nē), *n.* village near Jerusalem, now in NW Jordan.

beth el (beth′əl), *n.* 1 (in the Bible) a holy place. 2 church or chapel for seamen. [< Hebrew *bēthēl* house of God]

be think (bi thingk′), *v.,* **-thought, -think ing.** *—v.t.* **bethink oneself of, a** consider; reflect on: *I bethought myself of the need to study.* **b** remember: *You should bethink yourself of your duty to them.* *—v.i.* ARCHAIC. to deliberate; consider.

Beth le hem (beth′lə hem, beth′lē əm), *n.* 1 birthplace of Jesus, a town now in Jordan six miles south of Jerusalem. 36,000. 2 city in E Pennsylvania. 73,000.

be thought (bi thôt′), *v.* pt. and pp. of **bethink.**

Be thune (bə thün′), *n.* **Mary McLeod,** 1875-1955, American educator.

be tide (bi tīd′), *v.,* **-tid ed, -tid ing.** *—v.t.* happen to: *Woe betide you if you betray us.* *—v.i.* happen: *No matter what betides, the family will hold together.*

be times (bi tīmz′), *adv.* ARCHAIC. 1 early. 2 before it is too late. 3 in a short time; soon.

be to ken (bi tō′kən), *v.t.* be a sign or token of; indicate; show.

be took (bi tük′), *v.* pt. of **betake.**

be tray (bi trā′), *v.t.* 1 place in the hands of an enemy by treachery or disloyalty: *The fort was betrayed by its commander.* 2 be disloyal to (one's cause or leader); be unfaithful to. 3 disclose or reveal (secrets entrusted to one): *betray a friend's confidence.* 4 disclose unintentionally: *Her confusion betrayed the feelings she was trying to hide.* 5 show signs of; reveal: *a comment betraying lack of sympathy.* 6 lead into error; mislead; deceive: *I was betrayed by my own enthusiasm.* 7 seduce and desert. [Middle English *bitraien* < *be-* + *traien* betray < Old French *traïr* < Latin *tradere* hand over] **—be tray′er,** *n.*

be tray al (bi trā′əl), *n.* 1 a betraying. 2 a being betrayed.

be troth (bi trōᴛʜ′, bi trôth′), *v.t.* engage (two persons, one to the other) with a view to marriage.

be troth al (bi trō′ᴛʜəl, bi trô′thəl), *n.* a promise in marriage; engagement.

be trothed (bi trōᴛʜd′, bi trôtht′), *n.* person engaged to be married. *—adj.* engaged to be married.

bet ter[1] (bet′ər), *adj., comparative of* **good;** *adv., comparative of* **well**[1]**;** *n., v.* *—adj.* 1 more desirable, useful, or suitable than another: *He left for a better job.* 2 of superior quality: *better bread.* 3 larger; greater: *Four days is the better part of a week.* 4 improved in health; less sick: *The sick child is better today.* 5 **go one better,** do better than; outstrip; excel.
—adv. 1 more desirably, usefully, etc.; in a more excellent way: *Do better another time.* 2 in or to a higher degree; more completely: *I know her better than I know anyone else.* 3 more: *It is better than a mile to town.* 4 **better off,** in a better condition. 5 **had better,** ought to; will be wise to; should. 6 **think better of, a** think over and change one's mind about. **b** form a better opinion of (a person).
—n. 1 person, thing, or state that is better: *the better of two roads.* 2 Usually, **betters,** *pl.* one's superiors: *Listen to the advice of your betters.* 3 **for the better,** toward improvement or recovery. 4 **get the better of** or **have the better of,** be superior to; defeat.
—v.t. 1 make better; improve: *We can better that work by being more careful.* 2 do better than; surpass: *The other class cannot better our grades.* *—v.i.* 1 become better; improve: *The situation has bettered since yesterday.* 2 **better oneself,** improve one's position, condition, or circumstances.
[Old English *betera*]

bet ter[2] (bet′ər), *n.* bettor.

bet ter ment (bet′ər mənt), *n.* 1 a making better; improvement. 2 Usually, **better-**

ments, *pl.* an improvement of real estate property.

bet tor (bet′ər), *n.* person who bets. Also, **better.**

be tween (bi twēn′), *prep.* 1 in the space or time separating: *There is a distance of ten feet between the two trees.* 2 in the range or part separating: *She earned between ten and twelve dollars.* 3 from one part to the other of; joining; connecting: *a highway between cities.* 4 having to do with: *war between two countries.* 5 in regard to one or the other of: *We must choose between the two books.* 6 by the combined action of: *They caught twelve fish between them.* 7 in the combined possession of: *They own the property between them.* 8 **between you and me,** as a secret; confidentially. *—adv.* 1 in the space or time separating: *We could not see the moon, for a cloud came between.* 2 **in between, a** in the middle. **b** in the midst of; among. [Old English *betwēonum* < *be-* by + *twā* two] **—be tween′ness,** *n.*

➜ **between you and me.** When two pronouns follow a preposition in standard English both pronouns are in the objective case: *between you and me* (or *between you and her, between you and him, between you and us, between you and them*). ➜ See **among** for another usage note.

be tween times (bi twēn′tīmz′), *adv.* at intervals.

be twixt (bi twikst′), *prep., adv.* 1 ARCHAIC. between. 2 **betwixt and between,** in the middle; neither one nor the other. [Old English *betweox*]

Bev or **BeV** (bev), *n.* a billion electron volts, used as a unit for measuring energy in nuclear physics. [< *b(illion) e(lectron) v(olts)*]

bev a tron (bev′ə tron), *n.* particle accelerator in which protons are accelerated to energies of a billion or more electron volts.

bev el (bev′əl), *n., v.,* **-eled, -el ing** or **-elled, -el ling,** *adj.* *—n.* 1 a sloping edge or surface. There is often a bevel on a picture frame, on a mirror, or on a piece of plate glass. 2 any angle except a right angle. 3 instrument or tool consisting of a flat rule with a movable arm pivoted at one end, used for drawing angles or for adjusting the surfaces of work to a particular angle. *—v.t.* cut or slant to a bevel: *to bevel plate glass.* *—v.i.* slope; slant. *—adj.* slanting; oblique. [< Middle French *beveau*]

bev er age (bev′ər ij), *n.* liquid used or prepared for drinking, as milk, tea, coffee, beer, or wine. [< Old French *bevrage* < *bevre* to drink < Latin *bibere*]

bev y (bev′ē), *n., pl.* **bev ies.** 1 a small group of women or girls. 2 flock of birds, especially of larks or quails. 3 any small group. [origin uncertain]

be wail (bi wāl′), *v.t.* express great sorrow for; mourn. *—v.i.* wail; mourn.

be ware (bi wer′, bi war′), *v.i.* be wary or cautious; be on guard: *You must beware of swimming in a strong current. Beware lest you anger him.* *—v.t.* be on guard against: *Beware the dog!* [< phrase *be ware*]

be wil der (bi wil′dər), *v.t.* 1 confuse completely; perplex: *The child was bewildered by the crowds.* See **puzzle** for synonym study. 2 ARCHAIC. cause to lose one's way or bearings. **—be wil′der ing ly,** *adv.* **—be wil′der ment,** *n.*

be witch (bi wich′), *v.t.* 1 put under a spell; affect by witchcraft or magic. 2 charm; fascinate: *The ease and beauty of her style bewitch the reader.* **—be witch′ing ly,** *adv.* **—be witch′ment,** *n.*

be witch er y (bi wich′ər ē), *n.* 1 fact or power of bewitching. 2 charm; spell.

be wray (bi rā′), *v.t.* ARCHAIC. make known; reveal. [Middle English *bewreien* < *be-* + *wreien* < Old English *wrēgan* accuse]

bey (bā), *n., pl.* **beys.** 1 governor of a province or district of the Ottoman Empire. 2 (formerly) a title of respect for persons of rank in Turkey, Egypt, etc. 3 (formerly) a native ruler of Tunis. [< Turkish]

be yond (bi yond′), *prep.* 1 on or to the farther side of: *She lives beyond the sea.* 2 farther on than: *The school is beyond the last house.* 3 later than; past: *They stayed beyond the time set.* 4 out of the reach, range, or understanding of: *The meaning of this story is beyond me.* 5 more than; exceeding: *The price of the suit was beyond what I could pay.* 6 in addition to; besides: *I will do nothing beyond the job given me.* *—adv.* farther away: *Beyond were the hills.* *—n.* **the beyond** or **the great beyond,** life after death; hereafter. [Old English *begeondan* < *be-* at, near + *geondan* yond]

Bey routh (bā rüt′, bā′rüt), *n.* Beirut.

bez el (bez′əl), *n.* 1 a slope or sloping edge, especially of a chisel or other cutting tool. 2 the sloping sides or faces of a cut gem, especially those of the upper half. 3 the grooved ring or rim that holds a gem or a watch crystal in its setting. [< Old French *bizel*]

be zique (bə zēk′), *n.* a card game resembling pinochle, using 64 cards. [< French *bésigue*]

b.f. or **bf.,** (in printing) boldface.

bg., *pl.* **bgs.** bag.

bhang (bang), *n.* 1 variety of hemp grown in India. 2 preparation of dried hemp leaves and seed cases smoked or eaten as a narcotic and intoxicant in India. [ultimately < Sanskrit *bhaṅgā* hemp]

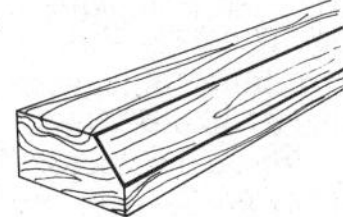

bevel (def. 1)

bevel (def. 3)

Bhar at (bur′ut), *n.* official name of India.

Bhu tan (bü tän′), *n.* country between Tibet and NE India. Bhutan's foreign affairs are partly under the control of the government of India. 1,000,000 pop.; 18,000 sq. mi. *Capital:* Thimbu.

Bhu tan ese (büt′n ēz′), *n., pl.* **-ese,** *adj.* *—n.* native or inhabitant of Bhutan. *—adj.* of Bhutan or its people.

bi-, *prefix.* 1 twice a ___: *Biannual = twice a year.* 2 doubly ___: *Bipinnate = doubly pinnate.* 3 two ___: *Bisect = divide into two parts.* 4 having two ___: *Biped = having two feet.* 5 once every two ___: *Bimonthly = once every two months.* [< Latin *bi-* < *bis* twice]

Bi, bismuth.

Bi a fra (bē ä′frə), *n.* region in S Nigeria, known as the Eastern Region, in rebellion against the central government from 1967 to 1970.

bi an nu al (bī an′yü əl), *adj.* occurring twice a year. **—bi an′nu al ly,** *adv.*

➜ **biannual, biennial.** *Biannual* means occurring twice a year; *biennial* means occurring once in two years: *Our doctor recommends a biannual visit to the dentist. The sophomores are taking the biennial intelligence exam this afternoon.*

hat, āge, fär; let, ēqual, tėrm;
it, īce; hot, ōpen, ôrder;
oil, out; cup, pu̇t, rüle;
ch, child; ng, long; sh, she;
th, thin; ŦH, then; zh, measure;

ə represents *a* in about, *e* in taken, *i* in pencil, *o* in lemon, *u* in circus.

< = from, derived from, taken from.

Biar ritz (byä rits′, bē′ə rits′), *n.* seaside resort in SW France. 25,000.

bi as (bī′əs), *n., adj., adv., v.,* **-ased, -as ing** or **-assed, -as sing.** *—n.* 1 a slanting or oblique line, especially across a woven fabric. 2 **on the bias,** diagonally across the weave: *cloth cut on the bias.* 3 tendency to favor one side too much; inclination or leaning based on prejudice. See **prejudice** for synonym study. 4 in the game of bowls: **a** the lopsided shape of a ball that makes it swerve when rolled. **b** the weight or force that makes it swerve. *—adj.* slanting across the threads of cloth; oblique; diagonal. *—adv.* obliquely. *—v.t.* give a bias to; influence, usually unfairly; prejudice. [< Middle French *biais* slant]

bi ased (bī′əst), *adj.* favoring one side too much; prejudiced.

bi ath lon (bī ath′lon), *n.* an Olympic contest combining a cross-country ski race with rifle marksmanship. [< *bi-* two + Greek *athlon* contest]

bi ax i al (bī ak′sē əl), *adj.* having two axes: *a biaxial crystal.*

bib (bib), *n.* 1 cloth worn under the chin to protect clothing, especially by small children at meals. 2 part of an apron or overalls above the waist. 3 anything similar to a bib in purpose or design. [Middle English *bibben* to drink]

Bib., 1 Bible. 2 Biblical.

bib and tucker, INFORMAL. clothes.

bib ber (bib′ər), *n.* a habitual drinker of alcoholic liquor. [< earlier *bib* to drink]

bi be lot (bib′lō; *French* bē blō′), *n.* a small object valued for its beauty, rarity, or interest. [< French]

Bi ble (bī′bəl), *n.* 1 the collection of sacred writings of the Christian religion, comprising the Old and New Testaments. 2 the form of the Old Testament accepted by the Jews. 3 the sacred writings of any religion: *The Koran is the Bible of the Moslems.* 4 **bible,** any book accepted as an authority: *Gray's "Manual," the botanist's bible, was most useful.* [< Old French < Medieval Latin *biblia* < Greek, plural of *biblion* book < *biblos* originally, papyrus]

bib li cal or **Bib li cal** (bib′lə kəl), *adj.* 1 of the Bible: *biblical literature.* 2 according to the Bible: *biblical history.* 3 in the Bible: *a biblical reference to Solomon.* **—bib′li cal ly, Bib′li cal ly,** *adv.*

biblio-, *combining form.* book or books: *Bibliophile = lover of books.* [< Greek *biblion* book]

bib li og ra pher (bib′lē og′rə fər), *n.* 1 compiler of a bibliography. 2 an expert in bibliography.

bib li o graph ic (bib′lē ə graf′ik), *adj.* bibliographical.

bib li o graph i cal (bib′lē ə graf′ə kəl), *adj.* of bibliography. **—bib′li o graph′i cal ly,** *adv.*

bib li og ra phy (bib′lē og′rə fē), *n., pl.* **-phies.** 1 list of books, articles, etc., about a particular subject or person. 2 list of books, articles, etc., by a certain author. 3 study of the authorship, editions, dates, etc., of books, manuscripts, articles, etc. 4 list of the books, articles, etc., consulted or referred to by an author in the preparation of an article or book.

bib li o phile (bib′lē ə fīl), *n.* lover of books, especially one who likes to collect books.

bib u lous (bib′yə ləs), *adj.* 1 fond of drinking alcoholic liquor. 2 showing the effects of drinking alcoholic liquor; drunk. 3 absorbent of moisture. [< Latin *bibulus* < *bibere* to drink] **—bib′u lous ly,** *adv.* **—bib′u lous ness,** *n.*

bi cam er al (bī kam′ər əl), *adj.* having or consisting of two legislative chambers. The Congress of the United States is bicameral; it consists of the Senate and the House of Representatives. [< *bi-* two + Latin *camera* chamber]

bi car bo nate (bī kär′bə nit, bī kär′ bə nāt), *n.* salt of carbonic acid formed by neutralizing one hydrogen ion.

bicarbonate of soda, sodium bicarbonate.

bi cen te nar y (bī′sen ten′ər ē, bī sen′tə ner′ē), *adj., n., pl.* **-nar ies.** *—adj.* bicentennial (def. 1). *—n.* a bicentennial.

bi cen ten ni al (bī′sen ten′ē əl), *adj.* 1 having to do with a period of 200 years or a 200th anniversary. 2 recurring every 200 years. *—n.* 1 a 200th anniversary. 2 the celebration of this.

bi ceps (bī′seps), *n., pl.* **-ceps** or **-ceps es.** any muscle having two heads or origins: **a** the large muscle in the front part of the upper arm, which bends the forearm. **b** the corresponding large muscle in the back of the thigh. [< Latin, two-headed < *bi-* two + *caput* head]

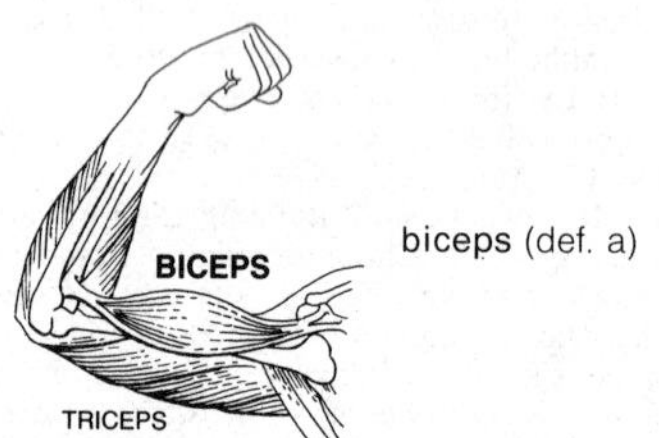

biceps (def. a)

bi chlo ride (bī klôr′īd, bī klôr′id; bī klōr′īd, bī klōr′id), *n.* dichloride.

bichloride of mercury, mercuric chloride.

bi chro mate (bī krō′māt), *n.* dichromate.

bick er (bik′ər), *v.i.* engage in a petty, noisy quarrel; squabble. *—n.* a petty, noisy quarrel. [Middle English *bikeren*]

bi col or (bī′kul′ər), *adj.* bicolored. *—n.* a two-colored blossom.

bi col ored (bī′kul′ərd), *adj.* having two colors.

bi con cave (bī kon′kāv, bī′kon kāv′), *adj.* concave on both sides.

bi con vex (bī kon′veks, bī′kon veks′), *adj.* convex on both sides.

bi cul tur al (bī kul′chər əl), *adj.* having two distinct cultures existing side by side.

bi cul tur al ism (bī kul′chər ə liz′əm), *n.* 1 policy that favors a country, province, etc., being bicultural. 2 practice or support of such a policy.

bi cus pid (bī kus′pid), *n.* a double-pointed premolar tooth that tears and grinds food. A human adult has eight bicuspids. See **incisor** for picture. *—adj.* having two points or cusps.

bi cy cle (bī′sik′əl, bī′sə kəl), *n., v.,* **-cled, -cling.** *—n.* a lightweight vehicle consisting of a metal frame with two wheels, one behind the other, a handlebar for steering, a seat for the rider, and pedals propelled by pressure of the feet. A motor bicycle is propelled by an engine. *—v.i.* ride or travel on a bicycle. [< *bi-* two + Greek *kyklos* circle, wheel] **—bi′cy cler,** *n.*

bi cy clist (bī′sik′list, bī′sə klist), *n.* person who rides a bicycle.

bid (bid), *v.,* **bade, bid** or (ARCHAIC) **bad, bid den** or **bid, bid ding,** *n.* *—v.t.* 1 tell (someone) what to do, where to go, etc.; command; order: *Do as I bid you. You bade me forget what is unforgettable. They were bidden to assemble.* 2 say or tell (a greeting, etc.); wish: *My friends came to bid me good-by.* 3 offer to pay (a certain price), especially at an auction: *She bid five dollars for the table.* 4 proclaim; declare: *She bade defiance to them all.* 5 state as the number of tricks or points one proposes to make or to win in some card games. 6 ARCHAIC. invite. 7 **bid in,** buy at auction to keep for the owner. 8 **bid up,** raise the price of by bidding more. *—v.i.* 1 offer a price; state a price: *Several companies will bid for the contract.* 2 **bid fair,** seem likely; have a good chance: *The plan bids fair to succeed.*
—n. 1 a bidding. 2 an offer to pay a certain price. 3 amount offered or stated: *My bid was $7.* 4 amount bid in a card game. 5 turn of a player to bid. 6 invitation. 7 an attempt to secure, achieve, or win: *He is making a great bid for popular support.*
[Old English *biddan* ask; meaning influenced by *bēodan* to offer, command] **—bid′der,** *n.*

b.i.d., (take) twice a day (used in doctors' prescriptions). [for Latin *bis in die*]

bid da ble (bid′ə bəl), *adj.* 1 doing what is ordered; obedient; docile. 2 on which a bid or bids can be made in a card game.

bid den (bid′n), *v.* a pp. of **bid.** *—adj.* invited.

bid ding (bid′ing), *n.* 1 command; order. 2 invitation. 3 the offering of a certain price for something, especially at an auction. 4 (in card games) the bids collectively. 5 **do one's bidding,** obey one.

bid dy[1] (bid′ē), *n., pl.* **-dies.** DIALECT. hen. [origin uncertain]

bid dy[2] (bid′ē), *n., pl.* **-dies.** a talkative old woman. [< the name *Biddy,* diminutive of *Bridget*]

bide (bīd), *v.,* **bode** or **bid ed, bid ed, bid ing.** *—v.i.* 1 remain or continue in some state or action; wait: *bide here a bit.* 2 ARCHAIC. dwell; reside. *—v.t.* ARCHAIC. put up with; endure; suffer. [Old English *bīdan*]

bi det (bi det′, bi dā′), *n.* a shallow porcelain bowl, usually with a nozzle and running water, used to bathe the genital and anal areas.

bi en ni al (bī en′ē əl), *adj.* 1 (of a plant) lasting two years; germinating in one year or growing season, and flowering, fruiting, and dying in the next year or growing season. 2 occurring every two years. *—n.* 1 plant that lives two years or seasons. Carrots and onions are biennials. 2 event that occurs every two years. [< Latin *biennium* a two-year period < *bi-* two + *annus* year] **—bi en′ni al ly,** *adv.* ➤ See **biannual** for usage note.

bier (bir), *n.* 1 a movable stand or framework on which a coffin or dead body is placed before burial. 2 such a stand together with the coffin. [Old English *bēr.* Related to *beran* BEAR[1].]

bi fid (bī′fid), *adj.* divided into two parts by a cleft; forked. [< Latin *bifidus* < *bi-* two + *findere* cleave] **—bi′fid ly,** *adv.*

bi fo cal (bī fō′kəl, bī′fō′kəl), *adj.* having two focuses. Bifocal lenses have two sections of different focal lengths, the upper for distant, the lower for near vision. *—n.* 1 **bifocals,** *pl.* pair of glasses having bifocal lenses. 2 a bifocal lens.

bi fur cate (*v.,* bī′fər kāt, bī fėr′kāt; *adj.* bī′fər kāt, bī fėr′kit), *v.,* **-cat ed, -cat ing,** *adj.* *—v.t., v.i.* divide into two branches. *—adj.* divided into two branches; forked. [< Medieval Latin *bifurcatum* forked < Latin *bifurcus* < *bi-* two + *furca* fork] **—bi′fur cate ly,** *adv.* **—bi′fur ca′tion,** *n.*

big (big), *adj.,* **big ger, big gest,** *adv.* *—adj.* 1 great in extent, amount, size, etc.; large: *a big room, a big book.* See **great** for synonym study. 2 grown up: *a big girl.* 3 important; great: *This is big news.* 4 of high position or standing: *The President is a big man.* 5 full; loud: *a big voice.* 6 filled; teeming: *eyes big with tears.* 7 generous; noble: *a big heart.* 8 boastful; pompous: *big talk.* 9 pregnant: *big with child.* *—adv.* INFORMAL. 1 boastfully: *He talks big.* 2 prosperously: *Things are going big.* [Middle English] **—big′ness,** *n.*

big a mist (big′ə mist), *n.* person married to more than one person at a time.

big a mous (big′ə məs), *adj.* 1 being married to more than one person at a time. 2 of or having to do with bigamy. **—big′a mous ly,** *adv.*

big a my (big′ə mē), *n.* practice or condition of having two wives or two husbands at the same time. Bigamy is illegal in most countries.

big bang theory, theory which maintains that the universe originated in a cosmic explosion of hydrogen, which became condensed into the galaxies.

big business, business and industry considered as one large, powerful group.

Big Dipper, group of seven bright stars in the constellation of Ursa Major, thought of as being arranged in the shape of a dipper.

big gish (big′ish), *adj.* somewhat big.

big-heart ed (big′här′tid), *adj.* kindly; generous.

big horn (big′hôrn′), *n., pl.* **-horns** or **-horn.** a wild, grayish-brown sheep of the Rocky Mountains, having thick, gracefully curved horns; Rocky Mountain sheep.

Big Horn, river flowing north from central Wyoming into the Yellowstone River in Montana. 336 mi.

Big Horn Mountains, range of the Rocky Mountains in N Wyoming and S Montana. Highest peak, 13,165 ft.

bight (bīt), *n.* 1 a long curve in a coastline, the shore of a river, or a range of mountains. 2 bay formed by this curve. 3 loop of rope; slack of rope between the fastened ends. [Old English *byht*]

hat, āge, fär; let, ēqual, tėrm;
it, īce; hot, ōpen, ôrder;
oil, out; cup, pu̇t, rüle;
ch, child; ng, long; sh, she;
th, thin; ᴛʜ, then; zh, measure;

ə represents *a* in about, *e* in taken, *i* in pencil, *o* in lemon, *u* in circus.

< = from, derived from, taken from.

big no ni a (big nō′nē ə), *n.* a tropical vine with clusters of showy, trumpet-shaped, orange-red flowers; trumpet vine; trumpet creeper. [< Abbé *Bignon,* librarian to Louis XIV]

big ot (big′ət), *n.* person who is bigoted; intolerant person. [< Middle French]

big ot ed (big′ə tid), *adj.* obstinately and unreasonably attached to a particular opinion, belief, party, etc., and intolerant of all who have different views; intolerant. **—big′ot ed ly,** *adv.*

big ot ry (big′ə trē), *n., pl.* **-ries.** bigoted conduct or attitude; intolerance.

big shot, SLANG. an important person.

big stick, military power wielded by a government as a means of coercion.

big time, SLANG. the top level in arts, sports, politics, industry, etc.

big top, 1 the largest tent of a circus. 2 INFORMAL. circus.

big tree, 1 giant sequoia. 2 redwood.

big wheel, SLANG. an influential person in a particular activity, industry, etc.

big wig (big′wig′), *n.* INFORMAL. an important person.

bike (bīk), *n., v.,* **biked, bik ing.** INFORMAL. *—n.* bicycle. *—v.i.* ride a bicycle.

bi ki ni (bə kē′nē), *n.* 1 a very scant two-piece bathing suit for women and girls. 2 **Bikini,** atoll in the Marshall Islands in the W Pacific, site of some U.S. atomic and hydrogen bomb tests.

bi la bi al (bī lā′bē əl), *adj.* formed by both lips; articulated by bringing the lips close together. *—n.* sound formed by both lips. *B, p, m,* and *w* are bilabials.

bi la bi ate (bī lā′bē at, bī lā′bē it), *adj.* having an upper and lower lip, as the corollas of flowers of the mint family.

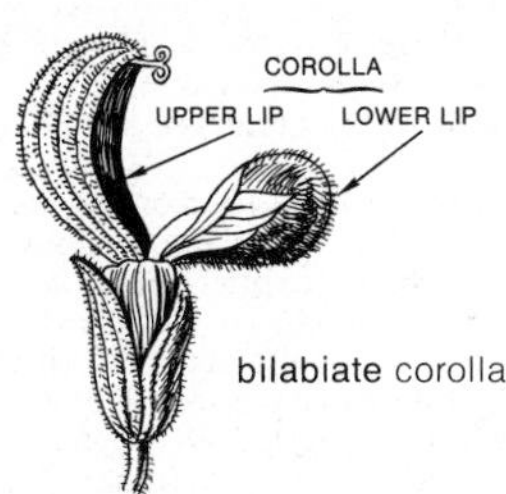

bilabiate corolla

bi lat er al (bī lat′ər əl), *adj.* 1 having two symmetrical sides. 2 on two sides. 3 binding both sides or parties: *The two nations signed a bilateral treaty.* **—bi lat′er al ly,** *adv.*

bilateral symmetry, (in zoology) a condition in which like parts are arranged in two halves, so that each half is the counterpart of the other, divisible in one plane only.

Bil ba o (bil bä′ō), *n.* seaport in N Spain. 401,000.

bil ber ry (bil′ber′ē, bil′bər ē), *n., pl.* **-ries.** 1 a small, edible, bluish-black berry much like a blueberry. 2 shrub that it grows on. [apparently < Scandinavian (Danish) *böllebær*]

bil bo¹ (bil′bō), *n., pl.* **-boes.** Usually, **bilboes,** *pl.* a long iron bar fastened down at one end by a lock with sliding shackles to confine the ankles of prisoners. [origin uncertain]

bil bo² (bil′bō), *n., pl.* **-boes.** ARCHAIC. a slender sword or rapier noted for the temper of its blade. [apparently short for *Bilbao,* Spain, famous for steel]

bile (bīl), *n.* 1 a bitter, greenish-yellow liquid secreted by the liver and stored in the gall bladder; gall. It aids digestion in the duodenum by neutralizing acids and emulsifying fats. 2 ill humor; bitterness of feeling; peevishness. [< French < Latin *bilem*]

bile duct, an excretory duct of the liver and gall bladder.

bilge (bilj), *n., v.,* **bilged, bilg ing.** *—n.* 1 bottom of a ship's hull. 2 the lowest internal part of a ship's hold. 3 bilge water. 4 the bulging part of a barrel. 5 INFORMAL. nonsense. *—v.t.* break in (the bottom of a ship). *—v.i.* 1 be broken or spring a leak in the bilge. 2 bulge; swell out. [variant of *bulge*]

bilge water, dirty water that collects in the bilge of a ship.

bil i ar y (bil′ē er′ē), *adj.* 1 of bile. 2 carrying bile: *a biliary duct.* 3 caused by trouble with the bile; bilious.

bi lin e ar (bī lin′ē ər), *adj.* of, consisting of, or involving two lines.

bi lin gual (bī ling′gwəl), *adj.* 1 able to speak another language as well or almost as well as one's own. 2 containing or written in two languages: *a bilingual dictionary.* *—n.* a bilingual person. **—bi lin′gual ly,** *adv.*

bil ious (bil′yəs), *adj.* 1 suffering from or caused by some trouble with bile or the liver. 2 having to do with bile. 3 peevish; bad-tempered. **—bil′ious ly,** *adv.* **—bil′ious ness,** *n.*

bil i ru bin (bil′ə rü′bin), *n.* the reddish-yellow pigment normally found in bile. [< Latin *bilis* bile + *ruber* red]

bil i ver din (bil′ə vėr′din), *n.* a green pigment in bile produced by the oxidation of bilirubin. [< Latin *bilis* bile + *viridis* green]

bilk (bilk), *v.t.* avoid payment of (a debt); defraud; cheat. *—n.* 1 a petty swindler. 2 fraud; deception. [origin uncertain] **—bilk′er,** *n.*

bill¹ (bil), *n.* 1 statement of money owed for work done, services rendered, or things supplied; account: *The electric company sends us a bill monthly.* 2 piece of paper money: *a dollar bill.* 3 a written or printed public notice, such as an advertisement, poster, or handbill. 4 a written or printed statement; list of items. 5 a theater program. 6 the entertainment in a theater. 7 a proposed law presented to a lawmaking body for its approval. 8 bill of exchange. 9 a written request or complaint presented to a court of law. 10 **fill the bill,** satisfy requirements. 11 **foot the bill,** pay or settle the bill. *—v.t.* 1 send a bill to: *The store will bill us on the first of the month.* 2 enter in a bill; charge in a bill: *Accounts are billed regularly.* 3 announce by bills or public notice. 4 post bills in or on. 5 list on a theatrical program. [< Medieval Latin *billa,* variant of *bulla* document, seal. See BULL².] **—bill′er,** *n.*

bill² (bil), *n.* 1 the horny part of the jaws of a bird; beak. 2 anything shaped like a bird's bill: *the bill of a turtle.* *—v.i.* 1 join beaks; touch bills. 2 **bill and coo,** kiss, caress, and talk as lovers do. [Old English *bile*]

bill³ (bil), *n.* 1 an old military weapon consisting of a staff ending in a hook-shaped blade. 2 billhook. [Old English *bil* sword]

bill board (bil′bôrd′, bil′bōrd′), *n.* signboard, usually outdoors, on which to display advertisements or post notices.

bil let¹ (bil′it), *n.* 1 a written order to provide board and lodging, especially for a soldier. 2 place where someone, especially a soldier, is lodged. 3 job; position. *—v.t.* 1 assign to quarters by billet: *Soldiers were billeted in all the houses of the village.* 2 provide quarters for; lodge. *—v.i.* have quarters. [< Old French *billette,* alteration of *bullette* certificate, ultimately < Latin *bulla* amulet]

bil let² (bil′it), *n.* 1 a thick piece of wood, especially one used for fuel. 2 bar of iron or steel. [< Old French *billette,* diminutive of *bille* log, tree trunk]

bil let-doux (bil′ē dü′, bil′ā dü′), *n., pl.* **bil lets-doux** (bil′ē düz′, bil′ā düz′). a love letter. [< French *billet doux*]

bill fold (bil′fōld′), *n.* a folding pocketbook for carrying paper money, cards, etc.; wallet.

bill head (bil′hed′), *n.* sheet of paper with the name and the address of a business firm printed at the top, and a blank space below for adding a bill.

bill hook (bil′hu̇k′), *n.* tool for pruning or cutting.

bil liard (bil′yərd), *adj.* of or for billiards. *—n.* carom.

bil liards (bil′yərdz), *n.* 1 game played with hard balls on an oblong table covered with cloth and having a raised, cushioned edge. A long stick called a cue is used to hit the balls. 2 any of several similar games. [< Middle French *billard,* diminutive of Old French *bille* log, tree trunk]

bill ing (bil′ing), *n.* the order in which the names of the performers, acts, etc., are listed in a playbill or similar advertisement.

bil lings gate (bil′ingz gāt′), *n.* vulgar, abusive language. [< *Billingsgate,* a gate and fish market in London where this type of language was common]

bil lion (bil′yən), *n., adj.* 1 (in the United States, Canada, and France) one thousand millions; 1,000,000,000. 2 (in Great Britain and Germany) one million millions; 1,000,000,000,000. [< French < *bi-* two (i.e., to the second power) + *(mi)llion* million]

bil lion aire (bil′yə ner′, bil′yə nar′), *n.* 1 person who has a billion or more dollars, pounds, francs, etc. 2 an extremely wealthy person.

bil lionth (bil′yənth), *adj., n.* 1 last in a series of a billion. 2 one, or being one, of a billion equal parts.

bill of attainder, act of a lawmaking body that deprives a person of property and civil rights, without benefit of judicial trial.

bill of exchange, a written order to a person, bank, or firm to pay a stated sum of money to a specified person or to his order; draft.

bill of fare, menu.

bill of goods, 1 a shipment of merchandise. 2 **sell a bill of goods,** SLANG. mislead or seek to mislead.

bill of health, an official certificate given to the master of a ship sailing from a port, stating whether or not there are infectious diseases on the ship or in the port.

bill of lading, receipt given by a ship, railroad, express agency, etc., showing a list of goods delivered to it for transportation.

bill of rights, 1 statement of the fundamental rights of the people of a state or nation. 2 **Bill of Rights,** the first ten amendments to the Constitution of the United States, adopted in 1791, which include a declaration of fundamental rights held by United States citizens.

bill of sale, a written statement transferring ownership of personal property from the seller to the buyer.

bil low (bil′ō), *n.* 1 a great, swelling wave or surge of the sea. 2 a great rolling or swelling mass of smoke, flame, air, etc. —*v.i.* 1 rise or roll in big waves; surge. 2 swell out; bulge: *The sheets on the clothesline billowed in the wind.* [< Scandinavian (Old Icelandic) *bylgja*]

bil low y (bil′ō ē), *adj.*, **-low i er, -low i est.** 1 rising or rolling in big waves. 2 swelling out; bulging.

bil ly (bil′ē), *n., pl.* **-lies.** 1 a policeman's club or stick. 2 any stick or club.

billy goat, a male goat.

bi lo bate (bī lō′bāt), *adj.* having or divided into two lobes: *a bilobate leaf.*

bi lo bat ed (bī lō′bā tid), *adj.* bilobate.

Bi lox i (bə luk′sē, bə lok′sē), *n.* city in SE Mississippi. 48,000.

bi met al (bī met′l), *n.* something consisting of two different metals. —*adj.* bimetallic.

bi me tal lic (bī′mə tal′ik), *adj.* 1 of or using two metals. 2 of or based on bimetallism.

bi met al lism (bī met′l iz′əm), *n.* use of both gold and silver as the basis of the money system of a nation. The amount in weight of each metal necessary to make coins having the same money value is fixed by law.

bi month ly (bī munth′lē), *adj., adv., n., pl.* **-lies.** —*adj.* 1 happening or appearing once every two months. 2 happening or appearing twice a month; semimonthly. —*adv.* 1 once every two months. 2 twice a month; semimonthly. —*n.* magazine or other periodical published bimonthly.

bin (bin), *n.* box or enclosed space for storing grain, coal, etc. [Old English *binn*]

bi nar y (bī′nər ē), *adj., n., pl.* **-nar ies.** —*adj.* consisting of two; involving two; dual. —*n.* 1 set of two things; pair; couple. 2 binary star. [< Late Latin *binarius* < Latin *bini* two at a time]

binary digit, 1 either of the digits 0 or 1 used in the binary system. 2 bit[4].

binary star, pair of stars that revolve around a common center of gravity.

binary system, system of numeration which counts only from 0 to 1 and then starts with a new place. In this system, the decimal number 1 is also noted as 1, but the decimal number 2 is noted as 10 (1 and 0), 3 as 11 (1 and 1), 4 as 100 (1 and 0 and 0), 5 as 101 (1 and 0 and 1), and so on.

bin au ral (bī nôr′əl), *adj.* 1 having to do with or using two speakers, or sources of sound reproduction or transmission, to give a three-dimensional auditory effect: *binaural broadcasting.* 2 of, having to do with, or used with both ears: *a binaural stethoscope.* 3 having two ears. [< Latin *bini* two at a time + English *aural*] **—bin au′ral ly,** *adv.*

bind (bīnd), *v.,* **bound, bind ing,** *n.* —*v.t.* 1 tie or fasten together; hold together: *The packing case was bound with metal tape.* 2 cause to stick together: *Tar will bind gravel and cement.* 3 hold by some force; restrain. 4 fasten (sheets of paper) into a cover; put a cover on (a book). 5 hold by a promise, duty, law, etc.; oblige: *A doctor is bound to help the sick.* 6 put under legal obligation: *He was bound over to keep the peace.* 7 put under legal obligation to serve as an apprentice: *bound out to be a carpenter.* 8 make (a bargain, contract, etc.) final so that it must be carried out: *A ten dollar deposit bound the bargain.* 9 put a bandage on: *bind up a wound.* 10 put a band or wreath around. 11 put a border or edge on to strengthen or ornament. 12 constipate. —*v.i.* stick together: *The gears will bind without oil.* —*n.* anything that binds or ties. [Old English *bindan*]

bind er (bīn′dər), *n.* 1 person who binds, especially a person who binds books. 2 anything that ties or holds together. 3 cover for holding loose sheets of paper together. 4 machine that cuts stalks of grain and ties them in bundles.

bind er y (bīn′dər ē), *n., pl.* **-er ies.** place where books are bound.

bind ing (bīn′ding), *n.* 1 the covering of a book. 2 strip protecting or ornamenting an edge. Binding is used on the seams of dresses. 3 the foot fastenings on a ski. —*adj.* 1 that binds, fastens, or connects. 2 having force or power to hold to a promise, duty, law, etc.; obligatory. **—bind′ing ly,** *adv.*

binding energy, energy necessary to break a molecule, atom, or nucleus into its smaller component parts.

bind weed (bīnd′wēd′), *n.* 1 convolvulus. 2 any plant with long runners that twine around fences, trees, or other plants.

bine (bīn), *n.* a twining, slender stem of a climbing plant, especially of the hop. [alteration of *bind,* noun]

Bi net (bi nā′), *n.* **Alfred,** 1857-1911, French psychologist, one of the inventors of the first intelligence tests.

binge (binj), *n.* INFORMAL. 1 a drunken spree. 2 a bout or spree of indulgence in anything. [origin uncertain]

bin go (bing′gō), *n.* game of chance derived from lotto. [origin uncertain]

bin na cle (bin′ə kəl), *n.* box or stand that contains a ship's compass, placed near the helm. [alteration of *bittacle,* ultimately < Latin *habitaculum* dwelling place < *habitare* dwell]

bi noc u lar (bə nok′yə lər, bī nok′yə lər), *adj.* 1 for both eyes at once: *a binocular microscope.* 2 using both eyes at once: *Most animals have binocular vision.* [< Latin *bini* two at a time + *oculi* eyes]

bi noc u lars (bə nok′yə lərz, bī nok′yələrz), *n.pl.* a double telescope joined as a unit for use with both eyes simultaneously, such as field glasses and opera glasses.

bi no mi al (bī nō′mē əl), *n.* 1 expression in algebra consisting of two terms connected by a plus or minus sign. $8a + 2b$ is a binomial. 2 scientific name of a plant or animal consisting of two terms, the first indicating the genus and the second the species. *Homo sapiens* is a binomial. —*adj.* consisting of two terms. [< Late Latin *binomius* having two names < Latin *bi-* two + *nomen* name] **—bi no′mi al ly,** *adv.*

binomial theorem, the algebraic theorem, invented by Sir Isaac Newton, for raising a binomial to any power. EXAMPLE: $(a + b)^2 = a^2 + 2ab + b^2$.

bio-, *combining form.* 1 life; living things: *Biology = the science of life.* 2 biological: *Biochemistry = biological chemistry.* [< Greek *bios* life]

bi o as say (bī′ō ə sā′, bī′ō as′ā), *n.* determination of the strength of a drug by comparing its effects on a test animal with those of a standard concentration of the substance. —*v.t.* determine (the strength of a drug) by this means.

bi o as tro naut ics (bī′ō as′trə nô′tiks), *n.* science that deals with the biological aspects of travel in outer space.

bi o chem i cal (bī′ō kem′ə kəl), *adj.* of or having to do with biochemistry. **—bi′ochem′i cal ly,** *adv.*

bi o chem ist (bī′ō kem′ist), *n.* an expert in biochemistry.

bi o chem is try (bī′ō kem′ə strē), *n.* science that deals with the chemical processes of living matter; biological chemistry.

bi o de grade (bī′ō di grād′), *v.t.,* **-grad ed, -grad ing.** break down (a detergent, etc.) by bacterial action. **—bi′o de grad′a ble,** *adj.*

bi o e col o gy (bī′ō ē kol′ə jē), *n.* branch of ecology dealing with plant and animal interrelationships.

bi o fla vo noid (bī′ō flā′və noid), *n.* any of a complex of substances, present in citrus fruits and other plant foods, that promote capillary resistance to hemorrhaging; formerly called vitamin P. [< *bio-* + Latin *flāvus* yellow + *-oid*]

biog., 1 biographical. 2 biography.

bi o gen e sis (bī′ō jen′ə sis), *n.* 1 theory that living things can be produced only by other living things. 2 production of living things from other living things. 3 history of the evolution of living organisms.

bi o ge net ic (bī′ō jə net′ik), *adj.* of or having to do with biogenesis. **—bi′o genet′i cal ly,** *adv.*

bi og ra pher (bī og′rə fər, bē og′rə fər), *n.* person who writes a biography.

bi o graph ic (bī′ə graf′ik), *adj.* biographical.

bi o graph i cal (bī′ə graf′ə kəl), *adj.* 1 of a person's life. 2 having to do with biography. **—bi′o graph′i cal ly,** *adv.*

bi og ra phy (bī og′rə fē, bē og′rə fē), *n., pl.* **-phies.** 1 an account of a person's life. 2 the part of literature that consists of biographies.

bi o log ic (bī′ə loj′ik), *adj., n.* biological.

bi o log i cal (bī′ə loj′ə kəl), *adj.* 1 of plant and animal life. 2 having to do with biology. 3 for use in or prepared by a biological laboratory: *biological serums.* 4 involving the use of disease germs, viruses, and other living organisms against an enemy: *biological weapons.* —*n.* drug prepared from plant or animal tissue. **—bi′o log′i cal ly,** *adv.*

binoculars

biological clock, an internal mechanism which controls the rhythm or cycle of various living functions and activities, such as photosynthesis in a plant.

biological warfare, warfare in which disease germs are used against people, animals, or crops.

hat, āge, fär; let, ēqual, tėrm;
it, īce; hot, ōpen, ôrder;
oil, out; cup, pu̇t, rüle;
ch, child; ng, long; sh, she;
th, thin; ᴛʜ, then; zh, measure;

ə represents *a* in about, *e* in taken, *i* in pencil, *o* in lemon, *u* in circus.

< = from, derived from, taken from.

bi ol o gist (bī ol′ə jist), *n.* an expert in biology.

bi ol o gy (bī ol′ə jē), *n.* 1 the scientific study of plant and animal life, including its origin, structure, activities, and distribution. Botany, zoology, and ecology are branches of biology. 2 the plant and animal life of a particular area or region. 3 the biological facts about a particular plant or animal.

bi o lu mi nes cence (bī′ō lü′mə nes′ns), *n.* phosphorescence or other emission of light by living organisms.

bi o lu mi nes cent (bī′ō lü′mə nes′nt), *adj.* showing bioluminescence.

bi o mass (bī′ō mas′), *n.* the total mass or weight of living material in a unit of area.

bi ome (bī′ōm), *n.* the plants and animals that make up a distinct natural community in any climatic region.

bi o me chan ics (bī′ō mə kan′iks), *n.* science that deals with the effects of forces on a living organism, especially the effects of gravity.

bi o met rics (bī′ə met′riks), *n.* branch of biology that deals with living things by measurements and statistics.

bi om e try (bī om′ə trē), *n.* biometrics.

bi on ics (bī on′iks), *n.* study of the anatomy and physiology of animals as a basis for new or improved electronic devices, systems, etc. [< *bio(logy)* + *(electro)nics*]

bi o phys i cal (bī′ō fiz′ə kəl), *adj.* of or having to do with biophysics.

bi o phys i cist (bī′ō fiz′ə sist), *n.* an expert in biophysics.

bi o phys ics (bī′ō fiz′iks), *n.* study of biology in relation to the laws of physics.

bi op sy (bī′op sē), *n., pl.* **-sies.** 1 the surgical removal of a sample of tissue from a living body for examination and diagnosis. 2 medical examination of this tissue. [< *bio-* + Greek *opsis* a viewing]

bi o sphere (bī′ə sfir), *n.* the region surrounding the earth that can support life, including the lithosphere, hydrosphere, and atmosphere.

bi o ta (bī ō′tə), *n.* the fauna and flora of a given region or period. [< Greek *biotē* life < *bioun* to live]

bi ot ic (bī ot′ik), *adj.* of or having to do with life or living things.

biotic potential, capacity of a living thing or species to reproduce and survive in an unlimited environment.

bi o tin (bī′ə tən), *n.* a crystalline acid of the vitamin B complex that promotes growth, found in liver, eggs, and yeast. *Formula:* $C_{10}H_{16}N_2O_3S$

bi o tite (bī′ə tīt), *n.* a black or dark-green mica, a silicate of aluminum and iron with magnesium and potassium. [< J. B. *Biot,* 1774-1862, French mineralogist]

bi par ti san (bī pär′tə zən), *adj.* of, representing, or supported by two political parties.

bi par ti san ship (bī pär′tə zən ship), *n.* support by two political parties.

bi par tite (bī pär′tīt), *adj.* 1 having to do with two peoples, nations, etc.: *a bipartite treaty between America and Canada.* 2 having two parts: *A clam has a bipartite shell.* 3 (in botany) divided into two parts nearly to the base: *a bipartite leaf.* **—bi par′tite ly,** *adv.*

bi par ti tion (bī′pär tish′ən), *n.* division into two parts.

bi ped (bī′ped), *n.* animal having two feet. Birds and men are bipeds. *—adj.* having two feet. [< Latin *bipedem* < *bi-* two + *pedem* foot]

bi plane (bī′plān′), *n.* airplane having two wings on each side of the fuselage, one above the other.

bi po lar (bī pō′lər), *adj.* 1 having two poles or opposite extremities. 2 of or found in both polar regions. 3 having or showing two opposite principles, sets of values, opinions, etc.

bi prism (bī′priz′əm), *n.* prism with a very obtuse angle, used to split a beam of light to obtain two images from a single source.

bi ra cial (bī rā′shəl), *adj.* of or having to do with two races: *biracial problems.*

bi ra di al (bī rā′dē əl), *adj.* having both a bilateral and a radial arrangement of parts: *biradial symmetry.* **—bi ra′di al ly,** *adv.*

birch (bėrch), *n.* 1 any of a genus of slender, hardy trees or shrubs of the same family as the hazelnut, having a smooth outer bark which peels off in thin layers. 2 the hard, close-grained wood of any of these trees or shrubs, often used in making furniture. 3 bundle of birch twigs or a birch stick, used for whipping. *—v.t.* whip with a birch or the like; flog. [Old English *bierce*]

birch bark (bėrch′bärk′), *n.* bark of a birch tree, used by some Indians to cover the framework of their canoes.

birch en (bėr′chən), *adj.* 1 of a birch tree. 2 made of birch wood. 3 having to do with the birch used in punishing.

bird (bėrd), *n.* 1 any of a class, Aves, of warm-blooded vertebrates that lay eggs, have a body covered with feathers, two legs, and the forelimbs modified to form wings with which most species fly in the air. 2 bird hunted for sport. 3 shuttlecock. 4 SLANG. person: *He's an odd bird.* 5 SLANG. a ballistic or guided missile. 6 clay pigeon. 7 **the bird,** a jeering or ridiculing. *—v.i.* watch wild birds; engage in bird watching. [Old English *bridd* young fowl] **—bird′like′,** *adj.*

bird bath (bėrd′bath′), *n., pl.* **-baths** (-baᴛʜz′, -baths′). a shallow basin raised off the ground and filled with water for birds to bathe in or drink.

bird brain (bėrd′brān′), *n.* SLANG. a shallow, foolish person.

bird call, 1 sound that a bird makes. 2 imitation of it. 3 instrument for imitating the call of a bird.

bird dog, dog trained to find birds or bring back birds shot by hunters.

biretta

bird house (bėrd′hous′), *n., pl.* **-hous es** (-hou′ziz). 1 a small box with a roof and one or more openings, raised off the ground for birds to nest in. 2 aviary.

bird ie (bėr′dē), *n., v.,* **bird ied, bird y ing.** *—n.* 1 a little bird. 2 score of one stroke less than par for any hole on a golf course. *—v.t.* score a birdie on (a hole).

bird lime (bėrd′līm′), *n.* a sticky substance smeared on twigs to catch small birds that alight on it.

bird man (bėrd′man′, bėrd′mən), *n., pl.* **-men** (-men′, -mən). 1 INFORMAL. aviator. 2 person who catches or sells birds, such as a fowler. 3 ornithologist.

bird of paradise, any of several birds living chiefly in New Guinea, noted for their magnificent plumage.

bird of paradise
7 in. long

bird of passage, 1 any migratory bird. 2 INFORMAL. person who roams from place to place.

bird of prey, any of a group of birds that hunt animals to eat their flesh, including eagles, hawks, owls, vultures, etc.

bird seed (bėrd′sēd′), *n.* mixture of small seeds often fed to caged birds.

bird's-eye (bėrdz′ī′), *adj.* 1 seen from above or from a distance: *You can get a bird's-eye view of the city from an airplane.* 2 general or brief: *a bird's-eye view of a problem.* 3 having markings somewhat like birds' eyes. **Bird's-eye maple** is a wood used in making furniture. *—n.* cotton cloth having markings somewhat like birds' eyes.

bird shot, a small size of lead shot, used in shooting birds.

bird watcher, person who observes and classifies wild birds in their natural environment. **—bird watching.**

bi reme (bī′rēm′), *n.* ship with two rows of oars on each side, one above the other, much used in the Mediterranean in ancient times. [< Latin *biremis* < *bi-* two + *remus* oar]

bi ret ta (bə ret′ə), *n.* a stiff, square cap with three (sometimes four) upright projecting ridges radiating to the crown from a central tassel or tuft, worn by Roman Catholic or Episcopal clergymen on certain occasions. [< Italian *berretta* < Popular Latin *birritta* < Late Latin *birrus* cloak]

Bir ken head (bėr′kən hed), *n.* city in W England, near Liverpool. 141,000.

Bir ming ham (bėr′ming əm *for 1;* bėr′ming ham *for 2*), *n.* 1 city in central England. 1,084,000. 2 city in central Alabama. 301,000.

birth (bėrth), *n.* 1 act of coming into life; fact of being born: *from birth till death.* 2 the bearing of young; childbirth: *Twins are born at one birth.* 3 beginning or origin: *the birth of a nation.* 4 a bringing forth: *the birth of a plan.* 5 natural inheritance: *a musician by birth.* 6 descent or family: *a person of Spanish birth.* 7 good family; noble descent: *a person of birth and breeding.* 8 that which is born; offspring; young. **9 give birth to, a** bring forth; bear. **b** be the origin or cause of. [Middle English *byrthe* < Scandinavian (Old Swedish) *byrth*]

birth control, 1 control of the birth rate by artificial means. 2 use of contraceptive methods or devices.

birth day (bėrth′dā′), *n.* 1 day on which a person was born. 2 the day or date of origin or beginning: *July 4, 1776, was the birthday of the United States.* 3 anniversary of the day on which a person was born, or on which something began.

birth mark (bėrth′märk′), *n.* spot or mark on the skin that was there at birth.

birth place (bėrth′plās′), *n.* 1 place where a person was born. 2 place of origin.

birth rate, proportion of the number of births per year to the total population or to some other stated number; natality.

birth right (bėrth′rīt′), *n.* rights, privileges, etc., belonging to a person because he is the eldest son, or because he was born in a certain country, or because of any other fact about his birth.

birth stone (bėrth′stōn′), *n.* gem associated with a certain month of the year. It is supposed to bring good luck when worn by a person born in its month.

Bi sa yan (bi sä′yən), *n.* Visayan.

Bi sa yas (bi sä′yəz), *n. pl.* Visayan Islands.

Bis cay (bis′kā, bis′kē), *n.* **Bay of,** bay north of Spain and west of France, part of the Atlantic.

bis cuit (bis′kit), *n., pl.* **-cuits** or **-cuit,** *adj.* —*n.* 1 U.S. a kind of bread leavened with baking powder, soda, or yeast and baked in small, round forms after either rolling and cutting or dropping. 2 BRITISH. **a** cracker. **b** cookie. 3 porcelain or other pottery after the first firing and before glazing; bisque^{2}. 4 a pale brown. —*adj.* pale-brown. [< Old French *bescuit* < *bes-* twice + *cuit* cooked]

bi sect (bī sekt′), *v.t.* 1 divide into two parts. 2 divide into two equal parts: *You can bisect a 90 degree angle into two 45 degree angles.* —*v.i.* divide in two; bifurcate. [< *bi-* two + Latin *sectum* cut]

bi sec tion (bī sek′shən), *n.* 1 act of bisecting. 2 place of bisecting. 3 one of two equal parts.

bi sec tor (bī sek′tər), *n.* 1 a straight line that bisects either an angle or another line. 2 anything that bisects.

bi sex u al (bī sek′shü əl), *adj.* 1 of or having to do with both sexes. 2 having the organs of both sexes in one individual plant or animal; hermaphroditic. 3 attracted to both sexes. —*n.* plant or animal that is bisexual. **—bi sex′u al ly,** *adv.*

bi sex u al i ty (bī sek′shü al′ə tē), *n.* bisexual condition or quality.

bish op (bish′əp), *n.* 1 a clergyman of the highest rank, especially in Catholic and Episcopal churches, who has certain spiritual duties and who administers the religious affairs of a church district or diocese. 2 a spiritual overseer or director in the early Christian church. 3 layman in charge of a ward in the Mormon church. 4 one of the pieces in the game of chess that move diagonally. [Old English *bisceop* < Popular Latin *ebiscopus,* variant of Latin *episcopus* < Greek *episkopos* overseer < *epi-* over + *skopos* watcher]

bish op ric (bish′əp rik), *n.* 1 position, office, or rank of bishop. 2 diocese. [Old English *bisceoprīce* < *bisceop* bishop + *rīce* dominion]

Bis marck (biz′märk), *n.* **1 Otto von,** 1815-1898, German prince and statesman who united the German States into an empire in 1871. 2 capital of North Dakota, in the S part. 35,000.

Bismarck Archipelago, group of islands in the W Pacific, northeast of New Guinea, governed by Australia. 167,000 pop.; 19,200 sq. mi.

bis muth (biz′məth), *n.* a brittle, reddish-white metallic element which occurs in nature as a free metal and in various ores, used in medicine and in making low-melting alloys. *Symbol:* Bi; *atomic number* 83. See pages 326 and 327 for table. [< German]

bi son (bī′sn, bī′zn), *n., pl.* **-son.** 1 a wild ox of North America, having a big, shaggy head, strong front legs, a high, large hump, and short, thick, curved horns; buffalo. 2 the wild ox of Europe, slightly larger than the American bison; aurochs; wisent. It is now almost extinct. [< Latin]

bisque^{1} (bisk), *n.* 1 a rich, thick soup made of cooked shellfish or game, or of strained vegetables. 2 ice cream containing powdered macaroons or crushed nuts. [< French]

bisque^{2} (bisk), *n.* biscuit (def. 3). [alteration of *biscuit*]

Bis sau (bi sou′), *n.* capital of Portuguese Guinea, a seaport on the Atlantic. 25,000.

bis ter or **bis tre** (bis′tər), *n.* 1 a dark-brown coloring matter made from soot. 2 a dark brown. [< French *bistre*]

bis tro (bis′trō; *French* bē strō′), *n., pl.* **-tros.** 1 (in France) a small, modest, neighborhood wine shop and restaurant. 2 INFORMAL. any bar or nightclub. [< French]

bi sul fate (bī sul′fāt), *n.* salt of sulfuric acid formed by neutralizing one hydrogen ion. Also **bisulphate.**

bi sul fide (bī sul′fīd, bī sul′fid), *n.* disulfide. Also, **bisulphide.**

bi sul phate (bī sul′fāt), *n.* bisulfate.

bi sul phide (bī sul′fīd, bī sul′fid), *n.* bisulfide.

bit^{1} (bit), *n.* 1 a small piece: *a bit of broken glass.* 2 a small amount: *a bit of work to do.* 3 INFORMAL. a short time: *stay for a bit.* 4 U.S. INFORMAL. $12\frac{1}{2}$ cents. A quarter is two bits. **5 a bit, a** a little; slightly: *I am a bit tired.* **b** somewhat: *a bit of a nuisance.* **6 bit by bit,** little by little. **7 do one's bit,** do one's share. [Old English *bita* piece bitten off < *bītan* to bite]

bit^{2} (bit), *v.* pt. and a pp. of **bite.**

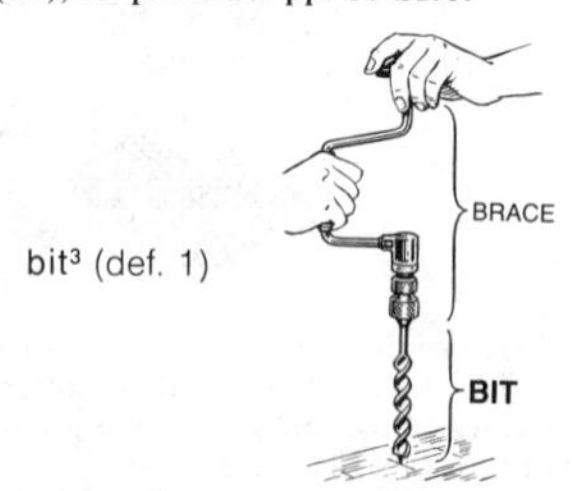

bit^{3} (def. 1)

bit^{3} (bit), *n., v.,* **bit ted, bit ting.** —*n.* 1 tool for boring or drilling that fits into a brace, electric drill, etc. 2 the biting or cutting end or part of a tool. 3 the part of a bridle that goes in a horse's mouth and to which the reins are attached. 4 anything that curbs or restrains. 5 the part of a key that goes into a lock and makes it turn. **6 champ at the bit,** be restless or impatient. —*v.t.* 1 put a bit in the mouth of; bridle. 2 curb; restrain. [Old English *bite* a bite < *bītan* to bite]

bit^{4} (bit), *n.* the basic unit of information in an electronic computer, equivalent to a choice between two possibilities, such as "yes" or "no." [< *bi(nary digi)t*]

bitch (bich), *n.* a female dog, wolf, fox, etc. [Old English *bicce*]

bite (bīt), *v.,* **bit, bit ten** or **bit, bit ing,** *n.* —*v.t.* 1 seize, cut into, or cut off with the teeth: *She bit the apple.* 2 cut; pierce: *The sword bit the knight's helmet.* 3 wound with teeth, fangs, a sting, etc.: *A mosquito bit me.* 4 cause a sharp, smarting pain to: *His fingers are bitten by frost.* 5 take a tight hold on; grip: *The jaws of a vise bite the wood they hold.* 6 eat into or corrode: *Acid bites metal.* —*v.i.* 1 take a bait; be caught: *The fish are biting well today.* 2 be taken in; be tricked. 3 cause injury by biting: *My dog never bites.* 4 nip; snap: *a dog biting at fleas.*

—*n.* 1 act of biting. 2 a piece bitten off; bit of food; mouthful: *Eat the whole apple, not just a bite.* 3 a light meal; snack: *Have a bite with me.* 4 a wound made by biting or stinging: *Mosquito bites itch.* 5 a sharp, smarting pain: *the bite of a cold wind.* 6 a cutting or wounding quality: *the bite of your sarcasm.* 7 tight hold: *the bite of a vise.* 8 action of acid in eating into a metal, etc. 9 manner in which the opposing teeth in the upper and lower jaws meet; occlusion.

[Old English *bītan*] **—bit′er,** *n.*

Bi thyn i a (bə thin′ē ə), *n.* ancient country in NW Asia Minor.

bit ing (bī′ting), *adj.* 1 sharp; cutting: *a biting wind.* 2 sarcastic; sneering: *a biting remark.* **—bit′ing ly,** *adv.*

bitt (bit), *n.* a strong post on a ship's deck, usually one of a pair, to which ropes, cables, etc., are fastened. [variant of *bit^{3}*]

bit ten (bit′n), *v.* a pp. of **bite.**

bit ter (bit′ər), *adj.* 1 having a sharp, harsh, unpleasant taste: *Quinine is bitter medicine.* 2 unpleasant to the mind or feeling; hard to admit or bear: *a bitter defeat. Failure is bitter.* 3 harsh or cutting: *bitter words.* 4 causing pain; sharp; severe: *a bitter wound, a bitter quarrel.* 5 expressing grief, pain, misery, etc.: *bitter tears.* 6 (of weather) very cold: *a bitter winter.* **7 to the bitter end, a** until the very last. **b** to death. —*adv.* bitterly: *a bitter cold day.* —*n.* that which is bitter; bitterness: *You must take the bitter with the sweet.* [Old English *biter.* Related to BITE.] **—bit′ter ly,** *adv.* **—bit′ter ness,** *n.*

bit tern (bit′ərn), *n.* any of several small herons found chiefly in marshes, characterized by a peculiar booming cry. [< Old French *butor*]

bit ter root (bit′ər rüt′, bit′ər rụ̇t′), *n.* a small plant of the same family as the purslane, with thick edible roots and showy pink flowers, found in the northern Rocky Mountains.

bit ters (bit′ərz), *n.pl.* 1 a liquid, usually alcoholic, in which a bitter herb, bark, or root has been steeped, used as a flavoring in certain cocktails and foods and sometimes as medicine. 2 a bitter, dark beer.

bit ter sweet (bit′ər swēt′), *n.* 1 a climbing plant of the nightshade family, with purple, blue, or white flowers and poisonous, scarlet berries. 2 a climbing vine of North America with greenish flowers and orange seedcases that open and show red seeds. 3 sweetness and bitterness mixed. —*adj.* 1 sweet and bitter mixed: *bittersweet chocolate.*

2 pleasant and painful at once: *bittersweet memories.*

bit ty (bit′ē), *adj.,* **-ti er, -ti est.** very small; tiny.

bi tu men (bə tü′mən, bə tyü′mən), *n.* any of a number of minerals that will burn, such as asphalt, petroleum, and naphtha. [< Latin]

bi tu mi nous (bə tü′mə nəs, bə tyü′mə nəs), *adj.* 1 containing or made with bitumen. 2 like bitumen.

bituminous coal, coal in which volatile matter constitutes more than 18 per cent and which therefore burns with much smoke and a yellow flame; soft coal.

bi va lence (bī vā′ləns), *n.* bivalent quality or condition.

bi va len cy (bī vā′lən sē), *n.* bivalence.

bi va lent (bī vā′lənt), *adj.* 1 having a valence of two; divalent. 2 having two valences. 3 double (applied to a pair of chromosomes united in synapsis). *—n.* a bivalent pair of chromosomes.

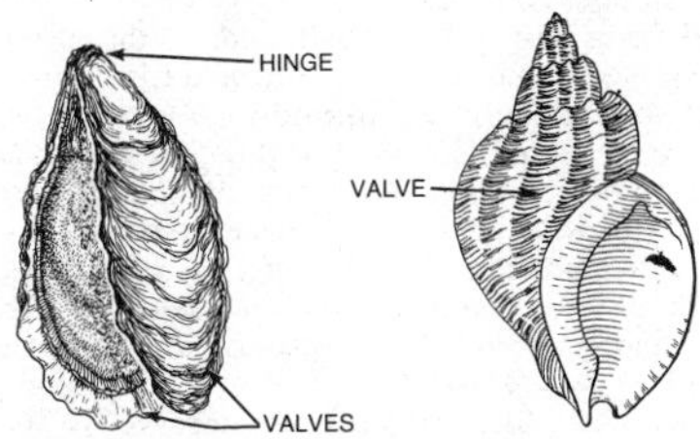

bivalve (def. 1)—left, an oyster with valves open, contrasted with a univalve (right), a whelk

bi valve (bī′valv′), *n.* 1 any mollusk whose shell consists of two parts hinged together so that it will open and shut like a book. Oysters and clams are bivalves. 2 any seed capsule, such as the pod of a pea, that splits into two halves. *—adj.* having two parts hinged together.

biv ouac (biv′wak, biv′ü ak), *n., v.,* **-ouacked, -ouack ing.** *—n.* a temporary, outdoor camp of soldiers, mountaineers, hikers, etc., usually without tents or with very small tents. *—v.i.* camp outdoors without tents. [< French]

bi week ly (bī wēk′lē), *adj., adv., n., pl.* **-lies.** *—adj.* 1 happening or appearing once every two weeks. 2 happening or appearing twice a week; semiweekly. *—adv.* 1 once every two weeks. 2 twice a week; semiweekly. *—n.* newspaper or other periodical published biweekly.

bi year ly (bī yir′lē), *adj., adv.* 1 twice a year; semiyearly. 2 every two years.

bi zarre (bə zär′), *adj.* strikingly odd in appearance or style; fantastic; grotesque. [< French < Spanish *bizarro* brave < Italian *bizzarro* angry < *bizza* anger] **—bi zarre′ly,** *adv.* **—bi zarre′ness,** *n.*

Bi zet (bē zā′), *n.* **Georges,** 1838-1875, French composer who wrote the opera *Carmen.*

Björn son (byœrn′sən), *n.* **Björnstjerne,** 1832-1910, Norwegian poet, novelist, and dramatist.

Bk, berkelium.

bk., 1 bank. 2 block. 3 book.

bkg., banking.

bks., 1 barracks. 2 books.

bkt., *pl.* **bkts.** 1 basket. 2 bracket.

bl., 1 bale. 2 barrel.

b.l. or **B/L,** bill of lading.

blab (blab), *v.,* **blabbed, blab bing,** *n.* INFORMAL. *—v.t., v.i.* tell (secrets); talk too much. *—n.* 1 blabbing talk; indiscreet chatter. 2 person who blabs. [Middle English]

blab ber (blab′ər), *n.* 1 person who blabs. 2 foolish talk. *—v.t., v.i.* blab.

black (blak), *adj.* 1 reflecting little or no light; having the color of coal or soot; opposite of white: *This print is black.* 2 Also, **Black.** having dark skin, eyes, and hair; having to do with or belonging to Negroes; Negro. 3 without any light; very dark: *The room was black as night.* 4 dirty; grimy: *hands black with soot.* 5 dismal; gloomy: *a black day, black news.* 6 sullen; angry: *a black look.* 7 evil; wicked: *a black lie.*
—n. 1 the darkest color; color of coal or soot; the opposite of white. 2 **in the black,** showing a profit (usually entered in black ink in account books). 3 a black paint, dye, or pigment. 4 black clothes, especially when worn as a sign of mourning. 5 Also, **Black.** person belonging to a dark-skinned ethnic group; Negro.
—v.t. 1 make black; blacken. 2 put blacking on (shoes, etc.). *—v.i.* become black.
black out, a become temporarily blind or unconscious. **b** darken completely. **c** suppress; withhold. **d** exclude from television reception.
[Old English *blæc*] **—black′er,** *n.* **—black′ly,** *adv.* **—black′ness,** *n.*

black a moor (blak′ə mùr), *n.* 1 a Negro. 2 a dark-skinned person.

black-and-blue (blak′ən blü′), *adj.* discolored from a bruise.

black and white, 1 writing or print: *I asked her to put her promise down in black and white.* 2 picture or sketch using only black and white.

black art, black magic.

black ball (blak′bôl′), *v.t.* 1 vote against; reject as a candidate for membership. 2 ostracize. *—n.* a vote against a person or thing. [from the practice of voting against a candidate by placing a black ball in the ballot box] **—black′ball′er,** *n.*

black bass, any of various game fishes of eastern and central North America that live in fresh water.

black bear, a large North American bear that has dense black fur and a tawny snout.

black belt, 1 section in a city or region inhabited mostly by Negroes. 2 strip of very rich black soil in Alabama and Mississippi. 3 the highest order in judo and karate.

black ber ry (blak′ber′ē, blak′bər ē), *n., pl.* **-ries,** *v.,* **-ried, -ry ing.** *—n.* 1 a small, black or dark-purple, sweet and juicy fruit of certain brambles of the rose family. 2 the thorny bush or vine that it grows on. *—v.i.* gather blackberries.

black bird (blak′bėrd′), *n.* 1 any of various American birds so named because the male is mostly black. The cowbird, grackle, and redwing are blackbirds. 2 a European thrush, the male of which is mostly black; merle.

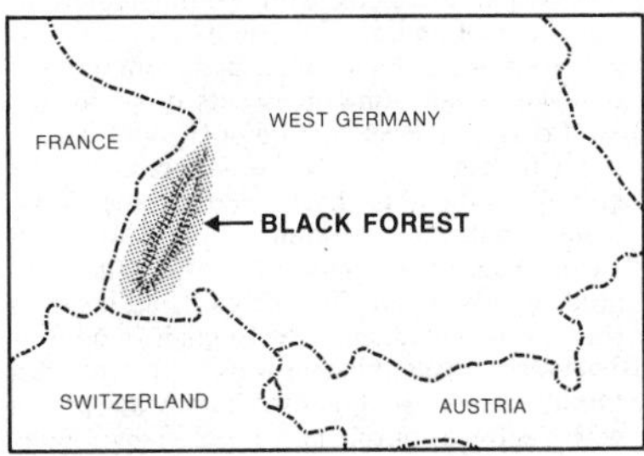

hat, āge, fär; let, ēqual, tėrm;
it, īce; hot, ōpen, ôrder;
oil, out; cup, pu̇t, rüle;
ch, child; ng, long; sh, she;
th, thin; ᴛʜ, then; zh, measure;

ə represents *a* in about, *e* in taken, *i* in pencil, *o* in lemon, *u* in circus.

< = from, derived from, taken from.

black board (blak′bôrd′, blak′bōrd′), *n.* a dark, smooth piece of slate, glass, or painted wood on which to write or draw with chalk or crayon.

black bod y (blak′bod′ē), *n.* a theoretical surface or body capable of completely absorbing all the radiation falling on it.

black book, book containing the names of people to be criticized or punished.

black box, INFORMAL. any self-contained electronic or automatic device for recording data, controlling a mechanical process, etc. One type is used to detect earthquakes and nuclear explosions and another is used in the automatic landing of aircraft.

black cap (blak′kap′), *n.* 1 a black raspberry. 2 any of various birds that have the top of the head black, such as the chickadee.

black code, U.S. laws passed in some southern states after the Civil War limiting the rights of the freed slaves, especially in employment.

Black Death, the bubonic plague that spread through Europe in the 1300's and destroyed one fourth of its population.

black en (blak′ən), *v.t.* 1 make black. 2 speak evil of: *blacken someone's character with false gossip.* *—v.i.* become black. **—black′en er,** *n.*

black eye, 1 a bruise around an eye. 2 INFORMAL. **a** a severe blow or rebuff: *The insult gave my pride a black eye.* **b** cause of disgrace or discredit. **c** disgrace or discredit.

black-eyed pea (blak′īd′), cowpea.

black-eyed Su san (sü′zn), a yellow daisylike flower of the composite family with yellow petals and a black or dark center.

black face (blak′fās′), *n.* 1 a Negro minstrel; actor made up as a Negro. 2 make-up for Negro parts in a show, etc. 3 INFORMAL. boldface.

Black feet (blak′fēt′), *n. pl. or sing.* Blackfoot (def. 1).

black fish (blak′fish′), *n., pl.* **-fish es** or **-fish.** 1 any of various dark-colored fishes, especially the tautog. 2 any of various small, black, toothed whales. 3 a small, edible freshwater fish of Alaska and Siberia.

black flag, Jolly Roger.

black fly, a small fly of the northern United States and Canada, with a black body. The female can inflict a very painful bite.

Black foot (blak′fu̇t′), *n., pl.* **-feet** or **-foot** for 1. 1 member of a tribe of American Indians that formerly lived in the northwestern United States and southern Canada and now live on reservations in Montana and in Alberta, Canada. 2 the Algonquian language of this tribe.

Black Forest, low mountains covered with forests in SW West Germany. Highest peak, 4900 ft.

black grouse, a large grouse of Europe and Asia. The male is black with white markings and a curled tail. The female is smaller and is brown and gray.

black guard (blag′ärd, blag′ərd), *n.* a low, contemptible man; scoundrel. —*v.t.* abuse with vile language; revile. —*v.i.* behave like a blackguard.

black guard ly (blag′ärd lē, blag′ərd lē), *adj.* of or like a blackguard.

Black Hand, U.S. a secret society organized to commit blackmail and crimes of violence.

black head (blak′hed′), *n.* a small, black-tipped lump of dead cells and oil plugging a pore of the skin, found especially on the face.

Black Hills, group of mountains in W South Dakota and NE Wyoming. The highest peak is Harney Peak, 7242 ft.

black humor, a morbid or bizarre form of humor, especially in novels and plays.

black ing (blak′ing), *n.* a black polish used on shoes, stoves, etc.

black ish (blak′ish), *adj.* somewhat black.

black jack (blak′jak′), *n.* 1 club with a flexible handle, used as a weapon. 2 Jolly Roger. 3 a small oak tree of the eastern United States that has a bark that is almost black. 4 the game of twenty-one. 5 ARCHAIC. a large drinking cup or jug, formerly made of leather. —*v.t.* 1 hit (a person) with a blackjack. 2 coerce.

black lead (led), graphite.

black leg (blak′leg′), *n.* 1 INFORMAL. swindler. 2 BRITISH. worker who takes a striker's job; strikebreaker.

black letter, a printing type with thick, heavy lines.

black list (blak′list′), *n.* list of persons or groups believed to deserve punishment, blame, suspicion, etc. Persons or groups on a blacklist are usually boycotted or cut off from membership, affiliation, employment, etc. —*v.t.* put on a blacklist.

black magic, evil magic; sorcery; witchcraft.

black mail (blak′māl′), *n.* 1 money or other advantage obtained by using threats, especially threats to reveal damaging secrets about a person or someone dear to him. 2 an attempt to extort money or other advantage in this way. —*v.t.* get or try to get blackmail from. [< *black* + *mail* rent, tribute, coin < Old French *maille* < *mail, medaille* coin, medal] —**black′mail′er,** *n.*

black mark, mark of criticism or punishment made against a person's name.

black market, 1 the selling of goods at illegal prices or in illegal quantities, violating price ceilings, rationing, etc. 2 place where such selling is done.

black mar ket eer (mär′kə tir′), person who deals on the black market.

Black Muslim, U.S. member of the Nation of Islam.

black out (blak′out′), *n.* 1 the extinguishing or concealing of all the lights of a city, district, etc., as a protection against an air raid. 2 the extinguishing of lights as the result of a power failure. 3 temporary blindness or unconsciousness resulting from lack of blood circulation in the brain. 4 a temporary failure of memory. 5 failure in radio reception due to jamming or to disturbances in the atmosphere or ionosphere. 6 the withholding of news or other information usually printed or broadcast. 7 the withholding of a particular television program.

Black Panther, U.S. member of a militant Negro organization seeking to achieve power and equality for Negroes by radical means.

black pepper, 1 a seasoning with a hot taste, made by grinding the whole dried berries of the pepper vine. 2 the vine itself.

Black pool (blak′pül), *n.* seaport in NW England. 150,000.

Black Power, power of collective Negro action used to achieve equality.

Black Prince, 1330-1376, Edward, Prince of Wales, son of Edward III of England.

Black Sea, inland sea between SE Europe and W Asia, connecting with the Mediterranean through the Bosporus, the Dardanelles, and the Aegean Sea. 164,000 sq. mi.

black sheep, person considered by his group or family to be a disgrace.

Black Shirt, 1 (formerly) a member of the Italian Fascist party, who wore a black shirt as part of his uniform. 2 member of any similar fascist organization.

black smith (blak′smith′), *n.* person who works with iron by heating it in a forge and hammering it into shape on an anvil. Blacksmiths mend tools and also make and fit horseshoes. [with reference to black metals, e.g., iron]

black snake (blak′snāk′), *n.* 1 a harmless snake of North America having a black color and smooth scales, often attaining a length of six feet. 2 a similar black, harmless snake differing in having ridged scales edged with white. 3 a long, heavy whip made of braided leather.

Black stone (blak′stōn, blak′stən), *n.* Sir **William,** 1723-1780, English legal writer and judge.

black tea, tea which has been allowed to wither and ferment in the air for some time before roasting.

black thorn (blak′thôrn′), *n.* 1 a thorny European shrub of the rose family, having white flowers and very small, black or dark-purple fruit. The fruit, and sometimes the shrub itself, is called *sloe.* 2 a walking stick or club made from the stem of this shrub.

black tie, 1 a black bow tie for wear with a dinner jacket or tuxedo. 2 formal evening dress that includes a black bow tie and dinner jacket or tuxedo, as opposed to full evening dress or tails.

black top (blak′top′), *n., v.,* **-topped, -topping.** —*n.* 1 asphalt mixed with crushed rock, used as a surface for roads, highways, airport runways, etc. 2 surface covered with this substance. —*v.t.* surface or pave (a road) with blacktop.

black walnut, 1 an oily, round, edible nut with a rough shell. 2 the tall North American walnut tree that it grows on. 3 its heavy, hard, strong, dark-brown wood, often used for furniture, woodwork, etc.

black widow, a very poisonous, small spider of the United States, having a glossy black, spherical body with a reddish mark in the shape of an hourglass on its underside. It gets its name from its color and from the fact that the female sometimes eats its mate.

blad der (blad′ər), *n.* 1 a soft, thin, elastic sac which stores the urine secreted by the kidneys until it is discharged by the body. 2 any similar sac in animals or plants. 3 a strong bag, often made of rubber, that will hold liquids or air. The rubber bag inside a football is a bladder. [Old English *blǣdre*]

blad der wort (blad′ər wėrt′), *n.* any of a family of insect-eating marsh or water plants with yellow or purple flowers. Some varieties float on the water by means of small bladders on the weak stems and leaves; others take root in mud.

blade (blād), *n.* 1 the cutting part of an edged tool or weapon, as distinguished from the handle. 2 sword. 3 swordsman. 4 a smart, dashing fellow. 5 leaf of grass. 6 the flat, wide part of a leaf, as distinguished from the stalk. 7 a flat, wide, leaflike part of any instrument or utensil, as an oar, a paddle, a spade, etc. 8 the wide, flat part of a bone. 9 the front, flat part of the tongue directly behind and around the tip. [Old English *blæd*] —**blade′like′,** *adj.*

blad ed (blā′did), *adj.* having a blade or blades.

blain (blān), *n.* an inflamed swelling or sore on the skin, such as a blister or a pustule. [Old English *blegen*]

Blaine (blān), *n.* **James Gillespie,** 1830-1893, American statesman.

Blake (blāk), *n.* **William,** 1757-1827, English poet and artist.

blam a ble (blā′mə bəl), *adj.* deserving blame; blameworthy. —**blam′a bly,** *adv.*

blame (blām), *v.,* **blamed, blam ing,** *n.* —*v.t.* 1 hold (a person or thing) responsible for something bad or wrong: *We blamed the fog for our accident.* 2 place responsibility for (something bad or wrong) on a person or thing: *They blamed the accident on me.* 3 find fault with: *The teacher will not blame us if we do our best.* See synonym study below. 4 **be to blame,** deserve to be blamed; be responsible. —*n.* 1 responsibility for something bad or wrong: *Carelessness deserves the blame for many mistakes.* 2 a finding fault; reproof. [< Old French *blasmer* < Latin *blasphemare* < Greek *blasphēmein,* ultimately < *blas-* false, slanderous + *phēmē* word. Doublet of BLASPHEME.] —**blam′er,** *n.*

Syn. *v.t.* 3 **Blame, censure, reproach** mean to find fault with. **Blame,** the least formal word, means to find fault with someone for doing something wrong: *The principal blamed him for his frequent absence from school.* **Censure,** less personal, adds to *blame* the idea of expressing disapproval, often publicly: *The Congress censured one of its members for his excessive absence from the Capitol.* **Reproach** adds to *blame* the idea of expressing one's feelings of displeasure or resentment, sometimes unjustly: *I reproached them for their ingratitude.*

blame less (blām′lis), *adj.* free from blame; faultless. See **innocent** for synonym study. —**blame′less ly,** *adv.* —**blame′less ness,** *n.*

blame wor thy (blām′wėr′ᴛʜē), *adj.* deserving blame; culpable. —**blame′wor′thi ness,** *n.*

blanch (blanch), *v.t.* 1 make white or pale:

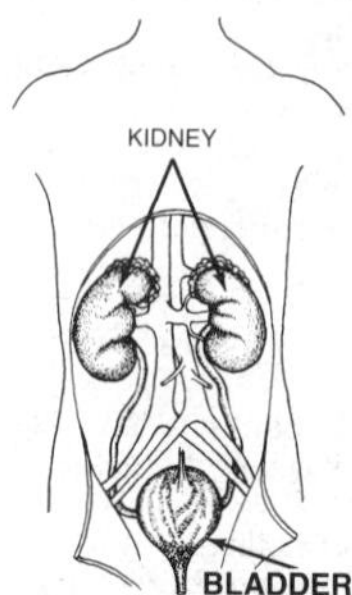

bladder (def. 1)

Old age blanched his hair. See **whiten** for synonym study. 2 whiten or prevent from becoming green by excluding the light, as the stems or leaves of plants such as celery or lettuce. 3 scald or boil so as to whiten, remove the skin, separate the grains or strands, etc.: *blanch almonds, blanch vegetables.* —*v.i.* turn white or pale: *blanch with fear.* [< Old French *blanchir* < *blanc* white]

blanc mange (blə mänzh′), *n.* a sweet dessert made of milk boiled and thickened with gelatin, cornstarch, etc., flavored and cooled in a mold. [< Old French *blanc-manger* white food]

bland (bland), *adj.* 1 gentle or soothing; balmy: *a bland summer breeze.* 2 smoothly agreeable and polite: *a bland smile.* 3 soothing to the palate or digestive tract; not irritating: *a bland diet of baby food.* [< Latin *blandus* soft] —**bland′ly,** *adv.* —**bland′ness,** *n.*

blan dish (blan′dish), *v.t., v.i.* persuade by gentle ways; coax; flatter. [< Old French *blandiss-,* a form of *blandir* < Latin *blandiri* flatter < *blandus* soft] —**blan′dish er,** *n.*

blan dish ment (blan′dish mənt), *n.* 1 a coaxing; flattery. 2 expression or action that coaxes or flatters.

blank (blangk), *n.* 1 space left empty or to be filled in: *Leave a blank if you can't answer the question.* 2 paper with spaces to be filled in: *an application blank.* 3 an empty or vacant place; void: *When I saw the hard test, my mind became a complete blank.* 4 dash marking an empty space for an omitted letter, word, etc. 5 a lottery ticket that does not win a prize. 6 **draw a blank,** be unsuccessful. 7 a piece of metal prepared to be stamped or filed into a coin, key, or the like. 8 a white spot in the center of a target; bull's-eye. 9 anything aimed at like a target. 10 cartridge containing gunpowder but no bullet or shot.
—*adj.* 1 not written or printed on: *blank sheets of paper.* 2 with spaces left for filling in: *a blank application form.* 3 empty; vacant: *a blank space, a blank mind.* See **empty** for synonym study. 4 without interest or meaning; dull: *a blank outlook for the future. There was a blank look on her face.* 5 lacking some usual feature: *blank cartridge.* A blank window has the usual frame but no opening.
—*v.t.* 1 (in games) to keep from scoring. 2 hide or obscure; blot *(out): His name had been blanked out.*
[< Old French *blanc* white, shining] —**blank′ly,** *adv.* —**blank′ness,** *n.*

blank check, 1 a signed check that allows the bearer to write in the amount. 2 INFORMAL. freedom or permission to do as one pleases; carte blanche.

blan ket (blang′kit), *n.* 1 a soft, heavy covering woven from wool, cotton, nylon, or other material, used to keep people or animals warm. 2 anything like a blanket: *A blanket of snow covered the ground.* —*v.t.* 1 cover with a blanket. 2 cover, hinder, or obscure: *The snow blanketed the ground.* —*adj.* covering several or all: *A blanket insurance policy insures a car against all kinds of accidents.* [< Old French *blankete* < *blanc* white]

blank verse, 1 unrhymed poetry having five iambic feet in each line: *Shakespeare's "Julius Caesar" is written in blank verse.* 2 any unrhymed poetry: *Walt Whitman wrote most of his poetry in blank verse.*

blare (bler, blar), *v.,* **blared, blar ing,** *n.* —*v.i.* make a loud, harsh sound: *The trumpets blared.* —*v.t.* utter harshly or loudly. —*n.* 1 a loud, harsh sound. 2 brilliance of color; glare. [< Middle Dutch *blaren*]

blar ney (blär′nē), *n., pl.* **-neys,** *v.* —*n.* smoothly flattering or coaxing talk. —*v.t., v.i.* flatter; coax. [< *Blarney Stone*]

Blarney Stone, stone built into a castle near Cork, Ireland. Anyone who kisses it is supposed to become skillful in flattering and coaxing people.

bla sé (blä zā′, blä′zā), *adj.* tired of pleasures; bored. [< French]

blas pheme (bla sfēm′), *v.t., v.i.,* **-phemed, -phem ing.** speak about (God, sacred things, etc.) with abuse or contempt; utter blasphemy. [< Old French *blasfemer* < Latin *blasphemare.* Doublet of BLAME.] —**blas-phem′er,** *n.*

blas phe mous (blas′fə məs), *adj.* uttering, containing, or showing blasphemy; profane. —**blas′phe mous ly,** *adv.* —**blas′phe-mous ness,** *n.*

blas phe my (blas′fə mē), *n., pl.* **-mies.** abuse or contempt for God or sacred things; profanity.

blast (blast), *n.* 1 a strong gust: *the icy blasts of winter.* 2 the blowing of a trumpet, horn, whistle, etc. 3 sound made by blowing a trumpet, horn, whistle, etc. 4 a strong current of air used in smelting iron, etc. 5 a blasting; explosion. 6 charge of dynamite, gunpowder, or some other explosive, that blows up rocks, earth, etc. 7 wave of high-pressure air that spreads out from an explosion. 8 cause of withering, blight, or ruin. 9 **full blast,** in full operation; at highest speed or largest capacity: *The carnival was going full blast.*
—*v.t.* 1 blow up (rocks, earth, etc.) with dynamite, gunpowder, or some other explosive. 2 cause to wither, blight or ruin; destroy: *A disease has blasted our grapes. His conviction for fraud blasted his reputation.* 3 blow (a trumpet, horn, whistle, etc.). —*v.i.* 1 be blighted. 2 blow up rocks, earth, etc., with dynamite, gunpowder, or some other explosives. 3 **blast off,** take off into rocket-propelled flight.
[Old English *blǣst*] —**blast′er,** *n.*

blast ed (blas′tid), *adj.* 1 blighted or ruined. 2 damned; cursed.

blast furnace, furnace in which ore is smelted, especially iron ore to produce pig iron, by forcing a strong current of air into the furnace from the bottom to make the intense heat required.

blas to coel or **blas to coele** (blas′tə-sēl′), *n.* the central cavity of a blastula.

blas to derm (blas′tə dėrm′), *n.* layer of cells formed by the growth of a fertilized egg. It later divides into three layers, from which all parts of the animal are formed. [< Greek *blastos* sprout, germ + *derma* skin]

blast off (blast′ôf′, blast′of′), *n.* a launching or taking off into rocket-propelled flight.

blast to mere (blast′tə mir), *n.* any of the cells or segments into which a fertilized egg first divides.

blas to my co sis (blas′tō mī kō′sis), *n.* a chronic disease of man or animals caused by a yeastlike fungus that may attack the skin, mouth, internal organs, etc.

blas to pore (blas′tə pôr, blas′tə pōr), *n.* the opening of the cavity of a gastrula.

blas tu la (blas′chə lə), *n., pl.* **-las, -lae** (-lē). an early stage in the development of an embryo of an animal, after the fertilization and cleavage of the ovum, consisting of a single layer of cells arranged spherically to enclose a cavity. [< New Latin < Greek *blastos* sprout, germ]

hat, āge, fär; let, ēqual, tėrm;
it, īce; hot, ōpen, ôrder;
oil, out; cup, pu̇t, rüle;
ch, child; ng, long; sh, she;
th, thin; ᴛʜ, then; zh, measure;

ə represents *a* in about, *e* in taken, *i* in pencil, *o* in lemon, *u* in circus.

< = from, derived from, taken from.

blas tu lar (blas′chə lər), *adj.* having to do with or resembling a blastula.

blat (blat), *v.,* **blat ted, blat ting.** INFORMAL. —*v.i.* cry like a calf or sheep; bleat. —*v.t.* say loudly and foolishly; blurt out. [variant of *bleat*]

bla tan cy (blāt′n sē), *n.* blatant quality; noisy or unpleasant obtrusiveness.

bla tant (blāt′nt), *adj.* 1 offensively loud or noisy; loud-mouthed. 2 showy in dress, manner, etc. 3 obvious; flagrant: *blatant hypocrisy, blatant lies.* [coined by Spenser, apparently < Latin *blatire* babble] —**bla′tant ly,** *adv.*

blath er (blaᴛʜ′ər), *n.* foolish talk; nonsense. —*v.i., v.t.* talk or utter foolishly; talk nonsense. [< Scandinavian (Old Icelandic) *bladhr*]

blath er skite (blaᴛʜ′ər skīt), *n.* INFORMAL. person who talks much and says little.

blaze[1] (blāz), *n., v.,* **blazed, blaz ing.** —*n.* 1 a bright flame or fire. See **flame** for synonym study. 2 a glow of brightness; intense light; glare. 3 a bright display: *a blaze of color.* 4 a sudden or violent outburst: *a blaze of temper.* —*v.i.* 1 burn with a bright flame; be on fire: *A fire was blazing in the fireplace.* 2 show bright colors or lights: *On New Year's Eve the big house blazed with lights.* 3 make a bright display. 4 burst out in anger or excitement. 5 **blaze away,** fire a gun, etc., continuously. —*v.t.* 1 cause to shine forth. 2 cause to blaze up. [Old English *blæse*]

blaze[2] (blāz), *n., v.,* **blazed, blaz ing.** —*n.* 1 mark made on a tree by chipping off a piece of bark to indicate a trail or boundary in a forest. 2 a white spot on an animal's forehead. —*v.t.* mark (a tree, trail, or boundary) by chipping off a piece of bark. [perhaps < Low German *bläse*]

blaze[3] (blāz), *v.t.,* **blazed, blaz ing.** make known; proclaim. [< Scandinavian (Old Icelandic) *blāsa*]

blaz er (blā′zər), *n.* a bright-colored or distinctively decorated jacket, sometimes worn as part of the uniform of a team or school.

bla zon (blā′zn), *v.t.* 1 make known; proclaim: *Big posters blazoned the wonders of the coming circus.* 2 decorate; adorn. 3 describe or paint (a coat of arms). 4 display; show. —*n.* 1 coat of arms, or a shield with a coat of arms on it. 2 description

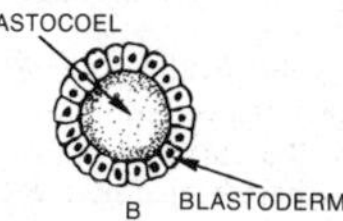

blastula
A, external view;
B, cross section

or painting of a coat of arms. 3 display; show. [< Old French *blason* shield] **—bla′zon er,** *n.*

bla zon ry (blā′zn rē), *n., pl.* **-ries.** 1 bright decoration or display. 2 coat of arms. 3 description or painting of a coat of arms.

bldg., *pl.* **bldgs.** building.

bleach (blēch), *v.t.* 1 whiten (linen, etc.) by washing and exposing to sunlight or by using chemicals. See **whiten** for synonym study. 2 remove some of the color of; lighten: *the sun had bleached my hair.* —*v.i.* become white; turn pale; lose color. —*n.* 1 any chemical used in bleaching. 2 act or process of bleaching. [Old English *blǣcean*] **—bleach′er,** *n.*

bleach ers (blē′chərz), *n.pl.* rows or tiers of low-priced, usually roofless seats at a baseball game or other outdoor sports event.

bleaching powder, 1 a white powder used for bleaching and disinfecting, made by treating slaked lime with chlorine; chlorinated lime; chloride of lime. 2 any powder used in bleaching.

bleak (blēk), *adj.* 1 exposed to cold and winds; bare; desolate: *bleak mountain peaks.* 2 chilly; cold; raw: *The bleak wind made him shiver.* 3 cheerless and depressing; dismal: *Lonely and ill, I faced a bleak future.* [Middle English *bleke* pale] **—bleak′ly,** *adv.* **—bleak′ness,** *n.*

blear (blir), *adj.* 1 (of the eyes) dim from water, tears, etc. 2 indistinct; dim. —*v.t.* 1 dim (the eyes) with tears, etc. 2 blur. [Middle English *bleren*]

blear-eyed (blir′īd′), *adj.* bleary-eyed.

blear y (blir′ē), *adj.,* **blear i er, blear i est.** 1 bleary-eyed. 2 indistinct in outline; blurred. **—blear′i ly,** *adv.* **—blear′i-ness,** *n.*

blear y-eyed (blir′ē īd′), *adj.* having eyes dim with water, tears, etc.

bleat (blēt), *n.* 1 the cry made by a sheep, goat, or calf. 2 a sound like this. —*v.i.* 1 make the cry of a sheep, goat, or calf. 2 make a sound like this. [Old English *blǣtan*] **—bleat′er,** *n.*

bleb (bleb), *n.* 1 blister. 2 bubble. [probably imitative]

bled (bled), *v.* pt. and pp. of **bleed.**

bleed (blēd), *v.,* **bled, bleed ing,** *n.* —*v.i.* 1 lose blood. 2 shed one's blood; suffer wounds or death. 3 lose sap, juice, etc., from a surface that has been cut or scratched, as a tree or vine. 4 feel great anguish, sorrow, or pity *(for).* 5 (of printed text, illustrations, etc.) extend to the edge of a page, leaving no margin. —*v.t.* 1 draw or let blood from: *Doctors used to bleed sick people as a method of treating diseases.* 2 **bleed white,** take all the power, strength, money, etc., of. 3 take sap, juice, etc., from. 4 INFORMAL. get money away from by extortion. 5 design or print (text, illustrations, etc.) so that they leave no margin. 6 drain slowly: *bleed the fluid from a hydraulic brake system.* 7 drain fluid slowly from: *bleed a hydraulic brake system.*
—*n.* 1 illustration or page that has no margin. 2 paper or printed matter trimmed off such a page. 3 a valve or tap.
[Old English *blēdan* < *blōd* blood]

bleed er (blē′dər), *n.* hemophiliac.

bleeding heart, a common garden plant of the same family as the Dutchman's-breeches, having drooping clusters of red, pink, or creamy-white heart-shaped flowers.

bleep (blēp), *n.* a short, high-pitched sound emitted as a signal or to obliterate undesirable words in a broadcast. —*v.i.* emit a bleep. **—bleep′er,** *n.*

blem ish (blem′ish), *n.* 1 a physical defect; stain, spot, or scar: *A mole is a blemish on a person's skin.* 2 something that mars completeness or perfection; imperfection; flaw. —*v.t.* 1 stain, spot, or scar. 2 injure or mar the completeness or perfection of. [< Old French *blemiss-,* a form of *blemir* make livid] **—blem′ish er,** *n.*

blench[1] (blench), *v.i.* draw back; shrink away; flinch. [Old English *blencan* deceive]

blench[2] (blench), *v.i., v.t.* turn white or pale; blanch. [variant of *blanch*]

blend (blend), *v.,* **blend ed** or (ARCHAIC) **blent, blend ing** *n.* —*v.t.* 1 mix together so thoroughly that the things mixed cannot be distinguished or separated. See **mix** for synonym study. 2 make by mixing several kinds together: *blend teas.* —*v.i.* 1 be or become blended: *Oil and water will not blend.* 2 shade into each other, little by little; merge: *The colors of the rainbow blend into one another.* 3 go well together; harmonize: *Brown and gold blend well.* —*n.* 1 a thorough mixture. 2 mixture of several kinds: *a blend of coffee.* 3 word made by fusing two words, often with a syllable in common; portmanteau word. *Smog* is a blend of *smoke* and *fog.* [Old English *blendan* to mix] **—blend′er,** *n.*

blende (blend), *n.* 1 sphalerite. 2 any of certain other sulfides. [< German *Blende*]

blen ny (blen′ē), *n., pl.* **-nies.** any of various small, saltwater fishes having a slender, tapering body, often found near rocky coasts. [< Latin *blennius* < Greek *blennos* slime]

blent (blent), *v.* ARCHAIC. a pt. and a pp. of **blend.**

bless (bles), *v.t.,* **blessed** or **blest, bless-ing.** 1 consecrate by a religious rite or prayer; make holy or sacred: *The bishop blessed the new church.* 2 ask God's favor for: *Bless these little children.* 3 wish good to; feel grateful to: *I bless you for your kindness.* 4 make happy or fortunate: *May this country always be blessed with freedom.* 5 call holy; praise; glorify: *Bless the Lord, O my soul.* 6 guard or protect from evil: *Heaven bless this house.* 7 make the sign of the cross over. [Old English *blētsian, blēdsian* consecrate (i.e., with blood) < *blōd* blood]

bless ed (bles′id, blest), *adj.* 1 holy; sacred. 2 bringing joy; joyful. 3 happy; fortunate. 4 enjoying the favor of heaven; beatified. 5 INFORMAL. annoying; confounded. **—bless′ed ly,** *adv.* **—bless′ed ness,** *n.*

Bless ed Sacrament (bles′id), the Eucharist.

Bless ed Virgin (bles′id), the Virgin Mary.

bless ing (bles′ing), *n.* 1 prayer asking God to show His favor; benediction: *A religious service often ends with a blessing.* 2 a giving of God's favor. 3 a brief prayer of thanks said before or sometimes after a meal. 4 a wish for happiness or success. 5 anything that makes one happy or contented; benefit: *A good temper is a great blessing.* 6 consent or approval.

blest (blest), *v.* a pt. and a pp. of **bless.** —*adj.* blessed.

blew (blü), *v.* pt. of **blow**[2] and **blow**[3].

blight (blīt), *n.* 1 disease of plants that causes leaves, stems, fruits, and tissues to wither and die. 2 bacterium, fungus, or virus that causes such a disease. 3 anything that withers hope or causes destruction or ruin. 4 decay; deterioration. —*v.t.* 1 cause to wither and die: *Mildew blighted the June roses.* 2 destroy; ruin: *The letter of rejection blighted all my hopes.* —*v.i.* be blighted; suffer from blight. [origin uncertain]

blimp (blimp), *n.* a nonrigid airship. [apparently < *Type B limp,* designation for "limp dirigible" in early experiments]

blimp—The gas-filled balloon provides lift. The motor behind the cabin moves the blimp forward.

blind (blīnd), *adj.* 1 not able to see; sightless. 2 difficult to see; hidden: *a blind curve on a highway.* 3 without the help of sight; by means of instruments instead of the eyes: *blind flying of an aircraft at night.* 4 without thought, judgment, or good sense: *blind fury, a blind guess.* 5 **blind to,** unable to understand, perceive, or appreciate: *She is blind to my arguments.* 6 with only one opening: *a blind canyon, a blind alley.* 7 without an opening: *a blind wall.* 8 of or for blind persons. 9 made without previous knowledge: *a blind purchase.*
—*adv.* without the help of sight: *to fly blind.*
—*v.t.* 1 make unable to see: *The bright lights blinded me for a moment.* 2 make difficult to see; cover; conceal. 3 rob of power to understand or judge.
—*n.* 1 something that keeps out light or hinders sight, as a window shade or shutter. 2 anything that conceals an action or purpose; pretext. 3 a hiding place for a hunter.
[Old English] **—blind′ly,** *adv.* **—blind′-ness,** *n.*

blind date, U.S. 1 date between two persons of opposite sex who have not previously met, arranged by someone else. 2 either of the two persons.

blind er (blīn′dər), *n.* either of two leather flaps on a horse's bridle to keep the horse from seeing sideways; blinker.

blind fold (blīnd′fōld′), *v.t.* cover the eyes of, especially with a bandage. —*adj.* 1 with the eyes covered. 2 reckless. —*n.* a cloth covering the eyes. [Middle English *blindfelled,* past tense < *blind* + *fellen* strike down]

blind man's buff (blīnd′manz buf′), game in which a blindfolded person tries to catch and identify one of several other players.

blind spot, 1 a point on the retina, not sensitive to light, where the optic nerve enters the eye. See **eye** for diagram. 2 matter on which a person does not know that he is prejudiced or poorly informed. 3 area of poor radio or television reception. 4 area of poor visibility: *There is a blind spot where the road dips on that steep curve.*

blind worm (blīnd′wėrm′), *n.* a small lizard of Europe and western Asia with a limbless, snakelike body and very tiny eyes.

blink (blingk), *v.i.* 1 look with the eyes

opening and shutting: *She blinked at the sudden light.* 2 close the eyes and open them again quickly; wink: *We blink every few seconds.* 3 shine with an unsteady light: *A little lantern blinked in the night.* —*v.t.* shut the eyes to; look with indifference at; ignore: *Don't blink the fact that time slips by.* —*n.* 1 a blinking. 2 **on the blink,** INFORMAL. not working properly: *Our television set is on the blink again.* 3 a sudden flash of light; gleam. 4 glimpse. [Middle English *blinken*]

blink er (bling′kər), *n.* 1 blinder. 2 device with flashing lights used as a warning signal or to send messages.

blintz (blints), *n.* blintze.

blin tze (blin′tsə), *n.* a thin, rolled pancake filled with cheese, fruit, jam, etc. [< Yiddish *blintse* < Ukrainian *blynci*]

blip (blip), *n.* a small spot or dot of light on a radar screen, showing the location of an object within its range. [imitative]

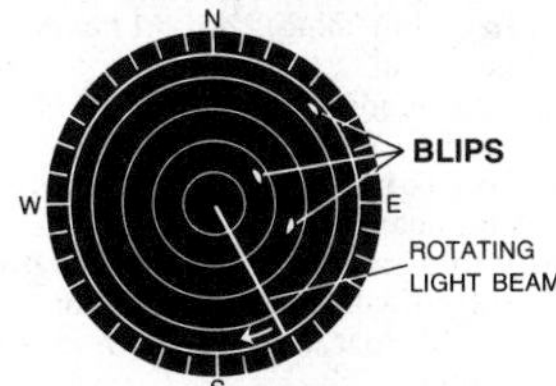

blip—The three blips on the radar screen indicate three objects. Distance from the radar is indicated by the circles. Those blips closest to the center are the nearest.

bliss (blis), *n.* great happiness or delight; perfect joy; ecstasy. See **happiness** for synonym study. [Old English *blīths* < *blīthe* blithe]

bliss ful (blis′fəl), *adj.* supremely happy; joyful. **—bliss′ful ly,** *adv.* **—bliss′ful ness,** *n.*

blis ter (blis′tər), *n.* 1 a small swelling in the skin filled with watery matter, often caused by burns or rubbing. 2 a similar swelling on the surface of a plant, on metal, on painted wood, or in glass. 3 bulge on the fuselage of an aircraft, often transparent, for an observer, navigator, or gunner. —*v.t.* 1 raise a blister or blisters on. 2 attack with sharp words. —*v.i.* become covered with blisters; have blisters. [< Old French *blestre*]

blister beetle, any of various beetles which are dried and powdered for use in raising blisters on the skin in medical treatment, especially the Spanish fly.

blister copper, impure copper with a black, blistered surface, obtained during smelting.

blis ter y (blis′tər ē), *adj.* blistering.

blithe (blīтн, blīth), *adj.* 1 happy and cheerful; gay; joyous. 2 heedless. [Old English *blīthe*] **—blithe′ly,** *adv.* **—blithe′ness,** *n.*

blithe some (blīтн′səm, blīth′səm), *adj.* blithe. **—blithe′some ly,** *adv.* **—blithe′some ness,** *n.*

blitz (blits), *n.* 1 blitzkrieg. 2 a sudden, violent attack using many airplanes and tanks. 3 any sudden, violent attack. —*v.t.* attack or overcome by a blitz. [short for *blitzkrieg*]

blitz krieg (blits′krēg′), *n.* warfare in which the offensive is extremely rapid, violent, and hard to resist. [< German *Blitzkrieg* lightning war]

bliz zard (bliz′ərd), *n.* 1 a blinding snowstorm with a very strong wind accompanied by intense cold. 2 a similar storm of windblown sand, dust, etc. [variant of dialectal *blizzer* a blow, shot]

bloat (blōt), *v.t.* 1 swell up; puff up; inflate: *Overeating bloated their stomachs.* 2 preserve (herring) by slightly salting and partially smoking. —*v.i.* become bloated; swell. —*n.* disorder of cattle, sheep, etc., characterized by a swelling of the stomach caused by eating green forage too rapidly or eating moist feed that ferments. [Middle English *blout* soft with moisture]

bloat er (blō′tər), *n.* herring preserved by slightly salting and partially smoking, softer and less dry than a kipper.

blob (blob), *n.* 1 a small, soft drop; sticky lump: *Blobs of wax covered the candlestick.* 2 a splash or daub of color. [perhaps imitative]

bloc (blok), *n.* 1 group of persons, companies, or nations combined for a purpose: *The farm bloc in Congress is a group from different political parties that favors laws to help farmers.* 2 an association of peoples or nations having common interests: *Poland and East Germany are a part of the eastern European bloc.* [< French]

block (blok), *n.* 1 a solid piece of wood, stone, metal, ice, etc., usually with one or more flat sides. 2 a shaped piece of wood, plastic, etc., with which children play at building. 3 obstruction; hindrance: *a traffic block, a mental block.* 4 U.S. space in a city or town that is bounded by streets on each side. 5 U.S. length of one side of a block in a city or town. 6 number of buildings close together. 7 a large, single building consisting of a number of stores or shops, each with its separate entrance to the street. 8 group of things of the same kind: *a block of ten seats in a theater.* 9 a short section of railroad track with signals for spacing trains. 10 a support for the neck of a person being beheaded. 11 platform where things are put up for sale at an auction. 12 casing with a hook or eye in which a pulley or pulleys are mounted. 13 mold on which something is shaped. 14 piece of wood, metal, or other material engraved for printing. 15 SLANG. a person's head. 16 an obstructing of a nerve, etc. 17 (in sports) a hindering of an opponent's play. 18 **go to the block, a** go to have one's head cut off. **b** be for sale at an auction. 19 **on the block,** up for sale, especially at an auction.

—*v.t.* 1 fill up so as to prevent passage or progress: *The country roads were blocked with snow.* 2 obstruct the way or course of; hinder: *The plans for expansion were blocked by a drop in the stock market.* 3 mount on a block. 4 shape with a mold: *Felt hats are blocked.* 5 (in sports and games) hinder (an opponent or his play). 6 prevent or postpone the passage of a bill in a legislature. 7 prevent (a nerve) from transmitting impulses. 8 **block in** or **block out,** plan or sketch roughly without filling in the details; outline. 9 **block up, a** fill up so as to prevent passage or progress. **b** raise on blocks. —*v.i.* (in sports and games) hinder an opponent or his play.

[< Old French *bloc* piece of wood]

block ade (blo kād′), *n., v.,* **-ad ed, -ad ing.** —*n.* 1 a blocking of a place by military means, especially with ships, to control who or what goes into or out of it: *In 1948-1949, the airlift defeated the Russian blockade of Berlin.* 2 **run the blockade,** dodge into or out of a port that is being blockaded. 3 a navy, army, etc., used to blockade a place. 4 anything that blocks up or obstructs. —*v.t.* 1 put under blockade. 2 block up; obstruct. **—block ad′er,** *n.*

hat, āge, fär; let, ēqual, tėrm;
it, īce; hot, ōpen, ôrder;
oil, out; cup, pu̇t, rüle;
ch, child; ng, long; sh, she;
th, thin; ᴛʜ, then; zh, measure;

ə represents *a* in about, *e* in taken, *i* in pencil, *o* in lemon, *u* in circus.

< = from, derived from, taken from.

block ade-run ner (blo kād′run′ər), *n.* ship that tries to make a run into or out of a port that is being blockaded.

block and tackle, combination of pulleys and ropes to lift or pull something.

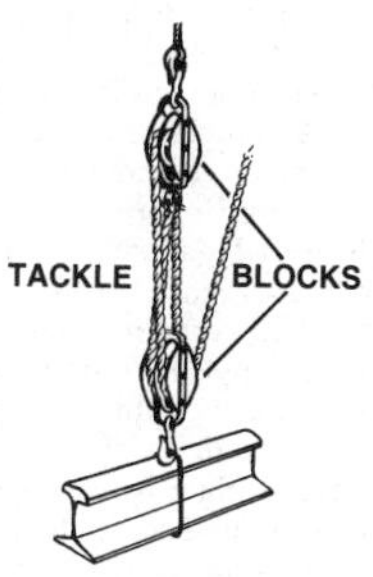

block and tackle

block bust er (blok′bus′tər), *n.* INFORMAL. 1 a very destructive aerial bomb that weighs two or more tons. 2 anything very large, forceful, or overwhelming. 3 U.S. a real-estate dealer who engages in blockbusting.

block bust ing (blok′bus′ting), *n.* U.S. practice by some real-estate dealers of causing residents of a block to sell their homes or property at low prices by exploiting their fear of impending racial integration.

block head (blok′hed′), *n.* a stupid person; fool.

block house (blok′hous′), *n., pl.* **-hous es** (-hou′ziz). 1 a small fort or building with loopholes to shoot from. 2 structure for protection against blast, heat, radiation, etc., during the firing of a rocket, missile, or nuclear weapon.

block ish (blok′ish), *adj.* very dull or stupid. **—block′ish ly,** *adv.* **—block′ish ness,** *n.*

block letter, 1 letter or type without serifs or hairlines. THIS LINE IS IN BLOCK LETTERS. 2 capital letter.

block signal, a signal to show whether or not a short section of railroad track ahead has a train on it.

block y (blok′ē), *adj.,* **block i er, block i est.** 1 like a block; chunky. 2 (of a photograph) having patches of light and shade.

Bloem fon tein (blüm′fon tān), *n.* city in the central part of the Republic of South Africa, the capital of Orange Free State. 146,000.

bloke (blōk), *n.* BRITISH SLANG. man; fellow. [origin unknown]

blond or **blonde** (blond), *adj.* 1 light in color: *blond hair, blond furniture.* 2 having yellow or light-brown hair, blue or gray eyes, and a fair skin. —*n.* person having blond hair, blue or gray eyes, and a fair skin. A man or boy of this sort is usually referred to as a blond. A woman or girl of this sort is usually referred to as a blonde. [< French] **—blond′ness, blonde′ness,** *n.*

blood (blud), *n.* 1 the liquid in the veins, arteries, and capillaries of vertebrates, normally appearing to be red, but actually consisting of a fluid pale-yellow plasma and semisolid red and white blood cells and platelets. Blood is circulated by the heart, carrying oxygen and digested food to all parts of the body and carrying away waste materials. 2 the corresponding liquid, colored or colorless, in animals other than vertebrates. 3 relationship by descent from a common ancestor; parentage; descent. 4 high lineage, especially royal lineage: *a prince of the blood.* 5 man of dash and spirit. 6 anger, fright, passion, etc.; temper; emotion: *Cruelty to animals makes my blood boil.* 7 bloodshed; slaughter. 8 **curdle one's blood,** frighten very much; horrify; terrify. 9 **draw blood,** inflict damage or pain. 10 **in cold blood,** without feeling; cruelly and deliberately. —*v.t.* give (troops) their first experience in actual warfare. [Old English *blōd*] **—blood′like′,** *adj.*

blood bank, 1 place for storage of blood to be used in transfusions. 2 the blood kept in storage.

blood bath, an indiscriminate slaughter of people; massacre.

blood brother, 1 brother by birth; real brother. 2 person who goes through a ceremony of mixing some of his blood with another person's.

blood cell, any of the cells or corpuscles contained in blood.

blood count, count of the number of red and white blood cells and the amount of hemoglobin in a sample of a person's blood to see if it is normal.

blood cur dling (blud′kėrd′ling), *adj.* terrifying; horrible.

blood ed (blud′id), *adj.* derived from ancestors of good blood; of good breed or pedigree.

blood feud, a very bitter feud marked by bloodshed.

blood fluke, schistosome.

blood group, any one of the groups into which human blood may be divided on the basis of the presence or absence of certain substances that cause red cells to clump together; blood type.

blood hound (blud′hound′), *n.* 1 any of a breed of large, powerful dogs with a keen sense of smell, used in tracking fugitives, etc. 2 SLANG. detective.

blood less (blud′lis), *adj.* 1 without bloodshed: *a bloodless victory.* 2 deficient in blood supply; pale. 3 without energy; spiritless. 4 cold-hearted; cruel. **—blood′less ly,** *adv.* **—blood′less ness,** *n.*

blood let ting (blud′let′ing), *n.* 1 act of opening a vein to take out blood. 2 bloodshed or blood bath; slaughter.

blood line (blud′līn′), *n.* 1 series of ancestors in a pedigree. 2 pedigree, family, or strain (applied especially to animals).

blood mo bile (blud′mō bēl′), *n.* a large motor vehicle with medical equipment and staff for collecting blood donated for use in blood transfusions.

blood money, 1 money paid to have somebody killed. 2 compensation paid to the relatives of a person who has been killed. 3 INFORMAL. money gained at the cost of another person's life, freedom, welfare, etc.

blood platelet, any of the colorless, round or oval disks in the blood of vertebrates, smaller than red blood cells, important in coagulation; thrombocyte; platelet.

blood poisoning, a diseased condition of the blood caused by the presence of toxins, bacteria, etc.; toxemia or septicemia.

blood pressure, pressure of the blood against the inner walls of the arteries, varying with the strength of the heartbeat, exertion, excitement, health, age, etc.

blood root (blud′rüt′, blud′rủt′), *n.* a wild plant of the same family as the poppy, that has a red root, orange-red sap, and a single white flower that blooms in early spring.

blood shed (blud′shed′), *n.* the shedding of blood; slaughter.

blood shot (blud′shot′), *adj.* red and inflamed from broken or swollen blood vessels: *bloodshot eyes.*

blood sport, any sport involving the killing of animals.

blood stain (blud′stān′), *n.* stain left by blood. —*v.t.* stain with blood.

blood stained (blud′stānd′), *adj.* 1 stained with blood. 2 guilty of murder or bloodshed.

blood stone (blud′stōn′), *n.* a semiprecious green variety of quartz with specks of red jasper scattered through it; heliotrope.

blood stream (blud′strēm′), *n.* blood as it flows through the body.

blood suck er (blud′suk′ər), *n.* 1 leech or other animal that sucks blood. 2 person who gets on at the expense of others; sponger. 3 extortioner.

blood suck ing (blud′suk′ing), *adj.* 1 that sucks blood. 2 extorting.

blood sugar, glucose in the blood, the presence of which in excessive quantities is a sign of diabetes.

blood test, examination of a sample of a person's blood to determine the type of blood, diagnose illness, etc.

blood thirst y (blud′thėr′stē), *adj.* eager for bloodshed; cruel and murderous: *a bloodthirsty pirate.* **—blood′thirst′i ly,** *adv.* **—blood′thirst′i ness,** *n.*

blood transfusion, transfusion (def. 2).

blood type, blood group.

blood-type (blud′tīp′), *v.t.*, **-typed, -typing.** classify (the blood) according to type or (persons) according to blood group.

blood vessel, any of the flexible tubes in the body through which the blood circulates. Arteries, veins, and capillaries are blood vessels.

blood y (blud′ē), *adj.*, **blood i er, blood i est,** *v.*, **blood ied, blood y ing.** —*adj.* 1 covered with blood; bleeding: *a bloody nose.* 2 stained with blood: *a bloody sword.* 3 with much bloodshed: *a bloody battle.* 4 eager for bloodshed; bloodthirsty. 5 BRITISH SLANG. cursed; confounded: *He is a bloody fool!* —*v.t.* 1 cause to bleed. 2 stain with blood. **—blood′i ly,** *adv.* **—blood′i ness,** *n.*

bloom[1] (blüm), *v.i.* 1 have flowers; produce flowers; blossom. 2 be in the condition or time of greatest health, vigor, or beauty; flourish. 3 glow with health and beauty. —*v.t.* cause to bloom. —*n.* 1 flower of a plant, especially an ornamental plant. 2 flowers collectively. 3 condition or time of flowering: *violets in bloom.* 4 condition or time of greatest health, vigor, or beauty: *the bloom of youth.* 5 a rosy tint of the cheek; glow of health and youth. 6 a delicate, powdery or downy coating on some fruits and leaves. [< Scandinavian (Old Icelandic) *blōm*] **—bloom′er,** *n.*

bloom[2] (blüm), *n.* 1 bar of iron or steel, rolled or hammered from an ingot. 2 an unmelted, spongy mass of wrought iron from the puddling furnace or forge. [Old English *blōma* lump]

bloom ers (blü′mərz), *n.pl.* 1 loose trousers, gathered at the knee, formerly worn by women and girls for physical training, sports, etc. 2 underwear made like these. [< Amelia J. *Bloomer,* 1818-1894, who first referred to them in a magazine she published]

bloom ing (blü′ming), *adj.* 1 having flowers; blossoming. 2 flourishing. 3 BRITISH SLANG. confounded; bloody: *not a blooming chance.* **—bloom′ing ly,** *adv.*

Bloom ing ton (blü′ming tən), *n.* city in E Minnesota, near Minneapolis. 82,000.

bloom y (blü′mē), *adj.*, **bloom i er, bloom i est.** covered with bloom, as a plum.

bloop er (blü′pər), *n.* SLANG. a foolish mistake; boner.

blos som (blos′əm), *n.* 1 flower, especially of a plant that produces fruit: *apple blossoms.* 2 condition or time of flowering: *a cherry tree in blossom.* —*v.i.* 1 have flowers; produce flowers. 2 open out; develop. [Old English *blōstma*]

blos som y (blos′ə mē), *adj.* full of blossoms.

blot (blot), *n.*, *v.*, **blot ted, blot ting.** —*n.* 1 a spot of ink or stain of any kind. 2 a spot upon one's character or reputation; blemish; disgrace. —*v.t.* 1 make blots on; stain; spot. 2 dry (ink) with blotting paper, sand, etc. 3 **blot out, a** cover up entirely; hide. **b** wipe out; destroy. —*v.i.* make a blot or blots. [Middle English]

blotch (bloch), *n.* 1 a large, irregular spot, stain, or blot. 2 place where the skin is red or broken out. —*v.t.* cover or mark with blotches. [perhaps a blend of *blot* and *botch*]

blotch y (bloch′ē), *adj.*, **blotch i er, blotch i est.** having blotches.

blot ter (blot′ər), *n.* 1 piece of blotting paper. 2 book for recording happenings or transactions as they take place. A police station blotter is a record of arrests and charges.

blotting paper, a soft, absorbent paper used to dry writing by soaking up ink.

blouse (blous, blouz), *n.* 1 a loose or fitted upper garment covering the body from the neck or shoulder to the waistline, worn by women and children as part of their outer clothing. 2 a loosely fitting garment for the upper part of the body: *Sailors wear blouses as a part of their uniform.* 3 a short, fitted coat worn as part of a military uniform. 4 kind of smock reaching to the knees, worn by European peasants and workmen to protect their clothes. [< French] **—blouse′like′,** *adj.*

blow[1] (blō), *n.* 1 a sudden hard hit or knock; stroke: *a blow with the fist, a blow with a hammer.* See synonym study below. 2 a sudden happening that causes misfortune or loss; severe shock; calamity: *His mother's death was a great blow to him.* 3 a sudden

hat, āge, fär; let, ēqual, tėrm;
it, īce; hot, ōpen, ôrder;
oil, out; cup, pu̇t, rüle;
ch, child; ng, long; sh, she;
th, thin; ᴛʜ, then; zh, measure;

ə represents *a* in about, *e* in taken, *i* in pencil, *o* in lemon, *u* in circus.

< = from, derived from, taken from.

attack or assault: *The army struck a swift blow at the enemy.* 4 **at one blow,** by one act or effort. 5 **come to blows,** start fighting. 6 **without striking a blow,** with no effort. [Middle English *blaw;* perhaps originally a special meaning of *blow*²]

Syn. 1 **Blow, stroke** mean a sudden hard hit. **Blow** emphasizes its force, violence, and heaviness: *She got a blow on the head.* **Stroke** emphasizes the sharpness and precision of a hit or its unexpectedness: *His scar was made by a sword stroke across the face.*

blow² (blō), *v.,* **blew, blown, blow ing,** *n.* —*v.i.* 1 produce a strong current of air: *Blow on the fire or it will go out.* 2 move in a current, especially rapidly or with power: *The wind blows.* 3 be driven or carried by a currrent of air: *Dust blew across the road.* 4 make a sound by a current of air or steam: *The whistle blows at noon.* 5 be out of breath. 6 INFORMAL. boast; brag. 7 melt: *The short circuit caused the fuse to blow.* 8 (of whales) spout water and air. —*v.t.* 1 drive or carry by a current of air: *The wind blew the curtains.* 2 force a current of air into, through, or against: *blow the fire into flames.* 3 empty or clear of obstructing matter by forcing air through: *The plumber blew the pipes.* 4 put out of breath; cause to pant. 5 form or shape by inflation; swell with air; puff up: *blow bubbles, blow glass.* 6 cause to make a sound by a current of air or steam: *blow a whistle.* 7 shatter or destroy by explosion: *The dynamite blew the wall to bits.* 8 melt: *The short circuit blew the fuse.* 9 publish or spread (news). 10 (of insects) lay eggs in: *Some flies blow fruit.* 11 U.S. SLANG. spend (money) recklessly.

blow off, get rid of (steam, energy, etc.) noisily or violently.

blow out, 1 extinguish or be extinguished by a current of air: *Blow out the candle.* 2 have or cause a blowout in: *The worn tire blew out.*

blow over, 1 pass by or over. 2 be forgotten.

blow up, 1 explode. 2 fill with air; inflate. 3 INFORMAL. become enraged. 4 INFORMAL. scold; abuse. 5 become stronger; arise: *A storm blew up suddenly.* 6 enlarge (a photograph).

—*n.* 1 act or fact of forcing air into, through, or against something; blast. 2 gale (def. 1). 3 a blowing of a wind instrument; blast. [Old English *blāwan*]

blow³ (blō), *n., v.,* **blew, blown, blow ing.** —*n.* 1 a state of blossoming; bloom. 2 display of blossoms. —*v.i.* blossom. [Old English *blōwan*]

blow by (blō′bī′), *n.* leakage of fuel, pressure, etc., between the piston and cylinder of an automobile.

blow-by-blow (blō′bī blō′), *adj.* described minutely; including every detail: *a blow-by-blow account of the fight.*

blow er (blō′ər), *n.* 1 person or thing that blows. 2 fan or other machine for forcing air into a building, furnace, mine, or other enclosed area.

blow fly (blō′flī′), *n., pl.* **-flies.** any of various two-winged flies that deposit their eggs on meat or in wounds.

blow gun (blō′gun′), *n.* tube through which a person blows something, such as arrows, darts, or dried beans; blowpipe.

blow hard (blō′härd′), *n.* SLANG. a noisy boaster; braggart.

blow hole (blō′hōl′), *n.* 1 nostril or hole for breathing, in the top of the head of whales, porpoises, and dolphins. 2 hole in the ice to which whales, seals, etc., come to breathe. 3 hole where air or gas can escape. 4 defect in a metal casting due to a bubble of air or gas. 5 defect; flaw.

blown (blōn), *adj.* 1 out of breath; exhausted. 2 flyblown. 3 shaped by blowing. 4 (of cattle, sheep, etc.) bloated. —*v.* pp. of **blow**² and **blow**³.

blow out (blō′out′), *n.* 1 the bursting of the casing of a tire, and of the inner tube, if any, caused by air pressure from inside. 2 a sudden or violent escape of air, steam, etc. 3 the melting of an electric fuse by a sudden overload in a circuit or line, causing a power failure. 4 SLANG. a big party or meal.

blow pipe (blō′pīp′), *n.* 1 tube for blowing air or gas into a flame to increase the heat. 2 blowgun. 3 a long metal tube used for blowing molten glass into the required shape.

blows y (blou′zē), *adj.,* **blows i er, blows i est.** blowzy.

blow torch (blō′tôrch′), *n.* a small, portable torch that shoots out a very hot alcohol or gasoline flame under pressure. A blowtorch is used to melt lead or solder, remove old paint, thaw frozen pipes, etc.

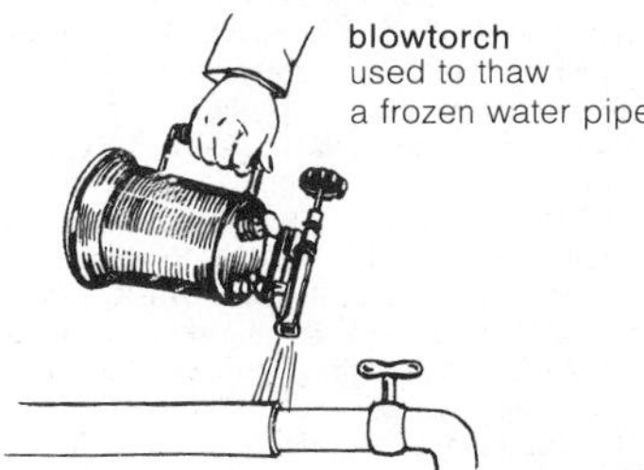
blowtorch used to thaw a frozen water pipe

blow up (blō′up′), *n.* 1 explosion. 2 INFORMAL. outburst of anger. 3 quarrel. 4 an enlargement of a photograph. 5 an expanded version.

blow y (blō′ē), *adj.,* **blow i er, blow i est.** windy: *a blowy day.*

blowz y (blou′zē), *adj.,* **blowz i er, blowz i est.** 1 lacking neatness; untidy; disheveled: *blowzy hair.* 2 red-faced and coarse-looking. Also, **blowsy.** —**blowz′i ly,** *adv.* —**blowz′i ness,** *n.*

blub ber (blub′ər), *n.* 1 fat of whales and some other sea animals, lying under the skin and over the muscles, from which oil is obtained. 2 extreme body fat. 3 noisy weeping. —*v.i.* weep noisily; sob. —*v.t.* 1 utter with tears; sob: *blubber out an apology.* 2 disfigure or swell with crying: *a face all blubbered.* —*adj.* swollen; thick: *blubber lips.* [Middle English *bluber*]

blu cher (blü′chər, blü′kər), *n.* shoe whose tongue and front part are made from one piece of leather. [< Field Marshal Gebhard von *Blücher,* 1742-1819, Prussian field marshal]

bludg eon (bluj′ən), *n.* a short club with a heavy end, used as a weapon. —*v.t.* 1 strike with a bludgeon. 2 bully or threaten. [origin unknown] —**bludg′eon er,** *n.*

blue (blü), *n., adj.,* **blu er, blu est,** *v.,* **blued, blu ing** or **blue ing.** —*n.* 1 the color of the clear sky in daylight, lying in the color spectrum between green and violet. 2 a lighter or darker shade of this color. 3 a blue pigment or dye. 4 blue cloth or clothing. 5 member of a company, team, crew, army, etc., having blue as its distinctive color. 6 **the blue,** a the sky. b the sea. 7 **out of the blue,** from an unforeseen source; from an unknown place; completely unexpectedly. 8 **the blue and the gray,** (in the Civil War) soldiers of the Union and Confederate armies respectively. —*adj.* 1 having the color of the clear sky in daylight or any variation of this color. 2 having a dull-bluish color; livid: *blue from cold, blue from a bruise.* 3 in low spirits; sad; gloomy. 4 strict in morals or religion; puritanical. 5 off-color; indecent.
—*v.t.* 1 make blue. 2 use bluing on.
[< Old French *bleu*] —**blue′ness,** *n.*

blue baby, infant born with a bluish skin, or cyanosis, caused by a defective heart.

Blue beard (blü′bird′), *n.* 1 a legendary character who murdered six of his wives and hid their bodies in a room which he forbade anyone to enter. 2 any man who marries women and murders them.

blue bell (blü′bel′), *n.* species of campanula with blue bell-shaped flowers; harebell.

blue ber ry (blü′ber′ē, blü′bər ē), *n., pl.* **-ries.** 1 a small, round, sweet, blue berry which tastes like the huckleberry but has smaller seeds. 2 shrub of the heath family that it grows on.

blue bird (blü′bėrd′), *n.* a small thrush of North America related to the robin. The male usually has a bright-blue back and wings and a chestnut-brown breast.

Blue Bird, member of the junior division of the Camp Fire Girls, for girls seven to nine years old.

blue blood, 1 aristocratic descent. 2 aristocrat.

blue-blood ed (blü′blud′id), *adj.* aristocratic.

blue bon net (blü′bon′it), *n.* 1 a lupine bearing blue flowers resembling sweet peas. 2 bachelor's-button. 3 Scotsman.

blue book, directory that lists socially prominent people.

blucher

blue bot tle (blü′bot′l), *n.* 1 any of several large blowflies having a steel-blue or green abdomen and a hairy body. 2 any similar fly. 3 bachelor's-button.

blue chip, 1 chip of the highest value in poker and certain other gambling games. 2 stock issued by a well-established company, usually high-priced and considered especially safe for investment.

blue coat (blü′kōt′), *n.* U.S. 1 policeman. 2 soldier in the Union army in the Civil War.

blue-col lar (blü′kol′ər), *adj.* of or having to do with industrial or factory work or workers.

blue fin (blü′fin′), *n.* a large tuna, im-

portant commercially and as a game fish.
blue fish (blü′fish′), *n., pl.* **-fish es** or **-fish.** 1 a saltwater food fish, bluish or greenish above and silvery below, of the Atlantic coast of North America, related to the mackerel. 2 any of several other bluish fishes.
blue flag, kind of iris that has blue flowers.
blue galaxy, a heavenly object outside of our own galaxy that is brighter than a quasar.
blue grass (blü′gras′), *n.* any of various grasses with bluish-green stems, valuable for pasturage, hay, and lawns.
blue-green algae (blü′grēn′), class of algae with a bluish pigment, consisting of one or more cells without definite nuclei.
blue gum, eucalyptus.
blue helmet, 1 the blue-colored helmet worn by members of the United Nations military force. 2 member of this force.
blue ing (blü′ing), *n.* bluing.
blue ish (blü′ish), *adj.* bluish.
blue jack et (blu′jak′it), *n.* sailor in the United States or British navy.
blue jay, a noisy, chattering jay of eastern North America with a prominent crest and bright-blue feathers on its back.
blue jeans, U.S. jeans, usually made of blue denim.
blue law, any very strict law regulating personal conduct. Laws prohibiting dancing or going to the theater on Sunday are blue laws.
Blue Nile, river flowing from E Africa into the Nile. 850 mi.
blue nose (blü′nōz′), *n.* INFORMAL. a prudish or puritanical person.
blue note, a somewhat flat note between the usual notes in jazz, especially a flatted third or seventh note, characteristic of the blues.
blue-pen cil (blü′pen′səl), *v.t.,* **-ciled, -cil ing** or **-cilled, -cil ling.** 1 change, cut down, or cross out with a pencil that makes a blue mark. 2 edit or censor.
blue point (blü′point′), *n.* a small oyster from the south shore of Long Island, usually eaten raw. [< *Blue Point,* Long Island]
blue print (blü′print′), *n.* 1 a photographic print of white lines on a blue background or blue lines on a white background, used chiefly in copying building plans, mechanical drawings, maps, etc. 2 a detailed plan for any enterprise. —*v.t.* make a blueprint of.
blue racer, a dark-blue, harmless variety of blacksnake found in the central United States.
blue ribbon, 1 ribbon of a blue color awarded to one that wins first prize in a contest. 2 the first prize; highest honor.
blue-rib bon (blü′rib′ən), *adj.* specially selected on the basis of education or other qualifications: *a blue-ribbon jury.*
Blue Ridge, the SE range of the Appalachian Mountains, extending from NW Maryland to N Georgia. Highest peak, 5964 ft.
blues (blüz), *n. pl.* 1 a slow, melancholy song with jazz rhythm that originated among American Negroes, usually in a major key but with the third and seventh (the blue notes) flatted optionally. 2 **the blues,** INFORMAL. low spirits.
blue-sky law (blü′skī′), INFORMAL. law to prevent the sale of worthless stocks and bonds. [probably in reference to the unclouded faith of the buyer of such stocks]
blue star, 1 a heavenly body that emits a faint light. 2 star located in a blue galaxy. 3 a blue galaxy.
blue stock ing (blü′stok′ing), *n.* woman who displays great interest in intellectual or literary subjects. [< the nickname *"Blue Stocking* Society" given to a group of English men and women who met about 1750 to discuss literature]
blue stone (blü′stōn′), *n.* 1 a bluish sandstone. 2 blue vitriol.
blu et (blü′it), *n.* any of several small North American plants with pale blue flowers. [< French *bleuet,* diminutive of *bleu* blue]
blue vitriol, a poisonous, blue, crystalline compound of copper and sulfuric acid, used in dyeing and printing, in electric batteries, and in sprays to destroy insects, fungi, etc.; copper sulfate; cupric sulfate; bluestone. *Formula:* $CuSO_4 \cdot 5H_2O$
blue whale, a blue-gray whale with yellowish underparts, sometimes growing to over 100 feet in length and weighing over 115 tons. It is the largest living animal; sulphurbottom.
bluff[1] (bluf), *n.* a high, steep bank or cliff, especially one on the shore of a sea, lake, or river. —*adj.* 1 rising with a straight, broad front; steep. 2 good-naturedly blunt, frank, or plain-spoken; rough and hearty. See **blunt** for synonym study. [probably < earlier Dutch *blaf* broad, flat] **—bluff′ly,** *adv.* **—bluff′ness,** *n.*
bluff[2] (bluf), *n.* 1 show of confidence or pretense of strength put on to deceive or mislead others. 2 **call one's bluff,** ask for proof or for action when pretense is suspected. 3 act of bluffing. 4 threat that cannot be carried out. 5 person who bluffs. —*v.t.* 1 deceive (a rival, opponent, etc.) by a show of pretended confidence; fool. 2 frighten with a threat that cannot be carried out: *He bluffed the robber with a toy gun.* —*v.i.* deceive or try to deceive someone by a bluff. [probably < Dutch *bluffen* brag] **—bluff′er,** *n.*
blu ing (blü′ing), *n.* a blue liquid or powder put in water when laundering to keep white clothes from turning yellow. Also, **blueing.**
blu ish (blü′ish), *adj.* somewhat blue. Also, **blueish.**
blun der (blun′dər), *n.* a stupid or careless mistake; bungle. —*v.i.* 1 make a stupid or careless mistake. 2 move clumsily or thoughtlessly; stumble. —*v.t.* 1 do clumsily or wrongly; bungle. 2 say or reveal clumsily, stupidly, or thoughtlessly; blurt out. [Middle English *blonderen* mix up] **—blun′der er,** *n.*

blunderbuss
(def. 1)

blun der buss (blun′dər bus), *n.* 1 a short gun with a wide muzzle and large bore, formerly used to shoot balls or slugs a very short distance without exact aim. 2 a blundering person. [alteration of Dutch *donderbus* thunder box]
blunt (blunt), *adj.* 1 without a sharp edge or point; dull: *a blunt knife, a blunt pencil.* See **dull** for synonym study. 2 abrupt in speech; outspoken; frank: *a blunt answer.* See synonym study below. 3 slow in perceiving or understanding. —*v.t., v.i.* make or become blunt. [Middle English] **—blunt′ly,** *adv.* **—blunt′ness,** *n.*
Syn. *adj.* 2 **Blunt, bluff, curt** mean abrupt in speaking or manner. **Blunt** implies frankness and plainness of speech without consideration for the feelings of others: *The chairman's blunt and tactless reply caused resentment.* **Bluff** suggests a frank and rough manner of speaking and acting combined with heartiness and genuineness: *Everyone likes the bluff sea captain.* **Curt** means rudely abrupt and brief: *A curt nod was the only notice he gave that he knew I was there.*
blur (blėr), *v.,* **blurred, blur ring,** *n.* —*v.t.* 1 make less clear in form or outline: *Mist blurred the hills.* 2 dim (the sight, perception, etc.): *Tears blurred her eyes.* 3 smear; smudge: *I blurred the writing by touching the ink before it was dry.* —*v.i.* become dim or indistinct: *His eyes blurred with tears.* —*n.* 1 a blurred condition; dimness. 2 thing seen dimly or indistinctly. 3 a smear; smudge. [perhaps a variant of *blear*]
blurb (blėrb), *n.* INFORMAL. a brief advertisement or description full of high praise, usually on the jacket of a book, album, etc. [supposedly coined in 1907 by Gelett Burgess, 1866-1951, American humorist]
blur ry (blėr′ē), *adj.,* **-ri er, -ri est.** 1 dim; indistinct. 2 full of smears and smudges.
blurt (blėrt), *v.t.* say suddenly or thoughtlessly: *blurt out the secret.* [imitative]
blush (blush), *v.i.* 1 become red in the face because of shame, modesty, confusion, etc.: *I used to be so shy that I blushed every time I was spoken to.* 2 be ashamed: *I blushed at your bad table manners.* 3 be or become red or rosy. —*v.t.* 1 make rosy; redden. 2 express or make known by blushing. —*n.* 1 a reddening of the face caused by shame, modesty, confusion, etc. 2 a rosy color or glow. 3 **at first blush,** on first glance; at first thought. [Old English *blyscan* redden]
blus ter (blus′tər), *v.i.* 1 storm noisily; blow violently: *The wind blustered around the house.* 2 talk noisily and violently: *He blusters in an attempt to hide his ignorance.* —*v.t.* 1 do or say noisily and violently. 2 make or get by blustering. —*n.* 1 a stormy blowing. 2 noisy and stormy commotion. 3 noisy and violent talk with empty threats or protests. [Middle English *blusteren,* perhaps < Low German *blüstern* blow violently] **—blus′ter er,** *n.*
blus ter y (blus′tər ē), *adj.* blustering.
blvd., boulevard.
b.m., board measure.
BMD, ballistic missile defense.
BMEWS (bē′myüz), *n.* Ballistic Missile Early Warning System.
BMR, basal metabolic rate.
B.O., 1 body odor. 2 box office.
bo a (bō′ə), *n.* 1 any of a family of large, tropical snakes which lack poisonous fangs, but kill their prey by crushing with their coils, as the anaconda, python, and boa constrictor. 2 a long scarf made of fur or feathers, worn around a woman's neck. [< Latin, a type of serpent]
boa constrictor, a large boa of tropical America, from 10 to 15 feet long.
boar (bôr, bōr), *n.* 1 an uncastrated male pig or hog. 2 wild boar. [Old English *bār*]
board (bôrd, bōrd), *n.* 1 a broad, thin piece of wood for use in building, etc. 2 a flat piece of wood or other material used for some

special purpose, as for drawing on, posting notices, etc. 3 tablet or frame on which pieces are moved in some games: *a backgammon board.* 4 pasteboard: *a book with covers of board.* 5 either of the rectangular pieces of strong pasteboard, used to make the hard covers of a book. 6 table to serve food on; table. 7 food served on a table, especially meals provided for pay at a boardinghouse, etc. 8 group of persons having the management or direction of some office or trust; council: *a firm's board of directors, a school board.* 9 side of a ship. 10 **the boards,** the stage of a theater. 11 **go by the board,** a fall over the side of a ship. b be given up, neglected, or ignored. 12 **on board,** on a ship, train, bus, airplane, etc. 13 **tread the boards,** act in a play.
—*v.t.* 1 cover, enclose, or close with boards. 2 provide with regular meals, or room and meals, for pay. 3 get on (a ship, train, bus, airplane, etc.). 4 come alongside of or against (a ship). —*v.i.* 1 get regular meals, or room and meals, for pay. 2 sail in a zigzag course against the wind; tack.
[Old English *bord*]

board er (bôr′dər, bōr′dər), *n.* 1 person who pays for meals, or for room and meals, at another's house. 2 one of the men assigned to go on board an enemy ship.

board foot, unit for measuring logs and lumber equal to the volume of a board one foot square and one inch thick; 144 cubic inches.

board ing (bôr′ding, bōr′ding), *n.* 1 boards. 2 structure made of boards.

board ing house (bôr′ding hous′, bōr′ding hous′), *n., pl.* **-hous es** (-hou′ziz). house where meals, or room and meals, are provided for pay.

boarding school, school where pupils are lodged and fed during the school term.

board measure, the system for measuring logs and lumber. The unit is the board foot.

board of health, U.S. department of a state and local government in charge of public health.

board of trade, 1 association of businessmen to protect, regulate, and advance their interests. 2 **Board of Trade,** department of the British government concerned with commerce and industry.

board walk (bôrd′wôk′, bōrd′wôk′), *n.* 1 a wide sidewalk or promenade, usually made of boards, near the water at a beach or shore resort. 2 any sidewalk made of boards.

boast (bōst), *v.i.* praise oneself; brag. See synonym study below. —*v.t.* 1 brag about. 2 display with pride or vanity: *Our town boasts many fine parks.* —*n.* 1 statement praising oneself; bragging words. 2 something to be proud of. [Middle English *bosten*] **—boast′er,** *n.* **—boast′ing ly,** *adv.*

Syn. *v.i.* **Boast, brag** mean to praise oneself. **Boast** means to talk too much about something one has done or about one's possessions, family, etc., even though there may be some reason to be proud: *She boasts about her grades in school.* **Brag** always suggests showing off and exaggerating: *He is always bragging about what he can do with a car.*

boast ful (bōst′fəl), *adj.* 1 speaking too well about oneself; boasting. 2 fond of boasting. **—boast′ful ly,** *adv.* **—boast′ful ness,** *n.*

boat (bōt), *n.* 1 a small, usually open vessel for traveling on water, propelled by oars, sails, or motor. 2 ship. 3 a boat-shaped dish for gravy, sauce, etc. 4 **in the same boat,** in the same position or condition; taking the same chances. 5 **miss the boat,** INFORMAL. miss an opportunity; lose one's chances. 6 **rock the boat,** INFORMAL. disturb or upset the way things are: *Your refusal to abide by the rules is rocking the boat.* —*v.i.* go in a boat; travel in a boat. —*v.t.* put or carry in a boat. [Old English *bāt*] **—boat′er,** *n.* **—boat′like′,** *adj.*

boat el (bō tel′), *n.* hotel at a marina, for use by boaters. [blend of *boat* and *hotel*]

boat hook, a metal hook on a pole, used for pulling or pushing a boat, raft, etc.

boat house (bōt′hous′), *n., pl.* **-hous es** (-hou′ziz). house or shed for sheltering a boat or boats.

boat ing (bō′ting), *n.* act or sport of going by boat, as in rowing or sailing.

boat load (bōt′lōd′), *n.* 1 as much or as many as a boat can hold or carry. 2 load that a boat is carrying.

boat man (bōt′mən), *n., pl.* **-men.** 1 man who rents out boats or takes care of them. 2 man who rows or sails boats for pay. 3 man who works on a boat.

boat swain (bō′sn; *less often* bōt′swān′), *n.* a ship's officer who is in charge of the anchors, ropes, rigging, etc., and directs some of the work of the crew. Also, **bo's'n, bosun.**

bob[1] (bob), *v.,* **bobbed, bob bing,** *n.* —*v.t.* cause to move up and down, or to and fro, with short, quick motions: *The bird bobbed its head up and down.* —*v.i.* 1 move the body, head, etc., with a bobbing motion. 2 **bob up,** appear suddenly or unexpectedly. 3 try to catch with the teeth something floating or hanging: *One game at the party was to bob for apples in a bowl of water.* —*n.* a short, quick motion up and down, or to and fro, especially of the head. [Middle English *bobben*]

bob[2] (bob), *n., v.,* **bobbed, bob bing.** —*n.* 1 a child's or woman's haircut that is fairly short and even all around the head. 2 a horse's docked tail. 3 weight at the end of a pendulum or plumb line. 4 float for a fishing line. 5 bobsled. —*v.t.* 1 cut (hair) short. 2 dock (an animal's tail). —*v.i.* fish with a bob. [Middle English *bobbe* bunch]

bob[3] (bob), *n., pl.* **bob.** BRITISH SLANG. shilling. [origin uncertain]

bob bin (bob′ən), *n.* 1 reel or spool for holding thread, yarn, etc., used in spinning, weaving, machine sewing, and lacemaking. 2 reel around which wire is coiled in electrical instruments. [< Middle French *bobine*]

bob bi net (bob′ə net′), *n.* a netting or lace made by machines. [< *bobbin* + *net*[1]]

bob ble (bob′əl), *v.,* **-bled, -bling.** —*v.i.* 1 move with a continual bobbing. 2 SLANG. blunder; fumble. —*v.t.* SLANG. fumble (a ball). —*n.* 1 movement of agitated water. 2 SLANG. blunder; fumble.

bob by (bob′ē), *n., pl.* **-bies.** BRITISH INFORMAL. policeman. [< *Bobby,* nickname for Sir *Robert* Peel, who founded the London police force]

bobby pin, a metal hairpin whose prongs close on and hold tightly to the hair.

bob by socks (bob′ē soks′), *n.pl.* U.S. socks reaching just above the ankle, worn especially by girls.

bob by sox er (bob′ē sok′sər), *n.* U.S. an adolescent girl, especially one in the 1940's who wore bobbysocks and enthusiastically followed every new fad.

hat, āge, fär; let, ēqual, tėrm;
it, īce; hot, ōpen, ôrder;
oil, out; cup, pu̇t, rüle;
ch, child; ng, long; sh, she;
th, thin; ᴛʜ, then; zh, measure;

ə represents *a* in about, *e* in taken, *i* in pencil, *o* in lemon, *u* in circus.

< = from, derived from, taken from.

bobcat—23 in. high at the shoulder

bob cat (bob′kat′), *n.* a small lynx of North America having a pale tan to reddish-brown coat with black spots.

bob o link (bob′ə lingk), *n.* a common North American songbird related to the blackbird, that lives in fields and meadows; reedbird. [imitative]

bob sled (bob′sled′), *n., v.,* **-sled ded, -sled ding.** —*n.* 1 a long sled with two sets of runners, a continuous seat, a steering wheel, and brakes. 2 two short sleds fastened together by a plank. —*v.i.* ride or coast on a bobsled.

bob stay (bob′stā′), *n.* rope, chain, or steel stay to hold a bowsprit down.

bob tail (bob′tāl′), *n.* 1 a short tail or a tail cut short. 2 horse or dog with its tail cut short. —*adj.* having a bobtail.

bob tailed (bob′tāld′), *adj.* 1 having a bobtail. 2 cut short; curtailed.

bob white (bob′hwīt′), *n.* any of various American quails, especially one having a grayish body with brown and white markings. Its call sounds somewhat like its name.

Boc cac ci o (bō kä′chē ō), *n.* **Giovanni,** 1313-1375, Italian poet and story writer.

boc cie (boch′ē), *n.* an Italian form of the game of bowls, played outdoors on a narrow, enclosed court. [< Italian *bocce,* plural of *boccia* ball]

bock (bok), *n.* bock beer.

bock beer, a strong, dark, somewhat sweet beer, usually brewed in the winter for use in the spring. [< German *Bockbier*]

bode[1] (bōd), *v.t.,* **bod ed, bod ing.** 1 be a sign of; indicate beforehand; portend; foreshadow: *The rumble of thunder boded rain.* 2 **bode ill,** be a bad sign. 3 **bode well,** be a good sign. [Old English *bodian* < *boda* messenger] **—bode′ment,** *n.*

bode[2] (bōd), *v.* a pt. of **bide.**

bod ice (bod′is), *n.* 1 the close-fitting upper part of a dress. 2 a wide girdle worn over a dress and laced up the front. [variant of *bodies,* plural of *body* (def. 13)]

-bodied, *combining form.* having a ___body: *Heavy-bodied = having a heavy body.*

bod i less (bod′ē lis), *adj.* without a body; incorporeal.

bod i ly (bod′l ē), *adj.* of or in the body; physical: *bodily pain.* —*adv.* 1 in person: *She is not with us bodily, but she is here in* *spirit.* 2 as a whole; all together; entirely: *The audience rose bodily to cheer the hero.*

bod kin (bod′kən), *n.* 1 a large, blunt needle with an eye, used for drawing tape or cord through a hem, loops, etc. 2 a long hairpin. 3 a pointed tool for making holes in cloth, etc. 4 a small dagger; stiletto. [Middle English *boydekyn* dagger]

bod y (bod′ē), *n., pl.* **bod ies,** *v.,* **bod ied, bod y ing.** —*n.* 1 the whole material or physical structure of a person, animal, or plant, whether living or dead. 2 the main part or trunk of an animal, apart from the head, limbs, or tail. 3 the main, central, or principal part of anything. 4 part of a vehicle which holds the passengers or the load. 5 fuselage of an airplane. 6 hull of a ship. 7 the main part of a speech or document, excluding the introduction, appendixes, etc. 8 group of persons or things considered together; collection of persons or things: *a body of troops, a body of laws.* 9 INFORMAL or DIALECT. person: *a good-natured body.* 10 a dead person or animal; corpse. 11 portion of matter; mass: *The stars and planets are heavenly bodies. A lake is a body of water.* 12 substantial quality; substance: *wine of good body. Thin soup lacks body.* 13 that part of a garment that covers the trunk above the waist. 14 **in a body,** as a unit; in a group. 15 **keep body and soul together,** keep barely alive.
—*v.t.* 1 provide with a body; give substance to; embody. 2 **body forth, a** give a real form to. **b** be a sign of; represent; typify. [Old English *bodig*]

bod y-build (bod′ē bild′), *n.* bodily structure; physique.

body check, (in hockey) a defensive play in which a player attempts to throw the carrier of the puck off stride by bumping him with his body.

bod y-check (bod′ē chek′), *v.t., v.i.* check or block with a body check.

body count, a daily count of the dead bodies on the battlefield as the basis of estimating enemy casualties.

bod y guard (bod′ē gärd′), *n.* 1 man or men who guard a person: *A bodyguard accompanies the President when he travels.* 2 retinue; escort.

body politic, a people forming a political group with an organized government.

body snatcher, person who steals corpses from graves, especially for the purpose of dissection.

body stocking, a lightweight, tight-fitting, one-piece undergarment for women that covers most of the body.

Boe o tia (bē ō′shə), *n.* district in ancient Greece, north of Athens. **—Boe o′tian,** *adj., n.*

Boer (bôr, bōr, bůr), *n.* person of Dutch descent living in South Africa. —*adj.* of or having to do with the Boers. [< Dutch *boer* farmer]

Boer War, war between Great Britain and the Boers, from 1899 to 1902.

bof fin (bof′ən), *n.* BRITISH SLANG. scientist engaged in research. [origin unknown]

bof fo (bof′ō), *adj.* U.S. SLANG. 1 funny: *boffo jokes.* 2 popular or successful: *a boffo movie.* [origin unknown]

bog (bog, bôg), *n., v.,* **bogged, bog ging.** —*n.* piece of wet, spongy ground, consisting chiefly of decayed or decaying moss and other vegetable matter, too soft to bear the weight of any heavy body on its surface; marsh; swamp. —*v.t., v.i.* 1 sink or get stuck in a bog. 2 **bog down,** sink in or get stuck so that one cannot get out without help: *She is bogged down with problems.* [< Irish or Scottish Gaelic, soft]

bo gey (bō′gē), *n., pl.* **-geys,** *v.* —*n.* 1 bogy. 2 (in golf) a score of one stroke over par for any hole on a course. 3 SLANG. an unidentified aircraft. —*v.t.* (in golf) play (a hole) in one stroke over par. [variant of *bogy*]

bo gey man (bō′gē man′, bůg′ē man′), *n., pl.* **-men.** a frightening imaginary creature; bogy.

bog gle (bog′əl), *v.,* **-gled, -gling,** *n.* —*v.i.* 1 hold back; raise difficulties or objections; hesitate. 2 be overwhelmed with wonder, shock, etc. 3 blunder. 4 jump with fright; shy. —*v.t.* 1 bungle; botch. 2 overwhelm with wonder, shock, etc. —*n.* a bungle; botch. [probably < Scottish *bogill* bogy]

bog gy (bog′ē, bôg′ē), *adj.,* **-gi er, -gi est.** soft and wet like a bog; marshy; swampy.

bo gie[1] (bō′gē, bůg′ē), *n.* bogy.

bo gie[2] (bō′gē), *n.* 1 assembly of the four rear wheels of a six-wheeled truck. 2 BRITISH. a low, strong, four-wheeled truck or cart. [origin unknown]

Bo go tá (bō′gə tä′), *n.* capital of Colombia, in the central part. 2,512,000.

bo gus (bō′gəs), *adj.* U.S. not genuine; counterfeit; sham. [origin unknown]

bo gy (bō′gē, bůg′ē), *n., pl.* **-gies.** 1 evil spirit; goblin. 2 person or thing, usually imaginary, that is feared without reason; bugbear; bugaboo. Also, **bogey, bogie.** [probably < obsolete *bog* bugbear]

Bohemia (def. 1)—the shaded area

Bo he mi a (bō hē′mē ə, bō hē′myə), *n.* 1 former country in central Europe, now a region of Czechoslovakia. 2 Also, **bohemia. a** an unconventional, carefree sort of existence. **b** place where artists, writers, etc., live in an unconventional, carefree way.

Bo he mi an (bō hē′mē ən, bō hē′myən), *adj.* 1 of Bohemia, its people, or their language. 2 Also, **bohemian.** carefree and unconventional. —*n.* 1 native or inhabitant of Bohemia. 2 language of Bohemia; Czech. 3 Also, **bohemian.** artist, writer, etc., who lives an unconventional, carefree sort of existence. 4 gypsy.

bo he mi an ism or **Bo he mi an ism** (bō hē′mē ə niz′əm, bō hē′myə niz′əm), *n.* a carefree, unconventional way of living.

Bohr (bôr, bōr), *n.* **Niels,** 1885-1962, Danish physicist who first stated the Bohr theory on the nature of the atom.

boil[1] (boil), *v.i., v.t.* 1 bubble up and give off steam or vapor when heated; turn from the liquid into the gaseous state. 2 cook by boiling: *boil eggs. The eggs are boiling.* 3 cleanse or sterilize by boiling: *boil drinking water.* 4 prepare by boiling and evaporation: *boil sugar.* 5 (of a container) have its contents boil: *The pot is boiling.* 6 be very excited; be stirred up: *She is boiling with anger.* See synonym study below. 7 move violently: *The stormy sea is boiling.* 8 **boil down, a** reduce the bulk of by boiling and evaporation: *boil down sauce.* **b** reduce by getting rid of unimportant parts: *boil down a report.* **c** INFORMAL. amount to when briefly stated: *It all boils down to this.* 9 **boil over, a** come to the boiling point and overflow. **b** be unable to control anger.
—*n.* 1 act of boiling. 2 condition of boiling or being boiled. 3 **come to a boil,** reach the boiling point.
[< Old French *boillir* < Latin *bullire* form bubbles < *bulla* bubble]

Syn. *v.i., v.t.* 6 **Boil, simmer, seethe,** when used figuratively, mean to be emotionally excited. **Boil** suggests being so stirred up by emotion, usually anger, that one's feelings are thought of as bubbling over: *Resentment was boiling in my breast.* **Simmer** suggests less intense emotion or greater control, so that one's feelings are just below the boiling point: *I was simmering with laughter.* **Seethe** suggests being violently stirred up, so that a person or a group of people is thought of as boiling and foaming: *The people seethed with discontent.*

boil[2] (boil), *n.* a painful, red swelling on the skin, formed by pus around a hard core, often caused by infection; furuncle. [Old English *bȳle*]

boil er (boi′lər), *n.* 1 tank for making steam to heat buildings or drive engines. 2 tank for heating and holding hot water. 3 container in which anything is heated or boiled.

boiling point, temperature at which a liquid boils. The boiling point of water at sea level is 212 degrees Fahrenheit or 100 degrees centigrade.

boil-off (boil′ôf′, boil′of′), *n.* loss of liquid fuel in a rocket by vaporization.

Boi se (boi′sē), *n.* capital of Idaho, in the SW part. 75,000.

bois ter ous (boi′stər əs), *adj.* 1 noisily cheerful; exuberant: *a boisterous game.* 2 rough and stormy; turbulent: *a boisterous wind.* 3 rough and noisy; clamorous: *a boisterous child.* [Middle English *boistrous*] **—bois′ter ous ly,** *adv.* **—bois′ter ous ness,** *n.*

bo la (bō′lə), *n., pl.* **bo las** (bō′ləz). weapon consisting of two or more stones or metal balls tied at the ends of long cords. South American cowboys throw it so that it winds around and entangles the animal aimed at. [< Spanish, ball < Latin *bulla* bubble]

bo las (bō′ləs), *n., pl.* **bo las** (bō′ləz), **bo las es** (bō′lə siz). bola.

bold (bōld), *adj.* 1 without fear; daring; brave: *a bold explorer.* 2 showing or requiring courage; daring: *a bold act.* 3 **make**

bold, take the liberty; dare. 4 too free in manner; impudent: *The bold child made faces at us as we passed.* See synonym study below. 5 sharp and clear to the eye; striking: *mountains in bold outline against the sky.* 6 steep; abrupt: *bold cliffs.* [Old English *bald*] **—bold′ly,** *adv.* **—bold′ness,** *n.*
Syn. 4 **Bold, brazen, forward** mean too free in manner. **Bold** suggests shamelessness and immodesty: *They were disconcerted by the girl's bold stare.* **Brazen** means defiantly and insolently shameless: *He is brazen about being expelled.* **Forward** suggests being too sure of oneself, too disrespectful of others, and inclined to push oneself forward: *His forward manner in the presence of older people made a very poor impression.*

bold face (bōld′fās′), *n.* a printing type with a thick face that prints blacker than ordinary type. **This sentence is in boldface.**

bole (bōl), *n.* stem or trunk of a tree. [< Scandinavian (Old Icelandic) *bolr*]

bo ler o (bə ler′ō), *n., pl.* **-ler os.** 1 a lively Spanish dance in $^{3}/_{4}$ time. 2 music for this dance. 3 a short, loose jacket coming barely to the waist. [< Spanish]

Bol eyn (bu̇l′ən, bu̇ lin′), *n.* **Anne,** 1507?-1536, the second wife of Henry VIII of England, mother of Queen Elizabeth I.

bo lide (bō′līd, bō′lid), *n.* a large meteor, usually one that explodes and falls in the form of meteorites. [< Latin *bolidem* < Greek *bolis* missile]

bol i var (bol′ə vər, bō lē′vär), *n., pl.* **bol i vars, bo li va res** (bō′lē vä′rās). the monetary unit of Venezuela, a silver coin equal to 100 centimos and worth about 23 cents. [< American Spanish *bolívar* < Simón *Bolívar*]

Bo lí var (bō lē′vär, bol′ə vər), *n.* **Simón,** 1783-1830, Venezuelan general and statesman, who led revolts against Spanish rule in South America. Bolivia is named after him.

Bo liv i a (bə liv′ē ə), *n.* country in W South America. 5,063,000 pop.; 424,000 sq. mi. *Capitals:* La Paz and Sucre. **—Bo liv′i an,** *adj., n.*

boll (bōl), *n.* the rounded seed pod or capsule of a plant, especially that of cotton or flax. [Old English *bolla* round vessel]

boll weevil, a small, grayish beetle with a long snout whose larva is hatched in and destructive to young cotton bolls.

boll worm (bōl′wėrm′), *n.* 1 a moth larva that feeds on cotton bolls. 2 corn earworm.

bo lo (bō′lō), *n., pl.* **-los.** a long, heavy, single-edged knife, used in the Philippines. [< Spanish (Philippines)]

bo lo gna (bə lō′nē, bə lō′nə), *n.* a large, lightly smoked sausage, usually made of beef, veal, and pork. [< *Bologna*]

Bo lo gna (bə lō′nyə), *n.* city in N Italy. 491,000.

bo lom e ter (bō lom′ə tər), *n.* instrument used to measure the intensity of radiant energy, especially of feeble radiation. [< Greek *bolē* ray + English *-meter*]

Bol she vik (bōl′shə vik, bol′shə vik), *n., pl.* **Bol she viks, Bol she vi ki** (bōl′shə vē′kē, bol′shə vē′kē), *adj.* *—n.* 1 member of the radical wing, led by Lenin, of the Russian Social Democratic Party that seized power in November 1917. The Bolsheviks became the Communist Party in March 1918. 2 member of the Communist Party of any country. 3 Also, **bolshevik.** an extreme radical. *—adj.* 1 of the Bolsheviks or Bolshevism. 2 Also, **bolshevik.** extremely radical. [< Russian *bol'shevik* < *bol'shie* greater (because of their temporary majority within the party in 1903)]

Bol she vism (bōl′shə viz′əm, bol′shə viz′əm), *n.* 1 doctrines and methods of the Bolsheviks. 2 Also, **bolshevism.** extreme radicalism.

Bol she vist or **bol she vist** (bōl′shə vist, bol′shə vist), *n., adj.* Bolshevik.

Bol she vis tic or **bol she vis tic** (bōl′shə vis′tik, bol′shə vis′tik), *adj.* of or like the Bolsheviks or bolsheviks.

bol ster (bōl′stər), *n.* 1 a long, firmly stuffed pillow, placed under the softer pillows on a bed or used as a back on a couch. 2 cushion or pad, often ornamental. *—v.t.* 1 support with a bolster. 2 keep from falling; support; prop. [Old English]

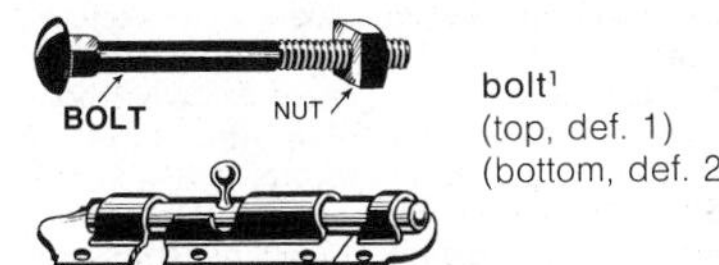

bolt[1]
(top, def. 1)
(bottom, def. 2)

bolt[1] (bōlt), *n.* 1 a metal rod with a head at one end and a screw thread for a nut at the other, used to fasten things together or hold them in place. 2 bar which may be slid or dropped into a bracket to lock a door, gate, etc. 3 a corresponding part of a lock, moved out and in by a key. 4 a sliding bar that opens and closes the breech of a breechloading rifle, especially one that ejects the used cartridge case and pushes a new one in position for firing. 5 a stout, short arrow with a thick head, made to be shot from a crossbow. **6 shoot one's bolt,** do as much or as well as one can. 7 discharge of lightning; thunderbolt. 8 a sudden start or rush, especially to get away. 9 roll of cloth or wallpaper. 10 U.S. refusal to support one's political party or its candidates.
—v.t. 1 fasten with a bolt. 2 swallow (food) quickly without chewing. 3 blurt out; say hastily. *—v.i.* 1 dash off; run away: *The horse bolted.* 2 U.S. break away from or refuse to support one's political party or its candidates. 3 move suddenly or swiftly; dart. *—adv.* **bolt upright,** stiff and straight. [Old English, arrow]

bolt[2] (bōlt), *v.t.* 1 sift through a cloth or sieve: *Bolt the flour to remove the bran.* 2 examine by sifting; search into carefully. [< Old French *buleter*]

bolt action, an action on the breech of a rifle consisting of a manually operated sliding bolt.

bolt er[1] (bōl′tər), *n.* 1 horse that runs away. 2 U.S. person who breaks away from or refuses to support his political party or its candidates. [< *bolt*[1]]

bolt er[2] (bōl′tər), *n.* cloth or sieve used for sifting flour, etc. [< *bolt*[2]]

Bol ton (bōlt′n), *n.* city in W England. 152,000.

bo lus (bō′ləs), *n.* 1 medicine in the form of a large roundish pill that can be swallowed, used especially in veterinary medicine. 2 lump of chewed food, ready to be swallowed. 3 any small, rounded mass. [< Late Latin < Greek *bōlos* lump]

bomb (bom), *n.* 1 projectile filled with a bursting charge or chemical and exploded by a fuse, by a time mechanism, or by impact. 2 any similar missile or device: *a tear gas bomb.* 3 **the Bomb,** the atomic bomb or nuclear weapons generally. 4 container filled with an insecticide, paint, toothpaste, etc., stored under pressure and ejected as spray or foam. 5 U.S. SLANG. a failure; flop. *—v.t.* hurl bombs at; drop bombs on: *bomb a target.* *—v.i.* attack with bombs. [< Italian *bomba* < Latin *bombus* a booming sound < Greek *bombos*]

hat, āge, fär; let, ēqual, tėrm;
it, īce; hot, ōpen, ôrder;
oil, out; cup, pu̇t, rüle;
ch, child; ng, long; sh, she;
th, thin; ᴛʜ, then; zh, measure;

ə represents *a* in about, *e* in taken, *i* in pencil, *o* in lemon, *u* in circus.

< = from, derived from, taken from.

bom bard (bom bärd′), *v.t.* 1 attack with heavy shellfire from artillery, rockets, or naval guns: *Tanks and howitzers bombarded enemy positions all morning.* 2 drop bombs on; bomb: *Aircraft bombarded the hydroelectric plant and destroyed it.* 3 keep attacking vigorously: *The lawyer bombarded the witness with question after question.* 4 strike (the nucleus of an atom) with a stream of fast-moving particles, radioactive rays, etc., to change the structure of the nucleus.

bom bar dier (bom′bər dir′), *n.* member of the crew of a bomber who operates the bombsight and the bomb-release mechanism.

bom bard ment (bom bärd′mənt), *n.* 1 an attack with heavy shellfire or with bombs. 2 a vigorous attack. 3 the striking of the nucleus of an atom with a stream of fast-moving particles.

bom bast (bom′bast), *n.* showy or high-flown language that is without much meaning. [< Old French *bombace* cotton wadding]

bom bas tic (bom bas′tik), *adj.* using many high-flown words with too little thought; high-sounding. **—bom bas′ti cal ly,** *adv.*

Bom bay (bom bā′), *n.* 1 seaport in W India, on the Arabian Sea. 5,534,000. 2 former state in W India.

bom ba zine (bom′bə zēn′, bom′bə zēn′), *n.* a twilled fabric with a silk warp and worsted filling, often dyed black. [< Middle French *bombasin*]

bomb bay, compartment in the fuselage of a bomber in which bombs are carried and from which they are dropped.

bomb er (bom′ər), *n.* 1 a combat airplane used to drop bombs on enemy troops, cities, factories, etc. 2 person who throws or drops bombs.

bom bi nate (bom′bə nāt), *v.i.,* **-nat ed, -nat ing.** hum; buzz. [ultimately < Latin *bombus.* See BOMB.]

bomb load (bom′lōd′), *n.* load of bombs carried by a bomber or other aircraft.

bomb proof (bom′prüf′), *adj.* strong enough to be safe from the effects of bombs and shells. *—n.* a bombproof shelter.

bomb shell (bom′shel′), *n.* 1 bomb (def. 1). 2 a sudden, unexpected happening, disturbing surprise.

bomb sight (bom′sīt′), *n.* instrument for determining the point in the flight of a bomber at which releasing a bomb will cause it to fall on the target.

bo na fide (bō′nə fīd′; bō′nə fī′dē), 1 in good faith; without deceit or fraud. 2 done in good faith; genuine. [< Latin]

bo nan za (bə nan′zə), *n.* 1 a rich mass of ore in a mine. 2 any rich source of profit. [< American Spanish < Spanish, fair weather, prosperity]

Bo na parte (bō′nə pärt), *n.* 1 **Napoleon,** 1769-1821, French general and emperor of France from 1804 to 1815. Also, **Napoleon I.** 2 his brother, **Jerome,** 1784-1860, king of Westphalia. 3 his brother, **Joseph,** 1768-1844, king of Naples and Spain. 4 his brother, **Louis,** 1778-1846, king of Holland. 5 his brother, **Lucien,** 1775-1840, statesman and diplomat.

bon ap pé tit (bôN nȧp pä tē′), FRENCH. good appetite.

bon bon (bon′bon′), *n.* a usually soft, fancy-shaped candy with a coating of fondant or chocolate and a filling of jelly, nuts, etc. [< French < *bon* good]

bond (bond), *n.* 1 anything that binds or fastens, as a rope, cord, or other band. 2 any force or influence that serves to unite people. See synonym study below. 3 **bonds,** *pl.* **a** chains; shackles. **b** ARCHAIC. imprisonment. 4 certificate of debt issued by a government or private company which promises to pay back with interest on a given future date the money borrowed from the buyer of the certificate. 5 a written agreement by which a person says he will pay a certain sum of money if he does not perform certain duties properly. 6 any agreement or binding engagement; compact. 7 person who acts as surety for another; security. 8 condition of goods placed in a warehouse until taxes are paid. 9 way of arranging bricks, stones, or boards to bind them together. 10 brick, stone, or board that binds together. 11 substance that binds together the other ingredients of a mixture: *Cement is the bond in concrete.* 12 (in chemistry) a unit of force by means of which atoms or groups of atoms are combined or joined together in a molecule, often represented in formulas by a dash (—) or a dot (•). A chemical bond usually consists of a pair of shared electrons. 13 bond paper.
—*v.t.* 1 issue bonds on; mortgage: *bond a railroad.* 2 provide surety against financial loss for: *bond an employee.* 3 convert into bonds: *bond a debt.* 4 put (goods) under bond. 5 bind or join firmly together. 6 arrange (bricks, etc.) so as to lock or bind them together. —*v.i.* hold together so as to give solidity, as bricks in a wall. [variant of *band*²] —**bond′a ble,** *adj.*
Syn. *n.* 2 **Bond, tie,** used figuratively, mean something that joins or unites people. **Bond** applies particularly to a connection that brings two people or a group so closely together that they may be considered as one: *The members of the club are joined by bonds of fellowship.* **Tie** applies particularly to a connection based on a sense of social obligation and is thus of a less voluntary nature: *family ties. When she went away, she severed all ties with her old life.*

bond age (bon′dij), *n.* 1 lack of freedom; slavery. 2 condition of being under some power or influence.

bond ed (bon′did), *adj.* 1 secured by bonds: *a bonded debt.* 2 put in a warehouse until taxes are paid: *bonded goods.*

bonded warehouse, warehouse where bonded goods are kept.

bond hold er (bond′hōl′dər), *n.* person who owns a bond or bonds issued by a government, company, etc.

bond man (bond′mən), *n., pl.* **-men.** 1 slave. 2 (in the Middle Ages) a serf.

bond paper, paper with a high rag content used for documents and the better grades of stationery.

bond servant, 1 servant who must work for a specified or indefinite period without pay. 2 slave.

bonds man (bondz′mən), *n., pl.* **-men.** 1 person who becomes responsible for another by giving a bond. 2 bondman.

bond wom an (bond′wu̇m′ən), *n., pl.* **-wom en.** a woman bondman.

bone (bōn), *n., v.,* **boned, bon ing,** *adj.* —*n.* 1 one of the distinct pieces making up the skeleton of a vertebrate animal. 2 the hard tissue forming the substance of the skeleton. 3 any of various similar animal substances, as the dentine of teeth, ivory, or whalebone. 4 strip of whalebone used to stiffen stays, etc. 5 a pale beige. 6 **bones,** *pl.* **a** U.S. SLANG. dice. **b** wooden clappers used in keeping time to music. **c** end man in a minstrel show. **d** skeleton. 7 **make no bones about,** INFORMAL. show no hesitation about; acknowledge readily. —*v.t.* 1 take bones out of: *bone fish.* 2 stiffen (garments) by putting whalebone or steel strips in. —*v.i.* SLANG. study hard: *bone up on algebra.* —*adj.* pale-beige. [Old English *bān*] —**bone′like′,** *adj.*

bone black (bōn′blak′), *n.* a black powder made by carbonizing bones in closed containers, used to remove color from liquids and as a coloring matter.

bone-dry (bōn′drī′), *adj.* very dry.

bone head (bōn′hed′), *n.* INFORMAL. a stupid person; blockhead.

bone less (bōn′lis), *adj.* 1 without bones. 2 without courage; cowardly.

bone meal, the coarser siftings of crushed or ground bones, used as fertilizer or added to feed for animals.

bone of contention, cause of a dispute; matter of controversy.

bon er (bō′nər), *n.* SLANG. a foolish mistake; stupid error; blunder; blooper.

bone set (bōn′set′), *n.* any of a genus of plants of the composite family with flat clusters of white, rose, or purple flowers.

bon fire (bon′fīr′), *n.* a large fire built outdoors. [earlier *bonefire* fire to burn bones]

bon go (bong′gō), *n., pl.* **-gos.** a small drum played with the fingers, especially in Latin-American and African music. Bongos usually come in pairs and are held between the knees. [< American Spanish *bongó*]

bongo drum, bongo.

bon ho mie or **bon hom mie** (bon′ə mē′), *n.* good nature; courteous and pleasant ways. [< French *bonhomie* < *bonhomme* good fellow]

bon i face (bon′ə fās, bon′ə fəs), *n.* 1 keeper of an inn. 2 owner of a hotel, restaurant, etc. [< *Boniface,* innkeeper in the play *The Beaux' Stratagem,* by George Farquhar, 1678-1707]

Bon i face (bon′ə fās, bon′ə fəs), *n.* **Saint,** A.D. 680?-755?, English monk who was a missionary in Germany.

bo ni to (bə nē′tō), *n., pl.* **-tos, -toes,** or **-to.** either of three saltwater fishes of the mackerel family, smaller than the related tunas, having edible flesh. [< Spanish, literally, pretty < Latin *bonus* good]

bon kers (bong′kərz), *adj.* BRITISH SLANG. crazy. [origin unknown]

bon mot (bôN mō′), *pl.* ***bons mots*** (bôN mōz′; bôN mō′), FRENCH. a clever saying; witty remark.

Bonn (bon), *n.* capital of West Germany, in the W part, on the Rhine. 299,000.

bon net (bon′it), *n.* 1 a head covering usually tied under the chin with strings or ribbons, worn by women and children. 2 cap worn by men and boys in Scotland. 3 headdress of feathers worn by North American Indians. 4 covering that protects a machine or chimney. 5 BRITISH. hood covering the engine of a car, truck, etc. [< Middle French]

bon ny or **bon nie** (bon′ē), *adj.,* **-ni er, -ni est.** 1 fair to see; rosy and pretty: *a bonny baby.* 2 gay or cheerful. [Middle English *bonne,* apparently < Old French *bone* good < Latin *bonus*] —**bon′ni ly,** *adv.* —**bon′ni ness,** *n.*

bon sai (bon′sī), *n., pl.* **-sai.** 1 a tree, dwarfed by controlling its root area and its food supply, used for decoration. 2 the art of growing dwarfed plants. [< Japanese]

bon spiel (bon′spēl′), *n.* a curling match or tournament. [perhaps < Dutch *bond* contract, league + *spel* game]

bon ton (bôN tôN′), FRENCH. 1 good style; fashion. 2 fashionable society. 3 good breeding.

bo nus (bō′nəs), *n.* something extra given in addition to what is due, especially an extra payment for services rendered. [< Latin, good]

bon vi vant (bôN vē väN′), *pl.* ***bons vi vants*** (bôN vē väN′). FRENCH. person who is fond of good food and luxury.

bon vo yage (bôN vwä yȧzh′), FRENCH. good-by; good luck; pleasant trip.

bon y (bō′nē), *adj.,* **bon i er, bon i est.** 1 of bone. 2 like bone. 3 full of bones: *bony fish.* 4 having large or prominent bones. 5 very thin. —**bon′i ness,** *n.*

boo (bü), *n., pl.* **boos,** *interj., v.* —*n., interj.* sound made to show dislike or contempt, or to frighten. —*v.i.* make such a sound. —*v.t.* shout "boo" at.

boob (büb), *n.* SLANG. a stupid person; fool; dunce. [< *booby*]

boo by (bü′bē), *n., pl.* **-bies.** 1 a dull, stupid person; fool. 2 any of various tropical and subtropical sea birds of the same family as the gannet. 3 person or team that does the worst in a game or contest. [< Spanish *bobo* < Latin *balbus* stammering]

booby hatch, 1 the covering over a hatchway on a boat. 2 SLANG. an insane asylum.

booby prize, prize given to the person or team that does the worst in a game or contest.

booby trap, 1 bomb or mine arranged to explode when a harmless-looking object to which it is attached is touched or moved by an unsuspecting person. 2 trick arranged to annoy some unsuspecting person.

boo by-trap (bü′bē trap′), *v.t.,* **-trapped, -trap ping.** catch with or in a booby trap.

boo dle (bü′dl), *n.* SLANG. 1 money from bribes; graft. 2 group; lot. [< Dutch *boedel* goods]

boog ie-woog ie (bu̇g′ē wu̇g′ē), *n.* form of blues played especially on the piano, marked by a repeating bass rhythm under a freely and elaborately varied melody. [origin unknown]

book (bu̇k), *n.* 1 a written or printed work of considerable length, especially on sheets of paper bound together between covers. 2 blank sheets bound together to form a volume in which to record business transactions, minutes of meetings, etc. 3 a main division of a literary work: *the books of the Bible.* 4 anything thought of as containing

hat, āge, fär; let, ēqual, tėrm;
it, īce; hot, ōpen, ôrder;
oil, out; cup, pu̇t, rüle;
ch, child; ng, long; sh, she;
th, thin; ᴛʜ, then; zh, measure;

ə represents *a* in about, *e* in taken, *i* in pencil, *o* in lemon, *u* in circus.

< = from, derived from, taken from.

lessons or instruction: *the book of nature.* 5 libretto. 6 script of a play. 7 record of bets, especially on a horse race. 8 number of tickets, stamps, checks, etc., fastened together like a book. 9 trick or a number of tricks forming a set in a card game. **10 the Book,** the Bible. **11 the books,** complete records of a business.
bring to book, a demand an explanation from. **b** rebuke.
by the book, by rule; accurately.
keep books, keep a record of business accounts.
like a book, with fullness or accuracy; completely.
one for the book, something exceptional or extraordinary.
—*v.t.* 1 enter, write, or register in a book or list. 2 make reservations for; engage (a place, passage, etc.). 3 make engagements for; engage: *The lecturer is booked for every night of the week.* 4 enter a charge against (a person) in a police record. —*v.i.* engage passage, a seat, a place, etc., beforehand.
—*adj.* 1 of or having to do with books: *a book salesman.* 2 according to account books: *a book profit.*
[Old English *bōc*] **—book′er,** *n.*
➤ **Book** refers especially to the contents, **volume** to the physical appearance. A *book* may be in two or more *volumes.*

book bind er (bu̇k′bīn′dər), *n.* person whose work or business is binding books.

book bind ing (bu̇k′bīn′ding), *n.* 1 the binding on a book. 2 act, art, or business of binding books.

book case (bu̇k′kās′), *n.* piece of furniture with shelves for holding books.

book club, a business organization that regularly supplies selected books to subscribers, usually at a reduced rate.

book end, a prop or support placed at the end of a row of books to held them upright.

book ie (bu̇k′ē), *n.* INFORMAL. bookmaker (def. 1).

book ish (bu̇k′ish), *adj.* 1 fond of reading or studying; studious. 2 knowing books better than real life. 3 stilted or pedantic. 4 of or having to do with books. **—book′ish ly,** *adv.* **—book′ish ness,** *n.*

book keep er (bu̇k′kē′pər), *n.* person who keeps a record of business accounts.

book keep ing (bu̇k′kē′ping), *n.* work of keeping a record of business accounts.

book let (bu̇k′lit), *n.* a small book, often with paper covers.

book mak er (bu̇k′mā′kər), *n.* 1 person who makes a business of taking bets on horse races or other contests at odds fixed by himself. 2 maker of books.

book mak ing (bu̇k′mā′king), *n.* 1 business of taking bets on horse races or other contests at odds fixed by the taker. 2 the writing, editing, or manufacture of books.

book mark (bu̇k′märk′), *n.* 1 something put between the pages of a book to mark the reader's place. 2 bookplate.

book mo bile (bu̇k′mə bēl′), *n.* a large motor vehicle serving as a traveling branch of a library.

Book of Common Prayer, book containing the prayers and services of the Church of England or, with some changes, the Episcopal Church.

Book of Mormon, a sacred book of the Church of Jesus Christ of Latter-day Saints, originally published in 1830.

book plate (bu̇k′plāt′), *n.* label with the owner's name or emblem printed on it, to paste in his books.

book review, article written about a book, especially a new one, discussing its merits, faults, etc.

book sell er (bu̇k′sel′ər), *n.* person whose business is selling books.

book shelf (bu̇k′shelf′), *n., pl.* **-shelves.** shelf for holding books.

book shop (bu̇k′shop′), *n.* bookstore.

book stall (bu̇k′stôl′), *n.* booth or stand, often outdoors, where books are sold.

book store (bu̇k′stôr′, bu̇k′stōr′), *n.* store where books are sold.

book value, value of anything as it appears on the account books of the owner. It may be higher or lower than the real or present value.

book worm (bu̇k′wėrm′), *n.* 1 person who is very fond of reading and studying. 2 any insect larva that feeds on the bindings or leaves of books.

Bool e an algebra (bü′lē ən), a mathematical system dealing with the relationship between sets, used to solve problems in logic, engineering, etc. [< George *Boole,* 1815-1864, English mathematician]

boom[1] (büm), *n.* 1 a deep, prolonged, hollow sound. 2 a rumbling or roaring: *the boom of cannon.* 3 a buzzing, humming, or droning. 4 sonic boom. 5 a sudden activity and increase in business, prices, or values of property; rapid growth. 6 a vigorous pushing or urging. 7 U.S. an increase in public favor, as of a political candidate or cause. —*v.i.* 1 make a deep, prolonged, hollow sound. 2 make a rumbling, humming, or droning noise. 3 burst into sudden activity; grow rapidly: *Business is booming.* —*v.t.* 1 utter with a deep, hollow sound. 2 push or urge vigorously: *The citizens' committee is booming the mayor for senator.* —*adj.* produced by a boom: *boom prices.* [imitative]

boom[2] (büm), *n.* 1 a long pole or beam, used to extend the bottom of a sail. **2 lower the boom,** INFORMAL. crack down; punish. 3 the lifting and guiding pole of a derrick. 4 a long metal arm for projecting a microphone above the angle of a camera. 5 chain, cable, or line of floating timbers stretched across a river or around an area of water to keep logs from floating away. [< Dutch, tree, pole]

boo me rang (bü′mə rang′), *n.* 1 a curved, rather flat piece of hard wood used as a weapon. One kind, made and used by Australian aborigines, can be thrown so as to curve in flight and return to the thrower. 2 anything that recoils or reacts to harm the doer or user. —*v.i.* act as a boomerang. [< native dialect of New South Wales]

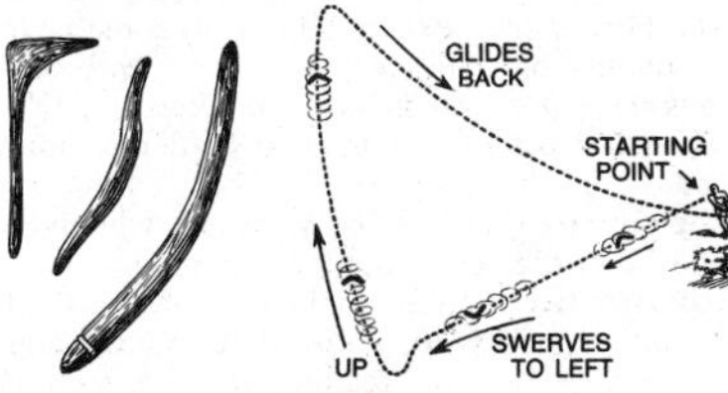

boomerang (def. 1)
left, three types of boomerangs; right, the path of a boomerang

boom town, town that has grown up suddenly, usually as a result of an increase in economic activity.

boon[1] (bün), *n.* 1 great benefit; blessing: *Those warm boots were a boon to me in the cold weather.* 2 ARCHAIC. something asked for or granted as a favor. [< Scandinavian (Old Icelandic) *bōn* petition]

boon[2] (bün), *adj.* 1 full of cheer; jolly; merry: *a boon companion.* 2 kindly; pleasant. [< Old French *bon* good < Latin *bonus*]

boon docks (bün′doks), *n.* U.S. SLANG. rough backwoods. [< Tagalog *bundók* mountain]

boon dog gle (bün′dog′əl), *v.,* **-gled, -gling,** *n.* U.S. INFORMAL. —*v.i.* do useless work. —*n.* a worthless work or product. [apparently coined by R. H. Link, American scoutmaster] **—boon′dog′gler,** *n.*

Boone (bün), *n.* **Daniel,** 1734-1820, American frontiersman who explored Kentucky.

boor (bu̇r), *n.* 1 a rude, bad-mannered person. 2 a clumsy person, especially from the country; bumpkin. 3 OBSOLETE. a farm laborer; peasant. [< Low German *bur* or Dutch *boer* farmer]

boor ish (bu̇r′ish), *adj.* like a boor; rude or rustic. **—boor′ish ly,** *adv.* **—boor′ish ness,** *n.*

boost (büst), *n.* 1 a push or shove that helps a person in rising or advancing. 2 an increase in degree, amount, price, pay, etc. —*v.t.* 1 lift or push upwards; raise. 2 help by speaking favorably of. 3 raise or improve: *boost prices, boost a person's spirits.* 4 increase the voltage in (an electric circuit). 5 U.S. SLANG. shoplift. [perhaps blend of *boom* and *hoist*]

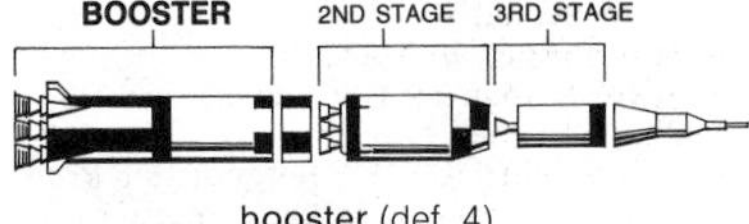

booster (def. 4)

boost er (bü′stər), *n.* 1 person or thing that boosts. 2 an accessory generator or other device for increasing the voltage in an electric circuit. 3 any of various rocket units or engines for providing initial or added thrust to an aircraft, missile, etc. 4 rocket used to launch a spacecraft, either as the only stage or as the first stage of a multistage rocket. 5 a radio-frequency amplifier between an antenna and a radio or television receiving set. 6 INFORMAL. a booster shot. 7 U.S. SLANG. shoplifter.

booster shot, a supplementary inoculation of vaccine or serum, given to continue the effectiveness of a previous inoculation.

boot[1] (büt), *n.* 1 a covering for the foot and lower part of the leg, usually of leather or rubber. 2 BRITISH. a high-cut shoe that covers the whole foot, including the ankle. 3 any sheath or case that resembles or suggests a boot. 4 an old instrument of torture used to crush a person's leg. 5 a protecting apron or cover for the driver of an open carriage. 6 a protective patch put inside a

tire. 7 BRITISH. an automobile trunk. 8 BRITISH. (formerly) a place for baggage in a coach. 9 a kick. 10 SLANG. a new recruit in training in the United States Navy or Marine Corps. 11 **the boot,** SLANG. dismissal.
—v.t. 1 put boots on; supply with boots. 2 give a kick to; drive or move by kicking. 3 kick (a football, etc.); punt. 4 INFORMAL. get rid of; dismiss. 5 misplay (the ball) in baseball. 6 SLANG. lose (an opportunity, etc.) through carelessness.
[< Old French *bote*]

boot² (büt), *n.* 1 ARCHAIC. profit; use; avail. 2 **to boot,** in addition; besides: *For my knife he gave me a compass and a dime to boot.* *—v.i.* ARCHAIC. be of use or profit; avail. [Old English *bōt* advantage]

boot black (büt′blak′), *n.* person whose work is shining shoes and boots.

boot camp, U.S. camp at which Navy or Marine Corps recruits are trained.

boot ed (bü′tid), *adj.* wearing boots.

boot ee (bü tē′, bü′tē), *n.* a baby's soft shoe, often knitted. Also, **bootie.**

Bo ö tes (bō ō′tēz), *n.* a northern constellation near Ursa Major that includes the star Arcturus.

booth (büth), *n., pl.* **booths** (büᴛʜz, büths), 1 a covered stall or similar place where goods are sold or shown at a fair, market, convention, etc. 2 a small, enclosed place for a telephone, motion-picture projector, etc. 3 a small, enclosed place for voting at elections. 4 a partly enclosed space in a restaurant, café, etc., containing a table and seats for a few persons. 5 a temporary shelter made of boards, boughs of trees, etc. [< Scandinavian (Old Danish) *bōth*]

Booth (büth), *n.* 1 **Edwin Thomas,** 1833-1893, American actor. 2 his brother, **John Wilkes,** 1839?-1865, American actor who assassinated Abraham Lincoln. 3 **William,** 1829-1912, English clergyman who founded the Salvation Army.

boot hill, U.S. cemetery in or near a frontier town of the old West.

boot ie (bü′tē), *n.* bootee.

boot jack (büt′jak′), *n.* device to help in pulling off boots.

boot leg (büt′leg′), *v.,* **-legged, -leg ging,** *adj., n.* U.S. *—v.t., v.i.* sell, transport, or make (goods, especially alcoholic liquor) unlawfully. *—adj.* sold, transported, or made unlawfully. *—n.* goods, especially alcoholic liquor, sold, transported, or made unlawfully. [from practice of smuggling liquor in boot legs] **—boot′leg′ger,** *n.*

boot less (büt′lis), *adj.* of no benefit or profit; useless. [< *boot*²] **—boot′less ly,** *adv.* **—boot′less ness,** *n.*

boot lick (büt′lik′), INFORMAL. *—v.t.* curry favor with; toady to; flatter excessively. *—v.i.* be a toady or slavish flatterer; fawn. **—boot′lick′er,** *n.*

boot mak er (büt′mā′kər), *n.* BRITISH. shoemaker.

boots (büts), *n., pl.* **boots.** BRITISH. servant, especially in a hotel, who shines shoes and boots and does similar tasks.

boot strap (büt′strap′), *n.* 1 loop of leather or cloth at the back of a boot by means of which it may be pulled onto the foot. 2 **by one's bootstraps,** by one's own efforts; without help from others.

boo ty (bü′tē), *n., pl.* **-ties.** 1 plunder taken from the enemy in war. 2 money, valuables, etc., seized by thieves or robbers; plunder. See **plunder** for synonym study. 3 gains; winnings; prize. [perhaps < Middle Dutch *botye*]

booze (büz), *n., v.,* **boozed, booz ing.** INFORMAL. *—n.* 1 any intoxicating liquor. 2 a drinking bout; spree. *—v.i.* drink heavily. [probably < Middle Dutch *busen* drink heavily] **—booz′er,** *n.*

booz y (bü′zē), *adj.,* **booz i er, booz i est.** INFORMAL. 1 somewhat drunk. 2 often drunk. **—booz′i ly,** *adv.* **—booz′i ness,** *n.*

bop¹ (bop), *n., v.,* **bopped, bop ping.** SLANG. *—n.* a blow with the hand, a club, etc. *—v.t.* hit; strike. [imitative]

bop² (bop), *n.* bebop.

bor., borough.

bo rac ic (bə ras′ik), *adj.* boric.

bor age (bėr′ij, bôr′ij, bor′ij), *n.* plant native to southern Europe, with hairy stems and leaves and blue or purplish flowers. It is used in salads, in flavoring beverages, and in medicine. [< Anglo-French *burage* < Late Latin *boraginem,* probably < Arabic *bū'araq,* a plant used to cause sweating]

bo rate (bôr′āt, bôr′it; bōr′āt, bōr′it), *n.* salt or ester of boric acid.

bo rax (bôr′aks, bōr′aks), *n.* a white crystalline powder having a sweetish alkaline taste, used as an antiseptic, as a cleansing agent, in fusing metals, and in making heat-resistant glass; sodium borate. *Formula:* $Na_2B_4O_7 \cdot 10H_2O$ [< Medieval Latin < Arabic *būraq*]

bo ra zon (bôr′ə zon), *n.* a crystalline compound of boron and nitrogen, as hard as diamond and having a higher melting point. *Formula:* BN

Bor deaux (bôr dō′), *n.* 1 seaport in SW France. 267,000. 2 a red or white wine made in the region near Bordeaux.

Bordeaux mixture, a liquid mixture of copper sulfate, lime, and water, used as a spray on trees and plants to kill insects, fungi, etc.

bor der (bôr′dər), *n.* 1 the side, edge, or boundary of anything, or the part near it: *the border of a lake.* See **edge** for synonym study. 2 line which separates one country, state, or province from another; frontier. 3 **the border,** the frontier between the United States and Mexico. 4 **the Border,** the region near the boundary between England and Scotland. 5 strip of ground planted with flowers, shrubs, etc., edging a garden, walk, or the like. 6 strip on the edge of anything for strength or ornament: *My handkerchief has a blue border.* *—v.t.* 1 form a boundary to; bound. 2 put a border on; edge. 3 **border on** or **border upon, a** touch at the border; be next to; adjoin. **b** come near in quality or character; verge on: *Such silly behavior borders on the ridiculous.* [< Old French *bordure* < *border* to border < *bord* side]

bor der er (bôr′dər ər), *n.* person who lives on the border of a country or region.

bor der land (bôr′dər land′), *n.* 1 land forming, or next to, a border. 2 an uncertain range, extent, or region: *the borderland between sleeping and waking.*

bor der line (bôr′dər līn′), *n.* a dividing line; boundary. *—adj.* 1 on a border or boundary. 2 in between; uncertain: *a borderline case of mumps.*

Border States, the slave states near free territory in the United States before the Civil War; Delaware, Maryland, Virginia, Kentucky, and Missouri.

border terrier, one of a breed of terriers having a slim body and a wiry coat, originally from the border country of northern England.

bore¹ (bôr, bōr), *v.,* **bored, bor ing,** *n.* *—v.i.* 1 make a hole by means of a tool that keeps turning, or by penetrating as a worm does in fruit; pierce; perforate; drill. 2 be bored; be suited for boring: *This wood bores easily.* 3 force a way through; push forward. *—v.t.* 1 make (a hole, passage, entrance, etc.) by pushing through or digging out. 2 bore a hole in; hollow out evenly. *—n.* 1 hole made by boring. 2 the hollow space inside a pipe, tube, or gun barrel. 3 caliber or internal diameter of a pipe, tube, or gun barrel. [Old English *borian*]

bore² (bôr, bōr), *v.,* **bored, bor ing,** *n.* *—v.t.* make weary by dull or tiresome behavior or conversation. *—n.* a dull, tiresome person or thing. [origin unknown]

bore³ (bôr, bōr), *v.* pt. of **bear**¹.

bore⁴ (bôr, bōr), *n.* a sudden, high tidal wave that rushes up a channel with great force. [< Scandinavian (Old Icelandic) *bāra* wave]

bo re al (bôr′ē əl, bōr′ē əl), *adj.* 1 of the north; northern. 2 of or having to do with Boreas.

Bo re as (bôr′ē əs, bōr′ē əs), *n.* 1 (in Greek myths) the north wind. 2 the north wind personified.

bore dom (bôr′dəm, bōr′dəm), *n.* a bored condition; weariness caused by dull, tiresome people or things.

bor er (bôr′ər, bōr′ər), *n.* 1 any of various insects or larvae that bore into wood, fruit, etc. 2 any of various mollusks, especially the shipworms, which bore through wood, etc. 3 tool for boring holes.

Bor gia (bôr′jə), *n.* 1 **Cesare,** 1476-1507, Italian cardinal and military leader, notorious for poisoning people. 2 his sister, **Lucrezia,** 1480-1519, who was also a notorious poisoner.

bo ric (bôr′ik, bōr′ik), *adj.* of or containing boron; boracic.

boric acid, a white, crystalline compound occurring in nature or made from borax, used as a mild antiseptic and in making cement, glass, soap, etc. *Formula:* H_3BO_3

born (bôrn), *adj.* 1 brought into life by birth; brought forth. 2 thought up; conceived. 3 by birth; natural: *a born athlete.* *—v.* a pp. of **bear**¹.

borne (bôrn, bōrn), *v.* a pp. of **bear**¹. *I have borne it as long as I can.*
➔ **borne. a Borne** is the past participle of *bear* in most of its meanings: *The ship was borne along by the breeze. The men had borne these burdens without complaint. She had borne herself with great dignity.* **b** In the sense give birth to, the past participle of *bear* is *borne* except in the very commonly used passive voice form when not followed by *by: She had borne five children. I was born in 1960.*

Bor ne o (bôr′nē ō), *n.* large island in the East Indies, between Java and the Philippines, divided into the states of Sabah and Sarawak (both members of the Federation of Malaysia), Brunei (a British protectorate), and Kalimantan (part of Indonesia). 5,788,000 pop.; 289,900 sq. mi.

Bo ro din (bôr′ə dēn), *n.* **Alexander,** 1834-1887, Russian composer.

bo ron (bôr′on, bōr′on), *n.* a nonmetallic element which occurs only in borax and other compounds, used in alloys, nuclear reactors,

hat, āge, fär; let, ēqual, tėrm;
it, īce; hot, ōpen, ôrder;
oil, out; cup, pu̇t, rüle;
ch, child; ng, long; sh, she;
th, thin; ᴛʜ, then; zh, measure;

ə represents *a* in about, *e* in taken, *i* in pencil, *o* in lemon, *u* in circus.

< = from, derived from, taken from.

etc. *Symbol:* B; *atomic number* 5. See pages 326 and 327 for table. [< *bor(ax)* + *(carb)on*]

bor ough (bėr′ō), *n.* 1 (in some states of the United States) an incorporated town with certain privileges, smaller than a city. 2 one of the five administrative divisions of New York City. 3 (in Alaska) a district similar to a county. 4 in Great Britain: **a** town with a municipal corporation and a charter that guarantees the right of local self-government. **b** district that sends representatives to Parliament. [Old English *burg*]

bor row (bor′ō, bôr′ō), *v.t.* 1 get (something) from another person with the understanding that it is to be returned. 2 take and use as one's own; adopt: *Rome borrowed many ideas from Greece.* 3 take from another language: *The word for the vegetable "squash" was borrowed from the Algonquian Indians.* 4 (in subtraction) take (one) from the digit immediately to the left and add its place value to the digit being subtracted from. *—v.i.* borrow something. [Old English *borgian* < *borg* pledge, surety] **—bor′row er,** *n.*

Bors (bôrs), *n.* **Sir,** (in Arthurian legends) a nephew of Lancelot and knight of the Round Table, who saw the Holy Grail.

borsch (bôrsh), *n.* a Russian soup consisting of meat stock, cabbage, and onions, colored red with beet juice and served with sour cream. [< Russian *borshch*]

borscht (bôrsht), *n.* borsch.

bor stal (bor′stəl), *n.* (in Great Britain) a reformatory. [< *Borstal,* village in southern England]

bor zoi (bôr′zoi), *n.* any of a breed of tall, slender, swift dogs with silky hair, developed in Russia; Russian wolfhound. [< Russian *borzoj* < *borzyj* swift]

bosh (bosh), *n., interj.* INFORMAL. nonsense. [< Turkish *boş* empty, worthless]

bosk y (bos′kē), *adj.,* **bosk i er, bosk i est.** 1 wooded. 2 shady. [< *busk* grove, dialectal variant of *bush*]

bo's'n (bō′sn), *n.* boatswain.

Bos ni a (boz′nē ə), *n.* region in W Yugoslavia, part of Bosnia-Herzegovina. **—Bos′ni an,** *adj., n.*

Bos ni a-Her ze go vi na (boz′nē ə hėr′tsə gə vē′nə), *n.* district in W Yugoslavia.

bos om (bu̇z′əm, bü′zəm), *n.* 1 the upper, front part of the human body; breast. 2 the part of a garment which covers the breast. 3 heart or feelings: *He kept the secret in his bosom.* 4 center or inmost part: *I did not tell it even in the bosom of my family.* 5 surface (of a sea, lake, river, the ground, etc.). *—adj.* close and trusted; intimate: *a bosom friend.* *—v.t.* cherish. [Old English *bōsm*]

bo son (bō′son), *n.* (in quantum mechanics) any of a class of elementary particles two or more of which can occupy the same state, including pi mesons and photons. [< Satyendra N. *Bose,* born 1894, Indian physicist + *(me)son*]

Bos phor us (bos′fər əs), *n.* Bosporus.

Bos por us (bos′pər əs), *n.* strait connecting the Black Sea and the Sea of Marmara. 18 mi. long. See **Dardanelles** for map.

boss[1] (bôs, bos), *n.* 1 person who hires, directs, or supervises workers; foreman, manager, or superintendent. 2 any person in charge; chief or master. 3 person who controls a political organization, especially a local one. *—v.t.* be the boss of; direct; control. *—adj.* master; chief. [< Dutch *baas* master]

boss[2] (bôs, bos), *n.* 1 a raised ornament of silver, ivory, or other material on a flat surface. 2 the enlarged part of a shaft on a machine. *—v.t.* decorate with ornamental nails, knobs, or studs. [< Old French *boce* swelling, hump]

bos sa no va (bä′sə nō′və), a dance music of Brazil that combines the rhythm of samba with jazz music. [< Portuguese (Brazil)]

bos sie (bos′sē′), *n.* bossy[3].

boss ism (bô′siz′əm, bos′iz′əm), *n.* U.S. control by political bosses.

boss y[1] (bô′sē, bos′ē), *adj.,* **boss i er, boss i est.** INFORMAL. fond of telling others what to do and how to do it; domineering. [< *boss*[1]] **—boss′i ness,** *n.*

boss y[2] (bô′sē, bos′ē), *adj.* decorated with bosses [< *boss*[2]]

bos sy[3] (bos′ē′), *n., pl.* **bos sies.** INFORMAL. a calf or cow. Also, **bossie.** [dialectal English *borse, boss* young calf]

Bos ton (bô′stən, bos′tən), *n.* seaport and capital of Massachusetts, on the Atlantic. 641,000.

Boston bull, Boston terrier.

Boston fern, variety of fern having long, drooping fronds, often grown as a house plant.

Bos to ni an (bô stō′nē ən, bo stō′nē ən), *adj.* of Boston, Massachusetts. *—n.* native or inhabitant of Boston.

Boston ivy, Japanese ivy.

Boston terrier, any of a breed of small terriers, brindled or black, with white markings and smooth, short hair; Boston bull.

Boston terrier
12 to 16 in. tall

bo sun (bō′sn), *n.* boatswain.

Bos well (boz′wel, boz′wəl), *n.* 1 **James,** 1740-1795, Scottish writer, biographer and friend of Samuel Johnson. 2 any author of a biography of a close friend.

bot (bot), *n.* larva of a botfly. [origin uncertain]

bot., 1 botanical. 2 botany.

bo tan ic (bə tan′ik), *adj.* botanical.

bo tan i cal (bə tan′ə kəl), *adj.* 1 having to do with plants and plant life. 2 having to do with botany. *—n.* drug made from roots, leaves, flowers, and other parts of plants. **—bo tan′i cal ly,** *adv.*

bot a nist (bot′n ist), *n.* an expert in botany.

bot a nize (bot′n īz), *v.,* **-nized, -niz ing.** *—v.i.* 1 study plants in their natural environment. 2 collect plants for study, classification, etc. *—v.t.* explore or examine the plant life of. **—bot′a niz′er,** *n.*

bot a ny (bot′n ē), *n.* 1 branch of biology that deals with plants and plant life; study of the structure, growth, classification, diseases, etc., of plants. 2 the plant life of a particular area: *the botany of Greenland.* 3 botanical facts or characteristics concerning a particular plant or group of plants: *the botany of roses.* [< Greek *botanē* plant]

Botany Bay, bay on the SE coast of Australia, near Sydney. A penal colony was formerly located there.

botch (boch), *v.t.* 1 spoil by unskillful work; bungle. 2 repair clumsily or imperfectly. *—n.* 1 a bungled piece of work. 2 a clumsy patch. [Middle English *bocchen*] **—botch′er,** *n.*

botch y (boch′ē), *adj.,* **botch i er, botch i est.** poorly made or done; botched.

bot fly (bot′flī′), *n., pl.* **-flies.** a two-winged fly whose larvae are parasites of horses, cattle, sheep, and sometimes man.

both (bōth), *adj.* the two; the one and the other: *Both houses are white.* *—pron.* the two together: *Both belong to me.* *—adv.* together or alike; equally: *He fears and hopes both at once.* *—conj.* together; alike; equally: *She is both strong and healthy.* [apparently < Old English *bā thā* both these]

➤ **Both** is used in informal English to emphasize the fact that two persons or places or things are involved in a situation: *The twins were both there.* Strictly speaking, the *both* is redundant, but it gives emphasis.

both er (boᴛʜ′ər), *n.* 1 much fuss or worry about small matters; trouble. 2 person or thing that causes worry, fuss, or trouble. *—v.i.* take trouble; concern oneself: *Don't bother about my breakfast; I'll eat what is here.* *—v.t.* cause trouble to; annoy; irritate: *Hot weather bothers me.* [origin unknown]

both er some (boᴛʜ′ər səm), *adj.* causing worry or fuss; troublesome; annoying.

Both ni a (both′nē ə), *n.* **Gulf of,** gulf between Sweden and Finland.

bo tree (bō), the sacred fig tree of India under which Buddha is said to have attained enlightenment; pipal. [< Singhalese *bo* < Pali *bodhi (taru)* perfect knowledge (tree)]

Bot swa na (bot swä′nə), *n.* country in S Africa, a member of the Commonwealth of Nations. Former name, **Bechuanaland.** 648,000 pop.; 222,000 sq. mi. *Capital:* Gaberones. See **South Africa** for map. **—Bot swa′nan,** *adj., n.*

Bot ti cel li (bot′ə chel′ē), *n.* **Sandro,** 1444?-1510, Italian painter.

bot tle (bot′l), *n., v.,* **-tled, -tling.** *—n.* 1 container for holding liquids, made of glass, plastic, etc., usually without handles and with a narrow neck which can be closed with a cap or stopper. 2 amount that a bottle can hold. 3 **the bottle,** alcoholic liquor. *—v.t.* 1 put into bottles: *bottle milk.* 2 hold in; keep back; control. 3 **bottle up,** hold in; keep back; control: *bottle up one's anger.* [< Old French *boteille* < Medieval Latin *butticula,* diminutive of Late Latin *buttis* cask, butt[4]] **—bot′tle like′,** *adj.* **—bot′tler,** *n.*

bottled gas, gas liquefied and stored under pressure in portable tanks.

bot tle ful (bot′l fu̇l), *n., pl.* **-fuls.** as much as a bottle will hold.

bot tle neck (bot′l nek′), *n.* 1 a narrow passageway or street. 2 person or thing that hinders progress; check. 3 situation in which progress is hindered.

bot tle nose (bot′l nōz′), *n.* any of various dolphins with a bottle-shaped nose.

bot tom (bot′əm), *n.* 1 the lowest part, place, or point; foot: *the bottom of the hill, the bottom of the basket.* 2 part on which anything rests; base: *The bottom of that cup is wet.* 3 ground or bed under a body of water: *the bottom of the sea.* 4 Often, **bottoms,** *pl.* the low land along a river, especially when the river is large and the level area is of considerable extent. 5 **bottoms,** *pl.* pajama trousers. 6 seat of a chair. 7 basis or origin: *We will get to the bottom of the mystery.* 8 the buttocks. 9 keel or hull of a ship. 10 ship. 11 **at bottom,** fundamentally. 12 **be at the bottom of,** be the cause or source of.
—*v.t.* 1 put a seat on. 2 get to the bottom of; understand fully. 3 set upon a foundation; base; rest.
—*adj.* 1 lowest or last: *bottom prices. I have spent my bottom dollar.* 2 underlying; fundamental. 3 of or at the bottom: *the bottom life in the ocean.* 4 living at or near the ocean bottom: *bottom fish.*
[Old English *botm*]

bot tom less (bot′əm lis), *adj.* 1 without a bottom. 2 so deep that the bottom cannot be reached; extremely deep. 3 unfathomable. —**bot′tom less ly,** *adv.*

bot u lism (boch′ə liz′əm), *n.* poisoning, frequently fatal, caused by a toxin secreted by a certain anaerobic bacterium sometimes present in foods not properly canned or preserved. [< Latin *botulus* sausage; originally attributed especially to sausages]

bou clé (bü klā′), *n.* 1 a knitted cloth having a surface with tiny loops and curls. 2 yarn used in making such a surface. [< French, buckled]

bou doir (bü′dwär, bü′dwôr), *n.* a lady's private bedroom, dressing room, or sitting room. [< French, literally, a place to sulk, < *bouder* sulk]

bouf fant (bü fänt′; *French* bü fäɴ′), *adj.* puffed out: *bouffant sleeves.* —*n.* a woman's puffed-out hairdo. [< French]

bough (bou), *n.* one of the branches of a tree, particularly one laden with blossoms or fruit. See **branch** for synonym study. [Old English *bōg* bough, shoulder]

bought (bôt), *v.* pt. and pp. of **buy.** *We bought apples from the farmer.*

bought en (bôt′n), *adj.* U.S. DIALECT. bought; not homemade: *Is that a boughten dress?*

bouil la baisse (bü′lyə bās′), *n.* a fish chowder highly seasoned with white wine, saffron, herbs, etc. [< French]

bouil lon (bu̇l′yon, bu̇l′yən), *n.* 1 a clear, thin soup or broth. 2 a liquid, nutritive medium used for growing cultures of bacteria. [< French < *bouillir* to boil]

boul der (bōl′dər), *n.* a large, detached rock whose edges have become rounded or worn by the action of water or weather. Also, **bowlder.** [short for *boulderstone* < Scandinavian (Swedish) *bullersten*]

Boulder Dam, former name of **Hoover Dam.**

boul e vard (bu̇l′ə värd, bü′lə värd), *n.* a broad street or avenue, often planted with trees. [< French, originally, the passage along a rampart < Middle Dutch *bolwerc.* Related to BULWARK.]

boulle (bül), *n.* buhl.

bounce (bouns), *v.,* **bounced, bounc ing,** *n.* —*v.i.* 1 spring into the air like a rubber ball: *The baby likes to bounce up and down on the bed.* 2 come or go noisily, angrily, etc.; burst or bound: *She bounced out of the room.* 3 leap; spring. 4 **bounce back,** begin anew, especially with vigor or enthusiasm. 5 INFORMAL. (of a check) be returned uncashed by the bank on which it is drawn because of insufficient funds in the account of the person who signed it. —*v.t.* 1 cause to bounce. 2 (of a communications satellite) relay or reflect (a signal, message, etc.). 3 SLANG. throw out; eject. 4 SLANG. discharge from work or employment.
—*n.* 1 a springing back; bound; rebound. 2 a sudden spring or leap. 3 a boasting; a bragging. 4 INFORMAL. energy; spirit: *I was in the hospital for a week, but now I am as full of bounce as ever.* 5 a heavy blow or thump. 6 SLANG. discharge from work or employment.
[Middle English *bunsen*]

bounc er (boun′sər), *n.* 1 one that bounces. 2 anything very large of its kind. 3 INFORMAL. braggart. 4 SLANG. a strong man hired by a night club, hotel, etc., to throw out disorderly persons.

bounc ing (boun′sing), *adj.* 1 that bounces. 2 big and strong. 3 vigorous; healthy: *a bouncing baby.* —**bounc′ing ly,** *adv.*

bouncing Bess (bes), bouncing Bet.

bouncing Bet (bet), a species of soapwort with pink or white flowers.

bound[1] (bound), *adj.* 1 under some obligation; tied down by circumstance, duty, etc.; obliged: *I feel bound by my promise.* 2 **bound up in** or **bound up with, a** closely connected with. **b** very devoted to. 3 certain; sure: *It is bound to get dark soon.* 4 U.S. INFORMAL. determined; resolved. 5 put in covers: *a bound book.* 6 tied fast; fastened: *bound hands.* 7 held by a chemical bond. —*v.* pt. and pp. of **bind.** *She bound the package with string.* [Middle English *bounden*]

bound[2] (bound), *v.i.* 1 spring back; bounce; rebound: *The rubber ball bounded from the wall.* 2 leap or spring lightly along; jump: *The deer bounds through the woods.* 3 leap or spring upward or onward. —*v.t.* cause to bound or rebound; bounce. —*n.* 1 a springing back; bounce; rebound. 2 a leaping or springing lightly along; jump. 3 a leap or spring upward or onward. [< Middle French *bondir* to leap, originally, resound, ultimately < Latin *bombus.* See BOMB.]

bound[3] (bound), *n.* 1 Usually, **bounds,** *pl.* a limiting line; boundary; limit: *Keep your hopes within bounds.* 2 **bounds,** *pl.* **a** land on or near a boundary. **b** area included within boundaries. 3 **out of bounds,** outside the area allowed by rules, custom, or law: *This town is out of bounds for soldiers.* —*v.t.* 1 form the boundary of; limit. 2 name the boundaries of: *Bound the state of Maine.* —*v.i.* share a boundary with; have its boundary *(on): Canada bounds on the United States.* [< Old French *bodne, bonde* < Medieval Latin *bodina*]

bound[4] (bound), *adj.* intending to go; on the way; going: *I am bound for home.* [< Scandinavian (Old Icelandic) *būinn* prepared]

bound ar y (boun′dər ē), *n., pl.* **-ar ies.** a limiting line or thing; limit; border: *the boundary between Canada and the United States.*

bound en (boun′dən), *adj.* 1 required; obligatory: *one's bounden duty.* 2 under obligation because of favors received; obliged.

bound er (boun′dər), *n.* INFORMAL. a rude, vulgar person; cad.

bound form, a linguistic form which does not occur alone or independently but is always part of a word, as *-s, -ly,* and *pre-.*

bound less (bound′lis), *adj.* 1 not limited; infinite: *Outer space is boundless.* 2 vast: *the boundless ocean.* —**bound′less ly,** *adv.* —**bound′less ness,** *n.*

boun te ous (boun′tē əs), *adj.* 1 given freely; generous. 2 plentiful; abundant. —**boun′te ous ly,** *adv.* —**boun′te ous ness,** *n.*

boun ti ful (boun′tə fəl), *adj.* 1 giving freely; generous. 2 plentiful; abundant. —**boun′ti ful ly,** *adv.* —**boun′ti ful ness,** *n.*

boun ty (boun′tē), *n., pl.* **-ties.** 1 a generous gift. 2 generosity in bestowing gifts; liberality. 3 reward; premium: *The state government gives a bounty for killing predatory animals.* [< Old French *bonté* < Latin *bonitatem* < *bonus* good]

bounty hunter, person who hunts fugitives from the law or harmful animals to collect the bounty for their capture.

bou quet (bō kā′, bü kā′ *for 1;* bü kā′ *for 2*), *n.* 1 bunch of flowers. 2 fragrance; aroma: *the bouquet of a wine.* [< Middle French, diminutive of Old French *bosc* wood]

bour bon (bėr′bən), *n.* kind of whiskey, distilled from a fermented grain mash containing at least 51 per cent corn. [< *Bourbon* County, Kentucky, where this whiskey was originally made]

Bour bon (bu̇r′bən; *occasionally* bėr′bən), *n.* 1 member of the royal family that ruled France from 1589 to 1792, and from 1814 to 1848. The Bourbons also ruled in Spain, Naples, and Sicily. 2 person who clings to old ideas and opposes any change; extreme conservative.

Bour bon ism (bu̇r′bə niz′əm), *n.* 1 support of the Bourbons. 2 political conservatism.

bour geois (bu̇r zhwä′, bu̇r′zhwä), *n., pl.* **-geois,** *adj.* —*n.* 1 person of the middle class, as distinguished from an aristocrat or a worker or peasant. 2 person who owns property or who is engaged in business or commerce, as an owner, partner, etc. —*adj.* 1 of or characteristic of the middle class. 2 like the middle class in appearance, way of thinking, etc.; ordinary; common: *bourgeois attitudes.* [< French < Medieval Latin *burgensis* town dweller, citizen < Late Latin *burgus* town. Doublet of BURGESS.]

bour geoi sie (bu̇r′zhwä zē′), *n.* 1 the middle class. 2 people of the middle class. 3 property owners and businessmen as a class, as contrasted with the working class or proletariat. [< French]

bourn[1] or **bourne**[1] (bôrn, bōrn), *n.* a small stream; brook. [Old English *burna*]

bourn[2] or **bourne**[2] (bôrn, bōrn, bu̇rn), *n.* ARCHAIC. 1 boundary; limit. 2 goal; aim. [< Middle French *bourne*]

Bourse (bu̇rs), *n.* the stock exchange in Paris, and in certain other European cities. [< French, originally, purse < Medieval Latin *bursa.* Doublet of BURSA, PURSE.]

bout (bout), *n.* 1 trial of strength or skill; contest: *a boxing bout.* 2 period spent in some particular way; spell: *a long bout of illness.* [variant of *bought* a bending, turn. Related to BOW[1].]

bou tique (bü tēk′), *n.* a small shop that specializes in stylish clothes and accessories for women or children. [< French < Greek *apothēkē.* See APOTHECARY.]

hat, āge, fär; let, ēqual, tėrm;
it, īce; hot, ōpen, ôrder;
oil, out; cup, pu̇t, rüle;
ch, child; ng, long; sh, she;
th, thin; ꟻH, then; zh, measure;

ə represents *a* in about, *e* in taken, *i* in pencil, *o* in lemon, *u* in circus.

< = from, derived from, taken from.

bou ton niere (büt′n er′), *n.* flower or flowers worn in a buttonhole. [< French *boutonnière* buttonhole]

bo vine (bō′vīn), *n.* 1 ox or cow. 2 any animal belonging to the genus of ruminant mammals that include domestic cattle, bison, water buffaloes, and the like. —*adj.* 1 of an ox or cow. 2 like an ox or cow; slow, dull, and stupid. 3 without emotion; stolid. 4 belonging to the genus of ruminant mammals that include the ox or cow. [< Late Latin *bovinus* < Latin *bovem* ox, cow]

bow[1] (bou), *v.i.* 1 bend the head or body in greeting, respect, worship, or submission. 2 give in; submit; yield. —*v.t.* 1 bend (the head or body) in greeting, respect, worship, or submission. 2 express by a bow: *He bowed his approval.* 3 usher with a bow or bows. 4 cause to stoop; bend: *The old man was bowed by age.*
bow and scrape, be too polite or slavish.
bow down, a weigh down: *bowed down with care.* b worship.
bow out, a withdraw: *She sprained her wrist and had to bow out of the tennis tournament.* b usher out.
—*n.* 1 a bending of the head or body in greeting, respect, worship, or submission. 2 **take a bow,** accept praise, applause, etc., for something done.
[Old English *būgan*] —**bow′er,** *n.*

bow[2] (bō), *n.* 1 weapon for shooting arrows, usually consisting of an arched strip of flexible wood with a string or cord stretched tight between the two ends. 2 a slender rod with horsehairs stretched on it, for playing a violin, cello, etc. 3 a curve; bend: *the bow of a person's lips.* 4 something curved; curved part: *A rainbow is a bow.* 5 a looped knot into which ribbons, shoelaces, etc., are tied. —*v.t.* 1 play (a violin, cello, etc.) with a bow. 2 curve; bend. —*v.i.* 1 have a curved shape; be bent. 2 use a bow on a violin, cello, etc. [Old English *boga*] —**bow′like′,** *adj.*

bow[3] (bou), *n.* the forward part of a ship, boat, or aircraft. See **aft** for picture. [probably < Middle Dutch *boegh* or Danish *bov.* Related to BOUGH.]

bowd ler ize (boud′lə rīz′, bōd′lə rīz′), *v.t.,* **-ized, -iz ing.** expurgate (a book or writing) by removing or altering words and passages thought to be improper. [< Thomas *Bowdler,* 1754-1825, who published an expurgated edition of Shakespeare's works in 1818] —**bowd′ler i za′tion,** *n.*

bow el (bou′əl), *n.* 1 a part of the intestines. 2 **bowels,** *pl.* a intestines. b the inner part; depths: *Miners dig for coal in the bowels of the earth.* c ARCHAIC. pity; tender feelings. [< Old French *boel* < Latin *botellum,* diminutive of *botulum* sausage]

bow er (bou′ər), *n.* 1 shelter of leafy branches. 2 summerhouse or arbor. [Old English *būr* dwelling]

bow er bird (bou′ər bėrd′), *n.* any of a family of birds of Australia and New Guinea, the males of which build bowers decorated to attract females.

bow er y (bou′ər ē), *adj.* leafy; shady.

Bow er y (bou′ər ē), *n.* street in New York City with cheap saloons, rooming houses, etc.

bow fin (bō′fin′), *n.* a freshwater fish found chiefly in the rivers of eastern North America.

bow ie knife (bō′ē, bü′ē), a heavy hunting knife with a long, single-edged blade, curved near the point, and carried in a sheath. [< Colonel James *Bowie,* 1799-1836, American pioneer who made it popular]

bow knot (bō′not′), *n.* slipknot with two loops and two ends that can be untied by pulling the ends.

bowl[1] (bōl), *n.* 1 a hollow, rounded dish, especially a wide one without handles. 2 amount that a bowl can hold. 3 a hollow, rounded part: *the bowl of a pipe.* 4 ARCHAIC. a large drinking cup. 5 ARCHAIC. drinking. 6 formation or structure shaped like a bowl. [Old English *bolla*] —**bowl′like′,** *adj.*

bowl[2] (bōl), *n.* 1 a large, heavy, lopsided or weighted ball used in bowls and certain other games. 2 a throw or rolling of a bowl in the game of bowls. —*v.i.* 1 play the game of bowls or of bowling. 2 roll or move along rapidly and smoothly: *Our car bowled along on the new highway.* —*v.t.* 1 roll or throw (a ball) in bowling, cricket, etc. 2 **bowl down,** knock down. 3 **bowl over,** a knock over. b INFORMAL. make helpless and confused. [< Old French *boule* < Latin *bulla* bubble, knob]

bowl der (bōl′dər), *n.* boulder.

bow leg (bō′leg′), *n.* 1 leg that curves outward in the middle and back in at its extremities. 2 an outward curve of the legs.

bow leg ged (bō′leg′id, bō′legd′), *adj.* having bowlegs.

bowl er (bō′lər), *n.* 1 person who bowls. 2 BRITISH. a derby hat.

bowline (def. 1)

bow line (bō′lən, bō′līn), *n.* 1 knot used to tie a loop that does not slip. 2 rope running forward from the edge of a square sail nearest the wind to the bow. It holds the sail steady when sailing into the wind.

bowl ing (bō′ling), *n.* 1 game played indoors, in which a heavy plastic ball is rolled down a wooden alley toward ten bottle-shaped wooden pins set up in a triangle; tenpins. 2 ninepins. 3 the game of bowls.

bowling alley, 1 a long, narrow lane for bowling. 2 building containing such lanes.

bowling green, a smooth, flat stretch of grass for playing bowls.

bowls (bōlz), *n.* game played on a bowling green in which bowls are rolled toward a stationary ball; lawn bowling.

bow man (bō′mən), *n., pl.* **-men.** archer.

Bow man's capsule (bō′mənz), a cup-shaped structure in the nephron for removing wastes from the kidney. [< William *Bowman,* 1816-1892, English anatomist]

bow shot (bō′shot′), *n.* 1 distance that a bow will shoot an arrow. 2 a shot from a bow.

bow sprit (bou′sprit′, bō′sprit′), *n.* pole or spar projecting forward from the bow of a ship. Ropes attached to the bowsprit help to steady sails and masts and hold the jib.

bow string (bō′string′), *n.* 1 a strong cord stretched from the ends of a bow, pulled back by the archer and then released to send the arrow forward. 2 cord like this.

bow tie (bō), a small necktie worn in a bowknot.

bow window (bō), a curved bay window.

box[1] (boks), *n.* 1 a rather stiff container to pack or put things in, usually rectangular and provided with a lid. 2 amount that a box can hold. 3 a small enclosed space in a theater, stadium, etc., containing chairs for spectators. 4 an enclosed space in a courtroom for a jury, witnesses, newspaper reporters, etc. 5 the driver's seat on a coach, carriage, etc. 6 a small shelter: *a box for a sentry.* 7 anything shaped or used like a box. 8 a hollow part that encloses or protects some piece of machinery. 9 (in baseball) place where the pitcher, batter, catcher, or coach stands. 10 box stall. 11 space in a newspaper, magazine, etc., set off by enclosing lines. 12 receptacle in a post office for a subscriber's mail. 13 BRITISH. gift; present. 14 U.S. INFORMAL. **the box,** television.
—*v.t.* 1 pack in a box; put into a box. 2 **box up** or **box in,** shut in; keep from getting out; confine.
[Old English < Late Latin *buxis* < Greek *pyxis*] —**box′er,** *n.* —**box′like′,** *adj.*

box[2] (boks), *n.* a blow with the open hand or the fist, especially on the ear. —*v.t.* 1 strike with such a blow. 2 fight (a person) with fists, especially as a sport. —*v.i.* fight with the fists, especially as a sport: *He had not boxed since he left school.* [origin unknown]

box[3] (boks), *n.* any of a genus of evergreen shrubs or small, bushy trees, much used for hedges, borders, etc. [< Latin *buxus* < Greek *pyxos*]

box car (boks′kär′), *n.* a railroad freight car enclosed on all sides, with a sliding door on either side.

box elder, a North American maple tree with compound leaves, often grown for shade or ornament.

box er (bok′sər), *n.* 1 man who fights with his fists as a sport, usually with padded gloves and according to definite rules. 2 a medium-sized dog with a smooth, fawn or brindle coat, related to the bulldog and terrier. 3 **Boxer,** member of a Chinese secret society which in 1900 tried to expel foreigners from China but was defeated by an international force of foreign soldiers.

box ing (bok′sing), *n.* act or sport of fighting with the fists.

Boxing Day, (in Great Britain) the first weekday after Christmas, a legal holiday, on which servants, postmen, errand boys, etc., receive Christmas boxes.

boxing glove, either of a pair of padded leather gloves worn when boxing.

box kite, a tailless kite consisting of two rectangular boxes with open ends, joined together lengthwise with a space between.

box office, 1 office or booth in a theater, hall, etc., where tickets of admission are sold. 2 money taken in at such a place.

box pleat, a double pleat with the cloth folded under at each side.

box score, a statistical summary of all the plays of a baseball game arranged in a table by the names of the players.

box seat, chair or seat in a box of a theater, stadium, hall, auditorium, etc.

box spring, a cloth-covered, boxlike frame containing bedsprings.

box stall, a separate compartment or stall

for a horse or other large animal in a stable or vehicle.

box wood (boks′wu̇d′), *n.* 1 the hard, fine-grained wood of the box. 2 the shrub or tree itself.

boy (boi), *n.* 1 a male child from birth to about eighteen. 2 bellboy. 3 a male servant. 4 INFORMAL. man; fellow. *—interj.* INFORMAL. exclamation of surprise, dismay, etc. [Middle English *boie* servant, helper < Old French *embuié* fettered, ultimately < Latin *in* + *boiae* fetters]

bo yar (bō yär′), *n.* member of a former high-ranking order of the Russian aristocracy abolished by Peter the Great. [< Russian *bojarin*]

boy cott (boi′kot), *v.t.* 1 combine against (a person, business, nation, etc.) in agreement not to buy from, sell to, or associate with and try to keep others from doing so for purposes of coercion, punishment, etc. 2 refuse to buy or use (a product, service, etc.). *—n.* act of boycotting. [< Captain Charles C. *Boycott,* 1832-1897, English land agent in Ireland whose tenants and neighbors boycotted him when he refused to lower rents] **—boy′cott er,** *n.*

boy friend (boi′frend′), *n.* INFORMAL. 1 a girl's sweetheart or steady male companion. 2 a male friend.

boy friend, boyfriend.

boy hood (boi′hu̇d), *n.* 1 time or condition of being a boy. 2 boys as a group: *the boyhood of the nation.*

boy ish (boi′ish), *adj.* 1 of a boy. 2 like a boy: *a boyish young man.* 3 like that of a boy: *the girl's boyish haircut.* 4 proper or suitable for boys: *boyish games.* **—boy′ish ly,** *adv.* **—boy′ish ness,** *n.*

Boyle (boil), *n.* **Robert,** 1627-1691, English scientist and philosopher, born in Ireland.

Boyle's law, (in physics) the statement that at a constant temperature the volume of a gas varies inversely with the pressure to which it is subjected. [< Robert *Boyle*]

boy scout, member of the Boy Scouts.

Boy Scouts, organization for boys that seeks to develop character, citizenship, usefulness to others, and outdoor skills.

boy sen ber ry (boi′zn ber′ē), *n., pl.* **-ries.** 1 a purple berry like a blackberry in size and shape, and like a raspberry in flavor. 2 plant of the rose family it grows on, developed as a cross between the loganberry and certain blackberries and raspberries. [< Rudolph *Boysen,* 1895-1950, American botanist who developed it]

b.p., boiling point.

Br, bromine.

br., 1 branch. 2 brand. 3 brother.

Br., 1 Britain. 2 British.

bra (brä), *n.* brassiere.

brace (brās), *n., v.,* **braced, brac ing.** *—n.* 1 clasp, clamp, or fastener for keeping objects in place or holding parts of a structure together. 2 device for supporting a weak back, curved shoulders, a weak joint, etc. 3 **braces,** *pl.* **a** metal clamps or wires used to straighten crooked teeth. **b** suspenders. 4 handle for a tool or drill used for boring. See **bit**[3] for picture. 5 a pair; couple: *a brace of ducks.* 6 either of these signs { } used to enclose words, figures, staffs in music, or a set in mathematics. 7 a leather thong that slides up and down the cord of a drum, used to regulate the tension of the skins and thus the pitch. *—v.t.* 1 give strength or firmness to; support: *We braced the roof with four poles.* 2 prepare (oneself): *I braced myself for the crash.* 3 give strength and energy to; refresh: *The mountain air braced us after the long climb.* 4 plant firmly; set down rigidly: *He braced his feet and stood ready for the attack.* *—v.i.* **brace up,** gather one's strength or courage anew. [< Old French, the two arms < Latin *bracchia,* plural of *bracchium* arm < Greek *brachīōn*]

brace and bit, tool for boring, consisting of a drill fitted into a handle.

brace let (brās′lit), *n.* band or chain worn for ornament around the wrist or arm. [< Middle French *bracelet,* diminutive of *bracel,* ultimately < Latin *bracchium* arm. See BRACE.]

brac er (brā′sər), *n.* 1 person or thing that braces. 2 (in archery, fencing, etc.) a guard for the wrist.

bra chi al (brak′ē əl, brā′kē əl), *adj.* 1 of or belonging to the arm: *the brachial artery.* 2 of or belonging to the forelimb of a vertebrate. 3 armlike.

bra chi ate (brak′ē āt, brā′kē āt), *v.i.,* **-at ed, -at ing.** move by swinging from branch to branch with the arms, as monkeys do. **—bra′chi a′tion,** *n.*

brach i o pod (brak′ē ə pod, brā′kē ə pod), *n.* any of phylum of sea animals characterized by bivalve shell and, coiled within the shell, a pair of arms covered with cilia for sweeping tiny food organisms into the mouth. [< Greek *brachīōn* arm + *podos* foot]

brach y ce phal ic (brak′ē sə fal′ik), *adj.* having a short, broad skull. [< Greek *brachys* short + *kephalē* head]

brac ing (brā′sing), *adj.* refreshing. *—n.* a brace or braces. **—brac′ing ly,** *adv.*

brack en (brak′ən), *n.* 1 a large, coarse fern common on hillsides, in woods, etc.; brake[4]. 2 thicket of these ferns. [Middle English *braken,* apparently < Scandinavian (Swedish) *bräken*]

brack et (brak′it), *n.* 1 a flat piece of stone, wood, or metal projecting from a wall as a support for a shelf, a statue, etc. 2 such a support, most often in the shape of a right triangle. 3 a small shelf supported by brackets. 4 (in architecture) any member designed to support a balcony, cornice, or other overhanging or projecting structure. 5 a gas or electric fixture projecting from a wall. 6 either of these signs [ ], used to enclose words, symbols, or figures. 7 parenthesis (def. 2). 8 any group thought of or mentioned together; class or category: *a family in a low income bracket.* *—v.t.* 1 support with a bracket or brackets. 2 enclose within brackets. 3 think of or mention together; group in the same class or category. 4 fire two shots, one beyond and one short of (a target) in order to find the range for artillery. [< Middle French *braguette* < *brague* breeches < Latin *bracae*]

bracket fungus, fungus on the trunks or stumps of trees that grows out horizontally like a rounded bracket.

brack ish (brak′ish), *adj.* 1 slightly salty. 2 distasteful. [< earlier *brack* brackish < Dutch *brak*] **—brack′ish ness,** *n.*

bract (brakt), *n.* a small leaf growing at the base of a flower or on a flower stalk. [< Latin *bractea* thin metal plate]

brad (brad), *n.* a small, thin nail with a small head. [< Scandinavian (Old Icelandic) *broddr* spike]

Brad dock (brad′ək), *n.* **Edward,** 1695-1755, British general, commander in America during the French and Indian War.

Brad ford (brad′fərd), *n.* 1 **William,** 1590-1657, Pilgrim leader and second governor of Plymouth colony. 2 city in N England. 292,000.

Brad ley (brad′lē), *n.* **Omar Nelson,** born 1893, American general.

brae (brā), *n.* SCOTTISH. slope; hillside.

brag (brag), *v.,* **bragged, brag ging,** *n.* *—v.i.* praise oneself or one's condition, action, or possessions; boast. See **boast** for synonym study. *—v.t.* boast of. *—n.* 1 a boast. 2 boastful talk. 3 thing that is boasted of. 4 braggart. [Middle English *braggen*] **—brag′ger,** *n.*

Bragg (brag), *n.* **Braxton,** 1817-1876, Confederate general in the Civil War.

brag ga do ci o (brag′ə dō′shē ō), *n., pl.* **-ci os.** 1 a boasting; bragging. 2 boaster; braggart. [< *Braggadocio,* boastful character in Spencer's *The Faerie Queene,* made up from the word *brag*]

brag gart (brag′ərt), *n.* person who brags much; boaster. *—adj.* vainly boastful; bragging.

Brahe (brä), *n.* **Tycho,** 1546-1601, Danish astronomer.

Brah ma (brä′mə *for 1;* brā′mə, brä′mə *for 2*), *n.* 1 in Hinduism: **a** the pervading soul of the universe. **b** the god of creation. Brahma is thought of as a trinity (Brahma the Creator, Vishnu the Preserver, Siva the Destroyer). **c** the creator, one of the gods of this trinity. 2 one of a breed of cattle usually having a large hump on the back, originally imported from India and related to the zebu. [< Sanskrit *bráhman* the Absolute and *brahmán* the Creator]

Brah man (brä′mən), *n.* 1 member of the priestly caste, the highest caste in India. 2 Brahma (def. 2). Also **Brahmin.**

Brah man ism (brä′mə niz′əm), *n.* the Hindu religious and social system.

Brah ma pu tra (brä′mə pü′trə), *n.* river flowing from S Tibet into the Ganges near the Bay of Bengal. 1800 mi.

Brah min (brä′mən), *n., pl.* **-min.** 1 Brahman (def. 1). 2 a cultured, intellectual person of the upper class.

Brahms (brämz), *n.* **Johannes,** 1833-1897, German composer.

braid (brād), *n.* 1 band formed by weaving together three or more strands of hair, ribbon, straw, etc.; plait. 2 a narrow band woven of silk, woolen, cotton, gold or silver thread, used to trim or bind clothing. 3 band or string for confining the hair. *—v.t.* 1 weave or twine together three or more strands of (hair, ribbon, straw, etc.). 2 make by braiding: *braid rugs.* 3 trim or bind (fabrics, garments, etc.) with braid. 4 confine (hair) with a band or string. [Old English *bregdan* to braid] **—braid′er,** *n.* **—braid′like′,** *adj.*

braid ing (brā′ding), *n.* 1 braid used as a trimming. 2 anything braided.

brail (bräl), *n.* one of the small ropes fastened to the edge of a sail, Used in drawing

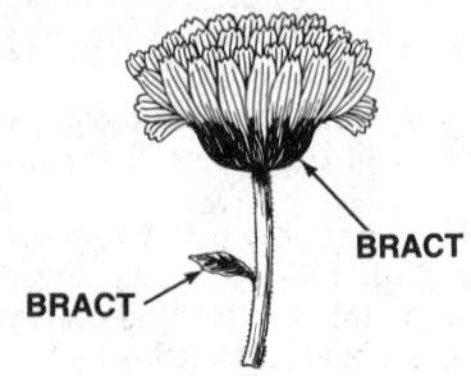

the sail up or in. [< Old French *braiel* < *braie* fastening < *brague* breeches. See BRACKET.]

Braille or **braille** (brāl), *n.* 1 system of writing for blind people in which the letters of the alphabet are represented by different arrangements of raised dots, read by touching them. 2 the letters themselves. [< Louis *Braille*, 1809-1852, French teacher of the blind, who invented this system]

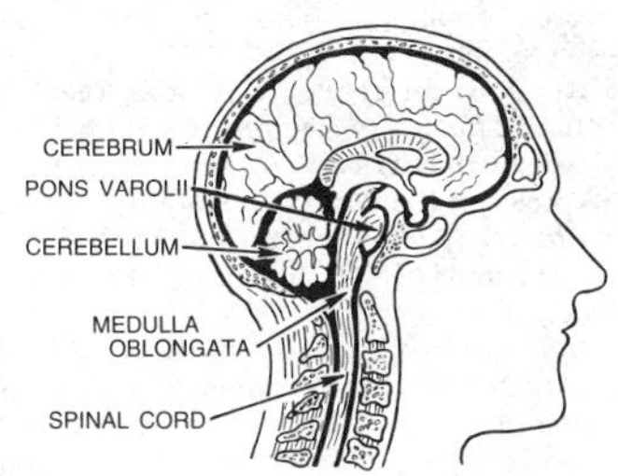

brain (def. 1)—parts of the human brain

brain (brān), *n.* 1 the soft, grayish and whitish mass of nerve cells and nerve fibers enclosed in the skull or head of vertebrate animals, and in man consisting of the cerebrum, cerebellum, pons Varolii, and medulla oblongata; encephalon. The brain is the organ of consciousness or mind and furnishes outgoing stimulation of muscles as a response to incoming sensory stimulation. 2 the part of the nervous system of invertebrates corresponding in position or function to the brain of vertebrates. 3 a large electronic system capable of solving complex problems, storing data, etc., with great speed. 4 the regulatory or guidance controls of any mechanical system, as a heating system, a rocket or guided missile, etc. 5 SLANG. a very intelligent person. 6 Often, **brains,** *pl.* mind; intelligence. 7 **cudgel one's brains** or **rack one's brains,** try very hard to think of something. —*v.t.* 1 kill by smashing the skull of. 2 SLANG. hit on the head. [Old English *brægen*]

brain cell, a nerve cell in the brain.

brain child (brān′chīld′), *n., pl.* **-children.** INFORMAL. any idea, composition, invention, or discovery.

brain drain, INFORMAL. depletion or shortage of scientists, technicians, and other skilled persons because of their emigration.

brain less (brān′lis), *adj.* 1 stupid; foolish. 2 without a brain. **—brain′less ly,** *adv.* **—brain′less ness,** *n.*

brain pan (brān′pan′), *n.* cranium.

brain stem, the base of the human brain lying beneath the cerebrum and the cerebellum, which connects the spinal cord with the forebrain.

brain storm (brān′stôrm′), *n.* 1 INFORMAL. a sudden inspiration. 2 a sudden and violent, but temporary, mental disturbance.

brain trust, group of experts consulted by an administrator or political leader.

brain wash (brān′wosh′, brān′wôsh′), *v.t.* indoctrinate by brainwashing.

brain wash ing (brān′wosh′ing, brān′wôsh′ing), *n.* process of systematically, forcibly, and intensively indoctrinating a person to destroy or weaken his beliefs and ideas, so that he becomes willing to accept different or opposite beliefs and ideas.

brain wave, 1 electric current produced by the rhythmic electric fluctuations between the parts of the brain. 2 INFORMAL. a sudden bright idea; brainstorm.

brain y (brā′nē), *adj.,* **brain i er, brain i est.** INFORMAL. intelligent; clever. **—brain′i ness.** *n.*

braise (brāz), *v.t.,* **braised, brais ing.** to brown (meat, etc.) quickly in fat and then cook long and slowly in a tightly covered pan with very little liquid. [< French *braiser*]

brake[1] (brāk), *n., v.,* **braked, brak ing.** —*n.* 1 device used to slow or stop the motion of a wheel or vehicle by friction, usually by pressing or scraping. 2 anything that retards or holds back; restraint. —*v.t.* 1 slow or stop by using a brake. 2 use a brake on. —*v.i.* use a brake or brakes. [perhaps < Old French *brac* arm]

brake[2] (brāk), *n.* 1 tool or machine for breaking up flax or hemp into fibers. 2 a baker's machine for kneading or rolling. [< Middle Dutch *braeke*]

brake[3] (brāk), *n.* thicket. [probably < Middle Low German]

brake[4] (brāk), *n.* bracken. [probably variant of *bracken*]

brake[5] (brāk), *v.* ARCHAIC. a pt. of **break.**

brake band, a flexible band which, when tightened against a brake drum, causes friction and resultant braking action.

brake drum, a metal cylinder revolving with a wheel or shaft, against which a brake band or shoe is pressed to create the friction necessary for retarding motion.

brake man (brāk′mən), *n., pl.* **-men.** member of a train crew who helps the engineer or conductor.

brake shoe, part of a brake mechanism on railroad cars, automobiles, and other vehicles; a shaped metal block which rubs against a wheel, drum, or other surface in motion to provide friction when the brakes are applied.

bram ble (bram′bəl), *n.* 1 any of a large genus of usually prickly shrubs and vines of the rose family, such as the blackberry and raspberry. 2 any rough, prickly shrub. [Old English *bræmbel,* variant of *brēmel* < *brōm* broom]

bram bly (bram′blē), *adj.,* **-bli er, -bli est.** 1 full of brambles: *a brambly field.* 2 like brambles; prickly: *a brambly bush.*

bran (bran), *n.* the broken coat of the grains of wheat, rye, etc., separated from the flour or meal by bolting and used as fodder and in cereal, bread, and other foods. [< Old French]

branch (branch), *n.* 1 the part of a tree, shrub, or other plant growing out from the trunk; any woody part of a tree above the ground except the trunk. See synonym study below. 2 any division that extends like the branch of a tree. 3 a line of family descent. 4 a tributary stream. 5 subdivision of a subject or field of study. 6 subdivision of a complex organization; department; section. 7 a local office of a business, a library, or the like. —*v.i.* 1 put out branches; spread in branches. 2 divide into branches. 3 **branch off,** go off a main road or route in a different direction; diverge. 4 **branch out, a** put out branches. **b** undertake fresh activities; enlarge one's field of operations. —*v.t.* divide into branches; spread out as branches. [< Old French *branche* < Late Latin *branca* paw] **—branch′less,** *adj.* **—branch′like′,** *adj.*

Syn. *n.* 1 **Branch, bough, limb** mean a part of a tree growing out from the trunk. **Branch** applies to any woody outgrowth, large or small, of a tree or shrub: *The branches waved in the breeze.* **Bough** often suggests any branch covered with blossoms, fruit, etc., especially when it has been cut from the tree: *Those boughs of flowering plum are beautiful on the table.* **Limb** applies to a main or large branch: *The wind broke a whole limb from the tree.*

hat, āge, fär; let, ēqual, tėrm;
it, īce; hot, ōpen, ôrder;
oil, out; cup, pu̇t, rüle;
ch, child; ng, long; sh, she;
th, thin; ᴛʜ, then; zh, measure;

ə represents *a* in about, *e* in taken, *i* in pencil, *o* in lemon, *u* in circus.

< = from, derived from, taken from.

bran chi o pod (brang′kē ə pod), *n.* any of a subclass of mainly freshwater crustaceans having an elongated body and numerous pairs of flat, leaflike appendages that serve as gills. Water fleas belong to this subclass. [< Greek *branchia* gills + *podos* foot]

brand (brand), *n.* 1 the quality or kind (of goods) as indicated by a mark, stamp, or label; a certain kind, grade, or make: *a brand of coffee.* 2 trademark. 3 an iron stamp for branding. 4 mark made by burning the hide (of cattle, horses, etc.) with a brand to identify them. 5 mark of disgrace; stigma. 6 piece of wood that is burning or partly burned on the hearth. 7 ARCHAIC. sword. —*v.t.* 1 mark by burning the skin or hide with a hot iron. In former times criminals were often branded. 2 put a mark of disgrace on; stigmatize: *branded as a traitor.* 3 single out: *Her hairstyle brands her as old-fashioned.* 4 impress upon: *events branded on one's memory.* [Old English] **—brand′er,** *n.*

Bran deis (bran′dīs), *n.* **Louis Dembitz,** 1856-1941, American jurist.

Bran den burg (bran′dən bėrg′), *n.* district in East Germany.

bran died (bran′dēd), *adj.* prepared, mixed, or flavored with brandy.

branding iron, a brand used for branding cattle, horses, etc.

bran dish (bran′dish), *v.t.* wave or shake threateningly; flourish. —*n.* a threatening shake; flourish. [< Old French *brandiss-,* a form of *brandir* to brand < *brand* sword]

brand name, 1 a distinctive name or symbol identifying a product; trade name. 2 product with a well-known trade name.

brand-new (brand′nü′, brand′nyü′), *adj.* very new; entirely new.

Brandt (brant; *German* bränt), *n.* **Willy,** born 1913, chancellor of West Germany since 1969.

bran dy (bran′dē), *n., pl.* **-dies,** *v.,* **-died, -dy ing.** —*n.* 1 a strong alcoholic liquor distilled from wine. 2 a similar alcoholic liquor distilled from fermented fruit juice, as of apples or peaches. —*v.t.* mix, flavor, or preserve with brandy. [< Dutch *brandewijn* burnt (that is, distilled) wine]

brant (brant), *n., pl.* **brants** or **brant.** either of two species of small, dark, wild geese that breed in arctic regions. [origin uncertain]

Braque (brák), *n.* **Georges,** 1882-1963, French painter, founder, with Picasso, of cubism.

brash (brash), *adj.* 1 showing lack of respect; impudent; saucy. 2 hasty; rash: *a brash act.* [origin uncertain] **—brash′ly,** *adv.* **—brash′ness,** *n.*

Bra sí lia (brə zē′lyə), *n.* capital of Brazil since 1960, in the central part. 545,000.

brass (bras), *n.* 1 a yellowish, malleable, ductile metal that is an alloy of copper and zinc in various proportions. 2 ornament, dish, or other thing made of brass. 3 Also, **brasses,** *pl.* **a** musical instruments made of metal and played by blowing into a cup-shaped mouthpiece. The trumpet, trombone, and French horn are brasses. **b** section of an orchestra or band composed of these instruments. 4 BRITISH SLANG. money. 5 INFORMAL. rude boldness; effrontery; impudence. 6 SLANG. **a** high-ranking military officers. **b** the officers or executives of any business. 7 a funeral monument consisting of a plate of brass incised with an effigy, coat of arms, inscriptions, etc. —*adj.* made of brass: *brass candlesticks.* [Old English *bræs*]

bras sard (bras′ärd, bra särd′), *n.* band worn above the elbow as a badge. [< French < *bras* arm]

brass bound (bras′bound′), *adj.* 1 INFORMAL. keeping strictly to rule. 2 bound with brass: *a brassbound box.*

brass hat, SLANG. a high-ranking military officer, especially a general or staff officer.

brass ie (bras′ē), *n., pl.* **brass ies.** a golf club with a wooden head, used for long shots off the fairway. Also, **brassy.**

bras siere (brə zir′), *n.* a woman's undergarment worn to support the breasts. [< French *brassière* bodice < *bras* arm]

brass knuckles, a metal bar or linked rings that fit across the knuckles, used as a weapon.

brass tacks, INFORMAL. the actual facts or details.

brass y (bras′ē), *adj.,* **brass i er, brass i est,** *n., pl.* **brass ies.** —*adj.* 1 of brass. 2 like brass. 3 loud and harsh: *a brassy voice.* 4 INFORMAL. shameless; impudent. —*n.* brassie. —**brass′i ly,** *adv.* —**brass′i ness,** *n.*

brat (brat), *n.* a spoiled, unpleasant, and annoying child. [origin uncertain]

Bra ti sla va (brä′ti slä′və), *n.* city in S Czechoslovakia, on the Danube. 279,000.

brat ty (brat′ē), *adj.,* **-ti er, -ti est.** INFORMAL. disobedient; fresh; impudent.

Braun (brôn; *German* broun), *n.* See **von Braun.**

bra va do (brə vä′dō), *n., pl.* **-does** or **-dos.** a show of courage or boldness without much real courage; defiant or blustering behavior. [< Spanish *bravada,* ultimately < *bravo.* See BRAVE.]

brave (brāv), *adj.,* **brav er, brav est,** *n., v.,* **braved, brav ing.** —*adj.* 1 without fear; having or showing courage in the face of danger. See synonym study below. 2 making a fine appearance; showy; splendid: *a brave display of flags.* 3 ARCHAIC. fine; excellent. —*n.* 1 brave people: *The United States has been called "the land of the free and the home of the brave."* 2 a North American Indian warrior. —*v.t.* 1 meet, face, or endure with courage and firmness of spirit. 2 dare; defy. [< Middle French < Italian *brave* bold < Spanish, wild < Popular Latin *brabus* < Latin *barbarus* foreigner. See BARBARIAN.] —**brave′ly,** *adv.* —**brave′ness,** *n.*

Syn. *adj.* 1 **Brave, courageous** mean showing no fear. **Brave** suggests being able to face danger boldly and with determination: *The brave girl went into the burning house to save a baby.* **Courageous** suggests having a strength and firmness of character that makes one able to fearlessly endure any trial or danger: *The courageous pioneers were not daunted by the perils of the journey westward.*

brav er y (brā′vər ē), *n., pl.* **-er ies.** 1 quality of being brave; fearlessness; boldness. See **courage** for synonym study. 2 fine clothes; finery. 3 ostentation; splendor.

bra vo[1] (brä′vō), *interj., n., pl.* **-vos.** —*interj.* well done! fine! excellent! —*n.* a cry of "bravo!" [< Italian or Spanish]

bra vo[2] (brä′vō, brā′vō), *n., pl.* **-voes** or **-vos.** a hired fighter or murderer. [< Italian, literally, wild]

bra vur a (brə vyůr′ə), *n.* 1 piece of music requiring great skill and spirit in the performer. 2 show of brilliant performance. 3 dash; spirit. [< Italian, bravery]

braw (brô, brä), *adj.* SCOTTISH. 1 making a fine appearance. 2 excellent; fine. [variant of *brave*]

brawl (brôl), *n.* a noisy and disorderly quarrel; fracas. —*v.i.* quarrel in a noisy and disorderly way. [Middle English *brallen*] —**brawl′er,** *n.*

brawn (brôn), *n.* 1 firm, strong muscles; muscle. 2 muscular strength. [< Old French *braon*]

brawn y (brô′nē), *adj.,* **brawn i er, brawn i est.** strong; muscular. —**brawn′i ness,** *n.*

bray (brā), *n.* 1 the loud, harsh cry or noise made by a donkey. 2 a sound like this. —*v.i.* 1 make a loud, harsh sound: *The trumpets brayed.* 2 utter with a loud, harsh voice. —*v.t.* utter in a loud, harsh sound. [< French *braire* cry out] —**bray′er,** *n.*

braze (brāz), *v.t.,* **brazed, braz ing.** solder with brass or other hard solder that has a high melting point. [probably < French *braser*]

bra zen (brā′zn), *adj.* 1 having no shame; shameless; impudent. See **bold** for synonym study. 2 loud and harsh; brassy. 3 made of brass. 4 like brass in color or strength. —*v.t.* 1 make shameless or impudent. 2 **brazen it out** or **brazen it through,** act as if one did not feel ashamed of it: *Although he was caught lying, he tried to brazen it out by telling another lie.* [Old English *bræsen* < *bræs* brass] —**bra′zen ly,** *adv.* —**bra′zen ness,** *n.*

bra zier[1] (brā′zhər), *n.* a large metal pan or tray to hold burning charcoal or coal. Braziers are used in some countries for heating rooms. [< Old French *brasier* < *breze* hot coals]

bra zier[2] (brā′zhər), *n.* person who works with brass. [Old English *brasian* to cover with brass < *bræs* brass]

Bra zil (brə zil′), *n.* country in South America. 92,238,000 pop.; 3,286,200 sq. mi. *Capital:* Brasilia. —**Bra zil′ian,** *adj., n.*

Brazil nut, a large, triangular, edible nut of a tree growing in Brazil.

Braz za ville (braz′ə vil), *n.* capital of the Republic of Congo, in the S part. 156,000.

breach (brēch), *n.* 1 an opening made by breaking down something solid, as a gap made in a wall or fortification. 2 a breaking or neglect (of a law, a trust, etc.); infraction; infringement: *For the guard to leave now would be a breach of duty.* 3 a breaking of friendly relations; quarrel. —*v.t.* break through; make an opening in: *The wall had been breached in several places.* [Old English *bræc* a break]

breach of promise, a breaking of a promise, especially a promise to marry.

breach of the peace, a public disturbance; riot.

bread (bred), *n.* 1 food made of flour or meal mixed with milk or water, with or without yeast or other leaven, usually kneaded and baked. 2 food in general. 3 means of keeping alive; food; livelihood. 4 **break bread, a** eat or share a meal. **b** administer or take Communion. —*v.t.* cover with bread crumbs before cooking. [Old English *brēad*] —**bread′less,** *adj.*

bread and butter, 1 bread spread with butter. 2 means of keeping alive; livelihood.

bread-and-but ter (bred′n but′ər), *adj.* 1 expressing thanks for hospitality: *a bread-and-butter letter.* 2 of or having to do with the essentials of life. 3 INFORMAL. commonplace.

bread bas ket (bred′bas′kit), *n.* 1 basket or tray for bread. 2 region that is a chief source of grain. 3 SLANG. the stomach.

bread fruit (bred′früt′), *n.* 1 a large, round or oval, starchy tropical fruit grown in the islands of the Pacific, much used for food. When baked, it tastes somewhat like bread. 2 tree that it grows on, of the same family as the mulberry.

bread line, line of people waiting to get food given as charity or relief.

bread stuff (bred′stuf′), *n.* 1 Also, **breadstuffs,** *pl.* grain, flour, or meal for making bread. 2 bread.

breadth (bredth, bretth), *n.* 1 distance from side to side of a surface; width. 2 piece of a certain width: *a breadth of cloth.* 3 freedom from narrowness in outlook; largeness (of mind, view, etc.): *A tolerant person usually has breadth of mind.* 4 spaciousness; extent. [Middle English *bredethe* < *brede* breadth, Old English *brǣdu* < *brād* broad]

bread win ner (bred′win′ər), *n.* person who earns a living for himself and those dependent on him.

break (brāk), *v.,* **broke** or (ARCHAIC) **brake, bro ken** or (ARCHAIC) **broke, break ing,** *n.* —*v.t.* 1 make come to pieces by a blow or pull: *How did you break your glasses?* See synonym study below. 2 destroy the evenness, wholeness, etc., of: *break a five-dollar bill, break step.* 3 damage; injure: *She broke her watch by winding it too tightly.* 4 fracture the bone of; dislocate: *break one's arm.* 5 crack the skin of; rupture: *The fall bruised me badly but didn't break the skin.* 6 fail to keep; act against; violate: *break a law, break a promise.* 7 decrease the force of; lessen: *The bushes broke her fall from the tree.* 8 put an end to; stop: *break one's fast, break a strike.* 9 stop for a time; interrupt: *break a journey.* 10 reduce in a rank; dismiss: *The captain was broken for neglect of duty.* 11 escape or become free from: *break jail. The boat broke its moorings in the storm.* 12 force open: *break the enemy's ranks.* 13 train to obey; tame: *break a colt.* 14 go beyond; exceed: *The speed of the new train has broken all records.* 15 dig or plow (ground), especially for the first time. 16 make known; reveal: *break the bad news gently.* 17 train (someone) away from a habit. 18 ruin financially; make bankrupt. 19 figure out; decipher: *break a code.* 20 stop the flow of electricity in (a circuit). —*v.i.* 1 come apart; crack; burst: *The plate broke into pieces when it fell on the floor.* 2 force one's way: *break loose from prison.* 3 come suddenly: *The storm broke within ten minutes.* 4 change suddenly: *The spell of rainy weather has broken. His voice broke with emotion.*

5 be crushed; give away: *The dog's heart broke when its master died.* 6 fail in strength: *His health was breaking fast.* 7 dawn; appear: *The day is breaking.* 8 decline suddenly and sharply: *The sick child's fever broke.* 9 (of fish) jump from the water. 10 break ranks or fall into disorder. 11 become bankrupt. 12 (in baseball) to curve or swerve abruptly. 13 (in racing) begin running from a starting position: *He breaks fast.*

break away, a start before the signal. b flee; escape. c change suddenly.

break down, a have an accident; fail to work. b become weak; collapse. c begin to cry. d analyze. e separate; decompose.

break in, a prepare for work or use. b enter by force: *The thieves broke in through the cellar.* c interrupt: *She broke in with a funny remark while the teacher was reading to us.*

break into, a enter by force: *A robber broke into the house.* b begin suddenly. c interrupt: *break into a conversation.*

break off, a stop suddenly. b stop being friends.

break out, a start suddenly: *War broke out.* b have pimples, rashes, etc., appear on the skin. c leave by force; escape. d burst out.

break up, a scatter. b put an end to; stop. c disturb greatly; upset.

break with, stop being friends with.

—*n.* 1 a broken place; gap; crack. 2 a forceful and sudden separation of parts; fracture; rupture. 3 a forcing one's way out. 4 an abrupt or marked change. 5 a pause in work, athletic practice, etc., for rest, relaxation, or refreshment. 6 (in verse) pause or interruption; caesura. 7 (in jazz playing) a short cadenza in which the soloist improvises without accompaniment. 8 point of separation between the different registers of a voice or of a wind instrument. 9 a sudden, sharp decline, especially in prices. 10 (in pool, billiards, etc.) the opening shot that separates the balls. 11 act or process of making an electric circuit incomplete. 12 SLANG. an awkward remark; mistake in manners. 13 SLANG. chance; opportunity.

[Old English *brecan*] **—break′a ble,** *adj.*

Syn. *v.t.* 1 **Break, shatter, smash** mean to make something come or go to pieces. **Break** means to divide something into two or more pieces by pulling, hitting, dropping, or striking it: *I broke the handle off a cup.* **Shatter** means to break suddenly into a number of pieces that fly in all directions: *I shattered the cup when I dropped it on the floor.* **Smash** means to break completely to pieces with sudden violence and noise: *I smashed the headlights when I hit the wall.*

break age (brā′kij), *n.* 1 a breaking; break. 2 amount of anything broken. 3 damage or loss caused by breaking. 4 allowance made for such damage or loss.

break down (brāk′doun′), *n.* 1 failure to work. 2 failure; collapse. 3 failure of health; weakness. 4 separation or division of a process into parts, steps, etc. 5 chemical decomposition or analysis.

break er (brā′kər), *n.* 1 wave that breaks into foam on the shore, on rocks, etc.; comber. See **wave** for synonym study. 2 person or thing that breaks, crushes, or destroys something.

break fast (brek′fəst), *n.* the first meal of the day. —*v.i.* eat breakfast. —*v.t.* provide with a breakfast. [< *break* + *fast*[2]]

break-in (brāk′in′), *n.* burglary.

break neck (brāk′nek′), *adj.* likely to cause a broken neck; very risky; dangerous.

break of day, dawn; daybreak.

break out (brāk′out′), *n.* 1 an escaping from a prison, etc. 2 breakthrough (def. 1).

break through (brāk′thrü′), *n.* 1 an offensive military operation through an enemy defensive system into the unorganized area in the rear. 2 an important achievement or a solution of a major problem hindering a scientific or technical undertaking.

break up (brāk′up′), *n.* 1 a scattering; separation. 2 a stopping; end.

break wa ter (brāk′wô′tər, brāk′wot′ər), *n.* wall or barrier to break the force of waves, especially one built to form or protect a harbor; pier.

breakwater

bream (brēm), *n., pl.* **breams** or **bream.** 1 a yellowish freshwater fish related to the carp, common in Europe. 2 any of several freshwater sunfishes of the United States. [< Middle French *brême*]

breast (brest), *n.* 1 the upper, front part of the human body between the shoulders and the stomach; chest. 2 the corresponding part in animals. 3 the upper, front part of a coat, dress, etc. 4 thing suggesting the human breast in shape or position; front or forward part. 5 gland of females that gives milk; mammary gland. 6 heart or feelings. 7 **make a clean breast of,** confess completely. —*v.t.* struggle with; advance against; face or oppose: *The experienced swimmer was able to breast the waves. She breasted every trouble as it came.* —*v.i.* press on confidently. [Old English *brēost*]

breast-beat ing (brest′bē′ting), *n.* a loud emotional, public display of grief, regret, etc.

breast bone (brest′bōn′), *n.* the thin, flat bone in the front of the chest attached by cartilages to the ribs; sternum. See **collarbone** for diagram.

Breas ted (bres′tid), *n.* **James Henry,** 1865-1935, American historian and Egyptologist.

breast-feed (brest′fēd′), *v.t., v.i.,* **-fed, -feed ing.** feed at the mother's breast rather than from a bottle; nurse.

breast plate (brest′plāt′), *n.* armor for the chest. See **armor** for picture.

breast stroke, a swimming stroke in which the swimmer is face downward and both arms are brought back under the water simultaneously from in front of the head to the sides, while the legs make a frog kick.

breast work (brest′wėrk′), *n.* a low, sometimes hastily built wall for defense.

breath (breth), *n.* 1 air drawn into and forced out of the lungs. 2 act of breathing. 3 moisture from breathing. 4 ability to breathe easily. 5 a single drawing in and forcing out of air from the body. 6 a slight movement in the air; light breeze. 7 time to breathe freely; pause or respite. 8 something said softly; whisper. 9 a slight trace or suggestion; hint: *This administration has not been marred by one breath of scandal.* 10 life. 11 (in phonetics) forming a sound without motion of the vocal cords, producing

hat, āge, fär; let, ēqual, tėrm;
it, īce; hot, ōpen, ôrder;
oil, out; cup, pu̇t, rüle;
ch, child; ng, long; sh, she;
th, thin; ᴛʜ, then; zh, measure;

ə represents *a* in about, *e* in taken, *i* in pencil, *o* in lemon, *u* in circus.

< = from, derived from, taken from.

such consonants as *h, s, f, p, t, k.* 12 fragrance given off by flowers, etc.

below one's breath or **under one's breath,** in a whisper.

catch one's breath, a gasp. b rest.

in the same breath, at the same time.

out of breath, short of breath.

[Old English *brǣth* odor, steam]

breath a bil i ty (brē′ᴛʜə bil′ə tē), *n.* 1 a being breathable. 2 permeability; porosity.

breath a ble (brē′ᴛʜə bəl), *adj.* fit or agreeable to breathe or be inhaled.

Breath a lyz er (breth′ə lī′zər), *n.* trademark for a type of drunkometer.

breathe (brēᴛʜ), *v.* **breathed, breath ing.** —*v.i.* 1 draw air into and send it out of the lungs; inhale and exhale; respire. 2 stop for breath; rest. 3 blow lightly or softly. 4 be alive; live. 5 **breathe again** or **breathe freely,** be relieved; feel easy. —*v.t.* 1 draw (air) into the lungs and force it out. 2 allow to rest and breathe. 3 put out of breath. 4 say softly; whisper: *Never breathe a word of this to anyone.* 5 (in phonetics) utter with the breath and not with the voice. 6 draw into the lungs; inhale. 7 send out from the lungs; exhale. 8 send out; impart; give: *The speech breathed new life into the team.* 9 be alive with; express: *words that breathe the truth.*

breath er (brē′ᴛʜər), *n.* 1 a short stop for breath; rest. 2 person or thing that breathes.

breath ing (brē′ᴛʜing), *n.* 1 respiration. 2 a single breath. 3 time needed for a single breath. 4 remark; utterance. 5 a slight breeze. 6 sound of the letter *h.*

breathing space, room or time enough to breathe easily; opportunity to rest.

breathing spell, time to catch one's breath; opportunity to rest.

breath less (breth′lis), *adj.* 1 out of breath. 2 holding one's breath because of fear, amazement, excitement, etc. 3 without breath; lifeless; dead. 4 without a breeze. **—breath′less ly,** *adv.* **—breath′less ness,** *n.*

breath tak ing (breth′tā′king), *adj.* thrilling; exciting. **—breath′tak′ing ly,** *adv.*

breath y (breth′ē), *adj.* (of the voice or singing) characterized by audible sounds of breathing.

brec ci a (brech′ē ə, bresh′ē ə), *n.* rock consisting of angular fragments of older rocks cemented together. [< Italian]

Brecht (brekt; *German* breʜt), *n.* **Bertolt,** 1898-1956, German playwright.

Breck in ridge (brek′ən rij), *n.* **John Cabell,** 1821-1875, American statesman and Confederate general, vice-president of the United States from 1857 to 1861.

bred (bred), *v.* pt. and pp. of **breed.**

breech (brēch), *n.* 1 the part of a gun behind the barrel. 2 the lower part; back part. 3 rump; buttocks. [< *breeches*]

breech cloth (brēch′klôth′, brēch′kloth′),

n., pl. **-cloths** (-klôꟻHz′, -klôths′; -kloꟻHz′, -kloths′). loincloth.

breech es (brich′iz, brē′chiz), *n.pl.* 1 short trousers fastened at or just below the knees. 2 trousers. [Old English *brēc,* plural of *brōc* leg covering]

breeches (def. 1) breeches buoy

breeches buoy, pair of short canvas trousers fastened to a belt or life preserver which slides along a rope on a pulley, used to rescue people from sinking ships or to transfer people from one ship to another.

breech load er (brēch′lō′dər), *n.* a breechloading gun.

breech load ing (brēch′lō′ding), *adj.* (of a gun) loaded at the rear end of the barrel instead of at the muzzle end.

breed (brēd), *v.,* **bred, breed ing,** *n.* —*v.t.* 1 produce (young). 2 raise or grow, especially under controlled conditions so as to get new or improved kinds: *breed new varieties of corn.* 3 be the cause of; produce: *Careless driving breeds accidents.* 4 bring up; train. 5 convert (nonfissionable material) into fissionable material. —*v.i.* 1 produce young: *Rabbits breed rapidly.* 2 be produced or caused. —*n.* 1 group of animals or plants within a species, developed by artificial selection and maintained by controlled propagation, having certain distinguishable characteristics, as of color, size, shape, etc.: *Jerseys and Guernseys are breeds of cattle.* 2 a line of descendants from a particular parentage. 3 kind; sort; type. [Old English *brēdan*]

breed er (brē′dər), *n.* 1 person who breeds animals: *a dog breeder.* 2 animal that produces offspring. 3 source; cause. 4 breeder reactor.

breeder reactor, reactor that produces at least as much fissionable material as it uses. In one type of reaction it consumes uranium and produces plutonium.

breed ing (brē′ding), *n.* 1 the producing of offspring. 2 the producing of animals or new types of plants, especially to get improved kinds. 3 upbringing or training; behavior; manners. 4 the producing in a reactor of at least as much fissionable material as is used.

breeze (brēz), *n., v.,* **breezed, breez ing.** —*n.* 1 a light, gentle wind. See **wind** for synonym study. 2 (in meteorology) a wind having a velocity of 4 to 31 miles per hour. 3 BRITISH INFORMAL. disturbance; quarrel. 4 INFORMAL. anything that is easily done. —*v.i.* INFORMAL. proceed easily or briskly. [< Old Spanish and Portuguese *briza* northeast wind]

breeze way (brēz′wā′), *n.* a roofed passage open at the sides between two separate buildings, such as a house and a garage.

breez y (brē′zē), *adj.,* **breez i er, breez i est.** 1 with light winds blowing. 2 lively and jolly; brisk. —**breez′i ly,** *adv.* —**breez′i ness,** *n.*

Brem en (brem′ən, brā′mən), *n.* city in N West Germany. 607,000.

Bren ner (bren′ər), *n.* mountain pass in the Alps between Austria and Italy. 4500 ft. high.

br'er (brėr), *n.* U.S. DIALECT. brother: *Br'er Rabbit and Br'er Fox.*

Bres lau (bres′lou, brez′lou), *n.* German name of **Wrocław.**

Brest (brest), *n.* 1 seaport in NW France. 154,000. 2 city in W Soviet Union. 74,000.

Brest Li tovsk (brest′ li tôfsk′), former name of Brest, in the Soviet Union.

breth ren (breꟻH′rən), *n.pl.* 1 the fellow members of a church, society, or religious order. 2 ARCHAIC. brothers.

Bret on (bret′n), *n.* 1 native or inhabitant of Brittany. 2 the Celtic language of Brittany. 3 **Cape,** the NE point of Nova Scotia. —*adj.* of or having to do with Brittany, its people, or their language.

breve (brēv), *n.* 1 a curved mark (˘) put over a vowel or syllable to show that it is short. 2 a musical note equal to two whole notes. [< Italian < Latin *brevem* short. Doublet of BRIEF.]

bre vet (brə vet′; *British* brev′it), *n., adj., v.,* **-vet ted, -vet ting** or **-vet ed, -vet ing.** —*n.* a commission promoting an army officer to a higher honorary rank without an increase in pay. —*adj.* having or giving rank by a brevet. —*v.t.* give rank by a brevet. [< Middle French diminutive of Old French *bref* letter. See BRIEF.]

bre vi ar y (brē′vē er′ē, brev′ē er′ē), *n., pl.* **-ar ies.** 1 book of prescribed prayers to be said daily by certain clergymen and religious of the Roman Catholic Church. 2 any similar book used in some other church. [< Latin *breviarium* summary < *brevis* short]

brev i ty (brev′ə tē), *n., pl.* **-ties.** 1 shortness in time. 2 shortness in speech or writing; conciseness. [< Latin *brevitatem* < *brevis* short]

brew (brü), *v.t.* 1 make (beer, ale, etc.) from malt, or malt and hops, or from other material by steeping, boiling, and fermenting. 2 make (a drink) by steeping, boiling, or mixing: *Tea is brewed in boiling water.* 3 bring about; plan; plot: *They are brewing some mischief.* —*v.i.* 1 make beer, ale, etc. 2 begin to form; gather: *Dark clouds show that a storm is brewing.* —*n.* 1 a drink that is brewed. 2 quantity brewed at one time. [Old English *brēowan*]

brew er (brü′ər), *n.* person who brews beer, ale, etc.

brewers' yeast, a selected strain of yeast used in brewing beer.

brew er y (brü′ər ē), *n., pl.* **-er ies.** place where beer, ale, etc., is brewed.

brew ing (brü′ing), *n.* 1 the preparing of a brew. 2 amount brewed at one time.

Brezh nev (brezh′nef), *n.* **Leonid I.,** born 1906, Russian political leader, first secretary of the Soviet Communist Party since 1964.

Bri and (brē äN′), *n.* **Aristide,** 1862-1932, French statesman.

bri ar[1] (brī′ər), *n.* brier[1].

bri ar[2] (brī′ər), *n.* brier[2].

bri ar wood (brī′ər wu̇d′), *n.* brierwood.

bri ar y (brī′ər ē), *adj.* briery.

bribe (brīb), *n., v.,* **bribed, brib ing.** —*n.* 1 money or other reward given or offered to a person to get him to do something dishonest or unlawful for the benefit of the giver. 2 a reward for doing something that a person does not want to do. —*v.t.* give or offer a bribe to. —*v.i.* use or practice bribery. [< Middle French, bit of bread given to a beggar] —**brib′a ble,** *adj.* —**brib′er,** *n.*

brib er y (brī′bər ē), *n., pl.* **-er ies.** 1 the giving or offering of a bribe. 2 the taking of a bribe.

bric-a-brac or **bric-à-brac** (brik′ə-brak′), *n.* interesting or curious trinkets used as decorations; small ornaments, such as vases, old china, or small statues. [< French *bric-à-brac*]

brick (brik), *n., pl.* **bricks** or **brick,** *adj., v.* —*n.* 1 block made chiefly of clay baked by sun or fire, used in building and paving. 2 substance of which these blocks consist: *as hard as brick.* 3 anything shaped like a brick. 4 INFORMAL. a good fellow; one who is generous and dependable. —*adj.* 1 made of bricks. 2 resembling brick. —*v.t.* build or pave with bricks; cover or fill with bricks. [< Middle Dutch *bricke*] —**brick′like′,** *adj.*

brick bat (brik′bat′), *n.* 1 piece of broken brick, especially one used as a missile. 2 INFORMAL. an insult.

brick lay er (brik′lā′ər), *n.* person whose work is building with bricks.

brick lay ing (brik′lā′ing), *n.* act or work of building with bricks.

brick-red (brik′red′), *adj.* yellowish-red or brownish-red.

brick work (brik′wėrk′), *n.* wall, foundation, or other structure built of bricks.

brick yard (brik′yärd′), *n.* place where bricks are made or sold.

brid al (brī′dl), *adj.* of or having to do with a bride or a wedding; nuptial: *a bridal veil.* —*n.* a wedding. [Old English *brȳdealo* bride ale]

bridal wreath, shrub of the rose family having long sprays of small, white flowers that bloom in the spring. It is a kind of spiraea.

bride (brīd), *n.* woman just married or about to be married. [Old English *brȳd*]

bride groom (brīd′grüm′, brīd′gru̇m′), *n.* man just married or about to be married; groom. [Old English *brȳdguma* < *brȳd* bride + *guma* man; influenced by *groom*]

brides maid (brīdz′mād′), *n.* a young, usually unmarried woman who attends the bride at a wedding.

bridge[1] (brij), *n., v.,* **bridged, bridg ing.** —*n.* 1 structure built over a river, road, railroad, etc., so that people, cars, trains, etc., can get across. 2 platform above the deck of a ship from which the officer in command directs the course of the ship. 3 the upper, bony part of the nose. 4 the curved central part of a pair of eyeglasses which rests on the nose. 5 a false tooth or teeth in a mounting fastened to adjacent natural teeth. 6 a thin, arched piece over which the strings of a violin or some other stringed instrument are stretched. 7 any other thing like a bridge in form or use. —*v.t.* 1 build a bridge over: *The engineers bridged the river.* 2 form a bridge over; extend over; span: *A log bridged the brook.* 3 make a way over (anything that hinders). [Old English *brycg*] —**bridge′a ble,** *adj.* —**bridge′like′,** *adj.*

bridge[2] (brij), *n.* a card game derived from whist, played with 52 cards by four people divided into two opposing pairs. The highest bidder names the trump suit or declares no trumps. Auction bridge and contract bridge are two kinds. [origin unknown]

bridge head (brij′hed′), *n.* 1 position obtained and held by advance troops within enemy territory, used as a starting point for further attack. 2 any position taken as a

hat, āge, fär; let, ēqual, tėrm;
it, īce; hot, ōpen, ôrder;
oil, out; cup, pu̇t, rüle;
ch, child; ng, long; sh, she;
th, thin; ᴛʜ, then; zh, measure;

ə represents *a* in about, *e* in taken, *i* in pencil, *o* in lemon, *u* in circus.

< = from, derived from, taken from.

foothold from which to make further advances. 3 fortification protecting the end of a bridge nearer to the enemy.

Bridge port (brij′pôrt, brij′pōrt), *n.* city in SW Connecticut, on Long Island Sound. 157,000.

Bridg es (brij′iz), *n.* **Robert (Seymour),** 1844-1930, English poet.

Bridg et (brij′it), *n.* **Saint,** A.D. 453-523, a patron saint of Ireland.

Bridge town (brij′toun), *n.* capital of Barbados. 12,000.

bridge-tun nel (brij′tun′l), *n.* causeway consisting of several bridges and underwater tunnels, designed to carry traffic across a large body of water.

bridge work (brij′wėrk′), *n.* false teeth in a mounting fastened to real teeth nearby.

bri dle (brī′dl), *n., v.,* **-dled, -dling.** —*n.* 1 the head part of a horse's harness, usually consisting of a headstall, bit, and reins and used to control him. 2 anything that holds back or controls; curb. —*v.t.* 1 put a bridle on. 2 hold back; check; control. —*v.i.* hold the head up high with the chin drawn back to express pride, vanity, scorn, or anger. [Old English *brīdel, brigdels* < *bregdan* to braid] **—bri′dler,** *n.*

bridle path, path for people riding horses.

brief (brēf), *adj.* 1 lasting only a short time: *a brief meeting.* See **short** for synonym study. 2 using few words; concise: *a brief announcement.* 3 curt; abrupt. —*n.* 1 a short statement; summary. 2 statement of the facts and the points of law of a case to be pleaded in court. 3 **briefs,** *pl.* short, close-fitting underpants. 4 **hold a brief for,** argue for; support; defend. 5 **in brief,** in few words. —*v.t.* 1 make a brief of; summarize. 2 furnish with a brief. 3 BRITISH. retain as a lawyer or counsel. 4 give a briefing to. [< Old French *bref* < Latin *brevem* short. Doublet of BREVE.] **—brief′ly,** *adv.* **—brief′ness,** *n.*

brief case (brēf′kās′), *n.* a flat container of leather or the like for carrying loose papers, books, drawings, etc., without folding.

brief ing (brē′fing), *n.* 1 a short summary of the details of a flight mission, given to the crew of a combat airplane just before it takes off. 2 any short summary of the details of something about to be undertaken. 3 summary of a current situation to inform or provide background.

bri er[1] (brī′ər), *n.* bush that has a thorny or prickly, woody stem. The blackberry and the wild rose are often called briers. Also, **briar.** [Old English *brēr*]

bri er[2] (brī′ər), *n.* 1 a white heath tree found in southern Europe. 2 a tobacco pipe made of brierwood. Also, **briar.** [< French *bruyère* heath]

bri er wood (brī′ər wu̇d′), *n.* 1 the wood of brier roots, used in making tobacco pipes. 2 pipe made from brierwood. Also, **briarwood.**

bri er y (brī′ər ē), *adj.* full of briers; thorny. Also, **briary.**

brig (brig), *n.* 1 a square-rigged ship with two masts. 2 prison on a warship. 3 SLANG. guardhouse. [short for *brigantine*]

Brig., 1 brigade. 2 Brigadier.

bri gade (bri gād′), *n.* 1 a military unit made up of headquarters troops and two or more regiments or battalions, commanded by a brigadier general or a colonel. 2 a large body of troops. 3 any group of people organized for a particular purpose: *The fire brigade successfully put out the fire.* [< French]

brig a dier (brig′ə dir′), *n.* brigadier general.

brigadier general, *pl.* **brigadier generals.** a commissioned officer in the army, air force, or Marine Corps, ranking next above a colonel and next below a major general.

brig and (brig′ənd), *n.* person who robs travelers on the road, especially one of a gang of robbers in mountain or forest regions; robber; bandit. [< Middle French < Italian *brigante* < *brigare* to fight]

brig and age (brig′ən dij), *n.* robbery; plundering.

brig an tine (brig′ən tēn′, brig′ən tīn), *n.* ship with two masts. The foremast is square-rigged; the mainmast is fore-and-aft-rigged. [< Middle French *brigantin* < Italian *brigantino* < *brigare* to fight]

bright (brīt), *adj.* 1 giving much light; shining: *a bright moon.* See synonym study below. 2 very light or clear: *a bright day.* 3 quick-witted; intelligent; clever: *a bright answer.* 4 vivid; glowing: *bright colors.* 5 lively or cheerful: *a bright smile.* 6 likely to turn out well; favorable; promising. 7 famous; glorious: *The knight was a bright example of courage in battle.* —*adv.* in a bright manner: *The fire shines bright.* [Old English *briht, beorht*] **—bright′ly,** *adv.* **—bright′ness,** *n.*

Syn. *adj.* 1 **Bright, radiant, brilliant** mean shining. **Bright** applies to anything thought of as giving out or reflecting light: *Her silver earrings are bright.* **Radiant** suggests shining with a light that comes from deep within the thing described: *The sun is a radiant body.* **Brilliant** means excessively bright and often suggests sparkling or flashing: *The water is brilliant in the sunlight.*

Bright (brīt), *n.* **John,** 1811-1889, English orator and statesman.

bright en (brīt′n), *v.i., v.t.* become or make bright or brighter: *The sky brightened. She brightened the room with flowers.*

Brigh ton (brīt′n), *n.* seaside resort in SE England. 162,000.

Bright's disease, a kidney disease characterized by albumin in the urine. [< Richard *Bright,* 1789-1858, British physician, who first described it]

brill (bril), *n., pl.* **brills** or **brill.** a European flatfish related to the turbot. [origin uncertain]

bril liance (bril′yəns), *n.* 1 great brightness; radiance; sparkle. 2 splendor; magnificence. 3 great ability. 4 (in music) clarity and vividness of sound.

bril lian cy (bril′yən sē), *n.* brilliance.

bril liant (bril′yənt), *adj.* 1 shining brightly; sparkling: *brilliant jewels, brilliant sunshine.* See **bright** for synonym study. 2 splendid; magnificent: *a brilliant performance.* 3 having great ability: *a brilliant musician.* 4 extremely favorable: *brilliant prospects.* 5 (in music) clear and vivid in tone. —*n.* 1 diamond or other gem cut to sparkle brightly. 2 the smallest regular size of type; 3½ point: This sentence is set in brilliant. [< French *brillant,* present participle of *briller* shine < Italian *brillare*] **—bril′liant ly,** *adv.*

bril lian tine (bril′yən tēn′), *n.* 1 an oily liquid used to make the hair glossy. 2 a glossy cloth of cotton and wool, resembling alpaca.

brim (brim), *n., v.,* **brimmed, brim ming.** —*n.* 1 edge of a cup, bowl, etc. 2 edge or border of anything; rim. 3 the projecting edge of something: *the brim of a hat.* 4 edge bordering water; water at the edge. —*v.t.* fill to the brim. —*v.i.* be full to the brim. [Middle English *brimme*] **—brim′less,** *adj.*

brim ful (brim′fu̇l′), *adj.* full to the brim; full to the very top.

brim stone (brim′stōn′), *n.* sulfur. [Middle English *brinston* < *brinn-* burn + *ston* stone]

Brin di si (brin′də zē), *n.* seaport in SE Italy. 71,000.

brin dle (brin′dl), *adj.* brindled. —*n.* 1 a brindled color. 2 a brindled animal.

brin dled (brin′dld), *adj.* gray, tan, or tawny with darker streaks and spots. [Middle English *brended*]

brine (brīn), *n.* 1 very salty water. Some pickles are kept in brine. 2 a salt lake, sea, or ocean. [Old English *brȳne*]

bring (bring), *v.t.,* **brought, bring ing.** 1 come with or carry (some thing or person) from another place: *Bring me a clean plate.* See synonym study below. 2 cause to come: *What brings you into town today?* 3 win over to a belief or action; influence; persuade; convince: *She was brought to agree by our arguments.* 4 sell for: *Meat brings a high price this time of year.* 5 present before a court of law: *They brought a charge against me.* 6 cause (a ship, etc.) to come or go into a certain position or direction: *bring by the board.*

bring about, cause to happen; cause: *The flood was brought about by a heavy rain.*

bring around or **bring round, a** restore to consciousness: *When I fainted, they brought me around.* **b** convince; persuade: *At first my parents refused to let me go to the party, but soon I brought them around and they let me go.*

bring forth, a give birth to; bear. **b** reveal; show: *New evidence was brought forth by the lawyer.*

bring forward, a reveal; show: *The judge ordered the prisoner to be brought forward.* **b** (in accounting or bookkeeping) carry over from one page to another.

bring off, carry out successfully.

bring on, cause to happen; cause: *My bad cold brought on pneumonia.*

bring out, a reveal; show: *The lawyer brought out new evidence at the trial.* **b** offer to the public.

bring over, convince; persuade: *Try to bring him over to our way of thinking.*

bring to, a restore to consciousness: *She fainted when she heard the news, but they finally brought her to.* **b** stop; check.

bring up, a care for in childhood. **b** educate or train, especially in behavior or manners. **c** suggest for action or discussion. **d** stop suddenly. **e** vomit.

[Old English *bringan*] **—bring′er,** *n.*

Syn. 1 **Bring, fetch** mean to come to a person or place with or carrying something. **Bring** means to come with someone or something from another place to the place where the speaker is: *I brought some cake* *home with me.* **Fetch** means to go and get someone or something: *Please take the car and fetch him.*

bring ing-up (bring′ing up′), *n.* 1 care given in childhood; upbringing. 2 education; training.

brink (bringk), *n.* 1 edge at the top of a steep place. 2 edge: *on the brink of ruin.* [Middle English]

brink man ship (bringk′mən ship), *n.* the maintaining or urging of a policy to the limits of safety before giving ground.

brin y (brī′nē), *adj.*, **brin i er, brin i est.** of or like brine; very salty: *a briny taste.* —**brin′i ness,** *n.*

bri o (brē′ō), *n.* liveliness and vigor of style. [< Italian]

bri oche (brē′ōsh, brē′osh), *n.* a very light roll raised with yeast, rich in butter and eggs. [< French]

bri quette or **bri quet** (bri ket′), *n.* a molded block of coal dust or charcoal used for fuel. [< French, diminutive of *brique* brick]

Bris bane (briz′bān, briz′bən), *n.* seaport in E Australia. 833,000.

brise-so leil (brēz′sō lā′), *n., pl.* **brises-so leil** (brēz′sō lā′), **brise-so leils.** (in architecture) any system of louvers, screens, etc., to keep out sun glare while admitting light and air. [< French, literally, sun breaker]

brisk (brisk), *adj.* 1 quick and active; lively: *a brisk walk.* 2 keen; sharp: *a brisk wind.* [perhaps variant of *brusque*] —**brisk′ly,** *adv.* —**brisk′ness,** *n.*

bris ket (bris′kit), *n.* 1 meat from the breast of an animal. See **beef** for diagram. 2 breast of an animal. [Middle English *brusket*]

bris ling (bris′ling), *n.* a sardinelike Norwegian fish, packed in oil and used for food. [< Norwegian]

bris tle (bris′əl), *n., v.,* **-tled, -tling.** —*n.* 1 one of the short, stiff hairs of a hog or wild boar, used to make brushes. 2 any short, stiff hair of an animal or plant. 3 a synthetic substitute for a hog's bristles. —*v.t.* 1 provide with bristles. 2 cause (hair) to stand up straight. —*v.i.* 1 stand up straight: *The angry dog's hair bristled.* 2 have one's hair stand up straight: *The frightened kitten bristled when it saw the dog.* 3 show that one is aroused and ready to fight: *The whole country bristled with indignation.* 4 be thickly set: *Our path bristled with difficulties.* [Middle English *brustel,* Old English *byrst* bristle] —**bris′tle like′,** *adj.*

bris tle tail (bris′əl tāl′), *n.* any of several wingless insects having two or three long, bristlelike appendages at the end of the abdomen.

bris tly (bris′lē), *adj.,* **-tli er, -tli est.** 1 rough with bristles or hair like bristles. 2 like bristles. 3 likely to bristle.

Bris tol (bris′tl), *n.* seaport in SW England, on the Avon River. 426,000.

Bristol board, a fine, smooth cardboard or pasteboard.

Bristol Channel, inlet of the Atlantic, between SW England and Wales. 85 mi. long.

Brit., 1 Britain. 2 Briticism. 3 British.

Brit ain (brit′n), *n.* Great Britain.

Bri tan ni a (bri tan′ē ə, bri tan′yə), *n.* 1 Great Britain. 2 the British Empire. 3 woman symbolizing Britain or the British Empire.

Britannia metal or **britannia metal,** a white alloy of tin, copper, and antimony, used in making tableware.

Bri tan nic (bri tan′ik), *adj.* British.

britch es (brich′iz), *n.pl.* INFORMAL. breeches.

Brit i cism (brit′ə siz′əm), *n.* word or phrase used especially by the British. *Lift* meaning *elevator* and *petrol* meaning *gasoline* are Briticisms.

Brit ish (brit′ish), *adj.* of Great Britain or its people. —*n.* 1 *pl. in use.* the people of Great Britain. 2 the English spoken in Great Britain.

British Columbia, province in SW Canada, on the Pacific. 2,190,000 pop.; 366,300 sq. mi. *Capital:* Victoria. *Abbrev.:* B.C.

British Commonwealth or **British Commonwealth of Nations,** Commonwealth of Nations.

British Empire, former empire consisting of all the countries and colonies owing allegiance to the British crown.

Brit ish er (brit′i shər), *n.* any British subject, especially an Englishman.

British Guiana, former British colony in N South America, now the country of Guyana.

British Honduras, British colony in Central America, southeast of Mexico. 130,000 pop.; 8600 sq. mi. *Capital:* Belmopan.

British Isles, Great Britain, Ireland, the Isle of Man, and other nearby islands. 61,178,000 pop.; 122,500 sq. mi.

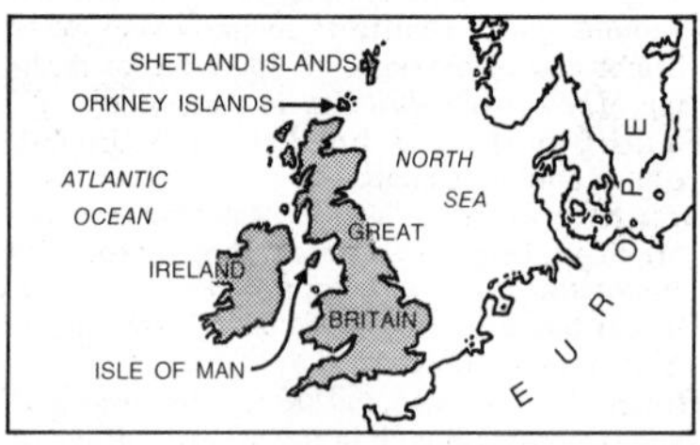

British Isles

British North Borneo, former British territory in NE Borneo, now called Sabah.

British thermal unit, unit for measuring heat, equal to the amount of heat necessary to raise one pound of pure water one degree Fahrenheit.

British West Indies, British islands in the West Indies, including the Bahamas and the British Virgin Islands.

Brit on (brit′n), *n.* 1 native or inhabitant of Great Britain or the former British Empire. 2 one of a Celtic people who inhabited southern Britain before the Roman conquest of Britain.

Brit ta ny (brit′n ē), *n.* peninsular region and former province in NW France. See **Burgundy** for map.

Brit ten (brit′n), *n.* **Benjamin,** born 1913, British composer.

brit tle (brit′l), *adj.* of rigid texture but very easily broken; breaking with a snap; fragile: *Thin glass and ice are brittle.* [Middle English *britel* < Old English *brēotan* to break] —**brit′tle ness,** *n.*

Br no (bėr′nō), *n.* city in central Czechoslovakia. 335,000. Also, *German* **Brünn.**

bro. or **Bro.,** brother.

broach (brōch), *v.t.* 1 begin conversation or discussion about; introduce: *broach a subject.* 2 open by making a hole: *broach a barrel of cider.* 3 enlarge and finish (a drilled hole) with a broach. —*n.* 1 a sharp, tapered tool for shaping or enlarging holes. 2 a sharp-pointed, slender rod on which meat is roasted; spit. 3 gimlet used in opening casks. 4 brooch. [< Old French *broche* < Latin *broccus* projecting] —**broach′er,** *n.*

broad (brôd), *adj.* 1 large across; wide: *Many cars can go on that broad road.* See **wide** for synonym study. 2 having wide range; extensive; vast: *broad experience.* 3 not limited or narrow; liberal; tolerant: *broad ideas.* 4 including only the most important parts; not detailed; general: *Give the broad outlines of what the speaker had to say.* 5 clear; full: *broad daylight.* 6 plain; plain-spoken. 7 coarse; not refined; gross: *broad jokes.* 8 pronounced with the vocal passage open wide. The *a* in *father* is broad. 9 indicating pronunciation by using one symbol for each phoneme, disregarding allophones: *a broad phonetic transcription.* —*adv.* 1 fully; widely: *broad awake.* 2 outspokenly. —*n.* 1 the broad part of anything. 2 U.S. SLANG. a woman or girl. [Old English *brād*] —**broad′ly,** *adv.* —**broad′ness,** *n.*

broad ax or **broad axe** (brôd′aks′), *n.* ax with a broad blade.

broad band (brôd′band′), *adj.* operating over a wide range of frequencies: *broadband radio transmission.*

broad-based (brôd′bāst′), *adj.* built on a broad base; having a wide range; not narrow or limited: *A broad-based economy relies on many products.*

broad bean, a smooth, kidney-shaped, edible seed borne in long pods by an Old World vetch; fava bean.

broad cast (brôd′kast′), *n., v.,* **-cast** or **-cast ed, -cast ing,** *adj., adv.* —*n.* 1 speech, news, music, drama, etc., transmitted by radio or television. 2 a transmitting by radio or television: *a nation-wide broadcast.* 3 a radio or television program. 4 a scattering or spreading widely. —*v.t.* 1 transmit (a message, news, music, etc.) by radio or television. 2 scatter or spread widely: *broadcast seed.* 3 disseminate widely; make generally known: *broadcast gossip.* —*v.i.* 1 transmit programs by radio or television. 2 take part in or supply an item of a radio or television program. —*adj.* 1 transmitted by radio or television. 2 scattered or spread widely. —*adv.* 1 so as to reach many radio or television receiving stations or sets in various directions. 2 over a wide surface. —**broad′cast′er,** *n.*

Broad-Church (brôd′chėrch′), *adj.* of or having to do with a party in the Anglican Church that seeks to avoid rigid definitions of dogma and ritual.

broad cloth (brôd′klôth′, brôd′kloth′), *n., pl.* **-cloths** (-klôᴛʜz′, -klôths′; -kloᴛʜz′, -kloths′). 1 a closely woven cloth with a smooth finish, of cotton, silk, rayon or other synthetic, used in making shirts, pajamas, dresses, etc. 2 a closely woven woolen cloth with a smooth finish, used in making suits, coats, and dresses.

broad en (brôd′n), *v.i., v.t.* become or make broad or broader; widen: *The river broadens at its mouth. Broaden the narrow road.*

broad-gauge (brôd′gāj′), *adj.* having railroad tracks more than 56½ inches apart.

broad jump, 1 a jump to cover as much ground as possible. 2 contest for the longest jump. —**broad jumper.**

broad loom (brôd′lüm′), *adj.* woven on a wide loom: *a broadloom carpet.* —*n.* material woven in this way.

broad-mind ed (brôd′mīn′did), *adj.* not prejudiced or bigoted; liberal; tolerant. **—broad′-mind′ed ly,** *adv.* **—broad′-mind′ed ness,** *n.*

broad side (brôd′sīd′), *n.* 1 the whole side of a ship above the water line. 2 all the guns that can be fired from one side of a ship. 3 the firing of all these guns at the same time. 4 INFORMAL. a violent attack; storm of abuse. 5 a broad surface or side, as of a house. 6 a large sheet of paper printed on one or both sides: *broadsides announcing a big sale.* —*adv.* with the side turned: *The ship drifted broadside to the pier.*

broad-spec trum (brôd′spek′trəm), *adj.* having a wide range of use or application: *a broad-spectrum drug.*

broad sword (brôd′sôrd′, brôd′sōrd′), *n.* sword with a broad, flat cutting blade.

broad tail (brôd′tāl′), *n.* skin or fur of a very young caracul lamb, with flat, wavy hair, used to make or trim garments.

Broad way (brôd′wā′), *n.* 1 street running northwest and southeast through New York City, part of which lies in the main theater district. 2 the New York commercial theater.

Brob ding nag i an (brob′ding nag′ē ən), *adj.* gigantic; huge. [< *Brobdingnag,* the land of the giants in Jonathan Swift's *Gulliver's Travels*]

bro cade (brō kād′), *n., v.,* **-cad ed, -cad ing.** —*n.* an expensive cloth woven with raised designs on it, used for clothing or upholstery. —*v.t.* weave or decorate with raised designs. [< Spanish *brocado*]

bro cad ed (brō kā′did), *adj.* woven or worked into a brocade.

broc co li (brok′l ē), *n., pl.* **-li.** 1 variety of cauliflower having green branching stems and flower heads. 2 its heads and stems, eaten as a vegetable. [< Italian, plural of *broccolo* sprout]

bro chette (brō shet′), *n.* a small spit or skewer used in cooking meat. [< French]

bro chure (brō shür′), *n.* pamphlet. [< French]

Brock ton (brok′tən), *n.* city in SE Massachusetts. 89,000.

bro gan (brō′gən), *n.* a strong work shoe made of heavy leather. [< Irish Gaelic *brōgan,* diminutive of *brōg* shoe]

brogue[1] (brōg), *n.* 1 an Irish accent or pronunciation of English. 2 a strongly marked accent or pronunciation peculiar to any dialect. [perhaps < *brogue*[2] in the sense of "the speech of those who call their shoes brogues"]

brogue[2] (brōg), *n.* 1 a shoe made for comfort and long wear, often with decorative perforations. 2 any coarse, strong shoe; brogan. [< Irish Gaelic *brōg* shoe]

broil[1] (broil), *v.t.* 1 cook by putting or holding directly over the fire or heat on a rack, or under it in a pan; grill. 2 make very hot. —*v.i.* 1 be very hot: *You will broil if you don't get out of this hot sun.* 2 be worked up with anger, impatience, etc. —*n.* broiled food. [perhaps < Old French *bruiller* burn]

broil[2] (broil), *n.* an angry quarrel or struggle; brawl. —*v.i.* quarrel; fight. [< Middle French *brouiller* to disorder]

broil er (broi′lər), *n.* 1 pan or rack for broiling. 2 a young chicken for broiling. 3 person or thing that broils.

broke (brōk), *v.* 1 pt. of **break.** *She broke her doll.* 2 ARCHAIC. a pp. of **break.** —*adj.* SLANG. without money.

bro ken (brō′kən), *v.* pp. of **break.** *The window was broken by a ball.* —*adj.* 1 separated into parts by a break; in pieces: *a broken cup.* 2 not in working condition; damaged: *a broken watch.* 3 rough; uneven: *broken ground, a broken voice.* 4 acted against; not kept: *a broken promise.* 5 imperfectly spoken: *The French girl speaks broken English.* 6 weakened in strength, spirit, etc.; tamed; crushed: *broken by failure.* 7 interrupted: *broken sleep.* 8 bankrupt; ruined: *a broken man.* **—bro′ken ly,** *adv.* **—bro′ken ness,** *n.*

bro ken-down (brō′kən doun′), *adj.* 1 shattered; ruined. 2 unfit for use.

bro ken-heart ed (brō′kən här′tid), *adj.* crushed by sorrow or grief; heartbroken. **—bro′ken-heart′ed ly,** *adv.*

bro ker (brō′kər), *n.* person who buys and sells stocks, bonds, grain, cotton, etc., for other people. [< Anglo-French *brocour* retailer of wine. Related to BROACH.]

bro ker age (brō′kər ij), *n.* 1 business or office of a broker. 2 money charged by a broker for his services.

bro mide (brō′mīd, brō′mid), *n.* 1 any compound of bromine with another element or radical, especially potassium bromide. 2 a drug used to induce sleep and as a tranquilizer. 3 INFORMAL. a commonplace idea; trite remark.

bro mid ic (brō mid′ik), *adj.* INFORMAL. commonplace; trite.

bro mine (brō′mēn′, brō′min), *n.* a dark, brownish-red, nonmetallic, liquid chemical element somewhat like chlorine and iodine, that gives off an irritating vapor. It is used in antiknock compounds for gasoline, in drugs, and in photography. *Symbol:* Br; *atomic number* 35. See pages 326 and 327 for table. [< Greek *brōmos* stench]

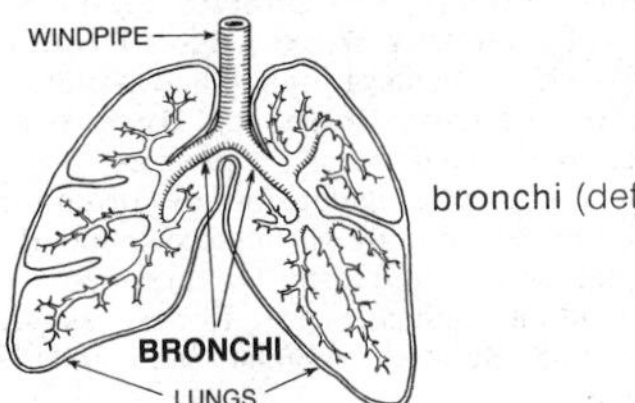

bronchi (def. 1)

bron chi (brong′kī), *n.pl.* of **bronchus.** 1 the two large, main branches of the windpipe, one going to each lung. 2 the smaller branching tubes in the lungs that finally divide into bronchioles. [< New Latin, plural of *bronchus* < Greek *bronchos* windpipe]

bron chi al (brong′kē əl), *adj.* of the bronchi or their branching tubes.

bronchial tubes, bronchi and their branching tubes.

bron chi ole (brong′kē ōl), *n.* a very small branch of the bronchi.

bron chit ic (brong kit′ik), *adj.* 1 of bronchitis. 2 having bronchitis.

bron chi tis (brong kī′tis), *n.* inflammation of the mucous membrane that lines the bronchial tubes, usually accompanied by a deep cough. It may be acute or chronic.

bron cho (brong′kō), *n., pl.* **-chos.** bronco.

bron chus (brong′kəs), *n.* sing. of **bronchi.**

bron co (brong′kō), *n., pl.* **-cos.** a wild or partly tamed horse of western North America. Also, **broncho.** [< American Spanish < Spanish, rough, rude]

hat, āge, fär; let, ēqual, tėrm;
it, īce; hot, ōpen, ôrder;
oil, out; cup, pu̇t, rüle;
ch, child; ng, long; sh, she;
th, thin; ᴛʜ, then; zh, measure;

ə represents *a* in about, *e* in taken,
i in pencil, *o* in lemon, *u* in circus.

< = from, derived from, taken from.

bron co bust er (brong′kō bus′tər), *n.* U.S. SLANG. person who breaks broncos to the saddle.

Bron të (bron′tē), *n.* 1 **Anne,** 1820-1849, English novelist. 2 her sister, **Charlotte,** 1816-1855, English novelist. 3 her sister, **Emily,** 1818-1848, English novelist.

bron to saur (bron′tə sôr), *n.* brontosaurus.

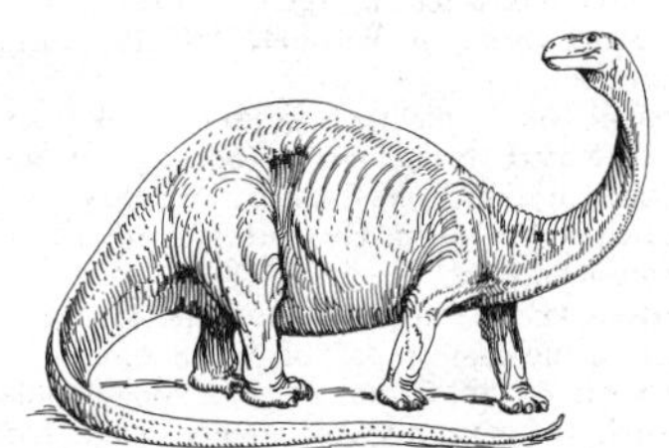
brontosaurus—60 ft. long; 14 ft. tall

bron to sau rus (bron′tə sôr′əs), *n., pl.* **-sau ri** (-sôr′ī), **-sau rus es.** a huge herbivorous dinosaur of America and other continents during the Jurassic and Cretaceous periods. [< Greek *brontē* thunder + *sauros* lizard]

Bronx (brongks), *n.* **The,** borough of New York City, the only one on the mainland. 1,472,000.

Bronx cheer, U.S. SLANG. raspberry (def. 3).

bronze (bronz), *n., adj., v.,* **bronzed, bronz ing.** —*n.* 1 a brown metal, an alloy of copper and tin. 2 a similar alloy of copper with zinc or other metals. 3 statue, medal, disk, etc., made of bronze. 4 a yellowish brown or reddish brown. —*adj.* 1 made of bronze. 2 yellowish-brown or reddish-brown. —*v.t., v.i.* make or become bronze in color or appearance: *The sailor was bronzed from the sun.* [< Middle French < Italian *bronzo* bell metal]

Bronze Age, the prehistoric period of human culture after the Stone Age, when bronze tools, weapons, etc., were used, lasting in different parts of Europe from about 3500 B.C. to about 1000 B.C. It was followed by the Iron Age.

bronz y (bron′zē), *adj.* 1 tinged with bronze color. 2 resembling bronze.

brooch (brōch, brüch), *n.* an ornamental pin having the point secured by a catch; broach. [variant of *broach,* noun]

brood (brüd), *n.* 1 the young birds hatched at one time in the nest or cared for together. 2 young animals or human beings who share the same mother or are cared for by the same person. 3 kind, type, or breed (of animals, things, etc.). —*v.i.* 1 (of birds) sit on eggs so as to hatch them; incubate. 2 cover or protect young with or as if with the wings.

3 think or worry a long time about some one thing. —*v.t.* 1 sit on (eggs) in order to hatch. 2 dwell on in thought: *For years he brooded vengeance.* 3 **brood on** or **brood over, a** keep thinking about. **b** hover over; hang close over. —*adj.* kept for breeding: *a brood mare.* [Old English *brōd*] —**brood′ing ly,** *adv.*

brood er (brü′dər), *n.* 1 a closed place that can be heated, used in raising chicks, etc. 2 person who broods. 3 hen hatching or ready to hatch eggs.

brood y (brü′dē), *adj.,* **brood i er, brood i est.** 1 brooding. 2 inclined to brood; moody. —**brood′i ness,** *n.*

brook[1] (bru̇k), *n.* a natural stream of water smaller than a river; creek. [Old English *brōc*]

brook[2] (bru̇k), *v.t.* put up with; endure; tolerate: *Her pride would not brook such insults.* [Old English *brūcan* to use]

Brooke (bru̇k), *n.* **Rupert,** 1887-1915, English poet.

brook let (bru̇k′lit), *n.* a little brook.

Brook lyn (bru̇k′lən), *n.* borough of New York City, on Long Island. 2,602,000.

Brooks (bru̇ks), *n.* **Gwendolyn,** born 1917, American poet.

brook trout, a freshwater, speckled game fish of the eastern part of North America.

broom (brüm, bru̇m), *n.* 1 a long-handled brush for sweeping, originally made from twigs of broom. 2 shrub of the pea family, with long, slender branches, small leaves, and yellow flowers. [Old English *brōm*]

broom corn (brüm′kôrn′, bru̇m′kôrn′), *n.* kind of sorghum resembling corn, with seed clusters growing on long, stiff stems used for making brooms.

broom stick (brüm′stik′, bru̇m′stik′), *n.* the long handle of a broom.

bros. or **Bros.,** brothers.

broth (brôth, broth), *n., pl.* **broths** (brôᴛʜz, brôths). 1 a thin soup made from water in which meat, fish, or vegetables have been boiled. 2 medium in which cultures of bacteria are grown. [Old English]

broth el (broth′əl, broᴛʜ′əl; brôth′əl, brôᴛʜ′əl), *n.* house of prostitution. [Middle English < Old English *brēothan* go to ruin]

broth er (bruᴛʜ′ər), *n., pl.* **broth ers** (or **breth ren** for 4, 5), *adj.* —*n.* 1 son of the same parents. 2 son only of the same mother or father; half brother. 3 a close friend, companion, or countryman. 4 a male fellow member of a church, union, association, fraternal order, society, etc. 5 a male member of a religious order who is not a priest: *a lay brother.* —*adj.* being in or of the same profession or calling: *brother officers.* [Old English *brōthor*] —**broth′er less,** *adj.* —**broth′er like′,** *adj.*

broth er hood (bruᴛʜ′ər hu̇d), *n.* 1 bond between brothers; feeling of brother for brother. 2 association of men with some common aim, characteristic, belief, profession, etc. 3 members of such an association; persons joined as brothers.

broth er-in-law (bruᴛʜ′ər in lô′), *n., pl.* **broth ers-in-law.** 1 brother of one's husband or wife. 2 husband of one's sister. 3 husband of the sister of one's wife or husband.

broth er ly (bruᴛʜ′ər lē), *adj.* 1 of a brother. 2 like a brother's; friendly; kindly. —*adv.* like a brother. —**broth′er li ness,** *n.*

brougham (brüm, brü′əm, brō′əm), *n.* a closed carriage or automobile having an outside seat for the driver. [< Lord *Brougham,* 1778-1868, British statesman]

brought (brôt), *v.* pt. and pp. of **bring.** *He brought my lunch today.*

brou ha ha (brü hä′hä), *n.* a confused uproar; hullabaloo. [< French]

brow (brou), *n.* 1 part of the face above the eyes; forehead: *a wrinkled brow.* 2 arch of hair over the eye; eyebrow. 3 ridge on which the eyebrow grows. 4 edge of a steep place; top of a slope. [Old English *brū*]

brow beat (brou′bēt′), *v.t.,* **-beat, -beat en, -beat ing.** frighten into doing something by overbearing looks or threats; bully; intimidate. —**brow′beat′er,** *n.*

brown (broun), *n.* 1 the color of toast, potato skins, or coffee; a dark and dusky color, inclining to red or yellow. 2 a brown pigment or dye. 3 brown cloth or clothing. —*adj.* 1 having a color like that of toast, potato skins, or coffee. 2 dark-skinned; tanned. —*v.t., v.i.* make or become brown. [Old English *brūn*] —**brown′ness,** *n.*

Brown (broun), *n.* **John,** 1800-1859, American Abolitionist who attempted to incite a slave rebellion but was captured at Harpers Ferry.

brown algae, class of multicellular marine algae, generally dark brown to olive green due to the presence of a brown pigment as well as chlorophyll. The kelps are brown algae.

brown bear, any bear having brown fur that lives in northern Europe, Asia, and North America, especially Alaska.

brown bet ty (bet′ē), baked pudding made of apples, sugar, and bread crumbs.

brown bread, 1 dark, steamed bread containing molasses. 2 bread made of dark flour, such as rye bread.

brown coal, lignite.

Browne (broun), *n.* 1 **Charles F.,** the real name of **Artemus Ward.** 2 Sir **Thomas,** 1605-1682, English physician and writer.

Brown i an movement or **Brownian motion** (brou′nē ən), (in physics) a constant, random, irregular motion often observed in very minute particles suspended in a liquid or a gas, caused by the impact of surrounding molecules. [< Robert *Brown,* 1773-1858, Scottish botanist, who first described it]

brown ie (brou′nē), *n.* 1 a good-natured elf or fairy, especially one supposed to help secretly at night. 2 **Brownie,** member of the junior division of the Girl Scouts, for girls from 7 to 9. 3 a small, flat, sweet chocolate cake, often containing nuts.

Brown ing (brou′ning), *n.* 1 **Elizabeth Barrett,** 1806-1861, English poet, wife of Robert Browning. 2 **Robert,** 1812-1889, English poet.

brown ish (brou′nish), *adj.* somewhat brown.

brown rice, rice that is not polished.

brown shirt, storm trooper.

brown stone (broun′stōn′), *n.* 1 a reddish-brown sandstone, used as a building material. 2 building, especially a house, having exterior walls built of this material.

brown study, condition of being absorbed in thought; serious reverie.

brown sugar, sugar that is not refined or only partly refined.

brown thrasher, a brown-and-white bird somewhat like a thrush, but more closely related to the mockingbird.

browse (brouz), *v.,* **browsed, brows ing,** *n.* —*v.i.* 1 feed on growing grass or the leaves and shoots of trees and shrubs by nibbling and eating here and there; graze. 2 read here and there in a book or in books. 3 pass the time looking at books in a library, bookstore, etc. —*v.t.* feed on (grass, twigs, or leaves); graze. —*n.* 1 the tender shoots of trees and shrubs; green food for cattle, etc. 2 act of browsing. [< Middle French *brouster*] —**brows′er,** *n.*

Broz (brōz), *n.* **Josip,** the real name of Marshal **Tito.**

Bruce (brüs), *n.* **Robert the Bruce,** 1274-1329, king of Scotland from 1306 to 1329, victor over the English at Bannockburn in 1314. Also, **Robert I.**

Bruck ner (bru̇k′nər; *German* bru̇k′nər), *n.* **Anton,** 1824-1896, Austrian composer.

Bruges (brüzh, brü′jiz), *n.* city in NW Belgium. 51,000.

bru in (brü′ən), *n.* bear[2] (def. 1). [< Middle Dutch, brown]

bruise (brüz), *n., v.,* **bruised, bruis ing.** —*n.* 1 injury to the body, caused by a fall or a blow, that breaks blood vessels without breaking the skin; contusion: *The bruise on my arm turned black and blue.* 2 injury to the outside of a fruit, vegetable, plant, etc. 3 hurt or injury to the feelings. —*v.t.* 1 injure the outside of. 2 hurt; injure: *Harsh words bruised my feelings.* 3 pound or crush (drugs or food). —*v.i.* become bruised: *My flesh bruises easily.* [fusion of Old English *brȳsan* to crush and Old French *bruisier* to break, shatter]

bruis er (brü′zər), *n.* INFORMAL. 1 a professional boxer. 2 a bully. 3 a very muscular person.

bruit (brüt), *v.t.* spread a report or rumor of: *News of their engagement was bruited about.* —*n.* ARCHAIC. report; rumor. [< Old French, a roar < *bruire* to roar]

brum ma gem (brum′ə jəm), INFORMAL. —*adj.* cheap and showy; tawdry. —*n.* anything cheap and showy. [alteration of *Birmingham,* England]

Brum mell (brum′əl), *n.* **George Bryan,** the real name of **Beau Brummell.**

brunch (brunch), *n.* meal taken late in the morning and intended to combine breakfast and lunch. [< *br(eakfast)* + *(l)unch*]

Brun dis i um (brun diz′ē əm), *n.* ancient seaport in SE Italy where Brindisi is now.

Bru nei (bru̇ nī′), *n.* 1 sultanate in N Borneo under British protection. 130,000 pop.; 2200 sq. mi. 2 its capital. 34,000.

Bru nel les chi (brü′nl es′kē), *n.* **Filippo,** 1377-1446, Italian architect.

bru nette or **bru net** (brü net′), *adj.* 1 dark in color: *brunette hair.* 2 having dark-brown or black hair, brown or black eyes, and dark skin. —*n.* person having brunette hair, brown or black eyes, and dark skin. [< French < *brun* brown]

Brünn (bryn), *n.* German name of **Brno.**

Bruns wick (brunz′wik), *n.* 1 city in NE West Germany. 225,000. 2 former state in NW Germany.

brunt (brunt), *n.* the main force or violence; hardest part: *the brunt of the hurricane.* [origin uncertain]

brush[1] (brush), *n.* 1 tool for cleaning, sweeping, scrubbing, painting, etc., made of bristles, hair, or wire set in a stiff back or fastened to a handle. 2 a brushing; a rub with a brush. 3 a light touch in passing. 4 a short, brisk fight or quarrel. 5 the bushy tail of an animal, especially of a fox. 6 piece of car-

bon, copper, etc., used to conduct the electricity from the revolving part of an electric motor or generator to the outside circuit. 7 art or skill of an artist.
—*v.t.* 1 clean, sweep, scrub, or paint with a brush; use a brush on. 2 wipe away; remove: *The child brushed the tears from his eyes.* 3 touch lightly in passing. 4 **brush aside,** put aside; refuse to consider. 5 **brush off,** INFORMAL. **a** refuse to see or listen to. **b** dismiss as unimportant; make light of. 6 **brush up on** or **brush up,** refresh one's knowledge of; review. —*v.i.* 1 move quickly. 2 touch (against) something lightly.
[< Old French *broisse*] —**brush′like′,** *adj.*

brush² (brush), *n.* 1 U.S. branches broken or cut off; brushwood. 2 shrubs, bushes, and small trees growing thickly in the woods; brushwood. 3 U.S. a thinly settled country; backwoods. [< Old French *brosse*]

brush fire war (brush′fīr′), warfare confined to a small area or occurring on a small scale.

brush off (brush′ôf′), *n.* INFORMAL. refusal to see or listen.

brush stroke (brush′strōk′), *n.* 1 movement of the brush when applying paint. 2 method of using brushstrokes in painting.

brush up (brush′up′), *n.* a refreshing of memory or a reviewing of knowledge, skill, etc.

brush wood (brush′wu̇d′), *n.* brush² (defs. 1 and 2).

brush work (brush′wėrk′), *n.* an artist's characteristic manner of using a brush in his paintings.

brush y¹ (brush′ē), *adj.,* **brush i er, brush i est.** like a brush; rough and shaggy. [< *brush*¹]

brush y² (brush′ē), *adj.,* **brush i er, brush i est.** covered with bushes, shrubs, etc. [< *brush*²]

brusque (brusk), *adj.* abrupt in manner or speech; blunt. [< French < Italian *brusco* coarse] —**brusque′ly,** *adv.* —**brusque′ness,** *n.*

Brus sels (brus′əlz), *n.* capital of Belgium, in the central part. 1,073,000.

Brussels sprouts, 1 variety of cabbage having many small heads growing along a stalk. 2 the heads of this plant, eaten as a vegetable.

Brussels sprouts (def. 1) about 2½ ft. tall

bru tal (brü′tl), *adj.* 1 like a brute; savagely cruel; inhuman. See **cruel** for synonym study. 2 rude and coarse; unrefined. 3 sensual. —**bru′tal ly,** *adv.*

bru tal i ty (brü tal′ə tē), *n., pl.* **-ties.** 1 brutal conduct; cruelty; savageness. 2 a cruel or savage act. 3 coarse behavior; sensuality.

bru tal ize (brü′tl īz), *v.,* **-ized, -iz ing.** —*v.t.* 1 make brutal: *War brutalizes many men.* 2 treat in a brutal or cruel manner. —*v.i.* become brutal. —**bru′tal i za′tion,** *n.*

brute (brüt), *n.* 1 mammal or reptile without power to reason. See **animal** for synonym study. 2 a cruel, coarse, or sensual person. —*adj.* 1 not possessing reason or understanding: *brute beasts.* 2 of or characteristic of animals as distinguished from man; dull; stupid. 3 cruel; coarse. 4 sensual. 5 lacking intelligence; not having sense or sensation: *the brute forces of nature.* [< Old French *brut* < Latin *brutum* heavy, dull]

brut ish (brü′tish), *adj.* 1 like a brute; cruel or coarse. 2 lacking restraint; sensual. —**brut′ish ly,** *adv.* —**brut′ish ness,** *n.*

Bru tus (brü′təs), *n.* **Marcus Junius,** 85-42 B.C., Roman political leader; one of the men who killed Julius Caesar.

Bry an (brī′ən), *n.* **William Jennings,** 1860-1925, American political leader and orator.

Bry ant (brī′ənt), *n.* **William Cullen,** 1794-1878, American poet.

Bryce (brīs), *n.* **James,** Viscount, 1838-1922, British statesman, diplomat, and writer.

Bryce Canyon National Park, national park in S Utah, famous for its oddly shaped colored rocks. 56 sq. mi.

bry ol o gy (brī ol′ə jē), *n.* branch of botany that deals with mosses and liverworts. [< Greek *bryon* moss]

bry o ny (brī′ə nē), *n., pl.* **-nies.** a climbing plant of the gourd family, having small, greenish flowers and red, white, or black berries. The roots of some kinds are used in medicine. [< Greek *bryōnia* < *bryein* to swell]

bry o phyte (brī′ə fīt), *n.* any of a division of nonflowering plants comprising the mosses and liverworts. [< Greek *bryon* moss + *phyton* plant]

bry o phyt ic (brī′ə fit′ik), *adj.* of or having to do with the bryophytes.

bry o zo an (brī′ə zō′ən), *n.* any of a phylum of minute, mosslike, aquatic invertebrates that form permanently attached colonies, reproduce by budding, and have distinct alimentary canals. —*adj.* of or belonging to this phylum.

Bry thon ic (bri thon′ik), *adj.* Cymric. —*n.* one of the two main divisions of the Celtic language (the other being Goidelic), including Breton, Cornish, and Welsh.

b.s., 1 balance sheet. 2 bill of sale.

B.S., Bachelor of Science.

B.S.A., Boy Scouts of America.

B.Sc., Bachelor of Science.

Bt. or **Bt,** Baronet.

Btu, B.t.u., or **B.T.U.,** British thermal unit or units.

bu., 1 bureau. 2 bushel or bushels.

bub ble (bub′əl), *n., v.,* **-bled, -bling.** —*n.* 1 a thin, round film of liquid enclosing air or gas. When water boils, it is full of bubbles. 2 pocket of air or gas in a liquid or solid. Sometimes there are bubbles in ice or glass. 3 act or process of bubbling. 4 sound of bubbling. 5 plan or idea that looks good, but soon goes to pieces. 6 bubbletop. —*v.i.* 1 have bubbles; make bubbles. 2 make sounds like water boiling: *The baby bubbled and cooed.* 3 **bubble over, a** overflow. **b** be very enthusiastic. —*v.t.* 1 cause to bubble. 2 ARCHAIC. swindle. [Middle English *bobel*] —**bub′bling ly,** *adv.*

bubble chamber, a small vessel filled with a superheated, pressurized liquid, especially hydrogen or propane, through which charged subatomic particles make a bubbly track by means of which they may be examined and identified.

hat, āge, fär; let, ēqual, tėrm;
it, īce; hot, ōpen, ôrder;
oil, out; cup, pu̇t, rüle;
ch, child; ng, long; sh, she;
th, thin; ᴛʜ, then; zh, measure;

ə represents *a* in about, *e* in taken, *i* in pencil, *o* in lemon, *u* in circus.

< = from, derived from, taken from.

bubble gum, a chewing gum that can be blown out through the lips so as to form a large bubble.

bub ble top (bub′əl top′), *n.* a transparent plastic top or canopy, often retractable, on an automobile or airplane; bubble.

bub bly (bub′lē), *adj.,* **-bli er, -bli est.** 1 full of bubbles. 2 lively: *bubbly humor.*

bu bo (byü′bō), *n., pl.* **-boes.** an inflammatory swelling of a lymph gland, especially in the groin or armpits. [< Late Latin < Greek *boubōn* swelling in the groin]

bu bon ic (byü bon′ik), *adj.* having or characterized by inflammatory swelling of the lymph glands.

bubonic plague, a serious contagious disease, accompanied by high fever, chills, and swelling of the lymph glands, usually carried to human beings by fleas from rats or squirrels.

buc cal (buk′əl), *adj.* 1 of the cheek. 2 of the mouth as a whole or the sides of the mouth. [< Latin *bucca* cheek, mouth]

buc ca neer (buk′ə nir′), *n.* a pirate, especially one who preyed upon Spanish vessels and colonies in America in the 1600's and 1700's. —*v.i.* act as a buccaneer; be a buccaneer. [< French *boucanier,* ultimately < Tupi *boucan* frame for curing meat (early Caribbean pirates preserved meat in this way)]

Bu ceph a lus (byü sef′ə ləs), *n.* the war horse of Alexander the Great.

Bu chan an (byü kan′ən, bə kan′ən), *n.* **James,** 1791-1868, the 15th president of the United States, from 1857 to 1861.

Bu cha rest (bü′kə rest′, byü′kə rest′), *n.* capital of Romania, in the S part. 1,475,000.

buck¹ (buk), *n.* 1 a male deer, goat, hare, rabbit, antelope, or sheep (but not applied to a male elk, moose, or red deer). 2 dandy. 3 INFORMAL. man. 4 buckskin. —*adj.* male: *a buck rabbit.* [fusion of Old English *buc* male deer, and *bucca* male goat]

buck² (def. 1)

buck² (buk), *v.i.* 1 (of horses) jump into the air with the back curved and come down with the front legs stiff: *My horse bucked violently.* 2 (of an automobile, motor, etc.) run unevenly; jerk, as when the fuel supply is low or the motor is cold. 3 INFORMAL. resist or oppose. 4 **buck up,** INFORMAL. cheer up; be brave, energetic, or enterprising. *—v.t.* 1 throw or attempt to throw (a rider) by bucking. 2 INFORMAL. fight against; resist stubbornly. 3 push or hit with the head; butt. 4 rush at; charge against; work against: *The swimmer bucked the current with strong strokes.* 5 (in football) charge into (the opposing line) with the ball. 6 **buck for,** strive earnestly for. *—n.* 1 a throw or attempt to throw (a rider) by bucking. 2 (in football) a charge made into the opponent's line with a ball. [special use of *buck*[1]] **—buck′er,** *n.*

buck[3] (buk), *n.* 1 sawhorse. 2 (in gymnastics) a padded, adjustable frame used for vaulting, etc. [short for *sawbuck*]

buck[4] (buk), *n.* **pass the buck,** INFORMAL. shift the responsibility, blame, work, etc., to someone else. [origin uncertain]

buck[5] (buk), *n.* U.S. SLANG. dollar. [origin uncertain]

Buck (buk), *n.* **Pearl,** 1892-1973, American novelist.

buck a roo (buk′ə rü′, buk′ə rü′), *n., pl.* **-roos.** U.S. cowboy. [alteration of Spanish *vaquero.* See VAQUERO.]

buck board (buk′bôrd′, buk′bōrd′), *n.* an open, four-wheeled carriage having a seat fastened to a platform of long, springy boards instead of a body and springs.

buck et (buk′it), *n.* 1 pail made of wood, metal, or plastic, used for carrying such things as water, milk, or coal. 2 bucketful. 3 scoop of a dredging machine. 4 one of the blades on the rotor of a gas or steam turbine. 5 SLANG. ship, car, etc., especially one that is old and slow. 6 **kick the bucket,** SLANG. die. *—v.t.* lift or carry in a bucket or buckets. *—v.i.* INFORMAL. 1 move fast. 2 move jerkily and irregularly. 3 drive forward hurriedly. [< Anglo-French *buket* washtub, pail, perhaps < Old English *būc* vessel, pitcher]

bucket brigade, line of persons formed to pass buckets of water one to another to put out a fire.

buck et ful (buk′it fu̇l), *n., pl.* **-fuls.** amount that a bucket can hold.

bucket seat, a small, low, single seat with a rounded back, used especially in sports cars, small airplanes, etc.

buck eye (buk′ī′), *n.* 1 tree or shrub of the same family as the horse chestnut, with showy clusters of small flowers, large divided leaves, and large brown seeds. 2 its seed.

Buck ing ham (buk′ing əm, buk′ing ham), *n.* 1 the first Duke of, 1592-1628, **George Villiers,** English politician and courtier. 2 the second Duke of, 1628-1687, his son, **George Villiers,** English politician and courtier. 3 Buckinghamshire.

Buckingham Palace, official London residence of all British sovereigns since 1837.

Buck ing ham shire (buk′ing əm shər, buk′ing əm shir), *n.* county in S England.

buck le (buk′əl), *n., v.,* **-led, -ling.** *—n.* 1 catch or clasp used to fasten together the ends of a belt, strap, etc. 2 a metal, plastic, etc., ornament for a shoe. 3 a bend, bulge, kink, or wrinkle. *—v.t.* 1 fasten together with a buckle. 2 bend out of shape; bulge, kink, or wrinkle: *The plaster has been buckled by the settling of the house.* 3 **buckle down to,** work hard at. *—v.i.* bend, bulge, or lose shape, especially under strain or pressure: *The front wheel of my bicycle buckled.* [< Old French *boucle* metal ring on a shield < Latin *bucculam* cheek strap on a helmet, diminutive of *bucca* cheek]

buck ler (buk′lər), *n.* 1 a small, round shield used to parry blows or thrusts. 2 means of protection; defense.

buck-pass ing (buk′pas′ing), *n.* U.S. SLANG. avoidance of responsibility, blame, work, etc., by shifting it to someone else.

buck private, SLANG. an enlisted man ranking below a private first class.

buck ram (buk′rəm), *n.* a coarse cloth made stiff with glue or something like glue, used for stiffening garments, binding books, etc. *—adj.* made of buckram. [< Old French *bouquerant,* ultimately < *Bokhara,* region in central Asia]

buck saw (buk′sô′), *n.* saw set in a light frame and held with both hands.

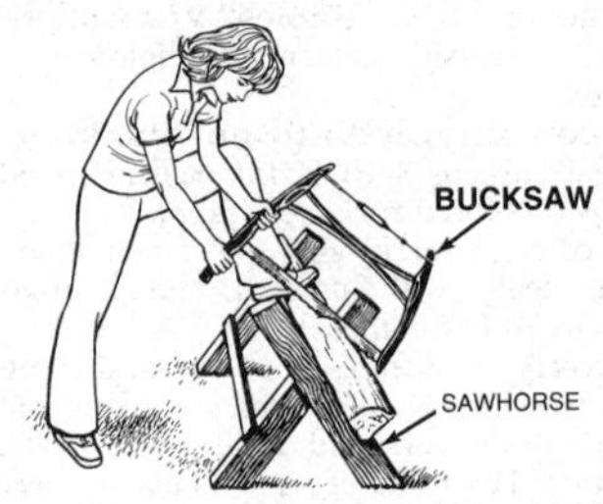

buck shot (buk′shot′), *n.* a large lead shot, usually fired from a shotgun, used for shooting large game, such as deer.

buck skin (buk′skin′), *n.* 1 a strong, soft leather, yellowish or grayish in color, made from the skins of deer or sheep. 2 **buckskins,** *pl.* clothing made of buckskin. 3 (in Western United States) horse having the color of buckskin.

buck thorn (buk′thôrn′), *n.* any of a genus of small, sometimes thorny trees or shrubs with clusters of black berries, each containing two to four tiny seeds.

buck tooth (buk′tüth′), *n., pl.* **-teeth.** tooth that sticks out beyond the rest.

buck toothed (buk′tütht′, buk′tüᴛʜd′), *adj.* having a protruding tooth or teeth.

buck wheat (buk′hwēt′), *n.* 1 plant with black or gray triangular seeds and fragrant white or pink-tinged flowers. 2 its seeds, used as food for animals or ground into flour. 3 meal, flour, or batter made from buckwheat.

bu col ic (byü kol′ik), *adj.* 1 of shepherds; pastoral: *bucolic poetry.* 2 rustic; rural: *a bucolic setting, bucolic wit.* *—n.* poem about shepherds. [< Latin *bucolicus* < Greek *boukolikos* < *boukolos* herdsman < *bous* cow] **—bu col′i cal ly,** *adv.*

bud (bud), *n., v.,* **bud ded, bud ding.** *—n.* 1 a small swelling on a plant consisting of a mass of growing tissue that develops into a flower, leaf, or branch. 2 a partly opened flower or leaf. 3 anything in an undeveloped state or beginning stage. 4 child or young girl. 5 a small swelling (in certain animals or plants of simple organic structure) that develops into a new individual of the same species; gemma: *the buds of yeast plants.* 6 **in bud,** budding: *The pear tree is in bud.* 7 **nip in the bud,** stop at the very beginning. *—v.i.* 1 put forth buds. 2 begin to grow or develop. 3 be like a bud in youth, beauty, or promise. *—v.t.* 1 cause to bud. 2 put forth as buds. 3 graft (a bud) from one kind of plant into the stem of a different kind, as a method of propagating a desired quality or variety. [Middle English *budde*] **—bud′der,** *n.* **—bud′like′,** *adj.*

Bu da pest (bü′də pest), *n.* capital of Hungary, on the Danube. 2,000,000.

Bud dha (bü′də, bu̇d′ə), *n.* 563?-483? B.C., a religious teacher of northern India and the founder of Buddhism. Also, **Gautama.**

Bud dhism (bü′diz əm, bu̇d′iz əm), *n.* religion based on the teachings of Buddha which maintains that right living will enable people to attain nirvana, a condition free from all desire and pain.

Bud dhist (bü′dist, bu̇d′ist), *n.* believer in Buddhism. *—adj.* having to do with Buddha or Buddhism.

Bud dhis tic (bü dis′tik, bu̇ dis′tik), *adj.* Buddhist.

bud dy (bud′ē), *n., pl.* **-dies.** 1 INFORMAL. comrade; pal. 2 U.S. INFORMAL. a little boy. 3 U.S. SLANG. brother.

budge (buj), *v.,* **budged, budg ing.** *—v.i.* move from one's place. *—v.t.* cause to move. [< French *bouger* stir]

budg er i gar (buj′ər i gär), *n.* a small, brightly colored parakeet, native to Australia. [< native Australian]

budg et (buj′it), *n., v.* *—n.* 1 estimate of the amount of money that will probably be received and spent for various purposes in a given time by a government, school, business, family, etc. 2 plan of procedure based on such an estimate. 3 allotment of expenditures for various items for a period of time. 4 stock or collection: *a budget of news.* *—v.t.* 1 make a plan for spending: *budget your time.* 2 put in a budget; allot: *She budgeted three dollars a week for school lunches.* *—v.i.* 1 draw up or prepare a budget. 2 arrange for in a budget. [< Middle French *bougette,* diminutive of *bouge* bag < Latin *bulga*]

budg et ar y (buj′ə ter′ē), *adj.* of a budget: *a budgetary deficit.*

budg ie (buj′ē), *n.* INFORMAL. budgerigar.

Bue nos Ai res (bwā′nəs er′ēz; bwā′nəs ar′ēz; bwā′nəs ī′rās), capital of Argentina, in the E part. 2,972,000.

buff (buf), *n.* 1 a dull yellow. 2 a strong, soft, dull-yellow leather having a fuzzy surface, made from oxhide, and used for belts, pouches, etc. 3 a soldier's coat made of this leather. 4 a polishing wheel or stick covered with leather. 5 INFORMAL. bare skin. 6 INFORMAL. a fan or devotee: *a football buff.* *—adj.* 1 dull-yellow. 2 made of buff leather. *—v.t.* 1 polish with a wheel or stick covered with leather. 2 polish; shine. [< Middle French *buffle* < Italian *bufalo.* See BUFFALO.]

buffalo (def. 2)—water buffalo
5 ft. high at the shoulder

buf fa lo (buf′ə lō), *n., pl.* **-loes, -los,** or **lo,** *v.* *—n.* 1 the bison of North America. 2 any of several kinds of oxen. The tame water buffalo of Asia and the wild Cape buffalo of Africa are two different kinds. *—v.t.* SLANG. 1 intimidate or overawe. 2 puzzle; mystify. [< Italian *bufalo* < Latin *bubalus* wild ox < Greek *boubalos*]

Buf fa lo (buf′ə lō), *n.* city in W New York State, a port on Lake Erie. 463,000.

Buffalo Bill (bil), 1846-1917, American frontier scout and showman. His real name was William F. Cody.

buffalo grass, a short native grass of central and western North America, often used for pasture.

buff er[1] (buf′ər), *n.* 1 a mechanical device for absorbing the force of a concussion, as a hydraulic bumper. 2 any person or thing that softens the shock of a blow. 3 buffer solution. 4 buffer state. *—v.t.* 1 soften or lessen the impact of. 2 treat with a buffer solution. [< earlier *buff* soften the shock of a blow < Old French *buffe* a blow]

buff er[2] (buf′ər), *n.* 1 stick or pad having a soft cloth or leather surface for polishing. 2 person who polishes. [< *buff*]

buffer solution, substance in a solution that makes the degree of acidity (hydrogen ion concentration) resistant to change when an acid or base is added.

buffer state, a small country lying between two larger countries that are enemies or competitors.

buffer zone, a neutral area established as a barrier between two adjoining enemy or rival areas.

buf fet[1] (buf′it), *n.* 1 a blow of the hand or fist. 2 a knock, stroke, or hurt. *—v.t.* 1 strike with the hand or fist. 2 knock about; strike repeatedly; beat back: *The waves buffeted me.* 3 fight or struggle against: *The boat buffeted the heavy waves caused by the storm.* *—v.i.* deal blows; struggle; contend. [< Old French, diminutive of *buffe* blow]

buf fet[2] (bu fā′, bu̇ fā′), *n.* 1 a low cabinet with a flat top for dishes and with shelves or drawers for silver and table linen; sideboard. 2 counter where food and drinks are served. 3 restaurant with such a counter. 4 meal at which guests serve themselves from food laid out on a table or sideboard. [< French]

buf foon (bu fün′), *n.* 1 person who amuses people with tricks, pranks, and jokes; clown. 2 person given to undignified or rude joking. [< French *bouffon* < Italian *buffone* < *buffa* jest]

buf foon er y (bu fü′nər ē), *n., pl.* **-er ies.** 1 tricks, pranks, and jokes of a clown. 2 undignified or rude joking.

buf foon ish (bu fü′nish), *adj.* like or characteristic of a buffoon.

bug (bug), *n., v.,* **bugged, bug ging.** *—n.* 1 any of the order of hemipterous insects that are wingless or have a front pair of wings thickened at the base, and have a pointed beak for piercing and sucking. Bedbugs, lice, and chinch bugs are **true bugs.** 2 any insect or other invertebrate somewhat like an insect. Ants, spiders, beetles, and flies are often called bugs. 3 bedbug. 4 INFORMAL. a disease germ or microbe: *the flu bug.* 5 INFORMAL. a mechanical defect; any structural fault or difficulty: *The new engine needed repair because of a bug in the design of the fuel system.* 6 INFORMAL. person who is very enthusiastic about something: *a basketball bug.* 7 INFORMAL. a very small microphone hidden in a room, a telephone, etc., for overhearing conversation. *—v.t.* 1 INFORMAL. hide a small microphone in (a room, telephone, etc.). 2 SLANG. annoy; irritate: *His constant grumbling bugs me.* [origin uncertain] **—bug′like′,** *adj.*

bug a boo (bug′ə bü), *n., pl.* **-boos.** bogy. [< obsolete *bug* bogy + *boo*]

bug bear (bug′ber′, bug′bar′), *n.* 1 bogy. 2 a difficulty, problem, or obstacle. 3 a pet hate

bug-eyed (bug′īd′), *adj.* SLANG. having eyes wide open and bulging, especially from wonder or excitement.

bug gy[1] (bug′ē), *n., pl.* **-gies.** U.S. 1 a light carriage, with or without a top, pulled by one horse and having a single large seat. 2 a baby's carriage. [origin uncertain]

bug gy[2] (bug′ē), *adj.,* **-gi er, -gi est.** 1 swarming with bugs. 2 SLANG. crazy.

bug house (bug′hous′), *n., pl.* **-hous es** (-hou′ziz), *adj.* SLANG. *—n.* asylum for lunatics. *—adj.* crazy.

bu gle (byü′gəl), *n., v.,* **-gled, -gling.** *—n.* a musical instrument like a small trumpet, made of brass or copper, and sometimes having keys or valves. Bugles are used in the military forces for sounding calls and orders, and for playing band music. *—v.i.* blow a bugle. *—v.t.* direct or summon by blowing on a bugle. [< Old French < Latin *buculus,* diminutive of *bos* ox; with reference to early hunting horns]

bu gler (byü′glər), *n.* 1 person who plays a bugle. 2 soldier who gives signals with a bugle.

bu gloss (byü′glos, byü′glôs), *n.* a European plant of the same family as the borage, with bristly leaves and stems and blue flowers. [< Middle French *buglosse*]

buhl (bül), *n.* wood inlaid with elaborate patterns of tortoise shell, ivory, brass, white metal, and other materials, used for furniture. Also, **boulle.** [< German *Buhl* < French *boulle* < André C. *Boulle,* 1642-1732, French cabinetmaker]

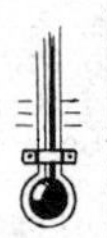

bulb—lily bulb (def. 1); thermometer bulb (def. 4); electric light bulb (def. 5)

build (bild), *v.,* **built** or (ARCHAIC) **build ed, build ing,** *n.* *—v.t.* 1 make (a more or less permanent structure) by putting materials together; construct: *Men build houses, bridges, ships, and machines.* 2 form or establish gradually; develop: *build a business, build an empire.* 3 establish on some foundation; base: *A lawyer builds his case on facts.* 4 **build up, a** form gradually; develop: *The firm has built up a wide reputation for fair dealing.* **b** fill with houses: *The hill overlooking the town has been built up in the last five years.* **c** increase or strengthen: *You must rest to build up your health.* *—v.i.* 1 follow the business of constructing buildings; make a structure: *He builds for a living.* 2 accept as a basis for argument, planning, or acting; reply; depend: *We can build on her honesty.* *—n.* form, style, or manner in which something is put together; structure: *An elephant has a heavy build.* [Old English *byldan* < *bold* dwelling]

build ed (bil′did), *v.* ARCHAIC. a pt. and a pp. of **build.**

build er (bil′dər), *n.* 1 person or animal that builds. 2 person whose business is constructing buildings or other structures.

build ing (bil′ding), *n.* 1 structure to house people, goods, machinery, or the like, such as a house, factory, barn, or store. See synonym study below. 2 business, art, or process of

hat, āge, fär; let, ēqual, tėrm;
it, īce; hot, ōpen, ôrder;
oil, out; cup, pu̇t, rüle;
ch, child; ng, long; sh, she;
th, thin; ᴛʜ, then; zh, measure;

ə represents *a* in about, *e* in taken,
i in pencil, *o* in lemon, *u* in circus.

< = from, derived from, taken from.

making houses, stores, bridges, ships, etc. **Syn.** 1 **Building, edifice, structure** mean something constructed. **Building,** the general word, has a wide range of uses because it does not suggest purpose, size, materials, etc.: *From the hill we could see the buildings in the city.* **Edifice** is a formal word, suggesting a large amd imposing building: *The cathedral is a handsome edifice.* **Structure** emphasizes the type of construction: *The new library is a fireproof structure.*

build-up (bild′up′), *n.* 1 an increasing of strength, size, rate, etc.: *a military build-up, a build-up of pressure.* 2 publicity to develop interest in a person, commodity, or the like: *The play has had a big build-up in the press.*

built (bilt), *v.* a pt. and a pp. of **build.**

built-in (bilt′in′), *adj.* 1 included in or provided for as part of the plan or design of anything; not movable or removable: *A built-in bookcase was fitted into one corner.* 2 having as a part of one's nature, or as an integral part: *a built-in sense of humor.*

Bu jum bur a (bü′jəm bu̇r′ə), *n.* capital of Burundi. 100,000. Also, **Usumbura.**

bulb (bulb), *n.* 1 a round, underground bud from which certain plants such as onions, tulips, and lilies grow. 2 any plant that has a bulb or grows from a bulb. The narcissus is a bulb. 3 the thick part of an underground stem resembling a bulb; tuber or corm: *a crocus bulb.* 4 any object with a rounded end or swelling part: *the bulb of a thermometer.* 5 the glass container surrounding the filament of an incandescent electric lamp or the electrodes of a fluorescent lamp. 6 an electron tube. 7 the medulla oblongata. [< Latin *bulbus* < Greek *bolbos*] **—bulb′less,** *adj.* **—bulb′like′,** *adj.*

bulb ar (bul′bər), *adj.* having to do with a bulb, especially the medulla oblongata: *bulbar poliomyelitis.*

bul bil (bul′bəl), *n.* an aerial bud with fleshy scales, growing in the leaf axils or taking the place of flowers. [< New Latin *bulbillus* < Latin *bulbus* bulb]

bulb ous (bul′bəs), *adj.* 1 shaped like a bulb; rounded and swelling: *a bulbous nose.* 2 having bulbs; growing from bulbs: *Daffodils are bulbous plants.*

bul bul (bu̇l′bu̇l), *n.* songbird of southern Asia and Africa, often mentioned in Persian poetry, of the same family as the thrush. [< Persian, nightingale < Arabic]

Bul gar (bul′gär, bu̇l′gär), *n.* Bulgarian.

Bul gar i a (bul ger′ē ə, bu̇l ger′ē ə), *n.* country in SE Europe, on the Black Sea. 8,467,000 pop.; 39,900 sq. mi. *Capital:* Sofia. See **Balkan States** for map.

Bul gar i an (bul ger′ē ən, bu̇l ger′ē ən), *adj.* of or having to do with Bulgaria, its people, or their language. *—n.* 1 native or inhabitant of Bulgaria. 2 the Slavic language of Bulgaria.

bulge (bulj), *v.,* **bulged, bulg ing,** *n.* *—v.i.*

swell outward; protrude: *My pockets bulged with candy.* —*v.t.* cause to swell outward: *The candy bulged my pockets.* —*n.* 1 an outward swelling; protuberance: *The force of the water caused a bulge in the dam.* 2 a temporary increase: *The graph shows a bulge in the birth rate.* [< Old French *boulge* bag < Latin *bulga*]

bul gur (bu̇l′gu̇r), *n.* a cereal food prepared from cracked wheat, eaten in the Middle East. [< Turkish]

bulg y (bul′jē), *adj.,* **bulg i er, bulg i est.** having a bulge or bulges. **—bulg′i ness,** *n.*

bulk (bulk), *n.* 1 size, especially large size: *An elephant has great bulk.* See **size**[1] for synonym study. 2 the largest part; main mass: *The oceans form the bulk of the earth's surface.* 3 **in bulk, a** transported or sold loose or by volume, not in packages, bottles, etc.: *In most markets you can buy fresh fruit in bulk.* **b** in large quantities: *Grain goes to the mill in bulk.* —*v.i.* 1 have size; be of importance. 2 grow large; swell. [< Scandinavian (Old Icelandic) *bulki* heap]

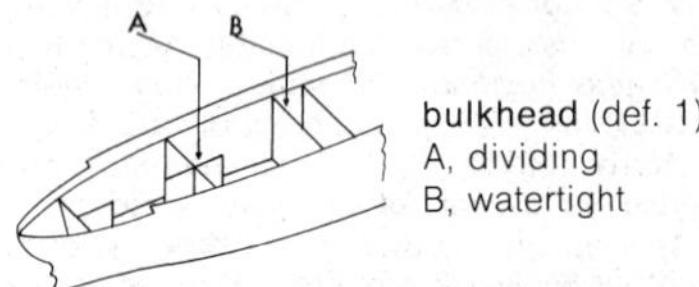

bulkhead (def. 1)
A, dividing
B, watertight

bulk head (bulk′hed′), *n.* 1 one of the upright partitions dividing a ship into compartments. 2 wall or partition built in a tunnel, conduit, etc., to hold back water, earth, rocks, air, etc. 3 a boxlike structure covering the top of a staircase or other opening. 4 a horizontal or inclined door leading from the outside of a house to the cellar.

bulk y (bul′kē), *adj.,* **bulk i er, bulk i est.** 1 taking up much space; large: *a bulky package.* 2 hard to handle; clumsy; unwieldy. **—bulk′i ly,** *adv.* **—bulk′i ness,** *n.*

bull[1] (bu̇l), *n.* 1 the uncastrated full-grown male of cattle. 2 **take the bull by the horns,** deal bravely and directly with a dangerous or difficult situation. 3 the male of the whale, elephant, seal, walrus, and other large mammals. 4 person whose size or loudness resembles that of a bull. 5 person who believes that prices, especially stock market prices, will rise, tries to raise prices, or buys stocks, bonds, commodities, etc., in the hope of rising prices. 6 U.S. SLANG. policeman. 7 SLANG. foolish talk; nonsense. 8 a bulldog. —*adj.* 1 male: *a bull moose.* 2 like a bull; large and strong. 3 roaring. —*v.t.* get by force; push: *bull one's way through a crowded street.* [Old English *bula*]

bull[2] (bu̇l), *n.* a formal announcement or official decree from the pope. [< Medieval Latin *bulla* < Latin, amulet, bubble]

bull[3] (bu̇l), *n.* an absurd and amusing mistake in language, especially one that is self-contradictory. EXAMPLE: If you don't receive this letter, write and let me know. [Middle English, falsehood]

bull., bulletin.

bull dog (bu̇l′dôg′, bu̇l′dog′), *n., adj., v.,* **-dogged, -dog ging.** —*n.* any of a breed of bold and fierce dogs, having a large head, short muzzle, strong muscular body of medium height, strong jaws, and short, smooth hair. —*adj.* like a bulldog's: *bulldog courage.* —*v.t.* (in the western United States) throw (a steer) to the ground by grasping its horns and twisting its neck.

bull doze (bu̇l′dōz′), *v.t.,* **dozed, -doz ing.** 1 INFORMAL. frighten, sometimes by violence or threats; bully. 2 move, clear, dig, or level with a bulldozer.

bull doz er (bu̇l′dō′zər), *n.* U.S. 1 a powerful crawler tractor with a wide, curved steel blade that moves rocks, earth, trees, brush, etc., used for grading, road building, clearing land, etc. 2 INFORMAL. person who bullies another, sometimes by violence or threats.

bul let (bu̇l′it), *n.* a shaped piece of lead, steel, or other metal to be shot from a pistol, rifle, or other small gun. [< Middle French *boulette,* diminutive of *boule* ball]

bul le tin (bu̇l′ə tən), *n.* 1 a short statement or account of late news or events, issued for the information of the public, especially by an authority: *a weather bulletin. Doctors issued a bulletin about the condition of the wounded president.* 2 magazine or newspaper appearing regularly, especially one published by a club or society for its members. [< Middle French < Italian *bullettino,* diminutive of *bulla* bull[2]]

bulletin board, board on which notices are posted.

bul let proof (bu̇l′it prüf′), *adj.* made so that a bullet cannot go through; resistant to bullets: *a bulletproof vest.*

bull fiddle, INFORMAL. contrabass.

bull fight (bu̇l′fīt′), *n.* fight between men and a bull in an arena, popular in Spain, Portugal, and parts of Latin America.

bull fight er (bu̇l′fī′tər), *n.* man who fights a bull in an arena.

bull fight ing (bu̇l′fī′ting), *n.* act or ritual of fighting a bull in an arena.

bull finch (bu̇l′finch′), *n.* a European and Asiatic songbird with a blue and gray back and light-red breast and a short, stout bill.

bull frog (bu̇l′frog′, bu̇l′frôg′), *n.* any of various large frogs of North America that make a loud, croaking noise.

bull head (bu̇l′hed′), *n.* 1 any of various American catfishes which have large, broad heads. 2 a stupid fellow.

bull head ed (bu̇l′hed′id), *adj.* stupidly stubborn; obstinate. **—bull′head′ed ly,** *adv.* **—bull′head′ed ness,** *n.*

bull horn (bu̇l′hôrn′), *n.* U.S. SLANG. 1 loudspeaker. 2 an electronic megaphone.

bul lion (bu̇l′yən), *n.* gold or silver in the form of ingots or bars. [< Anglo-French < Old French *bouillir* to boil; influenced by Old French *billon* debased metal]

bull ish (bu̇l′ish), *adj.* 1 like a bull in manner or temper. 2 trying or tending to raise prices in the stock market, etc. 3 optimistic. **—bull′ish ly,** *adv.* **—bull′ish ness,** *n.*

bull-mas tiff (bu̇l′mas′tif), *n.* a powerful, agile dog with a dense coat, a cross between a bulldog and a mastiff.

Bull Moose, member of the Progressive Party led by Theodore Roosevelt in the presidential election of 1912.

bull necked (bu̇l′nekt′), *adj.* having a thick neck.

bumblebee
about
life size

bull ock (bu̇l′ək), *n.* 1 a castrated bull; ox; steer. 2 (originally) a young bull. [Old English *bulluc* bull calf]

bull pen (bu̇l′pen′), *n.* a place outside the playing limits in which baseball relief pitchers warm up during a game.

bull ring (bu̇l′ring′), *n.* arena for bullfights.

Bull Run, stream in NE Virginia where two Civil War battles took place in 1861 and 1862. Both times the Confederate army defeated the Union army.

bull session, SLANG. a frank, informal discussion about any vitally interesting topic.

bull's-eye (bu̇lz′ī′), *n.* 1 center of a target. 2 shot that hits it. 3 any act or remark that successfully accomplishes its purpose. 4 a thick disk or hemispherical piece of glass in the deck or side of a ship to let in light. 5 a lens shaped like a half-sphere to concentrate light. 6 a small lantern with such a lens in its side. 7 (in architecture) any circular opening for light or air.

bull terrier, a strong, active, short-haired dog, developed from a cross between a bulldog and a terrier.

bull whip (bu̇l′hwip′, bu̇l′wip′), *n.* a long, heavy leather whip.

bul ly (bu̇l′ē), *n., pl.* **-lies,** *v.,* **-lied, -ly ing,** *adj.,* **-li er, -li est,** *interj.* —*n.* person who teases, frightens, threatens, or hurts smaller or weaker people. —*v.t.* frighten (into doing something) by noisy talk or threats; intimidate. —*v.i.* be a bully; be overbearing. —*adj.* INFORMAL. first-rate; excellent. —*interj.* INFORMAL. bravo! well done! [earlier, swashbuckler < Middle Dutch *boele* lover, brother]

bully beef, canned or pickled beef. [*bully* < French *bouilli* boiled beef]

bul ly rag (bu̇l′ē rag′), *v.t.,* **-ragged, -ragging.** INFORMAL. 1 attack with abusive language; bully. 2 tease.

bul rush (bu̇l′rush′), *n.* 1 any of a genus of tall, slender sedges that grows in or near water. 2 BRITISH. cattail. 3 (in the Bible) the papyrus of Egypt. [Middle English *bulrysche*]

bul wark (bu̇l′wərk), *n.* 1 person, thing, or idea that is a defense or protection. 2 wall of earth or other material for defense against an enemy; rampart. 3 breakwater. 4 Usually, **bulwarks,** *pl.* side of a ship extending like a fence above the deck. —*v.t.* 1 defend; protect. 2 provide with a bulwark or bulwarks. [Middle English *bulwerk*]

Bul wer-Lyt ton (bu̇l′wər lit′n), *n.* **Edward George,** 1803-1873, first Baron Lytton, English novelist, dramatist, and politician.

bum (bum), *n., v.,* **bummed, bum ming,** *adj.,* **bum mer, bum mest.** INFORMAL. —*n.* 1 an idle or dissolute person; loafer. 2 tramp; hobo. 3 a drunken spree. 4 **on the bum,** not functioning; out of order. —*v.t.* get (food, money, etc.) by sponging on others; beg: *bum a ride.* —*v.i.* 1 loaf around; idle about. 2 drink heavily. 3 sponge on others; beg. —*adj.* 1 of poor quality; worthless. 2 physically depressed. [short for earlier *bummer* loafer < German *Bummler*] **—bum′mer,** *n.*

bum ble (bum′bəl), *n., v.,* **-bled, -bling.** —*n.* an awkward mistake. —*v.i.* act in a bungling or awkward way. —*v.t.* do (something) in a clumsy, foolish way; bungle; botch. [origin uncertain]

bum ble bee (bum′bəl bē′), *n.* any of various large bees with thick, hairy bodies usually banded with gold, that live in small colonies in underground nests, old logs, etc., and make a loud, buzzing sound; humblebee.

bump (bump), *v.i.* 1 push, throw, or strike against something large or solid. 2 move by bumping against things: *Our car bumped along the rough road.* —*v.t.* 1 hit or come against heavily: *That truck bumped our car.* 2 U.S. INFORMAL. oust and take the place of (someone) on an airplane, in a job, etc., by exercising a higher priority, greater seniority, etc. 3 **bump into,** INFORMAL. meet by chance. 4 **bump off,** SLANG. kill. —*n.* 1 a heavy blow or knock. 2 a swelling caused by a bump. 3 any swelling or lump. 4 jolt or upward thrust of an airplane due to a rising current of air. [imitative]

bump er (bum′pər), *n.* 1 any device that protects against damage from bumping. 2 bar or bars of metal across the front and back of a car, bus, or truck that protect it from being damaged if bumped. 3 person or thing that bumps. 4 cup or glass filled to the brim. 5 INFORMAL. something unusually large of its kind. —*adj.* unusually large: *a bumper crop.*

bump kin (bump′kən), *n.* an awkward or naive person from the country. [perhaps < Middle Dutch *bommekyn* little barrel]

bump tious (bump′shəs), *adj.* unpleasantly assertive or conceited; arrogant and quarrelsome. [< *bump*] —**bump′tious ly,** *adv.* —**bump′tious ness,** *n.*

bump y (bum′pē), *adj.*, **bump i er, bump i est.** 1 having bumps; full of bumps: *a bumpy road.* 2 causing bumps; rough: *a bumpy ride.* —**bump′i ly,** *adv.* —**bump′i ness,** *n.*

bun (bun), *n.* 1 a small roll, often slightly sweetened and containing spice, raisins, etc. 2 hair coiled in the shape of a bun. [Middle English *bunne*]

bu na (bü′nə, byü′nə), *n.* a synthetic rubber made from butadiene, used in making automobile tires, etc. [< *bu(tadiene)* + *Na,* symbol for sodium]

bunch (bunch), *n.* 1 group of things of the same kind growing, fastened, placed, or thought of together: *a bunch of grapes, a bunch of sheep.* See **bundle** for synonym study. 2 INFORMAL. group of people: *They are a friendly bunch.* —*v.i.* come together in one place: *The sheep bunched in the shed to keep warm.* —*v.t.* bring together and make into a bunch. [probably < Old French *bonge* bundle] —**bunch′er,** *n.*

➔ **bunch.** Formal English limits the use of *bunch* to objects that grow together or can be fastened together: *a bunch of radishes, a bunch of flowers, a bunch of keys.* Informal English, however, clings to the older usage of *bunch,* applying it to a small collection of anything—including people: *A bunch of us met at the gym today for practice.*

Bunche (bunch), *n.* **Ralph Johnson,** 1904-1971, American educator and diplomat, winner of a Nobel Peace Prize in 1950.

bunch y (bun′chē), *adj.*, **bunch i er, bunch i est.** 1 having bunches. 2 growing in bunches. —**bunch′i ly,** *adv.* —**bunch′i ness,** *n.*

bun co (bung′kō), *n.*, *pl.* **-cos,** *v.* —*n.* 1 SLANG. a swindle or confidence game. —*v.t.* swindle. Also, **bunko.** [apparently < American Spanish *banca, banco* a card game < Italian *banca* bank]

bun combe (bung′kəm), *n.* bunkum.

Bund (bu̇nd; *German* bu̇nt), *n.* a former organization in the United States of persons with Nazi sympathies. [< German, association, society]

Bun des rat (bu̇n′dəs rät), *n.* the upper house of the federal legislature in West Germany.

Bun des tag (bu̇n′dəs täk), *n.* the lower house of the federal legislature in West Germany.

Bun des wehr (bu̇n′dəs vār′), *n.* the federal defense forces of West Germany.

bun dle (bun′dl), *n.*, *v.*, **-dled, -dling.** —*n.* 1 number of things tied or wrapped together. See synonym study below. 2 parcel; package. 3 number of things considered together; group; bunch. 4 group of muscle or nerve fibers bound closely together. —*v.t.* 1 wrap or tie together; make into a bundle. 2 send in a hurry; hustle: *The children were bundled off to school.* —*v.i.* 1 conduct a courtship, fully dressed, in bed, as in New England in colonial days. 2 go or leave in a hurry. 3 **bundle up,** dress warmly. [perhaps < Middle Dutch *bondel*] —**bun′dler,** *n.*

Syn. *n.* 1 **Bundle, bunch, parcel** mean a thing or things arranged for convenient handling. **Bundle** describes things of the same or different sizes and shapes bound or wrapped together, often clumsily: *We gave away several bundles of old newspapers and magazines.* **Bunch** describes things of the same kind bound together, usually closely and neatly: *I bought a bunch of flowers.* **Parcel** suggests one or more things wrapped and tied neatly for carrying or mailing: *I had too many parcels to carry on the bus.*

bung (bung), *n.* 1 stopper for closing the hole in the side or end of a barrel, keg, or cask. 2 bunghole. —*v.t.* 1 close the opening of with a bung. 2 **bung up,** **a** close with a stopper. **b** stop up; choke up. **c** SLANG. bruise. [probably < Middle Dutch *bonghe*]

bun ga low (bung′gə lō), *n.* a small house, usually of one story or a story and a half, with low, sweeping lines. [< Hindustani *banglā* of Bengal]

bun gee (bun′jē), *n.* a tension device, such as a set of springs, an elastic cable, or a rubber cord, used in an aircraft to assist in moving the controls. [origin unknown]

bung hole (bung′hōl′), *n.* hole in the side or end of a barrel, keg, or cask through which it is filled and emptied.

bun gle (bung′gəl), *v.*, **-gled, -gling,** *n.* —*v.t.* do or make (something) in a clumsy, unskillful way. —*n.* a clumsy, unskillful performance or piece of work. [imitative] —**bun′gler,** *n.* —**bun′gling ly,** *adv.*

bun ion (bun′yən), *n.* a painful, inflamed swelling on the foot, especially on the first joint of the big toe. [origin uncertain]

bunk[1] (bungk), *n.* 1 a narrow bed, one of two or more stacked one above another. 2 any place to sleep. —*v.i.* 1 sleep in a bunk; occupy a bunk. 2 sleep in rough quarters: *We bunked in a deserted house.* [origin uncertain]

bunk[2] (bungk), *n.* SLANG. insincere talk; nonsense; humbug. [short for *bunkum*]

bunk er (bung′kər), *n.* 1 place or bin for coal or oil, especially on a ship. 2 a sandy hollow or mound of earth on a golf course, forming an obstacle. 3 a fortified shelter, often part of a larger fortification, built partly or entirely below ground.

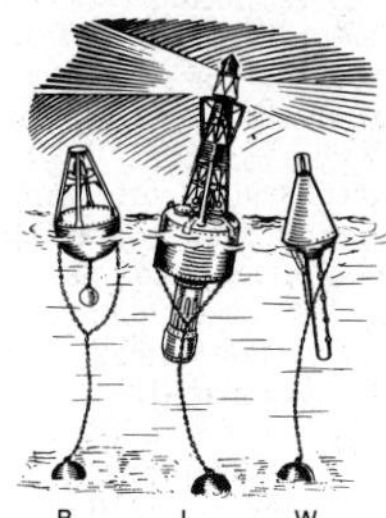

buoy (def. 1)
B, bell buoy
L, light buoy
W, whistle buoy

hat, āge, fär; let, ēqual, tėrm;
it, īce; hot, ōpen, ôrder;
oil, out; cup, pu̇t, rüle;
ch, child; ng, long; sh, she;
th, thin; ᴛʜ, then; zh, measure;

ə represents *a* in about, *e* in taken, *i* in pencil, *o* in lemon, *u* in circus.

< = from, derived from, taken from.

Bunker Hill, hill near Boston, Massachusetts, close to the site of an early battle of the Revolutionary War which took place on Breed's Hill, June 17, 1775.

bunk house (bungk′hous′), *n.*, *pl.* **-hous es** (-hou′ziz). a rough building with sleeping quarters or bunks, especially one provided for workers on a ranch, at a construction camp, etc.

bun ko (bung′kō), *n.*, *pl.* **-kos,** *v.t.* bunco.

bun kum (bung′kəm), *n.* insincere talk; nonsense; humbug. Also, **buncombe.** [alteration of *buncombe* < *Buncombe* County, North Carolina, whose congressman in 1819-1821 kept making long-winded and pointless speeches "for Buncombe"]

bun ny (bun′ē), *n.*, *pl.* **-nies.** a pet name for a rabbit. [perhaps < Scottish *bun* tail of a hare]

Bun sen burner (bun′sən), a gas burner with a very hot, blue flame, used in laboratories. Air is let in at the base and mixed with gas. [< Robert *Bunsen,* 1811-1899, German chemist, who invented it]

bunt[1] (bunt), *v.i.*, *v.t.* 1 push or tap (a baseball) lightly without a full swing of the bat so that it goes only a short distance. 2 strike with the head or horns, as a goat does; butt. 3 push; shove. —*n.* 1 act of bunting a baseball. 2 baseball that is bunted. 3 a push; shove. [perhaps variant of *butt*[3]] —**bunt′er,** *n.*

bunt[2] (bunt), *n.* the central, bellying part of a square sail. [origin uncertain]

bunt[3] (bunt), *n.* disease of wheat in which a parasitic fungus turns the kernels into foul-smelling black spores. [origin uncertain]

bun ting[1] (bun′ting), *n.* 1 a thin, loosely woven woolen or cotton cloth used for making flags and for patriotic decorations. 2 long pieces of cloth having the colors and designs of a flag, used to decorate buildings and streets on holidays and special occasions. 3 a baby's warm, hooded outer garment closed at the bottom. [perhaps Middle English *bonten* to sift (because the cloth was used for sifting)]

bun ting[2] (bun′ting), *n.* any of several small, usually brightly colored birds with stout bills, of the same family as the finches. [origin unknown]

bunt line (bunt′lən, bunt′līn′), *n.* rope fastened to the bottom of a sail, used to haul the sail up to the yard for furling. [< *bunt*[2]]

Bun yan (bun′yən), *n.* 1 **John,** 1628-1688, English clergyman and religious writer who wrote *Pilgrim's Progress.* 2 **Paul,** (in American folklore) a giant lumberjack with amazing strength.

Buo na par te (bwô′nä pär′tā), *n.* Bonaparte.

buoy (boi, bü′ē), *n.* 1 a floating object anchored on the water to warn against hidden rocks or shallows or to indicate the safe part of a channel. 2 life buoy. —*v.t.* 1 furnish with buoys; mark with a buoy. 2 **buoy up, a** hold up; keep from sinking. **b** support or encourage. [< Old French *boie* chain, fetter < Latin *boiae*]

buoy an cy (boi′ən sē, bü′yən sē), *n.* 1 power to float: *Balsa has more buoyancy than oak.* 2 power to keep things afloat: *Salt water has greater buoyancy than fresh water.* 3 a body's loss in weight when immersed in a fluid. 4 tendency to rise. 5 tendency to be hopeful and cheerful; light-heartedness: *Her buoyancy kept us from being downhearted.*

buoy ant (boi′ənt, bü′yənt), *adj.* 1 able to float: *Wood and cork are buoyant in water; iron and lead are not.* 2 able to keep things afloat: *Air is buoyant; helium-filled balloons float in it.* 3 tending to rise. 4 cheerful and hopeful; light-hearted: *Children are usually more buoyant than adults.* **—buoy′ant ly,** *adv.*

bur (bėr), *n., v.,* **burred, bur ring.** *—n.* 1 a prickly, clinging seedcase or flower of some plants. 2 plant or weed bearing burs. 3 person or thing that clings like a bur. —*v.t.* remove burs from. Also, **burr.** [probably < Scandinavian (Danish) *borre* burdock]

Bur bank (bėr′bangk), *n.* 1 **Luther,** 1849-1926, American naturalist who bred new varieties of plants. 2 city in S California. 89,000.

bur ble (bėr′bəl), *v.i.,* **-bled, -bling.** 1 make a bubbling noise. 2 speak in a confused, excited manner. [probably imitative]

bur bly (bėr′blē), *adj.* 1 full of bubbles; bubbly. 2 turbulent.

bur bot (bėr′bət), *n., pl.* **-bots** or **-bot.** a freshwater fish with an elongated, slender body, of the same family as the cod; eelpout. [< Middle French *bourbotte*]

bur den[1] (bėrd′n), *n.* 1 something carried; load (of things, care, work, duty, or sorrow). See **load** for synonym study. 2 a load too heavy to carry easily; heavy load: *Your debts are a burden that will bankrupt you.* 3 quantity of freight that a ship can carry; weight of a ship's cargo. —*v.t.* 1 put a burden on; load. 2 load too heavily; weigh down; oppress: *She was burdened with worries.* [Old English *byrthen.* Related to BEAR[1].]

bur den[2] (bėrd′n), *n.* 1 the main idea or message: *The way to achieve peace was the burden of the President's speech.* 2 a repeated verse in a song; chorus; refrain. [< Old French *bourdon* a humming, drone of a bagpipe]

burden of proof, obligation to establish a fact by proof.

bur den some (bėrd′n səm), *adj.* hard to bear; very heavy; oppressive: *The President's many duties are burdensome.* See **heavy** for synonym study. **—bur′den some ly,** *adv.* **—bur′den some ness,** *n.*

bur dock (bėr′dok′), *n.* a coarse weed of the composite family, with burs and broad leaves. [< *bur* + *dock*[4]]

bur eau (byu̇r′ō), *n., pl.* **bur eaus, bur eaux** (byu̇r′ōz). 1 chest of drawers for clothes, often having a mirror; dresser. 2 BRITISH. desk or writing table with drawers. 3 office for transacting business, giving out information, etc.: *a travel bureau.* 4 a division within a government department: *The United States Weather Bureau makes daily reports on weather conditions.* [< French, desk (originally cloth-covered) < Old French *burel,* diminutive of *bure* coarse woolen cloth < Late Latin *burra*]

bu reauc ra cy (byu̇ rok′rə sē), *n., pl.* **-cies.** 1 system of government by groups of officials, each dealing with its own kind of business under the direction of its chief. 2 the officials running government bureaus. 3 concentration of power in administrative bureaus. 4 excessive insistence on rigid routine, resulting in delay in making decisions or in carrying out requests; red tape.

bur eau crat (byu̇r′ə krat), *n.* 1 official in a bureaucracy. 2 a government official who insists on rigid routine. [< *bureau* + *(auto)crat*]

bur eau crat ic (byu̇r′ə krat′ik), *adj.* 1 having to do with a bureaucracy or a bureaucrat. 2 arbitrary. **—bur′eau crat′i cal ly,** *adv.*

bu rette or **bu ret** (byu̇ ret′), *n.* a graduated glass tube, usually with a tap at the bottom. It is used for accurately measuring out small amounts of a liquid or gas. [< French *burette*]

burg (bėrg), *n.* INFORMAL. town or city. Also, **burgh.** [variant of *borough*]

bur gee (bėr′jē), *n.* a small, swallow-tailed flag or pennant, used on merchant ships and yachts. [origin uncertain]

bur geon (bėr′jən), *v.i.* 1 grow or shoot forth; bud; sprout. 2 grow or develop rapidly; flourish: *New suburbs have burgeoned all around the city.* *—n.* a bud; sprout. [< Old French *burjon* a bud]

Bur ger (bėr′gər), *n.* **Warren Earl,** born 1907, chief justice of the United States Supreme Court since 1969.

bur gess (bėr′jis), *n.* 1 member of the lower house of the colonial legislature in Virginia or Maryland. 2 citizen of an English borough. [< Old French *burgeis* < Late Latin *burgensis* citizen. Doublet of BOURGEOIS.]

burgh (bėrg, bėr′ō), *n.* 1 a chartered town in Scotland. 2 burg. [Scottish variant of *borough*]

burgh er (bėr′gər), *n.* citizen of a burgh or town; citizen.

bur glar (bėr′glər), *n.* person who breaks into a house or other building, usually at night, to steal or commit some other crime. [< Anglo-French *burglour*]

bur glar ize (bėr′glə rīz′), *v.t.,* **-ized, -iz ing.** INFORMAL. break into (a building) to steal.

bur glar y (bėr′glər ē), *n., pl.* **-glar ies.** a breaking into a house or other building, usually at night, to steal or commit some other crime.

bur gle (bėr′gəl), *v.t.,* **-gled, -gling.** SLANG. burglarize.

bur go mas ter (bėr′gə mas′tər), *n.* mayor of a town in Austria, Belgium, Germany, or the Netherlands. [< Dutch *burgemeester* < *burg* borough + *meester* master]

Bur goyne (bər goin′, bėr′goin), *n.* **John,** 1722-1792, British general. His surrender at Saratoga in 1777 marked the turning point of the Revolutionary War.

Bur gun dy (bėr′gən dē), *n., pl.* **-dies** for 2, 3. 1 region in E France. Once an independent kingdom, it became a duchy and later a province of France. 2 a red or white wine made there. 3 any of certain similar wines made elsewhere. **—Bur gun di an** (bər gun′dē ən), *adj., n.*

bur i al (ber′ē əl), *n.* act of putting a dead body in a grave, in a tomb, or in the sea; burying. *—adj.* having to do with burying: *a burial service.* [Middle English *biriel* < *biriels* (understood as a plural form), Old English *byrgels* burying ground]

bur ied (ber′ēd), *v.* pt. and pp. of **bury.** *The dog buried his bone.*

bu rin (byu̇r′in), *n.* an engraver's pointed steel tool for cutting. [< French < Italian *burine*]

Burke (bėrk), *n.* **Edmund,** 1729-1797, British statesman and orator, born in Ireland.

burl (bėrl), *n.* 1 a small knot or lump in wool or cloth. 2 a large knot in maple, walnut, and some other woods. —*v.t.* dress (cloth), especially by removing knots and lumps. [< Old French *bourle* < Late Latin *burra* coarse wool]

bur lap (bėr′lap), *n.* a coarse fabric made from jute or hemp, often used to make bags for farm and factory products. A superior grade of burlap is used for curtains, wall coverings, upholstery, and clothing. [origin uncertain]

bur lesque (bər lesk′), *n., v.,* **-lesqued, -les quing,** *adj.* *—n.* 1 a literary or dramatic composition that treats a serious subject ridiculously or a trivial subject as if it were important: *Mark Twain's story, "A Connecticut Yankee in King Arthur's Court," is a burlesque of the legends about King Arthur.* 2 kind of vaudeville characterized by coarse, vulgar comedy and dancing. 3 a ridiculous imitation of something worthy or dignified; mockery: *By taking bribes the judge made a burlesque of his high office.* —*v.t.* imitate so as to make fun of. *—adj.* making people laugh; comically imitative. [< French < Italian *burlesco* < *burla* jest] **—bur les′quer,** *n.*

bur ley or **Bur ley** (bėr′lē), *n., pl.* **-leys.** kind of thin-leaved tobacco grown widely in Kentucky and North Carolina. [< *Burley,* a proper name]

bur ly (bėr′lē), *adj.,* **-li er, -li est.** great in bodily size; big and strong; sturdy: *a burly wrestler.* [Middle English *burli,* earlier *burlich, borlich,* Old English *borlice* nobly] **—bur′li ly,** *adv.* **—bur′li ness,** *n.*

Bur ma (bėr′mə), *n.* country in SE Asia, on the Bay of Bengal. 27,584,000 pop.; 261,800 sq. mi. *Capital:* Rangoon.

Bur mese (bėr′mēz′), *n., pl.* **-mese,** *adj.* *—n.* 1 native or inhabitant of Burma. 2 the chief language of Burma. *—adj.* of Burma, its people, or their official language.

burn[1] (bėrn), *v.,* **burned** or **burnt, burn ing,** *n.* *—v.i.* 1 be on fire; be very hot; blaze; glow: *The campfire burned all night.* 2 be destroyed or suffer death by fire. 3 become injured, charred, singed, scorched, etc., by fire, heat, or acid. See synonym study below. 4 feel hot: *Your forehead burns with fever.* 5 be very excited or eager: *burning with enthusiasm.* 6 be inflamed with anger, passion, etc.: *burn with fury.* 7 give light: *Lamps*

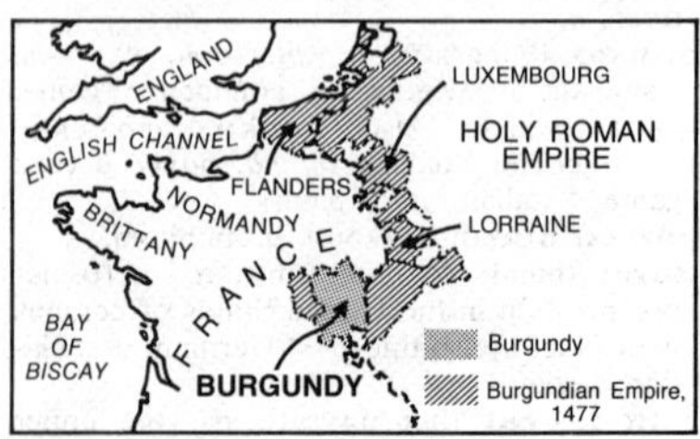

Burgundy (def. 1)

were burning in every room. 8 to sunburn: *My skin burns easily.* 9 (in chemistry) undergo combustion; oxidize rapidly. 10 (in nuclear physics) undergo fission or fusion. 11 (of a rocket engine) to fire or ignite. —*v.t.* 1 set on fire; cause to burn; ignite. 2 destroy by fire: *burn old papers.* 3 injure, char, singe, scorch, etc., by fire, heat, or acid: *I burned my hand on the hot iron.* See synonym study below. 4 make by fire, heat, or acid: *The cigar burned a hole in the rug.* 5 give a feeling of heat to: *Mustard and curry burn the tongue.* 6 inflame with anger, passion, etc. 7 produce, harden, glaze, etc., by fire or heat: *burn bricks, burn lime.* 8 use to produce heat: *Our furnace burns oil.* 9 use to produce energy: *burn uranium.* 10 (in chemistry) cause to undergo combustion; oxidize rapidly. 11 to sunburn: *The sun burned her face badly.* 12 cauterize.

burn down, **a** burn to the ground. **b** decrease in fuel or heat.

burn out, **a** destroy by burning. **b** cease to burn. **c** burn the inside of: *The warehouse was burned out.* **d** drive (a person) out by fire. **e** consume: *During the long race he burned out his brakes.*

burn up, **a** consume: *A large car burns up the gasoline.* **b** INFORMAL. make angry.

—*n.* 1 injury caused by fire, heat, or acid; burned place. 2 a sunburn. 3 **a** the firing of a rocket engine. **b** the period of firing.

[fusion of Old English *beornan* be on fire and Old English *bærnan* consume with fire] **—burn′a ble,** *adj.*

Syn. *v.i., v.t.* 3 **Burn, scorch, sear** mean to injure or be injured by fire, heat, or acid. **Burn,** the general word, suggests any degree of damage from slight injury to destruction: *The toast burned. I burned the toast.* **Scorch** means to burn the surface enough to discolor it, sometimes to damage the texture: *The cigarette scorched the paper. The blouse scorched because the iron was too hot.* **Sear** means to burn or scorch the surface by heat or acid enough to dry or harden it, and is applied particularly to burning the tissues of people or animals: *Wounds are seared to cauterize them. She seared the roast to brown it.*

➤ **burn.** The past tense and past participle of *burn* are either *burned* or *burnt. Burnt* is usual when the participle is used as an adjective: *The partially burnt papers gave them little help in solving the mystery.* Verb: *They hastily burned all the old letters before they left.*

burn[2] (bėrn), *n.* SCOTTISH. a small stream; brook. [Old English *burna*]

burn er (bėr′nər), *n.* 1 part of a lamp, stove, furnace, etc., from which the flame comes or where it is produced. 2 thing or part that burns or works by heat: *Some stoves are oil burners; others are gas burners.* 3 man whose work is burning something: *a charcoal burner.* 4 (in a jet engine) a combustion chamber.

burn ing (bėr′ning), *adj.* 1 glowing; hot. 2 vital or urgent: *a burning question.* **—burn′ing ly,** *adv.*

burning glass, a convex lens used to produce heat or set fire to a substance by focusing the sun's rays on it.

bur nish (bėr′nish), *v.t.* 1 make (metal) smooth and bright; polish (a surface) by rubbing until shiny: *burnish brass.* 2 make bright and glossy. —*n.* polish; luster. [< Old French *burniss-,* a form of *burnir* make brown, polish < *brun* brown] **—bur′nish er,** *n.*

burnoose
The burnoose consists of a piece of cloth which is draped about the head and body.

bur noose or **bur nous** (bər nüs′, bėr′nüs), *n.* a long cloak with a hood, worn by Moors and Arabs. [< French *burnous* < Arabic *burnus*]

burn out (bėrn′out′), *n.* 1 a failure due to burning or extreme heat. 2 in aerospace: **a** the dying out of the flame in a rocket engine as a result of its fuel being used up or intentionally shut off. **b** the time or position when such dying out occurs.

Burns (bėrnz), *n.* **Robert,** 1759-1796, Scottish poet.

burn sides or **Burn sides** (bėrn′sīdz), *n.pl.* sideburns, especially when long and heavy; muttonchops. [< Ambrose E. *Burnside,* 1824-1881, a Union general in the Civil War]

burnt (bėrnt), *v.* a pt. and a pp. of **burn**[1]. ➤ See **burn**[1] for usage note.

burn up (bėrn′up′), *n.* the consumption of fuel in a nuclear reactor.

burp (bėrp), INFORMAL. —*n.* a belch. —*v.i.* belch. —*v.t.* help (a baby) in the expulsion of gas from the stomach, as by patting on the back; cause to belch. [imitative]

burr[1] (bėr), *n.* 1 a bur. 2 a rough ridge or edge left by a tool on metal, wood, etc., after cutting, drilling, or punching it. 3 tool used by engravers, die makers, etc., to cut and shape metal. 4 tool with a head shaped like a bur, used by dentists in drilling. —*v.t.* bur. [variant of *bur*]

burr[2] (bėr), *n.* 1 a guttural or rough pronunciation of *r.* 2 a rough or dialectal pronunciation in which *r* sounds are prominent: *a Scottish burr.* 3 a whirring sound. —*v.i.* 1 pronounce *r* roughly. 2 make a whirring sound. —*v.t.* pronounce with a burr. [probably imitative]

Burr (bėr), *n.* **Aaron,** 1756-1836, American politician, vice-president of the United States from 1801 to 1805.

bur ro (bėr′ō, bůr′ō), *n., pl.* **-ros.** a donkey, usually a small one, used to carry loads or packs in the southwestern United States. [< Spanish < *burrico* small horse < Late Latin *buricus*]

Bur roughs (bėr′ōz), *n.* **John,** 1837-1921, American naturalist and writer.

bur row (bėr′ō), *n.* 1 hole dug in the ground by woodchucks, rabbits, and various other animals for refuge or shelter. 2 a similar dwelling, shelter, or refuge. —*v.i.* 1 dig a hole in the ground: *The mole quickly burrowed out of sight.* 2 live in burrows. 3 work a way into or under something: *She burrowed under the blankets.* 4 hide oneself. 5 search carefully or diligently: *She burrowed in the library for a book about Indian life.* —*v.t.* 1 make burrows in; dig: *Rabbits have burrowed the ground for miles around.* 2 hide in a burrow or something like a burrow: *The runaway burrowed himself in the haystack.* 3 make by burrowing: *Their dens are burrowed in the mountainside.* [Middle English variant of *borough*] **—bur′row er,** *n.*

hat, āge, fär; let, ēqual, tėrm;
it, īce; hot, ōpen, ôrder;
oil, out; cup, pu̇t, rüle;
ch, child; ng, long; sh, she;
th, thin; ᴛʜ, then; zh, measure;

ə represents *a* in about, *e* in taken, *i* in pencil, *o* in lemon, *u* in circus.

< = from, derived from, taken from.

bur sa (bėr′sə), *n., pl.* **-sae** (-sē′), **-sas.** sac of the body, especially one containing a lubricating fluid that reduces friction between a muscle or tendon and a bone; pouch or cavity. [< Medieval Latin, purse < Greek *byrsa* hide. Doublet of BOURSE, PURSE.]

bur sar (bėr′sər, bėr′sär), *n.* treasurer, especially of a college or university. [< Medieval Latin *bursarius* < *bursa.* See BURSA.]

bur sar y (bėr′sər ē), *n., pl.* **-sar ies.** 1 treasury, especially of a college or university. 2 a grant of money to a student at a college or university.

bur si tis (bər sī′tis), *n.* inflammation of a bursa, usually near the shoulder or hip.

burst (bėrst), *v.,* **burst, burst ing,** *n.* —*v.i.* 1 break in pieces from pressure; fly apart suddenly with force; explode: *The bomb burst.* 2 go, come, do, etc., by force or suddenly: *He burst into the room without knocking.* 3 be very full, as if ready to break open: *The barns were bursting with grain.* 4 give way; be about to give way from violent pain or emotion: *burst into tears.* 5 open or be opened suddenly or in full force: *The trees burst into bloom.* 6 act or change suddenly in a way suggesting a break or explosion: *She burst into loud laughter.* —*v.t.* 1 open suddenly or violently: *burst a lock, burst a door open.* 2 cause to break open or into pieces; shatter: *burst a blood vessel. The prisoner burst his chains.*

—*n.* 1 outbreak: *a burst of laughter.* 2 a sudden and violent issuing forth; sudden opening to view or sight. 3 a sudden display of activity or energy: *a burst of speed.* 4 act of bursting. 5 explosion of a shell, bomb, etc. 6 series of shots fired by one pressure on the trigger of an automatic weapon.

[Old English *berstan*]

bur then (bėr′ᴛʜən), *n., v.t.* ARCHAIC. burden[1].

Bu run di (bů rün′dē), *n.* country in central Africa, formerly part of Ruanda-Urundi. 3,500,000 pop.; 10,700 sq. mi. *Capital:* Bujumbura. See **Zaïre** for map.

bur y (ber′ē), *v.t.,* **bur ied, bur y ing.** 1 put (a dead body) in the earth, in a tomb, or in the sea. 2 perform a funeral service for. 3 cover up; hide: *The squirrels buried nuts under the dead leaves.* 4 absorb: *She buried herself in a book.* 5 forget: *I had long ago buried any memory of the accident.* 6 withdraw or cause to move to obscurity or retirement; *totally buried in the country.* [Old English *byrgan*] **—bur′i er,** *n.*

bus (bus), *n., pl.* **bus es** or **bus ses,** *v.,* **bused, bus ing** or **bussed, bus sing.** —*n.* 1 a large motor vehicle with seats inside and, formerly, also on the roof, used to carry many passengers between fixed stations along a certain route. 2 INFORMAL. an automobile or aircraft. —*v.t., v.i.* take or go by bus: *The city bused the children to school.*

They bus to work each morning. [short for *omnibus*]

bus., business.

bus boy (bus′boi′), *n.* a waiter's assistant, who brings bread and butter, fills glasses, carries off empty dishes, etc.

bus by (buz′bē), *n., pl.* **-bies.** a tall fur hat with a bag hanging from the top over the right side, worn by hussars and certain other corps in the British army. [probably < *Busby,* a proper name]

busby

bush (bu̇sh), *n.* 1 a woody plant smaller than a tree, often with many separate branches starting from or near the ground. Some bushes are used as hedges; others are cultivated for their fruit. 2 open forest or wild, unsettled land: *the bush of Australia.* 3 **beat around the bush,** approach a matter in a roundabout way; avoid coming straight to the point. —*v.i.* spread out like a bush; grow thickly. —*v.t.* cover with bushes. [Old English *busc* (found in place names)]

bush baby, galago.

bushed (bu̇sht), *adj.* INFORMAL. exhausted.

bush el (bu̇sh′əl), *n.* 1 unit of capacity for measuring grain, produce, and other dry things. It is equal to 4 pecks or 32 quarts. See **measure** for table. 2 container that holds a bushel. 3 INFORMAL. an indefinitely large quantity. [< Old French *boissiel,* diminutive of *boisse* a measure of grain]

Bu shi do or **bu shi do** (bü′shē dō), *n.* the moral code of the knights and warriors of feudal Japan; Japanese chivalry. [< Japanese < *bushi* warrior + *do* way]

bush ing (bu̇sh′ing), *n.* 1 a removable metal lining used to protect parts of machinery from wear. 2 a metal lining inserted in a hole, pipe, etc., to reduce its size. 3 a lining for a hole, to insulate one or more wires or other electrical conductors passing through. [< *bush* bushing < Middle Dutch *busse* box]

bush league, SLANG. 1 (in baseball) a minor league. 2 any insignificant or inexpert person, group, organization, etc.

bush man (bu̇sh′mən), *n., pl.* **-men.** 1 settler in the Australian bush. 2 **Bushman, a** member of a Kalahari Desert tribe of roving hunters who formerly lived in southern Africa. **b** language of this tribe.

bush mas ter (bu̇sh′mas′tər), *n.* the largest poisonous snake of Central and South America.

bush pilot, pilot who flies a small plane over relatively unsettled country, such as parts of Alaska and northern Canada.

bush whack (bu̇sh′hwak′), *v.i.* live or work in the bush or backwoods. —*v.t.* ambush or raid.

bush whack er (bu̇sh′hwak′ər), *n.* 1 person who lives or works in the bush or backwoods. 2 a guerrilla fighter.

bush y (bu̇sh′ē), *adj.,* **bush i er, bush i est.** 1 spreading out like a bush; growing thickly: *a bushy beard.* 2 overgrown with bushes. **—bush′i ness,** *n.*

bus i ly (biz′ə lē), *adv.* in a busy manner; actively.

busi ness (biz′nis), *n.* 1 one's particular occupation, profession, or trade; work: *A carpenter's business is building.* See **occupation** for synonym study. 2 action which requires time, attention, and labor: *Business comes before pleasure.* 3 **mean business,** INFORMAL. be in earnest; be serious: *When she says she is going to get good marks, she means business.* 4 matter; affair; concern: *I am tired of the whole business.* 5 activities of buying and selling; commercial dealings; trade: *This hardware store does a big business in tools.* 6 a commercial enterprise; industrial establishment: *They sold the bakery business for a million dollars.* 7 right to act; responsibility: *That is not your business.* 8 action in a play; thing done to make a play seem like real life. —*adj.* of or having to do with business: *A business office usually has typewriters and other business machines.* [Old English *bisignis* < *bisig* busy + *-nis* -ness]

business college, school that gives training in shorthand, typewriting, bookkeeping, and other commercial subjects.

business cycle, cycle of business activity of alternating stages of prosperity and recession or depression.

busi ness like (biz′nis līk′), *adj.* well-managed; practical.

business machine, a computer, duplicator, data-processing machine, or any other machine used in a business office to speed up operations.

busi ness man (biz′nis man′), *n., pl.* **-men.** 1 man in business, especially an executive. 2 man who runs a business.

busi ness wom an (biz′nis wu̇m′ən), *n., pl.* **-wom en.** 1 woman in business, especially an executive. 2 woman who runs a business.

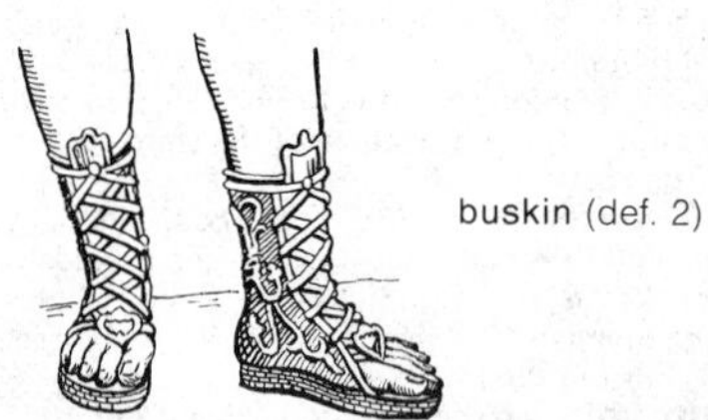
buskin (def. 2)

bus kin (bus′kən), *n.* 1 boot reaching to the calf or knee, worn in olden times. 2 a high shoe with a very thick sole, worn by Greek and Roman actors of tragedies. 3 tragic drama; tragedy. [perhaps < Old French *brousequin*]

bus man (bus′mən), *n., pl.* **-men.** conductor or driver of a bus.

bus man's holiday, holiday spent in doing what one does at one's daily work.

buss (bus), *v.t., v.i., n.* INFORMAL. kiss. [probably imitative]

bus ses (bus′iz), *n.* a pl. of **bus.**

bust[1] (bust), *n.* 1 piece of sculpture representing a person's head, shoulders, and upper chest. 2 the upper front part of the body. 3 a woman's bosom. [< French *buste* < Italian *busto* < Latin *bustum* funeral monument]

bust[2] (bust), SLANG. —*v.i.* 1 burst. 2 fail financially; become bankrupt. —*v.t.* 1 burst; break. 2 bankrupt; ruin. 3 punch; hit. 4 demote, especially as a punishment: *The corporal was busted to private.* 5 train to obey; tame: *bust a bronco.* 6 break up (a trust) into smaller companies. 7 arrest or jail. —*n.* 1 a burst. 2 a total failure; bankruptcy. 3 spree. [alteration of *burst*] **—bust′er,** *n.*

bus tard (bus′tərd), *n.* any of a family of large game birds with long legs and a heavy body, found on the dry, open plains of Africa, Europe, Asia, and Australia. [blend of Old French *bistarde* and *oustarde,* both < Latin *avis tarda* slow bird]

bus tle[1] (bus′əl), *v.,* **-tled, -tling,** *n.* —*v.i.* be noisily busy and in a hurry. —*v.t.* make (someone) hurry or work hard. —*n.* noisy or excited activity; commotion. See **stir**[1] for synonym study. [perhaps imitative] **—bus′tler,** *n.*

bustle[2]

bus tle[2] (bus′əl), *n.* (formerly) a pad, cushion, or small wire frame used to puff out the upper back part of a woman's skirt. [origin unknown]

bus y (biz′ē), *adj.,* **bus i er, bus i est,** *v.,* **bus ied, bus y ing.** —*adj.* 1 having plenty to do; not idle; working; active: *The principal of our school is a busy person.* See synonym study below. 2 full of work or activity: *a busy day, a busy street.* 3 in use: *Her telephone line was busy.* 4 prying into other people's affairs; meddling: *That inquisitive woman is always busy.* 5 INFORMAL. having too much color, design, or ornament: *a busy drawing, busy decoration.* —*v.t.* make busy; keep busy: *The bees busied themselves at making honey.* —*v.i.* be busy; occupy oneself. [Old English *bisig*] **—bus′y ness,** *n.*

Syn. *adj.* 1 **Busy, industrious, diligent** mean actively or attentively occupied. **Busy** means working steadily or at the moment: *He is such a busy man, it is hard to get an appointment with him.* **Industrious** means hard-working by nature or habit: *Bees and ants are industrious workers.* **Diligent** means hard-working at a particular thing, usually something one likes or especially wants to do: *She is a diligent mother, but a poor housekeeper.*

bus y bod y (biz′ē bod′ē), *n., pl.* **-bod ies.** person who pries into other people's affairs; meddler.

bus y work (biz′ē wėrk′), *n.* work assigned or done merely to fill time or to appear to be busy.

but (but; *unstressed* bət), *conj.* 1 on the other hand; yet: *It rained, but I went anyway.* See synonym study below. 2 unless; except that: *It never rains but it pours.* 3 other than; otherwise than: *We cannot choose but listen.* 4 who not; which not: *None sought his aid but were helped.* 5 that not: *He is not so sick* *but he can eat.* 6 that: *I don't doubt but she will come.* 7 **but that,** were it not that: *I would have come but that I felt too ill.* 8 **but what,** but that. *—prep.* 1 except; save: *I work every day but Sunday.* 2 other than: *No one replied but me.* *—adv.* no more than; only; merely: *He is but a boy.* *—n.* objection: *Not so many buts, please.* [Old English *būtan* without, unless < *be-* by + *ūtan* outside < *ūt* out]

Syn. *conj.* 1 **But, however** express a relationship in which two things or ideas are thought of as standing in contrast to each other. **But** expresses the contrast clearly and sharply by placing the two things or ideas side by side in perfect balance: *He is sick, but he can eat.* **However** is more formal, and suggests that the second idea should be compared and contrasted with the first: *We have not yet reached a decision; however, our opinion of your plan is favorable.*

➤ **but.** Two clauses connected by *but* should ordinarily be separated by a comma. The contrast in idea suggests the use of punctuation even when the clauses are relatively short: *I couldn't see the license number, but it was a New York plate.*

bu ta di ene (byü′tə dī′ēn, byü′tə dī ēn′), *n.* a colorless gas derived from petroleum by-products, used in making synthetic rubber. *Formula:* C_4H_6

bu tane (byü′tān, byü tān′), *n.* a colorless gas, a hydrocarbon, produced in petroleum refining, and much used as a fuel. *Formula:* C_4H_{10} [< *but(yl)* + *-ane*]

butch er (bu̇ch′ər), *n.* 1 person who cuts up and sells meat. 2 person whose work is killing animals for food. 3 a brutal killer; murderer. 4 U.S. vendor; peddler, especially one who sells magazines, candy, etc. on trains. 5 INFORMAL. person who botches or bungles. *—v.t.* 1 kill (animals) for food. 2 kill (people, wild animals, or birds) needlessly, cruelly, or in large numbers. 3 kill brutally; murder. 4 spoil by poor work: *Don't butcher that song by singing off key.* [< Old French *bochier* one who slaughters he-goats < *boc* he-goat, buck[1]] **—butch′er er,** *n.*

butch er bird (bu̇ch′ər bėrd′), *n.* any of various large shrikes that fasten their prey on thorns.

butch er y (bu̇ch′ər ē), *n., pl.* **-er ies.** 1 brutal killing; murder in large numbers. 2 a slaughterhouse. 3 a butcher shop. 4 a butcher's work; cutting up and selling meat.

but ler (but′lər), *n.* the head male servant in a household, in charge of the pantry and table service. [< Anglo-French variant of Old French *bouteillier* < *bouteille* bottle. See BOTTLE.]

butler's pantry, a small room between the kitchen and dining room, for use by a butler, serving maid, etc.

butt[1] (but), *n.* 1 the thicker end of a tool, weapon, ham, etc.: *the butt of a gun.* 2 end that is left; stub; stump: *a cigar butt.* [Middle English *but, bott.* Related to BUTTOCKS.]

butt[2] (but), *n.* 1 object of ridicule or scorn: *The new boy was the butt of many jokes.* 2 target. 3 (on a rifle, archery, or artillery range) a mound of earth or sawdust behind the target to stop shots. 4 **the butts,** place to practice shooting. *—v.i., v.t.* join end to end. [< Old French *bout* end and *but* aim]

butt[3] (but), *v.i.* 1 strike or push by knocking hard with the head: *A goat butts.* 2 **butt in,** SLANG. meddle; interfere. *—v.t.* strike with the head or horns; push or drive. *—n.* a push or blow with the head. [< Old French *bouter* to thrust]

butt[4] (but), *n.* 1 a large barrel for wine or beer. 2 a liquid measure equal to 126 U.S. gallons of wine or 108 U.S. gallons of ale. [< Old French *botte* < Late Latin *butta*]

butte (byüt), *n.* (in the western United States) a steep, flat-topped hill standing alone. [< French]

butte

but ter (but′ər), *n.* 1 the solid, yellowish fat separated from cream by churning, used chiefly for spreading on bread and in cooking. 2 any of various foods like butter in looks or use, as peanut butter. *—v.t.* 1 put butter on. 2 INFORMAL. flatter. 3 **butter up,** INFORMAL. flatter. [Old English *butere* < Latin *butyrum* < Greek *boutyron* < *bous* cow + *tyros* cheese] **—but′ter less,** *adj.*

but ter-and-eggs (but′ər ən egz′), *n.* a common European toadflax having showy yellow-and-orange flowers and growing as a weed in much of North America.

butter bean, 1 variety of the lima bean having small white or brown seeds, grown in the southern United States. 2 wax bean.

but ter cup (but′ər kup′), *n.* any of a genus of wild flowers, having bright-yellow, satiny flowers shaped like cups, and deeply divided leaves resembling a crow's foot; crowfoot.

but ter fat (but′ər fat′), *n.* the fat in milk. It can be made into butter.

but ter fin gered (but′ər fing′gərd), *adj.* INFORMAL. apt to let things drop or slip through one's fingers.

but ter fin gers (but′ər fing′gərz), *n.* INFORMAL. 1 a butterfingered person. 2 a careless or clumsy person.

but ter fish (but′ər fish′), *n., pl.* **-fish es** or **-fish.** any of several small, edible, silvery fishes of the Atlantic coast of North America, with slippery skins covered with mucus, oval bodies, and spiny fins.

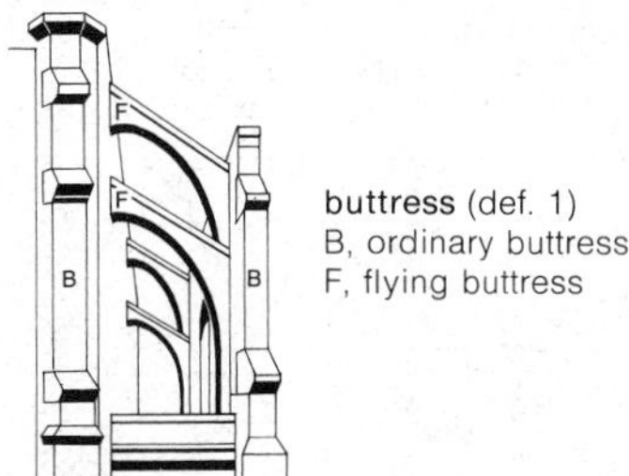

buttress (def. 1)
B, ordinary buttress
F, flying buttress

but ter fly (but′ər flī′), *n., pl.* **-flies.** 1 any of various insects with slender bodies and two pairs of large, usually brightly colored, overlapping wings. Butterflies fly mostly in the daytime. 2 person who suggests a butterfly by delicate beauty, bright clothes, fickleness, etc. [Old English *buterflēoge*]

butterfly fish, any of several fishes noted for their bright colors or for their broad fins somewhat resembling the wings of the butterfly.

butterfly weed, a North American milkweed with orange-colored flowers.

but ter milk (but′ər milk′), *n.* the sour liquid left after butter has been separated from cream. Milk can also be changed to buttermilk artificially.

but ter nut (but′ər nut′), *n.* 1 an oily kind of edible walnut grown in North America. 2 tree that bears butternuts.

but ter scotch (but′ər skoch′), *n.* candy made from brown sugar and butter. *—adj.* flavored with brown sugar and butter: *butterscotch pudding.*

but ter y[1] (but′ər ē), *adj.* 1 like butter. 2 containing or spread with butter. 3 given to flattery.

but ter y[2] (but′ər ē), *n., pl.* **-ter ies.** pantry. [< Old French *boterie* < *botte* butt[4]]

but tocks (but′əks), *n.pl.* the fleshy hind part of the body where the legs join the back; rump. [Old English *buttuc* end, small piece of land]

but ton (but′n), *n.* 1 a round, flat piece of metal, bone, glass, plastic, etc., fastened on garments to hold them closed or to decorate them. 2 knob used as a handle or a catch to take hold of, push, or turn so that it holds or closes something. 3 anything that resembles or suggests a button. The knob or disk pressed to ring an electric bell is called a button. 4 a young or undeveloped mushroom. *—v.t.* fasten the buttons of; close with buttons. *—v.i.* (of garments) be fastened or capable of being fastened with buttons. [< Old French *boton* < *bouter* to thrust] **—but′ton less,** *adj.* **—but′ton like′,** *adj.*

but ton hole (but′n hōl′), *n., v.,* **-holed, -hol ing.** *—n.* hole or slit through which a button is passed. *—v.t.* 1 make buttonholes in. 2 sew with the stitch used in making buttonholes. 3 hold in conversation or force to listen, as if holding someone by the buttonholes of his coat.

but ton hook (but′n hu̇k′), *n.* hook for pulling the buttons of shoes, gloves, etc., through the buttonholes.

but ton wood (but′n wu̇d′), *n.* the sycamore tree of North America.

but tress (but′ris), *n.* 1 a support built against a wall or building to strengthen it. 2 a support like this; prop. *—v.t.* 1 strengthen with a buttress. 2 support and strengthen. [< Old French *bouterez* (plural) < *bouter* thrust against]

bu tyl (byü′tl), *n.* a univalent hydrocarbon radical obtained from butane. *Formula:* C_4H_9- [< *but(yric acid)* + *-yl*]

butyl alcohol, any of four isomeric alcohols used as a solvent for resins, adhesives, varnishes, etc. *Formula:* C_4H_9OH

bu ty lene (byü′tl ēn′), *n.* a gaseous hydrocarbon of the ethylene series, often used in

hat, āge, fär; let, ēqual, tėrm;
it, īce; hot, ōpen, ôrder;
oil, out; cup, pu̇t, rüle;
ch, child; ng, long; sh, she;
th, thin; ᴛʜ, then; zh, measure;

ə represents *a* in about, *e* in taken, *i* in pencil, *o* in lemon, *u* in circus.

< = from, derived from, taken from.

making synthetic rubber. *Formula:* C_4H_8

bu tyr ic acid (byü tir′ik), an oily, colorless liquid that has an unpleasant odor, formed by fermentation in rancid butter, cheese, etc. *Formula:* $C_4H_8O_2$ [< Latin *butyrum* butter < Greek *boutyron*]

bux om (buk′səm), *adj.* (of a woman) plump and good to look at; healthy and cheerful. [Middle English *buhsum* < Old English *būgan* to bend] **—bux′om ly,** *adv.* **—bux′om ness,** *n.*

buy (bī), *v.,* **bought, buy ing,** *n.* —*v.t.* 1 get by paying a price, usually in money; purchase: *You can buy a pencil for five cents.* See synonym study below. 2 get in exchange for something else, or by making some sacrifice. 3 bribe: *It was charged that two members of the jury had been bought by the defendant.* 4 be sufficient to purchase or get: *Gold cannot buy health.* 5 **buy off,** get rid of by paying money to; bribe. 6 **buy out,** buy all the shares, rights, merchandise, etc., of. 7 **buy up,** buy all that one can of; buy. —*v.i.* buy things. —*n.* INFORMAL. 1 a bargain. 2 thing bought; purchase. [Old English *bycgan*]

Syn. *v.t.* 1 **Buy, purchase** mean to get something by paying a price. **Buy** is the general and informal word: *A person can buy anything in that store if he has the money.* **Purchase,** a somewhat more formal word, suggests buying after careful planning or negotiating or on a large scale: *The bank has purchased some property on which to construct a new building.*

buy er (bī′ər), *n.* 1 person who buys; purchaser; customer. 2 person whose work is buying goods for a department store or other business.

buzz (buz), *n.* 1 the humming sound made by flies, mosquitoes, or bees. 2 the low, confused sound of many people talking quietly. 3 whisper; rumor. 4 INFORMAL. a call on the telephone. 5 busy movement; stir.
—*v.i.* 1 make a steady, humming sound; hum loudly. 2 talk excitedly. 3 gossip. 4 (of places) be filled with the noise of conversation, etc. —*v.t.* 1 sound in a low, confused way. 2 utter or express by buzzing. 3 tell or spread (gossip); whisper. 4 signal with a buzzer: *She buzzed her secretary.* 5 INFORMAL. call (a person) by telephone. 6 fly an airplane very fast and low over (a place or person). 7 **buzz about,** move about busily.
[imitative]

buz zard (buz′ərd), *n.* 1 any of various large, heavy, slow-moving hawks. 2 turkey buzzard. [< Old French *busart,* ultimately < Latin *buteo* hawk]

buzz bomb, an aerial projectile that can be guided from land to a target where it explodes; robot bomb.

buzz er (buz′ər), *n.* 1 an electrical device that makes a buzzing sound as a signal. 2 thing that buzzes.

buzz saw, a circular saw.

B.V., Blessed Virgin.

B.W.I., British West Indies.

bx., *pl.* **bxs.** box.

by (bī), *prep.* 1 at the side or edge of; near; beside: *The garden is by the house.* 2 along; over; through: *go by the bridge.* 3 through the means, action, or use of: *a play by Shakespeare.* See synonym study below. 4 combined with in multiplication or relative dimensions: *a room ten by twenty feet.* 5 in the measure of: *eggs by the dozen.* 6 as soon as; not later than: *by six o'clock.* 7 during: *The sun shines by day.* 8 past: *She walked by the church.* 9 according to: *work by the rules.* 10 in relation to; concerning: *He did well by his children.* 11 to the extent of: *larger by half.* 12 taken separately as units or groups in a series: *two by two. Algebra must be mastered step by step.* 13 toward: *The island lies south by east from here.*
—*adv.* 1 at hand: *near by.* 2 past: *days gone by. The train rushed by.* 3 aside or away: *put something by.* 4 INFORMAL. at, in, or into another's house when passing: *Please come by and eat with me.* 5 **by and by,** after a while; before long; soon. 6 **by and large,** for the most part.
—*n.* 1 bye. 2 **by the by,** by the way.
[Old English *bi, be*]

Syn. *prep.* 3 **By, through, with** are seldom interchangeable, though all are used to connect to a sentence a word naming the agent that has performed an action or the means or instrument used to perform it. **By** is used before the word naming the agent in sentences with passive verbs: *My tooth was filled by the dentist.* Even when such a verb is only implied, the use of *by* identifies an agent: *a statement by the President, a picture by Titian, a story by Poe. By* is also used sometimes to imply means: *I travel by airplane.* **Through** is used to connect the word naming the means or the reason: *We found out through her. They complied with the robber's orders through fear.* **With** is used to connect the word naming the instrument: *We cut meat with a knife.*

by-, *prefix.* 1 secondary; minor; less important: *By-product* = *secondary product.* 2 near by: *Bystander* = *person standing near by.* 3 aside; side: *By-road* = *side road.* [Old English *bi-*]

by-and-by (bī′ən bī′), *n.* the future.

bye (bī), *n.* 1 in games or tournaments where opponents are drawn by pairs: **a** an unpaired status, entitling the contestant to the next round. **b** contestant who draws no opponent in a given round. 2 (in golf) the holes not played after one player has won. 3 (in cricket) a run made on a missed ball. 4 **by the bye,** incidentally. Also, **by.** [variant of *by*]

by-e lec tion (bī′i lek′shən), *n.* BRITISH. a special election; election held at a time other than that of the regular elections.

Byel o rus sia (byel′ə rush′ə), *n.* Byelorussian S.S.R. Also, **Belorussia, White Russia. —Byel′o rus′sian,** *adj., n.*

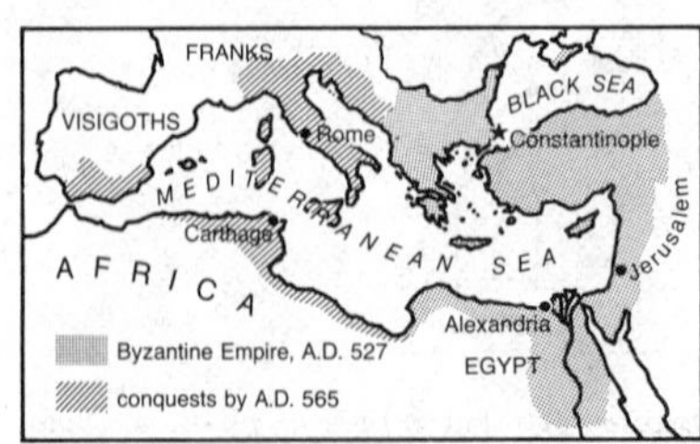

Byzantine Empire—The shaded areas show the Empire at its greatest extent.

Byelorussian S.S.R., one of the constituent republics of the U.S.S.R., in the W part, just east of Poland. 9,000,000 pop.; 80,200 sq. mi. *Capital:* Minsk.

by gone (bī′gôn′, bī′gon′), *adj.* gone by; past; former. —*n.* 1 **bygones,** *pl.* what is gone by and past. 2 the past.

by law (bī′lô′), *n.* 1 law made by a city, company, club, etc., for the control of its own affairs. 2 a secondary law or rule; not one of the main rules. [< Scandinavian (Danish) *bylov* < *by* town + *lov* law]

by-line (bī′līn′), *n.* line at the beginning of a newspaper or magazine article giving the name of the writer.

by-pass (bī′pas′), *n.* 1 road, channel, pipe, etc., providing a secondary passage to be used instead of the main passage. 2 (in electricity) a shunt. —*v.t.* 1 go around: *by-pass a city.* 2 provide a secondary passage for. 3 go over the head of (a superior, etc.) to a higher authority. 4 set aside or ignore (regulations, etc.) in order to reach a desired objective. 5 get away from; avoid; escape: *by-pass a question.* 6 (in military use) flank.

by-path (bī′path′), *n., pl.* **-paths** (-paᴛʜz′, -paths′). a side path; byway.

by-play (bī′plā′), *n.* action that is not part of the main action, especially on the stage.

by-prod uct (bī′prod′əkt), *n.* 1 a secondary product produced in addition to the main product: *Kerosene is a by-product of petroleum refining.* 2 a secondary result produced in doing something else.

Byrd (bėrd), *n.* **Richard Evelyn,** 1888-1957, American naval officer, aviator, and polar explorer.

by-road (bī′rōd′), *n.* a side road.

By ron (bī′rən), *n.* **George Gordon,** Lord, 1788-1824, English poet.

By ron ic (bī ron′ik), *adj.* of or like Byron or his poetry.

by stand er (bī′stan′dər), *n.* person who stands near or looks on but does not take part; onlooker; spectator.

by-street (bī′strēt′), *n.* a side street.

by way (bī′wā′), *n.* a side path or road; way which is little used.

by word (bī′wėrd′), *n.* 1 a common saying; proverb. 2 person or thing that becomes well known as a type of some characteristic. 3 object of contempt; thing scorned. [Old English *bīword*]

Byz an tine (biz′n tēn′, biz′n tīn, bi zan′tən), *adj.* 1 of or like the Byzantine Empire or Byzantium. 2 of or like a style of art or architecture developed in the Byzantine Empire, characterized by a circular dome over a square space, and the use of rich mosaics and frescoes. 3 of or having to do with the Eastern Church. —*n.* native or inhabitant of Byzantium.

Byzantine Empire, E part of the Roman Empire after the division in A.D. 395. The Byzantine Empire ended with the capture of its capital, Constantinople, by the Turks in 1453. Also, **Eastern Roman Empire.**

By zan ti um (bi zan′shē əm, bi zan′tē əm), *n.* ancient city on the site of modern Istanbul. It was renamed Constantinople when it became the capital of the Roman Empire in A.D. 330.

C c

C[1] or **c** (sē), *n., pl.* **C's** or **c's.** 1 the third letter of the English alphabet. 2 the Roman numeral for 100.

C[2] (sē), *n., pl.* **C's.** the first tone of the musical scale of C major.

C, 1 carbon. 2 central.

c., 1 Also, **ca.** about; approximately [for Latin *circa*]. 2 (in baseball) catcher. 3 cathode. 4 cent or cents. 5 center. 6 centimeter. 7 century. 8 chapter. 9 copyright. 10 cubic. 11 cup or cups. 12 carat.

C., 1 Cape. 2 Catholic. 3 Celsius. 4 Centigrade.

Ca, calcium.

ca., Also, **c.** about; approximately [for Latin *circa*].

C.A., 1 Central America. 2 chartered accountant. 3 chief accountant. 4 (in psychology) chronological age. 5 consular agent.

cab (kab), *n.* 1 automobile that can be hired with driver; taxicab. 2 carriage that can be hired with driver, usually pulled by one horse. 3 the enclosed part of a railroad engine where the engineer and fireman sit. 4 the enclosed part of a truck, crane, etc., where the driver or operator sits. [short for *cabriolet*]

ca bal (kə bal′), *n.* 1 a small group of people working or plotting in secret; faction. 2 intrigue; plot. [< French *cabale* < Medieval Latin *cabbala.* See CABALA.]

cab a la (kab′ə lə, kə bä′lə), *n.* 1 system of interpretation of the Scriptures based on the numerical rather than the alphabetical value of the letters of a word, developed in the Middle Ages by certain rabbis. 2 a mystical belief; secret doctrine. [< Medieval Latin *cabbala* < Hebrew *qabbālāh* tradition]

cab a lis tic (kab′ə lis′tik), *adj.* 1 having a mystical meaning; secret. 2 of or suitable for the Jewish cabala. **—cab′a lis′ti cal ly,** *adv.*

cab al ler o (kab′ə ler′ō, kab′ə lyer′ō), *n., pl.* **-ler os.** 1 (in Spain) a gentleman. 2 in the southwestern United States: **a** horseman. **b** an ardent admirer of women or of a particular woman. [< Spanish < Late Latin *caballarius* horseman. Doublet of CAVALIER, CHEVALIER.]

ca ban a (kə ban′ə), *n.* a small tentlike or cabinlike shelter, used especially on a beach for dressing or to provide shade. [< Spanish *cabaña* < Late Latin *capanna* hut. Doublet of CABIN.]

cab a ret (kab′ə rā′, kab′ə rā′), *n.* 1 restaurant with entertainment consisting of singing and dancing. 2 the entertainment. [< French < Middle Dutch *ca(m)bret,* ultimately < Latin *camera* vault. Related to CHAMBER.]

cab bage (kab′ij), *n.* 1 species of cole, with thick leaves closely folded into a round head that grows on a short stem. 2 its head, eaten either cooked or raw as a vegetable. [< Old French *caboche, caboce* < *bosse* mound; dent. Related to BOSS[2].]

cab by or **cab bie** (kab′ē), *n., pl.* **-bies.** INFORMAL. cabdriver.

cab driv er (kab′drī′vər), *n.* person who drives a taxicab.

cab in (kab′ən), *n.* 1 a small, roughly built house, usually having only one story. See **cottage** for synonym study. 2 a small house built for some special purpose: *a tourist cabin.* 3 a private room in a ship. 4 a room on a small boat containing the bunks. 5 place for passengers in an aircraft. [< Old French *cabane* < Late Latin *capanna.* Doublet of CABANA.]

cabin boy, boy or man whose work is waiting on the officers and passengers on a ship.

cabin class, class of passenger accommodations on a ship, lower than first class and higher than tourist class.

cabriolet (def. 2)

cab i net (kab′ə nit), *n.* 1 piece of furniture with shelves or drawers to hold articles for use or display: *a supply cabinet, a filing cabinet, a china cabinet, a phonograph cabinet.* 2 Also, **Cabinet.** group of advisers chosen by the head of a government to aid in administration. The Attorney General and the Secretary of Defense are members of the cabinet of the President of the United States. 3 ARCHAIC. a small, private room. [< Middle French]

cabinet government, 1 the system of governing by a cabinet headed by a prime minister, as in Great Britain. 2 government by this or a similar system.

cab i net mak er (kab′ə nit mā′kər), *n.* person whose work is making fine furniture and woodwork.

cab i net mak ing (kab′ə nit mā′king), *n.* business, work, or art of a cabinetmaker.

cab i net work (kab′ə nit wėrk′), *n.* 1 any beautifully made furniture or woodwork. 2 the making of such furniture or woodwork.

ca ble (kā′bəl), *n., v.,* **-bled, -bling.** *—n.* 1 a strong, thick rope, now usually made of wires twisted together. The cable by which a ship's anchor is raised and lowered is often made of chain. 2 an insulated bundle of wires for carrying an electric current. Telegraph messages are sent across the ocean by a waterproof, underwater cable. 4 cablegram. 5 cable's length. *—v.t.* 1 tie or fasten with a cable. 2 transmit (a message, news, etc.) across the ocean by underwater cable. 3 send a cablegram to. *—v.i.* communicate by cable. [< Old French < Late Latin *capulum* halter]

cable car, car pulled by a moving cable that is operated by an engine.

ca ble gram (kā′bəl gram), *n.* message sent across the ocean by underwater cable.

cable's length or **cable length,** unit of nautical measurement, 720 feet in the United States navy and 607.56 feet (about 100 fathoms) in the British navy.

ca ble way (kā′bəl wā′), *n.* apparatus in which a wire cable supports or conveys a moving load.

cab man (kab′mən), *n., pl.* **-men.** driver of a cab, especially a taxicab.

hat, āge, fär; let, ēqual, tėrm;
it, īce; hot, ōpen, ôrder;
oil, out; cup, pu̇t, rüle;
ch, child; ng, long; sh, she;
th, thin; ᴛʜ, then; zh, measure;
ə represents *a* in about, *e* in taken, *i* in pencil, *o* in lemon, *u* in circus.
< = from, derived from, taken from.

ca boose (kə büs′), *n.* 1 a small car, usually the last car, on a freight train in which the conductor and trainmen can work, rest, and sleep. 2 kitchen on the deck of a ship. [perhaps < Dutch *kabuyse* galley]

Cab ot (kab′ət), *n.* 1 **John,** 1450?-1498, Italian navigator who explored for England, discoverer of the North American continent in 1497. 2 his son, **Sebastian,** 1474?-1557, English navigator and explorer.

cab ri o let (kab′rē ə lā′), *n.* 1 formerly, an automobile resembling a coupe, but having a convertible top. 2 a light, one-horse, two-wheeled carriage, often with a folding top, seating two persons. [< French < *cabrioler* to caper]

ca ca o (kə kā′ō, kə kä′ō), *n., pl.* **-ca os.** 1 a small, tropical American, evergreen tree grown for its large, nutritious seeds. 2 the seeds of this tree, which are fermented, then washed to remove the sticky coating, and dried, used especially in making cocoa and chocolate. [< Spanish < Nahuatl *caca-uatl*]

cach a lot (kash′ə lot, kash′ə lō), *n.* sperm whale. [< French]

cache (kash), *n., v.,* **cached, cach ing.** *—n.* 1 a hiding place, especially of goods, treasure, food, etc. 2 the store of food or supplies hidden. *—v.t.* put or store in a cache; hide. [< French < *cacher* to hide]

ca chet (ka shā′, kash′ā), *n.* 1 a private seal or stamp, especially of an important or powerful person. 2 a distinguishing mark of quality or genuineness; stamp. 3 a stamped or printed slogan, design, etc., on mail. [< French < *cacher* to hide]

cach in na tion (kak′ə nā′shən), *n.* loud or immoderate laughter. [< Latin *cachinnationem* < *cachinnare* laugh loudly]

ca cique (kə sēk′), *n.* a native Indian chief or prince in the West Indies, Mexico, etc. [< Spanish < Arawakan]

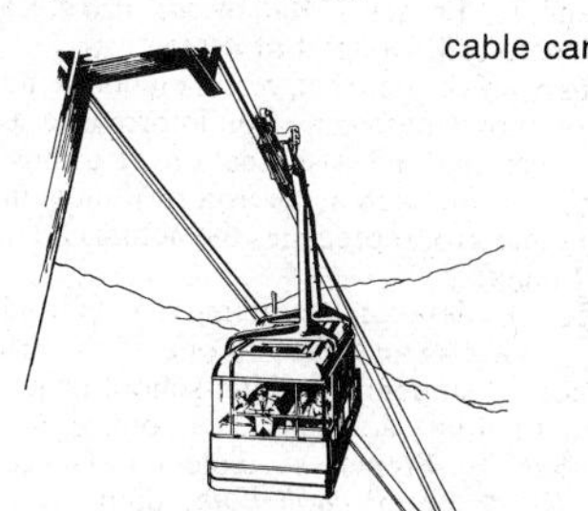

cable car

cack le (kak′əl), *n., v.,* **-led, -ling.** *—n.* 1 the shrill, broken sound that a hen makes, especially after laying an egg. 2 shrill, harsh, or broken laughter. 3 noisy chatter. *—v.i.* 1 (of a hen) make a shrill, broken sound, especially after laying an egg. 2 laugh in a shrill, harsh, or broken way. 3 chatter. *—v.t.* utter with or express by cackling. [Middle

English *cakelen;* imitative] **—cack′ler,** *n.*
cac o gen e sis (kak′ə jen′ə sis), *n.* low vitality and infertility in a breed, especially common in mixed breeds. [< Greek *kakos* bad + *genesis* origin]
ca coph o nous (kə kof′ə nəs), *adj.* harsh and clashing in sound; dissonant; discordant. **—ca coph′o nous ly,** *adv.*
ca coph o ny (kə kof′ə nē), *n., pl.* **-nies.** a harsh, clashing sound; dissonance; discord. [< Greek *kakophōnia* < *kakos* bad + *phōnē* sound]
cac tus (kak′təs), *n., pl.* **-tus es, -ti** (-tī). any of a family of plants, chiefly native to the hot, dry regions of America, with thick, fleshy stems, usually leafless, and bearing clusters of spines, and often with brightly colored flowers. [< Latin < Greek *kaktos*]
cad (kad), *n.* boy or man who does not act like a gentleman; ill-bred person. [< *caddie*]
ca dav er (kə dav′ər), *n.* a dead body; corpse. [< Latin < *cadere* to fall]
ca dav er ous (kə dav′ər əs), *adj.* 1 pale and ghastly. 2 thin and worn. 3 of or like a cadaver. **—ca dav′er ous ly,** *adv.*
cad die (kad′ē), *n., v.,* **-died, -dy ing.** *—n.* person who helps a golf player by carrying golf clubs, finding the ball, etc. *—v.i.* help a golf player in this way. Also, **caddy.** [< French *cadet* younger brother. See CADET.]
cad dis fly (kad′is), any of an order of slender, mothlike insects with two pairs of wings and long legs; trichopteran. [origin uncertain]
cad dish (kad′ish), *adj.* like a cad; ungentlemanly: *caddish manners.* **—cad′dish ly,** *adv.* **—cad′dish ness,** *n.*
caddis worm, larva of a caddis fly, used as bait in fishing and as fish food. It lives under water and forms a portable case for itself of sand, bits of leaves, or the like.
cad dy[1] (kad′ē), *n., pl.* **-dies.** a small box, can, or chest, often used to hold tea. [< Malay *kati* a small weight]
cad dy[2] (kad′ē), *n., pl.* **-dies,** *v.i.,* **-died, -dy ing.** caddie.
ca dence (kād′ns), *n.* 1 the measure or beat of music, dancing, marching, or any movement regularly repeating itself; rhythm: *the cadence of a drum.* 2 fall of the voice. 3 a rising and falling sound; modulation. 4 series of chords bringing part of a piece of music to an end. [< French < Italian *cadenza* < Latin *cadere* to fall. Doublet of CHANCE.]
ca den za (kə den′zə), *n.* an elaborate flourish or showy passage, often improvised, usually near the end of a section of a musical composition, such as an aria or a movement of a concerto. It precedes the actual cadence. [< Italian]
ca det (kə det′), *n.* 1 a young man in training for service as an officer in one of the armed forces. 2 student in a high-school or grade-school military academy. 3 a younger son or brother. [< French < dialectal (Gascony) *capdet* < Latin *capitellum,* diminutive of *caput* head]
ca det ship (kə det′ship), *n.* rank or position of a cadet.
cadge (kaj), *v.t., v.i.,* **cadged, cadg ing.** INFORMAL. beg shamelessly. [Middle English *caggen*] **—cadg′ er,** *n.*
ca di (kä′dē, kā′dē), *n.* a minor Moslem judge, usually of a town or village. [< Arabic *qāḍī* judge]
Cá diz (kə diz′, kā′diz), *n.* seaport in SW Spain. 138,000.
cad mi um (kad′mē əm), *n.* a soft, bluish-white, ductile metallic element resembling tin, which occurs only in combination with other elements and is used in plating to prevent corrosion and in making alloys. *Symbol:* Cd; *atomic number* 48. See pages 326 and 327 for table. [< Latin *cadmia* zinc ore < Greek *Kadmeia (gē)* Cadmean (earth)]
Cad mus (kad′məs), *n.* (in Greek legends) a Phoenician prince who killed a dragon and sowed its teeth, from which armed men sprang up who fought with each other until only five were left. These five helped Cadmus found the Greek city of Thebes.
cad re (kad′rē), *n.* 1 staff of officers and enlisted men of a military unit necessary to establish and train a new unit. 2 a similar group of trained men in another activity, especially a group that forms the core of an organization. 3 framework. [< French < Italian *quadro* < Latin *quadrum* square]
ca du ce us (kə dü′sē əs, kə dyü′sē əs), *n., pl.* **-ce i** (-sē ī). staff of Mercury, or Hermes, with two snakes twined around it and a pair of wings on top. The caduceus is often used as an emblem of the medical profession. [< Latin] **—ca du′ce an,** *adj.*
cae cal (sē′kəl), *adj.* cecal. **—cae′cal ly,** *adv.*
cae cum (sē′kəm), *n., pl.* **-ca** (-kə). cecum.
Caed mon (kad′mən), *n.* early English poet who lived about A.D. 670.
Cae sar (sē′zər), *n.* 1 **Gaius Julius,** 102?-44 B.C., Roman general, statesman, and historian. 2 title of the Roman emperors from Augustus to Hadrian, and later of the heir to the throne. 3 emperor. 4 dictator or tyrant.
Cae sa re a (sē′zə rē′ə, ses′ə rē′ə), *n.* small seaport in NW Israel. It was the ancient Roman capital of Judea.
Cae sar e an (si zer′ē ən, si zar′ē ən), *adj.* 1 of Julius Caesar. 2 of the Caesars. *—n.* Caesarean section. Also, **Caesarian, Cesarean, Cesarian.**
Caesarean section, operation by which a baby is removed from the uterus by cutting through the abdominal and uterine walls. [from the belief that Julius *Caesar* was born in this way]
Cae sar i an (si zer′ē ən, si zar′ē ən), *adj.* Caesarean.
cae si um (sē′zē əm), *n.* cesium.
cae sur a (si zhůr′ə, si zyůr′ə), *n., pl.* **-sur as, -sur ae** (-zhůr′ē, -zyůr′ē). a pause in a line of verse, generally agreeing with a pause required by the sense. The caesura is the chief pause if there is more than one. In Greek and Latin poetry the caesura regularly falls within a foot, not far from the middle of a line. In English poetry it usually comes near the middle of a line, either within or after a metrical foot. EXAMPLE: "To err is human, | to forgive, divine." Also, **cesura.** [< Latin, a cutting < *caedere* to cut]

caisson (defs. 1 and 2)

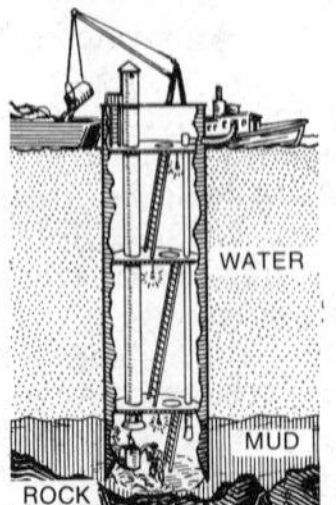

caisson (def. 3) The weight of the caisson forces it into sand and mud below the water. Air under pressure is then forced into the caisson, driving out the water and permitting workmen to enter through airtight compartments.

ca fé or **ca fe** (ka fā′, kə fā′), *n.* 1 place to buy and eat a meal; restaurant. 2 barroom. [< French *café* coffee, coffeehouse]
ca fé au lait (kȧ fā′ ō lā′), FRENCH. coffee with milk or cream.
caf e ter i a (kaf′ə tir′ē ə), *n.* restaurant where people wait on themselves. [< Mexican Spanish *cafetería* coffee shop < *café* coffee]
caf feine or **caf fein** (kaf′ēn, kaf′ē ən), *n.* a slightly bitter, stimulating drug found in coffee and tea. *Formula:* $C_8H_{10}N_4O_2{\cdot}H_2O$ [< French *caféine* < *café* coffee]
caf tan (kaf′tən, käf tän′), *n.* a long-sleeved, ankle-length tunic with a girdle, worn under the coat by men in Turkey, Egypt, etc. Also, **kaftan.** [< Turkish *kaftan*]
cage (kāj), *n., v.,* **caged, cag ing.** *—n.* 1 frame or place closed in with wires, strong iron bars, or wood. Birds and wild animals are kept in cages. 2 thing shaped or used like a cage. The car or closed platform of a mine elevator is a cage. 3 prison. 4 (in ice hockey, etc.) the network and frame forming the goal. 5 (in baseball) a place enclosed by a net for batting practice. 6 (in basketball) the basket or net where points are scored. *—v.t.* 1 put or keep in a cage. 2 (in sports) to put (the ball, puck, etc.) into the goal. [< Old French < Latin *cavea* < *cavus* hollow. Compare CAVE.]
cage ling (kāj′ling), *n.* bird kept in a cage.
cage y (kā′jē), *adj.,* **cag i er, cag i est.** INFORMAL. shrewd and cautious; sharp and wary. Also, **cagy. —cag′i ly,** *adv.* **—cag′i ness,** *n.*
Ca glia ri (kä′lyär ē), *n.* capital of Sardinia, on the S coast. 223,000.
cag y (kā′jē), *adj.,* **cag i er, cag i est.** cagey.
ca hoots (kə hüts′), *n.* SLANG. **in cahoots,** in partnership: *He did the mischief in cahoots with another.* [origin uncertain]
Cai a phas (kā′ə fəs, kī′ə fəs), *n.* high priest from A.D. 18? to 36 who presided at the trial of Jesus.
cai man (kā′mən), *n.* a large crocodilian of tropical America similar to an alligator. Also, **cayman.** [< Spanish *caimán*]
Cain (kān), *n.* 1 (in the Bible) the oldest son of Adam and Eve. He killed his brother Abel. 2 murderer. 3 **raise Cain,** SLANG. make a great disturbance.
ca ique or **ca ïque** (kä ēk′), *n.* 1 a long, narrow Turkish rowboat, much used on the Bosporus. 2 a small Mediterranean sailing ship. [< French *caïque* < Italian *caicco* < Turkish *kayik*]
Cai rene (kī′rēn′, kī rēn′), *n.* native or inhabitant of Cairo. *—adj.* of Cairo.
cairn (kern, karn), *n.* 1 pile of stones heaped up as a memorial, tomb, or landmark. 2 cairn terrier. [< Scottish Gaelic *carn* heap of stones]
cairn terrier, a small, long-haired terrier that originated in Scotland. It has a wiry coat.
Cai ro (kī′rō), *n.* capital of Egypt, in the NE part. 4,961,000.
cais son (kā′sn, kā′son), *n.* 1 wagon to carry ammunition, especially artillery shells. 2 box for ammunition. 3 a watertight box or chamber in which men can work under ground or water to make foundations for

bridges, dig tunnels, etc. 4 a watertight float used in raising sunken ships. [< French < Italian *cassone* < *cassa* chest < Latin *capsa* box]

caisson disease, severe pain, loss of physical control, and asphyxia, caused by changing too suddenly from high air pressure as in a caisson, to ordinary air pressure; the bends.

cai tiff (kā′tif), *n.* ARCHAIC. a mean, cowardly person. —*adj.* cowardly and mean. [< Old French *caitif,* ultimately < Latin *captivus* captive. Doublet of CAPTIVE.]

ca jole (kə jōl′), *v.t.,* **-joled, -jol ing.** persuade by pleasant words, flattery, or false promises; coax. [< French *cajoler*] —**ca jol′er,** *n.*

ca jol er y (kə jō′lər ē), *n., pl.* **-er ies.** persuasion by pleasant words, flattery, or false promises.

Ca jun (kā′jən), *n.* a descendant of the French who came to Louisiana from Acadia. [alteration of *Acadian*]

cake (kāk), *n., v.,* **caked, cak ing.** —*n.* 1 a baked mixture of flour, sugar, eggs, flavoring, and other things. 2 a flat, thin mass of dough baked or fried; a pancake or hoecake. 3 any small, flat mass of food fried on both sides: *a potato cake.* 4 a shaped mass of solid material: *a cake of soap, a cake of ice.* 5 **take the cake,** SLANG. **a** win first prize. **b** excel. —*v.t.* form into a solid mass; harden: *Water caked the powder as hard as a stone.* —*v.i.* take the form of cake or a flat, compact, hardened mass: *Mud cakes as it dries.* [probably < Scandinavian (Old Icelandic) *kaka*]

cake walk (kāk′wôk′), *n.* a dance with prancing high steps that developed from an earlier march or promenade for couples. A cake was the prize for the most original steps. —*v.i.* do a cakewalk. —**cake′ walk′er,** *n.*

cal., 1 calendar. 2 caliber. 3 calorie or calories.

Cal., California. The official abbreviation is **Calif.**

cal a bash (kal′ə bash), *n.* 1 a gourdlike fruit whose dried shell is used to make bottles, bowls, drums, pipes, and rattles. 2 the tropical tree of the same family as the bignonia that it grows on. 3 bottle, bowl, drum, pipe, or rattle made from such a dried shell. [< Middle French *calabasse*]

cal a boose (kal′ə büs, kal′ə büs′), *n.* INFORMAL. a jail; prison. [< Spanish *calabozo* dungeon]

Ca la bri a (kə lā′brē ə), *n.* 1 region in S Italy, forming the toe of the Italian peninsula. 2 ancient Roman district in SE Italy, now part of Apulia. —**Ca la′ bri an,** *adj., n.*

ca la di um (kə lā′dē əm), *n.* any of a genus of tropical American plants of the same family as the arum, with large, colorful leaves. [< Malay *keladi*]

Cal ais (ka lā′, kal′ā), *n.* seaport in N France, on the Strait of Dover; nearest French port to the coast of England. 75,000.

cal a mine (kal′ə mīn, kal′ə mən), *n.* compound of zinc oxide and ferric oxide, used in lotions to relieve skin irritations or sunburn. [< Medieval Latin *calamina* < Latin *cadmia.* See CADMIUM.]

ca lam i tous (kə lam′ə təs), *adj.* causing calamity; accompanied by calamity; disastrous. —**ca lam′i tous ly,** *adv.* —**ca lam′i tous ness,** *n.*

ca lam i ty (kə lam′ə tē), *n., pl.* **-ties.** 1 a great misfortune, such as a flood, a fire, the loss of one's sight or hearing. See **disaster** for synonym study. 2 serious trouble; misery. [< Latin *calamitatem*]

cal a mus (kal′ə məs), *n., pl.* **-mi** (-mī). 1 sweet flag. 2 its fragrant root, used in perfumes and medicines. 3 the quill of a feather. [< Latin < Greek *kalamos* reed]

ca lash (kə lash′), *n.* 1 a light, low carriage that usually has a folding top. 2 a folding top or hood. 3 a woman's silk hood or bonnet, worn in the 1700's and 1800's. [< French *calèche*]

calash (def. 1)

cal ca ne um (kal kā′nē əm), *n., pl.* **-ne a** (-nē ə). calcaneus.

cal ca ne us (kal kā′nē əs), *n., pl.* **-ne i** (-nē ī). the largest bone of the row of tarsal bones; the bone of the human heel. [< Late Latin, heel < Latin *calcem*]

cal car (kal′kär), *n., pl.* **cal car i a** (kal ker′ē ə, kal kar′ē ə). (in biology) a spur or spurlike projection. [< Latin < *calcem* heel]

cal car e ous (kal ker′ē əs, kal kar′ē əs), *adj.* of or containing lime, limestone, or calcium carbonate. [< Latin *calcarius* < *calcem* lime] —**cal car′e ous ly,** *adv.* —**cal car′e ous ness,** *n.*

cal cif e rol (kal sif′ə rôl′, kal sif′ə rōl′), *n.* a form of vitamin D (vitamin D_2) present in fish-liver oils, milk, and eggs, and produced by irradiating ergosterol. *Formula:* $C_{28}H_{44}O$

cal cif er ous (kal sif′ər əs), *adj.* yielding or containing calcite. [< Latin *calcem* lime + English *-ferous*]

cal ci fi ca tion (kal′sə fə kā′shən), *n.* 1 process of calcifying. 2 a calcified part. 3 the accumulation of calcium in certain soils.

cal ci fy (kal′sə fī), *v.t., v.i.,* **-fied, -fy ing.** make or become hard or bony by the deposit of calcium salts: *Cartilage often calcifies in older people.*

cal ci mine (kal′sə mīn, kal′sə mən), *n., v.,* **-mined, -min ing.** —*n.* a white or tinted liquid consisting of a lime solution, coloring matter, glue, etc., used on walls, ceilings, etc. —*v.t.* cover with calcimine. Also, **kalsomine.**

cal ci na tion (kal′sə nā′shən), *n.* 1 act or operation of calcining. 2 anything formed by calcining.

cal cine (kal′sīn, kal′sən), *v.,* **-cined, -cin ing.** —*v.t.* burn (something) to ashes or powder: *calcine bones.* —*v.i.* burn to ashes or powder.

cal cite (kal′sīt), *n.* mineral composed of calcium carbonate. It is the chief substance in limestone, chalk, and marble. *Formula:* $CaCO_3$

cal ci um (kal′sē əm), *n.* a soft, silvery-white metallic element. It is a part of limestone, chalk, milk, bone, etc. Calcium is used in alloys and its compounds are used in making plaster, in cooking, and as bleaching agents. *Symbol:* Ca; *atomic number* 20. See pages 326 and 327 for table. [< New Latin < Latin *calcem* lime]

calcium carbide, a heavy, gray substance that reacts with water to form acetylene gas. *Formula:* CaC_2

calcium carbonate, compound of cal-

hat, āge, fär; let, ēqual, tėrm;
it, īce; hot, ōpen, ôrder;
oil, out; cup, pu̇t, rüle;
ch, child; ng, long; sh, she;
th, thin; ᴛʜ, then; zh, measure;

ə represents *a* in about, *e* in taken, *i* in pencil, *o* in lemon, *u* in circus.

< = from, derived from, taken from.

cium occurring in rocks such as marble and limestone, in bones, shells, and teeth, and to some extent in plants. *Formula:* $CaCO_3$

calcium chloride, compound of calcium and chlorine, used on roads to settle dust or melt ice, and in refrigeration. *Formula:* $CaCl_2$

calcium hydroxide, slaked lime. *Formula:* $Ca(OH)_2$

calcium oxide, lime[1]. *Formula:* CaO

calcium phosphate, compound of calcium and phosphoric acid, used in medicine, in making enamels, etc. It is found in bones and as rock. *Formula:* $Ca_3(PO_4)_2$

cal cu la ble (kal′kyə lə bəl), *adj.* 1 that can be calculated. 2 reliable; dependable. —**cal′cu la bly,** *adv.*

cal cu late (kal′kyə lāt), *v.,* **-lat ed, -lat ing.** —*v.t.* 1 find out by adding, subtracting, multiplying, or dividing; compute: *calculate the cost of building a house.* 2 find out beforehand by any process of reasoning; estimate: *Calculate the day of the week on which New Year's Day will fall.* 3 plan or intend: *That remark was calculated to hurt her feelings.* —*v.i.* 1 depend; count: *You can calculate on earning $65 a week if you take the job.* 2 INFORMAL. think; suppose. [< Latin *calculatum* counted < *calculus* stone used in counting, diminutive of *calcem* stone, lime] —**cal′cu lat′ed ly,** *adv.*

cal cu lat ing (kal′kyə lā′ting), *adj.* 1 able to calculate: *a calculating machine.* 2 shrewd and careful. 3 scheming and selfish. —**cal′cu lat′ing ly,** *adv.*

cal cu la tion (kal′kyə lā′shən), *n.* 1 act of adding, subtracting, multiplying, or dividing to find a result; computation. 2 result found by calculating. 3 careful thinking; deliberate planning.

cal cu la tive (kal′kyə lā′tiv), *adj.* 1 having to do with calculation. 2 tending to be calculating.

cal cu la tor (kal′kyə lā′tər), *n.* 1 machine that calculates, especially one that solves difficult problems in calculation. 2 person who calculates.

cal cu lous (kal′kyə ləs), *adj.* caused by or containing a calculus (def. 2) or calculi.

cal cu lus (kal′kyə ləs), *n., pl.* **-li** (-lī), **-lus es.** 1 system of calculation in advanced mathematics, using algebraic symbols to solve problems dealing with changing quan ties. 2 stone or hard mass of mineral formed in the body because of a di condition. Gallstones are calculi. See CALCULATE.]

Cal cut ta (kal kut′ə), *n.* seap near the Bay of Bengal. It w capital of India. 3,159,000 *adj., n.*

cal dron (kôl′drən), boiler. Also, **cauld** *dron* < Late Lati hot]

Cal e do ni

name of Scotland. **—Cal′e do′ni an,** *adj., n.*

cal en dar (kal′ən dər), *n.* 1 table showing the months, weeks, and days of the year. A calendar shows the day of the week on which each day of the month falls. 2 system by which the beginning, length, and divisions of the year are fixed. 3 a list or schedule; record; register: *The clerk of the court announced the next case on the calendar.* 4 schedule of the order in which bills are considered on the floor of a legislative body. *—v.t.* enter in a calendar or list; register. [< Latin *kalendarium* account book < *kalendae* calends (the day bills were due)]

cal en der (kal′ən dər), *n.* machine in which cloth, paper, or similar material is smoothed and glazed by pressing between rollers. *—v.t.* make smooth and glossy by pressing in a calender. [< Middle French *calendre,* ultimately < Greek *kylindros* cylinder] **—cal′en der er,** *n.*

cal ends (kal′əndz), *n., pl. in form, sometimes sing. in use.* the first day of the month in the ancient Roman calendar. Also, **kalends.** [< Latin *kalendae*]

ca len du la (kə len′jə lə), *n.* 1 any of a small genus of composite herbs with yellow or orange flowers. 2 the flower of any of these herbs, used as medicine. [< New Latin < Latin *kalendae* calends]

calf[1] (kaf), *n., pl.* **calves** for 1, 2, and 4. 1 a young cow or bull. 2 a young elephant, whale, deer, seal, etc. 3 calfskin. 4 INFORMAL. a clumsy, silly boy or young man. 5 **kill the fatted calf,** prepare a feast to celebrate something or welcome someone; prepare an elaborate welcome. [Old English *cealf*]

calf[2] (kaf), *n., pl.* **calves.** the thick, fleshy part of the back of the leg below the knee. [< Scandinavian (Old Icelandic) *kālfi*]

calf skin (kaf′skin′), *n.* 1 skin of a calf. 2 leather made from it.

Cal ga ry (kal′gər ē), *n.* city in SW Canada. 361,000.

Cal houn (kal hün′), *n.* **John Caldwell,** 1782-1850, American statesman, vice-president of the United States from 1825 to 1832.

Cal i ban (kal′ə ban), *n.* 1 the beastlike slave in Shakespeare's play *The Tempest.* 2 any bestial or degraded man.

cal i ber (kal′ə bər), *n.* 1 the inside diameter of the barrel of a rifle, shotgun, or pistol. A .45-caliber revolver has a barrel with an [illegible] 2 the

We have a calico cat. [< *Calicut,* India]

Cal i cut (kal′ə kut), *n.* seaport in SW India. 306,000.

ca lif (kā′lif, kal′if), *n.* caliph.

Calif., the official abbreviation of California.

cal i fate (kal′ə fāt, kā′lə fāt), *n.* caliphate.

Cal i for nia (kal′ə fôr′nyə, kal′ə fôr′nē ə), *n.* 1 one of the Pacific states of the United States. 19,953,000 pop.; 158,700 sq. mi. *Capital:* Sacramento. *Abbrev.:* Calif. 2 **Gulf of,** arm of the Pacific between Lower California and the mainland of Mexico. 750 mi. long. **—Cal′i for′nian,** *adj., n.*

California Current, a cold ocean current originating in the northern Pacific and passing southward and then southwestward along the western coast of North America.

California poppy, 1 a small herb of the poppy family, having finely divided leaves and orange, yellow, or cream-colored flowers. 2 its flower.

cal i for ni um (kal′ə fôr′nē əm), *n.* a radioactive metallic element, produced artificially from curium, plutonium, or uranium. *Symbol:* Cf; *atomic number* 98. See pages 326 and 327 for table. [< *California*]

Ca lig u la (kə lig′yə lə), *n.* A.D. 12-41, Roman emperor from A.D. 37 to 41.

cal i pers (kal′ə pərz), *n.pl.* instrument used to measure the diameter or thickness of something. Also, **callipers.** [variant of *caliber*]

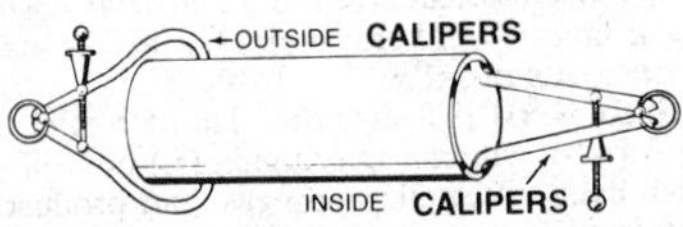

ca liph (kā′lif, kal′if), *n.* the former title of religious and political heads of some Moslem states. Also, **calif, khalif.** [< Old French *calife* < Arabic *khalīfa* successor]

cal iph ate (kal′ə fāt, kā′lə fāt), *n.* rank, reign, government, or territory of a caliph. Also, **califate.**

cal is then ic (kal′is then′ik), *adj.* of calisthenics. Also, **callisthenic.**

cal is then ics (kal′is then′iks), *n.* 1 *pl. in form and use.* exercises to develop a strong and graceful body, carried out by moving the body, without the use of special equipment. 2 *pl. in form, sing. in use.* the practice or art of calisthenic exercises. Also, **callisthenics.** [< Greek *kallos* beauty + *sthenos* strength]

calk[1] (kôk), *n.* 1 a projecting piece on a horseshoe that catches in the ground or ice to prevent slipping. 2 a sharp, projecting piece of metal on the bottom of a shoe to prevent slipping. *—v.t.* put calks on. [< Latin *calcem* heel or *calcar* spur]

calk[2] (kôk), *v.t.* caulk. **—calk′er,** *n.*

call (kôl), *v.t.* 1 speak or say in a loud voice; shout or cry out: *The nurse called the names of the next three patients.* 2 give a signal to: *The bugle called the men to assemble.* 3 rouse; waken: *Call me at seven o'clock.* 4 ask to come; summon: *He called us to help him.* See synonym study below. 5 ask to come; cause to come: *The assembly was called to order. My case will be called in court tomorrow.* 6 get; bring: *The space age has called into existence a whole new body of scientific and technical words.* 7 give a name to; name: *They called the new baby "John."* 8 read over aloud: *The teacher called the roll of the class.* 9 talk to by telephone; telephone: *Call me at the office.* 10 consider; estimate: *Everyone called the party a success.* 11 end; stop: *The ball game was called on account of rain.* 12 demand payment of: *The bank called my loan.* 13 demand for payment: *The company will call its bonds April first.* 14 U.S. INFORMAL. declare or describe in advance; predict. *—v.i.* 1 speak in a loud voice; shout or cry out: *He called from downstairs.* 2 (of a bird or animal) utter its characteristic noise or cry. 3 to telephone: *Did you call anyone today?* 4 make a short visit or stop: *She called and left a birthday card.* 5 demand a show of hands in poker.

call back, **a** ask (a person) to return; recall. **b** telephone to someone who has called earlier. **c** take back; retract.

call down, INFORMAL. scold.

call for, **a** go and get; stop and get. **b** need; require.

call in, **a** summon for advice or consultation. **b** withdraw from free action, circulation, or publicity. **c** collect as debts: *call in a mortgage.*

call off, **a** cancel. **b** say or read over aloud in succession. **c** order to withdraw.

call on or **call upon,** **a** pay a short visit to. **b** appeal to.

call out, **a** say in a loud voice; shout. **b** summon into service. **c** (in the armed forces) commission an officer temporarily for some special assignment or duty. **d** bring into play; elicit; evoke.

call up, **a** bring to mind; bring back. **b** telephone to. **c** draft into military service.

—n. 1 a shout or cry. 2 the characteristic noise or cry of a bird or other animal. 3 a signal given by sound: *Reveille and taps are bugle calls.* 4 invitation, request, command, or summons. 5 a telephone call. 6 a short visit or stop. 7 a claim or demand: *A busy person has many calls on his time.* 8 a need; occasion: *You have no call to meddle in other people's business.* 9 a demand for payment. 10 a notice requiring actors and stagehands to attend a rehearsal. 11 act of calling. 12 (in poker) the demand that all hands still active be shown after their players have matched the current bet. 13 (in square dancing) an instruction which is chanted or shouted. 14 a calling; vocation. 15 **on call,** **a** ready or available. **b** subject to payment on demand. 16 **within call,** near enough to hear a call. [unrecorded Old English *callian,* dialectal variant of *ceallian* to call]

Syn. *v.t.* 4 **Call, invite, summon** mean to ask or order someone to come. **Call** is the general and informal word: *The principal called the student leaders to her office.* **Invite** means to ask politely, and suggests giving a person a chance to do something he would like to do: *The principal invited the student leaders to come in and talk things over.* **Summon** means to call with authority, and is used especially of a formal calling up to duty or to some formal meeting: *The principal summoned the rebellious students to her office.*

cal la (kal′ə), *n.* 1 species of arum with a large, petallike, white, pink, or yellow leaf curled around a thick spike of yellow florets. 2 species of arum with heart-shaped leaves, which grows in marshes. [< New Latin]

calla lily, 1 calla (def. 1). 2 its blossom.

Cal la o (kä yä′ō, kä lyä′ō), *n.* seaport in W Peru, near Lima. 322,000.

call board (kôl′bôrd′, kôl′bōrd′), *n.* bulletin board in a theater, for posting hours of rehearsal, etc.

call boy (kôl′boi′), *n.* bellboy in a hotel, ship, etc.

cal ler (kô′lər), *n.* 1 person who makes a short visit. 2 person who calls out steps at a square dance. 3 person who calls.

cal lig ra pher (kə lig′rə fər), *n.* 1 person who writes by hand. 2 person who writes by hand beautifully.

cal li graph ic (kal′ə graf′ik), *adj.* having to do with calligraphy.

cal lig ra phy (kə lig′rə fē), *n.* 1 handwriting. 2 beautiful handwriting. [< Greek *kalligraphia* < *kallos* beauty + *graphein* write]

call ing (kô′ling), *n.* 1 occupation, profession, or trade. 2 invitation, command, or summons. 3 a spiritual or divine summons to a special service or office.

calling card, a small card with a person's name on it, used when visiting someone, in acknowledging gifts, etc.; visiting card.

cal li o pe (kə lī′ə pē; *for 1, also* kal′ē ōp), *n.* 1 a musical instrument having a series of steam whistles played by pushing keys. 2 **Calliope,** (in Greek myths) the Muse of eloquence and heroic poetry. [< Latin *Calliope* < Greek *Kalliope* < *kallos* beauty + *ops* voice]

cal li op sis (kal′ē op′sis), *n.* any of a number of annual species of coreopsis.

cal li pers (kal′ə pərz), *n.pl.* calipers.

cal lis then ic (kal′is then′ik), *adj.* calisthenic.

cal lis then ics (kal′is then′iks), *n.* calisthenics.

call loan, loan that must be paid back on demand.

call money, money borrowed that must be paid back on demand.

call number, set of numbers and letters assigned to a library book to identify it and find its location in the library.

cal los i ty (kə los′ə tē), *n., pl.* **-ties.** 1 callus (def. 1). 2 lack of feeling or sensitivity; hardness of heart.

cal lous (kal′əs), *adj.* 1 hard or hardened, as parts of the skin that are exposed to constant pressure and friction. 2 unfeeling; insensitive: *Only a callous person can see suffering without trying to relieve it.* **—cal′lous ly,** *adv.* **—cal′lous ness,** *n.*

cal loused (kal′əst), *adj.* made callous; hardened.

cal low (kal′ō), *adj.* 1 young and inexperienced: *a callow youth.* 2 not fully developed. 3 (of birds) without feathers sufficiently developed for flight. [Old English *calu* bald] **—cal′low ness,** *n.*

call-up (kôl′up′), *n.* a summoning of men to military training or duty.

cal lus (kal′əs), *n.* 1 a hard, thickened place on the skin. 2 a new growth to unite the ends of a broken bone. 3 substance that grows over the wounds of plants. *—v.i.* form or develop a callus. [< Latin]

calm (käm, kälm), *adj.* 1 not stormy or windy; not stirred up; quiet; still: *a calm sea.* 2 not excited; peaceful: *Although she was frightened, she answered with a calm voice.* See synonym study below. *—n.* 1 absence of wind or motion; quietness; stillness. 2 absence of excitement; peacefulness. 3 (in meteorology) a condition in which the wind has a velocity of less than one mile per hour. *—v.i.* become calm: *The crying baby soon calmed down.* *—v.t.* make calm: *I soon calmed the baby.* [< Old French *calme* < Italian *calma* time for rest < Greek *kauma* heat of the day] **—calm′ly,** *adv.* **—calm′ness,** *n.*

Syn. *adj.* 2 **Calm, composed, collected** mean not disturbed or excited. **Calm** means being or seeming to be completely undisturbed, showing no sign of being confused or excited: *Mother's calm behavior quieted the frightened boy.* **Composed** means calm as the result of having or having got command over one's thoughts and feelings and, sometimes, an inner peace: *She was composed at the funeral.* **Collected** emphasizes having control over one's actions, thoughts, and feelings, especially at times of danger or disturbance: *He was collected as he led the rescuers.*

cal o mel (kal′ə mel, kal′ə məl), *n.* a white, tasteless, crystalline powder, a compound of mercury and chlorine, used in medicine as a laxative; mercurous chloride. *Formula:* Hg_2Cl_2 [< Greek *kalos* beautiful + *melas* black]

ca lo ric (kə lôr′ik, kə lor′ik), *n.* heat. *—adj.* 1 having to do with heat. 2 of or having to do with calories. **—ca lo′ri cal ly,** *adv.*

cal or ie (kal′ər ē), *n., pl.* **-or ies.** 1 either of two units for measuring the amount of heat: **a small calorie,** the quantity of heat necessary to raise the temperature of a gram of water one degree centigrade. **b large calorie,** the quantity of heat necessary to raise the temperature of a kilogram of water one degree centigrade. 2 unit of the energy supplied by food, corresponding to the large calorie. An ounce of sugar will produce about one hundred such calories. 3 quantity of food capable of producing such an amount of energy. Also, **calory.** [< French < Latin *calor* heat]

cal o rif ic (kal′ə rif′ik), *adj.* 1 producing heat. 2 caloric.

cal o rim e ter (kal′ə rim′ə tər), *n.* apparatus for measuring the quantity of heat, as the specific heat of different substances or the heat of chemical combination.

cal or i met ric (kal′ər ə met′rik), *adj.* having to do with calorimetry. **—cal′or i met′ri cal ly,** *adv.*

cal o rim e try (kal′ə rim′ə trē), *n.* the quantitative measurement of heat.

cal or y (kal′ər ē), *n., pl.* **-or ies.** calorie.

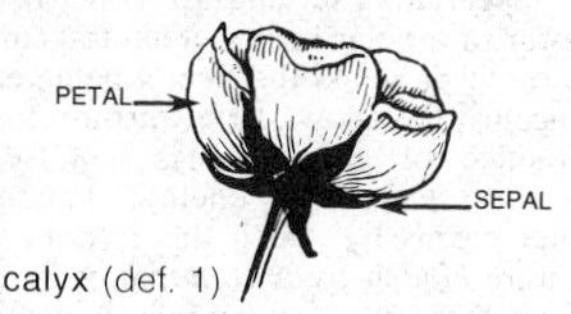

calyx (def. 1)

cal u met (kal′yə met, kal′yə met′), *n.* a long, ornamented tobacco pipe smoked by the American Indians in ceremonies as a symbol of peace; peace pipe. [< Canadian French, ultimately < Latin *calamus* reed < Greek *kalamos*]

ca lum ni ate (kə lum′nē āt), *v.t.,* **-at ed, -at ing.** say false and harmful things about; slander. **—ca lum′ni a′tor,** *n.*

ca lum ni a tion (kə lum′nē ā′shən), *n.* 1 act of calumniating. 2 calumny.

ca lum ni ous (kə lum′nē əs), *adj.* slanderous. **—ca lum′ni ous ly,** *adv.*

cal um ny (kal′əm nē), *n., pl.* **-nies.** a false statement made to injure someone's reputation; slander. [< Latin *calumnia.* Doublet of CHALLENGE.]

Cal var y (kal′vər ē), *n.* (in the Bible) a place near Jerusalem where Jesus died on the Cross; Golgotha.

calve (kav), *v.i.,* **calved, calv ing.** give birth to a calf. [Old English *calfian* < *cealf* calf]

hat, āge, fär; let, ēqual, tėrm;
it, īce; hot, ōpen, ôrder;
oil, out; cup, pu̇t, rüle;
ch, child; ng, long; sh, she;
th, thin; ᴛʜ, then; zh, measure;

ə represents *a* in about, *e* in taken, *i* in pencil, *o* in lemon, *u* in circus.

< = from, derived from, taken from.

Cal vert (kal′vərt), *n.* 1 Sir **George,** 1580?-1632, the first Lord Baltimore, an English noble who was responsible for founding the colony of Maryland. 2 his son, **Leonard,** 1606?-1647, the first governor of the colony of Maryland.

calves (kavz), *n.* pl. of **calf**[1] (defs. 1, 2, and 4) and **calf**[2].

Cal vin (kal′vən), *n.* **John,** 1509-1564, French leader of the Protestant Reformation at Geneva. The Puritans and Huguenots followed the teachings of Calvin.

Cal vin ism (kal′və niz′əm), *n.* the religious teachings of Calvin and his followers, especially the doctrine that God has ordained all things beforehand, including the salvation of man, who has fallen from his pure state, and that only the elect will be saved.

Cal vin ist (kal′və nist), *n.* person who follows the teachings of Calvin. *—adj.* having to do with Calvinism or Calvinists.

Cal vin is tic (kal′və nis′tik), *adj.* of Calvinism.

calx (kalks), *n., pl.* **calx es, cal ces** (kal′sēz′). an ashy substance left after a metal or a mineral has been thoroughly roasted, burned, etc. [< Latin, lime]

Cal y don (kal′ə don), *n.* city in the W part of ancient Greece.

Cal y do ni an (kal′ə dō′nē ən), *adj.* of Calydon. The **Calydonian boar** was a wild boar sent by Artemis to attack Calydon. Meleager finally killed it.

ca lyp so (kə lip′sō), *n., pl.* **-sos.** type of improvised song, usually about some matter of current interest, that originated in the British West Indies.

Ca lyp so (kə lip′sō), *n.* (in Greek legends) a sea nymph who detained Ulysses on her island for seven years on his way home from the Trojan War.

ca lyx (kā′liks, kal′iks), *n., pl.* **ca lyx es, cal y ces** (kal′ə sēz′, kā′lə sēz′). 1 the outer leaves that surround the unopened bud of a flower. The calyx is made up of sepals. 2 (in anatomy and zoology) a cuplike structure or organ. [< Latin < Greek *kalyx*]

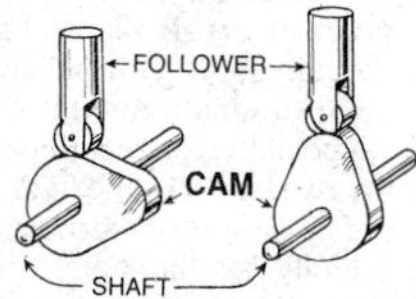

cam—As the cam turns with the shaft, the follower moves down (left) and up (right).

cam (kam), *n.* a noncircular wheel mounted on a shaft that changes a regular circular motion into an irregular circular motion or into a back-and-forth motion. Cams are used to vary the speed of some mechanisms or to change the direction of their movement. [< Dutch *kam* cog, comb]

Ca ma güey (kä′mä gwā′), *n.* city in central Cuba. 191,000.

ca ma ra der ie (kä′mə rä′dər ē), *n.* friendliness and loyalty among comrades; comradeship. [< French]

cam ass or **cam as** (kam′əs), *n.* plant of the lily family growing in western North America, having a sweet, edible bulb. [< Chinook jargon]

cam ber (kam′bər), *v.t., v.i.* bend or curve upward in the middle; arch slightly. *—n.* 1 an upward bend or curve in the middle; slight arch. 2 a slightly arching piece of timber. 3 the rise and fall of the curve of an airfoil of an aircraft. 4 a slight inward tilt of the bottom of the wheels of an automobile. [< Middle French *cambre* bent < Latin *camur* crooked]

cam bi um (kam′bē əm), *n.* layer of soft growing tissue between the bark and the wood of trees and shrubs. New bark and new wood grow from it. [< Medieval Latin, exchange < Latin *cambiare* to exchange]

Cam bo di a (kam bō′dē ə), *n.* country in SE Asia, formerly part of French Indochina. Its official name is **Khmer Republic.** 7,000,000 pop.; 69,900 sq. mi. *Capital:* Phnom Penh. See **Indochina** for map. **—Cam bo′di an,** *adj., n.*

Cam bri a (kam′brē ə), *n.* an old name of Wales.

Cam bri an (kam′brē ən), *n.* 1 the earliest geological period of the Paleozoic era. During this period there were large numbers of primitive, invertebrate water animals. See chart under **geology.** 2 the rocks formed during this period. 3 Welshman. *—adj.* 1 of or having to do with the Cambrian or its rocks. 2 Welsh.

cam bric (kām′brik), *n.* a fine, thin linen or cotton cloth. [< *Cambrai,* city in France]

cambric tea, drink made of hot water, milk, and sugar, sometimes flavored with a little tea.

Cam bridge (kām′brij), *n.* 1 city in E England. 100,000. 2 university located there. 3 city in E Massachusetts, near Boston. 100,000.

Cam den (kam′dən), *n.* city in SW New Jersey, on the Delaware. 103,000.

came (kām), *v.* pt. of **come.** *I came to school late this morning.*

cam el (kam′əl), *n.* either of two kinds of cud-chewing mammals with a long neck and cushioned feet, used as a beast of burden in the deserts of northern Africa and central Asia because they can go for a long time without drinking water. The dromedary, or Arabian camel, has one hump; the Bactrian camel has two humps. [< Latin *camelus* < Greek *kamēlos;* of Semitic origin]

cam el back (kam′əl bak′), *n.* 1 the back of a camel. 2 compound of reclaimed rubber with a small amount of crude rubber, used especially for recapping tires.

ca mel lia (kə mē′lyə, kə mē′lē ə), *n.* 1 any of a genus of shrubs or trees of the same family as the tea shrub, with glossy evergreen leaves and waxy white, red, pink, or mottled flowers shaped like roses. 2 the flower of any of these plants. [< George J. *Camellus,* 1661-1706, missionary in Luzon]

ca mel o pard (kə mel′ə pärd), *n.* giraffe. [< Greek *kamēlopardalis* < *kamēlos* camel + *pardalis* leopard]

Cam e lot (kam′ə lot), *n.* a legendary place in England where King Arthur had his palace and court.

camel's hair, 1 hair of a camel, used in making cloth, paintbrushes, etc. 2 cloth made of this hair or something like it.

Cam em bert (kam′əm ber), *n.* a rich, soft cheese. [< *Camembert,* a village in France]

cam e o (kam′ē ō), *n., pl.* **cam e os.** 1 a precious or semiprecious stone carved so that there is a raised design on a background usually of a different color. Agates, other stones having a layered structure, and sometimes shells, are used for cameos. 2 a dramatic sketch, performance, etc., that highlights a certain character or event. [< Italian]

cam er a (kam′ər ə), *n., pl.* **-er as** for 1 and 2, **-er as** or **-er ae** (-ər ē) for 3. 1 machine for taking photographs or motion pictures in which film or plates are exposed to light and the image is formed by means of a lens. 2 part of the transmitter which converts images into electronic impulses for television transmitting. 3 a judge's private office. 4 **in camera,** a in a judge's private office. b privately. [< Latin, arched chamber, arch < Greek *kamara.* Doublet of CHAMBER.]

cam er a man (kam′ər ə man′), *n., pl.* **-men.** man who operates a camera, especially a motion-picture or television camera.

Cam er oon (kam′ə rün′), *n.* country in W central Africa, including the former Cameroun and the southern portion of the former Cameroons. 5,836,000 pop.; 183,300 sq. mi. *Capital:* Yaoundé. See **Upper Volta** for map. Also, **Cameroun. —Cam′er oon′i-an,** *adj., n.*

Cam er oons (kam′ə rünz′), *n.* former British trust territory in W Africa, divided between Cameroon and Nigeria in 1961.

Cam er oun (kam′ə rün′), *n.* 1 Cameroon. 2 former French trust territory now included in Cameroon.

cam i sole (kam′ə sōl), *n.* a woman's undergarment that is like the top part of a slip. [< French]

Cam o ëns (kam′ō ens), *n.* **Luis de,** 1524-1580, Portuguese poet.

cam o mile (kam′ə mīl), *n.* chamomile.

cam ou flage (kam′ə fläzh), *n., v.,* **-flaged, -flag ing.** *—n.* 1 a disguise or false appearance serving to conceal. The white fur of a polar bear is a natural camouflage, for it prevents the bear's being easily seen against the snow. 2 (in warfare) the act or practice of giving things a false appearance to deceive the enemy. 3 materials or other means by which this is done: *The guns were hidden by a camouflage of earth and branches.* *—v.t.* give a false appearance to in order to conceal; disguise: *camouflage hurt feelings with laughter.* [< French < *camoufler* to disguise] **—cam′-ou flag′er,** *n.*

camp (kamp), *n.* 1 group of tents, huts, or other shelters where people live temporarily: *A marching army usually makes camp every night.* 2 place where one lives in a tent or hut or outdoors. 3 area where an army sets up temporary shelter. 4 persons living in a camp. 5 any tent, hut, or other shelter to live in temporarily: *Many people live in a camp near a lake in the summer.* 6 act of living an outdoor life with very simple shelter; camping. 7 group of people who agree or work together. 8 military life. 9 (in the western United States) a town that has sprung up in a mining area. 10 **break camp,** pack up tents and equipment. 11 **in the same camp,** in agreement; working together.
—v.i. 1 make a camp; put up tents, huts, or other shelters. 2 live in a camp for a time. 3 live simply without comforts for a time. 4 **camp out,** a live in the open in a tent or camp: *We camped out for a week.* b spend the night outdoors.
[< French < Italian *campo* < Latin *campus* field. Doublet of CAMPUS.]

cam paign (kam pān′), *n.* 1 series of related military operations for some special purpose: *The general planned a campaign to capture the enemy's most important city.* 2 series of connected activities to do or get something; planned course of action for some special purpose: *a campaign to raise money for a college, an advertising campaign, a campaign to elect someone to political office.* *—v.i.* take part in or serve in a campaign. [< French *campagne* open country (where military campaigns were undertaken), ultimately < Latin *campus* field] **—cam paign′er,** *n.*

Cam pa ni a (kam pā′nē ə), *n.* region in SW Italy. **—Cam pa′ni an,** *adj., n.*

cam pa ni le (kam′pə nē′lē), *n., pl.* **-ni les, -ni li** (-nē′lē). tower built to contain a bell or bells. It may be a separate building. [< Italian < *campana* bell < Late Latin]

cam pan u la (kam pan′yə lə), *n.* any of a genus of plants with bell-shaped blue, purple, pink, or white flowers, such as the bluebell and Canterbury bell; bellflower. [< Medieval Latin, diminutive of *campana* bell]

Cam pe che (käm pā′chā), *n.* 1 state in SE Mexico, in the Yucatán Peninsula. 2 seaport and capital of this state. 44,000.

camp er (kam′pər), *n.* 1 person who camps or camps out. 2 a vehicle fitted out for camping, such as a small trailer, or a trailer-like room attached to the bed of a pickup truck.

cam pe si no (käm pä sē′nō), *n., pl.* ***-nos.*** SPANISH. farmer or peasant.

camp fire (kamp′fīr′), *n.* 1 fire in a camp for cooking or warmth. 2 a social gathering of soldiers, scouts, etc.

campfire girl, member of the Camp Fire Girls.

Camp Fire Girls, organization for girls that seeks to develop health, character, citizenship, and usefulness to others.

camp ground (kamp′ground′), *n.* 1 place for camping, such as a public park with fireplaces, campsites, etc. 2 place where a camp meeting is held.

cam phor (kam′fər), *n.* a white, crystalline substance with a strong odor and a bitter taste, usually obtained from the camphor tree and used in medicine and to protect clothes from moths. *Formula:* $C_{10}H_{16}O$ [< Medieval Latin *camphora* < Arabic *kāfūr*]

cam phor at ed (kam′fə rā′tid), *adj.* containing camphor: *camphorated oil.*

camphor tree, an evergreen tree of the same family as the laurel, found in southeast Asia.

cam pi on (kam′pē ən), *n.* any of a genus of pinks with red, pink, or white flowers. [perhaps < Latin *campus* field]

camp meeting, a religious gathering held outdoors or in a tent, sometimes lasting several days.

cam po ree (kam′pə rē′), *n.* a gathering or outing by boy scouts or girl scouts of a district. [< *camp* + *(jamb)oree*]

camp site (kamp′sīt′), *n.* place where people camp.

camp stool (kamp′stül′), *n.* a lightweight folding seat.

cam pus (kam′pəs), *n.* grounds of a college, university, or school. [< Latin, field, plain. Doublet of CAMP.]

cam shaft (kam′shaft′), *n.* a rod or shaft on which a cam is fastened.

Ca mus (kȧ mʏ′), *n.* **Albert,** 1913-1960, French novelist and essayist.

can[1] (kan; *unstressed* kən), *auxiliary v., present sing.* and *pl.* **can,** *past* **could.** 1 be able to: *He can read rapidly.* 2 know how to: *She can run that machine.* 3 have the right to: *Anyone can cross the street here.* 4 be allowed to; may: *You can go if you want to.* [Old English, know, know how, can]

➔ **can, may.** In general informal usage *may* occurs rather rarely except in the sense of possibility: *It may be all right for her, but not for me. Can* is generally used for both permission and ability: *Can I go now? You can if you want to. I can go 80 miles an hour with my car.* This is in such general usage that it should be regarded as acceptable English in speaking and in informal writing. In formal English, however, some distinction is often made between the auxiliary *can,* implying ability, being able to, and *may,* implying permission: *You may go now. He can walk with crutches. You may if you can. May* also indicates possibility: *She may have been the one.*

can[2] (kan), *n., v.,* **canned, can ning.** —*n.* 1 a metal container, usually with a cover or lid: *a trash can, a paint can.* 2 amount that a can holds. 3 contents of a can. 4 a drinking cup. 5 U.S. SLANG. **a** a depth charge. **b** a destroyer. —*v.t.* 1 put in a can; preserve by putting in an airtight can or jar: *can fruit.* 2 U.S. SLANG. dismiss from a job; get rid of. 3 U.S. SLANG. do away with or cease doing (something): *Can the chatter.* [Old English *canne* vessel]

Can., 1 Canada. 2 Canadian.

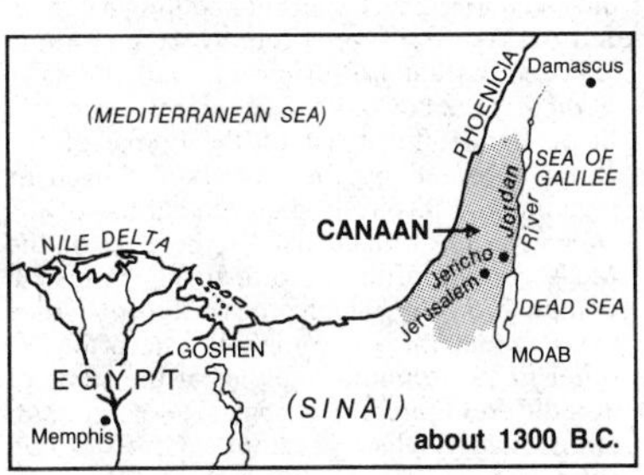

Canaan (def. 1)

Ca naan (kā′nən), *n.* 1 (in the Bible) a region between the Jordan River and the Mediterranean; Palestine. God promised Canaan to Abraham and his descendants. 2 land of promise.

Ca naan ite (kā′nə nīt), *n.* inhabitant of Canaan before it was conquered by the Hebrews.

Can a da (kan′ə də), *n.* country in the N part of North America, consisting of ten provinces and two territories and extending from the Atlantic to the Pacific and from the United States to the Arctic Ocean. It is a member of the Commonwealth of Nations. 21,681,000 pop.; 3,851,800 sq. mi. *Capital:* Ottawa.

Canada balsam, a sticky, yellow resin obtained from the balsam fir tree. It is used in making lacquers and varnishes, and for mounting objects on glass slides to be examined under a microscope.

Canada goose, a large, wild goose of North America, having a black head and neck, white throat, and a brownish-gray body with gray underparts.

Ca na di an (kə nā′dē ən), *adj.* of Canada or its people. —*n.* native or inhabitant of Canada.

Canadian French, the form of French spoken by French-speaking Canadians.

Canadian Shield, extensive rocky plateau rich in minerals, lying north of the Great Lakes in Canada; Laurentian Highlands.

ca naille (kə nāl′, ka nī′), *n.* the lowest class of people; rabble; riffraff. [< French < Italian *canaglia* < *cane* dog < Latin *canem*]

ca nal (kə nal′), *n.* 1 waterway dug across land for ships and small boats to go through or to carry water for irrigation. 2 tube in the body of an animal or in a plant that carries food, liquid, air, etc. 3 a long arm of a large body of water. [< Latin *canalis* trench, pipe < *canna* cane. Doublet of CHANNEL.]

canal boat (kənal′bōt′), *n.* a long, narrow boat used on canals.

can a lic u lus (kan′ə lik′yə ləs), *n., pl.* **-li** (-lī). a small canal or duct in the body. Canaliculi connect the small cavities in the bones. [< New Latin]

ca nal ize (kə nal′īz, kan′l īz), *v.t.,* **-ized, -iz ing.** 1 make a canal or canals through. 2 make into or like a canal. **—ca nal′i za′tion,** *n.*

Canal Zone, the Panama Canal and the land five miles on each side, governed by the United States. 50,000 pop.; 553 sq. mi. Also, **Panama Canal Zone.**

can a pé (kan′ə pā, kan′ə pē), *n.* cracker or thin piece of toast or bread spread with a seasoned mixture of olives, meat, fish, cheese, etc., and served as an appetizer. [< French, literally, couch, sofa. Related to CANOPY.]

ca nard (kə närd′), *n.* a false rumor; exaggerated report; hoax. [< French]

Ca nar ies (kə ner′ēz), *n.pl.* Canary Islands.

ca nar y (kə ner′ē), *n., pl.* **-nar ies,** *adj.* —*n.* 1 a small, yellow or greenish songbird, originally from the Canary Islands. It is a kind of finch and is often kept as a pet. 2 a light yellow. 3 a light, sweet white wine from the Canary Islands. —*adj.* light-yellow.

Canary Islands, group of Spanish islands in the Atlantic, near the NW coast of Africa. 944,000 pop.; 2800 sq. mi. *Capital:* Santa Cruz de Tenerife.

canary yellow, a light yellow.

ca nas ta (kə nas′tə), *n.* 1 a card game similar to rummy, played with two decks of cards plus four jokers. The players try to earn as many points as possible by melding sets of seven or more cards. 2 a seven-card set in this game. [< Spanish, literally, basket, ultimately < Latin *canistrum.* See CANISTER.]

Ca nav er al (kə nav′ər əl), *n.* **Cape,** former name of **Cape Kennedy.**

Can ber ra (kan′ber ə, kan′bər ə), *n.* capital of Australia, in the SE part. 135,000.

can can (kan′kan), *n.* a kind of dance marked by extravagant kicking and leaping. [< French]

can cel (kan′səl), *v.,* **-celed, -cel ing** or **-celled, -cel ling,** *n.* —*v.t.* 1 put an end to, set aside, or withdraw; do away with; stop: *cancel an appointment. She canceled her order for the books.* 2 make up for; compensate for; balance: *The little boy's sweet smile canceled his mischief.* 3 cross out; mark, stamp, or punch so that it cannot be used again: *cancel a stamp.* 4 in mathematics: **a** reduce (a fraction) by dividing both the numerator and the denominator by the same quantity. **b** reduce (an equation) by dividing both members by a common factor. —*n.* 1 a canceling. 2 a canceled part. [< Latin *cancellare* cross out with latticed lines < *cancelli* crossbars]

hat, āge, fär; let, ēqual, tėrm;
it, īce; hot, ōpen, ôrder;
oil, out; cup, pu̇t, rüle;
ch, child; ng, long; sh, she;
th, thin; ᴛʜ, then; zh, measure;

ə represents *a* in about, *e* in taken, *i* in pencil, *o* in lemon, *u* in circus.

< = from, derived from, taken from.

can cel la tion (kan′sə lā′shən), *n.* 1 a canceling. 2 a being canceled. 3 marks made when something is canceled or crossed out. 4 something that is canceled.

can cer (kan′sər), *n.* 1 a very harmful growth in the body; malignant tumor, formed by a change in the normal growth of cells, and tending to spread and destroy the healthy tissues and organs of the body. 2 any of several diseases characterized by such abnormal cell development. 3 an evil or harmful thing that tends to spread. 4 **Cancer, a** tropic of Cancer. **b** a northern constellation seen by ancient astronomers as having the rough outline of a crab. **c** the fourth sign of the zodiac; Crab. The sun enters Cancer about June 21. [< Latin, crab, tumor. Doublet of CANKER, CHANCRE.]

can cer ous (kan′sər əs), *adj.* 1 like cancer. 2 having cancer.

can de la (kan dē′lə), *n.* unit for measuring the strength or intensity of light, equal to 1/60 of the radiating power of one square centimeter of a black body at the temperature at which platinum solidifies; candle. It replaced the international candle in the United States in 1948. [< Latin, candle]

can de la bra (kan′dl ä′brə, kan′dl ā′brə), *n.* candelabrum.

can de la brum (kan′dl ä′brəm, kan′dl ā′brəm), *n., pl.* **-bra** or **-brums.** an ornamental candlestick with several branches for holding candles. [< Latin < *candela* candle]

can des cent (kan des′nt), *adj.* glowing with heat; incandescent.

can did (kan′did), *adj.* 1 saying openly what one really thinks; frank and sincere; outspoken: *a candid reply.* See **frank**[1] for synonym study. 2 fair; impartial: *a candid decision.* 3 unposed: *a candid photograph of children playing.* [< Latin *candidus* white < *candere* to shine] **—can′did ly,** *adv.* **—can′did ness,** *n.*

can di da cy (kan′də də sē), *n., pl.* **-cies.** fact or condition of being a candidate: *Please support my candidacy for the office of class treasurer.*

can di date (kan′də dāt, kan′də dit), *n.* 1 person who seeks, or is proposed for, some office or honor: *There are three candidates for president of the club.* 2 person who is studying for a degree: *a doctoral candidate.* 3 person applying for a position: *There were twenty candidates for the job.* [< Latin *candidatus* clothed in white (toga) < *candidus* white]

can di da ture (kan′də də chu̇r, kan′də dā′chər), *n.* BRITISH. candidacy.

candid camera, a small camera with a fast lens for photographing persons unposed and often unaware that their picture is being taken.

can died (kan′dēd), *adj.* 1 cooked in sugar; glazed with sugar: *candied sweet potatoes.* 2 made sweet or agreeable: *candied words of praise.* 3 preserved or encrusted with sugar: *candied ginger.*

can dle (kan′dl), *n., v.,* **-dled, -dling.** *—n.* 1 stick of wax or tallow with a wick in it, burned to give light. 2 anything shaped or used like a candle. Sulfur candles are burned to disinfect rooms. 3 either of two units, candela or international candle, for measuring the strength or intensity of light. 4 **burn the candle at both ends,** use up one's strength and resources rapidly. 5 **not hold a candle to,** not compare with. *—v.t.* test (eggs) for freshness by holding them in front of a light. [Old English *candel* < Latin *candela* < *candere* to shine] **—can′dler,** *n.*

can dle hold er (kan′dl hōl′dər), *n.* candlestick.

can dle light (kan′dl līt′), *n.* 1 light of a candle or candles. 2 time when candles are lighted; dusk; twilight. 3 artificial light.

can dle lit (kan′dl lit′), *adj.* lit by candlelight.

Can dle mas (kan′dl məs), *n.* February 2, a church festival in honor of the purification of the Virgin Mary and the presentation of the infant Jesus in the Temple. It is celebrated with lighted candles.

can dle pin (kan′dl pin′), *n.* 1 one of a set of thin, cylindrical bowling pins. 2 **candlepins,** *pl.* game of tenpins played with these bowling pins.

candle power, strength or intensity of light, measured in candles. One candle power is equal to 12.57 lumens.

can dle stick (kan′dl stik′), *n.* holder for a candle, to make it stand up straight; candleholder.

can dle wick (kan′dl wik′), *n.* wick of a candle.

can dor (kan′dər), *n.* 1 a saying openly what one really thinks; honesty in giving one's view or opinion; frankness and sincerity. 2 fairness; impartiality. [< Latin, whiteness < *candere* to shine]

can dour (kan′dər), *n.* BRITISH. candor.

can dy (kan′dē), *n., pl.* **-dies,** *v.,* **-died, -dy ing.** *—n.* 1 sugar or syrup, cooked and flavored, then cooled and made into small pieces for eating. Chocolate, butter, milk, nuts, fruits, etc., are often added. 2 piece of this: *Take a candy from the box.* *—v.t.* 1 turn into sugar. 2 cook in sugar; preserve by boiling in sugar. 3 make sweet or agreeable. *—v.i.* become sugar or covered with candied sugar: *this honey has candied.* [< French *(sucre) candi* (sugar) candy < Persian *qand* sugar]

can dy tuft (kan′dē tuft′), *n.* plant of the mustard family, with clusters of white, purple, pink, or red flowers.

cane (kān), *n., v.,* **caned, can ing.** *—n.* 1 stick to help a person in walking. 2 stick used to inflict punishment. 3 a long, jointed stem, such as that of the bamboo. 4 plant having such stems. Sugar cane, bamboo, and rattan are canes. 5 material made of such stems, used for furniture, chair seats, etc. 6 a slender stalk or stem. *—v.t.* 1 beat with a cane. 2 make or repair with material made of long, jointed stems. [< Latin *canna* reed < Greek *kanna*]

Ca ne a (kə nē′ə), *n.* capital of Crete, a seaport in the NW part. 38,000.

cane brake (kān′brāk′), *n.* thicket of cane plants.

cane sugar, sugar made from sugar cane.

ca nine (kā′nīn), *adj.* 1 of or like a dog: *canine faithfulness.* 2 like that of a dog: *The glutton had a canine appetite.* 3 of or belonging to the family of carnivorous mammals that includes dogs, foxes, jackals, and wolves. *—n.* 1 a dog. 2 any animal belonging to the canine family. 3 a canine tooth. [< Latin *caninus* < *canis* dog]

canine tooth, one of the four pointed teeth next to the incisors; cuspid. See **incisor** for diagram.

Ca nis Major (kā′nis), constellation southeast of Orion that contains Sirius, the brightest of the stars. [< Latin, literally, greater dog]

Ca nis Minor (kā′nis), constellation east of Orion, separated from Canis Major by the Milky Way. [< Latin, literally, lesser dog]

can is ter (kan′ə stər), *n.* 1 a small box or can, especially for tea, coffee, flour, or sugar. 2 cylinder or shell filled with metal fragments that is shot from a cannon. 3 the boxlike part of a gas mask that contains the filtering or chemical substance through which the air is breathed. [< Latin *canistrum* basket < Greek *kanastron*]

can ker (kang′kər), *n.* 1 a spreading sore, especially one in the mouth. 2 a fungous disease of plants, especially of fruit trees, that causes slow decay. 3 anything that causes rot or decay or destroys by a gradual eating away. 4 cankerworm. *—v.t., v.i.* infect or be infected with canker; decay; rot. [Old English *cancer* < Latin, crab, tumor. Doublet of CANCER, CHANCRE.]

can ker ous (kang′kər əs), *adj.* 1 of or like canker. 2 causing canker.

can ker worm (kang′kər wėrm′), *n.* caterpillar that eats away the leaves of trees and plants.

can na (kan′ə), *n.* 1 any of a genus of tropical or subtropical plants with large, pointed leaves and large red, pink, or yellow flowers. 2 the flower of any of these plants. [< Latin, reed]

can na bis (kan′ə bis), *n.* 1 hemp. 2 the dried flowering tops of the hemp from which marijuana and hashish are made. [< Latin]

canned (kand), *adj.* 1 put in a can; preserved by being put in airtight cans or jars: *canned peaches.* 2 SLANG. preserved on a phonograph record; recorded: *canned music.*

can nel (kan′l), *n.* cannel coal. [apparently variant of *candle*]

cannel coal, bituminous coal in large lumps that burns with a bright flame.

can nel lo ni (kan′ə lō′nē), *n.pl.* pasta for soup in the shape of thick tubes, usually stuffed with meat or cheese. [< Italian]

can ner (kan′ər), *n.* person who cans food.

can ner y (kan′ər ē), *n., pl.* **-ner ies.** factory where food is canned.

Cannes (kan, kanz; *French* kän), *n.* resort in SE France, on the Mediterranean. 67,000.

can ni bal (kan′ə bəl), *n.* 1 person who eats human flesh. 2 animal that eats others of its own kind. *—adj.* of or like cannibals. [< Spanish *Canibal* Carib < Arawak]

can ni bal ism (kan′ə bə liz′əm), *n.* practice of eating the flesh of one's own kind.

can ni bal is tic (kan′ə bə lis′tik), *adj.* of or characteristic of cannibals. **—can′ni bal is′ti cal ly,** *adv.*

can ni bal ize (kan′ə bə līz), *v.t.,* **-ized, -iz ing.** take usable parts from (a vehicle, piece of machinery, etc.) to assemble or repair another: *My brother cannibalized a baby carriage to get its wheels for a racing car.*

can ning (kan′ing), *n.* the preserving of food by cooking it and sealing it up in airtight cans or jars.

can non (kan′ən), *n., pl.* **-nons** or **-non.** 1 a large gun, especially one that is too large to be carried by hand and is fixed to the ground or mounted on a carriage. Artillery consists of cannons, such as howitzers and mortars. 2 cannon bone. [< Italian *cannone* < Latin *canna* reed, tube < Greek *kanna*]

can non ade (kan′ə nād′), *n., v.,* **-ad ed, -ad ing.** *—n.* a continued firing of cannons; barrage. *—v.t.* attack with or as if with cannons.

cannon ball (kan′ən bôl′), *n.* a large iron or steel ball, formerly fired from cannons.

cannon bone, (in horses, etc.) the bone between the hock and the fetlock.

can non eer (kan′ə nir′), *n.* artilleryman; gunner.

can not (kan′ot, ka not′, kə not′), *v.* can not.

➤ **cannot, can not.** Usage is divided, but *cannot* is by far the more common spelling. *Can not* should be used only if the negative is to be emphasized.

can ny (kan′ē), *adj.,* **-ni er, -ni est.** 1 shrewd and cautious in dealing with others. 2 thrifty. [< *can*[1]] **—can′ni ly,** *adv.* **—can′ni ness,** *n.*

ca noe (kə nü′), *n., v.,* **-noed, -noe ing.** *—n.* a light boat often tapered at both ends and moved with a paddle. *—v.i.* paddle a canoe; go in a canoe. [< Spanish *canoa* < Arawak]

ca noe ist (kə nü′ist), *n.* 1 person who paddles a canoe. 2 an expert in paddling a canoe.

can on[1] (kan′ən), *n.* 1 rule by which a thing is judged; standard; criterion: *the canons of good taste.* 2 law of a church; body of church law. 3 the official list of the books of the Bible accepted by the Christian church as genuine and inspired. 4 an official list of the saints. 5 any official list. 6 the part of the Mass coming after the offertory. 7 musical composition in which the different voice parts repeat the same melody one after another in strict imitation either at the same or at a different pitch. 8 a large size of type; 48 point. [Old English < Latin < Greek *kanōn* rule]

can on[2] (kan′ən), *n.* 1 member of a group of clergymen belonging to a cathedral chapter or other collegiate church. 2 member of a group of Roman Catholic clergymen living according to a certain rule. [< Old French < Late Latin *canonicus* clergyman < Latin *canon* canon[1]]

ca ñon (kan′yən), *n.* canyon.

ca non i cal (kə non′ə kəl), *adj.* 1 according to or prescribed by the laws of a church. 2 in the canon of the Bible. 3 authorized; accepted. **—ca non′i cal ly,** *adv.*

canonical hours, the seven periods of the day fixed by canon law for prayer and worship. There are matins (and lauds), prime, tierce, sext, nones, vespers, and complin.

ca non i cals (kə non′ə kəlz), *n.pl.* clothes worn by a clergyman at a church service.

can on ize (kan′ə nīz), *v.t.,* **-ized, -iz ing.** 1 declare (a dead person) to be a saint; place in the official list of saints: *Joan of Arc was canonized by the Roman Catholic Church in 1920.* 2 treat as a saint; glorify. 3 make or recognize as canonical. 4 authorize. **—can′on i za′tion,** *n.*

canon law, laws of a church governing ecclesiastical affairs.

Ca no pus (kə nō′pəs), *n.* the second brightest star in the sky, in the southern constellation Argo.

can o py (kan′ə pē), *n., pl.* **-pies,** *v.,* **-pied, -py ing.** *—n.* 1 a covering fixed over a bed, throne, entrance, etc., or carried on poles over a person. 2 a rooflike covering; shelter or shade. 3 sky. 4 the umbrellalike supporting area of a parachute. 5 the sliding transparent cover of the cockpit of a small aircraft. *—v.t.* cover with a canopy. [< Old French *canape* < Medieval Latin *canapeum* < Greek *kōnōpion* a couch with curtains of mosquito netting < *kōnōps* gnat]

canst (kanst), *v.* ARCHAIC. can[1]. "Thou canst" means "you can."

cant[1] (kant), *n.* 1 insincere talk; moral or religious statements that many people make, but few really believe or follow out. 2 the peculiar language of a special group, using many strange words; jargon; argot: *"Jug" is one of the words for "jail" in thieves' cant.* *—adj.* peculiar to a special group: *cant words of thieves.* *—v.i.* 1 use cant; talk in cant. 2 speak in the manner of a beggar; whine; beg. [< Latin *cantus* song]

cant[2] (kant), *n.* 1 a sloping, slanting, or tilting position; inclination. 2 a sudden pitch which causes a person or thing to overturn or fall. 3 a turning or tilting movement. *—v.t.* 1 give a slant or slope to; bevel. 2 put into a slant; tip; tilt: *The wind canted the ship to port.* 3 pitch with a sudden jerk: *The horse canted his rider into the stream.* *—v.i.* 1 tilt, pitch on one side, or turn over. 2 have a slanting position or direction. [< Old French < Popular Latin *cantus* corner, edge < Latin, tire of a wheel]

can't (kant), cannot or can not.

➤ **can't help (but).** In spite of the objection that it involves double negation, *can't* (or *cannot) help but* is an established informal usage: *I can't help but feel sorry about it.* In more formal usage this would be: *I cannot* (or *can't) help feeling sorry about it.*

can ta bi le (kän tä′bi lā), *adj.* (in music) in a smooth and flowing style; songlike. [< Italian]

Can ta brig i an (kan′tə brij′ē ən), *adj.* of Cambridge, England, or Cambridge University. *—n.* 1 native or inhabitant of Cambridge, England. 2 student or graduate of Cambridge University. [< Medieval Latin *Cantabrigia* Cambridge]

can ta loupe or **can ta loup** (kan′tl ōp), *n.* kind of muskmelon with a hard, rough rind and sweet, juicy, orange flesh. [< French *cantaloup* < Italian *Cantalupo* papal estate near Rome where first cultivated]

can tan ker ous (kan tang′kər əs), *adj.* hard to get along with because of a nature that is ready to make trouble and oppose anything suggested; ill-natured; quarrelsome. [Middle English *contecker* contentious person < *conteck* strife, quarreling < Anglo-French] **—can tan′ker ous ly,** *adv.* **—can tan′ker ous ness,** *n.*

can ta ta (kən tä′tə), *n.* musical composition consisting of a story or play which is sung by a chorus and soloists, but not acted. [< Italian < *cantare* sing < Latin]

can teen (kan tēn′), *n.* 1 a small container for carrying water or other drinks. 2 a place in a school, camp, factory, etc., where food, drinks, and other articles are sold or given out. 3 recreation hall for servicemen. 4 box of cooking utensils for use in camp. [< French *cantine* < Italian *cantina* wine cellar]

can ter (kan′tər), *v.t., v.i.* gallop gently. *—n.* a gentle gallop. [short for *Canterbury (gallop);* from the easy pace of pilgrims riding to Canterbury]

Can ter bur y (kan′tər ber′ē), *n.* city in SE England. Many pilgrims traveled there during the Middle Ages to visit the shrine of Saint Thomas à Becket. 33,000.

Canterbury bell, species of campanula with tall stalks of bell-shaped flowers, usually purplish-blue, pink, or white.

cant hook, pole with a movable hook at one end, used to grip and turn over logs.

can ti cle (kan′tə kəl), *n.* a short song, hymn, or chant used in religious services. [< Latin *canticulum* little song < *cantus* song]

Canticle of Canticles, (in the Douay Bible) The Song of Solomon.

Can ti cles (kan′tə kəlz), *n.* book of the Old Testament. It is also called **The Song of Solomon** or **The Song of Songs.**

can ti lev er (kan′tl ev′ər, kan′tl ē′vər), *n.* a large, projecting bracket or beam that is supported at one end only, especially one designed to bear a weight or structure over a space where supports cannot be placed or are not desired. *—v.t.* build (something) with cantilevers or a cantilever. *—v.i.* extend outward, as a cantilever. [origin uncertain]

cantilever bridge, bridge made of two cantilevers whose projecting ends meet but do not support each other.

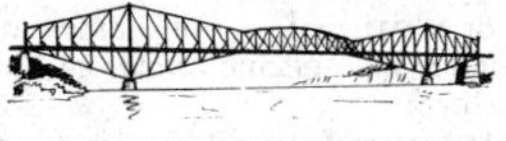

cantilever bridge

can tle (kan′tl), *n.* the part of a saddle that sticks up at the back. [< Old French *cantel* < Medieval Latin *cantellus* little corner]

can to (kan′tō), *n., pl.* **-tos.** one of the main divisions of a long poem. A canto of a poem corresponds to a chapter of a novel. [< Italian < Latin *cantus* song]

can ton (kan′tən, kan′ton, kan ton′), *n.* a small part or political division of a country. Switzerland is made up of 22 cantons. *—v.t.* allot quarters to or provide quarters for (soldiers, etc.). [< French < Italian *cantone* < *canto* corner < Popular Latin *cantus.* See CANT[2].]

Can ton (kan ton′ *for 1;* kan′tən *for 2*), *n.* 1 former name of **Kwangchow.** 2 city in NE Ohio. 110,000.

can ton al (kan′tə nəl), *adj.* of a canton.

Can ton ese (kan′tə nēz′), *n., pl.* **-ese,** *adj.* *—n.* 1 native or inhabitant of Canton, China. 2 the Chinese dialect spoken in or near Canton, China. *—adj.* of Canton, China, its people, or their dialect.

can ton ment (kan ton′mənt, kan tōn′mənt), *n.* place where soldiers live; quarters for soldiers.

can tor (kan′tər, kan′tôr), *n.* 1 man who leads the services in a synagogue. 2 man who leads the singing of a choir or congregation. [< Latin, singer < *canere* sing]

Ca nuck (kə nuk′), *n., adj.* SLANG. 1 Canadian. 2 French Canadian.

Ca nute (kə nüt′, kə nyüt′), *n.* 994?-1035, king of England from 1017? to 1035 who also was king of Denmark and Norway.

can vas (kan′vəs), *n.* 1 a strong cloth with a coarse weave made of cotton, flax, or hemp, used to make tents, sails, certain articles of clothing, etc. 2 something made of or covered with canvas. 3 **the canvas,** the floor of a boxing ring. 4 sail or sails. 5 piece of canvas on which an oil painting is painted. 6 an oil painting. 7 **under canvas, a** in tents. **b** with sails spread. *—adj.* made of canvas. [< Old French *canevas* < Latin *cannabis* hemp]

hat, āge, fär; let, ēqual, tėrm;
it, īce; hot, ōpen, ôrder;
oil, out; cup, pu̇t, rüle;
ch, child; ng, long; sh, she;
th, thin; ᴛʜ, then; zh, measure;

ə represents *a* in about, *e* in taken, *i* in pencil, *o* in lemon, *u* in circus.

< = from, derived from, taken from.

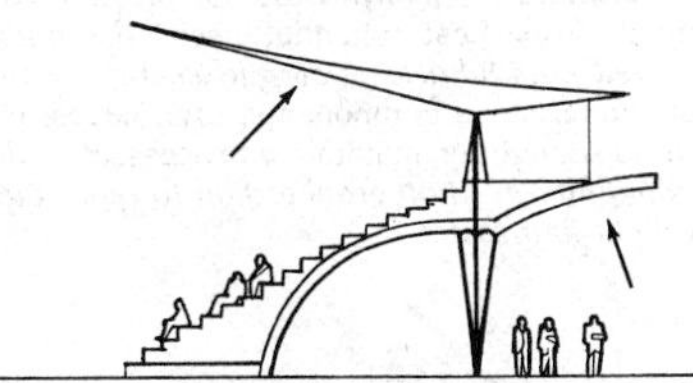

cantilever—two cantilevers shown in a cross section of a football grandstand

can vas back (kan′vəs bak′), *n.* a large wild duck of North America. The male has a reddish-brown head and neck and a grayish-white back.

can vass (kan′vəs), *v.t.* 1 go through (a city, district, etc.) asking for votes, orders, donations, etc.: *Salesmen canvassed the whole city for subscriptions to magazines.* 2 examine carefully; inspect: *She canvassed the papers, hunting for notices of jobs.* 3 examine and count the votes cast in an election. 4 discuss: *The city council canvassed the mayor's plan thoroughly.* *—v.i.* ask for votes, orders, donations, etc.: *The candidate canvassed right up to election day.* *—n.* 1 act or process of canvassing, especially a personal visiting of homes and stores in a district to sell something, ask for votes, etc. 2 discussion. [< obsolete verb *canvass* toss (someone) in a sheet, (later) shake out, discuss < *canvas*] **—can′vass er,** *n.*

can yon (kan′yən), *n.* a narrow valley with high, steep sides, usually with a stream at the bottom. Also, **cañon.** [< Mexican Spanish *cañón* narrow passage]

caou tchouc (kou chük′, kü′chu̇k), *n.* the gummy, coagulated juice of various tropical plants of the same family as the spurge, from which rubber is made; crude, natural rubber. [< Quechua *cauchuc* Indian rubber tree]

cap (kap), *n., v.,* **capped, cap ping.** *—n.* 1 a close-fitting covering for the head, with little or no brim but often with a visor. 2 a special head covering worn to show rank or occupation: *a nurse's cap.* 3 anything like a cap: *a bottle cap.* The top of a mushroom is called a cap. 4 the highest part; top: *the polar cap at the North Pole.* 5 a small quantity of explosive in a wrapper or covering. 6 **set one's cap for,** INFORMAL. try to get for a husband. *—v.t.* 1 put a cap on: *cap a bottle.* 2 put a top on; cover the top of: *Whipped cream capped the dessert.* 3 do or follow with something as good or better: *Each of the two* *clowns capped the other's last joke.* 4 form or serve as a cap, covering, or crown to; lie on top of. [Old English *cæppe* < Late Latin *cappa* cap, hood, mantle. Doublet of CAPE[1].] **—cap′less,** *adj.* **—cap′like′,** *adj.*

cap., 1 capacity. 2 capital. 3 capitalize. 4 *pl.* **caps.** capital letter.

ca pa bil i ty (kā′pə bil′ə tē), *n., pl.* **-ties.** 1 ability to learn or do; power or fitness; capacity: *the capability to master higher mathematics.* 2 **capabilities,** *pl.* undeveloped properties; potential uses: *the unexplored capabilities of atomic energy.* 3 the characteristics, components, etc., necessary to do something, maintain a process, etc.: *the capability of photographic film to reproduce a light impression.*

caparison (def. 1)

ca pa ble (kā′pə bəl), *adj.* 1 having fitness, power, or ability; able; efficient; competent: *a capable teacher.* See **able** for synonym study. 2 **capable of, a** having ability, power, or fitness for: *Some airplanes are capable of going 1000 miles per hour.* **b** open to; ready for: *a statement capable of many interpretations.* [< Late Latin *capabilis* < Latin *capere* take] **—ca′pa ble ness,** *n.* **—ca′pably,** *adv.*

ca pa cious (kə pā′shəs), *adj.* able to hold much; large and roomy; spacious: *a capacious closet.* **—ca pa′cious ly,** *adv.* **—ca-pa′cious ness,** *n.*

ca pac i tance (kə pas′ə təns), *n.* property of a capacitor that determines the amount of electrical charge it can receive and store; capacity.

ca pac i tate (kə pas′ə tāt), *v.t.,* **-tat ed, -tat ing.** make capable or fit; qualify.

ca pac i tor (kə pas′ə tər), *n.* device for receiving and storing a charge of electricity, consisting of two conducting surfaces or plates separated by a layer of insulation; condenser.

ca pac i ty (kə pas′ə tē), *n., pl.* **-ties.** 1 amount of room or space inside; largest amount that can be held by a container: *A gallon can has a capacity of 4 quarts.* 2 power of receiving and holding: *a theater with a seating capacity of 400.* 3 ability to learn or do; power or fitness: *a great capacity for learning.* 4 ability to withstand some force or perform some function: *the capacity of a metal to retain heat.* 5 the physical power or ability to produce: *the maximum capacity of a machine.* 6 maximum output: *Steel factories worked at capacity during the war.* 7 capacitance. 8 position or relation. A person may act in the capacity of guardian, trustee, voter, friend, etc. 9 legal power or qualification. [< Latin *capacitatem* < *capere* take]

cap and bells, cap trimmed with bells, worn by a jester.

cap and gown, a flat cap and loose gown, worn by teachers and students on certain occasions.

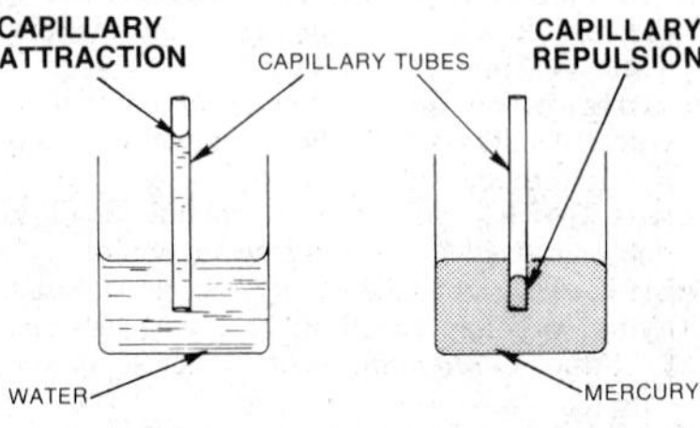

cap-a-pie or **cap-à-pie** (kap′ə pē′), *adv.* from head to foot; completely. [< Middle French *(de) cap à pied* (from) head to foot]

ca par i son (kə par′ə sən), *n.* 1 an ornamental covering for a horse. 2 any rich dress or outfit. *—v.t.* dress richly; fit out. [< Middle French *caparaçon* < Spanish *caparazón*]

cape[1] (kāp), *n.* an outer garment, or part of one, without sleeves, worn falling loosely from the shoulders and often fastened at the neck. [< French < Spanish *capa* < Late Latin *cappa* cap, hood. Doublet of CAP.]

cape[2] (kāp), *n.* point of land extending into the water. [< Old French *cap* < Provençal < Latin *caput* head]

Cape or **Cape of.** For names of capes look under the specific name, as **Horn** (for Cape Horn).

Cape Breton Island, island off the E coast of Canada, part of Nova Scotia. 167,000 pop.; 4000 sq. mi.

Cape buffalo, a large, fierce buffalo of southern Africa.

cap e lin (kap′ə lən), *n.* a small fish of the north Atlantic, used for food and as bait for cod. [< French]

Ca pel la (kə pel′ə), *n.* the brightest star in the constellation Auriga, one of the six brightest stars in the sky.

Cape of Good Hope, 1 See **Good Hope.** 2 province in the S part of the Republic of South Africa.

ca per[1] (kā′pər), *v.i.* leap or jump about playfully. *—n.* 1 a playful leap or jump. 2 prank; trick. 3 **cut a caper** or **cut capers, a** play or do a trick. **b** dance, leap, or jump about playfully. [probably short for *capriole*]

ca per[2] (kā′pər), *n.* 1 a low, prickly shrub of the Mediterranean region. 2 **capers,** *pl.* the green flower buds and unripe berries of this shrub, pickled and used for seasoning. [< Latin *capparis* < Greek *kapparis*]

Ca per na um (kə pėr′nē əm), *n.* town in ancient Palestine, on the Sea of Galilee.

Ca pet (kā′pit, kap′it), *n.* **Hugh,** A.D. 938?-996, king of France from A.D. 987 to 996.

Ca pe tian (kə pē′shən), *adj.* of or having to do with Hugh Capet or the kings named Capet who ruled in France from A.D. 987 to 1328. *—n.* member of the Capetian dynasty.

Cape town (kāp′toun′), *n.* Cape Town.

Cape Town, seaport near the S tip of Africa. The legislature for the Republic of South Africa meets there. 626,000.

Cape Verde Islands, group of islands west of Cape Verde, belonging to Portugal. *Capital:* Praia. 250,000 pop.; 1600 sq. mi.

cap il lar i ty (kap′ə lar′ə tē), *n.* 1 capillary attraction or repulsion. 2 quality of having or causing capillary attraction or repulsion.

cap il lar y (kap′ə ler′ē), *n., pl.* **-lar ies,** *adj.* *—n.* a blood vessel with a very slender, hairlike opening. Capillaries join the end of an artery to the beginning of a vein. *—adj.* 1 of or in the capillaries. 2 like a hair; very slender. [< Latin *capillaris* of hair, hairlike < *capillus* hair]

capillary attraction, the force that causes a liquid to rise in a narrow tube or when in contact with a porous substance. A plant draws up water from the ground and a paper towel absorbs water by means of capillary attraction.

capillary repulsion, the force that causes a liquid to be depressed when in contact with the sides of a narrow tube, as is mercury in a glass tube.

capillary tube, tube with a very slender, hairlike opening or bore.

cap i tal[1] (kap′ə təl), *n.* 1 city where the government of a country, state, or province is located. 2 capital letter. 3 amount of money or property that a company or a person uses in carrying on a business: *The Smith Company has a capital of $30,000.* 4 source of power or advantage; resources. 5 national or individual wealth as produced by industry and available for reinvestment in the production of goods. 6 in accounting: **a** the net worth of a business after the deduction of taxes and other liabilities. **b** the total investment in a business, often expressed as capital stock. 7 capitalists as a group. 8 **make capital of,** take advantage of; use to one's advantage: *He made capital of his father's fame to get the job.*
—adj. 1 of or having to do with capital. 2 important; leading. 3 main; chief. 4 of the best kind; excellent: *A maple tree gives capital shade.* 5 involving death; punishable by death: *Murder is a capital crime in many countries.* 6 in which the seat of government is located: *a capital city.*
[< Latin *capitalem* chief; punishable by death < *caput* head. Doublet of CATTLE, CHATTEL.]
➔ **Capital, capitol** are often confused. *Capital* always has the basic meaning of chief, head, first in its class or in importance. In the United States, *capitol* always applies only to a building in which a legislature meets: *There is a dome on the capitol in Sacramento, the capital of California.*

cap i tal[2] (kap′ə təl), *n.* the top part of a column or pillar. See **column** for diagram. [< Late Latin *capitellum,* diminutive of Latin *caput* head]

capital goods, goods, such as machinery, equipment, etc., that can be used in the production of other goods.

cap i tal ism (kap′ə tə liz′əm), *n.* an economic system based on the ownership of land, factories, and other means of production by private individuals or groups of individuals who compete with one another, using the hired labor of other persons, to produce goods and services that are offered on a free market for whatever profit may be obtainable.

cap i tal ist (kap′ə tə list), *n.* 1 person whose money and property are used in carrying on business. 2 a wealthy person. 3 person who favors or supports capitalism.

cap i tal is tic (kap′ə tə lis′tik), *adj.* 1 of or having to do with capitalism or capitalists. 2 favoring or supporting capitalism. **—cap′-i tal is′ti cal ly,** *adv.*

cap i tal i za tion (kap′ə tə lə zā′shən), *n.* 1 a capitalizing. 2 a being capitalized. 3 amount at which a company is capitalized; capital stock of a business.

cap i tal ize (kap′ə tə līz), *v.*, **-ized, -iz ing.** —*v.t.* 1 write or print with a capital letter. 2 set the capital of (a company) at a certain amount. 3 turn into capital; use as capital: *The company capitalized its reserve funds.* 4 provide or furnish with capital. —*v.i.* **capitalize on,** take advantage of; use to one's advantage: *capitalize on another's mistake.*

capital letter, the large form of a letter; A, B, C, D, etc., as distinguished from a, b, c, d, etc.

cap i tal ly (kap′ə tə lē), *adv.* very well; excellently.

capital punishment, the death penalty for a crime.

capital ship, a large warship, such as a battleship.

capital stock, capital used in carrying on a business. It is represented in shares.

cap i ta tion (kap′ə tā′shən), *n.* tax, fee, or charge of the same amount for every person. [< Late Latin *capitationem* poll tax < Latin *caput* head]

Cap i tol (kap′ə təl), *n.* 1 the building at Washington, D.C., in which Congress meets. 2 Also, **capitol.** the building in which a state legislature meets. 3 the ancient temple of Jupiter on the Capitoline Hill in Rome. 4 the Capitoline Hill. [< Latin *Capitolium* chief temple (of Jupiter) < *caput* head] ➤ See **capital**[1] for usage note.

Cap i to line (kap′ə tl īn), *n.* one of the seven hills on which ancient Rome was built. —*adj.* having to do with the Capitol at Rome or the hill on which it stood.

ca pit u late (kə pich′ə lāt), *v.i.*, **-lat ed, -lat ing.** surrender on certain terms or conditions: *The men in the fort capitulated on condition that they be allowed to go away unharmed.* [< Medieval Latin *capitulatum* arranged under headings or chapters < Latin *capitulum* small head < *caput* head] **—ca pit′u la′tor,** *n.*

ca pit u la tion (kə pich′ə lā′shən), *n.* 1 a surrender on certain terms or conditions. 2 agreement or condition. 3 summary.

Cap′n (kap′ən), *n.* Captain.

ca pon (kā′pon, kā′pən), *n.* rooster specially raised to be eaten. It is castrated and fattened. [Old English *capūn* < Latin *caponem*]

Cap pa do cia (kap′ə dō′shə), *n.* ancient Roman province in E Asia Minor.

Ca pri (kə prē′, kä′prē), *n.* small island in the Bay of Naples, Italy. 11,000 pop.; 5.5 sq. mi.

ca pric ci o (kə prē′chē ō), *n.*, *pl.* **-ci os.** a lively piece of music in a free, irregular style. [< Italian]

ca price (kə prēs′), *n.* 1 a sudden change of mind without reason; unreasonable notion or desire; whim. 2 tendency to change suddenly and without reason. 3 capriccio. [< French < Italian *capriccio,* literally, a shiver]

ca pri cious (kə prish′əs, kə prē′shəs), *adj.* likely to change suddenly without reason; changeable; fickle: *capricious weather.* **—ca pri′cious ly,** *adv.* **—ca pri′cious ness,** *n.*

Cap ri corn (kap′rə kôrn), *n.* 1 tropic of Capricorn. 2 a southern constellation seen by ancient astronomers as having the rough outline of a goat. 3 the 10th sign of the zodiac. The sun enters Capricorn about December 22. [< Latin *capricornus* < *caper* goat + *cornu* horn]

Cap ri cor nus (kap′rə kôr′nəs), *n.* Capricorn.

cap ri ole (kap′rē ōl), *n.*, *v.*, **-oled, -ol ing.** —*n.* 1 a high leap made by a horse without moving forward. 2 a leap or caper, as in dancing. —*v.i.* 1 (of a horse) make a high leap without moving forward. 2 leap; caper. [< French < Italian *capriola,* ultimately < Latin *caper* goat]

caps., capital letters.

cap si cum (kap′sə kəm), *n.* pepper (def. 4). [< New Latin < Latin *capsa* box]

cap size (kap sīz′, kap′sīz), *v.i., v.t.*, **-sized, -siz ing.** turn bottom side up; upset; overturn: *The sailboat nearly capsized in the squall. The rough waves capsized the rowboat.* [perhaps < Spanish *chapuzar* to duck, as under water, ultimately < Latin *sub* under + *puteus* pit]

cap stan (kap′stən), *n.* machine for lifting or pulling that revolves on an upright shaft or spindle, now usually operated by an engine. Sailors on old sailing ships hoisted the anchor or raised heavy sails by turning the capstan. [< Provençal *cabestan* < Latin *capistrum* halter < *capere* take]

capstan on large sailing vessel. As it is turned, it winds up the rope that hoists the anchor, or unwinds it.

capstan bar, pole used to turn a capstan.

cap stone (kap′stōn′), *n.* 1 the top stone or top layer of stones of a wall or other structure. 2 a finishing touch; climax.

cap su lar (kap′sə lər, kap′syə lər), *adj.* 1 of or having to do with a capsule. 2 shaped like a capsule.

cap sule (kap′səl, kap′syül), *n., adj., v.*, **-suled, -sul ing.** —*n.* 1 a small case or covering. Medicine is often given in capsules made of gelatin. 2 the enclosed front section of a rocket made to carry instruments, astronauts, etc., into space. In flight the capsule can separate from the rest of the rocket and go into orbit or be directed back to earth. 3 dry seedcase that opens when ripe. 4 a membrane enclosing an organ of the body; membranous bag or sac. 5 a concise summary. —*adj.* 1 very short; condensed or abridged: *a capsule comment.* 2 very small; miniature: *a capsule radio transmitter.* 3 of or having to do with a space capsule: *a capsule communicator.* —*v.t.* furnish with or enclose within a capsule. [< Latin *capsula,* diminutive of *capsa* box]

Capt., Captain.

cap tain (kap′tən), *n.* 1 head of a group; leader or chief: *Robin Hood was captain of his band.* 2 commander of a ship. 3 an army, air force, or marine officer ranking next below a major and next above a first lieutenant. 4 a navy officer ranking next below a rear admiral and next above a commander. 5 a police or fire department officer ranking next above a lieutenant. 6 leader of a team in sports. —*v.t.* lead or command as captain: *I will captain the swimming team next season.* [< Old French *capitaine* < Late Latin *capitaneus* chief < Latin *caput* head. Doublet of CHIEFTAIN.]

hat, āge, fär; let, ēqual, tėrm;
it, īce; hot, ōpen, ôrder;
oil, out; cup, pu̇t, rüle;
ch, child; ng, long; sh, she;
th, thin; ᴛʜ, then; zh, measure;

ə represents *a* in about, *e* in taken, *i* in pencil, *o* in lemon, *u* in circus.

< = from, derived from, taken from.

cap tain cy (kap′tən sē), *n.*, *pl.* **-cies.** rank, commission, or authority of a captain.

cap tain ship (kap′tən ship), *n.* captaincy.

cap tion (kap′shən), *n.* 1 title or heading at the head of a page, article, chapter, etc., or under a picture explaining it. 2 (in motion pictures) a subtitle. —*v.t.* put a caption on. [< Latin *captionem* a taking < *capere* take]

cap tious (kap′shəs), *adj.* 1 hard to please; faultfinding. 2 that entraps or entangles by subtlety: *captious arguments.* [< Latin *captiosus* < *capere* take] **—cap′tious ly,** *adv.* **—cap′tious ness,** *n.*

cap ti vate (kap′tə vāt), *v.t.*, **-vat ed, -vat ing.** hold captive by beauty, talent, or interest; charm; fascinate: *The children were captivated by the story.* **—cap′ti vat′ing ly,** *adv.* **—cap′ti va′tor,** *n.*

cap ti va tion (kap′tə vā′shən), *n.* 1 a captivating. 2 a being captivated. 3 charm; fascination.

cap tive (kap′tiv), *n.* person or animal captured and held against his will; prisoner. —*adj.* 1 made a prisoner; held against one's will: *The captive soldiers were shut up in a dungeon.* 2 captivated. 3 owned and controlled by another company. 4 of or belonging to a captive. [< Latin *captivus* < *capere* take. Doublet of CAITIFF.]

cap tiv i ty (kap tiv′ə tē), *n.*, *pl.* **-ties.** 1 condition of being in prison. 2 condition of being held against one's will: *Some animals cannot bear captivity, and die after a few weeks in a cage.*

cap tor (kap′tər), *n.* person who takes or holds a prisoner.

cap ture (kap′chər), *v.*, **-tured, -tur ing,** *n.* —*v.t.* 1 make a prisoner of; take by force, skill, or trickery; seize: *We captured butterflies with a net.* See **catch** for synonym study. 2 attract and hold; catch and keep: *capture a person's attention.* —*n.* 1 person or thing taken by force, skill, or trickery. 2 a capturing. 3 a being captured. [< Latin *captura* a taking < *capere* take]

cap u chin (kap′yə shən, kə pyü′shən), *n.* 1 a South American monkey with black hair on its head that looks like a hood. 2 **Capuchin,** a Franciscan monk belonging to an order that wears a long, pointed hood or cowl. [< Middle French < Italian *cappuccio* hood < *cappa* < Late Latin]

cap y ba ra (kap′ə bär′ə), *n.* a tailless rodent of South America. It is the world's largest rodent, growing up to two feet high and four feet long. [< Portuguese < Tupi]

car (kär), *n.* 1 a four-wheeled passenger vehicle driven by an internal-combustion engine; automobile. 2 a railroad car or streetcar. 3 any vehicle that moves on wheels. 4 the closed platform of an elevator, balloon, or airship for carrying passengers or cargo. 5 chariot. [< Old North French *carre* wagon < Medieval Latin *carra* < Latin *carrus*]

ca ra ba o (kär′ə bä′ō), *n., pl.* **-ba os.** water buffalo of the Philippines. [< Spanish < Malay *kĕrbau*]

car a bi neer or **car a bi nier** (kar′ə bə nir′), *n.* (in former times) a cavalry soldier with a carbine.

Car a cal la (kar′ə kal′ə), *n.* A.D. 188-217, Roman emperor from A.D. 211 to 217.

ca ra ca ra (kär′ə kär′ə), *n.* any of several vulturelike hawks of South and Central America and the southern United States. [< Spanish *caracará* < Tupi]

Ca ra cas (kə rä′kəs, kə rak′əs), *n.* capital of Venezuela, in the N part. 1,000,000.

car a cole (kar′ə kōl), *n., v.,* **-coled, -col ing.** —*n.* a half turn to the right or left, made by a horse and rider. —*v.i.* make such half turns; prance from side to side. [< French]

car a cul (kar′ə kəl), *n.* 1 a short, flat, loose, curly fur made from the skin of newborn or very young lambs of a breed of robust, fat-tailed Asian sheep. 2 any of this breed of sheep. Also, **karakul.** [< *Kara Kul,* lake in Turkestan]

ca rafe (kə raf′), *n.* a glass bottle for holding water, wine, coffee, etc., especially an ornamental one. [< French < Italian *caraffa* < Spanish *garrafa* < Arabic *gharrāf* drinking vessel]

car a gan a (kar′ə gan′ə), *n.* any of a genus of trees or shrubs of the pea family, native to Asia, having feathery, pale green foliage and yellow flowers appearing in early spring. [< New Latin]

car a mel (kar′ə məl, kär′məl), *n.* 1 sugar browned or burned over heat, used for coloring and flavoring food. 2 a small block of chewy candy flavored with this sugar. [< French < Spanish *caramelo*]

car a mel ize (kär′ə mə liz, kär′mə liz), *v.t., v.i.* **-ized, -iz ing.** change into caramel. —**car′a mel i za′tion,** *n.*

car a pace (kar′ə pās), *n.* shell or bony covering on the back of a turtle, armadillo, lobster, crab, etc. [< French < Spanish *carapacho*]

car at (kar′ət), *n.* 1 unit of weight for precious stones, equal to $^1/_5$ gram. 2 karat. [< Middle French < Italian *carato* < Arabic *qīrāt* < Greek *keration,* diminutive of *keras* horn]

car a van (kar′ə van), *n.* 1 group of merchants, pilgrims, etc., traveling together for safety through difficult or dangerous country. 2 the vehicles or beasts of burden used by such a group. 3 a closed truck or, formerly, a large, covered wagon, for moving goods; van. 4 BRITISH. trailer (def. 3). [< Old French *caravane* < Persian *kārwān*]

car a van sa ry (kar′ə van′sər ē), *n., pl.* **-ries.** 1 inn in the Orient where caravans stop to rest, usually surrounding a spacious court. 2 any large inn. [< Persian *kārwān-sarāī* < *kārwān* caravan + *sarāī* inn]

car a van se rai (kar′ə van′sə rī′, kar′ə van′sə rā′), *n.* caravansary.

car a vel (kar′ə vel), *n.* a small, fast sailing ship of the type used by Columbus with a broad bow and a high stern. [< French *caravelle* < Portuguese *caravela*]

car a way (kar′ə wā), *n.* 1 plant of the same family as parsley that yields fragrant, spicy seeds which are used to flavor bread, rolls, cakes, etc. 2 its seeds. [< Arabic *karawyā*]

car bide (kär′bīd, kär′bid), *n.* 1 compound of carbon with another element, usually a metal. 2 calcium carbide.

car bine (kär′bīn, kär′bēn′), *n.* a short, light rifle or musket. [< French *carabine*]

car bo hy drate (kär′bō hī′drāt), *n.* substance made from carbon dioxide and water by green plants in sunlight. Carbohydrates are composed of carbon, hydrogen, and oxygen. Sugar and starch are carbohydrates.

car bo lat ed (kär′bə lā′tid), *adj.* containing carbolic acid.

car bol ic acid (kär bol′ik), a very poisonous crystalline compound obtained from coal tar, used in solution as a disinfectant and antiseptic; phenol. *Formula:* C_6H_5OH

car bon (kär′bən), *n.* 1 a very common nonmetallic element which occurs in combination with other elements in all plants and animals. Diamonds and graphite are pure carbon in the form of crystals; coal and charcoal are mostly carbon in uncrystallized form. *Symbol:* C; *atomic number* 6. See pages 326 and 327 for table. 2 piece of carbon used in batteries, arc lamps, etc. 3 piece of carbon paper. 4 copy made with carbon paper. [< French *carbone* < Latin *carbonem* coal]

carbon 12, the most common isotope of carbon, now adopted in place of oxygen as the standard for determining the atomic weight of chemical elements. *Symbol:* C^{12}; *atomic number* 6; *mass number* 12.

carbon 14, a radioactive isotope of carbon produced by the bombardment of nitrogen atoms by neutrons. Since carbon 14 decays at a uniform rate, the extent of its decay in the wood, bone, etc., of animals and plants that have died is evidence of the age of archaeological finds or geological formations in which organic matter occurs. *Symbol:* C^{14}; *atomic number* 6; *mass number* 14.

car bo na ceous (kär′bə nā′shəs), *adj.* of, like, or containing carbon.

car bo na do (kär′bə nā′dō), *n., pl.* **-does** or **-dos.** an opaque, dark-colored, massive form of diamond, used for drills. It is found mostly in Brazil. [< Portuguese]

car bon ate (*v.* kär′bə nāt; *n.* kär′bə nāt, kär′bə nit), *v.,* **-at ed, -at ing,** *n.* —*v.t.* 1 saturate with carbon dioxide. Soda water is carbonated to make it bubble and fizz. 2 change into a carbonate. —*n.* salt or ester of carbonic acid. —**car′bon a′tion,** *n.*

carbon black, a smooth, black pigment of pure carbon, formed by deposits from incompletely burned gas, oil, etc., and used in the manufacture of rubber and printing inks.

carbon copy, 1 copy made with carbon paper. 2 anything that appears to duplicate something else: *His ideas are a carbon copy of his father's.*

carbon cycle, 1 (in physics) the series of thermonuclear reactions in incandescent stars that, beginning and ending with a carbon 12 atom, liberate atomic energy and transform hydrogen to helium. 2 (in biology) the circulation of carbon in nature, including photosynthesis of carbohydrates from atmospheric carbon dioxide by plants, the use of the plants as animal nutrients, and the return of the carbon to the atmosphere by respiration and decay.

caravel

carbon dating, method of dating organic, geological, or archaeological specimens by measuring the amount of disintegration of carbon 14 in the specimens; radiocarbon dating.

carbon dioxide, a heavy, colorless, odorless gas, present in the atmosphere or formed when any fuel containing carbon is burned, widely used for saturating water to form carbonated water (soda water), as Dry Ice, in fire extinguishers, etc. It is exhaled from an animal's lungs during respiration, and is used by plants in photosynthesis. *Formula:* CO_2

car bon ic (kär bon′ik), *adj.* of or containing carbon.

carbonic acid, acid made when carbon dioxide is dissolved in water. It gives the sharp taste to soda water. *Formula:* H_2CO_3

Car bon if er ous (kär′bə nif′ər əs), *n.* 1 the geological period of the Paleozoic era including the Pennsylvanian and Mississippian periods. During the Carboniferous warm, moist climate produced great forests of tree ferns, rushes, and conifers, whose remains formed the great coal beds. See chart under **geology.** 2 the rocks and coal beds formed during this period. —*adj.* 1 of or having to do with this period or its rocks. 2 **carboniferous,** (of rocks, etc.) containing or producing coal.

car bon ize (kär′bə nīz), *v.t.,* **-ized, -iz ing.** 1 change into carbon by burning; char. 2 cover or combine with carbon. —**car′bon i za′tion,** *n.*

carbon monoxide, a colorless, odorless, very poisonous gas, formed when carbon burns with an insufficient supply of air. It is part of the exhaust gases of automobile engines. *Formula:* CO

carbon paper, a thin paper having carbon or some other inky substance on one surface. It is used between sheets of paper to make a copy of what is written or typed on the upper sheet.

carbon tetrachloride, a colorless, nonflammable liquid, often used in fire extinguishers and in cleaning fluids. Its fumes are very dangerous if inhaled. *Formula:* CCl_4

car bon yl (kär′bə nil), *n.* a bivalent radical occurring in aldehydes, ketones, acids, etc. *Formula:* $-C{=}O$

Car bo run dum (kär′bə run′dəm), *n.* trademark for an extremely hard compound of carbon and silicon, used for grinding and polishing.

car box yl (kär bok′səl), *n.* a univalent radical existing in many organic acids. *Formula:* $-COOH$

car box yl ic acid (kär′bok sil′ik), any organic acid, all of which typically contain the carboxyl group.

car boy (kär′boi), *n.* a very large glass bottle, usually enclosed in basketwork or in a wooden box or crate to keep it from being broken. [< Persian *qarābah*]

car bun cle (kär′bung kəl), *n.* 1 a very painful, inflamed swelling under the skin caused by infection. A carbuncle discharges pus like a boil but is more serious in its effects. 2 a smooth, round garnet or other deep-red jewel. [< Latin *carbunculus* < *carbonem* coal]

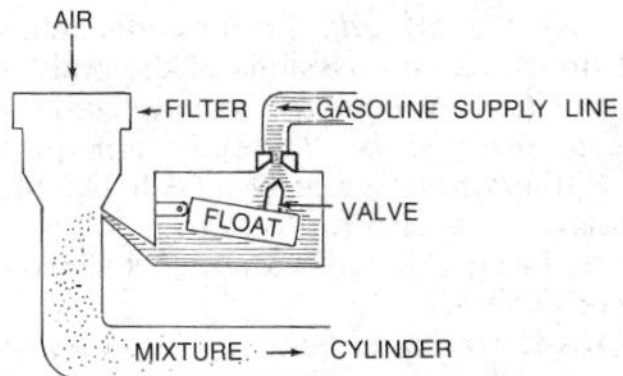

carburetor—A float and valve control the flow of gasoline, which sprays into the pipe and is mixed with air.

car bu re tor (kär′bə rā′tər, kär′byə-ret′ər), *n.* device for mixing air with a liquid fuel to produce an explosive vapor for ignition in an internal-combustion engine.

car bu ret tor (kär′byə ret′ər), *n.* BRITISH. carburetor.

car ca jou (kär′kə jü, kär′kə zhü), *n.* wolverine. [< Canadian French < Algonquian]

car cass (kär′kəs), *n.* 1 body of a dead animal. 2 INFORMAL. a human body, dead or living (now usually in ridicule or humor). 3 the shell or framework of any structure, such as a building or ship. [< Middle French *carcasse* < Italian *carcassa*]

car cin o gen (kär sin′ə jən), *n.* any substance or agent that produces cancer.

car cin o gen ic (kär sin′ə jen′ik), *adj.* 1 tending to cause cancer. 2 caused by cancer.

car ci no ma (kär′sə nō′mə), *n., pl.* **-mas, -ma ta** (-mə tə). any of various cancers of the skin, gland tissue, etc. [< Latin < Greek *karkinōma* < *karkinos* crab, cancer]

card[1] (kärd), *n.* 1 piece of stiff paper, thin cardboard, or plastic, usually small and rectangular: *an identification card, a credit card.* 2 a similar piece of stiff paper, often folded and decoratively designed, sent to persons on special occasions: *a get-well card, Christmas cards.* 3 a printed program of sporting or other events. 4 a series of items forming a program or list. 5 playing card. 6 **cards,** *pl.* **a** game or games played with a pack of playing cards. **b** a playing such a game or games. 7 a round piece of paper, etc., on which the 32 points of the compass are marked. 8 INFORMAL. an odd or amusing person. 9 **card up one's sleeve,** a plan held in reserve; extra help kept back until needed. 10 **in the cards** or **on the cards,** likely to happen; possible. 11 **put one's cards on the table,** show what one has or can do; be perfectly frank about something. —*v.t.* 1 provide with a card or cards. 2 put on a card. [< Middle French *carte* < Latin *charta.* Doublet of CHART.]

card[2] (kärd), *n.* a toothed tool or wire brush, such as that used to separate, clean, and straighten the fibers of wool before spinning or to clean the grooves of a metal file. —*v.t.* clean or comb with such a tool. [< Middle French *carde,* ultimately < Latin *carduus* thistle] **—card′er,** *n.*

Card., cardinal.

car da mom or **car da mum** (kär′də-məm), *n.* 1 a spicy seed used as seasoning and in medicine. 2 the East Indian plant that it grows on, of the same family as ginger. [< Latin *cardamomum*]

car da mon (kär′də mən), *n.* cardamom.

card board (kärd′bôrd′, kärd′bōrd′), *n.* a stiff material made of layers of paper pressed together, used to make cards, boxes, etc.

car di ac (kär′dē ak), *adj.* 1 of or having to do with the heart: *cardiac disease, cardiac arteries.* 2 having to do with the upper part of the stomach. —*n.* 1 person who has heart disease. 2 medicine that stimulates the heart. [< Latin *cardiacus* < Greek *kardiakos* < *kardia* heart]

Car diff (kär′dif), *n.* seaport and capital of Wales, in the SE part. 284,000.

car di gan (kär′də gən), *n.* a knitted jacket or sweater that buttons down the front. [< Earl of *Cardigan,* 1797-1868, British general]

car di nal (kärd′n əl), *adj.* 1 of first importance; chief; principal: *The cardinal value of his plan is that it is simple.* 2 bright, rich red. —*n.* 1 one of the high officials of the Roman Catholic Church, appointed by the Pope to the Sacred College as his counselors, and ranking next below him. 2 a bright, rich red. 3 a North American songbird, the male of which has bright-red feathers marked with a little gray and black. It is a kind of finch. 4 cardinal number. [< Latin *cardinalem* chief, having to do with a hinge < *cardinem* hinge, turning point] **—car′di nal ly,** *adv.*

car di nal ate (kärd′n ə lāt), *n.* 1 position or rank of cardinal. 2 the Sacred College of cardinals.

cardinal flower, 1 the bright-red flower of a North American plant. 2 the lobelia plant that it grows on.

car di nal i ty (kärd′n al′ə tē), *n.* the property of being expressible by a cardinal number.

cardinal number, number that shows how many are meant.

➤ **Cardinal numbers,** such as three, ten, 246, 9371, are the numbers used in counting. They are contrasted with **ordinal numbers,** like first, second, and 24th, which are used to indicate order or position in a series.

cardinal points, the four main directions of the compass; north, south, east, and west.

cardinal virtues, prudence, fortitude, temperance, and justice, considered by the ancient philosophers to be the basic qualities of a good character.

card ing (kär′ding), *n.* the cleaning and straightening of the fibers of wool, cotton, flax, etc., before spinning.

car di o gram (kär′dē ə gram), *n.* electrocardiogram.

car di o graph (kär′dē ə graf), *n.* electrocardiograph.

car di o graph ic (kär′dē ə graf′ik), *adj.* electrocardiographic.

car di ol o gist (kär′dē ol′ə jist), *n.* an expert in cardiology.

car di ol o gy (kär′dē ol′ə jē), *n.* branch of medicine dealing with the heart and the diagnosis and treatment of its diseases.

car di o vas cu lar (kär′dē ō vas′kyə lər), *adj.* of, having to do with, or affecting both the heart and the blood vessels.

card play er (kärd′plā′ər), *n.* person who plays cards.

cards (kärdz), *n.pl.* See def. 6 under **card**[1].

card sharp (kärd′shärp′), *n.* a dishonest professional cardplayer.

care (ker, kar), *n., v.,* **cared, car ing.** —*n.* 1 a troubled state of mind because of fear of what may happen; feeling anxious or uneasy because of one's obligations; worry: *Few people are completely free from care.* See synonym study below. 2 serious attention; heed: *Always drive a car with great care.* 3 object of worry, concern, or attention: *He has always been a care to his parents.* 4 watchful keeping; charge: *The child was left in my care.* 5 food, shelter, and protection: *Your child will have the best of care.*

have a care, be careful.

in care of, at the address of.

take care, be careful.

take care of, **a** take charge of; attend to. **b** watch over; be careful with. **c** INFORMAL. deal with.

—*v.i.* 1 be concerned; feel interest: *I care about music.* 2 like; want; wish: *A cat does not care to be washed.* 3 **care for, a** be fond of; like. **b** want; wish: *I don't care for any dessert tonight.* **c** take charge of; attend to. [Old English *caru*] **—car′er,** *n.*

Syn. *n.* 1 **Care, concern, solicitude** mean a troubled, worried, or anxious state of mind. **Care** suggests being burdened with heavy responsibilities or constant worries and fears: *It is care that has made her sick.* **Concern** suggests uneasiness over someone or something one likes or is interested in: *He expressed concern over her health.* **Solicitude** suggests great concern, often together with loving care: *Her friends wait on her with solicitude.*

CARE (ker, kar), *n.* Cooperative for American Remittances to Everywhere, Inc.

ca reen (kə rēn′), *v.i.* lean to one side or sway sharply; tilt; tip: *The ship careened in the strong wind.* —*v.t.* 1 lay (a ship) over on one side for cleaning, painting, repairing, etc. 2 cause to lean to one side or sway sharply: *The gale careened the sailboat.* [< Middle French *carène* keel < Latin *carina*]

ca reer (kə rir′), *n.* 1 a general course of action or progress through life: *It is interesting to read of the careers of great men and women.* 2 way of living; occupation; profession: *She planned to make law her career.* 3 a run at full speed; going with force; speed: *We were in full career when we struck the post.* —*v.i.* rush along wildly; dash: *The runaway horse careered through the streets.* —*adj.* following a certain occupation or profession throughout life: *a career diplomat.* [< Middle French *carrière* race course < Latin *carrus* wagon]

ca reer ist (kə rir′ist), *n.* person interested only in advancing his career, often at the expense of other people.

care free (ker′frē′, kar′frē′), *adj.* without worry; happy; gay.

care ful (ker′fəl, kar′fəl), *adj.* 1 thinking what one says; watching what one does; taking pains; watchful; cautious. See synonym study below. 2 showing care; done with thought or effort; exact; thorough. 3 full of care or concern; attentive: *She was careful of the feelings of others.* 4 ARCHAIC. anxious; worried. **—care′ful ly,** *adv.* **—care′ful ness,** *n.*

Syn. 1 **Careful, cautious, wary** mean watchful in speaking and acting. Careful means being observant and giving serious attention and thought to what one is doing, especially to details: *He is a careful driver.*

Cautious means very careful, looking ahead for possible risks or dangers, and guarding against them by taking no chances: *She is cautious about making promises.* **Wary** emphasizes the idea of being mistrustful and on the alert for danger or trouble: *He is wary of overfriendly people.*

care less (ker′lis, kar′lis), *adj.* 1 not thinking what one says; not watching what one does; not watchful or cautious: *One careless step may cost a life.* 2 done without enough thought or effort; not exact or thorough: *careless work.* 3 not troubling oneself; unconcerned; indifferent. 4 without worry; happy; gay. **—care′less ly,** *adv.* **—care′less ness,** *n.*

ca ress (kə res′), *n.* a gentle touch or stroke showing affection; tender embrace or kiss. *—v.t.* touch or stroke tenderly; embrace or kiss. [< Middle French *caresse* < Italian *carezza* < Latin *carus* dear] **—ca ress′a ble,** *adj.* **—ca ress′er,** *n.* **—ca ress′ing ly,** *adv.*

car et (kar′ət), *n.* a mark (∧) to show where something should be put in, used in writing or printing. [< Latin, there is wanting]

care tak er (ker′tā′kər, kar′tā′kər), *n.* person who takes care of another person, a place, or a thing, often for the owner or for another.

care worn (ker′wôrn′, ker′wōrn′; kar′wôrn′, kar′wōrn′), *adj.* showing signs of worry; tired or weary from care.

car fare (kär′fer′, kär′far′), *n.* money paid for riding on a bus, subway, in a taxicab, etc.

car go (kär′gō), *n., pl.* **-goes** or **-gos.** load of goods carried on a ship or aircraft; freight. [< Spanish < *cargar* load, ultimately < Latin *carrus* wagon]

car hop (kär′hop′), *n.* waiter or waitress who serves customers in their cars at a drive-in restaurant.

Car ib (kar′ib), *n.* 1 member of an Indian tribe of northeastern South America. 2 a language family found primarily in northeastern South America, and to a lesser extent in Central America and the West Indies.

Car ib be an (kar′ə bē′ən, kə rib′ē ən), *adj.* 1 of or having to do with the Caribbean Sea or the islands in it. 2 of or having to do with the Caribs (def. 1).

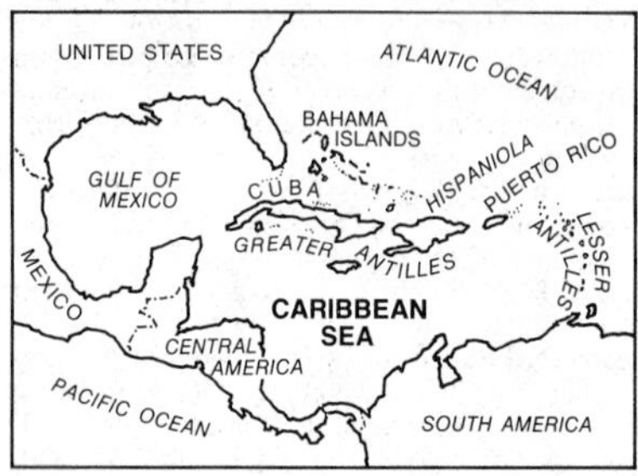

Caribbean Sea, sea bordered by Central America, the West Indies, and South America. 750,000 sq. mi.

ca ri be (kä rē′bā), *n.* piranha. [< Spanish, cannibal]

car i bou (kar′ə bü), *n., pl.* **-bous** or **-bou.** the reindeer of northern regions of the New World and Siberia. [< Canadian French < Algonquian *xalibu*]

caricature (def. 1) caricature of Abraham Lincoln

car i ca ture (kar′ə kə chůr, kar′ə kə chər), *n., v.,* **-tured, -tur ing.** *—n.* 1 picture, cartoon, or description that exaggerates the peculiarities of a person or the defects of a thing. 2 art of making such pictures, cartoons, or descriptions. 3 imitation or rendering of something by ridiculous exaggeration of flaws in the original. *—v.t.* make a caricature of. [< French < Italian *caricatura* < *caricare* overload, exaggerate < Late Latin *carricare* to load < Latin *carrus* wagon]

car i ca tur ist (kar′ə kə chůr′ist, kar′ə kə chər ist), *n.* person who makes caricatures.

car ies (ker′ēz, ker′ē ēz; kar′ēz, kar′ē ēz), *n.* decay of teeth, bones, or tissues. [< Latin]

car il lon (kar′ə lon, kar′ə lən, kə ril′yən), *n.* 1 set of bells arranged for playing melodies. 2 melody played on such bells. 3 part of an organ imitating the sound of bells. [< French, ultimately < Latin *quattuor* four (because it originally consisted of four bells)]

car il lon neur (kar′ə lə nėr′), *n.* person who plays a carillon.

Ca rin thi a (kə rin′thē ə), *n.* district in S Austria.

car i o ca (kar′ē ō′kə), *n.* 1 a dance of South America. 2 **Carioca,** native or inhabitant of Rio de Janeiro. [< Brazilian Portuguese]

car i ole (kar′ē ōl), *n.* 1 a small, one-horse carriage. 2 a covered cart. 3 a light, open sleigh drawn by one or two horses or sometimes by dogs. [< French]

car i ous (ker′ē əs, kar′ē əs), *adj.* having caries; decayed: *carious teeth.*

car load (kär′lōd′), *n.* as much as a car can hold or carry.

Carls bad (kärlz′bad), *n.* Karlsbad.

Carls bad Caverns (kärlz′bad), national park in SE New Mexico, famous for its huge limestone caverns.

Car lyle (kär līl′, kär′līl), *n.* **Thomas,** 1795-1881, Scottish essayist, historian, and philosopher.

Car mel (kär′məl), *n.* **Mount,** mountain in NW Israel. 1800 ft.

Car mel ite (kär′mə līt), *n.* a mendicant friar or nun of a Roman Catholic religious order founded in the 1100's on Mount Carmel.

car min a tive (kär min′ə tiv, kär′mə nā′tiv), *adj.* expelling gas from the stomach and intestines. *—n.* medicine that does this. [< Latin *carminatum* carded, cleansed]

car mine (kär′mən, kär′mīn), *n.* 1 a deep red with a tinge of purple. 2 a light crimson. 3 a crimson coloring matter found in cochineal, used to stain microscopic slides and formerly used as a dye. *—adj.* 1 deep-red with a tinge of purple. 2 light-crimson. [< Medieval Latin *carminium* < Arabic *qirmiz* the kermes insect + Latin *minium* red lead]

car nage (kär′nij), *n.* slaughter of a great number of people. [< Middle French < Italian *carnaggio,* ultimately < Latin *carnem* flesh]

car nal (kär′nl), *adj.* 1 of or connected with the appetites and passions of the body; sensual: *Gluttony and drunkenness have been called carnal vices.* 2 worldly; not spiritual. [< Latin *carnalis* < *carnem* flesh. Doublet of CHARNEL.] **—car′nal ly,** *adv.*

car nal i ty (kär nal′ə tē), *n.* 1 sensuality. 2 worldliness.

car na tion (kär nā′shən), *n.* 1 a red, white, or pink flower with a spicy fragrance. 2 plant, a species of pink, that it grows on. 3 a rosy pink. *—adj.* rosy-pink. [< Middle French < Italian *carnagione* flesh color < *carnaggio.* See CARNAGE.]

car nau ba wax (kär nou′bə), wax from the leaves of a Brazilian palm tree, used to make polishes, phonograph records, electric insulation, etc. [*carnauba* < Brazilian Portuguese, the tree < Tupi]

Car ne gie (kär nā′gē, kär′nə gē), *n.* **Andrew,** 1835-1919, American steel manufacturer and philanthropist, born in Scotland.

car nel ian (kär nē′lyən), *n.* a red or reddish-brown stone used in jewelry. It is a kind of quartz. Also, **cornelian.** [< Old French *corneline*]

car ni val (kär′nə vəl), *n.* 1 place of amusement or a traveling show having merry-go-rounds, games, sideshows, etc. 2 program of events: *There were many exhibitions of swimming and diving skill at the water carnival.* 3 feasting and merrymaking; noisy and unrestrained revels; celebration. 4 time of feasting and merrymaking just before Lent. [< Italian *carnevale,* alteration of *carnelevare* a leaving off of (eating) meat]

Car niv or a (kär niv′ər ə), *n.pl.* order of mammals comprising the carnivores.

car ni vore (kär′nə vôr, kär′nə vōr), *n.* 1 any of an order of mammals that feed chiefly on flesh, characterized by large, sharp canine teeth and including cats, dogs, lions, tigers, bears, and seals. 2 plant that eats insects.

car niv or ous (kär niv′ər əs), *adj.* 1 of or having to do with an order of mammals that feed chiefly on flesh. 2 using other animals as food; flesh-eating: *the strong carnivorous eagle.* 3 (of plants) having leaves specially adapted to trap insects for food. [< Latin *carnivorus* < *carnem* flesh + *vorare* devour] **—car niv′or ous ly,** *adv.* **—car niv′or ous ness,** *n.*

car no tite (kär′nə tīt), *n.* a yellowish, radioactive mineral found in the western and southwestern United States. It is a source of uranium, radium, and vanadium. [< Adolphe *Carnot,* 1839-1920, a French inspector general of mines]

car ol (kar′əl), *n., v.,* **-oled, -ol ing,** or **-olled, -ol ling.** *—n.* 1 song of joy. 2 hymn of joy sung at Christmas. 3 (in the Middle Ages) a dance done in a ring with accompaniment of song. *—v.i.* sing joyously; sing: *The birds were caroling in the trees.* *—v.t.* 1 sing joyously. 2 praise with carols. [< Old French *carole* < Latin *choraula* < Greek *choraulēs* flute player accompanying a choral dance < *choros* dance + *aulos* flute] **—car′ol er, car′ol ler,** *n.*

Car o li na (kar′ə lī′nə), *n.* 1 an early American colony on the Atlantic coast. The first settlers arrived in 1653, and the colony was officially divided into North Carolina and South Carolina in 1729. 2 either North Carolina or South Carolina. 3 **the Carolinas,** North Carolina and South Carolina.

Car o line Islands (kar′ə līn, kar′ə lin), group of over 500 islands in the W Pacific, east of the Philippines. They were formerly under Japanese supervision and are now under United States administration. 62,000 pop.; 380 sq. mi. See **Melanesia** for map.

Car o lin gi an (kar′ə lin′jē ən), *adj.* of or having to do with the second Frankish dynasty. It ruled in France from A.D. 751 to 987, in Germany from A.D. 751 to 911, and in Italy from A.D. 774 to 887. *—n.* member or one of the sovereigns of the Carolingian family or dynasty. Charlemagne was a Carolingian.

Car o lin i an (kar′ə lin′ē ən), *adj.* of North Carolina and South Carolina, or either of them. *—n.* native or inhabitant of North Carolina or South Carolina.

car om (kar′əm), *v.i.* 1 hit and bounce off. 2 make a carom. *—n.* 1 a hitting and bouncing off. 2 a shot in the game of billiards in which the ball struck with the cue hits two balls, one after the other. 3 a similar shot in other games. [short for *carambole* < Spanish *carambola* a carom in billiards]

car o tene (kar′ə tēn′), *n.* a red or yellow crystalline pigment found in the carrot and other plants, and in animal tissue, and converted by the body into vitamin A. *Formula:* $C_{40}H_{56}$ Also, **carotin.** [< Latin *carota* carrot]

ca rot en oid (kə rot′n oid), *n.* any of a group of yellow to dark-red pigments found in various plant and animal tissues. The group includes carotene.

ca rot id (kə rot′id), *n.* either of two large arteries, one on each side of the neck, that carry blood to the head. *—adj.* having to do with these arteries. [< Greek *karōtides* < *karos* stupor (state produced by compression of carotids)]

car o tin (kar′ə tən), *n.* carotene.

ca rous al (kə rou′zəl), *n.* a noisy revel or drinking party.

ca rouse (kə rouz′), *v.*, **-roused, -rous ing,** *n.* *—v.i.* drink heavily; take part in noisy revels. *—n.* a noisy revel or drinking party. [< obsolete adverb, completely < German *gar aus(trinken)* (drink) all up] **—ca rous′er,** *n.*

car ou sel (kar′ə sel′, kar′ə zel′), *n.* carrousel.

carp[1] (kärp), *v.t.* find fault; complain. [< Scandinavian (Old Danish) *karpa* to boast] **—carp′er,** *n.*

carp[2] (kärp), *n., pl.* **carps** or **carp.** 1 a bony, freshwater fish living in ponds and slow streams, that feeds mostly on plants and sometimes grows quite large. 2 any of a group of similar fishes, including goldfish, minnows, chub, and dace. [< Old French *carpe* < Late Latin *carpa*]

car pal (kär′pəl), *adj.* of the carpus. *—n.* bone of the carpus.

car park, BRITISH. parking lot.

Car pa thi an Mountains (kär pā′thē ən), mountain system in central Europe, extending in an arc from central Czechoslovakia to SW Romania. Highest peak, 8737 feet.

Car pa thi ans (kär pā′thē ənz), *n.pl.* Carpathian Mountains.

car pel (kär′pəl), *n.* a modified leaf which forms a pistil or part of a pistil of a flower. [< Greek *karpos* fruit]

Car pen tar i a (kär′pən ter′ē ə), *n.* **Gulf of,** large gulf on the N coast of Australia. 480 mi. long; 420 mi. wide.

car pen ter (kär′pən tər), *n.* person whose work is building and repairing, chiefly with wood. *—v.i.* do such work. [< Old North French *carpentier* < Latin *carpentarius* carriage maker < *carpentum* carriage]

car pen try (kär′pən trē), *n.* trade or work of a carpenter.

car pet (kär′pit), *n.* 1 a heavy, woven fabric for covering floors and stairs. 2 a covering made of this fabric. 3 anything like a carpet: *We walked on a carpet of grass.* 4 **on the carpet, a** under consideration or discussion. **b** INFORMAL. being scolded or rebuked. *—v.t.* cover or furnish with a carpet: *In the fall, the ground was carpeted with leaves.* [< Medieval Latin *carpeta, carpita* thick cloth < Popular Latin *carpire* card (wool) < Latin *carpere*]

car pet bag (kär′pit bag′), *n.* a traveling bag made of carpet.

car pet bag ger (kär′pit bag′ər), *n.* U.S. Northerner who went to the South to get political or other advantages during the time of disorganization that followed the Civil War.

carpet beetle or **carpet bug,** a small beetle whose larva destroys carpets, other fabrics, and furs.

car pet ing (kär′pə ting), *n.* 1 fabric for carpets. 2 carpets.

carp ing (kär′ping), *adj.* faultfinding; complaining. **—carp′ing ly,** *adv.*

car pool, arrangement for providing transportation, especially to and from work, in which the members of the pool rotate use of their own cars.

car port (kär′pôrt′, kär′pōrt′), *n.* shelter for automobiles, usually attached to a house and open on at least one side.

car pus (kär′pəs), *n., pl.* **-pi** (-pī). 1 wrist. 2 bones of the wrist. [< New Latin < Greek *karpos* wrist]

car rack (kar′ək), *n.* (in former times) a large sailing ship; galleon. [< Old French *carraque* < Arabic *qarāqīr* (plural)]

car ra geen or **car ra gheen** (kar′ə-gēn′), *n.* Irish moss. [< *Carragheen,* Ireland]

Car ra ra (kə rär′ə), *n.* city in NW Italy, famous for its fine white marble. 65,000.

car rel or **car rell** (kar′əl), *n.* a small enclosed place for individual study in a library, usually containing a desk and bookshelves. [< Medieval Latin *carola*]

car riage (kar′ij; *for 7, also* kar′ē ij), *n.* 1 vehicle that moves on wheels. Some carriages are pulled by horses and are used to carry people. 2 frame on wheels that supports a gun. 3 a moving part of a machine that supports some other part or object: *a typewriter carriage.* 4 manner of holding the head and body; bearing: *She has a queenly carriage.* See **bearing** for synonym study. 5 BRITISH. a railway passenger car. 6 the taking of persons or goods from one place to another; carrying; transporting. 7 cost or price of carrying. 8 management; way of handling. [< Old French *cariage* < *carier.* See CARRY.]

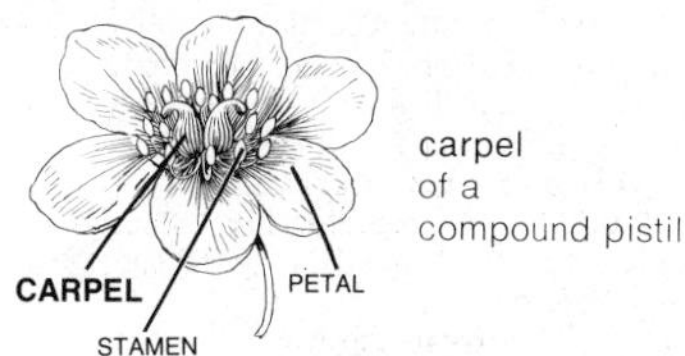

carpel of a compound pistil

carriage trade, the wealthy persons who are patrons of theaters, expensive restaurants and stores, etc., so called because such persons formerly drove in private carriages.

car ri er (kar′ē ər), *n.* 1 person or thing that carries something. A postman is a mail carrier. 2 thing designed to carry something in or on. 3 person or thing that carries or transmits a disease. Carriers are often healthy persons who are immune to a disease, but carry its germs. 4 carrier wave. 5 company that transports goods, people, etc., usually over certain routes, and according to fixed schedules. Bus systems, railways, airlines, and truck companies are carriers. 6 aircraft carrier. 7 carrier pigeon.

hat, āge, fär; let, ēqual, tėrm;
it, īce; hot, ōpen, ôrder;
oil, out; cup, pu̇t, rüle;
ch, child; ng, long; sh, she;
th, thin; ᴛʜ, then; zh, measure;

ə represents *a* in about, *e* in taken, *i* in pencil, *o* in lemon, *u* in circus.

< = from, derived from, taken from.

carrier pigeon, 1 homing pigeon. 2 one of a breed of large domestic pigeons.

carrier wave, a radio wave whose amplitude, frequency, or phase is modulated in order to transmit a signal, usually in broadcasting radio and television programs and sending telephone and telegraph messages.

car ri on (kar′ē ən), *n.* 1 dead and decaying flesh. 2 rottenness; filth. *—adj.* 1 dead and decaying. 2 feeding on dead and decaying flesh. 3 rotten; filthy. [< Old French *caroine* carcass < Popular Latin *caronia* < Latin *carnem* flesh. Doublet of CRONE.]

carrion crow, the common European crow that feeds on carrion.

Car roll (kar′əl), *n.* **Lewis,** 1832-1898, English writer, author of *Alice in Wonderland.* His real name was **Charles L. Dodgson.**

car rot (kar′ət), *n.* 1 plant of the same family as the parsley which has a long, tapering, orange-red root. 2 its root, which is eaten as a vegetable, either cooked or raw. [< Middle French *carotte* < Latin *carota* < Greek *karōton*]

car rot y (kar′ə tē), *adj.* 1 like a carrot in color; orange-red. 2 red-haired.

car rou sel (kar′ə sel′, kar′ə zel′), *n.* merry-go-round. Also, **carousel.** [< French]

car ry (kar′ē), *v.,* **-ried, -ry ing,** *n., pl.* **-ries.** *—v.t.* 1 take from one place to another: *Railroads carry coal from the mines to the factories.* See synonym study below. 2 bear or have with one: *carry an umbrella.* 3 bear the weight of; hold up; support; sustain: *Those rafters carry the roof.* 4 hold (one's body and head) in a certain way: *The trained soldier carries himself well.* 5 capture or win: *The governor didn't carry enough towns to get reelected.* 6 get (a motion or bill) passed or adopted: *The motion to adjourn the meeting was carried.* 7 continue; extend: *carry a road into the mountains.* 8 influence greatly; lead: *His acting carried the audience.* 9 have as a result; have as an attribute, property, etc.; involve: *Her judgment carries great weight.* 10 sing with correct pitch: *He can carry a tune.* 11 sing or play (a melody, theme, or part): *She will carry the soprano solos. The first violins carry the melody.* 12 keep in stock: *This store carries clothing for men.* 13 (of a newspaper, magazine, etc.) print an article in its pages: *The evening newspapers carried a review of the new play.*

14 keep on the account books of a business. 15 transfer (a number) from one place or column in the sum to the next. *—v.i.* 1 act as a bearer. 2 cover the distance; have the power of throwing or driving: *Your voice will carry to the back of the room. This gun will carry half a mile.*
carry away, arouse strong feeling in; influence beyond reason.
carry forward, a go ahead with; make progress with. b (in bookkeeping) reenter (an item or items already entered) on the next or a later page or column of an accounting record.
carry off, a win (a prize, honor, etc.). b succeed with. c be the death of; kill: *Pneumonia carried him off.*
carry on, a do; manage; conduct. b go ahead with; go on with after being stopped. c keep going; not stop; continue. d U.S. INFORMAL. behave wildly or foolishly.
carry out, get done; do; accomplish; complete: *She carried out her job well.*
carry over, a have left over; be left over. b keep until later; continue; extend.
carry through, a get done; do; accomplish; complete: *Most people could not have accomplished the task it was his destiny to carry through.* b bring through trouble; keep from being discouraged.
—n. 1 range of a gun, missile, etc. 2 portage. 3 place where portage is done. 4 method or position of carrying or holding: *a fireman's carry.* 5 (in golf) the distance a ball travels in the air before hitting the ground.
[< Old North French *carier* < Late Latin *carricare* < Latin *carrus* wagon, cart. Doublet of CHARGE.]
Syn. *v.t.* 1 **Carry, convey, transport** mean to take or bring from one place to another. **Carry,** the general word, suggests holding and moving a person or thing in or with something, such as a vehicle, container, or hands: *The cat carried its kittens away.* **Convey** suggests getting a person or thing to a place by some means or through some channel, and therefore is sometimes used figuratively in the sense of communicate: *Escalators convey people. Language conveys ideas.* **Transport** suggests conveying in a ship, plane, or vehicle: *Trucks transport freight.*

car ry all[1] (kar′ē ôl′), *n.* 1 a lightweight, covered, one-horse carriage for several passengers. 2 a closed passenger automobile having a bench along each side. 3 a station wagon. [alteration of *cariole*]

car ry all[2] (kar′ē ôl′), *n.* a large bag or basket. [< *carry* + *all*]

carrying charge, interest charged on a loan, a mortgage, or the balance owed on a purchase.

car ry-o ver (kar′ē ō′vər), *n.* 1 part left over. 2 item carried forward in an accounting record.

car sick (kär′sik′), *adj.* nauseated as a result of the motion of a car, train, etc. **—car′sick′ness,** *n.*

Car son (kär′sən), *n.* **Kit,** 1809-1868, American frontiersman, scout, and guide in the Far West.

Carson City, capital of Nevada, in the W part. 15,000.

cart (kärt), *n.* 1 vehicle with two wheels, used to carry heavy loads. Horses, donkeys, and oxen are often used to draw carts. 2 a light wagon, used to deliver goods. 3 a small vehicle on wheels, moved by hand: *a grocery cart.* 4 **put the cart before the horse,** reverse the accepted or usual order of things. *—v.t.* carry in a cart. [< Scandinavian (Old Icelandic) *kartr*]

cart age (kär′tij), *n.* 1 a carting or transporting. 2 cost or price of carting.

Car ta ge na (kär′tə jē′nə), *n.* 1 seaport in SE Spain, on the Mediterranean. 147,000. 2 seaport in NW Colombia. 319,000.

carte blanche (kärt′ blänch′; *French* kȧrt′bläNsh′), *pl.* **cartes blanches** (kärts′ blänch′; *French* kȧrt′bläNsh′). freedom to use one's own judgment; full authority. [< French, literally, blank paper]

car tel (kär tel′, kär′tl), *n.* 1 a large group of business firms that agree to operate as a monopoly, especially to regulate prices and production. 2 a written agreement between countries at war for the exchange of prisoners or for some other purpose. 3 (formerly) a written challenge to a duel. [< Middle French < Italian *cartello* little card]

car tel ize (kär tel′īz, kär′tl īz), *v.t., v.i.* **-ized, -iz ing.** 1 combine in a cartel. 2 join with other businesses to form a cartel. **—car′te li za′tion,** *n.*

cart er (kär′tər), *n.* man whose work is driving a cart or truck.

Car te sian (kär tē′zhən), *adj.* of or having to do with René Descartes, or with his doctrines or methods. *—n.* follower of Descartes' doctrines or methods. [< *Cartesius,* Latinized form of *Descartes*]

Cartesian coordinate, 1 either one of two numbers which determine the position of a point in a plane by its distance from two fixed intersecting lines. 2 any one of three numbers which determine the position of a point in space.

Cartesian product or **Cartesian set,** (in mathematics) the set of all ordered pairs that can be formed by matching each member of one set with each member of a second set in turn.

Car thage (kär′thij), *n.* city and seaport of ancient times in N Africa, founded by the Phoenicians. It was destroyed by the Romans in 146 B.C., rebuilt in 29 B.C., and finally destroyed by the Arabs in A.D. 698. See **Byzantine Empire** for map.

Car tha gin i an (kär′thə jin′ē ən), *adj.* of Carthage. *—n.* native or inhabitant of Carthage.

Car thu sian (kär thü′zhən), *n.* member of an austere order of monks founded by St. Bruno in 1084. *—adj.* of or having to do with this order.

Car ti er (kär tyā′, kär′tē ā′), *n.* **Jacques,** 1491-1557, French navigator who discovered the St. Lawrence River.

car ti lage (kär′tl ij), *n.* 1 a tough, elastic substance forming parts of the skeleton of vertebrates; gristle. Cartilage is more flexible than bone and not as hard. The external ear consists of cartilage and skin. 2 part formed of this substance. [< Latin *cartilago*]

car ti lag i nous (kär′tə laj′ə nəs), *adj.* 1 of or like cartilage; gristly. 2 having the skeleton formed mostly of cartilage: *Sharks are cartilaginous.*

car tog ra pher (kär tog′rə fər), *n.* maker of maps or charts.

car to graph ic (kär′tə graf′ik), *adj.* having to do with cartography or cartographers.

car tog ra phy (kär tog′rə fē), *n.* the making or study of maps or charts. [< Medieval Latin *carta* chart, map + English *-graphy*]

car ton (kärt′n), *n.* 1 box made of pasteboard or cardboard. 2 amount that a carton holds: *He could drink a carton of milk at one meal.* [< French, pasteboard < Italian *cartone* < *carta* paper]

car toon (kär tün′), *n.* 1 sketch or drawing that interests or amuses by showing persons, things, or events in an exaggerated way. 2 animated cartoon. 3 comic strip. 4 a full-size drawing of a design or painting, used as a model for a fresco, mosaic, tapestry, etc. *—v.t.* make a cartoon of. [< Italian *cartone* pasteboard; because drawn on heavy paper]

car toon ist (kär tü′nist), *n.* person who draws cartoons.

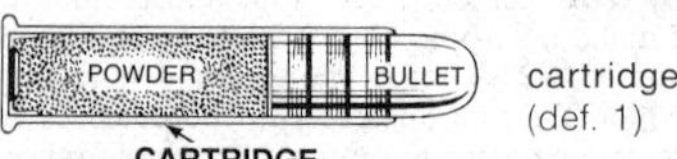

cartridge (def. 1)

car tridge (kär′trij) *n.* 1 case made of metal, plastic, or cardboard for holding gunpowder and a bullet or shot. 2 any case for insertion into a mechanical device which holds a supply of material for use therein. A cartridge may contain ink for a pen, a roll of photographic film, razor blades, etc. 3 unit holding the needle in the pickup of a phonograph. [alteration of French *cartouche* roll of paper]

cart wheel (kärt′hwēl′), *n.* 1 wheel of a cart. 2 a sideways handspring or somersault. 3 SLANG. a large coin, especially a silver dollar.

Cart wright (kärt′rīt), *n.* **Edmund,** 1743-1823, English clergyman, inventor of a power loom.

car un cle (kar′ung kəl, kə rung′kəl), *n.* a fleshy protuberance or process. [< Latin *caruncula* < *caro, carnis* flesh]

Ca ru so (kə rü′sō), *n.* **Enrico,** 1873-1921, Italian operatic tenor.

carve (kärv), *v.,* **carved, carv ing.** *—v.t.* 1 cut into slices or pieces: *carve the meat at the table.* 2 make by cutting; cut: *Statues are often carved from marble, stone, or wood.* 3 decorate with figures or designs cut on the surface: *The oak chest was carved with scenes from the Crusades.* 4 cut (a design, etc.) on or into a surface: *They carved their initials on the tree.* 5 make as if by cutting: *He ruthlessly carved himself a financial empire.* *—v.i.* cut up and serve meat at the table. [Old English *ceorfan*]

carv en (kär′vən), *adj.* ARCHAIC. carved.

carv er (kär′vər), *n.* 1 person who carves. 2 carving knife.

Car ver (kär′vər), *n.* **George Washington,** 1864?-1943, American botanist and chemist.

carv ing (kär′ving), *n.* 1 carved work; carved decoration: *a wood carving.* 2 act or art of a person or thing that carves.

carving knife, knife for cutting meat.

car y at id (kar′ē at′id), *n., pl.* **-ids, -i des** (-ə dēz′). statue of a woman used as a column. [< Latin *caryatides* < Greek *Karyatides women of Caryae,* village in Laconia]

car y op sis (kar′ē op′sis), *n.* a small dry seed fruit, especially of grasses. A grain of wheat is a caryopsis. [< Greek *karyon* nut + *opsis* appearance]

ca sa ba (kə sä′bə), *n.* kind of winter muskmelon with a yellow rind and edible flesh. Also, **cassaba.** [< *Kasaba,* near Izmir, Turkey]

Cas a blan ca (kas′ə blang′kə, kä′səbläng′kə), *n.* seaport in N Morocco, on the Atlantic. 1,320,000.

Ca sals (kä säls′), *n.* **Pablo,** 1876-1973, Spanish cellist.

Cas a no va (kaz′ə nō′və, kas′ə nō′və), *n.* 1 **Giovanni Jacopo,** 1725-1798, Italian adventurer. 2 man who has many affairs with women, especially an immoral adventurer.

cas cade (ka skād′), *n., v.,* **-cad ed, -cad ing.** —*n.* 1 a small waterfall. 2 anything like this: *Her dress had a cascade of ruffles down the front.* 3 series of pieces of apparatus serving to continue or develop a process. 4 series of reactions in which one causes or produces another. —*v.i.* fall, pour, or flow in a cascade. [< French < Italian *cascata* < Latin *casus* a falling. See CASE[1].]

Cascade Range, mountain range in NW United States, extending from N California to British Columbia. The highest peak is Mount Rainier, 14,408 feet.

cas car a (kas ker′ə, kas kar′ə), *n.* 1 buckthorn of the northwestern United States yielding cascara sagrada. 2 cascara sagrada.

cascara sa gra da (sə grä də), medicine prepared from the dried bark of the cascara, used as a laxative. [< Spanish *cáscara sagrada,* literally, sacred bark]

case[1] (kās), *n.* 1 instance; example: *a case of poor work.* See synonym study below. 2 condition; situation; state: *a case of poverty.* 3 the actual condition; real situation; true state: *He said he had done the work, but that was not the case.* 4 instance of a disease or injury: *a case of measles.* 5 person who is being treated by a doctor; patient. 6 matter for a court of law to decide. 7 statement of facts raising a point of view for a court of law to consider. 8 a convincing argument. 9 (in grammar) one of the forms of a noun, pronoun, or adjective used to show its relation to other words. *I* is the nominative case; *me* is the objective case; *my* is the possessive case. 10 relation shown by such a form. *I* is in the nominative case. 11 INFORMAL. a strange or unusual person.

in any case, under any circumstances; anyhow.

in case, if it should happen that; if; supposing.

in case of, if there should be; in the event of: *In case of fire walk quickly to the nearest door.*

in no case, under no circumstances; never. [< Old French *cas* < Latin *casus* a falling, chance; a grammatical case < *cadere* to fall]

Syn. 1 **Case, instance** mean example. **Case** applies to a fact, actual happening, situation, etc., that is typical of a general kind or class: *The accident was a case of reckless driving.* **Instance** applies to an individual case used to support a general idea or conclusion: *Going through a stop signal is an instance of his recklessness.*

➤ **case.** Writers often make unnecessary and ineffective use of expressions containing the word *case: Although I read many stories, in not one case was I satisfied with the ending. The author used the same plot before in the case of a short story about pioneer days. In many cases students did extensive research on their projects.* In the first sentence, *case* is entirely unnecessary. The second can be improved by dropping *the case of.* The third can be made less wordy and more emphatic by substituting *Many students* for *In many cases students.*

case[2] (kās), *n., v.,* **cased, cas ing.** —*n.* 1 thing to hold or cover something. 2 a covering; sheath: *Put the knife back in its case.* 3 box; crate: *There is a big case full of books in the hall.* 4 amount that a case can hold: *a case of ginger ale.* 5 frame. A window fits in a case. —*v.t.* 1 put in a case; cover with a case. 2 SLANG. look over carefully; inspect or examine: *The thieves cased the bank before the robbery.* [< Old French *casse* < Latin *capsa* box < *capere* to hold. Doublet of CASH[1], CHASE[3].]

case hard en (kās′härd′n), *v.t.* 1 harden (iron or steel) on the surface. 2 make callous or unfeeling.

case history, all the facts about a person or group which may be useful in deciding what medical or psychiatric treatment, social services, etc., are needed.

ca sein (kā′sēn′, kā′sē ən), *n.* protein present in milk and containing phosphorus, used in making plastics, adhesives, and certain kinds of paints. Cheese is mostly casein. [< Latin *caseus* cheese]

case knife, 1 knife carried in a case. 2 a table knife.

case mate (kās′māt), *n.* 1 a bombproof chamber in a fort or rampart, with openings through which cannon may be fired. 2 an armored enclosure protecting guns on a warship. [< Middle French < Italian *casamatta*]

case ment (kās′mənt), *n.* 1 window or part of a window which opens on hinges like a door. 2 any window. 3 a casing; covering; frame.

ca se ous (kā′se əs), *adj.* of or like cheese. [< Latin *caseus* cheese]

case work (kās′wėrk′), *n.* social work involving a thorough study of the problems of an individual or family as a basis for help or guidance.

case work er (kās′wėr′kər), *n.* person who does casework.

cash[1] (kash), *n.* 1 money in the form of coins and bills. 2 money, or something equivalent to money, such as a bank check, paid at the time of buying something. —*v.t.* 1 give cash for: *The bank will cash your five-dollar check.* 2 get cash for: *cash a check.* 3 **cash in,** a U.S. INFORMAL. change (poker chips, etc.) into cash. b SLANG. die. 4 **cash in on,** U.S. INFORMAL. a make a profit from. b take advantage of; use to advantage. [< French *caisse* < Provençal *caissa* < Latin *capsa* box, coffer. Doublet of CASE[2], CHASE[3].] —**cash′a ble,** *adj.*

cash[2] (kash), *n., pl.* **cash.** 1 coin of small value, used in China, India, etc. 2 a former Chinese copper coin with a square hole in it. [< Portuguese *caixa* < Tamil *kasu*]

cash-and-car ry (kash′ən kar′ē), *adj.* 1 with immediate payment for goods and without delivery service. 2 operated on this basis: *a cash-and-carry store.*

cash book (kash′bu̇k′), *n.* book in which a record is kept of money received and paid out.

cash crop, crop grown for sale, rather than for consumption on the farm.

cash ew (kash′ü, kə shü′), *n.* 1 a small, edible, kidney-shaped nut. 2 the tropical American tree that it grows on. [< Brazilian Portuguese *acajú* < Tupi *acayú*]

cash ier[1] (ka shir′), *n.* person who has charge of money in a bank, or in any business. [< French *caissier* treasurer < *caisse.* See CASH[1].]

cash ier[2] (ka shir′), *v.t.* dismiss from service for some dishonorable act; discharge in disgrace. [< Dutch *casseren* < Old French *casser* or *quasser* < Latin *quassare* to break]

cashier's check, check drawn by a bank on its own funds and signed by its cashier.

hat, āge, fär; let, ēqual, tėrm;
it, īce; hot, ōpen, ôrder;
oil, out; cup, pu̇t, rüle;
ch, child; ng, long; sh, she;
th, thin; ᴛʜ, then; zh, measure;

ə represents *a* in about, *e* in taken,
i in pencil, *o* in lemon, *u* in circus.

< = from, derived from, taken from.

cash mere (kash′mir, kazh′mir), *n.* 1 a fine, soft wool from a breed of long-haired goats of Tibet and Kashmir. 2 a costly kind of shawl made of this wool. 3 a fine, soft wool from sheep. 4 a fine, soft woolen cloth. [< variant of *Kashmir*]

cash on delivery, payment when goods are delivered.

cash register, machine which records and shows the amount of a sale. It usually has a drawer to hold money.

cas ing (kā′sing), *n.* 1 thing put around something; covering; case. The outermost part of a tire and the skin of a sausage are kinds of casings. 2 frame. A window fits in a casing.

ca si no (kə sē′nō), *n., pl.* **-nos.** 1 building or room for public shows, dancing, gambling, etc. 2 cassino. [< Italian, diminutive of *casa* house < Latin]

cask (kask), *n.* 1 barrel. A cask may be large or small, and is usually made to hold liquids. 2 amount that a cask holds. [< Spanish *casco* skull, helmet, cask of wine. Doublet of CASQUE.]

cas ket (kas′kit), *n.* 1 coffin. 2 a small box to hold jewels, letters, or other valuables.

Cas pi an Sea (kas′pē ən), inland sea between Europe and Asia in the Soviet Union and Iran, east of the Black Sea. 169,000 sq. mi. See **Assyria** for map.

casque (kask), *n.* 1 a piece of armor to cover the head; helmet. 2 (in zoology) any helmet-like structure. [< French < Spanish *casco.* Doublet of CASK.]

cas sa ba (kə sä′bə), *n.* casaba.

Cas san dra (kə san′drə), *n.* 1 (in Greek legends) a daughter of Hecuba and King Priam of Troy. Apollo gave her the gift of prophecy, but later in anger punished her by ordering that no one should believe her prophecies. 2 person who prophesies misfortune, but is not believed.

cas sa tion (ka sā′shən), *n.* annulment or reversal. [< Medieval Latin *cassationem* < Late Latin *cassare* annul]

Cas satt (kə sat′), *n.* **Mary,** 1845-1926, American painter.

cas sa va (kə sä′və), *n.* 1 a tropical plant of the same family as the spurge, with starchy roots; manioc. 2 a nutritious starch made from its roots. Tapioca is made from cassava. [< French *cassave* < Spanish *casabe*]

cas se role (kas′ə rōl′), *n.* 1 a covered baking dish in which food can be both cooked and served. 2 food cooked and served in such a dish, usually a mixture of meat, cheese, or vegetables in macaroni, rice, or mashed potatoes, and sauce. [< French]

cas sette (ka set′), *n.* 1 container holding magnetic tape for playing or recording sound automatically. 2 cartridge for film.

cas sia (kash′ə, kas′ē ə), *n.* 1 an inferior kind of cinnamon, made from the bark of a laurel tree of southern China. 2 the tree.

3 plant of the pea family yielding leaves and pods that are used in making senna. 4 the pods or their pulp. [Old English < Latin < Greek *kassia*]

cas si mere (kas′ə mir), *n.* a soft, lightweight, woolen cloth, sometimes used for men's suits. [variant of *cashmere*]

cas si no (kə sē′nō), *n.* a card game in which cards in the hand are matched with cards on the table. Also, **casino.** [variant of *casino*]

Cas si o pe ia (kas′ē ə pē′ə), *n.* 1 (in Greek legends) the mother of Andromeda. 2 constellation near the North Star, named after her.

Cassiopeia's Chair, group of five bright stars in the constellation Cassiopeia suggesting a chair.

cas sit e rite (kə sit′ə rīt′), *n.* dioxide of tin, found pure in nature, which is the chief source of tin; tinstone. *Formula:* SnO_2 [< Greek *kassiteros* tin]

Cas sius Lon gi nus (kash′əs lon jī′nəs; kas′ē əs lon jī′nəs), **Gaius,** died 42 B.C., one of the leaders of the conspiracy to assassinate Julius Caesar.

cas sock (kas′ək), *n.* a long outer garment, usually black, worn by a clergyman. [< French *casaque* < Italian *casacca*]

cas so war y (kas′ə wer′ē), *n., pl.* **-war ies.** a large bird of Australia and New Guinea like an ostrich, but smaller. Cassowaries run swiftly, but cannot fly. [< Malay *kĕsuari*]

cast (kast), *v.,* **cast, cast ing,** *n., adj.* —*v.t.* 1 throw, fling, or hurl. See **throw** for synonym study. 2 throw one end of (a fishing line) out into the water. 3 throw off; let fall; shed: *The snake cast its skin.* 4 direct or turn: *He cast a glance of surprise at me.* 5 deposit (a ballot); give (a vote). 6 to shape by pouring or squeezing into a mold to harden. Metal is first melted and then cast. 7 arrange: *She cast her plans into final form.* 8 in the theater: **a** assign the various parts of (a play). **b** select (an actor) for a part in a play. **c** fill (a part) by assigning an actor to it. 9 add; calculate. 10 calculate astrologically: *cast a horoscope.* —*v.i.* 1 throw. 2 calculate.
cast about, search or seek; look around.
cast aside, a throw or put away. **b** throw aside from use; discard.
cast away, a abandon. **b** to shipwreck.
cast down, a turn downward; lower. **b** make sad or discouraged.
cast off, a let loose; set free; untie from moorings: *cast off a boat.* **b** abandon or discard. **c** make the last row of stitches in knitting.
cast on, make the first row of stitches in knitting.
cast out, drive out forcibly; banish or expel.
cast up, a turn upward; raise (the eyes, head, etc.). **b** find the sum of; add up.
—*n.* 1 the distance a thing is thrown; throw. 2 act of throwing a fishing line. 3 a throw of dice. 4 the number of spots showing after a throw of dice. 5 thing made by casting; thing that is molded. 6 mold used in casting; mold. 7 a plaster cast used to support a broken bone while it is mending: *I had my arm in a cast for more than a month.* 8 the actors in a play. 9 outward form or look; appearance. 10 kind; sort: *a man of humble cast.* 11 a slight amount of color; tinge: *a white dress with a pink cast.* 12 a slight squint.
—*adj.* made by casting.
[< Scandinavian (Old Icelandic) *kasta*]

cas ta net (kas′tə net′), *n.* one of a pair of instruments held in the hand and clicked together to beat time for dancing or music. Castanets are made of hard wood or ivory. [< Spanish *castañeta* < Latin *castanea.* See CHESTNUT.]

castanet—a pair of castanets

cast a way (kast′ə wā′), *adj.* 1 thrown away; cast adrift. 2 outcast; rejected. —*n.* 1 person cast adrift at sea; shipwrecked person. 2 an outcast.

caste (kast), *n.* 1 one of the social classes into which Hindus are divided. By tradition, a Hindu is born into the caste of his father and cannot rise above it. 2 an exclusive social group; distinct class. 3 a social system having distinct classes separated by differences of birth, rank, wealth, or position. 4 the position which caste confers: *renounce caste.* 5 **lose caste,** lose social rank, status, or position. [< Portuguese *casta* race, class, animal species; perhaps < Germanic]

cas tel lat ed (kas′tl ā′tid), *adj.* 1 built like a castle; having turrets and battlements. 2 having many castles.

cast er (kas′tər), *n.* 1 a small wheel on a swivel set into the base of a piece of furniture or other object, such as a shopping cart. 2 shaker or bottle containing salt, mustard, vinegar, or other seasoning for table use. 3 stand or rack for such bottles. 4 person or thing that casts. Also, **castor** for 1-3.

cas ti gate (kas′tə gāt), *v.t.,* **-gat ed, -gat ing.** 1 censure, chasten, or punish in order to correct. 2 criticize severely. [< Latin *castigatum* chastened < *castus* pure] —**cas′ti ga′tion,** *n.* —**cas′ti ga′tor,** *n.*

Cas tile (ka stēl′), *n.* 1 region in N and central Spain, formerly a kingdom. 2 Castile soap.

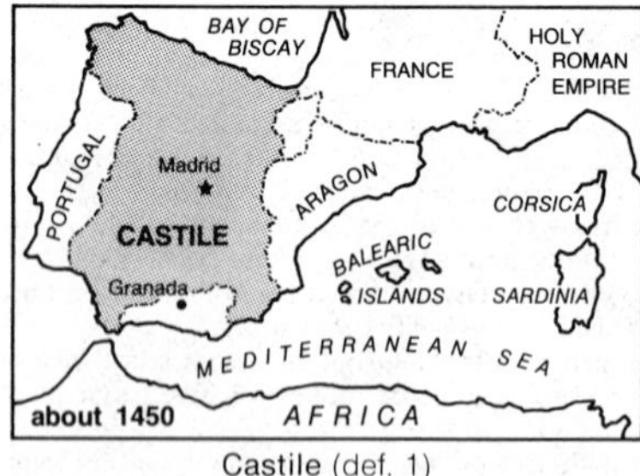

Castile (def. 1)

Castile soap or **castile soap,** a pure, hard soap made from olive oil and sodium hydroxide.

Cas til ian (ka stil′yən), *adj.* of Castile, its people, or their language. —*n.* 1 Castilian Spanish. 2 native or inhabitant of Castile.

Castilian Spanish, Spanish as spoken in Castile, the standard language of Spain.

cast ing (kas′ting), *n.* 1 thing shaped by being poured into a mold to harden. 2 act or process of shaping things by pouring into a mold. 3 assignment of the parts in a play, film, etc.

casting vote, a vote by the presiding officer to decide a question when the votes of an assembly, council, board, or committee are evenly divided.

cast iron, a hard, brittle form of iron containing carbon and silicon, made by remelting pig iron and running it into molds, used to make automobile engine blocks, etc.

cast-i ron (kast′ī′ərn), *adj.* 1 made of cast iron. 2 not yielding; hard: *cast-iron policies.* 3 hardy; strong: *a cast-iron stomach.*

cas tle (kas′əl), *n., v.,* **-tled, -tling.** —*n.* 1 a large building or group of buildings with thick walls, turrets, battlements, and other defenses against attack. 2 palace that once had defenses against attack. 3 a large and stately residence. 4 rook[2]. —*v.i.* in chess: **a** move the king two squares toward a rook and bring that rook to the square the king has passed over. **b** (of the king) be thus moved. —*v.t.* place in or as if in a castle. [< Latin *castellum,* diminutive of *castrum* fort. Doublet of CHÂTEAU.]

castle in the air, something imagined but not likely to come true; daydream.

Cas tle reagh (kas′əl rā), *n.* **Viscount,** 1769-1822, Robert Stewart, British statesman, born in Ireland.

cast off (kast′ôf′, kast′of′), *adj.* thrown away; abandoned; discarded: *castoff clothes.* —*n.* person or thing that has been cast off.

cas tor[1] (kas′tər), *n.* caster (defs. 1-3).

cas tor[2] (kas′tər), *n.* 1 an oily substance with a strong odor, secreted by beavers. It is used in making perfume and in medicines. 2 hat made of beaver fur. [< Latin, beaver < Greek *kastōr*]

Cas tor (kas′tər), *n.* 1 (in Greek and Roman myths) one of the twin sons of Zeus. Castor was mortal; his brother, Pollux, was immortal. 2 the fainter of the two bright stars in the constellation Gemini.

castor bean, seed of the castor-oil plant.

castor oil, a thick, yellow oil obtained from castor beans, used as a laxative and as a lubricant for machines.

cas tor-oil plant (kas′tər oil′), a tall, tropical plant of the same family as the spurge, from whose seeds castor oil is obtained.

cas trate (kas′trāt), *v.,* **-trat ed, -trat ing,** *n.* —*v.t.* 1 remove the testicles of; emasculate. An ox is a castrated bull. 2 mutilate or expurgate. —*n.* a castrated animal or person. [< Latin *castratum* castrated] —**cas tra′tion,** *n.*

Cas tries (ka strē′), *n.* capital of St. Lucia. 40,000.

Cas tro (kas′trō), *n.* **Fidel,** born 1927, premier of Cuba since 1959.

cas u al (kazh′ü əl), *adj.* 1 happening by chance; not planned or expected; accidental: *a casual meeting.* 2 without plan or method; careless: *a casual answer, a casual glance.* 3 uncertain; indefinite; indifferent; vague. 4 informal in manner; offhand: *casual manners, casual living.* 5 occasional or irregular: *casual labor, a casual laborer.* 6 designed for informal wear: *casual clothes.* —*n.* 1 a casual laborer. 2 soldier awaiting orders, transportation, etc., at a post or station to which he is not attached or assigned. [< Latin *casualis* < *casus* chance. See CASE[1].] —**cas′u al ly,** *adv.* —**cas′u al ness,** *n.*

cas u al ty (kazh′ü əl tē), *n., pl.* **-ties.** 1 member of the armed forces who has been wounded, killed, or captured as a result of enemy action. 2 person injured or killed in an accident or disaster: *The earthquake caused many casualties.* 3 accident, especially a fatal or serious one. 4 an unfortunate accident; mishap.

cas u ist (kazh′ü ist), *n.* 1 person who reasons cleverly but falsely, especially in regard to right and wrong. 2 person who decides questions of right and wrong in regard to conscience or conduct. [< French *casuiste* < Latin *casus* case]

cas u is tic (kazh′ü is′tik), *adj.* 1 of or like casuistry. 2 too subtle; sophistical. **—cas′u is′ti cal ly,** *adv.*

cas u ist ry (kazh′ü ə strē), *n., pl.* **-ries.** 1 clever but false reasoning, especially in regard to right and wrong. 2 the deciding of questions of right and wrong in regard to conscience or conduct.

ca sus bel li (kä′səs bel′ī; kä′səs bel′ē), LATIN. cause for war.

cat (kat), *n., v.,* **cat ted, cat ting.** *—n.* 1 a small, furry, four-footed, carnivorous mammal, often kept as a pet or for catching mice and rats. 2 any animal of the family that includes cats, lions, tigers, and leopards. 3 animal resembling a cat. 4 a mean, spiteful woman. 5 catfish. 6 cat-o'-nine-tails. 7 tackle for hoisting an anchor. 8 **bell the cat,** do something dangerous. 9 **let the cat out of the bag,** tell a secret. 10 **rain cats and dogs,** pour down rain very hard. *—v.t.* hoist (an anchor) and fasten it to a beam on the ship's side. [Old English *catt*] **—cat′like′,** *adj.*

Cat (kat), *n.* trademark for a Caterpillar crawler tractor.

cat., 1 catalogue. 2 catechism.

cata-, *prefix.* down; against, as in *catabolism.* Also, **cat-,** before vowels and *h,* as in *category, cathode.* [< Greek *kata-* < *kata* down]

cat a bol ic (kat′ə bol′ik), *adj.* of, having to do with, or exhibiting catabolism. **—cat′a bol′i cal ly,** *adv.*

ca tab o lism (kə tab′ə liz′əm), *n.* process of breaking down living tissues into simpler substances or waste matter, thereby producing energy; dissimilation. [< *cata-* + *(meta)bolism*]

cat a clysm (kat′ə kliz′əm), *n.* 1 a great flood, earthquake, or any sudden, violent change in the earth. 2 any violent change or upheaval: *Atomic warfare between nations would be a cataclysm for all mankind.* [< Greek *kataklysmos* flood < *kata-* down + *klyzein* to wash]

cat a clys mal (kat′ə kliz′məl), *adj.* cataclysmic.

cat a clys mic (kat′ə kliz′mik), *adj.* of or like a cataclysm; extremely sudden and violent. **—cat′a clys′mi cal ly,** *adv.*

cat a comb (kat′ə kōm), *n.* Usually, **catacombs,** *pl.* an underground gallery forming a burial place, especially a network of such galleries with recesses in which to place the dead. [< Late Latin *catacumbae,* plural]

cat a falque (kat′ə falk), *n.* stand or platform to support a coffin in which a dead person lies. [< French < Italian *catafalco* < Latin *cata-* down + *fala* tower]

Cat a lan (kat′l ən, kat′l an), *adj.* of Catalonia, its people, or their language. *—n.* 1 native or inhabitant of Catalonia. 2 the Romance language spoken in Catalonia. Also, **Catalonian.**

cat a lase (kat′l ās), *n.* enzyme found in most living cells which catalyzes the separation of hydrogen peroxide into gaseous oxygen and water.

cat a lep sy (kat′l ep′sē), *n.* condition usually associated with schizophrenia in which a person's muscles become more or less rigid, and his arms and legs maintain any position in which they are placed. [< Greek *katalēpsis,* literally, seizure < *kata-* down + *lambanein* seize]

cat a lep tic (kat′l ep′tik), *adj.* 1 of catalepsy. 2 having catalepsy. *—n.* person who has catalepsy.

Cat a li na Island (kat′l ē′nə), island resort off the SW coast of California, near Los Angeles; Santa Catalina. 20 mi. long.

cat a lo (kat′l ō), *n., pl.* **-loes** or **-los.** cattalo.

cat a log (kat′l ôg, kat′l og), *n., v.* *—n.* 1 list of items in some collection, either identifying each item very briefly or describing it more fully. A library has a catalog of its books, arranged in alphabetical order. A company sometimes prints a catalog with pictures and prices of the things that it sells. See **list** for synonym study. 2 volume or booklet issued by a college or university listing rules, courses to be given, etc. 3 any list or series: *a catalog of lies.* *—v.t.* 1 make a catalog of: *I cataloged all the insects in my collection.* 2 put in a catalog. *—v.i.* make a catalog. [< Old French < Late Latin *catalogus* a list < Greek *katalogos* < *kata-* down + *legein* to count] **—cat′a log′er,** *n.*

cat a logue (kat′l ôg, kat′l og), *n., v.,* **-logued, -logu ing.** catalog. **—cat′a logu′er,** *n.*

Cat a lo ni a (kat′l ō′nē ə), *n.* region in NE Spain.

Cat a lo ni an (kat′l ō′nē ən), *adj., n.* Catalan.

ca tal pa (kə tal′pə), *n.* tree of North America and Asia with large, heart-shaped leaves, clusters of bell-shaped flowers, and long pods. [< Creek *kutuhlpa*]

ca tal y sis (kə tal′ə sis), *n., pl.* **-ses** (-sēz′). the causing or speeding up of a chemical reaction by the presence of a catalyst. [< Greek *katalysis* dissolution < *kata-* down + *lyein* to loose]

cat a lyst (kat′l ist), *n.* 1 substance that causes or speeds up a chemical reaction while undergoing no permanent change in composition itself. Enzymes are important catalysts in digestion. 2 anything that brings about some change or changes without being directly affected itself: *The first successful heart transplant was the catalyst that sparked widespread scientific work in this field.*

cat a lyt ic (kat′l it′ik), *adj.* 1 of catalysis. 2 causing catalysis.

cat a lyze (kat′l īz), *v.t.,* **-lyzed, -lyz ing.** act upon by catalysis.

cat a lyz er (kat′l ī′zər), *n.* catalyst.

cat a ma ran (kat′ə mə ran′), *n.* 1 boat with two hulls side by side joined by crosspieces. 2 raft made of pieces of wood lashed together. [< Tamil *kattamaram* tied tree]

cat a mount (kat′ə mount), *n.* wildcat, such as a puma or lynx. [short for *catamountain* cat of (the) mountain]

Ca ta nia (kə tā′nyə, kä tä′nyä), *n.* seaport in E Sicily, Italy. 413,000.

cat a pult (kat′ə pult), *n.* 1 an ancient weapon for shooting stones, arrows, etc. 2 slingshot. 3 device for launching an airplane from the deck of a ship. *—v.t.* throw; hurl. *—v.i.* shoot up suddenly; spring. [< Latin *catapulta* < Greek *katapeltēs,* probably < *kata-* down + *pallein* to hurl]

cat a ract (kat′ə rakt′), *n.* 1 a large, steep waterfall. 2 a violent rush or downpour of water; flood. 3 an opaque condition in the lens of the eye, or its capsule, that develops from a cloudy film and may cause partial or

hat, āge, fär; let, ēqual, tėrm;
it, īce; hot, ōpen, ôrder;
oil, out; cup, pu̇t, rüle;
ch, child; ng, long; sh, she;
th, thin; ᴛʜ, then; zh, measure;

ə represents *a* in about, *e* in taken, *i* in pencil, *o* in lemon, *u* in circus.

< = from, derived from, taken from.

total blindness. [< Latin *cataracta* < Greek *kataraktēs* < *kata-* down + *arassein* to dash]

ca tarrh (kə tär′), *n.* an inflamed condition of a mucous membrane, usually that of the nose or throat, causing a discharge of mucus. [< Greek *katarrhous* < *kata-* down + *rhein* to flow]

ca tarrh al (kə tär′əl), *adj.* 1 like catarrh. 2 caused by catarrh.

ca tas tro phe (kə tas′trə fē), *n.* 1 a sudden, widespread, or extraordinary disaster; great calamity or misfortune. A big earthquake, flood, or fire is a catastrophe. See **disaster** for synonym study. 2 outcome, especially of a literary work; ending. The catastrophe of a tragedy usually brings death or ruin to the leading character. 3 a disastrous end; ruin. [< Greek *katastrophē* an overturning < *kata-* down + *strephein* to turn]

cat a stroph ic (kat′ə strof′ik), *adj.* of or caused by disaster; calamitous. **—cat′a stroph′i cal ly,** *adv.*

cat a to ni a (kat′ə tō′nē ə), *n.* condition associated with schizophrenia, characterized by mental stupor and muscular rigidity. [< *cata-* + Greek *tonos* tone]

Ca taw ba (kə tô′bə), *n.* 1 a light-red grape of North America. 2 a light wine made from it.

cat bird (kat′bėrd′), *n.* a grayish North American songbird of the same family as the mockingbird, with black on its head, wings, and tail. The catbird can make a sound like a cat mewing.

cat boat (kat′bōt′), *n.* sailboat with one mast set far forward and no jib.

cat burglar, burglar who enters by skillful feats of climbing.

cat call (kat′kôl′), *n.* a shrill cry or whistle to express disapproval. Actors who perform poorly are sometimes greeted by catcalls from the audience. *—v.i.* make catcalls. *—v.t.* attack with catcalls.

catapult (def. 1)—The very heavy bow was drawn by means of ropes and could send an arrow a great distance.

catch (kach), *v.,* **caught, catch ing,** *n., adj.* *—v.t.* 1 take and hold (someone trying to escape); seize; capture. See synonym study below. 2 attract and hold the attention of: *Bright colors catch the baby's eye.* 3 be affected or influenced by; become infected with; take: *Paper catches fire easily. I caught* *cold last week.* 4 reach or get to in time: *You have just five minutes to catch your train.* 5 grab or seize (something in flight): *He caught the ball in his glove.* 6 hear, see, or understand: *She tried hard to catch what the man across the room was saying.* 7 take notice of; discover: *He thought I wouldn't catch his error.* 8 entangle or grip: *A nail caught her sleeve.* 9 come upon suddenly; surprise: *Mother caught me just as I was hiding her birthday present.* 10 reach with a blow; hit; strike: *The stone caught me on the leg.* 11 check suddenly: *She caught her breath.* 12 catch up; overtake. *—v.i.* 1 become hooked, entangled, or fastened: *My dress caught in the door.* 2 become lighted; burn: *Tinder catches easily.* 3 be a catcher in baseball.

catch as catch can, grab or wrestle in any way.

catch at, a try to catch. **b** seize eagerly.

catch it, INFORMAL. be scolded or punished.

catch on, INFORMAL. **a** get the idea; understand. **b** become popular; be widely used or accepted.

catch up, a pick up suddenly; snatch; grab. **b** interrupt and annoy with criticisms or questions; heckle. **c** hold up in loops.

catch up with, come up even with a person or thing while going the same way; overtake: *The dog ran as fast as he could to catch up with the car.*

—n. 1 act of catching. 2 thing that catches. A fastener for a door or window is a catch. 3 thing caught: *A dozen fish is a good catch.* 4 INFORMAL. a desirable person to marry because of his or her wealth, position, etc. 5 game that consists of throwing and catching a ball. 6 act of receiving and holding a thrown, kicked, or batted ball. 7 (in music) a round. 8 a scrap or fragment of anything: *They sang catches of songs.* 9 a choking or stoppage of the breath: *He had a catch in his voice.* 10 INFORMAL. a hidden or tricky condition or meaning; some difficulty that does not appear on the surface: *There is a catch to that question.*

—adj. 1 getting one's attention; arousing one's interest: *Advertisements often contain catch phrases.* 2 tricky; deceptive: *a catch question.*

[< Old North French *cachier* to chase, hunt < Latin *captare* try to catch < *capere* take. Doublet of CHASE[1].]

Syn. *v.t.* **1 Catch, capture** mean to seize and hold someone or something. **Catch** suggests overtaking or taking something moving, fleeing, or hidden by force, surprise, or cleverness: *We caught the thief.* **Capture** suggests seizing or overtaking in spite of greater difficulty or obstacles: *The enemy captured the fort.*

catch all (kach′ôl′), *n.* container for odds and ends.

catch er (kach′ər), *n.* 1 person or thing that catches. 2 a baseball player who stands behind the batter to catch balls thrown by the pitcher and not hit by the batter.

catch ing (kach′ing), *adj.* 1 likely to spread from one to another; contagious; infectious: *Colds are catching.* 2 attractive or fascinating.

catch ment (kach′mənt), *n.* reservoir for catching water.

catch pen ny (kach′pen′ē), *adj., n., pl.* **-nies.** *—adj.* showy but worthless or useless; made to sell quickly. *—n.* a catchpenny article.

catch up (kech′əp, kach′əp), *n.* catsup.

catch word (kach′wėrd′), *n.* 1 word or phrase used again and again for effect; slogan: *"No taxation without representation" was a political catchword during the Revolutionary War.* 2 guide word.

catch y (kach′ē), *adj.,* **catch i er, catch i est.** 1 attractive and easy to remember: *a catchy tune.* 2 that is misleading; tricky; deceptive: *catchy questions.* **—catch′i ly,** *adv.* **—catch′i ness,** *n.*

cate (kāt), *n.* ARCHAIC. a delicacy; choice food. [variant of Middle English *acate* < Old French *acat* a purchase]

cat e chism (kat′ə kiz′əm), *n.* 1 book of questions and answers about religion, used for teaching religious doctrine. 2 set of questions and answers about any subject. 3 a long or formal set of questions. [< Greek *katēchismos* < *katēchizein* teach orally < *katēchein* < *kata-* thoroughly + *ēchein* to sound]

cat e chist (kat′ə kist), *n.* person who catechizes.

cat e chis tic (kat′ə kis′tik), *adj.* of a catechist or catechism. **—cat′e chis′ti cal ly,** *adv.*

cat e chize (kat′ə kīz), *v.t.,* **-chized, -chiz ing.** 1 teach by questions and answers. 2 question closely. [< Greek *katēchizein.* See CATECHISM.] **—cat′e chi za′tion,** *n.* **—cat′e chiz′er,** *n.*

cat e chu men (kat′ə kyü′mən), *n.* 1 person who is being taught the elementary principles of Christianity. 2 person who is being taught the fundamentals of any field of study. [< Greek *katēchoumenos* < *katēchein.* See CATECHISM.]

cat e go ric (kat′ə gôr′ik, kat′ə gor′ik), *adj.* categorical.

cat e go ri cal (kat′ə gôr′ə kəl, kat′ə gor′ə-kəl), *adj.* 1 without conditions or qualifications; positive. 2 of or in a category. **—cat′e go′ri cal ly,** *adv.*

cat e go rize (kat′ə gə rīz′), *v.t.,* **-rized, -riz ing.** put in a category; classify. **—cat′e go ri za′tion,** *n.*

cat e go ry (kat′ə gôr′ē, kat′ə gōr′ē), *n., pl.* **-ries.** group or division in a general system of classification; class: *She places all people into two categories: those she likes and those she dislikes.* [< Latin *categoria* < Greek *katēgoria* assertion < *kata-* down + *agoreuein* speak]

ca ter (kā′tər), *v.i.* 1 provide food, supplies, and sometimes service: *They run a restaurant and also cater for weddings and parties.* 2 provide what is needed or wanted: *The new magazine caters to boys by printing stories about aviation, athletics, and camping.* [verbal use of *cater* buyer of provisions < Old North French *acateor* < *acater* buy]

cat er-cor ner (kat′ər kôr′nər), *adj., adv.* cater-cornered. Also, **kitty-corner.**

cat er-cor nered (kat′ər kôr′nərd), *adj.* diagonal. *—adv.* diagonally. Also, **catty-cornered, kitty-cornered.** [< obsolete *cater* move diagonally (< French *quatre* four) + *cornered*]

ca ter er (kā′tər ər), *n.* person who provides food, supplies, and sometimes service for parties, weddings, etc.

cat er pil lar (kat′ər pil′ər), *n.* the wormlike larva of insects such as the butterfly and the moth. [< Old North French *catepelose* hairy cat < Popular Latin *catta pilosa*]

Cat er pil lar (kat′ər pil′ər), *n.* trademark for crawler tractors and other machinery.

cat er waul (kat′ər wôl), *v.i.* howl like a cat; screech. *—n.* such a howl or screech. [Middle English *caterwrawe* < *cater* cat + *wrawe* wail, howl]

cat fish (kat′fish′), *n., pl.* **-fish es** or **-fish.** any of several scaleless fishes with long, slender growths called barbels around the mouth that look somewhat like a cat's whiskers.

cat gut (kat′gut′), *n.* a tough string made from the dried and twisted intestines of sheep or other animals, used to string violins and tennis rackets, and formerly to stitch wounds. [perhaps alteration of earlier *kit* small violin + *gut*]

Cath., Catholic.

ca thar sis (kə thär′sis), *n.* 1 a purging. 2 an emotional purification or relief, usually by sharing in the experience of another. [< Greek *katharsis,* ultimately < *katharos* clean]

ca thar tic (kə thär′tik), *n.* a strong laxative. Epsom salts and castor oil are cathartics. *—adj.* strongly laxative.

Ca thay (ka thā′), *n.* ARCHAIC. China.

cat head (kat′hed′), *n.* beam on the side of a ship near the bow. The anchor is hoisted and fastened to it. [< *cat* (def. 7) + *head*]

ca the dral (kə thē′drəl), *n.* 1 the official church of a bishop. 2 a large or important church. *—adj.* 1 having a bishop's throne. 2 of or like a cathedral. [< Late Latin *cathedralis* of the (bishop's) chair < Greek *kathedra* chair < *kata-* down + *hedra* seat]

Cath er (kaᴛʜ′ər), *n.* **Willa Sibert,** 1876-1947, American novelist.

Cath er ine I (kath′ər ən), 1683?-1727, wife of Peter the Great and, after his death, empress of Russia from 1725 to 1727.

Catherine II, Catherine the Great.

Catherine of Aragon, 1485-1536, first wife of Henry VIII of England.

Catherine the Great, 1729-1796, empress of Russia from 1762 to 1796.

cath e ter (kath′ə tər), *n.* a slender rigid or flexible tube to be inserted into a passage or cavity of the body. A catheter may be used to remove urine from the bladder. [< Greek *kathetēr* < *kata-* down + *hienai* send]

cath ode (kath′ōd), *n.* 1 a negative electrode. Electrons flow from the cathode to the anode producing an electric current. The zinc case of a dry cell and the filament of a vacuum tube are cathodes. 2 the negative pole of any source of current. [< Greek *kathodos* a way down < *kata-* down + *hodos* way]

cathode rays, the invisible streams of electrons from the cathode in a vacuum tube. When cathode rays strike a solid substance, they produce X rays.

cath ode-ray tube (kath′ōd rā′), vacuum tube in which beams of high-speed electrons are passed through magnetic fields and deflected to a fluorescent screen on which movement of the beams is visible as spots or ribbons of light. Cathode-ray tubes are used in television receivers.

ca thod ic (kə thod′ik), *adj.* having to do with or resembling a cathode.

Cath o lic (kath′ə lik), *adj.* 1 of the Christian church governed by the pope; Roman Catholic. 2 of the ancient, undivided Christian church, or of its present representatives, including the Anglican, Orthodox, and Roman Catholic Churches. 3 **catholic, a** of interest or use to all people; including all; broad; universal. **b** having sympathies with all; broad-minded; liberal. **c** of the whole

Christian church. —*n.* member of a Catholic church, especially the Roman Catholic Church. [< Latin *catholicus* < Greek *katholikos* universal < *kata-* in respect to + *holos* whole]

Ca thol i cism (kə thol′ə siz′əm), *n.* 1 faith, doctrine, and organization of the Catholic Church. 2 **catholicism,** catholicity.

Cath o lic i ty (kath′ə lis′ə tē), *n.* 1 Catholicism. 2 **catholicity, a** broadness; universality. **b** broad-mindedness; liberalness.

ca thol i cize (kə thol′ə sīz), *v.t., v.i.* **-cized, -ciz ing.** make or become catholic or universal.

Cat i line (kat′l īn), *n.* 108?-62 B.C., leader of a conspiracy against the Roman republic.

cat i on (kat′ī′ən), *n.* 1 a positively charged ion that moves toward the negative pole in electrolysis. 2 atom or group of atoms having a positive charge. [coined by Faraday from Greek *kation* going down < *kata-* down + *ienai* go]

cat kin (kat′kən), *n.* the soft, downy or scaly spike of flowers, without petals, which grows on willows, birches, etc.; ament. [< Dutch *katteken* little cat]

Cat lin (kat′lin), *n.* **George,** 1796-1872, American artist who painted and wrote about American Indian life.

cat nap (kat′nap′), *n.* a short nap or doze.

cat nip (kat′nip), *n.* plant of the mint family with strongly scented leaves that cats like. [< *cat* + *nip,* variant of *nep* catnip < Latin *nepeta*]

Ca to (kā′tō), *n.* 1 **Marcus Porcius,** 234-149 B.C., Roman statesman and writer. He was called "the Elder" or "the Censor." 2 his great-grandson, **Marcus Porcius,** 95-46 B.C., Roman statesman, soldier, and Stoic philosopher, called "the Younger."

cat-o'-nine-tails (kat′ə nīn′tālz′), *n., pl.* **-tails.** whip consisting of nine pieces of knotted cord fastened to a handle. It was formerly used as a means of punishment in the navy.

cat's cradle, a child's game played with a string looped over the fingers of both hands.

cat's-eye (kats′ī′), *n.* a semiprecious gem, especially a variety of quartz showing beautiful changes of color suggesting a cat's eye.

Cats kill Mountains (kats′kil), range of Appalachian Mountains in SE New York State. Highest peak, 4204 feet.

Cats kills (kats′kilz), *n.pl.* Catskill Mountains.

cat's-paw or **cats paw** (kats′pô′), *n.* 1 person used by another to do something unpleasant or dangerous. 2 a light breeze that ruffles a small stretch of water.

cat sup (kech′əp, kat′səp), *n.* sauce made to use with meat, fish, etc. Tomato catsup is made of tomatoes, onions, salt, sugar, and spices. Also, **catchup, ketchup.**

Catt (kat), *n.* **Carrie Chapman,** 1859-1947, American leader of the women's suffrage movement.

cat tail (kat′tāl′), *n.* a tall, reedlike marsh plant with flowers in long, round, furry, brown spikes; flag[2].

cat ta lo (kat′l ō), *n., pl.* **-loes** or **-lo.** hybrid of the bison and the domestic cow. Also, **catalo.** [< *catt(le)* + *(buff)alo*]

cat tle (kat′l), *n.pl.* 1 animals of the same genus as the ox raised for meat, milk, hides, etc.; cows, bulls, steers, heifers, and calves. 2 (formerly) farm animals; livestock. 3 any despised people. [< Old North French *catel* < Medieval Latin *capitale* property, neuter of Latin *capitalem.* Doublet of CAPITAL[1], CHATTEL.]

cat tle man (kat′l mən), *n., pl.* **-men.** man who raises or takes care of cattle.

cat ty (kat′ē), *adj.,* **-ti er, -ti est.** 1 mean and spiteful. 2 catlike. 3 of cats. **—cat′ti ly,** *adv.* **—cat′ti ness,** *n.*

cat ty-cor nered (kat′ē kôr′nərd), *adj., adv.* cater-cornered.

Ca tul lus (kə tul′əs), *n.* **Gaius Valerius,** 87?-54? B.C., Roman lyric poet.

CATV, Community Antenna Television (a system of television reception using community antennas).

cat walk (kat′wôk′), *n.* a narrow place to walk on a bridge, near the ceiling of a stage, in an airship, etc.

Cau ca sia (kô kā′zhə, kô kā′shə), *n.* region in the SW Soviet Union, between the Black and Caspian Seas; Caucasus.

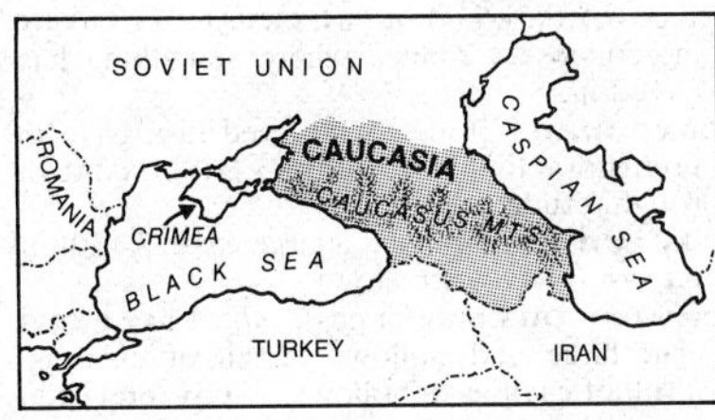

Cau ca sian (kô kā′zhən, kô kā′shən; kô kazh′ən, kô kash′ən), *n.* 1 member of the so-called white race, including the chief peoples of Europe, southwestern Asia, northern Africa, the Western Hemisphere, Australia, and New Zealand. 2 native or inhabitant of the Caucasus. —*adj.* 1 of or having to do with the so-called white race. 2 of or having to do with the Caucasus or its inhabitants.

Cau ca sus (kô′kə səs), *n.* 1 mountain range in SW Soviet Union, extending from the Black Sea to the Caspian Sea. The highest peak is 18,481 feet. 2 Caucasia.

cau cus (kô′kəs), *n.* 1 U.S. a meeting of members or leaders of a political party to make plans, choose candidates, or decide how to vote. 2 any similar meeting for the private discussion of policy. —*v.i.* hold a caucus. [probably < Algonquian *caucauasu* elder]

cau dal (kô′dl), *adj.* 1 of, at, or near the tail or the posterior end of an animal. 2 taillike. [< Latin *cauda* tail] **—cau′dal ly,** *adv.*

caudal fin, a fin located at the hind end of fishes. See **fin** for picture.

cau dex (kô′deks), *n., pl.* **-di ces** (-də sēz′), **-dex es.** the woody base of a perennial plant, which sends up new herbaceous stems each year in place of the old. [< Latin, trunk of a tree]

cau dil lo (kô dē′lyō; *Spanish* kou ᴛʜē′lyō, kou ᴛʜē′yō), *n., pl.* **-los.** a military leader or dictator in a Spanish-speaking country. [< Spanish < Latin *capitellum* little head]

cau dle (kô′dl), *n.* a warm drink for sick people, as wine or ale thickened with gruel or soaked bread, sweetened, and spiced. [< Old French *caudel* < Latin *calidus* warm]

caught (kôt), *v.* pt. and pp. of **catch.** *I caught the ball. The mouse was caught in a trap.*

caul (kôl), *n.* a portion of the membrane enclosing a child in the womb that is sometimes found clinging to the head at birth. It was supposed to bring good luck and to safeguard against drowning. [Old English *cawl* basket, net]

hat, āge, fär; let, ēqual, tėrm;
it, īce; hot, ōpen, ôrder;
oil, out; cup, pu̇t, rüle;
ch, child; ng, long; sh, she;
th, thin; ᴛʜ, then; zh, measure;

ə represents *a* in about, *e* in taken, *i* in pencil, *o* in lemon, *u* in circus.

< = from, derived from, taken from.

caul dron (kôl′drən), *n.* caldron.

cau li flow er (kô′lə flou′ər, kol′ē flou′ər), *n.* 1 species of cole, related to the cabbage, having a solid, white head with a few leaves around it. 2 its head, which is eaten as a vegetable. [half-translation of New Latin *cauliflora* < Latin *caulis* cabbage + *florem* flower]

cauliflower ear, INFORMAL. ear that has been misshapen by injuries received in boxing, etc.

caulk (kôk), *v.t.* fill up (a seam, crack, or joint) so that it will not leak; make watertight. Sailors caulk wooden boats with oakum and tar. Plumbers caulk joints in pipe with lead. Also, **calk.** [< Old French *cauquer* press in, tread < Latin *calcare* < *calcem* heel] **—caulk′er,** *n.*

caus al (kô′zəl), *adj.* 1 of a cause; acting as a cause. 2 having to do with cause and effect. 3 showing a cause or reason. *Because* is a causal conjunction. **—caus′al ly,** *adv.*

cau sal i ty (kô zal′ə tē), *n., pl.* **-ties.** 1 relation of cause and effect; principle that nothing can happen or exist without a cause: *a belief in causality.* 2 causal quality or agency.

cau sa tion (kô zā′shən), *n.* 1 a causing or a being caused. 2 whatever produces an effect; cause or causes. 3 relation of cause and effect; principle that nothing can happen or exist without a cause.

caus a tive (kô′zə tiv), *adj.* 1 being a cause; productive (of an effect). 2 expressing causation. In *enrich, en-* is a causative prefix. **—caus′a tive ly,** *adv.* **—caus′a tive ness,** *n.*

cause (kôz), *n., v.,* **caused, caus ing.** —*n.* 1 whatever produces an effect; person, thing, or event that makes something happen: *The flood was the cause of much damage.* See synonym study below. 2 reason or occasion for action; ground; motive: *cause for celebration.* See **reason** for synonym study. 3 good reason; reason enough: *He was angry without cause.* 4 subject or movement in which many people are interested and to which they give their support: *World peace is the cause she works for.* 5 matter for a court of law to decide; lawsuit. 6 **make common cause with,** join efforts with; side with; help and support. —*v.t.* produce as an effect; make happen; make do; bring about: *The fire caused much damage.* [< Latin *causa*] **—caus′er,** *n.*

Syn. *n.* 1 **Cause, occasion** mean whatever makes something happen. **Cause** applies to a thing, person, situation, action, etc., that brings about an effect sooner or later: *A poor foundation was the cause of the building's collapse.* **Occasion** applies to that which brings forth the effect by giving the opportunity for something to happen: *The earth-*

quake was the occasion of the building's collapse.

cause cé lè bre (kōz sā leb′rə), *pl.* ***causes cé lè bres*** (kōz sā leb′rə). FRENCH. 1 (in law) a famous case. 2 situation or episode attracting intense and widespread interest.

cause less (kôz′lis), *adj.* 1 without any known cause; happening by chance. 2 without good reason; not having reason enough. **—cause′less ly,** *adv.*

cau se rie (kō′zə rē′), *n.* 1 an informal talk or discussion; chat. 2 a short, informal written article. [< French]

cause way (kôz′wā′), *n.* 1 a raised road or path, usually built across wet ground or shallow water. 2 a main road; highway. *—v.t.* provide with a causeway. [Middle English *cauce weye* < *cauce* causeway (< Medieval Latin *calciata* paved) + *weye* way]

caus tic (kô′stik), *n.* substance that burns or destroys flesh; corrosive substance. *—adj.* 1 that burns or destroys flesh; corrosive. Lye is caustic soda or caustic potash. 2 very critical or sarcastic; stinging; biting: *The coach's caustic remarks made the football players angry.* [< Latin *causticus* < Greek *kaustikos* < *kaiein* to burn] **—caus′ti cal ly,** *adv.*

caustic potash, potassium hydroxide.

caustic soda, sodium hydroxide.

cau ter ize (kô′tə rīz′), *v.t.,* **-ized, -iz ing.** burn with a hot iron or a caustic substance. Doctors sometimes cauterize wounds to prevent bleeding or infection. **—cau′ter i za′tion,** *n.*

cau tion (kô′shən), *n.* 1 great care; regard for safety; unwillingness to take chances; prudence: *Use caution in crossing streets.* 2 a warning: *A sign with "Danger" on it is a caution.* 3 INFORMAL. a very unusual person or thing. *—v.t.* urge to be careful; warn. See **warn** for synonym study. [< Latin *cautionem* < *cavere* beware]

cau tion ar y (kô′shə ner′ē), *adj.* urging care; warning.

cau tious (kô′shəs), *adj.* very careful; taking care to be safe; not taking chances; prudent: *a cautious driver.* See **careful** for synonym study. **—cau′tious ly,** *adv.* **—cau′tious ness,** *n.*

Cav., Cavalry.

cav al cade (kav′əl kād′, kav′əl kād), *n.* 1 procession of persons riding on horses, in carriages, or in automobiles. 2 series of scenes or events: *a cavalcade of sports.* [< Middle French < Italian *cavalcata* < *cavalcare* ride horseback < Late Latin *caballicare* < Latin *caballus* horse]

cav a lier (kav′ə lir′), *n.* 1 horseman, mounted soldier, or knight. 2 a courteous gentleman. 3 a courteous escort for a lady. 4 **Cavalier,** person who supported Charles I of England in his struggle with Parliament from 1640 to 1649. *—adj.* 1 careless in manner; free and easy; offhand. 2 proud and scornful; haughty; arrogant. 3 **Cavalier,** of the Cavaliers. [< Italian *cavalliere* < Late Latin *caballarius* horseman. Doublet of CABALLERO, CHEVALIER.] **—cav′a lier′ly,** *adv.* **—cav′a lier′ness,** *n.*

cav al ry (kav′əl rē), *n., pl.* **-ries.** 1 (formerly) soldiers who fought on horseback. 2 branch of an army in which soldiers fought on horseback, now modernized and equipped with armored vehicles, especially tanks. [< Middle French *cavalerie* < Italian *cavalleria* knighthood, cavalry < *cavalliere.* See CAVALIER.]

cav al ry man (kav′əl rē mən), *n., pl.* **-men.** soldier in the cavalry.

cave (kāv), *n., v.,* **caved, cav ing.** *—n.* a hollow space underground, especially one with an opening in the side of a hill or mountain. *—v.i., v.t.* **cave in, a** fall in; sink. **b** cause to fall in; smash. **c** INFORMAL. give in; yield; submit. [< Old French < Latin *cava* hollow (places) < *cavus* hollow] **—cave′like′,** *adj.*

ca ve at (kā′vē at), *n.* 1 a legal notice given to a law officer or some legal authority not to do something until the person giving notice can be heard. 2 a warning. [< Latin, let him beware]

ca ve at emp tor (kā′vē at emp′tôr; kä′wē ät emp′tōr), LATIN. let the buyer beware; you buy at your own risk.

cave dweller, person who lived in a cave in prehistoric times.

cave-in (kāv′in′), *n.* INFORMAL. 1 a caving in; collapse. 2 place where something has caved in.

cave man, 1 man who lived in a cave in prehistoric times; troglodyte. 2 INFORMAL. a rough, crude man.

cav ern (kav′ərn), *n.* a large cave. [< Latin *caverna* < *cavus* hollow]

cav ern ous (kav′ər nəs), *adj.* 1 like a cavern; large and hollow. 2 full of caverns. 3 full of cavities or hollows. **—cav′ern ous ly,** *adv.*

cav i ar or **cav i are** (kav′ē är, kä′vē är), *n.* the salted eggs of sturgeon or of certain other large fish, eaten as an appetizer. [< French *caviar* < Italian *caviaro* < Turkish *havyar*]

cav il (kav′əl), *v.,* **-iled, -il ing** or **-illed, -il ling,** *n.* *—v.i.* find fault without good reason; raise trivial objections. *—n.* a trivial objection; petty criticism. [< Old French *caviller* < Latin *cavillari* to jeer] **—cav′il er, cav′il ler,** *n.*

cav i ta tion (kav′ə tā′shən), *n.* formation of cavities or hollows in a fluid substance, body structure, etc.

cav i ty (kav′ə tē), *n., pl.* **-ties.** 1 hollow place; hole: *a cavity in a tooth.* See **hole** for synonym study. 2 an enclosed space inside the body: *the abdominal cavity.*

ca vort (kə vôrt′), *v.* U.S. prance about; jump around: *The children cavorted about the field, racing and tumbling.*

Ca vour (kä vůr′), *n.* **Camillo Benso di,** 1810-1861, Italian statesman. He was a leader in making Italy a united nation.

ca vy (kā′vē), *n., pl.* **-vies.** any of a family of South American rodents, the best known being the guinea pig. [< Carib *cabiai*]

caw (kô), *n.* the harsh cry made by a crow or raven. *—v.i.* make this cry. [imitative]

Cawn pore (kôn′pôr, kôn′pōr), *n.* Kanpur.

Cax ton (kak′stən), *n.* **William,** 1422?-1491, first English printer. He was also an author and translator.

cay (kē, kā), *n.* key[2]. [< Spanish *cayo*]

cay enne (kī en′, kā en′), *n.* a very hot, biting powder made from the seeds or fruit of a pepper plant; red pepper. [< *Cayenne*]

Cay enne (kī en′, kā en′), *n.* capital of French Guiana, on the Atlantic. 25,000.

cayenne pepper, cayenne.

cay man (kā′mən), *n.* caiman.

Cay man Islands (kā′mən, kī män′), group of three islands in the Caribbean Sea NW of Jamaica, a colony of Great Britain. 9000 pop.; 100 sq. mi.

Ca yu ga (kā ü′gə, kī ü′gə), *n., pl.* **-ga** or **-gas.** member of a tribe of Iroquois Indians formerly living in western New York State.

cay use (kī yüs′, kī′üs), *n.* in the western United States: 1 pony bred by Indians. 2 any pony or horse. [< *Cayuse*]

Cay use (kī yüs′), *n., pl.* **-use** or **-us es.** member of a tribe of Indians of northeastern Oregon.

Cb, columbium.

CBC, Canadian Broadcasting Corporation.

CBS, Columbia Broadcasting System.

cc. or **c.c.,** cubic centimeter or cubic centimeters.

C clef, symbol in music that shows the position of middle C. It is called the alto clef when placed on the third line of the staff, and the tenor clef when placed on the fourth line of the staff. See **clef** for diagram.

Cd, cadmium.

cd., cord or cords.

C.D., civil defense.

Cdn., Canadian.

Ce, cerium.

cease (sēs), *v.,* **ceased, ceas ing.** *—v.i.* come to an end; stop: *The music ceased suddenly.* See **stop** for synonym study. *—v.t.* put an end or stop to: *Cease trying to do more than you can.* [< Old French *cesser* < Latin *cessare*]

cease-fire (sēs′fīr′), *n.* a halt in military operations, especially for the purpose of discussing peace.

cease less (sēs′lis), *adj.* going on all the time; never stopping; continual. **—cease′less ly,** *adv.* **—cease′less ness,** *n.*

Ce bu (sā bü′), *n.* 1 island in the central Philippines. 1700 sq. mi. 2 province including this island and adjacent small islands. 1,333,000 pop.; 1900 sq. mi. 3 seaport on this island. 351,000.

ce cal (sē′kəl), *adj.* of or having to do with the cecum or a cecum. Also **caecal.** **—ce′cal ly,** *adv.*

Ce ci lia (sə sē′lyə, sə sil′yə), *n.* **Saint,** died A.D. 230?, Roman Christian martyr, the patron saint of music.

Ce cro pi a moth (sə krō′pē ə), a large silkworm moth of eastern North America. Its larvae feed on trees and shrubs. [< New Latin *cecropia,* the species name < *Cecrops,* legendary founder of Athens and first king of Attica]

ce cum (sē′kəm), *n., pl.* **-ca** (-kə). 1 the first part of the large intestine, closed at one end. 2 any cavity closed at one end. Also, **caecum.** [< Latin *caecum* blind (thing)]

ce dar (sē′dər), *n.* 1 any of a genus of North African or Asian evergreen trees of the pine family, having wide-spreading branches, fragrant, durable, reddish wood, and erect cones. 2 any of several trees with similar wood. 3 wood of any of these trees, much used for lining clothes closets and making chests, cigar boxes, pencils, and posts. *—adj.* made of cedar. [< Latin *cedrus* < Greek *kedros*]

ce dar bird (sē′dər bėrd′), *n.* cedar waxwing.

Cedar Rapids, city in E Iowa. 111,000.

cedar waxwing, a small North American bird with a crest and small, red markings on its wings; cedarbird.

cede (sēd), *v.t.,* **ced ed, ced ing.** give up; surrender; hand over to another: *Spain ceded the Philippines to the United States.* [< Latin *cedere* yield, go]

ce di (sē′dē), *n.* the monetary unit of Ghana, a note equal to 100 pesewas and

hat, āge, fär; let, ēqual, tėrm;
it, īce; hot, ōpen, ôrder;
oil, out; cup, pu̇t, rüle;
ch, child; ng, long; sh, she;
th, thin; ᴛʜ, then; zh, measure;

ə represents *a* in about, *e* in taken, *i* in pencil, *o* in lemon, *u* in circus.

< = from, derived from, taken from.

worth about 98 cents. [< a native name]

ce dil la (sə dil′ə), *n.* mark somewhat like a comma (ç) put under *c* in certain words to show that it has the sound of *s* before *a, o,* or *u.* EXAMPLE: façade. [< earlier Spanish, diminutive of *ceda,* the letter *z* < Latin *zeta,* < Greek *zēta* (because it developed from a tiny *z* written beneath the *c*)]

ceil ing (sē′ling), *n.* 1 the inside, top covering of a room; surface opposite the floor. 2 the greatest height to which an aircraft can go under certain conditions. 3 distance from the earth to the lowest clouds. 4 an upper limit set for prices, wages, rents, etc. [Middle English *celynge*]

cel an dine (sel′ən dīn), *n.* 1 plant with yellow flowers of the same family as the poppy. 2 the **lesser celandine,** a plant closely related to the buttercup, with yellow flowers and heart-shaped leaves. [< Old French *celidoine*]

Cel e bes (sel′ə bēz′), *n.* large island in Indonesia, between Borneo and New Guinea. With adjacent small islands, 7,000,000 pop.; 73,000 sq. mi. Also, **Sulawesi.**

cel e brant (sel′ə brənt), *n.* 1 person who performs a ceremony or rite. 2 priest who performs Mass. 3 anyone who celebrates.

cel e brate (sel′ə brāt), *v.,* **-brat ed, -brat ing.** *—v.t.* 1 observe (a special time or day) with the proper ceremonies or festivities: *We celebrated my birthday with a party.* 2 perform publicly with the proper ceremonies and rites: *The priest celebrates Mass in church.* 3 make known publicly; proclaim. 4 praise; honor; laud. *—v.i.* 1 observe a festival or event with ceremonies or festivities: *On my birthday I was too sick to celebrate.* 2 INFORMAL. have a gay time. [< Latin *celebratum* observed by many < *celeber* frequented, crowded] **—cel′e bra′tor,** *n.*

cel e brat ed (sel′ə brā′tid), *adj.* much talked about; famous; well-known.

cel e bra tion (sel′ə brā′shən), *n.* 1 the observing of a feast, day, or special season; the honoring or recognizing of an event by religious ceremonies, festivities, etc.: *the celebration of Thanksgiving, the celebration of Washington's birthday.* 2 act of celebrating; making famous. 3 performance of a solemn ceremony: *the celebration of the Eucharist.*

ce leb ri ty (sə leb′rə tē), *n., pl.* **-ties.** 1 a famous person; person who is well known or much talked about. 2 a being well known or much talked about; fame.

ce ler i ty (sə ler′ə tē), *n.* swiftness of movement; speed; rapidity. [< Latin *celeritatem* < *celer* swift]

cel er y (sel′ər ē), *n.* 1 plant of the same family as the parsley, having long, crisp stalks with leaves at the top. 2 its stalks, which are eaten either raw or cooked as a vegetable. [< French *céleri,* ultimately < Greek *selinon*]

ce les ta (sə les′tə), *n.* a musical instrument with a keyboard, resembling a small, upright piano. The tones resemble the tinkle of small bells and are made by hammers hitting steel plates. [< French *célesta* < Latin *caelestem* heavenly]

ce les tial (sə les′chəl), *adj.* 1 of the sky; having to do with the heavens: *The sun, moon, planets, and stars are celestial bodies.* 2 of or belonging to heaven as the place of God and the angels; heavenly; divine. 3 very good or beautiful. [< Latin *caelestis* < *caelum* heaven] **—ce les′tial ly,** *adv.*

celestial equator, the great circle of the celestial sphere, the plane of which is perpendicular to the axis of the earth; equinoctial line.

celestial latitude, the angular distance of a heavenly body from the nearest point on the ecliptic.

celestial navigation, method of navigation in which the position of a ship or aircraft is calculated from the position of heavenly bodies.

celestial sphere, the imaginary sphere of infinite radius with the observer as its center, which appears to enclose the universe. To an observer on earth, the visible sky forms half of the celestial sphere.

ce li ac (sē′lē ak), *adj.* of or having to do with the abdominal cavity. Also, **coeliac.** [< Greek *koiliakos* < *koilia* intestines < *koilos* hollow]

celiac disease, a chronic digestive disorder of childhood, resulting in diarrhea, swelling of the abdomen, and stunted growth.

cel i ba cy (sel′ə bə sē), *n.* unmarried state; single life.

cel i bate (sel′ə bit, sel′ə bāt), *n.* an unmarried person, especially one who takes a vow to lead a single life. *—adj.* unmarried; single. [< Latin *caelibatus* < *caelibem* unmarried]

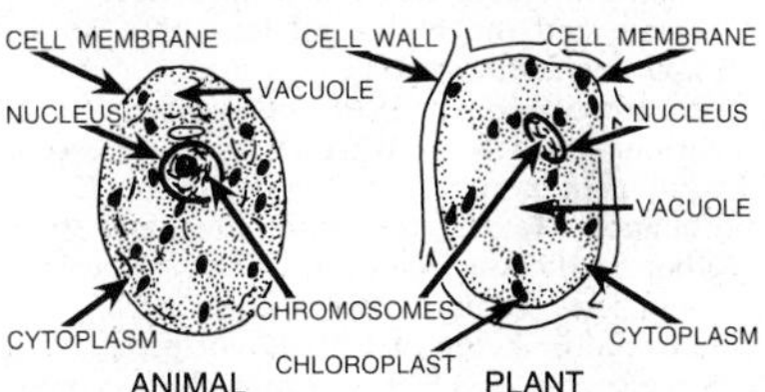

cell (def. 3)—two types, greatly magnified

cell (sel), *n.* 1 a small room in a prison, convent, or monastery. 2 any small, hollow place: *Bees store honey in the cells of a honeycomb.* 3 the basic unit of living matter of which all plants and animals are made. Cells are generally microscopic, contain a central nucleus with chromosomes surrounded by cytoplasm, and are enclosed by a cell wall or cell membrane. 4 container holding materials which produce electricity by chemical action. A battery consists of one or more cells. 5 a small group that acts as a political, social, or religious unit for a larger, sometimes revolutionary, organization. [< Latin *cella* small room] **—cell′-like′,** *adj.*

cel lar (sel′ər), *n.* 1 an underground room or rooms, usually under a building and often used for storing food or fuel. 2 such a room for wines. 3 supply of wines. [< Latin *cellarium* storeroom < *cella* small room]

cel lar age (sel′ər ij), *n.* 1 space in a cellar. 2 cellars. 3 a charge for storage in a cellar.

cell division, mitosis.

Cel li ni (chə lē′nē), *n.* **Benvenuto,** 1500-1571, Italian sculptor and artist in metalwork.

cel list (chel′ist), *n.* person who plays the cello; violoncellist.

cell membrane, the thin membrane that forms the outer surface of the protoplasm of a cell; plasma membrane.

cel lo (chel′ō), *n., pl.* **-los.** a musical instrument like a violin, but very much larger and with a lower tone; violoncello. It is held between the knees while being played. [< *(violon)cello*]

cel lo phane (sel′ə fān), *n.* a transparent substance made from cellulose, used as a wrapping to keep food, candy, tobacco, etc., fresh and clean. [< *cell(ul)o(se)* + Greek *phainein* to show]

cel lu lar (sel′yə lər), *adj.* 1 having to do with the cells. 2 made up of cells. All animal and plant tissue is cellular.

cel lu loid (sel′yə loid), *adj.* having to do with films or motion pictures.

Cel lu loid (sel′yə loid), *n.* trademark for a hard, transparent, combustible substance made from cellulose and treated with camphor. Combs, toilet articles, camera films, etc., are often made of white or colored celluloid.

cel lu lose (sel′yə lōs), *n.* substance that forms the walls of plant cells; the woody part of trees and plants. Wood, cotton, flax, and hemp are largely cellulose. Cellulose is used to make paper, rayon, plastics, explosives, etc. *Formula:* $(C_6H_{10}O_5)_n$ [< Latin *cellula* small room]

cellulose acetate, any of several compounds, formed from cellulose in the presence of acetic acid, used in making textiles, camera films, lacquers, varnishes, etc.

cellulose nitrate, nitrocellulose.

cell wall, the hard, transparent outer covering of a plant cell, made up mostly of cellulose and surrounding the cell membrane.

Cel si us scale (sel′sē əs), the official name of the centigrade scale. [< Anders *Celsius,* 1701-1744, Swedish astronomer, who devised it]

Celt (selt, kelt), *n.* member of a people to which the Irish, Scottish Highlanders, Welsh, Bretons, and Manx belong. The ancient Gauls and Britons were Celts. Also, **Kelt.**

Celt ic (sel′tik, kel′tik), *adj.* of the Celts or their language. *—n.* group of languages spoken by the Celts, including Irish, Gaelic, Welsh, Breton, and Manx. Also, **Keltic.**

cel tuce (sel′təs), *n.* a crisp, leafy type of lettuce with an edible stem that combines the flavors of celery and lettuce. [< *cel(ery)* + *(let)tuce*]

ce ment (sə ment′), *n.* 1 a fine, gray powder made by burning clay and limestone. 2 this substance mixed with water, sand, and gravel to form concrete, used to make sidewalks, streets, floors, and walls. Cement, sand, and water form mortar, used to hold stones and bricks together in the walls of buildings. 3 any soft substance that hardens and holds

cello
played with a bow or by plucking strings with the fingers

things together: *rubber cement.* 4 cementum. 5 substance used to fill cavities in teeth or to fasten fillings into them. 6 anything that joins together or unites. *—v.t.* 1 fasten together with cement. 2 spread cement over. 3 join firmly; unite. *—v.i.* become joined firmly; stick. [< Latin *caementum* chippings of stone < *caedere* to cut] **—ce′men ta′tion,** *n.* **—ce ment′er,** *n.*

ce men tum (sə men′təm), *n.* the bony tissue forming the outer crust of the root of a tooth.

cem e ter y (sem′ə ter′ē), *n., pl.* **-ter ies.** place for burying the dead; graveyard. [< Latin *coemeterium* < Greek *koimeterion,* originally, sleeping place < *koiman* lull to sleep]

cen., central.

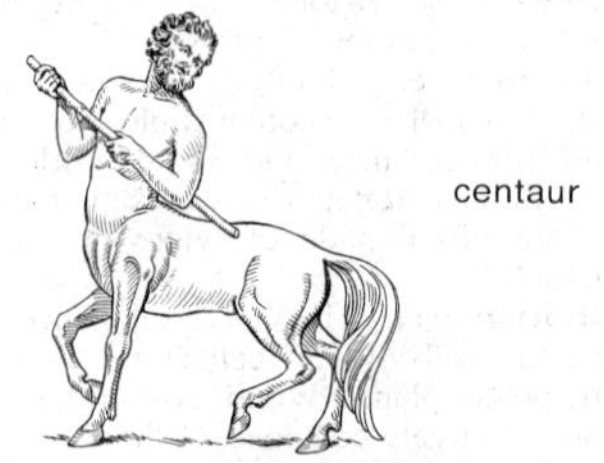
centaur

cen o bite (sen′ə bīt, sē′nə bīt), *n.* member of a religious group living in a monastery or convent. Also, **coenobite.** [< Late Latin *coenobita* < *coenobium* convent < Greek *koinobion* < *koinos* common + *bios* life]

cen o taph (sen′ə taf), *n.* monument erected in memory of a dead person who is buried elsewhere. [< Latin *cenotaphium* < Greek *kenotaphion* < *kenos* empty + *taphos* tomb]

Cen o zo ic (sen′ə zō′ik, sē′nə zō′ik), *n.* 1 the most recent and present era in geological history, during which mammals began to dominate the animal kingdom. See chart under **geology.** 2 the rocks formed in this era. *—adj.* of or having to do with this era or its rocks. [< Greek *kainos* new, recent + *zōē* life]

cen ser (sen′sər), *n.* container in which incense is burned, especially during religious ceremonies. [< Anglo-French *censer,* short for Old French *encensier,* ultimately < Latin *incensum* incense]

cen sor (sen′sər), *n.* 1 person who examines and, if necessary, changes letters, books, news reports, plays, motion pictures, etc., to make their content satisfactory to the government or to some organization. 2 (in ancient Rome) a magistrate who took the census and supervised the conduct of citizens. 3 person who tells others how they ought to behave. 4 person who likes to find fault. *—v.t.* examine or change as a censor; make changes in; take out part of (news reports, books, letters, motion pictures, etc.): *Two scenes in the movie were censored for being too violent.* [< Latin < *censere* appraise]

cen so ri al (sen sôr′ē əl, sen sōr′ē əl), *adj.* of or suitable for a censor.

cen so ri ous (sen sôr′ē əs, sen sōr′ē əs), *adj.* too ready to find fault; severely critical. **—cen so′ri ous ly,** *adv.* **—cen so′ri ous ness,** *n.*

cen sor ship (sen′sər ship), *n.* 1 act or system of censoring: *Censorship of news is common in time of war.* 2 position or work of a censor.

cen sur a ble (sen′shər ə bəl), *adj.* deserving censure; blamable. **—cen′sur a bly,** *adv.*

cen sure (sen′shər), *n., v.,* **-sured, -sur ing.** *—n.* 1 expression of disapproval; unfavorable opinion; criticism. 2 penalty, as a public rebuke or suspension from office. *—v.t.* express disapproval of; find fault with; criticize. See **blame** for synonym study. [< Latin *censura* < *censere* appraise] **—cen′sur er,** *n.*

cen sus (sen′səs), *n.* an official count of the people of a country or district. It is taken to find out the number of people, their age, sex, occupation, and many other facts about them and their property. [< Latin < *censere* appraise]

cent (sent), *n.* 1 unit of money in the United States and Canada, usually a coin of copper alloy worth $^1/_{100}$ of a dollar; penny. 2 unit of money equaling $^1/_{100}$ of the standard unit of currency in certain other countries. [< Latin *centum* hundred]

cent., 1 centigrade. 2 central. 3 century.

cen tare (sen′ter, sen′tar), *n.* centiare.

cen taur (sen′tôr), *n.* (in Greek myths) a monster that had the head, arms, and chest of a man, and the body and legs of a horse. [< Greek *kentauros*]

cen ta vo (sen tä′vō), *n., pl.* **-vos.** 1 any of various small coins worth $^1/_{100}$ of a peso or equivalent monetary unit in Argentina, Cuba, Ecuador, Mexico, the Philippines, and some other South American and Central American countries. 2 coin of Portugal, worth $^1/_{100}$ of an escudo. 3 coin of Brazil, worth $^1/_{100}$ of a cruzeiro. [< Spanish < Latin *centum* hundred]

cen te nar i an (sen′tə ner′ē ən), *n.* person who is 100 years old or more. *—adj.* 1 100 years old or more. 2 of 100 years.

cen ten ar y (sen ten′ər ē, sen′tə ner′ē; *British* sen tē′nər ē), *n., pl.* **-ar ies,** *adj.* *—n.* 1 a 100th anniversary. 2 celebration of the 100th anniversary. 3 period of 100 years; century. *—adj.* of or having to do with 100 years or a 100th anniversary. [< Latin *centenarius* of a hundred < *centum* hundred]

cen ten ni al (sen ten′ē əl, sen ten′yəl), *adj.* 1 of or having to do with 100 years or the 100th anniversary. 2 100 years old. *—n.* 1 a 100th anniversary: *The town is celebrating its centennial.* 2 celebration of the 100th anniversary. [< Latin *centum* hundred + English *(bi)ennial*] **—cen ten′ni al ly,** *adv.*

cen ter (sen′tər), *n.* 1 point within a circle or sphere equally distant from all points of the circumference or surface. 2 the middle point, place, or part: *the center of a room.* See **middle** for synonym study. 3 person, thing, or group in a middle position. 4 the main body of an army, not a part of the flanks. 5 point toward which people or things go, or from which they come; main point: *New York is one of the trade centers of the world.* 6 an offensive player who has the position between the guards in the line in football. He begins each scrimmage by passing the ball backward between his legs, to a back. 7 player who starts play in basketball, hockey, etc. 8 part of a lawmaking body that sits in front of the presiding officer. It is made up of the political groups having moderate opinions. 9 the people and parties holding moderate views. 10 mass of nerve cells closely connected and acting together; nerve center: *the respiratory center.* *—v.t.* 1 to place in or at a center. 2 concentrate; focus; rest: *All his hopes are centered on being promoted.* 3 mark or provide with a center: *a smooth lawn centered by a pool.* 4 (in football) to pass back (the ball) to begin a play. 5 (in soccer, hockey, etc.) to cross (the ball or puck) near the entrance to the goal. 6 grind or adjust (a lens) so that the optical center is at the geometrical center. *—v.i.* 1 collect or gather together at a center. 2 rest on; be concentrated; rest: *All his hopes centered on being promoted.* 3 be at a center. Also, BRITISH **centre.** [< Old French *centre* < Latin *centrum* < Greek *kentron* sharp point]

➤ **Center around** or **center about** is used informally to mean "focus upon": *The story centers around (or about) a robbery.* The formal expression is *center on* or *center upon.*

cen ter board (sen′tər bôrd′, sen′tər bōrd′), *n.* a movable keel of a sailboat. It is lowered through a slot in the bottom of a boat to prevent drifting to leeward.

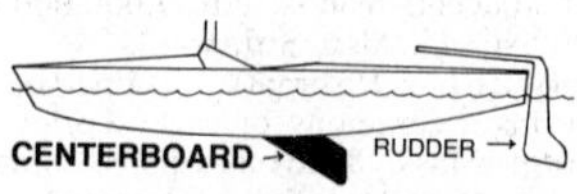

center field, (in baseball) the middle section of the outfield between left field and right field.

center fielder, a baseball player whose position is in center field.

center of gravity, point in a body around which its weight is evenly balanced.

center of mass, point in a body which moves as though it bore the entire mass of the body, usually identical with the center of gravity.

cen ter piece (sen′tər pēs′), *n.* an ornamental piece of glass, lace, etc., or an arrangement of flowers for the center of a dining table, buffet, mantel, etc.

cen tes i mal (sen tes′ə məl), *adj.* 1 100th. 2 divided into 100ths. [< Latin *centesimus* hundredth]

cen tes i mo (sen tes′ə mō *for 1,* chen tez′ə mō *for 2*), *n., pl.* **-mos** for 1, **-mi** (-mē) for 2. 1 any of various small coins worth $^1/_{100}$ of the basic monetary unit in Chile, Panama, Uruguay, etc. 2 coin of Italy, worth $^1/_{100}$ of a lira. [< Spanish *centésimo* and Italian *centesimo* < Latin *centesimus* hundredth]

centi-, *combining form.* 1 100: *Centigrade = 100 degrees.* 2 100th part of: *Centimeter = 100th part of a meter.* [< Latin *centum* hundred]

cen ti are (sen′tē er′, sen′tē ar′), *n.* $^1/_{100}$ of an are; one square meter. See **measure** for table. Also, **centare.**

cen ti grade (sen′tə grād), *adj.* of, based on, or according to a scale for measuring temperature on which 0 degrees marks the freezing point of water and 100 degrees marks the boiling point. The **centigrade thermometer** is marked off according to this scale. [< French < Latin *centum* hundred + *gradus* degree]

cen ti gram (sen′tə gram), *n.* unit of mass equal to $^1/_{100}$ of a gram. See **measure** for table.

cen ti gramme (sen′tə gram), *n.* BRITISH. centigram.

cen ti li ter (sen′tə lē′tər), *n.* unit of volume equal to $^1/_{100}$ of a liter. See **measure** for table.

cen ti li tre (sen′tə lē′tər), *n.* BRITISH. centiliter.

hat, āge, fär; let, ēqual, tėrm;
it, īce; hot, ōpen, ôrder;
oil, out; cup, pu̇t, rüle;
ch, child; ng, long; sh, she;
th, thin; ᴛʜ, then; zh, measure;

ə represents *a* in about, *e* in taken, *i* in pencil, *o* in lemon, *u* in circus.

< = from, derived from, taken from.

cen time (sän′tēm′), *n.* unit of money in France, Belgium, Switzerland, and countries of the French Community, a coin worth $^1/_{100}$ of a franc. [< French]

cen ti me ter (sen′tə mē′tər), *n.* unit of length equal to $^1/_{100}$ of a meter. See **measure** for table.

cen ti me ter-gram-sec ond (sen′tə-mē′tər gram′sek′ənd), *adj.* having to do with a system of measurement in which the centimeter is the unit of length, the gram is the unit of mass, and the second is the unit of time.

cen ti me tre (sen′tə mē′tər), *n.* BRITISH. centimeter.

cen ti mo (sen′tə mō), *n., pl.* **-mos.** any of various small coins worth $^1/_{100}$ of the basic monetary unit in Costa Rica, Spain, Paraguay, and Venezuela. [< Spanish *céntimo*]

cen ti pede (sen′tə pēd′), *n.* any of a class of flat, wormlike arthropods with many pairs of legs, the front pair of which are clawlike and contain poison glands; chilopod. Centipedes vary in length from an inch to nearly a foot. [< Latin *centipeda* < *centum* hundred + *pedem* foot]

CEN TO (sen′tō), *n.* Central Treaty Organization (an alliance of Turkey, Iran, Pakistan, and Great Britain). The United States, while not a member, is affiliated with CENTO.

cen tral (sen′trəl), *adj.* 1 of the center; being or forming the center. 2 at the center; near the center. 3 from the center; head: *the central library.* 4 equally distant from all points; easy to get to or from. 5 main; principal: *What is the central idea in this story?* 6 in anatomy and physiology: **a** of or designating the brain and spinal cord as a major division of the nervous system of vertebrates. **b** arising from or affecting these parts of the nervous system: *central anesthesia.* —*n.* 1 a telephone exchange. 2 a telephone operator. [< Latin *centralis* < *centrum.* See CENTER.] **—cen′tral ness,** *n.*

Central African Republic, country in central Africa, south of Chad, a member of the French Community. 2,080,000 pop.; about 240,000 sq. mi. *Capital:* Bangui. See **Zaïre** for map.

Central America, part of North America between Mexico and South America. Guatemala, El Salvador, Honduras, British Honduras, Nicaragua, Costa Rica, and Panama are in Central America. **—Central American.**

Central Intelligence Agency, agency of the United States government that deals with matters involving national security.

cen tral ism (sen′trə liz′əm), *n.* theory of centralizing control, especially in a government.

cen tral ist (sen′trə list), *n.* person who advocates or favors centralism. —*adj.* of centralists or centralism.

cen tral is tic (sen′trə lis′tik), *adj.* having to do with or favoring centralism.

cen tral i ty (sen tral′ə tē), *n.* central position or character.

cen tral i za tion (sen′trə lə zā′shən), *n.* 1 a coming or bringing to a center. 2 a gathering together at a center: *Centralization of medical services may prevent waste of effort.* 3 a bringing together under the control of a single authority: *the centralization of government under a dictator.*

cen tral ize (sen′trə līz), *v.,* **-ized, -iz ing.** —*v.t.* 1 bring to or toward a center; locate in a center. 2 gather together in a center; concentrate. 3 bring under the control of a single authority. —*v.i.* come together at one center.

cen tral ly (sen′trə lē), *adv.* at or near the center.

central nervous system, the part of the nervous system of vertebrates that consists of the brain and spinal cord. The nerves from the central nervous system control muscles.

Central Powers, Germany and Austria-Hungary during World War I, sometimes also including their allies, Turkey and Bulgaria.

Central Standard Time, the standard time in the central part of the United States and Canada. It is six hours behind Greenwich Time.

cen tre (sen′tər), *n., v.t., v.i.,* **-tred, -tring.** BRITISH. center.

cen tric (sen′trik), *adj.* central. **—cen′tri cal ly,** *adv.*

cen trif u gal (sen trif′yə gəl, sen trif′ə gəl), *adj.* 1 moving or tending to move away from a center. 2 making use of or acted upon by centrifugal force. [< Latin *centrum* center + *fugere* flee] **—cen trif′u gal ly,** *adv.*

centrifugal force, the inertia, or tendency to move in one direction, which causes a body turning around a center to move away from the center.

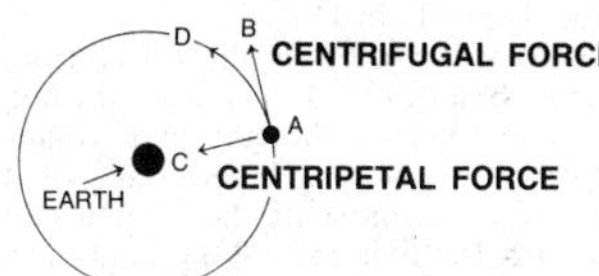

The tendency of the satellite A to move in a straight line toward B (centrifugal force) is overcome by the force exerted by gravity toward C (centripetal force), resulting in motion toward D.

cen trif u ga tion (sen trif′yə gā′shən), *n.* the separation of materials of different densities by centrifugal force.

cen tri fuge (sen′trə fyüj), *n., v.,* **-fuged, -fug ing.** —*n.* machine for separating two substances varying in density, as cream from milk or bacteria from a fluid, by means of centrifugal force. —*v.t.* 1 separate with a centrifuge. 2 rotate in a centrifuge; subject to a centrifugal force.

cen tri ole (sen′trē ōl), *n.* a minute granular particle within the centrosome of a cell which organizes the spindle fiber during mitosis. See **centrosome** for diagram.

cen trip e tal (sen trip′ə təl), *adj.* 1 moving or tending toward a center. 2 making use of or acted upon by centripetal force. [< Latin *centrum* center + *petere* seek] **—cen trip′e tal ly,** *adv.*

centripetal force, the force that tends to move things toward the center around which they are turning. Gravitation acts as a centripetal force. See picture above.

cen trist (sen′trist), *n.* (in several countries of continental Europe) member of a moderate political party whose political views are neither radical nor conservative.

centro-, *combining form.* center; central: *Centrosphere = center sphere.* [< Latin *centrum*]

cen troid (sen′troid), *n.* 1 the center of mass. 2 (in geometry) the point of intersection of the medians of a triangle.

cen tro mere (sen′trə mir), *n.* the point on a chromosome by which it is drawn to the pole during mitosis.

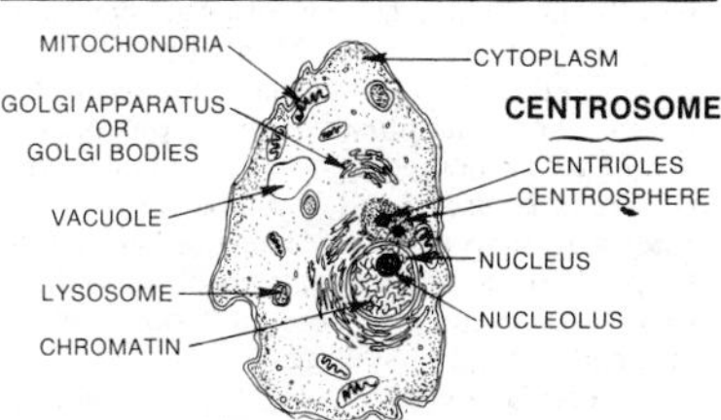

cen tro some (sen′trə sōm), *n.* a tiny body in a cell, usually found near the nucleus, that separates into two parts and attracts the divided chromosomes, one group to each part.

cen tro sphere (sen′trə sfir′), *n.* 1 mass of protoplasm around a centriole in a centrosome. See **centrosome** for diagram. 2 the central core of the earth.

cen trum (sen′trəm), *n., pl.* **-trums, -tra** (-trə). 1 a central part or center. 2 the body of a vertebra. The centrum is the solid part to which a bony arch and processes are attached. [< Latin, center]

cen tur i on (sen tu̇r′ē ən, sen tyu̇r′ē ən), *n.* commander of about 100 soldiers in the ancient Roman army.

cen tur y (sen′chər ē), *n., pl.* **-tur ies.** 1 each 100 years, counting from some special time, such as the birth of Christ. 2 period of 100 years. From 1824 to 1924 is a century. 3 group of 100 people or things. 4 body of soldiers in the ancient Roman army. Originally, it probably consisted of 100 soldiers. 5 division of the ancient Roman people for voting. Each century had one vote. [< Latin *centuria* < *centum* hundred]

➤ **centuries.** To name the century correctly, add one to the number of its hundred. Thus the nineteenth century began January 1, 1801, and continued through December 31, 1900, though popularly it is often considered as being from January 1, 1800, through December 31, 1899. Dates before Christ are figured like those after. The first century B.C. runs back from the birth of Christ through 100, the second century from 101 through 200, and so on.

century plant, a large, thick-leaved plant, a kind of agave which blooms at ten years or more and then dies, found in Mexico and the southwestern United States; aloe. It sometimes reaches forty feet in height, and is popularly believed to bloom only when 100 years old.

ceorl (cherl, kyerl), *n.* churl (def. 4). [Old English]

ce phal ic (sə fal′ik), *adj.* 1 of the head. 2 near, on, or in the head. 3 toward the head. [< Latin *cephalicus* < Greek *kephalikos* < *kephale* head]

cephalic index, the ratio of the greatest breadth of the skull to its greatest length from front to back, multiplied by 100. The cephalic index is used in anthropology and comparative anatomy.

ceph a lo chor date (sef′ə lō kôr′dāt), *n.* any of a subphylum of semitransparent, fishlike chordates, having a body pointed at both ends and a notochord running from the body through the indistinct head; lancelet.

ceph a lo pod (sef′ə lə pod), *n.* any of the most highly developed class of mollusks, having long, armlike tentacles around the mouth, a large head, a pair of large eyes, and a sharp, birdlike beak. Many can expel a dark, inklike fluid. Cuttlefish, squids, octopuses, and nautiluses are cephalopods. *—adj.* of or belonging to the cephalopods. [< Greek *kephale* head + *podos* foot]

ceph a lo spo rin (sef′ə lō spôr′ən, sef′ə-lō spōr′ən), *n.* any of a group of antibiotics related to penicillin, derived from a mold originally found in sewage.

ceph a lo tho rac ic (sef′ə lō thə ras′ik), *adj.* of or having to do with the cephalothorax.

ceph a lo tho rax (sef′ə lō thôr′aks, sef′ə-lō thōr′aks), *n.* the combined head and thorax of some animals, such as crabs and spiders.

Ce phe us (sē′fē əs, sē′fyüs), *n.* 1 (in Greek legends) an Ethiopian king, father of Andromeda. 2 a northern constellation between Cassiopeia and Draco.

ce ra ceous (sə rā′shəs), *adj.* of the nature of wax; waxy.

ce ram ic (sə ram′ik), *adj.* of or having to do with pottery, earthenware, porcelain, etc., or with making them. Ceramic articles are usually made of fired clay. *—n.* article made of pottery, earthenware, porcelain, etc. [< Greek *keramikos* < *keramos* potter's clay]

ce ram i cist (sə ram′ə sist), *n.* 1 an expert in ceramics. 2 manufacturer of ceramics.

ce ram ics (sə ram′iks), *n.* the art of making pottery, earthenware, porcelain, etc.

Cer ber us (sėr′bər əs), *n.* 1 (in Greek and Roman myths) a three-headed dog that guarded the entrance to Hades. 2 a surly, watchful guard.

Cerberus (def. 1)

cere (sir), *n.* a waxy-looking membrane through which the nostrils open near the beak of certain birds, especially parrots and birds of prey. [< Medieval Latin *cera* < Latin, wax]

cer e al (sir′ē əl), *n.* 1 any plant, usually a grass, that produces grain which is used as a food. Wheat, rice, corn, oats, and barley are cereals. 2 the grain. 3 food made from the grain, especially dried processed cereal grains commonly eaten at breakfast. *—adj.* of or having to do with grain or the grasses producing it: *cereal crops, cereal products.* [< Latin *Cerealem* having to do with *Ceres*]

cer e bel lar (ser′ə bel′ər), *adj.* of or having to do with the cerebellum.

cer e bel lum (ser′ə bel′əm), *n., pl.* **-bel-lums, -bel la** (-bel′ə). the part of the brain that controls the coordination of the muscles. It consists of a middle lobe and two lateral lobes and is located below the back part of the cerebrum. See **brain** for diagram. [< Latin, diminutive of *cerebrum* brain]

ce re bral (sə rē′brəl, ser′ə brəl), *adj.* 1 of the brain. A cerebral hemorrhage may cause paralysis. 2 of the cerebrum. 3 characterized by thought and reason rather than emotion or action: *Chess is a cerebral game.* **—ce-re′bral ly,** *adv.*

cerebral hemisphere, either of the two lobes of the cerebrum.

cerebral palsy, paralysis due to brain damage occurring before or at birth, marked by a lack of control of motor muscles that causes involuntary jerky movements.

cer e brate (ser′ə brāt), *v.i.,* **-brat ed, -brat ing.** use the brain; think.

cer e bra tion (ser′ə brā′shən), *n.* 1 action of the brain. 2 act of thinking.

cer e bro spi nal (sə rē′brō spī′nl, ser′ə-brō spī′nl), *adj.* of or having to do with both the brain and the spinal cord: *a cerebrospinal nerve.*

cerebrospinal fluid, the clear fluid normally present in the central of the three membranes, the meninges, enveloping the brain and spinal cord.

ce re brum (sə rē′brəm, ser′ə brəm), *n., pl.* **-brums, -bra** (-brə). 1 the part of the human brain that controls thought and voluntary muscular movements. It consists of two lobes which fill most of the cranial cavity. See **brain** for diagram. 2 the anatomically corresponding part of the brain of any vertebrate. 3 the brain. [< Latin]

cere cloth (sir′klôth′, sir′kloth′), *n., pl.* **-cloths** (-klôᴛʜz′, -klôths′; -kloᴛʜz′, -kloths′). 1 waxed cloth. 2 a waxed cloth in which a dead person is wrapped for burial.

cere ment (sir′mənt), *n.* Often, **cerements,** *pl.* cloth or garment in which a dead person is wrapped for burial.

cer e mo ni al (ser′ə mō′nē əl), *adj.* 1 of or having to do with ceremony. 2 very formal: *The President received his guests in a ceremonial way.* *—n.* the formal actions proper to an occasion. Bowing the head and kneeling are ceremonials of religion. **—cer′e mo′ni-al ly,** *adv.* **—cer′e mo′ni al ness,** *n.*

cer e mo ni al ism (ser′ə mō′nē ə liz′əm), *n.* adherence to or fondness for ceremonies, as in religion.

cer e mo ni ous (ser′ə mō′nē əs), *adj.* 1 full of ceremony. 2 very formal; extremely polite. **—cer′e mo′ni ous ly,** *adv.* **—cer′-e mo′ni ous ness,** *n.*

cer e mo ny (ser′ə mō′nē), *n., pl.* **-nies.** 1 a special act or set of acts to be done on special occasions such as weddings, funerals, graduations, or holidays: *a marriage ceremony.* See synonym study below. 2 very polite conduct; way of conducting oneself that follows all the rules of polite social behavior: *The old gentleman showed us to the door with a great deal of ceremony.* 3 attention to forms and customs; formality: *the traditional ceremony of the royal court.* 4 **stand on ceremony,** be too polite; be very formal. 5 an empty form; meaningless formality. [< Latin *caerimonia* rite]

Syn. 1 **Ceremony, rite** mean a set of dignified and usually traditional practices followed on special occasions. **Ceremony** applies to the observances or procedure used on religious, public, or other solemn occasions: *The graduation ceremony was inspiring.* **Rite** applies to a fixed ceremony, in which both the actions and the words are prescribed: *A priest administered the last rites to the dying man.*

Cer es (sir′ēz), *n.* 1 (in Roman myths) the goddess of agriculture and the harvest, identified with the Greek goddess Demeter. 2 the first and largest asteroid to be discovered.

cer e us (sir′ē əs), *n.* any of several cactuses of the southwestern United States and tropical America, having large, tubular flowers. [< Latin, wax candle < *cera* wax]

ce rise (sə rēs′, sə rēz′), *adj.* bright pinkish-red. *—n.* a bright, pinkish red. [< French, cherry]

cer i um (sir′ē əm), *n.* a grayish rare-earth metallic element which occurs only in combination with other elements, used in porcelain, glass, and alloys. *Symbol:* Ce; *atomic number* 58. See pages 326 and 327 for table. [< the asteroid *Ceres*]

cer met (sėr′met), *n.* an alloy of a heat-resistant compound and a metal, used in combustion chambers, turbojet engines, etc. Cermets combine the properties of ceramic and metallic materials. [< *cer(amic)* + *met(al)*]

CERN, European Council for Nuclear Research [for French *Conseil Européen pour la Recherche Nucléaire*].

cer tain (sėrt′n), *adj.* 1 without a doubt; sure: *It is certain that 2 and 3 do not make 6.* See **sure** for synonym study. 2 known but not named; some; particular: *A certain person gave our church $1000.* 3 settled; fixed: *at a certain hour.* 4 that can be depended on; reliable: *I have certain information that school will end a day earlier this year.* 5 sure to happen; inevitable. *—n.* **for certain,** surely; without a doubt. [< Old French < Latin *certus* sure, related to *cernere* decide] **—cer′tain ness,** *n.*

cer tain ly (sėrt′n lē), *adv.* without a doubt; surely.

➤ **certainly.** *Certainly* is often used as an intensive or as an affirmative answer to questions: *I'm certainly pleased that you came. Are you going to the football game Saturday? Certainly.*

cer tain ty (sėrt′n tē), *n., pl.* **-ties.** 1 a being certain; freedom from doubt: *The man's certainty was amusing, for we could all see that he was wrong.* 2 something certain; a sure fact: *The coming of spring and summer is a certainty.*

cer tes (sėr′tēz), *adv.* ARCHAIC. certainly; in truth. [< Old French, ultimately < Latin *certus* sure]

cer ti fi a ble (sėr′tə fī′ə bəl), *adj.* that can be certified.

cer tif i cate (*n.* sər tif′ə kit; *v.* sər tif′ə kāt), *n., v.,* **-cat ed, -cat ing.** *—n.* an official written or printed statement that declares something to be a fact. A birth certificate gives the date and place of a person's birth and the names of his parents. *—v.t.* 1 give a certificate to. 2 authorize by a certificate.

cer ti fi ca tion (sėr′tə fə kā′shən), *n.* 1 a certifying. 2 a being certified. 3 a certified statement.

cer ti fied (sėr′tə fīd), *adj.* 1 guaranteed. 2 having a certificate.

certified check, check whose value is guaranteed by the bank upon whose account it is drawn.

certified mail, U.S. letter or parcel whose delivery is recorded and certified by the postal service, for extra postage.

certified milk, milk guaranteed to meet certain official standards.

hat, āge, fär; let, ēqual, tėrm;
it, īce; hot, ōpen, ôrder;
oil, out; cup, pu̇t, rüle;
ch, child; ng, long; sh, she;
th, thin; ᴛʜ, then; zh, measure;

ə represents *a* in about, *e* in taken, *i* in pencil, *o* in lemon, *u* in circus.

< = from, derived from, taken from.

certified public accountant, accountant who has fulfilled the legal requirements and been given a state certificate to practice public accounting.

cer ti fy (sėr′tə fī), *v.t.,* **-fied, -fy ing.** 1 declare (something) true or correct by an official spoken, written, or printed statement. 2 guarantee the quality or value of. 3 assure; make certain. [< Late Latin *certificare* < Latin *certus* sure + *facere* make] **—cer′ti fi′er,** *n.*

cer ti o rar i (sėr′shē ə rer′ē, sėr′shē ərer′ī), *n.* an order from a higher court of law to a lower one, calling for the record of a case for review. [< Late Latin, be informed or made certain]

cer ti tude (sėr′tə tüd, sėr′tə tyüd), *n.* certainty; sureness.

ce ru le an (sə rü′lē ən), *adj.* sky-blue. *—n.* a sky-blue color. [< Latin *caeruleus* dark blue]

ce ru men (sə rü′mən), *n.* earwax. [< New Latin < Latin *cera* wax]

cer us site (sir′ə sit), *n.* natural lead carbonate, an ore of lead. *Formula:* $PbCO_3$ [< Latin *cerussa*]

Cer van tes (sər van′tēz′), *n.* **Miguel de,** 1547-1616, Spanish writer, author of *Don Quixote.*

cer vi cal (sėr′və kəl), *adj.* 1 of the neck. 2 of a cervix or necklike part.

cer vine (sėr′vīn, sėr′vən), *adj.* of or like a deer. [< Latin *cervus* deer]

cer vix (sėr′viks), *n., pl.* **cer vix es, cer vi ces** (sər vī′sēz′). 1 the neck, especially the back of the neck. 2 a necklike part of an organ, such as the narrow end of the uterus. [< Latin]

Ce sar e an or **Ce sar i an** (si zer′ē ən, si zar′ē ən), *adj., n.* Caesarean.

ce si um (sē′zē əm), *n.* a soft, silvery, metallic element of the alkali metal group which occurs as a minute part of various minerals. It is highly electropositive and is used in photoelectric cells. *Symbol:* Cs; *atomic number* 55. See pages 326 and 327 for table. Also, **caesium.** [< New Latin *caesium* < Latin *caesius* bluish-gray]

ces sa tion (se sā′shən), *n.* a ceasing; a stopping: *Both armies agreed on a cessation of the fighting.* [< Latin *cessationem* < *cessare* cease]

ces sion (sesh′ən), *n.* a handing over to another; ceding; giving up; surrendering. [< Latin *cessionem* < *cedere* to yield]

cess pool (ses′pül′), *n.* 1 a pool or pit for house drains to empty into. 2 any filthy place. [earlier *cesperalle* < Old French *souspirail* a vent]

ces tode (ses′tōd), *n.* any of a class of parasitic flatworms which may infest the intestinal tract of man and other vertebrates; tapeworm. [< Greek *kestos* girdle]

ce sur a (si zhu̇r′ə, si zyu̇r′ə), *n., pl.* **-sur as, -sur ae** (-zhu̇r′ē, -zyu̇r′ē). caesura.

Ce ta cea (sə tā′shə), *n.pl.* order of mammals comprising the cetaceans. [< New Latin < Latin *cetus* whale < Greek *ketos*]

ce ta cean (sə tā′shən), *n.* any of an order of mammals living in water, including whales, dolphins, and porpoises. *—adj.* of or belonging to the Cetacea.

ce ta ceous (sə tā′shəs), *adj.* cetacean.

Ce tus (sē′təs), *n.* constellation on or near the celestial equator.

Cé vennes (sā ven′), *n.* group of mountains in S France. Highest peak, 5753 ft.

Cey lon (si lon′), *n.* island country in the Indian Ocean, just off S India. Its official name is **Sri Lanka.** See **India** for map.

Cey lo nese (sē′lə nēz′), *adj., n., pl.* **-nese.** *—adj.* of Ceylon or its people. *—n.* native or inhabitant of Ceylon.

Cé zanne (sā zan′, sā zän′), *n.* **Paul,** 1839-1906, French painter.

Cf, californium.

cf., compare [for Latin, *confer*].

c.f.i. or **C.F.I.,** cost, freight, and insurance.

cg., centigram or centigrams.

cgm., centigram or centigrams.

c.g.s. or **C.G.S.,** centimeter-gram-second.

ch. or **Ch.,** 1 chain. 2 chaplain. 3 chapter. 4 child or children. 5 church.

cha-cha (chä′chä′), *n.* a ballroom dance with a fast, strongly marked rhythm, originally from Latin America. [< American Spanish *cha-cha-cha*]

Cha co (chä′kō), *n.* vast, low-lying plain in N Argentina, S Bolivia, and W Paraguay. about 200,000 sq. mi. Also, **Gran Chaco.**

Chad (chad), *n.* 1 **Lake,** lake in N central Africa. 5000 to 10,000 sq. mi. according to the season. 2 **Republic of,** country in N central Africa south of Libya, a member of the French Community. 3,500,000 pop.; 495,800 sq. mi. *Capital:* Fort-Lamy. See **Algeria** for map. 3 group of Hamitic languages spoken around the Lake Chad area.

chafe (chāf), *v.,* **chafed, chaf ing,** *n. —v.t.* 1 rub so as to wear away, scrape, or make sore: *The stiff collar chafed my neck.* 2 rub to make warm: *She chafed her cold hands.* 3 wear away by rubbing. 4 make angry: *Their teasing chafed me. —v.i.* 1 become worn away by rubbing. 2 become irritated by rubbing. 3 become angry: *I chafed under their teasing. —n.* a chafing; irritation. [< Old French *chaufer* to warm < Latin *calefacere* < *calere* be warm + *facere* make]

chaf er (chā′fər), *n.* any of a group of beetles including the June bugs and scarabs. [Old English *ceafor*]

chaff[1] (chaf), *n.* 1 husks of wheat, oats, rye, etc., especially when separated from grain by threshing. 2 hay or straw cut fine for feeding cattle. 3 worthless stuff; rubbish. [Old English *ceaf*]

chaff[2] (chaf), *v.t., v.i.* make fun of in a good-natured way to one's face; banter. *—n.* good-natured joking about a person to his face. [origin uncertain]

chaf fer (chaf′ər), *n.* a disputing about a price; bargaining. *—v.i.* dispute about a price; bargain. **—chaf′fer er,** *n.*

chaf finch (chaf′inch), *n.* a European songbird with a pleasant, short song, often kept as a cage bird.

chaff y (chaf′ē), *adj.* 1 full of chaff. 2 like chaff; worthless.

cha fing dish (chā′fing), pan with a heater under it, used to cook food at the table or to keep it warm.

Cha gall (shə gäl′), *n.* **Marc,** born 1887, Russian painter living in France.

cha grin (shə grin′), *n.* a feeling of disappointment, failure, or humiliation. *—v.t.* cause to feel chagrin. [< French, apparently < *chat* cat + *grigner* to purse (the lips)]

chain (chān), *n.* 1 series of metal or other links joined together. 2 series of things joined or linked together: *a mountain chain, a chain of events.* 3 anything that binds or restrains. 4 **chains,** *pl.* **a** bonds; fetters. **b** imprisonment or bondage. 5 a measuring instrument like a chain. A surveyor's chain is 66 feet long; an engineer's chain is 100 feet long. 6 number of similar restaurants, stores, theaters, etc., either owned and managed by a single company or affiliated with a company, but individually owned. 7 a number of atoms linked together like a chain, usually within an organic molecule. *—v.t.* 1 join together with a chain; fasten with a chain. 2 bind; restrain; fetter. 3 keep in prison; make a slave of. [< Old French *chaeine* < Latin *catena*] **—chain′like′,** *adj.*

chain gang, U.S. gang of convicts, etc., chained together while at work outdoors or on their way to work.

chain letter, letter which each person receiving is asked to copy and send to several others.

chain mail, kind of flexible armor used in the Middle Ages, made of metal rings linked together.

chain measure, system of measurement used by surveyors:

7.92 inches	= 1 link
100 links or 66 ft.	= 1 chain
10 chains	= 1 furlong
80 chains	= 1 mile

chain reaction, 1 a self-sustaining nuclear reaction occurring when a fissionable nucleus absorbs a neutron and splits, releasing atomic energy and additional neutrons. These neutrons split other fissionable nuclei releasing more energy and more neutrons. 2 any series of events or happenings, each caused by the preceding one or ones.

chain saw, a power saw with an endless chain of saw-toothed links, used in tree surgery, coal mining, and logging.

chain stitch, a stitch in sewing, crocheting, or embroidery, in which each stitch makes a loop through which the next stitch is taken. Many industrial bags are closed with chain stitches.

chain store, one of a group of stores operated within a chain.

chair (cher, char), *n.* 1 seat which has a back and, sometimes, arms, usually for one person. 2 seat of rank, dignity, or authority. 3 position or authority of a person who has such a seat: *Professor Smith occupies the chair of philosophy at this college.* 4 **take the chair, a** begin a meeting. **b** preside at or be in charge of a meeting. 5 chairman: *The chair called the meeting to order.* 6 sedan chair. *—v.t.* 1 put or carry in a chair. 2 put in a position of authority. 3 conduct as chairman: *chair a meeting.* 4 BRITISH. carry high up, as if in a chair: *The winning team chaired their captain.* [< Old French *chaiere* < Latin *cathedra* < Greek *kathedra.* See CATHEDRAL.]

chair lift, a series of chairs suspended from an endless cable to carry people, especially skiers, to the top of a slope or between two points.

chair man (cher′mən, char′mən), *n., pl.* **-men.** 1 person who presides at or is in charge of a meeting. 2 person at the head of a committee, board, or other organized body.

➜ **Chairman** may quite properly be used for either a man or a woman in charge of a meeting or committee. The forms of address are: *Mr. Chairman, Madame Chairman.*

chair man ship (cher′mən ship, char′-mən ship), *n.* 1 position of chairman. 2 length of time one is a chairman.

chair wom an (cher′wu̇m′ən, char′-wu̇m′ən), *n., pl.* **-wom en.** 1 woman who presides at or is in charge of a meeting. 2 woman at the head of a committee, board, or other organized body.

chaise (def. 1)

chaise (shāz), *n.* 1 a light, open carriage, usually with a folding top, especially a one-horse, two-wheeled carriage for two persons. 2 chaise longue. [< French]

chaise longue (shāz′ lông′; shāz′ long′), chair with a long seat and a back at one end, somewhat like a couch. [< French, long chair]

chaise lounge (shāz′ lounj′), chaise longue.

chal ced o ny (kal sed′n ē, kal′sə dō′nē), *n., pl.* **-nies.** any of a variety of fibrous quartz that consist of submicroscopic crystals, have a waxy luster, and occur in various colors and forms. A common kind is grayish or blue. Agate, onyx, carnelian, jasper, etc., are chalcedony. [< Latin *chalcedonius* < Greek *chalkedon*]

chal cid (kal′sid), *n.* any of a family of very small four-winged insects whose larvae live as parasites on other insects. [< Greek *chalkos* copper; in reference to its color]

chal co cite (kal′kə sīt), *n.* a shiny gray sulfide of copper. It is an important copper ore. *Formula:* Cu_2S [< Greek *chalkos* copper]

chal co py rite (kal′kə pī′rīt, kal′kə pir′īt), *n.* a yellow sulfide of copper and iron. It is an important copper ore. *Formula:* $CuFeS_2$

Chal da ic (kal dā′ik), *adj., n.* Chaldean.

Chal de a (kal dē′ə), *n.* ancient region in SW Asia, on either side of the lower part of the Euphrates river. See **Babylonia** for map.

Chal de an (kal dē′ən), *adj.* of or having to do with Chaldea, its people, or their language. —*n.* 1 native or inhabitant of Chaldea. The Chaldeans were a Semitic tribe closely related to the Babylonians. 2 language of Chaldea.

Chal dee (kal dē′, kal′dē), *adj., n.* Chaldean.

cha let (sha lā′, shal′ā), *n.* 1 a herdsman's hut or cabin in the Alps. 2 a Swiss house with wide, overhanging eaves. 3 any house like this. [< Swiss French, diminutive of Old French *chasel* dairy < Popular Latin *casale* < Latin *casa* house]

chal ice (chal′is), *n.* 1 cup or goblet. 2 cup that holds the wine used in the Communion service. 3 a cup-shaped blossom of a flower. [< Old French < Latin *calicem* cup]

chalk (chôk), *n.* 1 a soft, white or gray limestone, made up mostly of very small fossil sea shells. Chalk is used for making lime and for writing or drawing. 2 a white or colored substance like chalk, used for writing or drawing on a blackboard or chalkboard. 3 piece of this substance. 4 a record of credit given; tally. —*v.t.* 1 mark, write, or draw with chalk. 2 mix or rub with chalk; whiten with chalk. 3 score; record. 4 **chalk up, a** write down; record. **b** score. [Old English *ceale* < Latin *calcem* lime] **—chalk′like′,** *adj.*

chalk board (chôk′bôrd′, chôk′bōrd′), *n.* a smooth, hard surface, used for writing or drawing on with chalk or crayon.

chalk y (chô′kē), *adj.,* **chalk i er, chalk i est.** 1 of chalk; containing chalk. 2 like chalk; white as chalk: *The clown's face was chalky.* **—chalk′i ness,** *n.*

chal lenge (chal′ənj), *v.,* **-lenged, -leng ing,** *n.* —*v.t.* 1 call to a game or contest. 2 call to fight, especially in a duel. 3 call on (a person) to answer and explain: *A guard challenges everyone who comes near the fort.* 4 call in question; doubt; dispute: *I challenge your statement; you must prove it before I believe it.* 5 object to (a juror, vote, etc.): *The attorney for the defense challenged the juror.* 6 claim or command (effort, interest, feeling, etc.): *Preventing disease is a problem that challenges everyone's attention.* —*n.* 1 a call to a game or contest: *a challenge to a game of chess.* 2 a call to fight, especially in a duel. 3 a call to answer and explain: *"Who goes there?" was the sentry's challenge.* 4 a demand for proof of the truth of a statement; a doubting or questioning of the truth of a statement. 5 anything that claims or commands effort, interest, feeling, etc. 6 objection made to a juror, vote, etc.: *The judge upheld the challenge and dismissed the juror from duty.* [< Old French *chalenger* < Latin *calumniari* to slander < *calumnia* false accusation. Doublet of CALUMNY.] **—chal′lenge a ble,** *adj.* **—chal′leng er,** *n.*

chal lis or **chal lie** (shal′ē), *n.* a lightweight printed cloth of cotton, wool, or rayon, used for dresses, blouses, etc. [< French *challis*]

cha lyb e ate (kə lib′ē it, kə lib′ē āt), *adj.* containing salts of iron. —*n.* water, medicine, etc., containing salts of iron. [< Latin *chalybeius* (< *chalybs* steel < Greek *chalyps*) + English *-ate*[1]]

cham (kam), *n.* ARCHAIC. khan[1].

cham ber (chām′bər), *n.* 1 a room, especially a room in a house. 2 **chambers,** *pl.* **a** office of a lawyer or judge. **b** set of rooms in a building arranged for living or for offices. 3 bedroom. 4 hall where a legislature or a governing body meets. 5 group of lawmakers: *The Congress of the United States has two chambers, the Senate and the House of Representatives.* 6 group of people organized for some business purpose. 7 an enclosed space in the body of an animal or plant, or in some kinds of machinery. The heart has four chambers. The part of a gun that holds the charge is called the chamber. —*v.t.* provide with a chamber. —*adj.* of, having to do with, or performing chamber music. [< Old French *chambre* < Latin *camera* vault. Doublet of CAMERA.]

cham bered (chām′bərd), *adj.* having a chamber or chambers; divided into compartments.

cham ber lain (chām′bər lən), *n.* 1 person who manages the household of a king or great noble. 2 a high official of a royal court. 3 treasurer: *city chamberlain.* [< Old French *chamberlenc*]

Cham ber lain (chām′bər lən), *n.* 1 Sir **(Joseph) Austen,** 1863-1937, British statesman. 2 **Joseph,** 1836-1914, British statesman, father of Austen and Neville Chamberlain. 3 **(Arthur) Neville,** 1869-1940, British statesman, prime minister of Great Britain from 1937 to 1940.

cham ber maid (chām′bər mād′), *n.* maid who takes care of bedrooms in a house, hotel, or motel.

chamber music, music suited for performance in a room or small hall, such as music for a trio or quartet.

chamber of commerce, group of businessmen organized to protect and promote the business interests of a city, state, or country. .

chamber pot, a portable receptacle, used especially for urination in the bedroom.

cham bray (sham′brā), *n.* a cotton cloth woven from white and colored threads, used for dresses and men's shirts. It is a kind of gingham. [< *Cambrai,* town in France]

cha me le on (kə mē′lē ən, kə mē′lyən), *n.* 1 a small lizard that can change the color of its skin to blend with the surroundings. 2 a changeable or fickle person. [< Greek *chamaileōn* < *chamai* on the ground, dwarf + *leōn* lion]

cham fer (cham′fər), *n.* a slanting surface made by cutting off an edge or corner. —*v.t.* 1 cut off at an edge or corner to make a slanting surface. 2 make a groove or furrow in. [< Middle French *chamfrain*]

cham ois (sham′ē), *n., pl.* **-ois.** 1 a small, goatlike antelope that lives in the high mountains of Europe and southwestern Asia. 2 a soft leather made from its skin or the skin of sheep, goats, or deer. Also, **shammy** for 2. [< French < Late Latin *camocem*]

cham o mile (kam′ə mīl), *n.* plant of the composite family, with daisylike flowers, whose flowers and leaves are sometimes dried and used as medicine. Also, **camomile.** [< Late Latin *chamomilla, camomilla*]

champ[1] (champ), *v.t.* 1 bite and chew noisily. 2 bite and chew on impatiently: *The race horse champed its bit.* —*v.i.* make biting and chewing movements with the jaws and teeth: *champ with impatience.* Also, **chomp.** [perhaps imitative]

champ[2] (champ), *n.* INFORMAL. champion.

cham pagne (sham pān′), *n.* 1 a sparkling, bubbling white wine, sweet or dry, first made in Champagne. 2 a pale, brownish-yellow color. —*adj.* pale brownish-yellow.

Cham pagne (sham pān′), *n.* region in N France, formerly a province.

cham paign (sham pān′), *n.* a wide plain; level, open country. —*adj.* level and open. [< Old French *champaigne* < Late Latin *campania* < Latin *campus* field]

cham pi on (cham′pē ən), *n.* 1 person, animal, or thing that wins first place in a game or contest: *the swimming champion of the world.* 2 person who fights or speaks for another; person who defends a cause; defender; supporter: *a champion of peace.* —*adj.* that has won first place; ahead of all others: *a champion runner.* —*v.t.* fight for; speak in behalf of; defend; support: *All her life she has championed freedom.* [< Old French < Late Latin *campionem* < *campus* field (of battle)] **—cham′pi on less,** *adj.*

cham pi on ship (cham′pē ən ship), *n.* 1 position of a champion; first place. 2 defense; support.

hat, āge, fär; let, ēqual, tėrm;
it, īce; hot, ōpen, ôrder;
oil, out; cup, pu̇t, rüle;
ch, child; ng, long; sh, she;
th, thin; ᴛʜ, then; zh, measure;
ə represents *a* in about, *e* in taken, *i* in pencil, *o* in lemon, *u* in circus.
< = from, derived from, taken from.

Cham plain (sham plān′), *n.* 1 **Lake,** long, narrow lake between New York and Vermont, and extending into Canada. 125 mi. long; 600 sq. mi. 2 **Samuel de,** 1567?-1635, French explorer who founded Quebec and was the first French governor of Canada.

chance (chans), *n., v.,* **chanced, chanc ing,** *adj.* —*n.* 1 a favorable time; opportunity: *a chance to make some money.* 2 likelihood of anything happening; possibility or probability: *There's a good chance that you will be well enough to return to work next week.* 3 fate, fortune, or luck: *Chance led to the finding of gold in California.* 4 a happening; event: *I shall never forget the chance that befell me that day.* 5 a risk; gamble: *She took a big chance when she swam the swift river.* 6 (in baseball) any defensive fielding play which results in a putout, an assist, or an error. 7 ticket in a raffle or lottery.
by chance, accidentally.
on the chance, depending on the possibility.
on the off chance, depending on luck.
stand a chance, have favorable prospects.
—*v.i.* 1 have the fortune; happen: *I chanced to meet an old friend today.* See **happen** for synonym study. 2 **chance upon** or **chance on,** happen to find or meet. —*v.t.* take the risk of: *I will not chance driving in this blizzard.*
—*adj.* not expected or planned; accidental; casual: *a chance visit.*
[< Old French *cheance* < Popular Latin *cadentia* a falling < *cadere* to fall. Doublet of CADENCE.]

chan cel (chan′səl), *n.* the space around the altar of a church, used by the clergy and the choir. It is often separated from the rest of the church by a railing, lattice, or screen. See **apse** for diagram. [< Old French < Latin *cancelli* a grating]

chan cel ler y (chan′sə lər ē), *n., pl.* **-ler ies.** 1 position of a chancellor. 2 office of a chancellor.

chan cel lor (chan′sə lər), *n.* 1 the prime minister or other very high official of some European countries. 2 U.S. the chief judge of a court of chancery or equity. 3 any of various high British government officials, especially: **a** the Chancellor of the Exchequer. **b** the Lord Chancellor. 4 head or president of some universities. [< Anglo-French *chanceler* < Latin *cancellarius* officer stationed at tribunal < *cancelli* a grating, bars]

Chancellor of the Exchequer, the British cabinet minister responsible for financial affairs.

chan cel lor ship (chan′sə lər ship), *n.* 1 position or office of a chancellor. 2 term of office of a chancellor.

chan cer y (chan′sər ē), *n., pl.* **-cer ies.** 1 court of equity. 2 equity. 3 office where public records are kept. 4 office of a chancellor. 5 (in wrestling) a grip on the head. 6 **in chancery,** in a helpless position. [variant of *chancellery*]

chan cre (shang′kər), *n.* ulcer or sore with a hard base, the first lesion of syphilis. [< French < Latin *cancer.* Doublet of CANCER, CANKER.]

chanc y (chan′sē), *adj.,* **chanc i er, chanc i est.** subject to chance; uncertain; risky.

chan de lier (shan′də lir′), *n.* a branched fixture for lights, usually hanging from the ceiling. [< French < Latin *candelabrum.* See CANDELABRUM.]

chand ler (chand′lər), *n.* 1 maker or seller of candles. 2 dealer in groceries and supplies: *a ship chandler.* [< Anglo-French *chandeler* < Old French *chandeile* candle < Latin *candela*]

chand ler y (chand′lər ē), *n., pl.* **-ler ies.** 1 storeroom for candles. 2 warehouse, goods, or business of a chandler.

Chang chun (chäng′chu̇n′), *n.* city in NE China. 1,800,000.

change (chānj), *v.,* **changed, chang ing,** *n.* —*v.t.* 1 make different; modify: *She changed the room by painting the walls green.* See synonym study below. 2 put (something) in place of another; substitute: *change soiled clothes for clean ones.* 3 take in place of: *change a dollar bill for ten dimes.* 4 give and take; exchange: *I changed seats with my friend.* —*v.i.* 1 become different; vary: *The wind changed from east to west.* See synonym study below. 2 make an exchange: *We changed from a station wagon to a sedan.* 3 change one's clothes: *After swimming we went to the cabin and changed.* 4 transfer from one aircraft, train, bus, etc., to another. —*n.* 1 the substitution of one thing for another; a changing: *a change of scene.* 2 a changed condition: *Do you see any change in his behavior?* 3 lack of sameness; variety: *Let me drive for a change.* 4 thing to be used in place of another of the same kind: *She packed two changes of clothing for the trip.* 5 money returned to a person when he has given a larger amount than the price of what he buys. 6 money of smaller denomination given in place of money of larger denomination: *Can you give me change for a quarter?* 7 coins of small denomination: *I have a dollar bill and some change.* 8 **changes,** *pl.* different ways in which a set of bells can be rung. 9 **ring the changes, a** ring a set of bells in all its different ways. **b** do a thing in many different ways; say or wear the same thing in different ways.
[< Old French *changier* < Latin *cambiare*] —**chang′er,** *n.*
Syn. *v.t.* 1, *v.i.* 1 **Change, alter** mean to make or become different. **Change** suggests that the difference is fundamental and complete: *She used to be shy, but has changed since she went to college. Automobiles have greatly changed life in the United States.* **Alter** suggests a less drastic difference, limited to some particular: *alter the wording of a statement. My outlook on life has altered as I get older.*

change a bil i ty (chān′jə bil′ə tē), *n.* a changeable quality or condition.

change a ble (chān′jə bəl), *adj.* 1 that can change; likely to change; inconstant. 2 that can be changed; likely to be changed; alterable. 3 having a color or appearance that changes. Silk is changeable when it shows different colors in different lights. —**change′a ble ness,** *n.* —**change′a bly,** *adv.*

change ful (chānj′fəl), *adj.* full of changes; likely to change; changing. —**change′ful ly,** *adv.* —**change′ful ness,** *n.*

change less (chānj′lis), *adj.* not changing; not likely to change; constant. —**change′less ly,** *adv.* —**change′less ness,** *n.*

change ling (chānj′ling), *n.* 1 child secretly substituted for another. 2 (in fairy tales) a strange, stupid, or ugly child left by fairies in place of a child carried off by them.

change of life, menopause.

change o ver (chānj′ō′vər), *n.* 1 a shift to the manufacture of a new model, product, etc. 2 transfer of ownership or control.

change ringing, art of ringing a peal of bells in regularly varying order, so that all the possible combinations may be made.

Chang sha (chäng′shä′), *n.* city in S China. 703,000.

chan nel (chan′l), *n., v.,* **-neled, -nel ing** or **-nelled, -nel ling.** —*n.* 1 the bed of a stream, river, etc. 2 body of water joining two larger bodies of water: *the English Channel.* 3 the deeper part of a waterway: *There is shallow water on both sides of the channel in this river.* 4 passage for liquids; groove or canal. 5 the means by which something moves or is carried: *The information came through secret channels.* 6 a narrow band of radio or television frequencies. 7 course of action; field of activity: *She tried to find a suitable channel for her abilities.* —*v.t.* 1 form a channel in; wear or cut into a channel: *The river had channeled its way through the rocks.* 2 direct into a particular course: *Channel all your efforts into this one project, and you will succeed.* [< Old French *chanel* < Latin *canalem.* Doublet of CANAL.]

Channel Islands, British islands near the NW coast of France. The most important are Alderney, Guernsey, Jersey, and Sark. 121,000 pop.; 75 sq. mi.

chan nel ize (chan′ə līz), *v.t.,* **-ized, -iz ing.** to channel. —**chan′nel i za′tion,** *n.*

chan son (shäɴ sôɴ′), *n.* FRENCH. song.

chant (chant), *n.* 1 song: *an Indian war chant.* 2 a short, simple song in which several syllables or words are sung in one tone. Chants are sometimes used in church services. 3 psalm, prayer, or other song for chanting. 4 a singsong way of talking. —*v.t.* 1 sing: *chant a melody.* 2 sing to a chant, or in the manner of a chant. A choir chants psalms or prayers. 3 keep talking about; say over and over again. —*v.i.* sing or warble. [< Old French *chanter* sing < Latin *cantare,* frequentative of *canere* sing] —**chant′er,** *n.*

chan teuse (shäɴ tœz′), *n.* FRENCH. a woman singer.

chan tey (shan′tē, chan′tē), *n., pl.* **-teys.** song chanted by sailors, especially in rhythm with the motions of their work. Also, **chanty, shantey,** or **shanty.** [alteration of French *chanter* sing]

chan ti cleer (chan′tə klir), *n.* rooster. [< Old French *Chantecler,* the name of the cock in *Reynard the Fox*]

chan try (chan′trē), *n., pl.* **-tries.** 1 chapel attached to a church, used for the less important services. 2 endowment to pay for singing or saying of Masses for a person's soul.

chan ty (shan′tē, chan′tē), *n., pl.* **-ties.** chantey.

Cha nu kah (hä′nə kə), *n.* Hanukkah.

cha os (kā′os), *n.* 1 very great confusion; complete disorder: *The tornado left the town in chaos.* 2 Also, **Chaos.** the infinite space in which formless matter was thought to have existed before the ordered universe came into being. [< Latin < Greek]

cha ot ic (kā ot′ik), *adj.* very confused; completely disordered. **—cha ot′i cal ly,** *adv.*

chap[1] (chap), *v.,* **chapped, chap ping,** *n.* —*v.t., v.i.* crack open; make or become rough: *A person's lips often chap in cold weather. Cold weather chaps my skin.* —*n.* place where the skin is chapped. [Middle English *chappen* to cut]

chap[2] (chap), *n.* INFORMAL. fellow; man or boy. [short for *chapman*]

chap[3] (chap), *n.* Often, **chaps.** jaw; chop. [variant of *chop*[2]]

chap., 1 chapel. 2 chaplain. 3 chapter.

chap ar ral (chap′ə ral′, shap′ə ral′), *n.* (in the southwestern United States) a dense, often thorny thicket of low brushy vegetation. [< Spanish < *chaparro* evergreen oak]

chap book (chap′bu̇k′), *n.* a small book or pamphlet of popular tales, ballads, etc., formerly sold on the streets. [< *chap(man)* + *book*]

cha peau (sha pō′), *n., pl.* **-peaux** or **-peaus** (-pōz′). hat. [< French]

chap el (chap′əl), *n.* 1 a building for worship, not as large as a church. 2 a small place for worship in a larger building. 3 a room or building for worship in a palace, school, etc. 4 a religious service in a chapel, especially in a school or college. 5 (in Great Britain) a place for worship used by people who do not belong to the established church. [< Old French *chapele* < Medieval Latin *cappella* < Late Latin *cappa* cape; originally, the shrine in which the cape of Saint Martin of Tours was preserved]

chap e ron or **chap e rone** (shap′ə rōn′), *n., v.,* **-roned, -ron ing.** —*n.* 1 a person, especially a married or an older woman, who accompanies a young unmarried woman in public for the sake of propriety. 2 an older person who is present at a party or other social activity of young people to see that good taste is observed. —*v.t.* act as a chaperon to; escort. [< Old French *chaperon* hood, protector]

chap e ron age (shap′ə rō′nij), *n.* activities or protection of a chaperon.

chap fall en (chap′fô′lən, chop′fô′lən), *adj.* dejected, discouraged, or humiliated. Also, **chopfallen.**

chap lain (chap′lən), *n.* clergyman authorized or appointed to perform religious functions for a family, court, society, public institution, or unit in the armed forces. [< Old French *chapelain* minister of a chapel < Medieval Latin *capellanus* < *cappella.* See CHAPEL.]

chap lain cy (chap′lən sē), *n., pl.* **-cies.** position of a chaplain.

chap lain ship (chap′lən ship), *n.* chaplaincy.

chap let (chap′lit), *n.* 1 wreath worn on the head. 2 string of beads. 3 string of beads for keeping count in saying prayers, one third as long as a rosary. 4 prayers said with such beads. [< Old French *chapelet,* diminutive of *chapel* headdress]

chap let ed (chap′lə tid), *adj.* wearing a wreath on the head.

Chap lin (chap′lin), *n.* **Charles Spencer,** born 1889, British motion-picture comedian and producer, called "Charlie" Chaplin.

chap man (chap′mən), *n., pl.* **-men.** BRITISH. an itinerant trader; peddler. [Old English *cēapman* < *cēap* trade + *man* man]

Chap man (chap′mən), *n.* **George,** 1559?-1634, English poet and dramatist.

chaps (shaps, chaps), *n.pl.* strong leather trousers without a seat, worn over other trousers by cowboys. [short for Mexican Spanish *chaparajos*]

chap ter (chap′tər), *n.* 1 a main division of a book or other writing, dealing with a certain part of the story or subject. 2 anything like a chapter; part; section: *The development of radio is an interesting chapter in modern science.* 3 a local division of an organization, which holds its own meetings; branch of a club, society, etc. 4 group of clergymen, usually attached to a cathedral. 5 a meeting of such a group. —*v.t.* divide into chapters; arrange in chapters. [< Old French *chapitre* < Latin *capitulum,* diminutive of *caput* head]

chapter house, 1 the building where the chapter of a cathedral holds its meetings. 2 house of a college fraternity or sorority.

Cha pul te pec (chə pul′tə pek), *n.* fort on a rocky hill SW of the center of Mexico City. United States troops captured the fort in 1847 during the Mexican War.

char[1] (chär), *v.,* **charred, char ring,** *n.* —*v.t.* 1 reduce by burning to charcoal or carbon. 2 burn enough to blacken; scorch. —*v.i.* become reduced to charcoal. —*n.* 1 a charred substance. 2 charcoal. [perhaps < *charcoal*]

char[2] (chär), *n., v.,* **charred, char ring.** BRITISH. —*n.* 1 charwoman. 2 an odd job, especially of housework; chore. —*v.i.* 1 do odd jobs by the day or hour. 2 do odd jobs. Also, BRITISH **chare.** [Old English *cerr* a turn]

char[3] (chär), *n., pl.* **chars** or **char.** any of a group of active trout with small scales, including the brook trout and lake trout. [origin unknown]

char-a-banc (shar′ə bang′, shar′ə bangk′), *n.* BRITISH. a large motorbus, used for excursions. [< French *char à bancs* car with benches]

char ac ter (kar′ik tər), *n.* 1 all the qualities or features possessed; sort; nature: *He dislikes people of that character. The soil on the prairies is of a different character from that in the mountains.* 2 moral strength or weakness; the special way in which any person feels, thinks, and acts: *a person of shallow, changeable character.* See synonym study below. 3 moral firmness, self-control, or integrity: *It takes character to endure hardship for very long.* 4 the estimate formed of a person's qualities; reputation. 5 good reputation. 6 (in biology) a distinctive feature; trait; characteristic. The size and form of a given breed of dogs and the fragrance of a sweet pea are characters. 7 position or condition: *The treasurer of the club also serves in the character of secretary.* 8 person or animal in a play, poem, story, or book. 9 INFORMAL. person who attracts attention because he is strange or eccentric. 10 letter, mark, or sign used in writing or printing. A, a, %, +, −, 1, 2, and 3 are characters. 11 writing or printing of a certain style: *books in Gothic character.* 12 description of a person's qualities. 13 **in character,** as expected; natural or usual. 14 **out of character,** not as expected; not natural or usual. [< Latin < Greek *charaktēr* instrument for marking, distinctive mark < *charassein* engrave]

Syn. 2 **Character, personality, individuality** mean the qualities that make a person what he is. **Character** applies to the moral qualities that determine the way a person thinks, feels, and acts in the important matters of life, especially in relation to the principles of right and wrong. **Personality** applies to the personal qualities as voice, bearing, cordiality, etc., that determine the way he acts in his social and personal relations. **Individuality** applies to the particular qualities that make a person himself, an individual: *He has a weak character, but a winning personality and great individuality.*

char ac ter is tic (kar′ik tə ris′tik), *adj.* distinguishing from others; special; distinctive: *Bananas have their own characteristic smell.* —*n.* 1 a special quality or feature; whatever distinguishes one person or thing from others: *Cheerfulness is a characteristic that we admire in people. An elephant's trunk is its most unusual characteristic.* See **feature** for synonym study. 2 the whole number in a logarithm. In the logarithm 2.95424, the characteristic is 2 and the mantissa is .95424. **—char′ac ter is′ti cal ly,** *adv.*

char ac ter i za tion (kar′ik tər ə zā′shən), *n.* 1 a characterizing; description of characteristics. 2 creation of characters in a play, poem, story, or book.

char ac ter ize (kar′ik tə rīz′), *v.t.,* **-ized, -iz ing.** 1 describe the special qualities or features of (a person or thing); describe. 2 be a characteristic of; distinguish: *A camel is characterized by the hump on its back and its ability to go without water for several days.* 3 give character to: *The author characterized his heroine in a few short paragraphs.*

char ac ter less (kar′ik tər lis), *adj.* 1 without a character. 2 without distinction; uninteresting.

character sketch, 1 a literary profile of a person or a type, bringing out notable characteristics. 2 a brief impersonation on the stage.

char ac ter y (kar′ik tə rē), *n.* signs or symbols used to express ideas.

cha rade (shə rād′), *n.* Often, **charades,** *pl.* game in which one player acts out a word or phrase and the others try to guess what it is. [< French]

char coal (chär′kōl′), *n.* 1 a black, brittle form of carbon made by partly burning wood or bones in an airtight kiln. Charcoal is used as fuel and in filters. 2 stick, pencil, or crayon of charcoal for drawing. 3 a drawing made with such a charcoal stick, pencil, or crayon. [Middle English *charcole*]

chard (chärd), *n.* kind of beet whose large leaves are eaten as a vegetable; Swiss chard. [ultimately < Latin *carduus* thistle, artichoke]

chare (cher, char), *n., v.i.,* **chared, char ing.** BRITISH. char[2].

charge (chärj), *v.,* **charged, charg ing,** *n.* —*v.t.* 1 ask as a price; put on a price of: *The doctor charges ten dollars for an office call.* 2 put down as a debt to be paid: *This store*

will charge things that you buy and let you pay for them later. 3 put down as a debt against: *Please charge my account.* 4 load or fill: *He charged the gun with powder and shot.* 5 give an electric charge to (a storage battery, condenser, etc.). 6 give a task, duty, or responsibility to: *The law charges the police with serving and protecting citizens.* 7 give an order or command to; direct: *She charged us to keep the plan secret. The judge charged the jury to come to a fair decision.* 8 accuse of an offense or crime, especially in a court of law: *The driver was charged with speeding.* See synonym study below. 9 rush with force; attack; assault: *The soldiers charged the enemy.* 10 attribute (a fault, etc.) to a person. —*v.i.* 1 ask a price; demand payment: *This store does not charge for delivery.* 2 have put down as a debt to be paid: *We charge at the service station.* 3 rush with force; attack: *The captain gave the order to charge.*
charge off, a subtract as a loss. b put down as belonging: *A bad mistake must be charged off to experience.* c INFORMAL. dash away.
charge up, put down as belonging: *I charged it up to inexperience.*
—*n.* 1 price asked for or put on something. See **price** for synonym study. 2 a debt to be paid: *Taxes are a charge on property.* 3 amount needed to load or fill something. A gun is fired by exploding the charge of powder in the shell. 4 task; duty; responsibility: *Protecting citizens is the charge of the police.* 5 care; management: *Doctors and nurses have charge of sick people.* 6 person, persons, or thing under the care or management of someone: *Sick people are the charges of doctors and nurses.* 7 an order; command; direction: *a judge's charge to the jury.* 8 accusation: *He admitted the truth of the charge and paid a fine.* 9 an attack; forceful rush; assault: *The charge drove the enemy back.* 10 electric charge. **11 in charge,** having the care or management; in command: *The mate is in charge when the captain leaves the ship.* **12 in charge of,** a having the care or management of: *My sister is in charge of the office.* b under the care or management of. c in command of: *The corporal was in charge of the patrol.*
[< Old French *chargier* < Late Latin *carricare* to load < Latin *carrus* wagon. Doublet of CARRY.] **—chargeʹa ble,** *adj.*
Syn. *v.t.* 8 **Charge, accuse** mean to put blame on a person. **Charge** may suggest blame for some minor wrongdoing, such as breaking a rule, but it commonly suggests a serious offense, such as breaking a law, and making a formal statement before the proper authority: *He was charged with leaving the grounds without permission.* **Accuse** suggests making the charge directly to the person blamed and expressing disapproval, but not necessarily taking him before authority: *They accused me of lying.*

charge account, 1 system of purchasing on credit in which the customer agrees to pay his accumulated bills on presentation. 2 record kept at a store of things bought by a person on credit.

char gé d'af faires (shär zhāʹ də ferʹ; shär zhāʹ də farʹ), *pl.* **char gés d'af faires** (shär zhāzʹ də ferʹ; shär zhāzʹ də farʹ), official who takes the place of an ambassador, minister, or other diplomat. [< French]

charg er[1] (chärʹjər), *n.* 1 war horse. 2 person or thing that charges. 3 device that gives an electrical charge to storage batteries. [< *charge*]

charg er[2] (chärʹjər), *n.* ARCHAIC. a large, flat dish; platter. [ultimately < Old French *chargier* to load. See CHARGE.]

char i ly (cherʹə lē, charʹə lē), *adv.* 1 cautiously. 2 shyly. 3 stingily.

char i ness (cherʹē nis, charʹē nis), *n.* 1 caution. 2 shyness. 3 stinginess.

char i ot (charʹē ət), *n.* 1 a two-wheeled carriage pulled by horses. The chariot was used in ancient times for fighting, for racing, and in processions. 2 a four-wheeled carriage or coach. [< Old French < *char* wagon < Latin *carrus*]

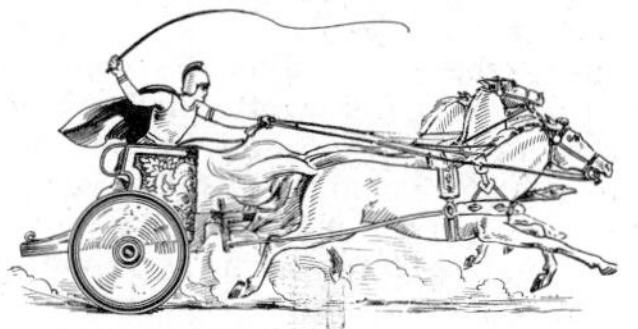

chariot (def. 1)—Roman chariot

char i ot eer (charʹē ə tirʹ), *n.* person who drives a chariot.

cha ris ma (kə rizʹmə), *n., pl.* **-ma ta** (-mə tə for 3.) 1 a mysterious power to fascinate and attract; great personal magnetism or glamor: *the charisma of a popular leader.* 2 sex appeal. 3 a spiritual gift or grace giving a person the power of prophesying, healing, etc. [< Greek]

char is mat ic (karʹiz matʹik), *adj.* having charisma; capable of inspiring great personal allegiance.

char i ta ble (charʹə tə bəl), *adj.* 1 generous in giving to poor, sick, or helpless people; benevolent and kind. 2 of or for charity. 3 kindly in judging people and their actions; lenient. **—charʹi ta ble ness,** *n.* **—charʹi ta bly,** *adv.*

char i ty (charʹə tē), *n., pl.* **-ties.** 1 a generous giving to the poor, or to organizations which look after the sick, the poor, and the helpless. 2 act or work of charity. 3 fund, institution, or organization for helping the sick, the poor, and the helpless. 4 kindness in judging people's faults. 5 love of one's fellow men. [< Old French *charite* < Latin *caritatem* affection < *carus* dear]

char la tan (shärʹlə tən), *n.* person who pretends to have more knowledge or skill than he really has; quack. [< French < Italian *ciarlatano* < *cerretano* person from *Cerreto (di Spoleto),* town in Italy where street hucksters were common in the Middle Ages]

char la tan ism (shärʹlə tə nizʹəm), *n.* the practices or methods of a charlatan; quackery.

char la tan ry (shärʹlə tən rē), *n.* charlatanism.

Char le magne (shärʹlə mān), *n.* A.D. 742-814, king of the Franks from A.D. 768 to 814 and emperor of the Holy Roman Empire from A.D. 800 to 814. He made many reforms in government and education in western Europe. Also, **Charles I, Charles the Great.**

Charles (chärlz), *n.* **1 Cape,** cape in SE Virginia, on the E side of Chesapeake Bay. **2 Charles River,** river in E Massachusetts, between Boston and Cambridge. 47 mi.

Charles I, 1 1600-1649, king of England from 1625 until he was convicted of treason and executed in 1649. 2 Charlemagne. 3 A.D. 823-877, king of France from A.D. 840 to 877. He was called "Charles the Bald." As emperor of the Holy Roman Empire from 875 to 877, he was known as Charles II.

hat, āge, fär; let, ēqual, tėrm;
it, īce; hot, ōpen, ôrder;
oil, out; cup, pu̇t, rüle;
ch, child; ng, long; sh, she;
th, thin; ᴛʜ, then; zh, measure;

ə represents *a* in about, *e* in taken, *i* in pencil, *o* in lemon, *u* in circus.

< = from, derived from, taken from.

4 1500-1558, king of Spain from 1516 to 1556. As emperor of the Holy Roman Empire from 1519 to 1556, he was known as Charles V.

Charles II, 1 1630-1685, king of England from 1660 to 1685. He was the son of Charles I. 2 Charles I (def. 3).

Charles IV, 1294-1328, king of France from 1322 to 1328. He was called "Charles the Fair."

Charles V, 1 Charles I (def. 4). 2 1337-1380, king of France from 1364 to 1380. He was called "Charles the Wise."

Charles XII, 1682-1718, king of Sweden from 1697 to 1718.

Charles Mar tel (mär telʹ), A.D. 690?-741, ruler of the Franks from A.D. 714 to 741, and grandfather of Charlemagne. His defeat of the Saracens near Tours in A.D. 732 prevented them from conquering western Europe.

Charles the Great, Charlemagne.

Charles ton (chärlzʹtən), *n.* 1 capital of West Virginia, in the W part. 72,000. 2 seaport in SE South Carolina. 67,000. 3 a lively ballroom dance, especially popular in the 1920's.

char ley horse (chärʹlē), INFORMAL. stiffness or cramp in a muscle, especially of the leg or arm.

Char lotte (shärʹlət), *n.* city in S North Carolina. 241,000.

Char lot te A ma li e (shär lotʹə ə mäʹlē-ə), seaport and capital of the Virgin Islands that belong to the United States. 12,000. Former name, **St. Thomas.**

char lotte russe (shärʹlət rüsʹ), dessert made of a mold of sponge cake filled with whipped cream or custard. [< French, Russian charlotte (a type of dessert)]

Char lottes ville (shärʹləts vil), *n.* city in central Virginia. 39,000.

Char lotte town (shärʹlət toun), *n.* capital of Prince Edward Island, Canada. 18,000.

charm (chärm), *n.* 1 power of delighting or fascinating; attractiveness: *Our grandmother did not lose her charm for us as she grew old.* 2 a pleasing quality or feature. 3 a small ornament or trinket worn on a bracelet, watch chain, etc. 4 word, verse, act, or thing supposed to have magic power to help or harm people. —*v.t.* 1 please greatly; delight; fascinate; captivate: *The storyteller charmed us with tales of adventure.* See synonym study below. 2 act on as if by magic. 3 give magic power to; protect as by a charm. —*v.i.* attract strongly; delight; be captivating. [< Old French *charme* < Latin *carmen* song, enchantment < *canere* sing] **—charmʹless,** *adj.*
Syn. *v.t.* 1 **Charm, attract, allure** mean to win a person by pleasing. **Charm** emphasizes winning and holding a person's attention and admiration by giving delight: *Her beautiful voice charms everyone.* **Attract**

emphasizes drawing attention and liking by being pleasing: *She attracts everyone she meets by her gracious manner.* **Allure** emphasizes attracting a person by appealing to the senses and feelings: *Bermuda allures many tourists from the United States.*

charmed (chärmd), *adj.* protected as by a charm: *The pilot led a charmed life in which he narrowly survived many accidents.*

charm er (chär′mər), *n.* one that charms, delights, or fascinates.

charm ing (chär′ming), *adj.* very pleasing; delightful; fascinating; attractive. **—charm′ing ly,** *adv.*

char nel (chär′nl), *n.* charnel house. *—adj.* 1 of or used for a charnel. 2 like a charnel; deathlike; ghastly. [< Middle French, ultimately < Latin *carnalem* carnal. Doublet of CARNAL.]

charnel house, place where dead bodies or bones are laid.

Char on (ker′ən, kar′ən), *n.* (in Greek myths) the boatman who ferried the spirits of the dead across the river Styx to Hades.

chart (chärt), *n.* 1 map used by sailors to show the coasts, rocks, and shallow places of the sea. The course of a ship is marked on a chart. See **map** for synonym study. 2 an outline map showing special conditions or facts: *a weather chart.* 3 sheet of information arranged in lists, pictures, tables, or diagrams. 4 such a list, table, picture, or diagram. 5 a graphic representation of any variable, such as temperature, pressure, production, or sales. *—v.t.* 1 make a chart of; show on a chart. 2 plan in detail: *She is now charting the course of her campaign.* [< Middle French *charte* < Latin *charta* leaf of paper < Greek *chartēs.* Doublet of CARD[1].] **—chart′less,** *adj.*

char ter (chär′tər), *n.* 1 a written grant by a government to a colony, a group of citizens, a corporation, etc., bestowing the right of organization, with other privileges, and specifying the form of organization. 2 a written order from the authorities of a society, giving to a group of persons the right to organize a new chapter, branch, or lodge. 3 document setting forth aims and purposes of a group of nations, organizations, or individuals in a common undertaking: *the Charter of the United Nations.* 4 a special right, privilege, or immunity. *—v.t.* 1 give a charter to. 2 hire: *charter a ship, charter a bus.* [< Old French *chartre* < Latin *chartula,* diminutive of *charta.* See CHART.] **—char′ter er,** *n.* **—char′ter less,** *adj.*

charter member, one of the original members of a club, society, or company.

Chart ism (chär′tiz′əm), *n.* 1 a reform movement whose members were chiefly workingmen, active in England especially from 1838 to 1848. 2 its principles and demands, set forth in a document called the "People's Charter."

Chart ist (chär′tist), *n.* adherent of Chartism. *—adj.* of or having to do with Chartism.

Char tres (shär′trə), *n.* city in N France. Its Gothic cathedral is over 700 years old. 34,000.

char treuse (shär trüz′, shär trüs′; *French* shär trœz′), *n.* 1 a light, yellowish green. 2 a green, yellow, or white liqueur first made by Carthusian monks. *—adj.* light yellowish-green. [< French, Carthusian]

char wom an (chär′wu̇m′ən), *n., pl.* **-wom en.** woman who is hired to clean and scrub homes, offices, and public buildings. [< *char*[2] + *woman*]

char y (cher′ē, char′ē), *adj.,* **char i er, char i est.** 1 showing caution; careful; wary: *The cat was chary of getting its paws wet.* 2 shy: *chary of strangers.* 3 sparing; stingy: *A jealous person is chary of praising others.* [Old English *cearig* sorrowful < *caru* care]

Cha ryb dis (kə rib′dis), *n.* 1 a dangerous whirlpool proverbially located in the strait between Sicily and Italy, opposite the rock Scylla. 2 (in Greek myths) a monster that sucked down ships.

chase[1] (chās), *v.,* **chased, chas ing,** *n.* *—v.t.* 1 run or follow after to catch or kill. 2 drive away. 3 run after; follow; pursue: *chase a ball.* 4 hunt. *—v.i.* INFORMAL. rush; hurry. *—n.* 1 act of chasing. 2 **give chase,** run after; pursue. 3 hunting as a sport; hunt: *We watched the chase.* 4 a hunted animal: *The chase escaped the hunter.* [< Old French *chacier* < Latin *captare.* Doublet of CATCH.]

chase[2] (chās), *v.,* **chased, chas ing,** *n.* *—v.t.* decorate (metal, etc.) with embossed or engraved work. *—n.* a rectangular metal frame to hold type that is ready to print or make plates from. [< French *châsse* a frame, case]

chase[3] (chās), *n.* a groove, furrow, or trench cut in a wall, the ground, etc., for a pipe or other conductor. [< French *chas,* originally, enclosure < Late Latin *capsum* < Latin *capere* take]

Chase (chās), *n.* **Salmon P.,** 1808-1873, American statesman, secretary of the treasury under Lincoln, and chief justice of the Supreme Court from 1864 to 1873.

chas er (chā′sər), *n.* 1 person or thing that chases. 2 hunter. 3 a small, speedy airplane or ship used to repel and pursue attacking craft. 4 gun on the bow or stern of a ship. It is used when chasing, or being chased by, another ship. 5 INFORMAL. a drink of water or some mild beverage taken after a drink of strong liquor.

chasm (kaz′əm), *n.* 1 a deep opening or crack in the earth; gap. 2 a wide difference of feelings or interests between people or groups: *The chasm between England and the American colonies finally led to the Revolutionary War.* [< Latin *chasma* < Greek]

chas seur (sha sėr′), *n.* 1 soldier of a group of cavalry or infantry equipped and trained to move rapidly. 2 hunter. 3 a uniformed attendant. [< French]

Chas si dim (has′ə dəm), *n.pl.* Hasidim.

chassis (def. 1)

chas sis (chas′ē, shas′ē), *n., pl.* **chas sis** (chas′ēz, shas′ēz). 1 the frame, wheels, and machinery of a motor vehicle that support the body. 2 the main landing gear that supports the body of an aircraft. 3 the base or frame for the parts of a radio or television set. 4 frame on which a gun carriage moves backward and forward. [< French *châssis*]

chaste (chāst), *adj.* 1 pure; virtuous. 2 decent; modest. 3 simple in taste or style; not excessively ornamented. [< Old French < Latin *castus* pure] **—chaste′ly,** *adv.* **—chaste′ness,** *n.*

chas ten (chā′sn), *v.t.* 1 punish to improve; discipline. 2 restrain from excess or crudeness; moderate. 3 make chaste in character or style; purify; refine. **—chas′ten er,** *n.*

chas tise (cha stīz′), *v.t.,* **-tised, -tis ing.** 1 inflict punishment or suffering on to improve; punish. 2 criticize severely; rebuke. [variant of *chasten*] **—chas tis′er,** *n.*

chas tise ment (cha stīz′mənt, chas′tiz-mənt), *n.* 1 punishment. 2 a severe criticism or rebuke.

chas ti ty (chas′tə tē), *n.* 1 purity; virtue. 2 decency; modesty. 3 simplicity of style or taste; absence of excessive decoration.

chas u ble (chaz′yə bəl, chas′yə bəl), *n.* a sleeveless outer vestment worn by the priest at Mass. [< Old French < Late Latin *casubula* < Latin *casa* house]

chat (chat), *n., v.,* **chat ted, chat ting.** *—n.* 1 easy, familiar talk. 2 any of several birds with a chattering cry. *—v.i.* talk in an easy, familiar way. [short for *chatter*]

châ teau (sha tō′), *n., pl.* **-teaux** (-tōz′). 1 a large country house in France or elsewhere in Europe. 2 a French castle. [< French < Latin *castellum* castle. Doublet of CASTLE.]

Cha teau bri and (sha tō′brē änd; *French* shä tō brē äN′), *n.* **François René de,** 1768-1848, French author and statesman.

chat e laine (shat′l ān), *n.* 1 mistress or lady of a castle. 2 clasp or chain worn at a woman's waist, to which keys, a purse, etc., are fastened. [< French *châtelaine*]

Chat ham (chat′əm), *n.* first **Earl of.** See **Pitt, William.**

Chat ta hoo chee River (chat′ə hü′chē), river flowing from N Georgia that forms the southern half of the boundary between Georgia and Alabama. 400 mi.

Chat ta noo ga (chat′n ü′gə), *n.* city in SE Tennessee, on the Tennessee River. 119,000.

chat tel (chat′l), *n.* 1 piece of property that is not real estate; any movable possession. Furniture, automobiles, and animals are chattels. 2 slave or bondman. [< Old French *chatel* < Latin *capitale,* neuter of *capitalis.* Doublet of CAPITAL[1], CATTLE.]

chat ter (chat′ər), *v.i.* 1 talk constantly, rapidly, and foolishly about unimportant things. 2 make quick, indistinct sounds: *Monkeys chatter.* 3 rattle together: *Cold can make a person's teeth chatter.* 4 (of a cutting tool) vibrate in cutting. *—v.t.* utter constantly, rapidly, and foolishly. 2 utter with quick, indistinct sounds. 3 cause to rattle together. *—n.* 1 quick, foolish talk about unimportant things. 2 quick, indistinct sounds: *the continual chatter of the sparrows.* 3 sound of rattling together: *the chatter of teeth.* [imitative] **—chat′ter er,** *n.*

chat ter box (chat′ər boks′), *n.* person who chatters.

Chat ter ton (chat′ər tən), *n.* **Thomas,** 1752-1770, English poet.

chat ty (chat′ē), *adj.,* **-ti er, -ti est.** 1 fond of friendly, familiar talk about unimportant things. 2 having the style or manner of friendly, familiar talk: *a chatty article about women's fashions in the newspaper.* **—chat′ti ly,** *adv.* **—chat′ti ness,** *n.*

Chau cer (chô′sər), *n.* **Geoffrey,** 1340?-1400, English poet, author of *The Canterbury Tales.*

chauf feur (shō′fər, shō fėr′), *n.* person whose work is driving an automobile, usually as the employee of a private person or company. —*v.t.* act as a chauffeur to; drive around. [< French, literally, stoker < *chauffer* to heat; the term arose in the days of steam automobiles]

chau tau qua or **Chau tau qua** (shə-tô′kwə), *n.* 1 an assembly for education and entertainment of adults by lectures, concerts, etc., held for several days. 2 **Chautauqua,** lake and village in SW New York where chautauquas were first held.

chau vin ism (shō′və niz′əm), *n.* 1 boastful, warlike patriotism; unreasoning enthusiasm for the military glory of one's country. 2 an excessive enthusiasm for one's sex, race, or group: *no lack of female chauvinism.* [< French *chauvinisme* < Nicolas *Chauvin,* an old soldier and enthusiastic admirer of Napoleon I]

chau vin ist (shō′və nist), *n.* 1 a boastful, warlike patriot. 2 person excessively enthusiastic about his or her sex, race, or group: *a male chauvinist.* —*adj.* chauvinistic.

chau vin is tic (shō′və nis′tik), *adj.* of chauvinism or chauvinists. **—chau′vin-is′ti cal ly,** *adv.*

cheap (chēp), *adj.* 1 costing little; low in price: *Eggs are cheap out in the country.* See synonym study below. 2 costing less than it is worth. 3 charging low prices: *a cheap market.* 4 costing little effort; easily obtained. 5 of little value; not worth respect; common: *cheap entertainment.* 6 **feel cheap,** feel inferior and ashamed. 7 (of money) obtainable at a low rate of interest. 8 reduced in value or purchasing power, as money depreciated by inflation: *cheap silver.* —*adv.* at a low price; at small cost: *I sold the car cheap to get rid of it.* [short for *good cheap* a good bargain; Old English *cēap* price, bargain] **—cheap′ly,** *adv.* **—cheap′-ness,** *n.*

Syn. *adj.* 1 **Cheap, inexpensive** mean costing little. **Cheap** means low in price, but often is used to express a demeaning attitude toward the thing and to suggest low quality worth no more or even less than the price: *I won't wear cheap shoes.* **Inexpensive** means not expensive, suggests a quality worth the price or even more, and usually expresses a more impersonal attitude: *This inexpensive car gives good gas mileage.*

cheap en (chē′pən), *v.t.* 1 make cheap; lower the price of. 2 cause to be thought little of. —*v.i.* become cheap. **—cheap′en er,** *n.*

cheap jack or **cheap-Jack** (chēp′jak′), INFORMAL. —*n.* a person who deals in cheap or worthless goods. —*adj.* worthless; useless; inferior.

cheap skate (chēp′skāt′), *n.* INFORMAL. a stingy, miserly person.

cheat (chēt), *v.i.* play or do business in a way that is not honest; practice deceit: *cheat at cards.* —*v.t.* deceive to further one's own purposes; trick; hoodwink; swindle; defraud: *cheat someone out of his money.* See synonym study below. —*n.* 1 person who is not honest and does things to deceive or trick others. 2 fraud; trick. [variant of *escheat*] **—cheat′er,** *n.*

Syn. *v.t.* **Cheat, trick** mean to gain or seek to gain an advantage by underhand means. **Cheat** means to do so by misrepresentation: *He cheated me by short-changing me.* **Trick** implies using a misleading device: *The FBI used fake plans to trick the spy.*

check (chek), *v.t.* 1 stop suddenly: *They checked their steps.* See **stop** for synonym study. 2 hold back; control; restrain: *check one's anger, check a forest fire.* See synonym study below. 3 repel or reverse: *check an enemy attack.* 4 examine or compare to prove true or right: *Check your answers with mine.* 5 mark (something found true or right). 6 leave or take for safekeeping: *check one's hat in the lobby. The hotel checked our baggage.* 7 mark in a pattern of squares. 8 U.S. send (baggage) to a particular place: *I shall check my bag through to Chicago.* 9 (in chess) put (an opponent's king) in a position of danger so that it must be moved or the danger avoided in some other way. —*v.i.* 1 correspond accurately when compared, usually with a duplicate or the original: *The two copies check.* 2 examine something to discover facts or prove true or right. 3 U.S. crack or split along crossing lines, as timber or a painted surface. 4 (in chess) move so that an opponent's king is in immediate danger.

check in, a arrive and register at a hotel, etc. **b** SLANG. die.

check off, mark as checked and found true or right.

check out, a U.S. pay one's bill at a hotel, store, etc., when leaving. **b** inspect or examine to see if in proper order, condition, etc.: *check out a plane before takeoff.* **c** prove right or true: *check out a fact or statement.* **d** SLANG. die.

check up, U.S. examine or compare to prove true or correct.

—*n.* 1 a sudden stop: *The storm warning put a check to our plans for a picnic.* 2 a holding back; control; restraint. 3 **in check,** held back; controlled. 4 any person, thing, or event that controls or holds back action. A rein used to prevent a horse from lowering his head is a check. 5 a rebuff; repulse; reverse. 6 examination or comparison to prove something true or right: *My work will be a check on yours.* 7 a mark (√) to show that something has been examined or compared. Usually this mark indicates that the thing is true or right. Sometimes, as on examinations, it indicates something false or wrong. 8 ticket or token given in return for a coat, hat, baggage, package, etc., to show the right to claim again later. 9 a written order directing a bank to pay money to the person named; cheque. 10 a written statement of the amount owed in a restaurant. 11 a pattern made of squares: *Do you want a check or a stripe for your new shirt?* 12 a single one of these squares: *The checks in this shirt are big.* 13 fabric having a pattern of squares. 14 U.S. a crack; split. 15 (in chess) the position of an opponent's king when it is in danger.

—*adj.* 1 used in checking. 2 marked in a pattern of squares.

—*interj.* 1 (in chess) a call in the game of chess warning that an opponent's king is in danger and must be moved. 2 INFORMAL. OK.

[< Old French *eschequier* < *eschec* a check at chess, ultimately < Persian *shāh* king, king at chess] **—check′a ble,** *adj.*

Syn. *v.t.* 2 **Check, restrain, curb** mean to hold someone or something back. **Check** suggests the use of some means that slows up or stands in the way of action or progress: *Deep mud checked the progress of the march.* **Restrain** suggests use of some force to keep down or within limits or to prevent completely: *A bystander restrained him from hitting the man.* **Curb** suggests use of a control that pulls back suddenly or keeps from acting freely: *His good sense curbed his impulse to hit the man.*

hat, āge, fär; let, ēqual, tėrm;
it, īce; hot, ōpen, ôrder;
oil, out; cup, pu̇t, rüle;
ch, child; ng, long; sh, she;
th, thin; ᴛʜ, then; zh, measure;
ə represents *a* in about, *e* in taken,
i in pencil, *o* in lemon, *u* in circus.
< = from, derived from, taken from.

check book (chek′bu̇k′), *n.* book of blank checks on a bank.

check er[1] (chek′ər), *v.t.* 1 to mark (something) in a pattern of squares of different colors. 2 mark off with patches different from one another: *The ground under the trees was checkered with sunlight and shade.* —*n.* 1 pattern of squares of different colors. 2 one of these squares. 3 one of the flat, round pieces used in the game of checkers. 4 the service tree. Also, BRITISH **chequer.** [< Old French *eschequier* chessboard < *eschec.* See CHECK.]

check er[2] (chek′ər), *n.* 1 person or thing that checks. 2 U.S. cashier in a self-service store or market. [< *check*]

check er ber ry (chek′ər ber′ē), *n., pl.* **-ries.** 1 the bright-red berry of the wintergreen plant. 2 the plant. 3 partridgeberry.

check er board (chek′ər bôrd′, chek′ər-bōrd′), *n.* board marked in a pattern of 64 squares of two alternating colors, used in playing checkers or chess; chessboard.

check ered (chek′ərd), *adj.* 1 marked in a pattern of squares of different colors. 2 marked in patches. 3 often changing; varied; irregular: *a checkered career.*

check ers (chek′ərz), *n.* game played by two people, each with 12 round, flat pieces to move on a checkerboard.

checking account, bank account against which checks may be drawn.

check list (chek′list′), *n.* list of names, titles, jobs, etc., arranged to form a ready means of reference, comparison, or checking.

check mate (chek′māt′), *v.,* **-mat ed, -mat ing,** *n.* —*v.t.* 1 (in chess) put (an opponent's king) in check from which his next move cannot free him, and so win the game. 2 defeat completely. 3 counteract a scheme or action of (an opponent), making it useless or ineffective. —*n.* 1 (in chess) a move that ends the game by putting the opponent's king in check so that he is unable to escape by his next move. 2 a complete defeat. [< Old French *eschec mat* < Persian *shāh māt* the king is dead]

check off (chek′ôf′, chek′of′), *n.* system of collecting union dues through wage deductions made by the employer on the union's behalf.

check out (chek′out′), *n.* a careful inspection of something before it is approved.

checkout counter, U.S. counter in a store where a cashier collects payment for merchandise purchased.

check point (chek′point′), *n.* place of inspection on a road, at a border, etc.

check rein (chek′rān′), *n.* 1 a short rein attached to the saddle or harness to keep a horse from lowering its head. 2 a short rein connecting the bit of one of a team of horses to the driving rein of the other.

check room (chek′rüm′, chek′ru̇m′), *n.*

place where coats, hats, baggage, packages, etc., can be left until called for later.

checks and balances, 1 U.S. limitations set on the powers of any branch of the government by requiring that each branch obtain the consent of the others to make its acts constitutional. 2 any system of limitations whereby contrary forces or powers are kept in balance.

check up (chek′up′), *n.* 1 a careful inspection. 2 a thorough physical examination.

Ched dar (ched′ər), *n.* kind of hard, white or yellow cheese. [< *Cheddar,* a village in England, where it was first made]

cheek (chēk), *n.* 1 side of the face below either eye. 2 **cheek by jowl, a** side by side; close together. **b** close; intimate. 3 something suggesting the human cheek in form or position, such as a jamb. 4 INFORMAL. saucy talk or behavior; impudence. [Old English *cēce*]

cheek bone (chēk′bōn′), *n.* bone just below either eye.

cheek y (chē′kē), *adj.,* **cheek i er, cheek i est.** saucy; impudent. **—cheek′i ly,** *adv.* **—cheek′i ness,** *n.*

cheep (chēp), *v.i.* make a short, sharp sound such as a young bird makes; chirp; peep. *—n.* a short, sharp sound such as a young bird makes; chirp; peep. [imitative] **—cheep′er,** *n.*

cheer (chir), *n.* 1 a shout of encouragement, approval, praise, etc. 2 joy or gladness; comfort; encouragement: *The warmth of the fire and a good meal brought cheer to our hearts again.* 3 food: *We enjoyed our Christmas cheer.* 4 state of mind; condition of feeling: *My friends encouraged me to be of good cheer.* 5 **What cheer?** How are you? *—v.t.* 1 urge on with cheers: *Everyone cheered our team.* 2 give joy or gladness to; comfort; encourage: *It cheered the old woman to have us visit her.* See synonym study below. 3 greet or welcome with cheers. *—v.i.* shout encouragement, approval, praise, etc.

cheer up, make or become happier; be glad; raise one's spirits.

—interj. **cheers,** word used in drinking to a person's health.

[< Old French *chere* face, cheer] **—cheer′er,** *n.*

Syn. *v.t.* 2 **Cheer, gladden** mean to raise a person's spirits. **Cheer** suggests either making a person feel less downhearted by giving comfort and encouragement (often *cheer up*) or putting him in high spirits by giving pleasure or joy: *The news cheered everyone.* **Gladden** suggests putting a person in good spirits by giving delight and making him feel happy: *Their son's success gladdened both their hearts.*

cheer ful (chir′fəl), *adj.* 1 full of cheer; joyful; glad: *a smiling, cheerful person.* 2 filling with cheer; pleasant; bright: *a cheerful, sunny room.* 3 willing: *a cheerful giver.* **—cheer′ful ly,** *adv.* **—cheer′ful ness,** *n.*

cheer lead er (chir′lē′dər), *n.* person who leads a group in organized cheering, especially at high-school or college athletic events.

cheer less (chir′lis), *adj.* without joy or comfort; gloomy; dreary. **—cheer′less ly,** *adv.* **—cheer′less ness,** *n.*

cheer y (chir′ē), *adj.,* **cheer i er, cheer i est.** cheerful; pleasant; bright; gay. **—cheer′i ly,** *adv.* **—cheer′i ness,** *n.*

cheese (chēz), *n.* 1 a solid food made from the curds of milk. 2 mass of this pressed or molded into a shape, often covered with a rind. [Old English *cēse* < Latin *caseus*] **—cheese′like′,** *adj.*

cheese burg er (chēz′bėr′gər), *n.* a hamburger sandwich with a slice of melted cheese on top of the meat.

cheese cake (chēz′kāk′), *n.* kind of cake or pie made of cottage cheese or cream cheese, cream, eggs, sugar, etc., baked together.

cheese cloth (chēz′klôth′, chēz′kloth′), *n., pl.* **-cloths** (-klôᴛʜz′, -klôths′; -kloᴛʜz′, -kloths′). a thin, loosely woven cotton cloth, originally used for wrapping cheese.

chees y (chē′zē), *adj.,* **chees i er, chees i est.** 1 of or like cheese. 2 SLANG. of low quality; inferior.

chee tah (chē′tə), *n.* a flesh-eating, spotted mammal of the cat family somewhat like a leopard, found in southern Asia and Africa. Cheetahs run very fast and can be trained to hunt deer and antelope. [< Hindustani *chītā*]

cheetah 2½ ft. high at the shoulder

chef (shef), *n.* 1 a head cook. 2 any cook. [< French < Old French. Doublet of CHIEF.]

chef-d'oeu vre (she dœ′vrə), *n., pl.* ***chefs-d'oeu vre*** (she dœ′vrə). FRENCH. masterpiece.

Che foo (chē′fü′, ju′fü′), *n.* seaport in NE China. 140,000.

Che khov (chek′ôf), *n.* **Anton,** 1860-1904, Russian author of short stories, plays, and novels.

che la (kē′lə), *n., pl.* **-lae** (-lē). the prehensile claw of a lobster, crab, scorpion, etc., resembling a pincer. [< Latin *chele* < Greek *chēlē* claw]

che late (kē′lāt), *adj.* having a chela or chelae.

che lo ni an (ki lō′nē ən), *adj.* of turtles and tortoises. *—n.* turtle; tortoise. [< Greek *chelōnē* tortoise]

chem., 1 chemical. 2 chemist. 3 chemistry.

chem ic (kem′ik), *adj.* ARCHAIC. 1 chemical. 2 of alchemy.

chem i cal (kem′ə kəl), *adj.* 1 of, having to do with, or in chemistry. 2 made by or used in chemistry. 3 working, operated, or done by using chemicals: *a chemical fire extinguisher.* *—n.* any substance obtained by or used in a chemical process. Sulfuric acid, sodium bicarbonate, and borax are chemicals.

chemical change, (in chemistry) a change in which one substance is converted into one or more substances with different properties.

chemical engineering, science or profession of using chemistry for industrial purposes.

chem i cal ly (kem′ik lē), *adv.* 1 according to chemistry. 2 by chemical processes.

chemical warfare, the technique or use of gases, flames, smoke, or any chemicals other than explosives as weapons.

chem i lu mi nes cence (kem′ə lü′mənes′ns), *n.* the production of light by chemical reaction, without a rise in temperature.

che mise (shə mēz′), *n.* 1 a loose, shirtlike undergarment worn by women and girls. 2 a loosely fitting dress without a belt. [< Old French < Late Latin *camisia* shirt]

chem ist (kem′ist), *n.* 1 an expert in chemistry. 2 BRITISH. druggist.

chem is try (kem′ə strē), *n., pl.* **-tries.** 1 science that deals with the properties, composition, structure, and interactions of matter, and the energy changes that accompany these interactions. 2 the application of this science to a certain subject: *the chemistry of foods, the chemistry of plant cells.*

chemo-, *combining form.* chemical; by chemical reaction: *Chemosynthesis = chemical synthesis.* [< *chemical*]

chem o re cep tor (kem′ō ri sep′tər), *n.* a nerve ending or sense organ that reacts to chemical stimulation, as the taste buds in the tongue.

chem o sphere (kem′ə sfir′), *n.* region of predominant photochemical activity in the outer stratosphere, the mesosphere, and the ionosphere. See **atmosphere** for diagram.

chem o ster i lant (kem′ō ster′ə lənt), *n.* a chemical substance that destroys the ability of an organism, such as an insect, to reproduce.

chem o syn the sis (kem′ō sin′thə sis), *n.* the formation by cells of carbohydrates from carbon dioxide and water with energy obtained from some chemical reaction, rather than from light, as in photosynthesis.

chem o tax is (kem′ō tak′sis), *n.* movement of a cell, organism, or part of an organism toward or away from a chemical substance.

chem o ther a peu tic (kem′ō ther′ə-pyü′tik), *adj.* having to do with treatment by chemotherapy. **—chem′o ther′a peu′ti cal ly,** *adv.*

chem o ther a py (kem′ō ther′ə pē), *n.* the treatment of disease and infection by chemicals that have a specific toxic effect on the disease-producing organisms.

che mot ro pism (ke mo′trə piz′əm), *n.* tendency of an organism or part of an organism to turn or bend in response to a chemical stimulus.

chem ur gist (kem′ər jist), *n.* an expert in chemurgy.

chem ur gy (kem′ər jē), *n.* branch of chemistry that deals with the use of farm and forest products, such as casein and cornstalks, for purposes other than food and clothing. [< *chem(istry)* + Greek *-ourgia* work]

Cheng tu (cheng′tü′), *n.* walled city in central China. 1,107,000.

che nille (shə nēl′), *n.* 1 a soft, velvety cord of cotton, silk, or wool, used in embroidery, fringe, etc. 2 fabric woven from this cord, used for rugs, bedspreads, housecoats, etc. [< French, literally, caterpillar; from its furry look]

che ong-sam (chē′ong säm′, chē′ong-sam′), *n.* a one-piece garment with a high, round collar and slits on the sides of the skirt, worn by women in China. [< Chinese (Canton) *cheong sam*]

Che ops (kē′ops), *n.* 2600? B.C., Greek name of Khufu, king of Egypt who built the largest of the Pyramids.

cheque (chek), *n.* BRITISH. check (def. 9).

cheq uer (chek′ər), *v.t., n.* BRITISH. checker[1].

Cheq uers (chek′ərz), *n.* the official country residence of the prime minister of Great Britain, in Buckinghamshire, northwest of London.

Cher bourg (sher′bu̇rg), *n.* seaport in NW

France, on the English Channel. 38,000.

cher ish (cher′ish), *v.t.* 1 hold dear; treat with affection; care for tenderly: *Parents cherish their children.* 2 keep in mind; cling to: *We all cherished the hope of their safe return from the dangerous journey.* See synonym study below. [< Middle French *cheriss-*, a form of *cherir* < *cher* dear < Latin *carus*]

Syn. 2 **Cherish, foster, harbor,** when applied to an idea or feeling, mean to keep it in mind and care for it. **Cherish** implies treasuring it and watching over it with loving care: *He cherished memories of college days.* **Foster** suggests nourishing an idea or feeling, and helping it to grow: *She tries to foster tolerance.* **Harbor** suggests letting in a bad idea or feeling and brooding over it: *He harbors resentment of criticism.*

Cher o kee (cher′ə kē′, cher′ə kē′), *n., pl.* **-kee** or **-kees** for 1. 1 member of a tribe of Iroquois Indians of the southern Appalachians, now living mostly in Oklahoma. 2 their Iroquoian language.

Cherokee rose, rose growing wild in the southern United States. It is an evergreen plant with glossy leaflets and fragrant white flowers.

che root (shə rüt′), *n.* a long, narrow cigar cut off square at both ends. [< French *cheroute* < Tamil *shuruṭṭu* roll]

cher ry (cher′ē), *n., pl.* **-ries,** *adj.* —*n.* 1 a small, round, edible, juicy fruit with a stone or pit in it. 2 tree of the rose family that it grows on. 3 wood of this tree. 4 a bright red. —*adj.* 1 made of the wood of the cherry tree. 2 bright-red. [Middle English *chery,* back formation from *cherys* < Old North French *cherise* < Popular Latin *ceresia* < Late Greek *kerasia* cherry tree < Greek *kerasos*] **—cher′ry like′,** *adj.*

chert (chėrt), *n.* an impure variety of granular quartz, consisting of submicroscopic crystals, similar to flint but lighter in color. [origin unknown]

cher ub (cher′əb), *n., pl.* **cher u bim** for 1 and 2, **cher ubs** for 3 and 4. 1 one of the second highest order of angels. 2 picture or statue of a child with wings, or of a child's head with wings but no body. 3 a beautiful, innocent, or good child. 4 person with a chubby, innocent face. [< Latin < Greek *cheroub* < Hebrew *kerūb*]

che ru bic (chə rü′bik), *adj.* 1 of or like a cherub; angelic. 2 innocent; good. 3 chubby. **—che ru′bi cal ly,** *adv.*

cher u bim (cher′ə bim, cher′yə bim), *n.* 1 a pl. of **cherub** (defs. 1 and 2). 2 (formerly) cherub.

cher vil (chėr′vəl), *n.* plant of the same family as the parsley. The leaves, roots, and seeds are used to flavor soups, salads, etc. [Old English *cerfille*]

Ches a peake (ches′ə pēk′), *n.* city in E Virginia. 90,000.

Chesapeake Bay, bay of the Atlantic, in Maryland and Virginia. 200 mi. long; from 4 to 40 mi. wide.

Chesh ire (chesh′ər, chesh′ir), *n.* county in W England. Also, **Chester.**

Cheshire cat, 1 the grinning cat in *Alice in Wonderland.* It faded away until finally only its grin was left. 2 any creature that grins fixedly.

chess (ches), *n.* game played by two people, with 16 pieces to move on a checkerboard. The object of the game is to checkmate the other's king. [< Old French *esches,* plural of *eschec.* See CHECK.]

chess board (ches′bôrd′, ches′bōrd′), *n.* checkerboard.

chess man (ches′man′, ches′mən), *n., pl.* **-men.** one of the pieces used in playing chess.

chest (chest), *n.* 1 the front surface of the human body between the neck and the abdomen. 2 the corresponding part of an animal. 3 thorax. 4 a large box with a lid, used for holding things: *a linen chest, a tool chest.* 5 piece of furniture with drawers. 6 a tight container for gas, steam, etc. 7 place where money belonging to a public institution is kept; treasury. 8 the money itself. [Old English *cest, cist* < Latin *cista* < Greek *kistē* box]

-chested, *combining form.* having a ___ chest: *Broad-chested = having a broad chest.*

Ches ter (ches′tər), *n.* 1 city in W England. 61,000. 2 Cheshire.

ches ter field (ches′tər fēld′), *n.* 1 a single-breasted overcoat with the buttons hidden and a velvet collar. 2 (in Great Britain and Canada) a sofa. [< the fourth Earl of *Chesterfield*]

Ches ter field (ches′tər fēld′), *n.* the fourth **Earl of,** 1694-1773, British statesman who wrote witty and instructive letters to his son containing directions about manners and etiquette.

Ches ter ton (ches′tər tən), *n.* **Gilbert Keith,** 1874-1936, English author and critic.

chest nut (ches′nut, ches′nət), *n.* 1 any of a genus of trees belonging to the same family as the beech, that bears sweet, edible nuts in prickly burs. 2 nut of any of these trees. 3 wood of any of these trees. 4 a reddish brown. 5 a reddish-brown horse. 6 the hard knob in the skin of a horse at the inner side of the foreleg. 7 INFORMAL. a stale joke or story. —*adj.* reddish-brown. [< obsolete *chesten* chestnut (< Old French *chastaigne* < Latin *castanea* < Greek *kastanea*) + *nut*]

che val-de-frise (shə val′də frēz′), *n., pl.* **chevaux-de-frise** (shə vō′də frēz′). 1 piece of wood with spikes sticking out, formerly used to hinder the advance of enemy cavalry. 2 row of spikes or broken glass on top of a wall. [< French, literally, horse of Friesland; first used by Frisians to make up for lack of cavalry]

che val glass (shə val′), a tall mirror mounted in a frame so that it swings between its supports. [*cheval* < French, horse, support]

chev a lier (shev′ə lir′), *n.* 1 ARCHAIC. knight. 2 member of the lowest rank in the Legion of Honor of France. [< Old French < Late Latin *caballarius* horseman. Doublet of CABALLERO, CAVALIER.]

chev i ot (shev′ē ət *for 1 and 2;* chev′ē ət, chē′vē ət *for 3*), *n.* 1 a rough, woolen cloth. 2 a cotton cloth like it. 3 **Cheviot,** a hardy breed of sheep with heavy bodies and fine, thick-set wool, that originated in the Cheviot Hills.

Chev i ot Hills (chev′ē ət, chē′vē ət), hills on the boundary between England and Scotland. Highest peak, 2676 ft.

chev ron (shev′rən), *n.* 1 a cloth design shaped like a ∧ or ∨, worn on the sleeve by noncommissioned officers, policemen, etc., as an indication of rank, length of service, or wounds in war. 2 design shaped like ∧, used in coats of arms and in architecture. [< Middle French, rafter < *chèvre* goat < Latin *capra*]

chew (chü), *v.t.* 1 crush or grind with the teeth or as if with the teeth. 2 think over; consider. —*v.i.* 1 use the teeth, or toothlike parts, to crush or grind something. 2 think something over; meditate. —*n.* 1 a chewing. 2 thing chewed; piece for chewing. [Old English *cēowan*] **—chew′a ble,** *adj.* **—chew′er,** *n.*

hat, āge, fär; let, ēqual, tėrm;
it, īce; hot, ōpen, ôrder;
oil, out; cup, pu̇t, rüle;
ch, child; ng, long; sh, she;
th, thin; ᴛʜ, then; zh, measure;

ə represents *a* in about, *e* in taken, *i* in pencil, *o* in lemon, *u* in circus.

< = from, derived from, taken from.

chewing gum, gum for chewing. It is usually chicle that has been sweetened and flavored.

che wink (chi wingk′), *n.* towhee. [imitative]

chew y (chü′ē), *adj.,* **chew i er, chew i est.** suitable for or requiring much chewing: *chewy caramels.* **—chew′i ness,** *n.*

Chey enne (shī an′, shī en′ *for 1 and 2;* shī en′ *for 3 and 4*), *n., pl.* **-enne** or **-ennes** for 3. 1 capital of Wyoming, in the SE part. 41,000. 2 **Cheyenne River,** river flowing from E Wyoming into the Missouri River in South Dakota. 290 mi. 3 member of an Algonquian tribe of Indians, now living in Montana and Oklahoma. 4 their language.

chg., *pl.* **chgs.** charge.

chi (kī), *n.* the 22nd letter of the Greek alphabet (Χ, χ), corresponding to the sound of *k* and the spelling *ch* in English.

Chiang Kai-shek (chyäng′ kī′shek′; chyang′ kī′shek′), born 1886, Chinese general and political leader, president of Nationalist China in 1948, and of its government on Taiwan since 1950.

Chi an ti (kē än′tē), *n.* a dry, red Italian wine. [< the *Chianti* Mountains in Italy]

Chi a pas (chē ä′päs), *n.* state in SE Mexico.

chi a ro scu ro (kē är′ə skyu̇r′ō), *n., pl.* **-ros.** 1 treatment of light and shade in a picture. 2 art using only light and shade in pictures. 3 a sketch in black and white. [< Italian, clear-dark]

chic (shēk, shik), *adj.* up-to-date in fashion; stylish. —*n.* style: *She is famous for her chic.* [< French]

Chi ca go (shə kô′gō, shə kä′gō), *n.* city in NE Illinois, on Lake Michigan. Chicago is the second largest city in the United States. 3,369,000.

chi can er y (shi kā′nər ē), *n., pl.* **-er ies.** low trickery; unfair practice. [< Middle French *chicanerie* < *chicaner* to quibble]

Chi ca no (chi kä′nō), *n.* an American of Mexican descent; Mexican American.

chi chi (shē′shē′), *adj.* 1 self-consciously or pretentiously ornate; arty. 2 overelegant; elaborately chic. [< French]

chick (chik), *n.* 1 a young chicken. 2 a young bird. 3 child. 4 SLANG. girl.

chick a dee (chik′ə dē′), *n.* a small bird of the titmouse family with black, white, and gray feathers, and usually a black head. Its cry sounds somewhat like its name. [imitative]

Chick a mau ga (chik′ə mô gə), *n.* a small creek flowing from NW Georgia into the

Tennessee River. The Confederates defeated the Union army there in 1863.

chick a ree (chik′ə rē′), *n.* the red squirrel of North America. [imitative]

Chick a saw (chik′ə sô), *n., pl.* **-saw** or **-saws** for 1. 1 member of a tribe of American Indians, now living in western Oklahoma. 2 their language.

chick en (chik′ən), *n.* 1 a young hen or rooster. 2 any hen or rooster. 3 flesh of a chicken used for food. 4 any young bird. 5 SLANG. a young person. 6 SLANG. person who is afraid, especially one who is cowardly. *—adj.* 1 SLANG. afraid of risk; cowardly. 2 young; small: *a chicken lobster.* [Old English *cīcen*]

chicken hawk, any of certain hawks that raid poultry yards.

chic ken-heart ed (chik′ən här′tid), *adj.* timid; cowardly.

chicken pox, a mild, contagious, viral disease, chiefly affecting children, accompanied by a rash on the skin; varicella.

chicken snake, one of several American snakes which eat chickens and eggs; rat snake.

chicken wire, light wire fence with mesh of about one inch.

chick pea (chik′pē′), *n.* 1 an annual plant of the pea family. Its short, puffy pods contain pealike seeds which are used for food. 2 one of these seeds.

chick weed (chik′wēd′), *n.* any of several genera of pinks that are common weeds and have small white flowers. The leaves and seeds of many kinds are eaten by birds.

chic le (chik′əl), *n.* a tasteless, gummy substance used in making chewing gum. It is the dried milky juice of a sapodilla tree of tropical America. [< Mexican Spanish < Nahuatl *tzictli*]

Chic o pee (chik′ə pē), *n.* city in S Massachusetts.

chic or y (chik′ər ē), *n., pl.* **-or ies.** 1 any of a genus of plants of the composite family with deep, hard roots and blue, purple, or white flowers, whose leaves are used as salad. 2 plant of this genus with bright-blue flowers; succory. 3 its root, roasted and used as a substitute for coffee or in a mixture with ground coffee. [< Middle French *chicoree* < Latin *cichoreum* < Greek *kichoreion*]

chid (chid), *v.* a pt. and a pp. of **chide.**

chide (chīd), *v.,* **chid ed, chid, chid ing.** *—v.t.* find fault with; reproach or blame; scold: *She chided the little girl for soiling her dress.* See **scold** for synonym study. *—v.i.* find fault; speak in rebuke: *The head nurse was always scolding and chiding.* [Old English *cīdan*] **—chid′er,** *n.* **—chid′ing ly,** *adv.*

chief (chēf), *n.* 1 head of a group; person highest in rank or authority; leader. 2 head of a tribe or clan. 3 **in chief,** at the head; of the highest rank or authority. *—adj.* 1 at the head; highest in rank or authority; leading. 2 most important; main: *the chief town in the county.* [< Old French *chief, chef* < Latin *caput* head. Doublet of CHEF.] **—chief′less,** *adj.*

chief executive, 1 head of the executive branch of a government or large corporation. 2 **Chief Executive,** the President of the United States or the governor of a state.

chief justice, 1 judge who acts as chairman of a group of judges in a court. 2 **Chief Justice,** the presiding judge of the United States Supreme Court.

chief ly (chēf′lē), *adv.* 1 for the most part; mainly; mostly: *This juice is made up chiefly of tomatoes.* 2 first of all; above all: *We visited Washington chiefly to see the Capitol and the White House.* *—adj.* of or proper to a chief: *his chiefly bearing, chiefly status.*

chief master sergeant, (in the U.S. Air Force) a noncommissioned officer who ranks next above a senior master sergeant.

chief of staff, 1 the senior officer of the staff of a general or admiral. 2 **Chief of Staff,** the senior officer of the Army or Air Force of the United States.

chief petty officer, (in the U.S. Navy) the highest noncommissioned rank.

chief tain (chēf′tən), *n.* 1 chief of a clan or tribe. 2 head of a group; leader. [< Old French *chevetaine* < Late Latin *capitaneus.* Doublet of CAPTAIN.]

chief tain cy (chēf′tən sē), *n., pl.* **-cies.** position or rank of a chieftain.

chief tain ship (chēf′tən ship), *n.* chieftaincy.

chif fon (shi fon′, shif′on), *n.* 1 a very thin silk or rayon cloth, used for dresses. 2 **chiffons,** *pl.* laces, ribbons, or finery. *—adj.* whipped light and fluffy: *chiffon pie.* [< French < *chiffe* rag]

chif fo nier (shif′ə nir′), *n.* a high chest of drawers, often having a mirror. [< French *chiffonnier* < *chiffon*]

chig ger (chig′ər), *n.* 1 larva of certain mites; chigoe. Chiggers stick to the skin and suck the blood, causing severe itching. 2 chigoe (def. 1). [alteration of *chigoe*]

chi gnon (shē′nyon; *French* shē nyôɴ′), *n.* a large knot or roll of hair worn at the back of the head by women. [< French]

chig oe (chig′ō), *n.* 1 flea of the West Indies, tropical South America, Africa, and India; chigger. The female burrows under the skin of people and animals, where it causes severe itching and sores. 2 chigger (def. 1). [< French *chique,* of West Indian origin]

Chi hua hua (chi wä′wä), *n.* 1 state in N Mexico. 2 its capital, in the central part. 364,000. 3 Also, **chihuahua.** a very small dog of an ancient Mexican breed, usually weighing from one to six pounds.

chil blain (chil′blān′), *n.* Usually, **chilblains,** *pl.* an itching sore or redness on the hands or feet caused chiefly by exposure to cold.

child (chīld), *n., pl.* **chil dren.** 1 a young boy or girl. 2 son or daughter. 3 baby; infant. 4 **with child,** pregnant. 5 descendant. 6 person like a child in nearness, affection, interest, etc. 7 an immature person; childish person. 8 result; product: *Invention is the child of necessity.* 9 person considered as the product of particular forces, influences, etc.: *a child of nature.* [Old English *cild*]

child bear ing (chīld′ber′ing, chīld′bar′ing), *n.* act of giving birth to children. *—adj.* able to bear children.

child bed (chīld′bed′), *n.* condition of a woman giving birth to a child.

childbed fever, infection of the genital tract occurring after childbirth.

child birth (chīld′bėrth′), *n.* act of giving birth to a child.

child hood (chīld′hůd), *n.* 1 condition of being a child. 2 time during which one is a child.

child ish (chīl′dish), *adj.* 1 of a child. 2 like a child. 3 not suitable for a grown person; weak; silly; foolish: *Crying for things you can't have is childish.* **—child′ish ly,** *adv.* **—child′ish ness,** *n.*

➤ **Childish, childlike** differ widely in their connotations when applied to adults, though both mean resembling or having the characteristics of a child. *Childish* is derogatory since it emphasizes characteristics which one might be expected to have outgrown: *Pouting when scolded is childish. Childlike,* however, emphasizes such characteristics as innocence, simplicity, and frankness and suggests regret that most adults have lost them: *He has a childlike love for a circus.*

child labor, work done by children in factories, business, etc., legally restricted in most of the United States.

child less (chīld′lis), *adj.* having no child. **—child′less ness,** *n.*

child like (chīld′līk′), *adj.* like or suitable to a child; innocent; frank; simple. **—child′like′ness,** *n.* ➤ See **childish** for usage note.

chil dren (chil′drən), *n.* pl. of **child.**

child's play, something very easy to do.

chil e (chil′ē), *n.* chili.

Chil e (chil′ē), *n.* country in SW South America, on the Pacific coast. 9,780,000 pop.; 286,400 sq. mi. *Capital:* Santiago. **—Chil′e an,** *adj., n.*

chil e con car ne (chil′ē kon kär′nē), chili con carne.

Chile saltpeter, sodium nitrate, found abundantly in Chile.

chil i (chil′ē), *n., pl.* **chil ies.** 1 a hot-tasting pod of red pepper, used for seasoning. 2 plant that it grows on, a tropical American shrub grown in the southern part of the United States. 3 chile con carne. Also, **chilli.** [< Mexican Spanish *chile* < Nahuatl *chilli*]

Chihuahua (def. 3)
7 in. high
at the shoulder

chili con carne (chil′ē kon kär′nē), a highly seasoned Mexican dish of chopped meat cooked with red peppers and, usually, kidney beans. Also, **chile con carne.** [< Spanish *chile con carne* chili with meat]

chili sauce, sauce made of red peppers, tomatoes, and spices, used on meat, fish, etc. Also, **chilli sauce.**

hat, āge, fär; let, ēqual, tėrm;
it, īce; hot, ōpen, ôrder;
oil, out; cup, pu̇t, rüle;
ch, child; ng, long; sh, she;
th, thin; ᴛʜ, then; zh, measure;

ə represents *a* in about, *e* in taken, *i* in pencil, *o* in lemon, *u* in circus.

< = from, derived from, taken from.

chill (chil), *n.* 1 an unpleasant coldness: *a chill in the air.* 2 a sudden coldness of the body with shivering. 3 a feeling cold; shivering. 4 lack of heartiness; unfriendliness. 5 a depressing influence; discouraging feeling. *—adj.* 1 unpleasantly cold: *a chill wind.* 2 cold in manner; unfriendly. 3 depressing; discouraging.
—v.i. 1 become cold; feel cold. 2 be affected with a sudden chill: *He chilled suddenly at seeing the ghost.* *—v.t.* 1 make cold. 2 cool without freezing. 3 depress; discourage. 4 harden (metal) on the surface by rapid cooling.
[Old English *ciele*] **—chill′ness,** *n.*

chil li (chil′ē), *n., pl.* **chil lies.** chili.

chill ing (chil′ing), *adj.* that chills. **—chill′ing ly,** *adv.*

chilli sauce, chili sauce.

chill y (chil′ē), *adj.,* **chill i er, chill i est.** 1 unpleasantly cool; rather cold: *a chilly day.* See **cold** for synonym study. 2 cold in manner; unfriendly: *a chilly greeting.* **—chill′i ly,** *adv.* **—chill′i ness,** *n.*

chi lo pod (kī′lə pod), *n.* any of a class of flat, elongated arthropods having one pair of long antennae, many body segments with one pair of long legs on most, and poison claws; centipede. [< Greek *cheilos* lip + *podos* foot]

chi maer a (kə mir′ə, kī mir′ə), *n.* chimera.

chime (chīm), *n., v.,* **chimed, chim ing.** *—n.* 1 set of bells tuned to a musical scale and played by hammers or simple machinery. 2 the musical sound made by a set of tuned bells. 3 agreement; harmony. *—v.i.* 1 ring out musically: *The bells chimed at midnight.* 2 agree; be in harmony. 3 **chime in, a** be in harmony; agree: *Her ideas chimed in perfectly with mine.* **b** break into a conversation. **c** join in. *—v.t.* 1 make musical sounds on (a set of tuned bells). 2 ring out: *The clock chimes midnight.* 3 say or utter in cadence or singsong. [< Old French *chimbe, cimble* < Latin *cymbalum.* See CYMBAL.] **—chim′er,** *n.*

chi mer a (kə mir′ə, kī mir′ə), *n.* 1 Also, **Chimera.** (in Greek myths) a monster with a lion's head, a goat's body, and a serpent's tail, supposed to breathe out fire. 2 a horrible creature of the imagination. 3 an absurd or impossible idea; wild fancy: *The hope of changing dirt to gold was a chimera.* 4 organism consisting of two or more tissues of different genetic composition, produced as a result of mutation, grafting, etc. Also, **chimaera.** [< Greek *chimaira* she-goat, chimera]

chi mer ic (kə mer′ik, kī mer′ik), *adj.* chimerical.

chi mer i cal (kə mer′ə kəl, kī mer′ə kəl), *adj.* 1 unreal; imaginary. 2 wildly fanciful; absurd; impossible: *chimerical schemes for getting rich.* **—chi mer′i cal ly,** *adv.*

chim ney (chim′nē), *n., pl.* **-neys.** 1 an upright structure of brick or stone, connected with a fireplace, furnace, etc., to make a draft and carry away smoke. 2 part of this that rises above a roof. 3 a glass tube placed around the flame of a lamp. 4 crack or opening in a rock, mountain, volcano, etc. [< Middle French *cheminée* < Late Latin *caminata* < Latin *caminus* oven < Greek *kaminos*] **—chim′ney less,** *adj.*

chimney corner, corner or side of a fireplace; place near the fire.

chimney piece, mantelpiece.

chimney pot, pipe of earthenware or metal fitted on top of a chimney to increase the draft.

chimney sweep, person whose work is cleaning out chimneys.

chimney swift, a small bird of North America with a short tail and long, narrow wings. It often builds its nest in unused chimneys.

chimp (chimp), *n.* INFORMAL. chimpanzee.

chim pan zee (chim′pan zē′, chim pan′zē), *n.* a manlike ape of equatorial Africa, smaller than a gorilla. It is probably the most intelligent ape. [< Bantu *(kivili)-chimpenze* ape]

chimpanzee 4½ ft. tall when standing

chin (chin), *n., v.,* **chinned, chin ning.** *—n.* 1 the front of the lower jaw below the mouth. 2 the lower surface of the face, below the mouth. 3 INFORMAL. a chat; gossip. *—v.t., v.i.* 1 **chin oneself,** hang by the hands from an overhead bar and pull oneself up until one's chin reaches the bar. 2 INFORMAL. chat; gossip. [Old English *cinn*] **—chin′less,** *adj.*

chi na (chī′nə), *n.* 1 a fine, white pottery baked by a special process, first used in China; porcelain. Colored designs can be baked into china and made permanent by glazing. 2 dishes, vases, ornaments, etc., made of china. 3 pottery dishes of any kind.

China (def. 1)

Chi na (chī′nə), *n.* 1 **People's Republic of,** country in E Asia, controlled by the Chinese Communists since 1949. 800,000,000 pop. (1972 estimate); 3,691,500 sq. mi. *Capital:* Peking. 2 **Republic of,** the non-Communist Chinese government on Taiwan, established in 1949; Nationalist China. *Capital:* Taipei.

chi na ber ry (chī′nə ber′ē), *n., pl.* **-ries.** 1 tree of the same family as the mahogany, native to Asia and widely cultivated in warm regions for its purplish flowers and yellow, berrylike fruits, and for shade; china tree. 2 its fruit. 3 soapberry of the southern United States, northern Mexico, and the West Indies.

Chi na man (chī′nə mən), *n., pl.* **-men.** UNFRIENDLY USE. 1 native or inhabitant of China. 2 person of Chinese descent.

China Sea, part of the Pacific Ocean east and southeast of Asia. Taiwan divides it into South China Sea and East China Sea.

Chi na town (chī′nə toun′), *n.* section of a city where Chinese live.

china tree, chinaberry.

chi na ware (chī′nə wer′, chī′nə war′), *n.* china.

chinch (chinch), *n.* 1 bedbug. 2 chinch bug. [< Spanish *chinche* < Latin *cimex* bedbug]

chinch bug, a small, black-and-white bug that does much damage to grain in dry weather.

chinchilla (def. 1) 15 in. long with tail

chin chil la (chin chil′ə), *n.* 1 a South American rodent that looks somewhat like a squirrel. 2 its very valuable soft, bluish-gray fur. 3 a thick woolen fabric woven in small, closely set tufts, used for overcoats. [< Spanish, probably < the native name in Peru]

chine (chīn), *n.* 1 backbone; spine. 2 piece of an animal's backbone with the meat on it, suitable for cooking. 3 ridge; crest. [< Old French *eschine*]

Chi nese (chī nēz′), *adj., n., pl.* **-nese.** *—adj.* of China, its people, or their language. *—n.* 1 native or inhabitant of China. 2 person of Chinese descent. 3 language of China.

Chinese Empire, China before it became a republic in 1912. It included Manchuria, Mongolia, Tibet, and Sinkiang.

Chinese lantern, lantern of thin colored paper that can be folded up.

Chinese puzzle, something that is very complicated and hard to solve. [named from the wood and metal puzzles with interlocking pieces invented by the Chinese]

Chinese Turkestan, Chinese district in central Asia, in Sinkiang.

Chinese Wall, Great Wall of China.

Ch'ing (ching), *n.* the dynasty of the Manchus, from 1644 to 1912. It was the last dynasty of the Chinese Empire.

chink[1] (chingk), *n.* a narrow opening; crack; slit: *Wind and snow came through the chinks between the logs of the cabin.* *—v.t.* fill up the chinks in. *—v.i.* come open in cracks; crack. [origin uncertain]

chink[2] (chingk), *n.* a short, sharp, ringing sound like coins or drinking glasses hitting together. *—v.i.* make a short, sharp, ringing sound. *—v.t.* cause to make such a sound: *He chinked the coins in his pocket.* [imitative]

Chin kiang (chin′kyang′), *n.* city in E China. 201,000.

chi no (chē′nō), *n.* 1 a cotton twill or duck fabric, used especially in making trousers. 2 **chinos,** *pl.* trousers made of this fabric. [< American Spanish]

chi nook (shə nu̇k′, chə nük′), *n.* 1 a warm, moist wind blowing from the sea to the land in winter and spring on the northern Pacific Coast. 2 a warm, dry wind that comes down the eastern slope of the Rocky Mountains. 3 the most important and largest species of Pacific salmon. [< *Chinook*]

Chi nook (shə nu̇k′, chə nük′), *n., pl.* **-nook** or **nooks** for 1. 1 member of a group of American Indian tribes living along the Columbia River in the northwestern United States. 2 their language.

Chinook jargon, a language used in trading in the Pacific Northwest, based on Chinook, with additional elements from French and English.

chin qua pin (ching′kə pin), *n.* 1 a dwarf chestnut tree, with edible nuts, ranging from Pennsylvania to Texas. 2 an evergreen tree of the same family, having a similar nut, and grown in California and Oregon. 3 nut of either tree. [< Algonquian]

chintz (chints), *n.* 1 a cotton cloth printed in patterns of various colors and often glazed. 2 a painted or stained calico formerly exported from India. [< Hindustani *chīṇt*]

chintz y (chint′sē), *adj.,* **chintz i er, chintz i est.** 1 of or like chintz. 2 SLANG. cheap and showy.

chin-up (chin′up′), *n.* the exercise of chinning oneself.

Chi os (kī′os, kē′os), *n.* 1 Greek island in the E Aegean Sea. 67,000 pop.; 354 sq. mi. 2 its capital. 24,000.

chip (chip), *n.,v.,* **chipped, chip ping.** —*n.* 1 a small, thin piece cut or broken off. 2 place where a small, thin piece has been cut or broken off. 3 a small, thin piece of food or candy. Potato chips are fried slices of potatoes. 4 a round, flat piece used for counting or to represent money in games. 5 strip of wood, palm leaf, or straw used in making baskets or hats. 6 piece of dried dung, used for fuel in some regions. 7 **chip off the old block,** boy who is much like his father. 8 **chip on one's shoulder,** INFORMAL. readiness to quarrel or fight. 9 **when the chips are down,** when the moment of decision or definite action arrives; in a crisis. —*v.i.* cut or break off in small, thin pieces: *This china chips easily.* —*v.t.* 1 separate (small pieces) by cutting or breaking: *chip old paint from a wall.* 2 shape by cutting at the surface or edge with an ax or chisel. 3 **chip in,** INFORMAL. **a** join with others in giving (money or help). **b** put in (a remark) when others are talking.
[Old English *(for)cippian* cut (off)]

chip munk (chip′mungk), *n.* a small, striped North American rodent of the same family as the squirrel; ground squirrel. [< Algonquian]

chipped (chipt), *adj.* (of meat) smoked and cut in very thin slices: *chipped beef.*

Chip pen dale (chip′ən dāl), *n.* **Thomas,** 1718?-1779, English furniture designer. —*adj.* in the style of graceful, ornate furniture designed by Thomas Chippendale.

chip per (chip′ər), *adj.* INFORMAL. lively and cheerful.

Chip pe wa (chip′ə wä, chip′ə wā, chip′əwə), *n., pl.* **-wa** or **-was.** Ojibwa.

chipping sparrow, a small sparrow of eastern and central North America.

chi rog ra phy (kī rog′rə fē), *n.* style or system of writing; handwriting. [< Greek *cheiros* hand + English *-graphy*]

Chi ron (kī′ron), *n.* (in Greek myths) a wise and kindly centaur, teacher of many Greek heroes. He was famous for his medical skill.

chi rop o dist (kə rop′ə dist, kī rop′ə dist), *n.* person who removes corns and treats other ailments of the feet; podiatrist.

chi rop o dy (kə rop′ə dē, kī rop′ə dē), *n.* work of a chiropodist; podiatry. [< Greek *cheir* hand + *podos* foot]

chi ro prac tic (kī′rə prak′tik), *n.* 1 treatment of diseases by manipulating the spine. 2 chiropractor. —*adj.* having to do with the treatment of diseases by manipulating the spine. [< Greek *cheir* hand + *praktikos* practical]

chi ro prac tor (kī′rə prak′tər), *n.* person who treats diseases by manipulating the spine.

chi rop ter (kī rop′tər), *n.* any of an order of mammals having forelimbs modified as wings; bat. [< Greek *cheir* hand + *pteron* wing]

chirp (chėrp), *n.* a short, sharp sound such as some small birds and insects make. —*v.i.* make a chirp: *The crickets chirped outside the house.* —*v.t.* utter with a chirp. [imitative] —**chirp′er,** *n.*

chirr (chėr), *v.i.* make a shrill, trilling sound: *The grasshoppers chirred in the fields.* —*n.* a shrill, trilling sound. Also, **churr.** [imitative]

chir rup (chir′əp, chėr′əp), *v.i., v.t.* chirp again and again: *I chirruped to my horse to make it go faster.* —*n.* the sound of chirruping. [alteration of *chirp*]

chi rur geon (kī rėr′jən), *n.* ARCHAIC. surgeon. [< Old French *cirurgien.* Doublet of SURGEON.]

chis el (chiz′əl), *n., v.,* **-eled, -el ing** or **-elled, el ling.** —*n.* a cutting tool with a sharp edge at the end of a strong blade, used to cut or shape wood, stone, or metal. —*v.t.* 1 cut or shape with a chisel. 2 SLANG. cheat; defraud. —*v.i.* SLANG. use unfair practices; cheat or swindle. [< Old French < Popular Latin *cisellum, caesellum,* ultimately < Latin *caedere* to cut] —**chis′el like′,** *adj.*

chis eled or **chis elled** (chiz′əld), *adj.* 1 cut, shaped, or wrought with a chisel. 2 having clear and sharp outlines, as if cut with a chisel.

chis el er or **chis el ler** (chiz′ə lər), *n.* 1 person or thing that chisels. 2 SLANG. a cheat.

Chis holm Trail (chiz′əm), famous western cattle trail from San Antonio, Texas, to Abilene, Kansas.

chit[1] (chit), *n.* 1 a signed note or ticket for a purchase, a meal, etc., that is to be paid for later. 2 letter or note. [short for *chitty* < Hindi *chiṭṭhī*]

chit[2] (chit), *n.* 1 child. 2 a saucy, forward girl. [origin uncertain]

chit chat (chit′chat′), *n.* 1 friendly, informal talk; chat. 2 idle talk; gossip.

chi tin (kīt′n), *n.* a horny substance forming the hard outer covering of beetles, lobsters, crabs, crickets, some fungi, etc. [< French *chitine* < Greek *chitōn* tunic]

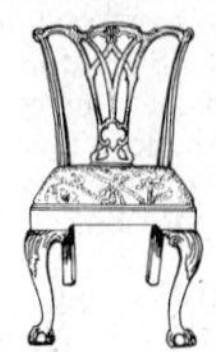

Chippendale chair

chi tin ous (kīt′n əs), *adj.* of or like chitin.

chit lings (chit′lingz), *n.pl.* chitterlings.

chiton (def. 1)

chi ton (kīt′n, kī′ton), *n.* 1 a long, loose garment worn next to the skin by men and women in ancient Greece. 2 any of a class of marine mollusks that adhere to rocks; amphineuran. They have bilateral symmetry and a shell of eight overlapping plates. [< Greek *chitōn*]

chit ter lings (chit′ər lingz), *n.pl.* parts of the small intestines of pigs, calves, etc., cooked as food; chitlings. [Middle English *cheterlingis*]

chiv al ric (shiv′əl rik, shə val′rik), *adj.* chivalrous.

chiv al rous (shiv′əl rəs), *adj.* 1 having the qualities of an ideal knight; brave, courteous, considerate, helpful, honorable, and devoted to the service of the weak and oppressed. 2 having to do with chivalry. —**chiv′al rous ly,** *adv.* —**chiv′al rous ness,** *n.*

chiv al ry (shiv′əl rē), *n.* 1 qualities of an ideal knight in the Middle Ages; bravery, honor, courtesy, protection of the weak, respect for women, generosity, and fairness to enemies. 2 rules and customs of knights in the Middle Ages; system of knighthood. 3 knights as a group. 4 gallant warriors or gentlemen. [< Old French *chevalerie* < *chevalier.* See CHEVALIER.]

chive (chīv), *n.* a perennial plant of the same genus as and similar to the onion, but having a very small bulb. Its long, slender leaves are used as seasoning. [< Old French < Latin *caepa* onion]

chla mys (klā′mis, klam′is), *n., pl.* **chla mys es, chla my des** (klam′ə dēz′). a short cloak worn by men in ancient Greece. [< Latin < Greek]

chlo ral (klôr′əl, klōr′əl), *n.* 1 a colorless, oily liquid made from chlorine and alcohol, used in making chloral hydrate and DDT. *Formula:* CCl_3CHO 2 chloral hydrate.

chloral hydrate, a colorless, crystalline drug formerly much used to quiet nervousness and produce sleep. *Formula:* $CCl_3CH(OH)_2$

chlo rate (klô′rāt′, klôr′it; klō′rāt′, klōr′it), *n.* salt of chloric acid.

chlo rel la (klə rel′ə), *n.* any of a genus of single-celled green algae regarded as a potential source of low-cost nutrients. [< New Latin]

chlo ric (klôr′ik, klōr′ik), *adj.* of or containing chlorine.

chloric acid, a colorless acid which occurs only in water solution and is a strong oxidizing agent. *Formula:* $HClO_3 \cdot 7H_2O$

chlo ride (klôr′īd, klôr′id; klōr′īd, klōr′id), *n.* 1 compound of chlorine with another element or a radical. Sodium chloride is a compound of sodium and chlorine. 2 salt or ester of hydrochloric acid.
chloride of lime, bleaching powder.
chlo rin ate (klôr′ə nāt, klōr′ə nāt), *v.t.,* **-at ed, -at ing.** combine or treat with chlorine, especially to disinfect. **—chlo′rin a′tion,** *n.*
chlorinated lime, bleaching powder.
chlo rine (klôr′ēn′, klôr′ən; klōr′ēn′, klōr′ən), *n.* a poisonous, greenish-yellow, gaseous element found chiefly in combination with sodium as common salt, used in bleaching and disinfecting, and in making plastics and a large number of other chemicals. Chlorine is bad-smelling and very irritating to the nose, throat, and lungs. *Symbol:* Cl; *atomic number* 17. See pages 326 and 327 for table. [< Greek *chloros* green]
chlo rite (klôr′īt′, klōr′īt′), *n.* salt of chlorous acid.
chlo ro form (klôr′ə fôrm, klōr′ə fôrm), *n.* a colorless, volatile liquid, used in refrigerants, propellants, plastics, and as an anesthetic and solvent. *Formula:* $CHCl_3$ *—v.t.* 1 make unconscious or unable to feel pain by giving chloroform. 2 kill with chloroform. [< *chlor(ine)* + *form(ic acid)*]
chlo ro phyll or **chlo ro phyl** (klôr′ə fil, klōr′ə fil), *n.* the coloring matter of the leaves and other green parts of plants occurring in small bodies (chloroplasts) within the cell. Chlorophyll is essential to plants for the manufacture of carbohydrates from carbon dioxide and water in the presence of light. [< Greek *chloros* green + *phyllon* leaf]
chlo ro plast (klôr′ə plast, klōr′ə plast), *n.* a specialized body in the cells of green plants that contains chlorophyll. See **cell** for diagram. [< Greek *chloros* green + *plastos* formed]
chlo ro sis (klə rō′sis), *n.* 1 a blanching or yellowing of plants because of inadequate formation of chlorophyll, usually resulting from a lack of iron or magnesium in the soil, or from a lack of light. 2 a form of anemia affecting young girls, characterized by a yellowish-green complexion. [< New Latin < Greek *chlōros* green]
chlo rous (klôr′əs, klōr′əs), *adj.* of or containing trivalent chlorine.
chlorous acid, an acid occurring only in solution or in the form of chlorites. *Formula:* $HClO_2$
chlor tet ra cy cline (klôr tet′rə sī′klən, klōr tet′rə sī′klən), *n.* Aureomycin.
chm. or **chmn.,** chairman.

chock (def. 2)

chock (chok), *n.* 1 block or wedge put under a barrel or wheel to keep it from rolling, or under something to keep it in place, such as a lifeboat on a ship's deck. 2 block with two arms curving inward for a rope to pass through. *—v.t.* 1 provide or fasten with chocks. 2 put (a boat) on chocks. *—adv.* as close or as tight as can be. [apparently < Old North French *choque* log]
chock a block (chok′ə blok′), *adj.* 1 with the blocks drawn close together. 2 jammed together; crowded; packed.
chock-full (chok′fu̇l′), *adj.* as full as can be; stuffed full. Also, **chuck-full.**
choc o late (chôk′lit, chôk′ə lit; chok′lit, chok′ə lit), *n.* 1 substance made by roasting and grinding cacao seeds. It has a strong, rich flavor and much value as food. 2 drink made of chocolate with hot milk or water and sugar. 3 candy made of chocolate. 4 a dark brown. *—adj.* 1 made of or flavored with chocolate. 2 dark-brown. [< Mexican Spanish < Nahuatl *chocolatl*]
Choc taw (chok′tô), *n., pl.* **-taw** or **taws** for 1. 1 member of a tribe of American Indians, now living mostly in Oklahoma. 2 their language.
choice (chois), *n., adj.,* **choic er, choic est.** *—n.* 1 act of choosing; selection: *careful in one's choice of friends.* 2 power or chance to choose: *I was given the choice between a radio and a camera.* 3 person or thing chosen: *This hat is my choice.* 4 thing among several things to be chosen; alternative: *Their action left no choice but war.* See synonym study below. 5 quantity and variety to choose from: *a wide choice of vegetables in the market.* 6 the best or finest part: *These flowers are the choice of my garden.* *—adj.* 1 of fine quality; excellent; superior: *a choice steak.* See **fine**[1] for synonym study. 2 carefully chosen: *choice arguments.* [< Old French *chois* < Germanic] **—choice′ly,** *adv.* **—choice′ness,** *n.*
Syn. *n.* 4 **Choice, alternative, preference, option** mean the thing to be chosen. **Choice,** the general and most informal word, emphasizes freedom in choosing: *My choice is the black puppy.* **Alternative** emphasizes limitation of the possibilities, usually to two but sometimes several, among which one must choose: *Your alternative to practicing the piano is to stop taking lessons.* **Preference** emphasizes choosing according to one's own liking: *Algebra was my preference among my classes last year.* **Option** emphasizes the right to choose granted by someone to another: *The court gave him two options, going to jail or paying a fine.*
choir (kwīr), *n.* 1 group of singers who perform or lead the musical part of a church service. 2 part of a church set apart for such a group. See **presbytery** for diagram. 3 any group of singers; chorus. 4 in music: **a** instruments of the same class in an orchestra: *the string choir, the brass choir.* **b** musicians playing such a class of instruments. 5 any of the nine orders of angels. *—v.i., v.t.* sing all together at the same time. [< Old French *cuer* < Latin *chorus.* Doublet of CHORUS.]
choir boy (kwīr′boi′), *n.* boy who sings in a choir; chorister.
choir mas ter (kwīr′mas′tər), *n.* director or conductor of a choir.
choke (chōk), *v.,* **choked, chok ing,** *n.* *—v.t.* 1 stop the breath of by squeezing or blocking up the throat; suffocate. 2 check or extinguish by cutting off the supply of air: *choke a fire.* 3 fill up or block; clog: *Sand is choking the river.* 4 reduce the supply of air to (an internal-combustion engine) to make a richer fuel mixture, especially when starting. 5 kill or injure (a plant) by depriving it of air and light or of room to grow. *—v.i.* 1 be unable to breathe. 2 be filled up or blocked.
choke back, hold back, control, or suppress: *I choked back a sharp cry.*
choke off, put an end to.

hat, āge, fär; let, ēqual, tėrm;
it, īce; hot, ōpen, ôrder;
oil, out; cup, pu̇t, rüle;
ch, child; ng, long; sh, she;
th, thin; ᴛʜ, then; zh, measure;

ə represents *a* in about, *e* in taken, *i* in pencil, *o* in lemon, *u* in circus.

< = from, derived from, taken from.

choke up, a block up; fill up; clog up. **b** fill with emotion; be or cause to be on the verge of tears.
—n. 1 act or sound of choking. 2 valve that reduces the supply of air to an internal-combustion engine. 3 a narrow or constricted part of a tube, etc., as in a chokebore. 4 choke coil.
[Old English *ācēocian*]
choke bore (chōk′bôr′, chōk′bōr′), *n.* 1 bore of a shotgun that narrows toward the muzzle to keep the shot from scattering too widely. 2 shotgun with such a bore.
choke cher ry (chōk′cher′ē), *n., pl.* **-ries.** 1 a bitter wild cherry of North America. 2 tree or shrub of the rose family that it grows on.
choke coil, coil of wire around a core of iron or air, used to control alternating currents in an electric circuit.
choke damp (chōk′damp′), *n.* a heavy, suffocating gas, mainly carbon dioxide, that gathers in mines, old wells, etc.
chok er (chō′kər), *n.* 1 person or thing that chokes. 2 something that fits tightly around the neck, such as a necklace or high collar.
chok y (chō′kē), *adj.,* **chok i er, chok i est.** 1 inclined to choke, especially with emotion. 2 tending to choke; suffocating: *a choky collar.*
chol er (kol′ər), *n.* an irritable disposition; anger. [< Late Latin *cholera* bile < Latin, cholera]
chol er a (kol′ər ə), *n.* 1 an acute, infectious, often fatal disease of the stomach and intestines, characterized by vomiting, cramps, and diarrhea; Asiatic cholera. 2 any of several diseases occurring chiefly in hot weather and causing acute diarrhea. [< Latin < Greek < *cholē* bile]
chol er ic (kol′ər ik), *adj.* 1 having an irritable disposition; easily made angry. 2 enraged; angry; wrathful: *a choleric outburst of temper.*
cho les te rol (kə les′tə rol′, kə les′tə rōl′), *n.* a white, crystalline substance important in metabolism, contained in all animal fats, bile, nervous tissue, blood, egg yolk, etc. *Formula:* $C_{27}H_{45}OH$ [< Greek *cholē* bile + *stereos* solid]
cho line (kō′lēn′, kol′ēn), *n.* constituent of the vitamin B complex, present in many animal and plant tissues, which prevents accumulation of fat in the liver. *Formula:* $C_5H_{15}NO_2$ [< Greek *cholē* bile]
cho lin es te rase (kō′lə nes′tə rās′, kol′ə nes′tə rās′), *n.* enzyme which prevents the accumulation of acetylcholine at the nerve endings by stimulating its hydrolysis.
chol la (choi′ə), *n.* a spiny, treelike cactus of the southwestern United States and Mexico. [< Mexican Spanish]
chomp (chomp), *v.t., v.i.* champ[1].
chon drich thi an (kon drik′thē ən), *n.* any of a class of fishes whose skeletons are

formed of cartilage and whose gills are thin and platelike; elasmobranch. Sharks and rays belong to this class. [< Greek *chondros* cartilage + *ichthys* fish]

Chon drich thy es (kon drik′thē ēz′), *n.pl.* class of fishes comprising the chondrichthians.

chon dri o some (kon′drē ə sōm), *n.* any of the mitochondria, or minute bodies contained in the form of rods, granules, and threads in the cytoplasm of cells. [< Greek *chondros* lump + *sōma* body]

choose (chüz), *v.,* **chose, cho sen, choos ing.** —*v.t.* 1 pick out; select from a number: *She chose a book from the library.* 2 prefer and decide; think fit: *I did not choose to go.* —*v.i.* make a choice: *You must choose for yourself.* [Old English *cēosan*] **—choos′er,** *n.*

choos y or **choos ey** (chü′zē), *adj.,* **choos i er, choos i est.** INFORMAL. particular or fussy. **—choos′i ness,** *n.*

chop[1] (chop), *v.,* **chopped, chop ping,** *n.* —*v.t.* 1 cut by hitting with something sharp: *chop wood with an ax.* See **cut** for synonym study. 2 cut into small pieces: *chop up cabbage for coleslaw.* 3 make by cutting: *The explorers chopped their way through the underbrush.* 4 (in tennis, baseball, cricket, etc.) swing at or hit with a downward stroke. —*v.i.* 1 make quick, sharp movements; jerk. 2 (in tennis, baseball, cricket, etc.) swing or hit with a downward stroke: *She chopped at the ball with her racket.* —*n.* 1 a cutting blow or stroke. 2 slice of lamb, pork, veal, etc., on a piece of rib, loin, or shoulder. 3 (in boxing) a sharp downward blow. 4 a short, irregular, broken motion of waves. [Middle English *choppen*]

chop[2] (chop), *n.* 1 jaw. 2 **chops,** *pl.* jaws or cheeks. [probably a special use of *chop*[1]]

chop[3] (chop), *v.i.,* **chopped, chop ping.** change suddenly; shift quickly; veer: *The wind chopped around from west to north.* [probably variant of obsolete *chap* buy and sell, exchange]

chop fall en (chop′fô′lən), *adj.* chapfallen.

chop house (chop′hous′), *n., pl.* **-hous es** (-hou′ziz). restaurant that makes a specialty of serving chops, steaks, etc.

Cho pin (shō′pan), *n.* **Frédéric François,** 1810-1849, Polish composer and pianist who lived in France.

chop per (chop′ər), *n.* 1 person who chops. 2 tool or machine for chopping. A short ax or a heavy knife are choppers. 3 SLANG. helicopter.

chop py[1] (chop′ē), *adj.,* **-pi er, -pi est.** 1 making quick, sharp movements; jerky. 2 moving in short, irregular, broken waves: *The sea is choppy today.* [< *chop*[1]] **—chop′pi ness,** *n.*

chop py[2] (chop′ē), *adj.,* **-pi er, -pi est.** changing suddenly; shifting quickly: *a choppy wind.* [< *chop*[3]]

chops (chops), *n.pl.* See def. 2 under **chop**[2].

chop sticks (chop′stiks′), *n.pl.* pair of small, slender sticks used by the Chinese, Japanese, and some other Orientals to raise food to the mouth. [< Chinese pidgin English *chop* quick + English *stick*[1]]

chop su ey (chop′ sü′ē), fried or stewed meat and vegetables cut up and cooked together in a sauce. It is usually served with rice. [< Chinese (Canton) *tsap sui* odds and ends]

cho ral (*adj.* kôr′əl, kōr′əl; *n. also* kə ral′, kə räl′), *adj.* 1 of a choir or chorus. 2 sung by a choir or chorus. —*n.* chorale. **—cho′ral ly,** *adv.*

cho rale (kə ral′, kə räl′; kôr′əl, kōr′əl), *n.* 1 a musical setting of a hymn. 2 a simple hymn sung in unison.

chord[1] (kôrd), *n.* combination of two or more musical notes sounded together, usually in harmony. [variant of *cord,* short for *accord,* noun]

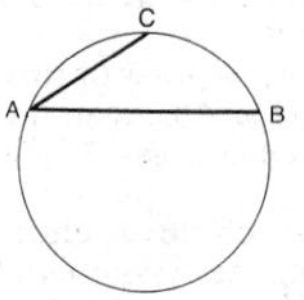

C
A
B

chord[2] (def. 1) AB and AC are chords.

chord[2] (kôrd), *n.* 1 a line segment connecting two points on a curve. 2 cord (def. 3). 3 string of a harp or other musical instrument. 4 emotion or feeling: *touch a sympathetic chord.* 5 a main, horizontal part of a bridge truss. 6 a straight line drawn across an airfoil from the leading to the trailing edge. [< Latin *chorda* < Greek *chordē* gut, string of a musical instrument. Doublet of CORD.]

chord al (kôr′dl), *adj.* in music: 1 of or having to do with the strings of an instrument. 2 of or having to do with chords.

Chor dat a (kôr′dā′tə), *n.pl.* phylum of animals comprising the chordates. [< New Latin]

chor date (kôr′dāt), *n.* any of a phylum of animals that have at some stage of development a dorsal nerve cord, a notochord, and pharyngeal gill slits and that include mammals, fishes, reptiles, birds, amphibians, and certain wormlike marine forms. —*adj.* of or belonging to this phylum.

chore (chôr, chōr), *n.* 1 an odd job; small task: *Feeding the dog was my daily chore.* 2 a difficult or disagreeable thing to do. [variant of *char*[2]]

cho re a (kô rē′ə, kō rē′ə), *n.* St. Vitus's dance. [< Greek *choreia* dance]

cho re o graph (kôr′ē ə graf, kōr′ē ə graf), *v.t.* arrange or design dancing for (a ballet, etc.).

cho re og ra pher (kôr′ē og′rə fər, kōr′ē-og′rə fər), *n.* planner or director of dances in a ballet, motion picture, or musical play.

cho re o graph ic (kôr′ē ə graf′ik, kōr′ē ə-graf′ik), *adj.* of or having to do with choreography. **—cho′re o graph′i cal ly,** *adv.*

cho re og ra phy (kôr′ē og′rə fē, kōr′ē-og′rə fē), *n.* 1 art of planning, designing, or directing dances and ballets. 2 dancing, especially ballet dancing. [< Greek *choreia* dance + English *-graphy*]

cho ric (kôr′ik, kōr′ik, kor′ik), *adj.* of or for a chorus, especially a chorus in an ancient Greek play.

cho ri on (kôr′ē on, kōr′ē on), *n.* the outermost membrane, enclosing the amnion, of the sac which envelops the embryo or fetus of the higher vertebrates. [< Greek]

cho ri on ic (kôr′ē on′ik, kōr′ē on′ik), *adj.* of, having to do with, or resembling the chorion.

cho ris ter (kôr′ə stər, kor′ə stər), *n.* 1 singer in a choir. 2 choirboy. 3 leader of a choir.

cho roid (kôr′oid′, kōr′oid′), *adj.* having to do with a delicate coat or membrane between the sclerotic coat and the retina of the eyeball. —*n.* choroid coat or membrane. See **eye** for diagram. [< Greek *choroeidēs* < *chorion* membrane]

chor tle (chôr′tl), *v.,* **-tled, -tling,** *n.* —*v.i., v.t.* chuckle or snort with glee. —*n.* a gleeful chuckle or snort. [blend of *chuckle* and *snort;* coined by Lewis Carroll] **—chor′tler,** *n.*

cho rus (kôr′əs, kōr′əs), *n.* 1 group of singers who sing together, such as a choir. 2 a musical composition to be sung by all singers together. 3 the repeated part of a song coming after each stanza; refrain. 4 anything sung by many people at once. 5 a saying by many at the same time: *My question was answered by a chorus of no's.* 6 **in chorus,** all together at the same time. 7 group of singers and dancers in a musical comedy or the like. 8 (in ancient Greek drama) an organized group of singers and dancers engaging in dialogue with the actors and commenting on the action on stage. —*v.t., v.i.* sing or speak all at the same time: *The audience chorused its approval by loud cheering. The birds were chorusing around me.* [< Latin < Greek *choros* a dance, band of dancers. Doublet of CHOIR.]

chorus girl, girl who sings and dances in a chorus of a musical comedy or review.

chose (chōz), *v.* pt. of **choose.** *She chose the red dress.*

cho sen (chō′zn), *v.* pp. of **choose.** *Have you chosen a book from the library?* —*adj.* picked out; selected from a group: *a carefully chosen target.*

Cho sen (chō′sen′), *n.* Japanese name of **Korea.**

Cho sen People (chō′zn), **The,** (in the Bible) the Israelites.

Chou (jō), *n.* a Chinese dynasty ruling from about 1027 B.C. to about 256 B.C., noted as the era of the philosophers Confucius, Laotse, and Mencius.

Chou En-lai (jō′ en′lī′), born 1898, Chinese Communist leader, premier of the People's Republic of China since 1949.

chough (chuf), *n.* a European crow, black with red feet and a red beak. [Middle English *choughe*]

chow[1] (chou), *n.* a medium-sized dog with a short, compact body, large head, thick coat, usually brown or black, and black tongue; chow chow. It was originally a Chinese breed. [short for *chow chow*]

chow[2] (chou), *n.* SLANG. 1 food. 2 the time when food is served. [short for *chowchow*]

chow chow (chou′chou′), *n.* 1 a Chinese mixed preserve. 2 any mixed pickles chopped up. [< Chinese pidgin English]

chow chow, chow[1]. [< Chinese pidgin English]

chow der (chou′dər), *n.* a thick soup or stew usually made of clams or fish with potatoes, onions, etc., and milk. [< French *chaudière* pot < Late Latin *caldaria* < Latin *calidus* hot]

chow mein (chou′ mān′), fried noodles served with a thickened stew of onions, celery, bean sprouts, egg, meat, etc. [< Chinese (Canton) *ch'au min* fried noodles]

Chr., 1 Christ. 2 Christian.

chrism (kriz′əm), *n.* consecrated oil, used by some churches in baptism and other sacred rites. [< Latin *chrisma* < Greek, ointment < *chriein* anoint]

Christ (krīst), *n.* 1 Jesus of Nazareth, whose life and teachings are the source of the Christian religion. 2 Also, **the Christ.** the Messiah. [Old English *Crist* < Latin *Christus* < Greek *christos* anointed]

Christ church (krīst′chėrch′), *n.* city in SE New Zealand. 260,000.

chris ten (kris′n), *v.t.* 1 give a first name to (a person) at baptism. 2 give a name to: *The new ship was christened before it was launched.* 3 baptize as a Christian. 4 INFORMAL. make the first use of. [Old English *cristnian* make Christian < *cristen* Christian < Latin *christianus* belonging to Christ]

Chris ten dom (kris′n dəm), *n.* 1 Christian countries; the Christian part of the world. 2 all Christians.

chris ten ing (kris′n ing), *n.* act or ceremony of baptizing and naming; baptism.

Chris tian (kris′chən), *n.* 1 person who believes in Christ and follows His teachings; person belonging to the religion of Christ. 2 INFORMAL. a decent person. *—adj.* 1 of Christ, His teachings, or the religion that bears His name. 2 believing in or belonging to the religion of Christ: *the Christian church, the Christian gospel.* 3 of Christians or Christianity. 4 showing a gentle, humble, helpful spirit: *Christian charity.* 5 INFORMAL. decent; respectable. 6 human; not animal. **—Chris′tian like′,** *adj.* **—Chris′tian ly,** *adj., adv.*

Christian X, 1870-1947, king of Denmark from 1912 to 1947.

Christian Church, Disciples of Christ.

Christian Era, time since the birth of Christ, in use in all predominantly Christian countries. A.D. is in the Christian Era; B.C. is before it.

Chris ti an i a (kris′chē an′ē ə, kris′tē-ä′nē ə), *n.* 1 former name of **Oslo.** 2 (in skiing) a skidding turn in which the skier keeps his skis parallel, shifts his weight forward and in the direction he wishes to turn, and springs just sufficiently to free his weight from the skis; Christie.

Chris ti an i ty (kris′chē an′ə tē), *n.* 1 the religion taught by Christ and His followers; Christian religion. 2 condition of being a Christian; Christian spirit or character. 3 all Christians; Christendom.

Chris tian ize (kris′chə nīz), *v.t.,* **-ized, -iz ing.** make Christian; convert to Christianity. **—Chris′tian i za′tion,** *n.* **—Chris′tian iz′er,** *n.*

Christian name, the personal name or names given at christening, as distinguished from the family name or surname; given name: *"John" is the Christian name of "John Smith."*

Christian Science, religion and system of healing founded by Mary Baker Eddy in 1866. It treats disease by mental and spiritual means.

Christian Scientist, believer in Christian Science.

Chris tie (kris′tē), *n.* Christiania (def. 2).

Christ like (krīst′līk′), *adj.* like Christ; like that of Christ; showing the spirit of Christ. **—Christ′like′ness,** *n.*

Christ mas (kris′məs), *n.* 1 the yearly celebration of the birth of Christ; December 25. 2 the season of Christmas. [Old English *Cristes mæsse* Christ's Mass]

Christmas club, group of bank accounts into which depositors, wishing to accumulate savings to be used for shopping before Christmas, make weekly deposits throughout the year.

Christmas Day, December 25.

Christmas Island, 1 island in the Indian Ocean, south of Java, governed by Australia. 3000 pop.; 60 sq. mi. 2 British island in the central Pacific, part of Gilbert and Ellice Islands colony. 400 pop.; 220 sq. mi.

Christ mas tide (kris′məs tīd′), *n.* the Christmas season.

Christ mas time (kris′məs tīm′), *n.* the Christmas season.

Christmas tree, an evergreen or artificial tree hung with decorations at Christmastime.

Chris to pher (kris′tə fər), *n.* **Saint,** died A.D. 250?, legendary Christian martyr. He is the patron saint of travelers.

chro mate (krō′māt), *n.* salt or ester of chromic acid.

chro mat ic (krō mat′ik), *adj.* 1 of color or colors. 2 progressing only by half steps instead of by the regular intervals of the musical scale: *There are twelve chromatic tones.* *—n.* (in music) an accidental. [< Latin *chromaticus* < Greek *chromatikos* < *chroma* color] **—chro mat′i cal ly,** *adv.*

chromatic aberration, failure of the different colors of light to meet in one focus when refracted through a convex lens.

chromatic scale, a musical scale that progresses by half steps.

chro ma tid (krō′mə tid), *n.* one of the halves into which a chromosome divides during cell division, and which develops into a complete new chromosome.

chro ma tin (krō′mə tən), *n.* a protein substance found throughout the nucleus of a cell which absorbs stains readily and draws together to form chromosomes during mitosis.

chro ma to graph ic (krō′mə tə graf′ik), *adj.* having to do with chromatography.

chro ma tog ra phy (krō′mə tog′rə fē), *n.* separation and analysis of mixtures of chemical compounds by the use of an adsorbing material, so that the different compounds become adsorbed in separate sections.

chro ma to phore (krō′mə tə fôr, krō′mə-tə fōr), *n.* one of the specialized pigment-bearing bodies in the cells of plants, such as a chloroplast or chromoplast.

chrome (krōm), *n., v.,* **chromed, chrom ing.** *—n.* 1 chromium. 2 the name given to several different paint pigments. 3 chrome steel. *—v.t.* cover or plate with chrome: *chromed steel.* [< French < Greek *chrōma* color]

chrome green, any of various green pigments containing chromium, used in paints and dyes and in textile printing.

chrome steel, a very hard, strong steel containing chromium.

chrome yellow, a yellow coloring matter made from lead chromate and used in some yellow paints.

chro mic (krō′mik), *adj.* of or containing chromium.

chro mite (krō′mīt), *n.* mineral containing iron and chromium. *Formula:* $FeCr_2O_4$

chro mi um (krō′mē əm), *n.* a grayish, hard, brittle metallic element that does not rust or become dull easily; chrome. Chromium is used to electroplate other metals, as part of stainless steel and other alloys, for making dyes and paints, in photography, etc. *Symbol:* Cr; *atomic number* 24. See pages 326 and 327 for table.

chro mo (krō′mō), *n., pl.* **-mos.** a colored picture printed from a series of stones or plates.

chro mo phore (krō′mō fôr, krō′mō fōr), *n.* a group of atoms which produce the color within the molecules of colored organic compounds. [< Greek *chrōma* color + *-phoros* carrying]

chro mo plast (krō′mə plast), *n.* a yellow or red body in the cytoplasm of a plant cell containing coloring matter. The colors of flowers and fruits are largely due to the presence of chromoplasts. [< Greek *chrōma* color + *plastos* formed]

chro mo so mal (krō′mə sō′məl), *adj.* of, having to do with, or resembling a chromosome or chromosomes.

chro mo some (krō′mə sōm), *n.* any of the rod-shaped bodies found in the nucleus of a cell that appear during cell division. Chromosomes are derived from the parents and carry the genes that determine heredity. See **cell** for diagram. [< Greek *chrōma* color + *soma* body]

chro mo sphere (krō′mə sfir′), *n.* 1 a red-hot layer of gas around the sun which can be seen only during a total eclipse. 2 a similar layer around a star.

chron., 1 chronological. 2 chronology.

Chron., Chronicles.

chron ic (kron′ik), *adj.* 1 lasting a long time: *Rheumatism is often a chronic disease.* 2 suffering long from an illness: *a chronic invalid.* 3 never stopping; constant; habitual: *a chronic liar.* [< Greek *chronikos* of time < *chronos* time] **—chron′i cal ly,** *adv.*

chro nic i ty (krə nis′ə tē), *n.* chronic condition, as of a disease.

chron i cle (kron′ə kəl), *n., v.,* **-cled, -cling.** *—n.* 1 record of events in the order in which they took place; history; story. 2 narrative; account. *—v.t.* 1 write the history of; tell the story of. 2 put on record.

chron i cler (kron′ə klər), *n.* writer of a chronicle; recorder; historian.

Chron i cles (kron′ə kəlz), *n.* either of two books of the Old Testament, called I and II Chronicles.

chron o graph (kron′ə graf), *n.* 1 instrument for measuring very short intervals of time accurately, such as a stopwatch. 2 instrument for recording the exact instant of an astronomical or other occurrence. [< Greek *chronos* time + English *-graph*]

chron o log i cal (kron′ə loj′ə kəl), *adj.* of or in accordance with chronology; arranged in the order in which the events happened: *In telling a story a person usually follows chronological order.* **—chron′o log′i cal ly,** *adv.*

chro nol o gist (krə nol′ə jist), *n.* an expert in chronology.

chro nol o gy (krə nol′ə jē), *n., pl.* **-gies.** 1 science of measuring time or periods of time and of determining the proper order and dates of events. 2 table or list that gives the exact dates of events arranged in the order in which they happened. 3 system of arranging time in periods and assigning dates to events; arrangement of the exact dates of events in the order in which they happened.

chro nom e ter (krə nom′ə tər), *n.* clock or watch that keeps very accurate time. A ship's chronometer is used in determining longitude.

chron o scope (kron′ə skōp), *n.* instrument for measuring very small intervals of time.

chrys a lid (kris′ə lid), *n.* chrysalis. *—adj.* of a chrysalis.

chrysalis (defs. 1 and 2) of a butterfly

chrys a lis (kris′ə lis), *n., pl.* **chrys a lis es, chry sal i des** (krə sal′ə dēz′). 1 the stage in the development of moths, butterflies, and most other insects between the larva and the adult, when the larva lives in a hard case or cocoon; pupa. 2 the case or cocoon. 3 stage of development or change. [< Latin < Greek *chrysallis* golden sheath of a butterfly < *chrysos* gold]

chry san the mum (krə san′thə məm), *n.* 1 any of a genus of plants of the composite family that have many-petaled round flowers of various colors and that bloom in the fall. The different varieties show a great range in the size and the form of the flower. 2 the flower of any of these plants. [< Latin < Greek *chrysanthemon* < *chrysos* gold + *anthemon* flower]

chrys o lite (kris′ə līt), *n.* olivine.

chrys o prase (kris′ə prāz), *n.* a light-green semiprecious stone; kind of chalcedony. [< Greek *chrysoprasos* < *chrysos* gold + *prason* leek]

chrys o tile (kris′ə til), *n.* a fibrous variety of serpentine. It is the most important type of asbestos. [< Greek *chrysos* gold + *tilos* lint, fiber]

chub (chub), *n., pl.* **chubs** or **chub.** 1 a thick freshwater fish of Europe, of the same family as the carp. 2 any of various small freshwater fishes of central and eastern United States and Canada. [Middle English *chubbe*]

chub by (chub′ē), *adj.,* **-bi er, -bi est.** round and plump: *chubby cheeks, a chubby child.* **—chub′bi ness,** *n.*

chuck[1] (chuk), *v.t.* 1 give a slight blow or tap; pat: *I chucked the baby under the chin.* 2 throw or toss: *She chucked the stones into the pond.* *—n.* 1 a slight blow or tap. 2 a throw or toss. [origin unknown]

chuck[2] (chuk), *n.* 1 device for holding a tool or piece of work in a lathe, drill, or other machine. 2 cut of beef between the neck and the shoulder that includes the first three ribs. See **beef** for diagram. [variant of *chock*]

chuck-full (chuk′fu̇l′), *adj.* chock-full.

chuck hole (chuk′hōl′), *n.* U.S. a deep depression or hole in a street or road.

chuck le (chuk′əl), *v.,* **-led, -ling,** *n.* *—v.i.* laugh softly or quietly, especially to oneself. *—n.* a soft laugh; quiet laughter. [probably < earlier *chuck* to make a clucking noise; imitative] **—chuck′ler,** *n.*

chuck le head (chuk′əl hed′), *n.* INFORMAL. a stupid person.

chuck le head ed (chuk′əl hed′id), *adj.* dull; stupid.

chuck wagon, (in the western United States) a wagon, now sometimes a truck, that carries food and cooking equipment for cowboys or harvest workers.

chuck wal la (chuk′wol′ə), *n.* a large, brownish lizard of the desert areas of the southwestern United States. [< Mexican Spanish *chacahuala*]

chug (chug), *n., v.,* **chugged, chug ging.** *—n.* a short, loud burst of sound: *the chug of a steam engine.* *—v.i.* 1 make short, loud bursts of sound. 2 INFORMAL. go or move with such sounds: *The old truck chugged along.* [imitative]

chuk ker or **chuk kar** (chuk′ər), *n.* one of the periods of play in polo, usually lasting 7½ minutes. [< Hindustani *chakar* a round < Sanskrit *chakra* wheel]

chum (chum), *n., v.,* **chummed, chum ming.** INFORMAL. *—n.* 1 a very close friend. 2 roommate. *—v.i.* 1 be very close friends. 2 room together. [perhaps short for *chamber mate* or *chamber fellow*]

chum my (chum′ē), *adj.,* **-mi er, -mi est.** INFORMAL. like a chum; very friendly; intimate. **—chum′mi ly,** *adv.* **—chum′mi ness,** *n.*

chump (chump), *n.* 1 INFORMAL. a foolish or stupid person; blockhead. 2 a short, thick block of wood. 3 a thick, blunt end. 4 SLANG. the head. [origin uncertain]

Chung king (chu̇ng′king′), *n.* city in central China, on the Yangtze River. 2,121,000.

chunk (chungk), *n.* a thick piece or lump: *a chunk of wood.* [variant of *chuck*[2]]

chunk y (chung′kē), *adj.,* **chunk i er, chunk i est.** 1 like a chunk; short and thick. 2 INFORMAL. stocky: *The child had a chunky build.* **—chunk′i ly,** *adv.* **—chunk′i ness,** *n.*

church (chėrch), *n.* 1 building for public Christian worship or religious services. 2 public worship of God in a church. 3 Usually, **Church.** group of Christians with the same beliefs and under the same authority; denomination: *the Methodist Church, the Presbyterian Church.* 4 a locally organized unit of a group of Christians for religious services. 5 **the Church,** all Christians. 6 organization of a church; ecclesiastical authority or power. 7 profession of a clergyman: *make the church one's career.* 8 any building, group, or organization like a church. *—adj.* of a church. *—v.t.* conduct or bring to church, as for a ceremony or service. [Old English *cirice* < Greek *kyriakon (dōma)* (house) of the Lord < *kyrios* lord < *kyros* power] **—church′less,** *adj.* **—church′-like′,** *adj.*

church go er (chėrch′gō′ər), *n.* person who goes to church regularly.

Church ill (chėr′chil, chėr′chəl), *n.* 1 **John.** See **Marlborough.** 2 **Winston,** 1871-1947, American novelist. 3 Sir **Winston,** 1874-1965, British statesman and writer, prime minister of Great Britain from 1940 to 1945 and from 1951 to 1955. 4 **Churchill River,** river flowing from central Saskatchewan, Canada, into Hudson Bay. 1000 mi.

church ly (chėrch′lē), *adj.* 1 of a church. 2 suitable for a church. **—church′li ness,** *n.*

church man (chėrch′mən), *n., pl.* **-men.** 1 clergyman. 2 member of a church.

Church of Christ, Scientist, the official name of the Christian Science Church.

Church of England, the Episcopal Church in England that is recognized as a national institution by the government; Anglican Church.

Church of Jesus Christ of Latter-day Saints, the official name of the Mormon Church.

church ward en (chėrch′wôrd′n), *n.* a lay official in the Church of England or the Protestant Episcopal Church who manages the business, property, and money of a church.

church wom an (chėrch′wu̇m′ən), *n., pl.* **-wom en.** a woman member of a church.

church yard (chėrch′yärd′), *n.* the ground around a church. Part of a churchyard is sometimes used as a burial ground.

churl (chėrl), *n.* 1 a rude, surly person; boor. 2 person of low birth; peasant. 3 person stingy in money matters; miser. 4 (in Anglo-Saxon and medieval England) a freeman of the lowest rank; ceorl. [Old English *ceorl*]

churl ish (chėr′lish), *adj.* rude or surly; bad-tempered: *a churlish reply.* **—churl′ish ly,** *adv.* **—churl′ish ness,** *n.*

churn (chėrn), *n.* 1 container or machine in which butter is made from cream or milk by stirring or shaking. 2 a violent stirring or shaking. *—v.t.* 1 stir or shake (cream or milk) in a churn. 2 make (butter) by using a churn. 3 stir violently; make foamy: *The ship's propeller churned the waves.* *—v.i.* 1 make butter with a churn. 2 become foamy: *The water churns in the rapids.* 3 move as if agitated or shaken: *The excited crowd churned about the speaker's platform.* [Old English *cyrn*] **—churn′er,** *n.*

churr (chėr), *v.i., n.* chirr.

chute (shüt), *n.* 1 an inclined trough, tube, etc., for dropping or sliding such things as mail, soiled clothes, or coal to a lower level. 2 rapids in a river; waterfall. 3 a steep slope or sloping passage. 4 INFORMAL. parachute. [apparently blend of French *chute* fall (of water) and English *shoot*]

chut ney (chut′nē), *n., pl.* **-neys.** a spicy sauce or relish made of fruits, herbs, pepper, etc. [< Hindustani *chatnī*]

chutz pah (hu̇ts′pə), *n.* SLANG. effrontery; impudence; gall. [< Yiddish *khutspe*]

chyle (kīl), *n.* a milky liquid composed of digested fat and lymph, formed from the chyme in the small intestine and carried from there into the veins. [< Greek *chylos* < *chein* pour]

chyme (kīm), *n.* a pulpy semiliquid mass into which food is changed by the action and secretions of the stomach. Chyme passes from the stomach into the small intestine. [< Greek *chymos* < *chein* pour]

CIA, Central Intelligence Agency.

ci bo ri um (sə bôr′ē əm, sə bōr′ē əm), *n., pl.* **-bo ri a** (-bôr′ē ə, -bōr′ē ə). 1 a covered container used to hold the sacred bread of the Eucharist. 2 a dome-shaped canopy over an altar. [< Latin < Greek *kiborion*]

ci ca da (sə kā′də, sə kä′də), *n.* a large insect, commonly called a locust, with two pairs of thin, transparent wings. The male produces a loud, shrill sound in hot, dry weather by vibrating membranes on the abdomen. [< Latin]

cic a trice (sik′ə tris), *n.* cicatrix.

cic a trix (sik′ə triks, sə kā′triks), *n., pl.* **cic a tri ces** (sik′ə trī′sēz′). 1 scar left by a healed wound. 2 scar left on a tree or plant by a fallen leaf, branch, etc. 3 scar on a seed where it was attached to the pod or seed container. [< Latin]

cic a trize (sik′ə trīz), *v.t., v.i.,* **-trized, -triz ing.** heal by forming a scar.

Cic e ro (sis′ə rō′), *n.* **Marcus Tullius,**

106-43 B.C., Roman orator, writer, and statesman. Also, **Tully.**

cic e ro ne (sis′ə rō′nē), *n.* guide for sightseers who shows and explains antiquities or curiosities of a place. [< Italian < the Roman orator *Cicero* (because guides are said to be talkative)]

Cic e ro ni an (sis′ə rō′nē ən), *adj.* resembling Cicero's classical literary style; eloquent.

Cid (sid), *n.* **the,** 1040?-1099, Spanish national hero who fought against the Moors.

-cide, *combining form.* 1 killing of: *Regicide = killing of a king.* 2 killer: *Pesticide = pest killer.* [< Latin *-cidium* a killing, and *-cida* killer, both < *caedere* kill]

ci der (sī′dər), *n.* 1 juice pressed out of apples, used as a drink and in making vinegar. 2 juice pressed from other fruits. [< Old French *sidre* < Late Latin *sicera* < Greek *sikera* < Hebrew *shēkār* liquor]

Cien fue gos (syen fwā′gōs), *n.* seaport in S central Cuba. 100,000.

C.I.F., CIF, or **c.i.f.,** cost, insurance, and freight.

ci gar (sə gär′), *n.* a tight roll of cured tobacco leaves for smoking. [< Spanish *cigarro*]

cig a rette or **cig a ret** (sig′ə ret′, sig′ə-ret′), *n.* a small roll of finely cut tobacco wrapped in a thin sheet of treated paper for smoking.

cil i a (sil′ē ə), *n.pl.* of **cil i um** (sil′ē əm). very small, hairlike projections on leaves, wings, insects, etc. Some microscopic animals use cilia to move themselves or to set up currents in the surrounding water. [< Latin]

cil i ar y (sil′ē er′ē), *adj.* 1 of or resembling cilia. 2 having to do with certain delicate structures of the eyeball.

cil i ate (sil′ē āt, sil′ē it), *adj.* provided with cilia. —*n.* any of a class of one-celled protozoans having cilia. Paramecia are ciliates.

cil i at ed (sil′ē ā′tid), *adj.* ciliate.

Ci li cia (sə lish′ə), *n.* 1 ancient country and Roman province on the SE coast of Asia Minor. 2 region in S Turkey. **—Ci li′cian,** *adj., n.*

Ci ma bu e (chē′mä bü′ā), *n.* **Giovanni,** 1240?-1302?, Florentine painter, sometimes called the father of modern painting.

Cim ar ron River (sim′ə rōn′, sim′ə-ron′), river flowing from NE New Mexico into the Arkansas River in Oklahoma. 650 mi.

Cim me ri an (sə mir′ē ən), *n.* one of a legendary people, described by Homer, said to live in perpetual mists and darkness. —*adj.* very dark and gloomy.

C. in C., commander in chief.

cinch (sinch), *n.* 1 a strong girth for fastening a saddle or pack on a horse. 2 INFORMAL. a firm hold or grip. 3 SLANG. something sure and easy: *It's a cinch we'll win the game.* —*v.t.* 1 fasten on with a cinch; bind firmly. 2 INFORMAL. get a firm hold on. 3 INFORMAL. make certain of. [< Spanish *cincha* < Latin *cingula* a band, belt < *cingere* bind]

cinquefoil (def. 2)

cin cho na (sin kō′nə), *n.* 1 an evergreen tree of the same family as the madder, native to the Andes Mountains and growing in the East Indies. 2 its valuable, bitter bark, from which quinine and other drugs are obtained; Peruvian bark. [< Countess *Cinchón,* 1576-1639, wife of a Spanish viceroy to Peru]

Cin cin nat i (sin′sə nat′ē, sin′sə nat′ə), *n.* city in SW Ohio, on the Ohio River. 453,000.

Cin cin na tus (sin′sə nā′təs), *n.* **Lucius Quinctius,** 519?-439? B.C., Roman patriot, dictator in 458 and 439 B.C. On both occasions, he defeated the enemies of Rome and promptly returned to his farm as a simple citizen.

cinc ture (singk′chər), *n., v.,* **-tured, -tur ing.** —*n.* 1 belt or girdle. 2 border or enclosure. —*v.t.* encircle; surround. [< Latin *cinctura* < *cingere* bind, gird]

cin der (sin′dər), *n.* 1 piece of burned-up wood or coal. 2 **cinders,** *pl.* **a** wood or coal partly burned but no longer flaming. **b** ashes. 3 slag, especially slag produced in making pig iron in the blast furnace. [Old English *sinder*]

cinder block, a rectangular building block of cement and finely ground coal cinders, usually hollow, used in walls and partitions.

Cin der el la (sin′də rel′ə), *n.* 1 girl in a fairy tale who is cruelly overworked by her stepmother but is rescued by her fairy godmother, and later marries a prince. 2 person whose real worth or beauty is not recognized.

cin e (sin′ə, sin′ē), *adj.* cinematographic; motion-picture: *a cine camera, cine art.* [short for *cinema*]

cin e ma (sin′ə mə), *n.* 1 a motion picture. 2 a motion-picture theater. 3 **the cinema,** motion pictures. [short for *cinematograph*]

cin e mat ic (sin′ə mat′ik), *adj.* having to do with motion pictures. **—cin′e mat′i cal ly,** *adv.*

cin e mat o graph (sin′ə mat′ə graf), *n.* 1 BRITISH. a motion-picture projector. 2 a motion-picture camera. [< Greek *kinematos* motion + English *-graph*]

cin e mat o graph ic (sin′ə mat′ə-graf′ik), *adj.* of or having to do with a cinematograph or cinematography.

cin e ma tog ra phy (sin′ə mə tog′rə fē), *n.* art and science of making motion pictures.

cin e rar i a (sin′ə rer′ē ə), *n.* 1 a small plant of the composite family with large, heart-shaped leaves and clusters of white, red, or purple flowers. 2 pl. of **cinerarium.**

cin e rar i um (sin′ə rer′ē əm), *n., pl.* **-rar i a.** place for keeping the ashes of cremated bodies. [< Latin < *cinerem* ashes]

cin e rar y (sin′ə rer′ē), *adj.* of or for ashes; used to hold the ashes of a cremated body.

cin na bar (sin′ə bär), *n.* 1 a reddish or brownish mineral that is the chief source of mercury; native mercuric sulfide. *Formula:* HgS 2 artificial mercuric sulfide, used as a red pigment in making paints, dyes, etc. 3 a bright red color; vermilion. —*adj.* bright-red; vermilion. [< Latin *cinnabaris*]

cin na mon (sin′ə mən), *n.* 1 spice made from the dried, reddish-brown inner bark of a laurel tree of the East Indies. 2 this bark. 3 tree yielding this bark. 4 a light, reddish brown. —*adj.* 1 flavored with cinnamon. 2 light reddish-brown: *a cinnamon bear.* [< Latin < Greek *kinnamon;* of Semitic origin]

cinque foil (singk′foil′), *n.* 1 any of a genus of plants of the rose family, having small, five-petaled yellow, white, or red flowers and leaves divided into five parts. 2 an ornamental design, especially in architecture, made of five connected semicircles or part circles. [< Latin *quinquefolium* < *quinque* five + *folium* leaf]

hat, āge, fär; let, ēqual, tėrm;
it, īce; hot, ōpen, ôrder;
oil, out; cup, pu̇t, rüle;
ch, child; ng, long; sh, she;
th, thin; ᴛʜ, then; zh, measure;

ə represents *a* in about, *e* in taken, *i* in pencil, *o* in lemon, *u* in circus.

< = from, derived from, taken from.

CIO or **C.I.O.,** Congress of Industrial Organizations, a group of labor unions organized on a permanent basis in 1938. The CIO merged with the AFL in 1955. See **AFL-CIO.**

ci on (sī′ən), *n.* scion (def. 2).

ci pher (sī′fər), *n.* 1 secret writing; code: *Part of the letter is in cipher.* 2 something in secret writing or code. 3 the key to a method of secret writing or a code. 4 zero; 0. 5 an Arabic numeral. 6 person or thing of no importance. 7 interlaced intitials; monogram. —*v.i.* do arithmetic; use figures. —*v.t.* 1 work by arithmetic. 2 express by characters of any kind, especially in code or secret writing. Also, **cypher.** [< Medieval Latin *ciphra* < Arabic *ṣifr* empty. Doublet of ZERO.]

cir ca (sėr′kə), *prep.* about; approximately: *Mohammed was born circa* A.D. *570.* [< Latin]

cir ca di an (sėr′kā′dē ən), *adj.* of or having to do with any biological process that recurs in a daily rhythm, such as the 24-hour cycle of sleep and wakefulness in man. [< Latin *circa* around + *dies* day]

Cir cas sia (sər kash′ə), *n.* region in SW Soviet Union, on the NE shore of the Black Sea. **—Cir cas′sian,** *adj., n.*

Cir ce (sėr′sē), *n.* 1 (in Greek legends) an enchantress who changed men into beasts. Ulysses withstood her spell and forced her to set free his companions, whom she had changed to swine. 2 any enchantress.

cir ci nate (sėr′sə nāt), *adj.* 1 rolled up into a coil. 2 (in botany) coiled from the tip toward the base. The new leaves of a fern are circinate. [< Latin *circinatus* made round] **—cir′ci nate ly,** *adv.*

cir cle (sėr′kəl), *n., v.,* **-cled, -cling.** —*n.* 1 a closed, curved line on which every point is equally distant from a fixed point within called the center. 2 a plane figure bounded by such a line. 3 halo, crown, or anything shaped like a circle or part of one. 4 ring. 5 set of seats in the balcony of a theater. 6 a complete series or course; period; cycle: *A year is a circle of 12 months.* 7 group of people held together by the same interests: *the family circle, a circle of friends.* See synonym study below. 8 sphere of influence, action, etc. 9 set of parts that form a connected whole: *the circle of the sciences.* 10 traffic circle.
—*v.t.* 1 go around in a circle; revolve around: *The moon circles the earth.* 2 form a circle around; surround; encircle. —*v.i.* 1 move in a circle: *The airplane circled before it landed.* 2 form a circle.
[< Old French *cercle* < Latin *circulus,* diminutive of *circus* ring] **—cir′cler,** *n.*

Syn. *n.* 7 **Circle, clique** mean a group of

people held together by a common tie. **Circle** applies to a group held together around a person or a common interest, cause, or occupation: *literary circles, academic circles.* **Clique** applies to a small, exclusive, sometimes snobbish, group, and often expresses an attitude of disapproval on the part of the speaker toward the group: *Every school has its cliques.*

cir clet (sėr′klit), *n.* 1 a small circle. 2 a round ornament worn on the head, neck, arm, or finger, especially a headband.

cir cuit (sėr′kit), *n.* 1 a going around; a moving around: *It takes a year for the earth to make its circuit of the sun.* 2 route over which a person or group makes repeated journeys at certain times. Some judges make a circuit, stopping at certain towns along the way to hold court. 3 the part of the country through which such journeys are made. 4 district under the jurisdiction of a circuit court. 5 distance around any space. 6 line enclosing any space. 7 space enclosed. 8 the complete path over which an electric current flows. 9 arrangement of wiring, tubes, etc., forming electrical connections; hookup. 10 number of theaters under the same management and presenting the same shows. *—v.t.* make a circuit of. *—v.i.* go in a circuit. [< Latin *circuitus* a going around < *circum* around + *ire* go]

circuit breaker, switch that automatically opens or interrupts an electric circuit under conditions of excessive current, voltage, temperature, etc.

circuit court, court whose judges regularly hold court at certain places in a district.

cir cu i tous (sər kyü′ə təs), *adj.* not direct; roundabout: *We took a circuitous route home to avoid poor roads.* **—cir cu′i tous ly,** *adv.* **—cir cu′i tous ness,** *n.*

circuit rider, preacher who rides from place to place over a circuit to preach. Methodist circuit riders were common in the 1800's.

cir cuit ry (sėr′kə trē), *n., pl.* **-ries.** 1 the science of electrical or electronic circuits. 2 the component parts of an electrical or electronic circuit.

cir cu i ty (sər kyü′ə tē), *n., pl.* **-ties.** 1 circuitous quality. 2 a roundabout manner of moving, acting, etc.

cir cu lar (sėr′kyə lər), *adj.* 1 round like a circle. 2 moving in a circle; going around a circle. 3 of or having to do with a circle. 4 sent to each of a number of people: *a circular letter.* 5 roundabout; indirect. 6 happening in a cycle, especially a repetitious cycle: *a circular chain of events.* *—n.* letter, notice, or advertisement sent to each of a number of people. **—cir′cu lar ly,** *adv.*

cir cu lar i ty (sėr′kyə lar′ə tē), *n., pl.* **-ties.** circular shape.

cir cu lar ize (sėr′kyə lə rīz′), *v.t.,* **-ized, -iz ing.** 1 send circulars to. 2 make circular or round. **—cir′cu lar i za′tion,** *n.* **—cir′cu lar iz′er,** *n.*

circular measure, system used for measuring circles:

60 seconds = 1 minute
60 minutes = 1 degree
90 degrees = 1 quadrant
4 quadrants or 360 degrees = 1 circle

circular saw, a thin disk with teeth in its edge, turned at high speed by machinery.

cir cu late (sėr′kyə lāt), *v.,* **-lat ed, -lat ing.** *—v.i.* 1 go around; pass from place to place or from person to person: *Water circulates in the pipes of a building. Money circulates as it goes from person to person. A newspaper circulates among people who read it.* 2 (of the blood) flow from the heart through the arteries and veins back to the heart. *—v.t.* 1 send around from person to person or from place to place: *circulate news of a holiday.* 2 put into the hands of readers; distribute: *This book has been circulated widely.* **—cir′cu la′tor,** *n.*

circulating library, library whose books can be rented or borrowed.

cir cu la tion (sėr′kyə lā′shən), *n.* 1 a going around; circulating: *Open windows increase the circulation of air in a room.* 2 flow of the blood from the heart through the arteries and veins back to the heart. 3 a sending around of books, papers, news, etc., from person to person or from place to place. 4 the number of copies of a book, newspaper, magazine, etc., that are sent out during a certain time.

cir cu la to ry (sėr′kyə lə tôr′ē, sėr′kyə lə-tōr′ē), *adj.* having to do with circulation. Arteries and veins are parts of the circulatory system of the human body.

circum-, *prefix.* in a circle; around: *Circumnavigate = navigate around.* [< Latin < *circus* circle, ring]

cir cum am bi ent (sėr′kə mam′bē ənt), *adj.* surrounding; encircling.

cir cum am bu late (sėr′kə mam′byə lāt), *v.t., v.i.,* **-lat ed, -lat ing.** go around (a place); circle by walking.

cir cum cen ter (sėr′kəm sen′tər), *n.* the center of a circle that is circumscribed around another figure. The circumcenter of a triangle is the center of the circle circumscribed about it.

cir cum cise (sėr′kəm sīz), *v.t.,* **-cised, -cis ing.** cut off the foreskin of. [< Latin *circumcisum* circumcised < *circum* around + *caedere* cut] **—cir′cum cis′er,** *n.*

cir cum ci sion (sėr′kəm sizh′ən), *n.* 1 act of circumcising. 2 a Jewish ritual in which a boy is circumcised when he is eight days old as a symbol of the covenant which, according to the Bible, God made with Abraham.

cir cum fer ence (sər kum′fər əns), *n.* 1 the boundary line of a circle or of certain other surfaces. Every point in the circumference of a circle is at the same distance from the center. 2 the distance around: *The circumference of the earth at the equator is almost 25,000 miles.* [< Latin *circumferentia* < *circum* around + *ferre* bear]

cir cum fer en tial (sər kum′fə ren′shəl), *adj.* of a circumference; located at or near the circumference.

cir cum flex (sėr′kəm fleks), *n.* a circumflex accent. *—adj.* 1 of or having a circumflex accent. 2 bending or winding around. [< Latin *circumflexum* bent around < *circum* around + *flectere* to bend]

circumflex accent, 1 (in the pronunciations in this book) a mark used over *o* to show that it is pronounced as in *order* (ôr′dər). 2 mark (ˆ or ⁀ or ˜) placed over a vowel to tell something about its pronunciation, as in the French word *fête.*

cir cum flu ent (sər kum′flü ənt), *adj.* flowing around; surrounding.

cir cum fuse (sėr′kəm fyüz′), *v.t.,* **-fused, -fus ing.** 1 pour or spread around. 2 surround; suffuse. **—cir′cum fu′sion,** *n.*

cir cum lo cu tion (sėr′kəm lō kyü′shən), *n.* 1 the use of several or many words instead of one or a few. 2 a roundabout expression: *"The wife of your father's brother" is a circumlocution for "Your aunt."*

cir cum loc u to ry (sėr′kəm lok′yə tôr′ē, sėr′kəm lok′yə tōr′ē), *adj.* marked by circumlocution; roundabout.

cir cum lu nar (sėr′kəm lü′nər), *adj.* 1 revolving about the moon. 2 surrounding the moon.

cir cum nav i gate (sėr′kəm nav′ə gāt), *v.t.,* **-gat ed, -gat ing.** sail around: *Magellan's ship circumnavigated the earth.* **—cir′cum nav′i ga′tor,** *n.*

cir cum nav i ga tion (sėr′kəm nav′ə-gā′shən), *n.* act of sailing around.

cir cum po lar (sėr′kəm pō′lər), *adj.* 1 around the North or South Pole: *circumpolar seas.* 2 around either pole of the heavens without sinking below the horizon: *a circumpolar star.*

cir cum scribe (sėr′kəm skrīb′, sėr′kəm-skrīb), *v.t.,* **-scribed, -scrib ing.** 1 draw a line around; mark the boundaries of; bound. 2 surround: *the atmosphere circumscribing the earth.* 3 limit; restrict: *A prisoner's activities are circumscribed.* 4 draw (a figure) around another figure so as to touch as many points as possible. 5 be so drawn around: *A circle that circumscribes a square touches the four corners of the square.* [< Latin *circumscribere* < *circum* around + *scribere* write]

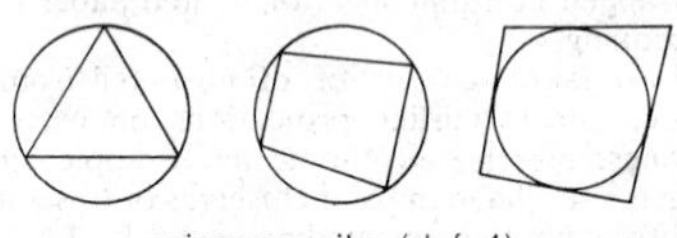

circumscribe (def. 4)
circumscribed figures

cir cum scrip tion (sėr′kəm skrip′shən), *n.* 1 a circumscribing. 2 a being circumscribed. 3 thing that circumscribes. 4 inscription around a coin, medal, etc. 5 outline; boundary. 6 space circumscribed. 7 limitation; restriction.

cir cum spect (sėr′kəm spekt), *adj.* watchful on all sides; cautious or prudent; careful. [< Latin *circumspectum* < *circum* around + *specere* look] **—cir′cum spect′ly,** *adv.* **—cir′cum spect′ness,** *n.*

cir cum spec tion (sėr′kəm spek′shən), *n.* caution or prudence; care.

cir cum stance (sėr′kəm stans), *n.* 1 condition that accompanies an act or event: *The place and the weather were the two circumstances that made our picnic a great success.* 2 fact or event: *It was a lucky circumstance that she found her money.* 3 unimportant details in a narration; full detail: *tell of one's adventures with great circumstance.* 4 ceremony; display: *The royal procession advanced with pomp and circumstance.* 5 **circumstances,** *pl.* **a** financial condition: *A rich person is in good circumstances; a poor person is in bad circumstances.* **b** the existing conditions or state of affairs: *forced by circumstances to resign.* 6 **under no circumstances,** never; no matter what the conditions are. 7 **under the circumstances,** because of these conditions; things being as they are or were. [< Latin *circumstantia* < *circumstare* surround < *circum* around + *stare* stand]

cir cum stan tial (sėr′kəm stan′shəl), *adj.* 1 depending on or based on circumstances: *Stolen jewels found in a person's possession are circumstantial evidence that he stole them.* 2 not essential; not important; incidental: *Minor details are circumstantial* *compared with the main fact.* 3 giving full and exact details; complete: *a circumstantial report of an accident.* **—cir′cum stan′tial ly,** *adv.*

cir cum stan ti ate (sėr′kəm stan′shē āt), *v.t.,* **-at ed, -at ing.** give the circumstances of; support or prove with details. **—cir′cum stan′ti a′tion,** *n.*

cir cum vent (sėr′kəm vent′), *v.t.* 1 get the better of or defeat by trickery; outwit: *circumvent the law.* 2 go around. 3 catch in a trap. [< Latin *circumventum* circumvented < *circum* around + *venire* come] **—cir′cum ven′tion,** *n.*

cir cus (sėr′kəs), *n.* 1 a traveling show of acrobats, clowns, horses, riders, and wild animals. 2 the performers who give the show or the performances they give. 3 the circular area, often covered by a large circular tent, with tiers of seats for spectators, in which such a performance is given. 4 INFORMAL. **a** an amusing person or thing. **b** a lively time. 5 (in ancient Rome) an arena with rows of seats around it, each row higher than the one in front of it. 6 BRITISH. a traffic circle. [< Latin, ring. Doublet of CIRQUE.]

cirque (sėrk), *n.* 1 a circular space. 2 a natural amphitheater encircled by heights, especially one in the mountains formed by erosion at the head of a glacier. 3 circlet; ring. [< Middle French < Latin *circus.* Doublet of CIRCUS.]

cir rho sis (sə rō′sis), *n.* a chronic disease of the liver marked by degeneration of the liver cells and excessive formation of connective tissue. [< New Latin < Greek *kirrhos* orange-yellow]

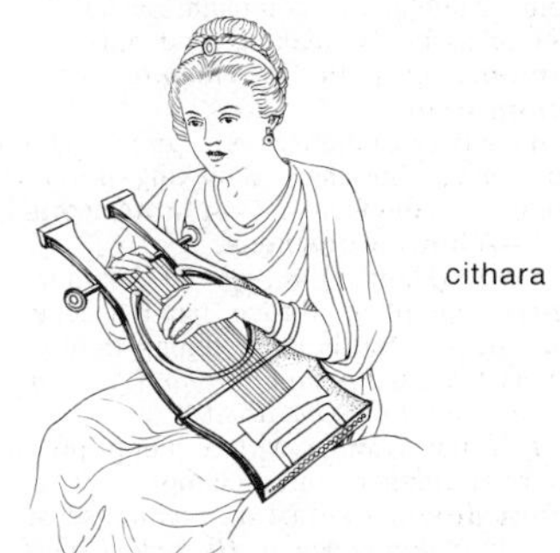
cithara

cir rhot ic (sə rot′ik), *adj.* 1 having cirrhosis. 2 resembling cirrhosis.

cir ri ped (sir′ə ped), *n.* any of a subclass of crustaceans having threadlike appendages instead of legs. Barnacles belong to this subclass. [< Latin *cirrus* curl + *pedem* foot]

cir ro cu mu lus (sir′ō kyü′myə ləs), *n.* cloud formation consisting of small, globular masses of white, fleecy clouds arranged in wavelike rows or groups, occurring at heights of 20,000 feet and above.

cir ro stra tus (sir′ō strā′təs), *n.* a thin, white, veillike cloud formation occurring at heights of 20,000 feet and above.

cir rus (sir′əs), *n., pl.* **cir ri** (sir′ī). 1 cloud formation consisting of thin, detached, featherlike, white clouds of ice crystals occurring at heights of 20,000 feet and above. 2 (in zoology) a slender process or appendage. 3 (in botany) a tendril. [< Latin, curl]

cis-, *prefix.* 1 on this side of; near, as in *cislunar.* 2 (in chemistry) having certain atoms on the same side of a plane: *a cis-isomeric compound.* [< Latin, on this side]

cis al pine (sis al′pīn, sis al′pin), *adj.* on the southern side of the Alps.

cis co (sis′kō), *n., pl.* **-coes** or **-cos.** a kind of whitefish found in the Great Lakes area; lake herring. [short for Canadian French *ciscoette,* perhaps < Ojibwa *siskawit*]

cis lu nar (si slü′nər), *adj.* in the moon's vicinity; between the earth and the moon: *cislunar space.*

Cis ter cian (si stėr′shən), *n.* member of a Benedictine order of monks and nuns founded in France in 1098. *—adj.* of or having to do with this order.

cis tern (sis′tərn), *n.* an artificial reservoir for storing water, especially a tank below ground. [< Latin *cisterna* < *cista* box]

cit., 1 citation. 2 cited. 3 citizen.

cit a del (sit′ə dəl, sit′ə del), *n.* 1 fortress commanding a city. 2 a strongly fortified place; stronghold. 3 a strong, safe place; refuge. [< Middle French *citadelle* < Italian *cittadella,* diminutive of *città* city < Latin *civitatem.* See CITY.]

ci ta tion (sī tā′shən), *n.* 1 quotation or reference given as an authority for facts or opinions. 2 act of citing. 3 honorable mention for bravery in war. 4 specific mention in an official dispatch. 5 commendation of a civilian for public service by some official or institution. 6 summons to appear before a court of law.

cite (sīt), *v.t.,* **cit ed, cit ing.** 1 quote (a passage, book, or author), especially as an authority: *I cited the encyclopedia to prove my statement.* See **quote** for synonym study. 2 refer to; mention as an example: *The lawyer cited another case similar to the one being tried.* 3 give honorable mention for bravery in war. 4 commend publicly for service to the community. 5 summon officially to appear before a court of law. 6 arouse to action; summon. [< Latin *citare* summon < *ciere* set in motion] **—cite′a ble,** *adj.*

cith ar a (sith′ər ə), *n.* an ancient musical instrument somewhat like a lyre. [< Latin < Greek *kithara.* Doublet of GUITAR, ZITHER.]

cit i fied (sit′ə fīd), *adj.* INFORMAL. having city ways or fashions.

cit i zen (sit′ə zən, sit′ə sən), *n.* 1 person who by birth or by choice is a member of a state or nation which gives him certain rights and claims his loyalty: *Many immigrants have become citizens of the United States.* 2 inhabitant of a city or town. 3 a civilian. [< Anglo-French *citisein,* alteration of Old French *citeain* < *cite.* See CITY.]

cit i zen ry (sit′ə zən rē, sit′ə sən rē), *n., pl.* **-ries.** citizens as a group.

cit i zen ship (sit′ə zən ship, sit′ə sən ship), *n.* 1 the duties, rights, and privileges of a citizen. 2 condition of being a citizen.

cit rate (sit′rāt), *n.* salt or ester of citric acid.

cit ric (sit′rik), *adj.* of or from citrus fruits.

citric acid, a white, odorless acid with a sour taste, found in the juice of oranges, lemons, limes, and similar fruits. It is used as a flavoring, as a medicine, and in making dyes. *Formula:* $C_6H_8O_7$

cit rine (sit′rən), *adj.* lemon-colored; pale-yellow. *—n.* a pale yellow.

cit ron (sit′rən), *n.* 1 a pale-yellow citrus fruit somewhat like a lemon but larger, with less acid and a thicker rind. 2 the shrub or small tree that it grows on. 3 its rind, candied and used in fruit cakes, plum pudding, candies, etc. [< Middle French < Italian *citrone* < Latin *citrus* citrus tree]

hat, āge, fär; let, ēqual, tėrm;
it, īce; hot, ōpen, ôrder;
oil, out; cup, pu̇t, rüle;
ch, child; ng, long; sh, she;
th, thin; ᴛʜ, then; zh, measure;

ə represents *a* in about, *e* in taken, *i* in pencil, *o* in lemon, *u* in circus.

< = from, derived from, taken from.

cit ro nel la (sit′rə nel′ə), *n.* 1 oil used in making perfume, soap, liniment, etc., and for keeping mosquitoes away. 2 a fragrant grass of southern Asia and Central America from which this oil is made.

cit rous (sit′rəs), *adj.* having to do with citrus fruits.

cit rus (sit′rəs), *n.* 1 any tree of the same family as the rue, bearing lemons, grapefruit, limes, oranges, and similar fruit. Citruses usually grow in warm climates. 2 Also, **citrus fruit.** fruit of such a tree, rich in vitamin C. *—adj.* of such trees. [< Latin]

cittern

cit tern (sit′ərn), *n.* an old instrument somewhat like the guitar, much used in the 1500's and 1600's.

cit y (sit′ē), *n., pl.* **cit ies,** *adj.* *—n.* 1 a large and important center of population and business activity. 2 division of local government in the United States having a charter from the state that fixes its boundaries and powers. A city is usually governed by a mayor and a board of aldermen or councilmen. 3 division of local government in Canada of the highest class. 4 (in Great Britain) a borough, usually the seat of a bishop, which has been granted the rank of "city" by royal authority. 5 people living in a city. 6 a city-state. *—adj.* 1 of a city. 2 in a city. [< Old French *cite* < Latin *civitatem* citizenship, state, city < *civis* citizen]

city editor, the newspaper editor in charge of collecting and editing local news.

city fathers, councilmen, aldermen, magistrates, or other leading men of a city.

city hall, the headquarters of the officials, bureaus, etc., of a city government.

city manager, person hired by a city council or commission to manage the government of a city.

city of David, 1 Jerusalem. 2 Bethlehem.

cit y-state (sit′ē stāt′), *n.* an independent state consisting of a city and the territories depending on it. Athens was a city-state in ancient Greece.

cit y wide (sit′ē wīd′), *adj.* covering an entire city; over all of a city.

Ciu dad Juá rez (syü däd′ hwä′rās), city in N Mexico, on the Rio Grande. 379,000.

Ciu dad Tru jil lo (syü däd′ trü hē′yō), former name of **Santo Domingo.**

civ et (siv′it), *n.* 1 a yellowish secretion produced by certain glands of the civet cat. It has a musky odor and is used in making perfume. 2 civet cat. [< Middle French *civette* < Italian *zibetto* < Arabic *zabād*]

civet cat, any of various small, usually spotted or striped mammals of Africa and Asia, having glands that produce civet.

civ ic (siv′ik), *adj.* 1 of a city. 2 of or having to do with citizens or citizenship: *Every person has some civic duties, such as obeying the laws, voting, and paying taxes.* [< Latin *civicus* < *civis* citizen] **—civ′i cal ly,** *adv.*

civ ics (siv′iks), *n.* study of the duties, rights, and privileges of citizens.

civ il (siv′əl), *adj.* 1 of a citizen or citizens; having to do with citizens: *civil duties.* 2 of or having to do with the government, state, or nation: *Police departments are civil institutions.* 3 occurring among citizens of one community, state, or nation: *civil strife.* 4 of a citizen in his ordinary capacity; not connected with the armed forces or the church: *a civil court, a civil marriage.* 5 polite; courteous: *Although he was in a hurry, the boy pointed out the way in a civil manner.* See **polite** for synonym study. 6 having to do with the private rights of individuals and with laws protecting these rights. Civil lawsuits deal with such things as contracts, ownership of property, and payment for personal injury. [< Latin *civilis* < *civis* citizen]

civil defense, a civilian emergency program for protecting people and property from enemy attack and natural disasters.

civil disobedience, refusal on principle to obey a law of the country or state, especially by not paying taxes or by refusing to serve in the armed forces.

civil engineer, person whose profession is civil engineering.

civil engineering, the planning and directing of the construction of bridges, roads, harbors, canals, dams, and other public works.

ci vil ian (sə vil′yən), *n.* person who is not in the armed forces. *—adj.* of civilians; not of the armed forces: *civilian clothes.*

ci vil i ty (sə vil′ə tē), *n., pl.* **-ties.** 1 polite behavior; courtesy. 2 act or expression of politeness or courtesy.

civ i li za tion (siv′ə lə zā′shən), *n.* 1 civilized condition; advanced stage in social development. 2 nations and peoples that have reached advanced stages in social development: *All civilization should be aroused against war.* 3 the culture and ways of living of a people or nation: *There are differences between Chinese civilization and our own.* 4 process of becoming civilized; improvement in culture. 5 a civilizing.

civ i lize (siv′ə līz), *v.t.,* **-lized, -liz ing.** 1 bring out of a savage or barbarian condition; train in culture, science, and art: *The Romans civilized a great part of their world.* 2 improve in culture and good manners; refine. **—civ′i liz′er,** *n.*

civ i lized (siv′ə līzd), *adj.* 1 advanced in social customs, art, and science. 2 of civilized nations or persons. 3 showing culture and good manners; refined: *a civilized attitude.*

civil law, 1 law that regulates and protects private rights and is controlled and used by civil courts, not military courts. 2 Roman law or a system of law based on Roman law, used in France and other European countries, and in parts of the United States and Canada, such as Louisiana and Quebec.

civil liberty, the freedom of a person to enjoy the rights guaranteed by the laws or constitution of a country without any undue restraint or interference by the government.

civ il ly (siv′ə lē), *adv.* 1 politely; courteously. 2 according to the civil law.

civil marriage, marriage performed by a government official, not by a clergyman.

civil rights, the rights of a citizen, especially the rights guaranteed to all citizens of the United States, regardless of race, color, or sex, by the 13th, 14th, 15th, 19th, and 24th amendments to the Constitution and certain acts of Congress.

civil servant, member of the civil service.

civil service, branch of government service concerned with affairs not military, naval, legislative, or judicial. All civilian government workers who are appointed rather than elected are in the civil service.

civil war, 1 war between opposing groups of one nation. 2 **Civil War, a** war between the northern and southern states of the United States from 1861 to 1865; War Between the States. **b** war between the English Parliament and the Royalists, from 1642 to 1646 and from 1648 to 1652.

ck., *pl.* **cks.** cask.

Cl, chlorine.

cl., 1 centiliter or centiliters. 2 class. 3 clerk.

clab ber (klab′ər), *n.* thick, sour milk. *—v.t., v.i.* thicken in souring; curdle. [< Irish *clabar* curds]

clack (klak), *v.i.* 1 make a short, sharp sound: *The train clacked over the rails.* 2 talk noisily; chatter. *—v.t.* cause to clack. *—n.* 1 a short, sharp sound: *We heard the clack of a typewriter.* 2 the noise of continuous speech; senseless chatter. [imitative] **—clack′er,** *n.*

clad (klad), *v.* a pt. and a pp. of **clothe.**

claim (klām), *v.t.* 1 say one has (a right, title, possession, etc.) and demand that others recognize it; assert one's right to: *claim a tract of land.* 2 demand as one's own or one's right: *Does anyone claim this pencil?* See **demand** for synonym study. 3 say strongly; declare as a fact; maintain: *I claimed that my answer was correct.* 4 require; call for; deserve: *Business claims her attention.* *—v.i.* 1 assert a right; put forward as a right or title. 2 assert a belief or opinion. *—n.* 1 demand for something due; assertion of a right. 2 right or title to something; right to demand something. 3 something that is claimed. 4 piece of public land which a settler or prospector marks out for himself. 5 declaration of something as a fact. 6 **jump a claim,** seize a piece of land claimed by another. 7 **lay claim to,** assert one's right to; claim: *lay claim to a piece of land.* [< Old French *claimer, clamer* < Latin *clamare* call, proclaim] **—claim′a ble,** *adj.* **—claim′er,** *n.*

claim ant (klā′mənt), *n.* person who makes a claim.

clair voy ance (kler voi′əns, klar voi′əns), *n.* 1 the supposed power of seeing or knowing about things that are out of sight. 2 exceptional insight.

clair voy ant (kler voi′ənt, klar voi′ənt), *adj.* 1 supposedly having the power of seeing or knowing things that are out of sight. 2 having exceptional insight. *—n.* person who has, or claims to have, the power of seeing or knowing things that are out of sight: *The clairvoyant claimed to be able to locate lost articles and to give news of faraway people.* [< French < *clair* clear + *voyant* present participle of *voir* to see] **—clair-voy′ant ly,** *adv.*

clam (klam), *n., v.,* **clammed, clam ming.** *—n.* 1 any of various mollusks somewhat like oysters, with a soft body and a shell in two hinged halves. Clams burrow in sand or mud along the seashore or at the edges of rivers, lakes, etc. Many kinds are edible. 2 the fleshy part of such a mollusk, eaten raw or cooked. *—v.i.* 1 go out after clams; dig for clams. 2 **clam up,** INFORMAL. stop talking; refuse to speak. [apparently special use of earlier *clam* pair of pincers; Old English *clamm* fetter] **—clam′like′,** *adj.*

clam bake (klam′bāk′), *n.* picnic where clams are baked or steamed. A clambake may be an elaborate meal, with much to eat besides clams.

clam ber (klam′bər), *v.i., v.t.* climb, using both hands and feet; climb awkwardly or with difficulty; scramble. *—n.* an awkward or difficult climb. [Middle English *clambren.* Related to CLIMB.] **—clam′ber er,** *n.*

clam my (klam′ē), *adj.,* **-mi er, -mi est.** 1 cold and damp. 2 soft, moist, and sticky. [Middle English *claymy*] **—clam′mi ly,** *adv.* **—clam′mi ness,** *n.*

clam or (klam′ər), *n.* 1 a loud noise or continual uproar; shouting. 2 a shout; outcry. 3 a noisy demand or complaint. *—v.i.* 1 make a loud noise or continual uproar; shout. 2 demand or complain noisily. *—v.t.* utter or assert by making loud noise. Also, **clamour.** [< Latin < *clamare* cry out] **—clam′or er,** *n.*

clam or ous (klam′ər əs), *adj.* 1 loud and noisy; shouting. 2 making noisy demands or complaints. **—clam′or ous ly,** *adv.* **—clam′or ous ness,** *n.*

clam our (klam′ər), *n., v.i., v.t.* clamor.

clamp (klamp), *n.* brace, band, wedge, or other device for holding things tightly together: *She used a clamp to hold the arm on the chair until the glue dried.*

—v.t. fasten together with a clamp; put in a clamp; strengthen with a clamp.

clamp down, INFORMAL. **a** impose strict control: *clamp down a 10 o'clock curfew.* **b** become more strict: *clamp down on speeders.*

[perhaps < Middle Dutch *klampe*]

clam shell (klam′shel′), *n.* 1 shell of a clam. 2 bucket, box, or the like, hinged like a clamshell, used in dredging and loading.

clan (klan), *n.* 1 group of related families that claim to be descended from a common ancestor. 2 group of people closely joined together by some common interest. [< Scottish Gaelic *clann* offspring, family < Latin *plantam* sprout, plant] **—clan′like′,** *adj.*

clan des tine (klan des′tən), *adj.* arranged or made in a stealthy or underhanded manner; concealed; secret: *a clandestine plan.* See **secret** for synonym study. [< Latin *clandestinus* < *clam* secretly] **—clan des′tine ly,** *adv.* **—clan des′tine-ness,** *n.*

clang (klang), *n.* a loud, harsh, ringing sound, as of metal being hit: *The clang of the fire bell aroused the town.* *—v.i.* make a clang. *—v.t.* 1 cause to make a clang. 2 strike together with a clang. [imitative]

hat, āge, fär; let, ēqual, tėrm;
it, īce; hot, ōpen, ôrder;
oil, out; cup, pu̇t, rüle;
ch, child; ng, long; sh, she;
th, thin; ᴛʜ, then; zh, measure;

ə represents *a* in about, *e* in taken, *i* in pencil, *o* in lemon, *u* in circus.

< = from, derived from, taken from.

clan gor (klang′ər, klang′gər), *n.* 1 a continued clanging. 2 clang. —*v.i.* make a clangor; clang. Also, **clangour.** [< Latin < *clangere* to ring]

clan gor ous (klang′ər əs, klang′gər əs), *adj.* clanging. **—clan′gor ous ly,** *adv.*

clarinet

clan gour (klang′ər, klang′gər), *n., v.i.* clangor.

clank (klangk), *n.* a sharp, harsh sound like the rattle of a heavy chain. —*v.i.* 1 make a sharp, harsh sound: *The tire chains clanked on bare highway.* 2 move with a clanking sound. —*v.t.* cause to clank. [probably imitative]

clan nish (klan′ish), *adj.* 1 having to do with a clan. 2 closely united; not liking outsiders. **—clan′nish ly,** *adv.* **—clan′nish ness,** *n.*

clans man (klanz′mən), *n., pl.* **-men.** member of a clan.

clap (klap), *v.,* **clapped, clap ping,** *n.* —*v.t.* 1 strike together loudly: *clap the cymbals, clap one's hands.* 2 applaud (a person, performance, etc.) by striking the hands together. 3 strike with a quick blow; slap: *clap a friend on the back.* 4 put or place quickly and effectively: *clapped into jail.* —*v.i.* 1 strike the hands together in applauding: *When the show was over, we all clapped.* 2 make a sharp, abrupt sound. —*n.* 1 a sudden noise, such as a single burst of thunder, the sound of the hands struck together, or the sound of a loud slap. 2 a loud, quick blow; slap: *a clap on the shoulder.* [Old English *clæppan*]

clap board (klab′ərd, klap′bôrd′, klap′bōrd′), *n.* a thin board, usually thicker along one edge than along the other, used to cover the outer walls of wooden buildings. Each board is made to overlap the one below it. —*v.t.* cover with clapboards. [half translation of Middle Dutch *klapholt* < *klappen* fit together + *holt* board]

clap per (klap′ər), *n.* 1 person or thing that claps. 2 the movable part inside a bell that strikes against and rings the outer part. 3 device for making noise.

clap trap (klap′trap′), *n.* empty talk or an insincere remark made just to get attention or applause. —*adj.* cheap and showy.

claque (klak), *n.* 1 group of persons hired to applaud in a theater. 2 group that applauds or follows another person for selfish reasons. [< French < *claquer* to clap]

Clar en don (klar′ən dən), *n.* Edward Hyde, the first **Earl of,** 1609-1674, British statesman and historian.

clar et (klar′ət), *n.* 1 kind of red wine. 2 a dark purplish red. —*adj.* dark purplish-red. [< Old French, light colored, diminutive of *cler* clear. See CLEAR.]

clar i fi ca tion (klar′ə fə kā′shən), *n.* 1 act or process of clarifying. 2 state of being clarified.

clar i fi er (klar′ə fī′ər), *n.* 1 substance used to clarify liquids. 2 a large metal pan used in clarifying the juice of sugar cane.

clar i fy (klar′ə fī), *v.,* **-fied, -fy ing.** —*v.t.* 1 make clearer; explain: *The teacher's explanation clarified the difficult instructions.* 2 make clear; purify: *The cook clarified the fat by heating it with a little water and straining it through cloth.* —*v.i.* become clear: *My mind suddenly clarified.* [< Old French *clarifier* < Late Latin *clarificare* < Latin *clarus* clear + *facere* make]

clar i net (klar′ə net′), *n.* a woodwind instrument, having a mouthpiece with a single reed and played by means of holes and keys. [< French *clarinette,* diminutive of *clarine* bell < Latin *clarus* clear]

clar i net ist or **clar i net tist** (klar′ə-net′ist), *n.* person who plays a clarinet.

clar i on (klar′ē ən), *adj.* clear and shrill: *a clarion sound or call.* —*n.* 1 a trumpet with clear, shrill tones. 2 sound made by this trumpet. 3 a clear, shrill sound like it. [< Medieval Latin *clarionem* < Latin *clarus* clear]

clar i ty (klar′ə tē), *n.* clearness.

Clark (klärk), *n.* 1 **George Rogers,** 1752-1818, American soldier and frontiersman. 2 his brother, **William,** 1770-1838, American soldier and explorer. He was a leader of the Lewis and Clark expedition from St. Louis to the mouth of the Columbia River from 1804 to 1806.

clash (klash), *n.* 1 a loud, harsh sound like that of two things running into each other, of striking metal, or of bells rung together but not in tune. 2 a strong disagreement; conflict: *a clash of opinion.* 3 a hostile encounter; collision. —*v.i.* 1 make a loud harsh sound of striking together. 2 come into contact with much violence and noise: *Their swords clashed together.* 3 come into conflict; disagree strongly: *The freshmen clashed with the sophomores.* 4 fail to harmonize: *Those red shoes clash with that green shirt and purple pants.* —*v.t.* 1 hit or strike with a clash. 2 throw, shut, etc., with a clash. [imitative] **—clash′er,** *n.*

clasp (klasp), *n.* 1 thing to fasten two parts or pieces together. A buckle on a belt is one kind of clasp. 2 a close hold with the arms. 3 a firm grip with the hand: *She gave my hand a warm clasp.* —*v.t.* 1 fasten together with a clasp. 2 hold closely with the arms; embrace. 3 grip firmly with the hand; grasp. [Middle English *claspen*] **—clasp′er,** *n.*

clasp knife, knife with a blade or blades folding into the handle, especially a large knife, with a single blade which, when open, may be secured in place by a catch.

class (klas), *n.* 1 group of persons or things alike in some way; kind; sort. 2 group of students taught together: *an art class.* 3 a meeting of such a group: *When I was absent I missed a great many classes.* 4 U.S. group of pupils entering a school together and graduating in the same year: *The class of 1970 graduated in 1970.* 5 rank or division of society: *the middle class.* 6 system of ranks or divisions in society. 7 high rank in society. 8 **the classes,** the higher ranks or divisions of society. 9 group of military draftees of the same age. 10 grade or quality: *First class is the best and most costly way to travel.* 11 SLANG. excellence; high style: *They have never really shown much class.* 12 (in zoology) a primary group of related animals ranking below a phylum and above an order. Crustaceans and insects are two classes in the phylum of arthropods. See **classification** for chart. 13 (in botany) a primary group of related plants ranking below either a division or subdivision and above an order. Monocotyledons and dicotyledons are two classes in the subdivision of angiosperms. See **classification** for chart.
—*v.t.* put in a class or group; classify. —*v.i.* be in a class or group.
[< Latin *classis* class, collection]

class., 1 classical. 2 classified.

class book (klas′bu̇k′), *n.* 1 book in which a teacher records the absences and keeps the grades of students. 2 an annual book usually published by the graduating class of a high school or college. It has pictures of the students, teachers, school buildings, etc.

class-con scious (klas′kon′shəs), *adj.* conscious of belonging to a particular social class and of being identified with its interests. **—class′-con′scious ness,** *n.*

clas sic (klas′ik), *n.* 1 author or artist of acknowledged excellence whose works serve as a standard, model, or guide: *Shakespeare is a classic.* 2 work of literature or art of the highest rank or quality: *Emily Brontë's "Wuthering Heights" is a classic.* 3 contest, match, or game of great importance: *The World Series is a baseball classic.* 4 **the classics,** the literature of ancient Greece and Rome. —*adj.* 1 of the highest rank or quality; serving as a standard, model, or guide; excellent; first-class. 2 of or having to do with the literature, art, and life of ancient Greece and Rome. 3 like this literature and art; simple, regular, and restrained. 4 (of fashion, clothes, etc.) simple in style; likely to remain in style for a long time. 5 famous in literature or history. [< Latin *classicus* of the highest class (of Romans) < *classis* class]

clas si cal (klas′ə kəl), *adj.* 1 classic (*adj.* defs. 1, 2, and 3). 2 acquainted with or having to do with the classics, especially the Greek and Roman classics: *classical studies, classical students.* 3 based on the classics: *"Ulysses" is perhaps the best of Tennyson's classical poems.* 4 being the original or traditional form of something; orthodox and sound, but not quite up to date: *classical physics.* 5 (in music) of high artistic quality and enjoyed especially by serious students of music. **—clas′si cal ly,** *adv.*

clas si cism (klas′ə siz′əm), *n.* 1 principles of the literature and art of ancient Greece and Rome, which include simplicity, regularity, restraint, and interest in forms. 2 the following of these principles. 3 knowledge of the literature of ancient Greece and Rome; classical scholarship. 4 idiom or form from Greek or Latin introduced into another language.

clas si cist (klas′ə sist), *n.* 1 follower of the principles of classicism in literature and art. 2 an expert in the classics. 3 person who urges the study of Greek and Latin.

clas si fi ca tion (klas′ə fə kā′shən), *n.* 1 act or process of arranging in classes or groups; grouping according to some system. 2 result of classifying; a systematic arrangement in groups or classes. 3 the arrangement of plants and animals into groups on the basis of ancestral relationship or structure.

clas si fi ca to ry (klas′ə fə kə tôr′ē, klas′ə fə kə tōr′ē), *adj.* of or having to do with classification.

clas si fied (klas′ə fīd), *adj.* 1 sorted or arranged in classes. A classified telephone directory lists names according to classes of business, services, and professions. 2 (of certain public documents of the United States) having a classification as secret, confidential, or restricted. 3 INFORMAL. secret.

classified ad, want ad.

clas si fy (klas′ə fī), *v.t.*, **-fied, -fy ing.** arrange in classes or groups; group according to some system: *Employees in the postal service classify letters and parcels according to the places where they are to go.* **—clas′si fi′a ble,** *adj.* **—clas′si fi′er,** *n.*

class interval, (in statistics) any of the arbitrary groups of equal and convenient size into which the possible values of a variable are often divided.

class less (klas′lis), *adj.* without classes; not divided into classes: *a classless society.*

class mate (klas′māt′), *n.* member of the same class in school.

class room (klas′rüm′, klas′rům′), *n.* room where classes are held; schoolroom.

class struggle, any conflict between divisions of society, especially between capital and labor.

clath rate (klath′rāt), *adj.* resembling a lattice; latticelike in form: *a clathrate crystal.* —*n.* a clathrate crystal. [< Latin *clathri* lattices]

clat ter (klat′ər), *n.* 1 a confused noise like that of many plates being struck together: *There was such a clatter in the kitchen that we could hardly hear one another talk.* 2 noisy talk. —*v.i.* 1 move or fall with confused noise; make a confused noise: *The horses clattered over the stones.* 2 talk fast and noisily; chatter. —*v.t.* cause to rattle or clatter. [Old English *clatrian*] **—clat′ter er,** *n.*

Clau di us I (klô′dē əs), 10 B.C.-A.D. 54, Roman emperor from A.D. 41 to 54.

clause (klôz), *n.* 1 part of a sentence having a subject and predicate. In "He came before we left," "He came" is a main clause that can stand alone as a sentence, and "before we left" is a subordinate clause that depends upon the main clause for completion of its meaning. A subordinate clause functions as a noun, adjective, or adverb. 2 a single provision of a law, treaty, or any other written agreement: *There is a clause in our lease that says we may not keep a dog in this building.* [< Old French < Medieval Latin *clausa* close of a period < Latin *claudere* close]

claus tro pho bi a (klô′strə fō′bē ə), *n.* an abnormal fear of enclosed spaces. [< Latin *claustrum* closed place + English *phobia*]

claus tro pho bic (klô′strə fō′bik), *adj.* of or having to do with claustrophobia.

cla vate (klā′vāt), *adj.* club-shaped. [< Latin *clava* club < *clavus* nail]

clave (klāv), *v.* ARCHAIC. a pt. of **cleave**².

clav i chord (klav′ə kôrd), *n.* a musical instrument with strings and a keyboard. The piano developed from it. [< Medieval Latin *clavichordium* < Latin *clavis* key + *chorda* string]

Classification of Animals and Plants

Each classification is subordinate to the one above it. The terms in **bold** type are the primary categories used in the complete classification of any organism. The indented terms in roman type are intermediate categories sometimes used in classifications. Categories that are parallel or identical in the animal and vegetable kingdoms appear opposite each other.

ANIMAL KINGDOM	VEGETABLE KINGDOM
subkingdom	
phylum	**division**
subphylum	subdivision
superclass	
class	**class**
subclass	subclass
order	**order**
suborder	suborder
family	**family**
subfamily	subfamily
tribe	tribe
genus	**genus**
subgenus	subgenus
species	**species**
subspecies or variety	subspecies or variety

clav i cle (klav′ə kəl), *n.* collarbone. [< Latin *clavicula* small key < *clavis* key; because of the shape of the bone]

cla vier (klə vir′), *n.* 1 keyboard or set of keys of a piano, organ, etc. 2 any musical instrument with a keyboard. The harpsichord and piano are two kinds of claviers. 3 a soundless keyboard used for practice. [ultimately < Latin *clavis* key]

claw (klô), *n.* 1 a sharp, hooked nail on a bird's or animal's foot. 2 foot with such sharp, hooked nails. 3 the pincers of a lobster, crab, etc. 4 anything like a claw, such as the part of a hammer used for pulling nails. —*v.t.* scratch, tear, seize, or pull with the claws or hands. —*v.i.* lay hold with the claws or hands; grasp or clutch. [Old English *clawu*] **—claw′like′,** *adj.*

claw hammer, hammer with one end of the head curved like a claw and forked for pulling nails.

clay (klā), *n.* 1 a stiff, sticky kind of earth, that can be easily shaped when wet and hardens after drying or baking. Bricks, dishes, and vases may be made from clay. 2 earth. 3 (in the Bible) the human body. [Old English *clǣg*] **—clay′like′,** *adj.*

clavichord
made in Germany about 1760

Clay (klā), *n.* **Henry,** 1777-1852, American statesman.

clay ey (klā′ē), *adj.*, **clay i er, clay i est.** 1 of, like, or containing clay. 2 covered or smeared with clay.

clay ish (klā′ish), *adj.* somewhat clayey.

clay more (klā′môr, klā′mōr), *n.* a heavy, two-edged broadsword, formerly used by Scottish Highlanders. [< Scottish Gaelic *claidheamh mor* great sword]

clay pigeon, a saucerlike clay target thrown in the air or released from the trap in trapshooting.

clean (klēn), *adj.* 1 free from dirt or filth; not soiled or stained: *clean clothes.* 2 pure or innocent; not corrupted; virtuous: *a clean heart.* 3 having clean habits: *Cats are clean animals.* 4 (of atomic weapons) causing little or no radioactive fallout. 5 fit for food: *Moslems and Jews do not consider pork a clean meat.* 6 clear, even, or regular: *a clean cut.* 7 well-shaped; trim: *a clean figure.* 8 clever; skillful: *a clean performance.* 9 complete or entire; total: *make a clean sweep.* 10 (of written or typed copy) free from errors or corrections; fair.
—*adv.* 1 completely or entirely; totally: *The horse jumped clean over the brook.* 2 in a clean manner; cleanly.
—*v.t.* make clean: *clean a room.* See synonym study below. —*v.i.* 1 undergo cleaning: *This room cleans easily because it doesn't have much furniture in it.* 2 do cleaning: *I am going to clean this morning.*
clean out, a make clean by emptying. **b** empty; use up. **c** SLANG. deprive of money: *cleaned out in the card game.*
clean up, a make clean by removing dirt, rubbish, etc. **b** put in order. **c** INFORMAL. finish; complete. **d** SLANG. make a profit.
[Old English *clǣne*]

Syn. —*v.t.* **Clean, cleanse** mean to make free from dirt or impurities. **Clean** means to remove dirt, impurities, or stains, especially from objects: *clean the windows, clean the streets.* **Cleanse** is sometimes applied to removing impurities by chemical or other technical processes: *Health experts are trying to cleanse the air in cities. We cleanse wounds.*

clean-cut (klēn′kut′), *adj.* 1 having clear, sharp outlines: *a clean-cut profile.* 2 distinct; definite: *a clean-cut statement of fact.* 3 having a neat and wholesome look: *a clean-cut young man.*

clean er (klē′nər), *n.* 1 person whose work is keeping buildings, windows, or other objects clean. 2 tool or machine for cleaning. 3 anything that removes dirt, grease, or stains. 4 dry cleaner.

clean-limbed (klēn′limd′), *adj.* having well-shaped limbs.

clean li ness (klen′lē nis), *n.* cleanness; habitual cleanness.

clean ly[1] (klen′lē), *adj.*, **-li er, -li est.** clean; habitually clean: *Our cat is a cleanly animal.* [Old English *clǣnlīc* < *clǣne* clean + *-līc* -ly[2]]

clean ly[2] (klēn′lē), *adv.* in a clean manner: *The butcher's knife cut cleanly through the meat.* [Old English *clǣnlīce* < *clǣne* clean + *-līc* -ly[1]]

clean ness (klēn′nis), *n.* clean condition or quality.

clean room, a sterilized and pressurized room for laboratory work.

cleanse (klenz), *v.t.*, **cleansed, cleans ing.** 1 make clean. See **clean** for synonym study. 2 make pure; purify. [Old English *clǣnsian* < *clǣne* clean] **—cleans′a ble,** *adj.*

cleans er (klen′zər), *n.* substance for cleaning or scouring.

clean-shav en (klēn′shā′vən), *adj.* with the facial hair or whiskers shaved off.

cleans ing (klen′zing), *n.* a making clean. *—adj.* that cleanses: *a cleansing agent.*

clean up (klēn′up′), *n.* 1 a cleaning up. 2 SLANG. an exceptional profit or gain, often acquired in a short period of time.

clear (klir), *adj.* 1 not cloudy, misty, or hazy; bright; light: *a clear day.* 2 easy to see through; transparent: *clear glass.* 3 having a pure, even color: *a clear blue.* 4 easily heard, seen, or understood; plain; distinct: *a clear idea, a clear voice.* 5 free from blemishes: *clear skin.* 6 sure; certain: *It is clear that it is going to rain.* 7 not blocked or obstructed; open: *a clear view.* 8 without touching; without being caught: *The ship was clear of the iceberg.* 9 free from blame or guilt; innocent: *a clear conscience.* 10 free from debts or charges: *clear profit.* 11 without limitation; complete: *the clear contrary.* 12 (of lumber) free from knots or other imperfections.
—v.t. 1 make clear; get clear: *clear the land of trees.* 2 remove to leave a space clear: *clear dishes from a table.* 3 pass by or over without touching or being caught: *The horse cleared the fence.* 4 make free from blame or guilt; prove to be innocent: *The jury's verdict cleared the accused.* 5 make as profit free from debts or charges. 6 get (a ship or cargo) free by meeting requirements on entering or leaving a port. 7 give authority to or for: *The control tower cleared the airplane for landing.* 8 certify as reliable for a position of trust or secrecy. 9 exchange (checks and bills) and settle accounts between different banks.
—v.i. 1 become clear: *It rained and then it cleared.* 2 of a ship: **a** meet all requirements by port authorities on entering or leaving a port. **b** leave a port after doing this. 3 settle a buisness account or certify a check as valid.
clear away or **clear off, a** remove to leave a space clear. **b** disappear; go away. **c** clear dishes, etc., from a table.
clear out, a make clear by throwing out or emptying. **b** INFORMAL. go away; leave.
clear up, a make or become clear. **b** put in order by clearing. **c** explain: *clear up a problem.* **d** become clear after a storm.
—adv. 1 in a clear manner. 2 completely; entirely: *We climbed clear to the top.*
—n. 1 a clear space. 2 **in the clear, a** between the outside parts; in interior measurement: *The house was 40 feet wide in the clear.* **b** free of guilt, blame, or suspicion; innocent. **c** free from limitations or encumbrances. **d** in plain text; not in cipher or code.
[< Old French *cler* < Latin *clarus*] **—clear′a ble,** *adj.* **—clear′er,** *n.* **—clear′ly,** *adv.* **—clear′ness,** *n.*

clear ance (klir′əns), *n.* 1 act of clearing. 2 a clear space; distance between things that pass by each other without touching. 3 a certifying for a position of trust or secrecy. 4 sale of goods at reduced prices. 5 the meeting of requirements to get a ship or cargo free on entering or leaving a port. 6 certificate showing this. 7 the exchanging of checks and bills and settling of accounts between different banks through a clearing house.

clear-cut (klir′kut′), *adj.* 1 having clear, sharp outlines. 2 clear; definite; distinct: *She had clear-cut ideas about how to do her work.*

clear-head ed (klir′hed′id), *adj.* having or showing a clear understanding. **—clear′-head′ed ly,** *adv.* **—clear′-head′ed ness,** *n.*

clear ing (klir′ing), *n.* 1 an open space of cleared land in a forest or in an area of dense undergrowth. 2 the exchanging of checks and bills and settling of accounts between different banks, usually through a clearing house.

clearing house, place where banks exchange checks and bills and settle their accounts. Only the balances are paid in cash.

clear-sight ed (klir′sī′tid), *adj.* 1 able to see clearly. 2 able to understand or think clearly; discerning. **—clear′-sight′ed ly,** *adv.* **—clear′-sight′ed ness,** *n.*

clear sto ry (klir′stôr′ē, klir′stōr′ē), *n., pl.* **-ries.** clerestory.

cleat (klēt), *n.* 1 strip of wood or iron fastened across anything for support or for sure footing: *The gangway had cleats to keep the passengers from slipping.* 2 a small, wedge-shaped block fastened to a spar, etc., as a support, check, or the like. 3 piece of wood or iron used for securing ropes or lines to a flagpole, a dock, etc. 4 piece of metal, wood, hard rubber, plastic, or stiff leather attached to the sole or heel of a shoe to prevent slipping. *—v.t.* 1 fasten to or with a cleat. 2 furnish with cleats. [Middle English *cleete*]

cleav age (klē′vij), *n.* 1 a cleaving or a being cleft; split; division. 2 the property of a crystal or rock of splitting along planes. 3 way in which something splits or divides. 4 (in biology) any of the series of divisions by which a fertilized egg develops into an embryo.

cleave[1] (klēv), *v.*, **cleft** or **cleaved** or **clove, cleft** or **cleaved** or **clo ven, cleav ing.** *—v.t.* 1 cut, divide, or split open. 2 pass through; pierce; penetrate: *The airplane cleft the clouds.* 3 make by cutting: *They cleft a path through the wilderness.* *—v.i.* 1 split, especially into layers. 2 pass; penetrate. [Old English *clēofan*] **—cleav′a ble,** *adj.*

cleave[2] (klēv), *v.i.*, **cleaved** or (ARCHAIC) **clave, cleav ing.** hold fast; cling; adhere: *cleave to an idea.* [Old English *cleofian*]

cleav er (klē′vər), *n.* a cutting tool with a heavy blade and a short handle. A butcher uses a cleaver to chop through meat or bone.

hat, āge, fär; let, ēqual, tėrm;
it, īce; hot, ōpen, ôrder;
oil, out; cup, pu̇t, rüle;
ch, child; ng, long; sh, she;
th, thin; ᴛʜ, then; zh, measure;

ə represents *a* in about, *e* in taken, *i* in pencil, *o* in lemon, *u* in circus.

< = from, derived from, taken from.

cleek (klēk), *n.* a golf club with a wooden head and a hitting surface with a greater slope than a brassie.

clef (klef), *n.* symbol in music indicating the pitch of the notes on a staff. [< French < Latin *clavem* key]

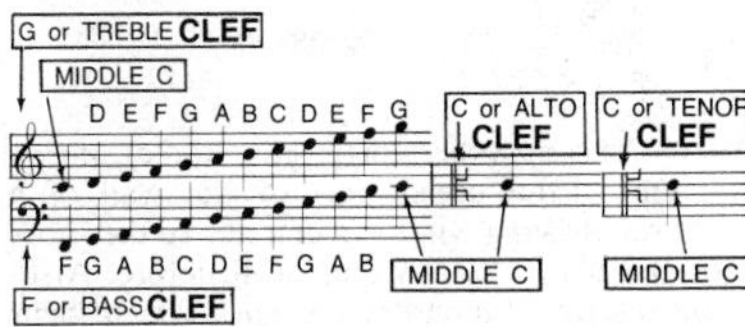

cleft (kleft), *v.* a pt. and a pp. of **cleave**[1]. *—adj.* split; divided: *a cleft stick.* *—n.* space or opening made by splitting; crack; fissure. [Old English *(ge)clyft*]

cleft palate, a narrow opening running lengthwise in the roof of the mouth, caused by failure of the two parts of the palate to join before birth.

cleis tog a mous (klī stog′ə məs), *adj.* having small, self-pollinating flowers that do not open in addition to regular flowers. [< Greek *kleistos* closed + *gamos* marriage]

clem a tis (klem′ə tis), *n., pl.* **-tis es** or **-tis.** any of a genus of climbing vines with clusters of fragrant white, red, pink, blue, or purple flowers. [< Latin < Greek *klēmatis* < *klema* vine branch]

Clem en ceau (klem′ən sō′), *n.* **Georges,** 1841-1929, French statesman, premier of France from 1906 to 1909 and from 1917 to 1920.

clem en cy (klem′ən sē), *n., pl.* **-cies.** 1 gentleness in the use of power or authority; mercy or leniency: *The judge showed clemency to the prisoner.* See **mercy** for synonym study. 2 mildness: *the clemency of the weather.*

Clem ens (klem′ənz), *n.* **Samuel Langhorne,** the real name of **Mark Twain.**

clem ent (klem′ənt), *adj.* 1 merciful toward those in one's power; lenient. 2 mild. [< Latin *clementem*] **—clem′ent ly,** *adv.*

Clem ent VII (klem′ənt), 1478-1534, pope from 1523 to 1534. He was Giulio de' Medici.

clench (klench), *v.t.* 1 close tightly together: *clench one's fists.* See synonym study below. 2 grasp firmly; grip tightly: *The player clenched the bat to swing at the ball.* 3 clinch (a nail, staple, etc.). *—n.* 1 a firm grasp; tight grip. 2 clinch of a nail, staple, etc. [Old English *(be)clencan* hold fast] **—clench′er,** *n.*

Syn. *v.t.* 1 **Clench, clinch** mean to hold fast or tightly. **Clench** emphasizes holding fast by closing tightly with the teeth, lips, etc., or grasping firmly with the fist: *clench* *one's teeth.* **Clinch** suggests fastening securely: *Clinch the nails to a board.*

Cle o pat ra (klē′ə pat′rə, klē′ə pā′trə), *n.* 69?-30 B.C., last queen of ancient Egypt, from 47 to 30 B.C.

clep sy dra (klep′sə drə), *n., pl.* **-dras, -drae** (-drē). device used by the ancients for measuring time by the flow of water, mercury, etc., through a small opening. [< Latin < Greek *klepsydra*]

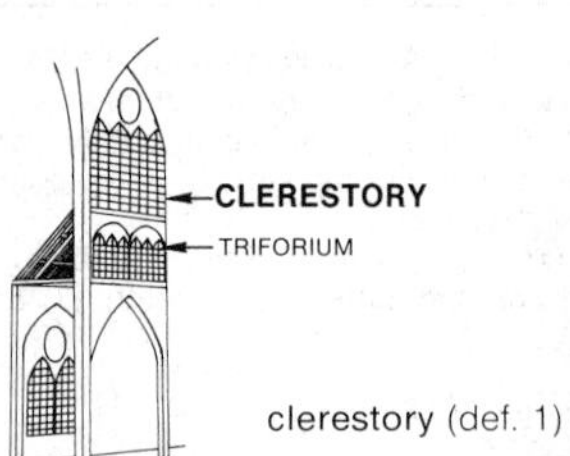

clerestory (def. 1)

clere sto ry (klir′stôr′ē, klir′stōr′ē), *n., pl.* **-ries.** 1 the upper part of the wall of a church, having windows in it above the roofs of the aisles. 2 any similar structure. Also, **clearstory.** [apparently < earlier *clere* clear + *story*²]

cler gy (klėr′jē), *n., pl.* **-gies.** persons ordained for religious work; ministers, pastors, priests, and rabbis. [< Old French *clergie* < *clerc.* See CLERK.]

cler gy man (klėr′jē mən), *n., pl.* **-men.** member of the clergy.

cler ic (kler′ik), *n.* 1 clergyman. 2 (in the Roman Catholic Church) a man who has undergone the rite preparatory to becoming a priest or monk. —*adj.* of a clergyman or the clergy; clerical. [< Latin *clericus.* Doublet of CLERK.]

cler i cal (kler′ə kəl), *adj.* 1 of a clerk or clerks; for clerks: *Keeping records and typing letters are clerical jobs in an office.* 2 of a clergyman or the clergy. 3 supporting the power or influence of the clergy in politics. —*n.* 1 clergyman. 2 Also, **Clerical.** supporter of the power or influence of the clergy in politics. 3 **clericals,** *pl.* the distinctive clothes worn by certain clergymen. **—cler′i cal ly,** *adv.*

cler i cal ism (kler′ə kə liz′əm), *n.* 1 power or influence of the clergy in politics. 2 support of such power or influence.

cler i cal ist (kler′ə kə list), *n.* person who supports clericalism.

clerk (klėrk; *British* klärk), *n.* 1 person employed in a store or shop to sell goods; salesman or saleswoman in a store. 2 person employed in an office to keep records or accounts, type letters, etc. 3 a public official who keeps the records and superintends the routine business of a court of law, legislature, town or country government, etc. 4 layman who has minor church duties. 5 ARCHAIC. clergyman. 6 ARCHAIC. person who can read and write; scholar. —*v.i.* work as a clerk. [partly Old English *clerc, cleric,* partly < Old French *clerc,* both < Latin *clericus* < Greek *klērikos* of an allotment < *klēros* lot, allotment; first applied (in the Septuagint) to the Levites, the service of God being the priest's lot. Doublet of CLERIC.]

clerk ly (klėrk′lē; *British* klärk′lē), *adj.* 1 of or like a clerk. 2 of the clergy. 3 ARCHAIC. scholarly.

clerk ship (klėrk′ship; *British* klärk′ship), *n.* position or work of a clerk.

Cler mont-Fer rand (kler môɴ fe räɴ′), *n.* city in central France. 149,000.

Cleve land (klēv′lənd), *n.* 1 city in NE Ohio, on Lake Erie. 751,000. 2 **(Stephen) Grover,** 1837-1908, the 22nd and 24th president of the United States, from 1885 to 1889 and from 1893 to 1897.

clev er (klev′ər), *adj.* 1 having a quick mind; bright; intelligent. See synonym study below. 2 skillful or expert in doing some particular thing: *a clever carpenter.* 3 showing skill or intelligence: *a clever trick, a clever answer.* 4 U.S. INFORMAL. good-natured; obliging. [Middle English *cliver*] **—clev′er ly,** *adv.* **—clev′er ness,** *n.*

Syn. 1 **Clever, ingenious** mean having a quick mind. **Clever** suggests a natural quickness in learning things and skill in using the mind: *He had no training, but was clever enough to become a good salesman.* **Ingenious** means quick to see ways of doing things and skillful in inventing: *Some ingenious person thought of the can opener.*

clev is (klev′is), *n.* a U-shaped piece of metal with a bolt or pin passing through the ends. A clevis may be used to fasten a whiffletree to a wagon or plow. [related to CLEAVE¹]

clew (klü), *n.* 1 clue (def. 1). 2 ball of thread or yarn. 3 a lower corner of a sail. 4 a metal ring fastened there to which lines are attached. —*v.t.* 1 raise or lower (a sail) by the clews. 2 coil into a ball. Also, **clue.** [Old English *cleowen*]

cli ché (klē shā′), *n.* 1 a timeworn expression or idea. "Father Time," "white as snow," and "cheeks like roses" are clichés. 2 a trite or overused plot, scene, effect, etc. [< French, past participle of *clicher* to stereotype]

click (klik), *n.* 1 a short, sharp sound like that of a key turning in a lock. 2 pawl. —*v.i.* 1 make a short, sharp sound. 2 SLANG. **a** come to an understanding; be in harmony; agree. **b** go well; be effective or successful: *This scene will click.* —*v.t.* cause to make a clicking noise: *I clicked my tongue.* [imitative]

cli ent (klī′ənt), *n.* 1 person, company, or organization for whom a lawyer, accountant, or other professional person acts. 2 customer. 3 person who is under the protection or patronage of another; dependent. [< Latin *clientem*] **—cli′ent less,** *adj.*

cli en tele (klī′ən tel′), *n.* 1 clients as a group. 2 customers. 3 dependents; following. 4 number of clients.

cliff (klif), *n.* a very steep slope of rock, clay, etc. [Old English *clif*] **—cliff′like′,** *adj.*

cliff dweller, 1 one of a group of prehistoric Indians in the southwestern United States, ancestors of the Pueblo Indians, who lived in caves or houses built into cliffs. 2 SLANG. person living in a large apartment house.

cliff dwelling, cave or house built in a cliff.

cliff hang er (klif′hang′ər), *n.* INFORMAL. a story, play, etc., based on unusually strong and sustained suspense.

cliff swallow, a North American swallow that builds a bottle-shaped nest of mud, straw, and feathers, and usually fastens it to a cliff or wall.

Clif ton (klif′tən), *n.* city in NE New Jersey. 82,000.

cli mac ter ic (klī mak′tər ik, klī′mak-ter′ik), *n.* 1 time when some important event occurs, changing the course of things; crucial period. 2 the period of life when the body becomes fundamentally changed, especially menopause. —*adj.* of or like a period when some important event or change occurs; crucial.

cli mac tic (klī mak′tik), *adj.* of or forming a climax: *the climactic scene of a play.* **—cli mac′ti cal ly,** *adv.*

cli mate (klī′mit), *n.* 1 the kind of weather a place has over a long period of time, based on conditions of heat and cold, moisture and dryness, clearness and cloudiness, wind and calm. 2 region with certain conditions of heat and cold, rainfall, wind, sunlight, etc.: *live in a dry climate.* 3 condition or feeling that exists at some time: *the climate of public opinion.* [< Latin *climatem* < Greek *klima* slope (of the earth) < *klinein* to incline]

cli mat ic (klī mat′ik), *adj.* of or having to do with climate. **—cli mat′i cal ly,** *adv.*

cli ma to log i cal (klī′mə tə loj′ə kəl), *adj.* of or having to do with climatology.

cli ma tol o gist (klī′mə tol′ə jist), *n.* an expert in climatology.

cli ma tol o gy (klī′mə tol′ə jē), *n.* science that deals with climate.

cli max (klī′maks), *n.* 1 the highest point; point of greatest interest; most exciting part. 2 orgasm. 3 arrangement of ideas in a rising scale of force and interest. 4 a plant or animal community that is relatively stable. —*v.t., v.i.* bring or come to a climax; be the climax (of). [< Late Latin < Greek *klimax* ladder < *klinein* to lean, incline]

climb (klīm), *v.,* **climbed** or (ARCHAIC) **clomb, climb ing,** *n.* —*v.i.* 1 go up, especially by using the hands or feet, or both; ascend: *climb up a ladder, climb over a fence.* 2 move upward; rise: *By noon the sun had climbed high overhead. The price of sugar has climbed during the past year.* 3 rise slowly or with steady effort: *It may take a poor person many years to climb from poverty to wealth.* 4 grow upward by holding on or entwining: *Some vines climb.* —*v.t.* 1 go up by using the hands or feet, or both; ascend: *She climbed the ladder.* See synonym study below. 2 grow upward on or twine around.

climb down, a go down, especially by using the hands and feet. **b** INFORMAL. give in; back down.

—*n.* 1 a climbing; ascent: *Our climb up the mountain took several hours.* 2 place to be climbed. 3 an increase: *a climb in price.* [Old English *climban*] **—climb′a ble,** *adj.*

Syn. *v.t.* 1 **Climb, ascend, mount** mean to go up. **Climb** suggests a need for effort: *This car will never climb that hill.* **Ascend,** a rather formal word, suggests a more steady or stately movement: *The queen ascended the steps to the throne.* **Mount** adds to *ascend,* the idea of getting on top of: *He mounted the horse.*

climb er (klī′mər), *n.* 1 person or thing that climbs. 2 INFORMAL. person who is always trying to get ahead socially. 3 a climbing plant; vine. 4 climbing iron.

climbing iron, one of a pair of frames with spikes, used for attaching to shoes to help in climbing.

clime (klīm), *n.* 1 country or region, especially one having pleasant conditions for living. 2 climate. [< Latin *clima*]

clinch (klinch), *v.t.* 1 make (a driven nail, a bolt, etc.) secure by flattening or bending over the end after it has passed through a plank, etc. See **clench** for synonym study. 2 fasten (things) together in this way. 3 fix firmly; settle decisively: *A deposit of five dollars clinched our bargain.* 4 clench. —*v.i.* 1 grasp one another tightly in boxing or wrestling; grapple: *When the boxers clinched, the crowd hissed.* 2 fasten a nail, bolt, etc., by clinching it. —*n.* 1 a tight grasp in boxing or wrestling. 2 fastening made by bending the end of a nail, bolt, etc. 3 kind of sailor's knot in which the end of the rope is lashed back. [variant of *clench*]

clinch er (klin′chər), *n.* 1 INFORMAL. a decisive argument, statement, etc. 2 tool for clinching nails, bolts, etc.

cline (klīn), *n.* a gradual variation in a particular inherited characteristic found across a series of adjacent populations of a group of related organisms. [< Greek *klinein* to lean, incline]

cling (kling), *v.*, **clung, cling ing,** *n.* —*v.i.* 1 stick or hold fast; adhere: *A vine clings to its support. We cling to the beliefs of our fathers.* 2 grasp; embrace. 3 keep near. —*n.* act of clinging. [Old English *clingan*]

cling stone (kling′stōn′), *n.* peach, plum, etc., whose stone clings to the fleshy part. —*adj.* having such a stone.

clin ic (klin′ik), *n.* 1 place where people can receive medical treatment, often free or at low cost. In the United States such a clinic is usually connected with a hospital or medical school. 2 place for medical treatment or study of certain people or diseases: *The children's clinic is open during school hours.* 3 practical instruction of medical students by examining or treating patients in the presence of the students. 4 place where practical instruction on any subject is given: *a football clinic, a reading clinic.* 5 class of students receiving medical or practical instruction. [< Greek *klinikos* physician who attends bedridden patients; literally, of a bed < *klinē* bed < *klinein* to lean, incline]

clin i cal (klin′ə kəl), *adj.* 1 of or having to do with a clinic. 2 used or performed in a sickroom, especially in a hospital. 3 of or having to do with the study of disease by observation of the patient rather than by experiment, autopsy, etc.: *clinical medicine.* 4 coldly impersonal; unemotional; detached. —**clin′i cal ly,** *adv.*

clinical thermometer, thermometer for measuring the temperature of the body.

cli ni cian (kli nish′ən), *n.* physician who practices or teaches in a clinic.

clink[1] (klingk), *n.* a light, sharp, ringing sound like that of drinking glasses hitting together. —*v.i.* make a clink. —*v.t.* cause to clink. [Middle English]

clink[2] (klingk), *n.* INFORMAL. prison. [apparently < name of a prison in London]

clink er (kling′kər), *n.* 1 a large, rough cinder left after coal has been burned in a furnace or forge. 2 a very hard brick. 3 mass of bricks fused together. 4 slag. [< Dutch *klinker* brick]

clink er-built (kling′kər bilt′), *adj.* made of boards or metal plates that overlap one another: *The lifeboat was clinker-built.*

cli nom e ter (klī nom′ə tər, klə nom′ə tər), *n.* instrument for measuring deviation from the horizontal.

Clin ton (klin′tən), *n.* 1 **De Witt,** 1769-1828, American political leader who promoted the building of the Erie Canal. 2 **George,** 1739-1812, American political leader, vice-president of the United States from 1805 to 1812.

Cli o (klī′ō), *n.* (in Greek myths) the Muse of history.

clip[1] (klip), *v.*, **clipped, clip ping,** *n.* —*v.t.* 1 trim with shears, scissors, or clippers; cut short; cut: *A sheep's fleece is clipped off to get wool.* 2 cut the hair or fleece of: *Our dog is clipped every summer.* 3 cut out of a magazine, newspaper, etc.: *clip a news item or recipe.* 4 omit syllables of (words) in pronouncing or writing; shorten or abbreviate. 5 damage (a coin) by cutting off the edge. 6 INFORMAL. hit or punch sharply. 7 INFORMAL. swindle or rob, especially by overcharging: *clip a customer.* —*v.i.* 1 INFORMAL. move fast. 2 cut pieces from a magazine, newspaper, etc. 3 cut or trim something with shears.
—*n.* 1 act of clipping. 2 anything clipped off, especially wool clipped from sheep at one time. 3 amount of wool clipped from sheep at one time. 4 Often, **clips,** *pl.* instrument for clipping. 5 piece clipped from a reel of film, a newspaper, etc.; clipping. 6 INFORMAL. a fast motion: *Our bus passed through the village at quite a clip.* 7 INFORMAL. a sharp blow or punch. 8 INFORMAL. one time; single occasion: *at one clip.*
[probably < Scandinavian (Old Icelandic) *klippa*]

clip[2] (klip), *v.*, **clipped, clip ping,** *n.* —*v.t.* hold tight; fasten: *clip papers together.* —*n.* 1 something used for clipping things together. A clip for papers is often made of a piece of bent wire. 2 in certain firearms: **a** a metal holder for cartridges. **b** the rounds it holds. [Old English *clyppan* encircle, embrace]

clip board (klip′bôrd′, klip′bōrd′), *n.* board with a heavy spring clip at one end for holding papers while writing.

clip per (klip′ər), *n.* 1 person who clips or cuts. 2 Often, **clippers,** *pl.* tool for cutting. 3 a large sailing ship built and rigged for speed.

clipper
(def. 2)
(def. 3)→

clip ping (klip′ing), *n.* 1 article, picture, or advertisement cut out of a newspaper, magazine, etc. 2 piece cut out of or from something else; cutting.

clique (klēk, klik), *n.*, *v.*, **cliqued, cli quing.** —*n.* a small, exclusive group of people within a larger group. See **circle** for synonym study. —*v.i.* INFORMAL. form or associate in a clique. [< French]

cli quish (klē′kish, klik′ish), *adj.* 1 like a clique. 2 tending to form a clique. —**cli′quish ly,** *adv.* —**cli′quish ness,** *n.*

cli tel lum (kli tel′əm, klī tel′əm), *n.* a glandular swelling around certain sections of an annelid from which a viscous fluid, which forms a cocoon for the eggs, is secreted. [< New Latin < Latin *clitellae* packsaddle]

cli tor is (klit′ər is, klī′tər is), *n.* a small, erectile organ of the female of most mammals located at the front of the vulva. It is homologous with the penis of the male. [< Greek *kleitoris*]

hat, āge, fär; let, ēqual, tėrm;
it, īce; hot, ōpen, ôrder;
oil, out; cup, pu̇t, rüle;
ch, child; ng, long; sh, she;
th, thin; ᴛʜ, then; zh, measure;

ə represents *a* in about, *e* in taken, *i* in pencil, *o* in lemon, *u* in circus.

< = from, derived from, taken from.

Clive (klīv), *n.* **Robert,** 1725-1774, British general and statesman in India. His victory at Plassey in 1757 helped to establish the British control of India.

clk., 1 clerk. 2 clock.

clo a ca (klō ā′kə), *n.*, *pl.* **-cae** (-sē). 1 sewer. 2 cavity in the body of birds, reptiles, amphibians, and most fishes, into which the intestinal, urinary, and generative canals open. 3 a similar cavity in certain invertebrates. [< Latin]

cloak (klōk), *n.* 1 a loose outer garment with or without sleeves; mantle. 2 anything that covers or conceals; outward show; mask. —*v.t.* 1 cover with a cloak. 2 cover up; conceal; hide. [< Old French *cloque* < Late Latin *clocca,* originally, bell. Doublet of CLOCHE, CLOCK[1].]

cloak-and-dag ger (klōk′ən dag′ər), *adj.* of or having to do with intrigue and adventure, as in melodrama or espionage.

cloak room (klōk′rüm′, klōk′ru̇m′), *n.* room where coats, hats, etc., can be left for a time; coatroom.

clob ber (klob′ər), *v.t.* SLANG. 1 strike or beat heavily. 2 defeat severely. [origin uncertain]

cloche (klōsh), *n.* a close-fitting hat for women. [< French, bell, ultimately < Late Latin *clocca.* Doublet of CLOAK, CLOCK[1].]

clock[1] (klok), *n.* instrument for measuring and showing time, especially one that is not carried around like a watch. —*v.t.* 1 measure or record the time of; time: *clock a horse race.* 2 record (time, distance, number, etc.) mechanically: *The racing car clocked 150 m.p.h.* —*v.i.* register on a time clock the beginning or end of a day's work; punch in or out. [< Middle Dutch *clocke* or Old French *cloque,* both < Late Latin *clocca* bell. Doublet of CLOAK, CLOCHE.] —**clock′er,** *n.* —**clock′like′,** *adj.*

clock[2] (klok), *n.* an ornamental pattern sewn or woven on the side of a stocking or sock, extending from the ankle up. [origin uncertain]

clock wise (klok′wīz′), *adv.*, *adj.* in the direction in which the hands of a clock rotate; from left to right.

clock work (klok′wėrk′), *n.* 1 the machinery by which a clock is run. 2 any similar machinery, consisting of gears, wheels, and springs, such as that which runs many mechanical toys. 3 **like clockwork,** with great regularity and smoothness.

clod (klod), *n.* 1 lump of earth; lump. 2 earth; soil. 3 a stupid person; blockhead. 4 boor. [Old English]

clod dish (klod′ish), *adj.* like a clod; stupid or boorish. —**clod′dish ness,** *n.*

clod hop per (klod′hop′ər), *n.* 1 a clumsy or awkward person. 2 **clodhoppers,** *pl.* large, heavy shoes.

clog (klog), *v.*, **clogged, clog ging,** *n.* *—v.t.* 1 fill up; choke up: *Greasy water clogged the drain.* 2 hinder; hold back; interfere with: *Heavy clothes clogged the swimmer's progress.* *—v.i.* 1 become filled or choked up. 2 dance by beating a heavy rhythm on the floor with wooden-soled shoes. *—n.* 1 anything that hinders or interferes. 2 any weight, such as a block of wood, fastened to the leg of an animal to hinder motion. 3 shoe with a thick, wooden sole. 4 clog dance. [Middle English *clogge* block]

clog dance, dance in which the dancer wears clogs to beat time.

cloi son né (kloi′zn ā′), *n.* a decorative enamel in which the patterns of the design are separated by thin metal strips fastened on the surface. *—adj.* enameled in this way: *a cloisonné bowl.* [< French]

cloister (def. 1)

clois ter (kloi′stər), *n.* 1 a covered walk, often along the wall of a building, with a row of pillars on the open side or sides. A cloister is sometimes built around the courtyard of a monastery, church, or college building. 2 place of religious retirement; convent or monastery. 3 a quiet place shut away from the world. *—v.t.* shut away in a quiet place. [< Old French *cloistre* < Latin *claustrum* closed place, lock < *claudere* to close]

clois tered (kloi′stərd), *adj.* 1 secluded. 2 having a cloister.

clois tral (kloi′strəl), *adj.* 1 of or suitable for a convent, monastery, etc. 2 like a cloister.

clomb (klōm), *v.* ARCHAIC. a pt. and a pp. of **climb.**

clone (klōn), *n.* group of plants or animals produced asexually from a single ancestor. [< Greek *klon* twig]

clop (klop), *n.*, *v.*, **clopped, clop ping.** *—n.* a sharp, hard sound such as that made by a horse's hoof on a paved road. *—v.i.* make such a sound. [imitative]

close[1] (klōz), *v.*, **closed, clos ing,** *n.* *—v.t.* 1 bring together or move the parts of so as to leave no opening; shut: *Close the door.* See synonym study below. 2 stop up; fill; block: *close a gap.* 3 bring together: *close the ranks of troops.* 4 bring to an end; finish: *close a debate.* 5 (in electricity) unite the parts of (a circuit) so as to make it complete. *—v.i.* 1 become shut: *The sleepy child's eyes are closing.* 2 come together: *The ranks closed.* 3 come to an end; finish: *The meeting closed with a speech by the president.* 4 come to terms; agree: *The labor union closed with the company.* 5 grapple.

close down, shut completely; stop.

close in, come near and shut in on all sides.

close out, sell in order to get rid of.

close up, a shut completely; stop up; block. **b** bring or come nearer together. **c** (of a wound) to heal.

—n. an end; finish.

[< Old French *clos-*, stem of *clore* to close < Latin *claudere*] **—clos′a ble,** *adj.* **—clos′er,** *n.*

Syn. *v.t.* 1 **Close, shut** mean to make not open. Close emphasizes the idea of leaving no opening, without suggesting the means or way: *Please close the window a little.* **Shut** means to close by pushing or pulling a door, lid, some part, etc., into place across the opening in order to keep out or in: *Please shut the door.*

close[2] (klōs), *adj.*, **clos er, clos est,** *adv.*, *n.* *—adj.* 1 with little space between; near together; near: *close teeth.* 2 fitting tightly; tight; narrow: *They live in very close quarters.* 3 having its parts near together; compact: *a close weave.* 4 intimate; dear: *a close friend.* 5 careful; exact: *a close translation.* 6 thorough; strict: *close attention.* 7 having little fresh air; stuffy: *a close room.* 8 hard to breathe. 9 near the surface; short: *a close haircut.* 10 stingy. 11 nearly equal; almost even: *a close contest.* 12 not fond of talking; keeping quiet about oneself; reserved. 13 secret; hidden. 14 closely confined; strictly limiting: *close quarters.* 15 restricted; limited. 16 hard to get; scarce. 17 closed; shut; not open. 18 (in phonetics) (of a vowel) pronounced with some part of the tongue brought near the palate, as the vowels in *leap* and *loop.*

—adv. near; closely.

—n. 1 an enclosed place. 2 grounds around a cathedral or abbey.

[< Old French *clos* < Latin *clausum* closed < *claudere* to close] **—close′ly,** *adv.* **—close′ness,** *n.*

close call (klōs), U.S. INFORMAL. a narrow escape from danger or an accident.

closed-cir cuit (klōzd′sėr′kit), *adj.* having to do with television broadcasting by wire or cable to a certain limited audience, as in a chain of theaters or a group of classrooms.

closed primary, U.S. primary in which only recognized party members may nominate candidates for their party.

closed season, any part of the year during which the hunting, fishing, or trapping of certain game is prohibited.

closed sentence, (in mathematics) a sentence which does not include a variable.

closed shop, factory or business that employs only members of labor unions.

closed syllable, syllable that ends in a consonant sound. EXAMPLE: *can-* in *candy.*

close-fist ed (klōs′fis′tid), *adj.* stingy; miserly.

close-grained (klōs′grānd′), *adj.* having a fine, close grain. Mahogany is a close-grained wood.

close-hauled (klōs′hôld′), *adj.* having sails set for sailing as nearly as possible in the direction from which the wind is blowing.

close-knit (klōs′nit′), *adj.* firmly united by affection or common interest: *a close-knit family.*

close-mouthed (klōs′mouŦHd′, klōs′-moutht′), *adj.* not fond of talking; reserved; reticent.

close quarters (klōs), 1 fighting or struggling close together. 2 place or position with little space.

close shave (klōs), INFORMAL. a narrow escape from danger or an accident.

clos et (kloz′it), *n.* 1 a small room for storing clothes or household supplies, such as canned food, china, or linen. 2 cupboard for holding china, linen, etc. 3 a small, private room for prayer, study, or interviews. 4 water closet. *—v.t.* shut up in a private room for a secret talk: *The president was closeted with his personal advisers for several hours.* [< Old French, diminutive of *clos.* See CLOSE[2].]

close-up (klōs′up′), *n.* 1 picture taken with a camera at close range. 2 a close view.

close-wo ven (klōs′wō′vən), *adj.* woven so that the threads are close together.

clo sure (klō′zhər), *n.* 1 a closing. 2 a being closed. 3 thing that closes. 4 the end; finish; conclusion. 5 cloture. 6 (in mathematics) a property of an operation on any two members of a set in which the result of the operation is also a member of the set.

clot (klot), *n.*, *v.*, **clot ted, clot ting.** *—n.* a half-solid lump; thickened mass: *A clot of blood formed in the cut and stopped the bleeding.* *—v.i.* form into clots; coagulate: *Milk clots when it turns sour.* *—v.t.* cause to clot; cover with clots. [Old English *clott*]

cloth (klôth, kloth), *n.*, *pl.* **cloths** (klôŦHz, klôths; kloŦHz, kloths), *adj.* *—n.* 1 material made from wool, cotton, silk, linen, hair, or other fiber, by weaving, knitting, or rolling and pressing. 2 piece of this material used for a special purpose: *a cloth for the table.* 3 the customary clothing worn by the members of a profession or trade. 4 the customary clothing worn by the clergy. 5 profession of a clergyman. 6 **the cloth,** clergymen; the clergy. 7 **made out of whole cloth,** INFORMAL. entirely false or imaginary. *—adj.* made of cloth. [Old English *clāth*]

clothe (klōŦH), *v.t.*, **clothed** or **clad, cloth ing.** 1 put clothes on; cover with clothes; dress. 2 provide with clothes. 3 cover: *The sun clothes the earth with light.* 4 provide; furnish; equip: *A judge is clothed with the authority of the state.* 5 express: *Her ideas are clothed in simple words.* [Old English *clāthian* < *clāth* cloth]

clothes (klōz, klōŦHz), *n.pl.* 1 coverings for a person's body; apparel; clothing; dress. See synonym study below. 2 bedclothes.

Syn. 1 **Clothes, clothing, apparel, dress, attire** refer to coverings for a person's body. **Clothes** is the most commonly used of these words: *His clothes were new.* **Clothing,** nearly as common, more often suggests large quantities than does *clothes: This store sells men's clothing.* **Apparel** is seldom used except in or about the clothing trades and then more frequently about women's clothes than men's: *There is a great variety in women's apparel this year.* **Dress** often suggests clothing suitable for some occasion or purpose: *evening dress.* **Attire** suggests rich or splendid clothing: *We need neat clothes, not fine attire.*

clothes horse (klōz′hôrs′, klōŦHz′hôrs′), *n.* 1 frame to hang clothes on to dry or air them. 2 U.S. SLANG. person who places too great a value on being well dressed.

clothes line (klōz′līn′, klōŦHz′līn′), *n.* rope or wire to hang clothes on to dry or air them.

clothes pin (klōz′pin′, klōŦHz′pin′), *n.* a wooden or plastic clip to hold clothes on a clothesline.

clothes press (klōz′pres′, klōŦHz′pres′), *n.* chest, cupboard, or closet in which to keep clothes.

clothes tree, an upright pole with branches on which to hang coats and hats.

hat, āge, fär; let, ēqual, tėrm;
it, īce; hot, ōpen, ôrder;
oil, out; cup, pu̇t, rüle;
ch, child; ng, long; sh, she;
th, thin; ᴛʜ, then; zh, measure;

ə represents *a* in about, *e* in taken, *i* in pencil, *o* in lemon, *u* in circus.

< = from, derived from, taken from.

cloth ier (klō′ᴛʜyər, klō′ᴛʜē ər), *n.* 1 seller or maker of clothing. 2 seller of cloth.

cloth ing (klō′ᴛʜing), *n.* 1 clothes; apparel; dress. See **clothes** for synonym study. 2 covering.

Clo tho (klō′thō), *n.* (in Greek and Roman myths) one of the three Fates. Clotho spins the thread of life.

clo ture (klō′chər), *n.* U.S. a limiting of debate by a legislature in order to get an immediate vote on the question being discussed; closure. [< French *clôture*]

cloud (kloud), *n.* 1 visible mass of condensed water droplets or ice particles floating in the air, usually at a height above the ground. 2 a visible mass of smoke or dust suspended in the air. 3 a great number of things moving close together: *a cloud of birds, a cloud of arrows.* 4 anything that darkens or dims. 5 a cause of suspicion or disgrace. 6 a blemish; streak; spot. 7 **in the clouds, a** far above the earth. **b** unrealistic or fanciful; not practical. **c** daydreaming; absent-minded. 8 **under a cloud, a** under suspicion; in disgrace. **b** in gloom or trouble. —*v.t.* 1 cover with a cloud or clouds. 2 to streak; spot. 3 make gloomy or troubled; darken; dim. 4 bring under suspicion or disgrace. —*v.i.* 1 grow or become cloudy: *The sky clouded over.* 2 become gloomy; darken; dim. [Old English *clūd* rock, hill] **—cloud′like′,** *adj.*

cloud burst (kloud′bėrst′), *n.* a sudden, violent rainfall.

cloud chamber, a large vessel with a glass dome, filled with vapor, especially a vapor of hydrogen and methyl alcohol, through which the paths of charged particles, such as protons and electrons, may be observed and photographed and thus identified.

cloud less (kloud′lis), *adj.* without a cloud; clear and bright; sunny. **—cloud′less ly,** *adv.* **—cloud′less ness,** *n.*

cloud let (kloud′lit), *n.* a little cloud.

cloud rack, group of broken clouds driven by the wind.

cloud y (klou′dē), *adj.,* **cloud i er, cloud i est.** 1 covered with clouds; having clouds in it: *a cloudy sky.* 2 of or like clouds. 3 not clear: *a cloudy liquid.* 4 streaked; spotted: *cloudy marble.* 5 not carefully thought out; confused; indistinct: *a cloudy notion.* 6 not cheerful; gloomy; frowning. **—cloud′i ly,** *adv.* **—cloud′i ness,** *n.*

clout (klout), *v.t.* INFORMAL. hit with the hand; rap; knock; cuff. —*n.* 1 INFORMAL. a hit with the hand; rap; knock; cuff. 2 INFORMAL. political force, power, or influence. 3 a white cloth target used in archery. 4 shot that hits this. 5 ARCHAIC. **a** cloth or rag. **b** garment. [Old English *clūt* small piece of cloth or metal]

clove[1] (klōv), *n.* 1 a strong, fragrant spice made from the dried flower buds of a tropical evergreen tree of the myrtle family. 2 the dried flower bud. 3 the tree. [< Old French *clou (de gilofre)* nail (of the clove tree); because of the shape]

clove[2] (klōv), *n.* a small, separate section of a bulb: *a clove of garlic.* [Old English *clufu*]

clove[3] (klōv), *v.* a pt. of **cleave**[1].

clove hitch, knot for tying a rope around a pole, spar, etc.

clo ven (klō′vən), *v.* a pp. of **cleave**[1]. —*adj.* split; divided.

cloven foot, cloven hoof.

clo ven-foot ed (klō′vən fu̇t′id), *adj.* cloven-hoofed.

cloven hoof, hoof divided into two parts. Cows have cloven hoofs. The Devil is traditionally pictured with cloven hoofs.

clo ven-hoofed (klō′vən hu̇ft′, klō′vən-hüft′), *adj.* 1 having cloven hoofs. 2 devilish.

clo ver (klō′vər), *n.* 1 any of a genus of low plants of the pea family, with leaves having three leaflets and sweet-smelling rounded heads of small red, white, yellow, or purple flowers. Clover is grown as food for horses and cattle and to improve the soil. 2 any similar plant of another genus of the pea family, such as sweet clover. 3 **in clover,** enjoying a life of pleasure and luxury without work or worry. [Old English *clāfre*]

clo ver leaf (klō′vər lēf′), *n., pl.* **-leafs** or **-leaves.** intersection of two highways, with one passing over the other, and with a series of curving ramps in the shape of a four-leaf clover that permit traffic to move from one highway to the other without having to cross in front of other traffic.

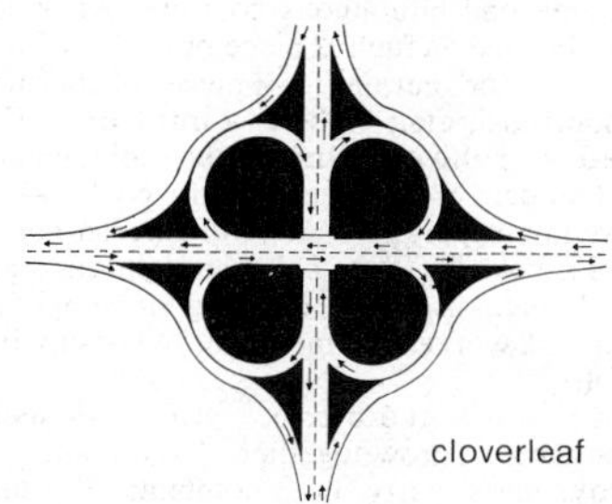
cloverleaf

Clo vis I (klō′vis), A.D. 465?-511, king of the Franks from A.D. 481 to 511, founder of the Merovingian dynasty.

clown (kloun), *n.* 1 person in a circus, carnival, etc., who amuses others by wearing funny costumes and make-up and by playing tricks and jokes. 2 person who acts like a clown; silly person. —*v.i.* act like a clown; play tricks and jokes; act silly. [origin uncertain]

clown er y (klou′nər ē), *n., pl.* **-er ies.** 1 tricks and jokes of a clown. 2 a clownish act.

clown ish (klou′nish), *adj.* like a clown; like a clown's. **—clown′ish ly,** *adv.* **—clown′ish ness,** *n.*

cloy (kloi), *v.t., v.i.* 1 make or become weary by too much, too sweet, or too rich food. 2 make or become weary by too much of anything pleasant. [Middle English *acloyen, ancloyen* drive a nail into, stop up, fill full < Old French *encloyer* < *en-* in + *clou* nail] **—cloy′ing ly,** *adv.* **—cloy′ing ness,** *n.*

club (klub), *n., v.,* **clubbed, club bing.** —*n.* 1 a heavy stick of wood, usually thicker at one end, used as a weapon. 2 stick or bat used in some games to hit a ball: *golf clubs.* 3 group of people joined together for some special purpose; association: *a tennis club.* 4 building, rooms, or facilities used by a club. 5 a figure shaped like this: ♣. 6 a playing card with one or more black, club-shaped figures. 7 **clubs,** *pl.* suit of such playing cards. —*v.t.* beat or hit with a club or something similar. —*v.i.* join together for some special purpose: *The children clubbed together to buy their parents an anniversary present.* [< Scandinavian (Old Icelandic) *klubba*]

club foot (klub′fu̇t′), *n., pl.* **-feet.** 1 a deformed foot, short and distorted. 2 deformity of the foot leaving the front part twisted and shortened, caused by faulty development before birth.

club foot ed (klub′fu̇t′id), *adj.* having a clubfoot.

club house (klub′hous′), *n., pl.* **-hous es** (-hou′ziz). building used by a club.

club moss, any of a family of plants that are either erect or creeping, usually mosslike, and have evergreen leaves; lycopod; lycopodium.

club steak, a small beefsteak cut from the tip of the loin.

cluck (kluk), *n.* 1 the sound that a hen makes in calling her chickens. 2 a sound like this. —*v.i.* 1 (of a hen) make a cluck when calling chickens. 2 make a sound like this. [imitative]

clue (klü), *n., v.,* **clued, clu ing** or **clue ing.** —*n.* 1 guide to the solving of a mystery or problem. 2 clew (defs. 2-4). —*v.t.* 1 indicate (something) by means of a clue. 2 INFORMAL. give a clue to. [variant of *clew*]

clum ber spaniel (klum′bər), *n.* kind of dog having a white coat with sparse orange or yellow markings, short legs, and a long, heavy body. [< *Clumber,* estate of the Duke of Newcastle in England]

clump (klump), *n.* 1 a small, closely gathered group; cluster: *a clump of trees.* 2 lump or mass: *a clump of earth.* 3 sound of heavy, clumsy walking. —*v.i.* 1 form a clump. 2 walk heavily and clumsily. —*v.t.* form into a clump. [probably < Middle Low German *klumpe*]

clump y (klum′pē), *adj.* 1 full of clumps. 2 like clumps. 3 heavy and clumsy.

clum sy (klum′zē), *adj.,* **-si er, -si est.** 1 stiff and awkward in moving; not graceful or skillful. See **awkward** for synonym study. 2 awkwardly done; tactless: *a clumsy apology.* 3 not well-shaped or well-made. [< earlier *clumse* be numb with cold] **—clum′si ly,** *adv.* **—clum′si ness,** *n.*

clung (klung), *v.* pt. and pp. of **cling.** *The child clung to his sister.*

clus ter (klus′tər), *n.* 1 number of things of the same kind growing or grouped together: *a cluster of grapes, a little cluster of houses.* 2 any group of persons or things. 3 sequence of two or more vowel or, especially, consonant sounds. *Str-* in *string* is a consonant cluster. —*v.i.* form into a cluster; group together closely: *The students clustered around their teacher.* —*v.t.* gather into a cluster. [Old English]

clutch[1] (kluch), *n.* 1 a tight grasp; hold: *I lost my clutch on the rope and fell.* 2 Often, **clutches,** *pl.* **a** a grasping claw, paw, hand, etc.: *The fish escaped from the bear's clutch.* **b** control; power: *a country in the clutches of a dictator.* 3 device in a machine for transmitting motion from one shaft to another or for disconnecting related moving parts. The clutch in an automobile is used to connect the engine with the transmission or to disconnect it from the transmission. 4 lever or pedal operating this device. —*v.t.* 1 grasp tightly; grip firmly: *The child clutched the blanket.* 2 seize eagerly; snatch. See **seize** for synonym study. —*v.i.* seize eagerly; snatch: *A drowning man will clutch at a straw.* [Old English *clyccan* bend, clench]

clutch[2] (kluch), *n.* 1 nest of eggs. 2 brood of chickens. 3 group of people or things. [< Scandinavian (Old Icelandic) *klekja*]

clut ter (klut′ər), *n.* 1 number of things scattered or left in disorder; litter. 2 confused noise; loud clatter; hubbub. —*v.t.* litter with things in confusion: *Her desk was all cluttered with old papers, strings, and other odds and ends.* —*v.i.* make a confused noise; clatter loudly. [variant of earlier *clotter* < *clot*]

Clyde (klīd), *n.* 1 **Clyde River,** river in S Scotland, flowing into the Firth of Clyde. 106 mi. 2 **Firth of,** deep inlet in SW Scotland. 64 mi. long.

Clydes dale (klīdz′dāl), *n.* kind of strong draft horse. [< *Clydesdale,* Scotland, where they were raised originally]

clyp e ate (klip′ē āt), *adj.* (in biology) shaped like a round shield or buckler. [< Latin *clypeus* round shield]

Cly tem nes tra (klī′təm nes′trə), *n.* (in Greek legends) the wife of Agamemnon. She killed him on his return from Troy and was afterwards slain by their son Orestes.

Cm, curium.

cm., centimeter or centimeters.

Cnos sus (nos′əs), *n.* Knossos.

co-, *prefix.* 1 with; together: *Coexist = exist together or with.* 2 joint: *Coauthor = joint author.* 3 equally: *Coextensive = equally extensive.* [< Latin, variant of *com-*]

Co, cobalt.

Co. or **co.,** 1 Company. 2 County.

CO or **C.O.,** 1 Commanding Officer. 2 INFORMAL. conscientious objector.

c/o or **c.o.,** in care of.

coach (kōch), *n.* 1 a large, four-wheeled, usually closed carriage with seats inside and often on top, formerly used in carrying passengers and mail. 2 a railroad car with seats for passengers at lower fares than sleeping accommodations. 3 bus. 4 a class of passenger accommodations on a commercial aircraft at lower rates than first class. 5 person who teaches or trains athletic teams, etc.: *a swimming coach.* 6 (in baseball) a person who directs base runners and the batter. 7 instructor who supervises the training of actors, singers, etc.: *a drama coach, a music coach.* 8 a private teacher who helps a student prepare for a special test. —*v.t.* 1 teach or train; instruct: *She coached me in chess. He coaches baseball.* 2 help to prepare for a special test. 3 carry in a coach. —*v.i.* 1 act as a coach: *He is coaching at a small college.* 2 to ride in a coach. [< Middle French *coche,* ultimately < Hungarian *kocsi (szekér)* (cart from) *Kocs,* a village in Hungary]

coach-and-four (kōch′ən fôr′, kōch′ən-fōr′), *n.* coach pulled by four horses.

coach dog, Dalmatian.

coach man (kōch′mən), *n., pl.* **-men.** man whose work is driving a coach or carriage.

co ad ju tor (kō aj′ə tər, kō′ə jü′tər), *n.* 1 assistant; helper. 2 bishop appointed to assist another bishop.

co ag u la ble (kō ag′yə lə bəl), *adj.* capable of being coagulated.

co ag u lant (kō ag′yə lənt), *n.* substance producing coagulation.

co ag u lase (kō ag′yə lās), *n.* enzyme that causes coagulation.

co ag u late (kō ag′yə lāt), *v.t., v.i.,* **-lat ed, -lat ing.** change from a liquid into a thickened mass; thicken: *Cooking coagulates the whites of egg. Blood from a cut coagulates.* [< Latin *coagulatum* curdled < *coagulum* means of curdling < *co-* together + *agere* drive] —**co ag′u la′tor,** *n.*

co ag u la tion (kō ag′yə lā′shən), *n.* 1 act or process of coagulating. 2 a coagulated mass.

Co a hui la (kō′ə wē′lə), *n.* state in NE Mexico.

coal (kōl), *n.* 1 a black, combustible mineral composed mostly of carbon, and formed in the earth from partly decayed vegetable matter under special conditions of great pressure, high humidity, and lack of air. Anthracite and bituminous coal are two kinds widely used as fuel. 2 piece or pieces of this mineral for burning. 3 piece of burning wood, coal, etc.; ember. 4 **haul over the coals** or **rake over the coals,** scold; blame. 5 charcoal. —*v.t.* supply with coal. —*v.i.* take in a supply of coal. [Old English *col*]

coal er (kō′lər), *n.* 1 ship, freight car, railroad, etc., used for carrying or supplying coal. 2 worker or merchant who supplies coal.

co a lesce (kō′ə les′), *v.i.,* **-lesced, -lesc ing.** 1 grow together. 2 unite into one body, mass, party, etc.; combine: *The thirteen colonies coalesced to form a nation.* [< Latin *coalescere* < *co-* together + *alescere* grow]

co a les cence (kō′ə les′ns), *n.* 1 a growing together. 2 union; combination.

co a les cent (kō′ə les′nt), *adj.* coalescing.

coal field (kōl′fēld′), *n.* region where beds of coal are found.

coal gas, 1 gas made from coal, used for heating and lighting. 2 gas given off by burning coal.

co a li tion (kō′ə lish′ən), *n.* 1 union; combination. 2 alliance of statesmen, political parties, etc., for some special purpose. In wartime several countries may form a temporary coalition against a common enemy. [< Medieval Latin *coalitionem* < Latin *coalescere.* See COALESCE.]

coal measures, strata containing coal.

coal oil, 1 kerosene. 2 petroleum.

coal scuttle, bucket for holding or carrying coal; hod.

coal tar, a black, sticky substance left after bituminous coal has been distilled to make coal gas. Coal tar is used to make roofing and paving materials and is a source of many organic chemicals used in dyes, medicines, paints, perfumes, etc.

coam ing (kō′ming), *n.* a raised edge around a hatch or opening in the deck of a ship to prevent water from running down below. [origin uncertain]

coati
4 ft. long
with tail

coarse (kôrs, kōrs), *adj.,* **coars er, coars est.** 1 made up of fairly large parts; not fine: *coarse sand.* 2 heavy or rough in appearance or texture: *Burlap is a coarse cloth.* 3 common; poor; inferior: *coarse food.* 4 not delicate or refined; crude; vulgar: *coarse manners.* See synonym study below. [adjectival use of *course,* noun, meaning "ordinary"] —**coarse′ly,** *adv.* —**coarse′ness,** *n.*

Syn. 4 **Coarse, vulgar** mean offensive to good taste. **Coarse** emphasizes the roughness and crudeness of what is said or done: *the coarse language of an army barracks.* **Vulgar** implies offensiveness to decency: *I thought the movie vulgar rather than artistic.*

coarse-grained (kôrs′grānd′, kōrs′-grānd′), *adj.* 1 having a coarse texture; made up of large, coarse fibers. 2 not delicate or refined; crude.

coars en (kôr′sən, kōr′sən), *v.t., v.i.* make or become coarse.

coast (kōst), *n.* 1 land along the sea; seashore. 2 region near a coast. 3 **the Coast,** (in the United States) the region along the Pacific. 4 a ride or slide downhill without the use of power. 5 a slope for sliding downhill on a sled, etc. 6 **The coast is clear.** No one is in the way; the danger is past. —*v.i.* 1 ride or slide without the use of effort or power: *coast downhill on a bicycle.* 2 move or advance with little effort or exertion: *coast along through school.* 3 sail from port to port along a coast. —*v.t.* 1 sail along or near the coast of. 2 sail from port to port of a coast. [< Old French *coste* < Latin *costa* side]

coast al (kō′stl), *adj.* of the coast; near or along a coast.

coastal plain, a flat stretch of land along a coast.

coast er (kō′stər), *n.* 1 person or thing that coasts. 2 ship that sails or trades along a coast. 3 sled to coast on. 4 roller coaster. 5 a little tray for holding a glass or bottle to protect the surface of a table, etc., from moisture.

coaster brake, brake in the hub of the rear wheel of a bicycle, worked by pushing back on the pedals.

coast guard, 1 group of men whose work is protecting lives and property along the coast of a country. 2 member of any such group. 3 **Coast Guard,** branch of the armed forces whose work is protecting lives and property and helping to prevent smuggling along the coasts of the United States. It is under the Navy Department in wartime and under the Department of Transportation in peacetime.

coast guards man (kōst′gärdz′mən), *n., pl.* **-men.** member of a coast guard; coast guard.

coast line (kōst′līn′), *n.* outline of a coast.

Coast Ranges, mountain system along the Pacific coast of North America. Highest peak, 19,850 ft.

coast ward (kōst′wərd), *adv., adj.* toward the coast.

coast wise (kōst′wīz′), *adv., adj.* along the coast.

coat (kōt), *n.* 1 an outer garment of cloth, fur, etc., with sleeves. 2 a natural outer covering: *a dog's coat of hair.* 3 a thin layer covering a surface; coating: *a coat of paint.* —*v.t.* 1 cover with a thin layer: *The old books were coated with dust.* 2 provide with a coat. [< Old French *cote*] —**coat′less,** *adj.*

co a ti (kō ä′tē), *n., pl.* **-tis** or **-ti.** a small mammal with a long body and tail and a flexible snout, somewhat like a raccoon, living in the southwestern United States, Mexico, and Central and South America. [< Tupi-Guarani]

coat ing (kō′ting), *n.* 1 layer covering a surface: *a coating of paint.* 2 cloth for making coats.

coat of arms, *pl.* **coats of arms.** 1 shield, or drawing of a shield, bearing designs symbolic of family history, used especially by noble families in Europe. 2 a somewhat similar device adopted as an emblem of authority by a government, city, or corporation.

coat of mail, *pl.* **coats of mail.** garment made of metal rings or plates, worn as armor.

coat room (kōt′rüm′, kōt′rụ̇m′), *n.* cloakroom.

coat tail (kōt′tāl′), *n.* 1 Usually, **coattails,** *pl.* the tails of a formal coat, jacket, etc. 2 **ride on (someone's) coattails,** advance in career or popularity by associating with a more successful or popular person.

co au thor (kō ô′thər), *n.* a joint author. —*v.t.* INFORMAL. write with the help of another.

coax (kōks), *v.t.* 1 persuade by soft words; influence by pleasant ways; cajole: *We coaxed our parents into letting us go to the movies.* 2 get by coaxing: *The baby-sitter coaxed a smile from the baby.* [< obsolete *cokes* a fool] **—coax′er,** *n.* **—coax′ing ly,** *adv.*

co ax i al (kō ak′sē əl), *adj.* having a common axis. **—co ax′i al ly,** *adv.*

coaxial cable, a cable of insulated conducting materials surrounding an insulated central conductor, used for simultaneously transmitting many telegraph, telephone, and television signals.

cob (kob), *n.* 1 corncob. 2 a strong horse with short legs. 3 a male swan. [Middle English *cobbe* stout man]

co balt (kō′bôlt), *n.* 1 a hard, silver-white metallic element with a pinkish tint, which occurs only in combination with other elements, used in making alloys, paints, etc. *Symbol:* Co; *atomic number* 27. See pages 326 and 327 for table. 2 a dark-blue coloring matter made from cobalt. [< German *Kobalt,* variant of *Kobold* goblin (because of miners' belief in the evil or mischievous effects of the substance)]

co bal tite (kō′bôl tīt), *n.* a silver-white mineral containing cobalt, arsenic, and sulfur. It is an important ore of cobalt. *Formula:* CoAsS

cobalt 60, a radioactive isotope of cobalt, produced by bombarding cobalt atoms with neutrons and used as a source of gamma rays in the treatment of cancer. *Symbol:* C^{60}; *atomic number* 27; *mass number* 60.

cob ble[1] (kob′əl), *v.t.,* **-bled, -bling.** 1 mend (shoes, etc.); repair; patch. 2 put together clumsily. [probably < *cobbler*[1]]

cob ble[2] (kob′əl), *n., v.,* **-bled, -bling.** —*n.* cobblestone. —*v.t.* pave with cobblestones. [perhaps diminutive of Middle English *cobbe* lump]

cob bler[1] (kob′lər), *n.* 1 person whose work is mending or making shoes. 2 a clumsy workman. [Middle English *cobeler*]

cob bler[2] (kob′lər), *n.* 1 U.S. a fruit pie baked in a deep dish, usually with a crust only on top. 2 an iced drink made of wine, fruit juice, etc. [origin unknown]

cob ble stone (kob′əl stōn′), *n.* a rounded stone formerly much used in paving.

Cob den (kob′dən), *n.* **Richard,** 1804-1865, British statesman and economist.

Cóbh (kōv), *n.* seaport in the S part of the Republic of Ireland. Former name, **Queenstown.** 6000.

CO BOL (kō′bôl), *n.* Common Business Oriented Language, a language for international use in programing data-processing machines.

co bra (kō′brə), *n.* a very poisonous snake of Asia and Africa. When excited, it flattens its neck so that the head takes on the appearance of a hood. [< Portuguese *cobra (de capello)* snake (with a hood)]

cob web (kob′web′), *n.* 1 a spider's web, or the stuff it is made of. 2 anything thin and slight or entangling like a spider's web. 3 any stale accumulation or obstruction. [Old English *(ātor)coppe* spider + *web*]

cob web by (kob′web′ē), *adj.* 1 of or like a cobweb. 2 covered with cobwebs.

co ca (kō′kə), *n.* 1 a large tropical shrub growing in South America, Java, and Ceylon, whose dried leaves are used to make cocaine and other alkaloids. 2 its dried leaves. [< Quechua *cuca*]

co caine or **co cain** (kō kān′, kō′kān), *n.* a white, bitter, crystalline drug obtained from dried coca leaves, used to deaden pain and as a stimulant. *Formula:* $C_{17}H_{21}NO_4$

coc coid (kok′oid), *adj.* of or like a coccus. —*n.* a coccoid microorganism.

coc cus (kok′əs), *n., pl.* **coc ci** (kok′sī). bacterium shaped like a sphere. [< New Latin < Greek *kokkos* seed]

coc cyx (kok′siks), *n., pl.* **coc cy ges** (kok sī′jēz′). 1 a small, triangular bone forming the lower end of the spinal column in man. 2 a similar part in certain animals and birds. [< Latin < Greek *kokkyx,* originally, cuckoo; because shaped like cuckoo's bill]

Co chin China (kō′chin, koch′in), former French colony in S Indochina, now part of South Vietnam.

coch i neal (koch′ə nēl′, koch′ə nēl), *n.* a bright-red dye made from the dried bodies of the females of a scale insect that lives on cactus plants of tropical America. [< French *cochenille*]

coch le a (kok′lē ə), *n., pl.* **-le ae** (-lē ē′). a spiral-shaped cavity of the inner ear, containing the nerve endings that transmit sound impulses along the auditory nerve. See **ear**[1] for diagram. [< Latin, snail < Greek *kochlias*]

coch le ar (kok′lē ər), *adj.* of the cochlea.

cock[1] (kok), *n.* 1 a male chicken; rooster. 2 the male of other birds. 3 faucet or valve used to regulate the flow of a liquid or gas. 4 hammer of a gun. 5 position of the hammer or firing pin of a gun when it is pulled back ready to fire. 6 weathercock. 7 leader; head; main person. —*v.t., v.i.* (of a gun) pull back the hammer or firing pin. [Old English *cocc*]

cock[2] (kok), *v.t.* turn or stick up, especially in a carefree, defiant, or inquiring manner: *The little bird cocked his eye at me.* —*n.* 1 an upward turn or bend of the eye, ear, hat, etc. 2 turn of the brim of a hat. [probably < *cock*[1]]

cock[3] (kok), *n.* a small, cone-shaped pile of hay, turf, etc., in a field. —*v.t.* pile in cocks. [Middle English *cocke*]

cock ade (ko kād′), *n.* knot of ribbon or a rosette worn on the hat as a badge.

cock-a-doo dle-doo (kok′ə dü′dl dü′), *n., pl.* **-doos.** imitation of a rooster's cry.

Cock aigne (ko kān′), *n.* an imaginary land of luxury and idleness. [< Old French *cokaigne* sugar cake]

hat, āge, fär; let, ēqual, tėrm;
it, īce; hot, ōpen, ôrder;
oil, out; cup, pụ̇t, rüle;
ch, child; ng, long; sh, she;
th, thin; ᴛʜ, then; zh, measure;

ə represents *a* in about, *e* in taken, *i* in pencil, *o* in lemon, *u* in circus.

< = from, derived from, taken from.

cock-and-bull story (kok′ən bụ̇l′), an absurd, incredible story.

cock a too (kok′ə tü′, kok′ə tü), *n., pl.* **-toos.** a large, brightly colored parrot of Australia, the East Indies, etc., with a crest which it can raise or lower. [< Dutch *kaketoe* < Malay *kakatua*]

cock a trice (kok′ə tris), *n.* (in old stories) a serpent whose look was supposed to cause death. A cockatrice was usually represented as part cock and part serpent. [< Old French *cocatris* (influenced by *coq* cock), ultimately < Latin *calcare* tread on]

cock boat (kok′bōt′), *n.* a small rowboat.

cock chaf er (kok′chā′fər), *n.* a large European beetle that destroys plants.

cock crow (kok′krō′), *n.* 1 the crowing of a rooster. 2 time when roosters begin to crow; dawn.

cocked hat (def. 1)

cocked hat, 1 hat with the brim turned up. 2 hat pointed in front and in back. 3 **knock into a cocked hat,** SLANG. destroy completely; defeat; ruin.

cock er el (kok′ər əl), *n.* a young rooster, not more than one year old.

cock er spaniel (kok′ər), one of a breed of small dogs with long, silky hair and drooping ears. [< *cock*[1], because it was used to hunt woodcock]

cock eye (kok′ī′), *n.* eye that squints.

cock eyed (kok′īd′), *adj.* 1 cross-eyed. 2 SLANG. tilted or twisted to one side. 3 SLANG. foolish; silly.

cock fight (kok′fīt′), *n.* fight between roosters or between gamecocks armed with steel spurs.

cock fight ing (kok′fī′ting), *n.* fighting by roosters or gamecocks for the entertainment of spectators.

cock horse (kok′hôrs′), *n.* rocking horse.

cock le[1] (kok′əl), *n., v.,* **-led, -ling.** —*n.* 1 a small, edible, saltwater mollusk with ridged, heart-shaped shells in two hinged halves. 2 one of these shells. 3 a small, light, shallow boat. 4 a bulge on the surface; wrinkle; pucker. 5 **cockles of one's heart,** the inmost part of one's heart or feelings. —*v.i., v.t.* curl or wrinkle up; pucker: *Paper sometimes cockles when you paste it.* [< Old French *coquille* < Latin *conchylium* < Greek *konchylion* < *konchē* conch]

cock le[2] (kok′əl), *n.* weed that grows in grain fields, such as the corn cockle, darnel, and cocklebur. [Old English *coccel*]

cock le bur (kok′əl bėr′), *n.* any of several weeds with spiny burs.

cock le shell (kok′əl shel′), *n.* 1 shell of the cockle. 2 a small, light, shallow boat; cockleboat.

cock ney (kok′nē), *n., pl.* **-neys,** *adj.* —*n.* 1 nickname for a native or inhabitant of the eastern section of London who speaks a particular dialect of English. 2 this dialect. —*adj.* 1 of or like this dialect. In cockney speech most h's at the beginning of words are not pronounced. 2 of or like cockneys. [Middle English *cokeney* cock's egg, pampered child, city fellow]

cock pit (kok′pit′), *n.* 1 place where the pilot sits in an airplane. 2 the open place in a boat where the pilot and passengers sit. 3 an enclosed place for cockfights. 4 scene of many fights or battles: *Belgium is often called the cockpit of Europe.* 5 rooms below the deck in warships of former times, used as quarters for junior officers, or as a hospital during battle.

cock roach (kok′rōch′), *n.* any of an order of nocturnal insects, usually brown with flattened oval bodies, some species of which are household pests inhabiting kitchens, areas around water pipes, etc. [< Spanish *cucaracha*]

cocks comb (koks′kōm′), *n.* 1 the fleshy, red crest on the top of a rooster's head. 2 a pointed cap somewhat like this, worn by a jester or clown. 3 amaranth with crested or feathery clusters of red, white, or yellow flowers. 4 OBSOLETE. coxcomb.

cock sure (kok′shůr′), *adj.* 1 too sure; overly confident. 2 perfectly sure; absolutely certain. —**cock′sure′ly,** *adv.* —**cock′sure′ness,** *n.*

cock swain (kok′sən, kok′swān′), *n.* coxswain.

cock tail (kok′tāl′), *n.* 1 a chilled drink of gin, whiskey, rum, vodka, etc., mixed with vermouth, fruit juices, sugar, bitters, etc. 2 an appetizer of juice: *a tomato-juice cocktail.* 3 shellfish served with a highly seasoned sauce as an appetizer. 4 any mixed fruits, diced and usually served in a glass.

cock y (kok′ē), *adj.,* **cock i er, cock i est.** INFORMAL. conceited or swaggering. —**cock′i ly,** *adv.* —**cock′i ness,** *n.*

co co (kō′kō), *n., pl.* **-cos.** 1 coconut palm. 2 coconut. Also, **cocoa.** [< Portuguese, grinning face]

co coa[1] (kō′kō), *n.* 1 powder made by roasting, grinding, and removing some fat from the kernels of cacao seeds. 2 drink made of this powder with milk or water and sugar. 3 the plant itself. 4 a dull-brown color, lighter than chocolate. —*adj.* 1 dull-brown. 2 of or having to do with cocoa. [variant of *cacao*]

co coa[2] (kō′kō), *n.* coco.

cocoa butter, a yellowish-white fat obtained from cacao seeds, used in making soap, cosmetics, etc.

co co nut or **co coa nut** (kō′kə nut′, kō′kə nət), *n.* the large, round, hard-shelled fruit of the coconut palm. Coconuts have a brown shell with a sweet, white, pulpy meat which is often shredded for use in cakes, puddings, and pies.

coconut milk, the sweet, clear or whitish liquid contained in a coconut.

coconut oil, oil obtained from coconuts, used for making soap, candles, etc.

coconut palm, a tall tropical palm tree on which coconuts grow; coco palm.

co coon (kə kün′), *n.* 1 case of silky thread spun by the larvae of various insects to live in while in the pupa stage. Most moth larvae form cocoons. Silk is obtained from the cocoons of silkworms. 2 any similar protective case or covering. [< French *cocon* < *coque* shell]

coco palm, coconut palm.

cod (kod), *n., pl.* **cods** or **cod.** a large, important food fish found in the cold parts of the northern Atlantic; codfish. [Middle English]

Cod (kod), *n.* **Cape,** a hook-shaped peninsula in SE Massachusetts.

c.o.d. or **C.O.D.,** cash on delivery; collect on delivery.

co da (kō′də), *n.* (in music) a passage introduced after the completion of the essential parts of a movement or composition, so as to form a more definite and satisfactory ending. [< Italian < Latin *cauda* tail]

cod dle (kod′l), *v.t.,* **-dled, -dling.** 1 treat tenderly; pamper: *coddle sick children.* 2 cook in hot water without boiling: *coddle an egg.* [origin uncertain]

code (kōd), *n., v.,* **cod ed, cod ing.** —*n.* 1 system of secret writing; arrangement of words, figures, etc., to keep a message short or secret. 2 a collection of laws arranged according to a system so that they can be understood and used. 3 any set of accepted manners or rules. A moral code is made up of the notions of right and wrong conduct held by a person, a group of persons, or a society. 4 system of signals for sending messages by telegraph, flags, etc. The Morse code is used in telegraphy. 5 genetic code. —*v.t.* change or put into a code. [< Old French < Latin *codex* codex. Doublet of CODEX.]

co deine or **co dein** (kō′dēn′, kō′dē ən), *n.* a white, crystalline drug obtained from opium or morphine, used to relieve pain, coughs, and to cause sleep. *Formula:* $C_{18}H_{21}NO_3$ [< Greek *kōdeia* poppy seed]

co dex (kō′deks), *n., pl.* **co di ces.** an ancient manuscript of the Scriptures or of a classical author. [< Latin, variant of *caudex* tree trunk, writing tablet, codex. Doublet of CODE.]

cod fish (kod′fish′), *n., pl.* **-fish es** or **-fish.** cod.

codg er (koj′ər), *n.* INFORMAL. an odd or peculiar person. [variant of *cadger*]

co di ces (kō′də sēz′, kod′ə sēz′), *n.* pl. of **codex.**

cod i cil (kod′ə səl), *n.* 1 (in law) something added to a will to change it, add to it, or explain it. 2 something added. [< Latin *codicillum,* diminutive of *codex*]

cod i fi ca tion (kod′ə fə kā′shən, kō′də fə kā′shən), *n.* arrangement of laws, etc., according to a system.

cod i fy (kod′ə fī, kō′də fī), *v.t.,* **-fied, -fy ing.** arrange (laws, etc.) according to a system: *The laws of France were codified from 1804 to 1810 by order of Napoleon I.* —**cod′i fi′er,** *n.*

cod lin (kod′lən), *n.* codling[1].

cod ling[1] (kod′ling), *n.* 1 a small, unripe apple. 2 a kind of long, tapering apple, usually for cooking. [Middle English *querdelyng*]

cod ling[2] (kod′ling), *n.* 1 a young or small cod. 2 hake.

codling moth, a small moth whose larvae destroy apples, pears, etc.

cod-liv er oil (kod′liv′ər), oil extracted from the liver of cod or of related species, used in medicine as a source of vitamins A and D.

co don (kō′don), *n.* 1 a three-letter code word representing a group of three chemical bases. 2 such a group, forming the arrangement for a specific amino acid in protein synthesis.

Co dy (kō′dē), *n.* **William F(rederick),** the real name of **Buffalo Bill.**

co ed or **co-ed** (kō′ed′), *n.* U.S. INFORMAL. a girl or woman student at a coeducational school.

co ed u ca tion (kō′ej ə kā′shən), *n.* education of boys and girls or men and women together in the same school or classes.

co ed u ca tion al (kō′ej ə kā′shə nəl), *adj.* 1 educating boys and girls or men and women together in the same school or classes. 2 having to do with coeducation. —**co′ed u ca′tion al ly,** *adv.*

co ef fi cient (kō′ə fish′ənt), *n.* 1 number or symbol put with and multiplying another. In *3x, 3* is the coefficient of *x,* and *x* is the coefficient of *3.* 2 (in physics) a ratio used as a multiplier to calculate the behavior of a substance under different conditions of heat, light, etc. —*adj.* cooperating.

coe la canth (sē′lə kanth), *n.* any of an order of fishes having rounded scales and lobed fins, formerly considered extinct. A coelacanth is similar to the primitive sea vertebrates which gave rise to all land vertebrates. [< Greek *koilos* hollow + *akantha* thorn, spine]

Coe len te rat a (si len′tə rā′tə), *n.pl.* phylum of invertebrates comprising the coelenterates. [< New Latin]

coe len te rate (si len′tə rāt′, si len′tər it), *n.* any of a phylum of aquatic invertebrates with radially symmetrical, saclike bodies, and a single internal cavity. Hydras, jellyfish, corals, and sea anemones belong to this phylum. —*adj.* of or belonging to this phylum. [< Greek *koilos* hollow + *enteron* intestine]

coe li ac (sē′lē ak), *adj.* celiac.

coe lom (sē′ləm), *n.* the body cavity of most many-celled animals, containing the heart, lungs, etc. [< Greek *koilōma* cavity < *koilos* hollow]

coen o bite (sen′ə bīt, sē′nə bīt), *n.* cenobite.

co en zyme (kō en′zīm), *n.* an organic substance, usually containing a mineral or vitamin, capable of attaching itself to and supplementing a specific protein to form an enzyme system.

co e qual (kō ē′kwəl), *adj.* equal in rank, degree, extent, etc. —*n.* person or thing that is equal with another. —**co e′qual ly,** *adv.*

co erce (kō ėrs′), *v.t.,* **-erced, -erc ing.** 1 compel; force: *The prisoner was coerced into confessing to the crime.* 2 control or restrain by force or authority. [< Latin *coercere* < *co-* together + *arcere* restrain] —**co erc′er,** *n.* —**co erc′i ble,** *adj.*

co er cion (kō ėr′shən, kō ėr′zhən), *n.* use of force; compulsion; constraint.

co er cive (kō ėr′siv), *adj.* using force; compelling; constraining. —**co er′cive ly,** *adv.* —**co er′cive ness,** *n.*

coes ite (kō′sīt), *n.* a very dense form of silica, produced by subjecting quartz to very high pressure. [< Loring *Coes,* Jr., born 1915, American chemist + *-ite*[2]]

co e val (kō ē′vəl), *adj.* 1 having the same age, date, or duration. 2 contemporary. —*n.* a contemporary. [< Late Latin *coaevus* < *co-* equal + *aevum* age] —**co e′val ly,** *adv.*

co ex ist (kō′ig zist′), *v.i.* exist together or at the same time: *Orange trees have coexisting fruit and flowers.*

hat, āge, fär; let, ēqual, tėrm;
it, īce; hot, ōpen, ôrder;
oil, out; cup, pu̇t, rüle;
ch, child; ng, long; sh, she;
th, thin; ŧʜ, then; zh, measure;
ə represents *a* in about, *e* in taken,
i in pencil, *o* in lemon, *u* in circus.
< = from, derived from, taken from.

co ex ist ence (kō′ig zis′təns), *n.* 1 existence together or at the same time. 2 condition or policy in which two opposing countries or powers coexist without war or interference with each other: *peaceful coexistence.*

co ex ist ent (kō′ig zis′tənt), *adj.* coexisting.

co ex tend (kō′ik stend′), *v.t., v.i.* extend equally or to the same limits.

co ex ten sion (kō′ik sten′shən), *n.* extension over an equal amount of space or time.

co ex ten sive (kō′ik sten′siv), *adj.* extending equally; extending over the same space or time. **—co′ex ten′sive ly,** *adv.*

cof fee (kô′fē, kof′ē), *n.* 1 a dark-brown drink made from the roasted and ground seeds of a tall, tropical evergreen shrub of the same family as the madder. 2 coffee beans. 3 the plant itself. 4 the color of coffee; a dark brown, darker than chocolate. *—adj.* having the color of coffee; dark-brown. [< Italian *caffè* < Turkish *kahveh* < Arabic *qahwa*]

coffee bean, seed of the coffee plant. Coffee beans are roasted and ground to make coffee.

cof fee house (kô′fē hous′, kof′ē hous′), *n., pl.* **-hous es** (-hou′ziz). place where coffee and other refreshments are served. In the 1600's and 1700's, London coffeehouses filled much the same place as modern clubs.

cof fee pot (kô′fē pot′, kof′ē pot′), *n.* container for making or serving coffee.

coffee shop, place where coffee, light refreshments, and inexpensive meals are served.

coffee table, a low table for serving coffee and other refreshments. It is often placed in front of a sofa.

cof fer (kô′fər, kof′ər), *n.* 1 box, chest, or trunk, especially one used to hold money or other valuable things. 2 an ornamental panel in a ceiling, etc. 3 cofferdam. 4 **coffers,** *pl.* treasury; funds. [< Old French *cofre* < Latin *cophinum* basket. See COFFIN.]

cof fer dam (kô′fər dam′, kof′ər dam′), *n.* structure of wooden piles and earth or sheets of steel forming a temporary dam, to expose an underwater area in order to build the foundations of a bridge, pier, etc.

cogwheel—two cogwheels. As one wheel turns, its teeth push against the teeth of the other wheel, causing it to turn.

cof fin (kô′fən, kof′ən), *n.* box into which a dead person is put to be buried; casket. [< Old French *cofin* basket < Latin *cophinum* < Greek *kophinos*]

cog[1] (kog), *n.* 1 one of a series of teeth on the edge of a wheel that transfers motion by locking into the teeth of a similar wheel. 2 cogwheel or gearwheel. [< Scandinavian (Swedish) *kugge*]

cog[2] (kog), *n.* projection, tenon, or tooth on one piece of wood that fits into a notch on another piece to make a joint. [variant of earlier *cock* to secure]

co gen cy (kō′jən sē), *n.* forcible quality; power of convincing.

co gent (kō′jənt), *adj.* having the power to convince; forcible or convincing: *The lawyer's cogent arguments convinced the jury.* See **valid** for synonym study. [< Latin *cogentem* < *co-* together + *agere* to drive] **—co′gent ly,** *adv.*

cog i tate (koj′ə tāt), *v.i., v.t.,* **-tat ed, -tat ing.** think over; consider with care; meditate; ponder. [< Latin *cogitatum* tossed around < *co-* (intensive) + *agitare* agitate] **—cog′i ta′tion,** *n.* **—cog′i ta′tor,** *n.*

cog i ta tive (koj′ə tā′tiv), *adj.* given to thinking; thoughtful; meditative. **—cog′i ta′tive ly,** *adv.*

co gnac (kō′nyak, kon′yak), *n.* a French brandy of superior quality. [< French < *Cognac,* town and region in France]

cog nate (kog′nāt), *adj.* 1 related by family or origin. English, Dutch, and German are cognate languages. 2 having a similar nature or quality. *—n.* anything related to another by having a common source. German *Wasser* and English *water* are cognates. [< Latin *cognatus* < *co-* together + *gnatus* born]

cog ni tion (kog nish′ən), *n.* 1 act of knowing; perception; awareness. 2 thing known, perceived, or recognized. [< Latin *cognitionem* < *cognoscere* perceive < *co-* (intensive) + *gnoscere* know]

cog ni tive (kog′nə tiv), *adj.* having to do with cognition. **—cog′ni tive ly,** *adv.*

cog ni zance (kog′nə zəns, kon′ə zəns), *n.* 1 knowledge; perception; awareness. 2 **take cognizance of,** take notice of; give attention to: *She took cognizance of her faults.* 3 in law: **a** an official notice. **b** right or power to deal with judicially. 4 jurisdiction; responsibility; charge. [< Old French *conoissance* < *conoistre* know < Latin *cognoscere.* See COGNITION.]

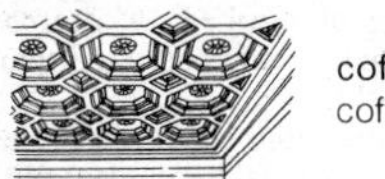

coffer (def. 2)
coffers in a ceiling

cog ni zant (kog′nə zənt, kon′ə zənt), *adj.* having cognizance; aware.

cog no men (kog nō′mən), *n.* 1 surname; family name; last name. 2 nickname. 3 any name. 4 (in ancient Rome) the third or family name of a person. [< Latin < *co-* with + *nomen* name]

co gno scen te (kō′nyō shen′tā), *n., pl.* **-ti** (-tē). person who is well-informed; connoisseur. [< Italian]

cog wheel (kog′hwēl′), *n.* wheel with teeth projecting from the rim for transmitting or receiving motion; gear; gearwheel.

co hab it (kō hab′it), *v.i.* live together as husband and wife do. **—co hab′i ta′tion,** *n.*

co here (kō hir′), *v.i.,* **-hered, -her ing.** 1 stick or hold together as parts of the same mass or substance: *Brick and mortar cohere.* 2 be logically connected; be consistent. [< Latin *cohaerere* < *co-* together + *haerere* cleave]

co her ence (kō hir′əns), *n.* 1 logical connection or relation; consistency; congruity. 2 a sticking together; tendency to hold together; cohesion.

co her en cy (kō hir′ən sē), *n.* coherence.

co her ent (kō hir′ənt), *adj.* 1 logically connected; consistent: *A sentence that is not coherent is hard to understand.* 2 sticking together; holding together. 3 (in physics) having waves with a high degree of similarity of phase, direction, and amplitude: *Lasers produce coherent light.* **—co her′ent ly,** *adv.*

co he sion (kō hē′zhən), *n.* 1 a sticking together; tendency to hold together: *Wet sand has more cohesion than dry sand.* 2 (in physics) the attraction between molecules of the same kind: *Drops of water are a result of cohesion.* 3 (in botany) the union of one part with another. [< Latin *cohaesum* pressed together]

co he sive (kō hē′siv), *adj.* tending to hold together; sticking together. **—co he′sive ly,** *adv.* **—co he′sive ness,** *n.*

co hort (kō′hôrt), *n.* 1 part of an ancient Roman legion. There were from 300 to 600 soldiers in each cohort, and ten cohorts in each legion. 2 group of soldiers. 3 any group, band, or company. 4 INFORMAL. associate or follower: *a cohort of the local political boss.* [< Latin *cohortem* court, enclosure. Doublet of COURT.]

coif (koif), *n.* cap or hood that fits closely around the head. *—v.t.* to cover with a coif or something like a coif. [< Old French *coife*]

coif fure (kwä fyu̇r′), *n.* 1 style of arranging the hair. 2 a covering for the hair; headdress. [< French]

coign (koin), *n.* a projecting corner. [variant of *coin*]

coign of vantage, a good location for watching or doing something.

coil[1] (koil), *v.t.* wind around and around in circular or spiral shape: *The snake coiled itself up.* *—v.i.* 1 wind oneself around; place or grow around something: *The snake coiled around a branch.* 2 move in a winding course. *—n.* 1 anything wound around and around in circular or spiral shape: *a coil of rope.* 2 one wind or turn of a coil. 3 series of connected pipes arranged in a coil or row, as in a radiator. 4 spiral of wire for conducting electricity. [< Old French *coillir* to collect < Latin *colligere*] **—coil′er,** *n.*

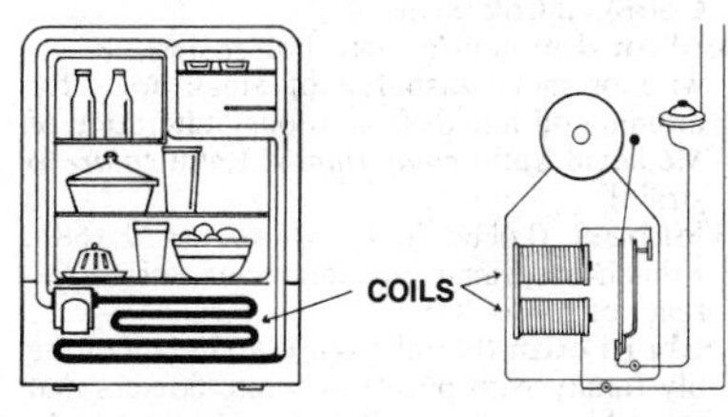

coil[1] (def. 3) coils in refrigerator

coil[1] (def. 4)—coils in electromagnet of electric bell

coil[2] (koil), *n.* ARCHAIC. a noisy disturbance; turmoil. [origin uncertain]

coin (koin), *n.* 1 piece of metal stamped and issued by a government for use as money. Pennies, nickels, dimes, and quarters are coins. 2 metal money. A government makes coin by stamping metal. 3 **pay back in his own coin,** treat him as he treated oneself or others. *—v.t.* 1 make (money) by stamping metal. 2 make (metal) into money. 3 make up; invent: *The word "chortle" was coined* *by Lewis Carroll.* [< Old French, corner < Latin *cuneus* wedge] **—coin′er,** *n.*

coin age (koi′nij), *n.* 1 the making of coins. 2 metal money; coins. 3 system of coins. The United States has a decimal coinage. 4 right of coining money. 5 act or process of making up; inventing: *the coinage of new words.* 6 word, phrase, etc., invented.

co in cide (kō′in sīd′), *v.i.,* **-cid ed, -cid ing.** 1 occupy the same place in space: *If these two triangles △ △ were placed one on top of the other, they would coincide.* 2 occupy the same time; occur at the same time: *The working hours of the two friends coincide.* 3 be just alike; correspond exactly; agree; concur: *Her opinion coincides with mine.* See **agree** for synonym study. [< Medieval Latin *coincidere* < Latin *co-* together + *in* upon + *cadere* fall]

co in ci dence (kō in′sə dəns), *n.* 1 the chance occurrence of two things at the same time or place in such a way as to seem remarkable, fitting, etc. 2 exact correspondence; agreement. 3 a coinciding.

co in ci dent (kō in′sə dənt), *adj.* 1 happening at the same time; coinciding. 2 occupying the same place or position. 3 in exact agreement. **—co in′ci dent ly,** *adv.*

co in ci den tal (kō in′sə den′tl), *adj.* 1 showing coincidence. 2 coincident. **—co-in′ci den′tal ly,** *adv.*

coir (koir), *n.* fiber obtained from the outer husks of coconuts, used to make rope, mats, etc. [< Malayalam *kāyar* cord]

co i tus (kō′ə təs), *n.* sexual intercourse. [< Latin]

coke (kōk), *n., v.,* **coked, cok ing.** *—n.* fuel made from bituminous coal that has been heated in an oven from which most of the air has been shut out. Coke burns with much heat and little smoke, and is used in furnaces, for melting metal, etc. *—v.t., v.i.* change into coke. [perhaps variant of dialectal *colk* (unburned) core (of wood)]

Coke (ku̇k, kōk), *n.* Sir **Edward,** 1552-1634, English lawyer and judge.

col-, *prefix.* form of **com-** before *l,* as in *collect.*

col., 1 colony. 2 column.

Col., 1 Colonel. 2 Colorado (official abbrev., **Colo.**). 3 Colossians.

col an der (kul′ən dər, kol′ən dər), *n.* a wire or metal dish full of small holes for draining off liquids from foods. [alteration of Medieval Latin *colatorium* < Latin *colare* to strain]

Col bert (kôl ber′), *n.* **Jean,** 1619-1683, French statesman and financier during the reign of Louis XIV.

col chi cum (kol′chə kəm), *n.* 1 plant of the lily family with purple or white flowers that resemble crocuses. 2 a bitter-tasting medicine for gout and rheumatism obtained from the dried seeds of this plant. [< Latin < Greek *kolchikon* < *Colchis*]

Col chis (kol′kis), *n.* ancient country on the E shore of the Black Sea. In Greek legends it is the country where the Golden Fleece was found by Jason and the Argonauts.

cold (kōld), *adj.* 1 much less warm than the body: *Snow and ice are cold.* See synonym study below. 2 having a relatively low temperature: *This coffee is cold.* 3 feeling cold or chilly: *Put on a sweater, or you will be cold.* 4 lacking in feeling; unfriendly: *a cold greeting.* 5 lacking in feeling, passion, or enthusiasm; indifferent: *a cold nature.* 6 faint; weak: *a cold scent.* 7 (in games, treasure hunts, etc.) far from what one is searching for. 8 suggesting coolness. Blue, green, and gray are called cold colors. *—n.* 1 lack of heat or warmth; low temperature. 2 a common viral infection of the mucous membrane of the nose and throat that may cause chills, fever, running at the nose, sore throat, sneezing, and coughing; common cold. 3 **catch cold** or **take cold,** become sick with a cold. 4 **in the cold** or **out in the cold,** all alone; neglected. [< Old English *cald*] **—cold′ly,** *adv.* **—cold′ness,** *n.*

Syn. *adj.* 1 **Cold, chilly, cool** mean having a low temperature. **Cold** means having low temperature, judged by the standard of normal body heat: *A cold wind is blowing.* **Chilly** means cold enough to be uncomfortable and make a person shiver a little: *Without my coat I feel chilly.* **Cool** means neither hot nor cold, but closer to cold: *After the hot day the evening seems cool.*

cold-blood ed (kōld′blud′id), *adj.* 1 having blood whose temperature varies with that of the surroundings. Snakes and turtles are called cold-blooded, but their blood is actually very close to the temperature of the air or water in which they live. 2 feeling the cold because of poor circulation. 3 lacking in feeling; cruel: *a cold-blooded murderer.* **—cold′-blood′ed ly,** *adv.* **—cold′-blood′ed ness,** *n.*

cold chisel, a strong, steel chisel for cutting cold metal.

cold cream, a creamy, soothing salve for softening or cleansing the skin.

cold cuts, slices of cooked or prepared meat, such as corned beef, salami, tongue, and ham, served cold.

cold frame, frame with a top of glass, plastic, etc., and no artificial heat, used out of doors to protect young or delicate plants from the cold.

cold front, the advancing edge of a cold air mass as it overtakes, passes under, and replaces a warmer one.

cold-heart ed (kōld′här′tid), *adj.* lacking in feeling; unsympathetic; unkind. **—cold′-heart′ed ly,** *adv.* **—cold′-heart′ed ness,** *n.*

cold light, light without heat. Phosphorescence and fluorescence are kinds of cold light.

cold pack, 1 something cold put on the body for medical purposes. 2 method of canning in which fruits and vegetables are put in jars or cans without cooking and then processed in boiling water or a pressure cooker to insure sterilization.

cold shoulder, 1 deliberately unfriendly or indifferent treatment; neglect. 2 **turn a cold shoulder to,** shun; avoid.

cold-shoul der (kōld′shōl′dər), *v.t.* treat in an unfriendly or indifferent way; turn a cold shoulder to.

cold sore, blister near or on the mouth, caused by a viral infection of the skin; fever blister.

cold steel, a steel weapon, such as a knife or sword.

cold storage, storage in a very cold place. Perishable foods are put in cold storage to preserve them.

cold sweat, perspiration accompanied by a chilly feeling, especially as produced by fear or nausea.

cold war, 1 conflict between nations for national advantage conducted by political, economic, and psychological means instead of direct military action. 2 **Cold War,** the contest for power between the communist nations headed by the Soviet Union and the nations of the West headed by the United States that began after World War II.

cold wave, period of very cold weather.

cole (kōl), *n.* any of a genus of plants of the mustard family, including cabbage, cauliflower, kale, rape, etc.; colewort. [Old English *cāl,* variant of *cāwel* < Latin *caulem* cabbage]

cole man ite (kōl′mə nīt), *n.* mineral consisting of hydrated calcium borate occurring in colorless to white crystals. Colemanite is the principal natural source of borax. *Formula:* $CA_2B_6O_{11} \cdot 5H_2O$ [< William T. *Coleman,* 1824-1893, civic leader of San Francisco]

co le op ter an (kō′lē op′tər ən, kol′ē-op′tər ən), *n.* any of the largest order of insects, usually having two pairs of wings, the forewings being hard and sheathlike, the hind wings membranous. Beetles, weevils, and fireflies belong to this order. [< Greek *koleos* sheath + *pteron* wing]

co le op ter ous (kō′lē op′tər əs, kol′ē-op′tər əs), *adj.* of or belonging to the coleopterans.

co le op tile (kō′lē op′təl, kol′ē op′təl), *n.* a tubular sheath covering the terminal bud of grasses for a short time after germination of the grains. [< Greek *koleos* sheath + *ptilon* feather]

Cole ridge (kōl′rij), *n.* **Samuel Taylor,** 1772-1834, English poet, literary critic, and philosopher.

cole slaw (kōl′slô′), *n.* salad made of finely shredded raw cabbage; slaw. [< Dutch *koolsla* cabbage salad]

co le us (kō′lē əs), *n.* any of a genus of plants of the mint family often grown for their showy, colorful leaves. [< Greek *koleos* sheath]

cole wort (kōl′wėrt′), *n.* 1 cole. 2 any kind of cabbage having a loosely packed head of curly leaves.

col ic (kol′ik), *n.* severe pains in the intestines. [< Late Latin *colicus* < Greek *kolikos* of the colon]

col ick y (kol′i kē), *adj.* 1 having colic. 2 of colic.

Co li gny or **Co li gni** (kô lē nyē′), *n.* **Gaspard de,** 1519-1572, French admiral and Huguenot leader.

col i se um (kol′ə sē′əm), *n.* 1 a large building or stadium for games, contests, etc. 2 **Coliseum,** Colosseum. [< Medieval Latin variant of Latin *colosseum.* See COLOSSEUM.]

co li tis (kō lī′tis, kə lī′tis), *n.* inflammation of the colon, often causing severe pain in the abdomen.

coll., 1 college. 2 colloquial.

col lab o rate (kə lab′ə rāt′), *v.i.,* **-rat ed, -rat ing.** 1 work together: *Two authors collaborated on that book.* 2 aid or cooperate traitorously. [< Latin *collaboratum* collaborated < *com-* with + *laborare* work]

col lab o ra tion (kə lab′ə rā′shən), *n.* 1 act of working together. 2 an aiding or cooperating traitorously.

col lab o ra tion ist (kə lab′ə rā′shə nist), *n.* collaborator (def. 2).

col lab o ra tive (kə lab′ə rā′tiv), *adj.* of or resulting from collaboration.

col lab o ra tor (kə lab′ə rā′tər), *n.* 1 person who works with another, usually in literary or scientific work. 2 person who aids or cooperates traitorously.

col lage (kə läzh′), *n.* 1 picture made by

hat, āge, fär; let, ēqual, tėrm;
it, īce; hot, ōpen, ôrder;
oil, out; cup, pu̇t, rüle;
ch, child; ng, long; sh, she;
th, thin; ᴛʜ, then; zh, measure;

ə represents *a* in about, *e* in taken, *i* in pencil, *o* in lemon, *u* in circus.

< = from, derived from, taken from.

pasting on a background such things as parts of photographs and newspapers, fabric, and string. 2 anything made of odd parts or pieces; composite. [< French, pasting, gluing < Greek *kolla* glue]

col la gen (kol′ə jən), *n.* the protein substance in the fibers of connective tissue, bone, and cartilage of vertebrates. Boiling with water converts collagen to gelatin. [< French *collagène* < Greek *kolla* glue]

col lapse (kə laps′), *v.,* **-lapsed, -laps ing,** *n.* —*v.i.* 1 shrink together suddenly; fall in; cave in: *Sticking a pin into the balloon caused it to collapse.* 2 break down; fail suddenly: *Both his health and his business collapsed within a year.* 3 (of lungs) become deflated. —*v.t.* fold or push together; cause to collapse: *collapse a telescope.* —*n.* 1 a falling or caving in; sudden shrinking together: *A heavy flood caused the collapse of the bridge.* 2 breakdown; failure. [< Latin *collapsum* fallen completely < *com-* completely + *labi* to fall]

col laps i ble (kə lap′sə bəl), *adj.* made so that it can be folded or pushed together into a smaller space: *a collapsible table.*

col lar (kol′ər), *n.* 1 the part of a coat, dress, or shirt that makes a band around the neck. 2 a separate or detachable band of linen, lace, or other material worn around the neck: *a fur collar.* 3 a leather or metal band for the neck of a dog or other pet animal. 4 a leather roll for a horse's neck to bear the weight of the loads he pulls. See **harness** for picture. 5 a colored stripe or other mark around an animal's neck. 6 a ring, disk, or flange on a rod, shaft, etc., that keeps a part from moving to the side. 7 a short pipe connecting two other pipes. —*v.t.* 1 put a collar on. 2 seize by the collar; capture. 3 INFORMAL. lay hold of; take. [< Latin *collarem* < *collum* neck] **—col′lar less,** *adj.* **—col′lar like′,** *adj.*

col lar bone (kol′ər bōn′), *n.* the bone connecting the breastbone and the shoulder blade; clavicle.

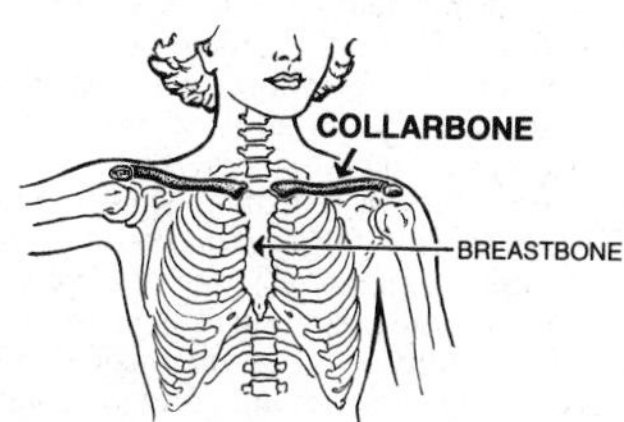

col lard (kol′ərd), *n.* 1 a kind of kale. 2 Usually, **collards,** *pl.* the fleshy leaves of this plant, cooked as greens. [alteration of *colewort*]

col late (kə lāt′, kol′āt), *v.t.,* **-lat ed, -lat ing.** 1 compare carefully. 2 arrange in order; put together. [< Latin *collatum* brought together < *com-* together + *latum* brought]

col lat er al (kə lat′ər əl), *adj.* 1 related but less important; secondary; indirect. 2 side by side; parallel. 3 in a parallel line of descent; descended from the same ancestors, but in a different line. Cousins are collateral relatives. 4 additional. 5 secured by stocks, bonds, etc. —*n.* 1 stocks, bonds, etc., pledged as security for a loan. 2 a collateral relative. [< Medieval Latin *collateralem* < Latin *com-* + *lateralem* lateral] **—col lat′er al ly,** *adv.*

col la tion (kə lā′shən), *n.* 1 a collating; careful comparison. 2 a light meal.

col la tor (kə lā′tər, kol′ā tər), *n.* person or machine that collates.

col league (kol′ēg′), *n.* fellow worker; fellow member of a profession, organization, etc.; associate. [< Middle French *collègue* < Latin *collega* < *com-* together + *legare* to delegate]

col lect[1] (kə lekt′), *v.t.* 1 bring together; gather together: *We collected sticks of wood to make a fire.* See **gather** for synonym study. 2 gather together for a set: *collect stamps for a hobby.* 3 ask and receive pay for (bills, debts, dues, taxes, etc.). 4 regain control of: *We soon collected ourselves after the slight accident.* —*v.i.* 1 come together; assemble: *A crowd soon collects at the scene of an accident.* 2 accumulate: *Dust collects on the furniture.* —*adj., adv.* to be paid for at the place of delivery: *a collect telegram. Telephone him collect.* [< Latin *collectum* gathered together < *com-* together + *legere* gather]

col lect[2] (kol′ekt), *n.* a short prayer used in certain church services. [< Medieval Latin *collecta* < *(oratio ad) collectam* (prayer on) assembly]

col lect a ble (kə lek′tə bəl), *adj.* collectible.

col lect ed (kə lek′tid), *adj.* 1 brought together; gathered together: *the author's collected works.* 2 under control; not confused or disturbed; calm. See **calm** for synonym study. **—col lect′ed ly,** *adv.* **—col lect′ed ness,** *n.*

col lect i ble (kə lek′tə bəl), *adj.* able to be collected. Also, **collectable.**

col lec tion (kə lek′shən), *n.* 1 act or practice of collecting: *The collection of these stamps took ten years.* 2 group of things gathered from many places and belonging together: *The library has a large collection of books.* 3 money collected for a religious or charitable purpose: *A church takes up a collection during services to help pay its expenses.* 4 mass or heap; accumulation: *There is a collection of dust in the attic.*

col lec tive (kə lek′tiv), *adj.* 1 of a group; as a group; taken all together; aggregate: *collective revenues of the government.* 2 of or derived from a number of persons taken or acting together; common: *collective wisdom of Congress.* 3 formed by collecting. 4 owned, worked, or managed on a cooperative basis; collectivized. —*n.* 1 collective noun. 2 a collective body; aggregate. 3 farm, factory, or other organization owned, worked, or managed cooperatively.

collective bargaining, negotiation about wages, hours, and working conditions between workers organized as a group and their employer or employers.

collective farm, farm operated and worked by a group cooperatively. The farm, its buildings, and its machinery may be owned communally by the group, by an institution, or, as in communist countries, by the state.

col lec tive ly (kə lek′tiv lē), *adv.* 1 as a group; all together. 2 in a singular form, but with a plural meaning.

collective noun, noun that is singular in form, but plural in meaning. *Crowd, people, troop,* and *herd* are collective nouns.

collective security, the guarantee by a group of countries of the security of each country in the group and the maintenance of peace by collective action against a country attacking any nation in the group.

col lec tiv ism (kə lek′ti viz′əm), *n.* a political and economic system in which the means of production of goods and services and the distribution of wealth is controlled by the people as a group or by the government.

col lec tiv ist (kə lek′ti vist), *n.* person who favors or supports collectivism. —*adj.* collectivistic.

col lec tiv is tic (kə lek′ti vis′tik), *adj.* of collectivism or collectivists.

col lec tiv i ty (kol′ek tiv′ə tē), *n.* people collectively, especially as forming a community or state.

col lec tiv ize (kə lek′ti vīz), *v.t.,* **-ized, -iz ing.** transfer ownership of, from an individual or individuals to the state or all the people collectively. **—col lec′tiv i za′tion,** *n.*

col lec tor (kə lek′tər), *n.* 1 person or thing that collects. 2 person hired to collect money owed. 3 device that collects electrical energy.

col lec tor ship (kə lek′tər ship), *n.* 1 office of a collector. 2 district covered by a collector.

col leen (kol′ēn′, kə lēn′), *n.* IRISH. girl. [< Irish *cailín,* diminutive of *caile* girl]

col lege (kol′ij), *n.* 1 institution of higher learning that gives degrees. 2 the academic department of a university for general instruction, as distinguished from the special, professional, or graduate schools. 3 school for special or professional instruction, as in medicine, pharmacy, agriculture, or music. 4 an organized association of persons having the same duties, privileges, and purposes: *a college of surgeons.* 5 building or buildings used by a college. —*adj.* of or associated with a college. [< Old French < Latin *collegium* fellowship of colleagues < *collega.* See COLLEAGUE.]

College of Cardinals, Sacred College.

col le gian (kə lē′jən, kə lē′jē ən), *n.* a college student.

col le giate (kə lē′jit, kə lē′jē it), *adj.* 1 of or like a college. 2 of or like college students.

col le gi um (kə lē′jē əm), *n., pl.* **-gi a** (-jē ə), group of officials acting as a ruling body. [< Latin. See COLLEGE.]

col len chy ma (kə leng′kə mə), *n.* living plant tissue with cells whose walls are thickened and usually elongated. [< Greek *kolla* glue + *en-* in + *chyma* what is poured]

col lide (kə līd′), *v.i.,* **-lid ed, -lid ing.** 1 come violently into contact; come together with force; crash: *Two large ships collided in the harbor.* 2 clash; conflict. [< Latin *collidere* < *com-* together + *laedere* strike]

col lie (kol′ē), *n.* one of a breed of large, intelligent, long-haired dogs used for tending sheep or kept as pets. [origin uncertain]

col lier (kol′yər), *n.* 1 ship for carrying coal. 2 a coal miner. [Middle English *colier* < *col* coal]

col lier y (kol′yər ē), *n., pl.* **-lier ies.** a coal mine and its buildings and equipment.

col li mate (kol′ə māt), *v.t.*, **-mat ed, -mat ing.** 1 bring into line; make parallel. 2 adjust accurately the line of sight of (a surveying instrument, telescope, etc.). [< New Latin *collimatum* brought into line, ultimately < Latin *com-* together + *lineare* make straight] **—col′li ma′tion,** *n.* **—col′-li ma′tor,** *n.*

col lin e ar (kə lin′ē ər), *adj.* lying in the same straight line.

Col lins (kol′ənz), *n.* **(William) Wilkie,** 1824-1889, English novelist.

col li sion (kə lizh′ən), *n.* 1 a violent rushing against; hitting or striking violently together; crash. 2 clash; conflict. [< Late Latin *collisionem* < Latin *collidere* collide]

col lo cate (kol′ō kāt), *v.t.*, **-cat ed, -cat ing.** 1 place together or side by side. 2 arrange.

col lo ca tion (kol′ō kā′shən), *n.* act of placing together; arrangement: *the collocation of words in a sentence.*

col lo di on (kə lō′dē ən), *n.* a gluelike solution of nitrocellulose in ether and alcohol that dries very rapidly and leaves a tough, waterproof, transparent film, used as a coating in photography and medicine. [< Greek *kollōdēs* gluey < *kolla* glue]

col loid (kol′oid), *n.* substance composed of particles that are extremely small but larger than most molecules. The particles in a colloid do not actually dissolve but remain suspended in a suitable gas, liquid, or solid. *—adj.* colloidal. [< Greek *kolla* glue]

col loi dal (kə loi′dl), *adj.* being, containing, or like a colloid. **—col loi′dal ly,** *adv.*

colloq., 1 colloquial. 2 colloquialism.

col lo qui al (kə lō′kwē əl), *adj.* used in everyday, informal talk, but not in formal speech or writing; conversational. Such expressions as *clip* for *punch* and *close call* for *a narrow escape* are colloquial. **—col-lo′qui al ly,** *adv.*

col lo qui al ism (kə lō′kwē ə liz′əm), *n.* 1 a colloquial word or phrase. 2 a colloquial style or usage.

col lo qui um (kə lō′kwē əm), *n., pl.* **-qui ums, -qui a** (-kwē ə). 1 meeting or conference, especially of scholars, scientists, etc., on a particular subject. 2 seminar. [< Latin]

col lo quy (kol′ə kwē), *n., pl.* **-quies.** a talking together; conversation; conference. [< Latin *colloquium* < *colloqui* talk together < *com-* with + *loqui* speak]

col lude (kə lüd′), *v.i.*, **-lud ed, -lud ing.** act together through a secret understanding; conspire in a fraud. [< Latin *colludere* < *com-* with + *ludere* play]

col lu sion (kə lü′zhən), *n.* a secret agreement for some wrong or harmful purpose; participation in a fraud or deceit. [< Latin *collusionem* < *colludere* collude]

col lu sive (kə lü′siv), *adj.* involving collusion; fraudulent. **—col lu′sive ly,** *adv.*

Colo., the official abbreviation of Colorado.

co logne (kə lōn′), *n.* a fragrant liquid, not so strong as perfume. [< French *(eau de) Cologne* (water of) Cologne]

Co logne (kə lōn′), *n.* city in W West Germany, on the Rhine. 866,000. Also, GERMAN **Köln.**

Co lom bi a (kə lum′bē ə), *n.* country in NW South America. 21,160,000 pop.; 439,800 sq. mi. *Capital:* Bogotá. **—Co lom′-bi an,** *adj., n.*

colonnade of an ancient Greek temple

Co lom bo (kə lum′bō), *n.* seaport and capital of Ceylon, on the W coast. 551,000.

co lon[1] (kō′lən), *n.* mark (:) of punctuation used before a series of items, explanations, long quotations, etc., to set them off from the rest of the sentence. [< Latin < Greek *kolon* limb, clause]

co lon[2] (kō′lən), *n., pl.* **co lons, co la** (kō′lə). the lower part of the large intestine. See **intestine** for diagram. [< Latin < Greek *kolon* part of the large intestine]

co lon[3] (kō lōn′), *n., pl.* **co lons, co lo nes** (kō lō′nās). 1 the monetary unit of Costa Rica, a bronze coin equal to 100 centimos and worth about 15 cents. 2 the monetary unit of El Salvador, a silver coin equal to 100 centavos and worth about 40 cents. [< American Spanish *colón* < *Colón* Columbus]

Co lón (kō lon′, kō lōn′), *n.* seaport in N Panama near the Atlantic end of the Panama Canal. 66,000.

colo nel (kėr′nl), *n.* a commissioned officer in the army, air force, or Marine Corps ranking next above a lieutenant colonel and next below a brigadier general. [< Middle French *coronel, colonel* < Italian *colonello* commander of a regiment < *colonna* military column < Latin *columna* column]

➤ **Colonel** is an example of a word whose pronunciation has survived a change in spelling. The word, from the French, developed two parallel forms, *colonel, coronel,* each pronounced in three syllables. For 150 years the word has been pronounced (kėr′nl), from the *coronel* form, but spelling has kept *colonel.*

colo nel cy (kėr′nl sē), *n., pl.* **-cies.** rank, commission, or authority of a colonel.

co lo ni al (kə lō′nē əl), *adj.* 1 of or having to do with a colony or colonies. 2 practicing colonialism; having colonies: *colonial powers.* 3 of or having to do with the thirteen British colonies which became the United States of America. 4 of the time when a nation was a colony: *colonial furniture.* *—n.* person living in a colony. **—co lo′ni al ly,** *adv.*

co lo ni al ism (kə lō′nē ə liz′əm), *n.* 1 the practice or policy of a nation that rules or seeks to rule weaker or economically dependent nations. 2 state of being a colony.

co lo ni al ist (kə lō′nē ə list), *n.* person or nation that favors or practices colonialism. *—adj.* of, having to do with, or favoring colonialism or colonialists.

col o nist (kol′ə nist), *n.* 1 person who lives in a colony; settler. 2 person who helps to found a colony.

col o nize (kol′ə nīz), *v.*, **-nized, -niz ing.** *—v.t.* 1 establish a colony or colonies in: *The English colonized New England.* 2 establish (persons) in a colony; settle in a colony. *—v.i.* form a colony; settle in a colony. **—col′o ni za′tion,** *n.* **—col′o niz′-er,** *n.*

col on nade (kol′ə nād′), *n.* series of columns set the same distance apart, usually supporting a roof, ceiling, cornice, etc. [< French < Italian *colonnata* < *colonna* column < Latin *columna*]

col on nad ed (kol′ə nā′did), *adj.* having a colonnade.

col o ny (kol′ə nē), *n., pl.* **-nies.** 1 group of people who leave their own country and go to settle in another land, but who still remain citizens of their original country. 2 the settlement made by such a group of people. 3 **the Colonies,** the thirteen British colonies that became the United States of America; New Hampshire, Massachusetts, Rhode Island, Connecticut, New York, New Jersey, Pennsylvania, Delaware, Maryland, Virginia, North Carolina, South Carolina, and Georgia. 4 territory distant from the country that governs it. 5 group of people from the same country or with the same occupation living as a group, especially in a certain part of a city: *the Italian colony in Boston, a colony of artists.* 6 group of animals or plants of the same species, living or growing together: *a colony of ants. Coral grows in colonies.* 7 mass of microorganisms arising from a single cell, living on or in a solid or partially solid medium. [< Latin *colonia* < *colonus* cultivator, settler < *colere* cultivate]

col o phon (kol′ə fon, kol′ə fən), *n.* 1 a small design or device of a publisher placed on the last page, the title page, or the spine of a book. 2 words or inscription placed at the end of a book, telling the name of the printer, the date of printing, sometimes the type used, etc. [< Greek *kolophon* summit, final touch]

col or (kul′ər), *n.* 1 sensation produced by the effect of waves of light striking the retina of the eye. Different colors are produced by rays of light having different wave lengths. See synonym study below. 2 red, yellow, blue, or any combination of them except black, white, or gray: *The color that results from mixing yellow and blue is green.* 3 a paint; dye or pigment. 4 coloring of the skin; complexion, especially ruddy complexion. 5 a flush caused by blushing. 6 the skin color of any people or race that is not white. 7 an outward appearance; show: *The lies had some color of truth.* 8 distinguishing quality; vividness: *Her gift for description adds color to her stories.* 9 character; tone. 10 in music: **a** quality of tone of a musical instrument; timbre. **b** quality or style of musical interpretation: *Her playing has color and vigor.* **11 colors,** *pl.* badge, ribbon, dress, etc., worn to show allegiance. **12 the colors, a** the flag of a nation, regiment, etc.: *Salute the colors.* **b** the ceremony of raising the flag in the morning and lowering it in the evening. **c** the nation represented by the flag, especially its armed forces: *Soldiers and sailors serve the colors.*

change color, 1 turn pale. 2 blush.

give color to or **lend color to,** cause to seem true or likely.

lose color, turn pale.

show one's true colors, 1 show oneself as one really is. 2 declare one's opinions or plans.

with flying colors, successfully; victoriously: *She passed the test with flying colors.*

—v.t. 1 give color to; put color on; change the color of. 2 make red in the face. 3 change to give a wrong idea; put in a false light: *The fisherman colored the facts to make his catch seem the biggest of all.* 4 give a distinguishing or vivid quality to: *Love of*

hat, āge, fär; let, ēqual, tėrm;
it, īce; hot, ōpen, ôrder;
oil, out; cup, pu̇t, rüle;
ch, child; ng, long; sh, she;
th, thin; ᴛʜ, then; zh, measure;

ə represents *a* in about, *e* in taken, *i* in pencil, *o* in lemon, *u* in circus.

< = from, derived from, taken from.

nature colored all of Wordsworth's writing. —*v.i.* 1 become red in the face; blush. 2 take on color; become colored: *My face colored in the sun.* Also, BRITISH **colour.** [< Latin] **—col′or er,** *n.*

Syn. *n.* 1 **Color, hue, shade** mean a sensation produced by the effect of waves of light striking the retina of the eye. **Color** is the general word: *Her dress is the color of grass.* **Hue** is poetic in the general meaning of color. Technically, *hue* means the quality of a color that gives the name: red, blue, etc. It is also used to suggest partial alteration of a color: *This pottery is blue with a greenish hue.* **Shade** applies to the darkness and lightness of color: *I like a blue car, but of a lighter shade than navy.*

col or a ble (kul′ər ə bəl), *adj.* 1 plausible. 2 pretended; deceptive.

Col o rad o (kol′ə rad′ō, kol′ə rä′dō), *n.* 1 one of the western states of the United States. 2,207,000 pop., 104,200 sq. mi. *Capital:* Denver. *Abbrev.:* Colo. 2 **Colorado River,** a river flowing from N Colorado through Utah, Arizona, Nevada, California, and NW Mexico into the Gulf of California. 1450 mi. b river flowing SE from central Texas into the Gulf of Mexico. 840 mi. 3 **Colorado Desert,** desert in SE California. 2000 sq. mi. **—Col′o rad′an,** *adj., n.*

Colorado Springs, city in central Colorado. The United States Air Force Academy is located there. 135,000.

col or ant (kul′ər ənt), *n.* a coloring substance, such as a pigment or dye.

col or a tion (kul′ə rā′shən), *n.* way in which a person or thing is colored; coloring: *The coloration of a chameleon can change.*

col or a tur a (kul′ər ə tu̇r′ə, kul′ər ə-tyu̇r′ə), *n.* 1 ornamental passages in music, such as trills or runs. 2 soprano who sings such passages. 3 music containing such passages. —*adj.* 1 suited for singing ornamental passages in music: *a coloratura soprano.* 2 (in vocal music) having ornamental passages. [< Italian < Late Latin, full of color < Latin *colorare* to color]

col or bear er (kul′ər ber′ər, kul′ər-bar′ər), *n.* person who carries the flag or colors; standardbearer.

col or-blind (kul′ər blīnd′), *adj.* unable to tell certain colors apart, especially red and green; unable to perceive certain colors or any colors. **—col′or-blind′ness,** *n.*

col or cast (kul′ər kast′), *n., v.,* **-cast** or **-cast ed, -cast ing.** —*n.* a television broadcast in color. —*v.t., v.i.* broadcast (a television program) in color.

col ored (kul′ərd), *adj.* 1 having color; not black or white. 2 having a certain kind of color. 3 of the black race or any race other than white. 4 tinged by prejudice, emotion, desire for effect, etc.; biased.

col or fast (kul′ər fast′), *adj.* resistant to loss or change of color: *colorfast material.*

color film, film for making photographs in color.

col or ful (kul′ər fəl), *adj.* 1 picturesque; vivid. 2 full of color. **—col′or ful ly,** *adv.* **—col′or ful ness,** *n.*

color guard, U.S. the honor guard of a military unit that carries or accompanies the flag during ceremonies, reviews, etc.

col or im e ter (kul′ə rim′ə tər), *n.* 1 instrument or device for measuring the shade, tint, brightness, and purity of a color. 2 device used in chemical analysis for comparing the color of a liquid with a standard color.

col or ing (kul′ə ring), *n.* 1 way in which a person or thing is colored; coloration. 2 substance used to color; pigment. 3 an outward or false appearance: *He lies with a coloring of truth.*

coloring matter, substance used to color; pigment.

col or ist (kul′ə rist), *n.* 1 artist who is skillful in painting with colors. 2 user of color.

col or less (kul′ər lis), *adj.* 1 without color. 2 without excitement or variety; uninteresting: *a colorless town.* **—col′or less ly,** *adv.* **—col′or less ness,** *n.*

color line, distinction in social or economic privileges drawn between members of different races on the basis of skin color.

co los sal (kə los′əl), *adj.* of huge size; gigantic; vast. **—co los′sal ly,** *adv.*

Col os se um (kol′ə sē′əm), *n.* a large amphitheater in Rome, completed in A.D. 80. The Colosseum was used for games and contests. Also, **Coliseum.** [< Latin *colosseum,* neuter of *colosseus* gigantic < *colossus.* See COLOSSUS.]

Co los sians (kə losh′ənz), *n.* book of the New Testament, written by the apostle Paul to the Christian people of Colossae, an ancient city of Asia Minor.

co los sus (kə los′əs), *n., pl.* **-los si** (-los′ī), **-los sus es.** 1 a huge statue. 2 anything huge; gigantic person or thing. [< Latin < Greek *kolossos* gigantic (Egyptian) statue]

Colossus of Rhodes, a huge statue of Helios made at Rhodes about 280 B.C. It was one of the seven wonders of the ancient world.

co los trum (kə los′trəm), *n.* the thin, yellowish milk secreted by a mammal for the first few days after the birth of young. It is especially rich in protein and helps establish both digestion and natural immunity. [< Latin]

col our (kul′ər), *n., v.t., v.i.* BRITISH. color.

col por teur (kol′pôr′tər, kol′pōr′tər), *n.* person who travels about and distributes Bibles, tracts, etc. [< French]

colt (kōlt), *n.* 1 a young horse, donkey, zebra, etc., especially a male less than four or five years old. 2 a young or inexperienced person. [Old English]

col ter (kōl′tər), *n.* a sharp blade or disk on a plow to cut the earth ahead of the plowshare. Also, **coulter.** [Old English *culter* knife < Latin, plowshare]

colt ish (kōl′tish), *adj.* like a colt; lively and frisky. **—colt′ish ly,** *adv.* **—colt′ish ness,** *n.*

colts foot (kōlts′fu̇t′), *n.* plant of the composite family with yellow flowers and large, heart-shaped leaves which were formerly much used in medicine.

Co lum bi a (kə lum′bē ə), *n.* 1 capital of South Carolina, in the central part. 114,000. 2 **Columbia River,** river flowing from British Columbia through E Washington and between Washington and Oregon into the Pacific. 1214 mi. 3 a name for the United States of America. Columbia is often represented as a woman dressed in red, white, and blue.

Co lum bi an (kə lum′bē ən), *adj.* 1 of or having to do with Columbia. 2 of or having to do with Christopher Columbus.

col um bine (kol′əm bīn), *n.* 1 any of a genus of plants of the same family as the buttercup, whose flowers have petals shaped like hollow spurs. Wild columbines have red-and-yellow or blue-and-white flowers. 2 **Columbine,** a woman character in comedy and pantomime, the sweetheart of Harlequin. [< Medieval Latin *columbina* < Latin, dove-like < *columba* dove]

co lum bi um (kə lum′bē əm), *n.* the former name of **niobium.** The name is still used in metallurgy. *Symbol:* Cb [< New Latin < *Columbia* the United States]

Co lum bus (kə lum′bəs), *n.* 1 **Christopher,** 1451?-1506, Italian navigator in the service of Spain who discovered America in 1492. 2 capital of Ohio, in the central part. 540,000. 3 city in W Georgia. 154,000.

Columbus Day, October 12, the anniversary of Columbus's discovery of America, observed as a legal holiday on the second Monday in October in most states of the United States.

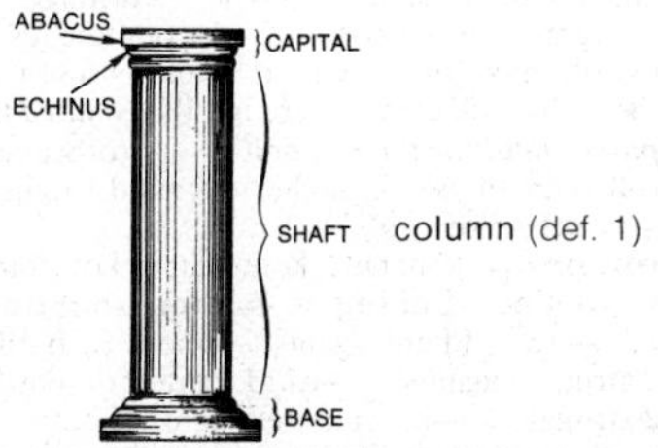

column (def. 1)

col umn (kol′əm), *n.* 1 a slender, upright structure; pillar. Columns are usually made of stone, wood, or metal, and are used as supports or ornaments to a building, but sometimes a column stands alone as a monument. 2 anything that seems slender and upright like a column: *a column of smoke, a long column of figures.* 3 arrangement of soldiers in several short rows one behind another. 4 line of ships or aircraft one behind another. 5 any similar line of persons, things, etc.: *A long column of cars followed the procession down the street.* 6 a narrow division of a page reading from top to bottom, kept separate by lines or by blank spaces. Some newspapers have eight columns on a page. 7 part of a newspaper or magazine used for a special subject or written by a special writer: *the sports column.* 8 a line or series of letters, figures, etc., arranged vertically. [< Latin *columna*]

co lum nar (kə lum′nər), *adj.* 1 like a column. 2 of or made of columns. 3 written or printed in columns.

col umned (kol′əmd), *adj.* 1 having columns. 2 formed into columns.

col umn ist (kol′əm nist, kol′ə mist), *n.* person who writes or selects and edits the material for a special column in a newspaper or magazine.

col za (kol′zə), *n.* 1 cole seed, especially rape seed. 2 oil made from these seeds, used as a fuel in lamps, as a lubricant, etc. [< Dutch *koolzaad,* literally, cabbage seed]

com-, *prefix.* with; together; altogether:

Commingle = mingle with one another. Compress = press together. See also **co-**, **col-**, **con-**, and **cor-**. [< Latin]

com., 1 commerce. 2 common.

Com., 1 Commissioner. 2 Committee.

co ma[1] (kō′mə), *n.* a prolonged unconsciousness caused by disease, injury, or poison. [< Greek *kōma*]

co ma[2] (kō′mə), *n., pl.* **-mae** (-mē). 1 a cloudlike mass around the nucleus of a comet. 2 tuft of hairs at the end of a seed. [< Latin < Greek *komē* hair]

Co man che (kə man′chē), *n., pl.* **-che** or **-ches** for 1, *adj.* —*n.* 1 member of a tribe of American Indians that formerly roamed from Nebraska to northern Mexico, and now live in Oklahoma. 2 their language. —*adj.* of this tribe.

com a tose (kom′ə tōs, kō′mə tōs), *adj.* in a stupor or coma; unconscious.

comb (kōm), *n.* 1 piece of metal, plastic, rubber, bone, etc., with teeth, used to arrange or straighten the hair or to hold it in place. 2 anything shaped or used like a comb, especially an instrument for combing wool or flax. 3 currycomb. 4 the red, fleshy crest on top of the head of chickens and some other fowls. 5 top of a wave rolling over or breaking. 6 honeycomb. —*v.t.* 1 arrange or straighten with a comb. 2 take out tangles in (wool, flax, etc.) with a comb. 3 search through; look everywhere in: *We combed the playground for the lost ball.* —*v.i.* (of waves) roll over or break at the top. [Old English] —**comb′like′**, *adj.*

com bat (*v.* kəm bat′, kom′bat; *n.* kom′bat), *v.,* **-bat ed, -bat ing** or **-bat ted, -bat ting,** *n.* —*v.t.* 1 fight against; oppose in battle. 2 struggle against. —*v.i.* 1 fight or do battle. 2 struggle. —*n.* 1 armed fighting between opposing forces; battle. 2 any fight or struggle; conflict. See **fight** for synonym study. [< Old French *combattre* < Late Latin *combattuere* < Latin *com-* together with + *battuere* beat]

com bat ant (kəm bat′nt, kom′bə tənt), *n.* one that takes part in combat; fighter. —*adj.* 1 fighting. 2 ready to fight; fond of fighting.

combat fatigue, state of nervous exhaustion that sometimes occurs among soldiers in active combat.

com bat ive (kəm bat′iv, kom′bə tiv), *adj.* ready to fight or oppose; fond of fighting; pugnacious. —**com bat′ive ly,** *adv.* —**com bat′ive ness,** *n.*

combe (küm, kōm), *n.* a narrow valley. Also, **coomb.** [Old English *cumb*]

comb er (kō′mər), *n.* 1 breaker. 2 person or thing that combs.

com bi na tion (kom′bə nā′shən), *n.* 1 a combining or a being combined; union. 2 thing made by combining; set of things combined together. 3 persons or groups joined together for some common purpose: *The farmers formed a combination to sell their crops at better prices.* 4 series of numbers or letters dialed in opening or closing a combination lock: *the combination of a safe.* 5 suit of underwear having the shirt and drawers in one piece. 6 in mathematics: **a** arrangement of individual items in groups so that each group has a certain number of items. **b** the groups thus formed. Possible two-letter combinations of *a, b,* and *c* are *ab, ac,* and *bc.* 7 union of substances to form a chemical compound.

com bi na tion al (kom′bə nā′shə nəl), *adj.* of or having to do with combination.

combination lock, lock which will not open until a movable dial has been turned to certain numbers or letters.

com bine (*v.* kəm bīn′; *n.* kom′bīn, *also* kəm bīn′ *for 1*), *v.,* **-bined, -bin ing,** *n.* —*v.t.* join together; unite: *combine forces.* See **join** for synonym study. —*v.i.* 1 unite or join; come together for a common purpose; form a combination. 2 unite to form a chemical compound: *Two atoms of hydrogen combine with one of oxygen to form water.* —*n.* 1 group of persons joined together for business or political purposes; combination. 2 U.S. machine for harvesting and threshing grain, soybeans, etc. It cuts the stalks and separates the grain from them as it moves across a field. [< Late Latin *combinare* < Latin *com-* together + *bini* two by two] —**com bin′a ble,** *adj.* —**com bin′er,** *n.*

comb ings (kō′mingz), *n.pl.* hairs removed by a comb.

combining form, form of a word used for combining with words or with other combining forms to make new words. EXAMPLES: *Psycho- + analysis = Psychoanalysis; kilo- + -meter = kilometer.*

comb jelly, ctenophore.

com bo (kom′bō), *n., pl.* **-bos.** U.S. INFORMAL. a small group of jazz musicians playing together regularly. [short for *combination*]

com bust (kəm bust′), *v.t., v.i.* burn up.

com bus ti bil i ty (kəm bus′tə bil′ə tē), *n.* flammability.

com bus ti ble (kəm bus′tə bəl), *adj.* capable of taking fire and burning; easily burned: *Gasoline is highly combustible.* —*n.* a combustible substance. —**com bus′ti bly,** *adv.*

com bus tion (kəm bus′chən), *n.* 1 act or process of burning; consumption or destruction by fire. 2 rapid oxidation accompanied by high temperature and usually by light. 3 slow oxidation not accompanied by high temperature and light. The cells of the body transform food into energy by this type of combustion. [< Latin *combustionem* < *comburere* burn up < *com-* up + *urere* burn]

combustion chamber, chamber in an internal-combustion or jet engine, furnace, rocket, etc., in which fuel is burned.

Comdr., Commander.

Comdt., Commandant.

come (kum), *v.i.,* **came, come, com ing.** 1 move toward; approach: *Come this way.* 2 arrive: *The train comes at noon.* 3 appear: *Light comes and goes.* 4 reach; extend: *The drapes come to the floor.* 5 take place; happen; occur: *Snow comes in winter.* 6 occur to the mind: *The solution of the problem has just come to me.* 7 be derived; issue: *Many English words came originally from Latin.* 8 be born; descend: *come from a poor family.* 9 be caused; result: *You see what comes of meddling.* 10 be brought; pass; enter: *come into use.* 11 turn out to be; become: *My wish came true.* 12 be available: *This soup comes in a can.* 13 be equal; amount: *The bill comes to $5.00.* 14 here! look! stop! behave!

come about, 1 take place; happen; occur. 2 turn around; change direction.

come around or **come round,** 1 return to consciousness or health; recover. 2 give in; yield; agree. 3 turn around; change direction or opinion.

come at, rush toward; attack.

come back, 1 return. 2 INFORMAL. return to a former condition or position.

come by, get; obtain; acquire.

come down, 1 be handed down or passed along. 2 lose position, rank, money, etc.

come down on, 1 INFORMAL. scold; blame. 2 attack suddenly.

come down with, become ill.

come forward, offer oneself for work or duty; volunteer.

come in, 1 arrive. 2 enter. 3 be brought into use; begin.

come in for, get; receive; acquire.

come into, inherit.

come off, 1 take place; happen; occur. 2 turn out to be. 3 finish in a certain manner: *come off with flying colors.*

come on, 1 find or meet by chance. 2 improve; develop; progress. 3 make an entrance onto the stage.

come out, 1 be revealed or shown. 2 take place in the end; result: *The ball game came out in our favor.* 3 be offered to the public. 4 put in an appearance. 5 declare oneself: *The candidate came out for lower taxes.* 6 make a debut.

come out with, 1 reveal; show. 2 offer to the public. 3 say; speak.

come through, 1 be successful; win; succeed. 2 last through successfully. 3 SLANG. hand over; pay.

come to, 1 return to consciousness. 2 anchor; stop.

come up, come into being; arise.

come upon, find or meet by chance.

[Old English *cuman*]

come back (kum′bak′), *n.* 1 INFORMAL. return to a former condition or position. 2 SLANG. a clever answer; sharp reply.

Com e con or **COM E CON** (kom′ə-kon), *n.* Council for Mutual Economic Assistance (the trade association of communist countries in eastern Europe).

co me di an (kə mē′dē ən), *n.* 1 actor in comedies; actor of comic parts. 2 person who amuses others with his funny talk and actions.

co me dic (kə mē′dik), *adj.* of the nature of comedy; comic.

co me di enne (kə mē′dē en′), *n.* actress in comedies; actress of comic parts. [< French *comédienne*]

come down (kum′doun′), *n.* INFORMAL. an unexpected loss of position, rank, etc.

com e dy (kom′ə dē), *n., pl.* **-dies.** 1 an amusing play or show having a happy ending. 2 such plays or shows as a class; branch of drama concerned with such plays. 3 an amusing happening; funny incident. 4 any literary work having a theme suited to comedy or using the methods of comedy. [< Latin *comoedia* < Greek *kōmōidia* < *kōmos* merrymaking + *ōidē* song]

come li ness (kum′lē nis), *n.* 1 pleasant appearance; attractiveness. 2 fitness; suitableness; propriety.

come ly (kum′lē), *adj.,* **-li er, -li est.** 1 pleasant to look at; attractive. 2 fitting; suitable; proper. [Old English *cȳmlic*]

come-on (kum′on′), *n.* INFORMAL. something that lures or entices; inducement.

com er (kum′ər), *n.* 1 person who comes. 2 INFORMAL. person who seems likely to succeed.

co mes ti ble (kə mes′tə bəl), *n.* Often, **comestibles,** *pl.* thing to eat; article of food. —*adj.* OBSOLETE. edible. [< Late Latin *comestibilis* < Latin *comestum* eaten up < *com-* + *edere* eat]

com et (kom′it), *n.* a bright heavenly body with a starlike center and often with a cloudy tail of light which revolves about the sun in an elliptical or, sometimes, a parabolic or hyperbolic orbit. [< Latin *cometa* < Greek *kometes* wearing long hair < *kome* hair]

come up pance (kum′up′əns), *n.* INFORMAL. one's just deserts.

com fit (kum′fit, kom′fit), *n.* piece of candy; sweetmeat. [< Old French *confit* < Latin *confectum.* See CONFECTION.]

com fort (kum′fərt), *v.t.* 1 ease the grief or sorrow of; cheer. See synonym study below. 2 give ease to; make comfortable. 3 (in law) help; support. —*n.* 1 anything that makes trouble or sorrow easier to bear; consolation. 2 person or thing that makes life easier or takes away hardship. 3 freedom from pain or hardship; ease. See **ease** for synonym study. 4 comforter for a bed. 5 (in law) help; support. [< Late Latin *confortare* strengthen < Latin *com-* + *fortis* strong] **—com′fort ing ly,** *adv.*

Syn. *v.t.* 1 **Comfort, console** mean to ease sorrow, trouble, or pain. **Comfort** means to ease the grief or sorrow of a person by making him more cheerful and giving him hope or strength: *Neighbors comforted the parents of the injured child.* **Console,** more formal, means to make grief or trouble easier to bear by doing something to lighten it or make the person forget it temporarily: *The pastor tried to console the grieving widow.*

com fort a ble (kum′fər tə bəl, kumf′tə-bəl), *adj.* 1 giving comfort: *A soft, warm bed is comfortable.* 2 in comfort; at ease; free from pain or hardship. 3 easy; tranquil; undisturbed: *a comfortable sleep.* 4 INFORMAL. enough for one's needs: *a comfortable income.* **—com′fort a ble ness,** *n.* **—com′fort a bly,** *adv.*

com fort er (kum′fər tər), *n.* 1 person or thing that gives comfort. 2 U.S. a padded or quilted covering for a bed. 3 a long, woolen scarf. 4 **the Comforter,** the Holy Spirit.

com fort less (kum′fərt lis), *adj.* 1 bringing no comfort or ease of mind. 2 having none of the comforts of life.

com fy (kum′fē), *adj.,* **-fi er, -fi est.** INFORMAL. comfortable.

com ic (kom′ik), *adj.* 1 causing laughter or smiles; amusing; funny. 2 of comedy; in comedies. —*n.* 1 comedian. 2 the amusing or funny side of literature, life, etc. 3 comic book. 4 **comics,** *pl.* comic strips; funnies. [< Latin *comicus* < Greek *kōmikos* < *kōmos* merrymaking]

com i cal (kom′ə kəl), *adj.* 1 amusing; funny. 2 INFORMAL. strange; odd. **—com′i cal ly,** *adv.* **—com′i cal ness,** *n.*

comic book, magazine of comic strips.

comic opera, an amusing light opera having dialogue as well as music.

comic strip, series of drawings presenting an adventure or a series of incidents.

Com in form (kom′in fôrm), *n.* an international Communist organization intended to coordinate the propaganda of Communist parties throughout the world, formed in 1947 and dissolved in 1956. [< *Com(munist) Inform(ation Bureau)*]

com ing (kum′ing), *n.* approach; arrival. —*adj.* 1 approaching; next: *this coming spring.* 2 INFORMAL. on the way to importance or fame.

Com in tern (kom′in tėrn′), *n.* the Third Communist International, an organization founded at Moscow in 1919 to spread communism, and dissolved in 1943. [< *Com(munist) Intern(ational)*]

com i ty (kom′ə tē), *n., pl.* **-ties.** courtesy; civility. [< Latin *comitatem* < *comis* friendly]

comity of nations, 1 respect shown by one nation for the laws and customs of another. 2 the nations practicing such a respect.

coml., commercial.

com ma (kom′ə), *n.* mark (,) of punctuation, used chiefly to show interruptions in the thought or in the grammatical structure of a sentence. [< Latin < Greek *komma* piece cut off < *koptein* to cut]

comma bacillus, the comma-shaped bacterium that causes Asiatic cholera.

comma fault, (in grammar) a comma between related main clauses not connected by a coordinate conjunction; comma splice.

com mand (kə mand′), *v.t.* 1 give an order to; direct. See synonym study below. 2 have authority or power over; be in control of; govern: *The captain commands his ship.* 3 have a position of control over; rise high above; overlook: *A hilltop commands the plain around it.* 4 be able to have and use: *He cannot command so large a sum of money.* 5 deserve and get; force to be given; exact: *Food commands a higher price when it is scarce.* —*v.i.* 1 give orders. 2 have power; rule; control: *Some people are born to command.* 3 be commander. 4 occupy a dominating position; stand overlooking.
—*n.* 1 an order; direction: *They obeyed the captain's command.* 2 authority; power; control: *The general is in command of the army.* 3 soldiers, ships, or region under an officer who has control or authority over them. 4 position of control or authority. 5 mastery or control by position. 6 outlook over; range of vision; prospect. 7 ability to have and use: *A good speaker or writer must have a command of words.*
[< Old French *comander* < Popular Latin *commandare,* alteration of Latin *commendare.* See COMMEND.]

Syn. *v.t.* 1 **Command, order, direct** mean to tell someone to do something. **Command** means to give an order with authority in a formal way: *The sentry commanded him to halt.* **Order** also means to tell with authority in a less official and more personal way: *I was ordered to behave.* **Direct** suggests giving instructions rather than a formal order: *She directed me to the bus stop.*

com man dant (kom′ən dant′, kom′ən-dänt′), *n.* 1 commander. 2 officer in command of a fort, naval yard, etc.

com man deer (kom′ən dir′), *v.t.* 1 seize (private property) for military or public use: *All automobiles in the town were commandeered by the army.* 2 INFORMAL. take by force.

com mand er (kə man′dər), *n.* 1 person who commands. 2 officer in charge of an army or a part of an army. 3 a navy officer ranking next below a captain and next above a lieutenant commander. 4 member of high rank in an order of knighthood or a society.

commander in chief, *pl.* **commanders in chief.** 1 person who has complete command of the armed forces of a country. In the United States, the President is the commander in chief. 2 officer commanding an army or navy.

com mand ing (kə man′ding), *adj.* 1 in command: *a commanding officer.* 2 controlling; powerful: *commanding influences.* 3 authoritative; impressive: *a commanding voice.* 4 having a position of control. **—com mand′ing ly,** *adv.*

hat, āge, fär; let, ēqual, tėrm;
it, īce; hot, ōpen, ôrder;
oil, out; cup, pu̇t, rüle;
ch, child; ng, long; sh, she;
th, thin; ᴛʜ, then; zh, measure;

ə represents *a* in about, *e* in taken, *i* in pencil, *o* in lemon, *u* in circus.

< = from, derived from, taken from.

com mand ment (kə mand′mənt), *n.* 1 (in the Bible) one of the ten laws that God gave to Moses. 2 any order, direction, or law.

com man do (kə man′dō), *n., pl.* **-dos** or **-does.** 1 soldier trained to make brief surprise raids in enemy territory. 2 group of such soldiers. [< Afrikaans *kommando*]

command performance, a stage performance, etc., given before royalty by request or order.

comma splice, comma fault.

comme il faut (kum′ ēl fō′), FRENCH. as it should be; proper.

com mem o rate (kə mem′ə rāt′), *v.,* **-rat ed, -rat ing.** 1 preserve the memory of: *Roman emperors built arches to commemorate their victories.* 2 honor the memory of: *Christmas commemorates Christ's birth.* [< Latin *commemoratum* remembered < *com-* + *memorare* bring to mind] **—com mem′o ra′tor,** *n.*

com mem o ra tion (kə mem′ə rā′shən), *n.* 1 act of commemorating. 2 service or celebration in memory of some person or event. 3 **in commemoration of,** to honor the memory of.

com mem o ra tive (kə mem′ə rā′tiv, kə-mem′ər ə tiv), *adj.* preserving or honoring the memory of some person, event, etc. —*n.* a postage stamp issued to commemorate some person, event, etc. **—com mem′o-ra′tive ly,** *adv.*

com mence (kə mens′), *v.,* **-menced, -menc ing.** —*v.i.* make a start; begin. —*v.t.* begin (an action); enter upon: *commence legal action.* See **begin** for synonym study. [< Old French *comencer* < Latin *com-* + *initiare* initiate] **—com menc′er,** *n.*

com mence ment (kə mens′mənt), *n.* 1 a beginning; start. 2 day when a school, college, or university awards diplomas and degrees. 3 ceremonies on this day.

com mend (kə mend′), *v.t.* 1 speak well of; praise. See **praise** for synonym study. 2 recommend. 3 hand over for safekeeping; entrust: *She commended the child to her aunt's care.* [< Latin *commendare* < *com-* + *mandare* commit, command]

com mend a ble (kə men′də bəl), *adj.* deserving praise or approval. **—com-mend′a bly,** *adv.*

com men da tion (kom′ən dā′shən), *n.* 1 praise; approval. 2 recommendation. 3 a handing over to another for safekeeping; entrusting.

com mend a to ry (kə men′də tôr′ē, kə-men′də tōr′ē), *adj.* 1 expressing approval; praising. 2 recommending.

com men sal (kə men′səl), *adj.* (of animals and plants) living with, on, or in the member of another species, but not as a parasite. —*n.* a commensal organism. [ultimately < *com-* + Latin *mensa* table] **—com men′sal ly,** *adv.*

com men sal ism (kə men′sə liz′əm), *n.* commensal existence or mode of living.

com men sur a ble (kə men′shər ə bəl, kə-men′sər ə bəl), *adj.* measurable by the same standard or scale of values. **—com-men′sur a ble ness,** *n.* **—com men′sur a-bly,** *adv.*

com men sur ate (kə men′shər it, kə-men′sər it), *adj.* 1 in the proper proportion; proportionate: *The pay should be commensurate with the work.* 2 of the same size or extent; equal. 3 commensurable. [< Late Latin *commensuratum* < Latin *com-* together + *mensura* measure] **—com-men′sur ate ly,** *adv.* **—com men′sur ate-ness,** *n.* **—com men′sur a′tion,** *n.*

com ment (kom′ent), *n.* 1 a short statement that explains, praises, or finds fault with something. 2 remark. 3 talk; gossip. *—v.i.* 1 make a comment or comments: *Everyone commented on my new hat.* 2 talk; gossip. [< Latin *commentum,* ultimately < *com-* up + *-minisci* think]

com men tar y (kom′ən ter′ē), *n., pl.* **-tar ies.** 1 series of notes explaining parts of a book; explanation. 2 series of comments: *a news commentary on television.* 3 an explanatory essay or treatise.

com men ta tor (kom′ən tā′tər), *n.* 1 writer of comments. 2 person who reports and comments on news, sporting events, plays, etc.: *a radio commentator.*

com merce (kom′ərs, kom′ėrs′), *n.* buying and selling, especially in large amounts between different places; business. See **trade** for synonym study. [< Middle French < Latin *commercium* < *com-* with + *mercem* wares]

com mer cial (kə mėr′shəl), *adj.* 1 having to do with commerce. 2 made to be sold for a profit. 3 supported or subsidized by a sponsor: *a commercial radio program.* *—n.* an advertising message on radio or television. **—com mer′cial ly,** *adv.*

commercial bank, an ordinary bank as distinguished from a savings bank or other specialized bank.

com mer cial ism (kə mėr′shə liz′əm), *n.* the methods, spirit, or attitude of commerce: *Making money is often the only object of commercialism.*

com mer cial is tic (kə mėr′shə lis′tik), *adj.* having to do with commercialism or commerce.

com mer cial ize (kə mėr′shə līz), *v.t.,* **-ized, -iz ing.** apply the methods and spirit of commerce to; make a matter of business or trade: *Charging admission to church services would commercialize religion.* **—com-mer′cial i za′tion,** *n.*

commercial paper, any negotiable draft, note, bill, or other instrument of credit given in the course of business.

commercial traveler, a traveling salesman.

com mie or **Com mie** (kom′ē), *n.* INFORMAL. communist.

com mi na tion (kom′ə nā′shən), *n.* threat; denunciation. [< Latin *comminationem* < *com-* with + *minari* threaten]

com min gle (kə ming′gəl), *v.t., v.i.,* **-gled, -gling.** mingle with one another; blend.

com mi nute (kom′ə nüt, kom′ə nyüt), *v.t.,* **-nut ed, -nut ing.** reduce to a powder or to small fragments; pulverize. [< Latin *comminutum* made very small < *com-* + *minus* less] **—com′mi nu′tion,** *n.*

com mis e rate (kə miz′ə rāt′), *v.t., v.i.,* **-rat ed, -rat ing.** feel or express sorrow for another's suffering or trouble; sympathize with; pity. [< Latin *commiseratum* pitied < *com-* + *miser* wretched] **—com mis′e-ra′tion,** *n.*

com mis e ra tive (kə miz′ə rā′tiv), *adj.* commiserating; compassionate.

com mis sar (kom′ə sär), *n.* 1 (formerly) head of a government department in the Soviet Union. 2 a Soviet government official representing the Communist Party in the army, etc. [< Russian *komissar*]

com mis sar i at (kom′ə ser′ē ət), *n.* 1 the department of an army that provides food and daily supplies for soldiers. 2 a food supply. 3 (formerly) any government department in the Soviet Union.

com mis sar y (kom′ə ser′ē), *n., pl.* **-sar ies.** 1 store handling food and supplies in a mining camp, lumber camp, army camp, etc. 2 deputy; representative. [< Medieval Latin *commissarius* < Latin *committere* commit]

com mis sion (kə mish′ən), *n.* 1 a written paper giving certain powers, privileges, and duties. 2 a written order giving rank and authority as an officer in the armed forces. 3 rank and authority given by such an order. 4 a giving of authority. 5 authority, power, or right given. 6 thing for which authority is given; task entrusted to a person. 7 group of people appointed or elected with authority to do certain things. 8 a committing; doing; performance: *the commission of a crime.* 9 percentage of the amount of business done, paid to the agent who does it: *She gets a commission of 10 per cent on all the sales she makes.* 10 service, use, or working order: *The car has been out of commission since the motor broke down.* *—v.t.* 1 give (a person) the power, right, or duty (to do something); give authority to; license; authorize; empower: *I commissioned a real estate agent to sell my house.* 2 give a commission to. 3 put into active service; make ready for use. A new warship is commissioned when it has the officers, sailors, and supplies needed for a voyage. [< Latin *commissionem* < *committere* commit]

commissioned officer, officer holding a commission and having the rank of second lieutenant or of ensign or above.

com mis sion er (kə mish′ə nər, kə-mish′nər), *n.* 1 member of a commission. 2 official in charge of some department of a government: *a health commissioner.*

commission merchant, person who buys or sells goods for others who pay him a commission.

com mis sure (kom′ə shür), *n.* any of the nerve fibers connecting corresponding parts of the brain or spinal cord. [< Latin *commissura* a joining]

com mit (kə mit′), *v.t.,* **-mit ted, -mit ting.** 1 do or perform (usually something wrong): *commit a crime.* 2 hand over for safekeeping; deliver: *commit oneself to the doctor's care.* See synonym study below. 3 send to prison or an asylum. 4 give over; carry over; transfer: *commit a poem to memory, commit thoughts to writing.* 5 reveal (one's opinion). 6 involve; pledge: *I would not commit myself in any way.* 7 refer to a committee for consideration. [< Latin *committere* < *com-* with + *mittere* send, put] **—com mit′ta ble,** *adj.*

Syn. 2 **Commit, consign, entrust** mean to hand over a person or thing. **Commit** means to hand over for custody or safekeeping: *The court committed the financial affairs of the orphan to a guardian.* **Consign** suggests formally handing over control of something, usually by signed documents: *His will consigned his share of the bonds to his sister.* **Entrust** means to commit with trust and confidence in the receiver: *I entrusted my door key to my neighbor.*

com mit ment (kə mit′mənt), *n.* 1 a committing. 2 a being committed. 3 a sending to prison or to an asylum. 4 order sending a person to prison or to an asylum. 5 a pledge; promise.

com mit tal (kə mit′l), *n.* commitment.

com mit tee (kə mit′ē), *n.* group of persons appointed or elected to do certain things.

com mit tee man (kə mit′ē mən), *n., pl.* **-men.** member of a committee.

committee of the whole, committee made up of all the members present.

com mit tee wom an (kə mit′ē wu̇m′ən), *n., pl.* **-wom en.** a woman member of a committee.

com mode (kə mōd′), *n.* 1 chest of drawers. 2 washstand. [< Middle French < Latin *commodus* convenient < *com-* with + *modus* measure]

com mo di ous (kə mō′dē əs), *adj.* 1 having plenty of room; spacious; roomy. 2 ARCHAIC. convenient; handy. [< Medieval Latin *commodiosus* < Latin *commodus.* See COMMODE.] **—com mo′di ous ly,** *adv.* **—com mo′di ous ness,** *n.*

com mod i ty (kə mod′ə tē), *n., pl.* **-ties.** 1 anything that is bought and sold: *Groceries are commodities.* 2 a useful thing.

com mo dore (kom′ə dôr, kom′ə dōr), *n.* 1 (formerly) an officer in the United States Navy ranking next below a rear admiral and next above a captain. 2 captain in the British navy in temporary command of a squadron. 3 title given to the president or head of a yacht club. [earlier *commandore,* perhaps < Dutch *commandeur* < French *commandeur* commander]

com mon (kom′ən), *adj.* 1 belonging equally to two or more persons or things; joint: *common property. The two triangles have a common base.* 2 of all; from all; by all; to all; general: *common knowledge, a common nuisance.* See **general** for synonym study. 3 often met with; usual; familiar: *Snow is common in cold countries.* See synonym study below. 4 without rank or position: *the common people. A common soldier is a private.* 5 below ordinary; having poor quality; inferior. 6 coarse; vulgar. 7 belonging to or representing the entire community; public: *a common council.* 8 belonging equally to two or more quantities: *a common factor.* 9 (in grammar) identical in form whether used as a subject or object. In *the man drove the car,* both *man* and *car* are in the common case rather than in the nominative or objective case respectively. *—n.* 1 Also, **commons,** *pl.* land owned or used by all the people of a town, village, etc. 2 **in common,** equally with another or others; owned, used, or done by both or all. [< Old French *comun* < Latin *communem* < *com-* together + *munia* duties] **—com′mon ness,** *n.*

Syn. *adj.* 3 **Common, ordinary** mean usual. **Common** means often met with or usual because shared by many people or things: *Colds are common in winter.* **Ordinary** means in agreement with the normal standards and order of things: *I use ordinary soap for shampoo.*

com mon al i ty (kom′ə nal′ə tē), *n., pl.*

-ties. 1 commonalty. 2 common quality.

com mon al ty (kom′ə nəl tē), *n., pl.* **-ties.** 1 the common people; persons without rank or title; middle and lower classes of society. 2 people as a group. 3 members of a corporation.

common carrier, company or person whose business is transporting goods or people. Railroads are common carriers.

common cold, a cold.

common denominator, 1 a common multiple of the denominators of a group of fractions: *12 is a common denominator of* $\frac{1}{2}$, $\frac{2}{3}$, *and* $\frac{3}{4}$. 2 quality, attribute, opinion, etc., shared by all in a group.

common divisor, number that will divide a group of numbers without a remainder: *2 is a common divisor of 4, 6, 8, and 10.*

com mon er (kom′ə nər), *n.* 1 one of the common people; person who is not a nobleman. 2 member of the House of Commons.

common fraction, fraction expressed as the ratio of two whole numbers. EXAMPLES: $\frac{1}{2}$. $\frac{7}{8}$.

common gender, (in grammar) a category of words that are either masculine or feminine. EXAMPLES: child, writer.

common law, law based on custom and usage and confirmed by the decisions of judges, as distinct from statute law.

com mon-law marriage (kom′ən lô′), a living together as husband and wife without having been married in a civil or religious ceremony.

com mon ly (kom′ən lē), *adv.* usually; generally.

Common Market, an association of Belgium, France, Italy, Luxembourg, the Netherlands, and West Germany, established in 1958 to eliminate tariffs among its members and have a common tariff for external commerce; European Economic Community. The Common Market agreed on terms for the entry of Great Britain, Denmark, and Ireland in 1973, with regular membership scheduled for 1978.

common multiple, number divisible by two or more numbers without a remainder: *12 is a common multiple of 2, 3, 4, and 6.*

common noun, name for any one of a class. *Boy* and *city* are common nouns. *John* and *Boston* are proper nouns.

com mon place (kom′ən plās′), *n.* 1 a common or everyday thing: *Fifty years ago broadcasting was a novelty; today it is a commonplace.* 2 an ordinary or obvious remark. *—adj.* not new or interesting; everyday; ordinary. See synonym study below. **—com′mon place′ness,** *n.*

Syn. *adj.* **Commonplace, trite, hackneyed** mean lacking in freshness and interest. **Commonplace** applies to ideas and words so everyday and ordinary that they are dull: *Most movie plots are commonplace.* **Trite** applies to ideas, words, and phrases that have become too familiar by overuse and are no longer interesting, such as *Necessity is the mother of invention.* **Hackneyed** applies especially to phrases used so much as to have lost almost all meaning, such as *last but not least.*

com mons (kom′ənz), *n., pl. in form, sometimes sing. in use.* 1 the common people; people who are not noblemen. 2 a dining hall or building where food is served to many at common tables. 3 **the Commons,** House of Commons.

common sense, good sense in everyday affairs; practical intelligence.

com mon sen si cal (kom′ən sen′sə kəl), *adj.* showing common sense; sensible; practical.

common stock, ordinary stock in a company. Common stock has no guaranteed rate of dividend and does not carry the privileges of preferred stock.

common time, (in music) meter consisting of four quarter notes to the measure.

com mon weal (kom′ən wēl′), *n.* 1 the general welfare; public good. 2 ARCHAIC. commonwealth.

com mon wealth (kom′ən welth′), *n.* 1 the people who make up a nation; citizens of a state. 2 a democratic state; republic. 3 any state of the United States, especially Kentucky, Massachusetts, Pennsylvania, and Virginia. 4 **Commonwealth,** government in England under Oliver Cromwell and later under his son. It lasted from 1649 to 1660, and included the Protectorate. 5 **the Commonwealth,** the Commonwealth of Nations.

Commonwealth of Nations, 1 association of the United Kingdom, the independent member states (such as Canada, Australia, New Zealand, India, Ceylon, Ghana, Nigeria, Cyprus), and various associated states, dependent territories, protectorates, and protected states; the Commonwealth. It was formerly called **British Commonwealth of Nations** or **British Commonwealth.** 704,150,000 pop.; 10,660,600 sq. mi. 2 (in former official use) the self-governing members of the Commonwealth of Nations, exclusive of the associated states, dependent territories, protectorates, and protected states.

com mo tion (kə mō′shən), *n.* 1 violent movement; agitation; turbulence: *the commotion of the storm.* 2 bustle or stir; confusion: *the commotion of the marketplace.*

com mu nal (kə myü′nl, kom′yə nəl), *adj.* 1 of a community; public. 2 owned jointly by all; used or participated in by all members of a group or community. 3 of a commune. **—com′mu nal ly,** *adv.*

com mune[1] (*v.* kə myün′; *n.* kom′yün), *v.,* **-muned, -mun ing,** *n.* *—v.i.* 1 talk intimately. 2 receive Holy Communion. *—n.* intimate talk; communion. [< Old French *communer* make common, share < *comun.* See COMMON.]

com mune[2] (kom′yün), *n.* 1 the smallest division for local government in France, Belgium, Italy, and several other European countries. 2 formerly: **a** a local unit of collective farms in Communist China. **b** the Russian mir. 3 **Commune, a** a revolutionary group that governed Paris from 1792 to 1794. **b** a similar group that governed Paris from March 18 to May 28, 1871. 4 U.S. group of people living together. [< Middle French, community, ultimately < Latin *communis.* See COMMON.]

com mu ni ca bil i ty (kə myü′nə kə bil′ə tē), *n.* quality of being communicable.

com mu ni ca ble (kə myü′nə kə bəl), *adj.* that can be communicated: *Ideas are communicable by words. Scarlet fever is a communicable disease.* **—com mu′ni ca ble ness,** *n.* **—com mu′ni ca bly,** *adv.*

com mu ni cant (kə myü′nə kənt), *n.* 1 person who receives Holy Communion. 2 person who informs or communicates. *—adj.* communicating.

com mu ni cate (kə myü′nə kāt), *v.,* **-cat ed, -cat ing.** *—v.t.* 1 give (information or news) by speaking, writing, etc.; talk, write, telephone, telegraph, etc. 2 pass along; transfer: *The stove communicated heat to the room.* See synonym study below. *—v.i.* 1 exchange information or news by speaking, writing, etc.; send and receive messages. 2 be connected: *The dining room communicates with the kitchen.* 3 receive Holy Communion. [< Latin *communicatum* shared, held in common < *communis* common. See COMMON.] **—com mu′ni ca′tor,** *n.*

hat, āge, fär; let, ēqual, tėrm;
it, īce; hot, ōpen, ôrder;
oil, out; cup, pu̇t, rüle;
ch, child; ng, long; sh, she;
th, thin; ᴛʜ, then; zh, measure;
ə represents *a* in about, *e* in taken, *i* in pencil, *o* in lemon, *u* in circus.
< = from, derived from, taken from.

Syn. *v.t.* 1, 2 **Communicate, impart** mean to pass something along. **Communicate** suggests merely that what is passed along becomes the common property of giver and receiver: *She communicated her wishes to me.* **Impart** emphasizes giving to another a share of what one has: *A teacher imparts knowledge to students.*

com mu ni ca tion (kə myü′nə kā′shən), *n.* 1 a giving or exchanging of information or news by speaking, writing, etc.: *People who are deaf often use sign language as a means of communication.* 2 information or news given in this way. 3 letter, message, etc., which gives information or news: *Your communication came in time to change all my plans.* 4 means of going from one place to another; passage; connection: *There is no communication between these two rooms.* 5 act or fact of passing along; transfer. 6 **communications,** *pl.* **a** system of communicating by telephone, telegraph, radio, television, etc. **b** system of routes or facilities for transporting military supplies, vehicles, and troops.

communications satellite, an artificial satellite that relays microwave signals between two points on earth.

com mu ni ca tive (kə myü′nə kā′tiv, kə myü′nə kə tiv), *adj.* ready to give information; talkative. **—com mu′ni ca′tive ly,** *adv.* **—com mu′ni ca′tive ness,** *n.*

com mun ion (kə myü′nyən), *n.* 1 act of sharing; a having in common. 2 exchange of thoughts and feelings; intimate talk; fellowship. 3 a close spiritual relationship. 4 group of people having the same religious beliefs. 5 **Communion,** Holy Communion. [< Latin *communionem* < *communis* common]

com mu ni qué (kə myü′nə kā′, kə myü′nə kā), *n.* an official bulletin, statement, or other communication. [< French]

com mu nism (kom′yə niz′əm), *n.* 1 an economic and social system based on the ownership of land, factories, and other means of production by the community as a whole or the state and in which the right of private individuals to hold property is partially or totally abolished. The state also has the right to control the distribution and consumption of the products of industry and, sometimes, the right of the individual to control his own labor is denied. 2 **Communism,** the political principles and practices of members of a Communist Party. [< French *communisme* < *commun* common]

➛ **Communism** and **socialism** are systems of social organization under which the means of production and distribution of goods are transferred from private hands to the government. Communism emphasizes replacing the existing social order by revolution; socialism seeks to establish itself by peaceful means, through election and legislation.

com mu nist (kom′yə nist), *n.* 1 person who favors and supports communism. 2 **Communist,** member of a Communist Party. *—adj.* 1 Also, **Communist.** communistic. 2 **Communist,** of or having to do with a Communist Party.

com mu nis tic (kom′yə nis′tik), *adj.* 1 of or having to do with communists or communism. 2 favoring communism. **—com′mu-nis′ti cal ly,** *adv.*

Communist Party, a political party which supports communism.

com mu ni ty (kə myü′nə tē), *n., pl.* **-ties.** 1 all the people living in the same place and subject to the same laws; people of any district or town. 2 group of people living together or sharing common interests: *a community of monks.* 3 **the community,** the public: *the approval of the community.* 4 ownership together; sharing together: *community of food supplies.* 5 all of the animals and plants sharing a common environment. 6 likeness; similarity; identity: *community of interests.*

community center, building where the people of a community meet for recreation, social purposes, etc.

community chest, fund of money contributed voluntarily by people to support charity and welfare in their community.

com mu nize (kom′yə nīz), *v.t.,* **-nized, -niz ing.** 1 make the property of the community. 2 cause to practice or adopt communism. **—com′mu ni za′tion,** *n.*

com mu tate (kom′yə tāt), *v.t.,* **-tat ed, -tat ing.** reverse the direction of (an electric current) by a commutator.

com mu ta tion (kom′yə tā′shən), *n.* 1 exchange; substitution. 2 reduction (of an obligation, penalty, etc.) to a less severe one: *a commutation of death sentence to life imprisonment.* 3 regular travel to and from work, especially between suburb and downtown, by public or private transportation. 4 a reversal of the direction of an electric current by a commutator.

commutation ticket, U.S. ticket sold at a reduced rate, entitling the holder to travel over a given route a certain number of times or during a certain period.

com mu ta tive (kom′yə tā′tiv), *adj.* of or having to do with a rule in mathematics that the order in which numbers are added or multiplied will not change the result of the operation. EXAMPLE: 2 + 3 will give the same result as 3 + 2.

com mu ta tor (kom′yə tā′tər), *n.* 1 device for reversing the direction of an electric current in the armature winding of a direct current generator or motor. 2 a revolving part in a generator or motor that carries the current to or from the brushes.

com mute (kə myüt′), *v.,* **-mut ed, -mut ing.** *—v.t.* 1 exchange; substitute. 2 change (an obligation, penalty, etc.) to a less severe one: *The governor commuted the prisoner's death sentence to one of life imprisonment.* 3 commutate. *—v.i.* U.S. travel regularly to and from work especially between suburb and downtown, by public or private transportation. [< Latin *commutare* < *com-* + *mutare* to change] **—com mut′a-ble,** *adj.*

com mut er (kə myü′tər), *n.* person who commutes.

Co mo (kō′mō), *n.* **Lake,** lake in N Italy. 30 mi. long; 56 sq. mi.

comp., 1 comparative. 2 compare. 3 composition. 4 compound.

com pact[1] (*adj.* kəm pakt′, kom′pakt; *v.* kəm pakt′; *n.* kom′pakt), *adj.* 1 firmly packed together; closely joined: *Cabbage leaves are folded into a compact head.* 2 having the parts neatly or tightly arranged within a small space: *a compact portable TV set.* 3 using few words; brief and well organized. *—v.t.* 1 pack firmly together; join closely; compress. 2 make by putting together firmly. 3 condense. *—n.* 1 a small case containing face powder or rouge. 2 compact car. [< Latin *compactum* confined < *com-* together + *pangere* fasten] **—com pact′ly,** *adv.* **—com pact′ness,** *n.*

com pact[2] (kom′pakt), *n.* agreement or contract. [< Latin *compactum* < *com-* together + *pacisci* make an agreement]

com pact car (kom′pakt), automobile that is smaller, usually cheaper, and more economical to operate than standard models.

com pac tion (kəm pak′shən), *n.* 1 act of making compact; compression. 2 condition of being compact.

com pan ion[1] (kəm pan′yən), *n.* 1 person who goes along with another; person who shares in what another is doing; comrade; associate. 2 person paid to live or travel with another as a friend and helper. 3 anything that matches or goes with another in kind, size, color, etc. 4 a member of the lowest rank in orders of knighthood. *—v.t.* be a companion to; go along with; accompany. [< Old French *compaignon* < Late Latin *companionem* < *companio* company < Latin *com-* together + *panis* bread]

com pan ion[2] (kəm pan′yən), *n.* 1 a covering over the top of a companionway. 2 companionway. [< Dutch *kampanje* quarterdeck]

com pan ion a ble (kəm pan′yə nə bəl), *adj.* pleasant as a companion; agreeable; sociable. **—com pan′ion a bly,** *adv.*

com pan ion ate (kəm pan′yə nit), *adj.* of or like companions.

companion cell, any of the small cells with large nuclei adjacent to the sieve tube in the phloem of vascular plants.

com pan ion ship (kəm pan′yən ship), *n.* association as companions; fellowship.

com pan ion way (kəm pan′yən wā′), *n.* stairway from the deck of a ship down to the rooms or area below.

com pa ny (kum′pə nē), *n., pl.* **-nies.** 1 group of people. See synonym study below. 2 group of people joined together for some purpose: *a business company, a company of actors.* 3 a gathering of persons for social purposes: *The children behave well in company.* 4 companion or companions: *You are known by the company you keep.* 5 companionship; fellowship. 6 one or more guests or visitors: *We often have company in the evening.* 7 a military unit made up of two or more platoons, usually commanded by a captain. It is usually part of a battalion or a regiment. 8 a ship's crew; officers and sailors of a ship. 9 a unit of firemen. 10 partners not named in the title of a firm. 11 **keep company, a** remain with for companionship. **b** go together. 12 **part company, a** go separate ways. **b** end companionship. [< Old French *compagnie* < *compain* companion < Late Latin *companio.* See COMPANION[1].]

Syn. 1 **Company, band, party** mean a group of people brought together in some way. **Company** is the word of widest application, as its long list of specific meanings in the entry above indicates. It is also the most general: *The chairman led the company in singing.* **Band** applies to a small group sharing a common purpose or lot: *A band of gypsies is in town.* **Party,** except as the political organization, applies to a small group joined for a specific purpose but for only a short time: *A rescue party started up the mountain.*

company union, 1 union of workers in one factory, store, etc., that is not part of a larger union. 2 union of workers dominated by the employer.

com par a ble (kom′pər ə bəl), *adj.* 1 able to be compared: *A fire is comparable with the sun; both give light and heat.* 2 fit to be compared: *A cave is not comparable to a house for comfort.* **—com′par a ble ness,** *n.* **—com′par a bly,** *adv.*

com par a tive (kəm par′ə tiv), *adj.* 1 that compares; of or having to do with comparison: *the comparative method of studying.* 2 measured by comparison with something else; relative: *Screens give us comparative freedom from flies.* 3 showing the second degree of comparison of an adjective or adverb. *Better* is the comparative form of *good.* *—n.* 1 the second degree of comparison of an adjective or adverb. 2 form or combination of words that shows this degree. *Fairer* and *more slowly* are the comparatives of *fair* and *slowly.* **—com par′a tive ly,** *adv.* **—com par′a tive ness,** *n.*

com par a tor (kəm par′ə tər, kom′pə-rā′tər), *n.* instrument for measuring small differences in parts of machinery, etc., by comparing the parts with some standard.

com pare (kəm per′, kəm par′), *v.,* **-pared, -par ing.** *n.* *—v.t.* 1 find out or point out how persons or things are alike and how they differ: *I compared the two books to see which one had the better pictures.* 2 consider as similar; liken: *The fins of a fish may be compared to the wings of a bird; both are used in moving.* 3 change the form of (an adjective or adverb) to show the comparative and superlative degree; name the positive, comparative, and superlative degrees of. 4 **not to be compared with, a** very different from. **b** not nearly so good as. *—v.i.* be considered like or equal; be compared: *Artificial light cannot compare with daylight for general use.* *—n.* **beyond compare,** without an equal; most excellent. [< French *comparer* < Latin *comparare* < *com-* with + *par* equal]

com par i son (kəm par′ə sən), *n.* 1 act or process of comparing; finding the likenesses and differences: *The teacher's comparison of the heart to a pump helped the students to understand its action.* 2 likeness; similarity: *There is no comparison between these two cameras; one is much better than the other.* 3 change in an adjective or adverb to show degrees. The three degrees of comparison are positive, comparative, and superlative. EXAMPLE: cold, colder, coldest; good, better, best; helpful, more helpful, most helpful. 4 **in comparison with,** compared with.

hat, āge, fär; let, ēqual, tėrm;
it, īce; hot, ōpen, ôrder;
oil, out; cup, pu̇t, rüle;
ch, child; ng, long; sh, she;
th, thin; ᴛʜ, then; zh, measure;

ə represents *a* in about, *e* in taken, *i* in pencil, *o* in lemon, *u* in circus.

< = from, derived from, taken from.

com part ment (kəm pärt′mənt), *n.* 1 a separate division or section; part of an enclosed space set off by walls or partitions. A ship's hold is often built in watertight compartments so that a leak will fill up only one compartment and not the whole ship. 2 any part, division, or section, as of a plant or animal, the mind, etc.

com part men tal ize (kom′pärt men′tl īz), *v.t.,* **-ized, -iz ing.** arrange in compartments, sections, or categories. **—com′part men′tal i za′tion,** *n.*

compass (def. 1) Even though the dial may be turned, the needle remains fixed on north.

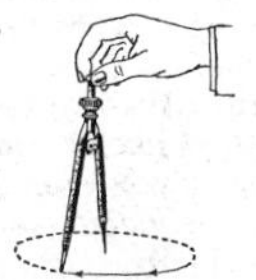
compass (def. 2) The sharply pointed arm remains fixed as the drawing arm revolves.

com pass (kum′pəs), *n.* 1 instrument for showing directions, consisting of a needle or compass card that points to the North Magnetic Pole. 2 Also, **compasses,** *pl.* instrument consisting of two legs hinged together at one end, used for drawing circles and curved lines and for measuring distances. 3 boundary; circumference: *within the compass of four walls.* 4 space within limits; extent; range: *There have been many scientific advancements within the compass of his lifetime.* See **range** for synonym study. 5 range of a voice or musical instrument. 6 **box the compass, a** name the points of the compass in order. **b** go all the way around and end where one started. *—v.t.* 1 make a circuit of; go around; move around. 2 form a circle around; hem in; surround. 3 accomplish; obtain. 4 plot; scheme. 5 grasp with the mind; understand completely. [< Old French *compas* < *compasser* divide equally < Latin *com-* with + *passus* step]

compass card, a circular card set beneath the needle of a compass showing the 32 points of direction and the degrees of the circle.

com pas sion (kəm pash′ən), *n.* feeling for another's sorrow or hardship that leads to help; sympathy; pity. See **pity** for synonym study. [< Latin *compassionem* < *compati* suffer with < *com-* with + *pati* suffer]

com pas sion ate (kəm pash′ə nit), *adj.* desiring to relieve another's suffering; sympathetic; pitying. **—com pas′sion ate ly,** *adv.*

com pat i bil i ty (kəm pat′ə bil′ə tē), *n.* ability to exist or get on well together; agreement; harmony.

com pat i ble (kəm pat′ə bəl), *adj.* able to exist or get on well together; agreeing; in harmony. [< Medieval Latin *compatibilem* < Latin *compati* suffer with. See COMPASSION.] **—com pat′i bly,** *adv.*

com pa tri ot (kəm pā′trē ət; *British* kəm pat′rē ət), *n.* one who is of the same country as another; a fellow countryman. *—adj.* of the same country.

com peer (kəm pir′, kom′pir), *n.* 1 an equal; peer. 2 companion; comrade. [< Old French *comper* < Latin *compar* equal to another < *com-* with + *par* equal]

com pel (kəm pel′), *v.t.,* **-pelled, -pel ling.** 1 drive or urge with force; force: *Rain compelled them to stop.* See synonym study below. 2 cause or get by force: *A policeman can compel obedience to the law.* [< Latin *compellere* < *com-* + *pellere* to drive] **—com pel′ling ly,** *adv.*

Syn. 1 **Compel, impel** mean to force. **Compel** means force a person to do something one wants or to give in to something: *It is impossible to compel a person to love his fellow men.* **Impel** means force to move forward, but is most often used figuratively to mean drive forward by strong desire: *Hunger impelled them to beg.*

com pend (kom′pend), *n.* compendium.

com pen di ous (kəm pen′dē əs), *adj.* brief but comprehensive; concise: *a compendious review of world history.* **—com pen′di ous ly,** *adv.* **—com pen′di ous ness,** *n.*

com pen di um (kəm pen′dē əm), *n., pl.* **-di ums, -di a** (-dē ə). summary that gives much information in a little space; concise treatise; condensation. [< Latin, a shortening < *compendere* weigh together < *com-* + *pendere* weigh]

com pen sate (kom′pən sāt), *v.,* **-sat ed, -sat ing.** *—v.t.* 1 make an equal return to; give an equivalent to: *The hunters gave the farmer $100 to compensate him for their damage to his field.* See **pay** for synonym study. 2 pay: *The company compensated her for extra work.* *—v.i.* 1 balance by equal weight, power, etc.; make up *(for)*: *Skill sometimes compensates for lack of strength.* 2 make amends. [< Latin *compensatum* balanced out < *com-* + *pensare* weigh < *pendere* weigh out] **—com′pen sa′tor,** *n.*

com pen sa tion (kom′pən sā′shən), *n.* 1 something given as an equivalent; something given to make up for a loss, injury, etc. 2 pay: *He said that equal compensation should be given to men and women for equal work.* 3 a balancing by equal power, weight, etc. 4 means for doing this. 5 increased size or activity of one part (of an organism or organ) to make up for loss or weakness of another part: *After one kidney was removed, the other became larger in compensation. The blind man developed especially sharp hearing as a compensation for his loss of sight.* 6 a compensating. 7 a being compensated.

com pen sa tive (kom′pən sā′tiv, kəm pen′sə tiv), *adj.* compensating.

com pen sa to ry (kəm pen′sə tôr′ē, kəm pen′sə tōr′ē), *adj.* compensating.

com pete (kəm pēt′), *v.i.,* **-pet ed, -pet ing.** 1 try hard to obtain something wanted by others; be rivals; contend. See **contend** for synonym study. 2 take part (in a contest): *Will you compete in the final race?* [< Latin *competere* < *com-* together + *petere* seek]

com pe tence (kom′pə təns), *n.* 1 ability; fitness: *No one doubted the guide's competence.* 2 enough money to provide a comfortable living. 3 legal power, capacity, or authority.

com pe ten cy (kom′pə tən sē), *n.* competence.

com pe tent (kom′pə tənt), *adj.* 1 properly qualified; able; fit: *a competent bookkeeper, competent to decide.* See **able** for synonym study. 2 legally qualified: *Two competent witnesses testified.* **—com′pe tent ly,** *adv.*

com pe ti tion (kom′pə tish′ən), *n.* 1 effort to obtain something wanted by others; rivalry: *competition among businesses for trade.* 2 contest.

com pet i tive (kəm pet′ə tiv), *adj.* of competition; having or based on competition; decided by competition: *a competitive examination for a job.* **—com pet′i tive ly,** *adv.* **—com pet′i tive ness,** *n.*

com pet i tor (kəm pet′ə tər), *n.* person who competes; rival.

com pi la tion (kom′pə lā′shən), *n.* 1 act of compiling. 2 book, list, etc., that has been compiled.

com pile (kəm pīl′), *v.t.,* **-piled, -pil ing.** 1 collect and bring together in one list or account. 2 make (a book, a report, etc.) out of various materials. [< Latin *compilare* pile up < *com-* together + *pilare* press] **—com pil′er,** *n.*

com pla cence (kəm plā′sns), *n.* complacency.

com pla cen cy (kəm plā′sn sē), *n.* a being pleased with oneself or what one has; self-satisfaction: *She solved the difficult puzzle easily and smiled with complacency.*

com pla cent (kəm plā′snt), *adj.* pleased with oneself or what one has; self-satisfied: *The winner's complacent smile annoyed the loser.* [< Latin *complacentem,* < *com-* + *placere* please] **—com pla′cent ly,** *adv.*

com plain (kəm plān′), *v.i.* 1 say that something is wrong; find fault. See synonym study below. 2 talk about one's pains, troubles, etc. 3 make an accusation or charge: *complain to the landlord about a noisy neighbor.* [< Old French *complaindre* < Late Latin *complangere* < Latin *com-* + *plangere* lament] **—com plain′er,** *n.* **—com plain′ing ly,** *adv.*

Syn. 1 **Complain, grumble** mean to express discontent. **Complain,** the general word, means to express discontent with something: *Complaining about the weather won't bring sunshine.* **Grumble** means to mutter complaints in a bad-tempered way: *Stop grumbling about the food.*

com plain ant (kəm plā′nənt), *n.* 1 person who complains. 2 person who brings a lawsuit against another; plaintiff: *The complainant accused the defendant of fraud.*

com plaint (kəm plānt′), *n.* 1 a complaining; finding fault. 2 accusation; charge. 3 a cause for complaining. 4 illness; ailment: *A cold is a very common complaint.*

com plai sance (kəm plā′zns, kom′plə zans), *n.* 1 obligingness; agreeableness; courtesy. 2 compliance.

com plai sant (kəm plā′znt, kom′plə zant), *adj.* 1 obliging; gracious; courteous. 2 compliant. [< French] **—com plai′sant ly,** *adv.*

com plect ed (kəm plek′tid), *adj.* complexioned.

➤ **Complected** (as in *dark-complected* and *light-complected*), though commonly used, especially in the United States, is not regarded as standard. The standard term is *complexioned.*

com ple ment (*n.* kom′plə mənt; *v.*

kom′plə ment), *n.* 1 something that completes or makes perfect. 2 number required to fill: *The ship now has its full complement of men, and no more can be taken on.* 3 word or group of words completing a predicate. In "The man is good," *good* is a complement. 4 amount needed to make an angle or an arc equal to 90 degrees. 5 (in mathematics) those members of a set that do not belong to a subset. 6 substance found in normal blood serum and protoplasm which combines with antibodies to destroy bacteria and other foreign bodies. *—v.t.* supply a lack of any kind; complete. See synonym study below. [< Latin *complementum* < *complere* to complete]

Syn. *v.t.* **Complement, supplement** mean to complete. **Complement** means to complete by supplying something that is missing but necessary to make a perfect whole: *The two texts complement each other; what is sketchily dealt with in either one is treated fully in the other.* **Supplement** means to add something to make better or bigger or richer in some way: *Outside reading supplements a person's education.*

➤ **complement, compliment.** *Complement* means something that completes or makes perfect, or a number required to fill (related to *complete*): *Education was the complement to her natural abilities. Compliment* has to do with politeness and praise: *Their progress deserved the principal's compliment.*

com ple men tal (kom′plə men′tl), *adj.* complementary.

com ple men tar y (kom′plə men′tər ē), *adj.* forming a complement; completing: *The four seasons are complementary parts of a year.*

complementary angle, either of two angles which together form an angle of 90 degrees.

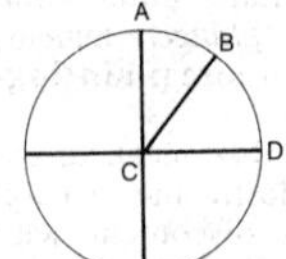

complementary angle
Angle ACB and angle BCD are complementary angles.

complementary colors, two colors whose reflected lights combine to produce white or gray. Red and green are complementary colors.

com plete (kəm plēt′), *adj., v.,* **-plet ed, -plet ing.** *—adj.* 1 with all the parts; whole; entire: *a complete set of Dickens's novels.* See synonym study below. 2 perfect: thorough: *a complete surprise.* 3 finished; done: *My homework is complete.* *—v.t.* 1 make up the full number or amount of; make whole or entire: *I completed the set of dishes by buying the cups and saucers.* 2 make perfect or thorough: *The good news completed my happiness.* 3 get done; finish: *She completed her homework before dinner.* [< Latin *completum* fulfilled, filled up < *com-* up + *-plere* fill] **—com plete′ly,** *adv.* **—com plete′ness,** *n.*

Syn. *adj.* 1 **Complete, entire** mean with all the parts. **Complete** implies that no part is missing: *I have the complete story now.* **Entire** implies wholeness and unbroken unity: *They gave the entire day to their work, foregoing lunch.*

com ple tion (kəm plē′shən), *n.* 1 act of completing; finishing. 2 condition of being completed: *The work is near completion.*

com plex (*adj.* kəm pleks′, kom′pleks; *n.* kom′pleks), *adj.* 1 made up of a number of parts: *A watch is a complex device. Hemoglobin is a complex chemical substance in the blood.* 2 complicated: *The instructions for building the radio were too complex for us to follow.* *—n.* 1 a complicated whole. 2 group of buildings, units, etc.: *the complex of buildings making up Rockefeller Center.* 3 group of repressed ideas associated with a past emotional disturbance so as to influence a person's present behavior to an abnormal degree. 4 a strong prejudice; unreasonable dislike or fear. [< Latin *complexum* comprised, embraced < *com-* together + *plectere* to twine] **—com plex′ly,** *adv.* **—com plex′ness,** *n.*

complex fraction, fraction having a fraction or mixed number in the numerator, in the denominator, or in both; compound fraction. EXAMPLES: $\frac{1^3/_4}{3}, \frac{1}{3^1/_2}, \frac{^3/_4}{1^7/_8}$.

com plex ion (kəm plek′shən), *n.* 1 color, quality, and general appearance of the skin, particularly of the face. 2 general appearance; nature; character.

com plex ioned (kəm plek′shənd), *adj.* having a certain kind of complexion: *dark-complexioned.*

com plex i ty (kəm plek′sə tē), *n., pl.* **-ties.** 1 a complex quality, condition, or structure: *The complexity of the road map puzzled the lost motorist.* 2 something complex; complication.

complex number, the sum of a real number and an imaginary number. EXAMPLE: $2 + 3\sqrt{-1}$

complex sentence, sentence having one main clause and one or more subordinate clauses. EXAMPLE: When the traffic light turns red, traffic stops.

com pli ance (kəm plī′əns), *n.* 1 a complying or doing as another wishes; yielding to a request or command. 2 tendency to yield to others. 3 **in compliance with,** complying with; according to.

com pli an cy (kəm plī′ən sē), *n.* compliance.

com pli ant (kəm plī′ənt), *adj.* complying; yielding; obliging. See **obedient** for synonym study. **—com pli′ant ly,** *adv.*

com pli cate (kom′plə kāt), *v.t.,* **-cat ed, -cat ing.** 1 make hard to understand, settle, cure, etc.; mix up; make complex; confuse. 2 make worse or more mixed up: *a headache complicated by eye trouble.* [< Latin *complicatum* folded together < *com-* together + *plicare* to fold]

com pli cat ed (kom′plə kā′tid), *adj.* hard to understand; involved; intricate. **—com′pli cat′ed ly,** *adv.* **—com′pli cat′ed ness,** *n.*

com pli ca tion (kom′plə kā′shən), *n.* 1 a complex or confused state of affairs that is hard to understand, settle, etc. 2 difficulty or problem added to one or more already existing: *Pneumonia was the complication we most feared.* 3 act or process of complicating.

com plic i ty (kəm plis′ə tē), *n., pl.* **-ties.** partnership in wrongdoing: *Knowingly receiving stolen goods in complicity in theft.* [< Middle French *complicité* < *complice* confederate < Late Latin *complicem* < Latin *com-* together + *plicare* to fold]

com pli ment (*n.* kom′plə mənt; *v.* kom′plə ment), *n.* 1 something good said about one; something said in praise of one's work, etc. 2 a courteous act: *The town paid the old artist the compliment of a large attendance at his exhibit.* 3 **compliments,** *pl.* greetings: *In the box of flowers was a card saying "With the compliments of a friend."* *—v.t.* 1 pay a compliment to; congratulate; praise: *The principal complimented me on my good grades.* 2 give something to (a person) as a polite attention. [< French < Italian *complimento* < Spanish *cumplimiento* < *cumplir* fulfill < Latin *complere* fill up, complete] ➤ See **complement** for usage note.

com pli men tar y (kom′plə men′tər ē), *adj.* 1 like or containing a compliment; praising. 2 U.S. given free: *a complimentary ticket to a concert.* **—com′pli men tar′i ly,** *adv.*

com plin (kom′plən), *n.* 1 last of the seven canonical hours. 2 the service for it, now usually following vespers. [< Old French *complie* < Latin *completa (hora)* completed (hour)]

com pline (kom′plən, kom′plīn), *n.* complin.

com ply (kəm plī′), *v.i.,* **-plied, -ply ing.** act in agreement with a request or command: *I will comply with the doctor's request.* [< Italian *complire* < Spanish *cumplir* < Latin *complere* fulfill, complete] **—com pli′er,** *n.*

com po nent (kəm pō′nənt), *n.* one of the parts that make up a whole; necessary part: *Because alcohol is a solvent, it is a component of many liquid medicines.* See **element** for synonym study. *—adj.* that composes; constituent: *Blade and handle are the component parts of a knife.* [< Latin *componentem* put together < *com-* together + *ponere* put]

com port (kəm pôrt′, kəm pōrt′), *v.t.* conduct (oneself) in a certain manner; behave: *Judges should comport themselves with dignity.* *—v.i.* agree; suit: *Bigotry does not comport with the position of judge.* [< Latin *comportare* < *com-* together + *portare* carry]

com port ment (kəm pôrt′mənt, kəm pōrt′mənt), *n.* bearing; behavior.

com pose (kəm pōz′), *v.,* **-posed, -pos ing.** *—v.t.* 1 make up; constitute: *The ocean is composed of salt water.* 2 put together; arrange or produce. 3 construct in words; write (prose, verse, etc.). 4 create or write (music). 5 set up (type) to form words and sentences. 6 arrange the parts of (a picture or painting). 7 get (oneself) ready; put in proper state: *compose oneself to read a book.* 8 calm (oneself or one's features): *Try to compose yourself before the doctor gets here.* 9 settle; adjust: *compose a dispute.* *—v.i.* 1 write music; be a composer. 2 write books, poems, etc.; be an author. 3 set up type in a printing office. [< Old French *composer* < *com-* together + *poser* put. See POSE[1].]

com posed (kəm pōzd′), *adj.* calm; quiet; self-controlled; tranquil. See **calm** for synonym study. **—com pos′ed ly,** *adv.* **—com pos′ed ness,** *n.*

com pos er (kəm pō′zər), *n.* 1 person or thing that composes. 2 writer of music.

com pos ite (kəm poz′it), *adj.* 1 made up of various parts; compound. 2 belonging to the composite family. *—n.* 1 any composite thing. 2 plant of the composite family. [< Latin *compositum* put together < *com-* together + *ponere* put. Doublet of COMPOST.] **—com pos′ite ly,** *adv.*

composite family, a very large plant

hat, āge, fär; let, ēqual, tėrm;
it, īce; hot, ōpen, ôrder;
oil, out; cup, pu̇t, rüle;
ch, child; ng, long; sh, she;
th, thin; ᴛʜ, then; zh, measure;

ə represents *a* in about, *e* in taken, *i* in pencil, *o* in lemon, *u* in circus.

< = from, derived from, taken from.

family comprising the most highly developed plants, including the daisy, aster, dandelion, marigold, and lettuce. The dicotyledonous plants of this family have a close head of many small flowers or florets.

composite number, number exactly divisible by some whole number other than itself or one; number that has more than two factors. 4, 6, and 9 are composite numbers; 2, 3, 5, and 7 are prime numbers.

com po si tion (kom′pə zish′ən), *n.* 1 the make-up of anything; what is in it: *The composition of this candy includes sugar, chocolate, and milk.* 2 a putting together of parts to form a whole, such as writing sentences, making pictures, and setting type in printing. 3 thing composed, such as a piece of music, a poem, or a painting. 4 a short essay written as a school exercise. 5 mixture of substances; compound: *The dentist filled my tooth with a composition of silver and mercury.* 6 agreement or compromise; settlement.

com pos i tor (kəm poz′ə tər), *n.* typesetter.

com pos men tis (kom′pəs men′tis), LATIN. of sound mind; sane.

com post (kom′pōst), *n.* mixture of decaying leaves, manure, etc., for improving and fertilizing soil. —*v.t.* make compost of (something). [< Old French < Latin *compositum* put together. Doublet of COMPOSITE.]

com po sure (kəm pō′zhər), *n.* calmness; quietness; self-control.

com pote (kom′pōt), *n.* 1 dish with a supporting stem for fruit, candy, etc. 2 stewed fruit. [< French]

com pound[1] (*adj.* kom′pound, kom pound′; *n.* kom′pound; *v.* kom pound′, kəm pound′), *adj.* 1 having more than one part: *a compound medicine, a compound molecule.* 2 formed by the joining of two or more words: *"Steamship" is a compound word.* 3 formed of many similar parts combined into a single structure: *The pineapple is a compound fruit. The housefly has a compound eye.* —*n.* 1 something made by combining parts; mixture: *Society is a compound of various groups.* 2 word made up of two or more words which keep their separate forms. "Blackbird" is a compound. 3 substance formed by chemical combination of two or more elements in definite proportions by weight: *Water is a compound of hydrogen and oxygen.* —*v.t.* 1 mix; combine: *The druggist compounds medicines.* 2 settle (a quarrel or a debt) by a yielding on both sides. 3 charge, pay, or increase by compound interest. 4 add to; increase; multiply: *I compounded my troubles by arguing with the teacher.* [< Old French *compondre* put together < Latin *componere* < *com-* together + *ponere* put] **—com pound′a ble,** *adj.* **—com pound′er,** *n.*

com pound[2] (kom′pound), *n.* an enclosed yard with buildings in it. [< Malay *kampong* village, enclosure]

compound eye, the eye of certain arthropods, composed of many visual units, such as the large lateral eyes of insects.

compound fraction, complex fraction.

compound fracture, fracture in which a broken bone cuts through the flesh.

compound interest, interest paid on both the original sum of money borrowed or invested and the interest added to it.

compound leaf, leaf composed of two or more leaflets on a common stalk.

compound microscope, microscope having more than one lens, such as one with an eyepiece and an objective.

compound number, quantity expressed in two or more kinds of units. EXAMPLES: 3 ft., 5 in.; 2 hr., 18 min., 40 sec.

compound sentence, sentence having two or more main clauses. EXAMPLE: The winds blew, the rains fell, and the water covered the earth.

com pre hend (kom′pri hend′), *v.t.* 1 understand the meaning of: *He comprehends the principles of an internal-combustion engine.* See synonym study below. 2 include; contain: *Her report comprehends all the facts.* See **include** for synonym study. [< Latin *comprehendere* < *com-* + *prehendere* seize] **—com′pre hend′i ble,** *adj.* **—com′pre hend′ing ly,** *adv.*

Syn. 1 Comprehend, apprehend mean to take hold of something mentally. **Comprehend** means to understand something fully and perfectly: *If you can use a word correctly, you comprehend it.* **Apprehend** means to see something of the meaning of a fact or idea but not all its relationships or implications, and therefore to understand it only partly: *I apprehend the word but cannot use it.*

com pre hen si bil i ty (kom′pri hen′sə bil′ə tē), *n.* intelligibility; comprehensible quality.

com pre hen si ble (kom′pri hen′sə bəl), *adj.* understandable; intelligible. **—com′pre hen′si bly,** *adv.*

com pre hen sion (kom′pri hen′shən), *n.* 1 act or power of understanding; ability to get the meaning: *Arithmetic is beyond the comprehension of a baby.* 2 act or fact of including. 3 comprehensiveness.

com pre hen sive (kom′pri hen′siv), *adj.* 1 of large scope or extent; including much: *The term's work ended with a comprehensive review.* 2 comprehending; understanding: *a comprehensive mind.* **—com′pre hen′sive ly,** *adv.* **—com′pre hen′sive ness,** *n.*

com press (*v.* kəm pres′; *n.* kom′pres), *v.t.* squeeze together; make smaller by pressure. —*n.* 1 pad of dry or wet cloth applied to some part of the body to create pressure or to reduce inflammation. 2 machine for compressing cotton into bales. [< Latin *compressare,* frequentative of *comprimere* < *com-* together + *premere* to press]

com pressed (kəm prest′), *adj.* 1 squeezed together; made smaller by pressure. 2 flattened.

compressed air, air put under extra pressure so that it has a great deal of force when released, especially to operate brakes, drills, etc., or to inflate tires.

com press i bil i ty (kəm pres′ə bil′ə tē), *n.* compressible quality.

com press i ble (kəm pres′ə bəl), *adj.* that can be compressed.

com pres sion (kəm presh′ən), *n.* 1 act or process of compressing. 2 compressed condition. 3 reduction in volume of a gas by the application of pressure, especially in the cylinder of an internal-combustion engine.

com pres sive (kəm pres′iv), *adj.* tending to compress; compressing.

com pres sor (kəm pres′ər), *n.* 1 person or thing that compresses. 2 machine for compressing air, gas, etc.

com prise (kəm prīz′), *v.t.,* **-prised, -pris ing.** 1 consist of; include: *The United States comprises 50 states.* See **include** for synonym study. 2 make up; compose; constitute: *Fifty states comprise the United States. The committee is comprised of five members.* [< Old French *compris,* past participle of *comprendre* < Latin *comprehendere.* See COMPREHEND.]

➤ **Comprise** has recently developed a meaning that is the reverse of its original one, perhaps by being confused with *compose.* Although some people insist that it can mean only "include," more people now use it to mean "be included in."

com pro mise (kom′prə mīz), *v.,* **-mised, -mis ing,** *n.* —*v.t.* 1 settle (a dispute) by agreeing that each will give up a part of what he demands. 2 expose to suspicion, danger, etc.: *compromise one's reputation.* —*v.i.* make a compromise. —*n.* 1 settlement of a dispute by a partial yielding on both sides. 2 result of such a settlement. 3 anything halfway between two different things. 4 an exposing to suspicion, danger, etc,; endangering. [< Old French *compromis* a compromise < Latin *compromissum* < *compromittere* promise together < *com-* together + *promittere* promise] **—com′pro mis′er,** *n.*

Comp ton (komp′tən), *n.* 1 **Arthur H(olly),** 1892-1962, American nuclear physicist. 2 city in SW California, near Los Angeles. 79,000.

comp trol ler (kən trō′lər), *n.* person employed to look after expenditures and accounts; controller. [variant of *controller*]

Comptroller General, *pl.* **Comptrollers General.** the chief accountant of the United States, head of the General Accounting Office.

comp trol ler ship (kən trō′lər ship), *n.* position or rank of a comptroller; controllership.

com pul sion (kəm pul′shən), *n.* 1 a compelling or a being compelled; use of force; force; coercion: *A contract signed under compulsion is not legal.* 2 impulse that is hard to resist: *A compulsion to steal is not normal.* [< Late Latin *compulsionem* < Latin *compellere.* See COMPEL.]

com pul sive (kəm pul′siv), *adj.* 1 compelling. 2 using compulsion. 3 of or having to do with compulsion: *a compulsive desire for neatness.* **—com pul′sive ly,** *adv.* **—com pul′sive ness,** *n.*

com pul sor y (kəm pul′sər ē), *adj.* 1 compelled; required: *Attendance at school is compulsory for children.* 2 compelling; using force. **—com pul′sor i ly,** *adv.*

com punc tion (kəm pungk′shən), *n.* 1 uneasiness of the mind because of wrongdoing; pricking of conscience; remorse. 2 a slight or passing regret. [< Late Latin *compunctionem* < Latin *compungere* to prick, sting < *com-* + *pungere* to prick]

com pu ta tion (kom′pyə tā′shən), *n.* 1 act or method of computing; calculation, especially in numbers. 2 amount computed.

com pu ta tion al (kom′pyə tā′shə nəl), *adj.* of or having to do with computation.

com pute (kəm pyüt′), *v.t.*, **-put ed, -put ing.** find out by using mathematical processes; calculate. [< Latin *computare* < *com-* up + *putare* reckon. Doublet of COUNT¹.] **—com put′a ble,** *adj.*

com put er (kəm pyü′tər), *n.* 1 machine which computes, especially an electronic machine that either solves problems when given certain coded data, or otherwise processes that data. 2 person skilled or trained in computing.

com put er ize (kəm pyü′tə rīz′), *v.t.*, **-ized, -iz ing.** adapt to a computer; operate by means of a computer. **—com put′er i-za′tion,** *n.*

com rade (kom′rad), *n.* 1 companion and friend. 2 person who shares in what another is doing; fellow worker; partner. 3 a fellow member of a union, political party, etc. [< Middle French *camarade* < Spanish *camarada* roommate < *cámara* room < Latin *camera*]

comrade in arms, *pl.* **comrades in arms,** a fellow soldier.

com rade ship (kom′rad ship), *n.* 1 friendship; fellowship. 2 condition of being a comrade.

com sat (kom′sat′), *n.* a communications satellite.

Comte (kôNt), *n.* **Auguste,** 1798-1857, French philosopher, founder of positivism.

con¹ (kon), *adv.* against: *The two debating teams argued the question pro and con.* —*n.* a reason against: *argue the pros and cons of an issue.* [short for Latin *contra* against]

con² (kon), *v.t.*, **conned, con ning.** 1 learn well enough to remember; study. 2 examine carefully; pore over. [Old English *cunnian* test, examine]

con³ (kon), *adj.*, *v.*, **conned, con ning.** SLANG. —*adj.* swindling: *a con man, a con game.* —*v.t.* dupe; swindle: *I was conned into buying an overpriced used car.* [short for *confidence game*]

con-, *prefix.* form of **com-** before *n,* as in *connote,* and before consonants except *b, h, l, m, p, r, w,* as in *concern.*

con., 1 against [for Latin *contra*]. 2 conclusion.

Con., Consul.

Con a kry (kon′ə krē), *n.* seaport and capital of Guinea, in the W part. 197,000. Also, **Konakri.**

con a mo re (kōn ä mōr′ā), ITALIAN. with love; with tenderness.

con cat e nate (kon kat′n āt), *v.*, **-nat ed, -nat ing,** *adj.* —*v.t.* link together. —*adj.* linked together. [< Latin *concatenatum* chained together < *com-* + *catena* chain] **—con cat′e na′tion,** *n.*

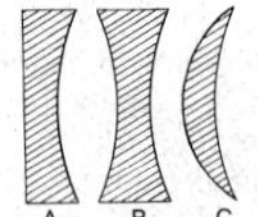

concave lenses:
A. plano-concave;
B. biconcave;
C, concavo-convex

con cave (kon kāv′, kon′kāv, kong′kāv), *adj.* hollow and curved like the inside of a circle or sphere; curving in. [< Latin *concavus* < *com-* + *cavus* hollow] **—con-cave′ly,** *adv.*

con cav i ty (kon kav′ə tē), *n.*, *pl.* **-ties.** 1 concave condition or quality. 2 a concave surface or thing; hollow.

con ca vo-con vex (kon kā′vō kon veks′), *adj.* concave on one side and convex on the other. In a concavo-convex lens, the concave face has the greater curvature.

con ceal (kən sēl′), *v.t.* 1 put or keep out of sight; hide. See **hide** for synonym study. 2 keep secret: *conceal one's identity.* [< Old French *conceler* < Latin *concelare* < *com-* + *celare* hide] **—con ceal′a ble,** *adj.* **—con-ceal′er,** *n.*

con ceal ment (kən sēl′mənt), *n.* 1 a concealing or keeping secret. 2 condition of being hidden or kept secret. 3 means or place for concealing.

con cede (kən sēd′), *v.*, **-ced ed, -ced ing.** —*v.t.* 1 admit as true; acknowledge: *I conceded that I had made a mistake.* 2 allow to have; grant; yield: *They conceded us the right to walk across their land.* —*v.i.* make a concession. [< Latin *concedere* < *com-* + *cedere* to yield] **—con ced′er,** *n.*

con ceit (kən sēt′), *n.* 1 too high an opinion of oneself or of one's ability, importance, etc.; vanity. See **pride** for synonym study. 2 a fanciful notion; witty thought or expression, often a far-fetched one. [< *conceive,* on analogy with *deceit*]

con ceit ed (kən sē′tid), *adj.* having too high an opinion of oneself or one's ability, importance, etc.; vain. **—con ceit′ed ly,** *adv.* **—con ceit′ed ness,** *n.*

con ceiv a ble (kən sē′və bəl), *adj.* that can be conceived or thought of; imaginable. **—con ceiv′a bly,** *adv.*

con ceive (kən sēv′), *v.*, **-ceived, -ceiv ing.** —*v.t.* 1 form in the mind; think up: *The Wright brothers conceived the design of the first successful motor-driven airplane.* See **imagine** for synonym study. 2 have (an idea or feeling). 3 put in words; express: *The warning was conceived in the plainest language.* 4 become pregnant with. —*v.i.* 1 have an idea or feeling; think; imagine: *We cannot conceive of such a thing happening.* 2 become pregnant. [< Old French *conceveir* < Latin *concipere* take in < *com-* + *capere* take] **—con ceiv′er,** *n.*

con cen trate (kon′sən trāt), *v.*, **-trat ed, -trat ing,** *n.* —*v.t.* 1 bring together in one place: *A convex lens is used to concentrate rays of light.* 2 make stronger; intensify: *An acid solution is concentrated when it has very much acid in it.* 3 remove rock, sand, etc., from (metal or ore). —*v.i.* 1 come together in one place. 2 pay close attention; focus the mind *(on* or *upon)*: *She concentrated upon the problem.* —*n.* something that has been concentrated. [< *con-* together + Latin *centrum* center] **—con′cen tra′tor,** *n.*

con cen trat ed (kon′sən trā′tid), *adj.* 1 brought together in one place. 2 (of liquids and solutions) made strong or stronger: *concentrated orange juice.*

con cen tra tion (kon′sən trā′shən), *n.* 1 a concentrating. 2 a being concentrated. 3 close attention: *He gave the problem his full concentration.* 4 amount of substance contained in a given quantity of a solution or mixture.

concentration camp, camp where political enemies, prisoners of war, and interned foreigners are held.

con cen tric (kən sen′trik), *adj.* having the same center: *concentric circles.* **—con-cen′tri cal ly,** *adv.*

con cen tric i ty (kon′sən tris′ə tē), *n.* quality or condition of being concentric.

Con cep ción (kōn′sep syōn′), *n.* city in S central Chile. 187,000.

con cept (kon′sept), *n.* idea of a class of objects; general notion; idea: *the concept of equality.* [< Latin *conceptum* < *concipere.* See CONCEIVE.]

con cep tion (kən sep′shən), *n.* 1 thought; idea; impression: *Your conception of the problem is different from mine.* 2 act or power of conceiving. 3 condition of being conceived. 4 design; plan. 5 a becoming pregnant.

con cep tu al (kən sep′chü əl), *adj.* having to do with concepts or general ideas. **—con-cep′tu al ly,** *adv.*

con cep tu al ize (kən sep′chü ə līz), *v.t.*, *v.i.*, **-ized, -iz ing.** form concepts or ideas about. **—con cep′tu al i za′tion,** *n.*

con cern (kən sėrn′), *v.t.* 1 have to do with; have an interest for; be the business or affair of: *The message is private; it concerns nobody but me.* 2 make anxious; cause to worry; trouble: *I was concerned about the accident.* 3 **concern oneself, a** take an interest; be busy. **b** be troubled or worried; be anxious or uneasy. —*n.* 1 whatever has to do with a person or thing; interest: *Keeping the checking account balanced is my wife's concern.* 2 troubled state of mind; worry; anxiety; uneasiness: *The mother's concern over her sick child kept her awake all night.* See **care** for synonym study. 3 a business company; firm. 4 relation; reference: *Children have little concern with politics.* [< Medieval Latin *concernere* relate to < Late Latin, mingle with, mix < Latin *com-* with + *cernere* sift, distinguish]

con cerned (kən sėrnd′), *adj.* 1 troubled; worried; anxious. 2 interested; affected; involved. 3 busy; occupied.

con cern ing (kən sėr′ning), *prep.* having to do with; regarding; relating to; about.

con cern ment (kən sėrn′mənt), *n.* 1 importance; interest. 2 worry. 3 affair.

con cert (*n.*, *adj.* kon′sərt; *v.* kən sėrt′), *n.* 1 a musical performance in which several musicians or singers take part. 2 agreement; harmony; union. 3 **in concert,** all together: *The rebels acted in concert.* —*adj.* used in concerts; for concerts. —*v.t.* arrange by agreement; plan or make together. [< French < Italian *concerto* < Latin *concertare* strive with < *com-* with + *certare* strive. Doublet of CONCERTO.]

con cert ed (kən sėr′tid), *adj.* 1 arranged by agreement; planned or made together; combined: *a concerted effort.* 2 (in music) arranged in parts for several voices or instruments. **—con cert′ed ly,** *adv.*

con cer ti na (kon′sər tē′nə), *n.* a small musical instrument somewhat like an accordion.

con cert mas ter (kon′sərt mas′tər), *n.* U.S. leader of the strings, usually the first violinist of an orchestra, assisting the conductor.

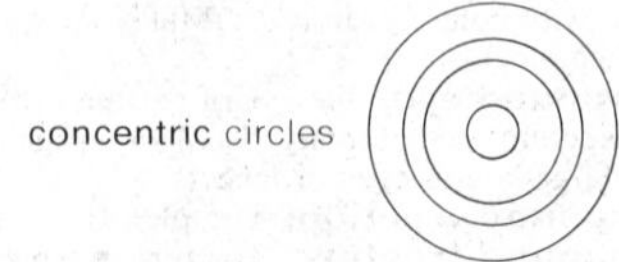

concentric circles

con cert meis ter (kôn tsert′mī′stər), *n.* concertmaster. [< German *Konzertmeister*]

con cer to (kən cher′tō), *n.*, *pl.* **-tos, -ti** (-tē). a long musical composition for one or more principal instruments, such as a violin or piano, accompanied by an orchestra. It usual-

hat, āge, fär; let, ēqual, tėrm;
it, īce; hot, ōpen, ôrder;
oil, out; cup, pu̇t, rüle;
ch, child; ng, long; sh, she;
th, thin; ᴛʜ, then; zh, measure;

ə represents *a* in about, *e* in taken, *i* in pencil, *o* in lemon, *u* in circus.

< = from, derived from, taken from.

ly has three movements. [< Italian. Doublet of CONCERT.]

con ces sion (kən sesh′ən), *n.* 1 a conceding; granting; yielding. 2 anything conceded or yielded; admission; acknowledgment. 3 something conceded or granted by a government or controlling authority; grant. Land or privileges given by a government to a business company are called concessions. 4 U.S. privilege or space leased for a particular use: *the hot-dog concession at the ball park.* [< Latin *concessionem* < *concedere.* See CONCEDE.]

con ces sion aire (kən sesh′ə ner′, kən-sesh′ə nar′), *n.* person, business company, etc., to whom a concession has been granted. [< French *concessionnaire*]

con ces sive (kən ses′iv), *adj.* 1 making or implying concession; yielding. 2 (in grammar) expressing concession. *Though* and *although* are concessive words.

conch (kongk, konch), *n., pl.* **conchs** (kongks), **conch es** (kon′chiz). 1 any of several mollusks of tropical waters having large, spiral shells. 2 its shell. [< Latin *concha* < Greek *konchē*]

con cha (kong′kə), *n.* the central, hollow part of the outer ear. [< Latin, conch]

con chol o gy (kong kol′ə jē), *n.* branch of zoology that deals with the shells of mollusks.

con ci erge (kon′sē ėrzh′; *French* kôɴ-syerzh′), *n.* 1 doorkeeper. 2 janitor. [< French]

con cil i ate (kən sil′ē āt), *v.t.,* **-at ed, -at ing.** 1 win over; soothe: *I conciliated the angry child with a candy bar.* 2 gain (good will, regard, favor, etc.) by friendly acts. 3 bring into harmony; reconcile. [< Latin *conciliatum* brought together, made friendly < *concilium.* See COUNCIL.] **—con cil′i-a′tor,** *n.*

con cil i a tion (kən sil′ē ā′shən), *n.* 1 a winning over or soothing; reconciling. 2 a being won over or soothed; being reconciled.

con cil i a to ry (kən sil′ē ə tôr′ē, kən sil′ē-ə tōr′ē), *adj.* tending to win over, soothe, or reconcile.

con cise (kən sīs′), *adj.* expressing much in few words; brief but full of meaning. See synonym study below. [< Latin *concisum* cut up, cut short < *com-* + *caedere* to cut] **—con cise′ly,** *adv.* **—con cise′ness,** *n.*

Syn. Concise, terse, succinct mean saying much in few words. **Concise,** applying to people or statements, implies that everything unnecessary has been cut out: *The secretary gave a concise report of the meeting.* **Terse,** applying chiefly to statements, implies conciseness that is both pointed and polished: *Lincoln's Gettysburg Address is terse.* **Succinct,** applying to people or statements, implies very compact conciseness: *"Blood, sweat, and tears" is a succinct description of war.*

con clave (kon′klāv, kong′klāv), *n.* 1 a private meeting. 2 (in the Roman Catholic Church) a private meeting of the cardinals for the election of a pope. [< Latin, room that can be locked < *com-* with + *clavis* key]

con clude (kən klüd′), *v.,* **-clud ed, -clud ing.** *—v.t.* 1 bring to an end; finish: *conclude a meeting.* See **end** for synonym study. 2 find out by thinking; reach or arrive at (a decision, judgment, or opinion) by reasoning; infer. See synonym study below. 3 arrange; settle: *conclude a peace treaty.* 4 decide; resolve: *I concluded not to go.* *—v.i.* 1 come to an end; finish; close: *The book concluded happily.* See **end** for synonym study. 2 come to a decision; decide. 3 arrive at an opinion or judgment; resolve. [< Latin *concludere* < *com-* up + *claudere* to close] **—con clud′er,** *n.*

Syn. *v.t.* 2 **Conclude, infer, deduce** mean to arrive at a decision. **Conclude** implies reaching a sound decision on the basis of the evidence at hand: *From the evidence, the jury concluded that the defendant was innocent.* **Infer** also suggests using the evidence at hand but does not necessarily imply that the decision is sound: *From your story we inferred that you went unwillingly.* **Deduce** implies an inference based either on good evidence or on some general principle: *Mother deduced from my loss of appetite what had happened to the cookies.*

con clu sion (kən klü′zhən), *n.* 1 final part; end. 2 the last main division of a speech, essay, etc. 3 decision, judgment, or opinion reached by reasoning; inference. 4 arrangement; settlement: *the conclusion of a peace treaty.* 5 a final result; outcome. 6 **in conclusion,** finally; lastly; to conclude. [< Latin *conclusionem* < *concludere.* See CONCLUDE.]

con clu sive (kən klü′siv), *adj.* decisive; convincing; final. **—con clu′sive ly,** *adv.* **—con clu′sive ness,** *n.*

con coct (kon kokt′, kən kokt′), *v.t.* 1 prepare by mixing with a variety of ingredients: *concoct a drink.* 2 make up; devise: *concoct an excuse.* [< Latin *concoctum* cooked together < *com-* together + *coquere* to cook] **—con coct′er,** *n.*

con coc tion (kon kok′shən, kən kok′shən), *n.* 1 act of concocting. 2 thing concocted.

con com i tance (kon kom′ə təns, kən-kom′ə təns), *n.* accompaniment.

con com i tant (kon kom′ə tənt, kən-kom′ə tənt), *adj.* accompanying; attending: *a concomitant result.* *—n.* an accompanying thing, quality, or circumstance; accompaniment. [< Latin *concomitantem* < *com-* + *comitari* accompany] **—con com′i tant-ly,** *adv.*

con cord (kon′kôrd, kong′kôrd), *n.* 1 agreement; harmony. 2 (in music) a harmonious combination of tones sounded together. 3 treaty. [< Old French < Latin *concordia* < *com-* together + *cordem* heart]

Con cord (kong′kərd), *n.* 1 town in E Massachusetts. The second battle of the Revolutionary War was fought there on April 19, 1775. 16,000. 2 capital of New Hampshire, in the S part. 30,000. 3 city in W California. 85,000.

con cord ance (kon kôrd′ns, kən kôrd′ns), *n.* 1 an alphabetical list of the principal words in a book or in the works of an author with references to the passages in which they occur. 2 agreement; harmony.

con cord ant (kon kôrd′nt, kən kôrd′nt), *adj.* agreeing; harmonious. **—con-cord′ant ly,** *adv.*

con cor dat (kon kôr′dat), *n.* 1 agreement; compact. 2 a formal agreement between a pope and a government about church affairs. [< French]

Concord grape, a large, sweet, bluish-black American variety of grape. [< *Concord,* Massachusetts]

con course (kon′kôrs, kon′kōrs; kong′-kôrs, kong′kōrs), *n.* 1 a running, flowing, or coming together: *the concourse of two rivers.* 2 crowd; throng. 3 place where crowds come: *the main concourse of a railroad station.* 4 boulevard or driveway. [< Old French *concours* < Latin *concursus* < *concurrere* run together. See CONCUR.]

con cres cence (kon kres′ns), *n.* a growing together of parts.

con crete (kon′krēt′, kon krēt′; *esp. for v.t. 2, v.i.* kon krēt′), *adj., n., v.,* **-cret ed, -cret ing.** *—adj.* 1 existing as an actual object, not merely as an idea or as a quality; real. All actual objects are concrete. *A painting is concrete; its beauty is abstract.* 2 not abstract or general; specific; particular: *The lawyer gave concrete examples of the prisoner's cruelty.* 3 naming a thing, especially something perceived by the senses: *"Sugar" and "people" are concrete nouns; "sweetness" and "humanity" are abstract nouns.* 4 made of concrete: *a concrete sidewalk.* 5 formed into a mass; solid; hardened. *—n.* mixture of crushed stone or gravel, sand, cement, and water that hardens as it dries. *—v.t.* 1 cover with concrete. 2 form or mix into a mass; harden into a mass. *—v.i.* become solid; solidify. [< Latin *concretum* grown together < *com-* + *crescere* grow] **—con crete′ly,** *adv.* **—con crete′ness,** *n.*

con cre tion (kon krē′shən), *n.* 1 a forming into a mass; solidifying. 2 a solidified mass; hard formation. Gallstones are concretions.

con cu bi nage (kon kyü′bə nij), *n.* 1 a living together of a man and a concubine. 2 a being a concubine.

con cu bine (kong′kyə bīn, kon′kyə bīn), *n.* 1 woman who lives with a man without being legally married to him. 2 (in certain polygamous societies) a wife having inferior rank, rights, etc. [< Latin *concubina* < *com-* with + *cubare* lie]

con cu pis cence (kon kyü′pə səns), *n.* sensual desire; lust.

con cu pis cent (kon kyü′pə sənt), *adj.* 1 eagerly desirous. 2 lustful; sensual. [< Latin *concupiscentem* < *com-* + *cupere* to desire]

con cur (kən kėr′), *v.i.,* **-curred, -cur ring.** 1 be of the same opinion; agree: *The judges all concurred in giving her the prize.* See **consent** for synonym study. 2 come together; happen at the same time; coincide. 3 work together; cooperate: *The events of your life concur to make you what you are.* [< Latin *concurrere* run together < *com-* + *currere* run]

con cur rence (kən kėr′əns), *n.* 1 the holding of the same opinion; agreement. 2 a happening at the same time. 3 a working together; cooperating. 4 (in geometry) a coming together; meeting at a point.

con cur rent (kən kėr′ənt), *adj.* 1 existing side by side; happening at the same time. 2 agreeing; consistent; harmonious. 3 working together; cooperating. 4 having equal authority or jurisdiction; coordinate. 5 coming together; meeting in a point.*—n.* a concurrent thing or event. **—con cur′rent-ly,** *adv.*

concurrent resolution, U.S. resolution

passed by both branches of a legislature, which expresses an opinion but does not have the force of law.

con cuss (kən kus′), *v.t.* shake or shock, as by a blow.

con cus sion (kən kush′ən), *n.* 1 a sudden, violent shaking; shock: *The concussion caused by the explosion broke many windows.* 2 injury to a soft part of the body, especially the brain, caused by a blow, fall, or other physical shock. [< Latin *concussionem* < *concutere* shake violently < *com-* + *quatere* shake]

con cus sive (kən kus′iv), *adj.* of or accompanied by concussion.

Con dé (kôɴ dā′), *n.* **Prince de.** See **Louis II of Bourbon.**

con demn (kən dem′), *v.t.* 1 express strong disapproval of; denounce: *We condemn cruelty to animals.* 2 pronounce guilty of crime or wrong; convict: *The accused was condemned.* 3 sentence; doom: *condemned to death.* 4 declare not sound or suitable for use: *This bridge was condemned because it is no longer safe.* 5 U.S. take for public use under special provision of the law: *These four blocks have been condemned to make a park.* [< Latin *condemnare* < *com-* + *damnare* cause loss to, condemn < *damnum* loss] **—con dem′na ble,** *adj.* **—con demn′er,** *n.*

con dem na tion (kon′dem nā′shən), *n.* 1 a condemning: *the condemnation of an unsafe bridge.* 2 a being condemned: *His condemnation made him an outcast.* 3 cause or reason for condemning.

con dem na to ry (kən dem′nə tôr′ē, kən dem′nə tōr′ē), *adj.* expressing condemnation; condemning.

con demned (kən demd′), *adj.* pronounced guilty of a crime or wrong.

con den sa tion (kon′den sā′shən), *n.* 1 a condensing. 2 a being condensed. 3 something condensed; condensed mass. A cloud is a condensation of water vapor in the atmosphere. 4 a changing of a gas or vapor to a liquid: *the condensation of steam into water.* 5 (in chemistry) a reaction in which two or more molecules unite to form a larger, denser, and more complex molecule, often with the separation of water or some other simple substance.

con dense (kən dens′), *v.,* **-densed, -dens ing.** *—v.t.* 1 make denser or more compact; compress. 2 make stronger; concentrate: *Light is condensed by means of lenses.* 3 change (a gas or vapor) to a liquid. 4 put into fewer words; express briefly: *She condensed the paragraph into one sentence.* *—v.i.* 1 become denser or more compact. 2 change from a gas or vapor to a liquid. If steam touches cold surfaces, it condenses into water. [< Latin *condensare* < *com-* together + *densus* thick] **—con den′sa ble,** *adj.*

condensed milk, a thick milk prepared by evaporating some of the water from sweetened cow's milk.

con dens er (kən den′sər), *n.* 1 person or thing that condenses something. 2 capacitor. 3 apparatus for changing gas or vapor into a liquid.

con de scend (kon′di send′), *v.i.* 1 come down willingly or graciously to the level of one's inferiors in rank: *The king condescended to eat with the beggars.* 2 grant a favor with a haughty or patronizing attitude. 3 stoop or lower oneself: *condescend to bribery.* [< Late Latin *condescendere* < Latin *com-* together + *descendere* descend]

con de scend ing (kon′di sen′ding), *adj.* 1 stooping to the level of one's inferiors. 2 patronizing. **—con′de scend′ing ly,** *adv.*

con de scen sion (kon′di sen′shən), *n.* 1 pleasantness to inferiors. 2 a haughty or patronizing attitude.

con dign (kən dīn′), *adj.* deserved; adequate; fitting: *condign punishment.* [< Middle French *condigne* < Latin *condignus* very worthy < *com-* + *dignus* worthy]

con di ment (kon′də mənt), *n.* something used to give flavor and relish to food, such as catsup and spices. [< Latin *condimentum* spice < *condire* put up, preserve]

con di tion (kən dish′ən), *n.* 1 state in which a person or thing is: *The condition of the house is better than when I bought it.* See **state** for synonym study. 2 physical fitness; good health: *Athletes must keep in condition.* 3 social position; rank: *Lincoln's parents were poor settlers of humble condition.* 4 thing on which something else depends; thing without which something else cannot be; requirement; prerequisite: *Ability and effort are conditions of success.* 5 something demanded as an essential part of an agreement. 6 **conditions,** *pl.* set of circumstances: *Icy roads make for poor driving conditions.* 7 (in mathematics) a requirement expressed by an open sentence. 8 (in grammar) a clause that expresses or contains a condition. 9 grade calling for reexamination or special work. 10 **on condition that,** if. *—v.t.* 1 put in good condition: *Exercise conditions your muscles.* 2 be a condition of: *Ability and effort condition success.* 3 subject to (a condition): *The gift to the boy was conditioned on his good behavior.* 4 require reexamination or special work of: *He was conditioned in Latin.* 5 shape the behavior of by repeated exposure to particular conditions, with which responses become associated: *This dog has been conditioned to expect food when he hears a bell.* *—v.i.* make conditions. [< Latin *condicionem* agreement < *condicere* agree < *com-* together + *dicere* say]

con di tion al (kən dish′ə nəl), *adj.* 1 depending on something else; not absolute; limited. "You may go if the sun shines" is a conditional promise. 2 expressing or containing a condition. "If the sun shines" is a conditional clause.

con di tion al ly (kən dish′ə nə lē), *adv.* under a condition or conditions: *She accepted conditionally.*

con di tioned (kən dish′ənd), *adj.* 1 put under a condition; subject to certain conditions. 2 produced by conditioning: *a conditioned response.*

conditioned reflex, a learned response which results from conditioning.

con di tion er (kən dish′ə nər), *n.* 1 device or substance that maintains or improves the quality of something. 2 air conditioner.

con dole (kən dōl′), *v.i.,* **-doled, -dol ing.** express sympathy; grieve; sympathize: *Their friends condoled with them at the funeral.* [< Latin *condolere* < *com-* with + *dolere* grieve, suffer]

con do lence (kən dō′ləns), *n.* expression of sympathy: *Their friends sent condolences.*

con do min i um (kon′də min′ē əm), *n.* 1 joint control, especially of two or more countries over the government of another country. 2 country or territory whose government is controlled jointly by two or more others. The Anglo-Egyptian Sudan was a condominium. 3 apartment house in which each apartment is purchased as a piece of real estate and separately valued for property tax purposes. [< New Latin < Latin *com-* with + *dominium* lordship]

con done (kən dōn′), *v.t.,* **-doned, -don ing.** forgive or overlook. [< Latin *condonare* < *com-* up + *donare* give] **—con′do na′tion,** *n.* **—con don′er,** *n.*

con dor (kon′dər), *n.* a large vulture with a ruffed neck and head bare of feathers. Condors live on high mountains in South America and California. [< Spanish *cóndor* < Quechua *cuntur*]

condor
4 ft. long,
wingspread up to
about 10 ft.

con duce (kən düs′, kən dyüs′), *v.i.,* **-duced, -duc ing.** be favorable; lead; contribute: *Darkness and quiet conduce to sleep.* [< Latin *conducere.* See CONDUCT.]

con du cive (kən dü′siv, kən dyü′siv), *adj.* favorable; helpful: *Exercise is conducive to health.* **—con du′cive ness,** *n.*

con duct (*n.* kon′dukt; *v.* kən dukt′), *n.* 1 way of acting; behavior: *win a medal for good conduct.* See synonym study below. 2 direction; management: *the conduct of an office.* *—v.t.* 1 act in a certain way; behave: *At home he is disorderly, but in company he conducts himself well.* 2 direct the course of; manage. See **manage** for synonym study. 3 direct (an orchestra, choir, etc.) as leader. 4 guide; lead. See **guide** for synonym study. 5 transmit (heat, electricity, etc.); be a channel for: *Metals conduct heat and electricity.* *—v.i.* 1 act as conductor, especially of an orchestra. 2 transmit heat, electricity, etc. 3 be the way; pass. [< Latin *conductum* < *conducere* to lead together < *com-* together + *ducere* lead. Doublet of CONDUIT.]

Syn. *n.* 1 **Conduct, behavior, deportment** mean way of acting. **Conduct** applies to a person's way of acting in general: *Your conduct is always admirable.* **Behavior** applies to the way of acting before and toward others, especially in a specific situation: *The students' behavior during the trip showed their consideration for others.* **Deportment** applies to way of acting according to a conventional code: *He was a model of deportment as a schoolboy.*

con duct ance (kən duk′təns), *n.* power of conducting electricity as affected by the shape, length, or material of the conductor. Its unit of measurement is the mho, or reciprocal of the ohm.

con duct i bil i ty (kən duk′tə bil′ə tē), *n.* power of conducting heat, electricity, etc.

con duct i ble (kən duk′tə bəl), *adj.* 1 that can conduct heat, electricity, etc. 2 that can be conducted.

con duc tion (kən duk′shən), *n.* 1 transmission of heat, electricity, etc., by the transferring of energy from one particle to another. 2 a conveying.

con duc tive (kən duk′tiv), *adj.* 1 having conductivity. 2 of conduction.

con duc tiv i ty (kon′duk tiv′ə tē), *n.* power of conducting heat, electricity, etc.

con duc tor (kən duk′tər), *n.* 1 person who conducts; leader or guide; director; manager. 2 director of an orchestra, chorus, etc. 3 person in charge of a railroad train, bus, etc., and its passengers. The conductor usually collects tickets or fares. 4 thing that transmits heat, electricity, light, sound, etc. Copper is a good conductor of heat and electricity.

con du it (kon′dü it, kon′dit), *n.* 1 channel or pipe for carrying liquids long distances. 2 pipe or underground passage for electric wires or cables. [< Old French < Medieval Latin *conductus* a leading, a pipe < Latin *conducere* to lead. Doublet of CONDUCT.]

cone (kōn), *n.* 1 a solid figure with a flat, circular base that tapers to a point at the top. 2 in geometry: **a** a surface traced by a moving straight line constantly touching a fixed plane curve and passing through a fixed point not on the curve. **b** the cone traced when the fixed plane curve is a circle, and a line connecting the vertex of the cone and the center of the base forms a right angle with the base; also called a **right circular cone.** 3 anything shaped like a cone: *an ice-cream cone, the cone of a volcano.* 4 a cone-shaped, scaly growth that bears the seeds on pine, cedar, fir, and other evergreen trees. 5 one of a group of cone-shaped cells of the retina of the eye that responds to light. [< Latin *conus* < Greek *konos* pine cone, cone]

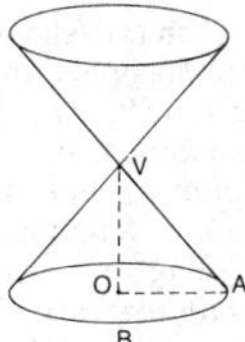

cone
(def. 2a)—V, fixed point or vertex; B, fixed plane curve or base.
(def. 2b)—If B is a circle, O is the center of B, and angle VOA is a right angle, then the cone is a right circular cone.

Con es to ga wagon (kon′ə stō′gə), a covered wagon with broad wheels, used especially by the American pioneers for traveling on soft ground or on the prairie. [< *Conestoga* Valley, Pennsylvania, where they were first built]

co ney (kō′nē), *n., pl.* **-neys.** cony.

conf., 1 compare [for Latin *confer*]. 2 conference.

con fab (kən fab′, kon′fab), *v.,* **-fabbed, -fab bing,** *n.* INFORMAL. —*v.i.* confabulate. —*n.* a confabulating; chat.

con fab u late (kən fab′yə lāt), *v.i.,* **-lat ed, -lat ing.** INFORMAL. talk together informally and intimately; chat. [ultimately < Latin < *com-* together + *fabulari* talk < *fabula* fable] **—con fab′u la′tion,** *n.*

con fect (kən fekt′), *v.t.* make up; devise; contrive: *confect a story.*

con fec tion (kən fek′shən), *n.* 1 piece of candy, candied fruit, jam, etc. 2 an elaborate hat, dress, etc. [< Latin *confectionem* < *confectum* prepared < *com-* up + *facere* make]

con fec tion er (kən fek′shə nər), *n.* person whose business is making or selling candies, ice cream, cakes, etc.

con fec tion er y (kən fek′shə ner′ē), *n., pl.* **-er ies.** 1 candies or sweets; confections. 2 business of making or selling confections. 3 place where confections, ice cream, cakes, etc., are made or sold.

Confed., Confederate.

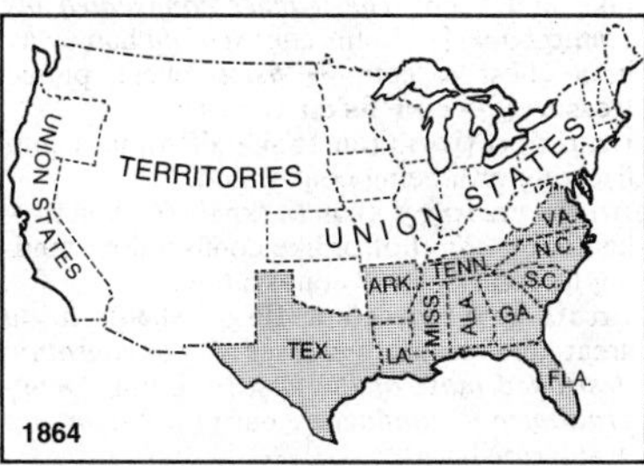

the Confederacy (def. 4)—the shaded area

con fed er a cy (kən fed′ər ə sē), *n., pl.* **-cies.** 1 union of countries or states; group of people joined together for a special purpose; confederation; federation. 2 league; alliance. 3 conspiracy. 4 **the Confederacy,** group of eleven southern states that seceded from the United States in 1860 and 1861.

con fed er ate (*n., adj.* kən fed′ər it; *v.* kən fed′ə rāt′), *n., adj., v.,* **-at ed, -at ing.** —*n.* 1 country, person, etc., joined with another for a special purpose; ally. 2 accomplice; partner in crime; accessory. 3 **Confederate,** person who lived in, supported, or fought for the Confederacy. —*adj.* 1 joined together for a special purpose; allied. 2 **Confederate,** of or belonging to the Confederacy: *the Confederate uniform.* —*v.t., v.i.* join together for a special purpose; ally. [< Late Latin *confoederatum* united in a league < Latin *com-* together + *foedus* league]

Confederate States of America, the Confederacy.

con fed e ra tion (kən fed′ə rā′shən), *n.* 1 act of joining together in a league or alliance. 2 a being united in a league or alliance. 3 group of countries, states, etc., joined together for a special purpose; league; alliance. 4 **the Confederation,** the union of the thirteen American states from 1781 to 1789 under the Articles of Confederation.

con fer (kən fėr′), *v.,* **-ferred, -fer ring.** —*v.i.* consult together; exchange ideas; talk things over: *The president often confers with his advisers.* See **consult** for synonym study. —*v.t.* give; award; bestow: *The general conferred a medal on the brave soldier.* See **give** for synonym study. [< Latin *conferre* < *com-* together + *ferre* bring] **—con fer′rer,** *n.*

con fer ee (kon′fə rē′), *n.* 1 U.S. person who takes part in a conference. 2 person on whom something is conferred. Also, **conferree.**

con fer ence (kon′fər əns), *n.* 1 meeting of interested persons to discuss a particular subject: *A conference was called to discuss getting a playground for the school.* 2 act of taking counsel; talking something over; consultation with a person or a group of persons: *The teacher was in conference with parents after school.* 3 association of schools, churches, etc., joined together for some special purpose.

con fer ment (kən fėr′mənt), *n.* conferral.

con fer ral (kən fėr′əl), *n.* a conferring; bestowal.

con fer ree (kon′fə rē′), *n.* conferee.

hat, āge, fär; let, ēqual, tėrm;
it, īce; hot, ōpen, ôrder;
oil, out; cup, pu̇t, rüle;
ch, child; ng, long; sh, she;
th, thin; ᴛʜ, then; zh, measure;

ə represents *a* in about, *e* in taken, *i* in pencil, *o* in lemon, *u* in circus.

< = from, derived from, taken from.

con fess (kən fes′), *v.t.* 1 own up to; acknowledge; admit: *confess a weakness for sweets. I confess you are right.* See **admit** for synonym study. 2 tell (one's sins) to a priest in order to obtain forgiveness. 3 hear (a person) tell his sins in order to obtain forgiveness. —*v.i.* 1 acknowledge or admit to a crime, fault, etc. 2 make known one's sins to a priest. 3 act as a confessor. [< Medieval Latin *confessare* < Latin *com-* + *fateri* confess]

con fess ed ly (kən fes′id lē), *adv.* by acknowledgment; admittedly.

con fes sion (kən fesh′ən), *n.* 1 an owning up; acknowledgment; admission. 2 admission of guilt. 3 the telling of one's sins to a priest in order to obtain forgiveness. 4 thing confessed. 5 acknowledgment of belief; profession of faith. 6 belief acknowledged; creed.

con fes sion al (kən fesh′ə nəl), *n.* 1 a small booth in which a priest hears confessions. 2 practice of confessing sins to a priest. —*adj.* of or having to do with confession.

con fes sor (kən fes′ər), *n.* 1 person who confesses. 2 priest who has the authority to hear confessions. 3 person who acknowledges belief.

con fet ti (kən fet′ē), *n.* bits of colored paper thrown about at carnivals, weddings, parades, etc. [< Italian, plural, comfits]

con fi dant (kon′fə dant′, kon′fə dant), *n.* person trusted with one's secrets, private affairs, etc.; close friend.

con fi dante (kon′fə dant′, kon′fə dant), *n.* a confidant.

con fide (kən fīd′), *v.,* **-fid ed, -fid ing.** —*v.t.* 1 tell as a secret: *He confided his troubles to his brother.* 2 hand over (a task, person, etc.) in trust; give to another for safekeeping: *The collection of dues is confided to the treasurer.* —*v.i.* 1 show trust by imparting secrets, private affairs, etc.: *She confided in her friend.* 2 put trust or have faith *(in): You can confide in his good faith.* [< Latin *confidere* < *com-* completely + *fidere* to trust] **—con fid′er,** *n.*

con fi dence (kon′fə dəns), *n.* 1 firm belief or trust; faith: *We have no confidence in a liar.* 2 firm belief in oneself and one's abilities; self-confidence. 3 boldness; too much boldness: *Although he could not swim, he dived into the water with confidence.* 4 a feeling of trust; assurance that a person will not tell others what is said: *The story was told to me in strict confidence.* 5 thing told as a secret. 6 (in a parliamentary form of government) trust, as expressed by the majority vote of a legislature, in the actions and policy of the prime minister and his cabinet.

confidence game, fraud in which the swindler persuades his victim to trust him.

confidence man, swindler who persuades his victim to trust him.

con fi dent (kon′fə dənt), *adj.* 1 firmly believing; certain; sure. See **sure** for synonym study. 2 sure of oneself and one's abilities. 3 too bold; too sure. —*n.* a close, trusted friend; confidant. —**con′fi dent ly,** *adv.*

con fi den tial (kon′fə den′shəl), *adj.* 1 told or written as a secret: *a confidential report.* 2 showing confidence. 3 trusted with secrets, private affairs, etc.: *a confidential secretary.* See **familiar** for synonym study. —**con′fi den′tial ly,** *adv.* —**con′fi den′tial ness,** *n.*

con fid ing (kən fī′ding), *adj.* trustful; trusting. —**con fid′ing ly,** *adv.*

con fig u ra tion (kən fig′yə rā′shən), *n.* the relative position of parts; manner of arrangement; form; shape; outline: *Geographers study the configuration of the surface of the earth.*

con fig u ra tion al (kən fig′yə rā′shə nəl), *adj.* of or having to do with configuration. —**con fig′u ra′tion al ly,** *adv.*

con fig u ra tive (kən fig′yər ə tiv, kən fig′yə rā′tiv), *adj.* configurational.

con fine (*v.* kən fīn′; *n.* kon′fīn), *v.,* **-fined, -fin ing,** *n.* —*v.t.* 1 keep within limits; restrict: *She confined her reading to biography.* 2 keep indoors; shut in. 3 imprison. 4 **be confined,** give birth to a child. —*n.* Often, **confines,** *pl.* boundary; border; limit: *These people have never been beyond the confines of their own valley.* [< Middle French *confiner* < *confins,* plural, bounds < Latin *confinium* < *com-* together + *finis* end, border] —**con fin′er,** *n.*

con fine ment (kən fīn′mənt), *n.* 1 a confining. 2 a being confined. 3 imprisonment. 4 period a mother is confined to bed during and after childbirth.

con firm (kən fėrm′), *v.t.* 1 prove to be true or correct; make certain: *confirm a rumor.* See synonym study below. 2 approve by formal consent; approve; consent to: *The Senate confirmed the treaty.* 3 make firmer; strengthen: *A sudden storm confirmed my decision not to leave.* 4 admit to full membership in a church or synagogue after required study and preparation. [< Latin *confirmare* < *com-* + *firmus* firm] —**con firm′a ble,** *adj.*

Syn. 1 **Confirm, corroborate, substantiate, authenticate** mean to prove to be true or genuine. **Confirm** implies removing doubt by means of facts or statements that cannot be doubted: *The Mayor confirmed the report that taxes would be reduced.* **Corroborate** implies the strengthening of proof by additional evidence or statements: *Finding the weapon corroborates the police theory.* **Substantiate** implies offering sufficient and solid evidence: *This theory has now been substantiated by the results of many experiments.* **Authenticate** implies the evidence of someone who knows: *Handwriting experts authenticated the will.*

con fir ma tion (kon′fər mā′shən), *n.* 1 a confirming. 2 thing that confirms; proof. 3 ceremony of admitting a person to full membership in a church or synagogue after required study and preparation.

con firm a to ry (kən fėr′mə tôr′ē, kən fėr′mə tōr′ē), *adj.* confirming.

con firmed (kən fėrmd′), *adj.* 1 firmly established; proved: *a confirmed rumor.* 2 habitual; constant; permanent: *a confirmed bachelor, a confirmed invalid.* 3 admitted to the full privileges of a church.

con fis cate (kon′fə skāt), *v.t.,* **-cat ed, -cat ing.** 1 seize for the public treasury: *The new government confiscated the property of all the deposed leaders.* 2 seize by authority; take and keep: *The teacher confiscated my comic book.* [< Latin *confiscatum* laid away in a chest < *com-* + *fiscus* chest, public treasury] —**con′fis ca′tor,** *n.*

con fis ca tion (kon′fə skā′shən), *n.* a confiscating or a being confiscated.

con fis ca to ry (kən fis′kə tôr′ē, kən fis′kə tōr′ē), *adj.* 1 of or like confiscation; tending to confiscate. 2 confiscating.

con fla gra tion (kon′flə grā′shən), *n.* a great and destructive fire: *A conflagration destroyed most of the city.* [< Latin *conflagrationem* < *conflagrare* burn up < *com-* up + *flagrare* burn]

con flict (*n.* kon′flikt; *v.* kən flikt′), *n.* 1 fight or struggle. See **fight** for synonym study. 2 direct opposition; disagreement; clash: *A conflict of opinions divided the members into two groups.* —*v.i.* be directly opposed; disagree; clash. [< Latin *conflictus* < *confligere* to clash < *com-* together + *fligere* strike]

con flu ence (kon′flü əns), *n.* 1 a flowing together: *the confluence of two rivers.* 2 place where two or more rivers, streams, etc., come together. 3 a coming together of people or things; throng.

con flu ent (kon′flü ənt), *adj.* flowing or running together; blending into one: *confluent rivers.* [< Latin *confluentem* < *com-* together + *fluere* flow]

con flux (kon′fluks), *n.* confluence.

con form (kən fôrm′), *v.i.* 1 act according to law or rule; be in agreement with generally accepted standards of business, conduct, or worship: *If you wish to be a member, you must conform to the rules of our club.* 2 become the same in form; correspond in form or character. 3 (in Great Britain) comply with the usages of the Church of England. —*v.t.* 1 make similar. 2 adapt; adjust. [< Latin *conformare* < *com-* + *forma* a shape] —**con form′er,** *n.*

con form a ble (kən fôr′mə bəl), *adj.* 1 similar. 2 adapted; adjusted. 3 in agreement; harmonious. 4 obedient; submissive: *conformable to another's wishes.* —**con form′a ble ness,** *n.* —**con form′a bly,** *adv.*

con for mal (kən fôr′məl), *adj.* 1 having the same scale in all directions at any given point: *a conformal map projection.* 2 (in mathematics) leaving unchanged the size of all angles.

con form ance (kən fôr′məns), *n.* act of conforming; conformity.

con for ma tion (kon′fôr mā′shən), *n.* 1 form of a thing resulting from the arrangement of its parts; structure; shape. 2 a symmetrical arrangement of the parts of a thing. 3 a conforming; adaptation.

con form ism (kən fôr′miz′əm), *n.* conformity.

con form ist (kən fôr′mist), *n.* 1 person who conforms. 2 (in Great Britain) a person who complies with the usages of the Church of England.

con form i ty (kən fôr′mə tē), *n., pl.* **-ties.** 1 action in agreement with generally accepted standards of business, conduct, or worship; fitting oneself and one's actions to the ideas of others; compliance. 2 likeness; similarity; correspondence. 3 obedience; submission. 4 (in Great Britain) compliance with the usages of the Church of England.

con found (kon found′, kən found′ *for 1, 2, 4, 5;* kon′found′ *for 3*), *v.t.* 1 confuse; mix up: *The shock confounded me.* 2 surprise and puzzle. 3 damn: *Confound your impudence.* 4 ARCHAIC. make uneasy and ashamed. 5 ARCHAIC. defeat; overthrow. [< Old French *confondre* < Latin *confundere* pour together, mix up, confuse] —**con found′er,** *n.*

con found ed (kon′foun′did, kən foun′did), *adj.* 1 damned. 2 hateful; detestable. —**con′found′ed ly,** *adv.*

con fra ter ni ty (kon′frə tėr′nə tē), *n., pl.* **-ties.** group of men united for some purpose or in a profession.

con frere (kon′frer), *n.* a fellow member; colleague. [< Old French < Medieval Latin *confrater* < Latin *com-* together + *frater* brother]

con front (kən frunt′), *v.t.* 1 meet face to face; stand facing. 2 face boldly; oppose. 3 bring face to face; place before: *The prosecuting attorney confronted the accused with the forged check.* [< Old French *confronter* < Medieval Latin *confrontare* < Latin *com-* together + *frontem* forehead] —**con′fron ta′tion,** *n.*

Con fu cian (kən fyü′shən), *adj.* of or having to do with Confucius, his teachings, or his followers. —*n.* follower of Confucius or his teachings.

Con fu cian ism (kən fyü′shə niz′əm), *n.* the moral teachings of Confucius and his followers.

Con fu cius (kən fyü′shəs), *n.* 551?-479 B.C., Chinese philosopher and moral teacher.

con fuse (kən fyüz′), *v.t.,* **-fused, -fus ing.** 1 throw into disorder; mix up. 2 bewilder; perplex: *So many people talking to me at once confused me.* 3 be unable to tell apart; mistake (one thing or person for another): *People often confuse this girl with her twin sister.* 4 make uneasy and ashamed; embarrass. See synonym study below. [< Latin *confusum* poured together, mixed up < *com-* together + *fundere* to pour] —**con fus′ing ly,** *adv.*

Syn. 4 **Confuse, embarrass, disconcert** mean to disturb a person. **Confuse** means to make so bewildered that one cannot think clearly or act sensibly: *Honking at a driver who has stalled his car often confuses him.* **Embarrass** means to make so self-conscious that one cannot talk or act naturally: *Meeting strangers embarrasses me.* **Disconcert** means to disturb so suddenly or badly that for a moment one loses his poise and ability to handle the situation: *The unexpected question disconcerted the speaker.*

con fus ed ly (kən fyü′zid lē, kən fyüzd′lē), *adv.* in a confused manner.

con fu sion (kən fyü′zhən), *n.* 1 act or fact of confusing. 2 confused condition; disorder: *There was confusion in the busy street after the accident.* 3 failure to distinguish clearly. 4 bewilderment. 5 uneasiness and shame.

con fu ta tion (kon′fyə tā′shən), *n.* 1 a confuting. 2 thing that confutes.

con fute (kən fyüt′), *v.t.,* **-fut ed, -fut ing.** 1 prove (an argument, testimony, etc.) to be false or incorrect: *The lawyer confuted the testimony of the witness by showing actual photographs of the accident.* 2 prove (a person) to be wrong; overcome by argument: *The speaker confuted his opponents by facts and logic.* [< Latin *confutare*] —**con fut′er,** *n.*

Cong., 1 Congregation. 2 Congregational. 3 Congress. 4 Congressional.

con ga (kong′gə), *n.* a fast Cuban ballroom dance, often performed by a line of dancers and requiring a kick on every fourth beat. [< American Spanish]

con geal (kən jēl′), *v.t., v.i.* 1 change from a liquid to a solid by freezing; freeze. 2 thicken; stiffen; coagulate. [< Old French *congeler* < Latin *congelare* < *com-* up + *gelare* to freeze] **—con geal′ment,** *n.*

con ge ner (kon′jə nər), *n.* person or thing of the same kind or class. [< Latin, of the same kind]

con gen ial (kən jē′nyəl), *adj.* 1 having similar tastes and interests; getting on well together: *congenial companions.* 2 agreeable; suitable: *congenial work.* [< *con-* + Latin *genialis* < *genius* spirit] **—con gen′ial ly,** *adv.*

con ge ni al i ty (kən jē′nē al′ə tē, kən-jē′nyal′ə tē), *n.* congenial quality.

con gen i tal (kən jen′ə təl), *adj.* 1 present at birth: *a congenital deformity.* 2 inborn; deep-seated: *congenital dislikes.* [< Latin *congenitus* born with < *com-* + *genitus* born] **—con gen′i tal ly,** *adv.*

con ger (kong′gər), *n.* a large ocean eel that is caught for food along the coasts of Europe. [< Latin < Greek *gongros*]

conger eel, conger.

con ger ies (kon′jər ēz), *n. sing. or pl.* collection; heap; mass. [< Latin < *congerere* bring together]

con gest (kən jest′), *v.t.* 1 fill too full; overcrowd: *a street congested with traffic.* 2 cause too much blood or mucus to gather in (one part of the body). *—v.i.* 1 become overcrowded. 2 become too full of blood or mucus. [< Latin *congestum* brought together < *com-* + *gerere* carry]

con ges tion (kən jes′chən), *n.* 1 an overcrowded or congested condition: *congestion of traffic.* 2 too much blood or mucus in one part of the body: *nasal congestion.*

con ges tive (kən jes′tiv), *adj.* 1 accompanied or produced by congestion. 2 causing congestion.

con glom er ate (*adj., n.* kən glom′ər it; *v.* kən glom′ə rāt′), *v.,* **-at ed, -at ing.** *—adj.* 1 made up of various parts or materials gathered into a mass. 2 gathered into a rounded mass; clustered. *—n.* 1 mixture of various materials or elements, clustered together without assimilation. 2 a miscellaneous group of unrelated corporations operating under a single ownership. 3 rock consisting of pebbles, gravel, etc., held together by a cementing material. *—v.t., v.i.* gather in a rounded mass; collect together. [< Latin *conglomeratum* rolled together < *com-* + *glomus* ball]

con glom e ra tion (kən glom′ə rā′shən), *n.* a mixed-up mass of various things or persons; mixture.

Con go (kong′gō), *n.* 1 **Congo River,** river in central Africa, flowing from SE Zaïre to the Atlantic. 2900 mi. Also, **Zaïre River.** 2 **Democratic Republic of the,** former name of **Zaïre,** country in central Africa. 3 **Republic of,** country in W central Africa on the Atlantic, a member of the French Community. 900,000 pop.; about 132,000 sq. mi. *Capital:* Brazzaville. See **Zaïre** for map.

congo eel, an eellike amphibian that has very small, weak legs; congo snake. Congo eels live in swampy regions in the southeastern United States.

Con go lese (kong′gə lēz′), *n., pl.* **-lese,** *adj.* *—n.* native or inhabitant of the Congo region or either of the Congo republics. *—adj.* of or having to do with any of these regions.

congo snake, congo eel.

con grat u late (kən grach′ə lāt), *v.t.,* **-lat ed, -lat ing.** express one's pleasure at the happiness or good fortune of; felicitate: *Congratulate the bride and groom.* [< Latin *congratulatum* congratulated < *com-* + *gratus* pleasing]

con grat u la tion (kən grach′ə lā′shən), *n.* 1 a congratulating. 2 **congratulations,** *pl.* expression of pleasure at another's happiness or good fortune.

con grat u la to ry (kən grach′ə lə tôr′ē, kən grach′ə lə tōr′ē), *adj.* expressing pleasure at another's happiness or good fortune: *a congratulatory note.*

con gre gate (kong′grə gāt), *v.i., v.t.,* **-gat ed, -gat ing.** come or bring together into a crowd or mass; assemble. [< Latin *congregatum* flocked together < *com-* + *gregem* flock] **—con′gre ga′tor,** *n.*

con gre ga tion (kong′grə gā′shən), *n.* 1 a coming together into a crowd or mass; assembling. 2 group of people gathered together for religious worship or instruction. 3 a gathering of people or things; assembly. 4 (in the Roman Catholic Church) a religious community or order with a common rule with or without solemn vows.

con gre ga tion al (kong′grə gā′shə nəl), *adj.* 1 of or done by a congregation. 2 **Congregational,** of Congregationalism or Congregationalists.

con gre ga tion al ism (kong′grə gā′shə-nə liz′əm), *n.* 1 system of church government in which each individual church governs itself. 2 **Congregationalism,** principles and system of organization of a Protestant denomination in which each individual church governs itself.

Con gre ga tion al ist (kong′grə gā′shə-nə list), *n.* 1 member of a Congregational church. 2 believer of Congregationalism. *—adj.* of or having to do with Congregationalism.

con gress (kong′gris), *n.* 1 the lawmaking body of a nation, especially of a republic. 2 **Congress, a** the national lawmaking body of the United States, consisting of the Senate and House of Representatives, with members elected from each state. **b** its session. 3 a formal meeting of representatives of interested groups to discuss some subject; conference: *a medical congress.* 4 a meeting. [< Latin *congressus* < *congredi* come together < *com-* together + *gradi* go]

con gres sion al (kən gresh′ə nəl), *adj.* 1 of or having to do with a congress. 2 Often, **Congressional,** of or having to do with Congress. **—con gres′sion al ly,** *adv.*

con gress man (kong′gris mən), *n., pl.* **-men.** Often, **Congressman.** member of Congress, especially of the House of Representatives.

Congress of Industrial Organizations, the CIO. See **AFL-CIO.**

con gress wom an (kong′gris wu̇m′ən), *n., pl.* **-wom en.** Often, **Congresswoman.** a woman member of Congress, especially of the House of Representatives.

Con greve (kon′grēv′, kong′grēv′), *n.* **William,** 1670-1729, English dramatist.

con gru ence (kən grü′əns, kong′grü əns), *n.* a being congruent.

con gru en cy (kən grü′ən sē, kong′grü ən-sē), *n.* congruence.

hat, āge, fär; let, ēqual, tėrm;
it, īce; hot, ōpen, ôrder;
oil, out; cup, pu̇t, rüle;
ch, child; ng, long; sh, she;
th, thin; ꟻH, then; zh, measure;

ə represents *a* in about, *e* in taken,
i in pencil, *o* in lemon, *u* in circus.

< = from, derived from, taken from.

con gru ent (kən grü′ənt, kong′grü ənt), *adj.* 1 (in geometry) coinciding exactly when superimposed; having the same size and shape: *congruent triangles.* 2 in harmony; agreeing. [< Latin *congruentem* coming together, agreeing] **—con gru′ent ly,** *adv.*

con gru i ty (kən grü′ə tē), *n., pl.* **-ties.** 1 a being congruous. 2 point of agreement. 3 (in geometry) the exact coincidence of lines, angles, figures, etc.

con gru ous (kong′grü əs), *adj.* 1 in harmony; agreeing. 2 fitting; appropriate. **—con′gru ous ly,** *adv.* **—con′gru ous-ness,** *n.*

con ic (kon′ik), *adj.* conical. *—n.* conic section.

con i cal (kon′ə kəl), *adj.* 1 shaped like a cone: *conical mountains.* 2 of a cone. **—con′i cal ly,** *adv.*

con ics (kon′iks), *n.* part of geometry dealing with conic sections.

conic section, a curve formed by the intersection of a plane with a right circular cone. Circles, ellipses, parabolas, and hyperbolas are conic sections.

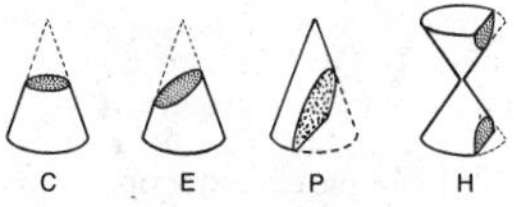

conic section—four types of conic sections: C, circle; E, ellipse; P, parabola; H, hyperbola

co nid i um (kə nid′ē əm), *n., pl.* **-nid i a** (-nid′ē ə), a one-celled, asexual spore produced in certain fungi. [< New Latin < Greek *konis* dust]

con i fer (kon′ə fər, kō′nə fər), *n.* any of a large order of trees and shrubs of the gymnosperm class, most of which are evergreen and all of which bear cones. The pine, fir, spruce, hemlock, larch, and yew are conifers. [< Latin, cone-bearing < *conus* cone + *ferre* to bear]

co nif er ous (kō nif′ər əs), *adj.* 1 bearing cones. 2 belonging to or having to do with the conifers.

conj., 1 conjugation. 2 conjunction.

con jec tur al (kən jek′chər əl), *adj.* 1 involving conjecture. 2 inclined to conjecture. **—con jec′tur al ly,** *adv.*

con jec ture (kən jek′chər), *n., v.,* **-tured, -tur ing.** *—n.* 1 formation of an opinion admittedly without sufficient evidence for proof; guessing. 2 a guess. *—v.t., v.i.* guess. See **guess** for synonym study. [< Latin *conjectura* < *conjicere* discuss, throw together < *com-* together + *jacere* throw] **—con-jec′tur a ble,** *adj.* **—con jec′tur er,** *n.*

con join (kən join′), *v.t., v.i.* join together; unite; combine. **—con join′er,** *n.*

con joint (kən joint′, kon′joint), *adj.* 1 joined together; united; combined.

2 formed by two or more in combination; joint. **—con joint′ly,** *adv.*

con ju gal (kon′jə gəl), *adj.* 1 of or having to do with marriage. 2 of husband and wife. [< Latin *conjugalis* < *conjuga* wife < *conjungere* join together < *com-* + *jungere* join] **—con′ju gal ly,** *adv.*

con ju gate (*v.* kon′jə gāt; *adj., n.* kon′jə-git, kon′jə gāt), *v.,* **-gat ed, -gat ing,** *adj., n.* —*v.t.* 1 give the forms of (a verb) according to a systematic arrangement. 2 join together; couple. —*v.i.* 1 give the conjugation of a verb. 2 (in biology) unite or fuse in conjugation. —*adj.* 1 joined together; coupled. 2 (in grammar) derived from the same root. —*n.* word derived from the same root as another. [< Latin *conjugatum* yoked together < *com-* + *jugum* yoke]

con ju ga tion (kon′jə gā′shən), *n.* 1 a systematic arrangement of the forms of a verb. 2 group of verbs having similar forms in such an arrangement. 3 act of giving the forms of a verb according to such an arrangement. 4 a joining together; coupling. 5 a being joined; combination. 6 **a** a kind of reproduction in which two one-celled organisms unite temporarily to exchange nuclear material and then separate, as in various protozoa. **b** the fusion of male and female gametes to form a zygote, as in various algae.

con ju ga tion al (kon′jə gā′shə nəl), *adj.* of or having to do with conjugation. **—con′ju ga′tion al ly,** *adv.*

con junct (kən jungkt′, kon′jungkt), *adj.* joined together; united. [< Latin *conjunctum* joined together < *com-* + *jungere* join]

con junc tion (kən jungk′shən), *n.* 1 word that connects words, phrases, clauses, or sentences. *And* and *but* are coordinate conjunctions; *both . . . and* and *either . . . or* are correlative conjunctions; *after* and *because* are subordinating conjunctions. 2 a joining together; union; combination: *Rain in conjunction with hot weather helped the crops grow.* 3 a coming together, especially of events or circumstances. 4 the apparent nearness of two or more heavenly bodies to each other.

con junc ti va (kon′jungk tī′və), *n., pl.* **-vas, -vae** (-vē). the mucous membrane that forms the inner surface of the eyelids and the front part of the eyeball. [< New Latin]

con junc tive (kən jungk′tiv), *adj.* 1 joining together; connective; uniting; combining. 2 joined together; joint; united; combined. 3 like a conjunction; like that of a conjunction. *Then* is a conjunctive adverb. 4 connecting words, phrases, or clauses in both meaning and construction. *And, also,* and *moreover* are conjunctive conjunctions. —*n.* a conjunctive word; conjunction. **—con junc′tive ly,** *adv.*

con junc ti vi tis (kən jungk′tə vī′tis), *n.* inflammation of the conjunctiva.

con junc ture (kən jungk′chər), *n.* 1 combination of events or circumstances. 2 a critical state of affairs; crisis.

con ju ra tion (kon′jə rā′shən), *n.* 1 an invoking by a sacred name; conjuring. 2 the practice of magic. 3 a magic form of words used in conjuring; magic spell. 4 ARCHAIC. a solemn appeal.

con jure (kon′jər, kun′jər *for v.t. 1-3, v.i.;* kən jür′ *for v.t. 4*), *v.,* **-jured, -jur ing.** —*v.t.* 1 compel (a spirit, devil, etc.) to appear or disappear by a set form of words. 2 cause to appear or happen as if by magic: *conjure up a whole meal in a jiffy.* 3 cause to appear in the mind: *conjure a vision.* 4 make a solemn appeal to; request earnestly; entreat. —*v.i.* 1 summon a devil, spirit, etc. 2 practice magic. 3 perform tricks by skill and quickness in moving the hands. [< Old French *conjurer* < Latin *conjurare* make a compact < *com-* together + *jurare* swear]

con jur er or **con jur or** (kon′jər ər, kun′jər ər), *n.* 1 person who performs tricks with quick, deceiving movements of the hands; juggler. 2 magician.

conk (kongk), SLANG. —*v.i.* **conk out,** break down; stall. —*v.t.* hit, especially on the head. —*n.* a blow on the head. [origin uncertain]

conk er (kong′kər), *n.* BRITISH. a horse chestnut.

Conn., Connecticut.

con nate (kon′āt), *adj.* 1 existing from birth or origin. 2 (in biology) united into one body, as leaves at the base. [< Latin *connatum* born with < *com-* + *nasci* be born] **—con′nate ly,** *adv.*

con nect (kə nekt′), *v.t.* 1 join (one thing to another); link (two things together); fasten together; unite: *connect a garden hose to a faucet. The telephone operator failed to connect us.* 2 think of (one thing) with (another); associate in the mind. 3 join in some business or interest; bring into some relation: *I am connected with the advertising division of the company.* —*v.i.* 1 be connected; become connected: *This room connects with that one.* 2 (of trains, buses, etc.) be scheduled so that passengers can change from one to another without delay. [< Latin *connectere* < *com-* together + *nectere* to tie] **—con nec′tor, con nect′er,** *n.*

con nect ed (kə nek′tid), *adj.* 1 joined together; fastened together. 2 joined in orderly sequence: *connected ideas.* 3 having ties and associates: *They are well connected socially.* **—con nect′ed ly,** *adv.*

Con nect i cut (kə net′ə kət), *n.* 1 one of the northeastern states of the United States. 3,032,000 pop.; 5000 sq. mi. *Capital:* Hartford. *Abbrev.:* Conn. 2 **Connecticut River,** river flowing between New Hampshire and Vermont, through Massachusetts and Connecticut, and into Long Island Sound. 407 mi.

connecting rod, bar connecting two or more moving parts in a machine, such as the rod which transmits motion from the piston to the crankshaft in an internal-combustion engine.

con nec tion (kə nek′shən), *n.* 1 act of connecting. 2 a being joined together or connected; union. 3 thing that connects; connecting part. 4 any kind of relation with another: *I have no connection with that firm.* 5 a linking of persons or things together; linking together of words or ideas in proper order. 6 group of people associated in some way. 7 an influential, wealthy, or prominent associate or friend: *I got a summer job through my friend's connection.* 8 the scheduled meeting of trains, ships, etc., so that passengers can change from one to the other without delay. 9 a related person; relative: *She is a connection of ours by marriage.* 10 a religious denomination. **11 in connection with,** together with; in regard to. Also, BRITISH **connexion.**

con nec tive (kə nek′tiv), *adj.* that connects; tending to connect. —*n.* 1 anything that connects. 2 word used to connect words, phrases, and clauses. Conjunctions and relative pronouns are connectives. **—con nec′tive ly,** *adv.*

connective tissue, tissue that connects, supports, or encloses other tissues and organs in the body.

con nex ion (kə nek′shən), *n.* BRITISH. connection.

con ning tower (kon′ing), tower on the deck of a submarine, used as an entrance and as a place for observation. [*conning,* present participle of obsolete *con* direct the steering of a ship < Old French *conduire* to conduct]

con nip tion (kə nip′shən), *n.* U.S. INFORMAL. fit of hysterical excitement. [origin uncertain]

con niv ance (kə nī′vəns), *n.* a conniving; pretended ignorance or secret encouragement of wrongdoing.

con nive (kə nīv′), *v.i.,* **-nived, -niv ing.** 1 avoid noticing something wrong; give aid to wrongdoing by not telling of it or by helping it secretly: *Some city officials connived at gambling.* 2 cooperate secretly: *The spy connived with the enemy.* [< Latin *connivere* shut the eyes, wink] **—con niv′er,** *n.*

con nois seur (kon′ə sėr′), *n.* a critical judge of art or of matters of taste; expert: *a connoisseur of antique furniture.* [< Old French < *connoistre* know < Latin *cognoscere.* See COGNITION.]

con no ta tion (kon′ə tā′shən), *n.* 1 a connoting. 2 what is suggested in addition to the literal meaning.

con no ta tive (kon′ə tā′tiv, kə nō′tə tiv), *adj.* 1 having connotation; connoting. 2 having to do with connotation. **—con′no ta tive ly,** *adv.*

con note (kə nōt′), *v.t.,* **-not ed, -not ing.** suggest in addition to the literal meaning; imply. *Portly, corpulent,* and *obese* all mean fleshy; but *portly* connotes dignity; *corpulent,* bulk; and *obese,* an unpleasant excess of fat. [< Medieval Latin *connotare* < Latin *com-* with + *notare* to note]

con nu bi al (kə nü′bē əl, kə nyü′bē əl), *adj.* of or having to do with marriage; conjugal. [< Latin *connubialem* < *connubium* marriage < *com-* with + *nubere* marry] **—con nu′bi al ly,** *adv.*

co noid (kō′noid), *adj.* shaped like a cone. —*n.* a cone-shaped figure.

co noi dal (kə noi′dl), *adj.* conoid.

con quer (kong′kər), *v.t.* 1 get by fighting; win in war: *conquer a country.* 2 overcome by force; defeat; vanquish; subdue: *conquer an enemy.* See **defeat** for synonym study. 3 get the better of; overcome: *conquer a bad habit.* —*v.i.* be victorious; be the conqueror. [< Old French *conquerre* < Latin *conquirere* < *com-* + *quaerere* seek] **—con′quer a ble,** *adj.*

con quer or (kong′kər ər), *n.* person who conquers; victor.

con quest (kon′kwest, kong′kwest), *n.* 1 act of conquering. See **victory** for synonym study. 2 thing conquered; land, people, etc., conquered. 3 person whose love or favor has been won. [< Old French *conqueste* < *conquerre.* See CONQUER.]

con quis ta dor (kon kwis′tə dôr, kon-kē′stə dôr), *n., pl.* **-dors, -do res** (-dôr′ēz). 1 a Spanish conqueror in North or South America during the 1500's. 2 conqueror. [< Spanish]

Con rad (kon′rad), *n.* **Joseph,** 1857-1924, British novelist, born in the Ukraine of Polish parents.

con san guin e ous (kon′sang gwin′ē əs),

hat, āge, fär; let, ēqual, tėrm;
it, īce; hot, ōpen, ôrder;
oil, out; cup, pu̇t, rüle;
ch, child; ng, long; sh, she;
th, thin; ᴛʜ, then; zh, measure;

ə represents *a* in about, *e* in taken, *i* in pencil, *o* in lemon, *u* in circus.

< = from, derived from, taken from.

adj. descended from the same parent or ancestor; related by blood. [< Latin *consanguineus* < *com-* together + *sanguinem* blood] **—con′san guin′e ous ly,** *adv.*

con san guin i ty (kon′sang gwin′ə tē), *n.* relationship by descent from the same parent or ancestor; relationship by blood.

con science (kon′shəns), *n.* 1 sense of right and wrong; ideas and feelings within a person that warn him of what is wrong. 2 **in conscience** or **in all conscience, a** reasonably; fairly. **b** surely; certainly. [< Latin *conscientia* < *conscire.* See CONSCIOUS.] **—con′science less,** *adj.*

conscience money, money paid by a person whose conscience bothers him because of some dishonesty.

con science-strick en (kon′shəns strik′-ən), *adj.* suffering from a feeling of having done wrong.

con sci en tious (kon′shē en′shəs), *adj.* 1 careful to do what one knows is right; controlled by conscience. 2 done with care to make it right; painstaking: *conscientious work.* **—con′sci en′tious ly,** *adv.* **—con′sci en′tious ness,** *n.*

conscientious objector, person whose beliefs do not let him take up arms in warfare.

con scion a ble (kon′shə nə bəl), *adj.* according to conscience; just. **—con′scion a bly,** *adv.*

con scious (kon′shəs), *adj.* 1 having experience; aware; knowing: *conscious of a sharp pain.* See synonym study below. 2 able to feel or perceive; awake: *About five minutes after fainting I became conscious again.* 3 known to oneself; felt: *conscious guilt.* 4 intentional; deliberate: *a conscious lie.* 5 self-conscious; shy; embarrassed. [< Latin *conscius* < *conscire* be conscious < *com-* + *scire* know] **—con′scious ly,** *adv.*

Syn. 1 **Conscious, aware** mean knowing that something exists. **Conscious** emphasizes the idea of realizing or knowing in one's mind that one sees, feels, hears, etc., something, either physically or emotionally: *I was conscious of great uneasiness.* **Aware** emphasizes the idea of merely noticing something one sees, smells, hears, tastes, feels, or is told: *I was aware that someone was talking, but not conscious of what was said.*

con scious ness (kon′shəs nis), *n.* 1 condition of being conscious; awareness. People and animals have consciousness; plants and stones do not. 2 all the thoughts and feelings of a person or group of people: *the moral consciousness of our generation.* 3 awareness of what is going on about one: *A severe emotional shock can make a person lose consciousness for a time.*

con script (*v.* kən skript′; *adj., n.* kon′skript), *v.t.* 1 compel by law to serve in the armed forces; draft. 2 take for government use: *The dictator proposed to conscript both capital and labor.* —*adj.* conscripted; drafted. —*n.* a conscripted soldier or sailor. [< Latin *conscriptum* enlisted < *com-* + *scribere* write]

con scrip tion (kən skrip′shən), *n.* 1 compulsory service of men in the armed forces; draft. 2 act or system of forcing contributions of money, labor, or other service to the government or as the government directs.

con se crate (kon′sə krāt), *v.,* **-crat ed, -crat ing,** *adj.* —*v.t.* 1 set apart as sacred; make holy; sanctify: *The new chapel in the church was consecrated by the bishop.* 2 make an object of veneration or cherished regard; hallow: *Time has consecrated these customs.* 3 devote to a purpose; dedicate: *She consecrated her life to helping the sick.* See **devote** for synonym study. —*adj.* ARCHAIC. consecrated. [< Latin *consecratum* made sacred < *com-* + *sacer* sacred] **—con′se cra′tor,** *n.*

con se cra tion (kon′sə krā′shən), *n.* 1 a consecrating. 2 a being consecrated. 3 ordination to a sacred office, especially to that of bishop.

con sec u tive (kən sek′yə tiv), *adj.* 1 following without interruption; successive: *Monday, Tuesday, and Wednesday are consecutive days of the week.* See **successive** for synonym study. 2 made up of parts that follow each other in logical order: *a consecutive account of an accident.* [< Latin *consecutum* followed closely < *com-* + *sequi* follow] **—con sec′u tive ly,** *adv.* **—con sec′u tive ness,** *n.*

con sen sus (kən sen′səs), *n.* general agreement; opinion of all or most of the people consulted. [< Latin < *consentire.* See CONSENT.]

con sent (kən sent′), *v.i.* give approval or permission; agree. See synonym study below. —*n.* approval; permission; assent. [< Latin *consentire* < *com-* with + *sentire* feel, think] **—con sent′er,** *n.*

Syn. *v.i.* **Consent, assent, concur** mean to agree. **Consent** means to agree *to* something by approving willingly or by giving in to the wishes of others: *I consented to run for president.* **Assent** means to agree *with* something by accepting it or expressing approval of it: *She assented to the suggested change in plans.* **Concur,** more formal, means to agree *with* others about something, by having the same opinion: *The majority concurred in the decision to raise the dues.*

con se quence (kon′sə kwens, kon′sə-kwəns), *n.* 1 result or effect; outcome: *The consequence of my fall was a broken leg.* See **effect** for synonym study. 2 a logical result; deduction; inference. 3 importance: *This matter is of little consequence.* See **importance** for synonym study. 4 importance in rank or position; distinction: *a person of great consequence.* 5 **take the consequences,** accept what happens because of one's action.

con se quent (kon′sə kwent, kon′sə-kwənt), *adj.* 1 following as an effect; resulting: *My long illness and consequent absence put me far behind in my work.* 2 following as a logical conclusion. 3 logically consistent. —*n.* 1 thing that follows something else; result; effect. 2 (in mathematics) the second term of a ratio. [< Latin *consequentem* < *com-* + *sequi* follow]

con se quen tial (kon′sə kwen′shəl), *adj.* 1 following as an effect; resulting. 2 self-important; pompous. **—con′se quen′tial ly,** *adv.* **—con′se quen′tial ness,** *n.*

con se quent ly (kon′sə kwent′lē, kon′sə-kwənt lē), *adv.* as a consequence; as a result; therefore. See **therefore** for synonym study.

con ser va tion (kon′sər vā′shən), *n.* 1 a preserving from harm or decay; protecting from loss or from being used up: *the conservation of forests.* 2 the official protection and care of forests, rivers, and other natural resources.

con ser va tion ist (kon′sər vā′shə nist), *n.* person who believes in and advocates conservation of the forests, rivers, and other natural resources of a country.

conservation of energy, (in physics) the principle that the total amount of energy in the universe, or in any closed system, does not vary, although energy can be changed from one form into another.

conservation of mass or **conservation of matter,** (in physics) the principle that the total mass of any closed system remains unchanged by reactions within the system. Thus, in a chemical reaction, matter is neither created nor destroyed but changed from one form of the substance to another.

con serv a tism (kən sėr′və tiz′əm), *n.* inclination to keep things as they are or return to what they were in the past; opposition to change, especially change in traditions.

con serv a tive (kən sėr′və tiv), *adj.* 1 inclined to keep things as they are or return to what they were in the past; opposed to change, especially any change in traditions. 2 not inclined to take risks; cautious; moderate: *conservative business methods.* 3 Often, **Conservative.** of or belonging to a political party that opposes major changes in national institutions. 4 free from novelties and fads: *clothes of a conservative style.* 5 having the power to preserve from harm or decay; conserving; preserving. 6 **Conservative,** of or having to do with a modern branch of Judaism regarded as being midway between Orthodox and Reform Judaism. —*n.* 1 person opposed to change. 2 Often, **Conservative.** member of a conservative political party, especially the Conservative Party in Great Britain or Canada. 3 means of preserving. **—con serv′a tive ly,** *adv.* **—con serv′a tive ness,** *n.*

Conservative Party, 1 a political party in Great Britain that favors existing national institutions or a return to some of those recently existing. 2 a similar political party in Canada.

con ser va toire (kən sėr′və twär′), *n.* school for instruction in music; conservatory. [< French]

con ser va tor (kon′sər vā′tər, kən sėr′və-tər), *n.* preserver; guardian.

con serv a to ry (kən sėr′və tôr′ē, kən-sėr′və tōr′ē), *n., pl.* **-ries.** 1 school for instruction in music. 2 greenhouse or glass-enclosed room for growing and displaying plants and flowers.

con serve (*v.* kən sėrv′; *n.* kon′sėrv′, kən-sėrv′), *v.,* **-served, -serv ing,** *n.* —*v.t.* 1 keep from harm or decay; protect from loss or from being used up; preserve. 2 preserve (fruit) in sugar, often as jam. —*n.* Often, **conserves,** *pl.* fruit preserved in sugar, often as jam. [< Latin *conservare* < *com-* with + *servare* to preserve] **—con serv′er,** *n.*

con sid er (kən sid′ər), *v.t.* 1 think about in order to decide: *Take time to consider the problem.* See synonym study below. 2 think to be; think of as; deem: *We consider Shakespeare a great poet.* 3 allow for; take into account: *This watch runs very well, if you consider how old it is.* 4 be thoughtful of (others and their feelings); respect. 5 think highly of; esteem. 6 ARCHAIC. look at carefully. —*v.i.* think carefully; reflect; ponder: *She considered fully before accepting the offer.* [< Latin *considerare,* originally, examine the stars < *com-* + *sideris* star; with reference to augury]

Syn. *v.t.* 1 **Consider, study, weigh** mean to think about something in order to decide. **Consider** means to think something over, to give it some careful thought before making a decision about it: *I considered going to college.* **Study** means to think out, to consider with serious attention to details: *He studied ways to support himself.* **Weigh** means to balance in the mind, to consider carefully both or all sides of an idea or action: *I weighed the idea of going to the local college.*

con sid er a ble (kən sid′ər ə bəl), *adj.* 1 worth thinking about; important: *a considerable responsibility.* 2 not a little; much: *a considerable sum of money.*

➜ **considerable, considerably.** More than with most adjective-adverb pairs, there is a tendency in speech to substitute the adjective *considerable* for the adverb *considerably.* In formal and informal writing the distinction is observed: *The teacher's explanation helped them considerably* (modifies verb *helped*). *The teacher's explanation was of considerable help to them* (modifies noun *help*).

con sid er a bly (kən sid′ər ə blē), *adv.* a good deal; much. ➜ See **considerable** for usage note.

con sid er ate (kən sid′ər it), *adj.* thoughtful of others and their feelings. See **thoughtful** for synonym study. **—con sid′er ate ly,** *adv.* **—con sid′er ate ness,** *n.*

con sid er a tion (kən sid′ə rā′shən), *n.* 1 act of thinking about in order to decide; attention; deliberation: *careful consideration given to a question.* 2 something thought of as a reason: *Price and quality are two considerations in buying anything.* 3 thoughtfulness for others and their feelings; regard; respect. 4 money or other payment; compensation. 5 importance. 6 **in consideration of, a** because of. **b** in return for. 7 **take into consideration,** allow for; take into account. 8 **under consideration,** being thought about.

con sid ered (kən sid′ərd), *adj.* carefully thought out: *in my considered opinion.*

con sid er ing (kən sid′ər ing), *prep.* taking into account; making allowance for: *Considering her age, the little girl reads well.* —*adv.* taking everything into account: *He does very well, considering.*

con sign (kən sīn′), *v.t.* 1 hand over; deliver: *The dog was consigned to the pound.* See **commit** for synonym study. 2 send; transmit: *We will consign the goods to you by express.* 3 set apart; assign. [< Latin *consignare* furnish with a seal < *com-* + *signum* seal] **—con sign′a ble,** *adj.*

con sign ee (kon′sī nē′), *n.* person or company to whom goods are consigned.

con sign er (kən sī′nər), *n.* consignor.

con sign ment (kən sīn′mənt), *n.* 1 act of consigning. 2 something consigned, especially a shipment sent to a person or company for safekeeping or sale. 3 **on consignment,** consigned to a person or company with the understanding that the goods will not be paid for until sold.

con sign or (kən sī′nər, kon′sī nôr′), *n.* person or company that consigns goods to another. Also, **consigner.**

con sist (kən sist′), *v.i.* 1 be made up; be formed: *A week consists of seven days.* 2 be in harmony; agree. 3 **consist in,** be contained in; be made up of: *He believes that happiness consists in being easily satisfied.* [< Latin *consistere* come to a stand, remain, exist < *com-* + *sistere* to stand]

con sist ence (kən sis′təns), *n.* consistency.

con sist en cy (kən sis′tən sē), *n., pl.* **-cies.** 1 degree of firmness or stiffness: *Frosting for a cake must be of the right consistency to spread easily without dripping.* 2 firmness; stiffness. 3 a keeping to the same principles, course of action, etc.: *consistency of purpose.* 4 agreement or harmony among the parts or elements of a thing; accordance.

con sist ent (kən sis′tənt), *adj.* 1 keeping or inclined to keep to the same principles, course of action, etc. 2 in agreement; in accord; in keeping; compatible: *Driving an automobile at high speed on a rainy night is not consistent with safety.* 3 (in mathematics) having at least one common solution, as of two or more equations or inequalities. **—con sist′ent ly,** *adv.*

con sis tor y (kən sis′tər ē), *n., pl.* **-tor ies.** 1 a church council or court, especially a council of the cardinals of the Roman Catholic Church presided over by the pope. 2 meeting of such a council or court. 3 place where it meets. [< Latin *consistorium* place of assembly < *consistere.* See CONSIST.]

con so la tion (kon′sə lā′shən), *n.* 1 a consoling. 2 a being consoled. 3 a comforting person, thing, or event. —*adj.* between losers in an earlier round of a tournament: *a consolation match.*

con sol a to ry (kən sol′ə tôr′ē, kən sol′ə-tōr′ē), *adj.* consoling; comforting.

con sole[1] (kən sōl′), *v.t.,* **-soled, -sol ing.** ease the grief or sorrow of; comfort: *I tried to console the lost child.* See **comfort** for synonym study. [< Middle French *consoler* < Latin *consolari* < *com-* + *solari* soothe] **—con sol′a ble,** *adj.* **—con sol′er,** *n.*

con sole[2] (kon′sōl), *n.* 1 part of an organ containing the manuals, stops, and pedals. 2 panel of buttons, switches, dials, etc., used to control electrical or electronic equipment in a computer, missile, etc. 3 a radio, television, or phonograph cabinet, made to stand on the floor. [< French, beam, support]

con sol i date (kən sol′ə dāt), *v.,* **-dat ed, -dat ing.** —*v.t.* 1 combine into one; unite: *The small farms were consolidated for greater efficiency.* 2 make solid or firm; solidify. 3 make secure; strengthen: *The Romans consolidated their conquest of Britain by building a wall to keep out the raiding Scots.* —*v.i.* 1 combine; merge: *The three banks consolidated and formed a single, large bank.* 2 become solid or firm. [< Latin *consolidatum* made solid < *com-* + *solidus* solid]

con sol i dat ed (kən sol′ə dā′tid), *adj.* united; combined: *consolidated efforts.*

consolidated school, school for pupils from several school districts.

con sol i da tion (kən sol′ə dā′shən), *n.* 1 a consolidating or a being consolidated; strengthening; combination. 2 a business merger.

con sols (kon′solz, kən solz′), *n.pl.* bonds of the government of Great Britain. [short for *consolidated annuities*]

con som mé (kon′sə mā′), *n.* a clear soup made by boiling meat in water. [< French]

con so nance (kon′sə nəns), *n.* 1 harmony; agreement; accordance. 2 harmony of sounds; simultaneous combination of tones in music that is agreeable to the ear.

con so nant (kon′sə nənt), *n.* 1 a speech sound formed by completely or partially stopping the breath. The two consonants in *ship* are spelled by the letters *sh* and *p.* 2 any letter or combination of letters representing such a sound. All the letters that are not vowels are consonants. —*adj.* 1 in agreement; in accord; harmonious. 2 harmonious in tone or sound. 3 consonantal. [< Latin *consonantem* harmonizing < *com-* together + *sonare* to sound] **—con′so nant ly,** *adv.*

con so nan tal (kon′sə nan′tl), *adj.* having to do with a consonant or its sound.

con sort (*n.* kon′sôrt; *v.* kən sôrt′), *n.* 1 husband or wife. The husband of a queen is sometimes called the prince consort. 2 ship accompanying another. 3 an associate. —*v.i.* 1 keep company; associate: *consorting with a rough gang.* 2 agree; accord. [< Middle French < Latin *consortem* sharer < *com-* with + *sortem* lot]

con sor ti um (kən sôr′shē əm), *n., pl.* **-ti a** (-shē ə). 1 partnership; association. 2 agreement among bankers of several nations to give financial aid to another nation. 3 group, association, etc., formed by such an agreement. [< Latin < *consortem* consort]

con spec tus (kən spek′təs), *n.* 1 a general or comprehensive view. 2 a short summary or outline of a subject; digest; résumé. [< Latin < *conspicere* look at. See CONSPICUOUS.]

con spic u ous (kən spik′yü əs), *adj.* 1 easily seen; clearly visible: *A traffic sign should be conspicuous.* See **prominent** for synonym study. 2 worthy of notice; remarkable: *Lincoln is a conspicuous example of a poor boy who succeeded.* [< Latin *conspicuus* visible < *conspicere* look at < *com-* + *specere* look] **—con spic′u ous ly,** *adv.* **—con spic′u ous ness,** *n.*

con spir a cy (kən spir′ə sē), *n., pl.* **-cies.** 1 act of conspiring; secret planning with others to do something unlawful or wrong, especially against a government, public personage, etc. 2 a plot or intrigue.

con spir a tor (kən spir′ə tər), *n.* person who conspires; plotter.

con spir a to ri al (kən spir′ə tôr′ē əl, kən-spir′ə tōr′ē əl), *adj.* having to do with conspiracy or conspirators.

con spire (kən spīr′), *v.,* **-spired, -spir ing.** —*v.i.* 1 plan secretly with others to do something unlawful or wrong; plot. See **plot** for synonym study. 2 act together: *All things conspired to make her birthday a happy one.* —*v.t.* plot (something evil or unlawful). [< Latin *conspirare,* originally, breathe together, < *com-* + *spirare* breathe] **—con-spir′er,** *n.*

const., (in mathematics) constant.

con sta ble (kon′stə bəl, kun′stə bəl), *n.* 1 a police officer, especially in a township, district, or rural area of the United States. 2 BRITISH. policeman. 3 a chief officer of a household, court, army, etc., especially in the Middle Ages. 4 keeper of a royal fortress or castle. [< Old French *conestable* < Late Latin *comes stabuli* count of the stable; later, chief household officer]

Con sta ble (kun′stə bəl), *n.* **John,** 1776-1837, English painter.

con stab u lar y (kən stab′yə ler′ē), *n., pl.*

hat, āge, fär; let, ēqual, tėrm;
it, īce; hot, ōpen, ôrder;
oil, out; cup, pu̇t, rüle;
ch, child; ng, long; sh, she;
th, thin; ᴛʜ, then; zh, measure;

ə represents *a* in about, *e* in taken, *i* in pencil, *o* in lemon, *u* in circus.

< = from, derived from, taken from.

-lar ies, *adj.* —*n.* 1 constables of a district or country. 2 police force organized like an army. —*adj.* of or having to do with constables.

Con stance (kon′stəns), *n.* **Lake,** lake in Switzerland, Austria, and Germany. 46 mi. long; 205 sq. mi.

con stan cy (kon′stən sē), *n.* 1 firmness in belief or feeling; steadfastness; determination. 2 faithfulness; loyalty. 3 a being always the same; absence of change.

con stant (kon′stənt), *adj.* 1 never stopping; continuous; incessant: *Three days of constant rain soaked everything.* 2 happening often or again and again; repeated: *The clock made a constant ticking sound.* 3 always the same; not changing: *If you walk due north, your direction is constant.* 4 faithful; loyal; steadfast: *a constant friend.* See **faithful** for synonym study. —*n.* 1 thing that is always the same; value or quantity that does not change. 2 a mathematical quantity assumed to be invariable throughout a given discussion. [< Latin *constantem* standing firm < *com-* + *stare* to stand] **—con′stant ly,** *adv.*

Con stan ța (kən stän′tsə), *n.* seaport in SE Romania, on the Black Sea. 172,000.

con stan tan (kon′stən tan), *n.* alloy of copper and nickel, used in rheostats and thermocouples.

Con stan tine (kon′stən tēn′), *n.* city in NE Algeria. 255,000.

Con stan tine I (kon′stən tēn′, kon′stən-tīn), Constantine the Great.

Constantine the Great, A.D. 288?-337, Roman emperor from A.D. 306 to 337, who granted liberty of worship to Christians and established the city of Constantinople.

Con stan ti no ple (kon′stan tə nō′pəl), *n.* former name of **Istanbul.** It was the capital of the Byzantine Empire and later the capital of Turkey. See **Byzantine Empire** for map.

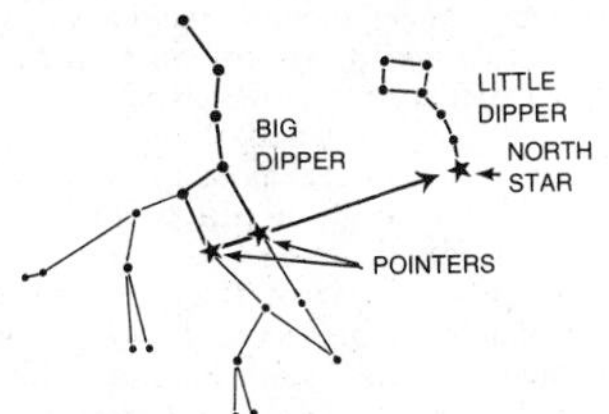

constellation (def. 1)—two constellations

con stel la tion (kon′stə lā′shən), *n.* 1 group of stars usually having a geometric shape. The Big Dipper is the easiest constellation to locate. 2 division of the heavens occupied by such a group. 3 a brilliant gathering. [< Late Latin *constellationem* < Latin *com-* together + *stella* star]

con ster na tion (kon′stər nā′shən), *n.* great dismay; paralyzing terror: *To our consternation the train rushed on toward the burning bridge.* See **dismay** for synonym study. [< Latin *consternationem* < *consternare* terrify]

con sti pate (kon′stə pāt), *v.t.,* **-pat ed, -pat ing.** cause constipation in. [< Latin *constipatum* pressed together < *com-* + *stipare* press. Doublet of COSTIVE.]

con sti pa tion (kon′stə pā′shən), *n.* condition in which it is difficult to empty the bowels.

con stit u en cy (kən stich′ü ən sē), *n., pl.* **-cies.** 1 the voters in a district; constituents: *The congressman was reelected to office by his constituency.* 2 this district. 3 group of supporters, customers, etc.

con stit u ent (kən stich′ü ənt), *adj.* 1 forming a necessary part; that composes: *Flour, liquid, salt, and yeast are constituent parts of bread.* 2 appointing; electing. 3 having the power to make or change a political constitution: *a constituent assembly.* —*n.* 1 part of a whole; necessary part; component. See **element** for synonym study. 2 voter: *The congresswoman received many letters from her constituents.*

con sti tute (kon′stə tüt, kon′stə tyüt), *v.t.,* **-tut ed, -tut ing.** 1 make up; form; comprise: *Seven days constitute a week.* 2 set up; establish: *Courts are constituted by law to dispense justice.* 3 give legal form to. 4 appoint; elect: *The group constituted one member as its leader.* [< Latin *constitutum* established < *com-* + *statuere* set up]

con sti tu tion (kon′stə tü′shən, kon′stə-tyü′shən), *n.* 1 way in which a person or thing is organized; nature; make-up: *A person with a good constitution is strong and healthy.* 2 system of fundamental principles according to which a nation, state, or group is governed: *The United States has a written constitution.* 3 document stating these principles. 4 **the Constitution,** the written set of fundamental principles by which the United States is governed. It was drawn up in 1787, ratified in 1788, and put into effect in 1789. Since then 26 amendments have been added to it. 5 an appointing, making, or forming. 6 a setting up; establishment.

con sti tu tion al (kon′stə tü′shə nəl, kon′stə tyü′shə nəl), *adj.* 1 of or in the constitution of a person or thing; inherent: *A constitutional weakness makes him subject to colds.* 2 of, in, or according to the constitution of a nation, state, or group: *The Supreme Court must decide whether this law is constitutional.* 3 adhering to or supporting a constitution: *a constitutional party.* 4 for one's health. —*n.* walk or other exercise taken for one's health.

con sti tu tion al i ty (kon′stə tü′shə-nal′ə tē, kon′stə tyü′shə nal′ə tē), *n.* accordance with the constitution of a nation, state, or group: *The constitutionality of the new law was disputed.*

con sti tu tion al ly (kon′stə tü′shə nə lē, kon′stə tyü′shə nə lē), *adv.* 1 in or by constitution; naturally. 2 according to the constitution.

constitutional monarchy, monarchy in which the ruler has only those powers given to him by the constitution and laws of the nation.

con sti tu tive (kon′stə tü′tiv, kon′stə-tyü′tiv), *adj.* 1 having power to establish or enact. 2 making up or forming a thing; constituent. 3 essential. **—con′sti tu′tive-ly,** *adv.*

con strain (kən strān′), *v.t.* 1 force; compel: *The principal was constrained to punish the rude child.* 2 confine; imprison. 3 repress; restrain. [< Old French *constreindre* < Latin *constringere* < *com-* together + *stringere* pull tightly] **—con strain′er,** *n.*

con strained (kən strānd′), *adj.* 1 forced. 2 restrained; stiff; unnatural: *a constrained smile.* **—con strain′ed ly,** *adv.*

con straint (kən strānt′), *n.* 1 a holding back of natural feelings; forced or unnatural manner; embarrassed awkwardness. 2 force; compulsion. 3 confinement. 4 restraint.

con strict (kən strikt′), *v.t.* draw together; contract; compress: *A tourniquet stops the flow of blood by constricting the blood vessels.* [< Latin *constrictum* constricted < *com-* together + *stringere* pull tightly]

con stric tion (kən strik′shən), *n.* 1 a constricting; compression; contraction. 2 a feeling of tightness; constricted condition: *a constriction in one's chest.* 3 a constricted part. 4 something that constricts.

con stric tive (kən strik′tiv), *adj.* contracting; compressing.

con stric tor (kən strik′tər), *n.* 1 any snake that kills its prey by squeezing it with its coils. The boa is a constrictor. 2 person or thing that constricts. 3 muscle that constricts a part of the body.

con struct (kən strukt′), *v.t.* 1 put together; fit together; build. See **make** for synonym study. 2 draw (a geometrical figure) so as to fulfill given conditions. [< Latin *constructum* piled up < *com-* + *struere* to pile] **—con-struc′tor,** *n.*

con struc tion (kən struk′shən), *n.* 1 act of constructing; building. 2 way in which a thing is constructed. 3 thing constructed; building. 4 arrangement, connection, or relation of words in a sentence, clause, phrase, etc. 5 meaning; explanation; interpretation: *You put an unfair construction on what I said.*

con struc tion al (kən struk′shə nəl), *adj.* having to do with construction.

con struc tion ist (kən struk′shə nist), *n.* person who gives a certain interpretation to laws, a constitution, etc.

con struc tive (kən struk′tiv), *adj.* 1 tending to construct; building up; helpful: *People appreciate constructive suggestions, not destructive criticisms.* 2 having to do with construction; structural. 3 not directly expressed; inferred. **—con struc′tive ly,** *adv.* **—con struc′tive ness,** *n.*

con strue (kən strü′), *v.t.,* **-strued, -stru ing.** 1 show the meaning of; explain; interpret: *Different judges may construe the same law differently.* 2 analyze the arrangement and connection of words in (a sentence, clause, phrase, etc.). [< Latin *construere* construct] **—con stru′a ble,** *adj.*

con sul (kon′səl), *n.* 1 official appointed by a government to live in a foreign city to look after the business interests of his own country and to protect citizens of his country who are traveling or living there. 2 either of the two chief magistrates of the ancient Roman republic. 3 one of the three chief magistrates of the French republic from 1799 to 1804. [< Latin, probably originally, one who consults the senate]

con su lar (kon′sə lər), *adj.* 1 of or belonging to a consul. 2 serving as a consul; having the duties of a consul.

con su late (kon′sə lit), *n.* 1 the official residence or the offices of a consul. 2 duties, authority, and position of a consul. 3 term of office of a consul. 4 Often, **Consulate.** government by consuls. France was governed by a consulate from 1799 to 1804.

consul general, *pl.* **consuls general.** consul of the highest rank stationed at an important place or having authority over several other consuls.

con sul ship (kon′səl ship), *n.* 1 duties, authority, and position of a consul. 2 term of office of a consul.

con sult (kən sult′), *v.t.* 1 seek information or advice from; refer to: *Consult a dictionary for the meaning of a word.* 2 take into consideration; have regard for: *A good teacher consults the interests of the class.* —*v.i.* exchange ideas; talk things over; confer: *I consulted with my lawyer.* See synonym study below. [< Latin *consultare* < *consulere* take counsel, consult] **—con sult′er,** *n.*

Syn. *v.i.* **Consult, confer** mean to talk something over with someone in order to make a decision. **Consult** means to talk over something of importance with another or others who are in a position to give wise advice: *She decided to consult with her attorney before buying the property.* **Confer** means to exchange ideas, opinions, or information with another, usually as an equal: *The manager conferred with the committee of employees.*

con sult ant (kən sult′nt), *n.* 1 person who gives professional or technical advice. 2 person who consults another.

con sul ta tion (kon′səl tā′shən), *n.* 1 act of consulting; seeking information or advice. 2 a meeting to exchange ideas or talk things over; conference.

con sult a tive (kən sul′tə tiv), *adj.* of or having to do with consultation; advisory.

con sume (kən süm′), *v.,* **-sumed, -sum ing.** —*v.t.* 1 use up; spend; expend: *A student consumes much of his time in studying.* 2 eat or drink up. 3 destroy; burn up: *A huge fire consumed the entire forest.* 4 waste (time, money, etc.); exhaust; squander. 5 **consumed with,** absorbed by (curiosity, envy, etc.). —*v.i.* waste away; be destroyed. [< Latin *consumere* < *com-* + *sumere* take up] **—con sum′a ble,** *adj.*

con sum er (kən sü′mər), *n.* 1 person who uses food, clothing, or anything grown or made by producers. 2 person or thing that consumes.

consumer goods, goods produced or used to satisfy human wants directly, as clothing or food.

con sum er ism (kən sü′mə riz′əm), *n.* 1 movement or trend toward increased protection of the consumer from faulty manufacturing processes in the production of goods, from misleading labeling, packaging, or promotion practices, and also toward protection of the environment from undue harm. 2 an aspect of capitalism which concentrates on producing and distributing goods for a market which must constantly be enlarged.

con sum mate (*v.* kon′sə māt; *adj.* kən sum′it), *v.,* **-mat ed, -mat ing,** *adj.* —*v.t.* 1 bring to completion; realize; fulfill: *My ambition was consummated when I won the first prize.* 2 fulfill the marriage union with the first act of sexual intercourse. —*adj.* in the highest degree; complete; perfect: *The paintings of great artists show consummate skill.* [< Latin *consummatum* brought to a peak < *com-* + *summa* peak] **—con sum′mate ly,** *adv.*

con sum ma tion (kon′sə mā′shən), *n.* completion; fulfillment.

con sump tion (kən sump′shən), *n.* 1 a consuming; using up; use: *We took along some food for consumption on our trip. The science of economics deals with the production, distribution, and consumption of wealth.* 2 amount used up: *The consumption of fuel oil is much greater in winter than in summer.* 3 a wasting disease of the body, especially tuberculosis of the lungs. [< Latin *consumptionem* < *consumere.* See CONSUME.]

con sump tive (kən sump′tiv), *adj.* 1 of, having, or likely to have consumption. 2 tending to consume; destructive; wasteful. —*n.* person who has consumption. **—con sump′tive ly,** *adv.* **—con sump′tive ness,** *n.*

cont., 1 containing. 2 contents. 3 continued.

Cont., Continental.

con tact (kon′takt), *n.* 1 condition of touching; a touch: *When two balls are in contact, one can be moved by touching the other.* 2 condition of being in communication: *The control tower lost radio contact with the airplane.* 3 connection: *The insurance salesman tried to make contacts with wealthy people. She has a useful contact in an advertising agency.* 4 connection between two conductors of electricity through which a current passes. 5 device or part for producing such a connection: *The electric light went out when the wire broke off at the contact.* —*adj., adv.* within sight of the ground: *contact flying, to fly contact.* —*v.t.* 1 INFORMAL. get in touch with; make a connection with. 2 cause to touch. —*v.i.* be in contact. [< Latin *contactus* < *contingere* touch closely < *com-* + *tangere* to touch]

contact lens, a very small plastic lens held in place on the front of the eyeball by the fluid of the eye.

contact print, a photographic print made by placing the negative and photographic paper in direct contact over a light.

con ta gion (kən tā′jən), *n.* 1 the spreading of disease by direct or indirect contact. 2 disease spread in this way; contagious disease. 3 means by which disease is spread. 4 the spreading of any influence from one to another: *At the cry of "Fire!" a contagion of fear swept through the audience.* [< Latin *contagionem* a touching < *contingere.* See CONTACT.]

con ta gious (kən tā′jəs), *adj.* 1 spreading by direct or indirect contact; catching: *Scarlet fever is a contagious disease.* 2 causing contagious diseases. 3 easily spreading from one to another: *Yawning is often contagious.* **—con ta′gious ly,** *adv.* **—con ta′gious ness,** *n.*

con tain (kən tān′), *v.t.* 1 have within itself; hold as contents; include: *This book contains much information.* See synonym study below. 2 be equal to: *A pound contains 16 ounces.* 3 control; hold back; restrain: *I contained my anger.* 4 be divisible by; be divisible by without a remainder: *12 contains 1, 2, 3, 4, 6, and 12.* [< Old French *contenir* < Latin *continere* hold together, hold in < *com-* + *tenere* to hold] **—con tain′a ble,** *adj.*

Syn. 1 **Contain, hold, accommodate** mean to have within itself or be capable of having and keeping. **Contain** emphasizes the idea of actually having something within itself as contents or parts: *The house contains five rooms.* **Hold,** although often used interchangeably with *contain,* suggests being capable of containing: *A paper bag won't hold water.* **Accommodate** means to hold conveniently or comfortably: *Most hotel rooms accommodate two people.*

con tain er (kən tā′nər), *n.* 1 box, can, jar, etc., used to hold or contain something. 2 amount that a container can hold.

con tain ment (kən tān′mənt), *n.* the confinement of a hostile or potentially hostile political or military force within existing geographical boundaries.

con tam i nant (kən tam′ə nənt), *n.* something that contaminates; pollutant.

con tam i nate (kən tam′ə nāt), *v.t.,* **-nat ed, -nat ing.** make impure by contact; defile; pollute: *Drinking water is contaminated when sewage seeps into the water supply.* [< Latin *contaminatum* contaminated] **—con tam′i na′tor,** *n.*

con tam i na tion (kən tam′ə nā′shən), *n.* 1 a contaminating or a being contaminated; pollution: *A sterile solution must be kept covered to avoid contamination.* 2 thing that contaminates; impurity.

con tam i na tive (kən tam′ə nā′tiv), *adj.* tending to contaminate.

contd., continued.

con temn (kən tem′), *v.t.* treat with contempt; scorn. [< Latin *contemnere* < *com-* + *temnere* to scorn] **—con temn′er,** *n.*

con tem plate (kon′təm plāt), *v.,* **-plat ed, -plat ing.** —*v.t.* 1 look at for a long time; gaze at. 2 think about for a long time; study carefully. 3 have in mind; consider; intend: *She is contemplating a trip to Europe.* —*v.i.* be absorbed in contemplation; meditate. [< Latin *contemplatum* surveyed < *com-* + *templum* temple, originally, restricted area marked off for the taking of auguries] **—con′tem pla′tor,** *n.*

con tem pla tion (kon′təm plā′shən), *n.* 1 a looking at or thinking about something for a long time. 2 deep thought; meditation: *sunk in contemplation.* 3 expectation or intention.

con tem pla tive (kon′təm plā′tiv, kən tem′plə tiv), *adj.* 1 deeply thoughtful; meditative. 2 devoted to religious meditation and prayer. **—con′tem pla′tive ly,** *adv.* **—con′tem pla′tive ness,** *n.*

con tem po ra ne ous (kən tem′pə rā′nē əs), belonging to the same period of time; contemporary: *The lives of Thomas Jefferson and Betsy Ross were contemporaneous.* **—con tem′po ra′ne ous ly,** *adv.* **—con tem′po ra′ne ous ness,** *n.*

con tem po rar y (kən tem′pə rer′ē), *adj., n., pl.* **-rar ies.** —*adj.* 1 belonging to or living in the same period of time: *Walt Whitman and Emily Dickinson were contemporary poets.* 2 of the same age or date: *contemporary trees.* 3 of or having to do with the present time; modern: *contemporary literature.* —*n.* 1 person living in the same period of time as another or others. 2 person or thing of the same age or date. [< *con-* together + Latin *temporarius* belonging to time < *tempus* time]

con tempt (kən tempt′), *n.* 1 the feeling that a person, act, or thing is mean, low, or worthless; scorn; despising; disdain: *We feel contempt for a cheat.* See **scorn** for synonym study. 2 a being scorned; disgrace: *A traitor is held in contempt by his countrymen.* 3 disobedience to or open disrespect for the rules or decisions of a court of law, a lawmaking body, etc. A person can be fined or put in jail for **contempt of court.** [< Latin

hat, āge, fär; let, ēqual, tėrm;
it, īce; hot, ōpen, ôrder;
oil, out; cup, pu̇t, rüle;
ch, child; ng, long; sh, she;
th, thin; ᴛʜ, then; zh, measure;

ə represents *a* in about, *e* in taken, *i* in pencil, *o* in lemon, *u* in circus.

< = from, derived from, taken from.

contemptus < *contemnere.* See CONTEMN.]

con tempt i ble (kən temp′tə bəl), *adj.* deserving contempt or scorn; held in contempt; mean; low; worthless: *a contemptible lie.* **—con tempt′i ble ness,** *n.* **—con tempt′i bly,** *adv.*

con temp tu ous (kən temp′chü əs), *adj.* showing contempt; scornful: *a contemptuous look.* **—con temp′tu ous ly,** *adv.* **—con temp′tu ous ness,** *n.*

con tend (kən tend′), *v.i.* 1 work hard against difficulties; fight; struggle: *The first settlers in America had to contend with sickness and lack of food.* 2 take part in a contest; compete: *Five runners were contending in the first race.* See synonym study below. 3 argue; dispute. *—v.t.* declare to be a fact; maintain as true; assert: *Columbus contended that the earth was round.* [< Latin *contendere* strain, strive < *com-* + *tendere* stretch] **—con tend′er,** *n.*

Syn. *v.i.* 2 **Contend, compete** mean to take part in a contest for something. **Contend** suggests struggling against opposition: *Our team is contending for the championship.* **Compete** emphasizes the rivalry involved and the prize to be won: *Only two of us are competing for the cup.*

con tent[1] (kon′tent), *n.* 1 Often, **contents,** *pl.* what is contained in anything; all things inside. 2 facts and ideas stated: *The content of his speech was good, but the form was not.* 3 amount contained; volume. 4 power of containing; capacity. 5 the subject matter or range of any field of study: *the content of our mathematics course.* [< Medieval Latin *contentum* something contained < Latin *continere.* See CONTAIN.]

➤ **content, contents.** *Content* is the more abstract: *the content of the course,* and is used when specifying the amount of an ingredient: *the moisture content. Contents* is the more concrete: *the contents of the box.*

con tent[2] (kən tent′), *v.t.* make easy in mind; satisfy; please: *Nothing contents that grumbling man.* See **satisfy** for synonym study. *—adj.* 1 satisfied; pleased; easy in mind: *Will you be content to wait until tomorrow?* 2 willing; ready: *I am not content to accept poor workmanship.* *—n.* contentment; satisfaction; ease of mind. [< Latin *contentum* contained, satisfied < *continere.* See CONTAIN.]

con tent ed (kən ten′tid), *adj.* satisfied; pleased; easy in mind. **—con tent′ed ly,** *adv.* **—con tent′ed ness,** *n.*

con ten tion (kən ten′shən), *n.* 1 statement or point that one has argued for; statement maintained as true: *Galileo's contention that the earth goes around the sun proved to be true.* 2 an arguing; disputing; quarreling: *Contention has no place in the classroom.* 3 argument; dispute; quarrel. 4 struggle; contest; competition. [< Latin *contentionem* < *contendere.* See CONTEND.]

con ten tious (kən ten′shəs), *adj.* 1 fond of arguing; given to disputing; quarrelsome. 2 characterized by contention: *a contentious campaign.* **—con ten′tious ly,** *adv.* **—con ten′tious ness,** *n.*

con tent ment (kən tent′mənt), *n.* ease of mind; a being pleased; satisfaction.

con tents (kon′tents), *n.pl.* See def. 1 of **content**[1].

con ter mi nous (kən tėr′mə nəs), *adj.* 1 having a common boundary; bordering. 2 coterminous. [< Latin *conterminus* < *com-* with + *terminus* boundary] **—con ter′mi nous ly,** *adv.*

con test (*n.* kon′test; *v.* kən test′), *n.* 1 trial of skill to see which can win. A game, a race, and a debate are contests. 2 a fight or struggle. 3 argument; dispute. *—v.t.* 1 fight for; struggle for: *The blackbirds contested one another for nesting territory.* 2 argue against; dispute about: *The lawyer contested the claim.* *—v.i.* try to win. [< Latin *contestari* call to witness < *com-* + *testis* witness] **—con test′a ble,** *adj.* **—con test′er,** *n.*

con test ant (kən tes′tənt), *n.* 1 person who contests; person who takes part in a contest. 2 person who contests election returns, a will, a judgment, etc.

con text (kon′tekst), *n.* parts directly before and after a word, sentence, etc., that influence its meaning. You can often tell the meaning of a word from its context. [< Latin *contextus* < *contexere* weave together < *com-* + *texere* weave]

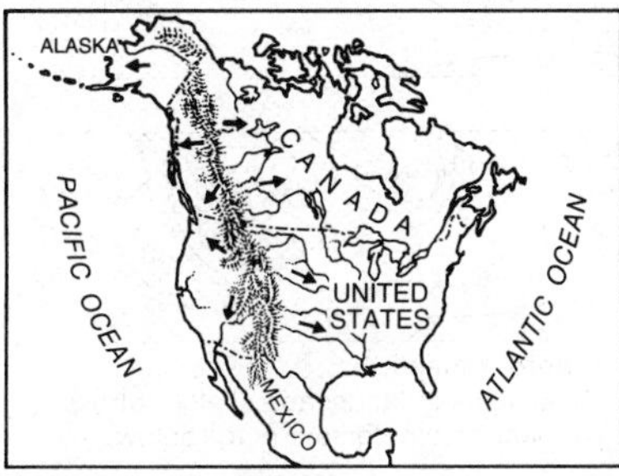

Continental Divide

con tex tu al (kən teks′chü əl), *adj.* having to do with the context; depending on the context. **—con tex′tu al ly,** *adv.*

con ti gu i ty (kon′tə gyü′ə tē), *n., pl.* **-ties.** 1 nearness: *The contiguity of the house and garage was a convenience in bad weather.* 2 contact. 3 a continuous mass; unbroken stretch.

con tig u ous (kən tig′yü əs), *adj.* 1 in actual contact; touching: *A fence showed where the two farms were contiguous.* 2 adjoining; near. [< Latin *contiguus* < *contingere* touch closely. See CONTACT.] **—con tig′u ous ly,** *adv.* **—con tig′u ous ness,** *n.*

con ti nence (kon′tə nəns), *n.* 1 control of one's actions and feelings; self-restraint; moderation. 2 chastity.

con ti nen cy (kon′tə nən sē), *n.* continence.

con ti nent[1] (kon′tə nənt), *n.* 1 one of the seven great masses of land on the earth. The continents are North America, South America, Europe, Africa, Asia, Australia, and Antarctica. 2 mainland. 3 **the Continent,** the mainland of Europe. It does not include the British Isles. [< Latin *(terram) continentem* connected or continuous (land), literally, holding in. See CONTINENT[2].]

con ti nent[2] (kon′tə nənt), *adj.* 1 showing restraint with regard to the desires or passions; using self-control; temperate. 2 chaste. [< Latin *continentem* holding in, refraining < *com-* in + *tenere* to hold] **—con′ti nent ly,** *adv.*

con ti nent al (kon′tə nen′tl), *adj.* 1 of, like, or like that of, a continent. 2 **Continental. a** belonging to or characteristic of the mainland of Europe; of or like that of the Continent: *Continental customs differ from those of England.* **b** of or having to do with the American colonies at the time of the Revolutionary War. *—n.* 1 **Continental, a** person living on the Continent; European. **b** soldier of the American army during the Revolutionary War. 2 piece of American paper money issued during the Revolutionary War. It was considered almost worthless by the time the war was over. 3 **not worth a continental,** INFORMAL. worthless. **—con′ti nent′al ly,** *adv.*

Continental Congress, either of two legislative assemblies representing the American colonies from 1774 to 1781. The Second Continental Congress adopted the Declaration of Independence in 1776.

Continental Divide, ridge in W North America which separates streams flowing toward the Pacific Ocean from those flowing toward the Atlantic or the Arctic Oceans; Great Divide. The Rocky Mountains form a major part of the Continental Divide.

continental drift, (in geology) the slow movement of the earth's land masses, thought to be caused by pressure that shifts them over the underlying molten material.

continental shelf, the shallow portion of sea bed that slopes gradually out from a continent to a depth of about 100 fathoms and ends in an abrupt descent to deeper water.

con tin gen cy (kən tin′jən sē), *n., pl.* **-cies.** 1 a happening or event depending on something that is uncertain; possibility: *The explorer carried supplies for every contingency.* 2 an accidental happening; unexpected event; chance. 3 uncertainty of occurrence; dependence on chance.

con tin gent (kən tin′jənt), *n.* 1 share of soldiers, laborers, etc., furnished to a force from other sources: *The United States sent a large contingent of troops to Europe in World War II.* 2 group that is part of a larger group: *The New York contingent sat together at the national convention.* 3 an accidental or unexpected event. *—adj.* 1 depending on something not certain; conditional: *Our plans for a picnic are contingent upon fair weather.* 2 liable to happen or not to happen; possible; uncertain: *contingent expenses.* 3 happening by chance; accidental; unexpected. [< Latin *contingentem* touching closely < *com-* + *tangere* to touch] **—con tin′gent ly,** *adv.*

con tin u al (kən tin′yü əl), *adj.* 1 never stopping: *the continual flow of the river.* 2 repeated many times; very frequent. **—con tin′u al ly,** *adv.*

➤ **continual, continuous.** *Continual* usually implies recurrence at regular or frequent intervals: *Ballet dancing requires continual practice. Continuous* means extending uninterruptedly in space or time: *a continuous procession of cars.*

con tin u ance (kən tin′yü əns), *n.* 1 a continuing; going on: *during the continuance of the strike.* 2 act of remaining; stay: *Public officials are paid during their continuance in office.* 3 time during which anything lasts;

duration. 4 continuation; sequel: *the continuance of a story.* 5 adjournment or postponement of legal proceedings until a future time.

con tin u a tion (kən tin′yü ā′shən), *n.* 1 act of going on with a thing after stopping; beginning again; resumption: *Continuation of the reading was difficult after so many interruptions.* 2 anything by which a thing is continued; added part: *The continuation of the story will appear in next month's magazine.* 3 act or fact of not stopping.

continuation school, an evening school for persons who have left elementary school or high school to go to work.

con tin ue (kən tin′yü), *v.,* **-tin ued, -tin u ing.** *—v.i.* 1 go on; keep up; keep on: *The road continues for miles.* 2 go on after stopping: *The class begged the teacher to continue with the reading.* 3 last; endure: *The queen's reign continued for 20 years.* See synonym study below. 4 stay: *The children must continue in school till the end of June.* *—v.t.* 1 go on with; keep on; keep up: *We continued our efforts to raise money for the hospital.* 2 go on with after stopping; begin again; resume: *I ate lunch and then continued my work.* 3 cause to last; maintain: *She continued the family tradition by going to law school.* 4 cause to stay; retain: *The voters continued the president in office for another term.* 5 put off until a later time; postpone; adjourn: *The judge continued the case until next month.* [< Latin *continuare* < *continuus* continuous < *continere* hold together. See CONTAIN.] **—con tin′u a ble,** *adj.*

Syn. *v.i.* 3 **Continue, last** mean to go on for a long time. **Continue** emphasizes the idea of going on and on without an end, usually without a break: *The extreme cold continued all winter.* **Last** emphasizes the idea of holding out, either in good condition or full strength or for an unusually long time: *Those flowers lasted for two weeks.*

con ti nu i ty (kon′tə nü′ə tē, kon′tə nyü′ə tē), *n., pl.* **-ties.** 1 condition or quality of being continuous. 2 a continuous or connected whole; uninterrupted succession; unbroken series. 3 a detailed plan of a motion picture; scenario. 4 (in radio or television) any connecting comments or announcements between the parts of a program.

con tin u ous (kən tin′yü əs), *adj.* without a stop or break; connected; unbroken; uninterrupted: *a continuous line, a continuous sound, continuous work.* **—con tin′u ous ly,** *adv.* **—con tin′u ous ness,** *n.* ➔ See **continual** for usage note.

con tin u um (kən tin′yü əm), *n., pl.* **-tin u a** (-tin′yü ə). 1 a continuous quantity, series, etc. 2 thing that remains the same. [< Latin]

con tort (kən tôrt′), *v.t.* twist or bend out of shape; distort: *The clown contorted his face.* [< Latin *contortum* contorted < *com-* + *torquere* to twist]

con tor tion (kən tôr′shən), *n.* 1 a twisting or bending out of shape; distorting. 2 a contorted condition; distorted form or shape.

con tor tion ist (kən tôr′shə nist), *n.* person who can twist or bend his body into odd and unnatural positions.

con tour (kon′tu̇r), *n.* 1 outline of a figure: *The contour of the Atlantic coast of America is very irregular.* See **outline** for synonym study. 2 line that defines or bounds anything. *—adj.* 1 showing the outline, especially of hills, valleys, etc.: *contour interval on a topographic map.* 2 following natural ridges and furrows to avoid erosion: *contour plowing.* 3 shaped to fit the contour of a particular object: *a contour chair, contour sheets.* *—v.t.* make an outline or contour of. [< French < Italian *contorno* < *contornare* encircle < Latin *com-* + *tornus* a turning lathe]

contour line, line on a map, showing height above or below sea level. All points on a contour line have the same elevation.

contour map, map showing heights at regular intervals above sea level by means of contour lines.

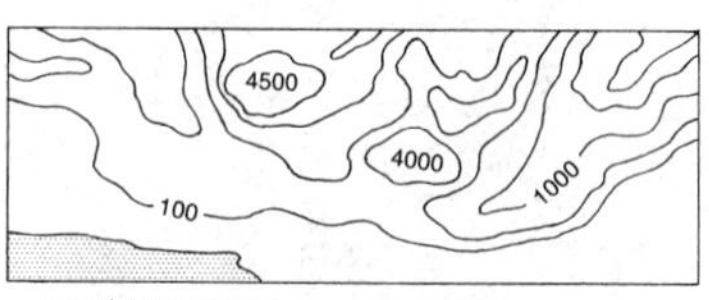

contour map
Mountains in landscape sketch (above) appear on the contour map (below).

contr., 1 contraction. 2 contractor.

contra-, *prefix.* in opposition; against: *Contradistinction = distinction by opposition or contrast.* [< Latin < *contra* against]

con tra band (kon′trə band), *n.* 1 goods imported or exported contrary to law; smuggled goods. 2 trading contrary to law; smuggling. 3 contraband of war. *—adj.* against the law; prohibited: *contraband trade.* [< Spanish *contrabando* < Italian < *contra-* against + *bando* edict, ban]

contraband of war, goods supplied by neutral nations to countries at war with one another which either warring country has the right to seize. Ammunition is always contraband of war.

con tra bass (kon′trə bās′), *n.* 1 the lowest bass instrument. 2 double bass. *—adj.* sounding an octave lower than the normal bass.

con tra bas soon (kon′trə bə sün′), *n.* a large bassoon, an octave lower in pitch than the ordinary bassoon; double bassoon.

con tra cep tion (kon′trə sep′shən), *n.* prevention of conception.

con tra cep tive (kon′trə sep′tiv), *adj.* of or for contraception. *—n.* means or device for preventing conception.

con tract (*v.t.* kən trakt′; *v.i.* kən trakt′ *for 1,* kon′trakt, kən trakt′ *for 2; n.* kon′trakt), *v.t.* 1 draw together; make shorter, narrower, or smaller: *contract a muscle. Wrinkling your forehead contracts your brows.* 2 shorten (a word, etc.) by omitting some of the letters or sounds: *In talking we often contract "do not" to "don't."* 3 bring on oneself; get; form: *contract bad habits, contract a disease.* *—v.i.* 1 become shorter, narrower, or smaller: *Wool fibers contract in hot water.* 2 make a contract; agree by contract: *The builder contracted to build the new library.* *—n.* 1 agreement. In a contract two or more people agree to do or not to do certain things. 2 a written agreement that can be enforced by law. 3 a formal agreement for marriage; betrothal. 4 contract bridge. [< Latin *contractum* drawn together < *com-* + *trahere* to draw]

contract bridge, variety of bridge in which the highest bidder can score toward a game only as many points as he promised to make in his bid.

con tract i ble (kən trak′tə bəl), *adj.* capable of being contracted.

con trac tile (kən trak′təl), *adj.* 1 capable of contracting: *Muscle is contractile tissue.* 2 producing contraction: *Cooling is a contractile force.*

contractile vacuole, vacuole in one-celled organisms that discharges its fluid by contracting.

con trac til i ty (kon′trak til′ə tē), *n.* ability to contract.

con trac tion (kən trak′shən), *n.* 1 act or process of contracting: *the contraction of liquids, gases, and solids caused by cold, the contraction of muscles.* 2 condition of being contracted. 3 something contracted; shortened form: *"Can't" is a contraction of "cannot."*

con trac tive (kən trak′tiv), *adj.* of or producing contraction.

con trac tor (kon′trak tər, kən trak′tər *for 1;* kən trak′tər *for 2*), *n.* 1 person who agrees to furnish materials or to do a piece of work for a certain price; person who makes a contract: *a building contractor.* 2 a thing that contracts, especially a muscle.

con trac tu al (kən trak′chü əl), *adj.* 1 of or having to do with a contract. 2 having the nature of a contract. **—con trac′tu al ly,** *adv.*

con tra dict (kon′trə dikt′), *v.t.* 1 say that (a statement, rumor, etc.) is not true; deny. See **deny** for synonym study. 2 deny the words of (a person); say the opposite of what (a person) has said. 3 be contrary to; disagree with: *His quick anger contradicted his previous statement that he never lost his temper.* [< Latin *contradictum* spoken against < *contra-* + *dicere* say] **—con′tra dict′a ble,** *adj.*

con tra dic tion (kon′trə dik′shən), *n.* 1 a denying of what has been said. 2 statement or act that contradicts another; denial. 3 disagreement. 4 inconsistency.

con tra dic tor y (kon′trə dik′tər ē), *adj.* 1 in disagreement; contradicting; contrary: *First reports of the election were so contradictory we could not tell who won.* 2 inclined to contradict. **—con′tra dic′tor i ly,** *adv.* **—con′tra dic′tor i ness,** *n.*

con tra dis tinc tion (kon′trə dis tingk′shən), *n.* distinction made by opposition or contrast: *Today we cross the continent in fast airplanes in contradistinction to the slow covered wagons of our ancestors.*

con trail (kon′trāl), *n.* trail of water vapor left by an aircraft flying at a high altitude; vapor trail. [< *con(densation) trail*]

con tra in di cate (kon′trə in′də kāt), *v.t.,* **-cat ed, -cat ing.** indicate (a medical treatment, etc.) as being inadvisable. **—con′tra in′di ca′tion,** *n.*

con tral to (kən tral′tō), *n., pl.* **-tos,** *adj.* *—n.* 1 the lowest female voice; alto. 2 singer with such a voice. 3 part in music for such a voice. *—adj.* of or for a contralto. [< Italian < *contra-* counter to + *alto* high]

con trap tion (kən trap′shən), *n.* INFORMAL. device or gadget; contrivance.

con tra pun tal (kon′trə pun′tl), *adj.* 1 of or having to do with counterpoint.

2 according to the rules of counterpoint. 3 polyphonic. [< Italian *contrappunto* counterpoint] **—con′tra pun′tal ly,** *adv.*

con tra pun tist (kon′trə pun′tist), *n.* person skilled in the rules and practice of counterpoint.

con tra ri e ty (kon′trə rī′ə tē), *n., pl.* **-ties.** 1 a being contrary. 2 something contrary; contrary fact or statement.

con tra ri wise (kon′trer ē wīz′), *adv.* 1 in the opposite way or direction. 2 on the contrary. 3 perversely.

con tra ry (kon′trer ē; *also for adj. 4* kən trer′ē), *adj., n., pl.* **-ries,** *adv.* —*adj.* 1 completely different: *Your taste in clothes is just contrary to my own.* 2 opposite in direction, position, etc.; counter: *a contrary force.* See **opposite** for synonym study. 3 unfavorable: *a contrary wind.* 4 opposing others; stubborn; perverse: *a contrary person, a contrary attitude.* —*n.* 1 fact or quality that is the opposite of something else; the opposite. 2 **on the contrary,** exactly opposite to what has been said. 3 **to the contrary,** with the opposite effect. —*adv.* in opposition. [< Anglo-French *contrarie* < Latin *contrarius* < *contra* against] **—con′tra ri ly,** *adv.* **—con′tra ri ness,** *n.*

con trast (*n.* kon′trast; *v.* kən trast′), *n.* 1 a great difference; striking difference; difference: *the contrast between black and white.* 2 person, thing, event, etc., that shows differences when compared with another: *Black hair is a sharp contrast to white skin.* —*v.t.* 1 compare (two things) so as to show their differences: *Contrast birds with fishes.* 2 put close together to heighten an effect by emphasizing differences. —*v.i.* 1 show differences when compared or put side by side: *The black and the gold contrast well in that design.* 2 form a contrast: *The strained language of his speeches contrasts oddly with the ease and naturalness of his letters.* [< French *contraste* < Italian *contrasto* < *contrastare* to contrast < Latin *contra-* against + *stare* stand] **—con trast′a ble,** *adj.*

con trast y (kon′tras′tē), *adj.* (of photographs) having very marked contrast between light and dark areas.

con tra vene (kon′trə vēn′), *v.t.,* **-vened, -ven ing.** 1 conflict with; oppose: *A dictatorship contravenes the liberty of individuals.* 2 contradict. 3 violate; infringe. [< Late Latin *contravenire* < Latin *contra-* against + *venire* come] **—con′tra ven′er,** *n.*

con tra ven tion (kon′trə ven′shən), *n.* 1 conflict; opposition. 2 contradiction. 3 violation; infringement.

con tre danse (kon′trə dans′), *n.* 1 dance in which the partners stand in two lines facing each other. 2 music written for such a dance. [< French < English *country-dance*]

con tre temps (kôɴ′trə täɴ′), *n., pl.* **-temps** (-täɴz′). an unlucky accident; embarrassing or awkward happening. [< French *contre-temps*]

contrib., contributor.

con trib ute (kən trib′yüt), *v.,* **-ut ed, -ut ing.** —*v.t.* 1 give (money, help, etc.) along with others; furnish as a share: *contribute to the Red Cross. Everyone was asked to contribute suggestions for the party.* 2 write (articles, stories, etc.) for a newspaper or magazine. —*v.i.* give or make a contribution. **contribute to,** help bring about: *A poor diet contributed to the child's illness.* [< Latin *contributum* bestowed together < *com-* + *tribuere* bestow, assign]

con tri bu tion (kon′trə byü′shən), *n.* 1 act of contributing; giving of money, help, etc., along with others. 2 money, help, etc., contributed; gift. 3 article, story, etc., written for a newspaper or magazine. 4 tax; levy.

con trib u tive (kən trib′yə tiv), *adj.* helping to bring about; contributing. **—con trib′u tive ly,** *adv.*

con trib u tor (kən trib′yə tər), *n.* 1 person or thing that contributes. 2 person who writes articles, stories, etc., for a newspaper or magazine.

con trib u to ry (kən trib′yə tôr′ē, kən trib′yə tōr′ē), *adj.* 1 helping to bring about; contributing: *The worker's carelessness was a contributory cause of the accident.* 2 having to do with or of the nature of a contribution.

con trite (kən trīt′, kon′trīt), *adj.* 1 broken in spirit by a sense of guilt; penitent. 2 showing deep regret and sorrow: *I wrote an apology in contrite words.* [< Latin *contritus* crushed < *com-* together + *terere* to rub, grind] **—con trite′ly,** *adv.* **—con trite′ness,** *n.*

con tri tion (kən trish′ən), *n.* 1 sorrow for one's sins or guilt; being contrite; penitence. 2 deep regret.

con triv ance (kən trī′vəns), *n.* 1 thing invented; mechanical device. 2 act or manner of contriving. 3 power or ability of contriving. 4 plan; scheme.

con trive (kən trīv′), *v.t.,* **-trived, -triv ing.** 1 plan with cleverness or skill; invent; design: *contrive a new kind of engine.* 2 plan; scheme; plot: *contrive a robbery.* 3 manage: *I will contrive to be there by ten o'clock.* 4 bring about. [< Old French *controver* < Late Latin *contropare* compare] **—con triv′er,** *n.*

con trived (kən trīvd′), *adj.* produced by contrivance; not natural; artificial.

con trol (kən trōl′), *v.,* **-trolled, -trol ling,** *n.* —*v.t.* 1 have power or authority over; direct: *A captain controls his ship and its crew.* 2 hold back; keep down; restrain: *I couldn't control my tears.* 3 regulate: *control prices and wages.* 4 check or verify (an experiment) by some standard of comparison. —*n.* 1 power to direct or guide; authority; direction: *A child is under its parents' control.* See **authority** for synonym study. 2 power or ability to restrain, check, or keep down: *She lost control of her temper.* 3 means of restraint; check: *The President's power to veto is a control over the legislation passed by Congress.* 4 device that regulates a machine. 5 **controls,** *pl.* the instruments and devices by which an aircraft, locomotive, car, etc., is operated. 6 individual or group serving as a standard of comparison for testing the results of a scientific experiment. 7 spirit that directs a medium in spiritualism. [< Old French *contreroller* < *contrerolle* register < *contre* against + *rolle* roll] **—con trol′la ble,** *adj.*

control equipment, experiment to test or verify the results of another experiment.

con trol ler (kən trō′lər), *n.* 1 comptroller. 2 person who controls, directs, or restrains: *air-traffic controller.* 3 device that regulates the speed, motion, power, etc., of a machine.

con trol ler ship (kən trō′lər ship), *n.* comptrollership.

control rod, mechanism containing neutron-absorbing material, used in a nuclear reactor to control the rate of a chain reaction.

control surface, a movable airfoil, such as a rudder, elevator, or aileron, used to guide or control an aircraft in flight.

control tower, tower at an airfield for controlling the traffic of aircraft taking off and landing.

hat, āge, fär; let, ēqual, tėrm;
it, īce; hot, ōpen, ôrder;
oil, out; cup, pu̇t, rüle;
ch, child; ng, long; sh, she;
th, thin; ᴛʜ, then; zh, measure;

ə represents *a* in about, *e* in taken, *i* in pencil, *o* in lemon, *u* in circus.

< = from, derived from, taken from.

con tro ver sial (kon′trə vėr′shəl), *adj.* 1 of or having to do with controversy. 2 open to controversy; debatable; disputed: *a controversial question.* 3 fond of controversy; argumentative. **—con′tro ver′sial ly,** *adv.*

con tro ver sial ist (kon′trə vėr′shə list), *n.* person who takes part in or is skilled in controversy.

con tro ver sy (kon′trə vėr′sē), *n., pl.* **-sies.** 1 an arguing a question about which differences of opinion exist. See **argument** for synonym study. 2 quarrel; wrangle. [< Latin *controversia* < *contra-* against + *versum* turned]

con tro vert (kon′trə vėrt′, kon′trə vėrt′), *v.t.* 1 dispute, deny, or oppose: *The statement of the last witness controverts the testimony of the first two.* 2 dispute about; discuss; debate. **—con′tro vert′er,** *n.* **—con′tro vert′i ble,** *adj.*

con tu ma cious (kon′tü mā′shəs, kon′tyə mā′shəs), *adj.* stubbornly rebellious; obstinately disobedient. **—con′tu ma′cious ly,** *adv.*

con tu ma cy (kon′tü mə sē, kon′tyə mə sē), *n., pl.* **-cies.** stubborn resistance to authority; obstinate disobedience. [< Latin *contumacia* < *contumacem* insolent < *com-* + *tumere* swell up]

con tu me li ous (kon′tü mē′lē əs, kon′tyə mē′lē əs), *adj.* contemptuously insolent; insulting. **—con′tu me′li ous ly,** *adv.*

con tu me ly (kən tü′mə lē, kən tyü′mə lē; kon′tü mə lē, kon′tyə mə lē), *n., pl.* **-lies.** 1 insolent contempt; insulting words or actions; humiliating treatment. 2 a humiliating insult. [< Latin *contumelia,* related to *contumacia* contumacy]

con tuse (kən tüz′, kən tyüz′), *v.t.,* **-tused, -tus ing.** injure without breaking the skin; bruise. [< Latin *contusum* beaten up < *com-* + *tundere* to beat]

con tu sion (kən tü′zhən, kən tyü′zhən), *n.* bruise.

co nun drum (kə nun′drəm), *n.* 1 riddle whose answer involves a pun or play on words. EXAMPLE: "When is a door not a door?" *Answer:* "When it's ajar." 2 any puzzling problem. [origin unknown]

con ur ban (kon′ėr′bən), *adj.* of or characterizing a conurbation.

con ur ba tion (kon′ər bā′shən), *n.* a grouping of urban communities.

con va lesce (kon′və les′), *v.i.,* **-lesced, -lesc ing.** recover health and strength after illness. [< Latin *convalescere* < *com-* + *valescere* grow strong < *valere* be strong]

con va les cence (kon′və les′ns), *n.* 1 the gradual recovery of health and strength after illness. 2 time during which one is convalescing.

con va les cent (kon′və les′nt), *adj.* recovering health and strength after ill-

ness. —*n.* person recovering after illness.
con vec tion (kən vek′shən), *n.* (in physics) the transfer of heat from one place to another by the circulation of currents of heated particles of a gas or liquid. [< Latin *convectionem* < *convehere* carry together < *com-* + *vehere* carry]
con vec tive (kən vek′tiv), *adj.* having to do with or resulting from convection.
con vec tor (kən vek′tər), *n.* device for heating air by convection.
con vene (kən vēn′), *v.*, **-vened, -ven ing.** —*v.i.* meet for some purpose; gather together; assemble: *Congress convenes in the Capitol at Washington, D.C., at least once a year.* —*v.t.* call together (members of an organization, etc.). [< Latin *convenire* < *com-* together + *venire* come] **—con ven′er,** *n.*
con ven ience (kən vē′nyəns), *n.* 1 fact or quality of being convenient: *The convenience of packaged goods increases their sale.* 2 comfort; advantage; accommodation: *Many stores have a delivery service for the convenience of shoppers.* 3 anything handy or easy to use; thing that saves trouble or work: *A folding table is a convenience in a small room.* 4 **at one's convenience,** so as to suit one as to time, place, or other conditions: *Write at your convenience.*
convenience food, dried or frozen food that can be stored and used at one's convenience, with a minimum of preparation, such as cake mixes, frozen pizzas, TV dinners, etc.
con ven ient (kən vē′nyənt), *adj.* 1 saving trouble; well arranged; easy to use: *use a convenient tool, live in a convenient house.* 2 easily done; not troublesome: *Will it be convenient for you to bring your lunch to school?* 3 within easy reach; handy: *meet at a convenient place.* 4 **convenient to,** INFORMAL. near. [< Latin *convenientem* coming together, fitting, suitable < *com-* together + *venire* come] **—con ven′ient ly,** *adv.*
con vent (kon′vent), *n.* 1 community of nuns or other persons dedicated to a religious life. 2 building or buildings in which they live. [< Latin *conventus* assembly < *convenire.* See CONVENE.]
con ven ti cle (kən ven′tə kəl), *n.* 1 a secret or unauthorized meeting, especially for religious worship. 2 place of such a meeting.
con ven tion (kən ven′shən), *n.* 1 a meeting for some purpose; gathering; assembly. A political party holds a convention to choose candidates for public offices. 2 delegates to a meeting or assembly. 3 general agreement; common consent; custom: *Convention governs how most people dress and wear their hair.* 4 custom or practice approved by general agreement; rule based on common consent: *Using the right hand to shake hands is a convention.* 5 agreement signed by two or more countries about matters less important than those in a treaty. [< Latin *conventionem* < *convenire.* See CONVENE.]
con ven tion al (kən ven′shə nəl), *adj.* 1 depending on conventions; customary: *"Good morning" is a conventional greeting.* See **formal** for synonym study. 2 acting or behaving according to commonly accepted and approved ways. 3 of the usual type or design; commonly used or seen: *conventional furniture.* 4 (in the arts) following custom and traditional models; formal: *The ode and the sonnet are conventional forms of English poetry.* **—con ven′tion al ly,** *adv.*
con ven tion al ism (kən ven′shə nə liz′əm), *n.* 1 tendency to follow conventional usages; adherence to custom. 2 something conventional; formal word, phrase, etc.
con ven tion al i ty (kən ven′shə nal′ə tē), *n., pl.* **-ties.** 1 conventional quality or character. 2 conventional behavior; adherence to custom. 3 a conventional custom, practice, or rule: *the conventionalities of an institution.*
con ven tion al ize (kən ven′shə nə līz), *v.t.*, **-ized, -iz ing.** make conventional. **—con ven′tion al i za′tion,** *n.*
con ven tu al (kən ven′chü əl), *adj.* of or like a convent.

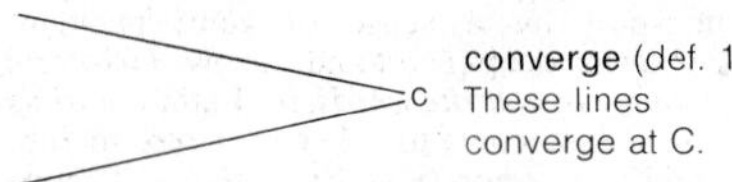

converge (def. 1) These lines converge at C.

con verge (kən vėrj′), *v.*, **-verged, -verg ing.** —*v.i.* 1 tend to meet in a point: *The sides of a road seem to converge in the distance.* 2 turn toward each other: *If you look at the end of your nose, your eyes converge.* 3 come together; center: *The interest of all the students converged upon the celebration.* —*v.t.* cause to converge. [< Late Latin *convergere* < Latin *com-* together + *vergere* to incline]
con ver gence (kən vėr′jəns), *n.* 1 act, process, or fact of converging; tendency to meet in a point. 2 point of converging. 3 the turning inward of the eyes in focusing on something very close to them. 4 the tendency in animals or plants not closely related to develop similar characteristics when living under the same conditions.
con ver gent (kən vėr′jənt), *adj.* converging.
con ver sant (kən vėr′sənt, kon′vər sənt), *adj.* familiar by use or study; acquainted: *conversant with many fields of study.*
con ver sa tion (kon′vər sā′shən), *n.* informal or friendly talk; exchange of thoughts by talking informally together.
con ver sa tion al (kon′vər sā′shə nəl), *adj.* 1 of, like, or having to do with conversation. 2 fond of conversation; good at conversation. **—con′ver sa′tion al ly,** *adv.*
con ver sa tion al ist (kon′vər sā′shə nə list), *n.* person who is fond of or who is good at conversation.
con verse[1] (*v.* kən vėrs′; *n.* kon′vėrs′), *v.*, **-versed, -vers ing,** *n.* —*v.i.* talk together in an informal way; chat. —*n.* conversation. [< Old French *converser* < Latin *conversari* live with, associate with < *convertere* turn around. See CONVERT.] **—con vers′er,** *n.*
con verse[2] (*adj.* kən vėrs′, kon′vėrs′; *n.* kon′vėrs′), *adj.* 1 opposite or contrary in direction or action. 2 reversed in order; turned about. —*n.* 1 thing that is opposite or contrary. 2 thing that is turned around: *"Honest but poor" is the converse of "Poor but honest."* [< Latin *conversum* turned around, converted]
con verse ly (kən vėrs′lē, kon′vėrs′lē), *adv.* if or when turned the other way around: *Six is more than five; conversely, five is less than six.*
con ver sion (kən vėr′zhən, kən vėr′shən), *n.* 1 a converting; a changing or turning; change: *Heat causes the conversion of water into steam.* 2 a change from unbelief to faith; change from one religion, party, etc., to another. 3 exchange into an equivalent: *the conversion of feet into inches.* 4 a taking and using unlawfully. 5 in football: **a** a kick, pass, or run, to score one or two extra points after a touchdown. **b** the point or points thus made.
con ver sion al (kən vėr′zhə nəl, kən vėr′shə nəl), *adj.* of or having to do with conversion.
con vert (*v.* kən vėrt′; *n.* kon′vėrt′), *v.t.* 1 turn to another use; change into an object or material of a different form, character, or function: *These machines convert cotton into cloth.* See **transform** for synonym study. 2 cause to change from unbelief to faith; change from one religion, political party, etc., to another: *French and Spanish missionaries converted some American Indians to the Christian religion.* 3 take and use unlawfully: *The dishonest treasurer converted the club's money to his own use.* 4 turn the other way around; invert; transpose. 5 exchange for an equivalent: *She converted her dollars into pounds upon arriving in London.* —*v.i.* 1 change from one belief, political party, etc., to another. 2 (in football) score a conversion. —*n.* person who has been converted. [< Latin *convertere* < *com-* around + *vertere* to turn]
con vert er (kən vėr′tər), *n.* 1 person or thing that converts. 2 a rotating device for changing alternating current into direct current or the reverse. 3 device in a radio or television receiver for changing from one range of frequency to another. 4 Bessemer converter.
con vert i bil i ty (kən vėr′tə bil′ə tē), *n.* quality of being convertible.
con vert i ble (kən vėr′tə bəl), *adj.* 1 that can be converted: *Wood is convertible into paper.* 2 (of an automobile) having a top that may be folded down. —*n.* automobile with a folding top. **—con vert′i bly,** *adv.*
con vert i plane (kən vėr′tə plān′), *n.* aircraft that operates like a conventional airplane in level flight, but which takes off and lands like a helicopter.
con vex (kon veks′, kon′veks), *adj.* curved out like the outside of a circle or sphere; curving out: *The lens of an automobile headlight is convex.* [< Latin *convexus*] **—con vex′ly,** *adv.* **—con vex′ness,** *n.*

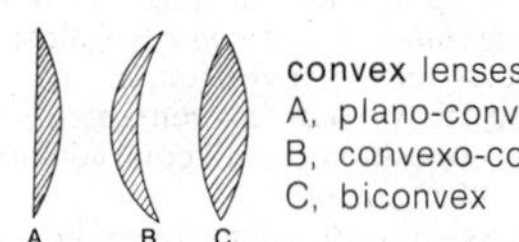

convex lenses: A, plano-convex; B, convexo-concave; C, biconvex

con vex i ty (kon vek′sə tē), *n., pl.* **-ties.** 1 convex condition or quality. 2 a convex surface or thing.
con vex o-con cave (kən vek′sō kon kāv′), *adj.* convex on one side and concave on the other. In a convexo-concave lens, the convex face has the greater curvature.
con vey (kən vā′), *v.t.* 1 take from one place to another; carry; transport: *A bus conveys passengers.* See **carry** for synonym study. 2 transmit; conduct: *A wire conveys an electric circuit.* 3 make known; communicate; express: *The speaker's words convey no meaning to me.* 4 transfer ownership of: *The old farmer conveyed his farm to his children.* [< Old French *conveier* < Latin *com-* with + *via* road. Doublet of CONVOY.] **—con vey′a ble,** *adj.*
con vey ance (kən vā′əns), *n.* 1 a carrying;

transmission; transportation. 2 thing that carries people and goods; vehicle. 3 communication. 4 transfer of ownership. 5 document showing such a transfer; deed.

con vey anc er (kən vā′ən sər), *n.* lawyer who investigates the ownership of property and prepares its conveyance.

con vey anc ing (kən vā′ən sing), *n.* preparation of a deed for the transfer of the ownership.

con vey or or **con vey er** (kən vā′ər), *n.* 1 person or thing that conveys. 2 a mechanical device that carries things from one place to another, especially by means of a moving, endless belt or chain.

con vict (*v.* kən vikt′; *n.* kon′vikt), *v.t.* 1 prove guilty. 2 declare guilty: *The jury convicted the accused of theft and arson.* —*n.* 1 person convicted by a court. 2 person serving a prison sentence for some crime. [< Latin *convictum* overcome, defeated < *com-* + *vincere* conquer]

con vic tion (kən vik′shən), *n.* 1 act of proving or declaring guilty. 2 condition of being proved or declared guilty. 3 act of convincing (a person). 4 a being convinced. 5 firm belief; certainty. See **belief** for synonym study.

con vince (kən vins′), *v.t.*, **-vinced, -vinc ing.** make a (person) feel sure; cause to believe; persuade by argument or proof: *The mistakes you made convinced me you had not studied your lesson.* See **persuade** for synonym study. [< Latin *convincere* < *com-* + *vincere* conquer] **—con vinc′er,** *n.* **—con vin′ci ble,** *adj.*

con vinc ing (kən vin′sing), *adj.* that convinces; persuasive; cogent: *a convincing argument.* **—con vinc′ing ly,** *adv.* **—con vinc′ing ness,** *n.*

con viv i al (kən viv′ē əl), *adj.* 1 fond of eating and drinking with friends; jovial; sociable. 2 of or suitable for a feast or banquet; festive. [< Latin *convivium* feast < *com-* with + *vivere* to live] **—con viv′i al ly,** *adv.*

con viv i al i ty (kən viv′ē al′ə tē), *n., pl.* **-ties.** 1 fondness for eating and drinking with friends; good fellowship. 2 eating and drinking with friends; festivity.

con vo ca tion (kon′və kā′shən), *n.* 1 a calling together; assembling by a summons. 2 assembly: *The convocation of clergymen passed a resolution condemning violence.*

con vo ca tion al (kon′və kā′shə nəl), *adj.* of, belonging to, or of the nature of a convocation.

con voke (kən vōk′), *v.t.*, **-voked, -vok ing.** call together; summon to assemble. [< Latin *convocare* < *com-* together + *vocare* to call] **—con vok′er,** *n.*

con vo lute (kon′və lüt), *adj., v.,* **-lut ed, -lut ing.** —*adj.* rolled up into a spiral shape with one part over another; coiled. —*v.t., v.i.* coil; twist. [< Latin *convolutum* rolled up < *com-* + *volvere* to roll] **—con′vo lute ly,** *adv.*

con vo lu tion (kon′və lü′shən), *n.* 1 a coiling, winding, or twisting together. 2 a coil; winding; twist. 3 an irregular fold or ridge on the surface of the brain.

con vol vu lus (kən vol′vyə ləs), *n., pl.* **-lus es, -li** (-lī). any of a genus of plants, usually vines, of the same family as the morning-glory, with flowers shaped like trumpets; bindweed. [< Latin]

con voy (*v.* kən voi′, kon′voi; *n.* kon′voi), *v.t.* accompany in order to protect; escort: *Warships convoy merchant ships during time of war.* —*n.* 1 an escort; protection: *The payroll was brought by truck under convoy of armed guards.* 2 warships, soldiers, etc., that convoy; protecting escort. 3 ship, fleet, supplies, etc., that are convoyed. [< Middle French *convoyer* < Old French *conveier.* Doublet of CONVEY.]

con vulse (kən vuls′), *v.t.*, **-vulsed, -vuls ing.** 1 shake violently: *An earthquake convulsed the island.* 2 cause violent disturbance in; disturb violently: *His face was convulsed with rage.* 3 throw into convulsions; shake with muscular spasms: *The sick child was convulsed before the doctor came.* 4 throw into fits of laughter; cause to shake with laughter: *The clown convulsed the audience with his funny acts.* [< Latin *convulsum* torn away < *com-* + *vellere* to tear]

con vul sion (kən vul′shən), *n.* 1 Often, **convulsions,** *pl.* a violent, involuntary contracting and relaxing of the muscles; spasm; fit. 2 a fit of laughter. 3 a violent disturbance: *The country was undergoing a political convulsion.*

con vul sive (kən vul′siv), *adj.* 1 violently disturbing. 2 having convulsions. 3 producing convulsions. **—con vul′sive ly,** *adv.* **—con vul′sive ness,** *n.*

co ny (kō′nē), *n., pl.* **-nies.** 1 rabbit fur. Cony is used to make or trim coats. 2 rabbit. 3 hyrax. 4 pika. Also, **coney.** [< Old French *conil* < Latin *cuniculus* rabbit]

coo (kü), *n., pl.* **coos,** *v.* —*n.* the soft, murmuring sound made by doves or pigeons. —*v.i.* 1 make a soft, murmuring sound. 2 murmur softly; speak in a soft, loving manner. —*v.t.* utter or express by cooing. [imitative] **—coo′er,** *n.*

coo ee (kü′ē), *n., interj.* a long, shrill signal call of the Australian aborigines, adopted by Australian colonists.

coo ey (kü′ē), *n., pl.* **-eys,** *interj.* cooee.

cook (ku̇k), *v.t.* 1 prepare (food, etc.) by using heat. 2 apply heat or fire to. 3 **cook up,** INFORMAL. **a** make up or prepare. **b** prepare falsely. —*v.i.* 1 prepare food for eating; act or work as cook. 2 undergo cooking; be cooked. 3 INFORMAL. happen; take place: *I turned to the news to find out what was cooking.* —*n.* person who cooks. [Old English *cōc* a cook < Latin *coquus*]

Cook (ku̇k), *n.* 1 **James,** 1728-1779, English navigator who explored the southern Pacific and the coasts of Australia and New Zealand. 2 **Mount,** mountain in S New Zealand; Aorangi. 12,349 ft.

cook book (ku̇k′bu̇k′), *n.* book of directions for cooking various kinds of food; book of recipes.

cook er (ku̇k′ər), *n.* apparatus, appliance, or container to cook things in.

cook er y (ku̇k′ər ē), *n., pl.* **-er ies.** art or occupation of cooking.

cook house (ku̇k′hous′), *n., pl.* **-hous es** (-hou′ziz). room or place for cooking.

cook ie (ku̇k′ē), *n.* a small, flat, sweet cake. Also, **cooky.** [< Dutch *koekje* little cake]

Cook Islands, group of islands in the S Pacific, northeast of and belonging to New Zealand. 21,000 pop.; about 93 sq. mi.

cook out (ku̇k′out′), *n.* a picnic, etc., where the food is cooked outdoors.

cook stove (ku̇k′stōv′), *n.* stove for cooking.

Cook Strait, channel between North and South Islands, New Zealand.

cook y (ku̇k′ē), *n., pl.* **cook ies.** cookie.

cool (kül), *adj.* 1 somewhat cold; more cold than hot: *a cool day.* See **cold** for synonym study. 2 allowing or giving a cool feeling: *cool, thin clothes.* 3 not excited; calm. 4 having little enthusiasm or interest; not cordial; indifferent: *a cool greeting.* 5 bold or impudent. 6 INFORMAL. without exaggeration or qualification: *a cool million dollars.* 7 SLANG. admirable; excellent. 8 (of colors) blue, green, or gray. —*n.* 1 something cool; cool part, place, or time: *in the cool of the evening.* 2 SLANG. calm restraint; presence of mind. —*v.t., v.i.* make or become cool. [Old English *cōl*] **—cool′ly,** *adv.* **—cool′ness,** *n.*

hat, āge, fär; let, ēqual, tėrm;
it, īce; hot, ōpen, ôrder;
oil, out; cup, pu̇t, rüle;
ch, child; ng, long; sh, she;
th, thin; ᴛʜ, then; zh, measure;

ə represents *a* in about, *e* in taken, *i* in pencil, *o* in lemon, *u* in circus.

< = from, derived from, taken from.

cool ant (kü′lənt), *n.* substance used to reduce heat in machinery.

cool er (kü′lər), *n.* 1 anything that cools. 2 apparatus or container that cools foods or drinks, or keeps them cool. 3 SLANG. jail.

cool-head ed (kül′hed′id), *adj.* not easily excited; calm. **—cool′-head′ed ly,** *adv.* **—cool′-head′ed ness,** *n.*

Coo lidge (kü′lij), *n.* **(John) Calvin,** 1872-1933, the 30th president of the United States, from 1923 to 1929.

coo lie (kü′lē), *n.* an unskilled, native laborer in China, India, etc. Also, **cooly.** [< Hindustani *qūlī*]

cool ish (kü′lish), *adj.* rather cool.

coo ly (kü′lē), *n., pl.* **-lies.** coolie.

coomb (küm, kōm), *n.* combe.

coon (kün), *n.* raccoon.

coon skin (kün′skin′), *n.* skin of a raccoon, used in making caps, coats, etc.

coop (küp, ku̇p), *n.* 1 a small cage or pen for chickens, rabbits, etc. 2 a narrow, confined place. —*v.t.* 1 keep or put in a coop. 2 confine, especially in a small space: *The children were cooped up indoors by the rain.* [Middle English *coupe* basket]

co-op (kō′op, kō op′), *n.* INFORMAL. cooperative.

coop., cooperative.

coop er (kü′pər, ku̇p′ər), *n.* man who makes or repairs barrels, casks, etc. —*v.t.* make or repair (barrels, casks, etc.). [perhaps < Middle Dutch *kuper* < Latin *cuparius* < *cupa* cask]

Coo per (kü′pər, ku̇p′ər), *n.* 1 **Anthony Ashley.** See **Shaftesbury.** 2 **James Fenimore,** 1789-1851, American novelist who wrote stories about Indian and frontier life, and about the sea. 3 **Peter,** 1791-1883, American philanthropist.

coop er age (kü′pər ij, ku̇p′ər ij), *n.* 1 work done by a cooper; business of a cooper. 2 price paid for such work. 3 shop where such work is done.

co op e rate (kō op′ə rāt′), *v.i.*, **-rat ed, -rat ing.** work together; unite in producing a result. [< Late Latin *cooperatum* worked together < *co-* + *operari* to work] **—co op′e ra′tor,** *n.*

co op e ra tion (kō op′ə rā′shən), *n.* 1 a working together; united effort or labor. 2 combination of persons for purposes of production, purchase, or distribution for their joint benefit.

co op e ra tive (kō op′ə rā′tiv, kō op′ər ə-tiv), *adj.* 1 wanting or willing to work together with others. 2 of, having to do with, or being a cooperative. —*n.* 1 cooperative store. 2 organization in which the profits and losses are shared by all members, such as a union of farmers for buying and selling their produce at the best price. 3 an apartment house owned and operated by the tenants. 4 apartment in such a building. —**co op′e ra′tive ly,** *adv.* —**co op′e ra′tive ness,** *n.*

cooperative store, store where merchandise is sold to members who share in the profits and losses according to the amounts they buy.

co-opt (kō opt′), *v.t.* (of a committee, etc.) add or elect (a new member). [< Latin *cooptare* < *co-* + *optare* choose]

co-op ta tion (kō′op tā′shən), *n.* a co-opting.

co or di nate (*v.* kō ôrd′n āt; *adj., n.* kō-ôrd′n it, kō ôrd′n āt), *v.,* **-nat ed, -nat ing,** *adj., n.* —*v.t.* 1 arrange in proper order or relation; harmonize; adjust: *Coordinating the movements of the arms and legs is the hardest part of learning to swim.* 2 make equal in importance; make coordinate. —*v.i.* 1 become coordinate. 2 act together or be arranged in the proper order or relation. —*adj.* 1 equal in importance; of equal rank. 2 made up of coordinate parts. 3 joining words, phrases, or clauses of equal grammatical importance. *And* and *but* are coordinate conjunctions. In the phrase "a cold, windy day," "cold" and "windy" are coordinate adjectives. —*n.* 1 a coordinate person or thing; equal. 2 (in mathematics) any of two or more numbers that define the position of a point, line, or plane by reference to a fixed figure, system of lines, etc. [< Medieval Latin *coordinatum* arranged in order < Latin *co-* + *ordinare* regulate, put in order] —**co or′di nate ly,** *adv.* —**co or′di nate ness,** *n.* —**co or′di na′tor,** *n.*

coordinate geometry, analytic geometry.

co or di na tion (kō ôrd′n ā′shən), *n.* 1 harmonious adjustment or working together: *Poor coordination in the hands makes drawing difficult.* 2 proper order or proper relation. 3 a putting or a being put into the same order or rank.

coot (küt), *n.* 1 a wading and swimming bird with short wings and webbed feet. 2 scoter. 3 INFORMAL. fool; simpleton. [Middle English *cote*]

coot ie (kü′tē), *n.* SLANG. louse.

cop[1] (kop), *n.* INFORMAL. policeman. [short for *copper*[2]]

cop[2] (kop), *v.t.,* **copped, cop ping.** SLANG. 1 capture; catch. 2 steal. 3 **cop out, a** back out; refuse to become involved. **b** plead guilty to the lesser of two charges. [probably < Old French *caper* seize < Latin *capere* take]

co pal (kō′pəl), *n.* resin from various tropical and semitropical trees of the same genus as frankincense, used chiefly in making varnish. [< Mexican Spanish < Nahuatl *kopalli*]

co part ner (kō pärt′nər), *n.* a fellow partner; associate.

co part ner ship (kō pärt′nər ship), *n.* partnership.

cope[1] (kōp), *v.i.,* **coped, cop ing.** fight with some degree of success; struggle on even terms; deal successfully: *I was busy but still able to cope with the extra work.* [< Old French *coper* to strike < *coup.* See COUP.]

cope[2] (kōp), *n., v.,* **coped, cop ing.** —*n.* 1 a long cape worn by priests during certain religious rites. 2 anything like a cope; cloaklike covering, such as a canopy, a high, arched roof, or the sky. —*v.t.* 1 cover with a cope or something like a cope. 2 provide with a coping or something like a coping. [< Medieval Latin *capa* cloak]

co peck (kō′pek), *n.* kopeck.

Co pen ha gen (kō′pən hā′gən, kō′pən-hä′gən), *n.* capital of Denmark and its largest city, in the E part of Zealand. 874,000.

Co per ni can (kə pėr′nə kən), *adj.* of or having to do with Copernicus or his system of astronomy.

Co per ni cus (kə pėr′nə kəs), *n.* **Nikolaus,** 1473-1543, Polish astronomer who demonstrated that the earth rotates on its axis and that the planets revolve around the sun (the **Copernican system**).

cope stone (kōp′stōn′), *n.* the top stone of a wall or building; stone used for or in a coping.

cop i er (kop′ē ər), *n.* 1 person who copies; imitator. 2 copyist. 3 duplicator.

co pi lot (kō′pī′lət), *n.* the assistant or second pilot in an aircraft.

cop ing (kō′ping), *n.* the top layer of a brick or stone wall, usually built with a slope to shed water. [< *cope*[2]]

coping saw, a narrow saw in a U-shaped frame, used to cut curves.

co pi ous (kō′pē əs), *adj.* 1 more than enough; plentiful; abundant: *a copious harvest.* 2 containing much matter. 3 containing many words. [< Latin *copiosus* < *copia* plenty < *co-* with + *ops* resources] —**co′pious ly,** *adv.* —**co′pi ous ness,** *n.*

co pla nar (kō plā′nər), *adj.* (of points, lines, figures) lying in the same plane. A circle is a set of coplanar points.

Co pland (kō′plənd), *n.* **Aaron,** born 1900, American composer.

co pol y mer (kō pol′i mər), *n.* compound formed by copolymerization.

co pol y mer ize (kō pol′i mə rīz′), *v.t., v.i.,* **-ized, -iz ing.** polymerize two or more substances. —**co pol′y mer i za′tion,** *n.*

cop per[1] (kop′ər), *n.* 1 a tough, reddish-brown, ductile metallic element which occurs in various ores. Copper resists rust and is an excellent conductor of heat and electricity. *Symbol:* Cu; *atomic number* 29. See pages 326 and 327 for table. 2 coin made of copper or bronze, especially a penny. 3 a large boiler or caldron. 4 a reddish brown. —*v.t.* cover or coat with copper. —*adj.* 1 of copper. 2 reddish-brown. [Old English *coper* < Latin *cuprum,* for earlier *aes Cyprium* metal of Cyprus]

cop per[2] (kop′ər), *n.* SLANG. policeman. [< *cop*[2]]

cop per as (kop′ər əs), *n.* a green, hydrated sulfate of iron, used in dyeing, in making ink, as a disinfectant, and in photography. *Formula:* $FeSO_4 \cdot 7H_2O$ [< Old French *couperose,* perhaps < Medieval Latin *(acqua) cuprosa* (water) of copper]

cop per head (kop′ər hed′), *n.* 1 a poisonous snake with a copper-colored head, found especially in the eastern United States, of the same family as the water moccasin and the rattlesnake. 2 **Copperhead,** person in the North who sympathized with the South during the Civil War.

cop per plate (kop′ər plāt′), *n.* 1 a thin, flat piece of copper on which a design, writing, etc., is engraved or etched. 2 an engraving, picture, or print made from a copperplate. 3 process of printing or engraving from copperplate.

cop per smith (kop′ər smith′), *n.* person who makes things out of copper.

copper sulfate, blue vitriol.

cop per y (kop′ər ē), *adj.* 1 of or containing copper. 2 like copper.

cop pice (kop′is), *n.* copse.

co pra (kō′prə), *n.* the dried meat of coconuts. Coconut oil is obtained from copra. [< Portuguese < Malayalam *koppara*]

copse (kops), *n.* thicket of small trees, bushes, shrubs, etc.; coppice. [< Old French *copeïz* a cut-over forest < *couper* to cut]

Copt (kopt), *n.* 1 native of Egypt descended from the ancient Egyptians. 2 member of the Coptic Church.

cop ter (kop′tər), *n.* INFORMAL. helicopter.

Cop tic (kop′tik), *adj.* of or having to do with the Copts. —*n.* a Hamitic language formerly spoken by the Copts, now used only in the rituals of the Coptic Church.

Coptic Church, the national Christian church of Egypt and formerly of Ethiopia.

cop u la (kop′yə lə), *n., pl.* **-las, -lae** (-lē). a linking verb, often some form of *be.* EXAMPLE: John *is* a boy. [< Latin, bond < *co-* together + *apere* fasten. Doublet of COUPLE.]
➤ A **copula** (linking verb) has little meaning of its own, but is used chiefly as a link between the subject of a sentence and a predicate noun or adjective that completes the thought: *Her mother is a lawyer. He will be angry. The grass became greener.* In these sentences *is, will be,* and *became* are the copulas.

cop u late (kop′yə lāt), *v.i.,* **-lat ed, -lat ing.** unite in sexual intercourse.

cop u la tion (kop′yə lā′shən), *n.* 1 sexual union. 2 a joining together; coupling.

cop u la tive (kop′yə lā′tiv, kop′yə lə tiv), *adj.* serving to couple or connect, especially to connect words or clauses: *"And" is a copulative conjunction. "Be" is a copulative verb.* —*n.* a copulative word. —**cop′u-la′tive ly,** *adv.*

cop y (kop′ē), *n., pl.* **cop ies,** *v.,* **cop ied, cop y ing.** —*n.* 1 thing made to be just like another; thing made on the pattern or model of another; duplicate; reproduction. 2 thing to be followed as a pattern or model. 3 one of a number of books, newspapers, magazines, pictures, etc., made at the same printing. 4 material ready to be set in type for a book, newspaper, or magazine. —*v.t.* 1 make a copy of: *Copy this page. She copied out the inscription in full.* 2 be like; follow as a model; imitate. —*v.i.* make a copy. [< Old French *copie* < Medieval Latin *copia* transcript < Latin, plenty. See COPIOUS.]

cop y book (kop′ē bůk′), *n.* book with models of handwriting to be copied in learning to write. —*adj.* commonplace; conventional; ordinary.

copy boy, person who takes copy from one desk to another or runs errands in a newspaper or magazine office.

hat, āge, fär; let, ēqual, tėrm;
it, īce; hot, ōpen, ôrder;
oil, out; cup, pu̇t, rüle;
ch, child; ng, long; sh, she;
th, thin; ᴛʜ, then; zh, measure;

ə represents *a* in about, *e* in taken, *i* in pencil, *o* in lemon, *u* in circus.

< = from, derived from, taken from.

cop y cat (kop′ē kat′), *n.* SLANG. person who imitates another.

copy desk, the desk in a newspaper office where news stories and articles are edited and prepared for publication.

cop y hold (kop′ē hōld′), *n.* in English law: 1 ownership of land proved by copy of the roll of a manorial court. 2 land held in this way.

cop y hold er (kop′ē hōl′dər), *n.* 1 person who reads manuscript aloud to a proofreader. 2 device for holding copy, as that used by a compositor in setting type. 3 (in English law) person who owns land by copyhold.

cop y ist (kop′ē ist), *n.* 1 person who makes written copies. 2 imitator.

cop y read er (kop′ē rē′dər), *n.* person who reads and edits copy for a newspaper.

cop y right (kop′ē rīt′), *n.* the exclusive right to publish a certain book, dramatic or musical composition, photograph, picture, etc., granted by a government for a certain number of years. *—v.t.* protect by getting a copyright.

cop y writ er (kop′ē rī′tər), *n.* writer of copy, especially for advertising.

co quet (kō ket′), *v.i.,* **-quet ted, -quet ting.** 1 flirt. 2 trifle.

co que try (kō′kə trē, kō ket′rē), *n., pl.* **-tries.** 1 flirting. 2 trifling.

co quette (kō ket′), *n.* woman who tries to attract men merely to please her vanity; flirt. [< French, feminine of *coquet,* diminutive of *coq* cock]

co quet tish (kō ket′ish), *adj.* 1 of a coquette. 2 like a coquette; like a coquette's. **—co quet′tish ly,** *adv.* **—co quet′tish ness,** *n.*

co qui na (kō kē′nə), *n.* a soft, porous, whitish limestone composed of fragments of sea shells and corals. [< Spanish, shellfish]

cor-, *prefix.* form of **com-** before *r,* as in *correct.*

cor., 1 corner. 2 corrected. 3 correction.

Cor., Corinthians.

co ra cle (kôr′ə kəl, kor′ə kəl), *n.* a small, light boat made by covering a wooden frame with waterproof material. [< Welsh *corwgl*]

co ra coid (kôr′ə koid, kor′ə koid), *n.* 1 bone between the shoulder blade and the breastbone in birds and reptiles. 2 a bony process extending from the shoulder blade to or toward the breastbone in mammals. *—adj.* of this bone or bony process. [< Greek *korakoeidēs* like a raven]

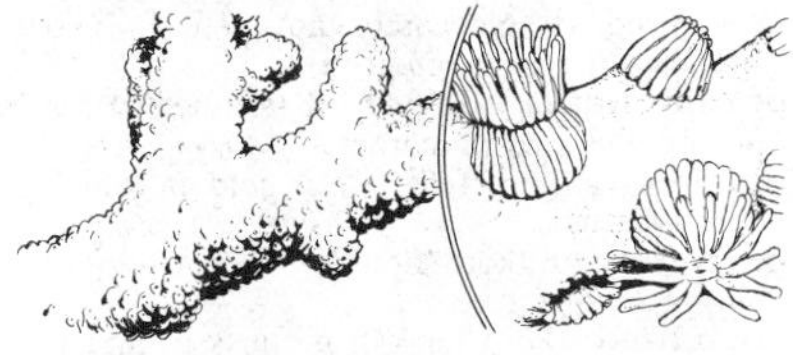

coral (def. 1), left—stony skeleton; coral (def. 2), right—enlarged section as it would appear with living polyps, some expanded and others contracted

co ral (kôr′əl, kor′əl), *n.* 1 a stony substance, mainly calcium carbonate, consisting of the skeletons of polyps. Reefs and small islands consisting of coral are common in tropical seas and oceans. Red, pink, and white coral are often used for jewelry. 2 polyp that secretes a skeleton of coral and forms large branching or rounded colonies by budding. 3 a deep pink or red. *—adj.* 1 made of coral. 2 deep-pink or red. [< Latin *corallum* < Greek *korallion*]

co ral line (kôr′ə lin, kor′ə lin), *adj.* of, having to do with, or like a coral. *—n.* organism resembling a coral, such as some red algae whose fronds contain calcium carbonate.

coral reef, reef consisting mainly of coral.

Coral Sea, part of the Pacific off NE Australia.

coral snake, a small, extremely poisonous American snake of the same family as the cobra, whose body is banded with alternating rings of red, yellow, and black.

cor bel (kôr′bəl), *n., v.,* **-beled, -bel ing** or **-belled, -bel ling.** *—n.* bracket of stone, wood, etc., on the side of a wall. It helps support a projecting ledge above. *—v.t.* furnish with or support by a corbel or corbels. [< Old French, diminutive of *corp* raven < Latin *corvus*]

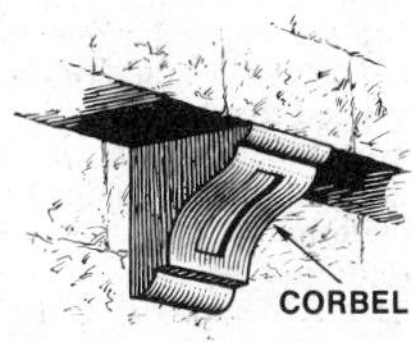

cord (kôrd), *n.* 1 a thick string; very thin rope. 2 anything resembling a cord, such as an electrical extension cord. 3 nerve, tendon, or other structure in an animal body that is somewhat like a cord, such as the spinal cord; chord. 4 ridge or ridged pattern on cloth. 5 cloth with such ridges on it, especially corduroy. 6 measure of cut wood equal to 128 cubic feet. A pile of wood 4 feet wide, 4 feet high, and 8 feet long is a cord. *—v.t.* 1 fasten or tie up with a cord or cords; provide with a cord or cords. 2 pile (wood) in cords. [< Old French *corde* < Latin *chorda* < Greek *chordē* gut. Doublet of CHORD².] **—cord′er,** *n.* **—cord′like′,** *adj.*

cord age (kôr′dij), *n.* 1 cords or ropes: *Most of the cordage on a sailing ship is in its rigging.* 2 quantity of wood measured in cords.

cor date (kôr′dāt), *adj.* heart-shaped. [< New Latin *cordatus* < Latin *cordem* heart] **—cor′date ly,** *adv.*

Cor day (kôr dā′), *n.* **Charlotte,** 1768-1793, Frenchwoman who assassinated Marat.

cord ed (kôr′did), *adj.* 1 having ridges on it; ribbed. 2 fastened with a cord; bound with cords. 3 (of wood) piled in cords.

Cor del ia (kôr dē′lyə), *n.* the loyal youngest daughter of Lear in Shakespeare's tragedy *King Lear.*

cor dial (kôr′jəl), *adj.* 1 warm and friendly in manner; hearty; sincere: *a cordial welcome.* 2 strengthening; stimulating. *—n.* 1 food, drink, or medicine that strengthens or stimulates. 2 liqueur. [< Medieval Latin *cordialem* < Latin *cordem* heart] **—cor′dial ly,** *adv.* **—cor′dial ness,** *n.*

cor di al i ty (kôr′jē al′ə tē, kôr jal′ə tē), *n., pl.* **-ties.** cordial quality or feeling; heartiness; warmth.

cor dil ler a (kôr dil′ər ə, kôr′də lyer′ə), *n.* system of mountain ranges; chain of mountains. 2 Often, **Cordilleras,** *pl.* **a** the main mountain system of a continent: *the Cordilleras of the Andes.* **b** system of mountain ranges extending from Alaska to Cape Horn. [< Spanish] **—cor dil′ler an,** *adj.*

cord ite (kôr′dīt), *n.* a smokeless gunpowder composed chiefly of nitroglycerin and nitrocellulose formed into cordlike lengths. [< *cord*]

cord less (kôrd′lis), *adj.* powered by electric cells and having no electric cord: *a cordless clock.*

cor do ba (kôr′də bə), *n.* the monetary unit of Nicaragua, a silver coin equal to 100 centavos and worth about 14 cents. [< Francisco de *Córdoba,* 1475-1526, Spanish explorer]

Cór do ba (kôr′də bə; *Spanish* kôr′ᴛʜō vä), *n.* 1 city in S Spain. 232,000. 2 city in central Argentina. 589,000. Also, **Cordova.**

cor don (kôrd′n), *n.* 1 line or circle of soldiers, policemen, forts, etc., enclosing or guarding a place. 2 cord, braid, or ribbon worn as an ornament or as a badge of honor. [< French]

cor don sa ni taire (kôr dôɴ′ sȧ nē ter′), *pl.* ***cor dons sa ni taires*** (kôr dôɴ′ sȧ nē ter′). FRENCH. 1 line of guards about a quarantined area. 2 a buffer zone. 3 (literally) sanitary cordon.

Cor do va (kôr′də və, kôr dō′və), *n.* Córdoba.

cor do van (kôr′də vən, kôr dō′vən), *adj.* of or having to do with a kind of soft leather. *—n.* 1 kind of soft, fine-grained leather. 2 shoe made of this leather. [< Spanish *cordobán* < *Córdoba,* Spain]

cor du roy (kôr′də roi′, kôr′də roi′), *n.* 1 a thick, cotton cloth with close, velvetlike ridges. 2 **corduroys,** *pl.* corduroy trousers. *—adj.* made of corduroy. [< *cord,* noun + obsolete *duroy,* a type of woolen cloth]

corduroy road, road made of logs laid crosswise, usually across low, wet land.

cord wain er (kôrd′wā nər), *n.* ARCHAIC. shoemaker. [< Anglo-French *cordewaner* < *cordewan* cordovan < Spanish *cordobán*]

cord wood (kôrd′wu̇d′), *n.* 1 wood sold by the cord. 2 firewood piled in cords. 3 wood cut in 4-foot lengths.

core (kôr, kōr), *n., v.,* **cored, cor ing.** *—n.* 1 the hard central part, containing the seeds, of fruits like apples and pears. 2 the central or most important part: *the core of a boil, the core of an argument.* 3 bar of soft iron or winding of iron wires forming the center of an electromagnet, induction coil, etc., and serving to increase and concentrate the induced magnetic field. 4 the central or innermost portion of the earth, below the mantle. *—v.t.* take out the core of: *The cook cored the apples.* [Middle English, apparently < Old French *cors* body < Latin *corpus*] **—cor′er,** *n.*

CORE (kôr, kōr), *n.* Congress of Racial Equality.

co re op sis (kôr′ē op′sis, kōr′ē op′sis), *n.* 1 any of a genus of herbs of the composite family, with yellow, red-and-yellow, or reddish flowers shaped like daisies. 2 its flower.

[< Greek *koris* bedbug + *opsis* appearance; from the shape of the seed]

co re spond ent (kō′ri spon′dənt), *n.* (in law) a person accused of adultery with a husband or wife who is being sued for divorce.

Cor fu (kôr′fyü, kôr fü′), *n.* Greek island in the Ionian Sea, just northwest of Greece. 102,000 pop.; 229 sq. mi.

co ri an der (kôr′ē an′dər, kōr′ē an′dər), *n.* 1 plant of the same family as the parsley, having a disagreeable odor but bearing aromatic fruits. 2 its seedlike fruit. The oil from the seeds is used as a flavoring and in medicine. [< Latin *coriandrum* < Greek *koriandron*]

Cor inth (kôr′inth, kor′inth), *n.* 1 seaport in S Greece. In ancient times, it was a center of commerce noted for its art and luxury. 18,000. 2 **Gulf of,** gulf separating the Peloponnesus from N Greece. 3 **Isthmus of,** narrow isthmus at the head of the Gulf of Corinth, connecting the Peloponnesus with N Greece. 4-8 mi. wide.

Co rin thi an (kə rin′thē ən), *adj.* 1 of or having to do with Corinth or its people. 2 of or having to do with the most elaborate of the three orders of Greek architecture. The capital of a Corinthian column is adorned with acanthus leaves. See **order** for picture. *—n.* native or inhabitant of Corinth.

Corinthian capital (def. 2)

Co rin thi ans (kə rin′thē ənz), *n.* either of two books of the New Testament, consisting of letters written by Saint Paul to the Christians of Corinth.

Cor i o la nus (kôr′ē ə lā′nəs, kor′ə-lā′nəs), *n.* Roman general of the 400's B.C. who was banished from Rome and later led an army in an unsuccessful attack on it.

co ri um (kôr′ē əm, kōr′ē əm), *n., pl.* **co ri a** (kôr′ē ə, kōr′ē ə). dermis. [< Latin, leather, skin, hide]

cork (kôrk), *n.* 1 the light, thick, elastic outer bark of the cork oak, used for bottle stoppers, floats for fishing lines, inner soles of shoes, and some floor coverings. 2 a shaped piece of cork: *the cork of a bottle.* 3 any stopper for a bottle, flask, etc., made of glass, rubber, etc. 4 an outer bark of woody plants, serving as a protective covering. *—v.t.* 1 stop up with a cork. 2 confine; restrain; check. 3 blacken with burnt cork. *—adj.* made of or with cork. [< Spanish *alcorque* < Arabic *al-qurq* the cork < Latin *corticem* cork; cortex]

Cork (kôrk), *n.* 1 county in the S part of the Republic of Ireland. 2 city in this county. 122,000.

cork er (kôr′kər), *n.* SLANG. person or thing of surpassing quality or size.

cork ing (kôr′king), *adj.* SLANG. excellent; outstanding; fine.

cork oak, the oak tree of the Mediterranean area, from which cork is obtained.

cork screw (kôrk′skrü′), *n.* tool used to pull corks out of bottles. *—adj.* shaped like a corkscrew; spiral. *—v.t., v.i.* INFORMAL. move or advance in a spiral or zigzag course.

cork tree, cork oak.

cork y (kôr′kē), *adj.,* **cork i er, cork i est.** of or resembling cork.

corm of a crocus partly cut away to show underlying layers

corm (kôrm), *n.* a fleshy, bulblike underground stem of certain plants, such as the crocus and gladiolus, that produces leaves and buds on the upper surface and roots on the lower. [< New Latin *cormus* < Greek *kormos* stripped tree trunk]

cor mor ant (kôr′mər ənt), *n.* 1 any of a family of large, and supposedly greedy, black sea birds with hooked bills and webbed feet. Tame cormorants are used in Asia to catch fish. 2 a greedy person. [< Old French *cormareng* < *corp* raven + *marenc* of the sea]

corn[1] (kôrn), *n.* 1 kind of grain that grows on large ears; maize; Indian corn. 2 plant, a species of cereal grass, that it grows on. 3 sweet corn. 4 any small, hard seed or grain, especially of cereal plants. 5 (in England) grain in general, especially wheat. 6 (in Scotland and Ireland) oats. 7 SLANG. something trite, outdated, or sentimental. *—v.t.* preserve (meat) with strong salt water or with dry salt. [Old English]

corn[2] (kôrn), *n.* a small, hard, shiny thickening of the outer layer of the skin, usually on a toe, caused by pressure or rubbing. [< Old French, horn < Latin *cornu*]

Corn Belt, area in the Middle West where corn is grown extensively. Nebraska, Iowa, Illinois, and Indiana are included in the Corn Belt.

corn borer, larva of a small moth, originally from the Old World, that destroys corn and other plants.

corn bread, bread made of corn meal.

corn cob (kôrn′kob′), *n.* 1 the elongated, central, woody part of an ear of corn, on which the kernels grow; cob. 2 a tobacco pipe with a bowl hollowed out of a piece of dried corncob.

corn cockle, weed, a species of pink, with red or white flowers and poisonous seeds that grows in grainfields.

corn crake, bird common in grainfields in Europe.

corn crib (kôrn′krib′), *n.* bin or small, ventilated building for storing unshelled corn.

cor ne a (kôr′nē ə), *n.* the transparent part of the outer coat of the eyeball. The cornea covers the iris and the pupil. See **eye** for diagram. [< Medieval Latin *cornea (tela)* horny (web) < Latin *cornu* horn]

cor ne al (kôr′nē əl), *adj.* of or having to do with the cornea.

corn ear worm (ir′wėrm′), large moth larva that feeds on ears of green corn; bollworm.

corned (kôrnd), *adj.* preserved with strong salt water or with dry salt: *corned beef.*

Cor neille (kôr nā′; *French* kôr ne′yə), *n.* **Pierre,** 1606-1684, French dramatist.

cor nel (kôr′nl), *n.* 1 (in Europe) a shrub or small tree of the same family as the dogwood, with yellow flowers and edible red berries. 2 (in North America) the dogwood. [< Old French *corneille,* ultimately < Latin *cornum*]

cor nel ian (kôr nē′lyən), *n.* carnelian.

cor ne ous (kôr′nē əs), *adj.* horny.

cor ner (kôr′nər), *n.* 1 point or place where lines or surfaces meet. 2 space between two lines or surfaces near where they meet; angle. 3 the place where two streets meet. 4 piece to form, protect, or decorate a corner. 5 place away from crowds; secret place. 6 place that is far away; region; part: *People have searched in all corners of the earth for gold.* 7 an awkward or difficult position; place from which escape is impossible: *driven into a corner.* 8 a buying up of the available supply of some stock or article to raise its price: *a corner in wheat.* 9 **cut corners, a** shorten the way by going across corners. **b** save money by reducing effort, time, labor, etc. 10 **turn the corner,** pass the worst or most dangerous point.
—adj. 1 at or on a corner: *a corner house.* 2 for a corner: *a corner cabinet.*
—v.t. 1 put in a corner; drive or force into a corner. 2 force into an awkward or difficult position; drive into a place from which escape is impossible. 3 buy up all or nearly all that is available of (something) to raise its price: *Some speculators have tried to corner silver.* *—v.i.* INFORMAL. (of an automobile) to round sharp corners at relatively high speeds without sway.
[< Old French *cornere* < Latin *cornu* horn]

cor nered (kôr′nərd), *adj.* without hope of escape or relief: *A cornered animal will fight.*

cor ner stone (kôr′nər stōn′), *n.* 1 stone at the corner of two walls that holds them together. 2 such a stone built into the corner of a building as its formal beginning. The laying of a cornerstone is often accompanied by ceremonies. 3 something of fundamental importance; foundation; basis: *The cornerstone of most religions is faith in God.*

cor ner ways (kôr′nər wāz′), *adv.* cornerwise.

cor ner wise (kôr′nər wīz′), *adv.* 1 with the corner in front; so as to form a corner. 2 from corner to corner; diagonally.

cor net (kôr net′ *for 1;* kôr′nit, kôr net′ *for 2*), *n.* 1 a musical wind instrument somewhat like a trumpet, usually made of brass. It has three valves that control the pitch. 2 piece of paper rolled into a cone and twisted at one end, used to hold candy, nuts, etc. [< Old French < Latin *cornu* horn]

cor net tist or **cor net ist** (kôr net′ist), *n.* person who plays a cornet.

corn field (kôrn′fēld′), *n.* field in which corn is grown.

corn flow er (kôrn′flou′ər), *n.* bachelor's-button.

corn husk (kôrn′husk′), *n.* husk of an ear of corn.

cor nice (kôr′nis), *n., v.,* **-niced, -nic ing.** *—n.* 1 an ornamental, horizontal molding along the top of a wall, pillar, building, etc. See **entablature** for diagram. 2 a molding around the walls of a room just below the ceiling or over the top of a window. *—v.t.* furnish or finish with a cornice. [< French *corniche* < Italian *cornice*]

Cor nish (kôr′nish), *adj.* of or having to do with Cornwall, its people, or the language formerly spoken by them. *—n.* a Celtic language spoken in Cornwall until the late 1700's.

Cor nish man (kôr′nish mən), *n., pl.* **-men.** native or inhabitant of Cornwall.

Corn Laws, series of laws restricting the importation of grain into England, repealed in 1846.

corn meal, meal made from ground-up corn; Indian meal.

corn pone, (in the southern United States) a flat loaf of corn meal shaped by hand. It is a simple kind of corn bread.

corn shock, a conical stack of cornstalks cut and set up on end together in a field.

corn silk, the glossy threads or styles at the end of an ear of corn.

corn stalk (kôrn′stôk′), *n.* stalk of corn.

corn starch (kôrn′stärch′), *n.* a starchy flour made from corn, used to thicken puddings, custard, gravies, etc.

corn sugar, sugar made from cornstarch.

corn syrup, syrup made from cornstarch.

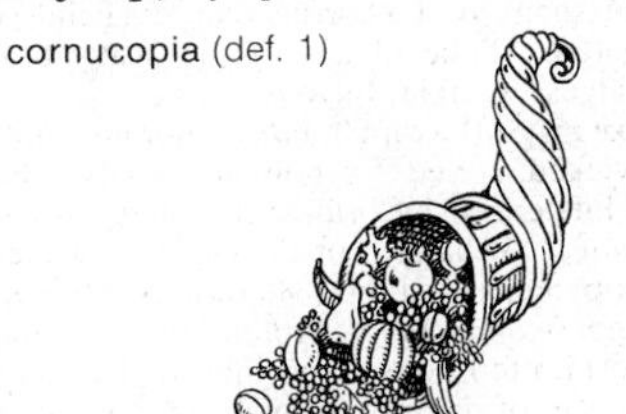

cornucopia (def. 1)

cor nu co pi a (kôr′nə kō′pē ə), *n.* 1 a horn-shaped container represented as overflowing with fruits, vegetables, and flowers; horn of plenty. 2 a horn-shaped container or ornament. [< Late Latin, for Latin *cornu copiae* horn of plenty]

Corn wall (kôrn′wôl), *n.* county in SW England.

Corn wal lis (kôrn wô′lis, kôrn wol′is), *n.* **Charles,** 1738-1805, British general who surrendered to Washington at Yorktown on October 19, 1781.

corn whiskey, whiskey distilled from corn.

corn y (kôr′nē), *adj.,* **corn i er, corn i est.** SLANG. trite, outdated, or sentimental.

co rol la (kə rol′ə), *n.* the internal envelope or floral leaves of a flower usually of some color other than green; the petals. See **bilabiate** for picture. [< Latin, garland, diminutive of *corona* crown]

co rol lar y (kôr′ə ler′ē, kor′ə ler′ē), *n., pl.* **-lar ies.** 1 something proved by inference from something else already proved. 2 inference; deduction. 3 a natural consequence or result: *Destruction and suffering were corollaries of the war.* [< Late Latin *corollarium* < Latin, money paid for a garland, gift < *corolla* garland]

co rol late (kôr′ə lāt, kor′ə lāt), *adj.* having or resembling a corolla.

co ro na (kə rō′nə), *n., pl.* **-nas, -nae** (-nē). 1 ring of light seen around the sun, moon, or other luminous body. 2 halo of light around the sun, visible to the naked eye only during an eclipse. 3 a crownlike part; crown. [< Latin, crown. Doublet of CROWN.]

co ro nach (kôr′ə nəH, kor′ə nəH), *n.* SCOTTISH and IRISH. dirge.

Co ro na do (kôr′ə nä′dō, kor′ə nä′dō), *n.* **Francisco Vásquez de,** 1510-1554, Spanish conquistador who explored the southwestern part of what is now the United States.

co ro na graph (kə rō′nə graf), *n.* instrument for observing the corona of the sun by means of lenses that produce an artificial solar eclipse.

co ro nal (*n.* kôr′ə nəl, kor′ə nəl; *adj. also* kə rō′nəl), *n.* 1 crown or coronet. 2 garland. *—adj.* of or having to do with a crown or a corona.

co ro nar y (kôr′ə ner′ē, kor′ə ner′ē), *adj., n., pl.* **-nar ies.** *—adj.* of or having to do with the coronary arteries. *—n.* coronary thrombosis.

coronary artery, either of the two arteries that supply blood to the muscular tissue of the heart.

coronary thrombosis or **coronary occlusion,** the stopping up of a coronary artery or one of its branches by a blood clot.

co ro na tion (kôr′ə nā′shən, kor′ə-nā′shən), *n.* ceremony of crowning a king, queen, emperor, etc.

co ro ner (kôr′ə nər, kor′ə nər), *n.* official of a local government whose principal function is to inquire in the presence of a jury into the cause of any death not clearly due to natural causes. [< Anglo-French *corouner* officer of the crown < *coroune.* See CROWN.]

co ro net (kôr′ə net′, kor′ə net′), *n.* 1 a small crown, especially one indicating a rank of nobility below that of the sovereign. 2 a circle of gold, jewels, or flowers worn around the head as an ornament.

Co rot (kô rō′), *n.* **Jean Baptiste Camille,** 1796-1875, French landscape painter.

Corp., 1 Corporal. 2 Corporation.

cor por al[1] (kôr′pər əl), *adj.* of the body: *corporal punishment.* [< Latin *corporalem* < *corpus* body] **—cor′por al ly,** *adv.*

cor por al[2] (kôr′pər əl), *n.* 1 the lowest-ranking noncommissioned officer in the army, ranking next below a sergeant and next above a private first class. He usually is in charge of a squad. 2 a noncommissioned officer of similar rank in the U.S. Marine Corps. [< French < Italian *caporale* < *capo* head < Latin *caput*]

cor por ate (kôr′pər it), *adj.* 1 forming a corporation; incorporated. 2 belonging to a corporation; of or having to do with a corporation. 3 united; combined. [< Latin *corporatum* formed into a body < *corpus* body] **—cor′por ate ly,** *adv.*

cor po ra tion (kôr′pə rā′shən), *n.* 1 group of persons who obtain a charter that gives them as a group certain legal rights and privileges distinct from those of the individual members of the group, such as the right to buy and sell and to own property, and limit their financial responsibility for the business. 2 group of persons with authority to act as a single person. The governing body of a college and the mayor and aldermen of a city are corporations.

cor po re al (kôr pôr′ē əl, kôr pōr′ē əl), *adj.* 1 of or for the body; bodily: *corporeal nourishment.* 2 material; tangible: *Land and money are corporeal things.* **—cor po′re al ly,** *adv.* **—cor po′re al ness,** *n.*

cor po re al i ty (kôr pôr′ē al′ə tē, kôr-pōr′ē al′ə tē), *n.* quality or condition of being corporeal.

corps (kôr, kōr), *n., pl.* **corps** (kôrz, kōrz). 1 branch of specialized military service: *the Quartermaster Corps, the Army Medical Corps.* 2 a military unit usually consisting of two or more divisions, plus supporting troops, usually commanded by a lieutenant general. It is smaller than an army. 3 group of people with special training, organized for working together: *a corps of nurses.*

hat, āge, fär; let, ēqual, tėrm;
it, īce; hot, ōpen, ôrder;
oil, out; cup, pu̇t, rüle;
ch, child; ng, long; sh, she;
th, thin; ᴛʜ, then; zh, measure;

ə represents *a* in about, *e* in taken, *i* in pencil, *o* in lemon, *u* in circus.

< = from, derived from, taken from.

[< French < Latin *corpus* body. Doublet of CORPSE, CORPUS.]

corps de bal let (kôr′ də ba lā′; *French* kôr də bȧ le′, group of ballet dancers, usually the members of a company other than the soloists. [< French]

corpse (kôrps), *n.* a dead human body. [< Old French *corps, cors* < Latin *corpus* body. Doublet of CORPS, CORPUS.]

corps man (kôr′mən, kōr′mən), *n., pl.* **-men.** 1 an enlisted man in the United States Navy or Army who performs medical duties or helps with the wounded. 2 member of any corps.

cor pu lence (kôr′pyə ləns), *n.* fatness.

cor pu len cy (kôr′pyə lən sē), *n.* corpulence.

cor pu lent (kôr′pyə lənt), *adj.* large or bulky of body; fat. **—cor′pu lent ly,** *adv.*

cor pus (kôr′pəs), *n., pl.* **-por a** (-pər ə). 1 a complete collection of writings on some subject or of some period, or of laws, etc. 2 any of various anatomical masses or parts of special character or function. 3 the body or material substance of anything. [< Latin, body. Doublet of CORPS, CORPSE.]

Cor pus Chris ti (kôr′pəs kris′tē), 1 feast of the Roman Catholic Church in honor of the Eucharist, celebrated on the first Thursday after Trinity Sunday. 2 city in S Texas. 205,000. [< Latin *corpus Christi* body of Christ]

cor pus cle (kôr′pus′əl, kôr′pə səl), *n.* 1 any of the cells that form a large part of the blood, lymph, etc. Red corpuscles carry oxygen to the tissues and remove carbon dioxide; some white corpuscles destroy disease germs. 2 a very small particle. [< Latin *corpusculum,* diminutive of *corpus* body]

cor pus cu lar (kôr pus′kyə lər), *adj.* of, like, or consisting of corpuscles.

cor pus de lic ti (kôr′pəs di lik′tī), 1 the actual facts that prove a crime or offense against the law has been committed. 2 body of a murdered person. [< Latin, body of the crime]

cor pus lu te um (kôr′pəs lü′tē əm), *pl.* **cor por a lu te a** (kôr′pər ə lü′tē ə). a yellow endocrine mass formed in the ovary from the ruptured sac left behind after the release of a mature ovum. [< New Latin, yellow body]

corr., 1 corrected. 2 corresponding.

cor ral (kə ral′), *n., v.,* **-ralled, -ral ling.** *—n.* 1 pen for keeping or for capturing horses, cattle, etc. 2 a circular camp formed by wagons for defense against attack. *—v.t.* 1 drive into or keep in a corral. 2 hem in; surround; capture: *The reporters corralled the candidate and asked him for a statement.* 3 form (wagons) into a circular camp. [< Spanish]

cor rect (kə rekt′), *adj.* 1 free from mistakes or faults; right: *the correct answer.* See synonym study below. 2 agreeing with a recognized standard, especially of good taste; proper: *correct manners.* —*v.t.* 1 change to what is right; remove mistakes or faults from: *Correct any misspellings that you find.* 2 alter or adjust to agree with some standard: *correct the reading of a barometer.* 3 point out or mark the errors of; check: *correct test papers.* 4 set right by punishing; find fault with to improve; punish: *The mother corrected the child for misbehaving.* 5 counteract or neutralize (something hurtful); cure; overcome; remedy: *Medicine can sometimes correct stomach trouble.* [< Latin *correctum* made straight < *com-* + *regere* to guide] **—cor rect′a ble,** *adj.* **—cor rect′ly,** *adv.* **—cor rect′ness,** *n.* **—cor rec′tor,** *n.*

Syn. *adj.* 1 **Correct, accurate, exact** mean without error or mistake. **Correct** adds nothing to that basic meaning: *I gave correct answers to the questions.* **Accurate** emphasizes the careful effort to make something agree exactly with the facts or with a model: *I gave an accurate account of the accident.* **Exact** emphasizes the complete agreement in every detail with the facts or with a model: *The painting is an exact copy of the original.*

cor rec tion (kə rek′shən), *n.* 1 act or process of correcting. 2 a change to correct an error or mistake. 3 punishment; rebuke; scolding. 4 amount added or subtracted to correct a result.

cor rec tion al (kə rek′shə nəl), *adj.* of or having to do with correction.

cor rec tive (kə rek′tiv), *adj.* tending to correct; setting right; making better: *Corrective exercises can make weak muscles strong.* —*n.* something that corrects or tends to correct. **—cor rec′tive ly,** *adv.*

Cor reg gio (kô rej′ō), *n.* **Antonio Allegri da,** 1494-1534, Italian painter.

Cor reg i dor (kə reg′ə dôr), *n.* fortified island at the entrance to Manila Bay, Philippines.

cor re late (kôr′ə lāt, kor′ə lāt), *v.,* **-lat ed, -lat ing.** —*v.t.* place in or bring into proper relation with one another; show the connection or relation between: *Try to correlate your knowledge of history with your knowledge of geography.* —*v.i.* be related one to the other; have a mutual relation: *The diameter and the circumference of a circle correlate.*

cor re la tion (kôr′ə lā′shən, kor′ə lā′shən), *n.* 1 the mutual relation of two or more things: *There is a close correlation between climate and crops.* 2 act or process of correlating. 3 condition of being correlated.

cor re la tion al (kôr′ə lā′shə nəl, kor′ə lā′shə nəl), *adj.* having to do with or using correlation.

cor rel a tive (kə rel′ə tiv), *adj.* 1 mutually dependent; so related that each implies the other. 2 having a mutual relation and commonly used together. Conjunctions used in pairs, such as *either . . . or* and *both . . . and,* are correlative. —*n.* 1 either of two things having a mutual relation and commonly used together. 2 either of a pair of correlative words. **—cor rel′a tive ly,** *adv.*

cor re spond (kôr′ə spond′, kor′ə spond′), *v.i.* 1 be in harmony; agree; harmonize; match: *My ideas on the subject correspond with yours.* See **agree** for synonym study. 2 be similar: *The fins of a fish correspond to the wings of a bird.* 3 exchange letters; write letters to each other. [< Medieval Latin *correspondere* < Latin *com-* together + *respondere* respond]

cor re spond ence (kôr′ə spon′dəns, kor′ə spon′dəns), *n.* 1 a being in harmony; agreement. 2 resemblance in structure or function; similarity. 3 exchange of letters; practice of letter writing. 4 letters: *Bring me the correspondence concerning that order.* 5 (in mathematics) a one-to-one relationship between sets.

correspondence course, set of lessons on a certain subject given by a correspondence school.

correspondence school, school that gives lessons by mail. Instructions, explanations, and questions are sent to the student, and he returns his written answers for correction or approval.

cor re spond ent (kôr′ə spon′dənt, kor′ə spon′dənt), *n.* 1 person who exchanges letters with another. 2 person employed by a newspaper, magazine, radio or television network, etc., to send news from a particular place or region. 3 person or company that has regular business with another in a distant place: *Many American banks have correspondents in European cities.* 4 thing that corresponds to something else; correlative. —*adj.* in agreement; corresponding.

cor re spond ing (kôr′ə spon′ding, kor′ə spon′ding), *adj.* 1 similar; matching. 2 in harmony; agreeing. 3 of or having to do with an exchange of letters, conduct of business correspondence, etc. **—cor′re spond′ing ly,** *adv.*

cor ri da (kôr rē′ᴛʜä), *n.* SPANISH. 1 a bullfight. 2 (literally) a running.

cor ri dor (kôr′ə dər, kôr′ə dôr; kor′ə dər, kor′ə dôr), *n.* 1 a long hallway; passage in a large building into which rooms open; passageway; hall. 2 a narrow strip of land connecting two parts of a country, or connecting an inland country with a seaport. [< French < Italian *corridore* < *correre* to run < Latin *currere*]

cor ri gen dum (kôr′ə jen′dəm, kor′ə jen′dəm), *n., pl.* **-da** (-də). error in a book, manuscript, etc., to be corrected. [< Latin, (thing) to be corrected]

cor ri gi ble (kôr′ə jə bəl, kor′ə jə bəl), *adj.* 1 that can be corrected. 2 yielding to correction; willing to be corrected. [< Medieval Latin *corrigibilem* < Latin *corrigere* to correct] **—cor′ri gi bly,** *adv.*

cor rob o rate (kə rob′ə rāt′), *v.t.,* **-rat ed, -rat ing.** make more certain; confirm; support: *Eyewitnesses corroborated my testimony in court.* See **confirm** for synonym study. [< Latin *corroboratum* strengthened < *com-* + *roborem* oak, strength] **—cor rob′o ra′tor,** *n.*

cor rob o ra tion (kə rob′ə rā′shən), *n.* 1 confirmation by additional proof. 2 something that corroborates; additional proof.

cor rob o ra tive (kə rob′ə rā′tiv, kə rob′ər ə tiv), *adj.* corroborating; confirming. **—cor rob′o ra′tive ly,** *adv.*

cor rob o ra to ry (kə rob′ər ə tôr′ē, kə rob′ər ə tōr′ē), *adj.* corroborative.

cor rode (kə rōd′), *v.,* **-rod ed, -rod ing.** —*v.t.* eat away gradually, especially by or as if by chemical action: *Moist air corrodes iron.* —*v.i.* become corroded. [< Latin *corrodere* < *com-* + *rodere* gnaw]

cor rod i ble (kə rō′də bəl), *adj.* capable of being corroded.

cor ro sion (kə rō′zhən), *n.* 1 act or process of corroding. 2 a corroded condition. 3 product of corroding. [< Latin *corrosionem* < *corrodere* corrode]

cor ro sive (kə rō′siv), *adj.* producing corrosion; tending to corrode. —*n.* substance that corrodes: *Most acids are corrosives.* **—cor ro′sive ly,** *adv.* **—cor ro′sive ness,** *n.*

corrosive sublimate, mercuric chloride.

cor ru gate (kôr′ə gāt, kor′ə gāt), *v.t.,* **-gat ed, -gat ing.** bend or shape (a surface or a thin sheet of material) into wavy folds or ridges; wrinkle; furrow: *The carton was made of corrugated cardboard.* [< Latin *corrugatum* wrinkled < *com-* + *ruga* wrinkle]

corrugated paper, paper or cardboard bent into a row of wavelike ridges, used as a protective wrapping for packages, etc.

cor ru ga tion (kôr′ə gā′shən, kor′ə gā′shən), *n.* 1 a corrugating. 2 a being corrugated. 3 one of a series of wavy folds or ridges; wrinkle; furrow.

cor rupt (kə rupt′), *adj.* 1 morally bad; evil; wicked. See synonym study below. 2 influenced by bribes; dishonest: *a corrupt judge.* 3 changed or damaged by inaccurate copying, insertions, alterations, etc.: *a corrupt manuscript.* 4 (of a language, dialect, form, etc.) considered inferior by some because of change in meaning or form, or deviation from standard usage. 5 ARCHAIC. rotten; decayed. —*v.t.* 1 make evil or wicked. 2 bribe. 3 make worse by changing; make incorrect. 4 cause (a form, meaning, dialect, etc.) to differ from standard usage. 5 make rotten or decayed. —*v.i.* become corrupt. [< Latin *corruptum* corrupted, broken < *com-* + *rumpere* to break] **—cor rupt′er, cor rup′tor,** *n.* **—cor rupt′ly,** *adv.* **—cor rupt′ness,** *n.*

Syn. *adj.* 1 **Corrupt, depraved** mean made morally bad. **Corrupt** implies loss of an earlier soundness or purity: *The Medical Association took away the license of the doctor because of his corrupt practices.* **Depraved** implies a complete deterioration of morals or taste: *This murder was committed by a depraved man.*

cor rupt i bil i ty (kə rup′tə bil′ə tē), *n.* corruptible quality.

cor rupt i ble (kə rup′tə bəl), *adj.* that can be corrupted. **—cor rupt′i ble ness,** *n.* **—cor rupt′i bly,** *adv.*

cor rup tion (kə rup′shən), *n.* 1 a making evil or wicked. 2 a being made evil or wicked. 3 evil conduct; wickedness. 4 bribery; dishonesty. 5 a changing for the worse; making impure or incorrect. 6 a causing (a form, meaning, dialect, etc.) to differ from standard usage: *the corruption of a language.* 7 rot; decay. 8 a corrupting influence; thing that causes corruption.

cor rup tive (kə rup′tiv), *adj.* tending to corrupt; causing corruption.

cor sage (kôr säzh′), *n.* 1 bouquet to be worn at a woman's waist or shoulder. 2 the upper part of a woman's dress. [< French < Old French *cors* bust, body < Latin *corpus*]

cor sair (kôr′ser, kôr′sar), *n.* 1 pirate. 2 a pirate ship. 3 privateer, especially a Saracen or Turkish privateer of the Barbary Coast. [< French *corsaire* < Medieval Latin *cursarius* runner < Latin *cursus* a run. Doublet of HUSSAR.]

corse (kôrs), *n.* ARCHAIC. corpse. [< Old French *cors* < Latin *corpus* body]

hat, āge, fär; let, ēqual, tėrm;
it, īce; hot, ōpen, ôrder;
oil, out; cup, pu̇t, rüle;
ch, child; ng, long; sh, she;
th, thin; ᴛʜ, then; zh, measure;

ə represents *a* in about, *e* in taken, *i* in pencil, *o* in lemon, *u* in circus.

< = from, derived from, taken from.

corselet

corse let (kôrs′lit), *n.* armor for the upper part of the body. Also, **corslet.**

cor set (kôr′sit), *n.* a woman's stiff, close-fitting undergarment, worn about the waist and hips to support or shape the body. *—v.t.* fit a corset on; dress in a corset. [< Old French, laced bodice < *cors* body < Latin *corpus*]

Cor si ca (kôr′sə kə), *n.* island in the Mediterranean, southeast of and belonging to France. 270,000 pop.; 3400 sq. mi. *Capital:* Ajaccio. **—Cor′si can,** *adj., n.*

cors let (kôrs′lit), *n.* corselet.

cor tege or **cor tège** (kôr tezh′, kôr-tāzh′), *n.* 1 procession: *a funeral cortege.* 2 group of followers, attendants, etc.; retinue. [< French *cortège* < Italian *corteggio* < *corte* court]

Cor tes (kôr′tez, kôr′tes), *n.* the national legislature of Spain or the national assembly of Portugal. [< Spanish and Portuguese < plural of *corte* court]

Cor tés or **Cor tez** (kôr tez′, kôr′tez), *n.* **Hernando,** 1485-1547, Spanish soldier who conquered Mexico.

cor tex (kôr′teks), *n., pl.* **-ti ces** (-tə sēz′), 1 the layer of gray matter which covers most of the surface of the brain. 2 the outer layer or wall of an internal organ: *the adrenal cortex.* 3 the part of the tissue of roots and stems of higher plants which lies outside the vascular tissue and inside the epidermis. In woody plants it becomes the bark. [< Latin, bark]

cor ti cal (kôr′tə kəl), *adj.* 1 of or having to do with a cortex, especially of the brain or kidneys. 2 consisting of cortex. **—cor′ti-cal ly,** *adv.*

cor ti coid (kôr′tə koid), *n.* any of a group of steroids, many of them hormones, produced by the cortex of the adrenal glands. They are important in metabolism.

cor ti co trop in (kôr′tə kō trop′ən), *n.* ACTH.

cor tin (kôrt′n), *n.* secretion from the cortex of the adrenal glands containing cortisone and other hormones.

cor ti sol (kôr′tə sōl), *n.* hydrocortisone.

cor ti sone (kôr′tə sōn, kôr′tə zōn), *n.* steroid hormone obtained from the cortex of the adrenal glands or produced synthetically, used in the treatment of arthritis and other ailments. *Formula:* $C_{21}H_{28}O_5$

co run dum (kə run′dəm), *n.* an extremely hard mineral consisting of aluminum oxide. The dark-colored variety is used for polishing and grinding. Sapphires and rubies are transparent varieties of corundum. *Formula:* Al_2O_3 [< Tamil *kurundam*]

cor us cate (kôr′ə skāt, kor′ə skāt), *v.i.,* **-cat ed, -cat ing.** give off flashes of light; sparkle; glitter. [< Latin *coruscatum* flashed < *coruscus* flashing] **—cor′us ca′tion,** *n.*

cor vée (kôr vā′), *n.* 1 unpaid or partly unpaid labor imposed by authorities on the residents of a district, as on roads. 2 unpaid work done by a peasant for his feudal lord. [< French]

cor vette or **cor vet** (kôr vet′), *n.* 1 a former warship with sails and only one tier of guns. 2 gunboat used against submarines. [< French]

cor vine (kôr′vīn, kôr′vən), *adj.* of or like a crow. [< Latin *corvus* crow]

Cor y bant (kôr′ə bant, kor′ə bant), *n., pl.* **Cor y ban tes** (kôr′ə ban′tēz, kor′ə-ban′tēz), **Cor y bants.** (in myths of Asia Minor) one of the attendants of the goddess Cybele. The Corybantes were known for their wild music and dancing.

Cor y ban tic (kôr′ə ban′tik, kor′ə ban′tik), *adj.* 1 of the Corybantes. 2 resembling the Corybantes or their rites.

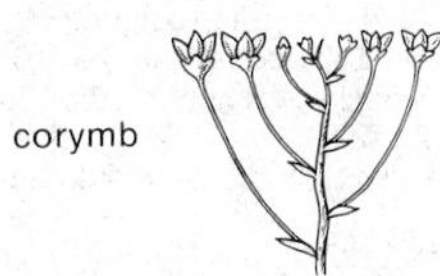
corymb

cor ymb (kôr′imb, kôr′im; kor′imb, kor′im), *n.* a flower cluster whose outer flowers blossom first and have longer pedicels than the inner flowers, so that together they form a round, rather flat cluster on top. Cherry blossoms are corymbs. [< Latin *corymbus* < Greek *korymbos* top, cluster]

cor y phée (kôr′ə fā′, kor′ə fā′), *n.* 1 (in some ballet companies) a dancer who dances in small ensembles, ranking just below a soloist, but above the corps de ballet. 2 any ballet dancer. [< French]

co ry za (kə rī′zə), *n.* a cold in the head; common cold. [< Late Latin < Greek *koryza* catarrh]

cos, cosine.

Co sa No stra (kō′zə nō′strə), U.S. the Mafia. [< Italian, literally, our affair]

co se cant (kō sē′kənt, kō sē′kant) *n.* (in trigonometry) 1 the ratio of the length of the hypotenuse of a right triangle to the length of the side opposite an acute angle. 2 the secant of the complement of a given angle or arc. See **secant** for diagram.

cosh (kosh), *n.* BRITISH SLANG. bludgeon or blackjack. *—v.t.* beat with a cosh. [perhaps < Romany *kosh* stick]

co sig na to ry (kō sig′nə tôr′ē, kō sig′nə-tōr′ē), *n., pl.* **-ries.** person who signs (a document, treaty, etc.) along with another or others.

co sine (kō′sīn), *n.* (in trigonometry) 1 the ratio of the length of the side adjacent to an acute angle of a right triangle to the length of the hypotenuse. 2 the sine of the complement of a given angle or arc. See **sine** for diagram.

cos met ic (koz met′ik), *n.* preparation for beautifying the skin, hair, nails, etc. Powder, lipstick, and face creams are cosmetics. *—adj.* beautifying the skin, hair, nails, etc. [< Greek *kosmētikos* of order, adornment < *kosmos* order]

cos me tol o gy (koz′mə tol′ə jē), *n.* work of a beautician; art of applying cosmetics.

cos mic (koz′mik), *adj.* 1 of or belonging to the cosmos; having to do with the whole universe: *Cosmic forces produce stars and meteors.* 2 vast: *a cosmic explosion.* **—cos′mi cal ly,** *adv.*

cosmic dust, fine particles of matter in outer space.

cosmic rays, rays of very short wavelengths and very great penetrating power that come to the earth from beyond the earth's atmosphere. See **radiation** for table.

cos mo drome (koz′mə drōm′), *n.* a Soviet launching site for spacecraft.

cos mog o ny (koz mog′ə nē), *n., pl.* **-nies.** 1 origin of the universe. 2 theory, system, or account of its origin. [< Greek *kosmogonia* < *kosmos* world + *gonos* birth]

cos mog ra pher (koz mog′rə fər), *n.* an expert in cosmography.

cos mo graph ic (koz′mə graf′ik), *adj.* of or having to do with cosmography.

cos mog ra phy (koz mog′rə fē), *n., pl.* **-phies.** 1 science that deals with the general appearance and structure of the universe. Cosmography includes astronomy, geography, and geology. 2 description of the general features of the earth or the universe.

cos mo log i cal (koz′mə loj′ə kəl), *adj.* of or having to do with cosmology.

cos mol o gist (koz mol′ə jist), *n.* an expert in cosmology.

cos mol o gy (koz mol′ə jē), *n.* science or theory of the universe, its parts, and its laws.

cos mo naut (koz′mə nôt), *n.* a Soviet astronaut.

cos mo pol i tan (koz′mə pol′ə tən), *adj.* 1 belonging to all parts of the world; not limited to any one country or its inhabitants; widely spread: *Music is a cosmopolitan art.* 2 free from national or local prejudices; feeling at home in all parts of the world. 3 (of animals and plants) widely distributed over the earth. *—n.* a cosmopolitan person or thing; person who feels at home in all parts of the world.

cos mo pol i tan ism (koz′mə pol′ə tə-niz′əm), *n.* cosmopolitan character or quality.

cos mop o lite (koz mop′ə līt), *n.* 1 a cosmopolitan person. 2 animal or plant found in all or many parts of the world. [< Greek *kosmopolitēs* < *kosmos* world + *politēs* citizen < *polis* city]

cos mos (koz′məs, koz′mos), *n., pl.* **-mos** or **-mos es** for 2 and 3. 1 the universe thought of as an orderly, harmonious system. 2 any complete system that is orderly and harmonious. 3 a tall, tropical American plant of the composite family, with showy flowers of many colors, that blooms in the fall or late summer. [< Greek *kosmos* order, world]

CO SPAR (kō′spär), *n.* Committee on Space Research.

Cos sack (kos′ak), *n.* one of a people living on the steppes in the southwestern Soviet Union, noted as horsemen. [< Russian *kazak* < Turkic, free man]

cos set (kos′it), *n.* a pet lamb; a pet. *—v.t.*

treat as a pet; pamper. [origin uncertain]

cost (kôst, kost), *n., v.,* **cost, cost ing.** *—n.* 1 price paid: *The cost of this watch was $10.* See **price** for synonym study. 2 loss or sacrifice: *The poor fox escaped from the trap at the cost of a leg.* 3 **at all costs** or **at any cost,** regardless of expense; by all means; no matter what must be done. 4 **costs,** *pl.* expenses of a lawsuit or case in court. *—v.t.* 1 be obtained at the price of: *This watch costs $10.* 2 cause the loss or sacrifice of: *The school play had cost much time and effort.* [< Old French < *coster* to cost < Latin *constare* stand together < *com-* + *stare* to stand]

cos tal (kos′tl, kôs′tl), *adj.* (in anatomy) having to do with a rib or the ribs. [< Late Latin *costalis* < Latin *costa* rib]

co-star (*n.* kō′stär; *v.* kō stär′, kō′stär), *n., v.,* **-starred, -star ring.** *—n.* a leading actor, singer, etc., appearing with another star in the same production. *—v.i., v.t.* star or be starred with.

cos tard (kos′tərd, kôs′tərd), *n.* 1 variety of large, English apple. 2 ARCHAIC. the head. [origin uncertain]

Cos ta Ri ca (kos′tə rē′kə; kôs′tə rē′kə), country in Central America, northwest of Panama. 1,680,000 pop.; 19,200 sq. mi. *Capital:* San José. **—Cos′ta Ri′can.**

cos ter (kos′tər, kôs′tər), *n.* costermonger.

cos ter mon ger (kos′tər mung′gər, kos′tər mong′gər; kôs′tər mung′gər, kôs′tər mong′gər), *n.* person who sells fruit, vegetables, fish, etc., from a handcart or stand in the street. [< *costard* + *-monger*]

cos tive (kos′tiv, kôs′tiv), *adj.* 1 constipated. 2 producing constipation. [< Old French < Latin *constipatum.* Doublet of CONSTIPATE.] **—cos′tive ly,** *adv.* **—cos′tive ness,** *n.*

cost li ness (kôst′lē nis, kost′lē nis), *n.* great cost; expensiveness.

cost ly (kôst′lē, kost′lē), *adj.,* **-li er, -li est.** 1 of great value; precious; valuable: *costly jewels.* 2 costing much: *costly mistakes.* See **expensive** for synonym study.

cost of living, the average price paid for food, rent, clothing, transportation, and other necessities by a person, family, etc., within a given period.

cost-of-liv ing index (kôst′əv liv′ing, kost′əv liv′ing), a comparative study of the cost of living, especially that made annually by the United States Bureau of Labor Statistics.

cos tume (*n.* kos′tüm, kos′tyüm; *v.* ko stüm′, ko styüm′), *n., v.,* **-tumed, -tum ing.** *—n.* 1 style of dress, outer clothing, etc., including the way the hair is worn, kind of jewelry worn, etc. 2 dress belonging to another time or place, worn on the stage, at masquerades, etc.: *The actors wore colonial costumes.* 3 a complete set of outer garments: *a street costume, a hunting costume.* *—v.t.* provide a costume or costumes for; dress. [< French < Italian < Popular Latin *consuetumen* custom. Doublet of CUSTOM.]

cos tum er (ko stü′mər, ko styü′mər), *n.* person who makes, sells, or rents costumes.

cos tum i er (ko stü′mē ər, ko styü′mē ər), *n.* costumer.

co sy (kō′zē), *adj.,* **-si er, -si est,** *n., pl.* **-sies.** cozy. **—co′si ly,** *adv.* **—co′si ness,** *n.*

cot[1] (kot), *n.* 1 a narrow, light bed. A cot is sometimes made of canvas stretched on a frame that folds together. 2 BRITISH. a child's crib. [< Hindustani *khāt*]

cot[2] (kot), *n.* 1 cottage. 2 cote. 3 a protective covering; sheath. [Old English]

cot, cotangent.

co tan gent (kō tan′jənt), *n.* (in trigonometry) 1 the ratio of the length of the adjacent side (not the hypotenuse) of an acute angle in a right triangle to the length of the opposite side. 2 the tangent of the complement of a given angle or arc. See **tangent** for diagram.

cote (kōt), *n.* shelter or shed for small animals, birds, etc. [Old English]

co ter ie (kō′tər ē), *n.* set or circle of close acquaintances; group of people who often meet socially. [< French]

co ter mi nous (kō tėr′mə nəs), *adj.* having the same boundaries or limits; coextensive. Also, **conterminous. —co ter′mi nous ly,** *adv.*

co til lion (kə til′yən), *n.* 1 a dance with complicated steps and much changing of partners, led by one couple. 2 an early French social dance for couples. 3 any large social dance. [< French *cotillon,* originally, petticoat]

co til lon (kə til′yən; *French* kô tē yôN′), *n.* cotillion.

Co to pax i (kō′tə pak′sē), *n.* volcano in the Andes Mountains in N Ecuador, the highest active volcano in the world. 19,498 ft.

Cots wolds (kots′wōldz, kots′wəldz), *n.pl.* range of hills in SW England. 310 sq. mi.

cot tage (kot′ij), *n.* 1 a small house, especially in the suburbs or the country. See synonym study below. 2 house at a summer resort. [< *cot*[2]]

Syn. 1 Cottage, cabin mean a small house. **Cottage** once applied only to a small, simple house lived in by poor people, but now applies to any small and simple house: *I live in a garden cottage.* **Cabin** applies to a small, roughly built house: *They live in a cabin in the woods.*

cottage cheese, a soft, white cheese made from the curds of sour skim milk.

cottage pudding, cake covered with a sweet sauce.

cot tag er (kot′ə jər), *n.* 1 person who lives in a cottage. 2 person who lives in a cottage at a summer resort.

cot ter[1] (kot′ər), *n.* 1 a pin or wedge that is inserted through a slot to hold small parts of machinery, etc., together. 2 cotter pin. [origin uncertain]

cot ter[2] or **cot tar** (kot′ər), *n.* a Scottish peasant who works for a farmer and is allowed to use a small cottage and a plot of land. [< Medieval Latin *cotarius* < *cota* < Old English *cot* cot[2]]

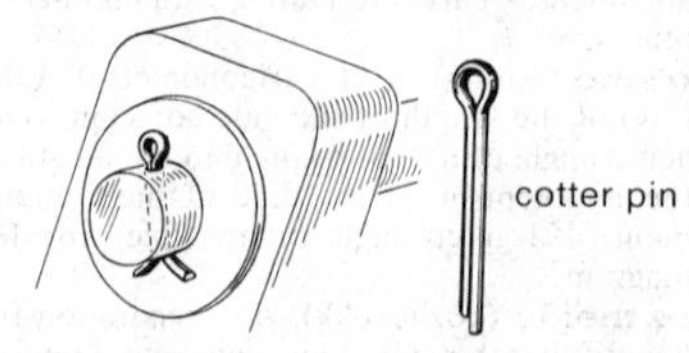

cotter pin, a split pin used as a cotter or locking device. Its ends are bent outward to keep it in its slot.

cot ton (kot′n), *n.* 1 the soft, white fibers in a fluffy mass around the seeds of a tall plant of the mallow family, used in making fabrics, thread, guncotton, etc. 2 the plant that produces these fibers. 3 crop of such plants. 4 thread made of cotton fibers. 5 cloth made of cotton thread. 6 any downy substance resembling cotton fibers, growing on other plants. *—adj.* made of cotton. *—v.i.* INFORMAL. 1 take a liking *(to): cotton to an idea.* 2 get on together; agree. [< Old French *coton* < Italian *cotone* < Arabic *quṭn*] **—cot′ton like′,** *adj.*

Cotton Belt, region in the southern United States where cotton is grown extensively.

cotton cake, mass of cottonseed after the oil has been pressed out, used as feed for livestock.

cotton candy, a light, fluffy candy made by spinning melted sugar.

cotton gin, machine for separating the fibers of cotton from the seeds; gin.

cot ton mouth (kot′n mouth′), *n., pl.* **-mouths** (-mouᴛʜz′). water moccasin.

cot ton seed (kot′n sēd′), *n., pl.* **-seeds** or **-seed.** seed of cotton, used for making cottonseed oil, fertilizer, cattle fodder, etc.

cottonseed oil, oil pressed from cottonseed, used for cooking, for making soap, etc.

cot ton tail (kot′n tāl′), *n.* any of several common American wild rabbits with fluffy, white fur on the underside of the tail.

cot ton wood (kot′n wu̇d′), *n.* 1 a North American tree of the same genus as the poplar, having cottonlike tufts of white hair on the tiny seeds. 2 its soft wood.

cotton wool, raw cotton, before or after picking.

cot ton y (kot′n ē), *adj.* 1 of cotton. 2 like cotton; soft; fluffy; downy.

cot y le don (kot′l ēd′n), *n.* an embryo leaf in the seed of a plant; the first leaf, or one of the first pair of leaves, growing from a seed; seed leaf. See **hypocotyl** for diagram. [< Latin < Greek *kotylēdōn* cup-shaped hollow < *kotyle* cup]

cot y le don ous (kot′l ēd′n əs), *adj.* having cotyledons.

couch (kouch), *n.* 1 a long seat, usually upholstered and usually having a back and arms; sofa. 2 bed or other structure made to sleep or rest on. 3 place to rest or sleep: *The deer sprang up from its grassy couch.* *—v.t.* 1 lay on a couch. 2 put in words; express: *Poets couch their ideas in beautiful language.* 3 lower into a level position ready to attack: *The knights couched their lances and prepared to charge.* *—v.i.* 1 lie down on a couch. 2 lie hidden ready to attack; lurk. [< Old French *couche* < *coucher* lay in place < Latin *collocare* < *com-* together + *locus* a place] **—couch′like′,** *adj.*

couch ant (kou′chənt), *adj.* (in heraldry) lying down, but with the head raised: *a lion couchant.*

couch grass, a coarse, weedlike grass whose stems creep underground and spread quickly in all directions.

cou gar (kü′gər), *n.* puma. [< French *couguar* < Tupi (Brazil) *guazuara*]

cough (kôf, kof), *v.i.* force air from the lungs with sudden effort and noise. *—v.t.* **cough up,** a expel from the throat by coughing. b SLANG. bring out; produce; give. *—n.* 1 act of coughing. 2 sound of coughing. 3 condition or symptom of repeated coughing. [Middle English *coghen*]

cough drop, a small tablet containing medicine to relieve coughs or hoarseness.

could (ku̇d), *v.* pt. of **can**[1]. *Once she could sing beautifully.* [Old English *cūthe;* the *l* was inserted on analogy with *should, would*]

➔ **could, might.** *Could* and *might,* originally the past tense forms of *can* and *may,* are now used chiefly to convey a shade of doubt, or a slight degree of possibility: *It might be all right for her, but it isn't for me. Perhaps I could write a poem, but I doubt it.*

could n't (ku̇d′nt), could not.

couldst (ku̇dst), *v.* ARCHAIC. could. "Thou couldst" means "You could."

cou lee (kü′lē), *n.* 1 a deep ravine or gulch that is usually dry in summer. 2 stream of lava. [< French *coulée* a flow]

cou lomb (kü lom′), *n.* unit of electrical quantity, equal to the quantity of electricity furnished by a current of one ampere in one second. [< Charles A. de *Coulomb,* 1736-1806, French physicist]

coul ter (kōl′tər), *n.* colter.

coun cil (koun′səl), *n.* 1 group of people called together to give advice, talk things over, or settle questions; assembly. 2 group of persons elected by citizens to make laws for and manage a city or town. 3 deliberation or consultation that takes place at the meeting of a council. 4 any body of delegates or representatives. [< Old French *concile* < Latin *concilium* < *com-* together + *calare* to call]

➤ **council, counsel.** *Council* is always a noun: *They called together a council* (group) *of the town's industrial leaders. Counsel* may be a noun or a verb: *She could always be counted on for good counsel* (advice). *Each side tried to get him as its counsel* (adviser). *I would prefer not to counsel* (advise) *you on that point.*

coun cil lor (koun′sə lər), *n.* councilor.

coun cil man (koun′səl mən), *n., pl.* **-men.** member of the council of a city or town.

coun ci lor (koun′sə lər), *n.* member of a council. Also, **councillor.**

coun sel (koun′səl), *n., v.,* **-seled, -sel ing** or **-selled, -sel ling.** —*n.* 1 act of exchanging ideas; talking things over; consultation. 2 carefully considered advice: *The lawyer's counsel was that we avoid a lawsuit.* See **advice** for synonym study. 3 lawyer or group of lawyers: *Each side of a case in a court has its own counsel.* 4 deliberate purpose; design; plan; scheme. 5 **keep one's own counsel,** not tell one's secrets. 6 **take counsel,** exchange ideas; talk things over; consult together. —*v.t.* 1 give advice to; advise. 2 recommend: *The doctor counseled operating at once.* —*v.i.* exchange ideas; consult together; deliberate. [< Old French *conseil* < Latin *consilium* < *consulere* consult] ➤ See **council** for usage note.

coun se lor or **coun sel lor** (koun′sə-lər), *n.* 1 person who gives advice; adviser. 2 lawyer. 3 instructor or leader in a summer camp.

count[1] (kount), *v.t.* 1 name numbers in order up to: *Wait till I count ten.* 2 add up; find the number of: *We counted the books and found there were fifty.* 3 include in counting; take into account. 4 think of as; consider: *I count myself fortunate in having good health.* —*v.i.* 1 name numbers in order: *She can count from one to ten in French.* 2 be included in counting; be taken into account. 3 have an influence; be of account or value: *Every vote counts in an election.* 4 depend; rely: *We count on your help.*

count for, be worth.

count in, INFORMAL. include: *Count me in on the picnic.*

count off, divide into equal groups by counting.

count out, **a** fail to consider or include. **b** declare (a fallen boxer) the loser when he fails to rise after 10 seconds have been counted.

—*n.* 1 an adding up; finding out how many: *The count showed that 5000 votes had been cast.* 2 the total number; amount. 3 ten seconds counted to give a fallen boxer time to get up before he is declared the loser. 4 (in law) each charge in a formal accusation: *The accused was found guilty on all four counts.* [< Old French *conter* < Latin *computare.* Doublet of COMPUTE.] —**count′a ble,** *adj.*

count[2] (kount), *n.* a European nobleman having a rank about the same as that of a British earl. [< Middle French *conte* < Old French < Latin *comitem* companion < *com-* with + *ire* go]

count down (kount′doun′), *n.* 1 period of time before the launching of a missile, rocket, etc. 2 the calling out of the minutes (and seconds, in the last stage) of this period as they pass.

coun te nance (koun′tə nəns), *n., v.,* **-nanced, -nanc ing.** —*n.* 1 expression of the face: *an angry countenance.* 2 face; features: *a noble countenance.* See **face** for synonym study. 3 approval; encouragement: *They gave countenance to our plan, but no active help.* 4 calmness; composure: *lose countenance.* 5 **keep one's countenance, a** be calm; not show feeling. **b** keep from smiling or laughing. —*v.t.* approve or encourage; sanction: *I will not countenance such a plan.* [< Old French *contenance* < Medieval Latin *continentia* demeanor < Latin, self-control < *continere.* See CONTAIN.] —**coun′te nanc er,** *n.*

count er[1] (koun′tər), *n.* 1 a long table in a store, restaurant, bank, etc., on which money is counted out, and across which goods, food, etc., are sold to customers. 2 thing used for counting, such as a round, flat disk. 3 an imitation coin. [< Old French *conteour* < *conter.* See COUNT[1].]

count er[2] (koun′tər), *n.* person or thing that counts. [< *count*[1]]

coun ter[3] (koun′tər), *adv.* in the opposite direction; opposed; contrary: *That wild idea runs counter to common sense.* —*adj.* opposite; contrary: *Your plans are counter to ours.* —*v.t.* 1 go or act counter to; oppose: *She countered my plan with one of her own.* 2 meet or answer (a move, blow, etc.) by another in return: *He ducked and countered a left to the jaw.* —*v.i.* 1 make a move or take a stand against some person, action, etc. 2 give a blow while receiving or blocking an opponent's blow. —*n.* 1 that which is opposite or contrary to something else. 2 blow given while receiving or blocking an opponent's blow. 3 a stiff piece inside the back of a shoe around the heel. 4 part of a ship's stern from the water line to the end of the curved part. [< Middle French *countre* < Latin *contra* against]

counter-, *prefix.* 1 in opposition to; against: *Counteract* = *act against.* 2 in return: *Counterattack* = *attack in return.* 3 corresponding: *Counterpart* = *corresponding part.* [< *counter*[3]]

coun ter act (koun′tər akt′), *v.t.* act against; neutralize the action or effect of; hinder: *counteract a fever with aspirin, counteract adverse publicity.*

coun ter ac tion (koun′tər ak′shən), *n.* action opposed to another action; hindrance; resistance.

coun ter ac tive (koun′tər ak′tiv), *adj.* tending to counteract. —*n.* something that counteracts.

coun ter at tack (koun′tər ə tak′), *n.* attack made to counter another attack. —*v.t., v.i.* attack in return.

coun ter bal ance (*n.* koun′tər bal′əns; *v.* koun′tər bal′əns), *n., v.,* **-anced, -anc ing.** —*n.* 1 weight balancing another weight; counterpoise. 2 influence, power, etc., balancing or offsetting another. —*v.t., v.i.* act as a counterbalance to; offset: *By studying, I was able to counterbalance my difficulty with arithmetic.*

coun ter check (koun′tər chek′), *n.* 1 something that restrains or opposes; obstacle. 2 check made upon a check; double-check for verification. —*v.t.* 1 restrain or oppose by some obstacle. 2 make a second check of; check again.

coun ter claim (*n.* koun′tər klām′; *v.* koun′tər klām′), *n.* an opposing claim; claim made by a person to offset a claim made against him. —*v.i.* ask for or make a counterclaim.

coun ter claim ant (koun′tər klā′mənt), *n.* person who makes a counterclaim.

coun ter clock wise (koun′tər klok′-wīz′), *adv., adj.* in the direction opposite to that in which the hands of a clock go.

coun ter cur rent (koun′tər kėr′ənt), *n.* current running in the opposite direction; opposing current.

coun ter es pi o nage (koun′tər es′pē ə-nij, koun′tər es′pē ə näzh′), *n.* measures taken to prevent or confuse enemy espionage.

coun ter feit (koun′tər fit), *v.t.* 1 copy (money, handwriting, pictures, etc.) in order to deceive or defraud; forge. 2 resemble closely. 3 pretend; dissemble: *I counterfeited interest to be polite.* —*n.* copy made to deceive or defraud and passed as genuine; forgery. —*adj.* 1 not genuine; sham. See **false** for synonym study. 2 pretended; dissembled. [< Old French *contrefait* imitated, past participle of *contrefaire* < *contre-* against + *faire* make] —**coun′ter feit′er,** *n.*

coun ter foil (koun′tər foil′), *n.* part of a check, receipt, etc., kept as a record; stub.

coun ter in sur gen cy (koun′tər in-sėr′jən sē), *n., pl.* **-cies.** defense and counterattack against guerrilla warfare and infiltration.

coun ter in tel li gence (koun′tər in-tel′ə jəns), *n.* system or activity of counteracting the intelligence or spy activities of an enemy.

coun ter ir ri tant (koun′tər ir′ə tənt), *n.* something used to produce irritation in one place in order to relieve disease or pain elsewhere.

coun ter man (koun′tər man′), *n., pl.* **-men.** person who serves at a counter, as in a store or lunchroom.

coun ter mand (koun′tər mand), *v.t.* 1 withdraw or cancel (an order, command, etc.). 2 recall or stop by a contrary order;

order back. [< Old French *contremander* < Latin *contra-* against + *mandare* order]

coun ter march (koun′tər märch′), *n.* a march in the opposite direction; a march back. —*v.i., v.t.* to march in the opposite direction; march back.

coun ter meas ure (koun′tər mezh′ər), *n.* measure or move taken to offset another.

coun ter of fen sive (koun′tər ə fen′siv), *n.* aggressive action on a large scale undertaken by a defending force to take the initiative from the attacking force.

coun ter pane (koun′tər pān′), *n.* an outer covering for a bed; bedspread. [alteration of *counterpoint* quilt < Old French *cuiltepointe* quilt stitched through]

coun ter part (koun′tər pärt′), *n.* 1 person or thing closely resembling another: *She is the counterpart of her twin sister.* 2 person or thing that complements or corresponds to another: *Night is the counterpart of day.* 3 copy; duplicate.

coun ter plot (koun′tər plot′), *n., v.,* **-plot ted, -plot ting.** —*n.* a plot to defeat another plot. —*v.i.* plot in opposition. —*v.t.* plot against (another plot or plotter).

coun ter point (koun′tər point′), *n.* 1 melody added to another as an accompaniment. 2 art of adding melodies to a given melody according to fixed rules. 3 polyphony. [< Middle French *contrepoint*]

coun ter poise (koun′tər poiz′), *n., v.,* **-poised, -pois ing.** —*n.* 1 weight balancing another weight. 2 influence, power, etc., balancing or offsetting another. 3 balance; equilibrium. —*v.t.* act as a counterpoise to; offset.

Counter Reformation, the reform movement within the Roman Catholic Church during the 1500's and 1600's designed to counter the effects of the Reformation.

coun ter rev o lu tion (koun′tər rev′ə lü′shən), *n.* revolution against a government established by a previous revolution.

coun ter rev o lu tion ar y (koun′tər-rev′ə lü′shə ner′ē), *adj., n., pl.* **-ar ies.** —*adj.* of or having to do with a counterrevolution. —*n.* person who takes part in or advocates a counterrevolution.

coun ter rev o lu tion ist (koun′tər-rev′ə lü′shə nist), *n.* a counterrevolutionary.

coun ter shaft (koun′tər shaft′), *n.* shaft that transmits motion from the main shaft to the working parts of a machine.

coun ter sign (koun′tər sīn′), *n.* 1 a sign or signal used in reply to another sign. 2 (in military use) password given in answer to the challenge of a sentinel. 3 signature added to another signature to confirm it. —*v.t.* sign (something already signed by another) to confirm it.

coun ter sig na ture (koun′tər sig′nə-chər), *n.* 1 act of countersigning. 2 signature added to another's signature to confirm it.

coun ter sink (koun′tər singk′), *v.,* **-sunk** (-sungk′), **-sink ing,** *n.* —*v.t.* 1 enlarge the upper part of (a hole) to make room for the head of a screw, bolt, etc. 2 sink the head of (a screw, bolt, etc.) into a hole so that it is even with or below the surface. —*n.* 1 tool for countersinking holes. 2 a countersunk hole.

coun ter spy (koun′tər spī′), *n., pl.* **-spies.** spy who works to uncover or oppose the activities of enemy spies.

coun ter ten or (koun′tər ten′ər), *n.* 1 an adult male voice, often falsetto, that is higher than the tenor. 2 singer with such a voice.

coun ter vail (koun′tər vāl′, koun′tər-vāl′), *v.t.* 1 make up for; compensate; offset. 2 avail against; counteract.

coun ter weight (koun′tər wāt′), *n.* weight that balances another weight.

counter word, word commonly used without reference to its exact meaning, as *terrific* and *wonderful.*

count ess (koun′tis), *n.* 1 wife or widow of a count or an earl. 2 lady whose rank is equal to that of a count or an earl.

count ing house (koun′ting hous′), *n., pl.* **-hous es** (-hou′ziz). building or office used for keeping accounts and doing business.

counting number, any whole number except 0.

counting room, room or office used as a countinghouse.

count less (kount′lis), *adj.* too many to count; very many; innumerable: *the countless sands of the seashore.*

coun tri fied (kun′tri fīd), *adj.* 1 looking or acting like a person from the country; rustic. 2 like the country; rural. Also, **country-fied.**

coun try (kun′trē), *n., pl.* **-tries,** *adj.* —*n.* 1 land, region, or district: *The country around the mining town was rough and hilly.* 2 all the land of a nation. 3 land where a person was born or where he is a citizen. 4 people of a nation. 5 land outside of cities and towns; rural district. 6 the public; the body of voters. —*adj.* 1 of the country; in the country; rural. 2 like the country. [< Old French *contree* < Popular Latin *contrata* region lying opposite < Latin *contra* against]

country club, club in the country near a city. It has a clubhouse and facilities for outdoor sports.

country cousin, a countrified relative pleased but confused by things in the city.

coun try-dance (kun′trē dans′), *n.* dance in which partners face each other in two long lines.

coun try fied (kun′trē fīd), *adj.* countrified.

coun try folk (kun′trē fōk′), *n.pl.* people who live in the country.

country gentleman, gentleman who lives on his estate in the country.

country house, home in the country.

coun try man (kun′trē mən), *n., pl.* **-men.** 1 man of one's own country; compatriot. 2 man who lives in the country; rustic.

coun try seat (kun′trē sēt′), *n.* residence or estate in the country, especially a fine one.

coun try side (kun′trē sīd′), *n.* 1 a rural area; country. 2 a certain section of the country. 3 its people.

coun try wide (kun′trē wīd′), *adj.* nationwide.

coun try wom an (kun′trē wům′ən), *n., pl.* **-wom en.** 1 woman of one's own country; compatriot. 2 woman who lives in the country; rustic.

coun ty (koun′tē), *n., pl.* **-ties.** 1 (in the United States) one of the districts into which a state is divided for the purposes of local government. It is the political unit next below the state. 2 (in Great Britain and Ireland) one of the districts into which the country is divided for administrative, judicial, and political purposes. The counties were formed as a result of historical events. 3 people of a county. 4 the officials of a county. [< Anglo-French *counté* territory of a count < *counte* count, variant of Old French *conte.* See COUNT[2].]

county farm, (formerly) a farm supported by a county, on which poor people were allowed to live and work.

county seat, U.S. town or city where the county government is located.

coup (kü), *n., pl.* **coups** (küz). 1 a sudden, brilliant action; unexpected, clever move; master stroke. 2 coup d'état. [< French, literally, a blow, stroke < Late Latin *colpus* < Greek *kolaphos*]

coup de grâce (kü′ də gräs′), *pl.* **coups de grâce** (kü′ də gräs′). 1 action that gives a merciful death to a suffering animal or person. 2 a finishing stroke. [< French, literally, stroke of grace]

coup d'é tat (kü′ dā tä′), *pl.* **coups d'é tat** (kü′ dā tä′). a sudden, decisive act in politics, usually bringing about a change of government unlawfully or by force. [< French, literally, stroke of state]

coupe (küp, kü pā′ *for 1;* kü pā′ *for 2*), *n.* 1 a closed, two-door automobile, usually seating two to six people. 2 a four-wheeled, closed carriage with a seat for two people inside and a seat for the driver outside. [< French *coupé,* past participle of *couper* to cut]

cou pé (kü pā′), *n.* coupe.

cou ple (kup′əl), *n., v.,* **-pled, -pling.** —*n.* 1 two things of the same kind that go together; pair: *a couple of tires.* See **pair** for synonym study. 2 INFORMAL. a small number; a few: *a couple of pencils.* 3 man and woman who are married, engaged, or paired together for a dance, party, game, etc. —*v.t.* 1 fasten or join together; join together in pairs. 2 (in electricity) connect by a coupling. [< Old French *cople* < Latin *copula* bond. Doublet of COPULA.]

cou pler (kup′lər), *n.* 1 person or thing that couples. 2 device used to join two railroad cars; coupling. 3 device in a pipe organ for coupling keys or keyboards so they can be played together.

cou plet (kup′lit), *n.* two successive lines of poetry, especially two that rhyme and have the same number of metrical feet. EXAMPLE: "Be not the first by whom the new are tried, Nor yet the last to lay the old aside."

cou pling (kup′ling), *n.* 1 a joining together. 2 device for joining together parts of machinery. 3 a railroad coupler. 4 device or arrangement for transferring electrical energy from one circuit to another.

cou pon (kü′pon, kyü′pon), *n.* 1 part of a ticket, advertisement, package, etc., that gives the person who holds it certain rights: *I saved the coupons from each box of soap to get free goblets.* 2 form for name and address to order goods, obtain information, etc. 3 a printed statement of interest due on a bond, which can be cut from the bond and presented for payment. [< French < *couper* to cut]

cour age (kėr′ij), *n.* 1 meeting danger without fear; bravery; fearlessness. See synonym study below. 2 **have the courage of one's convictions,** act as one believes one should. [< Old French *corage* < *cuer* heart < Latin *cor*]

Syn. 1 **Courage, bravery** mean fearlessness. **Courage** applies to moral strength that makes a person face any danger, trouble, or pain steadily and without showing fear: *The pioneer women faced the hardships of the westward trek with courage.* **Bravery** applies to a kind of courage that is shown by bold, fearless, daring action in the presence of

ica; prairie wolf. It is noted for loud howling at night. [< Mexican Spanish < Nahuatl *coyotl*]

coy pu (koi′pü), *n., pl.* **-pus** or **-pu.** a large water rodent of South America, having webbed hind feet; nutria. Its fur resembles beaver. [< Spanish *coipu*]

coz (kuz), *n.* INFORMAL. cousin.

coz en (kuz′n), *v.t., v.i.* deceive or trick; cheat; beguile. [perhaps < Italian *cozzonare* play the crafty knave] **—coz′en er,** *n.*

coz en age (kuz′n ij), *n.* practice of cozening; deception or trick; fraud.

co zy (kō′zē), *adj.,* **-zi er, -zi est,** *n., pl.* **-zies.** *—adj.* warm and comfortable; snug: *My favorite chair is in a cozy corner near the fireplace.* See **snug** for synonym study. *—n.* a padded cloth cover to keep a teapot warm. Also, **cosy.** [< Scandinavian (Norwegian) *koselig*] **—co′zi ly,** *adv.* **—co′zi ness,** *n.*

cp., 1 compare. 2 coupon.

c.p., 1 candle power. 2 chemically pure.

C.P., 1 chemically pure. 2 Common Prayer. 3 Communist Party.

C.P.A., Certified Public Accountant.

cpd., compound.

Cpl., Corporal.

cps, cycles per second.

Cr, chromium.

cr., credit.

crab[1] (krab), *n., v.,* **crabbed, crab bing.** *—n.* 1 crustacean that has a broad, flat body with a small abdomen or tail folded under, four pairs of legs, and one pair of pincers. Many kinds of crabs are edible. 2 any of various similar crustaceans such as a horseshoe crab. 3 machine for raising heavy weights. 4 a cross, ill-natured person. 5 **Crab,** Cancer. *—v.i.* 1 catch crabs for eating. 2 INFORMAL. find fault; complain; criticize. *—v.t.* INFORMAL. interfere with; spoil. [Old English *crabba*] **—crab′ber,** *n.* **—crab′like′,** *adj.*

crab[2] (krab), *n.* crab apple. [origin unknown]

crab apple, 1 any of various small, sour apples, used to make jelly. 2 a small, sour, wild apple. 3 tree that bears crab apples.

crab bed (krab′id), *adj.* 1 hard to read or decipher because irregular: *crabbed handwriting.* 2 crabby. **—crab′bed ly,** *adv.* **—crab′bed ness,** *n.*

crab by (krab′ē), *adj.,* **-bi er, -bi est.** INFORMAL. cross, peevish, or ill-natured.

crab grass (krab′gras′), *n.* a coarse grass that spreads rapidly and spoils lawns.

Crab Nebula, a white, expanding gaseous cloud in the constellation Taurus, that is a powerful source of radio waves.

crab wise (krab′wīz′), *adv., adj.* in the manner of a crab; sideways: *move crabwise.*

crack (krak), *n.* 1 split or opening made by breaking without separating into parts: *a crack in a cup.* 2 a narrow opening; chink: *I can see between the cracks in the old floorboards.* 3 a sudden, sharp noise: *the crack of a whip, the crack of loud thunder.* 4 INFORMAL. a hard, sharp blow. 5 INFORMAL. instant; moment: *We got up at the crack of dawn.* 6 INFORMAL. a try; effort; attempt. 7 SLANG. a funny or clever remark; joke. 8 SLANG. a nasty or sharp remark; gibe. *—v.i.* 1 break without separating into parts: *The glass cracked in the hot water.* 2 make a sudden, sharp noise; snap. 3 break with a sudden, sharp noise: *The tree cracked and fell.* 4 become harsh, broken, or shrill: *My voice cracked.* 5 INFORMAL. give way; break down. *—v.t.* 1 break without separating into parts; fracture: *crack a mirror.* 2 cause to make a sudden, sharp noise; snap: *crack a whip.* 3 break with a sudden, sharp noise: *crack nuts.* 4 hit with a sudden, sharp noise. 5 make (the voice) harsh, broken, or shrill. 6 break into: *crack a safe.* 7 break through: *crack the sound barrier.* 8 SLANG. tell or say (something funny or clever): *She cracked a joke.* 9 figure out the meaning of (a code); decipher. 10 separate (petroleum, coal tar, etc.) into various substances.

crack down, INFORMAL. take stern measures.

crack up, a crash; smash. **b** suffer a mental or physical collapse. **c** INFORMAL. praise: *That book is not what it is cracked up to be.* *—adj.* INFORMAL. excellent; first-rate: *a crack shot.* [Old English *cracian*]

crack brained (krak′brānd′), *adj.* crazy; insane.

crack down (krak′doun′), *n.* U.S. INFORMAL. act of taking stern measures or swift disciplinary action: *a crackdown against speeders.*

cracked (krakt), *adj.* 1 broken without separating into parts. 2 having harsh notes; lacking evenness; broken: *speak in a cracked voice.* 3 INFORMAL. crazy; insane.

crack er (krak′ər), *n.* 1 a thin, crisp biscuit or wafer. 2 firecracker. 3 U.S. DIALECT. a poor white person living in the hills and backwoods regions of Georgia, Florida, etc.

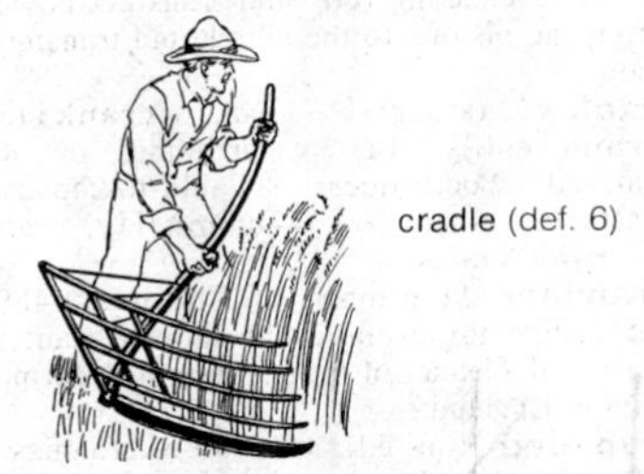
cradle (def. 6)

crack er-bar rel (krak′ər bar′əl), *adj.* U.S. having the plain, earthy, homespun quality of country people: *cracker-barrel humor.*

crack er jack (krak′ər jak′), SLANG. *—n.* person or thing of superior ability or grade. *—adj.* of superior ability or grade.

crack ing (krak′ing), *n.* process of breaking down heavy hydrocarbons in petroleum into lighter hydrocarbons, such as gasoline and jet fuel, by the application of heat, pressure, and a catalyst. Cracking is used in petroleum refining to increase the yield of gasoline.

crack le (krak′əl), *v.,* **-led, -ling,** *n.* *—v.i.* 1 make slight, sharp sounds: *A fire crackled in the fireplace.* 2 (of china, glass, etc.) become minutely cracked; craze. *—n.* 1 a slight, sharp sound, such as paper makes when crushed. 2 very small cracks on the surface of some kinds of china, glass, etc.

crack ling (krak′ling), *n.* 1 the making of slight, sharp sounds. 2 the crisp, browned skin or rind of roasted pork. 3 Usually, **cracklings,** *pl.* DIALECT. the crisp part left after lard has been fried out of hog's fat.

crack pot (krak′pot′), *n.* SLANG. a very eccentric or crazy person. *—adj.* eccentric or impractical: *crackpot ideas.*

crack up (krak′up′), *n.* 1 a crash; smashup. 2 INFORMAL. a mental or physical collapse; breakdown.

Crac ow (krak′ou, krā′kō), *n.* city in S Poland. 577,000. Also, POLISH **Kraków.**

cra dle (krā′dl), *n., v.,* **-dled, -dling.** *—n.*

hat, āge, fär; let, ēqual, tėrm;
it, īce; hot, ōpen, ôrder;
oil, out; cup, pu̇t, rüle;
ch, child; ng, long; sh, she;
th, thin; ᴛʜ, then; zh, measure;

ə represents *a* in about, *e* in taken, *i* in pencil, *o* in lemon, *u* in circus.

< = from, derived from, taken from.

cradle (def. 5)

1 a small bed for a baby, usually on rockers. 2 place where anything begins its growth: *The sea is thought to have been the cradle of life.* 3 frame to support a ship, aircraft, or other large object while it is being built, repaired, lifted, etc. 4 the part of the telephone that supports the receiver. 5 box on rockers to wash earth from gold or other metals. 6 frame fastened to a scythe for laying grain evenly as it is cut. *—v.t.* 1 put or rock in a cradle; hold as in a cradle. 2 shelter or train in early life. 3 support (a ship, etc.) in a cradle. 4 wash (earth from gold or other metals) in a cradle. 5 cut with a cradle scythe. [Old English *cradol*] **—cra′dle-like′,** *adj.*

cra dle song (krā′dl sông′, krā′dl song′), *n.* lullaby.

craft (kraft), *n.* 1 special skill: *The potter shaped the clay into a pitcher with great craft.* 2 trade or work requiring special skill. 3 members of a trade requiring special skill: *Carpenters belong to a craft.* 4 skill in deceiving others; slyness; trickiness: *By craft the gambler tricked them out of all their money.* 5 boats, ships, or aircraft. 6 a boat, ship, or aircraft. *—v.t.* work, make, or finish with skill or art: *woodwork crafted by expert cabinetmakers.* [Old English *cræft*]

crafts man (krafts′mən), *n., pl.* **-men.** 1 a skilled workman. 2 artist or professional whose work shows technical skill.

crafts man ship (krafts′mən ship), *n.* work or skill of a craftsman; craft.

craft union, a labor union made up of persons in the same craft. Unions of carpenters, plumbers, or bricklayers are craft unions.

craft y (kraf′tē), *adj.,* **craft i er, craft i est.** skillful in deceiving others; sly; tricky: *a crafty fox, a crafty schemer.* **—craft′i ly,** *adv.* **—craft′i ness,** *n.*

crag (krag), *n.* a steep, rugged rock or cliff rising above others. [< Celtic (Gaelic) *creag*]

crag ged (krag′id), *adj.* craggy.

crag gy (krag′ē), *adj.,* **-gi er, -gi est.** 1 having many crags; steep and rugged. 2 rough; uneven: *a craggy, weathered face.* **—crag′gi ness,** *n.*

crake (krāk), *n.* any of various rails with short bills, such as the corn crake. [< Scandinavian (Old Icelandic) *krāka* crow]

cram (kram), *v.,* **crammed, cram ming.** *—v.t.* 1 force into; force down; stuff: *I* *crammed all my clothes quickly into the bag.* 2 fill too full; crowd: *The hall was crammed, with many people standing.* 3 INFORMAL. stuff with knowledge or information. 4 INFORMAL. learn hurriedly. —*v.i.* 1 eat too fast or too much. 2 INFORMAL. try to learn too much in a short time. [Old English *cram-mian* < *crimman* to insert] —**cram′mer,** *n.*

cram be (kram′bē), *n.* 1 a broad-leaved plant of the mustard family grown in North Africa for its seeds, which yield an oil used in making synthetic rubber and plastics, in lubrication, etc. 2 sea kale. [< Greek *krambē* cabbage]

cramp (kramp), *v.t.* 1 shut into a small space. 2 cause to have a contraction or paralysis of muscles. 3 limit; restrict; restrain; hamper. 4 turn sharply to one side or the other; steer: *The driver had to cramp the front wheels to get out of the tight parking space.* 5 fasten together with a metal cramp; clamp. —*n.* 1 a sudden, painful contracting or pulling together of muscles, often from chill or strain. 2 paralysis of particular muscles as a result of using them too much. 3 **cramps,** *pl.* very sharp pains in the abdomen. 4 a metal bar bent at both ends, used for holding together blocks of stone, timbers, etc. 5 clamp. 6 something that confines or hinders; limitation; restriction. —*adj.* 1 confined; limited; restricted. 2 hard to read; difficult to understand. [< Middle Dutch *crampe* a cramp]

cram pon (kram′pon′), *n.* 1 a strong, iron bar with hooks at one end, used to lift heavy things; grapnel. 2 a spiked, iron plate on a shoe to prevent slipping, used in logging or mountain climbing. [< French]

cran ber ry (kran′ber′ē, kran′bər ē), *n., pl.* **-ries.** 1 a firm, sour, dark-red berry, used for jelly, sauce, etc. 2 the creeping shrub of the heath family that these berries grow on, found in marshes or bogs. [perhaps < Low German *kraanbere*]

crane (def. 1)

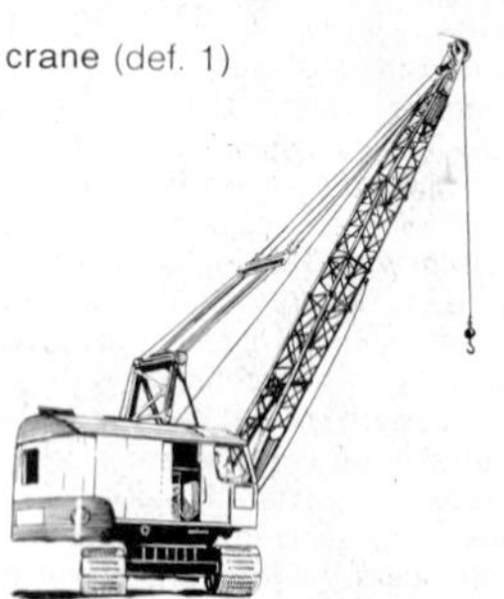

crane (krān), *n., v.,* **craned, cran ing.** —*n.* 1 machine with a long, swinging arm, for lifting and moving heavy weights. 2 a swinging metal arm in a fireplace, used to hold a kettle or pot over the fire. 3 any of a family of large wading birds with very long legs, neck, and bill. 4 any of various herons. —*v.t.* 1 move by, or as if by, a crane. 2 stretch (the neck) as a crane does, in order to see better. [Old English *cran*]

Crane (krān), *n.* **Stephen,** 1871-1900, American writer, author of *The Red Badge of Courage.*

cranes bill or **crane's-bill** (krānz′bil′), *n.* geranium.

cra ni al (krā′nē əl), *adj.* of or having to do with the skull; from the skull: *a cranial nerve.* —**cra′ni al ly,** *adv.*

cranial index, cephalic index.

cra ni ate (krā′nē it, krā′nē āt), *adj.* having a skull. —*n.* a craniate animal.

cra ni ol o gy (krā′nē ol′ə jē), *n.* science that deals with the size, shape, and other characteristics of skulls.

cra ni om e try (krā′nē om′ə trē), *n.* science of measuring skulls; measurement of skulls.

cra ni um (krā′nē əm), *n., pl.* **-ni ums, -ni a** (-nē ə). 1 the skull of a vertebrate. 2 the part of the skull enclosing the brain. [< Medieval Latin < Greek *kranion*]

crank (krangk), *n.* 1 part or handle of a machine connected at right angles to a shaft to transmit motion. 2 a queer notion or act; whim; caprice. 3 INFORMAL. **a** person with queer ideas or habits; person possessed by some idea, hobby, etc. **b** a cross or ill-tempered person. —*v.t.* work or start by means of a crank: *crank an engine.* —*v.i.* 1 turn a crank. 2 twist; wind. [Old English *cranc*]

crank case (krangk′kās′), *n.* a heavy, metal case forming the bottom of an internal-combustion engine. The crankcase of a gasoline engine contains lubricating oil and encloses the crankshaft, connecting rods, etc.

crank shaft (krangk′shaft′), *n.* shaft turning or turned by a crank. In an internal-combustion engine the crankshaft is attached to the connecting rods and transfers power from the pistons to the clutch and transmission.

crank y (krang′kē), *adj.,* **crank i er, crank i est.** 1 cross, irritable, or ill-natured. 2 odd; queer. 3 liable to capsize; unstable; shaky. —**crank′i ly,** *adv.* —**crank′i ness,** *n.*

Cran mer (kran′mər), *n.* **Thomas,** 1489-1556, first Protestant archbishop of Canterbury and a leader of the Protestant Reformation in England.

cran nied (kran′ēd), *adj.* full of crannies.

cran ny (kran′ē), *n., pl.* **-nies.** a small, narrow opening; crack; crevice; chink. [< Old French *cran* fissure]

crape (krāp), *n.* 1 crepe (def. 1). 2 piece of black crepe used as a sign of mourning.

crap pie (krap′ē), *n.* either of two small, North American freshwater fishes of the same family as the sunfish. [origin uncertain]

craps (kraps), *n.* U.S. a gambling game played with two dice. [< French, hazard (a dice game) < English *crabs* lowest throw in hazard]

crap shoot er (krap′shü′tər), *n.* U.S. person who plays craps.

crash[1] (krash), *n.* 1 a sudden, loud noise: *The dishes fell with a crash.* 2 a falling, hitting, or breaking with force and a loud noise; smash. 3 a fall to the earth or a bad landing of an aircraft. 4 sudden ruin; severe failure in business. —*v.i.* 1 make a sudden, loud noise. 2 fall, hit, or break with force and a loud noise; smash. 3 move or go with force and a loud noise: *The baseball crashed through the window.* 4 fall or land in such a way as to damage or wreck an aircraft; make a very bad landing. 5 be suddenly ruined; fail in business. —*v.t.* 1 hit or break with force and a loud noise: *He crashed the dishes to the floor.* 2 INFORMAL. go to (a party or dance) without being invited. 3 cause (an aircraft) to crash. —*adj.* to be carried out with all possible speed, at whatever cost: *a crash program.* [probably imitative] —**crash′er,** *n.*

crash[2] (krash), *n.* a coarse linen cloth, used for towels, curtains, upholstery, and clothing. [probably < Russian *krashenyj* colored, dyed]

Crash aw (krash′ô), *n.* **Richard,** 1612?-1649, English poet.

crash dive, a sudden, very rapid dive by a submarine.

crash-dive (krash′dīv′), *v.i.,* **-dived, -div ing.** make a crash dive.

crash helmet, a heavily padded head covering worn by automobile racers, etc.

crash-land (krash′land′), *v.t.* land (an airplane, etc.) in an emergency so that a crash results. —*v.i.* make a crash landing.

crash landing, an emergency landing of an airplane, etc., so that a crash results.

crass (kras), *adj.* 1 gross or stupid. 2 thick; coarse. [< Latin *crassus* thick] —**crass′ly,** *adv.* —**crass′ness,** *n.*

crate (krāt), *n., v.,* **crat ed, crat ing.** —*n.* a large frame or box made of wood, used to pack furniture, glass, fruit, etc., for shipping or storage. —*v.t.* pack in a crate. [< Latin *cratem* wickerwork. Doublet of GRATE[1].]

cra ter (krā′tər), *n.* 1 a bowl-shaped depression around the opening of a volcano. 2 a bowl-shaped hole: *The meteor crashed to earth, forming a huge crater.* 3 a round, ringlike elevation on the surface of the moon, resembling the crater of a volcano. [< Latin < Greek *kratēr* bowl]

Crater Lake, lake in the crater of an extinct volcano in SW Oregon, 6 mi. long; 5 mi. wide; 2000 ft. deep.

Crater Lake National Park, national park around Crater Lake. 251 sq. mi.

cra vat (krə vat′), *n.* necktie, especially a wide one. [< French *cravate,* special use of *Cravate* Croat (Croatian mercenaries in France wore these)]

crave (krāv), *v.t.,* **craved, crav ing.** 1 long for greatly; yearn for; desire strongly: *The thirsty man craved water.* 2 ask earnestly for; beg: *crave a favor, a problem craving solution.* [Old English *crafian* demand]

cra ven (krā′vən), *adj.* cowardly. —*n.* 1 coward. 2 **cry craven,** surrender; admit defeat. [< Old French *cravente* overcome < Popular Latin *crepantare* < Latin *crepare* crush; burst] —**cra′ven ly,** *adv.* —**cra′ven ness,** *n.*

crav ing (krā′ving), *n.* a strong desire; great longing; yearning. See **desire** for synonym study.

craw (krô), *n.* 1 crop of a bird or insect. 2 stomach of any animal. [Middle English *crawe*]

craw fish (krô′fish′), *n., pl.* **-fish es** or **-fish.** *v.* —*n.* crayfish. —*v.i.* U.S. INFORMAL. back out of something; retreat. [variant of *crayfish*]

crawl[1] (krôl), *v.i.* 1 move slowly by pulling the body along the ground: *Worms and snakes crawl.* 2 creep on hands and knees: *crawl through a hole.* 3 move slowly: *The heavy traffic crawled.* 4 swarm with crawling things: *The ground was crawling with ants.* 5 feel creepy: *My flesh crawled when I saw a big snake.* 6 move stealthily or slavishly. 7 swim with overarm strokes and rapid kicking of the feet. —*n.* 1 a crawling; slow movement. 2 a fast way of swimming by overarm strokes and rapid kicking of the feet. [apparently < Scandinavian (Old Icelandic) *krafla*] —**crawl′er,** *n.*

crawl[2] (krôl), *n.* enclosure made with stakes in shallow water, used to hold turtles, fish, etc. [< Afrikaans *kraal*

< Spanish *corral.* Doublet of CORRAL.]

crawler tractor, tractor that can travel over very rough ground on its two endless tracks.

crawl y (krô′lē), *adj.,* **crawl i er, crawl i est.** INFORMAL. feeling as if things are crawling over one's skin; creepy.

cray fish (krā′fish′), *n., pl.* **-fish es** or **-fish.** 1 any of numerous freshwater crustaceans looking much like a small lobster. 2 any of various similar but larger saltwater crustaceans, such as the spiny lobster. Also, **crawfish.** [< Old French *crevice* < Germanic. Related to CRAB[1].]

cray on (krā′on, krā′ən), *n.* 1 stick or pencil of chalk, charcoal, or a waxlike, colored substance, used for drawing or writing. 2 drawing made with a crayon or crayons. —*v.t., v.i.* draw with a crayon or crayons. [< French < *craie* chalk < Latin *creta*]

craze (krāz), *n., v.,* **crazed, craz ing.** —*n.* 1 something everybody is very much interested in for a short time; fad. —*v.t.* 1 make crazy; drive mad. 2 make tiny cracks all over the surface of (a dish, vase, etc.). —*v.i.* 1 become crazy; go mad. 2 become minutely cracked. [apparently < Old French *crasir* shatter]

cra zy (krā′zē), *adj.,* **-zi er, -zi est.** 1 having a diseased or injured mind; mad; insane. See synonym study below. 2 greatly distressed or shaken by strong emotion: *crazy with worry.* 3 of or suitable for a crazy person; unwise or senseless; foolish: *It was a crazy idea to jump out of such a high tree.* 4 INFORMAL. very eager or enthusiastic. 5 not strong or sound; shaky; frail. **6 like crazy,** SLANG. like mad: *When we saw the dog running toward us, we ran like crazy.* **—cra′zi ly,** *adv.* **—cra′zi ness,** *n.*

Syn. 1 **Crazy, mad, insane** mean showing characteristics of someone mentally ill. **Crazy** is the general word, applied commonly to any person who is mentally disturbed: *His absurd, incoherent statements made me wonder whether he was crazy.* **Mad** suggests being completely out of control or beyond reason, wildly foolish or reckless: *Such uncontrolled violence and wild ravings are to be expected of someone who is mad.* **Insane** suggests being utterly irrational or senseless: *He planned an insane revenge.* It is the legal term for a person who is adjudged not responsible for his actions because of mental disturbance: *The prisoner was found not guilty because she was insane.*

crazy bone, funny bone.

Crazy Horse, 1849?-1877, Sioux Indian chief who joined forces with Sitting Bull to defeat Custer in 1876.

crazy quilt, quilt made of pieces of cloth of various shapes, colors, and sizes, sewed together with no definite pattern.

creak (krēk), *v.i.* squeak loudly: *The hinges on the door creak when they need oil.* —*n.* a creaking noise. [Middle English *creken*]

creak y (krē′kē), *adj.,* **creak i er, creak i est.** likely to creak; creaking. **—creak′i ly,** *adv.* **—creak′i ness,** *n.*

cream (krēm), *n.* 1 the oily, yellowish part of milk which rises to the top when milk that is not homogenized is allowed to stand. Butter is made from cream. 2 food made of cream; food like cream: *ice cream, chocolate creams.* 3 an oily preparation put on the skin to make it smooth and soft. 4 a yellowish white. 5 the best or choicest part of anything: *the cream of the crop.* —*v.t.* 1 take or skim the cream from. 2 cook with cream, milk, or a sauce made of cream or milk with butter and flour. 3 make into a smooth mixture like cream. 4 put cream in. —*v.i.* form a thick layer like cream on the top; foam; froth. —*adj.* 1 containing cream or milk; resembling cream: *cream sauce, cream soup.* 2 yellowish-white. [< Old French *cresme* < Popular Latin *crama* cream and Latin *chrisma* ointment (< Greek *chrisma* < *chriein* anoint)]

cream cheese, a soft, white cheese made from cream, or milk and cream.

cream er (krē′mər), *n.* 1 a small pitcher for holding cream. 2 cream separator.

cream er y (krē′mər ē), *n., pl.* **-er ies.** 1 place where butter and cheese are made. 2 place where cream, milk, and butter are bought and sold. 3 place where milk is set for cream to rise.

cream of tartar, a white powder obtained from the deposit in wine casks and used in medicine and cooking, especially to make baking powder. *Formula:* $C_4H_5KO_6$

cream puff, a light pastry usually filled with whipped cream or custard.

cream y (krē′mē), *adj.,* **cream i er, cream i est.** 1 like cream; smooth and soft. 2 containing much cream. 3 yellowish-white. **—cream′i ly,** *adv.* **—cream′i ness,** *n.*

crease[1] (krēs), *n., v.,* **creased, creas ing.** —*n.* 1 line or mark made by folding or pressing cloth, paper, etc.; ridge; fold. 2 wrinkle. 3 (in hockey and certain other games) a small area marked off in front of a goal. —*v.t.* 1 make a crease or creases in. 2 graze with a bullet. —*v.i.* become creased or wrinkled. [earlier *creast,* variant of *crest*] **—creas′er,** *n.*

crease[2] (krēs), *n.* creese.

cre ate (krē āt′), *v.t.,* **-at ed, -at ing.** 1 cause to be; bring into being; make: *She created a garden in the desert.* 2 give rise to; cause: *create a disturbance.* 3 make by giving a new character, function, or status to: *create a man a knight.* [< Latin *creatum* made, produced]

cre a tine (krē′ə tən, krē′ə tēn′), *n.* a colorless, crystalline compound, found chiefly in the muscle tissue of vertebrate animals, which is involved with supplying energy for voluntary muscle contraction. *Formula:* $C_4H_9N_3O_2$ [< French *créatin*]

cre a tion (krē ā′shən), *n.* 1 a creating or a being created. 2 all things created; the world and everything in it; the universe. 3 thing created. 4 **the Creation,** the creating of the universe by God.

cre a tive (krē ā′tiv), *adj.* having the power to create; inventive. **—cre a′tive ly,** *adv.* **—cre a′tive ness,** *n.*

cre a tiv i ty (krē′ā tiv′ə tē), *n.* creative ability; being creative.

cre a tor (krē ā′tər), *n.* 1 person or thing that creates. 2 **the Creator,** God.

crea ture (krē′chər), *n.* 1 a living being; animal or person. 2 anything created: *a creature of the imagination.* 3 person who is strongly influenced or controlled by another.

creature comforts, things that give bodily comfort. Food, clothing, and shelter are creature comforts.

crèche (kresh, krāsh), *n.* 1 model of the Christ child in the manger, with attending figures, often displayed at Christmas. 2 day nursery. 3 asylum or hospital for foundlings. [< French, manger, crib]

cre dal (krē′dl), *adj.* creedal.

cre dence (krēd′ns), *n.* belief; credit: *Never give credence to gossip.* [< Medieval Latin *credentia* < Latin *credere* believe]

hat, āge, fär; let, ēqual, tėrm;
it, īce; hot, ōpen, ôrder;
oil, out; cup, pu̇t, rüle;
ch, child; ng, long; sh, she;
th, thin; ᴛʜ, then; zh, measure;

ə represents *a* in about, *e* in taken, *i* in pencil, *o* in lemon, *u* in circus.

< = from, derived from, taken from.

cre den tial (kri den′shəl), *n.* 1 something that gives or recommends credit or confidence. 2 **credentials,** *pl.* letters of introduction; references.

cred i bil i ty (kred′ə bil′ə tē), *n.* fact or quality of being credible.

cred i ble (kred′ə bəl), *adj.* worthy of belief; believable; reliable. [< Latin *credibilem* < *credere* believe] **—cred′i ble ness,** *n.* **—cred′i bly,** *adv.*

➤ **Credible, creditable,** and **credulous** are sometimes confused. *Credible* means believable: *The story is hardly credible; how could all that happen to one person? Creditable* means bringing honor or praise: *He turned in a creditable performance, though his heart was no longer in his acting. Credulous* means too ready to believe: *Credulous people are easily fooled and often swindled.*

cred it (kred′it), *n.* 1 belief in the truth of something; faith; trust: *put credit in what someone says.* 2 trust in a person's ability and intention to pay. 3 money in a person's account. 4 entry of money paid on account. 5 the right-hand side of an account where such entries are made. 6 delayed payment; time allowed for delayed payment. 7 reputation in money matters: *If you pay your bills on time, your credit will be good.* 8 favorable reputation; good name; honor: *a person of credit.* 9 honor; praise: *The person who does the work should get the credit.* 10 person or thing that brings honor or praise: *a credit to the community.* 11 entry on a student's record showing that he has passed a course of study. 12 unit of work entered in this way: *I need three credits to graduate.* 13 Usually, **credits,** *pl.* a listing of those who have contributed their skills to making a motion picture, play, etc. **14 do credit to,** bring honor or praise to. **15 give credit for,** **a** think that one has: *Give me credit for some brains.* **b** give recognition to: *Give him credit for the idea.* **16 on credit,** on a promise to pay later: *She bought a new car on credit.*

—*v.t.* 1 believe in the truth of; have faith in; trust. See synonym study below. 2 give credit in a bank account, etc. 3 enter on the credit side of an account. 4 put an entry on the record of (a student) showing that he has passed a course of study. **5 credit to,** ascribe to; attribute to: *The shortage of wheat was credited to lack of rain.* **6 credit with,** give recognition to: *I credit you with good sense for not panicking during the fire.* [< Middle French *crédit* < Italian *credito* < Latin *creditum* a loan < *credere* trust, entrust, believe]

Syn. *v.t.* 1 **Credit, accredit** mean to believe someone or something responsible for saying, doing, feeling, or causing something. **Credit** emphasizes the idea of believing, not always with enough reason or evidence: *You credit me with doing things I never thought of.*

Accredit emphasizes the idea of accepting because of some proof: *We accredit Peary with having discovered the North Pole.*

cred it a bil i ty (kred′ə tə bil′ə tē), *n.* quality of being creditable.

cred it a ble (kred′ə tə bəl), *adj.* bringing credit or honor: *a creditable record of perfect attendance.* —**cred′it a ble ness,** *n.* —**cred′it a bly,** *adv.* ➤ See **credible** for usage note.

credit card, card identifying its holder as entitled to charge the cost of goods or services.

cred i tor (kred′ə tər), *n.* person to whom money or goods are due; one to whom a debt is owed.

credit union, a cooperative association that makes loans to its members at low rates of interest.

cre do (krē′dō, krā′dō), *n., pl.* **-dos.** 1 creed. 2 Also, **Credo. a** the Apostles' Creed or the Nicene Creed. **b** music that accompanies either of these Creeds. [< Latin, I believe. Doublet of CREED.]

cre du li ty (krə dü′lə tē, krə dyü′lə tē), *n.* a too great readiness to believe.

cred u lous (krej′ə ləs), *adj.* too ready to believe; easily deceived. —**cred′u lous ly,** *adv.* —**cred′u lous ness,** *n.* ➤ See **credible** for usage note.

Cree (krē), *n., pl.* **Cree** or **Crees.** member of a tribe of American Indians living in Montana and in central and southern Canada.

creed (krēd), *n.* 1 a brief statement of the essential points of religious belief as approved by some church. 2 any statement of faith, principles, opinions, etc. 3 Also, **Creed.** the Apostles' Creed or the Nicene Creed. [Old English *crēda* < Latin *credo* I believe. Doublet of CREDO.]

creed al (krē′dl), *adj.* of or having to do with a creed or creeds; based on religious faith. Also, **credal.**

creek (krēk, krik), *n.* 1 a small stream. 2 a narrow bay, running inland for some distance. [Middle English *creke* Scandinavian (Old Icelandic) *kriki* nook]

Creek (krēk), *n., pl.* **Creek** or **Creeks.** member of a confederacy of American Indian tribes formerly living in Alabama and Georgia, now living in Oklahoma.

creel (krēl), *n.* 1 basket for holding fish that have been caught. 2 a basketlike trap to catch fish, lobsters, etc. [< Old French *creil* < Latin *craticulam* gridiron < *cratem* wickerwork]

creep (krēp), *v.,* **crept, creep ing,** *n.* —*v.i.* 1 move slowly with the body close to the ground or floor; crawl: *The cat was creeping toward the mouse.* 2 move slowly: *The traffic is creeping over the narrow bridge.* 3 move or behave in a timid, stealthy or servile manner: *The robbers crept toward their victims.* 4 grow along the ground or over a wall by means of clinging stems: *Ivy had crept up the wall of the old house.* 5 feel as if things were creeping over the skin. 6 slip slightly out of place: *The hall rug creeps until we pull it back.* —*n.* 1 a creeping; slow movement. 2 **the creeps,** INFORMAL. a feeling of horror, as if things were creeping over one's skin. 3 show deformation of a material, such as a metal, due to stress or increased temperature. [Old English *crēopan*]

creep er (krē′pər), *n.* 1 person or thing that creeps. 2 any plant that grows along a surface, sending out rootlets from the stem, such as the Virginia creeper and ivy. 3 any of a family of small birds that creep around on trees and bushes looking for food. 4 **creepers,** *pl.* **a** garment combining shirt and pants, worn by babies. **b** spiked iron plates worn on shoes to prevent slipping.

creep ing (krē′ping), *adj.* moving slowly and stealthily; progressing insidiously: *creeping inflation.*

creep y (krē′pē), *adj.,* **creep i er, creep i est.** 1 having a feeling of horror, as if things were creeping over one's skin; frightened. 2 causing such a feeling. 3 moving slowly; creeping. —**creep′i ly,** *adv.* —**creep′i ness,** *n.*

creese (krēs), *n.* dagger with a wavy blade, used by the Malays. Also, **crease, kris.** [< Malay *kĕris* dagger]

cre mate (krē′māt, kri māt′), *v.t.,* **-mat ed, -mat ing.** 1 burn (a dead body) to ashes instead of burying it. 2 burn. [< Latin *crematum* burned] —**cre′ma tor,** *n.*

cre ma tion (kri mā′shən), *n.* the burning of a dead body to ashes instead of burying it.

cre ma to ri um (krē′mə tôr′ē əm, krē′mə tōr′ē əm; krem′ə tôr′ē əm, krem′ə tōr′ē əm), *n., pl.* **-to ri ums, -to ri a** (-tôr′ē ə, -tōr′ē ə). crematory.

cre ma to ry (krē′mə tôr′ē, krē′mə tōr′ē; krem′ə tôr′ē, krem′ə tōr′ē), *n., pl.* **-ries,** *adj.* —*n.* 1 furnace for cremating. 2 building having such a furnace. —*adj.* of or having to do with cremating.

crème (krem), *n.* FRENCH. cream.

crème de menthe (krem′ də mäNT′), FRENCH. liqueur flavored with mint.

cre nate (krē′nāt), *adj.* with a scalloped edge: *Many leaves are crenate.* [< New Latin *crenatus* < Popular Latin *crena* notch] —**cre′nate ly,** *adv.*

cre na tion (kri nā′shən), *n.* crenate formation.

cren el ate (kren′l āt), *v.t.,* **-at ed, -at ing.** furnish with battlements. [< Old French *creneler* < *crenel* embrasure < Popular Latin *crena* notch] —**cren′el a′tion,** *n.*

cren el late (kren′l āt), *v.t.,* **-lat ed, -lat ing.** crenelate. —**cren′el la′tion,** *n.*

cre o dont (krē′ə dont), *n.* any of a suborder of extinct carnivorous mammals with small brains, regarded as the ancestors of the modern carnivores. [< Greek *kreōs* flesh + *odous, odontos* tooth]

Cre ole or **cre ole** (krē′ōl), *n.* 1 descendant of the early French or Spanish settlers in Louisiana. 2 the French language as spoken in Louisiana. 3 a French or Spanish person born in Latin America or the West Indies. 4 person who is part Negro and part Creole. —*adj.* 1 of or having to do with the Creoles. 2 cooked in sauce made of stewed tomatoes, peppers, etc. [< French *créole* < Spanish *criollo* < Portuguese *crioulo,* originally, brought up in one's house < *criar* bring up < Latin *creare* create]

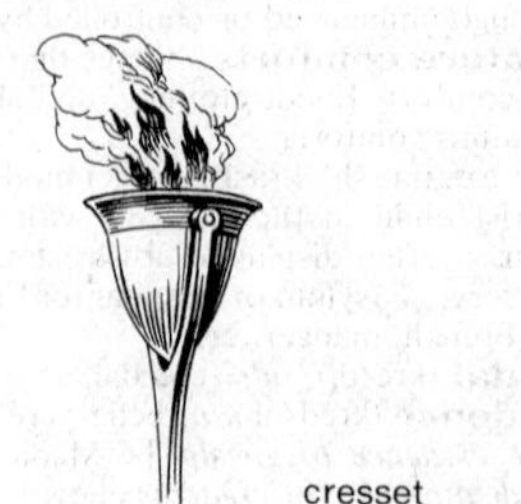

cresset

cre o sol (krē′ə sōl, krē′ə sol), *n.* a colorless to yellowish liquid obtained from beechwood tar and a certain resin, one of the active constituents of creosote. *Formula:* $C_8H_{10}O_2$ [< *creosote*]

cre o sote (krē′ə sōt), *n., v.,* **-sot ed, -sot ing.** —*n.* 1 an oily liquid with a penetrating odor, obtained by distilling wood tar, used to preserve wood and in cough medicine. 2 a similar substance obtained from coal tar. —*v.t.* treat with creosote. [originally, a meat preservative, < German *kreosot* < Greek *kreōs* flesh + *sōzein* to save]

crepe or **crêpe** (krāp), *n.* 1 a thin, light silk, cotton, rayon, or woolen cloth with a finely crinkled surface; crape. 2 crepe paper. [< French *crêpe* < Latin *crispa,* feminine of *crispus* curled]

crepe de Chine (krāp də shēn′), a soft, thin, medium-weight, silk crepe. [< French *crêpe de Chine* China crepe]

crepe paper, a thin, crinkled paper that looks like crepe, used for making decorations.

crepe rubber, a crude rubber with a crinkled surface, used for the soles of shoes.

crêpe su zette (krāp′ sü zet′), *pl.* **crêpes su zette** (krāps′ sü zet′), **crêpe su zettes** (krāp′ sü zets′). a thin pancake, usually rolled in fruit juice and brandy, and set ablaze when served. [< French]

crep i tate (krep′ə tāt), *v.i.,* **-tat ed, -tat ing.** crackle; rattle. [< Latin *crepitatum* crackled < *crepare* to crack] —**crep′i ta′tion,** *n.*

crept (krept), *v.* pt. and pp. of **creep.**

crenelate—crenelated wall

cre pus cu lar (kri pus′kyə lər), *adj.* 1 of twilight; resembling twilight; dim; indistinct. 2 (of certain birds, insects, etc.) appearing or flying at twilight. [< Latin *crepusculum* twilight]

cres. or **cresc.,** crescendo.

cre scen do (krə shen′dō), *adj., adv., n., pl.* **-dos.** —*adj., adv.* (in music) with a gradual increase in force or loudness. —*n.* 1 a gradual increase in force or loudness, especially in music. 2 (in music) a crescendo passage. [< Italian, literally, increasing]

cres cent (kres′nt), *n.* 1 shape of the moon in its first or last quarter. 2 anything that curves in a similar way. A curved street or row of houses is sometimes called a crescent. —*adj.* 1 shaped like the moon in its first or last quarter. 2 growing; increasing. [< Latin *crescentem* growing, increasing] —**cres′cent like′,** *adj.*

cre sol (krē′sōl, krē′sol), *n.* 1 any of three liquid or crystalline compounds having the same formula, obtained from coal tar, and used as a disinfectant and in resins. *Formula:* $CH_3C_6H_4OH$ 2 a mixture of these compounds. [variant of *creosol*]

cress (kres), *n.* any of several genera of plants of the mustard family whose leaves have a peppery taste and are used as a garnish or in salad. [Old English *cresse*]

cres set (kres′it), *n.* a metal container for burning oil, wood, etc., to give light. Cressets are mounted on poles or hung from above.

hat, āge, fär; let, ēqual, tėrm;
it, īce; hot, ōpen, ôrder;
oil, out; cup, pu̇t, rüle;
ch, child; ng, long; sh, she;
th, thin; ᴛʜ, then; zh, measure;

ə represents *a* in about, *e* in taken, *i* in pencil, *o* in lemon, *u* in circus.

< = from, derived from, taken from.

[< Old French *cresset, craisset* < *craisse* grease < Latin *crassus* fat, thick]

Cres si da (kres′ə də), *n.* (in medieval legends) a Trojan woman who was faithless to her lover, Troilus.

crest (krest), *n.* 1 comb, tuft, etc., on the head of a bird or other animal. 2 decoration of plumes or feathers worn on the top of a helmet. 3 decoration at the top of a coat of arms. A family crest is sometimes put on silverware, dishes, or stationery. 4 the top part; high point; peak; summit: *the crest of a wave, the crest of the hill, the crest of a career.* —*v.t.* 1 furnish with a crest. 2 reach the crest or summit of (a hill, wave, etc.). —*v.i.* (of waves) form or rise into a crest. [< Old French *creste* < Latin *crista* tuft] **—crest′-like′,** *adj.*

crest ed (kres′tid), *adj.* having a crest.

crest fall en (krest′fô′lən), *adj.* dejected; discouraged. **—crest′fall′en ly,** *adv.* **—crest′fall′en ness,** *n.*

Cre ta ceous (kri tā′shəs), *n.* 1 the last geological period of the Mesozoic era, characterized by the formation of chalk deposits. During this period flowering plants began to appear and dinosaurs became extinct. 2 the rocks formed during this period. See chart under **geology.** —*adj.* 1 of or having to do with the Cretaceous or its rocks. 2 **cretaceous,** like chalk; containing chalk. [< Latin *cretaceus* < *creta* chalk]

Crete (krēt), *n.* Greek island in the Mediterranean, southeast of Greece. *Capital:* Canea. 483,000 pop.; 3200 sq. mi. See **Adriatic Sea** for map. **—Cret′an,** *adj., n.*

cre tin (krēt′n), *n.* person affected with cretinism. [< French *crétin* < Swiss dialect < Latin *Christianus* Christian; came to mean "man," then "fellow," then "poor fellow"]

cre tin ism (krēt′n iz′əm), *n.* deficiency in the thyroid gland causing severe mental and physical retardation. It may be congenital or develop in infancy.

cre tin ous (krēt′n əs), *adj.* 1 of or having to do with a cretin. 2 of the nature of cretinism.

cre tonne (kri ton′, krē′ton), *n.* a strong cotton, linen, or rayon cloth with designs printed in colors on one or both sides. Cretonne is used for curtains, furniture covers, etc. [< French, probably < *Creton,* village in Normandy]

cre vasse (krə vas′), *n.* 1 a deep crack or crevice in the ice of a glacier, or in the ground after an earthquake. 2 break in the levee of a river, dike, or dam. [< French < Old French *crevace.* Doublet of CREVICE.]

crev ice (krev′is), *n.* a narrow split or crack; fissure. [< Old French *crevace* < Popular Latin *crepacia* < Latin *crepare* to crack. Doublet of CREVASSE.]

crew[1] (krü), *n.* 1 men needed to work a ship. 2 persons manning an aircraft. 3 any group of people working or acting together: *a crew of loggers, a maintenance crew.* 4 a band or company; group; crowd; gang. 5 the members of a rowing team. [< Old French *creüe* increase, recruit < *creistre* grow < Latin *crescere*]

crew[2] (krü), *v.* a pt. of **crow**[1].

crew cut, kind of very short haircut for men and boys.

crew el (krü′əl), *n.* 1 a loosely twisted, woolen yarn, used for embroidery. 2 embroidery done with this yarn. [origin uncertain]

crew man (krü′mən), *n., pl.* **-men.** member of a crew.

crib (krib), *n., v.,* **cribbed, crib bing.** —*n.* 1 a small bed with high barred sides to keep a baby from falling out. 2 rack or manger for horses and cows to eat from. 3 building or box for storing grain, salt, etc. 4 framework of logs or timbers used in building. The wooden lining inside a mine shaft is a crib. 5 INFORMAL. use of another's words or ideas as one's own; plagiarism. 6 INFORMAL. notes or helps that are unfair to use in doing schoolwork or in examinations. 7 a small room or house. 8 (in cribbage) a set of cards made up of two discards from each hand and scored by the dealer after the deal has been played. —*v.t.* 1 provide with a crib. 2 shut up in a small space. 3 INFORMAL. use (another's words or ideas) as one's own; plagiarize. —*v.i.* INFORMAL. use notes or helps unfairly in doing schoolwork. [Old English *cribb*] **—crib′ber,** *n.*

crest (def. 3)

crib bage (krib′ij), *n.* a card game for two to four people. The players keep score on a narrow board into which movable pegs fit.

crick (krik), *n.* a muscular cramp; painful stiffness of muscles. [origin uncertain]

Crick (krik), *n.* **Francis H. C.,** born 1916, British biochemist, one of the discoverers of the molecular structure of DNA.

crick et[1] (krik′it), *n.* any of a family of leaping insects of the same order as the grasshopper. Male crickets make a chirping noise by friction of the front wings. [< Old French *criquet* < *criquer* to creak, rattle]

crick et[2] (krik′it), *n.* 1 an outdoor game played by two teams of eleven players each, with a ball, a flattened bat, and a pair of wickets. Cricket is very popular in England. 2 INFORMAL. fair play; good sportsmanship. —*adj.* INFORMAL. according to good sportsmanship; fair; honest. —*v.i.* play the game of cricket. [< Old French *criquet* goal post, stick] **—crick′et er,** *n.*

crick et[3] (krik′it), *n.* a small, low, wooden stool. [origin uncertain]

cried (krīd), *v.* pt. and pp. of **cry.**

cri er (krī′ər), *n.* 1 official who shouts out public announcements, as in a court or in certain towns. 2 person who shouts out announcements of goods for sale. 3 person who cries or shouts.

cries (krīz), *n.* pl. of **cry.** —*v.* 3rd person singular, present tense of **cry.**

crime (krīm), *n.* 1 an act that is against the law. See synonym study below. 2 activity of criminals; violation of law. 3 an evil or wrong act. [< Old French < Latin *crimen* accusation, offense]

Syn. 1 Crime, offense mean an act that breaks a law. **Crime** applies particularly to an act that breaks a law that has been made for the public good, and is punishable by public law: *Murder and swindling are crimes.* **Offense** is more general, and applies to any act, not always serious, that breaks any moral, public, or social law: *Lying and cruelty are offenses.*

Cri me a (krī mē′ə), *n.* peninsula in the SW part of the Soviet Union in Europe, on the N coast of the Black Sea. **—Cri me′an,** *adj., n.*

crim i nal (krim′ə nəl), *n.* person guilty of a crime. —*adj.* 1 guilty of wrongdoing. 2 of or having to do with crime or its punishment: *criminal court, criminal law.* 3 like crime; wrong. **—crim′i nal ly,** *adv.*

crim i nal i ty (krim′ə nal′ə tē), *n., pl.* **-ties.** 1 fact or quality of being criminal; guilt. 2 a criminal act.

crim i no log i cal (krim′ə nə loj′ə kəl), *adj.* of or having to do with criminology.

crim i nol o gist (krim′ə nol′ə jist), *n.* an expert in criminology.

crim i nol o gy (krim′ə nol′ə jē), *n.* the scientific study of crime, its prevention and treatment, and criminals.

crimp[1] (krimp), *v.t.* 1 press into small, regular, narrow folds; make wavy: *The children crimped tissue paper to make paper flowers.* 2 hinder; cramp. —*n.* 1 something crimped; fold or wave. 2 act of crimping. 3 a waved or curled lock of hair. 4 **put a crimp in,** U.S. INFORMAL. interfere with; hinder. [< Low German *krimpen* shrink, wrinkle] **—crimp′er,** *n.*

crimp[2] (krimp), *n.* person who makes a business of forcing or tricking men into becoming sailors, soldiers, etc. —*v.t.* force or trick (men) into becoming sailors, soldiers, etc. [origin uncertain]

crimp y (krim′pē), *adj.,* **crimp i er, crimp i est.** having small, narrow folds; wavy.

crim son (krim′zən), *n.* a deep red. —*adj.* deep-red. —*v.t., v.i.* make or become deep-red. [< Italian *cremesino* < *cremisi, chermisi* the color crimson < Arabic *qirmizī* < *qirmiz* kermes]

cringe (krinj), *v.,* **cringed, cring ing,** *n.* —*v.i.* 1 shrink from danger or pain; crouch in fear. 2 try to get favor or attention by servile behavior: *The courtiers cringed before the king.* —*n.* act of cringing. [Middle English *crengen,* Old English *cringan* give way] **—cring′er,** *n.*

crin gle (kring′gəl), *n.* a small loop or ring of rope on the edge of a sail. The sail can be fastened by putting a rope through the cringle. [apparently < Low German *kringel,* diminutive of *kring* ring]

crin kle (kring′kəl), *v.,* **-kled, -kling,** *n.* —*v.t., v.i.* 1 wrinkle or ripple: *Crepe paper is crinkled.* 2 rustle. —*n.* 1 a wrinkle or ripple. 2 a rustle. [Middle English *crenklen* < Old English *crincan* to bend]

crin kly (kring′klē), *adj.,* **-kli er, -kli est.** full of crinkles.

cri noid (krī′noid, krin′oid), *n.* any of a class of echinoderms having a small, cup-shaped body with five branched feathery arms, usually anchored by a stalk; sea lily. —*adj.* of or belonging to this class. [< Greek *krinoeidēs* < *krinon* lily]

crin o line (krin′l ən), *n.* 1 a stiff cloth used

as a lining to hold a skirt out, make a coat collar stand up, etc. 2 petticoat of crinoline to hold a skirt out. 3 a hoop skirt. [< French < Italian *crinolino* < *crino* horsehair + *lino* thread]

crip ple (krip′əl), *n., v.,* **-pled, -pling.** —*n.* person or animal that cannot use his legs, arms, or body properly because of injury, deformity, or lack; lame person or animal. —*v.t.* 1 make a cripple of; make lame. See synonym study below. 2 damage; disable; weaken: *The ship was crippled by the storm.* [Old English *crypel.* Related to CREEP.] **—crip′pler,** *n.*

Syn. *v.t.* 1 **Cripple, disable** mean to deprive of the ability or power to carry on normal activities. **Cripple** means to deprive a person or animal of the use of a leg, foot, or arm: *He has been crippled since he broke his hip.* **Disable** means to deprive of the ability to work or act normally: *The man is disabled by a heart condition.*

cri sis (krī′sis), *n., pl.* **-ses** (-sēz′). 1 a deciding event: *a crisis in a person's career.* 2 state of danger or anxious waiting: *a domestic crisis, a monetary crisis.* See **emergency** for synonym study. 3 the turning point in a disease, toward life or death. [< Latin < Greek *krisis* < *krinein* decide]

crisp (krisp), *adj.* 1 hard and thin; breaking easily with a snap; brittle: *Dry toast and fresh celery are crisp.* 2 sharp and clear; bracing; brisk: *The fresh air was cool and crisp.* 3 clear-cut; decisive: *"Don't worry; I'll be back," was his crisp answer.* 4 curly and wiry: *crisp hair.* —*v.t., v.i.* make or become crisp. —*n.* 1 something crisp. 2 BRITISH. a potato chip. [Old English < Latin *crispus* curled] **—crisp′ly,** *adv.* **—crisp′ness,** *n.*

crisp y (kris′pē), *adj.,* **crisp i er, crisp i est.** crisp.

criss cross (kris′krôs′, kris′kros′), *v.t.* 1 mark or cover with crossed lines. 2 come and go across: *Buses and cars crisscross the city.* —*adj.* made or marked with crossed lines; crossed; crossing. —*adv.* crosswise. —*n.* mark or pattern of crossed lines. [Middle English *cristcross,* literally, Christ's cross]

Cris tó bal (kris tō′bəl), *n.* seaport in the N part of the Canal Zone, at the Atlantic end of the Panama Canal. 1000.

cri ter i a (krī tir′ē ə), *n.* a pl. of **criterion.**

cri ter i on (krī tir′ē ən), *n., pl.* **-ter i a** or **-ter i ons.** rule or standard for making a judgment; test: *Wealth is only one criterion of success.* See **standard** for synonym study. [< Greek *kritērion* < *krinein* decide, judge]

crit ic (krit′ik), *n.* 1 person who makes judgments of the merits and faults of books, music, pictures, plays, acting, etc.: *The artist's work was praised by the critics, but was not popular with the public.* 2 person whose profession is writing such judgments for a newspaper, magazine, etc. 3 person who disapproves or finds fault; faultfinder. [< Latin *criticus* < Greek *kritikos* able to decide < *krinein* decide, judge]

crit i cal (krit′ə kəl), *adj.* 1 inclined to find fault or disapprove: *a critical disposition.* 2 skilled as a critic. 3 coming from one who is skilled as a critic: *a critical judgment.* 4 belonging to the work of a critic: *critical essays.* 5 of a crisis; being important at a time of danger or difficulty: *the critical moment.* 6 full of danger or difficulty: *The patient was in a critical condition.* 7 (of supplies, labor, or resources) necessary for some work or project but existing in inadequate supply. 8 (in physics and chemistry) having to do with or constituting a point at which some action, property, or condition undergoes a decisive change: *critical velocity.* 9 (in nuclear physics) capable of sustaining a chain reaction. **—crit′i cal ly,** *adv.* **—crit′i cal ness,** *n.*

crocodile (def. 1)—20 to 30 ft. long

critical angle, the smallest possible angle of incidence that gives total reflection.

crit i cal i ty (krit′ə kal′ə tē), *n.* point at which a nuclear reactor becomes critical.

critical mass, the smallest amount of fissionable material that will support a self-sustaining chain reaction.

critical temperature, the highest temperature at which a gas can be liquefied by pressure alone.

crit i cise (krit′ə sīz), *v.i., v.t.,* **-cised, -cis ing.** criticize. **—crit′i cis′er,** *n.*

crit i cism (krit′ə siz′əm), *n.* 1 unfavorable remarks or judgments; disapproval; faultfinding: *I always seem to be the object of your criticism.* 2 the making of judgments; approving or disapproving; analysis of merits and faults: *Before I finish this theme, I would appreciate your criticisms of what I have written.* 3 art or principles of making careful judgments on the merits and faults of books, music, pictures, plays, acting, etc. 4 a critical comment, essay, review, etc. See **review** for synonym study.

crit i cize (krit′ə sīz), *v.,* **-cized, -ciz ing.** —*v.t.* 1 find fault with; disapprove: *Don't criticize them until you know all the circumstances.* 2 judge as a critic. —*v.i.* act or speak as a critic. Also, **criticise. —crit′i-ciz′er,** *n.*

cri tique (kri tēk′), *n.* 1 a critical essay or review: *Some newspapers have critiques of new books.* 2 art of criticism; criticism. [< French]

crit ter (krit′ər), *n.* U.S. DIALECT. creature.

croak (krōk), *n.* the deep, hoarse sound made by a frog, crow, or raven. —*v.i.* 1 make this sound. 2 be always prophesying evil; be dissatisfied; grumble. 3 SLANG. die. —*v.t.* utter in a deep, hoarse voice. [Middle English *croken* to croak] **—croak′er,** *n.*

croak y (krō′kē), *adj.,* **croak i er, croak i est.** 1 making a croaking sound. 2 given to croaking.

Cro at (krō′at), *n.* native or inhabitant of Croatia; Croatian.

Cro a tia (krō ā′shə), *n.* district in NW Yugoslavia that includes Slavonia. It is one of the constituent republics of Yugoslavia. *Capital:* Zagreb.

Cro a tian (krō ā′shən), *adj.* of or having to do with Croatia or the Croats. —*n.* 1 Croat. 2 the Slavic language of Croatia. Croatian and Serbian are virtually the same language written in different alphabets.

cro chet (krō shā′), *v.,* **-cheted** (-shād′), **-chet ing** (-shā′ing), *n.* —*v.t., v.i.* knit (sweaters, lace, etc.) with a single needle having a hook at one end. —*n.* knitting done in this way. [< Old French, diminutive of *croc* hook. Doublet of CROTCHET.] **—cro-chet′er** (krō shā′ər), *n.*

crock (krok), *n.* pot or jar made of earthenware. [Old English *crocca*]

crock er y (krok′ər ē), *n.* earthenware.

Crock ett (krok′it), *n.* **Davy,** 1786-1836, American hunter, scout, and Congressman, killed at the defense of the Alamo.

croc o dile (krok′ə dīl), *n.* 1 any of a family of large, lizardlike reptiles with thick skin, a long narrow head, and webbed hind feet. Crocodiles live in the rivers and marshes of the warm parts of Africa, Asia, Australia, and America. 2 any crocodilian. [< Latin *crocodilus* < Greek *krokodilos* crocodile, lizard]

crocodile tears, pretended or insincere grief. It is so called because of the story that crocodiles shed tears while eating their victims.

croc o dil i an (krok′ə dil′ē ən), *n.* any of an order of reptiles that includes crocodiles, alligators, etc. —*adj.* of or like a crocodile.

cro cus (krō′kəs), *n., pl.* **-cus es, -ci** (-sī). 1 any of a genus of small, hardy plants of the same family as the iris, that grow from a bulblike corm and have white, yellow, or purple flowers. Most crocuses bloom very early in the spring. 2 the flower of any of these plants. 3 a deep yellow; saffron. [< Latin < Greek *krokos*]

Croe sus (krē′səs), *n.* 1 died 546? B.C., king of Lydia from 560 to 546 B.C., famous for his great wealth. 2 any very rich person.

croft (krôft, kroft), *n.* BRITISH. 1 a small, enclosed field. 2 a very small rented farm. [Old English]

croft er (krôf′tər, krof′tər), *n.* BRITISH. person who rents and cultivates a very small farm.

crois sant (krä′sänt; *French* krwä säN′), *n.* a small roll of bread shaped like a crescent. [< French]

croix de guerre (krwä də ger′), a French medal given to soldiers for bravery under fire. [< French, war cross]

Cro-Mag non (krō mag′nən), *adj.* of or belonging to a group of prehistoric people who lived in southwestern Europe about 25,000 years ago. Considered of the same species as modern man, they used stone and bone implements, and some were skilled artists. —*n.* one of these people. [< *Cro-Magnon* cave, in southwestern France, where remains were found]

crom lech (krom′lek), *n.* 1 circle of upright stones built in prehistoric times. 2 a dolmen. [< Welsh < *crom* bent + *llech* (flat) stone]

Cromp ton (kromp′tən), *n.* **Samuel,** 1753-1827, English inventor.

Crom well (krom′wel, krom′wəl), *n.* 1 **Oliver,** 1599-1658, English general, statesman, and Puritan leader. He was Lord Protector of the Commonwealth from 1653 to 1658. 2 his son, **Richard,** 1626-1712, English soldier and politician. He was Lord Protector of the Commonwealth from 1658 to 1659. 3 **Thomas,** 1485?-1540, Earl of Essex, English statesman.

crone (krōn), *n.* a withered old woman. [< Middle Dutch *croonje* < Old French *carogne* carcass, hag. Doublet of CARRION.]

Cro nus (krō′nəs), *n.* (in Greek myths) a Titan who was the ruler of the universe until overthrown by his son Zeus. He was identified with the Roman god Saturn.

cro ny (krō′nē), *n., pl.* **-nies.** a very close friend; chum. [earlier *chrony* < Greek *chronios* lasting < *chronos* time]

crook (krůk), *v.t.* make a hook or curve in; bend: *I crooked my leg around the branch to keep from falling.* —*v.i.* bend or be bent; be turned from a right line. —*n.* 1 hook; bend; curve: *a crook in a stream.* 2 a hooked, curved, or bent part: *the crook of the elbow.* 3 a shepherd's staff, curved on its upper end into a hook. 4 INFORMAL. a dishonest person; thief or swindler. [apparently < Scandinavian (Old Icelandic) *krōkr*]

cross (def. 3)—different types of crosses

crook ed (krůk′id), *adj.* 1 not straight; curved; twisted. 2 dishonest; fraudulent. —**crook′ed ly,** *adv.* —**crook′ed ness,** *n.*

Crookes (krůks), *n.* Sir **William,** 1832-1919, English chemist and physicist.

crook neck (krůk′nek′), *n.* kind of squash with a long, curved neck.

croon (krün), *v.i., v.t.* 1 hum, sing, or murmur in a low tone: *I crooned to the baby.* 2 sing in a low, sentimental voice. —*n.* a low humming, singing, or murmuring. [apparently < Middle Dutch *krōnen* to murmur] —**croon′er,** *n.*

crop (krop), *n., v.,* **cropped, crop ping.** —*n.* 1 product grown or gathered for use, especially for use as food or fiber: *Wheat, corn, and cotton are three main crops of the United States.* 2 the whole amount (of wheat, corn, or the produce of any plant or tree) that one season yields: *The drought made the potato crop very small this year.* 3 anything like a crop; group; collection: *a crop of lies.* 4 act or result of cropping. A short haircut is a crop. 5 mark produced by clipping the ears. 6 a baglike swelling of a bird's or insect's food passage where food is prepared for digestion; craw. 7 a short whip with a loop instead of a lash. 8 handle of a whip. —*v.i.* 1 plant, cultivate, or yield a crop or crops. 2 **crop out** or **crop up, a** appear or come to the surface. **b** turn up unexpectedly. —*v.t.* 1 cut or bite off the top of: *Sheep had cropped the grass very short.* 2 cut short (the tail, ear, hair, edge of a book, etc.); clip. [Old English *cropp* sprout, craw]

crop land (krop′land′), *n.* land under cultivation for crops.

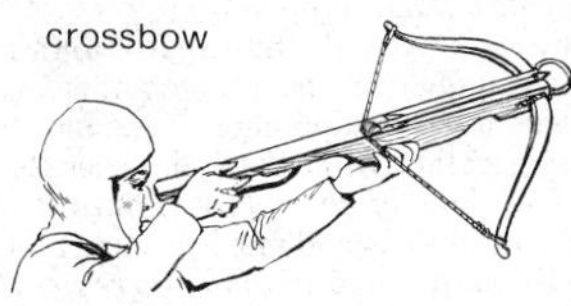

crop per (krop′ər), *n.* 1 person or thing that crops. 2 sharecropper. 3 **come a cropper,** INFORMAL. meet with misfortune; fail or collapse; come to grief.

crop rotation, way of conserving the fertility of soil by successively planting on the same ground different crops with varying food requirements that do not exhaust one constituent of the soil as a repeated crop does.

cro quet (krō kā′), *n.* an outdoor game played by driving wooden balls through wickets with mallets. [< French, dialectal variant of *crochet.* See CROCHET.]

cro quette (krō ket′), *n.* a small mass of chopped meat, fish, vegetables, etc., coated with crumbs and fried. [< French < *croquer* to crunch]

cro sier (krō′zhər), *n.* an ornamental staff carried by or before bishops or certain abbots. Also, **crozier.** [< Old French, crook bearer < *crosse* hook < Popular Latin *croccia* < Germanic]

cross (krôs, kros), *n.* 1 stick or post with another across it like a T or an X. 2 **the Cross, a** the cross on which Christ was crucified. **b** the sufferings and death of Christ; the Atonement. **c** the Christian religion. 3 thing, design, or mark shaped like a cross. A cross is the symbol of the Christian religion. A person who cannot write his name makes a cross instead. A soldier is sometimes given a cross for bravery in war. 4 a crossing; lying or going across. 5 burden of duty or suffering; trouble. 6 a mixing of kinds, breeds, or races. 7 result of such mixing; hybrid: *A mule is a cross between a horse and a donkey.* 8 (in boxing) a countering blow crossing over the opponent's lead. 9 **take the cross,** join a crusade.
—*v.t.* 1 draw a line across: *In writing you cross the letter "t".* 2 cancel by marking with a cross or by drawing a line or lines across: *cross off a name on a list. I crossed out the wrong word.* 3 put or lay across: *She crossed her arms.* 4 lie across; intersect: *Main Street crosses Market Street.* 5 go across; move across: *cross a bridge.* 6 meet and pass: *I crossed her on the stairs.* 7 make the sign of the cross on or over: *The priest crossed himself.* 8 oppose; hinder: *If anyone crosses him, he gets very angry.* 9 mix kinds, breeds, or races of: *A new plant is sometimes made by crossing two others.* —*v.i.* 1 lie across; intersect: *Parallel lines cannot cross.* 2 meet and pass: *Our letters crossed in the mail.*
—*adj.* 1 lying or going across; crossing: *cross streets.* 2 in a bad temper; peevish. 3 mixed in kind, breed, or race; crossbred; hybrid.
[Old English *cros* < Old Irish *cross* < Latin *crux.* Doublet of CRUX.] —**cross′ly,** *adv.* —**cross′ness,** *n.*

cross bar (krôs′bär′, kros′bär′), *n.* bar, line, or stripe going crosswise.

cross beam (krôs′bēm′, kros′bēm′), *n.* a large beam that crosses another or extends from wall to wall.

cross bill (krôs′bil′, kros′bil′), *n.* a small finch whose powerful bill has points that cross when the bill is closed.

cross bones (krôs′bōnz′, kros′bōnz′), *n.pl.* two large bones placed crosswise, usually below a skull, as a symbol of death.

cross bow (krôs′bō′, kros′bō′), *n.* a medieval weapon for shooting arrows, stones, etc., with a bow fixed across a wooden stock, and a groove in the middle to direct the arrows, stones, etc.

cross bow man (krôs′bō′mən, kros′bō′mən), *n., pl.* **-men.** soldier who uses a crossbow.

cross bred (krôs′bred′, kros′bred′), *adj.* produced by crossbreeding; hybrid.

cross breed (krôs′brēd′, kros′brēd′), *v.,* **-bred, -breed ing,** *n.* —*v.t., v.i.* breed by mixing kinds, breeds, or races. —*n.* individual or breed produced by crossbreeding. The loganberry is a crossbreed of a dewberry and the red raspberry.

hat, āge, fär; let, ēqual, tėrm;
it, īce; hot, ōpen, ôrder;
oil, out; cup, pủt, rüle;
ch, child; ng, long; sh, she;
th, thin; ᴛʜ, then; zh, measure;

ə represents *a* in about, *e* in taken, *i* in pencil, *o* in lemon, *u* in circus.

< = from, derived from, taken from.

cross buck (krôs′buk, kros′buk), *n.* a highway traffic sign consisting of two crosspieces forming an X to warn motorists that a railroad crossing is ahead.

cross-coun try (krôs′kun′trē, kros′kun′trē), *adj., adv.* 1 across fields or open country instead of by road: *a cross-country race.* 2 across an entire country, not merely a part: *fly cross-country from New York to Seattle.*

cross cur rent (krôs′kėr′ənt, kros′kėr′ənt), *n.* 1 current of air blowing across another. 2 an opposing tendency or trend: *the crosscurrents of political thought.*

cross cut (krôs′kut′, kros′kut′), *n., adj., v.,* **-cut, -cut ting.** —*n.* 1 a cut, course, or path going across. 2 a shortcut. —*adj.* 1 used or made for cutting across. 2 cut across. —*v.t.* cut across.

crosscut saw, saw used or made for cutting across the grain of wood.

crosse (krôs, kros), *n.* racket used in playing lacrosse. [< French]

cross-ex am i na tion (krôs′eg zam′ə nā′shən, kros′eg zam′ə nā′shən), *n.* 1 examination to check a previous examination, especially the questioning of a witness by the lawyer for the opposing side to test the truth of the witness's testimony. 2 a close or severe questioning.

cross-ex am ine (krôs′eg zam′ən, kros′eg zam′ən), *v.t., v.i.,* **-ined, -in ing.** 1 question closely (a witness for the opposing side) to check the truth of his testimony. 2 question closely or severely. —**cross′-ex am′in er,** *n.*

cross-eye (krôs′ī′, kros′ī′), *n.* strabismus, especially the form in which both eyes are turned toward the nose and cannot focus on the same point.

cross-eyed (krôs′īd′, kros′īd′), *adj.* having both eyes turned toward the nose, and unable to focus on the same point.

cross-fer ti li za tion (krôs′fėr′tl ə zā′shən, kros′fėr′tl ə zā′shən), *n.* fertilization of one flower by pollen from another; allogamy.

cross-fer ti lize (krôs′fėr′tl īz, kros′fėr′tl īz), *v.,* **-lized, -liz ing.** —*v.t.* cause the cross-fertilization of. —*v.i.* be subjected to cross-fertilization.

cross-file (krôs′fīl′, kros′fīl′), *v.i.,* **-filed, -fil ing.** U.S. file for nomination on more than one party's ticket during Congressional or other primaries.

cross fire (krôs′fīr′, kros′fīr′), *n.* 1 gunfire coming from two or more opposite directions so as to cross. 2 a verbal attack from two or more sources or directions.

cross-grained (krôs′grānd′, kros′grānd′),

adj. 1 having the grain in crossing directions, or irregular or gnarled, instead of straight: *cross-grained wood.* 2 hard to get along with; contrary.

cross hairs, fine strands stretched across the focal plane of an optical instrument for accurately defining the line of sight.

cross hatch (krôs′hach′, kros′hach′), *v.t., v.i.* mark or shade with two sets of parallel lines crossing each other.

cross hatch ing (krôs′hach′ing, kros′hach′ing), *n.* 1 the making of crosshatches. 2 the marking or shading made.

crosshatching (def. 2)

cross ing (krô′sing, kros′ing), *n.* 1 place where lines, tracks, etc., cross; intersection. 2 place at which a street, river, etc., may be crossed. 3 a going across, especially a voyage across water. 4 crossbreeding.

cross ing-o ver (krô′sing ō′vər, kros′ing-ō′vər), *n.* a mutual exchange of genes between homologous chromosomes during meiosis.

cross-leg ged (krôs′leg′id, krôs′legd′; kros′leg′id, kros′legd′), *adj.* 1 with one leg over the other and the knees together. 2 with the ankles crossed and the knees apart.

cross-match (krôs′mach′, kros′mach′), *v.i., v.t.* determine the compatibility of a donor's and recipient's (blood) before transfusion.

cross o ver (krôs′ō′vər, kros′ō′vər), *n.* 1 place at which a crossing is made. 2 anything that crosses over or connects, as a bridge over a highway. 3 crossing-over.

cross patch (krôs′pach′, kros′pach′), *n.* INFORMAL. a cross, bad-tempered person.

cross piece (krôs′pēs′, kros′pēs′), *n.* piece of wood, metal, etc., that is placed across something.

cross-pol li nate (krôs′pol′ə nāt, kros′pol′ə nāt), *v.,* **-nat ed, -nat ing.** —*v.t.* cause cross-pollination in. —*v.i.* be subjected to cross-pollination.

cross-pol li na tion (krôs′pol′ə nā′shən, kros′pol′ə nā′shən), *n.* transfer of pollen from the anther of one flower to the stigma of another. Insects and wind are agents of cross-pollination.

cross-pur pose (krôs′pėr′pəs, kros′pėr′pəs), *n.* 1 an opposing or contrary purpose. 2 **at cross-purposes, a** misunderstanding each other's purpose. **b** acting under such a misunderstanding.

cross-ques tion (krôs′kwes′chən, kros′kwes′chən), *v.t.* question closely or severely; cross-examine. —*n.* question asked in cross-examining.

cross-re fer (krôs′ri fėr′, kros′ri fėr′), *v.t., v.i.,* **-ferred, -fer ring.** 1 refer from one part to another. 2 make a cross-reference.

cross-ref er ence (krôs′ref′ər əns, kros′ref′ər əns), *n.* reference from one part of a book, index, etc., to another. "See **harness** for diagram" under **crupper** is a cross-reference.

cross road (krôs′rōd′, kros′rōd′), *n.* 1 road that crosses another. 2 road that connects main roads. 3 **crossroads,** *pl.* place where roads cross. 4 **at the crossroads,** in a situation where a choice must be made.

cross ruff (krôs′ruf′, kros′ruf′), *n.* (in card games) a play in which each of two partners leads a card that the other can trump. —*v.i.* trump cards in this way.

cross section, 1 act of cutting anything across: *She prepared slides for her microscope by making a series of thin cross sections of a carrot.* 2 piece cut in this way. 3 small selection of people, things, etc., with the same qualities as the entire group; representative sample.

cross-stitch (krôs′stich′, kros′stich′), *n.* 1 one stitch crossed over another, forming an X. 2 embroidery made with this stitch. —*v.t., v.i.* embroider or sew with one stitch crossed over another.

cross tie (krôs′tī′, kros′tī′), *n.* a heavy piece of timber or iron placed crosswise to form a foundation or support. The rails of a railroad track are fastened to crossties about a foot apart.

cross town (krôs′toun′, kros′toun′), *adj.* that runs across the town: *a crosstown bus.* —*adv.* across the town.

cross trees (krôs′trēz′, kros′trēz′), *n.pl.* two horizontal bars of wood or metal near the top of a ship's mast to support the upper shrouds.

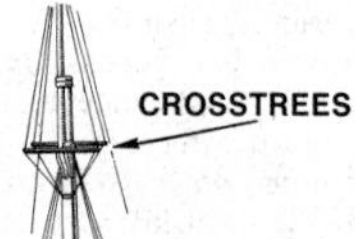

cross walk (krôs′wôk′, kros′wôk′), *n.* area marked with lines for pedestrians to cross a street.

cross way (krôs′wā′, kros′wā′), *n.* crossroad.

cross ways (krôs′wāz′, kros′wāz′), *adv.* crosswise.

cross wise (krôs′wīz′, kros′wīz′), *adv.* 1 so as to cross; across. 2 in the form of a cross. 3 opposite to what is required; wrongly.

cross word puzzle (krôs′wėrd′, kros′wėrd′), puzzle with sets of squares to be filled in with words, one letter to each square. Synonyms, definitions, or other clues are listed with numbers corresponding to the numbers in the squares.

crotch (kroch), *n.* 1 a forked piece or part; place where a tree, bough, etc., divides into two limbs or branches. 2 place where the human body divides into the two legs. [< French *croche* crook. Related to CROTCHET.]

crotched (krocht), *adj.* having a crotch; forked.

crotch et (kroch′it), *n.* 1 an odd notion; unreasonable whim. 2 a small hook or hooklike part. 3 BRITISH. a quarter note in music. [< Old French *crochet,* diminutive of *croc* hook. Doublet of CROCHET.]

crotch et y (kroch′ə tē), *adj.* full of odd notions or unreasonable whims. —**crotch′et i ness,** *n.*

cro ton (krōt′n), *n.* any of a genus of tropical Asian shrubs or trees of the same family as the spurge, having a strong odor. The seeds of one species yield an oil used in medicine as a cathartic. [< Greek *krotōn* castor-oil plant]

Croton bug, a small, pale yellowish-brown cockroach, commonly found in houses near damp places; water bug. [< *Croton* Reservoir, source of water for New York City, and source also of these bugs]

crouch (krouch), *v.i.* 1 stoop low with bent legs like an animal ready to spring. 2 shrink down in fear. 3 bow down in a timid or slavish manner; cower. —*v.t.* bend low. —*n.* 1 act or state of crouching. 2 a crouching position. [perhaps blend of *couch* and *crook*]

croup[1] (krüp), *n.* inflammation or diseased condition of the throat and windpipe, especially in children, characterized by a hoarse cough and difficult breathing. [< obsolete *croup* cry hoarsely, croak; imitative]

croup[2] (krüp), *n.* rump of a horse, etc.; crupper. See **horse** for picture. [< Old French *croupe*]

crou pi er (krü′pē ər), *n.* attendant at a gambling table who rakes in the money and pays the winners. [< French]

croup y (krü′pē), *adj.,* **croup i er, croup i est.** 1 sick with croup. 2 hoarse and having difficulty in breathing. 3 of croup; resembling croup.

crou ton (krü′ton), *n.* a small piece of toasted or fried bread, often served in soup. [< French *croûton* < *croûte* crust < Latin *crusta*]

crow[1] (krō), *n., v.,* **crowed** (or **crew** for 1), **crowed, crow ing.** —*n.* 1 the loud cry of a rooster. 2 a happy sound made by a baby. —*v.i.* 1 make the cry of a rooster. 2 make the happy sound of a baby. 3 show happiness and pride; boast: *The winning team crowed over its victory.* [Old English *crāwan* to crow]

crow[2] (krō), *n.* 1 any of several large, glossy, black birds that have a harsh cry or caw. 2 any similar and related bird, such as a raven, magpie, or jay. 3 crowbar. 4 **as the crow flies,** in a straight line; in or by the shortest way. 5 **eat crow,** be forced to do something very disagreeable and humiliating. [Old English *crāwe*]

Crow (krō), *n., pl.* **Crow** or **Crows.** member of a tribe of American Indians who formerly lived in Montana and Wyoming and now live in Montana.

crow bar (krō′bär′), *n.* a strong iron or steel bar, flattened into a wedge at one end for use as a lever.

crowd (kroud), *n.* 1 a large number of people together: *A crowd gathered to hear the speaker.* See synonym study below. 2 the common people; people in general; the masses: *Advertisements seek to appeal to the crowd.* 3 a large number of things together; multitude. 4 INFORMAL. group; set: *We are in the same crowd at school.* —*v.i.* 1 collect in large numbers. 2 press forward; force one's way: *crowd into the subway car.* —*v.t.* 1 fill; fill too full: *crowd a bus.* 2 push; shove. [Old English *crūdan* to press]

Syn. *n.* 1 **Crowd, throng, swarm** mean a large number of people together. **Crowd** applies to a large number of people standing close together without much order: *A crowd was waiting in the lobby.* **Throng** implies greater numbers and more pushing and pressing forward: *At Christmas there are throngs in the streets.* **Swarm** suggests a large, confused, moving mass: *A swarm of students gathered.*

crow foot (krō′fu̇t′), *n., pl.* **-foots.** 1 buttercup. 2 any of various other plants with deeply divided leaves somewhat resembling a crow's foot.

crown (kroun), *n.* 1 a head covering for a king, queen, etc.; diadem. 2 **the Crown,** the governing power and authority in a monarchy; royal power. 3 a king, queen, etc. 4 design or thing shaped like a crown. 5 wreath for the head; garland: *The winner of the race received a crown.* 6 honor; reward. 7 head. 8 the highest part; top: *the crown of the head.* See **top**[1] for synonym study. 9 the top part of a hat, cap, etc. 10 the highest state or quality of anything. 11 part of a tooth visible beyond the gum. 12 an artificial substitute for this part. 13 a British coin worth 5 shillings. 14 end of an anchor between the arms. 15 top of a root of a plant, from which the stem arises.
—v.t. 1 make king, queen, etc. 2 honor; reward. 3 be on top of; cover the highest part of: *A fort crowns the hill.* 4 make perfect or complete; add the finishing touch to: *Success crowned her efforts.* 5 put a crown on (a tooth). 6 make a king of (a checker that has advanced to the opponent's rearmost row).
—adj. of or having to do with a crown: *the crown jewels.*
[< Anglo-French *coroune* < Latin *corona* garland, wreath, crown. Doublet of CORONA.]

crown colony, colony under the control and authority of the British Crown, administered by a governor. Hong Kong is a crown colony.

crown glass, 1 a very clear glass used in optical instruments. 2 an old kind of window glass blown and whirled into round sheets with a thick place left in the middle by the glass blower's tube.

crown prince, the oldest living son of a king or queen; the male heir to the throne.

crown princess, 1 wife of a crown prince. 2 girl or woman who is heir to the throne.

crow's-feet (krōz′fēt′), *n.pl.* the tiny wrinkles at the outer corners of the eyes.

crow's-nest (krōz′nest′), *n.* 1 a small, enclosed platform near the top of a ship's mast, used by the lookout. 2 any similar platform ashore.

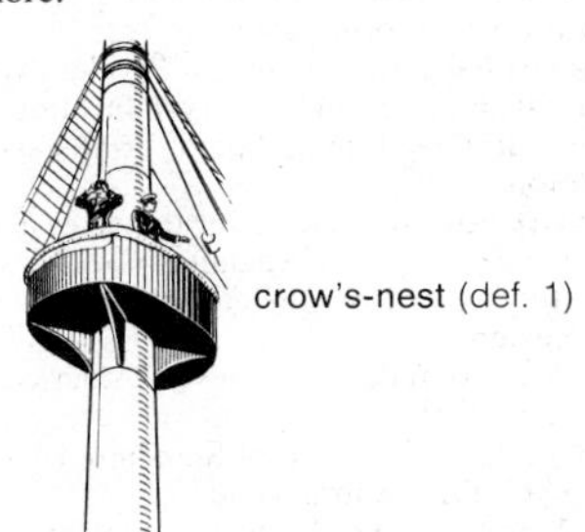
crow's-nest (def. 1)

cro zier (krō′zhər), *n.* crosier.

cru ces (krü′sēz′), *n.* a pl. of **crux.**

cru cial (krü′shəl), *adj.* 1 very important or decisive; critical. 2 very trying; severe. [< New Latin *crucialis* < Latin *crucem* cross; with reference to the fork of a road] **—cru′cial ly,** *adv.*

cru ci ble (krü′sə bəl), *n.* 1 container in which metals, ores, etc., can be melted. 2 a severe test or trial. [< Medieval Latin *crucibulum,* originally, night lamp]

cru ci fix (krü′sə fiks), *n.* cross with a figure of the crucified Christ on it. [< Late Latin *crucifixus* < *crucifigere* crucify. See CRUCIFY.]

cru ci fix ion (krü′sə fik′shən), *n.* 1 a crucifying. 2 a being crucified. 3 **Crucifixion,** a the crucifying of Christ on the cross. b picture, statue, etc., of this.

cru ci form (krü′sə fôrm), *adj.* shaped like a cross. **—cru′ci form′ly,** *adv.*

cru ci fy (krü′sə fī), *v.t.,* **-fied, -fy ing.** 1 put to death by nailing or binding the hands and feet to a cross. 2 persecute or torture. [< Old French *crucifier* < Late Latin *crucifigere* < Latin *crux, crucis* cross + *figere* fix, fasten] **—cru′ci fi′er,** *n.*

crude (krüd), *adj.,* **crud er, crud est.** 1 in a natural or raw state; unrefined. Oil, ore, sugar, etc., before being refined and prepared for use are crude. See **raw** for synonym study. 2 not mature; unripe; green. 3 rough; coarse: *a crude log cabin.* 4 lacking finish, grace, taste, or refinement; rude: *crude manners.* *—n.* crude oil. [< Latin *crudus* raw] **—crude′ly,** *adv.* **—crude′ness,** *n.*

cru di ty (krü′də tē), *n., pl.* **-ties.** 1 a being crude; lack of finish; roughness. 2 a crude action, thing, etc.

cru el (krü′əl), *adj.* 1 fond of causing pain to others and delighting in their suffering; not caring about the pain and suffering of others; hard-hearted. See synonym study below. 2 showing a cruel nature: *cruel acts.* 3 causing pain and suffering: *a cruel war.* [< Old French < Latin *crudelem* rough. Related to CRUDE.] **—cru′el ly,** *adv.* **—cru′el ness,** *n.*
Syn. 1 Cruel, brutal, pitiless mean willing to cause pain to people and animals. **Cruel** implies indifference to the physical or mental suffering of others and taking pleasure in causing or adding to it: *The cruel master mistreated his slaves. The cruel remark was difficult to forget.* **Brutal** suggests cruelty shown in acts of physical violence: *Brutal captors beat their prisoners.* **Pitiless** implies cold unwillingness to show mercy to those who are suffering: *The pitiless ruler refused to help the poor.*

cru el ty (krü′əl tē), *n., pl.* **-ties.** 1 a being cruel; readiness to give pain to others or to delight in their suffering. 2 a cruel act or acts.

cru et (krü′it), *n.* a glass bottle to hold vinegar, oil, etc., for the table. [< Old French, diminutive of *cruie* pot]

Cruik shank (krůk′shangk′), *n.* **George,** 1792-1878, English artist, famous for his caricatures.

cruise (krüz), *v.,* **cruised, cruis ing,** *n.* *—v.i.* 1 sail about from place to place on pleasure or business: *The cutter cruised along the shore looking for smugglers.* 2 journey or travel from place to place: *Taxis cruise, looking for passengers.* 3 travel in a car, airplane, boat, etc., at the speed at which it operates best. *—v.t.* 1 sail over or about: *Freighters and oil tankers cruise the oceans of the world.* 2 travel or journey over or about: *Patrol cars cruised the streets to keep the peace.* *—n.* act of sailing about from place to place on pleasure or business. [< Dutch *kruisen* to cross, cruise < *kruis* cross < Latin *crucem* cross]

cruis er (krü′zər), *n.* 1 warship with less armor and firepower, but greater speed than a battleship. 2 airplane, taxi, etc., that cruises. 3 motorboat having a cabin and equipped with facilities for living on board. 4 a police car used for patrolling streets and highways; patrol car.

crul ler (krul′ər), *n.* piece of rich, sweet dough fried brown in deep fat; twisted doughnut. [< Dutch *kruller* < *krullen* to curl]

crumb (krum), *n.* 1 a very small piece of bread, cake, etc., broken from a larger piece.

hat, āge, fär; let, ēqual, tėrm;
it, īce; hot, ōpen, ôrder;
oil, out; cup, pů t, rüle;
ch, child; ng, long; sh, she;
th, thin; ᴛʜ, then; zh, measure;

ə represents *a* in about, *e* in taken, *i* in pencil, *o* in lemon, *u* in circus.

< = from, derived from, taken from.

2 a little bit: *a crumb of comfort.* 3 the soft inside part of bread. *—v.t.* 1 break into crumbs; crumble. 2 cover with crumbs for frying or baking. 3 INFORMAL. brush or wipe the crumbs from (a tablecloth, etc.). *—v.i.* break into crumbs; crumble. [Old English *cruma*]

crum ble (krum′bəl), *v.,* **-bled, -bling.** *—v.t.* break into very small pieces or crumbs: *crumble dirt between your hands.* *—v.i.* 1 break into small pieces: *This cake crumbles too easily.* 2 fall to pieces; decay: *The old wall was crumbling away at the edges.*

crum bly (krum′blē), *adj.,* **-bli er, -bli est.** tending to crumble; easily crumbled. **—crum′bli ness,** *n.*

crumb y (krum′ē), *adj.,* **crumb i er, crumb i est.** 1 full of crumbs. 2 soft like the inside part of bread.

crum my (krum′ē), *adj.,* **crum mi er, crum mi est.** SLANG. disgusting; repulsive: *a crummy neighborhood.*

crum pet (krum′pit), *n.* a round, flat cake, thicker than a pancake, baked on a griddle. Crumpets are usually toasted and eaten while hot. [perhaps Old English *crompeht* a cake]

crum ple (krum′pəl), *v.,* **-pled, -pling,** *n.* *—v.t.* crush together; wrinkle: *She crumpled the paper into a ball.* *—v.i.* 1 become crumpled or crushed together. 2 fall down; collapse: *crumple to the floor in a faint.* *—n.* wrinkle made by crushing something together. [< Old English *crump* bent]

crunch (krunch), *v.t.* crush noisily with the teeth. *—v.i.* make or move with a crunching noise: *The hard snow crunched under our feet. The children crunched through the snow.* *—n.* 1 act or sound of crunching. 2 INFORMAL. critical or decisive point; crisis; crux: *matters coming to the crunch.* [imitative]

crunch y (krun′chē), *adj.,* **crunch i er, crunch i est.** INFORMAL. brittle and crackling.

crup per (krup′ər), *n.* 1 strap attached to the back of a harness and passed under a horse's tail to prevent the harness from slipping forward. See **harness** for diagram. 2 rump of a horse. [< Old French *cropiere* < *crope, croupe* croup[2]]

cru sade (krü sād′), *n., v.,* **-sad ed, -sad ing.** *—n.* 1 Often, **Crusade.** any one of the Christian military expeditions between the years 1096 and 1272 to recover the Holy Land from the Moslems. 2 war having a religious purpose and approved by the church. 3 a vigorous campaign against a public evil or in favor of some new idea: *a crusade against heart disease.* *—v.i.* take part in a crusade. [earlier *crusada* < Spanish *cruzada,* ultimately < Latin *crucem* cross]

cru sad er (krü sā′dər), *n.* 1 person who takes part in a crusade. 2 **Crusader,** person who took part in any of the Crusades to recover the Holy Land from the Moslems.

cruse (krüz, krüs), *n.* ARCHAIC. jug, pot, or bottle made of earthenware. [< Middle Dutch *croes*]

crush (krush), *v.t.* 1 squeeze together violently so as to break or bruise. 2 wrinkle or crease by wear or rough handling. 3 break into fine pieces by grinding, pounding, or pressing. 4 flatten by heavy pressure. 5 conquer or suppress; subdue: *crush a revolt.* —*v.i.* become crushed. —*n.* 1 act of crushing. 2 a being crushed. 3 a violent pressure like grinding or pounding: *the crush of the crowd.* 4 mass of people crowded close together. 5 INFORMAL. **a** a sudden, strong liking for a person. **b** object of a sudden, strong liking. [apparently < Old French *croissir* < Germanic] **—crush′a ble,** *adj.* **—crush′er,** *n.*

Cru soe (krü′sō), *n.* **Robinson.** See **Robinson Crusoe.**

crust (krust), *n.* 1 the hard, outside part of bread. 2 piece of this. 3 any hard, dry piece of bread. 4 rich dough rolled out thin and baked for pies. 5 any hard outside covering: *The frozen crust on the snow was thick enough for us to walk on it.* 6 the solid outer layer of the earth. 7 INFORMAL. nerve; impudence. —*v.t.* 1 cover with a crust. 2 form or collect into a crust; harden. —*v.i.* form or become covered with a crust. [< Latin *crusta* rind] **—crust′like′,** *adj.*

Crus ta cea (krus′tā′shə), *n.pl.* class of arthropods comprising the crustaceans. [< New Latin < Latin *crusta* shell, rind]

crus ta cean (krus′tā′shən), *n.* any of a class of arthropods with hard shells and jointed bodies and appendages, living mostly in the water. Crabs, lobsters, and shrimps are crustaceans. —*adj.* of or belonging to this class.

crus ta ceous (krus′tā′shəs), *adj.* 1 crustacean. 2 having a shell or crust. 3 of or like a crust.

crus tal (krus′tl), *adj.* of or having to do with a crust, especially of the earth or the moon.

crust y (krus′tē), *adj.,* **crust i er, crust i est.** 1 having a crust; hard: *crusty bread.* 2 harsh in manner, speech, etc.; crabbed; surly. **—crust′i ly,** *adv.* **—crust′i ness,** *n.*

crutch (kruch), *n.* 1 a support to help a lame person walk; a short stick that fits on the forearm and hand or a longer stick that fits under the arm. 2 anything like a crutch in shape or use; support; prop. [Old English *crycc*]

crux (kruks), *n., pl.* **crux es** or **cru ces.** 1 the essential part; most important point: *the crux of an argument.* 2 a puzzling or perplexing question; difficult point to explain. [< Latin, cross. Doublet of CROSS.]

cru zei ro (krü zār′ō), *n., pl.* **-ros.** the monetary unit of Brazil, equal to 100 centavos and worth about 18 cents. [< Portuguese]

cry (krī), *v.,* **cried, cry ing,** *n., pl.* **cries.** —*v.t.* 1 call loudly; shout. 2 sell by calling on the streets, etc.: *Peddlers cry their wares.* 3 **cry down,** make little of; speak of as unimportant or of little value; deprecate; disparage. 4 **cry for, a** ask earnestly for; beg for. **b** need very much. 5 **cry up,** praise; speak of as important or valuable. —*v.i.* 1 shed tears; weep. 2 make a sound that shows pain, fear, sorrow, etc. See synonym study below. 3 (of an animal) make its usual noise or call.
—*n.* 1 a loud call; shout: *a cry for help.* 2 spell of shedding tears; fit of weeping. 3 sound made by a person or animal that shows some strong feeling, such as pain, fear, anger, or sorrow; noise of grief, pain, etc. 4 noise or call of an animal: *the cry of hounds, the hungry cry of the wolf.* 5 call to action; slogan: *"Forward" was the army's cry as it attacked.* 6 call for help; appeal; entreaty. 7 call that means things for sale. 8 **in full cry,** in close pursuit.
[< Old French *crier* < Popular Latin *critare* < Latin *quiritare,* originally, implore the aid of the *Quirites* Roman citizens]
Syn. *v.i.* 2 **Cry, shout, bellow** mean to call loudly. **Cry** applies whether meaningless sounds or distinct words are used: *I cried out in sudden pain.* **Shout** applies when words are used and are called out at the top of one's voice: *I shouted upstairs.* **Bellow** applies when a cry is uttered in a loud, angry, bull-like voice: *I bellowed when I hit my thumb.*

cry ba by (krī′bā′bē), *n., pl.* **-bies.** person who cries easily or pretends to be hurt.

cry ing (krī′ing), *adj.* 1 that cries. 2 demanding attention; very bad: *The slums in that city are a crying shame.*

cry o bi ol o gy (krī′ō bī ol′ə jē), *n.* study of the effects of low temperatures on living things. [< Greek *kryos* frost + English *biology*]

cry o gen ic (krī′ō jen′ik), *adj.* of or having to do with low temperatures or with cryogenics.

cry o gen ics (krī′ō jen′iks), *n.* branch of physics dealing with the behavior of matter at extremely low temperatures.

cry o lite (krī′ə līt), *n.* fluoride of sodium and aluminum found in Greenland. It is used in aluminum refining, in making ceramics, etc. *Formula:* Na_3AlF_6 [< Greek *kryos* frost + English *-lite*]

cry o sur ger y (krī′ō sėr′jər ē), *n., pl.* **-ger ies.** surgery that uses extremely low temperatures to destroy or remove diseased tissue.

cry o tron (krī′ō tron), *n.* a very small electronic device used to replace vacuum tubes or transistors in computers. It is capable of losing practically all electrical resistance at temperatures below −420 degrees Fahrenheit.

crypt (kript), *n.* an underground room or vault. The crypt beneath the main floor of a church was formerly often used as a burial place. [< Latin *crypta* < Greek *kryptē* vault < *kryptos* hidden. Doublet of GROTTO.]

cryp tic (krip′tik), *adj.* having a hidden meaning; secret; mysterious: *a cryptic message.* [< Late Latin *crypticus* < Greek *kryptikos* < *kryptos* hidden] **—cryp′ti cal ly,** *adv.*

cryp ti cal (krip′tə kəl), *adj.* cryptic.

cryp to gam (krip′tə gam), *n.* an old term for a plant having no seeds, such as ferns and mosses. [< Greek *kryptos* hidden + *gamos* marriage]

cryp to gam ic (krip′tə gam′ik), *adj.* of cryptogams; resembling cryptogams.

cryp tog a mous (krip tog′ə məs), *adj.* cryptogamic.

cryp to gram (krip′tə gram), *n.* something written in secret code or cipher. [< Greek *kryptos* hidden + English *-gram*[1]]

cryp to graph (krip′tə graf), *n.* cryptogram.

cryp tog ra pher (krip tog′rə fər), *n.* an expert in cryptography.

cryp to graph ic (krip′tə graf′ik), *adj.* of or having to do with cryptography.

cryp tog ra phy (krip tog′rə fē), *n.* art or process of writing or deciphering secret codes or ciphers.

crys tal (kris′tl), *n.* 1 a clear, transparent mineral, a kind of quartz, that looks like ice. 2 piece of crystal cut for use or ornament. Crystals may be hung around lights or worn as beads. 3 glass of great brilliance and transparency, used especially in making drinking glasses, serving dishes, etc. 4 glasses, dishes, etc., made of crystal. 5 the transparent glass or plastic cover over the face of a watch. 6 a regularly shaped mass with angles and flat surfaces, into which many substances solidify: *Crystals of sugar can be distinguished from crystals of snow by their difference in form.* 7 a crystalline material such as quartz or Rochelle salt, with special electrical properties, used in radio and other electronic devices for rectification, demodulation, etc. —*adj.* 1 clear and transparent like crystal: *crystal spring water.* 2 made of crystal: *crystal beads.* [< Old French < Latin *crystallus* < Greek *krystallos* clear ice, ultimately < *kryos* frost] **—crys′tal like′,** *adj.*

crys tal line (kris′tl ən, kris′tl īn), *adj.* 1 made of crystals; solidified in the form of crystals: *Sugar and salt are crystalline.* 2 made of crystal. 3 clear and transparent like crystal.

crystalline lens, lens of the eye.

crys tal lize (kris′tl īz), *v.,* **-lized, -liz ing.** —*v.i., v.t.* 1 form into crystals; solidify into crystals: *Water crystallizes to form snow.* 2 form into definite shape: *Our vague ideas crystallized into a clear plan.* 3 coat with sugar. **—crys′tal liz′a ble,** *adj.* **—crys′tal li za′tion,** *n.*

crys tal log ra pher (kris′tl og′rə fər), *n.* an expert in crystallography.

crys tal log ra phy (kris′tl og′rə fē), *n.* science that deals with the form, structure, and properties of crystals.

crys tal loid (kris′tl oid), *adj.* like crystal. —*n.* substance capable of crystallization that, when dissolved in a liquid, forms a true solution.

crystal set, radio receiver that uses a crystal device instead of vacuum tubes to separate the signal from the carrier wave.

Cs, cesium.

C.S.A., Confederate States of America.

csc, cosecant.

CST or **C.S.T.,** Central Standard Time.

CT or **C.T.,** Central Time.

ct., 1 cent. *pl.* **cts.** 2 court.

Ct., Connecticut (official abbrev., **Conn.**).

cte noid (tē′noid, ten′oid), *adj.* having marginal projections like the teeth of a comb, as the scales of certain fishes. [< Greek *ktenos* comb]

cten o phore (ten′ə fôr, ten′ə fōr), *n.* any of a phylum of marine invertebrate animals resembling jellyfishes, having biradial symmetry, and swimming by means of eight rows of ciliated plates; comb jelly. [< Greek *ktenos* comb + *phorein* carry]

ctn, cotangent.

Cu, copper. [for Latin *cuprum*]

cu., cubic.

cub (kub), *n.* 1 a young bear, fox, lion, etc. 2 an inexperienced or awkward boy. 3 cub scout. [origin uncertain]

Cu ba (kyü′bə), *n.* country on the largest

hat, āge, fär; let, ēqual, tėrm;
it, īce; hot, ōpen, ôrder;
oil, out; cup, pu̇t, rüle;
ch, child; ng, long; sh, she;
th, thin; ᴛʜ, then; zh, measure;

ə represents *a* in about, *e* in taken, *i* in pencil, *o* in lemon, *u* in circus.

< = from, derived from, taken from.

island in the West Indies, south of Florida. 8,100,000 pop.; 44,200 sq. mi. *Capital:* Havana. See **Caribbean Sea** for map. **—Cu′ban,** *adj., n.*

cub by hole (kub′ē hōl′), *n.* a small, enclosed space. [< *cubby* (diminutive of earlier *cub* shed, coop) + *hole*]

cube (kyüb), *n., v.,* **cubed, cub ing.** *—n.* 1 solid figure with 6 square faces or sides, all equal. 2 anything shaped like a cube: *a cube of sugar.* 3 product obtained when a number is cubed: *The cube of 4 is 64.* *—v.t.* 1 make or form into the shape of a cube: *The beets we had for supper were cubed instead of sliced.* 2 use (a number) three times as a factor: *5 cubed is 125, because 5 × 5 × 5 = 125.* [< Latin *cubus* < Greek *kybos* cube, die] **—cube′like′,** *adj.*

cu beb (kyü′beb), *n.* the dried, unripe berry of a tropical shrub of the same family as the pepper, used as a spice and in medicine. Cubebs were formerly crushed and smoked in pipes and cigarettes for the treatment of catarrh. [< Old French *cubebe* < Arabic *kabāba*]

cube root, number that produces a given number when multiplied twice by itself: *The cube root of 125 is 5.*

cu bic (kyü′bik), *adj.* 1 shaped like a cube. 2 having length, breadth, and thickness. A cubic inch is the volume of a cube whose edges are each one inch long. The cubic content of a room is the number of cubic feet it contains. 3 having to do with or involving the cubes of numbers.

cu bi cal (kyü′bə kəl), *adj.* shaped like a cube; cubic. **—cu′bi cal ly,** *adv.*

cu bi cle (kyü′bə kəl), *n.* a very small room or compartment. [< Latin *cubiculum* bedroom < *cubare* to lie]

cubic measure, system of units, such as cubic foot and cubic centimeter, used for measuring volume. See **measure** for table.

cub ism (kyü′biz′əm), *n.* style of painting, drawing, and sculpture, developed in the early part of the 1900's, in which objects are represented by cubes and other geometric forms rather than by realistic details.

cub ist (kyü′bist), *n.* artist or sculptor whose art is based on cubism. *—adj.* of cubism or cubists.

cu bit (kyü′bit), *n.* an ancient measure of length, about 18 to 22 inches. [< Latin *cubitum* elbow, cubit]

cu boid (kyü′boid), *adj.* shaped like a cube; cubical. *—n.* something shaped like a cube.

cu boi dal (kyü boi′dl), *adj.* cuboid.

cub reporter, a young, inexperienced newspaper reporter.

cub scout, member of the junior division of the Boy Scouts. Cub scouts are 8 to 10 years of age.

cuck old (kuk′əld), *n.* husband of an unfaithful wife. *—v.t.* make a cuckold of. [< Old French *cucuault* < *coucou* cuckoo]

cuck oo (kü′kü; *esp. for n.* ku̇k′ü), *n., pl.* **cuck oos,** *adj.* *—n.* 1 bird whose call sounds much like its name. The common European cuckoo lays its eggs in the nests of other birds instead of hatching them itself. The American cuckoo builds its own nest and has a call less like the name. 2 the call of the cuckoo. *—adj.* SLANG. crazy; silly. [imitative]

cuckoo clock, clock with a little toy bird that makes a sound like that of the European cuckoo to mark intervals of time.

cu cul late (kyü′kə lāt, kyü kul′āt), *adj.* (in biology) having a hood; shaped like a hood. [< Late Latin *cucullatus* < Latin *cucullus* cap]

cu cum ber (kyü′kum bər), *n.* 1 a long, green vegetable of the gourd family, with firm flesh and many seeds inside, used in salads and for pickles. 2 vine it grows on. 3 **cool as a cucumber, a** very cool. **b** calm and unruffled; not excited. [< Old French *cocombre* < Latin *cucumerem*]

cu cur bit (kyü kėr′bit), *n.* gourd or any plant of the gourd family. [< Latin *cucurbita*]

cud (kud), *n.* mouthful of food brought back from the first stomach of cattle or other ruminant animals for a slow, second chewing in the mouth. [Old English *cudu, cwidu*]

cud dle (kud′l), *v.,* **-dled, -dling,** *n.* *—v.t.* hold closely and lovingly in one's arms or lap: *I cuddled the baby.* *—v.i.* lie close and snug; curl up: *The two puppies cuddled together near the stove.* *—n.* a hug; embrace. [origin uncertain]

cud dly (kud′lē), *adj.,* **-dli er, -dli est.** 1 given to cuddling. 2 pleasing to cuddle.

cud dy (kud′ē), *n., pl.* **-dies.** a small cabin on a boat. [origin uncertain]

cudg el (kuj′əl), *n., v.,* **-eled, -el ing** or **-elled, -el ling.** *—n.* 1 a short, thick stick used as a weapon; club. 2 **take up the cudgels for,** defend strongly. *—v.t.* beat with a cudgel. [Old English *cycgel*]

cue[1] (kyü), *n., v.,* **cued, cue ing** or **cu ing.** *—n.* 1 action, speech, or word which gives the signal for an actor, singer, musician, etc., to enter or to begin. 2 hint or suggestion as to what to do or when to act: *Take your cue from me at the party about when it is time to leave.* 3 part one is to play; course of action. 4 frame of mind; mood. *—v.t.* provide (a person) with a cue or hint. [perhaps a spelling for *q.*, abbreviation of Latin *quando* when (a word used in directions to actors)]

cue[2] (kyü), *n.* 1 a long, tapering stick used for striking the ball in billiards, pool, etc. 2 queue. [variant of *queue*]

cue ball, the ball, usually white, struck by the cue in billiards or pool.

cuff[1] (kuf), *n.* 1 band around the wrist, either attached to a sleeve or separate. 2 a turned-up fold around the bottom of a trouser leg. 3 handcuff. [Middle English *cuffe* glove]

cuff[2] (kuf), *v.t.* hit with the hand; slap. *—n.* a hit with the hand; slap. [origin unknown]

cuff link, link for the cuff of a shirt.

cu. ft., cubic foot or cubic feet.

cui bo no (kwē′ bō′nō; kī′ bō′nō), LATIN. 1 for whose benefit? 2 to what use or good purpose?

cu. in., cubic inch or cubic inches.

cuirass (def. 1)

cui rass (kwi ras′), *n.* 1 piece of armor for the body made of a breastplate and a plate for the back fastened together. 2 the breastplate alone. [< Middle French *cuirasse* < Italian *corazza* < Late Latin *coriacea (vestis)* (garment) of leather < Latin *corium* leather]

cui ras sier (kwir′ə sir′), *n.* a cavalry soldier wearing a cuirass.

cui sine (kwi zēn′), *n.* 1 style of cooking or preparing food; cooking; cookery: *Italian cuisine.* 2 food. [< Middle French < Latin *cocina,* variant of *coquina* kitchen < *coquere* to cook]

cuisse (kwis), *n.* piece of armor to protect the thigh. See **armor** for picture. [< French, thigh < Latin *coxa* hip]

cul-de-sac (kul′də sak′, ku̇l′də sak′), *n., pl.* **culs-de-sac** (kulz′də sak′, ku̇lz′də sak′), **cul-de-sacs.** street or passage open at one end only; blind alley. [< French, bottom of the sack]

cu lex (kyü′leks), *n., pl.* **-li ces** (-lə sēz′). any of a large genus of mosquitoes that includes the common mosquito of North America and Europe. [< Latin, gnat]

cu li nar y (kyü′lə ner′ē, kul′ə ner′ē), *adj.* 1 of or having to do with cooking or the kitchen. 2 used in cooking. [< Latin *culinarium* < *culina* kitchen]

cull (kul), *v.t.* 1 pick out; select: *The lawyer culled important facts from the mass of evidence.* 2 pick over; make selections from. *—n.* something picked out as inferior or worthless. Poor fruit, stale vegetables, and animals not up to standard are called culls. [< Old French *coillir* < Latin *colligere* collect] **—cull′er,** *n.*

culm[1] (kulm), *n.* small or refuse hard coal; slack. [Middle English]

culm[2] (kulm), *n.* the jointed stem characteristic of grasses, usually hollow. [< Latin *culmus* stalk]

cul mi nate (kul′mə nāt), *v.i.,* **-nat ed, -nat ing.** reach its highest point; reach a climax: *The Christmas party culminated in the distribution of the presents.* [< Late Latin *culminatum* crowned, topped < Latin *culminem* top]

cul mi na tion (kul′mə nā′shən), *n.* 1 the highest point; climax. 2 a reaching of the highest point.

cu lottes (kyü lots′), *n.pl.* a woman's skirt divided and sewed like trousers, but cut so full as to appear much like an ordinary skirt. [< French]

cul pa bil i ty (kul′pə bil′ə tē), *n.* a being culpable.

cul pa ble (kul′pə bəl), *adj.* deserving blame. [< Latin *culpabilem* < *culpa* fault] **—cul′pa ble ness,** *n.* **—cul′pa bly,** *adv.*

cul prit (kul′prit), *n.* 1 person guilty of a fault or crime; offender. 2 prisoner in court accused of a crime. [< Anglo-French abbreviation *cul. prit,* earlier *cul. prist; cul.* for culpable, and *prist,* variant of Old French *prest* ready (for trial), ultimately < Latin *praesto* I am ready]

cult (kult), *n.* 1 system of religious worship: *Buddhism includes many cults.* 2 great admiration for a person, thing, idea, etc; worship. 3 group showing such admiration; worshipers. [< Latin *cultus* worship < *colere* to till, cherish]

cul ti gen (kul′tə jən), *n.* 1 a cultivated plant of unknown origin, such as the cabbage. 2 cultivar.

cult ist (kul′tist), *n.* follower of a cult.

cul ti va bil i ty (kul′tə və bil′ə tē), *n.* quality or condition of being cultivable.

cul ti va ble (kul′tə və bəl), *adj.* that can be cultivated.

cul ti var (kul′tə vär, kul′tə vər), *n.* variety of plant produced by cultivation; cultigen. [< *culti(vated) var(iety)*]

cul ti vat a ble (kul′tə vā′tə bəl), *adj.* cultivable.

cul ti vate (kul′tə vāt), *v.t.*, **-vat ed, -vat ing.** 1 prepare and use (land) to raise crops by plowing it, planting seeds, and taking care of the growing plants; till. 2 help (plants) grow by labor and care. 3 loosen the ground around (growing plants) to kill weeds, etc. 4 improve or develop (the body, mind, or manners) by education or training. 5 give time, thought, and effort to; practice: *An artist cultivates his craft.* 6 seek the friendship of: *She cultivated people who could help her.* [< Medieval Latin *cultivatum* cultivated < *cultivus* under cultivation < Latin *colere* to till, cherish]

cul ti vat ed (kul′tə vā′tid), *adj.* 1 prepared and used to raise crops: *A field of wheat is cultivated land; a pasture is not.* 2 produced by cultivation; not wild: *Prize roses are cultivated flowers.* 3 improved or developed. 4 cultured; refined.

cul ti va tion (kul′tə vā′shən), *n.* 1 act of preparing land and growing crops by plowing, planting, and necessary care. 2 a being prepared by plowing, planting, etc. 3 improvement or development. 4 act of giving time and thought to improving and developing (the body, mind, or manners). 5 result of improvement or growth through education and experience; culture; refinement.

cul ti va tor (kul′tə vā′tər), *n.* 1 person or thing that cultivates. 2 tool or machine used to loosen the ground and destroy weeds.

cul tur al (kul′chər əl), *adj.* of or having to do with culture: *Music and art are cultural studies.* **—cul′tur al ly,** *adv.*

cul ture (kul′chər), *n., v.,* **-tured, -tur ing.** *—n.* 1 fineness of feelings, thoughts, tastes, manners, etc.; refinement. See **education** for synonym study. 2 civilization of a given people or nation at a given time; its customs, arts, conveniences, etc.: *the culture of the ancient Incas.* 3 development of the mind or body by education, training, etc. 4 preparation of land to raise crops by plowing, planting, and necessary care; cultivation. 5 the raising of bees, fish, silkworms, oysters, etc., by proper or special care. 6 growth of bacteria, etc., in specially prepared mediums for scientific study or medicinal use. 7 the resulting colony of growth. *—v.t.* 1 cultivate. 2 grow (bacteria, etc.) in a specially prepared medium. [< Middle French < Latin *cultura* a tending < *colere* to till, cherish]

cul tured (kul′chərd), *adj.* 1 having or showing culture; refined. 2 produced or raised by culture: *cultured pearls.*

cul tus (kul′təs), *n.* a religious cult. [< Latin. See CULT.]

cul ver in (kul′vər ən), *n.* 1 musket used in the Middle Ages. 2 a long, heavy cannon, used in the 1500′s and 1600′s. [< Middle French *coulevrine* < *couleuvre* serpent < Latin *colubra*]

cul vert (kul′vərt), *n.* a small channel for water to run under a road, railroad, canal, etc. [origin uncertain]

culvert

cum (kum, ku̇m), *prep.* with; together; including: *transfer of stocks cum dividend.* [< Latin]

cum ber (kum′bər), *v.t.* encumber. *—n.* encumbrance. [< Old French *combrer* impede < *combre* barrier]

Cum ber land (kum′bər lənd), *n.* 1 county in NW England. 2 **Cumberland River,** river flowing through SE Kentucky, N Tennessee, and W Kentucky into the Ohio River. 687 mi.

Cumberland Gap, pass in the Cumberland Mountains, where Virginia, Kentucky, and Tennessee meet. 1315 ft. high.

Cumberland Mountains, plateau of the Appalachian Mountains, extending from S West Virginia to N Alabama. Highest peak, 4000 feet.

Cumberland Plateau, Cumberland Mountains.

cum ber some (kum′bər səm), *adj.* hard to manage; clumsy, unwieldy, or burdensome: *The armor worn by knights seems cumbersome to us today.* **—cum′ber some ly,** *adv.* **—cum′ber some ness,** *n.*

cum brous (kum′brəs), *adj.* cumbersome. **—cum′brous ly,** *adv.* **—cum′brous ness,** *n.*

cum in (kum′ən), *n.* a small herb of the same family as the parsley, whose seedlike fruits are used in cookery and medicine. Also, **cummin.** [< Latin *cuminum* < Greek *kyminon*]

cum lau de (ku̇m lou′dē; kum lô′dē), with distinction (added to the diploma of a student who has done especially good academic work): *to graduate cum laude.* [< Latin, with praise]

cum mer bund (kum′ər bund), *n.* a broad sash worn around the waist. [< Hindustani *kamarband* < Persian *kamar* waist + *band* band, bandage]

cum min (kum′ən), *n.* cumin.

Cum mings (kum′ingz), *n.* **Edward Estlin,** 1894-1962, American poet.

cum quat (kum′kwot), *n.* kumquat.

cu mu late (kyü′myə lāt), *v.,* **-lat ed, -lat ing,** *adj. —v.t., v.i.* heap up; accumulate. *—adj.* heaped up. [< Latin *cumulatum* heaped up < *cumulus* heap] **—cu′mu la′tion,** *n.*

cu mu la tive (kyü′myə lə tiv, kyü′myə lā′tiv), *adj.* increasing or growing in amount, force, etc., by additions; accumulated. A cumulative dividend is one that must be added to future dividends if not paid when due. **—cu′mu la tive ly,** *adv.* **—cu′mu la tive ness,** *n.*

cu mu lo-nim bus (kyü′myə lō nim′bəs), *n., pl.* **-bus es, -bi** (-bī). a massive, vertical cloud formation having peaks that sometimes resemble mountains and sometimes spread out to resemble anvils, occurring at heights of between 1600 and over 20,000 feet; thundercloud.

cu mu lo-stra tus (kyü′myə lō strā′təs), *n., pl.* **-ti** (-tī). a cumulus cloud with its base spread out horizontally like a stratus cloud.

cu mu lous (kyü′myə ləs), *adj.* of or like cumulus clouds.

cu mu lus (kyü′myə ləs), *n., pl.* **-li** (-lī). 1 a vertical cloud formation consisting of detached clouds, rounded at the top and flat at the bottom, seen in fair weather and occurring at heights of between 1600 and 20,000 feet. 2 a heap; pile. [< Latin, heap]

cu ne ate (kyü′nē it, kyü′nē āt), *adj.* tapering to a point at the base; wedge-shaped: *a cuneate leaf.* [< Latin *cuneatum* < *cuneus* wedge]

cu ne i form (kyü nē′ə fôrm, kyü′nē ə fôrm), *adj.* 1 wedge-shaped. 2 composed of cuneiform characters or inscriptions: *cuneiform tablets. —n.* the wedge-shaped characters used in the writing of ancient Babylonia, Assyria, Persia, etc. [< Latin *cuneus* wedge + English *-form*]

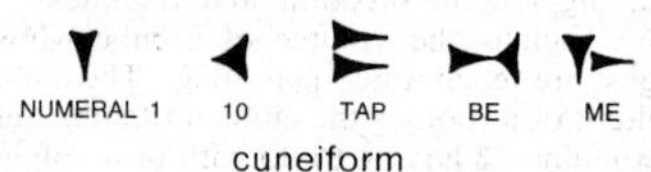

cuneiform

cun ner (kun′ər), *n.* a small, edible fish of the same family as the wrasse, found off the Atlantic coast. [origin uncertain]

cun ning (kun′ing), *adj.* 1 clever in deceiving; sly: *a cunning fox, a cunning thief.* See **sly** for synonym study. 2 skillful; clever: *The old watch was a fine example of cunning workmanship.* 3 INFORMAL. pretty and dear; cute: *a cunning baby. —n.* 1 slyness in getting what one wants; cleverness in deceiving one's enemies: *The fox has a great deal of cunning.* 2 skill; cleverness. [Old English *cunnung* < *cunnan* know (how). Related to CAN[1].] **—cun′ning ly,** *adv.* **—cun′ning ness,** *n.*

cup (kup), *n., v.,* **cupped, cup ping.** *—n.* 1 dish to drink from, usually with a handle. 2 as much as a cup holds; cupful. 3 thing shaped like a cup. The petals of some flowers form a cup. 4 an ornamental cup, vase, etc., given to the winner of a contest; trophy. 5 drink or food served in a cup. 6 cup used in Communion. 7 wine used in Communion. 8 something to endure or experience; fate: *the bitter cup of defeat.* 9 **in one's cups,** drunk. *—v.t.* 1 shape like a cup: *She cupped her hands to catch the ball.* 2 take or put in a cup. 3 take blood from (a person) by the process of cupping. [Old English *cuppe* < Late Latin *cuppa* < Latin *cupa* tub] **—cup′like′,** *adj.*

cup bear er (kup′ber′ər, kup′bar′ər), *n.* (formerly) a person who filled and served cups of wine at banquets.

cup board (kub′ərd), *n.* 1 closet or cabinet with shelves for dishes, food, etc. 2 any small closet.

cup cake (kup′kāk′), *n.* a small cake baked in a cup-shaped container.

cup ful (kup′fu̇l), *n., pl.* **-fuls.** as much as a cup holds. In cooking, a cupful equals a half pint.

Cu pid (kyü′pid), *n.* 1 (in Roman myths) the god of love, son of Mercury and Venus, identified with the Greek god Eros. Cupid is usually represented as a winged child with bow and arrows. 2 **cupid,** figure of a winged child used as a symbol of love: *the cupids on a valentine.*

cu pid i ty (kyü pid′ə tē), *n.* eager desire to possess something; greed. [< Latin *cupiditatem* < *cupidus* desirous < *cupere* long for, desire]

cu po la (kyü′pə lə), *n.* 1 a rounded roof; dome. 2 a small dome or tower on a roof. [< Italian < Late Latin *cupula,* diminutive of Latin *cupa* tub]

cup ping (kup′ing), *n.* use of a glass cup to create a partial vacuum to draw blood to or through the skin.

cu pre ous (kyü′prē əs), *adj.* 1 of or containing copper. 2 copper-colored. [< Latin *cupreus* < *cuprum* copper]

cu pric (kyü′prik), *adj.* of or containing divalent copper.

cupric sulfate, blue vitriol.

cu prous (kyü′prəs), *adj.* of or containing monovalent copper.

cu pule (kyü′pyül), *n.* 1 a cup-shaped membranous cover surrounding a fruit, as in the acorn. 2 any cup-shaped organ or part. [< Latin *cupula* cupola]

cur (kėr), *n.* 1 a dog of mixed breed; mongrel. 2 a surly, contemptible person. [Middle English *curre,* probably < Scandinavian (Old Icelandic) *kurra* snarl]

cur a bil i ty (kyůr′ə bil′ə tē), *n.* a being curable.

cur a ble (kyůr′ə bəl), *adj.* that can be cured. **—cur′a ble ness,** *n.* **—cur′a bly,** *adv.*

cu ra çao (kyůr′ə sō′), *n.* liqueur or cordial flavored with orange peel. [< *Curaçao*]

Cu ra çao (kyůr′ə sō′), *n.* the largest island of the Netherlands Antilles. 141,000 pop.; 210 sq. mi.

cu ra cy (kyůr′ə sē), *n., pl.* **-cies.** position, rank, or work of a curate.

cu rar e or **cu rar i** (kyů rär′ē), *n.* a poisonous, resinlike extract of certain tropical plants, used by some South American Indians as an arrow poison. Curare is used in medicine to relax muscles. [< Spanish *curaré* or Portuguese *curare* < Tupi]

cur ate (kyůr′it), *n.* clergyman who assists a pastor, rector, or vicar. [< Medieval Latin *curatus* < *cura* cure of souls < Latin *cura* care. Doublet of CURÉ.]

cur a tive (kyůr′ə tiv), *adj.* having the power to cure; tending to cure; curing. *—n.* means of curing; remedy. **—cur′a tive ly,** *adv.*

cu ra tor (kyü rā′tər), *n.* person in charge of all or part of a museum, library, art gallery, zoo, etc. [< Latin < *curare* care for < *cura* care]

curb (kėrb), *n.* 1 a raised border of concrete, stone, or wood along the edge of a pavement, around the top of a well, etc. 2 check; restraint: *put a curb on one's spending.* 3 chain or strap fastened to a horse's bit and passed under its lower jaw. When the reins are pulled tight, the curb checks the horse. 4 market that deals in stocks and bonds not listed on the regular stock exchange. *—v.t.* 1 hold in check; restrain: *My hunger was curbed by the snack.* See **check** for synonym study. 2 provide with a curb. [< Middle French *courbe* < Latin *curvus* bent, curved]

curb ing (kėr′bing), *n.* 1 material for making a curb. 2 a curb.

curb roof, roof having two slopes on each side.

curb side (kėrb′sīd′), *n.* area at or near a curb. *—adj.* at or near a curb.

curb stone (kėrb′stōn′), *n.* stone or stones forming a curb along the sides of a street.

cur cu li o (kėr′kyü′lē ō), *n., pl.* **-li os.** any of certain weevils that have long snouts and are very destructive of fruit. [< Latin]

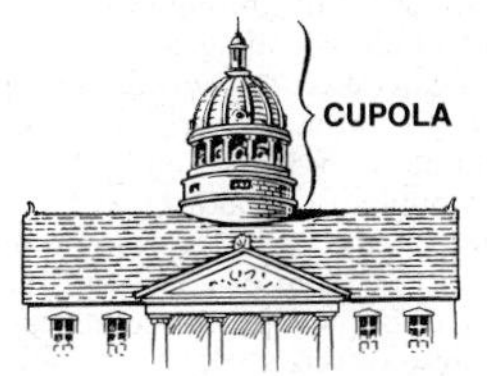

cupola (def. 2)

curd (kėrd), *n.* Often, **curds,** *pl.* the thick part of milk that separates from the watery part when milk sours. Cheese is made from curds. *—v.t., v.i.* form into curds; curdle. [Middle English *curd, crud*]

cur dle (kėr′dl), *v.t., v.i.,* **-dled, -dling.** 1 form into curds: *Milk curdles when kept too long.* 2 thicken.

curd y (kėr′dē), *adj.* 1 full of curds. 2 like curdled milk.

cure (kyůr), *v.,* **cured, cur ing,** *n.* *—v.t.* 1 make well; bring back to health: *cure a child of pneumonia.* See synonym study below. 2 get rid of: *cure a cold, cure a bad habit.* 3 preserve (bacon, fish, etc.) by drying, salting, smoking, pickling, etc. *—v.i.* be or become cured. *—n.* 1 act of curing. 2 means of curing; treatment intended to relieve or remove disease or any bad condition: *a cure for sore eyes, a cure for laziness.* 3 medicine that is a means of curing; remedy. 4 a successful medical treatment; restoration to health. 5 spiritual charge; religious care. 6 method or process of curing meat, fish, etc. [< Old French *curer* < Latin *curare* care for < *cura* care] **—cure′less,** *adj.* **—cur′er,** *n.*

Syn. *v.t.* 1 **Cure, heal, remedy** mean to make well or right. **Cure** applies particularly to bringing back to health after sickness or disease: *The new treatment cured his skin disease.* **Heal** means to make whole, and is used particularly of wounds, burns, etc.: *This medicine will heal that cut.* **Remedy** means to put right, and applies to curing or relieving any unhealthy physical or mental condition: *The operation remedied her twisted foot.*

cu ré (kyů rā′), *n.* a parish priest. [< French < Medieval Latin *curatus.* Doublet of CURATE.]

cure-all (kyůr′ôl′), *n.* remedy supposed to cure all diseases or ills; panacea.

cur few (kėr′fyü), *n.* 1 rule requiring certain persons to be off the streets or at home before a fixed time: *There is a 10 p.m. curfew for children in our city.* 2 the ringing of a bell at a fixed time every evening as a signal. In the Middle Ages, it was a signal to put out lights and cover fires. 3 bell ringing such a signal: *Every night at nine the curfew rang.* 4 time when a curfew begins. [< Old French *covrefeu* < *covrir* to cover + *feu* fire]

cur i a (kyůr′ē ə), *n., pl.* **cur i ae** (kyůr′ē ē). 1 **Curia,** group of high officials who assist the Pope in the government and administration of the Roman Catholic Church; papal court of the Roman Catholic Church. 2 a medieval council or court of law. 3 the meeting place of the ancient Roman senate. 4 one of the ten divisions of each of the three ancient Roman tribes. [< Latin]

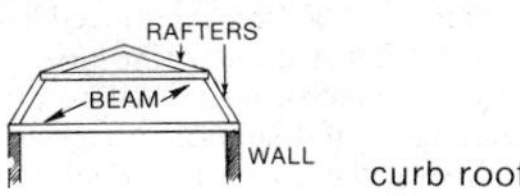

curb roof

hat, āge, fär; let, ēqual, tėrm;
it, īce; hot, ōpen, ôrder;
oil, out; cup, pút, rüle;
ch, child; ng, long; sh, she;
th, thin; ᴛʜ, then; zh, measure;

ə represents *a* in about, *e* in taken, *i* in pencil, *o* in lemon, *u* in circus.

< = from, derived from, taken from.

Cur ie (kyůr′ē, kyů rē′), *n.* 1 **Marie,** 1867-1934, French physicist and chemist, born in Poland. She and her husband Pierre discovered radium in 1898. 2 **Pierre,** 1859-1906, French physicist and chemist. 3 **curie,** unit for measuring the intensity of radioactivity.

cur i o (kyůr′ē ō), *n., pl.* **cur i os.** object valued as a curiosity; a strange, rare, or novel object: *Oriental curios.* [short for *curiosity*]

cur i os i ty (kyůr′ē os′ə tē), *n., pl.* **-ties.** 1 an eager desire to know: *He satisfied his curiosity about animals by visiting the zoo often.* 2 a being too eager to know: *Curiosity killed the cat.* 3 something arousing curiosity; novelty: *The intricate carving was a curiosity. His unexpectedly erratic behavior is a curiosity.* 4 a curious quality: *The president's childish behavior is of some curiosity.*

cur i ous (kyůr′ē əs), *adj.* 1 eager to know: *a curious student.* 2 too eager to know; prying: *Being so curious about other people's business might get you in trouble.* See synonym study below. 3 strange, odd, or unusual: *a curious old book.* 4 very odd; peculiar; eccentric: *curious notions.* [< Latin *curiosus* inquisitive, full of care < *cura* care] **—cur′i ous ly,** *adv.* **—cur′i ous ness,** *n.*

Syn. 2 **Curious, inquisitive, prying** mean eager to find out about things. **Curious** means eager to learn things, but sometimes suggests being too eager to know about other people's business: *I was curious to know who was visiting our neighbors.* **Inquisitive** suggests constantly asking questions to find out what one wants to know, especially about personal matters: *My roommate is too inquisitive about my dates.* **Prying** adds to *inquisitive* the idea of peeping and of busying oneself about other people's business: *I had prying neighbors.*

cur i um (kyůr′ē əm), *n.* a radioactive metallic element produced artificially from plutonium or americium. *Symbol:* Cm; *atomic number* 96. See pages 326 and 327 for table. [< Marie and Pierre *Curie*]

curl (kėrl), *v.t.* 1 twist into ringlets; roll into coils: *curl one's hair.* 2 twist out of shape; bend into a curve: *She curled her lip in a forced smile.* *—v.i.* 1 twist into rings; roll into coils: *hair that curls naturally.* 2 twist out of shape; bend into a curve: *Paper curls as it burns.* 3 rise in rings: *Smoke is curling slowly from the chimney.* 4 **curl up,** draw up one's legs: *I curled up on the sofa.* *—n.* 1 a curled lock of hair; ringlet. 2 anything like it. 3 a curling. 4 a being curled. [Middle English *curlen, crullen* < *crul* curly]

curl er (kėr′lər), *n.* 1 person or thing that curls. 2 device on which hair is twisted to make it curl.

cur lew (kėr′lü), *n., pl.* **-lews** or **-lew.** any of several wading birds of the same family as the sandpipers, with a long, thin bill curved downward. [< Old French *courlieu*]

curl i cue (kėr′lə kyü), *n.* a fancy twist, curl, or flourish: *Curlicues in handwriting often make it hard to read.*

curl ing (kėr′ling), *n.* game in which large, smooth, rounded stones with handles are slid along ice toward a target.

curling iron, instrument for curling or waving hair.

curl y (kėr′lē), *adj.,* **curl i er, curl i est.** 1 having a tendency to curl; curling; wavy. 2 having curls. **—curl′i ness,** *n.*

cur mudg eon (kər muj′ən), *n.* a rude, stingy, bad-tempered person; miser. [origin unknown]

cur rant (kėr′ənt), *n.* 1 a small, seedless raisin made from certain small, sweet grapes grown chiefly in the countries on the eastern Mediterranean and in California, used in puddings, cakes, and buns. 2 a small, sour, red, black, or white berry that grows in bunches on any of a genus of shrubs belonging to the same family as the saxifrage. It is used mainly for jelly and jam. 3 any of the shrubs this berry grows on. [< Anglo-French *(raisins de) Corauntz* raisins of Corinth]

cur ren cy (kėr′ən sē), *n., pl.* **-cies.** 1 money in actual use in a country: *Coins and paper money are currency in the United States.* 2 a being current, generally reported, and accepted; prevalence: *People who spread a rumor give it currency.* 3 general use or acceptance; common occurrence: *Words such as "couldst" and "thou" have little currency now.*

cur rent (kėr′ənt), *n.* 1 a flow of water, air, or any liquid; running stream: *a current of cold air. The current swept the stick down the river.* See **stream** for synonym study. 2 flow of electricity through a wire, etc. 3 rate or amount of such a flow, usually expressed in amperes. 4 course or movement (of events or of opinions); general direction: *the current of public opinion.* *—adj.* 1 of the present time: *current events, the current issue of a magazine.* 2 generally used or accepted; commonly occurring: *Long ago the belief was current that the earth was flat.* See synonym study below. 3 generally known and talked about; prevalent: *A rumor is current that school will close tomorrow.* [< Old French *curant, corant,* present participle of *corre* to run < Latin *currere*] **—cur′rent ness,** *n.*

Syn. *adj.* **2 Current, present, prevailing** mean generally used or occurring at a certain time. **Current** means commonly known, used, accepted, or occurring now unless another time is stated: *We read the daily newspapers to keep up with the current situation and developments in different parts of the world.* **Present** emphasizes the idea of being in this place at this time: *This dictionary records present English usage.* **Prevailing** emphasizes the idea of being strongest or most common at a given time and place: *"Foolish" is now the prevailing meaning of "silly." In one period the prevailing sense of "silly" was "helpless."*

cur rent ly (kėr′ənt lē), *adv.* 1 at the present time; now. 2 generally; commonly.

cur ri cle (kėr′ə kəl), *n.* a two-wheeled carriage drawn by two horses. [< Latin *curriculum.* Doublet of CURRICULUM.]

cur ric u lar (kə rik′yə lər), *adj.* of or having to do with a curriculum.

cur ric u lum (kə rik′yə ləm), *n., pl.* **-lums, -la** (-lə). 1 the whole range of studies offered in a school, college, etc., or in a type of school: *The American high-school curriculum includes English, mathematics, science, history, and foreign languages.* 2 program of studies leading to a particular degree, certificate, etc.: *the curriculum of the Law School.* [< Latin, course, race course, chariot, diminutive of *currus* chariot < *currere* to run. Doublet of CURRICLE.]

curriculum vi tae (vī′tē), a biographical summary; short account of a person's background, education, and professional career. [< Latin, course of one's life]

cur ri er (kėr′ē ər), *n.* 1 person who curries tanned leather. 2 person who curries horses, etc.

cur rish (kėr′ish), *adj.* of or like a cur; surly; contemptible. **—cur′rish ly,** *adv.*

cur ry[1] (kėr′ē), *v.t.,* **-ried, -ry ing.** 1 rub and clean (a horse, etc.) with a brush or currycomb. 2 prepare (tanned leather) for use by soaking, scraping, beating, coloring, etc. [< Old French *correier* put in order < *con-* altogether + *reier* arrange]

cur ry[2] (kėr′ē), *n., pl.* **-ries,** *v.,* **-ried, -ry ing.** *—n.* 1 a peppery sauce or powder of spices, seeds, vegetables, etc. Curry is a popular seasoning in India. 2 food flavored with curry. *—v.t.* prepare or flavor with curry. [< Tamil *kari* sauce]

cur ry comb (kėr′ē kōm′), *n.* comb or brush with metal teeth for rubbing and cleaning a horse. *—v.t.* use a currycomb on; brush with a currycomb.

curse (kėrs), *v.,* **cursed** or **curst, curs ing,** *n.* *—v.t.* 1 ask God, or a god, to bring evil or harm on. 2 bring evil or harm on; trouble greatly; torment: *cursed with blindness, cursed with a bad temper.* 3 swear at. *—v.i.* use profane language; swear; blaspheme. See synonym study below. *—n.* 1 the words that a person says when he asks God, or a god, to curse someone or something. 2 something that is cursed. 3 harm or evil that comes as if in answer to a curse. 4 cause of evil or harm. 5 word or words used in swearing. [Old English *cursian* < *curs* a curse] **—curs′er,** *n.*

Syn. *v.i.* **Curse, swear** mean to use profane language. **Curse** emphasizes anger or hatred, and implies a heartfelt wish to bring harm upon someone: *He cursed when the car almost hit him.* **Swear** suggests using holy names to punctuate one's speech or to express strong feelings: *She swore when she stubbed her toe.*

curs ed (kėr′sid, kėrst), *adj.* 1 under a curse. 2 deserving a curse; evil; hateful. Also, **curst. —curs′ed ly,** *adv.* **—curs′ed ness,** *n.*

cur sive (kėr′siv), *adj.* written with the letters joined together. Ordinary handwriting is cursive. *—n.* letter made to join other letters. [< Medieval Latin *cursivus* < Latin *cursus* a running < *currere* to run] **—cur′sive ly,** *adv.*

cur sor (kėr′sər), *n.* the sliding glass of a slide rule or optical instrument, having a fine hairline on it, used to facilitate computing or sighting. [< Latin, runner < *currere* to run]

cur so ri al (kėr sôr′ē əl, kėr sōr′ē əl), *adj.* 1 for running. 2 having legs fitted for running: *The ostrich is a cursorial bird.*

cur sor y (kėr′sər ē), *adj.* without attention to details; hasty and superficial: *Even a cursory reading of the letter showed many errors.* [< Latin *cursorius* of a race < *currere* to run] **—cur′sor i ly,** *adv.* **—cur′sor i ness,** *n.*

curst (kėrst), *adj.* cursed. *—v.* a pt. and a pp. of **curse.**

curt (kėrt), *adj.* rudely brief; short; abrupt: *a curt way of talking.* See **blunt** for synonym study. [< Latin *curtus* cut short] **—curt′ly,** *adv.* **—curt′ness,** *n.*

cur tail (kėr tāl′), *v.t.* cut short; cut off part of; reduce; lessen. See **shorten** for synonym study. [< obsolete *curtal,* adjective, cut short (especially of tails) < Old French *curtald* < *court* short < Latin *curtus* cut short] **—cur′tail′er,** *n.* **—cur′tail′ment,** *n.*

cur tain (kėrt′n), *n.* 1 cloth hung at windows or in doors for protection or ornament. 2 the drapery or hanging screen which separates the stage of a theater from the part where the audience sits. 3 the fall or closing of the curtain at the end of an act or scene. 4 thing that covers or hides: *a curtain of fog.* 5 part of a wall connecting two bastions, towers, etc. *—v.t.* 1 provide or shut off with a curtain or curtains; decorate with a curtain. 2 cover; hide. [< Old French *curtine* < Late Latin *cortina* < Latin *cohortem* enclosure, court]

curtain call, call for an actor, musician, etc., to return to the stage after a performance and acknowledge the applause of the audience.

curtain raiser, 1 a short play given before the main play in a theater. 2 a little thing used to introduce something bigger.

Cur tis (kėr′tis), *n.* **Charles,** 1860-1936, vice-president of the United States from 1929 to 1933.

Cur tiss (kėr′tis), *n.* **Glenn Hammond,** 1878-1930, American inventor and pioneer in aviation.

curt sey (kėrt′sē), *n., pl.* **-seys,** *v.i.* curtsy.

curt sy (kėrt′sē), *n., pl.* **-sies,** *v.,* **-sied, -sy ing.** *—n.* bow of respect or greeting by women and girls, made by bending the knees and lowering the body slightly. *—v.i.* make a curtsy. [variant of *courtesy*]

cu rule chair (kyůr′ül), a special seat that only certain of the highest magistrates or officials of ancient Rome were permitted to use. [*curule* < Latin *curulem* of the highest officials < *currus* (triumphal) chariot]

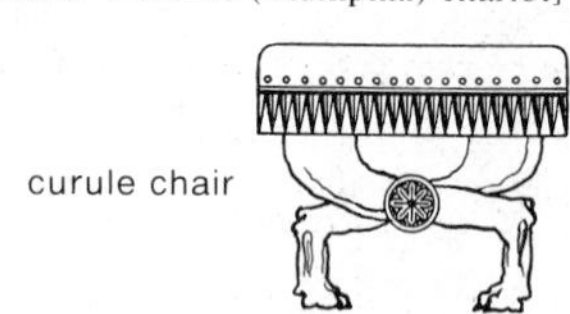
curule chair

cur va ceous (kėr′vā′shəs), *adj.* INFORMAL. (of a girl or woman) having a full figure; attractively well-developed.

cur va ture (kėr′və chər, kėr′və chůr), *n.* 1 a curving, especially abnormal curving: *curvature of the spine.* 2 a curved piece or part; curve. 3 the degree of curving; curve: *the curvature of the earth's surface.*

curve (kėrv), *n., v.,* **curved, curv ing,** *adj.* *—n.* 1 line that has no straight part. 2 something having the shape of a curve; bend: *The automobile had to slow down for the curves in the road.* 3 baseball pitched so that it curves away from the batter about the time it reaches home plate. *—v.t.* bend so as to form a curve. *—v.i.* 1 bend in a curve; move in the course of a curve: *The highway curved to the right.* 2 pitch a curve in baseball. *—adj.* curved. [< Latin *curvus* curved]

hat, āge, fär; let, ēqual, tėrm; it, īce; hot, ōpen, ôrder; oil, out; cup, pu̇t, rüle; ch, child; ng, long; sh, she; th, thin; ᴛʜ, then; zh, measure;

ə represents *a* in about, *e* in taken, *i* in pencil, *o* in lemon, *u* in circus.

< = from, derived from, taken from.

curved (kėrvd), *adj.* bent so as to form a curve.

cur vet (*n.* kėr′vit; *v.* kėr′vet′, kėr′vit), *n.*, *v.*, **-vet ted, -vet ting** or **-vet ed, -vet ing.** —*n.* leap in the air made by a horse. The forelegs are raised first and then the hind legs, so that all legs are off the ground for a second. —*v.i.* (of a horse) leap in this way. —*v.t.* make (a horse) leap in the air. [< Italian *corvetta,* diminutive of *corvo* curve < Latin *curvus* curved]

cur vi lin e al (kėr′və lin′ē əl), *adj.* curvilinear.

cur vi lin e ar (kėr′və lin′ē ər), *adj.* consisting of a curved line or lines; enclosed by curved lines.

curv y (kėr′vē), *adj.*, **curv i er, curv i est.** 1 INFORMAL. curvaceous. 2 having a curve or curves.

Cus co (kü′skō), *n.* Cuzco.

Cush (kush), *n.* (in the Bible) a country in NE Africa, probably Ethiopia.

cush ion (ku̇sh′ən), *n.* 1 a soft pillow or pad used to sit, lie, or kneel on. 2 anything that makes a soft place: *a cushion of moss.* 3 anything that eases the effect of or protects. Air or steam forms a protective cushion in some machines. *During her years of working she created a cushion of savings against sickness and retirement.* 4 the elastic padding on the sides of a billiard table. —*v.t.* 1 put or rest on a cushion; support with cushions. 2 provide with a cushion. 3 protect from sudden shocks with a cushion of air or steam. 4 soften or ease the effects of: *Nothing could cushion the shock of his father's death.* [< Old French *coussin,* perhaps < Popular Latin *culcinum* < Latin *culcita* hip] **—cush′ion like′,** *adj.*

cush ion craft (ku̇sh′ən kraft′), *n.* Hovercraft.

Cu shit ic (kə shit′ik), *n.* a group of Hamitic languages of Ethiopia and eastern Africa. —*adj.* of these languages.

cush y (ku̇sh′ē), *adj.*, **cush i er, cush i est.** SLANG. soft; comfortable; easy: *a cushy job.* [< Hindustani *khush* excellent + English *-y*[1]]

cusk (kusk), *n.* an edible fish of the same family as the cod. [origin unknown]

cusp (kusp), *n.* 1 a pointed end; point. A crescent has two cusps. 2 a blunt or pointed protuberance of the crown of a tooth. [< Latin *cuspidem*]

cus pid (kus′pid), *n.* canine tooth.

cus pi date (kus′pə dāt), *adj.* having a sharp, pointed end.

cus pi dat ed (kus′pə dā′tid), *adj.* cuspidate.

cus pi dor (kus′pə dôr), *n.* spittoon. [< Portuguese, spitter < *cuspir* to spit < Latin *conspuere*]

cuss (kus), INFORMAL. —*n.* 1 a curse. 2 an odd or troublesome person or animal. —*v.t., v.i.* curse. [variant of *curse*]

cuss ed (kus′id), *adj.* INFORMAL. 1 cursed. 2 stubborn. **—cuss′ed ly,** *adv.* **—cuss′ed-ness,** *n.*

cus tard (kus′tərd), *n.* a baked or boiled pudding of eggs, milk, sugar, etc. [variant of earlier *crustade* < Middle French *croustade,* ultimately < Latin *crusta* crust]

custard apple, 1 a heart-shaped tropical fruit with sweet, yellowish flesh. 2 tree that it grows on. 3 any tree or shrub of the same genus, such as the papaw.

Cus ter (kus′tər), *n.* **George Armstrong,** 1839-1876, United States Army officer in the Civil War and in many Indian wars.

cus to di al (kus tō′dē əl), *adj.* having to do with custody or custodians.

cus to di an (kus tō′dē ən), *n.* 1 person in charge; guardian; keeper: *the legal custodian of a child.* 2 person who takes care of a building or offices; janitor; caretaker: *a school custodian.*

cus to di an ship (kus tō′dē ən ship), *n.* position or duties of a custodian.

cus to dy (kus′tə dē), *n.*, *pl.* **-dies.** 1 watchful keeping; charge; care: *Parents have the custody of their young children.* 2 a being confined or detained; imprisonment. 3 **in custody,** in the care of the police; under arrest. 4 **take into custody,** arrest. [< Latin *custodia* < *custodem* guardian]

cus tom (kus′təm), *n.* 1 any usual action or practice; habit: *It was her custom to rise early every morning.* See synonym study below. 2 the accepted way of acting in a community or other group; convention; tradition. 3 habit maintained for so long that it has almost the force of law. 4 the regular business given by a customer to a particular store, shop, etc. 5 the customers of a store or shop. 6 **customs,** *pl.* **a** taxes paid to the government on things brought in from foreign countries. **b** department of the government that collects these taxes. 7 tax or service regularly due from feudal tenants to their lord. —*adj.* 1 made to order; custom-made: *custom clothes.* 2 making things to order; not selling ready-made goods: *a custom tailor.* [< Old French *custume* < Popular Latin *consuetumen* < Latin *consuescere* make customary < *com-* + *suescere* accustom. Doublet of COSTUME.]

Syn. *n.* 1 **Custom, habit, practice** mean a usual action or way of acting. **Custom** applies to an action or way of doing things that has become established by a person or a group as the result of being repeated over a period of time: *Eating hot dogs is an American custom.* **Habit** applies to an action that a person has repeated so often that he does it naturally and without thinking: *She had the habit of winding her watch before going to bed.* **Practice** applies to a usual or customary procedure that a person has established by deliberate choice: *Getting up early is his practice.*

cus tom ar y (kus′tə mer′ē), *adj.* 1 according to custom; as a habit; usual; habitual: *customary greetings.* See **usual** for synonym study. 2 holding or held by custom; established by custom: *customary law, customary rent.* **—cus′tom ar′i ly,** *adv.* **—cus′tom-ar′i ness,** *n.*

cus tom-built (kus′təm bilt′), *adj.* built to order; not ready-made.

cus tom er (kus′tə mər), *n.* 1 person who buys, especially a regular shopper at a particular store. 2 INFORMAL. person; fellow: *He can be a rough customer when he gets angry.*

custom house, a government building or office where taxes on things brought into a country are collected.

cus tom-made (kus′təm mād′), *adj.* made to order; made specially for an individual customer; not ready-made.

cut (kut), *v.*, **cut, cut ting,** *adj.*, *n.* —*v.t.* 1 divide, separate, open, or remove with something sharp: *cut meat, cut timber, cut one's nails.* See synonym study below. 2 pierce or wound with something sharp: *She cut her finger.* 3 make by cutting: *I cut a hole through the wall with an ax.* 4 make a recording on: *cut a record.* 5 have (teeth) grow through the gums. 6 reduce; decrease: *cut expenses.* 7 shorten by removing a part or parts: *cut a speech, cut the hedge, cut one's hair.* 8 go across; divide by crossing: *A brook cuts that field.* 9 hit or strike sharply: *The cold wind cut me to the bone.* 10 hit with a slicing stroke: *She cut the ball so that it bounded almost backward.* 11 hurt the feelings of: *The mean remark cut me.* 12 stop: *cut an engine.* 13 INFORMAL. refuse to recognize socially: *No one in the class cut the new boy although he was very unfriendly.* 14 INFORMAL. be absent from (a class, lecture, etc.): *We wanted to cut history when we heard there was going to be a test.* 15 make less sticky or stiff; dissolve: *Gasoline cuts grease and tar.* 16 draw (a card) at random from a pack. 17 divide (a pack of cards) at random. 18 INFORMAL. do; perform; make: *cut a caper.* —*v.i.* 1 make a cut, opening, channel, etc.: *This knife cuts well.* 2 be cut; admit of being cut: *Cheese cuts easily.* 3 go by a short cut: *cut through the woods to get home.* 4 cross: *A brook cuts through that field.* 5 stop photographing a scene in a motion picture or on television.

cut across, go straight across or through.

cut back, **a** reduce or curtail: *cut back production.* **b** (in football, hockey, etc.) go in a different direction suddenly. **c** shorten by cutting off the end (of a plant).

cut down, **a** cause to fall by cutting. **b** reduce; decrease.

cut in, **a** break in; interrupt: *cut in with a remark.* **b** interrupt a dancing couple to take the place of one of them. **c** move suddenly into a line, such as a vehicle into a line of moving traffic. **d** admit into a group or activity.

cut off, **a** remove by cutting. **b** shut off. **c** stop suddenly. **d** break; interrupt. **e** disinherit.

cut out, **a** remove by cutting. **b** take out; leave out. **c** take the place of; get the better of: *cut out a rival.* **d** make by cutting; make; form. **e** plan; map out: *She has her work cut out for her.* **f** stop doing, using, making, etc.: *Please cut out the noise.* **g** INFORMAL. go out suddenly: *We cut out of the party and went home.*

cut up, **a** cut to pieces. **b** INFORMAL. hurt. **c** SLANG. show off; play tricks.

—*adj.* 1 that has been cut: *a cut pie.* 2 shaped or formed by cutting. 3 reduced: *cut prices.* 4 **cut and dried,** **a** ready for use; arranged in advance. **b** dull; uninteresting.

—*n.* 1 wound or opening made by cutting. 2 passage, channel, etc., made by cutting or digging. 3 piece cut off or cut out: *a cut of meat.* 4 way in which a thing is cut; style; fashion. 5 reduction; decrease. 6 shortcut. 7 a sharp blow or stroke. 8 (in tennis, baseball, etc.) a slicing stroke. 9 action or speech that hurts the feelings; slight. 10 INFORMAL.

refusal to recognize socially. 11 INFORMAL. absence from a class, lecture, etc. 12 block or plate with a picture engraved on it, used in printing. 13 picture made from such a block or plate. 14 INFORMAL. share: *Each partner has a cut of the profits.* 15 a random division of a pack of playing cards.
[Middle English *cutten*]
Syn. *v.t.* 1 **Cut, chop, hack** mean to separate or remove with something sharp. **Cut** is the general word: *He cut a whistle from a willow branch.* **Chop** means to cut by hitting: *He chopped the wood.* **Hack** means to cut or chop roughly and unevenly, and often suggests that the implement should be sharper or its user more skilled: *You certainly hacked that roast when you carved it.*

cu ta ne ous (kyü tā′nē əs), *adj.* of or having to do with the skin; on the skin. [< New Latin *cutaneus* < Latin *cutis* skin]

cutaway (def. 1)

cut a way (kut′ə wā′), *n.* 1 man's coat for formal daytime wear with the lower part cut back in a curve or slope from the waist in front to the tails in back. 2 object, or a model or drawing of an object, having part of its covering removed to show a section of its working parts for examination. *—adj.* showing or representing an object in this way.

cut back (kut′bak′), *n.* reduction in output, expenditure, etc.: *Many factories made cutbacks when their orders were canceled.*

cute (kyüt), *adj.,* **cut er, cut est.** INFORMAL. 1 pretty and dear: *a cute baby.* 2 clever; shrewd: *a cute trick.* 3 consciously stylish or mannered: *cute dialogue.* [variant of *acute*] **—cute′ly,** *adv.* **—cute′ness,** *n.*

cut glass, glass shaped or decorated by grinding and polishing.

cu ti cle (kyü′tə kəl), *n.* 1 epidermis. 2 the hard skin around the sides and base of a fingernail or toenail. [< Latin *cuticula,* diminutive of *cutis* skin]

cu tin (kyüt′n), *n.* a waxy substance that is the chief ingredient of the outer skin of many plants. [< Latin *cutis* skin]

cu tis (kyü′tis), *n.* dermis. [< Latin]

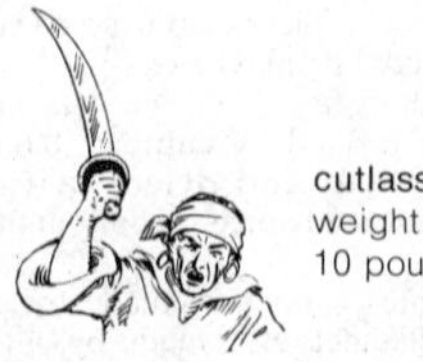
cutlass
weight about
10 pounds

cut lass or **cut las** (kut′ləs), *n.* a short, heavy, slightly curved sword. [< Middle French *coutelas* < *coutel* small knife < Latin *cultellus,* diminutive of *culter* plowshare, knife]

cut ler (kut′lər), *n.* person who makes, sells, or repairs knives, scissors, and other cutting instruments. [< Middle French *coutelier* < *coutel* small knife. See CUTLASS.]

cut ler y (kut′lər ē), *n.* 1 knives, scissors, and other cutting instruments. 2 knives, forks, spoons, etc., for table use. 3 business of a cutler.

cut let (kut′lit), *n.* 1 slice of meat cut from the leg or ribs for broiling or frying: *a veal cutlet.* 2 a flat, fried cake of chopped meat or fish; croquette. [< French *côtelette,* diminutive of *côte* rib < Latin *costa*]

cut off (kut′ôf′, kut′of′), *n.* 1 a short way across or through; shortcut. 2 a new passage cut by a river across a bend. 3 a stopping of the passage of a liquid, gas, etc., through a pipe or opening. 4 valve or other device that does this. *—adj.* at or in which anything is cut off: *a cutoff date.*

cut out (kut′out′), *n.* 1 shape or design to be cut out: *Some books for children have cutouts.* 2 device which releases exhaust gases from an engine directly into the air instead of through the muffler. 3 device for breaking or closing an electric current.

cut o ver (kut′ō′vər), *adj.* from which the trees have been cut: *They replanted the cutover land.*

cut purse (kut′pėrs′), *n.* pickpocket.

cut-rate (kut′rāt′), *adj.* 1 at reduced rates or prices: *cut-rate merchandise.* 2 offering goods or services at reduced prices or rates: *cut-rate stores.*

cut ter (kut′ər), *n.* 1 person who cuts: *A garment cutter cuts out clothes.* 2 tool or machine for cutting: *a meat cutter.* 3 a small, light sleigh, usually pulled by one horse. 4 a small sailboat with one mast. 5 a small, armed ship used to patrol a coast. 6 a ship's boat, used to carry people and supplies to and from the ship.

cutter (def. 3)

cut throat (kut′thrōt′), *n.* murderer. *—adj.* 1 murderous. 2 without mercy; relentless or severe.

cut ting (kut′ing), *n.* 1 thing cut off or cut out. 2 a small shoot cut from a plant to grow a new plant; slip. 3 a newspaper or magazine clipping. 4 place or way cut through high ground for a road, track, etc. *—adj.* 1 that cuts; sharp: *the cutting edge of a knife, a cutting wind.* 2 hurting the feelings; sarcastic: *a cutting remark.* **—cut′ting ly,** *adv.*

cut tle bone (kut′l bōn′), *n.* the hard internal shell of cuttlefish, used for making polishing powder and as food for canaries, etc.

cut tle fish (kut′l fish′), *n., pl.* **-fish es** or **-fish.** a saltwater mollusk that has eight short arms with suckers, two long tentacles, and a hard internal shell. When frightened, cuttlefish squirt out an inky fluid which is the source of sepia. [*cuttle* < earlier *codul,* Old English *cudele* cuttlefish]

cut up (kut′up′), *n.* SLANG. person who shows off or plays tricks.

cut wa ter (kut′wô′tər, kut′wot′ər), *n.* the front part of a ship's prow.

cut worm (kut′wėrm′), *n.* any of several night-feeding moth larvae that cut off the stalks of young plants near or below the ground.

Cu vi er (kyü′vē ā; *French* ky vyā′), *n.* **Georges,** 1769-1832, French naturalist who founded the science of comparative anatomy.

Cuz co (kü′skō), *n.* city in S Peru, once the capital of the Inca empire. 105,000. Also, **Cusco.**

CVA, cerebrovascular accident.

cwt., hundredweight [for Latin *centum* hundred and English *weight*].

-cy, *suffix added to nouns or adjectives to form nouns.* 1 office, position, or rank of _____: *Captaincy = rank of captain.* 2 quality, condition, or fact of being _____: *Bankruptcy = condition of being bankrupt.* [< Latin *-cia, -tia*]

cy an a mide (sī an′ə mīd, sī an′ə mid; sī′ə-nam′īd, sī′ə nam′id), *n.* 1 a white, crystalline compound prepared by the action of ammonia on cyanogen chloride and in other ways. *Formula:* HN:C:NH 2 a grayish powder obtained by heating calcium carbide to a very high temperature in the presence of nitrogen. It is used in fertilizers and for making other nitrogen compounds. *Formula:* CaNCN

cy an ic (sī an′ik), *adj.* 1 of cyanogen; containing cyanogen. 2 blue. [< Greek *kyanos* dark blue]

cy a nide (sī′ə nīd, sī′ə nid), *n., v.,* **-nid ed, -nid ing.** *—n.* salts of hydrocyanic acid, especially potassium cyanide, a powerful poison. Cyanide is used in making plastics and in extracting and treating metals. *—v.t.* treat with a cyanide.

cy an o gen (sī an′ə jən), *n.* 1 a colorless, poisonous, inflammable gas with the odor of bitter almonds. *Formula:* C_2N_2 2 a univalent radical (-CN) consisting of one atom of carbon and one of nitrogen, found in hydrocyanic acid.

cy a no sis (sī′ə nō′sis), *n.* blueness or lividness of the skin, caused by lack of oxygen in the blood.

cy a not ic (sī′ə not′ik), *adj.* of or affected with cyanosis.

Cyb e le (sib′ə lē), *n.* (in myths of Asia Minor) a nature goddess often identified with the Greek Rhea.

cy ber nate (sī′bər nāt), *v.t.,* **-nat ed, -nat ing.** automate.

cy ber na tion (sī′bər nā′shən), *n.* automation.

cy ber net ic (sī′bər net′ik), *adj.* of or having to do with cybernetics.

cy ber net ics (sī′bər net′iks), *n.* the comparative study of the nervous system and systems of mechanical and electronic control of machinery and mechanical devices in order to better understand communication and control in both types of systems. [< Greek *kybernētēs* steersman (< *kybernan* to steer) + English *-ics*]

cy borg (sī′bôrg), *n.* person or animal whose bodily functions are regulated or monitored by mechanical or electrical devices in a scientific experiment. [< *cyb(ernetic) org(anism)*]

cy cad (sī′kad), *n.* any of a family of large, tropical, palmlike plants with a cluster of long, fernlike leaves either rising from an underground stem or borne at the top of a thick columnlike trunk.

Cycads bear cones. [< New Latin *cycadem*]

Cyc la des (sik′lə dēz′), *n.pl.* group of Greek islands in the S Aegean Sea. 100,000 pop.; 1000 sq. mi.

cyc la mate (sik′lə māt, sī′klə māt), *n.* a white, crystalline powder with a very sweet taste, formerly much used as a sweetening agent.

cyc la men (sik′lə mən), *n.* plant of the same family as the primrose, with heart-shaped leaves and showy white, purple, pink, or crimson flowers, whose five petals bend backward. [< Latin *cyclaminos* < Greek *kyklaminos*]

cy cle (sī′kəl), *n., v.,* **-cled, -cling.** —*n.* 1 period of time or complete process of growth or action that repeats itself in the same order. The seasons of the year—spring, summer, autumn, and winter—make a cycle. 2 a complete set or series. 3 all the stories, legends, poems, etc., told about a certain hero or event: *There is a cycle of stories about the adventures of King Arthur and his knights.* 4 a very long period of time; age. 5 a complete alternation or reversal of an alternating electric current. The number of cycles per second is the measure of frequency. 6 bicycle, tricycle, or motorcycle. —*v.i.* 1 pass through a cycle; occur over and over again in the same order. 2 ride a bicycle, tricycle, or motorcycle. [< Late Latin *cyclus* < Greek *kyklos* wheel, circle, ring] **—cy′cler,** *n.*

cy clic (sī′klik, sik′lik), *adj.* 1 of a cycle. 2 moving or occurring in cycles. 3 of, having to do with, or containing an arrangement of atoms in a ring or closed chain. **—cy′cli cal ly,** *adv.*

cy cli cal (sī′klə kəl, sik′lə kəl), *adj.* cyclic.

cy clist (sī′klist), *n.* rider of a bicycle, tricycle, or motorcycle.

cy cloid (sī′kloid), *adj.* 1 like a circle. 2 **a** (of the scales of certain fishes) somewhat circular, with smooth edges. **b** (of a fish) having cycloid scales. —*n.* (in geometry) a curve traced by a point on the circumference or on a radius of a circle when the circle is rolled along a straight line and kept in the same plane.

CYCLOID

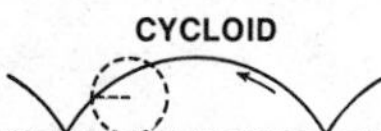

cy cloi dal (sī kloi′dl), *adj.* cycloid.

cy clom e ter (sī klom′ə tər), *n.* instrument that measures the distance that a wheel travels by recording the revolutions that it makes.

cy clone (sī′klōn), *n.* 1 storm moving around and toward a calm center of low pressure, which also moves. The motion of a cyclone is counterclockwise in the Northern Hemisphere and clockwise in the Southern Hemisphere. 2 a very violent windstorm; tornado. [< Greek *kyklōn* moving around in a circle < *kyklos* wheel, circle]

cy clon ic (sī klon′ik), *adj.* of or like a cyclone. **—cy clon′i cal ly,** *adv.*

cy clon i cal (sī klon′ə kəl), *adj.* cyclonic.

cy clo pae di a (sī′klə pē′dē ə), *n.* encyclopedia.

cy clo pae dic (sī′klə pē′dik), *adj.* encyclopedic.

Cy clo pe an (sī′klə pē′ən), *adj.* 1 of or having to do with the Cyclopes. 2 Also, **cyclopean.** huge; gigantic; massive.

cy clo pe di a (sī′klə pē′dē ə), *n.* encyclopedia.

cy clo pe dic (sī′klə pē′dik), *adj.* encyclopedic.

Cy clops (sī′klops), *n., pl.* **Cy clo pes** (sī klō′pēz). (in Greek legends) one of a race of giants, each having only one eye in the center of his forehead. [< Latin < Greek *Kyklōps* < *kyklos* circle + *ōps* eye]

cy clo ram a (sī′klə ram′ə), *n.* a large picture of a landscape, battle, etc., on the wall of a circular room. [< Greek *kyklos* circle + *horama* spectacle]

cy clo ram ic (sī′klə ram′ik), *adj.* having to do with or like a cyclorama.

cy clo sis (sī klō′sis), *n.* the streaming movement of protoplasm in a cell.

Cy clo sto ma ta (sī′klə stō′mə tə), *n.pl.* class of vertebrates comprising the cyclostomes.

cy clo stome (sī′klə stōm′), *n.* any of a class of slender, snakelike fishes, having a round, sucking mouth and no jaws. Lampreys and hagfishes belong to this class. —*adj.* of or belonging to this class. [< Greek *kyklos* circle + *stoma, stomatos* mouth]

cy clo tron (sī′klə tron), *n.* particle accelerator in which protons or other particles are accelerated in a spiral path away from their sources by an alternating electric field in a constant magnetic field. [< Greek *kyklos* circle + English *-tron*]

cyg net (sig′nit), *n.* a young swan. [< Old French *cigne* < Popular Latin *cicinum* < Latin *cygnus, cycnus* < Greek *kyknos*]

Cyg nus (sig′nəs), *n.* a northern constellation in the Milky Way, seen by ancient astronomers as having the rough outline of a swan; Swan. [< Latin *cygnus* swan]

cyl., 1 cylinder. 2 cylindrical.

cyl in der (sil′ən dər), *n.* 1 a solid figure bounded by two equal, parallel circles and by a curved surface, formed by moving a straight line of fixed length so that its ends always lie on the two parallel circles. 2 any long, round object, solid or hollow, with flat ends. Rollers and tin cans are cylinders. 3 the part of a revolver that contains chambers for cartridges. 4 the piston chamber of an internal-combustion engine. [< Latin *cylindrus* < Greek *kylindros* < *kylindein* to roll]

cy lin dric (sə lin′drik), *adj.* cylindrical.

cy lin dri cal (sə lin′drə kəl), *adj.* shaped like a cylinder; having the form of a cylinder. **—cy lin′dri cal ly,** *adv.*

cym bal (sim′bəl), *n.* one of a pair of brass or bronze plates, used as a musical instrument. Cymbals make a loud, ringing sound. [Old English *cimbal* < Latin *cymbalum* < Greek *kymbalon* < *kymbē* hollow of a vessel]

cym bal ist (sim′bə list), *n.* person who plays the cymbals.

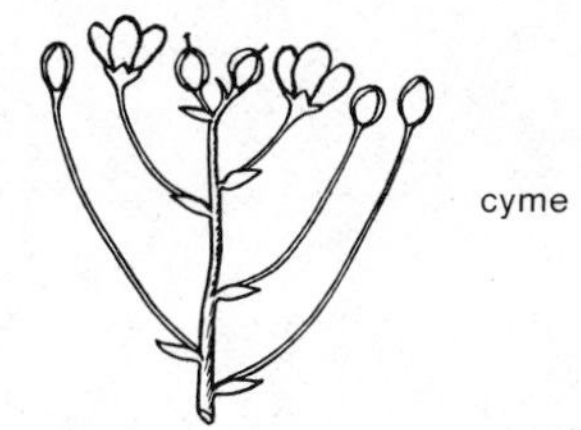

cyme

cyme (sīm), *n.* a flower cluster in which there is a flower at the top of the main stem and of each branch of the cluster. The flower in the center opens first. The sweet william has cymes. [< Latin *cyma* < Greek *kyma* something swollen, sprout < *kyein* be pregnant]

hat, āge, fär; let, ēqual, tėrm;
it, īce; hot, ōpen, ôrder;
oil, out; cup, pu̇t, rüle;
ch, child; ng, long; sh, she;
th, thin; ᴛʜ, then; zh, measure;

ə represents *a* in about, *e* in taken, *i* in pencil, *o* in lemon, *u* in circus.

< = from, derived from, taken from.

cy mose (sī′mōs, sī mōs′), *adj.* 1 having a cyme or cymes. 2 like a cyme.

Cym ric (kim′rik, sim′rik), *adj.* 1 Welsh. 2 of or having to do with the group of Celts that includes the Welsh, Cornish, and Bretons, or their languages; Brythonic. —*n.* Welsh.

Cym ry (kim′rē), *n.* 1 the Welsh people. 2 branch of the Celts that includes the Welsh, Cornish, and Bretons.

cyn ic (sin′ik), *n.* 1 person inclined to believe that the motives for people's actions are insincere and selfish. 2 a sneering, sarcastic person. 3 **Cynic,** member of a group of ancient Greek philosophers who taught that self-control is the essential part of virtue. They despised pleasure, money, and personal comfort. —*adj.* 1 cynical. 2 **Cynic,** of or having to do with the Cynics or their doctrines. [< Latin *cynicus* < Greek *kynikos* doglike < *kyon* dog]

cylinder (def. 1)

cylinder (def. 4)

cyn i cal (sin′ə kəl), *adj.* 1 doubting the sincerity and goodness of others. See synonym study below. 2 sneering; sarcastic. **—cyn′i cal ly,** *adv.* **—cyn′i cal ness,** *n.*

Syn. 1 Cynical, pessimistic mean doubting and mistrustful. **Cynical** emphasizes a tendency to doubt the honesty and sincerity of people and their motives for doing things: *It is difficult to make friends with a person who is cynical about friendship.* **Pessimistic** emphasizes a disposition to look on the dark side of things and expecting the unpleasant or worst to happen: *She has a very pessimistic attitude toward the value of this work.*

cyn i cism (sin′ə siz′əm), *n.* 1 cynical quality or disposition. 2 a cynical remark. 3 **Cynicism,** doctrines of the Cynics.

cy no sure (sī′nə shůr, sin′ə shůr), *n.* 1 center of attraction, interest, or attention. 2 something used for guidance or direction. 3 **Cynosure, a** the northern constellation Ursa Minor, which includes the North Star. **b** North Star. [< Latin *Cynosura* Cynosure < Greek *kynosoura* dog's tail < *kyōn* dog + *oura* tail]

Cyn thi a (sin′thē ə), *n.* 1 (in Greek and Roman myths) Artemis or Diana, regarded as the goddess of the moon. 2 the moon.

cy pher (sī′fər), *n., v.i., v.t.* cipher.

cy press (sī′prəs), *n.* 1 any of a genus of evergreen trees with hard wood and small, dark, scalelike leaves. 2 its wood, used for boards, shingles, and doors. [< Old French *cipres* < Latin *cypressus* < Greek *kyparissos*]

Cyp ri an (sip′rē ən), *adj.* of or having to do with Cyprus. —*n.* native or inhabitant of Cyprus.

cyp ri noid (sip′rə noid), *n.* any of a large family of freshwater fishes, including the carp, goldfish, bream, most freshwater minnows, etc. —*adj.* of or belonging to this family. [< Latin *cyprinus* carp]

Cyp ri ot (sip′rē ət), *n.* native or inhabitant of Cyprus. —*adj.* of or having to do with Cyprus.

Cyp ri ote (sip′rē ōt), *n., adj.* Cypriot.

cyp ri pe di um (sip′rə pē′dē əm), *n., pl.* **-di a** (-dē ə). any of several orchids that have drooping flowers with a protruding saclike lip, including the lady's-slipper and moccasin flower. [< New Latin]

Cy prus (sī′prəs), *n.* island and country in the E Mediterranean, south of Turkey, a member of the Commonwealth of Nations. 630,000 pop.; 3600 sq. mi. *Capital:* Nicosia. See **Adriatic Sea** for map.

Cyr a no de Ber ge rac (sir′ə nō′ də ber′zhə räk′). See **Bergerac.**

Cyr e na i ca (sir′ə nā′ə kə), *n.* 1 ancient country in N Africa, west of Egypt. 2 territory in E Libya. 330,000 sq. mi.

Cy re ne (sī rē′nē), *n.* city in ancient N Africa, west of Egypt, settled by the Greeks.

Cy ril lic (si ril′ik), *adj.* of or having to do with an ancient Slavic alphabet from which the Russian, Bulgarian, and Serbian alphabets have developed. [< St. *Cyril,* an apostle to the Slavs in the A.D. 800's, who is traditionally supposed to have invented it]

Cy rus (sī′rəs), *n.* 1 died 529 B.C., king of Persia from 558? to 529 B.C. and founder of the Persian empire. He was called "Cyrus the Great." 2 died 401 B.C., Persian military leader. He was called "Cyrus the Younger."

cyst (sist), *n.* 1 a small, abnormal, saclike growth in animals or plants, usually containing liquid and diseased matter produced by inflammation. 2 a saclike structure in animals or plants. [< New Latin *cystis* < Greek *kystis* pouch, bladder]

cyst ic (sis′tik), *adj.* 1 of or like a cyst. 2 having a cyst or cysts.

cystic fibrosis, a hereditary disease of the pancreas characterized by excessive secretion from internal organs and accompanying respiratory infection.

cys tine (sis′tēn′), *n.* a crystalline amino acid found in many proteins, especially keratin. *Formula:* $C_6H_{12}N_2O_4S_2$

cys ti tis (sis tī′tis), *n.* inflammation of the urinary bladder.

cys to scope (sis′tō skōp), *n.* instrument for examining the interior of the urinary bladder.

cys to scop ic (sis′tō skop′ik), *adj.* 1 having to do with a cystoscope. 2 performed with a cystoscope.

-cyte, *combining form.* cell: *Leucocyte = a white (blood) cell.* [< Greek *kytos* receptacle, cell]

cyto-, *combining form.* cell or cells: *Cytoplasm = protoplasm of a cell.* [< Greek *kytos* receptacle, cell]

cy to chem is try (sī′tō kem′ə strē), *n.* science of the chemistry of cells.

cy to chrome (sī′tə krōm), *n.* any of various pigments concerned with cellular respiration, important as catalysts in the oxidation process.

cy to ge net ics (sī′tō jə net′iks), *n.* branch of biology dealing with the relation of cells to heredity and variation.

cy to log ic (sī′tə loj′ik), *adj.* cytological.

cy to log i cal (sī′tə loj′ə kəl), *adj.* of or having to do with cytology. —**cy′to log′i cal ly,** *adv.*

cy tol o gist (sī tol′ə jist), *n.* an expert in cytology.

cy tol o gy (sī tol′ə jē), *n.* branch of biology that deals with the formation, structure, and function of cells.

cy to plasm (sī′tə plaz′əm), *n.* the living substance or protoplasm of a cell, outside of the nucleus.

cy to plas mic (sī′tə plaz′mik), *adj.* having to do with cytoplasm.

cy to sine (sī′tə sən, sī′tə sēn′), *n.* substance present in nucleic acid in cells. It is one of the pyrimidine bases of both DNA and RNA. *Formula:* $C_4H_5N_3O$

C.Z., Canal Zone.

czar (zär), *n.* 1 emperor. It was the title of the former emperors of Russia. 2 person having absolute power; autocrat: *the czar of the underworld.* Also, **tsar, tzar.** [< Russian *tsar* < Old Church Slavic *cēsarĭ* < Latin *Caesar* Caesar]

czar dom (zär′dəm), *n.* office, power, or territory of a czar.

czar e vitch (zär′ə vich), *n.* 1 the eldest son of a Russian czar. 2 son of a Russian czar. [< Russian *tsarevich*]

cza ri na (zä rē′nə), *n.* wife of a czar; Russian empress. Also, **tsarina, tzarina.** [< German *Zarin* (earlier *Czarin*), feminine of *Zar* < Russian *tsar.* See CZAR.]

czar ism (zär′iz′əm), *n.* autocratic government; absolutism; despotism.

czar ist (zär′ist), *adj.* of or having to do with a czar or czarism. —*n.* supporter of a czar or czars.

Czech (chek), *n.* 1 member of the most westerly branch of the Slavs. Bohemians, Moravians, and Silesians are Czechs. 2 their Slavic language; Bohemian. —*adj.* of or having to do with Czechoslovakia, its people, or the language of the Czechs.

Czech ish (check′ish), *adj.* Czech.

Czech o slo vak (chek′ə slō′vak, chek′ə slō′väk), *adj.* of or having to do with Czechoslovakia, its people, or their languages. —*n.* 1 native or inhabitant of Czechoslovakia. 2 either of the languages, Czech and Slovak, of Czechoslovakia.

Czech o slo va ki a (chek′ə slō vä′kē ə, chek′ə slō vak′ē ə), *n.* country in central Europe. 14,467,000 pop.; 49,400 sq. mi. *Capital:* Prague. See **Austria** for map. —**Czech′o slo va′ki an,** *adj., n.*

D d

D[1] or **d** (dē), *n., pl.* **D's** or **d's.** 1 the fourth letter of the English alphabet. 2 the Roman numeral for 500.

D[2] (dē), *n., pl.* **D's.** the second tone of the musical scale of C major.

D, 1 deuterium. 2 diameter. 3 didymium.

d., 1 date. 2 daughter. 3 day. 4 degree. 5 density. 6 died. 7 dime. 8 dollar. 9 English penny; pence: *2d. = 2.3 cents* [for Latin *denarius*].

D., 1 December. 2 Democrat. 3 Dutch.

D.A., District Attorney.

dab (dab), *v.,* **dabbed, dab bing,** *n.* —*v.t.* 1 touch lightly; pat with something soft or moist; tap: *I dabbed my face with a handkerchief.* 2 put on with light strokes: *dab ointment on a burn.* —*v.i.* 1 pat with something soft or moist. 2 strike lightly; peck. —*n.* 1 a quick, light touch or blow; pat or tap. 2 a small, soft or moist mass: *a dab of butter.* 3 a little bit. [Middle English *dabben*] **—dab′ber,** *n.*

dab ble (dab′əl), *v.,* **-bled, -bling.** —*v.t.* dip (hands, feet, etc.) in and out of water; splash. —*v.i.* do anything in a slight or superficial manner: *dabble at painting, dabble in the stock market.* [< Flemish *dabbelen*] **—dab′bler,** *n.*

dab chick (dab′chik′), *n.* any of various small grebes of Europe and North America. [origin uncertain]

da ca po (dä kä′pō), (in music) from the beginning (a direction to repeat a passage). [< Italian]

Dac ca (dak′ə), *n.* capital of Bangladesh. 557,000.

dace (dās), *n., pl.* **dac es** or **dace.** any of several small freshwater fish, of the same family as the carp. [Middle English *darse* < Old French *dars*]

da cha (dä′chə), *n.* (in Russia) a house in the country or suburbs. [< Russian]

dachs hund (däks′hu̇nt′, daks′hu̇nd′), *n.* a small hound with a long body, very short legs, and large, drooping ears. [< German *Dachshund* < *Dachs* badger + *Hund* dog]

Da cia (dā′shə), *n.* ancient Roman province in S Europe, comprising approximately the area of Romania.

Da cron (dā′kron, dak′ron), *n.* trademark for an artificial fiber or fabric that does not wrinkle or fade easily, used for shirts, dresses, suits, etc.

dac tyl (dak′təl), *n.* a metrical foot having one accented or long syllable followed by two unaccented or short syllables. EXAMPLE: "This′ is the | fo′rest pri | me′val. The | mur′mur ing | pines′ and the | hem′locks." [< Latin *dactylus* < Greek *daktylos* finger (by analogy, because of the length of the first finger joint). Doublet of DATE[2].]

dac tyl ic (dak til′ik), *adj.* 1 consisting of dactyls. 2 of dactyls.

dad (dad), *n.* INFORMAL. father.

Da da (dä′də), *n.* Dadaism.

Da da ism (dä′də iz′əm), *n.* movement in modern art rejecting and ridiculing all accepted standards and conventions. [< French *Dada,* originally a child's word for "hobbyhorse"]

dad dy (dad′ē), *n., pl.* **-dies.** INFORMAL. father.

dad dy-long legs (dad′ē lông′legz′, dad′ē long′legz′), *n., pl.* **-legs.** any of an order of spiderlike arachnids with a small body and long, thin legs; harvestman.

da do (dā′dō), *n., pl.* **-does** or **-dos.** the part of a pedestal between the base and the cap. [< Italian, cube, die]

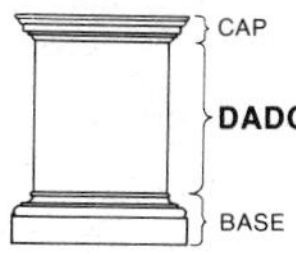

Daed a lus (ded′l əs), *n.* (in Greek legends) a skillful workman who constructed the Labyrinth in Crete; with his son Icarus he escaped from imprisonment in it by using wings he contrived of feathers fastened by wax.

dae mon (dē′mən), *n.* demon.

daf fo dil (daf′ə dil), *n.* 1 narcissus with yellow or white or partly white flowers that have a long, trumpet-shaped corona growing out from the center of the petals. 2 its flower. 3 a bright yellow. [earlier *affodill* < Latin *asphodelus.* See ASPHODEL.]

daff y (daf′ē), *adj.,* **daff i er, daff i est.** INFORMAL. daft.

daft (daft), *adj.* 1 without sense or reason; silly; foolish. 2 crazy; insane. [Old English *(ge)dæfte* gentle] **—daft′ly,** *adv.* **—daft′ness,** *n.*

da Gam a (də gam′ə; də gä′mə), **Vasco,** 1469?-1524, Portuguese navigator who discovered a route from Europe to India by sailing around southern Africa.

dag ger (dag′ər), *n.* 1 a small weapon with a short, pointed blade, used for stabbing. 2 sign (†) used in printing to refer the reader to a note someplace else in the book. [probably < obsolete *dag* to stab] **—dag′ger-like′,** *adj.*

da guerre o type (də ger′ə tīp, də ger′ē ə tīp), *n.* 1 an early method of photography by which the pictures were fixed on silvered metal plates made sensitive to light. 2 picture made in this way. [< French *daguerréotype* < Louis *Daguerre,* 1789-1851, its inventor]

dahl ia (dal′yə, däl′yə; *British* dāl′yə), *n.* 1 a tall plant of the composite family, with large, showy flowers that bloom in the autumn. 2 its flower. [< Anders *Dahl,* 1751-1789, Swedish botanist]

Da ho mey (də hō′mē), *n.* country in W Africa on the Atlantic. 2,640,000 pop.; 43,200 sq. mi. *Capital:* Porto-Novo. See **Upper Volta** for map. **—Da ho′me an, Da ho′mey an,** *adj., n.*

Dail Eir eann (dôl er′ən; doil er′ən), the lower house of parliament of the Republic of Ireland.

dai ly (dā′lē), *adj., adv., n., pl.* **-lies.** —*adj.* done, happening, or appearing every day, or every day but Sunday: *a daily paper.* —*adv.* every day; day by day: *deliver daily.* —*n.* newspaper printed every day, or every day but Sunday.

daily double, (in horse or dog racing) a combination bet in which the bettor attempts to pick the winners in two specified races, usually the first two, in the course of a day.

dai mio (dī′myō), *n., pl.* **-mio** or **-mios.** one of the feudal nobles of Japan. [< Japanese < Chinese *dai* great + *mio* name]

hat, āge, fär; let, ēqual, tėrm;
it, īce; hot, ōpen, ôrder;
oil, out; cup, pu̇t, rüle;
ch, child; ng, long; sh, she;
th, thin; ᴛʜ, then; zh, measure;

ə represents *a* in about, *e* in taken,
i in pencil, *o* in lemon, *u* in circus.

< = from, derived from, taken from.

dai myo (dī′myō), *n., pl.* **-myo** or **-myos.** daimio.

dain ty (dān′tē), *adj.,* **-ti er, -ti est,** *n., pl.* **-ties.** —*adj.* 1 having delicate beauty; fresh and pretty: *a dainty flower.* See **delicate** for synonym study. 2 delicate in tastes and feeling; particular: *dainty about one's eating.* 3 good to eat; delicious. —*n.* something very good to eat; a delicious bit of food. [< Old French *deinte* < Latin *dignitatem* worthiness. Doublet of DIGNITY.] **—dain′ti ly,** *adv.* **—dain′ti ness,** *n.*

dai quir i (dī′kər ē, dak′ər ē), *n.* cocktail made from rum, lime juice, and sugar. [< *Daiquirí,* town in Cuba]

Dai ren (dī′ren′), *n.* a former name of **Talien.**

dair y (der′ē), *n., pl.* **dair ies.** 1 room or building where milk and cream are kept and made into butter and cheese. 2 farm where milk and cream are produced and sometimes butter and cheese are made. 3 store or company that sells milk, cream, butter, and cheese. 4 business of producing milk and cream and making butter and cheese. [Middle English *daierie* < *daie* dairymaid (Old English *dǣge* maker of bread)]

dairy cattle, cows of certain breeds raised for the milk they produce.

dair y ing (der′ē ing), *n.* business of operating a dairy or dairy farm.

dair y maid (der′ē mād′), *n.* girl or woman who works in a dairy.

dair y man (der′ē mən), *n., pl.* **-men.** 1 man who works in a dairy. 2 man who owns or manages a dairy.

da is (dā′is; *British* dās), *n.* a raised platform at one end of a hall or large room for a throne, seats of honor, a lectern, etc. [< Old French *deis* < Latin *discus* quoit, dish < Greek *diskos.* Doublet of DESK, DISCUS, DISH, and DISK.]

dai sy (dā′zē), *n., pl.* **-sies.** 1 any of a genus of small plants of the composite family whose flowers or petals are usually white or pink around a yellow center. 2 a tall plant of the same genus as the chrysanthemum, whose flower heads have a yellow disk and white rays; the common "white daisy" of North America. 3 the flower of any of these plants. [Old English *dæges ēage* day's eye] **—dai′sy like′,** *adj.*

Da kar (dä kär′), *n.* seaport and capital of Senegal, on the Atlantic. 581,000.

Da ko ta (də kō′tə), *n.* 1 North Dakota or South Dakota. 2 the former territory of the United States that became North Dakota and South Dakota. 3 Sioux. **—Da ko′tan,** *adj., n.*

Da lai La ma (dä lī′ lä′mə), the chief priest of the religion of Lamaism in Tibet and Mongolia; Grand Lama.

dale (dāl), *n.* valley. [Old English *dæl*]

Da li (dä′lē), *n.* **Salvador,** born 1904, Spanish surrealist painter.

Dal las (dal′əs), *n.* city in NE Texas. 844,000.

dal li ance (dal′ē əns), *n.* 1 a dallying; trifling. 2 flirtation.

dal ly (dal′ē), *v.*, **-lied, -ly ing.** —*v.i.* 1 act in a playful manner. 2 flirt (with a person). 3 toy or trifle (with a thing or subject): *I dallied with the offer for days, but finally refused it.* See **trifle** for synonym study. 4 linger idly; loiter. —*v.t.* waste (time); idle: *dally the afternoon away.* [< Old French *dalier* to chat] **—dal′li er,** *n.*

Dal ma tia (dal mā′shə), *n.* region in W Yugoslavia, along the Adriatic.

Dal ma tian (dal mā′shən), *n.* 1 a large, short-haired dog, usually white with black or brown spots; coach dog. 2 native or inhabitant of Dalmatia. —*adj.* of Dalmatia or its people.

dal se gno (däl sā′nyō), (in music) from the sign (a direction to repeat the section starting at the sign). [< Italian]

Dal ton (dôlt′n), *n.* **John,** 1766-1844. English chemist, physicist, and meteorologist who contributed greatly to modern atomic theory.

dam[1] (dam), *n.*, *v.*, **dammed, dam ming.** —*n.* 1 wall built to hold back the water of a stream or any flowing water. 2 body of water held back by a dam. 3 anything resembling a dam. —*v.t.* 1 provide with a dam; hold back (water, etc.) by means of a dam. 2 hold back; block up. [Middle English *dame*]

dam[1] (def. 1)

dam[2] (dam), *n.* 1 the female parent of sheep, cattle, horses, or other quadrupeds. 2 a mother. [variant of *dame*]

dam age (dam′ij), *n.*, *v.*, **-aged, -ag ing.** —*n.* 1 harm or injury that lessens value or usefulness. 2 INFORMAL. cost; price; expense. 3 **damages,** *pl.* money claimed or paid by law to make up for some harm done to a person or his property. —*v.t.* harm or injure so as to lessen value or usefulness: *I damaged the canoe when I allowed the current to ram it against a rock.* See **harm** for synonym study. [< Old French < *dam* loss < Latin *damnum*]

dam a scene (dam′ə sēn′, dam′ə sēn′), *v.t.*, **-scened, -scen ing.** ornament (metal) with inlaid gold or silver or with a wavy design. [< Latin *Damascenus* < Greek *Damaskēnos* of Damascus]

Da mas cus (də mas′kəs), *n.* capital of Syria, in the SW part. It is one of the world's oldest cities, famous for its fine metalwork and brocades. 835,000.

Damascus steel, kind of ornamented steel with fine wavy lines, used in making sword blades; damask.

dam ask (dam′əsk), *n.* 1 a firm, shiny, reversible linen, silk, or cotton fabric with woven designs. 2 linen material of this type used especially for tablecloths and napkins. 3 a rose color; pink. 4 Damascus steel. —*adj.* 1 made of damask. 2 rose-colored; pink. 3 of or named after the city of Damascus. —*v.t.* 1 damascene. 2 weave with the design of damask fabric. [< Greek *Damaskos* Damascus]

dame (dām), *n.* 1 lady: *Dame Fortune, Dame Nature.* 2 in Great Britain: **a** title of honor given to a woman, corresponding to the rank of a knight. **b** the legal title of the wife or widow of a knight or baronet. 3 an elderly woman. 4 SLANG. woman. 5 ARCHAIC. the mistress of a household or of a school. [< Old French < Latin *domina* lady, mistress < *domus* house]

Dalmatian (def. 1) 20 in. high at the shoulder

Da mi en (dā′mē ən; *French* dȧ myaN′), *n.* **Father (Joseph de Veuster),** 1840-1889, Belgian Roman Catholic missionary.

damn (dam), *v.t.* 1 declare (something) to be bad or inferior; condemn. 2 cause to fail; ruin. 3 doom to hell. 4 swear or swear at by saying "damn"; curse. —*n.* 1 a saying of "damn"; curse. 2 a contemptible amount: *not worth a damn.* —*adv.* SLANG. very. [< Old French *damner* < Latin *damnare* condemn < *damnum* loss]

dam na ble (dam′nə bəl), *adj.* 1 abominable or outrageous; detestable. 2 deserving damnation. **—dam′na ble ness,** *n.* **—dam′na bly,** *adv.*

dam na tion (dam nā′shən), *n.* 1 a damning or a being damned; condemnation. 2 condemnation to eternal punishment. 3 curse.

damned (damd), *adj.* 1 cursed; abominable. 2 condemned as bad or inferior. 3 doomed to eternal punishment. —*adv.* SLANG. very.

Dam o cles (dam′ə klēz′), *n.* (in Greek legends) a courtier of the king of Syracuse, who glorified the happiness and riches of kings until the king placed him at a banquet with a sword suspended over his head by a single hair, to show him the constant peril of a king's life.

Da mon (dā′mən), *n.* (in Roman legends) a man who pledged his life to obtain leave for his condemned friend Pythias to go home to settle his affairs.

dam o sel or **dam o zel** (dam′ə zel), *n.* ARCHAIC. damsel.

damp (damp), *adj.* slightly wet; moist. See synonym study below. —*n.* 1 moisture. 2 thing that checks or deadens; damper: *Your illness cast a damp over the party.* 3 any poisonous or explosive gas that collects in mines, such as chokedamp or firedamp. —*v.t.* 1 make moist or slightly wet; dampen. 2 check or deaden: *Weariness damped the traveler's enthusiasm.* 3 (in music) stop the vibrations of (a string, etc.). [< Middle Dutch or Middle Low German, vapor] **—damp′ly,** *adv.* **—damp′ness,** *n.*

Syn. *adj.* **Damp, moist, humid** mean somewhat wet. **Damp** implies a slight degree of wetness and usually suggests that it is unpleasant or unwanted: *This house is damp in rainy weather.* **Moist** implies less wetness than *damp,* usually with no suggestion of unpleasantness: *Use a moist, not a damp, cloth.* **Humid** is used commonly to describe a high degree of moisture in the air: *In the East the air is humid in summer.*

damp en (dam′pən), *v.t.* 1 make damp; moisten. 2 cast a damp over; depress; discourage. —*v.i.* become damp. **—damp′en er,** *n.*

damp er (dam′pər), *n.* 1 person or thing that discourages or checks. 2 a movable plate to control the draft in a stove or furnace. 3 (in music) a device for checking vibration and reducing the volume of sound, especially of piano strings. 4 device for checking the vibration of a magnetic needle.

dam sel (dam′zəl), *n.* ARCHAIC. a young girl; maiden. [< Old French *dameisele,* ultimately < Latin *domina* lady]

dam sel fly (dam′zəl flī′), *n., pl.* **-flies.** any of a suborder of small insects similar to a dragonfly but having four wings that when at rest fold together vertically over the back; devil's darning needle.

dam son (dam′zən), *n.* 1 a small, blue, blackish, or dark-purple plum. 2 tree that it grows on. [< Latin *(prunum) damascenum* (plum) of Damascus]

Dan (dan), *n.* 1 in the Bible: **a** the fifth son of Jacob. **b** a Hebrew tribe descended from him, that migrated to northern Palestine. 2 village in the N part of ancient Palestine.

Dan., 1 Daniel. 2 Danish.

Da na (dā′nə), *n.* **Richard Henry,** 1815-1882, American writer, author of *Two Years Before the Mast.*

Da Nang (dä′ näng′), seaport in NE South Vietnam, on the South China Sea. 334,000.

dance (dans), *v.*, **danced, danc ing,** *n., adj.* —*v.i.* 1 move in rhythm, usually in time with music. 2 jump up and down; move in a lively way: *The little child danced with delight.* 3 bob up and down. —*v.t.* 1 do, perform, or take part in (a dance): *They danced a waltz.* 2 cause to dance: *He danced me around the room.* —*n.* 1 movement in rhythm, usually in time with music. 2 some special group of steps, such as the waltz, fox trot, etc. 3 party where people dance. 4 one round of dancing. 5 piece of music for dancing or in a dance rhythm. 6 movement up and down; lively movement. —*adj.* of dancing; for dancing. [< Old French *danser*]

danc er (dan′sər), *n.* 1 person who dances. 2 person whose occupation is dancing.

dan de li on (dan′dl ī′ən), *n.* a common weed of the composite family with deeply notched leaves and bright-yellow flowers that bloom in the spring. [< Middle French *dent de lion* lion's tooth; from its toothed leaves]

dan der (dan′dər), *n.* INFORMAL. **get one's dander up,** lose one's temper. [origin uncertain]

dan di fy (dan′də fī), *v.t.* **-fied, -fy ing.** make trim or smart like a dandy.

dan dle (dan′dl), *v.t.*, **-dled, -dling.** 1 move (a child, etc.) up and down on one's knees or in one's arms. 2 pet; pamper. [origin uncertain]

dan druff (dan′drəf), *n.* small, whitish scales of dead skin that flake off the scalp. [origin uncertain]

dan dy (dan′dē), *n., pl.* **-dies,** *adj.*, **-di er, -di est.** —*n.* 1 man who is too careful about his dress and appearance; fop. 2 INFORMAL. an excellent or first-rate thing. —*adj.* 1 of a dandy; too carefully dressed; foppish. 2 INFORMAL. excellent; first-rate. [perhaps < *Dandy,* a variant of *Andrew*]

dan dy ish (dan′dē ish), *adj.* like a dandy; foppish.

Dane (dān), *n.* 1 native or inhabitant of Denmark. 2 person of Danish descent.

Dane law (dān′lô′), *n.* 1 set of laws enforced by the Danes when they held northeast England in the A.D. 800's and 900's. 2 the part of England under these laws.

dan ger (dān′jər), *n.* 1 chance of harm; nearness to harm; risk; peril: *There is some danger in mountain climbing.* See synonym study below. 2 thing that may cause harm: *Hidden rocks are a danger to ships.* [< Old French *dangier,* ultimately < Latin *dominium* sovereignty < *dominus* master]

Syn. 1 Danger, peril mean threat of harm. **Danger** is the general word, always suggesting there is a definite chance of harm, but the harm is not always certain: *Miners at work are always in danger.* **Peril** means that great harm is very near at hand and probable: *When a mine caves in, the miners are in peril.*

dan ger ous (dān′jər əs), *adj.* likely to cause harm; not safe; risky. **—dan′ger ous ly,** *adv.* **—dan′ger ous ness,** *n.*

dan gle (dang′gəl), *v.,* **-gled, -gling.** *—v.i.* 1 hang and swing loosely: *The curtain cord dangles.* 2 hang about; follow: *The popular girl always had several people dangling after her.* *—v.t.* 1 hold or carry (a thing) so that it swings loosely: *The cat played with the string I dangled in front of it.* 2 cause to dangle. [probably < Scandinavian (Danish) *dangla*] **—dan′gler,** *n.*

dangling participle, participle not clearly connected with the word it modifies. In "Sitting on the porch, a beautiful moon can be seen," *sitting* is a dangling participle.

Dan iel (dan′yəl), *n.* 1 (in the Bible) a Hebrew prophet whose great faith in God kept him unharmed in a den of lions. 2 book in the Old Testament which tells about him.

Dan ish (dā′nish), *adj.* of or having to do with Denmark, its people, or their language. *—n.* 1 *pl. in use.* people of Denmark. 2 the Scandinavian language of Denmark. 3 a rich, flaky pastry made with yeast.

dank (dangk), *adj.* unpleasantly damp or moist: *The cave was dark, dank, and chilly.* [Middle English *danke*] **—dank′ly,** *adv.* **—dank′ness,** *n.*

d'An nun zi o (dä nün′tsē ō), *n.* **Gabriele,** 1863-1938, Italian poet, novelist, and dramatist.

dan seur (dan sėr′; *French* däɴ sœr′), *n.* a male dancer, especially in a ballet. [< French]

dan seuse (dan süz′; *French* däɴ sœz′), *n., pl.* **-seus es** (-sü′ziz; *French* -sœz′). a female dancer in a ballet. [< French]

Dan te (dan′tē, dän′tā), *n.* 1265-1321, Italian poet, author of the *Divine Comedy.*

Dan te A li ghie ri (dän′tā ä′lē gyer′ē), Dante.

Dan ton (dan′tən; *French* däɴ tôɴ′), *n.* **Georges Jacques,** 1759-1794, a leader in the French Revolution.

Dan ube River (dan′yüb), river flowing from S West Germany through Austria, Czechoslovakia, Hungary, Yugoslavia, Bulgaria, Romania, and the Soviet Union into the Black Sea. 1725 mi. **—Da nu′bi an,** *adj.*

Dan zig (dant′sig, dan′zig), *n.* seaport in N Poland, on the Baltic Sea. 370,000. Also, POLISH **Gdańsk.**

Daph ne (daf′nē), *n.* (in Greek myths) a nymph pursued by Apollo, whom she escaped by being changed into a laurel tree.

dap per (dap′ər), *adj.* 1 neat, trim, or spruce. 2 small and active. [< Middle Dutch, agile, strong] **—dap′per ly,** *adv.* **—dap′per ness,** *n.*

dap ple (dap′əl), *adj., v.,* **-pled, -pling,** *n.* *—adj.* marked with spots; spotted: *a dapple horse.* *—v.t., v.i.* mark or become marked with spots. *—n.* 1 a spotted appearance or condition. 2 animal with a spotted or mottled skin. [Middle English *dappel*]

D.A.R., Daughters of the American Revolution, a society of women who are descended from Americans who fought in the Revolutionary War.

Dar by and Joan (där′bē ən jōn′), a typical old married couple, contented and devoted to each other.

Dar da nelles (därd′n elz′), *n.* strait in NW Turkey which connects the Sea of Marmara with the Aegean Sea, and separates European from Asian Turkey. In ancient times it was called the Hellespont. 40 mi. long; 1-5 mi. wide.

dare (der, dar), *v.,* **dared** or (ARCHAIC) **durst, dared, dar ing,** *n.* *—v.i.* have courage; be bold; be bold enough: *You wouldn't dare!* *—v.t.* 1 have courage to try; not be afraid of; face or meet boldly: *The explorer dared the dangers of the icy north. She dared contradict the teacher.* See synonym study below. 2 meet and resist; face and defy: *dare the power of a dictator.* 3 challenge: *I dare you to jump.* *—n.* challenge. [Old English *dearr,* first person singular present indicative of *durran* to dare]

Syn. *v.t.* **1 Dare, venture** mean to be courageous or bold enough to do something. **Dare** emphasizes the idea of meeting fearlessly any danger or trouble, especially in doing something that is or seems important: *Only the firemen dared to enter the burning building.* **Venture** emphasizes the idea of being willing to take chances: *He ventured to cross the rickety bridge when none of the rest of us would.*

➤ **dare, dares.** Either *dare* or *dares* is used with the third person singular: *He dare not. He dares to do many reckless things.*

dare dev il (der′dev′əl, dar′dev′əl), *n.* a reckless person. *—adj.* recklessly daring.

dare say (der′sā′, dar′sā′), *v.t., v.i.* believe.

➤ **Daresay** is used only in the first person singular, present tense: *I daresay that fad will not last long.*

Dar es Sa laam (där es sə läm′), seaport and capital of Tanzania, on the Indian Ocean. 273,000.

hat, āge, fär; let, ēqual, tėrm;
it, īce; hot, ōpen, ôrder;
oil, out; cup, pu̇t, rüle;
ch, child; ng, long; sh, she;
th, thin; ᴛʜ, then; zh, measure;

ə represents *a* in about, *e* in taken, *i* in pencil, *o* in lemon, *u* in circus.

< = from, derived from, taken from.

Dar i en (der′ē en′, dar′ē en′), *n.* 1 **Gulf of,** gulf of the Caribbean Sea, between Panama and Colombia. 2 **Isthmus of,** a former name of the Isthmus of Panama.

dar ing (der′ing, dar′ing), *n.* courage to take risks; boldness. *—adj.* bold; fearless; courageous. **—dar′ing ly,** *adv.* **—dar′ing ness,** *n.*

Da ri us I (də rī′əs), 558?-486? B.C., king of Persia from 521 to 486? B.C., defeated by the Athenians at Marathon in 490 B.C.

dark (därk), *adj.* 1 without light; with very little light: *a dark night.* See synonym study below. 2 reflecting or radiating little light; nearly black: *dark clouds.* 3 not light-colored: *a dark complexion.* 4 gloomy; dull; dismal: *looking on the dark side of things.* 5 hard to understand or explain: *a dark chapter in a book.* 6 secret or hidden: *a dark plan.* 7 without knowledge or culture; ignorant: *a dark period in history.* 8 evil; wicked: *a dark deed.* 9 sad; sullen; frowning: *a dark look.*
—n. 1 absence of light. 2 night; nightfall. 3 **after dark,** after night has fallen. 4 a dark color. 5 obscurity. 6 secrecy. 7 ignorance. 8 **in the dark,** in ignorance; without knowledge or information.
[Old English *deorc*] **—dark′ly,** *adv.* **—dark′ness,** *n.*

Syn. *adj.* **1 Dark, dim** mean without light. **Dark** means without any light or with very little light: *The house is dark; not a light is on.* **Dim** means without enough light to see clearly or distinctly: *With only the fire burning, the room was dim.*

Dark Ages or **dark ages,** 1 the early part of the Middle Ages, from about A.D. 400 to about A.D. 1000, when learning and culture in western Europe were at a low ebb. 2 Middle Ages.

dark en (där′kən), *v.t., v.i.* make or become dark or darker. **—dark′en er,** *n.*

dark horse, 1 an unexpected winner about whom little is known. 2 person who is unexpectedly nominated for a political office.

dark ish (där′kish), *adj.* somewhat dark.

dark lantern, lantern whose light can be hidden by a cover or dark glass.

dark ling (därk′ling), *adv.* in the dark. *—adj.* dark; dim; obscure.

dark room (därk′rüm′, därk′ru̇m′), *n.* room cut off from all outside light, arranged for developing photographs. It usually has a very dim, colored light.

dark some (därk′səm), *adj.* 1 dark. 2 gloomy; somber.

dar ling (där′ling), *n.* 1 person or animal very dear to another; person or animal much loved. 2 a favorite. *—adj.* 1 very dear; much loved. 2 favorite. 3 INFORMAL. pleasing or attractive. [Old English *dēorling* < *dēore* dear]

Dar ling (där′ling), *n.* river in SE Australia, flowing southwest into the Murray River. 1160 mi.

Darm stadt (därm′shtät), *n.* city in central West Germany. 141,000.

darn[1] (därn), *v.t., v.i.* mend by making rows of stitches back and forth across a hole, torn place, etc. —*n.* 1 place mended by darning. 2 act of darning. [< dialectal Middle French *darner* < *darne* piece < Breton *darn*] **—darn′er,** *n.*

darn[2] (därn), *v.t., n., adv.* INFORMAL. damn. [variant of *damn*]

dar nel (där′nl), *n.* kind of grass with poisonous seeds which looks somewhat like rye and often grows as a weed in grain fields. [Middle English]

darning needle, 1 a long needle with a large eye for heavy thread, used for darning. 2 dragonfly.

dart (därt), *n.* 1 a slender, pointed weapon or short stick tipped with a sharp metal point. It may be thrown by hand, or shot from a blowgun. 2 **darts,** *pl.* a game in which darts are thrown at a target. 3 a sudden, swift movement; dash. 4 the stinger of an insect. 5 a short seam to make a garment fit better. 6 a sharp look, word, etc. —*v.t.* 1 throw or shoot suddenly and quickly; hurl; launch. 2 send suddenly: *She darted an angry glance at her sister.* 3 fit with a dart or darts: *dart the waistline of a dress.* —*v.i.* move suddenly and swiftly; dash; bolt: *The deer saw us and darted away.* [< Old French < Germanic]

dart er (där′tər), *n.* 1 animal or person that moves suddenly and swiftly. 2 a small freshwater fish, of the same family as the perch. 3 snakebird.

Dar win (där′wən), *n.* **Charles Robert,** 1809-1882, English naturalist, who formulated the theory of evolution through natural selection.

Dar win i an (där win′ē ən), *adj.* of Charles Darwin, Darwinism, or Darwinists. —*n.* person who believes in Darwinism.

Dar win ism (där′wə niz′əm), *n.* theory of evolution through natural selection developed by Charles Darwin, according to which natural selection results in the survival of some plant and animal forms but not others. Among a number of slight variations those best adapted to the environment survive, ultimately resulting in new, usually more complex species.

Dar win ist (där′wə nist), *adj., n.* Darwinian.

dash (dash), *v.t.* 1 throw, drive, or strike with violence: *In a fit of anger he dashed his ruler against the door.* 2 splash: *I dashed some paint on the canvas.* 3 strike violently so as to break; smash: *I dashed the bowl to bits on a rock.* 4 ruin or destroy: *Our hopes were dashed by the bad news.* 5 depress; discourage. 6 mix with a small amount of something else. 7 **dash off,** do, make, write, etc., quickly: *dash off a letter.* —*v.i.* 1 strike violently: *The waves dashed against the rocks.* 2 rush: *They dashed by in a car.* —*n.* 1 a splash: *the dash of waves against the rocks.* 2 rush: *make a dash for safety.* 3 a violent blow or stroke. 4 smash. 5 thing that depresses or discourages; check. 6 a small amount: *Put in just a dash of pepper.* 7 a short race: *the fifty-yard dash.* 8 energy; spirit; liveliness. 9 showy appearance or behavior. 10 a mark (—) used in writing or printing to show a break in sense, explanatory material, omitted letters or words, etc. 11 a long sound used in sending messages by telegraph or radiotelegraph. 12 dashboard. [Middle English *daschen*]

dash board (dash′bôrd′, dash′bōrd′), *n.* 1 panel with instruments, gauges, and certain controls in front of the driver in an automobile, aircraft, etc. 2 protection on the front of a wagon, boat, etc., that prevents mud or water from being splashed into it.

dashboard (def. 2)

dash er (dash′ər), *n.* 1 person or thing that dashes. 2 device for stirring the cream in a churn or in an ice-cream freezer.

da shi ki (də shē′kē), *n.* a loose, pullover shirt, often colorfully printed or embroidered, used for casual wear. [< an African word]

dash ing (dash′ing), *adj.* 1 full of energy and spirit; lively. 2 showy or stylish. **—dash′ing ly,** *adv.*

das tard (das′tərd), *n.* a mean coward; sneak. —*adj.* mean and cowardly; sneaking; dastardly. [Middle English]

das tard ly (das′tərd lē), *adj.* like a dastard; mean and cowardly; sneaking. **—das′tard li ness,** *n.*

dat., dative.

da ta (dā′tə, dat′ə), *n.pl.* of **datum.** facts from which conclusions can be drawn; things known or admitted; information. [< Latin, plural of *datum* (thing) given. Doublet of DIE[2].]

➤ **Data** is the plural of the seldom-used singular *datum.* When *data* refers to a group of facts as a unit, it is used with a singular verb in informal English: *The data we have collected is not enough to be convincing.* In formal English *data* is regarded as a plural: *The data we have collected are not enough to be convincing.*

data processing, the handling and storing of complex data by means of electronic computers.

date[1] (dāt), *n., v.,* **dat ed, dat ing.** —*n.* 1 time when something happens or happened; a particular day, month, or year: *July 4, 1776, is the date of the signing of the Declaration of Independence.* 2 statement of time: *There is a date stamped on every piece of United States money.* 3 period of time. 4 INFORMAL. appointment for a certain time. 5 INFORMAL. person of the opposite sex with whom a social appointment is made. 6 **out of date,** old-fashioned; not in present use. 7 **to date,** till now; yet. 8 **up to date, a** according to the latest style or idea; in fashion; modern. **b** up to the present time. —*v.t.* 1 mark the time of; put a date on: *date a letter.* 2 find out the date of; give a date to. 3 make old-fashioned or out of date. 4 INFORMAL. make a social appointment with (a person of the opposite sex). —*v.i.* 1 be dated; have a date on it. 2 belong to a certain period of time; have its origin: *The oldest house in town dates from the 1800's.* 3 be or become old-fashioned or out of date. [< French < Medieval Latin *data (epistola Romae)* (letter) given, in the sense of "written" (at Rome)] **—dat′a ble, date′a ble,** *adj.* **—dat′er,** *n.*

date[2] (dāt), *n.* 1 the oblong, fleshy, sweet fruit of the date palm. 2 date palm. [< Old French < Latin *dactylus* < Greek *daktylos* date, finger. Doublet of DACTYL.]

dat ed (dā′tid), *adj.* 1 marked with or showing a date. 2 out-of-date.

date less (dāt′lis), *adj.* 1 without a date; not dated. 2 endless; unlimited. 3 so old that it cannot be given a date. 4 old but enduring; ageless.

date line (dāt′līn′), *n., v.,* **-lined, -lin ing.** —*n.* line in a letter, newspaper, etc., giving the date and place of writing. —*v.t.* furnish with a dateline.

date line, International Date Line.

date palm, the palm tree on which dates grow.

da tive (dā′tiv), *adj.* showing the indirect object of a verb or the object of a preposition. Latin and some other languages have a dative case. In English, the dative function is expressed by word order or by a prepositional phrase: "Give *him* the book." "Give the book *to him.*" —*n.* 1 the dative case. 2 word in this case. [< Latin *dativus* of giving < *datus* a giving < *dare* give]

➤ **dative case.** Most English grammars now include the dative and the accusative cases under the general term *objective case.*

da tum (dā′təm, dat′əm), *n.* sing. of **data.** ➤ See **data** for usage note.

daub (dôb), *v.t.* 1 coat or cover with plaster, clay, mud, or any greasy or sticky substance. 2 apply (greasy or sticky substance) to a surface. 3 make dirty; soil; stain. 4 paint (something) unskillfully. —*v.i.* 1 daub something. 2 paint unskillfully. —*n.* 1 anything daubed on. 2 a badly painted picture. 3 act of daubing. 4 material for daubing, such as rough plaster or mortar. [< Old French *dauber* < Latin *dealbare* < *de-* + *albus* white] **—daub′er,** *n.*

Dau det (dō dā′), *n.* **Alphonse,** 1840-1897, French novelist, poet, and playwright.

daugh ter (dô′tər), *n.* 1 a female child or person in relation to her parents or parent. 2 a female descendant. 3 girl or woman attached to a country, cause, etc., as a child is to its parents. 4 anything thought of as a daughter in relation to its origin. —*adj.* 1 like a daughter. 2 of a daughter. 3 resulting from a primary division or segmentation: *a daughter chromosome.* [Old English *dohtor*]

daugh ter-in-law (dô′tər in lô′), *n., pl.* **daugh ters-in-law.** wife of one's son.

daugh ter ly (dô′tər lē), *adj.* 1 of a daughter. 2 like a daughter; like a daughter's. 3 proper for a daughter.

Dau mier (dō myā′), *n.* **Honoré,** 1808-1879, French caricaturist and painter.

daunt (dônt, dänt), *v.t.* 1 overcome with fear; frighten; intimidate. 2 lessen the courage of; discourage; dishearten. [< Old French *danter* < Latin *domitare* < *domare* to tame]

daunt less (dônt′lis, dänt′lis), *adj.* not to be frightened or discouraged; brave. **—daunt′less ly,** *adv.* **—daunt′less ness,** *n.*

dau phin (dô′fən), *n.* the oldest son of the king of France, used as a title from 1349 to 1830. [< Middle French, originally a family name]

dav en port (dav′ən pôrt, dav′ən pōrt), *n.* 1 a long, upholstered sofa, frequently convertible into a bed. 2 a writing desk with

hat, āge, fär; let, ēqual, tėrm;
it, īce; hot, ōpen, ôrder;
oil, out; cup, pu̇t, rüle;
ch, child; ng, long; sh, she;
th, thin; ᴛʜ, then; zh, measure;

ə represents *a* in about, *e* in taken, *i* in pencil, *o* in lemon, *u* in circus.

< = from, derived from, taken from.

drawers and a hinged shelf to write on. [probably < the maker's name]

Dav en port (dav′ən pôrt, dav′ən pōrt), *n.* city in E Iowa, on the Mississippi. 98,000.

Da vid (dā′vid *for 1;* dä vēd′ *for 2*), *n.* 1 died 970? B.C., Hebrew warrior, poet, and second king of Israel, from 1010? to 970? B.C., who succeeded Saul and organized the Jewish tribes into a national state. According to tradition, he wrote many Psalms of the Bible. 2 **Jacques Louis,** 1748-1825, French painter of classical and historical subjects.

da Vin ci (də vin′chē), **Leonardo,** 1452-1519, Italian painter, musician, sculptor, architect, engineer, and scientist.

Da vis (dā′vis), *n.* 1 **Jefferson,** 1808-1889, president of the Confederacy from 1861 to 1865. 2 **Richard Harding,** 1864-1916, American writer.

Davis Strait, strait in the Atlantic between Canada and Greenland. 200-500 mi. wide.

davit (def. 1) lifeboat suspended by a pair of davits

dav it (dav′it, dā′vit), *n.* 1 one of a pair of curved metal or wooden arms at the side of a ship, used to hold or lower a small boat. 2 crane for raising or lowering the anchor of a ship. [< Anglo-French *daviot*]

Da vy (dā′vē), *n.* Sir **Humphry,** 1778-1829, English chemist.

Davy Jones, spirit of the sea; the sailor's devil.

Davy Jones's locker, grave of those who die at sea; bottom of the ocean.

daw (dô), *n.* jackdaw. [Middle English *dawe*]

daw dle (dô′dl), *v.,* **-dled, -dling.** —*v.i.* waste time; idle; loiter; dally: *Don't dawdle over your work.* —*v.t.* waste by trifling: *I dawdled the afternoon away.* —*n.* 1 person who dawdles. 2 act of dawdling. [origin uncertain] —**daw′dler,** *n.*

Dawes (dôz), *n.* **Charles Gates,** 1865-1951, vice-president of the United States from 1925 to 1929.

dawn (dôn), *n.* 1 beginning of day; the first light in the east. 2 beginning: *Dinosaurs roamed the earth before the dawn of man.* —*v.i.* 1 grow bright or clear in the morning. 2 grow clear to the eye or mind: *It dawned on me that my friend wanted me to leave.* 3 begin; appear: *A new era of progress is dawning in Africa.* [short for Middle English *dawning,* probably < Scandinavian (Danish) *dagning.* Related to DAY.]

day (dā), *n.* 1 time of light between sunrise and sunset. 2 light of day; daylight. 3 the period of 24 hours of day and night; time it takes for the earth to make one rotation on its axis. 4 day or date set aside for a particular purpose or celebration: *a school day, a feast day.* 5 hours for work; workday: *a seven-hour day.* 6 time; period: *the present day, in days of old.* 7 period of life, activity, power, or influence: *Great Britain has had its day as a great colonial power.* 8 conflict; contest: *Our side won the day.* 9 victory: *The day is ours.* 10 **call it a day,** INFORMAL. stop work. [Old English *dæg*]

Day ak (dī′ak), *n.* one of a primitive people of central Borneo speaking a Malayan language. Also, **Dyak.**

day bed (dā′bed′), *n.* bed, usually narrow, with a low headboard and footboard convertible to a couch by day.

day book, 1 (in bookkeeping) a book in which a record is kept of each day's business. 2 diary.

day break (dā′brāk′), *n.* time when it begins to get light in the morning; dawn.

day camp, a summer camp for children, held during the daytime only.

day-care center (dā′ker′, dā′kar′), day nursery.

day coach, a railroad passenger car with seats only.

day dream (dā′drēm′), *n.* 1 dreamy thinking about pleasant things. 2 something imagined but not likely to come true. —*v.i.* think dreamily about pleasant things. —**day′-dream′er,** *n.*

day laborer, an unskilled or manual worker who is paid by the day.

day light (dā′līt′), *n.* 1 light of day. 2 daytime. 3 dawn; daybreak: *He was up at daylight in order to get an early start.* 4 publicity; openness. 5 **daylights,** *pl.* SLANG. vital parts; innards: *knock the daylights out of an enemy, scare the daylights out of someone.* 6 **see daylight,** INFORMAL. **a** understand. **b** approach the end of a hard or tiresome job.

day light-sav ing time (dā′līt′sā′ving), time that is one hour ahead of standard time. Clocks are set ahead one hour in the spring and back one hour in the fall.

day lily, any of a genus of plants of the lily family having large, short-lived yellow, orange, or sometimes red flowers.

day long (dā′lông′, dā′long′), *adj., adv.* through the whole day.

day nursery, nursery for the care of small children during the day.

Day of Atonement, Yom Kippur.

Day of Judgment, Judgment Day.

day school, 1 school held in the daytime. 2 a private school for students who live at home. 3 an elementary school held on weekdays.

day star (dā′stär′), *n.* 1 morning star. 2 sun.

day time (dā′tīm′), *n.* time when it is day and not night.

Day ton (dāt′n), *n.* city in SW Ohio. 244,000.

daze (dāz), *v.,* **dazed, daz ing,** *n.* —*v.t.* 1 make unable to think clearly; confuse; bewilder; stun: *The blow on my head dazed me.* 2 hurt (one's eyes) with light; dazzle: *The child was dazed by the bright sun.* —*n.* a dazed condition; bewilderment. [< Scandinavian (Old Icelandic) *dasask* become exhausted]

daz zle (daz′əl), *v.,* **-zled, -zling,** *n.* —*v.t.* 1 hurt (the eyes) with too bright light or with quick-moving lights. 2 overcome the sight or the mind of with anything very bright or splendid: *The children were dazzled by the richness of the palace.* —*n.* act or fact of dazzling; bewildering brightness. [< *daze*] —**daz′zler,** *n.*

daz zling (daz′ling), *adj.* brilliant or splendid. —**daz′zling ly,** *adv.*

d.c., direct current.

D.C., 1 da capo. 2 direct current. 3 District of Columbia.

D.D., Doctor of Divinity.

D-day (dē′dā′), *n.* 1 June 6, 1944, the day when the Allies landed in France in World War II. 2 day on which a previously planned military attack is to be made, or on which an operation is to be started.

D.D.S., Doctor of Dental Surgery.

DDT or **D.D.T.,** a very powerful, odorless insecticide. *Formula:* $C_{14}H_9Cl_5$ [< *d(ichloro)-d(iphenyl)-t(richloro-ethane),* the chemical name]

de-, *prefix.* 1 do the opposite of: *Decentralize = do the opposite of centralize.* 2 down; lower: *Depress = press down.* 3 away; off: *Derail = (run) off the rails.* 4 take away; remove: *Defrost = remove the frost.* 5 entirely; completely: *Despoil = spoil entirely.* [< Latin < *de* away from]

dea con (dē′kən), *n.* 1 officer of a Christian church who helps the minister in church duties not connected with preaching. 2 (in episcopal churches) member of the clergy next below a priest in rank. [Old English *diacon* < Latin *diaconus* < Greek *diakonos,* originally, servant]

dea con ess (dē′kə nis), *n.* woman who officially assists a minister in church work, visiting, etc.

de ac ti vate (dē ak′tə vāt), *v.t.,* **-vat ed, -vat ing.** remove from active service or use; make inactive. —**de ac′ti va′tion,** *n.*

dead (ded), *adj.* 1 no longer living; that has died. See synonym study below. 2 without life; inanimate. 3 like death: *in a dead faint.* 4 not active or productive; dull or quiet: *Summer is often a dead season in certain businesses.* 5 without force, power, spirit, or feeling: *a dead battery.* 6 no longer in use; obsolete: *dead languages.* 7 out of play: *a dead ball.* 8 INFORMAL. very tired; worn-out. 9 sure; certain: *a dead shot.* 10 complete; absolute: *a dead loss, dead silence.* 11 carrying no electrical charge; not connected to a source of power: *The telephone line is dead.*

—*adv.* 1 completely; absolutely: *dead wrong, dead tired.* 2 directly; straight: *dead ahead.*

—*n.* 1 **the dead,** person or persons no longer living. 2 time when there is the least life stirring: *the dead of night.*

[Old English *dēad*] —**dead′ness,** *n.*

Syn. *adj.* 1 **Dead, deceased, lifeless** mean without life. **Dead** emphasizes the idea of dying, and applies particularly to someone or something that was living or alive, but no longer is: *The flowers in my garden are dead.* **Deceased,** a technical word, applies only to a dead person: *The deceased man left no will.* **Lifeless** emphasizes the idea of being without life, and is used both of what now is or seems to be without life of any kind and of things that never had life: *a lifeless body, lifeless stones.*

dead beat (ded′bēt′), *n.* SLANG. 1 U.S. person who avoids paying for what he gets. 2 a lazy person; loafer.

dead center, position of the crank and connecting rod in an engine, at which they are in a straight line and the connecting rod has no power to turn the crank. Dead center occurs at each end of a stroke.

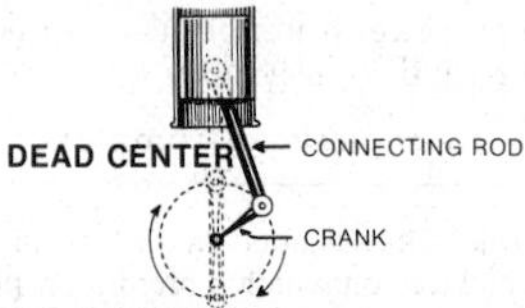

dead en (ded′n), *v.t.* 1 make dull or weak; lessen the intenseness or force of. 2 make soundproof: *deaden a room.*

dead end, 1 street, passage, etc., closed at one end. 2 a point beyond which progress, advancement, etc., is impossible.

dead-end (ded′end′), *adj.* 1 closed at one end. 2 having no opportunity for progress, advancement, etc.; fruitless: *a dead-end job.* 3 of the slums; tough: *a dead-end gang.*

dead eye (ded′ī′), *n.* a round, flat, wooden block used to fasten the shrouds of a ship.

dead fall (ded′fôl′), *n.* 1 trap for animals made so that a heavy weight falls upon and holds or kills the animal. 2 mass of fallen trees and underbrush.

dead head (ded′hed′), *n.* INFORMAL. person who rides on a train or bus, sees a game, etc., without paying.

dead heat, race that ends in a tie.

dead letter, 1 letter that cannot be delivered or returned because of a wrong address, not enough postage, etc. 2 law, rule, etc., that is no longer observed.

dead line (ded′līn′), *n.* 1 the latest possible time to do something: *April 15 is the deadline for filing individual income-tax returns.* 2 the time when all copy for a newspaper or the like must be in.

dead lock (ded′lok′), *n.* complete standstill: *Employers and strikers were at a deadlock; neither side would give in.* —*v.t., v.i.* bring or come to a complete standstill.

dead ly (ded′lē), *adj.,* **-li er, -li est,** *adv.* —*adj.* 1 causing or likely to cause death; fatal: *a deadly wound.* See **fatal** for synonym study. 2 like death; deathly: *deadly stillness.* 3 aiming or tending to kill or destroy; implacable: *deadly enemies.* 4 causing death of the soul: *deadly sins.* 5 INFORMAL. extreme; intense. 6 dull; boring: *a deadly lecture.* 7 absolutely accurate: *a deadly shot.* —*adv.* 1 like death; deathly: *deadly pale.* 2 extremely; intensely. 3 as if dead. **—dead′li ness,** *n.*

deadly nightshade, belladonna.

deadly sins, pride, covetousness, lust, anger, gluttony, envy, and sloth.

dead march, a funeral march.

dead pan (ded′pan′), *n., adj., adv., v.,* **-panned, -pan ning.** SLANG. —*n.* an expressionless face, person, or manner. —*adj.* showing no expression or feeling. —*adv.* in a deadpan manner. —*v.t., v.i.* act or perform in a deadpan manner.

dead reckoning, 1 calculation of the position of a ship or aircraft without observations of the sun, stars, etc., by using a compass and studying the navigator's record. 2 calculation of one's location by natural landmarks.

Dead Sea, salt lake between Israel and Jordan. 46 mi. long; 10 mi. wide. Its surface is the lowest on earth, almost 1300 ft. below sea level.

Dead Sea Scrolls, collection of ancient scrolls discovered in several caves near the Dead Sea. They contain the oldest known copies of most of the books of the Bible.

dead weight, 1 the weight of anything lifeless, rigid, and unyielding. 2 a very great or oppressive burden.

dead wood (ded′wu̇d′), *n.* 1 dead branches or trees. 2 useless people or things.

deaf (def), *adj.* 1 not able to hear. 2 not able to hear well. 3 not willing to hear; heedless: *The miser was deaf to all requests for money.* [Old English *dēaf*] **—deaf′ly,** *adv.* **—deaf′ness,** *n.*

deaf en (def′ən), *v.t.* 1 make deaf. 2 stun with noise. 3 drown out by a louder sound. 4 make soundproof; deaden. **—deaf′en ing ly,** *adv.*

deaf-mute (def′myüt′), *n.* person who is unable to hear and speak, usually because he has been deaf from birth or from childhood.

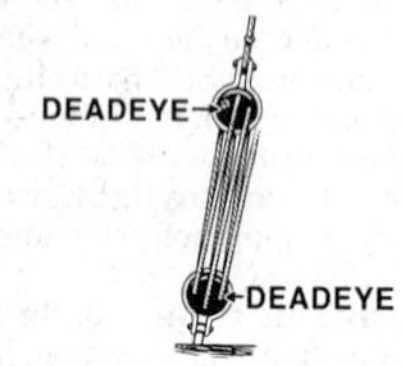

deal[1] (dēl), *v.,* **dealt, deal ing,** *n.* —*v.i.* 1 have to do: *Arithmetic deals with numbers.* 2 act; behave: *deal fairly with someone.* 3 occupy oneself; take action: *The courts deal with those who break the laws.* 4 carry on a business; buy and sell: *A butcher deals in meat.* 5 distribute playing cards: *It's your turn to deal.* -*v.t.* 1 give or deliver: *One fighter dealt the other a blow.* 2 give out among several: distribute. 3 distribute (playing cards).
—*n.* 1 INFORMAL. a business arrangement; bargain. 2 INFORMAL. distribution; arrangement; plan: *a new deal, a square deal.* 3 a secret or underhanded agreement. 4 in card playing: **a** the distribution of cards. **b** a player's turn to deal. **c** time during which one deal of cards is being played. **d** the cards held by the player; hand. 5 quantity; amount: *I took a deal of trouble.* 6 **a good deal** or **a great deal, a** a large part, portion or amount: *spend a great deal of money on entertainment.* **b** to a great extent or degree; much: *You are a good deal smarter than your friends.*
[Old English *dǣlan* < *dǣl* part, amount]

deal[2] (dēl), *n.* 1 board of pine or fir wood. 2 pine or fir wood. —*adj.* made of deal. [< Middle Low German or Middle Dutch *dele*]

deal er (dē′lər), *n.* 1 person who makes his living by buying and selling. 2 person who distributes the playing cards in a card game.

deal ing (dē′ling), *n.* 1 way of doing business. 2 way of acting; behavior toward others; conduct: *fair dealing.* 3 distribution of playing cards, etc. 4 **dealings,** *pl.* **a** business relations. **b** friendly relations.

dealt (delt), *v.* pt. and pp. of **deal**[1].

de am i nate (dē am′ə nāt), *v.t.,* **-nat ed, -nat ing.** alter (a compound) by removing the amino group $—NH_2$. **—de am′i na′tion,** *n.*

dean (dēn), *n.* 1 member of the faculty of a school, college, or university who has charge of the behavior or studies of the students. 2 head of a division or school in a college or university: *the dean of the law school.* 3 a high official of a church. A dean is often in charge of a cathedral. 4 member who has belonged to a group longest. [< Old French *deien* < Late Latin *decanus* master of ten < Latin *decem* ten]

dean er y (dē′nər ē), *n., pl.* **-er ies.** 1 position or authority of a dean. 2 residence or district of a dean.

dean ship (dēn′ship), *n.* position, office, or rank of a dean.

dear (dir), *adj.* 1 much loved; precious; beloved. 2 much valued; highly esteemed. *Dear* is used as a form of polite address at the beginning of letters: *Dear Sir.* 3 high in price; costly; expensive. See **expensive** for synonym study. —*n.* dear one; darling. —*adv.* 1 at a high price; very much; much. 2 with affection; fondly. —*interj.* exclamation of surprise, trouble, regret, etc. [Old English *dēore*] **—dear′ly,** *adv.* **—dear′ness,** *n.*

Dear born (dir′bərn, dir′bôrn), *n.* city in SE Michigan, near Detroit. 104,000.

Dearborn Heights, city in SE Michigan, near Detroit. 80,000.

dear ie (dir′ē), *n.* deary.

dearth (dėrth), *n.* 1 too small a supply; great scarcity or lack. See **scarcity** for synonym study. 2 scarcity of food; famine. [Middle English *derthe*]

dear y (dir′ē), *n., pl.* **dear ies.** INFORMAL. darling. Also, **dearie.**

death (deth), *n.* 1 act or fact of dying; the ending of any form of life in people, animals, or plants. 2 Often, **Death.** power that destroys life, often represented as a skeleton dressed in black and carrying a scythe. 3 any ending that is like dying: *the death of an empire.* 4 condition of being dead. 5 any condition like being dead. 6 cause of dying. 7 bloodshed; murder. 8 **at death's door,** almost dead; dying. 9 **put to death, a** kill or execute. **b** killed. 10 **to death,** beyond endurance; excessively: *She was bored to death.* [Old English *dēath*] **—death′like′,** *adj.*

death bed (deth′bed′), *n.* 1 bed on which a person dies. 2 the last hours of life. —*adj.* during the last hours of life: *The murderer made a deathbed confession.*

death blow (deth′blō′), *n.* 1 blow that kills. 2 thing that puts an end (to something).

death cup, a very poisonous mushroom that has a cuplike enlargement at the base of the stem.

death duty, BRITISH. inheritance tax.

death less (deth′lis), *adj.* never dying; living forever; immortal; eternal. **—death′less ly,** *adv.* **—death′less ness,** *n.*

death ly (deth′lē), *adj.* 1 like death: *a deathly pallor.* 2 causing death; deadly. —*adv.* 1 like death. 2 extremely: *deathly ill.*

death mask, a clay, wax, or plaster likeness of a person's face made from a cast taken after his death.

death rate, proportion of the number of deaths per year to the total population or to some other stated number.

death's-head (deths′hed′), *n.* a human skull, used as a symbol of death.

Death Valley, valley in E California, the lowest land in the Western Hemisphere. 276 ft. below sea level.

death watch (deth′woch′, deth′wôch′), *n.* 1 vigil kept beside a dying or dead person.

2 guard for a person about to be put to death. 3 any of several insects that make a ticking sound once believed to be an omen of death.

de ba cle (dā bä′kəl, di bak′əl), *n.* 1 a sudden downfall or collapse; disaster; overthrow. 2 the breaking up of ice in a river. 3 a violent rush of waters carrying debris. [< French *débâcle*]

de bar (di bär′), *v.t.,* **-barred, -bar ring.** bar out; shut out; prevent; prohibit. **—de bar′ment,** *n.*

de bark[1] (di bärk′), *v.i., v.t.* go or put ashore from a ship; disembark; land. [< French *débarquer* < *dé-* parting from + *barque* bark[3]] **—de′bar ka′tion,** *n.*

de bark[2] (dē bärk′), *v.t.* remove bark from (a tree). **—de bark′er,** *n.*

de base (di bās′), *v.t.,* **-based, -bas ing.** make low or lower; lessen the value of: *debase silver money by increasing the amount of alloy in it, debase oneself by one's evil actions.* **—de base′ment,** *n.* **—de bas′er,** *n.*

de bat a ble (di bā′tə bəl), *adj.* 1 capable of being debated; open to debate: *a debatable statement. Your conclusions are debatable.* 2 not decided; in dispute.

de bate (di bāt′), *v.,* **-bat ed, -bat ing,** *n.* *—v.t.* 1 discuss reasons for and against; deliberate. See **discuss** for synonym study. 2 argue about (a question, topic, etc.) in a public meeting. 3 think over in one's mind; consider: *I am debating buying a camera.* *—n.* 1 discussion of reasons for and against; argument: *There has been much debate as to which person should be class treasurer.* 2 a public argument for and against a question in a meeting. A formal debate is a contest between two sides to see which one has more skill in speaking and reasoning. [< Old French *debatre* < Latin *de-* completely + *battuere* to beat] **—de bat′er,** *n.*

de bauch (di bôch′), *v.t.* lead away from duty, virtue, or morality; corrupt or seduce. *—v.i.* indulge excessively in sensual pleasures, eating, drinking, etc. *—n.* 1 period or bout of excessive indulgence in sensual pleasures; excess in eating, drinking, etc. 2 debauchery. [< French *débaucher* entice from duty] **—de bauch′er,** *n.*

deb au chee (deb′ô chē′, deb′ô shē′), *n.* person who indulges himself excessively in sensual pleasures.

de bauch er y (di bô′chər ē), *n., pl.* **-er ies.** 1 excessive indulgence in sensual pleasures. 2 departure from duty, virtue, or morality; corruption.

de beak (dē bēk′), *v.t.* remove the beak of (a bird).

de ben ture (di ben′chər), *n.* 1 a written acknowledgment of a debt. 2 bond issued by a company acknowledging indebtedness for a sum on which interest is due until the principal is paid. [< Latin *debentur* there are owing < *debere* owe]

de bil i tate (di bil′ə tāt), *v.t.,* **-tat ed, -tat ing.** make weak or feeble; weaken: *A hot, wet climate can debilitate those who are not used to it.* See **weaken** for synonym study. **—de bil′i ta′tion,** *n.*

de bil i ty (di bil′ə tē), *n., pl.* **-ties.** a being weak; weakness; feebleness. [< Latin *debilitatem* < *debilis* weak]

deb it (deb′it), *n.* 1 entry of something owed in an account. 2 the left-hand side of an account where such entries are made. *—v.t.* 1 charge with or as a debt: *debit an account $500.* 2 enter on the debit side of an account. [< Latin *debitum.* Doublet of DEBT.]

deb o nair or **deb o naire** (deb′ə ner′, deb′ə nar′), *adj.* pleasant, courteous, and gay. [< Old French *debonaire* < *de bon aire* of good disposition] **—deb′o nair′ly,** *adv.* **—deb′o nair′ness,** *n.*

de bouch (di büsh′), *v.i.* 1 come out from a narrow or confined place into open country: *The soldiers debouched from the valley into the plain.* 2 come out; emerge. [< French *déboucher*] **—de bouch′ment,** *n.*

De bre cen (deb′re tsen), *n.* city in E Hungary. 155,000.

de brief (dē brēf′), *v.t.* question (an emissary, pilot, intelligence officer, etc.) on his return from a mission.

de bris or **dé bris** (də brē′, dā′brē′; *British* deb′rē′), *n.* 1 the remains of anything broken down or destroyed; ruins; rubbish: *the debris from an explosion.* 2 (in geology) a mass of large fragments worn away from rock: *the debris left by a glacier.* [< French *débris*]

Debs (debz), *n.* **Eugene Victor,** 1855-1926, American socialist leader.

debt (det), *n.* 1 something owed to another. 2 liability or obligation to pay or render something; indebtedness: *be in debt to the grocer, get out of debt.* 3 a sin; trespass. [< Old French *dete* < Latin *debitum* (thing) owed < *debere* originally, keep from having < *de-* away + *habere* have. Doublet of DEBIT.]

debt or (det′ər), *n.* person who owes something to another.

de bunk (di bungk′), INFORMAL. *—v.t.* 1 remove nonsense or sentimentality from. 2 prove false or incorrect; refute: *debunk a theory.* **—de bunk′er,** *n.*

De bus sy (də byü′sē; *French* də by sē′), *n.* **Claude A.,** 1862-1918, French composer.

de but or **dé but** (dā′byü, dā byü′), *n.* 1 a first public appearance: *a young actor's debut on the stage.* 2 the first formal appearance of a young woman in society. [< French *début*]

deb u tante or **dé bu tante** (deb′yə tänt, deb′yə tant, deb′yə tänt′), *n.* 1 a young woman during her first season in society. 2 woman making a debut. [< French *débutante*]

dec., 1 deceased. 2 decimeter.

Dec., December.

deca-, *combining form.* ten: *Decagram = ten grams.* [< Greek *deka-* < *deka*]

dec ade (dek′ād), *n.* 1 period of ten years. 2 group, set, or series of ten. [< Middle French *décade,* ultimately < Greek *deka* ten]

dec a dence (dek′ə dəns, di kād′ns), *n.* a falling off; growing worse; decline; decay: *The decadence of morals was one of the causes of the fall of Rome.* [< Middle French *décadence* < Medieval Latin *decadentia* < Latin *de-* + *cadere* to fall]

dec a dent (dek′ə dənt, di kād′nt), *adj.* falling off; growing worse; declining; decaying. *—n.* a decadent person. **—dec′a dent ly,** *adv.*

dec a gon (dek′ə gon), *n.* a plane figure having 10 angles and 10 sides. [< Greek *decagōnon* < *deka* ten + *gōnia* corner, angle]

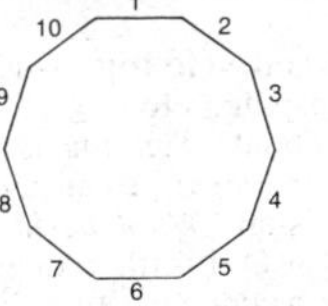

regular decagon

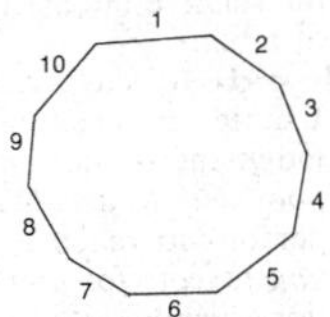

irregular decagon

hat, āge, fär; let, ēqual, tėrm;
it, īce; hot, ōpen, ôrder;
oil, out; cup, pu̇t, rüle;
ch, child; ng, long; sh, she;
th, thin; ᴛʜ, then; zh, measure;

ə represents *a* in about, *e* in taken, *i* in pencil, *o* in lemon, *u* in circus.

< = from, derived from, taken from.

dec a gram (dek′ə gram), *n.* unit of mass equal to 10 grams. See **measure** for table. Also, **dekagram.**

dec a gramme (dek′ə gram), *n.* BRITISH. decagram.

dec a he dron (dek′ə hē′drən), *n., pl.* **-drons, -dra** (-drə). a solid figure having ten flat surfaces. [< Greek *deka* ten + *hedra* base]

de cal (dē′kal, di kal′), *n.* design or picture to be transferred to glass, wood, etc., treated so that it will stick fast. [< *decal(comania)*]

de cal ci fy (dē kal′sə fī), *v.t.,* **-fied, -fy ing.** to remove lime or calcium from (bone, etc.). **—de cal′ci fi ca′tion,** *n.*

de cal co ma ni a (di kal′kə mā′nē ə), *n.* 1 decal. 2 process of decorating glass, wood, etc., by applying decals. [< French *décalcomanie* < *décalquer* transfer a tracing + *manie* mania]

dec a li ter (dek′ə lē′tər), *n.* unit of volume equal to 10 liters. See **measure** for table. Also, **dekaliter.**

dec a li tre (dek′ə lē′tər), *n.* BRITISH. decaliter.

Dec a logue or **Dec a log** (dek′ə lôg, dek′ə log), *n.* 1 (in the Bible) the Ten Commandments. 2 **decalogue** or **decalog,** any set of ten commandments or rules. [< Greek *dekalogos* < *deka* ten + *logos* word]

dec a me ter (dek′ə mē′tər), *n.* unit of length equal to 10 meters. See **measure** for table. Also, **dekameter.**

dec a me tre (dek′ə mē′tər), *n.* BRITISH. decameter.

de camp (di kamp′), *v.i.* 1 leave quickly and secretly; run away; flee: *The stranger decamped during the night, taking two horses.* 2 leave a camp; break camp. **—de camp′ment,** *n.*

de cant (di kant′), *v.t.* 1 pour off (liquor or a solution) gently without disturbing the sediment. 2 pour from one container to another. [< Medieval Latin *decanthare* < Latin *de-* + *canthus, cantus* edge]

de cant er (di kan′tər), *n.* a glass bottle with a stopper, used for serving wine or liquor.

de cap i tate (di kap′ə tāt), *v.t.,* **-tat ed, -tat ing.** cut off the head of; behead. [< Late Latin *decapitatum* beheaded < Latin *de-* + *capitem* head] **—de cap′i ta′tion,** *n.*

dec a pod (dek′ə pod), *n.* 1 any of an order of crustaceans having ten legs or arms, such as a lobster, crab, or crayfish. 2 any of a suborder of mollusks having ten arms or tentacles, such as a squid or cuttlefish. *—adj.* having ten legs, arms, or tentacles. [< Greek *deka* ten + *pous, podos* foot]

dec a stere (dek′ə stir), *n.* unit of volume equal to 10 steres, or 13.08 cubic yards. See **measure** for table. Also, **dekastere.**

dec a syl lab ic (dek′ə sə lab′ik), *adj.* having ten syllables: *a decasyllabic line.* *—n.* a decasyllable.

dec a syl la ble (dek′ə sil′ə bəl), *n.* a line of poetry having ten syllables.

de cath lon (di kath′lon), *n.* a track-and-field contest with ten different events held during two days, including racing, jumping, throwing the javelin, etc. The person who scores the most points for all ten parts is the winner. [< *deca-* ten + Greek *athlon* contest]

De ca tur (di kā′tər), *n.* 1 **Stephen,** 1779-1820, American naval officer. 2 city in central Illinois. 90,000.

de cay (di kā′), *v.i.* 1 become rotten; rot: *The old fruits and vegetables decayed.* See synonym study below. 2 grow less in power, strength, wealth, beauty, etc.: *The power of the Roman Empire was decaying at the time of Nero.* 3 (of radioactive substances) undergo transformation through the disintegration of component nuclei. 4 (of an orbiting earth satellite) slow down because of atmospheric friction. *—n.* 1 a rotting: *tooth decay.* 2 loss of power, strength, wealth, beauty, etc. 3 the transformation of a radioactive substance through the disintegration of its component nuclei. 4 reduction in speed of an orbiting earth satellite, caused by atmospheric friction. [< Old French *decair* < *de-* + *cair* to fall]

Syn. *v.i.* 1 **Decay, rot, decompose** mean to change from a good or healthy condition to a bad one. **Decay** emphasizes the idea of changing little by little through natural processes: *Tooth decay is accelerated by failure to brush the teeth.* **Rot,** more emphatic, emphasizes the idea of spoiling, and applies especially to plant and animal matter: *The fruit rotted on the vines.* **Decompose** emphasizes the idea of breaking down into original parts, by natural or chemical processes: *Bodies decompose after death.*

Dec can (dek′ən, de kan′), *n.* 1 peninsula that constitutes the S part of India. 2 plateau on this peninsula.

de cease (di sēs′), *n., v.,* **-ceased, -ceas ing.** *—n.* act or fact of dying; death. *—v.i.* die. [< Latin *decessus* < *decedere* depart < *de-* away + *cedere* go]

de ceased (di sēst′), *adj.* no longer living; dead. See **dead** for synonym study. *—n.* **the deceased,** a (particular) dead person or persons.

de ce dent (di sēd′nt), *n.* (in law) a dead person. [< Latin *decedentem*]

de ceit (di sēt′), *n.* 1 a making a person believe as true something that is false; deceiving, lying, or cheating. See synonym study below. 2 a dishonest trick; lie spoken or acted. 3 deceitfulness. [< Old French *deceite* < *deceveir.* See DECEIVE.]

Syn. 1 **Deceit, deception, guile** mean false or misleading representation. **Deceit** implies concealing or twisting the truth in order to mislead and gain advantage over others: *She was truthful and without deceit.* **Deception** applies to the act that gives a false or wrong idea, but does not always suggest a dishonest purpose: *A magician uses deception.* **Guile** suggests craftiness and slyness and deception by means of trickery: *He got what he wanted by guile, not work.*

de ceit ful (di sēt′fəl), *adj.* 1 ready or willing to deceive. 2 meant to deceive; deceiving; misleading. **—de ceit′ful ly,** *adv.* **—de ceit′ful ness,** *n.*

de ceive (di sēv′), *v.,* **-ceived, -ceiv ing.** *—v.t.* make (a person) believe as true something that is false; mislead. *—v.i.* use deceit; lie. [< Old French *deceveir* < Latin *decipere* ensnare, catch < *de-* + *capere* take] **—de ceiv′a ble,** *adj.* **—de ceiv′er,** *n.* **—deceiv′ing ly,** *adv.*

de cel e rate (dē sel′ə rāt′), *v.t., v.i.,* **-rat ed, -rat ing.** decrease the velocity (of); slow down. **—de cel′e ra′tion,** *n.* **—de cel′e ra′tor,** *n.*

De cem ber (di sem′bər), *n.* the 12th and last month of the year. It has 31 days. [< Latin < *decem* ten; because it was the tenth month in the early Roman calendar]

de cem vir (di sem′vər), *n., pl.* **-virs, -vir i** (-və rī′). 1 member of a council of ten magistrates in ancient Rome. 2 member of a council of ten men. [< Latin, singular of *decemviri* < *decem* ten + *viri* men]

de cem vir ate (di sem′vər it, di sem′və rāt′), *n.* 1 office or government of decemvirs. 2 council of decemvirs.

de cen cy (dē′sn sē), *n., pl.* **-cies.** 1 condition or quality of being decent. 2 propriety of behavior; conforming to the standard of good taste; decorum. 3 proper regard for modesty or delicacy; respectability. 4 **decencies,** *pl.* **a** suitable acts; proper observances. **b** things required for a proper standard of living.

de cen ni al (di sen′ē əl), *adj.* 1 of or for ten years. 2 happening every ten years. *—n.* a tenth anniversary or its celebration. [< Latin *decennium* decade < *decem* ten + *annus* year] **—de cen′ni al ly,** *adv.*

de cent (dē′snt), *adj.* 1 proper and right; suitable: *It is not decent to laugh at another's troubles.* 2 modest; free from vulgarity; not obscene. 3 having a good reputation; respectable: *decent people.* 4 good enough; fairly good: *I get decent marks at school.* 5 suitable to one's position; adequate: *She earns a decent living.* 6 not severe; rather kind: *The teacher was very decent to excuse my absence.* 7 dressed; not naked: *"Are you decent?" my sister called through the door.* [< Latin *decentem* becoming, fitting] **—de′cent ly,** *adv.* **—de′cent ness,** *n.*

de cen tral ize (dē sen′trə līz), *v.t.,* **-ized, -iz ing.** 1 spread or distribute (authority, power, etc.) among smaller groups or local governments. 2 reorganize (an industry, school system, etc.) into smaller units of management and operation. **—de cen′tral i za′tion,** *n.*

de cep tion (di sep′shən), *n.* 1 a deceiving. See **deceit** for synonym study. 2 a being deceived. 3 thing that deceives; illusion. 4 trick meant to deceive; fraud; sham; hoax; ruse. [< Late Latin *deceptionem* < Latin *decipere.* See DECEIVE.]

de cep tive (di sep′tiv), *adj.* 1 tending to deceive or mislead: *He played the piano with deceptive ease.* 2 meant to deceive. **—de cep′tive ly,** *adv.* **—de cep′tive ness,** *n.*

deci-, *combining form.* one tenth of: *Decigram = one tenth of a gram.* [< Latin *decimus* tenth < *decem* ten]

dec i bel (des′ə bəl), *n.* unit for measuring the relative intensity of sounds, equal to $^1/_{10}$ of a bel.

de cide (di sīd′), *v.,* **-cid ed, -cid ing.** *—v.t.* 1 settle (a question, dispute, etc.); give a judgment or decision about: *Fighting is a poor way to decide an argument.* 2 cause (a person) to reach a decision: *What decided you to vote for him?* *—v.i.* 1 settle a question, dispute, etc.; give a judgment or decision: *The court decided in favor of the defendant.* 2 make up one's mind; resolve. See synonym study below. [< Latin *decidere* cut off < *de-* + *caedere* to cut] **—de cid′a ble,** *adj.* **—de cid′er,** *n.*

Syn. *v.i.* 2 **Decide, determine, resolve** mean to make up one's mind regarding a course of action. **Decide** emphasizes the idea of thinking over the considerations for or against before reaching a conclusion: *I decided to take the position at the bank.* **Determine** suggests fixing one's mind firmly on a course of action: *I am determined to make a success of it.* **Resolve** further implies that one has promised to oneself to do or not to do something: *I resolved to do good work.*

de cid ed (di sī′did), *adj.* 1 clear or definite; unquestionable: *His height gave the basketball player a decided advantage.* 2 firm; determined; resolute: *a decided wish to go to college.* **—de cid′ed ness,** *n.*

de cid ed ly (di sī′did lē), *adv.* 1 without question; clearly; definitely. 2 in a determined manner; firmly.

de cid u ous (di sij′ü əs), *adj.* 1 shedding leaves annually. Maples, elms, and most oaks are deciduous trees. 2 falling off at a particular season or stage of growth: *deciduous leaves, deciduous horns, deciduous teeth.* [< Latin *deciduus* < *decidere* fall off < *de-* + *cadere* to fall] **—de cid′u ous ly,** *adv.* **—de cid′u ous ness,** *n.*

dec i gram (des′ə gram), *n.* unit of mass equal to one tenth of a gram. See **measure** for table.

dec i gramme (des′ə gram), *n.* BRITISH. decigram.

dec i li ter (des′ə lē′tər), *n.* unit of volume equal to one tenth of a liter. See **measure** for table.

dec i li tre (des′ə lē′tər), *n.* BRITISH. deciliter.

de cil lion (di sil′yən), *n.* 1 (in the United States, Canada, and France) 1 with 33 zeros following it. 2 (in Great Britain and Germany) 1 with 60 zeros following it. [< *deci-* + *(mi)llion*]

dec i mal (des′ə məl), *n.* 1 a decimal fraction. 2 number containing a decimal fraction. EXAMPLES: 75.24, 3.062, .7, .091. *—adj.* based upon ten or tenths; proceeding by tens. [< Latin *decimus* tenth] **—dec′i mal ly,** *adv.*

decimal fraction, fraction whose denominator is ten or a multiple of ten, expressed by placing a decimal point to the left of the numerator. EXAMPLES: .04 = $^4/_{100}$, .2 = $^2/_{10}$.

decimal point, period placed before a decimal fraction, as in 2.03, .623.

decimal system, system of numeration which is based on units of 10.

dec i mate (des′ə māt), *v.t.,* **-mat ed, -mat ing.** 1 destroy much of; kill a large part of: *War had decimated the tribe.* 2 take or destroy one tenth of. [< Latin *decimatum* decimated < *decem* ten] **—dec′i ma′tion,** *n.* **—dec′i ma′tor,** *n.*

dec i me ter (des′ə mē′tər), *n.* unit of length equal to one tenth of a meter. See **measure** for table.

dec i me tre (des′ə mē′tər), *n.* BRITISH. decimeter.

de ci pher (di sī′fər), *v.t.* 1 make out the meaning of (something that is not clear): *decipher someone's handwriting, decipher a mystery.* 2 interpret (secret writing) by using a key; change (something in cipher or code) to ordinary language; decode. **—de ci′pher a ble,** *adj.* **—de ci′pher ment,** *n.*

hat, āge, fär; let, ēqual, tėrm;
it, īce; hot, ōpen, ôrder;
oil, out; cup, pu̇t, rüle;
ch, child; ng, long; sh, she;
th, thin; TH, then; zh, measure;

ə represents *a* in about, *e* in taken, *i* in pencil, *o* in lemon, *u* in circus.

< = from, derived from, taken from.

de ci sion (di sizh′ən), *n.* 1 a making up of one's mind; resolution. 2 a settling of a question, dispute, etc.; a giving judgment. 3 judgment reached or given; verdict: *The jury brought in a decision of not guilty.* 4 firmness and determination: *She is a woman of decision who makes up her mind what to do and then does it.* [< Latin *decisionem* < *decidere.* See DECIDE.]

de ci sive (di sī′siv), *adj.* 1 having or giving a clear result; settling something beyond question or doubt: *The Battle of Saratoga was a decisive victory for the Americans.* 2 having or showing decision; resolute: *a decisive answer.* **—de ci′sive ly,** *adv.* **—de ci′sive ness,** *n.*

dec i stere (des′ə stir), *n.* unit of volume equal to one tenth of a stere, or .1308 cubic yard. See **measure** for table.

deck (dek), *n.* 1 one of the floors or platforms extending from side to side and often from end to end of a ship. Often the upper deck has no roof over it. 2 part or floor resembling this: *the deck of an airplane.* 3 a pack of playing cards. 4 **on deck, a** ready to do something. **b** (in baseball) next at bat. *—v.t.* 1 clothe in rich garments; array. 2 adorn; decorate: *deck the halls with holly.* 3 provide with a deck. [< Middle Dutch *dec* roof < *decken* to cover]

deck chair, a light folding chair with a canvas cover and often foot and arm rests.

deck hand (dek′hand′), *n.* sailor who works on deck; a common sailor.

deck le (dek′əl), *n.* deckle edge. [< German *Deckel*]

deckle edge, 1 the rough edge of untrimmed paper. 2 an imitation of it. **deck′le-edged′,** *adj.*

de claim (di klām′), *v.i.* 1 recite in public; make a formal speech. 2 speak in a loud and emotional manner; speak or write for effect. [< Latin *declamare* < *de-* + *clamare* to cry] **—de claim′er,** *n.*

dec la ma tion (dek′lə mā′shən), *n.* 1 act or art of declaiming; making formal speeches. 2 a formal speech or selection of poetry, prose, etc., for reciting. 3 loud and emotional talk.

de clam a to ry (di klam′ə tôr′ē, di klam′ə tōr′ē), *adj.* 1 having to do with declamation. 2 loud and emotional.

dec la ra tion (dek′lə rā′shən), *n.* 1 act of declaring: *a declaration of love.* 2 thing declared; open or public statement. 3 document containing a declaration. 4 statement of goods, etc., for taxation or customs. 5 (in bridge) a bid, especially the winning bid.

Declaration of Independence, the public statement adopted by the Second Continental Congress on July 4, 1776, in which the American colonies declared themselves free and independent of Great Britain.

de clar a tive (di klar′ə tiv), *adj.* making a statement; explaining. "I'm eating" and "The dog has four legs" are declarative sentences.

de clar a to ry (di klar′ə tôr′ē, di klar′ə tōr′ē), *adj.* 1 declarative. 2 that explains the law or the legal rights of parties in a dispute: *a declaratory judgment.*

de clare (di kler′, di klar′), *v.,* **-clared, -clar ing.** *—v.t.* 1 announce publicly or formally; make known; proclaim: *Congress has the power to declare war. That company has just declared a dividend on its stock.* See **announce** for synonym study. 2 say openly; state strongly; affirm: *I declare the story to be false.* See synonym study below. 3 make a statement of (goods, etc.) for taxation or customs. 4 (in bridge) announce (what suit) will be played as trumps. *—v.i.* make a declaration; proclaim (oneself): *The students declared themselves against cheating.* [< Latin *declarare* < *de-* + *clarare* make clear < *clarus* clear] **—de clar′er,** *n.*

Syn. *v.t.* 2 **Declare, assert** mean to state positively. **Declare** means to state firmly and openly: *The Continental Congress declared that the colonies were free and independent.* **Assert** means to state vigorously, but without proof and even in spite of proof that one is wrong: *You assert that you were not there, but ten people saw you.*

de clas si fy (dē klas′ə fī), *v.t.,* **-fied, -fy ing.** remove (documents, codes, etc.) from the list of restricted, confidential, or secret information.

de clen sion (di klen′shən), *n.* 1 in grammar: **a** the giving of the different forms of nouns, pronouns, and adjectives according to their case, number, and gender, usually in a given order, so far as such variations occur in the language to which the words belong. **b** the giving of variant forms of a word for case only. The declension of *who* is: nominative case, *who;* possessive case, *whose;* objective case, *whom.* **c** group of words whose endings for the different cases, etc., are alike. 2 a downward movement, bend, or slope. 3 a sinking into a lower or inferior condition; decline. 4 deviation from a standard. 5 a polite refusal. [ultimately < Latin *declinationem* < *declinare.* See DECLINE.]

de clen sion al (di klen′shə nəl), *adj.* of or belonging to declension.

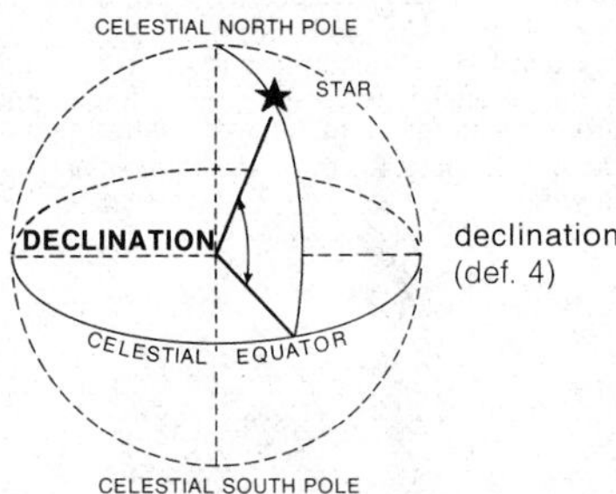

declination (def. 4)

dec li na tion (dek′lə nā′shən), *n.* 1 a downward bend or slope. 2 a polite refusal. 3 deviation of the needle of a compass from true north. 4 (in astronomy) the angular distance of a star, planet, etc., from the celestial equator. The declination of a star is used to locate its north or south position in the heavens.

de cline (di klīn′), *v.,* **-clined, -clin ing,** *n.* *—v.t.* 1 turn away from doing; refuse (to do something): *She declined to do as she was told.* See **refuse** for synonym study. 2 refuse politely: *He declined my offer of help.* 3 cause to bend or slope down. 4 give the different cases or case endings of (a noun, pronoun, or adjective); inflect. *—v.i.* 1 grow less in strength, power, value, etc.; grow worse; decay; deteriorate; degenerate: *Great nations have risen and declined.* 2 refuse something politely. 3 bend or slope down: *The hill declines to a fertile valley.* *—n.* 1 a losing of power, strength, value, etc.; growing worse; decay; deterioration: *the decline of the Roman Empire.* 2 a falling to a lower level; sinking: *a decline in prices.* 3 the last part of anything: *in the decline of a person's life.* 4 a wasting disease; consumption; tuberculosis of the lungs. 5 a downward incline or slope; declivity. [< Latin *declinare* < *de-* from + *clinare* to bend] **—de clin′a ble,** *adj.*

de cliv i ty (di kliv′ə tē), *n., pl.* **-ties.** a downward slope. [< Latin *declivitatem* < *declivis* sloping downward < *de-* + *clivus* slope]

de coct (di kokt′), *v.t.* extract desired substances from (herbs, etc.) by boiling. [< Latin *decoctum* cooked down < *de-* + *coquere* to cook]

de coc tion (di kok′shən), *n.* 1 act of boiling to extract some desired substance. 2 preparation made by boiling a substance in water or other liquid; extract obtained by boiling.

de code (dē kōd′), *v.t.,* **-cod ed, -cod ing.** translate (secret writing) from code into ordinary language. **—de cod′er,** *n.*

dé colle tage (dā′kol täzh′, dā′ko lə täzh′), *n.* 1 neck of a dress cut low so as to leave the neck and shoulders exposed. 2 a dress cut in this way. [< French]

dé colle té (dā′kol tā′, dā′ko lə tā′), *adj.* 1 low-necked. 2 wearing a low-necked gown. [< French]

de col or ize (dē kul′ə rīz′), *v.t.,* **-ized, -iz ing.** remove the color of.

de com mis sion (dē′kə mish′ən), *v.t.* take out of active service; retire: *decommission a ship.*

de com pose (dē′kəm pōz′), *v.,* **-posed, -pos ing.** *—v.t.* 1 separate (a substance) into what it is made of: *The prism decomposed the sunlight into its various colors.* 2 rot; decay. See **decay** for synonym study. *—v.i.* 1 (of a substance) become separated into its parts. 2 become rotten; decay.

de com po si tion (dē′kom pə zish′ən), *n.* 1 act or process of decomposing. 2 decay; rot.

de com press (dē′kəm pres′), *v.t.* 1 remove pressure from. 2 lessen the pressure of air on. **—de′com pres′sion,** *n.*

de con ges tant (dē′kən jes′tənt), *n.* drug used to relieve nasal congestion.

de con tam i nate (dē′kən tam′ə nāt), *v.t.,* **-nat ed, -nat ing.** 1 make free from poison gas or harmful radioactive agents. 2 free from any sort of contamination. **—de′con tam′i na′tion,** *n.*

de con trol (dē′kən trōl′), *v.,* **-trolled, -trol ling,** *n.* *—v.t.* remove controls from. *—n.* a removing of controls.

dé cor (dā kôr′), *n.* 1 decoration. 2 the overall arrangement of the decoration and furnishings of a room, house, store, office, etc. 3 scenery and furnishings on a stage setting. [< French]

dec o rate (dek′ə rāt′), *v.t.,* **-rat ed, -rat ing.** 1 improve by providing with something ornamental or becoming; adorn. See synonym study below. 2 paint or paper (a room, etc.). 3 give a medal, ribbon, or badge to (a person) as an honor. [< Latin *decoratum* adorned < *decorum* adornment]

Syn. 1 **Decorate, ornament, adorn** mean to add something to give or increase beauty. **Decorate** means to trim with flowers, evergreens, trinkets, etc., to add color, variety, or a festive appearance: *We decorated the Christmas tree.* **Ornament** suggests adding, often permanently, something which especially suits a thing and adds to its general effect and beauty: *Stained glass windows ornament the church.* **Adorn** suggests adding something which is beautiful itself and therefore increases the beauty of a thing or person: *She adorned her hair with flowers.*

dec o ra tion (dek′ə rā′shən), *n.* 1 thing used to decorate; ornament. 2 medal, ribbon, or badge given as an honor. 3 act or process of decorating.

Decoration Day, Memorial Day.

dec o ra tive (dek′ə rā′tiv, dek′rə tiv), *adj.* helping to adorn; ornamental; decorating. **—dec′o ra′tive ly,** *adv.* **—dec′o ra′tive ness,** *n.*

dec o ra tor (dek′ə rā′tər), *n.* 1 person who decorates. 2 interior decorator. 3 person whose work is painting or papering rooms, etc.

dec or ous (dek′ər əs, di kôr′əs, di kōr′əs), *adj.* acting properly; in good taste; well-behaved; dignified. [< Latin *decorus* < *decor* seemliness, comeliness] **—dec′or ous ly,** *adv.* **—dec′or ous ness,** *n.*

de co rum (di kôr′əm, di kōr′əm), *n.* 1 proper behavior; good taste in conduct, speech, dress, etc.: *act with decorum, observe decorum at church.* 2 observance or requirement of polite society: *a meeting completely lacking in decorum.* [< Latin, (that which is) seemly < *decor* seemliness]

de coy (*v.* di koi′; *n.* dē′koi, di koi′), *v.t.* 1 lure (wild birds, animals, etc.) into a trap or near the hunter. 2 lead or tempt (a person) into danger by trickery; entice. *—n.* 1 an artificial bird used to lure birds into a trap or near the hunter. 2 bird or other animal trained to lure others of its kind into a trap. 3 any person or thing used to lead or tempt into danger; lure; bait. [probably < Dutch *de kooi* the cage] **—de coy′er,** *n.*

de crease (*v.* di krēs′; *n.* dē′krēs, di krēs′), *v.,* **-creased, -creas ing,** *n.* *—v.t., v.i.* make or become less; lessen: *Decrease the dose of medicine as you feel better. Hunger decreases as one eats.* See synonym study below. *—n.* 1 a growing less; lessening: *Toward night there was a decrease of heat.* 2 amount by which a thing becomes less or is made less. 3 **on the decrease,** decreasing. [< Old French *decreiss-,* a form of *descreistre* < Latin *decrescere* < *de-* down + *crescere* grow] **—de creas′ing ly,** *adv.*

Syn. *v.t., v.i.* **Decrease, diminish, dwindle** mean to make or become less. **Decrease** suggests steadily going down little by little: *The rainfall is decreasing.* **Diminish** suggests becoming smaller in size, amount, or importance because someone or something keeps taking away a part: *The medical bills during my long sickness have diminished my savings.* **Dwindle** emphasizes the idea of wasting away, of becoming smaller and smaller until nothing is left: *Our savings have dwindled.*

de cree (di krē′), *n., v.,* **-creed, -cree ing.** *—n.* 1 something ordered or settled by authority; official decision. 2 a decision or order of a court or judge. 3 law of a church council, especially one settling a disputed point of doctrine. *—v.t.* 1 order or settle by authority: *Fate decreed that Ulysses should travel long and far.* 2 decide; determine. *—v.i.* decide; determine. [< Old French *decre* < Latin *decretum* < *de-* + *cernere* distinguish, separate]

dec re ment (dek′rə mənt), *n.* 1 a gradual decrease; slow loss. 2 amount lost by gradual decrease. [< Latin *decrementum* < *decrescere.* See DECREASE.]

de crep it (di krep′it), *adj.* 1 broken down or weakened by old age; old and feeble. 2 worn out or broken down from use. See **weak** for synonym study. [< Latin *decrepitum* broken down < *de-* + *crepare* to creak] **—de crep′it ly,** *adv.*

de crep i tude (di krep′ə tüd, di krep′ə tyüd), *n.* feebleness, usually from old age; decrepit condition; weakness.

de cre scen do (dē′krə shen′dō, dā′krə shen′dō), *n., pl.* **-dos,** *adj., adv.* in music: *—n.* 1 a gradual decrease in force or loudness; diminuendo. 2 passage to be played or sung with a decrescendo. *—adj., adv.* with a gradual decrease in force or loudness; diminuendo. [< Italian]

de cry (di krī′), *v.t.,* **-cried, -cry ing.** 1 express strong disapproval of; condemn; denounce: *The pacifist decried all forms of violence.* 2 make little of; try to lower the value of by slighting statements; disparage: *The lumber dealer decried the use of concrete for houses.* [< French *decrier* < *de-* + *crier* to cry] **—de cri′er,** *n.*

de cum bent (di kum′bənt), *adj.* 1 (of stems, branches, etc.) lying or trailing on the ground with the end tending to climb. 2 lying down; reclining. [< Latin *decumbentem* lying down]

decoy (def. 1)
wooden decoy attracting wild ducks

de cus sate (di kus′āt), *adj.* 1 crossed; intersecting. 2 (of leaves, etc.) arranged along the stem in pairs, each pair at right angles to the pair next above or below. [< Latin *decussatum*]

ded i cate (ded′ə kāt), *v.t.,* **-cat ed, -cat ing.** 1 set apart for a sacred or solemn purpose; consecrate: *The new altar was dedicated at a special service.* 2 celebrate the opening of (a bridge, institution, meeting, etc.) with an official ceremony. 3 give up wholly or earnestly to some person or purpose; devote: *The doctor dedicated his life to improving hospital care in his community.* See **devote** for synonym study. 4 address (a book, poem, etc.) to a friend or patron as a mark of affection, respect, gratitude, etc. [< Latin *dedicatum* affirmed, proclaimed < *de-* + *dicare* proclaim] **—ded′i ca′tor,** *n.*

ded i ca tion (ded′ə kā′shən), *n.* 1 a setting apart or a being set apart for a sacred or solemn purpose; consecration: *the dedication of a church.* 2 ceremony attending the official opening of something, as a building, institution, or convention: *the dedication of a new library wing.* 3 a giving up wholly or earnestly to some person or purpose; devotion. 4 words dedicating a book, poem, etc., to a friend or patron.

ded i ca tive (ded′ə kā′tiv), *adj.* dedicatory.

ded i ca to ry (ded′ə kə tôr′ē, ded′ə kə tōr′ē), *adj.* of dedication; as a dedication.

de dif fer en ti a tion (dē dif′ə ren′shē ā′shən), *n.* process in which cells, tissues, etc., lose their special form or function; loss of specialization.

de duce (di düs′, di dyüs′), *v.t.,* **-duced, -duc ing.** 1 reach (a conclusion) by reasoning; infer from a general rule or principle. See **conclude** for synonym study. 2 trace the course, descent, or origin of. [< Latin *deducere* < *de-* down + *ducere* to lead]

de duc i ble (di dü′sə bəl, di dyü′sə bəl), *adj.* that can be deduced or inferred.

de duct (di dukt′), *v.t.* take away from a sum or amount; subtract. See **subtract** for synonym study.

de duct i ble (di duk′tə bəl), *adj.* that can be deducted.

de duc tion (di duk′shən), *n.* 1 act of deducting; subtraction: *No deduction from one's pay is made for absence due to illness.* 2 amount deducted. 3 a reaching of conclusions by reasoning; inference. A person using deduction reasons from general laws to particular cases. EXAMPLE: All animals die; this cat is an animal; therefore, this cat will die. 4 thing deduced; conclusion.

de duc tive (di duk′tiv), *adj.* of or using deduction; reasoning by deduction. **—de duc′tive ly,** *adv.*

deed (dēd), *n.* 1 thing done; act. 2 a brave, skillful, or unusual act; feat. 3 performance; doing: *Deeds, not words, are needed.* 4 a written or printed statement of ownership. The buyer of real estate receives a deed to the property from the former owner. 5 **in deed,** in fact; actually. *—v.t.* transfer by deed. [Old English *dǣd*]

deem (dēm), *v.t., v.i.* form or have an opinion; think, believe, or consider. [Old English *dēman* < *dōm* judgment]

deep (dēp), *adj.* 1 going a long way down from the top or surface: *a deep well.* 2 going a long way back from the front: *The lot on which our house stands is 100 feet deep.* 3 from far down or back: *Take a deep breath.* 4 far down or back: *a deep cut.* 5 far on: *be deep in the study of physics.* 6 low in pitch: *a deep voice.* 7 hard to understand; requiring much thought and study: *a deep book.* 8 earnest; heartfelt: *deep sorrow.* 9 strong; great; intense; extreme: *a deep sleep.* 10 strong and dark in color; rich: *a deep red.* 11 in depth: *a tank 8 feet deep.* 12 with the mind fully taken up; absorbed: *deep in thought.* 13 going below the surface: *a speech of deep importance.* 14 wise; shrewd. 15 sly; crafty. 16 grave; serious: *in deep disgrace.* 17 much involved: *deep in debt.* *—adv.* 1 far down or back: *The men dug deep before they found water.* 2 well along in time; far on: *She studied deep into the night.* *—n.* 1 a deep place. 2 the most intense part: *the deep of winter.* 3 **the deep,** the sea. [Old English *dēop*] **—deep′ly,** *adv.* **—deep′ness,** *n.*

deep en (dē′pən), *v.t., v.i.* make or become deep or deeper.

hat, āge, fär; let, ēqual, tėrm;
it, īce; hot, ōpen, ôrder;
oil, out; cup, pu̇t, rüle;
ch, child; ng, long; sh, she;
th, thin; ᴛʜ, then; zh, measure;

ə represents *a* in about, *e* in taken, *i* in pencil, *o* in lemon, *u* in circus.

< = from, derived from, taken from.

deep-freeze (dēp′frēz′), *v.t.*, **-froze** (-frōz′) or **-freezed, -fro zen** (-frō′zn) or **-freezed, -freez ing.** freeze (food) and store it for later use.

deep-root ed (dēp′rü′tid, dēp′ru̇t′id), *adj.* 1 deeply rooted. 2 firmly fixed: *deep-rooted traditions.*

deep-sea (dēp′sē′), *adj.* of, belonging to, or in the deeper parts of the sea: *a deep-sea diver.*

deep-seat ed (dēp′sē′tid), *adj.* 1 far below the surface. 2 firmly fixed.

deep-set (dēp′set′), *adj.* 1 set deeply: *deep-set eyes.* 2 firmly fixed.

deep South or **Deep South,** the southeastern part of the United States, especially the states of South Carolina, Georgia, Alabama, Mississippi, and Louisiana.

deer (dir), *n., pl.* **deer.** 1 any of a family of hoofed, cud-chewing, herbivorous mammals that have antlers, borne chiefly by males, which are shed and regrown annually. Elk, moose, and caribou are deer. 2 any of the smaller species of these mammals, including the mule deer of America, the red deer of Europe and Asia, and the fallow deer of Europe. [Old English *dēor* animal] **—deer′like′,** *adj.*

deer hound (dir′hound′), *n.* dog of a Scottish breed, resembling a greyhound but larger and with a shaggy coat.

deer mouse, any of a genus of small American mice with white feet and large ears.

deer skin (dir′skin′), *n.* 1 skin of a deer. 2 leather made from it. 3 clothing made of this leather.

deer stalk er (dir′stô′kər), *n.* a close-fitting cap with earflaps, originally worn by hunters in stalking deer.

def., 1 defendant. 2 definition.

de face (di fās′), *v.t.*, **-faced, -fac ing.** spoil the appearance of; mar. [< Old French *defacer* < *de-* + *face* face] **—de face′ment,** *n.* **—de fac′er,** *n.*

Syn. Deface, disfigure mean to spoil the appearance of. **Deface** means to spoil the surface of something by blotting out an important detail, by scratching something in, by wearing down, etc.: *The inscription is too badly defaced to be read.* **Disfigure** suggests spoiling the beauty of a person or thing by permanent injury too deep or serious to remove: *The accident left her disfigured.*

de fac to (dē fak′tō), 1 in fact; in reality. 2 actually existing, whether lawful or not: *de facto racial segregation.* [< Latin, from the fact]

de fal cate (di fal′kāt, di fôl′kāt), *v.i.*, **-cat ed, -cat ing.** steal or misuse money trusted to one's care. [< Medieval Latin *defalcatum* lopped off, deducted < *de-* + *falcem* sickle] **—de fal′ca tor,** *n.*

de fal ca tion (dē′fal kā′shən, dē′fôl-kā′shən), *n.* 1 theft or misuse of money entrusted to one's care. 2 amount stolen or misused.

def a ma tion (def′ə mā′shən, dē′fə-mā′shən), *n.* a defaming or a being defamed; slander or libel.

de fam a to ry (di fam′ə tôr′ē, di fam′ə-tōr′ē), *adj.* that defames; slanderous or libelous.

de fame (di fām′), *v.t.*, **-famed, -fam ing.** attack the good name of; harm the reputation of; speak evil of; slander or libel. **—de-fam′er,** *n.*

de fault (di fôlt′), *n.* 1 failure to do something or to appear somewhere when due; neglect. If, in any contest, one side does not appear, it loses by default. 2 **in default of,** in the absence of; having no; lacking: *In default of evidence, the case was dismissed.* *—v.i.* fail to do something or appear somewhere when due. *—v.t.* fail to perform or pay when due. **—de fault′er,** *n.*

de feat (di fēt′), *v.t.* 1 win a victory over in a contest or conflict; overcome; vanquish: *defeat an army.* See synonym study below. 2 cause to fail; frustrate; thwart: *defeat someone's plans.* *—n.* 1 a defeating; an overcoming in a contest or conflict: *inflict a defeat upon an opponent.* 2 a being defeated; overthrow: *Napoleon's defeat at Waterloo.* [< Old French *desfait,* past participle of *desfaire* undo < Latin *dis-* un- + *facere* do]

Syn. *v.t.* 1 **Defeat, conquer, vanquish, overcome** mean to win a victory over someone or something. **Defeat** often means to win a victory temporarily: *We defeated Lincoln High School in debate yesterday.* **Conquer** emphasizes final achievement after a long effort in winning control over people, things, or feelings: *Some countries may be defeated, but never conquered.* **Vanquish** emphasizes completely overpowering another, usually in a single encounter: *The champion vanquished the challengers one by one.* **Overcome** emphasizes the idea of getting the better of someone or something, especially a habit or feeling: *She could not overcome her dislike for that man.*

de feat ism (di fē′tiz′əm), *n.* conduct tending to bring about acceptance of defeat.

de feat ist (di fē′tist), *n.* person who expects or admits defeat. *—adj.* having to do with or characterized by defeatism.

def e cate (def′ə kāt), *v.*, **-cat ed, -cat ing.** *—v.i.* to discharge or void intestinal waste. *—v.t.* clear of impurities; purify; refine. [< Latin *defaecatum* cleansed < *de-* from + *faeces* dregs] **—def′e ca′tion,** *n.*

de fect (*n.* dē′fekt, di fekt′; *v.* di fekt′), *n.* 1 a shortcoming or failing in a person or thing; fault or blemish. See synonym study below. 2 lack of something necessary for completeness; deficiency. *—v.i.* forsake one's own country, group, etc., for another, especially another that is opposed to it in political or social doctrine. [< Latin *defectus* lack < *deficere* fail < *de-* down + *facere* do] **—de fec′tion,** *n.* **—de fec′tor,** *n.*

Syn. 1 **Defect, flaw** mean an imperfection or fault. **Defect** is the general word, applying to any imperfection on the surface or in the make-up of a person or thing: *A hearing aid helps to overcome defects in hearing.* **Flaw** applies to a defect in structure: *a diamond without flaw, a flaw in character.*

de fec tive (di fek′tiv), *adj.* 1 having a defect or defects; not perfect or complete; faulty. 2 lacking one or more of the usual forms of grammatical inflection. *Ought* is a defective verb. 3 below normal in behavior or intelligence. *—n.* person who has some defect. **—de fec′tive ly,** *adv.* **—de-fec′tive ness,** *n.*

de fence (di fens′), *n.* BRITISH. defense.

de fend (di fend′), *v.t.* 1 guard from attack or harm; keep safe; protect: *defend a fort.* See **guard** for synonym study. 2 act, speak, or write in favor of; maintain: *defend one's rights.* 3 contest (a claim or lawsuit). 4 act or speak in behalf of (a person accused). [< Latin *defendere* ward off < *de-* + *fendere* to strike] **—de fend′er,** *n.*

de fend ant (di fen′dənt), *n.* person accused or sued in a court of law.

de fense (di fens′), *n.* 1 something that defends; means of guarding against attack or harm. 2 a guarding against attack or harm; defending or protecting. 3 action, speech, or writing in favor of something. 4 team or players defending a goal in a game. 5 a defendant and his lawyers. 6 answer of a defendant to an accusation or lawsuit against him. Also, BRITISH **defence.** [< Latin *defensa* < *defendere* defend]

de fense less (di fens′lis), *adj.* having no defense; unprotected. **—de fense′less ly,** *adv.* **—de fense′less ness,** *n.*

defense mechanism, any self-protective reaction by an organism, especially the shutting out of unpleasant emotions to avoid awareness of a situation.

de fen si ble (di fen′sə bəl), *adj.* 1 that can be defended. 2 justifiable. **—de fen′si bly,** *adv.*

de fen sive (di fen′siv), *adj.* 1 ready to defend; intended to defend; defending. 2 for defense: *defensive armor.* 3 of defense: *a defensive attitude.* *—n.* 1 position or attitude of defense. 2 thing that defends. 3 **on the defensive,** ready to defend, apologize, or explain. **—de fen′sive ly,** *adv.* **—de-fen′sive ness,** *n.*

de fer[1] (di fėr′), *v.t., v.i.*, **-ferred, -fer ring.** put off to some later time; delay; postpone: *defer an exam.* See **delay** for synonym study. [< Latin *differre.* Doublet of DIFFER.] **—de-fer′ra ble,** *adj.* **—de fer′rer,** *n.*

de fer[2] (di fėr′), *v.i.*, **-ferred, -fer ring.** yield in judgment or opinion: *defer to one's parents' wishes.* [< Middle French *déférer* < Latin *deferre* < *de-* down + *ferre* carry]

def er ence (def′ər əns), *n.* 1 a yielding to the judgment, opinion, wishes, etc., of another. 2 great respect. See **honor** for synonym study. 3 **in deference to,** out of respect for the wishes or authority of.

def e ren tial (def′ə ren′shəl), *adj.* showing deference; respectful. **—def′e ren′tial ly,** *adv.*

de fer ment (di fėr′mənt), *n.* a putting off; postponement; delay.

de fi ance (di fī′əns), *n.* 1 a defying; standing up against authority and refusing to recognize or obey it. 2 challenge to meet in a contest, to do something, or to prove something. 3 **in defiance of,** without regard for; in spite of.

de fi ant (di fī′ənt), *adj.* showing defiance; openly resisting. **—de fi′ant ly,** *adv.* **—de-fi′ant ness,** *n.*

de fi cien cy (di fish′ən sē), *n., pl.* **-cies.** 1 lack of something needed or required; incompleteness. 2 amount by which something is not sufficient; shortage.

de fi cient (di fish′ənt), *adj.* 1 not complete; defective: *His knowledge of geography is deficient.* 2 not sufficient in quantity, force, etc.; lacking: *This milk is deficient in fat.* *—n.* person or thing that is deficient. [< Latin *deficientem* lacking, failing < *de-* down + *facere* do] **—de fi′cient ly,** *adv.*

deficient number, a positive integer whose divisors have a sum less than twice the integer.

def i cit (def′ə sit), *n.* amount by which a sum of money falls short; shortage. [< Latin, it is wanting < *deficere* fail. See DEFECT.]

de fi er (di fī′ər), *n.* person who defies.

de file[1] (di fīl′), *v.t.,* **-filed, -fil ing.** 1 make filthy or dirty; make disgusting in any way. 2 destroy the purity or cleanness of (anything sacred); desecrate. 3 stain; dishonor. 4 ARCHAIC. ravish. [< Old French *defouler* trample down or violate] **—de file′ment,** *n.* **—de fil′er,** *n.*

de file[2] (di fīl′, dē′fīl), *v.,* **-filed, -fil ing,** *n.* —*v.i.* march in single file or a narrow column. —*n.* a steep and narrow valley. [< French *défiler*]

de fine (di fīn′), *v.t.,* **-fined, -fin ing.** 1 make clear the meaning of; explain: *A dictionary defines words.* 2 make clear; make distinct. 3 fix; settle. 4 settle the limits of: *define a boundary by treaty.* 5 characterize. [< Latin *definire* to limit < *de-* down + *finis* end] **—de fin′a ble,** *adj.* **—de fin′er,** *n.*

def i nite (def′ə nit), *adj.* 1 clear or exact; not vague: *Give a definite answer, either yes or no.* 2 having settled limits; limited; restricted. **—def′i nite ness,** *n.*

definite article, the article *the.* It is used to limit or restrict the sense of a noun *(The king died last night)* or to generalize its sense *(The dog is a domesticated animal).*

def i nite ly (def′ə nit lē), *adv.* 1 in a definite manner. 2 certainly: *Will you go? Definitely.*

def i ni tion (def′ə nish′ən), *n.* 1 act of making clear the meaning of a word. 2 statement that makes clear the meaning of a word. 3 formal or precise statement of the essential nature of anything. 4 power of making clear and distinct, especially the capacity of a lens to make the image of an object distinct to the eye. 5 clearness; distinctness. 6 accuracy with which sound or images are reproduced by a radio or television receiver.

de fin i tive (di fin′ə tiv), *adj.* 1 that decides or settles a question; conclusive; final: *She appealed to the Supreme Court for a definitive answer.* 2 authoritative; completely reliable. 3 limiting; defining. **—de fin′i tive ly,** *adv.* **—de fin′i tive ness,** *n.*

de flate (di flāt′), *v.,* **-flat ed, -flat ing.** —*v.t.* 1 let air or gas out of (a balloon, tire, football, etc.). 2 reduce (inflated prices, currency, etc.). 3 injure or destroy the conceit or confidence of. —*v.i.* become deflated. [probably < *de* + *(in)flate*] **—de fla′tor,** *n.*

de fla tion (di flā′shən), *n.* 1 a deflating. 2 a being deflated. 3 reduction of the amount of available money in circulation so that the value of money increases and prices go down.

de fla tion ar y (di flā′shə ner′ē), *adj.* of or having to do with deflation.

de flect (di flekt′), *v.t., v.i.* bend or turn aside; change direction: *The wind deflected the arrow's flight. The ball deflected from its straight course.* [< Latin *deflectere* < *de-* away + *flectere* to bend] **—de flec′tion,** *n.*

de flow er (dē flou′ər), *v.t.* 1 strip flowers from. 2 rob anything of beauty, excellence, etc.; ravage; desecrate. 3 to break the hymen of (a woman) during sexual intercourse, so that she is no longer a virgin.

De foe (di fō′), *n.* **Daniel,** 1660?-1731, English writer, author of *Robinson Crusoe.*

de fo li ant (di fō′lē ənt), *n.* a chemical agent used to strip trees or plants of their leaves.

de fo li ate (di fō′lē āt), *v.,* **-at ed, -at ing.** —*v.t.* strip (a tree or plant) of leaves. —*v.i.* be stripped of leaves. [< Late Latin *defoliatum* stripped of leaves < *de-* from + *folium* leaf] **—de fo′li a′tion,** *n.*

de fo rest (dē fôr′ist, dē for′ist), *v.t.* clear of trees or forests. **—de fo′rest a′tion,** *n.* **—de fo′rest er,** *n.*

De Fo rest (di fôr′ist, di for′ist), **Lee,** 1873-1961, American inventor who made improvements in radio and television.

de form (di fôrm′), *v.t.* 1 spoil the form or shape of; disfigure: *Constantly wearing shoes that are too tight may deform the feet.* 2 make ugly. —*v.i.* become deformed. **—de form′er,** *n.*

de for ma tion (dē′fôr mā′shən, def′ər mā′shən), *n.* 1 act of deforming. 2 deformed condition; disfigurement.

de formed (di fôrmd′), *adj.* 1 not properly formed; disfigured. 2 ugly.

de form i ty (di fôr′mə tē), *n., pl.* **-ties.** 1 part that is not properly formed; malformation. 2 condition of being improperly formed. 3 ugliness.

de fraud (di frôd′), *v.t.* take money, rights, etc., away from by fraud; cheat. **—de′frau da′tion,** *n.* **—de fraud′er,** *n.*

de fray (di frā′), *v.t.* pay (costs or expenses): *The expenses of national parks are defrayed by the taxpayers.* [< Middle French *desfraier* < *de-* out + *frais* costs] **—de fray′a ble,** *adj.* **—de fray′er,** *n.*

de fray al (di frā′əl), *n.* payment of costs or expenses.

de frost (di frôst′, di frost′), *v.t.* 1 remove frost or ice from. 2 thaw out.

de frost er (di frôs′tər, di fros′tər), *n.* device that removes frost or ice, either through heat or mechanically. Defrosters are used on automobile windshields, the wings of airplanes, in the freezing compartments of refrigerators, etc.

deft (deft), *adj.* quick and skillful in action; nimble: *the deft fingers of a surgeon.* See synonym study below. [variant of *daft*] **—deft′ly,** *adv.* **—deft′ness,** *n.*

Syn. Deft, dexterous, adroit mean skillful. **Deft,** usually confined to physical skill, suggests neatness and exceptional lightness and swiftness, particularly of the hands: *A surgeon must be deft in tying knots.* **Dexterous** usually suggests easy, quick, smooth movements and lightness and sureness of touch coming from practice *(She is a dexterous pianist),* although it occasionally suggests having quick intelligence. **Adroit** is used less often of physical skill than of mental quickness, resourcefulness, and cleverness in handling situations: *The adroit stewardess kept the passengers on the plane cheerful during the storm.*

de funct (di fungkt′), *adj.* no longer in existence; dead; extinct. [< Latin *defunctum* finished < *de-* + *fungi* perform]

de fuse (dē fyüz′), *v.t.,* **-fused, -fus ing.** remove the fuse from (a bomb, etc.).

de fy (di fī′), *v.t.,* **-fied, -fy ing.** 1 resist boldly or openly: *defy the law.* 2 be beyond the power of; withstand: *Granite defies weathering more than sandstone.* 3 challenge (a person) to do or prove something; dare. [< Old French *defier* distrust, have no faith in, oppose < Latin *dis-* + *fidus* faithful]

deg., degree or degrees.

de gas (dē gas′), *v.t.,* **-gassed, -gas sing.** remove gas from.

De gas (dā gä′; *French* də gä′), *n.* **(Hilaire Germain) Edgar,** 1834-1917, French impressionist painter.

de Gaulle (də gōl′), **Charles (André Joseph Marie),** 1890-1970, French general and political leader, president of France from 1959 to 1969.

de gauss (di gous′, di gôs′), *v.t.* neutralize the magnetic field of (a steel ship) so that explosive magnetic mines will not be attracted to its hull.

de gen er a cy (di jen′ər ə sē), *n.* degenerate condition or character.

de gen e rate (*v.* di jen′ə rāt′; *adj., n.* di jen′ər it), *v.,* **-rat ed, -rat ing,** *adj., n.* —*v.i.* 1 grow worse; decline in physical, mental, or moral qualities. 2 (in biology) sink to a lower type; lose the normal or more highly developed characteristics of one's race or kind. —*adj.* 1 that has degenerated; showing a decline in physical, mental, or moral qualities. 2 (in biology) that has lost the normal or more highly developed characteristics of its race or kind. —*n.* 1 person having a degenerate or unwholesome character. 2 a sexual pervert. [< Latin *degeneratum* away from one's kind < *de-* away + *generem* race, kind] **—de gen′e rate ly,** *adv.* **—de gen′e rate ness,** *n.*

de gen e ra tion (di jen′ə rā′shən), *n.* 1 process of degenerating. 2 a degenerate condition. 3 deterioration in tissues or organs caused by disease, injury, etc. 4 (in biology) a gradual change to a less highly developed or lower type.

de gen e ra tive (di jen′ə rā′tiv, di jen′ər ə tiv), *adj.* 1 tending to degenerate. 2 characterized by or showing degeneration: *degenerative changes in the tissues.*

de glu ti tion (dē′glü tish′ən, deg′lü tish′ən), *n.* act or power of swallowing. [< French *déglutition* < Latin *deglutire* < *de-* down + *glutire* to swallow]

deg ra da tion (deg′rə dā′shən), *n.* 1 a degrading. 2 a being degraded. 3 a degraded condition; debasement; degeneracy. 4 a wearing away by erosion.

de grade (di grād′), *v.t.,* **-grad ed, -grad ing.** 1 reduce in rank, especially as a punishment. 2 bring into dishonor or contempt. 3 lower in character or quality; debase. 4 wear down by erosion. [< Late Latin *degradare* < Latin *de-* down + *gradus* grade] **—de grad′er,** *n.*

de gree (di grē′), *n.* 1 a step in a scale; stage in a process: *By degrees the lake gets warm enough to swim in.* 2 step in a direct line of descent: *a cousin two degrees removed.* 3 amount; extent: *To what degree are you interested in reading?* 4 unit for measuring temperature: *The freezing point of water is 32 degrees (32°) Fahrenheit or 0 degrees (0°) centigrade.* 5 unit for measuring an angle or an arc of a circle. A degree is 1/90 of a right angle or 1/360 of the circumference of a circle.

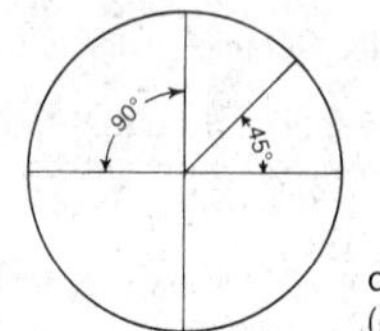

degree (def. 5)

hat, āge, fär; let, ēqual, tėrm;
it, īce; hot, ōpen, ôrder;
oil, out; cup, pu̇t, rüle;
ch, child; ng, long; sh, she;
th, thin; ᴛʜ, then; zh, measure;

ə represents *a* in about, *e* in taken, *i* in pencil, *o* in lemon, *u* in circus.

< = from, derived from, taken from.

6 position on the earth's surface or the celestial sphere as measured by degrees of latitude or longitude. 7 rank: *A princess is a lady of high degree.* 8 rank or title given by a college or university to a student whose work fulfills certain requirements, or to a noted person as an honor: *an A.B. degree, a D.D. degree.* 9 any of various grades conferred by a fraternal society, etc., upon its members. 10 (in grammar) one of the three stages in the comparison of adjectives or adverbs. The positive degree of *fast* is *fast;* the comparative degree is *faster;* the superlative degree is *fastest.* 11 (in algebra) rank as determined by an exponent or sum of exponents. a^3 and a^2b are terms of the third degree. 12 a relative condition, manner, way, or respect: *A bond and a stock may both be wise investments, each in its degree.* 13 (in law) the relative measure of the seriousness of a crime: *murder in the first degree.* 14 in music: **a** interval between any note of the scale and the next note. **b** line or space on the staff showing the position of the notes. **c** interval between two of these. 15 **to a degree, a** to a large amount; to a great extent. **b** somewhat; a little. [< Old French *degre* < Latin *de-* down + *gradus* grade]

de gree-day (di grē′dā′), *n.* unit representing one degree of deviation below a standard (usually 65 degrees) in the mean outdoor temperature for one day. It is used to determine fuel requirements.

de Groot (də grōt′), **Hugo.** See **Grotius.**

de hisce (dē his′), *v.i.*, **-hisced, -hisc ing.** (of an organ, seed pod, etc.) to burst open along a definite line so as to provide for discharge of the seeds or other contents. [< Latin *dehiscere* < *de-* away + *hiscere* be open, gape]

dehiscence of a seed pod left, closed right, open

de his cence (dē his′ns), *n.* the bursting open of an organ, pod, anther, etc., to discharge seeds, pollen, etc.

de his cent (dē his′nt), *adj.* dehiscing.

de horn (dē hôrn′), *v.t.* remove the horns from.

de hu man ize (dē hyü′mə nīz), *v.t.*, **-ized, -iz ing.** deprive of human qualities, interests, sympathy, etc. **—de hu′man i za′tion,** *n.*

de hu mid i fy (dē′hyü mid′ə fī), *v.t.*, **-fied, -fy ing.** remove moisture from (the air, etc.). **—de′hu mid′i fi er,** *n.*

de hy drate (dē hī′drāt), *v.*, **-drat ed, -drat ing.** *—v.t.* take water or moisture from; dry: *dehydrate vegetables.* *—v.i.* lose water or moisture. [< *de-* remove + Greek *hydros* water] **—de′hy dra′tion,** *n.*

de hy dro gen ase (dē hī′drə jə nās), *n.* enzyme that activates hydrogen and causes its removal, as from body tissue.

de hy dro gen ate (dē hī′drə jə nāt), *v.t.*, **-at ed, -at ing.** remove hydrogen from (a compound). **—de hy′dro gen a′tion,** *n.*

de ice (dē īs′), *v.t.*, **-iced, -ic ing.** prevent ice from forming on; remove ice from. **—de ic′er,** *n.*

de i fi ca tion (dē′ə fə kā′shən), *n.* 1 a deifying. 2 a being deified.

de i fy (dē′ə fī), *v.t.*, **-fied, -fy ing.** 1 make a god of. 2 worship or regard as a god: *deify wealth.* [< Old French *deifier* < Late Latin *deificare* < Latin *deus* god + *facere* make]

deign (dān), *v.i.* think fit; condescend. *—v.t.* condescend to give (an answer, a reply, etc.). [< Old French *deignier* < Latin *dignari* < *dignus* worthy]

de i on ize (dē ī′ə nīz), *v.t.*, **-ized, -iz ing.** purify (water) by removing salt ions. **—de i′on i za′tion,** *n.*

de ism (dē′iz′əm), *n.* belief in God on the evidence of reason and nature, and without accepting any particular religion.

de ist (dē′ist), *n.* person who believes in deism.

de i ty (dē′ə tē), *n., pl.* **-ties.** 1 one of the gods worshiped by a people or a tribe; god or goddess. 2 divine nature; being a god. 3 **the Deity,** God. [< Old French *deite* < Latin *deitatem* < *deus* god]

dé jà vu (dā zhä vʏ′), FRENCH. 1 illusion of having previously experienced something that one is actually experiencing for the first time. 2 (literally) already seen.

de ject ed (di jek′tid), *adj.* in low spirits; sad; discouraged. See **sad** for synonym study. [< Latin *dejectum* < *de-* down + *jacere* to throw] **—de ject′ed ly,** *adv.* **—de ject′ed ness,** *n.*

de jec tion (di jek′shən), *n.* lowness of spirits; sadness; discouragement: *Her face showed her dejection at missing the party.*

de jur e (dē ju̇r′ē), by right; according to law; legal. [< Latin, by law]

dek a gram (dek′ə gram), *n.* decagram.

De Kalb (di kalb′), Baron **Johann,** 1721-1780, German general in the American army during the Revolutionary War.

dek a li ter (dek′ə lē′tər), *n.* decaliter.

dek a me ter (dek′ə mē′tər), *n.* decameter.

dek a stere (dek′ə stir), *n.* decastere.

De Koo ning (də kü′ning), **Willem,** born 1904, American painter, born in the Netherlands.

del., 1 delegate. 2 delete. 3 delivery.

Del., Delaware.

De la croix (də lä krwä′), *n.* **(Ferdinand Victor) Eugène,** 1798?-1863, French painter.

de la Mare (də lə mer′; də lə mar′), **Walter (John),** 1873-1956, English poet and novelist.

De la ny (də lā′nē), *n.* **Martin Robinson,** 1812-1885, American abolitionist, physician, and army officer.

Del a ware (del′ə wer, del′ə war), *n.* 1 one of the southeastern states of the United States. 548,000 pop.; 2400 sq. mi. *Capital:* Dover. *Abbrev.:* Del. 2 **Delaware River,** river flowing from SE New York State between Pennsylvania and New Jersey into Delaware Bay. 296 mi. 3 member of a tribe of American Indians, most of whom formerly lived in the valley of the Delaware River. **—Del′a war′e an,** *adj., n.*

Delaware Bay, inlet of the Atlantic between Delaware and New Jersey, at the mouth of the Delaware River.

delft (def. 1)

de lay (di lā′), *v.t.* 1 put off till a later time: *We will delay the party for a week.* See synonym study below. 2 make late; keep waiting; hinder the progress of: *The accident delayed the train for two hours.* *—v.i.* be late; go slowly; stop along the way. *—n.* 1 act of delaying. 2 fact of being delayed. [< Old French *delaier* < *de-* + *laier* leave, let] **—de lay′er,** *n.*

Syn. *v.t.* 1 **Delay, defer, postpone** mean to put off doing something. **Delay** often suggests holding off or putting off indefinitely: *I delayed seeing the dentist.* **Defer** usually suggests deciding to put off until a better time: *I deferred going until I had more time.* **Postpone** suggests deferring until a definite time, after something has been done, learned, etc.: *I postponed going until next week.*

de le (dē′lē), *v.t., v.i.*, **-led, -le ing.** (in printing) delete.

de lec ta ble (di lek′tə bəl), *adj.* very pleasing; delightful. [< Latin *delectabilis* < *delectare.* See DELIGHT.] **—de lec′ta ble ness,** *n.* **—de lec′ta bly,** *adv.*

de lec ta tion (dē′lek tā′shən), *n.* great pleasure; delight; entertainment.

del e ga cy (del′ə gə sē), *n., pl.* **-cies.** 1 group of delegates; delegation. 2 the sending or appointing of a delegate.

del e gate (*n.* del′ə gāt, del′ə git; *v.* del′ə gāt), *n., v.*, **-gat ed, -gat ing.** *—n.* 1 person given power or authority to act for others; representative to a convention, meeting, etc. 2 representative of a territory in the United States House of Representatives. 3 member of the lower branch of the legislature in Maryland, Virginia, and West Virginia. *—v.t.* 1 appoint or send (a person) as a representative: *Each club delegated one member to attend the state meeting.* 2 give over to another so that he may act for one: *delegate responsibility to an employee.* [< Latin *delegatum* delegated < *de-* + *legare* send with a commission]

del e ga tion (del′ə gā′shən), *n.* 1 act of delegating. 2 fact of being delegated. 3 group of delegates.

de lete (di lēt′), *v.t., v.i.*, **-let ed, -let ing.** 1 strike out or take out (anything written or printed); cross out. 2 wipe out; erase. [< Latin *deletum* wiped out]

del e ter i ous (del′ə tir′ē əs), *adj.* causing harm; injurious. [< Greek *dēlētērios* < *dēleesthai* to hurt] **—del′e ter′i ous ly,** *adv.* **—del′e ter′i ous ness,** *n.*

de le tion (di lē′shən), *n.* 1 act of deleting. 2 a deleted part.

delft (delft), *n.* 1 kind of glazed earthenware made in the Netherlands, usually decorated in blue on a white background. 2 any pottery like this. [< *Delft*]

Delft (delft), *n.* city in SW Netherlands. 84,000.

delft ware (delft′wer′, delft′war′), *n.* delft.

Del hi (del′ē), *n.* 1 city in N India, former capital of India. 2,874,000. 2 New Delhi.

del i (del′ē), *n.* INFORMAL. delicatessen.

De li an (dē′lē ən), *adj.* of or belonging to Delos. —*n.* native or inhabitant of Delos.

de lib er ate (*adj.* di lib′ər it; *v.* di lib′ə rāt′), *adj., v.,* **-at ed, -at ing.** —*adj.* 1 carefully thought out beforehand; made or done on purpose; intended: *a deliberate lie.* See synonym study below. 2 slow and careful in deciding what to do; thoughtful; cautious. 3 not hurried; slow: *walk with deliberate steps.* See **slow** for synonym study. —*v.i., v.t.* 1 think over carefully; consider. 2 discuss reasons for and against something; debate. [< Latin *deliberatum* carefully weighed < *de-* + *librare* weigh] **—de lib′er ate ly,** *adv.* **—de lib′er ate ness,** *n.*

Syn. *adj.* 1 **Deliberate, intentional** mean done after thinking something over. **Deliberate** suggests full thought before acting: *The lawyer made a deliberate attempt to confuse the jury.* **Intentional** means done on purpose, with a definite end in mind: *His mean remark was intentional; he wanted to make you angry.*

de lib e ra tion (di lib′ə rā′shən), *n.* 1 careful thought: *After long deliberation, I decided not to go.* 2 discussion of reasons for and against something; debate: *the deliberations of Congress.* 3 slowness and care: *The hunter aimed his gun with great deliberation.*

de lib e ra tive (di lib′ə rā′tiv), *adj.* of or for deliberation; having to do with deliberation: *Congress is a deliberative body.* **—de lib′e ra′tive ly,** *adv.* **—de lib′e ra′tive ness,** *n.*

del i ca cy (del′ə kə sē), *n., pl.* **-cies.** 1 fineness of weave, quality, or make; slightness and grace: *the delicacy of lace, the delicacy of a flower, the delicacy of a baby's skin.* 2 fineness of feeling for small differences; sensitiveness: *delicacy of hearing or touch.* 3 need of care, skill, or tact: *a matter of great delicacy.* 4 thought or regard for the feelings of others; consideration. 5 a shrinking from what is offensive or not modest. 6 a being easily hurt or made ill; weakness. 7 a choice kind of food; dainty.

del i cate (del′ə kit), *adj.* 1 pleasing to the senses; light, mild, or soft: *delicate foods, delicate colors, a delicate fragrance.* See synonym study below. 2 of fine weave, quality, or make; easily torn; thin: *A spider's web is very delicate.* 3 requiring care, skill, or tact: *a delicate situation, a delicate question.* 4 very rapidly responding to slight changes of condition; finely sensitive: *delicate instruments, a delicate sense of touch.* 5 easily hurt or made ill; frail: *a delicate child.* 6 hard to appreciate; subtle: *a delicate point in reasoning.* 7 careful of the feelings of others; considerate; tactful. 8 avoiding anything that is offensive or immodest; fastidious. [< Latin *delicatus* pampered] **—del′i cate ly,** *adv.* **—del′i cate ness,** *n.*

Syn. 1 **Delicate, dainty** mean pleasing to the senses. **Delicate** suggests fineness or softness of texture, lightness in quality, or exactness and fineness in the making: *He does delicate work with water colors.* **Dainty** suggests smallness, perfection in the making, and a delicate beauty: *The baby wore a dainty dress.*

del i ca tes sen (del′ə kə tes′n), *n.* 1 *sing. in use.* store that sells prepared foods, such as cooked meats, smoked fish, cheese, salads, pickles, sandwiches, etc. 2 *pl. in use.* the foods sold at such a store. [< German *Delikatessen,* plural of *Delikatesse* delicacy]

de li cious (di lish′əs), *adj.* very pleasing or satisfying, especially to the taste or smell; delightful. See synonym study below. [< Latin *deliciae* a delight < *delicere* entice. See DELIGHT.] **—de li′cious ly,** *adv.* **—de li′cious ness,** *n.*

Syn. Delicious, luscious mean delighting the senses. **Delicious** means highly pleasing in flavor: *This dessert is delicious.* **Luscious** adds to *delicious* the suggestion of richness or sweetness: *a luscious apple pie.*

de light (di līt′), *n.* 1 great pleasure; joy. See **pleasure** for synonym study. 2 something which gives great pleasure. —*v.t.* please greatly. —*v.i.* have great pleasure: *Children delight in surprises.* [< Old French *delit* < *delitier* to charm < Latin *delectare* < *delicere* entice < *de-* + *lacere* entice]

de light ed (di lī′tid), *adj.* greatly pleased; very glad; joyful. **—de light′ed ly,** *adv.* **—de light′ed ness,** *n.*

de light ful (di līt′fəl), *adj.* very pleasing; giving joy. **—de light′ful ly,** *adv.* **—de light′ful ness,** *n.*

de light some (di līt′səm), *adj.* delightful.

De li lah (di lī′lə), *n.* 1 (in the Bible) a woman who betrayed Samson, her lover, to the Philistines. 2 a false, treacherous woman; temptress.

de lim it (di lim′it), *v.t.* fix the limits of; mark the boundaries of. **—de lim′i ta′tion,** *n.*

de lin e ate (di lin′ē āt), *v.t.,* **-at ed, -at ing.** 1 trace the outline of. 2 draw; sketch. 3 describe in words; portray. [< Latin *delineatum* delineated < *de-* + *linea* line] **—de lin′e a′tor,** *n.*

de lin e a tion (di lin′ē ā′shən), *n.* 1 act of delineating. 2 thing delineated; diagram, sketch, portrait, or description.

de lin quen cy (di ling′kwən sē), *n., pl.* **-cies.** 1 failure or neglect of a duty or obligation; guilt. 2 condition or habit of behaving unlawfully. 3 a fault; offense; misdeed.

de lin quent (di ling′kwənt), *adj.* 1 failing or neglecting a duty or obligation. 2 guilty of a fault or an offense. 3 due and unpaid; overdue: *delinquent taxes.* 4 having to do with delinquents. —*n.* a delinquent person; offender. [< Latin *delinquentem* failing, leaving off < *de-* off + *linquere* to leave] **—de lin′quent ly,** *adv.*

del i quesce (del′ə kwes′), *v.i.,* **-quesced, -quesc ing.** become liquid by absorbing moisture from the air: *Calcium chloride deliquesces readily.* [< Latin *deliquescere* < *de-* + *liquescere* become fluid < *liquere* be liquid]

del i ques cence (del′ə kwes′ns), *n.* act or process of deliquescing.

del i ques cent (del′ə kwes′nt), *adj.* becoming liquid by absorbing moisture from the air: *deliquescent crystals.*

de lir i ous (di lir′ē əs), *adj.* 1 temporarily out of one's senses; wandering in mind; raving. 2 wildly enthusiastic. 3 caused by delirium. **—de lir′i ous ly,** *adv.* **—de lir′i ous ness,** *n.*

de lir i um (di lir′ē əm), *n., pl.* **-lir i ums, -lir i a** (-lir′ē ə). 1 a temporary disorder of the mind that occurs during fevers, insanity, drunkenness, etc., characterized by restlessness, excitement, irrational talk, and hallucinations. 2 wild enthusiasm. [< Latin < *delirare* rave, be crazy < *de lira (ire)* (go) out of the furrow (in plowing)]

delirium tre mens (trē′mənz), violent tremblings and terrifying hallucinations, caused by prolonged and excessive drinking of alcoholic liquor. [< New Latin, trembling delirium]

De li us (dē′lē əs, dē′lyəs), *n.* **Frederick,** 1863-1934, English composer.

de liv er (di liv′ər), *v.t.* 1 carry and give out; distribute: *The postman delivers letters.* 2 hand over; give up: *deliver a fort to the enemy.* 3 give forth in words: *deliver a talk. The jury delivered its verdict.* 4 strike; throw: *deliver a blow.* 5 set free; rescue; save: *deliver an animal from a trap.* See **rescue** for synonym study. 6 help give birth. 7 help in the birth of: *deliver a baby.* 8 **deliver oneself of,** speak; give out. —*v.i.* make a delivery or deliveries. [< Old French *delivrer* < Late Latin *deliberare* set free < Latin *de-* away + *liber* free] **—de liv′er a ble,** *adj.* **—de liv′er er,** *n.*

de liv er ance (di liv′ər əns), *n.* 1 a setting free or a being set free; rescue; release. 2 a formal opinion or judgment.

de liv er y (di liv′ər ē), *n., pl.* **-er ies.** 1 a carrying and giving out of letters, goods, etc.: *There is one delivery of mail a day in our city.* 2 a giving up; handing over: *The captive was released upon the delivery of the ransom.* 3 manner of speaking; way of giving a speech, lecture, etc. 4 act or way of striking, throwing, etc. 5 a rescue; release. 6 a giving birth to a child; childbirth. 7 anything that is delivered, especially goods. 8 (in law) the formal handing over of property to another.

dell (del), *n.* a small, sheltered glen or valley, usually with trees in it. [Old English]

del la Rob bi a (del′ə rob′ē ə; *Italian* dāl′lā rōb′byä), **Luca,** 1400?-1482, Italian sculptor.

De los (dē′los), *n.* Greek island in the S Aegean Sea, one of the Cyclades. 2 sq. mi.

de louse (dē lous′, dē louz′), *v.t.,* **-loused, -lous ing.** remove lice from.

Del phi (del′fī), *n.* town in ancient Greece where a famous oracle of Apollo was located.

Del phi an (del′fē ən), *adj.* Delphic.

Del phic (del′fik), *adj.* 1 having to do with the oracle of Apollo at Delphi. 2 having a double meaning; obscure.

del phin i um (del fin′ē əm), *n.* larkspur. [< New Latin]

del Sar to (del sär′tō), **Andrea,** 1486-1531, Italian painter.

delta (def. 1) of the Mississippi River

del ta (del′tə), *n.* 1 deposit of earth and sand, usually three-sided, that collects at the mouths of some rivers. 2 the fourth letter of the Greek alphabet (Δ or δ). 3 any triangular space or figure. [< Greek]

delta ray, electron emitted when a fast-moving charged particle, such as an alpha particle, penetrates matter.

del ta-wing (del′tə wing′), *adj.* (of an aircraft) having wings in the shape of a triangle.

del toid (del′toid), *adj.* shaped like a delta; triangular. *—n.* a large triangular muscle of the shoulder by which the arm is raised.

de lude (di lüd′), *v.t.,* **-lud ed, -lud ing.** mislead the mind or judgment of; trick or deceive. [< Latin *deludere* < *de-* + *ludere* to play] **—de lud′er,** *n.*

del uge (del′yüj), *n., v.,* **-uged, -ug ing.** *—n.* 1 a great flood. See **flood** for synonym study. 2 **the Deluge,** (in the Bible) the Flood. 3 a heavy fall of rain. 4 any overwhelming rush: *Most stores have a deluge of orders just before Christmas.* *—v.t.* 1 flood or overflow. 2 overwhelm. [< Old French < Latin *diluvium* < *diluere* wash away < *dis-* away + *luere* to wash]

de lu sion (di lü′zhən), *n.* 1 a false belief or opinion: *She was under the delusion that she could pass any test without studying for it.* See **illusion** for synonym study. 2 a deluding. 3 a being deluded. 4 a fixed belief maintained in spite of unquestionable evidence to the contrary. People with mental disorders often have delusions. [< Latin *delusionem* < *deludere.* See DELUDE.]

de lu sion al (di lü′zhə nəl), *adj.* having to do with or characterized by delusions.

de lu sive (di lü′siv), *adj.* misleading the mind or judgment; deceptive. **—de lu′sive ly,** *adv.* **—de lu′sive ness,** *n.*

de lu sor y (di lü′sər ē), *adj.* delusive; deceptive.

de luxe (də lu̇ks, də luks), *adj.* of exceptionally good quality; elegant: *deluxe accommodations.*

de luxe (də lu̇ks′; də luks′), deluxe. [< French]

delve (delv), *v.i.,* **delved, delv ing.** 1 search carefully for information: *delve in books for facts to support a theory.* 2 ARCHAIC. dig. [Old English *delfan*] **—delv′er,** *n.*

Dem., 1 Democrat. 2 Democratic.

de mag net ize (dē mag′nə tīz), *v.t.,* **-ized, -iz ing.** deprive of magnetism. **—de mag′net i za′tion,** *n.* **—de mag′net iz′er,** *n.*

dem a gog (dem′ə gog, dem′ə gôg), *n.* demagogue.

dem a gog ic (dem′ə goj′ik, dem′ə gog′ik), *adj.* of or like a demagogue. **—dem′a gog′i cal ly,** *adv.*

dem a gog i cal (dem′ə goj′ə kəl, dem′ə gog′ə kəl), *adj.* demagogic.

dem a gogue (dem′ə gog, dem′ə gôg), *n.* a popular leader who stirs up the people by appealing to their emotions and prejudices in order to get power or further his own interests. [< Greek *demagōgos* < *demos* people + *agōgos* leader]

dem a gogu er y (dem′ə gog′ər ē, dem′ə gôg′ər ē), *n.* methods or principles of a demagogue.

dem a go gy (dem′ə gō′jē, dem′ə gog′ē, dem′ə gôg′ē), *n.* demagoguery.

de mand (di mand′), *v.t.* 1 ask for as a right: *The accused demanded a trial by jury.* See synonym study below. 2 ask for with authority: *The policeman demanded the names of the boys.* 3 ask to know or to be told: *demand an answer.* 4 call for; require; need: *Training a puppy demands patience.* *—n.* 1 act of demanding: *a demand for employment by the unemployed.* 2 thing demanded. 3 claim; requirement: *demands upon one's time.* 4 desire and ability to buy: *Because of the large crop, the supply of apples is greater than the demand.* 5 **in demand,** wanted: *Taxicabs are much in demand on rainy days.* 6 **on demand,** upon request; on being claimed: *a note payable on demand.* [< Latin *demandare* < *de-* + *mandare* to order] **—de mand′a ble,** *adj.* **—de mand′er,** *n.*

Syn. *v.t.* 1 **Demand, claim, require** mean to ask or call for something as a right or need. **Demand** emphasizes insisting on getting something a person has the right to call for: *I demand a fair hearing.* **Claim** emphasizes having, or stating one has, the right to get what is demanded: *Three different heirs claimed the inheritance.* **Require** emphasizes authority to make a demand: *The bank requires evidence of good character before a loan is granted.*

de mand ing (di man′ding), *adj.* making severe demands.

de mar cate (dē′mär kāt, di mär′kāt), *v.t.,* **-cat ed, -cat ing.** 1 set and mark the limits of. 2 separate; distinguish. [< Spanish *demarcar* < *de-* off + *marcar* to mark] **—de′mar ca′tion,** *n.*

dé marche (dā marsh′), *n.* FRENCH. 1 a plan of action. 2 a change of plans.

Dem a vend (dem′ə vend′), *n.* **Mount,** mountain peak in N Iran, the highest of the Elburz Mountains. 18,600 ft.

deme (dēm), *n.* 1 an administrative division or township in ancient Attica. 2 (in biology) a small group or population of organisms that interbreed, such as an anthill, all the frogs in a pond, etc. [< Greek *dēmos* deme, people]

de mean[1] (di mēn′), *v.t.* lower in dignity or standing; humble; degrade: *demean oneself by insulting a friend.* [< *de-* down + *mean*[2]]

de mean[2] (di mēn′), *v.t.* behave or conduct (oneself). [< Old French *demener* < *de-* + *mener* to lead]

de mean or (di mē′nər), *n.* way a person looks and acts; behavior; manner.

de ment ed (di men′tid), *adj.* mentally ill; insane; crazy. [< Latin *dementem* < *de-* out + *mentem* mind] **—de ment′ed ly,** *adv.* **—de ment′ed ness,** *n.*

de men tia (di men′shə), *n.* a partial or complete deterioration of mind. [< Latin]

dementia prae cox (prē′koks), schizophrenia. [< Latin, precocious insanity]

de mer it (dē mer′it), *n.* 1 fault or defect. 2 a mark against a person's record for unsatisfactory behavior or poor work. [< Medieval Latin *demeritum* < Latin *de-* + *merere* to merit]

de mesne (di mān′, di mēn′), *n.* 1 house and land belonging to a lord and used by him. 2 domain; realm. 3 district; region. 4 (in law) the possession of land as one's own. 5 real estate. [< Anglo-French variant of Old French *demeine* domain]

De me ter (di mē′tər), *n.* (in Greek myths) the goddess of agriculture, fruitfulness, and marriage, identified with the Roman goddess Ceres.

demi-, *prefix.* half; partial: *Demigod = a half god.* [< Old French *demi* < Latin *dimidius* < *dis-* apart + *medius* middle]

dem i god (dem′i god′), *n.* 1 a god who is partly human. Hercules was a demigod. 2 person so outstanding as to seem like a god.

dem i john (dem′i jon), *n.* a large bottle of glass or earthenware enclosed in wicker. [< French *dame-jeanne* Lady Jane, a popular name of the bottle]

de mil i ta rize (dē mil′ə tə rīz′), *v.t.,* **-rized, -riz ing.** free from military control. **—de mil′i ta ri za′tion,** *n.*

dem i mon daine (dem′i mon dān′), *n.* woman of the demimonde.

dem i monde (dem′i mond), *n.* class of women supported by lovers, and of questionable social standing and reputation. [< French, literally, half-world]

hat, āge, fär; let, ēqual, tėrm;
it, īce; hot, ōpen, ôrder;
oil, out; cup, pu̇t, rüle;
ch, child; ng, long; sh, she;
th, thin; ᴛʜ, then; zh, measure;
ə represents *a* in about, *e* in taken, *i* in pencil, *o* in lemon, *u* in circus.
< = from, derived from, taken from.

de mise (di mīz′), *n., v.,* **-mised, -mis ing.** *—n.* 1 death. 2 transfer of an estate by a will or lease. 3 transfer of royal power by death or abdication. *—v.t.* 1 transfer (an estate) by a will or lease. 2 transfer (royal power) by death or abdication. [< Old French, past participle of *desmettre* put away < *des-* away + *mettre* put]

dem i tasse (dem′i tas′), *n.* 1 a very small cup of black coffee. 2 a small cup for serving black coffee. [< French, literally, half-cup]

de mo bi lize (dē mō′bə līz), *v.t.,* **-lized, -liz ing.** remove from military service, status, or control: *demobilize an army.* **—de mo′bi li za′tion,** *n.*

de moc ra cy (di mok′rə sē), *n., pl.* **-cies.** 1 government that is run by the people who live under it. In a democracy the people rule either directly through meetings that all may attend, such as the town meetings in New England, or indirectly through the election of certain representatives. 2 country, state, or community having such a government. 3 the common people or their political power. 4 treatment of other people as one's equals: *The teacher's democracy made her popular among her pupils.* [< Greek *dēmokratia* < *dēmos* people + *kratos* rule]

dem o crat (dem′ə krat), *n.* 1 person who believes that a government should be run by the people who live under it. 2 person who treats other people as his equals. 3 **Democrat,** member of the Democratic Party.

dem o crat ic (dem′ə krat′ik), *adj.* 1 of a democracy; like a democracy. 2 of or having to do with the common people. 3 treating other people as one's equals. 4 **Democratic,** of or having to do with the Democratic Party. **—dem′o crat′i cal ly,** *adv.*

Democratic Party, one of the two main political parties in the United States, founded in 1828 by Democratic-Republicans.

demijohn

Dem o crat ic-Re pub li can (dem′ə krat′ik ri pub′lə kən), *adj.* of or having to do with an American political party of the early 1800's which opposed a strong central government. In 1828 it was renamed the Democratic Party. *—n.* member of this party.

de moc ra tize (di mok′rə tīz), *v.t., v.i.,* **-tized, -tiz ing.** make or become democratic. **—de moc′ra ti za′tion,** *n.*

De moc ri tus (di mok′rə təs), *n.* 460?-370? B.C., Greek philosopher.

de mod u late (dē moj′ə lāt), *v.t.,* **-lat ed, -lat ing.** (in electronics) to separate the sound wave or other signal being sent from the carrier wave by a demodulator; detect.

de mod u la tion (dē moj′ə lā′shən), *n.* (in electronics) the separation of the sound wave or other signal being sent from the carrier wave; detection.

de mod u la tor (dē moj′ə lā′tər), *n.* (in electronics) a vacuum tube or crystal that separates the sound wave or other signal being sent from the carrier wave; detector.

de mog ra pher (di mog′rə fər), *n.* an expert in demography.

de mo graph ic (dē′mə graf′ik, dem′ə-graf′ik), *adj.* of or having to do with demography. **—de′mo graph′i cal ly,** *adv.*

de mog ra phy (di mog′rə fē), *n.* science dealing with statistics of human populations, including size, distribution, diseases, number of births, deaths, etc. [< Greek *demos* people]

dem oi selle (dem′wä zel′), *n.* a young girl. [< French]

de mol ish (di mol′ish), *v.t.* 1 pull or tear down; destroy; raze: *Shells and bombs demolished the fortress.* See **destroy** for synonym study. 2 put an end to; ruin completely: *demolish a plan.* [< Middle French *démoliss-*, a form of *démolir* destroy < Latin *demoliri* tear down < *de-* + *moles* mass] **—de mol′ish er,** *n.* **—de mol′ish ment,** *n.*

dem o li tion (dem′ə lish′ən, dē′mə-lish′ən), *n.* a demolishing; destruction.

de mon (dē′mən), *n.* 1 an evil spirit; devil; fiend. 2 a very wicked or cruel person. 3 an evil influence. 4 person who has great energy or vigor. 5 an attendant or guiding spirit. 6 an inferior or minor Greek god. Also, **daemon.** [< Latin *daemon* < Greek *daimōn* divinity, spirit] **—de′mon like′,** *adj.*

de mon e tize (dē mon′ə tīz, dē mun′ə tīz), *v.t.,* **-tized, -tiz ing.** 1 deprive of its standard value as money. 2 withdraw from use as money. **—de mon′e ti za′tion,** *n.*

de mo ni ac (di mō′nē ak), *adj.* 1 of or like demons. 2 devilish; fiendish. 3 raging; frantic. 4 possessed by an evil spirit. *—n.* person supposed to be possessed by an evil spirit.

de mo ni a cal (dē′mə nī′ə kəl), *adj.* demoniac. **—de′mo ni′a cal ly,** *adv.*

de mon ic (di mon′ik), *adj.* 1 of evil spirits; caused by evil spirits. 2 influenced by a guiding spirit; inspired.

de mon ol o gy (dē′mə nol′ə jē), *n.* study of demons or of beliefs about demons.

de mon stra bil i ty (di mon′strə bil′ə tē, dem′ən strə bil′ə tē), *n.* demonstrable quality or condition.

de mon stra ble (di mon′strə bəl, dem′ən-strə bəl), *adj.* capable of being proved. **—de mon′stra ble ness,** *n.* **—de mon′-stra bly,** *adv.*

dem on strate (dem′ən strāt), *v.,* **-strat-ed, -strat ing.** *—v.t.* 1 show clearly; prove. 2 explain by carrying out experiments, or by using samples or specimens; show how (a thing) is done. 3 show the merits of (a thing for sale); advertise or make known by carrying out a process in public: *The salesman demonstrated the new washing machine.* 4 show (feeling) openly. *—v.i.* 1 take part in a parade or meeting to protest or to make demands. 2 display military strength to frighten or deceive an enemy. [< Latin *demonstratum* shown clearly < *de-* + *monstrare* to show]

dem on stra tion (dem′ən strā′shən), *n.* 1 clear proof: *a demonstration of ability.* 2 a showing or explaining something by carrying out experiments or by using samples or specimens. 3 a showing of the merits of a thing for sale; advertising or making known by carrying out a process in public: *the demonstration of a new sewing machine.* 4 an open show or expression of feeling: *a demonstration of joy.* 5 parade or meeting to protest or to make demands: *The tenants held a demonstration against the raise in rent.* 6 display of military strength to frighten or deceive an enemy. 7 (in logic) an argument or series of propositions that proves a conclusion. 8 (in mathematics) the process of proving that certain assumptions necessarily produce a certain result.

de mon stra tive (di mon′strə tiv), *adj.* 1 expressing one's affections freely and openly: *Demonstrative greetings embarrass me.* 2 (in grammar) pointing out the object referred to. *This, that, these, those* are called **demonstrative adjectives** or **pronouns,** according to their use in a sentence. Adjective: *This car was bought in May.* Pronoun: *This costs more than those.* 3 showing clearly; explanatory. 4 giving proof; conclusive. *—n.* pronoun or adjective that points out. **—de mon′stra tive ly,** *adv.* **—de mon′-stra tive ness,** *n.*

dem on stra tor (dem′ən strā′tər), *n.* 1 person or thing that demonstrates. 2 person who takes part in a demonstration. 3 vehicle, appliance, etc., that is used by a dealer in demonstrating the product to customers.

de mo ral ize (di môr′ə līz, di mor′ə līz), *v.t.,* **-ized, -iz ing.** 1 corrupt the morals or principles of; deprave: *The drug habit demoralizes its victims.* 2 weaken the spirit, courage, or discipline of; dishearten: *Lack of food demoralized the besieged soldiers.* 3 throw into confusion or disorder: *Threats of war demoralized the stock market.* **—de mo′ral-i za′tion,** *n.* **—de mo′ral iz′er,** *n.*

De mos the nes (di mos′thə nēz′), *n.* 384?–322 B.C., Athenian orator and statesman.

de mote (di mōt′), *v.t.,* **-mot ed, -mot ing.** put back to a lower grade; reduce in rank. [< *de-* + *(pro)mote*]

de mot ic (di mot′ik), *adj.* 1 of the common people; popular. 2 having to do with the Egyptian form of simplified writing derived from the hieratic character. *—n.* the standard spoken form of modern Greek. [< Greek *dēmotikos* < *dēmos* the people]

de mo tion (di mō′shən), *n.* 1 act of demoting. 2 fact of being demoted.

de mount (dē mount′), *v.t.* 1 remove from a mounting: *demount a photograph.* 2 take apart; dismount. *—v.i.* dismount. **—de-mount′a ble,** *adj.*

Demp ster (demp′stər), *n.* **Arthur Jeffrey,** 1886-1950, American physicist, born in Canada, who discovered the isotope uranium 235.

de mul cent (di mul′sənt), *adj.* soothing. *—n.* a soothing ointment. [< Latin *demulcentem* < *de-* + *mulcere* soothe]

de mur (di mėr′), *v.,* **-murred, -mur ring,** *n. —v.i.* 1 show disapproval or dislike; take exception; object. 2 (in law) enter a demurrer. 3 OBSOLETE. hesitate. *—n.* a demurring; objection; exception. [< Old French *demurer* < Latin *demorari* < *de-* + *morari* to delay]

de mure (di myůr′), *adj.,* **-mur er, -mur est.** 1 artificially proper; assuming an air of modesty; coy: *the demure smile of a flirt.* 2 reserved or composed in demeanor; serious and sober. See **modest** for synonym study. [< *de-* + Old French *meür* discreet, mature < Latin *maturus*] **—de mure′ly,** *adv.* **—de mure′ness,** *n.*

de mur rage (di mėr′ij), *n.* 1 failure to load or unload a ship, railroad car, etc., within the time specified. 2 payment made for this failure.

de mur rer (di mėr′ər), *n.* 1 person who objects. 2 objection. 3 (in law) a plea by a defendant that a lawsuit be dismissed because the facts, while true, do not sustain the plaintiff's claim, or because there is some legal defect in the claim.

den (den), *n., v.,* **denned, den ning.** *—n.* 1 cave, pit, or other place where a wild beast lives; lair. 2 place where thieves or the like have their headquarters. 3 a small, dirty room. 4 one's private room for reading, work, or relaxation, usually small and cozy. 5 group of eight to ten cub scouts. *—v.i.* 1 live in or as if in a den. 2 escape into or hide in a den. [Old English *denn*] **—den′like′,** *adj.*

Den., Denmark.

de nar i us (di ner′ē əs), *n., pl.* **-nar i i** (-ner′ē ī). an ancient Roman silver or gold coin. [< Latin, containing ten (here, ten times the value of an *as*[2]) < *deni* ten each. Doublet of DINAR, DENIER[2].]

de na tion al ize (dē nash′ə nə līz, dē-nash′nə līz), *v.t.,* **-ized, -iz ing.** deprive of national rights, scope, or character. **—de-na′tion al i za′tion,** *n.*

de na tur ant (dē nā′chər ənt), *n.* a denaturing substance or agent.

de na ture (dē nā′chər), *v.t.,* **-tured, -tur ing.** 1 change the nature of. 2 make unfit for eating or drinking without destroying its usefulness for other purposes: *denatured alcohol.* 3 change the properties of (a protein) by changing its structure, as by heat or the addition of chemicals. **—de na′tur-a′tion,** *n.*

de na zi fy (dē nät′sə fī, dē nat′sə fī), *v.t.,* **-fied, -fy ing.** rid of Nazi doctrines or Nazi influences. **—de na′zi fi ca′tion,** *n.*

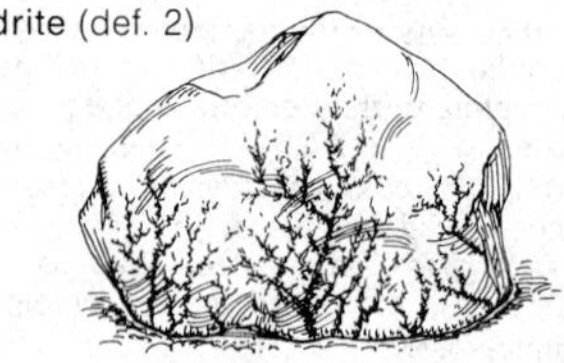
dendrite (def. 2)

den drite (den′drīt), *n.* 1 the branching part at the receiving end of a nerve cell. See **neuron** for diagram. 2 stone or mineral with branching, treelike markings. 3 a treelike marking. [< Greek *dendrites* of a tree < *dendron* tree]

den dro chron o log i cal (den′drō-kron′ə loj′ə kəl), *adj.* of or having to do with dendrochronology.

den dro chro nol o gy (den′drō krə nol′-ə jē), *n.* the study of annual rings in trees to establish dates and environmental conditions in the past.

Den eb (den′eb), *n.* star of the first magnitude in the northern constellation Cygnus.

den gue (deng′gā, deng′gē), *n.* an infectious

fever with severe pain in the head, joints, and muscles and usually skin rash, caused by a virus transmitted by an aëdes mosquito. [< Spanish < Swahili *kidinga*]

de ni al (di nī′əl), *n.* 1 a declaring that something is not true or valid: *Your denial is fruitless; we have proof.* 2 a saying that one does not hold to or accept: *a public denial of a belief.* 3 act of refusing a request; noncompliance. 4 a refusing to acknowledge; disowning: *Peter's denial of Christ.* 5 a doing without things that one wants; self-denial.

de ni er[1] (di nī′ər), *n.* person who denies. [< *deny*]

den ier[2] (den′yər, də nir′ *for 1;* də nir′ *for 2*), *n.* 1 unit of weight used to express the fineness of silk or synthetic yarn, as rayon or nylon, or other fiber, based on the number of .05 grams of weight in 450 meters of length. 2 an old French coin, originally silver, later having little value. [< Old French < Latin *denarius.* Doublet of DINAR, DENARIUS.]

den i grate (den′ə grāt), *v.t.,* **-grat ed, -grat ing.** blacken the reputation of (a person, etc.); defame. [< Latin *denigratum* blackened thoroughly < *de-* + *nigrare* blacken] **—den′i gra′tion,** *n.* **—den′i gra′tor,** *n.*

den im (den′əm), *n.* 1 a heavy, coarse cotton cloth with a diagonal weave, used for overalls, upholstery, sports clothes, etc. 2 **denims,** *pl.* overalls or pants made of this cloth. [< French *(serge) de Nîmes* (serge) from Nîmes, town in France]

de ni tri fy (dē nī′trə fī), *v.t.,* **-fied, -fy ing.** 1 remove nitrogen or its compounds from. 2 change (nitrates) by reduction into nitrites, nitrogen, or ammonia. **—de ni′tri fi ca′tion,** *n.*

den i zen (den′ə zən), *n.* 1 inhabitant or occupant of a place or region: *Fish are denizens of the sea.* 2 a foreign plant, animal, etc., that has been naturalized. [< Old French *denzein* < *denz* within < Medieval Latin *deintus* < Latin *de* from + *intus* within]

Den mark (den′märk), *n.* country in N Europe, between the Baltic Sea and the North Sea. 4,913,000 pop.; 16,600 sq. mi. *Capital:* Copenhagen.

de nom i nate (di nom′ə nāt), *v.t.,* **-nat ed, -nat ing.** give a name to; name. [< Latin *denominatum* named < *de-* + *nomen* name]

de nom i nate number (di nom′ə nit), number used with the name of the kind of unit, as 6 ft. or 9 lb.

de nom i na tion (di nom′ə nā′shən), *n.* 1 name for a group or class of things; name. 2 a religious group or sect: *Methodists and Baptists are two large Protestant denominations.* 3 class or kind of units: *Reducing 5/12, 1/3 and 1/6 to the same denomination gives 5/12, 4/12, and 2/12. The United States coin of the lowest denomination is a cent.* 4 act of naming.

de nom i na tion al (di nom′ə nā′shə nəl), *adj.* having to do with or controlled by some religious denomination; sectarian: *a denominational school.* **—de nom′i na′tion al ly,** *adv.*

de nom i na tion al ism (di nom′ə nā′shə nə liz′əm), *n.* 1 denominational principles. 2 division into denominations.

de nom i na tive (di nom′ə nā′tiv, di nom′ə nə tiv), *adj.* 1 giving a distinctive name; naming. 2 derived from a noun or an adjective. *To center* and *to whiten* are denominative verbs. *—n.* word derived from a noun or an adjective. **—de nom′i na′tive ly,** *adv.*

de nom i na tor (di nom′ə nā′tər), *n.* the number below the line in a fraction, stating the size of the parts in their relation to the whole: *In 3/4, 4 is the denominator, and 3 is the numerator.*

de no ta tion (dē′nō tā′shən), *n.* 1 meaning, especially the exact, literal meaning. The denotation of *home* is "place where one lives," but it has many connotations. 2 a denoting or marking out; indication. 3 mark; sign; symbol.

de no ta tive (di nō′tə tiv), *adj.* having the quality of denoting; indicative.

de note (di nōt′), *v.t.,* **-not ed, -not ing.** 1 be the sign of; indicate: *A fever usually denotes sickness. The symbol × denotes multiplication.* 2 be a name for; mean: *The word "stool" denotes a small chair without a back.* [< Latin *denotare* < *de-* + *nota* mark]

de noue ment or **dé noue ment** (dā′nü mäɴ′), *n.* 1 solution of a plot in a story, play, situation, etc. 2 outcome; end. [< French *dénouement* < *dénouer* untie]

de nounce (di nouns′), *v.t.,* **-nounced, -nounc ing.** 1 condemn publicly; express strong disapproval of. 2 give information against; accuse. 3 give formal notice of the termination of (a treaty, etc.). [< Old French *denoncer* < Latin *denuntiare* < *de-* + *nuntius* messenger] **—de nounce′ment,** *n.* **—de nounc′er,** *n.*

de no vo (dē nō′vō), LATIN. anew; starting again.

dense (dens), *adj.,* **dens er, dens est.** 1 having its parts closely packed together; thick: *a dense growth of weeds.* 2 very great; intense: *dense ignorance.* 3 stupid. 4 relatively opaque: *a dense photographic negative.* [< Latin *densus*] **—dense′ly,** *adv.* **—dense′ness,** *n.*

den si ty (den′sə tē), *n., pl.* **-ties.** 1 dense condition or quality; having parts very close together; compactness; thickness. 2 the quantity of matter in a unit of volume: *The density of lead is greater than the density of wood.* 3 the quantity of anything per unit area: *population density.* 4 stupidity. 5 relative opaqueness: *the density of a developed negative.*

dent (dent), *n.* 1 a hollow made by a blow or pressure: *The fall put a dent in my bicycle fender.* 2 a weak spot; start of a break, hole, or cut: *The purchase of a new car made a dent in our savings.* *—v.t.* make a dent in. *—v.i.* become dented: *Soft wood dents easily.* [Middle English *dente,* variant of *dint*]

den tal (den′tl), *adj.* 1 of or for the teeth. 2 of or for a dentist's work. 3 (of speech sounds) produced by placing the tip of the tongue against or near the back of the upper front teeth. *—n.* a dental sound. The sounds (t) and (d) are dentals. [< Latin *dentem* tooth] **—den′tal ly,** *adv.*

dental floss, a strong, waxed thread for cleaning between the teeth.

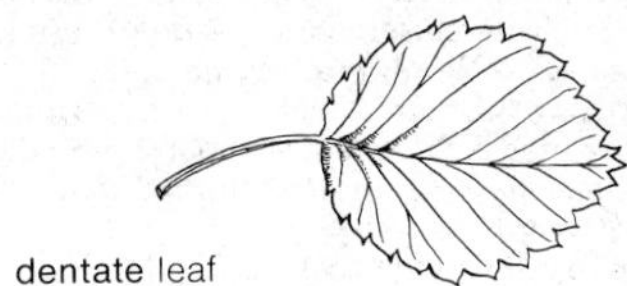
dentate leaf

den tate (den′tāt), *adj.* having toothlike projections; toothed; notched: *a dentate leaf.* **—den′tate ly,** *adv.*

dent corn, variety of Indian corn in which the kernels become indented on maturing.

hat, āge, fär; let, ēqual, tėrm;
it, īce; hot, ōpen, ôrder;
oil, out; cup, pu̇t, rüle;
ch, child; ng, long; sh, she;
th, thin; ᴛʜ, then; zh, measure;

ə represents *a* in about, *e* in taken, *i* in pencil, *o* in lemon, *u* in circus.

< = from, derived from, taken from.

den ti frice (den′tə fris), *n.* paste, powder, or liquid for cleaning the teeth. [< Latin *dentifricium* < *dentem* tooth + *fricare* to rub]

den tin (den′tən), *n.* dentine.

den tine (den′tēn′, den′tən), *n.* the hard, bony material beneath the enamel of a tooth, forming the main part of a tooth.

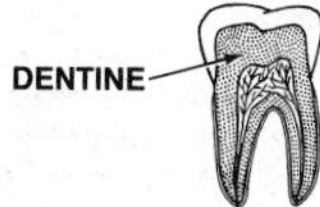

dentine shown in a cross section of a molar

den tist (den′tist), *n.* doctor whose work is the care of teeth. A dentist fills cavities in teeth, cleans, straightens or extracts them, and supplies artificial teeth.

den tist ry (den′tə strē), *n.* work, art, or profession of a dentist.

den ti tion (den tish′ən), *n.* 1 growth of teeth; teething. 2 kind, number, and arrangement of the teeth: *Dogs and wolves have the same dentition.*

den ture (den′chər), *n.* set of teeth, especially of artificial teeth.

de nude (di nüd′, di nyüd′), *v.t.,* **-nud ed, -nud ing.** 1 make bare; strip of clothing, covering, etc.: *trees denuded of their leaves.* 2 (in geology) lay (a rock, etc.) bare by erosion, etc. **—de′nu da′tion,** *n.*

de nun ci a tion (di nun′sē ā′shən), *n.* 1 expression of strong disapproval; public condemnation; denouncing: *the mayor's denunciation of crime.* 2 an informing against; accusation. 3 a formal notice of the intention to end a treaty, etc.

de nun ci a to ry (di nun′sē ə tôr′ē, di nun′sē ə tōr′ē), *adj.* condemning; accusing; threatening.

Den ver (den′vər), *n.* capital of Colorado, in the central part. 515,000.

de ny (di nī′), *v.,* **-nied, -ny ing.** *—v.t.* 1 declare (something) is not true: *I denied the charges against me.* See synonym study below. 2 say that one does not hold to or accept: *deny a belief.* 3 refuse to give or grant: *I could not deny her so small a favor.* 4 refuse to acknowledge; disown: *He denied his signature.* *—v.i.* **deny oneself,** do without the things one wants. [< Old French *denier* < Latin *denegare* < *de-* + *negare* say no]

Syn. *v.t.* 1 **Deny, contradict** mean to declare something not true. **Deny** means to state definitely that something is untrue: *She denied that she planned to leave town.* **Contradict** means to assert strongly that the truth is the opposite of what has been said: *He contradicted the testimony of the preceding witness.*

de o dar (dē′ə där), *n.* a cedar tree of the Himalayas, cultivated as a shade tree and for its very durable wood. [< Hindustani *deodār* < Sanskrit *devadāru* wood of the gods]

de o dor ant (dē ō′dər ənt), *n.* preparation that neutralizes unpleasant odors. *—adj.* that neutralizes unpleasant odors.

de o dor ize (dē ō′də rīz′), *v.t.,* **-ized, -iz ing.** destroy or neutralize the odor of. **—de o′dor i za′tion,** *n.* **—de o′dor iz′er,** *n.*

De o gra ti as (dē′ō grā′shē as), LATIN. thanks to God.

De o vo len te (dē′ō vō len′tē), LATIN. if God is willing.

de ox i dize (dē ok′sə dīz), *v.t.,* **-dized, -diz ing.** remove oxygen from (a chemical compound). **—de ox′i diz′er,** *n.*

de ox y gen ate (dē ok′sə jə nāt), *v.t.,* **-at ed, -at ing.** remove free oxygen from (water, etc.).

de ox y ri bo nu cle ic acid (dē ok′sə-rī′bō nü klē′ik, dē ok′sə rī′bō nyü klē′ik), a nucleic acid in the chromatin of all living cells that carries the genetic code; DNA. A single molecule consists of two parallel twisted chains of alternating units of phosphoric acid and deoxyribose, linked by crosspieces of the purine bases, adenine and guanine, and the pyrimidine bases, cytosine and thymine. Also, **desoxyribonucleic acid.**

de ox y ri bose (dē ok′sə rī′bōs), *n.* the sugar constituent of deoxyribonucleic acid. *Formula:* $C_5H_{10}O_4$

dep., 1 department. 2 deputy.

de part (di pärt′), *v.i.* 1 go away; leave: *The flight departs at 6:15.* See synonym study below. 2 turn away; change *(from): She departed from her usual way of working.* 3 die. *—v.t.* go away from: *He departed this life at the age of seventy.* [< Late Latin *departire* divide < Latin *de-* + *partem* part]

Syn. *v.i.* 1 **Depart, withdraw, retire** mean to go away or leave. **Depart** suggests going away from some definite place or person: *I departed from my home.* **Withdraw** suggests departing for a good reason: *I withdrew while they discussed my qualifications for the job.* **Retire** suggests prolonged or permanent change of condition: *retire from business.*

de part ed (di pär′tid), *n. sing. and pl.* Usually, **the departed,** a dead person or persons. *—adj.* 1 dead. 2 gone; past.

de part ment (di pärt′mənt), *n.* 1 a separate part of some whole; special branch; division: *the fire department of a city government.* 2 a main division of governmental administration: *the Department of Justice.* 3 a special division within a company, store, etc.: *the legal department, the furniture department.* 4 section within a university, college, or school, giving instruction in a certain field: *the history department.* 5 one of the administrative districts into which France is divided.

de part men tal (dē′pärt men′tl), *adj.* 1 having to do with a department. 2 divided into departments. **—de′part men′tal ly,** *adv.*

de part men tal ize (dē′pärt men′tl īz), *v.t.,* **-ized, -iz ing.** divide into departments. **—de′part men′tal i za′tion,** *n.*

department store, store that sells many different kinds of merchandise arranged in separate departments.

de par ture (di pär′chər), *n.* 1 act of going away; leaving. 2 a turning away; change: *a departure from our old custom.* 3 a starting on a new course of action or thought. 4 ARCHAIC. death.

de pend (di pend′), *v.i.* 1 be a result of; be controlled or influenced by something else: *The success of our picnic will depend partly upon the weather.* 2 get support; rely *(on* or *upon)* for help: *Children depend on their parents.* 3 rely *(on* or *upon);* trust: *You can depend on the timetable to tell you when trains leave.* See **rely** for synonym study. 4 hang down; be suspended. [< Latin *dependere* < *de-* from + *pendere* hang]

de pend a bil i ty (di pen′də bil′ə tē), *n.* reliability; trustworthiness.

de pend a ble (di pen′də bəl), *adj.* that can be depended on; reliable; trustworthy. **—de-pend′a ble ness,** *n.* **—de pend′a bly,** *adv.*

de pend ant (di pen′dənt), *adj., n.* dependent.

de pend ence (di pen′dəns), *n.* 1 fact or condition of being dependent: *the dependence of crops on good weather.* 2 a trusting or relying on another for support or help. 3 reliance; trust. 4 person or thing relied on.

de pend en cy (di pen′dən sē), *n., pl.* **-cies.** 1 country or territory controlled by another country: *The Virgin Islands is a dependency of the United States.* 2 dependent condition; dependence. 3 thing that depends on another.

de pend ent (di pen′dənt), *adj.* 1 relying on another for help, support, etc.: *A child is dependent on its parents.* 2 resulting from another thing; depending: *Good crops are dependent on the right kind of weather.* 3 under the control or rule of another; subject. 4 hanging down; pendent. 5 in mathematics: **a** (of a variable) relying on the values assumed by one or more independent variables. **b** (of an equation) that can be derived from another equation. $x + y = 3$ and $2x + 2y = 6$ are dependent equations. *—n.* person who is supported by another. Also, **dependant.**

dependent clause, subordinate clause.

de pict (di pikt′), *v.t.* 1 represent by drawing, painting, or carving; picture. 2 describe in words, music, etc.; portray. [< Latin *depictum* painted, portrayed < *de-* + *pingere* to paint] **—de pic′tion,** *n.*

dep i late (dep′ə lāt), *v.t.,* **-lat ed, -lat ing.** remove hair from. [< Latin *depilatum* shorn of hair < *de-* from + *pilus* hair] **—dep′i-la′tion,** *n.*

de pil a to ry (di pil′ə tôr′ē, di pil′ə tōr′ē), *n., pl.* **-ries.** liquid or other preparation for removing hair.

de plane (dē plān′), *v.i.,* **-planed, -plan ing.** get off an airplane after landing.

de plete (di plēt′), *v.t.,* **-plet ed, -plet ing.** empty or exhaust by drawing away or using up resources, strength, vitality, etc. [< Latin *depletum* emptied out < *de-* + *-plere* fill]

de ple tion (di plē′shən), *n.* a depleting or a being depleted; exhaustion.

de plor a ble (di plôr′ə bəl, di plōr′ə bəl), *adj.* 1 that is to be deplored; regrettable; lamentable: *a deplorable accident.* 2 wretched; miserable. **—de plor′a ble-ness,** *n.* **—de plor′a bly,** *adv.*

de plore (di plôr′, di plōr′), *v.t.,* **-plored, -plor ing.** be very sorry about; regret deeply; lament. [< Latin *deplorare* < *de-* + *plorare* weep]

de ploy (di ploi′), *v.t., v.i.* 1 spread out (troops, military units, etc.) from a column into a long battle line. 2 spread out or extend (anything). [< French *déployer* < *dé-* de- + *ployer* to fold] **—de ploy′ment,** *n.*

de po lar ize (dē pō′lə rīz′), *v.t.,* **-ized, -iz ing.** destroy or neutralize the polarity or polarization of. **—de po′lar i za′tion,** *n.* **—de po′lar iz′er,** *n.*

de po nent (di pō′nənt), *n.* 1 person who testifies, especially in writing, under oath. 2 (in Greek and Latin grammar) a verb passive in form but active in meaning. *—adj.* having passive form but active meaning. [< Latin *deponentem* putting down < *de-* + *ponere* put]

de pop u late (dē pop′yə lāt), *v.t.,* **-lat ed, -lat ing.** reduce the population of; deprive of inhabitants, wholly or in part. **—de-pop′u la′tion,** *n.* **—de pop′u la′tor,** *n.*

de port (di pôrt′, di pōrt′), *v.t.* 1 force to leave a country; banish; expel. An alien whose presence is undesirable or illegal is often deported and sent back to his native land. See **banish** for synonym study. 2 behave or conduct (oneself) in a particular manner: *The children deported themselves well.* [< Latin *deportare* < *de-* away + *portare* carry]

de por ta tion (dē′pôr tā′shən, dē′pōr-tā′shən), *n.* removal from a country by banishment or expulsion.

de por tee (dē′pôr tē′, dē′pōr tē′), *n.* person who is or has been deported.

de port ment (di pôrt′mənt, di pōrt′mənt), *n.* way a person acts; behavior; conduct.

de pose (di pōz′), *v.,* **-posed, -pos ing.** *—v.t.* 1 put out of office or a position of authority, especially a high one like that of king. 2 declare under oath; testify: *The witness deposed that she had seen the accused on the day of the murder.* *—v.i.* testify under oath. [< Old French *deposer* < *de-* down + *poser* put]

de pos it (di poz′it), *v.t.* 1 put down; lay down; leave lying: *He deposited his bundles on the table.* 2 leave lying as sediment: *The flood deposited a layer of mud in the streets.* 3 put in a place for safekeeping: *Deposit your money in the bank.* 4 place in the hands of another as a pledge to do something, in part payment for a purchase, etc. *—v.i.* make a deposit; settle. *—n.* 1 material laid down or left lying by natural means: *There is often a deposit of mud and sand at the mouth of a river.* 2 something put in a certain place for safekeeping. 3 money paid as a pledge to do something or to pay more later. 4 mass of some mineral in rock or in the ground. 5 act of depositing. 6 **on deposit, a** in a place for safekeeping. **b** in a bank. [< Latin *depositum* put away < *de-* + *ponere* put]

de pos i tar y (di poz′ə ter′ē), *n., pl.* **-tar ies.** 1 person or company that receives something for safekeeping; trustee. 2 depository; storehouse.

dep o si tion (dep′ə zish′ən, dē′pə zish′-ən), *n.* 1 act of putting out of office or a position of authority; removal from power. 2 the giving of testimony under oath. 3 testimony, especially a sworn statement in writing. 4 a depositing. 5 thing deposited; deposit.

de pos i tor (di poz′ə tər), *n.* 1 person who deposits. 2 person who deposits money in a bank.

de pos i to ry (di poz′ə tôr′ē, di poz′ə-tōr′ē), *n., pl.* **-ries.** 1 place where anything is stored for safekeeping; storehouse. 2 depositary; trustee.

de pot (dē′pō *for 1;* dep′ō *for 2-4*), *n.* 1 a railroad or bus station. 2 storehouse; warehouse. 3 place where military supplies are stored. 4 place where recruits are brought together and trained. [< French *dépôt*]

de prave (di prāv′), *v.t.,* **-praved,**

-prav ing. make bad; injure morally; corrupt; pervert. [< Latin *depravare* < *de-* + *pravus* crooked, wrong]

de praved (di prāvd′), *adj.* having very bad morals; corrupt; perverted. See **corrupt** for synonym study.

de prav i ty (di prav′ə tē), *n., pl.* **-ties.** 1 a being depraved; corruption. 2 a corrupt act; bad practice.

dep re cate (dep′rə kāt), *v.t.,* **-cat ed, -cat ing.** express strong diapproval of: *Lovers of peace deprecate war.* [< Latin *deprecatum* pleaded in excuse, averted by prayer <*de-* + *precari* pray] **—dep′re cat′ing ly,** *adv.*

dep re ca tion (dep′rə kā′shən), *n.* a strong expression of disapproval.

dep re ca to ry (dep′rə kə tôr′ē, dep′rə kə tōr′ē), *adj.* 1 deprecating. 2 apologetic.

de pre ci ate (di prē′shē āt), *v.,* **-at ed, -at ing.** *—v.t.* 1 lessen the value or price of. 2 speak slightingly of; belittle: *Some people depreciate the value of exercise.* *—v.i.* lessen in value: *The longer an automobile is driven the more it depreciates.* [< Latin *depretiatum* lessened in price < *de-* + *pretium* price]

de pre ci a tion (di prē′shē ā′shən), *n.* 1 a lessening or lowering in value: *Machinery undergoes depreciation as it is used or becomes obsolete.* 2 such a loss of value figured as the cost of doing business. 3 reduction in the value of money. 4 a belittling; disparagement.

de pre ci a tive (di prē′shē ā′tiv), *adj.* depreciatory.

de pre ci a to ry (di prē′shē ə tôr′ē, di prē′shē ə tōr′ē), *adj.* tending to depreciate.

dep re da tion (dep′rə dā′shən), *n.* act of plundering; robbery; ravaging. [< Latin *depraedationem* < *de-* + *praeda* booty]

de press (di pres′), *v.t.* 1 make sad or gloomy; cause to have low spirits: *I was depressed by the bad news.* 2 press down; push down; lower: *depress the keys of a piano.* 3 make less active; weaken: *Business is depressed.* 4 lower in amount or value: *depress stocks.* [< Latin *depressum* pressed down < *de-* + *premere* press] **—de press′ing ly,** *adv.*

de pres sant (di pres′nt), *n.* drug or other substance that slows or reduces the body's reactions and relaxes muscles.

de pressed (di prest′), *adj.* 1 gloomy; low-spirited; sad. See **sad** for synonym study. 2 pressed down; lowered. 3 (in botany and zoology) flattened down.

depressed area, region characterized by unemployment, poverty, etc.

de pres sion (di presh′ən), *n.* 1 a pressing down; sinking or lowering: *depression of mercury in a barometer.* 2 a depressed condition. 3 a low place; hollow: *depressions in the ground.* 4 sadness or gloominess; low spirits: *a fit of depression.* 5 form of psychosis, or a lesser mental disorder, often characterized by great despondency, gloominess, and inactivity. 6 a serious and usually extensive reduction of business activity: *Many people lose their jobs during times of business depression.*

de pres sive (di pres′iv), *adj.* tending to produce or characterized by depression.

de pres sor (di pres′ər), *n.* 1 person or thing that depresses. 2 muscle that pulls down a part. 3 instrument for pressing down some part or organ.

dep ri va tion (dep′rə vā′shən), *n.* 1 act of depriving. 2 condition of being deprived; loss; privation.

de prive (di prīv′), *v.t.,* **-prived, -priv ing.** 1 take away from by force; divest: *deprive a dictator of his power.* 2 keep from having or doing: *Worrying deprived me of sleep.* [< Old French *depriver* < *de-* + *priver* deprive]

dept., 1 department. 2 deputy.

depth (depth), *n.* 1 distance from top to bottom: *the depth of a hole, the depth of a lake.* 2 distance from front to back: *The depth of our playground is 250 feet.* 3 a deep place, especially of the sea. 4 the deepest or most central part: *the depths of the earth, the depth of the forest, the depths of despair.* 5 deep quality; deepness: *depth of understanding.* 6 deep understanding; profoundness: *The story has a good plot but it has no depth.* 7 lowness of pitch. 8 intensity of color, etc. [Middle English *depthe* < *dep* deep, Old English *dēop* deep]

depth charge or **depth bomb,** an explosive charge, used especially against submarines, dropped from a ship or aircraft and set to explode at a certain depth under water.

depth perception, the ability to judge the distance and relation of distant things to each other and to the observer.

dep u ta tion (dep′yə tā′shən), *n.* 1 group of persons sent to represent or act on behalf of others. 2 act of deputing.

de pute (di pyüt′), *v.t.,* **-put ed, -put ing.** 1 appoint to act on one's behalf; appoint as one's substitute or agent; delegate. 2 give (one's work, authority, etc.) to another; transfer. [< Latin *deputare* consider as < *de-* + *putare* think, count]

dep u tize (dep′yə tīz), *v.,* **-tized, -tiz ing.** *—v.t.* appoint as deputy. *—v.i.* act as deputy.

dep u ty (dep′yə tē), *n., pl.* **-ties,** *adj.* *—n.* 1 person appointed to do the work of or act in the place of another. 2 assistant to certain public officials: *a sheriff's deputy.* 3 representative in the lower house of certain legislatures. *—adj.* acting as a deputy.

De Quin cey (di kwin′sē), **Thomas,** 1785-1859, English essayist.

der., 1 derivation. 2 derivative.

de rail (dē rāl′), *v.t.* cause (a train, etc.) to run off the rails. *—v.i.* run off the rails. **—de rail′ment,** *n.*

de rail leur (di rā′lər), *n.* 1 a spring-driven mechanism on a bicycle that changes gears by causing the drive chain to move from one sprocket wheel to another. 2 a bicycle equipped with a derailleur. [< French]

de range (di rānj′), *v.t.,* **-ranged, -rang ing.** 1 disturb the order or arrangement of; throw into confusion. 2 make insane. **—de range′ment,** *n.*

derby (def. 3b)

Der by (dėr′bē; *British* där′bē), *n., pl.* **-bies.** 1 a famous horse race run every year since 1780 at Epsom Downs. 2 a horse race of similar importance: *the Kentucky Derby.* 3 **derby,** a any important race or competition. b a stiff hat with a rounded crown and a narrow brim; bowler. 4 city in central England. 220,000. [< the 12th Earl of *Derby,* died 1834, who founded the race]

der e lict (der′ə likt), *adj.* 1 abandoned, deserted, or left by an owner or guardian, as a ship at sea. 2 failing in one's duty; negligent. *—n.* 1 ship abandoned and afloat at sea. 2 a poor, homeless person who is unwilling or unable to care for himself. 3 any useless, discarded, or forsaken thing. [< Latin *derelictum* abandoned < *de-* + *re-* behind + *linquere* leave]

hat, āge, fär; let, ēqual, tėrm;
it, īce; hot, ōpen, ôrder;
oil, out; cup, pu̇t, rüle;
ch, child; ng, long; sh, she;
th, thin; ᴛʜ, then; zh, measure;

ə represents *a* in about, *e* in taken, *i* in pencil, *o* in lemon, *u* in circus.

< = from, derived from, taken from.

der e lic tion (der′ə lik′shən), *n.* 1 failure in one's duty; negligence. 2 abandonment; forsaking.

de ride (di rīd′), *v.t.,* **-rid ed, -rid ing.** make fun of; laugh at in scorn. See **ridicule** for synonym study. [< Latin *deridere* < *de-* + *ridere* to laugh] **—de rid′er,** *n.* **—de rid′ing ly,** *adv.*

de ri gueur (də rē gœr′), FRENCH. required by etiquette; according to custom; proper.

de ri sion (di rizh′ən), *n.* 1 scornful laughter; ridicule. 2 object of ridicule. [< Latin *derisionem* < *deridere.* See DERIDE.]

de ri sive (di rī′siv), *adj.* that ridicules; mocking: *derisive laughter.* **—de ri′sive ly,** *adv.* **—de ri′sive ness,** *n.*

de ri sor y (di rī′sər ē), *adj.* derisive.

deriv., 1 derivation. 2 derivative.

der i va tion (der′ə vā′shən), *n.* 1 act or fact of deriving. 2 condition of being derived. 3 origin; source. 4 system in a language for making words from another word or root by adding prefixes and suffixes and by other methods. EXAMPLE: *Quickness* = *quick* + suffix *-ness.* 5 statement or account of the formation and origin of a word; etymology.

de riv a tive (di riv′ə tiv), *adj.* coming from a source; not original; derived. *—n.* 1 something derived. 2 word formed by adding a prefix or suffix to another word. 3 a chemical substance obtained from another by modification or by partial substitution of components: *Acetic acid is a derivative of alcohol.* 4 (in mathematics) the instantaneous rate of change of a function with respect to its variable. **—de riv′a tive ly,** *adv.*

de rive (di rīv′), *v.,* **-rived, -riv ing.** *—v.t.* 1 obtain from a source; get; receive: *derive knowledge from reading books.* 2 trace (a word, custom, etc.) from or to a source or origin: *The word "December" is ultimately derived from the Latin word "decem," which means "ten."* 3 obtain by reasoning; deduce. 4 obtain (a chemical substance) from another. *—v.i.* come from a source or origin; originate. [< Latin *derivare* lead off, draw off < *de-* + *rivus* stream] **—de riv′a ble,** *adj.*

der ma (dėr′mə), *n.* dermis. [< Greek *derma, dermatos*]

der mal (dėr′məl), *adj.* of the skin.

der ma ti tis (dėr′mə tī′tis), *n.* inflammation of the skin.

der ma to log i cal (dėr′mə tə loj′ə kəl), *adj.* of or having to do with dermatology.

der ma tol o gist (dėr′mə tol′ə jist), *n.* an expert in dermatology.

der ma tol o gy (dėr′mə tol′ə jē). *n.* branch of medicine that deals with the skin, its structure, and its diseases.
der ma to sis (dėr′mə tō′sis), *n.* any skin disease.
der mis (dėr′mis), *n.* the sensitive layer of skin beneath the epidermis; derma; cutis; corium. See **epidermis** for diagram.
der o gate (der′ə gāt), *v.,* **-gat ed, -gat ing.** —*v.i.* 1 take away a part so as to impair it; detract: *The queen felt that summoning a parliament would derogate from her authority.* 2 become worse; degenerate. —*v.t.* take away (something) from a thing so as to impair it. [< Latin *derogatum* < *de-* away from + *rogare ask*] **—der′o ga′tion,** *n.*
de rog a tive (di rog′ə tiv), *adj.* derogatory.
de rog a to ry (di rog′ə tôr′ē, di rog′ə-tōr′ē), *adj.* having the effect of lowering in honor or estimation; disparaging: *a derogatory remark.* **—de rog′a to′ri ly,** *adv.*

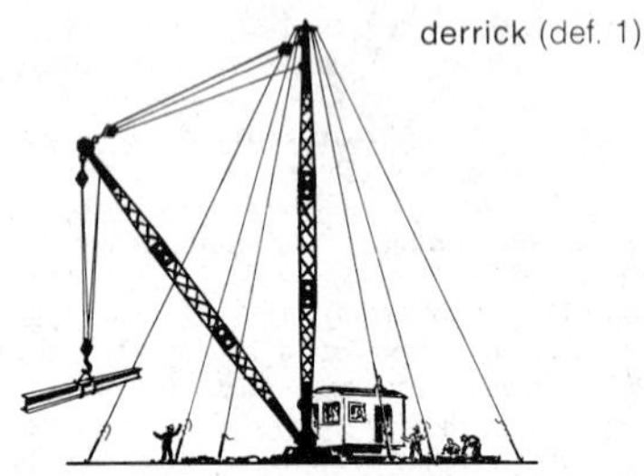
derrick (def. 1)

der rick (der′ik), *n.* 1 machine for lifting and moving heavy objects. A derrick has a long arm that swings at an angle from the base of an upright post or frame. 2 a tower-like framework over an oil well that holds the drilling and hoisting machinery. [earlier meaning "gallows" < *Derrick,* a hangman in London around 1600]
der ri ère or **der ri ere** (der′ē er′), *n.* the buttocks. [< French *derrière*]
der ring-do (der′ing dü′), *n.* daring deeds; heroic daring. [alteration of Middle English *dorryng don* daring to do]
der rin ger (der′ən jər), *n.* a short pistol of relatively large caliber. [< Henry *Deringer,* 1786-1868, American inventor]
der vish (dėr′vish), member of a Moslem mystical religious order that practices self-denial and devotion. Some dance and spin about violently. [< Turkish *derviş* < Persian *darvīsh*]
de sal i nate (dē sal′ə nāt), *v.t.,* **-nat ed, -nat ing.** desalt.
de salt (dē sôlt′), *v.t.* remove salt from: *desalt sea water.* **—de salt′er,** *n.*
des cant (*v.* des kant′, dis kant′; *n.* des′kant), *v.i.* 1 talk at great length; discourse: *She descanted upon the wonders of her trip to Europe.* 2 sing or play a melody with another melody. —*n.* 1 part music. 2 melody to be played or sung with another melody. 3 an extended comment; discourse. [< Old French *deschanter* < Medieval Latin *discantare* < Latin *dis-* + *cantus* song]
Des cartes (dā kärt′), *n.* **René,** 1596-1650, French philosopher and mathematician.
de scend (di send′), *v.i.* 1 go or come down from a higher to a lower place: *The river descends from the mountains to the sea.* 2 go or come down from an earlier to a later time: *a superstition descended from the Middle Ages.* 3 go from greater to less numbers; go from higher to lower on any scale: *75-50-25 form a series that descends.* 4 slope downward. 5 make a sudden attack: *The wolves descended on the sheep.* 6 be handed down from parent to child; pass by inheritance: *This land has been in our family for 150 years, descending from father to son.* 7 come down or spring from: *He is descended from pioneers.* 8 lower oneself; stoop: *In order to eat she descended to stealing.* —*v.t.* go or come down; move downward upon or along: *descend stairs. The trail descends the mountain.* [< Latin *descendere* < *de-* down + *scandere* to climb] **—de scend′a ble, de-scend′i ble,** *adj.*
de scend ant (di sen′dənt), *n.* 1 person born of a certain family or group: *a descendant of the Pilgrims.* 2 offspring; child, grandchild, great-grandchild, etc. You are a direct descendant of your parents, grandparents, great-grandparents, and earlier ancestors. —*adj.* going or coming down; descending.
de scend ent (di sen′dənt), *n., adj.* descendant.
de scent (di sent′), *n.* 1 a coming down or going down from a higher to a lower place: *the descent of a balloon.* 2 a downward slope. 3 way or passage down; means of descending. 4 a handing down from parent to child. 5 family line; ancestry: *of Italian descent.* 6 a sinking to a lower condition; decline; fall. 7 a sudden attack.
de scribe (di skrīb′), *v.t.,* **-scribed, -scrib ing.** 1 tell or write about; give a picture or account of in words: *The reporter described the accident.* 2 draw the outline of; trace: *The spinning top described a figure 8.* [< Latin *describere* < *de-* + *scribere* write] **—de scrib′a ble,** *adj.* **—de scrib′er,** *n.*
de scrip tion (di skrip′shən), *n.* 1 act of describing. 2 composition or account that describes or gives a picture in words. 3 kind; sort: *In the crowd there were people of every description.*
de scrip tive (di skrip′tiv), *adj.* using description; describing. **—de scrip′tive ly,** *adv.* **—de scrip′tive ness,** *n.*
de scry (di skrī′), *v.t.,* **-scried, -scry ing.** 1 catch sight of; be able to see; make out: *descry an island on the horizon.* 2 discover by observation; detect. [< Old French *descrier* proclaim < *des-* dis- + *crier* to cry]
des e crate (des′ə krāt), *v.t.,* **-crat ed, -crat ing.** treat or use without respect; disregard the sacredness of; profane. [< *de-* + *(con)secrate*] **—des′e crat′er, des′e-cra′tor,** *n.* **—des′e cra′tion,** *n.*
de seg re gate (dē seg′rə gāt), *v.,* **-gat ed, -gat ing.** —*v.t.* abolish racial segregation in: *desegregate a public school.* —*v.i.* become desegregated.
de seg re ga tion (dē seg′rə gā′shən), *n.* abolishment of the practice of racial segregation.
de sen si tize (dē sen′sə tīz), *v.t.,* **-tized, -tiz ing.** 1 make less sensitive. 2 (in photography) make less sensitive to light. **—de sen′si ti za′tion,** *n.* **—de sen′si tiz′-er,** *n.*
des ert[1] (dez′ərt), *n.* 1 a dry, barren region that is usually sandy and without trees. 2 region that is not inhabited or cultivated; wilderness. See synonym study below. —*adj.* 1 dry and barren. 2 not inhabited or cultivated; wild: *a desert island.* [< Late Latin *desertum* (thing) abandoned < Latin *deserere* abandon. See DESERT[2].]
Syn. *n.* 1,2 **Desert, wilderness** mean an uninhabited or uncultivated region. **Desert** usually emphasizes dryness or barrenness: *Deserts in Arizona and California have been made into farm land by irrigation. A desert island,* however, might be a verdant place which is merely deserted. **Wilderness** emphasizes lack of trails and roads in a region covered with dense vegetation: *Daniel Boone lived in Kentucky when it was still a wilderness.*
de sert[2] (di zėrt′), *v.t.* 1 go away and leave; abandon: *After the family deserted the farm, its buildings fell into ruin.* 2 forsake (a person, cause, etc.), especially in violation of an oath, obligation, or responsibility. 3 leave (military service) without permission and without intending to return. 4 fail (one) when needed: *His self-confidence deserted him after so many failures.* See synonym study below. —*v.i.* 1 run away from duty. 2 leave military service without permission. [< French *déserter* < Late Latin *desertare* < Latin *deserere* abandon < *de-* off + *serere* join] **—de sert′er,** *n.*
Syn. *v.t.* **Desert, forsake, abandon** mean to leave someone or something completely, either physically or mentally. **Abandon** implies little else, although in appropriate contexts it might gain overtones similar to *desert* and *forsake: abandon a blown-out tire, abandon one's vacation plans.* **Forsake,** a somewhat stilted word, may be used for rhetorical effect, especially of someone or something once regarded with affection: *forsake one's friends and home.* **Desert** is interchangeable with both *abandon* and *forsake* in defs. 1 and 4. Often, however, it carries the idea of violating an oath, obligation, or responsibility, as in defs. 2 and 3: *deserting one's children, a soldier's deserting his post.*
de sert[3] (di zėrt′), *n.* Usually, **deserts,** *pl.* what one deserves; suitable reward or punishment: *The reckless driver got his just deserts when his driver's license was revoked.* [< Old French *deserte,* past participle of *deservir.* See DESERVE.]
de ser tion (di zėr′shən), *n.* 1 act of deserting. 2 condition of being deserted. 3 a running away from duty, especially from military service.
de serve (di zėrv′), *v.,* **-served, -serv ing.** —*v.t.* have a claim or right to; be worthy of; merit: *A hard worker deserves good pay.* —*v.i.* be worthy: *He is a hard worker and deserves well.* [< Old French *deservir* < Latin *deservire* serve well < *de-* + *servire* serve] **—de serv′er,** *n.*
de serv ed ly (di zėr′vid lē), *adv.* according to what is deserved; justly; rightly.
de serv ing (di zėr′ving), *adj.* 1 that deserves; worthy (of something). 2 worth helping. —*n.* merit; deserts.
des ha bille (dez′ə bēl′), *n.* dishabille.
des ic cant (des′ə kənt), *n.* agent or drug that dries or desiccates.
des ic cate (des′ə kāt), *v.,* **-cat ed, -cat ing.** —*v.t.* 1 deprive of moisture or water; dry thoroughly. 2 preserve by drying thoroughly; dehydrate: *desiccated fruit.* —*v.i.* become dry; dry up. [< Latin *desiccatum* dried out < *de-* + *siccus* dry] **—des′ic ca′-tion,** *n.*
de sid e ra tum (di sid′ə rā′təm, di sid′ə-rä′təm), *n., pl.* **-ta** (-tə). something desired or needed. [< Latin]
de sign (di zīn′), *n.* 1 a drawing, plan, or sketch made to serve as a pattern from which to work: *a design for a machine.*

design (def. 2)

2 arrangement of detail, form, and color in painting, weaving, building, etc.: *a wallpaper design in tan and brown.* 3 art of making designs, patterns, or sketches: *Architects study to become skilled in design.* 4 piece of artistic work. 5 plan or scheme in mind to be carried out. See **plan** for synonym study. 6 plan or scheme of attack; crafty plan: *The thief had designs upon the safe.* 7 purpose; aim; intention: *Whether by accident or design, he overturned the lamp.* See **intention** for synonym study. 8 adaptation of means to a planned end; underlying plan or conception: *the evidence of design in a communication satellite.*
—*v.t.* 1 make a first sketch of; arrange form and color of; draw in outline: *design a dress.* 2 plan out; form in the mind; contrive: *The author of this detective story has designed an exciting plot.* 3 have in mind to do; purpose: *Did you design this result?* 4 set apart; intend: *That room was designed for a library.* —*v.i.* 1 make drawings, sketches, plans, etc. 2 form or fashion a work of art.
[< Middle French *desseign,* ultimately < Latin *designare* mark out < *de-* + *signum* mark]

des ig nate (*v.* dez′ig nāt; *adj.* dez′ig nit, dez′ig nāt), *v.,* **-nat ed, -nat ing,** *adj.* —*v.t.* 1 mark out; point out; indicate definitely; show: *Red lines designate main roads on this map.* 2 name; entitle: *The ruler of Iran is designated Shah.* 3 select for duty, office, etc.; appoint: *The President designated her as ambassador to Italy.* —*adj.* appointed; selected: *the bishop designate.* —**des′ig na′tor,** *n.*

des ig na tion (dez′ig nā′shən), *n.* 1 act of marking out; pointing out: *The designation of places on a map should be clear.* 2 a descriptive title; name: *"Your Honor" is a designation given to a judge.* 3 appointment to an office or position; selection for a duty.

de sign ed ly (di zī′nid lē), *adv.* on purpose; intentionally.

de sign er (di zī′nər), *n.* 1 person who designs. A dress designer makes patterns and sketches for women's clothes. 2 plotter; schemer.

de sign ing (di zī′ning), *adj.* 1 scheming; plotting. 2 showing plan or forethought. —*n.* art of making designs, patterns, sketches, etc.

de sir a bil i ty (di zī′rə bil′ə tē), *n.* quality or condition of being desirable.

de sir a ble (di zī′rə bəl), *adj.* worth wishing for; worth having; pleasing. —**de sir′a ble ness,** *n.* —**de sir′a bly,** *adv.*

de sire (di zīr′), *n., v.,* **-sired, -sir ing.** —*n.* 1 a wanting or longing; strong wish: *a desire for money.* See synonym study below. 2 an expressed wish; request: *I sent you, at your desire, the articles you wanted.* 3 thing wished for: *The desire of all nations is peace.* —*v.t.* 1 wish earnestly for; long for; crave: *desire wealth or fame.* See **wish** for synonym study. 2 express a wish for; ask for: *I desire a room for the night.* —*v.i.* have or feel a desire. [< Old French *desirer* to long for < Latin *desiderare*]

Syn. *n.* 1 **Desire, longing, craving** mean a strong wish. **Desire** applies to any strong wish for something a person thinks or hopes he can get: *She felt a great desire to see her birthplace again.* **Longing** applies to an earnest or enduring desire, often for something that is beyond reach: *the longing for the return of spring.* **Craving** applies to a desire so strong that it amounts to a need or hunger: *a craving for alcohol.*

de sir ous (di zī′rəs), *adj.* having or showing desire; desiring; wishing; eager: *desirous of going to Europe.*

de sist (di zist′), *v.i.* stop doing something; cease. [< Latin *desistere* < *de-* + *sistere* to stop]

desk (desk), *n.* 1 piece of furniture with a flat or sloping top on which to write or to rest books for reading. 2 any similar piece, such as a lectern or pulpit. 3 department of work at a certain location or at a desk: *the information desk of a library.* [< Medieval Latin *desca* < Italian *desco* < Latin *discus* quoit, dish < Greek *diskos.* Doublet of DAIS, DISCUS, DISH, and DISK.]

Des Moines (də moin′), 1 capital of Iowa, in the central part. 201,000. 2 **Des Moines River,** river flowing from SW Minnesota across Iowa into the Mississippi. 327 mi.

des o late (*adj.* des′ə lit; *v.* des′ə lāt), *adj., v.,* **-lat ed, -lat ing.** —*adj.* 1 laid waste; devastated; barren: *desolate land.* 2 not lived in; deserted: *a desolate house.* 3 unhappy; forlorn; wretched. See synonym study below. 4 left alone; solitary; lonely. 5 dreary; dismal: *a desolate life.* —*v.t.* 1 make unfit to live in; lay waste. 2 make unhappy: *We are desolated to hear that you are going away.* 3 deprive of inhabitants. [< Latin *desolatum* < *de-* + *solus* alone] —**des′o late ly,** *adv.* —**des′o late ness,** *n.*

Syn. *adj.* 3 **Desolate, disconsolate** mean unhappy and forlorn. **Desolate** emphasizes the feeling that one is left alone or separated from someone dear: *I was desolate when my mother died.* **Disconsolate** implies absence of hope, consolation, and comfort: *I was disconsolate when I lost my job and was unable to get another for several months.*

des o la tion (des′ə lā′shən), *n.* 1 act of making desolate; devastation. 2 a ruined, lonely, or deserted condition. 3 a desolate place. 4 lonely sorrow; sadness.

De So to (di sō′tō), **Hernando,** 1500?-1542, Spanish explorer in North America who discovered the Mississippi River.

des ox y ri bo nu cle ic acid (des ok′sə rī′bō nü klē′ik, des ok′sə rī′bō nyü klē′ik), deoxyribonucleic acid.

de spair (di sper′, di spar′), *n.* 1 loss of hope; a being without hope; a feeling that nothing good can happen to one; helplessness. 2 person or thing that causes despair. —*v.i.* lose hope; be without hope: *The doctors despaired of saving the sick man's life.* [< Old French *desperer* lose hope < Latin *desperare* < *de-* out of, without + *sperare* to hope]

de spair ing (di sper′ing, di spar′ing), *adj.* feeling, showing, or expressing despair; hopeless. See **hopeless** for synonym study. —**de spair′ing ly,** *adv.*

des patch (dis pach′), *v., n.* dispatch.

des pe ra do (des′pə rā′dō, des′pə rä′dō), *n., pl.* **-does** or **-dos.** a bold, reckless criminal; dangerous outlaw. [< earlier Spanish, despaired < Latin *desperatum*]

des per ate (des′pər it), *adj.* 1 not caring what happens because hope is gone; reckless because of despair: *Suicide is a desperate act.* 2 ready to run any risk: *a desperate robber.* 3 having little chance for hope or cure; very dangerous or serious: *a desperate illness.* 4 hopelessly bad: *desperate circumstances.* 5 hopeless. See **hopeless** for synonym study. [< Latin *desperatum* despaired, hopeless] —**des′per ate ly,** *adv.* —**des′per ate ness,** *n.*

hat, āge, fär; let, ēqual, tėrm;
it, īce; hot, ōpen, ôrder;
oil, out; cup, pu̇t, rüle;
ch, child; ng, long; sh, she;
th, thin; ᴛʜ, then; zh, measure;

ə represents *a* in about, *e* in taken, *i* in pencil, *o* in lemon, *u* in circus.

< = from, derived from, taken from.

des pe ra tion (des′pə rā′shən), *n.* 1 a hopeless and reckless feeling; readiness to run any risk: *They jumped out of the window in desperation when they saw that the stairs were on fire.* 2 despair.

des pi ca ble (des′pi kə bəl, des pik′ə bəl), *adj.* to be despised; contemptible: *a despicable liar.* [< Late Latin *despicabilem* < *despicere* despise] —**des′pi ca ble ness,** *n.* —**des′pi ca bly,** *adv.*

de spise (di spīz′), *v.t.,* **-spised, -spis ing.** look down on; feel contempt for; scorn. [< Old French *despis-,* a form of *despire* < Latin *despicere* < *de-* down + *specere* look at] —**de spis′er,** *n.*

de spite (di spīt′), *prep.* in spite of: *We went for a walk despite the rain.* —*n.* 1 insult or injury. 2 malice; spite. 3 contempt; scorn. 4 **in despite of,** in spite of. [< Old French *despit* < Latin *despectum* spite < *despicere* despise]

de spite ful (di spīt′fəl), *adj.* spiteful; malicious. —**de spite′ful ly,** *adv.*

de spoil (di spoil′), *v.t.* strip of possessions; rob; plunder. [< Latin *despoliare* < *de-* + *spolium* armor, booty] —**de spoil′er,** *n.* —**de spoil′ment,** *n.*

de spo li a tion (di spō′lē ā′shən), *n.* robbery; plundering.

de spond (di spond′), *v.i.* lose heart, courage, or hope. —*n.* despondency. [< Latin *despondere* < *de-* + *spondere* lose heart]

de spond ence (di spon′dəns), *n.* despondency.

de spond en cy (di spon′dən sē), *n.* loss of heart, courage, or hope; discouragement; dejection.

de spond ent (di spon′dənt), *adj.* having lost heart, courage, or hope; discouraged; dejected. —**de spond′ent ly,** *adv.*

des pot (des′pət, des′pot), *n.* 1 monarch having unlimited power; absolute ruler. 2 any person who exercises tyrannical authority; oppressor. [< Greek *despotēs* master]

des pot ic (des pot′ik), *adj.* of a despot; having unlimited power; tyrannical. —**des pot′i cal ly,** *adv.*

des pot ism (des′pə tiz′əm), *n.* 1 government by a despot. 2 tyranny or oppression.

des sert (di zėrt′), *n.* course of pie, cake, ice cream, cheese, fruit, etc., served at the end of a meal. [< Middle French < *desservir* clear the table < *des-* dis- + *servir* serve]

des ti na tion (des′tə nā′shən), *n.* 1 place to which a person or thing is going or is being sent. 2 a setting apart for a particular purpose or use; intention.

des tine (des′tən), *v.t.*, **-tined, -tin ing.** 1 set apart for a particular purpose or use; intend: *The prince was destined from birth to be a king.* 2 cause by fate: *My letter was destined never to reach her.* 3 **destined for,** intended to go to; bound for: *ships destined for England.* [< Old French *destiner* < Latin *destinare* fix, set < *de-* + *stare* to stand]

des ti ny (des′tə nē), *n., pl.* **-nies.** 1 what becomes of a person or thing in the end; one's lot or fortune. See **fate** for synonym study. 2 what will happen in spite of all later efforts to change or prevent it. 3 power that is believed to determine the course of events; fate.

des ti tute (des′tə tüt, des′tə tyüt), *adj.* 1 lacking necessary things such as food, clothing, and shelter. 2 **destitute of,** having no; without: *A bald head is destitute of hair.* [< Latin *destitutum* forsaken < *de-* away + *statuere* put, place]

des ti tu tion (des′tə tü′shən, des′tə-tyü′shən), *n.* 1 destitute condition; extreme poverty. See **poverty** for synonym study. 2 a being without; lack.

de stroy (di stroi′), *v.t.* 1 break to pieces; make useless; ruin; spoil: *Drought destroyed the corn crop.* See synonym study below. 2 put an end to; do away with: *A heavy rain destroyed all hope of a picnic.* 3 deprive of life; kill: *Fire destroys many trees every year.* 4 counteract the effect of; make void: *A child's confidence can be destroyed by correcting his every move.* [< Old French *destruire* < Latin *destruere* < *de-* + *struere* pile, build]

Syn. 1 **Destroy, demolish** mean to pull down or wreck the structure of something. **Destroy** means to make useless by breaking to pieces, taking apart, killing, or in any other of many ways: *The paintings were destroyed in the fire.* **Demolish** means to ruin by tearing down or smashing to pieces and applies only to things thought of as having been built up: *The city demolished many buildings to make room for the thruway.*

de stroy er (di stroi′ər), *n.* 1 person or thing that destroys. 2 a small, fast warship with guns, torpedoes, and other weapons.

de struct (di strukt′), *v.t., v.i.* blow up a rocket or other missile that fails to function properly. —*n.* the destructing of a rocket or missile. [back-formation < *destruction*]

de struct i bil i ty (di struk′tə bil′ə tē), *n.* quality of being destructible.

de struct i ble (di struk′tə bəl), *adj.* capable of being destroyed.

de struc tion (di struk′shən), *n.* 1 act of destroying. 2 condition of being destroyed; ruin. See **ruin** for synonym study. 3 thing that destroys. [< Latin *destructionem* < *destruere.* See DESTROY.]

de struc tive (di struk′tiv), *adj.* 1 destroying; causing destruction: *Fires and earthquakes are destructive. Termites are destructive insects.* 2 tearing down; not helpful; not constructive: *No one appreciates destructive criticism.* **—de struc′tive ly,** *adv.* **—de struc′tive ness,** *n.*

destructive distillation, the decomposition of a substance, such as wood or coal, by strong heat in a closed container, and the collection of the volatile matters evolved.

de struc tor (di struk′tər), *n.* 1 a furnace or incinerator for the burning of refuse. 2 something that destructs.

des ue tude (des′wə tüd, des′wə tyüd), *n.* disuse: *Many words once commonly used have fallen into desuetude.* [< Latin *desuetudo* < *de-* dis- + *suescere* accustom]

des ul to ry (des′əl tôr′ē, des′əl tōr′ē), *adj.* jumping from one thing to another; without aim or method; unconnected: *desultory reading.* [< Latin *desultorius* of a leaper, ultimately < *de-* down + *salire* to leap] **—des′ul to′ri ly,** *adv.* **—des′ul to′ri ness,** *n.*

de tach (di tach′), *v.t.* 1 loosen and remove; unfasten; separate: *She detached the trailer from the car.* 2 send away on special duty: *One squad of soldiers was detached to guard the road.* [< French *détacher* < *dé-* dis- + *(at)tacher* attach] **—de tach′a ble,** *adj.*

de tached (di tacht′), *adj.* 1 separate from others; isolated; unattached: *a row of detached houses.* 2 impartial. 3 reserved; aloof. **—de tach′ed ly,** *adv.* **—de tach′ed ness,** *n.*

de tach ment (di tach′mənt), *n.* 1 a taking apart; separation. 2 a standing apart; lack of interest; aloofness. 3 freedom from prejudice or bias; impartial attitude. 4 group of soldiers or ships sent on some special duty. 5 state of being on special duty: *soldiers on detachment.*

de tail (di tāl′, dē′tāl), *n.* 1 a small or unimportant part; item; particular: *the details of a report.* See **item** for synonym study. 2 a dealing with small things one by one: *An engineer must have a grasp of detail.* 3 a minute account; report of particulars. 4 a minor decoration or subordinate part in a building, picture, machine, etc. 5 act of selecting a small group for some special duty. 6 a small group selected for or sent on some special duty. 7 **in detail,** with all the details; part by part. —*v.t.* 1 tell fully; give the particulars of: *detail a plan.* 2 select for or send on special duty: *We were detailed to pick out a campsite.* [< French *détail* < *détaillir* cut in pieces < *de-* + *tailler* cut]

de tailed (di tāld′, dē′tāld), *adj.* 1 full of details and particulars. 2 minute; exact; particular.

de tain (di tān′), *v.t.* 1 keep from going; hold back; delay: *The heavy traffic detained us for almost an hour.* 2 keep from going away; hold as a prisoner: *The police detained the suspect for further questioning about the robbery.* 3 withhold. [< Old French *detenir* < Latin *detinere* < *de-* + *tenere* to hold] **—de tain′ment,** *n.*

de tect (di tekt′), *v.t.* 1 discover (a person) in the performance of some act: *The child was detected stealing cookies in the pantry.* 2 discover the presence, existence, or fact of: *detect any odor in the room, detect an error in the account.* 3 demodulate. [< Latin *detectum* uncovered < *de-* + *tegere* to cover]

de tect a ble (di tek′tə bəl), *adj.* capable of being detected.

de tect i ble (di tek′tə bəl), *adj.* detectable.

de tec tion (di tek′shən), *n.* 1 a finding out; discovery: *the detection of crimes.* 2 a being found out or discovered: *His detection will be a matter of only a few hours.* 3 demodulation.

de tec tive (di tek′tiv), *n.* member of a police force or other person whose work is finding information by investigation, to discover who committed a crime, etc. —*adj.* 1 having to do with detectives and their work: *a detective story.* 2 fitted for, skilled in, or used in detecting.

de tec tor (di tek′tər), *n.* 1 person or thing that detects. 2 demodulator.

dé tente (dā tänt′), *n.* FRENCH. the easing of tensions, especially between nations or political groups.

de ten tion (di ten′shən), *n.* 1 act of detaining; holding back. 2 condition of being detained. 3 a keeping in custody; confinement: *A jail is used for the detention of persons who have been arrested.* [< Late Latin *detentionem* < Latin *detinere.* See DETAIN.]

de ter (di tėr′), *v.t.*, **-terred, -ter ring.** discourage or prevent from acting or proceeding by fear or consideration of danger or trouble; hinder: *The extreme heat deterred us from going downtown.* [< Latin *deterrere* < *de-* from + *terrere* frighten] **—de ter′ment,** *n.*

de ter gen cy (di tėr′jən sē), *n.* detergent quality; cleansing power.

de ter gent (di tėr′jənt), *n.* 1 a synthetic substance, usually a chemical compound that acts like soap, used for cleansing. 2 any substance used for cleansing. Soap is a detergent. —*adj.* cleansing. [< Latin *detergentem* wiping off < *de-* + *tergere* wipe]

de ter i o rate (di tir′ē ə rāt′), *v.*, **-rat ed, -rat ing.** —*v.i.* become worse; lessen in value; depreciate: *Machinery deteriorates rapidly if it is not taken care of.* —*v.t.* make worse. [< Latin *deterioratum* worsened < *deterior* worse] **—de ter′i o ra′tion,** *n.*

de ter mi na ble (di tėr′mə nə bəl), *adj.* 1 capable of being settled or decided. 2 capable of being found out exactly.

de ter mi nant (di tėr′mə nənt), *adj.* determining; deciding. —*n.* 1 thing that determines. 2 (in mathematics) a certain number of quantities arranged in a square block whose value is the sum of all the products that can be formed from them according to certain rules.

de ter mi nate (di tėr′mə nit), *adj.* 1 with exact limits; fixed; definite. 2 settled; positive. 3 determined; resolute. 4 having flowers which arise from terminal buds and thus terminate a stem or branch; cymose. The forget-me-not has determinate inflorescence. **—de ter′mi nate ly,** *adv.* **—de ter′mi nate ness,** *n.*

de ter mi na tion (di tėr′mə nā′shən), *n.* 1 great firmness in carrying out a purpose; fixed purpose: *My determination was not weakened by the difficulties I met.* 2 a finding out the exact amount or kind, by weighing, measuring, or calculating: *determination of the gold in a sample of rock.* 3 a deciding; settling beforehand. 4 a being determined; settlement; decision. 5 result of finding out exactly; conclusion.

de ter mi na tive (di tėr′mə nā′tiv, di tėr′mə nə tiv), *adj.* determining. —*n.* thing that determines. **—de ter′mi na′tive ly,** *adv.* **—de ter′mi na′tive ness,** *n.*

de ter mine (di tėr′mən), *v.*, **-mined, -min ing.** —*v.i.* make up one's mind very firmly; resolve: *She determined to become the best Scout in her troop.* See **decide** for synonym study. —*v.t.* 1 find out exactly: *The captain determined the latitude and longitude of his ship's position.* 2 be the deciding fact in reaching a certain result: *Tomorrow's weather will determine whether we go to the beach or stay home.* 3 decide or settle beforehand; fix: *determine the date of a meeting.* 4 limit; define: *The meaning of a word is partly determined by its use in a particular sentence.* 5 settle; decide: *determine a dispute.* 6 fix the geometrical position of. 7 put an end to; conclude. [< Latin *determinare* set limits to < *de-* + *terminus* end]

de ter mined (di tėr′mənd), *adj.* 1 with one's mind firmly made up; resolved: *I was determined to go in spite of the storm.* 2 firm; resolute: *a determined effort.* **—de ter′mined ly,** *adv.* **—de ter′mined ness,** *n.*

de ter min er (di tėr′mə nər), *n.* 1 person or thing that determines; determinant. 2 a limiting adjective or modifier which precedes a noun or pronoun phrase. *A* in *a hat, the* in *the big house,* and *every* in *every little thing* are determiners.

de ter min ism (di tėr′mə niz′əm), *n.* 1 doctrine that human actions are the necessary results of antecedent causes. 2 doctrine that all events are determined by antecedent causes.

de ter min ist (di tėr′mə nist), *n.* person who believes in determinism.

de ter min is tic (di tėr′mə nis′tik), *adj.* of or having to do with determinism.

de ter rence (di tėr′əns, di ter′əns), *n.* 1 act or process of deterring. 2 a deterrent.

de ter rent (di tėr′ənt, di ter′ənt), *adj.* discouraging or hindering; deterring: *a deterrent influence.* *—n.* something that deters.

de test (di test′), *v.t.* dislike intensely; hate. See **hate** for synonym study. [< Latin *detestari* curse while calling the gods to witness < *de-* + *testis* witness] **—de test′er,** *n.*

de test a ble (di tes′tə bəl), *adj.* deserving to be detested; hateful. **—de test′a ble ness,** *n.* **—de test′a bly,** *adv.*

de tes ta tion (dē′tes′tā′shən), *n.* 1 an intense dislike; hatred. 2 a detested person or thing.

de throne (di thrōn′), *v.t.,* **-throned, -thron ing.** put off a throne or a high position; remove from ruling power; depose. **—de throne′ment,** *n.* **—de thron′er,** *n.*

de Tocque ville (də tôk′vil), **Alexis,** 1805-1859, French statesman and political writer.

det o nate (det′n āt), *v.t., v.i.,* **-nat ed, -nat ing.** explode with a loud noise: *The workmen detonated the dynamite. Suddenly the bomb detonated.* [< Latin *detonatum* thundered < *de-* + *tonare* to thunder] **—det′o na′tion,** *n.*

det o na tor (det′n ā′tər), *n.* fuse, percussion cap, or similar device used to set off an explosive.

de tour (dē′tůr, di tůr′), *n.* 1 road that is used when the main or direct road cannot be traveled. 2 a roundabout way or course. *—v.i.* use a detour. *—v.t.* cause to use a detour. [< French *détour* < *détourner* turn aside]

de tox i fy (dē tok′sə fī), *v.t.,* **-fied, -fy ing.** remove toxic or poisonous qualities from. **—de tox′i fi ca′tion,** *n.*

de tract (di trakt′), *v.i., v.t.* take away (a part) from a whole; remove (some of the quality or worth); withdraw: *The ugly frame detracts something from the beauty of the picture.* [< Latin *detractum* drawn away < *de-* + *trahere* to draw]

de trac tion (di trak′shən), *n.* 1 a taking away of some quality or worth; detracting. 2 a speaking evil of; belittling.

de trac tive (di trak′tiv), *adj.* 1 tending to detract. 2 speaking evil; belittling. **—de trac′tive ly,** *adv.*

de trac tor (di trak′tər), *n.* person who speaks evil of or belittles another.

de train (dē trān′), *v.i.* get off a railroad train. *—v.t.* put off from a railroad train. **—de train′ment,** *n.*

det ri ment (det′rə mənt), *n.* 1 loss, damage, or injury done, caused to, or sustained by a person or thing; harm: *She worked her way through college without detriment to her studies.* 2 something that causes loss, damage, or injury. [< Latin *detrimentum* < *deterere* wear away < *de-* + *terere* to wear]

det ri men tal (det′rə men′tl), *adj.* causing loss or damage; injurious; harmful. **—det′ri men′tal ly,** *adv.*

de tri tus (di trī′təs), *n.* 1 (in geology) an accumulation of small fragments such as sand, silt, etc., worn away from rock. 2 any disintegrated material. [< Latin, a rubbing away < *deterere.* See DETRIMENT.]

De troit (di troit′), *n.* 1 city in SE Michigan. 1,514,000. 2 **Detroit River,** river connecting Lake Erie and Lake St. Clair. 25 mi.

de trop (də trō′), FRENCH. 1 too much; too many. 2 unwelcome; in the way.

deuce (düs, dyüs), *n., v.,* **deuced, deuc ing,** *interj.* *—n.* 1 a playing card marked with a *2.* 2 the side of a die having two spots. 3 a dice throw of two aces. 4 in tennis: **a** a tie score of 40 each, or any subsequent tie score in a game. **b** a tie score of five or more games each in a set. *—v.t.* (in tennis) to even the score of (a game or set) at deuce. *—interj.* INFORMAL. exclamation of annoyance meaning "bad luck" or "the devil." [< Old French *deus* two < Latin *duos,* accusative of *duo* two]

deu ced (dü′sid, düst; dyü′sid, dyüst), INFORMAL. *adj.* devilish; excessive. *—adv.* devilishly; excessively. **—deu′ced ly,** *adv.*

de us ex ma chi na (dē′əs eks mak′ə-nə), LATIN. person, god, or event that comes just in time to solve a difficulty in a story, play, etc.

Deut., Deuteronomy.

deu ter i um (dü tir′ē əm, dyü tir′ē əm), *n.* isotope of hydrogen whose atoms have about twice the mass of ordinary hydrogen; heavy hydrogen. Deuterium occurs in heavy water. *Symbol:* D; *atomic number* 1; *mass number* 2. [< New Latin < Greek *deuteros* second]

deuterium oxide, heavy water.

deu te ron (dü′tə ron′, dyü′tə ron′), *n.* the nucleus of an atom of deuterium, consisting of one proton and one neutron.

Deu te ron o my (dü′tə ron′ə mē, dyü′tə-ron′ə mē), *n.* the fifth book of the Old Testament.

Deut sche mark (doi′chə), the monetary unit of Germany, a coin worth about 31 cents in West Germany and about 45 cents in East Germany.

de Va ler a (dev′ə ler′ə, dev′ə lir′ə), **Eamon,** born 1882, Irish political leader, former prime minister of the Republic of Ireland, president from 1959 to 1973.

de val u ate (dē val′yü āt), *v.t.,* **-at ed, -at ing.** devalue. **—de val′u a′tion,** *n.*

de val ue (dē val′yü), *v.t.,* **-val ued, -val u ing.** reduce the value of; fix a lower legal value on; devaluate: *devalue the pound.*

dev as tate (dev′ə stāt), *v.t.,* **-tat ed, -tat ing.** make desolate; lay waste; destroy; ravage: *A long war devastated the country.* [< Latin *devastatum* laid waste *de-* + *vastus* waste] **—dev′as tat′ing ly,** *adv.* **—dev′as ta′tion,** *n.* **—dev′as ta′tor,** *n.*

de Ve ga (də vā′gə), **Lope,** 1562-1635, Spanish dramatist and poet.

de vel op (di vel′əp), *v.i.* 1 come into being or activity; grow: *Plants develop from seeds.* 2 change in character through successive periods; evolve: *Land animals are believed to have developed from sea animals.* 3 become bigger, better, fuller, more useful, etc.: *Our business developed very slowly.* 4 (of an exposed or sensitized photographic film or plate) be treated with chemicals to bring out the latent image. 5 become known; become apparent. *—v.t.* 1 bring into being or activity: *Scientists have developed many new drugs to fight disease.* 2 cause to change in character through successive periods; evolve. 3 come to have: *I developed an interest in collecting stamps.* 4 make bigger, better, fuller, more useful, etc.: *Exercise develops the muscles.* 5 work out in greater detail: *Gradually we developed our plans for the club.* 6 treat (an exposed or sensitized photographic film or plate) with chemicals to bring out the latent image. 7 make known; reveal: *The investigation did not develop any new facts.* 8 (in music) elaborate (a theme or motive) by variation of rhythm, melody, harmony, etc. 9 bring forth; make more available: *develop the water power of an area.* 10 build on (open land) or rebuild (an old and often run-down area). [< French *développer* unwrap] **—de vel′op a ble,** *adj.*

hat, āge, fär; let, ēqual, tėrm;
it, īce; hot, ōpen, ôrder;
oil, out; cup, pu̇t, rüle;
ch, child; ng, long; sh, she;
th, thin; ᴛʜ, then; zh, measure;

ə represents *a* in about, *e* in taken, *i* in pencil, *o* in lemon, *u* in circus.

< = from, derived from, taken from.

de vel op er (di vel′ə pər), *n.* 1 person or thing that develops. 2 chemical used to bring out the latent image on a photographic film or plate. 3 person or company that develops land.

de vel op ment (di vel′əp mənt), *n.* 1 process of developing; growth. 2 outcome; result; new event: *The newspaper described the latest developments in the elections.* 3 a working out in greater and greater detail. 4 group of similar houses or apartment buildings built on open land or in place of old buildings. 5 a developing of a photograph.

de vel op men tal (di vel′əp men′tl), *adj.* of or having to do with development. **—de vel′op men′tal ly,** *adv.*

Dev e reux (dev′ə rü′), *n.* **Robert.** See **Essex.**

de vi ant (dē′vē ənt), *n.* a deviate. *—adj.* that deviates; deviating.

de vi ate (*v.* dē′vē āt; *n., adj. also* dē′vē it), *v.,* **-at ed, -at ing,** *n., adj.* *—v.i.* turn aside (from a way, course, rule, truth, etc.); diverge: *The mayor deviated from his custom and did not attend the parade.* See **diverge** for synonym study. *—v.t.* cause to turn aside; deflect. *—n.* an individual who shows a marked deviation from the norm. *—adj.* 1 characterized by a marked deviation from the standard or norm. 2 deviant. [< Late Latin *deviatum* turned aside < Latin *devius.* See DEVIOUS.] **—de′vi a′tor,** *n.*

de vi a tion (dē′vē ā′shən), *n.* 1 act of turning aside; swerving. 2 in statistics: **a** the difference between the mean of a set of values and one value in the set, used to measure variation from the norm. **b** amount of such difference. 3 divergence from a policy or course of action.

de vi a tion ism (dē′vē ā′shə niz′əm), *n.* a departing from party policies, especially from official Communist policies.

de vi a tion ist (dē′vē ā′shə nist), *n.* person who departs from party policies, especially from official Communist policies.

de vice (di vīs′), *n.* 1 something invented, devised, or fitted for a particular use or special purpose; mechanism or apparatus: *a device for automatically lighting a gas stove.* 2 a plan, scheme, or trick: *The child used the device of pretending illness to stay home from school.* 3 a drawing or figure used in a pattern or as an ornament. 4 picture or design on a coat of arms, often accompanied by a motto. 5 motto. 6 **leave to one's own devices,** leave to do as one thinks best. [< Old French *devis, devise* < *deviser* arrange. See DEVISE.]

dev il (dev′əl), *n., v.,* **-iled, -il ing** or **-illed, -il ling,** *interj.* —*n.* 1 **the Devil,** the supreme spirit of evil; the enemy of goodness; Satan. 2 any evil spirit; fiend; demon. 3 a wicked or cruel person. 4 a very clever, energetic, or reckless person. 5 an unfortunate or wretched person: *Would he do anything for a poor devil like me?* 6 printer's devil. 7 something very bad; an evil influence or power. 8 machine that has sharp teeth or spikes for tearing, cleaning, etc. 9 **give the devil his due,** be fair even to a bad or disliked person. 10 **raise the devil,** SLANG. make a great disturbance. 11 **the devil to pay,** much trouble ahead.
—*v.t.* 1 INFORMAL. bother or tease. 2 prepare (food) with hot or savory seasoning: *devil ham.*
—*interj.* **the devil!** exclamation used to express disgust, anger, surprise, etc.
[Old English *dēofol* < Late Latin *diabolus* < Greek *diabolos* slanderer < *diaballein* to slander < *dia-* against + *ballein* to throw]

dev iled (dev′əld), *adj.* highly seasoned: *deviled ham, deviled eggs.*

dev il fish (dev′əl fish′), *n., pl.* **-fish es** or **-fish.** 1 any of several large rays of warm seas that move by a flapping motion of broad fins; manta. 2 a large cephalopod, especially an octopus.

dev il ish (dev′ə lish), *adj.* 1 like a devil; worthy of the Devil; very evil: *a devilish temper.* 2 mischievous or daring. 3 INFORMAL. very great; extreme. —*adv.* INFORMAL. very; extremely. **—dev′il ish ly,** *adv.* **—dev′il ish ness,** *n.*

dev il-may-care (dev′əl mā ker′, dev′əl mā kar′), *adj.* very careless or reckless.

dev il ment (dev′əl mənt), *n.* devilish action or behavior; deviltry.

dev il ry (dev′əl rē), *n., pl.* **-ries.** deviltry.

devil's advocate, 1 (in the Roman Catholic Church) an official appointed to argue against a proposed beatification or canonization. 2 critic who argues either against a popular cause or for an unpopular cause.

devil's darning needle, dragonfly or damselfly.

devil's food cake, a rich, dark, chocolate cake.

Devil's Island, island off the coast of French Guiana, formerly used as a French penal colony.

dev il try (dev′əl trē), *n., pl.* **-tries.** 1 evil action; wicked mischief. 2 mischievous or daring behavior.

de vi ous (dē′vē əs), *adj.* 1 out of the direct way; winding; roundabout: *We took a devious route through side streets and alleys to avoid the crowded main street.* 2 straying from the right course; not straightforward: *His devious nature was shown in little lies and other dishonesties.* [< Latin *devius* turning aside < *de-* out of + *via* way] **—de′vi ous ly,** *adv.* **—de′vi ous ness,** *n.*

de vise (di vīz′), *v.,* **-vised, -vis ing,** *n.* —*v.t.* 1 think out; plan or contrive; invent: *I devised a way of raising boards up to my tree house by using a pulley.* 2 give or leave (land, buildings, etc.) by a will. —*n.* 1 a giving or leaving of land, buildings, etc., by a will. 2 a will or part of a will doing this. 3 land, buildings, etc., given or left in this way. [< Old French *deviser* dispose in portions, arrange, ultimately < Latin *dividere* divide]

de vis er (di vī′zər), *n.* person who devises; inventor.

de vi sor (di vī′zər, di vī′zôr), *n.* person who gives or leaves land, buildings, etc., by a will.

de vi tal ize (dē vī′tl īz), *v.,* **-ized, -iz ing.** 1 take the life of; kill. 2 make less vital; weaken; exhaust. **—de vi′tal i za′tion,** *n.*

de void (di void′), *adj.* entirely without; empty; lacking: *A well devoid of water is useless.* [< Old French *desvoidier* < *des-* dis- + *voidier* to empty]

de voir (də vwär′, dev′wär), *n.* 1 Usually, **devoirs,** *pl.* an act of civility or respect. 2 duty. [< Old French *deveir,* noun use of infinitive < Latin *debere* owe]

dev o lu tion (dev′ə lü′shən), *n.* 1 progression from stage to stage. 2 the transmitting or passing of property from person to person. 3 the passing on to a successor of any unexercised right. 4 the delegating (of duty, responsibility, etc.) to another. 5 (in biology) reversed evolution; degeneration. [< Medieval Latin *devolutionem* < Latin *devolvere.* See DEVOLVE.]

de volve (di volv′), *v.,* **-volved, -volv ing.** —*v.i.* be handed down to someone else; be transferred: *If the president is unable to handle his duties, they devolve upon the vice-president.* —*v.t.* transfer (duty, work, etc.) to someone else. [< Latin *devolvere* < *de-* down + *volvere* to roll]

Dev on (dev′ən), *n.* county in SW England.

De vo ni an (də vō′nē ən), *n.* 1 the geological period of the Paleozoic era, after the Silurian and before the Carboniferous, characterized by the appearance of amphibians, wingless insects, and seed-bearing plants. See chart under **geology.** 2 the rocks formed during this period. —*adj.* 1 of or having to do with Devon. 2 of or having to do with the Devonian or its rocks.

Dev on shire (dev′ən shər, dev′ən shir), *n.* Devon.

de vote (di vōt′), *v.t.,* **-vot ed, -vot ing.** 1 set apart for some person or purpose; give up: *That museum devotes one wing to modern art.* See synonym study below. 2 set apart and consecrate to God or to a sacred purpose. [< Latin *devotum* devoted < *de-* entirely + *vovere* to vow. Doublet of DEVOUT.]
Syn. 1 **Devote, dedicate, consecrate** mean to give something or someone up to a purpose. **Devote** emphasizes giving up seriously to a single purpose, shutting out everything else: *He devoted his time to study.* **Dedicate** emphasizes giving up or setting apart earnestly or solemnly for a serious or sacred use: *She dedicated her life to science.* **Consecrate** emphasizes setting the person or thing apart as sacred or glorified, by a solemn vow or ceremony: *A bishop consecrated the burial ground.*

de vot ed (di vō′tid), *adj.* very loyal; faithful: *a devoted friend.* **—de vot′ed ly,** *adv.* **—de vot′ed ness,** *n.*

dev o tee (dev′ə tē′), *n.* 1 person who is strongly devoted to something; enthusiast: *a devotee of the opera.* 2 person who is earnestly devoted to religion.

de vo tion (di vō′shən), *n.* 1 deep, steady affection; loyalty; faithfulness: *the devotion of a mother to her child.* 2 act of devoting. 3 condition of being devoted. 4 earnestness in religion; devoutness. 5 **devotions,** *pl.* worship, prayers, or praying.

de vo tion al (di vō′shə nəl), *adj.* having to do with religious devotion; used in worship. —*n.* a brief religious service. **—de vo′tion al ly,** *adv.*

de vour (di vour′), *v.t.* 1 eat (usually said of animals): *The lion devoured the zebra.* 2 eat like an animal; eat very hungrily: *The hungry boy devoured his dinner.* 3 consume, waste, or destroy: *The raging fire devoured the forest.* 4 swallow up; engulf. 5 take in with eyes or ears in a hungry, greedy way: *devour a new book.* 6 absorb wholly: *devoured by anxiety, devoured by curiosity.* [< Old French *devorer* < Latin *devorare* < *de-* down + *vorare* to gulp]

de vout (di vout′), *adj.* 1 having or showing reverence for God; religious. See **pious** for synonym study. 2 showing devotion: *a devout prayer.* 3 earnest; sincere; hearty: *devout thanks.* [< Old French *devot* < Latin *devotum.* Doublet of DEVOTE.] **—de vout′ly,** *adv.* **—de vout′ness,** *n.*

De Vries (də vrēs′), **Hugo,** 1848-1935, Dutch botanist.

dew (dü, dyü), *n.* 1 moisture from the air that condenses and collects in small drops on cool surfaces during the night. 2 any moisture in small drops, as tears or perspiration. 3 something fresh or refreshing like dew: *the dew of youth, the dew of sleep.* —*v.t.* wet with dew; moisten. [Old English *dēaw*]

dew ber ry (dü′ber′ē, dü′bər ē; dyü′ber′ē, dyü′bər ē), *n., pl.* **-ries.** 1 the sweet, black berry of various trailing vines, of the same genus as the blackberry. 2 any of these vines.

dew claw (dü′klô′, dyü′klô′), *n.* a small, useless hoof or toe on the feet of deer, pigs, dogs, etc.

dew drop (dü′drop′, dyü′drop′), *n.* a drop of dew.

Dew ey (dü′ē, dyü′ē), *n.* 1 **George,** 1837-1917 American admiral in the Spanish-American War. 2 **John,** 1859-1952, American philosopher and educator.

Dewey decimal system, system for classifying books, pamphlets, etc., in many libraries. Each subject and its subdivisions are assigned specific three-digit numbers and decimals. [< Melvil *Dewey,* 1851-1931, American librarian, who devised it]

dew fall (dü′fôl′, dyü′fôl′), *n.* 1 the formation or deposition of dew. 2 the time in the evening when this begins.

dew lap (dü′lap′, dyü′lap′), *n.* the loose fold of skin under the throat of cattle and some other animals.

dew lapped (dü′lapt′, dyü′lapt′), *adj.* having a dewlap.

DEW line, Distant Early Warning line, a chain of radar stations north of the Arctic Circle, designed to give the earliest possible warning of an air attack on the United States or Canada.

dew point, the temperature of the air at which dew begins to form.

dew y (dü′ē, dyü′ē), *adj.,* **dew i er, dew i est.** 1 wet with dew. 2 fresh or refreshing like dew. 3 of dew. **—dew′i ness,** *n.*

dex ter (dek′stər), *adj.* 1 of or on the right-hand side. 2 (in heraldry) situated on that part of an escutcheon to the right of the bearer. [< Latin, right]

dex ter i ty (dek ster′ə tē), *n.* 1 skill in using the hands or body. 2 skill in using the mind; cleverness.

dex ter ous (dek′stər əs), *adj.* 1 skillful in using the hands or body. See **deft** for synonym study. 2 having or showing skill in using the mind; clever. Also, **dextrous. —dex′ter ous ly,** *adv.* **—dex′ter ous ness,** *n.*

dex tral (dek′strəl), *adj.* 1 of the right hand; right-hand. 2 right-handed. **—dex′tral ly,** *adv.*

dex tral i ty (dek stral′ə tē), *n.* 1 state of being on the right side rather than the left. 2 right-handedness.

dex trin (dek′strən), *n.* a gummy substance obtained from starch, used as an adhesive, for sizing paper, etc.

dex trine (dek′strən, dek′strēn′), *n.* dextrin.

dextro-, *combining form.* toward the right: *Dextrorotatory = rotatory toward the right.* [< Latin *dexter*]

dex tro ro ta to ry (dek′strə rō′tə tôr′ē, dek′strə rō′tə tōr′ē), *adj.* 1 turning or causing to turn toward the right or in a clockwise direction. 2 (in physics and chemistry) characterized by turning the plane of polarization of light to the right, as a crystal, lens, or compound in solution.

dex trorse (dek′strôrs, dek strôrs′), *adj.* rising spirally from left to right: *the dextrorse stem of a vine.* [< Latin *dextrorsum* to the right < *dexter* to the right + *versum* turned] **—dex′trorse ly,** *adv.*

dex trose (dek′strōs), *n.* a crystalline sugar less sweet than cane sugar, occurring in many plant and animal tissues and fluids; grape sugar. It is a form of glucose. *Formula:* $C_6H_{12}O_6$

dex trous (dek′strəs), *adj.* dexterous.

dey (dā), *n., pl.* **deys.** a former title for rulers of Algiers, Tunis, and Tripoli. [< French < Turkish *dayı,* originally, maternal uncle]

DFC, Distinguished Flying Cross.

DFM, Distinguished Flying Medal.

dg., decigram or decigrams.

dhar ma (där′mə, dėr′mə), *n.* 1 (in Buddhism) the law. 2 (in Hinduism) correct behavior; virtue; righteousness. [< Sanskrit]

dhow

dhow (dou), *n.* a sailing ship that is used along the coasts of Arabia and east Africa. [< Arabic *dāw*]

di-[1], *prefix.* 1 twice; double; twofold, as in *dicotyledon.* 2 two; having two, as in *digraph.* 3 containing two atoms, etc., of the substance specified, as in *dioxide.* See also **dis-**[2]. [< Greek < *dis*]

di-[2], *prefix.* form of **dis-**[1] before *b, d, l, m, n, r, s, v,* and sometimes before *g* and *j,* as in *direct, divert.*

di-[3], *prefix.* form of **dia-** before vowels, as in *diorama.*

dia-, *prefix.* through; across; thoroughly, as in *diatonic.* Also, **di-** before vowels. [< Greek < *dia* through, apart]

di a be tes (dī′ə bē′tis, dī′ə bē′tēz), *n.* any of several diseases characterized by excessive production of urine, especially one involving a deficiency of insulin, characterized by excessive sugar in the blood and urine and by the inability of the body to absorb normal amounts of sugar and starch. [< Greek *diabētēs* a passer-through < *diabainein* pass through < *dia-* + *bainein* go]

di a bet ic (dī′ə bet′ik, dī′ə bē′tik), *adj.* 1 of or having to do with diabetes. 2 having diabetes. *—n.* person who has diabetes.

di a bol ic (dī′ə bol′ik), *adj.* 1 very cruel or wicked; devilish; fiendish. 2 having to do with the Devil or devils. [< Greek *diabolikos* < *diabolos.* See DEVIL.] **—di′a bol′i cal ly,** *adv.* **—di′a bol′i cal ness,** *n.*

di a bol i cal (dī′ə bol′ə kəl), *adj.* diabolic.

di ac o nal (dī ak′ə nəl), *adj.* of or having to do with a deacon. [< Latin *diaconus* deacon]

di ac o nate (dī ak′ə nit, dī ak′ə nāt), *n.* 1 rank or position of a deacon. 2 group of deacons.

di a crit ic (dī′ə krit′ik), *adj.* diacritical. *—n.* a diacritical mark. [< Greek *diakritikos* < *diakrinein* distinguish < *dia-* apart + *krinein* separate]

di a crit i cal (dī′ə krit′ə kəl), *adj.* 1 used to distinguish; distinctive. 2 used to distinguish sounds or values of letters.

diacritical mark, a small mark like ¨ ˆ ˜ ˊ or ˋ put on a letter to indicate pronunciation, accent, etc.

di a dem (dī′ə dem), *n.* 1 a crown. 2 an ornamental band of cloth formerly worn as a crown. 3 royal power or authority. [< Latin *diadema* < Greek *diadēma* < *diadein* bind across < *dia-* + *dein* bind]

di aer e sis (dī er′ə sis), *n., pl.* **-ses** (-sēz′). dieresis.

Dia ghi lev (dyä′gə lef), *n.* **Sergei Pavlovich,** 1872-1929, Russian ballet producer and director.

di ag nose (dī′əg nōs′, dī′əg nōz′), *v.t., v.i.,* **-nosed, -nos ing.** make a diagnosis of (a disease, etc.); identify a condition by observation.

di ag no sis (dī′əg nō′sis), *n., pl.* **-ses** (-sēz′). 1 act or process of identifying a disease by careful investigation of its symptoms: *X rays and blood samples were used in the diagnosis.* 2 a careful study of the facts about something to find out its essential features, faults, etc. 3 decision reached after a careful study of symptoms or facts. 4 (in biology) a statement of the determining characteristics of a genus, species, etc. [< Greek < *dia-* apart + *gignoskein* know]

di ag nos tic (dī′əg nos′tik), *adj.* 1 of or having value in diagnosis. 2 helping in diagnosis: *diagnostic tests.* **—di′ag nos′ti cal ly,** *adv.*

di ag nos ti cian (dī′əg no stish′ən), *n.* an expert in making diagnoses.

di ag o nal (dī ag′ə nəl), *n.* 1 a line segment connecting two corners that are not next to each other in a polygon or polyhedron; line that cuts across in a slanting direction. 2 any slanting part, course, or arrangement of things. 3 virgule. *—adj.* 1 taking the direction of a diagonal; slanting: *a diagonal stripe in cloth.* 2 having slanting lines, ridges, etc. 3 connecting two nonadjacent corners in a polygon or polyhedron: *a diagonal line.* [< Latin *diagonalis* < Greek *diagōnios* from angle to angle < *dia-* across + *gōnia* angle] **—di ag′o nal ly,** *adv.*

hat, āge, fär; let, ēqual, tėrm;
it, īce; hot, ōpen, ôrder;
oil, out; cup, pu̇t, rüle;
ch, child; ng, long; sh, she;
th, thin; ᴛʜ, then; zh, measure;

ə represents *a* in about, *e* in taken, *i* in pencil, *o* in lemon, *u* in circus.

< = from, derived from, taken from.

di a gram (dī′ə gram), *n.,v.,* **-gramed, -gram ing** or **-grammed, -gram ming.** *—n.* 1 drawing or sketch which gives an outline or general scheme of something and shows the relations of its various parts. 2 (in mathematics) figure used to aid in the proof of a geometrical proposition or as a mathematical representation. *—v.t.* put on paper, a blackboard, etc., in the form of a drawing or sketch; make a diagram of. [< Greek *diagramma* < *dia-* apart, out + *gramma* lines (of a drawing, etc.)]

di a gram mat ic (dī′ə grə mat′ik), *adj.* 1 in the form of a diagram. 2 in outline form only; sketchy. **—di′a gram mat′i cal ly,** *adv.*

di a gram mat i cal (dī′ə grə mat′ə kəl), *adj.* diagrammatic.

di al (dī′əl), *n., v.,* **-aled, -al ing** or **-alled, -al ling.** *—n.* 1 the graduated plate, disk, or face on which the readings of gauges, meters, and other measuring or recording instruments are shown by a pointer. 2 face of a clock graduated to show hours and minutes. 3 plate or disk with numbers or letters on it for tuning in to a radio or television station. 4 part of an automatic telephone, with letters and numbers, used in making telephone calls. 5 plate or disk on a lock with numbers or letters on it used for opening the lock. 6 sundial. *—v.t.* 1 tune in by using a radio or television dial: *I was trying to dial London on my shortwave radio.* 2 call or seek to call by operating a telephone dial: *You have dialed the wrong number.* 3 turn a dial in order to open a lock: *dial a combination.* *—v.i.* operate a dial. [apparently < Medieval Latin *(rota) dialis* daily (wheel) < Latin *dies* day]

dial., 1 dialect. 2 dialectal.

di a lect (dī′ə lekt), *n.* 1 form of speech characteristic of a class or region and differing from the standard language in pronunciation, vocabulary, and grammatical form. See **language** for synonym study. 2 one of a group of closely related languages: *Some of the dialects descended from the Latin language are French, Italian, Spanish, and Portuguese.* 3 words and pronunciations used by certain professions, classes of people, etc. *—adj.* dialectal. [< Latin *dialectus* < Greek *dialektos* discourse, conversation, ultimately < *dia-* between + *legein* speak]

di a lec tal (dī′ə lek′təl), *adj.* of a dialect; like that of a dialect. **—di′a lec′tal ly,** *adv.*

di a lec tic (dī′ə lek′tik), *n.* 1 Often, **dialectics,** *pl.* art or practice of logical discussion as a means of examining critically the truth of a theory or opinion. 2 discussion or debate on the basis of logic of the truth of an opinion or theory. 3 Often, **dialectics,** *pl.* a social, economic, or other change believed to result from the resolution of contradictory opposites. *—adj.* 1 having to do with dialectics; dialectical. 2 dialectal. [< Greek *dialektikē (technē)* dialectic (art) < *dialektos.* See DIALECT.]

di a lec ti cal (dī′ə lek′tə kəl), *adj.* dialectic.

dialectical materialism, a socialist doctrine that advocates a classless society emerging as the result of a long struggle between economic classes. It was developed by Karl Marx and Friedrich Engels from Georg Hegel's dialectic theory.

di a lec tol o gist (dī′ə lek tol′ə jist), *n.* an expert in dialectology.

di a lec tol o gy (dī′ə lek tol′ə jē), *n.* the study of dialects.

di a logue or **di a log** (dī′ə lôg, dī′ə log), *n.* 1 conversation between two or more persons. 2 conversation in a play, novel, story, etc. 3 airing of views; discussion. [< Greek *dialogos* < *dia-* between + *logos* speech]

dial tone, a humming sound heard on a dial telephone which indicates that a number may be dialed.

di al y sis (dī al′ə sis), *n., pl.* **-ses** (-sēz′). separation of colloids or large molecules from dissolved substances or small molecules, by application of the principle that small molecules diffuse readily through a membrane and colloids or large molecules not at all or very slightly. [< Greek < *dia-* apart + *lyein* to loose]

di a lyze (dī′ə līz), *v.t.,* **-lyzed, -lyz ing.** separate or obtain by dialysis.

diam., diameter.

di a mag net ic (dī′ə mag net′ik), *adj.* repelled by a magnet. **—di′a mag net′i cal ly,** *adv.*

di a mag net ism (dī′ə mag′nə tiz′əm), *n.* diamagnetic quality.

di am e ter (dī am′ə tər), *n.* 1 a line segment passing from one side to the other through the center of a circle, sphere, etc. 2 the length of such a line segment; measurement from one side to the other through the center; width; thickness: *The diameter of the earth is about 8000 miles.* [< Greek *diametros* < *dia-* + *metron* measure]

di a met ric (dī′ə met′rik), *adj.* 1 of or along a diameter. 2 exactly opposite.

di a met ri cal (dī′ə met′rə kəl), *adj.* diametric.

di a met ri cal ly (dī′ə met′rik lē), *adv.* 1 as a diameter. 2 directly; exactly; entirely: *diametrically opposed views.*

dia mond (dī′mənd, dī′ə mənd), *n.* 1 a colorless or tinted precious stone, formed of pure carbon in crystals. Diamond is the hardest natural substance known. Inferior diamonds are used to cut glass and metal, and in drill bits. 2 tool having a diamond tip for cutting glass. 3 a plane figure shaped like this: ◊ ; lozenge; rhombus. 4 a playing card marked with one or more red, diamond-shaped figures. 5 **diamonds,** *pl.* suit of such playing cards. 6 in baseball: **a** the area bounded by home plate and the three bases; infield. **b** the whole field. 7 a very small size of type; $4\frac{1}{2}$ point. This sentence is in diamond. [< Old French *diamant* < Medieval Latin *diamantem,* alteration of Latin *adamantem* adamant. Doublet of ADAMANT.] **—dia′mond-like′,** *adj.*

dia mond back (dī′mənd bak′, dī′ə mənd-bak′), *n.* 1 any of several large rattlesnakes having diamond-shaped markings on the back, found in the southern and western United States. 2 diamondback terrapin.

dia mond-backed (dī′mənd bakt′, dī′ə-mənd bakt′), *adj.* having the back marked with diamond-shaped figures.

diamondback terrapin, a diamond-backed turtle living in salt marshes along the Atlantic coast and the Gulf of Mexico.

Di an a (dī an′ə), *n.* (in Roman myths) goddess of the hunt and of the moon, and the protectress and helper of women, identified with the Greek goddess Artemis.

di a pa son (dī′ə pā′zn, dī′ə pā′sn), *n.* 1 a swelling musical sound. 2 the whole range of a voice or instrument. 3 a fixed standard of musical pitch. 4 either of two principal stops in an organ: **a open diapason,** a stop giving full, majestic tones. **b stopped diapason,** a stop giving powerful flutelike tones. [< Greek *dia pason (chordon)* across all (the notes of the scale)]

di a pause (dī′ə pôz), *n.* period of suspended development (as in some insects) during which physiological activity is very low.

diaper (def. 2)

di a per (dī′ə pər, dī′pər), *n.* 1 piece of cloth or other soft, absorbent material folded and used as underpants for a baby. 2 pattern of small, constantly repeated geometric figures. 3 a white cotton or linen cloth woven with such a pattern. *—v.t.* 1 put a diaper on: *diaper a baby.* 2 ornament with a diaper pattern. [< Old French *diapre, diaspre* < Medieval Latin *diasprum,* alteration of Latin *iaspidem* jasper]

di aph a nous (dī af′ə nəs), *adj.* transparent: *Gauze is a diaphanous fabric.* [< Greek *diaphanes* < *dia-* through + *phainein* to show] **—di aph′a nous ly,** *adv.* **—di-aph′a nous ness,** *n.*

di a phragm (dī′ə fram), *n.* 1 a partition of muscles and tendons in mammals which separates the cavity of the chest from the cavity of the abdomen and is important in respiration; midriff. 2 a thin dividing partition, as in a galvanic cell, or in some shellfish. 3 a thin disk that vibrates rapidly when receiving or producing sounds, used in telephones, loudspeakers, microphones, and other instruments. 4 disk with a hole in the center for controlling the amount of light entering a camera, microscope, etc. *—v.t.* furnish with a diaphragm. [< Greek *diaphragma* < *dia-* across + *phragma* fence]

di a phrag mat ic (dī′ə frag mat′ik), *adj.* having to do with or like a diaphragm. **—di′a phrag mat′i cal ly,** *adv.*

di ar ist (dī′ər ist), *n.* person who keeps a diary.

di ar rhe a (dī′ə rē′ə), *n.* condition of having too many watery movements of the bowels. [< Latin *diarrhoea* < Greek *diarrhoia* < *dia-* through + *rhein* to flow]

di ar rhe al (dī′ə rē′əl), *adj.* of or having to do with diarrhea.

di ar rhe ic (dī′ə rē′ik), *adj.* diarrheal.

di ar rhoe a (dī′ə rē′ə), *n.* diarrhea.

di ar y (dī′ər ē), *n., pl.* **-ar ies.** 1 account written down each day of what one has done, thought, etc., during the day. 2 book for keeping such a daily account, with a blank space for each day of the year. [< Latin *diarium* < *dies* day]

Di as (dē′äs), *n.* **Bartolomeu,** 1450?-1500, Portuguese navigator who discovered the Cape of Good Hope. Also, **Diaz.**

Di as por a (dī as′pər ə), *n.* 1 the scattering of the Jews after their captivity in Babylon. 2 Jews thus scattered. 3 the early Jewish Christians living outside Palestine. 4 **diaspora,** the scattering of any group; dispersion. [< Greek *diaspora* a scattering < *dia-* through + *speirein* sow]

di a stase (dī′ə stās), *n.* amylase, especially certain impure extracts from molds or germinating seeds. [< Greek *diastasis* separation]

di a stat ic (dī′ə stat′ik), *adj.* of or having to do with diastase.

di as to le (dī as′tl ē), *n.* the normal, rhythmical dilation of the heart, especially that of the ventricles. During diastole the chambers of the heart fill up with blood. [< Greek *diastolē* expansion < *dia-* apart + *stellein* to send]

di as tol ic (dī′ə stol′ik), *adj.* having to do with diastole.

di a stroph ic (dī′ə strof′ik), *adj.* of or like diastrophism.

di as tro phism (dī as′trə fiz′əm), *n.* the action of the forces that have caused the deformation of the earth's crust, producing mountains, continents, etc. [< Greek *diastrophē* distortion]

di a ther mic (dī′ə thėr′mik), *adj.* of or having to do with diathermy.

di a ther my (dī′ə thėr′mē), *n.* method of treating diseases by heating the tissues beneath the skin with high-frequency electric currents. [< Greek *dia-* through + *thermē* heat]

di a tom (dī′ə tom), *n.* any of a class of numerous microscopic, one-celled, aquatic algae that have hard shells composed mostly of silica. [< Greek *diatomos* cut in half]

di a to ma ceous (dī′ə tə mā′shəs), *adj.* of or having to do with diatoms or their fossil remains: *diatomaceous earth.*

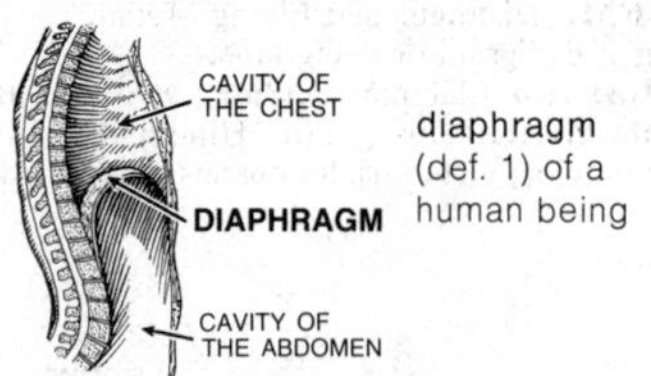

diaphragm (def. 1) of a human being

di a tom ic (dī′ə tom′ik), *adj.* having two atoms in each molecule.

di at o mite (dī at′ə mīt), *n.* earth consisting of the fossil remains of diatoms; diatomaceous earth; kieselguhr. It is used as an abrasive, insulator, filter, etc.

di a ton ic (dī′ə ton′ik), *adj.* of or using the eight tones of a standard major or minor musical scale without chromatic alteration. **—di′a ton′i cal ly,** *adv.*

diatonic scale, a standard major or minor musical scale of eight tones in the octave, with no chromatic intervals.

di a tribe (dī′ə trīb), *n.* speech or discussion

bitterly and violently directed against some person or thing; denunciation. [< Greek *diatribē* pastime, discourse < *dia-* away + *tribein* to wear]

Di az (dē′äs), *n.* **Bartholomew.** See **Dias.**

Dí az (dē′äs), *n.* **Porfirio,** 1830-1915, Mexican general, president of Mexico from 1877 to 1880 and from 1884 to 1911.

di az o (dī az′ō, dī ā′zō), *adj.* of or containing two nitrogen atoms, N_2, combined with a hydrocarbon radical.

di ba sic (dī bā′sik), *adj.* (of an acid) having two hydrogen atoms that can be replaced by two atoms or radicals of a base in forming salts.

dib ble (dib′əl), *n., v.,* **-bled, -bling.** —*n.* a pointed tool for making holes in the ground for seeds, bulbs, or young plants. —*v.t.* 1 make a hole in (the soil) with or as if with a dibble. 2 sow or plant (seeds, etc.) in this way. [origin uncertain]

dice (dīs), *n. pl. of* **die**[2], *v.,* **diced, dic ing.** —*n.* 1 small cubes marked on each side with a different number of spots (one to six), shaken and thrown from the hand or a box in playing some games and in gambling. 2 game played with dice. 3 any small cubes or square blocks. 4 **load the dice,** INFORMAL. decide or insure the outcome for or against something in advance. —*v.i.* 1 play with dice. 2 split into small fragments when broken. —*v.t.* 1 cut into small cubes: *dice carrots.* 2 make an ornament with a pattern of cubes or squares. [< Old French *des,* plural of *de* die[2]. See DIE[2].] **—dic′er,** *n.*

dice y (dī′sē), *adj.* BRITISH SLANG. 1 risky. 2 doubtful; uncertain.

di chlo ride (dī klôr′īd′, dī klôr′id; dī-klōr′īd′, dī klōr′id), *n.* chloride whose molecules contain two atoms of chlorine; bichloride.

di chot o mous (dī kot′ə məs), *adj.* 1 divided or dividing into two parts. 2 (in botany) branching by repeated divisions into two. **—di chot′o mous ly,** *adv.*

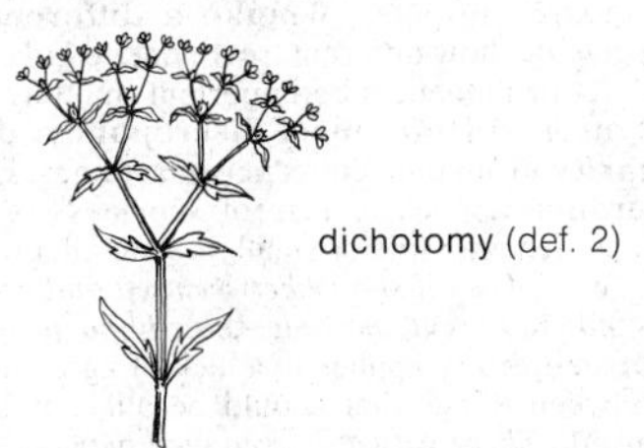
dichotomy (def. 2)

di chot o my (dī kot′ə mē), *n., pl.* **-mies.** 1 division of a whole into two parts. 2 (in botany) a branching by repeated divisions into two parts. 3 (in zoology) a branching in which each successive axis divides into two; repeated bifurcation, as of the veins. 4 (in logic) division or subdivision of a class into two mutually exclusive groups: *the dichotomy of the living and the nonliving.* [< Greek *dichotomia* < *dicha* in two + *temnein* to cut]

di chro ic (dī krō′ik), *adj.* 1 having or showing two colors. 2 (of a crystal) showing two different colors according to the direction of transmitted light, due to difference in the amount of absorption of the rays. 3 (of a solution) showing different colors for different concentrations, as a solution of chlorophyll.

di chro ism (dī′krō iz′əm), *n.* quality of being dichroic.

di chro mate (dī krō′māt), *n.* chromate whose molecules have two atoms of chromium; bichromate.

di chro mat ic (dī′krō mat′ik), *adj.* having or showing two colors.

di chro ma tism (dī krō′mə tiz′əm), *n.* dichromatic quality or condition.

dick ens (dik′ənz), *n., interj.* exclamation of surprise or annoyance.

Dick ens (dik′ənz), *n.* **Charles,** 1812-1870, English novelist.

Dick en si an (di ken′zē ən), *adj.* of, having to do with, or like the style of Charles Dickens or his writings.

dick er (dik′ər), *v.i., v.t.* trade by barter or by petty bargaining; haggle. —*n.* a petty bargain. [< *dicker,* noun, a lot of ten hides, ultimately < Latin *decuria* ten]

dick ey (dik′ē), *n., pl.* **-eys.** 1 a shirt front that can be detached. 2 an insert worn at the neck opening of a blouse, jacket, etc. 3 vestee. 4 a high collar on a shirt. 5 a child's bib or pinafore. 6 the driver's seat on the outside of a carriage. 7 seat at the back of a carriage for servants. Also, **dicky.** [< *Dick,* proper name]

Dick in son (dik′ən sən), *n.* **Emily,** 1830-1886, American poet.

Dick test (dik), test for susceptibility to scarlet fever, in which a reaction to the injection of the scarlet fever toxin indicates a lack of immunity. [< George F. *Dick,* 1881-1967, and Gladys *Dick,* 1881-1963, American bacteriologists, who developed it in 1923]

dick y (dik′ē), *n., pl.* **dick ies.** dickey.

di cot (dī′kot), *n.* dicotyledon.

di cot y le don (dī kot′l ēd′n), *n.* any of a class of flowering plants of the angiosperm subdivision, having two cotyledons or seed leaves in the embryo. Dicotyledons have leaves with a network of veins and flower parts in fours or fives. Many trees and most cultivated plants are dicotyledons.

di cot y le don ous (dī kot′l ēd′n əs), *adj.* having two cotyledons.

dict., dictionary.

dic ta (dik′tə), *n.* a pl. of **dictum.**

Dic ta phone (dik′tə fōn), *n.* trademark for an instrument that records and subsequently reproduces for transcription words spoken into it.

dic tate (*v.* dik′tāt, dik tāt′; *n.* dik′tāt), *v.,* **-tat ed, -tat ing,** *n.* —*v.t.* 1 say or read aloud to another person who writes down the words: *dictate a letter to a stenographer.* 2 command with authority; order in clear and definite terms: *The country that won the war dictated the terms of peace to the country that lost.* —*v.i.* 1 say or read something to be written down. 2 give a direction that must be carried out or obeyed; give orders. —*n.* command given with authority; order given by one in authority. [< Latin *dictatum* said often < *dicere* say]

dic ta tion (dik tā′shən), *n.* 1 act of saying or reading words aloud to another person who writes them down: *The pupils wrote at the teacher's dictation.* 2 words said or read aloud to be written down: *We have dictation in the first few minutes of our French class.* 3 act of giving orders or commanding with authority.

dic ta tor (dik′tā tər, dik tā′tər), *n.* 1 person exercising absolute authority, especially a person who, without having any claim through inheritance or free popular election, seizes control of a government. 2 (in Roman history) an official given absolute authority over the state in times of emergency. 3 person who dictates.

hat, āge, fär; let, ēqual, tėrm;
it, īce; hot, ōpen, ôrder;
oil, out; cup, pu̇t, rüle;
ch, child; ng, long; sh, she;
th, thin; ᴛʜ, then; zh, measure;

ə represents *a* in about, *e* in taken, *i* in pencil, *o* in lemon, *u* in circus.

< = from, derived from, taken from.

dic ta to ri al (dik′tə tôr′ē əl, dik′tə tōr′ē-əl), *adj.* 1 of or like that of a dictator; absolute: *dictatorial government.* 2 domineering; overbearing: *a dictatorial manner.* **—dic′ta to′ri al ly,** *adv.* **—dic′ta to′ri al-ness,** *n.*

dic ta tor ship (dik′tā tər ship, dik tā′tər-ship), *n.* 1 position or rank of a dictator. 2 term of a dictator; period of time a dictator rules. 3 absolute authority; power to give orders that must be obeyed. 4 country under the rule of a dictator.

dic tion (dik′shən), *n.* 1 manner of expressing ideas in words; choice or selection of words and phrases; style of speaking or writing. See synonym study below. 2 manner of pronouncing words; enunciation; articulation. [< Latin *dictionem* a saying < *dicere* say]

Syn. 1 **Diction, phraseology, wording** mean the way of using words. **Diction** applies mainly to the use of words and emphasizes the care and skill with which they are chosen: *The diction acceptable in speech is usually less formal than that required in writing.* **Phraseology** applies to the grouping of words, particularly as used by a particular group, profession, or individual: *I don't understand legal phraseology.* **Wording** applies to the use and grouping of words but emphasizes their special suitability for a given purpose: *I changed the wording of the telegram to make it clearer.*

dic tion ar y (dik′shə ner′ē), *n., pl.* **-ar ies.** 1 book containing a selection of the individual words of a language, or certain specified classes of them, usually arranged alphabetically and giving their spelling, pronunciation, meanings, use in context, synonyms, etymology, etc.: *a dictionary of the English language. This German-English dictionary translates German words into English.* 2 book of information or reference on any subject or branch of knowledge, the items of which are arranged in some stated order, often alphabetical: *a dictionary of architecture.*

Dic to graph (dik′tə graf), *n.* trademark for a machine capable of recording in one room sounds or conversation made in another by means of a transmitter so sensitive that no mouthpiece is needed.

dic tum (dik′təm), *n., pl.* **-tums** or **-ta.** 1 a formal comment; authoritative opinion: *The dictum of the critics was that the play was excellent.* 2 maxim; saying. [< Latin, (thing) said < *dicere* say]

did (did), *v.* pt. of **do**[1]. *I did my work.*

di dac tic (dī dak′tik, di dak′tik), *adj.* 1 intended to instruct: *Aesop's "Fables" are didactic stories; each one has a moral.* 2 inclined to instruct others; teacherlike: *The older brother was called "Professor"* because of his didactic manner. [< Greek *didaktikos* < *didaskein* teach] **—di dac′ti cal ly,** *adv.*

di dac ti cal (dī dak′tə kəl, di dak′tə kəl), *adj.* didactic.

di dac ti cism (dī dak′tə siz′əm, di dak′tə-siz′əm), *n.* didactic quality, character, or manner.

di dac tics (dī dak′tiks, di dak′tiks), *n.* science or art of giving instruction.

did dle (did′l), *v.t.,* **-dled, -dling.** INFORMAL. 1 cheat; swindle. 2 waste (time). [origin uncertain]

Di de rot (dē′də rō′), *n.* **Denis,** 1713-1784, French philosopher and encyclopedia editor.

did n't (did′nt), did not.

di do (dī′dō), *n., pl.* **-dos** or **-does.** INFORMAL. a mischievous or disorderly action; prank; trick. [origin uncertain]

Di do (dī′dō), *n.* (in Roman legends) a queen of Carthage. In Virgil's *Aeneid* she falls in love with Aeneas and kills herself when he goes away.

didst (didst), *v.* ARCHAIC. did. "Thou didst" means "You did."

di dym i um (dī dim′ē əm), *n.* mixture of the elements neodymium and praseodymium. [< New Latin < Greek *didymos* twin]

die[1] (dī), *v.i.,* **died, dy ing.** 1 stop living; become dead; cease to exist: *to die of disease. The flowers died from the heavy frost.* 2 lose force or strength; come to an end; stop: *My sudden anger died.* See synonym study below. 3 stop running or functioning: *The motor sputtered and died.* 4 INFORMAL. want very much; be very desirous: *I'm dying to go to Alaska.* 5 **die away** or **die down,** stop or end little by little: *The music died away.* 6 **die off,** die one after another until all are dead: *The whole herd of cattle died off in the epidemic.* [Middle English *dien*]

Syn. 1,2 **Die, perish** mean to stop living or existing. **Die,** the general word meaning to stop living, is also used figuratively of things that have been active in any way: *The noisy conversation of the class died down suddenly when the teacher came into the room.* **Perish,** more formal or literary than *die,* implies dying through violence or hardship, and used figuratively means to go out of existence permanently: *She feared that the unleashing of atomic power would cause civilization to perish.*

➤ **Die** is generally used with *of* before an illness: *He died of* (not *from* or *with*) *cancer.* However, *from* is sometimes used to express "from the effects of": *He died from a wound.*

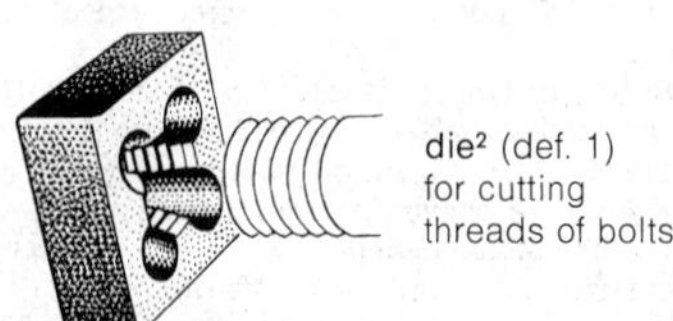

die[2] (def. 1) for cutting threads of bolts

die[2] (dī), *n., pl.* **dies** for 1, **dice** for 2. 1 tool or apparatus for shaping, cutting, punching, or stamping things, usually consisting of a metal block or plate cut in a way to fit its purpose. Dies are used for coining money and for raising printing up from the surface of paper. 2 one of a set of dice. 3 **the die is cast,** the decision is made and cannot be changed. [< Old French *de* < Latin *datum* (thing) given (that is, by fortune) < *dare* give. Doublet of DATA.]

di e cious (dī ē′shəs), *adj.* dioecious.

die-hard or **die hard** (dī′härd′), *adj.* resisting to the very end; refusing to give in. *—n.* person who refuses to give in.

di el drin (dī el′drən), *n.* a very poisonous insecticide obtained by the oxidation of aldrin with certain acids. *Formula:* $C_{12}H_8OCl_6$

di e lec tric (dī′i lek′trik), *adj.* (in electricity) nonconducting. *—n.* a dielectric substance, such as glass, rubber, or wood.

Dien Bien Phu (dyen′ byen′ fü′), town in NW Vietnam taken by Vietminh troops in 1954 in a decisive battle which ended French power in Vietnam.

di en ceph a lon (dī′en sef′ə lon), *n.* the posterior part of the forebrain, which connects the midbrain to the cerebrum.

di er e sis (dī er′ə sis), *n., pl.* **-ses** (-sēz′). two dots (¨) placed over the second of two consecutive vowels to indicate that the second vowel is to be pronounced in a separate syllable. EXAMPLES: *Noël, naïve.* Also, **diaeresis.** [< Greek *diairesis* separation, division < *diairein* divide < *dia-* apart + *hairein* take]

➤ **dieresis.** With prefixes, a hyphen is often used instead of a dieresis, especially in words with *re- (re-enlist).* In words of common occurrence, the tendency now is to use neither dieresis nor hyphen: *cooperation, zoology.* In the body of a word, however, the dieresis is still much used: *Chloë, Phaëthon.*

die sel or **Die sel** (dē′zl, dē′sl), *n.* 1 diesel engine. 2 a truck, locomotive, train, etc., with a diesel engine. *—adj.* 1 equipped with or run by a diesel engine: *a diesel tractor.* 2 of or for a diesel engine: *diesel fuel.* [< Rudolf *Diesel,* 1858-1913, German engineer who invented the diesel engine]

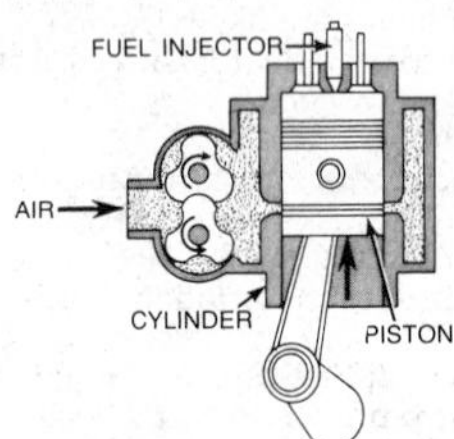

diesel engine—Air entering the cylinder is compressed by the piston and becomes very hot. A spray of oil sent into the air burns, causing a forceful expansion of the gas, which forces the piston down.

diesel engine or **Diesel engine,** an internal-combustion engine in which fuel oil vapor is ignited by heat from compression of air in the cylinder heads.

die sel ize or **Die sel ize** (dē′zl īz, dē′sl-īz), *v.t.,* **-ized, -iz ing.** equip with a diesel engine or engines.

Di es I rae (dī′ēz ī′rē; dē′äs ē′rī), a medieval Latin hymn describing the Day of Judgment and formerly sung at masses for the dead. [< Latin, day of wrath]

di et[1] (dī′ət), *n.* 1 the articles of food and drink in daily use by a person or animal, especially in relation to their quality and effects: *a balanced diet.* 2 a prescribed course of food, restricted in kind and limited in quantity, especially for medical reasons: *a reducing diet.* *—v.i.* eat according to prescribed rules; eat food restricted in kind and limited in quantity: *Don't give me any cake; I'm dieting.* *—v.t.* cause to diet. [< Old French *diete* < Latin *diaeta* < Greek *diaita* way of life] **—di′et er,** *n.*

di et[2] (dī′ət), *n.* 1 a formal assembly for discussion. 2 the national lawmaking body in certain countries, such as Switzerland and Japan. [< Medieval Latin *dieta* day's work, meeting of councilors < Latin *dies* day]

di e tar y (dī′ə ter′ē), *adj., n., pl.* **-tar ies.** *—adj.* having to do with diet: *Dietary rules tell what foods to eat for healthy living and how to prepare them.* *—n.* 1 allowance of food in a prison, hospital, etc. 2 system of diet.

di e tet ic (dī′ə tet′ik), *adj.* of or having to do with diet or dietetics. **—di′e tet′i cal ly,** *adv.*

di e tet ics (dī′ə tet′iks), *n.* science that deals with the amount and kinds of food needed by the body.

di e ti tian or **di e ti cian** (dī′ə tish′ən), *n.* an expert in planning meals that have the proper proportions of various kinds of food.

dif-, *prefix.* form of **dis-**[1] before *f,* as in *diffuse.*

diff., 1 difference. 2 different.

dif fer (dif′ər), *v.i.* 1 be not the same; be unlike; be different *(from): The twins differ from each other in their interests.* 2 have or express a different opinion; disagree: *I differed from him in the solution he offered. I never differ with your plans.* [< Latin *differre* set apart, differ < *dis-* apart + *ferre* carry. Doublet of DEFER[1].]

dif fer ence (dif′ər əns), *n.* 1 a being different: *the difference of night and day.* See synonym study below. 2 way of being different; point in which people or things are different. 3 amount by which one quantity is different from another; what is left after subtracting one number from another: *The difference between 6 and 15 is 9.* 4 condition of having a different opinion; disagreement. 5 quarrel; dispute. 6 **make a difference, a** give or show different treatment. **b** have an effect or influence; be important; matter.

Syn. *n.* 1 **Difference, discrepancy, disparity** mean unlikeness between things. **Difference** applies to lack of sameness or of any likeness, large or small, in a detail, quality, etc.: *The difference between red and green is not apparent to some color-blind people.* **Discrepancy** applies to a lack of agreement between things that should be alike or balanced: *There was a discrepancy between the two reports of the accident.* **Disparity** applies to inequality, suggesting that one thing is noticeably lower, smaller, etc., than the other: *There is a disparity between my expenses and my income.*

dif fer ent (dif′ər ənt), *adj.* 1 not alike; not like; unlike: *A boat is different from an automobile.* 2 not the same; separate; distinct: *I saw her three different times today.* 3 not like others or most others; unusual. **—dif′fer ent ly,** *adv.*

➤ **different.** The standard American usage with *different* is *from: Her second book was entirely different from her first.* Informal usage is divided, using *from* occasionally, sometimes *to* (which is a common British usage), and more often *than: She was different than any other girl I had ever known. Different than* is becoming more common when the object is a clause: *The house was a good deal different than I remembered it.*

dif fe ren ti a (dif′ə ren′shē ə), *n., pl.* **-ti ae**

(-shē ē). (in logic) the quality or condition that distinguishes one species from all the others of the same genus or class. [< Latin, difference]

dif fe ren tial (dif′ə ren′shəl), *adj.* 1 of a difference; showing a difference; depending on a difference: *The differential rates in freight charges are for carrying heavier packages longer distances.* 2 distinguishing; distinctive: *a differential feature peculiar to itself.* 3 having to do with distinguishing characteristics or specific differences: *A differential diagnosis attempts to distinguish between two similar diseases.* 4 (in mathematics) having to do with or involving differentials. 5 (in physics and mechanics) concerning the difference of two or more motions, pressures, etc. —*n.* 1 a differential duty, rate, charge, etc. 2 differential gear. 3 (in mathematics) the product of the derivative of a function containing one variable multiplied by the increment of the independent variable. —**dif′fe ren′tial ly,** *adv.*

differential calculus, branch of higher mathematics that investigates differentials, derivatives, and their relations.

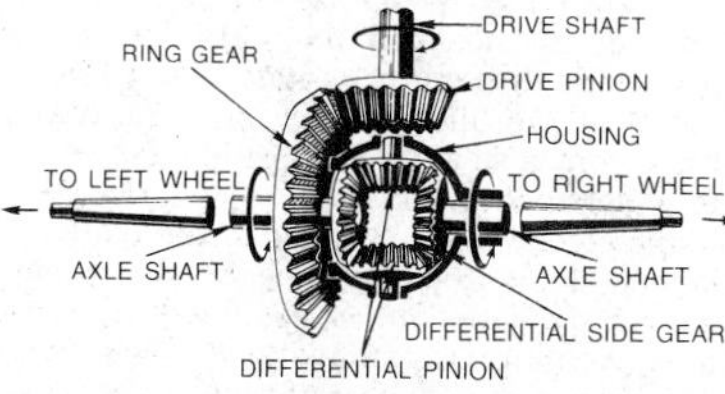

differential gear—When an automobile turns a corner, the axle shaft of the outside wheel rotates more rapidly than that of the inside wheel. The four pinions (of which only two are shown here) mesh with the two differential side gears, which are connected to the two axle shafts, permitting the wheels to rotate at different speeds.

differential gear, arrangement of gears in an automobile axle that allows one of the rear wheels to turn faster than the other in going around a corner or curve; differential.

dif fe ren ti ate (dif′ə ren′shē āt), *v.,* **-at ed, -at ing.** —*v.t.* 1 make different; cause to have differences: *Consideration for others differentiates good manners from mere politeness.* 2 tell the difference in or between; find or show to be different: *The botanist differentiated varieties of plants.* See **distinguish** for synonym study. 3 (in biology) make different in the process of growth or development; make unlike by modification. 4 (in mathematics) find the derivative of. —*v.i.* 1 become different. 2 tell the difference; find or show what is different. 3 (in biology) become differentiated or specialized: *The cells of an embryo differentiate into organs and parts as it grows.*

dif fe ren ti a tion (dif′ə ren′shē ā′shən), *n.* act, process, or result of differentiating; alteration; modification; distinction.

dif fi cult (dif′ə kult, dif′ə kəlt), *adj.* 1 hard to do, perform, carry out, or practice: *Cutting down the tree was difficult.* 2 hard to get along with; not easy to please or satisfy: *I found my new employer difficult.* 3 hard to understand; perplexing; puzzling: *Algebra is difficult for some students.* See **hard** for synonym study. 4 presenting obstacles or trouble: *a thing difficult to imagine, a place difficult of access.* 5 hard to persuade; unwilling. —**dif′fi cult ly,** *adv.*

dif fi cul ty (dif′ə kul′tē, dif′ə kəl tē), *n., pl.* **-ties.** 1 fact or condition of being difficult; degree to which something is difficult: *The difficulty of the job prevented us from finishing it on time.* 2 hard work; much effort: *The lame man walked with difficulty.* 3 something which stands in the way of getting things done; thing that is hard to do or understand. 4 trouble: *in difficulty with the police. Some children have difficulty learning how to spell.* 5 disagreement; quarrel. [< Latin *difficultatem* < *difficilis* hard < *dis-* + *facilis* easy]

dif fi dence (dif′ə dəns), *n.* lack of self-confidence; shyness.

dif fi dent (dif′ə dənt), *adj.* lacking in self-confidence; shy. [< Latin *diffidentem* < *dis-* + *fidere* to trust] —**dif′fi dent ly,** *adv.*

dif fract (di frakt′), *v.t.* break up by diffraction. [< Latin *diffractum* broken up < *dis-* + *frangere* to break]

dif frac tion (di frak′shən), *n.* 1 a spreading of light around an obstacle into a series of light and dark bands or into the colored bands of the spectrum. 2 a similar spreading of sound waves, electricity, etc.

diffraction grating, (in physics) a plate of glass or polished metal with very fine and close parallel lines, used to produce spectra by diffraction.

dif fuse (*v.* di fyüz′; *adj.* di fyüs′), *v.,* **-fused, -fus ing,** *adj.* —*v.t.* spread out so as to cover a large space or surface; scatter widely: *The sun diffuses light and heat.* —*v.i.* 1 scatter widely; spread. 2 mix together by spreading into one another, as one gas with another or one liquid with another. —*adj.* 1 not concentrated together at a single point; spread out: *diffuse light.* 2 using many words where a few would do; wordy: *a diffuse writer.* [< Latin *diffusum* poured forth < *dis-* + *fundere* to pour] —**dif fuse′ly,** *adv.* —**dif fuse′ness,** *n.* —**dif fus′er, dif fu′sor,** *n.*

dif fus i bil i ty (di fyü′zə bil′ə tē), *n.* quality of being diffusible.

dif fus i ble (di fyü′zə bəl), *adj.* capable of being diffused.

dif fu sion (di fyü′zhən), *n.* 1 act or fact of diffusing; a spreading widely; a scattering: *The invention of printing greatly increased the diffusion of knowledge.* 2 a being widely spread or scattered; diffused condition. 3 a mixing together of the atoms or molecules of gases, liquids, or solids by spreading into one another as a result of their random thermal motion. 4 the scattering of light resulting from its being reflected from a rough surface. 5 use of too many words; wordiness.

dif fu sive (di fyü′siv), *adj.* 1 tending to diffuse. 2 showing diffusion. —**dif fu′sive ly,** *adv.* —**dif fu′sive ness,** *n.*

dig (dig), *v.,* **dug, dig ging,** *n.* —*v.i.* 1 use a shovel, spade, hands, claws, or snout to make a hole or to turn over the ground. 2 **dig in,** INFORMAL. **a** dig trenches for protection. **b** work or study hard. 3 make a way by digging: *dig under a mountain, dig through a hill.* 4 make a careful search or inquiry (for information or into the works of some author). 5 INFORMAL. work or study hard. —*v.t.* 1 break up and turn over (ground) with a spade, etc. 2 make by digging and removing material; excavate: *dig a well, dig a cellar.* 3 get by digging: *dig potatoes, dig clams.* 4 make a thrust or stab into; prod. 5 SLANG. **a** understand; appreciate. **b** notice; observe. **c** like; admire.

hat, āge, fär; let, ēqual, tėrm;
it, īce; hot, ōpen, ôrder;
oil, out; cup, pu̇t, rüle;
ch, child; ng, long; sh, she;
th, thin; ᴛʜ, then; zh, measure;

ə represents *a* in about, *e* in taken, *i* in pencil, *o* in lemon, *u* in circus.

< = from, derived from, taken from.

—*n.* 1 a thrust or poke. 2 a sarcastic remark. 3 INFORMAL. an archaeological excavation. 4 **digs,** *pl.* INFORMAL. place to live. [Middle English *diggen*]

dig., digest.

di gest (*v.* də jest′, dī jest′; *n.* dī′jest), *v.t.* 1 change or break down (food) in the mouth, stomach, and intestines into materials which the body can assimilate, store, or oxidize and use as nourishment. 2 promote the digestion of (food). 3 understand and absorb mentally; think over or out; consider: *He likes to digest what he reads.* 4 make a brief statement of; summarize. 5 (in chemistry) soften or decompose by combinations of heat, moisture, pressure, or chemical action. —*v.i.* undergo digestion; be digested: *Our food digests slowly.* —*n.* a brief statement of what is in a longer book, article, or statement; summary. See **summary** for synonym study. [< Latin *digestum* separated, dissolved < *dis-* apart + *gerere* carry] —**di gest′er,** *n.*

di gest i bil i ty (də jes′tə bil′ə tē, dī jes′tə bil′ə tē), *n.* quality of being digestible.

di gest i ble (də jes′tə bəl, dī jes′tə bəl), *adj.* capable of being digested.

di ges tion (də jes′chən, dī jes′chən), *n.* 1 the digesting of food. 2 ability to digest food. 3 act of digesting (books, etc.).

di ges tive (də jes′tiv, dī jes′tiv), *adj.* 1 of or for digestion: *the digestive system.* 2 helping digestion: *digestive tablets.* —*n.* something that aids digestion. —**di ges′tive ly,** *adv.*

dig ger (dig′ər), *n.* 1 person or thing that digs. 2 tool for digging.

digger wasp, any of various wasps that dig nests in the ground.

dig gings (dig′ingz), *n.pl.* 1 mine, archaeological site, or other place where digging is being done. 2 material that is dug out. 3 INFORMAL. place to live.

dight (dīt), *v.t.,* **dight** or **dight ed, dight ing.** ARCHAIC. 1 dress; adorn. 2 equip. [Old English *dihtan* compose, arrange < Latin *dictare* dictate]

dig it (dij′it), *n.* 1 any of the figures 0, 1, 2, 3, 4, 5, 6, 7, 8, 9. (0 is sometimes excluded.) 2 finger or toe. [< Latin *digitus* finger]

dig it al (dij′ə təl), *adj.* 1 of, having to do with, or using a digit or digits. 2 digitate. 3 of, having to do with, or based on the principle of a digital computer. —*n.* 1 finger. 2 key of an organ, piano, etc., played with the fingers. —**dig′it al ly,** *adv.*

digital computer, a type of electronic calculating machine using numbers expressed as digits of some numerical system to solve problems which can be expressed mathematically.

dig i tal is (dij′ə tal′is, dij′ə tā′lis), *n.* 1 medicine used for stimulating the heart, obtained from the dried leaves of the common foxglove. 2 foxglove. [< Latin, of the finger < *digitus* finger; from shape of corolla]

digitate (def. 2) digitate leaf

dig i tate (dij′ə tāt), *adj.* 1 having separate or divided fingers or toes. 2 (in botany) having radiating divisions like fingers. **—dig′i tate′ly,** *adv.*

dig i ti grade (dij′ə tə grād′), *adj.* walking so that the toes are the only portion of the foot on the ground: *Dogs, cats, and horses are digitigrade animals.*

dig ni fied (dig′nə fīd), *adj.* having dignity of manner, style, or appearance; noble; stately. **—dig′ni fied′ly,** *adv.*

dig ni fy (dig′nə fī), *v.t.,* **-fied, -fy ing.** 1 give dignity to; make noble, worthwhile, or worthy. 2 give a high-sounding name or title to.

dig ni tar y (dig′nə ter′ē), *n., pl.* **-tar ies.** person who has high rank or a position of honor. A bishop is a dignitary of the church.

dig ni ty (dig′nə tē), *n., pl.* **-ties.** 1 proud and self-respecting character or manner; stateliness. 2 degree of worth, honor, or importance: *A judge should maintain the dignity of his position.* 3 a high office, rank, or title; position of honor: *the dignity of the presidency.* 4 worth; nobleness: *Honest work has dignity.* [< Old French *dignete* < Latin *dignitatem* < *dignus* worthy. Doublet of DAINTY.]

di graph (dī′graf), *n.* two letters used together to spell a single sound. EXAMPLES: *ea* in *each, th* in *with, sh* in *shop.*

di gress (də gres′, dī gres′), *v.i.* 1 turn aside from the main subject in talking or writing. See **diverge** for synonym study. 2 swerve. [< Latin *digressum* stepped aside < *dis-* + *gradi* to step]

di gres sion (də gresh′ən, dī gresh′ən), *n.* a digressing; turning aside from the main subject in talking or writing.

di gres sive (də gres′iv, dī gres′iv), *adj.* characterized by digression; tending to digress; digressing. **—di gres′sive ly,** *adv.* **—di gres′sive ness,** *n.*

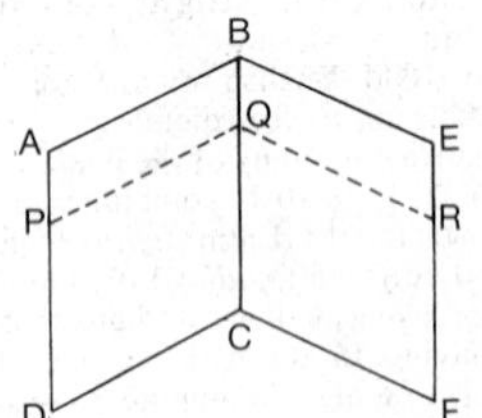

dihedral angle—The dihedral angle is angle PQR, which is formed by the intersecting planes ABCD and BEFC.

di he dral (dī hē′drəl), *adj.* having or formed by two intersecting plane surfaces: *a dihedral angle.* —*n.* the figure formed by two intersecting plane surfaces. [< *di-*[1] two + Greek *hedra* seat, base]

di hy brid (dī hī′brid), *adj.* having parents whose genetic make-up differs in two pairs of inheritable characters. —*n.* a dihybrid organism.

Di jon (dē zhôN′), *n.* city in E France. 145,000.

dike (dīk), *n., v.,* **diked, dik ing.** —*n.* 1 a bank of earth or a dam constructed to prevent flooding of low-lying lands by a river or the sea. 2 ditch or channel for water. 3 a low wall of earth or stone; causeway. 4 a long, usually narrow mass of igneous rock which was thrust, while molten, into a fissure in older rock. —*v.t.* 1 provide with a dike or dikes. 2 drain with a ditch or channel for water. —*v.i.* dig or build dikes. Also, **dyke.** [Old English *dīc.* Related to DITCH.] **—dik′er,** *n.*

di lap i dat ed (də lap′ə dā′tid), *adj.* fallen into ruin or disrepair; decayed through neglect. [< Latin *dilapidatum* scattered; ruined (as by hailstones) < *dis-* + *lapis* stone]

di lap i da tion (də lap′ə dā′shən), *n.* partial ruin; falling to pieces.

dil a ta tion (dil′ə tā′shən, dī′lə tā′shən), *n.* 1 dilation. 2 enlargement, expansion, or stretched condition of a part or an opening of the body.

di late (dī lāt′, də lāt′), *v.,* **-lat ed, -lat ing.** —*v.t.* make larger or wider: *When you take a deep breath, you dilate your nostrils.* See **expand** for synonym study. —*v.i.* 1 become larger or wider: *The pupil of the eye dilates when the light gets dim.* See **expand** for synonym study. 2 speak or write in a very complete or detailed manner. [< Latin *dilatare* < *dis-* apart + *latus* wide] **—di lat′a ble,** *adj.*

di la tion (dī lā′shən, də lā′shən), *n.* 1 act of dilating; enlargement; widening. 2 dilated condition. 3 a dilated part.

di la tor (dī lā′tər, də lā′tər), *n.* person or thing that dilates.

dil a to ry (dil′ə tôr′ē, dil′ə tōr′ē), *adj.* 1 tending to delay; not prompt. 2 causing delay. [< Latin *dilatorius* < *dilatum* brought apart < *dis-* apart + *latum* brought] **—dil′a to′ri ly,** *adv.* **—dil′a to′ri ness,** *n.*

di lem ma (də lem′ə), *n.* situation requiring a choice between two alternatives, which are or appear equally unfavorable; difficult choice. See **predicament** for synonym study. [< Greek *dilēmma* < *di-* two + *lēmma* premise]

dil et tante (dil′ə tänt′, dil′ə tan′tē), *n., pl.* **-tantes, -tan ti** (-tän′tē, -tan′tē), *adj.* —*n.* 1 person who follows some art or science as a pastime or without serious aim or study; dabbler. 2 lover of the fine arts. —*adj.* of or like a dilettante. [< Italian < *dilettare* to delight < Latin *delectare* to charm. See DELIGHT.]

dil et tant ism (dil′ə tän′tiz′əm, dil′ə tan′tiz′əm), *n.* quality or practice of a dilettante.

Dil i (dil′ē), *n.* capital of Portuguese Timor. 11,000.

dil i gence[1] (dil′ə jəns), *n.* constant and earnest effort to accomplish what is undertaken; industry.

dil i gence[2] (dil′ə jəns), *n.* a public stagecoach formerly used in France and other parts of Europe. [< French *(carosse de) diligence* fast (coach)]

dil i gent (dil′ə jənt), *adj.* 1 hard-working; industrious. See **busy** for synonym study. 2 careful and steady: *a diligent search.* [< Latin *diligentem* < *dis-* apart + *legere* choose] **—dil′i gent ly,** *adv.*

dill (dil), *n.* 1 plant of the same family as the parsley, whose spicy seeds or leaves are used to flavor pickles. 2 its seeds or leaves. [Old English *dile*]

dill pickle, a cucumber pickle flavored with dill.

dil ly dal ly (dil′ē dal′ē), *v.,* **-lied, -ly ing.** waste time; loiter; trifle. [reduplication of *dally*]

dil u ent (dil′yü ənt), *adj.* that dilutes; diluting. —*n.* a diluting agent.

di lute (də lüt′, dī lüt′), *v.,* **-lut ed, -lut ing,** *adj.* —*v.t.* 1 make weaker or thinner by adding water or some other liquid. 2 take away the strength or force of; weaken; lessen. —*v.i.* become diluted. —*adj.* weakened or thinned by the addition of water or some other liquid: *a dilute acid.* [< *dilutum* washed away < *dis-* + *luere* to wash] **—di lute′ness,** *n.* **—di lut′er,** *n.*

di lu tion (də lü′shən, dī lü′shən), *n.* 1 act of diluting. 2 fact or state of being diluted. 3 something diluted.

di lu vi al (də lü′vē əl, dī lü′vē əl), *adj.* 1 of or having to do with a flood. 2 made up of debris left by a flood or glacier. [< Latin *diluvium* deluge]

di lu vi an (də lü′vē ən, dī lü′vē ən), *adj.* diluvial.

dim (dim), *adj.,* **dim mer, dim mest,** *v.,* **dimmed, dim ming.** —*adj.* 1 not bright; not clear; not distinct: *dim light.* See **dark** for synonym study. 2 not clearly seen, heard, or understood; faint: *a dim view, a dim voice, a dim recollection.* 3 without luster; dull: *dim colors.* 4 not seeing, hearing, or understanding clearly: *Grandfather's eyesight is getting dim.* 5 INFORMAL. unfavorable: *She takes a dim view of our chances of winning the game.* —*v.t.* make dim: *He dimmed the car's headlights as another car approached.* —*v.i.* become dim. [Old English *dimm*] **—dim′ly,** *adv.* **—dim′ness,** *n.*

dim., 1 diminuendo. 2 diminutive.

dime (dīm), *n.* a copper and nickel coin of the United States and of Canada, worth 10 cents. Ten dimes make one dollar. [< Old French *disme* a tenth, tithe < Latin *decima (pars)* tenth (part) < *decem* ten]

di men sion (də men′shən), *n.* 1 measurement of length, breadth, or thickness: *She ordered wallpaper for a room of the following dimensions: 16 ft. long, 12 ft. wide, 9 ft. high.* 2 Also, **dimensions,** *pl.* size; extent; scope: *a project of large dimensions.* [< Latin *dimensionem* < *dis-* out + *metiri* to measure]

di men sion al (də men′shə nəl), *adj.* having to do with dimension or dimensions.

di men sion al i ty (də men′shə nal′ə tē), *n.* quality or condition of having or being within certain dimensions.

di mer ic (dī mer′ik), *adj.* dimerous.

dim er ism (dim′ə riz′əm), *n.* dimerous quality or nature.

dim er ous (dim′ər əs), *adj.* consisting of two parts or divisions.

dime store, U.S. store selling a large variety of low-priced articles; variety store.

dimin., 1 diminuendo. 2 diminutive.

di min ish (də min′ish), *v.t.* 1 make smaller; lessen; reduce. See **decrease** for synonym study. 2 lessen the importance, power, or reputation of; degrade. 3 (in architecture) to cause to taper. —*v.i.* 1 become smaller; lessen; decrease. See **decrease** for synonym study. 2 (in architecture) to taper. [ultimately < Latin *dis-* apart + *minus* less] **—di min′ish a ble,** *adj.*

di min ished (də min′isht), *adj.* (of a musical interval) smaller by a half step than the corresponding perfect or minor interval: *a diminished fifth.*

di min u en do (də min′yü en′dō), *n., pl.* **-dos,** *adj., adv.* decrescendo. [< Italian]

dim i nu tion (dim′ə nü′shən, dim′ə nyü′shən), *n.* a diminishing; lessening; reduction; decrease.

di min u tive (də min′yə tiv), *adj.* 1 very small; tiny; minute. See **little** for synonym study. 2 (in grammar) expressing smallness: *"Droplet" and "lambkin" have diminutive endings.* —*n.* 1 a small person or thing. 2 word or part of a word expressing smallness. The suffixes *-kin, -let,* and *-ling* are diminutives. —**di min′u tive ly,** *adv.* —**di min′u tive ness,** *n.*

dim i ty (dim′ə tē), *n., pl.* **-ties.** a thin cotton cloth woven with heavy threads in striped or checked arrangement, used for dresses, curtains, etc. [< Italian *dimiti,* plural < Greek *dimitos* of double thread]

dim mer (dim′ər), *n.* 1 person or thing that dims. 2 device that dims an electric light, especially automobile headlights.

di mor phic (dī môr′fik), *adj.* existing or occurring in two distinct forms.

di mor phism (dī môr′fiz′əm), *n.* the occurrence of two different forms of the same plant, animal, organ, substance, etc.

di mor phous (dī môr′fəs), *adj.* dimorphic.

dim ple (dim′pəl), *n., v.,* **-pled, -pling.** —*n.* 1 a small hollow or indented place formed in the surface of some part of a person's body, especially in the act of smiling. 2 any small, hollow place. —*v.t.* make or show dimples in. —*v.i.* form dimples. [Middle English *dympull*]

din (din), *n., v.,* **dinned, din ning.** —*n.* a continuing loud, confused noise. See **noise** for synonym study. —*v.i.* make a din. —*v.t.* 1 strike with a din. 2 say over and over again; repeat in a tiresome way. [Old English *dynn*]

di nar (di när′), *n.* 1 the monetary unit of several countries in the Mediterranean area, varying in value from six cents in Yugoslavia to $2.95 in Iraq, Jordan, and Kuwait. 2 coin worth one dinar. 3 any of various gold coins of ancient Arab countries. [< Arabic and Persian *dīnār* < Greek *denarion* < Latin *denarius.* Doublet of DENARIUS, DENIER[2].]

Di nar ic Alps (də nar′ik), range of the Alps in W Yugoslavia.

dine (dīn), *v.,* **dined, din ing.** —*v.i.* eat dinner. —*v.t.* give dinner to; give a dinner for. [< Old French *disner* to breakfast < Popular Latin *disjejunare* < *dis-* + *jejunium* fast[2]]

din er (dī′nər), *n.* 1 person who is eating dinner. 2 a railroad car in which meals are served; dining car. 3 restaurant shaped like such a car.

di nette (dī net′), *n.* a small dining room.

ding (ding), *v.t., v.i.* make the sound of a bell; ring continuously. —*n.* sound made by a bell. [imitative]

ding bat (ding′bat), *n.* U.S. SLANG. gadget.

ding-dong (ding′dông′, ding′dong′), *n.* sound made by a bell or anything like a bell; continuous ringing. —*adj.* INFORMAL. very vigorous; closely contested: *a ding-dong race.* [imitative]

din ghy (ding′ē), *n., pl.* **-ghies.** 1 a small rowboat. 2 a small boat used as a tender by a large boat. 3 a rowboat or sailing boat used in the East Indies. [< Hindustani *ḍingī*]

din gle (ding′gəl), *n.* a small, deep, shady valley. [origin uncertain]

din go (ding′gō), *n., pl.* **-goes.** a wolflike wild dog of Australia. [< native Australian name]

ding us (ding′əs), *n.* SLANG. thing whose name is unknown, unfamiliar, or forgotten. [< Dutch *dinges* < *ding* thing, object]

din gy (din′jē), *adj.,* **-gi er, -gi est.** lacking brightness or freshness; dirty-looking; dull. [origin uncertain] —**din′gi ly,** *adv.* —**din′gi ness,** *n.*

dining car, diner.

dining room, room in which dinner and other meals are served.

dink ey (ding′kē), *n., pl.* **-eys.** a small locomotive, used for pulling freight cars around in a railroad yard, for hauling logs, etc. [origin uncertain]

dink y (ding′kē), *adj.,* **dink i er, dink i est.** INFORMAL. small and insignificant. [origin uncertain]

din ner (din′ər), *n.* 1 the main meal of the day. 2 a formal meal in honor of some person or occasion. [< Old French *disner* dine; infinitive used as noun]

dinner jacket, a semiformal coat without tails, usually black with satin lapels, worn by men in the evening; jacket of a tuxedo.

din o flag el late (din′ə flaj′ə lāt), *n.* any of an order of tiny marine flagellates, some species of which produce a red, toxic substance poisonous to fish.

di no saur (dī′nə sôr), *n.* any of two orders of extinct reptiles, some of which grew to enormous size, that dominated the earth during the Mesozoic era. [< New Latin *dinosaurus* < Greek *deinos* terrible + *sauros* lizard]

di no sau ri an (dī′nə sôr′ē ən), *adj.* of or like a dinosaur. —*n.* dinosaur.

dint (dint), *n.* 1 force: *By dint of hard work the job was completed on schedule.* 2 dent. —*v.t.* make a dent in. [Old English *dynt*]

di oc e san (dī os′ə sən, dī′ə sē′sn), *adj.* of or having to do with a diocese. —*n.* bishop of a diocese.

di o cese (dī′ə sis, dī′ə sēs′), *n.* a church district under a bishop's authority; bishopric; see[2]. [< Late Latin *diocesis* < Greek *dioikēsis* province, diocese]

Di o cle tian (dī′ə klē′shən), *n.* A.D. 245-313, Roman emperor from A.D. 284 to 305.

di ode (dī′ōd), *n.* vacuum tube having two electrodes, especially a rectifier which permits the flow of electrons in one direction only. [< *di-*[1] two + *(electr)ode*]

di oe cious (dī ē′shəs), *adj.* having male and female flowers on separate plants of the same species. The asparagus and willow are dioecious. Also, **diecious.** [< Greek *di-* double + *oikos* house]

Di og e nes (dī oj′ə nēz′), *n.* 412?-323 B.C., Greek Cynic philosopher.

Di o me des (dī′ə mē′dēz), *n.* (in Greek legends) a Greek hero in the Trojan War.

Di o ny si a (dī′ə nish′ē ə, dī′ə nis′ē ə), *n. pl.* set of festivals in honor of Dionysus.

Di o ny sian (dī′ə nish′ən, dī′ə nis′ē ən), *adj.* having to do with Dionysus.

Di o ny si us (dī′ə nish′ē əs, dī′ə nis′ē əs), *n.* 430?-367 B.C., ruler of the ancient Greek city of Syracuse from 405 to 367 B.C. He was called "the Elder."

Di o ny sus (dī′ə nī′səs), *n.* (in Greek myths) the god of wine; Bacchus.

di o ram a (dī′ə ram′ə), *n.* 1 a three-dimensional scene viewed through a windowlike opening showing a foreground of sculptured figures of animals, men, etc., and surrounding objects, against a painted or modeled background. 2 picture that is usually looked at through a small opening, lighted

hat, āge, fär; let, ēqual, tėrm;
it, īce; hot, ōpen, ôrder;
oil, out; cup, pu̇t, rüle;
ch, child; ng, long; sh, she;
th, thin; ᴛʜ, then; zh, measure;

ə represents *a* in about, *e* in taken, *i* in pencil, *o* in lemon, *u* in circus.

< = from, derived from, taken from.

from above, the light being diminished or increased to represent changes in weather, etc. [< Greek *dia-* through + *horama* sight]

di o ram ic (dī′ə ram′ik), *adj.* having to do with or like a diorama.

di o rite (dī′ə rīt), *n.* a coarse-grained igneous rock consisting essentially of hornblende and feldspar. [< French < Greek *diorizein* distinguish]

Di os cur i (dī′ə skyu̇r′ī), *n.pl.* (in Greek and Roman myths) the twins Castor and Pollux.

di ox ide (dī ok′sīd, dī ok′sid), *n.* oxide having two atoms of oxygen for each molecule.

dip (dip), *v.,* **dipped** or **dipt, dip ping,** *n.* —*v.t.* 1 put under water or any liquid and lift quickly out again: *She dipped her hand into the clear pool.* See synonym study below. 2 make (a candle) by putting a wick over and over into hot tallow or wax. 3 take up in the hollow of the hand or with a pail, pan, or other container: *dip water from a bucket, dip up a sample of wheat.* 4 put (one's hand, a spoon, etc.) into to take out something. 5 lower and raise again quickly: *The ship's flag was dipped as a salute.* 6 dye by dipping in a liquid: *dip a dress.* 7 wash or clean by dipping in a liquid. 8 immerse in a solution for plating or galvanizing. 9 **dip into, a** read or look at for a short time; glance at: *dip into a book.* **b** engage in superficially: *dip into astronomy.* —*v.i.* 1 go under water and come quickly out again. 2 sink or drop down: *The bird dipped in its flight.* 3 slope downward: *The road dips into the valley.* 4 put one's hand, a spoon, etc., into something to take out its contents: *dip into a box of candy, dip into one's savings.*
—*n.* 1 a dipping of any kind, especially a quick plunge into and out of a tub of water, the sea, etc. 2 liquid in which to dip something for washing or cleaning. 3 a creamy mixture of foods eaten by dipping into with a cracker, piece of bread, etc. 4 a sudden drop: *a dip in a road, a dip in prices.* 5 candle made by dipping. 6 that which is taken out or up by dipping. 7 amount of slope down.
[Old English *dyppan*]

Syn. *v.t.* 1 **Dip, plunge, immerse** mean to put into a liquid. **Dip** emphasizes taking right out again after putting or lowering partly in or wholly under: *I dipped my handkerchief in the cool water.* **Plunge** emphasizes throwing or putting completely under, suddenly or with force: *I plunged the vegetables into boiling water.* **Immerse** emphasizes keeping completely under long enough to get thoroughly soaked: *I immersed my clothes in the soapy water.*

diph ther i a (dif thir′ē ə, dip thir′ē ə), *n.* an acute, infectious disease of the throat, usually accompanied by a high fever and the formation of a membranous substance that hinders respiration. It is caused by a bacillus. [< French *diphthérie* < Greek *diphthera* hide, leather; with reference to the tough membranous substance developed on the affected parts]

diph ther i al (dif thir′ē əl, dip thir′ē əl), *adj.* having to do with diphtheria.

diph the rit ic (dif′thə rit′ik, dip′thə-rit′ik), *adj.* 1 of or like diphtheria. 2 suffering from diphtheria.

diph thong (dif′thông, dif′thong; dip′-thông, dip′thong), *n.* 1 a vowel sound made up of two identifiable vowel sounds in immediate sequence and pronounced in one syllable, such as *ou* in *house* or *oi* in *noise.* Sometimes a diphthong is represented by only one letter, as *i* in *ice* or *u* in *abuse.* 2 two vowel letters joined together in printing, such as *æ* and *œ;* ligature. 3 digraph. [< Greek *diphthongos* < *di-* double + *phthongos* sound]

diph thon gal (dif thông′gəl, dif thong′gəl; dip thông′gəl, dip thong′gəl), *adj.* of or like a diphthong.

diph thong ize (dif′thông īz, dif′thong īz; dip′thông īz, dip′thong īz), *v.*, **-ized, -iz ing.** —*v.t.* change (a vowel or vowels) into a diphthong. —*v.i.* become a diphthong. **—diph′thong i za′tion,** *n.*

dip lo blas tic (dip′lō blas′tik), *adj.* having two germ layers, the ectoderm and endoderm, as coelenterates. [< Greek *diploos* double + *blastos* germ]

di plod o cus (də plod′ə kəs), *n.* any of a genus of very large plant-eating dinosaurs of the Upper Jurassic period of western North America. [< Greek *diploos* double + *dokos* wooden beam]

dip loid (dip′loid), *adj.* having two sets of chromosomes. —*n.* a diploid organism or cell. [< Greek *diploos* double]

di plo ma (də plō′mə), *n.* 1 certificate given by a school, college, or university which states that a person has completed a certain course of study or has been graduated after a certain amount of work. 2 any certificate that bestows certain rights, privileges, honors, etc. [< Latin < Greek *diplōma* paper folded double, ultimately < *diploos* double]

di plo ma cy (də plō′mə sē), *n., pl.* **-cies.** 1 the management of relations between nations, as in the negotiations of treaties, international agreements, etc. 2 skill in managing such relations. 3 skill in dealing with others; tact.

dip lo mat (dip′lə mat), *n.* 1 person skilled in diplomacy. Ambassadors, envoys, and chargé d'affaires are diplomats. 2 a tactful person.

dip lo mat ic (dip′lə mat′ik), *adj.* 1 of or having to do with diplomacy: *the diplomatic service.* 2 having or showing skill in dealing with others; tactful: *a diplomatic policeman, a diplomatic answer.* **—dip′lo mat′i cal ly,** *adv.*

diplomatic corps, all of the ambassadors, ministers, etc., of foreign nations at the capital of a country.

diplomatic immunity, special privileges accorded to diplomats and their families and staffs by international agreement, including freedom from arrest, search, and taxation.

di plo mat ist (də plō′mə tist), *n.* BRITISH. diplomat.

dip lo pod (dip′lə pod), *n.* any of a class of elongated, cylindrical anthropods having one pair of short antennae and many body segments, with two pairs of legs on most segments; millipede. [< Greek *diploos* double + *podos* foot]

dip needle, dipping needle.

di pole (dī′pōl), *n.* 1 two equal electric charges or magnetic poles of opposite sign which are separated by a specified distance, as in a molecule. 2 molecule or other object having two such charges or poles. 3 a radio or television antenna having two separated conducting rods one-half wave in length.

dip per (dip′ər), *n.* 1 person or thing that dips. 2 a cup-shaped container with a long handle for dipping water or other liquids. 3 any of various diving birds, such as the kingfisher. 4 **Dipper,** either of two groups of stars in the northern sky somewhat resembling the shape of a dipper; Big Dipper or Little Dipper. See **constellation** for diagram.

dipping needle, a suspended magnetic needle that indicates by its dip the direction of the earth's magnetism; dip needle.

dip so ma ni a (dip′sə mā′nē ə), *n.* an uncontrollable craving for alcoholic liquor. [< Greek *dipsa* thirst + *mania* mania]

dip so ma ni ac (dip′sə mā′nē ak), *n.* person who has dipsomania.

dip stick (dip′stik′), *n.* rod for measuring the level of liquid in a container, such as the oil in the crankcase of an internal-combustion engine.

dipt (dipt), *v.* a pt. and a pp. of **dip.**

dip ter an (dip′tər ən), *adj.* dipterous. —*n.* any of a large order of insects that have one pair of membranous wings, the usual second pair being replaced by small club-shaped organs. Mosquitoes, gnats, and houseflies belong to this order. [< Greek *di-* two + *pteron* wing]

dip ter ous (dip′tər əs), *adj.* of or belonging to the dipterans.

diptych (def. 1)

dip tych (dip′tik), *n.* 1 an ancient writing tablet consisting of two pieces hinged together. 2 pair of paintings or carvings on two panels hinged together. [< Greek *diptychos* folded double < *di-* twice + *ptychē* a fold]

dir., director.

Di rac (di rak′), *n.* **Paul Adrien Maurice,** born 1902, British physicist who helped to develop quantum mechanics.

dire (dīr), *adj.,* **dir er, dir est.** causing great fear or suffering; dreadful. [< Latin *dirus*] **—dire′ly,** *adv.* **—dire′ness,** *n.*

di rect (də rekt′, dī rekt′), *v.t.* 1 have authority or control over; manage or guide: *direct a play, direct a business.* See **manage** for synonym study. 2 instruct to do something; order: *We were directed to include return addresses on our applications.* See **command** for synonym study. 3 tell or show (a person) the way; inform or guide as to the right way or road: *Can you direct me to the airport?* 4 cause (a person or thing) to move, point, or turn toward a place or object; turn (the eyes, attention, etc.) to an aim, purpose, object, etc.: *Direct the hose at the flames.* 5 put the address on (a letter, package, etc.). 6 address (words, etc.) to a person: *To whom is your question directed?* 7 turn (a thing) straight to. —*v.i.* give directions; order.

—*adj.* 1 proceeding in a straight line without a stop or turn; straight: *a direct route.* 2 proceeding in an unbroken line of descent; lineal: *a direct heir.* 3 without anyone or anything in between; not through others; by oneself or itself; immediate: *direct influence. Selling door to door is direct selling.* See synonym study below. 4 straightforward: *a direct answer. He made a direct denial of the charge of cheating.* 5 exact: *the direct opposite.* 6 of or produced by the action of the people as voters, without intermediaries or representatives: *direct elections.*

—*adv.* directly: *This plane flies direct from Chicago to Los Angeles.*

[< Latin *directum* led straight < *dis-* + *regere* to guide] **—di rect′ness,** *n.*

Syn. *adj.* 3 **Direct, immediate** mean proceeding from one to another without a break. **Direct** means going straight from one to another in an unbroken line, though there may be many steps between: *Overwork and too great strain were the direct causes of his death.* **Immediate** means going from one thing to the next, without anything between: *A heart attack was the immediate cause of his death.*

direct current, an electric current that flows in one direction only.

direct discourse, a quoting of what a person says in his exact words. EXAMPLE: He said, "Let's go now."

di rec tion (də rek′shən, dī rek′shən), *n.* 1 a directing; managing or guiding: *the direction of a play or movie.* 2 order; command: *It was his direction that I prepare a report.* 3 Also, **directions,** *pl.* a knowing or telling what to do, how to do something, where to go., etc.; instructions: *Can you give me directions for driving to Chicago?* 4 address on a letter or package. 5 course taken by a moving body, such as a ball or a bullet. 6 any way in which one may face or point. North, south, east, and west are directions. 7 course along which something moves; line of action; tendency: *The town shows improvement in many directions.* See synonym study below.

Syn. 7 **Direction, trend, tendency** mean line or course of action. **Direction** applies when the course of action is set and steady: *The crime investigation has taken a new direction.* **Trend** applies when the course is more general and involves twistings and turnings: *The trend is toward higher wages and prices.* **Tendency** applies when the course is definite but the progress, though inclined in this direction, is uncertain: *The tendency is toward higher taxes.*

di rec tion al (də rek′shə nəl, dī rek′shə-nəl), *adj.* 1 of, having to do with, or indicating direction: *the directional signals of an automobile.* 2 sending or receiving radio signals in or from a particular direction: *a directional antenna.*

di rec tive (də rek′tiv, dī rek′tiv), *n.* a general instruction on how to proceed or act. —*adj.* directing; serving to direct.

di rec tiv i ty (də rek tiv′ə tē, dī′rek tiv′ə-tē), *n.* directional condition or quality.

di rect ly (də rekt′lē, dī rekt′lē), *adv.* 1 in a direct line or manner; straight: *This road runs directly north.* 2 exactly; absolutely: *directly opposite.* 3 at once; immediately: *Come home directly!*

direct object, (in grammar) word or words denoting the person or thing undergoing the action expressed by the verb. In "The boat struck a rock," *rock* is the direct object of the verb *struck*.

di rec tor (də rek′tər, dī rek′tər), *n.* 1 person who directs, rules, or guides. 2 person who plans and supervises the performance of a play or program on the stage or in radio, television, or motion pictures. 3 one of a group of persons who direct the affairs of a company or institution.

di rec tor ate (də rek′tər it, dī rek′tər it), *n.* 1 position of director. 2 group of directors.

di rec to ri al (də rek tôr′ē əl, də rek tōr′ē-əl; dī′rek tôr′ē əl, dī′rek tōr′ē əl), *adj.* having to do with a director or directorate.

di rec tor ship (də rek′tər ship, dī rek′tər-ship), *n.* position or term of office of a director.

di rec tor y (də rek′tər ē, dī rek′tər ē), *n., pl.* **-tor ies,** *adj.* —*n.* 1 list of names and addresses, usually in alphabetical order. A telephone book is a directory of people who have telephones. 2 group of directors; directorate. 3 **Directory,** group of five men that governed France from 1795 to 1799. —*adj.* serving to direct; directing; advisory.

direct primary, U.S. primary in which the candidates are chosen by direct vote instead of by party members at a convention.

di rec trix (də rek′triks, dī rek′triks), *n., pl.* **di rec trix es, di rec tri ces** (dī′rek trī′sēz). (in geometry) a fixed line used in determining a conic section.

direct tax, tax that must be paid directly by the taxed person, such as an income, property or inheritance tax.

dire ful (dīr′fəl), *adj.* dire; dreadful; terrible. —**dire′ful ly,** *adv.* —**dire′ful ness,** *n.*

dirge (dėrj), *n.* a funeral song or tune. [contraction of Latin *dirige* direct! (first word in office for the dead)]

dir ham (dir ham′), *n.* the monetary unit of Morocco, a coin or note worth about 20 cents. [< Arabic < Latin *drachma* drachma]

dir i gi ble (dir′ə jə bəl, də rij′ə bəl), *n.* airship, especially a rigid airship. —*adj.* capable of being directed. [< Latin *dirigere* to direct]

dirk (dėrk), *n.* dagger. —*v.t.* stab with a dirk. [origin unknown]

dirn dl (dėrn′dl), *n.* 1 an Alpine peasant girl's costume consisting of a blouse, a tight bodice, and a full, brightly colored skirt, gathered at the waist. 2 dress imitating such a costume. 3 skirt of this type. [< German dialectal *Dirndl* girl, diminutive of *Dirne* maid]

dirt (dėrt), *n.* 1 mud, dust, earth, or anything like them. Dirt soils whatever it touches. 2 loose earth or soil. 3 an unclean action, thought, or speech. 4 uncleanness; meanness. 5 INFORMAL. scandal; gossip. [Middle English *drit*]

dirt-cheap (dėrt′chēp′), *adj.* very cheap.

dirt farmer, INFORMAL. farmer who does his own farming, without hired help.

dirt y (dėr′tē), *adj.,* **dirt i er, dirt i est,** *v.,* **dirt ied, dirt y ing.** —*adj.* 1 soiled by dirt; unclean: *dirty hands.* See synonym study below. 2 that makes dirty; soiling: *a dirty job.* 3 not clean or pure in action, thought, or speech; low; base. 4 stormy or windy; rough: *dirty weather.* 5 not clear or pure in color: *a dirty red.* 6 causing a great amount of radioactive fallout: *dirty bombs.* —*v.t., v.i.* make or become dirty; soil. —**dirt′i ly,** *adv.* —**dirt′i ness,** *n.*

Syn. *adj.* 1 **Dirty, filthy, foul** mean unclean. **Dirty** means soiled in any way: *dirty shoes.* **Filthy,** expressing disgust, suggests being extremely dirty: *a filthy kitchen.* **Foul** implies still greater disgust and suggests being filled or covered with filth: *The water in the swamp is foul.*

Dis (dis), *n.* 1 (in Roman myths) the god of the lower world, identified with the Greek god Pluto. 2 Hades.

dis-[1], *prefix.* 1 opposite of; lack of; not: *Dishonest = not honest; opposite of honest. Discomfort = lack of comfort.* 2 do the opposite of: *Disentangle = do the opposite of entangle.* 3 apart; away, as in *dispel.* See also **di-**[2] and **dif-.** [< Latin]

dis-[2], *prefix.* form of **di-**[1] before *s,* as in *dissyllable.*

dis a bil i ty (dis′ə bil′ə tē), *n., pl.* **-ties.** 1 lack of ability or power: *The player's disability was caused by lameness.* 2 something that disables. 3 something that disqualifies.

dis a ble (dis ā′bəl), *v.t.,* **-bled, -bling.** 1 make unable; make unfit for use, action, etc., cripple. See **cripple** for synonym study. 2 disqualify legally. —**dis a′ble ment,** *n.*

dis a buse (dis′ə byüz′), *v.t.,* **-bused, -bus ing.** free from deception or error: *Education should disabuse people of foolish prejudices.*

di sac cha ride (dī sak′ə rīd′, dī sak′ər id), *n.* any of a group of carbohydrates, such as lactose, maltose, sucrose, and various other sugars, which hydrolysis changes into two monosaccharides or simple sugars.

dis ad van tage (dis′əd van′tij), *n.* 1 lack of advantage; unfavorable condition: *The shy child was at a disadvantage in school.* 2 loss or injury: *The candidate's enemies spread rumors that were to his disadvantage.*

dis ad van taged (dis′əd van′tijd), *adj.* lacking advantages; being in an unfavorable condition: *disadvantaged children.*

dis ad van ta geous (dis ad′vən tā′jəs), *adj.* causing disadvantage; unfavorable. —**dis ad′van ta′geous ly,** *adv.* —**dis-ad′van ta′geous ness,** *n.*

dis af fect (dis′ə fekt′), *v.t.* make unfriendly, disloyal, or discontented.

dis af fect ed (dis′ə fek′tid), *adj.* unfriendly, disloyal, or discontented.

dis af fec tion (dis′ə fek′shən), *n.* unfriendliness, disloyalty, or discontent: *Lack of food and supplies caused disaffection among the soldiers.*

dis a gree (dis′ə grē′), *v.i.,* **-greed, -gree ing.** 1 fail to agree; be different: *Your account of the accident disagrees with hers.* 2 have unlike opinions; differ: *Doctors sometimes disagree about the proper method of treating a patient.* 3 quarrel; dispute. 4 have a bad effect; be harmful: *Strawberries disagree with me.*

dis a gree a ble (dis′ə grē′ə bəl), *adj.* 1 not to one's liking; unpleasant. 2 not friendly; bad-tempered; cross. —**dis′a gree′a ble-ness,** *n.* —**dis′a gree′a bly,** *adv.*

dis a gree ment (dis′ə grē′mənt), *n.* 1 failure to agree; difference of opinion. 2 quarrel; dispute. 3 difference; unlikeness.

dis al low (dis′ə lou′), *v.t.* refuse to allow; deny the truth or value of; reject: *The court disallowed my claim to the property.*

dis al low ance (dis′ə lou′əns), *n.* a disallowing.

dis ap pear (dis′ə pir′), *v.i.* 1 pass from sight; stop being seen: *The dog disappeared around the corner.* See synonym study below. 2 pass from existence; stop being: *When spring comes, the snow disappears.*

Syn. 1 **Disappear, vanish, fade** mean to pass from sight. **Disappear,** the general term, means to pass out of sight slowly or quickly, gradually or suddenly: *He disappeared into the night.* **Vanish** means to disappear without a trace, usually suddenly, often in some strange or mysterious way: *The stranger vanished from town.* **Fade** means to disappear little by little: *The ship faded into the fog.*

hat, āge, fär; let, ēqual, tėrm;
it, īce; hot, ōpen, ôrder;
oil, out; cup, pu̇t, rüle;
ch, child; ng, long; sh, she;
th, thin; ŦH, then; zh, measure;

ə represents *a* in about, *e* in taken, *i* in pencil, *o* in lemon, *u* in circus.

< = from, derived from, taken from.

dis ap pear ance (dis′ə pir′əns), *n.* act of disappearing.

dis ap point (dis′ə point′), *v.t.* 1 fail to satisfy or please; leave wanting or expecting something. 2 fail to keep a promise to. 3 keep from happening; oppose and defeat.

dis ap point ment (dis′ə point′mənt), *n.* 1 state of being or feeling disappointed. 2 person or thing that causes disappointment. 3 act or fact of disappointing.

dis ap pro ba tion (dis ap′rə bā′shən), *n.* disapproval.

dis ap prov al (dis′ə prü′vəl), *n.* 1 opinion or feeling against; expression of an opinion against; dislike. 2 refusal to consent; rejection.

dis ap prove (dis′ə prüv′), *v.,* **-proved, -prov ing.** —*v.t.* 1 have or express an opinion against. 2 refuse consent to; reject: *The judge disapproved the verdict.* —*v.i.* show dislike *(of): Most children disapprove of going to school in the summer.* —**dis′ap-prov′ing ly,** *adv.*

dis arm (dis ärm′), *v.t.* 1 take weapons away from: *The police captured the robbers and disarmed them.* 2 remove anger or suspicion from; make friendly: *The speaker's honesty disarmed the angry crowd.* 3 make harmless: *disarm a bomb by removing the fuse.* —*v.i.* stop having an army, navy, etc.; reduce or limit armed forces or weapons: *The nations agreed to disarm.* —**dis arm′ing ly,** *adv.*

dis ar ma ment (dis är′mə mənt), *n.* 1 act of disarming. 2 reduction or limitation of a country's armed forces or weapons.

dis ar range (dis′ə rānj′), *v.t.,* **-ranged, -rang ing.** disturb the arrangement of; put out of order: *The wind disarranged my hair.* —**dis′ar range′ment,** *n.*

dis ar ray (dis′ə rā′), *n.* 1 lack of order; disorder; confusion. 2 disorder of clothing. —*v.t.* 1 put into disorder or confusion. 2 undress; strip.

dis as sem ble (dis′ə sem′bəl), *v.t.,* **-bled, -bling.** take apart: *disassemble a motor to repair it.*

dis as so ci ate (dis′ə sō′shē āt), *v.t.,* **-at ed, -at ing.** dissociate. —**dis′as so′ci-a′tion,** *n.*

dis as ter (də zas′tər), *n.* event that causes much suffering or loss; a sudden or great misfortune, such as a destructive fire or an earthquake. [< Middle French *désastre* unfavorable star, calamity < Latin *dis-* without + *astrum* star]

Syn. Disaster, calamity, catastrophe mean a great misfortune. **Disaster** applies to an event which happens suddenly or unexpectedly and causes much loss and suffering: *The failure of the bank was a disaster for the farmers.* **Calamity** applies especially to a disaster which causes intense suffering and grief to a great number: *The attack on Pearl Harbor was a calamity.* **Catastrophe** suggests a disaster which is final and complete, causing loss that can never be made up: *A modern war is a catastrophe.*

dis as trous (də zas′trəs), *adj.* bringing disaster; causing much suffering or loss. **—dis as′trous ly,** *adv.*

dis a vow (dis′ə vou′), *v.t.* deny that one knows about, approves of, or is responsible for; disclaim: *He disavowed any share in the plot.*

dis a vow al (dis′ə vou′əl), *n.* a disavowing; denial.

dis band (dis band′), *v.t.* break up (a band or company); dismiss from service: *disband an army.* *—v.i.* break ranks; become scattered. **—dis band′ment,** *n.*

dis bar (dis bär′), *v.t.,* **-barred, -bar ring.** deprive (a lawyer) of the right to practice law. **—dis bar′ment,** *n.*

dis be lief (dis′bi lēf′), *n.* lack of belief; refusal to believe. See **unbelief** for synonym study.

dis be lieve (dis′bi lēv′), *v.t.,* **-lieved, -liev ing.** have no belief in; refuse to believe. **—dis′be liev′er,** *n.*

dis bur den (dis bėrd′n), *v.t.* relieve of a burden: *The girl disburdened her mind by confessing what she had done.* **—dis bur′den ment,** *n.*

dis burse (dis bėrs′), *v.t.,* **-bursed, -burs ing.** pay out; expend. See **spend** for synonym study. [< Old French *desbourser* < *des-* dis- + *bourse* purse] **—dis burs′er,** *n.*

dis burse ment (dis bėrs′mənt), *n.* 1 a paying out. 2 money paid out.

disc (disk), *n.* disk.

dis card (*v.* dis kärd′; *n.* dis′kärd), *v.t.* 1 give up as useless or not wanted; throw aside. 2 get rid of (unwanted playing cards) by throwing them aside or playing them. 3 play (a card) that is neither of trump nor of the suit led. *—v.i.* throw out an unwanted card. *—n.* 1 act of throwing aside as useless or not wanted. 2 thing or things thrown aside as useless or not wanted. 3 cards thrown aside or played as not wanted. [< *dis-*[1] + *card*[1]]

dis cern (də zėrn′, də sėrn′), *v.t.* see clearly; perceive the difference between (two or more things); distinguish or recognize: *We discerned the island through the mist. I cannot discern the meaning of that paragraph.* [< Latin *discernere* < *dis-* off + *cernere* to separate] **—dis cern′er,** *n.*

dis cern i ble (də zėr′nə bəl, də sėr′nə bəl), *adj.* capable of being discerned. **—dis cern′i bly,** *adv.*

dis cern ing (də zėr′ning, də sėr′ning), *adj.* keen in seeing and understanding; with good judgment; shrewd. **—dis cern′ing ly,** *adv.*

dis cern ment (də zėrn′mənt, də sėrn′mənt), *n.* 1 keenness in seeing and understanding; good judgment; shrewdness. See **insight** for synonym study. 2 act of discerning.

dis charge (*v.* dis chärj′; *n.* dis chärj′, dis′chärj), *v.,* **-charged, -charg ing,** *n.* *—v.t.* 1 unload (cargo or passengers) from a ship, train, bus, etc.: *The ship discharged its passengers at the dock.* 2 fire off; shoot: *discharge a gun.* 3 release; let go; dismiss: *discharge a patient from a hospital, discharge a lazy employee, discharge a committee.* See **dismiss** for synonym study. 4 give off; let out: *The infection discharged pus.* 5 rid of an electric charge; withdraw electricity from. 6 perform (a duty, function, etc.): *discharge the duties of postman.* See **perform** for synonym study. 7 pay (a debt, etc.). 8 (in law) cancel or set aside (a court order). *—v.i.* 1 unload cargo or passengers from a ship, train, bus, etc. 2 (of a gun) go off. 3 come or pour forth: *The river discharges into a bay.* 4 lose an electric charge.
—n. 1 an unloading: *The discharge of this cargo will not take long.* 2 a firing off of a gun, a blast, etc. 3 a release; a letting go; a dismissing: *the discharge of a prisoner from jail.* 4 writing that shows a person's release or dismissal; certificate of release: *Many members of the armed services got discharges when the war ended.* 5 a giving off; letting out: *Lightning is a discharge of electricity from the clouds.* 6 thing given off or let out: *a watery discharge from the eye.* 7 performance: *Public officials should be honest in the discharge of their duties.* 8 payment: *the discharge of a debt.* 9 transference of electricity between two charged bodies when placed in contact or near each other. 10 rate of flow: *The discharge from the pipe is ten gallons a second.* **—dis charge′a ble,** *adj.* **—dis charg′er,** *n.*

dis ci ple (də sī′pəl), *n.* 1 believer in the thought and teaching of any leader; follower. See **follower** for synonym study. 2 (in the Bible) one of the followers of Jesus, especially one of the twelve Apostles. [< Latin *discipulus* pupil]

dis ci ple ship (di sī′pəl ship), *n.* 1 state of being a disciple. 2 time of being a disciple.

Disciples of Christ, a religious sect founded in the United States in 1809 that rejects all creeds and seeks to unite Christians on the basis of the New Testament alone; Christian Church.

dis ci pli nar i an (dis′ə plə ner′ē ən), *n.* person who enforces discipline or who believes in strict discipline. *—adj.* disciplinary.

dis ci pli nar y (dis′ə plə ner′ē), *adj.* 1 having to do with discipline: *disciplinary problems.* 2 for discipline; intended to improve discipline: *take disciplinary measures.*

dis ci pline (dis′ə plin), *n., v.,* **-plined, -plin ing.** *—n.* 1 training, especially training of the mind or character. 2 the training effect of experience, misfortune, etc. 3 a trained condition of order and obedience. 4 order among school pupils, soldiers, or members of any group. 5 a particular system of rules for conduct. 6 punishment; chastisement. *—v.t.* 1 bring to a condition of order and obedience; bring under control; train. 2 punish; chastise: *discipline a child for bad behavior.* [< Latin *disciplina* < *discipulus* pupil] **—dis′ci plin er,** *n.*

disc jockey, INFORMAL. disk jockey.

dis claim (dis klām′), *v.t.* 1 refuse to recognize as one's own; deny connection with: *The motorist disclaimed responsibility for the accident.* 2 give up all claim to: *She disclaimed any share in the inheritance.*

dis claim er (dis klā′mər), *n.* 1 a disclaiming; denial. 2 person who disclaims.

dis close (dis klōz′), *v.t.,* **-closed, -clos ing.** 1 open to view; uncover: *The window disclosed a beautiful landscape.* 2 make known; reveal: *This letter discloses a secret.* See **reveal** for synonym study. **—dis clos′er,** *n.*

dis clo sure (dis klō′zhər), *n.* 1 a disclosing. 2 thing disclosed.

dis cog ra phy (dis kog′rə fē), *n., pl.* **-phies.** list of phonograph disks or of writings about them.

dis coid (dis′koid), *adj.* having the form of a disk; disk-shaped.

dis coi dal (dis koi′dəl), *adj.* discoid.

dis col or (dis kul′ər), *v.t.* change or spoil the color of; stain: *Smoke and grime had discolored the building.* *—v.i.* become changed in color.

dis col or a tion (dis kul′ə rā′shən), *n.* 1 a discoloring. 2 a being discolored. 3 a stain.

dis com bob u late (dis′kəm bob′yə lāt), *v.t.,* **-lat ed, -lat ing.** INFORMAL. confuse; disconcert. [a coined word]

dis com fit (dis kum′fit), *v.t.* 1 defeat completely; rout. 2 defeat the plans or hopes of; frustrate. 3 embarrass greatly; confuse; disconcert. [< Old French *desconfit* discomfited < *des-* dis- + *confire* make, accomplish]

dis com fi ture (dis kum′fi chůr, dis kum′fi chər), *n.* 1 a complete defeat; rout. 2 defeat of plans or hopes; frustration. 3 confusion.

dis com fort (dis kum′fərt), *n.* 1 lack of comfort; uneasiness. 2 thing that causes discomfort; inconvenience. *—v.t.* make uncomfortable or uneasy.

dis com mode (dis′kə mōd′), *v.t.,* **-mod ed, -mod ing.** put to inconvenience. [< *dis-* + French *commode* convenient]

dis com pose (dis′kəm pōz′), *v.t.,* **-posed, -pos ing.** 1 disturb the self-possession of; confuse. 2 disarrange.

dis com po sure (dis′kəm pō′zhər), *n.* condition of being discomposed; confusion; uneasiness.

dis con cert (dis′kən sėrt′), *v.t.* 1 disturb the self-possession of; embarrass greatly; confuse: *I was disconcerted by this unexpected opposition.* See **confuse** for synonym study. 2 upset or frustrate (plans, etc.). **—dis′con cert′ing ly,** *adv.*

dis con nect (dis′kə nekt′), *v.t.* undo or break the connection of; separate; unfasten: *I pulled out the plug to disconnect the toaster.* **—dis′con nec′tion,** *n.*

dis con nect ed (dis′kə nek′tid), *adj.* 1 not connected; separate. 2 without order or connection; incoherent. **—dis′con nect′ed ly,** *adv.* **—dis′con nect′ed ness,** *n.*

dis con so late (dis kon′sə lit), *adj.* 1 without hope; forlorn; unhappy: *disconsolate over the death of a friend.* See **desolate** for synonym study. 2 causing discomfort; cheerless: *a long, disconsolate day.* [< Medieval Latin *disconsolatus* < Latin *dis-* + *consolari* to console] **—dis con′so late ly,** *adv.* **—dis con′so late ness,** *n.*

dis con tent (dis′kən tent′), *n.* lack of contentment; feeling of dissatisfaction. *—v.t.* dissatisfy; displease. *—adj.* discontented. **—dis′con tent′ment,** *n.*

dis con tent ed (dis′kən ten′tid), *adj.* not contented; showing discontent; dissatisfied. **—dis′con tent′ed ly,** *adv.* **—dis′con tent′ed ness,** *n.*

dis con tin u ance (dis′kən tin′yü əns), *n.* act of stopping or breaking off: *the discontinuance of electric service because of nonpayment of the bill.*

dis con tin ue (dis′kən tin′yü), *v.,* **-tin ued, -tin u ing.** *—v.t.* 1 cause to cease; put a stop to; break off; give up; stop: *The train has been discontinued.* 2 cease from;

cease to take, use, etc.: *They decided to discontinue the evening newspaper.* 3 terminate (a lawsuit) by request of the plaintiff or by his failure to continue it. *—v.i.* come to an end or stop; cease. **—dis′con tin′u a′tion,** *n.*

dis con ti nu i ty (dis′kon tə nü′ə tē, dis′kon tə nyü′ə tē), *n., pl.* **-ties.** 1 lack of connection. 2 break or gap in something.

dis con tin u ous (dis′kən tin′yü əs), *adj.* not continuous; having gaps or breaks; interrupted. **—dis′con tin′u ous ly,** *adv.*

dis cord (dis′kôrd), *n.* 1 disagreement of opinions and aims; dissension. 2 in music: **a** dissonance. **b** combination of two or more tones not in harmony with each other. 3 a clashing of sounds. 4 a harsh or unpleasing sound. [< Old French < *discorder* disagree < Latin *discordare* < *discordem* discordant < *dis-* apart + *cordem* heart]

dis cord ance (dis kôrd′ns), *n.* 1 discord of sounds. 2 disagreement.

dis cord an cy (dis kôrd′n sē), *n.* discordance.

dis cord ant (dis kôrd′nt), *adj.* 1 not in agreement; differing; disagreeing: *discordant views.* 2 not in harmony: *a discordant note in music.* 3 harsh; clashing: *the discordant sound of automobile horns honking in a traffic jam.* **—dis cord′ant ly,** *adv.*

dis co theque (dis′kə tek), *n.* night-club where phonograph records are played for dancing. [< French]

dis count (*v.* dis′kount, dis kount′; *n.* dis′kount), *v.t.* 1 deduct (a certain percentage) of the amount or cost: *The store discounts 2 per cent on all bills paid when due.* 2 allow for exaggeration, prejudice, or inaccuracy in (a statement, etc.); believe only part of. 3 leave out of account; disregard: *In his plans he discounted the expense.* 4 take (an expected event, etc.) into account beforehand, and so lessen its impact when it occurs. 5 buy, sell, or lend money on (a note, bill of exchange, etc.), deducting a certain percentage to allow for unpaid interest. *—v.i.* 1 sell goods at a discount: *Many stores do not discount at all.* 2 lend money, deducting the interest in advance. *—n.* 1 deduction from the amount or cost: *During the sale the dealer allowed a 10 per cent discount on all cash purchases.* 2 percentage charged for buying, selling, or lending money on (a note, bill of exchange, etc.). 3 interest deducted in advance. 4 **at a discount, a** at less than the regular price; below par. **b** easy to get because not in demand. **—dis′count a ble,** *adj.*

dis coun te nance (dis koun′tə nəns), *v.t.,* **-nanced, -nanc ing.** 1 refuse to approve; discourage. 2 make ashamed; embarrass greatly; disconcert.

discount house, a retail store or distributor that regularly sells merchandise for less than the manufacturer's list price, making its profit from a large sales volume with low overhead.

dis cour age (dis kėr′ij), *v.t.,* **-aged, -ag ing.** 1 lessen the courage or confidence of; dishearten: *Repeated failures discouraged him.* 2 try to prevent by disapproving; dissuade: *Her friends discouraged her from attempting such a dangerous swim.* 3 prevent or hinder: *Fear that it might rain discouraged us from camping out.* **—dis cour′ag ing ly,** *adv.*

dis cour age ment (dis kėr′ij mənt), *n.* 1 lack of spirit or confidence. 2 a disheartening influence. 3 act of discouraging.

dis course (*n.* dis′kôrs, dis′kōrs; *v.* dis kôrs′, dis kōrs′), *n., v.,* **-coursed, -cours ing.** *—n.* 1 a formal or extensive speech or writing: *Lectures and sermons are discourses.* 2 talk; conversation. *—v.i.* 1 speak or write formally or at length on some subject. 2 talk; converse. [< Latin *discursus* a running about < *dis-* + *cursus* a running]

dis cour te ous (dis kėr′tē əs), *adj.* not courteous; rude; impolite. **—dis cour′te ous ly,** *adv.* **—dis cour′te ous ness,** *n.*

dis cour te sy (dis kėr′tə sē), *n., pl.* **-sies.** 1 lack of courtesy; rudeness; impoliteness. 2 a rude or impolite act.

dis cov er (dis kuv′ər), *v.t.* 1 see or learn of for the first time; find out. See synonym study below. 2 ARCHAIC. make known; reveal. [< Old French *descovrir* < Late Latin *discooperire* uncover < Latin *dis-* + *cooperire* to cover] **—dis cov′er a ble,** *adj.* **—dis cov′er er,** *n.*

Syn. 1 **Discover, invent** mean to find something not known before. **Discover** means to find or find out something that already existed, but was not known about or had not been seen: *Pierre and Marie Curie discovered radium.* **Invent** means to make or work out something that did not exist before: *Thomas Edison invented the electric light bulb.*

dis cov er y (dis kuv′ər ē), *n., pl.* **-er ies.** 1 act of discovering. 2 something discovered.

dis cred it (dis kred′it), *v.t.* 1 cast doubt on; destroy belief, faith, or trust in: *The lawyer discredited the witness by proving that he had been bribed.* 2 refuse to believe; decline to trust or have faith in; disbelieve. 3 injure the good name or standing of; give a bad reputation to. *—n.* 1 loss of belief, faith, or trust; doubt: *cast discredit on a theory.* 2 loss of good name or standing: *bring discredit upon one's family.* 3 person or thing that causes loss of good name or standing; disgrace.

dis cred it a ble (dis kred′ə tə bəl), *adj.* bringing discredit; disgraceful. **—dis cred′it a bly,** *adv.*

dis creet (dis krēt′), *adj.* very careful and sensible in speech and action; having or showing good judgment; wisely cautious. [< Old French *discret* < Late Latin *discretus* discerning < Latin *discernere* discern] **—dis creet′ly,** *adv.* **—dis creet′ness,** *n.*

dis crep an cy (dis krep′ən sē), *n., pl.* **-cies.** 1 lack of consistency; difference. See **difference** for synonym study. 2 an example of inconsistency: *The lawsuit was lost because of discrepancies in the statements of the witnesses.*

dis crep ant (dis krep′ənt), *adj.* showing lack of harmony; disagreeing. [< Latin *discrepantem* sounding differently < *dis-* + *crepare* to sound] **—dis crep′ant ly,** *adv.*

dis crete (dis krēt′), *adj.* 1 distinct from others; separate. 2 consisting of distinct parts; discontinuous. [< Latin *discretum* separated < *dis-* off + *cernere* to separate] **—dis crete′ly,** *adv.* **—dis crete′ness,** *n.*

dis cre tion (dis kresh′ən), *n.* 1 quality of being discreet; great carefulness in speech or action; good judgment; wise caution: *Use your own discretion.* 2 freedom to decide or choose: *It is within the principal's discretion to punish a pupil.*

dis cre tion ar y (dis kresh′ə ner′ē), *adj.* with freedom to decide or choose; left to one's own judgment.

dis crim in a ble (dis krim′ə nə bəl), *adj.*

hat, āge, fär; let, ēqual, tėrm;
it, īce; hot, ōpen, ôrder;
oil, out; cup, pu̇t, rüle;
ch, child; ng, long; sh, she;
th, thin; ᴛʜ, then; zh, measure;

ə represents *a* in about, *e* in taken, *i* in pencil, *o* in lemon, *u* in circus.

< = from, derived from, taken from.

that can be discriminated or distinguished: *discriminable colors.*

dis crim i nate (*v.* dis krim′ə nāt; *adj.* dis krim′ə nit), *v.,* **-nat ed, -nat ing,** *adj.* *—v.i.* 1 make or see a difference; make a distinction: *discriminate between a mere exaggeration and a deliberate falsehood.* 2 accord a particular person, class, etc., distinctive (and usually unfair) treatment: *discriminate against people because of their race or beliefs.* *—v.t.* make or see a difference between; distinguish; differentiate: *discriminate good books from poor ones.* See **distinguish** for synonym study. *—adj.* having discrimination; making careful distinctions. [< Latin *discriminatum* separated < *discrimen* separation < *discernere.* See DISCERN.] **—dis crim′i nate ly,** *adv.* **—dis crim′i na′tor,** *n.*

dis crim i nat ing (dis krim′ə nā′ting), *adj.* 1 able to discriminate well; discerning. 2 that discriminates. **—dis crim′i nat′ing ly,** *adv.*

dis crim i na tion (dis krim′ə nā′shən), *n.* 1 the seeing or making of a distinction; noticing a difference between things. 2 power of detecting distinctions or differences; good judgment. 3 a difference in attitude or treatment shown to a particular person, class, etc.: *racial discrimination.*

dis crim i na tive (dis krim′ə nā′tiv), *adj.* 1 discriminating. 2 showing discrimination. **—dis crim′i na′tive ly,** *adv.*

dis crim i na to ry (dis krim′ə nə tôr′ē, dis krim′ə nə tōr′ē), *adj.* discriminative; showing partiality or prejudice.

dis cur sive (dis kėr′siv), *adj.* wandering from one subject to another; rambling. **—dis cur′sive ly,** *adv.* **—dis cur′sive ness,** *n.*

dis cus (dis′kəs), *n.* a heavy, circular plate, often of wood with a metal rim, thrown for distance in an athletic contest or as an exercise. [< Latin < Greek *diskos.* Doublet of DAIS, DESK, DISH, and DISK.]

dis cuss (dis kus′), *v.t.* 1 consider all sides of (a question in argument). See synonym study below. 2 talk over: *discuss the news.* [< Latin *discussum* shaken apart < *dis-* + *quatere* to shake]

Syn. 1 **Discuss, argue, debate** mean to talk something over with others in order to arrive at a conclusion. **Discuss** means considering all sides of a question: *We discussed* *the best road to take.* **Argue** suggests taking one side and bringing forward facts and reasons for it and against the others: *She argued for the imposition of a sales tax.* **Debate** suggests more formal arguing, often publicly, between clearly drawn up sides: *The question of federal aid to schools was hotly debated in the Senate.*

dis cus sant (dis kus′nt), *n.* person participating in a discussion.

dis cus sion (dis kush′ən), *n.* 1 examination or investigation of something by argument for and against. 2 act of discussing things; *a classroom discussion on modern art.*

dis dain (dis dān′), *v.t.* think unworthy of oneself or one's notice; regard or treat with contempt; scorn. —*n.* a disdaining; feeling of scorn. See **scorn** for synonym study. [< Old French *desdeignier* < *des-* dis- + *deignier* deign]

dis dain ful (dis dān′fəl), *adj.* feeling or showing disdain; scornful. **—dis dain′ful ly,** *adv.* **—dis dain′ful ness,** *n.*

dis ease (də zēz′), *n.* 1 condition of poor health; condition in which an organ, system, or part does not function properly; illness: *People, animals, and plants are all liable to disease.* 2 any particular illness: *Measles and chicken pox are two diseases of children.* [< Old French *desaise* < *des-* dis- + *aise* ease]

dis eased (də zēzd′), *adj.* having a disease; showing signs of sickness.

dis em bark (dis′em bärk′), *v.i., v.t.* go or put ashore from a ship; land from a ship. **—dis′em bar ka′tion,** *n.*

dis em bar rass (dis′em bar′əs), *v.t.* set free from something that holds back or entangles; disengage.

dis em bod ied (dis′em bod′ēd), *adj.* separated from the body: *Ghosts are usually thought of as disembodied spirits.*

dis em bow el (dis′em bou′əl), *v.t.,* **-eled, -el ing** or **-elled, -el ling.** take or rip out the bowels of; eviscerate. **—dis′em bow′el ment,** *n.*

dis en chant (dis′en chant′), *v.t.* set free from enchantment or illusion; disillusion. **—dis′en chant′ment,** *n.*

dis en cum ber (dis′en kum′bər), *v.t.* set free from encumbrances.

dis en fran chise (dis′en fran′chīz), *v.t.,* **-chised, -chis ing.** disfranchise. **—dis′en fran′chise ment,** *n.*

dis en gage (dis′en gāj′), *v.t.,* **-gaged, -gag ing.** 1 free or release from anything that holds; detach; loosen: *disengage the clutch. He disengaged his hand from that of the sleeping child.* 2 free from an engagement, pledge, or obligation. 3 (in military use) withdraw from combat or contact with (an enemy). **—dis′en gage′ment,** *n.*

dis en tan gle (dis′en tang′gəl), *v.t., v.i.* **-gled, -gling.** free from tangles or complications; untangle. **—dis′en tan′gle ment,** *n.*

dis e qui lib ri um (dis ē′kwə lib′rē əm), *n.* loss of equilibrium.

dis es tab lish (dis′e stab′lish), *v.t.* 1 deprive of the character of being established. 2 withdraw state recognition or support from (a church). **—dis′es tab′lish ment,** *n.*

dis es teem (dis′e stēm′), *v.t.* regard with scorn; dislike. —*n.* low regard; scorn; disfavor.

di seuse (dē zœz′), *n.* FRENCH. a woman entertainer who specializes in monologue.

dis fa vor (dis fā′vər), *n.* 1 unfavorable regard; dislike or disapproval. 2 condition of having lost favor or trust. —*v.t.* dislike or disapprove.

dis fig ure (dis fig′yər), *v.t.,* **-ured, -ur ing.** spoil the appearance of; mar the beauty of. See **deface** for synonym study. **—dis fig′ure ment,** *n.*

dis fran chise (dis fran′chīz), *v.t.,* **-chised, -chis ing.** 1 take the right to vote, hold office, etc., away from. 2 take any right or privilege away from. Also, **disenfranchise. —dis fran′chise ment,** *n.*

dis gorge (dis gôrj′), *v.,* **-gorged, -gorg ing.** —*v.i.* throw up the contents; empty; discharge. —*v.t.* 1 throw out from the throat; vomit forth. 2 pour forth; discharge. 3 give up unwillingly: *The robbers were forced to disgorge their plunder.*

dis grace (dis grās′), *n., v.,* **-graced, -grac ing.** —*n.* 1 loss of honor or respect; shame. See synonym study below. 2 loss of favor or trust: *The queen's former adviser is now in disgrace.* 3 person or thing that causes disgrace: *The rude boy was a disgrace to his parents.* —*v.t.* cause disgrace to; bring shame upon. **—dis grac′er,** *n.*

Syn. *n.* 1 **Disgrace, dishonor, ignominy** mean loss of good name or respect. **Disgrace** suggests losing the respect and approval of others: *He was in disgrace after his rude behavior.* **Dishonor** suggests losing one's self-respect and honor: *For neglect of duty he was stripped of his rank with dishonor.* **Ignominy** suggests being put to public shame and held in contempt: *the ignominy of being caught cheating in a game.*

dis grace ful (dis grās′fəl), *adj.* causing loss of honor or respect; shameful; dishonorable. **—dis grace′ful ly,** *adv.* **—dis grace′ful ness,** *n.*

dis grun tled (dis grun′tld), *adj.* in bad humor; discontented. [< *dis-*[1] + obsolete *gruntle* to grunt, grumble]

dis guise (dis gīz′), *v.,* **-guised, -guis ing,** *n.* —*v.t.* 1 change the dress or personal appearance of (anyone) so as to conceal identity or to resemble someone else: *The spy disguised herself as an old woman.* 2 alter the appearance of (anything) so as to mislead or deceive as to its nature; misrepresent: *disguise one's hate by a false show of friendliness. The pirates disguised their ship.* —*n.* 1 use of a changed or unusual dress and appearance in order to conceal one's identity. 2 clothes, actions, etc., used to conceal identity: *Glasses and a wig formed the spy's disguise.* 3 a false or misleading appearance; deception. 4 a disguised condition or form: *a blessing in disguise.* **—dis guis′er,** *n.*

dis gust (dis gust′), *n.* strong dislike; sickening dislike. See **dislike** for synonym study. —*v.t.* cause to feel disgust. [< Middle French *desgoust* < *desgouster* loathe < *des-* dis- + *goust* taste]

dis gust ed (dis gus′tid), *adj.* filled with disgust. **—dis gust′ed ly,** *adv.*

dis gust ing (dis gus′ting), *adj.* that disgusts; unpleasant; distasteful. **—dis gust′ing ly,** *adv.*

dish (dish), *n.* 1 a shallow and wide-topped container, such as a plate, platter, bowl, cup, or saucer, used for holding and serving food. 2 amount of food served in a dish. 3 food served. 4 thing shaped like a dish. —*v.t.* 1 put (food) into a dish for serving at the table: *dish up the dinner.* 2 shape like a dish; make concave. [Old English *disc* < Latin *discus* dish, discus. Doublet of DAIS, DESK, DISCUS, and DISK.]

dis ha bille (dis′ə bēl′), *n.* 1 informal, careless dress. 2 condition of being partly undressed. Also, **deshabille.** [< French *déshabillé* undressed]

dis har mo ny (dis här′mə nē), *n., pl.* **-nies.** lack of harmony; discord.

dish cloth (dish′klôth′, dish′kloth′), *n., pl.* **-cloths** (-klôᴛʜz′, -klôths′; -kloᴛʜz′, -kloths′). cloth to wash dishes with; dishrag.

dis heart en (dis härt′n), *v.t.* cause to lose hope; discourage; depress. **—dis heart′en ing ly,** *adv.* **—dis heart′en ment,** *n.*

di shev el (də shev′əl), *v.t.,* **-eled, -el ing** or **-elled, -el ling.** disarrange or rumple (hair, clothing, etc.). [< Old French *descheveler* < *des-* dis- + *chevel* hair]

di shev eled or **di shev elled** (də shev′əld), *adj.* 1 not neat; rumpled; mussed; untidy. 2 hanging loosely or in disorder: *disheveled hair.*

dis hon est (dis on′ist), *adj.* 1 not fair play; showing lack of honesty: *Lying, cheating, and stealing are dishonest.* 2 ready to cheat; not upright. 3 arranged to work in an unfair way. **—dis hon′est ly,** *adv.*

dis hon es ty (dis on′ə stē), *n., pl.* **-ties.** 1 lack of honesty. 2 a dishonest act.

dis hon or (dis on′ər), *n.* 1 loss of honor or reputation; shame; disgrace. See **disgrace** for synonym study. 2 person or thing that causes dishonor. 3 refusal or failure to pay a check, bill, etc. —*v.t.* 1 bring reproach or shame to; cause dishonor to. 2 refuse or fail to pay (a check, bill, etc.). **—dis hon′or er,** *n.*

dis hon or a ble (dis on′ər ə bəl), *adj.* without honor; shameful; disgraceful. **—dis hon′or a ble ness,** *n.* **—dis hon′or a bly,** *adv.*

dish rag (dish′rag′), *n.* dishcloth.

dish tow el (dish′tou′əl), *n.* towel to dry dishes with.

dish wash er (dish′wosh′ər, dish′wôsh′ər), *n.* 1 machine for washing dishes, pots, glasses, etc. 2 person who washes dishes, especially in a restaurant, etc.

dish wa ter (dish′wô′tər, dish′wot′ər), *n.* water in which dishes have been or are to be washed.

dis il lu sion (dis′i lü′zhən), *v.t.* set free from illusion; disenchant. —*n.* freedom from illusion. **—dis′il lu′sion ment,** *n.*

dis in cli na tion (dis in′klə nā′shən), *n.* slight dislike; unwillingness.

dis in cline (dis′in klīn′), *v.t., v.i.,* **-clined, -clin ing.** make or be unwilling.

dis in clined (dis′in klīnd′), *adj.* unwilling.

dis in fect (dis′in fekt′), *v.t.* destroy the disease germs in or on. **—dis′in fec′tion,** *n.* **—dis′in fec′tor,** *n.*

dis in fect ant (dis′in fek′tənt), *n.* a chemical solution, heat, or any agent used to destroy or inhibit the growth of disease germs. Alcohol, iodine, and carbolic acid are disinfectants. —*adj.* destroying disease germs: *a disinfectant soap.*

dis in gen u ous (dis′in jen′yü əs), *adj.* lacking in frankness; insincere. **—dis′in gen′u ous ly,** *adv.* **—dis′in gen′u ous ness,** *n.*

dis in her it (dis′in her′it), *v.t.* prevent from inheriting; deprive of an inheritance or the right to inherit.

dis in te grate (dis in′tə grāt), *v.,* **-grat ed, -grat ing.** —*v.t.* break up; separate into small parts or bits. —*v.i.* 1 become dis-

hat, āge, fär; let, ēqual, tėrm;
it, īce; hot, ōpen, ôrder;
oil, out; cup, pu̇t, rüle;
ch, child; ng, long; sh, she;
th, thin; ᴛʜ, then; zh, measure;

ə represents *a* in about, *e* in taken, *i* in pencil, *o* in lemon, *u* in circus.

< = from, derived from, taken from.

integrated; break up. 2 (of atomic nuclei) undergo disintegration. **—dis in′te gra′tor,** *n.*

dis in te gra tion (dis in′tə grā′shən), *n.* 1 a breaking up; separation into small parts or bits: *Rain and frost had caused the gradual disintegration of the rock.* 2 a change in the structure of an atomic nucleus by its emission of particles or rays. Disintegration occurs naturally in the nuclei of radioactive substances or can be induced in other substances by bombarding their nuclei with fast-moving particles or rays.

dis in ter (dis′in tėr′), *v.t.,* **-terred, -ter ring.** 1 take out of a grave or tomb; dig up. 2 bring to light; discover and reveal. **—dis′in ter′ment,** *n.*

dis in ter est (dis in′tər ist), *n.* lack of interest; indifference; unconcern.

dis in ter est ed (dis in′tər ə stid, dis in′tər es′tid), *adj.* 1 free from selfish motives; impartial; fair. 2 uninterested. **—dis in′ter est ed ly,** *adv.* **—dis in′ter est ed ness,** *n.*

➤ **Disinterested** and **uninterested** can be used to make a useful distinction of meaning. *Uninterested* means having no concern about the matter and paying no attention: *I find it difficult to entertain anyone so uninterested in everything I suggest doing.* In careful usage, *disinterested* means having no reason or desire to be anything but strictly impartial and fair: *A judge should be disinterested.* Increasingly, however, *disinterested* is being used with the meaning of *uninterested.* Because of this, it is wise to make sure that context makes the intended meaning of *disinterested* unmistakable.

dis join (dis join′), *v.t.* keep from joining; prevent from being joined; separate. *—v.i.* become separate.

dis joint (dis joint′), *v.t.* 1 take apart at the joints: *disjoint a chicken.* 2 break up; put out of order: *War disjoints a nation's affairs.* 3 put out of joint; dislocate. *—v.i.* come apart; be put out of joint. *—adj.* (in mathematics) having no common members. (0, 1, 2) and (3, 4, 5) are disjoint sets. (0, 1, 2) and (2, 3, 4) are not disjoint sets.

dis joint ed (dis join′tid), *adj.* 1 without proper connection; incoherent: *disjointed speech.* 2 taken apart at the joints. 3 out of joint. **—dis joint′ed ly,** *adv.* **—dis joint′ed ness,** *n.*

dis junc tion (dis jungk′shən), *n.* 1 a disjoining or a being disjoined; separation. 2 (in logic) a proposition which asserts that one or the other of two things is true but both cannot be true.

dis junc tive (dis jungk′tiv), *adj.* 1 causing separation; separating. 2 (in grammar) showing a choice or contrast between two ideas, words, etc. *But, yet, either. . .or,* etc., are disjunctive conjunctions. *Otherwise, else,* etc., are disjunctive adverbs. *—n.* a disjunctive conjunction.

disk (disk), *n.* 1 a round, flat, thin object shaped like a coin. 2 a round, flat surface that the sun, moon, and other planets seem to have. 3 a round, flat part in certain plants: *The yellow center of a daisy is a disk.* 4 (in anatomy and zoology) any round, flat part or structure, especially the masses of fibrous cartilage between the bodies of the vertebrae. 5 anything resembling a disk. 6 a phonograph record. *—v.t.* cultivate (ground) with a disk harrow. Also, **disc.** [< Latin *discus* discus < Greek *diskos.* Doublet of DAIS, DESK, DISCUS, and DISH.] **—disk′like′,** *adj.*

disk harrow, harrow with a row of sharp, revolving disks, used in preparing ground for planting or sowing.

disk jockey, INFORMAL. announcer for a radio program that consists chiefly of recorded popular music. Also, **disc jockey.**

dis like (dis līk′), *v.,* **-liked, -lik ing,** *n.* *—v.t.* not like; object to; have a feeling against. *—n.* a feeling of not liking; a feeling against. See synonym study below.

Syn. *n.* **Dislike, distaste, disgust** mean a feeling of not liking someone or something. **Dislike** is the general word, applying to any degree of this feeling: *I have a dislike for baseball and would rather play tennis.* **Distaste** applies to a fixed dislike for something one finds unpleasant or disagreeable: *a distaste for chocolate.* **Disgust** applies to a strong dislike for something that is disagreeable, sickening, or bad: *We feel disgust for bad odors or tastes.*

dis lo cate (dis′lō kāt), *v.t.,* **-cat ed, -cat ing.** 1 put out of joint: *I dislocated my shoulder when I fell.* 2 put out of order; disturb; upset.

dis lo ca tion (dis′lō kā′shən), *n.* 1 a dislocating. 2 a being dislocated.

dis lodge (dis loj′), *v.t.,* **-lodged, -lodg ing.** drive or force out of a place, position, etc.: *The workman used a crowbar to dislodge a heavy stone from the wall. Heavy gunfire dislodged the enemy from the fort.* **—dis lodg′ment,** *n.*

dis loy al (dis loi′əl), *adj.* not loyal; unfaithful. **—dis loy′al ly,** *adv.*

dis loy al ty (dis loi′əl tē), *n., pl.* **-ties.** 1 lack of loyalty; unfaithfulness: *disloyalty to one's country.* See synonym study below. 2 a disloyal act.

Syn. 1 **Disloyalty, treachery, treason** mean faithlessness. **Disloyalty** means unfaithfulness to the allegiance owed to persons, friends, one's country, or the like: *They reproached me with disloyalty to my school.* **Treachery** suggests some definite act of betraying trust while pretending to be loyal: *His secret collaboration with the opposition amounted to treachery.* **Treason** applies to treachery to one's country, shown by doing something openly to help the enemy: *As an American citizen, he was guilty of treason for broadcasting enemy propaganda.*

dis mal (diz′məl), *adj.* 1 dark and gloomy; dreary: *a damp, dismal cave.* 2 depressed; miserable: *Sickness or bad luck often makes a person feel dismal.* [< Old French *dis mal* evil days < Medieval Latin *dies mali*] **—dis′mal ly,** *adv.*

dis man tle (dis man′tl), *v.t.,* **-tled, -tling.** 1 strip (anything) of the necessary equipment, furniture, or apparatus. 2 pull down; take apart: *We had to dismantle the bookcases in order to fit them through the doorway.* **—dis man′tle ment,** *n.*

dis mast (dis mast′), *v.t.* take away or break down the mast or masts of: *The storm dismasted the ship.*

dis may (dis mā′), *n.* 1 sudden loss of courage because of fear of danger. See synonym study below. 2 lack of confidence because of unexpected difficulty; sudden apprehension.

disk (def. 1)

disk harrow

—v.t. paralyze with fear or hopelessness; trouble greatly; make afraid. [Middle English *desmayen* < *dis-* + Old French *esmaiier* perturb < Popular Latin *exmagare* weaken] **—dis may′ing ly,** *adv.*

Syn. *n.* 1 **Dismay, consternation** mean a feeling of being unnerved or overwhelmed by the thought of what is going to happen next. **Dismay** suggests loss of ability to face or handle something frightening, baffling, or upsetting: *They were filled with dismay when their son confessed he had robbed a store.* **Consternation** suggests dismay and dread so sudden or great that a person cannot think clearly or, sometimes, move: *To our consternation the child darted out in front of the speeding car.*

dis mem ber (dis mem′bər), *v.t.* 1 separate or divide into parts: *After the war the defeated country was dismembered.* 2 cut or tear the limbs from; divide limb from limb. **—dis mem′ber ment,** *n.*

dis miss (dis mis′), *v.t.* 1 send away; allow to go: *At noon the teacher dismissed the class.* See synonym study below. 2 remove from office or service: *We dismissed the painter because his work was so poor.* 3 put out of mind; stop thinking about: *Dismiss your troubles.* 4 refuse to consider (a complaint, plea, etc.) in a court of law. [< Latin *dismissum* sent away < *dis-* + *mittere* to send]

Syn. 1 **Dismiss, discharge, release** mean to let someone go from his job, duty, etc. **Dismiss** applies whether he is forced to go or permitted to do so: *After five days in the hospital, the patient was dismissed.* **Discharge** means to dismiss for incompetence or neglect of duty (except in military or legal use): *The manager discharged the bookkeeper.* **Release** emphasizes setting a person free from his obligation: *The soldier was released from duty for two days.*

dis miss al (dis mis′l), *n.* 1 act of dismissing. 2 condition or fact of being dismissed. 3 a written or spoken order dismissing someone.

dis mount (dis mount′), *v.i.* 1 get off a horse, bicycle, etc. *—v.t.* 1 throw or bring down from a horse; unhorse. 2 take (a thing) from its setting or support: *The cannons were dismounted for shipping.* 3 take apart; take to pieces: *dismount a typewriter to fix the keys.*

Dis ney (diz′nē), *n.* **Walt(er Elias),** 1901-1966, American motion-picture producer, especially of animated cartoons.

dis o be di ence (dis′ə bē′dē əns), *n.* refusal to obey; failure to obey.

dis o be di ent (dis′ə bē′dē ənt), *adj.* refusing to obey; failing to obey. **—dis′o be′di ent ly,** *adv.*

dis o bey (dis′ə bā′), *v.t., v.i.* refuse to obey; fail to obey. **—dis′o bey′er,** *n.*

dis o blige (dis′ə blīj′), *v.t.,* **-bliged,**

-blig ing. 1 neglect or refuse to oblige; refuse to do a favor for. 2 give offense to. 3 to inconvenience.

dis or der (dis ôr′dər), *n.* 1 lack of order; confusion. 2 a public disturbance; riot. 3 sickness; disease: *a stomach disorder.* —*v.t.* 1 put out of order; destroy the order of; throw into confusion. 2 cause sickness in.

dis or dered (dis ôr′dərd), *adj.* 1 not in order; disturbed. 2 sick.

dis or der ly (dis ôr′dər lē), *adj.* 1 not orderly; in confusion: *a disorderly retreat.* 2 causing disorder; making a disturbance; breaking rules; unruly: *a disorderly mob.* 3 against the law; contrary to good morals or decency: *disorderly conduct.* **—dis or′der li ness,** *n.*

dis or gan ize (dis ôr′gə nīz), *v.t.,* **-ized, -iz ing.** throw into confusion or disorder; upset the order and arrangement of. **—dis or′gan i za′tion,** *n.*

dis o ri ent (dis ôr′ē ent, dis ōr′ē ent), *v.t.* cause to lose one's bearings. **—dis o′ri en ta′tion,** *n.*

dis own (dis ōn′), *v.t.* refuse to recognize as one's own; cast off; renounce; repudiate.

dis par age (dis par′ij), *v.t.,* **-aged, -ag ing.** 1 speak slightingly of; belittle. 2 lower the reputation of; discredit. [< Old French *desparagier* match unequally < *des-* dis- + *parage* rank, lineage < *par* peer[1]] **—dis par′age ment,** *n.* **—dis par′ag ing ly,** *adv.*

dis par ate (dis′pər it), *adj.* distinct in kind; essentially different; unlike. [< Latin *disparatum* < *dis-* apart + *parare* get] **—dis′par ate ly,** *adv.* **—dis′par ate ness,** *n.*

dis par i ty (dis par′ə tē), *n., pl.* **-ties.** 1 lack of equality: *disparity in numbers.* 2 quality of being unlike; difference: *The disparity between the two teams made the outcome of the game a foregone conclusion.* See **difference** for synonym study.

dis pas sion ate (dis pash′ə nit), *adj.* free from emotion or prejudice; calm and impartial. **—dis pas′sion ate ly,** *adv.*

dis patch (dis pach′), *v.t.* 1 send off to some place or for some purpose: *The captain dispatched a boat to bring a doctor on board ship.* 2 get done promptly or speedily; settle; conclude. 3 kill. 4 INFORMAL. finish off; eat up. —*n.* 1 a sending off a letter, a messenger, etc., to a particular place or on a specified errand: *the dispatch of an embassy.* 2 a written message or communication, such as special news or government business: *a dispatch from the ambassador in France, dispatches from a war correspondent at the scene of the battle.* 3 promptness in doing anything; speed. 4 a putting to death; a killing. Also, **despatch.** [< Italian *dispacciare* or Spanish *despachar*]

dis patch er (dis pach′ər), *n.* person who dispatches. A train dispatcher is in charge of sending off the trains on schedule.

dis pel (dis pel′), *v.t.,* **-pelled, -pel ling.** drive away and scatter; disperse. See **scatter** for synonym study. [< Latin *dispellere* < *dis-* away + *pellere* to drive]

dis pen sa bil i ty (dis pen′sə bil′ə tē), *n.* quality of being dispensable.

dis pen sa ble (dis pen′sə bəl), *adj.* 1 that can be done without; unimportant. 2 capable of being dispensed or administered.

dis pen sar y (dis pen′sər ē), *n., pl.* **-sar ies.** place where medicines, medical care, and medical advice are given out.

dis pen sa tion (dis′pən sā′shən), *n.* 1 a giving out; distributing: *the dispensation of food and clothing to the flood victims.* 2 thing given out or distributed: *They gave thanks for the dispensations of Providence.* 3 rule; management: *England under the dispensation of Elizabeth I.* 4 management or ordering of the affairs of the world by Providence or Nature. 5 a religious system: *the Christian dispensation.* 6 official permission to disregard a rule.

dis pen sa to ry (dis pen′sə tôr′ē, dis pen′sə tōr′ē), *n., pl.* **-ries.** book that tells how to prepare and use medicines.

dis pense (dis pens′), *v.t.,* **-pensed, -pens ing.** 1 give out in portions or from a general stock; distribute. See **distribute** for synonym study. 2 carry out; put in force; apply: *Judges and courts of law dispense justice.* 3 prepare and give out (medicine). 4 **dispense with, a** do away with; make unnecessary. **b** do without; get along without. [< Latin *dispensare* < *dispensum* weighed out < *dis-* out + *pendere* weigh]

dis pens er (dis pen′sər), *n.* person or thing that dispenses.

dis per sal (dis pėr′səl), *n.* a scattering or a being scattered; dispersing: *the dispersal of a crowd.*

dis perse (dis pėrs′), *v.,* **-persed, -pers ing.** —*v.t.* 1 send or drive off in different directions; scatter. See **scatter** for synonym study. 2 divide (light) into rays of different colors. 3 scatter (particles of a colloid, etc.) throughout another substance or a mixture. —*v.i.* spread in different directions; scatter: *The crowd dispersed when it began raining.* [< Latin *dispersum* dispersed < *dis-* apart + *spargere* to scatter]

dis pers i ble (dis pėr′sə bəl), *adj.* that can be dispersed.

dis per sion (dis pėr′zhən, dis pėr′shən), *n.* 1 a dispersing. 2 a being dispersed. 3 the separation of light into its different colors.

dis per sive (dis pėr′siv), *adj.* dispersing; tending to disperse.

dis pir it (dis pir′it), *v.t.* lower the spirits of; discourage; depress; dishearten. **—dis pir′it ed ly,** *adv.* **—dis pir′it ed ness,** *n.*

dis place (dis plās′), *v.t.,* **-placed, -plac ing.** 1 take the place of; replace: *The automobile has displaced the horse and buggy.* 2 remove from a position of authority. 3 move from its usual place or position.

displaced person, person forced out of his own country by war, famine, political disturbance, etc.

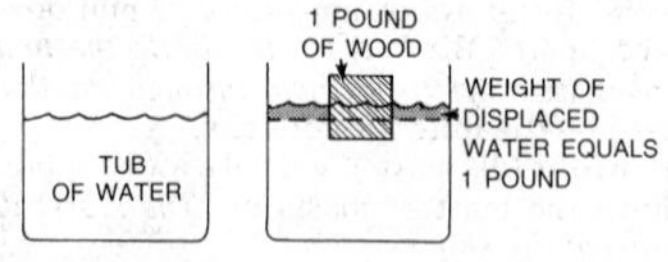

displacement (def. 3)
One cubic foot of cork (15.6 pounds), floating in water, displaces its own weight, but not its own volume.

dis place ment (dis plās′mənt), *n.* 1 a displacing. 2 a being displaced. 3 weight of the volume of water displaced by a ship or other floating object. This weight is equal to that of the floating object.

dis play (dis plā′), *v.t.* 1 expose to view; show. See synonym study below. 2 show in a special way, so as to attract attention: *The stores are displaying the new spring clothes in their windows.* 3 let appear unintentionally or incidentally; reveal: *She displayed her good nature by answering all our questions.* 4 spread out; unfold (a banner, sail, etc.). —*n.* 1 a showing; exhibition: *a display of bad temper.* See **show** for synonym study. 2 a showing off; ostentation: *A fondness for display led them to buy a new car every year.* 3 a planned showing of a thing, for some special purpose; exhibit: *a display of children's drawings.* [< Old French *despleier* < Latin *displicare* to scatter < *dis-* + *plicare* to fold]

Syn. *v.t.* 1 **Display, exhibit, evince** mean to show. **Display** implies showing something so that others may see it clearly and examine it: *They displayed their wedding presents on the table.* **Exhibit** implies showing something especially worth looking at and in a way that draws attention: *The museum is exhibiting a rare collection of coins.* **Evince** applies only to something that cannot be seen with the eyes, such as a feeling or quality: *He evinced obvious displeasure when he learned he would have to stay after school.*

dis please (dis plēz′), *v.,* **-pleased, -pleas ing.** —*v.t.* be disagreeable to; offend; annoy. —*v.i.* be disagreeable or offensive.

dis pleas ure (dis plezh′ər), *n.* the feeling of being displeased; annoyance; dislike.

dis port (dis pôrt′, dis pōrt′), *v.t., v.i.* amuse or entertain (oneself); play; sport: *bears disporting themselves in the water.* [< Old French *desporter* < *des-* dis- + *porter* carry]

dis pos a ble (dis pō′zə bəl), *adj.* 1 that can be disposed of after use. 2 at one's disposal; available.

dis pos al (dis pō′zəl), *n.* 1 a getting rid (of something): *the disposal of garbage.* 2 a giving away or selling: *Her will provided for the disposal of her property after her death.* 3 power or authority to dispose of or use something; control: *The trustees had the disposal of the estate.* 4 a dealing with; settling: *His disposal of the difficulty satisfied everybody.* 5 a putting in a certain order or position; arrangement: *a very tasteful disposal of flowers.* 6 **at one's disposal,** ready for one's use or service at any time; under one's control or management.

dis pose (dis pōz′), *v.,* **-posed, -pos ing.** —*v.t.* 1 put in the proper or desired order, position, etc.; arrange: *The flags were disposed in a straight line for the parade.* 2 arrange (matters); settle (affairs); determine. 3 make ready or willing; incline: *Shorter hours of work disposed him to take the new job.* 4 make liable or subject: *Getting your feet wet disposes you to catching cold.* —*v.i.* 1 **dispose of, a** get rid of. **b** give away: *dispose of clothing among the poor,* **c** sell: *dispose of a house for $35,000.* **d** eat or drink. **e** have available. 2 control the course of events; settle affairs; determine. [< Old French *disposer* < *dis-* + *poser* to place. See POSE[1].] **—dis pos′er,** *n.*

dis posed (dis pōzd′), *adj.* willing.

dis po si tion (dis′pə zish′ən), *n.* 1 one's habitual ways of acting toward others or of thinking about things; nature: *a cheerful disposition.* See synonym study below. 2 tendency; inclination: *a disposition to argue.* 3 a putting in a proper or desired order or position; arrangement: *the disposition of soldiers in battle.* 4 a disposing; settlement: *What disposition did the court make of the case?* 5 disposal.

Syn. 1 **Disposition, temperament** mean

hat, āge, fär; let, ēqual, tėrm;
it, īce; hot, ōpen, ôrder;
oil, out; cup, pu̇t, rüle;
ch, child; ng, long; sh, she;
th, thin; ᴛʜ, then; zh, measure;
ə represents *a* in about, *e* in taken, *i* in pencil, *o* in lemon, *u* in circus.
< = from, derived from, taken from.

the qualities that characterize a person as an individual. **Disposition** applies to the controlling mental or emotional quality that determines a person's natural or usual way of thinking and acting: *a quarrelsome disposition.* **Temperament** applies to the combined physical, emotional, and mental qualities that determine a person's whole nature: *an artistic temperament.*

dis pos sess (dis′pə zes′), *v.t.* 1 force to give up the possession of a house, land, etc.; oust: *The tenant was dispossessed for not paying rent.* 2 deprive. **—dis′pos ses′sor,** *n.*

dis pos ses sion (dis′pə zesh′ən), *n.* 1 a dispossessing. 2 a being dispossessed.

dis praise (dis prāz′), *v.,* **-praised, -prais ing,** *n.* —*v.t.* express disapproval of; speak against; blame. —*n.* expression of disapproval; blame. **—dis prais′er,** *n.* **—dis prais′ing ly,** *adv.*

dis proof (dis prüf′), *n.* 1 a disproving; refutation. 2 fact or reason that disproves something.

dis pro por tion (dis′prə pôr′shən, dis′prə pōr′shən), *n.* 1 lack of proper proportion. 2 something out of proportion. —*v.t.* make disproportionate.

dis pro por tion al (dis′prə pôr′shə nəl, dis′prə pōr′shə nəl), *adj.* not in proportion; disproportionate. **—dis′pro por′tion al ly,** *adv.*

dis pro por tion ate (dis′prə pôr′shə nit, dis′prə pōr′shə nit), *adj.* out of proportion; lacking in proper proportion. **—dis′pro por′tion ate ly,** *adv.* **—dis′pro por′tion ate ness,** *n.*

dis prove (dis prüv′), *v.t.,* **-proved, -prov ing.** prove false or incorrect; refute. **—dis prov′a ble,** *adj.*

dis put a ble (dis pyü′tə bəl, dis′pyə tə bəl), *adj.* liable to be disputed, questioned, or discussed; uncertain; questionable. **—dis put′a bly,** *adv.*

dis pu tant (dis′pyə tənt, dis pyüt′nt), *n.* person who takes part in a dispute or debate.

dis pu ta tion (dis′pyə tā′shən), *n.* 1 debate; discussion. 2 a dispute. 3 exercise in which parties attack and defend a thesis, as in medieval universities.

dis pu ta tious (dis′pyə tā′shəs), *adj.* fond of disputing; inclined to argue; contentious. **—dis′pu ta′tious ly,** *adv.* **—dis′pu ta′tious ness,** *n.*

dis put a tive (dis pyü′tə tiv), *adj.* disputatious.

dis pute (dis pyüt′), *v.,* **-put ed, -put ing,** *n.* —*v.i.* 1 give reasons or facts for or against something; argue; debate; discuss. 2 wrangle; quarrel. —*v.t.* 1 argue about; debate; discuss: *The lawyers disputed the case before the judge.* 2 call in question; argue against. 3 fight against; oppose; resist. 4 fight for the possession of; contest: *The soldiers disputed every inch of ground.* 5 try to win; compete for: *The losing team disputed the victory up to the last minute of play.* —*n.* 1 argument; debate. See **argument** for synonym study. 2 a quarrel. [< Latin *disputare* examine, discuss, argue < *dis-* apart + *putare* calculate] **—dis put′er,** *n.*

dis qual i fi ca tion (dis kwol′ə fə kā′shən), *n.* 1 a disqualifying. 2 a being disqualified. 3 something that disqualifies.

dis qual i fy (dis kwol′ə fī), *v.t.,* **-fied, -fy ing.** 1 make unfit; make unable to do something: *My broken leg disqualified me from sports last year.* 2 declare unfit or unable to do something; deprive of a right or privilege: *The principal disqualified two members of the team.*

dis qui et (dis kwī′ət), *v.t.* make uneasy or anxious; disturb. —*n.* uneasy feelings; anxiety. **—dis qui′et ing ly,** *adv.*

dis qui e tude (dis kwī′ə tüd, dis kwī′ə tyüd), *n.* uneasiness; anxiety.

dis qui si tion (dis′kwə zish′ən), *n.* a long or formal speech or writing about a subject; dissertation. [< Latin *disquisitionem* < *disquirere* inquire < *dis-* + *quaerere* seek]

Dis rae li (diz rā′lē), *n.* **Benjamin,** 1804-1881, Earl of Beaconsfield, British statesman and novelist, prime minister in 1868 and from 1874 to 1880.

dis re gard (dis′ri gärd′), *v.t.* 1 pay no attention to; take no notice of: *Disregarding the child's screams, the doctor cleaned and bandaged the cut.* 2 treat without proper regard or respect; slight. —*n.* 1 lack of attention; neglect: *disregard of the traffic laws.* 2 lack of proper regard or respect: *disregard for tradition.*

dis re gard ful (dis′ri gärd′fəl), *adj.* lacking in regard; neglectful; careless.

dis rel ish (dis rel′ish), *v.t., n.* dislike.

dis re pair (dis′ri per′, dis′ri par′), *n.* bad condition; need of repair.

dis rep u ta ble (dis rep′yə tə bəl), *adj.* 1 having a bad reputation. 2 not fit to be used or seen; in poor condition: *a disreputable old hat.* **—dis rep′u ta ble ness,** *n.* **—dis rep′u ta bly,** *adv.*

dis re pute (dis′ri pyüt′), *n.* loss or absence of reputation; discredit; disfavor.

dis re spect (dis′ri spekt′), *n.* lack of respect; rudeness; impoliteness.

dis re spect ful (dis′ri spekt′fəl), *adj.* showing no respect; lacking in courtesy to elders or superiors; rude; impolite. **—dis′re spect′ful ly,** *adv.* **—dis′re spect′ful ness,** *n.*

dis robe (dis rōb′), *v.t., v.i.,* **-robed, -rob ing.** undress.

dis rupt (dis rupt′), *v.t., v.i.* break or burst apart; break in pieces; shatter: *Slavery seemed likely to disrupt the Union.* [< Latin *disruptum* broken up < *dis-* + *rumpere* to break] **—dis rupt′er,** *n.*

dis rup tion (dis rup′shən), *n.* 1 a bursting apart; breaking in pieces; shattering. 2 a disrupted condition.

dis rup tive (dis rup′tiv), *adj.* causing disruption. **—dis rup′tive ly,** *adv.*

dis sat is fac tion (dis′sat i sfak′shən), *n.* a being dissatisfied; displeasure.

dis sat is fac tor y (dis′sat i sfak′tər ē), *adj.* causing dissatisfaction; unsatisfactory.

dis sat is fied (dis sat′i sfīd), *adj.* discontented; displeased.

dis sat is fy (dis sat′i sfī), *v.t.,* **-fied, -fy ing.** fail to satisfy; make discontented; displease.

dis sect (di sekt′, dī sekt′), *v.t.* 1 cut apart (an animal, plant, etc.) in order to examine or study the structure. 2 examine carefully part by part; criticize in detail; analyze. [< Latin *dissectum* cut apart < *dis-* + *secare* to cut] **—dis sec′tor,** *n.*

dis sect ed (di sek′tid, dī sek′tid), *adj.* cut into many lobes, as a leaf.

dis sec tion (di sek′shən, dī sek′shən), *n.* 1 act of cutting apart an animal, plant, etc., in order to examine or study the structure. 2 examination of something part by part; criticism in detail; analysis.

dis sem ble (di sem′bəl), *v.,* **-bled, -bling.** —*v.t.* 1 hide (one's real feelings, thoughts, plans, etc.); disguise: *She dissembled her anger with a smile.* 2 pretend; feign: *The bored listener dissembled an interest he didn't feel.* —*v.i.* conceal one's opinions, motives, etc. [alteration (patterned after *resemble*) of obsolete *dissimule* dissimulate] **—dis sem′bler,** *n.*

dis sem i nate (di sem′ə nāt), *v.t.,* **-nat ed, -nat ing.** scatter widely; spread abroad: *News is disseminated by means of television and radio.* [< Latin *disseminatum* scattered < *dis-* + *seminem* seed] **—dis sem′i na′tion,** *n.* **—dis sem′i na′tor,** *n.*

dis sen sion (di sen′shən), *n.* 1 disagreement in opinion that produces strife; discord. 2 a violent disagreement or quarrel.

dis sent (di sent′), *v.i.* 1 think differently; disagree: *Two of the judges dissented from the decision of the other three.* 2 withhold consent. 3 refuse to conform to the rules and beliefs of an established church. —*n.* 1 difference of opinion; disagreement. 2 declaration of disagreement of opinion about something. 3 refusal to conform to the rules and beliefs of an established church. [< Latin *dissentire* < *dis-* apart + *sentire* think, feel]

dis sent er (di sen′tər), *n.* 1 person who dissents. 2 **Dissenter,** (in England and Scotland) a Nonconformist.

dis sen tient (di sen′shənt), *adj.* dissenting from the opinion of the majority. —*n.* person who dissents.

dis ser ta tion (dis′ər tā′shən), *n.* a formal discussion of a subject, especially the thesis of a candidate for a doctor's degree. [< Latin *dissertationem* < *dissertare* discuss often < *disserere* discuss < *dis-* + *serere* join words]

dis serv ice (dis sėr′vis), *n.* bad treatment; injury; detriment.

dis sev er (di sev′ər), *v.t.* cut into parts; sever; separate. —*v.i.* separate. **—dis sev′er ment,** *n.*

dis sev er ance (di sev′ər əns), *n.* act or fact of dissevering; separation.

dis si dence (dis′ə dəns), *n.* disagreement in opinion, character, etc.; dissent.

dis si dent (dis′ə dənt), *adj.* disagreeing in opinion, character, etc.; dissenting. —*n.* person who disagrees or dissents. [< Latin *dissidentem* < *dis-* apart + *sedere* sit]

dis sim i lar (di sim′ə lər), *adj.* not similar; unlike; different. **—dis sim′i lar ly,** *adv.*

dis sim i lar i ty (di sim′ə lar′ə tē), *n., pl.* **-ties.** lack of similarity; unlikeness; difference.

dis sim i la tion (di sim′ə lā′shən), *n.* 1 act or process of making or becoming unlike. 2 catabolism. 3 the change in a speech sound making it less like a similar sound nearby, such as the change of the first *r* to *l* in Italian *pellegrino* from Latin *peregrinus,* both meaning "foreign."

dis sim u late (di sim′yə lāt), *v.,* **-lat ed, -lat ing.** —*v.t.* disguise or hide under a pretense; dissemble. —*v.i.* hide the truth;

dissemble. **—dis sim′u la′tion,** *n.* **—dis-sim′u la′tor,** *n.*

dis si pate (dis′ə pāt), *v.,* **-pat ed, -pat ing.** *—v.t.* 1 spread in different directions; scatter. 2 cause to disappear; dispel: *The sun dissipated the mists.* 3 spend foolishly; waste on things of little value; squander. *—v.i.* 1 scatter so as to disappear; disperse. 2 indulge excessively in sensual or foolish pleasures. [< Latin *dissipatum* scattered < *dis-* apart + *supare* to throw]

dis si pat ed (dis′ə pā′tid), *adj.* 1 indulging excessively in sensual or foolish pleasures; dissolute. 2 wasted. **—dis′si pat′ed ly,** *adv.* **—dis′si pat′ed ness,** *n.*

dis si pa tion (dis′ə pā′shən), *n.* 1 a scattering in different directions. 2 a wasting by misuse. 3 excessive indulgence in sensual or foolish pleasures; intemperance.

dis so ci ate (di sō′shē āt), *v.,* **-at ed, -at ing.** *—v.t.* 1 break the connection or association with; separate: *The new appointee to the Cabinet dissociated himself from his business in order to avoid a conflict of interest.* 2 (in chemistry) separate by dissociation. *—v.i.* 1 withdraw from association. 2 (in chemistry) to be subjected to dissociation. Also, **disassociate.** [< Latin *dissociatum* disunited < *dis-* apart + *socius* ally]

dis so ci a tion (di sō′sē ā′shən, di sō′shē-ā′shən), *n.* 1 a dissociating. 2 a being dissociated. 3 in chemistry: **a** the usually reversible changing of a substance into two or more simpler substances: *the dissociation of water into hydrogen and oxygen at high temperatures.* **b** separation of molecules of an electrolyte into constituent ions; ionization. Sodium and chlorine ions are formed by the dissociation of sodium chloride molecules in water. 4 (in psychology) separation of an idea or feeling from the main stream of consciousness. Also, **disassociation.**

dis so ci a tive (di sō′shē ā′tiv), *adj.* having to do with dissociation.

dis sol u bil i ty (di sol′yə bil′ə tē), *n.* fact or quality of being dissoluble.

dis sol u ble (di sol′yə bəl), *adj.* capable of being dissolved.

dis so lute (dis′ə lüt), *adj.* living an immoral life; loose in morals; licentious; dissipated. [< Latin *dissolutum* loosened, loose < *dis-* apart + *solvere* to loosen] **—dis′so lute′ly,** *adv.* **—dis′so lute′ness,** *n.*

dis so lu tion (dis′ə lü′shən), *n.* 1 a breaking up or ending of an association of any kind: *the dissolution of a partnership.* 2 a making or becoming liquid; dissolving. 3 the breaking up of an assembly by ending its session: *the dissolution of parliament.* 4 ruin; destruction: *dissolution of an empire.* 5 death.

dis solve (di zolv′), *v.,* **-solved, -solv ing,** *n.* *—v.t., v.i.* 1 change from a solid or gas to a liquid: *The warm air dissolved the ice.* 2 change into a solution: *Salt and sugar will dissolve in water.* See **melt** for synonym study. 3 break up; end: *dissolve a partnership.* 4 fade away: *The dream dissolved when she woke up.* 5 separate into parts; decompose. 6 (in motion pictures and television) fade or cause to fade gradually from the screen while the succeeding picture or scene slowly appears. *—n.* (in motion pictures and television) the gradual disappearing of a picture or scene while the succeeding picture or scene slowly appears. [< Latin *dissolvere* loosen, dissolve < *dis-* apart + *solvere* to loosen] **—dis solv′a ble,** *adj.* **—dis-solv′er,** *n.*

dis so nance (dis′n əns), *n.* 1 harshness and unpleasantness of sound. 2 (in music) the sound of two or more tones in a combination that is nonharmonic or that requires resolution; discord. 3 lack of harmony; disagreement.

dis so nant (dis′n ənt), *adj.* 1 harsh and unpleasant in sound; not harmonious; clashing. 2 (in music) marked by dissonance; discordant. 3 out of harmony with other conditions, persons, etc.; disagreeing. [< Latin *dissonantem* < *dis-* differently + *sonare* to sound] **—dis′so nant ly,** *adv.*

dis suade (di swād′), *v.t.,* **-suad ed, -suad ing.** 1 persuade not to do something. 2 advise against. [< Latin *dissuadere* < *dis-* against + *suadere* to urge]

dis sua sion (di swā′zhən), *n.* act of dissuading.

dis sua sive (di swā′siv), *adj.* attempting to dissuade; tending to dissuade. **—dis-sua′sive ly,** *adv.* **—dis sua′sive ness,** *n.*

dis syl lab ic (dis′sə lab′ik), *adj.* having two syllables. Also, **disyllabic. —dis′syl-lab′i cal ly,** *adv.*

dis syl la ble (dis′sil′ə bəl, di sil′ə bəl), *n.* word having two syllables, such as *about, bandage,* or *candy.* Also, **disyllable.**

dist., 1 distance. 2 distinguish. 3 distinguished. 4 district.

distaff (def. 1)—Fibers bound to the distaff are drawn out and twisted by the motion and weight of the spindle to make thread.

dis taff (dis′taf), *n.* 1 a stick, split at the tip, to hold wool or flax for spinning by hand. 2 staff on a spinning wheel for holding wool or flax. 3 woman's work or affairs. [Old English *distæf* < *dis-* flax + *stæf* staff]

distaff side, the mother's side of a family.

dis tal (dis′tl), *adj.* (in anatomy) away from the center or point of origin; terminal: *Fingernails are at the distal ends of fingers.* [< *dist(ant)* + *-al*[1]] **—dis′tal ly,** *adv.*

dis tance (dis′təns), *n., v.,* **-tanced, -tanc ing.** *—n.* 1 length of space between two points or objects: *the distance from the sun to the earth.* 2 a being far away: *Because of the lake's distance, we will have to stop overnight on the way.* 3 a place far away: *a light in the distance.* 4 time in between; interval. 5 (in music) the interval or difference between two tones. 6 coldness of manner; reserve. 7 remoteness in relation or degree; amount of difference: *the distance between a descendant and his ancestor. The distance in color of the two fabrics is very noticeable.* 8 **at a distance,** a long way: *The farm is at a distance from the road.* 9 **keep at a distance,** refuse to be friendly or familiar with; treat coldly. 10 **keep one's distance,** be not too friendly or familiar. *—v.t.* leave far behind; do much better than.

dis tant (dis′tənt), *adj.* 1 separated by a great length of space; far apart: *The sun is distant from the earth.* See synonym study below. 2 away: *The town is three miles distant.* 3 far apart in time: *in the distant future.* 4 far removed in relationship, likeness, etc.; not close: *a distant relative.* 5 not friendly; reserved: *a distant nod.* 6 situated at or involving motion from or to a remote point; not near: *a distant vision, a distant journey.* [< Latin *distantem* < *dis-* off + *stare* to stand] **—dis′tant ly,** *adv.* **—dis′tant ness,** *n.*

Syn. 1 Distant, far, remote mean not near. **Distant** suggests a considerable space unless the exact measure is stated: *I live in a distant city. The city is 10 miles distant from Chicago.* **Far** suggests a long but somewhat indefinite distance away; **remote** suggests a long distance from the center of things: *Vietnam is a far country; to Americans it used to be remote.*

dis taste (dis tāst′), *n.* dislike. See **dislike** for synonym study.

dis taste ful (dis tāst′fəl), *adj.* unpleasant; disagreeable; offensive: *a distasteful task.* **—dis taste′ful ly,** *adv.* **—dis taste′ful-ness,** *n.*

dis tem per (dis tem′pər), *n.* 1 an infectious viral disease of dogs and other animals, accompanied by fever, a short, dry cough, and a loss of strength. 2 any sickness of the mind or body; disorder; disease. 3 disturbance. 4 paint made by mixing the colors with eggs or glue instead of oil. Distemper is often used for painting on plaster walls. 5 method of painting with such a mixture. 6 a painting done in distemper. *—v.t.* 1 make unbalanced; disturb; disorder. 2 paint in distemper. [< Late Latin *distemperare* mix improperly < Latin *dis-* + *temperare* to temper]

dis tend (dis tend′), *v.t., v.i.* stretch out by pressure from within; swell out; expand: *The balloon was distended almost to the bursting point.* [< Latin *distendere* < *dis-* apart + *tendere* to stretch]

dis ten si ble (dis ten′sə bəl), *adj.* capable of being distended.

dis ten sion (dis ten′shən), *n.* distention.

dis ten tion (dis ten′shən), *n.* 1 a distending. 2 a being distended.

dis tich (dis′tik), *n.* two lines of verse forming a stanza, and usually making complete sense. EXAMPLE:

Those who in quarrels interpose
Must often wipe a bloody nose.

[< Greek *distichon* < *di-* two + *stichos* line]

dis till or **dis til** (dis til′), *v.,* **-tilled, -till ing.** *—v.t.* 1 heat (a liquid or solid) and condense the vapor or gas given off by cooling it, so as to obtain the substance or one of its constituents in a state of concentration or

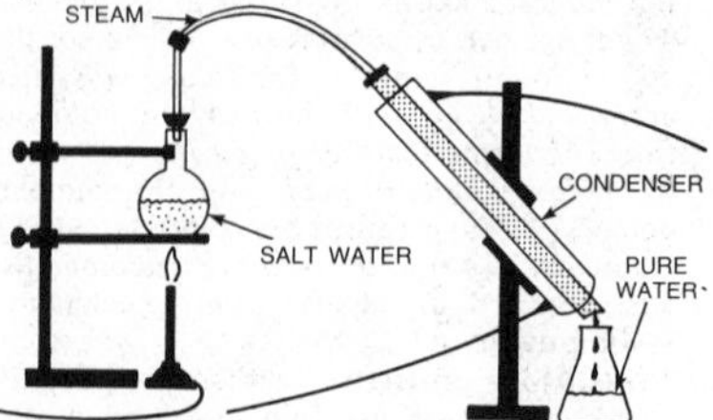

distill (def. 1)
Pure water is distilled from salt water by heating until the water turns to vapor. It is changed back to liquid form by cooling in the condenser.

hat, āge, fär; let, ēqual, tėrm;
it, īce; hot, ōpen, ôrder;
oil, out; cup, pu̇t, rüle;
ch, child; ng, long; sh, she;
th, thin; ᴛʜ, then; zh, measure;

ə represents *a* in about, *e* in taken, *i* in pencil, *o* in lemon, *u* in circus.

< = from, derived from, taken from.

purity: *distill water for drinking.* 2 obtain by distilling: *Gasoline is distilled from crude oil. Alcoholic liquor is distilled from grain mash.* 3 extract: *A jury must distill the truth from the testimony of witnesses.* 4 give off or let fall in drops: *Flowers distill nectar.* —*v.i.* 1 fall in drops; drip. 2 undergo distillation. 3 condense. [< Latin *distillare* < *de-* down + *stilla* drop]

dis til late (dis′tl it, dis′tl āt), *n.* a distilled liquid; something obtained by distilling.

dis til la tion (dis′tl ā′shən), *n.* 1 act of distilling. 2 process of distilling. 3 something distilled. 4 extract.

dis till er (dis til′ər), *n.* 1 person or thing that distills. 2 person or company that makes whiskey, rum, brandy, etc.

dis till er y (dis til′ər ē), *n., pl.* **-er ies.** place where distilling is done, especially where whiskey, rum, brandy, etc., are made; still.

dis tinct (dis tingkt′), *adj.* 1 not the same; separate: *She asked me about it three distinct times.* 2 different in quality or kind; distinctive: *Mice are distinct from rats.* 3 easily seen, heard, or understood; clear: *Large, distinct print is easy to read.* 4 unmistakable; definite; decided: *a distinct advantage.* [< Latin *distinctus* < *distinguere.* See DISTINGUISH.] **—dis tinct′ly,** *adv.* **—dis tinct′ness,** *n.*

dis tinc tion (dis tingk′shən), *n.* 1 a distinguishing from others; making a difference; discrimination: *She treated all her children alike without distinction.* 2 difference. 3 special quality or feature; point of difference. 4 honor. 5 mark or sign of honor. 6 excellence; superiority: *a man of distinction.*

dis tinc tive (dis tingk′tiv), *adj.* distinguishing from others; special; characteristic: *Policemen wear a distinctive uniform.* **—dis tinc′tive ly,** *adv.* **—dis tinc′tive ness,** *n.*

dis tin gué (dis′tang gā′, dis tang′gā), *adj.* looking important or superior; distinguished. [< French]

dis tin guish (dis ting′gwish), *v.t.* 1 recognize as different; tell apart. See synonym study below. 2 see or hear clearly; make out plainly; discern: *It is much too dark for me to distinguish the outline of the house.* 3 make different; be a special quality or feature of; differentiate: *The ability to talk distinguishes human beings from animals.* 4 make famous or well known; confer distinction on: *She distinguished herself by winning the Nobel prize.* —*v.i.* see or show the difference; discriminate: *distinguish between right and wrong.* [< Latin *distinguere* < *dis-* between + *stinguere* to prick]

Syn. *v.t.* 1 **Distinguish, differentiate, discriminate** mean to recognize or show the differences in or between things. **Distinguish** means to recognize the qualities and features of a thing that give it its special character and set it off from others: *I distinguished the violins from the cellos in the orchestra.* **Differentiate** means to point out the exact differences between one thing and others of the same class: *The teacher differentiated between Shakespeare's sonnets and Milton's.* **Discriminate** means to see the fine shades of difference between things: *Sometimes only experts can discriminate counterfeit bills from genuine money.*

dis tin guish a ble (dis ting′gwi shə bəl), *adj.* capable of being distinguished. **—dis tin′guish a bly,** *adv.*

dis tin guished (dis ting′gwisht), *adj.* 1 famous; well-known: *a distinguished artist.* See **eminent** for synonym study. 2 looking important or superior.

dis tort (dis tôrt′), *v.t.* 1 pull or twist out of shape; change the normal appearance of: *Rage distorted his face.* 2 give a twist or turn to (the mind, thoughts, views); misrepresent: *The driver distorted the facts of the accident to escape blame.* [< Latin *distortum* turned away, twisted < *dis-* + *torquere* to twist] **—dis tort′er,** *n.*

dis tor tion (dis tôr′shən), *n.* 1 a distorting; twisting out of shape: *Exaggeration is a distortion of the truth.* 2 condition of being distorted. 3 anything distorted: *a story full of distortions.* 4 a distorted form or image.

dis tract (dis trakt′), *v.t.* 1 turn aside or draw away (the mind, attention, etc.): *Noise distracts my attention from study.* 2 confuse; disturb. 3 make insane. [< Latin *distractum* drawn away < *dis-* + *trahere* to draw] **—dis tract′ed ly,** *adv.* **—dis tract′ing ly,** *adv.*

dis trac tion (dis trak′shən), *n.* 1 act of turning aside or drawing away the mind, attention, etc. 2 thing that draws away the mind, attention, etc. 3 confusion of mind; disturbance of thought: *The parents of the lost children scarcely knew what they were doing in their distraction.* 4 relief from continued thought, grief, or effort; amusement: *Movies and television are popular distractions.* 5 insanity; madness.

dis trac tive (dis trak′tiv), *adj.* distracting; tending to distract.

dis train (dis trān′), *v.t.* (in law) seize (goods) for unpaid rent or other debts. [< Old French *destreindre* < Latin *dis-* apart + *stringere* to draw]

dis trait (dis trā′), *adj.* not paying attention; absent-minded. [< French]

dis traught (dis trôt′), *adj.* 1 in a state of mental conflict and confusion; distracted. 2 crazed. [variant of obsolete *distract,* adjective, distracted]

dis tress (dis tres′), *n.* 1 great pain or sorrow; anxiety; trouble. See **sorrow** for synonym study. 2 something that causes distress; misfortune. 3 a dangerous condition; difficult situation: *A burning or sinking ship is in distress.* —*v.t.* 1 cause great pain or sorrow to; make unhappy. 2 subject to pressure, stress, or strain. [< Old French *distrece,* ultimately < Latin *districtum* drawn apart < *dis-* + *stringere* to draw] **—dis tress′ing ly,** *adv.*

dis tress ful (dis tres′fəl), *adj.* 1 causing distress; painful. 2 in great distress; suffering. **—dis tress′ful ly,** *adv.* **—dis tress′ful ness,** *n.*

dis trib u tar y (dis trib′yə ter′ē), *n., pl.* **-tar ies.** branch of a river that flows away from, rather than into, the main stream and never rejoins it.

dis trib ute (dis trib′yüt), *v.t.,* **-ut ed, -ut ing.** 1 give some of to each; divide and give out in shares; deal out: *distribute candy.* See synonym study below. 2 spread; scatter: *Distribute the paint evenly over the wall.* 3 divide into separate parts: *The children were distributed into three groups for the trip.* 4 arrange in classes; sort out: *The flowering plants are distributed into over 20 well-marked classes.* 5 sell (goods) to a particular market. [< Latin *distributum* divided < *dis-* apart, individually + *tribuere* assign] **—dis trib′ut a ble,** *adj.*

Syn. 1 **Distribute, dispense** mean to give out shares. **Distribute** means to divide into definite parts: *The dividends were distributed to the stockholders.* **Dispense** means to give out according to one's needs: *The Red Cross dispensed new clothing to the flood victims.*

dis tri bu tion (dis′trə byü′shən), *n.* 1 act of distributing: *After the contest the distribution of prizes to the winners took place.* 2 way of being distributed: *If some get more than others, there is an uneven distribution.* 3 thing distributed. 4 a distributing to consumers of goods grown or made by producers. 5 the area over which a particular thing is spread: *the distribution of a species of animal.* 6 (in statistics) a systematic arrangement of numerical data.

dis tri bu tion al (dis′trə byü′shə nəl), *adj.* of or having to do with distribution.

dis trib u tive (dis trib′yə tiv), *adj.* 1 of or having to do with distribution. 2 (in grammar) referring to each individual of a group considered separately. *Each, every, either,* and *neither* are distributive pronouns. 3 of or having to do with a rule that the same product results in multiplication when performed on a set of numbers as when performed on the members of the set individually. EXAMPLE: $3(4 + 5) = (3 \times 4) + (3 \times 5)$. **—dis trib′u tive ly,** *adv.* **—dis trib′u tive ness,** *n.*

dis trib u tor (dis trib′yə tər), *n.* 1 person or thing that distributes. 2 person or company that distributes goods to consumers. 3 part of a gasoline engine that distributes electric current to the spark plugs.

dis trict (dis′trikt), *n.* 1 part of a larger area; region: *a farming district.* 2 part of a country, state, or city marked off for electoral, administrative, judicial, or other purposes. *v.t.* divide into districts. [< Medieval Latin *districtus* district < Latin *districtum* drawn apart. See DISTRESS.]

district attorney, lawyer who prosecutes cases for the government within a federal or state district.

District of Columbia, district in E United States between Maryland and Virginia, governed by Congress and coextensive with the national capital, Washington. 757,000 pop.; 70 sq. mi. *Abbrev.:* D.C.

dis trust (dis trust′), *v.t.* have no confidence in; not trust; be suspicious of. —*n.* lack of trust or confidence; suspicion. See **suspicion** for synonym study.

dis trust ful (dis trust′fəl), *adj.* not trusting; suspicious. **—dis trust′ful ly,** *adv.* **—dis trust′ful ness,** *n.*

dis turb (dis tėrb′), *v.t.* 1 destroy the peace, quiet, or rest of. 2 break in upon with noise or change: *Do not disturb the baby; he is asleep.* 3 put out of order: *Someone has disturbed all my papers.* 4 make uneasy; trouble: *I was disturbed to hear of your illness.* 5 inconvenience: *Don't disturb yourself; I can do it.* [< Latin *disturbare* < *dis-* + *turba* commotion] **—dis turb′er,** *n.*

dis turb ance (dis tėr′bəns), *n.* 1 a disturbing. 2 a being disturbed. 3 thing that disturbs. 4 confusion; disorder. 5 uneasiness; trouble; worry.

di sul fide or **di sul phide** (dī sul′fīd, dī-sul′fīd), *n.* compound consisting of two atoms of sulfur combined with another element or radical; bisulfide.

dis un ion (dis yü′nyən), *n.* 1 separation; division. 2 lack of unity; disagreement; dissension.

dis u nite (dis′yü nīt′), *v.t.*, **-nit ed, -nit ing.** 1 separate; divide. 2 destroy the unity of; cause to disagree.

dis u ni ty (dis yü′nə tē), *n.* lack of unity; disunion; dissension.

dis use (*n.* dis yüs′; *v.* dis yüz′), *n., v.*, **-used, -us ing.** —*n.* lack of use; not being used: *Many words common in Shakespeare's time have fallen into disuse.* —*v.t.* discontinue the use or practice of.

di syl lab ic (dis′ə lab′ik), *adj.* dissyllabic. **—di′syl lab′i cal ly,** *adv.*

di syl la ble (di sil′ə bəl), *n.* dissyllable.

ditch (dich), *n.* a long, narrow place dug in the earth, usually for carrying off water. —*v.t.* 1 dig a ditch in or around. 2 drive or throw into a ditch: *The careless driver ditched his car.* 3 land (an airplane not equipped for the purpose) on water. 4 SLANG. get rid of. [Old English *dīc*] **—ditch′er,** *n.*

dith er (diᴛʜ′ər), *n.* INFORMAL. a confused, excited condition. [origin uncertain]

dith er y (diᴛʜ′ər ē), *adj.* INFORMAL. confused and excited; flustered.

dith y ramb (dith′ə ram′, dith′ə ramb′), *n.* 1 a Greek choral song in honor of Dionysus. 2 poem, speech, etc., that is full of wild emotion, enthusiasm, etc. [< Greek *dithyrambos*]

dith y ram bic (dith′ə ram′bik), *adj.* 1 of a dithyramb. 2 wild and vehement.

dit to (dit′ō), *n., pl.* **-tos,** *adv., v.* —*n.* 1 the same (used in lists, accounts, etc., to avoid repetition of a word or phrase appearing above). 2 ditto mark. 3 a copy; duplicate. —*adv.* INFORMAL. as said before; likewise. —*v.t.* copy; duplicate. [< Italian, said]

ditto mark, a small mark (") used to avoid repeating something written immediately above.

dit ty (dit′ē), *n., pl.* **-ties.** a short, simple song or poem. [< Old French *ditie* < Latin *dictatum* (thing) dictated]

ditty bag, a small bag, used especially by sailors, to hold needles, thread, buttons, soap, laundry, etc.

di u ret ic (dī′yü ret′ik), *adj.* causing an increase in the flow of urine. —*n.* a diuretic drug or agent. [< Late Latin *diureticus* < Greek *diourētikos* < *dia-* through + *ourein* urinate]

di ur nal (dī ėr′nl), *adj.* 1 occurring every day; daily. 2 of or belonging to the daytime: *the diurnal temperature.* 3 active only in the daytime: *Butterflies are diurnal.* 4 opening by day and closing by night, as certain flowers. [< Late Latin *diurnalis* < Latin *dies* day. Doublet of JOURNAL.] **—di ur′nal ly,** *adv.*

div., 1 dividend. 2 division.

di va (dē′və), *n.* prima donna. [< Italian < Latin, goddess]

di va gate (dī′və gāt), *v.i.*, **-gat ed, -gat ing.** wander about; stray from one place or subject to another. [< Latin *divagatum* wandered about < *dis-* + *vagari* wander] **—di′va ga′tion,** *n.*

di va lent (dī vā′lənt), *adj.* having a valence of two; bivalent.

di van (dī′van, də van′), *n.* a long, low, soft couch or sofa. [< Turkish *divān* < Persian *dēvān*]

dive (dīv), *v.*, **dived** or **dove, dived, div ing,** *n.* —*v.i.* 1 plunge, usually headfirst, into or under water. 2 dart out of sight suddenly; disappear: *The gopher dived into its hole.* 3 plunge the hand into anything to take something out: *He dived into his pockets and brought out a dollar.* 4 enter deeply or plunge (into a matter): *She dived into her work.* 5 plunge downward at a steep angle: *The hawk dived straight at the field mouse.* —*v.t.* cause to dive; direct into a dive. —*n.* 1 act of diving. 2 a downward plunge at a steep angle: *The submarine made a dive toward the bottom.* 3 INFORMAL. a cheap tavern or nightclub. [Old English *dȳfan*]

dive bomber, bomber that releases its bomb load just before it pulls out of a dive toward the target.

div er (dī′vər), *n.* 1 person or thing that dives. 2 person whose occupation is working or diving under water. 3 a diving bird, especially a loon.

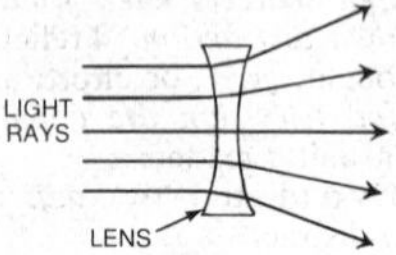

diverge (def. 1)—The lens causes the light rays to diverge.

di verge (də vėrj′, dī vėrj′), *v.*, **-verged, -verg ing.** —*v.i.* 1 move or lie in different directions from the same point; branch off: *Their paths diverged at the fork in the road.* See synonym study below. 2 differ; vary. —*v.t.* cause to diverge. [< Late Latin *divergere* < Latin *dis-* off + *vergere* to slope]

Syn. *v.i.* 1 **Diverge, deviate, digress** mean to turn or move in a different direction. **Diverge** means to branch out in different directions from a main or former course: *Our paths diverged when we left school.* **Deviate** means to turn aside in one direction from a normal or regular path, way of thinking or acting, rule, etc.: *The teacher deviated from custom and gave us no homework.* **Digress** applies to turning aside from the main subject while speaking or writing: *A reader may lose interest if an author digresses too much.*

di ver gence (də vėr′jəns, dī vėr′jəns), *n.* act or fact of diverging; a deviating or differing: *divergence from the rules, a wide divergence of opinion.*

di ver gen cy (də vėr′jən sē, dī vėr′jən sē), *n., pl.* **-cies.** divergence.

di ver gent (də vėr′jənt, dī vėr′jənt), *adj.* diverging; different. **—di ver′gent ly,** *adv.*

di vers (dī′vərz), *adj.* more than one; several different; various. [< Old French < Latin *diversum* turned aside, diverted]

di verse (də vėrs′, dī vėrs′), *adj.* 1 not alike; different: *diverse opinions.* 2 varied; diversified: *A person of diverse interests can talk on many subjects.* [variant of *divers*] **—di verse′ly,** *adv.* **—di verse′ness,** *n.*

di ver si fi ca tion (də vėr′sə fə kā′shən, dī vėr′sə fə kā′shən), *n.* 1 a diversifying. 2 a being diversified.

di ver si fy (də vėr′sə fī, dī vėr′sə fī), *v.*, **-fied, -fy ing.** —*v.t.* 1 make diverse; give variety to; vary: *diversify one's interests.* 2 invest in various types of (securities, etc.). —*v.i.* make diverse products.

di ver sion (də vėr′zhən, dī vėr′zhən), *n.* 1 a turning aside; diverting: *a diversion of trade from one country to another.* 2 distraction from work, care, etc.; amusement; entertainment; pastime: *Baseball is my favorite diversion.* 3 attack or feint intended to distract an opponent's attention from the point of main attack.

di ver sion ar y (də vėr′zhə ner′ē, dī-vėr′zhə ner′ē), *adj.* of or like a diversion or feint, especially in military tactics.

di ver si ty (də vėr′sə tē, dī vėr′sə tē), *n., pl.* **-ties.** 1 complete difference; unlikeness. 2 point of unlikeness. 3 variety: *a diversity of food on the table.*

di vert (də vėrt′, dī vėrt′), *v.t.* 1 turn aside: *A ditch diverted water from the stream into the fields.* 2 amuse; entertain: *Listening to music diverted me after a hard day's work.* [< Latin *divertere* < *dis-* aside + *vertere* turn]

di ver tic u lum (dī′vər tik′yə ləm), *n., pl.* **-la** (-lə). (in anatomy) an abnormal tubular sac or process branching off from a canal or cavity. [< Latin]

di ver tisse ment (də ver′tis mənt; *French* dē ver tēs mäɴ′), *n.* 1 amusement; entertainment. 2 a short ballet. [< French]

di vest (də vest′, dī vest′), *v.t.* 1 rid or strip, especially of clothing or any covering, ornament, etc.; unclothe. 2 force to give up; deprive: *A person in prison is divested of his right to vote.* [< Old French *desvestir* < *des-* dis- + *vestir* clothe]

di vide (də vīd′), *v.*, **-vid ed, -vid ing,** *n.* —*v.t.* 1 separate into parts: *A brook divides the field.* See **separate** for synonym study. 2 separate into equal parts: *When you divide 8 by 2, you get 4.* 3 give some of to each; share: *The children divided the candy.* 4 cause to disagree; cause to differ in feeling, opinion, etc.: *Jealousy divided us.* 5 separate (a legislature, etc.) into two groups in voting. 6 mark off in parts; graduate (a scale, instrument, etc.). 7 distinguish by kinds; sort out; classify. —*v.i.* 1 separate into parts; part: *The road divides and forms two roads.* 2 differ in feeling, opinion, etc.; disagree: *The school divided on the choice of a motto.* 3 vote by separating into two groups. —*n.* ridge of land between two regions drained by different river systems. [< Latin *dividere* < *dis-* apart + *-videre* to separate]

di vid ed (də vī′did), *adj.* 1 separated. 2 (of a leaf) cut to the base so as to form distinct portions. 3 disagreeing in feeling, opinion, etc. 4 having a partition or dividing strip between opposite lanes: *a divided highway.*

div i dend (div′ə dend), *n.* 1 number or quantity to be divided by another: *In 728 ÷ 16, 728 is the dividend.* 2 money earned as a profit by a company and divided among the owners or stockholders of the company. 3 share of such money. 4 part of the profits of an insurance company given to a person holding an insurance policy. [< Latin *dividendum* (thing) to be divided]

di vid er (də vī′dər), *n.* 1 person or thing that divides: *a concrete divider in the center of a parkway.* 2 **dividers,** *pl.* compass used for dividing lines, measuring distances, etc.

div i na tion (div′ə nā′shən), *n.* 1 act of foreseeing the future or discovering what is hidden or obscure by supernatural or magical means. 2 augury; prophecy. 3 a skillful guess.

di vine (də vīn′), *adj., n., v.,* **-vined,**

-vin ing. —*adj.* 1 of God or a god: *a divine act.* 2 given by or coming from God: *divine guidance.* 3 to or for God; sacred; holy: *divine worship.* 4 like God or a god; heavenly. 5 INFORMAL. excellent or delightful; unusually good or great. —*n.* clergyman who knows much about theology; minister; priest. —*v.t.* 1 foresee or foretell by inspiration, by magic, or by signs and omens; predict. 2 guess correctly. [< Old French *divin* < Latin *divinum* < *divus* deity] **—di vine′ly,** *adv.* **—di vine′ness,** *n.* **—di vin′er,** *n.*

Divine Office, the stated service of daily prayer.

divine right of kings, the right to rule, thought to have been given to kings by God, not by the consent of the governed.

diving bell

diving bell, a large, hollow container filled with air and open at the bottom, in which people can work under water.

diving suit, a waterproof suit with a helmet into which air can be pumped through a tube, worn by persons working under water.

divining rod, a forked stick supposed to be useful in locating underground water, oil, metal, etc., by dipping downward when held over a deposit of the substance sought.

di vin i ty (də vin′ə tē), *n., pl.* **-ties.** 1 a divine being; god or goddess. 2 **the Divinity,** God. 3 divine nature or quality. 4 study of God, religion, and divine things; theology.

di vis i bil i ty (də viz′ə bil′ə tē), *n.* quality of being divisible.

di vis i ble (də viz′ə bəl), *adj.* 1 capable of being divided. 2 capable of being divided without leaving a remainder: *12 is divisible by 1, 2, 3, 4, 6, and 12.*

di vi sion (də vizh′ən), *n.* 1 a dividing. 2 a being divided. 3 a giving some to each; sharing: *a fair division of the work.* 4 process of dividing one number by another. 5 thing that divides. A boundary or a partition is a division. 6 one of the parts into which a thing is divided; group; section: *the research division of a drug company.* 7 (in botany) the highest group of the vegetable kingdom; phylum. The plants in a division are thought to be related by descent from a common ancestral form. See **classification** for chart. 8 a military unit made up of several brigades or regiments plus supporting troops, usually commanded by a major general. It is smaller than a corps. 9 a tactical subdivision of a fleet or squadron, consisting of two or more ships, aircraft, etc., of the same type. 10 one of the parts into which a country, county, or other territory is divided for political, administrative, judicial, or military purposes. 11 a difference of opinion, thought, or feeling; disagreement. 12 separation of a legislative body into two groups for voting. [< Latin *divisionem* < *dividere* to divide]

di vi sion al (də vizh′ə nəl), *adj.* of or having to do with a division.

division of labor, distribution of separate small parts of a process among many workers, as on an assembly line, in order to facilitate mass production.

di vi sive (də vī′siv), *adj.* tending to cause division or disagreement. **—di vi′siveness,** *n.*

di vi sor (də vī′zər), *n.* 1 number or quantity by which another is to be divided: *In 728 ÷ 16, 16 is the divisor.* 2 number or quantity that divides another without a remainder.

di vorce (də vôrs′, də vōrs′), *n., v.,* **-vorced, -vorc ing.** —*n.* 1 the legal ending of a marriage. 2 separation: *In this country there is a complete divorce of government and religion.* —*v.t.* 1 end legally a marriage between. 2 get rid of by a divorce: *She divorced her husband.* 3 separate: *In sports, exercise and play are not divorced.* —*v.i.* separate by means of a divorce. [< Old French < Latin *divortium* divorce; separation < *divertere.* See DIVERT.] **—di vorce′ment,** *n.*

di vor cée (də vôr′sā′, də vōr′sā′), *n.* a divorced woman. [< French]

div ot (div′ət), *n.* a small piece of turf or earth dug up by a golf club in making too low a stroke. [origin uncertain]

di vulge (də vulj′, dī vulj′), *v.t.,* **-vulged, -vulg ing.** make known or tell openly (something private or secret); reveal. [< Latin *divulgare* make common < *dis-* + *vulgus* common people] **—di vulg′er,** *n.*

di vul gence (də vul′jəns), *n.* act of divulging; disclosure.

diving suit

div vy (div′ē), *v.t., v.i.,* **-vied, -vy ing.** SLANG. share or divide.

Dix ie (dik′sē), *n.* 1 the southern states of the United States. 2 a lively song about the South written in 1859, popular during the Civil War.

Dix ie crat (dik′sē krat), *n.* a Southern Democrat opposed to the civil rights program of the Truman Administration and of the 1948 platform of the Democratic Party.

diz en (diz′n, dī′zn), *v.t.* dress with gaudy clothes, ornaments, etc.; bedizen. [< Middle Dutch]

diz zy (diz′ē), *adj.,* **-zi er, -zi est,** *v.,* **-zied, -zy ing.** —*adj.* 1 likely to fall, stagger, or spin around because of a sensation that things about one are whirling; giddy. 2 confused; bewildered. 3 likely to make dizzy; causing dizziness: *The airplane climbed to a dizzy height.* 4 INFORMAL. foolish; stupid. —*v.t.* make dizzy. [Old English *dysig* foolish] **—diz′zi ly,** *adv.* **—diz′zi ness,** *n.*

hat, āge, fär; let, ēqual, tėrm;
it, īce; hot, ōpen, ôrder;
oil, out; cup, pu̇t, rüle;
ch, child; ng, long; sh, she;
th, thin; ꟻH, then; zh, measure;

ə represents *a* in about, *e* in taken, *i* in pencil, *o* in lemon, *u* in circus.

< = from, derived from, taken from.

Dja kar ta (jə kär′tə), *n.* seaport in NW Java, capital of Indonesia. 4,750,000. Also, **Jakarta.** Former name, **Batavia.**

Dji bou ti (ji bü′tē), *n.* seaport and capital of Afars and Issas, on the Gulf of Aden. 62,000. Also, **Jibuti.**

dkg., decagram or decagrams.

dkl., decaliter or decaliters.

dkm., decameter or decameters.

dl., deciliter or deciliters.

D layer, D Region.

D. Lit. or **D. Litt.,** 1 Doctor of Letters. 2 Doctor of Literature.

dm., decimeter or decimeters.

DMZ, demilitarized zone.

DNA, deoxyribonucleic acid.

Dne pro pe trovsk (nē′prō pi trôfsk′), *n.* city in SW Soviet Union, on the Dnieper. 863,000.

Dnie per River (nē′pər), river flowing from W Soviet Union into the Black Sea. 1400 mi.

Dnies ter River (nē′stər), river flowing from SW Soviet Union into the Black Sea. 850 mi.

do[1] (dü), *v.,* **did, done, do ing.** —*v.t.* 1 carry through to an end any action or piece of work; carry out; perform: *She did her work well.* See synonym study below. 2 complete; finish; end: *That's done.* 3 make; produce: *Walt Disney did a movie about the seven dwarfs.* 4 be the cause of; bring about: *Your work does you credit.* 5 render: *do homage, do justice.* 6 deal with; take care of: *do one's hair.* 7 be satisfactory enough for; serve: *It's a small house, but it will do us.* 8 work out; solve: *do a puzzle.* 9 cook: *The roast will be done in an hour.* 10 cover; traverse: *We did 50 miles in an hour.* 11 INFORMAL. cheat; trick. —*v.i.* 1 act; behave: *You have done wisely.* 2 get along; manage; fare: *My brother is doing well in his new job.* 3 be satisfactory; serve: *This hat will do.* 4 *Do* is used: **a** to ask questions: *Do you like milk?* **b** to emphasize a verb: *I do want to go.* **c** to stand for another verb already used: *My dog goes where I do.* **d** in expressions that contain *not: People talk; animals do not.* **e** in inverted constructions after the adverbs *rarely, hardly, little,* etc.: *Rarely did she laugh.*

do away with, a put an end to; abolish: *do away with a rule.* **b** kill.

do by, act or behave toward; treat.

do for, ruin or damage: *That fire means my business is done for.*

do in, a ruin. **b** INFORMAL. kill. **c** exhaust: *I was done in by the long hike.*

do up, a wrap up; tie up. **b** arrange: *do up one's hair.*

do without, get along without the thing mentioned or implied.

[Old English *dōn*]

Syn. *v.t.* 1 **Do, perform, accomplish**

mean to carry on an activity to its end. **Do** applies to almost every kind of act: *I did my homework after school so I could go to the game.* **Perform,** a rather formal word in this meaning, usually implies that the activity is completed and often suggests that it is one regularly engaged in: *She performed wonders by making all arrangements for the field trip in two hours.* **Accomplish** implies that the activity is carried out successfully: *Will tears accomplish more than reason did?*

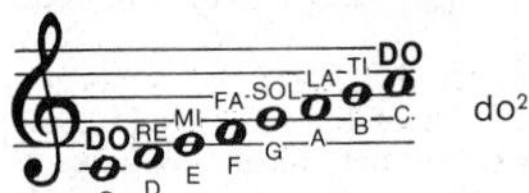

do[2]

do[2] (dō), *n.* (in music) the first and last tones of the diatonic scale. [< Italian]

do., ditto.

DOA, dead on arrival.

do a ble (dü′ə bəl), *adj.* that can be done.

dob bin (dob′ən), *n.* a slow, gentle, plodding horse, especially a farm horse. [variant of *Robin,* proper name]

Do ber man pin scher (dō′bər mən pin′shər), any of a breed of medium-sized, slender, alert dogs with short, dark, smooth hair. [< Ludwig *Dobermann,* German dog breeder of the 1800's + German *Pinscher* (apparently < English *pinch*)]

Do bru ja or **Do bru dja** (dō′brü jä), *n.* district in SE Romania, on the Black Sea.

dob son fly (dob′sən flī′), *n.* a large winged insect whose larva, hellgrammite, is often used as bait by anglers. [origin uncertain]

doc (dok), *n.* U.S. INFORMAL. doctor.

doc., document.

do cent (dō′snt), *n.* a lecturer at a college or university. [< earlier German *Docent*]

doc ile (dos′əl; *British* dō′sīl, dos′īl), *adj.* 1 easily managed or dealt with; obedient. See **obedient** for synonym study. 2 easily taught; willing to learn. [< Middle French < Latin *docilem* < *docere* teach] **—doc′ile ly,** *adv.*

do cil i ty (dō sil′ə tē), *n.* docile quality.

dock[1] (dok), *n.* 1 platform built on the shore or out from the shore to which ships or boats may be secured; wharf; pier. 2 water between two piers, permitting the entrance of ships. 3 place where a ship may be repaired, often built watertight so that the water may be kept high or pumped out. *—v.t.* 1 steer or direct (a ship) into a dock; tie up at a dock. 2 join (two spacecraft) while in space. *—v.i.* come into or moor at a dock: *The ship docked during the night.* [< Middle Dutch *docke*]

dock[2] (dok), *v.t.* 1 cut short or lessen by taking away a part: *My wages are docked if I am late to work.* 2 cut short; cut off the end of. Horses' and dogs' tails are sometimes docked. *—n.* the solid, fleshy part of an animal's tail. [Old English *-docca,* as in *finger-docca* finger muscle]

dock[3] (dok), *n.* the place where an accused person stands or sits in a court of law. [perhaps < Flemish *dok* pen]

dock[4] (dok), *n.* any of a group of large, coarse weeds of the same family as the buckwheat, with sour or bitter leaves and clusters of greenish flowers; sorrel. [Old English *docce*]

dock age[1] (dok′ij), *n.* 1 place to dock ships. 2 charge for using a dock. 3 the docking of ships. [< *dock*[1]]

dock age[2] (dok′ij), *n.* act of cutting down; act of cutting some off. [< *dock*[2]]

dock et (dok′it), *n.* 1 list of lawsuits to be tried by a court. 2 summary or list of court decisions. 3 any list of matters to be considered by some person or group. 4 label or ticket giving the contents of a package, document, etc. *—v.t.* 1 enter on a docket. 2 make a summary or list of (court decisions). 3 mark with a docket. [origin uncertain]

dock yard (dok′yärd′), *n.* place where ships are built, equipped, and repaired. A dockyard contains docks, workshops, and warehouses for supplies.

doc tor (dok′tər), *n.* 1 person licensed to treat diseases and physical or mental disorders; physician, surgeon, dentist, veterinarian, etc. 2 any person who treats diseases, as a medicine man. 3 person who has the highest degree given by a university: *a Doctor of Philosophy.* 4 ARCHAIC. a learned man; teacher. *—v.t.* INFORMAL. 1 treat disease in (a person, animal, etc.). 2 tamper with: *The dishonest cashier doctored the accounts.* 3 repair; mend. *—v.i.* be a doctor; practice medicine. [< Latin, teacher < *docere* teach]

doc tor al (dok′tər əl), *adj.* having to do with a doctor or doctorate.

doc tor ate (dok′tər it), *n.* a doctor's degree given by a university.

doc tri naire (dok′trə ner′, dok′trə nar′), *adj.* stubbornly trying to apply a theory without considering the actual circumstances. *—n.* a doctrinaire person.

doc tri nal (dok′trə nəl), *adj.* of or having to do with doctrine. **—doc′tri nal ly,** *adv.*

doc trine (dok′trən), *n.* 1 what is taught as true by a church, nation, or group of persons; belief: *Christian doctrine.* 2 body or system of principles in any department of knowledge. 3 any of these principles; dogma; tenet. [< Latin *doctrina* < *doctor.* See DOCTOR.]

doc u ment (*n.* dok′yə mənt; *v.* dok′yə ment), *n.* a written or printed paper or other object that gives information, evidence, etc., on any matter or subject under consideration. Letters, maps, and pictures are documents. *—v.t.* prove or support by means of documents or the like: *This theory is fully documented.* [< Latin *documentum* example, proof < *docere* to show, teach] **—doc′u men ta′tion,** *n.*

doc u men tar y (dok′yə men′tər ē), *adj., n., pl.* **-tar ies.** *—adj.* 1 consisting of documents; in writing, print, etc.: *The man's own letters were documentary evidence of his guilt.* 2 presenting or recording factual information in an artistic fashion: *a documentary film.* *—n.* a documentary motion picture, book, or radio or television program.

dod der[1] (dod′ər), *v.i.* be unsteady; tremble or shake from frailty. [origin uncertain]

dod der[2] (dod′ər), *n.* any of a genus of plants without leaves or chlorophyll that live as parasites by twining their threadlike stems around flax, clover, thyme, or other plants. [Middle English *doder*]

do dec a gon (dō dek′ə gon), *n.* a plane figure having 12 angles and 12 sides. [< Greek *dōdekagōnon* < *dōdeka* twelve + *gōnia* angle]

do dec a he dron (dō′dek ə hē′drən), *n., pl.* **-drons, -dra** (-drə). a solid figure having 12 faces. [< Greek *dōdekaedron* < *dōdeka* twelve + *hedra* seat, base]

Do dec a nese Islands (dō′dek ə nēs′, dō′dek ə nēz′), group of Greek islands in the Aegean Sea, off SW Turkey. 123,000 pop.; 1000 sq. mi.

dodge (doj), *v.,* **dodged, dodg ing,** *n.* *—v.i.* move or jump quickly to one side. *—v.t.* 1 avoid by moving or jumping to one side: *dodge a ball.* 2 avoid by cleverness; get away from by some trick: *dodge questions.* *—n.* 1 a sudden movement to one side. 2 a trick to cheat: *a clever dodge.* [origin uncertain]

dodg er (doj′ər), *n.* 1 person who dodges. 2 a shifty or dishonest person. 3 a small handbill. 4 a kind of corn bread.

Dodg son (doj′sən), *n.* **Charles L.** the real name of **Lewis Carroll.**

do do (dō′dō), *n., pl.* **-dos** or **-does.** a large, clumsy bird unable to fly, that became extinct in the 1600's. Dodos lived on Mauritius in the Indian Ocean. [< Portuguese *doudo* fool]

doe (dō), *n.* the female of a deer, antelope, rabbit, hare, and of most other animals whose male is called a buck. [Old English *dā*]

Doe (dō), *n.* **John.** See **John Doe.**

do er (dü′ər), *n.* person who does something, especially with energy and drive.

does (duz), *v.* third person singular, present indicative of **do**[1].

doe skin (dō′skin′), *n.* 1 skin of a doe. 2 leather made from it. 3 a smooth, soft woolen cloth, used for clothing.

does n't (duz′nt), does not.

do est (dü′ist), *v.* ARCHAIC. do[1]. "Thou doest" means "you do."

do eth (dü′ith), *v.* ARCHAIC. does.

doff (dof, dôf), *v.t.* 1 take off; remove: *He doffed his hat as the flag passed by.* 2 get rid of; throw aside. [contraction of *do off*]

dog (def. 8)

dog (dôg, dog), *n., v.,* **dogged, dog ging.** *—n.* 1 a carnivorous, domesticated mammal bred in a great number of varieties, and widely kept as pets and used for hunting and for guarding property. 2 any animal of the same family as the dog, including wolves, foxes, and jackals. 3 a male dog, fox, wolf, etc. 4 any of various animals somewhat like a dog, such as the prairie dog. 5 a low, contemptible man. 6 INFORMAL. man; fellow: *He is a gay dog.* 7 INFORMAL. outward show. 8 device to hold or grip something. 9 andiron. 10 **Dog,** either of two constellations, Canis Major **(Great Dog)** or Canis Minor **(Little Dog).** 11 **go to the dogs,** be ruined. *—v.t.* 1 hunt or follow like a dog; pursue: *Spies dogged his footsteps.* 2 worry

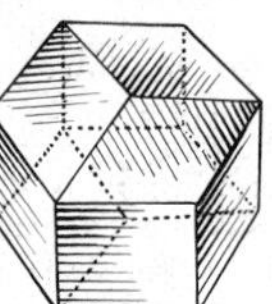

dodecahedron

as if by a dog; beset; afflict: *Injuries dogged the baseball team all season.* [Old English *docga*] **—dog′like′,** *adj.*

dog bane (dôg′bān′, dog′bān′), *n.* any of a genus of plants, many of them poisonous, with clusters of small, white or pink, bell-shaped flowers.

dog ber ry (dôg′ber′ē, dog′ber′ē), *n., pl.* **-ries.** 1 fruit of a North American species of dogwood. 2 the plant. 3 any of various other shrubs or trees, or their fruit, such as the mountain ash or one species of wild gooseberry.

dogcart (def. 2)

dog cart (dôg′kärt′, dog′kärt′), *n.* 1 a small cart pulled by dogs. 2 a small, open, horse-drawn carriage with two seats that are placed back to back.

dog catch er (dôg′kach′ər, dog′kach′ər), *n.* person whose work is to catch and detain stray dogs.

dog days, period of very hot and uncomfortable weather during July and August. [with reference to the rising of Sirius, the *Dog* Star]

doge (dōj), *n.* the chief magistrate of Venice or Genoa when they were republics. [< Italian *doge, doce* < Latin *ducem* leader. Doublet of DUCE, DUKE.]

dog-ear (dôg′ir′, dog′ir′), *n.* a folded-down corner of a page in a book. A dog-ear is often made to mark the place where the reader has stopped. *—v.t.* fold down the corner of (a page in a book). **—dog′-eared′,** *adj.*

dog-eat-dog (dôg′ēt dôg′, dog′ēt dog′), *adj.* characterized by ruthless practices; fierce; cutthroat.

dog face (dôg′fās′, dog′fās′), *n.* U.S. SLANG. a common soldier; infantryman.

dog fight (dôg′fīt′, dog′fīt′), *n.* 1 combat between individual fighter planes at close quarters. 2 brawl.

dog fish (dôg′fish′, dog′fish′), *n., pl.* **-fish es** or **-fish.** any of several kinds of small shark.

dog ged (dô′gid, dog′id), *adj.* not giving up; stubborn; persistent: *dogged determination.* [< *dog*] **—dog′ged ly,** *adv.* **—dog′ged-ness,** *n.*

dog ger el (dô′gər əl, dog′ər əl), *n.* very poor poetry; poetry that is not artistic in form or meaning. *—adj.* 1 of or like doggerel; crude; poor; not artistic. 2 (of verse) comic in style and irregular in form. [Middle English]

dog gie (dô′gē, dog′ē), *n.* 1 a little dog. 2 a pet name for a dog. Also, **doggy.**

dog gone (dôg′gôn′, dog′gon′), *adj.,* **-gon er, -gon est,** *adv., v.,* **-goned, -gon ing.** U.S. SLANG. *—adj.* damned; darned. *—adv.* very: *The test was doggone hard.* *—v.t.* to damn; darn.

dog gy (dô′gē, dog′ē), *adj.,* **-gi er, -gi est,** *n., pl.* **-gies.** *—adj.* 1 like a dog. 2 INFORMAL. outwardly showy. *—n.* doggie.

dog house (dôg′hous′, dog′hous′), *n., pl.* **-hous es** (-hou′ziz). 1 a small house or shelter for a dog. 2 **in the doghouse,** SLANG. out of favor.

do gie (dō′gē), *n.* (in the western United States and Canada) a motherless calf on the range or in a range herd. Also, **dogy.** [origin uncertain]

dog in the manger, INFORMAL. person who prevents others from using or enjoying something of no value to himself. [with reference to the fable of the dog who would not let the ox or horse eat the hay which he himself did not want]

dog ma (dôg′mə, dog′mə), *n.* 1 belief taught or held as true, especially by authority of a church; doctrine. 2 any system of established principles and tenets. 3 opinion asserted in a positive manner as if it were of the highest authority. [< Latin < Greek, opinion < *dokein* think]

dog mat ic (dôg mat′ik, dog mat′ik), *adj.* 1 of or having to do with dogma; doctrinal. 2 positive and emphatic in asserting opinions. 3 asserted in a positive and emphatic manner: *a dogmatic statement.* **—dog mat′i cal ly,** *adv.*

dog mat i cal (dôg mat′ə kəl, dog mat′ə-kəl), *adj.* dogmatic.

dog ma tism (dôg′mə tiz′əm, dog′mə-tiz′əm), *n.* positive and emphatic assertion of opinion.

dog ma tist (dôg′mə tist, dog′mə tist), *n.* person who asserts opinions as if they were authoritative.

dog ma tize (dôg′mə tīz, dog′mə tīz), *v.i.,* **-tized, -tiz ing.** assert opinions in a positive or authoritative manner; speak or write in a dogmatic way. **—dog′ma ti za′tion,** *n.*

do-good er (dü′gůd′ər), *n.* INFORMAL. person who is too eager to correct things or set things right.

dog rose, a wild rose of Europe with pink or white flowers and hooked spines.

Dog Star, 1 Sirius. 2 Procyon.

dog tag, INFORMAL. 1 a metal identification disk worn on a neck chain by a member of the armed forces. 2 a metal disk attached to a dog's collar.

dog-tired (dôg′tīrd′, dog′tīrd′), *adj.* very tired.

dog tooth violet (dôg′tüth′, dog′tüth′), any small plant of a genus of the lily family having a single yellow, white, or purple flower, and, in some species, mottled leaves; trout lily; adder's-tongue.

dog trot (dôg′trot′, dog′trot′), *n.* a gentle, easy trot.

dog watch (dôg′woch′, dôg′wôch′; dog′-woch′, dog′wôch′), *n.* a two-hour period of work on a ship. There are two dogwatches a day, one from 4 to 6 P.M. and the other from 6 to 8 P.M.

dog wood (dôg′wůd′, dog′wůd′), *n.* 1 tree with large white or pinkish flowers in the spring and red berries in the fall. 2 any shrub or tree of the same family as the dogwood.

do gy (dō′gē), *n., pl.* **-gies.** dogie.

Do ha (dō′hə), *n.* capital of Qatar. 100,000.

doi ly (doi′lē), *n., pl.* **-lies.** a small piece of linen, lace, paper, or plastic put under plates, bowls, vases, etc., on a table. [< *Doily,* name of an English dry-goods dealer of the 1700's]

do ings (dü′ingz), *n.pl.* 1 things done; actions. 2 behavior; conduct.

doit (doit), *n.* 1 a former Dutch copper coin worth about $\frac{1}{4}$ cent. 2 a small sum; trifle; bit: *No one cares a doit what he thinks.* [< Dutch *duit*]

do-it-your self (dü′it yər self′), *adj.* designed for use, construction, or assembly by an amateur.

hat, āge, fär; let, ēqual, tėrm;
it, īce; hot, ōpen, ôrder;
oil, out; cup, pu̇t, rüle;
ch, child; ng, long; sh, she;
th, thin; ᴛʜ, then; zh, measure;

ə represents *a* in about, *e* in taken, *i* in pencil, *o* in lemon, *u* in circus.

< = from, derived from, taken from.

dol ce (dōl′chā), *adj.* ITALIAN. sweet; soft.

dol ce far nien te (dōl′chā fär nyen′tā), ITALIAN. 1 pleasant idleness. 2 (literally) it is sweet doing nothing.

dol drums (dol′drəmz, dōl′drəmz), *n.pl.* 1 gloomy feeling; low spirits. 2 region of the ocean near the equator where the wind is very light or constantly shifting. When a sailing ship gets in the doldrums, it makes hardly any headway. [origin uncertain]

dole[1] (dōl), *n., v.,* **doled, dol ing.** *—n.* 1 portion of money, food, etc., given in charity. 2 a small portion. 3 relief money given by a government to unemployed workers. 4 a dealing out of money, food, etc., given in charity. 5 ARCHAIC. lot; fate. *—v.t.* 1 give as a dole; distribute in charity. 2 give in small portions. [Old English *dāl* part]

dole[2] (dōl), *n.* ARCHAIC. sorrow; grief. [< Old French *doel* < Late Latin *dolus*]

dole ful (dōl′fəl), *adj.* very sad or dreary; mournful; dismal. **—dole′ful ly,** *adv.* **—dole′ful ness,** *n.*

dole some (dōl′səm), *adj.* ARCHAIC. doleful.

dol i cho ce phal ic (dol′ə kō sə fal′ik), *adj.* having a long, narrow skull. [< Greek *dolichos* long + *kephalē* head]

doll (dol), *n.* 1 a child's toy made to look like a baby, child, or grown person. 2 a pretty child, girl, or woman. *—v.t., v.i.* **doll up,** INFORMAL. dress in a stylish or showy way: *all dolled up in evening dress.* [< *Doll,* nickname for *Dorothy*] **—doll′-like′,** *adj.*

dol lar (dol′ər), *n.* 1 the basic monetary unit of the United States and Canada, a coin or note equal to 100 cents. 2 the monetary unit of several other countries, varying in value from $1.19 in Australia to 18 cents in Hong Kong. 3 a silver coin or piece of paper money worth one dollar. [earlier *daler* < Low German < German *Joachimsthaler,* coin of St. Joachim's valley (in Bohemia), where it was first made]

dollar diplomacy, diplomacy that seeks chiefly to extend a country's business interests in other countries.

doll house (dol′hous′), *n., pl.* **-hous es** (-hou′ziz). a toy house for children to use in playing with dolls.

dol lop (dol′əp), *n.* INFORMAL. portion or serving, large or small: *cake with a dollop of whipped cream.* [origin uncertain]

doll y (dol′ē), *n., pl.* **doll ies,** *v.,* **doll ied, doll y ing.** *—n.* 1 a child's name for a doll. 2 a small, low frame on wheels, used to move heavy things. 3 platform on wheels on which a motion-picture or television camera can be moved about. *—v.t., v.i.* move on a dolly: *The camera dollied in for the final scene.*

dol man sleeve (dol′mən), sleeve of a dress or coat, close-fitting at the wrist and set deep into the garment's bodice rather than into a conventional armhole. [*dolman* < Turkish *dolama*]

dolmen

dol men (dol′mən), *n.* a prehistoric tomb made by laying a large, flat stone across several upright stones. [< French]

dol o mite (dol′ə mīt), *n.* a rock consisting mainly of calcium and magnesium carbonate. Much white marble is dolomite. [< D. G. de *Dolomieu,* 1750-1801, French geologist]

Dolomite Alps, Dolomites.

Dol o mites (dol′ə mīts), *n.pl.* range of the Alps in N Italy. Highest peak, 10,964 ft.

dol o mit ic (dol′ə mit′ik), *adj.* containing or consisting of dolomite.

do lor (dō′lər), *n.* sorrow; grief. [< Latin < *dolere* grieve]

dol or ous (dol′ər əs, dō′lər əs), *adj.* 1 full of or expressing sorrow; mournful. 2 causing or giving rise to sorrow; grievous; painful. **—dol′or ous ly,** *adv.* **—dol′or ous ness,** *n.*

dol phin (dol′fən), *n.* 1 any of various sea mammals of the same order as the porpoise and the whale, having an elongated, beaklike snout and remarkable intelligence. 2 porpoise. 3 either of two large, edible, saltwater fishes of the same family that change color when taken from the water. [< Old French *daulphin* < Latin *delphinus* < Greek *delphnos*]

dolt (dōlt), *n.* a dull, stupid person; blockhead. [apparently related to Old English *dol* dull]

dolt ish (dōl′tish), *adj.* like a dolt; dull and stupid. **—dolt′ish ly,** *adv.* **—dolt′ish ness,** *n.*

Dom (dom; *Portuguese* dōN), *n.* 1 title given to Benedictine and Carthusian monks. 2 (in Portugal and Brazil) title used before the Christian name of noblemen, cardinals, bishops, etc. [< Latin *dominum* lord, master]

-dom, *suffix forming nouns.* 1 *(added to nouns)* position, rank, or realm of a ______: *Kingdom = realm of a king.* 2 *(added to adjectives)* condition of being ______: *Freedom = condition of being free.* 3 *(added to nouns)* all those who are ______: *Heathendom = all those who are heathen.* [Old English *-dōm* state, rank < *dōm* law, judgment]

do main (dō mān′), *n.* 1 territory under the control of one ruler or government. 2 land owned by one person; estate. 3 (in law) the absolute ownership of land. 4 field of thought, action, etc.; sphere of activity: *the domain of science, the domain of religion.* 5 (in mathematics) the set whose members are considered as possible replacements for the variable in a given relation; replacement set. [< Middle French *domaine* < Latin *dominium* < *dominum* lord, master]

dome (dōm), *n., v.,* **domed, dom ing.** *—n.* 1 a large, rounded roof or ceiling on a circular or many-sided base; cupola. 2 something high and rounded: *the dome of a hill.* 3 ARCHAIC. a large house; mansion. *—v.t.* 1 cover with a dome. 2 shape like a dome. *—v.i.* rise or swell as a dome does. [< Middle French *dôme* < Provençal *doma* < Late Latin, roof, house < Greek *dōma* housetop] **—dome′like′,** *adj.*

Domes day Book (dümz′dā′), book containing the record of the value and ownership of the lands in England, made in 1086 at the order of William the Conqueror.

do mes tic (də mes′tik), *adj.* 1 of the home, household, or family affairs: *domestic problems, a domestic scene.* 2 attached to home; devoted to family life. 3 living with or under the care of man in or near his habitations; not wild; tame. Cats, dogs, cows, horses, pigs, and sheep are domestic animals. 4 of one's own country; not foreign: *domestic news.* 5 made in one's own country; native: *domestic woolens.* *—n.* servant in a household. [< Latin *domesticus* < *domus* house] **—do mes′ti cal ly,** *adv.*

do mes ti cate (də mes′tə kāt), *v.t.,* **-cat ed, -cat ing.** 1 change (animals, plants, etc.) from a wild to a tame or cultivated state. 2 make fond of home and family life. 3 cause to be or feel at home; naturalize. **—do mes′ti ca′tion,** *n.*

do mes tic i ty (dō′mes tis′ə tē), *n., pl.* **-ties.** 1 home and family life. 2 fondness for home and family life. 3 **domesticities,** *pl.* domestic affairs.

domestic science, home economics.

dom i cal (dō′mə kəl, dom′ə kəl), *adj.* 1 of or having a dome or domes. 2 resembling a dome.

dom i cile (dom′ə sīl, dom′ə səl), *n., v.,* **-ciled, -cil ing.** *—n.* 1 a dwelling place; house; home. 2 place of permanent residence. One may have several residences, but only one legal domicile at a time. *—v.t.* settle in a domicile. *—v.i.* dwell; reside. [< Latin *domicilium* < *domus* house]

dom i cil i ar y (dom′ə sil′ē er′ē), *adj.* having to do with a domicile.

dom i nance (dom′ə nəns), *n.* a being dominant; rule; control.

dom i nant (dom′ə nənt), *adj.* 1 most powerful or influential; controlling; ruling; governing. See synonym study below. 2 rising high above its surroundings; towering over: *Dominant hills sheltered the bay.* 3 (in music) based on or having to do with the dominant. 4 (in biology) of, having to do with, or designating a dominant character. *—n.* 1 (in music) the fifth tone of the diatonic scale; fifth. G is the dominant in the key of C. 2 dominant character. 3 the most extensive and characteristic species in a plant community, determining the type and abundance of other species in the community. **—dom′i nant ly,** *adv.*

Syn. *adj.* 1 **Dominant, predominant, paramount** mean uppermost. **Dominant** means ruling, and therefore having the most influence, power, or authority: *The President was the dominant figure at the Cabinet meeting.* **Predominant** means before others in influence, power, authority, and therefore principal or superior: *Love of liberty is predominant in struggles for independence.* **Paramount** means first in importance, authority, or rank, and therefore supreme: *It is of paramount importance that we finish the work on time.*

dome (def. 1) of a cathedral

dominant character, the one of any pair of contrasting characters that prevails in an animal or plant when both are present in the germ plasm. EXAMPLE: If a child inherits a gene for brown eyes from one parent and a gene for blue eyes from the other, it will have brown eyes, as brown eyes are dominant and blue eyes are recessive.

dom i nate (dom′ə nāt), *v.,* **-nat ed, -nat ing.** *—v.t.* 1 control or rule by strength or power. 2 rise high above; tower over: *The mountain dominates the city and its harbor.* *—v.i.* 1 exercise control; predominate; prevail. 2 hold a commanding position. [< Latin *dominatum* ruled < *dominum* lord, master] **—dom′i na′tor,** *n.*

dom i na tion (dom′ə nā′shən), *n.* act of dominating; the exercise of ruling power; control; rule.

dom i na tive (dom′ə nā′tiv), *adj.* dominating; controlling.

dom i neer (dom′ə nir′), *v.i.* rule or govern arbitrarily; assert one's authority or opinion in an overbearing way; tyrannize. *—v.t.* tyrannize over; dominate.

dom i neer ing (dom′ə nir′ing), *adj.* inclined to domineer; arrogant; overbearing: *a domineering attitude.* **—dom′i neer′ing ly,** *adv.* **—dom′i neer′ing ness,** *n.*

Dom i nic (dom′ə nik), *n.* **Saint,** 1170-1221, Spanish priest who founded an order of preaching friars in 1215 and an order of nuns in 1206.

Dom i ni ca (dom′ə nē′kə, də min′ə kə), *n.* one of the Windward Islands. *Capital:* Roseau. 70,000 pop.; 305 sq. mi.

Do min i can (də min′ə kən), *adj.* 1 of Saint Dominic or the religious orders founded by him. 2 of or having to do with the Dominican Republic. *—n.* 1 friar or nun belonging to the Dominican order. 2 native or inhabitant of the Dominican Republic.

Dominican Republic, country in the E part of the island of Hispaniola, in the West Indies. 4,174,000 pop.; 19,300 sq. mi. *Capital:* Santo Domingo.

dom i nie (dom′ə nē *for 1;* dom′ə nē, dō′mə nē *for 2*), *n.* 1 SCOTTISH. schoolmaster. 2 INFORMAL. clergyman. [< Latin *domine,* vocative of *dominum* lord, master]

do min ion (də min′yən), *n.* 1 power or right of governing and controlling; rule; control. 2 territory under the control of one ruler or government. 3 a self-governing territory. 4 **Dominion,** name formerly used for a self-governing country within the British Commonwealth. *—adj.* Often, **Dominion.** (in Canada) relating to the country as a whole; national in scope. [< Medieval Latin, alteration of Latin *dominium* ownership < *dominum* lord, master]

Dominion Day, July 1, a national holiday in Canada commemorating the establishment of the Dominion of Canada in 1867.

dom i no (dom′ə nō), *n., pl.* **-noes** or **-nos.** 1 **dominoes,** *pl.* game played with flat, oblong pieces of bone, wood, etc., that are either blank or marked with dots. Players try to match pieces having the same number of blanks or dots. 2 one of the pieces used in

domino (def. 3)

the game of dominoes. 3 a loose cloak with a small mask covering the upper part of the face, formerly worn as a disguise at masquerades. 4 the small mask. [< French]

Do mi tian (də mish′ən), *n.* A.D. 51-96, Roman emperor from A.D. 81 to 96.

Dom re my (dôN rə mē′), *n.* village in NE France, the birthplace of Joan of Arc.

don[1] (don), *v.t.,* **donned, don ning.** put on (clothing, etc.): *The knight donned his armor.* [contraction of *do on*]

don[2] (don), *n.* 1 **Don,** a Spanish title meaning Mr. or Sir: *Don Felipe.* 2 a Spanish gentleman; Spaniard. 3 a distinguished person. 4 a head, fellow, or tutor of a college at Oxford or Cambridge Univeristy. [< Spanish < Latin *dominum* lord, master]

Do ña (dō′nyä), *n.* 1 a Spanish title meaning Lady or Madam: *Doña Maria.* 2 **doña,** a Spanish lady.

do nate (dō′nāt), *v.t., v.i.,* **-nat ed, -nat ing.** give (money, help, etc.), especially to a fund or institution; contribute. **—do′na tor,** *n.*

Don a tel lo (don′ə tel′ō), *n.* 1386?-1466, Italian sculptor.

do na tion (dō nā′shən), *n.* 1 gift; contribution. 2 a giving; donating. [< Latin *donationem* < *donare* give < *donum* gift]

Don cas ter (dong′kas′tər; *British* dong′kə stər), *n.* city in central England. 84,000.

done (dun), *adj.* 1 finished or completed; through: *She is done with her homework.* 2 ended; over: *The play is done.* 3 INFORMAL. worn out; exhausted. 4 cooked: *I want my steak well done.* 5 conforming to custom or convention; proper; fitting: *Eating peas with a knife is not done.* —*v.* pp. of **do**[1]. *Have you done all your chores?*

do nee (dō nē′), *n.* person who has been given something as a gift.

Don e gal (don′i gôl, don i gôl′), *n.* county in the NW Republic of Ireland.

Do nets Basin (dō nets′), industrial and coal-producing region in the Soviet Union in Europe, SW of the Donets. 10,000 sq. mi.

Donets River, river in SW Soviet Union that flows into the Don River. 700 mi.

Don i zet ti (don′ə zet′ē), *n.* **Gaetano,** 1797-1848, Italian composer of operas.

don jon (dun′jən, don′jən), *n.* a large, strongly fortified tower of a medieval castle; keep. [variant of *dungeon*]

Don Juan (don wän′; don hwän′; don jü′ən), 1 a legendary Spanish nobleman who led a dissolute and immoral life. 2 man leading an immoral life; libertine.

don key (dong′kē, dung′kē), *n., pl.* **-keys.** 1 the domesticated ass or burro. 2 a stubborn person. 3 a silly fool; stupid person. 4 donkey engine. [origin uncertain]

donkey engine, a small, auxiliary steam engine which operates an anchor, heating system, etc.

Don na (don′ə), *n.* 1 an Italian title meaning Lady or Madam. 2 **donna,** an Italian lady.

Donne (dun), *n.* **John,** 1573-1631, English poet and clergyman.

don nish (don′ish), *adj.* like or characteristic of a university don; pedantic. **—don′nish ly,** *adv.* **—don′nish ness,** *n.*

don ny brook or **Don ny brook** (don′ē brůk′), *n.* a riot; brawl. [< *Donnybrook,* town in Ireland where an annual fair was suppressed in 1855 because of its wild brawls]

do nor (dō′nər), *n.* person who donates; giver; contributor: *a blood donor.*

do-noth ing (dü′nuth′ing), *n.* 1 person who lacks initiative or is reluctant to upset existing conditions by taking action. 2 idler. —*adj.* lacking initiative or reluctant to upset existing conditions by acting.

do-noth ing ism (dü′nuth′ing iz′əm), *n.* do-nothing policy or practice.

Don Qui xo te (don ki hō′tē; don kwik′sət), the chivalrous and idealistic, but also foolish and impractical hero of Cervantes' novel of the same name.

Don River (don), river in SW Soviet Union. 1325 mi.

don't (dōnt), do not.

doo dad (dü′dad), *n.* INFORMAL. a fancy, trifling ornament. [origin unknown]

doo dle (dü′dl), *v.,* **-dled, -dling,** *n.* —*v.i., v.t.* make drawings or marks absent-mindedly while talking or thinking. —*n.* drawing or mark made absent-mindedly. [apparently < dialectal English, to trifle] **—doo′dler,** *n.*

doo dle bug (dü′dl bug′), *n.* U.S. larva of the ant lion.

doo hick ey (dü′hik′ē), *n., pl.* **-eys.** INFORMAL. a thing; gadget; dingus. [a coined word]

doom (düm), *n.* 1 one's fortune or lot; fate. See **fate** for synonym study. 2 an unhappy or terrible fate; ruin or death: *As the ship sank they faced their doom.* 3 judgment; sentence: *The judge pronounced the guilty man's doom.* 4 (in Christian belief) end of the world; God's final judgment of mankind. —*v.t.* 1 condemn to an unhappy or terrible fate. 2 condemn by a judgment or sentence. 3 make a bad or unwelcome outcome certain: *The weather doomed our hopes for a picnic.* [Old English *dōm* law, judgment]

dooms day (dümz′dā′), *n.* Judgment Day.

door (dôr, dōr), *n.* 1 a movable part that turns on hinges or slides open and shut, used to close an opening in a wall. A room has at least one door through which one may enter or leave. 2 any movable part that suggests a door. 3 doorway. 4 room, house, or building to which a door belongs: *Her house is three doors down the street.* 5 any means by which to go in or out; way to get something; access: *Study is the door to knowledge.*

lay at the door of, blame for.

out of doors, not in a house or building; outside.

show (someone) the door, ask one to leave.

[Old English *duru* door, *dur* gate] **—door′like′,** *adj.*

door bell (dôr′bel′, dōr′bel′), *n.* bell inside a house connected to a button or handle on the outside of a door, rung as a signal for admittance.

door jamb (dôr′jam′, dōr′jam′), *n.* the upright piece forming the side of a doorway; doorpost.

door keep er (dôr′kē′pər, dōr′kē′pər), *n.* 1 person who guards a door. 2 doorman.

door knob (dôr′nob′, dōr′nob′), *n.* handle on a door.

hat, āge, fär; let, ēqual, tėrm;
it, īce; hot, ōpen, ôrder;
oil, out; cup, pu̇t, rüle;
ch, child; ng, long; sh, she;
th, thin; ᴛʜ, then; zh, measure;

ə represents *a* in about, *e* in taken, *i* in pencil, *o* in lemon, *u* in circus.

< = from, derived from, taken from.

door man (dôr′mən, dôr′man′; dōr′mən, dōr′man′), *n., pl.* **-men.** 1 man whose work is opening the door of a hotel, store, apartment house, etc., for people going in or out. 2 man who guards a door; doorkeeper.

door mat (dôr′mat′, dōr′mat′), *n.* mat placed near a door for wiping off the dirt from the bottom of one's shoes before entering.

door nail (dôr′nāl′, dōr′nāl′), *n.* 1 nail with a large head. 2 **dead as a doornail,** entirely dead.

door plate (dôr′plāt′, dōr′plāt′), *n.* a metal plate on a door with a name, number, etc., on it.

door post (dôr′pōst′, dōr′pōst′), *n.* doorjamb.

door sill (dôr′sil′, dōr′sil′), *n.* threshold.

door step (dôr′step′, dōr′step′), *n.* step, or one of a set of steps, leading from an outside door to the ground.

door way (dôr′wā′, dōr′wā′), *n.* 1 an opening in a wall where a door is. 2 way to get something; access.

door yard (dôr′yärd′, dōr′yärd′), *n.* yard near the door of a house; yard around a house.

dope (dōp), *n., v.,* **doped, dop ing.** —*n.* 1 SLANG. a narcotic drug, such as opium or morphine. 2 SLANG. information; forecast; prediction. 3 SLANG. a very stupid person. 4 oil, grease, etc., used to make machinery run smoothly. 5 a thick varnish or similar liquid applied to a fabric to strengthen or waterproof it. —*v.t.* SLANG. 1 give or apply dope to. 2 solve or figure out; forecast; predict. —*v.i.* SLANG. use dope. [< Dutch *doop* dipping sauce < *dopen* to dip] **—dop′er,** *n.*

dope ster (dōp′stər), *n.* U.S. SLANG. person who gathers information in order to predict the outcome of future events, as horse races or elections.

dope y (dō′pē), *adj.,* **dop i er, dop i est.** SLANG. 1 drugged; drowsy. 2 very stupid. Also, **dopy.** **—dop′i ness,** *n.*

Dop pler effect (dop′lər), (in physics) the apparent change in the frequency of waves when either the source of the waves or the observer moves toward or away from the other. [< Christian J. *Doppler,* 1803-1853, Austrian physicist]

dop y (dō′pē), *adj.,* **dop i er, dop i est.** dopey.

dor (dôr), *n.* any of various large beetles that fly with a buzzing sound. [Old English *dora*]

Do ré (dô rā′), *n.* **(Paul) Gustave,** 1832?-1883, French illustrator, painter, and sculptor.

Do ri an (dôr′ē ən, dōr′ē ən), *n.* member of a warlike Hellenic people who invaded the Peloponnesus, Crete, and Rhodes in the 1100's B.C. and put an end to Mycenaean culture. —*adj.* of or having to do with the Dorians.

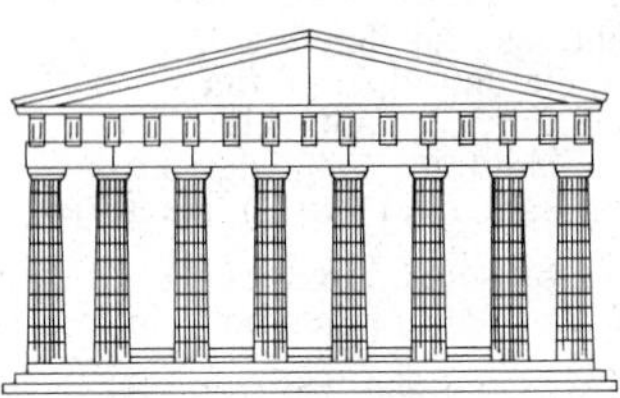

Doric (def. 1)—Doric temple

Do ric (dôr′ik, dor′ik), *adj.* 1 of or having to do with the oldest and simplest order of Greek architecture. The capital of a Doric column has a rounded molding. Also see **order** for picture. 2 Dorian.

dorm (dôrm), *n.* INFORMAL. dormitory.

dor man cy (dôr′mən sē), *n.* dormant condition.

dor mant (dôr′mənt), *adj.* 1 lying asleep; sleeping or apparently sleeping: *Bears and other animals that hibernate are dormant during the winter.* 2 in a state of rest or inactivity; not in motion, action, or operation; quiescent: *a dormant volcano.* See **inactive** for synonym study. 3 (of plants, bulbs, seeds, etc.) with development suspended; not growing. 4 used during a dormant period: *a dormant spray.* [< Old French, present participle of *dormir* to sleep < Latin *dormire*]

dormer (defs. 1 and 2)

dor mer (dôr′mər), *n.* 1 an upright window that projects from a sloping roof. 2 the projecting part of a roof that contains such a window. [< Old French *dormeor*]

dormer window, dormer (def. 1).

dor mi to ry (dôr′mə tôr′ē, dôr′mə tōr′ē), *n., pl.* **-ries.** 1 a building with many sleeping rooms. Colleges often provide dormitories where students live and study. 2 a sleeping room containing several beds. [< Latin *dormitorium* < *dormire* to sleep]

dor mouse (dôr′mous′), *n., pl.* **-mice.** any of a family of small Old World rodents that resemble squirrels and hibernate most of the winter.

dor sal (dôr′səl), *adj.* of, on, or near the back or upper surface of an organ, part, etc.: *a dorsal nerve.* [< Latin *dorsum* the back] **—dor′sal ly,** *adv.*

dorsal fin, a fin or finlike part or parts on the back of most aquatic vertebrates. See **fin** for picture.

Dor set (dôr′sit), *n.* county in S England.

Dor set shire (dôr′sit shər, dôr′sit shir), *n.* Dorset.

Dort mund (dôrt′mùnt), *n.* city in W West Germany. 649,000.

do ry (dôr′ē, dōr′ē), *n., pl.* **-ries.** rowboat with a narrow, flat bottom and high sides, often used by fishermen. [< native name in Honduras]

dos age (dō′sij), *n.* 1 amount of a medicine to be given or taken at one time. 2 the giving of medicine in doses. 3 the measured addition of ingredients to a substance to give it a certain strength or flavor.

dose (dōs), *n., v.,* **dosed, dos ing.** *—n.* 1 amount of a medicine to be given or taken at one time. 2 intensity or length of exposure to X rays, etc. 3 amount of anything given or taken at one time; portion: *a dose of flattery.* 4 portion of an ingredient added to a substance. 5 anything unpleasant to take or endure: *a dose of hard work.* *—v.t.* 1 give medicine to in doses; treat with medicine: *The doctor dosed the child with penicillin.* 2 administer in doses; divide into doses. [< Middle French < Greek *dosis* a giving < *didonai* give]

do sim e ter (dō sim′ə tər), *n.* small device a person may wear for measuring the doses of atomic radiation received over a given period of time.

Dos Pas sos (dəs pas′əs), **John,** 1896-1970, American novelist.

dos si er (dos′ē ā, dos′ē ər), *n.* collection of documents or papers about some subject or person. [< French, bundle of papers labeled on the back, ultimately < Latin *dorsum* back]

dost (dust), *v.* ARCHAIC. do[1]. "Thou dost" means "you do."

Dos to ev ski (dos′tə yef′skē), *n.* **Feodor,** 1821-1881, Russian novelist.

dot[1] (dot), *n., v.,* **dot ted, dot ting.** *—n.* 1 a tiny round mark; point. There is a dot over each *i* in this line. 2 a small spot: *a blue necktie with white dots.* 3 a short sound used in sending messages by telegraph or radio. 4 in music: **a** a tiny, round mark after a note or rest that makes it half again as long. **b** a similar mark placed over or under a note to indicate that it is to be played or sung staccato. 5 **on the dot,** INFORMAL. at exactly the right time; at the specified time. *—v.t.* 1 mark with a dot or dots. 2 be here and there in: *Trees and bushes dotted the lawn.* [Old English *dott* head of a boil] **—dot′ter,** *n.*

dot[2] (dot), *n.* dowry. [< Old French < Latin *dotem*]

dot age (dō′tij), *n.* a weak-minded and childish condition that sometimes accompanies old age; senility.

do tal (dō′tl), *adj.* of or having to do with a dowry.

dot ard (dō′tərd), *n.* person who is weak-minded and childish because of old age.

dote (dōt), *v.i.,* **dot ed, dot ing.** 1 be weak-minded and childish because of old age. 2 **dote on** or **dote upon,** be foolishly fond of; be too fond of. [Middle English *doten*] **—dot′er,** *n.*

doth (duth), *v.* ARCHAIC. does. "She doth" means "she does."

dot ing (dō′ting), *adj.* foolishly fond; too fond. **—dot′ing ly,** *adv.*

dot ter el (dot′ər əl), *n.* 1 a short-billed plover of Europe and Asia that is easily caught. 2 any related bird.

dot tle (dot′l), *n.* tobacco left in the bowl of a pipe after smoking. [Middle English *dottel* a plug, stopper]

dot ty (dot′ē), *adj.,* **-ti er, -ti est.** 1 INFORMAL. feeble-minded; half-witted; partly insane. 2 full of dots.

Dou ai or **Dou ay** (dü ā′), *n.* town in N France, where part of the Douay Bible was published in 1609. 28,000.

Douay Bible or **Douay Version,** an English translation of the Latin Vulgate Bible, used by English-speaking Roman Catholics.

dou ble (dub′əl), *adj., adv., n., v.,* **-bled, -bling.** *—adj.* 1 twice as much, as many, as large, as strong, etc.: *double pay, a double letter.* 2 for two: *a double bed.* 3 made of two like parts; in a pair: *double doors.* 4 having two unlike parts; having two meanings, characters, etc. The spelling *b-e-a-r* has a double meaning: *carry* and *a certain animal.* 5 insincere; deceitful; false: *a double tongue.* 6 having more than one set of petals: *Some roses are double; others are single.*
—adv. 1 twice; doubly. 2 two (of everything) instead of one: *The blow on the head made me see double.*
—n. 1 number or amount that is twice as much: *Four is the double of two.* 2 person or thing just like another. In a motion picture an actor often has a double to do the dangerous scenes. 3 a fold; bend. 4 a sharp backward bend or turn. 5 (in baseball) hit by which a batter gets to second base. 6 (in bridge) act of doubling a bid. 7 **doubles,** *pl.* game of tennis, etc., with two players on each side. 8 **on the double,** **a** quickly. **b** in double time.
—v.t. 1 make twice as much or twice as many. 2 fold; bend. 3 close together tightly; clench: *I doubled my fists in anger.* 4 go around: *The ship doubled Cape Horn.* 5 (in bridge) increase the points or penalties of (an opponent's bid). *—v.i.* 1 become twice as much or twice as many. 2 take the place of another; substitute. 3 serve two purposes; play two parts: *The maid doubled as cook.* 4 bend or turn sharply backward: *The fox doubled on its tracks to get away from the dogs.* 5 (in baseball) hit a double.
double back, **a** fold over. **b** go back the same way that one came.
double up, **a** fold up; curl up. **b** bend over: *double up with laughter.* **c** share room, bed, or quarters with another.
[< Old French *duble, doble* < Latin *duplus.* Doublet of DUPLE.] **—dou′bler,** *n.*

double bar, a double vertical line on a musical staff that marks the end of a movement or of an entire piece of music. See **bar** for diagram.

dou ble-bar reled (dub′əl bar′əld), *adj.* 1 having two barrels: *a double-barreled shotgun.* 2 having a two-fold purpose.

double bass
The four strings are played with a bow or by plucking with the fingers.

double bass, a deep-toned, stringed instrument shaped like a cello but much larger; bass viol; contrabass.

double bassoon, contrabassoon.

double boiler, pair of pans, one of which fits down into the other. The food in the upper pan is cooked by the heat from the boiling water in the lower pan.

dou ble-breast ed (dub′əl bres′tid), *adj.* (of clothing) overlapping across the breast. A double-breasted jacket usually has two rows of buttons.

dou ble-check (dub′əl chek′), *v.t., v.i.*

doublet (def. 1)

check twice: *double-check a report. Shall I double-check?* —*n.* a second check of something: *make a double-check.*

double chin, a soft fold of flesh under the chin.

double concave, concave on both sides.

double convex, convex on both sides.

double cross, INFORMAL. act of treachery.

dou ble-cross (dub′əl krôs′, dub′əl kros′), *v.t., v.i.* INFORMAL. promise to do one thing and then do another; be treacherous (to). **—dou′ble-cross′er,** *n.*

double dagger, mark (‡) used to refer the reader to another section or to a note in a book.

dou ble-deal er (dub′əl dē′lər), *n.* person guilty of double-dealing.

dou ble-deal ing (dub′əl dē′ling), *n.* a pretending to do one thing and then doing another; deceitful action or behavior. —*adj.* deceitful.

dou ble-deck er (dub′əl dek′ər), *n.* 1 bus, railroad car, ship, bed, etc., having two decks, floors, levels, or sections. 2 sandwich having two layers of filling between three slices of bread.

dou ble-edged (dub′əl ejd′), *adj.* 1 two-edged. 2 cutting or acting both ways.

dou ble-en ten dre (dub′əl än tän′drə; *French* dü blän tän′drə), *n.* word or expression with two meanings. One meaning is often indelicate or improper. [< obsolete French *double entendre* double meaning]

double entry, system of bookkeeping in which each transaction is written down twice, once on the credit side of the account and once on the debit side.

dou ble-faced (dub′əl fāst′), *adj.* two-faced.

dou ble head er (dub′əl hed′ər), *n.* 1 two games played one right after the other on the same day. 2 a railroad train pulled by two engines.

double jeopardy, U.S. (in law) the trying of a person a second time for an offense he was acquitted of at a previous legal trial. Double jeopardy is prohibited by the fifth amendment of the Constitution.

dou ble-joint ed (dub′əl join′tid), *adj.* having joints that let fingers, arms, legs, etc., bend in unusual ways.

double negative, statement having two negative words and expressing a negative meaning. EXAMPLE: *There wasn't no answer to my call = There was no answer to my call* or *There wasn't any answer to my call.*

dou ble-park (dub′əl pärk′), *v.t., v.i.* park (a car, etc.) beside another car that is occupying the parking space.

double play, a play in baseball in which two base runners are put out.

dou ble-quick (dub′əl kwik′), *n.* double time. —*adj.* very quick. —*adv.* in double-quick time. —*v.i.* march in double-quick step.

double star, two stars so close together that they look like one to the naked eye.

dou blet (dub′lit), *n.* 1 a man's close-fitting jacket. Men in Europe wore doublets from the 1400's to the 1600's. 2 pair of two similar or equal things; couple. 3 one of a pair. 4 one of two or more words in a language, derived from the same original source but coming by different routes. EXAMPLE: *fragile* and *frail.*

dou ble-talk (dub′əl tôk′), *n.* speech that is purposely meaningless, but seems meaningful because normal words and intonations are mixed in.

double time, 1 rate of marching in which 180 paces, each of 36 inches, are taken in a minute; double-quick. 2 double the usual rate of pay.

dou ble-time (dub′əl tīm′), *v.i.* **-timed, -tim ing.** march at double time.

dou ble tree (dub′əl trē′), *n.* crossbar on a carriage, wagon, plow, etc.

dou bloon (du blün′), *n.* a former Spanish gold coin. Its value varied from about $5 to about $16. [< Spanish *doblón* < *doble* double]

dou bly (dub′lē), *adv.* 1 twice as; twice. 2 two at a time.

doubt (dout), *v.t.* not believe or trust; not be sure of; feel uncertain about: *I doubt that he wrote the letter.* —*v.i.* be uncertain or undecided. —*n.* 1 difficulty in believing; lack of trust or confidence; uncertainty. See **suspicion** for synonym study. 2 an uncertain state of mind: *We were in doubt as to the right road.* 3 an uncertain condition of affairs: *The ship's fate is still in doubt.* 4 **beyond doubt,** surely; certainly. 5 **no doubt, a** surely; certainly. **b** probably. 6 **without doubt,** surely; certainly. [< Old French *douter* < Latin *dubitare*] **—doubt′a ble,** *adj.* **—doubt′er,** *n.* **—doubt′ing ly,** *adv.*

doubt ful (dout′fəl), *adj.* 1 full of doubt; not sure; uncertain. See synonym study below. 2 causing doubt; open to question or suspicion: *Her sly answers made her sincerity doubtful.* **—doubt′ful ly,** *adv.* **—doubt′ful ness,** *n.*

Syn. 1 Doubtful, dubious mean uncertain. **Doubtful** usually implies only lack of certainty: *I am doubtful about his ability to do that kind of work.* **Dubious** often implies suspicion: *I am dubious about his stories of early success.*

doubting Thomas, person who doubts everything. [< *Thomas,* the apostle who doubted Christ's resurrection]

doubt less (dout′lis), *adv.* 1 without doubt; surely. 2 probably. —*adj.* having no doubts; sure; certain. **—doubt′less ly,** *adv.* **—doubt′less ness,** *n.*

douche (düsh), *n., v.,* **douched, douch ing.** —*n.* 1 jet of water, antiseptic solution, etc., applied on or into any part of the body. 2 application of a douche. 3 spray, syringe, or other device for applying a douche. —*v.t.* apply a douche to. —*v.i.* take a douche. [< French]

dough (dō), *n.* 1 a soft, thick mixture of flour, milk, fat, and other materials for baking. Bread, biscuits, cake, and pie crust are made from dough. 2 any soft, thick mass like this. 3 INFORMAL. money. [Old English *dāg*] **—dough′like′,** *adj.*

dough boy (dō′boi′), *n.* U.S. INFORMAL. an infantryman in the United States Army during World War I.

dough nut (dō′nut′), *n.* a small cake of sweetened dough fried in deep fat, usually made in the shape of a ring.

dough ty (dou′tē), *adj.,* **-ti er, -ti est.** strong and bold; stout; brave; hearty. [Old English *dohtig* < *dugan* be of use] **—dough′ti ly,** *adv.* **—dough′ti ness,** *n.*

hat, āge, fär; let, ēqual, tėrm;
it, īce; hot, ōpen, ôrder;
oil, out; cup, pu̇t, rüle;
ch, child; ng, long; sh, she;
th, thin; ᴛʜ, then; zh, measure;

ə represents *a* in about, *e* in taken,
i in pencil, *o* in lemon, *u* in circus.

< = from, derived from, taken from.

dough y (dō′ē), *adj.,* **dough i er, dough i est.** of or like dough; soft and thick; pale and flabby.

Doug las (dug′ləs), *n.* **Stephen A.,** 1813-1861, American statesman who was the Democratic candidate for president against Abraham Lincoln in 1860.

Douglas fir, an evergreen tree of the pine family, often over 200 feet high, common in the western United States and in British Columbia. [< David *Douglas,* 1798-1834, Scottish botanist and explorer]

Doug lass (dug′ləs), *n.* **Frederick,** 1817-1895, American author, orator, and Abolitionist who was himself once a slave.

dour (du̇r, dour), *adj.* 1 gloomy or sullen: *a dour silence.* 2 stern; severe. [< Latin *durus* hard, stern] **—dour′ly,** *adv.* **—dour′ness,** *n.*

douse (dous), *v.,* **doused, dous ing.** —*v.t.* 1 plunge into water or any other liquid. 2 throw water over; drench. 3 INFORMAL. put out; extinguish: *Douse the candles.* 4 INFORMAL. take off; doff. 5 lower or slacken (a sail) in haste. —*v.i.* plunge or be plunged into a liquid. [origin uncertain]

dove[1] (duv), *n.* 1 pigeon, especially one of the smaller and undomesticated species. The dove is often a symbol of peace. 2 INFORMAL. person who is eager for peace; person who advocates a peaceful solution in a conflict. [Old English *dūfe-*. Related to DIVE.]

dove[2] (dōv), *v.* a pt. of **dive.**

dove cot (duv′kot′), *n.* dovecote.

dove cote (duv′kōt′), *n.* a small house or shelter for doves or pigeons.

Do ver (dō′vər), *n.* 1 seaport in SE England, the nearest English port to France. 36,000. 2 **Strait of,** narrow channel or strait between N France and SE England. 20 mi. wide. 3 capital of Delaware, in the central part. 17,000.

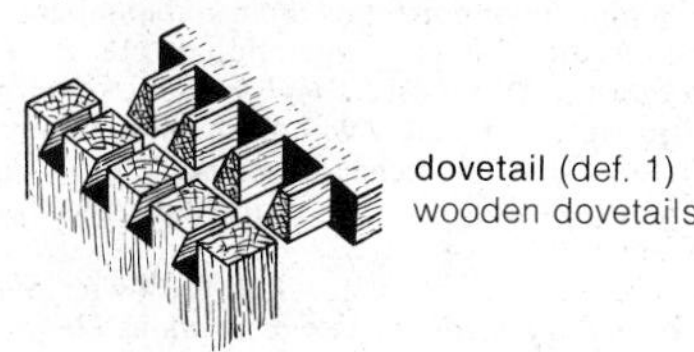
dovetail (def. 1) wooden dovetails

dove tail (duv′tāl′), *n.* 1 projection at the end of a piece of wood, metal, etc., that can be fitted into a corresponding opening at the end of another piece to form a joint. 2 the joint formed in this way. —*v.t.* fasten, join, or fit together with dovetails. —*v.i.* fit together exactly: *The various pieces of evidence dovetailed so completely that the mystery was solved at once.*

dov ish (duv′ish), *adj.* 1 like a dove. 2 INFORMAL. eager for peace; advocating a peaceful solution in a conflict.

dow a ger (dou′ə jər), *n.* 1 woman who holds some title or property from her dead husband: *The queen and her mother-in-law, the queen dowager, were both present.* 2 INFORMAL. a dignified, elderly woman, usually of high social position. [< Old French *douagere* < *douage* dower < *douer* endow < Latin *dotare* < *dotem* dowry]

dow dy (dou′dē), *adj.*, **-di er, -di est,** *n., pl.* **-dies.** —*adj.* poorly dressed; not neat; not stylish; shabby. —*n.* woman whose clothes are either shabby or not stylish. [origin uncertain] **—dow′di ly,** *adv.* **—dow′di ness,** *n.*

dow el (dou′əl), *n., v.,* **-eled, -el ing** or **-elled, -el ling.** —*n.* peg on a piece of wood, metal, etc., to fit into a corresponding hole on another piece, so as to form a joint fastening the two pieces together. —*v.t.* fasten with dowels. [Middle English *dowle*]

dow er (dou′ər), *n.* 1 a widow's share for life of her dead husband's property. 2 dowry. —*v.t.* provide with a dower; endow. [< Old French *douaire* < Medieval Latin *dotarium* < Latin *dotare* endow < *dotem* dowry]

down[1] (doun), *adv.* 1 from a higher to a lower place or condition: *They ran down from the top of the hill. I laid down the knife.* 2 in a lower place or condition: *Down in the valley the fog still lingers.* 3 to or in a place or condition thought of as lower: *She lives in New York, but goes down to Florida every winter.* 4 into or in a fallen or inferior position or condition: *You can't keep a good man down.* 5 from an earlier to a later time or person: *The story has come down through the years.* 6 from a larger to a smaller amount, degree, station, etc.: *everyone from the hotel manager down to the bellhop. The temperature has gone down.* 7 actually; really: *Stop talking, and get down to work.* 8 on paper; in writing: *Take down what I say.* 9 in cash when bought: *You can pay $10 down and the rest of the price later.* 10 into a heavier or more concentrated form: *The maple sap was boiled down to a syrup.* **11 down with,** put down; throw down: *Down with tyranny!*
—*prep.* down along, through, or into: *ride down a hill, walk down a street.*
—*adj.* 1 in a lower place or condition: *The sun is down.* 2 going or pointed down: *the down elevator.* 3 sick; ill: *She is down with a cold.* 4 sad; discouraged: *I felt down about my grades.* 5 (of a football) no longer in play. 6 behind an opponent by a certain number of points, etc. 7 in cash when bought: *We made a down payment on a television set.* **8 down and out,** completely without health, money, friends, etc.; wretched; forsaken. **9 down on,** INFORMAL. angry at; having a grudge against.
—*v.t.* 1 put, throw, or knock down: *She downed the medicine in one swallow. He was downed in a fight.* 2 defeat: *Our baseball team downed Lincoln High School.* —*v.i.* lie down; get down.
—*n.* 1 piece of bad luck: *the ups and downs of life.* 2 (in football) a play from scrimmage. A team has four downs to make at least ten yards. 3 a downward movement.
[Old English *adūne,* earlier *of dūne* from (the) hill]

down[2] (doun), *n.* 1 soft feathers: *the down of a young bird.* 2 soft hair or fluff: *the down on a boy's chin.* [< Scandinavian (Old Icelandic) *dūnn*]

down[3] (doun), *n.* Usually, **downs,** *pl.* rolling, grassy land. [Old English *dūn* hill]

down beat (doun′bēt′), *n.* in music: 1 the first beat in a measure. 2 the downward gesture of the conductor's hand to indicate this beat.

down cast (doun′kast′), *adj.* 1 directed downward: *downcast eyes.* 2 dejected; sad; discouraged.

Dow ney (dou′nē), *n.* city in SW California. 88,000.

down fall (doun′fôl′), *n.* 1 a coming to ruin; sudden overthrow; ruin: *the downfall of an empire.* 2 a heavy rain or snow.

DOWEL

down fall en (doun′fô′lən), *adj.* fallen; overthrown; ruined.

down grade (doun′grād′), *n., v.,* **-grad ed, -grad ing,** *adv.* —*n.* 1 a downward slope. **2 on the downgrade,** growing less in strength, power, value, etc.; declining. —*v.t.* lower in position, importance, reputation, etc.: *downgrade an employee. He downgrades people he does not like, in spite of their merits.* —*adv.* downward.

down heart ed (doun′här′tid), *adj.* in low spirits; discouraged; dejected; depressed. **—down′heart′ed ly,** *adv.* **—down′heart′ed ness,** *n.*

down hill (doun′hil′), *adv.* 1 down the slope of a hill; downward. **2 go downhill,** get worse. —*adj.* going or sloping downward: *a downhill race.*

Down ing Street (dou′ning), 1 street in London on which the official residence of the Prime Minister is located. 2 the British government.

down pour (doun′pôr′, doun′pōr′), *n.* a heavy rain.

down range (doun′rānj′), *adv., adj.* along a range in a direction away from the starting point: *The missile soared 2000 miles downrange.*

down right (doun′rīt′), *adj.* 1 thorough; complete: *a downright thief, a downright lie.* 2 plain; positive: *Her downright answer left no doubt as to what she thought.* —*adv.* thoroughly; completely: *They were downright rude to me.*

down shift (doun′shift′), *v.t., v.i.* to shift from a higher to a lower gear. —*n.* a shifting from a higher to a lower gear.

down stage (doun′stāj′), *adv., adj.* toward or at the front of the stage.

down stairs (doun′sterz′, doun′starz′), *adv.* 1 down the stairs. 2 on or to a lower floor. —*adj.* on a lower floor. —*n.* the lower floor or floors.

down stream (doun′strēm′), *adv., adj.* with the current of a stream; down a stream.

down swing (doun′swing′), *n.* 1 a downward movement or trend: *a sharp downswing in sales.* 2 a swinging down.

down-to-earth (doun′tə ėrth′), *adj.* not fanciful; matter-of-fact; practical; realistic.

down town (doun′toun′), *adv., adj.* to or in the central or main business section of a town or city. —*n.* the central or main business section of a town or city.

down trend (doun′trend′), *n.* a declining trend or tendency, especially in business activity.

down trod (doun′trod′), *adj.* downtrodden.

down trod den (doun′trod′n), *adj.* trampled upon; oppressed.

down turn (doun′tėrn′), *n.* downtrend.

down under, Australia and New Zealand.

down ward (doun′wərd), *adv., adj.* 1 toward a lower place or condition. 2 toward a later time.

down wards (doun′wərdz), *adv.* downward.

down wind (doun′wind′), *adj., adv.* in the same direction as the wind.

down y (dou′nē), *adj.,* **down i er, down i est.** 1 made or consisting of soft feathers or hair. 2 covered with soft feathers or hair. 3 like down; soft and fluffy. **—down′i ness,** *n.*

dow ry (dou′rē), *n., pl.* **-ries.** 1 money or property that a woman brings to her husband when she marries him. 2 natural gift, talent, or quality; natural endowment: *Good health and intelligence are a precious dowry.* Also, **dower.** [< Old French *douaire.* See DOWER.]

dowse (douz), *v.i.,* **dowsed, dows ing.** use a divining rod to locate water, etc. [origin unknown] **—dows′er,** *n.*

dox ol o gy (dok sol′ə jē), *n., pl.* **-gies.** hymn or statement praising God. One familiar doxology begins: "Praise God from whom all blessings flow." [< Greek *doxa* glory, praise + *logos* speaking]

Doyle (doil), *n.* Sir **Arthur Conan,** 1859-1930, English writer, author of the Sherlock Holmes detective stories.

doz., dozen or dozens.

doze (dōz), *v.,* **dozed, doz ing,** *n.* —*v.i.* 1 sleep lightly; be half asleep. **2 doze off,** fall into a doze. —*n.* a light sleep; nap. [perhaps < Scandinavian (Danish) *döse* make dull] **—doz′er,** *n.*

doz en (duz′n), *n., pl.* **-ens** or *(after a number)* **-en.** group of 12; 12. [< Old French *dozeine* < *douse* twelve < Latin *duodecim* < *duo* two + *decem* ten]

doz enth (duz′nth), *adj.* the 12th.

DP or **D.P.,** displaced person.

dpt., department.

dr., 1 debit. 2 dram or drams.

Dr. or **Dr,** Doctor.

Dr., 1 debtor. 2 Drive.

drab[1] (drab), *adj.,* **drab ber, drab best,** *n.* —*adj.* 1 lacking brightness or color; dull: *the drab houses of a dingy mining town.* 2 dull brownish-gray. —*n.* a dull brownish gray. [earlier *drap* kind of cloth < Old French. See DRAPE.] **—drab′ly,** *adv.* **—drab′ness,** *n.*

drab[2] (drab), *n.* 1 a dirty, untidy woman; slattern. 2 prostitute. [origin uncertain]

drachm (dram), *n.* 1 dram. 2 drachma.

drach ma (drak′mə), *n., pl.* **-mas, -mae** (-mē) or **-mai** (-mī). 1 the monetary unit of modern Greece, a note or coin equal to 100 lepta and worth about $3^{1}/_{3}$ cents. 2 an ancient Greek silver coin, varying in value. 3 a small ancient Greek weight. [< Latin < Greek *drachmē* handful. Doublet of DRAM.]

Dra co (drā′kō), *n.* a northern constellation, a part of which forms a semicircle around the Little Dipper; Dragon.

draft (draft), *n.* 1 current of air, especially in

a confined space, as a room or a chimney. 2 device for controlling a current of air in a furnace, fireplace, stove, etc. 3 plan; sketch. 4 a rough copy: *I made three different drafts of my theme before I had it in final form.* 5 selection of persons for some special purpose. Men needed as soldiers are supplied to the army by draft. 6 persons selected for some special purpose. 7 act of pulling loads. 8 the quantity pulled. 9 the pulling of a net to catch fish. 10 quantity of fish caught in a net at one time. 11 a heavy demand or drain on anything: *Her long illness was a draft on her resources.* 12 a written order from one person or bank to another, requiring the payment of a stated amount of money. 13 depth of water that a ship needs for floating; depth to which a ship sinks in water, especially when loaded. 14 a single act of drinking: *I emptied the glass at one draft.* 15 amount taken in a single drink; drink or dose. 16 the breathing in of air, smoke, etc. 17 air, smoke, etc., breathed in. 18 the drawing of beer, ale, etc., from a barrel when ordered. Beer is sold on draft and in cans or bottles. 19 (in masonry) a line or border chiseled at the edge of a stone to serve as a guide in leveling the surface.

—*v.t.* 1 make a plan or sketch of. 2 write out a rough copy of. 3 select for some special purpose, especially to conscript for military service. 4 draw off or away.

—*adj.* 1 used for or suited to pulling loads: *a draft animal.* 2 drawn up in rough or sketchy form: *a draft letter.* 3 drawn from a barrel when ordered: *draft beer.* Also, **draught.** [variant of *draught,* Middle English *draht* < Old English *dragan* to draw, drag] **—draft′er,** *n.*

draft ee (draf tē′), *n.* person who is drafted for military service.

drafts (drafts), *n.* the game of checkers. Also, BRITISH **draughts.**

drafts man (drafts′mən), *n., pl.* **-men.** person who makes plans or sketches. A draftsman draws designs or diagrams from which buildings and machines are made. Also, **draughtsman.**

drafts man ship (drafts′mən ship), *n.* work of a draftsman. Also, **draughtsmanship.**

draft y (draf′tē), *adj.,* **draft i er, draft i est.** 1 in a current of air. 2 having many currents of air: *a drafty room.* Also, **draughty. —draft′i ly,** *adv.* **—draft′i ness,** *n.*

drag (drag), *v.,* **dragged, drag ging,** *n.* —*v.t.* 1 pull along heavily or slowly; pull or draw along the ground: *A team of horses dragged the big log out of the forest.* See **draw** for synonym study. 2 pull a net, hook, harrow, etc., over or along for some purpose; search: *drag a lake for fish.* —*v.i.* 1 move along heavily or slowly: *The crippled animal dragged along.* 2 go too slowly: *Time drags when you have nothing to do.* 3 lag in the rear. 4 puff or inhale on a cigarette, pipe, or cigar. 5 U.S. SLANG. take part in a drag race.

drag in, bring (something irrelevant) into a discussion.

drag on or **drag out, a** make or be too slow. **b** make or last too long.

—*n.* 1 net, hook, harrow, etc., used in dragging. 2 act of dragging. 3 thing dragged. 4 anything that holds back; obstruction; hindrance. 5 a low, strong sled for carrying heavy loads. 6 a heavy harrow or other implement drawn over land to level it and break up clods. 7 device for slowing down the rotation of the wheels of a vehicle. 8 the force acting on a body in motion through a fluid in a direction opposite to the body's motion and produced by friction. 9 SLANG. influence. 10 SLANG. a puff or inhalation on a cigarette, pipe, or cigar. 11 SLANG. street: *the main drag.*

[< Scandinavian (Old Icelandic) *draga,* or Old English *dragan*] **—drag′ger,** *n.*

drag gle (drag′əl), *v.,* **-gled, -gling.** —*v.t.* make wet or dirty (a garment, etc.) by dragging it through mud, water, dust, etc. —*v.i.* 1 become wet or dirty by dragging through mud, water, dust, etc. 2 follow slowly; lag behind; straggle.

drag gy (drag′ē), *adj.,* **-gi er, -gi est.** dragging; slow-moving; boring.

drag net (drag′net′), *n.* 1 net pulled over the bottom of a river, pond, etc., to catch fish. 2 net used to catch small game. 3 a means of catching or gathering in: *criminals caught in the police dragnet.*

drag o man (drag′ə mən), *n., pl.* **-mans** or **-men.** (in the Orient) an interpreter. [< Medieval Greek *dragomanos* < Arabic *targumān* < Aramaic]

drag on (drag′ən), *n.* 1 (in old stories) a huge, fierce animal supposed to look like a snake with wings and claws, which often breathed out fire and smoke. 2 a fierce, violent person. 3 a very strict and watchful woman; a stern chaperon. 4 **Dragon,** Draco. [< Old French < Latin *draconem* < Greek *drakōn*] **—drag′on like′,** *adj.*

drag on fly (drag′ən flī′), *n., pl.* **-flies.** any of various large, harmless insects of the same order as damselflies, with long, slender bodies and two pairs of gauzy wings, which prey on flies, mosquitoes, etc.; darning needle; devil's darning needle.

dra goon (drə gün′), *n.* a mounted soldier trained to fight on foot or on horseback. —*v.t.* 1 force (into a course of action, etc.) by rigorous and harassing measures. 2 persecute or oppress. [< French *dragon* dragon, pistol, (later) soldier]

drag race, U.S. race between cars to determine which can accelerate faster over a given distance.

drain (drān), *v.t.* 1 draw off (a liquid) gradually: *That ditch drains water from the swamp.* 2 draw water or other liquid from; empty or dry by draining: *The farmers drained the swamps to get more land for crops.* 3 take away from slowly; use up little by little; exhaust: *The war drained the country of its people and money.* 4 empty by drinking; drink dry: *The thirsty hiker drained the canteen.* —*v.i.* 1 flow off gradually: *The water drains into a river.* 2 become gradually dry; dry by the flowing off of water: *Let the dishes drain on the sink.* 3 get rid of its surplus water; find an outlet for water: *Vast areas of the United States drain into the Gulf of Mexico.* —*n.* 1 channel, trench, or pipe for carrying off water or waste of any kind. 2 anything that drains: *a drain for pus from wounds.* 3 a slow taking away; a using up little by little; draining: *a drain on one's strength.* [Old English *drēahnian.* Related to DRY.] **—drain′er,** *n.*

drain age (drā′nij), *n.* 1 act or process of draining; gradual drawing off or flowing off of water. 2 system of channels or pipes for carrying off water or waste of any kind. 3 what is drained off.

drainage basin, area that is drained by a river and its tributaries.

drain pipe (drān′pīp′), *n.* pipe for carrying off water or other liquid.

hat, āge, fär; let, ēqual, tėrm;
it, īce; hot, ōpen, ôrder;
oil, out; cup, pu̇t, rüle;
ch, child; ng, long; sh, she;
th, thin; ᴛʜ, then; zh, measure;

ə represents *a* in about, *e* in taken, *i* in pencil, *o* in lemon, *u* in circus.

< = from, derived from, taken from.

drake (drāk), *n.* a male duck. [Middle English]

Drake (drāk), *n.* Sir **Francis,** 1540?-1596, English navigator; the first Englishman to sail around the world.

dram (dram), *n.* 1 a small weight. In apothecaries' weight, 8 drams make one ounce; in avoirdupois weight, 16 drams make one ounce. See **measure** for table. 2 fluid dram. 3 a small drink of intoxicating liquor. 4 a small amount of anything. Also, **drachm.** [< Old French *drame* < Latin *drachma.* Doublet of DRACHMA.]

dra ma (drä′mə, dram′ə), *n.* 1 composition in prose or verse written to be acted on a stage or before motion-picture or television cameras, etc., in which a story is told by means of dialogue and action; play. 2 the art of writing, acting, or producing plays. 3 branch of literature having to do with plays. 4 series of happenings in real life that seem like those of a play. 5 dramatic quality; action or excitement. [< Greek *drama, dramatos* play, deed < *dran* do]

Dram a mine (dram′ə mēn′), *n.* trademark for a drug used against motion sickness.

dra mat ic (drə mat′ik), *adj.* 1 of drama; having to do with plays. 2 seeming like a play; full of action or feeling; exciting. See synonym study below. 3 striking; impressive: *a dramatic combination of colors.* **—dra mat′i cal ly,** *adv.*

Syn. 2 **Dramatic, theatrical, melodramatic** often mean having qualities in real life that are suitable to plays or the stage. **Dramatic** suggests exciting the imagination and deeply moving the feelings: *The reunion of the returning veterans and their wives was dramatic.* **Theatrical** suggests artificial or cheap effects and calling directly on the feelings: *Her show of gratitude was theatrical.* **Melodramatic** emphasizes falseness and exaggeration, especially in trying to stir up the feelings: *The paper gave a melodramatic account of the child's rescue.*

dra mat ics (drə mat′iks), *n.* 1 *pl. in form, sing. in use.* art of acting or producing plays. 2 *pl. in form and use.* plays given by amateurs. 3 *pl. in form and use.* INFORMAL. tendency to show off.

dram a tis per so nae (dram′ə tis pər sō′nē), characters or actors in a play. [< Latin]

dram a tist (dram′ə tist), *n.* writer of plays; playwright.

dram a tize (dram′ə tīz), *v.t.,* **-tized, -tiz ing.** 1 make a drama of; arrange in the form of a play: *dramatize a novel.* 2 show or express in a dramatic way; make seem exciting and thrilling. **—dram′a ti za′tion,** *n.*

dram a tur gic (dram′ə tėr′jik), *adj.* having to do with dramaturgy.

dram a tur gy (dram′ə tėr′jē), *n.* art of writing or producing dramas. [< Greek *dra-*

matourgia < *drama* drama + *-ourgos* making < *ergon* work]

drank (drangk), *v.* pt. of **drink.**

drape (drāp), *v.,* **draped, drap ing,** *n.* —*v.t., v.i.* 1 cover or hang with cloth falling loosely in folds, especially as a decoration: *The buildings were draped with red, white, and blue bunting.* 2 arrange (clothes, hangings, etc.) to hang loosely in folds: *The designer draped the robe around the model's shoulders.* —*n.* cloth hung in folds: *There were heavy drapes at the windows.* [< Old French *drap* cloth < Late Latin *drappus*]

drap er (drā′pər), *n.* 1 BRITISH. dealer in cloth or dry goods. 2 person who drapes.

dra per y (drā′pər ē), *n., pl.* **-per ies.** 1 hangings or clothing arranged in folds, especially when hung as curtains. 2 the graceful arrangement of hangings or clothing. 3 cloths or fabrics; dry goods.

dras tic (dras′tik), *adj.* 1 acting with force or violence; vigorous. 2 vigorously effective; violent. [< Greek *drastikos* effective < *dran* do] —**dras′ti cal ly,** *adv.*

draught (draft), *n., v.t., adj.* draft. —**draught′er,** *n.*

draughts (drafts; *British* dräfts), *n.* BRITISH. drafts.

draughts man (drafts′mən), *n., pl.* **-men.** draftsman.

draughts man ship (drafts′mən ship), *n.* draftsmanship.

draught y (draf′tē), *adj.,* **draught i er, draught i est.** drafty.

Dra vid i an (drə vid′ē ən), *adj.* of or having to do with a group of intermixed races in southern India and in Ceylon. —*n.* 1 member of any of these races. 2 their languages, constituting a family that includes Tamil and Malayalam.

draw (drô), *v.,* **drew, drawn, draw ing,** *n.* —*v.t.* 1 cause to move by the use of force or effort; pull or drag; haul: *The horses drew the wagon.* See synonym study below. 2 pull out, up, or back: *She drew her hand from her pocket.* 3 cause to come out; take out; get out: *Draw a pail of water from the well.* 4 take out (a pistol, sword, etc.) for action. 5 take; get; receive: *Each partner draws $200 a week as salary.* 6 find out by reasoning; infer: *draw a conclusion.* 7 make; cause; bring: *Your actions draw praise or blame on yourself.* 8 attract: *A parade draws a crowd.* 9 make a picture or likeness of with pencil, pen, chalk, crayon, etc.: *draw a circle.* 10 describe: *fully drawn characters in a novel.* 11 write out in proper form; frame; draft: *draw a deed.* 12 write (an order to pay money): *draw a check.* 13 breathe in; inhale: *draw a deep breath.* 14 make the same score in (a game); finish with neither side winning. 15 make long or longer; stretch: *draw out a rubber band.* 16 make small or smaller; shrink. 17 sink to a depth of; need for floating: *A ship draws more water when it is loaded than when it is empty.* 18 take out the insides of: *The cook drew the chicken before cooking it.* 19 draw by lot; get by chance: *Each player in the game drew five cards.* 20 cause the flow of (blood, pus, etc.) to or through a part: *A hot poultice was used to draw the boil.* 21 temper (steel) by reheating. —*v.i.* 1 come or go; move: *We drew near the fire to get warm.* 2 take out a pistol, sword, etc., for action. 3 make a picture or likeness with pencil, pen, chalk, crayon, etc.; make drawings. 4 make a demand; be a drain: *The noisy students drew on the teacher's patience.* 5 become long or longer; stretch. 6 become small or smaller; shrink. 7 make a current of air to carry off smoke. 8 make the same score in a game; finish with neither side winning. 9 attract.

draw on, a come near; approach: *Evening drew on.* **b** take money or supplies from: *draw on the company for expenses.*

draw oneself up, stand up straight.

draw out, persuade to talk: *draw out a shy person.*

draw up, a arrange in order. **b** write out in proper form: *draw up a will.* **c** stop; pull up. —*n.* 1 act of drawing: *The gunman was quick on the draw.* 2 anything that attracts. 3 a tie in a game. If neither side wins, it is a draw. 4 a drawing of lots; lottery. 5 the lot drawn. 6 a part of a drawbridge that can be moved. 7 a small land basin into or through which water drains.

[Old English *dragan*]

Syn. *v.t.* 1 **Draw, drag, haul** mean to pull. **Draw** suggests smoothness or ease of movement: *I drew a chair to the table.* **Drag** suggests resistance and means to pull with force, sometimes slowly: *We dragged the piano from the corner of the room.* **Haul** suggests pulling or moving something very heavy, often in a large vehicle: *Two engines are needed to haul trains over the mountains.*

draw back (drô′bak′), *n.* anything that retards progress or takes from success or satisfaction; hindrance; disadvantage.

draw bar (drô′bär′), *n.* 1 bar on the back of a tractor to which implements are attached. 2 an iron rod with a hole at each end, formerly used as a coupling for railroad cars.

draw bridge (drô′brij′), *n.* bridge that can be entirely or partly lifted, lowered, or moved to one side. In old castles drawbridges were lifted to keep out enemies. A drawbridge over a river is lifted to let tall boats pass.

draw ee (drô ē′), *n.* person for whom an order to pay money is written.

drawer (drôr *for 1 and 4;* drô′ər *for 2 and 3*), *n.* 1 box with handles built to slide in and out of a table, desk, or bureau. 2 person or thing that draws. 3 person who writes an order to pay money. 4 **drawers,** *pl.* undergarment fitting over the legs and around the waist.

draw ing (drô′ing), *n.* 1 picture, sketch, plan, or design done with pencil, pen, chalk, crayon, etc. 2 act or art of making such a picture, sketch, etc.; representing objects by lines. 3 lottery.

drawing board, board on which paper can be fastened for drawing.

drawing card, person or thing that attracts people to a show, event, etc.

drawing room, 1 room for receiving or entertaining guests; parlor. 2 a private compartment for several people in a railroad sleeping car. 3 a formal reception. [short for *withdrawing room*]

draw knife (drô′nīf′), *n., pl.* **-knives.** a woodworking tool having a blade with a handle at each end, used to shave off surfaces by drawing toward the body; drawshave.

drawl (drôl), *v.t., v.i.* talk in a slow way; speak or say slowly, drawing out the vowels. —*n.* a slow way of talking; speech of someone who drawls. [apparently < Dutch *dralen* linger, delay] —**drawl′er,** *n.* —**drawl′ing ly,** *adv.*

drawn (drôn), *v.* pp. of **draw.** —*adj.* made tense; strained: *His face was drawn with pain.*

drawn butter, U.S. melted butter used as a sauce.

drawn work, ornamental work done by drawing threads from a fabric, the remaining portions usually being formed into patterns by needlework.

draw shave (drô′shāv′), *n.* drawknife.

draw string (drô′string′), *n.* string or cord run through the folded border of a bag, garment, etc., so that it can be tightened or loosened.

draw tube (drô′tüb′, drô′tyüb′), *n.* tube sliding within another tube, such as the tube carrying the eyepiece in a microscope.

dray (drā), *n.* a low, strong cart or wagon for carrying heavy loads. —*v.t.* transport or carry on a cart. [Old English *dræge* dragnet < *dragan* to draw]

dray age (drā′ij), *n.* 1 act of hauling a load on a dray. 2 charge for hauling a load on a dray.

dray man (drā′mən), *n., pl.* **-men.** man who drives a dray.

dread (dred), *v.t.* 1 fear greatly; feel terror or uneasiness about: *I dreaded my visits to the dentist. My cat dreads water.* 2 ARCHAIC. regard with awe. —*v.i.* feel great fear. —*n.* 1 great fear; feeling of terror or uneasiness, especially about what is to happen. See **fear** for synonym study. 2 person or thing inspiring fear. 3 ARCHAIC. awe. —*adj.* 1 dreaded; fearful; terrible. 2 held in awe; awe-inspiring. [Old English *drǣdan*]

dread ful (dred′fəl), *adj.* 1 causing dread; fearful; terrible. 2 very bad; very unpleasant: *a dreadful cold.* —**dread′ful ness,** *n.*

dread ful ly (dred′fə lē), *adv.* 1 in a dreadful manner. 2 very; exceedingly.

dread nought or **dread naught** (dred′nôt′), *n.* a large powerful battleship with heavy armor and large guns. [< *Dreadnought,* a British battleship launched in 1906, first of its type]

dream (drēm), *n., v.,* **dreamed** or **dreamt, dream ing.** —*n.* 1 images passing through the mind during sleep. 2 something as unreal as a dream. 3 condition in which a person has dreams. 4 something having great beauty or charm. 5 daydream; reverie. —*v.t.* 1 imagine mentally during sleep. 2 think of (something) as possible; imagine. 3 spend in

hat, āge, fär; let, ēqual, tėrm;
it, īce; hot, ōpen, ôrder;
oil, out; cup, pu̇t, rüle;
ch, child; ng, long; sh, she;
th, thin; ᴛʜ, then; zh, measure;

ə represents *a* in about, *e* in taken, *i* in pencil, *o* in lemon, *u* in circus.

< = from, derived from, taken from.

dreaming. 4 **dream up,** INFORMAL. create (an invention, etc.) mentally. —*v.i.* 1 have a dream or dreams. 2 have daydreams; form fancies. [Old English *drēam* joy, music] **—dream′less,** *adj.* **—dream′like′,** *adj.*

dream er (drē′mər), *n.* 1 person who dreams. 2 daydreamer. 3 an impractical person; visionary.

dream land (drēm′land′), *n.* 1 place where a person seems to be when he is dreaming. 2 an unreal place. 3 sleep.

dreamt (dremt), *v.* a pt. and a pp. of **dream.**

dream world, world of dreams or illusions.

dream y (drē′mē), *adj.,* **dream i er, dream i est.** 1 full of dreams. 2 like a dream; vague; dim. 3 fond of daydreaming; fanciful; impractical. 4 causing dreams; soothing. 5 SLANG. wonderful; exciting; attractive. **—dream′i ly,** *adv.* **—dream′i ness,** *n.*

drear (drir), *adj.* ARCHAIC. dreary.

drear y (drir′ē), *adj.,* **drear i er, drear i est.** 1 without cheer; dull; gloomy: *a cold, dreary day.* 2 ARCHAIC. sad; sorrowful. [Old English *drēorig*] **—drear′i ly,** *adv.* **—drear′i ness,** *n.*

dredge[1] (drej), *n., v.,* **dredged, dredg ing.** —*n.* 1 machine with a scoop or series of buckets for cleaning out or deepening a harbor or channel or for excavating. 2 apparatus with a net, used for gathering oysters, etc. It is dragged along the bottom of a river or the sea. 3 boat equipped for dredging. —*v.t.* 1 clean out, deepen, or excavate with a dredge. 2 bring up or gather with a dredge. 3 dig up; collect: *dredge up all the facts.* —*v.i.* use a dredge. [origin uncertain] **—dredg′er,** *n.*

dredge[2] (drej), *v.t.,* **dredged, dredg ing.** sprinkle: *dredge meat with flour.* [apparently < Middle English *dredge,* noun, grain mixture < Old French *dragie* sweetmeats < Latin *tragemata* < Greek, spices]

D region, the lowest region of the ionosphere; D layer. See **atmosphere** for diagram.

dregs (dregz), *n.pl.* 1 the solid bits of matter that settle to the bottom of a liquid: *the dregs of a coffee pot.* 2 the least desirable part. [< Scandinavian (Old Icelandic) *dregg,* singular]

Drei ser (drī′sər, drī′zər), *n.* **Theodore,** 1871-1945, American novelist.

drench (drench), *v.t.* 1 wet thoroughly; soak: *A heavy rain drenched the campers.* See **wet** for synonym study. 2 compel (an animal) to swallow a medicine. —*n.* 1 a thorough wetting; soaking. 2 something that drenches; solution for soaking. 3 draft of medicine given to an animal. [Old English *drencan* < *drincan* to drink]

Dres den (drez′dən), *n.* city in SE East Germany, on the Elbe River. 501,000.

Dresden china, kind of fine china originally made near Dresden.

dress (dres), *n., adj., v.,* **dressed** or **drest, dress ing.** —*n.* 1 an outer garment worn by women, girls, and babies. 2 an outer covering, as the feathers of birds. 3 clothes; clothing. See **clothes** for synonym study. 4 formal clothes: *in full dress.* 5 the outward form under which anything is presented.
—*adj.* 1 of or for a dress. 2 of or for formal dress: *a dress shirt.* 3 characterized by formal dress.
—*v.t.* 1 put clothes on. 2 put formal clothes on. 3 decorate; adorn: *dress a store window.* 4 make ready for use (food, skins, ore, timber, soil, etc.) by subjecting to some particular process: *dress a chicken, dress a sheepskin.* 5 comb, brush, and arrange (hair). 6 put medicine, bandages, etc., on (a wound or sore). 7 form in a straight line: *The soldiers dressed ranks.* 8 smooth; finish: *to dress leather.* 9 **dress down, a** scold; rebuke. **b** beat; thrash. —*v.i.* 1 put clothes on oneself. 2 put on formal clothes. 3 wear clothes properly and attractively: *Some people don't know how to dress.* 4 **dress up, a** put on one's best clothes. **b** put on formal clothes. [< Old French *dresser* arrange < Popular Latin *directiare* < Latin *directum* directed. See DIRECT.]

dres sage (dres′ij; *French* dre säzh′), *n.* the guiding of a horse through various paces, postures, etc., without using reins or noticeable signals. [< French]

dress circle, circle or section of seats in a theater, originally reserved for persons in formal dress.

dress er[1] (dres′ər), *n.* 1 person who dresses (himself, another person, a shop window, etc.). 2 tool or machine to prepare things for use.

dress er[2] (dres′ər), *n.* 1 piece of furniture with drawers for clothes and usually a mirror; bureau. 2 piece of furniture with shelves for dishes. 3 OBSOLETE. table on which to get food ready for serving. [< Middle French *dresseur* < *dresser* arrange. See DRESS.]

dress ing (dres′ing), *n.* 1 medicine, bandage, etc., put on a wound or sore. 2 mixture of bread crumbs, seasoning, etc., used to stuff chicken, turkey, etc. 3 sauce for salads, fish, meat, etc. 4 fertilizer. 5 act of one that dresses.

dress ing-down (dres′ing doun′), *n.* INFORMAL. 1 a scolding; rebuke. 2 a beating, thrashing.

dressing gown, a loose robe worn while dressing or resting.

dressing room, room in which to dress, especially one in a theater for actors to put on make-up and costume.

dressing table, table with a mirror, at which a person sits to comb the hair, put on make-up, etc.; vanity.

dress mak er (dres′mā′kər), *n.* person whose work is making dresses, etc.

dress mak ing (dres′mā′king), *n.* act or occupation of making dresses, etc.

dress parade, a formal parade of soldiers, sailors, etc., in dress uniform.

dress rehearsal, rehearsal of a play with costumes and scenery just as for a regular performance.

dress suit, a man's suit worn on formal occasions, especially in the evening.

dress y (dres′ē), *adj.,* **dress i er, dress i est.** INFORMAL. 1 fond of wearing showy clothes. 2 stylish; fashionable. **—dress′i ness,** *n.*

drest (drest), *v.* a pt. and a pp. of **dress.**

drew (drü), *v.* pt. of **draw.**

Drey fus (drā′fəs, drī′fəs), *n.* **Alfred,** 1859-1935, French army officer of Jewish birth who was convicted of treason in 1894, but was proved innocent in 1906.

drib ble (drib′əl), *v.,* **-bled, -bling,** *n.* —*v.i.* 1 flow in drops or small amounts; trickle; drip: *Gasoline dribbled from the leak in the tank.* 2 let saliva run from the mouth; drool. 3 (in various games) move a ball or advance with it by kicking or bouncing it rapidly so as to keep control of it. —*v.t.* 1 let flow in drops or small amounts; trickle. 2 (in various games) propel (a ball) by dribbling to keep control of it. —*n.* 1 a dropping; dripping; trickle. 2 a very light rain; drizzle. 3 act of dribbling a ball. [< dialectal *drib,* variant of *drip*] **—drib′bler,** *n.*

drib let (drib′lit), *n.* a small amount.

dried (drīd), *v.* pt. and pp. of **dry.**

dri er (drī′ər), *adj.* comparative of **dry.** —*n.* 1 person or thing that dries. 2 substance mixed with paint, varnish, ink, etc., to make it dry more quickly; dryer.

dries (drīz), *v.* third person singular, present tense of **dry.**

dri est (drī′ist), *adj.* superlative of **dry.**

drift (drift), *v.t.* 1 carry along by currents of water or air: *The wind drifted the boat onto the rocks.* 2 pile up; heap up: *The wind drifted the snow.* —*v.i.* 1 be carried along by currents of water or air: *A raft drifts if it is not steered.* 2 move or appear to move aimlessly: *People drifted in and out of the meeting.* 3 go along without knowing or caring where one is going: *Some people have a purpose in life; others just drift.* 4 be piled into heaps: *The snow is drifting.*
—*n.* 1 a drifting. 2 direction of drifting. 3 tendency or trend: *The drift of opinion was against war.* 4 direction of thought; meaning: *I did not quite get the drift of what you said.* 5 sand, gravel, rocks, etc., moved from one place and left in another by a river, glacier, etc. 6 snow, sand, etc., heaped up by the wind. 7 current of water or air caused by the wind. 8 the sideways movement of an aircraft or ship off its projected course due to cross-currents of air or water. 9 distance that a ship or aircraft is off course because of currents of air or water. 10 an almost horizontal passageway in a mine along a vein of ore, coal, etc.
[Middle English, a driving < Old English *drīfan* to drive] **—drift′er,** *n.*

drift age (drif′tij), *n.* 1 a drifting. 2 the distance drifted. 3 what has drifted; material that drifts around in water or is washed up on the shore.

drift wood (drift′wu̇d′), *n.* wood carried along by water or washed ashore.

drill[1] (dril), *n.* 1 tool or machine for boring holes. 2 teaching or training by having the

drill[1] (def. 1)
It has two handles so that it may be used vertically or horizontally. The cutting part, or bit, works like an auger.

learner do a thing over and over again for practice. See **exercise** for synonym study. 3 group instruction and training in physical exercises or in marching, handling a gun, and other duties of soldiers. 4 any of numerous marine snails that bore into and destroy oysters and other mollusks. —*v.t.* 1 bore a hole in; pierce with a drill. 2 teach by having the learner do a thing over and over. 3 cause to do military or physical exercises. —*v.i.* 1 use a drill; pierce with a drill. 2 be taught or trained by doing a thing over and over again. 3 take part in military or physical exercises. [< Dutch *dril* < *drillen* to bore (a hole)] **—drill′er,** *n.*

drill[2] (dril), *n.* 1 machine for planting seeds in rows. It makes a small hole or furrow, drops the seed, and then covers it. 2 a small furrow to plant seeds in. —*v.t.* plant in small furrows. [origin uncertain]

drill[3] (dril), *n.* a strong, twilled cotton or linen cloth, used for overalls, linings, etc.; drilling. [short for *drilling* < German *Drillich*]

drill[4] (dril), *n.* a black-faced baboon of western Africa, of the same genus as the mandrill but smaller. [probably < an African name]

drill ing (dril′ing), *n.* drill[3].

drill mas ter (dril′mas′tər), *n.* 1 officer who drills soldiers in marching, handling rifles, etc. 2 person who drills others in anything.

drill press, a machine tool for drilling holes, especially in metal.

dri ly (drī′lē), *adv.* dryly.

drink (dringk), *v.,* **drank** or (ARCHAIC) **drunk, drunk** or (ARCHAIC) **drunk en, drink ing,** *n.* —*v.t.* 1 swallow (water or other liquid). See synonym study below. 2 take and hold; absorb: *The dry ground drank up the rain.* 3 swallow the contents of (a cup, etc.): *Drink a cup of tea.* 4 **drink in,** take in through the senses with eagerness and pleasure: *Our ears drank in the music.* 5 **drink to,** drink in honor of; drink with good wishes for. —*v.i.* 1 swallow water or other liquid. 2 drink alcoholic liquor. 3 drink alcoholic liquor to excess. —*n.* 1 liquid swallowed or to be swallowed. 2 portion of a liquid: *Please give me a drink of milk.* 3 alcoholic liquor. 4 too much drinking of alcoholic liquor. [Old English *drincan*]

Syn. *v.t.* 1 **Drink, sip, imbibe** mean to swallow a liquid. **Drink** is the general word: *A person or animal must drink water in order to stay alive.* **Sip** means to drink little by little: *One should sip, not gulp, very hot liquids.* **Imbibe** is now more frequently used figuratively with the meaning "to absorb": *Her one desire is to imbibe more knowledge.*

drink a ble (dring′kə bəl), *adj.* fit to drink. —*n.* something to drink.

drink er (dring′kər), *n.* 1 person who drinks. 2 person who drinks alcoholic liquor often or too much.

Drink wa ter (dringk′wô′tər, dringk′-wot′ər), *n.* **John,** 1882-1937, English dramatist, poet, and critic.

drip (drip), *v.,* **dripped** or **dript, drip ping,** *n.* —*v.i.* 1 fall in drops. 2 be so wet that drops fall: *dripping with perspiration.* —*v.t.* let fall in drops. —*n.* 1 a falling in drops. 2 liquid that falls in drops. 3 part that projects to keep water off the parts below. 4 SLANG. person considered to be objectionable. [Old English *dryppan* < *dropa* a drop]

drip-dry (drip′drī′), *v.,* **-dried, -dry ing,** *adj.* —*v.i., v.t.* wash and hang to dry without wringing and with little or no ironing: *drip-dry a shirt.* —*adj.* that can be drip-dried; wash-and-wear.

dripping pan, pan put under roasting meat to catch the drippings.

drip pings (drip′ingz), *n.pl.* the melted fat and juice that have dripped down from meat while it was being cooked.

dript (dript), *v.* a pt. and a pp. of **drip.**

drive (drīv), *v.,* **drove, driv en, driv ing,** *n.* —*v.t.* 1 make go: *Drive the dog away.* 2 make go where one wishes; direct the movement of: *drive a car, drive a team of horses.* 3 carry in an automobile, carriage, etc.: *drive someone to the station.* 4 force; urge on: *Hunger drove them to steal.* 5 carry out with vigor; bring about: *drive a bargain.* 6 compel to work hard. 7 direct by a blow or thrust: *drive a nail into a board.* 8 set in motion; supply power for: *The wind drives the windmill.* 9 (in sports) hit very hard and fast: *drive a golf ball.* 10 get or make by drilling, boring, etc.: *drive a well.* 11 **drive at,** mean; intend: *What are you driving at?* 12 **let drive,** strike; aim: *The fighter let drive a left to the jaw.* —*v.i.* 1 direct the movement of an automobile, etc.: *Can you drive?* 2 go in an automobile, carriage, etc.: *drive through the mountains.* 3 work hard. 4 move along quickly; dash or rush with force: *The ship drove on the rocks.* 5 to aim; strike.

—*n.* 1 trip in an automobile, carriage, etc.: *a Sunday drive in the country.* See **ride** for synonym study. 2 road to drive on. 3 a driving force; pressure: *The craving for approval is a strong drive in people.* 4 vigor; energy: *a person with drive.* 5 a special effort of a group for some purpose; campaign: *a drive to get money for charity.* 6 (in sports) a very hard, fast hitting of a ball. 7 a military attack, often a large-scale, forceful attack. 8 act of driving: *a drive of cattle.* 9 the thing or things driven. 10 part that drives machinery. 11 the means by which power is transmitted to the wheels in a motor vehicle: *rear-wheel drive.* [Old English *drīfan*]

drive-in (drīv′in′), *adj.* arranged and equipped so that customers may drive in and be served or entertained while remaining seated in their cars: *a drive-in movie theater, a drive-in bank.* —*n.* place so arranged and equipped.

driv el (driv′əl), *v.,* **-eled, -el ing** or **-elled, -el ling,** *n.* —*v.i.* 1 let saliva run from the mouth; dribble; slaver. 2 talk in a stupid, foolish manner; talk nonsense. —*v.t.* say in a stupid, foolish manner. —*n.* 1 saliva running from the mouth. 2 silly talk; nonsense. [Old English *dreflian*] **—driv′el er, driv′el ler,** *n.*

driv en (driv′ən), *v.* pp. of **drive.**

driv er (drī′vər), *n.* 1 person or thing that drives. 2 person who drives an automobile, carriage, etc. 3 person who makes people under him work very hard. 4 a golf club with a wooden head, used in hitting the ball off the tee.

drive shaft, a shaft that transmits power from an engine to the various working parts of a machine, especially used as a device in an automobile connecting the transmission and the rear axle.

drive way (drīv′wā′), *n.* road to drive on, leading from a house, garage, or other building to the road.

driz zle (driz′əl), *v.,* **-zled, -zling,** *n.* —*v.i.* 1 rain gently, in very small drops like mist. 2 fall in fine drops. —*v.t.* shed or let fall in very small drops. —*n.* very small drops of rain like mist. [perhaps Middle English *dresen* to fall, Old English *drēosan*]

driz zly (driz′ə lē), *adj.,* **-zli er, -zli est.** having overcast skies and a light rain.

drogue (drōg), *n.* parachute for decelerating or stabilizing an aircraft while in flight. [variant of *drag*]

droll (drōl), *adj.* odd and amusing; quaint and laughable: *a monkey's droll tricks.* [< French *drôle*] **—droll′ness,** *n.*

droll er y (drō′lər ē), *n., pl.* **-er ies.** 1 something odd and amusing; laughable trick. 2 quaint humor. 3 a jesting; joking.

drol ly (drōl′lē), *adv.* amusingly.

drom e dar y (drom′ə der′ē, drum′ə-der′ē), *n., pl.* **-dar ies.** a swift camel with one hump and short hair, specially reared and trained for riding, found in parts of India, Arabia, and northern Africa; Arabian camel. [< Late Latin *dromedarius* < Greek *dromados (kamēlos)* running (camel) < *dromos* a running]

drone (drōn), *n., v.,* **droned, dron ing.** —*n.* 1 the male of certain bees, especially the honeybee, which has no sting and does no work. 2 a deep, continuous humming sound: *the drone of airplane motors.* 3 person not willing to work; idler; loafer. 4 a pilotless aircraft or vessel directed by remote control. 5 one of the bass pipes of a bagpipe, giving forth continuous tones. —*v.i.* 1 make a deep, continuous humming sound: *Bees droned among the flowers.* 2 talk in a dull, monotonous voice. 3 spend time idly; loaf. —*v.t.* say in a dull, monotonous voice: *drone a prayer.* [Old English *drān*]

drool (drül), *v.i.* 1 let saliva run from the mouth as a baby does; drivel. 2 SLANG. talk foolishly. —*n.* 1 saliva running from the mouth. 2 SLANG. foolish talk. [apparently alteration of *drivel*]

droop (drüp), *v.i.* 1 hang down; bend down. 2 become weak; lose strength and energy. 3 become discouraged or depressed; be sad and gloomy. —*v.t.* let hang down. —*n.* a drooping position. [< Scandinavian (Old Icelandic) *drūpa*] **—droop′ing ly,** *adv.*

droop y (drü′pē), *adj.,* **droop i er, droop i est.** 1 hanging down; drooping. 2 discouraged; depressed.

drop (drop), *n., v.,* **dropped** or **dropt, drop ping.** —*n.* 1 a small amount of liquid in a somewhat round shape: *a drop of rain, a drop of blood.* 2 a very small amount of liquid: *Take a few drops of this medicine.* 3 **drops,** *pl.* liquid medicine given in drops: *eye drops, nose drops.* 4 a very small amount of anything: *a drop of kindness.* 5 anything shaped like a drop. Some earrings or pieces of candy are called drops. 6 a sudden fall: *a drop in temperature, a drop in prices.* 7 distance down; length of a fall: *From the top of the cliff to the water is a drop of 200 feet.* 8 thing arranged to fall or let fall. A letter drop is a slot, usually with a hinged cover. A backdrop on a stage is called a drop. 9 act of letting bombs, supplies, etc., fall from an airplane.

—*v.i.* 1 fall in very small amounts. 2 fall suddenly: *The price of sugar will drop soon.* 3 fall: *It was so quiet you could hear a pin drop.* 4 fall dead, wounded, or tired out. 5 go lower; sink: *Her voice dropped to a whisper.* 6 pass into a less active or a worse condition: *drop off to sleep.* 7 come to an end or stop: *Let the matter drop.* 8 come casually or unexpectedly: *Drop in for a chat sometime.* 9 go with the current or tide: *The raft*

dropped down the river. 10 **drop off, a** go away; disappear. **b** go to sleep. **c** become less; fall; sink. 11 **drop out,** leave school or college before completing a course or a term. —*v.t.* 1 let fall in drops. 2 let fall suddenly. 3 cause to fall: *He dropped his opponent in the first round.* 4 let fall: *I dropped the package.* 5 cause to fall dead; kill. 6 make lower: *Please drop your voice.* 7 let go; dismiss: *Members who do not pay their dues will be dropped from the club.* 8 leave out; omit: *Drop the "e" in "drive" before adding "ing."* 9 stop; end: *The matter is not important; let's drop it.* 10 send (a letter, etc.): *Drop me a card. I'll drop a line to you.* 11 give or express casually: *drop a hint.* 12 set down from a ship, automobile, carriage, etc.: *She dropped her passengers at Main Street.* 13 (of animals) give birth to: *The mare dropped a colt.* 14 lose: *The team dropped four straight games.*
[Old English *dropa*] **—drop′like′,** *adj.*

drop-forge (drop′fôrj′, drop′fōrj′), *v.t.*, **-forged, -forg ing.** beat (hot metal) into shape with a very heavy hammer or weight. **—drop′-forg′er,** *n.*

drop hammer, a very heavy weight lifted by machinery and then dropped on the metal that is to be beaten into shape.

drop kick, kick given to a football just as it touches the ground after being dropped from the hands.

drop-kick (drop′kik′), *v.t.* give (a football) a drop kick.

drop leaf, a hinged table leaf that folds down when not in use.

drop let (drop′lit), *n.* a tiny drop.

drop out (drop′out′), *n.* student who leaves school or college before completing a course or term.

drop per (drop′ər), *n.* 1 a small glass tube with a hollow rubber cap at one end and a small opening at the other end from which a liquid can be made to fall in drops. 2 person or thing that drops.

drop pings (drop′ingz), *n.pl.* dung of animals and birds.

drop si cal (drop′sə kəl), *adj.* 1 of or like dropsy. 2 having dropsy.

drop sy (drop′sē), *n.* edema. [< Old French *idropisie* < Latin *hydropisis* < Greek *hydrōps* < *hydōr* water]

dropt (dropt), *v.* a pt. and a pp. of **drop.**

droshky

drosh ky (drosh′kē), *n., pl.* **-kies.** a low, four-wheeled, open carriage, formerly used in Russia. [< Russian *drozhki,* diminutive of *drogi* wagon]

dro soph i la (drō sof′ə lə), *n., pl.* **-lae** (-lē). any of a genus of fruit flies, especially a species frequently used in experimental studies of heredity. [< New Latin < Greek *drosos* dew + *philos* loving]

dross (drôs, dros), *n.* 1 waste or scum that comes to the surface of melting metals. 2 waste material; rubbish. [Old English *drōs*]

drought (drout), *n.* 1 a long period of dry weather; continued lack of rain. 2 lack of moisture; dryness. Also, **drouth.** [Old English *drūgath.* Related to DRY.]

➤ **drought, drouth.** Both forms are in good use, though *drought* is more usual in formal English.

drought y (drou′tē), *adj.,* **drought i er, drought i est.** 1 showing or suffering from drought. 2 lacking moisture; dry.

drouth (drouth), *n.* drought. ➤ See **drought** for usage note.

drouth y (drou′thē), *adj.,* **drouth i er, drouth i est.** droughty.

drove[1] (drōv), *v.* pt. of **drive.**

drove[2] (drōv), *n.* 1 group of cattle, sheep, hogs, etc., moving or driven along together; flock; herd. 2 many people moving along together; crowd. [Old English *drāf*]

drov er (drō′vər), *n.* 1 man who drives cattle, sheep, hogs, etc., to market. 2 dealer in cattle.

drown (droun), *v.i.* die under water or other liquid because of lack of air to breathe. —*v.t.* 1 kill by keeping under water or other liquid. 2 cover with water; flood. 3 be stronger or louder than; keep from being heard: *The boat's whistle drowned out what she was trying to tell us.* 4 get rid of: *try to drown one's sorrow in work.* [Old English *druncnian.* Related to DRINK.]

drowse (drouz), *v.,* **drowsed, drows ing,** *n.* —*v.i.* be sleepy; be half asleep. —*v.t.* 1 make sleepy. 2 pass (time) in drowsing. —*n.* a being half asleep; sleepiness. [Old English *drūsian* to sink]

drow sy (drou′zē), *adj.,* **-si er, -si est.** 1 half asleep; sleepy. See **sleepy** for synonym study. 2 making one sleepy. 3 caused by sleepiness. **—drow′si ly,** *adv.* **—drow′si ness,** *n.*

drub (drub), *v.t.,* **drubbed, drub bing.** 1 beat with a stick; whip soundly; thrash. 2 defeat by a large margin in a fight, game, contest, etc. [perhaps < Arabic *ḍaraba* he beat] **—drub′ber,** *n.*

drub bing (drub′ing), *n.* 1 a beating. 2 a thorough defeat.

drudge (druj), *n., v.,* **drudged, drudg ing.** —*n.* person who does hard, tiresome, or disagreeable work. —*v.i.* do hard, tiresome, or disagreeable work. [Middle English *druggen* to drudge] **—drudg′er,** *n.*

drudg er y (druj′ər ē), *n., pl.* **-er ies.** work that is hard, tiresome, or disagreeable.

drug (drug), *n., v.,* **drugged, drug ging.** —*n.* 1 substance (other than food) used as a medicine or as an ingredient in medicine, obtained from molds, parts of plants, parts of animals, minerals, etc., or prepared synthetically. Aspirin, antibiotics, and vitamins are drugs. 2 drug that brings drowsiness or sleep, or lessens pain by dulling the nerves; narcotic. Opium is a habit-forming drug. —*v.t.* 1 give drugs to, particularly drugs that are harmful or cause sleep. 2 mix a harmful or poisonous drug in (food or drink). 3 affect or overcome (the body or senses) in a way that is not natural: *drugged by exhaustion.* —*v.i.* take drugs, especially as a habitual practice. [< Middle French *drogue*] **—drug′less,** *adj.*

drug gist (drug′ist), *n.* 1 person who sells drugs, medicines, etc. 2 pharmacist.

drug on the market, article that is too abundant, is no longer in demand, or has too slow a sale.

drug store (drug′stôr′, drug′stōr′), *n.* store that sells drugs and other items.

dru id or **Dru id** (drü′id), *n.* member of a religious order of priests, prophets, and poets among the ancient Celts of Britain, Ireland, and Gaul before the acceptance of Christianity. The druids appear in Welsh and Irish legends as sorcerers and soothsayers. [< Old French *druide* < Latin *druidae* druids < Gaulish]

hat, āge, fär; let, ēqual, tėrm;
it, īce; hot, ōpen, ôrder;
oil, out; cup, pu̇t, rüle;
ch, child; ng, long; sh, she;
th, thin; ᴛʜ, then; zh, measure;

ə represents *a* in about, *e* in taken, *i* in pencil, *o* in lemon, *u* in circus.

< = from, derived from, taken from.

dru id ic or **Dru id ic** (drü id′ik), *adj.* of or having to do with the druids.

dru id i cal or **Dru id i cal** (drü id′ə kəl), *adj.* druidic.

dru id ism or **Dru id ism** (drü′ə diz′əm), *n.* the religion of the druids, or their beliefs and practices.

drum (drum), *n., v.,* **drummed, drum ming.** —*n.* 1 a musical instrument that makes a sound when it is beaten. A drum is a hollow cylinder with a covering stretched tightly over the ends, and is played with sticks, brushes, or the hands. 2 sound made by beating a drum. 3 any sound like this. 4 anything shaped somewhat like a drum. 5 a drum-shaped container to hold oil, food, etc. 6 a thick bar or cylinder on which something is wound in a machine: *a drum of cable.* 7 any of a family of large, spiny-finned American fishes that make a drumming sound. 8 eardrum. 9 the hollow part of the middle ear.
—*v.i.* 1 beat or play a drum. 2 beat, tap, or strike again and again. 3 sound like a drum; resound: *The noise drummed in my ears.* —*v.t.* 1 teach or drive into one's head by repeating over and over: *Algebra had to be drummed into me because I didn't understand it.* 2 **drum out of,** send away from in disgrace. 3 **drum up, a** call together. **b** get by asking again and again; obtain.
[< Dutch or Low German *tromme*] **—drum′like′,** *adj.*

drum beat (drum′bēt′), *n.* sound made when a drum is beaten.

drum head (drum′hed′), *n.* parchment or membrane stretched tightly over one or both ends of a drum. —*adj.* of or resembling a drumhead court-martial.

drumhead court-martial, court-martial on the battlefield or while troops are moving, held in order to try offenders without delay. [because a drumhead often served as a table]

drum lin (drum′lən), *n.* ridge or oval hill formed by glacial drift. [apparently diminutive of Scottish and Irish *drum* long, narrow hill or ridge]

drum major, leader of a marching band.

drum majorette, girl or woman who leads parades, twirling a baton; marjorette.

drum mer (drum′ər), *n.* 1 person who plays a drum. 2 U.S. INFORMAL. traveling salesman.

drum stick (drum′stik′), *n.* 1 stick for beating a drum. 2 the lower half of the leg of a cooked chicken, turkey, etc.

drunk (drungk), *adj.* 1 overcome by alcoholic liquor; intoxicated. 2 very much excited or affected: *drunk with power.* —*n.* 1 person who is drunk. 2 INFORMAL. spell of drinking alcoholic liquor. —*v.* 1 pp. of **drink.** 2 ARCHAIC. a pt. of **drink.**

drunk ard (drung′kərd), *n.* person who is often drunk.

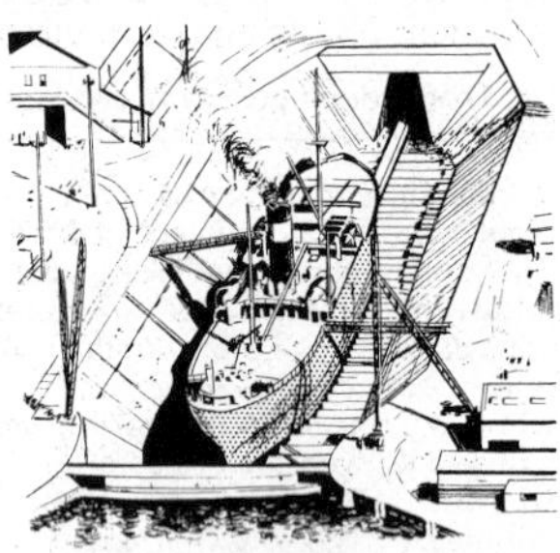

dry dock

drunk en (drung′kən), *adj.* 1 overcome by alcoholic liquor; drunk: *a drunken man.* 2 caused by or resulting from being drunk. 3 often drinking too much alcoholic liquor. —*v.* ARCHAIC. a pp. of **drink.** —**drunk′en ly,** *adv.* —**drunk′en ness,** *n.*

drunk om e ter (drung kom′ə tər), *n.* instrument for measuring the alcohol in the blood by analysis of the breath.

dru pa ceous (drü pā′shəs), *adj.* 1 like a drupe. 2 producing drupes.

drupe (drüp), *n.* fruit whose seed is contained in a hard pit or stone surrounded by soft, pulpy flesh; stone fruit. Cherries and peaches are drupes. [< New Latin *drupa* < Latin *druppa* very ripe olive < Greek *dryppa* olive]

drupe let (drüp′lit), *n.* one of the small drupes of which certain fruits, such as the raspberry, are made up.

dry (drī), *adj.,* **dri er, dri est,** *v.,* **dried, dry ing,** *n., pl.* **drys.** —*adj.* 1 not wet; not moist: *dry clothes.* 2 having little or no rain: *a dry climate.* 3 having little or no natural or ordinary moisture: *a dry tongue.* 4 not giving milk: *That cow has been dry for a month.* 5 containing no water or other liquid: *a dry fountain pen.* 6 wanting a drink; thirsty: *I'm awfully dry after that hike.* 7 not under, in, or on water: *dry land.* 8 not liquid; solid: *dry cargo.* 9 not shedding tears: *dry eyes.* 10 not fresh: *dry bread.* 11 showing no feeling; cold or restrained: *a dry answer.* 12 humorous in an unemotional or somewhat sarcastic way: *dry humor.* 13 not interesting; dull: *a dry subject.* 14 free from sweetness or fruity flavor: *dry wine.* 15 without butter: *dry toast.* 16 without mucus: *a dry cough.* 17 INFORMAL. forbidding the sale of alcoholic drinks: *a dry state.*

—*v.t.* 1 make dry: *dry dishes.* 2 wipe away: *dry one's tears.* 3 evaporate. —*v.i.* 1 become dry: *Clothes dry in the sun.* 2 evaporate.

dry up, a make or become completely dry. **b** SLANG. stop talking.

—*n.* U.S. INFORMAL. person who favors laws against making and selling alcoholic drinks. [Old English *drȳge*] —**dry′ness,** *n.*

dry ad or **Dry ad** (drī′əd, drī′ad), *n., pl.* **-ads, -a des** (-ə dēz). (in Greek myths) a nymph that lives in a tree; wood nymph; hamadryad. [< Greek *Dryades* dryads < *drys* tree]

dry cell, an electric cell in which the chemical producing the current is made into a paste with gelatin, sawdust, etc., so that its contents cannot spill.

dry-clean (drī′klēn′), *v.t.* clean (clothes, etc.) with naphtha, benzine, etc., instead of water.

dry cleaner, person or business that does dry cleaning.

dry cleaning, cleaning of fabrics without water, using liquids such as naphtha and benzine.

Dry den (drīd′n), *n.* **John,** 1631-1700, English poet, dramatist, and critic.

dry dock, dock built watertight so that the water may be pumped out or kept high. Dry docks are used for building or repairing ships.

dry-dock (drī′dok′), *v.t.* place in a dry dock. —*v.i.* go into dry dock.

dry er (drī′ər), *n.* 1 device or machine that removes water by heat, air, etc.: *a hair dryer.* 2 drier (def. 2).

dry-farm (drī′färm′), *v.t., v.i.* grow crops by dry farming.

dry farmer, person who does dry farming.

dry farming, way of farming land in regions where there is no irrigation and little rain by using methods which conserve the soil moisture and by raising crops which survive drought.

dry goods, cloth, ribbon, lace, and similar textile fabrics.

Dry Ice, trademark for a very cold, white solid formed when carbon dioxide is greatly compressed and then cooled. It is used for cooling because it changes from a solid back to a gas without becoming liquid.

dry ly (drī′lē), *adv.* in a dry manner. Also, **drily.**

dry measure, system of units, such as quart and peck, used for measuring the volume of grain, vegetables, fruit, or other solids. See **measure** for table.

dry point, 1 engraving made from a copper plate that has been engraved with a hard needle without using acid. 2 the needle used.

dry rot, 1 decay of seasoned wood, causing it to crumble to a dry powder, caused by various fungi. 2 disease of vegetables and fruits, caused by a fungus which dries and kills the tissue. 3 any of these fungi.

dry run, 1 a practice test or session. 2 any simulated firing practice, bombing approach, etc., without use of ammunition.

dry-shod (drī′shod′), *adj.* having dry shoes; without getting the feet wet.

d.s., 1 (in commerce) days after sight. 2 (in music) from the sign [for Italian *dal segno*].

D.S., Doctor of Science.

D.Sc., Doctor of Science.

D.S.C., Distinguished Service Cross.

D.S.M., Distinguished Service Medal.

D.S.O., Distinguished Service Order.

D.S.T. or **DST,** daylight-saving time.

d.t.'s, INFORMAL. delirium tremens.

du al (dü′əl, dyü′əl), *adj.* 1 consisting of two parts; double; twofold: *The automobile had dual controls.* 2 of two; showing two. [< Latin *dualis* < *duo* two] —**du′al ly,** *adv.*

du al ism (dü′ə liz′əm, dyü′ə liz′əm), *n.* 1 doctrine that mind and matter exist as two separate and distinct substances. 2 doctrine of principles in conflict, one good and one evil.

du al ist (dü′ə list, dyü′ə list), *n.* believer in dualism.

du al is tic (dü′ə lis′tik, dyü′ə lis′tik), *adj.* 1 having to do with or based on dualism. 2 dual.

du al i ty (dü al′ə tē, dyü al′ə tē), *n., pl.* **-ties.** dual condition or quality.

du al-pur pose (dü′əl pėr′pəs, dyü′əl-pėr′pəs), *adj.* 1 for two purposes: *a dual-purpose visit.* 2 (of cattle) raised for both meat and milk. 3 (of poultry) raised for both meat and eggs.

dub[1] (dub), *v.t.,* **dubbed, dub bing.** 1 give a title or nickname to; name; call. 2 make (a man) a knight by striking his shoulder lightly with a sword. 3 make smooth by cutting, rubbing, or scraping. [Old English *dubbian*]

dub[2] (dub), *v.t.,* **dubbed, dub bing.** add music, voices, or other sounds to (a motion-picture film, a radio or television broadcast, a recording, etc.). [short for *double*]

dub[3] (dub), *n., v.,* **dubbed, dub bing.** —*n.* SLANG. a clumsy, unskillful person. —*v.t., v.i.* do or play awkwardly; bungle. [perhaps < *dub*[1]]

Du bai (dü bī′), *n.* capital of the Union of Arab Emirates, in the E part. 60,000.

Du Bar ry (dü bar′ē; dyü bar′ē), **Countess,** 1746?-1793, French mistress of Louis XV of France who had great influence.

du bi e ty (dü bī′ə tē, dyü bī′ə tē), *n., pl.* **-ties.** 1 doubtfulness; uncertainty. 2 something which is doubtful.

du bi ous (dü′bē əs, dyü′bē əs), *adj.* 1 filled with or being in doubt; doubtful; uncertain: *a dubious compliment.* 2 feeling doubt; wavering or hesitating. See **doubtful** for synonym study. 3 of questionable character; probably bad: *a dubious scheme for making money.* [< Latin *dubiosus* < *dubius* doubtful] —**du′bi ous ly,** *adv.* —**du′bi ous ness,** *n.*

du bi ta ble (dü′bə tə bəl, dyü′bə tə bəl), *adj.* liable to doubt or question.

Dub lin (dub′lən), *n.* capital of the Republic of Ireland, in the E part. 569,000.

Du Bois (dü bois′), **W(illiam) E(dward) B(urghardt),** 1868-1963, American sociologist and author.

du cal (dü′kəl, dyü′kəl), *adj.* of or having to do with a duke or dukedom.

duc at (duk′ət), *n.* any of various gold or silver coins of different values, formerly used in Europe. [< Middle French < Italian *ducato,* ultimately < Latin *ducem* leader (because it bore the title of the ruler issuing it)]

du ce (dü′chā), *n.* 1 leader. 2 **Duce,** the title given to Benito Mussolini. [< Italian < Latin *ducem* leader. Doublet of DOGE, DUKE.]

duch ess (duch′is), *n.* 1 wife or widow of a duke. 2 woman with a rank equal to a duke's. [< Old French *duchesse* < *duc* duke. See DUKE.]

duch y (duch′ē), *n., pl.* **duch ies.** territory ruled by a duke or a duchess; dukedom.

duck[1] (duk), *n., pl.* **ducks** or **duck.** 1 any of various wild or tame swimming birds of the same family as geese and swans, with a short neck, short legs, webbed feet, and a broad, flat bill. 2 the female duck. The male is called a drake. 3 flesh of a duck used for food. 4 Often **ducks,** *pl.* BRITISH INFORMAL. a darling; pet. 5 SLANG. a fellow; chap. [Old English *dūce*] —**duck′like′,** *adj.*

duck[2] (duk), *v.i.* 1 dip or plunge suddenly under water and out again. 2 lower the head or bend the body suddenly to keep from being hit, seen, etc. 3 SLANG. get away; make off. —*v.t.* 1 plunge or dip in water momentarily. 2 lower (the head) or bend (the body) suddenly. 3 INFORMAL. get or keep away from; avoid; dodge. —*n.* 1 a sudden dip or plunge under water and out again. 2 a sudden lowering of the head or bending of

hat, āge, fär; let, ēqual, tėrm;
it, īce; hot, ōpen, ôrder;
oil, out; cup, pu̇t, rüle;
ch, child; ng, long; sh, she;
th, thin; ᴛʜ, then; zh, measure;

ə represents *a* in about, *e* in taken, *i* in pencil, *o* in lemon, *u* in circus.

< = from, derived from, taken from.

the body to keep from being hit, seen, etc. [Middle English *duken*]

duck[3] (duk), *n.* 1 a strong cotton or linen cloth, lighter and finer than canvas, used for small sails, tents, and clothing. 2 **ducks,** *pl.* trousers made of duck. [< Dutch *doek* cloth]

duck[4] (duk), *n.* an amphibious truck with a watertight body so that it may move through the water like a boat. [spelling for pronunciation of *DUKW,* its code name]

duck bill (duk′bil′), *n.* duckbilled platypus.

duckbilled platypus—about 1½ ft. long

duck billed platypus (duk′bild′), a small water mammal of Australia and Tasmania that lays eggs and has webbed feet and a bill somewhat like a duck's; platypus.

ducking stool, stool on which a person was tied and ducked into water as a punishment, used in early colonial America.

duck ling (duk′ling), *n.* a young duck.

duck pin (duk′pin′), *n.* 1 a short bowling pin, used in the game of duckpins. 2 **duckpins,** *pl.* game somewhat like bowling, but played with smaller balls and shorter pins.

duck weed (duk′wēd′), *n.* a very small stemless, aquatic plant, often forming a coating on the surface of the water.

duct (dukt), *n.* 1 tube, pipe, or channel for carrying liquid, air, etc. 2 a single pipe or channel for electric or telephone cables. 3 tube in the body for carrying a bodily fluid: *tear ducts.* [< Latin *ductus* a leading < *ducere* to lead] **—duct′less,** *adj.* **—duct′like′,** *adj.*

duc tile (duk′təl), *adj.* 1 capable of being hammered out thin or drawn out into a wire: *Gold and copper are ductile metals.* 2 capable of being easily molded or shaped; pliant: *Wax is ductile when it is warm.* 3 easily managed or influenced; docile.

duc til i ty (duk til′ə tē), *n.* ductile quality.

ductless gland, endocrine gland.

dud (dud), *n.* 1 shell of bomb that fails to explode. 2 SLANG. failure. 3 person or thing that is useless or inefficient. 4 **duds,** *pl.* INFORMAL. **a** clothes. **b** possessions; belongings. [Middle English *dudde*]

dude (düd, dyüd), *n.* 1 man who pays too much attention to his clothes; dandy. 2 (in the western parts of the United States and Canada) person raised in the city, especially an easterner who vacations on a ranch. [origin unknown]

dude ranch, ranch which is run as a tourist resort.

Du de vant (dʏd vän′), *n.* **Amandine,** the real name of **George Sand.**

dudg eon (duj′ən), *n.* 1 a feeling of anger or resentment. 2 **in high dudgeon,** very angry; resentful. [origin unknown]

dud ish (dü′dish, dyü′dish), *adj.* like that of a dude.

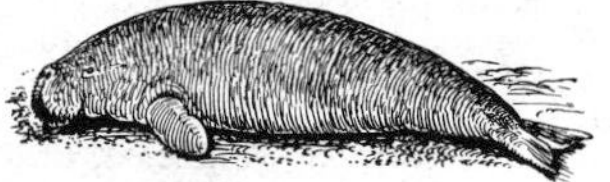

dugong—10 ft. long

Dud ley (dud′lē), *n.* **Robert.** See **Leicester.**

due (dü, dyü), *adj.* 1 owed as a debt; to be paid as a right: *The money due him for his work was paid today.* 2 proper; suitable; rightful: *due reward for good work.* 3 as much as needed; enough: *Use due care in crossing streets.* 4 promised to come or be ready; looked for; expected: *The train is due at noon. Your report is due tomorrow.* 5 (of notes, bills, etc.) becoming payable; having reached maturity; mature. 6 **due to, a** caused by: *The accident was due to careless driving.* **b** INFORMAL. because of; on account of: *The game was called off due to rain.* 7 **fall due,** be required to be paid. *—n.* 1 what is owed to a person; a person's right: *I am asking no more than my due.* 2 **dues,** *pl.* amount of money owed or to be paid to a club, etc., by a member; fee or tax for some purpose. 3 **give a person his due,** be fair to a person. *—adv.* straight; directly; exactly: *travel due west.* [< Old French *deü,* past participle of *devoir* owe < Latin *debere*]

ducking stool

du el (dü′əl, dyü′əl), *n., v.,* **-eled, -el ing** or **-elled, -el ling.** *—n.* 1 a formal fight between two persons armed with pistols or swords. Duels, intended to settle quarrels, avenge insults, etc., are fought in the presence of attendants called seconds. 2 any fight or contest between two opponents: *The two debate teams fought a duel of wits.* *—v.i.* fight a duel. [< Latin *duellum,* early fôrm of *bellum* war] **—du′el er,** *n.*

du el ist (dü′ə list, dyü′ə list), *n.* person who fights a duel or duels.

du en na (dü en′ə, dyü en′ə), *n.* 1 an elderly woman who is the governess and chaperon of young girls in a Spanish or Portuguese family. 2 governess or chaperon. [< earlier Spanish, married woman < Latin *domina* mistress]

du et (dü et′, dyü et′), *n.* 1 piece of music for two voices or instruments. 2 two singers or players performing together. [< Italian *duetto,* diminutive of *duo*]

duff (duf), *n.* a flour pudding boiled in a cloth bag. [variant of *dough*]

duf fel (duf′əl), *n.* 1 a coarse, woolen cloth with a thick nap. 2 camping equipment. [< Dutch < *Duffel,* town near Antwerp, Belgium]

duffel bag, a large canvas sack used by soldiers, campers, etc., for carrying clothing and other belongings.

duff er (duf′ər), *n.* INFORMAL. a clumsy, stupid, or incompetent person.

Du fy (dʏ fē′), *n.* **Raoul,** 1877-1953, French painter.

dug[1] (dug), *v.* pt. and pp. of **dig.**

dug[2] (dug), *n.* nipple; teat. [probably < Scandinavian (Danish) *dægge* suckle]

du gong (dü′gong), *n.* a large herbivorous sea mammal of the coastal waters of southern Asia and Australia, with flipperlike forelimbs and a forked tail; sea cow. It is of the same order as the manatee. [< Malay]

dug out (dug′out′), *n.* 1 a rough shelter or cave dug into the side of a hill, trench, etc., and often reinforced with logs, used for protection against bullets and bombs. 2 a small shelter at the side of a baseball field, used by players who are not at bat or not in the game. 3 a crude boat made by hollowing out a large log.

dui ker (dī′kər), *n.* any of various small South African antelopes. [< Afrikaans *duiker (bok)* diver (buck)]

Duis burg (dʏs′bu̇rk), *n.* city in W West Germany, at the point where the Ruhr and Rhine rivers meet. 458,000.

duke (dük, dyük), *n.* 1 nobleman of the highest title, ranking next below a prince and next above a marquis. 2 prince who rules a duchy. 3 **dukes,** *pl.* SLANG. hands or fists. [< Old French *duc* < Latin *ducem* leader. Doublet of DOGE, DUCE.]

duke dom (dük′dəm, dyük′dəm), *n.* 1 duchy. 2 title or rank of a duke.

dul cet (dul′sit), *adj.* soothing, especially to the ear; sweet or pleasing. [< Latin *dulcis*]

dulcimer

dul ci mer (dul′sə mər), *n.* a musical instrument with metal strings, played by striking the strings with two hammers. [< Old French *doulcemer, doulcemele* < Latin *dulcis* sweet + *melos* song]

dull (dul), *adj.* 1 not sharp or pointed; blunt: *a dull knife.* See synonym study below. 2 not bright or clear; lacking in vividness or intensity: *dull eyes, a dull day.* 3 slow in understanding; stupid: *a dull mind.* See **stupid** for synonym study. 4 having little feeling; insensitive. 5 not felt sharply; vague: *a dull pain.* 6 not interesting; tiresome; boring: *a dull book.* 7 having little life, energy, or spirit; not active: *The fur coat business is usually dull in the summer.* 8 lacking zest; depressed. *—v.t., v.i.* make or become dull. [Middle English *dul*] **—dull′ness, dul′ness,** *n.*

Syn. *adj.* 1 **Dull, blunt** mean without a sharp edge or point. **Dull** suggests that the object described has lost the sharpness it had or is not as sharp as it should be: *This knife is dull.* **Blunt** suggests that the edge or point is not intended to be sharp or keen: *The blunt side of a knife will not cut meat.*

dull ard (dul′ərd), *n.* person who is stupid and learns very slowly.

Dul les (dul′əs), *n.* **John Foster,** 1888-1959, American statesman, secretary of state from 1953 to 1959.

dull ish (dul′ish), *adj.* somewhat dull.

dul ly (dul′lē), *adv.* in a dull manner.

dulse (duls), *n.* any of several coarse, edible seaweeds that have red fronds. [< Irish and Scotch Gaelic *duileasg*]

Du luth (də lüth′), *n.* city in E Minnesota, on Lake Superior. 101,000.

du ly (dü′lē, dyü′lē), *adv.* 1 according to what is due; as due; rightly; suitably: *The documents were duly signed before a lawyer.* 2 when due; at the proper time: *The debt will be duly paid.*

Du mas (dü mä′, dü′mä), *n.* 1 **Alexandre,** 1802-1870, French novelist and dramatist. 2 his son, **Alexandre,** 1824-1895, French dramatist.

dumb (dum), *adj.* 1 not able to speak. 2 silenced for the moment by fear, surprise, shyness, etc.: *She was struck dumb with astonishment.* 3 unwilling to speak; not speaking; silent. 4 INFORMAL. slow in understanding; stupid. 5 not characterized by or accompanied by speech, words, or sound: *dumb gestures.* [Old English] **—dumb′ly,** *adv.* **—dumb′ness,** *n.*

dumbbell (def. 1)

dumb bell (dum′bel′), *n.* 1 a short bar of wood or iron with large, heavy balls or disks at the ends, generally used in pairs for lifting or swinging around to exercise the muscles of the arms, back, etc. 2 SLANG. a very stupid person.

dumb found (dum′found′), *v.t.* dumfound.

dumb show, pantomime.

dumb wait er (dum′wā′tər), *n.* 1 a box with shelves that can be pulled up or down a shaft, used to send dishes, food, rubbish, etc., from one floor of a building to another. 2 a stand to hold food, dishes, etc., placed near a dining table.

dum dum (dum′dum′), *n.* bullet having a soft or hollow nose that spreads out when it strikes, causing a serious wound. [from *Dum Dum,* arsenal near Calcutta, India]

dumdum bullet, dumdum.

dum found (dum′found′), *v.t.* amaze and make unable to speak; bewilder; confuse. Also, **dumbfound.** [< *dumb* + *(con)found*]

dum my (dum′ē), *n., pl.* **-mies,** *adj.* *—n.* 1 a life-size figure of a person used to display clothing in store windows, to shoot at in rifle practice, to tackle in football practice, etc. 2 an empty or imitation package or article used for display or advertising. 3 a sample volume with blank or partly printed pages to show size and general appearance. 4 an imitation; counterfeit. 5 INFORMAL. a stupid person; blockhead. 6 person who has nothing to say or who takes no active part in affairs. 7 person supposedly acting for himself, but really acting for another. 8 in card games: **a** a player whose cards are laid face up on the table and played by his partner. **b** hand of cards played in this way. *—adj.* 1 made to resemble the real thing; imitation: *dummy swords made of wood.* 2 acting for another while supposedly acting for oneself. [< *dumb*]

dump (dump), *v.t.* 1 empty out; throw down in a heap; unload in a mass: *The truck backed up to the hole and dumped the dirt in it.* 2 INFORMAL. get rid of; reject: *dump an unpopular candidate.* 3 sell in large quantities at a very low price or below cost, especially to do this in a foreign country at a price below that in the home country. *—v.i.* unload rubbish. *—n.* 1 place for throwing rubbish. 2 heap of rubbish. 3 SLANG. a dirty, shabby, or untidy place. 4 place for storing military supplies: *an ammunition dump.* [perhaps < Scandinavian (Danish) *dumpe* fall with a thud] **—dump′er,** *n.*

dump ling (dump′ling), *n.* 1 a rounded piece of dough, boiled or steamed and usually served with meat. 2 a small pudding made by enclosing fruit in a piece of dough and baking or steaming it.

dumps (dumps), *n.pl.* INFORMAL. 1 low spirits; gloomy feelings. 2 **in the dumps,** feeling gloomy or sad.

dump truck, truck which can be unloaded of waste, sand, etc., by tipping or by opening downward.

dump y (dum′pē), *adj.,* **dump i er, dump i est.** short and fat; squat. **—dump′i ly,** *adv.* **—dump′i ness,** *n.*

dun[1] (dun), *v.,* **dunned, dun ning,** *n.* *—v.t.* 1 demand payment of a debt from (someone) again and again. 2 pester or plague constantly. *—n.* 1 a demand for payment of a debt. 2 person repeatedly demanding payment of a debt. [< obsolete *dun* make a din < Scandinavian (Old Icelandic) *duna* to thunder]

dun[2] (dun), *adj.* dull, grayish-brown. *—n.* 1 a dull, grayish brown. 2 horse of a dun color. [Old English *dunn*]

Dun bar (dun′bär), *n.* **Paul Laurence,** 1872-1906, American poet.

Dun can (dung′kən), *n.* **Isadora,** 1878-1927, American dancer.

dunce (duns), *n.* 1 child slow at learning his lessons in school. 2 a stupid person. [< *Duns(man),* name applied in ridicule to any follower of John *Duns Scotus* by opponents of his ideas]

dunce cap, a tall, cone-shaped cap formerly worn as a punishment by a schoolchild slow in learning his lessons.

Dun dee (dun dē′), *n.* seaport in E Scotland. 182,000.

dun der head (dun′dər hed′), *n.* a stupid, foolish person; dunce; blockhead. [*dunder* of uncertain origin]

dune—a series of dunes

dune (dün, dyün), *n.* mound or ridge of loose sand heaped up by the wind. [< French < Middle Dutch]

dune buggy, a motor vehicle with very large tires, used on sand.

Dun e din (du nēd′n), *n.* seaport in SE New Zealand. 110,000 with suburbs.

dung (dung), *n.* waste matter from the intestines of animals, much used as a fertilizer. *—v.t.* put dung on as a fertilizer. [Old English]

dun ga ree (dung′gə rē′, dung′gə rē′), *n.* 1 a coarse cotton cloth, used for work clothes, sails, etc. 2 **dungarees,** *pl.* trousers, work clothes, or overalls made of this cloth. [< Hindi *dungrī*]

dung beetle, any of certain beetles that feed on or breed in dung.

dun geon (dun′jən), *n.* 1 a dark underground room or cell to keep prisoners in. 2 donjon. [< Old French *donjon*]

dung hill (dung′hil′), *n.* 1 heap of dung or refuse. 2 a vile place or person.

dunk (dungk), INFORMAL. *—v.t.* dip (something to eat) into a liquid: *dunk doughnuts into coffee.* *—v.i.* dip into water. [< Pennsylvania Dutch *dunken* to dip] **—dunk′er,** *n.*

Dun kirk (dun′kėrk′, dun kėrk′), *n.* seaport in N France where British forces crossed the English Channel to escape the German forces in 1940. 28,000.

dunlin
8 to 9 in. long

dun lin (dun′lən), *n., pl.* **-lins** or **-lin.** a small sandpiper of northern regions that has a broad black patch across the abdomen during the breeding season. [diminutive of *dun*[2]]

dun nage (dun′ij), *n.* 1 a loose packing of branches, mats, etc., placed around a cargo to protect it from damage by water or chafing. 2 baggage or clothes. [origin uncertain]

Dun sa ny (dun sā′nē), *n.* Lord **Edward,** 1878-1957, Irish writer.

Duns Sco tus (dunz skō′təs), **John,** 1265?-1308, English scholastic theologian and philosopher.

Dun stan (dun′stən), *n.* **Saint,** A.D. 925?-988, English churchman and statesman who served as archbishop of Canterbury.

du o (dü′ō, dyü′ō), *n., pl.* **du os.** 1 duet. 2 INFORMAL. pair. [< Italian < Latin, two]

du o dec i mal (dü′ō des′ə məl, dyü′ō-des′ə məl), *adj.* having to do with twelfths or twelve; expressed by twelves. *—n.* 1 one of a system of numerals, the base of which is twelve instead of ten. 2 one twelfth. 3 **duodecimals,** *pl.* system of counting by twelves.

du o de nal (dü′ō dē′nl, dyü′ō dē′nl; dü-od′ə nl, dyü od′ə nl), *adj.* of or having to do with the duodenum: *a duodenal ulcer.*

du o de num (dü′ō dē′nəm, dyü′ō dē′nəm; dü od′ə nəm, dyü od′ə nəm), *n., pl.* **-na** (-nə). the first part of the small intestine, beginning just below the stomach and extending to the jejunum. [< Medieval Latin < Latin *duodeni* twelve each; with reference to its length, about twelve finger breadths]

du o logue (dü′ə lôg, dü′ə log; dyü′ə lôg, dyü′ə log), *n.* 1 dialogue. 2 a dramatic piece in the form of a dialogue.

dup., duplicate.

dupe (düp, dyüp), *n., v.,* **duped, dup ing.** *—n.* 1 person easily deceived or tricked. 2 one who is being deluded or tricked.

—*v.t.* deceive or trick. [< French] **—dup′er,** *n.*

du ple (dü′pəl, dyü′pəl), *adj.* 1 double. 2 (in music) having two or a multiple of two beats to the measure. [< Latin *duplus* double. Doublet of DOUBLE.]

du plex (dü′pleks, dyü′pleks), *adj.* having two parts; double; twofold. —*n.* a duplex house or duplex apartment. [< Latin < *du-* two + *plicare* to fold]

duplex apartment, apartment having rooms on two floors.

duplex house, house built to accommodate two families.

du pli cate (*adj., n.* dü′plə kit, dyü′plə kit; *v.* dü′plə kāt, dyü′plə kāt), *adj., n., v.,* **-cat ed, -cat ing.** —*adj.* 1 exactly like something else: *We have duplicate keys for the front door.* 2 having two corresponding parts; twofold; double: *A person's lungs are duplicate, but he has only one heart.* 3 (in card games) having the same hands played by different players: *duplicate bridge.* —*n.* 1 one of two things exactly alike; an exact copy. 2 **in duplicate,** in two copies exactly alike. —*v.t.* 1 make an exact copy of; repeat exactly. 2 make double or twofold; double. [< Latin *duplicatum* made double < *du-* two + *plicare* to fold]

du pli ca tion (dü′plə kā′shən, dyü′plə-kā′shən), *n.* 1 a duplicating. 2 a being duplicated. 3 a duplicate copy.

du pli ca tive (dü′plə kā′tiv, dyü′plə-kā′tiv), *adj.* having the quality of doubling.

du pli ca tor (dü′plə kā′tər, dyü′plə-kā′tər), *n.* machine for making many exact copies of anything written, typed, or drawn.

du plic i ty (dü plis′ə tē, dyü plis′ə tē), *n., pl.* **-ties.** a secretly acting in one way and openly acting in another in order to deceive; deceitfulness.

Du quesne (dü kān′, dyü kān′), *n.* **Fort,** a former French fort built on the present site of Pittsburgh in 1754.

dur a bil i ty (dùr′ə bil′ə tē, dyùr′ə bil′ə-tē), *n.* lasting quality; ability to withstand wear.

dur a ble (dùr′ə bəl, dyùr′ə bəl), *adj.* 1 able to withstand wear, decay, etc.: *durable fabric.* 2 lasting a long time: *a durable peace.* [< Latin *durabilis* < *durare* to last, harden < *durus* hard] **—dur′a ble ness,** *n.* **—dur′a bly,** *adv.*

Du ral u min (dù ral′yə mən, dyù ral′yə-mən), *n.* trademark for a light, strong alloy of aluminum, copper, manganese, and magnesium.

dur a ma ter (dùr′ə mā′tər; dyùr′ə mā′-tər), the tough, fibrous membrane forming the outermost of the three coverings of the brain and spinal cord. [< Medieval Latin, literally, hard mother (that is, hard source)]

dur ance (dùr′əns, dyùr′əns), *n.* imprisonment. [< Old French, duration]

Du ran go (dü räng′gō), *n.* 1 state in NW Mexico. 2 its capital. 193,000.

du ra tion (dù rā′shən, dyù rā′shən), *n.* 1 length of time; time during which anything continues: *The storm was of short duration.* 2 **for the duration,** until the end, especially of a war: *She enlisted in the Women's Army Corps for the duration.*

Dur ban (dėr′bən, dėr′ban′), *n.* seaport in the SE part of the Republic of South Africa. 683,000.

dur bar (dėr′bär), *n.* an official court or reception held by a native prince of India or formerly, by a British governor or viceroy in India. [< Hindi *darbār* court]

Dü rer (dʏ′rər), *n.* **Albrecht,** 1471-1528, German painter and engraver.

du ress (dù res′, dyù res′; dùr′es, dyùr′es), *n.* 1 use of force; compulsion. The law does not require a person to fulfill a contract signed under duress. 2 imprisonment; confinement. [< Old French *duresse* < Latin *duritia* hardness < *durus* hard]

Dur ham (dėr′əm), *n.* 1 county in NE England. 2 city in N North Carolina. 95,000. 3 shorthorn.

dur i an (dùr′ē ən), *n.* 1 the bad-smelling but edible fruit of a tree of southeastern Asia, with a hard, prickly rind and cream-colored pulp. 2 the tree it grows on. [< Malay]

dur ing (dùr′ing, dyùr′ing), *prep.* 1 through the whole time of; throughout: *We played inside during the storm.* 2 at some time in; in the course of: *Come to see me during my office hours.* [present participle of obsolete *dure* to last < Latin *durare* < *durus* hard]

dur ra (dùr′ə), *n.* species of sorghum with slender stalks that produces grain. [< Arabic *dhura*]

durst (dėrst), *v.* ARCHAIC. a pt. of **dare.**

dur um (dùr′əm, dyùr′əm), *n.* a hard wheat from which the flour used in macaroni, spaghetti, etc., is made. [< Latin, neuter of *durus* hard]

durum wheat, durum.

Du se (dü′zā), *n.* **Eleonora,** 1859-1924, Italian actress.

dusk (dusk), *n.* 1 the darker stage of twilight; time just before dark. 2 shade; gloom. —*adj.* dark-colored; dusky. —*v.t., v.i.* make or become dusky. [Old English *dox* dark]

dusk y (dus′kē), *adj.,* **dusk i er, dusk i est.** 1 somewhat dark; dark-colored. 2 dim; obscure. 3 sad; gloomy. **—dusk′i ly,** *adv.* **—dusk′i ness,** *n.*

Düs sel dorf (dü′səl dôrf; *German* dʏs′əl-dôrf), *n.* city in W West Germany, on the Rhine River. 681,000.

dust (dust), *n.* 1 fine, dry earth: *Dust lay thick on the road.* 2 any fine powder: *The old papers had turned to dust.* 3 earth; ground. 4 cloud of dust floating in the air. 5 what is left of a dead body after decay. 6 low or humble condition. 7 a worthless thing. 8 BRITISH. ashes or refuse. 9 **bite the dust, a** fall dead or wounded. **b** be defeated, dismissed, or eliminated. 10 **shake the dust off one's feet,** go away feeling angry or scornful. 11 **throw dust in one's eyes,** deceive or mislead a person.
—*v.t.* 1 brush or wipe the dust from; get dust off: *dust the furniture.* 2 get dust on; soil with dust. 3 sprinkle (with dust, powder, etc.). [Old English *dūst*] **—dust′less,** *adj.* **—dust′like′,** *adj.*

dust bin (dust′bin′), *n.* BRITISH. receptacle for refuse; garbage can.

dust bowl, area, especially in the western plains of the United States and Canada, where dust storms are frequent and violent.

dust devil, a small whirlwind that stirs up a column of dust, leaves, etc., as it moves along.

dust er (dus′tər), *n.* 1 person or thing that dusts. 2 cloth, brush, etc., used to get dust off things. 3 apparatus for sifting or blowing dry poisons on plants to kill insects. 4 a long, light garment worn over the clothes to keep dust off them. 5 a similar garment worn by women as a dress, especially indoors.

dust jacket, an outer paper cover for protecting a book; jacket.

hat, āge, fär; let, ēqual, tėrm;
it, īce; hot, ōpen, ôrder;
oil, out; cup, pu̇t, rüle;
ch, child; ng, long; sh, she;
th, thin; ᴛʜ, then; zh, measure;

ə represents *a* in about, *e* in taken, *i* in pencil, *o* in lemon, *u* in circus.

< = from, derived from, taken from.

dust man (dust′man′, dust′mən), *n., pl.* **-men.** BRITISH. a garbage collector.

dust pan (dust′pan′), *n.* a flat, broad pan with a handle, onto which dust can be swept from the floor.

dust storm, a strong wind carrying clouds of dust across or from a dry region.

dust up (dust′up′), *n.* INFORMAL. a violent quarrel; commotion; disturbance.

dust y (dus′tē), *adj.,* **dust i er, dust i est.** 1 covered with dust; filled with dust. 2 like dust; dry and powdery. 3 having the color of dust; grayish. **—dust′i ly,** *adv.* **—dust′i ness,** *n.*

Dutch (duch), *adj.* 1 of or having to do with the Netherlands, its people, or their language. 2 German. 3 **go Dutch,** INFORMAL. have each person pay for himself. —*n.* 1 *pl. in use.* the people of the Netherlands. 2 the Germanic language of the Netherlands. 3 *pl. in use.* the people of Germany. The ancestors of the Pennsylvania Dutch came from Germany, not from the Netherlands. 4 SLANG. the German language. 5 **beat the Dutch,** INFORMAL. be very strange or surprising; outdo anything seen or heard of before. 6 **in Dutch,** SLANG. in trouble or disgrace. [< Middle Dutch *dutsch* Dutch, German]
➤ The various derogatory expressions compounded of Dutch, such as *Dutch courage* and *Dutch uncle,* are a legacy from the Dutch-English commercial rivalry of the 1600's and 1700's.

Dutch Borneo, former name of **Kalimantan.**

Dutch courage, INFORMAL. courage brought on by drinking alcoholic liquor.

Dutch door, door divided in two horizontally, so that one half may be open while the other is closed.

Dutch East Indies, islands in the East Indies formerly belonging to the Netherlands, now mostly in Indonesia. Also, **Netherlands East Indies.**

Dutch elm disease, a killing disease of elm trees, caused by fungus and carried by a beetle.

Dutch Guiana, Surinam.

Dutch man (duch′mən), *n., pl.* **-men.** 1 native or inhabitant of the Netherlands; Hollander; Netherlander. 2 SLANG. a German. 3 (in carpentry) a piece driven into an opening to close it, especially in a badly made joint.

Dutch man's-breech es (duch′mənz brich′iz), *n. sing. and pl.* 1 a creamy-white, fragrant wild flower with two slender projections, blossoming in the spring. 2 the plant which bears it, belonging to the same family as the bleeding heart.

Dutch New Guinea, a former name of **West Irian.**

Dutch oven, 1 a metal box that opens in front, used for roasting meat, etc., before an open fire or on top of a stove. 2 a heavy iron kettle with a close-fitting cover. Some Dutch ovens are covered with hot coals and used for baking. 3 a brick oven in which the walls are first heated, and food is put in to cook after the fire goes out or is removed.

Dutch treat, INFORMAL. meal or entertainment at which each person pays for himself.

Dutch uncle, INFORMAL. person who sternly criticizes or severely scolds another.

Dutch West Indies, Netherlands Antilles.

du te ous (dü′tē əs, dyü′tē əs), *adj.* dutiful; obedient. **—du′te ous ly,** *adv.* **—du′teous ness,** *n.*

du ti a ble (dü′tē ə bəl, dyü′tē ə bəl), *adj.* on which a duty or tax must be paid: *Imported perfumes are dutiable.*

du ti ful (dü′tə fəl, dyü′tə fəl), *adj.* 1 performing the duties required of one; obedient: *a dutiful child.* 2 required by duty; proceeding from or expressing a sense of duty: *dutiful words.* **—du′ti ful ly,** *adv.* **—du′tiful ness,** *n.*

du ty (dü′tē, dyü′tē), *n., pl.* **-ties.** 1 thing that is right to do; what a person ought to do; obligation: *It is your duty to obey the laws.* See synonym study below. 2 the binding force of what is right: *A sense of duty makes a person fulfill his obligations.* 3 action required by one's occupation or position; function; business: *the duties of a bookkeeper.* 4 proper behavior owed to an older or superior person; obedience and respect. 5 a tax, especially a tax on articles brought into or taken out of a country. 6 amount of work done or required; power or effectiveness, as of an engine; utility. 7 **off duty,** not at one's work or occupation. 8 **on duty,** at one's work or occupation. [< Anglo-French *dueté* < *du,* variant of Old French *deü.* See DUE.]

Syn. 1 **Duty, obligation** mean what a person ought to do. **Duty** applies to what a person ought to do at all times because it is legally or morally right: *Every person has a duty to his country.* **Obligation** applies more to what is required at a particular time by custom or by an agreement or contract: *A good citizen has certain obligations to society.*

du um vir (dü um′vər, dyü um′vər), *n., pl.* **-virs, -vir i** (-və rī′). either of two men who shared the same public office in ancient Rome. [< Latin < *duum virum* (one) of the two men]

du um vir ate (dü um′vər it, dyü um′vərit), *n.* 1 government by two men together. 2 any association of two in office or authority.

du ve tyn (dü′və tēn′), *n.* a soft, closely woven woolen cloth having a velvety finish. [< French *duvetine* < *duvet* down quilt]

D.V., 1 Douay Version. 2 God willing [for Latin *Deo volente*].

Dvi na River (dvē nä′), 1 river flowing from W Soviet Union into the Gulf of Riga. 640 mi. 2 river flowing from NW Soviet Union into the White Sea. 470 mi.

Dvoř ák (dvôr′zhäk), *n.* **Anton,** 1841-1904, Czech composer.

dwarf (dwôrf), *n., pl.* **dwarfs, dwarves** (dwôrvz), *adj., v.* —*n.* 1 person much below ordinary stature or size. See synonym study below. 2 animal or plant much below the ordinary height or size of its kind or related species. 3 (in fairy tales) an ugly little man with magic power. 4 any of a class of stars of small size and luminosity, including the sun. —*adj.* 1 much smaller than the usual size for its kind; miniature: *dwarf furniture.* 2 belonging to a species much smaller than related species: *a dwarf marigold.* —*v.t.* 1 keep from growing large; check in growth. 2 cause to look or seem small. —*v.i.* become dwarfed or smaller. [Old English *dweorg*] **—dwarf′ness,** *n.*

Syn. *n.* 1 **Dwarf, midget** mean a person very much smaller than normal. **Dwarf** applies particularly to a person whose growth has been stunted and who often has limbs that are very short compared with the head and body, which may be normal in size. **Midget** applies to a tiny person who is perfectly shaped and normal in every way except size.

dwarf ish (dwôr′fish), *adj.* like a dwarf; much smaller than usual. **—dwarf′ish ly,** *adv.* **—dwarf′ish ness,** *n.*

dwarf ism (dwôr′fiz′əm), *n.* condition or character of being a dwarf; a generally underdeveloped condition of growth, especially in the bony tissue of the limbs.

dwell (dwel), *v.i.,* **dwelt** or **dwelled, dwell ing.** 1 make one's home; live. 2 **dwell on** or **dwell upon,** a think, write, or speak about for a long time. b put stress on. [Old English *dwellan* delay] **—dwell′er,** *n.*

dwell ing (dwel′ing), *n.* place in which one lives; house; residence.

dwelling place, dwelling.

dwelt (dwelt), *v.* a pt. and a pp. of **dwell.**

dwin dle (dwin′dl), *v.t., v.i.,* **-dled, -dling.** make or become smaller and smaller; shrink; diminish. See **decrease** for synonym study. [ultimately Old English *dwīnan* waste away]

dwt., pennyweight or pennyweights.

DX, (in radio) distance or distant.

Dy, dysprosium.

dy ad (dī′ad), *n.* 1 group of two; couple. 2 one of the groups of chromosome pairs formed when a tetrad splits. [< Latin *dyadem* two]

dy ad ic (dī ad′ik), *adj.* having to do with a dyad.

Dy ak (dī′ak), *n.* Dayak.

dyb buk (dib′ük), *n.* (in Jewish folklore) a spirit, either a demon or the soul of a dead person, that takes possession of a living person. [< Hebrew *dibbūq* thing that adheres]

dye (dī), *n., v.,* **dyed, dye ing.** —*n.* 1 a coloring matter used to color cloth, hair, etc. A few dyes are derived from vegetable sources; most, however, are produced synthetically. 2 liquid containing such coloring matter: *a bottle of blue dye.* 3 color produced by such coloring matter. —*v.t.* 1 color (cloth, hair, etc.) by dipping in a liquid containing coloring matter. 2 color or stain: *The spilled grape juice dyed the tablecloth purple.* —*v.i.* become colored when treated with a dye: *This material dyes evenly.* [Old English *dēag*]

dyed-in-the-wool (dīd′n ᴛʜə wül′), *adj.* thoroughgoing; complete: *a dyed-in-the-wool conservative in politics.*

dye ing (dī′ing), *n.* the coloring of fabrics with dye.

dy er (dī′ər), *n.* person whose work or business is dyeing cloth, etc.

dye stuff (dī′stuf′), *n.* substance yielding a dye or used as a dye. Indigo and cochineal are dyestuffs.

dye wood (dī′wùd′), *n.* any wood, as logwood, yielding a coloring matter used for dyeing.

dy ing (dī′ing), *adj.* 1 about to die: *a dying old man.* 2 coming to an end: *the dying year.* 3 of death; at death: *dying words.* —*v.* ppr. of **die**[1].

dyke (dīk), *n., v.t., v.i.,* **dyked, dyk ing.** dike.

dy nam ic (dī nam′ik), *adj.* 1 having to do with energy or force in motion. 2 having to do with dynamics. 3 active; energetic: *a dynamic personality.* [< Greek *dynamikos* < *dynamis* power < *dynasthai* be powerful] **—dy nam′i cal ly,** *adv.*

dy nam i cal (dī nam′ə kəl), *adj.* dynamic.

dy nam ics (dī nam′iks), *n.* 1 *pl. in form, sing. in use.* branch of physics dealing with the motion of bodies and the action of forces on bodies either in motion or at rest. 2 *pl. in form, sing. in use.* science of force acting in any field. 3 *pl. in form and use.* the forces at work in any field: *the new dynamics of education.* 4 *pl. in form and use.* variation and contrast of force or loudness in the production of musical sounds.

dy na mism (dī′nə miz′əm), *n.* 1 any of various doctrines or philosophical systems which seek to explain the phenomena of nature by the action of some force. 2 dynamic quality; forcefulness.

dy na mite (dī′nə mīt), *n., v.,* **-mit ed, -mit ing.** —*n.* a powerful explosive made of nitroglycerin and certain other chemicals mixed with an absorbent material and pressed into round paper cylinders, or sticks. It is used in blasting rock, tree stumps, etc. —*v.t.* blow up or destroy, especially with dynamite. **—dy′na mit′er,** *n.*

dy na mo (dī′nə mō), *n., pl.* **-mos.** 1 generator, which turns mechanical energy into electrical energy. 2 motor, which turns electrical energy into mechanical energy. 3 INFORMAL. a dynamic person; live wire. [short for *dynamoelectric machine*]

dy na mo e lec tric (dī′nə mō i lek′trik), *adj.* having to do with the transformation of mechanical energy into electric energy, or electric energy into mechanical energy.

dy na mom e ter (dī′nə mom′ə tər), *n.* apparatus to measure force or power.

dy na mo met ric (dī′nə mō met′rik), *adj.* having to do with a dynamometer or with dynamometry.

dy na mom e try (dī′nə mom′ə trē), *n.* the measurement of force or power.

dy na mo tor (dī′nə mō′tər), *n.* a combined electric motor and dynamo for changing the voltage of an electric current.

dy nast (dī′nast, dī′nəst), *n.* 1 member or founder of a dynasty. 2 any ruler.

dy nas tic (dī nas′tik, də nas′tik), *adj.* having to do with a dynasty. **—dy nas′ti cally,** *adv.*

dy nas ty (dī′nə stē), *n., pl.* **-ties.** 1 succession of rulers who belong to the same family: *The Bourbon dynasty ruled France for more than 200 years.* 2 period of time during which a dynasty rules. [< Greek *dynasteia* power]

dyne (dīn), *n.* amount of force required to give a mass of one gram an acceleration of one centimeter per second for each second the force is applied. [< French < Greek *dynamis* power]

dys en ter ic (dis′ən ter′ik), *adj.* 1 of the nature of dysentery. 2 having dysentery.

dys en ter y (dis′n ter′ē), *n.* disease of the intestines, producing diarrhea with blood and mucus, caused by any of several microorganisms or by irritants. [< Greek *dysenteria* < *dys-* bad + *entera* intestines]

dys func tion (dis fungk′shən), *n.* a functional abnormality or impairment, as of an organ.

dys func tion al (dis fungk′shə nəl), *adj.* 1 having to do with dysfunction. 2 malfunctioning.

dys gen ic (dis jen′ik), *adj.* having to do with or causing degeneration in the type of offspring produced.

dys pep si a (dis pep′sē ə, dis pep′shə), *n.* indigestion. [< Greek < *dys-* bad + *peptein* digest]

dys pep tic (dis pep′tik), *adj.* 1 having to do with dyspepsia. 2 suffering from dyspepsia. 3 gloomy; pessimistic. —*n.* person who has dyspepsia. **—dys pep′ti cal ly,** *adv.*

dys pla sia (dis plā′zhə), *n.* abnormal development or growth of tissues, organs, etc. [< New Latin < Greek *dys-* bad + *plasis* a molding]

dys plas tic (dis plas′tik), *adj.* 1 having to do with displasia. 2 having displasia.

dysp ne a or **dysp noe a** (disp nē′ə), *n.* difficult or labored breathing. [< Greek *dys-* badly + *pnein* breathe]

dysp ne ic or **dysp noe ic** (disp nē′ik), *adj.* 1 of the nature of dyspnea. 2 having dyspnea.

dys pro si um (dis prō′sē əm, dis prō′shē-əm), *n.* a rare-earth metallic element found in various minerals which forms highly magnetic compounds. *Symbol:* Dy; *atomic number* 66. See pages 326 and 327 for table. [< New Latin < Greek *dysprositos* hard to get at]

dys tro phy (dis′trə fē), *n.* 1 defective nutrition. 2 defective development or degeneration. [< Greek *dys-* bad + *trophē* nourishment]

Dyu sham be (dyü shäm′bə), *n.* city in S Soviet Union, capital of Tadzhik S.S.R. 374,000.

dz., dozen or dozens.

hat, āge, fär; let, ēqual, tėrm;
it, īce; hot, ōpen, ôrder;
oil, out; cup, pu̇t, rüle;
ch, child; ng, long; sh, she;
th, thin; ᴛʜ, then; zh, measure;

ə represents *a* in about, *e* in taken, *i* in pencil, *o* in lemon, *u* in circus.

< = from, derived from, taken from.

E e

E[1] or **e** (ē), *n., pl.* **E's** or **e's.** the fifth letter of the English alphabet.

E[2] (ē), *n., pl.* **E's.** the third tone of the musical scale of C major.

e-, *prefix.* form of **ex-**[1] before consonants except *c, f, p, q, s, t,* as in *evaporate, emerge.*

E, 1 East or east. 2 Eastern or eastern. 3 einsteinium. 4 English.

ea., each.

each (ēch), *adj.* being one (of two or more persons, things, etc.) considered separately or one by one. See synonym study below. *—pron.* each one: *Each went his way. —adv.* for each; to each; apiece: *These pencils are ten cents each.* [Old English *ǣlc* < *ā* ever + *gelīc* alike]

Syn. *adj.* **Each, every** mean one and all (of a number or group). **Each** emphasizes that one and all of a number, or one and the other of two, are thought of singly, as individuals: *Each dog has a name* = any one of the dogs in the group has a name of its own. **Every,** relating to a group, means that one and all are included, with no exceptions: *Every dog has a name* = all the dogs in the group have names of their own.

➔ **each.** As a pronoun, *each* is singular: *Each of the three has a different instructor.*

each other, 1 each one the other one: *They struck each other.* 2 one another: *They struck at each other.*

ea ger (ē′gər), *adj.* 1 wanting very much; desiring very strongly. See synonym study below. 2 characterized by or showing keenness of desire or feeling: *eager looks.* [< Old French *aigre* < Latin *acer* keen] **—ea′ger ly,** *adv.* **—ea′ger ness,** *n.*

Syn. 1 **Eager, keen, anxious** mean strongly moved by desire or interest. **Eager** suggests being excited or impatient about something one wants to do or have: *The boys were eager to start building the clubhouse.* **Keen** is more informal and suggests being full of enthusiasm because of great interest or sharp desire: *The team is very keen to beat its old rival this year.* **Anxious** sometimes suggests fear of being disappointed and not getting what is wanted: *She is anxious that we should all like her new friend.*

eager beaver, U.S. INFORMAL. an overly hard-working, ambitious, or enthusiastic person.

eagle (def. 2)

ea gle (ē′gəl), *n.* 1 any of a group of large birds of prey of the same family as hawks, that have hooked beaks, keen eyesight, and powerful wings. The bald eagle is the national emblem of the United States. 2 figure or representation of an eagle, often used as an emblem on a flag, coat of arms, coin, stamp, etc. 3 standard bearing such a figure, especially the standard of the ancient Roman army. 4 a former gold coin of the United States, worth $10. 5 two strokes less than par for any hole on a golf course. 6 **Eagle,** Aquila. *—adj.* like that of an eagle: *the eagle eye of the scout.* [< Old French *egle* < Latin *aquila*]

ea glet (ē′glit), *n.* a young eagle.

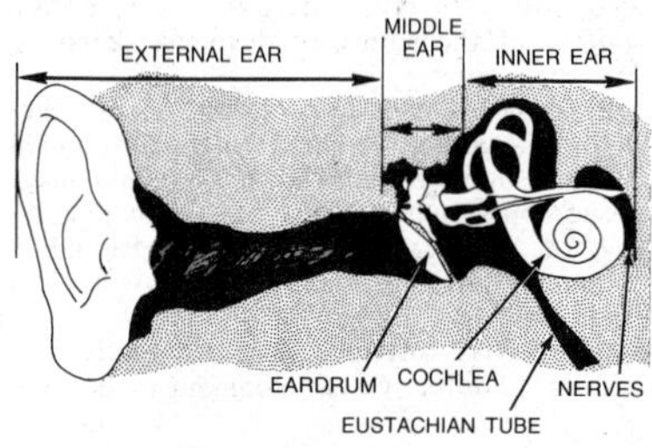

ear[1] (def. 1)

ear[1] (ir), *n.* 1 the part of the body by which human beings and other vertebrates hear; organ of hearing. It usually consists of the external ear, the middle ear, and the inner ear. 2 the outer part of the ear; auricle. 3 anything resembling the outer part of the ear in shape or position. 4 Also, **ears,** *pl.* sense of hearing. 5 ability to hear small differences in sounds: *a musician with a very good ear for pitch.* 6 a careful or favorable hearing; attention.

be all ears, INFORMAL. listen eagerly.

believe one's ears, credit what one hears.

play by ear, a play (a piece of music or a musical instrument) without using written music. **b** handle (a matter) without adequate preparation or guidance.

prick up one's ears, a point the ears upward. **b** give sudden attention: *I pricked up my ears when I heard my name mentioned.*

set by the ears, cause to disagree.

up to the ears, INFORMAL. thoroughly involved; almost overwhelmed.

[Old English *ēare*] **—ear′less,** *adj.* **—ear′like′,** *adj.*

ear[2] (ir), *n.* the part of a cereal plant, such as corn, wheat, oats, barley, or rye, which bears flowers from which grains develop. *—v.i.* grow ears; form ears. [Old English *ēar*]

ear ache (ir′āk′), *n.* pain in the ear.

ear drum (ir′drum′), *n.* a thin membrane across the middle ear that vibrates when sound waves strike it; tympanic membrane; tympanum. See **ear**[1] for diagram.

eared (ird), *adj.* having ears or earlike parts.

eared seal, any of a family of seals with very small ears, including the sea lion and the fur seal.

ear flap (ir′flap′), *n.* part of a cap that can be turned down over the ear to keep it warm.

ear ful (ir′fu̇l), *n., pl.* **-fuls.** INFORMAL. a startling or important disclosure.

earl (ėrl), *n.* 1 a British nobleman ranking below a marquis and above a viscount. 2 (in Anglo-Saxon England) a man of noble rank. [Old English *eorl*]

earl dom (ėrl′dəm), *n.* 1 lands ruled by an earl. 2 title or rank of an earl.

earless seal, hair seal.

ear lobe (ir′lōb′), *n.* 1 the hanging lower part of the external ear. 2 the fleshy fold beside the ear of some fowls.

ear ly (ėr′lē), *adv., adj.,* **-li er, -li est.** *—adv.* 1 near the beginning; in the first part: *The sun is not hot early in the day.* 2 before the usual or expected time: *Call me early.* 3 long ago; far back in time: *Horses were very small early in their development.* 4 before very long; in the near future; soon: *Spring may come early this year. —adj.* 1 of or occurring in the first part: *In his early years he liked ships.* 2 occurring before the usual or expected time: *We had an early dinner.* 3 happening far back in time: *early history.* 4 occurring in the near future: *Let us have an early reply.* [Old English *ǣrlīce* < *ǣr* ere + *-līce* -ly[1]] **—ear′li ness,** *n.*

early bird, INFORMAL. person who gets up or arrives early.

ear mark (ir′märk′), *n.* 1 mark made on the ear of an animal to show who owns it. 2 a special mark, quality, or feature that identifies a person or thing; sign. *—v.t.* 1 make an earmark on. 2 identify by a special mark, quality, or feature. 3 set aside for some special purpose.

ear muffs (ir′mufs′), *n.pl.* pair of coverings to put over the ears to protect them from the cold.

earn (ėrn), *v.t.* 1 receive for work or service; be paid: *She earns 25 dollars a day.* 2 do enough to get; do good enough work for; deserve: *He is paid more than he really earns.* 3 bring or get as deserved: *Her hard work earned her the respect of her teachers.* 4 gain as a profit or return: *Money well invested earns good interest.* [Old English *earnian*] **—earn′er,** *n.*

ear nest[1] (ėr′nist), *adj.* 1 strong and firm in purpose; eager and serious. 2 important: *"Life is real, life is earnest." —n.* **in earnest,** strong and firm in purpose; eager and serious. [Old English *eornost*] **—ear′nest ly,** *adv.* **—ear′nest ness,** *n.*

ear nest[2] (ėr′nist), *n.* 1 money given or something done at the time of a bargain as a pledge that the bargain will be carried out. 2 thing that shows what is to come; pledge; token. [Middle English *ernes,* alteration of Old French *erres,* plural < Latin *arra* < Greek *arrhabōn* < Hebrew *'ērābōn*]

earn ings (ėr′ningz), *n.pl.* money earned; wages or profits.

ear phone (ir′fōn′), *n.* receiver for a telephone, telegraph, radio, hearing aid, etc., that is fastened or placed over one or both ears.

ear ring (ir′ring′), *n.* ornament for the lobe of the ear.

ear shot (ir′shot′), *n.* distance at which the voice or other sound can be heard; range of hearing.

ear split ting (ir′split′ing), *adj.* overpoweringly loud; deafening.

earth (ėrth), *n.* 1 Also, **Earth.** the planet on which we live; the globe. The earth is the fifth largest planet in the solar system and the third in distance from the sun. See **solar system** for diagram. See synonym study below. 2 all the people who live on this planet. 3 this world as the place where man lives (often in contrast to heaven and hell). 4 dry land; ground: *the earth, the sea, and the sky.* 5 soil or dirt: *The earth in the garden is soft.* 6 hole of a fox or other burrowing animal. 7 a metallic oxide from which it is hard to remove the oxygen, such as alumina. 8 BRITISH. connection of an electrical conductor with the earth; ground. 9 **down to earth,** practical; realistic. 10 **run to earth, a** hunt or chase until caught. **b** look for until found. *—v.t.* cover with soil: *earth celery, earth up potatoes.* [Old English *eorthe*]

Syn. *n.* 1 **Earth, world, globe** mean the

hat, āge, fär; let, ēqual, tėrm;
it, īce; hot, ōpen, ôrder;
oil, out; cup, pu̇t, rüle;
ch, child; ng, long; sh, she;
th, thin; ᴛʜ, then; zh, measure;

ə represents *a* in about, *e* in taken, *i* in pencil, *o* in lemon, *u* in circus.

< = from, derived from, taken from.

planet on which we live. **Earth** applies to this planet in contrast to the other planets and sun, stars, etc.: *the gravitational attraction of the earth.* **World** applies to the earth as the home of man: *all the nations of the world.* **Globe** emphasizes the roundness of the earth: *Today a traveler can fly around the globe in a few hours.*

earth born (ėrth′bôrn′), *adj.* 1 born from the earth. 2 human; mortal.

earth bound (ėrth′bound′), *adj.* bound or limited to this earth.

earth en (ėr′thən), *adj.* 1 made of baked clay. 2 made of earth.

earth en ware (ėr′thən wer′, ėr′thən-war′), *n.* opaque pottery that is more porous than porcelain; crockery.

earth ling (ėrth′ling), *n.* inhabitant of the earth; human being; mortal.

earth ly (ėrth′lē), *adj.,* **-li er, -li est.** 1 having to do with the earth, not with heaven. See synonym study below. 2 possible: *Of what earthly use can that rubbish be?* **—earth′li ness,** *n.*

Syn. 1 **Earthly, terrestrial, worldly** mean having to do with the earth. **Earthly** is used in contrast to *heavenly* to describe things connected with life in this world: *acquire money and other earthly possessions.* **Terrestrial** is used particularly to refer to the earth as a planet, or to the land of the earth as opposed to water: *People are terrestrial beings; fish are aquatic beings.* **Worldly** emphasizes the pleasures, success, vanity, etc., of this life as contrasted with spiritual or religious values: *They enjoy parties, dances, and other worldly pleasures.*

earth quake (ėrth′kwāk′), *n.* a shaking or sliding of a portion of the earth's crust, caused by the sudden movement of masses of rock along a fault or by changes in the size and shape of masses of rock far beneath the earth's surface. Earthquakes are often associated with volcanic activity.

earth satellite, satellite of the earth, especially a man-made metal sphere or other structure launched by rockets into an orbit outside the earth's atmosphere.

earth science, any of the sciences dealing with the origin, composition, and physical features of the earth, such as geology, geography, meteorology, and oceanography.

earth shine (ėrth′shīn′), *n.* the faint light visible on the darker part of the moon, due to the light which the earth reflects on the moon.

earth ward (ėrth′wərd), *adv., adj.* toward the earth.

earth wards (ėrth′wərdz), *adv.* earthward.

earth work (ėrth′wėrk′), *n.* bank of earth piled up, especially as a fortification.

earth worm (ėrth′wėrm′), *n.* any of a class of annelid worms that live in the soil, especially a long, reddish-brown or grayish species with minute bristles on each segment that aid in locomotion; angleworm. Earthworms are useful in loosening soil and as bait for anglers. See **worm** for picture.

earth y (ėr′thē), *adj.,* **earth i er, earth i est.** 1 of earth or soil. 2 like earth or soil (in texture, color, etc.). 3 not spiritual; worldly. 4 not refined; coarse. **—earth′i-ness,** *n.*

ear wax (ir′waks′), *n.* the sticky, yellowish substance secreted by glands along the canal of the outer ear; cerumen.

ear wig (ir′wig′), *n.* any of an order of slender insects with short, leathery forewings and forcepslike appendages at the end of the abdomen, once thought to crawl into people's ears. [Old English *ēarwicga* < *ēare* ear + *wicga* insect]

ease (ēz), *n., v.,* **eased, eas ing.** *—n.* 1 freedom from pain or trouble; comfort. See synonym study below. 2 freedom from trying hard. 3 freedom from embarrassment; natural or easy manner. 4 **at ease, a** comfortable. **b** a military position, with the body relaxed and the feet apart. 5 **take one's ease,** make oneself comfortable; rest. *—v.t.* 1 make free from pain or trouble; relieve; soothe. 2 lessen; lighten: *Aspirin eased my headache.* 3 loosen: *This belt is too tight; ease it a notch or two.* 4 move slowly and carefully: *Ease the desk through the narrow door.* *—v.i.* 1 become less rapid, less tense, etc. 2 **ease off** or **ease up, a** lessen; lighten. **b** loosen. [< Old French *aise* comfort, opportunity < Popular Latin *adjaces* neighborhood < Latin *adjacentem* adjacent. See ADJACENT.] **—eas′er,** *n.*

Syn. *n.* 1 **Ease, comfort** mean freedom from strain. **Ease** suggests being relaxed or at rest: *When school is out, I am going to live a life of ease for a whole week.* **Comfort** suggests feeling well and contented and being well provided for: *Let others have money and fame; I want only comfort.*

ea sel (ē′zəl), *n.* a support or frame for holding an artist's canvas, blackboard, etc. [< Dutch *ezel* easel, literally, ass < Latin *asellus* small ass < *asinus* ass]

ease ment (ēz′mənt), *n.* (in law) a right held by one person to some limited use of land owned by another.

eas i ly (ē′zə lē), *adv.* 1 in an easy manner: *a job easily done.* 2 by far; without question: *He is easily the best singer in the choir.* 3 very likely; probably: *My candidate may easily be elected.*

eas i ness (ē′zē nis), *n.* 1 quality or condition of being easy. 2 carelessness or indifference.

east (ēst), *n.* 1 direction of the sunrise; direction just opposite west. 2 Also, **East.** the part of any country toward the east. 3 **the East, a** the part of the United States to the east of the Allegheny Mountains, especially New England. **b** the part of the United States that lies to the east of the Mississippi River, especially the states north of Maryland and the Ohio River. **c** the countries in Asia as distinguished from those in Europe and America; the Orient. **d** the Soviet Union and its satellites in eastern Europe. 4 **down East, a** New England. **b** the eastern part of New England; Maine. **c** in, to, or toward New England. *—adj.* 1 toward the east; farther toward the east. 2 coming from the east. 3 in the east. *—adv.* 1 toward the east. 2 **east of,** further east than. [Old English *ēast*]

East Anglia, early Anglo-Saxon kingdom in SE England, comprising modern Norfolk and Suffolk. See **Mercia** for map.

East Berlin, capital of East Germany, in the E part. 1,084,000.

east bound (ēst′bound′), *adj.* going east; bound eastward.

East China Sea, sea in the W Pacific between E China and the Ryukyu Islands, connected with the South China Sea by the Formosa Strait. 480,000 sq. mi.

Eas ter (ē′stər), *n.* the annual Christian festival on the first Sunday after the first full moon on or after March 21, celebrating Christ's resurrection; Easter Sunday. [Old English *ēastre,* originally, name of dawn goddess < *ēast* east]

Easter Island, island in the S Pacific, 2000 miles west of and belonging to Chile. 1200 pop.; 63 sq. mi.

Easter lily, lily with large, white, trumpet-shaped flowers. Easter lilies symbolize purity and are often used at Easter to decorate church altars.

east er ly (ē′stər lē), *adj., adv., n., pl.* **-lies.** *—adj., adv.* 1 toward the east. 2 from the east. *—n.* wind that blows from the east.

east ern (ē′stərn), *adj.* 1 toward the east. 2 from the east. 3 of the east; in the east. 4 **Eastern, a** of or in the eastern part of the United States. **b** Oriental. **c** of or having to do with Soviet Union and its allies in eastern Europe.

Eastern Church, group of Christian churches in eastern Europe, western Asia, and Egypt that consider the patriarch of Constantinople as head of the church; Greek Orthodox Church; Orthodox Church; Eastern Orthodox Church.

east ern er (ē′stər nər), *n.* 1 native or inhabitant of the east. 2 **Easterner,** native or inhabitant of the eastern part of the United States.

Eastern Hemisphere, the half of the world that includes Europe, Asia, Africa, and Australia.

east ern most (ē′stərn mōst), *adj.* farthest east.

Eastern Orthodox, of or having to do with the Eastern Church.

Eastern Orthodox Church, Eastern Church.

Eastern Roman Empire, Byzantine Empire.

Eastern Samoa, American Samoa.

Eastern Standard Time, the standard time in the eastern part of the United States and most of eastern Canada. It is five hours behind Greenwich Time.

Easter Sunday, the Sunday between March 22 and April 25 on which Easter is celebrated.

Eas ter tide (ē′stər tīd′), *n.* the week beginning with Easter Sunday.

East Germany, country in central Europe, comprising much of the eastern part of pre-World War II Germany. 17,075,000 pop.; 41,700 sq. mi. *Capital:* East Berlin. See **Austria** for map.

East Indian, 1 of or having to do with the East Indies. 2 native or inhabitant of the East Indies.

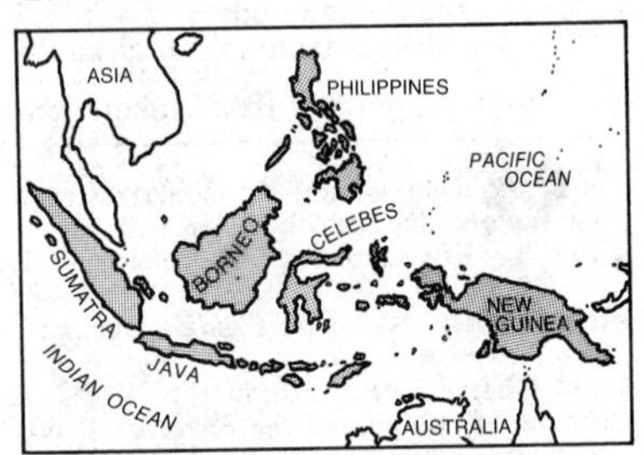

East Indies (def. 1)

East Indies, 1 the islands of the Malay Archipelago. 2 these islands, India, and SE Asia. 3 Indonesia.

East man (ēst′mən), *n.* **George,** 1854-1932, American inventor in the field of photography, manufacturer, and philanthropist.

east-north east (ēst′nôrth′ēst′), *n.* the point of the compass or the direction midway between east and northeast, two points or 22 degrees 30 minutes to the north of east.

East Orange, city in NE New Jersey. 75,000.

East Pakistan, former name of **Bangladesh.**

East Prussia, former German region on the Baltic Sea, divided after World War II between Poland and the Soviet Union.

East River, strip of water connecting Long Island Sound and New York Bay, between Manhattan and Long Island. 15 mi.

east-south east (ēst′south′ēst′), *n.* the point of the compass or the direction midway between east and southeast, two points or 22 degrees 30 minutes to the south of east.

east ward (ēst′wərd), *adv., adj.* toward the east. *—n.* an eastward part, direction, or point.

east ward ly (ēst′wərd lē), *adj., adv.* 1 toward the east. 2 from the east.

east wards (ēst′wərdz), *adv.* eastward.

eas y (ē′zē), *adj.,* **eas i er, eas i est,** *adv.* *—adj.* 1 not hard to do or get; that can be done or obtained with little effort: *an easy victory.* See synonym study below. 2 free from pain, discomfort, trouble, or worry; comfortable: *an easy life.* 3 giving comfort or rest: *an easy chair.* 4 not strict or harsh; not severe: *buy on easy terms.* 5 smooth and pleasant; not awkward: *easy manners.* 6 not steep; gradual: *an easy slope.* 7 not tight; loose: *an easy fit.* 8 not fast; not hurried; slow: *an easy pace.* *—adv.* INFORMAL. without much trouble; easily. [< Old French *aisier* put at ease < *aise,* noun. See EASE.]

Syn. *adj.* 1 **Easy, simple, effortless** mean that not much effort is needed to do, understand, use, solve, etc. **Easy** puts the emphasis on the little work that is needed: *Dinner was easy to prepare.* **Simple** emphasizes the fact that the job itself is not hard and so will be easy to do: *I can work out simple crossword puzzles.* **Effortless** suggests seeming to be easy or simple because the doer is skillful and expert from long practice: *the champion skater's effortless movements.*

eas y go ing (ē′zē gō′ing), *adj.* taking matters easily; not worrying.

easy mark, INFORMAL. person who is easily imposed upon.

eat (ēt), *v.,* **ate, eat en, eat ing** (see usage note below). *—v.t.* 1 chew and swallow (food): *Cows eat grass and grain.* 2 gnaw or devour: *Termites have eaten the posts and ruined the fence.* 3 destroy as if by eating; wear away; corrode: *This acid eats metal.* 4 **eat up,** use up; waste away: *Extravagant spending ate up our savings.* 5 make by eating: *Moths ate holes in my wool coat.* 6 INFORMAL. bother; annoy. *—v.i.* have a meal: *Where shall we eat?* [Old English *etan*] **—eat′er,** *n.*

➔ **eat.** Formerly the past tense form, spelled either *eat* or *ate,* was pronounced (et). This pronunciation is still common in England and in some parts of the United States, but is generally regarded as substandard in America.

eat a ble (ē′tə bəl), *adj.* fit to eat; edible. *—n.* **eatables,** *pl.* things fit to eat; food.

eat en (ēt′n), *v.* pp. of **eat.**

eau de Co logne (ō′ də kə lōn′), cologne. [< French, literally, water of Cologne]

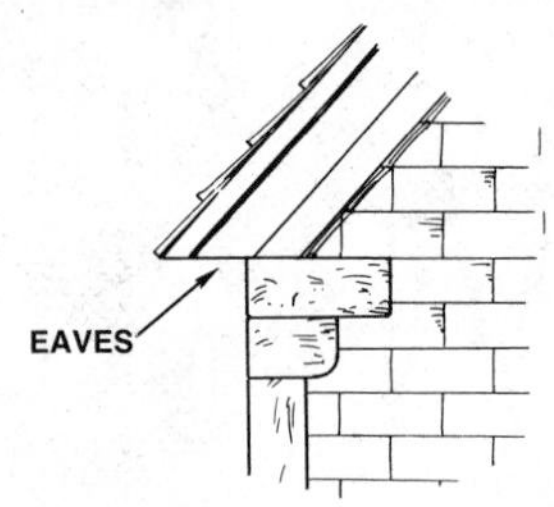

eaves (ēvz), *n.pl.* the lower edge of a roof that projects over the side of a building. [Old English *efes* edge]

eaves drop (ēvz′drop′), *v.i.,* **-dropped, -drop ping.** listen to talk one is not supposed to hear. [< *eavesdropper,* in the earlier sense of "one who stands under the eaves to listen"] **—eaves′drop′per,** *n.*

ebb (eb), *n.* 1 a flowing of the tide away from the shore; fall of the tide. 2 a growing less or weaker; decline; decay. 3 point of decline: *His fortunes were at an ebb.* *—v.i.* 1 flow out; fall: *The tide ebbed.* 2 grow less or weaker; decline: *My courage ebbed as I neared the haunted house.* [Old English *ebba*]

ebb tide, a flowing of the tide away from the shore.

eb on (eb′ən), ARCHAIC. *n., adj.* ebony.

eb on ite (eb′ə nīt), *n.* vulcanite.

eb on y (eb′ə nē), *n., pl.* **-on ies,** *adj.* *—n.* 1 a hard, durable, black wood, used for the black keys of a piano, for the backs and handles of brushes, for ornamental woodwork, etc. 2 any of a genus of tropical trees that yield this wood. *—adj.* 1 made of ebony. 2 like ebony; black; dark. [< Greek *ebenos* ebony < Egyptian *hbnj*]

E bro River (ē′brō; *Spanish* ā′vrō), river flowing from N Spain into the Mediterranean Sea. 465 mi.

e bul lience (i bul′yəns), *n.* great enthusiasm.

e bul lient (i bul′yənt), *adj.* 1 overflowing with excitement, liveliness, etc.; very enthusiastic. 2 boiling; bubbling. [< Latin *ebullientem* < *ex-* out + *bullire* to boil] **—e bul′lient ly,** *adv.*

eb ul li tion (eb′ə lish′ən), *n.* 1 a boiling or a bubbling up. 2 outburst (of feeling, etc.).

ec-, *prefix.* form of **ex-**[2] before consonants, as in *eccentric, eclectic, ecstasy.*

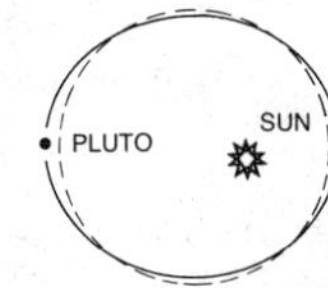

eccentric (def. 3) orbit of planet Pluto compared with a perfect circle

ec cen tric (ek sen′trik), *adj.* 1 out of the ordinary; not usual; odd; peculiar. 2 not having the same center: *These circles* ◎ *are eccentric.* 3 not perfectly circular: *The planets are in eccentric orbits around the sun.* 4 off center; having its axis set off center: *an eccentric wheel.* *—n.* 1 person who behaves in an unusual manner. 2 disk or wheel set off center so that it can change circular motion into back-and-forth motion. [< Medieval Latin *eccentricus* < Greek *ekkentros* off center < *ex-* out + *kentron* center] **—ec cen′tri cal ly,** *adv.*

ec cen tric i ty (ek′sen tris′ə tē), *n., pl.* **-ties.** 1 something strange or out of the ordinary; oddity; peculiarity. 2 eccentric condition; being unusual or out of the ordinary. 3 amount of deviation of the orbit of a planet from a perfect circle.

eccl. or **eccles.,** ecclesiastical.

Eccl. or **Eccles.,** Ecclesiastes.

Ec cle si as tes (i klē′zē as′tēz), *n.* book of the Old Testament, supposed to have been written by Solomon.

ec cle si as tic (i klē′zē as′tik), *n.* clergyman. *—adj.* ecclesiastical. [< Greek *ekklēsiastikos* < *ekklēsia* church, assembly < *ekkalein* call out, assemble < *ex-* out + *kalein* to call]

ec cle si as ti cal (i klē′zē as′tə kəl), *adj.* of or having to do with the church or the clergy. **—ec cle′si as′ti cal ly,** *adv.*

ec dy sis (ek′də sis), *n., pl.* **-ses** (-sēz′). the shedding of the outer covering or skin of certain animals, especially the shedding of the exoskeleton by arthropods. [< Greek *ekdysis* a stripping]

ECG, electrocardiogram.

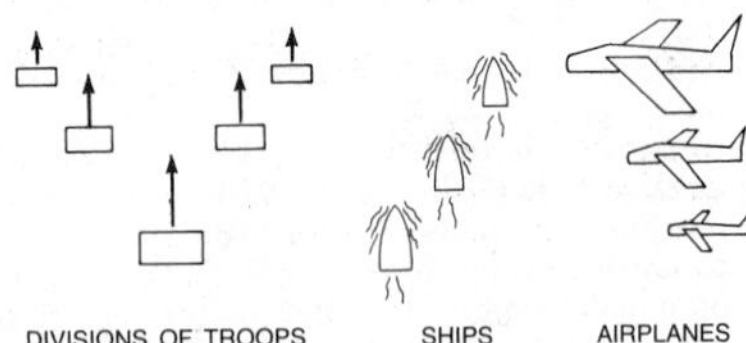

echelon (def. 1)

ech e lon (esh′ə lon), *n.* 1 arrangement of troops, ships, planes, etc., in a steplike formation. 2 level of command or authority designated as higher or lower. A unit of an army, such as a company, battalion, division, or corps, is an echelon. [< French *échelon* rung of a ladder]

e chid na (i kid′nə), *n., pl.* **-nas, -nae** (-nē). any of a family of small, egg-laying, ant-eating mammals of Australia, Tasmania, and New Guinea with long, slender snouts, no teeth, and a covering of spines; spiny anteater. [< Greek, viper]

e chi no derm (i kī′nə dėrm′), *n.* any of a

phylum of small sea animals usually with five arms arranged radially around a central disk and a body covering strengthened and supported by calcareous plates. Starfish and sea urchins belong to this phylum. [< Greek *echinos* sea urchin, originally, hedgehog + *derma* skin]

E chi no der ma ta (i kī′nə dėr′mə tə), *n.pl.* phylum of invertebrates comprising the echinoderms. [< New Latin]

e chi noid (i kī′noid), *n.* any of a class of echinoderms, having a hard, usually circular, shell of calcareous plates covered with minute, movable spines; sea urchin.

e chi nus (i kī′nəs), *n., pl.* **-ni** (-nī). 1 sea urchin. 2 a rounded molding at the top of a Doric column. See **column** for diagram. [< Latin < Greek *echinos*]

ech o (ek′ō), *n., pl.* **ech oes,** *v.* —*n.* 1 a sounding again; repetition of a sound or sounds produced by the reflection of the sound waves from some obstructing surface. You hear an echo when sound is sent back by a cliff or hill. 2 person who repeats the words or imitates the feelings, acts, ideas, or style of another. 3 a repeating the words or imitating the feelings, acts, ideas, or style of another. 4 a radio wave which has been reflected. The detection of radio wave reflection is the basis of radar, sonar, etc. 5 **Echo,** (in Greek myths) a nymph who pined away with love for Narcissus until only her voice was left. —*v.t., v.i.* 1 sound again; repeat or be repeated in sound: *The shout echoed through the valley.* 2 repeat or imitate what another says or does. [< Greek *ēchō*] **—ech′o er,** *n.*

e cho ic (e kō′ik), *adj.* 1 like an echo. 2 imitative in sound; onomatopoetic.

ech o lo ca tion (ek′ō lō kā′shən), *n.* method of finding the range and direction of objects by measuring the time it takes sound waves echoed from the objects to reflect back.

é clair (ā kler′, ā klar′), *n.* an oblong piece of pastry filled with whipped cream or custard and covered with icing. [< French, literally, lightning]

é clat (ā klä′), *n.* 1 a brilliant success. 2 fame; glory. 3 burst of applause or approval. [< French, literally, outburst]

ec lec tic (e klek′tik), *adj.* 1 selecting and using what seems best from various sources, systems, or schools of thought. 2 consisting of selections from various sources. —*n.* follower of an eclectic method. [< Greek *eklektikos* < *eklegein* pick out, select < *ex-* out + *legein* to pick] **—ec lec′ti cal ly,** *adv.*

ec lec ti cism (e klek′tə siz′əm), *n.* the use or support of eclectic methods.

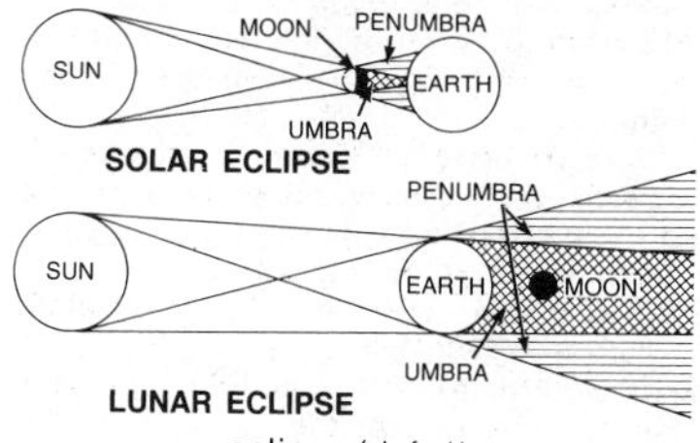

eclipse (def. 1)

e clipse (i klips′), *n., v.,* **e clipsed, e clips ing.** —*n.* 1 a complete or partial blocking of light passing from one heavenly body to another. A **solar eclipse** occurs when the moon passes between the sun and the earth. A **lunar eclipse** occurs when the moon enters the earth's shadow. 2 loss of importance or reputation. —*v.t.* 1 cut off or dim the light from; darken. 2 cast a shadow upon; obscure. 3 surpass; outshine: *Napoleon eclipsed other generals of his time.* [< Latin *eclipsis* < Greek *ekleipsis* < *ex-* out + *leipein* to leave]

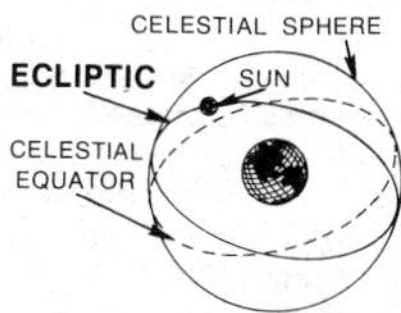

e clip tic (i klip′tik), *n.* path that the sun appears to travel in one year. It is that great circle of the celestial sphere which is cut by the plane containing the orbit of the earth. —*adj.* 1 of this circle. 2 having to do with an eclipse.

e clip ti cal (i klip′tə kəl), *adj.* ecliptic.

ec logue (ek′lôg, ek′log), *n.* a short poem about country life, often written as a dialogue between shepherds. [< Greek *eklogē* selection < *eklegein* pick out, select. See ECLECTIC.]

é cole (ā kôl′), *n.* FRENCH. school.

ec o log ic (ek′ə loj′ik, ē′kə loj′ik), *adj.* ecological.

ec o log i cal (ek′ə loj′ə kəl, ē′kə loj′ə kəl), *adj.* of or having to do with ecology. **—ec′o log′i cal ly,** *adv.*

e col o gist (ē kol′ə jist), *n.* an expert in ecology.

e col o gy (ē kol′ə jē), *n.* 1 branch of biology that studies the effect of environment upon the form, habits, and range of animals and plants and of their relation to each other. 2 branch of sociology that deals with the relations between human beings and their environment. [< German *Ökologie* < Greek *oikos* house + *-logia* study of]

econ., 1 economic. 2 economics. 3 economy.

e co nom ic (ē′kə nom′ik, ek′ə nom′ik), *adj.* 1 of or having to do with economics. Economic problems have to do with the production, distribution, and consumption of goods and services. 2 having to do with the management of the income, supplies, and expenses of a household, community, government, etc. 3 practical or utilitarian in application or use: *economic geography.*

e co nom i cal (ē′kə nom′ə kəl, ek′ə-nom′ə kəl), *adj.* avoiding waste; saving; thrifty. See synonym study below.

Syn. Economical, thrifty, frugal mean avoiding waste of money, time, work, etc. **Economical** implies prudent use of resources, large or small, which makes the best and fullest use of what is available: *She does more than others because she is economical of time and energy.* **Thrifty,** sometimes interchangeable with *economical,* implies the careful management of resources, hard work, and the regular putting aside of savings: *The thrifty boy saved part of his weekly salary to spend on his summer vacation.* **Frugal** implies the absence of all lavishness or extravagance in dress, diet, and the like, and the simplest kind of living: *A frugal person buys and uses food carefully.*

e co nom i cal ly (ē′kə nom′ik lē, ek′ə-nom′ik lē), *adv.* 1 in an economical manner. 2 from the point of view of economics.

e co nom ics (ē′kə nom′iks, ek′ə nom′iks), *n.* 1 *pl. in form, sing. in use.* science of the production, distribution, and consumption of goods and services. Economics deals with the material welfare of mankind and studies the problems of capital, labor, wages, prices, taxes, etc. 2 *pl. in form and use.* economic questions or affairs.

hat, āge, fär; let, ēqual, tėrm;
it, īce; hot, ōpen, ôrder;
oil, out; cup, pu̇t, rüle;
ch, child; ng, long; sh, she;
th, thin; ᴛʜ, then; zh, measure;

ə represents *a* in about, *e* in taken, *i* in pencil, *o* in lemon, *u* in circus.

< = from, derived from, taken from.

e con o mist (i kon′ə mist), *n.* an expert in economics.

e con o mize (i kon′ə mīz), *v.,* **-mized, -miz ing.** —*v.t.* manage so as to avoid waste; use to the best advantage. —*v.i.* cut down expenses. **—e con′o miz′er,** *n.*

e con o my (i kon′ə mē), *n., pl.* **-mies.** 1 a making the most of what one has; avoiding waste in the use of anything; thrift. 2 instance of this: *The economy of going without a vacation bought new furniture for the house.* 3 management of affairs and resources so as to avoid waste. 4 efficient arrangement of parts; organization; system. 5 system of managing the production, distribution, and consumption of goods: *feudal economy.* [< Latin *oeconomia* < Greek *oikonomia* < *oikonomos* one who manages a house < *oikos* house + *nemein* manage]

e co spe cies (ē′kō spē′shēz, ek′ō spē′-shēz), *n., pl.* **-cies.** (in biology) a group of organisms only somewhat fertile with organisms of related groups, usually considered equivalent to a species.

e co sys tem (ē′kō sis′təm, ek′ō sis′təm), *n.* system of ecological relationships upon which the life of any group of living organisms is based, such as food supply, weather, and natural enemies.

ec ru or **é cru** (ek′rü, ā′krü), *adj.* pale-brown; light-tan. —*n.* a pale brown; light tan. [< French *écru* raw, unbleached]

ec sta sy (ek′stə sē), *n., pl.* **-sies.** 1 condition of very great joy; thrilling or overwhelming delight: *The little girl was speechless with ecstasy over her new puppy.* 2 any strong feeling that completely absorbs the mind; uncontrollable emotion. See **rapture** for synonym study. 3 trance. [< Greek *ekstasis* distraction, trance < *existanai* put out of place < *ex-* out + *histanai* to place]

ec stat ic (ek stat′ik), *adj.* 1 full of ecstasy: *an ecstatic look of pleasure.* 2 caused by ecstasy: *an ecstatic mood.* **—ec stat′i cal ly,** *adv.*

ecto-, *combining form.* to or on the outside, as in *ectoderm, ectoplasm.* [< Greek *ekto-* < *ektos* outside]

ec to derm (ek′tə dėrm′), *n.* the outer layer of cells formed during the development of the embryos of animals. Skin, hair, nails, the enamel of teeth, and the essential parts of the nervous system, grow from the ectoderm.

ec to der mal (ek′tə dėr′məl), *adj.* of or having to do with the ectoderm.

ec to morph (ek′tə môrf), *n.* person with a relatively slender, thin, or spare body build developed from the ectodermal layer of the embryo.

ec to mor phic (ek′tə môr′fik), *adj.* of, like, or having to do with an ectomorph. **—ec′to mor′phi cal ly,** *adv.*

-ectomy, *combining form.* a surgical operation for removing a designated part of the body, as in *tonsillectomy.* [< Greek *ektomē* a cutting out]

ec to par a site (ek′tə par′ə sīt), *n.* parasite living on the outside parts of the host. Lice and fleas are ectoparasites.

ec to plasm (ek′tə plaz′əm), *n.* 1 the semiclear, somewhat rigid outer portion of the cytoplasm of a cell. 2 a supposed emanation from the body of a medium in a trance.

ec to plas mic (ek′tə plaz′mik), *adj.* of or having to do with ectoplasm.

Ec ua dor (ek′wə dôr), *n.* country in NW South America. 6,093,000 pop.; 104,500 sq. mi. *Capital:* Quito. **—Ec′ua do′ran, Ec′ua do′re an, Ec′ua do′ri an,** *adj., n.*

ec u men i cal (ek′yə men′ə kəl), *adj.* 1 general; universal. 2 of or representing the whole Christian Church: *an ecumenical council.* 3 promoting unity among all Christians or Christian denominations. Also, **oecumenical.** [< Latin *oecumenicus* < Greek *oikoumenikos* < *oikoumenē* (*gē*) inhabited (world), ultimately < *oikos* house] **—ec′u men′i cal ly,** *adv.*

ec u men ism (ek′yə men′iz′əm), *n.* 1 principle of worldwide Christian harmony and unity. 2 church movement in support of this principle.

ec ze ma (ek′sə mə, eg zē′mə), *n.* inflammation of the skin with itching and the formation of lesions which become scaly and encrusted from a watery discharge. [< Greek *ekzema* < *ex-* out + *zein* to boil]

-ed[1], *suffix forming the past tense of many verbs,* as in *wanted, tried, dropped.* [Old English *-de, -ede, -ode, -ade*]

-ed[2], 1 *suffix forming the past participle of many verbs,* as in *has echoed.* 2 *suffix forming adjectives from nouns:* **a** having ___: *Long-legged = having long legs.* **b** having the characteristics of ___: *Honeyed = having the characteristics of honey.* [Old English *-ed, -od, -ad*]

ed., 1 edited. 2 edition. 3 editor.

E dam (ē′dəm), *n.* Edam cheese.

Edam cheese, a round, mild-flavored, yellow cheese, originally made in the Netherlands, and usually having red wax on the outside. [< *Edam,* village in the Netherlands]

e daph ic (i daf′ik), *adj.* influenced by the soil, rather than by the climate. [< Greek *edaphos* bottom, ground]

Ed da (ed′ə), *n.* either of two books of Old Icelandic poems, myths, and legends compiled about 1200 to 1300.

Ed ding ton (ed′ing tən), *n.* Sir **Arthur Stanley,** 1882-1944, English astronomer and physicist.

ed dy (ed′ē), *n., pl.* **-dies,** *v.,* **-died, -dy ing.** *—n.* 1 water, air, smoke, etc., moving against the main current, especially when having a whirling motion; small whirlpool or whirlwind. 2 any similar current of fog or dust. 3 anything thought to resemble this: *eddies of controversy about war and peace.* *—v.i., v.t.* 1 move against the main current in a whirling motion; whirl. 2 move in circles. [perhaps < Scandinavian (Old Icelandic) *itha*]

Ed dy (ed′ē), *n.* **Mary Baker,** 1821-1910, American who founded Christian Science.

e del weiss (ā′dl vīs), *n.* a small Alpine plant of the composite family that has heads of very small, white flowers in the center of star-shaped clusters of leaves that are covered with a white fuzz. [< German *Edelweiss* < *edel* noble + *weiss* white]

e de ma (i dē′mə), *n., pl.* **-ma ta** (-mə tə). abnormal accumulation of a watery fluid in tissues or cavities of the body, often causing visible swelling; dropsy. [< New Latin < Greek *oidēma* < *oidein* to swell]

E den[1] (ēd′n), *n.* 1 (in the Bible) the garden where Adam and Eve first lived. 2 a delightful place; paradise.

E den[2] (ēd′n), *n.* Sir **Anthony,** born 1897, Earl of Avon, British statesman, prime minister of Great Britain from 1955 to 1957.

e den tate (ē den′tāt), *n.* any of an order of mammals that are toothless or lack incisors. Armadillos, sloths, and some anteaters belong to this order. *—adj.* toothless. [< Latin *edentatum* toothless < *ex-* out + *dentem* tooth]

edge (ej), *n., v.,* **edged, edg ing.** *—n.* 1 line or place where something ends; part farthest from the middle; side. See synonym study below. 2 the extreme border or margin of anything; brink: *the edge of a cliff, the edge of disaster.* 3 the thin side that cuts: *The knife had a very sharp edge.* 4 degree or sharpness of a blade. 5 sharpness; keenness: *The remark had a biting edge to it.* 6 INFORMAL. advantage: *have the edge in aircraft quality.* 7 **on edge, a** disturbed; irritated; tense. **b** eager; anxious. 8 **take the edge off,** take away the force, strength, or pleasure of. *—v.t.* 1 put an edge on; form an edge on: *edge a path with flowers.* 2 move little by little: *I edged my chair nearer to the fire.* *—v.i.* 1 move sideways: *She edged through the crowd.* 2 tilt a ski so that the edge cuts the snow. [Old English *ecg*]

Syn. *n.* 1 **Edge, border** mean the line or space that marks the boundary of something. **Edge** applies to a sharp line or very thin surface that marks the exact end of something: *the edge of the water.* **Border** applies to a line that marks the farthest limit of something or the space that runs along just inside the boundary or edge: *This handkerchief has a colored border.*

edged (ejd), *adj.* sharp.

edge ways (ej′wāz′), *adv.* with the edge forward; in the direction of the edge.

edge wise (ej′wīz′), *adv.* edgeways.

Edge worth (ej′wərth), *n.* **Maria,** 1767-1849, English novelist and essayist.

edg ing (ej′ing), *n.* thing forming an edge or put on along an edge; border or trimming for an edge: *an edging of lace.*

edg y (ej′ē), *adj.,* **edg i er, edg i est.** 1 impatient; irritable. 2 sharply defined: *edgy outlines.* **—edg′i ly,** *adv.* **—edg′i ness,** *n.*

ed i bil i ty (ed′ə bil′ə tē), *n.* fitness for eating.

ed i ble (ed′ə bəl), *adj.* fit to eat; eatable. *—n.* **edibles,** *pl.* things fit to eat; food. [< Late Latin *edibilis* < Latin *edere* eat]

e dict (ē′dikt), *n.* 1 decree or law proclaimed by a king or other ruler on his sole authority. See **proclamation** for synonym study. 2 any similar order or command. [< Latin *edictum* < *edicere* proclaim < *ex-* out + *dicere* say]

e dic tal (i dik′təl), *adj.* 1 of or like an edict. 2 commanded by edict.

ed i fi ca tion (ed′ə fə kā′shən), *n.* an edifying; moral improvement; spiritual benefit; instruction.

ed i fice (ed′ə fis), *n.* a building, especially a large or impressive one, such as a cathedral, palace, or temple. See **building** for synonym study. [< Old French < Latin *aedificium* < *aedificare* build < *aedis* a dwelling, temple + *facere* make]

ed i fy (ed′ə fī), *v.t.,* **-fied, -fy ing.** improve morally; benefit spiritually; instruct and uplift. [< Old French *edifier* < Latin *aedificare* build. See EDIFICE.] **—ed′i fi′er,** *n.*

e dile (ē′dīl), *n.* aedile.

Ed in burgh (ed′n bėr′ō; *British* ed′n bərə), *n.* 1 capital of Scotland, in the SE part. 468,000. 2 **Duke of.** See **Philip** (def. 3).

E dir ne (e dir′ne), *n.* city in NW Turkey; Adrianople. 46,000.

Ed i son (ed′ə sən), *n.* **Thomas Alva,** 1847-1931, American inventor.

ed it (ed′it), *v.t.* 1 prepare (another's writings, etc.) for publication or presentation by correcting errors, checking facts, etc.: *Scholars often edit Shakespeare's plays.* 2 have charge of (a newspaper, magazine, etc.) and decide what shall be printed in it. 3 revise or give final form to (motion-picture film, tape recordings, etc.) by such means as cutting and splicing. [< *edit(or)*]

edit., 1 edited. 2 edition. 3 editor.

e di tion (i dish′ən), *n.* 1 all the copies of a book, newspaper, etc., printed just alike and issued at or near the same time: *In the second edition of the book many of the errors in the first edition had been corrected.* 2 form in which a book is printed or published: *a one-volume edition of Shakespeare.* 3 an issue of the same newspaper, book, etc., published at different times with additions, changes, alterations, etc.: *the afternoon edition.*

ed i tor (ed′ə tər), *n.* 1 person who edits. 2 person who writes editorials. [< Late Latin, publisher < Latin *editum* published, given out < *ex-* out + *dare* give]

ed i to ri al (ed′ə tôr′ē əl, ed′ə tōr′ē əl), *n.* 1 article in a newspaper or magazine, giving the editor's or publisher's opinion on some subject. 2 a radio or television broadcast expressing the editorial opinion or attitude of the program, station, or network. *—adj.* 1 of or by an editor: *editorial work.* 2 of an editorial: *editorial comments.*

ed i to ri al ist (ed′ə tôr′ē ə list, ed′ə tōr′ē ə list), *n.* writer of editorials.

ed i to ri al ize (ed′ə tôr′ē ə līz, ed′ə tōr′ē ə līz), *v.i.,* **-ized, -iz ing.** 1 include comment and criticisms in news articles. 2 write an editorial. **—ed′i to′ri al i za′tion,** *n.* **—ed′i to′ri al iz′er,** *n.*

ed i to ri al ly (ed′ə tôr′ē ə lē, ed′ə tōr′ē ə lē), *adv.* 1 in an editorial manner. 2 in an editorial.

editor in chief, editor in charge of a newspaper, magazine, reference work, etc.

ed i tor ship (ed′ə tər ship), *n.* an editor's position, duties, or authority.

Ed mon ton (ed′mən tən), *n.* capital of Alberta, Canada, in the central part. 377,000.

E dom (ē′dəm), *n.* (in the Bible) a region in Palestine south of the Dead Sea. Also, **Idumaea, Idumea.**

E dom ite (ē′də mīt), *n.* native or inhabitant of Edom.

EDT, e.d.t., or **E.D.T.,** Eastern daylight time.

ed u ca ble (ej′ə kə bəl), *adj.* capable of being educated.

ed u cate (ej′ə kāt), *v.t.,* **-cat ed, -cat ing.**

1 develop in knowledge, skill, ability, or character by training, study, or experience; teach. 2 send to school; provide schooling for. 3 train for a particular calling or occupation. [< Latin *educatum* brought up, raised] **—ed′u cat′a ble,** *adj.*

educated guess, estimate, prediction, or opinion based on expert interpretation of incomplete data.

ed u ca tion (ej′ə kā′shən), *n.* 1 development in knowledge, skill, ability, or character by teaching, training, study, or experience; teaching; training. 2 knowledge, skill, ability, or character developed by teaching, training, study, or experience. See synonym study below. 3 study of the methods, principles, problems, etc., of teaching and learning.

Syn. 2 **Education, enlightenment, culture** mean the qualities and knowledge a person gets from study, teaching, and experience. **Education** emphasizes the training, knowledge, and abilities a person gets through teaching or study: *A person with education knows how to read with understanding.* **Enlightenment** emphasizes the insight and understanding that make a person free from prejudice and ignorance: *A person with enlightenment knows the value of education.* **Culture** emphasizes the combination of enlightenment and taste that results from complete education: *A person with culture appreciates good music and art.*

ed u ca tion al (ej′ə kā′shə nəl), *adj.* 1 of or having to do with education: *a state educational association.* 2 giving education; tending to educate; instructive: *an educational movie about Africa.* **—ed′u ca′tion al ly,** *adv.*

ed u ca tive (ej′ə kā′tiv), *adj.* 1 that educates; instructive. 2 of or having to do with education.

ed u ca tor (ej′ə kā′tər), *n.* 1 person whose profession is education; teacher. 2 leader in education; authority on methods and principles of education.

e duce (i düs′, i dyüs′), *v.t.,* **e duced, e duc ing.** bring out; draw forth; elicit: *The science teacher's questions educed many facts about home gardens.* [< Latin *educere* < *ex-* out + *ducere* to lead]

e duc i ble (i dü′sə bəl, i dyü′sə bəl), *adj.* that can be educed.

e duc tion (i duk′shən), *n.* 1 act of educing. 2 something educed.

Ed ward I (ed′wərd), 1239-1307, king of England from 1272 to 1307, son of Henry III. He was called Edward Longshanks.

Edward II, 1284-1327, king of England from 1307 to 1327, son of Edward I.

Edward III, 1312-1377, king of England from 1327 to 1377, son of Edward II.

Edward IV, 1442-1483, king of England from 1461 to 1470, and from 1471 to 1483, first king of the House of York.

Edward V, 1470-1483, king of England in 1483, son of Edward IV. He was murdered in the Tower of London.

Edward VI, 1537-1553, king of England from 1547 to 1553, son of Henry VIII and Jane Seymour.

Edward VII, 1841-1910, king of England from 1901 to 1910, son of Queen Victoria.

Edward VIII, 1894-1972, uncrowned king of England in 1936, son of George V. He abdicated to marry a commoner and received the title of Duke of Windsor.

Ed war di an (ed wär′dē ən), *adj.* 1 of or having to do with the reign or time of King Edward VII. 2 having characteristics considered typical of Edwardians, especially in manners, elegance, etc. *—n.* person who lived during the reign of Edward VII.

Ed wards (ed′wərdz), *n.* **Jonathan,** 1703-1758, American clergyman, theologian, and metaphysician.

Edward the Black Prince, 1330-1376, Prince of Wales, son of Edward III.

Edward the Confessor, 1004?-1066, king of England from 1042 to 1066.

-ee, *suffix added to verbs to form nouns.* 1 person who is ___: *Absentee = person who is absent.* 2 person who is ___ed: *Appointee = person who is appointed.* 3 person to whom something is ___ed: *Mortgagee = person to whom something is mortgaged.* 4 person who ___s: *Standee = person who stands.* [< Old French *-é* < Latin *-atum*]

E.E., Electrical Engineer.

EEG, 1 electroencephalogram. 2 electroencephalograph.

eel (ēl), *n., pl.* **eels** or **eel.** 1 any of several orders of long, slippery, snakelike, freshwater or saltwater fishes with continuous dorsal, caudal, and anal fins, including the morays and congers. 2 any of various other snakelike fishes, including the electric eel and lamprey. [Old English *ǣl*] **—eel′like′,** *adj.*

eel grass (ēl′gras′), *n.* U.S. a sea plant with long, narrow leaves, growing under water along the coasts of North America.

eel pout (ēl′pout′), *n.* 1 a small, eellike saltwater fish. 2 burbot.

eel worm (ēl′wėrm′), *n.* any of various small nematode worms, some injurious to plants.

e'en (ēn), *adv.* even.

e'er (er), *adv.* ever.

-eer, *suffix added to nouns to form nouns and verbs.* 1 person who directs or operates ___: *Auctioneer = person who directs an auction.* 2 person who produces ___: *Pamphleteer = person who produces pamphlets.* 3 be concerned or deal with, as in *electioneer.* [< French *-ier*]

eer ie or **eer y** (ir′ē), *adj.,* **eer i er, eer i est.** 1 causing fear because of strangeness or weirdness. See **weird** for synonym study. 2 timid because of superstition; fearful. [Middle English *eri,* variant of *erg,* Old English *earg* cowardly] **—eer′i ly,** *adv.* **—eer′i ness,** *n.*

ef-, *prefix.* form of **ex-**[1] before *f,* as in *effluent.*

ef face (ə fās′), *v.t.,* **-faced, -fac ing.** 1 rub out; blot out; wipe out; obliterate: *The inscriptions on many ancient monuments have been effaced by time.* See **erase** for synonym study. 2 keep (oneself) from being noticed; make inconspicuous: *The shy boy effaced himself by staying in the background.* [< Middle French *effacer* < *es-* away + *face* face] **—ef face′a ble,** *adj.* **—ef face′ment,** *n.* **—ef fac′er,** *n.*

ef fect (ə fekt′), *n.* 1 whatever is produced by a cause; something made to happen by a person or thing; result. See synonym study below. 2 power to produce results; force; validity: *This contract is of no effect.* 3 influence: *The medicine had an immediate effect.* 4 impression produced on the mind or senses: *The view gave the effect of a painting by Cézanne.* 5 something which produces such an impression: *The movie used many special effects with sounds and pictures.* 6 combination of color or form in a picture, etc.: *Sunshine coming through leaves makes a lovely effect.* 7 purport; intent; meaning: *She spoke to the effect that we must work harder.* 8 **effects,** *pl.* personal belongings including clothing, jewelry, etc.; goods. See **property** for synonym study.

for effect, for show; in order to impress or influence others.

give effect to, put in operation; make active.

in effect, 1 almost the same as; practically; virtually. 2 in force or operation; active.

take effect, begin to operate; become active.

—v.t. 1 make happen; bring about; produce as an effect. 2 make; construct.

[< Latin *effectus* < *efficere* work out, accomplish < *ex-* out + *facere* make] **—ef fect′er,** *n.*

Syn. *n.* 1 **Effect, consequence, result** mean something produced by a cause. **Effect** applies to what happens directly and immediately: *The effect of raising the speed limit from 35 to 55 miles per hour was that the number of accidents increased.* **Consequence** applies to what follows, but not directly or immediately: *As a consequence, there was a state investigation of highway conditions.* **Result** applies to what happens as a final effect or consequence: *The result was a new set of traffic regulations.*

➤ **Effect** and **affect** are often confused in writing, partly because they are pronounced very similarly or identically, and partly because *to affect* is synonymous with *to have an effect on.* But in the general vocabulary *affect* is used only as a verb, whereas *effect* is most commonly used as a noun: *Overwork has had a serious effect on (has seriously affected) his health.*

ef fec tive (ə fek′tiv), *adj.* 1 able to produce an effect: *an effective order.* See synonym study below. 2 producing the desired effect; getting results: *an effective medicine.* 3 in operation; active: *A federal law is effective as soon as the President signs the act.* 4 striking; impressive. 5 equipped and ready for fighting in the armed forces. *—n.* member of the armed forces equipped and ready to fight. **—ef fec′tive ly,** *adv.* **—ef fec′tive ness,** *n.*

Syn. *adj.* 1 **Effective, effectual, efficient** mean producing an effect. **Effective** applies to anyone or anything that can or does produce an effect: *Several new drugs are effective in treating serious diseases.* **Effectual** implies that the effect produced is desirable or decisive: *The Christmas Seal campaign is an effectual means of teaching the public about tuberculosis.* **Efficient** implies that the effect is produced without waste of time or energy: *A skilled surgeon is efficient.*

ef fec tor (ə fek′tər), *n.* muscle or gland capable of responding to a nerve impulse.

ef fec tu al (ə fek′chü əl), *adj.* 1 producing or capable of producing the desired effect: *Quinine is an effectual remedy for malaria.* See **effective** for synonym study. 2 valid. **—ef fec′tu al ly,** *adv.* **—ef fec′tu al ness,** *n.*

hat, āge, fär; let, ēqual, tėrm;
it, īce; hot, ōpen, ôrder;
oil, out; cup, pu̇t, rüle;
ch, child; ng, long; sh, she;
th, thin; ᴛʜ, then; zh, measure;

ə represents *a* in about, *e* in taken, *i* in pencil, *o* in lemon, *u* in circus.

< = from, derived from, taken from.

ef fec tu al i ty (ə fek′chü al′ə tē), *n.* quality of being effectual.

ef fec tu ate (ə fek′chü āt), *v.t.*, **-at ed, -at ing.** make happen; bring about; carry into effect; cause. **—ef fec′tu a′tion,** *n.*

ef fem i na cy (ə fem′ə nə sē), *n.* effeminate quality or character in a man or boy.

ef fem i nate (ə fem′ə nit), *adj.* 1 (of a man or boy) lacking in forceful qualities; showing weakness or softness. 2 characterized by weakness or delicacy. [< Latin *effeminatus* < *ex-* out of + *femina* woman] **—ef fem′i nate ly,** *adv.* **—ef fem′i nate ness,** *n.*

ef fen di (ə fen′dē), *n.* 1 a former Turkish title of respect meaning about the same as "Sir" or "Master." 2 (in countries of the Near East) person having this title; doctor, official, scholar, etc. [< Turkish *efendi*]

ef fer ent (ef′ər ənt), *adj.* carrying outward from a central organ or point. Efferent nerves carry impulses from the brain to the muscles. See **afferent** for diagram. [< Latin *efferentem* < *ex-* out + *ferre* carry] **—ef′fer ent ly,** *adv.*

ef fer vesce (ef′ər ves′), *v.i.*, **-vesced, -vesc ing.** 1 give off bubbles of gas; bubble: *Ginger ale effervesces.* 2 be lively and gay; be excited. [< Latin *effervescere* boil up < *ex-* out + *fervescere* begin to boil]

ef fer ves cence (ef′ər ves′ns), *n.* 1 act or process of bubbling. 2 liveliness and gaiety.

ef fer ves cent (ef′ər ves′nt), *adj.* 1 giving off bubbles of gas; bubbling. 2 lively and gay. **—ef′fer ves′cent ly,** *adv.*

ef fete (i fēt′), *adj.* no longer able to produce; worn out; exhausted: *an effete civilization.* [< Latin *effetus* worn out by bearing < *ex-* out + *fetus* having brought forth] **—ef fete′ly,** *adv.* **—ef fete′ness,** *n.*

ef fi ca cious (ef′ə kā′shəs), *adj.* producing the desired results; effective: *Vaccination is efficacious in preventing smallpox.* **—ef′fi ca′cious ly,** *adv.* **—ef′fi ca′cious ness,** *n.*

ef fi ca cy (ef′ə kə sē), *n., pl.* **-cies.** power to produce the effect wanted; effectiveness: *The efficacy of aspirin in relieving headaches is well known.* [< Latin *efficacia* < *efficere* accomplish < *ex-* + *facere* do, make]

ef fi cien cy (ə fish′ən sē), *n., pl.* **-cies.** 1 ability to produce the effect wanted without waste of time, energy, etc. 2 efficient operation: *Friction reduces the efficiency of a machine.* 3 ratio of the work performed or the energy generated by an engine, machine, etc., to the energy supplied to the engine, machine, etc.

ef fi cient (ə fish′ənt), *adj.* 1 able to produce the effect wanted without waste of time, energy, etc.; capable; competent. See **effective** for synonym study. 2 actually producing an effect: *Heat is the efficient cause in changing water to steam.* [< Latin *efficientem* < *ex-* + *facere* do, make] **—ef fi′cient ly,** *adv.*

ef fi gy (ef′ə jē), *n., pl.* **-gies.** 1 image or statue, usually of a person: *The dead man's monument bore his effigy.* 2 **burn in effigy** or **hang in effigy,** burn or hang an image of a person to show hatred or contempt. [< Latin *effigies* < *effingere* to fashion < *ex-* out + *fingere* to form]

ef flo resce (ef′lô res′, ef′lō res′), *v.i.*, **-resced, -resc ing.** 1 burst into bloom; blossom out; flower. 2 change either throughout or on the surface to a powder by loss of water of crystallization when exposed to air. 3 become covered with a crusty deposit when water evaporates. [< Latin *efflorescere* < *ex-* out + *florem* flower]

ef flo res cence (ef′lô res′ns, ef′lō res′ns), *n.* 1 act or process of bursting into bloom; flowering. 2 state or period of flowering: *The efflorescence of Romantic music occurred during the 1800's.* 3 mass of flowers. 4 anything like a mass of flowers. 5 a change that occurs when crystals lose their water of crystallization and become powder. 6 powder formed in this way. 7 deposit formed in this way. 8 formation of a crusty deposit when water evaporates from a solution. 9 eruption on the skin; rash.

ef flo res cent (ef′lô res′nt, ef′lō res′nt), *adj.* 1 bursting into bloom; flowering. 2 that changes from crystals into powder by losing water of crystallization when exposed to air. 3 covered with a deposit formed by efflorescence.

ef flu ence (ef′lü əns), *n.* 1 an outward flow, especially of light, electricity, magnetism, etc. 2 thing that flows out; emanation; efflux.

ef flu ent (ef′lü ənt), *adj.* flowing out or forth. *—n.* 1 something that flows out or forth; outflow. 2 stream flowing out of a larger stream, lake, reservoir, etc. [< Latin *effluentem* < *ex-* out + *fluere* to flow]

ef flu vi um (i flü′vē əm), *n., pl.* **-vi a** (-vē ə), **-vi ums.** vapor or odor, usually unpleasant. [< Latin, a flowing out]

ef flux (ef′luks), *n.* 1 an outward flow of water, etc. 2 effluence.

ef fort (ef′ərt), *n.* 1 use of energy and strength to do something; trying hard. See synonym study below. 2 a hard try; strong attempt. 3 result of effort; thing done with effort; achievement: *Works of art are artistic efforts.* 4 (in mechanics) a force upon a body due to a definite cause. A heavy body on an inclined plane is said to have an effort to fall vertically. [< Old French *esforcier* to force]

Syn. 1 **Effort, endeavor, application** mean active use of physical or mental power to do something. **Effort** implies trying hard, but not necessarily long or effectively: *I made an effort to finish my work today.* **Endeavor,** more formal, implies sincere and serious effort continued over some time: *By constant endeavor, he built a boat.* **Application** emphasizes continued effort and close attention to what one is doing: *By application to her studies she is making better grades.*

ef fort less (ef′ərt lis), *adj.* requiring or showing little or no effort; easy. See **easy** for synonym study. **—ef′fort less ly,** *adv.* **—ef′fort less ness,** *n.*

ef fron ter y (ə frun′tər ē), *n., pl.* **-ter ies.** shameless boldness; impudence; insolence: *My neighbor had the effrontery to say that I talk too much.* [< French *effronterie* < Old French *esfront* shameless < Latin *effrontem* < *ex-* out + *frontem* brow]

ef ful gence (i ful′jəns), *n.* a shining forth of light, etc.; great luster or brilliance; splendor.

ef ful gent (i ful′jənt), *adj.* shining brightly; radiant. [< Latin *effulgentem* < *ex-* forth + *fulgere* to shine] **—ef ful′gent ly,** *adv.*

ef fuse (i fyüz′), *v.t.*, **-fused, -fus ing.** pour out; spill; shed. [< Latin *effusum* poured out < *ex-* out + *fundere* pour]

ef fu sion (i fyü′zhən), *n.* 1 a pouring out, especially of a liquid: *There was an effusion of lava from the erupting volcano.* 2 unrestrained expression of feeling, etc., in talking or writing. 3 in medicine: **a** the escape of a fluid, such as blood or lymph, from its natural vessel into surrounding tissues or cavities. **b** the fluid that escapes.

ef fu sive (i fyü′siv), *adj.* 1 showing too much feeling; too demonstrative and emotional. 2 (in geology) formed by being poured out as lava on the surface of the earth: *Some igneous rocks are effusive.* 3 OBSOLETE. pouring out. **—ef fu′sive ly,** *adv.* **—ef fu′sive ness,** *n.*

eft[1] (eft), *n.* newt, especially an immature newt. [Old English *efete*]

eft[2] (eft), *adv.* ARCHAIC. eftsoon. [Old English]

EFTA, European Free Trade Association (an economic union of European countries not included in the Common Market).

eft soon (eft sün′), *adv.* ARCHAIC. 1 soon afterward. 2 again. [Old English *eftsōna* < *eft* again + *sōna* at once]

eft soons (eft sünz′), *adv.* ARCHAIC. eftsoon.

e.g., for example; for instance [for Latin *exempli gratia*].

➜ **E.g.** (not usually italicized) is regularly preceded by a comma or semicolon and followed by a comma or colon. It is now usually replaced by *for example.*

e gal i tar i an (ē gal′ə ter′ē ən), *n.* person who believes that all people are equal. *—adj.* believing that all people are equal. [< French *égalitaire* < *égalité* equality]

e gal i tar i an ism (ē gal′ə ter′ē ə niz′əm), *n.* belief in equality, especially in social equality.

e gest (i jest′), *v.t.* discharge; excrete: *egest waste matter.* [< Latin *egestum* carried outside < *ex-* out + *gerere* carry]

e ges tion (i jes′chən), *n.* 1 act or process of egesting. 2 something egested.

egg[1] (eg), *n.* 1 the round or oval body, covered with a shell or membrane, laid by the female of birds, many reptiles, amphibians, fishes, insects, and other animals that do not bring forth living young. Young animals hatch from these eggs. 2 the contents of an egg, especially a hen's egg, used as food. 3 anything shaped like a hen's egg. 4 egg cell; ovum. 5 INFORMAL. person: *a bad egg, a good egg.* [< Scandinavian (Old Icelandic)] **—egg′less,** *adj.* **—egg′like′,** *adj.*

egg[2] (eg), *v.t.* urge or encourage; incite: *We egged the team on when it was behind.* [< Scandinavian (Old Icelandic) *eggja* < *egg* edge]

egg and dart, a decorative pattern consisting of an egg-shaped ornament alternating with a dartlike, tonguelike, or anchorlike ornament. It is a characteristic decoration on the entablature of an Ionic column.

egg beat er (eg′bē′tər), *n.* utensil with revolving blades for beating air into uncooked eggs, cream, etc.

egg cell, a female reproductive cell; ovum.

egg head (eg′hed′), *n.* INFORMAL. an intellectual.

egg nog (eg′nog′), *n.* drink made of eggs beaten up with milk and sugar, often containing whiskey, brandy, or wine. [< *egg*[1] + *nog* strong ale]

egg plant (eg′plant′), *n.* 1 species of nightshade with large, oval, purple fruit. 2 its fruit, eaten as a vegetable.

egg shell (eg′shel′), *n.* 1 shell covering an egg. 2 a yellowish white. *—adj.* 1 like an eggshell; very thin and delicate; somewhat glossy. 2 yellowish-white.

e gis (ē′jis), *n.* aegis.

hat, āge, fär; let, ēqual, tėrm;
it, īce; hot, ōpen, ôrder;
oil, out; cup, pu̇t, rüle;
ch, child; ng, long; sh, she;
th, thin; ᴛʜ, then; zh, measure;

ə represents *a* in about, *e* in taken, *i* in pencil, *o* in lemon, *u* in circus.

< = from, derived from, taken from.

eg lan tine (eg′lən tīn, eg′lən tēn), *n.* sweetbrier. [< Middle French]

e go (ē′gō, eg′ō), *n., pl.* **e gos.** 1 the individual as a whole in his capacity to think, feel, and act; self. 2 INFORMAL. conceit. 3 part of the personality that is conscious of the environment and adapts itself to it. [< Latin, I]

e go cen tric (ē′gō sen′trik, eg′ō sen′trik), *adj.* self-centered; egoistic. —*n.* an egocentric person.

e go ism (ē′gō iz′əm, eg′ō iz′əm), *n.* 1 a seeking the welfare of oneself only; selfishness. 2 conceit. ➤ See **egotism** for usage note.

e go ist (ē′gō ist, eg′ō ist), *n.* 1 person who seeks the welfare of himself only; selfish person. 2 a conceited person.

e go is tic (ē′gō is′tik, eg′ō is′tik), *adj.* 1 seeking the welfare of oneself only; selfish. 2 talking too much about oneself; conceited. **—e′go is′ti cal ly,** *adv.*

e go is ti cal (ē′gō is′tə kəl, eg′ō is′tə kəl), *adj.* egoistic.

e go tism (ē′gə tiz′əm, eg′ə tiz′əm), *n.* 1 habit of thinking, talking, or writing too much of oneself; conceit. 2 selfishness.

➤ **Egotism, egoism** mean a habit of thinking about one's self. Although some people use them interchangeably, the words retain different meanings in careful usage. *Egotism* emphasizes conceit, boasting, and selfishness in talking about oneself and one's own affairs: *His egotism keeps him from having friends. Egoism* emphasizes looking at everyone and everything only as it affects oneself and one's own welfare, but does not suggest boasting or annoying conceit, nor always selfishness: *We forget the natural egoism of a genius when he is charming.*

e go tist (ē′gə tist, eg′ə tist), *n.* 1 person who thinks, talks, or writes about himself too much; conceited person. 2 a selfish person.

e go tis tic (ē′gə tis′tik, eg′ə tis′tik), *adj.* 1 characterized by egotism; conceited. 2 selfish. **—e′go tis′ti cal ly,** *adv.*

e go tis ti cal (ē′gə tis′tə kəl, eg′ə tis′tə kəl), *adj.* egotistic.

e gre gious (i grē′jəs), *adj.* 1 remarkably or extraordinarily bad; outrageous; flagrant: *an egregious blunder.* 2 remarkable; extraordinary. [< Latin *egregius* < *ex-* out + *gregem* herd, flock] **—e gre′gious ly,** *adv.* **—e gre′gious ness,** *n.*

e gress (ē′gres), *n.* 1 a going out: *The door was locked and no other egress was possible.* 2 a way out; exit; outlet: *The egress was plainly marked.* 3 right to go out. [< Latin *egressus* < *egredi* step out < *ex-* out + *gradi* to step, go]

e gret (ē′gret, eg′ret), *n.* 1 any of various herons which in mating season grow tufts of beautiful, long plumes. 2 one of its plumes; aigrette. [< Middle French *aigrette*]

E gypt (ē′jipt), *n.* country in NE Africa. Its official name is the **United Arab Republic.** 33,329,000 pop.; 386,200 sq. mi. *Capital:* Cairo. See **Algeria** for map.

E gyp tian (i jip′shən), *adj.* of or having to do with Egypt or its people. —*n.* 1 native or inhabitant of Egypt. 2 the Hamitic language of the ancient Egyptians.

Egyptian cotton, type of cotton having a long staple, much grown in the United States.

E gyp tol o gist (ē′jip tol′ə jist), *n.* an expert in Egyptology.

E gyp tol o gy (ē′jip tol′ə jē), *n.* the study of the monuments, history, language, etc., of ancient Egypt.

eh (ā), *interj.* 1 exclamation expressing doubt, surprise, or failure to hear exactly. 2 exclamation suggesting yes for an answer: *That's a good joke, eh?*

ei der (ī′dər), *n.* 1 any of a genus of large, northern sea ducks, usually black and white, with very soft feathers on their breasts; eider duck. The females line their nests with eiderdown plucked from their breasts. 2 eiderdown (def. 1). [< Scandinavian (Old Icelandic) *æthr*]

ei der down (ī′dər doun′), *n.* 1 the soft feathers from the breasts of eiders, used to stuff pillows and bed quilts, as trimming, etc.; eider. 2 quilt stuffed with these feathers.

eider duck, eider.

ei det ic (ī det′ik), *adj.* of or having to do with extremely clear images of previous optical impressions: *eidetic imagery.* [< Greek *eidetikos* < *eidos* form] **—ei det′i cal ly,** *adv.*

Eif fel (ī′fəl), *n.* **Alexandre Gustave,** 1832-1923, French engineer, designer of the Eiffel Tower.

Eiffel Tower, tower of wrought-iron framework in Paris. 984 ft.

eight (āt), *n.* 1 one more than seven; 8. 2 group of eight persons or things. 3 crew of eight rowers. —*adj.* being one more than seven. [Old English *eahta*]

eight ball, 1 (in pool) a black ball bearing a figure 8, which in certain varieties of the game carries a penalty unless pocketed last. 2 **behind the eight ball,** U.S. SLANG. in a very bad position.

eight een (ā′tēn′), *n., adj.* eight more than ten; 18.

eight een mo (ā tēn′mō), *n.* octodecimo.

eight eenth (ā′tēnth′), *adj., n.* 1 next after the 17th; last in a series of 18. 2 one, or being one, of 18 equal parts.

eight fold (āt′fōld′), *adj.* having eight parts or members.

eighth (ātth), *adj.* 1 next after the seventh; last in a series of 8. 2 being one of 8 equal parts. —*n.* 1 next after the seventh; last in a series of 8. 2 one of 8 equal parts. 3 (in music) an octave.

eighth note, (in music) a note played for one eighth as long a time as a whole note. See **note** for diagram.

eight i eth (ā′tē ith), *adj., n.* 1 next after the 79th; last in a series of 80. 2 one, or being one, of 80 equal parts.

eight y (ā′tē), *n., pl.* **eight ies,** *adj.* eight times ten; 80.

ei kon (ī′kon), *n.* icon.

Ein stein (īn′stīn), *n.* **Albert,** 1879-1955, American physicist, born in Germany, who developed the theory of relativity.

Einstein equation, equation expressing the relation of mass and energy: $E = mc^2$ (E = the energy in ergs; m = the mass in grams; c = the velocity of light in centimeters per second); mass-energy equation.

ein stein i um (īn stī′nē əm), *n.* a rare, radioactive element, produced artificially from plutonium or uranium. *Symbol:* Es; *atomic number* 99. See pages 326 and 327 for table. [< Albert *Einstein*]

Eir e (er′ə, ar′ə), *n.* Republic of Ireland.

Ei sen how er (ī′zn hou′ər), *n.* **Dwight D(avid),** 1890-1969, American general, the 34th president of the United States, from 1953 to 1961.

eis tedd fod (ā steᴛʜ′vod), *n., pl.* **eis tedd fods, eis tedd fod au** (ā′steᴛʜ vod′ī). a meeting of Welsh poets and musicians. [< Welsh, session < *eistedd* sit]

ei ther (ē′ᴛʜər, ī′ᴛʜər), *adj.* 1 one or the other of two: *Wear either hat, as you prefer.* 2 each of two: *On either side of the river lie cornfields.* —*pron.* 1 one or the other of two: *You may wear either.* 2 each of two: *Either is suitable for growing corn.* —*adv.* 1 any more than another: *If you do not go, I shall not go either.* 2 INFORMAL. word used to strengthen a negative in contradiction or retraction: *I've finished all my homework; no, I haven't either.* —*conj.* one or the other of two: *Either come in or go out.* [Old English *ǣgther* < *ǣghwæther* each of two < *ā* always + *gehwæther* each of two]

➤ **either.** *Either* is usually construed as singular, though its use as a plural seems to be increasing: *Either is good enough for me. Either Grace or Philip is* [or *are*] *expected.*

e jac u late (i jak′yə lāt), *v.t., v.i.,* **-lat ed, -lat ing.** 1 say suddenly and briefly; exclaim. 2 (in physiology) eject; discharge, especially semen. [< Latin *ejaculatum* thrown out < *ex-* out + *jacere* to throw]

e jac u la tion (i jak′yə lā′shən), *n.* 1 something said suddenly and briefly; exclamation. 2 (in physiology) ejection; discharge, especially of semen.

e jac u la to ry (i jak′yə lə tôr′ē, i jak′yə lə tōr′ē), *adj.* 1 said suddenly and briefly; containing exclamations. 2 (in physiology) ejecting; discharging, especially semen.

e ject (i jekt′), *v.t.* 1 throw out from within: *The volcano ejected lava and ashes.* 2 force out; drive out; expel: *The landlord ejected the tenant who did not pay his rent.* [< Latin *ejectum* thrown out < *ex-* out + *jacere* to throw] **—e ject′ment,** *n.* **—e jec′tor,** *n.*

e jec tion (i jek′shən), *n.* 1 an ejecting. 2 a being ejected. 3 something ejected: *Lava is a volcanic ejection.*

ejection seat, an airplane seat that in case of danger can be instantly ejected with its occupant and parachuted to earth.

eke[1] (ēk), *v.t., v.i.,* **eked, ek ing. 1 eke out, a** add to; increase: *The clerk eked out her regular wages by working evenings and Sundays.* **b** barely manage to make (a living). 2 ARCHAIC and DIALECT. increase; enlarge; lengthen. [Old English *ēcan* < *ēaca* addition]

eke[2] (ēk), *adv., conj.* ARCHAIC. also; moreover. [Old English *ēac*]

e kis tics (i kis′tiks), *n.* study of human settlements or communities. [< Greek *oikistēs* settler < *oikos* house]

el (el), *n.* 1 INFORMAL. elevated railroad. 2 ell[1]. 3 ell[2].

e lab or ate (*adj.* i lab′ər it, i lab′rit; *v.* i lab′ə rāt′), *adj., v.,* **-at ed, -at ing.** —*adj.* worked out with great care; having many details; complicated. See synonym study below. —*v.t.* 1 work out with great care; add details to: *She is elaborating her plans for the new addition to the house.* 2 make with labor; produce. —*v.i.* talk, write, etc., in great detail; give added details: *The witness was asked to elaborate upon one of his state-*

ments. [< Latin *elaboratum* worked out < *ex-* out + *labor* work] **—e lab′or ate ly,** *adv.* **—e lab′or ate ness,** *n.* **—e lab′or a-tor,** *n.*

Syn. *adj.* **Elaborate, studied, labored** mean worked out in detail. **Elaborate** emphasizes the idea of many details worked out with great care and exactness: *The elaborate decorations were perfect in every detail.* **Studied** emphasizes care in planning and working out details beforehand: *Her studied unconcern offended me.* **Labored** emphasizes great and unnatural effort to work out details: *The boy gave a labored excuse for arriving late at school.*

e lab o ra tion (i lab′ə rā′shən), *n.* 1 an elaborating. 2 a being elaborated. 3 something elaborated.

E laine (i lān′), *n.* (in Arthurian legends) a beautiful maiden who died for love of Lancelot.

El A la mein (el ä′lə mān′; el al′ə mān′), town on the coast of N Egypt where the British decisively defeated a German and Italian army in 1942.

E lam (ē′ləm), *n.* ancient country and empire just east of Babylonia, in what is now W Iran. It was conquered by the Assyrians in 640 B.C.

E lam ite (ē′lə mīt), *n.* native or inhabitant of Elam.

é lan (ā län′; *French* ā läɴ′), *n.* enthusiasm; liveliness; spirit. [< French]

e land (ē′lənd), *n.* either of two large, heavy, African antelopes of the same genus, with twisted horns. [< Dutch, elk]

e lapse (i laps′), *v.i.,* **e lapsed, e laps ing.** slip away; glide by; pass: *Many hours elapsed while I slept.* [< Latin *elapsum* slipped away < *ex-* away + *labi* to slip, glide]

e las mo branch (i las′mə brangk, i laz′-mə brangk), *n.* any of a class of fishes whose skeletons are formed of cartilage and whose gills are thin and platelike; chondrichthian. Sharks and rays belong to this class. [< Greek *elasmos* metal plate + *branchia* gills]

e las tic (i las′tik), *adj.* 1 having the quality of returning to its original size, shape, or position after being stretched, squeezed, bent, etc.: *Toy balloons, sponges, and steel springs are elastic.* 2 springing back; springy: *an elastic step.* 3 not permanently or easily depressed; buoyant: *Her elastic spirits kept her from being discouraged for long.* 4 easily changed to suit conditions; flexible; adaptable: *an elastic conscience.* —*n.* 1 tape, cloth, cord, etc., woven partly of rubber. 2 a rubber band. [< New Latin *elasticus* < Greek *elastos* ductile, driven < *elaunein* to drive] **—e las′ti cal ly,** *adv.*

e las tic i ty (i las′tis′ə tē, ē′las tis′ə tē), *n.* elastic quality: *Rubber has elasticity. "Good" and "evil" are words having much elasticity of meaning.*

e las ti cized (i las′tə sīzd), *adj.* woven or made with elastic.

e las to mer (i las′tə mər), *n.* any elastic, rubberlike substance. [< *elastic* + Greek *meros* a part]

e late (i lāt′), *v.t.,* **e lat ed, e lat ing.** raise the spirits of; make joyful or proud. [< Latin *elatum* carried away < *ex-* out, away + *latum* carried] **—e lat′er,** *n.*

e lat ed (i lā′tid), *adj.* in high spirits; joyful or proud. **—e lat′ed ly,** *adv.* **—e lat′ed-ness,** *n.*

el a ter (el′ə tər), *n.* 1 (in botany) an elastic filament for discharging and dispersing spores, as in liverworts. 2 any of a family of beetles which spring up with a click when laid on their backs. [< Greek *elatēr* driver < *elaunein* to drive]

e la tion (i lā′shən), *n.* high spirits; joy or pride: *She was filled with elation at having won the first prize.*

E layer, E region.

El ba (el′bə), *n.* Italian island between Italy and Corsica. Napoleon I was in exile there from 1814 to 1815. 29,000 pop.; 86 sq. mi.

El be (el′bə, elb), *n.* river flowing from NW Czechoslovakia through East Germany and West Germany into the North Sea. 725 mi.

El bert Peak (el′bərt), mountain in central Colorado, the highest in the Rocky Mountains. 14,431 ft.

el bow (el′bō), *n.* 1 joint between the upper and lower arm; bend of the arm. 2 anything like a bent arm in shape or position. A bent joint for connecting pipes or a sharp turn in a road or river may be called an elbow. 3 **out at the elbow,** ragged; shabby. 4 **rub elbows,** mingle: *rub elbows with different kinds of people.* —*v.t.* 1 push with the elbow; jostle. 2 make (one's way) by pushing: *He elbowed his way through the crowd.* —*v.i.* make one's way by pushing. [Old English *elnboga* < *eln* length of lower arm + *boga* bow²]

elbow grease, INFORMAL. hard work.

el bow room (el′bō rüm′, el′bō rům′), *n.* plenty of room; enough space to move or work in.

El brus (el′brüs, el′brüz), *n.* **Mount,** the highest mountain in Europe, located in SW Soviet Union in the Caucasus Mountains. 18,481 ft.

El burz Mountains (el bůrz′), mountain range in N Iran, south of the Caspian Sea. The highest peak, Mount Demavend, is 18,600 ft.

eld (eld), *n.* ARCHAIC. 1 old age. 2 ancient times. [Old English *eldo* < *eald* old]

eld er¹ (el′dər), *adj.* 1 born, produced, or formed before something else; older; senior: *my elder sister.* 2 prior in rank, validity, etc.: *an elder title to an estate.* 3 earlier; former: *in elder times.* —*n.* 1 Usually, **elders,** *pl.* person who is older than oneself; one's senior. 2 person of advanced years. 3 one of the older men of a tribe or community to whom age and experience have brought wisdom and judgment. 4 any of various officers in certain churches. 5 presbyter. 6 pastor or minister. 7 member of a higher priesthood in the Mormon church. [Old English *eldra,* comparative of *eald* old]

➤ **elder, eldest.** These archaic forms of *old* survive in formal English and are used, when speaking of persons, chiefly for members of the same family *(the elder brother, our eldest daughter)* and in some phrases *(an elder statesman).*

el der² (el′dər), *n.* any of a genus of shrubs or small trees of the same family as the honeysuckle, with flat clusters of white flowers and black or red berries. [Old English *ellern*]

el der ber ry (el′dər ber′ē), *n., pl.* **-ries.** 1 elder². 2 berry used in making wine, for pies, etc.

eld er ly (el′dər lē), *adj.* 1 somewhat old; beyond middle age. See **old** for synonym study. 2 of or having to do with persons in later life.

eld er ship (el′dər ship), *n.* 1 office or position of an elder in a church. 2 group or court of elders.

elder statesman, an older statesman or politician, usually no longer in office, who is turned to for advice.

eld est (el′dist), *adj.* oldest (of brothers and sisters or of a group). [Old English *eldesta,* superlative of *eald* old] ➤ See **elder** for usage note.

El do ra do (el′də rä′dō, el′də rā′dō), *n., pl.* **-dos.** El Dorado.

El Do ra do (el də rä′dō; el də rā′dō), *pl.* **-dos** 1 an imaginary city or region supposed to be full of gold and treasure, sought by early Spanish explorers in America. 2 any place said to be wealthy or where wealth is easily acquired. [< Spanish; literally, the gilded one]

elec., 1 electric. 2 electrical. 3 electricity.

e lect (i lekt′), *v.t.* 1 choose or select (a person) for an office, appointment, etc., from a number of candidates by voting. 2 choose; select: *We elected to play baseball.* —*v.i.* choose. —*adj.* 1 elected for an office, appointment, etc., but not yet installed: *the governor elect.* 2 specially chosen; selected. 3 chosen by God for salvation and eternal life. —*n.* **the elect, a** people selected or chosen by God for salvation and eternal life because He foresees their merit. **b** people who belong to a group with special rights and privileges. [< Latin *electum* chosen < *ex-* out + *legere* choose]

elect., 1 electric. 2 electrical. 3 electricity.

e lec tion (i lek′shən), *n.* 1 a choosing or selecting for an office, appointment, etc., by vote. 2 a being chosen or selected for an office, appointment, etc., by vote. 3 selection by God for salvation. 4 choice; selection or preference.

e lec tion eer (i lek′shə nir′), *v.i.* work for the success of a candidate or party in an election.

e lec tive (i lek′tiv), *adj.* 1 chosen by an election: *Senators are elective officials.* 2 filled by an election: *The office of President of the United States is an elective office.* 3 having the right to vote in an election. 4 based upon the principle of electing to office: *an elective government.* 5 open to choice; not required; optional: *Spanish is an elective subject in many high schools.* —*n.* subject or course of study which may be taken, but is not required. **—e lec′tive ly,** *adv.* **—e lec′tive ness,** *n.*

e lec tor (i lek′tər), *n.* 1 person who has the right to vote in an election. 2 member of the electoral college. 3 one of the princes who had the right to elect the emperor of the Holy Roman Empire.

e lec tor al (i lek′tər əl), *adj.* 1 of electors. 2 of an election. **—e lec′tor al ly,** *adv.*

electoral college, group of people chosen by the voters to elect the President and Vice-President of the United States.

electoral vote, the votes cast by the electoral college.

e lec tor ate (i lek′tər it), *n.* 1 the persons having the right to vote in an election. 2 territory under the rule of an elector of the Holy Roman Empire. 3 rank of an elector of the Holy Roman Empire.

electr-, *combining form.* form of **electro-** before vowels.

E lec tra (i lek′trə), *n.* (in Greek legends) the daughter of Agamemnon and Clytemnestra. Electra urged her brother, Orestes, to kill their mother and her lover in order to avenge the murder of their father.

hat, āge, fär; let, ēqual, tėrm;
it, īce; hot, ōpen, ôrder;
oil, out; cup, pu̇t, rüle;
ch, child; ng, long; sh, she;
th, thin; ᴛʜ, then; zh, measure;

ə represents *a* in about, *e* in taken, *i* in pencil, *o* in lemon, *u* in circus.

< = from, derived from, taken from.

e lec tric (i lek′trik), *adj.* 1 of or having to do with electricity. 2 charged with electricity: *an electric battery.* 3 run by electricity. 4 exciting; thrilling. —*n.* INFORMAL. automobile or railroad car run by electricity. [< New Latin *electricus* generated (by friction) from amber < Latin *electrum* amber < Greek *ēlektron*]

e lec tri cal (i lek′trə kəl), *adj.* electric.

e lec tri cal ly (i lek′trik lē), *adv.* by electricity.

electrical storm, thunderstorm.

electrical transcription, 1 a radio program broadcast from a special phonograph record. 2 a special phonograph record used for such a broadcast.

electric chair, 1 chair used in electrocuting criminals condemned to death. 2 sentence of death in such a chair.

electric charge, an accumulation of electricity in a storage battery, condenser, etc., which may again be discharged.

electric current, flow of electricity through a conductor or transmitter.

electric eel, a large, eellike fish of South America that can give strong electric shocks.

electric eye, photoelectric cell.

electric field, any space in which force due to an electric charge exists.

e lec tri cian (i lek′trish′ən, ē′lek trish′ən), *n.* person whose work is installing or repairing electric wiring, lights, motors, etc.

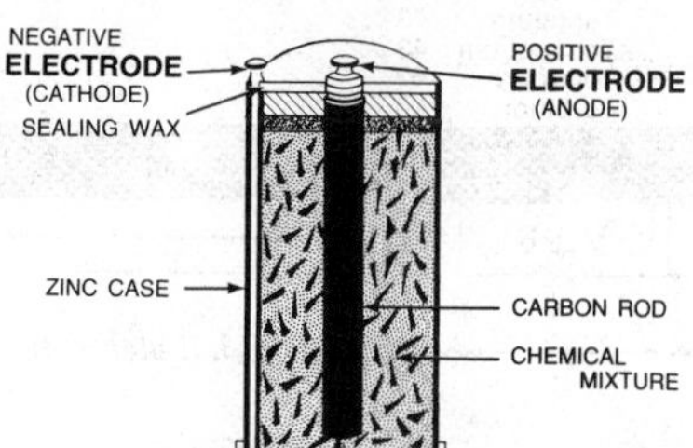

electrode—electrodes of a dry cell. The chemical mixture reacts with the zinc, causing positive ions to flow toward the carbon rod and electrons to flow toward the zinc. When the electrodes are connected in a circuit, an electric current leaves the cell at the cathode and returns to it at the anode.

e lec tric i ty (i lek′tris′ə tē, ē′lek tris′ə tē), *n.* 1 form of energy which can produce light, heat, magnetism, and chemical changes, and which can be generated by friction, induction, or chemical changes. Electricity is regarded as consisting of oppositely charged particles, electrons and protons, which may be at rest or moving about. Negative electricity is the form of electricity in which the electron is the elementary unit; positive electricity is that in which the proton is the elementary unit. 2 electric current. 3 branch of physics that deals with electricity.

electric light bulb, incandescent lamp.

electric ray, any of a family of flat-bodied fishes that stun or kill their prey by means of an electric shock; torpedo.

electric storm, thunderstorm.

e lec tri fi ca tion (i lek′trə fə kā′shən), *n.* 1 an electrifying. 2 a being electrified.

e lec tri fy (i lek′trə fī), *v.t.*, **-fied, -fy ing.** 1 charge with electricity. 2 equip for the use of electric power: *Some railroads once run by steam are now electrified.* 3 provide with electric power service: *Many rural areas will soon be electrified.* 4 give an electric shock to. 5 excite; thrill.

electro-, *combining form.* 1 electric ____: *Electromagnet = an electric magnet.* 2 electrically ____: *Electropositive = electrically positive.* 3 produced or operated by electricity, as in *electroplated.* [< Greek *ēlektron* amber]

e lec tro car di o gram (i lek′trō kär′dē ə gram), *n.* the tracing or record made by an electrocardiograph; cardiogram.

e lec tro car di o graph (i lek′trō kär′dē ə graf), *n.* instrument that detects and records the electrical impulses produced by the action of the heart with each beat; cardiograph. It is used to diagnose diseases of the heart.

e lec tro car di o graph ic (i lek′trō kär′dē ə graf′ik), *adj.* having to do with an electrocardiograph or electrocardiography.

e lec tro car di og ra phy (i lek′trō kär′dē og′rə fē), *n.* science or technique of using an electrocardiograph.

e lec tro chem i cal (i lek′trō kem′ə kəl), *adj.* of or having to do with electrochemistry. **—e lec′tro chem′i cal ly,** *adv.*

e lec tro chem is try (i lek′trō kem′ə strē), *n.* branch of chemistry that deals with chemical changes produced by electricity and the production of electricity by chemical changes.

e lec tro cute (i lek′trə kyüt), *v.t.*, **-cut ed, -cut ing.** kill or execute by the passage of a high voltage of electricity through the body. [< *electro-* + *(exe)cute*]

e lec tro cu tion (i lek′trə kyü′shən), *n.* a killing or execution by the passage of a high voltage of electricity through the body.

e lec trode (i lek′trōd), *n.* conductor by which electricity is brought into or out of a conducting medium, as either of the two terminals of a battery. The anode and cathode of an electric cell are electrodes. [< *electro-* + Greek *hodos* way]

e lec tro de pos it (i lek′trō di poz′it), *v.t.* deposit (a substance) by electrolysis.

e lec tro dep o si tion (i lek′trō dep′ə zish′ən), *n.* the depositing of a substance by electrolysis.

e lec tro dy nam ic (i lek′trō dī nam′ik), *adj.* 1 of or having to do with the force of electricity in motion. 2 of electrodynamics.

e lec tro dy nam ics (i lek′trō dī nam′iks), *n.* branch of physics that deals with the mutual influence of electric currents, the interaction of currents and magnets, and the influence of an electric current on itself.

e lec tro en ceph a lo gram (i lek′trō en sef′ə lə gram), *n.* a tracing made by an electroencephalograph.

e lec tro en ceph a lo graph (i lek′trō en sef′ə lə graf), *n.* instrument for measuring the electrical activity of the brain, used in the diagnosis and treatment of brain disorders.

e lec tro en ceph a lo graph ic (i lek′trō en sef′ə lə graf′ik), *adj.* of or having to do with an electroencephalograph or electroencephalography.

e lec tro en ceph a log ra phy (i lek′trō en sef′ə log′rə fē), *n.* science or technique of using an electroencephalograph.

e lec tro form (i lek′trə fôrm′), *v.t.* form (a substance) by electrodeposition on a mold.

e lec tro jet (i lek′trə jet), *n.* an electric current moving in an ionized layer in the upper atmosphere of the earth.

e lec tro ki net ics (i lek′trō ki net′iks), *n.* branch of physics that deals with electricity in motion.

e lec tro lu mi nes cence (i lek′trō lü′mə nes′ns), *n.* light produced without heat by passing an alternating current through a phosphorescent substance.

e lec tro lu mi nes cent (i lek′trō lu′mə nes′nt), *adj.* of or having to do with electroluminescence.

e lec trol y sis (i lek′trol′ə sis, ē′lek trol′ə sis), *n.* 1 decomposition of a chemical compound into its ions by the passage of an electrical current through a solution of it. 2 subjection of a chemical compound to such a process. 3 removal of excess hair, moles, etc., by destruction with an electrified needle.

e lec tro lyte (i lek′trə līt), *n.* 1 a chemical compound which ionizes when dissolved in a suitable liquid, or when melted, thus becoming a conductor for an electric current. Acids, bases, and salts are electrolytes. 2 solution that will conduct an electric current. [< *electro-* + Greek *lytos* soluble < *lyein* to loose]

e lec tro lyt ic (i lek′trə lit′ik), *adj.* of or having to do with electrolysis or with an electrolyte. **—e lec′tro lyt′i cal ly,** *adv.*

e lec tro lyze (i lek′trə līz), *v.t.*, **-lyzed, -lyz ing.** decompose by electrolysis.

e lec tro mag net (i lek′trō mag′nit), *n.* piece of soft iron that becomes a strong magnet temporarily when an electric current is passing through wire coiled around it.

e lec tro mag net ic (i lek′trō mag net′ik), *adj.* 1 of or caused by an electromagnet. 2 of electromagnetism. **—e lec′tro mag net′i cal ly,** *adv.*

electromagnetic spectrum, the entire range of the different types of electromagnetic waves, from the very long, low-frequency radio waves, through infrared and light waves, to the very short, high-frequency cosmic rays and X rays.

electromagnetic wave, wave of energy generated when an electric charge oscillates or is accelerated. Electromagnetic waves are light waves, radio waves, etc., according to their frequencies and wavelengths. See **radiation** for table.

e lec tro mag net ism (i lek′trō mag′nə tiz′əm), *n.* 1 magnetism produced by a current of electricity. 2 branch of physics that deals with electricity and magnetism.

e lec tro met al lur gy (i lek′trō met′l ėr′jē), *n.* the branch of metallurgy that deals with the application of electricity to metallurgical processes, such as the use of electricity as a source of heat in refining metals.

e lec trom e ter (i lek′trom′ə tər, ē′lek trom′ə tər), *n.* instrument for measuring differences in electric charge or potential.

e lec tro met ric (i lek′trə met′rik), *adj,* having to do with electrometry.

e lec trom e try (i lek′trom′ə trē, ē′lek-

Using the Periodic Table

The periodic table of the elements describes the atomic structure of each element and arranges elements having similar properties into groups. The discovery of the periodic law led to this arrangement in which the recurrent chemical properties of elements are displayed when the elements are arranged in the order of their atomic numbers.

Scientists have used the periodic table to predict the existence and chemical properties of unknown elements. Gallium, germanium, and scandium were predicted in this way long before they were discovered. The periodic table is also used as a reliable source for checking many kinds of information about the known elements.

Terms used on the periodic table:

atomic number, number indicating both the number of protons in the nucleus of an atom and the number of electrons that circle the nucleus of an atom. Hydrogen has one proton in its nucleus and one electron circling its nucleus.

group, vertical column including elements having similar chemical properties. Example: Group VIIA includes the most active elements, any of which combines directly with a metal to form a salt.

period, horizontal row including elements having similar atomic structures. The number of the period indicates the number of rings of electrons surrounding the nucleus of each atom of the elements in the period.

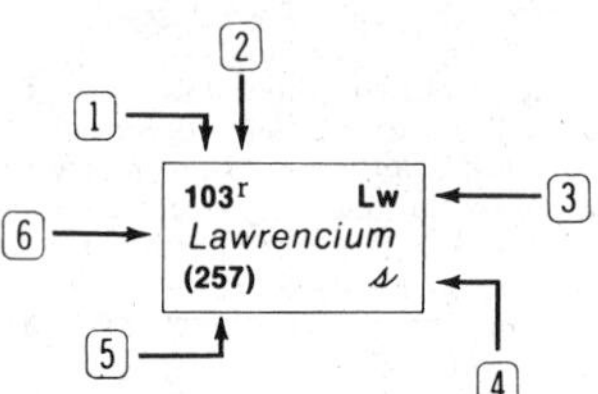

1 atomic number.
2 radioactive element.
3 chemical symbol.
4 form of pure element at 45°F under normal pressure: s=solid, l=liquid, g=gas.
5 atomic weight (parentheses indicate atomic weight of the most stable isotope).
6 name (italics indicate an element is artificially produced).

Chemical Elements and Their Atomic Numbers

Actinium	89	Cesium	55	Helium	2	Neodymium	60	Radium	88	Thallium	81
Aluminum	13	Chlorine	17	Holmium	67	Neon	10	Radon	86	Thorium	90
Americium	95	Chromium	24	Hydrogen	1	Neptunium	93	Rhenium	75	Thulium	69
Antimony	51	Cobalt	27	Indium	49	Nickel	28	Rhodium	45	Tin	50
Argon	18	Copper	29	Iodine	53	Niobium	41	Rubidium	37	Titanium	22
Arsenic	33	Curium	96	Iridium	77	Nitrogen	7	Ruthenium	44	Tungsten	74
Astatine	85	Dysprosium	66	Iron	26	Nobelium	102	Samarium	62	Uranium	92
Barium	56	Einsteinium	99	Krypton	36	Osmium	76	Scandium	21	Vanadium	23
Berkelium	97	Erbium	68	Lanthanum	57	Oxygen	8	Selenium	34	Xenon	54
Beryllium	4	Europium	63	Lawrencium	103	Palladium	46	Silicon	14	Ytterbium	70
Bismuth	83	Fermium	100	Lead	82	Phosphorus	15	Silver	47	Yttrium	39
Boron	5	Fluorine	9	Lithium	3	Platinum	78	Sodium	11	Zinc	30
Bromine	35	Francium	87	Lutetium	71	Plutonium	94	Strontium	38	Zirconium	40
Cadmium	48	Gadolinium	64	Magnesium	12	Polonium	84	Sulfur	16		
Calcium	20	Gallium	31	Manganese	25	Potassium	19	Tantalum	73		
Californium	98	Germanium	32	Mendelevium	101	Praseodymium	59	Technetium	43		
Carbon	6	Gold	79	Mercury	80	Promethium	61	Tellurium	52		
Cerium	58	Hafnium	72	Molybdenum	42	Protactinium	91	Terbium	65		

PERIODIC TABLE OF THE ELEMENTS

Group → / Period ↓	I·A	II·A	III·B	IV·B	V·B	VI·B	VII·B	VIII	
			← *Transitional elements*						
1 2 elements	1 H Hydrogen 1.00797 g								
	← LIGHT METALS *Alkali metals*	→ *Alkaline-Earth metals*							
			← *HEAVY METALS*						
2 8 elements	3 Li Lithium 6.939 s	4 Be Beryllium 9.0122 s							
3 8 elements	11 Na Sodium 22.9898 s	12 Mg Magnesium 24.312 s	← *Hard metals*				→	← *Ductile*	
4 18 elements	19 K Potassium 39.102 s	20 Ca Calcium 40.08 s	21 Sc Scandium 44.956 s	22 Ti Titanium 47.90 s	23 V Vanadium 50.942 s	24 Cr Chromium 51.996 s	25 Mn Manganese 54.9380 s	26 Fe Iron 55.847 s	27 Co Cobalt 58.9332 s
5 18 elements	37 Rb Rubidium 85.47 s	38 Sr Strontium 87.62 s	39 Y Yttrium 88.905 s	40 Zr Zirconium 91.22 s	41 Nb Niobium 92.906 s	42 Mo Molybdenum 95.94 s	43r Tc *Technetium* (99) s	44 Ru Ruthenium 101.07 s	45 Rh Rhodium 102.905 s
6 32 elements	55 Cs Cesium 132.905 s	56 Ba Barium 137.34 s	57-71 Lanthanides	72 Hf Hafnium 178.49 s	73 Ta Tantalum 180.948 s	74 W Tungsten 183.85 s	75 Re Rhenium 186.2 s	76 Os Osmium 190.2 s	77 Ir Iridium 192.2 s
7 17 known elements	87r Fr Francium (223) s	88r Ra Radium (226) s	89-103 Actinides						

57-71 Lanthanides (Rare Earths)	57 La Lanthanum 138.91 s	58 Ce Cerium 140.12 s	59 Pr Praseodymium 140.907 s	60 Nd Neodymium 144.24 s	61r Pm *Promethium* (147) s	62 Sm Samarium 150.35 s
89-103 Actinides	89r Ac Actinium (227) s	90r Th Thorium 232.038 s	91r Pa Protactinium (231) s	92r U Uranium 238.03 s	93r Np *Neptunium* (237) s	94r Pu *Plutonium* (242) s

trom′ə trē), *n.* the measurement of electricity by an electrometer.

e lec tro mo tive (i lek′trə mō′tiv), *adj.* 1 producing a flow of electricity. 2 of or having to do with electromotive force.

electromotive force, the force that causes a flow of electricity. It is the amount of energy derived from an electric source in one second when one unit of current is passing through the source, commonly measured in volts. Electromotive force is produced by differences in electrical charge or potential.

electromotive series, (in chemistry) a list of the metallic elements in the decreasing order of their tendencies to change to ions in solution, so that each metal displaces from solution those below it in the list and is displaced by those above it.

e lec tron (i lek′tron), *n.* an elementary particle charged with one unit of negative electricity and a very small mass. All atoms have electrons arranged about a nucleus. [< *electr(ic)* + *-on,* as in *ion*]

e lec tro neg a tive (i lek′trō neg′ə tiv), *adj.* 1 charged with negative electricity. 2 tending to pass to the anode in electrolysis. 3 tending to gain electrons; nonmetallic.

electron gun, the part of a cathode-ray tube that guides the flow and greatly increases the speed of electrons. In a television set or an oscilloscope, an electron gun directs a stream of electrons to the screen.

e lec tron ic (i lek′tron′ik, ē′lek tron′ik), *adj.* 1 of or having to do with electrons. 2 of or having to do with electronics. —**e lec′tron′i cal ly,** *adv.*

electronic brain, a complex electronic computer.

e lec tron ics (i lek′tron′iks, ē′lektron′iks), *n.* branch of physics that deals with the production, activity, and effects of electrons in motion in vacuum or through gases, especially with reference to industrial applications, as in vacuum tubes, etc.

electron lens, the electrodes or conductors which set up electric or magnetic fields by which a beam of electrons can be focused as light rays are by an optical lens.

electron microscope, microscope that uses beams of electrons instead of beams of light to project enlarged images upon a fluorescent surface or photographic plate. It has much higher power than any ordinary microscope.

electron optics, branch of electronics that deals with the control of beams of electrons by an electric or magnetic field in the same manner that lenses control a beam of light.

electron tube, vacuum tube.

electron volt, unit of electrical energy equal to the energy gained by an electron on going through a potential difference of one volt. One Bev equals one billion electron volts.

e lec tro pho re sis (i lek′trō fə rē′sis), *n.* the movement of colloidal particles resulting from the influence of an electric field. [< *electro-* + Greek *phorēsis* a carrying]

hat, āge, fär; let, ēqual, tėrm;
it, īce; hot, ōpen, ôrder;
oil, out; cup, pu̇t, rüle;
ch, child; ng, long; sh, she;
th, thin; ᴛʜ, then; zh, measure;

ə represents *a* in about, *e* in taken,
i in pencil, *o* in lemon, *u* in circus.

< = from, derived from, taken from.

e lec tro pho ret ic (i lek′trō fə ret′ik), *adj.* having to do with or produced by electrophoresis.

e lec troph or us (i lek′trof′ər əs, ē′lektrof′ər əs), *n., pl.* **-or i** (-ə rī′), a simple device for producing charges of electricity by means of induction. [< *electro-* + Greek *-phoros* bearing]

e lec tro plate (i lek′trə plāt′), *v.t.,* **-plat ed, -plat ing.** cover (silverware, printing plates, etc.) with a coating of metal by means of electrolysis. —**e lec′tro plat′er,** *n.*

e lec tro pos i tive (i lek′trō poz′ə tiv), *adj.* 1 charged with positive electricity. 2 tending to pass to the cathode in electrolysis. 3 tending to lose electrons; metallic.

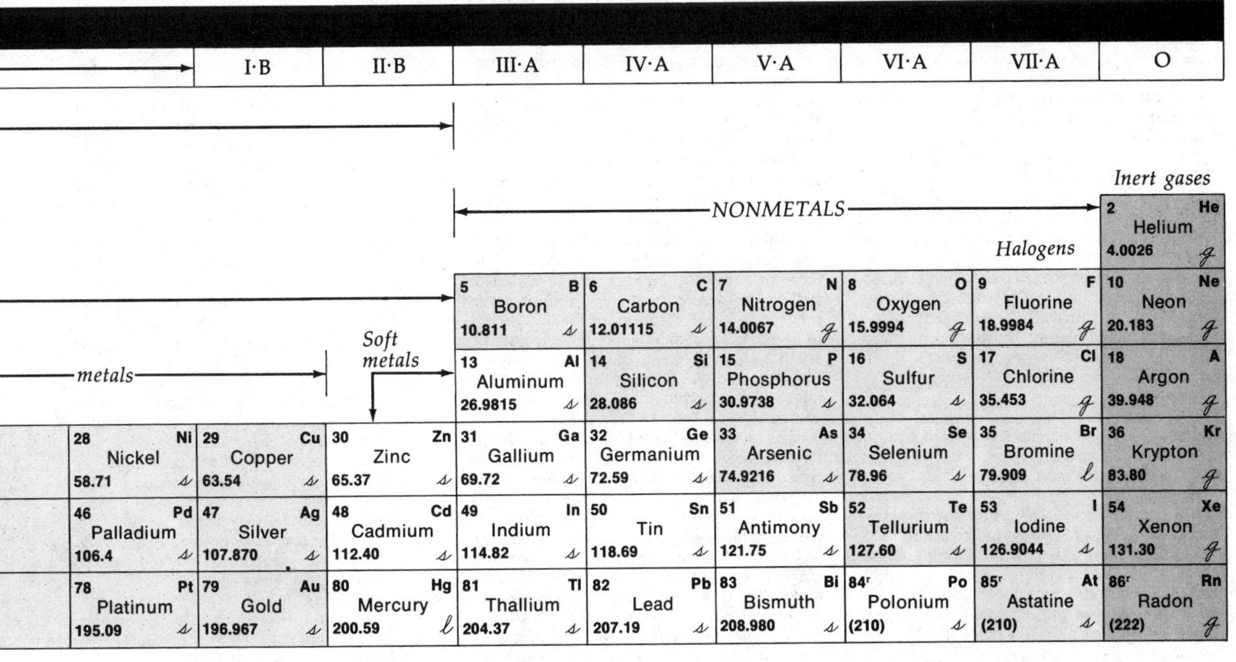

	I·B	II·B	III·A	IV·A	V·A	VI·A	VII·A	O
								2 He Helium 4.0026 g
			5 B Boron 10.811 s	6 C Carbon 12.01115 s	7 N Nitrogen 14.0067 g	8 O Oxygen 15.9994 g	9 F Fluorine 18.9984 g	10 Ne Neon 20.183 g
			13 Al Aluminum 26.9815 s	14 Si Silicon 28.086 s	15 P Phosphorus 30.9738 s	16 S Sulfur 32.064 s	17 Cl Chlorine 35.453 g	18 A Argon 39.948 g
28 Ni Nickel 58.71 s	29 Cu Copper 63.54 s	30 Zn Zinc 65.37 s	31 Ga Gallium 69.72 s	32 Ge Germanium 72.59 s	33 As Arsenic 74.9216 s	34 Se Selenium 78.96 s	35 Br Bromine 79.909 l	36 Kr Krypton 83.80 g
46 Pd Palladium 106.4 s	47 Ag Silver 107.870 s	48 Cd Cadmium 112.40 s	49 In Indium 114.82 s	50 Sn Tin 118.69 s	51 Sb Antimony 121.75 s	52 Te Tellurium 127.60 s	53 I Iodine 126.9044 s	54 Xe Xenon 131.30 g
78 Pt Platinum 195.09 s	79 Au Gold 196.967 s	80 Hg Mercury 200.59 l	81 Tl Thallium 204.37 s	82 Pb Lead 207.19 s	83 Bi Bismuth 208.980 s	84r Po Polonium (210) s	85r At Astatine (210) s	86r Rn Radon (222) g

63 Eu Europium 151.96 s	64 Gd Gadolinium 157.25 s	65 Tb Terbium 158.924 s	66 Dy Dysprosium 162.50 s	67 Ho Holmium 164.930 s	68 Er Erbium 167.26 s	69 Tm Thulium 168.934 s	70 Yb Ytterbium 173.04 s	71 Lu Lutetium 174.97 s
95r Am *Americium* (243) s	96r Cm *Curium* (247) s	97r Bk *Berkelium* (249) s	98r Cf *Californium* (251) s	99r E *Einsteinium* (254) s	100r Fm *Fermium* (253) s	101r Md *Mendelevium* (256) s	102r No *Nobelium* (254) s	103r Lw *Lawrencium* (257) s

e lec tro scope (i lek′trə skōp), *n.* device that indicates the presence of minute charges of electricity and shows whether they are positive or negative.

e lec tro scop ic (i lek′trə skop′ik), *adj.* of, having to do with, or done with an electroscope.

e lec tro shock therapy (i lek′trō-shok′), shock therapy by electrical means.

e lec tro stat ic (i lek′trō stat′ik), *adj.* 1 of or having to do with static electricity. 2 of or having to do with electrostatics. **—e lec′tro-stat′i cal ly,** *adv.*

electrostatic generator, device which produces high electrical charges, used as a particle accelerator.

e lec tro stat ics (i lek′trō stat′iks), *n.* branch of physics that deals with static electricity and charged objects.

e lec tro sur ger y (i lek′trō sėr′jər ē), *n.* surgical diathermy.

e lec tro ther a py (i lek′trō ther′ə pē), *n.* treatment of disease by electricity, as in diathermy.

e lec tro type (i lek′trə tīp), *n., v.,* **-typed, -typ ing.** *—n.* 1 a metal or composition plate used in printing. It is a copy of a page of type, an engraving, or the like, consisting of a thin shell of copper, lead, etc., deposited by electrolytic action in a wax or plastic mold of the original and backed with type metal. 2 print made from such a plate. *—v.t., v.i.* make such a plate or plates of. **—e lec′tro-typ′er,** *n.*

e lec tro va lence (i lek′trō vā′ləns), *n.* the number of electrons gained or lost by an atom when it becomes an ion.

e lec tro va lent (i lek′trō vā′lənt), *adj.* of or producing electrovalence.

e lec trum (i lek′trəm), *n.* a pale-yellow alloy of gold and silver, used by the ancients. [< Latin < Greek *ēlektron*]

e lec tu ar y (i lek′chü er′ē), *n., pl.* **-ar ies.** a medicinal paste of powdered drugs and syrup or honey. [< Late Latin *electuarium* < Greek *ekleikton* lozenge]

el ee mos y nar y (el′ə mos′ə ner′ē, el′ē ə-mos′ə ner′ē), *adj.* 1 of or for charity; charitable. 2 provided by charity; free. 3 dependent on charity; supported by charity. [< Late Latin *eleemosynarius* < Latin *eleemosyna* alms < Greek *eleēmosynē* mercy < *eleos*]

el e gance (el′ə gəns), *n.* 1 good taste; refined grace and richness; luxurious beauty. 2 something elegant.

el e gan cy (el′ə gən sē), *n., pl.* **-cies.** elegance.

el e gant (el′ə gənt), *adj.* 1 having or showing good taste; gracefully and richly refined; beautifully luxurious: *The palace had elegant furnishings.* See **fine**[1] for synonym study. 2 expressed with taste; correct and polished in expression or arrangement: *an elegant style of writing.* [< Old French < Latin *elegantem*] **—el′e gant ly,** *adv.*

el e gi ac (el′ə jī′ak, i lē′jē ak), *adj.* 1 of or suitable for an elegy. 2 sad; mournful; melancholy. 3 written in elegiacs. *—n.* (in Greek and Latin verse) a dactylic hexameter couplet, the second line having no unaccented syllables in the third and sixth feet:

—∪∪|—∪∪|—∪∪|—∪∪|—∪∪|—∪
—∪∪|—∪∪|— |—∪∪|—∪∪|—

el e gize (el′ə jīz), *v.t., v.i.,* **-gized, -giz ing.** write an elegy (about).

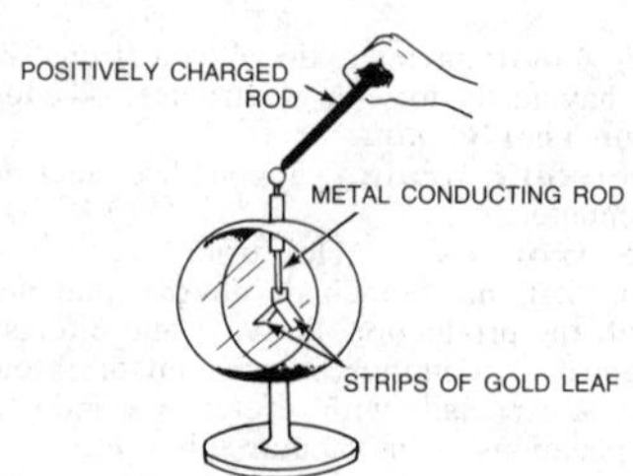

electroscope—When a positively charged rod touches the metal conducting rod, the strips of gold leaf repel each other. When a negative charge is brought into contact with the metal conducting rod, the strips of gold leaf come together again.

el e gy (el′ə jē), *n., pl.* **-gies.** 1 a mournful or melancholy poem, usually a lament for the dead. Milton's *Lycidas* and Shelley's *Adonais* are elegies. 2 poem written in elegiac meter. [< Greek *elegeia* < *elegos* mournful poem]

elem., elementary.

el e ment (el′ə mənt), *n.* 1 substance composed of atoms that are chemically alike and which cannot be separated into simpler parts by chemical means. Gold, iron, carbon, sulfur, oxygen, and hydrogen are among the 103 known elements. All matter is composed of either single elements or groups of elements. See pages 326 and 327 for table. 2 one of the basic parts of which anything is made up. See synonym study below. 3 a simple or necessary part to be learned first; first principle; rudiment: *teach the elements of grammar.* 4 one of the four substances —earth, water, air, and fire—that were once thought to be the fundamental constituents of matter. 5 **the elements,** the forces of the atmosphere, especially in bad weather: *The raging storm seemed to be a war of the elements.* 6 environment, sphere, or activity in which a particular person feels at home and able to do his best work or live to the full: *She was out of her element on the farm.* 7 the part that does the work in an electrical device. 8 (in military use) any unit or part of a larger group, formation, or maneuver. 9 in mathematics: **a** member of a set. **b** a very small part of a given magnitude similar in nature to the whole magnitude. **c** one of the lines, planes, points, etc., that make up a geometrical figure. 10 Often, **elements,** *pl.* bread and wine used in the Eucharist. [< Latin *elementum* rudiment, first principle]

Syn. 2 **Element, component, constituent, ingredient** mean one of the parts of which something is made up. **Element,** the general word, applies to any essential or basic part of something: *The Latin element in English is surprisingly large.* **Component** means a part of something that joins together with other parts to form a unit: *Quartz and feldspar are the chief components of granite.* **Constituent,** often used interchangeably with *component,* differs in suggesting active helping to form the whole instead of just being an inactive part: *The colors of the rainbow are the constituents of white light.* **Ingredient** suggests that the helping parts lose individual identity in a mixture or combination: *Milk, eggs, and flour are basic ingredients in making a cake.*

el e men tal (el′ə men′tl), *adj.* 1 of the forces of the atmosphere, especially of the weather: *The storm showed elemental fury in its violence.* 2 simple but powerful; natural: *Hunger is an elemental feeling.* 3 elementary. 4 of the four elements—earth, water, air, and fire. 5 of the forces of nature. Primitive peoples usually worship elemental gods, such as the sun, earth, or thunder. 6 of the nature of an ultimate constituent; not compounded; simple. 7 being a necessary or basic part. **—el′e men′tal ly,** *adv.*

el e men tar y (el′ə men′tər ē, el′ə men′-trē), *adj.* 1 of or dealing with the simple, necessary parts to be learned first; having to do with first principles; introductory. See synonym study below. 2 made up of only one chemical element; not a compound: *Silver is an elementary substance.* 3 having to do with a chemical element or elements. 4 elemental (def. 7). 5 of or having to do with basic or primary instruction. **—el′e men-tar′i ly,** *adv.*

Syn. 1 **Elementary, rudimentary, primary** mean having to do with the beginnings of something. **Elementary** emphasizes the idea of being basic, and applies to the first steps or beginning facts and principles of anything: *I learned addition and subtraction in elementary arithmetic.* **Rudimentary,** a formal word, means not yet developed beyond the first stage or beginning: *I have only a rudimentary knowledge of mathematics.* **Primary** emphasizes coming first in order or time: *Primary grades are the first three grades of elementary school.*

elementary particle, one of the fundamental units of which matter is composed; fundamental particle. Some of the many elementary particles known to exist are the electron, proton, neutron, neutrino, positron, photon, and meson.

elementary school, 1 school of six grades for pupils from about six to about twelve years of age, followed by junior high school. 2 school of eight grades for pupils from about six to about fourteen years, followed by a four-year high school.

el e phant (el′ə fənt), *n., pl.* **-phants** or **-phant.** either of a family of two massive, five-toed, herbivorous mammals, practically hairless, with long, muscular snouts or trunks, and large tusks developed from the upper incisor teeth. **African elephants,** the largest living land animals, have large ears and both the males and females have tusks. **Asian** or **Indian elephants** have smaller ears and the females often have no tusks. [< Latin *elephantus* < Greek *elephantos* elephant, ivory]

el e phan ti a sis (el′ə fan tī′ə sis), *n.* disease, usually caused by parasitic worms, characterized by inflammation and obstruction of the lymphatic vessels. Parts of the body, usually the legs, become greatly enlarged and the skin thickened and broken. [< Greek < *elephantos* elephant]

el e phan tine (el′ə fan′tēn′, el′ə fan′tīn), *adj.* 1 like an elephant in action or manner; clumsy and unwieldy. 2 of elephants.

elephant seal, sea elephant.

El eu sin i an (el′yə sin′ē ən), *adj.* of or having to do with Eleusis.

Eleusinian mysteries, the secret, religious ceremonies held yearly in ancient Greece at Eleusis in honor of the goddesses Demeter and Persephone.

E leu sis (i lü′sis), *n.* city in ancient Greece, near Athens.

el e vate (el′ə vāt), *v.t.,* **-vat ed, -vat ing.** 1 raise above the usual position, or above the level of surrounding objects; lift up. See **raise** for synonym study. 2 raise in rank or station; promote: *When the president of the company retired, the vice-president was elevated to his position.* 3 raise in quality: *Studying literature helps elevate one's critical ability.* 4 put in high spirits; make joyful or proud; elate. [< Latin *elevatum* raised up < *ex-* + *levare* lighten, raise]

el e vat ed (el′ə vā′tid), *adj.* 1 lifted up; raised; high. 2 dignified; lofty. 3 in high spirits; joyful; proud. —*n.* INFORMAL. elevated railroad.

elevated railroad, electric railroad that runs above street level on a supporting steel framework high enough for traffic to pass underneath; el.

el e va tion (el′ə vā′shən), *n.* 1 a raised place; high place: *A hill is an elevation.* 2 height above the earth's surface: *The airplane cruised at an elevation of 35,000 feet.* 3 height above sea level: *The elevation of Denver is 5300 feet.* 4 dignity; loftiness; nobility. 5 a raising; lifting up: *the elevation of Caesar from general to ruler of Rome.* 6 a being raised or lifted up. 7 a flat scale drawing of the front, rear, or side of a building, as distinguished from a ground plan. 8 the angular distance of a star, planet, etc., above the horizon.

el e va tor (el′ə vā′tər), *n.* 1 thing that raises or lifts up. 2 a moving platform, cage, or enclosed car to carry people and things up and down in a building, mine, etc. 3 grain elevator. 4 an adjustable, flat piece usually at the tail of an airplane by which the airplane may be caused to go up or down.

e lev en (i lev′ən), *n.* 1 one more than ten; 11. 2 a football or cricket team. —*adj.* being one more than ten. [Old English *endleofan* one left (over ten)]

e lev enth (i lev′ənth), *adj., n.* 1 next after the 10th; last in a series of 11. 2 one, or being one, of 11 equal parts.

eleventh hour, the latest possible moment.

el e von (el′ə von), *n.* a movable control surface on an aircraft or missile that functions as both an elevator and an aileron. [< *elev(ator)* + *(ailer)on*]

elf (elf), *n., pl.* **elves.** 1 a small, imaginary fairy, especially a male one, that is usually mischievous. 2 a small, mischievous person. [Old English *ælf*] —**elf′like′,** *adj.*

El Fai yum or **El Fai yûm** (el fī yüm′), city in N Egypt, SW of Cairo. 102,000.

elf in (el′fən), *adj.* 1 having to do with elves. 2 diminutive. 3 full of strange charm; fairylike.

elf ish (el′fish), *adj.* characteristic of elves; mischievous. Also, **elvish.** —**elf′ish ly,** *adv.* —**elf′ish ness,** *n.*

elf lock (elf′lok′), *n.* a tangled lock of hair, supposedly caused by elves.

El Gre co (el grek′ō; el grā′kō), 1541?-1614, Spanish painter born in Crete.

E li (ē′lī), *n.* (in the Bible) the Hebrew high priest who trained Samuel to become a religious leader.

E li a (ē′lē ə), *n.* pen name of Charles Lamb.

E li as (i lī′əs), *n.* (in the New Testament) Elijah.

e lic it (i lis′it), *v.t.* draw forth; bring out: *elicit the truth by discussion.* [< Latin *elicitum* lured out < *ex-* out + *lacere* entice]

➛ **Elicit, illicit** are not synonyms, but are sometimes confused because they are pronounced alike. **Elicit** is a formal verb meaning to draw out in a skillful way or with difficulty something that is being hidden or held back: *I succeeded in eliciting from her the facts concerning the accident.* **Illicit** is a formal adjective meaning unlawful or improper: *The police are trying to stop the illicit sale of drugs.*

e lic i ta tion (i lis′ə tā′shən), *n.* a drawing forth or a being drawn forth.

e lide (i līd′), *v.t.,* **e lid ed, e lid ing.** 1 omit or slur over (a vowel or syllable) in pronunciation. The *e* in *the* is elided in "th' enemy." 2 strike out; suppress. [< Latin *elidere* < *ex-* out + *laedere* to dash, strike]

el i gi bil i ty (el′ə jə bil′ə tē), *n., pl.* **-ties.** fitness to be chosen; qualification.

el i gi ble (el′ə jə bəl), *adj.* fit to be chosen; properly qualified; desirable: *Pupils had to pass in all subjects to be eligible for the school play.* —*n.* an eligible person. [< Late Latin *eligibilis* < Latin *eligere* pick out < *ex-* out + *legere* choose] —**el′i gi bly,** *adv.*

E li jah (i lī′jə), *n.* Hebrew prophet who lived in the 800's B.C.

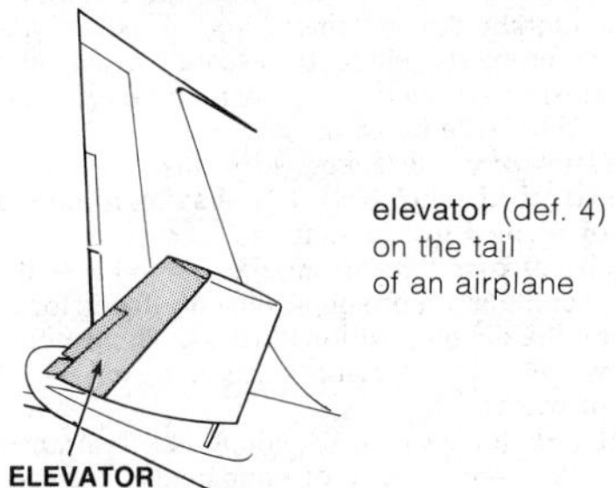

elevator (def. 4) on the tail of an airplane

e lim i nate (i lim′ə nāt), *v.t.,* **-nat ed, -nat ing.** 1 get rid of; remove. See **exclude** for synonym study. 2 set aside as irrelevant; omit; ignore: *The architect eliminated furniture, rugs, etc., in figuring the cost of the house.* 3 (in algebra) get rid of (an unknown quantity) in two or more equations by combining them. 4 expel (waste) from the body; excrete. [< Latin *eliminatum* turned out of doors, banished < *ex-* out + *liminis* threshold] —**e lim′i na′tor,** *n.*

e lim i na tion (i lim′ə nā′shən), *n.* 1 an eliminating. 2 a being eliminated.

e lim i na tive (i lim′ə nā′tiv), *adj.* tending or serving to eliminate.

El i ot (el′ē ət, el′yət), *n.* 1 **George,** 1819-1880, pen name of Mary Ann Evans, English novelist. 2 **John,** 1604-1690, American clergyman, a missionary among the American Indians. 3 **T(homas) S(tearns),** 1888-1965, British poet, essayist, and critic, born in the United States.

E lis (ē′lis), *n.* division of ancient Greece, in the Peloponnesus. Olympic games were held on the plain of Olympia in Elis. See **Peloponnesus** for map.

E li sha (i lī′shə), *n.* Hebrew prophet of the 800's B.C. who was taught by Elijah.

e li sion (i lizh′ən), *n.* suppression of a vowel or a syllable in pronouncing. Elision is often used in poetry where a word ending in a vowel is followed by a word beginning with a vowel, as in "th' inevitable hour." [< Latin *elisionem* < *elidere.* See ELIDE.]

e lite or **é lite** (i lēt′, ā lēt′), *n.* 1 the part that is best, most talented, etc., or is thought to be so (in a country, society, organization, etc.). 2 size of typewriter type, smaller than pica, having 12 characters to the inch. [< French *élite* < *élire* pick out < Latin *eligere.* See ELIGIBLE.]

hat, āge, fär; let, ēqual, tėrm;
it, īce; hot, ōpen, ôrder;
oil, out; cup, pu̇t, rüle;
ch, child; ng, long; sh, she;
th, thin; ᴛʜ, then; zh, measure;

ə represents *a* in about, *e* in taken, *i* in pencil, *o* in lemon, *u* in circus.

< = from, derived from, taken from.

e lix ir (i lik′sər), *n.* 1 substance supposed to have the power of changing lead, iron, etc., into gold or of lengthening life indefinitely. The alchemists of the Middle Ages sought for it. 2 cure-all. 3 medicine made of drugs or herbs mixed with alcohol and syrup. [< Medieval Latin < Arabic *al-iksīr*]

E liz a beth (i liz′ə bəth), *n.* city in NE New Jersey. 113,000.

Elizabeth I, 1533-1603, queen of England from 1558 to 1603, daughter of Henry VIII and Anne Boleyn.

Elizabeth II, born 1926, since 1952 queen of Great Britain and Northern Ireland, and head of the Commonwealth of Nations; daughter of George VI.

E liz a be than (i liz′ə bē′thən, i liz′ə-beth′ən), *adj.* of the time when Elizabeth I ruled England. —*n.* Englishman, especially a writer, of the time of Elizabeth I: *Shakespeare is a famous Elizabethan.*

Elizabethan sonnet, type of sonnet having three stanzas of four lines each, followed by a couplet, with the rhyme scheme *abab cdcd efef gg;* Shakespearian sonnet; English sonnet.

elk (elk), *n., pl.* **elks** or **elk.** 1 a large deer of northern Europe and Asia of the same genus as and closely resembling the moose, having broad, heavy antlers. 2 wapiti. [Old English *eolh*]

ell[1] (el), *n.* a former measure of length, equal to 45 inches in England, chiefly used in measuring cloth. Also, **el.** [Old English *eln* length of lower arm]

ell[2] (el), *n.* 1 the letter L, l. 2 an extension of a building at right angles to it; el.

Elles mere (elz′mir), *n.* large Canadian island northwest of Greenland. 76,600 sq. mi.

El ling ton (el′ing tən), *n.* **Edward Kennedy,** born 1899, American jazz composer, called "Duke" Ellington.

el lipse (i lips′), *n.* oval having both ends alike. It is the plane curve formed by the path of a point that moves so that the sum of its distances from two fixed points or foci remains the same. Any conic section formed by a cutting plane inclined to the base but not passing through the base is an ellipse. [< Latin *ellipsis*]

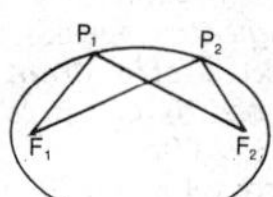

ellipse—F_1, F_2 are the two foci. P_1, P_2 are any points on the ellipse. The sum of the distances from any point on the ellipse to F_1 and F_2 is always the same. $F_1P_1 + P_1F_2 = F_1P_2 + P_2F_2$

el lip sis (i lip′sis), *n., pl.* **-ses** (-sēz′). 1 marks (. . . or * * *) used to show an omission in writing or printing. 2 omission of a word or words needed to complete the grammatical construction, but not the meaning, of a sentence. EXAMPLE: "She is as tall as her brother" instead of "She is as tall as her brother is tall." [< Latin < Greek *elleipsis* < *elleipein* come short, leave out]

el lip soid (i lip′soid), *n.* 1 a solid figure of which all plane sections are ellipses or circles. 2 any surface of such a solid. *—adj.* of an ellipsoid.

el lip tic (i lip′tik), *adj.* elliptical.

el lip ti cal (i lip′tə kəl), *adj.* 1 of or shaped like an ellipse. 2 of or showing ellipsis. **—el lip′ti cal ly,** *adv.*

El lis Island (el′is), small island in New York harbor where, from 1891 to 1954, immigrants were examined before entering the United States.

elm (elm), *n.* 1 any of a genus of large, deciduous trees, commonly grown for shade and ornament. Elms typically have alternate leaves and greenish-brown or purplish flowers without petals. 2 the hard, heavy wood of any of these trees. [Old English]

el o cu tion (el′ə kyü′shən), *n.* 1 art of speaking or reading clearly and expressively in public, including the use of the voice, gestures, etc. 2 manner of speaking or reading in public; delivery. [< Latin *elocutionem* < *eloqui* speak out]

el o cu tion ar y (el′ə kyü′shə ner′ē), *adj.* of or having to do with elocution.

el o cu tion ist (el′ə kyü′shə nist), *n.* person skilled in elocution.

elongate leaf (def. 1)

e lon gate (i lông′gāt, i long′gāt), *v.,* **-gat ed, -gat ing,** *adj. —v.t., v.i.* make or become longer; lengthen; extend; stretch: *A rubber band elongates easily. —adj.* 1 long and thin: *the elongate leaf of a willow.* 2 lengthened. [< Latin *elongatum* lengthened < *ex-* out + *longus* long]

e lon ga tion (ē′lông gā′shən, ē′long gā′shən), *n.* 1 a lengthening. 2 a lengthened part.

e lope (i lōp′), *v.i.,* **e loped, e lop ing.** 1 run away to get married. 2 escape. [< Anglo-French *aloper*] **—e lope′ment,** *n.* **—e lop′er,** *n.*

el o quence (el′ə kwəns), *n.* 1 flow of speech that has grace and force. 2 power to win by speaking; the art of using language so as to stir the feelings.

el o quent (el′ə kwənt), *adj.* 1 having eloquence. 2 very expressive: *eloquent eyes.* [< Latin *eloquentem* speaking out < *ex-* out + *loqui* speak] **—el′o quent ly,** *adv.*

El Pas o (el pas′ō), city in W Texas, on the Rio Grande. 322,000.

El Sal va dor (el sal′və dôr), country in W Central America. 3,534,000 pop.; 8300 sq. mi. *Capital:* San Salvador. Also, **Salvador.**

else (els), *adj.* 1 other than the person, place, thing, etc., mentioned; different; instead: *Will somebody else speak?* 2 in addition; more; besides: *The Browns are here; do you expect anyone else? —adv.* 1 differently: *How else can it be done?* 2 if not; otherwise: *Hurry, else you will be late.* [Old English *elles*]

➤ Because **else** follows the word (usually a pronoun) it modifies, it takes the sign of the possessive: *He finally decided the book was somebody else's.*

else where (els′hwer, els′hwar), *adv.* in, at, or to some other place; somewhere else.

e lu ci date (i lü′sə dāt), *v.t.,* **-dat ed, -dat ing.** make clear; explain; clarify. [< Late Latin *elucidatum* made clear < Latin *ex-* out + *lucidus* bright] **—e lu′ci da′tion,** *n.* **—e lu′ci da′tor,** *n.*

e lu ci da tive (i lü′sə dā′tiv), *adj.* explanatory.

e lude (i lüd′), *v.t.,* **e lud ed, e lud ing.** 1 avoid or escape by cleverness, quickness, etc.; slip away from; evade: *The sly fox eluded the dogs.* See **escape** for synonym study. 2 baffle: *The cause of cancer has eluded scientists.* [< Latin *eludere* < *ex-* out + *ludere* to play] **—e lud′er,** *n.*

e lu sion (i lü′zhən), *n.* an eluding; clever avoidance; evasion.

e lu sive (i lü′siv), *adj.* 1 hard to describe or understand; baffling: *an elusive idea.* 2 tending to elude or escape; evasive: *an elusive enemy.* **—e lu′sive ly,** *adv.* **—e lu′sive ness,** *n.*

e lu sor y (i lü′sər ē), *adj.* elusive.

e lu vi al (i lü′vē əl), *adj.* having to do with or formed by eluvium.

e lu vi um (i lü′vē əm), *n., pl.* **-vi a** (-vē ə). accumulation of soil or dust produced locally by the decomposition of rock or deposited by winds. [< New Latin < Latin *ex-* out + *luere* to wash]

el ver (el′vər), *n.* a young eel. [variant of *eelfare* the passage of young eels upstream]

elves (elvz), *n.* pl. of **elf.**

elv ish (el′vish), *adj.* elfish. **—elv′ish ly,** *adv.*

E ly sian (i lizh′ən), *adj.* 1 of or having to do with Elysium. 2 happy; delightful.

Elysian Fields, Elysium.

E ly sium (i lizh′əm, i liz′ē əm), *n.* 1 (in Greek myths) a place where heroes and virtuous people lived after death. 2 any place or condition of perfect happiness; paradise.

el y tron (el′ə tron), *n., pl.* **-tra** (-trə). either of a pair of hardened front wings that form a protective covering for the hind pair; wing case. Beetles and certain other insects have elytra. [< New Latin < Greek, sheath < *elyein* to wrap]

em (em), *n.* 1 the letter M, m. 2 unit for measuring the amount of print in a line, page, etc., originally the portion of a line occupied by the letter *m.* 3 a pica.

'em (əm), *pron. pl.* INFORMAL. them: *pick 'em up.*

em-[1], *prefix.* form of **en-**[1] before *b, p,* and sometimes *m,* as in *embark, employ.*

em-[2], *prefix.* form of **en-**[2] before *b, m, p, ph,* as in *emblem, emphasis.*

e ma ci ate (i mā′shē āt), *v.t.,* **-at ed, -at ing.** make unnaturally thin; cause to lose flesh or waste away: *A long illness had emaciated the patient.* [< Latin *emaciatum* made lean < *ex-* + *macies* leanness] **—e ma′ci a′tion,** *n.*

em a nate (em′ə nāt), *v.,* **-nat ed, -nat ing.** *—v.i.* originate from a person or thing as a source; come forth; spread out: *The rumor emanated from Chicago.* See **issue** for synonym study. *—v.t.* send out; emit. [< Latin *emanatum* flowed out < *ex-* out + *manare* to flow]

em a na tion (em′ə nā′shən), *n.* 1 an emanating. 2 anything that emanates: *Light and heat are emanations from the sun.*

em a na tive (em′ə nā′tiv), *adj.* emanating; characterized by emanation.

e man ci pate (i man′sə pāt), *v.t.,* **-pat ed, -pat ing.** release from slavery or restraint; set free: *emancipate women from old restrictions.* [< Latin *emancipatum* set free < *ex-* away + *manus* hand + *capere* to take]

e man ci pa tion (i man′sə pā′shən), *n.* a release from slavery or restraint.

Emancipation Proclamation, proclamation issued by Abraham Lincoln on January 1, 1863, declaring free all persons held as slaves in any state then in armed rebellion against the United States.

e man ci pa tor (i man′sə pā′tər), *n.* person who emancipates.

e mas cu late (i mas′kyə lāt), *v.t.,* **-lat ed, -lat ing.** 1 castrate. 2 destroy the force of; weaken. [< Latin *emasculatum* castrated < *ex-* out + *masculus* male]. **—e mas′cu la′tion,** *n.* **—e mas′cu la′tor,** *n.*

em balm (em bäm′, em bälm′), *v.t.* 1 treat (a dead body) with spices, chemicals, drugs, etc., to keep it from decaying. 2 keep in memory; preserve. 3 fill with sweet scent; perfume. [< Middle French *embaumer* < *en-* in + *baume* balm] **—em balm′er,** *n.*

em bank (em bangk′), *v.t.* protect, enclose, or confine with an embankment.

embankment (def. 1)

em bank ment (em bangk′mənt), *n.* 1 a raised bank of earth, stones, etc., used to hold back water, support a road, etc. 2 act or process of embanking.

em bar go (em bär′gō), *n., pl.* **-goes,** *v. —n.* 1 an order of a government forbidding merchant ships to enter or leave its ports: *During the War of 1812, Congress laid an embargo on commerce with Great Britain.* 2 any restriction put on commerce by law. 3 restriction; restraint; hindrance. *—v.t.* put under an embargo. [< Spanish < *embargar* restrain, ultimately < Latin *in-* + Popular Latin *barra* bar]

em bark (em bärk′), *v.i.* 1 go on board a ship or an aircraft: *Many people embark for Europe at New York harbor.* 2 begin an undertaking; set out; start: *embark upon a career. —v.t.* put on board a ship or an aircraft. [< Middle French *embarquer* < *en-* in + *barque* bark[3]] **—em bark′ment,** *n.*

em bar ka tion (em′bär kā′shən), *n.* an embarking.

em bar rass (em bar′əs), *v.t.* 1 disturb and confuse; make uneasy and ashamed; make self-conscious; disconcert: *She embarrassed me by asking me if I really liked her.* See **confuse** for synonym study. 2 hamper or hinder (persons, movements, etc.); impede. 3 make involved; complicate. 4 involve in financial difficulties; burden with debt. [< French *embarrasser,* literally, to block < *embarras* obstacle] **—em bar′rass ing ly,** *adv.*

hat, āge, fär; let, ēqual, tėrm;
it, īce; hot, ōpen, ôrder;
oil, out; cup, pu̇t, rüle;
ch, child; ng, long; sh, she;
th, thin; ᴛʜ, then; zh, measure;

ə represents *a* in about, *e* in taken, *i* in pencil, *o* in lemon, *u* in circus.

< = from, derived from, taken from.

em bar rass ment (em bar′əs mənt), *n.* 1 act of embarrassing. 2 condition of being embarrassed. 3 thing that embarrasses: *the embarrassment of forgetting a name.* 4 an excessive number or quantity from which it is difficult to select: *an embarrassment of riches, an embarrassment of friends.*

em bas sa dor (em bas′ə dər, em bas′ə-dôr), *n.* ambassador.

em bas sy (em′bə sē), *n., pl.* **-sies.** 1 ambassador and his staff of assistants. An embassy ranks next above a legation. 2 the official residence, offices, etc., of an ambassador in a foreign country. 3 position or duties of an ambassador. 4 person or group officially sent to a foreign government with a special errand. 5 a special errand; important mission; official message. [< Old French *embassee* < Italian *ambasciata* embassy; trip down into the valley, ultimately < Popular Latin *in* + *bassus* down]

em bat tle (em bat′l), *v.t.,* **-tled, -tling.** 1 prepare for battle; form into battle order. 2 fortify.

em bed (em bed′), *v.t.,* **-bed ded, -bed ding.** 1 fix or enclose in a surrounding mass; fasten firmly: *Precious stones are often found embedded in rock.* 2 plant in a bed: *He embedded the bulbs in a box of sand.* Also, **imbed.**

em bel lish (em bel′ish), *v.t.* 1 add beauty to; decorate; adorn; ornament. 2 make more interesting by adding real or imaginary details; elaborate: *embellish a story.* [< Old French *embelliss-*, a form of *embellir* embellish < *en-* in + *bel* handsome] **—em bel′lish ment,** *n.*

em ber[1] (em′bər), *n.* 1 piece of wood or coal still glowing in the ashes of a fire. 2 **embers,** *pl.* ashes in which there is still some fire. [Old English *ǣmerge*]

em ber[2] (em′bər), *adj.* of or having to do with the Ember days. [Old English *ymbren* Ember days]

Ember days, three days set apart for fasting and prayer by the Roman Catholic, Anglican, and some other churches. They are the Wednesday, Friday, and Saturday following the first Sunday in Lent, Whitsunday, September 14, and December 13.

em bez zle (em bez′əl), *v.t.,* **-zled, -zling.** steal (money, securities, etc., entrusted to one's care). [< Anglo-French *enbesiler* < *en-* + *beseler* destroy] **—em bez′zle ment,** *n.*

em bit ter (em bit′ər), *v.t.* make bitter: *embittered by constant failure.* **—em bit′ter ment,** *n.*

em bla zon (em blā′zn), *v.t.* 1 display conspicuously; picture in bright colors. 2 decorate; adorn: *The knight's shield was emblazoned with his coat of arms.* 3 praise highly; honor publicly. **—em bla′zon er,** *n.* **—em bla′zon ment,** *n.*

em bla zon ry (em blā′zn rē), *n., pl.* **-ries.** 1 brilliant decoration. 2 display of coats of arms.

em blem (em′bləm), *n.* 1 object or representation that stands for an invisible quality, idea, etc., by some connection of thought; sign of an idea; symbol: *The dove is an emblem of peace.* See synonym study below. 2 a heraldic device. [< Latin *emblema* inlaid work < Greek *emblēma* insertion < *en-* in + *ballein* to throw]

Syn. 1 **Emblem, symbol** mean something that stands for something else. **Emblem** applies to an object, or its likeness, that is especially suitable to suggest the nature of an idea, country, etc.: *The eagle is the emblem of the United States.* **Symbol,** often interchangeable with *emblem,* applies particularly to something chosen to stand for an idea or quality, without any thought of special fitness: *The skull and crossbones is a symbol of piracy.*

em blem at ic (em′blə mat′ik), *adj.* of or used as an emblem; symbolic.

em blem at i cal (em′blə mat′ə kəl), *adj.* emblematic.

em bod i ment (em bod′ē mənt), *n.* 1 that in which something is embodied; person or thing symbolizing some idea, quality, etc. 2 an embodying. 3 a being embodied.

em bod y (em bod′ē), *v.t.,* **-bod ied, -bod y ing.** 1 put into a form that can be seen; express in definite form: *A building embodies the idea of an architect.* 2 bring together in a single book, law, system, etc.; include; organize. 3 make part of an organized book, law, system, etc.; incorporate: *embody suggestions in a revised plan.*

em bold en (em bōl′dən), *v.t.* make bold; encourage.

em bo lism (em′bə liz′əm), *n.* obstruction of a blood vessel by an embolus.

em bo lus (em′bə ləs), *n., pl.* **-li** (-lī). a clot, air bubble, globule of fat, etc., that is carried in the bloodstream. It sometimes blocks a blood vessel. [< New Latin < Greek *embolos* peg < *emballein* throw in, insert]

em bon point (äɴ bôɴ pwaɴ′), *n.* FRENCH. fatness; plumpness.

em bos om (em bu̇z′əm, em bü′zəm), *v.t.* 1 surround; enclose; envelop. 2 embrace or cherish.

em boss (em bôs′, em bos′), *v.t.* 1 decorate with a design, pattern, etc., that stands out from the surface: *Our coins are embossed with letters and figures.* 2 cause to stand out from the surface: *The letters on the book's cover had been embossed.* **—em boss′er,** *n.* **—em boss′ment,** *n.*

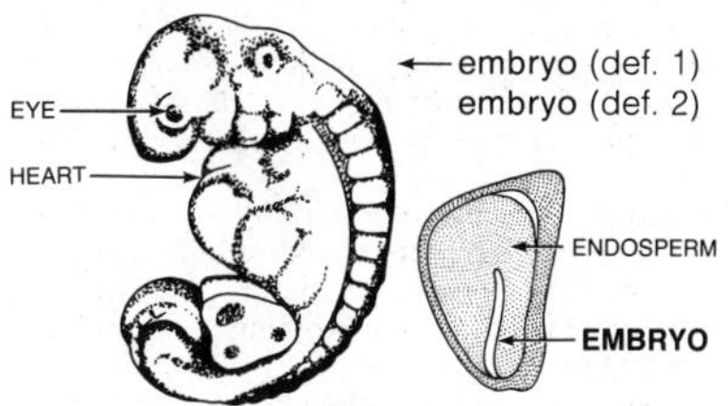

←embryo (def. 1)
embryo (def. 2)

em bou chure (äm′bə shu̇r′), *n.* 1 mouth of a river. 2 widening of a river valley into a plain. 3 mouthpiece of a wind instrument. 4 the shaping and use of the lips, tongue, etc., in playing such an instrument. [< French]

em bow er (em bou′ər), *v.t.* enclose in a shelter of leafy branches.

em brace (em brās′), *v.,* **-braced, -brac ing,** *n.* —*v.t.* 1 clasp or hold in the arms to show love or friendship; hug. 2 take up; take for oneself; accept: *She eagerly embraced the offer of a trip to Europe.* 3 take in; include; contain: *The cat family embraces cats, lions, tigers, and similar animals.* 4 surround; enclose. —*v.i.* hug one another: *We embraced when we met at the airport.* —*n.* a clasping in the arms; hug. [< Old French *embracer,* ultimately < Latin *in-* in + *brachium* arm] **—em brace′a ble,** *adj.* **—em brace′ment,** *n.* **—embrac′er,** *n.*

em bra sure (em brā′zhər), *n.* 1 an opening in a wall for a gun, with sides that spread outward to permit the gun to fire through a greater arc. 2 a slanting off of the wall at an oblique angle on the inner sides of a window or door. [< French]

em bro cate (em′brō kāt), *v.t.,* **-cat ed, -cat ing.** bathe and rub with liniment or lotion. [< Medieval Latin *embrocatum* bathed with lotion < Late Latin *embrocha* lotion]

em bro ca tion (em′brō kā′shən), *n.* 1 a bathing and rubbing with liniment or lotion. 2 liniment or lotion used.

em broi der (em broi′dər), *v.t.* 1 ornament (cloth, leather, etc.) with a raised design, pattern, etc., of stitches. 2 make (an ornamental design, pattern, etc.) on cloth, leather, etc., with stitches: *I embroidered a design on the vest.* 3 add imaginary details to; exaggerate. —*v.i.* do embroidery. [< *em-*[1] + *broider* embroider < Old French *broder*] **—em broi′der er,** *n.*

em broi der y (em broi′dər ē), *n., pl.* **-der ies.** 1 act or art of embroidering. 2 embroidered work or material; ornamental designs sewn in cloth, leather, etc., with a needle. 3 imaginary details; exaggeration.

em broil (em broil′), *v.t.* 1 involve (a person, country, etc.) in a quarrel. 2 throw (affairs, etc.) into a state of confusion. [< French *embrouiller* < *en-* in + *brouiller* to broil] **—em broil′ment,** *n.*

em brown (em broun′), *v.t.* tan; darken.

em bry o (em′brē ō), *n., pl.* **-bry os,** *adj.* —*n.* 1 animal during the period of its growth from the fertilized egg until its organs have developed so that it can live independently. The embryo of a mammal is usually called a fetus in its later stages (in human beings, more than three months after conception). 2 an undeveloped plant within a seed. 3 **in embryo,** in an undeveloped stage. —*adj.* undeveloped; embryonic. [< Medieval Latin < Greek *embryon* < *en-* in + *bryein* to swell]

em bry o log ic (em′brē ə loj′ik), *adj.* embryological.

em bry o log i cal (em′brē ə loj′ə kəl), *adj.* of or having to do with embryology. **—em′bry o log′i cal ly,** *adv.*

em bry ol o gist (em′brē ol′ə jist), *n.* an expert in embryology.

em bry ol o gy (em′brē ol′ə jē), *n.* branch of biology that deals with the formation and development of embryos.

em bry on ic (em′brē on′ik), *adj.* 1 of the embryo. 2 immature; undeveloped: *an embryonic leaf, an embryonic plan.*

em cee (em′sē′), *n., v.,* **-ceed, -cee ing.** U.S. INFORMAL. —*n.* master of ceremonies. —*v.t., v.i.* act as master of ceremonies of. [pronunciation of *M.C.*]

embrasure (def. 1)

e mend (i mend′), *v.t.* free (a faulty text, etc.) from faults or errors; correct. [< Latin *emendare* < *ex-* out of + *mendum, menda* fault. Doublet of AMEND.] **—e mend′a ble,** *adj.*

e men da tion (ē′men dā′shən, em′en-dā′shən), *n.* 1 an emending; correction. 2 a suggested change to free a faulty text, etc., from errors.

em er ald (em′ər əld), *n.* 1 a bright-green precious stone; transparent green beryl. 2 a bright green. *—adj.* bright-green. [< Old French *esmeralde* < Popular Latin *smaraldus* < Latin *smaragdus* < Greek *smaragdos*]

e merge (i mėrj′), *v.i.,* **e merged, e merg ing.** 1 come into view; come out; come up: *The sun emerged from behind a cloud.* 2 become known: *New facts emerged as a result of a second investigation.* See **issue** for synonym study. [< Latin *emergere* < *ex-* out + *mergere* to dip]

e mer gence (i mėr′jəns), *n.* act or fact of emerging.

e mer gen cy (i mėr′jən sē), *n., pl.* **-cies,** *adj. —n.* 1 a sudden need for immediate action: *I keep a box of tools in my car for use in an emergency.* 2 situation in which such a need arises: *a national emergency.* See synonym study below. *—adj.* for a time of sudden need: *an emergency brake, an emergency operation.*

Syn. *n.* 2 **Emergency, crisis** mean a trying or dangerous state of affairs. **Emergency** refers to a sudden or unexpected situation that calls for action without delay: *The failure of the city's electric power caused an emergency.* **Crisis** refers to a situation in which grave alternatives, sometimes life or death, hang in the balance and whose outcome will be decisive: *The floods brought on a crisis for the farmers.*

e mer gent (i mėr′jənt), *adj.* emerging.

e mer i tus (i mer′ə təs), *adj., n., pl.* **-ti** (-tī). *—adj.* honorably discharged; retired from active service, but still holding one's rank and title: *At the age of seventy, Professor Arnold became professor emeritus.* *—n.* person honorably discharged or retired from service. [< Latin *emeritus* having completed one's term of service < *ex-* to the end + *merere* serve]

e mer sion (i mėr′zhən, i mėr′shən), *n.* an emerging. [< Latin *emersionem* < *emergere.* See EMERGE.]

Em er son (em′ər sən), *n.* **Ralph Waldo,** 1803-1882, American essayist, poet, and philosopher.

em er y (em′ər ē), *n.* a hard, dark mineral, an impure corundum, used in powdered form to grind, smooth, and polish metals, stones, etc. [< Middle French *émeri* < Italian *smeriglio* < Popular Latin *smericulum* < Greek *smyris* abrasive powder]

e met ic (i met′ik), *adj.* causing vomiting. *—n.* medicine that causes vomiting. [< Late Latin *emeticus* < Greek *emetikos* < *emein* to vomit]

E.M.F., e.m.f., or **emf,** electromotive force.

em i grant (em′ə grənt), *n.* person who leaves his own country or region to settle in another. *—adj.* leaving one's own country or region to settle in another.

em i grate (em′ə grāt), *v.i.,* **-grat ed, -grat ing.** leave one's own country or region to settle in another. [< Latin *emigratum* moved out < *ex-* out + *migrare* to move]

➤ **emigrate, immigrate.** *Emigrate* means to move out of a country or region, *immigrate* to move into a country. One who *emigrates* from Norway might *immigrate* to the United States.

em i gra tion (em′ə grā′shən), *n.* 1 a leaving one's own country or region to settle in another. 2 body of emigrants.

ém i gré (em′ə grā; *French* ā mē grā′), *n., pl.* **-grés** (-grāz; *French* -grā′). 1 emigrant. 2 a royalist refugee from France during the French Revolution. 3 refugee from Russia during and after the Russian Revolution. [< French]

em i nence (em′ə nəns), *n.* 1 rank or position above all or most others; high standing. 2 a high place; high point of land. 3 **Eminence,** title of honor given to a cardinal in the Roman Catholic Church.

em i nent (em′ə nənt), *adj.* 1 above all or most others; outstanding; distinguished. See synonym study below. 2 conspicuous; noteworthy: *The judge was a man of eminent fairness.* 3 high; lofty. 4 standing out above other things; prominent. [< Latin *eminentem* standing out, prominent < *ex-* out + *minere* jut] **—em′i nent ly,** *adv.*

Syn. 1 **Eminent, prominent, distinguished** mean outstanding. **Eminent** implies standing high among or above all others of the same kind because of excellence in something: *Wordsworth and Coleridge were eminent English poets.* **Prominent** implies standing out from the crowd, and suggests being well known at least locally: *The president of that bank is a prominent man in his home town.* **Distinguished** implies being set off from others of the same kind because of outstanding qualities, and suggests being well known to the public: *President Eisenhower was also a distinguished general.*

➤ **Eminent, imminent.** *Eminent* means distinguished: *The new ambassador was eminent both as a diplomat and scholar. Imminent* means likely to happen soon: *Convinced that bankruptcy was imminent, the company president called a meeting of the directors.*

eminent domain, right of the government to take private property for public use. The owner must be paid for the property taken.

e mir (ə mir′), *n.* 1 an Arabian chief, prince, or military leader. 2 title of the descendants of Mohammed. 3 title of certain Turkish officials. Also, **amir.** [< Arabic *amīr*]

e mir ate (ə mir′it), *n.* 1 rank or authority of an emir. 2 territory governed by an emir. Also, **amirate.**

em is sar y (em′ə ser′ē), *n., pl.* **-sar ies.** 1 person sent on a mission or errand. 2 a secret agent; spy. [< Latin *emissarius* < *emittere.* See EMIT.]

e mis sion (i mish′ən), *n.* 1 act or fact of emitting. 2 thing emitted; discharge. [< Latin *emissionem* < *emittere.* See EMIT.]

e mis sive (i mis′iv), *adj.* emitting.

em is siv i ty (em′ə siv′ə tē), *n.* the relative ability of a surface to radiate energy.

e mit (i mit′), *v.t.,* **e mit ted, e mit ting.** 1 give off; send out; discharge: *The sun emits light and heat.* 2 put into circulation; issue. 3 utter; express. [< Latin *emittere* < *ex-* out + *mittere* send] **—e mit′ter,** *n.*

Em man u el (i man′yü əl), *n.* Christ. Also, **Immanuel.**

em mer (em′ər), *n.* species of wheat with a brittle central spike, grown especially as food for livestock. [< dialectal German *Emmer*]

em met (em′it), *n.* ARCHAIC. ant. [Old English *ǣmete*]

e mol lient (i mol′yənt), *adj.* softening or soothing. *—n.* something that softens and soothes: *Cold cream is an emollient for the skin.* [< Latin *emollientem* < *ex-* + *mollis* soft]

e mol u ment (i mol′yə mənt), *n.* profit from a job, office, or position; salary, fees, or wages. [< Latin *emolumentum* profit, ultimately < *ex-* out + *molere* to grind]

e mote (i mōt′), *v.i.,* **e mot ed, e mot ing.** 1 act, especially in an exaggerated manner. 2 show emotion. [back-formation < *emotion*]

e mo tion (i mō′shən), *n.* a strong feeling of any kind. Joy, grief, fear, hate, love, anger, and excitement are emotions. See **feeling** for synonym study. [< Middle French *émotion* < *émouvoir* stir up < Latin *emovere* < *ex-* out + *movere* move]

e mo tion al (i mō′shə nəl), *adj.* 1 of the emotions: *an emotional disorder.* 2 showing emotion: *an emotional reaction.* 3 appealing to the emotions: *an emotional plea for help.* 4 easily affected by emotion: *Emotional people are likely to cry if they read sad stories.* **—e mo′tion al ly,** *adv.*

e mo tion al ism (i mō′shə nə liz′əm), *n.* 1 tendency to display emotion too easily. 2 emotional quality or character. 3 appeal to the emotions.

e mo tive (i mō′tiv), *adj.* 1 showing or causing emotion. 2 having to do with the emotions. **—e mo′tive ly,** *adv.*

Emp., 1 emperor. 2 empress.

em pan el (em pan′l), *v.t.,* **-eled, -el ing** or **elled, -el ling.** impanel.

em pa thy (em′pə thē), *n.* (in psychology) the quality or process of entering fully, through imagination, into another's feelings or motives, into the meaning of a work of art, etc. [< Greek *empatheia* < *en-* in + *pathos* feeling]

Em ped o cles (em ped′ə klēz′), *n.* 490?-430? B.C., Greek philosopher.

em pen nage (em pen′ij), *n.* the tail assembly of an aircraft. [< French]

em per or (em′pər ər), *n.* 1 man who is the ruler of an empire. 2 ruler who has the title of "emperor." Japan has an emperor. [< Old French *empereor* < Latin *imperator* commander < *imperare* to command < *in-* in + *parare* to order]

em pha sis (em′fə sis), *n., pl.* **-ses** (-sēz′). 1 special force; stress; importance: *My high school puts much emphasis on studies that prepare its students for college.* 2 special force put on particular syllables, words, or phrases: *A speaker puts emphasis on important words by stressing them.* [< Latin < Greek < *emphainein* indicate < *en-* in + *phainein* to show]

em pha size (em′fə sīz), *v.t.,* **-sized, -siz ing.** give emphasis to; put emphasis on: *emphasize a word, emphasize a need.*

em phat ic (em fat′ik), *adj.* 1 said or done with force or stress; strongly expressed: *Her answer was an emphatic "No!"* 2 speaking with force or stress; expressing oneself strongly: *The emphatic speaker often pounded the table and shouted.* 3 attracting attention; very noticeable; striking: *The club made an emphatic success of its party.* 4 (in grammar) denoting a verbal construction that gives emphasis to the statement of the main verb. *Do come* and *did go* are the emphatic forms of *come* and *go.* [< Greek *emphatikos*

< *emphainein.* See EMPHASIS.] **—em phat′i cal ly,** *adv.*

em phy se ma (em′fə sē′mə), *n.* an abnormal enlargement of the air sacs in the lungs caused by a loss of elasticity in the walls of the air sacs and a resulting inability to expel carbon dioxide. Emphysema makes breathing difficult. [< Greek *emphysēma* swelling]

em pire (em′pīr), *n.* 1 group of countries or states under one ruler or government: *The Roman Empire consisted of many separate territories and different peoples.* 2 country that has an emperor or empress: *the Japanese Empire.* 3 absolute power; supreme authority. 4 a large business or group of businesses under the control of a single person, family, syndicate, etc. 5 **Empire,** of or having to do with a style of dress, furniture, etc., in fashion during the first French empire (1804-1815), characterized by formal and complex design. [< Old French < Latin *imperium* < *imperare.* See EMPEROR.]

em pir ic (em pir′ik), *n.* 1 person who lacks theoretical or scientific knowledge and relies entirely on practical experience. 2 quack. *—adj.* empirical. [< Latin *empiricus* < Greek *empeirikos* < *en-* in + *peira* experience]

em pir i cal (em pir′ə kəl), *adj.* 1 based on experiment and observation: *Chemistry is largely an empirical science.* 2 based entirely on practical experience, without regard to science or theory: *The quack doctor had only an empirical knowledge of medicine.* **—em pir′i cal ly,** *adv.*

empirical formula, formula used to indicate the simplest ratio of the number and kind of atoms in a chemical compound. It does not necessarily indicate the number of atoms in a molecule.

em pir i cism (em pir′ə siz′əm), *n.* 1 use of methods based on experiment and observation. 2 unscientific practice; quackery. 3 the philosophical theory that all knowledge is based on experience.

em pir i cist (em pir′ə sist), *n.* 1 experimenter. 2 quack. 3 philosopher who believes in empiricism.

em place (em plās′), *v.t.,* **-placed, -plac ing.** place into position.

em place ment (em plās′mənt), *n.* 1 space or platform for heavy weapons or equipment. 2 a placing in position.

em ploy (em ploi′), *v.t.* 1 give work and pay to; use the services of. See synonym study below. 2 make use of; use: *He employs his time wisely.* See **use** for synonym study. 3 engage the attention of; keep busy; occupy: *He employed himself in growing roses after he retired.* *—n.* service for pay; employment: *There are many workers in the employ of that firm.* [< Middle French *employer* < Latin *implicare* < *in-* in + *plicare* to fold. Doublet of IMPLICATE, IMPLY.] **—em ploy′a ble,** *adj.*

Syn. *v.t.* 1 **Employ, hire** mean to give work and pay to someone. **Employ** suggests regularity in the work: *The steel mill employs most of the men in the town.* **Hire** suggests temporary employment: *She hired a man to mow the lawn.*

em ploy ee, em ploy e, or **em ploy é** (em ploi′ē, em′ploi ē′; em plō′ē, em′plō ē′), *n.* person who works for some person or firm for pay.

em ploy er (em ploi′ər), *n.* person or firm that employs one or more persons.

em ploy ment (em ploi′mənt), *n.* 1 work; job: *His employment is sorting mail.* See **occupation** for synonym study. 2 act or process of employing: *the employment of a large staff.* 3 condition of being employed: *She enjoyed most her employment as babysitter.* 4 use: *The painter was clever in his employment of brushes and colors.*

em po ri um (em pôr′ē əm, em pōr′ē əm), *n., pl.* **-po ri ums, -po ri a** (-pôr′ē ə, -pōr′ē ə). 1 center of trade; marketplace. 2 a large store selling many different things. [< Latin < Greek *emporion* < *emporos* merchant, traveler < *en-* on + *poros* voyage]

em pow er (em pou′ər), *v.t.* 1 give power or authority to; authorize. 2 enable; permit.

em press (em′pris), *n.* 1 wife of an emperor. 2 woman who is the ruler of an empire.

em prise (em prīz′), *n.* ARCHAIC. 1 adventure. 2 knightly daring. [< Old French]

emp ty (emp′tē), *adj.,* **-ti er, -ti est,** *v.,* **-tied, -ty ing,** *n., pl.* **-ties.** *—adj.* 1 containing nothing; lacking the normal contents: *an empty purse.* 2 vacant; unoccupied: *an empty room.* See synonym study below. 3 not real; meaningless: *an empty promise, an empty threat.* 4 lacking knowledge and sense; foolish. 5 INFORMAL. hungry. 6 **empty of,** having no. *—v.t.* pour out or take out the contents of; make empty: *The hungry boy emptied his glass of milk quickly.* *—v.i.* 1 become empty: *The hall emptied after the concert.* 2 flow out; discharge: *The Mississippi River empties into the Gulf of Mexico.* *—n.* INFORMAL. something empty; empty container, freight car, etc. [Old English *ǣmtig* < *ǣmetta* leisure] **—emp′ti ly,** *adv.* **—emp′ti ness,** *n.*

Syn. *adj.* 1, 2 **Empty, vacant, blank** mean containing or occupied by nothing or no one. **Empty** means with nothing or with no one in it: *The house was empty when fire broke out.* **Vacant** means unoccupied or not occupied by the proper person or thing: *The children play baseball on the vacant lot.* A position or office becomes *vacant,* not empty: *The position of school principal is vacant just now.* **Blank** applies to a surface with nothing on it or with empty or vacant spaces: *My window faces a blank wall.*

emp ty-hand ed (emp′tē han′did), *adj.* having nothing in the hands; bringing or taking nothing, especially nothing of value.

empty set, (in mathematics) a set that has no members; null set. The set of natural numbers less than 0 is an empty set.

em pur pled (em pėr′pəld), *adj.* made purple; colored with purple.

em py e ma (em′pē ē′mə, em′pī ē′mə), *n.* pus in a body cavity: *empyema of the chest.* [< Greek *empyēma* < *en-* in + *pyon* pus]

em pyr e al (em pir′ē əl, em′pə rē′əl), *adj.* 1 of the empyrean; celestial; heavenly. 2 sublime; elevated.

em py re an (em′pə rē′ən), *n.* 1 the highest heaven; region of pure light. 2 the visible heavens; the sky. *—adj.* empyreal. [< Greek *empyrios* < *en-* in + *pyr* fire]

e mu (ē′myü), *n.* a large, flightless, swift-footed, three-toed Australian bird resembling an ostrich, but smaller. [apparently < Portuguese *ema*]

em u late (em′yə lāt), *v.t.,* **-lat ed, -lat ing.** 1 strive to equal or excel (a person, his achievements, or qualities); copy or imitate in order to equal or excel. 2 vie with; rival. [< Latin *aemulatum* rivaled < *aemulus* striving to equal] **—em′u la′tion,** *n.* **—em′u la′tor,** *n.*

em u la tive (em′yə lā′tiv), *adj.* trying to equal or excel.

hat, āge, fär; let, ēqual, tėrm;
it, īce; hot, ōpen, ôrder;
oil, out; cup, pu̇t, rüle;
ch, child; ng, long; sh, she;
th, thin; ᴛʜ, then; zh, measure;

ə represents *a* in about, *e* in taken, *i* in pencil, *o* in lemon, *u* in circus.

< = from, derived from, taken from.

em u lous (em′yə ləs), *adj.* wishing to equal or excel. **—em′u lous ly,** *adv.* **—em′u lous ness,** *n.*

e mul si fy (i mul′sə fī), *v.t.,* **-fied, -fy ing.** make or turn into an emulsion. **—e mul′si fi′a ble,** *adj.* **—e mul′si fi ca′tion,** *n.* **—e mul′si fi′er,** *n.*

e mul sion (i mul′shən), *n.* 1 mixture of liquids that do not dissolve in each other. In an emulsion one of the liquids contains minute droplets of the other evenly distributed throughout. 2 (in pharmacy) a milky liquid containing very tiny drops of fat, oil, etc. Cod-liver oil is made into an emulsion to improve its taste. 3 a coating on a camera film, plate, etc., that is sensitive to light. [< New Latin *emulsionem* < Latin *emulgere* milk out < *ex-* out + *mulgere* to milk]

e mul sive (i mul′siv), *adj.* 1 like an emulsion. 2 yielding an emulsion.

e mul soid (i mul′soid), *n.* colloid in which a solid exhibits a strong affinity for the liquid in which it is dispersed.

en (en), *n.* half the width of an em in printing.

en-[1], *prefix.* 1 cause to be ____; make ____: *Enfeeble = make feeble.* 2 put in ____; put on ____: *Enthrone = put on a throne.* 3 other meanings, as in *enact, encourage, entwine.* The addition of *en-* rarely changes the meaning of a verb except to make it more emphatic. See also **em-**[1]. [< Old French < Latin *in-*]

en-[2], *prefix.* in; on, as in *energy.* See also **em-**[2]. [< Greek]

-en[1], *suffix forming verbs from adjectives and nouns.* 1 cause to be ____; make ____: *Blacken = make black.* 2 cause to have ____: *Heighten = cause to have height.* 3 become ____: *Sicken = become sick.* 4 come to have ____; gain ____: *Lengthen = come to have length.* [Old English *-nian*]

-en[2], *suffix added to nouns to form adjectives.* made of ____: *Silken = made of silk.* [Old English]

-en[3], *suffix.* *-en* (or *-n*) ends the past participles of many strong verbs, as in *fallen, shaken, written, sworn.* [Old English]

-en[4], *suffix.* *-en* is used to form the plural of a few nouns, as in *children, oxen.* [Old English *-an*]

en a ble (en ā′bəl), *v.t.,* **-bled, -bling.** give ability, power, or means to; make able: *Rockets enable man to fly into outer space.*

emu
6 ft. tall

en act (en akt′), *v.t.* 1 pass (a bill) giving it validity as law; make into law. 2 decree; order. 3 represent (a play, scene, etc.) on the stage; play (a character or part); act out. **—en ac′tor,** *n.*

en act ment (en akt′mənt), *n.* 1 an enacting. 2 a being enacted. 3 a law.

e nam el (i nam′əl), *n., v.,* **-eled, -el ing** or **-elled, -el ling.** *—n.* 1 a glossy, usually opaque, glasslike substance melted and then cooled to make a smooth, hard surface on metal articles, pottery, etc., to protect or decorate them. 2 paint or varnish used to make a smooth, hard, glossy surface. 3 the smooth, hard, glossy outer layer of the teeth. 4 any smooth, hard, shiny coating or surface. *—v.t.* 1 cover or decorate with enamel. 2 form a hard, glossy surface upon. [< Anglo-French *enamayller* to enamel < *en-* on + *amayl* enamel] **—e nam′el er, e nam′el ler,** *n.* **—e nam′el like′,** *adj.*

e nam el ware (i nam′əl wer′, i nam′əl-war′), *n.* pots, pans, etc., made of metal coated with enamel.

e nam or (e nam′ər), *v.t.* 1 inflame or arouse to love; cause to fall in love. 2 charm; fascinate. [< Old French *enamourer* < *en-* in + *amour* love]

en bloc (en blok′; *French* äɴ blôk′), all together; in one lump. [< French]

enc., enclosure.

en camp (en kamp′), *v.i.* 1 make a camp. 2 live in a camp for a time. *—v.t.* put in a camp: *They were encamped in tents.* **—en camp′ment,** *n.*

en cap su late (en kap′sə lāt), *v.t., v.i.,* **-lat ed, -lat ing.** enclose or become enclosed in a capsule.

en case (en kās′), *v.t.,* **-cased, -cas ing.** 1 put into a case. 2 cover completely; enclose: *A cocoon encased the caterpillar.* Also, **incase. —en case′ment,** *n.*

en caus tic (en kô′stik), *n.* art or process of burning in the colors in painting, decorating, etc., by mixing the colors with wax and then applying heat.

-ence, *suffix forming nouns chiefly from verbs.* 1 act or fact of ____ing: *Abhorrence = act or fact of abhorring.* 2 quality or condition of being ____ent: *Prudence = quality of being prudent. Absence = condition of being absent.* Also, **-ency.** [< Old French < Latin *-entiam* -ency]

en ceinte (äɴ saɴt′), *adj.* FRENCH. pregnant.

en ce phal ic (en′sə fal′ik), *adj.* of or having to do with the brain.

en ceph a lit ic (en sef′ə lit′ik), *adj.* 1 having to do with or like encephalitis. 2 having encephalitis.

en ceph a li tis (en sef′ə li′tis), *n.* inflammation of the brain caused by injury, infection, poison, etc.

en ceph a lon (en sef′ə lon), *n.* the brain of a vertebrate. [< New Latin < Greek *enkephalos* < *en-* in + *kephalē* head]

en chain (en chān′), *v.t.* 1 fasten with a chain; put in chains; restrain; fetter. 2 hold fast (the attention); attach (the emotions) closely to an object. **—en chain′ment,** *n.*

en chant (en chant′), *v.t.* 1 use magic on; put under a spell; bewitch. 2 delight greatly; captivate; charm. [< Old French *enchanter* < Latin *incantare* < *in-* against + *cantare* to chant] **—en chant′er,** *n.*

en chant ing (en chan′ting), *adj.* very delightful; charming. **—en chant′ing ly,** *adv.*

en chant ment (en chant′mənt), *n.* 1 use of magic or sorcery. 2 a magic spell. 3 delight; rapture. 4 thing that delights or charms.

en chan tress (en chan′tris), *n.* 1 woman who practices magic; sorceress; witch. 2 a fascinating and bewitching woman.

en chi la da (en′chi lä′də), *n.* tortilla rolled around a filling of meat, cheese, etc., served with a peppery sauce. [< Mexican Spanish]

en ci pher (en sī′fər), *v.t.* put (a message, etc.) into cipher.

en cir cle (en sėr′kəl), *v.t.,* **-cled, -cling.** 1 form a circle around; surround: *Trees encircled the pond.* 2 go in a circle around: *The moon encircles the earth.* **—en cir′cle ment,** *n.*

en clave (en′klāv), *n.* country or portion of a country surrounded entirely or in part by the territory of another country. [< French < *enclaver* enclose]

en clit ic (en klit′ik), *n.* word or contraction pronounced as part of the preceding word. EXAMPLES: *s* in *Bert's here (= Bert is here), not* in *I cannot tell.* [< Late Latin *encliticus* < Greek *enklitikos* < *enklinein* lean on < *en-* in, on + *klinein* lean, incline]

en close (en klōz′), *v.t.,* **-closed, -clos ing.** 1 shut in on all sides; surround. 2 put a wall or fence around. 3 place in an envelope or package along with something else: *She enclosed a check.* 4 contain. Also, **inclose.**

en clo sure (en klō′zhər), *n.* 1 a space that is enclosed: *A corral is an enclosure for horses.* 2 thing that encloses. A wall or fence is an enclosure. 3 thing enclosed: *The order came with a $5 enclosure.* 4 an enclosing. 5 a being enclosed. Also, **inclosure.**

en code (en kōd′), *v.t.,* **-cod ed, -cod ing.** put (a message, etc.) into code; translate from ordinary language or symbols into code.

en co mi ast (en kō′mē ast), *n.* eulogist.

en co mi um (en kō′mē əm), *n., pl.* **-mi ums, -mi a** (-mē ə). a formal expression of high praise; eulogy. [< Late Latin < Greek *enkōmion* < *en-* in + *kōmos* revelry]

en com pass (en kum′pəs), *v.t.* 1 surround completely; encircle. 2 include; contain. **—en com′pass ment,** *n.*

en core (äng′kôr, äng′kōr; än′kôr, än′kōr), *interj., n., v.,* **-cored, -cor ing.** *—interj.* once more; again. *—n.* 1 a demand by the audience for the repetition of a song, etc., or for another appearance of the performer or performers. 2 the repetition of a song, etc., or the reappearance of a performer in response to such a demand. 3 an additional song, appearance, etc., by the performer. *—v.t.* call for the repetition of (a song, etc.) or the reappearance of (a performer, etc.): *The audience encored the singer by applauding.* [< French]

en coun ter (en koun′tər), *v.t.* 1 meet unexpectedly: *I encountered an old friend on the train.* 2 meet with (difficulties, opposition, etc.). 3 meet as an enemy; engage in conflict with. *—n.* 1 an unexpected meeting. 2 a meeting face to face. 3 a meeting of enemies; fight; battle. [< Old French *encontrer,* ultimately < Latin *in-* in + *contra* against]

en cour age (en kėr′ij), *v.t.,* **-aged, -ag ing.** 1 give courage, hope, or confidence to; urge on; hearten. 2 stimulate (persons or personal efforts) by helping or showing approval; support. 3 promote the development of; foster: *Sunlight encourages the growth of green plants.* **—en cour′ag ing ly,** *adv.*

en cour age ment (en kėr′ij mənt), *n.* 1 condition of being or feeling encouraged. 2 something that encourages. 3 act of encouraging.

en croach (en krōch′), *v.i.* 1 go beyond proper or usual limits; make gradual inroads on: *Over the years the sea has encroached upon the shore and submerged the beach.* 2 trespass upon the property or rights of another, especially stealthily or by gradual advances; intrude. See **intrude** for synonym study. [< Old French *encrochier* < *en-* in + *croc* hook] **—en croach′ment,** *n.*

en crust (en krust′), *v.t.* 1 cover or line with a crust or hard coating: *The inside of the kettle was encrusted with rust.* 2 decorate with a layer of costly material; embellish: *a gold crown encrusted with jewels. —v.i.* form a crust; form into a crust. Also, **incrust.**

en crus ta tion (en′kru stā′shən), *n.* incrustation.

en cum ber (en kum′bər), *v.t.* 1 hold back (from running, doing, etc.); hinder; hamper: *Heavy shoes encumber a runner in a race.* 2 block up; fill: *The neighboring yard was encumbered with old boxes and other rubbish.* 3 burden with weight, difficulties, cares, debt, etc.: *The farm was encumbered with a heavy mortgage.* Also, **incumber.** [< Old French *encombrer* < *en-* in + *combre* barrier]

en cum brance (en kum′brəns), *n.* 1 something useless or in the way; hindrance; burden. 2 claim, mortgage, etc., on property. Also, **incumbrance.**

-ency, variant of **-ence,** as in *dependency, frequency.* [< Latin *-entiam*]

ency. or **encyc.,** encyclopedia.

en cyc li cal (en sik′lə kəl, en sī′klə kəl), *n.* letter from the Pope to his bishops on a topic of interest to the whole Church. *—adj.* intended for wide circulation; general. [< Late Latin *encyclicus* < Greek *enkyklios* < *en-* in + *kyklos* circle]

en cy clo pae di a (en sī′klə pē′dē ə), *n.* encyclopedia.

en cy clo pae dic (en sī′klə pē′dik), *adj.* encyclopedic.

en cy clo pe di a (en sī′klə pē′dē ə), *n.* 1 book or set of books giving information on all branches of knowledge, usually with its articles arranged alphabetically. 2 book treating one subject very thoroughly, usually with its articles arranged alphabetically. Also, **cyclopedia** or **cyclopaedia.** [< New Latin *encyclopaedia* < Greek *enkyklopaideia,* for *enkyklios paideia* well-rounded education]

en cy clo pe dic (en sī′klə pē′dik), *adj.* 1 covering a wide range of subjects; possessing wide and varied information. 2 of or having to do with an encyclopedia. Also, **cyclopedic** or **cyclopaedic. —en cy′clo pe′di cal ly,** *adv.*

en cy clo pe dist (en sī′klə pē′dist), *n.* person who makes or compiles an encyclopedia.

en cyst (en sist′), *v.t., v.i.* enclose or become enclosed in a cyst or sac. **—en cyst′ment,** *n.*

end (end), *n.* 1 the last part; conclusion: *the end of the year, the end of a chapter.* 2 the part where a thing begins or stops: *the end of a road, the end of the table, a rope's end.* 3 purpose or goal; aim: *The end he had in mind was to skip a grade.* 4 final state; result; outcome: *It is hard to tell what the end of the battle will be.* 5 part left over; remnant. 6 death; destruction: *He met his end in the accident.* 7 an offensive or defensive player at either end of the line in football. 8 the

hat, āge, fär; let, ēqual, tėrm;
it, īce; hot, ōpen, ôrder;
oil, out; cup, pu̇t, rüle;
ch, child; ng, long; sh, she;
th, thin; ᴛʜ, then; zh, measure;

ə represents *a* in about, *e* in taken, *i* in pencil, *o* in lemon, *u* in circus.

< = from, derived from, taken from.

farthest or most distant part of any region: *the ends of the earth.*
at loose ends, a not settled or established. **b** in confusion or disorder.
end to end, with the ends placed so that they touch; endways.
in the end, in the long run; ultimately.
make both ends meet, spend no more than one has; live within one's income.
on end, a upright. **b** one after another: *It snowed for days on end.*
put an end to, do away with; stop.
—*v.t.* 1 bring to its last part; stop; finish. See synonym study below. 2 form the end of; be the end of: *This scene ends the play.* 3 destroy; kill. —*v.i.* 1 come to an end; finish. See synonym study below. 2 **end up,** wind up; come out: *end up in debt.*
[Old English *ende*]
Syn. *v.t., v.i.* 1 **End, conclude, finish** mean to bring or come to a close. **End** merely suggests stopping, whether at an appropriate place or not: *My vacation ended when school started.* **Conclude** suggests a formal closing, as of a speech, essay, action, piece of business, etc.: *Singing the national anthem will conclude the meeting.* **Finish** suggests bringing or coming to an approximate or intended end: *He has finished writing the report.*

en dan ger (en dān′jər), *v.t.* cause danger to; expose to loss or injury; imperil: *Fire endangered the hotel's guests.*

en dear (en dir′), *v.t.* make dear; inspire or create affection for. **—en dear′ing ly,** *adv.*

en dear ment (en dir′mənt), *n.* 1 an endearing. 2 thing that endears. 3 act or word showing love or affection; caress.

en deav or (en dev′ər), *v.i., v.t.* make an effort; try hard; attempt earnestly; strive: *A runner endeavors to win a race.* See **try** for synonym study. —*n.* an earnest attempt; hard try; effort. See **effort** for synonym study. [< *en-*[1] + Old French *devoir* duty]

en deav our (en dev′ər), *v.i., v.t., n.* BRITISH. endeavor.

en dem ic (en dem′ik), *adj.* 1 regularly found among a particular people or in a particular locality: *Cholera is endemic in India.* 2 (of plants or animals) indigenous to a certain locality. —*n.* an endemic disease. [< Greek *endēmos* native < *en-* in + *dēmos* people]

En di cott (en′də kot, en′də kət), *n.* **John,** 1588?-1665, first English colonial governor of the Massachusetts Bay Colony.

end ing (en′ding), *n.* 1 the last part; end: *The story has a sad ending.* 2 death. 3 letter or syllable added at the end of a word to form another word of different meaning or function; suffix. The common plural ending in English is *-s* or *-es.*

en dive (en′dīv, än′dēv), *n.* 1 species of chicory with broad, smooth leaves, used for salads; escarole. 2 variety of this plant with finely divided, curly leaves, used for salads. 3 variety of chicory whose leaves are blanched to look like very smooth white celery, used for salads; witloof. [< Old French < Medieval Greek *indivi* < Latin *intubum*]

end less (end′lis), *adj.* 1 having no end; never stopping; lasting or going on forever: *the endless rotation of the earth around the sun.* 2 seeming to have no end: *an endless scolding.* 3 with the ends joined; continuous: *The chain that drives the rear wheel of a bicycle is an endless chain.* **—end′less ly,** *adv.* **—end′less ness,** *n.*

end man, man at either end of a line of performers in a minstrel show who carries on a comic conversation with the interlocutor.

end most (end′mōst), *adj.* most distant; farthest.

endo-, *combining form.* within; inside; inner: *Endoderm = inner layer of cells.* [< Greek < *endon*]

en do car di um (en′dō kär′dē əm), *n.* the smooth membrane that lines the cavities of the heart.

en do carp (en′dō kärp), *n.* the inner layer of the pericarp of a fruit or ripened ovary of a plant. A peach stone is a hollow endocarp surrounding the seed. See **pericarp** for diagram. [< *endo-* + Greek *karpos* fruit]

en do crine (en′dō krən, en′dō krīn, en′dō krēn′), *adj.* of or having to do with the endocrine glands or the hormones they secrete. —*n.* 1 an endocrine gland. 2 its secretion. [< *endo-* + Greek *krinein* to separate]

endocrine gland, any of various glands that produce secretions that pass directly into the bloodstream or lymph instead of into a duct; ductless gland. They secrete hormones that influence or regulate other organs in the body. The thyroid and the pituitary are endocrine glands.

en do cri no log i cal (en′dō krī′nə loj′ə kəl), *adj.* of or having to do with endocrinology.

en do cri nol o gist (en′dō krī nol′ə jist, en′dō krə nol′ə jist), *n.* an expert in endocrinology.

en do cri nol o gy (en′dō krī nol′ə jē, en′dō krə nol′ə jē), *n.* science dealing with the endocrine glands, especially in their relation to bodily changes and disease.

en do derm (en′dō dėrm′), *n.* the inner layer of cells formed during development of animal embryos, from which the lining of the organs of the digestive system develops. [< *endo-* + Greek *derma* skin]

en do der mal (en′dō dėr′məl), *adj.* of or having to do with the endoderm or the endodermis.

en do der mis (en′dō dėr′mis), *n.* layer of cells which are united to form the inner boundary of the cortex and the sheath surrounding the vascular bundles of plants.

en dog a mous (en dog′ə məs), *adj.* of or having to do with endogamy.

en dog a my (en dog′ə mē), *n.* custom of marrying only within one's own clan or tribe.

en dog e nous (en doj′ə nəs), *adj.* growing from within; produced within. Cells or spores developing within a cell are endogenous.

en do morph (en′dō môrf), *n.* person with a relatively heavy body build developed from the endodermal layer of the embryo.

en do mor phic (en′dō môr′fik), *adj.* of, like, or having to do with an endomorph. **—en′do morph′i cal ly,** *adv.*

en do par a site (en′dō par′ə sīt), *n.* parasite living in the tissues or cavities of organisms. The tapeworm is an endoparasite.

en do plasm (en′dō plaz′əm), *n.* the inner portion of the cytoplasm of a cell.

en do plas mic (en′dō plaz′mik), *adj.* of or having to do with endoplasm.

end organ, a specialized structure at the distal end of a sensory or motor nerve. The retina is the end organ for vision.

en dorse (en dôrs′), *v.t.,* **-dorsed, -dors ing.** 1 write one's name on the back of (a check, note, or other document) as evidence of its transfer or assuring its payment. 2 approve; support: *Parents heartily endorsed the plan for a school playground.* Also, **indorse.** [alteration of Middle English *endossen* < Old French *endosser* < *en-* on + *dos* back] **—en dors′er,** *n.*

en dorse ment (en dôrs′mənt), *n.* 1 person's name or other writing on the back of a check, note, bill, or other document in evidence of its transfer or assuring its payment. 2 act of writing on the back of a check or other document. 3 approval; support. Also, **indorsement.**

en do skel e ton (en′dō skel′ə tən), *n.* the internal skeleton characteristic of vertebrates and allied forms.

en do sperm (en′dō spėrm′), *n.* food stored in the ovule or seed of a plant for the early nourishment of the embryo. See **embryo** for diagram.

en do spore (en′dō spôr, en′dō spōr), *n.* 1 the inner coat or wall of a spore of certain plants. 2 spore formed within a cell of certain bacteria.

en do the li um (en′dō thē′lē əm), *n., pl.* **-li a** (-lē ə). the tissue that lines blood vessels, lymphatic vessels, the heart, etc. It is a form of epithelium. [< New Latin < Greek *endon* within + *thēlē* nipple]

en do ther mic (en′dō thėr′mik), *adj.* of or having to do with a chemical change or reaction in which heat is absorbed.

en dow (en dou′), *v.t.* 1 give money or property to provide a permanent income for: *endow a college.* 2 provide from birth with some ability, quality, or talent: *Nature endowed her with both a good mind and good looks.* [< Old French *endouer* < *en-* on + *douer* endow]

en dow ment (en dou′mənt), *n.* 1 money or property given a person or institution to provide a permanent income. 2 inborn ability, quality, or talent. 3 act of endowing.

end point, 1 conclusion of a chemical process or reaction. 2 point in space where a line segment, etc., ends. 3 an object or goal.

end run, (in football) a play in which the ball carrier tries to advance the ball by running between the defensive end and the sideline.

end table, a small table suitable for placing beside a couch or chair.

en due (en dü′, en dyü′), *v.t.,* **-dued, -du ing.** 1 provide with a quality or power; furnish; supply. 2 clothe. Also, **indue.** [< Old French *enduire* < Latin *inducere* lead into, induce]

en dur a ble (en du̇r′ə bəl, en dyu̇r′ə bəl), *adj.* 1 that can be endured; bearable. 2 likely to endure or last. **—en dur′a bly,** *adv.*

en dur ance (en du̇r′əns, en dyu̇r′əns), *n.* 1 power to last and to withstand hard wear: *A runner must have great endurance to run 30 miles in a day.* 2 power to put up with, bear, or stand: *Her endurance of pain is remarkable.* 3 act or instance of enduring pain, hardship, etc. 4 duration.

en dure (en dur′, en dyur′), *v.,* **-dured, -dur ing.** —*v.i.* continue in existence; keep on; last: *Metal and stone endure for a long time.* —*v.t.* 1 put up with; bear; stand. See **bear**[1] for synonym study. 2 submit to; tolerate. [< Old French *endurer* < Latin *indurare* make hard < *in-* + *durus* hard]

en dur ing (en dur′ing, en dyur′ing), *adj.* lasting; permanent. See **lasting** for synonym study. —**en dur′ing ly,** *adv.*

end ways (end′wāz′), *adv.* 1 on end; upright. 2 with the end forward; in the direction of the end. 3 lengthwise. 4 with ends placed so that they touch; end to end.

end wise (end′wīz′), *adv.* endways.

En dym i on (en dim′ē ən), *n.* (in Greek myths) a beautiful youth loved by Selene.

end zone, (in football) the part of the field between each goal line and the corresponding end of the field.

ENE or **E.N.E.,** east-northeast.

en e ma (en′ə mə), *n.* injection of liquid into the rectum to flush the bowels. [< Greek < *en-* in + *hienai* send]

en e my (en′ə mē), *n., pl.* **-mies.** 1 person or group that hates and tries to harm another; adversary. See synonym study below. 2 a hostile force, nation, army, fleet, or air force; person, ship, etc., of a hostile nation. 3 anything harmful: *Frost is an enemy of flowers.* [< Old French *enemi* < Latin *inimicus* < *in-* not + *amicus* friendly]

Syn. 1 **Enemy, foe** mean an opposing or hostile person or group. **Enemy,** the common and general word, applies to any adversary and to any form of hostility shown: *Because of his unfair methods that businessman has many enemies.* **Foe,** now a somewhat literary word, suggests a dangerous adversary, actively or furtively demonstrating hostility: *The foes of the plan to move the city dump started a lawsuit against its supporters.*

en er get ic (en′ər jet′ik), *adj.* 1 full of energy; eager to work. 2 full of force; active; vigorous: *energetic reform measures.* —**en′er get′i cal ly,** *adv.*

en er gize (en′ər jīz), *v.t.,* **-gized, -giz ing.** give energy to; make active. —**en′er giz′er,** *n.*

en er gy (en′ər jē), *n., pl.* **-gies.** 1 will to work; vigor: *That boy is so full of energy that he cannot keep still.* 2 power to work or act; force: *All our energies were used in keeping the fire from spreading.* 3 capacity for doing work, such as lifting or moving an object. Atomic energy, kinetic energy, and potential energy are different forms of energy. *A steam engine changes heat into mechanical energy.* [< Late Latin *energia* < Greek *energeia* < *energēs* active < *en-* in + *ergon* work]

energy level, (in physics) one of the usually stable states of energy of a physical system. In the atom, electrons cluster about the nucleus in various energy levels.

en er vate (en′ər vāt), *v.t.,* **-vat ed, -vat ing.** lessen the vigor or strength of; weaken: *A hot, damp climate enervates people who are not used to it.* [< Latin *enervatum* weakened < *ex-* away + *nervus* sinew, nerve] —**en′er va′tion,** *n.*

en fa mille (äN fä mē′yə), FRENCH. with one's family; at home; informally.

en fant ter ri ble (äN fäN te rē′blə), FRENCH. 1 child whose behavior, questions, remarks, etc., embarrass older people. 2 person who is indiscreet or lacks a sense of responsibility.

en fee ble (en fē′bəl), *v.t.,* **-bled, -bling.** make feeble; weaken. —**en fee′ble ment,** *n.*

en fi lade (en′fə lād′), *n., v.,* **-lad ed, -lad ing.** —*n.* gunfire that sweeps from the side at a line of troops or a position held by them. —*v.t.* fire guns at (a line of troops or the position held by them) from the side. [< French]

en fold (en fōld′), *v.t.* 1 fold in; wrap up: *enfold oneself in a blanket.* 2 embrace; clasp: *enfold a puppy in one's arms.* Also, **infold.** —**en fold′er,** *n.* —**en fold′ment,** *n.*

en force (en fôrs′, en fōrs′), *v.t.,* **-forced, -forc ing.** 1 force obedience to; cause to be carried out; execute; administer: *Monitors help enforce school regulations.* 2 force; compel: *Illness enforced me to remain idle.* 3 urge with force; emphasize: *Graphic illustrations of crippling from arthritis enforced the seriousness of the disease.* —**en force′a ble,** *adj.* —**en forc′er,** *n.*

en force ment (en fôrs′mənt, en fōrs′mənt), *n.* an enforcing; putting into force.

en fran chise (en fran′chīz), *v.t.,* **-chised, -chis ing.** 1 give the rights of citizenship to, especially the right to vote: *The 19th amendment to the Constitution enfranchised American women.* 2 set free. —**en fran′chise ment,** *n.*

eng., 1 engineer. 2 engineering.

Eng., 1 England. 2 English.

engage (def. 3)

en gage (en gāj′), *v.,* **-gaged, -gag ing.** —*v.i.* 1 keep oneself busy; be occupied; be active; take part: *He engages in politics. They engaged in conversation.* 2 bind oneself; promise; pledge: *I will engage to be there on time.* 3 lock together; mesh: *The teeth of one gear engage with the teeth of the other.* —*v.t.* 1 keep busy; occupy: *Work engages much of my time.* 2 take for use or work; hire: *We engaged two rooms in the hotel. I engaged a carpenter to repair the porch.* 3 promise or pledge to marry: *He is engaged to my sister.* 4 catch and hold; attract: *Bright colors engage a baby's attention.* 5 bind by a promise or contract; pledge: *He engaged himself as an apprentice to a printer.* 6 fit into; lock together: *The teeth of geared wheels engage each other.* 7 start a battle with; attack: *The troops engaged their enemy.* [< Old French *engagier* < *en gage* under pledge]

en gaged (en gājd′), *adj.* promised or pledged to marry; betrothed.

en gage ment (en gāj′mənt), *n.* 1 an engaging. 2 a being engaged. 3 a promise; pledge: *I try to fulfill all my engagements.* 4 a promise or pledge to marry; betrothal. 5 appointment made to meet someone at a certain time. 6 period of being hired; time of use or work. 7 an encounter, fight, battle, etc., especially between two armed forces. See **battle** for synonym study.

en gag ing (en gā′jing), *adj.* very attractive; pleasing; charming: *an engaging smile.* —**en gag′ing ly,** *adv.* —**en gag′ing ness,** *n.*

En gels (eng′gəlz; *German* eng′əls), *n.* **Friedrich,** 1820-1895, German socialist writer.

en gen der (en jen′dər), *v.t.* 1 bring into existence; produce; cause: *Filth engenders disease.* 2 beget: *Violence engenders violence.* [< Old French *engendrer* < Latin *ingenerare* < *in-* in + *generare* create]

en gine (en′jən), *n.* 1 machine that changes energy from fuel, steam, water pressure, etc., into motion and power, used to apply power to some work, especially to start other machines moving. 2 a railroad engine; locomotive. 3 any machine; device or instrument: *Cannons are engines of war.* 4 fire engine. [< Old French *engin* skill < Latin *ingenium* inborn qualities, talent < *in-* in + *gen-,* root of *gignere* beget]

engine block, the main part of an engine, cast as a single unit, containing the cylinders.

en gi neer (en′jə nir′), *n.* 1 person who takes care of or runs engines. The man who runs a locomotive is an engineer. 2 an expert in engineering. 3 member of a military unit trained, equipped, and used for engineering work. —*v.t.* 1 plan, build, direct, or work as an engineer. 2 manage cleverly; guide skillfully: *She engineered the plan through to final approval against strong opposition.*

en gi neer ing (en′jə nir′ing), *n.* science, work, or profession of planning, building, or managing engines, machines, roads, bridges, canals, railroads, etc.

en gine ry (en′jən rē), *n.* engines or machines.

Eng land (ing′glənd), *n.* the largest division of Great Britain, in the S part. 46,254,000 pop.; 50,900 sq. mi. *Capital:* London.

Eng land er (ing′glən dər), *n.* an English person.

Eng lish (ing′glish), *adj.* of or having to do with England, its people, or their language. —*n.* 1 *pl. in use.* the people of England. 2 the language of England, including Old English or Anglo-Saxon, Middle English, and Modern English. Besides being spoken in the British Isles, English is also spoken in the United States, Canada, the Republic of South Africa, Australia, New Zealand, and many other places. 3 **english,** a spinning motion given to a ball by hitting, throwing, kicking, etc., on one side of its center. 4 a large size of type; 14 point. —*v.t.* translate into English; express in plain English. [Old English *Englisc* < *Engle* the English people]

English Channel, strait between England and France. 20-100 mi. wide.

English horn, a woodwind instrument re-

English horn

sembling an oboe, but larger and having a lower tone.

Eng lish man (ing′glish mən), *n., pl.* **-men.** 1 man who is a native or inhabitant of England. 2 one whose ancestry is English, as some Canadians and Australians.

English primrose, cowslip.

English setter, a long-haired, black-and-white hunting dog, sometimes having tan spots. It is trained to hunt with its nose pointed toward game.

English sonnet, Elizabethan sonnet.

English sparrow, a small, brownish-gray bird of the same family as the weaverbird, now very common in America; house sparrow.

English walnut, 1 a walnut tree from Asia, cultivated in Europe and North America. 2 its edible nut, used in candy, cakes, etc.

Eng lish wom an (ing′glish wu̇m′ən), *n., pl.* **-wom en.** 1 woman who is a native or inhabitant of England. 2 woman whose ancestry is English.

en gorge (en gôrj′), *v.,* **-gorged, -gorg ing.** —*v.t.* 1 swallow greedily. 2 glut; gorge. 3 congest with blood. —*v.i.* feed greedily. **—en gorge′ment,** *n.*

engr., 1 engineer. 2 engraved. 3 engraver. 4 engraving.

en graft (en graft′), *v.t.* 1 graft (a shoot, etc.) from one tree or plant into another. 2 fix in; implant. Also, **ingraft.**

en gram (en′gram), *n.* an enduring change, believed to occur in the protoplasm of nerve tissues in response to stimuli, which may account for the acquisition of skills, lasting memories, etc.

en grave (en grāv′), *v.t.,* **-graved, -grav ing.** 1 cut deeply in; carve in; carve artistically on a surface: *engrave initials on a ring.* 2 cut (a picture, design, map, etc.) in lines on a metal plate, block of wood, etc., for printing. 3 print from such a plate, block, etc. 4 fix firmly: *a face engraved in one's mind.*

en grav er (en grā′vər), *n.* person who engraves metal plates, blocks of wood, etc., for printing.

en grav ing (en grā′ving), *n.* 1 act or art of an engraver. 2 picture printed from an engraved plate, block, etc.; print.

en gross (en grōs′), *v.t.* 1 occupy wholly; take up all the attention of: *She was engrossed in a story.* 2 copy or write in large, clear letters. 3 write out in formal style; express in legal form. 4 buy all or much of (the supply of some commodity) so as to control prices. [(definitions 1,4) < *in gross* < French *en gros* in a lump; (definitions 2,3) < Anglo-French *engrosser* < *en-* in + *grosse* large writing, document] **—en gross′ment,** *n.*

en gulf (en gulf′), *v.t.* swallow up; overwhelm: *A wave engulfed the small boat.* **—en gulf′ment,** *n.*

en hance (en hans′), *v.t.,* **-hanced, -hanc ing.** make greater in quality, value, or importance; add to; heighten: *The gardens enhanced the beauty of the house.* [< Anglo-French *enhauncer,* variant of Old French *enhaucier* < *en-* on, up + *haucier* raise] **—en hance′ment,** *n.*

en har mon ic (en′här mon′ik), *adj.* (in music) having to do with notes on the scale with different names that have the same tone or sound on an instrument. EXAMPLE: C sharp and D flat.

e nig ma (i nig′mə), *n.* 1 a baffling or puzzling problem, situation, person, etc.: *The strange behavior of the child was an enigma even to her parents.* 2 a puzzling statement; riddle: *The philosopher seemed to speak in enigmas.* [< Latin *aenigma* < Greek *ainigma* < *ainissesthai* speak in riddles < *ainos* riddle, fable]

en ig mat ic (en′ig mat′ik, ē′nig mat′ik), *adj.* like an enigma or riddle; baffling; puzzling. **—en′ig mat′i cal ly,** *adv.*

en ig mat i cal (en′ig mat′ə kəl, ē′nig-mat′ə kəl), *adj.* enigmatic.

En i we tok (en′ē wē′tok), *n.* atoll in the Marshall Islands, site of United States atomic bomb tests from 1948 to 1958.

en join (en join′), *v.t.* 1 order, direct, or urge: *The father enjoined his children to be honest at all times.* 2 (in law) require or forbid by an authoritative command. [< Old French *enjoindre* < Latin *injungere* charge < *in-* on + *jungere* join] **—en join′er,** *n.*

en joy (en joi′), *v.t.* 1 have or use with joy; be happy with; take pleasure in. 2 have as an advantage or benefit: *I enjoy good health.* 3 **enjoy oneself,** have a good time; be happy.

en joy a ble (en joi′ə bəl), *adj.* that can be enjoyed; giving joy; pleasant. **—en joy′a ble ness,** *n.* **—en joy′a bly,** *adv.*

en joy ment (en joi′mənt), *n.* 1 an enjoying. 2 thing enjoyed. 3 pleasure; joy; delight. 4 a having as an advantage or benefit; possession or use: *Laws protect the enjoyment of our rights.*

en kin dle (en kin′dl), *v.t.,* **-dled, -dling.** kindle. **—en kin′dler,** *n.*

enl., 1 enlarged. 2 enlisted.

en lace (en lās′), *v.t.,* **-laced, -lac ing.** 1 wind about; encircle; enfold. 2 twine together; interlace.

en large (en lärj′), *v.,* **-larged, -larg ing.** —*v.t.* 1 make larger; increase in size: *enlarge a photograph.* See **increase** for synonym study. 2 **enlarge on,** talk or write about in more detail. —*v.i.* become larger; increase in size. **—en larg′er,** *n.*

en large ment (en lärj′mənt), *n.* 1 an enlarging. 2 a being enlarged. 3 thing that enlarges something else; addition. 4 anything that is an enlarged form of something else. 5 (in photography) a print that is made larger than the negative.

en light en (en līt′n), *v.t.* give truth and knowledge to; free from prejudice, ignorance, etc.; inform; instruct. **—en light′en er,** *n.*

en light en ment (en līt′n mənt), *n.* 1 an enlightening. 2 a being enlightened; information; instruction. See **education** for synonym study. 3 **the Enlightenment,** a philosophical movement in Europe in the 1700's that emphasized rationalism, intellectual freedom, and freedom from prejudice and superstition in social and political activity.

en list (en list′), *v.i.* 1 join a branch of the armed forces, especially voluntarily; enroll. 2 join in some cause or undertaking; give help or support. —*v.t.* 1 get to join a branch of the armed forces; induct. 2 get to join in some cause or undertaking; get the help or support of: *enlist the churches and schools to work for more city parks.* **—en list′er,** *n.*

enlisted man, man in the armed forces who is not a commissioned officer or warrant officer.

en list ment (en list′mənt), *n.* 1 an enlisting. 2 a being enlisted. 3 time for which a person enlists.

en liv en (en lī′vən), *v.t.* make lively, active, gay, or cheerful: *Bright curtains enliven a dull room.*

hat, āge, fär; let, ēqual, tėrm;
it, īce; hot, ōpen, ôrder;
oil, out; cup, pu̇t, rüle;
ch, child; ng, long; sh, she;
th, thin; ᴛʜ, then; zh, measure;

ə represents *a* in about, *e* in taken, *i* in pencil, *o* in lemon, *u* in circus.

< = from, derived from, taken from.

en masse (en mas′; *French* äɴ mȧs′), in a group; all together. [< French, in mass]

en mesh (en mesh′), *v.t.* catch in a net; enclose in meshes; entangle.

en mi ty (en′mə tē), *n., pl.* **-ties.** the feeling that enemies have for each other; hostility or hatred. [< Old French *enemistie* < Popular Latin *inimicitatem* < Latin *inimicus.* See ENEMY.]

en no ble (en nō′bəl), *v.t.,* **-bled, -bling.** 1 raise in the respect of others; make noble; dignify; exalt: *A good deed ennobles the person who does it.* 2 raise to a noble rank; give a title of nobility to. 3 make finer or more noble in nature; elevate: *His character had been ennobled through consideration of others.* **—en no′ble ment,** *n.*

en nui (än′wē), *n.* a feeling of weariness and discontent from lack of occupation or interest; boredom. [< French. Related to ANNOY.]

E noch (ē′nək), *n.* in the Bible: 1 the father of Methuselah. 2 the eldest son of Cain.

e nor mi ty (i nôr′mə tē), *n., pl.* **-ties.** 1 extreme wickedness; outrageousness: *the enormity of religious persecution.* 2 an extremely wicked crime; outrageous offense. 3 INFORMAL. great size, especially of a problem, job, etc.

e nor mous (i nôr′məs), *adj.* 1 extremely large; huge: *enormous animals, an enormous appetite.* See **huge** for synonym study. 2 extremely wicked; outrageous. [< Latin *enormis* < *ex-* out of + *norma* pattern] **—e nor′mous ly,** *adv.* **—e nor′mous ness,** *n.*

e nough (i nuf′), *adj.* as much or as many as needed or wanted; sufficient. See synonym study below. —*n.* quantity or number needed or wanted; sufficient amount: *I have had enough to eat.* —*adv.* 1 sufficiently; adequately: *Have you played enough?* 2 quite; fully: *I was willing enough to go.* 3 rather; fairly: *She talks well enough for a baby.* —*interj.* stop! no more! [Old English *genōg*]

Syn. *adj.* **Enough, sufficient, adequate** mean as much as is needed. **Enough** and its more formal equivalent, **sufficient,** mean as much as will fully satisfy a desire or need: *I have enough* (or *sufficient*) *money to pay the bill. She is not eating enough* (or *sufficient*) *food.* **Adequate** means as much as is needed to meet special, sometimes minimum, requirements: *To be healthy one must have an adequate diet.*

➔ **enough.** In sentences having a plural subject, the predicate adjective *enough* may be preceded by a plural or singular verb: *Five boxes of apples are enough for the camp. Five boxes of apples is enough for the camp.* The adjective *enough* may either precede or follow the noun it modifies: *We have enough room. We have room enough.*

e now (i nou′), *adj., n., adv.* ARCHAIC. enough.

en pas sant (äN pä säN′), FRENCH. in passing; by the way; incidentally.

en plane (en plān′), *v.*, **-planed, -plan ing.** —*v.i.* get on an airplane. —*v.t.* put on an airplane.

en quire (en kwīr′), *v.t., v.i.*, **-quired, -quir ing.** inquire.

en quir y (en kwī′rē, en′kwər ē), *n., pl.* **-quir ies.** inquiry.

en rage (en rāj′), *v.t.*, **-raged, -rag ing.** make very angry; make furious.

en rap port (äN rä pôr′), FRENCH. in sympathy; in agreement.

en rapt (en rapt′), *adj.* filled with great delight; rapt; enraptured.

en rap ture (en rap′chər), *v.t.*, **-tured, -tur ing.** move to rapture; fill with great delight.

en rich (en rich′), *v.t.* 1 make rich or richer: *An education enriches your mind. Decorations enrich a room.* 2 raise the nutritive value of (a food) by adding vitamins and minerals in processing. 3 make fertile; fertilize: *Compost enriches the soil.* **—en rich′ment,** *n.*

en roll or **en rol** (en rōl′), *v.*, **-rolled, -roll ing.** —*v.t.* 1 write in a roll or list; register. 2 make a member. —*v.i.* 1 have one's name written in a roll or list. 2 become a member. 3 enlist.

en roll ment or **en rol ment** (en rōl′mənt), *n.* 1 an enrolling. 2 number enrolled: *The school has an enrollment of 200 students.*

en route (än rüt′; en rüt′), on the way: *We shall stop at Philadelphia en route from New York to Washington.* [< French]

Ens., Ensign.

en sconce (en skons′), *v.t.*, **-sconced, -sconc ing.** 1 shelter safely; hide: *We were ensconced in the cellar during the tornado.* 2 settle comfortably and firmly: *The cat ensconced itself in the armchair.* [< *en-*[1] + *sconce* fortification, probably < Dutch *schans*]

en sem ble (än säm′bəl), *n.* 1 all the parts of a thing considered together; general effect. 2 a united performance of the full number of singers, musicians, etc.: *After the solo all the singers joined in the ensemble.* 3 group of musicians or the musical instruments used in such a performance: *Two violins, a cello, and a harp made up the string ensemble.* 4 set of clothes of which each item is chosen to match or complement the others; a complete, harmonious costume. [< French < Latin *insimul* at the same time < *in-* + *simul* at the same time]

en shrine (en shrīn′), *v.t.*, **-shrined, -shrin ing.** 1 enclose in a shrine: *A fragment of the Cross is enshrined in the cathedral.* 2 keep sacred; cherish: *memories enshrined in the heart.* **—en shrine′ment,** *n.*

en shroud (en shroud′), *v.t.* cover or hide; veil: *Fog enshrouded the ship.*

en sign (en′sīn, en′sən *for 1, 3, 4;* en′sən *for 2*), *n.* 1 a flag or banner: *The ensign of the United States is the Stars and Stripes.* 2 a navy officer ranking next below a lieutenant, junior grade, and next above a warrant officer. An ensign is the lowest commissioned officer in the United States Navy. 3 a former British army officer whose duty was carrying the flag. 4 sign of one's rank, position, or power; symbol of authority: *The ensign of the queen was her crown and scepter.* [< Old French *enseigne* < Latin *insignia.* Doublet of INSIGNIA.]

en si lage (en′sə lij), *n.* silage.

en sile (en sīl′, en′sīl), *v.t.*, **-siled, -sil ing.** 1 preserve (green fodder) in a silo. 2 make into silage.

en slave (en slāv′), *v.t.*, **-slaved, -slav ing.** make a slave or slaves of; take away freedom from. **—en slave′ment,** *n.* **—en slav′er,** *n.*

en snare (en sner′, en snar′), *v.t.*, **-snared, -snar ing.** catch in a snare; trap; snare. Also, **insnare.**

en sue (en sü′), *v.i.*, **-sued, -su ing.** 1 come after; follow. The ensuing year means the year following this. See **follow** for synonym study. 2 happen as a result: *I spent my allowance the first day, and a lean week ensued.* [< Old French *ensu-,* a form of *ensivre,* ultimately < Latin *in-* + *sequi* follow]

en sure (en shůr′), *v.t.*, **-sured, -sur ing.** 1 make sure or certain: *Careful planning and hard work ensured the success of the party.* 2 make sure of getting; secure: *A letter of introduction will ensure you an interview.* 3 make safe; protect: *Proper clothing ensured us against suffering from the cold.* 4 to guarantee against risk; insure. [< Anglo-French *enseurer* < *en-* + *seür* sure < Latin *securus*]

➤ **ensure, insure.** Although *ensure* and *insure* are interchangeable in most meanings, prevailing usage tends to differentiate them. *Ensure* is the usual spelling for "make sure or certain"; *insure,* for "arrange for money payment in case of loss, accident, or death": *These letters ensure your claims. He insured his car against theft.*

-ent, *suffix added to verbs.* 1 *(to form adjectives)* that ___s; ___ing: *Absorbent = that absorbs* or *absorbing.* 2 *(to form nouns)* one that ___s: *Correspondent = one that corresponds.* 3 *(to form adjectives)* other meanings, as in *competent, confident.* See also **-ant.** [< Latin *-entem*]

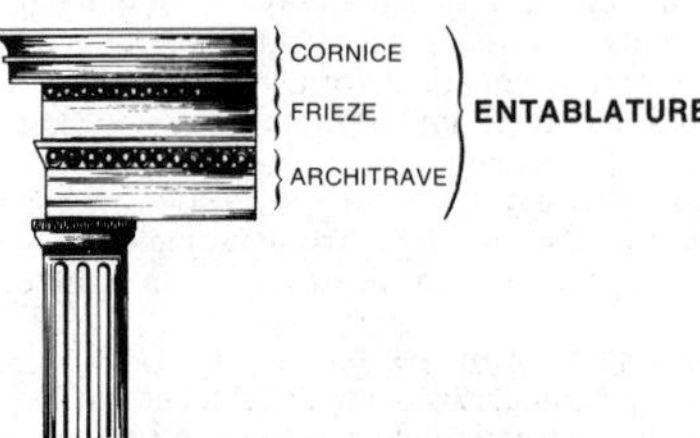

en tab la ture (en tab′lə chůr, en tab′lə-chər), *n.* part of a building resting on the top of columns. A classical entablature consisted of an architrave, frieze, and cornice. [< earlier French < Italian *intavolatura* < *in-* + *tavola* table]

en tail (en tāl′), *v.t.* 1 impose or require: *Owning an automobile entailed greater expense than we had expected.* 2 limit the inheritance of (property, etc.) to a specified line of heirs so that it cannot be left to anyone else. An entailed estate usually passes to the eldest son. —*n.* 1 an entailing. 2 an entailed inheritance. 3 the order of descent specified for an entailed estate: *Though the nobleman had quarreled with his heir, he could not break the entail and leave the estate to someone else.* [< *en-*[1] + Old French *taille* cutting, tax < *taillier* to cut] **—en tail′ment,** *n.*

en tan gle (en tang′gəl), *v.t.*, **-gled, -gling.** 1 get twisted up and caught; tangle: *I entangled my feet in the coil of rope and fell down.* 2 get into difficulty; involve: *The villain tried to entangle the hero in an evil scheme.* 3 perplex; confuse. **—en tan′gle ment,** *n.*

en tente (än tänt′), *n.* 1 an understanding; agreement between two or more governments. 2 parties to an understanding; governments that have made an agreement. [< French]

en tente cor diale (äN täNt′ kôr dyäl′), FRENCH. a friendly understanding or agreement, especially between two or more governments.

en ter (en′tər), *v.t.* 1 go into; come into: *enter a house. The bullet entered his heart.* 2 become a part or member of; join: *I entered the contest.* 3 cause to join or enter; obtain admission for; enroll: *Parents enter their children in school.* 4 begin; start: *After years of training, the doctor entered the practice of medicine.* 5 write or print in a book, list, etc.: *In a dictionary words are entered in alphabetical order.* 6 (in law) put in official form; make a formal record of; record: *The injured man entered a complaint in court.* 7 report (a ship or its cargoes) at the custom house. 8 **enter into, a** take part in; join in: *enter into a debate.* **b** form a part of: *Lead enters into the composition of pewter.* **c** consider; discuss: *enter into a question of law.* 9 **enter on** or **enter upon, a** begin; start: *enter on professional duties.* **b** take possession of: *enter upon an estate by inheritance.* —*v.i.* go in; come in: *Let them enter.* [< Old French *entrer* < Latin *intrare* < *intra* within]

en ter ic (en ter′ik), *adj.* intestinal. [< Greek *enterikos* < *enteron* intestine]

en te ri tis (en′tə rī′tis), *n.* inflammation of the intestines, usually accompanied by diarrhea, fever, etc.

en ter o coc cus (en′tər ə kok′əs), *n., pl.* **-coc ci** (-kok′sī). streptococcus usually found in the human intestine.

en ter prise (en′tər prīz), *n.* 1 an important, difficult, or dangerous plan to be tried; great or bold undertaking. 2 any undertaking; project; venture: *a business enterprise.* 3 readiness to try important, difficult, or dangerous plans; willingness to undertake great or bold projects. 4 the carrying on of enterprises; taking part in enterprises. [< Old French *entreprise* < *entre-* between + *prendre* to take]

en ter pris er (en′tər prī′zər), *n.* 1 person who carries on or takes part in enterprises. 2 entrepreneur.

en ter pris ing (en′tər prī′zing), *adj.* likely to start projects; ready to face difficulties. **—en′ter pris′ing ly,** *adv.*

en ter tain (en′tər tān′), *v.t.* 1 keep pleasantly interested; please or amuse: *The circus entertained the children.* See **amuse** for synonym study. 2 have as a guest: *She entertained ten people at dinner.* 3 take into the mind; consider: *entertain a foolish idea.* 4 hold in the mind; maintain: *entertain a hope of success.* —*v.i.* have guests; provide entertainment for guests: *He entertains a great deal.* [< Old French *entretenir* < *entre-* among + *tenir* to hold]

en ter tain er (en′tər tā′nər), *n.* 1 person who entertains. 2 singer, musician, dancer, etc., who performs in public, especially as a profession.

en ter tain ing (en′tər tā′ning), *adj.* interesting, pleasing, or amusing. **—en′ter tain′ing ly,** *adv.*

en ter tain ment (en′tər tān′mənt), *n.* 1 thing that interests, pleases, or amuses. A show or a circus is an entertainment. 2 act of entertaining. 3 condition of being entertained. 4 attention to the comfort and desires of guests; hospitality.

en thrall or **en thral** (en thrôl′), *v.t.*, **-thralled, -thrall ing.** 1 hold captive by beauty or interest; fascinate; charm. 2 make a slave of; enslave. **—en thrall′ment,** *n.*

en throne (en thrōn′), *v.t.*, **-throned, -thron ing.** 1 set on a throne. 2 place highest of all; exalt. 3 invest with authority, especially as a sovereign or as a bishop. **—en throne′ment,** *n.*

en thuse (en thüz′), *v.*, **-thused, -thus ing.** INFORMAL. *—v.i.* show enthusiasm. *—v.t.* fill with enthusiasm.

en thu si asm (en thü′zē az′əm), *n.* eager interest; zeal: *The pep talk filled us with enthusiasm.* [< Late Latin *enthusiasmus* < Greek *enthousiasmos* < *entheos* god-possessed < *en-* in + *theos* god]

en thu si ast (en thü′zē ast), *n.* 1 person who is filled with enthusiasm: *a football enthusiast.* 2 zealot; fanatic.

en thu si as tic (en thü′zē as′tik), *adj.* full of enthusiasm; eagerly interested: *an enthusiastic student.* **—en thu′si as′ti cal ly,** *adv.*

en tice (en tīs′), *v.t.*, **-ticed, -tic ing.** attract by arousing hopes or desires; tempt. See **lure** for synonym study. [< Old French *enticier* stir up, incite < *en-* in + Latin *titio* firebrand] **—en tice′ment,** *n.* **—en tic′ing ly,** *adv.*

en tire (en tīr′), *adj.* 1 having all the parts or elements; whole; complete. See **complete** for synonym study. 2 not broken; in one piece; having an unbroken outline. 3 (of leaves, shells, etc.) having an even margin; without notches. [< Old French *entir* < Latin *integer* < *in-* not + *tangere* to touch. Doublet of INTEGER.] **—en tire′ly,** *adv.* **—en tire′ness,** *n.*

en tire ty (en tīr′tē), *n.*, *pl.* **-ties.** 1 a being entire; wholeness; completeness. 2 a complete thing; the whole. 3 **in its entirety,** wholly; completely.

en ti tle (en tī′tl), *v.t.*, **-tled, -tling.** 1 give a claim or right *(to)*; qualify: *A ticket will entitle you to admission.* 2 give the title of; call by the name of: *The author entitles his book "Treasure Island."* **—en ti′tle ment,** *n.*

en ti ty (en′tə tē), *n.*, *pl.* **-ties.** 1 something that has a real and separate existence either actually or in the mind. Persons, mountains, languages, and beliefs are distinct entities. 2 being; existence. [< Medieval Latin *entitatem* < Latin *enti-*, a form of *ens* thing, being]

en tomb (en tüm′), *v.t.* place in a tomb; bury. **—en tomb′ment,** *n.*

en to mo log ic (en′tə mə loj′ik), *adj.* entomological.

en to mo log i cal (en′tə mə loj′ə kəl), *adj.* of or having to do with entomology. **—en′to mo log′i cal ly,** *adv.*

en to mol o gist (en′tə mol′ə jist), *n.* an expert in entomology.

en to mol o gy (en′tə mol′ə jē), *n.* branch of zoology that deals with insects. [< Greek *entomon* insect + English *-logy*]

en tou rage (än′tü räzh′), *n.* group of attendants; people usually accompanying a person; retinue: *a queen and her entourage.* [< French]

en tr'acte (än trakt′), *n.* 1 interval between two acts of a play, ballet, opera, etc. 2 music, dancing, or any entertainment performed during this interval. [< French]

en trails (en′trālz, en′trəlz), *n.pl.* 1 the inner parts of the body of a man or animal. 2 the intestines; bowels. [< Old French *entrailles* < Medieval Latin *intralia,* alteration of Latin *interanea* things inside < *inter* within]

en train (en trān′), *v.i.* get on a train. *—v.t.* put on a train.

en trance[1] (en′trəns), *n.* 1 act of entering: *The actor's entrance was greeted with applause.* 2 place by which to enter; door, passageway, etc. 3 freedom or right to enter; permission to enter; admission. [< Middle French < *entrer* enter. See ENTER.]

en trance[2] (en trans′), *v.t.*, **-tranced, -tranc ing.** 1 fill with joy or wonder; delight; charm. 2 put into a trance. [< *en-*[1] + *trance*] **—en trance′ment,** *n.* **—en tranc′ing ly,** *adv.*

en trant (en′trənt), *n.* 1 person who enters. 2 person who takes part in a contest. 3 a new member in a profession, club, association, etc.

en trap (en trap′), *v.t.*, **-trapped, -trap ping.** 1 catch in a trap. 2 bring into difficulty or danger; trick: *By clever questioning, the lawyer entrapped the witness into contradicting himself.* **—en trap′ment,** *n.*

en treat (en trēt′), *v.t.* ask or keep asking earnestly; beg and pray: *The prisoners entreated their captors to let them go.* Also, **intreat.** [< Old French *entraitier* < *en-* in + *traitier* to treat] **—en treat′ing ly,** *adv.*

en treat y (en trē′tē), *n.*, *pl.* **-treat ies.** an earnest request; prayer or appeal: *I gave in to the children's entreaties.*

en tre chat (än trə shä′), *n.* (in ballet) a leap in which the dancer points his feet and crosses them a number of times. [< French]

en tree or **en trée** (än′trā), *n.* 1 freedom or right to enter; access. 2 the main dish of food at dinner or lunch. 3 dish of food served before the roast or between the main courses at dinner. [< French *entrée*]

en trench (en trench′), *v.t.* 1 surround with a trench; fortify with trenches. 2 establish firmly: *a practice entrenched by long tradition.* 3 trespass; encroach; infringe: *entrench upon rights.* Also, **intrench.**

entrenchment (def. 3) in World War I

en trench ment (en trench′mənt), *n.* 1 an entrenching. 2 an entrenched position. 3 defense consisting of a trench and a rampart of earth or stone. Also, **intrenchment.**

en tre pôt (än′trə pō), *n.* warehouse for distribution of goods. [< French]

en tre pre neur (än′trə prə nėr′), *n.* person who organizes and manages a business or industrial enterprise, attempting to make a profit but taking the risk of a loss. [< French < *entreprendre* undertake]

en tro py (en′trə pē), *n.* 1 (in thermodynamics) a measure of the amount of energy that is not available for conversion into mechanical work. 2 (in physics) a measure of the degree of disorder of a system. [< German *Entropie* < Greek *en-* in + *tropē* a turning]

hat, āge, fär; let, ēqual, tėrm;
it, īce; hot, ōpen, ôrder;
oil, out; cup, pu̇t, rüle;
ch, child; ng, long; sh, she;
th, thin; ᴛʜ, then; zh, measure;

ə represents *a* in about, *e* in taken, *i* in pencil, *o* in lemon, *u* in circus.

< = from, derived from, taken from.

en trust (en trust′), *v.t.* 1 charge with a trust: *The club entrusted the newly elected treasurer with all of its money.* 2 give the care of; hand over for safekeeping: *While traveling, they entrusted their children to their grandparents.* See **commit** for synonym study. Also, **intrust.**

en try (en′trē), *n.*, *pl.* **-tries.** 1 act of entering: *Your sudden entry startled me.* 2 place by which to enter; way to enter, such as a lobby or vestibule. 3 thing written or printed in a book, list, etc. Each word explained in a dictionary is an entry or **entry word.** 4 person or thing that takes part in a contest. 5 (in law) the act of taking possession of lands by setting foot on them. 6 a giving of an account of a ship's cargo at a custom house.

en twine (en twīn′), *v.t.*, *v.i.*, **-twined, -twin ing.** 1 twine or become twined together. 2 twine or become twined around.

e nu cle ate (i nü′klē āt, i nyü′klē āt), *v.t.*, **-at ed, -at ing.** remove (a tumor, etc.) from its capsule or cover without cutting.

e nu mer a ble (i nü′mər ə bəl, i nyü′mər ə bəl), *adj.* that can be enumerated.

e nu me rate (i nü′mə rāt′, i nyü′mə rāt′), *v.t.*, **-rat ed, -rat ing.** 1 name one by one; list: *He enumerated the capitals of the 50 states.* 2 find out the number of; count. [< Latin *enumeratum* counted < *ex-* out + *numerus* number] **—e nu′me ra′tion,** *n.* **—e nu′me ra′tor,** *n.*

e nu me ra tive (i nü′mə rā′tiv, i nyü′mə rā′tiv), *adj.* that enumerates; having to do with enumeration.

e nun ci ate (i nun′sē āt), *v.*, **-at ed, -at ing.** *—v.i.* speak or pronounce words: *He enunciates very distinctly.* *—v.t.* 1 speak or pronounce; articulate: *Enunciate your words clearly.* 2 state definitely; announce: *enunciate a new theory.* [< Latin *enuntiatum* announced < *ex-* out + *nuntius* messenger] **—e nun′ci a′tor,** *n.*

e nun ci a tion (i nun′sē ā′shən), *n.* 1 articulation. 2 announcement.

en u re sis (en′yü rē′sis), *n.* the inability to control urination. [< New Latin < Greek *en-* in + *ourein* urinate]

env., envelope.

en vel op (en vel′əp), *v.t.* 1 wrap or cover; enfold. 2 hide; conceal: *Fog enveloped the village.* 3 surround; encircle: *envelop the enemy.* [< Old French *enveloper* < *en-* in + *voloper* to wrap] **—en vel′op ment,** *n.*

en ve lope (en′və lōp, än′və lōp), *n.* 1 a paper cover in which a letter or anything flat can be mailed, filed, etc. It can usually be folded over and sealed by wetting a gummed edge. 2 covering; wrapper. 3 any enclosing covering, such as a membrane or shell. 4 bag that holds the gas in a balloon or airship. [< French *enveloppe* < *enveloper* envelop]

en ven om (en ven′əm), *v.t.* 1 make poisonous. 2 fill with bitterness, hate, etc.

en vi a ble (en′vē ə bəl), *adj.* to be envied; worth having; desirable: *an enviable school record.* **—en′vi a ble ness,** *n.* **—en′vi a bly,** *adv.*

en vi ous (en′vē əs), *adj.* feeling or showing envy; full of envy: *envious of another's success.* **—en′vi ous ly,** *adv.* **—en′vi ous ness,** *n.*

en vi ron (en vī′rən), *v.t.* hem in; surround; enclose. [< Old French *environner* < *environ* around < *en-* in + *viron* circle]

en vi ron ment (en vī′rən mənt), *n.* 1 all the surrounding things, conditions, and influences affecting the development of living things. A person's character is influenced by the social environment around him. Differences in environment often account for differences in the same kind of plant found in different places. 2 surroundings: *an environment of poverty.* 3 condition of the air, water, soil, etc.; natural surroundings: *a pollution-free environment.*

en vi ron men tal (en vī′rən men′tl), *adj.* having to do with environment. **—en vi′ron men′tal ly,** *adv.*

en vi rons (en vī′rənz), *n.pl.* surrounding districts; suburbs or outskirts.

en vis age (en viz′ij), *v.t.,* **-aged, -ag ing.** form a mental picture of; visualize: *The architect envisaged the finished house from the plans.*

en vi sion (en vizh′ən), *v.t.* envisage.

en voi (en′voi, än′voi), *n.* envoy².

en voy¹ (en′voi, än′voi), *n.* 1 messenger or representative. 2 diplomat ranking next below an ambassador and next above a minister. 3 any person sent to represent a government or ruler for diplomatic purposes. [< French *envoyé,* past participle of *envoyer* send < Old French *envoier.* See ENVOY².]

en voy² (en′voi, än′voi), *n.* 1 a short stanza ending a poem. 2 a postscript to a literary work, often addressed to a friend or patron of the author. Also, **envoi.** [< Old French < *envoier* send < Latin *in via* on the way]

en vy (en′vē), *n., pl.* **-vies,** *v.,* **-vied, -vy ing.** *—n.* 1 feeling of discontent, dislike, or desire because another has what one wants. 2 the object of such feeling; person or thing envied. *—v.t.* 1 feel envy toward. See synonym study below. 2 feel envy because of: *envy a friend's success.* [< Old French *envie* < Latin *invidia,* ultimately < *invidere* look with enmity at < *in-* against + *videre* see] **—en′vy ing ly,** *adv.*

Syn. *v.t.* 1 **Envy, covet** mean to feel discontent about the good fortune of others. **Envy** implies resentment, jealousy, or even hatred directed toward them: *He envies famous people.* **Covet** implies a craving for the good fortune that is rightfully theirs: *He covets the fame that his brother has earned.*

en wrap (en rap′), *v.t.,* **-wrapped, -wrap ping.** wrap.

en wreathe (en rēᴛʜ′), *v.t.,* **-wreathed, -wreath ing.** wreathe around; encircle; surround.

en zy mat ic (en′zī mat′ik, en′zi mat′ik), *adj.* of or having to do with an enzyme or enzymes.

en zyme (en′zīm), *n.* a complex substance produced in living cells, either wholly or partially protein, that is able to cause or accelerate changes in other substances within a plant or animal without being changed itself. Enzymes such as pepsin help break down food so that it can be digested. [< German *Enzym,* ultimately < Greek *en-* in + *zyme* leaven]

E o cene (ē′ə sēn′), *n.* 1 the second epoch of the Tertiary period, after the Paleocene and before the Oligocene, during which the ancestors of many modern mammals appeared. See chart under **geology.** 2 the rocks formed during this epoch. *—adj.* of or having to do with this epoch or its rocks. [< Greek *ēōs* dawn + *kainos* recent]

e o hip pus (ē′ō hip′əs), *n.* any of an extinct genus of horses that lived in North America and Europe and was an ancestor of modern horses. About 11 inches high at the shoulder, it had, instead of hoofs, four toes on each front foot and three on each hind foot. [< Greek *ēōs* dawn + *hippos* horse]

E o li an or **e o li an** (ē ō′lē ən), *adj.* Aeolian.

e o lith (ē′ə lith), *n.* a roughly shaped stone tool belonging to a very early stage of human culture. [< Greek *ēōs* dawn + *lithos* stone]

e o lith ic (ē′ə lith′ik), *adj.* having to do with the stage of human culture, characterized by the use of eoliths.

e on (ē′ən, ē′on), *n.* a very long period of time; many thousands of years: *Eons passed before life existed on the earth.* Also, **aeon.** [< Latin *aeon* < Greek *aiōn* lifetime, age]

E os (ē′os), *n.* (in Greek myths) the goddess of the dawn, identified with the Roman goddess Aurora.

e o sin (ē′ə sən), *n.* a rose-red dye or stain made from coal tar, used in dyeing textiles, making red ink, etc. [< Greek *ēōs* dawn]

e o sine (ē′ə sən, ē′ə sēn′), *n.* eosin.

e o sin o phil (ē′ə sin′ə fil), *n.* cell containing granules which are easily stained by eosin or other acid dyes, especially a type of white blood cell.

EP, (of phonograph records) extended play.

E pam i non das (i pam′ə non′dəs), *n.* 418?-362 B.C., Greek general and statesman.

ep au let or **ep au lette** (ep′ə let), *n.* ornament on the shoulder of a uniform, now usually only as part of a military dress uniform. [< French *épaulette*]

é pée (ā pā′, e pā′), *n.* sword used in fencing and dueling, especially one with a sharp point and no cutting edge. [< French]

e phah (ē′fə), *n.* an ancient Hebrew unit of dry measure equal to a little more than a bushel. [< Hebrew *ēphāh*]

e phed rin (i fed′rən; *in chemistry, also* ef′ə drən), *n.* ephedrine.

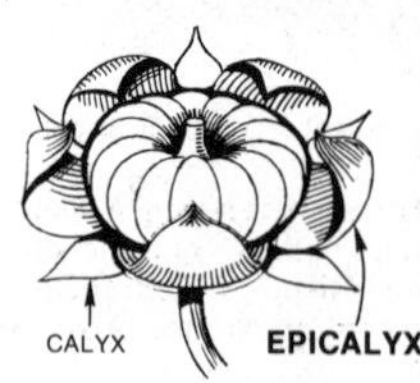

e phed rine (i fed′rən; *in chemistry, also* ef′ə drēn′, ef′ə drən), *n.* drug used to relieve hay fever, asthma, head colds, etc., by constricting mucous membranes and to stimulate the heart and the central nervous system. *Formula:* $C_{10}H_{15}ON$ [< Latin *ephedra* horsetail (a plant)]

e phem er a (i fem′ər ə), *n.pl.* things lasting for only a very short time.

e phem er al (i fem′ər əl), *adj.* 1 lasting for only a very short time; very short-lived; transitory. 2 lasting for only a day. [< Greek *ephēmeros* < *epi-* upon + *hēmera* day] **—e phem′er al ly,** *adv.*

e phem er id (i fem′ər id), *n.* any of an order of insects having a thin body, membranous forewings which are much larger than the hind wings and, usually, three long, delicate tails; mayfly. Ephemerids live only a day or two in the adult stage.

e phem er is (i fem′ər is), *n., pl.* **eph e mer i des** (ef′ə mer′ə dēz′). table showing the daily positions of a heavenly body. [< Greek *ephēmeris* diary, calendar < *ephēmeros.* See EPHEMERAL.]

E phe sian (i fē′zhən), *adj.* of Ephesus or its people. *—n.* native or inhabitant of Ephesus.

E phe sians (i fē′zhənz), *n.* book of the New Testament, written by Saint Paul to the Christians at Ephesus.

Eph e sus (ef′ə səs), *n.* Greek city of ancient times in what is now W Turkey.

eph od (ef′od, ē′fod), *n.* vestment worn by the ancient Hebrew high priests. [< Hebrew *ēphōd*]

eph or (ef′ôr, ef′ər), *n., pl.* **-ors, -o ri** (-ə rī′). one of five leading magistrates of ancient Sparta, elected yearly by the people to advise the king. [< Greek *ephoros* < *epi-* over + *horan* see]

E phra im (ē′frē əm, ē′frəm), *n.* 1 in the Bible: **a** the younger son of Joseph. **b** tribe of Israel descended from him. 2 the northern kingdom of ancient Israel.

E phra im ite (ē′frē ə mīt, ē′frə mīt), *n.* 1 member of the tribe of Ephraim. 2 inhabitant of the northern kingdom of ancient Israel.

epi-, *prefix.* on; upon; above; among: *Epicalyx = on the calyx. Epidermis = upon or above the dermis.* [< Greek *epi*]

ep ic (ep′ik), *n.* 1 a long narrative poem that tells the adventures and achievements of one or more great heroes, written in a dignified, majestic style, and often giving expression to the ideals of a nation or race. The *Odyssey* and *Beowulf* are epics. 2 a long novel, etc., having the qualities of an epic. 3 story or series of events worthy of being the subject of an epic. *—adj.* 1 of an epic. 2 majestic in style; heroic: *epic deeds.* [< Latin *epicus* < Greek *epikos* < *epos* story, word]

ep i ca lyx (ep′ə kā′liks, ep′ə kal′iks), *n.* ring of bracts at the base of a flower that looks like an outer calyx.

ep i car di um (ep′ə kär′dē əm), *n., pl.* **-di a** (-dē ə). the inner layer of the pericardium, which adheres to the heart.

ep i carp (ep′ə kärp), *n.* the outer layer of the pericarp of a fruit or ripened ovary of a plant; exocarp. The skin of a pear is its epicarp. See **pericarp** for diagram. [< *epi-* on + Greek *karpos* fruit]

ep i cen ter (ep′ə sen′tər), *n.* 1 point on the earth's surface directly above the true center of an earthquake. 2 any central or focal point.

ep i cot yl (ep′ə kot′l), *n.* the part of the stem or axis that is above the cotyledons in the embryo of a plant. [< *epi-* + Greek *kotylē* small vessel]

Ep ic te tus (ep′ik tē′təs), *n.* A.D. 60?-140?, Greek Stoic philosopher who taught at Rome.

ep i cure (ep′ə kyůr), *n.* person who has a refined taste in eating and drinking and who is very particular in choosing fine foods, wines, etc. [< *Epicurus*]

ep i cu re an (ep′ə kyů rē′ən), *adj.* 1 of, having to do with, or fit for an epicure: *an epicurean banquet.* 2 **Epicurean,** of Epicurus or his philosophy. *—n.* 1 epicure. 2 **Epicurean,** believer in the philosophy of Epicurus.

Ep i cu re an ism (ep′ə kyů rē′ə niz′əm), *n.* 1 philosophy or principles of Epicurus or his followers. 2 Also, **epicureanism.** belief in or practice of this philosophy.

Ep i cur us (ep′ə kyůr′əs), *n.* 342?-270 B.C., Greek philosopher who taught that pleasure is the highest good, but that true pleasure depends on self-control, moderation, and honorable behavior.

ep i dem ic (ep′ə dem′ik), *n.* 1 the rapid spread of a disease so that many people have it at the same time: *a flu epidemic.* 2 the rapid spread of an idea, fashion, etc. *—adj.* affecting many people at the same time; widespread: *an epidemic disease.* [< Greek *epidēmia* a stay, visit, prevalence (of a disease) < *epi-* among + *dēmos* people] **—ep′i dem′i cal ly,** *adv.*

ep i dem i cal (ep′ə dem′ə kəl), *adj.* epidemic.

ep i de mi o log ic (ep′ə dē′mē ə loj′ik), *adj.* 1 of or having to do with epidemiology. 2 having the character of an epidemic. **—ep′i de′mi o log′i cal ly,** *adv.*

ep i de mi o log i cal (ep′ə dē′mē ə loj′ə kəl), *adj.* epidemiologic.

ep i de mi ol o gist (ep′ə dē′mē ol′ə jist), *n.* an expert in epidemiology.

ep i de mi ol o gy (ep′ə dē′mē ol′ə jē), *n.* branch of medicine dealing with the causes, distribution, and control of the spread of diseases in a community.

ep i der mal (ep′ə dėr′məl), *adj.* of or having to do with the epidermis.

ep i der mis (ep′ə dėr′mis), *n.* 1 the outer, protective layer of the skin of vertebrate animals, covering the sensitive dermis; cuticle. 2 any of various outer layers of invertebrates. 3 a skinlike layer of cells in seed plants and ferns.

ep i gen e sis (ep′ə jen′ə sis), *n.* the development of the embryo from the substance of the egg by a series of new formations or successive differentiations.

ep i ge net ic (ep′ə jə net′ik), *adj.* of or produced by epigenesis.

ep i glot tal (ep′ə glot′l), *adj.* of or having to do with the epiglottis.

ep i glot tis (ep′ə glot′is), *n.* a thin, triangular plate of cartilage that covers the entrance to the windpipe during swallowing, so that food and drink do not get into the lungs.

ep i gram (ep′ə gram), *n.* 1 a short, pointed or witty saying. EXAMPLE: "Speech is silver, but silence is golden." See synonym study below. 2 a short poem ending in a witty or clever, and often satirical, turn of thought. EXAMPLE:

"Here lies our Sovereign Lord the King,
Whose word no man relies on,
Who never said a foolish thing,
Nor ever did a wise one."

[< Greek *epigramma* < *epigraphein* inscribe < *epi-* on + *graphein* write]

Syn. *n.* 1 **Epigram, paradox, aphorism, proverb** are all short, thoughtful sayings. An **epigram** is usually witty: *He knows the cost of everything, but the value of nothing.* A special type of epigram is the **paradox,** which makes a statement that, as it stands, contradicts fact or common sense or itself, and yet suggests a truth or at least a half truth: *All generalizations are false, including this one.* Closely related to the epigram is the **aphorism,** which is likely to be abstract and not necessarily witty: *Fools rush in where angels fear to tread.* A **proverb** is likely to make an observation on character or conduct and is the often-quoted, concrete expression of popular wisdom: *Still waters run deep.*

ep i gram mat ic (ep′ə grə mat′ik), *adj.* 1 like an epigram; short and witty. 2 of epigrams; full of epigrams. **—ep′i gram mat′i cal ly,** *adv.*

ep i gram mat i cal (ep′ə grə mat′ə kəl), *adj.* epigrammatic.

ep i gram ma tist (ep′ə gram′ə tist), *n.* person who makes epigrams.

e pig ra phy (i pig′rə fē), *n.* 1 inscriptions. 2 branch of knowledge that deals with the deciphering and interpretation of inscriptions.

ep i lep sy (ep′ə lep′sē), *n.* a chronic disorder of the nervous system, usually characterized by convulsions and unconsciousness, caused by a disturbance in the normal rhythm of brain cells. [< Greek *epilēpsia* seizure, ultimately < *epi-* on + *lambanein* seize, take]

ep i lep tic (ep′ə lep′tik), *adj.* 1 of or having to do with epilepsy. 2 having epilepsy. *—n.* person who has epilepsy.

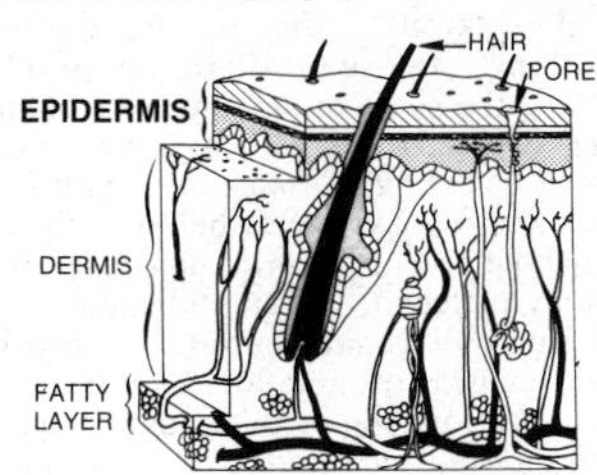

epidermis (def. 1)

ep i logue or **ep i log** (ep′ə lôg, ep′ə log), *n.* 1 a concluding section added to a novel, poem, etc., that rounds out or interprets the work. 2 speech or poem, addressed to the audience by one of the actors at the end of a play. 3 any concluding act or event. [< Greek *epilogos,* ultimately < *epi-* above + *legein* speak]

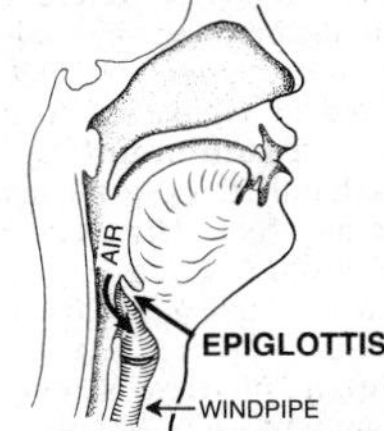

epiglottis—normal position for breathing. During swallowing, the epiglottis lowers and closes the windpipe.

ep i neph rin (ep′ə nef′rən), *n.* epinephrine.

ep i neph rine (ep′ə nef′rən, ep′ə nef′rēn′), *n.* adrenaline. [< *epi-* + Greek *nephros* kidney]

E piph a ny (i pif′ə nē), *n.* January 6, the anniversary of the coming of the Magi to honor the infant Jesus at Bethlehem. [< Late Latin *epiphania,* ultimately < Greek *epi-* + *phainein* to show]

hat, āge, fär; let, ēqual, tėrm;
it, īce; hot, ōpen, ôrder;
oil, out; cup, pu̇t, rüle;
ch, child; ng, long; sh, she;
th, thin; ᴛʜ, then; zh, measure;

ə represents *a* in about, *e* in taken, *i* in pencil, *o* in lemon, *u* in circus.

< = from, derived from, taken from.

ep i phyte (ep′ə fīt), *n.* any of various plants that grow on other plants for support, but draw nourishment from the air and rain instead of from their host; air plant. Many mosses, lichens, and orchids are epiphytes. [< *epi-* on + Greek *phyton* plant]

ep i phyt ic (ep′ə fit′ik), *adj.* growing as an epiphyte; having the characteristics of an epiphyte.

E pi rus (i pī′rəs), *n.* ancient country in the W part of the Balkan Peninsula. Part of it is now in Greece and part in Albania.

e pis co pa cy (i pis′kə pə sē), *n., pl.* **-cies.** 1 government of a church by bishops. 2 episcopate.

e pis co pal (i pis′kə pəl), *adj.* 1 of or having to do with a bishop or bishops. 2 governed by bishops. 3 **Episcopal,** of or having to do with the Church of England or with the Protestant Episcopal Church. [< Greek *episkopos* overseer < *epi-* + *skopos* watcher] **—e pis′co pal ly,** *adv.*

E pis co pa lian (i pis′kə pā′lyən, i pis′kə pā′lē ən), *n.* member of the Protestant Episcopal Church. *—adj.* Episcopal.

e pis co pate (i pis′kə pit, i pis′kə pāt), *n.* 1 position, rank, or term of office of a bishop. 2 bishopric. 3 bishops as a group.

ep i sode (ep′ə sōd), *n.* 1 an outstanding incident or experience in a person's life, in the history of a country, the world, an institution, etc. 2 an incidental set of events or actions separate from the main plot of a novel, story, etc. 3 (in music) a passage separated from and in contrast to the principal themes, especially in a sonata or fugue. [< Greek *epeisodion,* literally, accidental, coming in besides < *epi-* besides, on + *eis* in, into + *hodos* way]

ep i sod ic (ep′ə sod′ik), *adj.* like an episode; incidental. **—ep′i sod′i cal ly,** *adv.*

ep i sod i cal (ep′ə sod′ə kəl), *adj.* episodic.

e pis te mo log i cal (i pis′tə mə loj′ə kəl), *adj.* of or having to do with epistemology.

e pis te mol o gy (i pis′tə mol′ə jē), *n.* part of philosophy that deals with the origin, nature, and limits of knowledge. [< Greek *epistēmē* knowledge]

e pis tle (i pis′əl), *n.* 1 letter. Epistles are usually long, instructive, and written in formal or elegant language. 2 **Epistle, a** (in the Bible) any of the letters written by the Apostles to various churches and individuals. The Epistles make up 21 books of the New Testament. **b** selection from one of these, read as part of Mass or of the Anglican service of Holy Communion. [< Old French < Latin *epistola* < Greek *epistolē* < *epi-* to + *stellein* send]

e pis to lar y (i pist′l er′ē), *adj.* 1 carried on by or contained in letters. 2 of or suitable for writing letters. 3 composed in the form of letters: *an epistolary novel.*

ep i taph (ep′ə taf), *n.* a short statement in memory of a dead person, usually put on a gravestone or tombstone. [< Greek *epitaphion* funeral oration < *epi-* upon + *taphos* tomb]

ep i tha la mi on (ep′ə thə lā′mē ən), *n., pl.* **-mi a** (-mē ə). epithalamium.

ep i tha la mi um (ep′ə thə lā′mē əm), *n., pl.* **-mi ums, -mi a** (-mē ə). poem or song in honor of a bride, bridegroom, or newly married couple. [< Latin < Greek *epithalamion* < *epi-* upon + *thalamos* bridal chamber]

ep i the li al (ep′ə thē′lē əl), *adj.* of or having to do with the epithelium.

ep i the li um (ep′ə thē′lē əm), *n., pl.* **-li ums, -li a** (-lē ə). a thin layer of cells forming a tissue which covers the internal and external surfaces of the body, and which performs protective, secretive, or other functions. [< New Latin < Greek *epi-* on + *thēlē* nipple]

ep i thet (ep′ə thet), *n.* 1 a descriptive expression; word or phrase expressing some quality or attribute. In "crafty Ulysses" and "Richard the Lion-Hearted" the epithets are "crafty" and "the Lion-Hearted." 2 an insulting or contemptuous word or phrase used in place of a person's name. 3 the part of a scientific name of an animal or plant which denotes a species, variety, or other division of a genus. In *Pyrus malus* (the common apple), *malus* is the specific epithet. [< Greek *epitheton* added < *epi-* upon + *tithenai* to place]

ep i thet ic (ep′ə thet′ik), *adj.* of, having to do with, or like an epithet.

e pit o me (i pit′ə mē), *n.* 1 a condensed account; summary. An epitome contains only the most important points of a literary work, subject, etc. 2 person or thing that is typical or representative of something: *Solomon is often spoken of as the epitome of wisdom.* [< Greek *epitomē* < *epitemnein* cut short < *epi-* + *temnein* to cut]

e pit o mize (i pit′ə mīz), *v.t.,* **-mized, -miz ing.** 1 give an epitome of; summarize. 2 be typical or representative of: *Helen Keller epitomizes the human ability to overcome handicaps.*

ep i zo ot ic (ep′ə zō ot′ik), *adj.* (of diseases) temporarily common or prevalent among animals. *—n.* an epizootic disease.

e plu ri bus u num (ē plůr′ə bəs yü′nəm), LATIN. out of many, one. It is the motto inscribed on the official seal of the United States. It was once the official motto of the United States, but since 1956 the official motto has been "In God We Trust."

ep och (ep′ək, ē′pok), *n.* 1 period of time; era; age. 2 period of time in which striking things happened. 3 the starting point of such a period: *The invention of the steam engine marked an epoch in the evolution of industry.* 4 one of the divisions of time into which a geological period is divided: *the Recent epoch of the Quaternary period.* 5 (in astronomy) an arbitrarily chosen date or instant of time used as a reference point. [< Greek *epochē* a stopping, fixed point in time < *epechein* to stop < *epi-* up + *echein* to hold]

ep och al (ep′ə kəl), *adj.* 1 of or having to do with an epoch or epochs. 2 epoch-making. **—ep′och al ly,** *adv.*

ep och-mak ing (ep′ək mā′king, ē′pok-mā′king), *adj.* beginning an epoch; causing important changes.

ep o nym (ep′ō nim), *n.* person, real or imaginary, from whom a nation, tribe, place, etc., gets or is reputed to get its name: *Romulus is the eponym of Rome.* [< Greek *epōnymos* < *epi-* upon + *onyma* name]

ep on y mous (e pon′ə məs), *adj.* giving one's name to a nation, tribe, place, etc.

ep ox y (e pok′sē), *adj.* of or designating a large group of compounds containing oxygen as a bridge between two different atoms or radicals in a chain. Epoxy resins are used in the manufacture of plastics, adhesives, etc. [< *ep(i)-* + *oxy(gen)*]

ep si lon (ep′sə lon), *n.* the fifth letter of the Greek alphabet (E, ϵ).

Ep som (ep′səm), *n.* 1 town in SE England, near London. 71,000. 2 **Epsom Downs,** track near Epsom where England's famous horse race, the Derby, is run.

Epsom salts, a bitter, white, crystalline powder taken in water as a laxative; hydrated magnesium sulfate. *Formula:* $MgSO_4{\cdot}7H_2O$ [< *Epsom,* where it was first obtained from springs]

Ep stein (ep′stīn), *n.* Sir **Jacob,** 1880-1959, British sculptor, born in the United States.

eq., 1 equal. 2 equivalent.

eq ua bil i ty (ek′wə bil′ə tē, ē′kwə bil′ə-tē), *n.* equable condition or quality.

eq ua ble (ek′wə bəl, ē′kwə bəl), *adj.* changing little; uniform; even: *equable temperature, an equable disposition.* See **even**[1] for synonym study. **—eq′ua bly,** *adv.*

e qual (ē′kwəl), *adj., n., v.,* **e qualed, e qual ing** or **e qualled, e qual ling.** *—adj.* 1 the same in amount, size, number, value, degree, rank, etc.; as much; neither more nor less: *Ten dimes are equal to one dollar.* See synonym study below. 2 the same throughout; even; uniform: *an equal mixture.* 3 evenly matched; with no advantage on either side: *an equal contest.* 4 **equal to,** strong enough for; able to. 5 ARCHAIC. just; fair. *—n.* 1 person or thing that is equal: *In spelling she has no equal.* 2 an equal amount; equal number: *7 + 3 is the equal of 5 × 2.* *—v.t.* 1 be the same as: *Four times five equals twenty.* 2 make or do something equal to; match: *Our team equaled the other team's score, and the game ended in a tie.* [< Latin *aequalis* < *aequus* even, just]

Syn. *adj.* 1 **Equal, equivalent, tantamount** mean being the same or as much as. **Equal** applies to things that are exactly the same in any quality that can be measured or weighed: *The pieces of pie are equal.* **Equivalent** applies to things otherwise different but equal in a quality that cannot be physically measured: *A one-year course in high school may be regarded as equivalent to a college semester course.* **Tantamount,** applying only to immaterial things, means equivalent to another in effect: *His answer was tantamount to an insult.*

e qual i tar i an (i kwol′ə ter′ē ən), *adj., n.* egalitarian.

e qual i ty (i kwol′ə tē), *n., pl.* **-ties.** a being equal; sameness in amount, size, number, value, degree, rank, etc.

e qual ize (ē′kwə līz), *v.t.,* **-ized, -iz ing.** 1 make equal. 2 make even or uniform. **—e′qual i za′tion,** *n.*

e qual iz er (ē′kwə lī′zər), *n.* 1 person or thing that equalizes. 2 device for equalizing forces, pressures, etc.

e qual ly (ē′kwə lē), *adv.* in equal shares; in an equal manner; in or to an equal degree; so as to be equal.

e qua nim i ty (ē′kwə nim′ə tē, ek′wə-nim′ə tē), *n.* evenness of mind or temper; calmness; composure: *The speaker endured the insults of the heckler with equanimity.* [< Latin *aequanimitatem* < *aequus* even + *animus* mind, temper]

e quate (i kwāt′), *v.t.,* **e quat ed, e quat ing.** 1 state to be equal; put into the form of an equation. 2 make equal; consider, treat, or represent as equal.

e qua tion (i kwā′zhən, i kwā′shən), *n.* 1 statement of the equality of two quantities. EXAMPLES: $(4 \times 8) + 12 = 44$. $C = 2\pi r$. 2 expression using chemical formulas and symbols to show quantitatively the substances used and produced in a chemical change. In $HCl + NaOH = NaCl + H_2O$, HCl and NaOH are the reacting substances, and NaCl and H_2O are the resulting products, the sign = being read "produces" or "gives." 3 an equating. 4 a being equated.

e qua tor (i kwā′tər), *n.* 1 an imaginary circle around the middle of the earth, halfway between the North Pole and the South Pole. 2 a similarly situated circle on any heavenly body. 3 celestial equator. [< Medieval Latin *aequator (diei et noctis)* equalizer (of day and night) < Latin *aequare* make equal < *aequus* equal]

e qua to ri al (ē′kwə tôr′ē əl, ē′kwə tōr′ē-əl; ek′wə tôr′ē əl, ek′wə tōr′ē əl), *adj.* 1 of, at, or near the equator. 2 similar to conditions at or near the equator. **—e′qua to′ri-al ly,** *adv.*

Equatorial Guinea, country in W Africa, consisting of mainland Rio Muni and the island of Fernando Po. It was formerly known as **Spanish Guinea.** 300,000 pop.; 10,800 sq. mi. *Capital:* Santa Isabel.

eq uer ry (ek′wər ē), *n., pl.* **-ries.** 1 officer of a royal or noble household who has charge of the horses or who accompanies his master's carriage. 2 attendant upon a member of the British royal household. [< Old French *escuerie* stable]

e ques tri an (i kwes′trē ən), *adj.* 1 of horsemen or horsemanship; having to do with horseback riding, horses, or horseback riders: *equestrian skill.* 2 on horseback; mounted on a horse. An equestrian statue shows a person riding a horse. 3 having to do with or composed of knights. *—n.* rider or performer on horseback. [< Latin *equestris* of a horseman < *equus* horse]

e ques tri enne (i kwes′trē en′), *n.* a woman rider or performer on horseback. [< French]

equi-, *combining form.* 1 equal ___: *Equidistance = equal distance.* 2 equally ___: *Equidistant = equally distant.* [< Latin *aequus* equal]

e qui an gu lar (ē′kwē ang′gyə lər), *adj.* having all angles equal: *A square is equiangular.*

e qui dis tant (ē′kwə dis′tənt), *adj.* equally distant: *All points of the circumference of a circle are equidistant from the center.* **—e′qui dis′tant ly,** *adv.*

e qui lat er al (ē′kwə lat′ər əl), *adj.* having all sides equal. *—n.* figure having all sides equal. **—e′qui lat′er al ly,** *adv.*

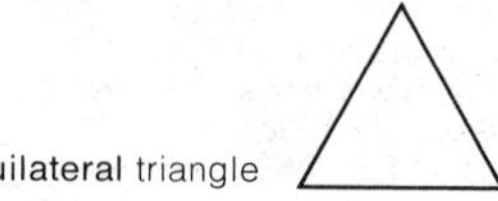
equilateral triangle

e quil i brant (i kwil′ə brənt), *n.* (in physics) a force or set of forces that counterbalances another force or set of forces.

e qui li brate (ē′kwə lī′brāt, i kwil′ə brāt), *v.t.,* **-brat ed, -brat ing.** bring into or keep in a state of equilibrium; balance. —*v.i.* be in equilibrium. **—e′qui li bra′tion,** *n.*

e qui lib ri um (ē′kwə lib′rē əm), *n.* 1 state of balance; condition in which opposing forces exactly balance or equal each other: *Scales are in equilibrium when the weights on each side are equal. After a time an equilibrium is established between parasite and host.* 2 mental poise: *She is a sensible person and will not let little annoyances upset her equilibrium.* [< Latin *aequilibrium* < *aequus* equal + *libra* balance]

e quine (ē′kwin), *adj.* 1 of horses. 2 like a horse; like that of a horse. —*n.* a horse. [< Latin *equinus* < *equus* horse]

e qui noc tial (ē′kwə nok′shəl), *adj.* 1 of, having to do with, or occurring at an equinox: *an equinoctial storm.* **Equinoctial points** are the two imaginary points in the sky where the sun crosses the celestial equator. 2 at or near the earth's equator: *Borneo is an equinoctial island.* —*n.* 1 the celestial equator. 2 storm occurring at or near the equinox.

equinoctial line, celestial equator.

e qui nox (ē′kwə noks), *n.* 1 either of the two times in the year when the center of the sun crosses the celestial equator, and day and night are of equal length in all parts of the earth, occurring about March 21 **(vernal equinox)** and about September 22 **(autumnal equinox).** 2 either of the two imaginary points in the sky at which the sun's path crosses the equator. [< Medieval Latin *equinoxium* < Latin *aequinoctium* < *aequus* equal + *nox, noctem* night]

e quip (i kwip′), *v.t.,* **e quipped, e quip ping.** 1 supply with all that is needed; fit out; provide. See **furnish** for synonym study. 2 array; dress. [< Middle French *equiper* < Old French *esquiper,* probably < Scandinavian (Old Icelandic) *skipa* to man (a ship) < *skip* ship]

eq ui page (ek′wə pij), *n.* 1 carriage. 2 carriage with its horses, driver, and servants. 3 equipment; outfit. 4 articles for personal ornament or use.

e quip ment (i kwip′mənt), *n.* 1 act of equipping; fitting out. 2 condition of being equipped. 3 what a person or thing is equipped with; outfit; furnishings; supplies.

e qui poise (ē′kwə poiz, ek′wə poiz), *n.* 1 equal distribution of weight or force; even balance. 2 a balancing force; counterbalance.

e qui po ten tial (ē′kwə pə ten′shəl), *adj.* (in physics) possessing the same or equal potential.

eq ui se tum (ek′wə sē′təm), *n., pl.* **-tums, -ta** (-tə). any of a genus of flowerless plants with jointed, green, cylindrical stems, either simple or branched, rough to the touch, and having scalelike leaves at each joint; horsetail. In a former geological period some equisetums grew in great, treelike forms. [< Latin *equisaetum* < *equus* horse + *saeta* (coarse) hair]

eq ui ta ble (ek′wə tə bəl), *adj.* 1 characterized by equity or fairness; fair; just: *Paying a person what he has earned is equitable.* 2 (in law) having to do with or dependent upon equity; valid in equity, as distinguished from common law and statute law. **—eq′ui ta ble ness,** *n.* **—eq′ui ta bly,** *adv.*

eq ui ta tion (ek′wə tā′shən), *n.* horseback riding; horsemanship. [ultimately < Latin *equus* horse]

eq ui ty (ek′wə tē), *n., pl.* **-ties.** 1 a being equal or fair; fairness; justice. 2 system of rules and principles as to what is fair or just that supplements common law and statute law by covering cases in which fairness and justice require a settlement not covered by law. 3 amount that a property is worth beyond what is owed on it.

e quiv a lence (i kwiv′ə ləns), *n.* condition of being equivalent; equality in value, force, significance, etc.

e quiv a len cy (i kwiv′ə lən sē), *n., pl.* **-cies.** equivalence.

e quiv a lent (i kwiv′ə lənt), *adj.* 1 the same in value, force, effect, meaning, etc.; equal: *Nodding your head is equivalent to saying yes.* See **equal** for synonym study. 2 equal in extent, but not having the same form: *A triangle and a square of equal area are equivalent.* 3 (in chemistry) equal in combining or reacting value to a (stated) quantity of another substance. —*n.* something equivalent. **—e quiv′a lent ly,** *adv.*

equivalent weight, the weight of a substance which will combine with or can replace one gram-atom of hydrogen or one-half gram-atom of oxygen.

e quiv o cal (i kwiv′ə kəl), *adj.* 1 having two or more meanings; intentionally vague or ambiguous: *His equivocal answer left us uncertain as to his real opinion.* See **obscure** for synonym study. 2 undecided; uncertain: *Nothing was proved because the result of the experiment was equivocal.* 3 questionable; suspicious: *The stranger's equivocal behavior made it unlikely that anyone would trust him.* [< Late Latin *aequivocus* ambiguous < Latin *aequus* equal + *vocare* to call] **—e quiv′o cal ly,** *adv.* **—e quiv′o cal ness,** *n.*

e quiv o cate (i kwiv′ə kāt), *v.i.,* **-cat ed, -cat ing.** use expressions of double meaning in order to mislead. **—e quiv′o ca′tor,** *n.*

e quiv o ca tion (i kwiv′ə kā′shən), *n.* 1 the use of expressions with double meaning in order to mislead. 2 an equivocal expression.

-er[1], *suffix forming nouns.* 1 *(added to verbs)* person or thing that ____s: *Admirer = a person who admires. Burner = thing that burns.* 2 *(added to nouns)* person living in ____: *New Yorker = a person living in New York. Villager = a person living in a village.* 3 *(added to nouns)* person who makes or works with ____: *Hatter = a person who makes hats.* 4 person or thing that is or has ____: *Six-footer = a person who is six feet tall.* [Old English *-ere,* ultimately < Latin *-arium* -ary]

-er[2], *suffix forming nouns from other nouns.* person or thing connected with ____: *Officer = person connected with an office.* [< Old French < Latin *-arium*]

-er[3], *suffix forming the comparative degree of adjectives and adverbs.* more: *Softer = more soft. Slower = more slow.* [Old English, *-or, -ra, -re*]

Er, erbium.

er a (ir′ə), *n.* 1 an age in history; historical period distinguished by certain important or significant happenings: *the Napoleonic era, the Romantic era.* 2 period of time starting from an important or significant happening, date, etc. The Christian era is the period of time reckoned from about four years after the birth of Christ. 3 one of the five major divisions of time in geological history. An era is usually divided into periods. [< Late Latin, variant of *aera* number, epoch, probably same word as Latin *aera* counters (for reckoning), plural of *aes* brass]

hat, āge, fär; let, ēqual, tėrm;
it, īce; hot, ōpen, ôrder;
oil, out; cup, pu̇t, rüle;
ch, child; ng, long; sh, she;
th, thin; ᴛʜ, then; zh, measure;

ə represents *a* in about, *e* in taken, *i* in pencil, *o* in lemon, *u* in circus.

< = from, derived from, taken from.

e rad i ca ble (i rad′ə kə bəl), *adj.* that can be eradicated.

e rad i cate (i rad′ə kāt), *v.t.,* **-cat ed, -cat ing.** 1 get rid of entirely; destroy completely; eliminate: *Yellow fever has been eradicated in the United States.* 2 pull out by the roots: *eradicate weeds.* [< Latin *eradicatum* rooted out < *ex-* out + *radicem* root] **—e rad′i ca′tor,** *n.*

e rad i ca tion (i rad′ə kā′shən), *n.* an eradicating; complete destruction.

e rad i ca tive (i rad′ə kā′tiv), *adj.* tending to eradicate.

e rase (i rās′), *v.t.,* **e rased, e ras ing.** 1 rub out; remove by rubbing or scraping: *He erased the wrong answer and wrote in the right one.* See synonym study below. 2 remove all trace of; blot out: *The blow on his head erased the details of the accident from his memory.* [< Latin *erasum* scraped out < *ex-* out + *radere* scrape] **—e ras′a ble,** *adj.*

Syn. 1 **Erase, expunge, efface** mean to remove something from a record of some kind. **Erase** means to remove all trace of something by scraping or rubbing: *I erased the faulty recording from the tape.* **Expunge** means to blot out something so that it seems never to have existed: *The judge ordered certain charges expunged from the record.* **Efface** means to wipe out the identity or existence of something by or as if by rubbing away its face: *Rain and wind effaced the inscription on the monument.*

e ras er (i rā′sər), *n.* 1 person or thing that erases. 2 implement, usually made of rubber or felt, for erasing marks made with pencil, ink, chalk, etc.

E ras mus (i raz′məs), *n.* 1466?-1536, Dutch scholar and religious teacher, a leader of the Renaissance movement.

e ra sure (i rā′shər, i rā′zhər), *n.* 1 an erasing. 2 an erased word, letter, etc. 3 place where a word, letter, etc., has been erased.

Er a to (er′ə tō), *n.* (in Greek myths) the Muse of lyric poetry and poetry about love.

er bi um (ėr′bē əm), *n.* a soft, lustrous, grayish, rare-earth metallic element which occurs as a minute part of various minerals, used in nuclear research. *Symbol:* Er; *atomic number* 68. See pages 326 and 327 for table. [< New Latin < *(Ytt)erby,* town in Sweden where it was found]

ere (er, ar), ARCHAIC. —*prep.* before. —*conj.* 1 before. 2 sooner than; rather than. [Old English *ǣr*]

Er e bus (er′ə bəs), *n.* (in Greek myths) a dark, gloomy place through which the dead passed on their way to Hades.

e rect (i rekt′), *adj.* 1 straight up; not bending; not tipping; upright: *an erect tree, stand*

erect. See **upright** for synonym study. 2 raised or directed upward; bristling; stiff: *The cat faced the dog with fur erect.* —*v.t.* 1 put straight up; set upright: *They erected a television antenna on the roof.* 2 put up; build: *That house was erected forty years ago.* 3 put together: *When the missing parts arrived we erected the machine.* 4 set up; establish; found: *erect an institution.* 5 (in geometry) to draw (a perpendicular to a given line); construct (a figure on a given base). [< Latin *erectum* directed upward < *ex-* up + *regere* to direct] —**e rect′ly,** *adv.* —**e rect′ness,** *n.*

e rec tile (i rek′təl), *adj.* that can be erected or set upright.

e rec tion (i rek′shən), *n.* 1 an erecting. 2 a being erected. 3 thing erected; building or other structure.

e rec tor (i rek′tər), *n.* person or thing that erects.

E region, region of the ionosphere which reflects low-frequency radio waves; E layer. See **atmosphere** for diagram.

ere long (er′lông′, er′long′; ar′lông′, ar′-long′), *adv.* ARCHAIC. before long; soon.

er e mite (er′ə mīt), *n.* hermit, especially a religious one. [< Greek *erēmitēs.* Doublet of HERMIT.]

e rep sin (i rep′sən), *n.* an enzyme complex that breaks down protein molecules, found in the intestinal juices. [< Latin *ereptum* set free + English *(pep)sin*]

Er furt (er′fůrt), *n.* city in SW East Germany. 195,000.

erg (ėrg), *n.* unit for measuring work or energy, equivalent to the amount of work done by a force of one dyne acting through a distance of one centimeter. [< Greek *ergon* work]

er go (ėr′gō), *adv., conj.* LATIN. therefore.

er gos te rol (ėr gos′tə rōl′, ėr gos′tə rol′), *n.* a steroid alcohol or sterol derived especially from yeast or ergot that turns into vitamin D when exposed to ultraviolet light and can be used for the prevention or curing of rickets. *Formula:* $C_{28}H_{44}O$ [< *ergo(t)* + *(chole)sterol*]

er got (ėr′gət, ėr′got), *n.* 1 disease of rye and other cereals in which the grains are replaced by blackish fungus growths. 2 growth produced by this disease. 3 medicine made from these growths, used to contract the uterus during childbirth. [< French]

Er hard (er′härt), *n.* **Ludwig,** born 1897, German statesman, chancellor of West Germany from 1963 to 1966.

Er ic son (er′ik sən), *n.* **Leif,** Viking chief and son of Eric the Red. He probably discovered North America about A.D. 1000.

Er ics son (er′ik sən), *n.* **John,** 1803-1889, American inventor and engineer, born in Sweden. He built the first ironclad warship, the *Monitor.*

Er ic the Red (er′ik), Viking chief who discovered Greenland about A.D. 982.

Er ie (ir′ē), *n.* 1 **Lake,** one of the five Great Lakes. 240 mi. long; 9940 sq. mi. 2 city in NW Pennsylvania on Lake Erie. 129,000. 3 member of a tribe of American Indians formerly living along the southern and eastern shores of Lake Erie.

Erie Canal, canal in New York State between Buffalo and Albany, connecting Lake Erie with the Hudson River. Parts of it are now abandoned, but most of it is included in the New York State Barge Canal System.

Er in (er′ən, ir′ən), *n.* Ireland.

E rin y es (i rin′ē ēz′), *n.pl. of* **E rin ys** (i rin′is, i rī′nis). (in Greek and Roman myths) the Furies.

Er is (ir′is, er′is), *n.* (in Greek myths) the goddess of strife and discord.

Er i tre a (er′ə trē′ə), *n.* northernmost province of Ethiopia, on the Red Sea, formerly an Italian colony. —**Er′i tre′an,** *adj., n.*

Er i van (er′ə vän′), *n.* Yerevan.

erl king (ėrl′king′), *n.* (in German and Scandinavian legends) a spirit or personification of natural forces, such as cold or storm, that does harm, especially to children. [< German *Erlkönig*]

er mine (ėr′mən), *n., pl.* **-mines** or **-mine.** 1 any of several kinds of weasel of northern regions which are brown in summer but white with a black-tipped tail in winter. 2 the soft, white fur of the winter phase, used for women's coats, trimming, etc. The official robes of English judges are trimmed with ermine as a symbol of purity and fairness. 3 position, rank, or duties of a judge. [< Old French, probably < Latin *(mus) Armenius* Armenian (rat)]

er mined (ėr′mənd), *adj.* 1 lined or trimmed with ermine. 2 clothed in ermine.

erne or **ern** (ėrn), *n.* kind of white-tailed European eagle that lives near the sea. [Old English *earn*]

e rode (i rōd′), *v.,* **e rod ed, e rod ing.** —*v.t.* 1 eat or wear away gradually; eat into: *Running water erodes soil and rocks.* 2 form by a gradual eating or wearing away: *The stream eroded a channel in the solid rock.* —*v.i.* be worn away or eaten out. [< Latin *erodere* < *ex-* away + *rodere* gnaw]

Er os (ir′os, er′os), *n.* (in Greek myths) the god of love, son of Aphrodite, identified by the Romans with Cupid.

e ro sion (i rō′zhən), *n.* 1 a gradual eating or wearing away by glaciers, running water, waves, or wind: *Trees help prevent the erosion of soil by running water.* 2 a being eaten or worn away. [< Latin *erosionem* < *erodere.* See ERODE.]

e ro sion al (i rō′zhə nəl), *adj.* 1 causing erosion. 2 produced by erosion.

e ro sive (i rō′siv), *adj.* causing erosion; eroding.

e rot ic (i rot′ik), *adj.* of or having to do with sexual passion or love. [< Greek *erōtikos* of Eros] —**e rot′i cal ly,** *adv.*

e rot i cism (i rot′ə siz′əm), *n.* erotic character or tendency.

err (ėr, er), *v.i.* 1 go wrong; make a mistake. 2 be wrong; be mistaken or incorrect. 3 do wrong; sin. [< Latin *errare* wander]

er rand (er′ənd), *n.* 1 a trip to do something for someone else: *The little boy goes to the store and runs other errands for his parents.* 2 what one is sent to do. 3 purpose or object of a trip. [Old English *ǣrende*]

er rant (er′ənt), *adj.* 1 traveling in search of adventure; wandering; roving: *an errant knight.* 2 straying from the proper course or place; astray: *errant sheep.* 3 wrong; mistaken. [< Old French *errer* to travel < Popular Latin *(it)erare* < Latin *iter* journey]

er rant ry (er′ən trē), *n., pl.* **-ries.** conduct or action like that of a knight-errant.

er ra ta (ə rā′tə, ə rä′tə), *n.* 1 plural of **erratum.** 2 errors and corrections in printing listed and inserted in a book.

er rat ic (ə rat′ik), *adj.* 1 not steady; uncertain; irregular: *An erratic clock is not dependable.* 2 queer; odd; eccentric: *erratic behavior.* 3 having no certain course; wandering: *an erratic star.* —*n.* (in geology) a boulder or mass of rock transported from its original site, as by glacial action. [< Latin *erraticus* < *errare* wander] —**er rat′i cal ly,** *adv.*

er ra tum (ə rā′təm, ə rä′təm), *n., pl.* **-ta.** error in writing or printing. [< Latin]

er ro ne ous (ə rō′nē əs), *adj.* containing error; wrong; mistaken; incorrect: *the erroneous belief that the earth is flat.* —**er ro′ne ous ly,** *adv.* —**er ro′ne ous ness,** *n.*

er ror (er′ər), *n.* 1 something wrong or incorrect; mistake: *There is an error in the date of his birth.* 2 condition of being wrong, mistaken, or incorrect: *You are in error; your answer is false.* 3 wrongdoing; sin. 4 a faulty play in catching or throwing a baseball that permits a batter who should have been put out to reach base or allows a runner to advance. 5 (in mathematics) the difference between the observed or approximate amount and the correct amount. [< Latin < *errare* wander] —**er′ror less,** *adj.*

er satz (er′zäts), *n.* a substitute or imitation, especially something inferior. —*adj.* substitute: *ersatz leather.* [< German *Ersatz* replacement]

Erse (ėrs), *n.* 1 Scottish Gaelic. 2 Irish Gaelic. —*adj.* of or in Scottish Gaelic or Irish Gaelic. [Scottish variant of *Irish*]

erst (ėrst), *adv.* ARCHAIC. formerly; long ago. [Old English *ǣrst,* superlative of *ǣr* ere]

erst while (ėrst′hwīl′), *adj.* former; past. —*adv.* ARCHAIC. in time past; formerly.

e ruct (i rukt′), *v.t., v.i.* belch. [< Latin *eructare* < *ex-* out + *ructare* belch]

e ruc tate (i ruk′tāt), *v.t., v.i.,* **-tat ed, -tat ing.** belch. —**e ruc′ta′tion,** *n.*

er u dite (er′ů dīt, er′yə dīt), *adj.* having much knowledge; scholarly; learned. [< Latin *eruditus* instructed < *ex-* + *rudis* rude] —**er′u dite′ly,** *adv.*

er u di tion (er′ů dish′ən, er′yə dish′ən), *n.* much knowledge acquired from study or reading; scholarship; learning.

e rupt (i rupt′), *v.i.* 1 burst forth: *Hot water erupted from the geyser.* 2 break out in an eruption: *Her skin erupted when she had measles.* 3 break through the gums: *When the baby was seven months old his teeth started to erupt.* —*v.t.* throw forth: *The volcano erupted lava and ashes.* [< Latin *eruptum* burst forth < *ex-* out + *rumpere* to burst]

e rup tion (i rup′shən), *n.* 1 a bursting forth; outbreak; outburst. 2 a throwing forth of lava, etc., from a volcano or of hot water from a geyser. 3 a breaking out with many small red spots on the skin; rash. 4 the red spots on the skin. 5 a breaking through the gums: *The eruption of teeth made the baby fretful.*

e rup tive (i rup′tiv), *adj.* 1 bursting forth; tending to burst forth. 2 causing the skin to break out. 3 of or formed by volcanic eruptions.

hat, āge, fär; let, ēqual, tėrm;
it, īce; hot, ōpen, ôrder;
oil, out; cup, pu̇t, rüle;
ch, child; ng, long; sh, she;
th, thin; ᴛʜ, then; zh, measure;

ə represents *a* in about, *e* in taken, *i* in pencil, *o* in lemon, *u* in circus.

< = from, derived from, taken from.

-ery, *suffix forming nouns.* 1 *(added to verbs)* place for ___ing: *Cannery = place for canning.* 2 *(added to nouns)* place for ___s: *Nunnery = place for nuns.* 3 *(added to nouns)* art or occupation of a ___: *Cookery = art or occupation of a cook.* 4 *(added to nouns)* condition of a ___: *Slavery = condition of a slave.* 5 *(added to nouns)* qualities, actions, etc., of a ___: *Knavery = qualities, actions, etc., of a knave.* 6 *(added to nouns)* group of ___s: *Machinery = group of machines.* [< Old French *-erie*]

er y sip e las (er′ə sip′ə ləs, ir′ə sip′ə ləs), *n.* an acute infectious disease that causes fever and a deep-red inflammation of the skin, caused by a streptococcus. [< Greek]

e ryth ro cyte (i rith′rō sīt), *n.* red blood cell. [< Greek *erythros* red + English *-cyte*]

e ryth ro cyt ic (i rith′rō sit′ik), *adj.* of or having to do with erythrocytes.

e ryth ro my cin (i rith′rō mī′sn), *n.* drug related to streptomycin, used against certain bacterial infections. [< Greek *erythros* red + *mykēs* fungus]

Es, einsteinium.

-es[1], *suffix.* form of **-s**[1] used chiefly after *s, z, sh, ch,* as in *asses, whizzes, bushes, witches;* in the plural of nouns ending in *-y* after a consonant, as in *dandies, duties, rubies;* and in some cases after *o,* as in *mosquitoes, potatoes, tomatoes.*

-es[2], *suffix.* form of **-s**[2] used after *s, z, sh, ch,* as in *dresses, buzzes, washes, touches,* and after certain vowels, as in *does, goes, hurries, magnifies.*

E sau (ē′sô), *n.* (in the Bible) the older son of Isaac and Rebecca, who sold his birthright to his twin brother Jacob.

es ca drille (es′kə dril′), *n.* (formerly) a small fleet of airplanes or warships, together with the equipment and men needed to keep them in use. [< French]

es ca late (es′kə lāt), *v.i., v.t.,* **-lat ed, -lat ing.** increase or expand by stages: *The commotion in the prison almost escalated into a riot.*

es ca la tion (es′kə lā′shən), *n.* 1 act of escalating. 2 condition of being escalated.

es ca la tor (es′kə lā′tər), *n.* a moving stairway made on the endless chain principle, so that the steps ascend or descend continuously, for carrying passengers up or down. [earlier *Escalator,* a trademark]

escalator clause, provision in a contract or treaty allowing an increase or decrease in wages, royalties, etc., under specified conditions.

es cal lop (e skol′əp, e skal′əp), *v.t.* scallop (def. 1).

es ca pade (es′kə pād, es′kə pād′), *n.* a breaking loose from rules or restraint; wild adventure or prank.

es cape (e skāp′), *v.,* **-caped, -cap ing,** *n., adj.* —*v.i.* 1 get out and away; get free; flee: *escape from prison.* 2 come out or find a way out from a container; leak: *Gas had been escaping from the cylinder all night.* 3 (in botany) to grow wild. —*v.t.* 1 get free from: *He thinks he will never escape hard work.* 2 keep free or safe from; avoid: *We all escaped the measles.* See synonym study below. 3 come out of without being intended: *A cry escaped her lips.* 4 fail to be noticed or remembered by: *I knew his face, but his name escaped me.* —*n.* 1 act of escaping: *His escape was aided by the thick fog.* 2 way of escaping: *There was no escape from the trap.* 3 relief from boredom, trouble, etc.: *find escape in mystery stories.* 4 outflow or leakage of gas, water, etc. —*adj.* providing a way of escape or avoidance: *escape literature.* [< Old French *escaper,* ultimately < Latin *ex-* out of + Late Latin *cappa* cloak]
Syn. *v.t.* 2 **Escape, evade, elude** mean to keep free from someone or something. **Escape** implies avoiding unpleasantness or danger by being out of its way or reach: *He escaped death in the collision by being thrown clear.* **Evade** means to avoid something by cleverness or trickery: *He used forged papers to evade military service.* **Elude** suggests slipperiness and quickness in getting away from trouble that is close: *The bandit eluded the posse that was following him.*

escape clause, clause that frees a signer of a contract from certain responsibilities under specified circumstances.

es cap ee (e skā′pē′, e skā′pē), *n.* person or animal that has escaped.

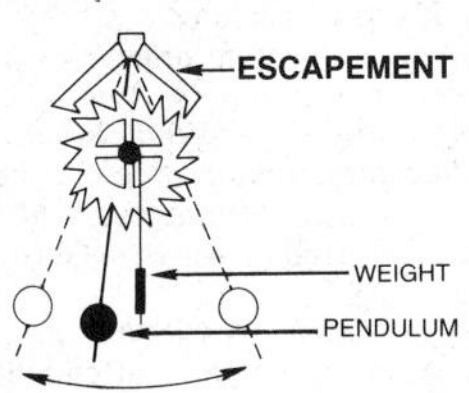

escapement (def. 1)—In a pendulum clock, the escapement coordinates the movement of the weight with that of the pendulum by preventing the weight from falling too fast. One tooth of the wheel escapes at each swing of the pendulum.

es cape ment (e skāp′mənt), *n.* 1 device in a timepiece by which the motion of the wheels and of the pendulum or balance wheel are accommodated to each other. 2 mechanism that controls the movement of a typewriter carriage.

escape velocity, the minimum speed that a moving object must reach to leave the gravitational field of the earth or other attracting body. A rocket traveling at 25,000 miles per hour can escape the pull of the earth without further power.

es cap ism (e skā′piz′əm), *n.* a habitual avoidance of unpleasant things by daydreaming or by entertainment.

es cap ist (ə skā′pist), *n.* person who habitually avoids unpleasant things by engaging in daydreams or entertainment. —*adj.* of or for escapists: *escapist literature.*

es car ole (es′kə rōl′), *n.* endive (def. 1). [< French]

es carp ment (e skärp′mənt), *n.* 1 a steep slope; cliff. 2 ground made into a steep slope as part of a fortification. [< French]

es cheat (es chēt′), *n.* 1 a reverting of the ownership of property to the state or to the lord of a manor when there are no legal heirs. 2 property whose ownership has so reverted. —*v.i.* revert to the state or to the lord of the manor. —*v.t.* transfer (the ownership of property) to the state. [< Old French *eschete,* ultimately < Latin *ex-* out + *cadere* to fall] **—es cheat′a ble,** *adj.*

es chew (es chü′), *v.t.* keep away from; avoid; shun: *eschew rich foods.* [< Old French *eschiver*]

es cort (*n.* es′kôrt; *v.* e skôrt′), *n.* 1 one or a group going with another to give protection, show honor, etc.: *an escort of ten airplanes.* 2 man who goes on a date with a woman: *Her escort to the party was a tall young man.* 3 act of going with another as an escort. —*v.t.* go with as an escort: *Warships escorted the troopship.* See **accompany** for synonym study. [< Middle French *escorte* < Italian *scorta* < *scorgere* to guide < Latin *ex-* out + *corrigere* set right]

escort carrier, an aircraft carrier of the smallest type.

es cri toire (es′krə twär′, es′krə twär), *n.* a writing desk. [< French]

es crow (es′krō, e skrō′), *n.* 1 deed, bond, or other written agreement held by a third person until certain conditions are met by two other parties. 2 **in escrow,** held by a third party in accordance with an agreement. [< Middle French *escroue* scrap, scroll]

es cu do (e skü′dō), *n., pl.* **-dos.** 1 the monetary unit of Chile, a coin equal to 100 centesimos and worth about $3^1/_2$ cents. 2 the monetary unit of Portugal, a coin equal to 100 centavos and worth about four cents. 3 a former gold or silver coin of Spain, Portugal, and their colonies, worth about $2. [< Spanish, Portuguese < Latin *scutum* shield]

es cu lent (es′kyə lənt), *adj.* suitable for food; edible. —*n.* anything that is fit for food, especially vegetables. [< Latin *esculentus* < *esca* food]

escutcheon with coat of arms

es cutch eon (e skuch′ən), *n.* shield or shield-shaped surface on which a coat of arms is put. [< Old French *escuchon* < Popular Latin *scutionem* < Latin *scutum* shield]

Es dras (ez′drəs), *n.* 1 either of the first two books of the Protestant Apocrypha. 2 either of two books in the Douay Bible corresponding to the books of Ezra and Nehemiah in the Protestant and Jewish Bibles.

-ese, *suffix added to nouns.* 1 *(to form adjectives)* of or having to do with ___: *Japanese = of Japan.* 2 *(to form nouns)* native or inhabitant of ___: *Portuguese = native or inhabitant of Portugal.* 3 *(to form nouns)* language of ___: *Chinese = language of China.* 4 *(to form nouns)* typical style or vocabulary of ___: *Journalese = typical style of journalists.* [< Old French *-eis* < Latin *-ensis* of or from (a place)]

ESE or **E.S.E.,** east-southeast.

es ker (es′kər), *n.* a winding ridge of sand, gravel, etc., believed to have been formed by streams flowing under or in glacial ice. [< Irish *eiscir*]

Es ki mo (es′kə mō), *n., pl.* **-mos** or **-mo** for 1, *adj.* —*n.* 1 member of a Mongoloid people living in the arctic regions of North America and northeastern Asia. 2 language of the Eskimos. *—adj.* of or having to do with the Eskimos or their language.

Es ki mo an (es′kə mō′ən), *adj.* Eskimo.

Eskimo dog, 1 any of a breed of strong, broad-chested dogs originating in Greenland and Labrador, having a shaggy outer coat and a woolly undercoat, used by the Eskimos for pulling sleds; husky. 2 any sled dog of North America; husky.

e so phag e al (ē′sə faj′ē əl), *adj.* of or connected with the esophagus.

e soph a gus (ē sof′ə gəs), *n., pl.* **-gi** (-jī). passage for food from the pharynx to the stomach; gullet. See **alimentary canal** for diagram. Also, **oesophagus.** [< Greek *oisophagos* < *oiso-* carry + *phagein* eat]

es o ter ic (es′ə ter′ik), *adj.* 1 understood only by a select few; intended for an inner circle of disciples, scholars, etc. 2 private; secret; confidential. [< Greek *esōterikos* < *esōterō,* comparative of *esō* within] **—es′o ter′i cal ly,** *adv.*

ESP, extrasensory perception.

esp., especially.

es pa drille (es′pə dril′; *French* es pə-drē′yə), *n.* a casual rope-soled shoe or sandal. [< French]

es pal ier (e spal′yər), *n.* 1 trellis or framework of stakes upon which fruit trees and shrubs are trained to grow. 2 plant or row of plants trained to grow up a wall or an espalier. *—v.t.* train or furnish with an espalier. [< French]

Es pa ña (e spä′nyä), *n.* SPANISH. Spain.

espec., especially.

es pe cial (e spesh′əl), *adj.* more than others; special: *my especial friend, of no especial value.*

es pe cial ly (e spesh′ə lē), *adv.* more than others; specially; chiefly.

Syn. Especially, particularly, principally mean in a manner or degree that is exceptional. **Especially** implies that it is exclusive or singular: *This book is designed especially for high-school students.* **Particularly** implies that it is foremost or most distinct: *All of my arithmetic problems are hard, but particularly this one.* **Principally** implies that it is prominent or prevailing: *Robberies occur principally at night.*

Es pe ran to (es′pə rän′tō, es′pə ran′tō), *n.* a simple artificial language for international use, whose vocabulary and grammar are based on forms common to the principal European languages. [< Dr. *Esperanto* (literally, one who hopes), pen name of Ludovic Lazarus Zamenhof, 1859-1917, Polish physician and language scholar, its inventor]

es pi al (e spī′əl), *n.* 1 act of spying. 2 observation. 3 discovery.

es pi o nage (es′pē ə nij, es′pē ə näzh), *n.* 1 the systematic use of spies or other secret agents by one country to gain military secrets, strategic information, etc., of other countries. 2 the use of spies to obtain secret information from another or others: *industrial espionage.* [< French *espionnage*]

es pla nade (es′plə nād′), *n.* 1 any open, level space used for public walks or drives, especially along a shore. 2 an open space separating a fortress from the houses of a town. [< French]

es pous al (e spou′zəl), *n.* 1 Also, **espousals,** *pl.* ceremony of becoming engaged or married. 2 an espousing; adoption (of a cause, etc.).

es pouse (e spouz′), *v.t.,* **-poused, -pous ing.** 1 marry. 2 take up or make one's own; adopt; embrace: *Late in life he espoused a new religion.* [< Old French *espouser* marry, betroth < Latin *sponsare* < *spondere* bind oneself] **—es pous′er,** *n.*

es pres so (e spres′ō), *n., pl.* **-sos.** a very strong black coffee made of coffee beans roasted black, and brewed under steam pressure, usually in a special machine. [< Italian *(caffè) espresso* pressured (coffee)]

es prit (e sprē′), *n.* FRENCH. lively wit; spirit.

es prit de corps (e sprē′ də kôr′), FRENCH. group spirit; comradeship: *The regiment had a strong esprit de corps.*

es py (e spī′), *v.,* **-pied, -py ing.** see at a distance; catch sight of; spy. [< Old French *espier*]

Esq. or **Esqr.,** Esquire.

-esque, *suffix forming adjectives from other adjectives or from nouns.* 1 in the ___ style; resembling the ___ style: *Romanesque = resembling the Roman style.* 2 like a ___; like that of a ___: *Statuesque = like a statue.* [< French < Italian *-esco* < Germanic. Related to -ISH.]

e squire (e skwīr′, es′kwīr), *n.* 1 (in the Middle Ages) a knight's attendant; squire. 2 Englishman ranking next below a knight. 3 **Esquire,** title of respect placed after a man's last name instead of *Mr.* before the name: *John Jones, Esquire = Mr. John Jones.* [< Old French *esquier* < Latin *scutarius* shield bearer < *scutum* shield]

ESRO, European Space Research Organization.

-ess, *suffix forming nouns from other nouns.* female ___: *Lioness = female lion.* [< Old French *-esse* < Latin *-issa* < Greek]

ESSA, Environmental Science Services Administration.

es say (*n.* es′ā, *also* e sā′ *for 2; v.* e sā′), *n.* 1 a literary composition written on a certain subject. An essay is usually shorter and more personal, but less methodical than a treatise. 2 a try; attempt. *—v.t.* try; attempt: *The student essayed his first solo flight.* [< Old French *essai* < Latin *exagium* a weighing < *ex-* out + *agere* do, act] **—es say′er,** *n.*

es say ist (es′ā ist), *n.* writer of essays.

Es sen (es′n), *n.* city in W West Germany. 706,000.

es sence (es′ns), *n.* 1 that which makes a thing what it is; necessary part or parts; important feature or features: *Being thoughtful of others is the essence of politeness.* 2 a concentrated substance that has the characteristic flavor, fragrance, or effect of the plant, fruit, etc., from which it is taken. Atropine is the essence of the belladonna plant. 3 solution of such a substance in alcohol. Essence of peppermint is a solution of peppermint in alcohol. 4 perfume. [< Latin *essentia* < *esse* be]

Es sene (es′ēn′, e sēn′), *n.* member of a monastic sect or brotherhood of Jews in Palestine from about 100 B.C. to about A.D. 100.

es sen tial (ə sen′shəl), *adj.* 1 needed to make a thing what it is; very important; necessary: *Good food and enough rest are essential to good health.* See **necessary** for synonym study. 2 of or making up the essence of a substance. 3 being or containing the essence, or fragrance, flavor, and medicinal qualities, of a plant or other material: *essential odors.* *—n.* an absolutely necessary element or quality; fundamental feature: *Learn the essentials first; then learn the details.* **—es sen′tial ly,** *adv.*

es sen ti al i ty (ə sen′shē al′ə tē), *n., pl.* **-ties.** 1 essential quality. 2 an essential element or point.

essential oil, a volatile oil having the characteristic fragrance or flavor of the plant or fruit from which it is extracted. It is used to make perfume and in flavoring.

Es sex (es′iks), *n.* 1 the second **Earl of,** 1567-1601, Robert Devereux, English soldier and courtier, executed for treason. 2 county in SE England. See **Mercia** for map.

-est, *suffix forming the superlative degree of adjectives and adverbs.* most: *Warmest = most warm.* [Old English *-est, -ost*]

est., 1 established. 2 estate. 3 estimated. 4 estuary.

E.S.T., EST, or **e.s.t.,** Eastern Standard Time.

es tab lish (e stab′lish), *v.t.* 1 set up on a firm or permanent basis: *establish a government, establish a business.* See **fix** for synonym study. 2 settle in a position; set up in a business: *A new doctor has established himself on our street.* 3 cause to be accepted and used for a long time: *establish a custom.* 4 show beyond dispute; prove: *establish a fact, establish a claim.* [< Old French *establiss-,* a form of *establir* establish < Latin *stabilire* make stable < *stabilis* stable] **—es tab′lish er,** *n.*

established church, church that is a national institution recognized and supported by the government. The Church of England is an established church.

es tab lish ment (e stab′lish mənt), *n.* 1 an establishing. 2 a being established. 3 something established. A household, business, church, or army is an establishment. 4 Usually, **the Establishment,** group that holds positions of influence or authority in a country, society, etc.

es tan cia (e stän′syä), *n.* a large ranch or estate in Latin America. [< Spanish, station]

es tate (e stāt′), *n.* 1 a large piece of land belonging to a person; landed property: *He has a beautiful estate with a country house and a swimming pool on it.* 2 that which a person owns; property; possessions. When a person dies, his estate is divided up among those to whom he has left it. 3 condition or stage in life: *A boy reaches man's estate at 21.* 4 class or group of people in a nation forming a social or political division. **The three estates** in France at the time of the French Revolution were the noblemen, clergymen, and common people. [< Old French *estat* < Latin *status* state. Doublet of STATE.]

Es tates-Gen er al (e stāts′jen′ər əl), *n.* States-General.

es teem (e stēm′), *v.t.* 1 have a very favorable opinion of; think highly of: *We esteem courage.* See **value** for synonym study. 2 think; consider: *Men have often esteemed happiness the greatest good.* *—n.* a very favorable opinion; high regard: *Courage is held in esteem.* [< Old French *estimer* < Latin *aestimare* to value]

es ter (es′tər), *n.* any of a group of organic compounds produced by the reaction of an acid and an alcohol, so that the acid hydrogen of the acid is replaced by the hydrocarbon radical of the alcohol. Animal and vegetable fats and oils are esters. [< German *Ester* < *Essigäther* vinegar ether]

es ter i fy (e ster′ə fī), *v.t.,* **-fied, -fy ing.**

change into an ester. **—es ter′i fi ca′tion,** *n.*

Es ther (es′tər), *n.* 1 (in the Bible) the Jewish wife of a Persian king, who saved her people from a massacre plotted by Haman. 2 book of the Old Testament that tells her story.

es thete (es′thēt), *n.* aesthete.

es thet ic (es thet′ik), *adj.* aesthetic. **—es thet′i cal ly,** *adv.*

es thet ics (es thet′iks), *n.* aesthetics.

Es tho ni a (es thō′nē ə, e stō′nē ə), *n.* Estonia. **—Es tho′ni an,** *adj., n.*

es ti ma ble (es′tə mə bəl), *adj.* 1 worthy of esteem; deserving high regard. 2 that can be estimated or calculated. **—es′ti ma bly,** *adv.*

es ti mate (*n.* es′tə mit, es′tə māt; *v.* es′tə māt), *n., v.,* **-mat ed, -mat ing.** *—n.* 1 judgment or opinion of the approximate worth, size, amount, etc.: *My estimate of the length of the room was 15 feet; it actually measured 14 feet, 9 inches.* 2 statement of what certain work will cost, made by one willing to do the work: *The painter's estimate for painting the house was $500.* *—v.t.* 1 form a judgment or opinion (about how much, how many, how good, etc.). 2 fix the worth, size, amount, etc., of, especially in a rough way; calculate approximately: *estimate one's losses, estimate the cost of a trip.* See synonym study below. [< Latin *aestimatum* valued, appraised] **—es′ti ma′tor,** *n.*

Syn. *v.t.* 2 **Estimate, appraise** mean to judge the measure, weight, or value of something. **Estimate** means to make a judgment regarding amount, number, value, or the like, under such circumstances that the result is not likely to be exactly right: *They estimated the tree to be thirty feet high.* **Appraise** means to make an expert judgment about some thing or things, and implies that the result given is correct or cannot be questioned: *The stolen necklace had been appraised at $15,000.*

es ti ma tion (es′tə mā′shən), *n.* 1 judgment or opinion: *In my estimation, your plan will not work.* 2 esteem; respect. 3 act or process of estimating.

es ti val (es′tə vəl, es tī′vəl), *adj.* of or having to do with summer. Also, **aestival.** [< Latin *aestivalis* < *aestivus* of summer < *aestas* summer]

es ti vate (es′tə vāt), *v.i.,* **-vat ed, -vat ing.** (in zoology) spend the summer in a dormant or torpid condition. Some snakes and rodents estivate. Also, **aestivate.** **—es′ti va′tion,** *n.*

Es to ni a (e stō′nē ə), *n.* Estonian S.S.R. Also, **Esthonia.**

Es to ni an (e stō′nē ən), *n.* 1 one of a Finnish people inhabiting the Estonian S.S.R. and neighboring parts of the Soviet Union. 2 the Finno-Ugric language of this people. *—adj.* of or having to do with the Estonian S.S.R., the Estonians, or their language.

Estonian S.S.R., one of the constituent republics of the U.S.S.R., in the W part, on the Baltic Sea. 1,400,000 pop.; 17,400 sq. mi. *Capital:* Tallinn.

es trange (e strānj′), *v.t.,* **-tranged, -trang ing.** 1 turn (a person) from affection to indifference, dislike, or hatred; make unfriendly; separate: *A quarrel had estranged him from his family.* 2 keep apart; keep away. [< Old French *estrangier* < Latin *extraneare* < *extraneus* strange, foreign]

es trange ment (e strānj′mənt), *n.* a turning away in feeling; becoming distant or unfriendly: *A misunderstanding had caused the estrangement of the two friends.*

es tro gen (es′trə jən), *n.* any of various hormones which induce a series of physiological changes in females, especially in the reproductive or sexual organs.

es tro gen ic (es′trə jen′ik), *adj.* 1 causing or promoting estrus. 2 of an estrogen or estrogens.

es trous cycle (es′trəs), the recurrent bodily changes in the sexual and other organs connected with the estrus in the female of the lower mammals.

es trus (es′trəs), *n.* 1 a periodically recurring state of sexual activity in most female mammals during which mating may take place; heat. 2 estrous cycle. [< Latin *oestrus* frenzy, gadfly < Greek *oistros* gadfly]

es tu ar ine (es′chü ər in), *adj.* 1 of or having to do with an estuary. 2 formed or deposited in an estuary.

es tu ar y (es′chü er′ē), *n., pl.* **-ar ies.** 1 a broad mouth of a river into which the tide flows. 2 inlet of the sea. [< Latin *aestuarium* < *aestus* tide]

esu, electrostatic unit or units.

-et, *suffix forming nouns from other nouns.* little ____: *Owlet = little owl.* [< Old French]

e ta (ā′tə, ē′tə), *n.* the seventh letter of the Greek alphabet (Η,η).

ETA, estimated time of arrival.

et al., 1 and others [for Latin *et alii*]. 2 and elsewhere [for Latin *et alibi*].

➤ **Et al.** (def. 1) means "and other (people)," and is not used to mean "and other things." For the latter, *etc.* is the abbreviation.

etc., et cetera.

➤ **etc., et cetera.** *Etc.,* usually read "and so forth," is most appropriately used in condensed references and in technical and business writing: *The case is suitable for prints, maps, blueprints, etc.*

et cet er a (et set′ər ə), and so forth; and others; and the rest; and so on; and the like. [< Latin] ➤ See **etc.** for usage note.

etch (ech), *v.t.* 1 engrave (a drawing or design) on a metal plate, glass, etc., by means of acid that eats away the lines. When filled with ink, the lines of the design will reproduce a copy on paper. 2 engrave a drawing or design on by means of acid: *The artist etched only a few copper plates.* 3 impress deeply; fix firmly: *Her face was etched in my memory.* *—v.i.* make etchings. [< Dutch *etsen* < German *ätzen.* Related to EAT.] **—etch′er,** *n.*

etch ing (ech′ing), *n.* 1 picture or design printed from an etched plate. 2 an etched plate; etched drawing or design. 3 art or process of engraving a drawing or design on a metal plate, glass, etc., by means of acid.

ETD, estimated time of departure.

e ter nal (i tėr′nl), *adj.* 1 without beginning or ending; lasting throughout all time; timeless. See synonym study below. 2 always and forever the same; immutable. 3 seeming to go on forever; constant: *When will we have an end to this eternal noise?* *—n.* **the Eternal,** God. [< Latin *aeternus,* ultimately < *aevum* age] **—e ter′nal ness,** *n.*

Syn. *adj.* 1 **Eternal, everlasting** mean lasting forever. **Eternal** emphasizes having neither a beginning nor an end: *Because a circle has no beginning or end, the wedding ring is a symbol of eternal love.* **Everlasting** does not imply the absence of a beginning but means having no end: *We wish for everlasting peace.*

Eternal City, Rome.

e ter nal ly (i tėr′nl ē), *adv.* 1 without beginning or ending; throughout all time. 2 always and forever. 3 constantly; incessantly.

hat, āge, fär; let, ēqual, tėrm;
it, īce; hot, ōpen, ôrder;
oil, out; cup, pu̇t, rüle;
ch, child; ng, long; sh, she;
th, thin; ᴛʜ, then; zh, measure;

ə represents *a* in about, *e* in taken,
i in pencil, *o* in lemon, *u* in circus.

< = from, derived from, taken from.

e ter ni ty (i tėr′nə tē), *n., pl.* **-ties.** 1 all time; all the past and all the future; time without beginning or ending. 2 the endless period after death. 3 a seemingly endless period of time. 4 eternal quality; endlessness.

eth ane (eth′ān), *n.* a colorless, odorless, flammable, gaseous hydrocarbon present in natural gas and coal gas, used as a refrigerant and as a fuel. *Formula:* C_2H_6 [< *ether*]

eth a nol (eth′ə nōl, eth′ə nol), *n.* ethyl alcohol. [< *ethan(e)* + *(alcoh)ol*]

e ther (ē′thər), *n.* 1 a colorless, volatile, flammable, sweet-smelling liquid, produced by the action of sulfuric acid on ethyl alcohol. Because its fumes cause unconsciousness when deeply inhaled, ether is used as an anesthetic. Ether is also used as a solvent for fats and resins. *Formula:* $(C_2H_5)_2O$ 2 the upper regions of space beyond the earth's atmosphere; clear sky. 3 an invisible, elastic substance formerly supposed to be distributed evenly through all space and to conduct light waves, electric waves, etc. 4 any of a group of organic compounds consisting of two hydrocarbon groups linked by an oxygen atom. Ethers are formed by the action of acids on alcohols. Also, **aether** for defs. 2 and 3. [< Latin *aether* < Greek *aithēr* upper air]

e the re al (i thir′ē əl), *adj.* 1 light; airy; delicate: *the ethereal beauty of a butterfly.* 2 not of the earth; heavenly. 3 of or having to do with the upper regions of space. Also, **aethereal.** **—e ther′e al ly,** *adv.* **—e ther′e al ness,** *n.*

e the re al ize (i thir′ē ə līz), *v.t.,* **-ized, -iz ing.** make ethereal.

e ther ize (ē′thə rīz′), *v.t.,* **-ized, -iz ing.** 1 make unconscious with ether fumes. 2 change into ether. **—e′ther i za′tion,** *n.*

eth ic (eth′ik), *adj.* ethical. *—n.* system of ethics. [< Latin *ethicus* < Greek *ēthikos* < *ēthos* character]

eth i cal (eth′ə kəl), *adj.* 1 having to do with standards of right and wrong; of ethics or morals. See **moral** for synonym study. 2 morally right: *ethical conduct.* 3 in accordance with formal or professional rules of right and wrong: *It is not considered ethical for a doctor to repeat a patient's confidences.* 4 (of drugs) that cannot be dispensed by a pharmacist without a doctor's prescription. **—eth′i cal ly,** *adv.*

eth ics (eth′iks), *n.* 1 *pl. in form, sing. in use.* the study of standards of right and wrong; the part of philosophy that deals with moral conduct, duty, and judgment. 2 *pl. in form and use.* formal or professional rules of right and wrong; system of conduct or behavior: *Medical ethics do not permit doctors to advertise.*

E thi o pi a (ē′thē ō′pē ə), *n.* 1 country in E

Africa; Abyssinia. 25,046,000 pop.; 471,800 sq. mi. *Capital:* Addis Ababa. See **Sudan** for map. 2 ancient region in NE Africa, south of Egypt.

E thi o pi an (ē′thē ō′pē ən), *adj.* 1 of or having to do with Ethiopia or its people. 2 ARCHAIC. Negro. —*n.* 1 native or inhabitant of Ethiopia. 2 (in ethnology) a member of one of the five races into which mankind was formerly divided, including the African Negro and the Negrito. 3 ARCHAIC. Negro.

E thi op ic (ē′thē op′ik, ē′thē ō′pik), *adj.* of or having to do with the ancient Semitic language of Ethiopia or the church using this language. —*n.* the ancient Semitic language of Ethiopia.

eth moid (eth′moid), *adj.* having to do with a bone situated in the walls and septum of the nose and containing numerous perforations for the filaments of the olfactory nerve. —*n.* the ethmoid bone. [< Greek *ēthmoeidēs* < *ēthmos* sieve + *eidos* form]

eth nic (eth′nik), *adj.* 1 of or having to do with the various racial or cultural groups of people and the characteristics, language, and customs of each; of, having to do with, or peculiar to a people. 2 of or having to do with people of foreign birth or descent: *There are many ethnic groups in our large cities.* —*n.* member of an ethnic group. [< Latin *ethnicus* < Greek *ethnikos* < *ethnos* nation] **—eth′ni cal ly,** *adv.*

eth ni cal (eth′nə kəl), *adj.* ethnic.

eth no cen tric (eth′nō sen′trik), *adj.* characterized by ethnocentrism.

eth no cen trism (eth′nō sen′triz′əm), *n.* practice of regarding one's own race or culture as superior to others.

eth no graph ic (eth′nə graf′ik), *adj.* having to do with ethnography. **—eth′no graph′i cal ly,** *adv.*

eth no graph i cal (eth′nə graf′ə kəl), *adj.* ethnographic.

eth nog ra phy (eth nog′rə fē), *n.* branch of anthropology that deals with the scientific description of various racial and cultural groups of people.

eth no log ic (eth′nə loj′ik), *adj.* ethnological.

eth no log i cal (eth′nə loj′ə kəl), *adj.* of or having to do with ethnology. **—eth′no log′i cal ly,** *adv.*

eth nol o gist (eth nol′ə jist), *n.* an expert in ethnology.

eth nol o gy (eth nol′ə jē), *n.* branch of anthropology that deals with the various racial or cultural groups of ancient or contemporary people, their origin and distribution, and their distinctive characteristics, customs, institutions, and culture.

eth yl (eth′əl), *n.* 1 a univalent radical present in many organic chemical compounds. Ordinary alcohol contains ethyl. *Formula:* $-C_2H_5$ 2 **Ethyl,** trademark for: **a** a poisonous, colorless compound usually containing tetraethyl lead, used in gasoline to reduce knocking. *Formula:* $Pb(C_2H_5)_4$ **b** gasoline containing this compound. [< *ether*]

ethyl alcohol, ordinary alcohol, a colorless, volatile liquid made by the fermentation of grain, sugar, etc.; ethanol. *Formula:* C_2H_5OH

eth yl ene (eth′ə lēn′), *n.* a colorless, flammable gas with an unpleasant odor, used as an anesthetic, in making organic compounds, and for coloring and ripening citrus fruits. *Formula:* C_2H_4

ethylene glycol, glycol.

e ti o log ic (ē′tē ə loj′ik), *adj.* etiological.

e ti o log i cal (ē′tē ə loj′ə kəl), *adj.* of or having to do with etiology. **—e′ti o log′i cal ly,** *adv.*

e ti ol o gy (ē′tē ol′ə jē), *n.* 1 science that deals with origins or causes. 2 theory of the causes of disease. 3 cause or causes of a disease. [< Greek *aitiologia* < *aitia* cause + *-logia* -logy]

et i quette (et′ə ket), *n.* 1 conventional rules for conduct or behavior in polite society. 2 formal rules or conventions for governing conduct in a profession, official ceremony, etc.: *diplomatic etiquette.* [< French *étiquette,* originally, ticket]

Et na (et′nə), *n.* **Mount,** active volcano in NE Sicily. 10,758 ft. Also, **Aetna.**

E ton (ēt′n), *n.* an English school for boys, at Eton, a town near London.

Eton collar, a broad, stiff collar worn outside the coat collar.

E to ni an (ē tō′nē ən), *adj.* of or having to do with Eton. —*n.* student or former student at Eton.

Eton jacket

Eton jacket, a short, black coat with broad lapels. The jacket comes to the waist and is not made to button.

E trur i a (i trůr′ē ə), *n.* ancient country in W central Italy.

E trur i an (i trůr′ē ən), *adj., n.* Etruscan.

E trus can (i trus′kən), *adj.* of or having to do with Etruria, its people, their language, art, or customs. —*n.* 1 native or inhabitant of Etruria. 2 language of Etruria.

et seq., and the following; and that which follows [for Latin *et sequens*].

-ette, *suffix forming nouns from other nouns.* 1 little ____: *Kitchenette = a little kitchen.* 2 female ____: *Usherette = a female usher.* 3 substitute for ____: *Leatherette = a substitute for leather.* [< French, feminine of *-et* -et]

é tude (ā tüd′, ā tyüd′), *n.* 1 study. 2 piece of music intended to develop skill in technique. 3 composition of a similar type, having artistic quality, and intended for public performance. [< French]

ETV, educational television.

et y mo log i cal (et′ə mə loj′ə kəl), *adj.* of or having to do with etymology. **—et′y mo log′i cal ly,** *adv.*

et y mol o gist (et′ə mol′ə jist), *n.* an expert in etymology.

et y mol o gy (et′ə mol′ə jē), *n., pl.* **-gies.** 1 the derivation of a word. 2 account or explanation of the origin and history of a word. 3 study dealing with linguistic changes, especially with individual word origins. [< Greek *etymologia* < *etymon* the original sense or form of a word (neuter of *etymos* true, real) + *-logos* treating of]

eu-, *prefix.* good; well; true, as in *eugenic, eucalyptus.* [< Greek]

Eu, europium.

Eu boe a (yü bē′ə), *n.* the largest island in the Aegean Sea, near Greece and belonging to it. 166,000 pop.; 1600 sq. mi. **—Eu boe′an,** *n., adj.*

eu ca lyp tus (yü′kə lip′təs), *n., pl.* **-tus es, -ti** (-tī). any of a genus of tall evergreen trees of the myrtle family, found mainly in Australia and neighboring islands; gum tree. It is valued for its timber and for a medicinal oil made from its leaves. [< New Latin < Greek *eu-* well + *kalyptos* covered; with reference to the covering on the bud]

Eu char ist (yü′kər ist), *n.* 1 sacrament of sharing in the Lord's Supper as a part of church service; Holy Communion. 2 the consecrated bread and wine used in this sacrament. [< Late Latin *eucharistia* < Greek, thankfulness, the Eucharist < *eucharistos* thankful < *eu-* good + *charis* grace]

Eu cha ris tic (yü′kə ris′tik), *adj.* of or having to do with the Eucharist.

eu chre (yü′kər), *n.* a card game for two, three, or four players, using the 32 (or 28, or 24) highest cards in the pack. The object is to win a majority of the five tricks. [origin uncertain]

Eu clid (yü′klid), *n.* Greek mathematician who wrote a famous book on geometry about 300 B.C.

Eu clid e an or **Eu clid i an** (yü klid′ē ən), *adj.* of Euclid or his principles of geometry.

Eu gene (yü jēn′), *n.* city in W Oregon. 76,000.

eu gen ic (yü jen′ik), *adj.* 1 having to do with eugenics. 2 coming of good stock. [< Greek *eugenēs* wellborn < *eu-* well + *genos* birth] **—eu gen′i cal ly,** *adv.*

eu gen i cist (yü jen′ə sist), *n.* 1 an expert in eugenics. 2 advocate of eugenics.

eu gen ics (yü jen′iks), *n.* science of improving the human race by a careful selection of parents in order to develop healthier and more intelligent children.

Eu gé nie (œ zhā nē′), *n.* 1826-1920, wife of Napoleon III, empress of France from 1853 to 1871.

eu ge nist (yü′jə nist), *n.* eugenicist.

eu gle na (yü glē′nə), *n.* any of a genus of one-celled protozoans classified as flagellates that are spindle-shaped and usually green, with one flagellum. They are easily grown in a culture for study. [< Greek *eu-* good + *glēnē* pupil of the eye]

eu gle noid (yü glē′noid), *adj.* of, having to do with, or like a euglena.

eu lo gist (yü′lə jist), *n.* person who eulogizes.

eu lo gis tic (yü′lə jis′tik), *adj.* of or like a eulogy; praising very highly. **—eu′lo gis′ti cal ly,** *adv.*

eu lo gis ti cal (yü′lə jis′tə kəl), *adj.* eulogistic.

eu lo gize (yü′lə jīz), *v.t.,* **-gized, -giz ing.** praise very highly; extol. **—eu′lo giz′er,** *n.*

eu lo gy (yü′lə jē), *n., pl.* **-gies.** 1 speech or writing in praise of a person or thing, especially a set oration in honor of a deceased person. 2 high praise. [< Greek *eulogia* < *eu-* well + *legein* speak]

Eu men i des (yü men′ə dēz′), *n.pl.* (in Greek and Roman myths) the Furies.

eu nuch (yü′nək), *n.* 1 a castrated man. 2 a castrated man in charge of a harem or the household of an Oriental ruler. [< Greek *eunouchos* < *eunē* bed + *echein* keep, be in charge of]

eu phe mism (yü′fə miz′əm), *n.* 1 use of a mild or indirect expression instead of one that is harsh or unpleasantly direct. 2 word or expression used in this way. "Pass away" is a common euphemism for "die." [< Greek *euphēmismos* < *euphēmizein* speak with fair words < *eu-* good + *phēmē* speaking < *phanai* speak]

eu phe mis tic (yü′fə mis′tik), *adj.* using mild or indirect words instead of harsh or unpleasant ones. **—eu′phe mis′ti cal ly,** *adv.*

eu phon ic (yü fon′ik), *adj.* 1 of or having to do with euphony. 2 euphonious.

eu pho ni ous (yü fō′nē əs), *adj.* pleasing to the ear; sounding agreeable; harmonious. **—eu pho′ni ous ly,** *adv.* **—eu pho′ni ous ness,** *n.*

eu pho ni um (yü fō′nē əm), *n.* a brass musical instrument like a tuba, but having a mellower, deeper tone.

eu pho ny (yü′fə nē), *n., pl.* **-nies.** 1 pleasing effect to the ear; agreeable sound; agreeableness of speech sounds as uttered or combined in utterance. 2 tendency to change sounds so as to favor ease of utterance. [< Greek *euphōnia* < *eu-* good + *phōnē* sound]

eu phor bi a (yü fôr′bē ə), *n., pl.* **-bi a** or **-bi as.** spurge. [< New Latin < Latin *euphorbea,* an African plant]

eu pho ri a (yü fôr′ē ə, yü fōr′ē ə), *n.* a feeling of happiness and bodily well-being. [< Greek < *eu-* good + *pherein* to bear]

eu phor ic (yü fôr′ik, yü for′ik), *adj.* having to do with or characterized by euphoria.

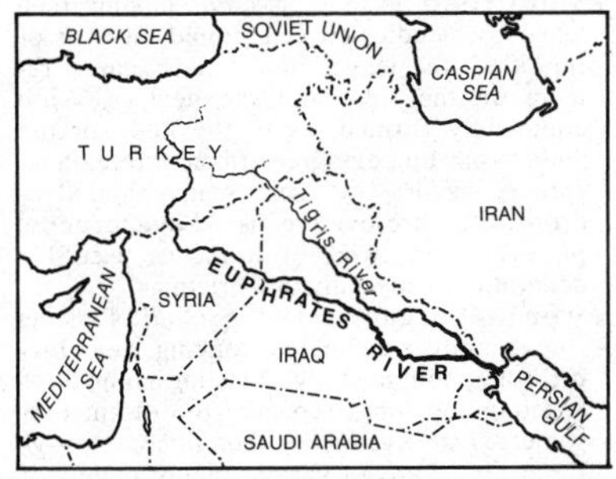

Eu phra tes River (yü frā′tēz), river in SW Asia, flowing from E Turkey through Syria and Iraq. It joins the Tigris River in SE Iraq before flowing into the Persian Gulf. 1700 mi.

Eu phros y ne (yü fros′n ē), *n.* (in Greek myths) one of the three Graces.

Eur., 1 Europe. 2 European.

Eur a sia (yu̇r ā′zhə, yu̇r ā′shə), *n.* Europe and Asia, thought of as a single continent.

Eur a sian (yu̇r ā′zhən, yu̇r ā′shən), *n.* person of mixed European and Asian parentage. *—adj.* 1 of or having to do with Eurasia or its people. 2 of mixed European and Asian parentage.

Eur at om (yu̇r at′əm′), *n.* the European Atomic Energy Community, an organization that pools the nuclear-power developments of France, West Germany, Italy, Belgium, the Netherlands, and Luxembourg.

eu re ka (yu̇ rē′kə), *interj.* I have found it! (an exclamation of triumph at any discovery). [< Greek *heurēka* < *heuriskein* to find; the reputed exclamation of Archimedes when he discovered the means of determining the proportion of base metal in the golden crown of the king of Syracuse]

Eu rip i des (yu̇ rip′ə dēz′), *n.* 480?-406? B.C., Greek dramatist.

Eu ro pa (yu̇ rō′pə), *n.* (in Greek myths) a Phoenician princess loved by Zeus. He took the form of a white bull and carried her off on his back to Crete.

Eur ope (yu̇r′əp), *n.* continent east of the North Atlantic Ocean and west of Asia 651,907,000 pop.; 4,065,000 sq. mi.

Eur o pe an (yu̇r′ə pē′ən), *adj.* of or having to do with Europe or its people. *—n.* 1 native or inhabitant of Europe. 2 person of European descent.

euphonium

European Economic Community, the Common Market.

Eur o pe an ize (yu̇r′ə pē′ə nīz), *v.t.,* **-ized, -iz ing.** make European in appearance, habit, way of life, etc.

European plan, U.S. system of charges to guests in a hotel by which the price covers the room, but not the meals.

eu ro pi um (yu̇ rō′pē əm), *n.* a soft, grayish, rare-earth metallic element which occurs only in combination with other elements. Europium compounds are used in coating color television screens. *Symbol:* Eu; *atomic number* 63. See pages 326 and 327 for table. [< Latin *Europa* Europe]

Eu ryd i ce (yu̇ rid′ə sē′), *n.* (in Greek myths) the wife of Orpheus.

eu ryp ter id (yü rip′tər id), *n.* any of an extinct order of crustaceans of the Paleozoic era, varying in size from a few inches to six feet. [< Greek *eurys* broad + *pteron* wing]

Eus ta chi an tube (yü stā′kē ən, yü stā′shən), a slender canal between the pharynx and the middle ear, which equalizes the air pressure on the two sides of the eardrum. See **ear**[1] for diagram. [< Bartolommeo *Eustachio,* 1520?-1574, Italian anatomist]

eu tec tic (yü tek′tik), *adj.* that may be easily melted, as an alloy or mixture whose melting point is lower than that of any other alloy or mixture composed of the same ingredients. [< Greek *eutēktos* easily melting < *eu-* well + *tēkein* melt]

Eu ter pe (yü tėr′pē), *n.* (in Greek myths) the Muse of music and lyric poetry.

eu tha na sia (yü′thə nā′zhə), *n.* a painless killing, especially to end a painful and incurable disease; mercy killing. [< Greek < *eu-* easy, good + *thanatos* death]

hat, āge, fär; let, ēqual, tėrm;
it, īce; hot, ōpen, ôrder;
oil, out; cup, pu̇t, rüle;
ch, child; ng, long; sh, she;
th, thin; ᴛʜ, then; zh, measure;

ə represents *a* in about, *e* in taken, *i* in pencil, *o* in lemon, *u* in circus.

< = from, derived from, taken from.

eu then ics (yü then′iks), *n.* science or art of improving the human race by controlling the environment or living conditions. [< Greek *euthenein* thrive, flourish]

Eux ine Sea (yük′sən), ancient name for the Black Sea.

ev, electron volts.

e vac u ate (i vak′yü āt), *v.t.,* **-at ed, -at ing.** 1 leave empty; withdraw from: *The tenants evacuated the building.* 2 withdraw; remove: *evacuate civilians from a war zone.* 3 clear out the contents of; empty (a container). 4 make empty: *evacuate the stomach.* [< Latin *evacuatum* emptied out < *ex-* out + *vacuus* empty] **—e vac′u a′tor,** *n.*

e vac u a tion (i vak′yü ā′shən), *n.* 1 a leaving empty; withdrawal from; act or process of evacuating. 2 removal; withdrawal. 3 a making empty. 4 discharge.

e vac u ee (i vak′yü ē′, i vak′yü ē′), *n.* person who is removed to a place of greater safety.

e vade (i vād′), *v.t.,* **e vad ed, e vad ing.** 1 get away from by trickery; avoid by cleverness; elude: *The thief evaded his pursuers and escaped.* See **escape** for synonym study. 2 avoid by indefinite or misleading statements: *The witness tried to evade an embarrassing question by saying he couldn't remember.* 3 elude or baffle (efforts, etc.). [< Latin *evadere* < *ex-* away + *vadere* go] **—e vad′a ble,** *adj.* **—e vad′er,** *n.*

e val u ate (i val′yü āt), *v.t.,* **-at ed, -at ing.** find out the value or the amount of; estimate the worth or importance of; appraise.

e val u a tion (i val′yü ā′shən), *n.* 1 an evaluating. 2 an estimated value; valuation.

e val u a tive (i val′yü ā′tiv), *adj.* of or capable of evaluation.

ev a nesce (ev′ə nes′), *v.i.,* **-nesced, -nescing.** disappear gradually; fade away; vanish. [< Latin *evanescere* < *ex-* out + *vanus* insubstantial]

ev a nes cence (ev′ə nes′ns), *n.* 1 a fading away; vanishing. 2 tendency to disappear or fade away.

ev a nes cent (ev′ə nes′nt), *adj.* gradually disappearing; soon passing away; vanishing.

e van gel (i van′jəl), *n.* 1 (in Christian belief) good news of the saving of mankind through Christ. 2 any good news. 3 evangelist. 4 **Evangel,** any of the four Gospels. [< Late Latin *evangelium* < Greek *euangelion* good tidings < *eu-* good + *angellein* announce < *angelos* messenger]

e van gel ic (ē′van jel′ik, ev′ən jel′ik), *adj.* evangelical.

e van gel i cal (ē′van jel′ə kəl, ev′ən jel′ə-kəl), *adj.* 1 of or according to the four Gospels or the New Testament. 2 of or having to do with the Protestant churches that emphasize Christ's atonement and man's salvation by faith as the most important parts of Christianity. Methodists and Baptists are evangelical; Unitarians and Universalists are not. 3 evangelistic. —*n.* 1 person who maintains evangelical doctrines; Protestant. 2 member of an evangelical church or party. **—e′van gel′i cal ly,** *adv.*

e van gel i cal ism (ē′van jel′ə kə liz′əm, ev′ən jel′ə kə liz′əm), *n.* 1 doctrines of an evangelical church. 2 adherence to such doctrines.

e van gel ism (i van′jə liz′əm), *n.* 1 a preaching of the Gospel; earnest effort for the spread of the Gospel. 2 belief in the doctrines of an evangelical church or party; evangelicalism.

e van gel ist (i van′jə list), *n.* 1 preacher of the Gospel. 2 a traveling preacher who stirs up religious feeling in revival services or camp meetings; revivalist. 3 **Evangelist,** writer of any of the four Gospels; Matthew, Mark, Luke, or John.

e van gel is tic (i van′jə lis′tik), *adj.* of or by an evangelist or evangelists. **—e van′gel is′ti cal ly,** *adv.*

e van gel ize (i van′jə līz), *v.t.,* **-ized, -iz ing.** 1 preach the Gospel to. 2 convert to Christianity by preaching. **—e van′gel i za′tion,** *n.*

Ev ans (ev′ənz), *n.* **Mary Ann,** the real name of **George Eliot.**

Ev ans ton (ev′ən stən), *n.* city in NE Illinois, near Chicago. 80,000.

Ev ans ville (ev′ənz vil), *n.* city in SW Indiana, on the Ohio River. 139,000.

e vap o rate (i vap′ə rāt′), *v.,* **-rat ed, -rat ing.** —*v.i.* 1 change from a liquid into a vapor: *Boiling water evaporates rapidly.* 2 give off moisture. 3 vanish; disappear. —*v.t.* 1 remove water or other liquid from: *Heat is used to evaporate milk.* 2 cause to change into a vapor: *Heat evaporates water.* [< Latin *evaporatum* evaporated < *ex-* out + *vapor* vapor]

evaporated milk, a thick, unsweetened, canned milk, prepared by evaporating some of the water from ordinary milk.

e vap o ra tion (i vap′ə rā′shən), *n.* 1 a changing of a liquid into vapor. 2 a being changed into vapor. 3 removal of water or other liquid. 4 disappearance.

e vap o ra tive (i vap′ə rā′tiv), *adj.* causing or having to do with evaporation.

e vap o ra tor (i vap′ə rā′tər), *n.* apparatus for removing water or other liquid from a substance.

e va sion (i vā′zhən), *n.* 1 a getting away from something by trickery; avoiding by cleverness: *Evasion of one's duty is contemptible.* 2 an attempt to escape an argument, a charge, a question, etc.: *The prisoner's evasions of the lawyer's questions convinced the jury of his guilt.* 3 means of evading; trick or excuse used to avoid something. [< Late Latin *evasionem* < Latin *evadere.* See EVADE.]

e va sive (i vā′siv, i vā′ziv), *adj.* tending or trying to evade: *"Perhaps" is an evasive answer.* **—e va′sive ly,** *adv.* **—e va′sive ness,** *n.*

eve (ēv), *n.* 1 evening or day before a holiday or some other special day: *Christmas Eve.* 2 time just before something happens: *The campaign ended on the eve of the election.* 3 ARCHAIC. evening. [variant of *even*²]

Eve (ēv), *n.* (in the Bible) the first woman, the wife of Adam.

e ven¹ (ē′vən), *adj.* 1 having the same height everywhere; level; flat; smooth: *Even country has no hills.* See **level** for synonym study. 2 at the same level; in the same plane or line: *The snow was even with the windowsill.* 3 keeping about the same; uniform; regular: *The car travels with an even motion.* See synonym study below. 4 no more or less than; equal: *They divided the money in even shares.* 5 that can be divided by 2 without a remainder: *2, 4, 6, 8, and 10 are even numbers.* 6 neither more nor less; exact: *Twelve apples make an even dozen.* 7 owing nothing: *When he paid all of his debts, he was even.* 8 equally balanced; in equilibrium. 9 not easily disturbed or angered; calm. 10 fair; impartial.
—*v.t.* make level or equal; make even: *She evened the edges by trimming them.* —*v.i.* become equal or comparable.
—*adv.* 1 in an even manner; evenly. 2 just; exactly: *She left even as you came.* 3 indeed: *He is ready, even eager, to go.* 4 fully; quite: *He was faithful even unto death.* 5 though one would not expect it; as one would not expect: *Even the least noise disturbs her.* 6 still; yet: *You can do even better if you try.*
break even, INFORMAL. have equal gains and losses.
even if, in spite of the fact that; although: *I will come, even if it rains.*
even though, although.
get even, a owe nothing. **b** have revenge.
[Old English *efen*] **—e′ven er,** *n.* **—e′ven ly,** *adv.* **—e′ven ness,** *n.*
Syn. *adj.* 3 **Even, uniform, equable** mean always the same. **Even** emphasizes being regular and steady in motion, action, quality, etc.: *the even hum of the motor.* **Uniform** emphasizes sameness in form or character throughout all parts of a substance, series, course, etc.: *We should have uniform traffic laws.* **Equable** suggests freedom from sudden alterations: *A watch has equable movement.*

e ven² (ē′vən), *n.* ARCHAIC. evening. [Old English *ǣfen*]

e ven hand ed (ē′vən han′did), *adj.* impartial; fair; just.

eve ning (ēv′ning), *n.* 1 the last part of day and early part of night; time between sunset and bedtime. 2 the last part: *Old age is the evening of life.* —*adj.* in, of, or for the evening. [Old English *ǣfnung* < *ǣfnian* become evening < *ǣfen* evening]

evening dress, formal clothes worn in the evening.

evening gown, a woman's evening dress.

evening primrose, any of a genus of tall American herbs with spikes of fragrant white, yellow, or pink flowers that open in the evening.

evening star, a bright planet seen in the western sky after sunset. Venus is often the evening star.

e ven song (ē′vən sông′, ē′vən song′), *n.* vespers. [Old English *ǣfensang*]

e vent (i vent′), *n.* 1 a happening, especially an important happening: *The discovery of polio vaccine was a great event in medicine.* See synonym study below. 2 result; outcome; consequence: *We made careful plans and awaited the event.* 3 one item or contest in a program of sports. 4 **at all events** or **in any event,** in any case; whatever happens. 5 **in the event of,** if there should be; in case of; if there is. 6 **in the event that,** if it should happen that; supposing: *In the event that the roads are icy, we shall not come.* [< Latin *eventus* < *evenire* come out < *ex-* out + *venire* come]
Syn. 1 **Event, incident, occurrence** mean a happening. **Event** applies particularly to a happening of some importance: *Her graduation from college was an event I did not want to miss.* **Incident** applies to a happening of less or little importance: *My unexpected meeting with a boy I used to know was an amusing incident.* **Occurrence** is the general word for any happening, event, or incident: *Going to school is an everyday occurrence.*

e vent ful (i vent′fəl), *adj.* 1 full of events; having many unusual events: *The class spent an eventful day touring the zoo.* 2 having important results; important: *The discovery of atomic energy began an eventful period in history.* **—e vent′ful ly,** *adv.* **—e vent′ful ness,** *n.*

e ven tide (ē′vən tīd′), *n.* ARCHAIC. evening.

e ven tu al (i ven′chü əl), *adj.* coming in the end; final; ultimate: *After several failures, his eventual success surprised us.*

e ven tu al i ty (i ven′chü al′ə tē), *n., pl.* **-ties.** a possible occurrence or condition; possibility: *We hope for rain, but we are ready for the eventuality of a drought.*

e ven tu al ly (i ven′chü ə lē), *adv.* in the end; finally.

e ven tu ate (i ven′chü āt), *v.i.,* **-at ed, -at ing.** come out in the end; happen finally; result.

ev er (ev′ər), *adv.* 1 at any time: *Is she ever at home?* 2 at all times; always; forever: *ever at your service.* 3 by any chance; in any case; at all: *What did you ever do to make him so angry?* 4 **ever so,** INFORMAL. very. [Old English *ǣfre*]

Ev er est (ev′ər ist), *n.* **Mount,** mountain in the Himalayas on the border between Tibet and Nepal, the highest in the world. 29,028 ft.

ev er glade (ev′ər glād), *n.* 1 a large tract of low, wet ground partly covered with tall grass; large swamp or marsh; glade. 2 **the Everglades,** a swampy region in S Florida. 140 mi. long; 50 mi. wide.

ev er green (ev′ər grēn′), *adj.* having green leaves or needles all year round. In trees of this kind, the leaves of the past season remain on the tree until the new ones are completely formed, as in the holly or the pine. —*n.* 1 an evergreen plant or tree. Pine, spruce, cedar, ivy, box, many rhododendrons, etc., are evergreens. 2 **evergreens,** *pl.* evergreen twigs or branches used for decoration, especially at Christmas.

ev er last ing (ev′ər las′ting), *adj.* 1 lasting forever; never ending or stopping. See **eternal** for synonym study. 2 lasting a long time. 3 lasting too long; repeated too often; tiresome: *his everlasting quibbles.* —*n.* 1 eternity. 2 any of various plants, mainly of the composite family, whose flowers keep their shape and color when dried; immortelle. 3 the flower of any of these plants. 4 **the Everlasting,** God. **—ev′er last′ing ly,** *adv.* **—ev′er last′ing ness,** *n.*

ev er more (ev′ər môr′, ev′ər mōr′), *adv.* for always; always; forever. —*n.* **for evermore,** for all time; for eternity.

e ver sion (i vėr′zhən, i vėr′shən), *n.* 1 a turning of an organ, structure, etc., inside out. 2 a being turned inside out. [< Latin *eversionem* < *evertere* evert]

e vert (i vėrt′), *v.i.* turn inside out or outward, as the eyelids. [< Latin *evertere* < *ex-* out + *vertere* to turn]

ev ery (ev′rē), *adj.* 1 being one of the entire number of persons or things; each and all: *Every written word is made of letters.* See **each** for synonym study. 2 all possible: *We showed him every consideration.* 3 **every now and then,** from time to time; again and again. 4 **every other,** every second: *The milkman makes deliveries every other day.* 5 **every which way,** INFORMAL. in all directions; in disorder. [Middle English *everich* < Old English *ǣfre ǣlc* ever each]

ev ery bod y (ev′rə bud′ē, ev′rē bod′ē), *pron.* every person; everyone: *Everybody likes the new principal.*

ev ery day (ev′rē dā′), *adj.* 1 of every day; daily: *Accidents are everyday occurrences.* 2 for every ordinary day; not for Sundays or holidays: *She wears everyday clothes to work.* 3 not exciting; usual.

➔ **Everyday** is one word when it is an adjective, two words when *day* is a noun modified by *every: This was an everyday occurrence. Every day seemed a year.*

ev ery one (ev′rē wun, ev′rē wən), *pron.* each one; everybody: *Everyone took his purchases home.*

➔ **everyone.** *Everyone* is usually written as one word, but when *one* is stressed or emphasized, it is written as two: *Everyone wants to attend the concert. Winning this game depends upon every one of you.*

ev ery thing (ev′rē thing), *pron.* every thing; all things. —*n.* something extremely important; very important thing: *This news means everything to us.*

➔ **Everything** is one word when it is a noun or pronoun, two words when *thing* is stressed or emphasized: *Everything was in its place. She meant everything to him. Food, water, clothes—every thing that Midas touched turned to gold.*

ev ery where (ev′rē hwer, ev′rē hwar), *adv.* in every place; in all places: *We looked everywhere for our lost dog.*

e vict (i vikt′), *v.t.* expel by a legal process from land, a building, etc.; eject: *The tenant was evicted by the sheriff for not paying his rent.* [< Latin *evictum* overcome, ejected < *ex-* out + *vincere* conquer] **—e vic′tor,** *n.*

e vic tion (i vik′shən), *n.* an evicting or a being evicted; expulsion.

ev i dence (ev′ə dəns), *n., v.,* **-denced, -denc ing.** —*n.* 1 anything that shows what is true and what is not; facts; proof: *The evidence showed that he had not been near the place.* See synonym study below. 2 facts established and accepted in a court of law. Before deciding a case, the judge or jury hears all the evidence given by both sides. 3 indication; sign: *A smile gives evidence of pleasure.* 4 **in evidence,** easily seen or noticed: *Poverty is much in evidence in the city slums.* —*v.t.* make easy to see or understand; show clearly; prove: *His smiles evidenced his pleasure.*

Syn. *n.* 1 **Evidence, testimony, proof** mean that which tends to demonstrate the truth or falsity of something. **Evidence** applies to facts that indicate, without fully proving, that something is so: *Running away was evidence of his guilt.* **Testimony** applies to any speech or action which serves as evidence of something: *His testimony contradicted that of the preceding witness.* **Proof** means evidence so full and convincing as to leave no doubt or little doubt: *The signed receipt is proof that the letter was delivered.*

ev i dent (ev′ə dənt), *adj.* easy to see or understand; clear; plain: *He has brought her a kitten, to her evident joy.* [< Latin *evidentem* < *ex-* out + *videre* see]

ev i den tial (ev′ə den′shəl), *adj.* 1 of or serving as evidence; based on evidence. 2 like evidence; giving evidence.

ev i dent ly (ev′ə dənt lē), *adv.* plainly; clearly; apparently.

e vil (ē′vəl), *adj.* 1 morally bad; wrong; sinful; wicked: *an evil life, an evil character.* See **bad** for synonym study. 2 causing harm or injury; harmful: *an evil plan.* 3 unfortunate. 4 due to bad character or conduct: *an evil reputation.* —*n.* 1 bad or evil quality; wickedness. 2 thing that causes harm or injury. [Old English *yfel*] **—e′vil ly,** *adv.* **—e′vil ness,** *n.*

e vil do er (ē′vəl dü′ər), *n.* person who does evil.

e vil do ing (ē′vəl dü′ing), *n.* a doing evil.

evil eye, power that some people are supposed to have of inflicting injury by a look.

e vil-mind ed (ē′vəl mīn′did), *adj.* having an evil mind; wicked; malicious.

Evil One, the Devil; Satan.

e vince (i vins′), *v.t.,* **e vinced, e vinc ing.** 1 show clearly; manifest: *The dog evinced its dislike of strangers by growling.* See **display** for synonym study. 2 show that one has (a certain quality, trait, etc.). [< Latin *evincere* < *ex-* out + *vincere* conquer]

e vin ci ble (i vin′sə bəl), *adj.* capable of proof; demonstrable.

e vis ce rate (i vis′ə rāt′), *v.t.,* **-rat ed, -rat ing.** 1 remove the bowels from; disembowel: *eviscerate a chicken.* 2 deprive of something essential. [< Latin *evisceratum* disemboweled < *ex-* out + *viscera* viscera] **—e vis′ce ra′tion,** *n.*

ev o ca ble (ev′ə kə bəl), *adj.* that can be evoked or called forth.

ev o ca tion (ev′ə kā′shən), *n.* an evoking or calling forth.

e voc a tive (i vok′ə tiv, i vō′kə tiv), *adj.* tending to evoke. **—e voc′a tive ness,** *n.*

e voke (i vōk′), *v.t.,* **e voked, e vok ing.** call forth; bring out; elicit: *A good joke evokes a laugh.* [< Latin *evocare* < *ex-* out + *vocare* to call]

ev o lu tion (ev′ə lü′shən), *n.* 1 any process of formation or growth; gradual development: *the evolution of the modern steamship from the first crude boat.* 2 something evolved; product of development. 3 theory that all existing species, genera, orders, etc., of animals and plants developed from a few simple forms of life, if not from one, by modification of characteristics in successive generations, by mutation, hybridization, selection, etc. 4 a planned movement of ships or soldiers. 5 movement that is a part of a definite plan, design, or series: *the graceful evolutions of that ballet dancer.* 6 a releasing; giving off; setting free: *the evolution of heat from burning coal.* 7 (in mathematics) the extraction of roots from powers.

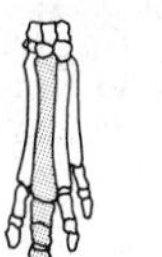
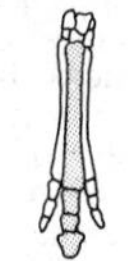

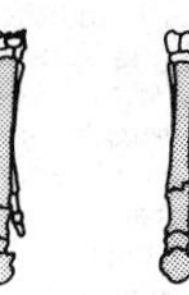

evolution (def. 3)
of the horse's forefoot from four toes to a single toe (hoof). The toe which became the hoof is shaded.

hat, āge, fär; let, ēqual, tėrm;
it, īce; hot, ōpen, ôrder;
oil, out; cup, pu̇t, rüle;
ch, child; ng, long; sh, she;
th, thin; ᴛʜ, then; zh, measure;

ə represents *a* in about, *e* in taken, *i* in pencil, *o* in lemon, *u* in circus.

< = from, derived from, taken from.

[< Latin *evolutionem* < *evolvere.* See EVOLVE.]

ev o lu tion al (ev′ə lü′shə nəl), *adj.* evolutionary.

ev o lu tion ar y (ev′ə lü′shə ner′ē), *adj.* 1 having to do with evolution or development. 2 in accordance with the theory of evolution.

ev o lu tion ism (ev′ə lü′shə niz′əm), *n.* the biological doctrine of evolution.

ev o lu tion ist (ev′ə lü′shə nist), *n.* believer and supporter of the theory of evolution.

e volve (i volv′), *v.,* **e volved, e volv ing.** —*v.t.* 1 develop gradually; work out; unfold: *The boys evolved a plan for earning money during their summer vacation.* 2 develop by a process of growth and change to a more highly organized condition. 3 release; give off; set free. —*v.i.* be developed by evolution. [< Latin *evolvere* < *ex-* out + *volvere* to roll] **—e volve′ment,** *n.*

ev zone (ev′zōn), *n.* member of a special corps of infantrymen in the Greek army, known for its valor and picturesque uniform. [< Greek *euzōnos* dressed for exercise < *eu-* well + *zōnē* girdle]

ewe (yü), *n.* a female sheep. [Old English *ēowu*]

ewer and basin

ew er (yü′ər), *n.* a wide-mouthed water pitcher. [< Anglo-French variant of Old French *eviere, aiguiere* < Latin *aquarius* for drawing water < *aqua* water]

ex (eks), *prep.* 1 out of. Ex elevator means free of charges until the time of removal from the grain elevator. 2 without; not including. Ex dividend stocks are stocks on which the purchaser will not receive the next dividend to be paid. [< Latin]

ex-[1], *prefix.* 1 former; formerly: *Ex-president = former president.* 2 out of; from; out: *Express = press out.* 3 thoroughly; utterly: *Exterminate = terminate (finish or destroy) thoroughly.* See also **e-** and **ef-.** [< Latin < *ex* out of, without]

ex-[2], *prefix.* from; out of, as in *exodus.* Also, **ec-** before consonants. [< Greek]

ex., 1 examined. 2 example.

Ex., Exodus.

ex ac er bate (eg zas′ər bāt, ek sas′ər bāt), *v.t.,* **-bat ed, -bat ing.** 1 make worse or aggravate (pain, disease, anger, etc.). 2 irritate (a person's feelings). [< Latin *exacerbatum* made harsh < *ex-* completely +

acerbus harsh, bitter] **—ex ac′er ba′tion,** *n.*

ex act (eg zakt′), *adj.* 1 without any mistake; correct; accurate; precise: *an exact measurement, the exact amount.* See **correct** for synonym study. 2 strict; severe; rigorous. 3 characterized by or using strict accuracy: *A scientist should be an exact thinker.* *—v.t.* 1 demand and get; force to be paid: *If he does the work, he can exact payment for it.* 2 call for; need; require: *A hard piece of work exacts effort and patience.* [< Latin *exactum* weighed accurately < *ex-* out + *agere* weigh] **—ex act′ness,** *n.*

ex act ing (eg zak′ting), *adj.* 1 requiring much; making severe demands; hard to please: *An exacting teacher will not permit careless work.* 2 requiring effort, care, or attention: *Flying an airplane is exacting work.* **—ex act′ing ly,** *adv.* **—ex act′ing ness,** *n.*

ex ac tion (eg zak′shən), *n.* 1 an exacting: *The ruler's repeated exaction of money left the people very poor.* 2 thing exacted. Taxes, fees, etc., forced to be paid are exactions.

ex act i tude (eg zak′tə tüd, eg zak′tə tyüd), *n.* exactness.

ex act ly (eg zakt′lē), *adv.* 1 in an exact manner; accurately; precisely. 2 just so; quite right.

ex ag ge rate (eg zaj′ə rāt′), *v.,* **-rat ed, -rat ing.** *—v.t.* 1 make (something) greater than it is; overstate: *He exaggerated the dangers of the trip in order to frighten them into not going.* 2 increase or enlarge abnormally: *The artist exaggerated parts of the drawing to make them clearer.* *—v.i.* say or think something is greater than it is; go beyond the truth: *He always exaggerates when he tells about things he has done.* [< Latin *exaggeratum* heaped up < *ex-* up + *agger* to heap] **—ex ag′ge ra′tor,** *n.*

ex ag ge ra tion (eg zaj′ə rā′shən), *n.* 1 an exaggerated statement; overstatement. 2 an exaggerating.

ex alt (eg zôlt′), *v.t.* 1 make high in rank, honor, power, character, or quality; elevate: *We exalt a man when we elect him President of our country.* 2 fill with pride, joy, or noble feeling. 3 praise; honor; glorify. [< Latin *exaltare* < *ex-* up + *altus* high] **—ex alt′er,** *n.*

ex al ta tion (eg′zôl tā′shən), *n.* 1 an exalting. 2 a being exalted. 3 elation of mind or feeling; rapture.

ex am (eg zam′), *n.* INFORMAL. examination.

ex am i na tion (eg zam′ə nā′shən), *n.* 1 an examining. 2 a being examined. See **investigation** for synonym study. 3 test of knowledge or qualifications; list of questions; test. 4 answers given in such a test. 5 (in law) an interrogation, especially of a witness.

ex am i na tion al (eg zam′ə nā′shə nəl), *adj.* of or having to do with examination.

ex am ine (eg zam′ən), *v.t.,* **-ined, -in ing.** 1 look at closely and carefully; inspect: *The doctor examined the wound.* 2 test the knowledge or qualifications of; ask questions of; test: *examine doctoral candidates.* 3 question (a witness) formally; interrogate. [< Latin *examinare* < *examen* a weighing < *exigere* weigh accurately < *ex-* out + *agere* weigh] **—ex am′in er,** *n.*

ex am i nee (eg zam′ə nē′), *n.* person who is being examined.

ex am ple (eg zam′pəl), *n.* 1 one thing taken to show what others are like; case that shows something: *New York is an example of a busy city.* See synonym study below. 2 person or thing to be imitated; model; pattern: *Lincoln is a good example for boys to follow.* See **model** for synonym study. 3 problem in arithmetic, etc. 4 warning to others: *The sergeant made an example of the soldiers who shirked their duty by ordering them to clean up the barracks.* 5 **for example,** as an example; for instance. 6 **set an example,** behave for others to imitate; give, show, or be a model of conduct. [< Old French < Latin *exemplum,* originally, that which is taken out (i.e., a sample) < *eximere* take out < *ex-* out + *emere* take]

Syn. 1 Example, sample mean something representing the whole of which it is a part. **Example** applies to any person or thing that shows what the type or kind is like or how a general rule works: *This chair is an example of period furniture.* **Sample** applies to one thing, part, or piece taken out of a group or class to show the quality of the whole: *She looked carefully at all the samples of material before buying any.*

ex arch (ek′särk), *n.* in the Eastern church: **a** a patriarch's deputy. **b** a bishop ranking below a patriarch and above a metropolitan. [< Greek *exarchos* leader, chief]

ex as pe rate (eg zas′pə rāt′), *v.t.,* **-rat ed, -rat ing.** irritate very much; annoy extremely; make angry: *The little boy's constant noise exasperated his father.* [< Latin *exasperatum* irritated < *ex-* completely + *asper* rough] **—ex as′pe rat′ing ly,** *adv.*

ex as pe ra tion (eg zas′pə rā′shən), *n.* extreme annoyance; irritation; anger.

exc., 1 excellent. 2 except.

Ex cal i bur (ek skal′ə bər), *n.* (in Arthurian legends) the magic sword of King Arthur.

ex ca the dra (eks kə thē′drə; eks kath′ə drə), 1 with authority. 2 spoken with authority. [< Latin, from the chair]

ex ca vate (ek′skə vāt), *v.t.,* **-vat ed, -vat ing.** 1 make a hollow in; hollow out: *The tunnel was made by excavating the side of a mountain.* 2 make by digging; dig: *The workmen excavated a tunnel through solid rock.* 3 dig out; scoop out: *Steam shovels excavated the dirt.* 4 uncover by digging: *They excavated an ancient buried city.* [< Latin *excavatum* hollowed out < *ex-* out + *cavus* hollow] **—ex′ca va′tor,** *n.*

ex ca va tion (ek′skə vā′shən), *n.* 1 an excavating. 2 an excavated space.

ex ceed (ek sēd′), *v.t.* 1 be more or greater than: *The sum of 5 and 7 exceeds 10.* 2 do more than; go beyond: *exceed the speed limit.* 3 be superior to; surpass; outdo. *—v.i.* excel. [< Latin *excedere* < *ex-* out + *cedere* go]

ex ceed ing (ek sē′ding), *adj.* very great; unusual. *—adv.* exceedingly.

ex ceed ing ly (ek sē′ding lē), *adv.* very greatly; extremely.

ex cel (ek sel′), *v.,* **-celled, -cel ling.** *—v.t.* be better than; do better than. See synonym study below. *—v.i.* be better than others; do better than others: *He excels in mathematics.* [< Latin *excellere* < *ex-* out + *-cellere* to rise]

Syn. *v.t.* **Excel, surpass, outdo** mean to be better in quality or action. **Excel** suggests being outstanding in merit or achievement: *He excelled his classmates in history.* **Surpass** suggests being better than someone else in some specified way: *She surpasses her sister in history.* **Outdo** suggests doing better than others, or better than has been done before: *The runner outdid his previous record for the race.*

ex cel lence (ek′sə ləns), *n.* unusually good quality; being better than others; superiority: *The inn was famous for the excellence of its food.*

ex cel len cy (ek′sə lən sē), *n., pl.* **-cies.** 1 excellence. 2 **Excellency,** title of honor used in addressing or speaking to or of a high official, such as a governor, ambassador, or bishop.

ex cel lent (ek′sə lənt), *adj.* of unusually good quality; better than others; superior. **—ex′cel lent ly,** *adv.*

ex cel si or (*adj.* ek sel′sē ôr; *n.* ek sel′sē ər), *adj.* LATIN. ever upward; higher. "Excelsior" is the motto of New York State. *—n.* fine, curled shavings of soft wood used for packing dishes, glassware, and other breakable articles. [< Latin, comparative of *excelsus* high < *ex-* out + *-cellere* to rise]

ex cept (ek sept′), *prep.* leaving out; other than; but: *every day except Sunday.* *—v.t.* take or leave out; exclude: *Those who passed the first test were excepted from the second.* *—v.i.* make objection; object. *—conj.* 1 only; but: *I would have had a perfect score except I missed the last question.* 2 ARCHAIC. unless. [< Latin *exceptum* taken out, excepted < *ex-* out + *capere* take]

➤ **Except** and **accept** are often confused because they are similar in sound. *Accept,* always a verb, means "receive": *He accepted the gift.* As a verb, *except* means either "omit" or "exclude": *We can call his career brilliant if we except that one serious blunder.* As a preposition, *except* means "but": *Everyone except John went home.*

ex cept ing (ek sep′ting), *prep.* leaving out; other than; except; but. *—conj.* ARCHAIC. unless.

ex cep tion (ek sep′shən), *n.* 1 a leaving out; excepting: *I like all my studies, with the exception of German.* 2 person or thing left out: *She praised the pictures, with two exceptions.* 3 an unusual instance; case that does not follow the rule. 4 objection: *a statement liable to exception.* 5 **take exception, a** object. **b** be offended.

ex cep tion a ble (ek sep′shə nə bəl), *adj.* liable to exception; objectionable. **—ex cep′tion a bly,** *adv.*

ex cep tion al (ek sep′shə nəl), *adj.* out of the ordinary; unusual: *This warm weather is exceptional for January. He has exceptional ability as a leader.* **—ex cep′tion al ly,** *adv.*

ex cerpt (*n.* ek′sėrpt′; *v.* ek sėrpt′), *n.* passage taken out of a book, etc.; quotation; extract. *—v.t.* take out (passages) from a book, etc.; quote. [< Latin *excerptum* plucked out < *ex-* + *carpere* to pluck]

ex cess (*n.* ek ses′, *sometimes* ek′ses; *adj.* ek′ses, ek ses′), *n.* 1 part that is too much; more than enough; surplus: *Pour off the excess.* 2 condition of exceeding what is usual or necessary; superabundance. 3 amount or degree by which one thing is greater than another: *The excess of 7 over 5 is 2.* 4 action that goes beyond what is necessary or just: *The soldiers burned and robbed houses and committed other excesses.* 5 eating or drinking too much; over-indulgence; intemperance: *His excesses shortened his life.* 6 **in excess of,** more than. 7 **to excess,** too much. *—adj.* extra: *excess baggage on an airplane.* [< Latin *excessum* < *excedere.* See EXCEED.]

ex ces sive (ek ses′iv), *adj.* too much; too great; going beyond what is necessary or right. See synonym study below. **—ex ces′sive ly,** *adv.* **—ex ces′sive ness,** *n.*

Syn. Excessive, exorbitant, inordinate mean exceeding a right or proper limit. **Excessive** means going beyond what is right or normal in amount or extent: *She spends an excessive amount of time telephoning.* **Exorbitant** applies particularly to unreasonable prices or demands: *He asked an exorbitant rent for the house.* **Inordinate** emphasizes lack of restraint in desires: *He has an inordinate appetite.*

exch., exchange.

ex change (eks chānj′), *v.,* **-changed, -chang ing,** *n.* —*v.t.* 1 give (one thing) for another; change: *She would not exchange her house for a palace.* 2 give in trade for something regarded as equivalent: *I will exchange two dimes for twenty pennies.* 3 give and receive (things of the same kind): *exchange letters.* 4 replace or have replaced (a purchase): *We can exchange no yard goods.* —*v.i.* make an exchange.
—*n.* 1 an exchanging: *a fair exchange.* 2 act or process of bartering, interchanging, etc.: *an exchange of prisoners, an exchange of blows.* 3 person or thing given or received in exchange for another, or as a substitute. 4 place where people trade. Stocks are bought, sold, and traded in a stock exchange. 5 a central station or office. A telephone exchange handles telephone calls. 6 system of settling accounts between debtors and creditors without actual transference of money. Documents called bills of exchange represent money values given and received instead of money. 7 a changing the money of one country into the money of equivalent value of another. 8 fee charged for settling accounts or changing money. 9 rate at which money is given or received in return for the currency of the same or a foreign country.
[< Old French *eschangier,* ultimately < Latin *ex-* out + *cambiare* to change] —**ex change′a ble,** *adj.* —**ex chang′er,** *n.*

ex change a bil i ty (eks chān′jə bil′ə tē), *n.* state of being exchangeable.

exchange student, student participating in a program of trading students between countries or institutions.

ex cheq uer (eks chek′ər, eks′chek ər), *n.* 1 treasury, especially of a state or nation. 2 **Exchequer, a** department of the British government in charge of its finances and the public revenues. **b** offices of this department. 3 INFORMAL. finances; funds. [< Old French *eschequier* chessboard; because accounts were kept on a table covered with a cloth marked in squares]

ex cise[1] (ek′sīz, ek′sīs), *n.* tax on the manufacture, sale, or use of certain articles made, sold, or used within a country. [apparently < Middle Dutch *excijs* < Old French *acceis* tax, ultimately < Latin *ad-* to + *census* tax]

ex cise[2] (ek sīz′), *v.t.,* **-cised, -cis ing.** cut out; remove. [< Latin *excisum* excised < *ex-* out + *caedere* cut]

ex ci sion (ek sizh′ən), *n.* a cutting out; removal.

ex cit a bil i ty (ek sī′tə bil′ə tē), *n.* quality of being excitable.

ex cit a ble (ek sī′tə bəl), *adj.* 1 that can be excited; easily excited. 2 (in physiology) sensitive to or capable of responding to stimuli. —**ex cit′a ble ness,** *n.* —**ex cit′a bly,** *adv.*

ex ci ta tion (ek′sī tā′shən), *n.* 1 an exciting. 2 a being excited.

ex cite (ek sīt′), *v.t.,* **-cit ed, -cit ing.** 1 stir up the feelings of; rouse: *The news of war excited everybody.* 2 arouse: *Her new bicycle excited envy.* 3 stir to action; stimulate: *Do not excite the dog.* 4 affect (an organ, tissue, etc.) so that its usual activity is aroused or intensified. 5 produce an electric or magnetic field in (a dynamo, cyclotron, etc.). 6 displace one or more electrons of (an atom) to a higher level of energy. [< Latin *excitare* < *excitum* excited < *ex-* out + *ciere* to set in motion] —**ex cit′er,** *n.*

ex cit ed (ek sī′tid), *adj.* stirred up; arouse. —**ex cit′ed ly,** *adv.*

ex cite ment (ek sīt′mənt), *n.* 1 an excited condition. 2 thing that excites. 3 an exciting; arousing.

ex cit ing (ek sī′ting), *adj.* causing excitement; arousing. —**ex cit′ing ly,** *adv.*

ex claim (ek sklām′), *v.i., v.t.* say or speak suddenly in surprise or strong feeling; cry out. [< Latin *exclamare* < *ex-* out + *clamare* cry out]

ex cla ma tion (ek′sklə mā′shən), *n.* 1 something exclaimed; interjection. *Ah!* and *oh!* are exclamations. 2 an exclaiming.

exclamation mark or **exclamation point,** mark (!) of punctuation used after a word, phrase, or sentence to show that it was exclaimed.

ex clam a to ry (ek sklam′ə tôr′ē, ek sklam′ə tōr′ē), *adj.* using, containing, or expressing exclamation.

ex clude (ek sklüd′), *v.t.,* **-clud ed, -clud ing.** 1 shut out; keep out. See synonym study below. 2 drive out and keep out; expel; banish. [< Latin *excludere* < *ex-* out + *claudere* to shut] —**ex clud′a ble,** *adj.* —**ex clud′er,** *n.*

Syn. 1 Exclude, eliminate mean to keep out. **Exclude** emphasizes keeping someone or something from coming into a place, into consideration, etc.: *The government excludes immigrants who have certain diseases.* **Eliminate** emphasizes putting out something already in, by getting rid of it or shutting it off from attention: *He eliminated fear from his thinking.*

ex clu sion (ek sklü′zhən), *n.* 1 act of excluding. 2 condition of being excluded.

ex clu sive (ek sklü′siv, ek sklü′ziv), *adj.* 1 each shutting out the other. "Tree" and "animal" are exclusive terms since a thing cannot be both. 2 shutting out all or most others: *exclusive attention to instructions.* 3 not divided or shared with others; single; sole: *an exclusive right to an invention.* 4 very selective in choosing friends, members, patrons, etc.: *an exclusive club.* 5 **exclusive of,** excluding; leaving out; not counting or considering: *There are 26 days in that month, exclusive of Sundays.* —**ex clu′sive ly,** *adv.* —**ex clu′sive ness,** *n.*

ex cog i tate (ek skoj′ə tāt), *v.t.,* **-tat ed, -tat ing.** think out; devise; contrive. —**ex cog′i ta′tion,** *n.*

ex com mu ni cate (ek′skə myü′nə kāt), *v.t.,* **-cat ed, -cat ing.** cut off formally from membership in the church; shut out from communion with the church. —**ex′com mu′ni ca′tor,** *n.*

ex com mu ni ca tion (ek′skə myü′nə kā′shən), *n.* 1 a formal cutting off from membership in the church; prohibition from participating in any of the rites of the church. 2 an official statement announcing this.

ex co ri ate (ek skôr′ē āt, ek skōr′ē āt), *v.t.,* **-at ed, -at ing.** 1 strip or rub off the skin of; make raw and sore; abrade. 2 denounce violently. [< Late Latin *excoriatum* stripped of skin < Latin *ex-* off + *corium* hide, skin] —**ex co′ri a′tion,** *n.*

hat, āge, fär; let, ēqual, tėrm;
it, īce; hot, ōpen, ôrder;
oil, out; cup, pu̇t, rüle;
ch, child; ng, long; sh, she;
th, thin; ᴛʜ, then; zh, measure;

ə represents *a* in about, *e* in taken, *i* in pencil, *o* in lemon, *u* in circus.

< = from, derived from, taken from.

ex cre ment (ek′skrə mənt), *n.* waste matter that is discharged from the body, especially from the intestines. [< Latin *excrementum* < *excretum.* See EXCRETE.]

ex cre men tal (ek′skrə men′tl), *adj.* of or like excrement.

ex cres cence (ek skres′ns), *n.* 1 an unnatural growth. Warts are excrescences on the skin. 2 a natural outgrowth. Fingernails are excrescences.

ex cres cent (ek skres′nt), *adj.* forming an unnatural growth or a disfiguring addition. [< Latin *excrescentem* < *ex-* out + *crescere* grow]

ex cre ta (ek skrē′tə), *n.pl.* waste matter discharged from the body.

ex crete (ek skrēt′), *v.t.,* **-cret ed, -cret ing.** separate (waste matter) from the blood or tissues and discharge it from the body: *The sweat glands excrete sweat.* [< Latin *excretum* sifted out < *ex-* out + *cernere* to sift]

ex cre tion (ek skrē′shən), *n.* 1 act or process of discharging waste matter from the body. 2 the waste matter discharged.

ex cre to ry (ek′skrə tôr′ē, ek′skrə tōr′ē), *adj.* excreting; having the task of discharging waste matter from the body.

ex cru ci ate (ek skrü′shē āt), *v.t.,* **-at ed, -at ing.** cause great suffering to; pain very much; torture. [< Latin *excruciatum* tortured < *ex-* out + *cruciare* torture, crucify < *crucem* cross] —**ex cru′ci a′tion,** *n.*

ex cru ci at ing (ek skrü′shē ā′ting), *adj.* 1 causing great suffering; very painful; torturing. 2 excessively elaborate; extreme: *excruciating politeness.* —**ex cru′ci at′ing ly,** *adv.*

ex cul pate (ek′skul pāt, ek skul′pāt), *v.t.,* **-pat ed, -pat ing.** free from blame; prove innocent. [< Latin *ex-* out + *culpa* guilt] —**ex′cul pa′tion,** *n.*

ex cul pa to ry (ek skul′pə tôr′ē, ek skul′pə tōr′ē), *adj.* exculpating.

ex cur rent (ek skėr′ənt), *adj.* 1 giving exit. 2 having the axis prolonged so as to form an undivided main stem or trunk, as in the spruce tree.

ex cur sion (ek skėr′zhən, ek skėr′shən), *n.* 1 a short journey taken for interest or pleasure, often by a number of people together: *Our club went on an excursion to the mountains.* 2 trip on a train, ship, aircraft, etc., at fares lower than those usually charged. 3 group of people who go on an excursion. 4 a wandering from the subject; deviation; digression. 5 (in physics) the departure of a body from its main position or proper course. [< Latin *excursionem* < *ex-* out + *cursus* a running]

ex cur sion ist (ek skėr′zhə nist, ek skėr′shə nist), *n.* person who goes on an excursion.

ex cur sive (ek skėr′siv), *adj.* off the subject; rambling. —**ex cur′sive ly,** *adv.* —**ex cur′sive ness,** *n.*

ex cuse (*v.* ek skyüz′; *n.* ek skyüs′), *v.*, **-cused, -cus ing,** *n.* —*v.t.* 1 offer a reason or apology for; try to remove the blame of: *She excused her own faults by blaming others.* 2 be a reason or explanation for; clear of blame: *Sickness excuses absence from school.* 3 pardon or forgive: *Excuse me, I have to go now.* See synonym study below. 4 free from duty or obligation; let off: *Those who passed the first test will be excused from the second one.* 5 not demand or require; dispense with: *We will excuse your presence.* 6 **excuse oneself, a** ask to be pardoned. **b** ask permission to leave. —*n.* 1 a real or pretended reason or explanation. 2 apology given. 3 act of excusing. [< Latin *excusare* < *ex-* away + *causa* cause] **—ex cus′a ble,** *adj.* **—ex cus′a bly,** *adv.* **—ex cus′er,** *n.*

Syn. *v.t.* 3 **Excuse, pardon, forgive** mean to free from blame or punishment. **Excuse** means to overlook less important errors and faults: *He excused our failure to reply.* **Pardon** is used in a similar manner, but it can also mean to free from punishment due for serious faults, wrongdoing, or crimes: *The governor pardoned him and restored his civil rights.* **Forgive** suggests more personal feeling, and emphasizes giving up all wish to punish for wrong done: *I am sure his rudeness was unintentional, and I forgive him for it.*

exec., 1 executive. 2 executor.

ex e cra ble (ek′sə krə bəl), *adj.* abominable; detestable. **—ex′e cra ble ness,** *n.* **—ex′e cra bly,** *adv.*

ex e crate (ek′sə krāt), *v.*, **-crat ed, -crat ing.** —*v.t.* 1 feel intense loathing for; abhor; detest. 2 pronounce a curse upon. —*v.i.* curse. [< Latin *exsecratum* declared accursed < *ex-* out + *sacer* sacred] **—ex′e-cra′tor,** *n.*

ex e cra tion (ek′sə krā′shən), *n.* 1 act of execrating. 2 a curse: *The mob shouted angry execrations at the assassin.* 3 person or thing execrated.

ex e cute (ek′sə kyüt), *v.t.*, **-cut ed, -cut ing.** 1 carry out; do: *The nurse executed the doctor's orders.* See **perform** for synonym study. 2 put into effect; enforce: *Congress makes the laws; the President executes them.* 3 put to death according to a legal sentence or decree: *The murderer was executed.* 4 make according to a plan or design: *The same artist executed that painting and that statue.* 5 perform or play (a piece of music). 6 make (a deed, lease, contract, will, etc.) legal by signing, sealing, etc. [< Latin *exsecutum* followed out < *ex-* out + *sequi* follow] **—ex′e cut′er,** *n.*

ex e cu tion (ek′sə kyü′shən), *n.* 1 a carrying out (of a plan, purpose, command, etc.); doing. 2 a putting into effect; enforcing. 3 way of carrying out or doing; degree of skill in executing something. 4 manner of performing or playing a piece of music. 5 a putting to death according to a legal sentence or decree. 6 a making according to a plan or design. 7 a making legal by signing, sealing, etc. 8 a written order from a court of law directing a judgment to be carried out. 9 **do execution,** have a destructive effect; have an effective action.

ex e cu tion er (ek′sə kyü′shə nər), *n.* person who puts someone to death according to a legal sentence or decree.

ex ec u tive (eg zek′yə tiv), *adj.* 1 having to do with carrying out or managing affairs: *The head of a school has an executive position.* 2 for or by an executive or executives. 3 having the duty and power of putting the laws into effect: *The President of the United States is the head of the executive branch of the government.* —*n.* 1 person who carries out or manages affairs. 2 person, group, or branch of government that has the duty and power of putting the laws into effect. **—ex-ec′u tive ly,** *adv.*

Executive Mansion, U.S. 1 the White House in Washington, D.C. 2 the official residence of the governor in some states.

executive session, meeting or session of a legislative body in which it serves as a council to the executive.

ex ec u tor (eg zek′yə tər *for 1;* ek′sə-kyü′tər *for 2*), *n.* 1 person named in a will to carry out the provisions of the will. 2 person who performs or carries out something.

ex ec u trix (eg zek′yə triks), *n.*, *pl.* **ex ec u trix es, ex ec u tri ces** (eg zek′yə-trī′sēz′). a woman executor.

ex e ge sis (ek′sə jē′sis), *n.*, *pl.* **-ses** (-sēz′). 1 a scholarly explanation or interpretation of the Bible or of a passage in the Bible: *an exegesis of the parable.* 2 explanation or interpretation of a word, sentence, etc.; explanatory note. [< Greek *exēgēsis* < *exegeesthai* interpret < *ex-* out + *hegeesthai* to lead, guide]

ex e gete (ek′sə jēt′), *n.* person skilled in exegesis; interpreter.

ex em plar (eg zem′plər, eg zem′plär), *n.* 1 person or thing worth imitating; good model or pattern: *Justice Oliver Wendell Holmes was the exemplar of the humane jurist.* 2 archetype. 3 a typical case; example. [< Latin < *exemplum.* See EXAMPLE.]

ex em plar y (eg zem′plər ē, eg′zəm-pler′ē), *adj.* 1 worth imitating; serving as a model or pattern: *exemplary conduct.* 2 serving as a warning to others: *exemplary punishment.* 3 serving as an example; typical. **—ex-em′plar i ly,** *adv.* **—ex em′plar i ness,** *n.*

ex em pli fi ca tion (eg zem′plə fə kā′-shən), *n.* 1 a showing by example; being an example. 2 example.

ex em pli fy (eg zem′plə fī), *v.t.*, **-fied, -fy ing.** show by example; be an example of: *Knights exemplified courage and courtesy.*

ex empt (eg zempt′), *v.t.* make free (from a duty, obligation, rule, etc., to which others are subject); release: *be exempted from the final examination.* —*adj.* freed from a duty, obligation, rule, etc., to which others are subject; released: *School property is exempt from all taxes.* [< Latin *exemptum* taken out < *ex-* out + *emere* take]

ex emp tion (eg zemp′shən), *n.* 1 act of exempting. 2 freedom from a duty, obligation, rule, etc.; release. See synonym study below. 3 instance of such a release or a cause permitting one: *income-tax exemptions.*

Syn. 2 **Exemption, immunity** mean freedom from obligations, duties, rules, etc., imposed on others. **Exemption** implies freeing a person or thing from a legal obligation or rule: *exemption from jury duty.* **Immunity** implies freedom from restrictions and penalties: *Ambassadors have immunity from prosecution under the laws of the United States.*

ex er cise (ek′sər sīz), *n.*, *v.*, **-cised, -cis ing.** —*n.* 1 active use of the body or mind for their improvement or as a means of training for any kind of activity. See synonym study below. 2 something that gives practice and training or causes improvement: *Study the lesson, and then do the exercises at the end.* 3 active use; application: *Safety requires the exercise of care.* 4 Often, **exercises,** *pl.* ceremony: *The opening exercises in our Sunday school are a song and a prayer.* —*v.t.* 1 make active use of; employ; apply: *When you vote you exercise your right as a citizen. Exercise caution in crossing streets.* 2 give exercise to; train; drill. 3 carry out in action; perform: *The mayor exercises the duties and powers of his office.* 4 bring into effect; exert: *What others think exercises a great influence on most of us.* 5 occupy the attention of. 6 make uneasy; worry, trouble, or annoy: *When her plan failed, she was greatly exercised.* —*v.i.* take exercise; go through exercises. [< Old French *exercice* < Latin *exercitium* < *exercere* keep busy < *ex-* out + *arcere* prevent] **—ex′er cis′a-ble,** *adj.* **—ex′er cis′er,** *n.*

Syn. *n.* 1 **Exercise, practice, drill** mean active use of physical or mental power for training or improvement. **Exercise** implies repeated use of mental or physical powers to develop strength, health, and energy: *Exercise of the mind increases its power.* **Practice** implies action repeated often and regularly to develop skill or gain perfection, especially in the use of a particular power: *Learning to play the piano well takes much practice.* **Drill** implies constant repetition of a particular kind of exercise to discipline the body or mind and develop correct habits: *drill in spelling.*

ex ert (eg zėrt′), *v.t.* 1 put into use or action; bring into effect; use: *exert both strength and skill, exert authority.* 2 **exert oneself,** make an effort; try hard; strive. [< Latin *exsertum* thrust out < *ex-* out + *serere* attach]

ex er tion (eg zėr′shən), *n.* 1 strenuous action; effort: *The exertions of the firemen kept the fire from spreading.* 2 a putting into action; active use; use: *exertion of authority.*

ex e unt (ek′sē ənt), *v.i.* LATIN. they go out (a stage direction for two or more actors to leave the stage).

ex fo li ate (eks fō′lē āt), *v.*, **-at ed, -at ing.** —*v.i.* come off in scales or layers (of bone, skin, minerals, etc.). —*v.t.* throw off in scales or layers. **—ex fo′li a′tion,** *n.*

ex fo li a tive (eks fō′lē ā′tiv), *adj.* exfoliating.

ex gra ti a (eks grā′shē ə), LATIN. from grace or favor, rather than from legal right: *an ex gratia payment.*

ex ha la tion (eks′hə lā′shən), *n.* 1 an exhaling. 2 something exhaled.

ex hale (eks hāl′), *v.*, **-haled, -hal ing.** —*v.t.* 1 breathe out: *We exhale air from our lungs.* 2 give off (air, vapor, smoke, odor, etc.). 3 change into vapor; evaporate. —*v.i.* 1 breathe out air or vapor. 2 pass off as vapor; rise like vapor: *Sweet odors exhale from the flowers.* [< Latin *exhalare* < *ex-* out + *halare* breathe]

ex haust (eg zôst′), *v.t.* 1 empty completely: *exhaust an oil well.* 2 use up; consume: *exhaust one's money, exhaust one's strength.* 3 tire very much: *The long, hard climb up the hill exhausted us.* 4 drain of strength, resources, etc.: *exhaust the soil. The long war exhausted the country.* 5 draw off: *exhaust the air in a jar.* 6 leave nothing important to be found out or said about; study or treat thoroughly: *Her book about tulips exhausted the subject.* —*v.i.* be discharged; go forth: *Gases from an automobile exhaust through a pipe.* —*n.* 1 the escape of used steam, spent gases, etc., from an engine. 2 pipe or other means for used steam, spent gases, etc., to escape from an engine. 3 duct through which used air passes, especially in an air-conditioning system. 4 the used steam, spent gases, used air, etc., that escape. [< Latin *exhaustum* drawn off < *ex-* out, off + *haurire* draw]

ex haust ed (eg zô′stid), *adj.* 1 used up. 2 worn out; very tired. See **tired** for synonym study.

ex haust i bil i ty (eg zô′stə bil′ə tē), *n.* quality of being exhaustible.

ex haust i ble (eg zô′stə bəl), *adj.* that can be exhausted.

ex haus tion (eg zôs′chən), *n.* 1 act of exhausting. 2 condition of being exhausted. 3 extreme fatigue; weariness.

ex haus tive (eg zô′stiv), *adj.* 1 tending to exhaust or drain of strength, resources, etc. 2 leaving out nothing important; thorough; comprehensive: *an exhaustive examination.* **—ex haus′tive ly,** *adv.* **—ex haus′tive ness,** *n.*

ex haust less (eg zôst′lis), *adj.* that cannot be exhausted; inexhaustible.

exhaust manifold, the pipe or set of pipes in an internal-combustion engine that conveys the spent gases from the cylinders to the exhaust pipe.

exhaust pipe, the pipe in an engine which carries away used steam or spent gases, as the pipe in an automobile engine from the exhaust manifold to the muffler, and sometimes including the tail pipe.

ex hib it (eg zib′it), *v.t.* 1 let be seen; show plainly; display: *He exhibits interest whenever you talk about dogs.* See **display** for synonym study. 2 show publicly; put on display: *He hopes to exhibit his paintings in New York.* 3 show in court as evidence. *—n.* 1 show; display. 2 an exhibiting; public showing. 3 thing or things shown publicly. See synonym study below. 4 document, object, etc., shown in court as evidence. [< Latin *exhibitum* held out, displayed < *ex-* out + *habere* hold]

Syn. *n.* 3 **Exhibit, exhibition** mean a public show. **Exhibit** applies particularly to an object or collection of things put on view that is usually part of a larger show: *His calf was part of the school's exhibit at the county fair.* **Exhibition** applies to a showing of art or art objects or to a public show of any kind having many parts: *The city holds an exhibition of all its different products every year.*

ex hib it er (eg zib′ə tər), *n.* exhibitor.

ex hi bi tion (ek′sə bish′ən), *n.* 1 an exhibiting; display: *an exhibition of bad manners.* 2 a public show: *The art school holds an exhibition every year.* See **exhibit** for synonym study. 3 thing or things shown publicly; exhibit.

ex hi bi tion ism (ek′sə bish′ə niz′əm), *n.* 1 an excessive tendency to seek attention or to show off one's abilities. 2 tendency toward indecent display.

ex hi bi tion ist (ek′sə bish′ə nist), *n.* person given to exhibitionism.

ex hi bi tion is tic (ek′sə bish′ə nis′tik), *adj.* 1 of or having to do with exhibitionism. 2 tending toward exhibitionism.

ex hib i tor (eg zib′ə tər), *n.* person, company, or group that exhibits. Also, **exhibiter.**

ex hil a rate (eg zil′ə rāt′), *v.t.,* **-rat ed, -rat ing.** make merry or lively; put into high spirits; cheer: *The joy of the holiday season exhilarates us all.* [< Latin *exhilaratum* made merry < *ex-* thoroughly + *hilaris* merry]

ex hil a ra tion (eg zil′ə rā′shən), *n.* 1 a being or feeling exhilarated; high spirits; lively joy. 2 an exhilarating.

ex hil a ra tive (eg zil′ə rā′tiv), *adj.* tending to exhilarate.

ex hort (eg zôrt′), *v.t.* urge strongly; advise or warn earnestly: *The preacher exhorted his congregation to live better lives.* [< Latin *exhortari* < *ex-* + *hortari* urge strongly] **—ex hort′er,** *n.*

ex hor ta tion (eg′zôr tā′shən, ek′sôr tā′shən), *n.* 1 strong urging; earnest advice or warning. 2 speech, sermon, etc., that exhorts.

ex hor ta tive (eg zôr′tə tiv), *adj.* exhortatory.

ex hor ta to ry (eg zôr′tə tôr′ē, eg zôr′tə tōr′ē), *adj.* intended to exhort; exhorting; urging; admonitory.

ex hu ma tion (eks′hyə mā′shən), *n.* act of exhuming.

ex hume (eks hyüm′, eg zyüm′), *v.t.,* **-humed, -hum ing.** 1 dig (a dead body) out of a grave or the ground; disinter. 2 bring to light; reveal. [< Medieval Latin *exhumare* < Latin *ex-* out of + *humus* ground] **—ex hum′er,** *n.*

ex i gence (ek′sə jəns), *n.* exigency.

ex i gen cy (ek′sə jən sē), *n., pl.* **-cies.** 1 situation demanding prompt action or attention; urgent case; emergency. 2 Often, **exigencies,** *pl.* an urgent need; demand for prompt action or attention: *The exigencies of business kept him from taking a vacation.*

ex i gent (ek′sə jənt), *adj.* 1 demanding prompt action or attention; urgent; pressing. 2 demanding a great deal; exacting. [< Latin *exigentem* < *ex-* out + *agere* to drive] **—ex′i gent ly,** *adv.*

ex i gu i ty (ek′sə gyü′ə tē), *n.* scantiness; smallness.

ex ig u ous (eg zig′yü əs, ek sig′yü əs), *adj.* scanty in measure or number; extremely small. [< Latin *exiguus* scanty, originally, weighed out (sparingly)] **—ex ig′u ous ly,** *adv.*

ex ile (eg′zīl, ek′sīl), *v.,* **-iled, -il ing,** *n.* *—v.t.* 1 force (a person) to leave his country or home, often by law as a punishment; banish. 2 remove (oneself) from one's country or home for a long time. See **banish** for synonym study. *—n.* 1 person who is exiled. 2 condition of being exiled; banishment. 3 any prolonged absence from one's own country. [< Old French *exilier* < Latin *exiliare* < *exilium* period or place of exile]

ex ist (eg zist′), *v.i.* 1 have being; be: *The world has existed a long time.* 2 be real: *He believes that ghosts exist.* 3 have life; live: *A person cannot exist without air.* 4 be found; occur: *Cases exist of persons who have no sense of smell.* [< Latin *exsistere* < *ex-* forth + *sistere* to stand]

ex ist ence (eg zis′təns), *n.* 1 being: *When we are born, we come into existence.* 2 a being real: *Most people do not now believe in the existence of ghosts.* 3 life: *Drivers of racing cars lead a dangerous existence.* 4 occurrence; presence. 5 all that exists. 6 thing that exists; a being.

ex ist ent (eg zis′tənt), *adj.* 1 that exists; existing. 2 now existing; of the present time; current.

ex is ten tial (eg′zi sten′shəl, ek′si sten′shəl), *adj.* of or having to do with existentialism.

ex is ten tial ism (eg′zi sten′shə liz′əm, ek′si sten′shə liz′əm), *n.* philosophy which holds that reality consists of living and that man makes himself what he is and is responsible to himself alone.

hat, āge, fär; let, ēqual, tėrm;
it, īce; hot, ōpen, ôrder;
oil, out; cup, pu̇t, rüle;
ch, child; ng, long; sh, she;
th, thin; ᴛʜ, then; zh, measure;

ə represents *a* in about, *e* in taken, *i* in pencil, *o* in lemon, *u* in circus.

< = from, derived from, taken from.

ex is ten tial ist (eg′zi sten′shə list, ek′si sten′shə list), *adj.* having to do with existentialism. *—n.* person who believes in existentialism.

ex it (eg′zit, ek′sit), *n.* 1 way out: *The theater had six exits.* 2 a going out; departure. 3 act of leaving the stage: *The actor made a graceful exit.* *—v.i.* 1 go out; leave. 2 LATIN. he goes out (a stage direction for an actor to leave the stage). [< Latin, he goes out < *ex-* out + *ire* go]

ex li bris (eks lī′bris; eks lē′bris), 1 from the library (of). 2 bookplate. [< Latin, from the books]

exo-, *prefix.* outside; outer: *Exoskeleton = outer skeleton.* [< Greek *exō* without]

ex o bi ol o gy (ek′sō bī ol′ə jē), *n.* study of life on other planets or celestial bodies.

ex o bi o ta (ek′sō bī ō′tə), *n.pl.* animal and plant life outside the earth or its atmosphere. [< New Latin *exo-* + Greek *bios* life]

ex o carp (ek′sō kärp), *n.* epicarp.

ex o crine (ek′sə krīn, ek′sə krən), *adj.* (of a gland) secreting outwardly, through a duct or into a cavity. [< *exo-* + Greek *krinein* to separate]

ex o dus (ek′sə dəs), *n.* 1 a going out; departure, usually of a large number of people. 2 **the Exodus,** the departure of the Israelites from Egypt under Moses. 3 **Exodus,** the second book of the Old Testament, containing an account of this departure. [< Latin *Exodus* (def. 3) < Greek *exodos* < *ex-* out + *hodos* way]

ex of fi ci o (eks ə fish′ē ō), because of one's office: *The Vice-President is, ex officio, the presiding officer of the Senate.* [< Latin]

ex og a mous (ek sog′ə məs), *adj.* of or having to do with exogamy.

ex og a my (ek sog′ə mē), *n.* custom of marrying only outside of one's own tribe or group. [< *exo-* + Greek *gamos* marriage]

ex og e nous (ek soj′ə nəs), *adj.* 1 (in botany) having stems that grow by the addition of layers of wood on the outside under the bark. 2 originating from the outside; caused by external conditions.

ex on e rate (eg zon′ə rāt′), *v.t.,* **-rat ed, -rat ing.** free from blame; prove or declare innocent: *Witnesses to the accident completely exonerated the truck driver.* [< Latin *exoneratum* freed from burden < *ex-* off + *onerem* burden] **—ex on′e ra′tion,** *n.*

ex on e ra tive (eg zon′ə rā′tiv), *adj.* tending to exonerate.

ex or bi tance (eg zôr′bə təns), *n.* a being exorbitant.

ex or bi tant (eg zôr′bə tənt), *adj.* exceeding what is customary, proper, or reasonable; unreasonably excessive: *One dollar is an exorbitant price for a pack of bubble gum.* See **excessive** for synonym study. [< Latin *exorbitantem* going out of the track < *ex-* out of + *orbita* track] **—ex or′bi tant ly,** *adv.*

ex or cise (ek′sôr sīz), *v.t.,* **-cised, -cis ing.** 1 drive out (an evil spirit) by prayers, ceremonies, etc. 2 free (a person or place) from an evil spirit. Also, **exorcize.** [< Late Latin *exorcizare* < Greek *exorkizein* < *ex-* + *horkizein* bind by oath < *horkos* oath] **—ex′or cis′er,** *n.*

ex or cism (ek′sôr siz′əm), *n.* 1 an exorcising. 2 the prayers, ceremonies, etc., used in exorcising.

ex or cist (ek′sôr sist), *n.* person who exorcises.

ex or cize (ek′sôr sīz), *v.t.,* **-cized, -ciz ing.** exorcise.

ex or di al (eg zôr′dē əl, ek sôr′dē əl), *adj.* 1 of an exordium. 2 introductory.

ex or di um (eg zôr′dē əm, ek sôr′dē əm), *n., pl.* **-di ums, -di a** (-dē ə). 1 the beginning. 2 the introductory part of a speech, treatise, etc. [< Latin < *ex-* + *ordiri* begin]

ex o skel e ton (ek′sō skel′ə tən), *n.* any hard, external covering or structure which protects or supports the body, such as the shells of turtles and lobsters.

ex o sphere (ek′sō sfir), *n.* the outermost region of the atmosphere beyond the ionosphere. See **atmosphere** for diagram.

ex o ter ic (ek′sə ter′ik), *adj.* 1 capable of being understood by the general public. 2 not belonging to an inner circle of disciples, scholars, etc. 3 popular; commonplace. [< Greek *exōterikos* < *exōtero* farther outside < *exō* outside]

ex o ther mic (ek′sō thėr′mik), *adj.* of or indicating a chemical change accompanied by a liberation of heat.

ex ot ic (eg zot′ik), *adj.* 1 from a foreign country; not native: *We saw many exotic plants at the flower show.* 2 fascinating or interesting because strange or different: *an exotic tropical island.* —*n.* an exotic person or thing. [< Greek *exōtikos* < *exō* outside < *ex* out of] **—ex ot′i cal ly,** *adv.*

ex ot i cism (eg zot′ə siz′əm), *n.* 1 condition or quality of being exotic. 2 something exotic.

ex o tox in (ek′sō tok′sən), *n.* toxin secreted by a living microorganism.

exp., 1 expenses. 2 export. 3 express.

ex pand (ek spand′), *v.t.* 1 make larger; increase in size; enlarge; swell. See synonym study below. 2 spread out; open out; unfold; extend: *A bird expands its wings before flying.* 3 express in fuller form or greater detail: *expand a mathematical equation. The writer expanded one sentence into a paragraph.* —*v.i.* 1 grow or become larger. See synonym study below. 2 unfold; open out. [< Latin *expandere* < *ex-* out + *pandere* to spread. Doublet of SPAWN.] **—ex pand′a ble,** *adj.* **—ex pand′er,** *n.*

Syn. *v.t., v.i.* 1 **Expand, swell, dilate** mean to make or become larger. **Expand** implies spreading out or opening out in any or all directions: *Heat expands metal. Our country expanded with the addition of new territory.* **Swell** implies growing bigger, usually from pressure inside or from having something added: *His abscessed tooth made his face swell.* **Dilate** implies widening, and applies particularly to circular or hollow things: *The doctor dilates the pupils of your eyes when he examines them.*

ex panse (ek spans′), *n.* 1 a large, open or unbroken space or stretch; wide, spreading surface: *The Pacific Ocean is a vast expanse of water.* 2 amount or distance of expansion.

ex pan si bil i ty (ek span′sə bil′ə tē), *n.* capacity for expanding.

ex pan si ble (ek span′sə bəl), *adj.* that can be expanded.

ex pan sile (ek span′səl), *adj.* 1 capable of expanding. 2 of or having to do with expansion.

ex pan sion (ek span′shən), *n.* 1 an expanding: *Heat caused the expansion of the gas.* 2 a being expanded; increase in size, volume, etc.: *The expansion of the factory made room for more machines.* 3 an expanded part or form: *That book is an expansion of a magazine article.* 4 anything that is spread out; expanse. 5 amount or degree of expansion. 6 (in mathematics) the fuller development of an indicated operation: *The expansion of* $(a+b)^3$ *is* $a^3 + 3a^2b + 3ab^2 + b^3$.

ex pan sion ism (ek span′shə niz′əm), *n.* policy of expansion, as of territory or currency.

ex pan sive (ek span′siv), *adj.* 1 capable of expanding; tending to expand: *expansive gases.* 2 capable of causing expansion: *expansive force of heat.* 3 expanding over a large surface or space; wide; spreading: *an expansive lake.* 4 taking in much or many things; having a wide range; broad; extensive: *an expansive view of history.* 5 showing one's feelings freely and openly; unrestrained; demonstrative. **—ex pan′sive ly,** *adv.* **—ex pan′sive ness,** *n.*

ex par te (eks pär′tē), 1 from one side only. 2 in the interest of only one side. [< Latin]

ex pa ti ate (ek spā′shē āt), *v.i.,* **-at ed, -at ing.** write or talk much *(on): She expatiated on the thrills of her trip to Hawaii.* [< Latin *expatiatum* digressed < *ex-* out + *spatium* space] **—ex pa′ti a′tion,** *n.* **—ex pa′ti a′tor,** *n.*

ex pa tri ate (*v.* ek spā′trē āt; *n., adj.* ek spā′trē it, ek spā′trē āt), *v.,* **-at ed, -at ing,** *n., adj.* —*v.t.* 1 force to leave one's country; banish; exile. 2 withdraw (oneself) from one's country; renounce one's citizenship. —*n.* an expatriated person; exile. —*adj.* expatriated. [ultimately < Latin *ex-* out of + *patria* fatherland] **—ex pa′tri a′tion,** *n.*

ex pect (ek spekt′), *v.t.* 1 think something will probably come or happen; look forward to. See synonym study below. 2 look forward to with reason or confidence: *I shall expect to find that job finished by Saturday.* 3 count on as necessary or right: *A nation expects support from its allies.* 4 INFORMAL. think; suppose; guess. —*v.i.* **be expecting,** be pregnant. [< Latin *exspectare* < *ex-* out + *specere* to look] **—ex pect′a ble,** *adj.*

Syn. *v.t.* 1 **Expect, anticipate** mean to look forward to a future event. **Expect** implies some certainty or confidence that it will occur: *He expects to take a vacation in May.* **Anticipate** means to look forward with pleasure or dread to something which one expects to occur: *He anticipates a wonderful vacation.*

ex pect ance (ek spek′təns), *n.* expectation.

ex pect an cy (ek spek′tən sē), *n., pl.* **-cies.** 1 expectation. 2 something expected or that can be expected.

ex pect ant (ek spek′tənt), *adj.* 1 having expectations; looking for; expecting. 2 showing expectation: *an expectant smile.* —*n.* person who expects something. **—ex pect′ant ly,** *adv.*

ex pec ta tion (ek′spek tā′shən), *n.* 1 an expecting; anticipation. 2 a being expected. 3 something expected. 4 good reason for expecting something; prospect: *He has expectations of inheriting money from a rich uncle.*

ex pec tor ant (ek spek′tər ənt), *adj.* causing or helping the discharge of phlegm, etc. —*n.* medicine that promotes expectoration.

ex pec to rate (ek spek′tə rāt′), *v.,* **-rat ed, -rat ing.** —*v.t.* cough up and spit out (phlegm, etc.); spit. —*v.i.* spit. [< Latin *expectoratum* cast out from the breast < *ex-* out of + *pectorem* breast]

ex pec to ra tion (ek spek′tə rā′shən), *n.* 1 act of expectorating. 2 expectorated matter.

ex pe di ence (ek spē′dē əns), *n.* expediency.

ex pe di en cy (ek spē′dē ən sē), *n., pl.* **-cies.** 1 a helping to bring about a desired result; desirability or fitness under the circumstances; usefulness. 2 personal advantage; self-interest: *The salesman was influenced more by the expediency of making a sale than by the needs of the buyer.*

ex pe di ent (ek spē′dē ənt), *adj.* 1 helping to bring about a desired result; desirable or suitable under the circumstances; useful; advantageous. 2 giving or seeking personal advantage; based on self-interest. —*n.* means of bringing about a desired result: *Having no packaged mix, I made a cake by the expedient of mixing my own ingredients.* **—ex pe′di ent ly,** *adv.*

ex pe dite (ek′spə dīt), *v.t.,* **-dit ed, -dit ing.** 1 make easy and quick; hasten the progress of; speed up: *If everyone will help, it will expedite matters.* 2 do or perform quickly. 3 issue officially; dispatch. [< Latin *expeditum* freed from entanglement < *ex-* out + *pedem* foot]

ex pe dit er (ek′spə dī′tər), *n.* person who is responsible for supplying raw materials or delivering finished products on schedule. Also, **expeditor.**

ex pe di tion (ek′spə dish′ən), *n.* 1 journey for some special purpose. A voyage of discovery or a march against the enemy is an expedition. 2 the people, ships, etc., making such a journey. 3 efficient and prompt action; speed.

ex pe di tion ar y (ek′spə dish′ə ner′ē), *adj.* of, having to do with, or making up an expedition: *an expeditionary army.*

ex pe di tious (ek′spə dish′əs), *adj.* efficient and prompt. **—ex′pe di′tious ly,** *adv.* **—ex′pe di′tious ness,** *n.*

ex pe di tor (ek′spə dī′ter), *n.* expediter.

ex pel (ek spel′), *v.t.,* **-pelled, -pel ling.** 1 drive out with much force; force out; eject: *When we exhale we expel air from our lungs.* 2 put (a person) out; dismiss permanently: *A boy who cheats or steals may be expelled from school.* [< Latin *expellere* < *ex-* out + *pellere* to drive] **—ex pel′la ble,** *adj.*

ex pend (ek spend′), *v.t.* use up; spend: *expend time and money on a project.* See **spend** for synonym study. [< Latin *expendere* < *ex-* + *pendere* weigh, pay. Doublet of SPEND.] **—ex pend′er,** *n.*

ex pend a bil i ty (ek spen′də bil′ə tē), *n.* quality or condition of being expendable.

ex pend a ble (ek spen′də bəl), *adj.* 1 that can be expended or used up. 2 in military use: **a** normally used up in service, battle, etc. **b** worth giving up or sacrificing for strategic reasons. —*n.* Usually, **expendables,** *pl.* expendable persons or things.

ex pend i ture (ek spen′də chůr, ek spen′də chər), *n.* 1 a using up; spending: *To keep such a large house in good repair requires the expenditure of much money, time, and effort.* 2 amount of money, etc., spent; expense: *Limit your expenditures to what is necessary.*

ex pense (ek spens′), *n.* 1 amount of money, etc., spent; cost; charge: *The expense of the trip for the youngest child was slight. He traveled at his uncle's expense.* 2 an expending; paying out of money; outlay: *A boy at college puts his father to considerable expense.* 3 cause of spending: *Running an automobile is an expense.* 4 **expenses,** *pl.* **a** charges incurred in doing something. **b** money to repay such charges: *A traveling salesman often receives expenses besides his salary.* 5 loss or sacrifice: *The town was captured at great expense to the victors.* **6 at the expense of, a** so as to be paid for by. **b** with the loss or sacrifice of.

expense account, record of expenditure charged to or reimbursed by an employer or company, especially for travel.

ex pen sive (ek spen′siv), *adj.* costly; high-priced. **—ex pen′sive ly,** *adv.* **—ex pen′sive ness,** *n.*

Syn. Expensive, costly, dear mean costing much. **Expensive** implies that the price is more than one can afford or than the thing is worth: *He had a very expensive pocketknife which cost $10.* **Costly** implies that the price, though very high, is justified by the worth of the article: *A diamond is costly.* **Dear** implies that the price is higher than usual: *Meat is dear this week.*

ex per i ence (ek spir′ē əns), *n., v.,* **-enced, -enc ing.** *—n.* 1 what happens or has happened to one; anything or everything met with, observed, done, felt, or lived through: *We had many pleasant experiences on our trips. People often learn by experience.* 2 all of the actions, events, or states, which make up the life of a person, a community, a race, etc.: *Nothing in human experience has prepared man for space travel.* 3 knowledge or skill gained by observing, doing, or living through things; practice: *Have you had any experience in this kind of work?* *—v.t.* have happen to one; meet with; live through; feel. See synonym study below. [< Latin *experientia* < *ex-* out + *peri* to try]

Syn. *—v.t.* **Experience, undergo** mean to go through something in life. **Experience** implies either pleasantness or unpleasantness, brevity or length, importance or unimportance: *Visiting India was the greatest thrill I ever experienced.* **Undergo** implies unpleasantness, pain, or danger: *I had to undergo disappointment and failure before experiencing success.*

ex per i enced (ek spir′ē ənst), *adj.* 1 having experience; taught by experience. 2 skillful or wise because of experience: *an experienced nurse.*

ex per i en tial (ek spir′ē en′shəl), *adj.* having to do with or based on experience.

ex per i ment (*v.* ek sper′ə ment; *n.* ek sper′ə mənt), *v.i.* 1 try something in order to find out about it; make trials or tests: *That painter is experimenting with different paints to get the color he wants.* *—n.* 1 trial or test to find out or discover something unknown, to verify a hypothesis, or to illustrate some known truth. See **trial** for synonym study. 2 a conducting of such trials or tests; experimentation: *Scientists test out theories by experiments.* **—ex per′i ment′er,** *n.*

ex per i men tal (ek sper′ə men′tl), *adj.* 1 based on experiments: *Chemistry is an experimental science.* 2 used for experiments: *A new variety of wheat was developed at the experimental farm.* 3 for testing or trying out: *experimental attempts to fly.* 4 based on experience, not on theory or authority. **—ex per′i men′tal ly,** *adv.*

ex per i men ta tion (ek sper′ə men tā′shən), *n.* an experimenting: *Cures for diseases are often found by experimentation on animals.*

ex pert (*n.* ek′spėrt′; *adj.* ek spėrt′, ek′spėrt′), *n.* a very skillful person; person who knows a great deal about some special thing. *—adj.* 1 very skillful; knowing a great deal about some special thing. See synonym study below. 2 of or from an expert; requiring or showing special skill: *expert workmanship, expert testimony.* [< Latin *expertum* tried, tested < *ex-* out + *-periri-* to try] **—ex pert′ly,** *adv.* **—ex pert′ness,** *n.*

Syn. *adj.* 1 **Expert, proficient, skilled** mean having the training and knowledge to do a special thing well. **Expert** implies having mastery or unusual ability: *He is an expert chemist.* **Proficient** implies being very good at doing something, but not having complete mastery or unusual ability: *She is proficient at sewing.* **Skilled** implies knowing thoroughly how to do something, and being competent at doing it: *He is a skilled mechanic.*

ex pert ise (ek′spər tēz′), *n.* expert knowledge or opinion.

ex pi a ble (ek′spē ə bəl), *adj.* that can be expiated.

ex pi ate (ek′spē āt), *v.t.,* **-at ed, -at ing.** pay the penalty of; make amends for a wrong, sin, etc.; atone for. [< Latin *expiatum* atoned completely < *ex-* completely + *piare* appease < *pius* devout] **—ex′pi a′tor,** *n.*

ex pi a tion (ek′spē ā′shən), *n.* 1 a making amends for a wrong, sin, etc.; atonement. 2 means of atonement; amends.

ex pi a to ry (ek′spē ə tôr′ē, ek′spē ə tōr′ē), *adj.* expiating; atoning.

ex pi ra tion (ek′spə rā′shən), *n.* 1 a coming to an end; termination: *the expiration of a lease.* 2 a breathing out; exhalation.

ex pir a to ry (ek spī′rə tôr′ē, ek spī′rə tōr′ē), *adj.* of or having to do with breathing out or exhalation.

ex pire (ek spīr′), *v.,* **-pired, -pir ing.** *—v.i.* 1 come to an end: *You must obtain a new automobile license when your old one expires.* 2 die. 3 breathe out; exhale. *—v.t.* breathe out (air); exhale. [< Latin *exspirare* < *ex-* out + *spirare* breathe]

ex pi ry (ek spī′rē, ek′spər ē), *n., pl.* **-ries.** 1 expiration. 2 dying; death.

ex plain (ek splān′), *v.t.* 1 make plain or clear; tell how to do. 2 tell the meaning of; interpret. See synonym study below. 3 give reasons for; account for. 4 **explain away,** nullify or deprive of force by giving reasons. 5 **explain oneself, a** make one's meaning plain or clear. **b** give reasons for one's behavior. *—v.i.* give an explanation. [< Latin *explanare* make plain < *ex-* out + *planus* plain, flat] **—ex plain′a ble,** *adj.* **—ex plain′er,** *n.*

Syn. *v.t.* 1, 2 **Explain, interpret** mean to make plain or understandable. **Explain** means to make clear something that is not understood: *He explained the problem in arithmetic.* **Interpret** means to explain or bring out more than the obvious meaning of something by using special knowledge, unusual understanding, or imagination: *She interpreted the poem for us.*

hat, āge, fär; let, ēqual, tėrm;
it, īce; hot, ōpen, ôrder;
oil, out; cup, půt, rüle;
ch, child; ng, long; sh, she;
th, thin; ᴛʜ, then; zh, measure;

ə represents *a* in about, *e* in taken, *i* in pencil, *o* in lemon, *u* in circus.

< = from, derived from, taken from.

ex pla na tion (ek′splə nā′shən), *n.* 1 an explaining; clearing up a difficulty or mistake. 2 something that explains.

ex plan a to ry (ek splan′ə tôr′ē, ek splan′ə tōr′ē), *adj.* that explains; serving or helping to explain: *Read the explanatory part of the lesson before you try to do the problems.* **—ex plan′a to′ri ly,** *adv.*

ex ple tive (ek′splə tiv), *n.* 1 syllable, word, or phrase used for filling out a sentence or a line of verse, without adding to the sense. In "There is a book on the table," *there* is an expletive. 2 oath or exclamation; interjection. "Damn" and "My goodness" are expletives. *—adj.* filling out a sentence or line of verse; completing. [< Late Latin *expletivus* < Latin *explere* fill up < *ex-* out + *plere* fill]

ex pli ca ble (ek splik′ə bəl, ek′splə kə bəl), *adj.* that can be explained.

ex pli cate (ek′splə kāt), *v.t.,* **-cat ed, -cat ing.** 1 develop (a principle, doctrine, etc.). 2 make clear the meaning of (anything); explain. [< Latin *explicatum* unfolded < *ex-* out + *plicare* to fold] **—ex′pli ca′tor,** *n.*

ex pli ca tion (ek′splə kā′shən), *n.* explanation.

ex pli ca tive (ek′splə kā′tiv, ek splik′ə tiv), *adj.* explicatory.

ex pli ca to ry (ek′splə kə tôr′ē, ek′splə kə tōr′ē), *adj.* that explains.

ex plic it (ek splis′it), *adj.* 1 clearly expressed; distinctly stated; definite: *He gave such explicit directions that everyone understood them.* 2 not reserved; frank; outspoken. [< Latin *explicitum* unfolded, explained < *ex-* out + *plicare* to fold] **—ex plic′it ly,** *adv.* **—ex plic′it ness,** *n.*

ex plode (ek splōd′), *v.,* **-plod ed, -plod ing.** *—v.i.* 1 burst with a loud noise; blow up: *The building was destroyed when the defective boiler exploded.* 2 burst or expand violently because of the pressure produced by the sudden generation of one or more gases, as by gunpowder, nitroglycerin, or a nuclear reaction. 3 burst forth noisily or violently: *The audience exploded with laughter. Racial tensions exploded into riots.* *—v.t.* 1 cause to explode: *Many boys explode firecrackers on the Fourth of July.* 2 cause to be rejected; destroy belief in; discredit: *Columbus helped to explode the theory that the earth is flat.* [< Latin *explodere* drive (an actor) off (the stage) by clapping; hiss < *ex-* out + *plaudere* to clap]

ex ploit (*n.* ek′sploit, ek sploit′; *v.* ek sploit′), *n.* a bold, unusual act; daring deed. *—v.t.* 1 make use of; turn to practical account: *A mine is exploited for its minerals.* 2 make unfair or selfish use of: *Nations used to exploit their colonies, taking as much wealth out of them as they could.* [< Old

French *esploit* < Popular Latin *explicitum* achievement < Latin, an unfolding < *ex-* out + *plicare* to fold] **—ex ploit′a ble,** *adj.* **—ex ploit′er,** *n.*

ex ploi ta tion (ek′sploi tā′shən), *n.* 1 use: *the exploitation of the ocean as a source for food.* 2 selfish or unfair use: *exploitation of child labor.*

ex plo ra tion (ek′splə rā′shən), *n.* 1 a traveling in little-known lands or seas for the purpose of discovery. 2 a going over carefully; looking into closely; examining.

ex plor a tive (ek splôr′ə tiv, ek splōr′ə-tiv), *adj.* 1 exploratory. 2 inclined to make explorations.

ex plor a to ry (ek splôr′ə tôr′ē, ek-splōr′ə tōr′ē), *adj.* of or having to do with exploration.

ex plore (ek splôr′, ek splōr′), *v.*, **-plored, -plor ing.** *—v.t.* 1 travel over (little-known lands or seas) for the purpose of discovery: *Admiral Byrd explored the land around the South Pole.* 2 go over carefully; look into closely; examine: *The surgeon explored the wound.* See **search** for synonym study. *—v.i.* carry out a methodical searching operation: *Some geologists explore for oil.* [< Latin *explorare* investigate, originally, cry out (at sight of game or enemy) < *ex-* out + *plorare* to cry]

ex plor er (ek splôr′ər, ek splōr′ər), *n.* person who explores.

ex plo sion (ek splō′zhən), *n.* 1 an exploding; blowing up: *the explosion of a bomb.* 2 a loud noise caused by this: *People five miles away heard the explosion.* 3 a noisy bursting forth; outbreak; outburst: *explosions of anger.* 4 a sudden or rapid increase or growth: *urban explosion, population explosion.*

ex plo sive (ek splō′siv, ek splō′ziv), *adj.* 1 of or for explosion; tending to explode: *Gunpowder is explosive.* 2 tending to burst forth noisily: *an explosive temper.* *—n.* 1 an explosive substance: *Explosives are used in making fireworks.* 2 (in phonetics) a stop. **—ex plo′sive ly,** *adv.* **—ex plo′sive-ness,** *n.*

ex po nent (ek spō′nənt), *n.* 1 person or thing that explains, interprets, etc. 2 person or thing that stands as an example, type, or symbol of something: *Lincoln is a famous exponent of self-education.* 3 person who argues for a policy, program, etc.; advocate. 4 small number written above and to the right of an algebraic symbol or quantity to show how many times the symbol or quantity is to be used as a factor; index. EXAMPLES: $2^2 = 2 \times 2$; $a^3 = a \times a \times a$. [< Latin *exponentem* putting forth, expounding < *ex-* forth + *ponere* put]

ex po nen tial (ek′spō nen′shəl), *adj.* having to do with algebraic exponents; involving unknown or variable quantities as exponents. **—ex′po nen′tial ly,** *adv.*

ex port (*v.* ek spôrt′, ek spōrt′; ek′spôrt, ek′spōrt; *n., adj.* ek′spôrt, ek′spōrt), *v.t.* send (goods) out of one country for sale and use in another: *The United States exports automobiles.* *—n.* 1 article exported: *Cotton is an important export of the United States.* 2 act or fact of exporting: *the export of wool from Great Britain.* *—adj.* of, having to do with, or adapted to exportation. [< Latin *exportare* < *ex-* away + *portare* carry] **—ex port′a ble,** *adj.*

ex por ta tion (ek′spôr tā′shən, ek′spōr-tā′shən), *n.* 1 an exporting. 2 article exported.

ex port er (ek spôr′tər, ek spōr′tər; ek′spôr tər, ek′spōr tər), *n.* person or company whose business is exporting.

ex pose (ek spōz′), *v.t.*, **-posed, -pos ing.** 1 lay open; leave without shelter or protection; uncover: *exposed to enemy gunfire, expose to ridicule. The excavation exposed some ancient ruins.* 2 show openly; display; exhibit: *expose goods for sale in a store.* 3 make known; show up; reveal: *expose a plot.* 4 put out without shelter; abandon: *The ancient Spartans exposed babies that they did not want.* 5 allow light to reach and act on (a photographic film or plate). [< Old French *exposer* < *ex-* forth + *poser* put] **—ex-pos′er,** *n.*

ex po sé (ek′spō zā′), *n.* a showing up of crime, dishonesty, fraud, etc. [< French]

ex po si tion (ek′spə zish′ən), *n.* 1 a public show or exhibition. A world's fair is an exposition. 2 a detailed explanation. 3 speech or writing explaining a process, thing, or idea. 4 (in music) the first section of a movement, as of a sonata, in which the principal themes are presented.

ex pos i tor (ek spoz′ə tər), *n.* person or thing that explains or expounds.

ex pos i to ry (ek spoz′ə tôr′ē, ek spoz′ə-tōr′ē), *adj.* explanatory.

ex post fac to (eks′ pōst′ fak′tō), made or done after something, but applying to it. An **ex post facto law** is one which applies to actions committed before the law was passed. [< Medieval Latin, from what is done afterwards]

ex pos tu late (ek spos′chə lāt), *v.i.*, **-lat ed, -lat ing.** reason earnestly with a person, protesting against something he means to do or has done; remonstrate in a friendly way: *The teacher expostulated with the student about his poor work.* [< Latin *expostulatum* demanded < *ex-* + *postulare* demand] **—ex pos′tu la′tor,** *n.*

ex pos tu la tion (ek spos′chə lā′shən), *n.* earnest protest; friendly remonstrance: *The teacher's expostulations failed, for the student made no effort to improve his work.*

ex pos tu la to ry (ek spos′chə lə tôr′ē, ek-spos′chə lə tōr′ē), *adj.* of or containing expostulation.

ex po sure (ek spō′zhər), *n.* 1 an exposing: *Anyone would dread public exposure of all his faults.* 2 a being exposed: *Exposure to the rain has ruined this machinery.* 3 position in relation to the sun and wind. A house with a southern exposure is open to sun and wind from the south. 4 time during which light reaches and acts on a photographic film or plate. 5 part of a photographic film for one picture. 6 a putting out without shelter; abandoning.

ex pound (ek spound′), *v.t.* 1 make clear; explain, interpret, etc. 2 set forth or state in detail. [< Old French *espondre* < Latin *exponere* < *ex-* forth + *ponere* put] **—ex-pound′er,** *n.*

ex-pres i dent (eks′prez′ə dənt), *n.* a former president; living person who once was president.

ex press (ek spres′), *v.t.* 1 put into words; state: *Try to express ideas clearly.* 2 show by look, voice, or action; reveal: *Your smile expresses joy.* 3 show by a sign, figure, etc.; indicate: *The sign × expresses multiplication.* 4 send by some quick means: *Express this trunk to Chicago.* 5 press out; squeeze out: *express the juice from grapes to make wine.* 6 **express oneself,** say or show what one thinks.
—adj. 1 clearly stated; plain; definite: *It was his express wish that we should go without him.* 2 for a particular purpose; special: *She came for the express purpose of seeing you.* 3 exact; precise: *He is the express image of his father.* 4 having to do with express: *an express company.* 5 traveling fast and making few or no intermediate stops: *an express train.* 6 designed for traveling at high speeds without stopping: *an express highway.*
—n. 1 a quick or direct means of sending things. Packages and money can be sent by express in trains, airplanes, etc. 2 system or company that carries packages, money, etc. 3 things sent by express. 4 train, bus, elevator, etc., traveling fast and making few or no intermediate stops. 5 a special messenger or message sent for a particular purpose.
—adv. by express; directly.
[< Latin *expressum* pressed out < *ex-* out + *premere* press] **—ex press′er,** *n.*

ex press i ble (ek spres′ə bəl), *adj.* that can be expressed.

ex pres sion (ek spresh′ən), *n.* 1 a putting into words; expressing: *the expression of an idea.* 2 word or group of words used as a unit: *"Shake a leg" is a slang expression.* 3 a showing by look, voice, or action: *A sigh is an expression of sadness.* 4 indication of feeling, spirit, character, etc.; look that shows feeling: *The baby had a happy expression on his face.* 5 a bringing out the meaning or beauty of something read, spoken, sung, played, etc.: *Try to read with more expression.* 6 a showing by a sign, figure, etc. 7 any combination of constants, variables, and symbols expressing some mathematical operation or quantity. 8 a pressing out: *the expression of oil from plants.* **—ex-pres′sion less,** *adj.*

ex pres sion ism (ek spresh′ə niz′əm), *n.* style of painting, sculpture, etc., characterized by free expression of the artist's reactions, often distorting nature or reality.

ex pres sion ist (ek spresh′ə nist), *n.* artist who uses expressionism. *—adj.* of or having to do with expressionism.

ex pres sion is tic (ek spresh′ə nis′tik), *adj.* of or having to do with expressionism or expressionists.

ex pres sive (ek spres′iv), *adj.* 1 serving as a sign or indication; expressing: *"Alas" is a word expressive of sadness.* 2 full of expression; having much feeling, meaning, etc. 3 of or having to do with expression. **—ex-pres′sive ly,** *adv.* **—ex pres′sive ness,** *n.*

ex press ly (ek spres′lē), *adv.* 1 in an express manner; plainly; definitely; clearly: *The package is not for you; you are expressly forbidden to touch it.* 2 for the express purpose; on purpose; specially: *You ought to talk to her, since she came expressly to see you.*

ex press man (ek spres′mən), *n., pl.* **-men.** person who collects or delivers articles for an express company.

ex press way (ek spres′wā′), *n.* highway built for motor-vehicle travel at high speeds.

ex pro pri ate (ek sprō′prē āt), *v.t.*, **-at ed, -at ing.** 1 take (land, possessions, etc.) from the owner, especially for public use. A city can expropriate land for a public park. 2 put (a person) out of possession; dispossess. [< Medieval Latin *expropriatum* taken from one's own < Latin *ex-* away from + *proprius* one's own] **—ex pro′pri a′tion,** *n.* **—ex pro′pri a′tor,** *n.*

ex pul sion (ek spul′shən), *n.* 1 an expelling; forcing out: *expulsion of air from the lungs.* 2 a being expelled; being forced out: *Expulsion from school is a punishment for bad behavior.* [< Latin *expulsionem* < *expellere.* See EXPEL.]

ex pul sive (ek spul′siv), *adj.* forcing out; expelling.

ex punge (ek spunj′), *v.t.,* **-punged, -pung ing.** remove completely; blot out; erase: *The secretary was directed to expunge certain accusations from the record.* See **erase** for synonym study. [< Latin *expungere* < *ex-* out + *pungere* to prick] **—ex pung′er,** *n.*

ex pur gate (ek′spər gāt), *v.t.,* **-gat ed, -gat ing.** remove objectionable passages or words from (a book, letter, etc.). [< Latin *expurgatum* purged out < *ex-* out + *purgare* to purge] **—ex′pur ga′tion,** *n.* **—ex′pur ga′tor,** *n.*

ex qui site (ek′skwi zit, ek skwiz′it), *adj.* 1 very lovely; delicate: *Those violets are exquisite.* 2 sharp; intense: *exquisite pain, exquisite joy.* 3 of highest excellence; most admirable: *She has exquisite taste and manners.* 4 keenly sensitive: *an exquisite ear for music.* —*n.* person (usually a man) who is too fastidious in dress, etc.; dandy; fop. [< Latin *exquisitus* sought out < *ex-* out + *quaerere* seek] **—ex′qui site ly,** *adv.* **—ex′qui site ness,** *n.*

ext., 1 extension. 2 extract.

ex tant (ek′stənt, ek stant′), *adj.* still existing; not destroyed or lost: *Some of Washington's letters are extant.* [< Latin *exstantem* standing out, existing < *ex-* out + *stare* to stand]

ex tem po ra ne ous (ek stem′pə rā′nē əs), *adj.* 1 spoken or done without preparation; offhand. 2 made for the occasion: *an extemporaneous shelter against a storm.* 3 (of a speech) carefully prepared, though usually not written out and never committed to memory. [< Late Latin *extemporaneus* < Latin *ex tempore* on the spur of the moment] **—ex tem′po ra′ne ous ly,** *adv.* **—ex tem′po ra′ne ous ness,** *n.*

ex tem po rar y (ek stem′pə rer′ē), *adj.* extemporaneous. **—ex tem′po rar′i ly,** *adv.*

ex tem por e (ek stem′pər ē), *adv.* on the spur of the moment; without preparation; offhand: *Each pupil will be called on to speak extempore.* —*adj.* impromptu. [< Latin *ex tempore*]

ex tem po rize (ek stem′pə rīz′), *v.i., v.t.,* **-rized, -riz ing.** 1 speak, play, sing, or dance, composing as one goes along; improvise: *The pianist was extemporizing.* 2 prepare offhand; make for the occasion: *The campers extemporized a shelter for the night.* **—ex tem′por i za′tion,** *n.*

ex tend (ek stend′), *v.t.* 1 stretch out: *extend your hand.* 2 continue or prolong in time, space, or direction: *I am extending my vacation another week.* See **lengthen** for synonym study. 3 increase or enlarge: *They plan to extend their research in that field.* 4 give; grant: *extend help to poor people.* 5 exert (oneself); strain. —*v.i.* continue in time, space, or direction: *The beach extends for miles in both directions.* [< Latin *extendere* < *ex-* out + *tendere* to stretch] **—ex tend′er,** *n.*

ex tend i ble (ek sten′də bəl), *adj.* extensible.

ex ten si bil i ty (ek sten′sə bil′ə tē), *n.* quality of being extensible.

ex ten si ble (ek sten′sə bəl), *adj.* that can be extended.

ex ten sion (ek sten′shən), *n.* 1 an extending; stretching. 2 a being extended. 3 an extended part; addition. 4 range; extent. 5 telephone connected with the main telephone or with a switchboard but in a different location. 6 the provision of courses of study by a university or college to people unable to take courses in the regular session. 7 (in physics) that property of a body by which it occupies a portion of space.

ex ten sion al (ek sten′shə nəl), *adj.* having to do with extension or extent.

extension cord, length of electric cord fitted with a plug and a socket, used to connect a short cord to an outlet or other source of power.

ex ten sive (ek sten′siv), *adj.* 1 of great extent; large: *an extensive park.* 2 far-reaching; affecting many things; comprehensive: *extensive changes.* 3 depending on the use of large areas: *extensive agriculture.* **—ex ten′sive ly,** *adv.* **—ex ten′sive ness,** *n.*

ex ten sor (ek sten′sər, ek sten′sôr), *n.* muscle that when contracted extends or straightens out a limb or other part of the body.

ex tent (ek stent′), *n.* 1 size, space, length, amount, or degree to which a thing extends; range: *Freight trains and motor trucks carry goods through the whole extent of the country. The extent of a judge's power is limited by law.* 2 something extended; extended space.

ex ten u ate (ek sten′yü āt), *v.t.,* **-at ed, -at ing.** 1 make the seriousness of (guilt, a fault, an offense, etc.) seem less; excuse in part. 2 make thin or weak; diminish. [< Latin *extenuatum* made thin, diminished < *ex-* out + *tenuis* thin] **—ex ten′u a′tor,** *n.*

ex ten u a tion (ek sten′yü ā′shən), *n.* 1 an extenuating: *The lawyer pleaded his client's youth in extenuation of the crime.* 2 something extenuating; partial excuse.

ex ter i or (ek stir′ē ər), *n.* an outer surface or part; outward appearance; outside: *The exterior of the house was made of brick. The gruff old man has a harsh exterior but a kind heart.* —*adj.* 1 on the outside; outer: *The skin of an apple is its exterior covering.* 2 coming from without; happening outside: *exterior influences.* [< Latin, comparative of *exterus* outside < *ex* out of] **—ex ter′i or ly,** *adv.*

exterior angle, 1 any of the four angles formed outside two lines intersected by a straight line. See **interior angle** for diagram. 2 angle formed by a side of a polygon and the extension of an adjacent side.

ex ter mi nate (ek stėr′mə nāt), *v.t.,* **-nat ed, -nat ing.** destroy completely: *This poison will exterminate rats.* [< Latin *exterminatum* driven out < *ex-* out of + *terminus* boundary]

ex ter mi na tion (ek stėr′mə nā′shən), *n.* complete destruction.

ex ter mi na tor (ek stėr′mə nā′tər), *n.* person or thing that exterminates, especially a person whose business is exterminating fleas, cockroaches, bedbugs, rats, etc.

ex ter nal (ek stėr′nl), *adj.* 1 on the outside; outer. 2 entirely outside; coming from without: *the external air.* 3 to be used only on the outside of the body: *Liniment and rubbing alcohol are external remedies.* 4 having existence outside one's mind. 5 easily seen but not essential; superficial: *Going to church is an external act of worship.* 6 having to do with international affairs; foreign: *War affects a nation's external trade.* —*n.* 1 an outer surface or part; outside. 2 **externals,** *pl.* clothing, manners, or other outward acts or appearances: *He judges people by mere externals.* [< Latin *externus* outside < *ex* out of] **—ex ter′nal ly,** *adv.*

hat, āge, fär; let, ēqual, tėrm;
it, īce; hot, ōpen, ôrder;
oil, out; cup, pu̇t, rüle;
ch, child; ng, long; sh, she;
th, thin; ᴛʜ, then; zh, measure;

ə represents *a* in about, *e* in taken, *i* in pencil, *o* in lemon, *u* in circus.

< = from, derived from, taken from.

external ear, the outer part of the ear on the side of the head, including the passage leading to the middle ear; outer ear. See **ear**[1] for diagram.

external respiration, the exchange of oxygen and carbon dioxide between the environment and the respiratory organs; breathing.

ex tinct (ek stingkt′), *adj.* 1 no longer existing: *The dinosaur is an extinct animal.* 2 no longer active; extinguished: *an extinct volcano.* [< Latin *exstinctum* extinguished]

ex tinc tion (ek stingk′shən), *n.* 1 an extinguishing: *The sudden extinction of the lights left the room in darkness.* 2 a being extinguished; extinct condition. 3 a doing away with completely; wiping out; destruction: *Physicians are working toward the extinction of disease.*

ex tin guish (ek sting′gwish), *v.t.* 1 put out; quench: *Water extinguished the fire.* 2 bring to an end; snuff out; destroy: *A government may extinguish liberty but not the love of liberty.* 3 eclipse or obscure by superior brilliancy; outshine. 4 annul (a right, claim, etc.); nullify. [< Latin *exstinguere* < *ex-* out + *stinguere* quench] **—ex tin′guish a ble,** *adj.* **—ex tin′guish er,** *n.*

ex tir pate (ek′stər pāt, ek stėr′pāt), *v.t.,* **-pat ed, -pat ing.** 1 remove completely; destroy totally: *extirpate a disease, extirpate poverty.* 2 tear up by the roots. [< Latin *exstirpatum* uprooted < *ex-* out + *stirps* root] **—ex′tir pa′tion,** *n.* **—ex′tir pa′tor,** *n.*

ex tir pa tive (ek′stər pā′tiv), *adj.* tending to extirpate.

ex tol or **ex toll** (ek stōl′, ek stol′), *v.t.,* **-tolled, -tol ling.** praise highly; commend. [< Latin *extollere* < *ex-* up + *tollere* to raise] **—ex tol′ler,** *n.* **—ex tol′ment,** *n.*

ex tort (ek stôrt′), *v.t.* obtain (money, a promise, etc.) by threats, force, fraud, or illegal use of authority. [< Latin *extortum* twisted out < *ex-* + *torquere* twist] **—ex tort′er,** *n.*

ex tor tion (ek stôr′shən), *n.* 1 an extorting: *Very high interest on loans is considered extortion and is forbidden by law.* 2 something extorted.

ex tor tion ate (ek stôr′shə nit), *adj.* 1 much too great; exorbitant: *an extortionate price.* 2 characterized by extortion: *extortionate demands.* **—ex tor′tion ate ly,** *adv.*

ex tor tion er (ek stôr′shə nər), *n.* extortionist.

ex tor tion ist (ek stôr′shə nist), *n.* person who is guilty of extortion.

ex tor tive (ek stôr′tiv), *adj.* extortionary.

ex tra (ek′strə), *adj.* beyond what is usual, expected, or needed; additional: *extra pay, extra favors.* —*n.* 1 something extra; anything beyond what is usual, expected, or needed: *a new car equipped with many extras.* 2 an additional charge. 3 a special edition of a newspaper. 4 person who is employed by the day to play minor parts in motion pictures. 5 INFORMAL. an additional worker. —*adv.* beyond the usual, proper, or expected amount or degree; unusually: *extra fine quality.* [probably short for *extraordinary*]

extra-, *prefix.* outside ____; beyond ____: *Extraordinary = outside the ordinary.* [< Latin < *extra* outside]

ex tra cel lu lar (ek′strə sel′yə lər), situated or taking place outside of a cell or cells.

ex tract (*v.* ek strakt′; *n.* ek′strakt), *v.t.* 1 pull out or draw out, usually with some effort: *extract a tooth, extract iron from the earth.* 2 obtain by pressing, squeezing, etc.: *extract oil from olives.* 3 deduce; infer: *extract a principle from a collection of facts.* 4 derive; obtain: *extract pleasure from a party.* 5 take out (a passage) from a book, speech, etc. 6 calculate or find (the root of a number). —*n.* 1 passage taken out of a book, speech, etc.; excerpt. 2 a concentrated preparation of a substance. Vanilla extract, made from vanilla beans, is used as flavoring. 3 (in pharmacy) a dry substance made from a drug, plant, etc., by dissolving the active ingredients and then evaporating the solvent. [< Latin *extractum* drawn out < *ex-* out + *trahere* draw] **—ex trac′tor,** *n.*

ex tract a ble or **ex tract i ble** (ek-strak′tə bəl), *adj.* that can be extracted.

ex trac tion (ek strak′shən), *n.* 1 an extracting: *the extraction of a tooth.* 2 a being extracted. 3 origin; descent: *Miss Del Rio is of Spanish extraction.* 4 something that has been extracted.

ex trac tive (ek strak′tiv), *adj.* 1 extracting; tending to extract. 2 that can be extracted. 3 deriving products from nature, as agriculture or mining. —*n.* an extractive substance.

ex tra cur ric u lar (ek′strə kə rik′yə lər), *adj.* outside the regular course of study: *Football, dramatics, and debating are extracurricular activities in our high school.*

ex tra dite (ek′strə dīt), *v.t.,* **-dit ed, -dit ing.** 1 give up or deliver (a fugitive or prisoner) to another state, nation, or authority for trial or punishment: *If an escaped prisoner of the state of Ohio is caught in Indiana, he can be extradited from Indiana to Ohio.* 2 obtain the surrender of (such a person). **—ex′tra dit′a ble,** *adj.*

ex tra di tion (ek′strə dish′ən), *n.* surrender of a fugitive or prisoner by one state, nation, or authority to another for trial or punishment. [< French < Latin *ex-* out + *traditionem* a delivering up < *tradere* to trade]

ex tra ga lac tic (ek′strə gə lak′tik), *adj.* outside our own galaxy: *extragalactic distances.*

ex tra mur al (ek′strə myůr′əl), *adj.* 1 occurring outside the boundaries of a college, school, etc.: *extramural activities.* 2 having to do with informally arranged competition between colleges: *extramural sports.*

ex tra ne ous (ek strā′nē əs), *adj.* 1 from outside; not belonging or proper to a thing; foreign: *Sand or some other extraneous matter had got into the butter.* 2 not part of what is under consideration; not essential: *extraneous remarks.* [< Latin *extraneus* < *extra* outside. Doublet of STRANGE.] **—ex tra′ne ous ly,** *adv.* **—ex tra′ne ous ness,** *n.*

ex traor di nar y (ek strôr′də ner′ē; *esp. for 2* ek′strə ôr′də ner′ē), *adj.* 1 beyond what is ordinary; very unusual or remarkable; exceptional: *Eight feet is an extraordinary height for a person.* 2 ranking below the regular class of officials; special. An **envoy extraordinary** is one sent on a special mission. **—ex traor′di nar′i ly,** *adv.*

ex trap o late (ek strap′ə lāt), *v.t., v.i.,* **-lat ed, -lat ing.** calculate or infer from what is known something that is possible but unknown; predict from facts. [< *extra-* + *(inter)polate*] **—ex trap′o la′tion,** *n.*

ex tra sen sor y perception (ek′strə-sen′sər ē), the perceiving of thoughts, actions, etc., through other than the normal senses.

ex tra ter res tri al (ek′strə tə res′trē əl), *adj.* outside the earth or its atmosphere.

ex tra ter ri to ri al (ek′strə ter′ə tôr′ē əl, ek′strə ter′ə tōr′ē əl), *adj.* 1 having to do with freedom from the jurisdiction of the country that a person is in. Any ambassador to the United States has certain extraterritorial privileges. 2 beyond territorial limits or jurisdiction. **—ex′tra ter′ri to′ri al ly,** *adv.*

ex tra ter ri to ri al i ty (ek′strə ter′ə-tôr′ē al′ə tē, ek′strə ter′ə tōr′ē al′ə tē), *n.* privilege of having extraterritorial rights.

ex trav a gance (ek strav′ə gəns), *n.* 1 careless and lavish spending; wastefulness: *His extravagance kept him always in debt.* 2 a going beyond the bounds of reason; excess: *The extravagance of the claims in the advertisement caused me to doubt the worth of the product.* 3 an extravagant action, idea, purchase, etc.

ex trav a gant (ek strav′ə gənt), *adj.* 1 spending carelessly and lavishly; wasteful: *An extravagant person has extravagant tastes and habits.* 2 beyond the bounds of reason; excessive: *an extravagant price, extravagant praise.* [< Medieval Latin *extravagantem* < Latin *extra-* outside + *vagari* to wander] **—ex trav′a gant ly,** *adv.*

ex trav a gan za (ek strav′ə gan′zə), *n.* a fantastic play, piece of music, literary composition, etc. Musical comedies having elaborate scenery, gorgeous costumes, etc., are extravaganzas. [< Italian *estravaganza*]

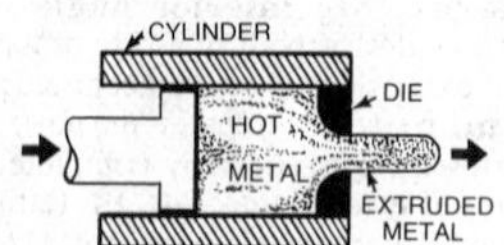

extrude (def. 2)—Cutaway drawing of cylinder shows the shaping of metal by extruding it. Hot metal is compressed in a cylinder and forced through a die; the extruded metal will have the shape of the die opening.

ex tra ve hic u lar (ek′strə vi hik′yə lər), *adj.* outside a spacecraft.

ex treme (ek strēm′), *adj.,* **-trem er, -trem est,** *n.* —*adj.* 1 of the highest degree; much more than usual; very great; very strong: *extreme joy, extreme peril.* 2 going to the greatest possible lengths; very severe; very violent: *extreme measures, an extreme case.* 3 at the very end; farthest possible; last: *the extreme north.* —*n.* 1 something extreme; one of two things as far or as different as possible from each other: *Love and hate are two extremes of feeling.* 2 the highest degree: *Joy is happiness in the extreme.* 3 the first or last term in a proportion or series: *In the proportion, 2 is to 4 as 8 is to 16, 2 and 16 are the extremes; 4 and 8 are the means.* 4 **go to extremes,** do or say too much. [< Latin *extremus,* superlative of *exterus* outside < *ex* out of] **—ex treme′ly,** *adv.* **—ex treme′ness,** *n.*

extreme unction, sacrament of the Roman Catholic Church, given by a priest to a dying person or one in danger of death; anointing of the sick. It consists of anointing with oil and reciting special prayers.

ex trem ism (ek strē′miz′əm), *n.* tendency or disposition to go to extremes.

ex trem ist (ek strē′mist), *n.* person who goes to extremes; supporter of extreme doctrines or practices.

ex trem i ty (ek strem′ə tē), *n., pl.* **-ties.** 1 the very end; farthest possible place; last part or point. 2 **extremities,** *pl.* the hands and feet. 3 very great danger or need: *In their extremity the people on the sinking ship bore themselves bravely.* 4 an extreme degree: *Joy is the extremity of happiness.* 5 an extreme action or measure: *The soldiers were forced to the extremity of firing their rifles to scatter the angry mob.*

ex tri ca ble (ek′strə kə bəl), *adj.* that can be extricated.

ex tri cate (ek′strə kāt), *v.t.,* **-cat ed, -cat ing.** set free (from entanglements, difficulties, embarrassing situations, etc.); release: *He extricated his younger brother from the barbed-wire fence.* [< Latin *extricatum* freed from perplexities < *ex-* out of + *tricae* perplexities] **—ex′tri ca′tion,** *n.*

ex trin sic (ek strin′sik), *adj.* 1 not essential or inherent; caused by external circumstances. 2 outside of a thing; coming from without; external. 3 originating outside the part upon which it acts: *the extrinsic muscles of the legs.* [< Latin *extrinsecus* from outside] **—ex trin′si cal ly,** *adv.*

ex trorse (ek strôrs′), *adj.* (in botany) turned or facing outward, as anthers which face and open away from the axis of the flower. [< Late Latin *extrorsum* < Latin *extra-* outside + *versum* turned]

ex tro ver sion (ek′strə vėr′zhən, ek′strə-vėr′shən), *n.* tendency to be more interested in what is going on around one than in one's own thoughts and feelings.

ex tro vert (ek′strə vėrt′), *n.* person more interested in what is going on around him than in his own thoughts and feelings; person tending to act rather than think. [< *extro-* outside (variant of *extra-*) + Latin *vertere* to turn]

ex tro vert ed (ek′strə vėr′tid), *adj.* characterized by extroversion.

ex trude (ek strüd′), *v.,* **-trud ed, -trud ing.** —*v.t.* 1 thrust out; push out: *extrude toothpaste from the tube.* 2 shape (metal, plastics, rubber, or ceramics) by forcing through dies. —*v.i.* stick out; protrude. [< Latin *extrudere* < *ex-* out + *trudere* to thrust]

ex tru sion (ek strü′zhən), *n.* 1 an extruding. 2 a being extruded; expulsion. 3 something extruded.

hat, āge, fär; let, ēqual, tėrm;
it, īce; hot, ōpen, ôrder;
oil, out; cup, pu̇t, rüle;
ch, child; ng, long; sh, she;
th, thin; ᴛʜ, then; zh, measure;

ə represents *a* in about, *e* in taken, *i* in pencil, *o* in lemon, *u* in circus.

< = from, derived from, taken from.

ex tru sive (ek strü′siv), *adj.* tending to extrude.

ex u ber ance (eg zü′bər əns), *n.* 1 a being exuberant; great abundance. 2 luxuriant growth.

ex u ber ant (eg zü′bər ənt), *adj.* 1 very abundant; overflowing; lavish: *exuberant joy, an exuberant welcome.* 2 profuse in growth; luxuriant: *the exuberant vegetation of the jungle.* 3 abounding in health and spirits; overflowing with good cheer: *an exuberant young man.* [< Latin *exuberantem* growing luxuriantly < *ex-* thoroughly + *uber* fertile] **—ex u′ber ant ly,** *adv.*

ex u da tion (ek′syə dā′shən), *n.* 1 an exuding. 2 something exuded.

ex ude (eg züd′, ek syüd′), *v.,* **-ud ed, -ud ing.** *—v.i.* come out in drops; ooze: *Sweat exudes from the pores in the skin.* *—v.t.* 1 send out in drops: *Some trees exude sap in the spring.* 2 give forth; emit: *exude self-confidence.* [< Latin *exsudare* < *ex-* out + *sudare* to sweat]

ex ult (eg zult′), *v.i.* be very glad; rejoice greatly. [< Latin *exsultare* leap out or up < *ex-* forth + *saltare* to leap] **—ex ult′ing ly,** *adv.*

ex ult ant (eg zult′nt), *adj.* rejoicing greatly; exulting; triumphant: *an exultant shout.* **—ex ult′ant ly,** *adv.*

ex ul ta tion (eg′zul tā′shən, ek′sul tā′shən), *n.* an exulting; great rejoicing; triumph.

ex urb (ek′sėrb′), *n.* town or area in exurbia.

ex ur ban ite (ek′sėr′bə nīt), *n.* person who has moved out of a large city to the region between the suburbs and the country, and whose way of living is a mixture of urban and rural elements. [< *ex-* + *(sub)urbanite*]

ex ur bi a (ek sėr′bē ə), *n.* region between a city's suburbs and the country.

ex u vi ate (eg zü′vē āt, ek sü′vē āt), *v.i., v.t.,* **-at ed, -at ing.** cast off or shed skin, shell, feathers, etc.; molt. [< Latin *exuviae* stuffed skins] **—ex u′vi a′tion,** *n.*

-ey, *suffix forming adjectives from nouns.* full of ___; containing ___; like ___: *Clayey = like or containing clay.* [variant of *-y*[1]]

Eyck (īk), *n.* 1 **Hubert van,** 1366?-1426, Flemish painter. 2 his brother, **Jan van,** 1385?-1440, also a painter.

eye (ī), *n., v.,* **eyed, ey ing** or **eye ing.** *—n.* 1 the part of the body by which human beings and animals see; organ of sight. 2 the colored part of the eye; iris. 3 region surrounding the eye: *The blow gave him a black eye.* 4 any organ that is sensitive to light. 5 Often, **eyes,** *pl.* sense of seeing; vision; sight: *A jet pilot must have good eyes.* 6 ability to see small differences in things: *an eye for color.* 7 look; glance. 8 a watchful look; careful regard. 9 Often, **eyes,** *pl.* way of thinking or considering; point of view; opinion; judgment: *Stealing is a crime in the eyes of the law.* 10 thing shaped like, resembling, or suggesting an eye. The little buds on potatoes, the hole for thread in a needle, and the loop in which a hook fastens are all called eyes. 11 the relatively calm, clear area at the center of a hurricane.

an eye for an eye, punishment as severe as the offense.

catch one's eye, attract one's attention.

in the public eye, **a** often seen in public. **b** widely known.

keep an eye on, look after; watch carefully.

lay eyes on or **set eyes on,** look at; see.

make eyes at, flirt with.

open one's eyes, make one see what is really happening.

see eye to eye, agree entirely; have exactly the same opinion.

shut one's eyes to, refuse to see or consider; ignore.

with an eye to, for; considering.

—v.t. look at; watch; observe: *The dog eyed the stranger.*

[Old English *ēage*] **—eye′like′,** *adj.*

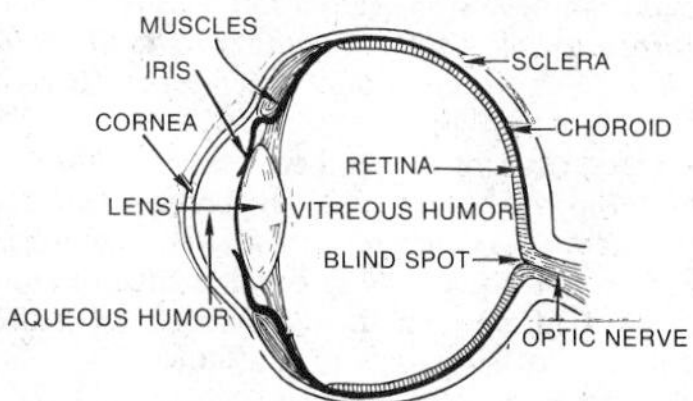

eye (def. 1) of a human being

eye ball (ī′bôl′), *n.* the ball-shaped part of the eye without the surrounding lids and bony socket.

eye brow (ī′brou′), *n.* 1 arch of hair above the eye. 2 the bony ridge that it grows on.

eye-catch er (ī′kach′ər), *n.* INFORMAL. anything striking; attraction.

eye-catch ing (ī′kach′ing), *adj.* INFORMAL. 1 striking; appealing. 2 conspicuous; clearly visible.

eye cup (ī′kup′), *n.* a small cup with a rim shaped to fit over the socket of the eye, used in washing the eyes or putting medicine in them.

eye drop per (ī′drop′ər), *n.* dropper used to apply liquid medicine to the eyes.

eye ful (ī′fu̇l), *n., pl.* **-fuls.** 1 as much as the eye can see at one time. 2 INFORMAL. a good look. 3 SLANG. a good-looking person.

eye glass (ī′glas′), *n.* 1 a lens to aid poor vision. 2 **eyeglasses,** *pl.* pair of such lenses, mounted in a frame, to correct defective eyesight; glasses; spectacles. 3 eyepiece.

eye hole (ī′hōl′), *n.* 1 the bony socket for the eyeball. 2 peephole. 3 a round opening for a pin, hook, rope, etc., to go through.

eye lash (ī′lash′), *n.* 1 one of the hairs on the edge of the eyelid. 2 fringe of such hairs.

eye less (ī′lis), *n.* 1 without eyes. 2 blind.

eye let (ī′lit), *n.* 1 a small, round hole for a lace or cord to go through. 2 a metal ring around such a hole to strengthen it. 3 peephole. 4 a small, round hole with stitches around it, used to make a pattern in embroidery.

eye lid (ī′lid′), *n.* the movable fold of skin, upper or lower, containing muscles by means of which one can shut and open the eyes.

eye-o pen er (ī′ō′pə nər), *n.* INFORMAL. a surprising happening or discovery; startling piece of information.

eye piece (ī′pēs′), *n.* lens or set of lenses in a telescope, microscope, etc., nearest to the eye of the user.

eye shot (ī′shot′), *n.* eyesight (def. 2).

eye sight (ī′sīt′), *n.* 1 power of seeing; sight. 2 range of vision; view.

eye sore (ī′sôr′, ī′sōr′), *n.* something unpleasant to look at.

eye spot (ī′spot′), *n.* a simple light receptor, consisting of a group of pigmented cells, found in certain lower animals.

eye stalk (ī′stôk′), *n.* (in zoology) the stalk or peduncle upon which the eye is borne in lobsters, shrimp, etc.

eye strain (ī′strān′), *n.* a tired or weak condition of the eyes caused by using them too much, reading in a dim light, etc.

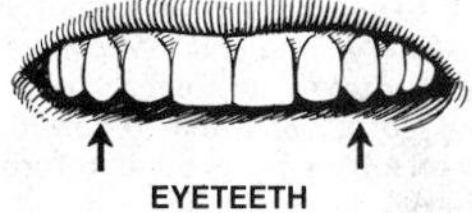
EYETEETH

eye tooth (ī′tüth′), *n., pl.* **-teeth.** an upper canine tooth.

eye wash (ī′wosh′, ī′wôsh′), *n.* 1 a liquid preparation to clean or heal the eyes. 2 SLANG. deceiving flattery; insincere excuse.

eye wit ness (ī′wit′nis), *n.* person who actually sees or has seen some act or happening, and thus can give testimony concerning it.

eyr ie or **eyr y** (er′ē, ar′ē, *or* ir′ē), *n., pl.* **eyr ies.** aerie.

E ze ki el (i zē′kē əl, i zē′kyəl), *n.* 1 Hebrew prophet who lived in the sixth century B.C. 2 book of the Old Testament containing his prophecies.

Ez ra (ez′rə), *n.* 1 Hebrew scribe who led a revival of Judaism in the 300's or 400's B.C. 2 book of the Old Testament that tells about him.

F f

F[1] or **f** (ef), *n.*, *pl.* **F's** or **f's.** the sixth letter of the English alphabet.
F[2] (ef), *n.*, *pl.* **F's.** the fourth tone of the musical scale of C major.
f, 1 focal length. 2 forte.
F, 1 fluorine. 2 (in genetics) filial generation.
f., 1 farad. 2 female. 3 feminine. 4 folio. 5 (and the) following (page, section, etc.). 6 forte. 7 franc.

facade (def. 1) of a church

F., 1 Fahrenheit. 2 February. 3 French. 4 Friday.
fa (fä), *n.* (in music) the fourth tone of the diatonic scale. [< Italian]
Fa bi an (fā′bē ən), *adj.* 1 using stratagem and delay to wear out an opponent; cautious; slow. 2 of or having to do with the Fabian Society. —*n.* member or supporter of the Fabian Society. [< *Fabius Maximus*]
Fabian Society, an English socialist society, founded in 1884, that favors the adoption of socialism by gradual reform rather than by revolution.
Fa bi us Max i mus (fā′bē əs mak′sə-məs), died 203 B.C., Roman general who wore out Hannibal's army by constantly harassing it without risking a battle.
fa ble (fā′bəl), *n.*, *v.*, **-bled, -bling.** —*n.* 1 a short story made up to teach a useful lesson, especially one in which animals or things are the speakers or actors. 2 an untrue story; falsehood. 3 legend or myth. —*v.i.* tell or write fables. —*v.t.* make up (a story, etc.); fabricate. [< Old French < Latin *fabula* narrative, tale < *fari* speak] **—fa′bler,** *n.*
fa bled (fā′bəld), *adj.* 1 celebrated or described in fables, legends, or myths: *the fabled Greek gods and goddesses.* 2 made-up; fictitious.
Fa bre (fä′bər; *French* fä′brə), *n.* **Jean Henri,** 1823-1915, French entomologist.
fab ric (fab′rik), *n.* 1 any of various materials manufactured by weaving, as broadcloth, canvas, flannel, or tweed, or by knitting, as jersey and lisle. 2 texture, whether smooth or rough, loose or close, etc.: *suits and dresses made of cloths of different fabric.* 3 way in which a thing is put together; framework or structure: *Unwise loans weakened the financial fabric of the bank.* [< Latin *fabrica* workshop < *faber* worker. Doublet of FORGE[1].]
fab ri cate (fab′rə kāt), *v.t.*, **-cat ed, -cat ing.** 1 make (anything that requires skill); build or manufacture. 2 make by fitting together standardized parts: *Automobiles are fabricated from parts made in different factories.* 3 make up; invent (a story, lie, excuse, etc.). **—fab′ri ca′tor,** *n.*
fab ri ca tion (fab′rə kā′shən), *n.* 1 a fabricating. 2 something fabricated.
Fab ri koid (fab′rə koid), *n.* trademark for a waterproof fabric resembling leather, used for bindings of books, traveling bags, automobile upholstery, etc.
fab u list (fab′yə list), *n.* person who tells, writes, or makes up fables.
fab u lous (fab′yə ləs), *adj.* 1 not believable; amazing: *That antique shop asks fabulous prices.* 2 of or belonging to a fable; imaginary: *The phoenix is a fabulous bird.* 3 like a fable. 4 INFORMAL. wonderful; exciting. **—fab′u lous ly,** *adv.* **—fab′u lous-ness,** *n.*
fa cade or **fa çade** (fə säd′), *n.* 1 the front part of a building. 2 any side of a building that faces a street or an open space. 3 outward appearance: *a facade of honesty.* [< French *façade*]
face (fās), *n.*, *v.*, **faced, fac ing.** —*n.* 1 the front part of the head, extending from the top of the forehead to the chin, and including (in man) the eyes, nose, mouth, and cheeks. See synonym study below. 2 look; expression: *His face was sad.* 3 an ugly or funny look made by twisting the face: *She made a face at me.* 4 the front part; the right side; surface: *the face of a clock, the whole face of the earth.* 5 outward appearance. 6 boldness; impudence; effrontery; audacity. 7 dignity; self-respect; personal importance: *To most people, loss of face is humiliating.* 8 the stated value: *The face of the note was $100, but $73 was all that anybody would pay for it.* 9 the vertical or steep side of a cliff, bank, etc.: *the face of a rock.* 10 any of the planes or surfaces that bound a solid figure. A cube has six faces. 11 (in mining) the end of a tunnel, drift, or other excavation, especially where work is in progress.
face to face, **a** with faces toward each other. **b** in the actual presence.
in the face of, **a** in the presence of. **b** in spite of.
fly in the face of, disobey openly; defy.
on the face of it, by its own evidence; obviously: *This action, on the face of it, looks bad.*
to one's face, in one's presence; openly; boldly.
—*v.t.* 1 have the front toward; be opposite to: *The house faces the street.* 2 turn the face toward: *Moslems face the east when they pray.* 3 cause to face. 4 meet face to face; stand before; front; confront: *The teacher faced the class.* 5 meet bravely or boldly: *The survivors of the storm faced an acute shortage of food and water.* 6 present itself to: *A crisis faced us.* 7 cover or line with a different material: *a wooden house faced with brick.* 8 cover the inside or outside edges of cuffs, a collar, etc., with the same or different material for protection or trimming. 9 smooth the surface of (stone, etc.). 10 **face down,** face fearlessly; meet boldly. 11 **face up to,** meet boldly; take full cognizance of. —*v.i.* have the face (toward); look. [< Old French < Popular Latin *facia* < Latin *facies* form, related to *facere* make, do]
Syn. *n.* 1 **Face, countenance** mean the front part of the head. **Face** emphasizes the physical nature or the features: *That girl has a pretty face.* **Countenance** emphasizes the looks, especially as they reveal a person's thoughts, feelings, or character: *He has a cheerful countenance.*
face card, king, queen, or jack of playing cards.
face-lift ing (fās′lif′ting), *n.* 1 operation to tighten the skin of the face, remove wrinkles, etc. 2 INFORMAL. a superficial change to improve appearance or modernize.

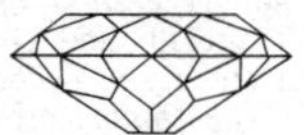
facet (def. 1)
gem with facets

fac et (fas′it), *n.*, *v.*, **-et ed, -et ing** or **-et ted, -et ting.** —*n.* 1 any one of the small, polished, flat surfaces of a cut gem. 2 any one of several sides or views. 3 one of the individual external visual units of a compound eye. —*v.t.* cut facets on. [< French *facette*]
fa ce tious (fə sē′shəs), *adj.* 1 having the habit of joking; being slyly humorous. 2 said in fun; not to be taken seriously. [< Latin *facetia* jest < *facetus* witty] **—fa ce′tious-ly,** *adv.* **—fa ce′tious ness,** *n.*
face-to-face (fās′tə fās′), *adj.* direct; personal: *a face-to-face talk.* —*adv.* in direct contact: *face-to-face with danger.*
face value, 1 value stated on a bond, check, note, bill, etc.; par value. 2 apparent worth, meaning, etc.: *Honest advertisements can be taken at their face value.*
fa cial (fā′shəl), *adj.* 1 of the face. 2 for the face. —*n.* massage or treatment of the face. **—fa′cial ly,** *adv.*
fac ile (fas′əl), *adj.* 1 easily done, used, etc.; taking little effort: *a facile task, facile methods.* 2 moving, acting, working, etc., easily or rapidly: *a facile hand, a facile tongue, a facile pen.* 3 of easy manners or temper; agreeable; yielding: *Her facile nature adapted itself to any company.* [< French < Latin *facilis* easy < *facere* do] **—fac′ile ly,** *adv.*
fa cil i tate (fə sil′ə tāt), *v.t.*, **-tat ed, -tat ing.** make easy; lessen the labor of; help bring about; assist; expedite: *A vacuum cleaner facilitates my housework.* **—fa cil′i-ta′tion,** *n.*
fa cil i ty (fə sil′ə tē), *n.*, *pl.* **-ties.** 1 absence of difficulty; ease: *Long practice enabled the storekeeper to add up long columns of figures with facility.* 2 power to do anything easily and quickly; skill in using the hands or mind. 3 Usually, **facilities,** *pl.* something that makes an action easy; aid; convenience: *Ropes, swings, and sand piles are facilities for play.* 4 easygoing quality; tendency to yield to others.
fac ing (fā′sing), *n.* 1 a covering of different material for ornament, protection, etc.: *a wooden house with a brick facing.* 2 material put around the inside or outside edge of cloth to protect or trim it. 3 **facings,** *pl.* cuffs, collar, and trimmings of a military coat.
fac sim i le (fak sim′ə lē), *n.*, *v.*, **-led, -le ing.** —*n.* 1 an exact copy or likeness; perfect reproduction. 2 an electronic process for transmitting printed matter and photographs by wire or radio and reproducing them on paper at the receiving set. 3 **in facsimile,** exactly. —*v.t.* make a facsimile of. [< Latin *fac* make! + *simile* similar, like]
fact (fakt), *n.* 1 thing known to be true or to have really happened: *Many scientific facts are based on actual observation.* 2 what has really happened or is the case; reality: *The fact of the matter is, I did not go.* 3 something said or supposed to be true or to have really happened: *We doubted his facts.* 4 crime or

offense: *an accessory after the fact.* 5 OBSOLETE. deed; act. 6 **as a matter of fact,** in fact. 7 **in fact,** truly; really. [< Latin *factum* (thing) done < *facere* do. Doublet of FEAT.]

fac tion (fak′shən), *n.* 1 group of persons in a political party, church, club, etc., acting together or having a common purpose. 2 strife or quarreling among the members of a political party, church, club, neighborhood, etc. [< Latin *factionem* party, class, originally, a doing < *facere* do. Doublet of FASHION.]

fac tion al (fak′shə nəl), *adj.* 1 having to do with factions. 2 causing faction.

fac tion al ism (fak′shə nə liz′əm), *n.* condition characterized by faction; tendency to factional differences.

fac tious (fak′shəs), *adj.* 1 fond of stirring up disputes; quarrelsome. 2 of or caused by faction. **—fac′tious ly,** *adv.* **—fac′tious ness,** *n.*

fac ti tious (fak tish′əs), *adj.* developed by effort; not natural; artificial: *His factitious smile convinced me that he was not sincere.* [< Latin *factitius* < *facere* do. Doublet of FETISH.] **—fac ti′tious ly,** *adv.* **—fac ti′tious ness,** *n.*

fac tor (fak′tər), *n.* 1 circumstance, fact, or influence that tends to produce a result: *Endurance is an important factor of success in sports.* 2 any of the numbers, algebraic expressions, etc., which, when multiplied together, form a product: *5, 3, and 4 are factors of 60.* 3 person who does business for another; agent. 4 agent managing a trading post. 5 gene. *—v.t.* separate or resolve into factors. [< Latin, doer < *facere* do]

fac to ri al (fak tôr′ē əl, fak tōr′ē əl), *adj.* (in mathematics) of or having to do with a factor. *—n.* the product of an integer multiplied by all the integers from one to that integer. EXAMPLE: The factorial of 4 is $4 \times 3 \times 2 \times 1 = 24$, and is symbolized 4!.

fac tor y (fak′tər ē), *n., pl.* **-tor ies.** 1 building or group of buildings where things are manufactured. 2 a trading post in a foreign country for merchants and factors.

fac to tum (fak tō′təm), *n.* servant or other person employed to do all kinds of work. [< New Latin < Latin *fac* do! + *totum* the whole]

fac tu al (fak′chü əl), *adj.* concerned with fact; consisting of facts; actual; real. **—fac′tu al ly,** *adv.*

fac ul ty (fak′əl tē), *n., pl.* **-ties.** 1 power of the mind or body; capacity; capability: *the faculty of hearing, the faculty of memory. Old people sometimes lose their faculties.* 2 power or ability to do some special thing, especially a power of the mind: *She has a great faculty for arithmetic.* 3 the teachers of a school, college, or university. 4 department of learning in a university: *the faculty of theology, the faculty of medicine.* 5 members of a profession: *The medical faculty is made up of doctors, surgeons, etc.* [< Latin *facultatem* < *facilis.* See FACILE.]

fad (fad), *n.* something everybody is very much interested in for a short time; craze; rage: *No one plays that game anymore; it was only a fad.* [origin uncertain]

fad dish (fad′ish), *adj.* 1 inclined to follow fads. 2 like a fad.

fad dist (fad′ist), *n.* person devoted to a fad; person who takes up new fads.

fade (fād), *v.,* **fad ed, fad ing,** *n.* *—v.i.* 1 become less bright; lose color: *My blue dress faded when it was washed.* 2 lose freshness or strength; wither: *The flowers in her garden faded at the end of the summer.* 3 die away; disappear little by little: *The sound of the train faded after it went by.* See **disappear** for synonym study. 4 in motion pictures, radio, and television: **a fade in,** become slowly more distinct or louder. **b fade out,** become slowly less perceptible. *—v.t.* cause to fade: *Sunlight faded the new curtains.* *—n.* a fading in or out. [< Old French *fader* < *fade* pale, weak]

fade less (fād′lis), *adj.* not fading; permanent. **—fade′less ly,** *adv.*

fade-out (fād′out′), *n.* 1 the gradual fading from the screen of a scene in a motion picture or television show. 2 a gradual disappearance.

fae cal (fē′kəl), *adj.* fecal.

fae ces (fē′sēz), *n.pl.* feces.

fa er ie or **fa er y** (fā′ər ē, fer′ē, far′ē), *n., pl.* **-er ies,** *adj.* ARCHAIC. *—n.* 1 fairyland. 2 fairy. *—adj.* fairy. [variant of *fairy*]

Faer oe Islands (fer′ō, far′ō), group of Danish islands in the N Atlantic, between Great Britain and Iceland. 39,000 pop.; 540 sq. mi. Also, **Faroe Islands.**

Faer o ese (fer′ō ēz′, far′ō ēz′), *adj., n., pl.* **-ese.** *—adj.* of the Faeroe Islands, their people, or their language. *—n.* 1 native or inhabitant of the Faeroe Islands. 2 the Scandinavian language of the Faeroe Islands.

fag (fag), *v.,* **fagged, fag ging,** *n.* *—v.t.* tire by work; weary: *The horse was fagged.* *—v.i.* 1 work hard or until wearied: *He fagged away at his arithmetic.* 2 act as a fag. *—n.* 1 drudgery. 2 drudge. 3 BRITISH. boy who waits on an older boy in certain schools. 4 SLANG. cigarette. [Middle English *fagge* fag end]

fag end, 1 the last part or remnant of anything, after the best part has been used: *the fag end of a cigar.* 2 the coarse, unfinished end of a piece of cloth. 3 an untwisted end of rope.

fag got (fag′ət), *n., v.t.* fagot.

fag got ing (fag′ə ting), *n.* fagoting.

fag ot (fag′ət), *n.* 1 bundle of sticks or twigs tied together for fuel. 2 bundle of iron rods or pieces of iron or steel to be welded. *—v.t.* 1 tie or fasten together into a fagot or fagots. 2 ornament with fagoting. [< Old French]

fag ot ing (fag′ə ting), *n.* an ornamental zigzag stitch used for loosely joining two finished edges.

Fahr., Fahrenheit.

Fahr en heit (far′ən hīt), *adj.* of, based on, or according to a scale for measuring temperature on which 32 degrees marks the freezing point of water and 212 degrees marks the boiling point of water at standard atmospheric pressure. The **Fahrenheit thermometer** is marked off according to this scale. [< Gabriel D. *Fahrenheit,* 1686-1736, German physicist, who introduced this scale]

fai ence (fī äns′, fā äns′; *French* fī äɴs′), *n.* a glazed, highly colored and decorated earthenware or porcelain, usually of fine quality. [< French *faïence* < *Faenza,* commune in northern Italy]

fail (fāl), *v.i.* 1 not succeed; be unable to do or become what is wanted, expected, or attempted; come to nothing: *After a long drought, the crops failed.* 2 be lacking or absent; be not enough; fall short: *When our supplies failed, we had no food.* 3 lose strength; grow weak; die away: *The sick man's heart was failing.* 4 be unable to pay what one owes; become bankrupt: *That company will fail.* 5 be unsuccessful in an examination, etc.; receive a mark of failure.

hat, āge, fär; let, ēqual, tėrm;
it, īce; hot, ōpen, ôrder;
oil, out; cup, pu̇t, rüle;
ch, child; ng, long; sh, she;
th, thin; ᴛʜ, then; zh, measure;

ə represents *a* in about, *e* in taken, *i* in pencil, *o* in lemon, *u* in circus.

< = from, derived from, taken from.

—v.t. 1 not do; neglect: *He failed to follow our advice.* 2 be of no use or help to when needed: *When I wanted his help, he failed me.* 3 give the mark of failure to (a student). *—n.* **without fail,** without failing to do, happen, etc.; surely; certainly. [< Old French *faillir,* ultimately < Latin *fallere* deceive]

fail ing (fā′ling), *n.* 1 failure. 2 fault; defect. See **fault** for synonym study. *—prep.* in the absence of; lacking; without: *Failing good weather, the tennis match will be played indoors.*

faille (fīl, fāl), *n.* a soft, ribbed cloth of silk, rayon, cotton, or acetate. [< French]

fail-safe (fāl′sāf′), *adj.* 1 having a built-in safety device that is automatically activated in case of some failure or malfunction. 2 designating a procedure by which a bomber is prevented from completing its mission in case of a reversal of orders.

fail ure (fā′lyər), *n.* 1 a being unable to do or become what is wanted, expected, or attempted; not succeeding; failing. 2 a not doing; neglecting. 3 a being lacking or absent; being not enough; falling short: *a failure of supplies.* 4 a losing strength; becoming weak; dying away; decline; deterioration: *failure of eyesight.* 5 bankruptcy. 6 person or thing that has failed: *The picnic was a failure because it rained.*

fain (fān), ARCHAIC. *—adv.* gladly; willingly. *—adj.* 1 willing, but not eager. 2 obliged. 3 glad. 4 eager. [Old English *fægen*]

faint (fānt), *adj.* 1 not clear or plain; hardly perceptible; dim; indistinct: *faint colors, a faint idea.* 2 weak; feeble; faltering: *a faint voice.* 3 done feebly or without zest: *a faint attempt.* 4 about to faint or lose consciousness; dizzy and weak. 5 lacking courage; cowardly: *a faint heart.* *—v.i.* 1 lose consciousness temporarily. 2 ARCHAIC. grow weak; lose courage: *"Ye shall reap, if ye faint not."* *—n.* a temporary loss of consciousness, often brought on by great hunger, sudden fear, illness, etc. [< Old French *feint,* past participle of *feindre.* See FEIGN.] **—faint′ly,** *adv.* **—faint′ness,** *n.*

faint heart ed (fānt′här′tid), *adj.* lacking courage to carry a thing through; cowardly; timid. **—faint′heart′ed ly,** *adv.* **—faint′heart′ed ness,** *n.*

fair[1] (fer, far), *adj.* 1 not favoring one more than others; just; honest: *a fair judge.* See synonym study below. 2 according to the rules: *fair play.* 3 not good and not bad; average; passable: *There is a fair crop of wheat this year.* 4 giving promise of success; favorable: *a fair prospect.* 5 not dark; light: *A blond person has fair hair and skin.* 6 not cloudy or stormy; clear or sunny: *The weather will be fair today.* 7 pleasing to see; beautiful: *a fair lady.* 8 gentle: *fair words.* 9 without spots or stains; clean: *She made a fair copy of her essay.* 10 easily read; plain: *fair handwriting.* 11 not obstructed; open:

a fair view of the ocean. 12 seeming good at first, but not really so: *His fair promises proved false.*
—*adv.* 1 in a fair manner; honestly: *play fair.* 2 **bid fair,** seem likely; have a good chance.
—*n.* ARCHAIC. woman; sweetheart.
[Old English *fæger*] —**fair′ness,** *n.*
Syn. *adj.* 1 **Fair, just, impartial** mean not showing favor in making judgments. **Fair** implies equal consideration of all sides without being swayed by personal feelings or interests: *The umpire is fair even to players he dislikes.* **Just** emphasizes acting only according to what is right or lawful: *A judge's decisions must be just.* **Impartial** emphasizes absence of prejudices regarding the matter at issue: *We need someone impartial to settle this quarrel.*

fair[2] (fer, far), *n.* 1 a display of products, goods, etc., of a certain region or group, at which prizes are often given for the best farm products, livestock, etc., and entertainment may also be offered: *a county fair.* 2 a periodical gathering of buyers and sellers, often held in a certain place at regular times during the year. 3 entertainment and sale of articles; bazaar: *Our church held a fair to raise money for charity.* [< Old French *feire* < Medieval Latin *feria* holiday < Latin *feriae* holidays, festival]

fair ball, a batted ball in baseball that is not a foul, permitting the batter to start around the bases.

Fair banks (far′bangks′, fer′bangks′), *n.* city in central Alaska. 15,000.

Fair Deal, name given by President Harry S. Truman to his domestic policy, particularly during and after the 1948 Presidential campaign.

Fair fax (fer′faks, far′faks), *n.* **Thomas,** third Baron, 1612-1671, English general.

fair game, 1 animals or birds that it is lawful to hunt. 2 a suitable object of pursuit or attack.

fair ground (fer′ground′, far′ground′), *n.* place outdoors where fairs are held.

fair ing (fer′ing, far′ing), *n.* an outer structure or surface of an aircraft, ship, etc., which reduces air or water resistance.

fair ish (fer′ish, far′ish), *adj.* fairly good, well, or large.

fair ly (fer′lē, far′lē), *adv.* 1 in a fair manner. 2 to a fair degree; tolerably. 3 justly; honestly. 4 moderately; rather: *She is a fairly good pupil, neither bad nor very good.* 5 absolutely; positively: *He was fairly beside himself with anger.* 6 clearly.

fair-mind ed (fer′mīn′did, far′mīn′did), *adj.* not prejudiced; just; impartial. —**fair′-mind′ed ness,** *n.*

fair sex, women.

fair-spo ken (fer′spō′kən, far′spō′kən), *adj.* speaking smoothly and pleasantly; civil; courteous.

fair-trade (fer′trād′, far′trād′), *v.t.*, **-trad ed, -trad ing.** 1 set a minimum retail price on (a trademarked product). 2 sell (a trademarked product) in accordance with a fair trade agreement.

fair trade agreement, agreement which permits United States manufacturers to set minimum price levels on products.

fair way (fer′wā′, far′wā′), *n.* 1 an unobstructed passage or way. 2 a safe route or channel for ships in a harbor, river, etc. 3 the part of a golf course between the tee and putting green, where the grass is kept short.

fair-weath er (fer′weᴛʜ′ər, far′weᴛʜ′ər), *adj.* 1 of or fitted for fair weather. 2 weakening or failing in time of need: *a fair-weather friend.*

fair y (fer′ē, far′ē), *n., pl.* **fair ies,** *adj.* —*n.* a supernatural being supposed to possess magical powers and to have great influence for good or evil over the affairs of people; fay; sprite. In modern stories, fairies are usually described as very small and sometimes very lovely and delicate; in medieval stories, however, they are often of full human size. —*adj.* 1 of fairies. 2 like a fairy; lovely and delicate. [< Old French *faerie* < *fae.* See FAY.] —**fair′y like′,** *adj.*

fair y land (fer′ē land′, far′ē land′), *n.* 1 the home of the fairies. 2 an enchanting and pleasant place.

fairy ring, a ring of grass differing in color from the grass surrounding it, caused by the growth of certain fungi.

fairy tale, 1 story about fairies or other beings with magic powers. 2 an untrue story; falsehood; lie.

Fai sal I (fī′səl), 1885-1933, king of Syria in 1920 and king of Iraq from 1921 to 1933. Also, **Feisal.**

fait ac com pli (fe tȧ kôɴ plē′), FRENCH. an accomplished fact; thing done and therefore no longer worth opposing.

faith (fāth), *n.* 1 belief without proof; trust: *We have faith in our friends.* 2 belief in God, religion, or spiritual things. 3 what is believed; doctrine or tenet. 4 a system of religion; creed: *the Christian faith.* 5 a being loyal; faithfulness.
break faith, break one's promise.
in bad faith, dishonestly.
in faith, truly; indeed.
in good faith, honestly; sincerely.
keep faith, keep one's promise.
—*interj.* truly; indeed.
[< Old French *feit* < Latin *fides* < *fidere* to trust]

faith ful (fāth′fəl), *adj.* 1 worthy of trust; doing one's duty; keeping one's promise; loyal: *a faithful friend, a faithful servant.* See synonym study below. 2 true to fact; accurate: *a faithful account of what happened.* 3 ARCHAIC. full of faith; trusting; believing. —*n.* **the faithful, a** true believers. **b** loyal followers or supporters of any cause, political party, etc. —**faith′ful ly,** *adv.* —**faith′ful ness,** *n.*
Syn. *adj.* 1 **Faithful, loyal, constant** mean true to a person or thing. **Faithful** emphasizes being true to a person or thing to which one is bound by a promise, a pledge, honor, or love: *He is a faithful comrade.* **Loyal** adds to *faithful* the idea of wanting to stand by and fight for the person or thing, even against heavy odds: *His many friends were loyal during his trial.* **Constant** implies steadfast devotion to friends or loved ones: *No two friends were more constant than Damon and Pythias.*

faith less (fāth′lis), *adj.* 1 failing in one's duty; breaking one's promises; not loyal; false: *A traitor is faithless.* 2 that cannot be trusted; not reliable. 3 without faith; unbelieving. —**faith′less ly,** *adv.* —**faith′less ness,** *n.*

fake (fāk), *v.,* **faked, fak ing,** *n., adj.* —*v.t.* 1 make, invent, or tamper with in order to deceive: *The picture was faked by pasting together two photographs.* 2 give intentionally a false impression of; pretend: *fake an illness.* —*v.i.* practice deception; produce a fake. —*n.* 1 anything made to seem other than what it actually is; fraud; deception: *The beggar's limp was a fake.* 2 person who fakes. —*adj.* intended to deceive; false: *The firm forbids its salespeople to use fake testimonials.* [origin uncertain] —**fak′er,** *n.*

fak er y (fā′kər ē), *n., pl.* **-er ies.** INFORMAL. deceit; fraud.

fa kir (fə kir′, fā′kər), *n.* 1 a Moslem holy man who lives by begging. 2 dervish. 3 a Hindu ascetic. Fakirs sometimes do extraordinary things, such as lying upon sharp knives. [< Arabic *faqīr* poor (man)]

Fa lange (fā′lanj, fə lanj′; *Spanish* fä-läng′ʜä), *n.* a Spanish fascist group holding power in Spain since the Spanish civil war, 1936-1939.

Fa lan gist (fə lan′jist), *n.* member of the Falange.

fal cate (fal′kāt), *adj.* curved like a sickle; hooked. [< Latin *falcatus* < *falcem* sickle]

falchion
(def. 1)

fal chion (fôl′chən), *n.* 1 sword having a short, broad blade with an edge that curves sharply to the point. 2 any sword. [< Old French *fauchon,* ultimately < Latin *falcem* sickle]

fal con (fôl′kən, fal′kən, fô′kən), *n.* 1 any of various hawks trained to hunt and kill other birds and small game. In the Middle Ages, hunting with falcons was a popular sport. 2 the female peregrine. 3 any of a family of swift-flying hawks having short, curved, notched bills and long claws and wings. [< Late Latin *falconem* < Latin *falcem* sickle (because of the hooked talons)]

fal con er (fôl′kə nər, fal′kə nər, fô′kə nər), *n.* 1 person who hunts with falcons; hawker. 2 person who breeds and trains falcons for hunting.

fal con ry (fôl′kən rē, fal′kən rē, fô′kən-rē), *n.* 1 sport of hunting with falcons. 2 the training of falcons to hunt.

fal de ral (fäl′də räl′), *n.* 1 a flimsy thing; trifle. 2 nonsense; rubbish. Also, **folderol.** [originally, nonsense syllables used as refrain in songs]

Falk land Islands (fôk′lənd, fôlk′lənd), group of islands in the S Atlantic, east of the Strait of Magellan, administered by Great Britain but claimed also by Argentina. 2000 pop.; 4600 sq. mi. *Capital:* Stanley. See **Chile** for map.

fall (fôl), *v.,* **fell, fall en, fall ing,** *n.* —*v.i.* 1 drop or come down from a higher place; pass downward under the influence of gravity; descend freely: *The snow falls fast. Leaves fall from the trees.* 2 come down suddenly from an erect position: *He fell on his knees.* 3 hang down: *Her curls fell upon her shoulders.* 4 be directed downward: *She blushed, and her eyes fell.* 5 do wrong; sin; become bad or worse: *Adam and Eve were tempted and fell.* 6 lose position, power, dignity, etc.; be taken by any evil: *The ruler fell from the people's favor.* 7 be captured, overthrown, or destroyed: *The fort fell to the*

hat, āge, fär; let, ēqual, tėrm;
it, ice; hot, ōpen, ôrder;
oil, out; cup, pu̇t, rüle;
ch, child; ng, long; sh, she;
th, thin; ᴛʜ, then; zh, measure;

ə represents *a* in about, *e* in taken, *i* in pencil, *o* in lemon, *u* in circus.

< = from, derived from, taken from.

enemy. 8 drop wounded or dead; be killed: *Many men fell in that battle.* 9 pass into some condition, position, etc.; become: *He fell sick. The rent falls due on Monday.* 10 come as if by dropping; arrive: *When night falls, the stars appear.* 11 come by chance or lot: *Our choice fell on him.* 12 come to pass; happen; occur: *Christmas falls on Sunday this year.* 13 pass by inheritance: *The money fell to the only son.* 14 have proper place or position: *The accent of "farmer" falls on the first syllable.* 15 become lower or less: *Prices fell sharply. The water in the river has fallen two feet. Her voice fell.* 16 be divided: *The story falls into five parts.* 17 look sad or disappointed: *His face fell at the news.* 18 to slope downward: *The land falls gradually to the beach.* 19 be directed: *The light falls on my book.*

fall back, go toward the rear; retreat; recede.

fall back on, a go back to for safety. **b** turn to for help or support.

fall behind, fail to keep up; lose ground.

fall for, SLANG. **a** be deceived by. **b** fall in love with.

fall in, a take a place in a military formation and come to a position of attention. **b** meet. **c** agree. **d** collapse toward the inside: *The building fell in.*

fall off, become less; drop.

fall on, attack.

fall out, a leave a place in a military formation. **b** stop being friends; quarrel. **c** turn out; happen.

fall through, fail: *His plans fell through.*

fall to, a begin. **b** begin to attack, eat, etc.

fall under, belong under; be classified as.

fall upon, attack.

—n. 1 a dropping from a higher place; coming down by the force of gravity: *The fall from his horse broke his shoulder.* 2 amount that comes down: *We had a heavy fall of snow last winter.* 3 distance that anything drops or comes down: *The fall of the river here is two feet.* 4 Usually, **falls,** *pl.* fall of water; waterfall. 5 a coming down suddenly from an erect position: *The child had a bad fall.* 6 a hanging down; dropping. 7 a becoming bad or worse. 8 capture, overthrow, or destruction. 9 proper place or position: *the fall of an accent.* 10 a becoming lower or less: *a fall in prices, the fall of the tide.* 11 a downward slope. 12 autumn. 13 way of throwing or being thrown in wrestling. 14 contest in wrestling. 15 **falls,** *pl.* apparatus used in lowering and raising a ship's boat. 16 **ride for a fall,** act so as to invite danger or trouble. 17 **the Fall,** the sin of Adam and Eve in yielding to temptation and eating the forbidden fruit.

[Old English *feallan*]

fal la cious (fə lā′shəs), *adj.* 1 that causes disappointment; deceptive; misleading: *a fallacious peace.* 2 logically unsound; erroneous: *fallacious reasoning.* **—fal la′cious ly,** *adv.* **—fal la′cious ness,** *n.*

fal la cy (fal′ə sē), *n., pl.* **-cies.** 1 a false idea; mistaken belief; error: *It is a fallacy to suppose that riches always bring happiness.* 2 mistake in reasoning; misleading or unsound argument. [< Latin *fallacia* < *fallacem* deceptive < *fallere* deceive]

fall en (fô′lən), *v.* pp. of **fall.** *—adj.* 1 dropped: *fallen arches.* 2 face down; down on the ground; down flat: *a fallen tree.* 3 degraded. 4 overthrown or destroyed. 5 dead.

fall guy, INFORMAL. person left to face the blame or consequences of something; scapegoat.

fal li bil i ty (fal′ə bil′ə tē), *n.* fallible condition or quality.

fal li ble (fal′ə bəl), *adj.* 1 liable to be deceived or mistaken; liable to err. 2 liable to be erroneous, inaccurate, or false: *Strong emotion can make human judgment fallible.* [< Medieval Latin *fallibilis* < Latin *fallere* deceive] **—fal′li bly,** *adv.*

fall ing-out (fô′ling out′), *n., pl.* **fallings-out.** disagreement or quarrel.

falling star, meteor.

fall line, 1 line that marks the end of layers of hard rock of a plateau and the beginning of a softer rock layer of a plain. There are many waterfalls and rapids along this line. 2 **Fall Line,** a fall line running north and south to the east of the Appalachian Mountains.

Fal lo pi an tubes (fə lō′pē ən), pair of slender tubes through which ova from the ovaries pass to the uterus. [< Gabriel *Fallopius,* 1523-1562, Italian anatomist, who described them]

fall out (fôl′out′), *n.* the radioactive particles or dust that fall to the earth after a nuclear explosion.

fal low[1] (fal′ō), *adj.* 1 plowed and left unseeded for a season or more. 2 (of the mind) uncultivated or inactive. *—n.* 1 land plowed and left unseeded for a season or more. 2 the plowing of land without seeding it for a season in order to destroy weeds, improve the soil, etc.; inactive period. *—v.t.* plow and break up (land) without seeding. [Old English *fealg*] **—fal′low ness,** *n.*

fal low[2] (fal′ō), *adj.* pale yellowish-brown. [Old English *fealu*]

fallow deer, a small European deer with a yellowish coat that is spotted with white in the summer.

Fall River, city in SE Massachusetts. 97,000.

false (fôls), *adj.,* **fals er, fals est,** *adv. —adj.* 1 contrary to what is true; not correct; wrong: *false statements.* 2 not truthful; lying: *a false witness.* 3 not loyal; not faithful; deceitful: *a false friend.* 4 used to deceive; deceiving: *false weights.* 5 (in music) not true in pitch: *a false note.* 6 not real; artificial: *false diamonds.* See synonym study below. 7 based on wrong notions; ill-founded: *false pride.* 8 (in biology) inaccurately so called, usually because of a deceptive resemblance to another species. One name for the locust tree is "false acacia." *—adv.* 1 in a false manner. 2 **play one false,** deceive or betray one. [< Latin *falsus* < *fallere* deceive] **—false′ly,** *adv.* **—false′ness,** *n.*

Syn. *adj.* 6 **False, counterfeit** mean not real or genuine. **False** does not necessarily suggest that an imitation is intended to deceive: *The false front of the building partially hid its pitched roof.* **Counterfeit** always suggests a dishonest attempt to make the imitation closely resemble the genuine: *Much counterfeit money is in circulation.*

false bottom, bottom in a trunk or drawer that is used to form a secret or a supplementary compartment.

false colors, 1 flag of another country. 2 false pretenses.

false face, a funny or ugly mask; mask.

false hood (fôls′hu̇d), *n.* 1 a false statement; lie. See **lie**[1] for synonym study. 2 quality of being false; falsity. 3 something false. 4 a making of false statements; lying.

false ribs, ribs unattached to the breastbone. Human beings have five pairs of false ribs.

false step, 1 a wrong step; stumble. 2 blunder; mistake.

fal set to (fôl set′ō), *n., pl.* **-tos,** *adj., adv. —n.* 1 an artificially high-pitched voice, especially in a man. 2 person who sings with such a voice. *—adj.* of or for such a voice; singing in a falsetto. *—adv.* in a falsetto. [< Italian]

fal si fi ca tion (fôl′sə fə kā′shən), *n.* 1 a falsifying; change made to deceive. 2 a being falsified.

fal si fy (fôl′sə fī), *v.,* **-fied, -fy ing.** *—v.t.* 1 make false; change to deceive; misrepresent: *The cheat falsified his bowling score.* 2 prove to be false; disprove. *—v.i.* make false statements; lie. **—fal′si fi′er,** *n.*

fal si ty (fôl′sə tē), *n., pl.* **-ties.** 1 a being false: *Education reveals the falsity of superstitions.* 2 something false; falsehood.

Fal staff (fôl′staf), *n.* Sir **John,** a fat, jolly, swaggering soldier, brazen and without scruples, in three of Shakespeare's plays.

falt boat (fält′bōt′), *n.* a light, collapsible boat similar to a kayak. [< German *Faltboot,* literally, folding boat]

fal ter (fôl′tər), *v.i.* 1 hesitate in action from lack of courage; draw back; waver: *The soldiers faltered for a moment as their captain fell.* See **hesitate** for synonym study. 2 move unsteadily; stumble; totter. 3 come forth in hesitating, broken sounds: *Her voice faltered as she described her fall from the bicycle.* *—v.t.* speak in hesitating or broken words; stammer; stutter: *Greatly embarrassed, he faltered out his thanks.* *—n.* 1 act of faltering. 2 a faltering sound. [Middle English *faltren*] **—fal′ter er,** *n.* **—fal′ter ing ly,** *adv.*

fame (fām), *n.* 1 fact or condition of being very well known; having much said or written about one; renown. 2 what is said about one; reputation. [< Latin *fama* report, rumor, reputation < *fari* speak]

famed (fāmd), *adj.* famous; renowned.

fa mil ial (fə mil′yəl, fə mil′ē əl), *adj.* of, having to do with, or characteristic of a family.

fa mil iar (fə mil′yər), *adj.* 1 known from constant association; well-known: *a familiar face. French is as familiar to him as English.* 2 of everyday use; common; ordinary: *A knife is a familiar tool.* 3 well-acquainted; versed: *He is familiar with French.* 4 extremely close; intimate: *Those familiar friends know each other very well.* See synonym study below. 5 informal; unceremonious: *a familiar attitude.* 6 too friendly; presuming; forward. *—n.* 1 an intimate friend or close acquaintance. 2 spirit or demon supposed to serve a particular person. A black cat was thought to be a witch's familiar. [< Latin *familiaris* < *familia.* See FAMILY.] **—fa mil′iar ly,** *adv.*

Syn. *adj.* 4 **Familiar, intimate, confidential** mean personally near or close. **Familiar** suggests an easy, informal relationship that comes of long or close acquaintance: *I feel very familiar with my cousins.* **Intimate** suggests a very close personal relationship based on affection or common interests: *They have been intimate friends since childhood.* **Confidential** suggests mutual trust and willingness to share personal secrets or private affairs: *The twin sisters had always lived on the most intimate and confidential terms.*

fa mil iar i ty (fə mil′yar′ə tē), *n., pl.* **-ties.** 1 close acquaintance; knowledge; intimacy. 2 thing done or said in a familiar way: *She dislikes such familiarities as the use of her first name by people that she has just met.* 3 lack of formality or ceremony.

fa mil ia rize (fə mil′yə rīz′), *v.t.,* **-rized, -riz ing.** 1 make (a person) well acquainted with something; accustom: *Before playing the new game, familiarize yourself with the rules.* 2 make well known: *Exploration in space has familiarized the word "astronaut."* **—fa mil′iar i za′tion,** *n.*

fam i ly (fam′ə lē), *n., pl.* **-lies.** 1 parents and their children thought of as a group. 2 children of a father and mother; offspring. 3 group of people living in the same house. 4 all of a person's relatives. 5 group of related people; tribe or clan. 6 group of related animals or plants, ranking below an order and above a genus. Lions, tigers, and leopards belong to the cat family. See **classification** for chart. 7 any group of related or similar things. [< Latin *familia* household < *famulus* servant]

family name, the last name of all the members of a certain family; surname.

family tree, 1 diagram showing the relationships and descent of all the members and ancestors of a family; genealogical chart. 2 all the members of a family line.

fam ine (fam′ən), *n.* 1 lack of food in a place; time of starving: *Many people died during the famine in India.* 2 starvation. 3 a great lack; scarcity; shortage: *a coal famine.* [< Old French < *faim* hunger < Latin *fames*]

fam ish (fam′ish), *v.i., v.t.* 1 be or make extremely hungry; starve. 2 starve to death.

fa mous (fā′məs), *adj.* 1 very well-known; much talked about or written about; noted; celebrated. See synonym study below. 2 INFORMAL. excellent; first-rate. **—fa′mous ly,** *adv.*

Syn. 1 **Famous, renowned, noted** mean very well known. **Famous** implies being widely and usually favorably known: *A great crowd of people greeted the famous statesman.* **Renowned** implies great and enduring fame, glory, and honor: *Marie Curie was a renowned scientist.* **Noted** implies being well-known or especially noticed for some particular thing: *A noted architect designed the store.* ➔ See **notorious** for usage note.

fan[1] (fan), *n., v.,* **fanned, fan ning.** *—n.* 1 instrument or device that produces an artificial breeze for cooling the skin, blowing dust or odors away, etc. 2 such a device of stiff paper, feathers, etc., to be held in the hand, which is folded or spread out into part of a circle. 3 such an instrument consisting of a series of revolving blades, turned by an electric motor or the belt from the drive shaft of an automobile. 4 anything spread out like an open fan. 5 machine for winnowing grain, etc. *—v.t.* 1 stir (the air) with a fan. 2 direct a current of air toward with a fan or anything like a fan: *Fan the fire to make it burn faster.* 3 drive away with a fan, etc.: *She fanned the flies from the sleeping child.* 4 stir up; arouse: *Bad treatment fanned their dislike into hate.* 5 spread out like an open fan: *He fanned the cards.* 6 winnow (grain, etc.). *—v.i.* 1 (in baseball) to strike out. 2 **fan out,** spread out like an open fan. [Old English *fann* < Latin *vannus*] **—fan′like′,** *adj.* **—fan′ner,** *n.*

fan[2] (fan), *n.* INFORMAL. 1 a regular spectator or enthusiastic follower of baseball, movies, television, etc. 2 an enthusiastic admirer of an actor, writer, etc. [short for *fanatic*]

fa nat ic (fə nat′ik), *n.* person who is carried away beyond reason by his feelings or beliefs, especially in religion or politics. *—adj.* unreasonably enthusiastic or zealous, especially in religion or politics. [< Latin *fanaticus* inspired by divinity < *fanum* temple]

fa nat i cal (fə nat′ə kəl), *adj.* fanatic. **—fa nat′i cal ly,** *adv.*

fa nat i cism (fə nat′ə siz′əm), *n.* excessive or unreasonable enthusiasm; extreme zeal, especially in matters of religion or politics.

fan belt, a reinforced rubber belt behind the radiator of an automobile engine that is rotated by the drive shaft and serves to turn the generator and radiator fan.

fan cied (fan′sēd), *adj.* imagined; imaginary: *a fancied insult.*

fan ci er (fan′sē ər), *n.* person who has a liking for or is especially interested in something: *a dog fancier.*

fan ci ful (fan′sə fəl), *adj.* 1 showing fancy in design; quaint or odd in construction or appearance: *a fanciful decoration.* 2 led by fancy; using fancies; imaginative. 3 suggested by fancy; imaginary; unreal: *A story about a child taking a trip to the planet Venus is fanciful.* **—fan′ci ful ly,** *adv.* **—fan′ci ful ness,** *n.*

fan cy (fan′sē), *v.,* **-cied, -cy ing,** *n., pl.* **-cies,** *adj.,* **-ci er, -ci est.** *—v.t.* 1 picture to oneself; imagine; conceive: *Can you fancy yourself on the moon?* 2 have an idea or belief; suppose: *I fancy that is right, but I am not sure.* 3 be fond of; like: *I fancy the idea of having a picnic.*
—n. 1 power to imagine; imagination; fantasy: *Dragons, fairies, and giants are creatures of fancy.* See **imagination** for synonym study. 2 something imagined. 3 something supposed; idea; notion: *That's just a fancy; don't believe it.* 4 a liking; fondness: *They took a great fancy to each other.* 5 a liking that lasts only a short time. 6 critical judgment in matters of art, and the like; taste.
—adj. 1 made or arranged especially to please; valued for beauty rather than use; decorated; ornamental. 2 requiring much skill: *fancy skating.* 3 chosen to please the fancy or one's special taste, etc.: *fancy fruit.* 4 much too high: *fancy prices.* 5 bred for special excellence.
[contraction of *fantasy*] **—fan′ci ly,** *adv.* **—fan′ci ness,** *n.*

fancy dress, costume arranged according to the wearer's fancy, worn at a masquerade.

fan cy-free (fan′sē frē′), *adj.* not in love; not bound to anyone; able to center one's affection and attention upon whomever one wishes.

fan cy work (fan′sē wėrk′), *n.* ornamental needlework; embroidery, crocheting, etc.

fan dan go (fan dang′gō), *n., pl.* **-gos.** 1 a lively Spanish or Spanish-American dance in three-quarter time. 2 music for such a dance. [< Spanish]

fane (fān), *n.* ARCHAIC. temple; church. [< Latin *fanum* temple]

fan fare (fan′fer, fan′far), *n.* 1 a short tune or call played on trumpets, bugles, hunting horns, or the like. 2 a loud show of activity, talk, etc.; showy flourish. [< French]

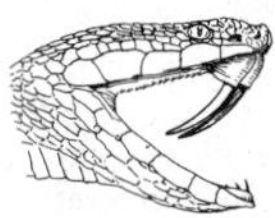

fang (def. 3) fangs of a rattlesnake

fang (fang), *n.* 1 a long, pointed tooth with which an animal grasps, holds, or tears its prey. 2 **fangs,** *pl.* the canine teeth of dogs, wolves, tigers, etc. 3 one of the long, hollow or grooved teeth of a poisonous snake with which it injects venom. 4 a long, slender, tapering part of anything, such as the prong of a fork. [Old English, something caught, prey]

fanged (fangd), *adj.* having fangs.

fan jet (fan′jet′), *n.* 1 turbofan. 2 aircraft powered by a turbofan.

fan light (fan′līt′), *n.* 1 a semicircular window with bars spread out like an open fan. 2 any semicircular or other window over a door.

fantail (def. 2)

fan tail (fan′tāl′), *n.* 1 tail, end, or part spread out like an open fan. 2 pigeon, goldfish, or other animal whose tail spreads out like an open fan. 3 the slender, overhanging part of the stern of some ships.

fan-tan (fan′tan′), *n.* 1 a Chinese gambling game played by betting on the number of coins under a bowl. 2 a card game in which the player who gets rid of his cards first wins the game. [< Chinese *fan t'an* repeated divisions]

fan ta si a (fan tā′zhē ə, fan tā′zhə, fan tā′zē ə), *n.* 1 a musical composition following no fixed form or style. 2 medley of well-known airs connected by interludes. [< Italian]

fan tas tic (fan tas′tik), *adj.* 1 very odd or queer; wild and strange in shape or manner; due to unrestrained fancy: *The firelight cast weird, fantastic shadows on the walls.* 2 very fanciful; capricious; eccentric; irrational: *The idea that machines could be made to fly seemed fantastic a hundred years ago.* 3 existing only in the imagination; imaginary; unreal: *Superstition causes fantastic fears.* 4 INFORMAL. unbelievably good, quick, high, etc.: *That store charges fantastic prices.* **—fan tas′ti cal ly,** *adv.* **—fan tas′ti cal ness,** *n.*

fan tas ti cal (fan tas′tə kəl), *adj.* fantastic.

fan ta sy (fan′tə sē, fan′tə zē), *n., pl.* **-sies.** 1 play of the mind; product of the imagination; fancy. 2 picture existing only in the mind; any strange mental image or illusion.

Fantasies seem real to a delirious person. 3 a wild, strange fancy. 4 caprice; whim. 5 (in music) fantasia. Also, **phantasy.** [< Old French *fantasie* < Latin *phantasia* < Greek, appearance, image, ultimately < *phainein* to show]

FAO, Food and Agricultural Organization (of the United Nations).

far (fär), *adj., adv.,* **far ther** or **fur ther, far thest** or **fur thest.** *—adj.* 1 not near; distant: *a far country. Your birthday is not far from mine.* See **distant** for synonym study. 2 more distant; the remoter of two: *the far side of the hill.* 3 extending to a great distance; long: *a far journey.* *—adv.* 1 a long way; a long way off in time or space. 2 very much: *It is far better to go by train.* 3 to an advanced distance, point, or degree: *He studied far into the night.*
as far as, to the distance, point, or degree that.
by far, very much.
far and away, very much.
far and near, everywhere.
far and wide, everywhere; even in distant parts.
how far, to what distance, point, or degree; how much.
in so far as, to the extent that.
so far, a to this or that point. **b** until now or then.
so far as, to the extent that.
[Old English *feorr*]

far ad (far′əd), *n.* unit of electrical capacitance equivalent to the capacitance of a condenser that, when charged with one coulomb, gives a potential of one volt. [< Michael *Faraday*]

far a day (far′ə dā, far′ə dē), *n.* unit of quantity of electricity that, in electrolysis, is necessary to deposit one gram atom of a univalent element, or about 96,500 coulombs. [< Michael *Faraday*]

Far a day (far′ə dā, far′ə dē), *n.* **Michael,** 1791-1867, English physicist and chemist.

fa rad ic (fə rad′ik), *adj.* of or having to do with induced currents of electricity.

far a way (fär′ə wā′), *adj.* 1 far away; distant; remote: *faraway places.* 2 dreamy: *a faraway look.*

farce (färs), *n.* 1 a play full of ridiculous happenings, absurd actions, and unreal situations, meant to be very funny. 2 kind of humor found in such plays; broad humor. 3 a ridiculous mockery; absurd pretense; sham: *The trial was a mere farce.* [< French, literally, stuffing < Old French *farcir* to stuff < Latin *farcire*]

far ci cal (fär′sə kəl), *adj.* of or like a farce; ridiculous; absurd. **—far′ci cal ly,** *adv.*

far ci cal i ty (fär′sə kal′ə tē), *n.* farcical quality or character.

far cry, a long way: *a far cry from home, a far cry from what we had hoped.*

far del (fär′dl), *n.* ARCHAIC. bundle; burden. [< Old French]

fare (fer, far), *n., v.,* **fared, far ing.** *—n.* 1 the money paid to ride in a taxi, bus, train, airplane, etc. 2 passenger. 3 food: *dainty fare.* *—v.i.* 1 eat food; be fed: *We fared very well at Grandmother's.* 2 get along; get on; do: *She is faring well in school.* 3 turn out; happen: *It will fare hard with you if you ignore the parking ticket.* 4 ARCHAIC. go; travel. [Old English *faran* go, travel]

Far East, China, Japan, and other parts of E Asia, including Korea and E Siberia. **—Far Eastern.**

fare-thee-well (fer′thē wel′, far′thē wel′), *n.* **to a fare-thee-well,** to the last point or utmost degree; completely.

fare well (fer′wel′, far′wel′), *interj.* 1 good luck; good-by. 2 expression of good wishes at parting. *—n.* 1 good luck; good-by. 2 expression of good wishes at parting. 3 departure; leave-taking. *—adj.* of farewell; parting; last: *a farewell kiss.*

far fetched (fär′fecht′), *adj.* not closely related to the topic; remotely connected; forced; strained.

far-flung (fär′flung′), *adj.* covering a large area; widely spread.

fa ri na (fə rē′nə), *n.* 1 flour or meal made from grain, potatoes, beans, nuts, etc., and used as cereal or in puddings, etc. 2 starch. [< Latin < *far,* a kind of wheat, coarse meal]

far i na ceous (far′ə nā′shəs), *adj.* consisting of flour or meal; starchy; mealy.

farm (färm), *n.* 1 piece of land used to raise crops or animals. 2 tract of water where certain animals are raised, especially for food: *an oyster farm.* 3 U.S. a minor-league baseball team belonging to or associated with a major-league club. Young players are usually sent to a farm to gain experience. *—v.i.* raise crops or animals on a farm either to eat or to sell: *Her father farms for a living.* *—v.t.* 1 cultivate (land); till: *He farms forty acres.* 2 take proceeds or profits of (a tax, undertaking, etc.) on paying a fixed sum. 3 let the labor or services of (a person) for hire. 4 **farm out, a** let for hire. **b** assign to a baseball team in a minor league. [< Old French *ferme* fixed rent or charge < *fermer* fasten, fix on, decide < Latin *firmare* make firm < *firmus* firm]

farm er (fär′mər), *n.* 1 person who owns or works on a farm. 2 person who takes a contract for the collection of taxes by agreeing to pay a certain sum to the government.

farm hand (färm′hand′), *n.* person who works on a farm.

farm house (färm′hous′), *n., pl.* **-hous es** (-hou′ziz). house to live in on a farm.

farm ing (fär′ming), *n.* 1 occupation or business of raising crops or animals on a farm; agriculture. 2 practice of letting out the collection of a public revenue. 3 condition of being let out at a fixed sum.

farm land (färm′land′, färm′lənd), *n.* land suitable for or used for raising crops or grazing.

farm stead (färm′sted), *n.* farm with its buildings.

farm yard (färm′yärd′), *n.* yard connected with the farm buildings or enclosed by them.

far o (fer′ō, far′ō), *n.* a gambling game played by betting on the order in which certain cards will appear. [apparently alteration of *Pharaoh*]

Far oe Islands (fer′ō, far′ō), Faeroe Islands.

far-off (fär′ôf′, fär′of′), *adj.* far away; distant; remote.

far-out (fär′out′), *adj.* SLANG. 1 very unconventional: *a far-out sport.* 2 very abstruse: *far-out research.* 3 extreme: *a far-out reactionary.*

far ra go (fə rā′gō, fə rä′gō), *n., pl.* **-goes.** a confused mixture; hodgepodge; jumble. [< Latin, mixed fodder, ultimately < *far* grits]

Far ra gut (far′ə gət), *n.* **David Glasgow,** 1801-1870, American admiral on the Union side during the Civil War.

far-reach ing (fär′rē′ching), *adj.* having a wide influence or effect; extending far; extensive.

hat, āge, fär; let, ēqual, tėrm;
it, īce; hot, ōpen, ôrder;
oil, out; cup, pu̇t, rüle;
ch, child; ng, long; sh, she;
th, thin; ᴛʜ, then; zh, measure;

ə represents *a* in about, *e* in taken, *i* in pencil, *o* in lemon, *u* in circus.

< = from, derived from, taken from.

far ri er (far′ē ər), *n.* 1 blacksmith who shoes horses. 2 veterinarian. [< Middle French *ferrier* < Latin *ferrarius* < *ferrum* iron]

far row (far′ō), *n.* litter of pigs. *—v.i.* give birth to a litter of pigs. *—v.t.* give birth to (pigs). [Old English *fearh*]

far see ing (fär′sē′ing), *adj.* 1 able to see far. 2 looking ahead; planning wisely for the future.

far sight ed (fär′sī′tid), *adj.* 1 seeing distant things more clearly than near ones because the parallel light rays entering the eye come to a focus behind, rather than on, the retina; not seeing nearby objects clearly; hyperopic. 2 looking ahead; planning wisely for the future; shrewd; prudent. **—far′sight′ed ly,** *adv.* **—far′sight′ed ness,** *n.*

far ther (fär′ᴛʜər), *comparative of* **far.** *—adj.* 1 more distant; more remote: *Three miles is farther than two.* 2 more; additional: *Do you need farther help?* *—adv.* 1 at or to a greater distance: *Go no farther.* 2 at or to a more advanced point: *That scientist has investigated the subject farther than any other scholar in the field.* 3 in addition; also.
➤ **farther, further.** In formal English a distinction is often made between *farther* and *further,* confining the first to expressions of physical distance and the second to abstract relationships of degree or quantity: *He lives farther from town than I do. She needs further schooling.* In informal English the distinction is not usually kept.

far ther most (fär′ᴛʜər mōst), *adj.* most distant; farthest.

far thest (fär′ᴛʜist), *superlative of* **far.** *—adj.* 1 most distant or remote. 2 longest. *—adv.* 1 to or at the greatest distance. 2 most.

far thing (fär′ᴛʜing), *n.* a former British coin worth a fourth of a British penny. [Old English *fēorthung* < *fēortha* fourth]

farthingale

far thin gale (fär′ᴛʜing gāl), *n.* a hoop skirt or framework for extending a woman's skirt, worn in England from about 1550 to about 1650. [< Middle French *verdugale,* ultimately < Latin *viridis* green]

Far West, the part of the United States between the Rocky Mountains and the Pacific Ocean.

f.a.s. or **F.A.S.,** free alongside ship (delivery to the ship without charge to the buyer).

fas ces (fas′ēz′), *n.pl. of* **fas cis** (fas′is). bundle of rods or sticks containing an ax with the blade projecting, carried before a Roman magistrate as a symbol of authority. [< Latin, bundles]

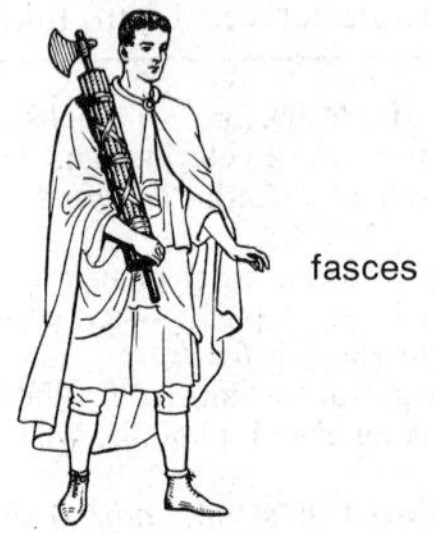
fasces

fas ci a (fash′ē ə), *n., pl.* **fas ci ae** (fash′ē ē). 1 band; fillet; long, flat strip. 2 a usually thin sheet of fibrous connective tissue covering, supporting, or binding together a muscle, part, or organ. [< Latin]

fas ci al (fash′ē əl), *adj.* 1 of a fascia. 2 consisting of fasciae.

fas ci cle (fas′ə kəl), *n.* 1 a small bundle. 2 a close cluster of flowers, leaves, etc. 3 part of a volume published in installments. [< Latin *fasciculus,* diminutive of *fascis* bundle]

fas ci cled (fas′ə kəld), *adj.* arranged in a fascicle.

fas cic u lar (fə sik′yə lər), *adj.* of or like a fascicle.

fas ci nate (fas′n āt), *v.t.,* **-nat ed, -nat ing.** 1 attract very strongly; enchant by charming qualities; charm: *The actress's beauty and cleverness fascinated everyone.* 2 hold motionless by strange power, by terror, etc.: *Snakes are said to fascinate small birds.* [< Latin *fascinatum* bewitched < *fascinum* a spell]

fas ci nat ing (fas′n ā′ting), *adj.* irresistibly attractive; enchanting; charming. **—fas′ci nat′ing ly,** *adv.*

fas ci na tion (fas′n ā′shən), *n.* 1 a fascinating. 2 a being fascinated. 3 irresistible attraction; charm; enchantment.

fas ci na tor (fas′n ā′tər), *n.* 1 person or thing that fascinates. 2 a crocheted scarf worn as a head covering by women.

fas cine (fa sēn′), *n.* bundle of long sticks tied together, used to line trenches, strengthen earthworks, etc. [< French]

fas cism or **Fas cism** (fash′iz′əm), *n.* 1 the principles or methods of a government or a political party favoring rule by a dictator, with strong control of industry and labor by the central government, great restrictions upon the freedom of individuals, and extreme nationalism and militarism. 2 **fascism,** any movement favoring such a system of government. 3 **Fascism,** the form of government in Italy from 1922 to 1943, under Benito Mussolini. [< Italian *fascismo* < *fascio* bundle (as political emblem) < Latin *fascis*]

fas cist or **Fas cist** (fash′ist), *n.* 1 member of a political party favoring the principles and methods of fascism. 2 **Fascist,** member of a strongly nationalistic political party that seized control of the Italian government in 1922 under the leadership of Benito Mussolini. 3 **fascist,** person who favors and supports fascism. *—adj.* of or having to do with fascism or fascists.

fas cis tic or **Fas cis tic** (fa shis′tik), *adj.* fascist.

fash ion (fash′ən), *n.* 1 way a thing is made, shaped, or done; manner: *walk in a peculiar fashion.* 2 the prevailing custom; a current usage, especially one characteristic of a particular place or period of time. See synonym study below. 3 polite society; fashionable people. 4 **after a fashion** or **in a fashion,** in some way or other; not very well. *—v.t.* 1 make, shape, or form: *He fashioned a whistle out of a piece of wood.* See **make** for synonym study. 2 adapt; accommodate. [< Old French *façon* < Latin *factionem* a doing. Doublet of FACTION.] **—fash′ion er,** *n.*

Syn. *n.* 2 **Fashion, style** mean custom in dress, manners, living arrangements, speech, etc. **Fashion** applies to the custom prevailing at a particular time or among a particular group: *It is no longer the fashion to curtsy in greeting people.* **Style** often applies to a distinctive fashion or to a fashion based on good taste rather than custom: *That dress has such a good style it will be fashionable for years.*

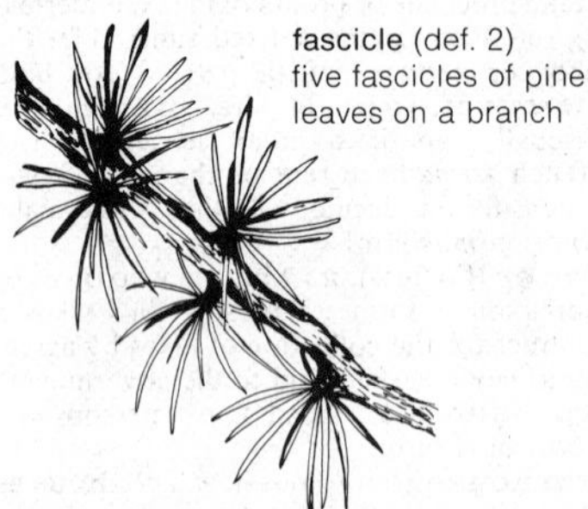
fascicle (def. 2) five fascicles of pine leaves on a branch

fash ion a ble (fash′ə nə bəl), *adj.* 1 following the fashion; in fashion; stylish. 2 of, like, or used by people who set the styles. **—fash′ion a ble ness,** *n.* **—fash′ion a bly,** *adv.*

fast[1] (fast), *adj.* 1 moving quickly; acting or doing with speed; rapid; swift: *a fast runner.* See **quick** for synonym study. 2 indicating a time later than the correct time: *My watch is fast.* 3 too gay or wild; not restrained in pleasures. 4 firm and secure; tight: *a fast hold on a rope.* 5 loyal; steadfast: *They have been fast friends for years.* 6 that will not fade easily: *Good cloth is dyed with fast color.* 7 adapted for speed: *a fast track.* 8 with greater than average speed, force, etc.: *a fast pitcher.* 9 firmly fixed or attached; tightly shut or locked: *a fast window.* 10 (of a film, lens, etc.) making a short exposure possible.

—adv. 1 quickly; rapidly; swiftly. 2 firmly; securely; tightly: *Bolt the door fast.* 3 thoroughly; soundly; completely: *The baby is fast asleep.* 4 ARCHAIC. close; near. 5 **play fast and loose,** be tricky, insincere, or unreliable.

[Old English *fæst*]

fast[2] (fast), *v.i.* go without food; eat little or nothing; go without certain kinds of food: *Some Christians fast during Lent.* *—n.* 1 a fasting. 2 day or time of fasting. 3 **break one's fast,** eat the first food of the day. [Old English *fæstan*]

fast back (fast′bak′), *n.* automobile with a roof that slopes down the rear in an unbroken convex curve.

fas ten (fas′n), *v.t.* 1 tie, lock, or make hold together in any way; fix firmly in place; secure: *fasten a dress, fasten a door.* 2 attach; connect: *He tried to fasten the blame upon his companions.* 3 direct intently; fix: *The dog fastened his eyes on the stranger.* 4 **fasten on** or **fasten upon,** take hold of; seize. *—v.i.* become fixed or fastened together.

fas ten er (fas′n ər), *n.* 1 person who fastens. 2 attachment, device, etc., used to fasten a door, garment, etc. A zipper is a fastener.

fas ten ing (fas′n ing), *n.* device used to fasten things together; fastener.

fas tid i ous (fa stid′ē əs), *adj.* hard to please; dainty in taste; easily disgusted. [< Latin *fastidiosus* < *fastidium* loathing] **—fas tid′i ous ly,** *adv.* **—fas tid′i ous ness,** *n.*

fast ness (fast′nis), *n.* 1 a strong, safe place; stronghold. 2 a being fast or firm; firmness. 3 a being quick or rapid; swiftness.

fat (fat), *n., adj.,* **fat ter, fat test,** *v.,* **fat ted, fat ting.** *—n.* 1 a white or yellow oily substance formed in animal tissue, made up chiefly of carbon, hydrogen, and oxygen. 2 a similar substance found in plants, especially in some seeds. 3 either of these substances used in cookery. 4 animal tissue composed mainly of fat. 5 any of a class of organic compounds of which the natural fats are mixtures, comprising an important group of animal foods. Fats contain carbon, hydrogen, and oxygen, but no nitrogen, and are chiefly compound esters of several acids. They are insoluble in water but dissolve in ether, chloroform, and benzine. 6 something inessential or superfluous; excess. 7 **live off the fat of the land,** have the best of everything. *—adj.* 1 consisting of or containing fat; oily: *fat meat.* 2 in a well-fed condition; fleshy; plump: *a fat baby, a fat pig.* 3 too fat; obese; corpulent. See synonym study below. 4 containing much of some constituent; fertile: *fat land.* 5 yielding much money; profitable: *a fat job.* 6 affording good opportunities. 7 full of good things; plentifully supplied; plentiful. 8 thick; broad. 9 dull; stupid. *—v.t.* make fat; fatten. *—v.i.* become fat. [Old English *fætt*] **—fat′like′,** *adj.* **—fat′ly,** *adv.* **—fat′ness,** *n.*

Syn. *adj.* 3 **Fat, stout, portly** mean having too much flesh. **Fat** commonly applies to any degree from healthy, well-fed plumpness to ugly, unhealthy excess of weight: *The fat man had difficulty walking up the flight of stairs.* **Stout** emphasizes thickness and bulkiness, suggesting firm rather than flabby flesh, but is often used as a euphemism for "too fat": *She calls herself stylishly stout.* **Portly** suggests stately stoutness: *The retired admiral is a portly old gentleman.*

fa tal (fā′tl), *adj.* 1 causing death: *fatal accidents.* See synonym study below. 2 causing destruction or ruin: *The loss of all our money was fatal to our plans.* 3 important; decisive: *At last the fatal day for the contest arrived.* 4 influencing fate. The three goddesses who controlled the fate of mankind were called the **fatal sisters.** [< Latin *fatalis* < *fatum.* See FATE.] **—fa′tal ly,** *adv.*

Syn. 1 **Fatal, deadly, mortal** mean causing death or capable of causing death. **Fatal** applies to what has caused death or will certainly cause it: *Many diseases are no* *longer fatal.* **Deadly** applies to something that is likely to cause death: *Cyanide is a deadly poison.* **Mortal** applies to something that is the direct cause of death: *His wound was mortal.*

fa tal ism (fā′tl iz′əm), *n.* 1 belief that fate controls everything that happens. 2 acceptance of everything that happens because of this belief.

fa tal ist (fā′tl ist), *n.* believer in fatalism.

fa tal is tic (fā′tl is′tik), *adj.* 1 of or having to do with fatalism or fatalists. 2 accepting things and events as inevitable. **—fa′tal-is′ti cal ly,** *adv.*

fa tal i ty (fā tal′ə tē, fə tal′ə tē), *n., pl.* **-ties.** 1 a fatal accident or happening; death: *Careless driving habits cause thousands of fatalities every year.* 2 a fatal influence or effect; deadliness: *Doctors are trying to reduce the fatality of diseases.* 3 liability to disaster. 4 condition of being controlled by fate; inevitable necessity; destiny: *We struggle against fatality in vain.*

fat back (fat′bak′), *n.* salt pork from the upper part of a side of pork.

fate (fāt), *n.* 1 power supposed to fix beforehand and control what is to happen. Fate is beyond any person's control. 2 what is caused by fate: *Drowning was his sad fate.* 3 one's lot or fortune; what happens to a person, group, etc.: *He deserved a better fate.* See synonym study below. 4 what becomes of a person or thing: *The jury decided the fate of the accused.* 5 death or ruin. 6 **Fates,** *pl.* (in Greek and Roman myths) the three goddesses who controlled human life; Clotho, Lachesis, and Atropos; Parcae. [< Latin *fatum* (thing) spoken (that is, by the gods) < *fari* speak]

Syn. 3 **Fate, destiny, doom** mean a person's predetermined and inevitable fortune or lot in life. **Fate** emphasizes the inevitable, irrational, and often cruel power that determines what becomes of a person or thing: *The fate of Joan of Arc was death.* **Destiny,** often used interchangeably with *fate,* suggests a fate all laid out beforehand and not to be changed: *Washington's destiny was to be President.* **Doom** applies to an unhappy or awful end brought about by fate: *The condemned man met his tragic doom.*

fat ed (fā′tid), *adj.* 1 controlled by fate. 2 destined; predestined.

fate ful (fāt′fəl), *adj.* 1 controlled by fate. 2 determining what is to happen; important; decisive: *a fateful battle.* 3 showing what will happen according to fate; prophetic: *fateful words.* 4 causing death, destruction, or ruin; disastrous. **—fate′ful ly,** *adv.* **—fate′ful-ness,** *n.*

fath., fathom.

fa ther (fä′ᴛʜər), *n.* 1 a male parent. 2 **Father,** a God. b the First Person of the Trinity. 3 person who is like a father. 4 a male ancestor; forefather. 5 man who did important work as a maker or leader: *the founding father of an organization.* 6 **the fathers,** the leading men of a city or an assembly. 7 **Father,** title of respect used in addressing a priest or other clergyman. 8 clergyman having this title. 9 title of respect for an old man. 10 senator of ancient Rome. 11 **the fathers,** the chief writers and teachers of the Christian Church during the first six centuries A.D.
—*v.t.* 1 be the father of. 2 take care of as a father does; act as a father to. 3 be the cause of; make; originate.
[Old English *fæder*]

fa ther hood (fä′ᴛʜər hu̇d), *n.* condition of being a father.

fa ther-in-law (fä′ᴛʜər in lô′), *n., pl.* **fa thers-in-law.** father of one's husband or wife.

fa ther land (fä′ᴛʜər land′), *n.* 1 one's native country. 2 land of one's ancestors.

fa ther less (fä′ᴛʜər lis), *adj.* 1 without a father living. 2 without a known father.

fa ther ly (fä′ᴛʜər lē), *adj.* 1 of a father. 2 like a father; like a father's. **—fa′ther li-ness,** *n.*

Father's Day, the third Sunday in June, set apart in the United States in honor of fathers.

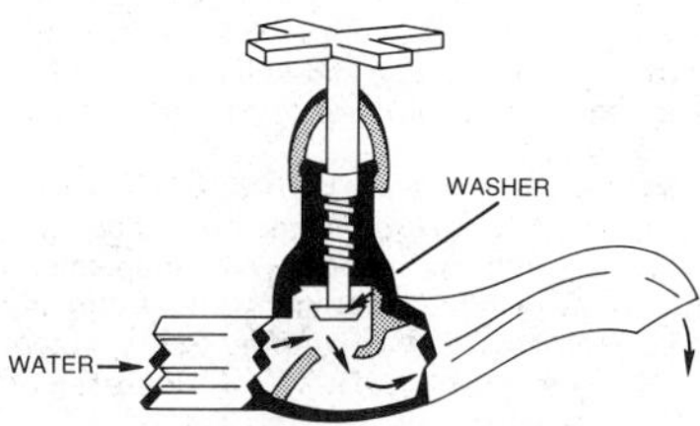

faucet—partly cut away to show water flow when the handle is turned to raise the disk-shaped washer. When the washer is screwed down over the circular opening the water flow stops.

fath om (faᴛʜ′əm), *n., pl.* **fath oms** or **fath om,** *v.* —*n.* unit of measure equal to 6 feet, used mostly in measuring the depth of water and the length of ships' ropes, cables, etc. —*v.t.* 1 measure the depth of (water); sound. 2 get to the bottom of; understand fully. [Old English *fæthm* width of the outstretched arms]

fath om a ble (faᴛʜ′ə mə bəl), *adj.* 1 that can be fathomed. 2 understandable.

Fa thom e ter (fa ᴛʜom′ə tər), *n.* trademark for a type of sonic depth finder.

fath om less (faᴛʜ′əm lis), *adj.* 1 too deep to be measured; bottomless. 2 impossible to be fully understood.

fa tigue (fə tēg′), *n., v.,* **-tigued, -ti guing,** *adj.* —*n.* 1 weariness caused by hard work or effort. 2 task or exertion producing weariness. 3 a weakening (of metal) caused by long-continued use or strain. 4 a temporary decrease in the capacity of an organ or cell to function after excessive activity. 5 fatigue duty. 6 **fatigues,** *pl.* work clothes or uniform worn during fatigue duty. —*v.t.* 1 make weary or tired; cause fatigue in; tire. 2 weaken (metal) by much use or strain. —*v.i.* become fatigued. —*adj.* having to do with fatigue. [< Middle French < *fatiguer* to tire < Latin *fatigare*]

fatigue duty, nonmilitary work done by members of the armed forces, such as cleaning up the camp or repairing roads.

Fa ti ma (fə tē′mə, fat′ə mə), *n.* A.D. 606?-632, favorite daughter of Mohammed.

fat ling (fat′ling), *n.* calf, lamb, kid, or pig fattened to be killed for food.

fat-sol u ble (fat′sol′yə bəl), *adj.* that can be dissolved in fats or in solvents for fats.

fat ten (fat′n), *v.t.* 1 make fat, especially to feed animals for market. 2 make productive; enrich (soil). —*v.i.* grow or become fat. **—fat′ten er,** *n.*

fat ty (fat′ē), *adj.,* **-ti er, -ti est.** 1 of or containing fat: *fatty tissues.* 2 like fat; oily; greasy. **—fat′ti ly,** *adv.* **—fat′ti ness,** *n.*

fatty acid, any of a group of organic acids, some of which, such as stearic acid, are found in animal and vegetable fats and oils.

hat, āge, fär; let, ēqual, tėrm;
it, īce; hot, ōpen, ôrder;
oil, out; cup, pu̇t, rüle;
ch, child; ng, long; sh, she;
th, thin; ᴛʜ, then; zh, measure;

ə represents *a* in about, *e* in taken, *i* in pencil, *o* in lemon, *u* in circus.

< = from, derived from, taken from.

fa tu i ty (fə tü′ə tē, fə tyü′ə tē), *n., pl.* **-ties.** self-satisfied stupidity; idiotic folly; silliness.

fat u ous (fach′ü əs), *adj.* stupid but self-satisfied; foolish; silly. See **foolish** for synonym study. [< Latin *fatuus*] **—fat′u ous ly,** *adv.* **—fat′u ous ness,** *n.*

fau bourg (fō′bu̇r, fō′bu̇rg; *French* fō-bür′), *n.* in France: a suburb. b district in a city. [< Old French *fors bourg* outside town]

fau ces (fô′sēz′), *n.pl.* cavity at the back of the mouth, leading into the pharynx. [< Latin]

fau cet (fô′sit), *n.* device containing a valve for controlling the flow of water or other liquid from a pipe or a container holding it, by opening or closing; spigot. [< Old French *fausset* < *fausser* bore through, originally, break < Latin *falsare* falsify < *falsus* false]

Faulk ner (fôk′nər), *n.* **William,** 1897-1962, American writer, especially of regional novels and stories of the South.

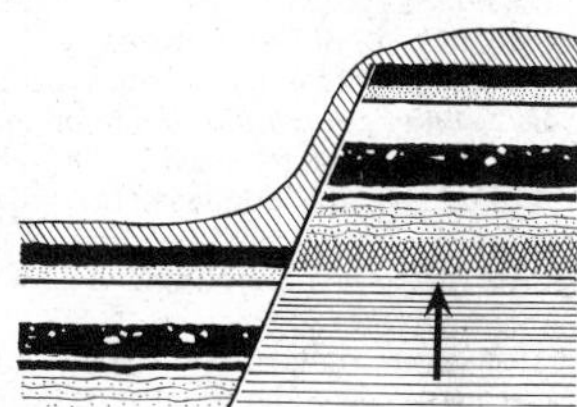

fault (def. 5)—In the fault shown above in cross section, a mass of rock was pushed upward.

fault (fôlt), *n.* 1 something that is not as it should be; flaw; defect. See synonym study below. 2 a failure in what is attempted; mistake; error. 3 misdeed or offense. 4 cause for blame; responsibility. 5 a break in the earth's crust, with the mass of rock on one side of the break pushed up, down, or sideways. 6 failure to serve the ball properly or into the right place in tennis and similar games.
at fault, a deserving blame; wrong. b uncertain.
find fault, find mistakes; complain.
find fault with, object to; criticize.
to a fault, too much; excessively: *generous to a fault.*
—*v.i.* 1 (of rock strata) undergo a fault or faults. 2 commit a fault or faults. —*v.t.* 1 (of rock strata) cause a fault or faults in. 2 find fault with: *We could not fault him on his knowledge of algebra.*
[< Old French *faute* < Popular Latin *fallitus,* ultimately < Latin *fallere* deceive]

Syn. *n.* 1 **Fault, failing** mean a defect of character, personality, habits, etc. **Fault** suggests a lack of something essential to perfection: *Laziness is his greatest fault.* **Failing**

suggests a weakness which may be excusable: *Her slowness in reading is a failing that can be corrected.*

fault find er (fôlt′fīn′dər), *n.* person who finds fault; person who complains.

fault find ing (fôlt′fīn′ding), *n.* act of finding fault. *—adj.* finding fault; complaining; pointing out faults.

fault less (fôlt′lis), *adj.* without a single fault or defect; free from blemish or error; perfect. **—fault′less ly,** *adv.* **—fault′less ness,** *n.*

fault y (fôl′tē), *adj.,* **fault i er, fault i est.** having faults; containing blemishes or errors; wrong; imperfect. **—fault′i ly,** *adv.* **—fault′i ness,** *n.*

faun

faun (fôn), *n.* (in Roman myths) a minor god that lived in fields and woods, represented as a man but having the pointed ears, small horns, tail, and sometimes the legs, of a goat. [< Latin *Faunus*]

fau na (fô′nə), *n., pl.* **-nas, -nae** (-nē′). the animals or animal life of a particular region or time: *the fauna of Australia, the fauna of the Carboniferous period.* [< New Latin < Late Latin *Fauna,* a rural goddess, the wife of *Faunus* faun]

fau nal (fô′nl), *adj.* of or having to do with a fauna or faunas.

Faust (foust), *n.* (in German legends) a man who sold his soul to the devil in return for youth, knowledge, and magic powers.

Fau vism (fō′viz′əm), *n.* style of painting developed in France in the early 1900's, characterized by the use of brilliant colors and bold designs. [< French *Fauvisme,* ultimately *fauves* wild beasts]

Fau vist (fō′vist), *adj.* of or having to do with Fauvism. *—n.* a Fauvist painter.

faux pas (fō′ pä′; fō′ pä′), *pl.* **faux pas** (fō′ päz′; fō′ päz′). slip in speech, conduct, manners, etc.; breach of etiquette; blunder; gaffe. [< French, literally, false step]

fava bean (fä′və, fā′və), broad bean. [< Italian *fava* < Latin *faba* bean]

fa vor (fā′vər), *n.* 1 act of kindness: *Will you do me a favor?* 2 exceptional kindness. 3 liking; approval: *They will look with favor on your plan.* See synonym study below. 4 condition of being liked, accepted, or approved: *A fashion in favor this year may be out of favor next year.* 5 more than fair treatment: *He divided the candy among the children without favor to any one.* 6 gift to show fondness; token: *The knight wore his lady's favor on his arm.* 7 a small token given to every guest at a party, dinner, etc. 8 letter; note: *your favor of the 15th.* 9 ARCHAIC. appearance; look. 10 ARCHAIC. face; countenance. 11 **curry favor,** seek favor by insincere flattery, constant attention, etc. 12 **in favor of, a** on the side of; supporting. **b** to the advantage of; helping. **c** to be paid to: *write a check in favor of the bank.* 13 **in one's favor,** for one; to one's benefit. *—v.t.* 1 show kindness to; oblige: *Favor us with a song.* 2 like; approve; prefer. 3 give more than fair treatment to. 4 be on the side of; support. 5 be to the advantage of; help; aid. 6 treat gently: *The dog favors his sore foot when he walks.* 7 look like: *The girl favors her mother.* Also, BRITISH **favour.** [< Latin < *favere* show kindness to] **—fa′vor er,** *n.*

Syn. *n.* 3 **Favor, good will** mean an attitude of friendly approval. **Favor** applies when the feeling is not outwardly expressed: *The manager looked on the new clerk with favor.* **Good will** applies when the feeling is expressed outwardly and actively: *The audience showed its good will toward the singer by its applause.*

fa vor a ble (fā′vər ə bəl), *adj.* 1 favoring; approving: *a favorable answer.* 2 being to one's advantage; helping; advantageous: *a favorable wind.* 3 boding well; promising: *The weather looks favorable.* See synonym study below. **—fa′vor a ble ness,** *n.* **—fa′vor a bly,** *adv.*

Syn. 3 **Favorable, auspicious** mean promising or giving signs of turning out well. **Favorable** implies that the conditions are right for a successful outcome: *It was a favorable time for our trip, since business was light.* **Auspicious** implies that the signs point to a lucky or successful outcome: *The popularity of her first book was an auspicious beginning of her career.*

fa vor ite (fā′vər it), *adj.* liked better than others. *—n.* 1 person or thing preferred above others. 2 person treated with special favor. 3 person, horse, etc., believed to have the best chance of winning a contest.

favorite son, a Presidential candidate supported chiefly by his own state delegation in the party's national convention.

fa vor it ism (fā′vər ə tiz′əm), *n.* 1 a favoring a certain one or some more than others; having favorites. 2 a being a favorite.

fa vour (fā′vər), *n., v.t.* BRITISH. favor.

Fawkes (fôks), *n.* **Guy,** 1570-1606, English conspirator, leader in a plot to blow up the king and the Houses of Parliament.

fawn[1] (fôn), *n.* 1 a young deer, especially one less than a year old. 2 a light, yellowish brown. *—adj.* light yellowish-brown. [< Old French *faon* young animal, ultimately < Latin *fetus* fetus] **—fawn′like′,** *adj.*

fawn[2] (fôn), *v.i.* 1 try to get favor or notice by slavish acts: *Many flattering relatives fawned on the rich old man.* 2 (of dogs, etc.) show fondness by crouching, wagging the tail, licking the hand, etc. [Old English *fagnian* < *fægen* fain] **—fawn′er,** *n.* **—fawn′ing ly,** *adv.*

fay (fā), *n.* fairy. [< Old French *fae, fee,* ultimately < Latin *fatum.* See FATE.]

faze (fāz), *v.t.,* **fazed, faz ing.** INFORMAL. discompose; disturb; worry. [Old English *fēsian* to drive]

➔ **Faze** is almost always used negatively: *His original failure did not faze him. Nothing fazes her self-confidence.*

FBI or **F.B.I.,** Federal Bureau of Investigation (a bureau of the United States Department of Justice, established to investigate violations of federal laws and safeguard national security).

FCC or **F.C.C.,** Federal Communications Commission.

F clef, bass clef.

FDA or **F.D.A.,** Food and Drug Administration.

FDIC, Federal Deposit Insurance Corporation.

FDR, Franklin Delano Roosevelt.

Fe, iron [for Latin *ferrum*].

fe al ty (fē′əl tē), *n., pl.* **-ties.** 1 loyalty and duty owed by a vassal to his feudal lord: *The nobles swore fealty to the king.* 2 loyalty; faithfulness; allegiance. [< Old French *feauté* < Latin *fidelitatem.* Doublet of FIDELITY.]

fear (fir), *n.* 1 a feeling that danger or evil is near; being afraid. See synonym study below. 2 condition of fearing (something). 3 cause for fear; danger; chance: *There is no fear of our losing.* 4 an uneasy feeling; anxious thought; concern: *a fear for one's life.* 5 awe; reverence. 6 **for fear of** (a thing), in order to prevent (that thing) from occurring. *—v.t.* 1 be afraid of; regard with fear. 2 feel concern for or about: *She fears that the children will be sick.* 3 have awe or reverence for: *Fear God.* *—v.i.* 1 feel fear. 2 have an uneasy feeling or anxious thought; feel concern. [Old English *fǣr* peril] **—fear′er,** *n.*

Syn. *n.* 1 **Fear, dread, alarm** mean the painful feeling experienced when danger or harm threatens. **Fear** means a feeling of being afraid: *The knight felt no fears in the midst of battle.* **Dread** applies to great fear experienced from knowing that something unpleasant or frightening will or might happen: *He has a dread of losing his job.* **Alarm** implies fright upon the awareness of danger: *The explosion caused alarm.*

Fear (fir), *n.* **Cape,** cape in SE North Carolina.

fear ful (fir′fəl), *adj.* 1 causing fear; terrible; dreadful: *a fearful explosion.* 2 feeling fear; frightened; afraid: *fearful of the dark.* 3 showing fear; caused by fear: *fearful cries.* 4 INFORMAL. very bad, unpleasant, ugly, etc.: *a fearful cold.* **—fear′ful ly,** *adv.* **—fear′ful ness,** *n.*

fear less (fir′lis), *adj.* without fear; afraid of nothing; brave; daring. **—fear′less ly,** *adv.* **—fear′less ness,** *n.*

fear some (fir′səm), *adj.* 1 causing fear; frightful: *a fearsome sight.* 2 afraid; timid: *She was fearsome of danger.* **—fear′some ly,** *adv.* **—fear′some ness,** *n.*

fea si bil i ty (fē′zə bil′ə tē), *n.* feasible quality.

fea si ble (fē′zə bəl), *adj.* 1 that can be done or carried out easily; possible without difficulty or damage; practicable: *The committee selected the plan that seemed most feasible.* See **possible** for synonym study. 2 likely; probable: *The witness's explanation of the accident sounded feasible.* 3 suitable; convenient: *The road was too rough to be feasible for travel by automobile.* [< Old French *faisable,* ultimately < Latin *facere* do] **—fea′si ble ness,** *n.* **—fea′si bly,** *adv.*

feast (fēst), *n.* 1 an elaborate meal prepared for some special occasion, usually a joyous one. See synonym study below. 2 an unusually delicious or abundant meal. 3 something that gives pleasure or joy: *a feast for the eyes.* 4 a religious festival or celebration: *Christmas and Easter are the most important Christian feasts.* *—v.i.* eat a rich meal; have a feast. *—v.t.* 1 provide a rich meal for. 2 give pleasure or joy to; delight: *We feasted our eyes on the sunset.* [< Old French < Latin *festa* festal ceremonies] **—feast′er,** *n.*

Syn. *n.* 1 **Feast, banquet** mean an elaborate meal with many guests. **Feast** empha-

hat, āge, fär; let, ēqual, tėrm;
it, īce; hot, ōpen, ôrder;
oil, out; cup, pu̇t, rüle;
ch, child; ng, long; sh, she;
th, thin; ᴛʜ, then; zh, measure;

ə represents *a* in about, *e* in taken, *i* in pencil, *o* in lemon, *u* in circus.

< = from, derived from, taken from.

sizes the abundance, fineness, and richness of the food and drink: *We went to the wedding feast.* **Banquet** applies particularly to a formal dinner given in rich surroundings: *A banquet was given to honor the retiring president.*

feast day, 1 day set aside for a celebration or festivity. 2 a religious festival.

feat (fēt), *n.* 1 a great or unusual deed; act showing great skill, strength, or daring; achievement. 2 ARCHAIC. action; deed. [< Old French *fait* < Latin *factum* (thing) done. Doublet of FACT.]

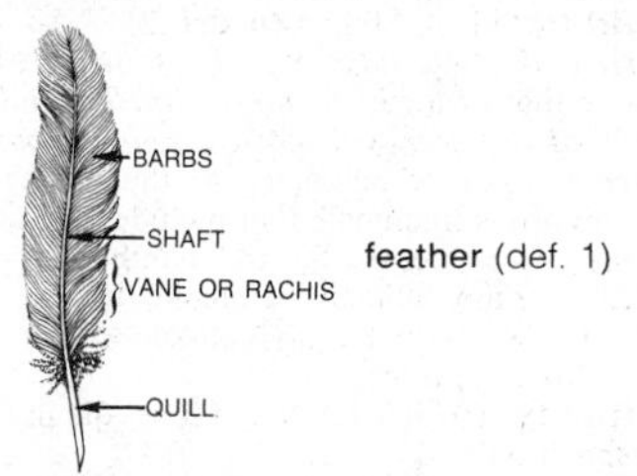

feather (def. 1)

feath er (feᴛʜ′ər), *n.* 1 one of the light, thin growths that cover a bird's skin, usually consisting of a partly hollow shaft bearing flat vanes formed of many parallel barbs. 2 attire. 3 kind; character: *birds of a feather.* 4 something like a feather in shape or lightness. 5 a featherlike tuft or fringe of hair. 6 projection, rib, or flange on a shaft or other mechanical part. 7 feather or feathers attached to the end of an arrow to direct its flight. 8 act of feathering an oar. 9 **feather in one's cap,** something to be proud of. —*v.t.* 1 supply or cover with feathers: *feather an arrow.* 2 turn (an oar) after a stroke so that the blade is flat and keep it that way until the next stroke begins. 3 turn (the blade of an airplane propeller) to decrease wind resistance. —*v.i.* 1 move like feathers. 2 grow like feathers.
[Old English *fether*] **—feath′er less,** *adj.* **—feath′er like′,** *adj.*

feather bed, 1 a very soft, warm mattress filled with feathers. 2 bed with such a mattress.

feath er bed ding (feᴛʜ′ər bed′ing), *n.* the practice on the part of some labor unions of forcing employers to hire more men than are needed for a particular job.

feath er brain (feᴛʜ′ər brān′), *n.* a silly, foolish, weak-minded person.

feath er brained (feᴛʜ′ər brānd′), *adj.* silly; foolish; weak-minded.

feath ered (feᴛʜ′ərd), *adj.* having feathers; covered with feathers.

feath er edge (feᴛʜ′ər ej′), *n.* a very thin, easily damaged edge.

feath er edged (feᴛʜ′ər ejd′), *adj.* having a very thin, easily damaged edge.

feath er stitch (feᴛʜ′ər stich′), *n.* a zigzag embroidery stitch. —*v.i.* make zigzag embroidery stitches. —*v.t.* decorate with such stitches.

feath er weight (feᴛʜ′ər wāt′), *n.* 1 a very light thing or person. 2 an unimportant person or thing. 3 boxer who weighs more than 118 and less than 126 pounds. 4 the lightest weight a horse can carry in a handicap race.

feath er y (feᴛʜ′ər ē), *adj.* 1 having feathers; covered with feathers; feathered. 2 like feathers; soft. 3 light; flimsy. **—feath′er i ness,** *n.*

fea ture (fē′chər), *n., v.,* **-tured, -tur ing.** —*n.* 1 part of the face. The eyes, nose, mouth, chin, and forehead are features. 2 **features,** *pl.* the face. 3 form or cast of the face. 4 a distinct part or quality; thing that stands out and attracts attention: *The main features of southern California are the climate and the scenery.* See synonym study below. 5 a main attraction, especially a full-length motion picture. 6 a special article, comic strip, etc., in a newspaper. —*v.t.* 1 be a feature of. 2 make a feature of: *The local newspapers featured the President's visit.* 3 INFORMAL. be like in features; favor. [< Old French *feture* < Latin *factura* a doing, making < *facere* do, make]
Syn. *n.* 4 **Feature, characteristic, trait** mean a distinguishing quality. **Feature** applies to a quality or detail that stands out and attracts attention: *the striking geological features of the Grand Canyon.* **Characteristic** applies to a quality or feature that helps to distinguish the character or nature of a person, thing, or class from others: *The use of slang is a characteristic of his writing.* **Trait** applies particularly to a distinguishing feature of mind or disposition: *Cheerfulness is his finest trait.*

fea ture less (fē′chər lis), *adj.* without features; not distinctive.

Feb., February.

feb ri fuge (feb′rə fyüj), *n.* anything which reduces fever. —*adj.* curing or lessening fever. [< French]

fe brile (fē′brəl, feb′rəl), *adj.* 1 of fever; feverish. 2 caused by fever. [< Medieval Latin *febrilis* < Latin *febris* fever]

Feb ru ar y (feb′rü er′ē, feb′yü er′ē), *n., pl.* **-ar ies.** the second month of the year. It has 28 days except in leap years, when it has 29. [< Latin *Februarius* < *februa,* plural, the Roman feast of purification celebrated on February 15]

fe cal (fē′kəl), *adj.* having to do with feces. Also, **faecal.**

fe ces (fē′sēz), *n.pl.* 1 waste matter discharged from the intestines; excrement. 2 dregs; sediment. Also, **faeces.** [< Latin *faeces* dregs]

feck less (fek′lis), *adj.* 1 futile; ineffective. 2 SCOTTISH. spiritless; worthless. [< *feck* vigor, variant of *fect,* short for *effect*] **—feck′less ly,** *adv.* **—feck′less ness,** *n.*

fe cund (fē′kənd, fek′ənd), *adj.* 1 able to produce much; productive: *Edison had a fecund mind.* 2 capable of producing offspring or vegetable growth abundantly; prolific: *the fecund earth of the tropical jungles.* [< Latin *fecundus*]

fe cun date (fē′kən dāt, fek′ən dāt), *v.t.,* **-dat ed, -dat ing.** 1 make fruitful or productive. 2 fertilize. **—fe′cun da′tion,** *n.*

fe cun di ty (fi kun′də tē), *n.* a being fertile; productiveness; fertility.

fed (fed), *v.* 1 pt. and pp. of **feed.** 2 **fed up,** SLANG. bored or disgusted.

fed., 1 federal. 2 federation.

fed er al (fed′ər əl), *adj.* 1 formed by an agreement between states establishing a central government to handle their common affairs while the states keep separate control of local affairs: *Switzerland and the United States both became nations by federal union.* 2 of or having to do with the central government formed in this way: *Congress is the federal lawmaking body of the United States.* 3 Also, **Federal.** of or having to do with the central government of the United States, not of any state or city alone. 4 **Federal, a** of or having to do with the Federal Party. **b** supporting the Union during the Civil War. —*n.* **Federal,** supporter or soldier of the Union during the Civil War. [< Latin *foederis* a compact, league] **—fed′er al ly,** *adv.*

fed er al ism (fed′ər ə liz′əm), *n.* 1 the federal principle of government. 2 support of this principle. 3 **Federalism,** principles of the Federal Party.

fed er al ist (fed′ər ə list), *n.* 1 **Federalist,** member of the Federal Party. 2 supporter of the federal principle of government.

Federalist Party, Federal Party.

fed er al ize (fed′ər ə līz), *v.t.,* **-ized, -iz ing.** 1 unite into a federal union. 2 put under the control of the federal government. **—fed′er al i za′tion,** *n.*

Federal Party, a political party in the United States from about 1791 to about 1816 that favored the adoption of the Constitution and a strong central government. Also, **Federalist Party.**

Federal Reserve System, U.S. the federal system of banks, consisting of a central bank **(Federal Reserve Bank)** in each of twelve districts and supervised by a board of seven members **(Federal Reserve Board)** appointed by the President. The Federal Reserve System regulates the loans and reserves of member banks and influences the flow of credit and currency in the country.

Federal Trade Commission, U.S. commission of five members appointed by the President to investigate and enforce laws against unfair business practices and violations of federal laws regulating trade.

fed e rate (*v.* fed′ə rāt′; *adj.* fed′ər it), *v.,* **-rat ed, -rat ing,** *adj.* —*v.t., v.i.* form into a union or federation. —*adj.* formed into a federation; federated.

fed e ra tion (fed′ə rā′shən), *n.* 1 union in a league; formation of a political unity out of a number of separate states, etc. 2 union by agreement, often a union of states, nations, groups, etc.; league: *a federation of students.*

fed e ra tive (fed′ə rā′tiv), *adj.* of or having to do with a federation; like a federation; forming a federation.

fe do ra (fi dôr′ə, fi dōr′ə), *n.* a man's low, soft felt hat with a curved brim, having the crown creased lengthwise. [< *Fédora,* a play by Victorien Sardou, 1831-1908, French playwright]

fee (fē), *n., v.,* **feed, fee ing.** —*n.* 1 money asked or paid for some service or privilege; charge: *Doctors and lawyers receive fees for their services.* 2 a small present of money; tip. 3 in the Middle Ages: **a** the right to keep and use land. **b** fief. 4 an inherited estate in land. 5 ownership. 6 (in law) an estate of land that may be passed on to the owner's heirs. 7 **hold in fee,** own. —*v.t.* give a fee to. [< Anglo-French variant of Old French *fieu, fief* < Germanic]

fee ble (fē′bəl), *adj.,* **-bler, -blest.** 1 lacking strength; weak; frail: *a feeble old man.*

2 lacking in energy or force; ineffective: *a feeble light, a feeble cry.* See **weak** for synonym study. [< Old French *feble* < Latin *flebilis* lamentable < *flere* weep] **—fee′ble·ness,** *n.* **—fee′bly,** *adv.*

fee ble-mind ed (fē′bəl min′did), *adj.* weak in mind; lacking normal intelligence. **—fee′ble-mind′ed ly,** *adv.* **—fee′ble-mind′ed ness,** *n.*

feed (fēd), *v.,* **fed, feed ing,** *n.* *—v.t.* 1 give food to: *It's time to feed the baby.* 2 give as food: *Feed this grain to the chickens.* 3 supply with material: *feed a machine.* 4 satisfy; gratify: *Praise fed his vanity.* 5 nourish; sustain: *She fed her curiosity by reading all kinds of books.* 6 (in the theater) supply (another actor) with cues. 7 **feed on** or **feed upon, a** live at the expense of; prey on. **b** derive satisfaction, support, etc., from. *—v.i.* (of animals) to eat: *Cows feed on hay.* *—n.* 1 food for animals; allowance of food for an animal. See synonym study below. 2 INFORMAL. meal for a person. 3 a feeding. 4 a supplying a machine, or the like, with material. 5 the material supplied. 6 part of a machine that supplies material. [Old English *fēdan* < *fōda* food]

Syn. *n.* 1 **Feed, fodder** mean food for animals. Feed applies to food for both animals and fowls: *Give the chickens their feed.* **Fodder** applies to coarse or dried feed, like alfalfa, hay, corn, or other plants fed to horses, cattle, pigs, or sheep: *Put some fodder in the bins.*

feed back (fēd′bak′), *n.* 1 process by which a system, machine, etc., regulates itself by feeding back to itself part of its output. 2 (in biology) a process whereby the course of a reaction is controlled by the activity of some of the products of the reaction.

feed er (fē′dər), *n.* 1 person or thing that feeds. 2 person or device that supplies food to a person or animal. 3 steer, lamb, etc., to be or being fattened for slaughtering. 4 thing or person that supplies another with material.

feel (fēl), *v.,* **felt, feel ing,** *n.* *—v.t.* 1 put the hand or some other part of the body on or against; touch: *Feel this cloth.* 2 try to find or make (one's way) by touch: *He felt his way across the room when the lights went out.* 3 test or examine by touching: *feel a person's pulse.* 4 find out by touching: *Feel how cold my hands are.* 5 be aware of: *He felt the cool breeze.* 6 have in one's mind; experience: *I felt pain.* 7 be influenced or affected by: *The ship feels her helm.* 8 think; believe; consider: *I feel that we shall win.* 9 **feel like,** INFORMAL. have a desire or preference for. 10 **feel out,** find out from in a cautious way: *Feel him out on this matter.* 11 **feel up to,** think one is capable of: *I don't feel up to doing my arithmetic just now.* *—v.i.* 1 search by touch; grope: *He felt in his pockets for a dime.* 2 have the feeling of being; be: *She feels sure.* 3 give the feeling of being; seem: *The air feels cold.* 4 have pity or sympathy: *She feels for all who suffer.* 5 have a feeling: *Try to feel more kindly toward her.*
—n. 1 touch: *I like the feel of silk.* 2 quality sensed by touch; way that something seems to the touch: *Wet soap has a greasy feel.* 3 the sense of touch. 4 sensation; feeling: *the satisfying feel of accomplishment.* [Old English *fēlan*]

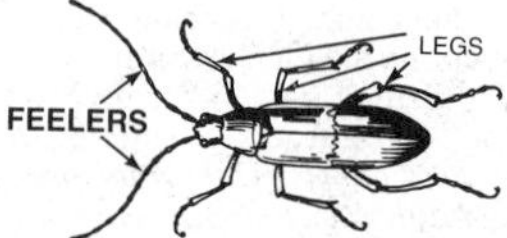

feeler (def. 1)—feelers of a beetle

feel er (fē′lər), *n.* 1 a special part of an animal's body for sensing by touch. An insect's antennae are its feelers. 2 remark, hint, question, or suggestion made to find out what others are thinking or planning. 3 person or thing that feels.

feel ing (fē′ling), *n.* 1 act or condition of one that feels. 2 sense of touch. 3 a being conscious; awareness; sensation. 4 state of mind in which joy, sorrow, fear, anger, or any similar sensation is felt; emotion. See synonym study below. 5 **feelings,** *pl.* tender or sensitive side of one's nature: *You hurt his feelings when you yell at him.* 6 the capacity for emotion; sensibility: *She was guided by feeling rather than thought.* 7 sensitivity to the higher or more refined emotions: *His work shows both feeling and taste.* 8 pity; sympathy: *Have you no feeling?* 9 opinion; idea: *Her feeling was that right would win.* *—adj.* that feels; sensitive; emotional. **—feel′ing ly,** *adv.*

Syn. *n.* 4 **Feeling, emotion, passion** mean a pleasant or painful sensation produced in a person in reaction to a stimulus of some kind. **Feeling** is the general word: *He had a feeling of hope.* **Emotion** means a strong and moving feeling: *She was overwhelmed with emotion and couldn't speak for a moment.* **Passion** means violent emotion, usually overcoming the power to think clearly and taking complete possession of a person: *In a passion of rage he killed her.*

feet (fēt), *n.pl.* of **foot.** 1 **sit at one's feet,** be a pupil or admirer of. 2 **stand on one's own feet,** be independent. 3 **sweep off one's feet, a** make very enthusiastic. **b** impress or overwhelm.

feign (fān), *v.t.* 1 put on a false appearance of; make believe; pretend: *Some animals feign death when in danger.* 2 make up to deceive; invent falsely: *feign an excuse.* *—v.i.* make oneself appear; pretend (to be): *He isn't sick; he is only feigning.* [< Old French *feign-,* a form of *feindre* feign < Latin *fingere* to form] **—feign′er,** *n.*

feint (fānt), *n.* 1 a false appearance; pretense: *The boy made a feint of studying hard, though actually he was listening to the radio.* 2 movement intended to deceive; sham attack; pretended blow. *—v.i.* make a feint: *The fighter feinted with his right hand and struck with his left.* [< French *feinte* < *feindre* feign]

Fei sal (fī′səl), *n.* Faisal I.

feld spar (feld′spär′), *n.* any of a group of crystalline minerals composed of silicate of aluminum, combined with potassium, sodium, calcium, and barium, used in making glass and pottery. Also, **felspar.** [alteration (influenced by *spar*[3]) of German *Feldspat,* literally, field spar]

fe lic i tate (fə lis′ə tāt), *v.t.,* **-tat ed, -tat ing.** express good wishes to formally; congratulate: *The young woman's friends felicitated her upon her promotion.*

fe lic i ta tion (fə lis′ə tā′shən), *n.* a formal expression of good wishes; congratulation.

fe lic i tous (fə lis′ə təs), *adj.* 1 well chosen for the occasion; appropriate; well-worded; apt: *The poem was full of striking and felicitous phrases.* 2 having a gift for apt speech. **—fe lic′i tous ly,** *adv.* **—fe lic′i tous ness,** *n.*

fe lic i ty (fə lis′ə tē), *n., pl.* **-ties.** 1 great happiness; bliss. See **happiness** for synonym study. 2 good fortune; blessing. 3 a pleasing ability in expression; appropriateness or gracefulness: *The famous writer phrased his ideas with felicity.* 4 an unusually appropriate or graceful expression; well-chosen phrase. [< Latin *felicitatem* < *felicem* happy]

fe lid (fē′lid), *n.* feline (*n.* def. 2).

fe line (fē′līn), *adj.* 1 of a cat: *feline eyes.* 2 like that of a cat: *feline stealth. The Indian stalked the deer with noiseless, feline movements.* 3 of or belonging to the family of carnivorous mammals that includes the cats, lions, tigers, leopards, and panthers. *—n.* 1 cat. 2 any animal belonging to the cat family. [< Latin *felinus* catlike < *felis* cat] **—fe′line ly,** *adv.*

fe lin i ty (fi lin′ə tē), *n.* feline quality or disposition.

fell[1] (fel), *v.* pt. of **fall.**

fell[2] (fel), *v.t.* 1 cause to fall; knock, cut, or strike down: *One blow felled him to the ground.* 2 cut down (a tree). 3 turn down and stitch one edge of (a seam) over the other. *—n.* 1 all the trees cut down in one season. 2 seam made by felling. [Old English *fellan* < *feallan* to fall] **—fell′a ble,** *adj.*

fell[3] (fel), *adj.* 1 fierce; savage; ruthless: *a fell blow.* 2 deadly; destructive. [< Old French *fel* < *felon* felon[1]]

fell[4] (fel), *n.* skin or hide of an animal; pelt. [Old English]

fel lah (fel′ə), *n., pl.* **fel la hin** (fel′ə hēn′). peasant or laborer in Egypt and other Arabic-speaking countries. [< Arabic *fallāh*]

fell er[1] (fel′ər), *n.* 1 person or thing that fells. 2 part attached to a sewing machine to fell seams.

fell er[2] (fel′ər), *n.* DIALECT. fellow.

fel loe (fel′ō), *n.* felly.

fel low (fel′ō; *often* fel′ə *for n. 2 and 4*), *n.* 1 a male person; man or boy. 2 INFORMAL. a young man courting a young woman; beau. 3 a person; anybody; one: *What can a fellow do?* 4 a friendly term of address for a dog, horse, etc. 5 a contemptible person. 6 companion; comrade; associate. 7 one of the same class or rank; equal; peer: *The world has not his fellow.* 8 the other one of a pair; mate; match. 9 a graduate student who has a fellowship from a university or college. 10 member of a learned society. 11 **hail fellow well met,** very friendly. *—adj.* being in the same or a like condition, class, etc.; united by the same work, interests, aims, etc.: *fellow citizens, fellow sufferers.* [Old English *fēolaga* < Scandinavian (Old Icelandic) *fēlagi* partner (literally, fee-layer)]

fellow man, fellow or kindred human being.

fel low ship (fel′ō ship), *n.* 1 condition or quality of being a fellow; companionship; friendship. 2 community of interest, sentiment, etc. 3 a being one of a group; membership. 4 group of people having similar tastes, interests, etc.; brotherhood. 5 position or money given by a university or college to a graduate student to enable him to continue his studies.

fellow traveler, person sympathizing with or supporting the programs of a political movement or party, especially the Communist Party, though not a member.

hat, āge, fär; let, ēqual, tėrm;
it, īce; hot, ōpen, ôrder;
oil, out; cup, pu̇t, rüle;
ch, child; ng, long; sh, she;
th, thin; ᴛʜ, then; zh, measure;

ə represents *a* in about, *e* in taken, *i* in pencil, *o* in lemon, *u* in circus.

< = from, derived from, taken from.

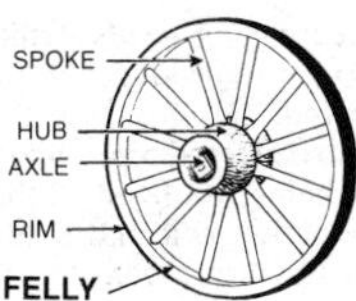

fel ly (fel′ē), *n., pl.* **-lies.** the circular rim of a wheel into which the outer ends of the spokes are inserted. Also, **felloe.** [Old English *felg*]

fel on[1] (fel′ən), *n.* person who has committed a felony; criminal. Murderers and thieves are felons. *—adj.* wicked; cruel. [< Old French < Popular Latin *fellonem*]

fel on[2] (fel′ən), *n.* a very painful inflammation of a finger or toe, usually near the nail; whitlow. [perhaps < Latin *fel* gall]

fe lo ni ous (fə lō′nē əs), *adj.* 1 having to do with a felony; criminal. 2 very wicked; villainous. **—fe lo′ni ous ly,** *adv.* **—fe lo′ni ous ness,** *n.*

fel o ny (fel′ə nē), *n., pl.* **-nies.** 1 crime more serious than a misdemeanor. Murder, burglary, and rape are felonies. 2 **compound a felony,** accept money not to prosecute a crime, etc.

fel spar (fel′spär′), *n.* feldspar.

felt[1] (felt), *v.* pt. and pp. of **feel.**

felt[2] (felt), *n.* 1 cloth that is not woven but made by rolling and pressing together wool, hair, or fur, used to make hats, slippers, pads, etc. 2 something made of felt, especially, a hat. 3 any material that resembles felt. *—adj.* made of felt. *—v.t.* 1 make into felt; mat or press (fibers, threads, etc.) together. 2 cover with felt. [Old English]

felt ing (fel′ting), *n.* 1 felted cloth. 2 act or process of making felt. 3 materials of which felt is made.

felucca

fe luc ca (fə luk′ə), *n.* a long, narrow, relatively fast ship moved by oars or lateen sails, or both, used along the coast of the Mediterranean Sea and the Red Sea. [< Italian]

fem., feminine.

fe male (fē′māl), *n.* 1 person of the sex that may conceive and bring forth young; woman or girl. See **woman** for synonym study. 2 animal belonging to the sex that produces eggs or may bring forth young. 3 in botany: **a** flower having a pistil or pistils and no stamens. **b** plant bearing only flowers with pistils. *—adj.* 1 of or having to do with women or girls: *female suffrage.* 2 belonging to the sex that produces eggs or may bring forth young. 3 consisting of women and girls: *female company.* 4 (in botany) having pistils but not stamens; pistillate. 5 designating some part of a machine, connection, etc., into which a corresponding part fits. [< Old French *femelle* < Latin *femella,* diminutive of *femina* woman; form influenced by *male*]

fem i nine (fem′ə nən), *adj.* 1 of women or girls. 2 like a woman; womanly. 3 (of a man) effeminate. 4 of or belonging to the female sex. 5 (in grammar) of the gender to which nouns and adjectives referring to females belong. *Actress, queen,* and *cow* are feminine nouns. *—n.* 1 the feminine gender. 2 word or form in the feminine gender. [< Latin *femininus* < *femina* woman] **—fem′i nine ly,** *adv.* **—fem′i nine ness,** *n.*

feminine rhyme, rhyme of two syllables of which the second is unstressed (as in *motion, notion*), or of three syllables of which the second and third are unstressed (as in *happily, snappily*).

fem i nin i ty (fem′ə nin′ə tē), *n.* 1 feminine quality or condition. 2 women; womankind.

fem i nism (fem′ə niz′əm), *n.* 1 doctrine of increased rights and activities for women in their economic, social, political, and private life. 2 movement to secure these rights.

fem i nist (fem′ə nist), *n.* person who believes in or favors feminism. *—adj.* believing in or favoring feminism.

fem i nis tic (fem′ə nis′tik), *adj.* feminist.

femme fa tale (fäm′ fä täl′), *pl.* ***femmes fa tales*** (fäm′ fä täl′). FRENCH. a dangerously seductive woman; seductress.

fem or al (fem′ər əl), *adj.* of, having to do with, or in the region of the femur.

fe mur (fē′mər), *n., pl.* **fe murs, fem or a** (fem′ər ə). 1 thighbone. See **fibula** for picture. 2 the third section (from the body) of the leg of an insect. [< Latin *femur, femoris* thigh]

fen (fen), *n.* low, marshy land covered wholly or partially with shallow, often stagnant water. [Old English *fenn*]

fence (fens), *n., v.,* **fenced, fenc ing.** *—n.* 1 railing, wall, or similar barrier around a yard, garden, field, farm, etc., to mark a boundary or to prevent people or animals from going out or coming in. 2 **on the fence,** doubtful; hesitating. 3 person who buys and sells stolen goods. 4 place where stolen goods are bought and sold. *—v.t.* put a fence around; keep out or in with a fence; enclose with a fence. *—v.i.* 1 fight with long, slender swords or foils. 2 evade giving answers or making admissions; parry questions. [variant of *defence*] **—fence′less,** *adj.* **—fenc′er,** *n.*

fenc ing (fen′sing), *n.* 1 art or sport of fighting with swords or foils. 2 material for fences. 3 fences.

fend (fend), *v.i.* **fend for oneself,** provide for oneself; get along by one's own efforts. *—v.t.* **fend off,** ward off; keep off. [variant of *defend*]

fend er (fen′dər), *n.* 1 anything that keeps or wards something off. 2 a metal frame over the wheel of a car, truck, bicycle, motorcycle, etc., that protects the wheel and reduces splashing in wet weather. 3 a metal bar or frame on the front or rear of a locomotive, streetcar, etc., to lessen damage in case of collision. 4 device at the front of a locomotive, etc., to reduce injury to an animal or person in case of collision. 5 a metal bar, frame, or screen in front of a fireplace to keep hot coals and sparks from the room. 6 rope, log, etc., put between a boat and the landing to prevent damage to the side when docking. [variant of *defender*]

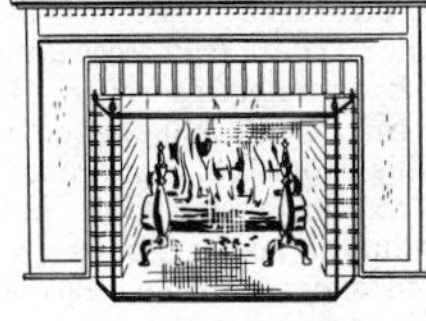

fender (def. 5)

fen es tra tion (fen′ə strā′shən), *n.* 1 arrangement of windows in a building, especially to provide light for the interior. 2 the use of windows as decorative elements of a facade. [< Latin *fenestra* window]

Fe ni an (fē′nē ən, fē′nyən), *n.* 1 member of an Irish secret organization founded in the United States about 1858 for the purpose of overthrowing English rule in Ireland. 2 member of a group of warriors famous in Irish legend. *—adj.* of or having to do with the Fenians.

fen nec (fen′ek), *n.* a small desert fox of North Africa and Syria, having large, pointed ears. [< Arabic *fanak*]

fen nel (fen′l), *n.* 1 a tall, perennial European plant with yellow flowers, of the same family as the parsley. 2 its fragrant seeds, used in medicine and cooking. [Old English *fenol,* ultimately < Latin *fenum* hay]

fen ny (fen′ē), *adj.* 1 marshy; boggy. 2 growing or living in fens. [Old English *fennig* < *fenn* fen]

feoff (fēf), *n.* fief.

FEPC, Fair Employment Practices Committee.

fer al (fir′əl), *adj.* 1 having reverted from domestication back to the original wild or untamed state. 2 wild; untamed. 3 brutal; savage. [< Latin *fera* wild beast < *ferus* wild]

fencing (def. 1)

fer-de-lance (fer′də läns′), *n.* a large, very poisonous pit viper of tropical America. [< French, iron (tip) of a lance]

Fer di nand I (fėrd′n and), died 1065, Spanish ruler of Castile and León, emperor of Spain from 1056 to 1065.

Ferdinand V, 1452-1516, king of Castile, 1474-1504, and of all Spain, 1506-1516. He and his queen, Isabella I, encouraged Christopher Columbus in his voyages.

fer ment (*v.* fər ment′; *n.* fėr′ment), *v.i.* 1 undergo or produce a gradual chemical change in which bacteria, yeast, etc., change sugar into alcohol and produce carbon dioxide. Vinegar is formed when cider ferments. 2 be excited; seethe with agitation or unrest. *—v.t.* 1 cause to ferment. Enzymes help ferment animal and vegetable matter. 2 cause unrest in; excite; agitate. *—n.* 1 substance that causes others to ferment.

Yeast and pepsin are ferments. 2 a chemical change caused by a ferment; fermentation. 3 social, industrial, political, or other unrest or agitation. [< Latin *fermentare* < *fermentum* leaven] **—fer ment′a ble,** *adj.*

fer men ta tion (fėr′men tā′shən), *n.* 1 act or process of fermenting. 2 a chemical change in an organic compound caused by a ferment. 3 agitation or ferment.

fer mi (fėr′mē, fer′mē), *n.* unit of length in nuclear physics, equal to 10^{-13} centimeters. [< Enrico *Fermi*]

Fer mi (fer′mē), *n.* **Enrico,** 1901-1954, American physicist, born in Italy, who directed the first controlled chain reaction in 1942.

fer mi on (fėr′mē on, fer′mē on), *n.* (in quantum mechanics) any of a class of elementary particles, only one of which can occupy a given state at one time, including protons, neutrons, and electrons. [< Enrico *Fermi*]

fer mi um (fėr′mē əm, fer′mē əm), *n.* a radioactive metallic element produced artificially from plutonium or uranium. *Symbol:* Fm; *atomic number* 100. See pages 326 and 327 for table. [< Enrico *Fermi*]

fern (fėrn), *n.* any of a class of plants resembling seed plants in having true roots, stems, feathery leaves, and vascular tissue, but lacking flowers and reproducing by means of spores grown in clusters instead of by seeds. Maidenhair and bracken are ferns. [Old English *fearn*] **—fern′like′,** *adj.*

Fer nán dez (fər nan′dez), *n.* **Juan,** 1538?-1602?, Spanish navigator who explored the western coast of South America.

Fer nan do Po (fər nan′dō pō′), island in the Gulf of Guinea, part of Equatorial Guinea. 80,000 pop.; 780 sq. mi.

fern er y (fėr′nər ē), *n., pl.* **-er ies.** place where ferns are grown.

fern y (fėr′nē), *adj.* 1 of ferns. 2 like ferns. 3 overgrown with ferns.

fe ro cious (fə rō′shəs), *adj.* 1 savagely cruel or destructive; fierce. See **fierce** for synonym study. 2 INFORMAL. extremely intense: *a ferocious headache.* [< Latin *ferocem* fierce] **—fe ro′cious ly,** *adv.* **—fe ro′cious ness,** *n.*

fe roc i ty (fə ros′ə tē), *n., pl.* **-ties.** savage cruelty; fierceness.

-ferous, *suffix added to nouns to form adjectives.* producing; containing; conveying, as in *metalliferous.* [< Latin *-fer* (< *ferre* to bear) + English *-ous*]

Fer ra ra (fə rär′ə), *n.* city in NE Italy. 156,000.

fer ret (fer′it), *n.* 1 a white or yellowish-white domesticated form of the European polecat, used for killing rats and driving rabbits from their holes. 2 species of weasel of western North America with black feet. *—v.t.* 1 hunt with ferrets. 2 drive from, off, or out of a place. 3 hunt; search: *The detectives ferreted out new evidence.* *—v.i.* 1 hunt with ferrets. 2 search about; rummage. [< Old French *fuiret,* ultimately < Latin *fur* thief] **—fer′ret er,** *n.*

fer ric (fer′ik), *adj.* of or containing iron, especially trivalent iron. [< Latin *ferrum* iron]

ferric oxide, a reddish-brown compound of iron and oxygen found naturally as hematite and produced chemically as a powder for use as a pigment, abrasive, etc.; iron oxide. *Formula:* Fe_2O_3

Fer ris wheel (fer′is), a large, upright wheel rotating about a fixed axis, with swinging seats hanging from its rim, used in carnivals, amusement parks, at fairs, etc. [< George W. G. *Ferris,* 1859-1896, American engineer, the inventor]

ferro-, *combining form.* 1 alloy of iron and ____: *Ferrochromium = alloy of iron and chromium.* 2 that contains iron; iron: *Ferroconcrete = concrete that contains iron.* [< Latin *ferrum* iron]

fer ro al loy (fer′ō al′oi), *n.* alloy of iron with another element such as tungsten, manganese, chromium, or vanadium.

fer ro chro mi um (fer′ō krō′mē əm), *n.* alloy of iron and chromium.

fer ro con crete (fer′ō kon′krēt, fer′ō kon krēt′), *n.* reinforced concrete.

fer ro mag net ic (fer′ō mag net′ik), *adj.* able to become highly magnetic in a relatively weak magnetic field, as iron, steel, cobalt, and nickel.

fer ro man ga nese (fer′ō mang′gə nēs′, fer′ō mang′gə nēz′), *n.* alloy of iron, manganese, and sometimes carbon, used for making tough steel.

fer rous (fer′əs), *adj.* of or containing iron, especially divalent iron.

fer ru gi nous (fə rü′jə nəs), *adj.* 1 of or containing iron; like that of iron. 2 reddish-brown like rust. [< Latin *ferruginus* < *ferruginem* iron rust < *ferrum* iron]

fer rule (fer′əl, fer′ül), *n.* a metal ring or cap put around the end of a cane, wooden handle, umbrella, etc., to strengthen it or to prevent splitting and wearing. Also, **ferule.** [earlier *verrel* < Old French *virelle* < Latin *viriola* little bracelet]

fer ry (fer′ē), *v.,* **-ried, -ry ing,** *n., pl.* **-ries.** *—v.t.* 1 carry (passengers, vehicles, and goods) in a boat back and forth across a river or narrow stretch of water. 2 go across in a ferryboat. 3 carry back and forth across a wide stretch of water in an airplane. 4 fly (an airplane) to a destination for delivery. *—v.i.* travel by ferryboat. *—n.* 1 ferryboat. 2 place where boats carry people and goods across a river or narrow stretch of water. 3 system for flying aircraft to a destination for delivery. [Old English *ferian* to carry < *fær* trip, fare]

fer ry boat (fer′ē bōt′), *n.* boat used for ferrying passengers, vehicles, and goods.

fer ry man (fer′ē mən), *n., pl.* **-men.** 1 man who owns or has charge of a ferry. 2 man who works on a ferry.

fer tile (fėr′tl), *adj.* 1 able to bear seeds, fruit, young, etc.; capable of reproduction. 2 capable of developing into a new individual; fertilized: *Chicks hatch from fertile eggs.* 3 able to produce much; producing crops easily: *Fertile soil yields good crops.* 4 producing ideas; creative: *a fertile mind.* See synonym study below. [< Latin *fertilis* < *ferre* to bear] **—fer′tile ly,** *adv.* **—fer′tile ness,** *n.*

Syn. 4 **Fertile, productive** mean able to produce much. **Fertile** emphasizes the power of producing and applies to things in which seeds or ideas can take root and grow: *The seed fell on fertile ground. He has a fertile imagination.* **Productive** suggests bringing forth in abundance: *Those fruit trees are very productive. He is a productive writer.*

Fertile Crescent, crescent-shaped strip of land extending from the E shore of the Mediterranean to the Persian Gulf, known for its great fertility in ancient times.

fer til i ty (fər til′ə tē), *n.* 1 the bearing, or abundant bearing, of seeds, fruits, crops, or young. 2 power to produce: *the fertility of an inventor's mind.*

fer ti li za tion (fėr′tl ə zā′shən), *n.* 1 a fertilizing. 2 a being fertilized. 3 the union of a male reproductive cell and a female reproductive cell to form a cell that will develop into a new individual.

fer ti lize (fėr′tl īz), *v.t.,* **-lized, -liz ing.** 1 make fertile; make able to produce much: *A crop of alfalfa fertilized the soil by adding nitrates to it.* 2 unite with (an egg cell) in fertilization; impregnate. 3 put fertilizer on: *fertilize a lawn.* **—fer′ti liz′a ble,** *adj.*

fer ti liz er (fėr′tl ī′zər), *n.* 1 substance such as manure, chemicals, etc., spread over or put into the soil to supply nutrients missing from the soil. 2 person or thing that fertilizes.

fer ule[1] (fer′əl, fer′ül), *n., v.,* **-uled, -ul ing.** *—n.* stick or ruler for punishing children by striking them, especially on the hand. *—v.t.* punish with a stick or ruler. [< Latin *ferula* rod]

fer ule[2] (fer′əl, fer′ül), *n.* ferrule.

fer ven cy (fėr′vən sē), *n.* fervor.

fer vent (fėr′vənt), *adj.* 1 showing great warmth of feeling; very earnest; ardent: *fervent devotion.* 2 hot; glowing; intense. **—fer′vent ly,** *adv.*

fer vid (fėr′vid), *adj.* 1 full of strong feeling; intensely emotional; ardent; spirited. 2 intensely hot. **—fer′vid ly,** *adv.* **—fer′vid ness,** *n.*

fer vor (fėr′vər), *n.* 1 great warmth of feeling; intense emotion; enthusiasm or earnestness; ardor: *patriotic fervor.* 2 intense heat. [< Latin < *fervere* to boil]

fer vour (fėr′vər), *n.* BRITISH. fervor.

fes cue (fes′kyü), *n.* any of a genus of tough perennial grasses growing in tufts, found in temperate regions and used for pasture or lawns. [< Old French *festu* < Latin *festuca* straw]

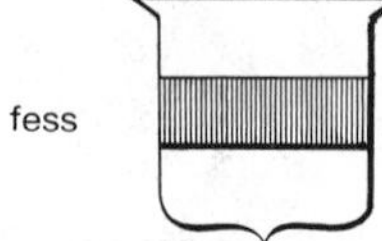
fess

fess or **fesse** (fes), *n.* (in heraldry) a wide, horizontal band across the middle of a shield. [< Old French *fesse, faisse* < Latin *fascia* band]

-fest, *combining form.* meeting, occasion, contest, or game, characterized by ____, as in *songfest.* [< German *Fest* feast]

fes tal (fes′tl), *adj.* of a feast, festival, or holiday; gay; festive; joyous: *A wedding or a birthday is a festal occasion.* [< Latin *festum* feast] **—fes′tal ly,** *adv.*

fes ter (fes′tər), *v.i.* 1 form pus: *The neglected wound festered and became very painful.* 2 cause soreness or pain; rankle: *Resentment festered in his mind.* 3 decay; rot. *—v.t.* 1 cause pus to form in. 2 cause to rankle: *Time festered the insult to his pride.* *—n.* sore that forms pus; small ulcer. [< Old French *festre* < Latin *fistula* ulcer]

fes ti val (fes′tə vəl), *n.* 1 day or special time of rejoicing or feasting, often in memory of some great happening: *Christmas and Easter are two festivals of the Christian church.* 2 celebration or entertainment, often at recurring periods: *Every year the city has a music festival during the first week in May.* *—adj.* of or having to do with a festival.

[< Medieval Latin *festivalis,* ultimately < Latin *festum* feast]

Festival of Lights, Hanukkah. It is celebrated by lighting candles for each of the eight days.

fes tive (fes′tiv), *adj.* of or suitable for a feast, festival, or holiday; gay; merry; joyous: *A birthday or a wedding is a festive occasion.* **—fes′tive ly,** *adv.* **—fes′tive-ness,** *n.*

fes tiv i ty (fe stiv′ə tē), *n., pl.* **-ties.** 1 festive activity; thing done to celebrate: *The festivities on the Fourth of July included a parade and fireworks.* 2 gaiety; merriment. 3 festival.

festoon (def. 1)

fes toon (fe stün′), *n.* 1 a string or chain of flowers, leaves, ribbons, etc., hanging in a curve between two points: *The bunting was draped on the wall in colorful festoons.* 2 a carved or molded ornament like this on furniture, pottery, architectural work, etc. *—v.t.* 1 decorate with festoons. 2 form into festoons; hang in curves. [< French *feston* < Italian *festone*]

fe tal (fē′tl), *adj.* 1 of or having to do with a fetus. 2 like that of a fetus. Also, **foetal.**

fetch (fech), *v.t.* 1 go to another place and bring back; go and get; bring. See **bring** for synonym study. 2 cause to come; succeed in bringing. 3 be sold for: *These eggs will fetch a good price.* 4 INFORMAL. deal or strike (a blow, etc.); hit: *He fetched him one on the nose.* 5 draw or take (a breath). 6 give (a groan, sigh, etc.). 7 (of a ship) reach; arrive at. *—v.i.* 1 (of ships) take a course; move; go. 2 **fetch up,** arrive; stop. *—n.* 1 act of fetching. 2 trick; stratagem. [Old English *feccan*] **—fetch′er,** *n.*

fetch ing (fech′ing), *adj.* INFORMAL. attractive; charming. **—fetch′ing ly,** *adv.*

fete or **fête** (fāt; *French* fet), *n., v.,* **fet ed, fet ing** or **fêt ed, fêt ing.** *—n.* festival or party, especially an elaborate one and often one held outdoors. *—v.t.* honor with a fete; entertain: *The engaged couple were feted by their friends.* [< French *fête* feast]

fet ich (fet′ish, fē′tish), *n.* fetish.

fet id (fet′id, fē′tid), *adj.* smelling very bad; stinking. [< Latin *foetidus* < *foetere* to stink] **—fet′id ly,** *adv.* **—fet′id ness,** *n.*

fet ish (fet′ish, fē′tish), *n.* 1 any material object worshiped by primitive people for its supposed magic powers. 2 anything regarded with unreasoning reverence or blind devotion: *Some people make a fetish of stylish clothes.* 3 an inanimate object or a part of the body which is a source of sexual stimulation. Also, **fetich.** [< French *fétiche* < Portuguese *feitiço* charm, originally adjective, artificial < Latin *factitius.* Doublet of FACTITIOUS.]

fet ish ism (fet′ə shiz′əm, fē′tə shiz′əm), *n.* 1 belief in or worship of fetishes. 2 an abnormal condition in which an inanimate object or a part of the body is a source of sexual stimulation.

fet lock (fet′lok), *n.* 1 tuft of hair above a horse's hoof on the back part of its leg. 2 the part of a horse's leg where this tuft grows. See **horse** for picture. [Middle English *fetlak, fitlok*]

fet ter (fet′ər), *n.* 1 chain or shackle for the feet to prevent escape. 2 Usually, **fetters,** *pl.* anything that shackles or binds; restraint. *—v.t.* 1 bind with fetters; chain the feet of. 2 bind; restrain: *Fetter your temper.* [Old English *feter.* Related to FOOT.]

fet tle (fet′l), *n.* state of readiness for action; physical condition; trim: *The horse is in fine fettle and should win the race.* [Middle English *fettelen* prepare, gird up < Old English *fetel* belt]

fe tus (fē′təs), *n.* an animal embryo during the later stages of its development in the womb or in the egg, especially a human embryo more than three months old. Also, **foetus.** [< Latin]

feud[1] (fyüd), *n.* 1 a long and deadly quarrel between families, tribes, etc., often passed down from generation to generation. 2 bitter hatred or contention between two persons, groups, etc. See **quarrel** for synonym study. *—v.i.* carry on a feud. [variant of Middle English *fede* < Old French *feide* < Old High German *fēhida* enmity]

feud[2] (fyüd), *n.* a feudal estate; fief. [< Medieval Latin *feudum;* of Germanic origin]

feu dal (fyü′dl), *adj.* 1 of or having to do with feudalism. 2 of or having to do with feuds or fiefs. **—feu′dal ly,** *adv.*

feu dal ism (fyü′dl iz′əm), *n.* 1 the social, economic, and political system of western Europe in the Middle Ages. Under this system vassals gave military and other services to their lord in return for his protection and the use of the land. 2 any similar social, economic, or political system.

feu dal is tic (fyü′dl is′tik), *adj.* 1 of or having to do with feudalism. 2 tending toward feudalism; favoring feudalism.

feudal system, feudalism.

feu da to ry (fyü′də tôr′ē, fyü′də tōr′ē), *adj., n., pl.* **-ries.** *—adj.* 1 owing feudal allegiance or services to a lord. 2 holding or held as a feudal estate or fief. *—n.* 1 a feudal vassal. 2 a feudal estate; fief.

fe ver (fē′vər), *n.* 1 an unhealthy condition in which the body temperature is higher than normal (usually 98.6 degrees Fahrenheit in people), often accompanied by rapid pulse and weakness. 2 any disease that causes or is accompanied by fever. 3 an excited, restless condition; agitation. 4 current fad or enthusiasm for something or for some person. [Old English *fēfer* < Latin *febris*] **—fe′ver-less,** *adj.*

fetish (def. 1)

fever blister, cold sore.

fe vered (fē′vərd), *adj.* 1 having fever. 2 excited; restless.

fe ver few (fē′vər fyü′), *n.* a bushy, perennial European herb with small, white, daisylike flowers, formerly used in medicine. It is a species of chrysanthemum.

fe ver ish (fē′vər ish), *adj.* 1 having fever. 2 having a slight degree of fever. 3 caused by fever: *a feverish thirst.* 4 causing fever: *a feverish climate.* 5 infested with fever: *a feverish swamp.* 6 excited; restless.

hat, āge, fär; let, ēqual, tėrm;
it, īce; hot, ōpen, ôrder;
oil, out; cup, pu̇t, rüle;
ch, child; ng, long; sh, she;
th, thin; ᴛʜ, then; zh, measure;

ə represents *a* in about, *e* in taken,
i in pencil, *o* in lemon, *u* in circus.

< = from, derived from, taken from.

—fe′ver ish ly, *adv.* **—fe′ver ish ness,** *n.*

fever sore, cold sore.

few (fyü), *adj.* not many; amounting to a small number: *There are few men in our neighborhood over six feet tall.* *—n.* 1 a small number: *Winter in New England does not have many warm days, only a few.* 2 **the few,** the minority. 3 **quite a few,** INFORMAL. a good many. [Old English *fēawe*] **—few′ness,** *n.*

➤ **fewer, less** both imply a comparison with what is larger. *Fewer* refers only to number and things that are counted: *Fewer cars were on the road. There were fewer than sixty present.* In formal usage *less* refers only to amounts or quantities considered as wholes: *less sugar, less tact. Less* commonly takes the place of *fewer,* especially before *than: Less than twenty men were present.*

fey (fā), *adj.* 1 elfin; fairylike. 2 behaving as if doomed or enchanted. 3 fated to die. [Old English *fǣge*]

fez (fez), *n., pl.* **fez zes.** a brimless felt cap with a flat top, usually red, ornamented with a long, black tassel, formerly the national headdress of the Turks. [< *Fez,* Morocco]

Fez (fez), *n.* city in N Morocco. 235,000.

ff, fortissimo.

ff., 1 folios. 2 (and the) following (pages, sections, etc.); and what follows.

FHA, Federal Housing Administration.

fi a cre (fē ä′kər; *French* fyä′krə), *n.* a small, four-wheeled carriage for hire; horse-drawn cab. [< French]

fi an cé (fē′än sā′, fē än′sā), *n.* man engaged to be married. [< French]

fi an cée (fē′än sā′, fē än′sā), *n.* woman engaged to be married. [< French]

fi as co (fē as′kō), *n., pl.* **-cos** or **-coes.** a complete or ridiculous failure; humiliating breakdown. [< Italian, literally, flask]

fi at (fī′ət, fī′at), *n.* an authoritative order or command; decree. [< Latin, let it be done]

fiat money, U.S. paper currency made legal tender by the decree of the government, but not based on or convertible into coin.

fib (fib), *n., v.,* **fibbed, fib bing.** *—n.* a lie about some trivial matter. See **lie**[1] for synonym study. *—v.i.* tell such a lie. [perhaps < obsolete *fibble-fabble* < *fable*] **—fib′-ber,** *n.*

fi ber (fī′bər), *n.* 1 any of the very fine, long threadlike pieces of which many organic and some inorganic materials consist; a threadlike part; thread: *A muscle is made up of many fibers.* 2 a similar structure of artificial origin: *a fiber of rayon, a plastic fiber. Synthetic fibers are produced chemically.* 3 substance made up of threads or threadlike parts: *Hemp fiber can be spun into rope or woven into a coarse cloth.* 4 texture: *cloth of coarse fiber.* 5 character; nature: *A person of strong moral fiber can resist temptation.* 6 one of the narrow elongated cells found in the bast of plants. 7 a slender, threadlike root of a plant. Also, **fibre.** [< Old French *fibre* < Latin *fibra*]

fi ber board (fī′bər bôrd′, fī′bər bōrd′), *n.* a building material made by compressing wood fibers and other material into flat sheets.

fi ber fill (fī′bər fil′), *n.* a synthetic fiber used for filling or padding cushions, mattresses, etc.

Fi ber glas (fī′bər glas′), *n.* trademark for fiberglass.

fi ber glass (fī′bər glas′), *n.* very fine, flexible filaments of glass used for insulating materials or woven into fabrics; spun glass.

fi bre (fī′bər), *n.* fiber.

fi bril (fī′brəl), *n.* 1 a small or very slender fiber. 2 one of the hairs on the roots of some plants.

fi bril lar (fī′brə lər), *adj.* of, having to do with, or like fibrils.

fi bril late (fī′brə lāt), *v.i.*, **-lat ed, -lat ing.** undergo fibrillation.

fi bril la tion (fī′brə lā′shən), *n.* tremor in a muscle, especially a condition in the heart characterized by independent action of individual muscle fibers.

fi brin (fī′brən), *n.* a white, tough, elastic, fibrous protein formed by the action of thrombin on fibrinogen when blood clots.

fi brin o gen (fī brin′ə jen), *n.* protein found in the blood, lymph, etc., which interacts with thrombin to form fibrin in the coagulation of blood.

fi bri nol y sin (fī′brə nol′ə sn), *n.* enzyme that can cause fibrin to dissolve, formed by the action of certain bacteria.

fi brin ous (fī′brə nəs), *adj.* 1 composed of or having fibrin. 2 like fibrin.

fi bro blast (fī′brə blast), *n.* one of the cells in which connective tissue is immediately formed.

fi broid (fī′broid), *adj.* made up of or resembling fibers or fibrous tissue, as a tumor.

fi bro sis (fī brō′sis), *n.* an excessive growth of fibrous connective tissue in an organ or part of the body.

fi brous (fī′brəs), *adj.* 1 made up of fibers; having fibers. 2 like fiber; stringy. 3 having a splintery or threadlike surface when fractured: *fibrous minerals.*

fiddler crab shell width up to $1^2/_3$ in.

fi bro vas cu lar bundle (fī′brō vas′kyə lər), a vascular bundle surrounded by elongate fibers. Leaf veins are fibrovascular bundles.

fib u la (fib′yə lə), *n., pl.* **-lae** (-lē′), **-las.** 1 the outer and thinner of the two bones in the human lower leg. It extends from knee to ankle. 2 a similar bone in the hind leg of animals. [< Latin, clasp, brooch]

fib u lar (fib′yə lər), *adj.* of or having to do with the fibula.

-fic, *suffix forming adjectives from nouns, adjectives, and verbs.* making; causing: *Pacific = making peace. Terrific = causing terror.* [< Latin *-ficus* < *facere* do, make]

FICA, Federal Insurance Contributions Act (a federal act dealing with the tax paid toward social security).

-fication, *suffix forming nouns, usually corresponding to verbs in* **-fy.** a making or doing: *Falsification = a falsifying or making false.* [< Latin *-ficationem* < *-ficare* < *facere* do, make]

Fich te (fiH′tə), *n.* **Johann Gottlieb,** 1762-1814, German philosopher.

fich u (fish′ü), *n.* a triangular piece of muslin, lace, etc., worn by women as a covering for the neck, throat, and shoulders. [< French]

fick le (fik′əl), *adj.* 1 likely to change or give up a loyalty, attachments, etc., without reason; inconstant: *a fickle friend.* 2 likely to change in nature; uncertain: *fickle weather.* [Old English *ficol* deceitful] **—fick′le ness,** *n.*

fic tion (fik′shən), *n.* 1 the type of literature that consists of novels, short stories, and other prose writings that tell about imaginary people and happenings. 2 something imagined or made up: *He exaggerates so much it is impossible to separate fact from fiction.* 3 an imaginary account or statement; made-up story. 4 something acted upon as a fact, in spite of its possible falsity. It is a legal fiction that a corporation is a person. [< Latin *fictionem* < *fingere* to form, fashion]

fic tion al (fik′shə nəl), *adj.* of, having to do with, or of the nature of, fiction. **—fic′tion al ly,** *adv.*

fic tion al ize (fik′shə nə līz), *v.t.*, **-ized, -iz ing.** give a fictitious form to; make fiction out of: *The famous trial was fictionalized in this novel.* **—fic′tion al i za′tion,** *n.*

fic ti tious (fik tish′əs), *adj.* 1 not real; imaginary; made-up: *Characters in novels are usually fictitious.* 2 assumed in order to deceive; false: *a fictitious name.* **—fic ti′tious ly,** *adv.* **—fic ti′tious ness,** *n.*

fid (fid), *n.* 1 a heavy, square bar used to support a topmast. 2 a hard pin like a spike, for separating strands of rope in splicing. [origin uncertain]

fid dle (fid′l), *n., v.,* **-dled, -dling.** —*n.* 1 INFORMAL. violin. 2 **fit as a fiddle,** in excellent physical condition. —*v.i.* 1 INFORMAL. play on a violin. 2 make aimless movements; play nervously; toy: *The embarrassed boy fiddled with his hat.* —*v.t.* 1 INFORMAL. play (a piece of music) on a violin. 2 trifle: *He fiddled away the whole day doing absolutely nothing.* [Old English *fithele*] **—fid′dler,** *n.*

fiddler crab, any of a genus of small, burrowing crabs found along coasts in warm regions. The male has one much enlarged claw.

fid dle stick (fid′l stik′), INFORMAL. —*n.* the bow with which a violin is played. —*interj.* **fiddlesticks,** nonsense! rubbish!

Fi de lis mo (fi′de lēz′mō), *n.* policies and practices of Fidel Castro, premier of Cuba, and of his followers, especially the dissemination of communism in Latin-American countries. [< Spanish]

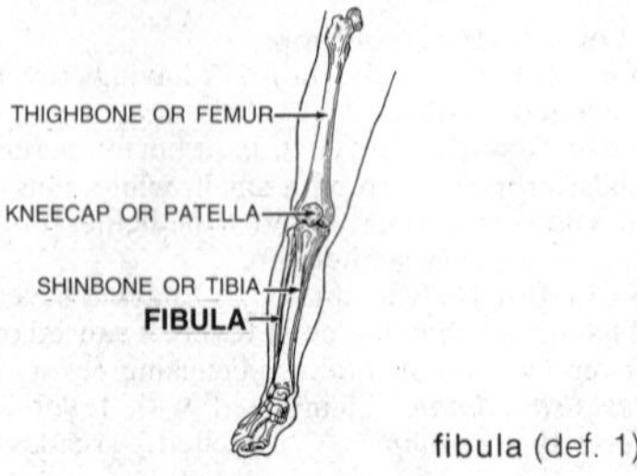

fibula (def. 1)

Fi de lis ta (fi′de lē′stä), *n.* supporter of Fidel Castro or Fidelismo. [< Spanish]

fi del i ty (fī del′ə tē, fə del′ə tē), *n., pl.* **-ties.** 1 steadfast faithfulness; loyalty. 2 exactness, as in a copy; accuracy. 3 the ability of a radio transmitter or receiver or other device to transmit or reproduce an electric signal or sound accurately. [< Latin *fidelitatem* < *fidelis* faithful < *fides* faith. Doublet of FEALTY.]

fidg et (fij′it), *v.i.* move about restlessly; be uneasy: *My little brother fidgets if he has to sit still a long time.* —*v.t.* make uneasy; worry. —*n.* 1 condition of being restless or uneasy. 2 person who moves about restlessly. 3 **the fidgets,** fit of restlessness or uneasiness. [< obsolete *fidge* move restlessly]

fidg et y (fij′ə tē), *adj.* restless; uneasy.

fi du ci ar y (fə dü′shē er′ē, fə dyü′shē er′ē), *adj., n., pl.* **-ar ies.** —*adj.* 1 held in trust: *fiduciary estates.* 2 holding in trust. A fiduciary possessor is legally responsible for what belongs to another. 3 of a trustee; of trust and confidence: *A guardian acts in a fiduciary capacity.* 4 depending upon public trust and confidence for its value. Paper money that cannot be redeemed in gold or silver is fiduciary currency. —*n.* trustee. [< Latin *fiduciarius* < *fiducia* trust < *fidere* to trust]

fie (fī), *interj.* for shame! shame! [< Old French *fi*]

fief (fēf), *n.* piece of land held on condition of giving military and other services to the feudal lord owning it, in return for his protection and the use of the land; feudal estate; feud; fee. Also, **feoff.** [< Old French; of Germanic origin]

field (fēld), *n.* 1 Often, **fields,** *pl.* piece of land with few or no trees; stretch of open land; open country. 2 piece of cleared land used for crops or for pasture. 3 piece of land used for some special purpose: *a baseball field.* 4 land yielding some product: *a coal field.* 5 battle. 6 region where certain military or other operations are carried on, especially a battlefield. 7 a flat space; broad surface: *A field of ice surrounds the North Pole.* 8 surface on which something is pictured or painted; background: *the field of a coat of arms.* 9 range of opportunity or interest; sphere of activity or operation: *the field of electronics.* 10 (in physics) the space throughout which a force operates. A magnet has a magnetic field around it. 11 space or area in which things can be seen through a telescope, microscope, etc. 12 (in television) the entire screen area occupied by an image. 13 area where contests in jumping, throwing, etc., are held. 14 all those in a game, contest, or outdoor sport. 15 all those in a game or contest except one or more specified: *bet on one horse against the field.* 16 a defensive football, baseball, etc., team. 17 (in mathematics) any set, as the set of all real numbers, which has two operations called addition and multiplication. For each operation, the set is closed, associative, and commutative, has an identity element and inverses (the zero element being excluded for multiplication), and is distributive of multiplication over addition. 18 **take the field,** begin a battle, campaign, game, etc.
—*v.t.* 1 (in baseball, cricket, etc.) stop or catch (a batted ball). 2 send (a player, team, etc.) to the field. —*v.i.* (in baseball, cricket, etc.) act as a fielder.

—*adj.* 1 of or having to do with a field or fields; used in the field. 2 inhabiting or growing in open country or fields. [Old English *feld*]

Field (fēld), *n.* 1 **Cyrus West,** 1819-1892, American financier who planned the first telegraph cable across the Atlantic. 2 **Eugene,** 1850-1895, American poet and journalist.

field army, a military unit made up of two or more corps plus supporting troops, commanded by a general. It is the largest tactical military unit.

field artillery, artillery capable of being moved and used against ground forces and installations.

field day, 1 day for athletic contests and outdoor sports. 2 day when soldiers perform drills, mock fights, etc. 3 day of unusual activity, display, or success.

field er (fēl′dər), *n.* (in baseball, cricket, etc.) a player who stops or catches the ball. A fielder is stationed around or outside the diamond in baseball.

field glasses or **field glass,** small binoculars for use outdoors.

field goal, 1 (in football) a goal counting three points, made by a place kick or drop kick. 2 (in basketball) a basket scored while the ball is in play, counting two points.

field gun, cannon mounted on a carriage for use in the field; fieldpiece.

field hockey, the game of hockey played on a field.

field hospital, a temporary hospital on or near a battlefield.

field house, 1 a building near an athletic field, used by athletes for storing equipment, for dressing rooms, etc. 2 a large building that is used for various athletic events.

Field ing (fēl′ding), *n.* **Henry,** 1707-1754, English novelist.

field magnet, magnet used to produce or maintain a magnetic field, especially in a dynamo or electric motor.

field marshal, an army officer ranking next below the commander in chief in the British, French, German, and some other armies.

field mouse, any of various species of mice living in fields and meadows.

field officer, an army officer ranking above a captain and below a brigadier general. Colonels, lieutenant colonels, and majors are field officers.

field piece (fēld′pēs′), *n.* field gun.

field test, test of a new product under conditions of actual use.

field-test (fēld′test′), *v.t.* test (a new product) under conditions of actual use.

field trial, 1 test of the performance of hunting dogs in the field. 2 field test.

field trip, trip away from school to give students special opportunities for observing important or historic places, things, etc.

field work (fēld′wėrk′), *n.* a temporary fortification for defense made by soldiers in the field.

field work, scientific or technical work done in the field by surveyors, geologists, linguists, sociologists, etc.

fiend (fēnd), *n.* 1 an evil spirit; devil; demon. 2 **the Fiend,** the Devil. 3 a very wicked or cruel person. 4 INFORMAL. **a** person who gives himself up to some harmful habit: *a dope fiend.* **b** person who spends an excessive amount of time in some game, pastime, etc.: *a bridge fiend.* [Old English *fēond* enemy, hater] **—fiend′like′,** *adj.*

fiend ish (fēn′dish), *adj.* very cruel or wicked; devilish: *fiendish tortures, a fiendish yell.* **—fiend′ish ly,** *adv.* **—fiend′ish ness,** *n.*

fierce (firs), *adj.,* **fierc er, fierc est.** 1 savagely cruel and wild; ferocious: *a fierce lion.* See synonym study below. 2 vehemently raging; violent: *a fierce wind, fierce anger.* 3 very eager or active; ardent: *a fierce determination to win.* 4 SLANG. very bad, unpleasant, etc. [Old French *fers, fiers* < Latin *ferus* wild] **—fierce′ly,** *adv.* **—fierce′ness,** *n.*

Syn. 1 **Fierce, ferocious, savage** mean wild and cruel. **Fierce** suggests an extremely violent temper or manner: *He was a fierce fighter.* **Ferocious** suggests a very cruel or brutal appearance or disposition: *That man looks ferocious.* **Savage** suggests the lack of all civilized restraint or compassion: *He has a savage temper.*

fie ry (fī′rē, fī′ər ē), *adj.,* **fie ri er, fie ri est.** 1 consisting of fire; containing fire; burning; flaming. 2 like fire; very hot; glowing; flashing: *a fiery red, fiery heat.* 3 full of feeling or spirit; ardent: *a fiery speech.* 4 easily aroused or excited: *a fiery temper.* 5 highly flammable. 6 inflamed: *a fiery sore.* [Middle English < Old English *fyr* fire] **—fie′ri ly,** *adv.* **—fie′ri ness,** *n.*

fi es ta (fē es′tə), *n.* 1 a religious festival, such as one honoring a saint's memory. In Spain and Latin-American countries fiestas are held with colorful ceremonies and festivities. 2 holiday or festivity. [< Spanish, feast]

fife
15½ in. long
with six
finger holes

fife (fīf), *n., v.,* **fifed, fif ing.** —*n.* a small, shrill musical instrument like a flute, played by blowing. Fifes and drums are used to make music for marching. —*v.t., v.i.* play on a fife. [< German *Pfeife* pipe] **—fif′er,** *n.*

Fife (fīf), *n.* county in E Scotland.

fif teen (fif′tēn′), *n.* 1 five more than ten; 15. 2 of fifteen players, as in Rugby. —*adj.* being five more than ten. [Old English *fīftēne*]

fif teenth (fif′tēnth′), *adj., n.* 1 next after the 14th; last in a series of 15. 2 one, or being one, of 15 equal parts.

fifth (fifth), *adj.* 1 next after the fourth; last in a series of 5. 2 being one of 5 equal parts. —*n.* 1 next after the fourth; last in a series of 5. 2 one of 5 equal parts. 3 bottle to hold one-fifth of a gallon (four-fifths of a quart), usually of an alcoholic beverage. 4 contents of such a bottle. 5 in music: **a** the fifth tone from the keynote of the diatonic scale; the dominant. **b** interval between such tones. **c** combination of such tones. [alteration of Old English *fīfta*]

Fifth Avenue, street in New York City, with fine shops and residences, often used as a symbol of wealth, elegance, fashion, etc.

fifth column, persons living within a country who secretly aid its enemies by sabotage, espionage, etc.

fifth columnist, member of a fifth column.

fifth ly (fifth′lē), *adv.* in the fifth place.

fifth wheel, INFORMAL. person or thing that is not needed.

hat, āge, fär; let, ēqual, tėrm;
it, īce; hot, ōpen, ôrder;
oil, out; cup, pu̇t, rüle;
ch, child; ng, long; sh, she;
th, thin; ᴛʜ, then; zh, measure;

ə represents *a* in about, *e* in taken, *i* in pencil, *o* in lemon, *u* in circus.

< = from, derived from, taken from.

fif ti eth (fif′tē ith), *adj., n.* 1 next after the 49th; last in a series of 50. 2 one, or being one, of 50 equal parts.

fif ty (fif′tē), *n., pl.* **-ties,** *adj.* five times ten; 50. [Old English *fīftig*]

fif ty-fif ty (fif′tē fif′tē), *adj., adv.* INFORMAL. in two equal parts; with two equal shares; half-and-half; even: *a fifty-fifty chance of winning, go fifty-fifty on expenses.*

fig (fig), *n.* 1 any of a genus of trees and shrubs of the same family as the mulberry, that grow in warm regions. 2 the small, soft, sweet, pear-shaped fruit of one species of this genus. Figs are sometimes eaten fresh or canned, but usually are dried like dates and raisins. 3 a very small amount: *I don't care a fig for his opinion.* [< Old French *figue* < Provençal *figa,* ultimately < Latin *ficus* fig]

fig., 1 figurative. 2 figuratively. 3 figure.

fight (fīt), *n., v.,* **fought, fight ing.** —*n.* 1 a violent struggle; contest; battle. See synonym study below. 2 an angry dispute; quarrel. 3 power or will to fight; fighting spirit: *There was not much fight in the defeated army.* 4 a boxing match. 5 **show fight,** resist; be ready to fight. —*v.i.* 1 take part in a fight; have a fight. 2 **fight shy of,** keep away from; avoid. —*v.t.* 1 take part in a fight against; struggle against. 2 carry on (a fight, conflict, etc.). 3 **fight it out,** fight until one side wins. 4 get or make by fighting: *He had to fight his way through the crowd.* 5 cause to fight. [Old English *feoht*]

Syn. *n.* 1 **Fight, combat, conflict** mean a struggle or battle between opposing forces. **Fight** suggests a close, unregulated, and often hand-to-hand struggle between two or more opponents: *The boys of the gang had a big fight.* **Combat** applies particularly to an organized contest or battle between two armed forces: *The marines went into combat against the enemy entrenched along the shore.* **Conflict** emphasizes clashing or collision between opposing forces, often drawn out and hard to resolve: *The UN General Assembly discussed the conflict in the Middle East.*

fight er (fī′tər), *n.* 1 one that fights. 2 soldier. 3 a professional boxer. 4 a small, fast, and highly maneuverable airplane, used mainly for attacking enemy airplanes or strafing ground forces.

fig ment (fig′mənt), *n.* something imagined; made-up story. [< Latin *figmentum* < *fingere* to form, fashion]

fig u ra tion (fig′yə rā′shən), *n.* 1 form; shape. 2 a forming; shaping. 3 representation by a likeness or symbol.

fig ur a tive (fig′yər ə tiv), *adj.* 1 using words out of their literal or ordinary meaning to add beauty or force. 2 having many figures of speech; characterized by the use of metaphors, similes, etc. Much poetry is figurative. 3 representing by a likeness or symbol; symbolic: *Baptism is a figurative cer-*

emony; it represents cleansing by washing away sin. **—fig′ur a tive ly,** *adv.* **—fig′ur a tive ness,** *n.*

fig ure (fig′yər; *British* fig′ər), *n., v.,* **-ured, -ur ing.** *—n.* 1 symbol standing for a number. 1, 2, 3, 4, etc., are figures. 2 **figures,** *pl.* calculations using figures; arithmetic. 3 amount or value given in figures; price; estimate: *Ask for a lower figure.* 4 form enclosing a surface or space: *Circles and cubes are geometric figures.* 5 form or shape: *In the darkness she saw dim figures moving.* See **form** for synonym study. 6 person considered from the point of view of appearance, manner, etc.: *The poor old woman was a figure of distress.* 7 person or character noticed or remembered: *Benjamin Franklin is a great figure in American history.* 8 an artificial representation of the human form in sculpture, painting, drawing, etc., usually of the whole or greater part of the body. 9 image; likeness. 10 drawing, diagram, or other illustration supplementing the text of a book, etc. 11 design or pattern: *Wallpaper often has figures on it.* 12 outline traced by movements: *figures made by an airplane.* 13 set of movements in dancing or skating. 14 figure of speech.
—v.t. 1 use numbers to find out (the answer to some problem); show by figures; calculate. 2 **figure out,** **a** find out by using figures; calculate. **b** think out; understand. 3 show by a figure; represent in a diagram. 4 decorate with a figure or pattern. 5 INFORMAL. think; consider. *—v.i.* 1 use figures to find out the answer to some problem; compute. 2 **figure on,** **a** depend on; rely on. **b** consider as part of a plan or undertaking. 3 be conspicuous; appear; be notable: *The names of great leaders figure in the story of human progress.*
[< Old French < Latin *figura* < *fingere* to form] **—fig′ur er,** *n.*

fig ured (fig′yərd), *adj.* 1 decorated with a design or pattern; not plain. 2 shown by a figure, diagram, or picture. 3 (in music) having accompanying chords of the bass part indicated by figures.

figure eight, 1 a flight maneuver in which an aircraft flies a path resembling a horizontal 8. 2 an evolution in figure skating in which the skater traces a single line resembling an 8.

figurehead (def. 2)

fig ure head (fig′yər hed′), *n.* 1 person who is the head of a business, government, etc., in name only, without real authority or responsibility. 2 statue or carving decorating the bow of a ship.

figure of speech, expression in which words are used out of their literal meaning or out of their ordinary use to add beauty or force. Similes and metaphors are figures of speech. EXAMPLES: Time is a thief. He fought like a lion. A volley of cheers greeted him.

fig u rine (fig′yə rēn′), *n.* a small, ornamental figure made of stone, pottery, metal, etc.; statuette.

fig wort (fig′wėrt′), *n.* any of a genus of tall, coarse herbs with small, bell-shaped flowers that are divided into two lips, have a disagreeable odor, and are greenish, purple, or yellow.

Fi ji (fē′jē), *n.* 1 Fiji Islands. 2 native of these islands. 3 country including these islands, a member of the Commonwealth of Nations. 514,000 pop.; 7000 sq. mi. *Capital:* Suva. **—Fi′ji an,** *adj., n.*

Fiji Islands, group of islands in the S Pacific, composing the country of Fiji, north of New Zealand. See **Australasia** for map.

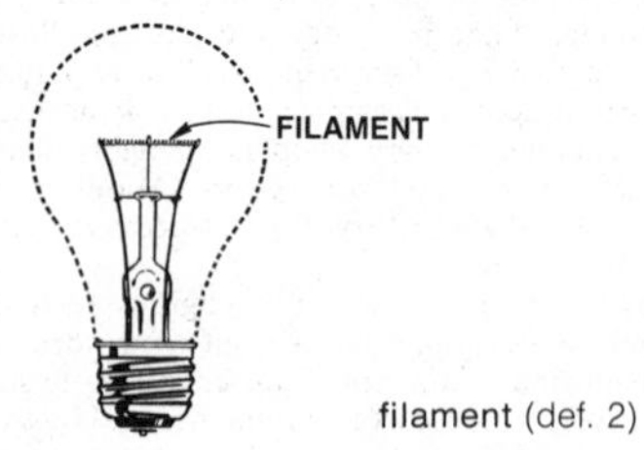

filament (def. 2)

fil a ment (fil′ə mənt), *n.* 1 a very fine thread; very slender, threadlike part. 2 the threadlike wire that becomes incandescent by the passage of a current in an electric light bulb. 3 the heated wire that acts as the negative electrode in a vacuum tube. See **vacuum tube** for diagram. 4 (in botany) the stalklike part of a stamen that supports the anther. See **stamen** for picture. [< Late Latin *filamentum* < Latin *filum* thread]

fil a men tous (fil′ə men′təs), *adj.* 1 threadlike. 2 having filaments.

fi lar i a (fi ler′ē ə, fi lar′ē ə), *n., pl.* **-lar i ae** (-ler′ē ē, -lar′ē ē). any of a family of threadlike, parasitic nematode worms, whose larvae develop in mosquitoes and other arthropods and are transmitted to the blood and tissues of man and other vertebrates, causing such diseases as elephantiasis. [< New Latin < Latin *filum* thread]

fi lar i al (fi ler′ē əl, fi lar′ē əl), *adj.* 1 of or belonging to the filariae. 2 of the nature of or caused by filariae.

fil a ri a sis (fil′ə rī′ə sis), *n.* a diseased condition caused by the presence of filariae in the blood, tissues, and especially lymph vessels.

fil bert (fil′bərt), *n.* 1 a sweet, thick-shelled kind of cultivated hazelnut. 2 tree or shrub it grows on. [< Saint *Philibert,* French Benedictine priest of the A.D. 600's (because the nuts ripen near his feast day, August 20)]

filch (filch), *v.t.* steal in small quantities; pilfer. See **steal** for synonym study. [origin uncertain] **—filch′er,** *n.*

file[1] (fīl), *n., v.,* **filed, fil ing.** *—n.* 1 container, drawer, folder, etc., for keeping memorandums, letters, or other papers in order. 2 set of papers kept in order. 3 row of persons, animals, or things one behind another. 4 **in file,** one after another; in succession: *ships sailing in file.* 5 **on file,** in a file; put away and kept in order. *—v.t.* 1 put away (papers, etc.) in order, for future reference. 2 place among the records of a court, public office, etc.: *The deed to our house is filed with the county clerk.* 3 send (a news story) by wire. *—v.i.* 1 march or move in a file. 2 make written application for a position, as a candidate, etc. [< Middle French *fil* thread (< Latin *filum*) and *file* row (ultimately < Late Latin *filare* spin a thread)] **—fil′er,** *n.*

file[2] (fīl), *n., v.,* **filed, fil ing.** *—n.* tool of steel or other metal having one or more of its surfaces covered with many small ridges or teeth, used to smooth rough materials or wear away hard substances. *—v.t.* smooth or wear away with a file. [Old English *fīl*] **—fil′er,** *n.*

file clerk, person whose work is taking care of the files in an office.

fi let (fi lā′, fil′ā), *n.* 1 fillet of fish or meat. 2 net or lace having a square mesh. *—v.t.* fillet (fish or meat). [< French]

fi let mi gnon (fi lā′ mē′nyon; fi lā′ minyon′; *French* fē le′ mē nyôN′), a small, round, thick piece of choice beef, cut from the tenderloin. [< French, literally, dainty filet]

fil i al (fil′ē əl), *adj.* of a son or daughter; due from a son or daughter toward a mother or father: *filial affection.* [< Late Latin *filialis* < Latin *filius* son and *filia* daughter] **—fil′i al ly,** *adv.*

filial generation, (in genetics) any generation of offspring of a hybrid. F_1, F_2, F_3, etc., mean the first, second, third, etc., filial generations.

fil i bus ter (fil′ə bus′tər), *n.* 1 the deliberate hindering of the passage of a bill in a legislature by long speeches or other means of delay. 2 any of the persons, especially certain citizens of the United States, who unlawfully initiated or supported revolts against South American governments during the 1800's in order to enrich themselves. *—v.i.* 1 deliberately hinder the passage of a bill by long speeches or other means of delay. 2 fight against another country without the authorization of one's government; act as a freebooter. *—v.t.* deliberately hinder the passage of (a bill) by long speeches or other means of delay. [< Spanish *filibustero* < Dutch *vrijbuiter.* See FREEBOOTER.] **—fil′i bus′ter er,** *n.*

fil i form (fil′ə fôrm), *adj.* threadlike.

fil i gree (fil′ə grē), *n.* 1 very delicate, lacelike, ornamental work of gold or silver wire. 2 any similar ornamental openwork. 3 anything very lacy, delicate, or fanciful. *—adj.* 1 ornamented with filigree. 2 delicate. [< French *filigrane* < Italian *filigrana* < Latin *filum* thread + *granum* grain]

fil ings (fī′lingz), *n.pl.* small pieces of iron, wood, etc., which have been removed by a file.

Fil i pi no (fil′ə pē′nō), *n., pl.* **-nos.** native or inhabitant of the Philippines. *—adj.* Philippine.

fill (fil), *v.t.* 1 make full; put into until there is room for nothing more: *fill a cup.* 2 take up all the space in; spread throughout: *The crowd filled the hall.* 3 satisfy the hunger or appetite of. 4 supply with all that is needed or wanted for: *The druggist filled the doctor's prescription.* 5 stop up or close by putting something in; put a filling in: *A dentist fills decayed teeth.* 6 hold and do the duties of (a position, office, etc.); occupy: *fill the office of governor.* 7 supply a person for or appoint a person to (a position, office, etc.): *fill a judgeship.* 8 (of the wind) stretch out (a sail) by blowing fully into it. *—v.i.* become full: *The hall filled rapidly.*

fill in, **a** fill with something put in. **b** complete by filling: *fill in a traffic ticket.* **c** put in to complete something; insert. **d** act as a substitute: *The understudy filled in for the vacationing star.*

fill out, **a** make or grow larger; swell. **b** make or grow rounder. **c** supply what is needed in.

fill up, fill; fill completely.

—*n.* 1 enough to fill something. 2 all that is needed or wanted: *Eat and drink your fill; there is plenty for all of us.* 3 something that fills. Earth and rock used to level uneven land is called fill. [Old English *fyllan* < *full* full]

fil ler (fil′ər), *n.* 1 person or thing that fills. 2 something used to fill a cavity, stop a gap, complete a load or charge, make bulk, etc. 3 liquid or paste used to fill the pores, cracks, etc., of a surface before applying paint, varnish, or other finish. 4 a short item used on a newspaper page to fill space for which no news stories or advertisements are available. 5 a similar item or an ornament used to fill space on the page of a book, magazine, etc.

fil let (fil′it; *usually* fi lā′, fil′ā *for n. 1 and v.t. 1*), *n.* 1 slice of fish or meat without bones or fat; filet. 2 a narrow band, ribbon, etc., worn around the head to hold the hair in place or as an ornament. 3 a narrow band or strip of any material. Fillets are often used between moldings, the flutes of a column, etc. 4 (in anatomy) a band of fibers, especially of white nerve fibers in the brain. —*v.t.* 1 cut (fish or meat) into fillets. When a fish is filleted, the flesh is cut away from the skeleton. Also, **filet.** 2 bind or decorate with a narrow band, ribbon, strip, etc. [< Old French *filet,* diminutive of *fil* thread < Latin *filum*]

fill ing (fil′ing), *n.* 1 thing put in to fill something: *a filling in a tooth, cake filling.* 2 the woof in woven fabric.

filling station, place where gasoline and oil for motor vehicles are sold; gas station; service station.

fil lip (fil′əp), *v.t.* 1 strike with the fingernail snapped from the end of the thumb: *He filliped me under the chin.* 2 toss or cause to move by striking in this way: *He filliped a speck of lint from the sleeve of his coat.* 3 rouse, revive, or stimulate. —*n.* 1 a quick, slight stroke with the fingernail snapped from the end of the thumb. 2 thing that rouses, revives, or stimulates: *The relishes served as a fillip to my appetite.* [probably imitative]

Fill more (fil′môr, fil′mōr), *n.* **Millard,** 1800-1874, the 13th president of the United States, from 1850 to 1853.

fil ly (fil′ē), *n., pl.* **-lies.** a young female horse, donkey, etc., especially one less than four or five years old. [< Scandinavian (Old Icelandic) *fylja.* Related to FOAL.]

film (film), *n.* 1 a very thin layer, sheet, surface, or coating, often of liquid. Oil poured on water will spread and make a film. 2 roll or sheet of thin, flexible material, such as cellulose acetate, used in making photographs. This roll or sheet is coated with an emulsion that is sensitive to light. 3 motion picture: *a foreign film.* 4 a thin skin or membranous layer. —*v.t.* 1 cover with or as if with a film: *Tears filmed her eyes.* 2 make a motion picture of: *They filmed "Hamlet."* 3 photograph for motion pictures: *They filmed the scene three times.* —*v.i.* 1 be or become covered with or as if with a film: *Her eyes filmed over with tears.* 2 be photographed for motion pictures. [Old English *filmen*] —**film′like′,** *adj.*

film badge, badge containing photographic film that records amounts of radiation exposure. It is worn by a person at an atomic plant or wherever there is a danger of exposure to radiation.

film strip (film′strip′), *n.* series of still pictures printed on a reel of 35 millimeter film, used especially in teaching to project each picture separately on a screen.

film y (fil′mē), *adj.,* **film i er, film i est.** 1 of or like a film; very thin. 2 covered with or as if with a film; dim; hazy. —**film′i ness,** *n.*

fil ter (fil′tər), *n.* 1 device for straining substances in suspension from a liquid or gas by passing the liquid or gas slowly through felt, paper, sand, charcoal, or other porous media. A filter is used to remove impurities from drinking water. 2 felt, paper, sand, charcoal, or other material through which the liquid or gas passes in a filter. 3 any of various devices for removing dust, smoke, germs, etc., from the air. 4 filter tip. 5 device for allowing only certain light rays, frequencies, etc., to pass while blocking all others. A yellow filter placed in front of a camera lens allows less blue light to reach the film. —*v.i.* pass or flow very slowly: *Water filters through sandy soil and into the well.* —*v.t.* 1 put through a filter; strain. 2 act as a filter for. 3 remove by a filter: *Filter out all the dirt before using this water.* [< Medieval Latin *filtrum* felt; of Germanic origin] —**fil′ter er,** *n.*

fil ter a bil i ty (fil′tər ə bil′ə tē), *n.* quality of being filterable.

fil ter a ble (fil′tər ə bəl), *adj.* 1 that can be filtered. 2 capable of passing through a filter which arrests most microorganisms: *a filterable virus.* Also, **filtrable.**

filter paper, porous paper used by chemists and others for filtering.

filter tip, 1 cigarette with an attached filter for removing impurities from the smoke before it is inhaled. 2 the filter itself.

filth (filth), *n.* 1 foul, disgusting dirt; muck: *The alley was filled with garbage and filth.* 2 obscene words or thoughts; vileness; moral corruption. [Old English *fȳlth* < *fūl* foul]

filth y (fil′thē), *adj.,* **filth i er, filth i est.** 1 very dirty; foul. See **dirty** for synonym study. 2 vile; obscene; corrupt; indecent. —**filth′i ly,** *adv.* —**filth′i ness,** *n.*

fil tra ble (fil′trə bəl), *adj.* filterable.

fil trate (fil′trāt), *n., v.,* **-trat ed, -trat ing.** —*n.* liquid that has been passed through a filter. —*v.t., v.i.* pass through a filter.

fil tra tion (fil trā′shən), *n.* 1 a filtering. 2 a being filtered.

fin (fin), *n.* 1 one of the movable winglike or fanlike parts of a fish's or other aquatic animal's body, used for propelling, steering, and balancing the body in water. 2 thing shaped or used like a fin. Some aircraft have fins to help stabilize them in flight. See **airplane** for picture. 3 flipper (def. 2). 4 any of certain thin, flat, lateral projections in various mechanisms: *the cooling fins of a radiator.* [Old English *finn*] —**fin′like′,** *adj.*

fi na gle (fə nā′gəl), *v.,* **-gled, -gling.** INFORMAL. —*v.t.* 1 get (something) by trickery or fraud. 2 cheat; swindle. —*v.i.* use trickery; practice fraud. [origin uncertain] —**fi na′gler,** *n.*

fi nal (fī′nl), *adj.* 1 at the end; coming last; with no more after it: *the final syllable of a word.* See **last**[1] for synonym study. 2 the last possible; ultimate: *the final goal of all things, the final truth.* 3 deciding completely; settling the question; not to be changed; definitive: *A decision of the Supreme Court is final.* 4 having to do with or expressing end or purpose: *a final clause.* —*n.* 1 something final. The last examination of a school term is a final. 2 Often, **finals,** *pl.* the last or deciding set in a series of contests, examinations, etc. [< Latin *finalis* < *finis* end]

hat, āge, fär; let, ēqual, tėrm;
it, īce; hot, ōpen, ôrder;
oil, out; cup, pu̇t, rüle;
ch, child; ng, long; sh, she;
th, thin; ᴛʜ, then; zh, measure;

ə represents *a* in about, *e* in taken, *i* in pencil, *o* in lemon, *u* in circus.

< = from, derived from, taken from.

fi na le (fə nä′lē, fi nal′ē), *n.* 1 the concluding part of a piece of music or a play. 2 the last part; end. [< Italian]

fi nal ist (fī′nl ist), *n.* person who takes part in the last or deciding set in a series of contests, examinations, etc.

fi nal i ty (fī nal′ə tē, fə nal′ə tē), *n., pl.* **-ties.** 1 condition of being final, finished, or settled. 2 something final; final act, speech, etc.

fi nal ize (fī′nl īz), *v.t.,* **-ized, -iz ing.** 1 make final or conclusive. 2 complete.

fi nal ly (fī′nl ē), *adv.* 1 at the end; at last. 2 in such a way as to decide or settle the question.

fi nance (fə nans′, fī′nans, fī nans′), *n., v.,* **-nanced, -nanc ing.** —*n.* 1 science or conduct of monetary business or affairs: *to study finance.* 2 system by which the income of a nation, state, corporation, etc., is raised and managed; management of revenue and expenditure. 3 **finances,** *pl.* financial resources of a nation, state, corporation, or individual; money; funds; revenues. —*v.t.* 1 provide money or credit for: *finance a new business.* 2 manage the finances of. —*v.i.* conduct or engage in financial operations. [< Old French, end, settlement of a debt, ultimately < *fin* end < Latin *finis*]

finance company, a business firm that loans money on interest, especially to finance the purchase of goods on credit or installment payments.

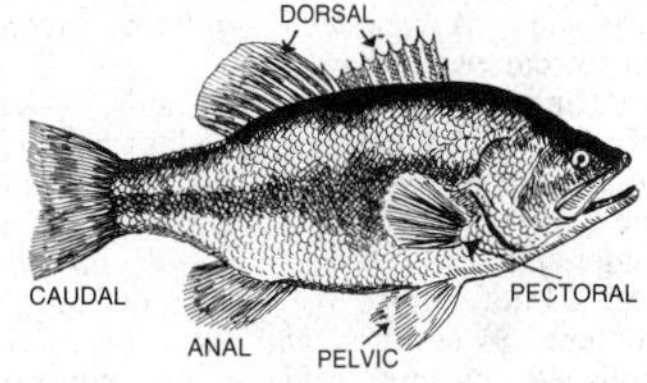

fin (def. 1)—fins of a bass

fi nan cial (fə nan′shəl, fī nan′shəl), *adj.* 1 of or having to do with money matters. See synonym study below. 2 having to do with the management of large sums of public or private money. —**fi nan′cial ly,** *adv.*

Syn. 1 **Financial, monetary, fiscal** mean having to do with money. **Financial** means having to do with money matters in general: *the nation's financial policy.* **Monetary** applies to coined or printed money as such: *The United States has a decimal monetary system.* **Fiscal** means having to do with the funds and financial affairs of a government, institution, or corporation: *The fiscal year of the United States government begins on July 1.*

fin an cier (fin′ən sir′, fī′nən sir′), *n.* 1 person occupied or skilled in finance. 2 person who is active in matters involving large sums of money. [< French]

fin back (fin′bak′), *n.* rorqual.

finch (finch), *n.* any of a family of small songbirds that have cone-shaped bills for cracking seeds. Sparrows, buntings, grosbeaks, canaries, and cardinals are finches. [Old English *finc*]

find (fīnd), *v.,* **found, find ing,** *n.* —*v.t.* 1 come upon by chance; happen on; meet with: *He found a dime in the road.* 2 look for and get: *Please find my hat for me.* 3 discover; learn: *We found that he could not swim.* 4 see; know; feel; perceive: *He found that he was growing sleepy.* 5 get; get the use of: *Can you find time to do this?* 6 arrive at; reach: *Water finds its level.* 7 decide and declare: *The jury found the accused man guilty.* 8 gain or recover the use of: *find one's tongue.* 9 provide; supply: *find food and lodging for a friend.* 10 **find oneself,** learn one's abilities and how to make good use of them. 11 **find out,** learn about; discover. —*v.i.* arrive at a judgment or verdict: *The jury found against the accused man.*
—*n.* 1 act or instance of finding; discovery. 2 something found, especially something exciting or valuable.
[Old English *findan*]

find er (fīn′dər), *n.* 1 person or thing that finds. 2 a small, extra lens on the outside of a camera that shows what is being photographed. 3 a small telescope attached to a larger one to help find objects more easily.

fin-de-siè cle (fan′də sye′klə; *French* faɴ′də sye′klə), *adj.* of or characteristic of the closing years of the 1800's. From about 1880 to 1910, *fin-de-siècle* was used to mean up-to-date or overelegant. [< French *fin de siècle* end of the century]

find ing (fīn′ding), *n.* 1 discovery; find. 2 thing found or discovered. 3 decision reached after an examination or inquiry, as the verdict of a jury. 4 **findings,** *pl.* the tools and supplies (other than the basic materials) used by a shoemaker, dressmaker, or other craftsman: *A jeweler's findings include swivels, clasps, and wire.*

fine[1] (fīn), *adj.,* **fin er, fin est,** *adv.* —*adj.* 1 of very high quality; very good; excellent: *a fine sermon, a fine view, a fine scholar.* See synonym study below. 2 very thin or slender: *fine wire.* 3 sharp: *a tool with a fine edge.* 4 not coarse or heavy; delicate in structure or texture: *fine lace, fine flour.* 5 polished; elegant; refined: *fine manners.* 6 subtle: *The law makes fine distinctions.* 7 too ornate; showy: *fine writing.* 8 good-looking; handsome: *a fine young man.* 9 clear; bright: *fine weather.* 10 without impurities. Fine gold is gold not mixed with any other metal. 11 having a stated proportion of gold or silver in it. A gold alloy that is 925/1000 fine is 92.5 per cent gold. —*adv.* INFORMAL. very well; excellently. [< Old French *fin* perfected, finished, ultimately < Latin *finire* to finish] **—fine′ly,** *adv.* **—fine′ness,** *n.*

Syn. *adj.* 1 **Fine, choice, elegant** mean of very high quality. **Fine** is the general word: *He does fine work.* **Choice** applies to something that seems fine to a discriminating taste: *Our store offers a choice selection of imported wines.* **Elegant** applies to something that is both choice and rich or luxurious: *The designer was noted for his elegant styles in gowns.*

fine[2] (fīn), *n., v.,* **fined, fin ing.** —*n.* 1 sum of money paid as a punishment for breaking a law or regulation. 2 **in fine, a** finally. **b** in a few words; briefly. —*v.t.* make to pay a fine. [< Old French *fin* settlement, payment < Medieval Latin *finis* < Latin, end]

fi ne[3] (fē′nā), *n.* end (a direction marking the end of a musical passage that has to be repeated). [< Italian]

fine arts, the arts which are concerned with the beautiful or which appeal to the faculty of taste, sometimes taken to include poetry, music, drama, and the dance, but now usually applied in a more restricted sense to the arts of design, as painting, sculpture, and architecture.

fine-drawn (fīn′drôn′), *adj.* 1 drawn out until very small or thin. 2 very subtle: *a fine-drawn distinction.*

fin er y (fī′nər ē), *n., pl.* **-er ies.** showy clothes, ornaments, etc. [< *fine*[1]]

fine spun (fīn′spun′), *adj.* 1 spun or drawn out until very small or thin. 2 very subtle.

fi nesse (fə nes′), *n., v.,* **-nessed, -ness ing.** —*n.* 1 delicacy of execution; subtlety of craftsmanship; refined and graceful skill: *the finesse of a great violinist.* 2 the skillful handling of a delicate situation to one's advantage; subtle or tactful strategy: *A successful diplomat must be a master of finesse.* 3 attempt to take a trick in bridge, whist, etc., with a lower card while holding a higher card, in the hope that the card or cards between may not be played. —*v.i.* 1 use finesse. 2 make a finesse in card playing. —*v.t.* 1 bring or change by finesse. 2 make or attempt a finesse with (a card). [< French < *fin* fine[1]]

fin ger (fing′gər), *n.* 1 one of the five slender divisions that end the hand, especially the four excluding the thumb. 2 part of a glove that covers a finger. 3 anything shaped or used like a finger; thing that reaches out and touches: *a long finger of light.* 4 width of a finger; $^{3}/_{4}$ inch. 5 length of a finger; $4^{1}/_{2}$ inches. 6 **put one's finger on,** point out exactly. 7 **twist around one's little finger,** manage easily; control completely. —*v.t.* 1 touch or handle with the fingers; use the fingers on. 2 perform or mark (a passage of music) with a certain fingering. 3 U.S. SLANG. point out (a prospective victim, loot, etc.) to a criminal. 4 pilfer or filch. [Old English] **—fin′ger like′,** *adj.*

finger alphabet, system of signs made with the fingers to represent letters of the alphabet, used by deaf-mutes to communicate; manual alphabet.

fin ger board (fin′gər bôrd′, fing′gər-bōrd′), *n.* 1 strip of wood on the neck of a violin, guitar, etc., against which the strings are pressed by the fingers of the player. 2 keyboard of a piano, organ, etc.

finger bowl, a small bowl to hold water for rinsing the fingers after or during a meal.

fin ger ing (fing′gə ring), *n.* 1 a touching or handling with the fingers; way of using the fingers. 2 the action or way of using the fingers in playing a musical instrument. 3 signs marked on a piece of music to show how the fingers are to be used in playing it.

fin ger ling (fing′gər ling), *n.* a small fish, especially a fish less than one year old.

fin ger nail (fing′gər nāl′), *n.* a hard layer of horn on the upper side of the end of each finger.

finger painting, 1 method of painting pictures or designs with thickened water colors on large sheets of paper, using fingers or hands instead of brushes. 2 picture or design painted in this way.

fin ger print (fing′gər print′), *n.* impression made with ink, etc., of the markings on the inner surface of the last joint of a finger or thumb. A person can be identified by his fingerprints because no two fingers have identical markings. —*v.t.* take the fingerprints of.

fin ger tip (fing′gər tip′), *n.* 1 tip of a finger. 2 **have at one's fingertips,** have thorough familiarity with; know well.

fin i al (fin′ē əl, fī′nē əl), *n.* 1 ornament on top of a roof, corner of a tower, end of a pew in church, etc. 2 the highest point. [originally, variant of *final*]

fin i cal (fin′ə kəl), *adj.* finicky. [apparently < *fine*[1]] **—fin′i cal ly,** *adv.* **—fin′i cal ness,** *n.*

fin ick ing (fin′ə king), *adj.* finicky.

fin ick y (fin′ə kē), *adj.* too dainty or particular; too precise; fussy. **—fin′ick i ness,** *n.*

fin is (fin′is, fī′nis), *n.* the end; conclusion. [< Latin]

fin ish (fin′ish), *v.t.* 1 bring (action, speech, etc.) to an end; reach the end of. See **end** for synonym study. 2 bring (work, affairs, etc.) to completion; complete: *He started the race but did not finish it.* 3 use up completely: *finish a spool of thread.* 4 prepare the surface of in some way: *finish cloth with nap.* 5 perfect in detail; polish. —*v.i.* 1 come to an end: *There was so little wind that the sailboat race didn't finish until after dark.* See **end** for synonym study. 2 **finish off, a** complete. **b** overcome completely; destroy; kill. 3 **finish up, a** complete. **b** use up completely. 4 **finish with, a** complete. **b** stop being friends with; have nothing to do with.
—*n.* 1 end; close; conclusion: *fight to a finish.* 2 way in which the surface is prepared: *a smooth finish on furniture.* 3 polished condition or quality; perfection. 4 something used to finish something else. 5 polish or refinement in manners, speech, etc.
[< Old French *feniss-,* a form of *fenir* to finish < Latin *finire*] **—fin′ish er,** *n.*

fin ished (fin′isht), *adj.* 1 ended or completed. 2 brought to the highest degree of excellence; perfected; polished.

finishing school, a private school that prepares young women for social life rather than for business or a profession, and gives chiefly arts courses.

Fin is terre (fin′i ster′), *n.* **Cape,** cape at the westernmost point of N Spain.

fi nite (fī′nīt), *adj.* 1 having limits or bounds; not infinite: *Human understanding is finite.* 2 having definite grammatical person, number, and tense; not an infinitive, participle, or gerund. In "Before going to work, he stopped to mail the letter," *stopped* is a finite verb; *going* and *to mail* are not finite. 3 in mathematics: **a** (of a number) that can be reached or passed in counting. **b** (of a magnitude) less than infinite and greater than infinitesimal. **c** (of a set) having a limited number of elements. —*n.* what is finite; something finite. [< Latin *finitus,* ultimately < *finis* end] **—fi′nite ly,** *adv.* **—fi′nite ness,** *n.*

hat, āge, fär; let, ēqual, tėrm;
it, īce; hot, ōpen, ôrder;
oil, out; cup, pu̇t, rüle;
ch, child; ng, long; sh, she;
th, thin; ᴛʜ, then; zh, measure;

ə represents *a* in about, *e* in taken, *i* in pencil, *o* in lemon, *u* in circus.

< = from, derived from, taken from.

fin i tude (fin′ə tüd, fin′ə tyüd; fī′nə tüd, fī′nə tyüd), *n.* condition of being finite.

fink (fingk), *n.* SLANG. 1 informer. 2 strikebreaker. 3 an undesirable or inferior person. [origin uncertain]

Fin land (fin′lənd), *n.* 1 country in N Europe, east of Sweden. 4,707,000 pop.; 130,100 sq. mi. *Capital:* Helsinki. 2 **Gulf of,** part of the Baltic Sea, south of Finland. 260 mi. long.

Fin land er (fin′lən dər), *n.* Finn (def. 1).

fin less (fin′lis), *adj.* without fins.

Finn (fin), *n.* 1 native or inhabitant of Finland. 2 member of those peoples that speak Finnish or a related language.

fin nan had die (fin′ən had′ē), smoked and dried haddock. [originally *Findon haddock* < *Findon,* village in Scotland + *haddock*]

finnan haddock, finnan haddie.

finned (find), *adj.* having a fin or fins.

Finn ish (fin′ish), *adj.* of or having to do with Finland, its people, or their language. —*n.* 1 the people of Finland. 2 the Finno-Ugric language of Finland.

Fin no-U gric (fin′ō ü′grik), *adj.* 1 of or having to do with the Finns and the Ugrians. 2 designating or having to do with a family of languages of eastern Europe and western Asia, including Finnish, Estonian, Lapp, Hungarian, etc. —*n.* this family of languages.

fin ny (fin′ē), *adj.,* **-ni er, -ni est.** 1 abounding with fish: *the finny world.* 2 having fins. 3 like a fin.

fiord (fyôrd, fyōrd), *n.* a long, narrow bay of the sea bordered by steep cliffs. Norway has many fiords. Also, **fjord.** [< Norwegian]

fip ple (fip′əl), *n.* plug at the mouth of certain wind instruments (recorders, flageolets, etc.) with a narrow slit through which the breath is directed toward the edge of a side opening. [perhaps < Scandinavian (Icelandic) *flipi* a horse's lip]

fipple flute, flageolet, recorder, or other flutelike instrument utilizing a fipple.

fir (fėr), *n.* 1 any of a genus of evergreen trees of the pine family, having the needles distributed evenly around the branch. Some firs reach a height of 300 feet and are valued for their timber. Small firs are often used for Christmas trees. The needles of fir trees have a pleasant smell. 2 the wood of any of these trees. [Old English *fyrh*]

fire (fīr), *n., v.,* **fired, fir ing.** —*n.* 1 flame, heat, and light caused by something burning; blaze. 2 something burning. 3 destruction by burning, especially the destructive burning of a large mass, such as a building or a forest. 4 fuel burning or arranged so that it will burn quickly: *A fire was laid in the fireplace.* 5 something that suggests a fire because it is hot, glowing, brilliant, or light: *the fire of lightning, an insane fire in his eye, the fire in a diamond.* 6 heat of feeling; passion, fervor, enthusiasm, or excitement: *a man full of fire and courage.* 7 burning pain; fever; inflammation: *the fire of a wound.* 8 severe trial or trouble. 9 the shooting or discharge of guns, etc.: *The enemy's fire sent thousands of bullets against us.* 10 a plying with questions, criticisms, protests, etc.
between two fires, attacked from both sides.
catch fire, a begin to burn. **b** arouse enthusiasm.
hang fire, a be slow in going off or acting. **b** be delayed.
lay a fire, build a fire so that it is ready to be lit.
miss fire, a fail to go off; misfire. **b** fail to do what was attempted.
on fire, a burning. **b** full of a feeling or spirit like fire; excited.
open fire, begin shooting.
play with fire, meddle with something dangerous.
under fire, a exposed to shooting from the enemy's guns. **b** attacked; blamed.
—*v.t.* 1 make burn; set on fire. 2 supply with fuel; tend the fire of: *fire a furnace, fire up the boiler.* 3 dry by heat; bake: *Bricks are fired to make them hard.* 4 make hot, red, glowing, etc. 5 arouse; excite; inflame: *Stories of adventure fire the imagination.* 6 discharge (a gun, etc.). 7 discharge or propel (a missile, etc.) from or as if from a gun, etc.; shoot: *fire a rocket. The hunter fired small shot at the birds.* 8 INFORMAL. throw; hurl: *fire a stone, fire a ball.* 9 **fire off,** INFORMAL. send in haste and anger: *fire off a memo to the chairman.* 10 INFORMAL. dismiss from a job, etc. —*v.i.* 1 begin to burn; burst into flame. 2 grow hot, red, glowing, etc. 3 shoot: *The soldiers fired from the fort.* 4 be discharged; go off with an explosion: *This gun won't fire.* 5 **fire away,** INFORMAL. begin or start, especially to talk rapidly or ask repeated questions; go ahead. 6 **fire up, a** start a fire in a furnace, boiler, etc.: *The men did not have time to fire up.* **b** become angry or excited; lose one's temper. [Old English *fȳr*] —**fir′er,** *n.*

fire alarm, 1 signal that a fire has broken out. 2 device that gives such a signal.

fire arm (fīr′ärm′), *n.* gun, pistol, or other weapon to shoot with. It is usually one that can be carried and used by one person.

fire ball (fīr′bôl′), *n.* 1 the great, luminous cloud of hot gases, water vapor, and dust produced by a nuclear explosion. 2 anything that looks like a ball of fire, such as a ball of lightning. 3 a large, brilliant meteor.

fire boat (fīr′bōt′), *n.* boat equipped with apparatus for putting out fires on a dock, ship, etc.

fire bomb, an incendiary bomb, such as one containing napalm.

fire-bomb (fīr′bom′), *v.t.* attack with a fire bomb or fire bombs.

fire box (fīr′boks′), *n.* 1 box or chamber for the fire in a furnace, boiler, etc. 2 box with a device for giving the alarm in case of fire.

fire brand (fīr′brand′), *n.* 1 piece of burning wood. 2 person who stirs up unrest, strife, rebellion, etc.; agitator.

fire break (fīr′brāk′), *n.* strip of land that has been cleared of trees or on which the sod has been turned over so as to prevent the spreading of a forest fire or a prairie fire.

fire brick (fīr′brik′), *n.* brick that can stand great heat, used to line furnaces and fireplaces.

fire bug (fīr′bug′), *n.* INFORMAL. person who purposely sets houses or property on fire; incendiary.

fire clay, clay capable of resisting high temperatures, used for making crucibles, firebricks, etc.

fire company, group of men organized to put out fires.

fire control, control of the aim, range, time, and volume of fire of projectiles or rockets, now commonly by automatic tracking and computing devices: *The jet plane was equipped with a radar system for fire control.*

fire crack er (fīr′krak′ər), *n.* a paper roll containing an explosive and a fuse, used as a firework to explode with a loud noise.

fire-cure (fīr′kyu̇r′), *v.t.,* **-cured, -cur ing.** prepare and age (tobacco) for use by hanging over open fires to dry. Fire-cured tobacco is usually dark in color and has a noticeably smoky flavor.

fire damp (fīr′damp′), *n.* 1 gas formed in coal mines, consisting chiefly of methane, that is dangerously explosive when mixed with certain proportions of air. 2 the explosive mixture thus formed.

fire department, a municipal department organized and equipped to put out and prevent fires.

fire dog (fīr′dôg′, fīr′dog′), *n.* andiron.

fire drill, drill for firemen, a ship's crew, pupils in a school, etc., to train them for duties or for orderly exit in case of fire.

fire-eat er (fīr′ē′tər), *n.* 1 entertainer who pretends to eat fire. 2 person who is too ready to fight or quarrel.

fire engine, truck with a machine for throwing water, chemicals, etc., to put out fires; fire truck.

fire escape, stairway, ladder, etc., in or on a building, to use when the building is on fire.

fire extinguisher, a portable container filled with chemicals which, when sprayed upon fire, extinguish it.

fire fly (fīr′flī′), *n., pl.* **-flies.** any of various winged insects having organs that produce light, especially any of a family of nocturnal beetles that give off flashes of light which can be seen when they fly at night; lightning bug.

fire house (fīr′hous′), *n., pl.* **-hous es** (-hou′ziz). building where apparatus for putting out fires is kept; fire station. Firemen usually live there when on duty.

fire irons, tools, such as a poker, tongs, and shovel, for tending a fire in a fireplace.

fire less cooker (fīr′lis), an insulated container that stays hot a long time without heat from outside, used to cook food or keep it hot.

fire light (fīr′līt′), *n.* light from a fire, as on a hearth.

fire man (fīr′mən), *n., pl.* **-men.** 1 man who belongs to a fire company, trained to put out fires. 2 man whose work is looking after fires in a furnace, boiler, locomotive, etc.

Fi ren ze (fē ren′dzā), *n.* Italian name of **Florence.**

fire place (fīr′plās′), *n.* place built to hold a fire. Indoor fireplaces are usually made of brick or stone, with a chimney leading up from them.

fire plug (fīr′plug′), *n.* hydrant.

fire pow er (fīr′pou′ər), *n.* 1 ability to deliver fire. 2 the amount of fire delivered by a military unit or by a particular weapon.

fire proof (fīr′prüf′), *adj.* that will not burn; almost impossible to burn. —*v.t.* make fireproof.

fire sale, a sale at very low prices of goods that have been damaged in a fire.

fire screen, screen to be placed in front of a fire as protection against heat or flying sparks.

fire side (fīr′sīd′), *n.* 1 space around a fireplace or hearth. 2 home; hearth. 3 home life. *—adj.* informal: *a fireside chat.*

fire station, firehouse

fire tower, tower from which forest rangers can watch for forest fires and give the alarm.

fire trap (fīr′trap′), *n.* building or other structure that could burn very easily and would be hard to get out of if it were on fire.

fire truck, fire engine.

fire wall, a fireproof wall for confining a possible fire.

fire ward en (fīr′wôrd′n), *n.* official whose duty is preventing and putting out fires in forests, camps, etc.

fire wa ter (fīr′wô′tər, fīr′wot′ər), *n.* strong alcoholic drink. *Firewater* is a translation of the North American Indians' name for whiskey, gin, rum, etc.

fire weed (fīr′wēd′), *n.* any of various weeds which often appear on land recently burned over.

fire wood (fīr′wu̇d′), *n.* wood for burning as fuel.

fire work (fīr′wėrk′), *n.* 1 a firecracker, skyrocket, etc., that makes a loud noise or a beautiful, fiery display at night. 2 **fireworks,** *pl.* **a** a firework display. **b** INFORMAL. an outburst or display of fiery emotions, as a heated controversy. **c** INFORMAL. any spectacular display: *the soprano's coloratura fireworks.*

firing line, 1 line where soldiers are stationed to shoot at the enemy, a target, etc. 2 soldiers on such a line. 3 the foremost position in a controversy, campaign for a cause, etc.

firing pin, the part of the mechanism of a firearm, cannon, etc., that sets off the primer which explodes the charge.

firing squad, 1 a small detachment of troops assigned to shoot to death a condemned person. 2 a detachment assigned to fire the salute at a military burial service.

fir kin (fėr′kən), *n.* 1 quarter of a barrel, used in Great Britain as a measure of capacity. 2 a small wooden cask for liquids, fish, butter, etc. [Middle English *ferdekyn*]

firm[1] (fėrm), *adj.* 1 not yielding easily to pressure or force; solid; hard: *firm flesh.* See synonym study below. 2 not easily moved or shaken; tightly fastened or fixed in place: *a tree firm in the earth.* 3 not easily changed; determined; resolute; positive: *a firm purpose.* 4 not changing; staying the same; steady; constant: *a firm price.* *—v.t., v.i.* make or become firm: *The company is firming up its financial plans. Profits are rising and prices are firming up.* [< Old French *ferme* < Latin *firmus*] **—firm′ly,** *adv.* **—firm′ness,** *n.*

Syn. *adj.* 1 **Firm, hard, solid** mean not yielding easily to pressure or force. **Firm** implies being so tough or stiff that it cannot be easily bent, squeezed, or pulled out of shape: *His muscles are firm.* **Hard** implies a surface difficult to dent or penetrate: *The ground is too hard to dig.* **Solid** implies being so strong, uniformly dense, firm, or hard as to withstand all pressure or force: *We build houses on solid ground.*

firm[2] (fėrm), *n.* 1 company or partnership of two or more persons in business together. 2 name or title used by such a company or partnership: *the firm of Black and Sons.* 3 any business concern. [< Italian *firma* signature < Latin *firmare* make firm < *firmus* firm[1]]

fir ma ment (fėr′mə mənt), *n.* arch of the heavens; sky. [< Latin *firmamentum,* ultimately < *firmus* firm[1]]

first (fėrst), *adj.* 1 preceding the second; designating the number or member in a series coming before all others. 2 coming before all others; earliest or foremost in time, order, position, rank, etc.: *He is first in his class.* 3 playing or singing the chief part or the part highest in musical pitch: *first violin.* 4 designating the lowest gear ratio of a standard automobile transmission; low. *—adv.* 1 before all others; before anything else: *Women and children go first.* 2 before some other thing or event: *First bring me the chalk.* 3 for the first time: *when I first visited Italy.* 4 rather; sooner: *I'll go to jail first.* *—n.* 1 the one which precedes the second; the first number or member in a series. 2 person, thing, place, etc., that is first. 3 the winning position in a race, etc. 4 (in baseball) first base. 5 beginning. 6 the first day of the month: *I'll see you on the first.* 7 the first or lowest gear in an automobile or similar machine; low. [Old English *fyrst*]

first aid, emergency treatment given to an injured or sick person before a doctor comes.

first-aid (fėrst′ād′), *adj.* of or for first aid: *a first-aid kit.*

first base, 1 in baseball: **a** the base that must be touched first by a runner. **b** position of the fielder covering the area near this base. 2 **get to first base,** INFORMAL. make the first step toward success. **—first baseman.**

first-born (fėrst′bôrn′), *adj.* born first; oldest. *—n.* the first-born child.

first class, 1 the best and most expensive passenger accommodations offered for travel by ship, airplane, or train. 2 class of mail that includes letters, post cards, etc., sealed against postal inspection.

first-class (fėrst′klas′), *adj.* 1 of the first or best quality; excellent. 2 of or having to do with first class. *—adv.* in or by first class.

first hand (fėrst′hand′), *adj., adv.* from the original source; direct.

first lady, the official hostess (usually the wife) of the President of the United States, the governor of a state, etc.

first lieutenant, a commissioned officer in the army, air force, or marines ranking next below a captain and next above a second lieutenant.

first ling (fėrst′ling), *n.* 1 the first of its kind. 2 the first product or result. 3 the first offspring of an animal.

first ly (fėrst′lē), *adv.* in the first place; before anything else; first.

first person, form of a pronoun or verb used to refer to the speaker or writer and those he includes with himself. *I, me, my,* and *we, us, our* are pronouns of the first person.

first quarter, 1 period of time between the new moon and the first half moon. 2 phase of the moon represented by the first half moon after the new moon. See **phase** for diagram.

first-rate (fėrst′rāt′), *adj.* of the highest class; very good; excellent. *—adv.* INFORMAL. very well; excellently.

first sergeant, (in the U.S. Army and Marine Corps) a master sergeant in direct charge of a company or similar unit under the commissioned officer in command.

first-strike (fėrst′strīk′), *adj.* 1 (of a nuclear weapon or force) intended for use only in an initial attack. 2 limited to the power to strike first; not retaliatory: *first-strike capability.*

first string, the players who usually make up the starting line-up in a game, distinguished from alternates or substitutes.

first-string (fėrst′string′), *adj.* 1 of or having to do with a first string. 2 first-rate.

firth (fėrth), *n.* 1 a narrow arm of the sea. 2 estuary of a river. [< Scandinavian (Old Icelandic) *fjörthr.* Related to FIORD.]

fis cal (fis′kəl), *adj.* 1 of or having to do with financial matters; financial. See **financial** for synonym study. 2 having to do with public finance: *the government's fiscal policy.* [< Latin *fiscalis* < *fiscus* purse] **—fis′cally,** *adv.*

fiscal year, time between one yearly settlement of financial accounts and another.

fish (fish), *n., pl.* **fish es** or **fish,** *v.* *—n.* 1 any of a superclass of cold-blooded vertebrates that live in the water, have gills instead of lungs for breathing, and are usually covered with scales and equipped with fins for swimming. Most fishes lay eggs in the water; others produce living young. 2 any of numerous other animals living in water, as a shellfish. 3 a fish or any part of a fish used for food. 4 INFORMAL. person; fellow: *He is an odd fish.* 5 a long strip of iron or wood used to strengthen a joint, etc. *—v.i.* 1 catch fish; try to catch fish. 2 try for something as if with a hook: *The boy fished with a stick for his watch, which had fallen through a grating.* 3 search: *She fished in her purse for a coin.* 4 try to get, often by indirect or underhand means: *She fished for compliments.* *—v.t.* 1 catch or try to catch: *fish trout. The chimpanzee fished the banana within reach.* 2 try to catch fish in: *He fished the stream for trout.* 3 search through as by fishing. 4 find and pull: *He fished an old map out of a box.* [Old English *fisc*] **—fish′like′,** *adj.*

➤ **fish.** The usual plural is *fish* except in speaking of different kinds or species: *He had a string of eight fish. Most of the income of the island is from these fishes: cod, halibut, and swordfish.*

fish and chips, fried pieces of fish and French-fried potatoes.

fish cake or **fish ball,** shredded cooked fish, especially codfish, and mashed potatoes shaped into a cake or ball and fried.

fish er (fish′ər), *n.* 1 fisherman. 2 animal that catches fish for food. 3 a slender, arboreal, carnivorous mammal of the same family as and resembling the weasel. 4 its dark-brown fur.

fish er man (fish′ər mən), *n., pl.* **-men.** 1 person who fishes, especially one who makes his living by catching fish. 2 ship used in fishing.

fish er y (fish′ər ē), *n., pl.* **-er ies.** 1 business or industry of catching fish. 2 place for catching fish. 3 place for breeding fish.

fish hawk, osprey.

fish hook (fish′hu̇k′), *n.* a barbed hook used for catching fish.

fish ing (fish′ing), *n.* the catching of fish for a living or for pleasure.

fishing ground, place where fish are plentiful.

fishing rod, a long, light, slender pole with

a line and hook attached to it, and often having a reel, used in catching fish.

fishing tackle, rods, lines, hooks, etc., used in catching fish.

fish ladder, waterway built as an ascending series of little pools to enable fish to pass over a dam or falls on their way to spawning grounds upstream; fishway.

fish line (fish′līn′), *n.* cord used with a fishhook for catching fish.

fish mon ger (fish′mung′gər, fish′mong′-gər), *n.* dealer in fish.

fish plate (fish′plāt′), *n.* plate used to fasten two rails or beams together end to end.

fish pond (fish′pond′), *n.* pond in which fish are stocked to be sold.

fish stick, a boneless piece of cod, haddock, perch, etc., dipped in batter and breaded, usually sold in frozen form.

fish story, INFORMAL. an exaggerated, unbelievable story.

fish tail (fish′tāl′), *adj.* like a fish's tail in shape or action.

fish way (fish′wā′), *n.* fish ladder.

fish wife (fish′wīf′), *n., pl.* **-wives.** 1 woman who uses coarse and abusive language. 2 woman who sells fish.

fish y (fish′ē), *adj.,* **fish i er, fish i est.** 1 like a fish in smell, taste, or shape. 2 of fish. 3 full of fish. 4 INFORMAL. of questionable character; doubtful; unlikely: *a fishy excuse.* 5 without expression or luster; dull. **—fish′i ly,** *adv.* **—fish′i ness,** *n.*

fis sile (fis′əl), *adj.* 1 that can be split or divided; cleavable. 2 fissionable. [< Latin *fissilis* < *findere* cleave]

fis sion (fish′ən), *n.* 1 a splitting apart; division into parts. 2 method of reproduction in which the body of the parent divides spontaneously to form two or more independent individuals. Many simple animals and plants reproduce by fission. 3 the splitting of an atomic nucleus into two parts, especially when bombarded by a neutron; nuclear fission. Fission releases huge amounts of energy when the nuclei of heavy elements, especially uranium and plutonium, are split. Fission is used to induce the chain reaction in an atomic bomb. *—v.t., v.i.* split or divide. [< Latin *fissionem* < *findere* cleave]

fis sion a ble (fish′ə nə bəl), *adj.* capable of nuclear fission; fissile.

fission bomb, atomic bomb.

fis sip ar ous (fi sip′ər əs), *adj.* 1 reproducing by fission. 2 splitting or tending to split apart. [< Latin *fissum* cleft + *parere* give birth]

fis sure (fish′ər), *n., v.,* **-sured, -sur ing.** *—n.* 1 a long, narrow opening; split; crack: *a fissure in a rock.* 2 a splitting apart; division into parts. *—v.t.* split apart; divide into parts. *—v.i.* become split or cleft. [< Latin *fissura* < *findere* cleave]

fist (fist), *n.* 1 hand closed tightly with the fingers doubled into the palm. 2 INFORMAL. hand. 3 INFORMAL. grasp; clutches. 4 symbol (☞) used in printing. [Old English *fȳst*] **—fist′like′,** *adj.*

fist ful (fist′fu̇l), *n., pl.* **-fuls.** handful: *a fistful of money.*

fist ic (fis′tik), *adj.* INFORMAL. having to do with boxing.

fist i cuffs (fis′tə kufs′), *n.pl.* 1 a fight with the fists. 2 blows with the fists.

fis tu la (fis′chə lə), *n., pl.* **-las, -lae** (-lē′). a tubelike abnormal passage connecting the surface of the body with some internal cavity or organ, caused by a wound, abscess, disease, etc. [< Latin, pipe, ulcer]

fis tu lar (fis′chə lər), *adj.* having to do with a fistula.

fis tu lous (fis′chu̇ ləs), *adj.* fistular.

fit[1] (fit), *adj.,* **fit ter, fit test,** *v.,* **fit ted** or **fit, fit ting,** *n., adv.* *—adj.* 1 having the right or necessary qualities; well adapted for a purpose; suitable: *Grass is a fit food for cows; it is not fit for men.* See synonym study below. 2 right; proper: *It is fit that we give thanks.* 3 in good physical condition; healthy and strong: *He is now well and fit for work.* 4 qualified or competent: *choose the fittest candidate.* 5 ready; prepared: *fit for active service.*

—v.t. 1 be suited or suitable to; be fit for: *a punishment that fits the crime.* 2 have the right size or shape for: *The dress fitted her.* 3 cause to fit; make fit: *Father was fitting new seat covers on our car. He fit the words to the music.* 4 make ready; prepare: *fit men for active duty in the army.* 5 supply with everything needed; equip: *fit out a room, fit a store with counters.* *—v.i.* 1 have the right size or shape: *Does this glove fit?* 2 ARCHAIC. be fit. 3 be harmonious or appropriate; belong; agree: *At camp I didn't fit anywhere. She fits in well with her age group. He fit perfectly into the new teaching system.*

—n. 1 way that something fits: *the fit of a coat, a tight fit.* 2 thing that fits: *This coat is a good fit.*

—adv. **see fit** or **think fit,** prefer and decide; choose.

[Middle English *fyt*] **—fit′ly,** *adv.* **—fit′ness,** *n.*

Syn. *adj.* 1 **Fit, suitable, appropriate** mean having the right qualities for something. **Fit** emphasizes the quality of having all that is necessary for a purpose: *That shack is not fit to live in.* **Suitable** suggests having the right or proper requirements for a definite occasion or situation: *The lawyer found a suitable office.* **Appropriate** suggests special readiness or fitness for a purpose or activity: *The verdict of the jury was announced with appropriate solemnity.*

fit[2] (fit), *n.* 1 a sudden, sharp attack of disease: *a fit of colic.* 2 a sudden attack characterized by loss of consciousness or by convulsions: *a fainting fit, a fit of epilepsy.* 3 any sudden, sharp attack: *In a fit of anger he hit his friend.* 4 a short period of doing some one thing; spell: *a fit of coughing, a fit of laughter.* 5 **by fits** or **by fits and starts,** irregularly; starting, stopping, beginning again, and so on. [Old English *fitt* conflict]

fitch (fich), *n.* 1 the polecat of Europe. 2 its fur, yellowish with dark markings. [perhaps < Middle Dutch *fisse*]

fitch et (fich′it), *n.* fitch.

fitch ew (fich′ü), *n.* fitch.

fit ful (fit′fəl), *adj.* going on and then stopping for a while; irregular: *a fitful sleep.* [< *fit*[2]] **—fit′ful ly,** *adv.* **—fit′ful ness,** *n.*

fit ter (fit′ər), *n.* 1 person whose work is fitting clothes on people. 2 person who supplies and fixes anything necessary for some purpose: *a pipe fitter.* 3 person who adjusts parts of machinery. 4 person or thing that fits.

fit ting (fit′ing), *adj.* proper and right; suitable. See synonym study below. *—n.* 1 a trying on of unfinished clothes to see if they will fit. 2 anything with which something is fitted by way of furnishing, equipping, etc. 3 **fittings,** *pl.* furnishings; fixtures: *fittings for an office, gas fittings.* **—fit′ting ly,** *adv.* **—fit′ting ness,** *n.*

Syn. *adj.* **Fitting, becoming, seemly**

hat, āge, fär; let, ēqual, tėrm;
it, īce; hot, ōpen, ôrder;
oil, out; cup, pu̇t, rüle;
ch, child; ng, long; sh, she;
th, thin; ᴛʜ, then; zh, measure;

ə represents *a* in about, *e* in taken, *i* in pencil, *o* in lemon, *u* in circus.

< = from, derived from, taken from.

mean right and proper. **Fitting** means right and proper for the purpose or nature of a thing, the character or mood of a person, and the atmosphere or spirit of an occasion: *It is a fitting evening for a dance.* **Becoming** emphasizes being right or proper in appearance, conduct, or speech: *Gentleness is becoming in a nurse.* **Seemly** emphasizes being right and proper as judged by rules for conduct or behavior, as well as by good taste: *Swearing is not seemly in a girl.*

Fitz ger ald (fits jer′əld), *n.* **F(rancis) Scott (Key),** 1896-1940, American novelist and short-story writer.

Fitz Ger ald (fits jer′əld), *n.* **Edward,** 1809-1883, English poet and translator.

five (fīv), *n.* 1 one more than four; 5. 2 set of five persons or things. 3 team of five basketball players. *—adj.* being one more than four. [Old English *fīf*]

five-and-dime (fīv′ən dīm′), *n.* U.S. INFORMAL. dime store.

five-and-ten (fīv′ən ten′), *n.* U.S. INFORMAL. dime store.

five fold (fīv′fōld′), *adj.* 1 five times as much or as many. 2 having five parts. *—adv.* five times as much or as many.

Five Nations, a former confederacy of Iroquois Indian tribes, consisting of the Mohawk, Oneida, Onondaga, Cayuga, and Seneca tribes.

five-year plan (fīv′yir′), any of a series of government plans listing the economic goals of a country to be reached in five years.

fix (fiks), *v.,* **fixed, fix ing,** *n.* *—v.t.* 1 make firm; fasten tightly: *We fixed the post in the ground. The boy fixed the spelling of the word in his mind.* See synonym study below. 2 settle; set: *He fixed the price at one dollar.* 3 direct or hold (the eyes, one's attention, etc.) steadily: *I fixed my eyes on the painting.* 4 make stiff or rigid: *eyes fixed in death.* 5 put or place definitely: *She fixed the blame on the person who did the damage.* 6 treat to prevent fading or otherwise changing: *A dye or photograph is fixed with chemicals.* 7 put in order; set right; arrange: *fix one's hair.* 8 mend; repair: *fix a watch.* 9 **fix up.** INFORMAL. **a** mend; repair: *They moved to the country and fixed up an old farmhouse.* **b** put in order; arrange. 10 prepare (a meal, food, etc.): *fix dinner.* 11 put in a condition or position favorable to oneself or unfavorable to one's opponents, especially by bribery: *fix a jury, fix a game.* 12 INFORMAL. get revenge upon; get even with; punish. 13 (in chemistry) to make stable by decreasing or destroying volatility, fluidity, etc. To fix nitrogen is to change it from a gas into a compound that can be used, such as a fertilizer or explosive. 14 prepare or preserve (an organism, tissue, etc.) for microscopic study. 15 castrate or spay (an animal). *—v.i.* 1 become firm; be fastened tightly. 2 be directed or held steadily. 3 become stiff or rigid. 4 **fix on**

or **fix upon,** decide on; choose; select. —*n.* INFORMAL. 1 position hard to get out of; awkward state of affairs: *The boy who cried "Wolf" got himself into a bad fix.* 2 position of a ship, aircraft, radio transmitter, etc., as determined by obtaining radio signals or other signals from two or more given points. 3 the determining of such a position. 4 position or condition that has been fixed, especially by bribery. 5 a determined position or opinion: *get a fix on the villain's identity.* 6 a narcotic or an injection of a narcotic, such as heroin.
[< Old French *fixer* < *fixe* fixed < Latin *figere* to fix] **—fix′a ble,** *adj.* **—fix′er,** *n.*

Syn. *v.t.* 1 **Fix, establish, settle** mean to set something or someone firmly in position. **Fix** (most often used of things) emphasizes setting something so firmly or solidly that it is hard to change or move: *We fixed the stove in place.* **Establish** (most often used of groups, institutions, businesses, etc.) means to set up firmly or permanently: *They established a partnership.* **Settle** (used of people or affairs) means to put in a steady, ordered, or permanent position, place, or condition: *They settled their father's estate.*

fix ate (fik′sāt), *v.,* **-at ed, -at ing.** —*v.t.* 1 make fixed so as to establish a habit. 2 concentrate (one's attention) on something. —*v.i.* 1 become fixed or fixated. 2 have or develop an abnormal attachment or prejudice.

fix a tion (fik sā′shən), *n.* 1 act or process of fixing. 2 condition of being fixed. 3 treatment to prevent something from fading or otherwise changing: *the fixation of a photographic film.* 4 an abnormal attachment or prejudice.

fix a tive (fik′sə tiv), *n.* 1 substance used to prevent something from fading or otherwise changing. 2 liquid sprayed on pastels, charcoal drawings, etc., to fix the loose particles. —*adj.* that prevents fading or change.

fixed (fikst), *adj.* 1 not movable; made firm; stationary. 2 definitely assigned; settled; set: *fixed charges for taxicabs.* 3 not moving; steady: *a fixed gaze.* 4 prearranged privately or dishonestly: *a fixed horse race.* 5 in chemistry: **a** entered in a stable compound, as an element. **b** not volatile: *a fixed oil or acid.* 6 provided, especially with money: *The widow was left comfortably fixed.*

fix ed ly (fik′sid lē), *adv.* in a fixed manner; without change; intently.

fix ed ness (fik′sid nis), *n.* a being fixed.

fixed star, star whose position in relation to other stars appears not to change. Fixed stars are so far from earth that many thousands of years must pass before man can see that they have moved.

fix ings (fik′singz), *n.pl.* INFORMAL. trimmings: *We had turkey and all the fixings for Thanksgiving dinner.*

fix i ty (fik′sə tē), *n., pl.* **-ties.** 1 fixed condition or quality. 2 something fixed.

fix ture (fiks′chər), *n.* 1 thing put in place to stay: *a bathroom fixture.* 2 person or thing that stays in one place, job, etc. 3 a fixing. 4 a being fixed.

fiz (fiz), *v.i.,* **fizzed, fiz zing,** *n.* fizz.

fizz (fiz), *v.i.* 1 make a hissing or sputtering sound. 2 effervesce. —*n.* 1 a hissing sound; bubbling. 2 an effervescent drink, such as champagne, soda water, etc. [imitative]

fiz zle (fiz′əl), *v.,* **-zled, -zling,** *n.* —*v.i.* 1 make a hissing sound that dies out weakly: *The firecracker just fizzled instead of exploding with a bang.* 2 INFORMAL. make a fiasco of something, especially after a good start. 3 INFORMAL. **fizzle out,** end in failure; fail. —*n.* 1 a fizzling or hissing; sputtering. 2 INFORMAL. failure; fiasco.

fizz y (fiz′ē), *adj.,* **fizz i er, fizz i est.** that fizzes.

fjord (fyôrd, fyōrd), *n.* fiord.

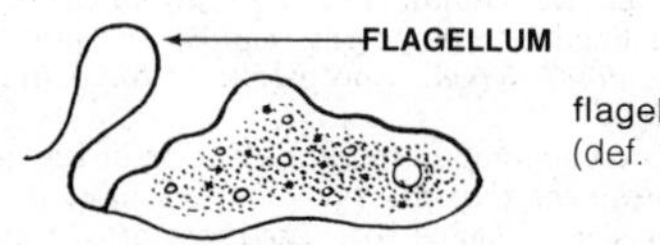

flagellum (def. 1)

Fl, fluorine.

fl., 1 florin. 2 flourished. 3 fluid.

Fla., Florida.

flab (flab), *n.* 1 flaccid flesh; excessive weight. 2 excess of anything: *cut the flab out of the story, executive flab in the company administration.* [shortened < *flabby*]

flab ber gast (flab′ər gast), *v.t.* INFORMAL. make speechless with surprise; astonish greatly; amaze. [origin uncertain]

flab by (flab′ē), *adj.,* **-bi er, -bi est.** 1 lacking firmness; soft; flaccid: *flabby cheeks.* See **limp**[2] for synonym study. 2 lacking force; feeble: *flabby arguments.* [variant of earlier *flappy* < *flap*] **—flab′bi ly,** *adv.* **—flab′bi ness,** *n.*

flac cid (flak′sid, flas′id), *adj.* 1 hanging or lying loose or in wrinkles; flabby: *flaccid muscles.* 2 limp or weak: *a flaccid will.* [< Latin *flaccidus* < *flaccus* flabby] **—flac′cid ly,** *adv.*

flac cid i ty (flak sid′ə tē, fla sid′ə tē), *n.* flaccid quality or condition.

flack[1] (flak), *n.* INFORMAL. a press agent. [origin uncertain]

flack[2] (flak), *n.* flak.

flack er y (flak′ər ē), *n.* INFORMAL. publicity; propaganda. [< flack[2]]

flac on (flak′ən; *French* flȧ kôN′), *n.* a small bottle with a stopper, used for perfume, smelling salts, etc. [< French]

flag[1] (flag), *n.,v.,* **flagged, flag ging.** —*n.* 1 piece of cloth varying in size, color, and design, but most frequently oblong or square, attached by one edge to a staff or halyard, used as a standard, ensign, or signal: *the flag of the United States, the red flag showing danger.* 2 hook (def. 11). —*v.t.* 1 put a flag or flags over or on; decorate with flags. 2 stop or signal, especially by waving a flag: *flag a train, flag down a cab.* 3 communicate by a flag: *flag a message.* [perhaps < *flag*[3]]

flag[2] (flag), *n.* 1 iris with blue, purple, yellow, or white flowers and sword-shaped leaves. 2 sweet flag. 3 cattail. 4 the flower of any of these plants. [perhaps < Scandinavian (Danish) *flæg*]

flag[3] (flag), *v.i.,* **flagged, flag ging.** 1 get tired; grow weak; droop: *After you do the same thing for a long time, your interest flags.* 2 hang down; flap about loose. [perhaps < Scandinavian (Old Icelandic) *flakka* flutter]

flag[4] (flag), *n., v.,* **flagged, flag ging.** —*n.* flagstone. —*v.t.* pave with flagstones. [< Scandinavian (Old Icelandic) *flaga* slab]

Flag Day, June 14, the anniversary of the day in 1777 when the Second Continental Congress adopted the Stars and Stripes as the flag of the United States.

flag el lant (flaj′ə lənt, flə jel′ənt), *n.* 1 person who whips or is whipped. 2 a religious fanatic who whips himself for religious discipline or for penance.

flag el late (flaj′ə lāt; *adj., n. also* flaj′ə lət), *v.,* **-lat ed, -lat ing,** *adj., n.* —*v.t.* beat or scourge with a whip or the like; whip; flog. —*adj.* 1 like a whip; long, thin, and flexible. 2 having flagella. —*n.* any of a class of protozoans that have one or more flagella serving as organs of locomotion and for obtaining food. Euglenas belong to this class.

flag el lat ed (flaj′ə lā′tid), *adj.* flagellate.

flag el la tion (flaj′ə lā′shən), *n.* a whipping; flogging.

fla gel lum (flə jel′əm), *n., pl.* **-la** (-lə), **-lums.** 1 a long, whiplike tail or part which is an organ of locomotion in certain cells, bacteria, protozoa, etc. 2 runner of a plant. 3 whip. [< Latin, diminutive of *flagrum* whip]

flageolet

flag eo let (flaj′ə let′), *n.* a small wind instrument somewhat like a flute, with a mouthpiece at one end, six main finger holes, and sometimes keys. [< French]

flag ging (flag′ing), *n.* 1 flagstones. 2 pavement made of flagstones.

fla gi tious (flə jish′əs), *adj.* scandalously wicked; shamefully vile; infamous. [< Latin *flagitiosus* < *flagitium* shame] **—fla gi′tious ly,** *adv.* **—fla gi′tious ness,** *n.*

flag man (flag′mən), *n., pl.* **-men.** person who signals with a flag or lantern at a railroad crossing, etc.

flag officer, a naval officer entitled to display a flag on his ship indicating his rank or command. An admiral, vice-admiral, rear admiral, or officer in command of a fleet or squadron is a flag officer.

flag of truce, a white flag used as a sign of surrender or of a desire to confer with the enemy.

flag on (flag′ən), *n.* 1 container for liquids, usually having a handle, a spout, and a cover. 2 a large bottle, holding about two quarts. 3 contents of a flagon. [< Old French *flacon, flascon* < Late Latin *flasconem.* Related to FLASK.]

flag pole (flag′pōl′), *n.* pole from which a flag is flown; flagstaff.

fla gran cy (flā′grən sē), *n.* flagrant nature or quality.

fla grant (flā′grənt), *adj.* 1 glaringly offensive; notorious; outrageous; scandalous: *a flagrant crime.* 2 glaring: *a flagrant error.* [< Latin *flagrantem* burning, blazing] **—fla′grant ly,** *adv.*

fla gran te de lic to (flə gran′tē di lik′tō), in flagrante delicto.

flag ship (flag′ship′), *n.* ship that carries the officer in command of a fleet or squadron and displays his flag.

hat, āge, fär; let, ēqual, tėrm;
it, īce; hot, ōpen, ôrder;
oil, out; cup, pu̇t, rüle;
ch, child; ng, long; sh, she;
th, thin; ᴛʜ, then; zh, measure;

ə represents *a* in about, *e* in taken, *i* in pencil, *o* in lemon, *u* in circus.

< = from, derived from, taken from.

flag staff (flag′staf′), *n.* flagpole.

flag station, a railroad station where trains stop only when signaled or to discharge passengers.

flag stone (flag′stōn′), *n.* a large, flat stone, used for paving paths, etc.

flag stop, a place where a bus, train, etc., stops for passengers or freight when flagged.

flag-wav ing (flag′wā′ving), *n.* 1 the waving of the flag of one's country to excite patriotic feelings in others. 2 any similar attempt to arouse popular enthusiasm for a cause.

flail (flāl), *n.* instrument for threshing grain by hand, consisting of a wooden handle at the end of which a stouter and shorter pole or club is fastened so as to swing freely. —*v.t.* 1 strike with a flail. 2 beat; thrash. [< Old French *flaiel* < Latin *flagellum* whip]

flair (fler, flar), *n.* 1 natural talent: *a flair for making clever rhymes.* 2 keen perception: *That trader has a flair for bargains.* [< Old French, scent < *flairer* to smell < Latin *fragrare*]

flak (flak), *n.* 1 shellfire from antiaircraft cannon. 2 INFORMAL. criticism. Also, **flack.** [< German *Fl.A.K.*, abbreviation of *Fl(ieger)a(bwehr)k(anone)* antiaircraft cannon]

flake (flāk), *n., v.,* **flaked, flak ing.** —*n.* 1 a small, light mass; soft, loose bit: *a flake of snow.* 2 a flat, thin piece or layer: *a flake of rust.* —*v.i.* come off in flakes; separate into flakes: *Dirty, gray spots showed where the paint had flaked off.* —*v.t.* 1 break or separate into flakes. 2 cover or mark with flakes. 3 form into flakes. [perhaps < Scandinavian (Old Icelandic) *flakna* chip off] **—flake′like′,** *adj.*

flak y (flā′kē), *adj.,* **flak i er, flak i est.** 1 consisting of flakes. 2 easily broken or separated into flakes. **—flak′i ly,** *adv.* **—flak′i ness,** *n.*

flam beau (flam′bō), *n., pl.* **-beaux** or **-beaus** (-bōz). 1 a flaming torch. 2 a large, decorated candlestick. [< French]

flam boy ance (flam boi′əns), *n.* flamboyant nature or quality.

flam boy an cy (flam boi′ən sē), *n.* flamboyance.

flamboyant (def. 2) window decorated with flamboyant design

flam boy ant (flam boi′ənt), *adj.* 1 gorgeously brilliant; flaming; showily striking: *flamboyant colors.* 2 very ornate; much decorated; florid: *flamboyant architecture.* 3 given to display; ostentatious; showy. 4 having wavy lines or flamelike curves: *flamboyant designs.* [< French] **—flam boy′ant ly,** *adv.*

flame (flām), *n., v.,* **flamed, flam ing.** —*n.* 1 one of the glowing tongues of light, usually red or yellow, that shoot out from a blazing fire. 2 a burning gas or vapor. 3 a burning with flames; blaze. See synonym study below. 4 something like flame. 5 brilliance; luster. 6 a bright light. 7 a burning feeling; ardor; zeal. 8 INFORMAL. sweetheart. —*v.i.* 1 rise up in flames; blaze. 2 grow hot, red, etc.: *Her cheeks flamed.* 3 shine brightly; give out a bright light; flash. 4 have or show a burning feeling. 5 burst out quickly and hotly; be or act like a flame. —*v.t.* subject to a flame; heat in a flame: *flame a test tube.* [< Latin *flamma*] **—flame′like′,** *adj.*

Syn. *n.* 3 **Flame, blaze** mean a bright burning or fire. **Flame** applies to a fire burning brightly and quickly: *The dying fire suddenly burst into flame.* **Blaze** applies to a hotter, brighter, and more steady fire: *The whole room was lighted by the blaze in the fireplace.*

fla men co (flə meng′kō), *n., pl.* **-cos.** style of Spanish Gypsy dance, originally of Andalusia, performed with castanets to fast, fiery, vigorous rhythms. [< Spanish, literally, Flemish (applied to the Gypsies' dance celebrating their departure from Germany, later confused with Flanders)]

flame out (flām′out′), *n.* the sudden failure of a jet aircraft engine to function, especially while in flight.

flame proof (flām′prüf′), *adj.* 1 not liable to combustion. 2 not liable to burn when in contact with flames.

flame test, test to identify certain elements by the color of their salts when heated in the flame of a Bunsen burner.

flame throw er (flām′thrō′ər), *n.* weapon or device that shoots forth a stream of burning fuel from the nozzle of a metal tube connected to tanks of fuel and compressed air.

flam ing (flā′ming), *adj.* 1 burning with flames; on fire. 2 like a flame; very bright; brilliant. 3 showing or arousing strong feeling; violent; vehement.

fla min go (flə ming′gō), *n., pl.* **-gos** or **-goes.** any of a family of large, web-footed, aquatic tropical birds with very long legs and neck, a heavy, bent bill, and feathers that vary from pink to scarlet. [< Portuguese < Spanish *flamenco,* literally, Flemish (from comparing the ruddy complexion of Flemings to the bird's color)]

flam ma bil i ty (flam′ə bil′ə tē), *n.* flammable quality or condition; inflammability.

flam ma ble (flam′ə bəl), *adj.* easily set on fire; inflammable.

Flan ders (flan′dərz), *n.* region in N Europe. It is now divided among Belgium, France, and the Netherlands. See **Burgundy** for map.

flange (flanj), *n., v.,* **flanged, flang ing.** —*n.* a projecting edge, collar, or rim on a wheel, pulley, pipe, or other object, used to keep an object in place, fasten it to another, strengthen it, etc. —*v.t.* provide with a flange. [perhaps ultimately < Old French *flanchir* to bend]

flank (flangk), *n.* 1 the fleshy or muscular part of the side of an animal or person between the ribs and the hip. 2 piece of beef cut from this part. See **beef** for diagram. 3 side of a mountain, building, etc. 4 the far right or the far left side of an army, fleet, or fort. —*v.t.* 1 be at the side of: *A garage flanked the house.* 2 get around the far right or the far left side of. 3 attack from or on the side. —*v.i.* 1 occupy a position on a flank or side. 2 present the flank or side. [< Old French *flanc* < Germanic]

flank er (flang′kər), *n.* 1 person or thing that flanks. 2 flankerback.

flank er back (flang′kər bak′), *n.* (in football) an offensive back who lines up on either flank, closer to the sidelines than his teammates.

flan nel (flan′l), *n.* 1 a soft, warm, woolen or worsted fabric having a nap on both sides. 2 a similar fabric made of cotton, especially a strong fabric with a long, soft nap, usually on one side only. 3 **flannels,** *pl.* **a** clothes, especially trousers, made of flannel. **b** woolen underwear. 4 flannelette. —*adj.* made of flannel. [Middle English *flaunneol*]

flannel board, board covered with flannel or felt, to which material with similar backing will adhere without glue. Flannel boards are often used in teaching.

flan nel ette or **flan nel et** (flan′l et′), *n.* a soft, warm, cotton cloth with a fuzzy nap that looks like flannel.

flap (flap), *v.,* **flapped, flap ping,** *n.* —*v.i.* 1 swing or sway about loosely and with some noise: *The sails flapped in the wind.* 2 fly by moving wings up and down: *The bird flapped away.* —*v.t.* 1 cause to swing or sway loosely. 2 move (wings, arms, etc.) up and down; beat. 3 strike noisily with something broad and flat. —*n.* 1 a flapping motion. 2 noise caused by flapping. 3 a blow from something broad and flat. 4 a broad, flat piece, usually hanging or fastened at one edge only: *His coat had flaps on the pockets.* 5 a hinged section on an airfoil of an airplane, especially a wing, which can be moved to assist a take-off or a landing. [Middle English *flappe*]

flap jack (flap′jak′), *n.* pancake.

flap per (flap′ər), *n.* 1 something that flaps. 2 a young bird just able to fly. 3 a rather forward and unconventional young woman of the 1920's.

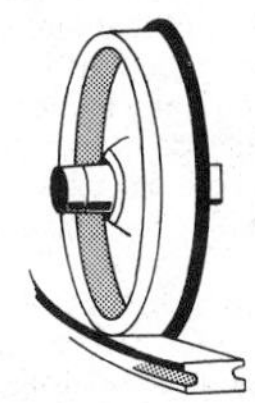
flange on a railroad car wheel

flare (fler, flar), *v.,* **flared, flar ing,** *n.* —*v.i.* 1 flame up briefly or unsteadily, sometimes with smoke. 2 shine; glow. 3 spread out in the shape of a bell: *The sides of a ship flare from the keel to the deck.* 4 **flare up** or **flare out,** burst out into open anger, violence, etc.; flame up. —*v.t.* signal by lights: *The rocket flared a warning.* —*n.* 1 a bright, brief, unsteady flame: *The flare of a match showed us his face.* 2 a dazzling light that burns for a short time, used for signaling, lighting up a battlefield, etc. 3 a sudden eruption of gases on the surface of the sun. 4 a sudden outburst of zeal, temper, rage, etc. 5 a spreading out into a bell shape. 6 part that spreads

out: *the flare of a skirt.* [origin uncertain]
flare-up (fler′up′, flar′up′), *n.* 1 outburst of flame. 2 INFORMAL. a sudden outburst of anger, violence, etc.
flar ing (fler′ing, flar′ing), *adj.* 1 burning with a broad, irregular flame. 2 gaudy. 3 spreading gradually outward in form or shape.
flash (flash), *n.* 1 a sudden, brief light or flame: *a flash of lightning.* See synonym study below. 2 a sudden, brief feeling or display: *a flash of hope, a flash of wit.* 3 a very brief time; instant. 4 a showy display. 5 a brief news report, usually received by teletype, or given over the radio or television. 6 flashbulb. 7 **flash in the pan,** a sudden, showy attempt or effort that fails or is not followed by further efforts.
—*v.i.* 1 give out a sudden, brief light or flame: *Lightning flashed in the sky.* 2 give out or reflect brilliant, flickering light; gleam: *Her eyes flashed with happiness.* 3 come suddenly; pass quickly: *A train flashed by. A thought flashed across his mind.* —*v.t.* 1 give out by flashes: *The lighthouse flashes signals twice a minute.* 2 cause to flash. 3 give out or send out like a flash: *Her eyes flashed defiance.* 4 send by telegraph, radio, etc.; communicate by flashes: *flash the news across the country.* 5 flood or flush with water. 6 display shortly or quickly: *flash a card.* 7 INFORMAL. show off: *flash one's jewelry.*
—*adj.* flashy.
[Middle English *flaschen* to splash]
—flash′er, *n.*
Syn. *n.* 1 **Flash, glitter, sparkle** mean a sudden or briefly gleaming light. **Flash** means a sudden, bright light that disappears immediately: *a single flash of light from the signal tower.* **Glitter** means a bright and wavering light reflected from a shining, hard surface: *the glitter of coins on the table.* **Sparkle** means light shooting out in many tiny, brief, brilliant flashes like sparks: *the sparkle of waves in the sunlight.*
flash back (flash′bak′), *n.* a break in the continuous series of events of a novel, motion picture, etc., to introduce some earlier event or scene.
flash bulb (flash′bulb′), *n.* a glass bulb containing a wire filament, and aluminum or zirconium foil, which produces a brilliant flash of light when electrically ignited, used in taking photographs indoors or at night.
flash burn, a severe burn caused by instantaneous radiation, such as that from an atomic bomb.
flash card (flash′kärd′), *n.* one of a series of cards bearing a letter, word, number, simple problem, or picture. In drills in elementary reading, arithmetic, etc., the teacher displays a flashcard briefly and the student gives a quick answer.
flash cube (flash′kyüb′), *n.* a cubical device containing a set of four small flashbulbs which, when attached to a camera, can be used to take several photographs in quick succession.
flash fire, a very sudden, violent fire, especially one that spreads rapidly through underbrush.
flash flood, a very sudden, violent flooding of a river, stream, etc.
flash gun, (in photography) an apparatus for holding and setting off a flashbulb.
flash ing (flash′ing), *n.* pieces of sheet metal used around windows, chimneys, in roof joints, etc., to make them watertight.
flash lamp, flashbulb.
flash light (flash′līt′), *n.* 1 a portable electric light, operated by batteries. 2 light that flashes, used in a lighthouse or for signaling. 3 flashbulb.
flash point, temperature at which the vapor given off from a flammable substance will ignite momentarily in air, in the presence of a small flame.
flash y (flash′ē), *adj.*, **flash i er, flash i est.** 1 brilliant or sparkling, especially in a superficial way or for a short time; flashing. 2 pretentiously or vulgarly showy; gaudy; tawdry. See **gaudy** for synonym study. **—flash′i ly,** *adv.* **—flash′i ness,** *n.*
flask (flask), *n.* 1 any bottle-shaped container, especially one having a narrow neck, used in laboratories for heating liquids, etc. 2 a small glass, plastic, or metal bottle with flat sides, made to be carried in the pocket. 3 box or frame for holding the sand, etc., used as a mold in a foundry. [Old English *flasce*]
flat[1] (flat), *adj.*, **flat ter, flat test,** *n.*, *adv.*, *v.*, **flat ted, flat ting.** —*adj.* 1 smooth and level; even; plane: *flat land.* 2 at full length; horizontal: *The storm left the trees flat on the ground.* 3 not very deep or thick: *A plate is flat.* 4 with little air in it; deflated: *a flat tire.* 5 not to be changed; positive; absolute: *a flat refusal.* 6 not varied; fixed: *A flat rate has no extra charges.* 7 neither more nor less; exact: *a flat ten seconds.* 8 without much life, interest, flavor, etc.; dull: *a flat voice. Plain food tastes flat.* 9 not shiny or glossy: *a flat yellow.* 10 without appearance of relief or projection in a painting. 11 not clear or sharp in sound. 12 in music: **a** below the true pitch; too low in pitch. **b** one half step or half tone below natural pitch. **c** (of a key) having sharps in the signature. 13 (of the letter *a*) having the sound it has in *man,* as contrasted with the *a* in *father.*
—*n.* 1 something flat. 2 flatboat. 3 the flat part: *The palm of an open hand is the flat.* 4 land that is flat and level. 5 swamp. 6 a shallow box or basket. 7 flatcar. 8 a piece of theatrical scenery. 9 INFORMAL. a tire with little air in it. 10 in music: **a** a tone or note that is one half step or half tone below natural pitch. **b** a sign (♭) for this. **11 flats,** *pl.* a pair of women's shoes with heels that are not built up.
—*adv.* 1 (in music) below the true pitch: *sing flat.* 2 in a flat manner; flatly. 3 exactly: *Time for the race is two minutes flat.* 4 **fall flat,** fail completely. 5 **flat out,** at maximum speed or effort.
—*v.t.* 1 make flat; flatten. 2 (in music) to lower (a note), especially by one half step. —*v.i.* 1 become gradually flat or level. 2 (in music) to sound below the true pitch.
[< Scandinavian (Old Icelandic) *flatr*]
—flat′ly, *adv.* **—flat′ness,** *n.*
flat[2] (flat), *n.* apartment. [alteration of Old English *flet, flett*]
flat boat (flat′bōt′), *n.* a large boat with a flat bottom, formerly much used for carrying goods on a river or canal.
flat-bot tomed (flat′bot′əmd), *adj.* having a flat bottom: *a flat-bottomed boat.*
flat car (flat′kär′), *n.* a railroad freight car without a roof or sides.
flat fish (flat′fish′), *n.*, *pl.* **-fish es** or **-fish.** any of an order of marine food fishes having a very compressed body, which swim on one side when adult, with both eyes on the upper side of the head; flounder; fluke. Halibut, sole, and turbot are flatfishes.
flat foot (flat′fu̇t′), *n.*, *pl.* **-feet** for 1 and 2, **-foots** for 3. 1 foot with a flattened arch so that the entire sole touches the ground. 2 condition in which the feet have flattened arches. 3 SLANG. policeman.
flat-foot ed (flat′fu̇t′id), *adj.* 1 having feet with flattened arches. 2 INFORMAL. firm; uncompromising. 3 **catch flat-footed,** catch off guard. **—flat′-foot′ed ness,** *n.*
flat i ron (flat′ī′ərn), *n.* a small household appliance with a flat bottom surface which is heated and used for pressing clothes, etc.; iron.
flat land (flat′land′), *n.* level land, not broken by hills and valleys.
flat let (flat′lit), *n.* BRITISH. a small apartment.
flat-out (flat′out′), *adj.* absolute; outright: *flat-out lies.*
flat ten (flat′n), *v.t.*, *v.i.* 1 make or become flat. 2 **flatten out,** spread out flat. **—flat′ten er,** *n.*
flat ter (flat′ər), *v.t.* 1 praise too much or beyond the truth; compliment insincerely. 2 exaggerate the good points of: *This photograph flatters her.* 3 try to please or win over by flattering words or actions; fawn upon. 4 cause to be pleased or feel honored. 5 **flatter oneself, a** be pleased to know or think. **b** overestimate oneself. —*v.i.* use flattery. [Middle English *flateren* to float, fawn upon. Related to FLUTTER.] **—flat′ter er,** *n.* **—flat′ter ing ly,** *adv.*
flat ter y (flat′ər ē), *n.*, *pl.* **-ter ies.** 1 act of flattering. 2 praise that is too much or untrue; adulation.
flat tish (flat′ish), *adj.* somewhat flat.
flat top (flat′top′), *n.* INFORMAL. aircraft carrier.
flat u lence (flach′ə ləns), *n.* 1 excessive gas in the stomach or intestines. 2 pompous speech or behavior.
flat u lent (flach′ə lənt), *adj.* 1 having excessive gas in the stomach or intestines. 2 causing gas in the stomach or intestines. 3 pompous in speech or behavior. [< French < Latin *flatus* a blowing < *flare* to blow] **—flat′u lent ly,** *adv.*
flat ware (flat′wer′, flat′war′), *n.* 1 knives, forks, and spoons. 2 plates, platters, saucers, and other flat or nearly flat dishes.
flat ways (flat′wāz′), *adv.* with the flat side forward, upward, or touching another surface.
flat work (flat′wėrk′), *n.* household linens, such as sheets, towels, and napkins, that do not require hand ironing but can be ironed on a mangle.
flat worm (flat′wėrm′), *n.* any of a phylum of worms with thin, usually flat, bilaterally symmetrical bodies, that live in water or as parasites in or on some animals; platyhelminth. Tapeworms and planarians are flatworms.
Flau bert (flō ber′, flō bar′), *n.* **Gustave,** 1821-1880, French novelist.
flaunt (flônt, flänt), *v.t.* show off to impress others; display ostentatiously. —*v.i.* 1 parade oneself boastfully, impudently, or defiantly in the public view. 2 wave gaily or proudly: *banners flaunting in the breeze.* —*n.* a flaunting. [origin uncertain] **—flaunt′ing ly,** *adv.*
➔ **Flaunt, flout** are sometimes confused. *Flaunt* means to display boldly and brazenly, regardless of what people may think: *flaunt one's wealth. Flout* means to mock or treat

with contempt: *flout school rules.* Confusion arises because one may *flaunt* one thing in order to *flout* another: *She flouted the custom of wearing simple dresses to the office by flaunting her red satin cocktail dress.*

flau tist (flô′tist), *n.* flutist.

fla vor (flā′vər), *n.* 1 taste, especially a characteristic taste or a noticeable element in the taste of a thing: *Chocolate and vanilla have different flavors.* See **taste** for synonym study. 2 flavoring. 3 a characteristic or particular quality: *Stories about ships have a flavor of the sea.* 4 aroma; odor. *—v.t.* 1 give added taste to; season: *The onion flavors the whole stew.* 2 give an exciting quality to: *Adventures flavored the explorer's life.* [< Old French *flaur* odor < Popular Latin *flator* < Latin *flare* to blow] **—fla′vor less,** *adj.*

fla vor ful (flā′vər fəl), *adj.* having flavor and interest.

fla vor ing (flā′vər ing), *n.* thing used to give a particular taste to food or drink: *chocolate flavoring.*

fla vor some (flā′vər səm), *adj.* full of flavor; flavorful.

fla vour (flā′vər), *n., v.t.* BRITISH. flavor.

flaw[1] (flô), *n.* 1 a defective place; crack: *A flaw in the dish caused it to break.* 2 a slight defect; fault; blemish. See **defect** for synonym study. *—v.t., v.i.* make or become defective. [< Scandinavian (Swedish) *flaga*]

flaw[2] (flô), *n.* 1 gust of wind; sudden squall. 2 a short period of rough weather. [origin uncertain]

flaw less (flô′lis), *adj.* without a flaw; perfect. **—flaw′less ly,** *adv.* **—flaw′less ness,** *n.*

flax (flaks), *n.* 1 a slender, upright plant with small, narrow leaves, blue or white flowers, and slender stems about two feet tall. 2 the threadlike fibers into which the stems of this plant separate. Flax is spun into thread and woven into linen. [Old English *fleax*]

flax en (flak′sən), *adj.* 1 made of flax. 2 like the color of flax; pale-yellow.

flax seed (flaks′sēd′), *n.* seed of flax, used to make linseed oil and in medicine; linseed.

flay (flā), *v.t.* 1 strip off the skin or outer covering of; skin. 2 scold severely; criticize without pity or mercy. [Old English *flēan*] **—flay′er,** *n.*

F layer, F region.

flea (flē), *n.* any of an order of small, wingless, jumping insects that live as parasites in the fur of dogs, cats, and other animals and feed on their blood. [Old English *flēah*]

flea bane (flē′bān′), *n.* any of a genus of plants belonging to the composite family supposed to drive away or destroy fleas.

flea-bit ten (flē′bit′n), *adj.* bitten by or infested with fleas.

flea market, an outdoor market dealing in odd items, junk, cheap antiques, etc.

fleck (flek), *n.* 1 spot or patch of color, light, etc.; small mark; speckle: *Freckles are brown flecks on the skin.* 2 a small particle; speck. *—v.t.* mark with spots or patches of color, light, etc.; speckle: *The bird's breast is flecked with brown.* [perhaps < Scandinavian (Old Icelandic) *flekkr*]

flec tion (flek′shən), *n.* 1 a bending: *the flection of a reed in the wind.* 2 a bent part; bend. 3 (in physiology) flexion. [< Latin *flexionem* < *flectere* to bend]

fled (fled), *v.* pt. and pp. of **flee.**

fledge (flej), *v.,* **fledged, fledg ing.** *—v.i.* (of a young bird) grow the feathers needed for flying. *—v.t.* provide or cover with feathers. [Old English *(un)fligge* unfledged]

fledg ling or **fledge ling** (flej′ling), *n.* 1 a young bird that has just grown feathers needed for flying. 2 a young, inexperienced person.

flee (flē), *v.,* **fled, flee ing.** *—v.i.* 1 run away from or as from danger; get away by running. 2 go quickly; move swiftly. 3 pass away; cease to be; vanish. *—v.t.* run away from; get away from by running. [Old English *flēon*] **—fle′er,** *n.*

fleece (flēs), *n., v.,* **fleeced, fleec ing.** *—n.* 1 wool that covers the skin of a sheep or similar animal. 2 the amount of wool shorn from a sheep at one time. 3 something like a fleece: *a fleece of hair.* *—v.t.* 1 cut the fleece from. 2 strip of money or belongings; rob or cheat. [Old English *flēos*] **—fleec′er,** *n.*

fleec y (flē′sē), *adj.,* **fleec i er, fleec i est.** 1 like a fleece; soft, woolly, and white: *fleecy clouds.* 2 covered with fleece or wool. 3 made of fleece. **—fleec′i ness,** *n.*

fleer (flir), *v.i., v.t., n.* jeer. [Middle English *fleryen, fliren*]

fleet[1] (flēt), *n.* 1 group of warships under one command. 2 the entire navy of a nation or allied nations. 3 group of ships or boats sailing together: *a fleet of fishing boats.* 4 group of airplanes, automobiles, or the like, moving or working together: *a fleet of trucks.* [Old English *flēot* < *flēotan* to float]

fleet[2] (flēt), *adj.* 1 swiftly moving; rapid. 2 not lasting; evanescent. *—v.i.* pass swiftly; move rapidly. [probably < Scandinavian (Old Icelandic) *fliōtr* swift] **—fleet′ly,** *adv.* **—fleet′ness,** *n.*

fleur-de-lis (def. 1)

fleet admiral, the naval officer of the highest rank in the United States Navy, entitled to an insigne or flag bearing five stars.

fleet ing (flē′ting), *adj.* passing swiftly; soon gone; transitory: *a fleeting smile.* **—fleet′ing ly,** *adv.*

Flem ing (flem′ing), *n.* 1 native or inhabitant of Flanders. 2 native or inhabitant of Belgium, especially northern Belgium, whose native language is Flemish. 3 Sir **Alexander,** 1881-1955, Scottish bacteriologist who discovered penicillin.

Flem ish (flem′ish), *adj.* of or having to do with Flanders, its people, or their language. *—n.* 1 the people of Flanders. 2 their Low German language, closely related to Dutch, and one of the official languages of Belgium.

flesh (flesh), *n.* 1 the soft tissue of the body that covers the bones and is covered by skin, consisting mostly of muscles and fat. 2 tissue or muscles of animals, regarded as an article of food; meat. 3 fatness; plumpness. 4 the body, not the soul or spirit; the physical side of human nature, as distinguished from the spiritual or moral side. 5 the human race; mankind. 6 all living creatures. 7 family or relatives by birth. 8 the soft or edible part of fruits or vegetables. 9 color of a white person's skin; pinkish white with a little yellow. 10 **flesh and blood, a** family or relatives by birth; child or relative by birth. **b** a human body. 11 **in the flesh, a** alive. **b** in person. *—v.t.* 1 feed (a hound or hawk) with flesh. 2 excite (to passion, bloodshed, etc.) by a foretaste: *flesh raw soldiers.* 3 **flesh out,** give body or substance to. *—v.i.* INFORMAL. become fleshy. [Old English *flǣsc*] **—flesh′less,** *adj.*

hat, āge, fär; let, ēqual, tėrm;
it, īce; hot, ōpen, ôrder;
oil, out; cup, pu̇t, rüle;
ch, child; ng, long; sh, she;
th, thin; ᴛʜ, then; zh, measure;

ə represents *a* in about, *e* in taken,
i in pencil, *o* in lemon, *u* in circus.

< = from, derived from, taken from.

flesh-col ored (flesh′kul′ərd), *adj.* pinkish-white with a tinge of yellow; of the color of a white person's skin.

flesh fly, any of a family of flies whose larvae feed on decaying flesh.

flesh ly (flesh′lē), *adj.,* **-li er, -li est.** 1 of the flesh; bodily. 2 sensual. 3 worldly. **—flesh′li ness,** *n.*

flesh pot (flesh′pot′), *n.* 1 a pot for cooking meat. 2 **fleshpots,** *pl.* good food and living; luxuries.

flesh wound, wound that merely injures the flesh; slight wound.

flesh y (flesh′ē), *adj.,* **flesh i er, flesh i est.** 1 having much flesh; plump; fat. 2 of flesh; like flesh. 3 pulpy: *a fleshy peach.* **—flesh′i ness,** *n.*

Fletch er (flech′ər), *n.* **John,** 1579-1625, English dramatist who wrote many plays with Francis Beaumont.

fleur-de-lis (flėr′də lē′, flėr′də lēs′), *n., pl.* **fleurs-de-lis** (flėr′də lēz′). 1 design or device used in heraldry to represent a lily (originally supposed to represent an iris). 2 the coat of arms of the royal family of France. 3 the iris flower or plant. [< Middle French, lily flower]

flew (flü), *v.* pt. of **fly**[2]. *The bird flew high in the air.*

flex (fleks), *v.t.* bend: *He flexed his stiff arm slowly.* [< Latin *flexum* bent < *flectere* to bend]

flex i bil i ty (flek′sə bil′ə tē), *n.* flexible quality.

flex i ble (flek′sə bəl), *adj.* 1 easily bent; not stiff; bending without breaking: *Leather, rubber, and wire are flexible.* 2 easily adapted to fit various conditions: *The actor's flexible voice accommodated itself to every emotion.* 3 easily managed; willing to yield to influence or persuasion. See synonym study below. **—flex′i bly,** *adv.*

Syn. 3 **Flexible, pliant, limber** mean bent or bending easily. **Flexible** means capable of being bent or twisted easily and without breaking, or, used figuratively, of being adaptable: *Great thinkers have flexible minds.* **Pliant** means inherently tending to bend or, figuratively, to yield easily to an influence: *He was too weak and pliant to make up his own mind.* **Limber,** used chiefly of the body, means having flexible muscles and joints and suggests easy movement: *A dancer has limber legs.*

flex ile (flek′səl), *adj.* flexible.

flex ion (flek′shən), *n.* 1 in physiology; **a** a bending of a joint in the body by the action of flexors. **b** a being bent in this way. 2 BRITISH. flection.

flex or (flek′sər), *n.* any muscle that when contracted bends a joint in the body.

flex ure (flek′shər), *n.* 1 a flexing. 2 a being flexed. 3 a bent part or thing; bend; curve.

flib ber ti gib bet (flib′ər tē jib′it), *n.* 1 a frivolous, flighty person. 2 chatterbox. [probably imitative]

flick (flik), *n.* 1 a quick, light blow; sudden, snapping stroke: *the flick of a whip.* 2 the light, snapping sound of such a blow or stroke. 3 a streak or splash. —*v.t.* 1 strike lightly with a quick, snapping blow: *He flicked the dust from his shoes with a handkerchief.* 2 make a sudden, snapping stroke with: *The boys flicked wet towels at each other.* —*v.i.* move quickly and lightly; flutter. [probably imitative]

flick er[1] (flik′ər), *v.i.* 1 shine or burn with a wavering, unsteady light or flame: *A dying fire flickered on the hearth.* 2 move quickly and lightly in and out or back and forth: *We heard the birds flicker among the leaves.* —*v.t.* cause to flicker. —*n.* 1 a wavering, unsteady light or flame. 2 a dying spurt of energy, emotion, etc.: *a flicker of enthusiasm.* 3 a quick, light movement: *the flicker of an eyelash.* 4 a brief flash; spark. [Old English *flicorian*] **—flick′er ing ly,** *adv.*

flick er[2] (flik′ər), *n.* any of a genus of woodpeckers, especially a large, common woodpecker of eastern North America, with a brownish back and yellow markings on its wings and tail; yellow hammer. [perhaps imitative of its call]

flied (flīd), *v.* a pt. and pp. of **fly**[2] (*v.i.* def. 8). *The batter flied to center field.*

fli er (flī′ər), *n.* 1 person or thing that flies. 2 pilot of an airplane; aviator. 3 a very fast train, ship, bus, etc. 4 INFORMAL. a reckless financial venture. 5 a small handbill. Also, **flyer.**

flies (flīz), *n. pl.* of **fly**[1] and **fly**[2].

flight[1] (flīt), *n.* 1 act or manner of flying: *the flight of a bird across the sky.* 2 distance a bird, bullet, airplane, etc., can fly. 3 group of things flying through the air together: *a flight of pigeons.* 4 U.S. a tactical unit of the Air Force consisting of two or more airplanes. 5 trip in an aircraft, especially a scheduled trip on an airline. 6 airplane that makes a scheduled trip. 7 a swift movement. 8 a soaring above or beyond the ordinary: *a flight of fancy.* 9 set of stairs or steps from one landing or story of a building to the next. [Old English *flyht.* Related to FLY[2].]

flight[2] (flīt), *n.* 1 act of fleeing; running away; escape. 2 **put to flight,** force to flee. 3 **take to flight,** flee. [Middle English *fliht.* Related to FLEE.]

flight engineer, member of the crew of certain aircraft responsible for the craft's mechanical performance in flight.

flight less (flīt′lis), *adj.* unable to fly, as ostriches, emus, and kiwis.

flight line, portion of an airfield which includes hangars and service buildings, but not runways or their approaches.

flight path, course taken by an aircraft, missile, etc.

flight y (flī′tē), *adj.,* **flight i er, flight i est.** 1 likely to have sudden fancies; full of whims; frivolous. 2 slightly crazy; lightheaded. **—flight′i ly,** *adv.* **—flight′i ness,** *n.*

flim flam (flim′flam′), *n., v.,* **-flammed, -flam ming.** INFORMAL. —*n.* 1 nonsense; rubbish. 2 a low trick; deception. —*v.t.* cheat or trick. [origin uncertain]

flim sy (flim′zē), *adj.,* **-si er, -si est,** *n., pl.* **-sies.** —*adj.* 1 lacking material strength; not solid or substantial; light and thin; slight; frail: *Muslin is too flimsy to be used for sails.* 2 lacking seriousness or sense; feeble; shallow: *a flimsy excuse.* —*n.* 1 a thin paper used by reporters. 2 a newspaper report on this paper. [perhaps < alteration of *film* + *-sy,* as in *clumsy*] **—flim′si ly,** *adv.* **—flim′si ness,** *n.*

flinch (flinch), *v.i.* 1 withdraw or hold back from difficulty or danger; shrink. See **shrink** for synonym study. 2 react by wincing: *I flinched when the doctor gave me a shot.* —*n.* 1 act of drawing back. 2 game played with cards bearing numbers from 1 to 14. [probably < Old French *flenchir* to bend] **—flinch′er,** *n.*

flin ders (flin′dərz), *n.pl.* small pieces; fragments; splinters. [perhaps < Scandinavian (Norwegian) *flindra*]

fling (fling), *v.,* **flung, fling ing,** *n.* —*v.t.* 1 throw with force; throw: *fling a stone.* 2 put suddenly or violently: *fling him into jail.* 3 throw aside; discard; abandon. —*v.i.* 1 move hastily or violently; rush; dash: *She flung out of the room.* 2 plunge or kick. —*n.* 1 a throw. 2 a plunge or kick. 3 time of doing as one pleases: *He had his fling when he was young; now he must work.* 4 a lively Scottish dance. 5 **have a fling at,** INFORMAL. **a** try; attempt. **b** make scornful remarks about. [perhaps < Scandinavian (Old Icelandic) *flengja* flog]

flint (flint), *n.* 1 a very hard, gray or brown granular quartz which makes a spark when struck against steel. 2 piece of this used with steel to light fires, explode gunpowder, etc. 3 anything very hard or unyielding. [Old English]

Flint (flint), *n.* city in SE Michigan. 193,000.

flint glass, a brilliant, heavy glass containing lead, potassium or sodium, and silicon, used for lenses, dishes, etc.

flint lock (flint′lok′), *n.* 1 gunlock in which a flint striking against steel makes sparks that explode the gunpowder. Flintlocks were used on guns from the 1600's to the 1800's. 2 musket, rifle, or pistol with such a gunlock.

flint y (flin′tē), *adj.,* **flint i er, flint i est.** 1 made of flint; containing flint. 2 like flint; very hard; unyielding. **—flint′i ly,** *adv.* **—flint′i ness,** *n.*

flip (flip), *v.,* **flipped, flip ping,** *n., adj.,* **flip per, flip pest.** —*v.t.* 1 toss or move with a snap of a finger and thumb: *He flipped a coin on the counter.* 2 move with a jerk or toss: *flip the pages of a book.* —*v.i.* 1 flick: *I flipped at a fly with a towel.* 2 turn or move with a jerk: *The branch flipped back.* 3 U.S. SLANG. get excited; go wild. —*n.* 1 a flipping; snap; smart tap: *The cat gave the kitten a flip on the ear.* 2 a sudden jerk or movement. 3 a hot drink containing beer, ale, cider, or the like, with sugar and spice. —*adj.* INFORMAL. flippant. [probably imitative]

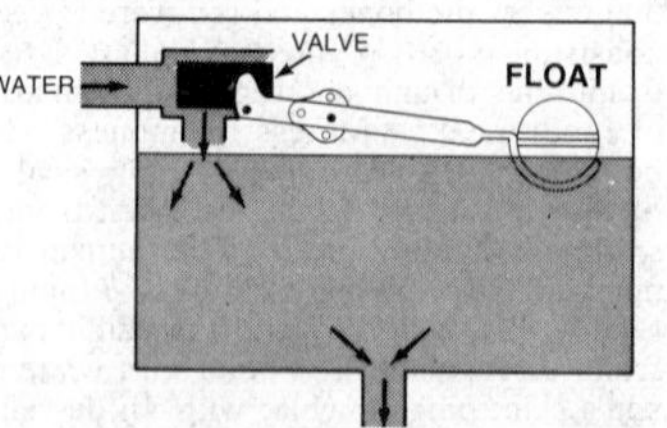

float (def. 5) regulating water level. As water is used, the float drops, opening the valve and permitting more water to enter the tank.

flip-flop (flip′flop′), *n.* 1 INFORMAL. a turnabout; reversal. 2 a switching unit used in electronic equipment, which changes physical states, frequencies, etc., upon certain impulses.

flip pan cy (flip′ən sē), *n., pl.* **-cies.** flippant quality or behavior.

flip pant (flip′ənt), *adj.* smart or pert in speech or manner; not respectful; impertinent; saucy: *a flippant answer.* **—flip′pant ly,** *adv.*

flip per (flip′ər), *n.* 1 a broad, flat limb especially adapted for swimming. Seals have flippers. 2 a molded rubber attachment for the human foot, used as an aid in swimming, especially by skin divers; fin.

flirt (flėrt), *v.i.* 1 play at making love; make love without meaning it. 2 trifle; toy: *He flirted with the idea of going to Europe, even though he couldn't afford it.* 3 move quickly to and fro; flutter: *The bird flirted from one branch to another.* —*v.t.* 1 give a brisk, sudden motion to; flutter: *She flirted her fan impatiently.* 2 toss; jerk. —*n.* 1 person who makes love without meaning it. 2 a quick movement or flutter: *With a flirt of its tail the squirrel ran off.* 3 toss; jerk. [origin uncertain]

flir ta tion (flėr tā′shən), *n.* 1 act of flirting. 2 a love affair that is not serious.

flir ta tious (flėr tā′shəs), *adj.* 1 inclined to flirt. 2 having to do with flirtation. **—flir ta′tious ly,** *adv.* **—flir ta′tious ness,** *n.*

flit (flit), *v.,* **flit ted, flit ting,** *n.* —*v.i.* 1 fly lightly and quickly; flutter: *Birds flitted from tree to tree.* 2 pass lightly and quickly; dart: *Thoughts flitted through his head.* —*n.* a light, quick movement; flutter. [perhaps < Scandinavian (Old Icelandic) *flytja*]

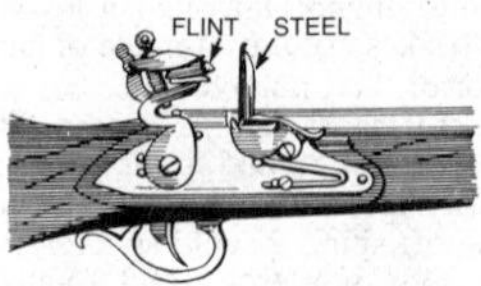

flintlock (def. 1)

flitch (flich), *n.* side of a hog salted and cured; side of bacon. [Old English *flicce*]

flit ter (flit′ər), *v.i., v.t., n.* flutter.

fliv ver (fliv′ər), *n.* SLANG. a small, cheap automobile, especially one that is no longer new. [origin unknown]

float (flōt), *v.i.* 1 stay on top of or be held up by air, water, or other liquid. 2 move with a moving liquid; drift: *The log floated out to sea.* 3 rest or move in a liquid, the air, etc. 4 move aimlessly. —*v.t.* 1 cause to float. 2 cover with liquid; flood. 3 set going (a company, scheme, etc.); launch. 4 sell (securities): *float an issue of stock.*

—*n.* 1 anything that stays up or holds up something else in water, such as a raft or life preserver. 2 cork on a fish line that supports the line and bobs when a fish bites the hook. 3 an air-filled organ that supports an aquatic animal or plant. 4 pontoon of an aircraft. 5 a hollow, metal ball that floats on and regulates the level, supply, or outlet of a liquid in a tank, boiler, etc. 6 a low, flat car that carries something to be shown in a parade. 7 drink consisting of ginger ale or a similar beverage with ice cream in it.

hat, āge, fär; let, ēqual, tėrm;
it, īce; hot, ōpen, ôrder;
oil, out; cup, pu̇t, rüle;
ch, child; ng, long; sh, she;
th, thin; ᴛʜ, then; zh, measure;

ə represents *a* in about, *e* in taken, *i* in pencil, *o* in lemon, *u* in circus.

< = from, derived from, taken from.

[Old English *flotian* < *flot* body of water. Related to FLEET.] **—float′a ble,** *adj.*

float er (flō′tər), *n.* 1 person or thing that floats. 2 INFORMAL. person who often changes his place of living, working, etc. 3 person who votes illegally in more than one place. 4 (in sports) a ball thrown or hit so as to travel slowly and appear to hang in the air, usually on a slightly arched course.

float ing (flō′ting), *adj.* 1 that floats. 2 not fixed; not staying in one place; moving around: *a floating population.* 3 not permanently invested, but ready for use as occasion demands: *floating capital.* 4 composed of sums of varying amounts due within a short time; not funded: *the floating debt of a business.* 5 of a machine part connected or hung so that it functions without causing vibration.

floating island, dessert made of boiled custard with meringue or whipped cream on it.

floating ribs, the lowest two pairs of human ribs, not attached to the breastbone.

floc cu late (flok′yə lāt), *v.t., v.i.,* **-lat ed, -lat ing.** form into flocculent masses; form compound masses of particles, as a cloud or a chemical precipitate. **—floc′cu la′tion,** *n.*

floc cu lence (flok′yə ləns), *n.* condition of being flocculent.

floc cu lent (flok′yə lənt), *adj.* 1 like bits of wool. 2 made up of soft, woolly masses. 3 covered with a soft, woolly substance. [< Latin *floccus* tuft of wool]

flock[1] (flok), *n.* 1 group of animals of one kind keeping, feeding, or moving together, especially sheep, goats, or birds. 2 a large group; crowd. 3 people of the same church group. —*v.i.* go or gather in a flock; come crowding: *The children flocked around the ice-cream stand.* [Old English *flocc*]

flock[2] (flok), *n.* 1 tuft of wool or cotton. 2 waste wool or cotton used to stuff mattresses and cushions. 3 finely powdered wool or cloth used in making wallpaper. —*v.t.* 1 stuff with flock. 2 cover or coat with flock. [< Old French *floc* < Latin *floccus*]

floe (flō), *n.* 1 field or sheet of floating ice. 2 a floating piece broken off from such a field or sheet. [< Scandinavian (Norwegian) *flo*]

flog (flog, flôg), *v.t.,* **flogged, flog ging.** whip very hard; beat with a whip, stick, etc. [perhaps English school slang for Latin *flagellare* to whip] **—flog′ger,** *n.*

flood (flud), *n.* 1 a great flow of water over what is usually dry land. See synonym study below. 2 **the Flood,** (in the Bible) the flood that covered the earth in the time of Noah; the Deluge. 3 a large amount of water; ocean, sea, lake, or river. 4 a great outpouring of anything: *a flood of light, a flood of words.* 5 rise of the tide; flow. —*v.t.* 1 flow over; cover with a great flow of water: *The river flooded our fields.* 2 fill much fuller than usual; fill to overflowing. 3 put much water on. 4 fill, cover, or overcome like a flood: *The rich man was flooded with requests for money. The room was flooded with moonlight.* 5 cause or allow too much fuel to flow into (the carburetor of a motor), so that the motor fails to start. —*v.i.* 1 pour out or stream like a flood. 2 flow like a flood. 3 become covered or filled with water. 4 (of a motor) receive too much fuel into the carburetor. [Old English *flōd*]

Syn. *n.* 1 **Flood, deluge, inundation** mean a great flow of water. **Flood** applies particularly to a great flow of water over land usually dry, caused by the rising and overflowing of a river or other body of water: *Floods followed the melting of mountain snow.* **Deluge** applies to a great and usually destructive flood or to a heavy downpour: *Livestock drowned in the deluge.* **Inundation** means an overflow, not necessarily harmful, covering everything around: *Crops were destroyed by the inundation of the fields.*

flood control, the practice of attempting to prevent or lessen damage caused by floods by the use of dams, levees, dikes, extra outlets, etc., or by reforestation.

flood gate (flud′gāt′), *n.* 1 gate in a canal, river, stream, etc., to control the flow of water. 2 thing that controls the flow or passage of anything.

flood light (flud′līt′), *n., v.,* **-light ed** or **-lit** (-lit′), **-light ing.** —*n.* 1 lamp that gives a broad beam of light. 2 a broad beam of light from such a lamp. —*v.t.* illuminate by a floodlight or floodlights.

flood plain (flud′plān′), *n.* plain bordering a river and made of sediment deposited during floods.

flood tide, the flowing of the tide toward the shore; rise of the tide.

flood wa ter (flud′wô′tər, flud′wot′ər), *n.* water flooding dry land.

floor (flôr, flōr), *n.* 1 the inside bottom covering of a room. 2 a flat surface at the bottom: *the floor of the ocean.* 3 story of a building: *I took the elevator to the fifth floor.* 4 the level supporting surface in other structures: *the floor of a bridge.* 5 any large, level surface: *a forest floor of pine needles and cones.* 6 part of a room or hall where members of a lawmaking body, etc., sit and from which they speak. 7 right or privilege to speak in a lawmaking body, etc. At a meeting, the chairman decides who has the floor. 8 the main part of an exchange, where buying and selling of stocks, bonds, etc., is done. 9 INFORMAL. (of prices, amounts, etc.) the lowest level. —*v.t.* 1 put a floor in or on. 2 knock down. 3 INFORMAL. defeat. 4 INFORMAL. confuse or puzzle completely: *be floored by a problem.* [Old English *flōr*]

floor board (flôr′bôrd′, flōr′bōrd′), *n.* 1 one of the strips of wood used in a wooden floor. 2 Usually, **floorboards,** *pl.* the floor of an automobile.

floor ing (flôr′ing, flōr′ing), *n.* 1 floor. 2 floors. 3 material for making or covering floors, such as wood, linoleum, or tile.

floor leader, U.S. member of a lawmaking body chosen to direct the members who belong to his political party.

floor show, entertainment consisting of music, singing, dancing, etc., presented at a night club, hotel, etc.

floor walk er (flôr′wô′kər, flōr′wô′kər), *n.* person employed in a large store to direct the work of salesclerks and give assistance to customers.

flooz ie or **flooz y** (flü′zē), *n., pl.* **flooz ies.** SLANG. woman or girl of loose morals. [origin unknown]

flop (flop), *v.,* **flopped, flop ping,** *n.* —*v.i.* 1 move loosely or heavily; flap around clumsily: *The fish flopped helplessly on the deck.* 2 fall, drop, or move heavily or clumsily: *The tired boy flopped down into a chair.* 3 change or turn suddenly. 4 INFORMAL. fail: *His first business venture flopped completely.* —*v.t.* drop or throw with a sudden bump or thud. —*n.* 1 a flopping. 2 a dull, heavy sound made by flopping. 3 INFORMAL. failure: *His last book was a flop.* [variant of *flap*] **—flop′per,** *n.*

flop house (flop′hous′), *n., pl.* **-hous es** (-hou′ziz). a cheap, run-down hotel or rooming house for vagrant and homeless persons.

flop py (flop′ē), *adj.,* **-pi er, -pi est.** INFORMAL. tending to flop; flopping: *a floppy hat.* **—flop′pi ly,** *adv.* **—flop′pi ness,** *n.*

flo ra (flôr′ə, flōr′ə), *n.* plants or plant life of a particular region or time: *the flora of California, the flora of the Carboniferous period.* [< New Latin < *Flora*]

Flo ra (flôr′ə, flōr′ə), *n.* (in Roman myths) the goddess of flowers.

flo ral (flôr′əl, flōr′əl), *adj.* 1 of or having to do with flowers. 2 resembling flowers. [< Latin *florem* flower] **—flo′ral ly,** *adv.*

Flo rence (flôr′əns, flor′əns), *n.* city in central Italy. 459,000. Also, ITALIAN **Firenze.**

Flo ren tine (flôr′ən tēn′, flor′ən tēn′), *adj.* of or having to do with Florence. —*n.* native or inhabitant of Florence.

Flo res (flôr′es, flōr′es), *n.* 1 island in Indonesia, east of Timor. 902,000 pop.; 6600 sq. mi. 2 island in the W Azores. 7000 pop., 55 sq. mi.

flo res cence (flô res′ns, flō res′ns), *n.* 1 act of blossoming. 2 condition of blossoming. 3 period of blossoming. [< New Latin *florescentia* < Latin *florescere* begin to flower < *florere* flourish]

flo res cent (flô res′nt, flō res′nt), *adj.* blossoming; flowering.

flo ret (flôr′it, flōr′it), *n.* 1 a small flower; floweret. 2 (in botany) one of the small flowers in a flower head of a composite plant, such as the aster.

flo ri bun da (flôr′ə bun′də, flōr′ə bun′də), *n.* a hybrid rose which bears many blossoms upon a low, bushy plant. [< New Latin < Latin *florem* flower]

flo ri cul tur al (flôr′ə kul′chər əl, flōr′ə-kul′chər əl), *adj.* having to do with floriculture.

flo ri cul ture (flôr′ə kul′chər, flōr′ə-kul′chər), *n.* cultivation of flowers or flowering plants, especially ornamental plants.

flo ri cul tur ist (flôr′ə kul′chər ist, flōr′ə-kul′chər ist), *n.* an expert in floriculture.

flo rid (flôr′id, flor′id), *adj.* 1 highly colored with red; ruddy: *a florid complexion.* 2 elaborately ornamented; showy; ornate: *florid language, florid architecture.* [< Latin *floridus* < *florem* flower] **—flo′rid ly,** *adv.* **—flo′rid ness,** *n.*

Flo ri da (flôr′ə də, flor′ə də), *n.* one of the southeastern states of the United States. 6,789,000 pop.; 58,600 sq. mi. *Capital:* Tallahassee. *Abbrev.:* Fla. **—Flor′i dan, Flo-rid′i an,** *adj., n.*

Florida Keys, chain of small islands south of Florida.

Florida Strait, strait connecting the Atlantic with the Gulf of Mexico, between S Florida and the Bahama Islands and Cuba.

flo rid i ty (flô rid′ə tē, flō rid′ə tē), *n.* quality or condition of being florid.

flo rin (flôr′ən, flor′ən), *n.* 1 an English coin worth ten pence. 2 a gold coin issued at Florence in 1252. 3 any of various gold or silver coins used in different countries of Europe since then, such as the Dutch guilder. [< Old French < Italian *fiorino* Florentine coin marked with a lily < *fiore* flower < Latin *florem*]

flo rist (flôr′ist, flōr′ist, flor′ist), *n.* 1 person who sells flowers and plants. 2 person who cultivates flowers, especially for sale.

floss (flôs, flos), *n.* 1 short, loose, silk fibers. 2 a shiny, untwisted silk thread made from such fibers. It is used for embroidery. Waxed floss is used for cleaning between the teeth. 3 soft, silky fluff or fibers. Milkweed pods contain white floss. [apparently < French *floche*]

floss y (flô′sē, flos′ē), *adj.,* **floss i er, floss i est.** 1 of floss. 2 like floss. 3 INFORMAL. fancy; glamorous; highly decorated.

flo ta tion (flō tā′shən), *n.* 1 act or process of floating. 2 condition of keeping afloat. 3 a getting started or established. 4 a selling or putting on sale. 5 process of obtaining a specific mineral from crushed ore by agitating it in water with chemicals which cause one group of particles to collect air bubbles and float to the top where they may be skimmed off.

flo til la (flō til′ə), *n.* 1 a small fleet. 2 fleet of small ships. [< Spanish, diminutive of *flota* fleet]

flot sam (flot′səm), *n.* 1 wreckage of a ship or its cargo found floating on the sea. 2 **flotsam and jetsam, a** wreckage or cargo found floating on the sea or washed ashore. **b** odds and ends; useless things. [< Anglo-French *floteson* < Old French *floter* to float]

flounce[1] (flouns), *v.,* **flounced, flounc ing,** *n.* —*v.i.* 1 go with an angry or impatient fling of the body: *She flounced out of the room in a rage.* 2 make floundering movements; twist and turn; jerk. —*n.* 1 an angry or impatient fling of the body. 2 a floundering movement; twisting and turning; jerk. [perhaps < Scandinavian (Swedish dialect) *flunsa* plunge]

flounce[2] (flouns), *n., v.,* **flounced, flounc ing.** —*n.* a wide strip of cloth, gathered along the top edge and sewed to a dress, skirt, etc., for trimming; a wide ruffle. —*v.t.* trim with a flounce or flounces. [variant of earlier *frounce* wrinkle < Old French *froncir* to fold, wrinkle]

floun der[1] (floun′dər), *v.i.* 1 struggle awkwardly without making much progress; plunge about: *The horses were floundering in the deep snowdrifts.* 2 be clumsy or confused and make mistakes: *The frightened girl could only flounder through her song.* —*n.* a floundering. [perhaps blend of *founder* and *blunder*]

floun der[2] (floun′dər), *n., pl.* **-ders** or **-der.** flatfish, especially any of two families of flatfish that are much used for food. [< Middle French *flondre,* perhaps < Scandinavian (Norwegian) *flundra*]

flour (flour), *n.* 1 the fine, powdery meal made by grinding and sifting the kernels of wheat or other grain, used to make bread, rolls, cake, etc. 2 any fine, soft powder. —*v.t.* cover or sprinkle with flour. [special use of *flower* (i.e., the flower, or finest part, of the meal)]

flour ish (flėr′ish), *v.i.* 1 grow or develop with vigor; do well; thrive. 2 be in the best time of life or activity: *Shakespeare flourished during Queen Elizabeth's reign.* 3 make a showy display. —*v.t.* wave in the air; brandish: *He flourished the letter when he saw us.* —*n.* 1 a waving about: *remove one's hat with a flourish.* 2 an extra ornament or curve in handwriting. 3 (in music) a showy trill or passage. 4 a showy display. 5 a being in the best time of life or activity. [< Old French *floriss-,* a form of *florir* to flourish < Latin *florere* to bloom < *florem* flower] **—flour′ish ing ly,** *adv.*

flourish (def. 2) flourishes in a signature

flour y (flou′rē), *adj.* 1 of or like flour. 2 covered or white with flour or powder.

flout (flout), *v.t.* treat with contempt or scorn; scoff at; mock: *The foolish boy flouted his mother's advice.* —*v.i.* show contempt or scorn; scoff. —*n.* a contemptuous speech or act; mockery; scoffing. [variant of *flute,* verb] **—flout′er,** *n.* **—flout′ing ly,** *adv.* ➤ See **flaunt** for usage note.

flow (flō), *v.i.* 1 run like water; move in a current or stream. See synonym study below. 2 pour out; pour along. 3 move easily or smoothly; glide. 4 hang loose and waving: *Her long hair flowed in the wind.* 5 be plentiful; be full and overflowing: *a land flowing with milk and honey.* 6 flow in; rise. —*n.* 1 current; stream. 2 any smooth, steady movement: *a rapid flow of speech.* 3 act or way of flowing. 4 rate of flowing. 5 the flowing of the tide toward the shore; rise of the tide. 6 an overflooding. 7 (in physics) the directional movement in a current or stream that is a characteristic of all fluids, as air or electricity. [Old English *flōwan*]

Syn. *v.i.* 1 **Flow, gush, stream** mean to run or pour out or along. **Flow** emphasizes the continuous forward movement of running or pouring water: *Water flowed over the sidewalks.* **Gush** means to rush out or flow forth suddenly in considerable quantity from an opening: *Water gushed from the broken pipe.* **Stream** means to pour forth steadily from a source, always in the same direction: *Tears streamed from her eyes.*

flow chart, diagram or chart showing the flow of supplies, equipment, information, etc., in an industrial, military, or other operation.

flow er (flou′ər), *n.* 1 part of a plant that produces the seed; blossom. A flower is a shortened branch with modified leaves called petals. In botanical use, a flower consists normally of pistil, stamens, corolla, and calyx in regular series, any one or more of which may be absent. 2 plant grown for its blossoms. 3 any of several kinds of reproductive structures in lower plants, such as the mosses. 4 the finest part: *The flower of the country's youth.* 5 condition or time of having flowers: *an orchard in flower.* 6 condition or time of greatest health, vigor, or beauty; prime: *a man in the flower of life.* 7 **flowers,** *pl.* a chemical substance in the form of a fine powder, obtained especially as the result of condensation after sublimation: *flowers of sulfur.* —*v.i.* 1 have flowers; produce flowers; bloom. 2 come into or be in one's prime; flourish. —*v.t.* cover or decorate with flowers. [< Old French *flour* < Latin *florem*] **—flow′er less,** *adj.* **—flow′er like′,** *adj.*

flow ered (flou′ərd), *adj.* 1 having flowers. 2 covered or decorated with flowers.

flow er et (flou′ər it), *n.* floret.

flower girl, 1 a young girl carrying flowers before the bride at a wedding ceremony. 2 girl who sells flowers.

flower head, a dense cluster of florets growing from a stem, as on the dandelion, chrysanthemum, sunflower, or other composite plants.

flow er ing (flou′ər ing), *adj.* having flowers.

flow er pot (flou′ər pot′), *n.* pot to hold soil for a plant to grow in.

flow er y (flou′ər ē), *adj.,* **-er i er, -er i est.** 1 having many flowers. 2 containing many fine words and fanciful expressions: *a flowery speech.* **—flow′er i ly,** *adv.* **—flow′er i ness,** *n.*

flow ing (flō′ing), *adj.* 1 moving in a current or stream: *flowing water.* 2 moving easily or smoothly: *flowing words.* 3 hanging loosely: *flowing robes.* **—flow′ing ly,** *adv.*

flow me ter (flō′mē′tər), *n.* any of various devices for measuring the volume or rate of flow of a liquid or gas.

flown (flōn), *v.* pp. of **fly**[2].

fl. oz., fluid ounce or fluid ounces.

flu (flü), *n.* influenza.

flub (flub), *v.,* **flubbed, flub bing,** *n.* INFORMAL. —*v.t.* do (something) very clumsily; spoil; botch. —*v.i.* perform badly; fail. —*n.* failure in performance; botch. [origin unknown]

fluc tu ate (fluk′chü āt), *v.i.,* **-at ed, -at ing.** 1 rise and fall; change continually; vary irregularly; waver; vacillate: *The temperature fluctuates from day to day. His emotions fluctuated between hopefulness and despair.* 2 move in waves. [< Latin *fluctuatum* moving as a wave < *fluctus* wave < *fluere* to flow]

fluc tu a tion (fluk′chü ā′shən), *n.* 1 a rising and falling; continual change; irregular variation; wavering. 2 a wavelike motion.

flue (flü), *n.* 1 tube, pipe, or other enclosed passage for conveying smoke, hot air, etc., outside a structure or from one part of it to another. A chimney often has several flues. 2 pipe or tube for conveying heat to water in certain kinds of steam boilers. 3 flue pipe. 4 the air passage in such a pipe. [origin unknown]

flu en cy (flü′ən sē), *n.* 1 a smooth, easy flow: *fluency of speech.* 2 easy, rapid speaking or writing; volubility.

flu ent (flü′ənt), *adj.* 1 flowing smoothly or easily: *speak fluent French.* 2 speaking or writing easily and rapidly. See synonym study below. 3 not fixed or stable; fluid. [< Latin *fluentem* < *fluere* to flow] **—flu′ent ly,** *adv.*

Syn. 2 **Fluent, glib, voluble** mean speaking easily. **Fluent** suggests speaking or writing both easily and well: *a fluent lecturer.* **Glib** suggests speaking too smoothly and easily to be sincere: *a glib liar.* **Voluble** suggests speaking so much and continuously that it is boring: *Detained by a voluble talker, I was late.*

flue pipe, an organ pipe in which the sound is made by a current of air striking the mouth or opening in the pipe.

fluff (fluf), *n.* 1 soft, light, downy particles: *Woolen blankets often have fluff on them.* 2 a soft, light, downy mass: *The little kitten looked like a fluff of fur.* 3 INFORMAL. a

hat, āge, fär; let, ēqual, tėrm;
it, īce; hot, ōpen, ôrder;
oil, out; cup, pu̇t, rüle;
ch, child; ng, long; sh, she;
th, thin; ᴛʜ, then; zh, measure;

ə represents *a* in about, *e* in taken, *i* in pencil, *o* in lemon, *u* in circus.

< = from, derived from, taken from.

mistake in reading, speaking, etc., as on the stage or on radio or television. —*v.t.* 1 shake or puff out (hair, feathers, etc.) into a soft, light, downy mass. 2 SLANG. make a mistake in reading, speaking, etc. (a line or passage). —*v.i.* 1 become fluffy. 2 SLANG. make a mistake in reading, speaking, etc. [origin uncertain]

fluff y (fluf′ē), *adj.*, **fluff i er, fluff i est.** 1 soft and light like fluff: *a fluffy shawl.* 2 covered or filled with fluff; downy; fleecy: *fluffy baby chicks.* **—fluff′i ness,** *n.*

flu id (flü′id), *n.* any liquid or gas; any substance that flows. Water, mercury, air, and oxygen are fluids. See **liquid** for synonym study. —*adj.* 1 in the state of a fluid; like a fluid; flowing: *She poured the fluid mass of hot candy into a dish to harden.* 2 of or having to do with fluids. 3 changing easily; not fixed, firm, or stable: *a fluid situation.* 4 flowing smoothly; fluent. 5 liquid: *fluid assets.* [< Latin *fluidus* < *fluere* to flow] **—flu′id ly,** *adv.* **—flu′id ness,** *n.*

fluid dram, one eighth of a fluid ounce. See **measure** for table.

flu id ic (flü id′ik), *adj.* of or having to do with fluids or fluidics.

flu id ics (flü id′iks), *n.* science or technology of using tiny jets of a gas or a liquid rather than electronic circuits for sensing, amplifying, or controlling functions.

flu id i ty (flü id′ə tē), *n.* fluid condition or quality.

flu id ize (flü′ə dīz), *v.t.*, **-ized, -iz ing.** make fluid or liquid. **—flu′id i za′tion,** *n.*

fluid ounce, measure for liquids. In the United States, 16 fluid ounces = 1 pint. See **measure** for table.

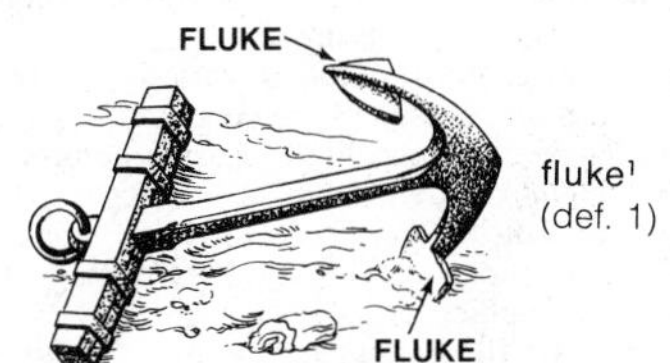

fluke[1] (def. 1)

fluke[1] (flük), *n.* 1 the flat, three-cornered piece at the end of each arm of an anchor, which catches in the ground and holds the anchor fast. 2 the barbed head of an arrow, harpoon, etc. 3 either of the two halves of a whale's tail. [perhaps special use of *fluke*[3] (because of its shape)]

fluke[2] (flük), *n., v.,* **fluked, fluk ing.** INFORMAL. —*n.* 1 a lucky shot in billiards or pool. 2 a lucky chance; fortunate accident. —*v.t.* 1 make or hit by a lucky shot in billiards or pool. 2 get by chance or accident. [origin uncertain]

fluke[3] (flük), *n.* 1 flatfish. 2 any of a class of parasitic flatworms shaped somewhat like a flatfish; trematode. [Old English *flōc* flatfish]

fluk y (flü′kē), *adj.*, **fluk i er, fluk i est.** INFORMAL. 1 obtained by chance rather than by skill. 2 uncertain: *fluky weather.*

flume (flüm), *n.* 1 a deep and very narrow valley with a stream running through it. 2 a large, inclined trough or chute through which water is channeled for transporting logs, furnishing power, etc. [< Old French *flum* < Latin *flumen* river < *fluere* to flow]

flum mer y (flum′ər ē), *n., pl.* **-mer ies.** 1 pudding made of milk, eggs, flour, sugar, etc. 2 an empty compliment; nonsense. [< Welsh *llymru*]

flum mox (flum′əks), *v.t.* INFORMAL. bring to confusion; bewilder. [origin unknown]

flung (flung), *v.* pt. and pp. of **fling.**

flunk (flungk), INFORMAL. —*v.t.* 1 fail (a test, course in school, etc.): *He flunked his history examination but passed all the others.* 2 cause to fail. 3 mark or grade as having failed. —*v.i.* 1 fail in a test, course in school, etc. 2 give up; back out.

flunk out, INFORMAL. dismiss or be dismissed from school, college, etc., for failing work.

—*n.* a flunking; failure.

[origin uncertain]

flunk ey (flung′kē), *n., pl.* **-eys.** flunky.

flunk y (flung′kē), *n., pl.* **flunk ies.** 1 a flattering, fawning person; toady. 2 footman. [perhaps alteration of *flanker* one posted on the flank of a person or group < *flank*]

flu o resce (flü′ə res′), *v.i.*, **-resced, -resc ing.** give off light by fluorescence; become fluorescent.

flu o res ce in (flü′ə res′ē ən), *n.* an orange-red, crystalline powder that forms a greenish-yellow, fluorescent, alkaline solution, used in making dyes. *Formula:* $C_{20}H_{12}O_5$

flu o res cence (flü′ə res′ns), *n.* 1 a giving off of light by a substance exposed to X rays, ultraviolet rays, or certain other rays, which continues only as long as exposure to these rays continues. 2 property of a substance that causes this. It is an ability to transform radiation so as to emit rays of a different wavelength or color. 3 light given off in this way. [< Latin *fluor* a flowing < *fluere* to flow]

flu o res cent (flü′ə res′nt), *adj.* that gives off light by fluorescence. Fluorescent substances glow in the dark when exposed to X rays.

fluorescent lamp, an electric lamp consisting of a tube in which a coating of fluorescent powder exposed to ultraviolet rays gives off a light that is cooler and less glaring than incandescent light.

fluor i date (flu̇r′ə dāt), *v.t.*, **-dat ed, -dat ing.** add small amounts of a fluorine compound to (drinking water), especially to decrease tooth decay in children. **—fluor′i da′tion,** *n.*

flu o ride (flü′ə rīd′, flü′ər id), *n.* compound of fluorine and another element or radical.

fluor i nate (flu̇r′ə nāt), *v.t.*, **-nat ed, -nat ing.** 1 fluoridate. 2 combine or cause to react with fluorine. **—fluor′i na′tion,** *n.*

flu o rine (flü′ə rēn′, flü′ər ən), *n.* a pale yellow, pungent, poisonous gaseous element which occurs only in combination with certain other elements and is the most reactive of all the chemical elements. It is used in small amounts in water to prevent tooth decay. *Symbol:* F or Fl; *atomic number* 9. See pages 326 and 327 for table. [< *fluor(ite)*]

flu o rite (flü′ə rīt′), *n.* a transparent or translucent, crystalline mineral composed of calcium and fluorine that occurs in many colors; fluorspar. It is used for fusing metals, making glass, etc. *Formula:* CaF_2 [< Latin *fluor* a flowing < *fluere* to flow]

flume (def. 2)

flu or o car bon (flü′ər ə kär′bən), *n.* any of a group of compounds of fluorine and carbon used as solvents, lubricants, refrigerator gases, etc.

fluor o scope (flu̇r′ə skōp), *n.* device with a fluorescent screen for examining objects by exposing them to X rays or other radiations, the parts of the object not penetrated by the rays casting shadows on the screen.

fluor o scop ic (flu̇r′ə skop′ik), *adj.* of or having to do with the fluoroscope or with fluoroscopy.

fluo ros co py (flu̇ ros′kə pē), *n.* the use of a fluoroscope.

flu or spar (flü′ər spär′), *n.* fluorite.

flur ry (flėr′ē), *n., pl.* **-ries,** *v.,* **-ried, -ry ing.** —*n.* 1 a sudden gust: *A flurry of wind upset the small sailboat.* 2 a light fall of rain or snow. 3 a sudden commotion: *a flurry of alarm.* 4 a sudden, short-lived fluctuation of prices, buying or selling, etc., on a stock or commodity exchange. —*v.t.* make nervous and excited; fluster: *Noise in the audience flurried the actor so that he forgot his lines.* —*v.i.* become flustered or excited. [ultimately imitative]

flush[1] (flush), *v.i.* 1 become red suddenly; blush; glow. 2 rush suddenly; flow rapidly: *Embarrassment caused the blood to flush to her cheeks.* 3 fly or start up suddenly. —*v.t.* 1 cause to blush or glow: *Exercise flushed his face.* 2 send a sudden flow of water over or through: *The city streets were flushed to make them clean.* 3 make joyful and proud; excite: *The team was flushed with its first victory.* 4 make even; level. 5 cause to fly or start up suddenly: *flush a partridge.*

—*n.* 1 a rosy glow or blush. 2 a sudden rush; rapid flow. 3 an excited condition or feeling; sudden rush of joyous pride, etc.: *the flush of victory.* 4 a sudden, fresh growth: *April brought the first flush of grass.* 5 glowing vigor; freshness: *the first flush of youth.* 6 fit of feeling very hot.

—*adj.* 1 forming an unbroken line (with a surface, etc.); even; level: *The edge of the new shelf must be flush with the old one.* 2 well supplied; having plenty: *The rich man was always flush with money.* 3 abundant; plentiful: *Money is flush when times are good.* 4 liberal; lavish. 5 prosperous. 6 glowing; ruddy. 7 direct; square. 8 full of vigor; lusty. 9 very full; flooded: *The reservoir was flush.*

—*adv.* 1 so as to be level; evenly. 2 directly; squarely: *The boxer hit his opponent flush on the nose.*

[Middle English *flusshen*]

flush[2] (flush), *n.* (in cards) a hand all of one suit. [< Middle French *flus* < Latin *fluxus* flow]

flus ter (flus′tər), *v.t.* make nervous and

excited; confuse. —*n.* nervous excitement; confusion. [< Scandinavian (Old Icelandic) *flaustr* bustle]

flute (flüt), *n., v.,* **flut ed, flut ing.** —*n.* 1 a long, slender, pipelike musical instrument, played by blowing across a hole near one end and by stopping holes along the tube with the fingers. 2 an organ stop with a flutelike tone. 3 a long, round groove, especially one of a parallel series cut in a column. 4 a decorative fine groove or crimp pressed into a fabric, as in a ruffle or pleating on a garment. —*v.i.* 1 play on a flute. 2 sing or whistle so as to sound like a flute. —*v.t.* 1 play (a melody, etc.) on a flute. 2 sing, whistle, say, etc., in flutelike tones. 3 make long, round grooves in: *flute a pillar.* [< Old French *fleüte, flaüte* < Provençal *flauta*] —**flute′like′,** *adj.*

flut ed (flü′tid), *adj.* having long, round grooves.

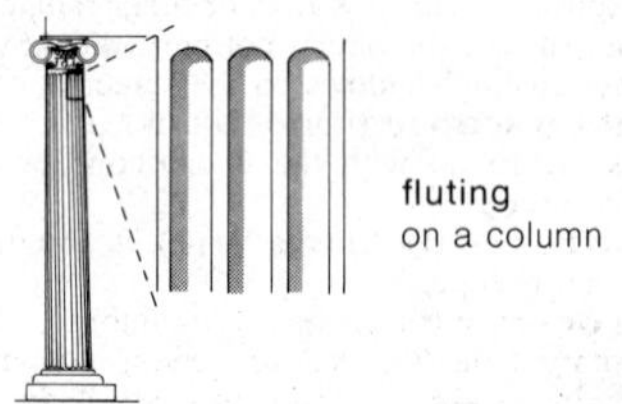

fluting on a column

flut ing (flü′ting), *n.* decoration consisting of long, round grooves.

flut ist (flü′tist), *n.* person who plays a flute. Also, **flautist.**

flut ter (flut′ər), *v.i.* 1 wave back and forth quickly and lightly: *The flag fluttered in the breeze.* 2 move or flap the wings rapidly without flying or with short flights: *The chickens fluttered excitedly when they saw the dog.* 3 come or go with a trembling or wavy motion: *The young birds fluttered to the ground.* 4 move about restlessly; flit. 5 move quickly and unevenly; tremble: *Her hands fluttered.* 6 beat feebly and irregularly: *The patient's pulse fluttered.* —*v.t.* 1 cause to flutter. 2 confuse; excite. —*n.* 1 a fluttering. 2 a confused or excited condition. 3 a rapid rise and fall in the sound pitch of a phonograph, film, or tape recording caused by slight variations in the speed at which the recording is played. Also, **flitter.** [Old English *flotorian.* Related to FLEET[2].] —**flut′ter er,** *n.*

flutter kick, a swimming movement in which the legs are moved alternately in short, rapid up-and-down kicks, as in the crawl.

flut ter y (flut′ər ē), *adj.* apt to flutter; fluttering.

flu vi al (flü′vē əl), *adj.* of, found in, or produced by a river: *A delta is a fluvial deposit.* [< Latin *fluvialis* < *fluvius* river < *fluere* to flow]

flux (fluks), *n.* 1 a flow; a flowing. 2 a flowing in of the tide. 3 continuous change: *New words and meanings keep the English language in a state of flux.* 4 an abnormal and excessive discharge of liquid matter from the body. 5 rosin or other substance used in soldering, welding, etc., to clean the surfaces of metals and help them join. 6 rate of flow of a fluid, heat, etc., across a certain surface or area. —*v.t.* 1 cause an abnormal discharge of liquid matter in; purge. 2 heat with a substance that helps metals or minerals melt together. —*v.i.* melt together. [< Latin *fluxus* < *fluere* to flow]

flute (def. 1)

flux ion (fluk′shən), *n.* 1 a flowing; flow. 2 discharge.

fly[1] (flī), *n., pl.* **flies.** 1 housefly. 2 any of an order of insects that have one pair of transparent wings, including houseflies, mosquitoes, and gnats. 3 any insect with transparent wings, such as a mayfly. 4 fishhook with feathers, silk, tinsel, etc., on it to make it look like an insect. 5 **fly in the ointment,** a small thing that spoils something else or lessens its value. [Old English *flēoge* < *flēogan* fly[2]]

fly[2] (flī), *v.,* **flew, flown, fly ing** for 1-7; **flied, fly ing** for 8; *n., pl.* **flies.** —*v.i.* 1 move through the air with wings. 2 float or wave in the air; flutter. 3 travel in an aircraft. 4 pilot an aircraft. 5 move swiftly; go rapidly: *The ship flies before the wind.* 6 run away; flee. 7 **fly off,** leave suddenly; break away. 8 bat a baseball high in the air. —*v.t.* 1 cause to float or wave in the air: *fly a kite.* 2 travel over in an aircraft: *We flew the Pacific in record time.* 3 pilot (an aircraft). 4 carry in an aircraft: *They flew a large number of rare animals from Africa.* 5 flee from; shun. 6 **fly at,** attack violently. 7 **let fly, a** shoot or throw: *The hunter let fly an arrow.* **b** say violently. —*n.* 1 flap to cover buttons, a zipper, etc., on clothing. 2 flap forming the door of a tent. 3 piece of canvas forming an extra, outer top for a tent. 4 width of a flag from the staff to the end. 5 part of a flag farthest from the staff. 6 BRITISH. a light, public carriage for passengers. 7 baseball batted high in the air. 8 act of flying; flight. 9 **flies,** *pl.* space above a stage in a theater. 10 **on the fly, a** while still in the air; before touching the ground. **b** INFORMAL. hurriedly: *I had my lunch on the fly.* [Old English *flēogan*]

fly a ble (flī′ə bəl), *adj.* 1 that can be flown. 2 suitable for flying.

fly blow (flī′blō′), *n., v.,* **-blew, -blown, -blow ing.** —*n.* the egg or young larva of a blowfly deposited in or on meat, etc. —*v.t.* 1 deposit eggs or larva in or on (meat, etc). 2 spoil; taint. —*v.i.* deposit eggs or larva in or on meat, etc.

fly blown (flī′blōn′), *adj.* 1 tainted by the eggs or larvae of flies. 2 spoiled; tainted.

fly by (flī′bī′), *n., pl.* **-bys.** 1 flight of a space vehicle close to a planet or other heavenly body. 2 flyover.

fly-by-night (flī′bī nīt′), *adj.* not to be trusted; not reliable; irresponsible. —*n.* INFORMAL. person who avoids paying his debts by leaving secretly at night.

fly-cast ing (flī′kas′ting), *n.* sport of fishing with rod and line, using an artificial fly as bait.

fly catch er (flī′kach′ər), *n.* any of various birds that catch flies and other insects while flying, especially a family of perching birds with small, weak feet, short necks, and large heads with broad, flattened bills hooked at the tip. The kingbird and phoebe are common types.

fly er (flī′ər), *n.* flier.

fly ing (flī′ing), *adj.* 1 that flies. 2 short and quick; hasty: *a flying visit.* 3 organized for rapid movement or prompt action: *a flying squad.* —*n.* action of piloting or traveling in an aircraft.

flying boat, seaplane with a boatlike hull and floats under its wings.

flying buttress, an arched support or brace built between the wall of a building and a supporting column to bear some of the weight of the roof. See **buttress** for picture.

flying colors, success; victory: *The team finished the tournament with flying colors.*

flying disk, flying saucer.

Flying Dutchman, 1 a legendary Dutch sea captain condemned to sail the seas until the Day of Judgment. 2 his ghostlike ship, supposed to appear to mariners near the Cape of Good Hope in storms, and regarded as a bad omen.

flying field, a small tract of land where aircraft can land or take off. It is much smaller and has fewer facilities than an airport.

flying fish, any of a family of tropical marine fishes having winglike pectoral fins which enable them to glide for some distance through the air after leaping from the water.

flying jib, a small, triangular sail attached to the jib boom or the flying jib boom in front of the regular jib. See **jib**[1] for picture.

flying machine, aircraft.

flying saucer, an unidentified, often disklike object, reported seen in the sky over many different parts of the world, especially since about 1947; flying disk.

flying squirrel, any of various squirrels that can make long, gliding leaps through the air. Their front and hind legs are connected by winglike folds of skin.

fly leaf (flī′lēf′), *n., pl.* **-leaves.** a blank sheet of paper at the beginning or end of a book, pamphlet, etc.

fly o ver (flī′ō′vər), *n.* a mass flight of aircraft in formation over a city, reviewing stand, etc., usually as a display of air power; fly-by.

fly pa per (flī′pā′pər), *n.* paper covered with a sticky or poisonous substance, used to catch or kill flies.

fly past (flī′past′), *n.* flyover.

fly speck (flī′spek′), *n.* 1 a tiny spot left by a fly. 2 any tiny speck. —*v.t.* mark with flyspecks.

fly trap (flī′trap′), *n.* any of several plants which trap insects, especially the Venus's-flytrap and the pitcher plant.

fly way (flī′wā′), *n.* route usually followed by migrating birds.

fly weight (flī′wāt′), *n.* boxer who weighs not more than 112 pounds.

fly wheel (flī′hwēl′), *n.* a heavy wheel attached to a machine to keep it and its parts moving at an even speed. See **steam engine** for diagram.

fm., fathom.

Fm, fermium.

FM or **F.M.,** frequency modulation.

f number, (in photography) the focal length of a lens divided by its effective diameter. An f/4 lens is one in which the diameter of the widest effective opening is $^1/_4$ of its focal length (f).

fo., folio.

foal (fōl), *n.* a young horse, donkey, etc.; colt

or filly. —*v.t., v.i.* give birth to (a foal). [Old English *fola*]

foam (fōm), *n.* 1 mass of very small bubbles formed in a liquid by agitation, fermentation, boiling, etc.; froth. 2 a frothy mass formed in the mouth as saliva or on the skin of animals as sweat: *The dog with foam around its mouth is suffering from rabies.* 3 a spongy, flexible material made from plastics, rubber, etc., by solidification of the material around air bubbles. —*v.i.* 1 form or gather foam; froth. 2 break into foam; emit foam, especially to froth at the mouth. —*v.t.* 1 cause to foam. 2 give (plastic, rubber, etc.) a spongy, flexible texture by solidifying it around trapped air or gas bubbles. [Old English *fām*] **—foam′like′,** *adj.*

foam rubber, a soft, spongy foam of natural or synthetic rubber used for mattresses, cushions, etc.

foam y (fō′mē), *adj.,* **foam i er, foam i est.** 1 covered with foam; foaming. 2 made of foam. 3 like foam. **—foam′i ly,** *adv.* **—foam′i ness,** *n.*

fob[1] (fob), *n.* 1 a small pocket in trousers or breeches for holding a watch, etc. 2 a short watch chain, ribbon, etc., that hangs out of such a pocket. 3 ornament worn at the end of such a chain, ribbon, etc. [perhaps < Low German *fobke* little pocket]

fob[2] (fob), *v.t.,* **fobbed, fob bing.** 1 deceive by a trick; cheat. 2 **fob off, a** put off or deceive by a trick. **b** palm off or get rid of by a trick. [perhaps < Middle English *fobbe, foppe* fool]

f.o.b. or **F.O.B.,** free on board.

fo cal (fō′kəl), *adj.* of or having to do with a focus. **—fo′cal ly,** *adv.*

focal distance, focal length.

fo cal ize (fō′kə līz), *v.t.,* **-ized, -iz ing.** 1 bring into focus; focus. 2 localize (an infection, etc.) at a particular site of activity. **—fo′cal i za′tion,** *n.*

focal length, distance from the optical center of a lens or mirror to the principal point of focus.

Foch (fôsh), *n.* **Ferdinand,** 1851-1929, French marshal, commander in chief of the Allied armies during World War I.

fo ci (fō′sī), *n.* a pl. of **focus.**

fo'c'sle (fōk′səl), *n.* forecastle.

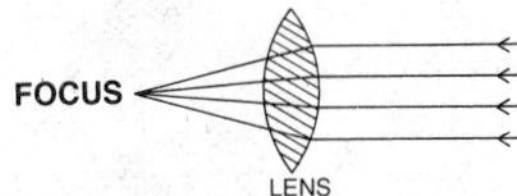

focus (def. 1)—Rays of light are brought to a focus by the lens.

fo cus (fō′kəs), *n., pl.* **-cus es** or **-ci,** *v.,* **-cused, -cus ing** or **-cussed, -cus sing.** —*n.* 1 point at which rays of light, heat, etc., meet, diverge, or seem to diverge after being reflected from a mirror, bent by a lens, etc. 2 focal length. 3 the correct adjustment of a lens, the eye, etc., to make a clear image: *If my camera is not brought into focus, the photograph will be blurred.* 4 the central point of attraction, attention, activity, etc.: *The new baby was the focus of attention.* 5 (in geometry) a fixed point used in determining a conic section. A parabola has one focus while an ellipse or a hyperbola has two foci. —*v.t.* 1 bring (rays of light, heat, etc.) to a focus. 2 adjust (a lens, the eye, etc.) to make a clear image. 3 make (an image, etc.) clear by adjusting a lens, the eye, etc. 4 concentrate or direct: *When studying, he focused his mind on his lessons.* —*v.i.* 1 converge to a focus. 2 adjust the eye or an optical instrument for clear vision: *Focus upon some distant object.* [< Latin, hearth]

fod der (fod′ər), *n.* coarse food for horses, cattle, etc. Hay and cornstalks with their leaves are fodder. See **feed** for synonym study. —*v.t.* give fodder to. [Old English *fōdor* < *fōda* food]

foe (fō), *n.* 1 person or group that hates and seeks to injure another; enemy. See **enemy** for synonym study. 2 enemy in battle or war. 3 anything that harms or is likely to injure. [Old English *fāh* hostile]

foehn (fān; *German* fœn), *n.* a warm, dry wind that blows down the leeward slope of a mountain, especially in the Alps. [< German *Föhn*]

foe man (fō′mən), *n., pl.* **-men.** ARCHAIC. enemy in war; adversary.

foe tal (fē′tl), *adj.* fetal.

foe tus (fē′təs), *n.* fetus.

fog (fog, fôg), *n., v.,* **fogged, fog ging.** —*n.* 1 cloud of fine drops of water just above the earth's surface, in which visibility is very poor; a low cloud or thick mist. 2 a darkened condition of the atmosphere, or a substance in the atmosphere that causes this. 3 a confused or puzzled condition. 4 (in photography) a grayish cloud or veil obscuring part or all of a developed film, plate, or print. —*v.t.* 1 cover with fog. 2 make misty or cloudy; darken; dim. 3 confuse; puzzle. —*v.i.* 1 become covered with fog. 2 become misty or cloudy. [probably < Scandinavian (Danish) *fog* spray, shower, drift]

fog bank, a dense mass of fog seen at a distance.

fog bound (fog′bound′, fôg′bound′), *adj.* prevented from sailing or moving by fog.

fo gey (fō′gē), *n., pl.* **-geys.** fogy.

fog gy (fog′ē, fôg′ē), *adj.,* **-gi er, -gi est.** 1 having much fog; misty. 2 not clear; dim; blurred. 3 confused; puzzled. **—fog′gi ly,** *adv.* **—fog′gi ness,** *n.*

fog horn (fog′hôrn′, fôg′hôrn′), *n.* 1 horn that warns ships in foggy weather. 2 a loud, harsh voice.

fog light, a special light on an automobile for use in heavy fog. Its beam, of low intensity and position, causes less reflection and glare than that of the white headlight.

fo gy (fō′gē), *n., pl.* **-gies.** old-fashioned person; person who is behind the times or lacks enterprise. [origin uncertain]

fo gy ism (fō′gē iz′əm), *n.* habits or practices of a fogy.

foi ble (foi′bəl), a weak point; weakness: *Talking too much is one of her foibles.* [< French, older form of *faible* feeble]

foil[1] (foil), *v.t.* 1 prevent from carrying out plans, attempts, etc.; get the better of; outwit or defeat: *The hero foiled the villain.* 2 prevent (a scheme, plan, etc.) from being carried out or from succeeding. [< Old French *fouler* trample, full (cloth) < Medieval Latin *fullare*]

foil[2] (foil), *n.* 1 metal beaten, hammered, or rolled into a very thin sheet: *Candy is sometimes wrapped in foil to keep it fresh.* 2 anything that makes something else look or seem better by contrast. 3 a very thin layer of polished metal, placed under a gem, especially an inferior or imitation gem, to give it more color or sparkle. 4 (in architecture) a leaflike ornament, especially an arc or rounded space between cusps. 5 leaf of a plant. [< Old French *foille* < Latin *folia* leaves]

hat, āge, fär; let, ēqual, tėrm;
it, īce; hot, ōpen, ôrder;
oil, out; cup, pu̇t, rüle;
ch, child; ng, long; sh, she;
th, thin; ᴛʜ, then; zh, measure;

ə represents *a* in about, *e* in taken, *i* in pencil, *o* in lemon, *u* in circus.

< = from, derived from, taken from.

foil[3] (foil), *n.* 1 a long, narrow sword with a knob or button on the point to prevent injury, used in fencing. 2 **foils,** *pl.* the sport or skill of fencing with such a sword. [origin uncertain]

foist (foist), *v.t.* palm off as genuine; impose by fraud: *The dishonest shopkeeper foisted inferior goods on his customers.* [probably < dialectal Dutch *vuisten* take in hand < *vuist* fist]

fold[1] (fōld), *v.t.* 1 bend or double over on itself. One folds a letter or a napkin. 2 bring together with the parts in or around one another: *You fold your arms.* 3 bend until close to the body: *A bird folds its wings.* 4 put the arms around and hold tenderly: *A mother folds her child to her breast.* 5 wrap; enclose: *He folded the pills in a blue paper.* 6 add (an ingredient) to a mixture in cooking by gently turning one part over another with strokes of a spoon: *fold in beaten egg whites.* —*v.i.* 1 become folded. 2 fail in business, etc; fold up.
fold up, a make or become smaller by folding. **b** INFORMAL. fail in business, etc.
—*n.* 1 layer of something folded; pleat. 2 mark or line made by folding. 3 act or process of folding. 4 (in geology) a bend in a layer of rock.
[Old English *faldan, fealdan*]

fold[2] (fōld), *n.* 1 pen to keep sheep in. 2 sheep kept in a pen. 3 group sharing a common belief or cause, especially a church or congregation. —*v.t.* put or keep (sheep) in a pen. [Old English *falod*]

-fold, *suffix forming adjectives and adverbs.* 1 ___times as many; ___times as great: *Tenfold = ten times as many.* 2 formed or divided into ___parts: *Manifold = formed into many parts.* [Old English *-feald.* Related to FOLD[1].]

fold er (fōl′dər), *n.* 1 holder for papers, made by folding a piece of stiff paper once. 2 pamphlet made of one or more folded sheets. 3 person or thing that folds.

fol de rol (fol′də rol′), *n.* falderal.

fold out (fōld′out′), *n.* an extra long illustrated page that has to be folded to fit into a book, magazine, etc., and unfolded to be read.

fo li a ceous (fō′lē ā′shəs), *adj.* 1 of or

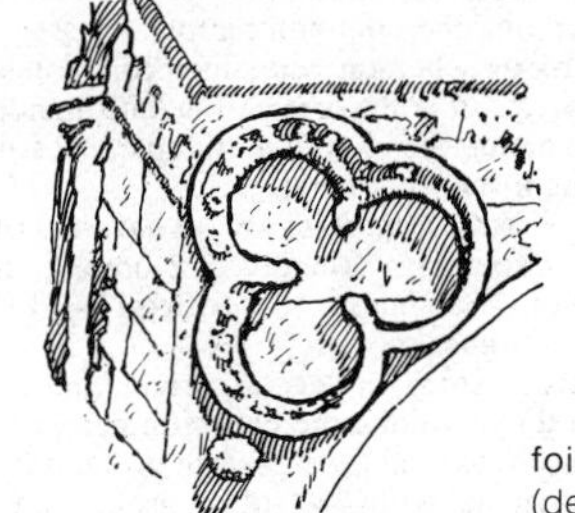

foil[2] (def. 4)

having to do with leaves; leaflike; leafy. 2 made of thin layers.

fo li age (fō′lē ij), *n.* 1 leaves of a plant. 2 decoration made of carved or painted leaves, flowers, etc. [< Middle French *feuillage* < *feuille* leaf < Latin *folia* leaves]

fo li ate (*adj.* fō′lē it, fō′lē āt; *v.* fō′lē āt), *adj., v.,* **-at ed, -at ing.** —*adj.* having leaves; covered with leaves. —*v.i.* 1 put forth leaves. 2 split into thin layers. —*v.t.* 1 decorate with leaflike ornaments. 2 number the folios or leaves of (a volume). [< Latin *foliatum* < *folia* leaves]

fo li a tion (fō′lē ā′shən), *n.* 1 process of putting forth of leaves. 2 a being in leaf. 3 decoration with leaflike ornaments or foils.

fo lic acid (fō′lik), a constituent of the vitamin B complex, found in green leaves and animal tissue, thought to be useful in treating anemia. *Formula:* $C_{19}H_{19}N_7O_6$ [< Latin *folium* leaf]

fo li o (fō′lē ō), *n., pl.* **-li os,** *adj.* —*n.* 1 a large sheet of paper folded once to make two leaves, or four pages, of a book, etc. 2 volume consisting of sheets folded once (that is, with four pages to each sheet); volume having pages of the largest size. A folio is usually any book more than 11 inches in height. 3 the size of a folio book. 4 (in printing) the page number of a book, etc. 5 leaf of a book, manuscript, etc., numbered on the front side only. —*adj.* having to do with or having the form of a folio: *The encyclopedia was in twenty volumes folio.* [< Latin, ablative of *folium* leaf]

fo li o late (fō′lē ə lāt), *adj.* of or consisting of leaflets.

folk (fōk), *n., pl.* **folk** or **folks,** *adj.* —*n.* 1 people: *Most city folk know very little about farming.* 2 tribe or nation. 3 the common people of a nation, etc. 4 **folks,** *pl.* **a** people. **b** INFORMAL. members of one's own family; relatives: *How are all your folks?* —*adj.* of or having to do with the common people, their beliefs, legends, customs, etc.: *folk laws, folk tunes.* [Old English *folc*]

folk dance, 1 dance originating and handed down among the common people. 2 music for it.

folk etymology, popular misconception of the origin of a word that often results in a modification of its sound or spelling. EXAMPLE: Old French *crevice* became English *crayfish,* influenced by *fish.*

folk lore (fōk′lôr′, fōk′lōr′), *n.* the traditional beliefs, legends, customs, etc., of a people, tribe, etc.

folk lor ist (fōk′lôr′ist, fōk′lōr′ist), *n.* an expert in the study of folklore.

folk medicine, the traditional medical maxims, remedies, and methods prevalent among the people of a region.

folk music, music originating and handed down among the common people.

folk singer, person who sings folk songs.

folk song, 1 song originating and handed down among the common people. 2 song imitating a real folk song.

folk sy (fōk′sē), *adj.,* **-si er, -si est.** INFORMAL. 1 sociable; friendly. 2 simple; unpretentious; common. **—folk′si ly,** *adv.* **—folk′si ness,** *n.*

folk tale, story or legend originating and handed down among the common people.

folk way (fōk′wā′), *n.* custom or habit that has grown up within a social group and is very common among the members of this group.

fol li cle (fol′ə kəl), *n.* 1 a small cavity, sac, or gland in the body. Hairs grow from follicles. 2 (in botany) a dry, one-celled fruit formed of a single carpel, that splits open along one seam only, as the fruit of a milkweed. [< Latin *folliculus* small bag, diminutive of *follis* bellows]

fol li cle-stim u lat ing hormone (fol′ə kəl stim′yə lā′ting), a hormone of the pituitary gland that stimulates the growth of the Graafian follicles of the ovaries.

fol lic u lar (fə lik′yə lər), *adj.* consisting of or like follicles.

fol lic u late (fə lik′yə lāt), *adj.* provided with or consisting of follicles.

fol low (fol′ō), *v.t.* 1 go or come after: *April follows March.* 2 result from: *Misery follows war.* 3 go along: *Follow this road to the corner.* 4 go along with; accompany: *My dog followed me to school.* 5 pursue: *The dogs followed the fox.* 6 act according to; take as a guide; obey: *Follow her advice.* 7 keep the eyes or attention on: *I could not follow that bird's flight.* 8 keep the mind on; keep up with and understand: *Try to follow my meaning.* 9 take as one's work; be concerned with: *follow the profession of lawyer.* —*v.i.* 1 go or come after someone or something else: *He leads; we follow.* See synonym study below. 2 occur as a consequence; result: *If you eat too much candy, a stomach ache will follow.*

follow out, carry out to the end: *follow out a plan of attack.*

follow through, continue a stroke, motion, plan, etc., through to the end.

follow up, **a** follow closely and steadily. **b** carry out to the end: *follow up an idea.* **c** act upon with energy: *follow up a suggestion.*

—*n.* act of following.

[Old English *folgian*]

Syn. *v.i.* 1 **Follow, succeed, ensue** mean to come or go after another. **Follow** is the general word: *He has come to take his new job, but his wife will follow later.* **Succeed** means to come next in order of time, and usually suggests taking the place of someone or something: *He succeeded to the presidency of the company when his father retired.* **Ensue,** a formal word, means to follow as a result or conclusion: *A lasting friendship ensued from our working together during the war.*

➔ **follow.** The idiom is *followed by,* not *followed with: Supper was followed by games and dancing.*

fol low er (fol′ō ər), *n.* 1 person or thing that follows. 2 person who follows the ideas or beliefs of another. See synonym study below. 3 attendant; servant. 4 gear, wheel, or other machine part that is given motion by another part.

Syn. 2 **Follower, adherent, disciple** mean someone who follows another, his beliefs, a cause, etc. **Follower** is the general word: *Men who promise riches always find followers among unthinking people.* **Adherent,** more formal, implies active and loyal support to a belief, cause, party, etc., and sometimes personal devotion to the leader: *Adherents of a political party will rarely switch over to another party.* **Disciple** emphasizes both devotion to a person as leader and teacher and firm belief in his teachings: *The disciples of Karl Marx spread his ideas throughout Europe.*

fol low ing (fol′ō ing), *n.* 1 group of followers; attendants. 2 **the following,** persons, things, items, etc., now to be named, related, described, etc. —*adj.* 1 that follows; next after: *the following day.* 2 that now follows; that is immediately to be named, described, etc.

fol low-up (fol′ō up′), *n.* 1 act of following up. 2 any action or thing, such as a second or third visit, appeal, letter, etc., designed to be a further effort in achieving some goal. —*adj.* sent or used as a follow-up: *a follow-up circular.*

fol ly (fol′ē), *n., pl.* **-lies.** 1 a being foolish; lack of sense; unwise conduct. 2 a foolish act, practice, or idea; something silly. 3 a costly but foolish undertaking. [< Old French *folie* < *fol* foolish. See FOOL.]

Fol som man (fol′səm), a Stone Age man thought to have lived in North America at the end of the most recent glacial period. [< *Folsom,* town in New Mexico, where relics were discovered]

fo ment (fō ment′), *v.t.* 1 stir up (trouble, rebellion, etc.); instigate: *Three sailors were fomenting a mutiny on the ship.* 2 apply warm water, hot cloths, etc., to (a hurt or pain). [< Late Latin *fomentare* < *fomentum* a warm application < Latin *fovere* to warm] **—fo ment′er,** *n.*

fo men ta tion (fō′men tā′shən), *n.* 1 a stirring up; instigation. 2 application of moist heat. 3 a hot, moist application.

fond (fond), *adj.* 1 **fond of,** having a liking for: *fond of children.* 2 loving; affectionate: *a fond look.* 3 loving foolishly or too much; doting. 4 cherished: *fond hopes.* 5 ARCHAIC. foolish. [Middle English *fonned,* past participle of *fonnen* be foolish < *fonne* fool] **—fond′ly,** *adv.* **—fond′ness,** *n.*

fon dant (fon′dənt), *n.* 1 a creamy confection used as a filling or coating for other candies. 2 a candy consisting mainly of fondant. [< French, literally, melting < *fondre* melt]

fon dle (fon′dl), *v.t.,* **-dled, -dling.** handle or treat lovingly; pet; caress. **—fon′dler,** *n.*

fon due (fon′dü, fon dü′), *n.* a dish made of melted cheese, eggs, butter, etc., into which crackers or small pieces of toast are dipped and eaten. [< French]

font[1] (def. 1)

font[1] (font), *n.* 1 basin holding water for baptism. 2 basin for holy water. 3 fountain; source. [< Latin *fontem* spring]

font[2] (font), *n.* (in printing) a complete set of type of one size and style. [< Middle French *fonte* < *fondre* melt]

Fon taine bleau (fon′tən blō, fon′tən blō′), *n.* 1 town in N France, site of a palace formerly used by the French kings. 18,000. 2 forest near this town.

fon ta nel or **fon ta nelle** (fon′tə nel′), *n.* any of the soft spots, closed by membrane and later to be filled by bone, on the head of an infant or fetus. [< Middle French *fontanelle,* originally diminutive of *fontaine* fountain]

Foo chow (fü′chou′), *n.* seaport in SE China. 616,000. Also, **Minho.**

food (füd), *n.* 1 anything that animals or people eat or drink that enables them to live and grow; whatever supplies nourishment. See synonym study below. 2 what is eaten; solid nutriment: *Give him food and drink.* 3 anything that plants take in that enables them to live and grow. 4 a particular kind or article of food: *breakfast foods.* 5 anything that causes growth: *Books are food for the mind.* 6 anything that sustains or serves for consumption in any way: *food for thought.* [Old English *fōda*]

Syn. 1 **Food, provisions, ration** mean that which is intended to be eaten or drunk. **Food** is the general word, applying to any substance which nourishes people or plants: *Milk is a valuable food.* **Provisions,** usually restricted to human food, means a supply of food, either for immediate use or stored away: *I must buy provisions for the holidays.* **Ration,** also usually restricted to human food, means a fixed allowance of food for a particular period or that amount of food allowed under some system of rationing: *weekly rations of meat.*

food chain, group of organisms so interrelated that each member of the group feeds upon the one below it and is in turn eaten by the organism above it.

food poisoning, poisoning caused by consuming foods that are poisonous in themselves or that contain certain bacteria, bacterial toxins, or certain chemicals. Botulism is a severe form of food poisoning.

food stuff (füd′stuf′), *n.* 1 material for food. Grain and meat are foodstuffs. 2 any nutritionally valuable element in food, as protein or carbohydrate.

food vacuole, vacuole containing food particles, found in certain protozoans, such as amoebas. It serves as a simple digestive system. See **amoeba** for diagram.

fool (fül), *n.* 1 person without sense or judgment; person who acts unwisely; stupid or silly person. 2 (in the Middle Ages) a jester. 3 dupe. 4 a feeble-minded or idiotic person. *—v.i.* 1 act like a fool for fun; play; joke: *I was only fooling.* 2 **fool around,** INFORMAL. waste time foolishly. *—v.t.* 1 make a fool of; deceive; trick: *You can't fool me.* 2 **fool away,** INFORMAL. waste (time) foolishly. 3 **fool with,** INFORMAL. meddle foolishly with: *Stop fooling with that machine.* [< Old French *fol* fool, madman, probably < Late Latin *follis* empty-headed < Latin *follis* bag, bellows]

fool er y (fü′lər ē), *n., pl.* **-er ies.** 1 a foolish action, performance, or thing. 2 habit or practice of acting foolishly.

fool har dy (fül′här′dē), *adj.,* **-di er, -di est.** foolishly bold; rash; reckless. **—fool′har′di ly,** *adv.* **—fool′har′di ness,** *n.*

fool ish (fü′lish), *adj.* 1 without sense or judgment; unwise; stupid or silly. See synonym study below. 2 ridiculous; absurd. **—fool′ish ly,** *adv.* **—fool′ish ness,** *n.*

Syn. 1 **Foolish, silly, fatuous** mean without sense and may be applied either to people or their actions. **Foolish** means showing lack of common sense and judgment: *It is foolish to keep late hours every night.* **Silly** suggests little intelligence because of pointless actions or speech: *It would be silly to sit in the middle of the highway.* **Fatuous** means stupid but completely self-satisfied: *After his boring speech, the fatuous speaker received almost no applause.*

fool proof (fül′prüf′), *adj.* so safe or simple that even a fool can use or do it.

fools cap (fülz′kap′), *n.* 1 writing paper in sheets from 12 to 13 ½ inches wide and 15 to 17 inches long, originally watermarked with a fool's cap. 2 fool's cap.

fool's cap, cap or hood, usually with bells on it, worn by the fool or jester of a king or lord.

fool's errand, a foolish or useless undertaking.

fool's gold, mineral that looks like gold, especially an iron pyrite.

fool's paradise, condition of happiness based on false beliefs or hopes.

foot (fu̇t), *n., pl.* **feet,** *v.* *—n.* 1 the end part of a leg; part that a person, animal, or thing stands on. 2 an organ present in some invertebrates, especially the muscular, ventral protuberance of the mollusks, used for locomotion. 3 part opposite the head of something; end toward which the feet are put: *the foot of a bed.* 4 the lowest or underlying part; bottom; base: *the foot of a hill.* 5 part of a stocking that covers the foot. 6 infantrymen; infantry. 7 unit of length, equal to twelve inches. See **measure** for table. 8 one of the parts into which a line of poetry is divided. This line has four feet: "The boy | stood on | the burn|ing deck." 9 lower edge or bottom of a sail. 10 thing or part resembling an animal's foot: *the foot of a chair.*

on foot, a standing or walking. b going on; in progress: *There's mischief on foot.*

put one's best foot forward, INFORMAL. a do one's best. b try to make a good impression.

put one's foot down, make up one's mind and act firmly.

put one's foot in it, INFORMAL. get into trouble by meddling; be extremely tactless in words or actions; blunder.

under foot, in the way.

with one foot in the grave, almost dead; dying.

—v.t. 1 walk: *The boys footed the whole ten miles.* 2 add up: *Foot this column of numbers.* 3 INFORMAL. pay (a bill, etc.). 4 walk or dance on; set foot on; tread. 5 make or renew the foot of (a stocking, etc.) *—v.i.* Also, **foot it.** a go on foot; walk. b dance. c move fast; hurry.

[Old English *fōt*]

foot age (fu̇t′ij), *n.* length in feet.

foot-and-mouth disease (fu̇t′n-mouth′), an acute, contagious virus disease of cattle and some other hoofed animals, causing fever and blisters in the mouth and around the hoofs; hoof-and-mouth disease. It rarely occurs in man.

foot ball (fu̇t′bôl′), *n.* 1 game played with a large, inflated, oval leather ball by two teams of eleven players each on a field with a goal at each end. The players try to score by carrying the ball over the goal line by a run or pass, or by kicking it through the goal posts. 2 ball used in this game or in Rugby. 3 the spherical ball used in soccer. 4 BRITISH. Rugby. 5 BRITISH. soccer. 6 person or thing that is kicked or tossed about: *The pollution issue became a political football in the election campaign.*

hat, āge, fär; let, ēqual, tėrm;
it, īce; hot, ōpen, ôrder;
oil, out; cup, pu̇t, rüle;
ch, child; ng, long; sh, she;
th, thin; ᴛʜ, then; zh, measure;

ə represents *a* in about, *e* in taken, *i* in pencil, *o* in lemon, *u* in circus.

< = from, derived from, taken from.

foot ball er (fu̇t′bô′lər), *n.* a football player.

foot board (fu̇t′bôrd′, fu̇t′bōrd′), *n.* 1 board or small platform on which to support the feet or to stand. 2 an upright piece across the foot of a bed.

foot brake, brake worked by pressing with the foot, as on an automobile.

foot bridge (fu̇t′brij′), *n.* bridge for pedestrians only.

foot-can dle (fu̇t′kan′dl), *n.* unit for measuring illumination, equal to the amount of light produced by a candle on a surface at a distance of one foot.

foot-drag ging (fu̇t′drag′ing), *n.* U.S. INFORMAL. sluggishness, hesitation, or delay; stalling.

foot ed (fu̇t′id), *adj.* having a foot or feet: *an animal footed like a goat.*

-footed, *combining form.* having a ____ foot or feet: *Club-footed = having a club foot. Four-footed animal = animal having four feet.*

foot fall (fu̇t′fôl′), *n.* 1 sound of steps coming or going. 2 footstep.

foot gear (fu̇t′gir′), *n.* shoes, boots, etc.

foot hill (fu̇t′hil′), *n.* a low hill at the base of a mountain or mountain range.

foot hold (fu̇t′hōld′), *n.* 1 place to put a foot; support for the feet; surface to stand on: *He climbed the steep cliff by getting footholds in cracks in the rock.* 2 a firm footing or position: *It is hard to break a habit after it has a foothold.*

foot ing (fu̇t′ing), *n.* 1 a firm and secure placing or position of the feet: *He lost his footing and fell down on the ice.* 2 place to put a foot; foothold. 3 a firm place or position. The footing for the foundation of a house extends below ground which might be affected by frost. 4 basis of understanding; position or standing: *The United States and Canada are on a friendly footing.* 5 an adding up a column of figures. 6 amount found by adding up such a column; sum; total. 7 a moving on the feet; walking, dancing, etc.

foot less (fu̇t′lis), *adj.* 1 without a foot or feet. 2 without support; not substantial. 3 INFORMAL. awkward, helpless, or inefficient.

foot lights (fu̇t′līts′), *n.pl.* 1 row of lights at the front of a stage. 2 profession of acting; the stage; theater.

foot lock er (fu̇t′lok′ər), *n.* a small chest for personal belongings, usually kept at the foot of one's bed, as in a barracks.

foot loose (fu̇t′lüs′), *adj.* free to go anywhere or do anything.

foot man (fu̇t′mən), *n., pl.* **-men.** a male servant who answers the bell, waits on the table, goes with an automobile or carriage to open the door, etc. Footmen usually wear a kind of uniform.

foot mark (fu̇t′märk′), *n.* footprint.

foot note (fu̇t′nōt′), *n., v.,* **-not ed, -not ing.** —*n.* note or comment at the bottom of a page referring to something on the page. —*v.t.* furnish with a footnote or footnotes.

foot pad (fu̇t′pad′), *n.* ARCHAIC. a highway robber who goes on foot only.

foot path (fu̇t′path′), *n., pl.* **-paths** (-paᴛʜz′, -paths′). a narrow path for pedestrians only.

foot-pound (fu̇t′pound′), *n.* unit of work or energy equal to the work done by a force of one pound that moves an object one foot in the direction of the force applied.

foot-pound-sec ond (fu̇t′pound′sek′-ənd), *adj.* of a system of units in which the foot, pound, and second are considered the basic units of length, mass, and time.

foot print (fu̇t′print′), *n.* mark or impression made by a foot; footmark; footstep.

foot race (fu̇t′rās′), *n.* race on foot; a running race.

foot rest (fu̇t′rest′), *n.* support to rest the feet on.

foot rule, a wooden, metal, or plastic ruler one foot long.

foot soldier, infantryman.

foot sore (fu̇t′sôr′, fu̇t′sōr′), *adj.* having sore or tender feet, especially from much walking; footworn.

foot step (fu̇t′step′), *n.* 1 a person's step. 2 distance covered in one step. 3 sound of steps coming or going. 4 footprint. 5 step on which to go up or down. **6 follow in someone's footsteps,** do as someone else has done.

foot stool (fu̇t′stül′), *n.* a low stool on which to place the feet when seated.

foot way (fu̇t′wā′), *n.* path for pedestrians only.

foot wear (fu̇t′wer′, fu̇t′war′), *n.* shoes, slippers, stockings, etc.

foot work (fu̇t′wėrk′), *n.* way of using the feet: *Footwork is important in boxing and dancing.*

foot worn (fu̇t′wôrn′, fu̇t′wōrn′), *adj.* 1 worn by feet: *a footworn path.* 2 footsore.

foo zle (fü′zəl), *v.,* **-zled, -zling,** *n.* —*v.t.* do clumsily; bungle (a stroke in golf, etc.). —*n.* a clumsy failure, especially a badly played stroke in golf. [origin uncertain]

fop (fop), *n.* a vain man who is very fond of fine clothes and has affected manners; dandy. [Middle English *foppe, fop*]

fop per y (fop′ər ē), *n., pl.* **-per ies.** behavior or dress of a fop.

fop pish (fop′ish), *adj.* 1 of a fop; suitable for a fop. 2 vain; affected. **—fop′pish ly,** *adv.* **—fop′pish ness,** *n.*

for (fôr; *unstressed* fər), *prep.* 1 in place of: *We used boxes for chairs.* 2 in support of; in favor of: *I am for giving everyone an equal opportunity.* 3 representing; in the interest of: *A lawyer acts for his client.* 4 in consideration of; in return for: *These apples are twelve for a dollar.* 5 with the object or purpose of taking, achieving, or obtaining: *He went for a walk.* 6 in order to become, have, keep, get to, etc.: *The navy trains men for sailors. He ran for his life.* 7 in search of: *She is hunting for her cat.* 8 in order to get to: *He has just left for New York.* 9 meant to belong to or to be used by or with; suited to: *a box for gloves, books for children.* 10 with a feeling toward: *She has an eye for beauty. We longed for home.* 11 with respect or regard to: *It is warm for April. Eating too much is bad for one's health.* 12 because of; by reason of: *He was punished for stealing.* 13 in honor of: *A party was given for her.* 14 as far as: *We walked for a mile.* 15 as long as; throughout; during: *He worked for an hour.* 16 as being: *They know it for a fact.* 17 in spite of: *For all his faults, we like him still.* 18 in proportion to: *For one poisonous snake there are many harmless ones.* 19 to the amount of: *His father gave him a check for $20.* **20 for (one) to,** that one will, should, must, etc.: *My lawyer has some legal papers for me to sign. It is time for us to go.* 21 showing equality between objects: *word for word. The prisoners were exchanged man for man.* **22 Oh! for,** I wish that I might have.
—*conj.* because: *We can't go, for it is raining.* [Old English]

for-, *prefix.* away; opposite; completely (often in a wrong or negative sense), as in *forbid, forswear.* [Old English]

for., 1 foreign. 2 forestry.

fo rage (fôr′ij, for′ij), *n., v.,* **-raged, -rag ing.** —*n.* 1 hay, grain, or other food for horses, cattle, etc. 2 a hunting or searching for food or provisions. —*v.i.* 1 hunt or search for food. 2 search about; hunt; rummage. —*v.t.* 1 supply with food; feed. 2 get by hunting or searching about; root out. 3 get or take food from. 4 plunder: *The soldiers foraged the villages near their camp.* [< Old French *fourage* < *fuerre* fodder < Germanic] **—fo′rag er,** *n.*

fo ra men (fə rā′mən), *n., pl.* **fo ram i na** (fə ram′ə nə), **fo ra mens.** an opening, orifice, or short passage, as in a bone or in the covering of the ovule of a plant. [< Latin < *forare* bore a hole]

fo ra min i fer (fôr′ə min′ə fər, for′ə-min′ə fər), *n.* any of an order of usually marine protozoans that have calcareous or chitinous shells with tiny holes in them. [< New Latin < Latin *foramen* an opening + *ferre* to bear]

fo ram i nif er al (fə ram′ə nif′ər əl), *adj.* consisting of, containing, or having to do with the foraminifers.

fo ram i nif er ous (fə ram′ə nif′ər əs), *adj.* 1 having perforations, pores, or foramina. 2 foraminiferal.

for as much as (fôr′əz much′ az), in view of the fact that; because; since.

fo ray (fôr′ā, for′ā), *n.* a raid for plunder. —*v.t.* lay waste; plunder; pillage. [< Old French *forrer* to forage]

for bade or **for bad** (fər bad′), *v.* pt. of **forbid.**

for bear[1] (fôr ber′, fôr bar′), *v.i.,* **-bore, -borne, -bear ing.** 1 hold back; keep from doing, saying, using, etc.: *I forbore telling her the truth because I knew it would upset her.* 2 be patient; control oneself. [Old English *forberan*] **—for bear′er,** *n.* **—for bear′ing ly,** *adv.*

for bear[2] (fôr′ber, fôr′bar), *n.* forebear.

for bear ance (fôr ber′əns, fôr bar′əns), *n.* 1 act of forbearing. 2 patience; self-control. See **patience** for synonym study.

for bid (fər bid′), *v.t.,* **-bade** or **-bad, -bid den** or **-bid, -bid ding.** 1 not allow (a person or persons) to do something; make a rule against; prohibit. See synonym study below. 2 keep from happening; prevent: *God forbid it!* 3 command to keep away from; exclude from: *I forbid you the house.* [Old English *forbēodan*]

Syn. 1 **Forbid, prohibit** mean to not allow to do something. **Forbid** implies an order or rule that is often direct or personal, and suggests expected obedience: *His father forbade him to smoke.* **Prohibit** implies a formal regulation against something, usually by law or official action, and suggests power to enforce it: *Picking flowers in this park is prohibited.*

for bid den (fər bid′n), *adj.* not allowed; against the law or rules; prohibited. —*v.* a pp. of **forbid.**

for bid ding (fər bid′ing), *adj.* causing fear or dislike; looking dangerous or unpleasant: *The coast was rocky and forbidding.* **—for bid′ding ly,** *adv.*

for bore (fôr bôr′, fôr bōr′), *v.* pt. of **forbear**[1].

for borne (fôr bôrn′, fôr bōrn′), *v.* pp. of **forbear**[1].

force (fôrs, fōrs), *n., v.,* **forced, forc ing.** —*n.* 1 active power; strength: *The speeding car struck the tree with great force.* 2 strength used against a person or thing; violence or coercion. 3 capacity to control, influence, persuade, convince, etc.; power: *He writes with force.* See **power** for synonym study. 4 power or might, especially military power, of a ruler, realm, etc.: *an army superior in fighting force.* 5 group of people working or acting together: *our office force.* 6 group of soldiers, sailors, policemen, etc. 7 cause that produces, changes, or stops the motion of a body. 8 meaning or significance of a word, sentence, etc. 9 binding power; validity, as of a law or contract: *The force of some laws has to be tested in court.* **10 forces,** *pl.* army, navy, etc.; armed forces. **11 by main force,** by using full strength. **12 in force, a** in effect or operation; legally binding; valid. **b** with full strength.
—*v.t.* 1 make (a person) act against his will; make do by force. 2 make or drive by force: *He forced his way into the house.* 3 get or take by force. 4 impose or impress by force: *force one's views on another.* 5 break open or through by force. 6 urge to violent effort. 7 make by an unusual or unnatural effort; strain. 8 hurry the growth or development of (flowers, fruits, a child's mind, etc.). 9 (in baseball) cause (a runner) to be put out by requiring him to try to advance to the next base.
[< Old French, ultimately < Latin *fortis* strong] **—force′less,** *adj.* **—forc′er,** *n.*

forced (fôrst, fōrst), *adj.* 1 made, compelled, or driven by force; enforced: *forced labor.* 2 done by unusual effort: *a forced march.* 3 not natural; strained: *a forced smile.*

force ful (fôrs′fəl, fōrs′fəl), *adj.* having much force; powerful, vigorous, or effective; strong. **—force′ful ly,** *adv.* **—force′ful ness,** *n.*

force meat (fôrs′mēt′, fōrs′mēt′), *n.* chopped and seasoned meat or fish, used for stuffing, etc. [< *force* (variant of obsolete *farce* stuff) + *meat*]

for ceps (fôr′seps, fôr′səps), *n., pl.* **-ceps.** pair of small pincers or tongs used by surgeons, dentists, etc., for seizing, holding, and

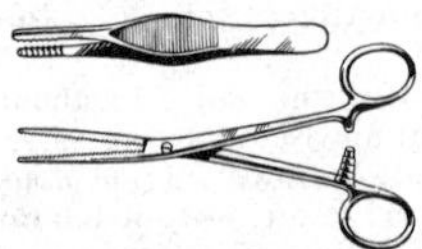

forceps—two kinds used in surgery

forecastle (def. 1)

pulling. [< Latin, tongs < *formus* hot + *capere* take]

force pump, pump which delivers liquid under pressure, especially one with a valveless piston whose action forces liquid through a pipe. See **pump**[1] for diagram.

for ci ble (fôr′sə bəl, fōr′sə bəl), *adj.* 1 made or done by force; using force: *a forcible entrance into a house.* 2 having or showing force; powerful or effective: *a forcible speaker.* **—for′ci ble ness,** *n.* **—for′ci bly,** *adv.*

ford (fôrd, fōrd), *n.* place where a river or other body of water is shallow enough to be crossed by wading or driving through the water. *—v.t.* cross (a river, etc.) at a ford. [Old English] **—ford′a ble,** *adj.*

Ford (fôrd, fōrd), *n.* 1 **Gerald R(udolph),** born 1913, vice-president of the United States, since 1973. 2 **Henry,** 1863-1947, American automobile manufacturer.

fore[1] (fôr, fōr), *adj.* at, near, or toward the front; forward: *The fore wall of a house faces the street.* *—adv.* at or toward the bow or front: *Several of the crew went fore.* *—n.* 1 the forward part; front. See **aft** for picture. 2 **to the fore,** to the front; into full view. [Old English]

fore[2] (fôr, fōr), *interj.* (in golf) a shout of warning to persons ahead on the fairway who are liable to be struck by the ball. [perhaps short for *before*]

fore-, *prefix.* 1 front; in front; at or near the front: *Forepaw = a front paw.* 2 before; beforehand: *Foregoing = going before.* [Old English]

fore and aft, 1 at or toward both bow and stern of a ship. 2 fore-and-aft.

fore-and-aft (fôr′ən aft′, fōr′ən aft′), *adj.* lengthwise on a ship; from bow to stern; placed lengthwise.

fore arm[1] (fôr′ärm′, fōr′ärm′), *n.* the part of the arm between the elbow and wrist. [< *fore-* + *arm*[1]]

fore arm[2] (fôr ärm′, fōr ärm′), *v.t.* prepare for trouble ahead of time; arm beforehand. [< *fore-* + *arm*[2], verb]

fore bear (fôr′ber, fôr′bar; fōr′ber, fōr′bar), *n.* ancestor; forefather. Also, **forbear.** [< *fore-* + *be* + *-er*[1]]

fore bode (fôr bōd′, fōr bōd′), *v.,* **-bod ed, -bod ing.** *—v.t.* 1 give warning of; predict: *Those black clouds forebode a storm.* 2 have a feeling that (something bad is going to happen); anticipate. *—v.i.* conjecture; forecast. **—fore bod′er,** *n.*

fore bod ing (fôr bō′ding, fōr bō′ding), *n.* 1 prediction; warning. 2 a feeling that something bad is going to happen; presentiment.

fore brain (fôr′brān′, fōr′brān′), *n.* the front part of the brain composed of the telencephalon and the diencephalon; prosencephalon. It includes the cerebrum, thalamus, and hypothalamus.

fore cast (fôr′kast′, fōr′kast′), *v.,* **-cast** or **-cast ed, -cast ing,** *n.* *—v.t.* 1 estimate or see beforehand; predict on the basis of observations, study, or experience: *Cooler weather is forecast for tomorrow.* 2 be a prediction of. 3 plan or decide ahead. *—n.* statement of what is coming; prediction or estimate of a future event or situation: *stock-market forecasts.* **—fore′cast′er,** *n.*

fore cas tle (fōk′səl, fôr′kas′əl, fōr′kas′əl), *n.* 1 the upper deck in front of the foremast. 2 the sailors' quarters in the forward part of a merchantman. Also, **fo'c'sle.**

fore close (fôr klōz′, fōr klōz′), *v.,* **-closed, -clos ing.** *—v.t.* 1 shut out; prevent; exclude: *foreclose objections.* 2 take away the right to redeem (a mortgage). When the conditions of a mortgage are not met, the holder can foreclose and have the property sold to satisfy his claim. *—v.i.* take away the right to redeem a mortgage.

fore clo sure (fôr klō′zhər, fōr klō′zhər), *n.* act of foreclosing a mortgage or taking away the right of a mortgager to redeem his property.

fore court (fôr′kôrt′, fōr′kōrt′), *n.* 1 a front or outer court. 2 part of a tennis court near the net.

fore deck (fôr′dek′, fōr′dek′), *n.* part of the main deck nearest the bow.

fore doom (fôr düm′, fōr düm′), *v.t.* doom beforehand.

fore fa ther (fôr′fä′ᴛʜər, fōr′fä′ᴛʜər), *n.* ancestor; progenitor.

fore fend (fôr fend′, fōr fend′), *v.t.* forfend.

fore fin ger (fôr′fing′gər, fōr′fing′gər), *n.* finger next to the thumb; index finger.

fore foot (fôr′fu̇t′, fōr′fu̇t′), *n., pl.* **-feet.** 1 one of the front feet of an animal having four or more feet. 2 the forward end of a ship's keel.

fore front (fôr′frunt′, fōr′frunt′), *n.* place of greatest importance, activity, etc.; foremost part; extreme front: *the forefront of battle.*

fore gath er (fôr gaᴛʜ′ər, fōr gaᴛʜ′ər), *v.i.* forgather.

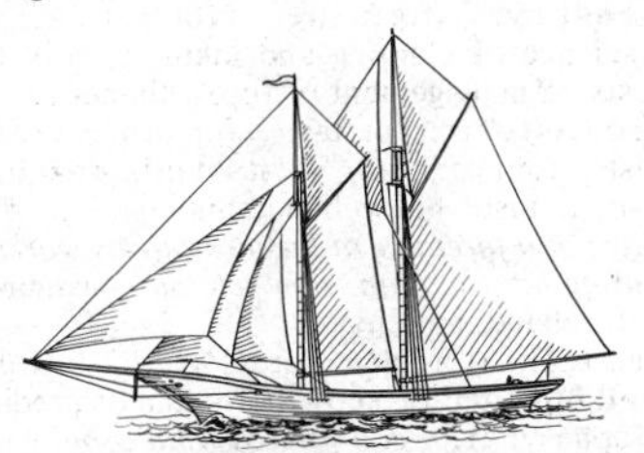
fore-and-aft rigged ship

fore go[1] (fôr gō′, fōr gō′), *v.t.,* **-went, -gone, -go ing.** forgo. **—fore go′er,** *n.*

fore go[2] (fôr gō′, fōr gō′), *v.i., v.t.,* **-went, -gone, -go ing.** go before; precede. [Old English *foregān*]

fore go ing (fôr′gō′ing, fōr′gō′ing), *adj.* going before; preceding.

fore gone[1] (fôr gôn′, fôr gon′; fōr gôn′, fōr gon′), *v.* pp. of **forego**[1].

fore gone[2] (fôr′gôn, fôr′gon; fōr′gôn, fōr′gon), *adj.* 1 known or decided beforehand; inevitable: *a foregone conclusion.* 2 that has gone before; previous. *—v.* pp. of **forego**[2].

fore ground (fôr′ground′, fōr′ground′), *n.* 1 the part of a picture or scene nearest the observer; the part in the front. 2 **in the foreground,** conspicuous.

fore hand (fôr′hand′, fōr′hand′), *n.* 1 stroke in tennis and other games made with the palm of the hand turned forward. 2 position in front or above. *—adj.* done or made with the palm of the hand turned forward.

hat, āge, fär; let, ēqual, tėrm;
it, īce; hot, ōpen, ôrder;
oil, out; cup, pu̇t, rüle;
ch, child; ng, long; sh, she;
th, thin; ᴛʜ, then; zh, measure;

ə represents *a* in about, *e* in taken,
i in pencil, *o* in lemon, *u* in circus.

< = from, derived from, taken from.

fore hand ed (fôr′han′did, fōr′han′did), *adj.* 1 providing for the future; prudent. 2 done beforehand; early. 3 forehand. **—fore′hand′ed ly,** *adv.* **—fore′hand′ed ness,** *n.*

fore head (fôr′id, for′id, fôr′hed′), *n.* 1 the part of the face above the eyes; brow. 2 a front part.

fo reign (fôr′ən, for′ən), *adj.* 1 outside one's own country: *She has traveled much in foreign countries.* 2 coming from outside one's own country: *a foreign ship, a foreign language, foreign money.* 3 having to do with other countries; carried on or dealing with other countries: *foreign affairs, foreign policy, foreign trade.* 4 not belonging; not related: *Sitting still is foreign to that child's nature.* 5 not belonging naturally to the place where found: *a foreign object in the eye.* [< Old French *forain* < Late Latin *foranus* on the outside < Latin *foras* outside] **—fo′reign ness,** *n.*

fo reign er (fôr′ə nər, for′ə nər), *n.* person from another country; alien.

foreign legion, part of an army made up largely of soldiers who are volunteers from other countries.

fore judge (fôr juj′, fōr juj′), *v.t., v.i.,* **-judged, -judg ing.** judge beforehand; prejudge.

fore know (fôr nō′, fōr nō′), *v.t.,* **-knew** (-nü′, -nyü′), **-known** (-nōn′), **-know ing.** know beforehand.

fore knowl edge (fôr′nol′ij, fōr′nol′ij; fôr nol′ij, fōr nol′ij), *n.* knowledge of a thing before it exists or happens.

fore land (fôr′land′, fōr′land′), *n.* headland; promontory.

fore leg (fôr′leg′, fōr′leg′), *n.* one of the front legs of an animal having four or more legs.

fore limb (fôr′lim′, fōr′lim′), *n.* one of the front limbs of an animal having four or more limbs.

fore lock (fôr′lok′, fōr′lok′), *n.* lock of hair that grows just above the forehead.

fore man (fôr′mən, fōr′mən), *n., pl.* **-men.** 1 man in charge of a group of workers or of some part of a factory. 2 chairman of a jury, who announces the verdict.

fore mast (fôr′mast′, fōr′mast′; *Nautical* fôr′məst, fōr′məst), *n.* mast nearest the bow of a ship. See **masthead** for picture.

forehand (def. 1) tennis stroke

fore most (fôr′mōst, fōr′mōst), *adj.* 1 first. 2 chief; leading; most notable. *—adv.* 1 first: *He stumbled and fell head foremost.* 2 in the first place; firstly. [Old English *formest;* spelling influenced by *fore*[1] and *most*]

fore name (fôr′nām′, fōr′nām′), *n.* first name.

fore named (fôr′nāmd′, fōr′nāmd′), *adj.* named or mentioned before.

fore noon (fôr′nün′, fōr′nün′), *n.* time between early morning and noon; part of the day from sunrise to noon.

fo ren sic (fə ren′sik), *adj.* of or used in a court of law or in public debate. *—n.* a spoken or written exercise in argumentation. [< Latin *forensis* < *forum* forum] **—fo-ren′si cal ly,** *adv.*

fore or dain (fôr′ôr dān′, fōr′ôr dān′), *v.t.* ordain beforehand; predestine.

fore or di na tion (fôr′ôr də nā′shən, fōr′ôr də nā′shən), *n.* an ordaining beforehand; predestination.

fore part (fôr′pärt′, fōr′pärt′), *n.* the front part; early part.

fore paw (fôr′pô′, fōr′pô′), *n.* a front paw.

fore quar ter (fôr′kwôr′tər, fōr′kwôr′tər), *n.* a front leg, shoulder, and nearby ribs of beef, lamb, pork, etc.

fore reach (fôr rēch′, fōr rēch′), *v.i.* move ahead quickly, as a ship does after coming into the wind. *—v.t.* 1 move ahead of; pass. 2 get the better of.

fore run (fôr run′, fōr run′), *v.t.,* **-ran** (-ran′), **-run, -run ning.** 1 run in front of; precede. 2 be a sign or warning of (something to come); foreshadow. 3 forestall.

fore run ner (fôr′run′ər, fōr′run′ər), *n.* 1 person who is sent ahead to prepare for and announce another's coming; herald; harbinger. 2 sign or warning that something is coming: *Black clouds are forerunners of a storm.* 3 predecessor or ancestor.

fore sail (fôr′sāl′, fōr′sāl′; *Nautical* fôr′səl, fōr′səl), *n.* 1 the principal sail on the foremast of a schooner. 2 the lowest sail on the foremast of a square-rigged ship.

fore saw (fôr sô′, fōr sô′), *v.* pt. of **foresee.**

fore see (fôr sē′, fōr sē′), *v.* **-saw, -seen, -see ing.** *—v.t.* see or know beforehand; anticipate. *—v.i.* use foresight. [Old English *foresēon*] **—fore see′a ble,** *adj.* **—fore-se′er,** *n.*

fore seen (fôr sēn′, fōr sēn′), *v.* pp. of **foresee.**

fore shad ow (fôr shad′ō, fōr shad′ō), *v.t.* indicate beforehand; be a warning of: *Those dark clouds foreshadow a storm.* **—fore-shad′ow er,** *n.*

fore shank (fôr′shangk′, fōr′shangk′), *n.* meat on the upper part of the forelegs of cattle.

fore sheet (fôr′shēt′, fōr′shēt′), *n.* 1 one of the ropes or sheets used to hold a foresail in place. 2 **foresheets,** *pl.* space in the forward part of an open boat.

fore shore (fôr′shôr′, fōr′shōr′), *n.* part of the shore between the high-water mark and low-water mark.

fore short en (fôr shôrt′n, fōr shôrt′n), *v.t.* shorten (lines, objects, etc.) in a drawing or painting in order to give the impression of depth and distance to the eye.

fore show (fôr shō′, fōr shō′), *v.t.,* **-showed, -shown** (-shōn′), **-show ing.** show beforehand; foretell; foreshadow.

fore sight (fôr′sīt′, fōr′sīt′), *n.* 1 power to see or know beforehand what is likely to happen. 2 careful thought for the future; prudence. See **prudence** for synonym study. 3 a looking ahead; view into the future.

fore sight ed (fôr′sī′tid, fōr′sī′tid; fôr′sī′-tid, fōr′sī′tid), *adj.* having or showing foresight. **—fore′sight′ed ly,** *adv.* **—fore′-sight′ed ness,** *n.*

fore skin (fôr′skin′, fōr′skin′), *n.* fold of skin that covers the end of the penis; prepuce.

fo rest (fôr′ist, for′ist), *n.* 1 a large area of land covered with trees; thick woods; woodland. 2 the trees themselves. *—adj.* of or in a forest. *—v.t.* plant with trees; change into a forest. [< Old French < Late Latin *forestis (silva)* outer (woods) < Latin *foris* outside]

fore stage (fôr′stāj′, fōr′stāj′), *n.* area of a theater stage in front of the curtain.

fore stall (fôr stôl′, fōr stôl′), *v.t.* 1 prevent by acting first: *The owner forestalled a strike by starting to negotiate early with the union.* 2 act sooner than; get ahead of: *By settling the deal over the telephone, he had forestalled all his competitors.* [Middle English *forstallen* < Old English *foresteall* prevention] **—fore-stall′er,** *n.*

fo rest a tion (fôr′ə stā′shən, for′ə stā′-shən), *n.* the planting or taking care of forests.

fore stay (fôr′stā′, fōr′stā′), *n.* rope or cable reaching from the top of a ship's foremast to the bowsprit. The forestay helps to support the foremast.

fo rest ed (fôr′ə stid, for′ə stid), *adj.* covered with trees; thickly wooded.

fo rest er (fôr′ə stər, for′ə stər), *n.* 1 person in charge of a forest to guard against fires, look after growing timber, etc. 2 person, bird, animal, etc., that lives in a forest.

fo rest ry (fôr′ə strē, for′ə strē), *n.* 1 science of planting and taking care of forests. 2 management of forest timber.

fore taste (*n.* fôr′tāst′, fōr′tāst′; *v.* fôr-tāst′, fōr tāst′), *n., v.,* **-tast ed, -tast ing.** *—n.* a taste beforehand; anticipation: *The boy got a foretaste of business life by working during his vacation from school.* *—v.t.* taste beforehand; anticipate.

fore tell (fôr tel′, fōr tel′), *v.t.* **-told, -tell ing.** tell or show beforehand; predict; prophesy: *Who can foretell what a baby will do next?* **—fore tell′er,** *n.*

fore thought (fôr′thôt′, fōr′thôt′), *n.* 1 previous thought or consideration; a planning beforehand. 2 careful thought for the future; prudence; foresight: *A little forethought will often save you much trouble afterwards.*

fore to ken (*v.* fôr tō′kən, fōr tō′kən; *n.* fôr′tō′kən, fōr′tō′kən), *v.t.* indicate beforehand; be an omen of. *—n.* indication of something to come; omen.

fore told (fôr tōld′, fōr tōld′), *v.* pt. and pp. of **foretell.**

fore top (fôr′top′, fōr′top′; *Nautical* fôr′təp, fōr′təp), *n.* platform at the top of the bottom section of a foremast.

fore-top gal lant (fôr′top gal′ənt, fōr′top-gal′ənt; *Nautical* fôr′tə gal′ənt, fōr′tə-gal′ənt), *adj.* next above the fore-topmast on the forward mast of a square-rigged ship.

fore-top mast (fôr′top′mast′, fōr′top′-mast′; *Nautical* fôr′top′məst, fōr′top′məst), *n.* mast next above the foremast.

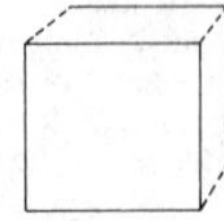

foreshortened—All of the broken lines in the cube are foreshortened.

fore-top sail (fôr′top′sāl′, fōr′top′sāl′; *Nautical* fôr′top′səl, fōr′top′səl), *n.* sail set on the fore-topmast and next above the foresail.

for ev er (fər ev′ər), *adv.* 1 without ever coming to an end; for always; for ever: *Nobody lives forever.* 2 all the time; always; continually: *She is forever telling me that I should take more exercise.*

for ev er more (fər ev′ər môr′, fər ev′ər-mōr′), *adv.* forever.

fore warn (fôr wôrn′, fōr wôrn′), *v.t.* warn beforehand.

fore went (fôr went′, fōr went′), *v.* pt. of **forego.**

fore wing (fôr′wing′, fōr′wing′), *n.* one of the front wings of an insect having four wings.

fore wom an (fôr′wum′ən, fōr′wum′ən), *n., pl.* **-wom en.** 1 woman who supervises a group of workers, as in a factory, etc. 2 chairwoman of a jury.

fore word (fôr′wėrd′, fōr′wėrd′), *n.* a brief introduction or preface to a book, speech, etc. See **introduction** for synonym study.

for feit (fôr′fit), *v.t.* lose or have to give up by one's own act, neglect, or fault: *He forfeited his life by his careless driving.* *—n.* 1 thing lost or given up because of some act, neglect, or fault; penalty; fine. 2 loss or giving up of something as a penalty. *—adj.* lost or given up as a penalty. [< Old French *forfait* a forfeit < *forfaire* transgress, do wrong] **—for′feit a ble,** *adj.* **—for′feit er,** *n.*

for fei ture (fôr′fi chər), *n.* 1 loss by forfeiting. 2 thing forfeited.

for fend (fôr fend′), *v.t.* 1 defend, secure, or protect. 2 ARCHAIC. ward off; avert; prevent. Also, **forefend.**

for gath er (fôr gaᴛʜ′ər), *v.i.* 1 gather together; assemble; meet. 2 meet by accident. 3 be friendly; associate. Also, **foregather.**

for gave (fər gāv′), *v.* pt. of **forgive.**

forge[1] (fôrj, fōrj), *n., v.,* **forged, forg ing.** *—n.* 1 an open fireplace or hearth with a bellows attached, used for heating metal very hot to be hammered into shape. 2 a blacksmith's shop; smithy. 3 place where wrought iron is made directly from the ore. *—v.t.* 1 shape (metal) by heating in a forge and then hammering. 2 make, shape, or form. 3 make or write (something false) to deceive; counterfeit: *forge a passport.* 4 sign (another's name) falsely to deceive. *—v.i.* 1 work at a forge. 2 commit forgery. [< Old French, ultimately < Latin *fabrica* workshop. Doublet of FABRIC.] **—forg′er,** *n.*

forge[2] (fôrj, fōrj), *v.i.,* **forged, forg ing.** move forward slowly but steadily. [origin uncertain]

forg er y (fôr′jər ē, fōr′jər ē), *n., pl.* **-er ies.** 1 act or crime of forging another person's name or making or writing something false. Forgery is punishable by law. 2 something forged: *The painting was a forgery.*

for get (fər get′), *v.,* **-got, -got ten** or **-got, -get ting.** *—v.t.* 1 let go out of the mind; fail to remember: *He forgot the poem which he had memorized.* 2 fail to think of; fail to do, take, notice, etc.: *I forgot to call the dentist. He had forgotten his umbrella.* 3 neglect; disregard; slight. 4 **forget oneself, a** think of others before oneself; be unselfish. **b** forget what one should do or be; say or do something improper. *—v.i.* be forgetful. [Old English *forgietan*] **—for get′ta ble,** *adj.* **—for get′ter,** *n.*

hat, āge, fär; let, ēqual, tėrm;
it, īce; hot, ōpen, ôrder;
oil, out; cup, pu̇t, rüle;
ch, child; ng, long; sh, she;
th, thin; ᴛʜ, then; zh, measure;

ə represents *a* in about, *e* in taken, *i* in pencil, *o* in lemon, *u* in circus.

< = from, derived from, taken from.

for get ful (fər get′fəl), *adj.* 1 apt to forget; having a poor memory. 2 neglectful; heedless. 3 causing to forget. **—for get′ful ly,** *adv.* **—for get′ful ness,** *n.*

for get-me-not (fər get′mē not′), *n.* 1 any of a genus of small plants of the same family as the borage, with hairy stems and curving spikes of small blue, pink, or white flowers. 2 the flower of any of these plants.

forg ing (fôr′jing, fōr′jing), *n.* piece of metal that has been forged.

for give (fər giv′), *v.t.,* **-gave, -giv en, -giv ing.** 1 give up the wish to punish; not have hard feelings at or toward; pardon; excuse: *She forgave her brother for breaking her tennis racket. Please forgive my mistake.* See **excuse** for synonym study. 2 give up all claim to; not demand payment for: *forgive a debt.* [Old English *forgiefan*] **—for giv′a ble,** *adj.* **—for giv′er,** *n.*

for giv en (fər giv′ən), *v.* pp. of **forgive.**

for give ness (fər giv′nis), *n.* 1 act of forgiving; pardon. 2 willingness to forgive.

for giv ing (fər giv′ing), *adj.* that forgives; willing to forgive. **—for giv′ing ly,** *adv.* **—for giv′ing ness,** *n.*

for go (fôr gō′), *v.t.,* **-went, -gone, -go ing.** do without; give up: *forgo the movies to study.* Also, **forego.** [Old English *forgān*]

for gone (fôr gôn′, fôr gon′), *v.* pp. of **forgo.**

for got (fər got′), *v.* a pt. and a pp. of **forget.**

for got ten (fər got′n), *v.* a pp. of **forget.**

fork (fôrk), *n.* 1 implement consisting of a long handle and two or more long, pointed prongs, or tines, used for carrying, lifting, pitching, digging, etc.: *a hay fork, a fork for spreading manure.* 2 instrument with two or more prongs used for holding food, carrying it to the mouth, etc. 3 anything shaped like a fork. 4 the place where a tree, road, or stream divides into branches: *They parted at the fork of the road.* 5 one of the branches into which anything is divided: *Take the right fork of the road.* —*v.t.* 1 lift, throw, dig, etc., with a fork: *fork weeds.* 2 make in the shape or form of a fork. 3 **fork out, fork over,** or **fork up,** SLANG. hand over; pay out. —*v.i.* have a fork or forks; divide into forks: *There is a garage where the road forks.* [Old English *forca* pitchfork < Latin *furca*] **—fork′like′,** *adj.*

forked (fôrkt; *sometimes* fôr′kid), *adj.* 1 having a fork or forks; divided into branches: *a forked stick.* 2 zigzag: *forked lightning.*

fork ful (fôrk′fu̇l), *n., pl.* **-fuls.** as much as a fork will hold.

fork lift, device often attached to one end of a truck or other vehicle, with horizontal metal prongs that can be inserted under a load to lift it or put it down.

for lorn (fôr lôrn′), *adj.* 1 left alone and neglected; deserted; abandoned. 2 wretched in feeling or looks; unhappy. 3 hopeless; desperate. 4 bereft *(of): forlorn of hope.* [Old English *forloren*] **—for lorn′ly,** *adv.* **—for lorn′ness,** *n.*

forlorn hope, 1 a dangerous or desperate enterprise. 2 undertaking almost sure to fail. 3 party of soldiers selected for a very dangerous job. [alteration of Middle Dutch *verloren hoop,* literally, lost troop]

form (fôrm), *n.* 1 appearance apart from color or materials; external shape of anything. See synonym study below. 2 shape of body; body of a person or animal, considered with regard to its shape or external appearance. 3 way in which a thing exists, takes shape, or shows itself; condition; character: *Water appears also in the forms of ice, snow, and steam.* 4 kind; sort; variety: *Heat, light, and electricity are forms of energy.* 5 way of doing something; manner; method: *He is a fast runner, but his form in running is bad.* 6 a set way of doing something: *Shaking hands is a form.* 7 a set or fixed order of words; customary wording. 8 method of procedure or outward behavior prescribed by usage, etiquette, etc.; formality: *It is considered bad form to be a poor loser.* 9 merely outward observance; empty ceremony. 10 document with printing or writing on it and blank spaces to be filled in: *To get a driver's license you must fill out a form.* 11 an orderly arrangement of parts. The effect of a work of literature, art, or music comes from its form as well as its content. 12 thing that gives shape to something; mold. 13 good condition of body or mind: *Athletes exercise to keep in form.* 14 (in grammar) any of the ways in which a word is spelled or pronounced to show its different meanings. *Boys* is the plural form of *boy. Saw* is the past form of *see. My* and *mine* are the possessive forms of *I.* 15 grade in school. 16 a long seat; bench. 17 (in printing) type fastened in a frame ready for printing or making plates. —*v.t.* 1 give shape to; make; fashion: *The cook formed the dough into loaves.* 2 become: *Water forms ice when it freezes.* 3 make up; compose: *Parents and children form a family.* 4 organize; establish: *We formed a club.* 5 develop: *Form good habits while you are young.* 6 arrange in some order: *The soldiers formed themselves into lines.* —*v.i.* 1 be formed; take shape: *Clouds form in the sky.* 2 assume a certain form: *The dancers formed into three groups.* [< Old French *forme* < Latin *forma*]

Syn. *n.* 1 **Form, shape, figure** mean the appearance of something apart from the color or the material of which it consists. **Form** suggests an appearance dependent on a certain distribution and arrangement of parts: *the form of a leaf.* **Shape** suggests both the outline and the bulk of something: *the shape of the head.* **Figure** applies only to the outline of an object: *geometrical figures.*

-form, *suffix forming adjectives.* 1 having the form of ___: *Cruciform = having the form of a cross.* 2 having ___ form or forms: *Multiform = having many forms.* [< Latin *-formis* < *forma* form]

for mal (fôr′məl), *adj.* 1 with strict attention to outward forms and ceremonies; not familiar and homelike; stiff: *a formal greeting.* 2 according to set customs or rules: *a formal invitation.* See synonym study below. 3 done, used, etc., as a formality only; routine. 4 done with the proper forms; clear and definite: *A written contract is a formal agreement to do something.* 5 very regular; symmetrical; orderly. 6 having to do with the form, not the content of a thing: *formal criticism.* 7 (of language) conforming to established convention in grammar, syntax, and pronunciation. 8 essential. —*n.* 1 a formal dance, party, or other affair. 2 gown worn to a formal affair. **—for′mal ly,** *adv.*

Syn. *adj.* 2 **Formal, conventional** mean in keeping with outward and usual forms and rules. **Formal** implies strict attention to prescribed forms and procedures: *A judge has a formal manner in a court of law.* **Conventional** implies paying attention to generally accepted forms and customs of social behavior, and often suggests lack of originality: *She wrote a conventional note of sympathy.*

for mal de hyde (fôr mal′də hīd), *n.* a colorless gas with a sharp, irritating odor, used in a water solution as a disinfectant and preservative. *Formula:* HCHO [< *form(ic acid)* + *aldehyde*]

for ma lin (fôr′mə lən), *n.* solution of formaldehyde in water.

for mal ism (fôr′mə liz′əm), *n.* strict observance of outward forms and ceremonies, especially in religious worship.

for mal ist (fôr′mə list), *n.* person inclined to formalism.

for mal is tic (fôr′mə lis′tik), *adj.* of formalism or formalists. **—for′mal is′ti cal ly,** *adv.*

for mal i ty (fôr mal′ə tē), *n., pl.* **-ties.** 1 procedure required by custom or rule; outward form; ceremony. 2 strict attention to outward forms and customs: *The king received his visitors with much formality.* 3 stiffness of manner, behavior, or arrangement.

for mal ize (fôr′mə līz), *v.,* **-ized, -iz ing.** —*v.t.* 1 make formal. 2 give a definite form to. —*v.i.* be formal. **—for′mal iz′er,** *n.*

for mat (fôr′mat), *n.* 1 shape, size, and general arrangement of a book, magazine, etc. 2 the design, plan, or arrangement of anything: *the format of a television show.* [< French < Latin *(liber) formatus* (book) formed (in a special way)]

for ma tion (fôr mā′shən), *n.* 1 a forming. 2 a being formed. 3 way in which something is formed; arrangement; structure: *The logical formation of his ideas made him a clear lecturer.* 4 thing formed: *Clouds are formations of tiny drops of water in the sky.* 5 an assembling or arrangement of troops in a certain way: *battle formation.* 6 series of layers or deposits of the same kind of rock or mineral.

form a tive (fôr′mə tiv), *adj.* 1 having to do with formation or development; forming; molding: *Home and school are the chief formative influences in a child's life.* 2 used to form words. Words are made from other words by adding formative endings, such as *-ly* and *-ness.* 3 that can produce new cells or tissues: *formative tissue.* **—form′a tive ly,** *adv.* **—form′a tive ness,** *n.*

form class, (in linguistics) a class of words or other forms in a language which share some grammatical feature, as all plural feminine nouns.

for mer[1] (fôr′mər), *adj.* 1 the first mentioned of two: *Canada and the United States are in North America; the former country lies north of the latter.* 2 earlier in time; past; bygone: *In former times, cooking was done in fireplaces instead of stoves.* [Middle English *formere,* a comparative patterned on *formest* foremost]

form er[2] (fôr′mər), *n.* person or thing that forms. [< *form*]

for mer ly (fôr′mər lē), *adv.* at an earlier time; some time ago; previously.

form fit ting (fôrm′fit′ing), *adj.* fitting closely the body's contour; close-fitting.

For mi ca (fôr mī′kə), *n.* trademark for a plastic covering resistant to water, heat, and most chemicals, much used on kitchen and bathroom surfaces, tables and other furniture, etc.

for mic acid (fôr′mik), a colorless, pungent liquid that is irritating to the skin, formerly obtained from ants, spiders, nettles, etc., and now made synthetically for use in dyeing, finishing textiles, etc. *Formula:* HCOOH [< Latin *formica* ant]

for mi da bil i ty (fôr′mə də bil′ə tē), *n.* formidable quality.

for mi da ble (fôr′mə də bəl), *adj.* hard to overcome; hard to deal with; to be dreaded: *a formidable opponent.* [< Latin *formidabilis* < *formidare* to dread < *formido* terror, dread] **—for′mi da ble ness,** *n.* **—for′mi da bly,** *adv.*

form less (fôrm′lis), *adj.* without definite or regular form; shapeless. **—form′less ly,** *adv.* **—form′less ness,** *n.*

form letter, letter so worded that it may be sent to many different people; letter copied from a pattern.

For mo sa (fôr mō′sə), *n.* Taiwan. **—For mo′san,** *adj., n.*

Formosa Strait, strait between Formosa and China. Also, **Taiwan Strait.**

for mu la (fôr′myə lə), *n., pl.* **-las** or **-lae.** 1 a set form of words, especially one which by much use has partly lost its literal meaning: *"How do you do?" is a polite formula.* 2 statement of religious belief or doctrine: *The Apostles' Creed is a formula of Christian faith.* 3 rule for doing something, especially as used by those who do not know the reason on which it is based. 4 recipe or prescription: *a formula for making soap.* 5 mixture, especially one for feeding a baby, made according to a recipe or prescription. 6 expression showing by chemical symbols the composition of a compound: *The formula for water is* H_2O. 7 expression in algebraic symbols of a rule or principle: $(a+b)^2 = a^2 + 2ab + b^2$ *is an algebraic formula.* 8 a definite plan or method: *a formula for settling a strike.* [< Latin, diminutive of *forma* form]

for mu lae (fôr′myə lē), *n.* a pl. of **formula.**

for mu la ic (fôr′myə lā′ik), *adj.* based on or consisting of formulas.

for mu la rize (fôr′myə lə rīz′), *v.t.,* **-rized, -riz ing.** formulate.

for mu lar y (fôr′myə ler′ē), *n., pl.* **-lar ies,** *adj.* *—n.* 1 collection of formulas. 2 a set form of words; formula. 3 (in pharmacy) a book of formulas for standard preparations used in medicines. *—adj.* having to do with formulas.

for mu late (fôr′myə lāt), *v.t.,* **-lat ed, -lat ing.** 1 state definitely or systematically: *A church may formulate its doctrines in a creed.* 2 express in a formula; reduce to a formula. **—for′mu la′tion,** *n.* **—for′mu la′tor,** *n.*

for ni cate (fôr′nə kāt), *v.i.,* **-cat ed, -cat ing.** commit fornication. [ultimately < Latin *fornicem* brothel] **—for′ni ca′tor,** *n.*

for ni ca tion (fôr′nə kā′shən), *n.* sexual intercourse between unmarried persons.

for sake (fôr sāk′), *v.t.,* **-sook, -sak en, -sak ing.** give up; leave alone; leave; abandon. See **desert**[2] for synonym study. [Old English *forsacan* < *for-* away + *sacan* to dispute]

for sak en (fôr sā′kən), *v.* pp. of **forsake.** *—adj.* deserted; abandoned.

for sook (fôr su̇k′), *v.* pt. of **forsake.**

for sooth (fôr süth′), *adv.* ARCHAIC. in truth; indeed. [Old English *forsōth* < *for* for + *sōth* sooth, truth]

For ster (fôr′stər), *n.* **Edward Morgan,** 1879-1969, English novelist.

for swear (fôr swer′, fôr swar′), *v.,* **-swore, -sworn, -swear ing.** *—v.t.* 1 renounce on oath; swear or promise solemnly to give up: *forswear smoking.* 2 deny solemnly or on oath. 3 perjure (oneself). *—v.i.* be untrue to one's sworn word or promise; commit perjury.

for swore (fôr swôr′, fôr swōr′), *v.* pt. of **forswear.**

for sworn (fôr swôrn′, fôr swōrn′), *adj.* untrue to one's sworn word or promise; perjured. *—v.* pp. of **forswear.**

for syth i a (fôr sith′ē ə, fôr sī′thē ə), *n.* 1 any of a genus of shrubs of the olive family, having many bell-shaped, yellow flowers. The flowers appear in early spring before the leaves do. 2 the flower of any of these plants. [< New Latin < William *Forsyth,* 1737-1804, British horticulturist]

fort (fôrt, fōrt), *n.* 1 a strong building or enclosed area that can be defended against attack; fortified place; fortress. 2 **hold the fort,** make a defense. 3 a permanent U.S. Army post. [< Middle French < Latin *fortis* strong]

Fort-de-France (fôr′də fräns′), *n.* capital of Martinique in the W part. 99,000.

forte[1] (fôrt, fōrt), *n.* something a person does very well; strong point: *Cooking is her forte.* [< French, feminine of *fort* strong < Latin *fortis*]

for te[2] (fôr′tā), in music: *—adj.* loud; strong. *—adv.* loudly; strongly. [< Italian, strong < Latin *fortis*]

forth (fôrth, fōrth), *adv.* 1 forward; onward: *From that day forth he lived alone.* 2 into view or consideration; out: *The sun came forth from behind the clouds.* 3 away. 4 **and so forth,** and so on; and the like. [Old English]

Forth (fôrth, fōrth), *n.* 1 **Firth of,** a deep inlet of the North Sea, in SE Scotland. 48 mi. long. 2 **Forth River,** river in central Scotland flowing into the Firth of Forth.

forth com ing (fôrth′kum′ing, fōrth′kum′-ing), *adj.* 1 about to appear; approaching: *The forthcoming week will be busy.* 2 ready when wanted; available: *She needed help, but none was forthcoming.* *—n.* appearance; approach.

forth right (*adj.* fôrth′rīt′, fōrth′rīt′; *adv. also* fôrth′rīt′, fōrth′rīt′), *adj.* frank and outspoken; straightforward; direct. *—adv.* 1 straight ahead; directly forward. 2 at once; immediately. **—forth′right′ly,** *adv.* **—forth′right′ness,** *n.*

forth with (fôrth′with′, fôrth′wiᴛʜ′; fōrth′with′, fōrth′wiᴛʜ′), *adv.* at once; immediately.

for ti eth (fôr′tē ith), *adj., n.* 1 next after the 39th; last in a series of 40. 2 one, or being one, of 40 equal parts.

for ti fi ca tion (fôr′tə fə kā′shən), *n.* 1 a fortifying. 2 thing used in fortifying; fort, wall, ditch, etc. 3 a fortified place. 4 art or science of building military defenses.

for ti fy (fôr′tə fī), *v.,* **-fied, -fy ing.** *—v.t.* 1 strengthen against attack; provide with forts, walls, etc. 2 give support to; strengthen. 3 enrich with vitamins and minerals: *fortify bread.* *—v.i.* build forts, walls, etc.; protect a place against attack. [< Middle French *fortifier* < Late Latin *fortificare* < Latin *fortis* strong + *facere* to make] **—for′ti fi er,** *n.*

for tis si mo (fôr tis′ə mō), in music: *—adj.* very loud. *—adv.* very loudly. [< Italian, superlative of *forte* strong]

for ti tude (fôr′tə tüd, fôr′tə tyüd), *n.* courage in facing pain, danger, or trouble; firmness of spirit. See **patience** for synonym study. [< Latin *fortitudo* strength < *fortis* strong]

Fort Knox, military reservation in N Kentucky, site of the most important United States gold depository.

Fort-La my (fôrt′lä mē′), *n.* capital of Chad, in the S part. 133,000.

Fort Lau der dale (lô′dər dāl), city in SE Florida. 140,000.

fort night (fôrt′nīt, fôrt′nit), *n.* two weeks. [Middle English *fourtenight* fourteen nights]

fort night ly (fôrt′nīt lē), *adv., adj., n., pl.* **-lies.** *—adv.* once in every two weeks. *—adj.* appearing or happening once in every two weeks. *—n.* a periodical published every two weeks.

FOR TRAN (fôr′tran), *n.* a machine language using algebraic notation for programing a computer. [< *FOR(MULA) TRAN(SLATION)*]

for tress (fôr′tris), *n.* a large, permanently fortified place or building; large fort or fortification. [< Old French *forteresse* < *fort* strong < Latin *fortis*]

for tu i tous (fôr tü′ə təs, fôr tyü′ə təs), *adj.* happening by chance; accidental: *a fortuitous meeting.* [< Latin *fortuitus* < *forte* by chance] **—for tu′i tous ly,** *adv.* **—for tu′i tous ness,** *n.*

for tu i ty (fôr tü′ə tē, fôr tyü′ə tē), *n., pl.* **-ties.** 1 fact or condition of being accidental; accidental character. 2 chance or accident.

for tu nate (fôr′chə nit), *adj.* 1 having good luck; lucky. See synonym study below. 2 bringing good luck; having favorable results: *He made a fortunate decision when he went into advertising.* **—for′tu nate ly,** *adv.*

Syn. 1 **Fortunate, lucky** mean having good luck. **Fortunate** suggests being favored by circumstances rather than mere chance: *You are fortunate in having such a fine family.* **Lucky** suggests the idea of pure chance or accident: *He is lucky that he missed his train the day it was wrecked.*

for tune (fôr′chən), *n.* 1 a great deal of money or property; riches; wealth: *He made a fortune in oil.* 2 what happens to a person by chance; luck or chance: *Fortune was against us; we lost.* 3 good luck; prosperity; success. 4 what is going to happen to a person; fate: *Gypsies often claim that they can tell people's fortunes.* [< Latin *fortuna*]

hat, āge, fär; let, ēqual, tėrm;
it, īce; hot, ōpen, ôrder;
oil, out; cup, pu̇t, rüle;
ch, child; ng, long; sh, she;
th, thin; ᴛʜ, then; zh, measure;

ə represents *a* in about, *e* in taken, *i* in pencil, *o* in lemon, *u* in circus.

< = from, derived from, taken from.

fortune hunter, 1 person who tries to get a fortune by marrying someone rich. 2 anybody who seeks wealth.

for tune tell er (fôr′chən tel′ər), *n.* person who claims to be able to tell what is going to happen to people.

for tune tell ing (fôr′chən tel′ing), *n.* a telling or a claiming to tell what will happen in the future. *—adj.* telling or claiming to tell what will happen in the future.

Fort Wayne (wān), city in NE Indiana. 178,000.

Fort Worth (wėrth), city in N Texas. 393,000.

for ty (fôr′tē), *n., pl.* **-ties,** *adj.* four times ten; 40. [Old English *fēowertig*]

for ty-five (fôr′tē fīv′), *n.* a .45 caliber revolver or automatic pistol.

for ty-nin er (fôr′tē nī′nər), *n.* person who went to California in 1849 to seek gold during the gold rush that had started there in 1848.

forty winks, INFORMAL. a short nap.

fo rum (fôr′əm, fōr′əm), *n., pl.* **fo rums, fo ra** (fôr′ə, fōr′ə). 1 the public square or market place of an ancient Roman city, often used for public assemblies, judicial proceedings, etc. 2 assembly for the discussion of questions of public interest. 3 court of law; tribunal. [< Latin]

for ward (fôr′wərd), *adv.* 1 toward the front; onward; ahead: *Forward, march!* See synonym study below. 2 to the front. 3 into view or consideration; out: *In his talk he brought forward several new ideas.* *—adj.* 1 near the front: *the forward part of a ship.* 2 advanced; far ahead: *A child of four years who can read is forward for his age.* 3 ready; eager: *He knew his lesson and was forward with his answers.* 4 impudent; bold. See **bold** for synonym study. 5 directed ahead; onward: *a forward movement.* 6 having to do with the future; prospective: *forward buying of grain.* *—v.t.* 1 help along: *He forwarded his friend's plan.* 2 send on further: *Please forward my mail to my new address.* *—n.* player whose position is in the front line of his team in games such as basketball, hockey, or soccer. [Old English *forweard*] **—for′ward er,** *n.* **—for′ward ly,** *adv.* **—for′ward ness,** *n.*

Syn. *adv.* 1 **Forward, onward** mean toward the front or a point ahead. **Forward** suggests looking or moving toward what lies ahead, or in the future: *We must look forward, not backward.* **Onward** suggests moving or progressing toward a definite point, place, or goal: *The boat sailed onward toward the shore.*

forward pass, (in football) a pass thrown to an eligible receiver in the direction of the opponents' goal.

for wards (fôr′wərdz), *adv.* forward.

for went (fôr went′), *v.* pt. of **forgo.**

fos sa (fos′ə), *n., pl.* **fos sae** (fos′ē). a usually elongated shallow depression or cavity in a bone, etc. [< Latin, ditch]

fosse (fôs, fos), *n.* ditch, trench, or moat. [< Old French < Latin *fossa* ditch]

fos sil (fos′əl), *n.* 1 anything found in the strata of the earth which is recognizable as the hardened remains or traces of an animal or plant of a former geological age. Fossils of ferns are sometimes found in coal. 2 a very old-fashioned person, set in his ways. *—adj.* 1 forming a fossil; of the nature of a fossil: *fossil remains.* 2 dug out of the earth: *fossil fuels.* 3 very old-fashioned; not modern: *fossil ideas.* [< French *fossile* < Latin *fossilis* dug up < *fodere* to dig]

fos sil if er ous (fos′ə lif′ər əs), *adj.* containing fossils.

fos sil ize (fos′ə līz), *v.t., v.i.,* **-ized, -iz ing.** 1 change into a fossil. 2 make or become antiquated, set, stiff, or rigid. **—fos′sil i za′tion,** *n.*

fos ter (fô′stər, fos′tər), *v.t.* 1 help the growth or development of; encourage: *Our city fosters libraries, parks, and playgrounds.* 2 care for fondly; cherish. See **cherish** for synonym study. 3 bring up; help to grow; make grow; rear. *—adj.* in the same family, but not related by birth. A **foster child** is a child brought up by a person or persons who are not his parents. A **foster father, foster mother,** and **foster parent** are persons who bring up the child of another. A **foster brother** or **foster sister** is a boy or girl brought up with another child or children of different parents. [Old English *fōstrian* nourish < *fōster* nourishment. Related to FOOD.] **—fos′ter er,** *n.*

Fos ter (fô′stər, fos′tər), *n.* **Stephen Collins,** 1826-1864, American composer.

fought (fôt), *v.* pt. and pp. of **fight.**

foul (foul), *adj.* 1 containing or covered with filth; very dirty, nasty, or smelly: *foul air.* See **dirty** for synonym study. 2 very wicked; vile: *a foul crime.* 3 offending modesty or decency; obscene; profane: *foul language.* 4 done against the rules; unfair. 5 hitting against: *One boat was foul of the other.* 6 tangled up; caught: *The sailor cut the foul rope.* 7 (of a ship) having the bottom covered with seaweed, barnacles, etc. 8 clogged up: *The fire will not burn because the chimney is foul.* 9 rainy or stormy: *foul weather.* 10 INFORMAL. very unpleasant or objectionable. 11 contrary to the rules of a game or sport; not observing recognized usages, etc.; not fair: *a foul stroke at billiards.* 12 (in baseball) of or having to do with the foul lines or foul balls.

—v.t. 1 make dirty; soil; defile: *Mud fouls things.* 2 dishonor; disgrace: *a name fouled by misdeeds.* 3 make a foul against. 4 hit (a foul ball). 5 hit against: *One boat fouled the other.* 6 get tangled up with; catch: *The rope they threw fouled our anchor chain.* 7 clog up: *Grease fouled the drain.* 8 cover (a ship's bottom) with seaweed, barnacles, etc. *—v.i.* 1 become dirty; soil. 2 make a foul. 3 hit a foul ball. 4 get tangled up; catch: *The anchor fouled on the seaweed.*

—n. 1 (in football, basketball, etc.) an unfair play; thing done contrary to the rules. 2 foul ball. 3 collision or entanglement.

—adv. 1 (in baseball) so that it is foul: *The line drive curved foul at the last minute.* 2 **run foul of, a** hit against and get tangled up with. **b** get into trouble or difficulties with. [Old English *fūl*] **—foul′ly,** *adv.* **—foul′ness,** *n.*

fou lard (fu̇ lärd′), *n.* 1 a soft, lightweight fabric of silk, rayon, or cotton with a printed pattern, used for neckties, dresses, etc. 2 necktie or handkerchief made from this material. [< French]

foul ball, (in baseball) a batted ball that lands outside the foul lines.

foul line, 1 (in baseball) either one of two straight lines extending from home plate through first base and third base to the limits of the playing field. 2 line or mark which may not be stepped on or over in a broad jump, throwing the javelin, etc.

foul mouthed (foul′mouᴛʜd′, foul′moutht′), *adj.* using obscene, profane, or vile language.

foul play, 1 unfair play; thing or things done against the rules. 2 treachery or violence.

foul shot, free throw.

found[1] (found), *v.* pt. and pp. of **find.**

found[2] (found), *v.t.* 1 set up; establish: *The Pilgrims founded a colony at Plymouth.* 2 rest for support; base: *He founded his claim on facts.* [< Old French *fonder* < Latin *fundare* < *fundus* bottom]

found[3] (found), *v.t.* melt and mold (metal); make of molten metal; cast. [< Middle French *fondre* < Latin *fundere*]

foun da tion (foun dā′shən), *n.* 1 part on which the other parts rest for support; base: *the foundation of a house.* See **base**[1] for synonym study. 2 basis: *This report has no foundation in fact.* 3 a founding or establishing. 4 a being founded or established. 5 institution founded and endowed. 6 fund given to support an institution. 7 part on which other parts are overlaid. 8 a woman's corset, girdle, etc., usually having a brassiere attached.

foun da tion al (foun dā′shə nəl), *adj.* of or having to do with a foundation.

foun der[1] (foun′dər), *v.i.* 1 fill with water and sink: *The ship foundered in the storm.* 2 fall down; stumble: *His horse foundered.* 3 break down; fail. *—v.t.* 1 cause to fill with water and sink. 2 cause (a horse) to break down, fall lame, etc. [< Old French *fondrer* < *fond* bottom < Latin *fundus*]

found er[2] (foun′dər), *n.* person who founds or establishes something. [< *found*[2]]

found er[3] (foun′dər), *n.* person who casts metals. [< *found*[3]]

found ling (found′ling), *n.* baby or little child found abandoned.

found ry (foun′drē), *n., pl.* **-ries.** 1 place where metal is melted and molded; place where things are made of molten metal. 2 act of melting and molding metal; making things of molten metal.

fount[1] (fount), *n.* 1 fountain. 2 source; origin. [probably short for *fountain*]

fount[2] (font), *n.* BRITISH. font[2].

foun tain (foun′tən), *n.* 1 water flowing or rising into the air in a spray. 2 pipes through which the water is forced and the basin built to receive it. 3 spring or source of water. 4 place to get a drink: *a water fountain.* 5 source; origin: *Solomon was a fountain of wisdom.* 6 container to hold a steady supply of ink, oil, etc. [< Old French *fontaine* < Late Latin *fontana,* originally feminine of *fontanus* of a spring < Latin *fontem* spring]

foun tain head (foun′tən hed′), *n.* 1 fountain or spring from which a stream flows; source of a stream. 2 an original source of anything.

fountain pen, pen for writing that gives a steady supply of ink from a rubber or plastic tube.

four (fôr, fōr), *n.* 1 one more than three; 4.

2 a set of four persons or things. 3 **on all fours,** **a** on all four feet. **b** on hands and knees. *—adj.* being one more than three. [Old English *fēower*]

four-flush (fôr′flush′, fōr′flush′), *v.i.* SLANG. be a four-flusher; bluff.

four-flush er (fôr′flush′ər, fōr′flush′ər), *n.* SLANG. person who pretends to be more or other than he really is; bluffer. [< a poker term meaning to bluff with a hand having only four cards of a suit, instead of the five necessary to make a flush]

four fold (fôr′fōld′, fōr′fōld′), *adj.* 1 four times as much or as many. 2 having four parts. *—adv.* four times as much or as many.

four-foot ed (fôr′fu̇t′id, fōr′fu̇t′id), *adj.* having four feet; quadruped.

four-hand ed (fôr′han′did, fōr′han′did), *adj.* 1 for four players. 2 (in music) for four hands or two players.

Four-H clubs or **4-H clubs,** a national system of clubs to teach agriculture, community service, home economics, and personality development to children in rural areas. Its aim is the improvement of head, heart, hands, and health.

four hundred, the most fashionable or exclusive social set. [because the social register once listed only *four hundred* names]

four-in-hand (fôr′in hand′, fōr′in hand′), *n.* 1 necktie tied in a slip knot with the ends left hanging. 2 carriage pulled by four horses driven by one person. 3 team of four horses driven by one person.

four-o'clock (fôr′ə klok′, fōr′ə klok′), *n.* 1 a small plant with red, white, or yellow trumpet-shaped flowers that open late in the afternoon and close in the morning. 2 its flower.

four pence (fôr′pəns, fōr′pəns), *n.* 1 four British pennies. 2 a former British silver coin worth four British pennies.

four-post er (fôr′pō′stər, fōr′pō′stər), *n.* bed with four tall corner posts for supporting a canopy or curtains.

four ra gère (fu̇r′ä zher′), *n.* a braided cord worn as part of a uniform, usually looped around the left shoulder. It indicates an award to a unit or a branch of service. [< French]

four score (fôr′skôr′, fōr′skōr′), *adj., n.* four times twenty; 80.

four some (fôr′səm, fōr′səm), *n.* 1 group of four people. 2 (in golf, etc.) a game played by four people, two on each side. 3 the players.

four square (fôr′skwer′, fôr′skwar′; fōr′skwer′, fōr′skwar′), *adj.* 1 square. 2 frank; outspoken. 3 not yielding; firm. *—adv.* 1 in a square form. 2 without yielding; firmly.

four teen (fôr′tēn′, fōr′tēn′), *n., adj.* four more than ten; 14.

four teenth (fôr′tēnth′, fōr′tēnth′), *adj., n.* 1 next after the 13th; last in a series of 14. 2 one, or being one, of 14 equal parts.

fourth (fôrth, fōrth), *adj.* 1 next after the third; last in a series of 4. 2 being one of 4 equal parts; quarter. *—n.* 1 next after the third; last in a series of 4. 2 one of 4 equal parts; quarter. 3 in music: **a** the fourth tone from the keynote of a diatonic scale. **b** interval between such tones. **c** the harmonic combination of such tones.

fourth dimension, dimension in addition to length, width, and thickness. Time has been thought of as a fourth dimension.

fourth estate, newspapers or newspaper workers; the press.

fourth ly (fôrth′lē, fōrth′lē), *adv.* in the fourth place.

Fourth of July, Independence Day.

four-wheel (fôr′hwēl′, fōr′hwēl′), *adj.* having four wheels; running on four wheels.

four-wheeled (fôr′hwēld′, fōr′hwēld′), *adj.* four-wheel.

fo ve a (fō′vē ə), *n., pl.* **-ve ae** (-vē ē′), (in biology) a small, often round depression or pit. Vision is much more acute at the fovea than at other portions of the retina. [< Latin, pit]

fo ve al (fō′vē əl), *adj.* 1 of a fovea. 2 situated in a fovea.

fowl (foul), *n., pl.* **fowls** or **fowl.** 1 any bird. 2 any of several kinds of large birds used for food, such as the chicken, turkey, duck, and goose. 3 a full-grown hen or rooster. 4 flesh of a fowl used for food. *—v.i.* hunt, shoot, catch, or trap wild birds. [Old English *fugol*]

fowl er (fou′lər), *n.* person who hunts, shoots, catches, or traps wild birds.

fowling piece, a lightweight shotgun especially for shooting wild birds.

fox (foks), *n.* 1 any of several wild, carnivorous mammals of the dog family, which are smaller than wolves, have pointed muzzles and bushy tails, and are known for their craftiness. 2 the fur of any of these mammals. 3 a cunning or crafty person. *—v.t.* 1 INFORMAL. trick by being sly and crafty; deceive. 2 discolor; stain. *—v.i.* 1 act slyly and craftily. 2 become discolored or stained. [Old English] **—fox′like′,** *adj.*

Fox (foks), *n., pl.* **Fox** or **Fox es** for 1. 1 member of an Algonquian tribe formerly of Wisconsin but now living mainly in Iowa. 2 **Charles James,** 1749-1806, British statesman and orator. 3 **George,** 1624-1691, English religious leader who founded the Society of Friends about 1650.

fox fire (foks′fīr′), *n.* the phosphorescent light emitted by decaying timber, caused by fungi.

fox glove (foks′gluv′), *n.* 1 any of a genus of plants of the same family as the figwort, with tall spikes of large, drooping, bell-shaped, purple or white flowers; digitalis. 2 the flower of any of these plants.

fox hole (foks′hōl′), *n.* hole in the ground large enough for one or two soldiers, dug for protection against enemy fire.

fox hound (foks′hound′), *n.* any of a breed of large, swift hunting dogs with a keen sense of smell, bred and trained to hunt foxes.

fox tail (foks′tāl′), *n.* 1 tail of a fox. 2 any of various grasses with soft, brushlike spikes of flowers.

fox terrier, any of a breed of small dogs including both smooth and wire-haired varieties, formerly trained to drive foxes from their holes, but now kept mainly as pets.

fox trot, 1 a ballroom dance of American origin in $^{4}/_{4}$ time, characterized by both slow and fast steps. 2 music for it. 3 a gait (of a horse, etc.) between a trot and a walk, made up of short steps.

fox-trot (foks′trot′), *v.i.,* **-trot ted, -trot ting.** dance the fox trot.

fox y (fok′sē), *adj.,* **fox i er, fox i est.** 1 like a fox; sly; crafty. 2 discolored; stained. **—fox′i ly,** *adv.* **—fox′i ness,** *n.*

foy er (foi′ər, foi′ā), *n.* 1 an entrance hall used as a lounging room in a theater, apartment house, or hotel; lobby. 2 an entrance hall. [< French, ultimately < Latin *focus* hearth]

fp, f.p., or **F.P.,** freezing point.

FPC, Federal Power Commission.

fpm or **f.p.m.,** feet per minute.

FPO, (in the U.S. Navy) Fleet Post Office.

fps or **f.p.s.,** 1 feet per second. 2 foot-pound-second.

Fr, francium.

fr., 1 fragment. 2 franc. 3 from.

Fr., 1 Father. 2 France. 3 French. 4 Friar. 5 Friday.

Fra (frä), *n.* Brother. It is used as the title of a monk or friar. [< Italian *fra,* short for *frate* brother < Latin *frater*]

fra cas (frā′kəs), *n.* a noisy quarrel or fight; uproar; brawl. [< French]

frac tion (frak′shən), *n.* 1 ratio of two numbers, shown by a horizontal or diagonal line separating the quantities and representing the division of one number by another: *$^{1}/_{2}$, $^{2}/_{3}$, $^{3}/_{4}$, $^{5}/_{6}$, and $^{7}/_{8}$ are fractions.* 2 a very small part, amount, etc.; fragment. [< Late Latin *fractionem* < Latin *frangere* to break]

frac tion al (frak′shə nəl), *adj.* 1 having to do with fractions. 2 forming a fraction: *440 yards is a fractional part of a mile.* 3 small by comparison; insignificant. 4 (in chemistry) of or designating a method for separating a mixture into its component parts based on certain differences in boiling points, solubility, etc., of these parts: *fractional oxidation.* **—frac′tion al ly,** *adv.*

fractional distillation, (in chemistry) the separation of two or more volatile liquids having different boiling points, by heating them so as to vaporize them successively and collecting the more volatile first.

frac tion ate (frak′shə nāt), *v.t.,* **-at ed, -at ing.** in chemistry: 1 separate (a mixture) by distillation, crystallization, etc., into its ingredients or into portions having different properties. 2 obtain by this process. **—frac′tion a′tion,** *n.* **—frac′tion a′tor,** *n.*

frac tious (frak′shəs), *adj.* 1 easily made angry; cross; fretful; peevish. 2 hard to manage; unruly. [< *fraction* (in obsolete sense of discord, brawling)] **—frac′tious ly,** *adv.* **—frac′tious ness,** *n.*

frac ture (frak′chər), *n., v.,* **-tured, -tur ing.** *—n.* 1 a breaking of a bone or cartilage. 2 a breaking. 3 a being broken. 4 result of breaking; a break; crack. 5 in mineralogy: **a** way in which a mineral breaks. **b** appearance of the surface of a freshly broken mineral. *—v.t.* 1 break; crack. 2 cause a fracture in (a bone, etc.): *The boy fractured his arm.* *—v.i.* undergo fracture; crack. [< Latin *fractura* < *frangere* to break]

frae (frā), SCOTTISH. *—prep.* from. *—adv.* fro.

frag ile (fraj′əl), *adj.* easily broken, damaged, or destroyed; delicate; frail. [< Latin *fragilis,* related to *frangere* to break. Doublet of FRAIL.] **—frag′ile ly,** *adv.*

fra gil i ty (frə jil′ə tē), *n.* fragile quality; delicacy; frailness.

frag ment (*n.* frag′mənt; *v.* frag ment′), *n.* 1 piece of something broken; part broken off. 2 an incomplete or disconnected part: *fragments of a conversation.* 3 part of an incomplete or unfinished work. *—v.t., v.i.* break or divide into fragments. [< Latin *fragmentum* < *frangere* to break]

frag men tal (frag men′tl), *adj.* fragmentary.

frag men tar y (frag′mən ter′ē), *adj.* made up of fragments; incomplete or disconnected: *fragmentary remains of a temple, fragmentary evidence.* **—frag′men tar′i ness,** *n.*

frag men ta tion (frag′mən tā′shən), *n.* process of breaking into many pieces.

fragmentation bomb, a bomb, grenade, etc., that throws bits of metal in all directions as it bursts.

frag ment ize (frag′mən tīz), *v.t.,* **-ized, -iz ing.** break into fragments.

fra grance (frā′grəns), *n.* a sweet smell; pleasing odor; aroma; perfume.

fra grant (frā′grənt), *adj.* having or giving off a pleasing odor; sweet-smelling. [< Latin *fragrantem*] **—fra′grant ly,** *adv.*

frail (frāl), *adj.* 1 slender and not very strong; weak. 2 easily broken or giving way. 3 morally weak; liable to yield to temptation. [< Old French *fraile* < Latin *fragilis* fragile. Doublet of FRAGILE.] **—frail′ly,** *adv.* **—frail′ness,** *n.*

frail ty (frāl′tē), *n., pl.* **-ties.** 1 a being frail; weakness. 2 moral weakness; liability to yield to temptation. 3 fault caused by moral weakness.

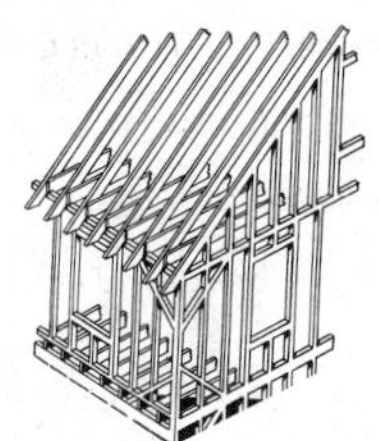

frame (def. 1) part of the frame of a house

frame (frām), *n., v.,* **framed, fram ing.** *—n.* 1 structure which serves as an underlying support or skeleton of something; framework: *the frame of a house.* 2 any structure. 3 body; build of the body: *a man of heavy frame.* 4 skeleton. 5 way in which a thing is put together. 6 an established order; plan; system. 7 shape or form. 8 border in which a thing is set: *a window frame.* 9 one of the individual pictures on a strip of motion-picture film. 10 one image transmitted by television. 11 one turn at bowling. 12 any of ten small squares for recording the score for each turn at bowling. 13 machine constructed on or within a framework.

—v.t. 1 shape or form; fashion: *frame one's life according to a noble pattern.* 2 put together; plan; make: *Thomas Jefferson helped to frame the Constitution.* 3 put a border around; enclose with a frame: *frame a picture.* 4 SLANG. make seem guilty by some false arrangement: *frame an innocent person.* [Old English *framian* to profit < *fram* forth] **—fram′er,** *n.*

frame house, house made of a wooden framework covered with boards.

frame of mind, way one is thinking or feeling; mood.

frame of reference, the standards by which a person compares something to form an attitude, make a judgment or analysis, etc.

frame-up (frām′up′), *n.* INFORMAL. 1 a secret and dishonest arrangement made beforehand. 2 arrangement made to have a person falsely accused.

frame work (frām′wėrk′), *n.* 1 support or skeleton; stiff part that gives shape to a thing: *A bridge often has a steel framework.* 2 way in which a thing is put together; structure or system.

fram ing (frā′ming), *n.* 1 frame or system of frames. 2 way in which a thing is put together.

franc (frangk), *n.* 1 the monetary unit of various European and African countries. The French franc is worth about $19\frac{1}{2}$ cents, the Belgian franc about $2\frac{1}{4}$ cents, and the Swiss franc about 26 cents. 2 coin or note worth one franc. [< Old French < Latin *Francorum Rex* king of the Franks, on early coins]

France (frans, fräns), *n.* 1 country in W Europe. 51,200,000 pop.; 213,000 sq. mi. *Capital:* Paris. 2 **Anatole,** 1844-1924, French author.

fran chise (fran′chīz), *n., v.,* **-chised, -chis ing.** *—n.* 1 privilege or right granted by a government to an individual or individuals: *The city granted the company a franchise to operate buses in the city.* 2 right to vote: *The United States gave women the franchise in 1920.* 3 privilege of selling the products of a manufacturer in a given area. *—v.t.* grant a franchise to. [< Old French < *franc* free. See FRANK[1].] **—fran′chis er,** *n.*

fran chis ee (fran′chī zē′), *n.* person who holds a franchise.

Fran cis (fran′sis), *n.* **Saint,** *(Saint Francis of Assisi),* 1181?-1226, Italian founder of the Franciscan order of friars.

Francis I, 1 1494-1547, king of France from 1515 to 1547. 2 title of Francis II as emperor of Austria.

Francis II, 1768-1835, last emperor of the Holy Roman Empire, from 1792 to 1806. As Francis I, he was the first emperor of Austria, from 1804 to 1835.

Fran cis can (fran sis′kən), *adj.* of Saint Francis of Assisi or the religious order founded by him in 1209. *—n.* friar belonging to the Franciscan order.

Francis Ferdinand, 1863-1914, archduke of Austria whose assassination at Sarajevo contributed to the outbreak of World War I.

Francis Joseph I, 1830-1916, emperor of Austria from 1848 to 1916, also king of Hungary and Bohemia.

fran ci um (fran′sē əm), *n.* a radioactive metallic element produced artificially from actinium or thorium. *Symbol:* Fr; *atomic number* 87. See pages 326 and 327 for table. [< New Latin < *France*]

Franck (frängk), *n.* **César,** 1822-1890, French composer, born in Belgium.

Fran co (frang′kō), *n.* **Francisco,** born 1892, Spanish general, ruler of Spain since 1936.

Franco-, *combining form.* 1 of France; of the French: *Francophile = friend of France or the French.* 2 French and ___: *Franco-German = French and German.* [< Medieval Latin *Francus* Frank, French]

fran co lin (frang′kə lən), *n.* any of several genera of partridges found in Africa, Asia, and southern Europe whose meat is considered a great delicacy. [< French]

Fran co ni a (frang kō′nē ə), *n.* 1 a former duchy of S Germany. 2 district of West Germany in N Bavaria.

Fran co phile (frang′kə fīl, frang′kə fil), *adj.* friendly to the French or to France. *—n.* person friendly to the French or to France.

fran gi bil i ty (fran′jə bil′ə tē), *n.* quality or condition of being frangible.

fran gi ble (fran′jə bəl), *adj.* breakable. [< French < Medieval Latin *frangibilis* < Latin *frangere* to break]

fran gi pan i (fran′jə pan′ē), *n.* 1 perfume made from, or imitating the odor of, the flower of the red jasmine. 2 red jasmine. [< French *frangipane*]

frank[1] (frangk), *adj.* 1 free in expressing one's real thoughts, opinions, and feelings; not hiding what is in one's mind; open. See synonym study below. 2 clearly manifest; undisguised; plain: *frank mutiny.* *—v.t.* 1 send (a letter, package, etc.) without charge. 2 mark (a letter, package, etc.) for free mailing. *—n.* 1 mark to show that a letter, package, etc., is to be sent without charge. 2 right to send letters, packages, etc., without charge. [< Old French *franc* free, sincere (originally, a Frank) < Germanic] **—frank′ly,** *adv.* **—frank′ness,** *n.*

Syn. *adj.* 1 **Frank, outspoken, candid** mean not afraid to say what one thinks or feels. **Frank** suggests expressing oneself openly, hiding or keeping back nothing: *He was frank to admit that he had not studied the lesson carefully.* **Outspoken** suggests being ready or even eager to speak out, often bluntly: *He was outspoken in his criticism.* **Candid** suggests being unwilling to conceal the truth, however unpleasant it may be: *He was candid about his best friend's dishonesty.*

frank[2] (frangk), *n.* INFORMAL. frankfurter.

Frank (frangk), *n.* member of a group of West Germanic tribes that conquered Gaul in the A.D. 500's.

Frank en stein (frang′kən stīn), *n.* 1 student of medicine in a novel by Mary Shelley, who creates a monster that he cannot control. 2 the monster itself. 3 anything that causes the ruin of its creator.

Frank fort (frangk′fərt), *n.* 1 capital of Kentucky, in the N part. 22,000. 2 Frankfurt am Main.

Frankfort on the Main (mān), Frankfurt am Main.

Frank furt (frangk′fərt, frängk′fůrt), *n.* Frankfurt am Main.

Frankfurt am Main (frängk′fůrt äm mīn′), city in central West Germany. 691,000.

frank furt er (frangk′fər tər), *n.* a reddish smoked sausage made of beef and pork, or of beef alone; wiener. Frankfurters in rolls are called hot dogs. [< German *Frankfurter* of or from Frankfurt]

frank in cense (frang′kən sens), *n.* a fragrant gum resin from certain Asian or African trees of the same family as myrrh. It gives off a sweet, spicy odor when burned. [< Old French *franc encens* pure incense]

Frank ish (frang′kish), *adj.* of or having to do with the Franks. *—n.* the language of the Franks (def. 1).

frank lin (frang′klən), *n.* in England: **a** a freeholder. **b** (in the 1300's and 1400's) a landowner of free birth who ranked next below the gentry. [Middle English *francoleyn,* ultimately < Medieval Latin *francus* free]

Frank lin (frang′klən), *n.* 1 **Benjamin,** 1706-1790, American statesman, author, scientist, printer, and inventor. 2 district in N canada that includes Baffin Island and several arctic peninsulas and islands.

hat, āge, fär; let, ēqual, tėrm;
it, īce; hot, ōpen, ôrder;
oil, out; cup, pův, rüle;
ch, child; ng, long; sh, she;
th, thin; ᴛʜ, then; zh, measure;

ə represents *a* in about, *e* in taken, *i* in pencil, *o* in lemon, *u* in circus.

< = from, derived from, taken from.

Franklin stove, U.S. stove for heating a room, resembling an iron fireplace, devised by Benjamin Franklin.

fran tic (fran′tik), *adj.* very much excited; wild with rage, fear, pain, grief, etc. [< Old French *frenetique* < Latin *phreneticus* < Greek *phrenitikos* < *phrenitis* inflammation of the brain, frenzy < *phrēn* mind] —**fran′ti cal ly, fran′tic ly,** *adv.* —**fran′tic ness,** *n.*

frappe (frap), *n.* 1 a flavored milk drink into which ice cream has been beaten. 2 frappé.

frap pé (fra pā′), *adj., n., pl.* **-pés.** U.S. —*adj.* iced; cooled. —*n.* 1 fruit juice sweetened and partially frozen or shaken with finely cracked ice. 2 any frozen or iced food or drink. [< French, chilled, beaten]

Fra ser River (frā′zər), river in SW British Columbia, Canada, flowing into the Pacific. 695 mi.

fra ter nal (frə tėr′nl), *adj.* 1 of or having to do with brothers or a brother; brotherly. 2 having to do with a fraternal order. 3 having to do with fraternal twins. [< Medieval Latin *fraternalis* < Latin *fraternus* brotherly < *frater* brother] —**fra ter′nal ly,** *adv.*

fra ter nal ism (frə tėr′nl iz′əm), *n.* condition or character of being fraternal.

fraternal twins, twins of the same or opposite sex coming from two separately fertilized egg cells rather than from one egg cell as identical twins do.

fra ter ni ty (frə tėr′nə tē), *n., pl.* **-ties.** 1 group of men or boys joined together for fellowship or for some other purpose. There are student fraternities in many American colleges. 2 group having the same interests, kind of work, etc. 3 fraternal feeling.

frat er nize (frat′ər nīz), *v.i.,* **-nized, -niz ing.** 1 associate in a brotherly way; be friendly. 2 associate in a friendly way with the citizens of a hostile nation during occupation of their territory. —**frat′er ni za′tion,** *n.* —**frat′er niz′er,** *n.*

frat ri cid al (frat′rə sī′dl, frā′trə sī′dl), *adj.* 1 having to do with fratricide. 2 having to do with the killing of relatives or fellow citizens: *A civil war is a fratricidal struggle.*

frat ri cide (frat′rə sīd, frā′trə sīd), *n.* 1 act of killing one's own brother or sister. 2 person who kills his own brother or sister.

Frau (frou), *n., pl.* ***Frau en*** (frou′ən), GERMAN. 1 Mrs. 2 wife.

fraud (frôd), *n.* 1 dishonest dealing; trickery; cheating: *obtain a prize by fraud.* 2 (in law) any deliberate misrepresentation of the truth or a fact used to take money, rights, etc., away from a person or persons. 3 a dishonest act, statement, etc.; something which is not what it seems to be; trick. 4 INFORMAL. impostor. [< Old French *fraude* < Latin *fraudem*]

fraud u lence (frô′jə ləns, frô′dyə ləns), *n.* a being fraudulent.

fraud u len cy (frô′jə lən sē, frô′dyə lən-sē), *n., pl.* **-cies.** fraudulence.

fraud u lent (frô′jə lənt, frô′dyə lənt), *adj.* 1 guilty of fraud; cheating; dishonest. 2 intended to deceive: *a fraudulent offer.* 3 done by fraud; obtained by trickery. —**fraud′u lent ly,** *adv.*

fraught (frôt), *adj.* loaded or filled *(with): The attempt to climb Mount Everest was fraught with danger.* [originally past participle of obsolete *fraught* to load < *fraught* a load, freight < Middle Dutch or Middle Low German *vracht* freight]

Fräu lein (froi′līn), *n., pl.* **-lein.** GERMAN. 1 Miss. 2 an unmarried woman; young lady.

Fraun ho fer lines (froun′hō′fər), dark lines in the solar spectrum caused by the absorption of some of the light by gaseous elements. [< Joseph von *Fraunhofer,* 1787-1826, German optician and physicist]

fray[1] (frā), *v.t.* 1 cause to separate into threads; make ragged or worn along the edge. 2 wear away; rub. —*v.i.* become frayed; ravel out or wear through. [< Middle French *frayer* < Latin *fricare* to rub]

fray[2] (frā), *n.* a noisy quarrel; brawl. [variant of *affray*]

fraz zle (fraz′əl), *v.,* **-zled, -zling,** *n.* —*v.t., v.i.* 1 wear to shreds; fray; ravel. 2 tire out; weary. —*n.* INFORMAL. a frazzled condition. [perhaps blend of *fray*[1] and obsolete *fazle* tangle]

FRB or **F.R.B.,** Federal Reserve Board.

freak (frēk), *n.* 1 something very queer or unusual: *A green leaf growing in the middle of a rose would be called a freak of nature.* 2 animal, plant, or person that has developed abnormally: *A circus often has a sideshow of freaks.* 3 a sudden change of mind without reason; odd notion or fancy. —*adj.* very queer or unusual. —*v.i.* **freak out,** SLANG. **a** be under the influence of a drug that distorts reality, such as LSD. **b** break away from the bounds of convention. [origin uncertain]

freak ish (frē′kish), *adj.* full of freaks; very queer or unusual. —**freak′ish ly,** *adv.* —**freak′ish ness,** *n.*

freak out (frēk′out′), *n.* SLANG. a being under the influence of a drug that distorts reality, such as LSD.

freck le (frek′əl), *n., v.,* **-led, -ling.** —*n.* a small, light-brown spot on the skin, often caused by exposure to the sun. —*v.t.* make freckles on; cover with freckles. —*v.i.* become marked or spotted with freckles. [Middle English *frakles* freckles, variant of *fraknes* < Scandinavian (Old Icelandic) *freknur*]

freck led (frek′əld), *adj.* marked with freckles.

freck ly (frek′lē), *adj.* covered with freckles.

Fred er ick I (fred′ər ik), 1 Frederick Barbarossa. 2 1657-1713, king of Prussia from 1701 to 1713.

Frederick II, 1 1194-1250, German king who was emperor of the Holy Roman Empire from 1220 to 1250 and also king of Sicily. 2 Frederick the Great.

Frederick IX, 1899-1972, king of Denmark from 1947 to 1972.

Frederick Bar ba ros sa (bär′bə ros′ə), 1123?-1190, Frederick I, German king who was emperor of the Holy Roman Empire from 1155 to 1190.

Fred er icks burg (fred′riks bėrg′), *n.* city in NE Virginia, where the Confederate army under General Robert E. Lee defeated the Union army in 1862. 14,000.

Frederick the Great, 1712-1786, third king of Prussia, from 1740 to 1786; Frederick II.

Frederick William, 1620-1688, elector of Brandenburg from 1640 to 1688. He helped make Prussia a strong state.

Fred er ic ton (fred′rik tən), *n.* capital of New Brunswick, in SE Canada. 39,000.

free (frē), *adj.,* **fre er, fre est,** *adv., v.,* **freed, free ing.** —*adj.* 1 not under another's control; not a captive or slave; having liberty; able to do, act, or think as one pleases. 2 showing liberty; caused by liberty: *free speech.* 3 not held back, fastened, or shut up; released; loose: *free to come and go.* 4 not hindered: *a free step.* 5 clear; open: *water having a free passage.* 6 without cost or payment: *These tickets are free.* 7 without paying a tax, toll, or duty: *free importation of goods.* 8 exempt from trade restrictions; open to all traders: *a free port.* 9 exempt or immune from, or not subject to, something harmful or undesirable: *free from difficulty, air free of dust.* 10 done, given, or made willingly or spontaneously: *He made him a free offer of his services.* 11 abundant: *a rose that is a free bloomer.* 12 not following rules, forms, or words exactly; not strict: *a free translation.* 13 saying what one thinks; frank: *He is too free with criticism.* 14 not restrained enough by manners or morals. 15 not combined with something else: *Oxygen exists free in air.*

free and easy, paying little attention to rules and customs.

free from or **free of,** without; having no; lacking.

free with, giving or using freely; generous, liberal, or lavish with: *free with one's money.*

make free with, use as if one owned or had complete rights.

—*adv.* 1 without cost or payment: *Children under 12 can attend free.* 2 in a free manner; freely.

—*v.t.* 1 make free; liberate. 2 let loose; release. See **release** for synonym study. 3 clear, disengage, or disentangle: *free a gas of impurities, free oneself of a charge.*

[Old English *frēo*] —**free′ly,** *adv.* —**free′ness,** *n.*

free association, a linkage or sequence of ideas, one suggesting another regardless of logical connection.

free board (frē′bôrd′, frē′bōrd′), *n.* the vertical distance, or the surface of the hull, between the water line and the deck or gunwale of a ship.

free boot er (frē′bü′tər), *n.* pirate; buccaneer. [< Dutch *vrijbuiter* < *vrij* free + *buit* booty]

free boot ing (frē′bü′ting), *n.* piracy; buccaneering.

free born (frē′bôrn′), *adj.* 1 born free, not in slavery. 2 of or suitable for people born free.

free city, city having an independent government and forming a sovereign state.

freed man (frēd′mən), *n., pl.* **-men.** man freed from slavery.

free dom (frē′dəm), *n.* 1 condition of being free. 2 power to do, say, or think as one pleases; liberty: *freedom of religion, political freedom.* See synonym study below. 3 free use: *We gave our guest the freedom of the house.* 4 too great liberty; lack of restraint. 5 ease of movement or action. 6 exemption or release from unfavorable or undesirable conditions: *freedom from fear.* 7 a special immunity or privilege possessed by a city, corporation, etc.

Syn. 2 **Freedom, liberty** mean being able to act without interference or control by another. **Freedom** emphasizes the power to exercise rights, powers, and the like: *Every person should have the freedom to worship God as he chooses.* **Liberty** emphasizes absence of external restraint and compulsion on an individual: *Freedom of speech does not mean liberty to gossip or tell lies.*

freedom fighter, person who bears arms against or otherwise actively opposes a dictatorial government.

freedom ride, U.S. a bus ride taken by a group of Negroes and whites across southern states to challenge racial segregation in interstate public travel. **—freedom rider.**

free electron, electron that is detached from an atom and can therefore move from atom to atom, as in a conductor of electricity or heat.

free enterprise, the right of private business to select and operate undertakings for profit with little control or regulation by the government; private enterprise.

free fall, 1 the motion of a body in flight through space when it is not acted upon by any force except the gravity of planetary bodies. A body is weightless during free fall. 2 the part of a parachute jump before a parachute is opened.

free flight, the flight of a rocket, missile, etc., after thrust has terminated.

free-float ing (frē′flō′ting), *adj.* 1 floating or moving without an attachment: *a free-floating astronaut.* 2 not established; unfounded; unproven: *a free-floating theory.* 3 not bound or committed; independent.

free-for-all (frē′fər ôl′), *n.* fight, race, etc., open to all or in which everybody participates.

free form, a linguistic form which occurs alone or independently, as distinguished from a bound form. EXAMPLES: *cold, street, eaten.*

free hand (frē′hand′), *adj.* done by hand without using instruments, measurements, etc.: *freehand drawing.*

free hand ed (frē′han′did), *adj.* generous; liberal.

free hold (frē′hōld′), *n.* 1 piece of land held for life or with the right to transfer it to one's heirs. 2 the holding of land in this way.

free hold er (frē′hōl′dər), *n.* person who has a freehold.

free lance, 1 writer, artist, etc., who sells his work to anyone who will buy it. 2 soldier in the Middle Ages who fought for any person, group, or state that would pay him.

free-lance (frē′lans′), *v.,* **-lanced, -lanc ing,** *adj.* —*v.i.* work as a free lance. —*adj.* of, having to do with, or done by a free lance. **—free′-lanc′er,** *n.*

free-liv ing (frē′liv′ing), *adj.* 1 living in a free or unrestrained manner. 2 in biology: **a** living free from and independent of a host; not parasitic. **b** able to live and move about independently; not sessile.

free load (frē′lōd′), *v.i.* INFORMAL. get something at another's expense, such as a free trip, tickets, accommodations, food, etc. **—free′load′er,** *n.*

free man (frē′mən), *n., pl.* **-men.** 1 person who is not a slave or a serf. 2 person who has civil or political freedom; citizen.

free market, an economic market in which prices are controlled by supply and demand, without governmental regulation or restriction.

Free ma son (frē′mā′sn), *n.* member of a worldwide secret society (the Free and Accepted Masons), whose purpose is mutual aid and fellowship; Mason.

Free ma son ry (frē′mā′sn rē), *n.* 1 principles or doctrines of the society of Freemasons; Masonry. 2 members of this society. 3 **freemasonry,** common understanding and sympathy based on similar experiences.

free on board, (of goods, etc.) placed on a freight car, truck, or other means of transportation at a point specified by the seller, without charge to the buyer, but with all further transportation being at the buyer's expense.

free press, the publishing of newspapers and magazines without censorship or control by the government.

free radical, (in chemistry) an organic compound in which some of the valence electrons are not paired.

free sia (frē′zhə), *n.* any of a genus of South African plants of the same family as the iris, grown for their clusters of fragrant white, rose, salmon, or yellow flowers. Freesias are grown from bulbs. [< New Latin < F. H. T. *Freese,* 1795?-1876, German botanist]

free silver, the free coinage of silver, especially at a fixed 16-to-1 ratio with gold; making silver into coins for anybody who brings it to the mint.

free soil, U.S. (before the Civil War) territory in which slaveholding was prohibited.

Free-Soil Party (frē′soil′), an American political party that was opposed to extending slavery into territories not yet admitted as states. It existed from 1848 to 1856.

free-spo ken (frē′spō′kən), *adj.* speaking freely; saying what one thinks; frank.

free stand ing (frē′stan′ding), *adj.* standing or able to stand without supports or attachments: *a freestanding building.*

Free State, U.S. (before the Civil War) any state in which slavery did not exist.

free stone (frē′stōn′), *n.* 1 stone, such as limestone or sandstone, that can easily be cut without splitting. 2 fruit having a stone that is easily separated from the pulp. Certain kinds of peaches and plums are freestones. 3 stone of such a fruit.

free style (frē′stīl′), *adj.* unrestricted as to style, method, or manner: *a freestyle swimmer.* —*n.* a freestyle race or figure-skating contest.

free-swing ing (frē′swing′ing), *adj.* 1 suspended or mounted so as to swing without hindrance, as a pendulum. 2 unrestrained, as by caution or tact.

free think er (frē′thing′kər), *n.* person who forms his opinions, especially on religion, independently of authority or tradition.

free throw, (in basketball) an unhindered shot from about 15 feet away from the basket, awarded to a player fouled by a member of the opposing team, and worth one point; foul shot.

Free town (frē′toun), *n.* seaport and capital of Sierra Leone, in the W part. 171,000.

free trade, international trade free from protective duties and subject only to tariff for revenue.

free trad er (frē′trā′dər), *n.* person who favors the system of free trade.

free verse, poetry not restricted by the usual conventions of meter, rhyme, etc., and often emphasizing variation of cadence and rhythm.

free way (frē′wā′), *n.* a high-speed highway on which no tolls are charged.

free wheel er (frē′hwē′lər), *n.* a freewheeling person.

free wheel ing (frē′hwē′ling), *adj.* 1 (of a car, bicycle, etc.) coasting freely. 2 acting freely or without restraint.

free will (frē′wil′), *adj.* of one's own accord; voluntary: *a freewill offering.*

free will, will free from outside restraints; voluntary choice; freedom of decision.

free world or **Free World,** the nations of the world that are not under communist control.

hat, āge, fär; let, ēqual, tėrm;
it, īce; hot, ōpen, ôrder;
oil, out; cup, pu̇t, rüle;
ch, child; ng, long; sh, she;
th, thin; ᴛʜ, then; zh, measure;

ə represents *a* in about, *e* in taken,
i in pencil, *o* in lemon, *u* in circus.

< = from, derived from, taken from.

freeze (frēz), *v.,* **froze, fro zen, freez ing,** *n.* —*v.i.* 1 harden by cold; turn into a solid by removal of heat. Water becomes ice when it freezes. 2 become very cold: *The weather suddenly froze.* 3 be killed or injured by frost. 4 become covered or clogged with ice: *The pipes froze.* 5 become fixed to something by freezing. 6 become stiff and unfriendly: *At my question he immediately froze.* 7 be chilled with fear, etc.: *She froze at the sight of the ghostly hand.* 8 become motionless. —*v.t.* 1 harden by cold; turn into ice: *freeze ice cream.* 2 make very cold; chill: *The north wind froze the spectators.* 3 kill or injure by frost. 4 cover or clog with ice. 5 fix to something by freezing; set fast in ice. 6 make stiff and unfriendly. 7 chill with fear, etc.: *The howling of the wolves froze him with terror.* 8 fix (prices, wages, rents, etc.) at a definite level, usually by governmental decree. 9 make (funds, bank balances, etc., of foreign ownership) unusable and inaccessible by governmental decree. 10 (in medicine) to chill (a part of the body) until anesthetized. 11 **freeze on to,** INFORMAL. hold on tightly to; become attached to; take to. 12 **freeze out,** INFORMAL. force out; exclude. —*n.* 1 a freezing. 2 a being frozen. 3 period during which there is freezing weather. [Old English *frēosan*]

freeze-dry (frēz′drī′), *v.t.,* **-dried, -dry ing.** dehydrate by freezing the moisture content to ice and evaporating the ice by subjecting it to microwaves in a vacuum. Freeze-dried substances keep without refrigeration.

freez er (frē′zər), *n.* 1 machine to freeze ice cream. 2 a refrigerator cabinet for freezing foods or storing frozen foods. 3 anything that freezes.

freezing point, temperature at which a liquid freezes. The freezing point of water at sea level is 32 degrees Fahrenheit or 0 degrees centigrade.

F region, region of the ionosphere above the E region, which reflects high-frequency radio waves; F layer. See **atmosphere** for diagram.

Frei burg (frī′bėrg′; *German* frī′bu̇rk), *n.* city in S West Germany. 166,000.

freight (frāt), *n.* 1 load of goods carried on a train, truck, ship, or aircraft. 2 the carrying of goods on a train, ship, aircraft, or truck. 3 charge for this. 4 train or ship for carrying goods. 5 load; burden. —*v.t.* 1 load with freight. 2 carry as freight. 3 send as freight. 4 load; burden; oppress. [< Middle Dutch or Middle Low German *vrecht*]

freight age (frā′tij), *n.* 1 the carrying of goods on a train, truck, ship, or aircraft. 2 charge for this. 3 the load carried; freight.

freight car, a railroad car for carrying freight.

freight er (frā′tər), *n.* ship or aircraft that carries mainly freight.

freight lin er (frāt′lī′nər), *n.* BRITISH. an express freight train.

freight train, a railroad train of freight cars; freight.

Fre mont (frē′mont), *n.* city in W California. 101,000.

Fré mont (frē′mont), *n.* **John Charles,** 1813-1890, American explorer, general, and political leader.

French (french), *adj.* of or having to do with France, its people, or their language. *—n.* 1 *pl. in use.* the people of France. 2 their Romance language. 3 **Daniel Chester,** 1850-1931, American sculptor. [Old English *Francisc* < *Franca* Frank]

French and Indian War, war between Great Britain and France, fought in North America from 1754 to 1763. The French were greatly aided by Indian allies.

French Canada, the part of Canada inhabited mainly by French Canadians, especially the province of Quebec.

French Canadian, 1 Canadian whose ancestors came from France. 2 of or having to do with French Canadians.

French Community, association formed in 1958 that includes France, her overseas territories, and many of her former colonies.

French doors, pair of doors hinged at the sides and opening in the middle. They have panes of glass like a window.

French dressing, a salad dressing made of olive oil, vinegar, salt, spices, etc.

French Equatorial Africa, former French colony comprising the present countries of Central African Republic, Chad, Congo, and Gabon.

French fries, potatoes cut into thin strips and fried in deep fat until crisp on the outside.

French-fry (french′frī′), *v.t.,* **-fried, -fry ing.** fry in deep fat.

French Guiana, French territory in N South America. 44,000 pop.; 35,100 sq. mi. *Capital:* Cayenne.

French Guinea, former French colony in W Africa, now the country of Guinea.

French horn, a brass wind instrument that has a mellow tone.

French i fy (fren′chə fī), *v.t.,* **-fied, -fy ing.** make French or like the French.

French India, former French possessions, now part of India.

French Indochina, former French territory in SE Asia, south of China, comprising the present countries of Cambodia, Laos, North Vietnam, and South Vietnam.

French leave, act of leaving without ceremony, permission, or notice; secret or hurried departure.

French man (french′mən), *n., pl.* **-men.** native or inhabitant of France.

French Oceania, former name of **French Polynesia.**

French Polynesia, overseas territory of France in the E part of the South Pacific, including the Society Islands, Marquesas Islands, and other island groups. 116,000 pop.; 1500 sq. mi. *Capital:* Papeete.

French Revolution, revolution in France from 1789 to 1799 which ousted the monarchy and set up a republic.

French Somaliland, former name of **Afars and Issas.**

French Sudan, former French colony in NW Africa, now the country of Mali.

French toast, slices of bread dipped in a mixture of egg and milk and then fried in a small quantity of fat.

French West Africa, former federation of French colonies comprising the present countries of Guinea, Dahomey, Ivory Coast, Mali, Mauritania, Niger, Senegal, and Upper Volta.

French West Indies, group of French islands in the West Indies. They include Guadeloupe, Martinique, and lesser islands. 699,000 pop.; 1100 sq. mi.

French windows, pair of long windows like doors, hinged at the sides and opening in the middle.

French wom an (french′wu̇m′ən), *n., pl.* **-wom en.** woman who is a native or inhabitant of France.

fre net ic (frə net′ik), *adj.* 1 excessively excited; frenzied. 2 insane. Also, **phrenetic.** [variant of *frantic*] **—fre net′i cal ly,** *adv.*

fren zied (fren′zēd), *adj.* greatly excited; frantic. **—fren′zied ly,** *adv.*

fren zy (fren′zē), *n., pl.* **-zies,** *v.,* **-zied, -zy ing.** *—n.* 1 state of near madness; frantic condition. 2 condition of very great excitement. *—v.t.* drive (a person) to frenzy. [< Old French *frenesie* < Latin *phrenesis,* ultimately < Greek *phrēn* mind]

Fre on (frē′on), *n.* trademark for any of a group of nearly odorless, colorless, gaseous carbon compounds, each of which has one or more atoms of fluorine, used as a refrigerant, aerosol propellant, solvent, and fire-extinguishing agent.

freq., 1 frequent. 2 frequentative. 3 frequently.

fre quence (frē′kwəns), *n.* frequency.

French horn—
It has three
valves for
changing pitch.

fre quen cy (frē′kwən sē), *n., pl.* **-cies.** 1 rate of occurrence: *The flashes of light came with a frequency of three per minute.* 2 a frequent occurrence: *The frequency of his visits began to annoy us.* 3 in physics: **a** the number of times that any regularly repeated event, as a vibration, occurs in a given unit of time. **b** number of complete cycles per second of an alternating current or other electric wave. Different radio and television stations broadcast at different frequencies so that their signals can be received distinctly. 4 (in statistics) the number of cases of the data under consideration falling within a particular class interval.

frequency distribution, in statistics: 1 an arrangement of data to show the number of times an event occurs in a particular way. 2 table or graph depicting such an arrangement.

frequency modulation, 1 a deliberate modulation of the frequency of the transmitting wave in broadcasting in order to agree with the changes in the sounds or images being transmitted. Frequency modulation reduces static. 2 a broadcasting system, relatively free of static, using this method of modulation.

fre quent (*adj.* frē′kwənt; *v.* fri kwent′, frē′kwənt), *adj.* 1 occurring often, near together, or every little while: *In my part of the country storms are frequent in March.* 2 that does a thing often; regular; habitual: *He is a frequent caller at our house.* *—v.t.* go often to; be often in: *Frogs frequent ponds, streams, and marshes.* [< Latin *frequentem*] **—fre quent′er,** *n.*

fre quen ta tive (fri kwen′tə tiv), *adj.* expressing frequent repetition of an action. *Waggle* is a frequentative verb from *wag.* *—n.* a frequentative verb or verbal form.

fre quent ly (frē′kwənt lē), *adv.* often; repeatedly. See **often** for synonym study.

fres co (fres′kō), *n., pl.* **-coes** or **-cos,** *v.,* **-coed, -co ing.** *—n.* 1 act or art of painting with water colors on damp, fresh plaster. 2 picture or design so painted. *—v.t.* paint with water colors on damp, fresh plaster. [< Italian, cool, fresh]

fresh[1] (fresh), *adj.* 1 newly made, grown, or gathered: *fresh footprints, fresh vegetables.* 2 not known, seen, or used before; new; recent. 3 additional; further: *After her failure she made a fresh start.* 4 not salty: *Rivers are usually fresh water.* 5 not spoiled; not stale: *Is this milk fresh?* 6 not artificially preserved: *Fresh foods usually have more flavor than canned ones.* 7 not tired out; vigorous; lively: *Put in fresh horses.* 8 not faded or worn; bright: *The party was fresh in her memory.* 9 looking healthy or young. 10 cool; refreshing: *a fresh breeze.* 11 fairly strong; brisk: *A fresh wind is more than a breeze.* 12 not experienced; unsophisticated. *—adv.* freshly; newly. [Old English *fersc;* but influenced in form by Old French *freis,* feminine *fresche* < Germanic] **—fresh′ly,** *adv.* **—fresh′ness,** *n.*

fresh[2] (fresh), *adj.* INFORMAL. too bold; impudent; forward. [< German *frech* impudent]

fresh en (fresh′ən), *v.t.* make fresh: *The rest freshened my spirits.* *—v.i.* 1 become fresh. 2 clean, wash, or groom oneself: *freshen up before dinner.* **—fresh′en er,** *n.*

fresh et (fresh′it), *n.* 1 flood caused by heavy rains or melted snow. 2 stream or rush of fresh water flowing into the sea. [< *fresh* flood, stream, or pool of fresh water + *-et*]

fresh man (fresh′mən), *n., pl.* **-men.** 1 student in the first year of high school or college. 2 beginner.

fresh wa ter (fresh′wô′tər, fresh′wot′ər), *adj.* 1 of or living in water that is not salty: *a freshwater fish.* 2 not used to sailing on the sea. 3 having little experience; unskilled.

Fres no (frez′nō), *n.* city in central California. 166,000.

fret[1] (fret), *v.,* **fret ted, fret ting,** *n.* *—v.i.* 1 be peevish, unhappy, discontented, or worried: *A baby frets in hot weather. Don't fret over your mistakes.* 2 become gnawed or corroded; waste away. *—v.t.* 1 make peevish, unhappy, discontented, or worried; harass; vex; provoke. 2 eat or wear away. 3 make or form by wearing away. 4 agitate or ruffle. *—n.* condition of worry or discontent; peevish complaining. [Old English *fretan* eat] **—fret′ter,** *n.*

fret[2] (fret), *n., v.,* **fret ted, fret ting.** *—n.* an ornamental pattern made of straight lines bent or combined at angles. *—v.t.* decorate with fretwork. [< Old French *frete*]

fret[3] (fret), *n.* any of a series of ridges of wood, ivory, or metal on the fingerboard of a guitar, banjo, etc., showing where to put the fingers in order to produce certain tones. [origin uncertain]

fret ful (fret′fəl), *adj.* 1 apt to fret; peevish, unhappy, discontented, or worried. 2 agitated; seething: *the fretful sea.* 3 gusty: *the fretful wind.* **—fret′ful ly,** *adv.* **—fret′ful ness,** *n.*

fret saw, saw with a long, slender blade and fine teeth, used to cut thin wood into patterns.

fret ted (fret′id), *adj.* having frets. *—v.* pt. and pp. of **fret**[1] and **fret**[2].

fret work (fret′wėrk′), *n.* ornamental openwork or carving.

Freud (froid), *n.* **Sigmund,** 1856-1939, Austrian physician who developed a theory and technique of psychoanalysis.

Freud i an (froi′dē ən), *adj.* of or having to do with Freud or his teachings. *—n.* person who believes in Freud's teachings or follows his technique of psychoanalysis.

Freud i an ism (froi′dē ə niz′əm), *n.* Freudian theories or doctrines.

Frey (frā), *n.* (in Scandinavian myths) the god of love, peace, and plenty, and giver of wealth.

Frey a (frā′ə), *n.* (in Scandinavian myths) the goddess of love and beauty.

F.R.G.S., Fellow of the Royal Geographical Society.

Fri., Friday.

fri a bil i ty (frī′ə bil′ə tē), *n.* condition of being friable.

fri a ble (frī′ə bəl), *adj.* easily crumbled; crumbly: *Dry soil is friable.* [< Latin *friabilis* < *friare* crumble] **—fri′a ble ness,** *n.*

fri ar (frī′ər), *n.* man who belongs to one of certain religious brotherhoods of the Roman Catholic Church. The Franciscans, Dominicans, Carmelites, and Augustinians are the four great orders of friars. [< Old French *frere* < Latin *frater* brother] ➔ See **monk** for usage note.

fri ar y (frī′ər ē), *n., pl.* **-ar ies.** 1 building or buildings where friars live; monastery. 2 brotherhood of friars.

fric as see (frik′ə sē′), *n., v.,* **-seed, -see ing.** *—n.* chicken or other meat cut up, stewed, and served in a sauce made with its own gravy. *—v.t.* prepare (meat) in this way. [< French *fricassée*]

fric a tive (frik′ə tiv), in phonetics: *—adj.* pronounced by forcing the breath through a narrow opening formed by placing the tongue or lips near or against the palate, teeth, etc.; spirant. *F, v, s,* and *z* are fricative consonants. *—n.* a fricative consonant; spirant. [< Latin *fricatum* rubbed, scraped]

fric tion (frik′shən), *n.* 1 a rubbing of one object against another; rubbing: *Matches are lighted by friction.* 2 resistance to motion of surfaces that touch; resistance of a body in motion to the air, water, etc., through which it travels or to the surface on which it travels: *Oil reduces friction.* 3 conflict of differing ideas, opinions, etc.; disagreement; clash: *Constant friction between the two nations brought them dangerously close to war.* [< Latin *frictionem* < *fricare* to rub] **—fric′tion less,** *adj.*

fric tion al (frik′shə nəl), *adj.* 1 of or having to do with friction. 2 moved or caused by friction. **—fric′tion al ly,** *adv.*

friction tape, a cotton tape saturated with an adhesive and moisture-repelling substance. It is used especially to protect electric wires, conductors, etc.

Fri day (frī′dē, frī′dā), *n.* 1 the sixth day of the week, following Thursday. 2 servant of Robinson Crusoe. 3 any faithful servant or devoted follower. [Old English *Frīgedæg* < *Frīge* of Frigg or Freya + *dæg* day]

fridge (frij), *n.* BRITISH INFORMAL. refrigerator.

fried (frīd), *adj.* cooked in hot fat. *—v.* pt. and pp. of **fry**[1].

fried cake (frīd′kāk′), *n.* a small cake fried in deep fat. Doughnuts and crullers are friedcakes.

friend (frend), *n.* 1 person who knows and likes another. 2 person who favors and supports: *She was a generous friend to the poor.* 3 person who belongs to the same side or group: *Are you friend or foe?* 4 **Friend,** Quaker. 5 **be friends with,** be a friend of. 6 **make friends with,** become a friend of. [Old English *frēond,* originally present participle of *frēogan* to love]

friend less (frend′lis), *adj.* without friends. **—friend′less ness,** *n.*

friend ly (frend′lē), *adj.,* **-li er, -li est,** *adv.* *—adj.* 1 of a friend; having the attitude of a friend; kind: *a friendly teacher.* 2 like a friend; like a friend's: *a friendly greeting.* 3 on good terms; not hostile: *friendly relations between countries.* 4 wanting to be a friend: *a friendly dog.* 5 favoring and supporting; favorable: *His talk was friendly to labor.* *—adv.* in a friendly manner; as a friend. **—friend′li ness,** *n.*

Friendly Islands, Tonga.

friend of the court, amicus curiae.

friend ship (frend′ship), *n.* 1 condition of being friends. 2 a liking between friends. 3 friendliness.

fri er (frī′ər), *n.* fryer.

Fries land (frēz′lənd), *n.* district in the N Netherlands.

frieze[1] (frēz), *n.* 1 a horizontal band of decoration around a room, building, mantel, etc. 2 a horizontal band, often ornamented with sculpture, between the cornice and architrave of a building. See **entablature** for diagram. [< French *frise*]

frieze[2] (frēz), *n.* a thick woolen cloth with a shaggy nap on one side. [< Middle French *frise* < Middle Dutch *vriese*]

frigate (def. 1)

frig ate (frig′it), *n.* 1 a fast, three-masted, sailing warship of medium size, much used from 1750 to 1850. 2 a small escort vessel, equipped to destroy submarines. [< French *frégate* < Italian *fregata*]

frigate bird, any of a genus of tropical sea birds that steal other birds' food and have long wings and great power of flight; man-of-war bird or man-o'-war bird; man-of-war hawk.

Frigg (frig), *n.* (in Scandinavian myths) the wife of Odin and goddess of the sky.

Frig ga (frig′ə), *n.* Frigg.

hat, āge, fär; let, ēqual, tėrm;
it, īce; hot, ōpen, ôrder;
oil, out; cup, pu̇t, rüle;
ch, child; ng, long; sh, she;
th, thin; ᴛʜ, then; zh, measure;

ə represents *a* in about, *e* in taken, *i* in pencil, *o* in lemon, *u* in circus.

< = from, derived from, taken from.

fright (frīt), *n.* 1 sudden and extreme fear; sudden terror or alarm. 2 INFORMAL. person or thing that is ugly, shocking, or ridiculous. *—v.t.* frighten; terrify. [Old English *fryhto*]

fright en (frīt′n), *v.t.* 1 fill with fright; make afraid; scare or terrify. See synonym study below. 2 drive or force by terrifying: *The sudden noise frightened the deer away.* *—v.i.* become afraid. **—fright′en ing ly,** *adv.*

Syn. *v.t.* 1 **Frighten, scare, alarm** mean to fill with fear. **Frighten** means to fill with a sudden, startling, often very great, fear: *The rattlesnake frightened me.* **Scare** particularly suggests suddenly giving sharp fear or terror to a timid person or animal, making him shrink and tremble or turn and run: *The firecrackers scared the puppy.* **Alarm** means to fill suddenly with excited fear and anxiety: *Her failure to come home at midnight alarmed us.*

fright ened (frīt′nd), *adj.* filled with fright; afraid. See **afraid** for synonym study.

fright ful (frīt′fəl), *adj.* 1 causing fright or horror; dreadful; terrible. 2 horrible to contemplate; ugly; shocking. 3 INFORMAL. disagreeable; unpleasant. 4 INFORMAL. very great: *I'm in a frightful hurry.* **—fright′ful ly,** *adv.* **—fright′ful ness,** *n.*

frig id (frij′id), *adj.* 1 very cold: *a frigid climate.* 2 cold in feeling or manner: *a frigid greeting.* [< Latin *frigidus* < *frigere* be cold] **—frig′id ly,** *adv.* **—frig′id ness,** *n.*

fri gid i ty (fri jid′ə tē), *n.* condition of being frigid.

Frigid Zone, either of the two polar regions, north of the arctic circle and south of the antarctic circle. See **zone** for diagram.

fri jol (frē′hōl), *n., pl.* **fri joles** (frē′hōlz, fri hō′lēz; *Spanish* frē hō′lās). kind of bean much used for food in Mexico and the southwestern United States. [< Spanish]

fri jole (frē′hōl, fri hō′lē), *n., pl.* **fri joles** (frē′hōlz, fri hō′lēz; *Spanish* frē hō′lās). frijol.

frill (fril), *n.* 1 ruffle: *Her fancy blouse had frills around the neck and down the front.* 2 thing added merely for show; useless ornament; affectation of dress, manner, speech, etc. 3 fringe of feathers, hair, etc., around the neck of a bird or animal. *—v.t.* put a ruffle on; adorn with ruffles. [origin uncertain]

frill y (fril′ē), *adj.,* **frill i er, frill i est.** full of frills; like frills.

fringe (frinj), *n., v.,* **fringed, fring ing,** *adj.* *—n.* 1 border or trimming made of threads, cords, etc., either loose or tied together in small bunches. 2 anything like this; border: *A fringe of hair hung over her forehead.* 3 anything thought of as marginal rather than central: *He belongs to the radical fringe of the labor movement.* *—v.t.* 1 make a fringe for. 2 be a fringe for; border: *Bushes fringed the road.* *—adj.* 1 of the border or outside: *a fringe district.* 2 apart from the main purpose; secondary: *the fringe provisions of a* *contract.* [< Old French *frenge,* ultimately < Latin *fimbria*]

fringe benefit, any benefit given by an employer to his employees in addition to wages and compensations required by law. Medical insurance, paid holidays and vacations, and recreational facilities are fringe benefits.

frip per y (frip′ər ē), *n., pl.* **-per ies.** 1 cheap, showy clothes; gaudy ornaments. 2 a showing off; foolish display; pretended refinement. [< Middle French *friperie,* ultimately < Old French *frepe* rag]

Fris bee (friz′bē), *n.* trademark for a saucer-shaped disk, usually made of colored plastic, that is skimmed into the air. Frisbees are used as toys and in playing various games.

Fris co (fris′kō), *n.* INFORMAL. San Francisco.

Fri sian (frizh′ən), *adj.* of or having to do with Friesland, its people, or their language. *—n.* 1 native or inhabitant of Friesland or certain nearby islands. 2 a language spoken in Friesland and certain nearby islands. Frisian is a West Germanic dialect.

frisk (frisk), *v.i.* run and jump about playfully; skip and dance joyously; frolic. *—v.t.* SLANG. search (a person) for concealed weapons, stolen goods, etc., by running a hand quickly over his clothes. [originally adjective < Middle French *frisque* frisky] **—frisk′er,** *n.*

frisk y (fris′kē), *adj.,* **frisk i er, frisk i est.** playful; lively. **—frisk′i ly,** *adv.* **—frisk′i ness,** *n.*

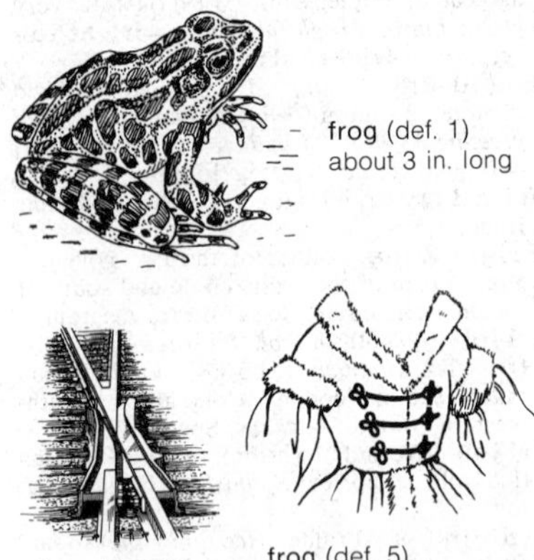

frog (def. 1) about 3 in. long

frog (def. 3)

frog (def. 5) three frogs on a dress

frit il lar y (frit′l er′ē), *n., pl.* **-lar ies.** 1 any of a genus of bulbous plants of the lily family, having drooping, bell-shaped flowers spotted with dark green or purple. 2 any of several genera of butterflies with spots on both the upper sides and undersides of their wings. [< New Latin *Fritillaria* < Latin *fritillus* dice box; with reference to the checkered markings on the petals]

frit ter[1] (frit′ər), *v.t.* 1 waste little by little: *He frittered away both time and energy reading worthless books.* 2 cut or tear into small pieces; break into fragments. [< earlier *fritters* fragments; origin uncertain] **—frit′ter er,** *n.*

frit ter[2] (frit′ər), *n.* sliced fruit, vegetables, meat, or fish covered with batter and fried. [< Middle French *friture,* ultimately < Latin *frigere* to fry]

fri vol i ty (fri vol′ə tē), *n., pl.* **-ties.** 1 a being frivolous; silly behavior; trifling. 2 a frivolous act or thing.

friv o lous (friv′ə ləs), *adj.* 1 lacking in seriousness or sense; silly: *Frivolous behavior is out of place in church.* 2 of little worth or importance; trivial. [< Latin *frivolus*] **—friv′o lous ly,** *adv.* **—friv′o lous ness,** *n.*

frizz or **friz** (friz), *v.,* **frizzed, friz zing,** *n., pl.* **friz zes.** *—v.t., v.i.* form into small, crisp curls; curl. *—n.* hair curled in small, crisp curls or a very close crimp. [apparently < French *friser*]

friz zle[1] (friz′əl), *v.,* **-zled, -zling,** *n.* *—v.t., v.i.* form (hair) into small, crisp curls. *—n.* a small, crisp curl. [probably < French *friser* to curl]

friz zle[2] (friz′əl), *v.,* **-zled, -zling,** *n.* *—v.i.* make a hissing, sputtering noise when cooking; sizzle. *—v.t.* fry or broil until crisp. *—n.* a hissing, sputtering noise; sizzle. [probably blend of *fry* and *sizzle*]

friz zly (friz′lē), *adj.,* **-zli er, -zli est.** full of small, crisp curls; curly.

friz zy (friz′ē), *adj.,* **-zi er, -zi est.** frizzly.

fro (frō), *adv.* 1 from; back. 2 **to and fro,** first one way and then back again; back and forth. [< Scandinavian (Old Icelandic) *frā.* Related to FROM.]

frock (frok), *n.* 1 a woman's or girl's dress. 2 a loose outer garment; smock. 3 robe worn by a clergyman. 4 a woolen jersey worn by sailors. *—v.t.* clothe in a frock. [< Old French *froc;* of Germanic origin]

frock coat, a man's coat reaching approximately to the knees, and equally long in front and in back.

Froe bel (frœ′bəl), *n.* **Friedrich,** 1782-1852, German educator who originated the kindergarten.

frog (frog, frôg), *n.* 1 any of various small, tailless amphibians, having a smooth skin and powerful web-footed hind legs for leaping, and being more aquatic and more agile than a toad. Frogs hatch from eggs as tadpoles and live in the water until they grow legs. 2 animal like this, such as a tree frog. 3 arrangement of a rail where a railroad track crosses or branches from another which guides the flanges of the wheels over the gaps, thus helping the train to stay on its track. 4 a triangular pad of elastic, horny substance in the middle of the bottom of a foot of a horse, donkey, etc. 5 an ornamental fastener on a garment, consisting of a loop and a button which passes through it. 6 **frog in the throat,** slight hoarseness caused by soreness or swelling in the throat. [Old English *frogga*] **—frog′like′,** *adj.*

frog kick, a swimming movement in which the legs are first bent outward at the knees, then extended, then brought together, as in the breast stroke.

frog man (frog′man, frôg′man), *n., pl.* **-men.** person trained and equipped with Aqua-Lungs for underwater operations of various kinds. Most of the world's navies now have frogmen.

frog march (frog′märch′, frôg′märch′), *v.t.* carry (a refractory prisoner) by having him held face downward by four men, each of whom grasps one of his limbs.

Frois sart (froi′särt; *French* frwä sär′), *n.* **Jean,** 1337?-1410?, French chronicler and poet.

frol ic (frol′ik), *n., v.,* **-icked, -ick ing.** *—n.* 1 a merry prank; play; fun. 2 a joyous game or party. *—v.i.* play about joyously; have fun together; make merry: *The children frolicked with the puppy.* [originally adjective < Dutch *vrolijk* gay < Middle Dutch *vro* glad] **—frol′ick er,** *n.*

frol ic some (frol′ik səm), *adj.* full of fun; playful; merry.

from (from, frum; *unstressed* frəm), *prep.* 1 out of: *a train from New York.* 2 out of the possession of: *Take the book from her.* 3 starting at; beginning with: *from that time forward.* 4 because of; by reason of: *act from a sense of duty. He is suffering from a cold.* 5 given, sent, etc., by: *The cut in his finger was from a knife.* 6 as being unlike; as distinguished from: *Anyone can tell apples from oranges.* 7 off: *She took a book from the table.* [Old English *fram, from*]

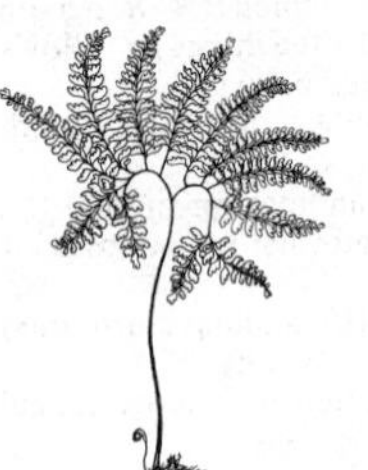

frond (def. 1) of a maidenhair fern

frond (frond), *n.* 1 the leaf of a fern, palm, or cycad. 2 a leaflike part which includes both stem and foliage, as the thallus of a lichen. [< Latin *frondem* leaf]

frond ed (fron′did), *adj.* having fronds.

front (frunt), *n.* 1 the first part; foremost part: *the front of a car.* 2 part that faces forward: *the front of a dress.* 3 the front face or part of a building. 4 thing fastened or worn on the front. 5 battlefront. 6 sphere of activity combining different groups in a political or economic battle: *the labor front.* 7 land facing a street, river, etc. 8 manner of looking or behaving: *a genial front.* 9 INFORMAL. an outward appearance of wealth, importance, etc.: *The newcomer put up an impressive front.* 10 INFORMAL. person or thing that serves as a cover for unlawful activities, for a pressure group, etc.: *The club was just a front for gangster activities.* 11 forehead. 12 face. 13 the dividing surface between two dissimilar air masses: *A cold front is moving toward this area from Canada.* 14 a call to a bellboy to come to the main part of the hotel lobby or to the desk. 15 **in front of,** in a place or position before (a person or thing); before.

—adj. 1 of, on, in, or at the front. 2 (in phonetics) pronounced by raising the tongue against or near the forward part of the hard palate. The *e* in *bee* is a front vowel.

—v.t. 1 have the front toward; face: *Her house fronts the park.* 2 be in front of. 3 meet face to face; meet as an enemy; defy; oppose. *—v.i.* 1 have the front in a certain direction: *Most houses front on the street.* 2 INFORMAL. serve as a cover for a pressure group, an illegal activity, etc.

[< Latin *frontem,* literally, forehead]

front age (frun′tij), *n.* 1 front of a building or of a lot. 2 length of this front. 3 direction that the front of a building or lot faces. 4 land facing a street, river, etc. 5 land between a building and a street, river, etc.

fron tal (frun′tl), *adj.* 1 of, on, in, or at the front: *a frontal attack.* 2 of or in the region of the forehead: *frontal bone.* —*n.* bone of the forehead. —**fron′tal ly,** *adv.*

Fron te nac (fron′tə nak′; *French* frônt-nȧk′), *n.* Comte **Louis de Buade de,** 1622?-1698, French general, colonial governor of French Canada from 1672 to 1682 and from 1689 to 1698.

fron tier (frun tir′, frun′tir, fron′tir), *n.* 1 the farthest part of a settled country, where the wilds begin; border of inhabited regions. 2 part of a country next to another country; border. 3 an uncertain or undeveloped region: *the frontiers of science.* —*adj.* of or on the frontier. [< Old French *frontiere* < *front* front < Latin *frontem*]

fron tiers man (frun tirz′mən), *n., pl.* **-men.** man who lives on the frontier.

fron tis piece (frun′ti spēs, fron′ti spēs), *n.* illustration facing the title page of a book or of a division of a book. [< French *frontispice* < Late Latin *frontispicium,* literally, looking at the forehead < Latin *frontem* forehead + *specere* to look]

front lash (frunt′lash′), *n.* U.S. reaction that offsets or reverses an unfavorable reaction.

front let (frunt′lit), *n.* 1 band or ornament worn on the forehead. 2 forehead of an animal.

front man, 1 person who officially represents a group or organization. 2 person who fronts for another.

front-page (frunt′pāj′), *adj.* suitable for the front page of a newspaper; important: *front-page news.*

front-run ner (frunt′run′ər), *n.* the leading contender at a given moment in any contest.

front-run ning (frunt′run′ing), *adj.* leading in a race or contest.

frosh (frosh), *n., pl.* **frosh.** U.S. INFORMAL. freshman at a college or school.

frost (frôst, frost), *n.* 1 a freezing condition; very cold weather, when the temperature is below the point at which water freezes. 2 act or process of becoming frozen. 3 moisture frozen on or in a surface; feathery crystals of ice formed when water vapor in the air condenses at a temperature below freezing: *frost on windows.* 4 coldness of manner or feeling; frigidity. —*v.t.* 1 cover with frost. 2 cover with anything that suggests frost: *The cook frosted the cake with icing.* 3 give a frostlike surface to (glass, etc.). 4 kill or injure by frost or freezing. —*v.i.* become covered with frost. [Old English. Related to FREEZE.] —**frost′less,** *adj.* —**frost′like′,** *adj.*

Frost (frôst, frost), *n.* **Robert (Lee),** 1875-1963, American poet.

frost bite (frôst′bīt′, frost′bīt′), *n., v.,* **-bit** (-bit′), **-bit ten, -bit ing.** —*n.* damage to or destruction of tissue in a part of the body caused by freezing. —*v.t.* injure (a part of the body) by frostbite; harm by severe cold.

frost bit ten (frôst′bit′n, frost′bit′n), *adj.* affected by frostbite. —*v.* pp. of **frostbite.**

frost ed (frô′stid, fros′tid), *adj.* 1 covered with frost. 2 having a surface like frost. 3 iced: *a frosted cake.* 4 frozen.

frost ing (frô′sting, fros′ting), *n.* 1 mixture of sugar and some liquid, often with the beaten whites of eggs, flavoring, etc., to cover a cake; icing. 2 a dull, rough finish on glass, metal, etc.

frost y (frô′stē, fros′tē), *adj.,* **frost i er, frost i est.** 1 cold enough for frost; freezing: *a frosty morning.* 2 covered with frost: *The glass is frosty.* 3 covered with anything like frost. 4 cold and unfriendly; with no warmth of feeling: *a frosty greeting.* 5 hoary. —**frost′i ly,** *adv.* —**frost′i ness,** *n.*

froth (frôth, froth), *n.* 1 foam. 2 foaming saliva coming from the mouth, caused by disease, exertion, etc. 3 something light or trifling; trivial notions, talk, etc. —*v.i.* give out froth; foam. —*v.t.* 1 cover with foam. 2 cause to foam by beating, pouring, etc. [Middle English *frothe* < Scandinavian (Old Icelandic) *frotha*]

froth y (frô′thē, froth′ē), *adj.,* **froth i er, froth i est.** 1 foamy. 2 light or trifling; unimportant: *frothy conversation.* —**froth′i ly,** *adv.* —**froth′i ness,** *n.*

frou frou (frü′frü′), *n.* 1 a rustling or swishing sound, as of a silk dress. 2 INFORMAL. fancy or fussy trimmings or the like; frills. [< French]

fro ward (frō′wərd, frō′ərd), *adj.* not easily managed; willful; contrary. [< *fro* + *-ward*] —**fro′ward ly,** *adv.* —**fro′ward ness,** *n.*

frown (froun), *n.* 1 a wrinkling of the forehead, usually in deep thought, disapproval, anger, etc. 2 any expression or show of disapproval. —*v.i.* 1 wrinkle the forehead to show disapproval, anger, etc. See synonym study below. 2 look displeased or angry. 3 look with disapproval: *frown on a scheme.* —*v.t.* express by frowning: *He frowned his disapproval.* [< Old French *froignier* to frown] —**frown′ing ly,** *adv.*

Syn. *v.i.* 1 **Frown, scowl** mean to produce a forbidding look by lowering or drawing the eyebrows together. **Frown** suggests a stern look indicating strong anger or mild displeasure: *The teacher frowned when the boy came in late.* **Scowl** suggests a sullen look indicating bad humor: *He is a disagreeable person, always scowling.*

frow sy (frou′zē), *adj.,* **-si er, -si est.** frowzy.

frow zy (frou′zē), *adj.,* **-zi er, -zi est.** 1 dirty and untidy; slovenly. 2 smelling bad; musty. [origin uncertain] —**frow′zi ness,** *n.*

froze (frōz), *v.* pt. of **freeze.**

fro zen (frō′zn), *adj.* 1 hardened by cold; turned into ice. 2 very cold. 3 preserved by being subjected to low temperatures: *frozen foods.* 4 killed or injured by frost. 5 covered or clogged with ice. 6 cold and unfeeling: *a frozen heart.* 7 too frightened or stiff to move: *frozen to the spot in horror.* 8 temporarily forbidden to be sold or exchanged: *frozen assets.* 9 (of a price, rent, wage, etc.) fixed at a particular amount or level. —*v.* pp. of **freeze.**

FRS, Federal Reserve System.

F.R.S., Fellow of the Royal Society.

frt., freight.

fruc ti fi ca tion (fruk′tə fə kā′shən), *n.* 1 a forming or bearing of fruit. 2 the fruit of a plant.

fruc ti fy (fruk′tə fī), *v.,* **-fied, -fy ing.** —*v.i.* bear fruit. —*v.t.* make fruitful or productive; cause to bear fruit; fertilize. [< Latin *fructificare* < *fructus* fruit + *facere* make]

fruc tose (fruk′tōs), *n.* sugar present in many fruits, honey, etc.; fruit sugar; levulose. It is sweeter than glucose or sucrose. *Formula:* $C_6H_{12}O_6$ [< Latin *fructus* fruit]

fru gal (frü′gəl), *adj.* 1 avoiding waste; tending to avoid unnecessary spending; saving; thrifty: *a frugal housekeeper.* See **economical** for synonym study. 2 costing little; barely sufficient: *He ate a frugal supper of bread and milk.* [< Latin *frugalis* < *frugi* temperate, useful, ultimately < *fructus* fruit, produce. See FRUIT.] —**fru′gal ly,** *adv.*

hat, āge, fär; let, ēqual, tėrm;
it, īce; hot, ōpen, ôrder;
oil, out; cup, pu̇t, rüle;
ch, child; ng, long; sh, she;
th, thin; ᴛʜ, then; zh, measure;

ə represents *a* in about, *e* in taken,
i in pencil, *o* in lemon, *u* in circus.

< = from, derived from, taken from.

fru gal i ty (frü gal′ə tē), *n., pl.* **-ties.** avoidance of waste; thrift.

fruit (früt), *n.* 1 a juicy or fleshy edible product of a tree, bush, shrub, or vine which is usually sweet and consists of the seed and its covering. Apples, pears, oranges, bananas, peaches, and plums are fruits. 2 (in botany) the matured ovary of a seed plant, consisting of the seeds, the tissues connected with them, and their covering. Pea pods, acorns, cucumbers, and grains of wheat are fruits. 3 the useful product of plants: *the fruits of the earth.* 4 result of anything; product. —*v.i., v.t.* have or produce fruit. [< Old French < Latin *fructus* fruit, produce < *frui* enjoy, make use of] —**fruit′like′,** *adj.*

fruit age (frü′tij), *n.* 1 a having or producing fruit. 2 crop of fruit; fruit. 3 product; result.

fruit cake (früt′kāk′), *n.* a rich cake usually containing raisins, currants, and other fruits and sometimes nuts and spices.

fruit er er (frü′tər ər), *n.* dealer in fruit.

fruit fly, any of various small flies, especially drosophila, whose larvae feed on decaying fruits and vegetables.

fruit ful (früt′fəl), *adj.* 1 producing much fruit. 2 producing much of anything; prolific: *a fruitful mind.* 3 having good results; bringing benefit or profit: *a fruitful plan.* —**fruit′ful ly,** *adv.* —**fruit′ful ness,** *n.*

fru i tion (frü ish′ən), *n.* 1 condition of having results; fulfillment; attainment: *After years of hard work his plans came to fruition.* 2 pleasure that comes from possession or use; enjoyment. 3 condition of producing fruit. [< Late Latin *fruitionem* enjoyment < Latin *frui* enjoy]

fruit less (früt′lis), *adj.* 1 having no results; of no use; unsuccessful; futile: *a fruitless search.* 2 producing no fruit; barren. —**fruit′less ly,** *adv.* —**fruit′less ness,** *n.*

fruit sugar, fructose.

fruit y (frü′tē), *adj.,* **fruit i er, fruit i est.** resembling fruit; having the taste, smell, etc., of fruit.

frump (frump), *n.* woman who is frumpish.

frump ish (frum′pish), *adj.* shabby and out of style in dress; dowdy.

frump y (frum′pē), *adj.,* **frump i er, frump i est.** frumpish.

Frun ze (frün′zə), *n.* 1 city in SW Soviet Union, capital of Kirghiz S.S.R. 431,000. 2 **Mikhail Vasilievich,** 1885-1925, Soviet military commander.

frus trate (frus′trāt), *v.t.,* **-trat ed, -trat ing.** 1 make useless or worthless; bring to nothing; foil; defeat. 2 prevent from accomplishing; thwart; oppose: *frustrated in one's ambition.* See synonym study below. [< Latin *frustratum* disappointed < *frustra* in vain]

Syn. 2 **Frustrate, thwart, baffle** mean to keep from accomplishing some purpose. **Frustrate** implies making a person's efforts and plans seem useless: *The police frustrated* *the bandits' attempt to rob the bank.* **Thwart** implies blocking his efforts: *The sudden storm thwarted the men trying to reach the wrecked plane.* **Baffle** implies confusing or bewildering him so that he can proceed no further: *The absence of clues baffled the police.*

frus tra tion (fru strā′shən), *n.* 1 a frustrating. 2 a being frustrated.

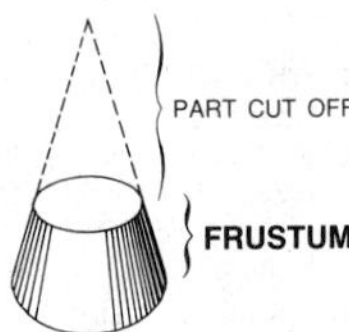

frus tum (frus′təm), *n., pl.* **-tums, -ta** (-tə). part of a cone-shaped solid left after the top has been cut off by a plane parallel to the base. [< Latin, piece]

fry[1] (frī), *v.,* **fried, fry ing,** *n., pl.* **fries.** —*v.t., v.i.* cook in hot fat in a deep or shallow pan, often over a flame: *fry potatoes. These fish are small and will soon fry.* —*n.* 1 dish of something fried; fried food. 2 an outdoor social gathering at which food, usually fish, is fried and eaten. [< Old French *frire* < Latin *frigere*]

fry[2] (frī), *n., pl.* **fry.** 1 the young of fish. 2 small adult fish living together in large groups or schools. 3 young creatures; offspring; children. [< Old French *frai* spawn]

fry er (frī′ər), *n.* 1 chicken intended for frying. 2 pan used for frying. Also, **frier.**

FSH, follicle-stimulating hormone.

ft., 1 foot or feet. 2 fort.

FTC, Federal Trade Commission.

ft.-lb., foot-pound.

fuch sia (fyü′shə), *n.* 1 any of a genus of ornamental shrubs of the same family as the evening primrose, bearing showy pink, red, or purple flowers that droop from the stems. 2 a purplish red. —*adj.* purplish-red. [< New Latin *Fuchsia* < Leonard *Fuchs,* 1501-1566, German botanist]

fuch sin (fük′sən), *n.* a coal tar occurring as a greenish solid which forms deep-red or purplish-red solutions, formerly used as a dye. [< *fuchs(ia)*]

fuch sine (fük′sən, fük′sēn′), *n.* fuchsin.

fud dle (fud′l), *v.t.,* **-dled, -dling.** 1 make stupid with drink. 2 confuse; muddle. [origin uncertain]

fud dy-dud dy (fud′ē dud′ē), *n., pl.* **-dies.** INFORMAL. a fussy or stuffy, usually elderly, person with out-of-date tastes and manners.

fudge[1] (fuj), *n.* 1 a soft candy made of sugar, milk, chocolate, butter, etc. 2 nonsense. [origin uncertain]

fudge[2] (fuj), *v.,* **fudged, fudg ing.** —*v.t.* put together in a clumsy, makeshift, or dishonest way; fake. —*v.i.* 1 be dishonest; cheat. 2 evade the fulfillment of an obligation. [origin uncertain]

Fueh rer (fyür′ər; *German* fʏ′rər), *n.* Führer.

fu el (fyü′əl), *n., v.,* **-eled, -el ing** or **-elled, -el ling.** —*n.* 1 coal, wood, oil, or any other material that can be burned to produce useful heat or power. 2 atomic matter producing heat by fission or fusion, as in a reactor. 3 anything that feeds or inflames feeling, excitement, etc. —*v.t.* 1 supply with fuel. 2 act as a driving force for; support. —*v.i.* get fuel. [< Old French *feuaile,* ultimately < Latin *focus* hearth]

fuel cell, device which produces electricity directly from a chemical reaction between oxygen and a gaseous fuel such as hydrogen or carbon monoxide.

fuel injection, the pumping of vaporized fuel under pressure into the cylinders of an internal-combustion engine, either to increase the force of combustion, or to achieve a more economical rate of fuel consumption. Fuel injection is used in rockets and aircraft and has replaced the carburetor in certain automobiles.

fuel oil, oil used for fuel, especially one used as a substitute for coal, made from crude petroleum.

fuel pump, pump in an engine that forces the liquid fuel from the tank to the carburetor or combustion chamber.

fu ga cious (fyü gā′shəs), *adj.* passing quickly; fleeting; transitory. [< Latin *fugacem* < *fugere* flee]

fu gal (fyü′gəl), *adj.* in music: 1 in the style of a fugue. 2 of or having to do with a fugue.

fu gi tive (fyü′jə tiv), *n.* 1 person who is fleeing or who has fled from danger, an enemy, justice, etc. 2 exile; refugee. —*adj.* 1 fleeing or having fled; runaway. 2 passing swiftly; fleeting: *fugitive bliss.* 3 moving from place to place; roving. [< Latin *fugitivus* < *fugere* flee] —**fu′gi tive ly,** *adv.* —**fu′gi tive ness,** *n.*

fugue (fyüg), *n.* a contrapuntal musical composition based on one or more short themes in which different voices or instruments repeat the same melody with slight variations. [< French < Italian *fuga* < Latin, flight < *fugere* flee]

Füh rer (fʏ′rər), *n.* GERMAN. leader. It was the title given to Adolf Hitler. Also, **Fuehrer.**

Fu ji (fü′jē), *n.* Fujiyama.

Fu ji ya ma (fü′jē yä′mə), *n.* extinct volcano in S Japan, near Tokyo. It is the highest mountain in Japan. 12,395 ft.

Fu kien (fü′kyen′), *n.* province in SE China.

Fu ku o ka (fü′kü ō′kä), *n.* seaport in Japan, in N Kyushu. 807,000.

-ful, *suffix added to nouns to form adjectives or other nouns.* 1 full of ____: *Cheerful = full of cheer.* 2 showing ____: *Careful = showing care.* 3 having a tendency to ____: *Harmful = having a tendency to harm.* 4 enough to fill a ____: *Cupful = enough to fill a cup.* 5 that can be of ____: *Useful = that can be of use.* 6 having the qualities of ____: *Masterful = having the qualities of a master.* [Old English < adjective *full*[1] full]

ful crum (ful′krəm), *n., pl.* **-crums, -cra** (-krə). support on which a lever turns or rests in moving or lifting something. See **lever** for diagram. [< Latin, bedpost < *fulcire* to support]

ful fill or **ful fil** (fu̇l fil′), *v.t.,* **-filled, -fill ing.** 1 carry out (a promise, prophecy, etc.); cause to happen or take place; accomplish; realize. 2 perform or do (a duty); obey (a command, law, etc.); execute; discharge. 3 satisfy (a requirement, condition, etc.); serve (a purpose). 4 bring to an end; finish or complete (a period of time, work, etc.): *fulfill a contract.* [Old English *fullfyllan* < *full* full[1] + *fyllan* to fill]

ful fill ment or **ful fil ment** (fu̇l fil′mənt), *n.* a fulfilling; completion; performance; accomplishment.

full[1] (fu̇l), *adj.* 1 able to hold no more; with no empty space; filled: *a full cup.* 2 complete in number, size, extent, etc.; entire: *a full supply.* 3 of the greatest size, amount, extent, volume, etc.: *a full mile.* 4 more than enough to satisfy; well supplied; abundant. 5 having eaten or drunk one's fill. 6 well filled out; plump; round: *a full face.* 7 having wide folds or much cloth: *a full skirt.* 8 strong, sonorous, and distinct: *a full voice.* 9 (of brothers and sisters) born of the same father and mother: *He is full brother to the present king.* 10 **full of, a** filled with. **b** absorbed by; completely taken up with. —*adv.* 1 completely; entirely. 2 straight; directly: *The blow hit him full in the face.* 3 **full well,** very well. —*n.* 1 the greatest degree; completeness: *We discussed the matter to the full.* 2 **in full, a** to or for the complete amount. **b** not abbreviated or shortened. —*v.t.* make with wide folds or much cloth. [Old English]

full[2] (fu̇l), *v.t.* clean and thicken (cloth) by beating and washing or a similar process. [< Old French *fouler,* ultimately < Latin *fullo* fuller]

full back (fu̇l′bak′), *n.* a football player who is a member of the offensive backfield and usually lines up between the halfbacks.

full blast, INFORMAL. in full operation; at highest speed or largest capacity.

full-blood ed (fu̇l′blud′id), *adj.* 1 of pure or unmixed race, breed, or strain; thoroughbred: *a full-blooded Indian.* 2 vigorous; hearty.

full-blown (fu̇l′blōn′), *adj.* 1 in full bloom. 2 completely developed or matured.

full-bod ied (fu̇l′bod′ēd), *adj.* having considerable strength, flavor, etc.

full dress, the formal clothes worn in the evening or on important occasions.

full-dress (fu̇l′dres′), *adj.* of or characterized by the wearing of full dress: *a full-dress parade.*

full er (fu̇l′ər), *n.* person whose work is cleaning and thickening cloth. [Old English *fullere* < Latin *fullo* fuller]

Full er (fu̇l′ər), *n.* **R(ichard) Buckminster,** born 1895, American inventor, architect, and engineer.

fuller's earth, a soft, claylike mixture used for removing grease from cloth and for refining mineral, vegetable, and animal oils.

Ful ler ton (fu̇l′ər tən), *n.* city in SW California. 86,000.

full-fledged (fu̇l′flejd′), *adj.* 1 fully developed. 2 of full rank or standing.

full-grown (fu̇l′grōn′), *adj.* fully grown; mature.

full house, a poker hand made up of three cards of one kind and two of another, such as three sixes and two kings.

full-length (fu̇l′lenkth′, fu̇l′length′), *adj.* 1 showing the entire human body: *a full-length portrait.* 2 of the full or normal length; not short.

full moon, the moon seen from the earth as a whole circle. See **phase** for diagram.

full ness (fu̇l′nis), *n.* condition of being full. Also, **fulness.**

full-rigged (fu̇l′rigd′), *adj.* 1 having three or four masts, all completely square-rigged. 2 completely equipped.

full-scale (fu̇l′skāl′), *adj.* 1 having the same size and proportion as the original: *a full-scale reproduction of a painting.* 2 not limited; using all resources; complete; all-out: *a* *full-scale investigation, a full-scale offensive.*

full-time (fu̇l′tīm′), *adj., adv.* for the usual or normal length of working time.

ful ly (fu̇l′ē), *adv.* 1 completely; entirely: *fully satisfied.* 2 abundantly; plentifully: *fully equipped.* 3 quite; exactly: *fully cognizant.*

ful mar (fu̇l′mər), *n.* a sea bird related to the petrel, inhabiting northern regions. [probably < Scandinavian (Old Icelandic) *fūlmārr* < *fūll* foul + *mār* sea gull]

ful mi nate (ful′mə nāt), *v.,* **-nat ed, -nat ing,** *n.* —*v.t.* 1 thunder forth (censure, threats, decrees, etc.). 2 denounce violently; censure strongly. 3 cause to explode violently. —*v.i.* 1 utter strong censure or denunciation; thunder: *The newspapers fulminated against the crime wave.* 2 explode violently. —*n.* (in chemistry) a violent explosive. [< Latin *fulminatum* struck with lightning < *fulminis* lightning, related to *fulgere* to shine] **—ful′mi na′tion,** *n.* **—ful′mi na′tor,** *n.*

ful ness (fu̇l′nis), *n.* fullness.

ful some (fu̇l′səm, ful′səm), *adj.* so much as to be disgusting; offensive, especially from being overdone: *fulsome praise.* [< *full* + *-some*[1]] **—ful′some ly,** *adv.* **—ful′some ness,** *n.*

Ful ton (fu̇lt′n), *n.* **Robert,** 1765-1815, American inventor and civil engineer who built the first successful steamboat.

fu ma role (fyü′mə rōl′), *n.* hole or vent in the earth's crust in a volcanic region, from which steam and hot gases issue. [< Italian *fumarola* ultimately < Latin *fumus* smoke, vapor]

fum ble (fum′bəl), *v.,* **-bled, -bling,** *n.* —*v.i.* 1 feel or grope about clumsily; search awkwardly: *He fumbled about in the darkness for the doorknob.* 2 handle something awkwardly. 3 (in sports) to drop a ball unintentionally, especially in attempting to catch or hold onto it. —*v.t.* 1 handle (something) awkwardly or with nervous clumsiness. 2 (in sports) to let (a ball) drop instead of catching or holding onto it. —*n.* 1 an awkward attempt to find or handle something. 2 failure to catch or hold onto a ball. [origin uncertain] **—fum′bler,** *n.*

fume (fyüm), *n., v.,* **fumed, fum ing.** —*n.* 1 Often, **fumes,** *pl.* vapor, gas, or smoke, especially if harmful, strong, or odorous: *The fumes from the automobile exhaust nearly choked him.* 2 fit of anger; angry or irritable mood. —*v.i.* 1 give off fumes. 2 pass off in fumes. 3 let off one's rage in angry comments; show anger or irritation: *He fumed about the slowness of the train.* —*v.t.* treat with fumes: *fumed oak.* [< Old French *fum* < Latin *fumus* smoke]

fu mi gant (fyü′mə gənt), *n.* substance used for fumigating.

fu mi gate (fyü′mə gāt), *v.t.,* **-gat ed, -gat ing.** disinfect or purify with fumes; expose to fumes: *They fumigated the building to kill the cockroaches.* **—fu′mi ga′tion,** *n.* **—fu′mi ga′tor,** *n.*

fun (fun), *n., v.,* **funned, fun ning.** —*n.* 1 merry play; playfulness; amusement. 2 **for fun** or **in fun,** as a joke; playfully. 3 **make fun of** or **poke fun at,** laugh at; ridicule. —*v.i.* INFORMAL. make fun or sport; indulge in fun; joke. [probably originally variant of obsolete verb *fon* befool]

func tion (fungk′shən), *n.* 1 proper work; normal action or use; purpose: *The function of the stomach is to help digest food.* 2 duty or office; employment. 3 a formal public or social gathering for some purpose, such as a wedding. 4 a mathematical quantity whose value depends on, or varies with, the value given to one or more variable quantities: *The area of a circle is a function of its radius.* 5 anything likened to a mathematical function. 6 (in grammar) the way in which a word or phrase is used in a sentence. —*v.i.* perform a function or one's functions; work; be used; act: *One of the older students can function as teacher.* [< Latin *functionem* < *fungi* perform]

func tion al (fungk′shə nəl), *adj.* 1 of a function or functions. 2 having or carrying out a function; working. 3 useful in many ways. 4 having function as the primary basis of design: *functional furniture.* 5 (in medicine) of or having to do with the function of an organ rather than its structure: *a functional disease.* **—func′tion al ly,** *adv.*

func tion ar y (fungk′shə ner′ē), *n., pl.* **-ar ies.** an official.

function word, word that expresses mainly a relationship between the grammatical elements of a sentence. Prepositions, conjunctions, and auxiliary verbs are function words.

fund (fund), *n.* 1 sum of money set aside for a special purpose: *The school has a fund of $2000 to buy books with.* 2 **funds,** *pl.* **a** money at a person's disposal. **b** money. 3 stock or store ready for use; supply: *There is a fund of information in a library.* —*v.t.* 1 set aside a sum of money to pay the interest on (a debt). 2 change (a debt) from a short term to a long term, at a fixed rate of interest. [< Latin *fundus* bottom, a piece of land]

fun da ment (fun′də mənt), *n.* 1 foundation; basis. 2 buttocks. 3 anus. [< Latin *fundamentum* < *fundare* to found[2] < *fundus* bottom]

fun da men tal (fun′də men′tl), *adj.* 1 of or forming a foundation or basis; essential; basic: *Reading is a fundamental skill.* 2 in music: **a** having to do with the lowest note of a chord. **b** designating a chord of which the root is the lowest note. —*n.* 1 something fundamental; essential part: *the fundamentals of grammar.* 2 (in music) the lowest note of a chord. 3 (in physics) that component of a wave which has the greatest wave length or lowest frequency. **—fun′da men′tal ly,** *adv.*

fun da men tal ism (fun′də men′tl iz′əm), *n.* 1 the belief that the words of the Bible were inspired by God and should be believed and followed literally. 2 movement in certain Protestant churches upholding this belief.

fun da men tal ist (fun′də men′tl ist), *n.* person who believes in fundamentalism. —*adj.* of or having to do with fundamentalism.

fundamental particle, elementary particle.

Fun dy (fun′dē), *n.* **Bay of,** inlet of the Atlantic in SE Canada, between Nova Scotia and New Brunswick.

fu ner al (fyü′nər əl), *n.* 1 ceremonies performed when a dead person's body is buried or cremated. A funeral usually includes a religious service and taking the body to the place where it is buried or cremated. 2 procession taking a dead person's body to the place where it is buried or cremated. —*adj.* of a funeral; suitable for a funeral: *a funeral procession.* [< Late Latin *funeralis* of a funeral < Latin *funeris* funeral, death]

funeral home or **funeral parlor,** place of business having rooms for embalming, funeral services, etc.

hat, āge, fär; let, ēqual, tėrm;
it, īce; hot, ōpen, ôrder;
oil, out; cup, pu̇t, rüle;
ch, child; ng, long; sh, she;
th, thin; ᴛʜ, then; zh, measure;

ə represents *a* in about, *e* in taken,
i in pencil, *o* in lemon, *u* in circus.

< = from, derived from, taken from.

fu ne rar y (fyü′nə rer′ē), *adj.* of a funeral or burial: *A funerary urn holds the ashes of a dead person's body.*

fu ner e al (fyü nir′ē əl), *adj.* 1 of or suitable for a funeral. 2 gloomy; dismal; sad. **—fu ner′e al ly,** *adv.*

fun gal (fung′gəl), *adj.* fungous.

fun gi (fun′jī), *n.* a pl. of **fungus.**

fun gi cid al (fun′jə sī′dl), *adj.* that destroys fungi.

fun gi cide (fun′jə sīd), *n.* any substance that destroys fungi.

fun gi stat ic (fun′jə stat′ik), *adj.* stopping the development or growth of a fungus without killing it.

fun go (fung′gō), *n., pl.* **-goes.** a fly ball batted for practice by tossing it up and hitting it before it falls. [origin unknown]

fun goid (fung′goid), *adj.* resembling a fungus; having spongy, unhealthful growths. —*n.* a fungoid plant.

fun gous (fung′gəs), *adj.* 1 of a fungus or fungi; like a fungus. 2 growing or springing up suddenly like a mushroom. 3 caused by a fungus.

fungus (def. 1)
fungi growing
on a tree

fun gus (fung′gəs), *n., pl.* **fun gi** or **fun gus es,** *adj.* —*n.* 1 any of a subdivision of plants without flowers, leaves, or chlorophyll that get their nourishment from dead or living organic matter and reproduce by spores and division. Mushrooms, yeasts, toadstools, smuts, rusts, molds, and mildews are fungi. 2 something that grows or springs up rapidly like a mushroom. —*adj.* fungous. [< Latin]

fu nic u lar (fyü nik′yə lər), *adj.* hanging from or operated by a rope. —*n.* funicular railway. [< Latin *funiculus,* a thin rope, diminutive of *funis* rope]

funicular railway, type of railway used on steep grades, in which two counterbalanced cars are linked by a cable so that when one moves down the other moves up.

funk (fungk), INFORMAL. —*n.* condition of panic or fear. —*v.t.* 1 be afraid of. 2 shrink from; shirk. —*v.i.* flinch or shrink through fear; try to back out of anything. [origin uncertain]

funk y (fung′kē), *adj.,* **funk i er, funk i est.** 1 shrinking in fear; timid. 2 U.S. SLANG. in jazz: **a** having a flavor or sound like that of the blues; wistful and sad. **b** earthy; unpretentious.

fun nel (fun′l), *n., v.,* **-neled, -nel ing** or **-nelled, -nel ling.** —*n.* 1 a tapering utensil with a wide, cone-shaped mouth ending in a tube, used to prevent spilling in pouring liquids, powder, grain, etc., into containers with small openings. 2 anything shaped like a funnel: *a funnel of smoke.* 3 smokestack or chimney on a steamship or steam engine. 4 flue or stack for carrying off smoke, etc., or for ventilation or lighting. —*v.t., v.i.* pass or feed through or as if through a funnel. [< Old French *fonel,* ultimately < Late Latin *fundibulum* < Latin *infundibulum* < *in-* in + *fundere* pour]

funnel (def. 1)

funnel (def. 2)
tornado funnel

fun nies (fun′ēz), *n.pl.* 1 comic strips; comics. 2 section of a newspaper carrying comic strips.

fun ny (fun′ē), *adj.,* **-ni er, -ni est.** 1 causing laughter; amusing. See synonym study below. 2 INFORMAL. strange; odd. 3 INFORMAL. questionable or underhanded: *There is some funny business going on there.* —**fun′ni ly,** *adv.* —**fun′ni ness,** *n.*

Syn. 1 Funny, laughable mean such as to cause laughter or amusement. **Funny** implies almost any degree of amusement from a hearty laugh to a faint smile: *The clown's antics were funny.* **Laughable** implies laughter, often scornful laughter: *His fine airs are laughable.*

funny bone, place at the bend of the elbow over which the ulnar nerve passes; crazy bone. When it is struck, a sharp, tingling sensation is felt in the arm and hand.

fur (fėr), *n., v.,* **furred, fur ring,** *adj.* —*n.* 1 the short, fine, soft hair covering the skin of many animals. 2 pelt of certain animals, with such hair on it, dressed and treated. Fur is used to make, cover, trim, or line clothing. 3 Usually, **furs,** *pl.* garment made of fur. 4 a coating of foul or waste matter like fur, as on the tongue of a sick person. —*v.t.* 1 make, cover, trim, or line with fur. 2 coat with foul or waste matter like fur. 3 put furring on (a wall, floor, etc.) —*adj.* made of fur: *a fur collar.* [< Old French *fourrer* to line with skins, encase < *feurre* sheath, case] —**fur′less,** *adj.* —**fur′like′,** *adj.*

fur., 1 furlong. 2 furnished.

fur be low (fėr′bə lō), *n.* bit of elaborate trimming: *frills and furbelows on a dress.* —*v.t.* trim in a fussy, elaborate way. [< Provençal *farbélla*]

fur bish (fėr′bish), *v.t.* 1 brighten by rubbing or scouring; polish: *furbish a rusty sword.* 2 restore to good condition; make usable again: *Before going to France, he furbished up his half-forgotten French.* [< Old French *forbiss-,* a form of *forbir* to polish] —**fur′bish er,** *n.*

fur cate (*adj.* fėr′kāt, fėr′kit; *v.* fėr′kāt), *adj., v.,* **-cat ed, -cat ing.** —*adj.* forked. —*v.i.* form a fork; divide into branches. [< Late Latin *furcatum* forked, cloven < Latin *furca* pitchfork] —**fur ca′tion,** *n.*

Fur ies (fyůr′ēz), *n.pl.* (in Greek and Roman myths) the three spirits of revenge who pursued those who had not atoned for their crimes; Eumenides; Erinyes.

fur i ous (fyůr′ē əs), *adj.* 1 full of wild, fierce anger. 2 intensely violent; raging: *a furious storm.* 3 of unrestrained energy, speed, etc.: *furious activity.* [< Latin *furiosus* < *furia* fury] —**fur′i ous ly,** *adv.* —**fur′i ous ness,** *n.*

furl (fėrl), *v.t.* roll up; fold up: *furl a sail.* —*v.i.* become rolled or gathered up in a spiral or twisted form; curl. —*n.* 1 a furling. 2 a roll, coil, or curl of anything furled. [< Middle French *ferler*]

fur long (fėr′lông, fėr′long), *n.* measure of distance equal to one eighth of a mile; 220 yards. See **measure** for table. [Old English *furlang* < *furh* furrow + *lang* long]

fur lough (fėr′lō), *n.* leave of absence, especially one granted to a soldier. —*v.t.* give leave of absence to. [< Dutch *verlof*]

fur nace (fėr′nis), *n.* 1 an enclosed chamber or box in which fuel is burned to heat buildings, melt metals, make glass, etc. 2 a very hot place. [< Old French *fornais, fornaise* < Latin *fornacem* kiln, oven]

fur nish (fėr′nish), *v.t.* 1 supply with something necessary, useful, or wanted; provide: *The sun furnishes heat.* See synonym study below. 2 supply (a room, house, etc.) with furniture, equipment, etc. [< Old French *furniss-,* a form of *furnir* accomplish < Germanic] —**fur′nish er,** *n.*

Syn. 1 Furnish, equip mean to provide or supply what is needed or appropriate. **Furnish** is a general word applying to the provision of anything necessary, useful, or desirable: *Furnish one good reason for your decision.* **Equip** means to supply whatever is needed for some particular occupation or function: *We equipped the kitchen with new appliances. He is not equipped to translate Latin.*

fur nish ings (fėr′ni shingz), *n.pl.* 1 furniture or equipment for a room, house, etc. 2 accessories of dress; articles of clothing: *men's furnishings.*

fur ni ture (fėr′nə chər), *n.* 1 movable articles needed or useful in a room, house, etc. Beds, chairs, tables, and desks are furniture. 2 articles needed to equip something; equipment.

fur or (fyůr′ôr), *n.* 1 wild enthusiasm or excitement. 2 craze; mania. 3 a rage; fury. [< Latin *furere* to rage]

fu rore (fyůr′ôr, fyů rôr′ē), *n.* furor. [< Italian < Latin *furor*]

furred (fėrd), *adj.* 1 having fur. 2 made, covered, trimmed, or lined with fur. 3 wearing fur. 4 coated with waste matter.

fur ri er (fėr′ē ər), *n.* 1 dealer in furs. 2 person whose work is preparing furs or making and repairing fur coats, etc.

fur ri er y (fėr′ē ər ē), *n., pl.* **-er ies.** business or work of a furrier.

fur ring (fėr′ing), *n.* 1 fur used to make, cover, trim, or line clothing. 2 a coating of foul or waste matter like fur. 3 the fastening of thin strips of wood or other material to beams, walls, etc., to make a level support for laths, plaster, etc., or to provide space for air. 4 the strips or other material so used.

fur row (fėr′ō), *n.* 1 a long, narrow groove or track cut in the earth by a plow. 2 any long, narrow groove or track: *Heavy trucks made deep furrows in the muddy road.* 3 wrinkle: *a furrow in one's brow.* —*v.t.* 1 plow. 2 make furrows in. 3 make wrinkles in; wrinkle: *The old man's face was furrowed with age.* —*v.i.* make a furrow or furrows. [Old English *furh*]

furrow (def. 1)—furrows cut by plowshares

fur ry (fėr′ē), *adj.,* **-ri er, -ri est.** 1 of fur; consisting of fur. 2 covered with fur. 3 soft like fur. —**fur′ri ness,** *n.*

fur seal, any of various species of eared seals that have a thick, soft underfur of great value.

fur ther (fėr′ŦHər), *adj., adv., comparative of* **far,** *v.* —*adj.* 1 more distant; farther: *on the further side.* 2 more; additional: *Do you need further help?* —*adv.* 1 at or to a greater distance: *Seek no further for happiness.* 2 to a more advanced point; to a greater extent: *Inquire further into the matter.* 3 also; in addition; besides: *say further.* —*v.t.* help forward; promote: *Let us further the cause of peace.* See **promote** for synonym study. [Old English *furthra,* adjective, *furthor,* adverb < *forth* forth] —**fur′ther er,** *n.* ➔ See **farther** for usage note.

fur ther ance (fėr′ŦHər əns), *n.* act of furthering; helping forward; advancement.

fur ther more (fėr′ŦHər môr, fėr′ŦHər mōr), *adv.* in addition; moreover; also.

fur ther most (fėr′ŦHər mōst), *adj.* most distant or remote; furthest.

fur thest (fėr′ŦHist), *adv., adj., superlative of* **far.** —*adv.* most distant; farthest. —*adj.* 1 most distant; farthest. 2 to the greatest degree or extent; most.

fur tive (fėr′tiv), *adj.* 1 done quickly and with stealth to avoid being noticed; secret: *a furtive glance into the forbidden room.* 2 sly; stealthy: *She had a furtive manner.* [< Latin *furtivus* < *furtum* theft < *fur* thief] —**fur′tive ly,** *adv.* —**fur′tive ness,** *n.*

fu run cle (fyůr′ung kəl), *n.* boil[2]. [< Latin *furunculus,* diminutive of *fur* thief]

fur y (fyůr′ē), *n., pl.* **fur ies.** 1 wild, fierce anger; rage. 2 violence; fierceness: *the fury of a battle.* 3 a raging or violent person. 4 **Fury** (in Greek and Roman myths) any one of the three Furies. [< Latin *furia*]

furze (fėrz), *n.* 1 a low, prickly, evergreen shrub of the pea family, having yellow flowers, common on waste lands in Europe; gorse; whin. 2 its flower. [Old English *fyrs*]

fuse[1] (fyüz), *n., v.,* **fused, fus ing.** —*n.* a slow-burning wick or other device used to set off a shell, bomb, a blast of gunpowder, or other explosive charge. —*v.t.* furnish with a fuse. Also, **fuze.** [< Italian *fuso* tube < Latin *fusus* spindle]

fuse[2] (fyüz), *n., v.,* **fused, fus ing.** —*n.* wire or strip of easily fusible metal inserted in an

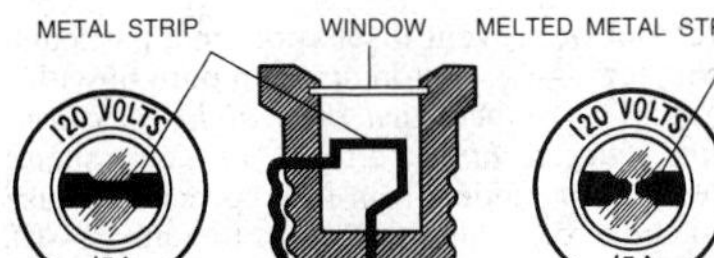

fuse²—This plug fuse screws into an electric circuit. When an overload of current melts the metal strip (as at the right), the fuse must be replaced to restore the circuit.

electric circuit that melts and breaks the connection when the current becomes dangerously strong. *—v.t.* 1 join together by melting; melt. See **melt** for synonym study. 2 blend; unite. *—v.i.* 1 become melted; melt together: *The wax from the two candles fused as they burned.* 2 become blended; unite. [< Latin *fusum* poured, melted]

fu see (fyü zē′), *n.* 1 a large-headed match that will burn in a wind. 2 flare that burns with a red light, used as a warning signal to traffic on railroads or highways. Also, **fuzee.** [< French *fusée*]

fu se lage (fyü′sə läzh, fyü′sə lij), *n.* body of an airplane, to which the wings, tail, etc., are fastened. The fuselage holds the passengers, crew, and cargo. See **airplane** for picture. [< French < *fuselé* spindle-shaped < Latin *fusus* spindle]

fu sel oil (fyü′zəl), an acrid, poisonous, oily liquid, consisting mainly of amyl alcohol, that occurs in alcoholic liquors when they are not distilled enough. [< German *Fusel* bad liquor]

fu si bil i ty (fyü′zə bil′ə tē), *n.* condition or quality of being fusible.

fu si ble (fyü′zə bəl), *adj.* that can be fused or melted.

fu si form (fyü′zə fôrm), *adj.* rounded and tapering from the middle toward each end; shaped like a spindle.

fu sil (fyü′zəl), *n.* a light flintlock musket. [< Middle French, steel for tinder box, ultimately < Latin *focus* hearth]

fu sil ier or **fu sil eer** (fyü′zə lir′), *n.* 1 (formerly) a soldier armed with a fusil. 2 soldier belonging to any of several British regiments formerly armed with fusils.

fu sil lade (fyü′zə lād′), *n., v.,* **-lad ed, -lad ing.** *—n.* 1 a rapid or continuous discharge of many firearms at the same time. 2 something that resembles a fusillade: *The reporters greeted the mayor with a fusillade of questions.* *—v.t.* attack or shoot down by a fusillade. [< French]

fu sion (fyü′zhən), *n.* 1 a melting together; melting; fusing: *Bronze is made by the fusion of copper and tin.* 2 a blending; union: *A third party was formed by the fusion of independent Republicans and Democrats.* 3 a fused mass. 4 the combining of two atomic nuclei to produce a nucleus of greater mass; nuclear fusion. Fusion releases tremendous amounts of energy and is used to produce the reaction in a hydrogen bomb. [< Latin *fusionem* < *fundere* pour, melt]

fusion bomb, hydrogen bomb.

fuss (fus), *n.* much bother about small matters; useless talk and worry; attention given to something not worth it. *—v.i.* make a fuss; be in a bustle: *She fussed about her work nervously.* *—v.t.* make nervous or worried; bother. [origin uncertain] **—fuss′er,** *n.*

fuss y (fus′ē), *adj.,* **fuss i er, fuss i est.** 1 inclined to fuss; hard to please; very particular: *A sick person is likely to be fussy about his food.* 2 elaborately made; much trimmed: *a fussy dress.* 3 full of details; requiring much care: *a fussy job.* **—fuss′i ly,** *adv.* **—fuss′i ness,** *n.*

fus tian (fus′chən), *n.* 1 a coarse, heavy cloth made of cotton and flax, used for clothing in Europe throughout the Middle Ages. 2 a thick cotton cloth like corduroy. 3 speech or writing made up of pompous, high-sounding words and phrases. *—adj.* 1 made of fustian. 2 pompous and high-sounding. [< Old French *fustaigne* < Medieval Latin *fustaneum* < Latin *fustis* stick of wood]

fus tic (fus′tik), *n.* 1 wood of a tropical American tree that yields a yellow dye. 2 the tree, of the same family as the mulberry. 3 the dye. [< French *fustoc* < Spanish]

fust y (fus′tē), *adj.,* **fust i er, fust i est.** 1 having a stale smell; musty. 2 too old-fashioned; out-of-date. [< earlier *fust,* noun, a mold or moldy smell < Old French *fust* wine cask < Latin *fustis* cudgel] **—fust′i ly,** *adv.* **—fust′i ness,** *n.*

fut., future.

fu tile (fyü′tl, fyü′tīl), *adj.* 1 not successful; useless; ineffectual: *He fell down after making futile attempts to keep his balance.* See **vain** for synonym study. 2 not important; trifling. [< Latin *futilis* pouring easily, worthless < *fundere* pour] **—fu′tile ly,** *adv.*

fu til i ty (fyü til′ə tē), *n., pl.* **-ties.** 1 uselessness; ineffectiveness. 2 unimportance. 3 futile action, event, etc.

fut tock (fut′ək), *n.* one of the curved timbers that form part of a compound rib or frame in the framework of a ship's hull. [perhaps contraction of *foot hook*]

fu ture (fyü′chər), *n.* 1 time to come; time to be. 2 the events of the future; what is to come; what will be. 3 chance of success or prosperity: *a young man with a future.* 4 the future tense or a verb form in this tense. 5 **futures,** *pl.* commodities and stocks bought or sold to be received or delivered at a future date. *—adj.* 1 that is to come; that will be; coming. 2 (in grammar) of or expressing the future tense: *One future form of "go" is "will go."* 3 occurring or experienced after death: *our future state.* [< Latin *futurus* about to be, future participle of *esse* be] **—fu′ture less,** *adj.*

hat, āge, fär; let, ēqual, tėrm;
it, īce; hot, ōpen, ôrder;
oil, out; cup, pu̇t, rüle;
ch, child; ng, long; sh, she;
th, thin; ᴛʜ, then; zh, measure;

ə represents *a* in about, *e* in taken, *i* in pencil, *o* in lemon, *u* in circus.

< = from, derived from, taken from.

future perfect, 1 designating or belonging to a tense that expresses past time with respect to some point in future time, as in *Next month he will have left.* 2 such a tense. 3 a verb form in such a tense.

future tense, 1 tense that expresses action taking place in the future, constructed in English with *shall* or *will.* 2 a verb form in the future tense.

fu tur ism (fyü′chə riz′əm), *n.* 1 movement in art originating and flourishing in Italy in the early 1900's, characterized by attempts to express the sensation of movement and growth in objects, not their appearance at some particular moment. 2 a similar tendency in literature and music.

fu tur ist (fyü′chər ist), *n.* person who favors futurism.

fu tu ris tic (fyü′chə ris′tik), *adj.* 1 of or like futurism. 2 of or relating to the future; not traditional; advanced. **—fu′tu ris′ti cal ly,** *adv.*

fu tur i ty (fyü tu̇r′ə tē, fyü tyu̇r′ə tē), *n., pl.* **-ties.** 1 future. 2 a future state or event. 3 quality, condition, or fact of being future.

fuze (fyüz), *n.* fuse¹.

fu zee (fyü zē′), *n.* fusee.

fuzz (fuz), *n.* loose, light, fluffy matter; fine fibers, hair, etc.; fine down: *the fuzz on a caterpillar.* *—v.t.* make fuzzy. *—v.i.* become fuzzy. [perhaps imitative]

fuzz y (fuz′ē), *adj.,* **fuzz i er, fuzz i est.** 1 of fuzz. 2 like fuzz. 3 covered with fuzz. 4 blurred; indistinct: *a fuzzy photograph.* **—fuzz′i ly,** *adv.* **—fuzz′i ness,** *n.*

fwd., forward.

-fy, *suffix forming verbs chiefly from adjectives.* 1 make ___; cause to be ___: *Simplify = make simple.* 2 become ___: *Solidify = become solid.* [< Old French *-fier* < Latin *-ficare* < *facere* do, make]

G g

G[1] or **g** (jē), *n., pl.* **G's** or **g's.** 1 the seventh letter of the English alphabet. 2 unit of force exerted on a body by the pull of gravity. The force exerted on a body at the earth's surface is 1 G. An accelerating body may experience a force of several G's.

G[2] (jē), *n., pl.* **G's.** the fifth tone of the musical scale of C major.

G or **G.,** 1 German. 2 gravity. 3 Gulf.

g, acceleration of gravity.

g., 1 gauge. 2 gram or grams. 3 gravity.

Ga, gallium.

Ga., Georgia.

G.A., 1 General Agent. 2 General Assembly.

gab (gab), *v.,* **gabbed, gab bing,** *n.* INFORMAL. —*v.i.* talk too much; chatter; gabble. —*n.* idle talk; chatter; gabble. [perhaps < Scandinavian (Old Icelandic) *gabba*]

gab ar dine (gab′ər dēn′, gab′ər dēn′), *n.* 1 a closely woven wool, cotton, or rayon cloth with small, diagonal ribs on its surface, used for raincoats, suits, etc. 2 gaberdine (def. 1). [< Spanish *gabardina*]

gab ble (gab′əl), *v.,* **-bled, -bling,** *n.* —*v.i.* talk rapidly with little or no meaning; jabber. —*n.* rapid talk with little or no meaning. [probably imitative] **—gab′bler,** *n.*

gab bro (gab′rō), *n., pl.* **-bros.** any of a group of granular igneous rocks, greenish-gray to black, containing pyroxene and triclinic feldspar. [< Italian]

gab by (gab′ē), *adj.,* **-bi er, -bi est.** INFORMAL. very talkative; garrulous.

gab er dine (gab′ər dēn′, gab′ər dēn′), *n.* 1 a man's long, loose outer garment or cloak, worn in the Middle Ages. 2 gabardine (def. 1).

Ga be ro nes (gä′bə rō′nēz), *n.* capital of Botswana, in the SE part. 14,000.

gab fest (gab′fest′), *n.* U.S. INFORMAL. a lengthy, informal talk or gathering to talk.

ga bi on (gā′bē ən), *n.* 1 cylinder of wicker filled with earth, formerly used as a military defense. 2 a metal cylinder filled with stones, used in building dams, supporting bridge foundations, etc. [< Middle French < Italian *gabbione*]

ga ble (gā′bəl), *n.* 1 end of a ridged roof, with the three-cornered piece of wall that it covers. 2 an end wall with a gable. 3 a triangular ornament or canopy over a door, window, etc. [< Old French < Scandinavian (Old Icelandic) *gafl*] **—ga′ble like′,** *adj.*

gable (def. 1)

ga bled (gā′bəld), *adj.* built with a gable or gables; having or forming gables.

gable roof, roof that forms a gable at one or both ends.

Ga bon (gȧ bôN′), *n.* country in W central Africa, on the Atlantic. 500,000 pop.; 102,000 sq. mi. *Capital:* Libreville.

Gab o nese (gab′ə nēz′), *adj., n., pl.* **-nese.** —*adj.* of Gabon, its people, or their languages. —*n.* native or inhabitant of Gabon.

Ga bri el (gā′brē əl), *n.* (in the Bible) an archangel who acts as God's messenger.

gad[1] (gad), *v.i.,* **gad ded, gad ding.** move about restlessly; go about looking for pleasure or excitement. [Middle English *gadden*] **—gad′der,** *n.*

gad[2] (gad), *n.* goad.

gad a bout (gad′ə bout′), *n.* INFORMAL. person who moves about restlessly or goes about looking for pleasure or excitement. —*adj.* rambling; wandering.

gad fly (gad′flī′), *n., pl.* **-flies.** 1 fly that bites cattle, horses, and other animals. The horsefly and botfly are two kinds. 2 person who goads others to action by irritating or annoying remarks.

gadg et (gaj′it), *n.* INFORMAL. a small mechanical device or contrivance; any ingenious device: *A can opener is a kitchen gadget.* [origin uncertain]

gadg et ry (gaj′ə trē), *n.* 1 gadgets: *electronic gadgetry.* 2 the inventing, making, and using of gadgets.

gad o lin i um (gad′l in′ē əm), *n.* a highly magnetic, rare-earth metallic element which occurs in combination with certain minerals. *Symbol:* Gd; *atomic number* 64. See pages 326 and 327 for table. [< Johann *Gadolin,* 1760-1852, Finnish chemist]

Gads den (gadz′dən), *n.* city in NE Alabama. 54,000.

Gadsden Purchase, region south of the Gila River in what is now Arizona and New Mexico, bought by the United States from Mexico in 1853.

gad wall (gad′wôl), *n., pl.* **-walls** or **-wall.** a freshwater duck of the Northern Hemisphere and Africa, with mottled, grayish-brown plumage. [origin unknown]

Gae a (jē′ə), *n.* (in Greek myths) the earth goddess and mother of the Titans.

Gael (gāl), *n.* 1 a Scottish Highlander. 2 Celt born or living in Scotland, Ireland, or the Isle of Man.

Gael ic (gā′lik), *adj.* of or having to do with the Gaels or their language. —*n.* 1 language of the Gaels. 2 Irish.

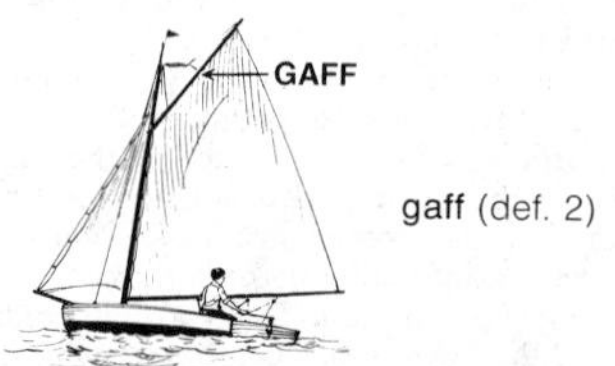

gaff (def. 2)

gaff (gaf), *n.* 1 a strong hook on a handle or barbed spear for pulling large fish out of the water. 2 spar or pole used to extend the upper edge of a fore-and-aft sail. 3 **stand the gaff,** SLANG. hold up well under strain or punishment. —*v.t.* hook or pull (a fish) out of the water with a gaff. [< Old French *gaffe*]

gaffe (gaf), *n.* a blunder; faux pas. [< French]

gaf fer (gaf′ər), *n.* an old man. [alteration of *godfather*]

gag (gag), *n., v.,* **gagged, gag ging.** —*n.* 1 something put into a person's mouth to keep him from talking or crying out. 2 anything used to silence a person; restraint or hindrance to free speech. 3 INFORMAL. amusing remark or trick; joke: *The comedian's gags made the audience laugh.* 4 (in a legislative body) a law or ruling designed to restrict or prevent discussion on a particular subject. —*v.t.* 1 stop up the mouth of with a gag: *The robbers tied the watchman's arms and gagged him.* 2 force to keep silent; restrain or hinder from free speech. 3 cause to choke or strain in an effort to vomit. —*v.i.* choke or strain in an effort to vomit; retch. [probably imitative]

ga ga (gä′gä), *adj.* SLANG. foolish or crazy. [< French]

Ga ga rin (gə gär′ən), *n.* **Yuri,** 1934-1968, Soviet cosmonaut. He was the first human being to travel in outer space.

gage[1] (gāj), *n., v.,* **gaged, gag ing.** —*n.* 1 pledge to fight; challenge. 2 glove or other object thrown down as a challenge to combat. 3 pledge; security. —*v.t.* ARCHAIC. pledge; wager. [< Middle French < Germanic]

gage[2] (gāj), *n., v.t.,* **gaged, gag ing.** gauge.

Gage (gāj), *n.* **Thomas,** 1721-1787, commander-in-chief of the British army in America at the beginning of the Revolutionary War.

gag man (gag′man′), *n., pl.* **-men.** person who invents comic lines and situations for comedians.

gai e ty (gā′ə tē), *n., pl.* **-ties.** 1 a being gay; cheerful liveliness; joyousness; merriment. 2 gay entertainment. 3 bright appearance; showiness: *gaiety of dress.* Also, **gayety.**

gai ly (gā′lē), *adv.* 1 in a gay manner; merrily; happily. 2 brightly; showily: *gaily dressed.* Also, **gayly.**

gain (gān), *v.t.* 1 come to have; get; obtain: *The king gained possession of more lands.* 2 get as an increase, addition, advantage, or profit: *How much did I gain by that?* 3 be the victor in; win: *The stronger army gained the battle.* 4 get to; arrive at; reach: *The swimmer gained the shore.* 5 run too fast by: *The clock gains a minute a day.* 6 **gain on,** come closer to; catch up with: *One boat is gaining on another.* 7 **gain over,** persuade to join one's side. —*v.i.* 1 make a gain or profit. 2 make progress; become better: *The sick child is gaining and will soon be well.* 3 improve in effect.
—*n.* 1 act of gaining or getting anything. 2 what is gained; increase, addition, or advantage: *a gradual gain in speed, a gain of ten per cent over last year's earnings.* 3 getting wealth: *Greed is love of gain.* 4 **gains,** *pl.* profits; earnings; winnings.
[< Middle French *gagner* < Germanic]

gain er (gā′nər), *n.* 1 person or thing that gains. 2 a fancy dive in which the diver turns a back somersault in the air.

gain ful (gān′fəl), *adj.* bringing in money or advantage; profitable. **—gain′ful ly,** *adv.* **—gain′ful ness,** *n.*

gain ly (gān′lē), *adj.* graceful; shapely; comely: *a gainly lad.* [< earlier *gain* nimble < Scandinavian (Old Icelandic) *gegn*]

gain said (gān′sed′), *v.* pt. and pp. of **gainsay.**

gain say (gān′sā′), *v.t.,* **-said, -say ing.** deny; contradict; dispute. [Middle English *gainsayen* < *gain-* against (Old English *gegn-*) + *sayen* say] **—gain′say′er,** *n.*

Gains bor ough (gānz′bėr′ō; *British* gānz′bə rə), *n.* **Thomas,** 1727-1788, English painter.

gainst or **'gainst** (genst, gānst), *prep.* ARCHAIC. against.

gait (gāt), *n.* 1 the manner of walking or running: *He has a lame gait because of an injured foot.* 2 (of horses) any one of various manners of stepping or running, as the gallop, trot, pace, etc. [< Scandinavian (Old Icelandic) *gata* way]

gait ed (gā′tid), *adj.* trained when to use different gaits: *a gaited horse.*

gai ter (gā′tər), *n.* 1 an outer covering for the lower leg or ankle, made of cloth, leather, etc., for outdoor wear. 2 shoe with an elastic strip in each side. [< French *guêtre* < Germanic]

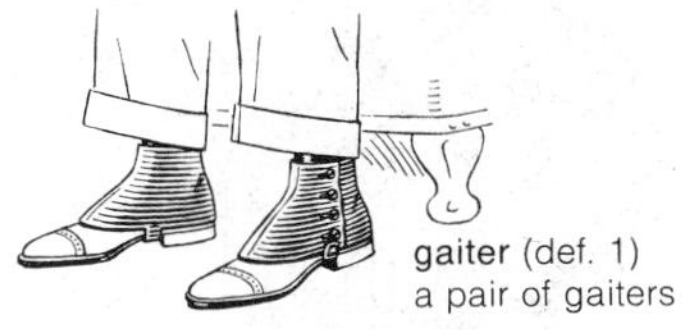
gaiter (def. 1) a pair of gaiters

gal[1] (gal), *n.* U.S. INFORMAL. girl.

gal[2] (gal), *n.* unit for measuring gravity, equal to one centimeter per second per second. [< *Gal(ileo)*]

gal., gallon. *pl.* **gal.** or **gals.**

Gal., Galatians.

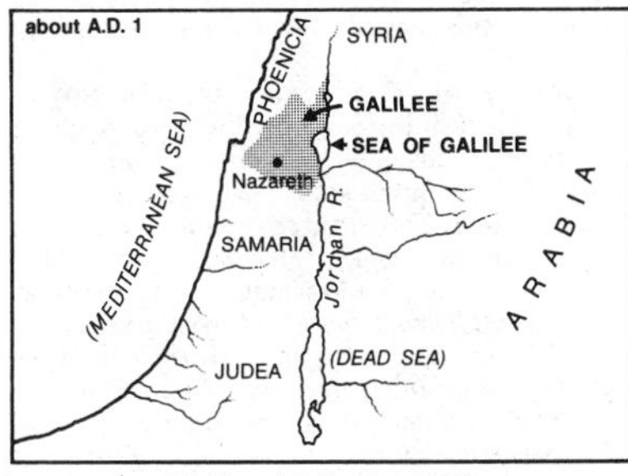

Galilee (defs. 1 and 2)

ga la (gā′lə, gal′ə), *adj.* of festivity; festive. —*n.* a festive occasion; festival. [< Italian < Old French *gale* merriment < Germanic]

ga la bi a or **ga la bi ya** (gə lä′bē ə), *n.* a flowing white robe worn in Egypt and many parts of Africa. [< Arabic *gallābīya*]

ga lac tic (gə lak′tik), *adj.* of or having to do with the Milky Way or with other galaxies.

ga lac tose (gə lak′tōs), *n.* a white, crystalline monosaccharide, found in combined form in lactose, pectins, gums, and certain other substances. *Formula:* $C_6H_{12}O_6$

ga lac to se mi a (gə lak′tō sē′mē ə), *n.* disease of infants caused by lack of an enzyme necessary for the digestion of galactose.

ga la go (gə lā′gō), *n., pl.* **-gos.** any of several species of small, furry, nocturnal primates of the African forests; bush baby. They move very nimbly on trees and have a childlike cry. [< a native name]

Gal a had (gal′ə had), *n.* (in Arthurian legends) the noblest and purest knight of King Arthur's Round Table, who found the Holy Grail.

Ga lá pa gos Islands (gə lä′pə gəs, gə lä′pə gōs), group of islands in the Pacific, west of and belonging to Ecuador. 3000 pop.; 2900 sq. mi.

Gal a te a (gal′ə tē′ə), *n.* (in Greek legends) an ivory statue of a maiden, carved by Pygmalion. When he fell in love with the statue, Aphrodite gave it life.

Ga la tia (gə lā′shə), *n.* ancient country in central Asia Minor that later became a Roman province. **—Ga la′tian,** *adj., n.*

Ga la tians (gə lā′shənz), *n.* book of the New Testament, written by Saint Paul.

gal ax y (gal′ek sē), *n., pl.* **-ax ies.** 1 system or aggregate of stars, cosmic dust, and gas held together by gravitation. Each galaxy holds many solar systems, and there are billions of galaxies in the universe. 2 **Galaxy,** the Milky Way. 3 a brilliant or splendid group, especially of beautiful women or distinguished persons. [< Greek *galaxias* < *galaktos* milk]

gale (gāl), *n.* 1 a very strong wind. 2 (in meteorology) a wind having a velocity of 32 to 63 miles per hour. 3 breeze. 4 a noisy outburst. [origin uncertain]

Ga len (gā′lən), *n.* **Claudius,** A.D. 138?-201?, Greek physician and writer.

ga le na (gə lē′nə), *n.* a metallic, gray mineral containing lead and sulfur. It is the chief source of lead. *Formula:* PbS [< Latin]

Ga li cia (gə lish′ə), *n.* 1 region in central Europe, now divided between Poland and the Soviet Union. 2 former kingdom in NW Spain. **—Ga li′cian,** *adj., n.*

Gal i le an (gal′ə lē′ən), *adj.* of or having to do with Galilee or its people. —*n.* 1 native or inhabitant of Galilee. 2 **the Galilean,** Jesus.

Gal i lee (gal′ə lē′), *n.* 1 region in N Israel that was a Roman province in the time of Christ. 2 **Sea of,** a small, freshwater lake in NE Israel; Sea of Tiberias; Lake of Gennesaret. 14 mi. long.

Gal i le o (gal′ə lē′ō, gal′ə lā′ō), *n.* 1564-1642, Italian astronomer, physicist, mathematician, and inventor.

gall[1] (gôl), *n.* 1 bile of animals. 2 anything very bitter or harsh. 3 bitterness; hate. 4 SLANG. too great boldness; impudence. [Old English *gealla*]

gall[2] (gôl), *v.t.* 1 make sore by rubbing: *The rough strap galled the horse's skin.* 2 annoy; irritate. —*v.i.* become sore by rubbing. —*n.* 1 a sore spot on the skin caused by rubbing, especially one on a horse's back. 2 cause of annoyance or irritation. [< Latin *galla* gall[3]]

gall[3] (gôl), *n.* an abnormal growth that forms on the leaves, stems, or roots of plants, caused by insects, parasitic bacteria, or fungi. The galls of oak trees are the source of tannin. [Old French *galle* < Latin *galla*]

gal lant (*adj.* gal′ənt *for 1-3,* gə lant′, gal′ənt *for 4; n.* gal′ənt, gə lant′), *adj.* 1 noble in spirit or in conduct: *King Arthur was a gallant knight.* 2 brave and high-spirited; heroic: *a gallant antagonist.* 3 grand; splendid; stately: *a gallant ship with sails spread.* 4 very polite and attentive to women. —*n.* 1 a spirited or courageous man. 2 man who is very polite and attentive to women. 3 man who wears showy, stylish clothes. 4 lover; paramour. [< Old French *galant,* present participle of *galer* make merry < *gale* merriment] **—gal′lant ly,** *adv.* **—gal′lant ness,** *n.*

gal lant ry (gal′ən trē), *n., pl.* **-ries.** 1 noble spirit or conduct; bravery. 2 great politeness and attention to women. 3 a gallant act or speech. 4 ARCHAIC. gay appearance; showy display.

Gal la tin (gal′ə tin), *n.* **Albert,** 1761-1849, American statesman, secretary of the treasury from 1801 to 1813.

gall bladder, sac attached to the liver, in which excess bile is stored until needed. See **liver**[1] for diagram.

gal le on (gal′ē ən, gal′yən), *n.* a large, high ship with three or four decks, used especially in the 1400's and 1500's. [< Spanish *galeón* < *galea* galley]

gal ler y (gal′ər ē), *n., pl.* **-ler ies.** 1 a hall or long, narrow passage, often with windows along one side. 2 balcony looking down into a large hall or room. 3 the highest balcony of a theater. 4 people who sit there. 5 group of people watching or listening. 6 a covered walk or porch. 7 an underground passage. 8 room or building used to show collections of pictures and statues. 9 collection of works of art. 10 room or building used for a special purpose, such as taking photographs or practicing shooting. 11 **play to the gallery,** try to get the praise or favor of the common people by doing or saying what will please them. [< Old French *galeria* < Italian *galleria* < Medieval Latin *galilea* church porch]

hat, āge, fär; let, ēqual, tėrm;
it, īce; hot, ōpen, ôrder;
oil, out; cup, pu̇t, rüle;
ch, child; ng, long; sh, she;
th, thin; ᴛʜ, then; zh, measure;

ə represents *a* in about, *e* in taken, *i* in pencil, *o* in lemon, *u* in circus.

< = from, derived from, taken from.

galley (def. 1)

gal ley (gal′ē), *n., pl.* **-leys.** 1 a long, narrow ship propelled by both oars and sails, used in medieval times in the Mediterranean. 2 a large warship of the ancient Greeks and Romans with one or more banks of oars. 3 a large rowboat. 4 kitchen of a ship or airplane. 5 (in printing) a long, narrow tray for holding type that has been set. 6 galley proof. [< Old French *galee,* ultimately < Medieval Greek *galea*]

galley proof, (in printing) a proof printed from type in a galley.

galley slave, 1 slave or criminal forced or condemned to row a galley. 2 drudge.

gall fly (gôl′flī′), *n., pl.* **-flies.** any of various flies or other insects that deposit their eggs in plants, causing galls to form.

Gal lic (gal′ik), *adj.* 1 of or having to do with Gaul or its people: *Caesar's Gallic Wars.* 2 French: *Gallic wit.*

gal lic acid (gal′ik), an organic acid obtained especially from galls on plants, used in making ink and dyes, in tanning, etc. *Formula:* $C_7H_6O_5 \cdot H_2O$

gal li cism or **Gal li cism** (gal′ə siz′əm), *n.* a French idiom or expression.

gal li gas kins (gal′ə gas′kənz), *n.pl.* 1 kind of loose hose or breeches worn in the

galleon

1500's and 1600's. 2 BRITISH DIALECT. leggings. [alteration of Middle French *(à la) greguesque* (in the) Greek fashion]

gal li mau fry (gal′ə mô′frē), *n., pl.* **-fries.** a confused jumble; hodge-podge. [< Middle French *galimafrée*]

gal li na ceous (gal′ə nā′shəs), *adj.* of or belonging to an order of birds that nest on the ground and fly only short distances. Chickens, turkeys, pheasants, grouse, partridges, etc., are gallinaceous birds. [< Latin *gallinaceus* < *gallina* hen < *gallus* cock]

gall ing (gô′ling), *adj.* that galls; chafing; irritating.

gal li nule (gal′ə nül, gal′ə nyül), *n.* any of certain long-toed wading birds of the same family as the rail. [< New Latin *gallinula* < Latin *gallina* hen]

Gal lip o li (gə lip′ə lē), *n.* peninsula in NW Turkey, forming the N shore of the Dardanelles. 60 mi. long.

gal li pot (gal′ə pot), *n.* a small pot or jar of glazed earthenware used especially by druggists to hold medicine, salve, etc. [< *galley* + *pot*]

gal li um (gal′ē əm), *n.* a rare grayish-white metallic element similar to mercury, with a melting point slightly above room temperature and high boiling point, used in thermometers. *Symbol:* Ga; *atomic number* 31. See pages 326 and 327 for table. [< New Latin]

gallium ar se nide (är′sə nīd), a crystalline compound of gallium and arsenic, used as a semiconductor. *Formula:* GaAs

gal li vant (gal′ə vant), *v.i.* 1 go about seeking pleasure; gad about. 2 flirt. [perhaps < *gallant*]

gall nut (gôl′nut′), *n.* a nutlike gall on plants.

gal lon (gal′ən), *n.* unit of measure for liquids equal to 4 quarts. The United States gallon equals 231 cubic inches. The British gallon equals 277.274 cubic inches. See **measure** for table. [< Old French *galon*]

gal lon age (gal′ə nij), *n.* amount in gallons.

gal lop (gal′əp), *n.* 1 the fastest gait of a horse or other four-footed animal. In a gallop, all four feet are off the ground together once in each stride. 2 a ride at a gallop. 3 a rapid rate. —*v.i.* 1 ride at a gallop. 2 go at a gallop. 3 go very fast; hurry. —*v.t.* cause to go at a gallop: *gallop a horse.* [< Middle French *galop* < *galoper* < Germanic. Doublet of WALLOP.] **—gal′lop er,** *n.*

gal lows (gal′ōz), *n., pl.* **-lows es** or **-lows.** 1 a wooden structure usually consisting of a crossbar on two upright posts, used for hanging criminals. 2 punishment by hanging. [Middle English *galwes, galghes,* Old English *galga*]

gall stone (gôl′stōn′), *n.* a pebblelike mass of cholesterol, mineral salts, etc., that sometimes forms in the gall bladder or its duct. When one or more gallstones stop the flow of bile, a painful illness results.

Gal lup (gal′əp), *n.* **George Horace,** born 1901, American statistician and specialist in surveys of public opinion.

gall wasp, any of a family of wasps which cause galls on plants.

gal op (gal′əp), *n.* 1 a lively dance in duple time. 2 the music for it. —*v.i.* dance a galop. [< French]

ga lore (gə lôr′, gə lōr′), *adv.* in abundance: *Every town has automobiles galore.* [< Irish *go leōr* to sufficiency]

ga losh es (gə losh′iz), *n.pl.* rubber or plastic overshoes covering the ankles, worn in wet or snowy weather. [< Old French *galoche*]

gals., gallons.

Gals wor thy (gôlz′wėr′ᴛʜē), *n.* **John,** 1867-1933, English novelist and playwright.

Gal ton (gôlt′n), *n.* Sir **Francis,** 1822-1911, English scientist noted for his researches in heredity and meteorology.

ga lumph (gə lumf′), *v.i.* gallop in a clumsy way: *cows galumphing home.* [coined by Lewis Carroll < *gallop*]

Gal va ni (gäl vä′nē), *n.* **Luigi,** 1737-1798, Italian physician who discovered that electricity can be produced by chemical action.

gal van ic (gal van′ik), *adj.* 1 of, caused by, or producing an electric current by chemical action; voltaic. 2 startling; galvanizing: *galvanic activity.* **—gal van′i cal ly,** *adv.*

gal va nism (gal′və niz′əm), *n.* 1 electricity produced by chemical action. 2 branch of physics dealing with this. 3 use of such electricity for medical purposes.

gal va nize (gal′və nīz), *v.t.,* **-nized, -niz ing.** 1 apply an electric current produced by chemical action to. 2 arouse suddenly; startle. 3 cover (iron or steel) with a thin coating of zinc to prevent rust. [< Luigi *Galvani*] **—gal′va ni za′tion,** *n.* **—gal′va niz′er,** *n.*

gal va nom e ter (gal′və nom′ə tər), *n.* instrument for detecting, measuring, and determining the direction of a small electric current.

gal va no met ric (gal′və nə met′rik, gal van′ə met′rik), *adj.* having to do with or measured by a galvanometer.

gal va no scope (gal′və nō skōp, gal van′ō skōp), *n.* instrument for detecting very small electric currents and showing their direction.

Gal ves ton (gal′və stən), *n.* seaport in SE Texas. 62,000.

Gal way (gôl′wā), *n.* 1 county in W Republic of Ireland, on the Atlantic. 2 seaport and the county seat of Galway. 25,000.

Ga ma (gä′mə, gam′ə), *n.* **Vasco da.** See **da Gama.**

Gam bet ta (gam bet′ə), *n.* **Léon,** 1838-1882, French statesman.

Gam bi a (gam′bē ə), *n.* **The,** country in W Africa, a member of the Commonwealth of Nations. 379,000 pop.; 4000 sq. mi. *Capital:* Bathurst. **—Gam′bi an,** *adj., n.*

gam bit (gam′bit), *n.* 1 way of opening a game of chess by sacrificing a pawn or a piece to gain some advantage. 2 any opening move or action, especially one intended to gain some advantage. [< Italian *gambetto* a tripping up < *gamba* leg. See GAMBOL.]

gam ble (gam′bəl), *v.,* **-bled, -bling,** *n.* —*v.i.* 1 play games of chance for money. 2 take a risk; take great risks in business or speculation. —*v.t.* 1 risk (money or other things of value). 2 **gamble away,** lose or squander by gambling: *gamble away a fortune.* —*n.* a risky act or undertaking. [probably related to GAME.]

gam bler (gam′blər), *n.* 1 person who gambles a great deal. 2 person whose occupation is gambling.

gam boge (gam bōj′, gam büzh′), *n.* a gum resin from certain tropical trees of southeastern Asia, used as a yellow pigment and as a cathartic. [< New Latin *gambogium* < *Cambodia*]

gam bol (gam′bəl), *n.* a running and jumping about in play; caper; frolic. —*v.i.* run and jump about in play; frolic: *Lambs gamboled in the meadow.* [earlier *gambade* < Middle French < Italian *gambata* < *gamba* leg < Late Latin *camba* < Greek *kampē* a bend]

gam brel (gam′brəl), *n.* 1 hock of a horse or other animal. 2 gambrel roof. [< Middle French *gamberel* < *gambe* leg]

gambrel roof

gambrel roof, roof having two slopes on each side. The lower slope is steeper than the upper one.

gam bu si a (gam byü′zē ə, gam byü′sē ə), *n.* a small American fish of the same order as the guppy that feeds largely on mosquito larvae, and is used in various parts of the world in the control of malaria. [< American Spanish]

game[1] (gām), *n., adj.,* **gam er, gam est,** *v.,* **gamed, gam ing.** —*n.* 1 way of playing; pastime; amusement: *a game of tag.* See **play** for synonym study. 2 things needed to play a game: *This store sells games.* 3 contest with certain rules: *a football game.* One person or side tries to win it. 4 a single round in a game: *The winner won three games out of five.* 5 the score in a game: *At the end of the first quarter the game was 14 to 7 in our favor.* 6 number of points required to win. 7 a particular manner of playing a game: *Our quarterback is playing a good game today.* 8 activity or undertaking that is carried on like a game: *the game of diplomacy.* 9 INFORMAL. any activity, vocation, etc., in which there is competition: *the acting game, the insurance game.* 10 plan; scheme: *They tried to trick us, but we saw through their game.* 11 wild animals, birds, or fish hunted or caught for sport or for food. 12 flesh of wild animals or birds used for food. 13 **make game of,** make fun of; laugh at; ridicule. 14 **play the game,** be fair; follow the rules; be a good sport. 15 **the game is up,** the plan or scheme has failed.
—*adj.* 1 having to do with game, hunting, or fishing: *Game laws protect wildlife.* 2 brave; plucky: *The losing team put up a game fight.* 3 having spirit or will enough: *The explorer was game for any adventure.*
—*v.t., v.i.* gamble.
[Old English *gamen* joy] **—game′ly,** *adv.* **—game′ness,** *n.*

game[2] (gām), *adj.* INFORMAL. lame; crippled; injured: *a game leg.* [origin uncertain]

game cock (gām′kok′), *n.* a rooster bred and trained for fighting.

game fish, fish that fights to get away when hooked.

game fowl, fowl of a breed trained for fighting.

game keep er (gām′kē′pər), *n.* person employed to take care of the wild animals and birds on an estate or in a certain district and prevent anyone from stealing them or killing them without permission.

games man ship (gāmz′mən ship), *n.* skill in using ploys to gain an advantage in a game, contest, etc.

game some (gām′səm), *adj.* full of play;

ready to play; sportive; playful. **—game′some ly,** *adv.*

game ster (gām′stər), *n.* gambler.

gam ete (gam′ēt, gə mēt′), *n.* a mature reproductive cell capable of uniting with another to form a fertilized cell that can develop into a new plant or animal; an egg or sperm cell; germ cell. [< New Latin *gameta* < Greek *gametē* wife, *gametēs* husband < *gamos* marriage]

ga met ic (gə met′ik), *adj.* of or having to do with gametes.

ga me to cyte (gə mē′tō sīt), *n.* cell that produces gametes by division.

gam e to gen e sis (gam′ə tō jen′ə sis), *n.* formation of gametes.

ga me to phyte (gə mē′tō fīt), *n.* the individual plant or generation of a plant which produces gametes.

game warden, official whose duty is to enforce the game laws in a certain district.

gam in (gam′ən), *n.* 1 a neglected child left to roam about the streets. 2 a small, lively person. [< French]

ga mine (ga mēn′), *n.* 1 a neglected girl left to roam about the streets. 2 a small, lively girl. [< French]

gam ing (gā′ming), *n.* the playing of games of chance for money; gambling.

gam ma (gam′ə), *n.* the third letter of the Greek alphabet (Γ, γ).

gamma globulin, component of human blood plasma containing many antibodies which protect against infectious diseases.

gamma radiation, gamma rays.

gamma ray, electromagnetic wave of very high frequency given off spontaneously by radium and other radioactive substances. Gamma rays are like X rays, but have a shorter wave length. Deadly gamma rays are emitted by the nuclei of excited atoms in atomic explosions. See **radiation** for table.

gam mer (gam′ər), *n.* ARCHAIC. an old woman. [alteration of *godmother*]

gam mon[1] (gam′ən), *n.* INFORMAL. nonsense; humbug. *—v.i.* talk nonsense, especially to deceive. *—v.i.* deceive; hoax. [probably related to Middle English and Old English *gamen* game[1]]

gam mon[2] (gam′ən), *n.* 1 the lower end of a side of bacon. 2 a smoked or cured ham. [< Old French *gambon* < *gambe* leg < Late Latin *camba.* See GAMBOL.]

-gamous, *combining form.* 1 marrying: *Bigamous = marrying twice.* 2 joined or joining: *Heterogamous = having to do with the joining of unequal gametes.* [< Greek *-gamos* < *gamos* marriage]

gam ut (gam′ət), *n.* 1 the whole series of notes on the musical scale. 2 the major scale. 3 the whole range of anything: *During the day I ran the gamut of feeling from hope to despair.* [contraction of Medieval Latin *gamma ut* < *gamma G* the lowest tone + *ut* (later *do*) the first note of the scale]

gam y (gā′mē), *adj.,* **gam i er, gam i est.** 1 having a strong taste or smell like the flesh of wild animals or birds. 2 brave; plucky. **—gam′i ly,** *adv.* **—gam′i ness,** *n.*

-gamy, *combining form.* 1 marriage: *Polygamy = plural marriage.* 2 condition of being joined together: *Allogamy = the condition of being joined in cross-fertilization.* [< Greek *-gamia* < *gamos* marriage]

gan der (gan′dər), *n.* 1 a male goose. 2 SLANG. a long look. [Old English *gandra*]

Gan dhi (gän′dē, gan′dē), *n.* **1 Indira,** born 1917, prime minister of India since 1966. **2 Mohandas K.,** 1869-1948, Hindu political, social, and religious leader in India, known as "Mahatma Gandhi."

gan dy dancer (gan′dē), SLANG. 1 member of a railroad section gang. 2 a seasonal or itinerant laborer. [origin uncertain]

gang[1] (gang), *n.* 1 group of people acting or going around together, especially a group engaged in some improper, unlawful, or criminal activity: *a gang of thieves.* 2 group of people working together under one foreman: *A gang of workmen was mending the road.* 3 set of similar tools or machines arranged to work together: *a gang of saws.* *—v.i.* INFORMAL. form a gang. *—v.t.* 1 INFORMAL. attack in a gang. **2 gang up on,** INFORMAL. oppose or attack as a group. [Old English, a going]

gang[2] (gang), *v.i.* SCOTTISH. walk or go. [Old English *gangan*]

Gan ges River (gan′jēz′), river flowing across N India and Bangladesh into the Bay of Bengal. It is regarded as sacred by the Hindus. 1550 mi.

gang land (gang′land′, gang′lənd), *n.* the world of gangsters.

gan gli a (gang′glē ə), *n.* a pl. of **ganglion.**

gan gling (gang′gling), *adj.* awkwardly tall and slender; lank and loosely built.

gan gli on (gang′glē ən), *n., pl.* **-gli a** or **-gli ons.** group of nerve cells forming a nerve center, especially outside of the brain or spinal cord. [< Greek]

gan gli on ic (gang′glē on′ik), *adj.* 1 having to do with a ganglion or ganglia. 2 having or characterized by ganglia.

gan gly (gang′glē), *adj.,* **-gli er, -gli est.** gangling.

gang plank (gang′plangk′), *n.* a movable bridge used in getting on and off a ship, etc.; gangway.

gang plow, plow or set of plows having several plowshares that operate simultaneously.

gan grene (gang′grēn′, gang grēn′), *n., v.,* **-grened, -gren ing.** *—n.* death and decay of tissue when the blood supply of a part of a living person or animal is cut off by injury, infection, or freezing; mortification; necrosis. *—v.t.* cause gangrene in. *—v.i.* be or become affected with gangrene; decay. [< Latin *gangraena*]

gan gre nous (gang′grə nəs), *adj.* of or having gangrene; decaying.

gang ster (gang′stər), *n.* member of a gang of criminals, roughs, etc.

gang ster ism (gang′stə riz′əm), *n.* 1 the commission of crimes by members of an organized gang. 2 gangsters or their crimes. 3 crime; delinquency.

Gang tok (gang′tok), *n.* capital of Sikkim, in the S part. 12,000.

gangue (gang), *n.* the worthless earthy or stony matter in a mineral deposit; matrix in which an ore is found. [< French < German *Gang* vein of ore]

gang way (gang′wā′), *n.* 1 passageway. 2 passageway on a ship. 3 gangplank. *—interj.* INFORMAL. get out of the way! stand aside and make room!

gan net (gan′it), *n.* a large, fish-eating sea bird of the same family as the booby, that resembles a goose but has a sharper bill, long, pointed wings, and a shorter tail. [Old English *ganot*]

gan oid (gan′oid), *adj.* (of fishes) having hard scales of bone overlaid with enamel. *—n.* a ganoid fish. Sturgeons and garfish are ganoids. [< French *ganoïde* < Greek *ganos* brightness + *eidos* form]

hat, āge, fär; let, ēqual, tėrm;
it, īce; hot, ōpen, ôrder;
oil, out; cup, pu̇t, rüle;
ch, child; ng, long; sh, she;
th, thin; ᴛʜ, then; zh, measure;

ə represents *a* in about, *e* in taken, *i* in pencil, *o* in lemon, *u* in circus.

< = from, derived from, taken from.

gant let[1] (gônt′lit, gant′lit, gänt′lit), *n.* gauntlet[1].

gant let[2] (gônt′lit, gant′lit, gänt′lit), *n.* gauntlet[2].

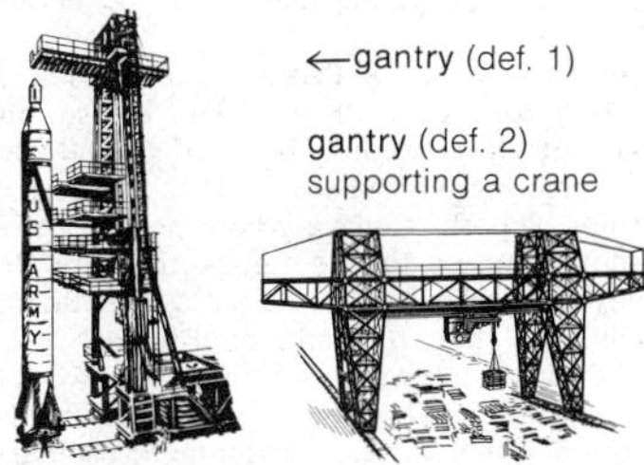

gan try (gan′trē), *n., pl.* **-tries.** 1 a movable framework used for erecting and servicing vertically mounted rockets or missiles. 2 a bridgelike framework for supporting a suspended movable crane, light signals over railroad tracks, etc. [probably < Old North French *gantier* < Latin *cantherius* rafter, frame]

Gan y mede (gan′ə mēd′), *n.* (in Greek and Roman myths) a beautiful youth who became cupbearer to the gods of Olympus.

gaol (jāl), *n., v.t.* BRITISH. jail. **—gaol′er,** *n.*

gap (gap), *n.* 1 a broken place; opening: *a gap in a fence.* 2 an empty part; unfilled space; blank: *The record is not complete; there are several gaps in it.* 3 a wide difference of opinion, character, etc. 4 a pass through mountains. 5 space between two electrodes, such as that in the spark plug of a gasoline engine, across which an electric spark jumps. [Middle English < Old Icelandic. Related to GAPE.]

gape (gāp, gap), *v.,* **gaped, gap ing,** *n.* *—v.i.* 1 open wide: *A deep hole in the earth gaped before us.* 2 open the mouth wide; yawn. 3 stare with the mouth open. *—n.* 1 a wide opening. 2 act of opening the mouth wide; yawning. 3 an open-mouthed stare. 4 **the gapes, a** fit of yawning. **b** disease of birds and poultry, caused by a nematode worm. [Middle English < Old Icelandic *gapa*] **—gap′er,** *n.* **—gap′ing ly,** *adv.*

gar (gär), *n., pl.* **gars** or **gar.** any of a family of fishes with long slender bodies covered with hard scales and long, narrow jaws; garfish. [Old English *gār* spear]

G.A.R., Grand Army of the Republic.

ga rage (gə räzh′, gə räj′), *n., v.,* **-raged, -rag ing.** *—n.* 1 place where automobiles are kept. 2 shop for repairing automobiles. *—v.t.* put or keep in a garage. [< French]

ga rage man (gə räzh′man′, gə räj′man′), *n., pl.* **-men.** man who works in a garage, especially an automobile mechanic.

garb (gärb), *n.* 1 the way one is dressed.

2 clothing. 3 outward covering, form, or appearance. —*v.t.* clothe. [< Middle French *garbe* < Italian *garbo* grace]

gar bage (gär′bij), *n.* 1 scraps of food to be thrown away; waste animal or vegetable matter from a kitchen, store, etc. 2 INFORMAL. anything of no value. [Middle English]

gar ble (gär′bəl), *v.t.*, **-bled, -bling.** 1 make unfair or misleading selections from (facts, statements, writings, etc.); omit parts of, often in order to misrepresent. 2 confuse or mix up (statements, words, letters, etc.) unintentionally. [< Middle French *garbeler* to sift < Italian *garbellare* < Arabic *gharbala,* probably < Late Latin *cribellare,* ultimately < Latin *cribrum* sieve] **—gar′bler,** *n.*

gar çon (gär sôɴ′), *n., pl.* **-çons** (-sôɴ′). FRENCH. 1 a young man; boy. 2 servant. 3 waiter.

Gar da (gär′dä), *n.* **Lake,** the largest lake in Italy, in the N part, E of Milan. 143 sq. mi.

gar den (gärd′n), *n.* 1 piece of ground used for growing vegetables, herbs, flowers, or fruits. 2 park or place where people go for amusement or to see things that are displayed: *the botanical garden.* 3 a fertile and delightful spot; well-cultivated region. —*v.i.* take care of a garden; make a garden; work in a garden. —*adj.* 1 growing or grown in a garden; for a garden. 2 common; ordinary. [< Old North French *gardin* < Germanic] **—gar′den like′,** *adj.*

gar den er (gärd′nər), *n.* 1 person employed to take care of a garden, lawn, etc. 2 person who makes a garden or works in a garden.

Garden Grove, city in SW California, near Los Angeles. 121,000.

gar de nia (gär dē′nyə, gär dē′nē ə), *n.* 1 an evergreen shrub or small tree of the same family as the madder, bearing fragrant white flowers with smooth, waxy petals. 2 its flower. [< Alexander *Garden,* 1730-1791, Scottish botanist]

Gar field (gär′fēld′), *n.* **James A.,** 1831-1881, the 20th president of the United States. He was assassinated in 1881, his first year in office.

gar fish (gär′fish′), *n., pl.* **-fish es** or **-fish.** gar.

Gar gan tu a (gär gan′chü ə), *n.* a good-natured giant in a satire by Rabelais. He was a tremendous eater and drinker.

gar gan tu an or **Gar gan tu an** (gär-gan′chü ən), *adj.* enormous; gigantic; huge.

gar gle (gär′gəl), *v.*, **-gled, -gling,** *n.* —*v.i.* wash or rinse the throat with a liquid kept in motion by the outgoing breath. —*v.t.* wash or rinse with a gargle. —*n.* liquid used for gargling. [probably < Middle French *gargouiller* < *gargouille* throat]

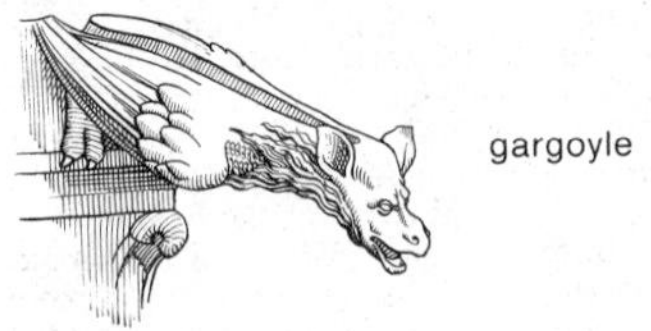

gargoyle

gar goyle (gär′goil), *n.* spout for carrying off rain water, ending in a grotesque figure of a head that projects from the gutter of a building. [< Middle French *gargouille* throat, waterspout]

Gar i bal di (gar′ə bôl′dē), *n.* **Giuseppe,** 1807-1882, Italian patriot and general.

gar ish (ger′ish, gar′ish), *adj.* 1 excessively bright; glaring: *a garish yellow.* 2 obtrusively bright in color; gaudy: *a garish suit.* 3 adorned to excess. [ultimately < obsolete *gaure* to stare] **—gar′ish ly,** *adv.* **—gar′ish ness,** *n.*

gar land (gär′lənd), *n.* wreath or string of flowers, leaves, etc. —*v.t.* 1 decorate with garlands. 2 form into garlands. [< Old French *garlande*]

Gar land (gar′lənd), *n.* city in NE Texas. 81,000.

gar lic (gär′lik), *n.* 1 plant of the same genus as the onion, whose pungent, strong-smelling bulb is composed of small sections called cloves. 2 its bulb, used to season meats, salads, etc. [Old English *gārlēac* < *gār* spear + *lēac* leek]

gar lick y (gär′lə kē), *adj.* smelling or tasting of garlic.

gar ment (gär′mənt), *n.* any article of clothing. —*v.t.* clothe. [< Old French *garnement* < *garnir* fit out]

gar ner (gär′nər), *v.t.* 1 gather and store away: *Wheat is cut and garnered at harvest time.* 2 collect or deposit. —*n.* 1 storehouse for grain. 2 a store of anything. [< Old French *gernier, grenier* < Latin *granarium* granary]

Gar ner (gär′nər), *n.* **John Nance,** 1868-1967, vice-president of the United States from 1933 to 1941.

gar net (gär′nit), *n.* 1 a hard, glassy silicate mineral occurring in many varieties. A common, deep-red, transparent variety is used as a gem and as an abrasive. 2 a deep red. —*adj.* deep-red. [Middle English *gernet* < Old French *grenat* of pomegranate color < *(pomme) grenate* pomegranate] **—gar′net like′,** *adj.*

garnet paper, paper coated with finely crushed garnets held by glue, used like sandpaper for polishing.

gar nish (gär′nish), *n.* 1 something laid on or around food as a decoration: *The turkey was served with a garnish of cranberries and parsley.* 2 decoration; trimming. —*v.t.* 1 decorate (food). 2 decorate; trim. 3 warn or notify by a garnishment. [< Old French *garniss-,* a form of *garnir* provide, defend < Germanic. Related to WARN.] **—gar′nish er,** *n.*

gar nish ee (gär′ni shē′), *v.t.* **-nish eed, -nish ee ing.** 1 withhold (a person's money or property) by legal authority in payment of a debt. If a creditor garnishees a debtor's salary, a certain portion of the salary is withheld and paid to the creditor. 2 notify (a person) not to hand over money or property belonging to the defendant in a lawsuit until the plaintiff's claims have been settled: *The debtor's employer was garnisheed.*

gar nish ment (gär′nish mənt), *n.* 1 decoration; trimming. 2 a legal notice warning a person to hold in his possession property that belongs to the defendant in a lawsuit until the plaintiff's claims have been settled. 3 the withholding of a person's money or property by legal authority in payment of a debt.

gar ni ture (gär′nə chər), *n.* decoration; trimming; garnish.

Ga ronne River (gȧ rôn′), river in SW France. 357 mi.

ga rotte (gə rot′, gə rōt′), *n., v.t.,* **-rot ted, -rot ting.** garrote.

gar ret (gar′it), *n.* 1 space in a house just below a sloping roof; attic. 2 room or apartment in such a place. [< Old French *garite* < *garir* defend]

Gar rick (gar′ik), *n.* **David,** 1717-1779, English actor and theater manager.

gar ri son (gar′ə sən), *n.* 1 group of soldiers stationed in a fort, town, etc., to defend it. 2 place that has a garrison. —*v.t.* 1 station soldiers in (a fort, town, etc.) to defend it. 2 occupy (a fort, town, etc.) as a garrison. [< Old French *garison* < *garir* defend]

Gar ri son (gar′ə sən), *n.* **William Lloyd,** 1805-1879, American editor and reformer who opposed slavery.

garrison state, country organized in a military way in time of peace as well as of war.

gar rote (gə rot′, gə rōt′), *n., v.,* **-rot ed, -rot ing.** —*n.* 1 a method of executing a person by strangling him with an iron collar. The collar is fastened to a post and tightened by a screw. 2 the iron collar used for this type of execution. 3 strangulation, especially in order to rob. 4 any device used to strangle. —*v.t.* 1 execute by garroting. 2 strangle and rob; strangle. Also, **garotte.** [< Spanish] **—gar rot′er,** *n.*

gar ru li ty (gə rü′lə tē), *n.* 1 talkativeness. 2 wordiness.

gar ru lous (gar′ə ləs, gar′yə ləs), *adj.* 1 talking too much; talkative. 2 using too many words; wordy. [< Latin *garrulus* < *garrire* to chatter] **—gar′ru lous ly,** *adv.* **—gar′ru lous ness,** *n.*

gar ter (gär′tər), *n.* 1 band or strap to hold up a stocking or sock. It is usually elastic. 2 **Garter. a Order of the,** the oldest and most important order of knighthood in Great Britain, established about 1348. **b** badge of this order. **c** membership in it. —*v.t.* fasten with a garter. [< Old French *gartier* < *garet* bend of the knee]

garter snake, any of a genus of small, harmless, brownish or greenish snakes with light yellow stripes that run along their bodies.

Gar y (ger′ē, gar′ē), *n.* city in NW Indiana, on Lake Michigan. 175,000.

gas (gas), *n., pl.* **gas es,** *v.,* **gassed, gas sing.** —*n.* 1 substance that is not a solid or a liquid; substance that has no shape or size of its own and can expand without limit. Oxygen and nitrogen are gases at ordinary temperatures. 2 any gas or mixture of gases except air. 3 any mixture of gases that can be burned for cooking, heating, or illuminating purposes, obtained from coal and other substances. 4 any gas used as an anesthetic, such as nitrous oxide. 5 a chemical substance in the form of a gas that poisons, suffocates, or stupefies, such as tear gas. 6 INFORMAL. gasoline. 7 SLANG. empty or boasting talk. —*v.t.* 1 supply with gas. 2 treat with gas; use gas on. Some kinds of seeds are gassed to hasten sprouting. 3 injure or kill by poisonous gas. 4 INFORMAL. supply with gasoline. —*v.i.* 1 give off gas. 2 SLANG. talk idly or in a boasting way. [alteration of Greek *chaos* chaos; coined by J. B. van Helmont, 1577-1644, Flemish physicist]

gas chamber, a hermetically sealed room in which a poison gas is released. It is used to execute criminals condemned to death.

Gas con (gas′kən), *n.* 1 native of Gascony. Gascons were famous in legend for their boastfulness. 2 **gascon,** boaster. —*adj.* 1 of Gascony or its people. 2 **gascon,** boastful.

gas con ade (gas′kə nād′), *n., v.,* **-ad ed,**

-ad ing. —*n.* extravagant boasting. —*v.i.* boast extravagantly.

Gas co ny (gas′kə nē), *n.* region, formerly a province, in SW France.

gas e ous (gas′ē əs), *adj.* in the form of gas; of or like a gas: *Steam is water in a gaseous condition.*

gas fitter, person whose work is putting in and repairing pipes and fixtures for the use of gas.

gash (gash), *n.* a long, deep cut or wound. —*v.t.* make a long, deep cut or wound in. [earlier *garsh* < Old North French *garser* scarify]

gas hold er (gas′hol′dər), *n.* gasometer.

gas house (gas′hous′), *n., pl.* **-hous es** (-hou′ziz). gasworks.

gas i fy (gas′ə fī), *v.,* **-fied, -fy ing.** —*v.t.* produce gas from or change into gas. —*v.i.* become gas. **—gas′i fi ca′tion,** *n.* **—gas′i fi′er,** *n.*

Gas kell (gas′kəl), *n.* **Elizabeth,** 1810-1865, English novelist.

gasket (def. 2)

gas ket (gas′kit), *n.* 1 ring or strip of rubber, metal, plaited hemp, etc., packed around a piston, pipe joint, etc., to keep a liquid or a gas from escaping. 2 cord or small rope used to secure a furled sail on a yard. [origin uncertain]

gas light (gas′līt′), *n.* 1 light made by burning gas. 2 lamp which burns gas.

gas lit (gas′lit′), *adj.* lit by gaslight.

gas mask, helmet or mask that covers the mouth and nose and is supplied with a filter containing chemicals to neutralize poisonous gas or smoke. The wearer breathes only filtered air.

gas o line or **gas o lene** (gas′ə lēn′, gas′ə lēn′), *n.* a colorless, liquid mixture of hydrocarbons which evaporates and burns very easily, now obtained chiefly in the distillation of crude petroleum or from gas formed in the earth. Gasoline is used as a fuel, solvent, cleansing agent, etc.

gasoline engine, U.S. an internal-combustion engine using gasoline for fuel.

gas om e ter (ga som′ə tər), *n.* 1 container, such as a large cylindrical tank, for storing household gas. 2 container for holding and measuring any gas.

gasp (gasp), *v.i.* 1 try hard to get one's breath with open mouth, as if out of breath or surprised. 2 breathe with gasps; pant. —*v.t.* utter with gasps. —*n.* 1 trying hard to get one's breath with open mouth. 2 **at the last gasp, a** about to die. **b** about to come to an end. [< Scandinavian (Old Icelandic) *geispa* yawn]

Gas pé Peninsula (ga spā′), peninsula in SE Canada, in Quebec province, extending into the Gulf of St. Lawrence. 150 mi. long.

gas ser (gas′ər), *n.* 1 a natural gas well. 2 SLANG. something extraordinary.

gas station, filling station.

gas sy (gas′ē), *adj.,* **-si er, -si est.** 1 full of gas; containing gas. 2 like gas. **—gas′si ness,** *n.*

gas tric (gas′trik), *adj.* 1 of or having to do with the stomach. 2 near the stomach. [< Greek *gastros* stomach]

gastric juice, the thin, nearly clear digestive fluid secreted by glands in the lining of the stomach. It contains pepsin and other enzymes and hydrochloric acid.

gas trin (gas′trən), *n.* hormone that promotes secretion of gastric juice.

gas tri tis (ga strī′tis), *n.* inflammation of the stomach, especially of its mucous membrane.

gas troc ne mi us (gas′trok nē′mē əs), *n., pl.* **-mi i** (-mē ī). the chief muscle of the calf of the leg, that gives it its bulging form. [< New Latin < Greek *gastroknemia* calf < *gastros* belly + *knēmē* leg]

gas tro en te rol o gist (gas′trō en′tə rol′ə jist), *n.* an expert in gastroenterology.

gas tro en te rol o gy (gas′trō en′tə rol′ə jē), *n.* branch of medicine dealing with the stomach and intestines.

gas tro in tes ti nal (gas′trō in tes′tə nəl), *adj.* of or having to do with the stomach and intestines.

gas tro nom ic (gas′trə nom′ik), *adj.* of or having to do with gastronomy. **—gas′tro nom′i cal ly,** *adv.*

gas tro nom i cal (gas′trə nom′ə kəl), *adj.* gastronomic.

gas tron o my (ga stron′ə mē), *n.* art or science of good eating. [< Greek *gastronomia* < *gastros* stomach + *nomos* law]

gas tro pod (gas′trə pod), *n.* any of a class of mollusks having eyes and feelers on a distinct head, usually a shell that is spiral or cone-shaped, and a muscular foot used for locomotion. Snails, slugs, and whelks are gastropods. —*adj.* of such mollusks. [< Greek *gastros* stomach + *podos* foot]

gas trop o dous (ga strop′ə dəs), *adj.* having to do with or like the gastropods.

gas tro vas cu lar (gas′trō vas′kyə lər), *adj.* serving for both digestive and circulatory functions.

gas tru la (gas′trù lə), *n., pl.* **-lae** (-lē′). stage in the development of all many-celled animals, when the embryo is usually saclike and composed of two layers of cells. [< New Latin, diminutive of Greek *gastros* stomach]

gas tru lar (gas′trù lər), *adj.* having to do with a gastrula or gastrulation.

gas tru late (gas′trə lāt), *v.i.,* **-lat ed, -lat ing.** to be in or have a gastrula stage. **—gas′tru la′tion,** *n.*

gas turbine, turbine which uses for its motive power the gas obtained by the combustion of a fuel.

gas works (gas′wėrks′), *n. pl. or sing.* an industrial plant which manufactures household gas; gashouse.

gat[1] (gat), *v.* ARCHAIC. a pt. of **get.**

gat[2] (gat), *n.* SLANG. revolver or automatic pistol. [short for *Gatling gun*]

gate (gāt), *n.* 1 a movable frame or door to close an opening in a wall or fence. It turns on hinges or slides open and shut. 2 an opening in a wall or fence where a gate is; gateway. 3 the part of a building containing the gate or gates, with the adjoining towers, walls, etc. 4 way to go in or out; way to get to something. 5 door or valve to stop or control the flow of water in a pipe, dam, canal, lock, etc. 6 number of people who pay to see a contest, exhibition, performance, etc. 7 the total amount of money received from them: *The two teams divided a gate of $3250.* [Old English *geat*] **—gate′less,** *adj.* **—gate′like′,** *adj.*

gate-crash er (gāt′krash′ər), *n.* INFORMAL. person who attends parties, gatherings, etc., without an invitation; uninvited guest.

gate house (gāt′hous′), *n., pl.* **-hous es** (-hou′ziz). house at or over a gate, used as the keeper's quarters.

gate leg table (gāt′leg′), table with drop leaves supported by legs set in gatelike frames which may be swung back to allow the leaves to be shut down.

hat, āge, fär; let, ēqual, tėrm;
it, īce; hot, ōpen, ôrder;
oil, out; cup, pu̇t, rüle;
ch, child; ng, long; sh, she;
th, thin; ᴛʜ, then; zh, measure;

ə represents *a* in about, *e* in taken, *i* in pencil, *o* in lemon, *u* in circus.

< = from, derived from, taken from.

gate post (gāt′pōst′), *n.* post on either side of a gate. A swinging gate is fastened to one gatepost and closes against the other.

Gates (gāts), *n.* **Horatio,** 1728-1806, American general in the Revolutionary War.

gate way (gāt′wā′), *n.* 1 an opening in a wall or fence where a gate is. 2 way to go in or out; way to get to something.

gath er (gaᴛʜ′ər), *v.t.* 1 bring into one place; collect. See synonym study below. 2 pick and collect from the place of growth: *The farmers gathered their crops.* 3 get or gain little by little: *The train gathered speed as it left the station.* 4 collect (oneself, one's strength, energies, thoughts, etc.) for an effort. 5 put together in the mind; conclude; infer: *I gather from your words that you are really upset.* 6 pull together in folds and stitch: *The dressmaker gathered the skirt at the waist.* 7 draw into wrinkles; pucker: *She gathered her brows in a frown.* 8 draw together or closer: *Gather your robe around you.* —*v.i.* 1 come together; assemble: *A crowd gathered at the scene of the accident.* 2 form a mass; collect: *Tears gathered in her eyes. Clouds gathered as the storm approached.* 3 come to a head and form pus: *A boil is a painful swelling that gathers under the skin.* 4 **gather up, a** pick up and put together. **b** pull together; bring into a smaller space.
—*n.* one of the folds between the stitches when cloth is gathered.
[Old English *gaderian*] **—gath′er er,** *n.*

Syn. *v.t.* 1 **Gather, collect, assemble** mean to bring together. **Gather** means simply to bring together: *I gathered the scattered papers.* **Collect** often adds the idea of bringing together according to a definite plan: *I collected clothes for the rummage sale.* **Assemble** implies bringing together as a whole for a definite purpose: *She assembled the slides for her illustrated lecture.*

gath er ing (gaᴛʜ′ə ring), *n.* 1 a group of people met together; assembly: *There was a family gathering at Thanksgiving time.* See **meeting** for synonym study. 2 swelling that comes to a head and forms pus.

Gat ling gun (gat′ling), an early type of machine gun consisting of a revolving cluster of barrels around a central axis. [< Richard J. *Gatling,* 1818-1903, American inventor]

Ga tun (gä tün′), *n.* 1 town in N Panama Canal Zone. 1000. 2 large dam near there. $1^1/_2$ mi. long. 3 **Gatun Lake,** artificial lake formed by Gatun Dam. 164 sq. mi.

gauche (gōsh), *adj.* lacking grace or tact; awkward. [< French, literally, left] **—gauche′ly,** *adv.* **—gauche′ness,** *n.*

gau che rie (gō′shə rē′, gō′shər ē), *n.* 1 a being awkward or tactless. 2 an awkward or tactless movement, act, etc.

gau cho (gou′chō), *n., pl.* **-chos.** cowboy on the southern plains of South America, usually of mixed Spanish and Indian descent. [< American Spanish]

gaud (gôd), *n.* a showy ornament; trinket. [apparently < Anglo-French *gaude* < *gaudir* rejoice < Latin *gaudere*]

gaud y (gô′dē), *adj.,* **gaud i er, gaud i est.** too bright and gay to be in good taste; cheap and showy. **—gaud′i ly,** *adv.* **—gaud′i ness,** *n.*

Syn. Gaudy, flashy, showy mean done for display. **Gaudy** suggests loud colors and overdone ornament: *a gaudy purple dress.* **Flashy** suggests an eye-catching and dazzling but cheap display: *a flashy necktie.* **Showy** suggests a striking display, but not necessarily a flashy or gaudy one: *Peacocks are showy birds.*

gauge (gāj), *n., v.,* **gauged, gaug ing.** *—n.* 1 a standard measure or a scale of standard measurements used for the measure of such things as the capacity of a barrel, the thickness of sheet iron, the diameter of a wire, etc. 2 instrument for measuring. A steam gauge measures the pressure of steam. 3 means of estimating or judging. 4 size; capacity; extent. 5 diameter of the bore of a firearm, especially a shotgun. 6 distance between the rails of a railroad. Standard gauge between rails is $56\frac{1}{2}$ inches. 7 the relative position of one sailing ship to another either nearer or farther from the wind. 8 the fineness of a knitted fabric as expressed in the number of loops per $1\frac{1}{2}$ inches: *51-gauge stockings.* *—v.t.* 1 measure accurately; find out the exact measurement of with a gauge. 2 determine the capacity or content of (a cask, etc.). 3 estimate; judge: *It was difficult to gauge the character of the stranger.* Also, **gage.** [< Old North French *gauger*] **—gauge′a ble,** *adj.*

gaug er (gā′jər), *n.* 1 person or thing that gauges. 2 official who measures the contents of barrels of taxable liquor. 3 collector of excise taxes.

Gau guin (gō gaN′), *n.* **Paul,** 1848-1903, French painter.

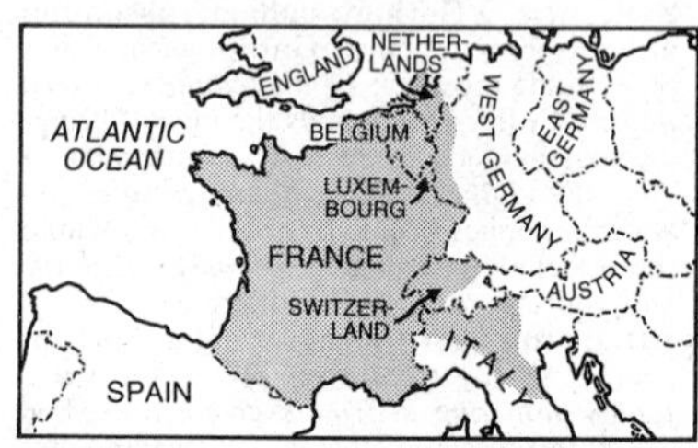

Gaul (def. 1), about 300 B.C., shown by the shaded area on a modern map

Gaul (gôl), *n.* 1 ancient region of W Europe. It included what is now France, Belgium, and Luxembourg, and parts of Switzerland, Germany, the Netherlands, and N Italy. 2 one of the Celtic inhabitants of ancient Gaul. 3 Frenchman.

Gaul ish (gô′lish), *adj.* of or having to do with ancient Gaul or the Gauls. *—n.* the Celtic language of the ancient Gauls.

Gaull ist (gō′list), *n.* (in France) a political follower and supporter of Charles de Gaulle, during and after World War II.

gaunt (gônt, gänt), *adj.* 1 very thin and bony; with hollow eyes and a starved look: *Hunger and suffering had made him gaunt.* See **thin** for synonym study. 2 looking bare and gloomy; desolate. [origin uncertain] **—gaunt′ly,** *adv.* **—gaunt′ness,** *n.*

Gaunt (gônt, gänt), *n.* **John of,** 1340-1399, Duke of Lancaster, English soldier and statesman. He was the founder of the royal house of Lancaster.

gaunt let[1] (gônt′lit, gänt′lit), *n.* 1 a former punishment or torture in which the offender had to run between two rows of men who struck him with clubs or other weapons as he passed. 2 **run the gauntlet, a** pass between two rows of men each of whom strikes the runner as he passes. **b** be exposed to unfriendly attacks or severe criticism. Also, **gantlet.** [< Swedish *gatlopp* a running through a lane]

gaunt let[2] (gônt′lit, gänt′lit), *n.* 1 a stout, heavy glove usually of leather covered with plates of iron or steel, that was worn as part of medieval armor. See **armor** for diagram. 2 a stout, heavy glove with a wide, flaring cuff often covering part of the arm, used in fencing, riding, etc. 3 the wide, flaring cuff. 4 **take up the gauntlet, a** accept a challenge. **b** take up the defense of a person, opinion, etc. 5 **throw down the gauntlet,** challenge. Also, **gantlet.** [< Middle French *gantelet,* diminutive of *gant* glove < Germanic]

gaur (gour), *n.* a large, wild ox of India, Burma, and Malaya, with a broad, protuberant forehead and long, curved, sharp horns. [< Hindustani]

gauss (gous), *n.* the unit of magnetic induction in the centimeter-gram-second system. [< Karl F. *Gauss*]

Gauss (gous), *n.* **Karl Friedrich,** 1777-1855, German mathematician and astronomer.

Gau ta ma (gô′tə mə, gou′tə mə), *n.* Buddha.

gauze (gôz), *n.* 1 a very thin, light cloth, easily seen through. Gauze is often used for bandages. 2 a thinly woven open material resembling this fabric: *Wire gauze is used for screens.* [< Middle French *gaze*] **—gauze′like′,** *adj.*

gauz y (gô′zē), *adj.,* **gauz i er, gauz i est.** like gauze; thin and light as gauze. **—gauz′i ness,** *n.*

gave (gāv), *v.* pt. of **give.**

gav el (gav′əl), *n.* a small mallet used by a chairman to signal for attention or order, or by an auctioneer to announce that the bidding is over. [origin uncertain]

ga vi al (gā′vē əl), *n.* any of a family of large, harmless crocodilians of southern Asia that have long, extremely slender snouts. [< French < Hindustani *ghaṛiyāl*]

ga votte (gə vot′), *n.* 1 an old French dance somewhat like a minuet but much more lively. 2 the music for it. [< French]

G.A.W., Guaranteed Annual Wage.

Ga wain (gä′wān, gä′win), *n.* (in Arthurian legends) knight of the Round Table and nephew of King Arthur.

gawk (gôk), INFORMAL. *—v.i.* stare idly, rudely, or stupidly. *—n.* an awkward person; clumsy fool. [origin uncertain]

gawk y (gô′kē), *adj.,* **gawk i er, gawk i est.** awkward; clumsy. **—gawk′i ly,** *adv.* **—gawk′i ness,** *n.*

gay (gā), *adj.* 1 happy and full of fun; merry. 2 bright-colored; showy: *a gay dress.* 3 fond of pleasures. 4 dissipated; immoral. 5 of or having to do with homosexuals; homosexual. [< Old French *gai*] **—gay′ness,** *n.*

Gay (gā), *n.* **John,** 1685-1732, English poet and dramatist.

gay e ty (gā′ə tē), *n., pl.* **-ties.** gaiety.

Gay-Lus sac (gā lʏ sȧk′), *n.* **Joseph Louis,** 1778-1850, French chemist.

gay ly (gā′lē), *adv.* gaily.

gaz., 1 gazette. 2 gazetteer.

Ga za (gä′zə), *n.* capital and largest city of the Gaza Strip, once an important city of the Philistines. 38,000.

Gaza Strip, land area in W Palestine between Israel and the Mediterranean Sea.

gaze (gāz), *v.,* **gazed, gaz ing,** *n.* *—v.i.* look long and steadily. See synonym study below. *—n.* a long, steady look. [probably < Scandinavian (dialectal Norwegian) *gasa*] **—gaz′er,** *n.*

Syn. *v.i.* **Gaze, stare** mean to look long and steadily at someone or something. **Gaze** emphasizes looking steadily in wonder, delight, or interest: *For hours I sat gazing at the stars.* **Stare** emphasizes looking steadily and directly at someone in curiosity, rudeness, surprise, or stupidity: *The child stared at the stranger for a few minutes before answering his question.*

ga ze bo (gə zē′bō), *n., pl.* **-bos** or **-boes.** a summer house, balcony, projecting window, etc., that overlooks a fine view. [supposedly < *gaze,* on the pattern of Latin future tenses in *-bo*]

gaze hound (gāz′hound′), *n.* a hunting dog that chases by sight rather than by scent, such as the whippet or greyhound.

ga zelle (gə zel′), *n., pl.* **-zelles** or **-zelle.** any of a genus of small, swift, graceful antelope of Africa and Asia, having soft, lustrous eyes. [< French < Arabic *ghazāl*] **—ga zelle′like′,** *adj.*

ga zette (gə zet′), *n., v.,* **-zet ted, -zet ting.** *—n.* 1 newspaper. 2 an official government journal containing lists of appointments, promotions, etc. *—v.t.* publish, list, or announce in a gazette. [< French < Italian *gazzetta*]

gavel used by a judge

gaz et teer (gaz′ə tir′), *n.* 1 dictionary of geographical names. Names of places, seas, mountains, etc., are arranged alphabetically. 2 writer for a gazette.

G.B., Great Britain.

GCA, ground-controlled approach (of aircraft).

G clef, treble clef.

Gd, gadolinium.

Gdańsk (gə dänsk′), *n.* Polish name of **Danzig.**

gds., goods.

Gdy nia (gə din′yə), *n.* seaport in N Poland. 182,000.

Ge, germanium.

gear (gir), *n.* 1 wheel having teeth that fit into the teeth of another wheel; cogwheel; gear-

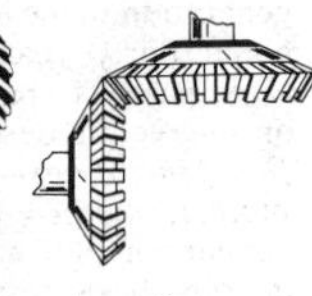

gear (defs. 1 and 2)—three kinds of gears
A, to change the speed of axle rotation
B, with angled teeth to run more quietly
C, to transmit motion at right angles

wheel. If the wheels are of different sizes they will turn at different speeds. 2 set of such wheels working together to transmit power or change the direction of motion in a machine. Power is transmitted from the motor of an automobile to the wheels by means of gears. 3 any arrangement of gears or moving parts considered as a unit in a larger mechanism: *a steering gear.* 4 equipment needed for some purpose. Harness, household goods, tools, tackle, and rigging are various kinds of gear. 5 clothes; apparel. 6 **in gear,** connected to the motor, etc. 7 **out of gear,** disconnected from the motor, etc. 8 **shift gears,** change from one gear to another; connect a motor, etc., to a different set of gears. *—v.t.* 1 connect by gears: *The motor is geared to the rear wheels of the automobile.* 2 provide with gear; equip. 3 make fit; adjust; adapt: *The steel industry was geared to the needs of war.* *—v.i.* fit or work together; mesh: *The cogs gear smoothly.* [apparently < Scandinavian (Old Icelandic) *gervi, görvi*] **—gear′less,** *adj.*

gear box (gir′boks′), *n.* an automobile transmission.

gear ing (gir′ing), *n.* 1 set of gears, chains, or parts of machinery for transmitting motion or power; gear. 2 act of fitting a machine with gears.

gear shift (gir′shift′), *n.* device for connecting a motor to any of several sets of gears in a transmission.

gear wheel (gir′hwēl′), *n.* cogwheel; gear.

geck o (gek′ō), *n., pl.* **geck os** or **geck oes.** any of a family of small, nocturnal, insect-eating lizards of warm climates, harmless to man, with adhesive pads on their feet for walking on ceilings, walls, etc. [< Malay *gekok*]

gee (jē), *interj., v.,* **geed, gee ing.** *—interj.* 1 word of command to horses, oxen, etc., directing them to turn to the right. 2 exclamation or mild oath. *—v.t., v.i.* turn to the right.

geese (gēs), *n.* pl. of **goose.**

gee zer (gē′zər), *n.* SLANG. an odd or eccentric man, especially an old one. [dialectal pronunciation of *guiser* someone in disguise, mummer]

ge füll te fish (gə fil′tə), cooked fish minced with bread crumbs, eggs, etc., and served in the form of balls or cakes. [< Yiddish *gefilte fish*]

ge gen schein (gā′gən shīn′), *n.* a faint light seen in the heavens of the tropics near the apparent path of the sun at a point exactly opposite the sun. [< German *Gegenschein,* literally, counter glow]

Ge hen na (gə hen′ə), *n.* 1 hell. 2 place of torment or misery.

Gei ger counter (gī′gər), an electronic device which detects and counts ionizing particles, consisting of a tube with two electrodes between which a high potential difference is maintained, used to measure radioactivity, test cosmic-ray particles, etc. [< Hans *Geiger,* 1882-1947, German physicist]

Gei ger-Mül ler counter (gī′gər mul′ər), an improved, more sensitive form of the Geiger counter.

gei sha (gā′shə, gē′shə), *n., pl.* **-sha** or **-shas.** a Japanese girl trained to be a professional entertainer and companion for men. [< Japanese]

gel (jel), *n., v.,* **gelled, gel ling.** *—n.* a jellylike or solid material formed from a colloidal solution. When glue sets, it forms a gel. *—v.i.* form a gel. Egg white gels when it is cooked. [short for *gelatin*]

gel a tin or **gel a tine** (jel′ə tən), *n.* 1 an odorless, tasteless protein substance like glue or jelly, obtained by boiling animal tendons, bones, hoofs, etc. It dissolves easily in hot water and is used in making jellied desserts and salads, glue, camera film, etc. 2 any of various vegetable substances having similar properties. 3 preparation or product in which gelatin is the essential constituent. [< French *gélatine* < Italian *gelatina* < *gelata* jelly < *gelare* to jell, freeze < Latin]

ge lat i nous (jə lat′n əs), *adj.* 1 of or like jelly. 2 of, like, or containing gelatin. **—ge lat′i nous ly,** *adv.* **—ge lat′i nous ness,** *n.*

ge la tion (jə lā′shən), *n.* solidification by cooling; freezing.

geld (geld), *v.t.,* **geld ed** or **gelt** (gelt), **geld ing.** remove the testicles of (a horse or other animal); castrate. [< Scandinavian (Old Icelandic) *gelda* < *geldr* barren]

geld ing (gel′ding), *n.* a gelded horse or other animal.

gel id (jel′id), *adj.* cold as ice; frosty; frozen. [< Latin *gelidus* < *gelu* cold] **—gel′id ly,** *adv.*

ge lid i ty (jə lid′ə tē), *n.* extreme cold; frigidity.

gel ig nite (jel′ig nīt), *n.* explosive made with nitroglycerin, wood pulp, and potassium or sodium nitrate. [< *gel(atin)* + Latin *ignis* fire]

gem (jem), *n., v.,* **gemmed, gem ming.** *—n.* 1 a precious or semiprecious stone, especially when cut or polished for ornament; jewel. Diamonds and rubies are gems. 2 person or thing that is very precious, beautiful, etc.: *The gem of her collection was a rare Persian stamp.* 3 kind of muffin made of coarse flour. *—v.t.* set or adorn with gems or as if with gems: *Stars gem the sky.* [< Old French *gemme* < Latin *gemmam* gem, bud] **—gem′like′,** *adj.*

Ge ma ra (gə mär′ə, gə môr′ə), *n.* a rabbinical commentary on the Mishna, and with it forming the Talmud. [< Aramaic *gemārā* completion]

Geiger counter
The probe detects amount of radiation, which is shown on the dial.

hat, āge, fär; let, ēqual, tėrm;
it, īce; hot, ōpen, ôrder;
oil, out; cup, pu̇t, rüle;
ch, child; ng, long; sh, she;
th, thin; ᴛʜ, then; zh, measure;

ə represents *a* in about, *e* in taken, *i* in pencil, *o* in lemon, *u* in circus.

< = from, derived from, taken from.

gem i nate (*v.* jem′ə nāt; *adj.* jem′ə nit, jem′ə nāt), *v.,* **-nat ed, -nat ing,** *adj.* *—v.t.* make double; combine into pairs. *—v.i.* become double. *—adj.* combined in a pair or pairs; coupled. [< Latin *geminatum* doubled < *geminus* twin] **—gem′i na′tion,** *n.*

Gem i ni (jem′ə nī), *n.pl.* 1 a northern constellation containing the two bright stars Castor and Pollux. 2 the third sign of the zodiac. The sun enters Gemini about May 21. 3 Castor and Pollux, the twin sons of Zeus. [< Latin, Twins]

gem ma (jem′ə), *n., pl.* **gem mae** (jem′ē). 1 a bud. 2 a budlike reproductive body in some plants, such as liverworts and mosses, that becomes detached from the plant and can develop into a new individual. [< Latin, bud]

gem mate (jem′āt), *v.,* **-mat ed, -mat ing,** *adj.* *—v.i.* put forth buds; reproduce by budding. *—adj.* having buds; reproducing by buds. **—gem ma′tion,** *n.*

gem mol o gy (je mol′ə jē), *n.* the study of gems, their origins, uses, etc.

gem mule (jem′yül), *n.* 1 a small bud. 2 a budlike reproductive body in sponges.

gem ol o gy (je mol′ə jē), *n.* gemmology.

gems bok (gemz′bok′), *n.* a large antelope of southwestern Africa, having long, nearly straight horns and a long, tufted tail. [< Afrikaans < German *Gemsbock* < *Gemse* chamois + *Bock* buck]

gem stone (jem′stōn′), *n.* a precious or semiprecious stone, capable of being cut and polished to make a gem.

ge müt lich (gə mʏt′liʜ), *adj.* GERMAN. congenial; cozy.

-gen, *combining form.* 1 something produced or growing, as *acrogen.* 2 something that produces, as *allergen, nitrogen.* [< Greek *-genēs,* ultimately < *gignesthai* be born]

gen., 1 general. 2 genitive.

Gen., 1 General. 2 Genesis.

gen darme (zhän′därm), *n., pl.* **-darmes** (-därmz). policeman in France and several other European countries who has had military training. [< Middle French < Old French *gens d'armes* men of arms]

gen dar me rie (zhän′där mər ē; *French* zhäɴ därm rē′), *n.* body of gendarmes. [< French]

gen der (jen′dər), *n.* 1 the grouping of nouns into certain classes, such as masculine, feminine, or neuter. 2 one of such classes. 3 sex: *the female gender.* [< Old French *gendre* < Latin *generis* kind, sort, class]

➔ **gender.** Many languages have special endings for masculine, feminine, and neuter nouns and for adjectives modifying them, but English abandoned this system several hundred years ago. Now, except in pronouns and a few nouns with endings such as *-ess, -us, -a, -or, -trix, -eur, -euse (actress, mistress, alumnus, alumna, actor, aviatrix, masseur, masseuse)* gender is indicated only by the meaning of the word: *man—woman, nephew—niece, rooster—hen.*

gene (jēn), *n.* a minute part of a chromosome, consisting essentially of DNA, that influences the inheritance and development of some character; factor. The genes inherited from its parents determine what kind of a plant or animal will develop from a fertilized egg cell. [< German *Gen,* ultimately < Greek *genea* breed, kind]

ge ne a log i cal (jē′nē ə loj′ə kəl, jen′ē ə-loj′ə kəl), *adj.* having to do with genealogy. A genealogical table or chart is called a family tree. **—ge′ne a log′i cal ly,** *adv.*

ge ne al o gist (jē′nē al′ə jist, jē′nē ol′ə-jist; jen′ē al′ə jist, jen′ē ol′ə jist), *n.* person who makes a study of or traces genealogies.

ge ne al o gy (jē′nē al′ə jē, jē′nē ol′ə jē; jen′ē al′ə jē, jen′ē ol′ə jē), *n., pl.* **-gies.** 1 account of the descent of a person or family from an ancestor or ancestors. 2 descent of a person or family from an ancestor; pedigree; lineage. 3 the making or investigation of accounts of descent; study of pedigrees. [< Greek *genealogia* < *genea* breed, generation + *-logos* treating of]

gen er a (jen′ər ə), *n.* a pl. of **genus.**

gen er al (jen′ər əl), *adj.* 1 of all; for all; from all: *A government takes care of the general welfare.* See synonym study below. 2 common to many or most; not limited to a few; widespread: *There is a general interest in sports.* 3 not detailed; sufficient for practical purposes: *general instructions.* 4 not special; not limited to one kind, class, department, or use: *A general reader reads different kinds of books.* 5 indefinite; vague: *She referred to her trip in a general way.* 6 of or for all those forming a group: *"Cat" is a general term for cats, lions, and tigers.* 7 of or having to do with a whole region or an entire body: *a general election.* 8 chief; of highest rank: *The Attorney General is the head of the Justice Department.*

—n. 1 a high army officer in command of many soldiers: *Hannibal was a famous general.* 2 a military officer ranking above a colonel, such as a lieutenant general or a major general. 3 (in the United States Army and Air Force) an officer ranking next below a General of the Army or a General of the Air Force and next above lieutenant general. 4 (in the United States Marine Corps) an officer of the highest rank. 5 (in the British Army) an officer ranking next below a field marshal and next above a lieutenant general. 6 a general fact, idea, principle, or statement. 7 **in general,** for the most part; usually; commonly. 8 head of a religious order. 9 ARCHAIC. people as a group; the public. [< Latin *generalis* of a (whole) class < *genus, generis* kind, sort, class]

Syn. *adj.* 1 **General, common, popular** mean belonging or relating to all or to most. **General** means applying to or done by all of a group or class, or most of it: *As a general rule, male birds are more conspicuously marked than female ones.* **Common** means shared by all the members of a group or class, or most of them: *English is the common language in the United States.* **Popular** means belonging to or prevailing among the people: *Various polls are supposed to find out popular opinions.*

General Assembly, 1 legislature of certain states of the United States. 2 the main deliberative body of the United Nations, made up of delegates from every member nation.

General Court, legislature of Massachusetts or New Hampshire.

gen er al is si mo (jen′ər ə lis′ə mō), *n., pl.* **-mos.** commander in chief of all the military forces in certain countries. [< Italian, superlative of *generale* general]

gen er al i ty (jen′ə ral′ə tē), *n., pl.* **-ties.** 1 a general or vague statement; word or phrase not definite enough to have much meaning or value: *The candidates spoke only in generalities; not once did they say what they would do if elected.* 2 a general principle or rule: *"Nothing happens without a cause" is a generality.* 3 the greater part; main body; mass: *The generality of people must work for a living.* 4 general quality or condition: *A rule of great generality has very few exceptions.*

gen er al i za tion (jen′ər ə lə zā′shən), *n.* 1 act or process of generalizing: *Don't be hasty in generalization; be sure you have the necessary facts first.* 2 a general idea, statement, principle, or rule.

gen er al ize (jen′ər ə līz), *v.,* **-ized, -iz ing.** *—v.t.* 1 make into one general statement; bring under a common heading, class, or law. 2 infer (a general rule) from particular facts. 3 state in a more general form; extend in application: *The statement that $5 + 3 = 8$ and $50 + 30 = 80$ can be generalized to the form $5a + 3a = 8a$.* 4 bring into general use or knowledge; popularize. 5 make general; give a general form or character to. *—v.i.* 1 infer a general rule from particular facts; make general inferences. 2 talk or write indefinitely or vaguely; use generalities. **—gen′er al iz′er,** *n.*

gen er al ly (jen′ər ə lē), *adv.* 1 in most cases; usually: *He is generally on time.* 2 for the most part; widely: *It was once generally believed that the earth is flat.* 3 in a general way; without giving details; not specially: *Generally speaking, our coldest weather comes in January.*

General of the Air Force, general of the highest rank in the United States Air Force, wearing the insigne of five stars.

General of the Army, general of the highest rank in the United States Army, wearing the insigne of five stars.

general practitioner, physician who does not specialize in any single field of medicine.

gen er al ship (jen′ər əl ship), *n.* 1 ability as a general; skill in commanding an army. 2 skillful management; leadership. 3 rank, commission, authority, or term of office of a general.

general staff, group of high army officers who assist a chief of staff of a division or larger unit in making plans for war or national defense.

general store, store that carries a wide variety of goods for sale.

gen e rate (jen′ə rāt′), *v.t.,* **-rat ed, -rat ing.** 1 cause to be; bring into being; produce: *Burning coal can generate steam. The steam can generate electricity by turning an electric generator.* 2 produce (offspring). 3 (in mathematics) form (a line, surface, figure, or solid) by moving a point, line, etc. [< Latin *generatum* brought forth, engendered < *generem* kind, sort, class]

gen e ra tion (jen′ə rā′shən), *n.* 1 all the people born about the same period. Parents belong to one generation and their children to the next. 2 the time from the birth of one generation to the birth of the next generation; about thirty years. 3 the offspring of the same parent or parents, regarded as one step or degree in descent: *The picture showed four generations—great-grandmother, grandmother, mother, and baby.* 4 a group of similar complex mechanical devices differing in some basic respect from previous or succeeding models. First-generation computers used vacuum tubes, which were replaced by transistors in second-generation computers. 5 production of offspring. 6 production by natural or artificial processes; generating: *Steam and water power are used for the generation of electricity.*

gen e ra tive (jen′ə rā′tiv), *adj.* 1 having to do with the production of offspring. 2 having the power of producing.

generative grammar, (in linguistics) a set of rules for producing all the grammatically correct sentences of a language.

gen e ra tor (jen′ə rā′tər), *n.* 1 machine that changes mechanical energy into electrical energy and produces either direct or alternating current. 2 apparatus for producing gas or steam. 3 person or thing that generates.

gen e ra trix (jen′ə rā′triks), *n., pl.* **gen e ra tri ces** (jen′ər ə trī′sēz). (in mathematics) a point, line, etc., whose motion produces a line, surface, figure, or solid. [< Latin]

ge ner ic (jə ner′ik), *adj.* 1 characteristic of a genus, kind, or class: *Cats and lions show generic differences.* 2 having to do with a class or group of similar things; general; not specific or special: *"Liquid" is a generic term, but "milk" is a specific term.* **—ge ner′i cal ly,** *adv.*

gen e ros i ty (jen′ə ros′ə tē), *n., pl.* **-ties.** 1 a being generous; willingness to share with others; unselfishness. 2 nobleness of heart or of mind; willingness to forgive. 3 generous behavior; generous act.

gen er ous (jen′ər əs), *adj.* 1 willing to share with others; unselfish: *a generous giver.* 2 noble and forgiving; not mean. 3 large; plentiful: *A quarter of a pie is a generous piece.* 4 fertile: *generous fields.* [< Latin *generosus* of noble birth, high-minded < *generis* birth, class, kind] **—gen′er ous ly,** *adv.* **—gen′er ous ness,** *n.*

gen e sis (jen′ə sis), *n., pl.* **-ses** (-sēz′) for 2. 1 **Genesis,** the first book of the Old Testament. Genesis gives an account of the creation of the world. 2 origin; creation; coming into being: *the genesis of an idea.* [< Latin < Greek *gignesthai* be born]

gen et (jen′it), *n.* jennet.

ge net ic (jə net′ik), *adj.* 1 having to do with origin and natural growth. 2 of or having to do with genetics. 3 of or having to do with genes. **—ge net′i cal ly,** *adv.*

ge net i cal (jə net′ə kəl), *adj.* genetic.

genetic code, the various combinations of nucleotides which may occur in the DNA or RNA molecule of a chromosome. The genetic code determines the make-up of genes.

ge net i cist (jə net′ə sist), *n.* an expert in genetics.

ge net ics (jə net′iks), *n.* branch of biology dealing with the principles of heredity and variation in animals and plants of the same or related kinds.

Ge ne va (jə nē′və), *n.* 1 city in SW Switzerland. 172,000. 2 **Lake,** long, narrow lake in SW Switzerland and E France; Lake Leman. 45 mi. long; 225 sq. mi. **—Ge ne′van,** *adj., n.*

Geneva Convention, an international agreement establishing rules for the treatment of prisoners of war, the wounded, etc., first formulated at Geneva, Switzerland, in 1864.

Gen ghis Khan (jeng′gis kän′), 1162-1227, Mongol conqueror of central Asia. Also, **Jenghis Khan.**

gen ial[1] (jē′nyəl), *adj.* 1 smiling and pleasant; cheerful and friendly; kindly: *a genial welcome.* 2 helping growth; pleasantly warming; comforting: *a genial climate.* [< Latin *genialis,* literally, belonging to the genius < *genius*] **—gen′ial ly,** *adv.* **—gen′ial ness,** *n.*

ge ni al[2] (jə nī′əl), *adj.* (in anatomy) of or having to do with the chin. [< Greek *geneion* chin < *genys* jaw]

ge ni al i ty (jē′nē al′ə tē), *n.* genial quality or behavior.

gen ic (jen′ik), *adj.* of, produced by, or like a gene.

-genic, *combining form.* 1 producing; having to do with production: *Carcinogenic = producing cancer.* 2 suitable for; suitable for production or reproduction by: *Photogenic = suitable for photography.* [-*gen* + -*ic*]

ge nic u late (jə nik′yə lit, jə nik′yə lāt), *adj.* 1 having kneelike joints or bends. 2 bent at a joint like the knee. **—ge nic′u late ly,** *adv.*

ge nie (jē′nē), *n., pl.* **-nies** or **-ni i.** (in Moslem mythology) a spirit or jinni. [< French *génie* < Arabic *jinnī*] ➤ See **genius** for usage note.

ge ni i (jē′nē ī), *n.* 1 a pl. of **genius** (defs. 6, 8). 2 a pl. of **genie.**

gen i tal (jen′ə təl), *adj.* having to do with reproduction or the sex organs. *—n.* **genitals,** *pl.* the external sex organs. [< Latin *genitalis,* ultimately < *gignere* beget]

gen i ta lia (jen′ə tā′lyə, jen′ə tā′lē ə), *n.pl.* genitals. [< Latin]

gen i ti val (jen′ə tī′vəl), *adj.* of or in the genitive case.

gen i tive (jen′ə tiv), *adj.* showing possession, source, or origin. *Mine, our, his,* and *their* are in the genitive case, or, as is usually said for English words, the possessive case. *—n.* 1 the genitive case. 2 word or construction in the genitive case. [< Latin *genitivus* of origin, ultimately < *gignere* beget]

gen i to u ri nar y (jen′ə tō yůr′ə ner′ē), *adj.* having to do with the genital and urinary organs or functions.

gen ius (jē′nyəs, jē′nē əs), *n., pl.* **gen ius es** for 1-5, 7 (or **ge ni i** for 6, 8). 1 very great natural power of mind. 2 person having such power: *Shakespeare was a genius.* 3 person with an intelligence quotient of 140 or more. 4 great natural ability of some special kind: *Mozart had a genius for composing music.* 5 the special character or spirit of a person, nation, age, language, etc. 6 a guardian spirit of a person, place, institution, etc. 7 person who powerfully influences another: *an evil genius.* 8 spirit or jinni; genie. [< Latin, tutelary spirit, male generative power, ultimately < *gignere* beget]

➤ **genius, genie. Genius,** although in modern use most commonly meaning very great natural power of mind, also means a spirit giving a special character to a language, period, place, etc., or influencing or guarding the destiny of a person: *"Guardian angel" and "good genius" are much the same thing.* **Genie,** also meaning a spirit, applies specifically to a supernatural creature in Moslem mythology: *"The Arabian Nights" tells about the genie of Aladdin's lamp.*

Gen nes ar et (jə nes′ər et), *n.* **Lake of,** Sea of Galilee.

Gen o a (jen′ō ə), *n.* seaport in NW Italy. 842,000.

gen o cid al (jen′ə sī′dl), *adj.* having to do with genocide.

gen o cide (jen′ə sīd), *n.* the extermination of a cultural or racial group. [< Greek *genos* race + -*cide*]

Gen o ese (jen′ō ēz′), *adj., n., pl.* **-ese.** *—adj.* of Genoa or its people. *—n.* native or inhabitant of Genoa. Also, **Genovese.**

gen ome (jē′nōm), *n.* 1 the sum of all the chromosomes within each nucleus of any species. 2 a haploid set of chromosomes with their genes. [< *gen(e)* + Greek -*oma* group, mass]

gen o type (jen′ə tīp), *n.* 1 the genetic make-up of an organism as distinguished from its physical appearance or phenotype. 2 group of organisms each having the same combinations of hereditary characteristics.

gen o typ ic (jen′ə tip′ik), *adj.* of or having to do with a genotype. **—gen′o typ′i cally,** *adv.*

gen o typ i cal (jen′ə tip′ə kəl), *adj.* genotypic.

Gen o vese (jen′ə vēz′), *adj., n., pl.* **-vese.** Genoese.

gen re (zhän′rə), *n.* 1 kind, sort, or style, especially in art or literature: *Poe was the originator of a genre of detective story.* 2 style or kind of painting that represents scenes from ordinary life. [< French < Latin *generem*]

gens (jenz), *n., pl.* **gen tes** (jen′tēz′). group of families in ancient Rome that claimed the same ancestor and were united by a common name and common religious ceremonies: *Julius Caesar was a member of the Julian gens.* [< Latin]

Gen ser ic (jen′sər ik, gen′sər ik), *n.* A.D. 395?-477, king of the Vandals, conqueror of northern Africa and Italy.

gent (jent), *n.* INFORMAL. man. [short for *gentleman*]

Gent (gent), *n.* Ghent.

gen teel (jen tēl′), *adj.* 1 belonging or suited to polite society. 2 polite; well-bred; fashionable; elegant. 3 artificially polite and courteous. [< Middle French *gentil* < Latin *gentilis.* Doublet of GENTILE, GENTLE, JAUNTY.] **—gen teel′ly,** *adv.* **—genteel′ness,** *n.*

gen tian (jen′shən), *n.* any of a large family of plants with funnel-shaped flowers, usually stemless leaves, and bitter juice. Gentians have blue, white, red, or yellow flowers. [< Latin *gentiana*]

gen tile or **Gen tile** (jen′tīl), *n.* 1 person who is not a Jew. 2 heathen; pagan. 3 (among Mormons) a person who is not a Mormon. *—adj.* 1 not Jewish. 2 heathen; pagan. 3 (among Mormons) of or having to do with those outside the Mormon community. [< Late Latin *gentilis* foreign < Latin, of a people, national. Doublet of GENTEEL, GENTLE, JAUNTY.]

gen til i ty (jen til′ə tē), *n., pl.* **-ties.** 1 gentle birth; being of good family and social position. 2 good manners. 3 refinement. 4 Usually, **gentilities,** *pl.* pretended refinements.

gen tle (jen′tl), *adj.,* **-tler, -tlest,** *v.,* **-tled, -tling.** *—adj.* 1 not severe, rough, or violent; mild: *a gentle tap.* See synonym study below. 2 soft; low: *a gentle sound.* 3 not too much or too fast; not harsh or extreme; moderate: *gentle heat, a gentle slope.* 4 kindly; friendly: *a gentle disposition.* 5 easily handled or managed: *a gentle dog.* 6 of good family and social position; wellborn. 7 having or showing good manners; refined; polite. 8 ARCHAIC. noble; gallant. *—v.t.* treat in a soothing way; make quiet or gentle: *The rider gentled his excited horse.* [< Old French *gentil* < Latin *gentilis* of the (same) family, national < *gentem* family, nation. Doublet of GENTEEL, GENTILE, JAUNTY.] **—gen′tleness,** *n.*

Syn. *adj.* 1 **Gentle, mild, meek** mean not harsh, rough, or violent. **Gentle** emphasizes control of strength or force, and suggests being pleasant or pleasing in some definite way, such as by being soft, tender, calm, or kindly: *The nurse is gentle in touch, manner, and voice.* **Mild** emphasizes being by nature agreeable and devoid of harshness, severity, etc.: *He is a mild man and seldom gets angry.* **Meek** emphasizes being patient and humble, and often suggests being afraid to act otherwise: *The meek little clerk tries to please everyone.*

gen tle folk (jen′tl fōk′), *n.pl.* people of good family and social position.

gen tle man (jen′tl mən), *n., pl.* **-men.** 1 man of good family and social position. 2 a well-bred man. 3 man of fine feelings or instincts, shown by behavior and consideration for others. 4 a polite term for any man: *"Gentlemen" is often used in speaking or writing to a group of men.* **—gen′tle manlike′,** *adj.*

gen tle man ly (jen′tl mən lē), *adj.* like a gentleman; suitable for a gentleman; well-bred; polite. **—gen′tle man li ness,** *n.*

gentleman's agreement or **gentlemen's agreement,** an informal agreement that is not legally binding. The people or countries that make it are bound only by their promise to keep it.

gen tle wom an (jen′tl wům′ən), *n., pl.* **-wom en.** 1 woman of good family and social position. 2 a well-bred woman; lady. 3 a woman attendant of a lady of rank.

gent ly (jent′lē), *adv.* 1 in a gentle way; tenderly; softly: *Handle the baby gently.* 2 gradually: *a gently sloping hillside.*

gen try (jen′trē), *n.* 1 people of good family and social position, belonging to the upper class of society. The English gentry are next below the nobility. 2 people of any particular class: *the sporting gentry.* [alteration of *gentrice* < Old French *genterise,* ultimately < *gentil.* See GENTLE.]

gen u flect (jen′yə flekt), *v.i.* bend the knee as an act of reverence or worship. [< Medieval Latin *genuflectere* < Latin *genu* knee + *flectere* bend] **—gen′u flec′tion,** *n.*

gen u ine (jen′yü ən), *adj.* 1 actually being what it seems or is claimed to be; real; true: *genuine leather, a genuine diamond.* See synonym study below. 2 without pretense; sin-

hat, āge, fär; let, ēqual, tėrm;
it, īce; hot, ōpen, ôrder;
oil, out; cup, pu̇t, rüle;
ch, child; ng, long; sh, she;
th, thin; ᴛʜ, then; zh, measure;

ə represents *a* in about, *e* in taken, *i* in pencil, *o* in lemon, *u* in circus.

< = from, derived from, taken from.

Geological time

CENOZOIC ERA	QUATERNARY PERIOD	*Recent Epoch*	Began 11,000 years ago. Glaciers recede and Ice Age ends. Continued uplift of W coast of North America. Man lives in and controls all parts of the world, domesticating animals and cultivating plants. Climate mild to warm.
		Pleistocene Epoch	Began 2,000,000 years ago. Mountain building and general uplift of land in W United States. Four periods of glaciation erode the land and form many lake basins, including the Great Lakes. Man develops and becomes dominant. Many large mammals become extinct. Modern plants develop. Climate cold to mild.
	TERTIARY PERIOD	*Pliocene Epoch*	Began 12,000,000 years ago. Volcanic activity and mountain building continue. General uplift of continents. Land bridge emerges between North and South America. Mammals continue development, migrate between continents, and remain dominant. First manlike apes appear. Lush vegetation decreases as climate becomes cooler.
		Miocene Epoch	Began 25,000,000 years ago. Volcanic activity and mountain building in W North America and in Europe. Probable land bridge between North America and Asia. Mastodons appear in North America. Forests decrease while grasses develop and cover vast plains. Grazing mammals appear and flourish as a result. Climate mild to cool.
		Oligocene Epoch	Began 40,000,000 years ago. Land is generally low. Volcanic activity in W United States. Mountain building as Alps and Himalayas begin to rise. Modern mammals develop and become dominant. First apes appear. Forests widespread. Climate mild.
		Eocene Epoch	Began 60,000,000 years ago. Seas cover little of the land. Extensive erosion of Rocky Mountain highlands. Mammals flourish; small ancestors of many modern mammals appear (cats, elephants). Flowering plants widespread. Tropical and subtropical forests. Climate mild.
		Paleocene Epoch	Began 70,000,000 years ago. Shallow inland seas gradually drain. Continued mountain building in W North America, followed by erosion. Small, primitive mammals abundant. Modern toothless birds develop. First primates appear. Flowering plants dominant. Climate mild.
MESOZOIC ERA	CRETACEOUS PERIOD		Began 135,000,000 years ago. Last great covering of major parts of continents. Chalk deposited. Coal swamps formed in W North America. Mountain building in W parts of North and South America. Dinosaurs, flying reptiles, and ammonites develop, then become extinct. Mammals still insignificant in size and number compared to reptiles. Flowering plants and hardwood trees develop, become abundant. Climate cool.
	JURASSIC PERIOD		Began 180,000,000 years ago. Land is low with swampy areas and inland seas. Mountain building in W North America. Birds and flying reptiles appear. Dinosaurs are abundant. Small mammals and modern insects (bees, ants) develop. Conifers and cycads are dominant plants. Climate mild and humid.
	TRIASSIC PERIOD		Began 230,000,000 years ago. Volcanic activity and faulting in E North America. Arid conditions in W United States. First dinosaurs and primitive mammals appear. Land and marine reptiles abundant. Conifers and cycads grow in thick forests. Climate mild and dry.
PALEOZOIC ERA	PERMIAN PERIOD		Began 260,000,000 years ago. Inland seas drain. Deserts and salt basins are common in Northern Hemisphere. Glaciation in Southern Hemisphere. Mountain building in E United States. Marine invertebrates and amphibians decrease. Reptiles increase. Many swamp plants become extinct. Climate warm and dry.
	CARBONIFEROUS PERIOD: PENNSYLVANIAN PERIOD		Began 310,000,000 years ago. Large inland seas. Mountain building in E United States. Amphibians abundant. Reptiles appear. Large insects common. Thick fernlike vegetation in coal-forming, swampy forests. Coal formed in E North America and Europe during Carboniferous periods. Climate warm and very humid.
	CARBONIFEROUS PERIOD: MISSISSIPPIAN PERIOD		Began 350,000,000 years ago. Shallow seas and swampy lowlands widespread. Some mountain building and volcanic activity in New England area. Amphibians, sharks, and bony fishes abundant. Winged insects appear. Conifer, fern, and lichen forests develop in swampy lowlands. Climate warm and humid.
	DEVONIAN PERIOD		Began 400,000,000 years ago. Shallow seas widespread. Europe and North America probably part of same continent mass. Mountain building and local volcanic activity in E North America. Fishes increase in size and diversity. Lungfish develop; first amphibians appear; wingless insects appear. First forests grow in swamps of E New York and Pennsylvania. Seed-bearing plants develop. Climate hot and humid.
	SILURIAN PERIOD		Began 425,000,000 years ago. Shallow seas less extensive over the land. Evaporation leaves salt beds in E United States. Mountain building in Europe at end of period. Air-breathing animals (water scorpions) appear. Primitive fishes highest form of life. First land plants (mosses) appear. Climate mild and dry.
	ORDOVICIAN PERIOD		Began 500,000,000 years ago. Volcanic activity on E and W coasts. Much of the land is covered by seas. First appearance of corals, clams, cephalopods, and bryozoans. First vertebrates (primitive fishes) appear. All animal phyla known today are represented by Ordovician fossil forms. Climate mild.
	CAMBRIAN PERIOD		Began 600,000,000 years ago. Seas flood inland and recede, leveling the land and depositing sedimentary rock. No major mountain ranges present in North America. Marine invertebrates develop shells. Common fossils are trilobites (insectlike sea animals), brachiopods, and snails. Algae abundant. Climate mild.
PRECAMBRIAN ERA: PROTEROZOIC ERA			Later Precambrian rocks (about 1 to 2 billion years old) have their sedimentary features mostly preserved and record periods of glaciation, mountain building, volcanic activity, and erosion. Uranium, copper, iron, nickel, graphite, and limestone are some economic deposits of this era. Simple marine plants (algae, fungi, and bacteria) develop. Evidence of some simple marine animals (sponges and wormlike animals). Climate warm to cool.
PRECAMBRIAN ERA: ARCHEOZOIC ERA			Early Precambrian rocks (about 3½ billion years old) are now much altered and consist of granites and other partially melted rocks. They preserve a record of volcanic activity, mountain building, and erosion. First known life exists. Climate variable, but temperatures were such that water was a liquid rather than a solid or gas.

cere; frank: *genuine sorrow.* [< Latin *genuinus* native, natural, ultimately < *gignere* beget] **—gen′u ine ly,** *adv.* **—gen′u ine ness,** *n.*

Syn. 1 **Genuine, authentic** mean being what it is claimed to be. **Genuine** emphasizes absence of artificiality, adulteration, or any spurious quality: *The table is genuine mahogany, not wood stained to look like it.* **Authentic** emphasizes absence of fraud or counterfeiting: *That is his authentic signature, not a forgery.*

ge nus (jē′nəs), *n., pl.* **gen er a** or **ge nus es.** 1 any group of similar things; kind; sort; class. 2 group of related animals or plants ranking below a family and above a species. The scientific name of an animal or plant consists of the genus written with a capital letter and the species written with a small letter. EXAMPLE: *Homo sapiens.* See **classification** for chart. 3 (in logic) a class or group of individuals divided into subordinate groups called species. [< Latin]

geo-, *combining form.* earth; of the earth: *Geology = science of the earth.* [< Greek *geō-* < *gē* earth]

ge o cen tric (jē′ō sen′trik), *adj.* 1 viewed or measured from the earth's center. 2 having or representing the earth as a center. **—ge′o cen′tri cal ly,** *adv.*

ge o cen tri cal (jē′ō sen′trə kəl), *adj.* geocentric.

ge o chem i cal (jē′ō kem′ə kəl), *adj.* of or having to do with geochemistry.

ge o chem ist (jē′ō kem′ist), *n.* an expert in geochemistry.

ge o chem is try (jē′ō kem′ə strē), *n.* science dealing with the chemical changes in, and the composition of, the earth's crust.

ge o chron o log i cal (jē′ō kron′ə loj′ə kəl), *adj.* of or having to do with geochronology.

ge o chro nol o gy (jē′ō krə nol′ə jē), *n.* science of determining the time or length of existence of geological formations and of geological periods.

ge ode (jē′ōd), *n.* 1 rock usually having a cavity lined with crystals or other mineral matter. 2 the cavity itself. [< Greek *geōdēs* earthy < *gē* earth + *eidos* form]

ge o des ic (jē′ə des′ik), *adj.* 1 geodetic. 2 having a curve like the curvature of the earth: *a geodesic dome.* —*n.* the shortest line between two points on a surface.

ge od e sist (jē od′ə sist), *n.* an expert in geodesy.

ge od e sy (jē od′ə sē), *n.* 1 branch of applied mathematics dealing with the measurement of the earth and of large areas on the surface of the earth. 2 branch of surveying dealing with such measurements. [< Greek *geōdaisia* < *gē* earth + *daiein* divide]

ge o det ic (jē′ə det′ik), *adj.* having to do with geodesy; geodesic: *a geodetic surveyor.* **—ge′o det′i cal ly,** *adv.*

Geof frey of Monmouth (jef′rē), 1100?-1154, Welsh historian who chronicled the life of King Arthur and his court.

geog., 1 geographer. 2 geography.

ge og ra pher (jē og′rə fər), *n.* an expert in geography.

ge o graph ic (jē′ə graf′ik), *adj.* geographical.

ge o graph i cal (jē′ə graf′ə kəl), *adj.* 1 of or having to do with geography. 2 of, having to do with, or characteristic of a particular region. **—ge′o graph′i cal ly,** *adv.*

geographical mile, nautical mile.

ge og ra phy (jē og′rə fē), *n., pl.* **-phies.** 1 study of the earth's surface, climate, continents, countries, peoples, industries, and products. 2 the surface features of a place or region: *the geography of New England.* [< Greek *geōgraphia* < *gē* earth + *graphein* describe]

geol., geology.

ge o log ic (jē′ə loj′ik), *adj.* geological.

ge o log i cal (jē′ə loj′ə kəl), *adj.* of or having to do with geology. **—ge′o log′i cal ly,** *adv.*

ge ol o gist (jē ol′ə jist), *n.* an expert in geology.

ge ol o gy (jē ol′ə jē), *n., pl.* **-gies.** 1 science that deals with the earth's crust, the layers of which it is composed, and their history. 2 features of the earth's crust in a place or region; rocks, rock formation, etc., of a particular area: *the geology of North America.*

geom., 1 geometric. 2 geometry.

ge o mag net ic (jē′ō mag net′ik), *adj.* of or having to do with the magnetism of the earth.

ge o mag net ism (jē′ō mag′nə tiz′əm), *n.* 1 the magnetism of the earth. 2 science concerned with the magnetism of the earth.

ge om e ter (jē om′ə tər), *n.* geometrician.

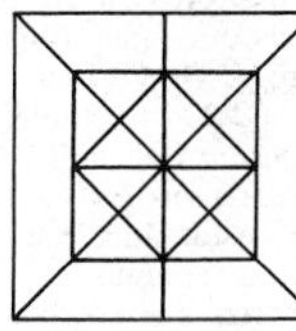

geometric (def. 2) designs based on the circle and the square

ge o met ric (jē′ə met′rik), *adj.* 1 of geometry; according to the principles of geometry: *geometric proof.* 2 consisting of straight lines, circles, triangles, etc.; regular and symmetrical: *a geometric design.* **—ge′o met′ri cal ly,** *adv.*

ge o met ri cal (jē′ə met′rə kəl), *adj.* geometric.

geometrical progression, geometric progression.

ge om e tri cian (jē om′ə trish′ən, jē′ə mə trish′ən), *n.* an expert in geometry.

geometric mean, the mean of a number *(n)* of positive quantities produced by taking the *n*th root of their product: *The geometric mean of the two quantities of 16 and 4 is the square root of their product, or 8.*

geometric progression, sequence of numbers in which each number is multiplied by the same factor in order to obtain the following number. 2, 4, 8, 16, and 32 form a geometric progression. So also do 3125, 625, 125, 25, 5, 1, $^{1}/_{5}$, and $^{1}/_{25}$.

ge om e trid (jē om′ə trid), *n.* any of a family of slender gray or greenish moths whose larvae have legs at the ends of the body, causing them to travel with a looping motion and to be called measuring worms or inchworms. —*adj.* of or having to do with a geometrid.

ge om e try (jē om′ə trē), *n., pl.* **-tries.** branch of mathematics which studies the relationship of points, lines, angles, and surfaces of figures in space; the mathematics of space. Geometry includes the definition, comparison, and measurement of squares, triangles, circles, cubes, cones, spheres, and other plane and solid figures. [< Greek *geōmetria* < *gē* earth + *-metria* measuring]

ge o mor pho log i cal (jē′ō môr′fə loj′ə kəl), *adj.* of or having to do with geomorphology.

hat, āge, fär; let, ēqual, tėrm;
it, īce; hot, ōpen, ôrder;
oil, out; cup, pu̇t, rüle;
ch, child; ng, long; sh, she;
th, thin; ᴛʜ, then; zh, measure;

ə represents *a* in about, *e* in taken, *i* in pencil, *o* in lemon, *u* in circus.

< = from, derived from, taken from.

ge o mor phol o gist (jē′ō môr fol′ə jist), *n.* an expert in geomorphology.

ge o mor phol o gy (jē′ō môr fol′ə jē), *n.* study of the surface features of the earth, their arrangement, origin, development, etc.

ge o phys i cal (jē′ō fiz′ə kəl), *adj.* of or having to do with geophysics.

ge o phys i cist (jē′ō fiz′ə sist), *n.* an expert in geophysics.

ge o phys ics (jē′ō fiz′iks), *n.* study of the relations between the physical features of the earth and the forces that change or produce them. Geophysics includes geology, meteorology, oceanography, seismology, and similar sciences.

ge o po lit i cal (jē′ō pə lit′ə kəl), *adj.* having to do with geopolitics. **—ge′o po lit′i cal ly,** *adv.*

ge o pol i ti cian (jē′ō pol′ə tish′ən), *n.* an expert in geopolitics.

ge o pol i tics (jē′ō pol′ə tiks), *n.* study of government and its policies as affected by physical geography.

George (jôrj), *n.* 1 **David Lloyd.** See **Lloyd George.** 2 **Henry,** 1839-1897, American economist. 3 **Saint,** died A.D. 303?, Christian martyr, the patron saint of England. 4 **Lake,** lake in E New York State. 36 mi. long.

George I, 1 1660-1727, king of England from 1714 to 1727. He was the first king of the house of Hanover. 2 1845-1913, king of Greece from 1863 to 1913.

George II, 1 1683-1760, king of England from 1727 to 1760. 2 1890-1947, king of Greece from 1922 to 1923 and from 1935 to 1947.

George III, 1738-1820, king of England from 1760 to 1820. He was the grandson of George II.

George IV, 1762-1830, king of England from 1820 to 1830. He was the son of George III.

George V, 1865-1936, king of England from 1910 to 1936. He was the son of Edward VII.

George VI, 1895-1952, king of England from 1936 to 1952. He was the son of George V and brother of Edward VIII.

George town (jôrj′toun), *n.* 1 seaport and capital of Guyana. 195,000, with suburbs. 2 seaport in Malaysia, on Penang. 235,000. Also, **Penang.**

George Town, Georgetown (def. 2).

geor gette (jôr jet′), *n.* a thin, fine, transparent, silk cloth with a slightly wavy surface, used for dresses, etc. [< name of French modiste]

Geor gia (jôr′jə), *n.* 1 one of the southeastern states of the United States. 4,590,000 pop.; 58,900 sq. mi. *Capital:* Atlanta. *Abbrev.:* Ga. 2 Georgian S.S.R.

Geor gian (jôr′jən), *adj.* 1 of or having to

do with the four Georges, kings of England from 1714 to 1830. 2 having to do with the style of architecture, art, or decoration during this period. 3 of or having to do with the state of Georgia or its people. 4 of or having to do with the Georgian S.S.R., its inhabitants, or their language. —*n.* 1 native or inhabitant of the state of Georgia. 2 native or inhabitant of the Georgian S.S.R. 3 person, especially a writer, of the time of the first four Georges in England.

Georgian Bay, the NE part of Lake Huron, in central Ontario.

Georgian S.S.R., one of the constituent republics of the U.S.S.R., in the SW part, on the Black Sea. 4,700,000 pop.; 26,900 sq. mi. *Capital:* Tbilisi.

ge o sci ence (jē′ō sī′əns), *n.* any science dealing with the earth, as geology, geophysics, and geochemistry.

ge o sphere (jē′ō sfir), *n.* lithosphere.

ge o ther mal (jē′ō thėr′məl), *adj.* of or having to do with the internal heat of the earth: *geothermal electricity.*

ge o trop ic (jē′ō trop′ik), *adj.* affected by geotropism; responding to gravity.

ge ot ro pism (jē ot′rə piz′əm), *n.* response by various organisms to the action of gravity. **Positive geotropism** is a tendency to move down into the earth, as plant roots do. **Negative geotropism** is a tendency to move upward. [< *geo-* + Greek *tropē* a turning]

ger., gerund.

Ger., 1 German. 2 Germany.

ge ra ni um (jə rā′nē əm), *n.* 1 any of a genus of cultivated or wild plants, usually having deeply notched leaves and showy white, pink, red, or purple flowers; cranesbill. 2 the flower of any of these plants. 3 pelargonium. [< Latin < Greek *geranion* < *geranos* crane; from resemblance of seed pod to crane's bill]

ger bil (jėr′bəl), *n.* any of various genera of small rodents with long hind legs, native to Old World desert regions. Some species of gerbils are used in scientific research and are kept as pets. [< French *gerbille*]

ger fal con (jėr′fal′kən, jėr′fôl′kən, jėr′fô′kən), *n.* gyrfalcon.

ger i at ric (jer′ē at′rik), *adj.* for or having to do with elderly people, old age, and geriatrics. [< Greek *geras* old age + *iatros* physician]

ger i a tri cian (jer′ē ə trish′ən), *n.* an expert in geriatrics.

ger i at rics (jer′ē at′riks), *n.* branch of medicine dealing with the study of aging, old age, and its diseases.

germ (jėrm), *n.* 1 a microscopic animal or plant, especially one which causes disease; microbe: *the scarlet fever germ.* 2 the earliest form of a living thing; seed; bud; spore. 3 the beginning of anything; origin: *Counting is the germ of arithmetic.* [< French *germe* < Latin *germen* sprout] —**germ′less,** *adj.* —**germ′like′,** *adj.*

ger man (jėr′mən), *adj.* 1 having the same parents. Children of the same father and mother are **brothers-german** or **sisters-german.** 2 being a child of one's uncle or aunt. A **cousin-german** is a first cousin. [< Old French *germain* < Latin *germanus,* related to *germen* sprout]

Ger man (jėr′mən), *adj.* of Germany, its people, or their language. —*n.* 1 native or inhabitant of Germany. 2 language of Germany. German is also the official language of Austria and one of the official languages of Switzerland. 3 **german, a** dance with complicated steps and frequent changing of partners; cotillion. **b** party at which it is danced.

ger man der (jər man′dər), *n.* 1 any of a genus of plants of the mint family, usually having dense spikes of small flowers. 2 a species of speedwell. [< Medieval Latin *germandrea*]

ger mane (jər mān′), *adj.* closely connected; to the point; pertinent. [variant of *german*]

Ger man ic (jər man′ik), *adj.* 1 German. 2 of or having to do with the people of northwestern Europe, such as the Germans, Scandinavians, and English, whose related languages form a branch of Indo-European. 3 of these languages or the branch they form. 4 Teutonic. —*n.* branch of the Indo-European language family, customarily divided into **East Germanic** (Gothic), **North Germanic** (the Scandinavian languages), and **West Germanic** (English, Frisian, Dutch, German).

ger ma ni um (jər mā′nē əm), *n.* a brittle, silver-white metalloid element which occurs in zinc ores, used as a semiconductor in transistors and other electronic devices. *Symbol:* Ge; *atomic number* 32. See pages 326 and 327 for table. [< New Latin < Latin *Germania* Germany]

German measles, a contagious virus disease resembling measles, but less serious; rubella; rubeola.

German shepherd, a large, strong, intelligent dog of a breed developed in Germany, often trained to work with soldiers and police or to guide blind persons; police dog; Alsatian.

German silver, nickel silver.

Ger man town (jėr′mən toun), *n.* NW section of Philadelphia, formerly a separate town. The British defeated Washington there in 1777.

Ger ma ny (jėr′mə nē), *n.* former country in central Europe divided after World War II into West Germany and East Germany, with parts of it going to Poland and the Soviet Union. Its capital was Berlin.

germ cell, 1 an egg or sperm cell; gamete. 2 a primitive cell from which an egg or sperm cell develops.

ger mi cid al (jėr′mə sī′dl), *adj.* capable of killing germs.

ger mi cide (jėr′mə sīd), *n.* any substance that kills germs, especially disease germs. Disinfectants and fungicides are germicides.

ger mi nal (jėr′mə nəl), *adj.* 1 of or like germs or germ cells. 2 in the earliest stage of development.

ger mi nate (jėr′mə nāt), *v.,* **-nat ed, -nat ing.** —*v.i.* begin to grow or develop; sprout: *Seeds germinate in the spring.* —*v.t.* cause to grow or develop. [< Latin *germinatum* sprouted < *germen* sprout] —**ger′mi na′tor,** *n.*

ger mi na tion (jėr′mə nā′shən), *n.* a starting to grow or develop; a sprouting.

ger mi na tive (jėr′mə nā′tiv), *adj.* capable of germinating.

Ger mis ton (jėr′mə stən), *n.* city in NE Republic of South Africa, near Johannesburg. 197,000.

germ layer, any of the three primary layers of cells, the ectoderm, mesoderm, or endoderm, which become further differentiated as the embryo develops.

germ plasm, 1 the germ cells of an organism. 2 the hereditary substance in germ cells, now known to consist of the chromosomes, that is transmitted to the offspring.

germ theory, the theory that infectious diseases are caused and spread by germs.

germ warfare, the spreading of germs to produce disease among the enemy in time of war.

Ge ron i mo (jə ron′ə mō), *n.* 1829-1909, Apache Indian chief.

ge ron to log i cal (jə ron′tl oj′ə kəl), *adj.* of or having to do with gerontology.

ger on tol o gist (jer′on tol′ə jist), *n.* an expert in gerontology.

ger on tol o gy (jer′on tol′ə jē), *n.* branch of science dealing with the phenomena and problems of old age. [< Greek *gerontos* old man]

Ger ry (ger′ē), *n.* **Elbridge,** 1744-1814, vice-president of the United States from 1813 to 1814.

ger ry man der (ger′ē man′dər, jer′ē-man′dər), U.S. —*v.t.* 1 arrange the political divisions of (a state, county, etc.) to give one political party an unfair advantage in elections. 2 manipulate unfairly. —*n.* 1 act of gerrymandering. 2 an election district or other political division resulting from gerrymandering. [< Elbridge *Gerry* + *(sala)mander;* while he was governor of Massachusetts (1810-1812), Gerry's party redistricted the state, and Essex County was divided so that one district became roughly salamander-shaped]

Gersh win (gėrsh′wən), *n.* **George,** 1898-1937, American composer.

ger und (jer′ənd), *n.* 1 (in English grammar) a verb form ending in *-ing,* and used as a noun. 2 (in Latin grammar) a form of the verb occurring as a noun in all cases except the nominative. [< Late Latin *gerundium,* ultimately < Latin *gerere* to bear]

➔ The English **gerund,** ending in *-ing,* has the same form as the present participle but differs in use. Gerund: *Running a hotel appealed to him.* Participle: *Running around the corner, I bumped into a policeman.* A gerund may take an object *(running a hotel)* or a complement *(being a hero),* and it may serve in any of the functions of a noun. Subject: *Looking for an apartment always fascinated her.* Direct object: *He taught dancing.* Predicate noun: *Seeing is believing.* Adjective use: *a fishing boat* (a boat for fishing, not a boat that fishes). Object of a preposition: *By running, I was able to catch the bus.*

ge run di al (jə run′dē əl), *adj.* 1 of a gerund. 2 used as a gerund.

ge run dive (jə run′div), *n.* a Latin verb form used as an adjective, frequently expressing the idea of necessity.

ges so (jes′ō), *n.* 1 a plasterlike coating used to cover the surface of picture frames, furniture, etc., before painting or inlaying them. It is made by heating a mixture of glue and powdered chalk or whiting. 2 a preparation of plaster of Paris or gypsum for use in painting and sculpture. [< Italian < Latin *gypsum* gypsum]

gest or **geste** (jest), *n.* ARCHAIC. 1 story or romance in verse. 2 story; tale. 3 feat; exploit. [< Old French *geste* < Latin *gesta* deeds < *gerere* carry on, accomplish]

Ge stalt (gə shtält′), *n.* school of psychology that emphasizes the fact that a whole may be something more than the sum of its parts, and that the parts as a whole are often modified by their relationships to it and to one another. [< German, form, configuration]

Ge sta po (gə stä′pō, gə shtä′pō), *n.* an official organization of secret police in Nazi Germany. [< German < *Ge(heime) Sta(ats)po(lizei)* secret state police]

ges tate (jes′tāt), *v.t.*, **-tat ed, -tat ing.** 1 carry in the womb during pregnancy. 2 form and develop (a project, idea, plan, etc.) in the mind. [< Latin *gestatum* carried about < *gerere* to bear]

ges ta tion (je stā′shən), *n.* 1 a having young developing in the uterus; pregnancy. 2 period of pregnancy. 3 formation and development of a project, idea, plan, etc., in the mind.

ges tic u late (je stik′yə lāt), *v.i.*, **-lat ed, -lat ing.** make or use gestures to show ideas or feelings. [< Latin *gesticulatum* gesticulated, ultimately < *gestus* gesture] **—ges tic′u la′tor,** *n.*

ges tic u la tion (je stik′yə lā′shən), *n.* 1 a making lively or excited gestures. 2 a lively or excited gesture: *His wild gesticulations showed that he was losing his temper rapidly.*

ges tic u la tive (je stik′yə lā′tiv), *adj.* making or using gestures.

ges ture (jes′chər), *n.*, *v.*, **-tured, -tur ing.** *—n.* 1 movement of any part of the body, to help express an idea or a feeling: *A speaker often makes gestures with his hands or arms to stress something that he is saying.* 2 the use of such movements. 3 anything said or done to impress or influence others: *Her refusal was merely a gesture; she really wanted to go.* *—v.i.* make a gesture or gestures; use gestures. *—v.t.* express by a gesture or gestures. [< Medieval Latin *gestura* < Latin *gestus* gesture < *gerere* to bear]

Ge sund heit (gə zünt′hīt), *interj.* your health! People often say "Gesundheit" when someone sneezes. [< German]

get (get), *v.*, **got, got** or **got ten, get ting,** *n.* *—v.t.* 1 come to have; obtain; acquire: *I got a new coat yesterday. He got first prize in the spelling contest.* See synonym study below. 2 catch; get hold of; seize: *He got the heavy box by the end and hoisted it up.* 3 find out by calculation or experiment: *get the answer to the problem.* 4 bring: *Get me a drink.* 5 INFORMAL. stir up; move. 6 cause to be or do: *Get the windows open. They got the fire under control.* 7 persuade; influence: *Try to get her to come, too.* 8 make ready; prepare: *I helped mother get dinner.* 9 INFORMAL. possess: *What have you got in your hand?* 10 INFORMAL. be obliged; need (with *have* and *had*): *We have got to win.* 11 INFORMAL. hit; strike: *The wild throw got the runner in the back as he slid into third base.* 12 INFORMAL. kill. 13 INFORMAL. puzzle; annoy: *This question gets me.* 14 SLANG. **a** understand: *Do you get me?* **b** hear. 15 (of animals) beget; procreate. *—v.i.* 1 reach; arrive: *Your letter got here yesterday. I got home early last night.* 2 be; become: *get sick, get nervous.* 3 come or go.

get about, **a** go from place to place. **b** spread; become widely known.

get across, INFORMAL. make clear, understood, or appreciated.

get around, **a** go from place to place. **b** become widely known; spread. **c** overcome. **d** deceive; trick.

get at, **a** reach. **b** find out. **c** INFORMAL. tamper with; influence with money or threats.

get away, **a** go away. **b** escape. **c** start, as in a race.

get away with, INFORMAL. take or do something and escape safely.

get back, **a** return. **b** recover.

get back at, SLANG. take revenge on.

get behind, support; endorse.

get by, INFORMAL. **a** pass. **b** not be noticed or caught. **c** manage.

get in, **a** go in. **b** put in. **c** arrive. **d** become friendly or familiar *(with).*

get it, INFORMAL. be scolded or punished.

get off, **a** come down from or out of. **b** take off. **c** escape punishment. **d** help to escape punishment. **e** start, as in a race. **f** say or express: *get off a joke.* **g** deliver: *get off a speech.*

get on, **a** go up on or into. **b** put on. **c** advance. **d** manage. **e** succeed. **f** agree.

get out, **a** go out. **b** take out. **c** go away. **d** escape. **e** help to escape. **f** become known. **g** publish.

get out of, **a** escape. **b** help to escape.

get over, **a** recover from. **b** overcome. **c** make clear or convincing.

get there, succeed.

get through, finish.

get together, INFORMAL. **a** bring or come together; meet; assemble. **b** come to an agreement.

get up, **a** get out of bed; arise. **b** stand up. **c** prepare; arrange. **d** dress up. **e** go ahead: *"Get up!" she commanded the horse.*

—n. 1 the return of a ball difficult to reach or hit, as in tennis. 2 (of animals) offspring. [Middle English *geten* < Scandinavian (Old Icelandic) *geta*]

Syn. *v.t.* 1 **Get, obtain, acquire** mean to come to have something. **Get** applies to gaining possession in any fashion, with or without effort: *I got a new car. He got a bad reputation after speeding through town.* **Obtain** usually suggests spending effort to get something one wants: *I obtained permission to go.* **Acquire** emphasizes possession by continued efforts: *I acquired a reading knowledge of German.*

➔ **Get** is increasingly used as an informal emphatic passive auxiliary: *We all got punished.*

ge ta (ge′tə), *n.pl.* wooden clogs worn by the Japanese. [< Japanese]

get a way (get′ə wā′), *n.* 1 act of getting away; escape. 2 a start from a complete stop: *a racing car's fast getaway.* 3 the start of a race, dramatic performance, etc.

Geth sem a ne (geth sem′ə nē), *n.* (in the Bible) a garden near Jerusalem, the scene of Jesus's agony, betrayal, and arrest.

get ter (get′ər), *n.* 1 person who gets. 2 a chemically active substance, such as magnesium, ignited in vacuum tubes to remove traces of gas.

get-to geth er (get′tə geᴛʜ′ər), *n.* an informal social gathering or party.

Get tys burg (get′ēz bėrg′), *n.* town in S Pennsylvania. One of the important battles of the Civil War was fought there July 1, 2, and 3, 1863. 7000.

get-up (get′up′), *n.* INFORMAL. 1 way a thing is put together; arrangement or style. 2 dress or costume.

get-up-and-go (get′up′ən gō′), *n.* INFORMAL. energy; initiative.

gew gaw (gyü′gô), *n.* a showy trifle; gaudy, useless ornament or toy; bauble. *—adj.* showy but trifling. [Middle English *giuegoue*]

gey ser (gī′zər), *n.* 1 spring that spouts a column of hot water and steam into the air at frequent intervals. 2 anything that spurts or gushes like a geyser. [< Icelandic *Geysir,* name of such a spring in Iceland < *geysa* to gush]

G-force (jē′fôrs′, jē′fōrs′), *n.* the force exerted on a person or object by gravity, or by changes in speed or direction.

hat, āge, fär; let, ēqual, tėrm;
it, īce; hot, ōpen, ôrder;
oil, out; cup, pu̇t, rüle;
ch, child; ng, long; sh, she;
th, thin; ᴛʜ, then; zh, measure;

ə represents *a* in about, *e* in taken, *i* in pencil, *o* in lemon, *u* in circus.

< = from, derived from, taken from.

GG or **G.G.,** gamma globulin.

Gha na (gä′nə), *n.* country in W Africa, a member of the Commonwealth of Nations. 8,546,000 pop.; 92,100 sq. mi. *Capital:* Accra. **—Gha nai an** (gä′nē ən, gä nā′ən), **Gha ni an** (gä′nē ən), *adj., n.*

ghast ly (gast′lē), *adj.*, **-li er, -li est,** *adv.* *—adj.* 1 causing terror; horrible; shocking: *Murder is a ghastly crime.* 2 like a dead person or ghost; deathly pale: *That very sick man looked ghastly.* 3 INFORMAL. very bad: *a ghastly failure.* *—adv.* in a ghastly manner. [Old English *gāstlic* ghostly < *gāst* ghost] **—ghast′li ness,** *n.*

ghat (gôt), *n.* in India: 1 steps or stairway leading down to a river. 2 a mountain pass. [< Hindustani *ghāṭ*]

Ghats (gôts), *n.pl.* mountain ranges along the E and W coasts of S India. Highest peak, 8000 ft.

ghee (gē), *n.* (in India) a liquid butter clarified by boiling, made from the milk of buffaloes and cows. [< Hindustani *ghī*]

Ghent (gent), *n.* city in NW Belgium, on the Scheldt River. 152,000. Also, **Gent.**

gher kin (gėr′kən), *n.* 1 a small, prickly cucumber often used for pickles. 2 the plant it grows on. 3 any young, green cucumber used for pickles. [< Dutch *gurken,* plural of *gurk* < Slavic]

ghet to (get′ō), *n., pl.* **-tos.** 1 (formerly) a section of a city where Jews were required to live. 2 section of a city where any racial or other minority group lives. [< Italian]

Ghib el line (gib′ə lən, gib′ə lēn′), *n.* member of the imperial and aristocratic political party of medieval Italy, that supported the Holy Roman Emperors and was opposed by the Guelphs.

Ghi ber ti (gē ber′tē), *n.* **Lorenzo,** 1378?-1455, Italian sculptor and goldsmith.

ghil lie (gil′ē), *n.* gillie.

ghost (gōst), *n.* 1 spirit of a dead person. It is supposed to live in another world and appear to living people as a pale, dim, shadowy form. 2 anything pale, dim, or shadowy like a ghost: *a ghost of a smile. We didn't have a ghost of a chance to win.* 3 the spirit, as distinct from the body; soul. 4 **give up the ghost,** die. 5 INFORMAL. ghostwriter. 6 a secondary or multiple image resulting from the reflection of a transmitted television signal. *—v.t.*

geyser (def. 1)

1 haunt as a ghost does. 2 INFORMAL. be a ghostwriter for. —*v.i.* 1 go about like a ghost. 2 INFORMAL. be a ghostwriter. —*adj.* deserted; forsaken. [Old English *gāst*] —**ghost′like′**, *adj.*

ghost ly (gōst′lē), *adj.*, **-li er, -li est.** 1 like a ghost; pale, dim, and shadowy. 2 ARCHAIC. spiritual. —**ghost′li ness**, *n.*

ghost town, a once-flourishing town that has become empty and lifeless.

ghost write (gōst′rīt′), *v.t., v.i.,* **-wrote** (-rōt′), **-writ ten** (-rit′n), **-writ ing.** write (something) for another person who pretends to be the author.

ghost writ er (gōst′rī′tər), *n.* person who writes something for another person who pretends to be the author.

ghoul (gül), *n.* 1 (in Oriental stories) a horrible demon that robs graves and feeds on corpses. 2 person who robs graves or corpses. 3 person who enjoys what is revolting, brutal, and horrible. [< Arabic *ghūl*]

ghoul ish (gü′lish), *adj.* like a ghoul; revolting, brutal, and horrible. —**ghoul′ish ly,** *adv.* —**ghoul′ish ness,** *n.*

GHQ or **G.H.Q.,** General Headquarters.

GI or **G.I.** (jē′ī′), *adj., n., pl.* **GI's** or **G.I.'s** (jē′īz′). —*adj.* 1 government issue: *GI shoes, GI socks.* 2 INFORMAL. conforming to regulations; standard: *GI uniforms.* 3 of, having to do with, or for a member of the armed forces: *a GI loan.* —*n.* INFORMAL. 1 an enlisted soldier in the United States Army; serviceman. 2 member or former member of any of the armed forces of the United States. [< the initial letters of the phrase "Government Issue"]

GI or **G.I.,** 1 gastrointestinal. 2 general issue. 3 government issue.

gi ant (jī′ənt), *n.* 1 an imaginary being having human form, but larger and more powerful than a man. 2 person or thing of great size, strength, or importance. —*adj.* like a giant; huge: *a giant potato.* [< Old French *geant* < Latin *gigantem* < Greek *gigas*]

gi ant ess (jī′ən tis), *n.* a female giant.

gi ant ism (jī′ən tiz′əm), *n.* 1 condition of being a giant. 2 gigantism.

giant panda, panda (def. 1).

giant sequoia, a very large evergreen tree of California, belonging to the same family as the redwood, often growing to a height of over 300 feet; sequoia; big tree.

giant star, a very bright star of vast size and low density, such as Arcturus.

giaour (jour), *n.* a Moslem term for a person who does not believe in the Moslem religion. [< Turkish *giaur*]

gib ber (jib′ər, gib′ər), *v.i.* chatter senselessly; talk in a confused, meaningless way: *The monkeys gibbered angrily at each other.* —*n.* senseless chattering. [imitative]

gib be rel lic acid (jib′ə rel′ik), a plant hormone, first discovered in a fungus, that increases size and the rate of growth. *Formula:* $C_{19}H_{22}O_6$ [< New Latin *Gibberella,* name of the fungus]

gib be rel lin (jib′ə rel′ən), *n.* any of a group of hormones that are synthesized in the protoplasm of plants and that increase the rate and amount of growth. Gibberellic acid is a gibberellin.

gib ber ish (jib′ər ish, gib′ər ish), *n.* senseless chatter; confused, meaningless talk or writing.

gib bet (jib′it), *n.* 1 an upright post with a projecting arm at the top, from which the bodies of criminals were hung after execution. 2 gallows. —*v.t.* 1 hang on a gibbet. 2 hold up to public scorn or ridicule. 3 put to death by hanging. [< Old French *gibet,* diminutive of *gibe* club]

gibbon
about 3 ft. tall

gib bon (gib′ən), *n.* any of various small apes of southeastern Asia and the East Indies that live in trees and have very long arms and no tail. [< French]

Gib bon (gib′ən), *n.* **Edward,** 1737-1794, English historian.

gib bos i ty (gi bos′ə tē), *n., pl.* **-ties.** 1 gibbous condition. 2 protuberance; swelling.

gib bous (gib′əs), *adj.* 1 curved out; humped. 2 (of a heavenly body) so illuminated as to be convex on both margins. A gibbous moon is more than half full but less than full. See **phase** for diagram. 3 humpbacked. [< Latin *gibbosus* < *gibbus* hump] —**gib′bous ly,** *adv.* —**gib′bous ness,** *n.*

Gibbs (gibz), *n.* **Josiah Willard,** 1839-1903, American mathematician and physicist, whose theories form the basis of modern physical chemistry.

gibe (jib), *v.,* **gibed, gib ing,** *n.* —*v.i.* speak sneeringly; jeer; scoff; sneer. —*n.* a jeer; taunt; sneer. Also, **jibe.** [perhaps < Old French *giber* handle roughly < *gibe* staff] —**gib′er,** *n.* —**gib′ing ly,** *adv.*

gib let (jib′lit), *n.* Usually, **giblets,** *pl.* the heart, liver, or gizzard of a fowl. [< Old French *gibelet* stew of game]

Gi bral tar (jə brôl′tər), *n.* 1 seaport and fortress on a high rock on the Mediterranean Sea, near the S tip of Spain. It is a British colony. 26,000 pop.; $1^7/_8$ sq. mi. 2 **Rock of,** the large rock on which this fortress stands. 3 a strongly fortified place; impregnable fortress or stronghold. 4 **Strait of,** strait between Africa and Europe, connecting the Mediterranean Sea with the Atlantic. $8^1/_2$ to 23 mi. wide.

gid dy (gid′ē), *adj.,* **-di er, -di est.** 1 having a whirling feeling in one's head; dizzy. 2 likely to make dizzy; causing dizziness: *a giddy dance.* 3 never or rarely serious; frivolous; fickle: *a giddy person.* [Old English *gydig* mad, possessed (by an evil spirit) < *god* a god] —**gid′di ly,** *adv.* —**gid′di ness,** *n.*

Gide (zhēd), *n.* **André,** 1869-1951, French novelist and critic.

Gid e on (gid′ē ən), *n.* (in the Bible) a hero of Israel who defeated the Midianites and was a judge of Israel for forty years.

gie (gē), *v.t., v.i.* SCOTTISH AND DIALECT. give.

gift (gift), *n.* 1 something given freely; present: *a birthday gift.* See synonym study below. 2 act of giving freely: *The house came to him by gift from an aunt.* 3 power or right of giving: *The job is within his gift.* 4 natural ability; special talent: *a gift for painting.* [Middle English *gifte* < Scandinavian. Related to GIVE.]

Syn. 1 **Gift, present** mean something given to express friendship, admiration, interest, etc. **Gift** usually applies to what is given to a person, organization, or institution to benefit it: *The university received a gift of a million dollars.* **Present** always suggests a personal connection and applies to what is given a friend, relative, or other close person: *We bought a wedding present for our cousin.*

gift ed (gif′tid), *adj.* having natural ability or special talent; unusually able: *Beethoven was a gifted composer.*

gift-wrap (gift′rap′), *v.t.,* **-wrapped, -wrap ping.** wrap (a parcel, gift, etc.) in fancy paper and with decorative trimmings.

gig[1] (gig), *n.* 1 a light, open, two-wheeled carriage drawn by one horse. 2 a long, light ship's boat moved by oars or sails. [origin uncertain]

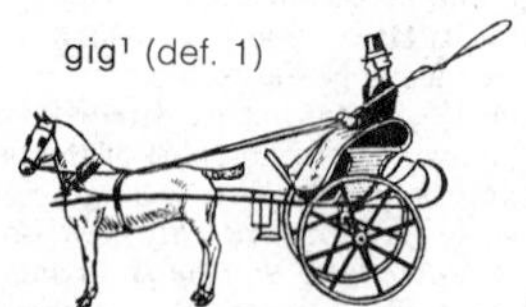

gig[1] (def. 1)

gig[2] (gig), *n., v.,* **gigged, gig ging.** —*n.* a fish spear. —*v.t.* spear (fish) with a gig. [origin uncertain]

gig[3] (gig), *n.* SLANG. 1 a gathering or meeting of jazz or rock musicians. 2 a single engagement or playing time of a jazz or rock group, or solo entertainer. 3 any work or interest that is habitual.

giga-, *combining form.* one billion: *Gigavolt = one billion volts.* [< Greek *gigas* giant]

gi gan tic (jī gan′tik), *adj.* 1 of, having to do with, or like a giant: *In folklore, Paul Bunyan was a gigantic lumberjack.* 2 huge; enormous. [< Greek *gigantos*] —**gi gan′ti cal ly,** *adv.*

gi gan tism (jī gan′tiz′əm), *n.* 1 abnormal growth or size of the body or part of the body, usually caused by malfunction of the pituitary gland. 2 condition of being a giant.

gig a volt (jig′ə vōlt′), *n.* one billion volts.

gig gle (gig′əl), *v.,* **-gled, -gling,** *n.* —*v.i.* laugh in a silly or undignified way. —*n.* a silly or undignified laugh. [imitative] —**gig′gler,** *n.* —**gig′gling ly,** *adv.*

gig gly (gig′lē), *adj.* having the habit of giggling: *a giggly pupil.*

gig o lo (jig′ə lō), *n., pl.* **-los.** man who is paid for being a woman's dancing partner, escort, or lover. [< French]

gig ot (jig′ət), *n.* 1 a leg-of-mutton sleeve. 2 leg of mutton, veal, etc. [< French]

Gi la monster (hē′lə), a large, poisonous lizard of the southwestern United States and northern Mexico, which has a thick tail, a heavy, clumsy body, and is covered with beadlike, orange-and-black scales. [< *Gila* River]

Gila River, river flowing from SW New Mexico across S Arizona into the Colorado River. 630 mi.

Gil bert (gil′bərt), *n.* 1 Sir **Humphrey,** 1539?-1583, English navigator who explored the coast of Newfoundland. 2 Sir **William Schwenck,** 1836-1911, English dramatist and librettist, who collaborated with Sir Arthur Sullivan in writing comic operas.

Gilbert and El lice Islands (el′is),

British colony in the central Pacific which includes a large number of small islands near the equator. Colonial headquarters are on Tarawa. 60,000 pop.; 374 sq. mi.

gild[1] (gild), *v.t.*, **gild ed** or **gilt, gild ing.** 1 cover with a thin layer of gold or similar material; make golden. 2 make (something) look bright and pleasing. 3 make (something) seem better than it is. [Old English *-gyldan* < *gold* gold]

gild[2] (gild), *n.* guild.

Gilded Age, U.S. the period between 1865 and 1900, noted for its showy wealth.

gild ing (gil′ding), *n.* 1 a thin layer of gold or similar material with which a thing is gilded. 2 a gilded thing or surface. 3 an attractive coating; veneer: *a gilding of politeness.*

Gil e ad (gil′ē əd), *n.* 1 region in ancient Palestine, east of the Jordan River. 2 **Mount,** mountain in NW Jordan, northeast of the Dead Sea. 3596 ft.

Gil e ad ite (gil′ē ə dīt), *n.* 1 native or inhabitant of Gilead. 2 member of a branch of the tribe of Manasseh.

gill[1] (gil), *n.* 1 part of the body of a fish, tadpole, crab, etc., by which it breathes in water. Oxygen passes in and carbon dioxide passes out through the thin membranous walls of the gills. 2 **gills,** *pl.* **a** the fine, thin, leaflike structures on the underside of a mushroom. **b** the flesh under a person's jaws. **c** wattle[2]. [probably < Scandinavian (Danish) *gjelle*]

gill[2] (jil), *n.* a small measure for liquids, equal to one fourth of a pint, or about half a cup. See **measure** for table. [< Old French *gille* a wine measure]

gil lie (gil′ē), *n.* 1 man who goes with and helps a hunter or fisherman in the Scottish Highlands. 2 follower; servant. 3 a sports shoe for women with laces that tie about the ankle. Also, **ghillie, gilly.** [< Scottish Gaelic *gille* lad]

gill net, net in which fish trying to pass through are caught by their gills.

gill slit, one of the openings in the pharynx of a fish, certain amphibians, etc., that serve as channels for the passage of water to the exterior.

gil ly (gil′ē), *n., pl.* **-lies.** gillie.

gil ly flow er (jil′ē flou′ər), *n.* any of various flowers that have a spicy fragrance, such as the wallflower, stock, and carnation. [alteration of Old French *gilofre* clove < Medieval Latin *caryophyllum* < Greek *karyophyllon* < *karyon* nut + *phyllon* leaf]

gilt[1] (gilt), *adj.* gilded. *—n.* 1 a thin layer of gold or similar material with which a surface is gilded. 2 gilding; veneer. *—v.* a pt. and a pp. of **gild**[1].

gilt[2] (gilt), *n.* a young sow or female pig. [< Scandinavian (Old Icelandic) *gyltr*]

gilt-edge (gilt′ej′), *adj.* gilt-edged.

gilt-edged (gilt′ejd′), *adj.* 1 having gilded edges. 2 of the very best quality: *Gilt-edged securities are the safest kind to invest in.*

gim bals (jim′bəlz, gim′bəlz), *n.pl.* device consisting of a pair of pivoting rings, one within the other and with axes at right angles to each other, for keeping an object horizontal, as a ship's compass by counteracting the roll and pitch of a ship. [earlier *gimmal* interlocking rings < Old French *gemel* twin < Latin *gemellus*]

gim crack (jim′krak′), *n.* a showy, useless trifle; knickknack. *—adj.* showy but useless. [origin uncertain]

gim crack er y (jim′krak′ər ē), *n., pl.* **-er ies.** gimcracks collectively.

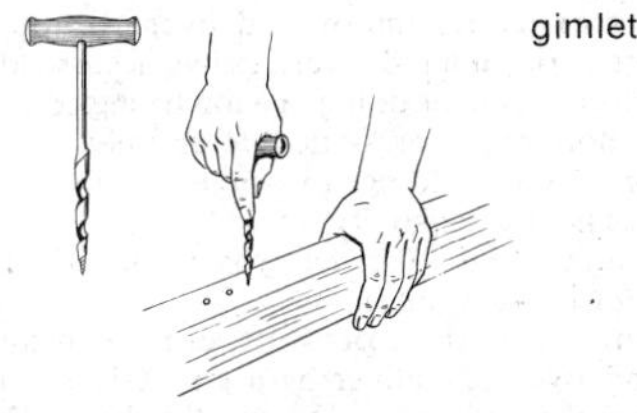

gim let (gim′lit), *n.* a small tool with a screw point on one end and a cross handle on the other, for boring holes. [< Old French *guimbelet*]

gim let-eyed (gim′lit īd′), *adj.* having sharp and piercing eyes.

gim mick (gim′ik), *n.* SLANG. 1 any small device, especially one used secretly or in a tricky manner. 2 a hidden or tricky condition in a plan, etc.; catch. 3 idea, scheme, or stunt to attract attention. [origin unknown]

gimp[1] (gimp), *n.* a braidlike trimming made of silk, worsted, or cotton, sometimes stiffened with wire, used on garments, curtains, furniture, etc. [< French *guimpe*]

gimp[2] (gimp), *n.* SLANG. 1 a lame step or walk; limp. 2 person who limps. [origin uncertain]

gimp y (gim′pē), *adj.* SLANG. lame; limping; halting.

gin[1] (jin), *n.* a strong, colorless alcoholic drink, distilled mostly from grain and usually flavored with juniper berries. [short for *geneva* < Dutch *genever* juniper, ultimately < Latin *juniperus*]

gin[2] (jin), *n., v.,* **ginned, gin ning.** *—n.* 1 cotton gin. 2 a trap; snare. *—v.t.* 1 separate (cotton) from its seeds. 2 trap; snare. [< Old French *engin* engine. See ENGINE.] **—gin′ner,** *n.*

gin[3] (jin), *n.* gin rummy.

gin ger (jin′jər), *n.* 1 spice made from the pungent root of a cultivated tropical plant. It is used for flavoring and in medicine. 2 its root, often preserved in syrup or candied. 3 the plant. 4 INFORMAL. liveliness; energy. [Old English *gingifer* < Medieval Latin *gingiber* < Latin *zingiberi* < Greek *zingiberis*]

ginger ale, a carbonated soft drink flavored with ginger.

ginger beer, drink similar to ginger ale, but made with fermenting ginger.

gin ger bread (jin′jər bred′), *n.* 1 cake flavored with ginger and sweetened with molasses. 2 something showy and elaborate; tasteless ornamentation. Cheap carvings glued on furniture are gingerbread. *—adj.* showy; gaudy.

gin ger ly (jin′jər lē), *adv.* with extreme care or caution. *—adj.* extremely cautious or wary. **—gin′ger li ness,** *n.*

gin ger snap (jin′jər snap′), *n.* a thin, crisp cookie flavored with ginger and sweetened with molasses.

gin ger y (jin′jər ē), *adj.* 1 like ginger; hot and sharp; spicy. 2 light reddish- or brownish-yellow.

ging ham (ging′əm), *n.* a cotton cloth made from colored threads. Its patterns are usually in stripes, plaids, or checks. [< French *guingan* < Malay *ginggang* striped]

gin gi vi tis (jin′jə vī′tis), *n.* inflammation of the gums. [< Latin *gingiva* gum]

ging ko (ging′kō, jing′kō), *n., pl.* **-koes.** ginkgo.

gink go (ging′kō, jing′kō), *n., pl.* **-goes.** a large, ornamental tree native to China and Japan, with fan-shaped leaves and edible nuts; maidenhair tree. [< Japanese *ginkyo*]

hat, āge, fär; let, ēqual, tėrm;
it, īce; hot, ōpen, ôrder;
oil, out; cup, pu̇t, rüle;
ch, child; ng, long; sh, she;
th, thin; ᴛʜ, then; zh, measure;

ə represents *a* in about, *e* in taken, *i* in pencil, *o* in lemon, *u* in circus.

< = from, derived from, taken from.

gin rummy, a card game like rummy, usually played by two persons. Players form sequences and matching combinations and may lay down their hands when their unmatched cards total ten points or less.

gin seng (jin′seng), *n.* 1 a low plant of the same family as ivy, grown in China and North America, and having a thick, branched, aromatic root. 2 this root, much used in medicine by the Chinese. [< Chinese *jên shên*]

Gior gio ne (jôr jō′nā), *n.* 1478?-1511, Italian painter of frescoes and other paintings.

Giot to (jot′ō), *n.* 1266?-1337, Italian painter and architect whose works mark the beginning of the Renaissance in painting.

gip sy or **Gip sy** (jip′sē), *n., pl.* **-sies,** *adj., v.i.,* **-sied, -sy ing.** gypsy.

gipsy moth, gypsy moth.

gi raffe (jə raf′), *n.* a large African mammal that chews its cud and has a very long neck, long legs, and a spotted skin. Giraffes are the tallest living animals. [< Italian *giraffa* < Arabic *zarāfah*]

Gi rau doux (zhē rō dü′), *n.* **Jean,** 1882-1944, French dramatist.

gird (gėrd), *v.t.,* **gird ed** or **girt, gird ing.** 1 put a belt or girdle around. 2 fasten with a belt or girdle: *gird up one's clothes.* 3 surround; enclose. 4 get ready: *gird oneself to face an examination.* 5 clothe; furnish; endue. [Old English *gyrdan*]

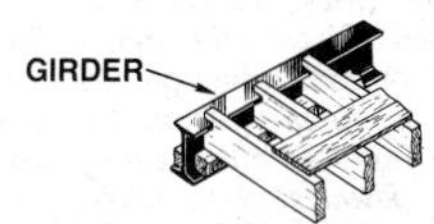

gird er (gėr′dər), *n.* a horizontal beam of steel, concrete, or wood used as a main support. The weight of a floor is usually supported by girders. A tall building or big bridge often has steel girders for its frame.

gir dle (gėr′dl), *n., v.,* **-dled, -dling.** *—n.* 1 belt, sash, cord, etc., worn around the waist. 2 anything that surrounds or encloses: *a girdle of trees around the pond.* 3 a light corset worn about the hips or waist. 4 ring made around a tree trunk, etc., by cutting the bark. *—v.t.* 1 put a girdle on or around. 2 surround; encircle: *Wide roads girdle the city.* 3 cut away the bark so as to make a ring around (a tree, branch, etc.). [Old English *gyrdel* < *gyrdan* gird] **—gir′dler,** *n.*

girl (gėrl), *n.* 1 a female child from birth to about eighteen. 2 a young, unmarried woman. 3 a female servant. 4 INFORMAL. sweetheart. 5 INFORMAL. woman. [Middle English *gurle, girle* child, young person]

girl friend (gėrl′frend′), *n.* INFORMAL. 1 boy's sweetheart or steady female companion. 2 a female friend.

girl guide, member of the **Girl Guides,** a British organization for girls similar to the Girl Scouts.

girl hood (gėrl′hu̇d), *n.* 1 time or condition of being a girl. 2 girls as a group: *the girlhood of the nation.*

girl ish (gėr′lish), *adj.* 1 of a girl. 2 like a girl. 3 like that of a girl. 4 proper or suitable for girls. **—girl′ish ly,** *adv.* **—girl′ishness,** *n.*

girl scout, member of the Girl Scouts.

Girl Scouts, organization for girls that seeks to develop health, character, citizenship, usefulness to others, and various skills.

Gi ronde (jə rond′; *French* zhē rôɴd′), *n.* estuary in SW France. 45 mi.

Gi ron dist (jə ron′dist), *n.* member of a French political party of moderate republicans from 1791 to 1793.

girt[1] (gėrt), *v.* a pt. and a pp. of **gird.**

girt[2] (gėrt), *v.t.* 1 put a belt, girdle, or girth around; gird. 2 fasten with a belt, girdle, or girth. [variant of *girth*]

girth (gėrth), *n.* 1 the measure around anything: *a man of large girth, the girth of a tree.* 2 strap or band that keeps a saddle, pack, etc., in place on a horse's back. See **harness** for picture. 3 girdle. *—v.t.* 1 fasten with a strap or band. 2 surround; girdle. *—v.i.* measure a certain amount in girth. [< Scandinavian (Old Icelandic) *gjörth* girdle. Related to GIRD.]

gis mo (giz′mō), *n., pl.* **-mos.** gizmo.

gist (jist), *n.* the essential part; real point; main idea; substance of a longer statement: *The gist of the superintendent's long speech was that we should build a new school.* [< Old French *gist* (it) lies (in), depends (on) < Latin *jacet* it lies]

git tern (git′ərn), *n.* an old musical instrument with wire strings, somewhat like a guitar. [< Old French *guiterne,* ultimately < Greek *kithara* cithara]

give (giv), *v.,* **gave, giv en, giv ing,** *n. —v.t.* 1 hand over as a gift; make a present of: *give money to charity.* See synonym study below. 2 hand over: *Give me that pencil.* 3 hand over in return for something; pay: *She can give as much as $3 for the wagon.* 4 let have; cause to have: *Don't give the teacher any trouble. Give me permission to leave.* 5 deal; administer: *to give medicine. Some boys give hard blows, even in play.* 6 offer; present: *give a recital, give a lecture. This newspaper gives a full story of the game.* 7 put forth; utter: *He gave a cry of pain.* 8 furnish; supply; provide: *give more light, give a party, give aid to the enemy.* 9 yield; produce: *cows giving milk. This farm gives good crops.* 10 exhibit; show: *give signs of life.* 11 make; do: *give a start.* 12 dedicate; devote: *give attention.* 13 sacrifice: *give one's life. —v.i.* 1 make a gift or present: *We give to several charities.* 2 yield to force or pressure: *The lock gave when I pushed hard against the door.*

give away, **a** give as a present. **b** hand over (a bride) to a bridegroom. **c** cause to be known; reveal; betray.

give back, return.

give in, stop fighting and admit defeat; yield.

give it to, INFORMAL. punish or scold.

give off, send out; put forth.

give out, **a** send out; put forth. **b** distribute. **c** make known. **d** become used up or worn out.

give over, **a** hand over; deliver. **b** stop.

give up, **a** hand over; deliver; surrender. **b** stop having or doing. **c** stop trying. **d** have no more hope for. **e** devote entirely.

—n. 1 a yielding to force or pressure. 2 resilience; elasticity.

[Middle English *given, yiven,* Old English *giefan*] **—giv′er,** *n.*

Syn. *v.t.* 1 **Give, present, confer** mean to hand over or deliver as a gift. **Give** is the general word: *She gave me this book.* **Present** means to give in a formal way, often with ceremony: *The Chamber of Commerce presented a trophy to the football team.* **Confer** means to present graciously, particularly as an honor or favor: *The university conferred an honorary degree on the distinguished journalist.*

give-and-take (giv′ən tāk′), *n.* 1 an even or fair exchange. 2 good-natured banter; exchange of talk.

give a way (giv′ə wā′), *n.* INFORMAL. 1 something revealed or made known unintentionally. 2 something given away or sold at a cheap price to promote business or good relations. 3 a radio or television show in which contestants receive prizes.

giv en (giv′ən), *adj.* 1 that has been stated; fixed; specified: *You must finish the test in a given time.* 2 having a fondness or habit; inclined; disposed: *He is given to boasting.* 3 assigned as a basis of calculating, reasoning, etc.; assumed: *The given radius being 4 ft., find the circumference.* 4 executed, dated, and delivered: *This document given under my hand, February 1, 1787. —v.* pp. of **give.**

given name, name given to a person in addition to his family name. *Jane* is the given name of *Jane Smith.*

Gi za or **Gi zeh** (gē′zə), *n.* town in NE Egypt, near Cairo, the Pyramids, and the Sphinx. 250,000.

giz mo (giz′mō), *n., pl.* **-mos.** U.S. SLANG. a gadget; device; contraption. Also, **gismo.**

giz zard (giz′ərd), *n.* 1 a bird's second stomach, where the food from the first stomach is ground up. The gizzard usually contains bits of sand or gravel. 2 INFORMAL. stomach or viscera. [Middle English *giser* < Old French *guiser,* ultimately < Latin *gigeria* cooked entrails of a fowl]

Gk., Greek.

gla brous (glā′brəs), *adj.* without hair or down; smooth: *Nasturtiums have glabrous stems.* [< Latin *glabrum* smooth]

gla cé (gla sā′), *adj.* 1 covered with sugar, frosting, or icing; candied. 2 frozen. 3 finished with a glossy surface. [< French]

gla cial (glā′shəl), *adj.* 1 of ice or glaciers; having much ice or many glaciers. 2 of or having to do with a glacial epoch or period. 3 made by the pressure and movement of ice or glaciers. 4 like ice; very cold; icy. [< Latin *glacialis* < *glacies* ice] **—gla′cially,** *adv.*

glacial epoch, 1 any of the times when much of the earth was covered with glaciers; ice age. 2 the most recent time when much of the Northern Hemisphere was covered with glaciers; Ice Age; Pleistocene.

glacial period, period that includes the glacial epochs.

gla ci ate (glā′shē āt), *v.t.,* **-at ed, -at ing.** 1 cover with ice or glaciers. 2 act on by ice or glaciers. **—gla′ci a′tion,** *n.*

gla cier (glā′shər), *n.* a large mass of ice moving very slowly down a mountain or along a valley, or spreading slowly over a large area of land. Glaciers are formed over many years from snow on high ground wherever winter snowfall exceeds summer melting. [< French]

Glacier National Park, national park in NW Montana, in the Rocky Mountains, noted for its many glaciers and lakes. 1600 sq. mi.

gla ci ol o gist (glā′shē ol′ə jist, glā′sēol′ə jist), *n.* an expert in glaciology.

gla ci ol o gy (glā′shē ol′ə jē, glā′sē ol′əjē), *n.* science that deals with glaciers and glacial action.

gla cis (glā′sis, glas′is), *n.* 1 a gentle slope. 2 (in fortification) a bank of earth, having a gradual downward slope toward the field or open country. [< French]

glad[1] (glad), *adj.,* **glad der, glad dest.** 1 feeling joy, pleasure, or satisfaction; happy; pleased: *She is glad to be well again.* See synonym study below. 2 bringing joy; pleasant: *The glad news made her happy.* 3 bright; gay: *The glad sunshine cheered us.* 4 willing; ready: *I am always glad to help my friends.* [Old English *glæd* bright, shining] **—glad′ly,** *adv.* **—glad′ness,** *n.*

Syn. 1 **Glad, happy** mean feeling pleasure or joy. **Glad** suggests feeling pleasure or delight: *She was glad that everything was going so well.* **Happy** suggests feeling deeply and fully contented and at peace: *He will never be happy until he has paid all his debts.*

glad[2] (glad), *n.* INFORMAL. gladiolus.

glad den (glad′n), *v.t.* make glad. See **cheer** for synonym study. *—v.i.* ARCHAIC. become glad.

glade (glād), *n.* 1 a small, open space in a wood or forest. 2 everglade. [probably related to GLAD[1]]

glad i a tor (glad′ē ā′tər), *n.* 1 slave, captive, or paid fighter who fought at the public shows in the arenas in ancient Rome. 2 a skilled contender in any fight or struggle. [< Latin < *gladius* sword]

glad i a to ri al (glad′ē ə tôr′ē əl, glad′ē ətōr′ē əl), *adj.* of or having to do with gladiators or their combats.

glad i o la (glad′ē ō′lə, glə dī′ə lə), *n.* gladiolus.

glad i o lus (glad′ē ō′ləs, glə dī′ə ləs), *n., pl.* **-li** (-lī), **-lus es.** 1 any of a genus of plants of the same family as the iris, that grow from bulblike, underground stems and have sword-shaped leaves and spikes of large, handsome flowers in various colors. 2 the flower of any of these plants. [< Latin, diminutive of *gladius* sword]

glad some (glad′səm), *adj.* 1 glad; joyful; cheerful. 2 causing gladness; pleasant; delightful. **—glad′some ly,** *adv.* **—glad′some ness,** *n.*

Glad stone (glad′stōn, glad′stən), *n.* 1 **William Ewart,** 1809-1898, British statesman who was prime minister four times. 2 Gladstone bag.

Gladstone bag, a traveling bag that opens flat into two equal compartments. [< William Ewart *Gladstone*]

glam or (glam′ər), *n.* mysterious fascination; alluring charm; magic attraction: *The glamor of Hollywood draws many young people there every year.* Also, **glamour.** [Scottish alteration of *grammar* occult learning; magic spell]

glam or ize (glam′ə rīz′), *v.t.,* **-ized, -iz ing.** 1 make (someone or something) glamorous. 2 invest with glory or romance. **—glam′ori za′tion,** *n.*

glam or ous (glam′ər əs), *adj.* full of glamor; fascinating; charming: *a glamorous*

hat, āge, fär; let, ēqual, tėrm;
it, īce; hot, ōpen, ôrder;
oil, out; cup, pu̇t, rüle;
ch, child; ng, long; sh, she;
th, thin; ᴛʜ, then; zh, measure;

ə represents *a* in about, *e* in taken, *i* in pencil, *o* in lemon, *u* in circus.

< = from, derived from, taken from.

job in a foreign city. **—glam′or ous ly,** *adv.* **—glam′or ous ness,** *n.*

glam our (glam′ər), *n.* glamor.

glance (glans), *n., v.,* **glanced, glanc ing.** *—n.* 1 a quick look directed at someone or something. See synonym study below. 2 a flash of light; gleam. 3 a deflected motion; swift, slanting movement or impact. 4 a passing reference; brief allusion. *—v.i.* 1 look quickly: *glance at a page, glance out the window.* 2 flash with light; gleam: *glancing eyes.* 3 hit and go off at a slant: *The spear glanced against the wall and missed the target.* 4 make a short reference and go on to something else. [variant of Middle English *glacen* to glance < Old French *glacier* to slip, ultimately < Latin *glacies* ice] **—glanc′ing ly,** *adv.*

Syn. *n.* 1 **Glance, glimpse** mean a quick look. **Glance** applies to a look directed at someone or something: *She gave him only a glance.* **Glimpse** applies to a short, quick, imperfect view, such as can be seen in a glance: *I caught a glimpse of him as he turned the corner.*

gland (gland), *n.* 1 organ in the body by which certain substances are separated from the blood and changed into some secretion for use in the body, such as bile, or into a product to be discharged from the body, such as sweat. The liver, the kidneys, the pancreas, and the thyroid are glands. 2 any of various structures similar to glands, such as the lymph nodes. [< French *glande* < Latin *glandem* acorn] **—gland′like′,** *adj.*

glan ders (glan′dərz), *n.* a serious, contagious, bacterial disease of horses, mules, etc., accompanied by fever, swellings beneath the lower jaw, and a profuse discharge from the nostrils.

glan du lar (glan′jə lər, glan′dyə lər), *adj.* 1 of or like a gland. 2 having glands. 3 made up of glands. **—glan′du lar ly,** *adv.*

glan du lous (glan′jə ləs, glan′dyə ləs), *adj.* glandular.

glans (glanz), *n., pl.* **glan des** (glan′dēz′). the head of the penis or of the clitoris. [< Latin, acorn]

glare (gler, glar), *n., v.,* **glared, glar ing,** *adj. —n.* 1 a strong, bright light; light that shines so brightly that it hurts the eyes. 2 a bright, smooth surface, such as a sheet of ice. 3 a fierce, angry stare. 4 too great brightness and showiness. *—v.i.* 1 give off a strong, bright light; shine so brightly as to hurt the eyes. 2 stare fiercely and angrily. 3 be too bright and showy. *—v.t.* express by a fierce, angry stare. *—adj.* bright and smooth: *glare ice.* [Middle English *glaren*]

glar ing (gler′ing, glar′ing), *adj.* 1 very bright; shining so brightly that it hurts the eyes; dazzling. 2 staring fiercely and angrily. 3 too bright and showy. 4 very easily seen; conspicuous: *a glaring fault.* **—glar′ing ly,** *adv.*

glar y (gler′ē, glar′ē), *adj.,* **glar i er, glar i est.** dazzling; glaring.

Glas gow (glas′gō, glas′kō), *n.* the largest city and chief seaport in Scotland, on the Clyde River. 908,000.

glass (glas), *n.* 1 a hard, brittle substance that is usually transparent, made by melting sand with soda ash, potash, lime, or other substances. Windows are made of glass. 2 container to drink from made of glass. 3 amount a glass can hold; glassful: *drink a glass of water.* 4 mirror. 5 any of various structures or implements made of glass, such as a lens, telescope, thermometer, windowpane, or watch crystal. 6 things made of glass; glassware. 7 **glasses,** *pl.* **a** eyeglasses; spectacles. **b** field glasses; binoculars. *—adj.* 1 made of glass: *a glass dish.* 2 with glass put in it; covered with glass. *—v.t.* 1 cover or protect with glass. 2 reflect. [Old English *glæs*] **—glass′like′,** *adj.*

glass blowing, art or process of shaping glass objects by blowing air from the mouth through a tube into a blob of molten glass at the other end of the tube. **—glass blower.**

glass ful (glas′fu̇l), *n., pl.* **-fuls.** as much as a glass holds.

glass ine (gla sēn′), *n.* a thin, strong, nearly transparent, glazed paper, used for packaging.

glass mak ing (glas′mā′king), *n.* art or process of making glass.

glass snake, a limbless, snakelike lizard of the southeastern and central United States. Its tail breaks off very easily.

glass ware (glas′wer′, glas′war′), *n.* articles made of glass.

Glas we gian (glas wē′jən, glas wē′jē ən), *adj.* of Glasgow. *—n.* native or inhabitant of Glasgow.

glass wool, glass spun in very fine threads, with a texture resembling loose fibers of wool, used for insulation, etc.

glass y (glas′ē), *adj.,* **glass i er, glass i est.** 1 like glass; smooth; easily seen through. 2 having a fixed, stupid stare. **—glass′i ly,** *adv.* **—glass′i ness,** *n.*

Glau ber's salt (glou′bərz, glô′bərz), hydrated sodium sulfate, used in dyeing and as a laxative and diuretic. *Formula:* $Na_2SO_4 \cdot 10H_2O$ [< Johann R. *Glauber,* 1604-1668, German chemist]

glau co ma (glô kō′mə, glou kō′mə), *n.* a disease of the eye common in old age in which increasing internal pressure causes damage resulting in a gradual loss of sight. [< Greek *glaukōma* < *glaukos* gray, silvery]

glau cous (glô′kəs), *adj.* 1 light bluish-green. 2 covered with a whitish, powdery or waxy substance, as plums and grapes are. [< Greek *glaukos* gray, silvery]

glaze (glāz), *v.,* **glazed, glaz ing,** *n. —v.t.* 1 put glass in; cover with glass. Pieces of glass cut to the right size are used to glaze windows and picture frames. 2 make a smooth, glassy surface or glossy coating on (china, food, etc.). *—v.i.* become smooth, glassy, or glossy. *—n.* 1 a smooth, glassy surface or glossy coating: *the glaze on a china cup.* 2 substance used to make such a surface or coating on things. [Middle English *glasen* < *glas* glass] **—glaz′er,** *n.*

gla zier (glā′zhər), *n.* person whose work is putting glass in windows, picture frames, etc.

glaz ing (glā′zing), *n.* 1 work of a glazier. 2 glass set or to be set in frames. 3 substance used to make a smooth, glassy surface or glossy coating on things. 4 such a surface or coating.

gleam (glēm), *n.* 1 flash or beam of light: *the gleam of headlights.* 2 a short or faint light: *the gleam of shining metal.* See synonym study below. 3 a short appearance; faint show: *After one gleam of hope, all was discouraging and dark.* *—v.i.* 1 flash or beam with light: *A candle gleamed in the dark.* 2 shine with a short or faint light: *gleaming jewelry.* 3 appear suddenly; be shown briefly. [Old English *glǣm*]

Syn. *n.* 2 **Gleam, glimmer** mean a faint, unsteady ray of light. **Gleam** applies to a light shining weakly and often intermittently against surrounding darkness: *At the end of the passage they saw a gleam of light.* **Glimmer** applies to a light which is fainter and more wavering than a *gleam: We saw the glimmer of a distant light through the trees.*

glean (glēn), *v.t.* 1 gather (grain) left on a field by reapers. 2 gather little by little: *glean information.* *—v.i.* gather grain left on a field by reapers. [< Old French *glener* < Late Latin *glennare*] **—glean′er,** *n.*

glean ing (glē′ning), *n.* Usually, **gleanings,** *pl.* anything that is gleaned.

glebe (glēb), *n.* 1 portion of land assigned to a parish church clergyman. 2 ARCHAIC. earth, soil, or land. [< Latin *gleba* lump, clod]

glee (glē), *n.* 1 a being merry and gay; lively joy; great delight. 2 song for three or more voices singing different parts, usually without accompaniment. [Old English *glēo*]

glee club, group, often of men only, organized for singing songs.

glee ful (glē′fəl), *adj.* filled with glee; merry and gay; joyous. **—glee′ful ly,** *adv.* **—glee′ful ness,** *n.*

glee man (glē′mən), *n., pl.* **-men.** ARCHAIC. a singer; minstrel.

glee some (glē′səm), *adj.* gleeful.

glen (glen), *n.* a small, narrow valley. [< Scottish Gaelic *gleann*]

Glen dale (glen′dāl), *n.* city in SW California, near Los Angeles. 133,000.

glengarry

glen gar ry (glen gar′ē), *n., pl.* **-ries.** a Scottish cap with straight sides and a creased top, often having short ribbons at the back. [< *Glengarry,* valley in Scotland]

Glenn (glen), *n.* **John,** born 1921, American astronaut. He was the first American to orbit the earth, in 1962.

glib (glib), *adj.,* **glib ber, glib best.** speaking or spoken too smoothly and easily to be believed: *a glib sales talk. No one believed his glib excuses.* See **fluent** for synonym study. [probably < Frisian *glibberig* slippery] **—glib′ly,** *adv.* **—glib′ness,** *n.*

glide (glīd), *v.,* **glid ed, glid ing,** *n. —v.i.* 1 move along smoothly, evenly, and easily: *Birds, ships, dancers, and skaters glide.* See **slide** for synonym study. 2 pass gradually, quietly, or imperceptibly: *The years glided* *past.* 3 come down slowly at a slant without using a motor. Under favorable circumstances, an airplane can glide about a mile for every thousand feet that it is above the ground. 3 (in music) pass from one tone to another without a break; slur. —*n.* 1 a smooth, even, easy movement. 2 (of an airplane) a coming down slowly at a slant without using a motor. 3 (in music) a slur. 4 (in phonetics) a sound made in passing from one speech sound to another, such as the *y* often heard between the *i* and *r* in *fire.* [Old English *glīdan*]

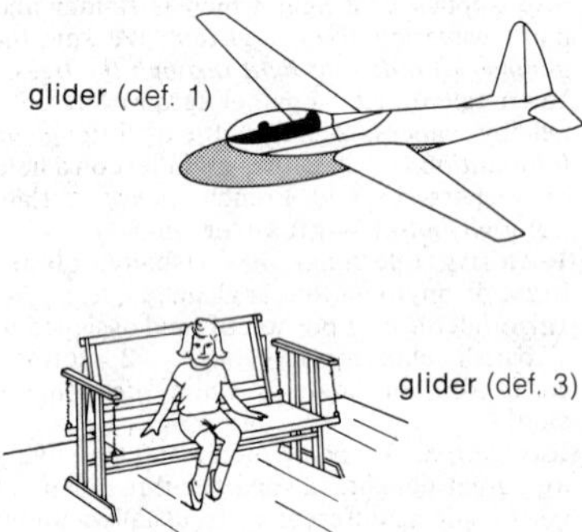

glider (def. 1)

glider (def. 3)

glid er (glī′dər), *n.* 1 a motorless aircraft that is kept in the air by rising air currents. 2 person or thing that glides. 3 a swinging seat suspended on a frame. Gliders are usually placed on porches or outdoors.

glim mer (glim′ər), *n.* 1 a faint, unsteady light. See **gleam** for synonym study. 2 a faint idea or feeling: *The doctor's report gave us only a glimmer of hope.* —*v.i.* 1 shine with a faint, unsteady light: *The candle glimmered and went out.* 2 appear faintly or dimly. [Middle English *glemeren.* Related to GLEAM.]

glim mer ing (glim′ər ing), *n.* glimmer.

glimpse (glimps), *n., v.,* **glimpsed, glimps ing.** —*n.* 1 a short, quick view: *I caught a glimpse of the falls as our train went by.* See **glance** for synonym study. 2 a short, faint appearance: *There were glimpses of truth in what he said.* —*v.t.* catch a short, quick view of. —*v.i.* look quickly; glance. [Middle English *glimsen.* Related to GLIMMER.]

Glin ka (gling′kə), *n.* **Mikhail Ivanovich,** 1804-1857, Russian composer.

glint (glint), *n.* 1 a gleam or flash of light: *The glint in her eye showed that she was angry.* 2 a short or momentary appearance. —*v.i.* 1 shine with a flashing light; gleam; glitter. 2 glance aside. [Middle English *glynten*]

glis san do (gli sän′dō), *adj., n., pl.* **-di** (-dē), **-dos.** in music: —*adj.* performed with a gliding effect. A pianist plays a glissando passage by running one finger rapidly over the white keys or the black keys on a piano. —*n.* part performed with a gliding effect; glissando passage. [in imitation of Italian < French *glissant* sliding]

glis ten (glis′n), *v.i.* shine with a twinkling light; glitter; sparkle: *The stars glistened in the sky.* —*n.* a glitter; sparkle. [Old English *glisnian*]

glis ter (glis′tər), *v.i., n.* ARCHAIC. glisten.

glit ter (glit′ər), *v.i.* 1 shine with a bright, sparkling light: *Her jewels glittered.* 2 be bright and showy. —*n.* 1 a bright, sparkling light. See **flash** for synonym study. 2 brightness; showiness. [< Scandinavian (Old Icelandic) *glitra*]

glit ter y (glit′ər ē), *adj.* glittering.

gloam ing (glō′ming), *n.* evening twilight; dusk. [Old English *glōmung* < *glom* twilight]

gloat (glōt), *v.i.* gaze intently; ponder with satisfaction: *The miser gloated over his gold.* [probably < Scandinavian (Old Icelandic) *glotta* smile scornfully] **—gloat′er,** *n.* **—gloat′ing ly,** *adv.*

glob (glob), *n.* a shapeless mass; blob.

glob al (glō′bəl), *adj.* 1 of the earth as a whole; worldwide. 2 shaped like a globe; spherical. **—glob′al ly,** *adv.*

glo bate (glō′bāt), *adj.* shaped like a globe.

globe (glōb), *n.* 1 anything having the form of a sphere. See **ball**[1] for synonym study. 2 the earth; world. See **earth** for synonym study. 3 sphere with a map of the earth or sky on it. 4 anything rounded like a globe, such as an electric light bulb. [< Middle French < Latin *globus*]

globe fish (glōb′fish′), *n., pl.* **-fish es** or **-fish.** any of various spiny, warm-water fishes that when disturbed can inflate into a ball-shaped form.

globe trot (glōb′trot′), *v.i.,* **-trot ted, -trot ting.** travel widely over the world, usually for sightseeing.

globe trot ter (glōb′trot′ər), *n.* person who globetrots.

glo bin (glō′bən), *n.* a protein substance formed in the decomposition of hemoglobin. [< Latin *globus* globe]

glo bose (glō′bōs, glō bōs′), *adj.* globular. **—glo′bose ly,** *adv.*

glob u lar (glob′yə lər), *adj.* 1 shaped like a globe or globule; round; spherical. 2 consisting of globules.

glob ule (glob′yül), *n.* a very small sphere or ball; tiny drop: *globules of sweat.*

glob u lin (glob′yə lən), *n.* any of a group of proteins, found in plant and animal tissue, which are insoluble in pure water but soluble in dilute salt solutions and in weak acids and alkalis. Globulin is a protein component of blood plasma.

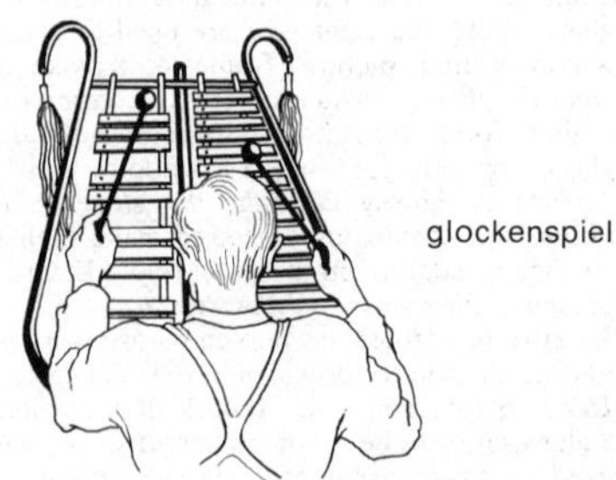

glockenspiel

glock en spiel (glok′ən spēl′), *n.* a percussion instrument consisting of a series of tuned metal bells, bars, or tubes mounted in a frame and struck with two hammers. [< German *Glockenspiel* < *Glocke* bell + *Spiel* play]

glom (glom), *v.t.,* **glommed, glom ming.** SLANG. **glom on to,** take hold of; latch on to.

glom er ate (glom′ər it), *adj.* clustered together; collected into a rounded mass. [< Latin *glomeratum* < *glomus* ball]

glo mer u lar (glə mer′ə lər, glə mer′yə lər), *adj.* of or like a glomerule.

glom e rule (glom′ə rül′), *n.* 1 any compact cluster. 2 (in botany) a cyme condensed into a headlike cluster, as in the dogwood.

glo mer u lus (glə mer′ə ləs, glə mer′yə ləs), *n., pl.* **-li** (-lī). tuft of capillaries in the tubules of the kidney, serving to filter out waste products from the blood. [< New Latin < Latin *glomus* ball]

gloom (glüm), *n.* 1 deep shadow; darkness; dimness. 2 dark thoughts and feelings; low spirits; sadness. 3 a dejected or sad look. —*v.i.* 1 be or become dark, dim, or dismal. 2 be in low spirits; feel sad. 3 look sad or dismal. [Middle English *gloumen* look sullen]

gloom y (glü′mē), *adj.,* **gloom i er, gloom i est.** 1 full of gloom; dark; dim: *a gloomy winter day.* 2 in low spirits; sad; melancholy: *a gloomy mood.* 3 causing low spirits; discouraging; dismal: *a gloomy scene of poverty.* **—gloom′i ly,** *adv.* **—gloom′i ness,** *n.*

Glo ri a (glôr′ē ə, glōr′ē ə), *n.* 1 Also, **gloria, a** song of praise to God. **b** the music for it. 2 one of three songs of praise to God, beginning "Glory be to God on high" (**Gloria in Excelsis**) "Glory be to the Father" (**Gloria Patri**) and "Glory be to Thee, O Lord" (**Gloria Tibi**) forming part of the Communion service or Mass. [< Latin]

glo ri fy (glôr′ə fī, glōr′ə fī), *v.t.,* **-fied, -fy ing.** 1 give glory to; make glorious: *glorify a hero.* 2 praise; worship: *We sing hymns to glorify God.* 3 make more beautiful or splendid than it usually appears. 4 exalt to the glory of heaven. **—glo′ri fi ca′tion,** *n.* **—glo′ri fi′er,** *n.*

glo ri ous (glôr′ē əs, glōr′ē əs), *adj.* 1 having or deserving glory; illustrious. 2 giving glory: *a glorious victory.* 3 magnificent; splendid: *a glorious day. The children had a glorious time at the fair.* **—glo′ri ous ly,** *adv.* **—glo′ri ous ness,** *n.*

glo ry (glôr′ē, glōr′ē), *n., pl.* **-ries.** *v.,* **-ried, -ry ing.** —*n.* 1 great praise and honor given to a person or thing by others; fame. 2 something that brings praise and honor; source of pride and joy. 3 adoring praise and thanksgiving. 4 brightness; splendor. 5 condition of greatest magnificence, splendor, or prosperity. 6 splendor and bliss of heaven; heaven. 7 a halo, especially as represented in art. 8 **go to glory,** die. 9 **in one's glory,** having one's greatest satisfaction or enjoyment. —*v.i.* be proud; rejoice. [< Old French *glorie* < Latin *gloria*]

gloss[1] (glôs, glos), *n.* 1 a smooth, shiny surface; luster: *Varnished furniture has a gloss.* 2 an outward appearance or surface that covers wrong underneath. —*v.t.* 1 put a smooth, shiny surface on. 2 **gloss over,** make (something wrong) seem right by passing over it lightly; smooth over: *gloss over a mistake.* [probably < Scandinavian (Old Icelandic) *glossi* to gleam]

gloss[2] (glôs, glos), *n.* 1 word inserted between the lines or in the margin of a text to explain or give the equivalent of a foreign or difficult word. 2 explanation; comment. 3 glossary. 4 translation inserted between the lines of a text printed in a foreign language. —*v.t.* comment on; explain. —*v.i.* make glosses; comment. [< Latin *glossa* hard word that needs explaining < Greek, literally, tongue] **—gloss′er,** *n.*

gloss., glossary.

glos sar i al (glo ser′ē əl, glo sar′ē əl; glô-ser′ē əl, glô sar′ē əl), *adj.* 1 having to do with a glossary. 2 like a glossary.

glos sar y (glos′ər ē, glôs′ər ē), *n., pl.*

-sar ies. 1 list of special, technical, or difficult words, usually in alphabetical order, with explanations or comments: *a glossary to Shakespeare's plays. Textbooks sometimes have glossaries at the end.* 2 a vocabulary or dictionary of limited scope: *a glossary of Scottish words, a glossary of the mining and mineral industry.*

gloss y (glô′sē, glos′ē), *adj.,* **gloss i er, gloss i est.** smooth and shiny. **—gloss′i ly,** *adv.* **—gloss′i ness,** *n.*

glot tal (glot′l), *adj.* 1 of the glottis. 2 (in phonetics) produced in the glottis. *H* in *hope* is a glottal sound.

glot tis (glot′is), *n.* the opening at the upper part of the windpipe, between the vocal cords. [< Greek *glōttis* < *glōtta* tongue]

Glouces ter (glos′tər, glôs′tər), *n.* 1 city in SW England, on the Severn River. 90,000. 2 seaport and fishing center in NE Massachusetts. 28,000. 3 Gloucestershire.

Glouces ter shire (glos′tər shər, glos′tər-shir; glôs′tər shər, glôs′tər shir), *n.* county in SW England.

glove (gluv), *n., v.,* **gloved, glov ing.** *—n.* 1 a covering for the hand, usually with separate places for each of the four fingers and the thumb. 2 a boxing glove. 3 a padded leather glove worn by baseball players in the field. *—v.t.* 1 cover with a glove; provide with gloves. 2 serve as a glove for. [Old English *glōf*] **—glove′less,** *adj.*

glov er (gluv′ər), *n.* person who makes or sells gloves.

glow (glō), *v.i.* 1 shine because of heat; be red-hot or white-hot. 2 give off light without heat. 3 show a warm color; look warm; be red or bright: *Her cheeks glowed as she danced.* 4 look or be eager: *Her eyes glowed at the thought of a trip.* *—n.* 1 the shine from something that is red-hot or white-hot. 2 a similar shine without heat. 3 a bright, warm color; brightness. 4 a warm feeling or color of the body. 5 an eager look on the face: *a glow of interest.* 6 warmth of feeling or passion; ardor: *He was filled with the glow of faith in God.* [Old English *glōwan*]

glow er (glou′ər), *v.i.* stare angrily; scowl fiercely: *The rivals glowered at each other.* *—n.* an angry stare; fierce scowl. [Middle English *gloren*] **—glow′er ing ly,** *adv.*

glow ing (glō′ing), *adj.* 1 shining from something that is red-hot or white-hot. 2 bright: *glowing colors.* 3 showing a warm color: *glowing cheeks.* 4 eager; animated: *a glowing description.* **—glow′ing ly,** *adv.*

glow worm (glō′wėrm′), *n.* any insect larva or insect which glows in the dark. Fireflies develop from some glowworms.

glox in i a (glok sin′ē ə), *n.* a tropical American plant of the same family as the African violet, with large white, red, or purple bell-shaped flowers, frequently cultivated as a house plant. [< Benjamin P. *Gloxin,* German botanist of the 1700's]

gloze (glōz), *v.t.,* **glozed, gloz ing.** smooth over; explain away: *Her friends glozed over her faults.* [< Old French *gloser* < Latin *glossa.* See GLOSS².]

glu ca gon (glü′kə gon), *n.* hormone secreted by the pancreas that raises the blood sugar level by stimulating the breakdown of glycogen to glucose, used medically in the treatment of diabetes and tumors.

glu cose (glü′kōs), *n.* 1 kind of sugar occurring in plant and animal tissues. Carbohydrates are present in the blood mainly in the form of glucose. Glucose is about half as sweet as cane sugar. *Formula:* $C_6H_{12}O_6$ 2 syrup made from starch. [< French < Greek *gleukos* sweet wine]

glu co side (glü′kə sīd), *n.* glycoside, especially one containing glucose.

glue (glü), *n., v.,* **glued, glu ing.** *—n.* 1 substance used to stick things together, made by boiling the hoofs, skins, and bones of animals in water. 2 any similar sticky substance made of casein, rubber, etc.; adhesive. *—v.t.* 1 stick together with glue. 2 fasten tightly; attach firmly. [< Old French *glu, glus* < Late Latin *glutem*] **—glue′like′,** *adj.*

glue y (glü′ē), *adj.,* **glu i er, glu i est.** 1 like glue; sticky. 2 full of glue; smeared with glue.

glum (glum), *adj.,* **glum mer, glum mest.** gloomy; dismal; sullen: *a glum look.* See **sullen** for synonym study. [related to GLOOM] **—glum′ly,** *adv.* **—glum′ness,** *n.*

glume (glüm), *n.* a chaffy bract at the base of the spikelet of grasses, sedges, etc. [< Latin *gluma* hull, husk]

glut (glut), *v.,* **glut ted, glut ting,** *n.* *—v.t.* 1 fill full; feed or satisfy fully: *A year of working aboard ship glutted my appetite for adventure.* 2 supply more than there is a demand for: *The prices for wheat dropped when the market was glutted with it.* *—n.* 1 a full supply; great quantity. 2 too great a supply. [probably < obsolete *glut,* noun, glutton < Old French]

glu ta mate (glü′tə māt), *n.* salt or ester of glutamic acid.

glu tam ic acid (glü tam′ik), a white, crystalline amino acid found in plant and animal proteins, especially in seeds and beets. *Formula:* $C_5H_9NO_4$ [*glut(en)* + *am(ide)* + *-ic*]

glu te al (glü tē′əl, glü′tē əl), *adj.* of or having to do with the gluteus or glutei.

glu ten (glüt′n), *n.* the tough, sticky, elastic protein substances in the flour of wheat and other grains. [< Latin, glue]

glu te nous (glüt′n əs), *adj.* 1 like gluten. 2 containing much gluten.

glu te us (glü tē′əs), *n., pl.* **-te i** (-tē ī). any of the three large muscles of the buttocks. [< New Latin < Greek *gloutos* buttock]

glu ti nous (glüt′n əs), *adj.* like glue; sticky. **—glu′ti nous ly,** *adv.* **—glu′ti nous-ness,** *n.*

glut ton (glut′n), *n.* 1 a greedy eater; person who eats too much. 2 person who never seems to have enough of something: *a glutton for punishment.* 3 the European name for the wolverine. [< Old French *glouton* < Latin *gluttonem*]

glut ton ous (glut′n əs), *adj.* 1 greedy about food; having the habit of eating too much. 2 greedy. **—glut′ton ous ly,** *adv.* **—glut′ton ous ness,** *n.*

glut ton y (glut′n ē), *n., pl.* **-ton ies.** excess in eating.

glyc e ride (glis′ə rīd′, glis′ər id), *n.* ester of glycerol.

glyc er in or **glyc er ine** (glis′ər ən), *n.* a colorless, syrupy, sweet liquid obtained from fats and oils. Glycerin is used in ointments, lotions, antifreeze solutions, and explosives. *Formula:* $C_3H_5(OH)_3$ [< French *glycérine* < Greek *glykeros* sweet]

glyc e rol (glis′ə rōl′, glis′ə rol′), *n.* glycerin.

gly cine (glī′sēn′, glī sēn′), *n.* a colorless, sweet-tasting, crystalline amino acid formed when gelatin or various other animal substances are boiled in the presence of alkalis. *Formula:* $C_2H_5NO_2$

hat, āge, fär; let, ēqual, tėrm;
it, īce; hot, ōpen, ôrder;
oil, out; cup, pu̇t, rüle;
ch, child; ng, long; sh, she;
th, thin; ᴛʜ, then; zh, measure;

ə represents *a* in about, *e* in taken, *i* in pencil, *o* in lemon, *u* in circus.

< = from, derived from, taken from.

gly co gen (glī′kə jən), *n.* a starchlike carbohydrate stored in the liver and other animal tissues. It is changed into glucose when needed. [< Greek *glykys* sweet + English *-gen*]

gly col (glī′kōl, glī′kol), *n.* a colorless, sweet-tasting alcohol obtained from various ethylene compounds and used as an antifreeze, as a solvent, in making lacquers, etc.; ethylene glycol. *Formula:* $C_2H_4(OH)_2$

gly col y sis (glī kol′ə sis), *n.* process by which a carbohydrate, such as glucose, is broken down to an acid.

gly co side (glī′kə sīd, glī′kə sid), *n.* any of a large group of organic compounds which yield a sugar, often glucose, and another substance on hydrolysis in the presence of various ferments or enzymes or a dilute acid; glucoside.

gm., gram or grams.

G-man (jē′man′), *n., pl.* **-men.** INFORMAL. a special agent of the United States Department of Justice; agent of the FBI. [short for *Government man*]

GMT or **G.M.T.,** Greenwich mean time.

gnarl (närl), *n.* knot in wood; hard, rough lump: *Wood with gnarls is hard to cut.*

gnarled (närld), *adj.* containing gnarls; knotted; twisted: *The farmer's gnarled hands grasped the plow firmly.* [variant of *knurled*]

gnarl y (när′lē), *adj.* gnarled.

gnash (nash), *v.t.* 1 strike or grind together: *gnash one's teeth.* 2 bite by gnashing the teeth; bite upon. [Middle English *gnasten*]

gnat (nat), *n.* any of various small, two-winged flies. Most gnats are bloodsucking and give bites that itch. [Old English *gnætt*]

gnath ic (nath′ik), *adj.* of or having to do with the jaw. [< Greek *gnathos* jaw]

gnaw (nô), *v.,* **gnawed, gnawed** or **gnawn, gnaw ing.** *—v.t.* 1 bite at and wear away: *A mouse has gnawed the cover of this box.* 2 make by biting: *A rat can gnaw a hole through wood.* 3 wear away; consume; corrode. 4 trouble; harass; torment. *—v.i.* 1 to bite: *gnaw at a bone.* 2 torment as if by biting: *The feeling of guilt gnawed at my conscience day and night.* [Old English *gnagan*] **—gnaw′er,** *n.* **—gnaw′ing ly,** *adv.*

gnawn (nôn), *v.* a pp. of **gnaw.**

gneiss (nīs), *n.* any of various very dense rocks consisting of coarse layers of quartz and feldspar alternating with layers of any of several other minerals. [< German *Gneis*]

gnome (nōm), *n.* (in folklore) a dwarf supposed to live in the earth and guard treasures of precious metals and stones. [< French < New Latin *gnomus;* coined by Paracelsus]

gno mic (nō′mik, nom′ik), *adj.* full of maxims or instructive sayings; aphoristic; sententious. [< Greek *gnōmikos* < *gnōmē* judgment, opinion]

gnom ish (nō′mish), *adj.* resembling or suggesting a gnome.

gno mon (nō′mon), *n.* rod, pointer, or triangular piece on a sundial, etc., that shows the time of day by casting its shadow on a marked surface. [< Greek *gnōmōn* indicator < *gignoskein* know]

Gnos tic (nos′tik), *adj.* of or having to do with Gnosticism or the Gnostics. —*n.* believer in Gnosticism. [< Greek *gnōstikos* of knowledge < *gignoskein* know]

Gnos ti cism (nos′tə siz′əm), *n.* a mystical religious and philosophical doctrine of early Christian times, according to which spiritual knowledge, rather than faith, was essential to salvation.

gno to bi ote (nō′tō bī′ōt), *n.* a germ-free animal infected with one or more microorganisms in order to study the microorganism in a controlled situation. [< Greek *gnōtos* known + *biotē* life]

GNP or **G.N.P.,** gross national product.

gnu (nü, nyü), *n., pl.* **gnus** or **gnu.** a large African antelope with an oxlike head, curved horns, high shoulders, and a long tail; wildebeest. [< Kaffir *nqu*]

go (gō), *v.,* **went, gone, go ing,** *n., pl.* **goes,** *adj.* —*v.i.* 1 move along: *Cars go on the road.* 2 move away; leave: *Don't go yet.* See synonym study below. 3 be in motion or action; act; work; run: *Electricity makes the washing machine go.* 4 get to be; become: *go mad.* 5 be habitually; be: *go hungry.* 6 proceed; advance: *go to New York.* 7 be current: *A rumor went through the town.* 8 be known: *She went under a false name.* 9 put oneself: *Don't go to any trouble for me.* 10 extend; reach: *His memory does not go back that far.* 11 pass: *Summer had gone. Vacation goes quickly.* 12 be given: *First prize goes to the winner.* 13 be sold: *The painting goes to the highest bidder.* 14 tend; lead: *This goes to show that you must work harder.* 15 turn out; have a certain result: *How did the game go?* 16 have its place; belong: *This book goes on the top shelf.* 17 make a certain sound: *The cork went "pop!"* 18 have certain words; be said: *How does that song go?* 19 refer; appeal: *go to court.* 20 carry an action to a given point: *go as high as $50.* 21 contribute to a result: *the items which go to make up the total.* 22 die: *My grandmother went peacefully in the night.* 23 break down; give way; fail: *My eyesight is going. The engine in the old car finally went.* 24 begin or come into action: *Here goes!* 25 linger; wait: *another hour to go.* 26 be permitted or accepted: *Anything goes.* —*v.t.* 1 make a bid or bet of; wager; stake: *I'll go another $5.* 2 carry on as far as; go to the point of. 3 INFORMAL. put up with; stand: *I can't go modern art.*

as they (people or things) **go,** considering how others are.

go about, a be busy at; work on. **b** move from place to place. **c** turn about; change direction.

go along, cooperate.

go around, a satisfy everyone; give some for all. **b** move from place to place.

go at, a attack. **b** take in hand with energy; work at.

go back of, INFORMAL. investigate.

go back on, INFORMAL. not be faithful or loyal to; betray.

go behind, investigate the real or hidden reasons for.

go by, a pass. **b** be guided by; follow. **c** be known by.

go down, a descend; decline; sink. **b** be defeated; lose.

go for, a try to get. **b** favor; support. **c** INFORMAL. attack. **d** be taken or considered as. **e** INFORMAL. be attracted to.

go in for, INFORMAL. take part in; spend time and energy at.

go into, a enter into a condition or activity. **b** be contained in. **c** investigate.

go in with, join; share with.

go it, INFORMAL. go fast.

go off, a leave; depart. **b** be fired; explode. **c** take place; happen.

go on, a go ahead; continue. **b** happen. **c** behave. **d** manage.

go out, a go to a party, show, etc. **b** stop burning. **c** give sympathy. **d** go on strike.

go over, a look at carefully. **b** do again; repeat. **c** read again. **d** INFORMAL. succeed.

go through, a go to the end of; do all of. **b** undergo; experience. **c** search. **d** be accepted or approved.

go through with, carry out to the end; complete.

go together, a harmonize; match. **b** keep steady company as sweethearts.

go under, a be ruined; fail. **b** be overwhelmed or sunk.

go up, a rise; ascend. **b** increase. **c** be built; be raised.

go with, a go steadily with; accompany. **b** belong with; go well with.

go without, do without; not have.

let go, a allow to escape. **b** give up one's hold. **c** give up. **d** fail to keep in good condition.

let oneself go, a give way to one's feelings or desires. **b** fail to keep oneself in good condition.

—*n.* 1 act of going. 2 INFORMAL. try; attempt; chance: *Let's have another go at this problem.* 3 something successful; a success: *He made a go of the new store.* 4 INFORMAL. spirit; energy. 5 INFORMAL. state of affairs; way things are. 6 INFORMAL. fashion; style; rage. 7 **no go,** INFORMAL. useless; worthless. 8 **on the go,** INFORMAL. busily occupied; active or restless.

—*adj.* U.S. INFORMAL. in perfect order and ready to proceed: *All systems are go for the rocket launching.*

[Old English *gān*] **—go′er,** *n.*

Syn. *v.i.* 2 **Go, leave** mean to move away from a point or place. **Go,** the opposite of *come,* emphasizes the movement involved: *She comes and goes as she pleases.* **Leave** emphasizes the departure from the place where one is (or has been): *He has left home. The boat left yesterday.*

Go a (gō′ə), *n.* former Portuguese colony on the SW coast of India. In 1961 it became a part of India.

goad (gōd), *n.* 1 a sharp-pointed stick for driving cattle; gad. 2 anything which drives or urges one on. —*v.t.* drive or urge on; act as a goad to: *Hunger goaded him to steal a loaf of bread.* [Old English *gād*]

go-a head (gō′ə hed′), *n.* INFORMAL. permission to go ahead or begin; authority to proceed.

goal (gōl), *n.* 1 place where a race ends. 2 place to which players in certain games try to advance a ball or puck in order to make a score. 3 act of advancing a ball or puck to this place. 4 score or points won by reaching this place. 5 something for which an effort is made; something desired; aim: *The goal of her ambition was to be a great doctor.* [Middle English *gol*] **—goal′less,** *adj.*

goal ie (gō′lē), *n.* goalkeeper.

goal keep er (gōl′kē′pər), *n.* player who guards the goal to prevent scoring in certain games; goalie; goaltender.

goal line, line marking the goal in a game.

goal post, one of a pair of posts with a bar across them, forming a goal in football, soccer, lacrosse, hockey, etc.

goal tend er (gōl′ten′dər), *n.* goalkeeper.

goat (gōt), *n., pl.* **goats** or **goat.** 1 a cud-chewing mammal with hollow horns and usually a beard, similar and related to sheep but stronger, less timid, and more active, found domesticated in all parts of the world. 2 any of certain related mammals, as the mountain goat. 3 INFORMAL. scapegoat. 4 **get one's goat,** INFORMAL. make a person angry or annoyed; tease a person. [Old English *gāt*] **—goat′like′,** *adj.*

goatee

goat ee (gō tē′), *n.* a pointed, trimmed beard on a man's chin.

goat herd (gōt′hėrd′), *n.* person who tends goats.

goat skin (gōt′skin′), *n.* 1 skin of a goat. 2 leather made from it. 3 container made from this leather, used especially for holding wine.

goat suck er (gōt′suk′ər), *n.* any of a family of birds with flat heads, wide mouths, and long wings, that fly at night and feed on flying insects; nightjar. A whippoorwill is a goatsucker.

gob[1] (gob), *n.* SLANG. sailor in the United States Navy. [origin uncertain]

gob[2] (gob), *n.* INFORMAL. lump; mass. [< Old French *gobe*]

gob bet (gob′it), *n.* lump; mass. [< Old French *gobet,* diminutive of *gobe* gob[2]]

gob ble[1] (gob′əl), *v.,* **-bled, -bling.** —*v.t.* 1 eat fast and greedily; swallow quickly in big pieces. 2 **gobble up,** INFORMAL. seize upon eagerly. —*v.i.* eat fast and greedily. [< *gob*[2]]

gob ble[2] (gob′əl), *v.,* **-bled, -bling,** *n.* —*v.i.* make the throaty sound of a male turkey or a sound like it. —*n.* the throaty sound that a male turkey makes. [imitative]

gob ble dy gook or **gob ble de gook** (gob′əl dē gu̇k′), *n.* INFORMAL. speech or writing which is hard to understand because it is full of long, involved sentences and big words. [a coined word]

gob bler (gob′lər), *n.* a male turkey.

Gob e lin (gob′ə lən), *adj.* of, having to do with, or made at the Gobelin factory and dye works at Paris: *Gobelin tapestries.* —*n.* a Gobelin tapestry.

go-be tween (gō′bi twēn′), *n.* person who goes back and forth between others with messages, proposals, suggestions, etc.; intermediary.

Go bi (gō′bē), *n.* desert in E Asia. Most of it is in Mongolia. 500,000 sq. mi.

gob let (gob′lit), *n.* 1 a drinking glass with a base and stem. 2 ARCHAIC. a hollow drinking bowl without a handle. [< Old French *gobelet,* diminutive of *gobel* cup]

gob lin (gob′lən), *n.* (in folklore) a mischievous sprite or elf in the form of an ugly-looking dwarf. [< Old French *gobelin*

< Medieval Latin *Gobelinus,* name of a local spirit]

go by (gō′bē), *n., pl.* **-bies** or **-by.** any of a family of bony fishes living near seacoasts. The ventral fins of gobies are united to form a suction cup by which they cling to rocks. [< Latin *gobius, cobius* gudgeon < Greek *kōbios*]

go-by (gō′bī′), *n.* INFORMAL. a going by or casting off; intentional neglect; slight: *He gave me the go-by.*

go cart or **go-cart** (gō′kärt′), *n.* **1** a low seat on wheels to take a small child around on; stroller. **2** a small framework with casters in which children may learn to walk; walker. **3** a light carriage.

God (god), *n.* **1** the Supreme Being worshiped in most religions as the maker and ruler of the world. **2 god, a** a being that is thought to have supernatural or superhuman powers and considered worthy of worship. **b** a male god. **c** likeness or image of a god; idol. **d** person or thing greatly admired and respected. [Old English]

god child (god′child′), *n., pl.* **-chil dren** (-chil′drən). child whom a grown-up person sponsors at its baptism.

God dard (god′ərd), *n.* **Robert Hutchings,** 1882-1945, American physicist who pioneered modern rocketry.

god daugh ter (god′dô′tər), *n.* a female godchild.

god dess (god′is), *n.* **1** a female god. **2** a very beautiful or charming woman.

god fa ther (god′fä′THər), *n.* man who sponsors a child when it is baptized. Often the position of a godfather is mainly an honorary one.

god head (god′hed′), *n.* **1** divine nature; divinity. **2 Godhead,** God.

god hood (god′hůd), *n.* divine character; divinity.

Go di va (gə dī′və), *n.* **Lady,** wife of an English nobleman, who lived in the 1000's. According to legend, she rode naked through Coventry to get her husband to grant relief to the people from a burdensome tax.

god less (god′lis), *adj.* **1** not believing in God; not religious. **2** ungodly; wicked; evil. **—god′less ly,** *adv.* **—god′less ness,** *n.*

god like (god′līk′), *adj.* **1** like God or a god; divine. **2** suitable for God or a god. **—god′like′ness,** *n.*

god ling (god′ling), *n.* a little god; a minor or petty deity.

god ly (god′lē), *adj.,* **-li er, -li est.** obeying, loving, and fearing God; religious; pious; devout. **—god′li ness,** *n.*

god moth er (god′muTH′ər), *n.* woman who sponsors a child when it is baptized. Often the position of a godmother is mainly an honorary one.

god par ent (god′per′ənt, god′par′ənt), *n.* godfather or godmother.

God's acre, churchyard with graves in it; burial ground; cemetery.

god send (god′send′), *n.* something unexpected and very welcome, as if sent from God; sudden piece of good luck.

god son (god′sun′), *n.* a male godchild.

God speed (god′spēd′), *n.* a wish of success to a person starting on a journey or undertaking.

Godt haab (gôt′hôp), *n.* capital of Greenland. 5000.

god wit (god′wit), *n.* any of a genus of wading birds somewhat like a snipe, having long, curving bills and slender legs.

goes (gōz), third person singular, present tense of **go.**

Goe thals (gō′thəlz), *n.* **George W.,** 1858-1928, American general and army engineer in charge of building the Panama Canal.

Goe the (gā′tə; *German* gœ′tə), *n.* **Johann Wolfgang von,** 1749-1832, German poet, prose writer, and dramatist.

go-get ter (gō′get′ər), *n.* INFORMAL. an energetic, aggressive person who tries hard for and usually gets what he is after.

go-get ting (gō′get′ing), *adj.* INFORMAL. aggressive and enterprising.

gog gle (gog′əl), *v.,* **-gled, -gling,** *adj., n.* *—v.i.* **1** roll one's eyes; stare with bulging eyes. **2** roll; bulge: *The children's eyes goggled as the magician pulled a rabbit out of the empty hat.* *—adj.* rolling; bulging: *A frog has goggle eyes.* *—n.* **goggles,** *pl.* large, close-fitting eyeglasses to protect the eyes from light, dust, etc. [Middle English *gogelen*]

gog gle-eyed (gog′əl īd′), *adj.* having rolling, bulging, or staring eyes.

Gogh (gō, gôk), *n.* See **Van Gogh.**

Go gol (gō′gol), *n.* **Nikolai,** 1809-1852, Russian writer of novels and short stories.

Goi del ic (goi del′ik), *adj.* of or having to do with the Gaels or their languages. *—n.* the Gaelic branch of Celtic, including Irish, Scottish Gaelic, and Manx.

go ing (gō′ing), *n.* **1** a going away; leaving: *Her going was very sudden.* **2** condition of the ground or road for walking or riding: *The going is bad on a muddy road.* *—adj.* **1** moving; acting; working; running: *Set the clock going.* **2** that goes well; operating with success: *His business is a going concern.* **3** in existence; existing; to be had; current or prevalent: *the going price for gold.* **4 be going to,** will; be about to: *It is going to rain soon.* **5 get going,** INFORMAL. make a start; begin: *Better get going on that report if you want to finish it today.* **6 going on,** almost; nearly: *It is going on four o'clock.*

go ing-o ver (gō′ing ō′vər), *n.* a close, searching inspection.

go ings-on (gō′ingz on′), *n.pl.* actions or events: *the goings-on at the convention.*

goi ter or **goi tre** (goi′tər), *n.* enlargement of the thyroid gland which is often seen as a large swelling in the front of the neck, usually caused by a diet with too little iodine. [< French *goitre,* ultimately < Latin *guttur* throat]

goi trous (goi′trəs), *adj.* **1** having goiter. **2** of or like goiter.

Go Kart, trademark for a low frame on wheels powered by a small gasoline engine, used for racing.

Gol con da (gol kon′də), *n.* **1** city in the south part of ancient India, famed for its wealth and diamond cutting. **2** mine or other source of great wealth.

gold (gōld), *n.* **1** a shiny, bright-yellow, ductile and malleable, precious metallic element which resists rust and other chemical changes. Gold is used for jewelry and has long been used as a commercial medium of exchange. *Symbol:* Au; *atomic number* 79. See pages 326 and 327 for table. **2** coins made of gold. **3** money in large sums; wealth. **4** a bright, beautiful, or precious thing or material: *a heart of gold.* **5** the color of gold; a bright yellow. *—adj.* **1** made of gold. **2** of or like gold. **3** bright-yellow. [Old English]

gold beat er (gōld′bē′tər), *n.* person whose work is beating gold into thin plates or gold leaf.

hat, āge, fär; let, ēqual, tėrm;
it, īce; hot, ōpen, ôrder;
oil, out; cup, pu̇t, rüle;
ch, child; ng, long; sh, she;
th, thin; TH, then; zh, measure;

ə represents *a* in about, *e* in taken, *i* in pencil, *o* in lemon, *u* in circus.

< = from, derived from, taken from.

gold brick (gōld′brik′), INFORMAL. *—v.i.* **1** avoid duties by any evasion or excuse, such as pretended illness. **2** swindle. *—n.* person, especially in the armed forces, who avoids duty or shirks work. **—gold′brick′er,** *n.*

Gold Coast, region in W Africa, a former British colony, now largely included in Ghana.

gold digger, SLANG. woman who schemes to get money from men.

gold en (gōl′dən), *adj.* **1** made or consisting of gold: *a golden medal.* **2** containing or yielding gold: *a golden region or country.* **3** shining like gold; bright-yellow: *golden hair.* **4** very good; excellent; extremely favorable, valuable, or important: *a golden opportunity.* **5** very prosperous and flourishing. **6** having to do with the fiftieth year or event in a series. **—gold′en ly,** *adv.* **—gold′en ness,** *n.*

Golden Age or **golden age, 1** (in Greek and Roman myths) the first and best age of mankind, an era of idyllic peace, prosperity, and happiness. **2** the period in which a nation, etc., is at its highest state of prosperity, or in which some human art or activity is at its most excellent.

golden calf, 1 (in the Bible) an idol made of gold, set up by the Israelites in the wilderness. **2** wealth thought of much too highly.

golden eagle, a large, fierce eagle of the Northern Hemisphere with golden-brown feathers on the top of the head and the back of the neck.

gold en eye (gōl′dən ī′), *n., pl.* **-eyes** or **-eye.** a diving duck with black and white feathers, living in northern regions.

Golden Fleece, (in Greek legends) a fleece of gold taken from a ram. It was guarded by a dragon until Jason and the Argonauts carried it away with the help of Medea.

Golden Gate, strait forming the entrance to San Francisco Bay from the Pacific.

golden glow, a tall plant of the composite family with globe-shaped yellow flowers.

Golden Horn, inlet of the Bosporus in European Turkey, forming the inner harbor of Istanbul.

golden mean, avoidance of extremes; safe, sensible way of doing things; moderation.

golden retriever, a medium-sized dog with a golden, water-resistant coat, used in hunting to retrieve game, especially waterfowl.

gold en rod (gōl′dən rod′), *n.* any of a genus of plants of the composite family which bloom in the late summer or early autumn and have many small, yellow flowers on tall, slender stalks.

golden rule, rule of conduct which states that a person should treat others as he would have them treat him.

golden wedding, the 50th anniversary of a wedding.

gold-filled (gōld′fild′), *adj.* made of a cheap metal covered with a layer of gold.

gold finch (gōld′finch′), *n.* 1 a small American songbird of the same family as the sparrow. The male is yellow marked with black. 2 a European songbird of the same family with a patch of yellow on its wings.

gold fish (gōld′fish′), *n., pl.* **-fish es** or **-fish.** a small, usually reddish-golden fish of the same family as the carp, often kept in garden pools or in glass bowls indoors.

Gol ding (gōl′ding), *n.* **William,** born 1911, English novelist.

gold leaf, gold beaten into very thin sheets, used in gilding.

gold mine, 1 mine where ore yielding gold is obtained. 2 INFORMAL. source of something of great value: *a gold mine of ideas.*

gold rush, a sudden rush of people to a place where gold has just been found.

gold smith (gōld′smith′), *n.* person who makes or sells things made of gold.

Gold smith (gōld′smith′), *n.* **Oliver,** 1728?-1774, British poet, novelist, and dramatist, born in Ireland.

gold standard, use of gold as the standard of value for the money of a country. The nation's unit of money value is declared by the government to be equal to and exchangeable for a certain amount of gold.

golf (golf, gôlf), *n.* game played on an outdoor course with a small, hard ball and a set of golf clubs. The player tries to hit the ball into each of a series of holes with as few strokes as possible. *—v.i.* play this game. [Middle English] **—golf′er,** *n.*

golf club, 1 any of several long-handled clubs having wooden or iron heads, used in playing golf. 2 group of people joined together for the purpose of playing golf. 3 buildings, land, etc., used by such a group.

golf course or **golf links,** place where golf is played, having tees, greens, and fairways.

Gol gi apparatus or **Gol gi bodies** (gol′jē), network or structure found in the cytoplasm of many cells, thought to have a secretory function. See **centrosome** for diagram. [< Camillo *Golgi,* 1844-1926, Italian anatomist]

Gol go tha (gol′gə thə), *n.* 1 (in the Bible) Calvary. 2 place of burial.

Go li ath (gə lī′əth), *n.* 1 (in the Bible) a Philistine giant whom David killed with a stone from a sling. 2 any huge, extremely strong man.

gol ly (gol′ē), *interj.* exclamation of wonder, pleasure, joy, etc.

Go mor rah or **Go mor rha** (gə môr′ə, gə mor′ə), *n.* (in the Bible) a wicked city destroyed, together with Sodom, by fire from heaven.

Gom pers (gom′pərz), *n.* **Samuel,** 1850-1924, American labor leader, born in England.

go nad (gō′nad, gon′ad), *n.* organ in which reproductive cells develop in the male or female; sex gland. Ovaries and testicles are gonads. [< New Latin *gonades,* plural < Greek *gonē* seed < *gignesthai* be produced]

go nad al (gō′nad əl, gon′ad əl), *adj.* of or having to do with gonads.

Gon court (gôɴ kür′), *n.* 1 **Edmond de,** 1822-1896, French author and artist. 2 his brother, **Jules de,** 1830-1870, French author and artist. The Goncourt brothers wrote many novels together.

gon do la (gon′dl ə), *n.* 1 a long, narrow boat with a high peak at each end, rowed or poled by a single oar. It is used on the canals of Venice. 2 a railroad freight car which has low sides and no top. 3 car suspended beneath the body of an airship which holds the passengers, instruments, etc. [< Italian]

gondola (def. 1)

gon do lier (gon′dl ir′), *n.* person who rows or poles a gondola.

gone (gôn, gon), *adj.* 1 moved away; left. 2 lost: *We had given you up for gone.* 3 dead. 4 used up; consumed: *Is all the candy gone?* 5 failed; ruined. 6 weak; faint: *a gone feeling.* 7 **far gone,** much advanced; deeply involved. 8 **gone on,** INFORMAL. in love with. *—v.* pp. of **go.**

gon er (gô′nər, gon′ər), *n.* INFORMAL. person or thing that is dead, ruined, or past help.

gon fa lon (gon′fə lən), *n.* flag or banner hung from a crossbar instead of a pole, often having several streamers. Gonfalons were used especially by medieval Italian republics. [< Italian *gonfalone*]

gong (gông, gong), *n.* 1 a large piece of metal shaped like a bowl or saucer which makes a loud noise when struck. A gong is a kind of bell. 2 (in music) a metal disk with a turned-up rim, which makes a loud noise when struck. [< Malay]

gon o coc cus (gon′ə kok′əs), *n., pl.* **-coc ci** (-kok′sī). bacterium that causes gonorrhea.

gon or rhe a or **gon or rhoe a** (gon′ə-rē′ə), *n.* a contagious venereal disease caused by the gonococcus that results in inflammation of the genital, urinary, and certain other organs. [< Greek *gonorrhoia* < *gonos* seed + *rhoia* a flow]

gon or rhe al or **gon or rhoe al** (gon′ə-rē′əl), *adj.* 1 having to do with gonorrhea. 2 having gonorrhea.

goo (gü), *n.* SLANG. thick, sticky matter.

goo ber (gü′bər), *n.* INFORMAL. (in the southern United States) a peanut. [< a Bantu word]

good (gu̇d), *adj.,* **bet ter, best,** *n., interj., adv. —adj.* 1 having high quality; superior: *a good piece of work. A craftsman insists on good tools.* 2 as it ought to be; right; proper; satisfactory: *good health, good weather. Do what seems good to you.* 3 in good condition: *his good leg, a good motor.* 4 that does what is right; well-behaved: *a good girl.* 5 kind; friendly: *Say a good word for me.* 6 desirable: *a good book for children.* 7 honorable; worthy: *my good friend, a good reputation.* 8 just: *a good king.* 9 devout; loyal: *a good member of the Church.* 10 reliable; dependable: *good judgment.* 11 real; genuine: *It is hard to tell counterfeit money from good money.* 12 agreeable; pleasant: *Have a good time.* 13 beneficial; advantageous; useful: *drugs good for a fever.* 14 satisfying; enough; full: *a good meal.* 15 skillful; clever: *a good manager, be good at arithmetic.* 16 effective in communication; accepted: *good English.* 17 valid; sound: *good reasons, a good contract.* 18 fairly great; more than a little: *work a good while.* 19 **as good as,** almost the same as; almost; practically. 20 **good for, a** able to do, live, or last. **b** able to pay or contribute. 21 **make good, a** make up for; pay for. **b** fulfill; carry out. **c** succeed in doing. **d** succeed. **e** prove.
—n. 1 benefit; advantage; use: *work for the common good.* 2 that which is good: *find the good in people.* 3 a good thing. 4 good people. 5 **for good** or **for good and all,** forever; finally; permanently. 6 **to the good,** on the side of profit or advantage; in one's favor.
—interj. that is good!
—adv. INFORMAL. 1 well. 2 **good and,** very: *Get the water good and hot.*
[Old English *gōd*]
➤ **good, well.** *Good* is an adjective; *well* is either an adjective or an adverb: *I feel good* and *I feel well* (adjectives) are both used, but have different connotations (*good* implying actual bodily sensation, *well* referring to the state of not being ill). In nonstandard English *good* is often used adverbially in place of *well: The engine's running pretty good now.*

good afternoon, form of greeting or farewell said in the afternoon; hello or good-by.

Good Book, the Bible.

good-by, good by, good-bye, or **good bye** (gu̇d′bī′), *interj., n., pl.* **-bys** or **-byes.** farewell. [contraction of *God be with ye*]

good day, form of greeting or farewell said in the daytime; hello or good-by.

good evening, form of greeting or farewell said in the evening; hello or good-by.

good fellow, a companionable person.

good-fel low ship (gu̇d′fel′ō ship), *n.* 1 pleasant companionship. 2 friendly fellowship.

good-for-noth ing (gu̇d′fər nuth′ing), *adj.* worthless; useless. *—n.* person who is disreputable or useless.

Good Friday, the anniversary of Christ's crucifixion, observed on the Friday before Easter.

good-heart ed (gu̇d′här′tid), *adj.* kind and generous. **—good′-heart′ed ly,** *adv.* **—good′-heart′ed ness,** *n.*

Good Hope, Cape of, cape near the SW tip of Africa.

good-hu mored (gu̇d′hyü′mərd, gu̇d′yü′-mərd), *adj.* having good humor; cheerful; pleasant; amiable. **—good′-hu′mored ly,** *adv.* **—good′-hu′mored ness,** *n.*

good ish (gu̇d′ish), *adj.* 1 rather good. 2 fairly great; considerable.

good-look ing (gu̇d′lu̇k′ing), *adj.* having a pleasing appearance; handsome or pretty.

good ly (gu̇d′lē), *adj.,* **-li er, -li est.** 1 of good quality; excellent: *a goodly land.* 2 good-looking: *a goodly youth.* 3 considerable; rather large; fairly great: *a goodly quantity.* **—good′li ness,** *n.*

good man (gu̇d′mən), *n., pl.* **-men.** ARCHAIC. 1 master of a household; husband. 2 title of respect for a man ranking below a gentleman: *Goodman Brown.*

good morning, (form of greeting or farewell said in the morning; hello or good-by.

good-na tured (gu̇d′nā′chərd), *adj.* having a pleasant disposition; kindly; cheerful; obliging. **—good′-na′tured ly,** *adv.* **—good′-na′tured ness,** *n.*

Good Neighbor Policy, a diplomatic policy, first sponsored by the United States in 1933, to encourage friendly relations and mutual defense among the nations of the Western Hemisphere.

hat, āge, fär; let, ēqual, tėrm;
it, īce; hot, ōpen, ôrder;
oil, out; cup, pu̇t, rüle;
ch, child; ng, long; sh, she;
th, thin; ᴛʜ, then; zh, measure;

ə represents *a* in about, *e* in taken, *i* in pencil, *o* in lemon, *u* in circus.

< = from, derived from, taken from.

good ness (gu̇d′nis), *n.* 1 quality or condition of being good. 2 excellence; virtue. See synonym study below. 3 kindness; friendliness. 4 valuable quality; best part. *—interj.* exclamation of surprise.

Syn. *n.* 2 **Goodness, virtue** mean excellence in character. **Goodness** applies to moral excellence that seems inborn: *Her goodness is shown by the many good deeds she does.* **Virtue** applies to moral excellence that is acquired by consciously developing particular qualities of character or by consciously following high moral principles: *He is a man of the highest virtue.*

good night, form of farewell said at night.

goods (gu̇dz), *n.pl.* 1 personal property; belongings. See **property** for synonym study. 2 thing or things for sale; wares. 3 material for clothing; cloth. 4 SLANG. what is needed to do something. 5 BRITISH. freight. 6 **get the goods on** or **have the goods on,** find out or know something bad about.

Good Samaritan, 1 (in the Bible) a traveler who rescued another traveler who had been beaten and robbed by thieves. 2 person who is unselfish in helping others.

Good Shepherd, Jesus.

good-sized (gu̇d′sīzd′), *adj.* somewhat large.

good-tem pered (gu̇d′tem′pərd), *adj.* easy to get along with; cheerful; agreeable. **—good′-tem′pered ly,** *adv.*

good turn, a kind or friendly act; favor.

gopher (def. 1) about 8 in. long with tail

good wife (gu̇d′wīf′), *n., pl.* **-wives.** ARCHAIC. 1 mistress of a household. 2 title of respect for a woman ranking below a lady: *Goodwife Brown.*

good will, 1 kindly or friendly feeling. See **favor** for synonym study. 2 cheerful consent; willingness. 3 the good reputation that a business has with its customers.

good y[1] (gu̇d′ē), *n., pl.* **good ies,** *interj., adj.* INFORMAL. *—n.* something very good to eat; piece of candy or cake. *—interj.* exclamation of pleasure. *—adj.* making too much of being good; good in a weak way.

good y[2] (gu̇d′ē), *n., pl.* **good ies.** ARCHAIC. an old woman of humble station. [variant of *goodwife*]

Good year (gu̇d′yir), *n.* **Charles,** 1800-1860, American who invented vulcanized rubber.

good y-good y (gu̇d′ē gu̇d′ē), *adj., n., pl.* **-good ies.** *—adj.* making too much of being good; good in an affected or artificial way. *—n.* person who makes too much of being good.

goo ey (gü′ē), *adj.,* **goo i er, goo i est.** SLANG. like goo; sticky.

goof (güf), SLANG. *—v.i.* make a stupid mistake; blunder. *—n.* 1 a blunder. 2 simpleton; fool.

goof y (gü′fē), *adj.,* **goof i er, goof i est.** SLANG. silly. **—goof′i ly,** *adv.* **—goof′i ness,** *n.*

goon (gün), *n.* SLANG. 1 ruffian hired to disrupt labor disputes. 2 a stupid person.

goose (güs), *n., pl.* **geese** for 1-4, **goos es** for 5. 1 a wild or tame web-footed swimming bird, of the same family as and similar to a duck, but larger and having a longer neck. 2 a female goose. The male is called a gander. 3 flesh of a goose used for food. 4 a silly person. 5 a tailor's smoothing iron with a curved handle like a goose's neck. 6 **cook one's goose,** INFORMAL. ruin one's reputation, plan, chances, etc. [Old English *gōs*] **—goose′like′,** *adj.*

Goose Bay, large military air base in Labrador, built in World War II.

goose ber ry (güs′ber′ē, güs′bər ē; güz′ber′ē, güz′bər ē), *n., pl.* **-ries.** 1 a small, sour berry somewhat like a currant but larger, used to make pies, tarts, jam, etc. 2 the thorny bush that it grows on, of the same genus as the currant.

goose egg, SLANG. (in athletic and other contests) a zero, indicating a miss or a failure to score.

goose flesh (güs′flesh′), *n.* a rough condition of the skin, like that of a plucked goose, caused by cold or fear; goose pimples.

goose foot (güs′fu̇t′), *n., pl.* **-foots.** any of a family of plants with coarse leaves, clusters of very small flowers, and dry, seedlike fruits. Beets and spinach are goosefoots.

goose neck (güs′nek′), *n.* something long and curved like a goose's neck, such as an iron hook, a movable support for a lamp, or a curved connecting pipe.

goose pimples, gooseflesh.

goose step, a marching step in which the leg is swung high with straight, stiff knee.

goose-step (güs′step′), *v.i.,* **-stepped, -step ping.** march with a goose step.

G.O.P. or **GOP,** Grand Old Party.

go pher (gō′fər), *n.* 1 any of a family of burrowing rodents of North America with large cheek pouches and long claws, especially on the front feet. 2 any of a genus of ground squirrels of the western plains of the United States. 3 any of a genus of burrowing land tortoises of the southern United States. [< French *gaufre,* literally, honeycomb; with reference to burrowing]

gopher snake, a blue-black snake of the southern United States; indigo snake.

Gor di an knot (gôr′dē ən), 1 a complicated knot tied by **Gordius,** a legendary king of Phrygia, to be undone only by the person who should rule Asia. Alexander the Great cut it with a sword. 2 an intricate or baffling problem. 3 **cut the Gordian knot,** find and use a quick, easy way out of a difficulty.

Gor don (gôrd′n), *n.* **Charles George,** 1833-1885, British general in China and Egypt.

gorilla (def. 1) standing height of male up to 6 ft.

gore[1] (gôr, gōr), *n.* blood that is shed; thick blood; clotted blood. [Old English *gor* dirt, dung]

gore[2] (gôr, gōr), *v.t.,* **gored, gor ing.** wound with a horn or tusk: *The angry bull gored the farmer in the leg.* [Middle English *goren* < Old English *gār* spear]

gore[3] (gôr, gōr), *n., v.,* **gored, gor ing.** *—n.* a long, triangular or tapering piece of cloth put or made in a skirt, sail, etc., to give greater width or change the shape. *—v.t.* put or make a gore in. [Old English *gāra* angular point]

Gor gas (gôr′gəs), *n.* **William Crawford,** 1854-1920, American army physician and sanitation expert.

gorge (def. 1)

gorge (gôrj), *n., v.,* **gorged, gorg ing.** *—n.* 1 a deep, narrow valley, usually steep and rocky, especially one with a stream. 2 contents of a stomach. 3 **make one's gorge rise,** fill one with great disgust or anger. 4 mass stopping up a narrow passage: *An ice gorge blocked the river.* 5 ARCHAIC. throat. *—v.i.* eat greedily until full. *—v.t.* 1 stuff with food: *He gorged himself with cake at the party.* 2 fill full. [< Old French, throat < Popular Latin *gorgam* throat, jaws < Latin *gurges* abyss, whirlpool] **—gorg′er,** *n.*

gor geous (gôr′jəs), *adj.* richly colored; splendid: *a gorgeous sunset.* [< Old French *gorgias* fashionable, suitable for adorning the neck] **—gor′geous ly,** *adv.* **—gor′geous ness,** *n.*

gor get (gôr′jit), *n.* piece of armor for the throat. See **armor** for picture. [< Old French *gorgete,* diminutive of *gorge* throat]

Gor gon (gôr′gən), *n.* 1 (in Greek myths) any of three sisters having snakes for hair and faces so horrible that anyone who looked at them turned to stone. 2 **gorgon,** a very ugly or terrible person, especially a repulsive woman.

go ril la (gə ril′ə), *n.* 1 the largest and most powerful anthropoid ape, found in the forests of central Africa. It is chiefly arboreal and vegetarian in diet. 2 SLANG. a strong and brutal man. [< Greek *gorillas,* plural, probably < an African word]

Gor ki or **Gor ky** (gôr′kē), *n.* 1 **Maxim,** 1868-1936, Russian writer of novels, stories, and plays. 2 Also, **Gorkiy.** city in W Soviet Union, on the Volga River. 1,170,000. Former name, **Nizhni Novgorod.**

gor mand ize (gôr′mən dīz), *v.i., v.t.,* **-ized, -iz ing.** stuff oneself with food; eat very greedily; gorge. **—gor′mand iz′er,** *n.*

gorse (gôrs), *n.* furze. [Old English *gorst*]

gor y (gôr′ē, gōr′ē), *adj.,* **gor i er, gor i est.** 1 covered with gore; bloody. 2 with much bloodshed: *a gory accident.* **—gor′i ly,** *adv.* **—gor′i ness,** *n.*

Gothic (def. 1) style of cathedral

gosh (gosh), *interj.* exclamation or mild oath. [altered pronunciation of *God*]

gos hawk (gos′hôk′), *n.* a large, powerful, short-winged hawk, formerly much used in falconry. [Old English *gōshafoc* < *gōs* goose + *hafoc* hawk]

Go shen (gō′shən), *n.* 1 (in the Bible) a fertile part of Egypt where the Israelites lived before the Exodus. 2 any land of plenty and comfort.

gos ling (goz′ling), *n.* a young goose.

gos pel (gos′pəl), *n.* 1 the teachings of Jesus and the Apostles, especially concerning the coming of the Messiah in the person of Christ, of salvation through the Atonement, and of the kingdom of God. 2 **Gospel, a** any one of the first four books of the New Testament, by Matthew, Mark, Luke, and John. **b** part of one of these books read during a religious service. 3 anything earnestly believed or taken as a guide for action. 4 the absolute truth: *She takes the doctor's words for gospel.* —*adj.* 1 of, like, or having to do with the gospel. 2 in agreement with the gospel; evangelical. 3 characterized by evangelical fervor; spreading the gospel: *gospel music, gospel hymns.* [Old English *gōdspel* good tidings (i.e., of the Nativity) < *gōd* good + *spel* spell[2]]

Gos plan (gos′plän′), *n.* the official Soviet planning agency in charge of programs for economic and industrial development.

gos sa mer (gos′ə mər), *n.* 1 film or thread of cobweb spun by small spiders, which is seen floating in the air in calm weather. 2 a very thin, light cloth or coat. 3 anything very light and thin. —*adj.* like gossamer; very light and thin; filmy. [Middle English *gossomer* goose summer, name for "Indian summer," as the season for goose and cobwebs]

gos sa mer y (gos′ə mər ē), *adj.* like gossamer; very light and thin.

gos sip (gos′ip), *n.* 1 idle talk, not always true, about other people and their affairs. 2 person who gossips a great deal. —*v.i.* repeat what one knows or hears about other people and their affairs. [Old English *godsibb,* originally, godparent < *god* God + *sibb* relative] **—gos′sip er,** *n.*

gos sip y (gos′ə pē), *adj.* 1 fond of gossip. 2 full of gossip.

got (got), *v.* pt. and a pp. of **get.**

➤ **Have got** or **has got** sometimes is used as the equivalent of *have* or *has* alone: as an auxiliary verb denoting obligation *(I've got to study now)* or with the present tense meaning of "own; possess" *(Have you got a pencil?)* In speech, *got* was added because *have* almost disappears when unstressed. That problem is not present in writing, where *got* is often avoided as unnecessary. See also usage note at **gotten.**

Gö te borg (yœ′tə bôrg′), *n.* seaport in SW Sweden. 447,000. Also, **Gothenburg.**

Goth (goth), *n.* member of a Germanic people who invaded the Roman Empire in the A.D. 200's, 300's, and 400's. The Goths settled mainly in southern and eastern Europe.

Goth en burg (got′n bėrg′, goth′ən bėrg′), *n.* Göteborg.

Goth ic (goth′ik), *n.* 1 style of architecture using pointed arches, flying buttresses, and high, steep roofs, developed in western Europe during the Middle Ages from about 1150 to 1550. 2 the East Germanic language of the Goths. 3 a square-cut style of type without serifs, used in printing. This sentence is in Gothic. —*adj.* 1 of Gothic architecture. 2 of the Goths or their language. 3 of or having to do with a type of literature that emphasizes the supernatural and the grotesque, usually having a medieval setting.

Got land (got′lənd), *n.* Swedish island in the Baltic between Sweden and Latvia. 54,000 pop.; 1200 sq. mi.

got ten (got′n), *v.* a pp. of **get.**

➤ In Great Britain, **gotten** has been largely superseded by *got.* In America, apart from the usages treated at the note for **got,** above, **got** and **gotten** are freely interchangeable as past participles, the choice depending mainly on rhythm or emphasis: *They could have gotten* (or *got*) *here by now. In the past I have gotten* (or *got*) *a good meal here.* EXCEPTIONS: *We've got* (not *gotten*) *to support this plan. She's now got* (not *gotten*) *an apartment in town.*

gouache (gwäsh), *n.* 1 method of painting with opaque water colors obtained by mixing pigments with water and gum. 2 a color made in this way. 3 a painting made by this method. [< French]

Gou da (gü′də), *n.* a mild yellow cheese made from whole milk in the shape of a thick, flat disk. [< *Gouda,* city in the Netherlands, where it was first made]

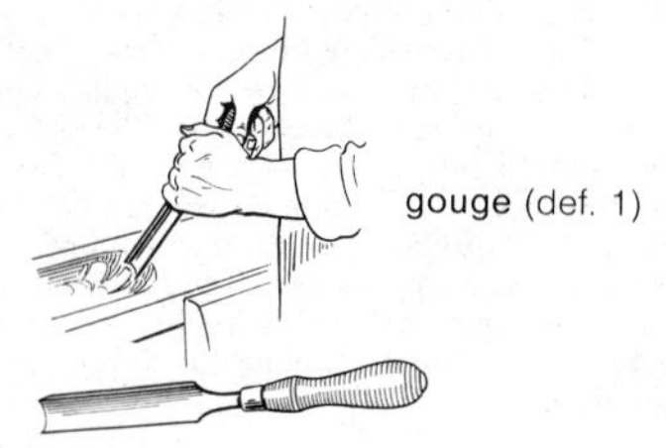
gouge (def. 1)

gouge (gouj), *n., v.,* **gouged, goug ing.** —*n.* 1 chisel with a curved, hollow blade, used for cutting round grooves or holes in wood. 2 groove or hole made by gouging. 3 INFORMAL. a trick; cheat; swindle. —*v.t.* 1 cut with a gouge. 2 dig out; tear out; force out. 3 INFORMAL. trick; cheat; swindle. [< Old French < Late Latin *gulbia*] **—goug′er,** *n.*

gou lash (gü′läsh), *n.* stew made of beef or veal and vegetables, usually highly seasoned. [< Hungarian *gulyás (hús)* herdsman's (meat)]

Gou nod (gü′nō), *n.* **Charles François,** 1818-1893, French composer.

gourd (gôrd, gōrd, gůrd), *n.* 1 any of various fleshy fruits with hard rinds and many flat seeds. Gourds are often dried and hollowed out for use as cups, bottles, bowls, etc. 2 any of certain vines of the gourd family on which gourds grow. 3 cup, bowl, bottle, etc., made from the dried shell of a gourd. [< Old French *gourde,* ultimately < Latin *cucurbita*] **—gourd′like′,** *adj.*

gourde (gůrd), *n.* the monetary unit of Haiti, a coin equal to 100 centimes and worth about 20 cents. [< French]

gourd family, group of dicotyledonous vines with hairy or prickly branched tendrils, large leaves, and fruits which usually have rinds and spongy, seedy interiors. Cucumbers, squashes, melons, and pumpkins belong to the gourd family.

gour mand (gůr′mənd), *n.* 1 person who is fond of good eating; gourmet. 2 OBSOLETE. person who eats to excess; glutton. [< Middle French, probably related to *gourmet*]

gour met (gůr′mā), *n.* person who is expert in judging and choosing fine foods, wines, etc. [< French < Old French *groumet* wine taster]

gout (gout), *n.* 1 a painful disease, characterized by inflammation of the joints, especially of the big toe. 2 drop, splash, or clot: *gouts of blood.* [< Old French *goute* < Latin *gutta* a drop]

gout y (gou′tē), *adj.,* **gout i er, gout i est.** 1 diseased or swollen with gout. 2 of gout; caused by gout. 3 causing gout. **—gout′i ness,** *n.*

gov., 1 government. 2 governor.

Gov., Governor.

gov ern (guv′ərn), *v.t.* 1 direct or manage with authority; rule or control. See **rule** for synonym study. 2 exercise a directing or restraining influence over; determine or guide: *the motives governing a person's decision.* 3 hold back; restrain; check: *Govern your temper.* 4 be a rule or law for: *the principles governing a case.* 5 (in grammar) require (a word) to be in a certain case or mood; require (a certain case or mood). 6 control automatically the speed of (a machine). —*v.i.* exercise the function of government; rule. [< Old French *governer* < Latin *gubernare* < Greek *kybernan* to steer] **—gov′ern a ble,** *adj.*

gov ern ance (guv′ər nəns), *n.* government; rule; control.

gov ern ess (guv′ər nis), *n.* woman who teaches and trains children in their home.

gov ern ment (guv′ərn mənt, guv′ər mənt), *n.* 1 rule or authority over a country, state, district, etc.; authoritative direction of the affairs of state: *federal government, municipal government.* 2 act or process of ruling and directing or controlling the actions and affairs of a people, state, etc.: *All government is difficult.* 3 person or persons ruling a country, state, district, etc.; administration or ministry. In the United States, the government often means the President, his cabinet, and his administrative assistants; in Great Britain, it may mean the cabinet. 4 system according to which a nation or community is governed: *republican government, civil government.* 5 country, state, district, etc., ruled: *Most governments are represented in the United Nations.* 6 political science. 7 rule, control, or management: *the government of one's conduct.* 8 (in grammar) the influence of one word in determining the case or mood of another.

gov ern men tal (guv′ərn men′tl, guv′ər-men′tl), *adj.* of or having to do with government. **—gov′ern men′tal ly,** *adv.*

gov er nor (guv′ər nər, guv′nər), *n.* 1 official elected as the executive head of a state of the United States. 2 official appointed to govern a province, colony, city, fort, etc. 3 person who manages or directs a club, society, institution, etc. A club often has a board of governors. 4 an automatic device that controls the supply of fuel or power and keeps a machine going at a certain speed. 5 BRITISH SLANG. one's father.

governor general, *pl.* **governors general,** governor who has subordinate or deputy governors under him, as in some countries of the Commonwealth of Nations.

gov er nor ship (guv′ər nər ship, guv′nər-ship), *n.* position, duties, or term of office of governor.

Governors Island, small island in upper New York Bay, belonging to the United States government.

govt. or **Govt.,** government.

gown (goun), *n.* 1 a woman's dress, especially a formal or evening dress. 2 a loose outer garment worn by college graduates, judges, clergymen, lawyers, and others to show their position, profession, etc. 3 nightgown or dressing gown. 4 members of a university: *arguments between town and gown.* —*v.t., v.i.* put a gown on; dress in a gown. [< Old French *goune* < Late Latin *gunna*] **—gown′less,** *adj.*

Go ya (gô′yə), *n.* **Francisco (José de),** 1746-1828, Spanish painter and etcher.

G.P., general practitioner.

G.P.O., 1 General Post Office. 2 Government Printing Office.

G.Q., General Quarters.

gr., 1 grade. 2 grain or grains. 3 gram or grams. 4 gross.

Gr., 1 Grecian. 2 Greece. 3 Greek.

Graaf i an follicle (grä′fē ən), one of the small, fluid-filled sacs or cavities in an ovary that contains an ovum. [< Regnier de *Graaf,* 1641-1673, Dutch physician]

grab (grab), *v.,* **grabbed, grab bing,** *n.* —*v.t.* 1 seize suddenly; snatch: *I grabbed the child before she fell.* 2 take possession of in an unscrupulous manner: *grab land.* 3 get or take in a hurry: *grab a sandwich, grab a shower.* —*n.* 1 a snatching; sudden seizing: *He made a grab at the butterfly.* 2 something which is grabbed. 3 a mechanical device for firmly holding something that is to be lifted or raised. [probably < Middle Dutch *grabben*] **—grab′ber,** *n.*

grab bag, 1 bag containing various unseen and unknown objects from which a person can take out one. 2 INFORMAL. any varied assortment.

Grac chi (grak′ī), *n.pl.* **the,** Gaius Gracchus and Tiberius Gracchus.

Grac chus (grak′əs), *n.* **1 Gaius (Sempronius),** 153?-121 B.C., Roman political and social reformer. **2 Tiberius (Sempronius),** 163?-133 B.C., his brother, who shared with him in the effort to bring political and social reform to Rome.

grace (grās), *n., v.,* **graced, grac ing.** —*n.* 1 beauty of form, movement, or manner; pleasing or agreeable quality; charm, ease, or elegance. 2 good will; favor. 3 mercy or pardon. 4 the favor and love of God: *fall from grace.* 5 a short prayer of thanks given before or after a meal. 6 favor shown by granting a delay. 7 time of the delay: *Most firms allow three days' grace after a bill is due.* 8 virtue or excellence. 9 behavior put on to seem attractive: *little airs and graces.* 10 **Grace,** title of a duke, duchess, or archbishop. 11 grace note. 12 **Graces,** *pl.* (in Greek myths) three sister goddesses who give beauty, charm, and joy to people and nature.

in one's bad graces, disfavored or disliked by.

in one's good graces, favored or liked by.

with bad grace, unpleasantly; unwillingly.

with good grace, pleasantly; willingly.

—*v.t.* 1 give or add grace to; adorn: *A vase of flowers graced the room.* 2 give grace or honor to: *The queen graced the ball with her presence.* 3 add grace notes to.

[< Old French < Latin *gratia* favor, thanks < *gratus* pleasing]

grace ful (grās′fəl), *adj.* having or showing grace; beautiful in form, movement, or manner; pleasing; agreeable: *A good dancer must be graceful. She thanked them with a graceful speech.* **—grace′ful ly,** *adv.* **—grace′fulness,** *n.*

grace less (grās′lis), *adj.* 1 without grace; ugly in form, movement, or manner: *awkward, graceless movements.* 2 without any sense of what is right or proper; impolite: *That boy is a graceless rascal.* **—grace′less ly,** *adv.* **—grace′less ness,** *n.*

grace note, (in music) a note or group of notes not essential to the harmony or melody, added for ornament; appoggiatura.

gra cious (grā′shəs), *adj.* 1 pleasant and kindly; courteous: *She welcomed her guests in a gracious manner which made them feel at ease.* See **kind**[1] for synonym study. 2 pleasant and kindly to people of lower social position: *The queen greeted the crowd with a gracious smile.* 3 merciful; kindly. —*interj.* exclamation of surprise. **—gra′cious ly,** *adv.* **—gra′cious ness,** *n.*

grack le (grak′əl), *n.* any of several large blackbirds with shiny, black feathers. [< Latin *graculus* jackdaw]

grad., 1 graduate. 2 graduated.

gra da tion (grā dā′shən), *n.* 1 a change by steps or stages; gradual change: *Our acts show gradation between right and wrong.* 2 step, stage, or degree in a series: *There are many gradations between poverty and wealth. The rainbow shows gradations of color.* 3 act or process of grading.

gra da tion al (grā dā′shə nəl), *adj.* having to do with or exhibiting gradation. **—gra da′tion al ly,** *adv.*

grade (grād), *n., v.,* **grad ed, grad ing.** —*n.* 1 any one division of elementary school or high school, arranged according to the pupils' progress and covering a year's work: *the seventh grade.* 2 the pupils in any one of these divisions. 3 **the grades,** U.S. elementary school. 4 step or stage in a course or process. 5 degree in rank, quality, or value: *Grade A milk is the best milk.* 6 group of persons or things having the same rank, quality, or value. 7 U.S. number or letter that shows how well one has done: *Her grade in English is B.* 8 slope of a road or railroad track. 9 amount of slope. 10 a hybrid animal, especially a cross between native stock and a superior breed. 11 **make the grade,** INFORMAL. be successful.

—*v.t.* 1 place in classes; arrange in grades; sort: *These apples are graded by size.* 2 give a grade to: *The teacher graded the papers.* 3 make more nearly level: *The road up the steep hill was graded.* —*v.i.* 1 change gradually; go through a series of steps, stages, or degrees: *Red and yellow grade into orange.* 2 be of a particular grade or quality.

[< Latin *gradus* step, degree]

grade crossing, place where a railroad crosses a highway, street, or other railroad on the same level.

grad er (grā′dər), *n.* 1 person or thing that grades. 2 student who is in a certain grade at school: *a sixth grader.* 3 machine that levels uneven or bumpy ground.

hat, āge, fär; let, ēqual, tėrm;
it, īce; hot, ōpen, ôrder;
oil, out; cup, pu̇t, rüle;
ch, child; ng, long; sh, she;
th, thin; ᴛʜ, then; zh, measure;

ə represents *a* in about, *e* in taken,
i in pencil, *o* in lemon, *u* in circus.

< = from, derived from, taken from.

grade school, U.S. elementary school.

grade separation, an intersection of highways, railroads, etc., on different levels, with ramps from one level to another, so that traffic going in one direction crosses over or under traffic going in a cross direction.

gra di ent (grā′dē ənt), *n.* 1 rate of upward or downward slope of a road, railroad track, etc.: *steep gradients.* 2 the sloping part of a road, railroad, etc.; grade. 3 rate at which a variable quantity, such as temperature or pressure, changes in value. —*adj.* going up or down gradually. [< Latin *gradientem* walking, going < *gradus* step, degree]

grad u al (graj′ü əl), *adj.* happening by small steps or degrees; changing step by step; moving little by little: *a gradual slope. A child's growth into an adult is gradual.* [< Medieval Latin *gradualis* < Latin *gradus* step, degree] **—grad′u al ly,** *adv.* **—grad′u al ness,** *n.*

grad u al ism (graj′ü ə liz′əm), *n.* principle or method of gradual, as opposed to immediate, change.

grad u al ist (graj′ü ə list), *n.* advocate of gradualism. —*adj.* of gradualism or gradualists: *a gradualist approach.*

grad u ate (*v.* graj′ü āt; *n., adj.* graj′ü it), *v.,* **-at ed, -at ing,** *n., adj.* —*v.i.* 1 finish a course of study at a school, college, or university and receive a diploma or other document saying so. 2 change gradually. —*v.t.* 1 give a diploma to for finishing a course of study: *He was graduated with honors.* 2 mark out in equal spaces for measuring: *My ruler is graduated in inches.* 3 arrange in regular steps, stages, or degrees: *The federal income tax is graduated so that people who make more money pay a higher rate of taxes.* —*n.* 1 person who has graduated and has a diploma. 2 container marked with degrees for measuring. —*adj.* 1 that has graduated: *a graduate student.* 2 of or for graduates: *a graduate school.* [< Medieval Latin *graduatum* graduated < Latin *gradus* step, degree] **—grad′u a′tor,** *n.*

➔ **graduate.** Except in formal writing, the passive form *to be graduated from* is now generally replaced by the active form: *She graduated from Smith in 1961.*

grad u a tion (graj′ü ā′shən), *n.* 1 a graduating from a school, college, or university. 2 ceremony of graduating; graduating exercises. 3 division into equal spaces. 4 mark or set of marks to show degrees for measuring. 5 arrangement in regular steps, stages, or degrees.

graf fi to (grə fē′tō), *n., pl.* **-ti** (-tē). a drawing or writing scratched or scribbled on a wall or other surface. [< Italian]

graft[1] (graft), *v.t.* 1 insert (a shoot or bud from one kind of tree or plant) into a slit in another closely related kind of tree or plant, so that it will grow there permanently; engraft. 2 produce or improve (a fruit, flower, etc.) by grafting. 3 do grafting on (a plant or tree). 4 transfer (a piece of skin, bone, etc.) from one part of the body to another, or to a new body, so that it will grow there permanently. *—v.i.* 1 insert a graft or grafts. 2 become grafted. *—n.* 1 shoot or bud used in grafting. 2 place on a tree or plant where the shoot or bud is inserted. 3 tree or plant that has had a shoot or bud grafted on it. 4 act or process of grafting. 5 piece of skin, bone, etc., transferred in grafting. [< Middle French *grafe* scion, stylus (the inserted shoot was thought to resemble a writing tool) < Latin *graphium* stylus < Greek *grapheion* < *graphein* write] **—graft′er,** *n.*

graft[2] (graft), *n.* 1 dishonest gains or unlawful profits made by a person in and through his official position, especially in connection with politics or government business. 2 money dishonestly and improperly taken. *—v.i.* make money by dishonest or unlawful means. [origin uncertain] **—graft′er,** *n.*

gra ham (grā′əm), *adj.* made from whole-wheat flour that has not been sifted: *graham crackers.* [< Sylvester *Graham,* 1794-1851, American reformer of dietetics]

Gra ham (grā′əm), *n.* **Martha,** born 1893, American dancer and choreographer.

Grail (grāl), *n.* (in medieval legends) the cup or dish used by Christ at the Last Supper, and by one of His followers to catch the last drops of Christ's blood at the Cross; Holy Grail. [< Old French *graal* < Medieval Latin *gradalis* bowl, cup]

grain (grān), *n.* 1 a single seed of wheat, corn, oats, and similar cereal grasses. In botanical usage a grain is not a seed but a fruit. 2 seeds or seedlike fruits of such plants in the mass: *grind grain.* 3 plants that these seeds or seedlike fruits grow on: *a field of grain.* 4 one of the tiny bits of which sand, salt, sugar, etc., are made up. 5 the smallest United States and British unit of weight. One pound avoirdupois equals 7000 grains; one pound troy equals 5760 grains. See **measure** for table. 6 the smallest possible amount; tiniest bit: *There isn't a grain of truth in the charge.* 7 arrangement or direction of fibers in wood, layers in stone, etc. Wood and stone split along the grain. 8 the little lines and other markings in wood, marble, etc.: *That mahogany table has a fine grain.* 9 quality of a substance due to the size, character, or arrangement of its constituent particles; texture: *a stone of coarse grain.* 10 the rough surface of leather. It is on the side of the skin from which the hair has been removed. 11 natural character; disposition: *Laziness went against her grain.* 12 **with a grain of salt,** with some reservation or allowance: *His claims must be taken with a grain of salt.* *—v.t.* 1 paint to look like the grain of wood, marble, etc. 2 form (sugar, powder, etc.) into grains; granulate. 3 remove the hair from (a skin or skins). 4 soften and raise the grain of (leather). *—v.i.* form grains; crystallize into grains.
[< Old French < Latin *granum* grain, seed] **—grain′er,** *n.* **—grain′less,** *adj.* **—grain′like′,** *adj.*

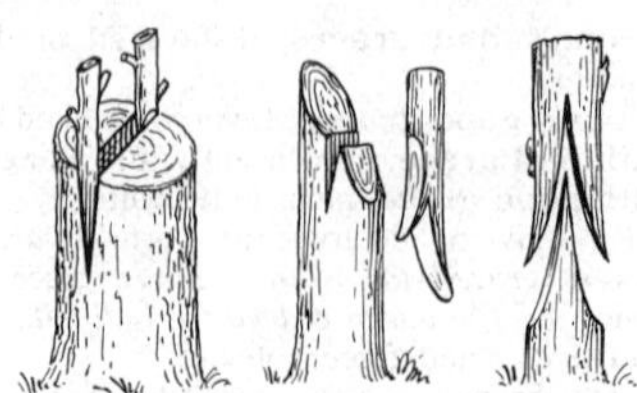

graft¹ (defs. 1, 2, and 3)—three types. The pieces are tied or taped together and kept moist until they join.

grain alcohol, ethyl alcohol, often made by the fermentation of grain.

grained (grānd), *adj.* 1 having little lines and markings. 2 painted to look like the grain in wood, marble, etc.

grain elevator, building for storing grain.

grain field (grān′fēld′), *n.* field in which grain grows.

grain y (grā′nē), *adj.,* **grain i er, grain i est.** 1 like the grain of wood, marble, etc. 2 granular. **—grain′i ness,** *n.*

gram (gram), *n.* the basic unit of mass in the metric system, approximately equal to the mass of one cubic centimeter of water at 39.2 degrees Fahrenheit or 4 degrees centigrade. See **measure** for table. Also, BRITISH **gramme.** [ultimately < Greek *gramma* small weight, (originally) something written < *graphein* write]

-gram[1], *combining form.* something drawn or written; message: *Cablegram = a cable message.* [< Greek *gramma*]

-gram[2], *combining form.* 1 ____grams: *Kilogram = a thousand grams.* 2 ____of a gram: *Centigram = one hundredth of a gram.* [< *gram*]

gra ma (grä′mə), *n.* any of a genus of low pasture grasses abundant in the western and southwestern United States. [< Spanish]

gram atom, mass of an element in grams that equals numerically the element's atomic weight: *A gram atom of oxygen is 16 grams.*

gram-a tom ic weight (gram′ə tom′ik), gram atom.

gra mer cy (grə mėr′sē), *interj.* ARCHAIC. 1 many thanks; thank you. 2 exclamation of surprise. [< Old French *grant merci*]

gram i ci din (gram′ə sīd′n, gra mis′ə dən), *n.* antibiotic obtained from soil bacteria which is too toxic for introduction into the bloodstream but is used locally for certain infections of the skin or throat. [< *Gram (= positive bacteria)* + *-cide*]

gram mar (gram′ər), *n.* 1 the scientific study and classification of the forms, uses, classes, and sounds of words in a particular language. 2 the systematic study comparing the forms and constructions of two or more languages. 3 the systematic study comparing present with past forms and usage of a language. 4 a treatise or book on one of these subjects. 5 rules describing the use of words in a language. 6 the use of words according to these rules. 7 the elements of any subject: *the grammar of painting.* [< Old French *grammaire* < Latin *grammatica* < Greek *grammatikē (technē)* (art) of letters < *gramma* letter, something written < *graphein* write]

gram mar i an (grə mer′ē ən), *n.* an expert in grammar.

grammar school, 1 (in the United States) an elementary school. 2 (in Great Britain) a secondary school that prepares students for a university.

gram mat i cal (grə mat′ə kəl), *adj.* 1 according to the correct use of words: *grammatical English.* 2 of grammar: *a grammatical mistake.*

gram mat i cal ly (grə mat′ik lē), *adv.* according to the rules and principles of grammar; as regards grammar.

gramme (gram), *n.* BRITISH. gram.

gram-mo lec u lar (gram′mə lek′yə lər), *adj.* of or having to do with a gram molecule.

gram-molecular weight, gram molecule.

gram molecule, mass of an element or compound in grams that equals numerically the element's or compound's molecular weight; mole: *A gram molecule of oxygen gas is 32 grams.*

Gram-neg a tive bacteria (gram′neg′ə tiv), bacteria that do not stain when treated with certain purple dyes. [< Hans C. J. *Gram,* 1853-1938, Danish bacteriologist, who discovered a method of classifying bacteria by using stains]

Gram o phone (gram′ə fōn), *n.* trademark for a type of phonograph.

Gram pi an Hills (gram′pē ən), low mountains across central Scotland, dividing the Highlands from the Lowlands. The highest peak, Ben Nevis, is 4406 ft.

Gram pi ans (gram′pē ənz), *n.pl.* Grampian Hills.

Gram-pos i tive bacteria (gram′poz′ə tiv), bacteria that stain when treated with certain purple dyes. [< Hans C. J. *Gram.* See GRAM-NEGATIVE BACTERIA.]

gram pus (gram′pəs), *n.* 1 a large mammal of the same family as the dolphin having a blunt nose, inhabiting oceans and seas through much of the world. 2 killer whale. [alteration of Old French *graspeis* < Medieval Latin *crassus piscis* fat fish]

gra na (grä′nə), *n.* pl. of **granum.**

Gra na da (grə nä′də), *n.* 1 district in S Spain. 2 its chief city, the last stronghold of the Moors until they were driven out of Spain in 1492. 170,000.

gran ar y (gran′ər ē, grā′nər ē), *n., pl.* **-ar ies.** 1 storehouse for grain after it is threshed. 2 region producing much grain. [< Latin *granarium* < *granum* grain]

Gran Cha co (grän′chä′kō). See **Chaco.**

grand (grand), *adj.* 1 large and of fine appearance: *grand mountains.* 2 of very high or noble quality; dignified: *a very grand palace, grand music, a grand old man.* See synonym study below. 3 highest or very high in rank; chief: *grand marshal, grand rabbi.* 4 great; important; main: *the grand staircase.* 5 complete; comprehensive: *grand total.* 6 INFORMAL. very satisfactory; very pleasing: *a grand time, grand weather.* *—n.* 1 SLANG. a thousand dollars. 2 grand piano. [< Old French *grant, grand* < Latin *grandis* big] **—grand′ly,** *adv.* **—grand′ness,** *n.*
Syn. *adj.* 2 **Grand, stately, noble** mean great, dignified, and impressive. **Grand** implies imposing magnitude and splendor: *Milton's grand style.* **Stately** emphasizes dignity and impressiveness: *a stately Spanish galleon, the stately rhythm of processional music.* **Noble** implies lofty grandeur: *The Statue of Liberty is a noble sight.*

gran dam (gran′dam), *n.* ARCHAIC. 1 grandmother. 2 an old woman. [< Anglo-French *graund dame,* literally, great lady]

gran dame (gran′dām), *n.* ARCHAIC. grandam.

Grand Army of the Republic, or-

hat, āge, fär; let, ēqual, tėrm;
it, īce; hot, ōpen, ôrder;
oil, out; cup, pu̇t, rüle;
ch, child; ng, long; sh, she;
th, thin; TH, then; zh, measure;

ə represents *a* in about, *e* in taken, *i* in pencil, *o* in lemon, *u* in circus.

< = from, derived from, taken from.

ganization of men who served in the Union Army or Navy during the Civil War, founded in 1866 and disbanded in 1956, after its last member died.

grand aunt (grand′ant′), *n.* aunt of one's father or mother; great-aunt.

Grand Bank or **Grand Banks,** shoal off the SE coast of Newfoundland, important for cod fishing. 500 mi. long.

Grand Canyon, deep gorge of the Colorado River, in N Arizona. 217 mi. long; over 1 mi. deep.

Grand Canyon National Park, national park including the Grand Canyon and the surrounding region. 1000 sq. mi.

grand child (grand′chīld′), *n., pl.* **-chil dren.** child of one's son or daughter.

Grand Cou lee (kü′lē), large dam on the Columbia River, in E Washington.

grand daugh ter (grand′dô′tər), *n.* daughter of one's son or daughter.

grand duchess, 1 wife or widow of a grand duke. 2 lady equal in rank to a grand duke. 3 princess of the ruling house of Russia before 1917.

grand duchy, territory under the rule of a grand duke or grand duchess.

grand duke, 1 prince who rules a small state or country called a grand duchy. A grand duke ranks just below a king. 2 prince of the ruling house of Russia before 1917.

grande dame (gräNd däm′), *pl.* ***grandes dames*** (gräNd däm′). FRENCH. a great lady, usually of a certain age and dignity.

gran dee (gran dē′), *n.* 1 a Spanish or Portuguese nobleman of the highest rank. 2 person of high rank or great importance. [< Spanish and Portuguese *grande*]

gran deur (gran′jər, gran′ju̇r), *n.* 1 magnificence or splendor of appearance, style of living, etc. 2 quality of being grand or imposing; majesty; nobility. [< French]

grand fa ther (grand′fä′THər), *n.* 1 father of one's father or mother. 2 any forefather.

grandfather clause, U.S. clause added to the constitutions of seven Southern states which discriminated against Negroes in qualifications for voting, declared void in 1915 by the United States Supreme Court.

grandfather clock, grandfather's clock.

grand fa ther ly (grand′fä′THər lē), *adj.* of, like, or characteristic of a grandfather.

grandfather's clock, clock in a tall, wooden case, which stands on the floor.

Grand Gui gnol (grän gē nyôl′), 1 a small theater in Paris which was famous for its horror plays. 2 Also, **grand guignol.** something designed to shock and horrify.

gran dil o quence (gran dil′ə kwəns), *n.* the use of lofty or pompous words.

gran dil o quent (gran dil′ə kwənt), *adj.* using lofty or pompous words. [< Latin *grandiloquus* < *grandis* grand + *loqui* speak] **—gran dil′o quent ly,** *adv.*

gran di ose (gran′dē ōs), *adj.* 1 grand in an imposing or impressive way; magnificent. 2 grand in a showy or pompous way; not really magnificent, but trying to seem so. [< French < Italian *grandioso*] **—gran′di ose ly,** *adv.*

gran di os i ty (gran′dē os′ə tē), *n.* the quality or condition of being grandiose.

grand jury, jury of from 6 to 23 persons chosen to investigate accusations of crime and decide whether there is enough evidence for a trial in court.

Grand Lama, Dalai Lama.

grand larceny, theft in which the value of the property taken equals or is more than a certain amount, in most states between $25 and $50.

grand ma (grand′mä′, gram′mä′, gram′ə), *n.* INFORMAL. grandmother.

grand mal (gräN mal′), attack of epilepsy characterized by severe convulsions. [< French, literally, great sickness]

grand march, ceremony at a ball in which the guests march around the ballroom in couples.

Grand Master, head of an order of knighthood, a lodge, etc.

grand moth er (grand′muTH′ər), *n.* 1 mother of one's father or mother. 2 any ancestress.

grand moth er ly (grand′muTH′ər lē), *adj.* of, like, or characteristic of a grandmother.

grand neph ew (grand′nef′yü; *British* grand′nev′yü), *n.* son of one's nephew or niece; great-nephew.

granny knot   square knot

grand niece (grand′nēs′), *n.* daughter of one's nephew or niece; great-niece.

Grand Old Party, the Republican Party in the United States.

grand opera, a musical drama, having a serious and often tragic theme, in which all the speeches are sung or recited to the accompaniment of an orchestra.

grand pa (grand′pä′, gram′pä′, gram′pə), *n.* INFORMAL. grandfather.

grand par ent (grand′per′ənt, grand′par′ənt), *n.* grandfather or grandmother.

grand piano, a large piano mounted on legs and having horizontal strings in a flat, harp-shaped wooden case.

Grand Rapids, city in SW Michigan. 198,000.

grand sir (grand′sėr′), *n.* ARCHAIC. grandsire.

grand sire (grand′sīr′), *n.* ARCHAIC. 1 grandfather. 2 forefather. 3 an old man.

grand slam, a winning all the tricks in a hand of bridge.

grand son (grand′sun′), *n.* son of one's son or daughter.

grand stand (grand′stand′), *n.* the principal seating place for people at an athletic field, racetrack, parade, etc.

grandstand play, U.S. INFORMAL. something done to attract the attention of an audience.

grand tour, an extended tour of continental Europe, formerly considered an essential part of the education of young men of the British aristocracy.

grand un cle (grand′ung′kəl), *n.* uncle of one's father or mother; great-uncle.

grange (grānj), *n.* 1 farm with its barns and other buildings. 2 **Grange, a** an association of farmers for the improvement of their welfare, founded in 1867. **b** a local branch of this organization. [< Old French < Medieval Latin *granica* < Latin *granum* grain]

grang er (grān′jər), *n.* 1 farmer. 2 **Granger,** member of the Grange.

gran ite (gran′it), *n.* a hard, igneous rock made of grains of other rocks, chiefly quartz and feldspar, much used for buildings and monuments. [< Italian *granito* grained < *grano* grain < Latin *granum*]

gran ite ware (gran′it wer′, gran′it war′), *n.* ironware covered with gray enamel.

gra nit ic (grə nit′ik), *adj.* of or like granite.

gra niv or ous (grə niv′ər əs), *adj.* eating or feeding on grain or seeds. [< Latin *granum* grain + *vorare* devour]

gran ny or **gran nie** (gran′ē), *n., pl.* **-nies.** INFORMAL. 1 grandmother. 2 an old woman. 3 a fussy person.

granny knot, knot differing from a square knot in having the ends crossed in the opposite way. It is easily jammed and often fails to hold under strain.

grant (grant), *v.t.* 1 give what is asked; allow: *grant a request, grant permission.* 2 admit to be true; accept without proof; concede: *I grant that you are right so far.* 3 bestow or confer (a right, etc.) by formal act; transfer or convey (the ownership of property), especially by deed or writing. 4 **take for granted, a** assume to be true; regard as proven or agreed to: *We take for granted the existence of atoms.* **b** accept as probable: *We took for granted that the sailor could swim.* —*n.* 1 thing granted, such as a gift of money, a privilege, a right, or a tract of land. 2 act of granting. [< Old French *granter, creanter* to promise, authorize, ultimately < Latin *credere* to trust] **—grant′a ble,** *adj.* **—grant′er,** *n.*

Grant (grant), *n.* **Ulysses S(impson),** 1822-1885, Union general during the Civil War, and 18th president of the United States, from 1869 to 1877.

grant ee (gran′tē′), *n.* person to whom a grant is made.

grant-in-aid (grant′in ād′), *n., pl.* **grants-in-aid.** 1 grant of money by one unit of government to another to help it carry out some public service or program. 2 grant of money to a person or institution, especially a school, to help defray the cost of a particular project.

grant or (gran′tər, gran′tôr′), *n.* person who makes a grant.

gran u lar (gran′yə lər), *adj.* 1 consisting of or containing grains or granules; grainy: *granular stone.* 2 resembling grains or granules. **—gran′u lar ly,** *adv.*

gran u lar i ty (gran′yə lar′ə tē), *n.* granular condition or quality.

gran u late (gran′yə lāt), *v.,* **-lat ed, -lat ing.** —*v.t.* 1 make into grains; form grains or granules. 2 roughen the surface of. —*v.i.* 1 become granular. 2 develop granulations. Wounds granulate in healing.

gran u lat ed (gran′yə lā′tid), *adj.* 1 formed into grains or granules: *granulated sugar.* 2 roughened on the surface: *granulated glass, granulated leather.*

gran u la tion (gran′yə lā′shən), *n.* 1 formation into grains or granules. 2 a roughening on the surface. 3 granule on a roughened surface.

gran ule (gran′yül), *n.* 1 a small grain. 2 a small bit or spot like a grain. [< Late Latin *granulum,* diminutive of Latin *granum* grain]

gran u lo cyte (gran′yə lō sīt), *n.* any of

several types of white blood cells whose cytoplasm contains granules.

gran u lose (gran′yə lōs), *adj.* granular.

gra num (grā′nəm), *n., pl.* **-na.** one of the very small, disk-shaped granules within the chloroplasts of plant cells. They contain chlorophyll. [< Latin, grain]

grape (grāp), *n.* 1 a small, round, berrylike fruit, red, purple, or pale-green, growing in bunches or clusters on any of a genus of woody vines. Grapes usually have several seeds, and are eaten raw or made into raisins, jelly, and wine. 2 grapevine. 3 grapeshot. [< Old French, bunch of grapes < *graper* pick grapes < *grape* hook] **—grape′like′,** *adj.*

grape fruit (grāp′früt′), *n.* 1 a pale-yellow, roundish citrus fruit like an orange, but larger and not as sweet. 2 tree it grows on.

grape shot (grāp′shot′), *n.* cluster of small iron balls formerly used as a projectile for cannon.

grape sugar, dextrose.

grape vine (grāp′vīn′), *n.* 1 vine that grapes grow on. 2 INFORMAL. way in which news or rumors are mysteriously spread. 3 INFORMAL. a baseless rumor.

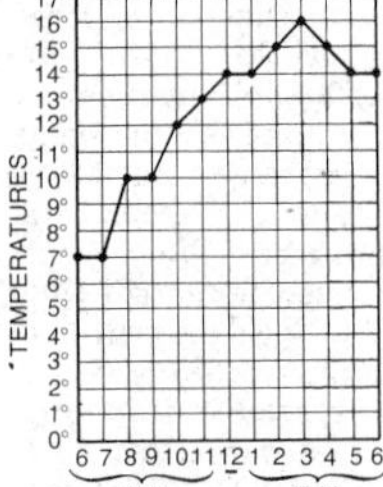

graph (def. 1) of the temperature of a winter day for 12 hours

graph (graf), *n.* 1 a symbolic diagram, used in mathematics, chemistry, etc., in which a system of one or more curves, lines, etc., shows how one quantity depends on or changes with another. 2 (in mathematics) a curve or other line representing the mathematical relations of the elements in an equation or function. —*v.t.* make a graph of. [short for *graphic formula*]

-graph, *combining form.* 1 instrument that writes, draws, records, etc.: *Seismograph = instrument that records earthquake data.* 2 something written, drawn, recorded, etc.: *Autograph = something written by oneself.* [< Greek *-graphos* < *graphein* write]

graph eme (graf′ēm′), *n.* (in linguistics) the smallest distinctive unit of the written language; any form of a letter or combination of letters that represents a speech sound.

graph ic (graf′ik), *adj.* 1 producing by words the effect of a picture; lifelike; vivid: *a graphic description of a battle.* 2 of or about graphs and their use. 3 shown by a graph: *a graphic record of school attendance for a month.* 4 of or about drawing, painting, engraving, or etching. 5 of or used in handwriting: *graphic symbols.* 6 written; inscribed. —*n.* an etching, drawing, lithograph, etc.; any work of the graphic arts. [< Latin *graphicus* < Greek *graphikos* < *graphein* write] **—graph′i cal ly,** *adv.*

graph i cal (graf′ə kəl), *adj.* graphic.

graphic arts, the arts or techniques of printing, engraving, etching, lithography, etc., sometimes including drawing and painting.

graph ics (graf′iks), *n.* 1 art or science of drawing, especially by mathematical principles, as in mechanical drawing. 2 science of calculating by means of graphs, diagrams, etc.

graph ite (graf′īt), *n.* a soft, black form of carbon with a metallic luster, used for lead in pencils, for lubricating machinery, etc.; black lead; plumbago. [< German *Graphit* < Greek *graphein* write]

gra phit ic (grə fit′ik), *adj.* having to do with or of the nature of graphite.

graph o log i cal (graf′ə loj′ə kəl), *adj.* of or having to do with graphology: *graphological analysis.*

graph ol o gist (gra fol′ə jist), *n.* an expert in graphology.

graph ol o gy (gra fol′ə jē), *n.* the study of handwriting, especially as a means of analyzing a person's character.

graph paper, paper ruled in squares, for making graphs, diagrams, etc.

-graphy, *combining form.* 1 process of writing, describing, or recording: *Cryptography = the process of writing in code.* 2 a descriptive science: *Geography = descriptive science of the earth.* [< Greek *-graphia* < *graphein* write]

grap nel (grap′nəl), *n.* 1 instrument with one or more hooks for seizing and holding something; grapple; grappling iron. 2 a small anchor with three or more highly curved and pointed hooks. [Middle English *grapenel* < Old French *grapin* or *grapil* hook]

grap ple (grap′əl), *v.,* **-pled, -pling,** *n.* —*v.t.* seize and hold fast; grip or hold firmly. —*v.i.* 1 struggle by seizing one another; fight closely: *The wrestlers grappled in the center of the ring.* 2 try to overcome, solve, or deal (with a problem, question, etc.). 3 use a grapnel. —*n.* 1 a seizing and holding fast; firm grip or hold. 2 grapnel. [< Old French *grapil* a hook] **—grap′pler,** *n.*

grappling iron, grapnel.

grap to lite (grap′tə līt), *n.* any of a group of small, extinct, invertebrate animals which lived in various forms of colonies, especially abundant during the Ordovician period. The presence of its fossil is a common means of dating rocks and rock formations. [< Greek *graptos* marked + English *-lite*]

grap y (grā′pē), *adj.,* **grap i er, grap i est.** of, having to do with, or made of grapes.

grasp (grasp), *v.t.* 1 seize and hold firmly with the fingers, claws, etc. See **seize** for synonym study. 2 hold firmly as with the hand; grip. 3 clutch at; seize greedily: *grasp an opportunity.* 4 lay hold of with the mind; understand: *She grasped my meaning at once.* 5 **grasp at, a** try to take hold of. **b** accept eagerly. —*n.* 1 a seizing and holding tightly; clasp of the hand. 2 power of seizing and holding; reach: *Success is within her grasp.* 3 firm hold or control; possession; mastery. 4 understanding: *a good grasp of mathematics.* [Middle English *graspen*] **—grasp′a ble,** *adj.* **—grasp′er,** *n.*

grasp ing (gras′ping), *adj.* greedy; avaricious. **—grasp′ing ly,** *adv.* **—grasp′ing ness,** *n.*

grass (gras), *n.* 1 any of various plants whose leaves or blades and stalks are eaten by horses, cattle, sheep, etc. 2 any of a family of plants that have jointed stems and long, narrow leaves and, usually, a small, dry, one-seeded fruit. Wheat, corn, sugar cane, and bamboo are grasses. 3 land covered with grass; pasture. 4 SLANG. marijuana. —*v.t.* cover with grass. —*v.i.* 1 feed on growing grass; graze. 2 produce grass. [Old English *græs.* Related to GREEN, GROW.] **—grass′less,** *adj.* **—grass′like′,** *adj.*

Grasse (gräs), *n.* **François Joseph Paul, Comte de,** 1722-1788, French admiral, commander of the fleet that supported Washington at the siege of Yorktown in the Revolutionary War.

grass hop per (gras′hop′ər), *n.* any of two families of winged insects with strong hind legs for jumping, often damaging crops. Locusts and katydids are grasshoppers.

grass land (gras′land′), *n.* land with grass on it, used for pasture.

grass roots, the ordinary citizens of a region or state, especially those in the rural areas, taken all together: *The senator is sure he will get support from the grass roots.*

grass snake, any of certain small, harmless, grayish-green snakes living in meadows.

grass widow, woman divorced or separated from her husband.

grass widower, man divorced or separated from his wife.

grapnel (def. 2)

grass y (gras′ē), *adj.,* **grass i er, grass i est.** 1 covered with grass. 2 of or like grass. **—grass′i ness,** *n.*

grate[1] (grāt), *n., v.,* **grat ed, grat ing.** —*n.* 1 framework of iron bars to hold burning fuel in a furnace, fireplace, etc. 2 fireplace. 3 framework of bars over a window or opening; grating. —*v.t.* furnish with a grate or grating. [< Medieval Latin *grata, crata* lattice < Latin *cratis* hurdle. Doublet of CRATE.] **—grate′like′,** *adj.*

grate[2] (grāt), *v.,* **grat ed, grat ing.** —*v.i.* 1 have an annoying or unpleasant effect: *Rude manners and loud voices grate on me.* 2 make a harsh, jarring noise by rubbing; sound harshly: *The door grated on its old, rusty hinges.* —*v.t.* 1 wear down or grind off in small pieces: *grate cheese.* 2 rub harshly together: *grate the teeth.* 3 fret; annoy; irritate. [< Old French *grater* < Germanic]

grate ful (grāt′fəl), *adj.* 1 feeling kindly because of a favor received; wanting to do a favor in return; thankful. 2 pleasing; welcome: *A breeze is grateful on a hot day.* [< obsolete *grate* agreeable (< Latin *gratus*) + *-ful*] **—grate′ful ly,** *adv.* **—grate′ful ness,** *n.*

grat er (grā′tər), *n.* 1 person or thing that grates. 2 instrument with a rough surface for grating: *a nutmeg grater.*

grat i fi ca tion (grat′ə fə kā′shən), *n.* 1 a gratifying. 2 a being gratified. 3 something that satisfies or pleases.

grat i fy (grat′ə fī), *v.t.,* **-fied, -fy ing.** 1 give pleasure to; please: *Flattery gratifies a vain person.* 2 give satisfaction to; satisfy; indulge: *gratify one's hunger with a large meal.* See **humor** for synonym study. [< Latin *gratificari* < *gratus* pleasing + *facere* make, do] **—grat′i fi′er,** *n.* **—grat′i fy′ing ly,** *adv.*

grat ing[1] (grā′ting), *n.* framework of parallel or crossed bars. Windows in a prison, bank, or ticket office usually have gratings over them. [< *grate*[1]]

hat, āge, fär; let, ēqual, tėrm;
it, īce; hot, ōpen, ôrder;
oil, out; cup, pu̇t, rüle;
ch, child; ng, long; sh, she;
th, thin; ᴛʜ, then; zh, measure;

ə represents *a* in about, *e* in taken, *i* in pencil, *o* in lemon, *u* in circus.

< = from, derived from, taken from.

grat ing[2] (grā′ting), *adj.* 1 unpleasant; annoying; irritating. 2 harsh or jarring in sound. [< *grate*[2]] **—grat′ing ly,** *adv.*

grat is (grat′is, grā′tis), *adv., adj.* for nothing; free of charge. [< Latin, ablative plural of *gratia* favor]

grat i tude (grat′ə tüd, grat′ə tyüd), *n.* kindly feeling because of a favor received; desire to do a favor in return; thankfulness.

gra tu i tous (grə tü′ə təs, grə tyü′ə təs), *adj.* 1 freely given or obtained; free. 2 without reason or cause; unnecessary; uncalled-for: *a gratuitous insult.* **—gra tu′i tous ly,** *adv.* **—gra tu′i tous ness,** *n.*

gra tu i ty (grə tü′ə tē, grə tyü′ə tē), *n., pl.* **-ties.** 1 present of money in return for services; tip. Gratuities are given to waiters, porters, servants, etc. 2 present; gift.

gra va men (grə vā′mən), *n., pl.* **-va min a** (-vam′ə nə). 1 grievance. 2 (in law) the burden or essential part of a charge or complaint. [< Late Latin, inconvenience < Latin *gravare* to load, burden < *gravis* heavy]

grave[1] (grāv), *n.* 1 hole dug in the ground where a dead body is to be buried. 2 mound or monument over it. 3 any place of burial: *a watery grave.* 4 death. [Old English *græf.* Related to GRAVE[3].]

grave[2] (grāv), *adj.,* **grav er, grav est,** *n.* *—adj.* 1 earnest; thoughtful; serious: *People are grave in church.* 2 not gay; dignified; solemn: *grave music, a grave ceremony.* 3 important; weighty; momentous: *a grave decision.* 4 somber: *grave colors.* 5 having a grave accent. 6 (in phonetics) low in pitch; not acute. *—n.* grave accent. [< Middle French < Latin *gravis* heavy, serious] **—grave′ly,** *adv.* **—grave′ness,** *n.*

grave[3] (grāv), *v.t.,* **graved, grav en** or **graved, grav ing.** 1 engrave; carve. 2 impress deeply; fix firmly. [Old English *grafan*]

grave[4] (grāv), *v.t.,* **graved, grav ing.** clean (a ship's bottom) and cover with tar. [origin uncertain]

gra ve[5] (grä′vā), in music: *—adj.* slow and solemn in tempo. *—adv.* slowly and solemnly. [< Italian < Latin *gravis* serious, heavy]

grave accent (grāv), mark (\`) placed over a vowel to show quality of sound, as in French *père;* syllabic value, as in *belovèd;* secondary stress, as in àdvertisement; or a low or falling tone, as in ancient Greek.

grave dig ger (grāv′dig′ər), *n.* person whose work is digging graves.

grav el (grav′əl), *n., v.,* **-eled, -el ing** or **-elled, -el ling,** *adj.* *—n.* 1 pebbles and rock fragments coarser than sand, much used for roads and paths. 2 small, hard substances formed in the bladder and kidneys. 3 disease in which these occur. *—v.t.* lay or cover with gravel. *—adj.* rough; harsh; gravelly. [< Old French *gravele,* diminutive of *grave* sand, seashore]

grave less (grāv′lis), *adj.* without a grave; unburied.

grav el ly (grav′ə lē), *adj.* 1 having much gravel. 2 of or like gravel. 3 rough; rasping; grating: *a gravelly voice.*

grav en (grā′vən), *adj.* engraved; carved: *graven images.* *—v.* a pp. of **grave**[3].

grav er (grā′vər), *n.* 1 tool for cutting, engraving, etc. 2 engraver.

Graves (grāvz), *n.* **Robert,** born 1895, British poet, novelist, and critic.

grave stone (grāv′stōn′), *n.* stone that marks a grave; headstone.

grave yard (grāv′yärd′), *n.* 1 cemetery. 2 place where old or useless objects are discarded: *an automobile graveyard.*

graveyard shift, INFORMAL. the working hours between midnight and the morning shift.

grav id (grav′id), *adj.* pregnant. [< Latin *gravidus* < *gravis* heavy] **—grav′id ly,** *adv.* **—grav′id ness,** *n.*

gra vim e ter (grə vim′ə tər), *n.* device used to measure gravity at the earth's surface.

grav i met ric (grav′ə met′rik), *adj.* of or having to do with a gravimeter.

grav i tate (grav′ə tāt), *v.i.,* **-tat ed, -tat ing.** 1 move or tend to move by the force of gravity. 2 settle down; sink; fall: *The sand and dirt in the water gravitated to the bottom of the bottle.* 3 tend to go; be strongly attracted: *The attention of the audience gravitated to the stage as the lights dimmed.*

grav i ta tion (grav′ə tā′shən), *n.* 1 the attraction of one body for another, or the effective force of one body moving toward another; the tendency of every particle of matter toward every other particle, of which the fall of bodies to the earth or the tendency of the sun, moon, stars, and other bodies of the universe to move toward one another are instances. 2 a moving or tendency to move caused by this force. 3 a settling down; sinking; falling. 4 a natural tendency toward some point or object of influence: *the gravitation of people to the cities.*

grav i ta tion al (grav′ə tā′shə nəl), *adj.* of or having to do with gravitation. **—grav′i ta′tion al ly,** *adv.*

grav i ta tive (grav′ə tā′tiv), *adj.* 1 of or having to do with gravitation. 2 tending or causing to gravitate.

grav i ty (grav′ə tē), *n., pl.* **-ties.** 1 the natural force that causes objects to move or tend to move toward the center of the earth, caused by the gravitation of the earth. Gravity causes objects to have weight. 2 the force of attraction that makes objects move or tend to move toward each other; gravitation. 3 heaviness; weight: *I balanced the long pole at its center of gravity.* 4 seriousness; earnestness. 5 serious or critical character; importance: *The gravity of the situation was greatly increased by threats of war.* 6 lowness of pitch. [< Latin *gravitatem* < *gravis* heavy]

gra vure (grə vyu̇r′, grā′vyu̇r), *n.* 1 photogravure or rotogravure. 2 plate or print produced by either of these processes. [< French < *graver* engrave]

gra vy (grā′vē), *n., pl.* **-vies.** 1 juice that comes out of meat in cooking. 2 sauce for meat, potatoes, etc., made from this juice, often by thickening it with flour. 3 SLANG. easy gain or profit. [Middle English *grave*]

gray (grā), *n.* 1 color made by mixing black and white. 2 a gray pigment or dye. 3 gray cloth or clothing. 4 a gray horse. *—adj.* 1 having a color between black and white: *Ashes and lead are gray.* 2 having gray hair. 3 old; ancient. 4 dark; gloomy; dismal: *a gray day.* *—v.t., v.i.* make or become gray. Also, **grey.** [Old English *grǣg*] **—gray′ly,** *adv.* **—gray′ness,** *n.*

Gray (grā), *n.* 1 **Asa,** 1810-1888, American botanist. 2 **Thomas,** 1716-1771, English poet.

gray beard (grā′bird′), *n.* an old man.

gray eminence, person who wields power or exerts influence privately or secretly.

gray hound (grā′hound′), *n.* greyhound.

gray ish (grā′ish), *adj.* somewhat gray.

gray ling (grā′ling), *n.* any of a genus of freshwater fishes of northern regions which somewhat resemble salmon and trout but have much larger dorsal fins.

gray matter, 1 the grayish tissue in the brain and spinal cord that contains nerve cells and some nerve fibers. 2 INFORMAL. intelligence; brains.

gray mullet, any of a family of bluish-silver food fishes found in salt and fresh water.

Graz (gräts), *n.* city in SE Austria. 253,000.

graze[1] (grāz), *v.,* **grazed, graz ing.** *—v.i.* feed on growing grass. Cattle and sheep graze. *—v.t.* 1 put (cattle, sheep, etc.) to feed on growing grass or a pasture. 2 tend or look after (cattle, sheep, etc.) while they are grazing. [Old English *grasian* < *græs* grass] **—graz′er,** *n.*

graze[2] (grāz), *v.,* **grazed, graz ing,** *n.* *—v.t.* 1 touch lightly in passing; rub lightly against: *The car grazed the garage door.* 2 scrape the skin from: *The bullet grazed his shoulder.* *—n.* 1 a grazing. 2 a slight wound or abrasion made by grazing. [origin uncertain]

gra zier (grā′zhər), *n.* person who grazes or feeds cattle to sell them.

graz ing (grā′zing), *n.* the growing grass that cattle, sheep, etc., feed on; pasture.

grease (*n.* grēs; *v.* grēs, grēz), *n., v.,* **greased, greas ing.** *—n.* 1 soft, melted animal fat. 2 any thick, oily substance. 3 shorn, uncleaned wool. *—v.t.* 1 rub grease on: *grease a cake pan.* 2 cause to run smoothly by greasing; lubricate: *Please grease my car.* 3 SLANG. give money to as a bribe or tip. [< Old French *graisse,* ultimately < Latin *crassus* fat] **—greas′er,** *n.*

grease paint (grēs′pānt′), *n.* mixture of tallow or grease and a pigment, used by actors in painting their faces.

grease wood (grēs′wu̇d′), *n.* a stiff, prickly shrub of the same family as the goosefoot, with narrow leaves, growing in alkaline regions in the western parts of the United States and Canada.

greas y (grē′sē, grē′zē), *adj.,* **greas i er, greas i est.** 1 smeared with grease; having grease on it. 2 containing much grease: *greasy food.* 3 like grease; smooth and slippery. **—greas′i ly,** *adv.* **—greas′i ness,** *n.*

great (grāt), *adj.* 1 large in extent, amount, size, or number; big: *a great house, a great crowd.* See synonym study below. 2 more than is usual; much: *great pain, great kindness, great ignorance.* 3 high in rank; important; remarkable; famous: *a great composer, a great event, a great achievement.* 4 most important; main; chief: *the great attraction.* 5 noble; generous: *great deeds.* 6 much in use; favorite: *That is a great habit of his.* 7 very much of a: *a great talker.* 8 INFORMAL. very good; fine: *We had a great time at the party.* 9 INFORMAL. skillful; expert: *She's great at skiing.* [Old English *grēat*] **—great′ness,** *n.*

Syn. 1 Great, large, big mean above average in size or measure. **Great** applies particularly to size and degree: *We saw the great redwoods* (size). *They are trees of great age* (degree). **Large** applies particularly to size and quantity but not to degree: *We saw many large trees.* **Big** applies particularly to size and weight: *A redwood is a big tree, very heavy and thick.*

great auk, a large, black-and-white, flightless sea bird formerly of North Atlantic shores, now extinct.

great-aunt (grāt′ant′), *n.* grandaunt.

Great Barrier Reef, the longest coral reef in the world, in the S Pacific along the NE coast of Australia. 1250 mi.

Great Basin, region in the W United States in which rivers and lakes have no outlet to the ocean, including most of Nevada and parts of Utah, California, Oregon, Wyoming, and Idaho. 210,000 sq. mi.

Great Bear, Ursa Major.

Great Bear Lake, lake in Northwest Territories, Canada. 12,275 sq. mi.

Great Britain, England, Scotland, and Wales. Great Britain is the largest island of Europe. 51,283,000 pop.; 88,700 sq. mi. See **British Isles** for map.

great circle, 1 any circle on the surface of a sphere having its plane passing through the center of the sphere. The equator is one of the great circles of the earth. 2 an arc of such a circle; the line of shortest distance between two points on the earth's surface.

great coat (grāt′kōt′), *n.* a heavy overcoat.

Great Dane
32 in. high
at shoulder

Great Dane, one of a breed of very large, powerful, short-haired dogs.

Great Divide, 1 Continental Divide. 2 **cross the Great Divide,** U.S. INFORMAL. die.

Greater Antilles, Cuba, Hispaniola, Puerto Rico, and Jamaica, the largest islands in the West Indies.

great-grand child (grāt′grand′child′), *n., pl.* **-chil dren** (-chil′drən). grandchild of one's son or daughter.

great-grand daugh ter (grāt′grand′dô′tər), *n.* granddaughter of one's son or daughter.

great-grand fa ther (grāt′grand′fä′ᴛʜər), *n.* grandfather of one's father or mother.

great-grand moth er (grāt′grand′muᴛʜ′ər), *n.* grandmother of one's father or mother.

great-grand par ent (grāt′grand′per′ənt, grāt′grand′par′ənt), *n.* great-grandfather or great-grandmother.

great-grand son (grāt′grand′sun′), *n.* grandson of one's son or daughter.

great heart ed (grāt′här′tid), *adj.* 1 noble; generous. 2 brave; fearless. **—great′heart′ed ness,** *n.*

Great Lakes, series of lakes between the United States and Ontario, Canada; Lakes Ontario, Erie, Huron, Michigan, and Superior. 94,700 sq. mi.

great ly (grāt′lē), *adv.* 1 in a great manner. 2 much.

great-neph ew (grāt′nef′yü; *British* grāt′nev′yü), *n.* grandnephew.

great-niece (grāt′nēs′), *n.* grandniece.

Great Plains, semiarid region just east of the Rocky Mountains in the United States and SW Canada.

Great Russian, member of a group of Slavic people living in the central part of the Soviet Union in Europe.

Great Salt Lake, shallow lake in NW Utah. Its water is much saltier than ocean water. 75 mi. long; 1000 to 1500 sq. mi.

great seal, the most important seal of a country or state, stamped on official documents as proof of their approval by the government.

Great Slave Lake, lake in Northwest Territories, Canada. 10,700 sq. mi.

Great Smoky Mountains, mountain range in E Tennessee and W North Carolina, part of the Appalachian Mountains. Highest peak, 6642 ft. Also, **Smoky Mountains.**

Great Smoky Mountains National Park, national park that includes most of the Great Smoky Mountains.

Great Spirit, deity worshiped by certain tribes or groups of North American Indians.

great-un cle (grāt′ung′kəl), *n.* granduncle.

Great Wall of China, a stone wall about 1500 miles long on the boundary between N and NW China and Mongolia; Chinese Wall. It was begun in the 200's B.C. to defend China against attack by nomads from the north.

Great White Way, the brightly lighted theater district along Broadway in New York City.

greave (grēv), *n.* Often, **greaves,** *pl.* armor for the leg below the knee. See **armor** for picture. [< Old French *greves,* plural]

grebe (grēb), *n.* any of a family of ducklike diving birds, having feet not completely webbed, a pointed bill, and short wings and tail. Its breast feathers are used to trim hats, etc. [< French *grèbe*]

Gre cian (grē′shən), *adj.* Greek. *—n.* 1 a Greek. 2 an expert in the Greek language or literature.

Gre co (grek′ō, grā′kō), *n.* **El.** See **El Greco.**

Greco-, *combining form.* 1 Greece; Greek things: *Grecophile = a lover of Greece or Greek things.* 2 Greek and ___: *Greco-Roman = Greek and Roman.* [< Latin *Graeco-* < Greek *Graikos* a Greek]

Gre co phile (grē′kō fil, grē′kō fil), *n.* person who loves Greece or Greek things.

Greece (grēs), *n.* country in SE Europe, on the Mediterranean. 8,736,000 pop.; 50,900 sq. mi. *Capital:* Athens. See **Adriatic Sea** for map.

greed (grēd), *n.* a wanting to get more than one's share; greedy behavior; greedy desire: *a miser's greed for money.* [back-formation < *greedy*]

greed y (grē′dē), *adj.,* **greed i er, greed i est.** 1 eager for gain, wealth, and the like; avaricious. 2 having a very great desire to possess something. 3 wanting to eat or drink a great deal in a hurry; piggish. [Old English *grǣdig*] **—greed′i ly,** *adv.* **—greed′i ness,** *n.*

Greek (grēk), *adj.* of Greece, its people, or their language. *—n.* 1 native or inhabitant of Greece. 2 language of Greece, considered classical in the form used until about A.D. 200. Greek is one of the oldest Indo-European languages spoken today. [Old English *Grēcas,* plural < Latin *Graeci,* plural of *Graecus* a Greek < Greek *Graikos*]

Greek cross, cross whose four arms are of the same length and form right angles.

Greek fire, substance easily set on fire whose flames could not be put out by water, used in warfare in ancient and medieval times.

Greek Orthodox Church, 1 Eastern Church. 2 the part of the Eastern Church forming the established church in Greece.

Gree ley (grē′lē), *n.* **Horace,** 1811-1872, American journalist, politician, and anti-slavery leader.

green (grēn), *n.* 1 the color of most growing plants, grass, and the leaves of trees in summer; color in the spectrum between yellow and blue. 2 a green pigment or dye. 3 green cloth or clothing. 4 ground covered with grass; grassy land. 5 **greens,** *pl.* **a** green leaves and branches used for decoration. **b** leaves and stems of plants used for food: *beet greens, salad greens.* 6 a putting green of a golf course. 7 **the Green,** the national color of the Republic of Ireland.

—adj. 1 having the color green; of the color green: *green paint. Emeralds are green.* 2 covered with growing plants, grass, leaves, etc.: *green fields.* 3 characterized by growing grass, etc.; not wintry: *a green Christmas.* 4 not ripe; not fully grown: *green apples.* 5 not dried, cured, seasoned, or otherwise prepared for use: *green tobacco, green wood.* 6 not trained or experienced; not mature in age, judgment, etc.: *a green crew on a ship.* 7 easily fooled; easy to trick or cheat; naïve. 8 full of life and strength: *green old age.* 9 recent; fresh; new: *a green wound.* 10 having a pale, sickly color because of fear, jealousy, or sickness.

—v.t., v.i. make or become green.

[Old English *grēne.* Related to GRASS.] **—green′ness,** *n.*

green algae, class of bright grass-green algae living mainly in fresh water. Green algae have definite nuclei and chloroplasts.

green back (grēn′bak′), *n.* piece of United States paper money, especially a legal-tender note, having the back printed in green. Greenbacks were originally issued in 1862 without any gold or silver reserve behind them.

Green Bay, 1 inlet of Lake Michigan extending into NE Wisconsin. 120 mi. long. 2 port in E Wisconsin at the head of this bay. 88,000.

green belt (grēn′belt′), *n.* section partially or completely surrounding a town or a city with trees, parks, etc., in which building is restricted or prohibited.

Green Beret, member of the Special Forces of the United States Army, a unit trained in unconventional warfare. Special Forces men wear green berets.

green bri er (grēn′brī′ər), *n.* 1 any of a large genus of woody vines of the lily family with prickly stems, umbrella-shaped clusters of flowers, and blackish or red berries; smilax. 2 a climbing vine of this genus with thick green leaves and small greenish flowers, grown in the eastern United States.

green corn, Indian corn, especially the ears in the tender stage; sweet corn.

hat, āge, fär; let, ēqual, tėrm;
it, īce; hot, ōpen, ôrder;
oil, out; cup, pu̇t, rüle;
ch, child; ng, long; sh, she;
th, thin; ᴛʜ, then; zh, measure;

ə represents *a* in about, *e* in taken, *i* in pencil, *o* in lemon, *u* in circus.

< = from, derived from, taken from.

Greene (grēn), *n.* 1 **Graham,** born 1904, British novelist. 2 **Nathanael,** 1742-1786, American general in the Revolutionary War.

green er y (grē′nər ē), *n., pl.* **-er ies.** 1 green plants, grass, or leaves; verdure. 2 greenhouse.

green-eyed (grēn′īd′), *adj.* 1 having green eyes. 2 jealous.

green gage (grēn′gāj′), *n.* a large plum having a light-green skin and pulp and a fine flavor. [< *green* + Sir William *Gage,* English botanist, who introduced it into England from France about 1725]

green gland, one of a pair of excretory organs located in the head of certain crustaceans, as the lobster.

green gro cer (grēn′grō′sər), *n.* BRITISH. person who sells fresh vegetables and fruit.

green gro cer y (grēn′grō′sər ē), *n., pl.* **-cer ies.** BRITISH. store that sells fresh vegetables and fruit.

green horn (grēn′hôrn′), *n.* INFORMAL. 1 person without training or experience. 2 person easy to trick or cheat.

green house (grēn′hous′), *n., pl.* **-hous es** (-hou′ziz). building with a glass roof and glass sides, kept warm for growing plants; hothouse; greenery.

green ing (grē′ning), *n.* apple with a yellowish-green skin when ripe.

green ish (grē′nish), *adj.* somewhat green.

Green land (grēn′lənd, grēn′land′), *n.* arctic island northeast of North America. It is the largest island in the world and belongs to Denmark. 54,000 pop.; 839,800 sq. mi. *Capital:* Godthaab.

green light, 1 a green traffic signal which indicates that vehicles or pedestrians may proceed. 2 INFORMAL. permission to go ahead with something.

green ling (grēn′ling), *n.* any of a genus of large fishes found around rocks and kelp in the northern Pacific, used for food.

green manure, green, leafy plants, such as clover or alfalfa, plowed under to enrich the soil.

Green Mountains, part of the Appalachian Mountains extending north and south through Vermont. Highest peak, 4393 ft.

green pepper, the unripe fruit of a red pepper plant. It is used as a vegetable, for stuffing, etc.

Green River, river flowing from W Wyoming into the Colorado River in SE Utah. 730 mi.

green room (grēn′rüm′, grēn′ru̇m′), *n.* room in a theater for the use of performers when they are not on the stage.

Greens bor o (grēnz′bėr′ō), *n.* city in N North Carolina. 144,000.

green soap, a soft soap used in treating skin diseases, cleansing wounds, etc.

green stick fracture (grēn′stik′), fracture in which the bone is bent and only partly broken.

green sward (grēn′swôrd′), *n.* green grass; turf.

green tea, tea made from leaves dried by machine without fermentation, thus retaining some of the green color.

green thumb, a remarkable ability to grow flowers, vegetables, etc.

green turtle, a large sea turtle with a green shell, used for food.

Green wich (gren′ich), *n.* borough in SE London, England, the former site of a famous observatory. Longitude is measured east and west of Greenwich. 226,000.

Greenwich Time, the standard time used in Great Britain and the basis for setting standard time elsewhere, reckoned by setting noon as the time the sun is directly overhead at the meridian which passes through Greenwich, England.

Greenwich Village, section of New York City, famous as a district where artists, writers, etc., live.

green wood (grēn′wu̇d′), *n.* forest in spring and summer when the trees are green with leaves.

greet (grēt), *v.t.* 1 speak or write to in a friendly, polite way; address in welcome; hail: *She greeted us at the door.* 2 respond to: *His speech was greeted with cheers.* 3 present itself to; meet: *When she opened the door, a strange sight greeted her eyes.* [Old English *grētan*] **—greet′er,** *n.*

greet ing (grē′ting), *n.* 1 act or words of a person who greets another; welcome. 2 **greetings,** *pl.* friendly wishes on a special occasion: *Season's greetings.*

gre gar i ous (grə ger′ē əs, grə gar′ē əs), *adj.* 1 living in flocks, herds, or other groups: *Sheep and cattle are gregarious, raccoons are not.* 2 fond of being with others: *Hermits are not gregarious.* 3 of or having to do with a flock or crowd. [< Latin *gregarius* < *gregem* flock] **—gre gar′i ous ly,** *adv.* **—gre gar′i ous ness,** *n.*

Gre go ri an (grə gôr′ē ən, grə gōr′ē ən), *adj.* 1 of Pope Gregory I. 2 of Pope Gregory XIII.

Gregorian calendar, calendar now in use in the United States and most other countries, introduced by Pope Gregory XIII in 1582. According to this calendar, the ordinary year has 365 days, and leap year has 366 days. It is a correction of the Julian calendar.

Gregorian chant, vocal music having free rhythm and a limited scale, introduced by Pope Gregory I and still sometimes used in the Roman Catholic Church. It is usually sung without an accompaniment.

Greg or y (greg′ər ē), *n.* Lady **Augusta,** 1852-1932, Irish playwright.

Gregory I, Saint, A.D. 540?-604, pope from A.D. 590 to 604. He was called "Gregory the Great."

Gregory VII, 1020?-1085, pope from 1073 to 1085; Hildebrand.

Gregory XIII, 1502-1585, pope from 1572 to 1585.

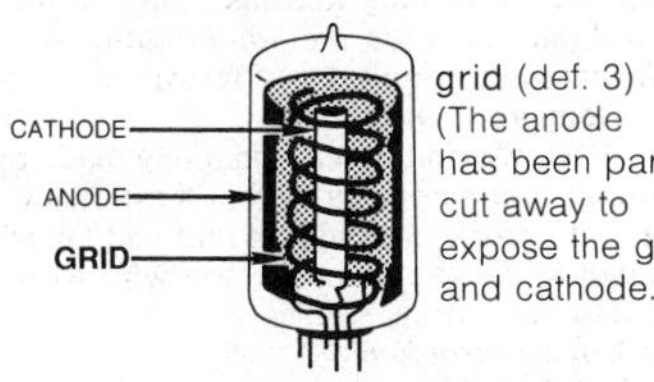

grid (def. 3) (The anode has been partly cut away to expose the grid and cathode.)

grem lin (grem′lən), *n.* an imaginary creature that causes trouble in an aircraft, its engines, parts, etc. [origin uncertain]

Gre na da (grə nā′də), *n.* one of the Windward Islands in the West Indies. 106,000 pop.; 133 sq. mi. *Capital:* St. George's.

gre nade (grə nād′), *n.* 1 a small bomb, which is thrown by hand or fired by a rifle: *The soldiers threw grenades into the enemy's trenches.* 2 a round, glass bottle filled with chemicals which scatter as the glass breaks. Fire grenades are thrown on fires to extinguish them. [< Middle French < Old French *(pomme) grenate* pomegranate]

gren a dier (gren′ə dir′), *n.* 1 (formerly) a soldier who threw grenades. 2 (later) a member of a specially chosen unit of foot soldiers. 3 (now) a member of a special regiment of guards in the British army.

gren a dine (gren′ə dēn′, gren′ə dēn′), *n.* 1 syrup made from pomegranate or red currants, used to flavor or color cocktails, etc. 2 a thin, openwork fabric of wool, silk, cotton, or rayon, used for women's dresses. [< French]

Gren fell (gren′fel), *n.* Sir **Wilfred Thomason,** 1865-1940, English physician and missionary in Labrador.

Gre no ble (grə nō′bəl), *n.* city in SE France. 162,000.

Gren ville (gren′vil), *n.* 1 **George,** 1712-1770, British statesman. 2 Sir **Richard,** 1541?-1591, English naval commander.

Gret na Green (gret′nə), village in S Scotland where many runaway couples from England were married.

grew (grü), *v.* pt. of **grow.**

grew some (grü′səm), *adj.* gruesome.

grey (grā), *n., adj., v.t., v.i.* gray.

Grey (grā), *n.* 1 **Charles,** Earl, 1764-1845, British statesman, prime minister of England from 1830 to 1834. 2 Sir **Edward,** 1862-1933, Viscount of Fallodon, British statesman. 3 Lady **Jane,** 1537-1554, great-granddaughter of Henry VII of England, executed as a usurper to the crown of England.

grey hound (grā′hound′), *n.* a tall, slender hunting dog with a long nose, a smooth coat, sharp sight, and the ability to run very swiftly. Also, **grayhound.** [alteration of Old English *grīghund*]

grib ble (grib′əl), *n.* a small, marine crustacean with seven pairs of legs, that bores into submerged timbers. [origin uncertain]

grid (grid), *n.* 1 framework of parallel iron bars with spaces between them; grating; gridiron. 2 the lead plate in a storage battery. 3 electrode consisting of parallel wires or a screen which controls the flow of electrons from cathode to anode in a vacuum tube. 4 arrangement of vertical and horizontal lines to determine the coordinates of given points or to locate points for which the coordinates are known. 5 the numbered squares drawn on maps and used for map references. 6 a football field. [shortened form of *gridiron*]

grid dle (grid′l), *n.* a heavy, flat plate, usually of metal, on which to cook pancakes, bacon, etc. [< Old North French *gredil* < Late Latin *craticulum.* Doublet of GRILL[1].]

grid dle cake (grid′l kāk′), *n.* pancake.

grid i ron (grid′ī′ərn), *n.* 1 grill for broiling. 2 any framework or network that looks like a gridiron. 3 a football field. 4 structure above the stage of a theater, from which scenery is manipulated. [Middle English, alteration (influenced by *iron*) of *gredire, gredile* griddle

< Old North French *gredil.* See GRIDDLE.]

grief (grēf), *n.* 1 great sadness caused by trouble or loss; heavy sorrow. See **sorrow** for synonym study. 2 **come to grief,** have trouble; fail. 3 cause of sadness or sorrow. [< Old French < *grever.* See GRIEVE.]

Grieg (grēg), *n.* **Edvard,** 1843-1907, Norwegian composer.

griev ance (grē′vəns), *n.* a real or imagined wrong; reason for being angry or annoyed; cause for complaint.

grieve (grēv), *v.,* **grieved, griev ing.** —*v.i.* feel grief; be very sad. —*v.t.* cause to feel grief; make very sad. [< Old French *grever* < Latin *gravare* to burden < *gravis* heavy] **—griev′er,** *n.* **—griev′ing ly,** *adv.*

griev ous (grē′vəs), *adj.* 1 hard to bear; causing great pain or suffering; severe: *grievous cruelty.* 2 very evil or offensive; outrageous: *Murder is a grievous crime in most societies.* 3 causing grief: *a grievous loss.* 4 full of grief; showing grief: *a grievous cry.* **—griev′ous ly,** *adv.* **—griev′ous ness,** *n.*

grif fin or **grif fon** (grif′ən), *n.* a mythical creature with the head, wings, and forelegs of an eagle, and the body, hind legs, and tail of a lion. Also, **gryphon.** [< Old French *grifon* < Popular Latin *gryphonem* < Latin *gryphus, gryps* < Greek]

Grif fith (grif′əth), *n.* **D(avid) W(ark),** 1875-1948, American motion-picture director and producer.

grig (grig), *n.* DIALECT. 1 cricket. 2 grasshopper. 3 a cheerful, lively person. [origin uncertain]

grill[1] (gril), *n.* 1 a cooking utensil with parallel iron bars or wires for broiling meat, fish, etc.; gridiron. 2 dish of broiled meat, fish, etc. 3 restaurant or dining room that specializes in serving broiled meat, fish, etc. —*v.t.* 1 cook by holding near the fire; broil. 2 torture with heat. 3 question severely and persistently: *The detectives grilled several suspects concerning the burglary.* [< French *gril* < Old French *greil, grail* < Latin *craticulum,* diminutive of *cratis* latticework. Doublet of GRIDDLE.] **—grill′er,** *n.*

grill[2] (gril), *n.* grille.

grille
left, on balcony
right, on window

grille (gril), *n.* an openwork, metal structure or screen, used as a gate, door, window, or to cover the opening in front of the radiator of an automobile; grating. [< French]

grill work (gril′wėrk′), *n.* pattern of grilles.

grilse (grils), *n., pl.* **grilse.** a young salmon that is returning from the sea to fresh water for the first time. [Middle English]

grim (grim), *adj.,* **grim mer, grim mest.** 1 without mercy; stern, harsh, or fierce: *grim, stormy weather.* 2 not yielding; not relenting: *a grim resolve.* 3 looking stern, fierce, or harsh. 4 horrible; frightful; ghastly: *grim jokes about death.* [Old English *grimm* fierce] **—grim′ly,** *adv.* **—grim′ness,** *n.*

gri mace (grə mās′, grim′is), *n., v.,* **-maced, -mac ing.** —*n.* a twisting of the face; ugly or funny smile: *a grimace caused by pain.* —*v.i.* make grimaces. [< Middle French] **—gri mac′er,** *n.*

gri mal kin (grə mal′kən, grə môl′kən), *n.* 1 cat. 2 an old female cat. 3 a spiteful old woman. [probably < *gray* + *Malkin,* diminutive of *Maud,* proper name]

grime (grīm), *n., v.,* **grimed, grim ing.** —*n.* dirt rubbed deeply and firmly into a surface: *the grime on a coal miner's hands.* —*v.t.* cover with grime; make very dirty. [< Flemish *grijmen* begrime]

Grimm (grim), *n.* **Jakob,** 1785-1863, and his brother, **Wilhelm,** 1786-1859, German philologists and collectors of fairy tales.

grim y (grī′mē), *adj.,* **grim i er, grim i est.** covered with grime; very dirty. **—grim′i ly,** *adv.* **—grim′i ness,** *n.*

griffin

grin (grin), *v.,* **grinned, grin ning,** *n.* —*v.i.* 1 smile broadly. 2 draw back the lips and show the teeth in anger, pain, scorn, etc.: *A snarling dog grins.* —*v.t.* show, make, or express by smiling broadly: *She grinned approval.* —*n.* 1 a broad smile. 2 act of showing the teeth in anger, pain, scorn, etc. [Old English *grennian*] **—grin′ner,** *n.*

grind (grīnd), *v.,* **ground, grind ing,** *n.* —*v.t.* 1 crush into bits or powder: *That mill grinds corn into meal and wheat into flour. Your back teeth grind food.* 2 crush by harshness or cruelty: *The slaves were ground down by their masters.* 3 sharpen, smooth, or wear by rubbing on something rough: *I ground the ax on the grindstone.* 4 make a harsh sound by rubbing; grate: *grind one's teeth in anger.* 5 force by rubbing or pressing: *grind one's heel in the dirt.* 6 work by turning a crank: *grind a coffee mill.* 7 produce by turning a crank: *The old man ground out music on the hand organ.* —*v.i.* 1 rub harshly; grate. 2 INFORMAL. work or study long and hard.
—*n.* 1 act of grinding. 2 something made by grinding: *a fine grind of coffee.* 3 INFORMAL. long, hard work or study. 4 dull and laborious work. 5 INFORMAL. person who works long and hard at his studies.
[Old English *grindan*]

grind er (grīn′dər), *n.* 1 person or thing that grinds. 2 person or machine that sharpens tools. 3 molar.

grind stone (grīnd′stōn′), *n.* a flat, round stone set in a frame and turned by hand, foot, or a motor. It is used to sharpen tools, such as axes and knives, or to smooth and polish things.

grin go (gring′gō), *n., pl.* **-gos.** (in Spain and Spanish America) an unfriendly term for a foreigner, especially an American or Englishman. [< Spanish, alteration of *griego* Greek]

grip (grip), *n., v.,* **gripped, grip ping.** —*n.* 1 a firm hold; seizing and holding tight; tight grasp. 2 power of gripping: *the grip of a bear.* 3 thing for gripping something. 4 part to take hold of; handle. 5 a certain way of gripping the hand as a sign of belonging to some secret society. 6 a small suitcase or handbag. 7 firm control: *in the grip of poverty.* 8 mental grasp; understanding. 9 grippe. 10 **come to grips, a** fight hand to hand; struggle close together. **b** work hard and seriously; struggle. —*v.t.* 1 take a firm hold on; seize and hold tight. 2 get and keep the interest and attention of: *An exciting story grips you.* [Old English *gripe* < *grīpan* to grasp] **—grip′less,** *adj.* **—grip′per,** *n.*

gripe (grīp), *v.,* **griped, grip ing,** *n.* —*v.t.* 1 clutch or grasp tightly; pinch. 2 oppress; distress. 3 INFORMAL. annoy; irritate. 4 cause pain in the intestines of: *Too much unripe fruit can gripe a person.* —*v.i.* 1 have pain in the intestines. 2 cause such pain. 3 INFORMAL. complain. —*n.* 1 a fast hold; gripping; clutch. 2 grasp; control. 3 **gripes,** *pl.* sharp, intermittent pain in the intestines. 4 INFORMAL. complaint. [Old English *grīpan*] **—grip′er,** *n.*

grippe (grip), *n.* influenza. Also, **grip.** [< French, literally, seizure]

grip ping (grip′ing), *adj.* that grips; that catches and holds the attention or interest. **—grip′ping ly,** *adv.*

grip py (grip′ē), *adj.* INFORMAL. having the grippe; characterized by the grippe.

grip sack (grip′sak′), *n.* U.S. INFORMAL. a traveling bag; valise.

Gri sel da (grə zel′də), *n.* heroine of several medieval romances, famed for her meekness and patience when cruelly treated by her husband.

gris ly (griz′lē), *adj.,* **-li er, -li est.** causing horror; frightful; horrible; ghastly. [Old English *grislic*] **—gris′li ness,** *n.*

grist (grist), *n.* 1 grain to be ground. 2 grain that has been ground; meal or flour. 3 **grist to one's mill** or **grist for one's mill,** source of profit or advantage to one. [Old English *grīst,* related to *grindan* to grind]

gris tle (gris′əl), *n.* cartilage, especially when found in meat. [Old English]

gris tly (gris′lē), *adj.,* **-tli er, -tli est.** of, containing, or like gristle; cartilaginous. **—gris′tli ness,** *n.*

grist mill (grist′mil′), *n.* mill for grinding grain.

grit (grit), *n., v.,* **grit ted, grit ting.** —*n.* 1 very fine bits of gravel or sand. 2 a coarse sandstone. 3 courage; pluck; endurance. —*v.t., v.i.* grate; grind: *She gritted her teeth and plunged into the cold water.* [Old English *grēot*]

grits (grits), *n.pl.* 1 corn, oats, wheat, etc., husked and coarsely ground. Grits are eaten boiled. 2 U.S. coarsely ground corn or hominy cooked as a cereal.

grindstone

hat, āge, fär; let, ēqual, tėrm;
it, īce; hot, ōpen, ôrder;
oil, out; cup, pu̇t, rüle;
ch, child; ng, long; sh, she;
th, thin; ᴛʜ, then; zh, measure;

ə represents *a* in about, *e* in taken,
i in pencil, *o* in lemon, *u* in circus.

< = from, derived from, taken from.

grit ty (grit′ē), *adj.,* **-ti er, -ti est.** 1 of or containing grit; like grit; sandy. 2 INFORMAL. courageous; plucky. **—grit′ti ness,** *n.*

griz zled (griz′əld), *adj.* 1 grayish; gray. 2 gray-haired. [< *grizzle* gray < Old French *grisel,* diminutive of *gris* gray]

griz zly (griz′lē), *adj.,* **-zli er, -zli est,** *n., pl.* **-zlies.** *—adj.* grayish; gray. *—n.* grizzly bear.

grizzly bear, a large, fierce, gray or brownish-gray bear of the mountains of northwestern North America.

gro., gross (12 dozen).

groan (grōn), *n.* sound made deep in the throat that expresses grief, pain, or disapproval; deep, short moan. *—v.i.* 1 give a groan or groans. 2 be loaded or overburdened: *The table groaned with food.* *—v.t.* express by groaning: *He groaned his disapproval.* [Old English *grānian*] **—groan′er,** *n.*

groat (grōt), *n.* 1 an old English silver coin worth fourpence. 2 a very small sum. [< Middle Dutch *groot,* literally thick (coin)]

groats (grōts), *n.pl.* hulled grain; hulled and crushed grain. [Old English *grotan,* plural]

gro cer (grō′sər), *n.* person who sells food and household supplies. [< Old French *grossier* wholesaler < Medieval Latin *grossarius* < Late Latin *grossus* coarse (of food) < Latin, thick, gross]

gro cer y (grō′sər ē), *n., pl.* **-cer ies.** 1 store that sells food and household supplies. 2 **groceries,** *pl.* articles of food and household supplies sold by a grocer.

grog (grog), *n.* 1 drink made of rum or any other strong alcoholic liquor, diluted with water. 2 any strong alcoholic drink. [supposedly < Old *Grog,* nickname of Edward Vernon, 1684-1757, a British admiral who ordered his seaman to dilute their rum, so called from his breeches of *grogram* cloth]

grog ger y (grog′ər ē), *n., pl.* **-ger ies.** BRITISH. saloon.

grog gy (grog′ē), *adj.,* **-gi er, -gi est.** INFORMAL. 1 not steady; shaky: *A blow on the head made me groggy.* 2 drunk; intoxicated. **—grog′gi ly,** *adv.* **—grog′gi ness,** *n.*

grog ram (grog′rəm), *n.* a coarse cloth made of silk, of wool, or of combinations of these with mohair. [< French *gros grain* coarse grain]

grog shop (grog′shop′), *n.* BRITISH. saloon.

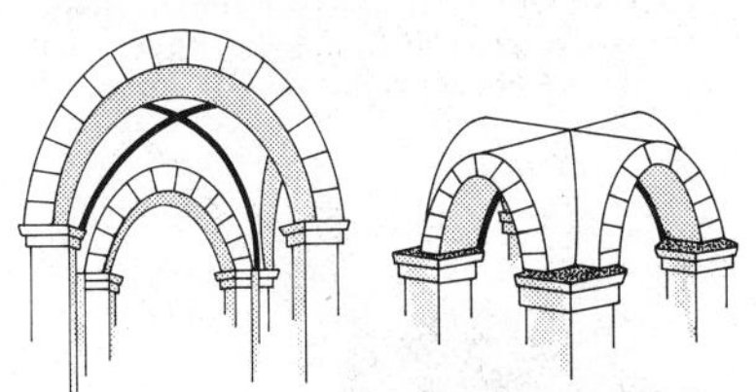

groin (def. 2)—groins shown from the inside and outside of the vaults. (The groins are indicated by heavy lines.)

groin (groin), *n.* 1 the hollow on either side of the body where the thigh joins the abdomen. 2 the curved edge where two vaults of a roof intersect. *—v.t.* form into or build with groins: *groined vaults.* [Middle English *grynde,* influenced by *loin*]

grom met (grom′it), *n.* 1 a metal eyelet. 2 ring of rope, used as an oarlock, to hold a sail on its stays, etc. [< obsolete French *gromette* curb of bridle]

Gro my ko (grō mē′kō), *n.* **Andrei Andreievich,** born 1909, Soviet diplomat.

Gro ning en (grō′ning ən), *n.* city in N Netherlands. 169,000.

groom (grüm), *n.* 1 man or boy whose work is taking care of horses. 2 bridegroom. 3 any of several officers of the English royal household. 4 ARCHAIC. manservant. *—v.t.* 1 feed, rub down, brush, and generally take care of (a horse, dog, etc.). 2 take care of the appearance of; make neat and tidy. 3 prepare (a person) for an office: *The lawyer was being groomed as a candidate for mayor.* [Middle English *grome* boy]

grooms man (grümz′mən), *n., pl.* **-men.** man who attends the bridegroom at a wedding.

groove (grüv), *n., v.,* **grooved, groov ing.** *—n.* 1 a long, narrow channel or furrow, especially one cut by a tool: *My desk has a groove for pencils. The plate rests in a groove on the rack.* 2 any similar channel; rut: *Wheels leave grooves in a dirt road.* 3 a fixed way of doing things: *It is hard to get out of a groove.* 4 **in the groove,** SLANG. **a** showing great skill; first-rate. **b** fashionable; up-to-date. *—v.t.* make a groove in: *The counter of the sink is grooved so that the water will run off.* [probably < Middle Dutch *groeve* furrow, ditch]

groov y (grü′vē), *adj.,* **groov i er, groov i est.** SLANG. first-rate; excellent; perfect.

grope (grōp), *v.,* **groped, grop ing.** *—v.i.* 1 feel about with the hands: *I groped for a flashlight when the lights went out.* 2 search blindly and uncertainly: *The detectives groped for some clue to the mysterious crime.* *—v.t.* find by feeling about with the hands; feel (one's way) slowly: *The blind man groped his way to the door.* [Old English *grāpian*] **—grop′ing ly,** *adv.*

Gro pi us (grō′pē əs), *n.* **Walter,** 1883-1969, German architect.

gros beak (grōs′bēk′), *n.* any of several colorful finches with large, stout, cone-shaped bills. [< French *grosbec* < *gros* large + *bec* beak]

gro schen (grō′shən), *n., pl.* **-schen.** 1 unit of money in Austria, a bronze coin worth $^{1}/_{100}$ of a schilling. 2 a small nickel coin used in Germany, worth 10 pfennigs. 3 a small silver coin varying in value, formerly used in Germany. [< German *Groschen*]

gros grain (grō′grān′), *n.* a closely woven silk or rayon cloth with heavy cross threads and a dull finish, used for ribbons, etc. [variant of *grogram*]

gross (grōs), *adj., n., pl.* **gross es** for 1, **gross** for 2, *v.* *—adj.* 1 with nothing taken out; whole; entire. Gross receipts are all the money taken in before costs are deducted. 2 very easily seen; glaring; flagrant: *gross misconduct. She makes gross errors in pronouncing words.* 3 coarse; vulgar: *gross manners.* 4 too big and fat; overfed. 5 thick; heavy; dense: *the gross growth of a jungle.* 6 lacking in culture or discrimination; without education or refinement: *gross taste in literature.* 7 concerned with large masses or outlines; general. *—n.* 1 the whole sum; total amount. 2 twelve dozen; 144. 3 **in the gross, a** as a whole; in bulk. **b** wholesale. *—v.t.* make a gross profit of; earn a total of: *gross $20,000 per year.* [< Old French *gros* < Latin *grossus* thick] **—gross′ly,** *adv.* **—gross′ness,** *n.*

gross national product, the total monetary value of all the goods and services produced in a nation during a certain period of time.

gross ton, 2240 pounds.

grot (grot), *n.* ARCHAIC. grotto.

gro tesque (grō tesk′), *adj.* 1 odd or unnatural in shape, appearance, manner, etc.; fantastic; queer: *pictures of dragons and other grotesque monsters.* 2 ridiculous; absurd: *The monkey's grotesque antics made the children laugh.* 3 (of painting or sculpture) in or resembling the grotesque. *—n.* painting, sculpture, etc., combining designs, ornaments, figures of persons or animals, etc., in a fantastic or unnatural way, much used in the Renaissance. [< French < Italian *grottesco,* literally, of caves, cavelike < *grotta.* See GROTTO.] **—gro tesque′ly,** *adv.* **—gro tesque′ness,** *n.*

Gro ti us (grō′shē əs), *n.* **Hugo,** 1583-1645, Dutch jurist and statesman, considered the founder of international law. Also, **de Groot.**

grot to (grot′ō), *n., pl.* **-toes** or **-tos.** 1 cave or cavern. 2 an artificial cave made for coolness and pleasure. [< Italian *grotto, grotta* < Latin *crypta* < Greek *krypte* vault. Doublet of CRYPT.]

grouch (grouch), INFORMAL. *—n.* 1 a surly, ill-tempered mood; fit of grumbling or complaining. 2 a surly, ill-tempered person; person who tends to grumble or complain. *—v.i.* grumble or complain in a surly, ill-tempered way. [< Old French *groucher* to murmur, grumble. Doublet of GRUDGE.]

grouch y (grou′chē), *adj.,* **grouch i er, grouch i est.** INFORMAL. tending to grumble or complain; surly; ill-tempered. **—grouch′i ly,** *adv.* **—grouch′i ness,** *n.*

ground[1] (ground), *n.* 1 the solid part of the earth's surface. 2 soil; earth; dirt. 3 Often, **grounds,** *pl.* any piece of land or region used for some special purpose: *fishing grounds, picnic grounds.* 4 **grounds,** *pl.* land, lawns, and gardens around a house, school, etc. 5 **grounds,** *pl.* small bits that sink to the bottom of a drink such as coffee or tea; dregs; sediment. 6 Often, **grounds,** *pl.* foundation for what is said, thought, claimed, or done; basis; reason: *There is no ground for complaining of his conduct. On what grounds do you say that is true?* 7 underlying surface; background: *The cloth has a blue pattern on a white ground.* 8 the solid bottom underlying a body of water. 9 the connection of an electrical conductor with the earth. 10 connection in a radio, television set, etc., for the conductor that leads to the ground.

above ground, alive.

break ground, a dig; plow. **b** begin building.

cover ground, a go over a certain distance or area. **b** do a certain amount of work, etc.

from the ground up, completely; entirely; thoroughly.

gain ground, a go forward; advance; prog-

ress. **b** become more common or widespread. **c** (in military use) to conquer ground from an opponent.
give ground, retreat; yield.
hold one's ground, keep one's position; not retreat or yield.
lose ground, a go backward; retreat; yield. **b** become less common or widespread.
run into the ground, INFORMAL. carry to an extreme; overdo.
shift one's ground, change one's position; use a different defense or argument.
stand one's ground, keep one's position; refuse to retreat or yield.
—adj. 1 of, on, at, or near the ground. 2 living or growing in, on, or close to the ground.
—v.t. 1 put on the ground; cause to touch the ground. 2 fix firmly; establish: *Her beliefs are grounded on facts.* 3 instruct in the first principles or elements: *The class is well grounded in arithmetic.* 4 furnish with a background. 5 connect (an electric wire or other conductor) with the earth. 6 keep (a pilot or an aircraft) from flying. *—v.i.* 1 run aground; hit the bottom or shore: *The boat grounded in shallow water.* 2 (in baseball) hit a bouncing or rolling ball. 3 **ground out,** (in baseball) be put out at first base on hitting a grounder.
[Old English *grund* bottom]

ground[2] (ground), *v.* pt. and pp. of **grind.**

ground cover, low plants, shrubbery, etc., planted for ornament or to enrich the soil and prevent the topsoil from eroding or blowing away.

ground crew, mechanics and other nonflying personnel responsible for the conditioning and maintenance of aircraft.

ground effect machine, Hovercraft.

ground er (groun′dər), *n.* baseball hit so as to bounce or roll along the ground.

ground floor, 1 the first floor of a building, nearest to the ground. 2 the beginning or most advantageous position of a venture.

ground glass, 1 glass with the surface roughened so that it is not transparent. 2 glass that has been ground to powder.

ground hog (ground′hôg′, ground′hog′), *n.* woodchuck.

Ground hog Day (ground′hôg′, ground′-hog′), February 2, the day when the groundhog is believed to come out of his hole. If the sun is shining and he sees his shadow, he goes back in his hole and winter continues for six more weeks.

ground less (ground′lis), *adj.* without foundation, basis, or reason: *a groundless rumor.* **—ground′less ly,** *adv.* **—ground′less ness,** *n.*

ground ling (ground′ling), *n.* 1 plant or animal that lives close to the ground. 2 fish that lives at the bottom of the water. 3 spectator or reader who has poor critical taste.

ground loop, an uncontrolled, abrupt turn made by an aircraft while moving along the ground.

ground mass (ground′mas′), *n.* the crystalline, granular, or glassy base of a porphyry, in which the more prominent crystals are embedded.

ground nut (ground′nut′), *n.* 1 any of various plants having edible tubers or nutlike underground seeds, such as the peanut. 2 the edible tuber, pod, etc., of such a plant.

ground pine, 1 a low, creeping evergreen, a kind of club moss, used for Christmas decorations, etc. 2 a European herb of the mint family with a resinous smell.

ground plan, 1 plan of a floor of a building. 2 the first or fundamental plan.

ground rule, one of a basic set of rules regulating the conduct of any activity.

ground sel (ground′səl), *n.* any of a large genus of plants of the composite family, with small heads of usually yellow flowers. The seeds of some kinds are used for bird food. [Old English *grundeswelge* < *grund* ground + *swelgan* to swallow]

ground sill (ground′sil), *n.* a horizontal timber used as a foundation; lowest part of a wooden framework; sill.

ground squirrel, any of various species of burrowing squirrels, such as the chipmunk.

ground state, that state of energy of an atom in which the electrons are as near to the nucleus as possible; state of lowest energy.

ground swell, 1 a broad, deep wave or swell of the ocean caused by a distant storm or earthquake. 2 a great rise or increase in the amount, degree, or force of anything.

ground water, water that flows or seeps downward and saturates the soil, supplying springs and wells. The upper level of this saturated zone is called the water table.

ground wave, radio wave that travels along, or near, the ground.

ground wire, wire connecting electric wiring, a radio, etc., with the ground.

ground work (ground′wėrk′), *n.* foundation; basis.

ground zero, the point on the surface of land or water directly above or below the center of a nuclear explosion.

group (grüp), *n.* 1 number of persons, animals, or things together: *A group of children were playing tag.* 2 number of persons, animals, or things belonging or classed together: *Wheat, rye, and oats belong to the grain group.* 3 a military unit made up of two or more battalions of supporting personnel, usually commanded by a colonel. 4 an air-force unit smaller than a wing and composed of two or more squadrons. 5 in chemistry: **a** a radical. **b** in the periodic table, a vertical column including elements having similar properties. 6 (in mathematics) a set of elements that has one operation and includes the properties of closure, identity element, inverse, and of being associative. *—v.t.* 1 form into a group. 2 put in a group; arrange in groups. *—v.i.* form a group; be part of a group. [< French *groupe* < Italian *gruppo;* of Germanic origin]

group er (grü′pər), *n., pl.* **-ers** or **-er.** any of various large food fishes of warm seas. [< Portuguese *garupa*]

group ing (grü′ping), *n.* 1 a placing or manner of being placed in a group or groups. 2 persons or things forming a group.

grouse[1] (grous), *n., pl.* **grouse.** any of a family of brown game birds with feathered legs. The prairie chicken, ruffed grouse, and sage grouse are different kinds of grouse. [origin unknown]

grouse[2] (grous), *v.,* **groused, grous ing,** *n.* INFORMAL. *—v.i.* grumble; complain. *—n.* complaint. [origin unknown] **—grous′er,** *n.*

grout (grout), *n.* 1 a thin mortar used to fill cracks, etc. 2 kind of plaster for finishing walls and ceilings. *—v.t.* fill up or finish with grout. [Old English *grūt* coarse meal]

grove (grōv), *n.* group of trees standing together. An orange grove is an orchard of orange trees. [Old English *grāf*]

grov el (gruv′əl, grov′əl), *v.i.,* **-eled, -el ing** or **-elled, -el ling.** 1 lie face downward; crawl at someone's feet; cringe: *When the dog saw the whip, he groveled before his master.* 2 abase or humble oneself: *I will apologize when I am wrong, but I will grovel before no one.* 3 enjoy low, mean, or contemptible things. [Middle English *groveling,* originally an adverb, in a prone position] **—grov′el er, grov′el ler,** *n.*

grow (grō), *v.,* **grew, grown, grow ing.** *—v.i.* 1 become bigger by taking in food, as plants and animals do; develop toward full size or age: *Plants grow from seeds.* 2 **grow up, a** become full-grown; become an adult. **b** come into being; be produced; develop. 3 exist; thrive: *Few trees grow in the desert.* 4 become bigger; increase: *Her fame grew. His business has grown fast.* 5 sprout; spring; arise. 6 come to be; become: *grow rich. It grew cold.* 7 become attached or united by growth: *The vine has grown fast to the wall.* *—v.t.* 1 cause to grow; produce; raise: *grow corn.* 2 allow to grow; develop: *grow a beard.* 3 **grow on** or **grow upon,** have an increasing effect or influence on: *The habit grew on me.* 4 **grow out of, a** grow too large for; outgrow: *grow out of childish habits. She grew out of her dress.* **b** result from; develop from: *Several ideas grew out of the discussion.* [Old English *grōwan.* Related to GRASS.]

grow er (grō′ər), *n.* 1 person who grows something: *a fruit grower.* 2 plant that grows in a certain way: *a quick grower.*

growing pains, 1 pains in the limbs or joints during childhood and youth, formerly supposed to be caused by growing. They are now often considered a symptom of rheumatic or other disorders. 2 troubles that arise when something new is just developing.

growl (groul), *v.i.* 1 make a deep, low, angry sound: *The dog growled at the stranger.* 2 complain angrily; grumble. 3 rumble: *Thunder growled in the distance.* *—v.t.* express by growling: *The dog growled its suspicion of the stranger.* *—n.* 1 a deep, low, angry sound; deep, warning snarl. 2 an angry complaint; grumble. 3 a rumble. [probably imitative] **—growl′er,** *n.*

grown (grōn), *adj.* 1 arrived at full growth. 2 covered with a growth. *—v.* pp. of **grow.**

grown-up (grōn′up′), *adj.* adult: *grown-up manners.* *—n.* an adult.

grouse[1]
ruffed grouse
17 in. long

growth (grōth), *n.* 1 process of growing; development. 2 amount grown; increase: *one year's growth.* 3 what has grown or is growing: *A thick growth of bushes covered the ground.* 4 an abnormal mass of tissue formed in or on the body. A tumor is a growth. 5 origin; source: *a plant of foreign growth.*

growth hormone, hormone secreted by the anterior lobe of the pituitary gland which controls the growth of the body.

growth ring, annual ring.

hat, āge, fär; let, ēqual, tėrm;
it, īce; hot, ōpen, ôrder;
oil, out; cup, pu̇t, rüle;
ch, child; ng, long; sh, she;
th, thin; ᴛʜ, then; zh, measure;

ə represents *a* in about, *e* in taken, *i* in pencil, *o* in lemon, *u* in circus.

< = from, derived from, taken from.

grub (grub), *n., v.,* **grubbed, grub bing.** —*n.* 1 a soft, thick, wormlike larva of an insect, especially that of a beetle. 2 person who toils; drudge. 3 SLANG. food. —*v.i.* 1 dig in the ground: *Pigs grub for roots.* 2 toil; drudge. 3 search or rummage about. —*v.t.* 1 root out of the ground; dig up: *It took the farmer weeks to grub the stumps on his land.* 2 rid (ground) of roots, etc. [Middle English *grubben* to dig, root up] —**grub′ber,** *n.*

grub by (grub′ē), *adj.,* **-bi er, -bi est.** 1 dirty; grimy; slovenly. 2 infested with grubs. —**grub′bi ly,** *adv.* —**grub′bi-ness,** *n.*

grub stake (grub′stāk′), *n., v.,* **-staked, -stak ing.** INFORMAL. —*n.* food, equipment, money, etc., supplied to a prospector on the condition of sharing in whatever he finds. —*v.t.* supply with a grubstake. —**grub′stak′er,** *n.*

grudge (gruj), *n., v.,* **grudged, grudg ing.** —*n.* feeling of anger or dislike against because of a real or imaginary wrong; ill will. See **spite** for synonym study. —*v.t.* 1 feel anger or dislike toward (a person) because of (something); envy the possession of. 2 give or let have unwillingly. [< Old French *groucher* to murmur, grumble. Doublet of GROUCH.] —**grudg′er,** *n.* —**grudg′ing ly,** *adv.*

gru el (grü′əl), *n., v.,* **-eled, -el ing** or **-elled, -el ling.** —*n.* a thin, almost liquid food made by boiling oatmeal, etc., in water or milk. Gruel is often given to those who are sick or old. —*v.t.* tire out completely; exhaust. [< Old French]

gru el ing or **gru el ling** (grü′ə ling), *adj.* very tiring; exhausting: *The marathon is a grueling contest.* —*n.* an exhausting or very tiring experience.

grue some (grü′səm), *adj.* causing fear or horror; horrible; revolting. Also, **grewsome.** [Middle English *gruen* to shudder] —**grue′some ly,** *adv.* —**grue′someness,** *n.*

gruff (gruf), *adj.* 1 deep and harsh; hoarse: *a gruff voice.* 2 rough, rude, or unfriendly; bad-tempered: *a gruff manner.* [< Dutch *grof*] —**gruff′ly,** *adv.* —**gruff′ness,** *n.*

grum ble (grum′bəl), *v.,* **-bled, -bling,** *n.* —*v.i.* 1 mutter in discontent; complain in a bad-tempered way; find fault. See **complain** for synonym study. 2 make a low, heavy sound like far-off thunder; rumble. —*v.t.* express by grumbling. —*n.* 1 a mutter of discontent; bad-tempered complaint. 2 a rumble. [perhaps < Middle Dutch *grommelen*] —**grum′bler,** *n.*

grump (grump), *v.i.* to sulk. —*n.* a grumpy person. [imitative]

grump y (grum′pē), *adj.,* **grump i er, grump i est.** surly; ill-humored; gruff: *Grumpy people find fault with everything.* —**grump′i ly,** *adv.* —**grump′i ness,** *n.*

Grun dy (grun′dē), *n.* Usually, **Mrs. Grundy.** person who supervises the manners and morals of others; social censorship personified. [< a person referred to with the question "What will Mrs. Grundy say?" in the play *Speed the Plough* by the English dramatist Thomas Morton, 1764-1838]

grun ion (grun′yən), *n.* a small fish, one of the silversides, found along the coast of southern California. [< American Spanish *gruñón*]

grunt (grunt), *n.* 1 the deep, hoarse sound that a hog makes. 2 sound like this: *I lifted the barbell with a grunt.* 3 any of a family of edible sea fishes that grunt when taken out of the water. 4 SLANG. soldier or marine who fights at the front; infantryman. —*v.i.* make the deep, hoarse sound of a hog. —*v.t.* say with this sound: *The sullen girl grunted her apology.* [Old English *grunnettan* < *grunian* to grunt] —**grunt′er,** *n.*

Gru yère (gri yer′, grü yer′), *n.* variety of firm, light-yellow cheese made from whole milk. [< *Gruyère,* district in Switzerland]

gryph on (grif′ən), *n.* griffin.

GSA, General Services Administration.

G-suit (jē′süt′), *n.* suit worn by a pilot or astronaut to counteract the effects of forces greater than the force of gravity and to prevent blackout. [< *g(ravity) suit*]

GSUSA, Girl Scouts of the United States of America.

gt., 1 drop [for Latin *gutta*]. 2 great.

Gt. Br. or **Gt. Brit.,** Great Britain.

Gua da la ja ra (gwä′dl ə här′ə), *n.* city in W central Mexico. 1,196,000.

Gua dal ca nal (gwä′dl kə nal′), *n.* one of the Solomon Islands in the W Pacific. The Japanese were defeated there by United States forces in 1942 and 1943. 18,000 pop.; 2500 sq. mi.

Gua dal quiv ir River (gwä′dl kwiv′ər; *Spanish* gwä′ᴛʜäl kē vir′), river flowing from S Spain into the Atlantic. 374 mi.

Gua de loupe (gwä′dl üp′), *n.* two islands in the West Indies which, with dependent islands, constitute an overseas department of France. 313,000 pop.; 657 sq. mi. *Capital:* Basse-Terre.

Guam (gwäm), *n.* island in the W Pacific, east of the Philippines, belonging to the United States. 87,000 pop.; 209 sq. mi. *Capital:* Agaña.

gua na co (gwä nä′kō), *n., pl.* **-cos, -co.** a wild South American mammal, of the same family as the camel, which is similar in size and appearance to the llama. [< Spanish < Quechua *huanacu*]

gua nine (gwä′nēn′, gwä′nən), *n.* substance present in nucleic acid in cells. It is one of the purine bases of DNA and RNA. *Formula:* $C_5H_5N_5O$ [< *guano,* a source of this substance]

gua no (gwä′nō), *n., pl.* **-nos.** 1 waste matter from sea birds or bats, used as a fertilizer. Guano from sea birds is found especially on islands near Peru. 2 any comparable fertilizer, such as one made from fish. [< Spanish < Quechua *huanu* dung]

Guan tá na mo Bay (gwän tä′nə mō), inlet of the Caribbean Sea in SE Cuba, site of a United States naval base.

Gua ra ni (gwä′rä nē′), *n., pl.* **-ni** or **-nis** for 1, **-nis** or **-nies** for 3. 1 member of a group of Indian tribes of central South America. 2 language of these tribes, belonging to the Tupi-Guarani family of languages. 3 **guarani,** the monetary unit of Paraguay, a note equal to 100 centimos and worth about $^4/_5$ of a cent.

guar an tee (gar′ən tē′), *n., v.,* **-teed, -tee ing.** —*n.* 1 a promise or pledge to replace or repair a purchased product, return the money paid, etc., if the product is not as represented: *We have a one-year guarantee on our new car.* 2 guaranty. 3 guarantor. 4 person to whom a guarantee is given. 5 something having the force or effect of a guaranty: *Wealth is no guarantee of happiness.* —*v.t.* 1 stand back of; give a guarantee for: *This company guarantees its clocks for a year.* 2 undertake to secure for another: *The landlady will guarantee us possession of the house by May.* 3 make secure; protect: *Her insurance guaranteed her against money loss in case of fire.* 4 promise (to do something); pledge that (something) has been or will be: *The salesman guaranteed to prove every statement he made. Wealth does not guarantee happiness.* [probably variant of *guaranty*]

guar an tor (gar′ən tôr, gar′ən tər), *n.* person who makes or gives a guarantee or guaranty.

guar an ty (gar′ən tē), *n., pl.* **-ties,** *v.,* **-tied, -ty ing.** —*n.* 1 a pledge or promise by which a person gives security for the payment of a debt or the performance of an obligation by another person; guarantee. 2 property, money, or goods given or taken as security. 3 act or fact of giving security. 4 guarantor. —*v.t.* guarantee. [< Anglo-French *guarantie* < *guarantir* to warrant < Old French *guarant* a warrant; of Germanic origin. Doublet of WARRANTY.]

guard (gärd), *v.t.* 1 keep safe; watch over carefully; defend; protect. See synonym study below. 2 keep in check; prevent from getting out; hold back: *Guard the prisoners.* 3 try to keep (an opponent) from scoring. —*v.i.* take precautions: *guard against errors.* —*n.* 1 person or group that guards; defender; protector. A soldier or group of soldiers guarding a person or place is a guard. 2 anything that gives protection; contrivance or appliance to protect against injury, loss, etc. 3 careful watch: *The watchdog kept guard over the house.* 4 defense; protection. 5 position of defense in boxing, fencing, or cricket. 6 arms or weapons held in a position of defense. 7 person who opens and closes the doors or gates on a train; brakeman. 8 BRITISH. conductor of a railroad train, streetcar, etc. 9 an offensive player at either side of the center in football. 10 player stationed near the center of the court in basketball. 11 **guards,** *pl.* certain groups of soldiers in the British army, especially those attached to the royal household. 12 **off guard** or **off one's guard,** unprepared to meet a sudden attack; unwary. 13 **on guard** or **on one's guard,** ready to defend or protect; watchful.
[< Old French *garde* a guard < *garder, guarder* to guard; of Germanic origin. Related to WARD.] —**guard′er,** *n.*

Syn. *v.t.* 1 **Guard, defend, protect** mean to keep safe. **Guard** implies watching over carefully: *The dog guarded the child night and day.* **Defend** implies resisting danger or attack: *She defended her little brother against the bully.* **Protect** implies warding off danger or harm: *Proper food protects a person's health.*

guard cell, one of the two specialized kidney-shaped cells of the plant epidermis that control the size of the stomata by expanding and contracting.

guard ed (gär′did), *adj.* 1 kept safe; carefully watched over; defended; protected. 2 careful; cautious: *"Maybe" was his guarded answer to my question.* **—guard′ed ly,** *adv.* **—guard′ed ness,** *n.*

guard hair, the long, coarse hair in the fur of a mammal.

guard house (gärd′hous′), *n., pl.* **-hous es** (-hou′ziz). 1 building used by soldiers on guard. 2 building used as a jail for soldiers.

guard i an (gär′dē ən), *n.* 1 person or thing that guards; protector; defender. 2 person appointed by law to take care of the affairs of someone who is young or cannot take care of them himself; trustee; warden; keeper; guard. *—adj.* protecting: *a guardian angel.*

guard i an ship (gär′dē ən ship), *n.* position or care of a guardian.

guard of honor, honor guard.

guard rail (gärd′rāl′), *n.* rail or railing for protection, such as at the side of a highway or staircase.

guard room (gärd′rüm′, gärd′rům′), *n.* 1 room used by soldiers on guard. 2 room used as a jail for soldiers.

guards man (gärdz′mən), *n., pl.* **-men.** 1 guard. 2 soldier who belongs to the National Guard.

Gua te ma la (gwä′tə mä′lə), *n.* country in NW Central America. 5,400,000 pop.; 42,000 sq. mi. *Capital:* Guatemala City. **—Gua′te ma′lan,** *adj., n.*

Guatemala City, capital of Guatemala, in the central part. 769,000.

gua va (gwä′və), *n.* 1 a tropical American tree or shrub of the myrtle family, with a yellow or red, round or pear-shaped fruit. 2 its fruit, used for jelly, jam, etc. [< Spanish *guayaba;* of Arawakan origin]

Guay a quil (gwī′ə kēl′), *n.* seaport in W Ecuador. 836,000.

gua yu le (gwä yü′lē), *n.* a small shrub of the composite family growing in the Mexican desert and cultivated in California, Texas, and Arizona. Rubber is obtained from its juice. [< Mexican Spanish < Nahuatl *cuauhuli*]

gu ber na to ri al (gü′bər nə tôr′ē əl, gü′-bər nə tōr′ē əl; gyü′bər nə tôr′ē əl, gyü′bər-nə tōr′ē əl), *adj.* of a governor; having to do with a governor. [< Latin *gubernator* governor, originally, pilot < *gubernare* govern, pilot]

guck (guk), *n.* INFORMAL. 1 a slimy substance: *pour red guck on the salad, clean the guck out of the gutters.* 2 anything unpleasant, especially something unappetizing: *serve guck to the passengers for lunch.* 3 something left over and useless; waste: *The astronauts released the guck into outer space.* [perhaps a blend of *goo* and *muck*]

gudg eon (guj′ən), *n.* 1 a small Eurasian freshwater fish of the same family as the carp, that is easy to catch and is often used for bait. 2 any of several other small fishes. [< Old French *goujon,* ultimately < Latin *gobius* < Greek *kōbios*]

Guelph or **Guelf** (gwelf), *n.* member of a political party that supported the popes in their struggle with the emperors of the Holy Roman Empire in medieval Italy. The Guelphs opposed the Ghibellines.

gue non (gə non′; *French* gə nôN′), *n.* any of various long-tailed monkeys of Africa. [< French]

guer don (gėrd′n), *n., v.t.* reward. [< Old French *guerdoner* to reward < *guerdon* a reward < Old High German *widarlōn* repayment]

gue ril la (gə ril′ə), *n.* guerrilla.

Guern sey (gėrn′zē), *n., pl.* **-seys** for 2. 1 one of the Channel Islands. 46,000 pop.; 25 sq. mi. 2 one of a breed of tan-and-white dairy cattle which give rich, cream-colored milk. Guernseys originally came from this island.

guer ril la (gə ril′ə), *n.* member of a band of fighters who harass the enemy by sudden raids, ambushes, the plundering of supply trains, etc. Guerrillas are not part of a regular army. *—adj.* of or by guerrillas: *a guerrilla attack.* Also, **guerilla.** [< Spanish, diminutive of *guerra* war; of Germanic origin]

guess (ges), *v.t.* 1 form an opinion of without really knowing: *guess the height of a tree.* See synonym study below. 2 get right or find out by guessing: *guess the answer to a riddle.* 3 think; believe; suppose: *I guess she is really sick after all.* *—v.i.* form an opinion without really knowing: *Do you know this or are you just guessing? We guessed at her weight.* *—n.* 1 opinion formed without really knowing. 2 a guessing. [Middle English *gessen,* probably < Scandinavian (Middle Danish) *getse*] **—guess′er,** *n.*

Syn. *v.t.* 1 **Guess, conjecture, surmise** mean form or express an opinion without knowing enough. **Guess** suggests forming an opinion on the basis of what one thinks likely, without really knowing for certain: *I guessed the distance to the nearest town.* **Conjecture** suggests having some evidence, but not enough for proof: *The scholars conjectured that the poem had once existed in a longer form.* **Surmise** suggests having little or no evidence beyond what one merely suspects: *Were you able to surmise her thoughts?*

guess ti mate (*n.* ges′tə mit, ges′tə māt; *v.* ges′tə māt), *n., v.,* **-mat ed, -mat ing.** INFORMAL. *—n.* an estimate based on conjecture. *—v.i.* make a guesstimate. *—v.t.* to estimate by conjecture. [blend of *guess* and *estimate*]

guess work (ges′wėrk′), *n.* work, action, or results based on guessing; guessing.

guest (gest), *n.* 1 person who is received and entertained at another's home, club, etc.; visitor. See **visitor** for synonym study. 2 person staying at a hotel, motel, boarding house, etc. 3 person invited to one of a series of programs, concerts, lectures, etc., for a single appearance or performance. 4 animal, especially an insect, that lives in the nests of other animals. *—adj.* 1 of or for guests: *a guest room, guest towels.* 2 being a guest: *a guest conductor.* *—v.i.* be a guest; appear or perform as a guest: *to guest on a TV show.* [< Scandinavian (Old Icelandic) *gestr*]

guest-star (gest′stär′), *v.i.,* **-starred, -star ring.** be a guest star; perform a leading part on a show as a guest.

guff (guf), *n.* SLANG. 1 empty talk; nonsense: *a paragraph of irrelevant guff.* 2 back talk; lip: *take no guff from anyone. Don't give me any more of your guff.* [imitative]

guf faw (gu fô′), *n.* burst of loud, coarse laughter. *—v.i.* laugh loudly and coarsely. [imitative]

Gui a na (gē ä′nə, gē an′ə), *n.* region in N South America, divided into Guyana, Surinam, and French Guiana. **—Gui a′nan,** *adj., n.*

guid ance (gīd′ns), *n.* 1 a guiding; leadership; direction: *Under my mother's guidance, I learned how to swim.* 2 thing that guides. 3 studies and counseling given to students to help them solve their problems, plan their education, and choose careers. 4 regulation of the path of an unmanned aircraft, rocket, or other missile in flight by means of radar, computers, radio signals, etc.

guide (gīd), *v.,* **guid ed, guid ing,** *n.* *—v.t.* 1 show the way; lead; direct. See synonym study below. 2 direct the movement or course of: *guide a ship through a storm.* 3 direct in any course of action: *guide someone in the choice of a career.* *—v.i.* act as a guide. *—n.* 1 person or thing that shows the way, leads, or directs; leader; director: *Tourists and hunters sometimes hire guides.* 2 part of a machine for directing or regulating motion or action. 3 guidebook. 4 guidepost. 5 something which marks a position or serves to guide the eye. [< Middle French *guider;* of Germanic origin] **—guid′a ble,** *adj.* **—guid′er,** *n.*

Syn. *v.t.* 1 **Guide, lead, conduct** mean to show the way. **Guide** implies continued direction by one who knows the course: *The Indian scout guided the explorers through the mountain pass.* **Lead** implies showing the way by going in advance: *The dog led his master to the injured man.* **Conduct** implies leading or escorting someone to a place: *She conducted the speaker to the platform.*

guide book (gīd′bůk′), *n.* book of directions and information, especially one for travelers, tourists, etc.

guided missile, missile that can be guided in flight to its target by means of radio signals from the ground or by automatic devices inside the missile which direct its course.

guide line (gīd′līn′), *n.* Usually, **guidelines,** *pl.* guide, principle, or policy for determining a future course of action: *adopt new guidelines for the national defense.*

guide post (gīd′pōst′), *n.* 1 post with signs and directions on it. A guidepost where roads meet tells travelers what places each road goes to and how far it is to each place. 2 anything that serves as a guide; guideline.

guide word, word put at the top of a page as a guide to the contents of the page; catchword. The guide words for these two pages are *guard hair* and *gum.*

gui don (gīd′n, gī′don), *n.* 1 a small flag or streamer carried as a guide by soldiers, or used for signaling. 2 flag, streamer, or pennant of a company, regiment, etc. 3 soldier who carries the guidon. [< Italian *guidone* < *guidare* to direct]

guild (gild), *n.* 1 association or society formed by people having the same interests, work, etc., for some useful or common purpose: *the hospital guild of a church.* 2 (in the Middle Ages) an association of merchants in a town or of persons in a particular trade or craft, formed to keep standards high, promote their business interests, protect themselves, etc. Also, **gild.** [< Scandinavian (Old Icelandic) *gildi*]

guil der (gil′dər), *n.* 1 the monetary unit of the Netherlands equal to 100 Netherlands cents and worth about 31 U.S. cents. 2 a silver coin having this value; gulden. [alteration of *gulden*]

guild hall (gild′hôl′), *n.* 1 hall in which a guild meets. 2 BRITISH. a town hall or city hall.

guilds man (gildz′mən), *n., pl.* **-men.** member of a guild.

guile (gīl), *n.* crafty deceit; sly tricks; cunning: *By guile the fox got the cheese from the crow.* See **deceit** for synonym study. [< Old

hat, āge, fär; let, ēqual, tėrm;
it, īce; hot, ōpen, ôrder;
oil, out; cup, pu̇t, rüle;
ch, child; ng, long; sh, she;
th, thin; ᴛʜ, then; zh, measure;

ə represents *a* in about, *e* in taken, *i* in pencil, *o* in lemon, *u* in circus.

< = from, derived from, taken from.

French; of Germanic origin. Related to WILE.]

guile ful (gīl′fəl), *adj.* crafty and deceitful; sly and tricky. **—guile′ful ly,** *adv.* **—guile′ful ness,** *n.*

guile less (gīl′lis), *adj.* without guile; honest; frank; straightforward. **—guile′less ly,** *adv.* **—guile′less ness,** *n.*

guil le mot (gil′ə mot), *n.* any of a genus of arctic diving birds of the same family as the auks, with narrow, pointed bills. [< French < *Guillaume* William]

guil lo tine (*n.* gil′ə tēn′; *v.* gil′ə tēn′), *n., v.,* **-tined, -tin ing.** *—n.* machine for beheading people by means of a heavy blade that slides down between two grooved posts. It was used during the French Revolution. *—v.t.* behead with a guillotine. [< French < Joseph I. *Guillotin,* 1738-1814, French physician who proposed its use]

guilt (gilt), *n.* 1 fact or condition of having done wrong; being guilty; being to blame. 2 guilty action or conduct; crime; offense; wrongdoing. 3 a feeling of having done wrong or being to blame. [Old English *gylt* offense]

guilt less (gilt′lis), *adj.* free from guilt; not guilty; innocent. See **innocent** for synonym study.

guilt y (gil′tē), *adj.,* **guilt i er, guilt i est.** 1 having done wrong; deserving to be blamed and punished: *The jury pronounced the prisoner guilty of theft.* 2 knowing or showing that one has done wrong: *The one who committed the crime had a guilty conscience and a guilty look.* **—guilt′i ly,** *adv.* **—guilt′i ness,** *n.*

guimpe (gimp, gamp), *n.* blouse worn under a dress or jumper and showing at the neck or at the neck and arms. A guimpe is usually worn with a low-necked dress. [< French]

guin ea (gin′ē), *n.* 1 a British gold coin, not made since 1813, worth 21 shillings. 2 amount equal to 21 shillings, formerly used in Great Britain in stating prices, fees, etc. [< *Guinea,* because the coins were originally made of gold from Guinea]

Guin ea (gin′ē), *n.* 1 country in W Africa on the Atlantic. 3,920,000 pop.; 95,200 sq. mi. *Capital:* Conakry. 2 **Gulf of,** large gulf of the Atlantic in W Africa. **—Guin′e an,** *adj., n.*

guinea fowl
about 1½ ft. long

guinea fowl, any of a family of plump birds native to Africa, especially a domesticated species having dark-gray feathers with small, white spots. Its flesh and its eggs are eaten.

guinea hen, 1 guinea fowl. 2 a female guinea fowl.

guinea pig, 1 a small, plump, harmless rodent with short ears and a short tail or no tail, a domesticated cavy. Guinea pigs make good pets and are often used for laboratory experiments. 2 any person or thing serving as a subject for experiment or observation.

Guin e vere (gwin′ə vir), *n.* (in Arthurian legends) King Arthur's queen, who was loved by Lancelot.

guise (gīz), *n.* 1 style of dress; garb: *The spy went in the guise of a monk and was not recognized by the enemy.* 2 outward appearance; aspect; semblance: *Her theory is nothing but an old idea in a new guise.* 3 assumed appearance; pretense: *Under the guise of friendship he plotted treachery.* [< Old French; of Germanic origin. Related to WISE².]

guillotine

Guise (gēz), *n.* 1 **Duke of,** 1519-1563, François de Lorraine, French general. 2 **Duke of,** 1550-1588, Henri de Lorraine, French general who opposed the Huguenots.

gui tar (gə tär′), *n.* a musical instrument usually having six strings, played with the fingers or with a pick. [< French *guitare* < Spanish *guitarra* < Greek *kithara* cithara. Doublet of CITHARA, ZITHER.]

Gui zot (gē zō′), *n.* **François,** 1787-1874, French historian and statesman.

Guj a rat or **Guj e rat** (gu̇j′ə rät′), *n.* state in W India.

Guj a ra ti or **Guj e ra ti** (gu̇j′ə rä′tē), *n.* the Indic language of Gujarat and adjoining parts of India.

gu lar (gyü′lər), *adj.* of, having to do with, or situated on the throat. [< Latin *gula* throat]

gulch (gulch), *n.* a very deep, narrow ravine with steep sides, especially one marking the course of a stream or torrent. [origin uncertain]

gul den (gu̇l′dən), *n., pl.* **-dens** or **-den.** guilder. [< Dutch and German, literally, golden (coin)]

gules (gyülz), *n., adj.* (in heraldry) red. [< Old French *gueules,* earlier *goules* red fur neckpiece]

gulf (gulf), *n.* 1 a large bay; arm of an ocean or sea extending into the land. 2 a very deep break or cut in the earth; chasm. 3 separation too great to be closed; wide gap: *The quarrel created a gulf between the old friends.* 4 something that swallows up; whirlpool. [< Old French *golfe* < Italian *golfo,* ultimately < Greek *kolpos,* originally, bosom] **—gulf′like′,** *adj.*

Gulf States, Texas, Louisiana, Mississippi, Alabama, and Florida, the states bordering on the Gulf of Mexico.

Gulf Stream, current of warm water in the Atlantic. It flows out of the Gulf of Mexico, north along the E coast of the United States, and then northeast across the Atlantic toward the British Isles. 50 mi. wide.

guinea pig (def. 1)
about 6 in. long

gulf weed (gulf′wēd′), *n.* an olive-brown seaweed having many berrylike sacs that keep it afloat.

gull¹ (gul), *n.* any of a family of graceful, gray-and-white birds with long wings, webbed feet, and thick, strong beaks, which live on or near large bodies of water. [Middle English, probably < Celtic (Cornish) *guilan*]

gull² (gul), *v.t.* deceive; cheat. *—n.* person who is easily deceived or cheated. [origin uncertain]

Gul lah (gul′ə), *n.* 1 one of a group of Negroes living along the coast of South Carolina and Georgia, and on the islands off the coast. 2 dialect of English spoken by the Gullahs.

guitar

gul let (gul′it), *n.* 1 esophagus. 2 throat. [< Old French *goulet,* ultimately < Latin *gula* throat]

gul li bil i ty (gul′ə bil′ə tē), *n.* a being gullible; tendency to be easily deceived or cheated.

gul li ble (gul′ə bəl), *adj.* easily deceived or cheated. [< *gull²*] **—gul′li bly,** *adv.*

Gul li ver (gul′ə vər), *n.* **Lemuel,** hero of voyages to four imaginary regions in Jonathan Swift's satire *Gulliver's Travels.*

gul ly (gul′ē), *n., pl.* **-lies,** *v.,* **-lied, -ly ing.** *—n.* a narrow gorge; small ravine; ditch made by heavy rains or running water. *—v.t.* make gullies in. [probably variant of *gullet*]

gulp (gulp), *v.t.* 1 swallow eagerly or greedily. 2 keep in; choke back: *The disappointed boy gulped down a sob.* *—v.i.* gasp or choke: *The spray of cold water made me gulp.* *—n.* 1 act of swallowing. 2 amount swallowed at one time; mouthful. [imitative] **—gulp′er,** *n.*

gum¹ (gum), *n., v.,* **gummed, gum ming.** *—n.* 1 a sticky juice given off by certain trees and plants that hardens in the air and dissolves in water. Gum is used to make mucilage, candy, drugs, etc. 2 any similar secretion, such as resin, gum resin, etc. 3 preparation of such a substance for use in industry or the arts. 4 gum tree. 5 gumwood. 6 chewing gum. 7 the sticky substance on the back of a stamp, the flap of an envelope, etc.; mucilage. 8 rubber. 9 **gums,** *pl.* rubber overshoes.
—v.t. 1 smear, stick together, or stiffen with gum. 2 make sticky; clog with something sticky. 3 **gum up,** SLANG. mess up; put out of order. *—v.i.* 1 give off gum; form gum. 2 become sticky; become clogged with something sticky.
[< Old French *gomme* < Latin *gummi* < Greek *kommi*] **—gum′like′,** *adj.*

gum² (gum), *n.* Often, **gums,** *pl.* the firm

flesh around the teeth. [Old English *gōma* palate]

gum am mo ni ac (ə mō′nē ak), gum resin used for medicines and as a cement for porcelain.

gum arabic, gum obtained from acacia trees, used in making candy, medicine, and mucilage.

gum bo (gum′bō), *n., pl.* **-bos.** 1 the okra plant. 2 its sticky pods. 3 soup usually made of chicken and rice and thickened with these pods. 4 kind of fine soil that contains much silt and becomes very sticky when wet. [< a Bantu dialect]

gum boil (gum′boil′), *n.* a small abscess on the gums.

gum drop (gum′drop′), *n.* a stiff, jellylike piece of candy made of gum arabic, gelatin, etc., sweetened and flavored.

gum my (gum′ē), *adj.,* **-mi er, -mi est.** 1 sticky like gum. 2 covered with gum. 3 giving off gum. **—gum′mi ness,** *n.*

gump tion (gump′shən), *n.* INFORMAL. 1 lively initiative; energy; resourcefulness. 2 common sense; good judgment. [origin uncertain]

gum resin, a natural mixture of gum and resin, obtained from or given off by certain plants. Asafetida and myrrh are gum resins.

gum shoe (gum′shü′), *n., v.,* **-shoed, -shoe ing.** *—n.* 1 a rubber overshoe. 2 **gumshoes,** *pl.* sneakers. 3 SLANG. detective. *—v.i.* SLANG. go around quietly and secretly.

gum tragacanth, tragacanth.

gum tree, 1 any of various trees of several families that yield gum, such as the sweet gum, sour gum, and eucalyptus. 2 eucalyptus.

gum wood (gum′wu̇d′), *n.* wood of a gum tree.

gun (gun), *n., v.,* **gunned, gun ning.** *—n.* 1 weapon with a metal tube for shooting bullets, shot, etc. A rifle or cannon is a gun. Pistols and revolvers are called guns in ordinary speech. 2 anything resembling a gun in use or shape. 3 the shooting of a gun as a signal or salute. 4 the throttle of an aircraft, automobile, etc. 5 an expert in using a gun.
big gun, INFORMAL. an important person.
go great guns, INFORMAL. move vigorously or successfully ahead; advance at full speed: *The team was going great guns in the second half of the game.*
jump the gun, a start too soon; start before the signal to do so. b get a head start on one's opposition.
spike one's guns, make one powerless; frustrate one's plans.
stick to one's guns, keep one's position; refuse to retreat or yield.
—v.i. 1 shoot with a gun; hunt with a gun: *He went gunning for rabbits.* 2 speed; accelerate: *The driver gunned away home. The motorcycle gunned through the streets.* *—v.t.* 1 shoot at with a gun; kill or wound with a gun. 2 put at high speed; accelerate: *The pilot gunned the engine for a sharp climb.*
[< Scandinavian *Gunna,* short for *Gunnhildr,* woman's name]

gun boat (gun′bōt′), *n.* a small warship that can be used in shallow water.

gunboat diplomacy, the ready use by a country of its military power to enforce diplomatic agreements with other countries.

gun cot ton (gun′kot′n), *n.* an explosive made by treating cotton or other cellulose fibers with a mixture of nitric and sulfuric acids.

gun fight (gun′fīt′), *n.* fight in which guns are used.

gun fight er (gun′fī′tər), *n.* person who engages in gunfights.

gun fire (gun′fīr′), *n.* the shooting of a gun or guns.

gung-ho (gung′hō′), *adj.* INFORMAL. eager; enthusiastic. [< Chinese, work together]

gunk (gungk), *n.* INFORMAL. an unpleasantly sticky mess. [probably imitative]

gun lock (gun′lok′), *n.* the part of a gun that controls the hammer and fires the charge.

gun man (gun′mən), *n., pl.* **-men.** man who uses a gun to rob or kill.

gun met al (gun′met′l), *n.* 1 a dark-gray alloy used for chains, buckles, handles, etc. 2 a dark gray. 3 kind of bronze formerly used for making guns.

gun nel[1] (gun′l), *n.* gunwale.

gun nel[2] (gun′l), *n.* any of a genus of small, eel-shaped fishes, especially a species found in the northern Atlantic. [origin uncertain]

gun ner (gun′ər), *n.* 1 man trained to fire artillery; soldier who handles and fires cannon. 2 (in the U.S. Navy) a warrant officer in charge of a ship's guns. 3 person who hunts with a gun.

gun ner y (gun′ər ē), *n.* 1 the construction and management of large guns. 2 use of guns; shooting of guns. 3 guns collectively.

gun ning (gun′ing), *n.* hunting with a gun.

gun ny (gun′ē), *n., pl.* **-nies.** 1 a strong, coarse fabric made of jute, used for sacks, bags, etc. 2 gunnysack. [< Hindustani *gōnī*]

gun ny sack (gun′ē sak′), *n.* sack, bag, etc., made of gunny.

gun point (gun′point′), *n.* 1 the tip or point of a gun barrel. 2 **at gunpoint,** being threatened by a gun; with a gun pointed at one.

gun pow der (gun′pou′dər), *n.* powder that explodes when brought into contact with fire, used in guns, fireworks, and blasting. Modern gunpowder is made of saltpeter, sulfur, and charcoal.

gun run ning (gun′run′ing), *n.* the bringing of guns and ammunition into a country illegally.

gun ship (gun′ship′), *n.* an armed helicopter.

gun shot (gun′shot′), *n.* 1 shot fired from a gun. 2 the shooting of a gun. 3 distance that a gun will shoot: *The deer was within gunshot.*

gun-shy (gun′shī′), *adj.* 1 afraid of the sound of a gun. 2 suspicious; wary.

gun smith (gun′smith′), *n.* person whose work is making or repairing small guns.

gun stock (gun′stok′), *n.* the wooden support or handle to which the barrel of a gun is fastened.

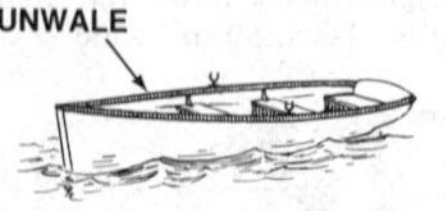

gun wale (gun′l), *n.* the upper edge of the side of a ship or boat. Also, **gunnel.** [< *gun* + *wale* a plank; because formerly used to support the guns]

gup py (gup′ē), *n., pl.* **-pies.** a very small, brightly colored fish of tropical fresh water, often kept in aquariums. The female bears live young instead of laying eggs. [< Robert J. L. *Guppy,* British scientist of the 1800's, who supplied the first specimens for public viewing]

Gup ta (gup′tə), *n.* member of a Hindu dynasty that ruled India from the A.D. 300's to 500's. The reign of the Guptas is sometimes called the golden age of Hindu culture.

gur gle (gėr′gəl), *v.,* **-gled, -gling,** *n.* *—v.i.* 1 flow or run with a bubbling sound: *Water gurgles when it is poured out of a bottle.* 2 make a bubbling sound: *The baby gurgled happily.* *—v.t.* express with a gurgle. *—n.* a bubbling sound. [perhaps imitative]

Gur kha (gu̇r′kə), *n.* member of a Nepalese Hindu people famous as soldiers.

gur nard (gėr′nərd), *n., pl.* **-nards** or **-nard.** any of various sea fishes with spiny fins, bony plates on the head, and three fingerlike feelers on the pectoral fins. [< Old French *gornart*]

gu ru (gü′rü, gu̇ rü′), *n.* 1 a religious teacher or guide in Hinduism. 2 any spiritual leader or guide. 3 any leader, as in the political, literary, or musical field. [< Hindustani *gurū*]

gush (gush), *v.i.* 1 rush out suddenly; pour out: *Oil gushed from the new well.* See **flow** for synonym study. 2 INFORMAL. talk in a way that shows too much silly or sentimental feeling: *All the children gushed about the new puppy.* *—v.t.* give forth suddenly or very freely: *The wound gushed blood.* *—n.* 1 rush of water or other liquid from an enclosed place: *If you get a deep cut, there is usually a gush of blood.* 2 INFORMAL. talk that shows too much silly or sentimental feeling. [probably imitative]

gush er (gush′ər), *n.* 1 an oil well which gives oil in large quantities without pumping. 2 INFORMAL. a gushy person.

gush ing (gush′ing), *adj.* 1 that gushes. 2 gushy.

gush y (gush′ē), *adj.,* **gush i er, gush i est.** showing too much silly or sentimental feeling. **—gush′i ness,** *n.*

gus set (gus′it), *n.* 1 a triangular piece of material inserted in a garment to give greater strength or more room. 2 bracket or plate used to reinforce the joints of a structure. [< Old French *gousset* < *gousse* husk]

gus sy (gus′ē), *v.t., v.i.,* **-sied, -sy ing.** SLANG. Usually, **gussy up.** dress up attractively or showily. [origin unknown]

gust (gust), *n.* 1 a sudden, violent rush of wind: *A gust upset the small sailboat.* 2 a sudden burst of rain, smoke, sound, etc. 3 a sudden bursting forth of anger, enthusiasm, or other feeling: *Gusts of laughter greeted the clown.* [< Scandinavian (Old Icelandic) *gustr*]

gus ta tion (gə stā′shən), *n.* 1 act of tasting. 2 ability to taste.

gus ta to ry (gus′tə tôr′ē, gus′tə tōr′ē), *adj.* of the sense of taste; having to do with tasting: *Eating fine foods gives gustatory pleasure.* [< Latin *gustus* taste]

Gus ta vus I (gə stā′vəs, gə stä′vəs), 1496-1560, king of Sweden from 1523 to 1560.

Gustavus II, Gustavus Adolphus.

Gustavus IV, 1778-1837, king of Sweden from 1792 to 1809.

Gustavus V, 1858-1950, king of Sweden from 1907 to 1950.

Gustavus VI, 1882-1973, king of Sweden from 1950 to 1973.

Gustavus A dol phus (ə dol′fəs), 1594-1632, king of Sweden from 1611 to 1632.

gus to (gus′tō), *n., pl.* **-tos.** 1 hearty enjoyment; keen relish: *The hungry girl ate her* *dinner with gusto.* 2 liking or taste. [< Italian and Spanish, taste < Latin *gustus*]

gust y (gus′tē), *adj.*, **gust i er, gust i est.** 1 coming in gusts; windy; stormy. 2 marked by outbursts: *gusty laughter.* **—gust′i ly,** *adv.* **—gust′i ness,** *n.*

gut (gut), *n., adj., v.,* **gut ted, gut ting.** *—n.* 1 the whole alimentary canal or one of its parts, such as the intestines or stomach. 2 **guts,** *pl.* **a** entrails; bowels. **b** SLANG. pluck; courage. 3 catgut. 4 a narrow channel or gully. 5 Usually, **guts,** *pl.* INFORMAL. the essential part or parts: *the guts of a story.* *—adj.* INFORMAL. vital; basic or fundamental: *a gut reaction or experience, gut political issues.* *—v.t.* 1 remove the entrails of; disembowel. 2 destroy the inside of: *Fire gutted the building and left only the brick walls standing.* 3 INFORMAL. remove an essential part of: *to gut a foreign aid program.* [Old English *guttas,* plural]

Gu ten berg (güt′n bėrg′), *n.* **Johann,** 1398?-1468, German printer. He is supposed to have been the first European to print from movable type.

gut less (gut′lis), *adj.* INFORMAL. 1 lacking courage; cowardly. 2 without vitality.

guts i ly (gut′sə lē), *adv.* SLANG. 1 boldly. 2 lustily.

guts y (gut′sē), *adj.*, **guts i er, guts i est.** SLANG. 1 full of guts; bold: *a gutsy fighter.* 2 full of vitality; lusty: *a gutsy singer.* Also, **gutty.**

gut ta-per cha (gut′ə pėr′chə), *n.* substance resembling rubber, made from the thick, milky juice of certain tropical trees of the same family as the sapodilla, used in dentistry, in insulating electric wires, etc. [< Malay *getah percha*]

gut ta tion (gə tā′shən), *n.* loss of water by a plant in the form of droplets, usually from the leaf. [< Latin *gutta* drop]

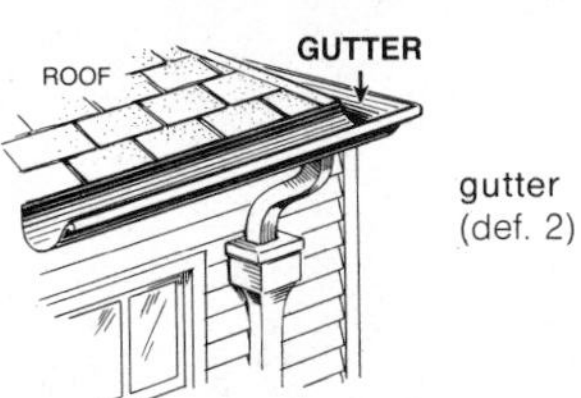

gutter (def. 2)

gut ter (gut′ər), *n.* 1 channel or ditch along the side of a street or road to carry off water; low part of a street beside the sidewalk. 2 channel or trough along the lower edge of a roof to carry off rain water. 3 channel; groove: *the gutters on either side of a bowling alley.* 4 a low, poor, or wretched place: *a child of the gutter.* *—adj.* INFORMAL. 1 base or vulgar. 2 cheap; sensational. *—v.t.* form gutters in; furnish with gutters. *—v.i.* 1 flow or melt in streams: *Water guttered down the side of the hill. The candle guttered so that the melted wax ran down its sides.* 2 become channeled. [< Old French *goutiere,* ultimately < Latin *gutta* drop]

gut ter snipe (gut′ər snīp′), *n.* INFORMAL. 1 urchin who lives in the streets. 2 any ill-bred person.

gut tur al (gut′ər əl), *adj.* 1 of the throat. 2 formed in the throat; harsh: *The visitor from Germany spoke in a deep, guttural voice.* 3 formed between the back of the tongue and the soft palate. The *g* in *go* is a guttural sound. *—n.* sound formed between the back of the tongue and the soft palate. The sound *k* is a guttural in the word *cool.* [< Latin *guttur* throat] **—gut′tur al ly,** *adv.* **—gut′tur al ness,** *n.*

gut ty (gut′ē), *adj.*, **-ti er, -ti est.** SLANG. gutsy.

guy[1] (gī), *n., v.,* **guyed, guy ing.** *—n.* rope, chain, or wire attached to something to steady or secure it. *—v.t.* steady or secure with a guy or guys. [< Old French *guie* < *guier* to guide]

guy[2] (gī), *n., v.,* **guyed, guy ing.** INFORMAL. *—n.* fellow. *—v.t.* make fun of; tease. [< *Guy* Fawkes; his effigy, called a *guy,* was burned each year on November 5, the anniversary of his attempt to blow up Parliament]

Guy an a (gī an′ə), *n.* country in N South America, a member of the Commonwealth of Nations, formerly the colony of British Guiana. 763,000 pop.; 83,000 sq. mi. *Capital:* Georgetown.

Guy a nese (gī′ə nēz′), *adj., n., pl.* **-nese.** *—adj.* of or having to do with Guyana or its people. *—n.* native or inhabitant of Guyana.

guy ot (gē ō′), *n.* seamount. [< Arnold *Guyot,* 1807-1884, Swiss-American geologist]

guz zle (guz′əl), *v.t., v.i.,* **-zled, -zling.** drink or eat greedily; drink or eat too much: *guzzle soda, guzzle sardines and bananas.* [probably < Old French *gosiller* to vomit] **—guz′zler,** *n.*

gym (jim), *n.* INFORMAL. gymnasium.

gym kha na (jim kä′nə), *n.* a sports contest or meet. [alteration (influenced by *gymnastic*) of Hindustani *gend-khāna* racket court, ball house]

gym na si um (jim nā′zē əm), *n., pl.* **-si ums, -si a** (-zē ə). room, building, etc., fitted up for physical exercise or training and for indoor athletic sports. [< Latin, gymnastic school, school < Greek *gymnasion* < *gymnazein* to exercise (naked) < *gymnos* naked]

Gym na si um (jim nā′zē əm; *German* gim nä′zē ům), *n.* a secondary school in Germany and certain other European countries that prepares students for the universities.

gym nast (jim′nast), *n.* an expert in gymnastics.

gym nas tic (jim nas′tik), *adj.* having to do with physical exercise or activities. **—gym nas′ti cal ly,** *adv.*

gym nas tics (jim nas′tiks), *n.pl.* exercises for developing the muscles and improving physical fitness and health, such as are done in a gymnasium.

gym no sperm (jim′nə spėrm′), *n.* any of a subdivision of plants of the spermatophyte division, having the seeds exposed, not enclosed in an ovary or fruit. The pine, fir, and spruce are gymnosperms. [< Greek *gymnospermos* having the seeds exposed < *gymnos* naked + *sperma* seed]

gym no sper mous (jim′nə spėr′məs), *adj.* belonging to the gymnosperms.

gy nan dro morph (ji nan′drə môrf, jī nan′drə môrf), *n.* (in zoology) an organism in which one part or side of the body has male characteristics and the other female characteristics. [< Greek *gynē* woman + *andros* man + *morphē* form]

gy ne co log ic (gī′nə kə loj′ik, jī′nə kə loj′ik, jin′ə kə loj′ik), *adj.* of or having to do with gynecology. **—gy′ne co log′i cal,** *adj.*

gy ne col o gist (gī′nə kol′ə jist, jī′nə kol′ə jist, jin′ə kol′ə jist), *n.* an expert in gynecology.

gy ne col o gy (gī′nə kol′ə jē, jī′nə kol′ə jē, jin′ə kol′ə jē), *n.* branch of medicine that deals with the functions and diseases specific to women, especially those of the reproductive system. [< Greek *gynē, gynaikos* woman + English *-logy*]

hat, āge, fär; let, ēqual, tėrm;
it, īce; hot, ōpen, ôrder;
oil, out; cup, pu̇t, rüle;
ch, child; ng, long; sh, she;
th, thin; ᴛʜ, then; zh, measure;

ə represents *a* in about, *e* in taken, *i* in pencil, *o* in lemon, *u* in circus.

< = from, derived from, taken from.

gy noe ci um (jī nē′sē əm, jə nē′sē əm), *n., pl.* **-ci a** (-sē ə). pistil or pistils of a flower. [< New Latin < Greek *gynē* woman + *oikion* house]

gyp (jip), *v.,* **gypped, gyp ping,** *n.* SLANG. *—v.t.* cheat; swindle. *—n.* 1 a cheating; swindle. 2 person who cheats; swindler. [short for *gypsy*] **—gyp′per,** *n.*

gyp soph i la (jip sof′ə lə), *n.* any of a genus of pinks with many small, fragrant, white or pink flowers on delicate, branching stalks with few leaves. [< New Latin < Greek *gypsos* gypsum + *philos* fond of]

gyp sum (jip′səm), *n.* mineral used to make fertilizer and plaster of Paris; hydrous calcium sulfate. Alabaster is one form of gypsum. *Formula:* $CaSO_4{\cdot}2H_2O$ [< Latin < Greek *gypsos*]

gyp sy (jip′sē), *n., pl.* **-sies,** *adj., v.,* **-sied, -sy ing.** *—n.* 1 Also, **Gypsy.** person belonging to a wandering group of people having dark skin and black hair, who originally came from India. 2 **Gypsy,** language of the gypsies; Romany. 3 person who looks or lives like a gypsy. *—adj.* 1 of gypsies: *gypsy music.* 2 resembling a gypsy. 3 INFORMAL. working independently or illegally: *gypsy truckers.* *—v.i.* live or act like a gypsy. Also, **gipsy.** [ultimately < *Egyptian* (from the belief that gypsies came from Egypt)]

gypsy cab, U.S. taxicab that cruises for fares even though it is licensed only to pick up passengers who call for a cab.

gypsy moth, a brownish or white moth whose larvae damage trees by eating their leaves. Also, **gipsy moth.**

gy rate (jī′rāt, jī rāt′), *v.i.,* **-rat ed, -rat ing.** move in a circle or spiral; whirl; rotate: *A spinning top gyrates.* [< Latin *gyrus* circle < Greek *gyros*] **—gy′ra tor,** *n.*

gy ra tion (jī rā′shən), *n.* circular or spiral motion; whirling; rotation.

gy ra to ry (jī′rə tôr′ē, jī′rə tōr′ē), *adj.* gyrating.

gyr fal con (jėr′fôl′kən, jėr′fal′kən, jėr′fô′kən), *n.* a large falcon of the Arctic which appears in any of several color phases. Also, **gerfalcon.** [< Old French *gerfaucon*]

gyrfalcon
about 2 ft. long

gy ro (jī′rō), *n., pl.* **-ros.** INFORMAL. 1 gyroscope. 2 gyrocompass.

gyro-, *combining form.* circle; spiral, as in *gyroscope.* [< Greek *gyros*]

gy ro com pass (jī′rō kum′pəs), *n.* compass using a motor-driven gyroscope instead of a magnetic needle. It points to true north instead of the North Magnetic Pole and is not affected by nearby objects of iron or steel.

gy ro scope (jī′rə skōp), *n.* instrument consisting of a heavy, rotating wheel or disk mounted so that its axis can turn freely in one or more directions. A spinning gyroscope tends to resist any change in the direction of its axis, no matter which way its base is turned. Gyroscopes are used to keep ships, airplanes, and guided missiles steady.

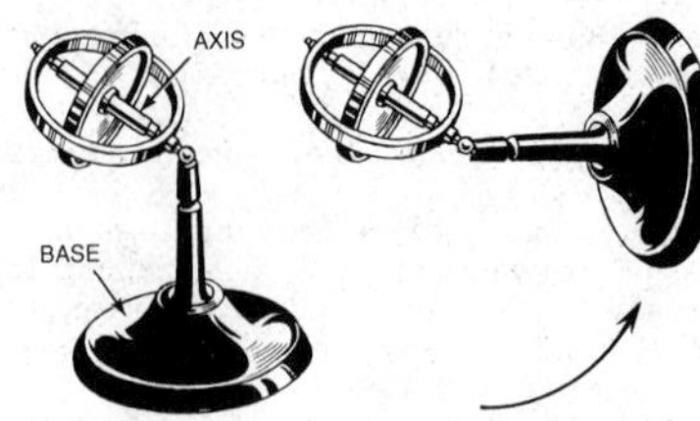

gyroscope
The end of the axis is on a bearing. As the base is moved, the rotating axis stays in the same position.

gy ro scop ic (jī′rə skop′ik), *adj.* having to do with a gyroscope.

gy ro sta bi liz er (jī′rō stā′bə lī′zər), *n.* device that uses a gyroscope for stabilizing a ship, airplane, etc., by counteracting its rolling motion.

gy rus (jī′rəs), *n., pl.* **-ri** (-rī). (in anatomy) a convolution, especially of the brain. [< Latin, circle]

gyve (jīv), *n., v.,* **gyved, gyv ing.** ARCHAIC. —*n.* a shackle, especially for the leg; fetter. —*v.t.* fetter; shackle. [Middle English]

H h

H or **h** (āch), *n., pl.* **H's** or **h's.** the eighth letter of the English alphabet.

H, hydrogen.

h. or **H.,** 1 hard. 2 henry. 3 hour.

ha (hä), *interj.* 1 exclamation of surprise, joy, triumph, suspicion, etc. 2 sound of a laugh or laughter. Also, **hah.**

Haar lem (här′ləm), *n.* city in the W Netherlands, near Amsterdam. 172,000.

Hab ak kuk (hab′ə kuk, hə bak′ək), *n.* 1 a Hebrew prophet and poet, perhaps of the late 600's B.C. 2 book of the Old Testament.

Ha ba na (ä vä′nä), *n.* See **La Habana.**

ha be as cor pus (hā′bē əs kôr′pəs), writ or order requiring that a prisoner be brought before a judge or into court to decide whether he is being held lawfully. The right of habeas corpus is a protection against unjust imprisonment. [< Medieval Latin, you may have the person]

hab er dash er (hab′ər dash′ər), *n.* dealer in the things men wear, such as hats, ties, shirts, socks, etc. [perhaps < Anglo-French *hapertas,* a kind of cloth]

hab er dash er y (hab′ər dash′ər ē), *n., pl.* **-er ies.** 1 store where men's shirts, ties, socks, etc., are sold. 2 articles sold there.

hab er geon (hab′ər jən), *n.* 1 a short coat of mail without sleeves. 2 hauberk. [< Old French *haubergeon,* diminutive of *hauberc.* See HAUBERK.]

ha bil i ment (hə bil′ə mənt), *n.* 1 **habiliments,** *pl.* articles of clothing; garments. 2 dress; attire. [< Old French *habillement* < *abiller* prepare, fit out]

hab it (hab′it), *n.* 1 tendency to act in a certain way or to do a certain thing; usual way of acting; custom; practice. 2 a particular practice, custom, or usage: *the habit of brushing your teeth twice a day.* See **custom** for synonym study. 3 the distinctive dress or costume worn by members of a religious order. Monks and nuns sometimes wear habits. 4 a woman's garment for horseback riding. 5 condition of body or mind: *The runner was of lean habit.* 6 the characteristic form, mode of growth, etc., of an animal or plant: *The honeysuckle has a twining habit.* —*v.t.* put a habit or garment on; dress. [< Old French < Latin *habitus* < *habere* have]

hab it a bil i ty (hab′ə tə bil′ə tē), *n.* a being habitable.

hab it a ble (hab′ə tə bəl), *adj.* fit to live in; able to be inhabited: *make a house habitable.* **—hab′it a ble ness,** *n.* **—hab′it a bly,** *adv.*

hab it ant (hab′ə tənt *for 1;* hab′ə tənt; *French* à bē täɴ′ *for 2*), *n.* 1 inhabitant. 2 farmer of French descent in Canada or Louisiana.

hab i tat (hab′ə tat), *n.* 1 place where an animal or plant naturally lives or grows: *The jungle is the habitat of monkeys.* 2 dwelling place; habitation. [< Latin, it inhabits]

hab i ta tion (hab′ə tā′shən), *n.* 1 place to live in; home; dwelling. 2 an inhabiting.

hab it-form ing (hab′it fôr′ming), *adj.* (of a drug, etc.) causing the user to crave it and depend on it.

ha bit u al (hə bich′ü əl), *adj.* 1 done by habit; caused by habit: *a habitual smile, habitual courtesy.* 2 being or doing something by habit; regular; steady: *a habitual reader.* 3 often done, seen, used, occurring, etc.; usual; customary: *a habitual sight.* **—ha bit′u al ly,** *adv.* **—ha bit′u al ness,** *n.*

ha bit u ate (hə bich′ü āt), *v.t.,* **-at ed, -at ing.** make used; accustom: *The pioneers were habituated to the hardship of frontier life.* **—ha bit′u a′tion,** *n.*

hab i tude (hab′ə tüd, hab′ə tyüd), *n.* 1 characteristic condition of body or mind. 2 habit; custom.

ha bit u é (hə bich′ü ā′), *n.* person who has the habit of going to any place frequently: *a habitué of the theater.* [< French]

Habs burg (haps′bėrg′; *German* häps′bu̇rk), *n.* Hapsburg.

ha chures (hə shu̇rz′, hash′u̇rz), *n.pl.* short lines used as shading to represent the slopes of mountains and hills on maps. [< French *hachure* hatch³]

ha ci en da (hä sē en′də), *n.* in Spanish America: 1 a large ranch or landed estate. 2 the principal dwelling on such a ranch or estate. [< Spanish < Latin *facienda* (things) to be done < *facere* do]

hack¹ (hak), *v.t.* cut roughly or unevenly; deal cutting blows to. See **cut** for synonym study. —*v.i.* 1 make rough or uneven cuts. 2 give frequent, short, dry coughs. —*n.* 1 a rough cut. 2 a cut or notch. 3 a short, dry cough. [Old English *-haccian*] **—hack′er,** *n.*

hack² (hak), *n.* 1 carriage or coach for hire; hackney. 2 INFORMAL. taxicab. 3 horse for hire. 4 an old or worn-out horse. 5 horse for ordinary riding. 6 person hired to do routine work, especially literary work. 7 a plodding, faithful, but undistinguished worker in an organization: *The party hacks got out the vote on election day.* —*adj.* 1 working merely for money; hired; drudging. 2 done merely for money. 3 hackneyed. —*v.i.* 1 INFORMAL. drive a taxicab. 2 ride on horseback over roads. [short for *hackney*]

hack a more (hak′ə môr, hak′ə mōr), *n.* halter, especially one used in breaking horses. [< Spanish *jáquima*]

hack ber ry (hak′ber′ē, hak′bər ē), *n., pl.* **-ries.** 1 any of a genus of North American trees of the same family as the elm that have small, edible, cherrylike fruit. 2 the fruit. 3 wood of any of these trees.

hack le¹ (hak′əl), *n.* 1 one of the long, slender feathers on the neck of a rooster, pigeon, peacock, etc. 2 the neck plumage of any of these birds. 3 **hackles,** *pl.* hairs on the back of a dog's neck that can become erect. 4 **raise the hackles,** INFORMAL. arouse anger; make mad. 5 comb used in splitting and combing out the fibers of flax, hemp, etc. [Middle English *hakell.* Related to HECKLE.]

hack le² (hak′əl), *v.t.,* **-led, -ling.** cut roughly; hack. [< *hack*¹]

hack man (hak′mən), *n., pl.* **-men.** driver of a hack.

hack ma tack (hak′mə tak′), *n.* tamarack. [< Algonquian]

hack ney (hak′nē), *n., pl.* **-neys,** *adj., v.* —*n.* 1 horse for ordinary riding or driving. 2 carriage or coach for hire. —*adj.* 1 hired. 2 hackneyed. —*v.t.* use too often; make commonplace. [Middle English *hakeney* < *Hackney,* a borough of London, formerly a town supposedly famous for its horses]

hack neyed (hak′nēd), *adj.* used too often; commonplace: *"White as snow" is a hackneyed comparison.* See **commonplace** for synonym study.

hat, āge, fär; let, ēqual, tėrm;
it, īce; hot, ōpen, ôrder;
oil, out; cup, pu̇t, rüle;
ch, child; ng, long; sh, she;
th, thin; ᴛʜ, then; zh, measure;

ə represents *a* in about, *e* in taken,
i in pencil, *o* in lemon, *u* in circus.

< = from, derived from, taken from.

hack saw (hak′sô′), *n.* saw for cutting metal, consisting of a narrow, fine-toothed blade fixed in a frame.

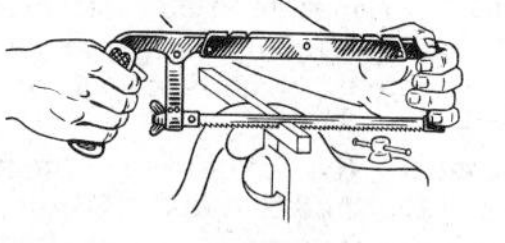
hacksaw

hack work (hak′wėrk′), *n.* tiresome, routine work, especially literary work.

had (had; *unstressed* həd, əd), *v.* pt. and pp. of **have.**

had dock (had′ək), *n., pl.* **-docks** or **-dock.** a food fish of the northern Atlantic, of the same family as and resembling the cod but usually smaller. [Middle English *haddok*]

Ha des (hā′dēz′), *n.* 1 in Greek myths: **a** the home of the dead, a gloomy place below the earth. **b** god of the lower world, identified with the Roman god Pluto. 2 Also, **hades.** INFORMAL. hell.

hadj (haj), *n.* hajj.

had ji (haj′ē), *n.* Moslem who has made the pilgrimage to Mecca. Also, **hajji.** [< Arabic *ḥājjī*]

had n't (had′nt), had not.

Ha dri an (hā′drē ən), *n.* A.D. 76-138, Roman emperor from A.D. 117 to 138.

hadst (hadst), *v.* ARCHAIC. had. "Thou hadst" means "you had."

hae (hā, ha), *v.t.* SCOTTISH. have.

hae mo glo bin (hē′mə glō′bən, hem′ə-glō′bən), *n.* hemoglobin.

haf ni um (haf′nē əm), *n.* a silvery metallic element which occurs in zirconium ores and is used to make filaments for incandescent lamps. *Symbol:* Hf; *atomic number* 72. See pages 326 and 327 for table. [< *Hafnia,* Latin name for Copenhagen]

haft (haft), *n.* handle, especially that of a knife, sword, dagger, etc. —*v.t.* furnish with a handle or hilt; set in a haft. [Old English *hæft*]

hag (hag), *n.* 1 a very ugly old woman, especially one who is vicious or malicious. 2 witch. [Middle English *hagge*]

Ha gar (hā′gär, hā′gər), *n.* (in the Bible) an Egyptian slave of Abraham's wife Sarah. She and her son Ishmael were driven into the desert because of Sarah's jealousy.

hag fish (hag′fish′), *n., pl.* **-fish es** or **-fish.** a small, eel-shaped, saltwater fish that attaches itself to other fish by its round mouth. It belongs to the same class as the lamprey.

Hag ga dah or **Hag ga da** (hə gä′də), *n., pl.* **-doth** (-dōth). 1 story or legend in the Talmud that explains the law. 2 the legendary, nonlegal part of the Talmud. 3 the religious text read at the Seder feast on the first two nights of Passover. [< Hebrew *haggādāh* story]

Hag ga i (hag′ē ī, hag′ī), *n.* 1 a Hebrew prophet who wrote about 520 B.C. 2 book of the Old Testament.

hag gard (hag′ərd), *adj.* looking worn from pain, fatigue, worry, hunger, etc.; careworn; gaunt. [perhaps < Old French *hagard*] **—hag′gard ly,** *adv.* **—hag′gard ness,** *n.*

hag gis (hag′is), *n.* pudding eaten especially in Scotland, made from the heart, lungs, and liver of a sheep or calf, chopped up and mixed with suet, oatmeal, onions, and seasonings and boiled in the stomach of the animal. [Middle English *hagas*]

hag gle (hag′əl), *v.,* **-gled, -gling,** *n.* *—v.i.* dispute, especially about a price or the terms of a bargain. *—v.t.* mangle in cutting; hack. *—n.* act of haggling. [< Scottish *hag* to chop < Scandinavian (Old Icelandic) *höggva*] **—hag′gler,** *n.*

Hag i og ra pha (hag′ē og′rə fə, hā′jē-og′rə fə), *n.pl.* the third and last division of the Biblical canon recognized by the Jews, usually comprising Psalms, Proverbs, Job, Canticles, Ruth, Lamentations, Ecclesiastes, Esther, Daniel, Ezra, Nehemiah, and 1 and 2 Chronicles. [< Late Greek, holy writings]

hag i og ra pher (hag′ē og′rə fər, hā′jē-og′rə fər), *n.* writer of lives of the saints or on sacred subjects.

hag i og ra phy (hag′ē og′rə fē, hā′jē-og′rə fē), *n.* branch of literature that deals with the lives and legends of the saints. [< Greek *hagios* holy + *graphos* thing written]

hag i ol o gy (hag′ē ol′ə jē, hā′jē ol′ə jē), *n., pl.* **-gies.** 1 hagiography. 2 list of saints.

Hague (hāg), *n.* **The,** unofficial capital of the Netherlands, in the SW part. The official capital is Amsterdam. Also, DUTCH **'s-Gravenhage.** 551,000.

hah (hä), *interj.* ha.

Hahn (hän), *n.* **Otto,** 1879-1968, German chemist, known for his work on atomic fission.

Hai fa (hī′fə), *n.* seaport in NW Israel. 215,000.

Haig (hāg), *n.* **Douglas,** Earl, 1861-1928, commander in chief of the British army in World War I.

hai ku (hī′kü), *n.* a very brief poem of three lines and containing only 17 syllables. [< Japanese]

hail[1] (hāl), *n.* 1 small, round pieces of ice formed in thunderclouds and falling like rain; hailstones. 2 a shower resembling hail: *a hail of bullets.* *—v.i.* fall in hail: *Sometimes it hails during a thunderstorm.* *—v.t.* throw, hurl, or send down in a shower with considerable force like hail in a storm. [Old English *hægel*]

hail[2] (hāl), *v.t.* 1 shout in welcome to; greet; cheer. 2 greet as; call: *They hailed him leader.* 3 call loudly to; shout to: *After our car stalled, we hailed passing cars to beg a ride.* *—v.i.* 1 call out in order to attract attention. 2 **hail from,** come from. *—n.* 1 a shout of welcome; greeting: cheer. 2 a loud call; shout. 3 **within hail,** near enough to hear a call or shout. *—interj.* greetings! welcome!: *Hail to the winner!* [earlier *be hail!* < Scandinavian (Old Icelandic) *heill* healthy] **—hail′er,** *n.*

Hail Mary, Ave Maria.

Hai le Se las sie (hī′lē sə las′ē; hī′lē sə-läs′ē), born 1891, emperor of Ethiopia from 1930 to 1936 and since 1941.

hail stone (hāl′stōn′), *n.* ball or pellet of hail.

hail storm (hāl′stôrm′), *n.* storm with hail.

Hai nan (hī′nän′), *n.* island off the SE coast of China in the South China Sea. 2,800,000 pop.; 13,000 sq. mi.

Hai phong (hī′fông′), *n.* seaport in North Vietnam, near the Gulf of Tonkin east of Hanoi. 369,000.

hair (her, har), *n.* 1 a fine, threadlike, pigmented growth from the skin of people and animals. 2 mass of such growths. 3 a fine, threadlike growth from the outer layer of plants. 4 hair's-breadth. 5 **not turn a hair,** not show any sign of being disturbed or embarrassed. 6 **split hairs,** make excessively fine distinctions. [Old English *hǣr*] **—hair′less,** *adj.* **—hair′like′,** *adj.*

hair breadth (her′bredth′, her′bretth′; har′bredth′, har′bretth′), *adj., n.* hair's-breadth.

hair brush (her′brush′, har′brush′), *n.* a stiff brush for smoothing and dressing the hair.

hair cell, cell with very fine hairlike processes, found in an organ in the inner ear.

hair cloth (her′klôth′, her′kloth′; har′-klôth′, har′kloth′), *n., pl.* **-cloths** (-klôᴛʜz′, -klôths′; -kloᴛʜz, -kloths′). a scratchy fabric made of cotton and horsehair or camel's hair, used to cover furniture, stiffen garments, etc.

hair cut (her′kut′, har′kut′), *n.* act or manner of cutting the hair.

hair do (her′dü′, har′dü′), *n., pl.* **-dos.** way of arranging the hair.

hair dress er (her′dres′ər, har′dres′ər), *n.* person whose work is arranging or cutting women's hair.

hair dress ing (her′dres′ing, har′dres′-ing), *n.* act or process of cutting and arranging someone's hair.

hair line (her′līn′, har′līn′), *n.* 1 a very thin line. 2 the irregular outline where hair growth ends on the head or forehead. *—adj.* very narrow or close: *The base runner disputed the umpire's hairline decision.*

hair piece (her′pēs′, har′pēs′), *n.* 1 toupee. 2 a small wig worn by women as a hair accessory.

hair pin (her′pin′, har′pin′), *n.* a small, thin piece of metal, plastic, etc., usually U-shaped, used by women and girls to keep their hair in place. *—adj.* shaped like a hairpin: *a hairpin turn.*

hair-rais er (her′rā′zər, har′rā′zər), *n.* something that causes fear or terror.

hair-rais ing (her′rā′zing, har′rā′zing), *adj.* making the hair stand on end; terrifying. **—hair′-rais′ing ly,** *adv.*

hair's-breadth or **hairs breadth** (herz′bredth′, herz′bretth′; harz′bredth, harz′bretth′), *adj.* very narrow; extremely close. *—n.* a very narrow space or distance. Also, **hairbreadth.**

hair seal, any of a family of seals without external ears, having coarse hair with no soft underlying fur, and little hunted for its pelt; earless seal.

hair shirt, a rough shirt or girdle made of horsehair, worn as a penance.

hair split ting (her′split′ing, har′split′ing), *n.* a making too fine distinctions. *—adj.* making too fine distinctions.

hair spring (her′spring′, har′spring′), *n.* a fine, hairlike spring that regulates the motion of the balance in a watch or clock.

hair trigger, trigger that operates by very slight pressure.

hair y (her′ē, har′ē), *adj.,* **hair i er, hair i est.** 1 covered with hair; having much hair. 2 of or like hair. **—hair′i ness,** *n.*

Hai ti (hā′tē), *n.* 1 country in the W part of the island of Hispaniola, in the West Indies. 4,867,000 pop.; 10,700 sq. mi. *Capital:* Port-au-Prince. 2 former name of Hispaniola.

Hai ti an (hā′tē ən, hā′shən), *adj.* of or having to do with Haiti, its people, or their language. *—n.* 1 native or inhabitant of Haiti. 2 the native language of Haiti, a dialect of French.

hajj (haj), *n.* pilgrimage to Mecca, required of every Moslem at least once in his life. Also, **hadj.** [< Arabic *ḥajj*]

haj ji (haj′ē), *n.* hadji.

hake (hāk), *n., pl.* **hakes** or **hake.** any of several marine food fishes related to the cod but more slender. [perhaps < Scandinavian (Norwegian) *hakefisk,* literally, hook fish]

Hak luyt (hak′lüt), *n.* **Richard,** 1552?-1616, English geographer and historian.

Ha ko da te (hä′kō dä′tā), *n.* seaport in N Japan. 252,000.

Ha la cha (hä läн′ä), *n., pl.* **Ha la chas, Ha la choth** (hä′läн ōth′). the body of traditional or oral law of the Jews, supplementing or interpreting the law of the Scripture. [< Hebrew *hălākhāh* rule to go by]

ha la tion (hā lā′shən, ha lā′shən), *n.* (in photography) effect of excess of light on some part of a negative.

halberd
held by a soldier

hal berd (hal′bərd), *n.* weapon of the 1400's and 1500's used both as a spear and a battle-ax. [< Middle French *hallebarde* < Italian *alabarda*]

hal berd ier (hal′bər dir′), *n.* (formerly) a soldier armed with a halberd.

hal bert (hal′bərt), *n.* halberd.

hal cy on (hal′sē ən), *adj.* calm; peaceful; tranquil. *—n.* ARCHAIC. bird supposed to breed in a nest on the sea and calm the water, identified with the kingfisher. [< Latin < Greek *halkyōn*]

halcyon days, 1 fourteen days of calm weather. 2 a quiet, happy period.

Hal dane (hôl′dān), *n.* **J(ohn) B(urdon) S(anderson),** 1892-1964, British geneticist, biochemist, and author.

hale[1] (hāl), *adj.,* **hal er, hal est.** free from infirmity; strong and well; healthy. [Old English *hāl*]

hale[2] (hāl), *v.t.,* **haled, hal ing.** 1 compel to go. 2 drag by force. [< Old French *haler,* of Germanic origin. Doublet of HAUL.]

Hale (hāl), *n.* 1 **Edward Everett,** 1822-1909, American author. 2 **Nathan,** 1755-1776, American patriot hanged as a spy by the British.

Ha le a ka la (hä′lā ä′kä lä′), *n.* extinct volcano on the island of Maui, Hawaii, that has the largest extinct crater in the world. 19 sq. mi.; 10,032 ft. high.

Haleakala National Park, national park on the island of Maui, Hawaii, including Haleakala.

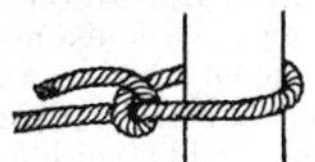

half hitch

half (haf), *n., pl.* **halves,** *adj., adv.* —*n.* 1 one of two equal parts. 2 one of two nearly equal parts: *Which is the bigger half?* 3 one of two equal periods in certain games. 4 **by half,** by far. —*adj.* 1 forming a half; being or making half of. 2 not complete; being only part of: *A half truth is often no better than a lie.* —*adv.* 1 to half of the full amount or degree: *a glass half full of milk.* 2 not completely; partly: *speak half aloud.* 3 almost; nearly: *The injured mountain climber was half dead from hunger when he was found.* 4 **not half bad,** fairly good. [Old English *healf*]

half-and-half (haf′ən haf′), *adj.* half one thing and half another. —*adv.* in two equal parts. —*n.* 1 mixture of milk and cream. 2 BRITISH. mixture of ale and porter.

half back (haf′bak′), *n.* 1 (in football) an offensive back who runs with the ball, blocks for another back, or goes downfield as a pass receiver. 2 (in rugby, soccer, etc.) player who is stationed behind the forward line.

half-baked (haf′bākt′), *adj.* 1 INFORMAL. not fully worked out; incomplete. 2 not cooked enough. 3 INFORMAL. not experienced; showing poor judgment.

half blood, relationship between persons who are related through one parent only.

half-blood (haf′blud′), *n.* 1 half-breed. 2 person related to another through one parent only.

half-plane

half-plane—The plane A is divided into two half-planes by the line T.

half-blood ed (haf′blud′id), *adj.* 1 having parents of different races. 2 related through only one parent.

half boot, boot reaching about halfway to the knee.

half-breed (haf′brēd′), *n.* person whose parents are of different races.

half brother, brother related through one parent only.

half-caste (haf′kast′), *n.* 1 person who has one European parent and one Asian parent; Eurasian. 2 half-breed.

half cock, position of the hammer of a gun when it is pulled back halfway. At half cock the trigger is locked and the gun cannot be fired.

half-cocked (haf′kokt′), *adj.* 1 (of a gun) at the position of half cock. 2 **go off half-cocked,** act or speak without sufficient thought or preparation.

half crown, a former British coin worth $2\frac{1}{2}$ shillings.

half dollar, a coin of the United States and Canada, worth 50 cents.

half eagle, a former gold coin of the United States, worth $5.00.

half gainer, dive in which the diver springs off the board facing forward, does a half somersault backwards, and enters the water headfirst, facing the board.

half heart ed (haf′här′tid), *adj.* lacking courage, interest, or enthusiasm; not earnest. —**half′heart′ed ly,** *adv.* —**half′heart′ed ness,** *n.*

half hitch, knot formed by passing the end of a rope under and over its standing part and then inside the loop.

half hour, 1 30 minutes. 2 the halfway point in an hour.

half-hour (haf′our′), *adj.* of a half hour; lasting a half hour. —**half′-hour′ly,** *adv.*

half-life (haf′līf′), *n.* length of time it takes for half the atoms of a particular radioactive substance to disintegrate. The half-life of a particular radioactive substance is always the same, and it is used to measure radioactivity and as the principal characteristic in distinguishing one substance from another.

half-line (haf′līn′), *n.* (in geometry) the part of a line on one side of a fixed point of the line that extends indefinitely; ray.

half-mast (haf′mast′), *n.* position halfway or part way down from the top of a mast, staff, etc.; half-staff. A flag is lowered to half-mast as a mark of respect for someone who has died or as a signal of distress.

half-moon (haf′mün′), *n.* 1 moon when only half of its surface appears bright. 2 something shaped like a half moon or crescent.

half nelson, (in wrestling) a hold applied by hooking one arm under an opponent's armpit and putting a hand on the back of his neck.

half note, (in music) a note played for one half as long a time as a whole note. See **note** for diagram.

half pen ny (hā′pə nē, hāp′nē), *n., pl.* **half pence** (hā′pəns), **half pen nies,** *adj.* —*n.* a British coin worth half a penny. —*adj.* 1 worth only a halfpenny. 2 having little value; trifling.

half-plane (haf′plān′), *n.* (in geometry) the part of a plane on one side of a fixed line of the plane.

half sister, sister related through one parent only.

half sole, sole of a shoe or boot from the toe to the instep.

half-sole (haf′sōl′), *v.t.,* **-soled, -sol ing.** put a new half sole or half soles on (shoes, etc.).

half sovereign, a former British gold coin worth ten shillings.

half-staff (haf′staf′), *n.* half-mast.

half step, difference in pitch between two adjacent keys on a piano; semitone.

half-tim bered (haf′tim′bərd), *adj.* having walls of wooden framework with the spaces filled by plaster, stone, or brick.

half time, the time between two halves of a game.

half tone (haf′tōn′), *n.* 1 a process in photoengraving in which gradations in tone in the original photograph, painting, etc., are reproduced in a series of very fine dots. 2 picture made by this process. 3 (in art, photography, etc.) a tone intermediate between the extreme lights and extreme shades.

half tone, half step.

half-track or **half track** (haf′trak′), *n.* a military motor vehicle with wheels in front and short tracks in the rear, used to carry troops and weapons.

hat, āge, fär; let, ēqual, tėrm;
it, īce; hot, ōpen, ôrder;
oil, out; cup, pu̇t, rüle;
ch, child; ng, long; sh, she;
th, thin; ᴛʜ, then; zh, measure;

ə represents *a* in about, *e* in taken, *i* in pencil, *o* in lemon, *u* in circus.

< = from, derived from, taken from.

half way (haf′wā′), *adv.* 1 half the way; half the required distance: *The rope reached only halfway around the tree.* 2 one half: *The lesson is halfway finished.* 3 **meet halfway** or **go halfway,** do one's share to agree or be friendly with. —*adj.* 1 midway: *a halfway stop in a journey.* 2 not going far enough; incomplete: *Fires cannot be prevented by halfway measures.*

half-wit (haf′wit′), *n.* 1 a feeble-minded person. 2 a stupid, foolish person.

half-wit ted (haf′wit′id), *adj.* 1 feeble-minded. 2 very stupid; foolish.

hal i but (hal′ə bət, hol′ə bət), *n., pl.* **-buts** or **-but.** any of a family of large flatfishes much used for food, found in the northern Atlantic and Pacific Oceans. [Middle English *halybutte* < *haly* holy + *butte* flatfish; because it was eaten on holy days]

Hal i car nas sus (hal′ə kär nas′əs), *n.* city built by the ancient Greeks in the SW part of Asia Minor, site of the Mausoleum.

hal ide (hal′īd, hal′id; hā′līd, hā′lid), *n.* any compound of a halogen with another element or radical. Sodium chloride is a halide.

hal i dom (hal′ə dəm), *n.* ARCHAIC. 1 a holy place; sanctuary. 2 a holy relic. [Old English *hāligdōm* < *hālig* holy + *-dōm* -dom]

hal i dome (hal′ə dōm), *n.* ARCHAIC. halidom.

Hal i fax (hal′ə faks), *n.* 1 seaport in SE Canada, the capital of Nova Scotia. 87,000. 2 city in central England. 93,000.

hal ite (hal′īt, hā′līt), *n.* rock salt. [< New Latin *halites* < Greek *hals* salt]

hal i to sis (hal′ə tō′sis), *n.* bad or offensive breath. [< New Latin < Latin *halitus* breath]

hall (hôl), *n.* 1 way for going through a building; passageway; hallway. 2 passageway or room at the entrance of a building; vestibule. 3 a large room for holding meetings, parties, banquets, etc. 4 a main room for common use, especially in a castle, palace, or other large dwelling. 5 building for public business, assemblies, etc. 6 building used by a school, college, or university for residence, teaching, etc. 7 the large common dining room in English universities. 8 residence of an English landowner. [Old English *heall*]

hal lah (hä′lə), *n., pl.* **hal lahs, hal loth** (hä lōt′). loaf of white bread, usually shaped like a braid, eaten by Jews on the Sabbath and holidays. [< Hebrew *hallah*]

half-track

Hal le (hä′lə), *n.* city in SW East Germany. 264,000.

Hal leck (hal′ək), *n.* **Fitz-Greene,** 1790-1867, American poet.

hal le lu jah or **hal le lu iah** (hal′ə-lü′yə), *interj.* praise ye the Lord! —*n.* song of praise. Also, **alleluia.** [< Hebrew *halēlūyāh* praise be Jehovah]

Hal ley's comet (hal′ēz), comet seen about every 76 years. It was last seen in 1910. [< Edmund *Halley,* 1656-1742, English astronomer who first predicted the year of its return]

hal liard (hal′yərd), *n.* halyard.

hall mark (hôl′märk′), *n.* 1 an official mark indicating standard of purity, put on gold or silver articles. 2 mark or sign of genuineness or good quality: *Courtesy and self-control are hallmarks of a gentleman.* —*v.t.* put a hallmark on. [< Goldsmiths' *Hall* in London, where the stamping of gold or silver articles was legally regulated + *mark*[1]]

hal lo (hə lō′), *interj., n., pl.* **-los,** *v.* —*interj.* 1 a call or shout to attract attention. 2 a call of greeting or surprise. —*n.* a shout or call. —*v.i.* shout; call. [variant of *halloo*]

hal loa (hə lō′), *interj., n., v.i.* hallo.

hal loo (hə lü′), *interj., n., pl.* **-loos,** *v.* —*interj., n.* 1 a shout to make hounds run faster. 2 hallo. —*v.i.* hallo. [probably < Old French *halloer* to shout (in pursuit)]

hal low (hal′ō), *v.t.* 1 make holy; make sacred; sanctify. 2 honor as holy or sacred. [Old English *hālgian* < *hālig* holy]

hal lowed (hal′ōd; *in church use, often* hal′ō id), *adj.* 1 made holy; sacred; consecrated: *A churchyard is hallowed ground.* 2 honored or observed as holy.

Hal low een or **Hal low e'en** (hal′ō ēn′, hol′ō ēn′), *n.* evening of October 31, before All Saints' Day. [short for *Allhallow-even*]

Hal low mas (hal′ō məs, hal′ō mas), *n.* All Saints' Day.

hal lu ci nate (hə lü′sn āt), *v.t., v.i.,* **-nat ed, -nat ing.** affect or be affected with hallucinations.

hal lu ci na tion (hə lü′sn ā′shən), *n.* 1 a seeing or hearing things that exist only in a person's imagination. Hallucinations may occur as a result of certain mental illnesses, acute alcoholism, the taking of certain drugs, etc. 2 an imaginary thing seen or heard. [< Latin *hallucinationem* < *hallucinari* to wander (in the mind) < Greek *haluein*]

hal lu ci na to ry (hə lü′sn ə tôr′ē, hə-lü′sn ə tōr′ē), *adj.* 1 having to do with or like hallucination. 2 characterized by hallucination. 3 hallucinogenic.

hal lu cin o gen (hə lü′sn ə jen), *n.* a drug such as LSD or marijuana, that produces or tends to produce hallucinations.

hal lu cin o gen ic (hə lü′sn ə jen′ik), *adj.* of, producing, or tending to produce hallucinations: *hallucinogenic drugs.*

hall way (hôl′wā′), *n.* 1 passage in a building; corridor; hall. 2 passageway or room at the entrance of a building.

ha lo (hā′lō), *n., pl.* **-los** or **-loes,** *v.* —*n.* 1 ring of light around the sun, moon, a star, or other luminous body, caused by the refraction of light through ice crystals suspended in the air. 2 a golden circle or disk of light represented about the head of a saint or angel in pictures or statues; nimbus. 3 glory or glamour that surrounds an idealized person or thing: *A halo of romantic adventure surrounds King Arthur and his knights.* —*v.t.* surround with a halo. [< Latin *halos* < Greek *halōs* disk; threshing floor (with reference to circular path of the oxen)] —**ha′lo like′,** *adj.*

hal o gen (hal′ə jən), *n.* any of the chemical elements iodine, bromine, chlorine, fluorine, and astatine. The halogens are electronegative, nonmetallic elements and combine directly with most metals to form salts. [< Greek *halos* salt + English *-gen*]

hal o gen a tion (hal′ə jə nā′shən), *n.* the addition of a halogen to an organic compound.

ha log e ton (hə loj′ə ton), *n.* a common weed, a species of goosefoot, that grows on the ranges of the western United States, where it kills a considerable number of livestock. [< New Latin < Greek *halos* salt + *geitōn* neighbor]

Hals (häls), *n.* **Frans,** 1580?-1666, Dutch painter.

Hal sey (hôl′zē), *n.* **William Frederick,** 1882-1959, American admiral in World War II.

halt[1] (hôlt), *v.i.* stop for a time: *The hikers halted and rested from their climb.* —*v.t.* cause to halt; stop: *The company halted operations during the strike.* —*n.* 1 a stop for a time. 2 **call a halt,** order a stop. [< French *halte* < German *Halt* < *halten* to stop, hold]

halt[2] (hôlt), *v.i.* 1 be in doubt; hesitate; waver: *Shyness made her halt as she talked.* 2 be faulty or imperfect. 3 ARCHAIC. be lame or crippled; limp. —*adj.* lame; crippled; limping. [Old English *haltian*] —**halt′ing-ly,** *adv.*

hal ter[1] (hôl′tər), *n.* 1 rope, strap, etc., with a noose or headstall by which horses, etc., are led or tied. 2 rope for hanging a person; noose. 3 death by hanging. 4 a woman's brief blouse which fastens behind the neck and across the back. —*v.t.* put a halter on; tie with a halter. [Old English *hælftre*]

hal tere or **hal ter**[2] (hal′tər), *n., pl.,* **hal ter es** (hal tir′ēz). either of two club-shaped organs in dipterous insects that take the place of a pair of posterior wings and help in balancing the body. [< Greek *haltēr* dumbbell-like weight for balance in leaping < *hallesthai* to leap]

halve (hav), *v.t.,* **halved, halv ing.** 1 divide into two equal parts; share equally. 2 cut in half; reduce to half: *The new machine will easily halve the time and cost of doing the work by hand.* [Middle English *halven, halfen* < *half*]

halves (havz), *n.pl.* of **half.** **1 by halves, a** not completely; partly. **b** in a half-hearted way. **2 go halves,** share equally.

hal yard (hal′yərd), *n.* rope or tackle used on a ship to raise or lower a sail, yard, flag, etc. Also, **halliard.** [Middle English *hallyer* < *hale*[2]*;* form influenced by *yard*[2]]

ham (ham), *n., v.,* **hammed, ham ming.** —*n.* 1 meat from the upper part of a hog's hind leg, usually salted and smoked. 2 the upper part of an animal's hind leg, used for food. 3 Often, **hams,** *pl.* back of the thigh; thigh and buttock. 4 part of the leg back of the knee. 5 SLANG. actor or performer who plays poorly and in an exaggerated manner. 6 INFORMAL. an amateur radio operator. —*v.i., v.t.* SLANG. play (a part) poorly and in an exaggerated manner. [Old English *hamm*]

hammer (def. 7)

Ham (ham), *n.* (in the Bible) the second son of Noah, supposed by legend to be the ancestor of African races.

ham a dry ad (ham′ə drī′əd, ham′ə-drī′ad), *n.* dryad. [< Greek *Hamadryades,* plural < *hama* together (with) + *dryados* nymph < *drys* tree]

Ha man (hā′mən), *n.* (in the Bible) a Persian minister who plotted to kill the Jews but was stopped by Queen Esther and hanged.

ham burg (ham′bėrg′), *n.* hamburger.

Ham burg (ham′bėrg′; *German* häm′bu̇rk), *n.* city in N West Germany, on the Elbe River. 1,817,000.

ham burg er (ham′bėr′gər), *n.* 1 ground beef, usually shaped into round, flat cakes and fried or broiled. 2 sandwich made with hamburger, usually in a roll or bun. [< German *Hamburger* of Hamburg]

hame (hām), *n.* either of two curved pieces on either side of the collar in a horse's harness, to which the traces are fastened. [< Middle Dutch]

Ha mil car Bar ca (hə mil′kär bär′kə; ham′əl kär bär′kə), died 228? B.C., Carthaginian general, father of Hannibal.

Ham il ton (ham′əl tən), *n.* **1 Alexander,** 1757-1804, American statesman, the first Secretary of the Treasury. 2 city in SE Canada, near the W end of Lake Ontario. 298,000. 3 capital of Bermuda. 3000.

Ham il to ni an (ham′il tō′nē ən), *adj.* of, having to do with, or agreeing with the principles of Alexander Hamilton. —*n.* follower of Alexander Hamilton.

Ham ite (ham′īt), *n.* 1 descendant of Ham. 2 member of various ethnic groups in northern and eastern Africa, including the Berbers and the ancient Egyptians.

Ha mit ic (ha mit′ik, hə mit′ik), *adj.* 1 of the Hamites. 2 of or having to do with a group of languages in northern and eastern Africa, including ancient Egyptian, Berber, Coptic, etc.

ham let (ham′lit), *n.* a small village; little group of houses in the country. [< Old French *hamelet,* diminutive of *hamel* village, of Germanic origin. Related to HOME.]

Ham let (ham′lit), *n.* 1 play by Shakespeare, first printed in 1603. 2 the principal character in this play, a prince of Denmark, who avenges his father's murder.

Ham mar skjöld (ham′ər shu̇ld′), *n.* **Dag,** 1905-1961, Swedish statesman, secretary general of the United Nations from 1953 to 1961.

ham mer (ham′ər), *n.* 1 tool with a metal head set crosswise on a handle, used to drive nails and to beat metal into shape. 2 a machine in which a heavy block of metal is used for beating, striking, etc.: *a steam hammer.* 3 a small mallet used by auctioneers to indicate by a rap the sale of an article. 4 one of the padded mallets for striking the string of a piano. 5 the part of the firing mechanism of a gun that is released by the tripper so that it strikes the percussion cap of a cartridge or pushes the firing pin and explodes the charge. 6 malleus. 7 a metal ball attached to a length

hat, āge, fär; let, ēqual, tėrm;
it, īce; hot, ōpen, ôrder;
oil, out; cup, pu̇t, rüle;
ch, child; ng, long; sh, she;
th, thin; ᴛʜ, then; zh, measure;

ə represents *a* in about, *e* in taken, *i* in pencil, *o* in lemon, *u* in circus.

< = from, derived from, taken from.

of steel wire with a handle on the other end, thrown for distance in athletic contests. 8 **hammer and tongs,** with all one's force and strength.
—*v.t.* 1 drive, hit, or work with a hammer. 2 beat into shape with a hammer. 3 fasten by using a hammer. 4 hit again and again. 5 force by repeated efforts. 6 work out with much effort. —*v.i.* 1 strike blows with a hammer. 2 **hammer at,** work hard at; keep working at. 3 **hammer away,** keep working hard. 4 **hammer out, a** form or forge with a hammer; shape by beating. **b** work out with much effort; contrive; devise.
[Old English *hamor*] —**ham′mer er,** *n.* —**ham′mer like′,** *adj.*

hammer and sickle, symbol of a sickle and hammer crossed, representing the laborer and the farmer, used on the flag of the Soviet Union.

Ham mer fest (häm′ər fest′), *n.* seaport in N Norway. It is the northernmost town in Europe. 6000.

ham mer head (ham′ər hed′), *n.* any of a genus of fierce sharks with wide heads which extend in flat processes bearing the eyes. As a result, a hammerhead looks somewhat like a double-headed hammer.

ham mer less (ham′ər lis), *adj.* having no hammer or no visible hammer. A hammerless pistol has its hammer covered.

ham mer lock (ham′ər lok′), *n.* (in wrestling) a hold in which an opponent's arm is twisted and held behind his back.

Ham mer stein (ham′ər stīn), *n.* **Oscar,** 1895-1960, American writer of musical plays.

ham mer toe (ham′ər tō′), *n.* toe in which the first joint nearest the instep is longer than usual so that the toe bends upward at an angle.

ham mock (ham′ək), *n.* a hanging bed or couch made of canvas, netted cord, etc., suspended by cords or ropes at both ends. [< Spanish *hamaca* < Arawak]

Ham mond (ham′ənd), *n.* city in NW Indiana. 108,000.

Ham mu ra bi (ham′u̇ rä′bē), *n.* king of Babylon who lived about 1800 B.C. and made a famous code of laws, called the Code of Hammurabi, for his people.

ham my (ham′ē), *adj.,* **-mi er, -mi est.** SLANG. acting like a ham.

Hamp den (hamp′dən, ham′dən), *n.* **John,** 1594-1643, British statesman.

ham per[1] (ham′pər), *v.t.* hold back; obstruct in action; hinder; restrain. [Middle English *hampren*]

ham per[2] (ham′pər), *n.* a large container, often a wicker basket, usually having a cover: *a picnic hamper.* [variant of earlier *hanaper* < Old French *hanapier* < *hanap* cup]

Hamp shire (hamp′shər, hamp′shir), *n.* county in S England that includes the administrative counties of Southampton and the Isle of Wight. Also, **Hants.**

Hamp ton (hamp′tən), *n.* 1 **Wade,** 1818-1902, Confederate general in the Civil War. 2 seaport in SE Virginia. 121,000.

Hampton Roads, channel in SE Virginia connecting the James River with Chesapeake Bay. The battle between the *Merrimac* and the *Monitor* took place there in 1862.

ham ster (ham′stər), *n.* a small rodent of Europe and Asia, with a short tail and large cheek pouches. Hamsters are used in scientific research and are often kept as pets. [< German *Hamster*]

ham string (ham′string′), *n., v.,* **-strung** or **-stringed, -string ing.** —*n.* 1 either of two tendons at the back of the knee in human beings. 2 the great tendon at the back of the hock in a four-footed animal. See **horse** for picture. —*v.t.* 1 cripple by cutting the hamstring. 2 destroy the activity, efficiency, etc., of; cripple; disable.

ham strung (ham′strung′), *v.* a pt. and a pp. of **hamstring.**

Ham sun (ham′sən; *Norwegian* häm′su̇n), *n.* **Knut,** 1859-1952, Norwegian novelist.

Han (hän), *n.* 1 **Han River,** river in central China, flowing into the Yangtze River at Wuhan. 900 mi. 2 a Chinese dynasty (202 B.C.-A.D. 220) marked by the introduction of Buddhism, the extension of Chinese rule over Mongolia, and the revival of letters.

Han cock (han′kok), *n.* 1 **John,** 1737-1793, American statesman, the first signer of the Declaration of Independence. 2 **Winfield Scott,** 1824-1886, Union general in the Civil War.

hand (hand), *n.* 1 the end part of the arm, below the wrist, with which a person grasps and holds objects. 2 end of any limb that grasps, holds, or clings, such as the hind foot of a monkey, the chela of a crustacean, or the foot of a hawk. 3 something resembling a hand in shape, appearance, or use: *The hands of a clock or watch show the time.* 4 sign (☞) drawing attention to something. 5 a hired worker who uses his hands: *a factory hand.* 6 member of a ship's crew; sailor. 7 **hands,** *pl.* possession; control: *Important evidence fell into the hands of the defense attorney.* 8 part or share in doing something: *He had no hand in the matter.* 9 side: *At her left hand stood two men.* 10 style of handwriting: *He writes in a clear hand.* 11 a person's signature. 12 skill; ability: *This painting shows the hand of a master.* 13 person, with reference to action, skill, or ability: *She is a great hand at thinking up new games.* 14 round of applause or clapping: *The crowd gave the winner a big hand.* 15 promise of marriage. 16 the breadth of a hand; 4 inches: *This horse is 18 hands high.* 17 cards held by a player in one round of a card game. 18 a single round in a card game. 19 player in a card game.
at first hand, from direct knowledge or experience.
at hand, a within reach; near. **b** ready.
at second hand, from the knowledge or experience of another; not directly.
at the hand of or **at the hands of,** through the act or deed of.
by hand, by using the hands, not machinery: *embroidered by hand.*
change hands, pass from one person to another.
force one's hand, make a person act prematurely or do something he dislikes.
from hand to mouth, without providing for the future: *Many poor people are forced to live from hand to mouth.*
give a hand, help.
hand and foot, a sparing no pain; diligently. **b** completely; thoroughly.
hand and glove or **hand in glove,** in close relations; intimate.
hand in hand, a holding hands. **b** together.
hands down, easily: *She won the contest hands down.*
hand to hand, close together; at close quarters.
have one's hands full, be very busy; be able to do no more.
in hand, a under control. **b** in one's possession; ready: *cash in hand.* **c** going along; being done.
lay hands on, a get hold of; seize. **b** arrest. **c** attack; harm. **d** bless by touching with the hands.
lend a hand, help.
off one's hands, out of one's care or charge.
on hand, a within reach; near; close. **b** ready: *have cash on hand.* **c** present: *I will be on hand again tomorrow.*
on the one hand, from this point of view.
on the other hand, from the opposite point of view.
out of hand, a out of control: *His temper was getting out of hand.* **b** at once.
show one's hand, reveal one's real intentions.
take in hand, a bring under control. **b** consider; deal with.
to hand, a within reach; near; close. **b** in one's possession.
turn one's hand to, work at.
wash one's hands of, have no more to do with; refuse to be responsible for.
—*v.t.* 1 give with the hand; pass along: *Please hand me a spoon.* 2 help with the hand: *I handed the old woman into the bus.*
hand down, a pass along: *The story was handed down from father to son.* **b** announce (a legal decision, opinion, etc.).
hand in, give; deliver.
hand it to, INFORMAL. give credit or praise to.
hand on, pass along.
hand out, give out; distribute.
hand over, give to another; deliver.
—*adj.* of, for, by, or in the hand: *a hand mirror, hand weaving.*
[Old English] —**hand′like′,** *adj.*

hand bag (hand′bag′), *n.* 1 a woman's small bag for money, keys, cosmetics, etc.; purse. 2 a small traveling bag to hold clothes, etc.

hand ball (hand′bôl′), *n.* 1 game played by hitting a small ball against a wall with the hand. 2 ball used in this game.

hand bar row (hand′bar′ō), *n.* frame with two handles at each end by which it is carried.

hand bill (hand′bil′), *n.* notice, advertisement, etc., usually printed on one page, that is to be handed out to people.

hand book (hand′bu̇k′), *n.* 1 a small book of directions or reference, especially in some field of study; manual: *a handbook on birds.* 2 book for recording bets. 3 place where bets are taken.

hand breadth (hand′bredth′, hand′bretth′), *n.* breadth of a hand, used as a measure. It varies from $2^1/_2$ to 4 inches. Also, **hand's-breadth.**

hand car (hand′kär′), *n.* a light, open, four-wheeled car moved along railroad tracks by pumping a handle up and down, used by workmen who maintain the tracks.

hand cart (hand′kärt′), *n.* a small cart pulled or pushed by hand; barrow.

hand clasp (hand′klasp′), *n.* the grasp of a person's hand in friendship, agreement, greeting, etc.

hand craft (hand′kraft′), *n.* handicraft. —*v.t.* make or work by hand.

hand cuff (hand′kuf′), *n.* one of a pair of metal rings joined by a short chain and fastened around the wrists to keep a person from using his hands. —*v.t.* put handcuffs on.

-handed, *combining form.* 1 having a certain kind of hand, as in *left-handed.* 2 using a certain number of hands: *a two-handed stroke.*

Han del (han′dl), *n.* **George Frederick,** 1685-1759, English composer, born in Germany.

hand ful (hand′fu̇l), *n., pl.* **-fuls.** 1 as much or as many as the hand can hold. 2 a small number or quantity. 3 INFORMAL. person or thing that is hard to manage.

hand gun (hand′gun′), *n.* pistol.

hand hold (hand′hōld′), *n.* place to put the hands.

hand i cap (han′dē kap′), *n., v.,* **-capped, -cap ping.** —*n.* 1 something that puts a person at a disadvantage; hindrance: *A sore throat was a handicap to the singer.* 2 race, contest, game, etc., in which the poorer contestants are given certain advantages and the better ones are given certain disadvantages, so that all have an equal chance to win. 3 the disadvantage or advantage given in such a race, contest, game, etc.: *A runner with a 5-yard handicap in a 100-yard race has to run either 105 yards or 95 yards.* —*v.t.* 1 put at a disadvantage; hinder: *A lame arm handicapped our pitcher.* 2 give a handicap to. [< *hand in cap;* apparently with reference to an old wagering game] **—hand′i cap′per,** *n.*

hand i craft (han′dē kraft′), *n.* 1 skill with the hands. 2 trade or art requiring skill with the hands. 3 artifact made with the hands. Also, **handcraft.** [alteration of *handcraft,* patterned after *handiwork*]

hand i crafts man (han′dē krafts′mən), *n., pl.* **-men.** person skilled with his hands in a trade or art; craftsman.

hand i work (han′dē wėrk′), *n.* 1 work done by a person's hands. 2 work which a person has done himself. [Old English *handgeweorc*]

hand ker chief (hang′kər chif), *n.* 1 a soft, usually square, piece of cloth used for wiping the nose, face, hands, eyes, etc., or carried or worn as an ornament. 2 kerchief.

han dle (han′dl), *n., v.,* **-dled, -dling.** —*n.* 1 a part of a thing made to be held or grasped by the hand. 2 something like a handle. 3 **fly off the handle,** INFORMAL. get angry or excited; lose one's temper or self-control. 4 SLANG. title or name. —*v.t.* 1 touch, feel, hold, or move with the hand; use the hands on: *She handled the old volumes carefully to avoid tearing the pages.* 2 manage; direct: *The captain handles his crew well.* 3 deal with; treat: *The teacher handled problems of discipline with ease without disturbing the class.* 4 deal with in speech or writing. 5 deal in; trade in: *That store handles meat and groceries.* —*v.i.* behave or act when handled: *This car handles easily.* [Old English < *hand* hand]

han dle bar (han′dl bär′), *n.* Often, **handlebars,** *pl.* the curved steering bar on a bicycle, motorcycle, etc.

han dler (han′dlər), *n.* 1 person or thing that handles. 2 person who helps to train or manage a boxer. 3 person who shows dogs or cats in a contest.

hand made (hand′mād′), *adj.* made by hand, not by machine.

hand maid (hand′mād′), *n.* 1 a female servant. 2 a female attendant. 3 person or thing that serves; servant.

hand maid en (hand′mād′n), *n.* handmaid.

hand-me-down (hand′mē doun′), *n.* something handed down from one person to another, such as a used garment. —*adj.* second-hand.

hand off (hand′ôf′, hand′of′), *n.* (in football) the handing of the football from one player to another, usually from the quarterback to a running back.

hand organ, a large, portable music box that is made to play tunes by turning a crank; barrel organ.

hand out (hand′out′), *n.* INFORMAL. 1 portion of food, clothing, or money handed out: *The beggar asked for a handout.* 2 a news story or piece of publicity issued to the press by a business organization, government agency, etc.

hand-picked (hand′pikt′), *adj.* 1 picked by hand. 2 carefully selected. 3 unfairly selected.

hand rail (hand′rāl′), *n.* railing used as a guard or as a support to the hand on a stairway, platform, etc.

hand saw (hand′sô′), *n.* saw used with one hand.

hand's-breadth (handz′bredth′, handz′-bretth′), *n.* handbreadth.

hand sel (han′səl), *n.* 1 gift given in token of good wishes at New Year's or to one entering a new job, house, etc. 2 first experience of anything; foretaste. Also, **hansel.** [Old English *handselen* giving of the hand (i.e., to confirm a bargain)]

hand set (hand′set′), *n.* telephone that has the receiver and mouthpiece on the same handle.

hand shake (hand′shāk′), *n.* act of clasping and shaking each other's hands in friendship, agreement, greeting, etc.

hand signal, position of a driver's hand and arm to tell other drivers he expects to slow down, stop, turn right, or turn left.

hand some (han′səm), *adj.,* **-som er, -som est.** 1 pleasing in appearance; good-looking. We usually say that a man is handsome, but that a woman is pretty or beautiful. See **beautiful** for synonym study. 2 fairly large; considerable: *A thousand dollars is a handsome sum of money.* 3 generous; liberal: *a handsome gift of one hundred dollars.* 4 gracious; proper. [Middle English *handsom* easy to handle, ready at hand < *hand* + *-some*[1]] **—hand′some ly,** *adv.* **—hand′some ness,** *n.*

hand spike (hand′spīk′), *n.* bar used as a lever, especially on a ship.

hand spring (hand′spring′), *n.* spring or leap in which a person lands on one or both hands and then back on his feet, making a complete turn of the body.

hand-to-hand (hand′tə hand′), *adj.* close together; at close quarters.

hand-to-mouth (hand′tə mouth′), *adj.* not providing for the future; having nothing to spare; not thrifty: *a hand-to-mouth existence.*

hand work (hand′wėrk′), *n.* work done by hand, not by machinery.

hand wo ven (hand′wō′vən), *adj.* woven or produced by means of a loom worked by hand.

hand writ ing (hand′rī′ting), *n.* 1 writing done by hand; writing done with pen, pencil, etc. 2 manner or style of writing.

hand writ ten (hand′writ′n), *adj.* written with the hand, or one's own hand.

hand y (han′dē), *adj.,* **hand i er, hand i est.** 1 easy to reach or use; saving work; useful; convenient. 2 skillful with the hands; dexterous. 3 easy to handle or manage. **—hand′i ly,** *adv.* **—hand′i ness,** *n.*

Han dy (han′dē), *n.* **W(illiam) C.,** 1873-1958, American jazz composer.

hand y man (han′dē man′), *n., pl.* **-men.** man who can do many kinds of odd jobs.

hang (hang), *v.,* **hung** or *(especially for execution or suicide; see usage note below)* **hanged, hang ing,** *n.* —*v.t.* 1 fasten or attach (something) to something above; suspend: *Hang your hat on the hook.* 2 fasten so as to swing or turn freely: *hang a door on its hinges.* 3 put to death by hanging with a rope around the neck. 4 bend down or forward; droop: *He hung his head in shame.* 5 cover or decorate with things that are fastened to something above: *hang a window with curtains. The walls were hung with pictures.* 6 attach (paper, etc.) to walls. 7 fasten in the proper position or angle: *hang the blade of a scythe.* 8 keep (a jury) from making a decision or reaching a verdict. One member can hang a jury by refusing to agree with the others when a verdict must be unanimous. —*v.i.* 1 be fastened or suspended from above; dangle: *The swing hangs from a tree. The folds of her evening gown hang gracefully.* 2 be fastened at the side, as on a hinge or pivot, so as to swing or turn freely: *The door hangs badly.* 3 die by hanging, especially as a form of capital punishment. 4 bend downward or forward; lean. 5 depend: *His future hangs on your decision.* 6 hold fast for support; cling. 7 be doubtful or undecided; hesitate; waver. 8 fail to agree, as a jury. 9 loiter; linger: *hang about a place.* 10 rest, float, or hover in the air. 11 be wearisome or tedious: *Time hangs on my hands.*

hang back, be unwilling to go forward; be backward.

hang on, **a** hold tightly. **b** be unwilling to let go, stop, or leave. **c** consider or listen to very carefully: *She hung on the teacher's every word.*

hang out, **a** lean out. **b** SLANG. live or stay.

hang over, **a** be about to happen to; threaten. **b** INFORMAL. remain from an earlier time or condition.

hang together, **a** stick together; support each other. **b** be coherent or consistent: *The story does not hang together.*

hang up, **a** put on a hook, peg, etc. **b** put a

handspring

telephone receiver back in place. **c** hold back; delay; detain.
—*n.* **1** way that a thing hangs: *She changed the hang of her skirt.* **2** INFORMAL. way of using or doing: *Riding a bicycle is easy after you get the hang of it.* **3** INFORMAL. idea; meaning: *After studying an hour I finally got the hang of the lesson.* **4** a trifle: *not care a hang.*
[Old English *hangian*]
➤ **hanged, hung.** In formal English, the principal parts of *hang* when referring to the death penalty are *hang, hanged, hanged;* in other senses they are *hang, hung, hung: They hanged the renegade from the ship's yardarm. They hung the rifle over the fireplace mantel.* Informal usage does not keep this distinction, using *hang, hung, hung* in all senses.

hang ar (hang′ər), *n.* **1** shed for airplanes or airships. **2** shed.

Hang chow (hang′chou′), *n.* seaport in E China. 800,000.

hang dog (hang′dôg′, hang′dog′), *adj.* ashamed or sneaking.

hang er (hang′ər), *n.* **1** thing on which something else is hung. **2** a specially shaped piece of wood, wire, plastic, etc., with a hook at the top, on which a coat, dress, skirt, etc., is hung. **3** loop, ring, etc., attached to something to hang it up by. **4** person who hangs things. **5** tool or machine that hangs things. **6** kind of short, light sword formerly worn by sailors on their belts.

hang er-on (hang′ər on′, hang′ər ôn′), *n., pl.* **hang ers-on. 1** follower or dependent. **2** an undesirable follower.

hang ing (hang′ing), *n.* **1** death by hanging with a rope around the neck. **2** Often, **hangings,** *pl.* thing that hangs from a wall, bed, etc. Curtains and draperies are hangings. —*adj.* **1** that hangs: *a hanging basket of flowers.* **2** leaning over or down; overhanging. **3** located on a height or steep slope: *hanging gardens.* **4** deserving to be punished by hanging: *a hanging crime.*

hang man (hang′mən), *n., pl.* **-men.** public executioner who puts condemned criminals to death by hanging them.

hang nail (hang′nāl′), *n.* bit of skin that hangs partly loose near the edge of a fingernail.

hang out (hang′out′), *n.* SLANG. place one lives in or goes to often.

hang o ver (hang′ō′vər), *n.* **1** INFORMAL. something that remains from an earlier time or condition. **2** SLANG. headache, nausea, etc., resulting from drinking too much alcoholic liquor.

hang-up (hang′up′), *n.* SLANG. problem, worry, etc., that a person cannot get rid of.

hank (hangk), *n.* **1** coil or loop. **2** skein. **3** skein of yarn containing a definite number of yards. [apparently < Scandinavian (Old Icelandic) *hönk*]

han ker (hang′kər), *v.i.* have a longing or craving; yearn. [origin uncertain] —**han′ker er,** *n.*

han ker ing (hang′kə ring), *n.* a longing; craving.

Han kow (han′kou′), *n.* former city in E China, now part of Wuhan.

han ky-pan ky (hang′kē pang′kē), *n.* INFORMAL. trickery; underhand dealing. [origin uncertain]

Han ni bal (han′ə bəl), *n.* 247-183? B.C., Carthaginian general who fought the Romans and invaded Italy.

Han no ver (han′ō vər), *n.* Hanover (def. 1).

Ha noi (hä noi′), *n.* capital of North Vietnam, in the central part. 415,000.

Han o ver (han′ō vər), *n.* **1** city in N West Germany. 518,000. Also, **Hannover. 2** former province of Prussia. **3** the royal family that ruled England from 1714 to 1901.

Han o ver i an (han′ō vir′ē ən), *adj.* of or having to do with the royal house of Hanover. —*n.* supporter or member of the house of Hanover.

hanse (hans), *n.* **1** a medieval guild of a town. **2 Hanse,** Hanseatic League. [< Old High German *hansa* band]

Han se at ic (han′sē at′ik), *adj.* of or having to do with the Hanseatic League.

Hanseatic League, a medieval league of towns in Germany and nearby countries for the promotion and protection of commerce.

han sel (han′səl), *n.* handsel.

Han sen's disease (han′sənz), leprosy. [< G. Armauer *Hansen,* 1841-1912, Norwegian physician]

hansom

han som (han′səm), *n.* a two-wheeled cab for two passengers, drawn by one horse. The driver sits on a seat high up behind the cab, and the reins pass over the roof. [< Joseph *Hansom,* 1803-1882, British architect, who designed such cabs]

Han son (han′sən), *n.* **Howard Harold,** born 1896, American composer, conductor, and educator.

Hants (hants), *n.* Hampshire.

Ha nuk kah (hä′nə kə; *Hebrew* HÄ′nù kä), *n.* a yearly Jewish festival commemorating the rededication of the temple in Jerusalem after a victory of the Jews over the Syrians in 165 B.C.; Festival of Lights. It lasts for eight days, mostly in December. Also, **Chanukah.** [< Hebrew *hănukkāh* dedication]

Han yang (hän′yäng′), *n.* former city in E China, now part of Wuhan.

hao le (hou′lā, hou′lē), *n.* (in Hawaii) a foreigner, especially a Caucasian. [< Hawaiian]

hap (hap), *n., v.,* **happed, hap ping.** ARCHAIC. —*n.* chance; luck. —*v.i.* happen. [< Scandinavian (Old Icelandic) *happ*]

hap haz ard (hap′haz′ərd), *adj.* not planned; random: *Haphazard answers are usually wrong.* See **random** for synonym study. —*adv.* by chance; at random. —*n.* chance: *Events seemed to happen at haphazard.* —**hap′haz′ard ly,** *adv.* —**hap′haz′ard ness,** *n.*

hap less (hap′lis), *adj.* unlucky; unfortunate. —**hap′less ly,** *adv.* —**hap′less ness,** *n.*

hap loid (hap′loid), *adj.* **1** having the gametic number of sets of chromosomes or half as many as in the somatic cells of the species. **2** monoploid. —*n.* **1** a haploid organism or cell. **2** monoploid. [< Greek *haplous* single]

hap ly (hap′lē), *adv.* ARCHAIC. by chance; perhaps.

hap pen (hap′ən), *v.i.* **1** come about; take place; occur: *Nothing interesting happens here.* See synonym study below. **2** be or take place by chance: *Accidents will happen.* **3** have the fortune; chance: *I happened to sit beside her at the party.* **4** be done: *Something has happened to this lock; the key won't turn.* **5 happen on, a** meet. **b** find: *She happened on a dime while looking for her ball.* [Middle English *happenen* < *hap*]
Syn. 1 Happen, chance, occur mean to take place or come about. **Happen,** the general word, suggests coming either by chance or according to design: *The accident happened suddenly.* **Chance** emphasizes happening without apparent reason: *There chanced to be someone there I knew.* **Occur,** more formal, is particularly used when definite or specific events are spoken of: *The accident occurred at the intersection.*

hap pen ing (hap′ə ning), *n.* **1** something that happens; event; occurrence. **2** Also, **Happening.** a staged scene in which paintings, music, etc., are combined to produce a single artistic effect.

hap pen stance (hap′ən stans), *n.* a chance occurrence; accident.

hap pi ly (hap′ə lē), *adv.* **1** in a happy manner: *She lives happily with her family.* **2** by luck; with good fortune; fortunately: *Happily, I saved you from falling.* **3** aptly; appropriately: *His letter of congratulation was happily phrased.*

hap pi ness (hap′ē nis), *n.* **1** a being happy; gladness. See synonym study below. **2** good luck; good fortune. **3** aptness; appropriateness.
Syn. 1 Happiness, felicity, bliss mean a feeling of satisfaction and pleasure. **Happiness** is the common and general word: *His promotion brought him happiness.* **Felicity** means great or joyous happiness: *I wish you felicity in marriage.* **Bliss** implies the highest degree of happiness: *They are in a state of bliss now that they are engaged.*

hap py (hap′ē), *adj.,* **-pi er, -pi est. 1** feeling pleasure and joy; glad; contented. See **glad** for synonym study. **2** showing that one is glad; showing pleasure and joy: *a happy smile, a happy look.* **3** pleased: *I am happy to accept your invitation.* **4** lucky; fortunate: *By a happy chance, I found the lost money.* **5** clever and fitting; successful and suitable; appropriate: *a happy way of expressing an idea.* [Middle English < *hap*]

hap py-go-luck y (hap′ē gō luk′ē), *adj.* taking things easily as they come; trusting to luck.

Haps burg (haps′bėrg′; *German* häps′-bürk), *n.* member of a German princely family prominent since about 1100. The Hapsburgs were rulers of the Holy Roman Empire from 1438 to 1806, of Austria from 1804 to 1918, of Hungary and Bohemia from 1526 to 1918, and of Spain from 1516 to 1700. Also, **Habsburg.**

har a-kar i (har′ə kar′ē, hä′rə kä′rē), *n.* hara-kiri.

har a-kir i (har′ə kir′ē, hä′rə kir′ē), *n.* suicide committed by ripping open the abdomen

hat, āge, fär; let, ēqual, tėrm;
it, īce; hot, ōpen, ôrder;
oil, out; cup, pu̇t, rüle;
ch, child; ng, long; sh, she;
th, thin; ᴛʜ, then; zh, measure;
ə represents *a* in about, *e* in taken, *i* in pencil, *o* in lemon, *u* in circus.
< = from, derived from, taken from.

with a knife. It was the national form of honorable suicide in Japan for the warrior class. Also, **hari-kari.** [< Japanese, belly cut]

ha rangue (hə rang′), *n., v.,* **-rangued, -rangu ing.** —*n.* 1 a noisy, vehement speech. 2 a long, pompous, formal speech. —*v.t.* address (someone) with a harangue. —*v.i.* deliver a harangue. [< Middle French] **—ha rangu′er,** *n.*

har ass (har′əs, hə ras′), *v.t.* 1 trouble by repeated attacks; harry: *Pirates harassed the villages along the coast.* 2 distress with annoying labor, care, misfortune, etc.; disturb; worry; torment. See **worry** for synonym study. [< French *harasser* < Old French *harer* set a dog on < *hare* a shout to excite dogs to attack] **—har′ass ment,** *n.*

Har bin (här′bēn′, här′bən), *n.* city in NE China. 1,600,000.

har bin ger (här′bən jər), *n.* one that goes ahead to announce another's coming; forerunner: *The robin is a harbinger of spring.* —*v.t.* announce beforehand; foretell. [< Old French *herbergere* provider of shelter (hence, one who goes ahead), ultimately < *herberge* lodging, of Germanic origin. Related to HARBOR.]

har bor (här′bər), *n.* 1 area of deep water protected from winds, currents, etc., forming a place of shelter for ships and boats. A harbor may have loading and unloading facilities for passengers and cargo. See synonym study below. 2 any place of shelter. —*v.t.* 1 give shelter to; give a place to hide: *The dog's shaggy hair harbors fleas.* 2 have and keep in the mind: *He harbored plans for revenge on his enemies.* See **cherish** for synonym study. —*v.i.* take shelter or refuge. Also, BRITISH **harbour.** [Middle English *herebeorg* lodgings < Old English *here* army + *beorg* shelter] **—har′bor er,** *n.* **—har′bor less,** *adj.*

Syn. *n.* 1 **Harbor, port** mean place of shelter for ships. **Harbor** emphasizes shelter, and applies to a protected body of water on a coast: *Many yachts are in the harbor.* **Port** applies particularly to a harbor where commercial ships dock for loading and unloading: *The ship arrived in port.*

har bor age (här′bə rij), *n.* 1 shelter for ships and boats. 2 any shelter.

harbor master, officer who has charge of a harbor or port and enforces the rules respecting it.

harbor seal, a common, spotted hair seal of northern coasts; sea calf.

har bour (här′bər), *n., v.t., v.i.* BRITISH. harbor.

hard (härd), *adj.* 1 solid and firm to the touch; not soft: *a hard nut.* See **firm**[1] for synonym study. 2 firmly formed; tight: *a hard knot.* 3 needing much ability, effort, or time; difficult or troublesome: *a hard problem, a hard job, a hard man to get on with.* See synonym study below. 4 acting or done with energy, persistence, etc.: *a hard worker.* 5 vigorous or violent: *a hard storm, a hard run.* 6 hardy; durable; tough: *hard goods.* 7 causing much pain, trouble, care, etc.; bad; severe: *a hard illness, a hard winter, hard times.* 8 INFORMAL. wicked; disreputable: *a hard character.* 9 not pleasant; harsh; ugly: *a hard face, a hard laugh.* 10 harsh in style, outline, or execution. 11 not yielding to influence; stern; unfeeling: *a hard master, a hard heart.* 12 strict in terms: *drive a hard bargain.* 13 not visionary; practical. 14 real and significant: *hard facts, hard news.* 15 containing mineral salts that keep soap from forming suds: *hard water.* 16 containing much alcohol: *hard liquor.* 17 sounded like the *c* in *corn* or the *g* in *get,* rather than like the soft *c* and *g* in *city* and *gem.* 18 in coin rather than paper currency: *hard money.* 19 in coins, bills, or actual money as distinguished from other property: *hard cash.* 20 (of money) backed by gold or silver, not merely government credit. 21 (of X rays) having great penetrating power. 22 (of a missile site or missile) situated underground so as to be practically safe from enemy aerial attack.

hard and fast, that cannot be changed or broken; strict: *hard and fast rules.*

hard of hearing, somewhat deaf.

hard put, having much difficulty or trouble.

hard up, INFORMAL. needing money or anything very badly.

—*adv.* 1 so as to be hard, solid, or firm: *The river is frozen hard.* 2 firmly; tightly: *Don't hold hard.* 3 with difficulty: *breathe hard.* 4 with steady effort or much energy: *They tried hard to lift the log.* 5 with vigor or violence: *It is raining hard.* 6 so as to cause trouble, pain, care, etc.; severely; badly; harshly: *It will go hard with you if you are lying.* 7 earnestly; intently: *look hard at a person.* 8 close; near: *The house stands hard by the bridge.* 9 to the extreme limit; fully: *The ship turned hard aport.*

[Old English *heard*]

Syn. *adj.* 3 **Hard, difficult** mean needing much effort or ability. **Hard** is the general word meaning not easy to do, understand, handle, etc.: *We have a hard lesson to learn.* **Difficult** emphasizes needing special ability or skill, shrewdness, or good judgment in order to accomplish, understand, handle, or deal with something hard: *Studies in college are more difficult than those in high school.*

hard back (härd′bak′), *n.* book with hardbound covers.

hard-bit ten (härd′bit′n), *adj.* stubborn; unyielding.

hard-boiled (härd′boild′), *adj.* 1 (of an egg) boiled until the white and yolk are firm. 2 INFORMAL. not easily influenced by the feelings; tough; rough.

hard bound (härd′bound′), *adj.* (of books) bound in leather, boards, or cloth, rather than in flexible paper.

hard coal, anthracite.

hard core, the firm, unyielding, central part, resistant to exterior pressures or change. **—hard′-core′,** *adj.*

hard en (härd′n), *v.t.* 1 make hard; solidify. 2 make capable of endurance; accustom. 3 make unfeeling or pitiless: *The miser hardened his heart to the pleas of the beggar.* —*v.i.* 1 become hard: *When the candy cooled, it hardened.* 2 become capable of endurance: *When he returned from a summer at camp, he had hardened and become fit.* 3 become hard in feeling or emotion. **—hard′en er,** *n.*

hard hack (härd′hak′), *n.* shrub of the rose family, a spiraea, with dense clusters of small pink, purple, or white flowers and woolly leaves and branches.

hard hat, type of helmet worn by construction workers as protection against falling objects.

hard head ed (härd′hed′id), *adj.* 1 not easily excited or deceived; practical; shrewd. 2 stubborn; obstinate. **—hard′head′ed ly,** *adv.* **—hard′head′ed ness,** *n.*

hard heart ed (härd′här′tid), *adj.* without pity; cruel; unfeeling. **—hard′heart′ed ly,** *adv.* **—hard′heart′ed ness,** *n.*

hard-hit ting (härd′hit′ing), *adj.* INFORMAL. vigorous; aggressive; powerful.

har di hood (här′dē hůd), *n.* 1 boldness; daring. 2 audacity; effrontery. 3 sturdiness or robustness.

Har ding (här′ding), *n.* **Warren Gamaliel,** 1865-1923, the 29th president of the United States, from 1921 to 1923.

hard labor, hard work in addition to imprisonment.

hard-land (härd′land′), *v.t., v.i.* crash-land a spacecraft, instruments, etc., on a body in outer space.

hard ly (härd′lē), *adv.* 1 only just; not quite; barely: *We hardly had time to eat breakfast.* 2 not quite: *He is hardly strong enough to lift that trunk.* 3 probably not: *They will hardly come in all this rain.* 4 with trouble or effort: *a hardly fought game.* 5 in a hard manner; harshly; severely: *deal hardly with a person.*

hard ness (härd′nis), *n.* 1 condition of being hard. 2 the comparative capacity of one mineral to scratch or be scratched by another mineral, as measured on the Mohs' scale.

hard palate, the bony front part of the roof of the mouth.

hard pan (härd′pan′), *n.* 1 hard, firm, often clayey subsoil through which roots cannot grow; pan. 2 hard, unbroken ground. 3 a solid foundation; bedrock.

hard rubber, vulcanite.

hard sauce, butter and sugar creamed together and flavored, used on cakes, puddings, etc.

hard sell, INFORMAL. a forceful and direct method of selling a product; high-pressure salesmanship.

hard-shell (härd′shel′), *adj.* 1 having a hard shell. 2 INFORMAL. rigid and uncompromising.

hard-shelled (härd′sheld′), *adj.* hard-shell.

hard ship (härd′ship), *n.* something hard to bear; hard condition of living: *Hunger, cold, and sickness were among the hardships of pioneer life.*

hard tack (härd′tak′), *n.* a very hard, dry biscuit that resists spoiling, eaten by sailors; ship biscuit; sea biscuit.

hard top (härd′top′), *n.* a passenger car with a rigid metal or plastic top but with window space comparable to that of a convertible.

hard ware (härd′wer′, härd′war′), *n.* 1 articles made from metal. Locks, hinges, nails, screws, knives, tools, etc., are hardware. 2 military weapons or equipment, such as guns, tanks, aircraft, or missiles. 3 a part or parts of an electronic computer, teaching machine, nuclear reactor, etc.

hard wheat, wheat having a hard kernel and high gluten content, used in making bread, macaroni, etc.

hard wood (härd′wůd′), *n.* 1 any hard, compact wood. 2 tree that has broad leaves, or does not have needles. Oak, cherry, maple, ebony, mahogany, etc., are hardwoods. 3 wood of such a tree. —*adj.* having or made of such wood: *a hardwood floor.*

har dy (här′dē), *adj.,* **-di er, -di est.** 1 able to bear hard treatment, fatigue, etc.; strong; robust: *hardy frontier settlers.* 2 able to withstand the cold of winter in the open air: *The*

hat, āge, fär; let, ēqual, tėrm;
it, īce; hot, ōpen, ôrder;
oil, out; cup, pu̇t, rüle;
ch, child; ng, long; sh, she;
th, thin; ᴛʜ, then; zh, measure;

ə represents *a* in about, *e* in taken, *i* in pencil, *o* in lemon, *u* in circus.

< = from, derived from, taken from.

hardy plants were able to grow in the open air throughout the year. 3 bold; daring. 4 too bold; rash. **—har/di ly,** *adv.* **—har/di ness,** *n.*

Har dy (här/dē), *n.* **Thomas,** 1840-1928, English novelist and poet.

hare (her, har), *n., pl.* **hares** or **hare.** any of various gnawing mammals that resemble and are of the same order as rabbits but are much larger, have longer ears, long hind legs, and do not live in burrows. The jack rabbit is a hare; the cottontail is a rabbit. [Old English *hara*]

hare bell (her/bel/, har/bel/), *n.* bluebell.

hare brained (her/brānd/, har/brānd/), *adj.* giddy, heedless, or reckless.

hare lip (her/lip/, har/lip/), *n.* deformity caused when parts of the upper lip fail to grow together before birth. It resembles the lip of a hare.

hare lipped (her/lipt/, har/lipt/), *adj.* having a harelip.

har em (her/əm, har/əm), *n.* 1 part of a Moslem house where the women live; seraglio. 2 its occupants; the wives, female relatives, and female servants of a Moslem household. [< Arabic *harīm*]

Har greaves (här/grēvz/), *n.* **James,** 1722?-1778, Englishman who invented the spinning jenny.

har i cot (har/ə kō), *n.* string bean. [< French]

har i-kar i (har/ē kar/ē), *n.* hara-kiri.

hark (härk), *v.i.* 1 listen, hearken. 2 **hark back,** go back; turn back: *His ideas hark back twenty years.* [Middle English *herkien*]

hark en (här/kən), *v.i., v.t.* hearken.

Har lem (här/ləm), *n.* 1 **Harlem River,** river channel in New York City connecting the East and the Hudson rivers. 8 mi. 2 northeastern section of Manhattan, bordering the Harlem and East rivers.

har le quin (här/lə kwən, här/lə kən), *n.* 1 **Harlequin,** character in comedy and pantomime, the lover of Columbine. He is usually masked and wears a costume of varied colors. 2 a mischievous person; buffoon. *—adj.* varied in color; many-colored. [< Middle French < Old French *Hellequin* a demon]

har le quin ade (här/lə kwə nād/, här/lə kə nād/), *n.* a pantomime or play in which Harlequin is the leading player.

har lot (här/lət), *n.* prostitute. [< Old French, vagabond]

har lot ry (här/lə trē), *n.* prostitution.

harm (härm), *n.* 1 something that causes pain, loss, etc.; injury; damage. 2 evil; wrong. *—v.t.* do harm to; damage; injure; hurt. See synonym study below. [Old English *hearm*]

Syn. *v.t.* **Harm, damage** mean hurt or injure a person or thing. **Harm** suggests inflicting pain, loss, or suffering of any kind: *Unfounded and malicious rumors harmed his reputation.* **Damage** means to hurt or harm so as to lessen the value, usefulness, or appearance of a person or thing: *The furniture was damaged in the fire.*

harm ful (härm/fəl), *adj.* causing harm; injurious; hurtful. **—harm/ful ly,** *adv.* **—harm/ful ness,** *n.*

harm less (härm/lis), *adj.* causing no harm; not harmful; innocuous. **—harm/less ly,** *adv.* **—harm/less ness,** *n.*

har mon ic (här mon/ik), *adj.* 1 having to do with harmony in music. 2 having to do with fainter and higher tones heard along with the main tones. 3 musical. 4 in harmony. 5 (in physics) of or designating any of the frequencies making up a wave or alternating current, which are integral multiples of the fundamental frequency. *—n.* 1 overtone. 2 tone produced on a stringed instrument by a light pressure at a point on a string. **—har mon/i cal ly,** *adv.*

har mon i ca (här mon/ə kə), *n.* a small, oblong musical instrument with several metal reeds which are caused to vibrate by air from the player's mouth controlled by the tongue and lips; mouth organ. [originally *armonica* (a different instrument), coined by Benjamin Franklin, ultimately < Latin *harmonia.* See HARMONY.]

har mon ics (här mon/iks), *n.* science of musical sounds.

har mo ni ous (här mō/nē əs), *adj.* 1 agreeing in feelings, ideas, or actions; getting along well together; amicable. 2 arranged so that the parts are orderly or pleasing; going well together; congruous: *A beautiful painting has harmonious colors.* 3 sweet-sounding; musical; melodious. **—har mo/ni ous ly,** *adv.* **—har mo/ni ous ness,** *n.*

har mo ni um (här mō/nē əm), *n.* a small organ with metal reeds. [< French]

har mo nize (här/mə nīz), *v.,* **-nized, -niz ing.** *—v.t.* 1 bring into harmony, accord, or agreement; make harmonious. 2 add tones to (a melody) to make successive chords in music. *—v.i.* 1 be in harmony or agreement. 2 sing or play in harmony. **—har/mo ni za/tion,** *n.* **—har/mo niz/er,** *n.*

har mo ny (här/mə nē), *n., pl.* **-nies.** 1 agreement of feeling, ideas, or actions; getting on well together: *The two brothers lived and worked in perfect harmony.* 2 an orderly or pleasing arrangement of parts; going well together; congruity: *In a beautiful landscape there is harmony of the different colors.* 3 the sounding together of musical tones in a chord. 4 structure of a piece of music in relation to the chords of which it consists, as distinguished from melody and rhythm. 5 study of chords in music and relating them to successive chords. 6 sweet or musical sound; music. 7 a grouping of passages on the same subject from different stories or accounts, showing their points of agreement: *a harmony of the Gospels.* [< Latin *harmonia* < Greek, concord, a joining < *harmos* joint]

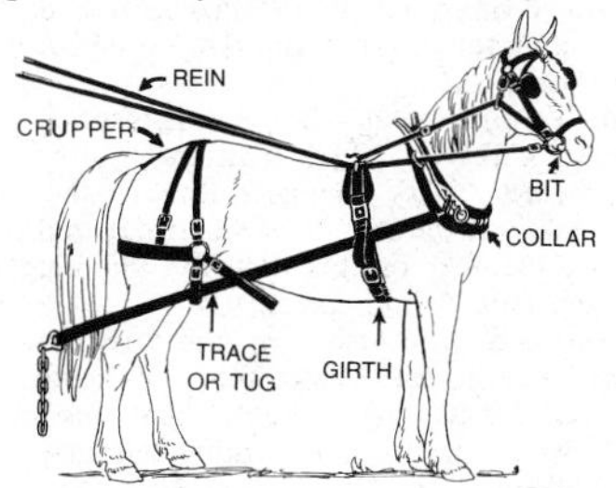

harness (def. 1)

har ness (här/nis), *n.* 1 a combination of leather straps, bands, and other pieces used to hitch a horse or other animal to a carriage, wagon, plow, etc. 2 any similar arrangement of straps, bands, etc., especially a combination of straps by which a parachute is attached to a person. 3 ARCHAIC. armor for a knight, warrior, or horse. 4 **in harness,** in or at one's regular work. *—v.t.* 1 put harness on. 2 cause to produce power. Water in a stream is harnessed by building a dam and installing turbines for the water to turn. 3 ARCHAIC. put armor on. [< Old French *harneis* tackle, gear]

Har old I (har/əld), died 1040, king of England from 1035 to 1040.

Harold II, 1022?-1066, last Saxon king of England, in 1066. He was defeated by William I.

harp

harp (härp), *n.* a large, stringed musical instrument played by plucking the strings with the fingers. *—v.t.* play (music) on the harp. *—v.i.* **harp on,** keep on tiresomely talking or writing about; refer continually to. [Old English *hearpe*] **—harp/er,** *n.* **—harp/like/,** *adj.*

Har pers Ferry (här/pərz), town in NE West Virginia. John Brown's raid on a government arsenal was made there in 1859.

harp ist (här/pist), *n.* person who plays the harp; harper.

har poon (här pün/), *n.* a barbed spear with a rope tied to it, used for catching whales and other sea animals. It is thrown by hand or fired from a gun. *—v.t.* strike, catch, or kill with a harpoon. [< Middle French *harpon* < *harper* to grip] **—har poon/er,** *n.*

harp si chord (härp/sə kôrd), *n.* a stringed musical instrument resembling a piano, used especially from about 1550 to 1750. It has a weak and tinkling sound because the strings are plucked by leather or quill points instead of being struck by hammers. [< earlier French *harpechorde* < *harpe* harp + *chorde* string]

Har py (här/pē), *n., pl.* **-pies.** 1 (in Greek and Roman myths) any of various filthy, greedy monsters with women's heads and birds' bodies. 2 **harpy,** a cruel, greedy person; person who preys upon others. [< Greek *harpyia*]

har que bus (här/kwə bəs), *n.* an old form of portable gun used before muskets were invented. Also, **arquebus.** [< Middle French *arquebuse*]

har ri dan (har′ə dən), *n.* a bad-tempered, disreputable old woman. [probably < French *haridelle* a worn-out horse]

har ri er[1] (har′ē ər), *n.* 1 a small hound resembling the English foxhound, used to hunt hares. 2 a cross-country runner. [apparently < *hare*]

har ri er[2] (har′ē ər), *n.* 1 person who harries. 2 any of a genus of slender hawks that feed on small animals, especially the marsh hawk. [< *harry*]

Har ris (har′is), *n.* **Joel Chandler,** 1848-1908, American writer, author of the Uncle Remus tales.

Har ris burg (har′is bėrg′), *n.* capital of Pennsylvania, in the S part. 68,000.

Har ri son (har′ə sən), *n.* 1 **Benjamin,** 1833-1901, the 23rd president of the United States, from 1889 to 1893. 2 his grandfather, **William Henry,** 1773-1841, the ninth president of the United States, in 1841.

har row (har′ō), *n.* a heavy frame with iron teeth or upright disks, used by farmers to break up plowed ground into finer pieces, cover seeds with earth, etc. See **disk harrow** for picture. *—v.t.* 1 draw a harrow over (land, etc.). 2 hurt; wound. 3 cause pain or torment to; distress. [Middle English *harwe*] **—har′row er,** *n.*

Har row (har′ō), *n.* 1 borough of London, England. 206,000. 2 an old and famous boys' boarding school located there.

har row ing (har′ō ing), *adj.* that harrows; very painful or distressing.

har ry (har′ē), *v.,* **-ried, -ry ing.** *—v.t.* 1 raid and rob with violence; lay waste; pillage. 2 keep troubling; worry; torment. *—v.i.* make predatory raids. [Old English *hergian* < *here* army]

harsh (härsh), *adj.* 1 unpleasantly rough to the touch; coarse in texture: *a harsh towel.* 2 unpleasantly rough to the taste; astringent: *a harsh flavor.* 3 unpleasing to the eye: *a harsh painting.* 4 disagreeably rough to the ear; jarring: *a harsh voice.* 5 without pity; unfeeling; cruel; severe: *a harsh man.* 6 rugged; bleak: *a harsh coast.* [Middle English *harsk* < Scandinavian (Danish) *harsk* rancid] **—harsh′ly,** *adv.* **—harsh′ness,** *n.*

hart (härt), *n., pl.* **harts** or **hart.** a male deer, especially the male European red deer after its fifth year; stag. [Old English *heorot*]

Harte (härt), *n.* **(Francis) Bret,** 1836-1902, American writer of short stories.

har te beest (här′tə bēst′, härt′bēst′), *n., pl.* **-beests** or **-beest.** either of two large, swift African antelopes of the same genus, with ringed, curved horns bent backward at the tips. [< Afrikaans, hart beast]

Hart ford (härt′fərd), *n.* capital of Connecticut, in the central part. 158,000.

harts horn (härts′hôrn′), *n.* form of ammonia used as smelling salts.

har um-scar um (her′əm sker′əm, har′əm skar′əm), *adj.* too hasty; reckless; rash. *—adv.* recklessly; rashly. *—n.* a reckless, rash person. [apparently < earlier *hare* frighten + *scare*]

Ha run al-Ra shid (hä rün′ äl rä shēd′), A.D. 763?-809, caliph of Baghdad from A.D. 786 to 809. He is the leading character of *The Arabian Nights.*

ha rus pex (hə rus′peks, har′ə speks), *n., pl.* **ha rus pi ces** (hə rus′pə sēz′). priest or soothsayer in ancient Rome who predicted the future by looking at the entrails of sacrificed animals. [< Latin < *haru-* entrails + *specere* inspect]

har vest (här′vist), *n.* 1 a reaping and gathering in of grain and other food crops. 2 time or season of the harvest, usually in the late summer or early autumn. 3 one season's yield of any natural product; crop: *the oyster harvest.* 4 result; consequences: *She is reaping the harvest of her years of study.* *—v.t.* 1 gather in and bring home for use (the grain or other ripe crop): *harvest wheat.* 2 gather the crop from. 3 win or undergo as a result or consequence. *—v.i.* gather in crops. [Old English *hærfest*]

har vest er (här′və stər), *n.* 1 person who works in a harvest field. 2 machine for harvesting crops, especially grain.

har vest man (här′vist mən), *n., pl.* **-men.** 1 daddy-longlegs. 2 man who harvests.

harvest moon, the full moon at harvest time or nearest the autumnal equinox, about September 23.

Har vey (här′vē), *n.* **William,** 1578-1657, English physician who discovered that blood circulates through the body.

Harz Mountains (härts), low mountain range in East Germany and West Germany. Highest peak, 3747 ft.

has (haz; *unstressed* həz, əz), *v.* third person singular, present indicative of **have.**

has-been (haz′bin′), *n.* INFORMAL. person or thing whose best days are past.

Has dru bal (haz′drü bəl), *n.* died 207 B.C., Carthaginian general, brother of Hannibal.

ha sen pfef fer (hä′zn fef′ər, hä′zn-pfef′ər), *n.* a stew made from rabbit marinated in vinegar, wine, etc. [< German *Hasenpfeffer* < *Hase* hare + *Pfeffer* pepper]

hash (hash), *n.* 1 mixture of cooked meat, potatoes, and other vegetables, chopped into small pieces and fried or baked. 2 mixture; jumble. 3 mess; muddle. 4 any presentation of old material worked over. 5 **settle one's hash,** INFORMAL. subdue or silence one completely; put an end to one. *—v.t.* 1 chop into small pieces. 2 make a mess or muddle of. 3 **hash over,** INFORMAL. discuss or review; reminisce about. [< French *hacher* < *hache* ax]

hash eesh (hash′ēsh′), *n.* hashish.

Hash em ite or **Hash im ite** (hash′ə-mīt), *adj.* of or having to do with the royal dynasty of the kingdoms of Jordan and Iraq. *—n.* member of this dynasty, claiming descent from Mohammed.

hash ish (hash′ēsh′), *n.* the dried flowers, top leaves, and tender parts of hemp prepared for use as a narcotic, and smoked or chewed for its intoxicating effect. Also, **hasheesh.** [< Arabic *hashīsh* dried hemp leaves]

Ha sid ic (hə sid′ik), *adj.* of or having to do with the Hasidim or with Hasidism. Also, **Hassidic.**

Has i dim (has′i dim; *Hebrew* HÄ sē′dim), *n.pl.* of **Has id** (has′id; *Hebrew* HÄ sēd′). members of a Jewish sect founded in the 1700's in Poland. Hasidim believe in mysticism and emphasize religious piety and devotion over formal learning. [< Hebrew *hasidhim* pious ones]

Has i dism (has′i diz′əm, hä′si diz′əm), *n.* the movement, philosophy, or rituals of Hasidim.

has n't (haz′nt), has not.

hasp on a door

hasp (hasp), *n.* clasp or fastening for a door, window, trunk, box, etc., especially a hinged metal clasp that fits over a staple or into a hole and is fastened by a peg, padlock, etc. [Middle English *haspe*]

Has sid ic (hə sid′ik), *adj.* Hasidic.

has sle (has′əl), *n., v.,* **-sled, -sling.** INFORMAL. *—n.* struggle or contest. *—v.i.* struggle; tussle. [apparently < southern United States dialectal *hassle* pant, breathe noisily]

has sock (has′ək), *n.* 1 a thick cushion or cushioned footstool to rest the feet on, sit on, or kneel on. 2 tuft or bunch of coarse grass; tussock. [Old English *hassuc* coarse grass]

hast (hast), *v.* ARCHAIC. have. "Thou hast" means "you have."

haste (hāst), *n., v.,* **hast ed, hast ing.** *—n.* 1 a trying to be quick; hurrying: *All his haste was of no use.* See **hurry** for synonym study. 2 quickness without thought or care; rashness: *Haste makes waste.* 3 condition of being obliged to act quickly on account of having very little time: *be breathless with haste.* 4 **make haste,** be quick; hurry: *Make haste or you will miss your train.* *—v.t., v.i.* hasten. [< Old French]

has ten (hā′sn), *v.t.* 1 cause to be quick; urge on; speed; hurry: *hasten everyone off to bed.* 2 cause to go faster; accelerate: *hasten a process.* *—v.i.* be quick; go fast: *hasten to explain.* **—has′ten er,** *n.*

Has tings (hā′stingz), *n.* 1 **Warren,** 1732-1818, British statesman, first governor general of India, from 1773 to 1785. 2 seaport in SE England, where William I defeated the Saxons to become king of England in 1066. 74,000.

hast y (hā′stē), *adj.,* **hast i er, hast i est.** 1 done or made in a hurry; quick: *a hasty glance.* 2 not well thought out; rash: *a hasty decision.* 3 easily angered; quick-tempered: *a hasty old gentleman.* 4 done or uttered in sudden anger or irritation: *hasty words.* **—hast′i ly,** *adv.* **—hast′i ness,** *n.*

hasty pudding, 1 U.S. mush made of corn meal. 2 BRITISH. mush made of flour or oatmeal.

hat (hat), *n., v.,* **hat ted, hat ting.** *—n.* a covering for the head, usually with a crown and a brim and usually worn outdoors.

pass the hat, take up a collection.

take off one's hat to, remove the hat, as a salute or sign of respect; honor.

throw one's hat into the ring, INFORMAL. enter a contest, especially for election to public office.

under one's hat, INFORMAL. as a secret; to oneself.

—v.t. provide with a hat; put a hat on.

[Old English *hætt*] **—hat′less,** *adj.*

hat band (hat′band′), *n.* band around the crown of a hat, just above the brim.

hatch[1] (hach), *v.t.* 1 bring forth (young) from an egg or eggs: *A hen hatches chickens.* 2 keep (an egg or eggs) warm until the young come out: *The heat of the sun hatches turtles' eggs.* 3 arrange; plan. 4 plan secretly; plot; scheme. *—v.i.* 1 come out from the egg: *Three of the chickens hatched today.* 2 develop to be young animals; bring forth young: *Not all eggs hatch properly.* *—n.* 1 act of hatching. 2 the brood hatched. [Middle English *hacchen*] **—hatch′er,** *n.*

hat, āge, fär; let, ēqual, tėrm;
it, īce; hot, ōpen, ôrder;
oil, out; cup, pu̇t, rüle;
ch, child; ng, long; sh, she;
th, thin; ᴛʜ, then; zh, measure;

ə represents *a* in about, *e* in taken, *i* in pencil, *o* in lemon, *u* in circus.

< = from, derived from, taken from.

hatch[2] (hach), *n.* 1 an opening in a ship's deck through which the cargo is loaded. 2 opening in the floor or roof of a building, etc. 3 a trap door covering such an opening. [Old English *hæcc* gate, wicket]

hatch[3] (hach), *v.t.* draw, cut, or engrave fine parallel lines on: *With a sharp pencil the artist hatched certain parts of the picture to darken and shade them.* —*n.* one of such a set of lines. [< Old French *hacher* chop, hatch < *hache* ax]

hatch er y (hach′ər ē), *n., pl.* **-er ies.** place for hatching eggs of fish, hens, etc.

hatch et (hach′it), *n.* 1 a small ax with a short handle, for use with one hand. 2 tomahawk. 3 **bury the hatchet,** stop quarreling or fighting; make peace. 4 **dig up the hatchet,** make war. [< Old French *hachette,* diminutive of *hache* ax] **—hatch′et like′,** *adj.*

hatch et-faced (hach′it fāst′), *adj.* having a sharp, narrow face.

hatchet man, INFORMAL. person employed or used to destroy the opponents or the character and standing of opponents of one's party or group.

hatch ing (hach′ing), *n.* fine, parallel lines drawn, cut, or engraved close together.

hatchment

hatch ment (hach′mənt), *n.* a square tablet set diagonally, bearing the coat of arms of a dead person. [earlier *atcheament, achement,* variant of *achievement*]

hatch way (hach′wā′), *n.* hatch of a ship, building, etc.

hate (hāt), *v.,* **hat ed, hat ing,** *n., adj.* —*v.t.* 1 dislike very strongly; detest. See synonym study below. 2 be very unwilling; dislike: *I hate to study.* —*v.i.* feel hatred. —*n.* 1 a very strong feeling of dislike; detestation. 2 object of intense dislike. —*adj.* characterized by or showing hate: *hate letters.* [Old English *hatian*] **—hat′er,** *n.*

Syn. *v.t.* 1 **Hate, detest, abhor** mean to dislike someone or something intensely. **Hate** implies very strong dislike and hostility, and often the desire to hurt or harm: *The prisoners hated the cruel guards.* **Detest** suggests strong or deep fixed dislike mixed with scorn: *I detest a coward.* **Abhor** suggests a profound dislike that makes one shudder or shrink away from someone or something: *I abhor filth of any kind.*

hate ful (hāt′fəl), *adj.* 1 causing hate; to be hated: *hateful behavior.* See synonym study below. 2 feeling hate; showing hate: *a hateful comment.* **—hate′ful ly,** *adv.* **—hate′ful ness,** *n.*

Syn. 1 **Hateful, odious, obnoxious** mean causing strong dislike or hate. **Hateful** applies especially to what is actually hated: *A bully does hateful things.* **Odious** applies to what excites strong displeasure or offense: *Conditions in the slums are odious.* **Obnoxious** means being so disagreeable or annoying to a person that he cannot stand the sight or thought of what is described: *His disgusting table manners made him obnoxious to us.*

hath (hath), *v.* ARCHAIC. has. "He hath" means "he has."

hat pin (hat′pin′), *n.* a long pin used by women to fasten a hat to their hair.

hat rack (hat′rak′), *n.* rack or shelf to put hats on.

ha tred (hā′trid), *n.* very strong dislike; hate; animosity.

hat ter (hat′ər), *n.* person who makes or sells hats.

Hat ter as (hat′ər əs), *n.* **Cape,** cape on an island off E North Carolina.

hau berk (hô′bərk), *n.* a long coat of mail or military tunic worn in the 1100's and 1200's; habergeon. [< Old French *hauberc* < Germanic]

haugh ty (hô′tē), *adj.,* **-ti er, -ti est.** too proud and scornful of others: *a haughty glance, haughty words.* See synonym study below. [Middle English *haute* < Middle French *haut* < Latin *altus* high] **—haugh′ti ly,** *adv.* **—haugh′ti ness,** *n.*

Syn. 1 **Haughty, arrogant** mean offensively proud. **Haughty** means feeling oneself superior to others and showing it by treating them with cold indifference and scorn: *A haughty person is often unpopular.* **Arrogant** implies a disposition to treat those considered inferior with overbearing rudeness: *the arrogant manners of a dictator.*

haul (hôl), *v.t.* 1 pull or drag with force: *The heavy logs were loaded on wagons and hauled to the mill by horses.* See **draw** for synonym study. 2 transport; carry: *Trucks, trains, and ships haul freight.* 3 change the course of (a ship). —*v.i.* 1 pull or tug: *The skipper hauled at the heavy sail.* 2 change; shift: *The wind hauled around to the east.* 3 **haul off, a** draw back one's arm to give a blow. **b** turn a ship away from an object. 4 **haul up,** turn a ship nearer to the direction of the wind. —*n.* 1 act of hauling; hard pull. 2 load hauled: *Powerful trucks are used for heavy hauls.* 3 distance or route over which a load is hauled. 4 amount won, taken, etc., at one time; catch: *a good haul of fish.* [< Old French *haler.* Doublet of HALE[2].] **—haul′er,** *n.*

haul age (hô′lij), *n.* 1 act of hauling. 2 charge made for hauling.

haunch (hônch, hänch), *n.* 1 hip (def. 1). 2 **haunches,** *pl.* the hindquarters of an animal: *The dog sat on his haunches.* 3 the leg and loin of a deer, sheep, or other animal, used for food. [< Old French *hanche*]

haunt (hônt, hänt), *v.t.* 1 go often to; visit frequently. 2 be often with; come often to: *Memories of his youth haunted the old man.* 3 visit frequently and habitually with manifestations of influence and presence: *People say ghosts haunt that old house.* —*v.i.* stay or remain usually (in a place). —*n.* place often gone to or visited: *The swimming pool was the children's favorite haunt on hot summer days.* 2 DIALECT. ghost. [< Old French *hanter*] **—haunt′ing ly,** *adv.*

haunt ed (hôn′tid, hän′tid), *adj.* visited by ghosts.

haus to ri um (hô stôr′ē əm, hô stōr′ē əm), *n., pl.* **haus to ri a** (hô stôr′ē ə, hô stōr′ē ə). one of the small roots of parasitic plants through which they absorb nourishment. [< New Latin < Latin *haustor* drainer < *haurire* draw (water)]

haut boy (hō′boi, ō′boi), *n.* oboe. [< Middle French *hautbois* < *haut* high + *bois* wood; with reference to its high notes]

haute cou ture (ōt kü ᴛʏʀ′), FRENCH. 1 the most notable fashion designers and dressmaking establishments of the world, as those of Paris. 2 the products of these designers and establishments.

haute cui sine (ōt kwē zēn′), FRENCH. 1 cooking as a fine art, especially as practiced by acknowledged master chefs. 2 food that is prepared in this way.

hau teur (hō tėr′, ō tėr′), *n.* a being proud and overbearing; haughtiness. [< French < *haut* high]

Ha van a (hə van′ə), *n.* 1 capital of Cuba, a seaport on the NW coast. 1,009,000. Also, SPANISH **La Habana.** 2 cigar made from Cuban tobacco.

have (hav; *unstressed* həv, əv), *v.,* **had, hav ing,** *n.* —*v.t.* 1 hold in one's hand, in one's keeping, or in one's possession: *The pitcher throws the ball to the player who has the bat. We have a big house and farm. He has a cheerful disposition.* See synonym study below. 2 be forced; be compelled; be obliged: *Men have to eat. He will have to go now because his work begins.* 3 cause (somebody to do something or something to be done): *She will have the car washed for you.* 4 take; get: *Have a seat.* 5 show by action: *have the courage to fight.* 6 experience: *have a pain, have fear.* 7 engage in; carry on; perform: *Have a talk with him.* 8 allow; permit: *She won't have any noise while she is reading.* 9 maintain; assert: *They will have it so.* 10 keep; retain: *He has the directions in mind.* 11 know; understand: *He has no Latin.* 12 hold in mind: *have an idea.* 13 be in a certain relation to: *She has three brothers.* 14 INFORMAL. hold an advantage over: *You have him there.* 15 SLANG. outwit or cheat. 16 become the father or mother of: *have a baby.* 17 *Have* is used with past participles to express completed action (the perfect tense). *They have come. She had gone before. I have called her. They will have seen her by Sunday.*

have at, attack; hit.

have done, be through; stop: *Let's have done with this quarreling.*

have had it, SLANG. **a** become disgusted; become fed up. **b** reach an end; lose something that one has had.

have it, a will; make happen: *As luck would have it, we missed the train.* **b** receive a thrashing or punishment: *If I catch you, I'll let you have it.* **c** discover or hit upon an answer, solution, etc. **d** INFORMAL. find oneself in certain (good or bad) circumstances: *You never had it so good.*

have it in for, INFORMAL. have a grudge against; try to get revenge on.

have it out, fight or argue until a question is settled.

have on, be wearing.

have to do with, a be connected with; be related to: *Botany has to do with the study of plants.* **b** be a companion, partner, or friend of; associate with.

—*n.* INFORMAL. person, group, or country that has much property or wealth. [Old English *habban*]

Syn. *v.t.* 1 **Have, hold, own** mean to possess or be in possession of something. **Have** is the general word: *He has many friends.* **Hold** emphasizes having control over or keeping: *He holds the office of treasurer. He cannot hold a friend long.* **Own** suggests having a right, especially a legal right, to hold a thing as property: *He owns a farm. In the United States a person cannot own another person.* ➤ See **of** for usage note.

ha ven (hā′vən), *n.* 1 harbor or port. 2 place of shelter and safety. [Old English *hæfen*]

have-not (hav′not′), *n.* INFORMAL. person, group, or country that has little or no property or wealth.

have n't (hav′ənt), have not.

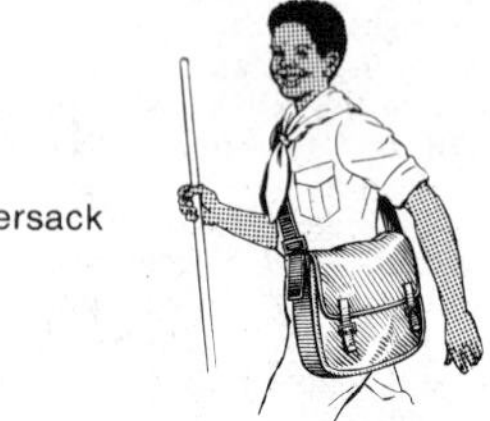

haversack

hav er sack (hav′ər sak), *n.* bag used by soldiers and hikers for carrying food, utensils, etc., when on a march or hike. [< French *havresac* < German *Habersack* oat sack]

Ha ver sian canal (hə vėr′shən), a tiny cylindrical hollow in a bone, through which blood vessels, lymphatics, connective tissues, and nerves run. [< Clopton *Havers,* 1650-1702, English anatomist]

hav oc (hav′ək), *n.* 1 very great destruction or injury; devastation; ruin: *Tornadoes, severe earthquakes, and plagues create widespread havoc.* 2 **play havoc with,** injure severely; ruin; destroy. [< Anglo-French *havok,* variant of Old French *havot* plundering, devastation]

Ha vre (hä′vər, hä′vrə), *n.* See **Le Havre.**

haw[1] (hô), *n.* 1 the red berry of the hawthorn. 2 hawthorn. [Old English *haga*]

haw[2] (hô), *interj., n.* a stammering sound between words. —*v.i.* make this sound; stammer. [imitative]

haw[3] (hô), *interj., n.* word of command to horses, oxen, etc., directing them to turn to the left. —*v.i.* turn to the left. [origin uncertain]

Ha wai i (hə wī′ē), *n.* 1 state of the United States in the N Pacific, consisting of the Hawaiian Islands. 770,000 pop.; 6400 sq. mi. *Capital:* Honolulu. 2 the largest of the Hawaiian Islands. 63,000 pop.; 4000 sq. mi.

Ha wai ian (hə wī′yən), *adj.* of or having to do with Hawaii, its people, or their language. —*n.* 1 native or inhabitant of Hawaii. 2 the Polynesian language of Hawaii.

Hawaiian guitar, a specially tuned guitar in which the length and pitch of the strings are altered by sliding a metal bar over them.

Hawaiian Islands, group of islands in the N Pacific, forming the state of Hawaii. Former name, **Sandwich Islands.**

Hawaii Standard Time, Alaska Standard Time.

Hawaii Volcanoes National Park, large national park on the island of Hawaii which includes Mauna Loa.

hawk[1] (hôk), *n.* 1 any of various birds of prey that hunt in the daytime, especially a genus of short-winged ones, which includes the goshawk. Hawks have strong hooked beaks, powerful feet with long claws, broad wings, and keen sight. Some hawks are trained to hunt and kill other birds and small animals. 2 any of various similar birds such as a buzzard or kite. 3 person who preys on others. 4 INFORMAL. person who advocates a warlike or military solution in a conflict. —*v.i.* 1 hunt with trained hawks. 2 hunt on the wing as a hawk does. —*v.t.* pursue or attack on the wing as a hawk does. [Old English *heafoc*] **—hawk′like′,** *adj.*

hawk[2] (hôk), *v.t.* 1 carry (goods) about and offer them for sale by shouting: *Peddlers hawked their wares in the street.* 2 spread (a report) around. [< *hawker*[1]]

hawk[3] (hôk), *v.i.* clear the throat noisily. —*v.t.* raise (phlegm, etc.) from the throat by hawking. —*n.* a noisy clearing of the throat. [probably imitative]

hawk er[1] (hô′kər), *n.* person who carries his wares around and offers them for sale by shouting; peddler. [probably < Middle Low German *haker.* Related to HUCKSTER.]

hawk er[2] (hô′kər), *n.* person who hunts with trained hawks; falconer. [< *hawk*[1]]

hawk-eyed (hôk′īd′), *adj.* having sharp eyes like a hawk.

Haw kins (hô′kinz), *n.* Sir **John,** 1532-1595, English admiral and slave trader in the West Indies.

hawk ish (hô′kish), *adj.* 1 like a hawk. 2 INFORMAL. advocating a warlike or military solution in a conflict.

hawk moth, any of various large, swift moths having narrow wings and long, stout bodies; sphinx.

hawks bill (hôks′bil′), *n.* hawksbill turtle.

hawksbill turtle, a sea turtle having a mouth shaped somewhat like a hawk's beak and a shell made of overlapping horny plates which provide tortoise shell.

hawk weed (hôk′wēd′), *n.* any of a genus of plants of the composite family, somewhat like chicory, having small yellow, orange, or red flowers.

hawse (defs. 1 and 2)

hawse (hôz, hôs), *n.* 1 part of a ship's bow having holes for hawsers or cables to pass through. 2 one of these holes; hawsehole. 3 space between the bow of a ship and her anchors when moored. [< Scandinavian (Old Icelandic) *hāls* neck]

hawse hole (hôz′hōl′, hôs′hōl′), *n.* hole in a ship's bow for a hawser to pass through.

haw ser (hô′zər, hô′sər), *n.* a large, stout rope or thin steel cable, used for mooring or towing ships. [< Old French *haucier* to hoist < Popular Latin *altiare* < Latin *altus* high]

haw thorn (hô′thôrn), *n.* any of a large genus of thorny shrubs or small trees of the rose family, having clusters of fragrant white, red, or pink flowers and small, red, applelike berries; haw; thorn apple. [Old English *hagathorn* < *haga* hedge + *thorn* thorn]

Haw thorne (hô′thôrn), *n.* **Nathaniel,** 1804-1864, American novelist and short-story writer.

hay (hā), *n.* 1 grass, alfalfa, clover, etc., cut and dried for use as food for cattle, horses, etc. 2 **make hay,** cut and dry grass, alfalfa, clover, etc., for hay. —*v.i.* cut and dry grass, alfalfa, clover, etc., for hay. —*v.t.* supply with hay. [Old English *hēg.* Related to HEW.]

Hay (hā), *n.* **John,** 1838-1905, American statesman, diplomat, and author, secretary of state from 1898 to 1905.

hay cock (hā′kok′), *n.* a small, cone-shaped pile of hay in a field.

Hay dn (hīd′n), *n.* **Franz Joseph,** 1732-1809, Austrian composer.

Hayes (hāz), *n.* 1 **Helen,** born 1900, American actress. 2 **Rutherford B.,** 1822-1893, the 19th president of the United States, from 1877 to 1881.

hay fever, allergy caused by the pollen of ragweed, trees, grasses, and other plants, characterized by sneezing, a running nose, and itching of the nose, throat, and eyes; pollinosis.

hay field (hā′fēld′), *n.* field in which grass, alfalfa, clover, etc., are grown for hay.

hay fork (hā′fôrk′), *n.* 1 pitchfork. 2 a mechanical device equipped with hooks for moving hay into or out of a hayloft.

hay loft (hā′lôft′, hā′loft′), *n.* place in a barn or stable where hay is stored; haymow.

hay mak er (hā′mā′kər), *n.* 1 person who tosses and spreads hay to dry after it is cut. 2 SLANG. a hard, swinging, upward blow with the fist.

hay mow (hā′mou′), *n.* 1 hayloft. 2 heap of hay stored in a barn or stable.

hay rack (hā′rak′), *n.* 1 rack or frame for holding hay to be eaten by cattle, horses, etc. 2 framework on a wagon used in hauling hay, straw, etc. 3 wagon and framework together.

hay rick (hā′rik′), *n.* haystack.

hay ride (hā′rīd′), *n.* outing in a wagon partly filled with hay.

hay seed (hā′sēd′), *n.* 1 grass seed, especially that shaken out of hay. 2 small bits of chaff, etc., that fall from hay. 3 U.S. SLANG. an awkward person from the country; bumpkin; yokel.

hay stack (hā′stak′), *n.* a large pile of hay outdoors.

Hay ward (hā′wərd), *n.* city in W California. 93,000.

hay wire (hā′wīr′), *n.* wire used to tie up bales of hay. —*adj.* SLANG. 1 out of order; wrong. 2 confused or crazy.

haz ard (haz′ərd), *n.* 1 chance of harm; risk; danger; peril: *Mountain climbing is full of hazards.* 2 chance: *take a hazard, games of hazard.* 3 pond, ditch, bush, or any other obstruction in a golf course that can trap a ball. 4 an old and complicated dice game. —*v.t.* 1 take a chance with; risk; venture: *I would hazard my life on his honesty.* 2 expose to risk: *hazard life for a friend.* [< Old French *hasard* game of dice < Arabic *az-zahr* the die]

haz ard ous (haz′ər dəs), *adj.* full of risk; dangerous; perilous. **—haz′ard ous ly,** *adv.* **—haz′ard ous ness,** *n.*

haze[1] (hāz), *n.* 1 a small amount of mist, smoke, dust, etc., in the air: *A thin haze veiled* *the distant hills.* 2 slight confusion; vagueness. [origin uncertain]

haze[2] (hāz), *v.t.,* **hazed, haz ing.** force (freshmen, fraternity initiates, etc.) to do humiliating or ridiculous tasks; bully. [< Middle French *haser* irritate, annoy] —**haz′er,** *n.*

ha zel (hā′zəl), *n.* 1 any of several shrubs or small trees related to the birch, having small, edible nuts with rough husks and smooth light-brown shells. 2 a light brown. *—adj.* light-brown. [Old English *hæsel*]

ha zel nut (hā′zəl nut′), *n.* 1 nut of a hazel. 2 hazel (def. 1).

Haz litt (haz′lit), *n.* **William,** 1778-1830, English critic and essayist.

ha zy (hā′zē), *adj.,* **-zi er, -zi est.** 1 full of haze; misty; smoky: *a hazy sky.* 2 slightly confused; vague; obscure: *a hazy idea.* —**ha′zi ly,** *adv.* —**ha′zi ness,** *n.*

H.B.M., 1 Her Britannic Majesty. 2 His Britannic Majesty.

H-bomb (āch′bom′), *n.* hydrogen bomb.

H.C., House of Commons.

HCF, H.C.F., or **h.c.f.,** highest common factor.

hd., *pl.* **hds.** head.

hdkf., *pl.* **hdkfs.** handkerchief.

hdqrs., headquarters.

he (hē; *unstressed* ē, i), *pron., nominative* **he,** *possessive* **his,** *objective* **him;** *pl. nominative* **they,** *possessive* **theirs** or **their,** *objective* **them;** *n., pl.* **he's.** *—pron.* 1 boy, man, or male animal spoken about or mentioned before. 2 anyone: *He who hesitates is lost.* *—n.* a male: *Is your dog a he or a she?* [Old English *hē*]

He, helium.

HE, high explosive.

H.E., 1 His Eminence. 2 His Excellency.

head (hed), *n., pl.* **heads** for 1-8, 10-29, **head** for 9; *adj., v.* *—n.* 1 the top part of the human body containing the brain, eyes, nose, ears, and mouth. 2 the corresponding part of an animal's body. 3 the top part of anything: *the head of a pin, the head of a bed, the head of a page.* 4 the front part of anything: *the head of a procession, the head of a comet.* 5 the chief person; leader; commander; director. 6 headmaster. 7 position of leadership; chief importance; command or direction: *at the head of the administration.* 8 person: *Kings and queens are crowned heads.* 9 one or ones; individual or individuals. Ten cows are ten head of cattle. 10 anything rounded like a head: *a head of cabbage.* 11 flower head. 12 the part of a boil or pimple where pus is about to break through the skin. 13 the striking or cutting part of a tool or implement: *the head of a hammer, the head of a golf club.* 14 piece of skin stretched tightly over the end of a drum, tambourine, etc. 15 either end of a barrel or cask. 16 mind; understanding: *A bank teller must have a good head for figures.* 17 topic; point: *He arranged his speech under four main heads.* 18 crisis or conclusion; decisive point: *His sudden refusal brought matters to a head.* 19 strength or force gained little by little: *As more people joined, the movement gathered head.* 20 pressure of water, gas, etc.: *a full head of steam.* 21 source of a river or stream. 22 foam; froth: *the head on a glass of beer.* 23 the line or lines at the top of a newspaper article; headline. 24 the forward part of a ship, including the bow. 25 lavatory, especially on a ship or boat. 26 body of water at a height above a particular level. 27 headland. 28 **heads,** *pl.* the top side of a coin. 29 (in grammar) a word which has the same function as the phrase in which it occurs. In *very fresh milk* the head is *milk.*
give someone his head, let someone do as he pleases.
go to one's head, **a** affect one's mind. **b** make one dizzy. **c** make one conceited.
hang one's head, be ashamed and show that one is.
head over heels, **a** in a somersault. **b** hastily; rashly. **c** completely; thoroughly: *head over heels in love.*
keep one's head, stay calm; not get excited.
keep one's head above water, avoid failure, loss, defeat, death, etc.
lose one's head, get excited; lose one's self-control.
make head or tail of, understand.
on one's head or **upon one's head,** on one's responsibility.
out of one's head or **off one's head,** INFORMAL. crazy; insane.
over one's head, **a** beyond one's power to understand. **b** passing over a person without giving him a chance to act.
put heads together or **lay heads together,** plan or plot together.
take it into one's head, **a** get the idea. **b** plan; intend.
turn one's head, make one conceited.
—adj. 1 at the head, top, or front: *the head division of a parade.* 2 coming from in front: *a head sea, head tides.* 3 chief; leading; commanding; directing: *the head clerk in a store.*
—v.t. 1 be or go at the head, top, or front of: *head a parade.* 2 cause to move or face in a certain direction: *head a boat toward shore.* 3 be the head or chief of; lead; command; direct: *head a business.* 4 put a head on; furnish with a head: *head a letter with a date.* 5 cut off the head of; behead. 6 go around the head of (a stream, lake, etc.): *The explorer headed the river instead of crossing it.* 7 **head off, a** get in front of and turn back or aside: *The cowboys tried to head off the stampeding herd.* **b** prevent; forestall: *He tried to head off possible trouble by taking extreme care in what he did.* *—v.i.* 1 move or go in a certain direction: *It's getting late, we'd better head for home.* 2 form a head; come to a head.
[Old English *hēafod*] —**head′like′,** *adj.*

head ache (hed′āk′), *n.* 1 pain in the head. 2 INFORMAL. something which causes great bother, annoyance, etc.

head ach y (hed′ā′kē), *adj.* INFORMAL. of, like, or caused by a headache.

head band (hed′band′), *n.* band of cloth, ribbon, etc., worn around the head.

head board (hed′bôrd′, hed′bōrd′), *n.* board or frame at the head or upper end of anything: *the headboard of a bedstead.*

head cheese (hed′chēz′), *n.* a jellied loaf formed of parts of the head and feet of hogs cut up, cooked, and seasoned.

head dress (hed′dres′), *n.* 1 a covering or decoration for the head. 2 way of wearing or arranging the hair.

head ed (hed′id), *adj.* 1 having a head. 2 having a heading.

-headed, *combining form.* 1 having a ____ head: *Long-headed = having a long head.* 2 having ____ heads: *Two-headed = having two heads.*

head er (hed′ər), *n.* 1 person, tool, or machine that puts on or takes off heads of barrels, pins, nails, etc. 2 a harvesting machine that cuts off the heads of grain and puts them in a storage box or wagon. 3 INFORMAL. a plunge, dive, or fall headfirst: *He slipped and took a header over the pool's edge.* 4 beam forming part of the framework around an opening in a floor or roof, placed so as to fit between two long beams and support the ends of short ones.

hat, āge, fär; let, ēqual, tėrm;
it, īce; hot, ōpen, ôrder;
oil, out; cup, pu̇t, rüle;
ch, child; ng, long; sh, she;
th, thin; ᴛʜ, then; zh, measure;

ə represents *a* in about, *e* in taken,
i in pencil, *o* in lemon, *u* in circus.

< = from, derived from, taken from.

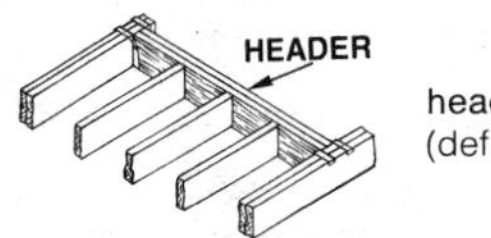

header (def. 4)

head first (hed′fėrst′), *adv.* 1 with the head first. 2 hastily; rashly. *—adj.* done or going with the head first.

head fore most (hed′fôr′mōst, hed′fōr′-mōst), *adv.* headfirst.

head gate, 1 an upstream gate of a lock in a canal or river. 2 floodgate of a race, sluice, irrigation ditch, etc.

head gear (hed′gir′), *n.* 1 covering for the head; a hat, cap, helmet, etc. 2 the parts of a harness which fit around an animal's head.

head hunt er (hed′hun′tər), *n.* member of a primitive tribe who cuts off the heads of his enemies and preserves them as a sign of victory, manhood, etc.

head hunt ing (hed′hun′ting), *n.* the practice of headhunters.

head ing (hed′ing), *n.* 1 something used as a head, top, or front. 2 something written or printed at the top of a page, such as a letterhead. 3 title of a page, chapter, topic, etc. 4 direction in which an aircraft or ship is moving.

head land (hed′lənd, hed′land′), *n.* point of high land jutting out into water; cape; promontory.

head less (hed′lis), *adj.* 1 having no head. 2 without a leader. 3 without brains; foolish; stupid.

head light (hed′līt′), *n.* a bright light at the front of an automobile, locomotive, etc.

head line (hed′līn′), *n., v.,* **-lined, -lin ing.** *—n.* 1 words printed in heavy type at the top of a newspaper or magazine article telling what it is about. 2 line printed at the top of a page giving the running title, page number, etc.; running head. 3 **headlines,** *pl.* publicity: *The invention got headlines everywhere.* *—v.t.* 1 furnish (a news story, etc.) with a headline. 2 give publicity to: *The newspapers headlined the story of the astronauts' trip to the moon.* 3 list or be listed in as the main attraction. *—v.i.* be the main attraction.

head lin er (hed′lī′nər), *n.* INFORMAL. actor or performer whose name is given prominence in advertisements, playbills, etc.

head lock (hed′lok′), *n.* (in wrestling) a hold in which the opponent's head is gripped and held between one's body and arm.

head long (hed′lông, hed′long), *adv.*

1 with the head first: *plunge headlong into the sea.* 2 with great speed and force: *rush headlong into the crowd.* 3 in too great a rush; without stopping to think: *The boy ran headlong across the busy street.* —*adj.* 1 done or going headfirst: *a headlong plunge.* 2 done, caused by, or characterized by great speed and force: *a headlong course.* 3 violently or suddenly rash; reckless: *One should not make a headlong decision about something important.* [Middle English *hedlong,* alteration of earlier *hedling* < *hed* head + *-ling,* adverb suffix expressing direction]

head man (hed′man′, hed′mən), *n., pl.* **-men.** chief; leader.

head mas ter (hed′mas′tər), *n.* man in charge of a school, especially of a private school; principal.

head mis tress (hed′mis′tris), *n.* woman in charge of a school, especially of a private school.

head most (hed′mōst), *adj.* most advanced; first.

head-on (hed′on′, hed′ôn′), *adj., adv.* with the head or front first: *a head-on collision, collide head-on.*

head phone (hed′fōn′), *n.* earphone held against one or both ears by a band over the head.

head piece (hed′pēs′), *n.* 1 helmet worn with a suit of armor. 2 any covering for the head. 3 headphone. 4 head; mind; intellect. 5 ornament or decoration at the head of a page, chapter, etc.

head pin (hed′pin′), *n.* the front pin of the triangle of pins in the game of bowling; kingpin.

head quar ters (hed′kwôr′tərz), *n.pl. or sing.* 1 place from which the chief or commanding officer of an army, police force, etc., sends out orders. 2 place from which any organization is controlled and directed; main office.

head race (hed′rās′), *n.* race, flume, or channel that brings water to a mill wheel.

head rest (hed′rest′), *n.* support for the head, as on a dentist's chair.

head-re straint (hed′rē strānt′), *n.* padded support for the head to hit if thrown forward and back in a collision, especially a rear-end collision.

head room (hed′rüm′, hed′rům′), *n.* a clear space overhead; clearance.

head set (hed′set′), *n.* pair of headphones used by telephone and radio operators, etc.

head ship (hed′ship), *n.* position of head; chief authority; leadership.

heads man (hedz′mən), *n., pl.* **-men.** a public executioner who puts condemned persons to death by cutting off their heads.

head stall (hed′stôl′), *n.* the part of a bridle or halter that fits around a horse's head.

head stand (hed′stand′), *n.* a balancing upon the head, with the hands placed in front of the head on the mat or ground.

head start, 1 advantage or lead allowed someone at the beginning of a race. 2 advantage gained by beginning something before somebody else.

head stock (hed′stok′), *n.* 1 part of a machine that contains the revolving or working parts. 2 part of a lathe that holds the spindle.

head stone (hed′stōn′), *n.* 1 stone set at the head of a grave; gravestone. 2 cornerstone of a building.

head stream (hed′strēm′), *n.* stream that is the source of a larger stream.

head strong (hed′strông′, hed′strong′), *adj.* 1 rashly or foolishly determined to have one's own way; hard to control or manage; obstinate: *a headstrong child, a headstrong horse.* 2 showing rash or foolish determination to have one's own way: *headstrong actions.*

head wait er (hed′wā′tər), *n.* man in charge of the waiters in a restaurant, hotel, etc.

head wa ters (hed′wô′tərz, hed′wot′ərz), *n.pl.* the sources or upper parts of a river.

head way (hed′wā′), *n.* 1 motion forward; progress: *The ship could make no headway against the strong wind and tide.* 2 progress with work, etc.; advance. 3 a clear space overhead in a doorway or under an arch, bridge, etc.; clearance. 4 interval of time between two trains, streetcars, ships, etc., going in the same direction over the same route.

head wind, wind blowing from the direction in which a ship, etc., is moving.

head word (hed′wėrd′), *n.* 1 word serving as a heading or title of a paragraph, article, dictionary entry, etc. 2 (in grammar) a word around which clusters of modifiers are built. In *the small boy, very glad, is running fast,* the words *boy, running,* and *glad* are headwords.

head work (hed′wėrk′), *n.* mental work; effort with the mind; thought.

head y (hed′ē), *adj.,* **head i er, head i est.** 1 hasty; rash; headlong. 2 apt to affect the head and make one dizzy; intoxicating. **—head′i ly,** *adv.* **—head′i ness,** *n.*

heal (hēl), *v.t.* 1 make whole, sound, or well; bring back to health; cure (a disease or wound). See **cure** for synonym study. 2 free from anything bad. 3 get rid of (anything bad). —*v.i.* become whole or sound; get well; return to health; be cured: *The fractured bone soon healed.* [Old English *hǣlan* < *hāl* whole] **—heal′er,** *n.*

health (helth), *n.* 1 a being well; freedom from sickness. 2 condition of body or mind: *She is in poor health.* 3 sound condition; well-being; welfare: *the safety and health of the whole state.* 4 a toast drunk in honor of a person with a wish that he may be healthy and happy: *We all drank a health to the bride.* [Old English *hǣlth* < *hāl* whole]

health ful (helth′fəl), *adj.* 1 giving health; good for the health: *healthful exercise, a healthful diet.* 2 having good health; healthy. **—health′ful ly,** *adv.* **—health′ful ness,** *n.*

➤ **healthful, healthy.** Though these words are often used interchangeably, many writers and speakers distinguish between them by using *healthful* to mean "giving health" and *healthy* to mean "having good health." Places and food are *healthful;* persons and animals are *healthy.*

health y (hel′thē), *adj.,* **health i er, health i est.** 1 having good health; in a sound condition; well: *a healthy baby.* 2 showing good health: *a healthy appearance.* 3 giving health; good for the health; healthful: *healthy exercise.* **—health′i ly,** *adv.* **—health′i ness,** *n.* ➤ See **healthful** for usage note.

heap (hēp), *n.* 1 pile of many things thrown or lying together in a confused way; mass: *a heap of stones, a sand heap.* 2 INFORMAL. a large amount: *a heap of trouble.* —*v.t.* 1 form into a heap; gather in heaps; amass: *She heaped the dirty clothes beside the washing machine.* 2 give generously or in large amounts: *The man heaped insults upon his enemy.* 3 fill full or more than full; load: *heap a plate with food.* —*v.i.* become heaped or piled. [Old English *hēap*] **—heap′er,** *n.*

hear (hir), *v.,* **heard, hear ing.** —*v.t.* 1 perceive by the ear: *hear voices, hear a bell.* See synonym study below. 2 listen to: *You must hear what he has to say.* 3 listen to with favor; grant: *Lord, hear my prayer.* 4 give a formal hearing to, as a king, a judge, a teacher, or an assembly does. 5 attend and listen to (a lecture, musical performance, etc.). 6 find out by hearing: *hear news.* **7 hear out,** listen to till the end. **8 will not hear of,** will not listen to, think of, agree to, or allow. —*v.i.* 1 be able to perceive by the ear: *He cannot hear well.* 2 listen: *The town crier shouted "Hear ye!"* 3 receive news or information: *Have you heard from your friend in Los Angeles?* [Old English *hēran*] **—hear′er,** *n.*

Syn. *v.t.* 1 **Hear, listen** mean to perceive by the ear. **Hear** applies to the physical act of receiving sound through the ear: *Do you hear a noise?* **Listen** means to pay attention to a sound and try to hear or understand it: *I heard you talking but did not listen to what you said.*

heard (hėrd), *v.* pt. and pp. of **hear.**

hear ing (hir′ing), *n.* 1 sense by which sound is perceived: *My hearing is poor.* 2 act or process of taking in sound, listening, or receiving information: *Hearing the good news made her happy.* 3 a formal or official listening, especially to evidence and arguments: *The judge gave both sides a hearing in court.* 4 chance to be heard: *Give us a hearing.* 5 distance that a sound can be heard; earshot: *talk freely in the hearing of others.*

hearing aid, a small, electronic device which amplifies sounds, worn in or directly behind the ear by people who cannot hear well.

heark en (här′kən), *v.i.* pay attention to what is said; listen attentively; listen. Also, **harken.** [Old English *heorcnian*]

hear say (hir′sā′), *n.* common talk; gossip or rumor.

hearse (hėrs), *n.* automobile, carriage, etc., for carrying a dead person to his grave. [Middle English *herse* framework over a bier for candles < Old French *herce,* ultimately < Latin *hirpicem* frame like a harrow]

Hearst (hėrst), *n.* **William Randolph,** 1863-1951, American editor and publisher of newspapers and magazines.

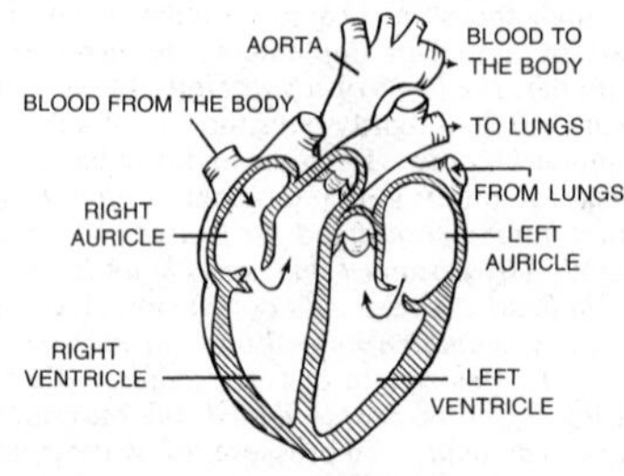

heart (def. 1)

heart (härt), *n.* 1 the hollow, muscular organ that pumps the blood throughout the body by contracting and relaxing. 2 feelings; mind; soul: *He knew in his heart that he was wrong.* 3 source of the emotions, especially of love: *give one's heart to someone.* 4 person loved

hat, āge, fär; let, ēqual, tėrm;
it, īce; hot, ōpen, ôrder;
oil, out; cup, pu̇t, rüle;
ch, child; ng, long; sh, she;
th, thin; ᴛʜ, then; zh, measure;

ə represents *a* in about, *e* in taken, *i* in pencil, *o* in lemon, *u* in circus.

< = from, derived from, taken from.

or praised: *group of stout hearts.* 5 kindness; sympathy: *Have you no heart?* 6 spirit; courage; enthusiasm: *The losing team still had plenty of heart.* 7 the innermost part; middle; center: *in the heart of the forest.* 8 the main part; most important or vital part: *the very heart of the matter.* 9 figure shaped like this: ♥. 10 a playing card marked with one or more red, heart-shaped figures. 11 **hearts,** *pl.* suit of such playing cards. 12 **hearts,** *pl.* game in which the players try to get rid of cards of this suit.

after one's own heart, just as one likes it; pleasing one perfectly.

at heart, in one's deepest thoughts or feelings.

by heart, a by memory: *I learned the poem by heart.* **b** from memory: *I can recite the poem by heart.*

eat one's heart out, feel great sorrow, grief, or worry.

have one's heart in the right place, mean well; have good intentions.

heart and soul, with all one's affections and energies.

in one's heart of hearts, in one's deepest thoughts or feelings.

lose one's heart (to), fall in love (with).

take heart, be encouraged.

take to heart, think seriously about; be deeply affected by.

wear one's heart on one's sleeve, show one's feelings quite plainly.

with all one's heart, a sincerely. **b** gladly.

[Old English *heorte*]

heart ache (härt′āk′), *n.* great sorrow or grief; deep pain.

heart attack, a sudden failure of the heart to function properly, sometimes resulting in death. It can be caused by coronary thrombosis, arteriosclerosis, high blood pressure, etc.

heart beat (härt′bēt′), *n.* pulsation of the heart, including one complete contraction and relaxation.

heart block, an abnormal condition of the heart, characterized by independent beating of the ventricles in relation to that of the auricles.

heart break (härt′brāk′), *n.* a crushing sorrow or grief.

heart break ing (härt′brā′king), *adj.* crushing with sorrow or grief. **—heart′-break′ing ly,** *adv.*

heart bro ken (härt′brō′kən), *adj.* crushed by sorrow or grief. **—heart′bro′ken ly,** *adv.* **—heart′bro′ken ness,** *n.*

heart burn (härt′bėrn′), *n.* a burning feeling in the esophagus caused by a rising up of acid from the stomach.

heart burn ing (härt′bėr′ning), *n.* rankling discontent, especially from a hidden feeling of envy or jealousy.

-hearted, *combining form.* having a ___ heart: *Hardhearted = having a hard heart. Kindhearted = having a kind heart.*

heart en (härt′n), *v.t.* cheer up; encourage: *This good news will hearten you.*

heart felt (härt′felt′), *adj.* with deep feeling; sincere; genuine: *heartfelt sympathy.*

hearth (härth), *n.* 1 stone or brick floor of a fireplace, often extending into the room. 2 fireside; home: *The travelers began to long for their own hearths.* 3 the lowest part of a blast furnace, where the molten metal and slag collects. [Old English *heorth*]

hearth side (härth′sīd′), *n.* fireside; home.

hearth stone (härth′stōn′), *n.* 1 stone forming a hearth. 2 fireside; home.

heart i ly (här′tl ē), *adv.* 1 in a warm, friendly way; sincerely: *express good wishes very heartily.* 2 with courage, spirit, or enthusiasm; vigorously: *set to work heartily.* 3 with a good appetite: *eat heartily.* 4 very; completely: *My mother was heartily tired when she came home from work.*

heart i ness (här′tē nis), *n.* hearty quality.

heart land (härt′land′, härt′lənd), *n.* any area or region that is the center of, or vital to, a country, industry, institution, etc.

heart less (härt′lis), *adj.* 1 without kindness or sympathy; unfeeling; cruel. 2 without courage, spirit, or enthusiasm. **—heart′-less ly,** *adv.* **—heart′less ness,** *n.*

heart-lung machine (härt′lung′), machine that pumps oxygenated blood through the body while the heart is drained of blood during certain operations.

heart-rend ing (härt′ren′ding), *adj.* causing mental anguish; very distressing. **—heart′-rend′ing ly,** *adv.*

hearts ease or **heart's-ease** (härts′ēz′), *n.* 1 peace of mind; tranquillity. 2 pansy, especially the wild pansy.

heart sick (härt′sik′), *adj.* sick at heart; very depressed; very unhappy.

heart sore (härt′sôr′, härt′sōr′), *adj.* feeling or showing grief; grieved.

heart-strick en (härt′strik′ən), *adj.* struck to the heart with grief; shocked with fear; dismayed.

heart strings (härt′stringz′), *n.pl.* deepest feelings; strongest affections.

heart-struck (härt′struk′), *adj.* heart-stricken.

heart throb (härt′throb′), *n.* 1 throb or pulsation of the heart. 2 passionate or sentimental emotion. 3 SLANG. sweetheart.

heart-to-heart (härt′tə härt′), *adj.* without reserve; frank; sincere.

heart-whole (härt′hōl′), *adj.* 1 not in love; heart-free. 2 hearty; sincere.

heart wood (härt′wu̇d′), *n.* the central, nonliving wood in the trunk of a tree, harder and more solid than the newer sapwood that surrounds it.

heart y (här′tē), *adj.,* **heart i er, heart i est,** *n., pl.* **heart ies.** *—adj.* 1 warm and friendly; genuine; sincere: *We gave our friends a hearty welcome.* 2 strong and well; vigorous: *The old man was still hale and hearty at eighty.* 3 full of energy and enthusiasm; unrestrained: *a loud, hearty laugh.* 4 with plenty to eat; abundant: *A hearty meal satisfied his hunger.* 5 having a good appetite: *a hearty eater.* 6 nourishing: *hearty food.* *—n.* 1 a fellow sailor. 2 a brave and good comrade.

heat (hēt), *n.* 1 condition of being hot; high temperature; hotness; warmth: *the heat of a fire.* 2 degree of hotness; temperature: *red heat, white heat, animal heat.* 3 sensation or perception of hotness or warmth, such as is experienced from nearness to fire. 4 (in physics) a form of energy that consists of the motion of the molecules of a substance, capable of being transmitted from one body to another by conduction, convection, or radiation. The effects of absorbed heat on a body are increase of temperature, expansion or increase of volume, and possible change of state, as of a solid to a liquid, or of a liquid to a gas. 5 hot weather or a hot season: *the heat of summer.* 6 warmth or intensity of feeling; violence; excitement. 7 the hottest point; most violent or active state: *In the heat of the argument he lost his temper.* 8 SLANG. pressure; coercion; torture. 9 a single intense effort: *do a thing at a heat.* 10 section of a race, consisting of a complete running of the course: *He won the first heat, but lost the final race.* 11 one operation of heating in a furnace or a forge. 12 a periodically recurring condition of sexual excitement in female animals; estrus. 13 period of time that this excitement lasts, when the female will mate with the male.

—v.t. 1 make hot or warm. 2 fill with strong feeling; inflame; excite. *—v.i.* 1 become hot or warm. 2 be filled with strong feeling; become excited.

[Old English *hǣtu.* Related to HOT.] **—heat′less,** *adj.*

heat ed (hē′tid), *adj.* 1 angry, excited, or violent: *a heated argument.* 2 hot. **—heat′-ed ly,** *adv.*

heat er (hē′tər), *n.* stove, furnace, radiator, or other apparatus that gives heat or warmth.

heat exchanger, device by means of which heat is transferred from one fluid to another in order that it may be utilized or eliminated, as in an atomic power plant. The radiator is a common heat exchanger.

heat exhaustion, condition caused by excessive exposure to heat, characterized by a cold, clammy skin and general symptoms of shock.

heath (hēth), *n.* 1 open, waste land with heather or low bushes growing on it, but few or no trees; moor. 2 heather. 3 any of a genus of low shrubs of the heath family, that are similar to heather and grow on heaths. [Old English *hǣth*] **—heath′like′,** *adj.*

Heath (hēth), *n.* **Edward,** born 1916, British statesman, prime minister since 1970.

hea then (hē′ᴛʜən), *n., pl.* **-thens** or **-then,** *adj.* *—n.* 1 person who does not believe in the God of the Bible; person who is not a Christian, Jew, or Moslem; pagan. See synonym study below. 2 people who are heathens. 3 person without religion or culture; unenlightened person. *—adj.* 1 of or having to do with heathens; not Christian, Jewish, or Moslem. 2 not religious or cultured; unenlightened. [Old English *hǣthen*]

Syn. *n.* 1 **Heathen, pagan** mean someone whose religion is not Christian and, usually, neither Jewish nor Moslem. **Heathen** is applied particularly to those whose religions are regarded as primitive and unenlightened: *The heathens worshiped idols.* **Pagan** is used especially of the religions of Greece, Rome, and other nations of antiquity: *The pagans believed in many gods.*

hea then dom (hē′ᴛʜən dəm), *n.* 1 heathen worship or ways. 2 heathen lands or people.

hea then ish (hē′ᴛʜə nish), *adj.* 1 having to do with heathens. 2 like heathens; uncivilized; barbarous. **—hea′then ish ly,** *adv.*

hea then ism (hē′ᴛʜə niz′əm), *n.* 1 heathen worship or ways. 2 lack of religion or culture; barbarism.

heath er (heᴛʜ′ər), *n.* a low, evergreen

shrub of the heath family, with stalks of small, purple or pink, bell-shaped flowers, covering many heaths of Scotland and England; heath. [Middle English *hathir*]

heath er y (heᴛʜ′ər ē), *adj.* 1 of or like heather. 2 covered with heather.

heath family, a widely distributed group of shrubs, often with evergreen leaves, including the heath, azalea, rhododendron, huckleberry, blueberry, etc.

heating element, part of an electrical device that provides heat, such as the set of exposed wires in a toaster.

heat lightning, flashes of light so distant that the thunder cannot be heard, seen near the horizon, especially on hot summer evenings.

heat shield, a coating or covering of special material on the nose cone of a missile or spacecraft to absorb or diffuse heat induced by friction when it reenters the earth's atmosphere.

heat stroke (hēt′strōk′), *n.* collapse or sudden illness with high fever and dry skin caused by exposure to excessive heat, as from the infrared rays of the sun.

heat wave, period of very hot weather.

heave (hēv), *v.,* **heaved** or **hove, heav ing,** *n., interj.* —*v.t.* 1 lift with force or effort; hoist: *He heaved the heavy box into the wagon.* 2 lift and throw; cast: *heave a stone.* 3 give (a sigh, groan, etc.) with a deep, heavy breath. —*v.i.* 1 pull with force or effort; haul: *They heaved on the rope.* 2 rise and fall alternately: *The waves heaved in the storm.* 3 breathe hard; pant; gasp. 4 vomit or try to vomit; retch. 5 (of a ship) move or turn in a certain direction or way. 6 be raised, thrown, or forced up; rise; swell; bulge: *The ground heaved from the earthquake.* 7 **heave in sight,** come into view. 8 **heave to,** stop a ship; stop. —*n.* 1 act or fact of heaving: *With a mighty heave, we pushed the boat into the water.* 2 **heaves,** *pl.* disease of horses characterized by difficult breathing, coughing, and heaving of the flanks. —*interj.* **heave ho!** sailors' cry when pulling up the anchor, etc. [Old English *hebban*] —**heav′er,** *n.*

heav en (hev′ən), *n.* 1 (in Christian and some other religious use) the place where God and the angels live and where the blessed go after death. 2 **Heaven,** God; Providence: *It was the will of Heaven.* 3 place or condition of greatest happiness. 4 Usually, **heavens,** *pl.* the upper air or sky in which the sun, moon, and stars seem to be set. 5 **for heaven's sake** or **good heavens!** exclamation of surprise or protest. 6 **move heaven and earth,** do everything possible. [Old English *heofon*]

heav en ly (hev′ən lē), *adj.* 1 of or in heaven; divine; holy: *God is our heavenly Father.* 2 like heaven; suitable for heaven; very happy, beautiful, or excellent: *a heavenly spot, heavenly peace.* 3 of or in the heavens: *The sun, moon, stars, planets, and comets are heavenly bodies.* —**heav′en li ness,** *n.*

heav en ward (hev′ən wərd), *adv., adj.* toward heaven.

heav en wards (hev′ən wərdz), *adv.* heavenward.

Heav i side layer (hev′ē sīd), layer of the ionosphere which reflects low-frequency radio waves; E region. See **atmosphere** for diagram. [< Oliver *Heaviside,* 1850-1925, British physicist]

heav y (hev′ē), *adj.,* **heav i er, heav i est,** *adv., n., pl.* **heav ies.** —*adj.* 1 hard to lift or carry; of great weight: *a heavy load.* See synonym study below. 2 having much weight for its size; of high specific gravity: *Osmium is the heaviest metal.* 3 of more than usual weight for its kind: *heavy silk.* 4 of great amount, force, or intensity; greater than usual; large: *a heavy rain, a heavy crop, a heavy sea, a heavy vote.* 5 doing or being such to an unusual degree: *a heavy buyer, a heavy smoker.* 6 hard to endure: *heavy taxes.* 7 hard to deal with, manage, etc.; trying or difficult in any way: *We had a difficult trip over heavy roads of mud and sand. Heavy soil is hard to work.* 8 hard to digest: *heavy food.* 9 weighted down; laden: *air heavy with moisture, eyes heavy with sleep.* 10 causing sorrow; gloomy: *heavy news.* 11 sorrowful; sad: *a heavy heart.* 12 grave; serious; sober; somber: *a heavy part in a play.* 13 cloudy; overcast: *a heavy sky.* 14 broad; thick; coarse: *a heavy line, heavy features.* 15 clumsy; sluggish; slow: *a heavy walk.* 16 uninteresting; dull; ponderous: *heavy reading.* 17 loud and deep: *the heavy roar of cannon.* 18 in military use: **a** heavily armed or equipped: *heavy tanks.* **b** of large size: *heavy artillery.* 19 not risen enough: *heavy bread.* 20 in chemistry and physics: **a** indicating an isotope possessing a greater atomic weight than another of the same element. **b** indicating a compound containing such isotopes. 21 pregnant.
—*adv.* 1 in a heavy manner; heavily. 2 **hang heavy,** pass slowly and uninterestingly: *The time hung heavy on his hands.*
—*n.* 1 INFORMAL. **a** villain in a play. **b** actor who plays such parts. 2 heavyweight (def. 2). [Old English *hefig* < *hebban* heave] —**heav′i ly,** *adv.* —**heav′i ness,** *n.*
Syn. *adj.* 1 **Heavy, weighty, burdensome** mean of great weight. **Heavy,** when used figuratively, suggests something pressing down on or weighing down the mind or feelings: *The President of the United States has heavy responsibilities.* **Weighty** is used chiefly figuratively, applying to something of great importance: *He made a weighty announcement.* **Burdensome** refers chiefly to something that is difficult to do or puts a strain on the one doing it: *The extra work was burdensome.*

heav y-du ty (hev′ē dü′tē, hev′ē dyü′tē), *adj.* durably built to withstand hard use, strain, etc.: *heavy-duty tires.*

heav y-foot ed (hev′ē fu̇t′id), *adj.* 1 stepping heavily; clumsy. 2 with tired feet.

heav y-hand ed (hev′ē han′did), *adj.* 1 clumsy; awkward: *heavy-handed humor.* 2 treating others harshly; oppressive. —**heav′y-hand′ed ly,** *adv.* —**heav′y-hand′ed ness,** *n.*

heav y-heart ed (hev′ē här′tid), *adj.* in low spirits; sad; gloomy. —**heav′y-heart′ed ly,** *adv.* —**heav′y-heart′ed ness,** *n.*

heavy hydrogen, deuterium.

heavy industry, industry that manufactures products, such as machines or steel, for use by other industries.

heav y set (hev′ē set′), *adj.* built heavily; broad; stocky.

heavy water, water formed of oxygen and deuterium; deuterium oxide. Heavy water is much like ordinary water, but is about 1.1 times as heavy and has a higher freezing point. It occurs in very small amounts in ordinary water. *Formula:* D_2O

heav y weight (hev′ē wāt′), *n.* 1 person or thing of more than average weight. 2 athlete who competes in the heaviest weight class, especially a boxer who weighs 175 pounds or more. 3 INFORMAL. person who has much intelligence or importance.

Heb., Hebrew or Hebrews.

heb dom a dal (heb dom′ə dəl), *adj.* weekly. [< Latin *hebdomadem* seven, seven days, ultimately < Greek *hepta* seven] —**heb dom′a dal ly,** *adv.*

He be (hē′bē), *n.* (in Greek myths) the goddess of youth.

He bra ic (hi brā′ik), *adj.* of or having to do with the Hebrews or their language or culture.

He bra ism (hē′brā iz′əm), *n.* 1 a Hebrew usage or idiom. 2 Hebrew character, spirit, thought, or practice.

He bra ist (hē′brā ist), *n.* an expert in the Hebrew language and literature.

He bra is tic (hē′brā is′tik), *adj.* Hebraic.

He brew (hē′brü), *n.* 1 Jew; Israelite. 2 the ancient Semitic language of the Jews, in which most of the Old Testament was written. 3 one of the present-day official languages of Israel, a modern form of ancient Hebrew. The other official language is Arabic. —*adj.* 1 Jewish. 2 of or having to do with ancient or modern Hebrew. [< Latin *Hebraeus* < Greek *Hebraios* < Aramaic *'Ebrai* < Hebrew *'Ibhrī,* literally, one from beyond (the river)]

Hebrew calendar, Jewish calendar.

He brews (hē′brüz), *n.* book of the New Testament, supposedly written by Saint Paul to Christians of Hebrew ancestry at Rome.

Heb ri de an (heb′rə dē′ən), *adj.* of or having to do with the Hebrides. —*n.* native or inhabitant of the Hebrides.

Heb ri des (heb′rə dēz′), *n.pl.* group of Scottish islands off NW Scotland. 48,000 pop.; 2900 sq. mi.

He bron (hē′brən), *n.* ancient town in W Jordan, near Jerusalem. 43,000.

Hec a te (hek′ə tē), *n.* (in Greek myths) the goddess of the moon, earth, and lower world. She was later associated with magic and witchcraft.

hec a tomb (hek′ə tōm, hek′ə tüm, hek′ə tom), *n.* 1 (in ancient Greece or Rome) a great public sacrifice of 100 oxen at one time. 2 any great slaughter. [< Latin *hecatombe* < Greek *hekatombē* < *hekaton* hundred + *bous* ox]

heck le (hek′əl), *v.t.,* **-led, -ling.** interrupt and annoy (a speaker, etc.) by asking many bothersome questions, jeering, or making loud remarks. [Middle English *hekelen.* Related to HACKLE[1].] —**heck′ler,** *n.*

hect-, *combining form.* form of **hecto-** before vowels, as in *hectare.*

hec tare (hek′ter, hek′tar), *n.* unit of area in the metric system, equal to 100 ares, 10,000 square meters, or 2.471 acres. See **measure** for table.

hec tic (hek′tik), *adj.* 1 very exciting; characterized by great activity, confusion, etc.: *We had a hectic time getting to school the morning after the big snowstorm.* 2 much excited. 3 flushed. 4 feverish. 5 showing the signs of tuberculosis; consumptive. [< Late Latin *hecticus* < Greek *hektikos* habitual, consumptive < *hexis* habit] —**hec′ti cal ly,** *adv.*

hecto-, *combining form.* 1 hundred: *Hectogram = hundred grams.* 2 many: *Hec-*

tograph = *machine that makes many copies.* [< French < Greek *hekaton*]

hec to gram (hek′tə gram), *n.* unit of mass equal to 100 grams. See **measure** for table.

hec to gramme (hek′tə gram), *n.* BRITISH. hectogram.

hec to graph (hek′tə graf), *n.* machine for making many copies of a page of writing, a drawing, etc., by transferring it to a surface coated with gelatin, from which copies are made. —*v.t.* make copies of with a hectograph.

hec to li ter (hek′tə lē′tər), *n.* unit of volume equal to 100 liters. See **measure** for table.

hec to li tre (hek′tə lē′tər), *n.* BRITISH. hectoliter.

hec to me ter (hek′tə mē′tər), *n.* unit of length equal to 100 meters. See **measure** for table.

hec to me tre (hek′tə mē′tər), *n.* BRITISH. hectometer.

hec tor (hek′tər), *n.* a bragging, bullying fellow. —*v.t.* 1 bluster; bully. 2 tease. —*v.i.* 1 act in a blustering, domineering way. 2 tease. [< *Hector*]

Hec tor (hek′tər), *n.* (in Greek legends) a son of Hecuba and Priam and the bravest of the Trojan warriors. He was killed by Achilles.

Hec u ba (hek′yə bə), *n.* (in Greek legends) the wife of Priam and the mother of Hector, Paris, and Cassandra.

he'd (hēd; *unstressed* ēd, id, hid). 1 he had. 2 he would.

hedge (hej), *n., v.,* **hedged, hedg ing.** —*n.* 1 a thick row of bushes or small trees, planted as a fence or boundary. 2 any barrier or boundary. 3 means of protection or defense. 4 act of hedging. —*v.t.* 1 put a hedge around. 2 enclose or separate with a hedge. 3 reduce one's possible losses on (a bet, risk, etc.) by betting or speculating on both sides. 4 **hedge in, a** hem in; surround on all sides. **b** keep from getting away or moving freely. —*v.i.* 1 avoid giving a direct answer or taking a definite stand; evade questions or problems. 2 bet on both sides to reduce one's possible losses. [Old English *hecg*] —**hedg′er,** *n.*

hedge hog (hej′hog′, hej′hôg′), *n.* 1 any of a genus of small nocturnal, insectivorous mammals of Europe, Asia, and Africa, that have spines on their backs. 2 any of several similar animals, such as the porcupine.

hedge hop (hej′hop′), *v.t., v.i.,* **-hopped, -hop ping.** fly (an airplane) very low over the ground, especially in short, repeated flights for dusting crops, bombing, etc. —**hedge′hop′per,** *n.*

hedge row (hej′rō′), *n.* a thick row of bushes or small trees forming a hedge.

He djaz (he jaz′, he jäz′), *n.* Hejaz.

he don ism (hēd′n iz′əm), *n.* 1 belief that pleasure or happiness is the greatest thing in life. 2 living only for pleasure. [< Greek *hēdonē* pleasure]

he don ist (hēd′n ist), *n.* person who believes in or practices hedonism.

he don is tic (hēd′n is′tik), *adj.* of or having to do with hedonists or hedonism.

heed (hēd), *v.t.* give careful attention to; take notice of; mind: *Now heed what I say.* —*v.i.* pay careful attention; take notice. —*n.* careful attention; regard: *He paid no heed to their advice.* [Old English *hēdan*] —**heed′er,** *n.*

heed ful (hēd′fəl), *adj.* careful; attentive: *heedful of advice.* —**heed′ful ly,** *adv.* —**heed′ful ness,** *n.*

heed less (hēd′lis), *adj.* careless; thoughtless: *heedless haste.* —**heed′less ly,** *adv.* —**heed′less ness,** *n.*

hee haw (hē′hô′), *n.* 1 the braying sound made by a donkey. 2 a loud, coarse laugh. —*v.i.* 1 make the braying sound of a donkey. 2 laugh loudly and coarsely.

heel[1] (hēl), *n.* 1 the back part of a person's foot, below the ankle. 2 the part of a stocking or shoe that covers the heel. 3 the part of a shoe or boot that is under the heel or raises the heel. 4 the part of the hind leg of certain vertebrate animals that corresponds to a person's heel. 5 anything shaped, used, or placed at an end like a heel, such as an end crust of bread, the rind of cheese, the rear end of a ship's keel, or the lower end of a rudder, mast, or piece of timber. 6 INFORMAL. a hateful person.
at heel, near the heels; close behind.
cool one's heels, INFORMAL. be kept waiting a very long time.
down at the heel or **down at the heels, a** with the heel of the shoe worn down. **b** shabby; poor.
kick up one's heels, have a good time.
take to one's heels, run away.
turn on one's heel, turn around quickly; turn away.
—*v.t.* 1 follow closely; run at the heels of. 2 put a heel or heels on (shoes, etc.). —*v.i.* 1 follow closely at a person's heels: *A well-trained dog heels at the command of his master.* 2 touch the ground with the heel. [Old English *hēla*] —**heel′less,** *adj.*

heel[2] (hēl), *v.i.* lean over to one side; tilt; tip: *The ship heeled as it turned.* —*v.t.* cause (a ship, etc.) to lean over to one side; tilt; tip. —*n.* act of heeling. [Old English *hieldan* < *heald* inclined]

heft (heft), INFORMAL. —*n.* 1 weight; heaviness. 2 U.S. the greater part; bulk. —*v.t.* 1 lift; heave. 2 judge the weight of by lifting. [< *heave;* patterned on *weft* < *weave*]

hedgehog (def. 1)—about 9 in. long

heft y (hef′tē), *adj.,* **heft i er, heft i est.** INFORMAL. 1 weighty; heavy: *a hefty load.* 2 substantial; considerable: *a hefty bill for repairs.* 3 big and strong. —**heft′i ly,** *adv.* —**heft′i ness,** *n.*

He gel (hā′gəl), *n.* **Georg Wilhelm Friedrich,** 1770-1831, German philosopher.

he gem o ny (hi jem′ə nē, hej′ə mō′nē), *n., pl.* **-nies.** political domination, especially the leadership or domination of one state over the others in a group; leadership. [< Greek *hēgemonia* < *hēgemōn* leader < *hegeisthai* to lead]

He gi ra (hi jī′rə, hej′ər ə), *n.* 1 flight of Mohammed from Mecca to Medina in A.D. 622. The Moslems use a calendar reckoned from this date. 2 the Moslem era. 3 **hegira,** departure; flight. Also, **Hejira.** [< Medieval Latin < Arabic *hijra* flight]

Hei del berg (hī′dl bėrg′), *n.* city in S West Germany, site of a famous university. 122,000.

Heidelberg man, a prehistoric man of the Pleistocene epoch, reconstructed from a human lower jawbone found in 1907 near Heidelberg.

hat, āge, fär; let, ēqual, tėrm;
it, īce; hot, ōpen, ôrder;
oil, out; cup, pu̇t, rüle;
ch, child; ng, long; sh, she;
th, thin; ᴛʜ, then; zh, measure;

ə represents *a* in about, *e* in taken, *i* in pencil, *o* in lemon, *u* in circus.

< = from, derived from, taken from.

heif er (hef′ər), *n.* a young cow that has not had a calf. [Old English *hēahfore*]

Hei fetz (hī′fits), *n.* **Jascha,** born 1901, American violinist, born in Russia.

heigh (hī, hā), *interj.* sound made to attract attention, give encouragement, express surprise, etc.

heigh-ho (hī′hō′, hā′hō′), *interj.* sound made to express surprise, joy, sadness, weariness, boredom, etc.

height (hīt), *n.* 1 measurement from top to bottom; how high a thing is; how tall a person is; how far up a thing goes; elevation above ground, sea level, etc.: *the height of a mountain.* See synonym study below. 2 a fairly great distance up: *rising at a height above the valley.* 3 a high point or place: *a mountain height.* 4 the highest part; top. 5 the highest point; greatest degree: *Fast driving on icy roads is the height of folly.* [Old English *hiehthu,* related to *hēah* high]
Syn. 1 Height, altitude mean extent or distance above a level. **Height** is the general term for any such distance, great or small: *What is the height of the Empire State Building?* **Altitude** applies chiefly to height above a given level, especially sea level or the earth's surface: *The plane quickly lost altitude.*

height en (hīt′n), *v.t.* 1 make high or higher. 2 make stronger or greater: *Wax applied to a wood floor heightens the shine.* —*v.i.* 1 become high or higher. 2 become stronger or greater.

Hei ne (hī′nə), *n.* **Heinrich,** 1797-1856, German poet and prose writer.

hei nous (hā′nəs), *adj.* very wicked; extremely offensive; hateful. [< Old French *haïnos,* ultimately < *haïr* to hate; of Germanic origin] —**hei′nous ly,** *adv.* —**hei′nous ness,** *n.*

heir (er, ar), *n.* 1 person who receives or has the right to receive someone's property or title after that one dies; person who inherits property. 2 person who inherits anything; person who receives or has something from someone before him. [< Old French < Latin *heres* heir] —**heir′less,** *adj.*

heir apparent, *pl.* **heirs apparent.** person who will be heir if he lives longer than the one holding the property or title: *The king's oldest son is heir apparent to the throne.*

heir ess (er′is, ar′is), *n.* 1 a woman or girl heir. 2 woman or girl inheriting great wealth.

heir loom (er′lüm′, ar′lüm′), *n.* any piece of personal property that has been handed down from generation to generation: *This clock is a family heirloom.* [< *heir* + *loom,* originally, implement]

heir presumptive, *pl.* **heirs presumptive.** person who will be heir unless a nearer relative is born.

heir ship (er′ship, ar′ship), *n.* position or

rights of an heir; right of inheritance; inheritance.

Hei sen berg (hī′zən bėrg, hī′zən bėrk′), *n.* **Werner,** born 1901, German atomic physicist.

heist (hīst), SLANG. *—v.t., v.i.* rob or steal. *—n.* a robbery or theft. [alteration of *hoist*]

He jaz (he jaz′, he jäz′), *n.* former country in NW Arabia, now part of Saudi Arabia. Also, **Hedjaz.**

He ji ra or **he ji ra** (hi jī′rə, hej′ər ə), *n.* Hegira.

held (held), *v.* pt. and pp. of **hold**¹.

Hel e na (hel′ə nə), *n.* capital of Montana, in the W part. 23,000.

Hel en of Troy (hel′ən), (in Greek legends) a very beautiful Greek woman, the wife of King Menelaus of Sparta. Her kidnaping by Paris caused the Trojan War.

hel i cal (hel′ə kəl), *adj.* of, having to do with, or having the form of a helix; spiral.

hel i ces (hel′ə sēz′), *n.* a pl. of **helix.**

hel i coid (hel′ə koid), *n.* (in geometry) a surface in the form of a coil or screw. *—adj.* shaped like a coil; spiral.

hel i coi dal (hel′ə koi′dl), *adj.* helicoid.

hel i con (hel′ə kon, hel′ə kən), *n.* a large, circular bass tuba.

Hel i con (hel′ə kon, hel′ə kən), *n.* **Mount,** mountain in S Greece. The ancient Greeks considered it sacred to the Muses. 5738 ft.

hel i copt (hel′ə kopt, hē′lə kopt), *v.i., v.t.* to helicopter.

hel i cop ter (hel′ə kop′tər, hē′lə kop′tər), *n.* type of aircraft without wings, lifted from the ground and supported in the air by one or more horizontal propellers or rotors. *—v.i.* travel by helicopter. *—v.t.* send or carry by helicopter. [< French *hélicoptère* < Greek *helix, helikos* spiral + *pteron* wing]

helio-, *combining form.* sun: *Helioscope = device for looking at the sun.* [< Greek *hēlios* sun]

he li o cen tric (hē′lē ō sen′trik), *adj.* 1 viewed or measured from the center of the sun. 2 having or representing the sun as a center.

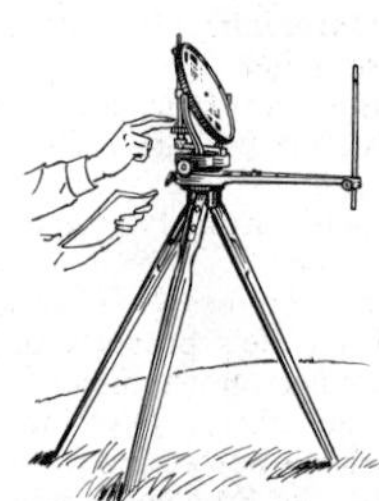
heliograph (def. 1) used by armies in the late 1800's

he li o graph (hē′lē ə graf′), *n.* 1 device for signaling by means of a movable mirror which flashes beams of sunlight to a distance. The flashes of the mirror represent the dots and dashes of the Morse code. 2 apparatus for taking photographs of the sun. *—v.t., v.i.* signal or communicate by heliograph.

He li op o lis (hē′lē op′ə lis), *n.* 1 city in the N part of ancient Egypt, now a ruin near Cairo. 2 ancient Greek name of **Baalbek.**

He li os (hē′lē os), *n.* (in Greek myths) the god of the sun, pictured driving a chariot drawn by four horses through the heavens. He was later identified with Apollo and with the Roman god Sol.

he li o trope (hē′lē ə trōp, hē′lyə trōp), *n.* 1 any of a genus of plants of the same family as borage, having clusters of small, fragrant purple or white flowers. 2 a pinkish purple. 3 bloodstone. *—adj.* pinkish-purple. [< Greek *hēliotropion* < *hēlios* sun + *-tropos* turning]

he li o trop ic (hē′lē ə trop′ik, hē′lē ə trō′pik), *adj.* (in botany) turning or bending in response to sunlight.

he li ot ro pism (hē′lē ot′rə piz′əm), *n.* phototropism in which a plant turns or bends in response to sunlight.

hel i pad (hel′ə pad′), *n.* a small area for helicopters to take off or land on.

hel i port (hel′ə pôrt′, hel′ə pōrt′), *n.* airport designed for use by helicopters.

he li um (hē′lē əm), *n.* a colorless, odorless, inert gaseous element that will not burn, occurring in small amounts in the air, in natural gas, etc., and also produced artificially. Helium is, next to hydrogen, the lightest gas, and is used in place of flammable gases to inflate balloons and airships, in electric welding, and, in the liquid state, as a refrigerant. *Symbol:* He; *atomic number* 2. See pages 326 and 327 for table. [< New Latin < Greek *hēlios* sun]

he lix (hē′liks), *n., pl.* **hel i ces** or **he lix es.** 1 anything having a spiral, coiled form such as a screw thread, a watch spring, or a snail shell. 2 a spiral ornament. 3 rim of the outer ear. 4 (in geometry) the curve traced by a straight line on a plane that is wrapped around a cylinder, as the thread of a screw. [< Latin < Greek, a spiral]

hell (hel), *n.* 1 (in Christian and some other religious use) the place where devils and evil spirits live and where wicked persons are punished after death. 2 the powers of evil. 3 abode of the dead; Hades. 4 any place or condition of wickedness, torment, or misery. 5 something very difficult or unpleasant. [Old English]

he'll (hēl; *unstressed* hil), 1 he will. 2 he shall.

Hel las (hel′əs), *n.* Greece.

hell bend er (hel′ben′dər), *n.* a large, aquatic salamander, common in the Ohio River and its tributaries.

hell bent (hel′bent′), *adj.* INFORMAL. firmly determined.

hell cat (hel′kat′), *n.* 1 a mean, spiteful woman; vixen. 2 witch.

hel le bore (hel′ə bôr, hel′ə bōr), *n.* 1 any of a genus of European plants of the same family as the buttercup, with showy flowers that bloom before spring. 2 the root of any of these plants, which is dried and used in medicine. 3 a tall plant of the lily family, with clusters of purple or white flowers. 4 its root, used in medicine or as a powder to kill insects. [< Greek *helleboros*]

Hel lene (hel′ēn), *n.* a Greek. [< Greek *Hellenes* a tribe of Thessaly]

Hel len ic (he len′ik, he lē′nik), *adj.* 1 Greek. 2 of Greek history, language, or culture from 776 B.C. to the death of Alexander the Great in 323 B.C.

helmet (defs. 1 and 2) helmets worn by a knight, a football player, and an astronaut

Hel len ism (hel′ə niz′əm), *n.* 1 ancient Greek culture or ideals; national character or spirit of the ancient Greeks. 2 adoption or imitation of Greek speech, ideals, or customs.

Hel len ist (hel′ə nist), *n.* 1 scholar skilled in the ancient Greek language, literature, and culture. 2 person who uses or imitates Greek language, ideals, or customs, especially a Jew who after the capture of Jerusalem in 586 B.C. came under Greek influence.

Hel len is tic (hel′ə nis′tik), *adj.* 1 of or having to do with Greek history, language, and culture after the death of Alexander the Great in 323 B.C. 2 of or having to do with Hellenists.

Hel len ize (hel′ə nīz), *v.,* **-ized, -iz ing.** *—v.t.* make Greek in character. *—v.i.* use or imitate the Greek language, ideals, or customs. **—Hel′len i za′tion,** *n.*

hell er (hel′ər), *n.* SLANG. person who creates mischief and excitement.

Hel les pont (hel′i spont), *n.* ancient name for the Dardanelles.

hell gram mite (hel′grə mīt), *n.* the aquatic larva of a dobsonfly, often used for fish bait. [origin uncertain]

hel lion (hel′yən), *n.* INFORMAL. a mischievous, troublesome person.

hell ish (hel′ish), *adj.* 1 fit to have come from hell; devilish; fiendish. 2 of hell; infernal. **—hell′ish ly,** *adv.* **—hell′ish ness,** *n.*

Hell man (hel′mən), *n.* **Lillian,** born 1905, American dramatist.

hellbender—1 to 2 ft. long

hel lo (he lō′, hə lō′), *interj., n., pl.* **-los,** *v.* *—interj.* a call or exclamation used to attract attention, express greeting, answer the telephone, etc. *—n.* a call or shout: *The girl gave a loud hello to let us know where she was.* *—v.i.* say or call "hello"; shout; call. Also, **hollo, holloa.** [variant of *hallo*]

helm¹ (def. 1)

helm¹ (helm), *n.* 1 handle or wheel by which a ship is steered. 2 the steering apparatus of a ship, including the wheel, rudder, and connecting parts. 3 position of control or guidance: *Upon the President's death, the Vice-President took the nation's helm.* *—v.t.* guide with a helm; steer. [Old English *helma*]

helm² (helm), *n.* ARCHAIC. helmet. [Old English]

hel met (hel′mit), *n.* 1 a covering to protect the head. Football players wear plastic helmets. 2 a piece of armor for the head.

Knights wore helmets as a part of their armor. 3 anything that resembles a helmet in shape, appearance, or position. [< Old French; of Germanic origin] **—hel′met like′,** *adj.*

hel minth (hel′minth), *n.* a worm, especially an intestinal worm, such as the tapeworm, roundworm, etc. [< Greek *helminthos*]

helms man (helmz′mən), *n., pl.* **-men.** man who steers a ship; pilot.

Hé lo ïse (ā lō ēz′), *n.* 1101?-1164?, lover of Pierre Abélard, who had been her teacher. When they were separated, she became a nun.

hel ot (hel′ət, hē′lət), *n.* 1 slave; serf. 2 **Helot,** member of a class of slaves or serfs in ancient Sparta. [< Latin *Helotes,* plural < Greek *Heilōtes*]

hel ot ism (hel′ə tiz′əm, hē′lə tiz′əm), *n.* serfdom like that of ancient Sparta.

hel ot ry (hel′ə trē, hē′lə trē), *n.* 1 helots; slaves. 2 serfdom; slavery.

help (help), *v.t.* 1 provide with what is needed or useful: *help a hospital with one's money. My father helped me with my homework.* See synonym study below. 2 relieve (a person) in want, trouble, or distress. 3 assist in bringing about; further: *remedies that help digestion.* 4 be of service or advantage to: *Her knowledge of French helped her in Quebec.* 5 make better; relieve or cure: *This medicine will help your cough.* 6 prevent; stop: *It can't be helped.* 7 avoid; keep from: *I can't help yawning.* 8 give food to; serve with food: *Help yourselves to some cake.* —*v.i.* 1 give aid or assistance: *We could finish the job faster if you would help.* 2 **help but,** fail to; avoid: *I can't help but admire her endurance.* 3 **help out,** help in doing or getting; be helpful.
—*n.* 1 thing done or given in helping: *Your advice is a great help.* 2 a helping or a being helped; aid; assistance: *I need some help with my work. The dying woman was beyond help.* 3 person or thing that helps; helper: *A sewing machine is a help in making clothes.* 4 a hired helper or group of hired helpers. 5 means of making better; remedy: *The medicine was a help.*
[Old English *helpan*]
Syn. *v.t.* 1 **Help, aid, assist** mean to give support by providing something needed or useful. **Help** is the common and general word for any kind of support: *She helps her mother at home.* **Aid** implies that the support is needed: *These scholarships are designed to aid students who cannot pay full tuition.* **Assist** suggests standing by to serve in any way needed, especially in a subordinate capacity: *Several nurses and an anesthesiologist assisted the doctor during the operation.*
➔ See **can't** for usage note.

help er (hel′pər), *n.* 1 person who helps, especially someone employed as assistant to another in doing some kind of work. 2 thing that helps.

help ful (help′fəl), *adj.* giving help; useful; serviceable. **—help′ful ly,** *adv.* **—help′ful ness,** *n.*

help ing (hel′ping), *n.* portion of food served to a person at one time.

helping verb, auxiliary verb.

help less (help′lis), *adj.* 1 not able to help oneself: *a helpless cripple.* 2 having no help from others; without help, protection, etc. **—help′less ly,** *adv.* **—help′less ness,** *n.*

help mate (help′māt′), *n.* companion and helper; wife or husband.

help meet (help′mēt′), *n.* helpmate.

Hel sing fors (hel′sing fôrz, hel′sing fôrs), *n.* Swedish name of **Helsinki.**

Hel sin ki (hel′sing kē), *n.* seaport and capital of Finland, in the S part. 534,000.

hel ter-skel ter (hel′tər skel′tər), *adv.* with headlong, disorderly haste; pell-mell: *The children ran helter-skelter when the dog rushed at them.* —*adj.* carelessly hurried; disorderly; confused. —*n.* noisy and disorderly haste, confusion, etc. [perhaps imitative rhyme]

helve (helv), *n.* handle of a tool or weapon, such as an ax or hammer. [Old English *hielfe*]

Hel ve tia (hel vē′shə), *n.* 1 ancient country that included most of modern Switzerland. 2 Latin name of Switzerland. **—Hel ve′tian,** *adj., n.*

hem[1] (hem), *n., v.,* **hemmed, hem ming.** —*n.* 1 border or edge on a garment; edge made on cloth by folding it over and sewing it down. 2 border; edge. —*v.t.* 1 fold over and sew down the edge of (cloth). 2 **hem in, hem around,** or **hem about, a** surround on all sides. **b** keep from getting away or moving freely. [Old English *hemm*] **—hem′mer,** *n.*

hem[2] (hem), *interj., n., v.,* **hemmed, hem ming.** —*interj., n.* sound like clearing the throat, used to attract attention or show doubt or hesitation. —*v.i.* 1 make this sound. 2 hesitate in speaking. 3 **hem and haw, a** hesitate in speaking. **b** stall or put off. [imitative]

hem- or **hema-,** *combining form.* blood: *Hemagglutination = agglutination of blood.* [< Greek *haima*]

he mag glu ti na tion (hē′mə glüt′n ā′shən), *n.* a clumping together of the red blood cells.

he mal (hē′məl), *adj.* 1 of or having to do with the blood or blood vessels. 2 having to do with or on the side of the body containing the heart and principal blood vessels.

he-man (hē′man′), *n., pl.* **-men.** INFORMAL. a virile, rugged man.

hem a tite (hem′ə tīt, hē′mə tīt), *n.* a widely distributed mineral which is an important iron ore, occurring in crystalline, massive, or granular form, and reddish-brown when powdered. *Formula:* Fe_2O_3 [< Greek *haimatitēs* bloodlike]

hemato- *combining form.* blood: *Hematology = study of blood.* [< Greek *haima, haimatos*]

hem a tol o gy (hem′ə tol′ə jē, hē′mə tol′ə jē), *n.* branch of medicine that deals with the structure, functions, and diseases of the blood and the organs that produce the constituents of the blood.

he ma to ma (hē′mə tō′mə, hem′ə tō′mə), *n.* tumor or swelling composed of blood.

heme (hēm), *n.* a deep-red pigment containing iron, obtained from hemoglobin.

hemi-, *prefix.* half: *Hemisphere = half sphere.* [< Greek]

hem i chor date (hem′ē kôr′dāt), *n.* any of a subphylum of small, wormlike, marine chordates having three body regions and a notochord limited to the front part of the body.

Hem ing way (hem′ing wā), *n.* **Ernest,** 1899-1961, American novelist and short-story writer.

hem i ple gi a (hem′ə plē′jē ə), *n.* paralysis of only one side of the body. [< Greek < *hemi-* half + *plēgē* stroke]

he mip ter an (hi mip′tər ən), *n.* any of a large order of insects that have pointed beaks for piercing and sucking, usually two pairs of

hat, āge, fär; let, ēqual, tėrm;
it, īce; hot, ōpen, ôrder;
oil, out; cup, pu̇t, rüle;
ch, child; ng, long; sh, she;
th, thin; ᴛʜ, then; zh, measure;
ə represents *a* in about, *e* in taken, *i* in pencil, *o* in lemon, *u* in circus.
< = from, derived from, taken from.

wings, and have young differing little from adults. Bedbugs, chinch bugs, and stinkbugs belong to this order. —*adj.* of or belonging to this order. [< *hemi-* + Greek *pteron* wing]

he mip ter ous (hi mip′tər əs), *adj.* of or belonging to the hemipterans.

hem i sphere (hem′ə sfir), *n.* 1 one half of a sphere or globe formed by a plane passing through the center. 2 half of the earth's surface: *the Western Hemisphere, the Eastern Hemisphere, the Northern Hemisphere, the Southern Hemisphere.* 3 area of action, life, or thought; sphere. 4 cerebral hemisphere.

hem i spher ic (hem′ə sfir′ik, hem′ə sfer′ik), *adj.* hemispherical.

hem i spher i cal (hem′ə sfir′ə kəl, hem′ə sfer′ə kəl), *adj.* 1 shaped like a hemisphere. 2 of a hemisphere. **—hem′i spher′i cal ly,** *adv.*

hem i stich (hem′ə stik), *n.* half of a line of verse, especially the part of a verse preceding or following the main caesura. [< Greek *hemi-* half + *stichos* row]

hem line (hem′līn′), *n.* border of a garment; hem.

hem lock (hem′lok), *n.* 1 a poisonous plant of the same family as parsley, with spotted reddish-purple stems, finely divided leaves, and small white flowers. 2 poison made from it. 3 any of a genus of evergreen trees of the pine family, with small cones, drooping branches, and reddish bark. The bark of one species is used in tanning. 4 the wood of any of these trees. [Old English *hymlice*]

he mo glo bin (hē′mə glō′bən, hem′ə glō′bən), *n.* substance in the red corpuscles of the blood of vertebrates made up of iron and protein, that carries oxygen from the lungs to the tissues and carries carbon dioxide from the tissues to the lungs. Also, **haemoglobin.**

he mol y sis (hi mol′ə sis), *n.* process of dissolution of the red blood cells, with the liberation of hemoglobin.

he mo lyt ic (hē′mə lit′ik, hem′ə lit′ik), *adj.* tending to dissolve the red blood cells: *hemolytic anemia.*

he mo phil i a (hē′mə fil′ē ə, hem′ə fil′ē ə), *n.* an inherited disorder of the blood in which clotting does not occur normally, making it difficult to stop bleeding even after the slightest injury. It affects only males but is inherited from the mother. [< Greek *haima* blood + *philia* affection, tendency]

he mo phil i ac (hē′mə fil′ē ak, hem′ə fil′ē ak), *n.* person who has hemophilia.

he mo phil ic (hē′mə fil′ik, hem′ə fil′ik), *adj.* 1 of or having hemophilia. 2 (of certain bacteria) flourishing in blood or a medium containing blood.

hem or rhage (hem′ər ij), *n., v.,* **-rhaged, -rhag ing.** —*n.* discharge of blood, especially a heavy discharge from a damaged blood vessel. A nosebleed is a mild hemorrhage. —*v.i.* have a hemorrhage; lose much blood.

[< Greek *haimorrhagia* < *haima* blood + *rhegnynai* to break, burst]

hem or rhag ic (hem′ə raj′ik), *adj.* of or having to do with hemorrhage.

hem or rhoids (hem′ə roidz′), *n.pl.* painful swellings formed by the dilation of blood vessels near the anus; piles. [< Greek *haimorrhoides* < *haima* blood + *rhein* to flow]

he mo stat ic (hē′mə stat′ik, hem′ə-stat′ik), *adj.* 1 stopping hemorrhage; styptic. 2 having to do with the stopping of bleeding.

hemp (hemp), *n.* 1 a tall annual plant of the same family as the mulberry, native to Asia and extensively cultivated elsewhere for its tough fibers, which are made into heavy string, rope, coarse cloth, etc.; cannabis. 2 the tough fibers obtained from the bark of this plant. 3 hashish or some other narcotic drug obtained from this plant. [Old English *henep*]

hemp en (hem′pən), *adj.* 1 made of hemp. 2 like hemp.

hem stitch (hem′stich′), *v.t., v.i.* make (an openwork pattern) on the edge of cloth by drawing out a few parallel threads and sewing the remaining threads into a series of little groups. —*n.* 1 the stitch used. 2 ornamental needlework made by hemstitching. —**hem′stitch′er,** *n.*

hen (hen), *n.* 1 a mature female domestic fowl: *a hen and her chicks.* 2 female of other birds: *a hen sparrow.* 3 a female fish or shellfish, such as a lobster. 4 SLANG. a woman. [Old English *henn*]

hen bane (hen′bān′), *n.* a coarse, bad-smelling poisonous plant of the nightshade family, having sticky, hairy leaves and clusters of yellowish-brown flowers.

hence (hens), *adv.* 1 as a result of this; therefore: *The king died, and hence his son became king.* 2 from now; from this time onward: *years hence.* 3 from here; away: *"Go hence, I pray thee."* —*interj.* go away! *"Hence! foul fiend."* [Middle English *hennes* < Old English *heonan* + *-s,* adverb ending]

➔ **Hence** is a more formal word than *consequently, therefore,* and *so that: They performed a series of experiments, all successful; hence their theory is well supported.*

hence forth (hens′fôrth′, hens′fōrth′), *adv.* from this time on; from now on.

hence for ward (hens′fôr′wərd), *adv.* henceforth.

hench man (hench′mən), *n., pl.* **-men.** 1 a trusted attendant or follower. 2 an obedient, unscrupulous follower. [Middle English *henxstman,* originally, a groom < Old English *hengest* horse + *man* man]

hen e quen or **hen e quin** (hen′ə kin), *n.* 1 a yellow fiber from leaves of an agave of Yucatán, used for making twine, ropes, coarse fabrics, etc. 2 plant that yields this fiber. [< Spanish *henequén,* perhaps < Maya]

Hen gist (heng′gist, hen′jist), *n.* died A.D. 488, a chief of the Jutes. He and his brother Horsa are said to have invaded England and founded the kingdom of Kent.

hen house (hen′hous′), *n., pl.* **-hous es** (-hou′ziz). house for poultry.

Hen ley (hen′lē), *n.* **William Ernest,** 1849-1903, English poet and critic.

hen na (hen′ə), *n.* 1 a dark, reddish-brown dye used especially on the hair. 2 a small, thorny tree or shrub of the same family as the loosestrife, native to Asia and Africa and bearing numerous small, fragrant white flowers, from whose leaves this dye is made. It is much used as a hedge in India. 3 a reddish brown. —*adj.* reddish-brown. —*v.t.* dye or color with henna. [< Arabic *hinnā′*]

hen ner y (hen′ər ē), *n., pl.* **-ner ies.** farm, building, or yard where poultry is kept or raised.

hen peck (hen′pek′), *v.t.* domineer over or rule (one's husband).

hen ry (hen′rē), *n., pl.* **-ries** or **-rys.** the unit of inductance. When a current varying at the rate of one ampere per second induces an electromotive force of one volt, the circuit has an inductance of one henry. [< Joseph *Henry*]

Hen ry (hen′rē), *n.* 1 **Joseph,** 1797-1878, American physicist. 2 **O.,** 1862-1910, American writer of short stories. His real name was William Sydney Porter. 3 **Patrick,** 1736-1799, American Revolutionary patriot, orator, and statesman. 4 **Cape,** cape in SE Virginia at the entrance to Chesapeake Bay.

Henry I, 1 1068-1135, king of England from 1100 to 1135. 2 1008?-1060, king of France from 1031 to 1060.

Henry II, 1 1133-1189, king of England from 1154 to 1189 and first of the Plantagenet line of kings. 2 1519-1559, king of France from 1547 to 1559.

Henry III, 1 1207-1272, king of England from 1216 to 1272. 2 1551-1589, king of France from 1574 to 1589.

Henry IV, 1 1367-1413, king of England from 1399 to 1413. 2 1553-1610, king of France from 1589 to 1610. He was known as "Henry of Navarre." 3 1050-1106, king of Germany and emperor of the Holy Roman Empire from 1056 to 1106.

Henry V, 1387-1422, king of England from 1413 to 1422.

Henry VI, 1421-1471, king of England from 1422 to 1461 and from 1470 to 1471.

Henry VII, 1457-1509, king of England from 1485 to 1509 and first of the Tudor line of kings.

Henry VIII, 1491-1547, king of England from 1509 to 1547 and father of Edward VI, Mary I, and Elizabeth I. He established the Church of England with himself as its head.

Hen son (hen′son), *n.* **Matthew,** 1867-1955, American explorer, who accompanied Admiral Robert Peary in the discovery of the North Pole in 1909.

hep (hep), *adj.* U.S. SLANG. hip². [origin uncertain]

hep ar in (hep′ər ən), *n.* glucoside present in the liver and other animal tissues, that prevents the blood from clotting. Heparin is used in the treatment of thrombosis. [< Greek *hēpar, hēpatos* liver]

he pat ic (hi pat′ik), *adj.* of or having to do with the liver. [< Latin *hepaticus* < Greek *hēpatikos* < *hēpar, hēpatos* liver]

he pat i ca (hi pat′ə kə), *n.* any of a genus of low plants of the same family as the buttercup, with delicate purple, pink, or white flowers that bloom early in the spring; liverwort.

hep a ti tis (hep′ə tī′tis), *n.* 1 inflammation of the liver. 2 a contagious virus disease characterized by inflammation of the liver, fever, and usually jaundice.

He phaes tus (hi fes′təs), *n.* (in Greek myths) the god of fire and metalworking, identified with the Roman god Vulcan.

Hep ple white (hep′əl hwīt), *n.* style of furniture having graceful curves and slender lines. —*adj.* of or like this style of furniture. [< George *Hepplewhite,* died 1786, English furniture designer]

hepta-, *combining form.* seven, as in *heptameter.* [< Greek *hepta*]

hep ta gon (hep′tə gon), *n.* a plane figure having seven angles and seven sides. [< Greek *hepta* seven + *gōnia* angle]

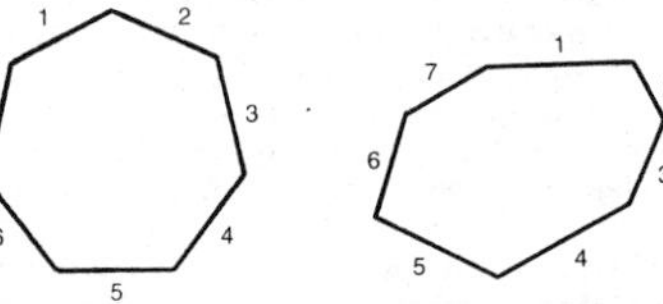

regular heptagon irregular heptagon

hep tag o nal (hep tag′ə nəl), *adj.* having the form of a heptagon.

hep tam e ter (hep tam′ə tər), *n.* line of verse having seven metrical feet. EXAMPLE: And thrice′ he rout′ed all′ his foes′, and thrice′ he slew′ the slain′.

her (hėr; *unstressed* hər, ər), *pron.* objective case of **she.** *I like her.* —*adj.* possessive form of **she.** of her; belonging to her; done by her: *her book, her work.* [Old English *hire*]

Her a (hir′ə), *n.* (in Greek myths) a goddess who was the wife of Zeus and queen of the gods and men, identified with the Roman goddess Juno. She was the special goddess of women and marriage. Also, **Here.**

Her a cles (her′ə klēz′), *n.* Hercules.

Her a cli tus (her′ə klī′təs), *n.* 540?-475 B.C., Greek philosopher.

Her a kles (her′ə klēz′), *n.* Hercules.

her ald (her′əld), *n.* 1 (formerly) an official who carried messages, made announcements, arranged and supervised tournaments and other public ceremonies, and regulated the use of armorial bearings. 2 person who carries messages and makes announcements; messenger. 3 forerunner; harbinger: *Dawn is the herald of day.* 4 (in Great Britain, etc.) an official who has authority over coats of arms and keeps a record of families that have them. —*v.t.* 1 bring news of; announce. 2 go before and announce the coming of. [< Old French *herault;* ultimately of Germanic origin]

he ral dic (he ral′dik), *adj.* of or having to do with heraldry or heralds.

her ald ry (her′əl drē), *n., pl.* **-ries.** 1 science or art dealing with coats of arms. Heraldry determines a person's right to use a coat of arms, traces family descent, designs coats of arms for new countries, etc. 2 coat of arms. 3 ceremony or pomp connected with the life of noble families.

herb (ėrb, hėrb), *n.* 1 plant whose leaves or stems are used for medicine, seasoning, food, or perfume. Sage, mint, and lavender are herbs. 2 a flowering plant whose stem above ground usually does not become woody as that of a tree or shrub does. Herbs can be annual, such as corn, biennial, such as the onion, but most are perennial, such as the rose. [< Latin *herba*] —**herb′like′,** *adj.*

her ba ceous (hėr bā′shəs), *adj.* 1 of or like an herb; soft and not woody: *a herbaceous stem.* 2 having the texture, color, etc., of an ordinary leaf; green: *a herbaceous flower.* [< Latin *herbaceus* < *herba*]

herb age (ėr′bij, hėr′bij), *n.* 1 grass and other low-growing plants covering a large extent of ground, especially as used for pasture; herbs collectively. 2 the green leaves and soft stems of plants.

hat, āge, fär; let, ēqual, tėrm;
it, īce; hot, ōpen, ôrder;
oil, out; cup, pu̇t, rüle;
ch, child; ng, long; sh, she;
th, thin; ᴛʜ, then; zh, measure;

ə represents *a* in about, *e* in taken, *i* in pencil, *o* in lemon, *u* in circus.

< = from, derived from, taken from.

herb al (hėr′bəl, ėr′bəl), *adj.* having to do with, consisting of, or made from herbs. —*n.* book on the kinds, qualities, uses, etc., of herbs or plants.

herb al ist (hėr′bə list, ėr′bə list), *n.* person who gathers or deals in herbs, especially medicinal herbs.

her bar i um (hėr′ber′ē əm, hėr′bar′ē əm), *n., pl.* **-bar i ums, -bar i a** (-ber′ē ə, -bar′ē ə). 1 collection of dried plants systematically arranged. 2 room or building where such a collection is kept. [< Late Latin < Latin *herba* herb. Doublet of ARBOR[1].]

Her bert (hėr′bərt), *n.* 1 **George,** 1593-1633, English poet. 2 **Victor,** 1859-1924, American composer, born in Ireland.

her bi ci dal (hėr′bə sī′dl), *adj.* having the characteristics of a herbicide.

her bi cide (hėr′bə sīd), *n.* a poisonous chemical used to destroy weeds; weed-killer.

her bi vore (hėr′bə vôr, hėr′bə vōr), *n.* any of a large group of animals that feed chiefly on plants. The ungulates are herbivores.

her biv or ous (hėr′biv′ər əs), *adj.* 1 feeding on grass or other plants. 2 of or belonging to the herbivores. [< New Latin *herbivorus* < Latin *herba* herb + *vorare* devour]

herb y (ėr′bē, hėr′bē), *adj.* 1 having many herbs; grassy. 2 of or like herbs.

Her cu la ne um (hėr′kyə lā′nē əm), *n.* city in the SW part of ancient Italy, near Naples, buried with Pompeii by an eruption of Mount Vesuvius in A.D. 79.

her cu le an or **Her cu le an** (hėr′kyü′lē ən, hėr′kyə lē′ən), *adj.* 1 having great strength, courage, or size; very powerful: *a herculean warrior.* 2 requiring great strength, courage, or size; very hard to do: *a herculean task.* 3 **Herculean,** of or having to do with Hercules.

Her cu les (hėr′kyə lēz′), *n.* 1 (in Greek and Roman myths) a son of Zeus, a hero who possessed such great strength and courage that he was able to perform twelve extraordinary labors imposed on him by Hera. 2 Also, **hercules.** any person of great strength, courage, or size. 3 a northern constellation near Lyra. Also, **Heracles, Herakles.**

herd (hėrd), *n.* 1 group of animals of one kind, especially cows, horses, elephants, or other large animals, keeping, feeding, or moving together. 2 a large number of people; crowd: *a herd of ragged children.* 3 the common people. 4 **ride herd on,** keep within bounds; control strictly. —*v.i.* 1 join together; flock together. 2 go in a herd; form a herd or herds. —*v.t.* 1 collect into a herd; form into a flock, herd, or group. 2 tend, drive, or take care of (cattle, sheep, etc.). [Old English *heord*]

herd er (hėr′dər), *n.* herdsman.

herds man (hėrdz′mən), *n., pl.* **-men.** man who takes care of a herd, especially of cattle.

here (hir), *adv.* 1 in this place; at this place: *Leave it here.* 2 to this place: *Come here.* 3 at this point in time; now: *Here the speaker paused.* 4 in this present life or condition. 5 who or which is here (used to call attention to a person or thing): *My friend here can help you.* 6 **here and there,** in this place and that; at intervals. 7 **here's to you!** a wish for health or success. 8 **neither here nor there,** not to the point; off the subject; unimportant. —*n.* 1 this place: *Where do we go from here?* 2 this life. —*interj.* 1 answer showing that one is present when roll is called. 2 exclamation used to call attention to some person or thing: *"Here! take away the dishes."* [Old English *hēr*]

Her e (hir′ē), *n.* Hera.

here a bout (hir′ə bout′), *adv.* about this place; around here; near here.

here a bouts (hir′ə bouts′), *adv.* hereabout.

here af ter (hir af′tər), *adv.* 1 after this; in the future. 2 in life after death. —*n.* 1 the future. 2 the life or time after death.

here at (hir at′), *adv.* 1 when this happened; at this time. 2 because of this.

here by (hir bī′), *adv.* by this; by this means; in this way: *The license said, "You are hereby given the right to hunt and fish in Dover County."*

he red i ta ble (hə red′ə tə bəl), *adj.* that can be inherited.

her e dit a ment (her′ə dit′ə mənt), *n.* (in law) any property that can be inherited.

he red i tar y (hə red′ə ter′ē), *adj.* 1 passing by inheritance from generation to generation: *"Prince" and "princess" are hereditary titles.* 2 holding a position, title, etc., by inheritance: *The queen of England is a hereditary ruler.* 3 transmitted or capable of being transmitted by means of genes from parents to offspring: *Color blindness is hereditary.* 4 derived from one's parents or ancestors: *a hereditary custom, a hereditary enemy to a country.* 5 of or having to do with inheritance or heredity: *hereditary descent.*

he red i ty (hə red′ə tē), *n., pl.* **-ties.** 1 the transmission of physical or mental characteristics from parent to offspring by means of genes. 2 qualities or characteristics of body or mind that have come to offspring from parents. 3 tendency of offspring to be like the parents. [< Latin *hereditatem* < *heredem* heir]

Here ford (hėr′fərd, her′ə fərd), *n.* 1 county in W England, east of Wales. 2 one of a breed of reddish-brown beef cattle developed in this county, having a white face and white markings under the body.

Her e ford shire (her′ə fərd shər, her′ə-fərd shir), *n.* Hereford (def. 1).

here in (hir in′), *adv.* 1 in this place; in this passage, book, etc. 2 in this matter; in this way.

here in af ter (hir′in af′tər), *adv.* afterward in this document, statement, etc.

here in be fore (hir in′bi fôr′, hir in′bi-fōr′), *adv.* before in this document, statement, etc.

here in to (hir in′tü), *adv.* 1 into this place. 2 into this matter.

here of (hir ov′, hir uv′), *adv.* of this; about this.

here on (hir on′, hir ôn′), *adv.* 1 on this. 2 immediately after this.

here's (hirz), here is.

her e sy (her′ə sē), *n., pl.* **-sies.** 1 a religious doctrine or opinion rejected by the authorities of a church as contrary to the established beliefs of that church. 2 opinion or doctrine opposed to what is generally accepted as authoritative. 3 the holding of such an opinion or doctrine. [< Old French *heresie* < Latin *haeresis* < Greek *hairesis* a taking, choosing < *hairein* choose, take]

her e tic (her′ə tik), *n.* 1 member of a church who adopts religious doctrines or opinions contrary to the established beliefs of his church. 2 person who maintains opinions or doctrines on any subject contrary to those generally accepted as authoritative. —*adj.* heretical.

he ret i cal (hə ret′ə kəl), *adj.* 1 of or having to do with heresy or heretics. 2 containing heresy; characterized by heresy. —**he ret′i-cal ly,** *adv.*

here to (hir tü′), *adv.* to this place, thing, document, etc.

here to fore (hir′tə fôr′, hir′tə fōr′), *adv.* before this time; until now.

here un der (hir un′dər), *adv.* 1 under this. 2 under authority of this.

here un to (hir′un tü′), *adv.* to this place, thing, document, etc.; hereto.

here up on (hir′ə pon′, hir′ə pôn′), *adv.* 1 upon this thing, point, subject, or matter. 2 immediately after this.

here with (hir wiᴛʜ′, hir with′), *adv.* 1 with this. 2 by this means; in this way.

her it a bil i ty (her′ə tə bil′ ə tē), *n.* heritable quality or condition.

her it a ble (her′ə tə bəl), *adj.* 1 capable of being inherited: *heritable diseases, heritable tendencies.* 2 capable of inheriting.

her it age (her′ə tij), *n.* what is handed down from one generation to the next; inheritance: *The heritage of freedom is precious to Americans.* [< Old French < *heriter* inherit < Late Latin *hereditare* < Latin *hereditatem* heredity]

her maph ro dite (hər maf′rə dīt), *n.* animal or plant having both male and female reproductive organs. —*adj.* of or like a hermaphrodite. [< Greek *Hermaphroditos,* son of Hermes and Aphrodite, who became united in body with a nymph]

her maph ro dit ic (hər maf′rə dit′ik), *adj.* of or like a hermaphrodite; bisexual.

her maph ro dit ism (hər maf′rə dī-tiz′əm), *n.* condition of a hermaphrodite.

Her mes (hėr′mēz), *n.* (in Greek myths) a god who was the messenger of Zeus and the other gods. He led the souls of the dead to Hades and was the god of travel and commerce, science and invention, and eloquence, luck, and cunning. He was also the patron of thieves and gamblers, and was identified with the Roman god Mercury.

her met ic (hər met′ik), *adj.* closed tightly so that air cannot get in or out; airtight. [< Medieval Latin *hermeticus* < *Hermes Trismegistus,* the supposed author of a work on magic and alchemy who discovered a means of making things airtight] —**her-met′i cal ly,** *adv.*

her met i cal (hər met′ə kəl), *adj.* hermetic.

her mit (hėr′mit), *n.* person who goes away from other people and lives by himself; recluse. A hermit often lives a religious life. [< Old French *hermite* < Late Latin *eremita* < Greek *erēmitēs* < *erēmia* desert < *erēmos* uninhabited. Doublet of EREMITE.] —**her′mit like′,** *adj.*

her mit age (hėr′mə tij), *n.* 1 dwelling place of a hermit. 2 a solitary or secluded dwelling place.

hermit crab, any of a genus of crabs with soft bodies that live in the empty shells of snails, whelks, etc., as a means of protection.

hermit thrush, a brown thrush of North America, with spotted breast and reddish tail, noted for its song.

Her mon (hėr′mən), *n.* **Mount,** mountain in the Anti-Lebanon range, on the border between Lebanon and Syria. 9200 ft.

her ni a (hėr′nē ə), *n., pl.* **-ni as, -ni ae** (-nē-ē). protrusion of some tissue or organ of the body, especially a part of the intestine, through the wall of the cavity which should hold it in; rupture. [< Latin]

her ni al (hėr′nē əl), *adj.* of or having to do with hernia.

her o (hir′ō), *n., pl.* **her oes.** 1 person admired for bravery, great deeds, or noble qualities: *George Washington is one of our great heroes.* 2 person admired for contribution to a particular field: *heroes of science.* 3 the most important male person in a story, play, poem, motion picture, etc. 4 (in Greek legends) a man of superhuman strength, courage, or ability, especially a warrior, favored by the gods. Hercules and Achilles were heroes. [< Latin *heros* < Greek *hērōs*]

Her o (hir′ō), *n.* (in Greek legends) a priestess of Aphrodite. Her lover, Leander, swam the Hellespont nightly to visit her and was drowned. Hero killed herself on learning of his death.

Her od (her′əd), *n.* 1 73?-4 B.C., king of Judea from 37? to 4 B.C. Jesus was born during his reign. He was called "Herod the Great." 2 his son, **Herod An ti pas** (an′tə-pas), died A.D. 40, ruler of Galilee from 4 B.C. to A.D. 40.

He ro di as (hə rō′dē əs), *n.* 14? B.C.-after A.D. 40, the second wife of Herod Antipas. She and her daughter Salome brought about the death of John the Baptist.

He rod o tus (hə rod′ə təs), *n.* 484?-425? B.C., Greek historian. He is called the father of history.

he ro ic (hi rō′ik), *adj.* 1 of, like, or suitable for a hero, his deeds, or his qualities; brave, great, or noble. 2 of or about heroes and their deeds; epic: *The "Iliad" and the "Odyssey" are heroic poems.* 3 using extreme things to get a necessary result; unusually daring or bold: *Only heroic measures could save the town from the flood.* 4 unusually large; larger than life size: *a heroic statue.* **—he ro′i cal ly,** *adv.*

he ro i cal (hi rō′ə kəl), *adj.* heroic.

heroic couplet, two successive rhyming lines of poetry in iambic pentameter.

he ro ics (hi rō′iks), *n.pl.* words or actions that seem grand or noble, but are only for effect.

heroic verse, a poetic form used in heroic and other long poems. English heroic verse is in iambic pentameter.

her o in (her′ō ən), *n.* a toxic, habit-forming, narcotic drug derived from morphine. [< German]

her o ine (her′ō ən), *n.* 1 woman or girl admired for her bravery, great deeds, or noble qualities. 2 the most important female person in a story, play, poem, motion picture, etc.

her o ism (her′ō iz′əm), *n.* 1 actions and qualities of a hero or heroine; great bravery; daring courage. 2 a doing something noble at great cost to oneself; a very brave act.

her on (her′ən), *n.* any of a family of wading birds with long necks, bills, and legs but short tails. Herons feed on fish, frogs, etc. [< Old French *hairon;* of Germanic origin]

her on ry (her′ən rē), *n., pl.* **-ries.** place where herons come annually in large numbers and build their nests.

hero worship, the idolizing of individuals or their memory, especially of persons thought of as heroes.

her pes (hėr′pēz), *n.* any of various viral diseases causing spreading blisterlike blotches on the skin or mucous membrane. [< Greek *herpēs* shingles < *herpein* to creep]

her pe tol o gist (hėr′pə tol′ə jist), *n.* an expert in herpetology.

her pe tol o gy (hėr′pə tol′ə jē), *n.* branch of zoology dealing with reptiles and amphibians. [< Greek *herpeton* reptile < *herpein* to creep]

Herr (her), *n., pl.* ***Her ren*** (her′ən). GERMAN. 1 Mr.; Sir. 2 gentleman.

Her rick (her′ik), *n.* **Robert,** 1591-1674, English poet.

her ring (her′ing), *n., pl.* **-rings** or **-ring.** any of a family of fishes, especially a small, bony food fish of the northern Atlantic, having spineless fins, the ventral fins back of the pectoral fins, no scales on the head, and no fleshy fin back of the dorsal fin. The grown fish are eaten fresh, salted, or smoked, and the young are canned as sardines. [Old English *hǣring*]

herringbone

her ring bone (her′ing bōn′), *adj., n., v.,* **-boned, -bon ing.** *—adj.* having a zigzag pattern or arrangement like the spine of a herring. *—n.* a zigzag pattern, arrangement, or stitch. *—v.t., v.i.* embroider or sew with a herringbone stitch; make a herringbone pattern.

Her ri ot (e ryō′), *n.* **Édouard,** 1872-1957, French statesman, three times premier of France.

hers (hėrz), *pron.* possessive form of **she.** the one or ones belonging to her: *This money is hers. Your answers are wrong; hers are right.*

her self (hər self′), *pron.* 1 the emphatic form of **she** or **her.** *She did it herself.* 2 the reflexive form of **her.** *She hurt herself.* 3 her real or true self: *She is so tired that she is not herself today.*

hertz (hėrts), *n.* unit of frequency in the centimeter-gram-second system, equivalent to one cycle per second. [< Heinrich R. *Hertz,* 1857-1894, German physicist]

Hertz i an waves (hert′sē ən), electromagnetic radiation, such as the waves used in communicating by radio. Hertzian waves are produced by irregular fluctuations of electricity in a conductor.

Her ze go vi na (her′tsə gə vē′nə), *n.* region in W Yugoslavia, formerly a province of Austria-Hungary, now part of Bosnia-Herzegovina.

he's (hēz; *unstressed* ēz, iz, hiz), 1 he is. 2 he has.

He si od (hē′sē əd, hes′ē əd), *n.* Greek poet who lived in the 700's B.C.

hes i tance (hez′ə təns), *n.* hesitancy.

hes i tan cy (hez′ə tən sē), *n., pl.* **-cies.** 1 tendency to hesitate; indecision. 2 an instance of this; hesitation.

hes i tant (hez′ə tənt), *adj.* tending to hesitate; doubtful; undecided. **—hes′i tant ly,** *adv.*

hes i tate (hez′ə tāt), *v.i.,* **-tat ed, -tat ing.** 1 fail to act promptly; hold back because one feels doubtful or undecided; show that one has not yet made up one's mind. See synonym study below. 2 feel that perhaps one should not; be unwilling; not want: *I hesitated to interrupt you.* 3 stop for an instant; pause: *He hesitated before asking the question.* 4 speak with short stays and pauses. [< Latin *haesitatum* stuck fast < *haerere* stick fast] **—hes′i tat′ing ly,** *adv.*

Syn. 1 **Hesitate, falter, waver** mean to fail to act promptly and resolutely. **Hesitate** emphasizes holding back because of doubt or indecision: *I hesitated about taking the new job.* **Falter** suggests losing courage and hesitating or giving way after starting to act: *I went to apologize, but faltered at the door.* **Waver** suggests not holding firmly to a decision or course of action: *I said I would help but wavered when I saw how much there was to do.*

hes i ta tion (hez′ə tā′shən), *n.* 1 a hesitating; doubt; indecision. 2 a speaking with short stops or pauses; stammering.

Hes per i an (he spir′ē ən), *adj.* of or having to do with the land of the west, or where the sun sets; western. [< Greek *Hesperos* Hesperus, originally adjective, of the evening, western]

Hes per i des (he sper′ə dēz′), *n.pl.* in Greek myths: 1 the nymphs who guarded the golden apples of Hera. 2 garden at the western extremity of the earth where these apples were kept.

Hes per us (hes′pər əs), *n.* Venus, when it appears as the evening star.

Hesse (hes, hes′ə), *n.* state in central West Germany.

Hes se (hes′ə), *n.* **Hermann,** 1877-1962, German novelist and poet.

Hes sian (hesh′ən), *adj.* of Hesse or its people. *—n.* 1 native or inhabitant of Hesse. 2 a German soldier hired by England to fight against the Americans during the Revolutionary War.

Hessian fly, a small fly whose larvae are very destructive to wheat.

hest (hest), *n.* ARCHAIC. behest; command. [alteration of Old English *hǣs*]

Hes ti a (hes′tē ə), *n.* (in Greek myths) the goddess of the hearth, identified with the Roman goddess Vesta.

het (het), *v.t., v.i.* DIALECT. 1 heated; pt. and pp. of **heat.** 2 **het up,** heated up; excited; riled.

hetero-, *combining form.* of more than one kind; other; different: *Heterogamete = different or other gamete.* [< Greek]

het er o chro mat ic (het′ər ə krō mat′ik), *adj.* having a complex pattern of more than one color.

het er o dox (het′ər ə doks), *adj.* 1 rejecting generally accepted beliefs or doctrines, especially in a religion; departing from an acknowledged standard; not orthodox. 2 holding opinions not in accord with some acknowledged standard. [< Greek *heterodoxos* < *heteros* other + *doxa* opinion]

het er o dox y (het′ər ə dok′sē), *n., pl.* **-dox ies.** 1 rejection of generally accepted beliefs or doctrines, especially in a religion. 2 belief or doctrine not in agreement with what is generally accepted.

het er o dyne (het′ər ə dīn′), *adj., v.,* **-dyned, -dyn ing.** *—adj.* receiving radio

hat, āge, fär; let, ēqual, tėrm;
it, īce; hot, ōpen, ôrder;
oil, out; cup, pu̇t, rüle;
ch, child; ng, long; sh, she;
th, thin; ᴛʜ, then; zh, measure;

ə represents *a* in about, *e* in taken, *i* in pencil, *o* in lemon, *u* in circus.

< = from, derived from, taken from.

waves by combining the signal-carrying current with a current of different frequency generated in the receiving set, in such a way that audible beats are produced. —*v.i.* produce sounds by a heterodyne system.

het er o ga mete (het′ər ō gə mēt′), *n.* either of two gametes, differing in character or behavior, which can unite with the other to form a zygote. A large, nonmotile egg and a small, motile sperm are heterogametes.

het e rog a mous (het′ə rog′ə məs), *adj.* 1 reproducing by the union of unlike gametes. 2 characterized by the alternation of two types of sexual reproduction in successive generations. 3 having flowers or florets of two sexually different kinds.

het e rog a my (het′ə rog′ə mē), *n.* 1 condition of being heterogamous. 2 heterogenesis.

het er o ge ne i ty (het′ər ə jə nē′ə tē), *n.* a being heterogeneous.

het er o ge ne ous (het′ər ə jē′nē əs, het′ər ə jē′nyəs), *adj.* 1 different in kind or nature; unlike; varied: *a heterogeneous group of people.* 2 composed of unlike parts or elements; miscellaneous: *a heterogeneous collection.* [< Medieval Latin *heterogeneus,* ultimately < Greek *heteros* other + *genos* kind] **—het′er o ge′ne ous ly,** *adv.*

het er o gen e sis (het′ər ə jen′ə sis), *n.* alternation of generations.

het er o nym (het′ər ə nim′), *n.* word spelled the same as another but having a different sound and meaning. EXAMPLE: *lead,* to conduct, and *lead,* a metal. [< *hetero-* + *(homo)nym*]

het e rop ter an (het′ə rop′tər ən), *adj.* heteropterous. —*n.* a heteropterous insect.

het e rop ter ous (het′ə rop′tər əs), *adj.* of, having to do with, or belonging to the order of hemipterous insects that comprises the true bugs. [< *hetero-* + Greek *pteron* wing]

het er o sex u al (het′ər ə sek′shü əl), *adj.* 1 (in biology) of or having to do with the different sexes. 2 having to do with, or manifesting sexual feeling for a person of the opposite sex. —*n.* a heterosexual person.

het er o sex u al i ty (het′ər ə sek′shü al′ə tē), *n.* 1 sexual feeling for a person of the opposite sex. 2 sexual behavior toward a person of the opposite sex.

het e ro sis (het′ə rō′sis), *n.* (in genetics) an increase in vigor of growth, fertility, size, or other characteristics, resulting from crossbreeding; hybrid vigor. [< Greek, alteration < *heteros* another, different]

het er o troph (het′ər ə trof), *n.* organism that cannot manufacture its own food, but is dependent upon complex organic substances for nutrition. Animals and some plants are heterotrophs.

het er o troph ic (het′ər ə trof′ik), *adj.* of or having to do with a heterotroph. [< *hetero-* + Greek *trophē* nourishment]

het er o zy gote (het′ər ə zī′gōt, het′ər ə zig′ōt), *n.* (in genetics) an animal or plant whose chromosomes contain both genes of a contrasting pair and which, therefore, does not always breed true to type.

het er o zy gous (het′ər ə zī′gəs), *adj.* of or having to do with a heterozygote.

het man (het′mən), *n., pl.* **-mans.** a Cossack leader or chief. [< Polish < Middle High German *heuptman,* literally, headman]

heu ris tic (hyu̇ ris′tik), *adj.* helping to find out or discover; stimulating investigation or research. [< German *heuristisch* < Greek *heuriskein* find out] **—heu ris′ti cal ly,** *adv.*

hew (hyü), *v.,* **hewed, hewed** or **hewn, hew ing.** —*v.t.* 1 cut with an ax, sword, etc.; chop: *He hewed down the tree.* 2 cut into shape; form by cutting with an ax, etc.: *hew stone for building, hew logs into beams.* —*v.i.* hold firmly *(to);* stick fast or cling *(to): hew to the rules.* [Old English *hēawan*] **—hew′er,** *n.*

HEW, Health, Education, and Welfare (a department of the U.S. government).

hewn (hyün), *v.* hewed; a pp. of **hew.**

hex (heks), U.S. —*v.t.* practice witchcraft on; bewitch. —*n.* 1 witch. 2 a magic spell. [< Pennsylvania German *hexe* < German *Hexe* witch]

hex-, *combining form.* form of **hexa-** before vowels, as in *hexose.*

hexa-, *combining form.* six, as in *hexameter.* [< Greek *hex* six]

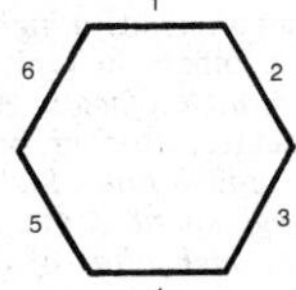

regular hexagon

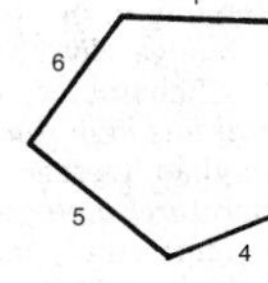

irregular hexagon

hex a gon (hek′sə gon), *n.* a plane figure having six angles and six sides. [< Greek *hex* six + *gōnia* angle]

hex ag o nal (hek sag′ə nəl), *adj.* 1 having the form of a hexagon. 2 having a hexagon as base or cross section. **—hex ag′o nal ly,** *adv.*

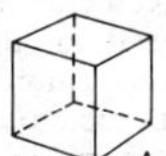

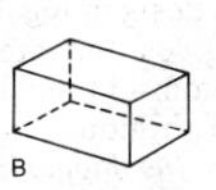

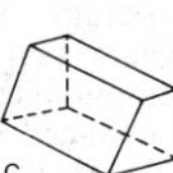

hexahedron—A, regular; B, C, irregular

hex a he dron (hek′sə hē′drən), *n., pl.* **-drons, -dra** (-drə). a solid figure having six faces. [< Greek *hex* six + *hedra* base]

hex am e ter (hek sam′ə tər), *n.* line of verse having six metrical feet. EXAMPLE: "This′ is the | fo′rest pri | me′val. The | mur′mur ing | pines′ and the | hem′locks."

hex ane (hek′sān, hek sān′), *n.* any of five colorless, volatile, liquid isomeric hydrocarbons derived from petroleum and used as solvents. *Formula:* C_6H_{14}

hex a pod (hek′sə pod), *n.* a true insect; arthropod having six feet. —*adj.* having six feet. [< Greek *hex* six + *podos* foot]

hex ose (hek′sōs), *n.* any of a class of simple sugars that contain six carbon atoms in the molecule, such as glucose and fructose.

hey (hā), *interj.* sound made to attract attention, to express surprise or other feeling, or to ask a question.

hey day (hā′dā′), *n.* period of greatest strength, vigor, spirits, prosperity, etc. [origin uncertain]

Hez e ki ah (hez′ə kī′ə), *n.* 740?-692? B.C., king of Judah from about 720 to 692 B.C.

Hf, hafnium.

hf., half.

HF, H.F., or **h.f.,** high frequency.

Hg, mercury [for New Latin *hydrargyrum* mercury].

hg., hectogram or hectograms.

hgt., height.

H.H., 1 Her Highness. 2 His Highness. 3 His Holiness.

hhd., hogshead.

hi (hī), *interj.* a call of greeting; hello.

H.I., Hawaiian Islands.

Hi a le ah (hī′ə lē′ə), *n.* city in SE Florida, near Miami. 102,000.

hi a tus (hī ā′təs), *n., pl.* **-tus es** or **-tus.** 1 an empty space; space from which something necessary to completeness is missing; gap. A lost or erased part of a manuscript is a hiatus. 2 the coming together of two vowel sounds without an intervening consonant sound, as in *preeminent.* [< Latin, gap < *hiare* to gape]

Hi a wath a (hī′ə woth′ə, hē′ə woth′ə), *n.* the young Indian brave who is the hero of Longfellow's poem *The Song of Hiawatha.*

hi ba chi (hi bä′chē), *n., pl.* **-chi** or **-chis.** a small, portable, cast-iron, potlike container, covered by a grill, used for burning charcoal for cooking or heating. [< Japanese]

hi ber nal (hī bėr′nl), *adj.* of or having to do with winter; wintry.

hi ber nate (hī′bər nāt), *v.i.,* **-nat ed, -nat ing.** spend the winter in a state like sleep or in an inactive condition, as bears, woodchucks, and some other wild animals do. [< Latin *hibernatum* wintered < *hibernus* wintry] **—hi′ber na′tion,** *n.* **—hi′ber na′tor,** *n.*

Hi ber ni a (hī bėr′nē ə), *n.* Latin name for Ireland. **—Hi ber′ni an,** *n., adj.*

hi bis cus (hə bis′kəs, hī bis′kəs), *n.* any of a genus of herbs, shrubs, or trees of the mallow family, with large red, pink, or white flowers that are usually bell-shaped. [< Latin]

hic cough (hik′up), *n., v.i.* hiccup.

hic cup (hik′up, hik′əp), *n., v.,* **-cupped, -cup ping.** —*n.* 1 an involuntary catching of the breath with a sharp, clicking sound, caused by a muscular spasm of the diaphragm. 2 **hiccups,** *pl.* condition of having one hiccup after another. —*v.i.* 1 have the hiccups. 2 make the sound of a hiccup. [probably imitative]

hic ja cet (hik jā′sit), 1 LATIN. here lies. These words often begin an epitaph on a tombstone. 2 epitaph.

hick (hik), *n.* INFORMAL. 1 person who lives in the country, in a small town, or in a backward community. 2 an ignorant, unsophisticated person. [< *Hick,* nickname for *Richard*]

hick or y (hik′ər ē), *n., pl.* **-or ies.** 1 any of a genus of North American trees of the same family as the walnut, bearing a hard nut with an edible, sweet kernel. 2 the tough, hard wood of any of these trees. 3 switch, stick, etc., of this wood. [alteration of Algonquian *pohickery,* a species of walnut]

hid (hid), *v.* pt. and a pp. of **hide**[1].

hi dal go (hi dal′gō), *n., pl.* **-gos.** a Spanish nobleman ranking below a grandee. [< Spanish]

hid den (hid′n), *adj.* put or kept out of sight; concealed; secret. —*v.* a pp. of **hide**[1].

hide[1] (hīd), *v.,* **hid, hid den** or **hid, hid ing.**

—*v.t.* 1 put or keep out of sight; conceal: *Hide it where no one else will know where it is.* See synonym study below. 2 cover up; shut off from sight: *Clouds hide the sun.* 3 keep secret: *She hid her disappointment.* —*v.i.* hide oneself: *I'll hide, and you find me.* [Old English *hȳdan*] —**hid′er,** *n.*

Syn. *v.t.* 1 **Hide, conceal** mean to put or keep something out of sight. **Hide** is the general word: *I hid the present under my bed.* **Conceal** is more formal and usually suggests hiding with a purpose or keeping under cover: *She concealed the note in her dress.*

hide[2] (hīd), *n., v.,* **hid ed, hid ing.** —*n.* 1 skin of an animal, either raw or tanned. See **skin** for synonym study. 2 INFORMAL. a person's skin. —*v.t.* INFORMAL. beat; thrash. [Old English *hȳd*]

hide[3] (hīd), *n.* an old English measure of land, usually about 120 acres. [Old English *hīgid*]

hide-and-seek (hīd′n sēk′), *n.* a children's game in which all but one of the players hide and he tries to find them.

hide a way (hīd′ə wā′), *n.* 1 place in which to hide; place of concealment. 2 a secluded spot; retreat.

hide bound (hīd′bound′), *adj.* 1 narrow-minded and stubborn. 2 with the skin sticking close to the bones.

hid e ous (hid′ē əs), *adj.* very ugly; frightful; horrible. [< Old French *hideus* < *hide* fear, horror] —**hid′e ous ly,** *adv.* —**hid′e-ous ness,** *n.*

hide-out (hīd′out′), *n.* a secluded place for hiding or being alone.

hid ing[1] (hī′ding), *n.* 1 a being hidden; concealment. 2 place to hide. [< *hide*[1]]

hid ing[2] (hī′ding), *n.* INFORMAL. a beating; thrashing. [< *hide*[2]]

hie (hī), *v.,* **hied, hie ing** or **hy ing.** —*v.i.* go quickly; hasten; hurry. —*v.t.* cause to hasten. [Old English *hīgian*]

hi e rarch (hī′ə rärk), *n.* person who has religious rule or authority; chief priest or church official.

hi e rar chal (hī′ə rär′kəl), *adj.* of or having to do with a hierarch.

hi e rar chic (hī′ə rär′kik), *adj.* hierarchical.

hi e rar chi cal (hī′ə rär′kə kəl), *adj.* of, having to do with, or belonging to a hierarchy. —**hi′e rar′chi cal ly,** *adv.*

hi e rar chy (hī′ə rär′kē), *n., pl.* **-chies.** 1 organization of persons or things arranged one above the other according to rank, class, or grade. 2 government by priests or church officials. 3 group of church officials of different ranks. In the hierarchy of the church, archbishops have more authority than bishops. [< Medieval Latin *hierarchia* < Greek *hieros* sacred + *archos* ruler]

hi e rat ic (hī′ə rat′ik), *adj.* 1 of or having to do with the priestly class; priestly. 2 of or having to do with a form of Egyptian writing used by the early priests in their records. Hieratic writing is a simplified form of hieroglyphics. [< Latin *hieraticus* < Greek *hieratikos,* ultimately < *hieros* sacred] —**hi′e-rat′i cal ly,** *adv.*

hi er o glyph (hī′ər ə glif), *n.* hieroglyphic.

hi er o glyph ic (hī′ər ə glif′ik), *n.* 1 picture, character, or symbol standing for a word, idea, or sound; hieroglyph. The ancient Egyptians used hieroglyphics instead of an alphabet like ours. 2 letter or word that is hard to read. 3 **hieroglyphics,** *pl.* **a** system of writing that uses hieroglyphics. **b** writing that is hard to read. 4 a secret symbol. —*adj.* 1 of or written in hieroglyphics. 2 hard to read. [< Late Latin *hieroglyphicus* < Greek *hieroglyphikos* < *hieros* sacred + *glyphē* a carving] —**hi′er o glyph′i cal ly,** *adv.*

hi-fi (hī′fī′), *n.* 1 high fidelity. 2 equipment for this. —*adj.* of or for high fidelity.

hig gle (hig′əl), *v.i.,* **-gled, -gling.** haggle. [apparently alteration of *haggle*] —**hig′-gler,** *n.*

hig gle dy-pig gle dy (hig′əl dē pig′əl dē), *adv.* in jumbled confusion. —*adj.* jumbled; confused.

high (hī), *adj.* 1 of more than usual height; tall: *a high tower.* See synonym study below. 2 rising to a specified extent: *The mountain is 20,000 feet high.* 3 far above the ground or some base: *an airplane high in the air.* 4 extending to or done from a height: *a high leap, a high dive.* 5 above others in rank, quality, character, etc.: *a high official. A general has high rank.* 6 greater, stronger, or better than average; great: *a high price, high temperature, high winds, high speed.* 7 most important; chief; main: *the high altar of a church.* 8 extreme of its kind; serious; grave: *high crimes.* 9 expensive; costly: *Strawberries are high in winter.* 10 not low in pitch; shrill; sharp: *a high voice, a high note.* 11 advanced to its peak: *high summer.* 12 haughty; arrogant: *a high manner.* 13 slightly tainted: *Game is often eaten after it has become high.* 14 happily excited: *high spirits.* 15 INFORMAL. **a** slightly drunk. **b** exhilarated or dazed under the influence of a drug. 16 designating an arrangement of gears that gives the greatest speed in an automobile, etc. 17 highly developed; more advanced in structure, intelligence, etc.: *the higher algae, the higher apes.* 18 more difficult or advanced: *higher mathematics.* 19 said with a part of the tongue raised high in the mouth. The *i* in *pit* and the *u* in *put* are high vowels. 20 **high and dry, a** up out of water. **b** all alone; without help; stranded.

—*adv.* 1 at or to a high point, place, rank, amount, degree, pitch, price, etc.: *He sings too high.* 2 **high and low,** everywhere. 3 **run high,** become heated; reach a high pitch: *Tempers ran high at election time.*

—*n.* 1 a high point, level, position, etc.: *Food prices reached a new high last month.* 2 arrangement of gears to give the greatest speed, as in an automobile. 3 area of relatively high barometric pressure. 4 U.S. INFORMAL. high school. 5 SLANG. exhilaration or stupor caused by a drug. 6 **on high, a** high above; up in the air. **b** in heaven. [Old English *hēah*]

Syn. *adj.* 1 **High, lofty, tall** mean of more than usual height. **High** applies to things, not people: *High hills surround the valley.* **Lofty** also applies to things and suggests an impressive height: *We saw the lofty Mount Shasta, snow-capped and rising over 14,000 feet.* **Tall** applies to both people and things, and suggests slenderness or narrowness as well as height: *He is a tall man. The corn grows tall here.*

A KINGLY
GIFT OF AN
OFFERING TABLE
TO
RA-HORUS
THE GREAT
GOD
LORD OF
HEAVEN

hieroglyphic (def. 1)
Egyptian hieroglyphics

high ball[1] (hī′bôl′), *n.* U.S. whiskey, brandy, etc., mixed with soda water or ginger ale and served with ice in a tall glass.

high ball[2] (hī′bôl′), U.S. —*n.* signal for a railroad train to proceed or increase its speed. —*v.i.* INFORMAL. move, travel, or advance rapidly: *The motorcycles highballed toward the curve.*

high blood pressure, hypertension.

high born (hī′bôrn′), *adj.* of noble birth.

high boy (hī′boi′), *n.* a tall chest of drawers on legs from 18 inches to 2 feet high.

high bred (hī′bred′), *adj.* 1 of superior breeding or stock. 2 well-mannered; very refined.

high brow (hī′brou′), INFORMAL. —*n.* person who cares or who claims to care a great deal about knowledge and culture. —*adj.* of or suitable for a highbrow.

high chair (hī′cher′, hī′char′), *n.* chair with a high seat and a tray, used for feeding babies.

High-Church (hī′chėrch′), *adj.* of or having to do with a party in the Anglican communion that lays great stress on church and priestly authority, ceremonial observances, and the Catholicism of the church.

High Churchman, person who favors High-Church practices.

high command, 1 the highest headquarters of a military force. 2 the top leadership of any organization.

High Commissioner or **high commissioner,** in the Commonwealth of Nations, the chief representative of one Commonwealth country to another.

high er-up (hī′ər up′), *n.* INFORMAL. person occupying a superior position.

high explosive, explosive, such as dynamite, that forms gas rapidly when detonated and shatters its container with great force.

high fa lu tin or **high fa lu ting** (hī′fə-lüt′n), *adj.* INFORMAL. high-sounding; pompous. [origin uncertain]

high fidelity, reproduction of sound by a radio or phonograph with as little distortion of the original sound as possible. —**high′-fi-del′i ty,** *adj.*

high fli er (hī′flī′ər), *n.* person who is extravagant or has pretentious ideas, ambitions, etc. Also, **highflyer.**

high-flown (hī′flōn′), *adj.* 1 aspiring or extravagant: *high-flown ideas.* 2 attempting to be elegant or eloquent: *high-flown compliments.*

high fly er (hī′flī′ər), *n.* highflier.

high frequency, (in electronics) a frequency ranging from 3 to 30 megacycles per second. —**high′-fre′quen cy,** *adj.*

High German, the literary and official language of Germany and Austria and one of the official languages of Switzerland. It developed from the dialects of central and southern Germany.

high-grade (hī′grād′), *adj.* of fine quality; superior.

high-hand ed (hī′han′did), *adj.* acting or done in a bold, arbitrary way; domineering; overbearing. —**high′-hand′ed ly,** *adv.* —**high′-hand′ed ness,** *n.*

high hat, top hat.
high-hat (hī′hat′), *v.,* **-hat ted, -hat ting,** *adj.* U.S. SLANG. —*v.t* treat as inferior; snub. —*adj.* 1 snobbish. 2 stylish or grand.
High Holidays, the Jewish holidays of Rosh Hashana and Yom Kippur.
high horse, an arrogant or condescending attitude, disposition, etc.
high jack (hī′jak′), *v.t.* hijack. —**high′-jack′er,** *n.*
high jinks (jinks), INFORMAL. noisy fun; lively or boisterous behavior.

high jump (def. 2)

high jump, 1 an athletic contest or event to determine how high each contestant can jump. 2 the jump itself. —**high jumper.**
high land (hī′lənd), *n.* 1 country or region that is higher and hillier than the neighboring country; land high above sea level. 2 **Highlands,** *pl.* mountainous region in N and W Scotland. —*adj.* of or in a highland or the Highlands.
high land er (hī′lən dər), *n.* 1 inhabitant of a highland. 2 **Highlander,** native or inhabitant of the Highlands of Scotland.
Highland fling, a lively dance of the Highlands of Scotland.
high light (hī′līt′), *v.,* **-light ed, -light ing,** *n.* —*v.t.* 1 cast a bright light on. 2 emphasize (parts of a painting, photograph, etc.) with lighting, certain colors, etc. 3 make prominent; focus on. —*n.* 1 effect or representation of bright light. 2 part of a painting, photograph, etc., in which light is represented as falling with greatest intensity. 3 the most prominent or interesting part, event, scene, etc.
high ly (hī′lē), *adv.* 1 in a high degree; very; very much: *highly amusing.* 2 very favorably: *spoke highly of his friend.* 3 at a high rate or price. 4 in or to a high position or rank.
High Mass, a complete ritual of Mass with music, the burning of incense, etc. The priest, assisted by a deacon and subdeacon, chants the service.
high-mind ed (hī′mīn′did), *adj.* 1 having or showing high principles and feelings. 2 ARCHAIC. proud. —**high′-mind′ed ly,** *adv.* —**high′-mind′ed ness,** *n.*
high ness (hī′nis), *n.* 1 a being high; height. 2 **Highness,** title of honor given to members of royal families: *The Prince of Wales is addressed as "Your Highness."*
high noon, fully noon; exactly midday.
high-oc tane (hī′ok′tān), *adj.* (of gasoline) having a high percentage of octane or a high octane number.
high-pitched (hī′picht′), *adj.* 1 of high tone or sound; shrill. 2 having a steep slope.
high-pow ered (hī′pou′ərd), *adj.* having much power: *a high-powered car.*
high-pres sure (hī′presh′ər), *adj., v.,* **-sured, -sur ing.** —*adj.* 1 having, using, or resisting a pressure (of steam, etc.) that is greater than the normal or that of the air. 2 having a high barometric pressure. 3 using strong, vigorous methods: *a high-pressure salesman.* —*v.t.* use strong, vigorous methods on in selling, etc.: *high-pressure a customer.*
high priest, 1 a chief priest. 2 head of the ancient Jewish priesthood. 3 an outstanding leader or authority.
high relief, carving or sculpture in which the figures project well out from the background.
high-rise (hī′rīz′), *adj.* having many stories; very tall. —*n.* a high-rise building.
high road (hī′rōd′), *n.* 1 a main road; highway. 2 a direct and easy way.
high school, school attended after the elementary school or junior high school; secondary school. High school consists of grades 9 through 12 or 10 through 12. —**high′-school′,** *adj.*
high seas, the open ocean. The high seas are outside the jurisdiction of any country.
high-sound ing (hī′soun′ding), *adj.* having an imposing or pretentious sound.
high-spir it ed (hī′spir′ə tid), *adj.* 1 proud. 2 courageous. 3 spirited; fiery. —**high′-spir′it ed ly,** *adv.* —**high′-spir′it ed-ness,** *n.*
high spirits, happiness; cheerfulness; gaiety.
high-strung (hī′strung′), *adj.* very sensitive or nervous; easily excited.
hight (hīt), *adj.* ARCHAIC. named; called. [Middle English *highte*]
high tail (hī′tāl′), *v.i.* INFORMAL. run quickly; hurry.
high-ten sion (hī′ten′shən), *adj.* having or using a high voltage.
high-test (hī′test′), *adj.* 1 passing very difficult requirements and tests. 2 having a very low boiling point. High-test gasoline, used in some automobiles, quickly forms a vapor in the engine.
high tide, 1 the highest level of the tide. 2 time when the tide is highest. 3 the highest point.
high time, time just before it is too late: *It is high time he began to study.*
high-toned (hī′tōnd′), *adj.* 1 having a high character or high principles. 2 pretentiously stylish and exclusive.
high treason, treason against one's ruler, state, or government.
high-wa ter mark (hī′wô′tər, hī′wot′ər), 1 the highest level reached by a body of water. 2 any highest point.
high way (hī′wā′), *n.* 1 a public road. 2 a main road or route. 3 a direct line or way to some end.
high way man (hī′wā′mən), *n., pl.* **-men.** (in former times) man who robbed travelers on a public road.
hi jack (hī′jak′), *v.t.* rob or take by force (goods in transit, an airplane in flight, etc.). Also, **highjack.** [origin uncertain] —**hi′-jack′er,** *n.*
hike (hīk), *v.,* **hiked, hik ing,** *n.* —*v.i.* 1 take a long walk; tramp or march. 2 draw or pull (up). —*v.t.* INFORMAL. 1 raise, move, or draw with a jerk; hitch: *Hike up your socks.* 2 raise; increase: *hike wages.* —*n.* 1 a long walk; tramp or march. 2 INFORMAL. increase: *a hike in prices.* [perhaps related to *hitch*] —**hik′er,** *n.*
hi lar i ous (hə ler′ē əs, hə lar′ē əs; hī ler′ē-əs, hī lar′ē əs), *adj.* very merry; noisily gay. —**hi lar′i ous ly,** *adv.* —**hi lar′i ous-ness,** *n.*
hi lar i ty (hə lar′ə tē, hī lar′ə tē), *n.* great merriment; noisy gaiety. [< Latin *hilaritatem* < *hilaris* gay]
Hil de brand (hil′də brand), *n.* name of Pope Gregory VII before he became pope.
hill (hil), *n.* 1 a raised part of the earth's surface, smaller than a mountain. 2 a little heap or pile. 3 a little heap of soil put over and around the roots of a plant or cluster of

hat, āge, fär; let, ēqual, tėrm;
it, īce; hot, ōpen, ôrder;
oil, out; cup, pu̇t, rüle;
ch, child; ng, long; sh, she;
th, thin; ᴛʜ, then; zh, measure;

ə represents *a* in about, *e* in taken, *i* in pencil, *o* in lemon, *u* in circus.

< = from, derived from, taken from.

plants. 4 plant or plants so surrounded. —*v.t.* 1 put a little heap of soil over and around. 2 form into a little heap. [Old English *hyll*] —**hill′er,** *n.*
Hil lar y (hil′ər ē), *n.* Sir **Edmund,** born 1919, New Zealand mountain climber who climbed Mount Everest in 1953.
hill bil ly (hil′bil′ē), *n., pl.* **-lies,** *adj.* INFORMAL —*n.* person who lives in the backwoods or a mountain region, especially in the southern United States. —*adj.* of, having to do with, or characteristic of hillbillies: *hillbilly music.*
hill ock (hil′ək), *n.* a little hill.
hill side (hil′sīd′), *n.* side of a hill.
hill top (hil′top′), *n.* top of a hill.
hill y (hil′ē), *adj.,* **hill i er, hill i est.** 1 having many hills. 2 like a hill; steep. —**hill′i ness,** *n.*
hilt (hilt), *n.* 1 handle of a sword, dagger, or tool. 2 **to the hilt,** thoroughly; completely. —*v.t.* furnish with a hilt. [Old English]
hi lum (hī′ləm), *n., pl.* **-la** (-lə). 1 mark or scar on a seed at the point of attachment to the seed vessel. The eye of a bean is a hilum. 2 place in a gland or other organ where blood vessels, nerves, and ducts enter and leave. [< Latin, a trifle]
him (him; *unstressed* im), *pron.* objective case of **he.** *Take him home.* [Old English, dative of *hē* he]
Him a la yan (him′ə lā′ən, hə mä′lyən), *adj.* of or having to do with the Himalayas.
Him a la yas (him′ə lā′əz, hə mä′lyəz), *n.pl.* mountain system extending about 1600 miles from the Pamirs in Pakistan eastward through India, Nepal, Sikkim, Bhutan, and the southern Chinese border. Its highest peak is Mount Everest.
him self (him self′; *except when following a pause,* im self′), *pron.* 1 the emphatic form of **he** or **him.** *He did it himself.* 2 the reflexive form of **him.** *He cut himself.* 3 his real or true self: *He feels like himself again.*
Hi na ya na (hē′nə yä′nə), *n.* the traditional form of Buddhism, observed chiefly in Burma, Cambodia, Ceylon, Laos, Thailand, and Vietnam, which reveres Buddha as a great human teacher but not as a divine being. [< Sanskrit *hīnayāna,* literally, small vehicle]
hind[1] (hīnd), *adj.,* **hind er, hind most** or **hind er most.** back; rear: *the hind legs of an animal.* [Middle English, perhaps < *hinder*[2]]
hind[2] (hīnd), *n., pl.* **hinds** or **hind.** a female deer, especially a female red deer in and after its third year. [Old English]
hind[3] (hīnd), *n.* ARCHAIC. 1 a farm worker. 2 peasant. [Old English *hīne,* plural, domestic servant]
hind brain (hīnd′brān′), *n.* the back part of the brain composed of the metencephalon and myelencephalon; rhombencephalon. It includes the cerebellum and the medulla oblongata.

Hin de mith (hin′də mith; *German* hin′də-mit), *n.* **Paul,** 1895-1963, German composer.

Hin den burg (hin′dən bėrg′), *n.* **Paul von,** 1847-1934, German general and field marshal, president of Germany from 1925 to 1934.

hin der[1] (hin′dər), *v.t.* keep back; hold back; get in the way of; make difficult; hamper. See **prevent** for synonym study. *—v.i.* get in the way; be a hindrance. [Old English *hindrian*] **—hin′der er,** *n.*

hind er[2] (hīn′dər), *adj.* hind[1]. [Old English]

hind er most (hīn′dər mōst), *adj.* hindmost.

Hin di (hin′dē), *n.* 1 an Indo-European vernacular language of northern India, comprising various dialects. 2 form of Hindustani used by educated Hindus and now regarded as the official language of India.

hind most (hīnd′mōst), *adj.* farthest back; nearest the rear; last.

Hin doo (hin′dü), *n., pl.* **-doos,** *adj.* Hindu.

hind quar ter (hīnd′kwôr′tər), *n.* 1 the rear half of a side of beef, veal, lamb, etc., including the leg, loin, and one or more ribs. 2 **hindquarters,** *pl.* the rear part of an animal's body, including the lower back, buttocks, and thighs; haunches.

hin drance (hin′drəns), *n.* 1 person or thing that hinders. See **obstacle** for synonym study. 2 act of hindering.

hind sight (hīnd′sīt′), *n.* 1 ability to see, after the event is over, what should have been done. 2 sight nearest the breech in a firearm.

Hin du (hin′dü), *n., pl.* **-dus,** *adj.* *—n.* 1 native or inhabitant of India. 2 person who believes in Hinduism. *—adj.* having to do with the Hindus, their language, or their religion. Also, **Hindoo.** [< Persian *Hindū* < *Hind* India]

Hin du ism (hin′dü iz′əm), *n.* the religious and social system of the Hindus. The caste system and the worship of many gods are parts of Hinduism.

Hin du Kush Mountains (hin′dü kush′), mountain range in NE Afghanistan and NW Pakistan. Highest peak, 25,263 ft.

Hin du stan (hin′də stän′, hin′də stan′), *n.* 1 a Persian name for India. 2 part of India north of the Deccan. 3 the Republic of India.

Hin du sta ni (hin′də stä′nē, hin′də-stan′ē), *adj.* of or having to do with India, its people, or their languages. *—n.* the commonest language of northern India. It is now used as a lingua franca throughout India. A Persian-Arabic form, Urdu, is one of the major languages of Pakistan.

hinge (hinj), *n., v.,* **hinged, hing ing.** *—n.* 1 joint on which a door, gate, cover, lid, etc., swings back and forth. 2 a natural joint doing similar work: *the hinge of the knee, the hinge of a clam.* 3 that on which something turns or depends; central principle; critical point. *—v.t.* furnish with hinges; attach by hinges. *—v.i.* 1 hang or turn on a hinge. 2 depend: *The success of the picnic hinges on the kind of weather we will have.* [Middle English *heng*]

hin ny (hin′ē), *n., pl.* **-nies.** a hybrid animal resembling a mule that is the offspring of a male horse and a female ass. [< Latin *hinnus*]

hint (hint), *n.* 1 a slight sign; indirect suggestion: *A small black cloud gave a hint of a coming storm.* 2 a very slight amount. *—v.t.* 1 give a slight sign of; suggest indirectly. See synonym study below. 2 **hint at,** give a hint of; suggest. [apparently < archaic *hent* to seize, Old English *hentan*] **—hint′er,** *n.*

Syn. *v.t.* 1 **Hint, intimate, insinuate** mean to suggest indirectly. **Hint** means to convey an idea in a roundabout way: *She hinted that she wanted to go to bed by saying, "Do you often stay up this late?"* **Intimate** means to suggest something in a delicate manner, so that others understand without being told outright: *He intimated that he will accept if he is invited.* **Insinuate** means to suggest or hint something unkind or nasty in a sly or underhand way: *Are you insinuating that I am a liar?*

hin ter land (hin′tər land′), *n.* 1 land or district behind a coast. 2 region far from towns and cities; thinly settled country.

hip[1] (hip), *n.* 1 the fleshy part of the human body that covers the hip joint, extending from just below the waist to the upper thigh. 2 hip joint. 3 a similar part in animals, where the hind leg joins the body. [Old English *hype*]

hip[2] (hip), *n.* seedcase containing the ripe seed of a rosebush. [Old English *hēope*]

hip[3] (hip), *adj.* U.S. SLANG. having up-to-date knowledge; informed; hep. [variant of *hep*]

hip bone (hip′bōn′), *n.* either of the two wide, irregular bones, which, with the lower backbone, form the pelvis.

hip joint, joint formed by the upper thighbone and the pelvis.

hipped (hipt), *adj.* U.S. SLANG. having the mind full of a certain subject; obsessed.

hip pie (hip′ē), *n.* person who rejects all conventional standards of behavior, dress, etc. Hippies often live in groups and act with complete freedom. [< *hip*[3]]

hip po (hip′ō), *n., pl.* **-pos.** INFORMAL. hippopotamus.

Hip poc ra tes (hi pok′rə tēz′), *n.* 460?-377? B.C., Greek physician, called the father of medicine.

Hip po crat ic oath (hip′ə krat′ik), oath attributed to Hippocrates, describing the duties and obligations of a physician. It is usually taken by those about to become physicians.

Hip po crene (hip′ə krēn′, hip′ə krē′nē), *n.* fountain on Mt. Helicon, sacred to the Muses and regarded as a source of poetic inspiration.

hip po drome (hip′ə drōm), *n.* 1 (in ancient Greece and Rome) an oval track for horse races and chariot races, surrounded by tiers of seats for spectators. 2 arena or building for a circus, rodeo, etc. [< Greek *hippodromos* < *hippos* horse + *dromos* race course]

hippopotamus (def. 1)
about 13 ft. long

hip po pot a mus (hip′ə pot′ə məs), *n., pl.* **-mus es, -mi** (-mī). 1 a massive herbivorous, amphibious, African mammal with a thick-skinned, hairless body, short legs, and a large head and mouth. Hippopotamuses are even-toed ungulates, related to swine; river horse. 2 a smaller similar mammal of the same family. [< Greek *hippopotamos* < *hippos* horse + *potamos* river]

hip roof, roof with sloping ends and sides.

hip roof

hip ster (hip′stər), *n.* U.S. SLANG. person who keeps up with new, unconventional, or the latest ideas, styles, attitudes, etc.; person who is or is considered hip.

hire (hīr), *v.,* **hired, hir ing,** *n.* *—v.t.* 1 agree to pay for the temporary use of (a thing) or the work or services of (a person). See **employ** for synonym study. 2 give the temporary use of (a thing) or the work or services of (a person) in return for payment. *—v.i.* **hire out,** give one's work in return for payment. *—n.* 1 payment for the use of a thing or the work or services of a person. 2 a hiring. 3 **for hire,** for use or work in return for payment. [Old English *hȳrian*] **—hir′er,** *n.*

hire ling (hīr′ling), *n.* person who works only for money, without interest or pride in the work.

hire-pur chase (hīr′pėr′chəs), *n.* BRITISH. 1 a purchase made on the installment plan. 2 installment plan.

Hir o hi to (hir′ō hē′tō), *n.* born 1901, emperor of Japan since 1926.

Hir o shi ge (hir′ō shē′ge), *n.* **Ando,** 1797-1858, Japanese painter.

Hir o shi ma (hir′ō shē′mə), *n.* seaport in W Japan, largely destroyed by the first military use of the atomic bomb on August 6, 1945. 541,000.

hir sute (hėr′süt), *adj.* hairy. [< Latin *hirsutus*] **—hir′sute ness,** *n.*

his (hiz; *unstressed* iz), possessive form of **he.** *adj.* of him; belonging to him: *This is his book.* *—pron.* the one or ones belonging to him: *The others are not his.* [Old English, genitive of *hē* he]

His pa ni a (hi spā′nē ə, hi spā′nyə), *n.* 1 Latin name for Spain and Portugal. 2 a literary name for Spain.

His pan ic (hi span′ik), *adj.* 1 Spanish. 2 Latin American.

His pan io la (his′pə nyō′lə), *n.* the second largest island in the West Indies, between Cuba and Puerto Rico. It is divided into the Dominican Republic and Haiti. 9,192,000 pop.; 29,500 sq. mi. Former name, **Haiti.** See **Caribbean Sea** for map.

hiss (his), *v.i.* 1 make a sound like *ss: Air or steam rushing out of a small opening hisses. Geese and snakes hiss.* 2 show disapproval or scorn by hissing. *—v.t.* 1 show disapproval of or scorn for by hissing. 2 force or drive by hissing: *They hissed him off the stage.* 3 say or show by hissing. *—n.* 1 the sound of hissing. 2 a hissing sound as an expression of disapproval or scorn. [imitative] **—hiss′er,** *n.*

hist (hist), *interj.* be still! listen!

hist., 1 historian. 2 history.

his ta mine (his′tə mēn′, his′tə mən), *n.* an amine released by the body in allergic reactions that lowers the blood pressure, used in the diagnosis and treatment of various allergies. *Formula:* $C_5H_9N_3$

his to gram (his′tə gram), *n.* (in statistics) a graph of a frequency distribution in which

hat, āge, fär; let, ēqual, tėrm;
it, īce; hot, ōpen, ôrder;
oil, out; cup, pu̇t, rüle;
ch, child; ng, long; sh, she;
th, thin; ᴛʜ, then; zh, measure;

ə represents *a* in about, *e* in taken, *i* in pencil, *o* in lemon, *u* in circus.

< = from, derived from, taken from.

vertical rectangles or columns are constructed with the width of each rectangle being a class interval and the height a distance corresponding to the frequency in that class interval. [< Greek *histos* web + English *-gram*]

his to log i cal (his′tə loj′ə kəl), *adj.* of or having to do with histology. **—his′to log′i cal ly,** *adv.*

his tol o gist (hi stol′ə jist), *n.* an expert in histology.

his tol o gy (hi stol′ə jē), *n.* 1 branch of biology that deals with the structure, especially the microscopic structure, of the tissues of animals and plants. 2 the tissue structure of an animal or plant. [< Greek *histos* web, tissue]

his to ri an (hi stôr′ē ən, hi stōr′ē ən), *n.* 1 person who writes about history. 2 scholar who is an authority on history.

his to ric (hi stôr′ik, hi stor′ik), *adj.* 1 famous or important in history: *Plymouth Rock is a historic spot.* 2 historical.

his to ri cal (hi stôr′ə kəl, hi stor′ə kəl), *adj.* 1 of or having to do with history. 2 according to history; based on history. 3 known to be real or true; in history, not in legend. 4 famous in history; historic. **—his to′ri cal ly,** *adv.* **—his to′ri cal ness,** *n.*

historical present, the present tense used in describing past events to make them seem more vivid.

his to ric i ty (his′tə ris′ə tē), *n.* quality of being true as history; real existence or occurrence.

his to ri og ra pher (hi stôr′ē og′rə fər, hi stōr′ē og′rə fər), *n.* 1 historian. 2 the official historian of a court, public institution, etc.

his to ri og ra phy (hi stôr′ē og′rə fē, hi stōr′ē og′rə fē), *n.* 1 study of the writing of history. 2 the writing of history. 3 written history.

his tor y (his′tər ē), *n., pl.* **-tor ies.** 1 story or record of important past events connected with a person or a nation. 2 a known past: *This ship has an interesting history.* 3 all past events considered together; course of human affairs. 4 a recording and explaining of past events. 5 branch of knowledge or study that deals with the record and interpretation of past events. 6 statement of what has happened; account. 7 case history. [< Latin *historia* < Greek, inquiry, record, history. Doublet of STORY[1].]

his tri on ic (his′trē on′ik), *adj.* 1 having to do with actors or acting. 2 theatrical; insincere. [< Latin *histrionicus* < *histrionem* actor] **—his′tri on′i cal ly,** *adv.*

his tri on ics (his′trē on′iks), *n. sing. or pl.* 1 dramatic representation; theatricals; dramatics. 2 a theatrical or insincere manner, expression, etc.

hit (hit), *v.,* **hit, hit ting,** *n.* *—v.t.* 1 give a blow to; strike; knock: *He hit the ball with the bat.* See **beat** for synonym study. 2 come against with force: *She hit her head against the shelf.* 3 get to (what is aimed at): *Her second arrow hit the bull's-eye.* 4 come upon; meet with; reach or find: *We hit the right road in the dark.* 5 have a painful effect on; affect severely: *The stockbroker was hard hit by the fall in stocks.* 6 attack or criticize sharply: *The reviews hit the new play.* 7 agree with; suit exactly; please: *This hits my fancy.* 8 reach or touch directly and effectively. *—v.i.* 1 give a blow or blows: *When I become angry my first impulse is to hit.* 2 knock or strike with force: *The ball hit against the window.* 3 ignite the mixture in a cylinder of an internal-combustion engine: *hit on all cylinders.* 4 make a base hit in baseball.

hit it off, get along well together; agree.

hit off, **a** imitate. **b** represent or describe cleverly.

hit on or **hit upon,** **a** come on; meet with; get to: *We hit upon a plan for making money.* **b** find, especially by accident; guess correctly: *He finally hit upon a solution to his problem.*

hit or miss, with no plan; haphazardly; at random.

—n. 1 a blow; stroke. 2 a getting to what is aimed at. 3 a sharp attack or criticism. 4 a successful attempt, performance, or production: *The new play is the hit of the season.* 5 base hit. 6 a stroke of luck or chance.

[< Scandinavian (Old Icelandic) *hitta*] **—hit′ter,** *n.*

hit-and-run (hit′n run′), *adj.* 1 of, having to do with, or caused by a driver who hits a person or vehicle and drives away without stopping to see what happened. 2 characterized by the tactic of carrying out a series of military actions suddenly and disappearing as quickly. 3 having to do with a play in baseball in which a base runner starts for the next base as the pitcher throws the ball and the batter tries to hit it.

hit-and-run driver, a motorist who fails to stop after hitting another vehicle or a pedestrian.

hitch (hich), *v.t.* 1 fasten with a hook, ring, rope, strap, etc.: *She hitched her horse to a post.* 2 harness to a wagon, carriage, etc.: *The farmer hitched up his team and drove to town.* 3 move or pull with a jerk: *He hitched his chair nearer to the fire.* 4 INFORMAL. get (a ride) by hitchhiking. *—v.i.* 1 become fastened or caught; fasten; catch: *A knot made the rope hitch.* 2 move with a jerk; move jerkily. 3 limp; hobble. *—n.* 1 a fastening; catch: *The hitch joining the plow to the tractor is broken.* 2 kind of knot used for temporary fastening. 3 a short, sudden pull or jerk: *The sailor gave his trousers a hitch.* 4 limp; hobble. 5 obstacle; hindrance: *A hitch in their plans made them miss the train.* 6 period of time, especially a period of service in the armed forces. [Middle English *hychen*]

hitch hike (hich′hīk′), *v.i.,* **-hiked, -hik ing.** travel by walking and getting free rides from passing automobiles, trucks, etc. **—hitch′hik′er,** *n.*

hith er (hiᴛʜ′ər), *adv.* 1 to this place; here. 2 **hither and thither,** here and there. *—adj.* on or toward this side; nearer. [Old English *hider*]

hith er most (hiᴛʜ′ər mōst), *adj.* nearest.

hith er to (hiᴛʜ′ər tü′), *adv.* until now: *a fact hitherto unknown.*

hith er ward (hiᴛʜ′ər wərd), *adv.* toward this place; hither.

hith er wards (hiᴛʜ′ər wərdz), *adv.* hitherward.

Hit ler (hit′lər), *n.* **Adolf,** 1889-1945, German National Socialist leader, born in Austria, dictator of Germany from 1933 to 1945.

hit-or-miss (hit′ər mis′), *adj.* not planned; random; haphazard.

Hit tite (hit′īt), *n.* 1 member of an ancient people in Asia Minor and Syria. Their civilization existed from about 2000 B.C. until about 1200 B.C. They were conquered by the Assyrians. 2 the Indo-European language of the Hittites, preserved in cuneiform and hieroglyphic writing. *—adj.* of or having to do with the Hittites or their language.

hive (hīv), *n., v.,* **hived, hiv ing.** *—n.* 1 house or box for honeybees to live in; beehive. 2 a large number of bees living in such a place. 3 a busy, swarming place full of people or animals. 4 a swarming crowd. *—v.t.* 1 put (bees) in a hive. 2 store up (honey) in a hive. 3 lay up for future use. *—v.i.* 1 live close together as bees do. 2 go into a hive. [Old English *hȳf*]

hives (hīvz), *n.* condition in which the skin itches and shows raised patches of red; urticaria. It is usually caused by an allergy to some food or drug.

hl., hectoliter or hectoliters.

hm., hectometer or hectometers.

H.M., 1 Her Majesty. 2 His Majesty.

H.M.S., 1 Her Majesty's Service. 2 Her Majesty's Ship. 3 His Majesty's Service. 4 His Majesty's Ship.

ho (hō), *interj.* 1 exclamation of surprise, joy, or scornful laughter. 2 exclamation to attract attention.

Ho, holmium.

hoar (hôr, hōr), *adj.* hoary. *—n.* hoarfrost. [Old English *hār*]

hoard (hôrd, hōrd), *v.t., v.i.* save and store away (money, goods, etc.) for preservation or future use: *A squirrel hoards nuts for the winter.* *—n.* what is saved and stored away for preservation or future use; things stored. [Old English *hordian*] **—hoard′er,** *n.*

hoard ing (hôr′ding, hōr′ding), *n.* BRITISH. 1 a temporary board fence around a building that is being put up or repaired. 2 billboard. [< Old French *hourd* scaffold, of Germanic origin]

hoar frost (hôr′frôst′, hôr′frost′; hōr′frôst′, hōr′frost′), *n.* the white, feathery crystals of ice formed when dew freezes; white frost; rime.

hoar hound (hôr′hound′, hōr′hound′), *n.* horehound.

hoarse (hôrs, hōrs), *adj.,* **hoars er, hoars est.** 1 sounding rough and deep: *the hoarse croak of the bullfrog.* 2 having a rough voice: *A bad cold has made me hoarse.* [Old English *hās*] **—hoarse′ly,** *adv.* **—hoarse′ness,** *n.*

hoar y (hôr′ē, hōr′ē), *adj.,* **hoar i er, hoar i est.** 1 white or gray. 2 white or gray with age. 3 old; ancient. **—hoar′i ness,** *n.*

ho at zin (hō at′sən), *n.* a brightly colored, crested South American bird, somewhat smaller than a pheasant. [< Mexican Spanish *uatzin* < Nahuatl]

hoax (hōks), *n.* a mischievous trick, especially a made-up story passed off as true. *—v.t.* play a mischievous trick on; deceive in jest or in malice. [probably alteration of *hocus*] **—hoax′er,** *n.*

hob[1] (hob), *n.* 1 shelf at the back or side of a fireplace, on which to keep food, etc., warm. 2 a round, slender peg used as a target in quoits and similar games. 3 a hard metal tool with a spiral thread, used for cutting gears, tools, etc. [origin uncertain]

hob[2] (hob), *n.* 1 hobgoblin or elf. 2 **play hob** or **raise hob,** INFORMAL. cause trouble. [Middle English < *Hob,* nickname for *Robin* or *Robert*]

Ho bart (hō′bärt, hō′bərt), *n.* capital of Tasmania, in the S part. 148,000.

Hobbes (hobz), *n.* **Thomas,** 1588-1679, English philosopher.

hob ble (hob′əl), *v.,* **-bled, -bling,** *n.* —*v.i.* 1 walk awkwardly or lamely; limp. 2 move unsteadily. —*v.t.* 1 cause to walk awkwardly or limp. 2 tie the legs of (a horse, etc.) together in order to prevent free motion. 3 hinder. —*n.* 1 an awkward walk; limp. 2 rope or strap used to hobble a horse, etc. [Middle English *hobelen*] —**hob′bler,** *n.*

hob ble de hoy (hob′əl dē hoi′), *n.* an awkward, clumsy boy.

hobble skirt, a woman's skirt that is very narrow below the knees.

hob by (hob′ē), *n., pl.* **-bies.** something a person especially likes to work at or study which is not his main business or occupation; any favorite pastime, topic of conversation, etc. [short for *hobbyhorse*]

hob by horse (hob′ē hôrs′), *n.* 1 stick with a horse's head, used as a toy horse by children. 2 rocking horse. 3 hobby. [< *Hobby,* nickname for *Robin* or *Robert* + *horse*]

hob by ist (hob′ē ist), *n.* person who is much interested in a hobby or hobbies.

hob gob lin (hob′gob′lən), *n.* 1 goblin or elf. 2 bogy.

hob nail (hob′nāl′), *n.* a short nail with a large head to protect the soles of heavy boots and shoes.

hob nailed (hob′nāld′), *adj.* having hobnails.

hob nob (hob′nob′), *v.i.,* **-nobbed, -nob bing.** 1 be on familiar terms; associate intimately. 2 drink together. [from drinking phrase *hob or nob* give or take] —**hob′-nob′ber,** *n.*

ho bo (hō′bō), *n., pl.* **-bos** or **-boes.** U.S. 1 person who wanders about and lives by begging or doing odd jobs; tramp. 2 a migratory workman. [origin uncertain]

Hob son's choice (hob′sənz), choice of taking the thing offered or nothing. [< Thomas *Hobson,* about 1594-1631, English liveryman who compelled each customer to take the horse nearest to the stable door or none]

Ho Chi Minh (hō′ chē′ min′), 1890?-1969, Vietnamese political leader, president of North Vietnam from 1954 to 1969.

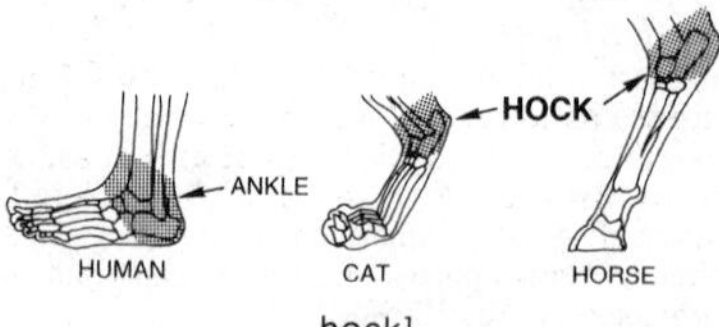

hock[1]

hock[1] (hok), *n.* joint in the hind leg of a horse, cow, etc., above the fetlock joint, corresponding to the ankle of man. [Old English *hōh*]

hock[2] (hok), SLANG. —*v.t., v.i.* pawn. —*n.* 1 pawn. 2 **in hock, a** in pawn. **b** in debt. [perhaps < Dutch *hok* pen, jail]

hock[3] (hok), *n.* kind of white Rhine wine. [short for *Hockamore,* alteration of *Hochheimer* < *Hochheim,* Germany]

hock ey (hok′ē), *n.* 1 game played on ice by two teams of six players each wearing skates and carrying hooked sticks with which they try to drive a black rubber disk, the puck, across the opposing team's goal; ice hockey. 2 a similar game played on a field with curved sticks and a small ball by two teams of eleven players each; field hockey. [perhaps < Old French *hoquet* (shepherd's) crook]

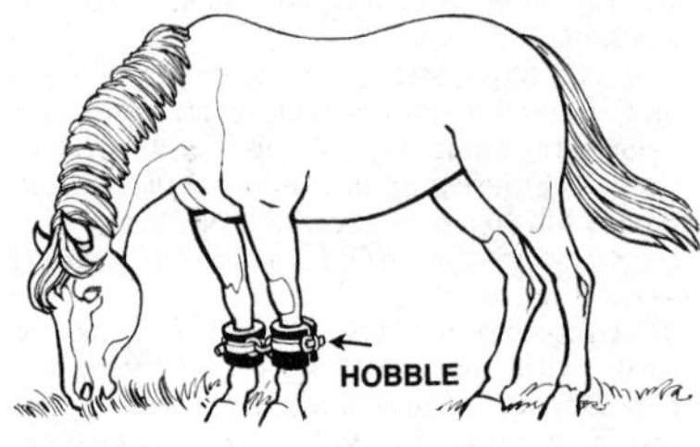

hobble (def. 2)

ho cus (hō′kəs), *v.t.,* **-cused, -cus ing** or **-cussed, -cus sing.** 1 play a trick on; hoax; cheat. 2 stupefy with drugs. 3 put drugs in (alcoholic drink). [short for *hocus-pocus*]

ho cus-po cus (hō′kəs pō′kəs), *n.* 1 a meaningless form of words used in performing magic tricks. 2 sleight of hand; magic. 3 trickery; deception. Also, **hokey-pokey.** [origin uncertain]

hod (def. 1)
used to carry mortar

hod (hod), *n.* 1 trough or tray set crosswise on top of a long, straight handle that is rested on the shoulder and used for carrying bricks, mortar, etc., up ladders, etc. 2 coal scuttle. [< Middle Dutch *hodde*]

hodge podge (hoj′poj′), *n.* a disorderly mixture; mess; jumble. Also, **hotchpotch.** [< Old French *hochepot* ragout]

hoe (hō), *n., v.,* **hoed, hoe ing.** —*n.* tool with a thin blade set across the end of a long handle, used for loosening soil, cutting weeds, etc. —*v.t.* loosen, dig, or cut with a hoe. —*v.i.* use a hoe. [< Old French *houe*] —**hoe′like′,** *adj.* —**ho′er,** *n.*

hoe cake (hō′kāk′), *n.* U.S. kind of bread made of corn meal.

hoe down (hō′doun′), *n.* U.S. 1 a noisy, lively square dance. 2 music for such a dance.

Hoff mann (hôf′män), *n.* **Ernst Theodor Wilhelm,** 1776-1822, German writer, musician, and painter.

hog (hog, hôg), *n., v.,* **hogged, hog ging.** —*n.* 1 pig. 2 an adult pig weighing more than 120 pounds, raised for its meat. 3 any animal of the same family as the pig. 4 INFORMAL. a stingy, grasping, gluttonous, or filthy person. 5 **go the whole hog,** INFORMAL. go to the limit; do something thoroughly. —*v.t.* SLANG. take more than one's share of. [Old English *hogg*]

ho gan (hō′gän′), *n.* dwelling used by the Navaho Indians. Hogans are built with logs and mounded over with earth. [< Navaho *hoghan* house]

Ho garth (hō′gärth), *n.* **William,** 1697-1764, English painter and engraver.

hog back (hog′bak′, hôg′bak′), *n.* (in geology) a low, sharp ridge with steep sides.

hog gish (hog′ish, hôg′ish), *adj.* 1 very selfish or greedy. 2 filthy. —**hog′gish ly,** *adv.* —**hog′gish ness,** *n.*

hog nose snake (hog′nōz′, hôg′nōz′), any of a genus of harmless North American snakes with upturned snouts. Hognose snakes hiss, while dilating and flattening the head when alarmed.

hogs head (hogz′hed, hôgz′hed), *n.* 1 a large barrel or cask. In the United States, a hogshead contains from 63 to 140 gallons. 2 a liquid measure equal to 63 gallons.

hog-tie (hog′tī′, hôg′tī′), *v.t.,* **-tied, -ty ing.** U.S. 1 tie all four feet, or the feet and hands, together; tie securely. 2 hinder; hold back.

hog wash (hog′wosh′, hôg′wôsh′), *n.* 1 refuse given to hogs; swill. 2 worthless stuff; nonsense.

Hoh en stau fen (hō′ən stou′fən; *German* hō′ən shtou′fən), *n.* member of a German princely family which ruled Germany from 1138 to 1208 and 1215 to 1254, and Sicily from 1194 to 1268.

Hoh en zol lern (hō′ən zol′ərn; *German* hō′ən tsôl′ərn), *n.* member of a German princely family, prominent since the Middle Ages. The kings of Prussia from 1701 to 1918 and the emperors of Germany from 1871 to 1918 were Hohenzollerns.

hoi pol loi (hoi′ pə loi′), the common people; the masses. [< Greek]

hoist (hoist), *v.t.* raise on high; lift up, often with ropes and pulleys: *hoist a flag, hoist sails.* —*n.* 1 a hoisting; lift; boost. 2 elevator or other apparatus for hoisting heavy loads. [earlier *hoise, hysse,* of unknown origin. Related to Dutch *hijsen.*]

hoi ty-toi ty (hoi′tē toi′tē), *interj.* exclamation showing surprise and some contempt. —*adj.* 1 giddy; flighty. 2 inclined to put on airs; haughty.

ho key-po key (hō′kē pō′kē), *n., pl.* **-keys.** hocus-pocus.

Hok kai do (hō kī′dō), *n.* the second largest island in Japan. 5,172,000 pop.; 30,100 sq. mi.

ho kum (hō′kəm), *n.* SLANG. 1 outworn melodramatic material or crude humor introduced into a play or the like for emotional effect or the laughs it may bring. 2 humbug; nonsense; bunk. [perhaps < *hocus*]

Ho ku sai (hō kü sī′), *n.* **Katsushika,** 1760-1849, Japanese painter and book illustrator.

Hol bein (hōl′bīn, hol′bīn), *n.* 1 **Hans,** 1460?-1524, German painter, called "the Elder." 2 his son, **Hans,** 1497-1543, German painter and maker of woodcuts, called "the Younger."

hold[1] (hōld), *v.,* **held, hold ing,** *n.* —*v.t.* 1 take in the hands or arms and keep; grasp and keep: *Please hold my hat.* 2 keep up or support with the hands or arms; keep from falling: *The boy was left awkwardly holding the baby.* 3 keep in some position or condition; cause to stay: *Hold the paper steady while you draw.* 4 keep from acting; hold back: *Hold your breath.* 5 keep back; detain; delay: *hold a letter for additional postage.*

6 keep; retain: *This package will be held until called for.* 7 keep by force against an enemy; defend: *Hold the fort.* 8 oblige (a person) to adhere to a promise, etc. 9 keep or have within itself; contain: *Those canisters hold sugar and flour.* See **contain** for synonym study. 10 be capable of containing; have room for: *How much water will this cup hold? This basket holds two bushels.* 11 have and take part in; carry on together: *Shall we hold a meeting of the club?* 12 have and keep as one's own; enjoy the use of; possess: *He holds much property in the city.* See **have** for synonym study. 13 have (a rank, position, etc.); occupy (an office): *That man has held the office of mayor for eight years.* 14 keep or have in the mind; regard as true; believe: *She holds a good opinion of you.* 15 think; consider: *People once held that the world was flat.* 16 think a certain way about; feel toward: *Wise men are held in honor.* 17 bear or carry in a certain position or attitude: *hold oneself erect.* 18 satisfy; suffice: *This meal should hold you until tomorrow.* 19 decide legally: *The court holds him guilty.* 20 keep on singing or playing (a musical note). *—v.i.* 1 remain fast or firm; not break, loosen, or give way: *The dike held during the flood.* 2 remain in a specified state; continue in a course; last; persist: *The frost still holds.* 3 maintain one's grasp on anything; cling: *The wind was so strong I had to hold onto the rail.* 4 maintain one's position against opposition or attack; hold out. 5 remain faithful or firm; adhere: *She held to her promise.* 6 be true; be in force or effect: *The rule holds in all cases.* 7 keep the same; keep on; continue: *The weather held warm.*

hold back, a keep back; keep from acting; restrain. **b** avoid disclosing.

hold down, a keep down; keep under control; repress. **b** INFORMAL. have and keep: *hold down a job.*

hold forth, a talk, preach, or harangue. **b** offer.

hold in, a keep in; keep back. **b** restrain oneself; keep silence.

hold off, a keep off or at a distance; keep from attacking. **b** keep from acting; keep away or aloof.

hold on, a keep one's hold. **b** keep on; continue. **c** INFORMAL. stop! wait a minute!

hold out, a keep up; continue; last. **b** keep resisting; not give in. **c** offer; present. **d** INFORMAL. keep back (something expected or due): *hold out on a promise.*

hold over, a keep for further action or consideration; postpone: *The bill has been held over until next year.* **b** stay in office beyond the regular term.

hold up, a keep from falling; support. **b** maintain; keep up: *Prices have been holding up pretty well.* **c** show; display. **d** continue; last: *If this wind holds up, we can go sailing.* **e** stop; withhold. **f** stop by force and rob: *I was held up in the alley.*

hold with, a side with. **b** agree with. **c** approve of.

—n. 1 act or manner of grasping or holding; grasp or grip: *release one's hold. You must take a better hold if you are to pull your weight.* 2 way of holding an opponent in wrestling. 3 thing to hold by: *The face of the cliff had enough holds for a good climber.* 4 thing to hold something else with. 5 a controlling force or influence: *A habit has a hold on you.* 6 a holding back; delay: *a hold in the launching of a missile.* 7 order to delay or temporarily halt something. 8 symbol (𝄐 or 𝄑) above or below a musical note or rest indicating that it is to be held for a longer time; pause. 9 ARCHAIC. fort; stronghold. **10 lay hold of** or **take hold of, a** seize; grasp: *They took hold of each other's hands.* **b** get control or possession of. **11 take hold,** become attached; take root. [Old English *healdan*]

hold² (hōld), *n.* interior of a ship or airplane where the cargo is carried. A ship's hold is below the deck. [variant of *hole*]

hold back (hōld′bak′), *n.* 1 thing that holds back; restraint; hindrance. 2 a restraining or preventing of action. 3 something withheld, especially money or wages.

hold er (hōl′dər), *n.* 1 person or thing that holds something. 2 person who owns, possesses, or occupies property, such as an owner or tenant. 3 thing to hold something else with: *a napkin holder.* 4 person legally entitled to receive payment on, or negotiate, a note, bill, etc.

hold fast (hōld′fast′), *n.* thing used to hold something else in place, such as a catch, hook, or clamp.

hold ing (hōl′ding), *n.* 1 piece of land or property. 2 Often, **holdings,** *pl.* property in stocks or bonds.

holding company, company that owns stocks or bonds of other companies and often controls them.

hold out (hōld′out′), *n.* INFORMAL. 1 person or group that refuses to accept terms, submit, or comply with a trend, order, etc. 2 refusal to accept terms, submit, or comply.

hold o ver (hōld′ō′vər), *n.* 1 person who continues to hold an office after his term has expired. 2 person or thing that remains behind from a former period.

hold up (hōld′up′), *n.* 1 INFORMAL. act of stopping by force and robbing. 2 a stopping.

hole (hōl), *n., v.,* **holed, hol ing.** *—n.* 1 an open place; opening: *a hole in a sock.* See synonym study below. 2 a hollow place in something solid. 3 a hollow place in the earth in which an animal lives; burrow. 4 a small, dark, dirty place. 5 INFORMAL. flaw; defect: *There's a hole in your argument.* 6 INFORMAL. position hard to get out of; embarrassing position. 7 a small, round, hollow place on a green, into which a golf ball is hit. 8 one of the divisions of a golf course, measured from tee to hole (def. 7). A regular golf course consists of 18 holes. 9 cove or small harbor. **10 in the hole,** in debt or financial difficulties. **11 pick holes in,** find fault with; criticize.

—v.t. 1 make holes in. 2 hit or drive (a golf ball) into a hole.

hole out, hit a golf ball into a hole.

hole up, a go or put into a hole. **b** go or put into hiding for a time.

[Old English *hol*] **—hole′less,** *adj.*

Syn. *n.* **1 Hole, cavity** mean an open or hollow place in something. **Hole** is the common word applying to an opening in or through anything: *Fire burned a hole in the roof. He bored a hole in the tree.* **Cavity** is chiefly scientific or technical, and applies only to a hollow space inside a solid mass or body, often with an opening at the surface: *The dentist filled several cavities in my teeth.*

hole y (hō′lē), *adj.* full of holes.

hol i day (hol′ə dā), *n.* 1 day free of work; day of pleasure and enjoyment. 2 day on which, either by law or custom, ordinary business is suspended: *Labor Day is a holiday in the United States.* 3 Often, **holidays,** *pl.* vacation. 4 holy day; religious festival.

hat, āge, fär; let, ēqual, tėrm;
it, īce; hot, ōpen, ôrder;
oil, out; cup, pu̇t, rüle;
ch, child; ng, long; sh, she;
th, thin; ᴛʜ, then; zh, measure;

ə represents *a* in about, *e* in taken,
i in pencil, *o* in lemon, *u* in circus.

< = from, derived from, taken from.

—adj. of or suited to a holiday; gay. *—v.i.* spend a holiday or vacation: *We holidayed in Great Britain last summer.* [Old English *hāligdæg* holy day] **—hol′i day′er,** *n.*

ho li ness (hō′lē nis), *n.* 1 quality or condition of being holy. 2 **Holiness,** title used in speaking to or of the Pope.

Hol ins hed (hol′inz hed, hol′in shed), *n.* **Raphael,** died 1580?, English chronicler.

ho lis tic (hō lis′tik), *adj.* taking in the whole of something; overall; inclusive. [< Greek *holos* whole]

hol land (hol′ənd), *n.* a linen or linen-and-cotton cloth used for window shades, upholstery, etc. It is usually light-brown and sometimes glazed. [< *Holland,* where it was first made]

Hol land (hol′ənd), *n.* the Netherlands.

hol lan daise sauce (hol′ən dāz), *n.* a creamy yellow sauce made from egg yolks, butter, lemon juice, and seasoning. [< French *sauce hollandaise,* literally, Holland sauce]

Hol land er (hol′ən dər), *n.* Dutchman.

Holland gin, Hollands.

Hol lands (hol′əndz), *n.* a strong gin made in Holland; schnapps.

hol ler (hol′ər), INFORMAL. *—v.i., v.t.* cry or shout loudly. *—n.* a loud cry or shout. [variant of *hollo*]

hol lo (hə lō′, hol′ō), *interj., n., pl.* **-los,** *v.i.* hello.

hol loa (hə lō′, hol′ō), *interj., n., v.i.* hello.

hol low (hol′ō), *adj.* 1 having nothing, or only air, inside; with a hole inside; not solid; empty: *A tube or pipe is hollow.* 2 bowl-shaped or cup-shaped: *a hollow dish for vegetables.* 3 as if coming from something hollow; deep and dull: *a hollow voice, a hollow groan.* 4 deep and sunken: *A starving person has hollow eyes and cheeks.* 5 not real or sincere; false: *hollow promises, hollow joys.* 6 hungry.

—n. 1 a hollow place; hole: *a hollow in the road.* 2 a low place between hills; valley: *Sleepy Hollow.*

—v.t. 1 make by hollowing; bend or dig out to a hollow shape. 2 make hollow. **3 hollow out,** form by hollowing. *—v.i.* become hollow.

—adv. INFORMAL. 1 thoroughly. **2 beat all hollow,** beat completely.

[Old English *holh*] **—hol′low ly,** *adv.* **—hol′low ness,** *n.*

hol low ware (hol′ō wer′, hol′ō war′), *n.* bowls, cups, dishes, etc., usually of silver, as contrasted with flatware.

hol ly (hol′ē), *n., pl.* **-lies.** 1 any of a genus of evergreen trees or shrubs with shiny, sharp-pointed leaves and bright-red berries; ilex. 2 the leaves and berries of any of these plants. Some species are often used as Christmas decorations. [Old English *holegn*]

hol ly hock (hol′ē hok), *n.* 1 a tall plant of the mallow family, with large, showy flowers of various colors that grow along tall, stiff, leafy stems; rose mallow. 2 its flower. [Middle English *holihoc* < *holi* holy + *hoc* mallow]

Hol ly wood (hol′ē wu̇d), *n.* 1 district of Los Angeles where many motion pictures are made. 2 the American motion-picture industry. 3 city in SE Florida. 107,000.

holm (hōm), *n.* 1 an evergreen oak of southern Europe with leaves like those of the holly; holm oak; ilex. 2 its hard wood. [Old English *holegn* holly]

Holmes (hōmz), *n.* 1 **Oliver Wendell,** 1809-1894, American author, humorist, and physician. 2 his son, **Oliver Wendell,** 1841-1935, American lawyer, an associate justice of the United States Supreme Court from 1902 to 1932. 3 **Sherlock.** See **Sherlock Holmes.**

hol mi um (hōl′mē əm), *n.* a rare-earth metallic element which occurs in combination with certain minerals. Its compounds are highly magnetic. *Symbol:* Ho; *atomic number* 67. See pages 326 and 327 for table. [< New Latin < *(Stock)holm,* near where it was found]

holm oak, holm.

hol o caust (hol′ə kôst), *n.* 1 complete destruction by fire, especially of animals or human beings. 2 great or wholesale destruction. 3 a sacrificial offering all of which is burned. [< Greek *holokaustos* < *holos* whole + *kaustos* burned]

Hol o cene (hol′ə sēn′), *adj., n.* Recent. [< Greek *holos* whole + *kainos* recent]

hol o gram (hol′ə gram), *n.* a photographic negative made by exposing a film or plate to two sources of coherent light, one a laser beam, the other light reflected from an object lit by a laser beam. When light is passed through this negative, the object reappears in three-dimensional detail. [< Greek *holos* whole]

hol o graph (hol′ə graf), *adj.* wholly written in the handwriting of the person in whose name it appears: *a holograph will.* —*n.* a holograph manuscript, letter, document, etc. [< Greek *holographos* < *holos* whole + *graphe* a writing]

hol o graph ic (hol′ə graf′ik), *adj.* (of a will) written, dated, and signed entirely in the handwriting of the person in whose name it appears.

ho log ra phy (hō log′rə fē), *n.* photography using laser beams to produce holograms.

hol o thu ri an (hol′ə thu̇r′ē ən, hō′lə-thu̇r′ē ən), *n.* any of a class of echinoderms, having an elongated, leathery body covered with very small calcareous plates; sea cucumber. [< Greek *holothourion,* kind of sea polyp]

Hol stein (hōl′stīn, hōl′stēn′), *n.* one of a breed of large, black-and-white dairy cattle, originally of Holland and Friesland. [< *Holstein,* region in North Germany]

Hol stein-Frie sian (hōl′stīn frē′zhən, hōl′stēn′frē′zhən), *n.* Holstein.

hol ster (hōl′stər), *n.* a leather case for a pistol, attached to a person's belt or for a rifle, attached to a horseman's saddle. [< Dutch]

ho ly (hō′lē), *adj.,* **-li er, -li est,** *n., pl.* **-lies.** —*adj.* 1 specially belonging to or devoted to God. 2 set apart for God's service; coming from God. 3 set apart for religious use or observance; sacred. See synonym study below. 4 declared sacred by religious use and authority. 5 like a saint; spiritually perfect; very good; pure in heart; devout; pious. 6 worthy of reverence. 7 INFORMAL. awesome; terrible: *Those children are holy terrors.* —*n.* a holy place. [Old English *hālig*]
Syn. *adj.* 3 **Holy, sacred** mean set apart for worship or reverence. **Holy** implies an inherent quality that makes someone or something worthy of worship: *God is holy. Jerusalem and Mecca are Holy Cities.* **Sacred** implies a quality given by dedicating or consecrating something to religious uses, making it worthy of reverence: *Churches are sacred. The Bible, Talmud, and Koran are sacred writings.*

Holy Alliance, agreement made by the rulers of Russia, Austria, and Prussia in 1815 to act and cooperate according to Christian principles.

Holy City, any city considered sacred by the adherents of a religion. Jerusalem, Rome, and Mecca are Holy Cities.

Holy Communion, 1 sacrament of sharing in or receiving the consecrated bread and wine commemorating the passion and death of Christ; Communion; Eucharist. 2 celebration in which this sacrament is received.

holy day, a religious festival, especially one not occurring on Sunday. Ash Wednesday and Good Friday are holy days.

holy day of obligation, (in the Roman Catholic Church) a day on which everyone is required to abstain from certain kinds of work and to attend religious services.

Holy Father, a title of the Pope.

Holy Ghost, spirit of God; third person of the Trinity; Holy Spirit.

Holy Grail, Grail.

Holy Land, Palestine.

holy of holies, 1 the holiest place. 2 the inner shrine of the Jewish Tabernacle and Temple.

holy orders, 1 the rite or sacrament of ordination. 2 the rank or position of an ordained Christian minister or priest. 3 the three higher ranks or positions in the Roman Catholic and Anglican churches. Bishops, priests, and deacons are members of holy orders.

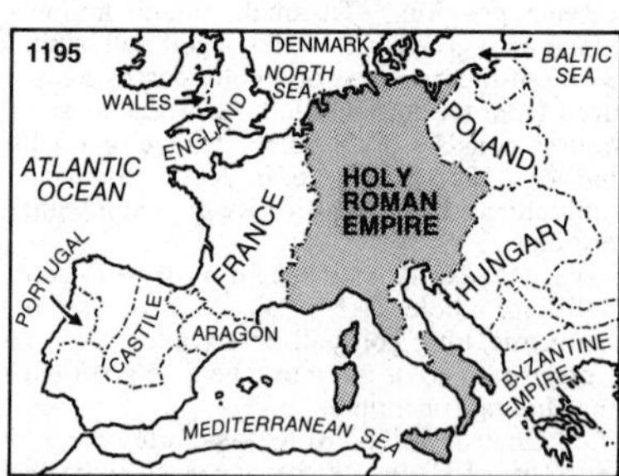

Holy Roman Empire, a loosely organized empire in western and central Europe regarded both as the continuation of the Roman Empire and as the temporal form of a universal dominion whose spiritual head was the Pope. It began with the coronation of Otto the Great (A.D. 962) or, according to some, with the coronation of Charlemagne (A.D. 800) and ended when Francis II renounced the imperial crown (1806).

Holy Saturday, Saturday before Easter.

Holy See, 1 office or jurisdiction of the Pope. 2 the Pope's court.

Holy Sepulcher, tomb at Jerusalem where Christ's body is believed to have lain between His burial and the Resurrection.

Holy Spirit, Holy Ghost.

ho ly stone (hō′lē stōn′), *n., v.,* **-stoned, -ston ing.** —*n.* piece of soft sandstone used for scrubbing the decks of ships. —*v.t., v.i.* scrub with a holystone.

Holy Synod, the church council that governs an Orthodox church.

Holy Thursday, the Thursday before Easter; Maundy Thursday.

holy water, water blessed by a priest for religious uses.

Holy Week, the week before Easter.

Holy Writ, the Bible.

hom age (hom′ij, om′ij), *n.* 1 dutiful respect; reverence: *Everyone paid homage to the great leader.* See **honor** for synonym study. 2 (in the Middle Ages) a formal acknowledgment by a vassal that he owed loyalty and service to his lord. 3 thing done or given to show such acknowledgment. [< Old French < Medieval Latin *hominaticum* < Latin *homo, hominem* man]

hom bre (ôm′brā), *n.* SLANG. man; fellow. [< Spanish]

hom burg (hom′bėrg′), *n.* a man's soft felt hat with a slightly rolled brim, and the crown creased lengthwise. [< *(Bad) Homburg,* German resort where it was first worn]

home (hōm), *n., adj., adv., v.,* **homed, hom ing.** —*n.* 1 place where a person or family lives; one's own house or dwelling place: *a beautiful home.* 2 a family or other group living together: *a happy home.* 3 place where a person was born or brought up; one's own town or country. 4 place where a thing is native or very common; habitat: *Alaska is the home of fur seals.* 5 place where a person can rest and be safe. 6 place where people who are homeless, poor, old, sick, blind, etc., may live; benevolent or charitable institution. 7 the goal which one tries to reach in various games. 8 home plate. 9 **at home, a** in one's own home or country. **b** at ease; comfortable. **c** ready to receive visitors.
—*adj.* 1 having to do with one's own home or country. 2 reaching its goal; effective: *a home thrust in argument.* 3 of or belonging to headquarters; principal: *the home office of a company.*
—*adv.* 1 at, to, or toward one's own home or country: *Go home.* 2 to the place where it belongs; to the thing aimed at: *strike home.* 3 to the heart or center; deep in: *drive a nail home.* 4 **bring home,** make clear, emphatic, or realistic.
—*v.i.* 1 go home. 2 (of birds) return home. 3 have a home; dwell. —*v.t.* 1 bring, carry, or send home. 2 provide with a home. 3 **home in on,** (of a guided missile) locate and move in a straight line toward (the target).
[Old English *hām*] —**home′less,** *adj.*
➤ **home, house.** In general usage *home* refers to any place that is the center of one's family affections; *house* refers only to a building. In real-estate advertising and the like, *home* is frequently used in place of *house* because of its favorable connotations.

home base, home plate.

home bod y (hōm′bod′ē), *n., pl.* **-bod ies.** person who prefers the pleasures of his home and family to outside attractions.

home bred (hōm′bred′), *adj.* bred or reared at home; native; domestic.

home-brew (hōm′brü′), *n.* beer or other alcoholic liquor made at home.

home com ing (hōm′kum′ing), *n.* 1 a com-

hat, āge, fär; let, ēqual, tėrm;
it, īce; hot, ōpen, ôrder;
oil, out; cup, pu̇t, rüle;
ch, child; ng, long; sh, she;
th, thin; ᴛʜ, then; zh, measure;
ə represents *a* in about, *e* in taken, *i* in pencil, *o* in lemon, *u* in circus.
< = from, derived from, taken from.

ing or returning home. 2 a returning to one's school, college, etc.

home economics, science and art that deals with the management of a household; domestic science. Home economics includes housekeeping, budgeting of finances, preparation of food, child care, etc.

home front, civilian activity in support of the armed forces.

home-grown (hōm′grōn′), *adj.* grown or made at home; domestic: *home-grown vegetables.*

home land (hōm′land′), *n.* country that is one's home; one's native land.

home like (hōm′līk′), *adj.* familiar, comfortable, or friendly; suggesting or resembling home.

home ly (hōm′lē), *adj.,* **-li er, -li est.** 1 not good-looking; having ordinary appearance or features; plain. See **ugly** for synonym study. 2 suited to home life; simple; everyday: *homely pleasures, homely food.* 3 of plain manners; unpretentious: *a simple, homely man.* **—home′li ness,** *n.*

home made (hōm′mād′), *adj.* made at home: *homemade bread.*

home mak er (hōm′mā′kər), *n.* woman who manages a home and its affairs; housewife.

home mak ing (hōm′mā′king), *n.* work of a homemaker.

ho me o path (hō′mē ə path, hom′ē ə path), *n.* person who practices or advocates homeopathy.

ho me o path ic (hō′mē ə path′ik, hom′ē-ə path′ik), *adj.* of or like homeopathy; practicing or advocating homeopathy.

ho me op a thy (hō′mē op′ə thē, hom′ē-op′ə thē), *n.* method of treating disease by drugs, given in very small doses, which would in large doses produce in a healthy person symptoms similar to those of the disease. [< Greek *homoios* similar + English *-pathy*]

ho me o sta sis (hō′mē ə stā′sis, hom′ē ə-stā′sis), *n.* (in physiology) the tendency of an organism to maintain internal equilibrium of temperature, fluid content, etc., by the regulation of its bodily processes. [< Greek *homoios* similar + *stasis* position]

ho me o stat ic (hō′mē ə stat′ik, hom′ē ə-stat′ik), *adj.* of or having to do with homeostasis.

home own er (hōm′ō′nər), *n.* person who owns his own home.

home plate, the marker or the flat, hard rubber slab beside which a player stands to bat the ball in baseball, and to which he must return, after getting on base, in order to score; home base.

hom er (hō′mər), *n.* 1 INFORMAL. home run. 2 homing pigeon. *—v.i.* INFORMAL. hit a home run.

Ho mer (hō′mər), *n.* 1 the great epic poet of ancient Greece. According to legend, Homer lived about the 800's B.C. and was the author of the *Iliad* and the *Odyssey.* 2 **Winslow,** 1836-1910, American painter.

home range, a definite area over which an animal roams.

Ho mer ic (hō mer′ik), *adj.* 1 written by or ascribed to Homer: *Homeric poems.* 2 of or having to do with Homer. 3 in the style of Homer. 4 of or having to do with the age in Greek life from about 1200 to about 800 B.C. **—Ho mer′i cal ly,** *adv.*

Homeric laughter, loud, hearty laughter, such as Homer describes.

home room (hōm′rüm′, hōm′ru̇m′), *n.* U.S. 1 classroom where members of a class meet to answer roll call, hear announcements, etc. 2 period during which this class meets.

home rule, management of the affairs of a country, district, or city by its own people; local self-government.

home run, a hit in baseball which allows the batter to round the bases without a stop and reach home plate to score a run.

home sick (hōm′sik′), *adj.* overcome by sadness because of being far away from home; ill with longing for home. **—home′-sick′ness,** *n.*

home spun (hōm′spun′), *adj.* 1 spun or made at home. 2 made of homespun cloth. 3 not polished; plain; simple: *homespun manners.* *—n.* 1 cloth made of yarn spun at home. 2 a strong, loosely woven cloth similar to it.

home stead (hōm′sted′), *n.* 1 house with its buildings and grounds; farm with its buildings. 2 U.S. parcel of 160 acres of public land granted to a settler under certain conditions by the United States government. 3 the place of one's dwelling or home. *—v.t.* take up and occupy as a homestead.

home stead er (hōm′sted′ər), *n.* 1 person who has a homestead. 2 settler granted a homestead by the United States government.

home stretch (hōm′strech′), *n.* 1 the straight part of a race track between the last turn and the finish line. 2 the last part of anything.

home ward (hōm′wərd), *adv., adj.* toward home.

home wards (hōm′wərdz), *adv.* homeward.

home work (hōm′wėrk′), *n.* 1 work done at home. 2 lesson to be studied or prepared outside the classroom.

home y (hō′mē), *adj.,* **hom i er, hom i est.** homelike. **—hom′ey ness,** *n.*

hom i cid al (hom′ə sī′dl, hō′mə sī′dl), *adj.* 1 having to do with homicide. 2 murderous. **—hom′i cid′al ly,** *adv.*

hom i cide (hom′ə sīd, hō′mə sīd), *n.* 1 a killing of one human being by another. Intentional homicide is murder. 2 person who kills another human being. [< Old French, ultimately < Latin *homo* man + *-cidium* act of killing or *-cida* killer]

hom i let ic (hom′ə let′ik), *adj.* 1 having to do with sermons or homiletics. 2 like or characteristic of a homily. **—hom′i let′i-cal ly,** *adv.*

hom i let ics (hom′ə let′iks), *n.* art of composing and preaching sermons.

hom i ly (hom′ə lē), *n., pl.* **-lies.** 1 sermon, usually on some part of the Bible. 2 serious moral talk or writing that warns, urges, or advises. [< Greek *homilia* < *homilos* a throng, assembly]

homing pigeon, pigeon trained to fly home from great distances carrying written messages; carrier pigeon.

hom i nid (hom′ə nid), *adj.* resembling or having to do with any of a family of primates that includes man. Man is the only hominid still extant. *—n.* a hominid animal.

hom i noid (hom′ə noid), *adj., n.* humanoid.

hom i ny (hom′ə nē), *n.* whole or coarsely ground hulled corn, usually eaten boiled. [short for *rockahominy* < Algonquian *rokehamen* parched corn]

ho mo (hō′mō), *n., pl.* **ho mi nes** (hom′ə-nēz′). LATIN. 1 man. 2 ***Homo,*** (in zoology) the genus of primate mammals comprising man, including one extant species, *Homo sapiens,* and various extinct species known from fossil remains.

homo-, *combining form.* the same; equal: *Homogenous = of the same origin.* [< Greek < *homos* same]

ho mog e nate (hə moj′ə nāt), *n.* a homogenized substance, especially tissue that has been homogenized for study or analysis.

ho mo ge ne i ty (hō′mə jə nē′ə tē, hom′ə-jə nē′ə tē), *n.* quality or condition of being homogeneous.

ho mo ge ne ous (hō′mə jē′nē əs, hō′mə-jē′nyəs; hom′ə jē′nē əs, hom′ə jē′nyəs), *adj.* 1 of the same kind, nature, or character; similar. 2 made up of similar elements or parts; of uniform nature or character throughout: *The population of the island was homogeneous because there were no foreigners there.* 3 (in mathematics) of the same degree or dimensions. [< Medieval Latin *homogeneus* < Greek *homogenēs* < *homos* same + *genos* kind] **—ho′mo ge′ne ous ly,** *adv.* **—ho′mo ge′ne ous ness,** *n.*

ho mog e nize (hə moj′ə nīz), *v.t.,* **-nized, -niz ing.** make homogeneous. In **homogenized milk** the fat is distributed evenly throughout the milk and does not rise to the top in the form of cream. **—ho mog′e ni-za′tion,** *n.* **—ho mog′e niz′er,** *n.*

ho mog e nous (hō moj′ə nəs), *adj.* (in biology) corresponding in structure because of a common origin: *homogenous organs.*

hom o graft (hom′ə graft, hō′mə graft), *n.* tissue from one individual grafted on an individual of the same species.

hom o graph (hom′ə graf, hō′mə graf), *n.* word having the same spelling as another word, but a different origin and meaning. *Bass* (bas) meaning "a kind of fish," and *bass* (bās) meaning "a male singing voice," are homographs. [< Greek *homographos* < *homos* same + *graphē* a writing]

hom o graph ic (hom′ə graf′ik), *adj.* having to do with homographs.

ho mol o gize (hō mol′ə jīz), *v.,* **-gized, -giz ing.** *—v.t.* make homologous; show the correspondence of. *—v.i.* be homologous; correspond.

ho mol o gous (hō mol′ə gəs), *adj.* 1 corresponding in position, proportion, value, structure, etc. 2 (in biology) corresponding in type of structure and in origin. The wing of a bird and the foreleg of a horse are homologous. 3 (in chemistry) belonging to a series where successive members differ regularly in formula, especially a series of organic compounds differing by multiples of $-CH_2$, as the alcohols. [< Greek *homologos* agreeing < *homos* same + *logos* reasoning, relation]

hom o logue (hom′ə lôg, hom′ə log), *n.* a homologous thing, organ, or part.

ho mol o gy (hō mol′ə jē), *n., pl.* **-gies.** 1 correspondence in position, proportion, value, structure, etc. 2 (in biology) correspondence in type of structure and in origin. 3 (in chemistry) the relation of the compounds forming a homologous series.

hom o nym (hom′ə nim, hō′mə nim), *n.* 1 word having the same pronunciation and spelling as another word, but a different origin and meaning. *Mail,* meaning "letters," and *mail,* meaning "armor" are homonyms. 2 homograph. 3 homophone. [< Greek *homōnymos* < *homos* same + *onyma* name]

ho mo nym ic (hō′mə nim′ik, hom′ə-nim′ik), *adj.* of or having to do with homonyms.

hom o phone (hom′ə fōn, hō′mə fōn), *n.* 1 word having the same pronunciation as another word, but a different origin and meaning. *Ate* and *eight* are homophones. 2 letter or symbol representing the same sound as another. The letters *c* and *k* are homophones in the word *cork.* [< Greek *homophōnos* < *homos* same + *phōnē* sound]

hom o phon ic (hom′ə fon′ik, hō′mə-fon′ik), *adj.* 1 having the same sound. 2 in music: **a** in unison. **b** having one part or melody predominating.

ho moph o nous (hō mof′ə nəs), *adj.* homophonic.

ho moph o ny (hō mof′ə nē, hom′ə fō′nē), *n.* 1 sameness of sound. 2 homophonic music.

ho mop ter an (hō mop′tər ən), *n.* any of an order of insects having mouthparts adapted for piercing and sucking and wings of the same thickness and texture throughout. Aphids and cicadas belong to this order. *—adj.* of or belonging to this order. [< *homo-* + Greek *pteron* wing]

ho mop ter ous (hō mop′tər əs), *adj.* of or belonging to the homopterans.

Ho mo sa pi ens (hō′mō sā′pē enz; hō′-mō sap′ē enz), the species including all existing races of mankind; human beings; man. [< New Latin, literally, intelligent man]

ho mo sex u al (hō′mə sek′shü əl), *adj.* having to do with or manifesting sexual feelings for a person of the same sex. *—n.* a homosexual person.

ho mo sex u al i ty (hō′mə sek′shü al′ə-tē), *n.* 1 sexual feelings for a person of the same sex. 2 sexual activity with a person of the same sex.

ho mo zy gote (hō′mə zī′gōt, hō′mə zig′ōt; hom′ə zī′gōt, hom′ə zig′ōt), *n.* (in genetics) an animal or plant whose chromosomes contain an identical pair of genes and which, therefore, always breed true to type.

ho mo zy gous (hō′mə zī′gəs, hom′ə-zī′gəs), *adj.* of or having to do with a homozygote. **—ho′mo zy′gous ly,** *adv.*

ho mun cu lus (hō mung′kyə ləs), *n., pl.* **-li** (-lī). a little man; dwarf. [< Latin, diminutive of *homo* man]

Hon., 1 Honorable. 2 Honorary.

Ho nan (hō′nan′, hō′nän′), *n.* province in E China.

Hon do (hon′dō), *n.* Honshu.

Hon dur as (hon dùr′əs, hon dyùr′əs), *n.* country in N Central America. 2,582,000 pop.; 43,300 sq. mi. *Capital:* Tegucigalpa. **—Hon dur′an,** *adj., n.*

hone (hōn), *n., v.,* **honed, hon ing.** *—n.* a fine-grained whetstone on which to sharpen cutting tools, especially razors. *—v.t.* sharpen on a hone. [Old English *hān* stone] **—hon′er,** *n.*

Hon eg ger (hon′ə gər; *French* ō ne ger′), *n.* **Arthur,** 1892-1955, French composer.

hon est (on′ist), *adj.* 1 not lying, cheating, or stealing; fair and upright; truthful: *an honest man.* 2 without lying, cheating, or stealing: *honest profits.* 3 not hiding one's real nature; frank; open: *She has an honest face.* 4 not mixed with something of less value; genuine; pure: *honest goods.* 5 bringing honor; creditable. 6 respectable. 7 ARCHAIC. chaste; virtuous. [< Old French *honeste* < Latin *honestus* < *honos* honor]

hon est ly (on′ist lē), *adv.* 1 in an honest way; with honesty. 2 indeed; really.

hon es ty (on′ə stē), *n.* 1 honest behavior; honest nature; honest quality. See synonym study below. 2 freedom from deceit or fraud; straightforwardness.

Syn. 1 **Honesty, integrity** mean the quality of being honorable and upright in character and actions. **Honesty** emphasizes fairness and uprightness in relations with others, and refusal to steal, lie, cheat, or misrepresent: *She shows honesty in all her business affairs.* **Integrity** applies more directly to character than to actions, and means soundness of character and possession of very high standards of right and wrong: *A man of integrity can be trusted.*

hon ey (hun′ē), *n., pl.* **hon eys,** *adj., v.,* **hon eyed** or **hon ied, hon ey ing.** *—n.* 1 a thick, sweet, yellow or golden liquid made for food by bees from the nectar they collect from flowers. 2 the nectar of flowers. 3 something sweet, delicious, or delightful; sweetness: *the honey of flattery.* 4 darling; dear. *—adj.* 1 of or like honey; sweet. 2 lovable; dear. *—v.t.* 1 sweeten with or as if with honey. 2 talk sweetly to; flatter. *—v.i.* talk sweetly. [Old English *hunig*] **—hon′ey-like′,** *adj.*

hon ey bee (hun′ē bē′), *n.* any of a genus of bees that produce honey, especially the domestic bee.

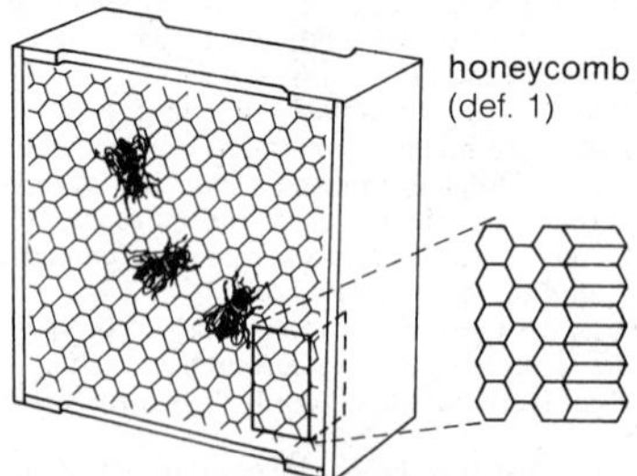
honeycomb (def. 1)

hon ey comb (hun′ē kōm′), *n.* 1 structure of wax containing rows of six-sided cells made by honeybees to store honey, pollen, and their eggs. 2 anything resembling this. *—adj.* like, or arranged in the form of, a honeycomb: *a honeycomb weave of cloth.* *—v.t.* 1 make or pierce with many holes like a honeycomb: *The old castle was honeycombed with passageways.* 2 weaken or harm by spreading through: *That city is honeycombed with crime.*

hon ey dew (hun′ē dü′, hun′ē dyü′), *n.* 1 a sweet substance that oozes from the leaves of certain plants in hot weather. 2 a sweet substance on leaves, secreted by tiny insects such as aphids or leaf hoppers, or a fungus. 3 honeydew melon.

honeydew melon, variety of muskmelon with sweet, green flesh and a smooth, pale-greenish skin.

hon eyed (hun′ēd), *adj.* 1 sweetened with honey. 2 laden with honey. 3 sweet as honey. *—v.* a pt. and a pp. of **honey.** Also, **honied.**

hon ey moon (hun′ē mün′), *n.* 1 holiday spent together by a newly married couple. 2 the first month of marriage. 3 a period of good feeling or good relations. *—v.i.* spend or have a honeymoon. **—hon′ey moon′-er,** *n.*

hon ey suck le (hun′ē suk′əl), *n.* 1 any of a genus of upright or climbing shrubs or vines, natives of the temperate parts of both hemispheres, having opposite leaves and white, yellow, or red, often fragrant, tubular flowers, which are succeeded by sweetish red or purple berries. The woodbine is a kind of honeysuckle. 2 any of various similar plants.

Hong kong (hong′kong′, hông′kông′), *n.* Hong Kong.

Hong Kong (hong′ kong′, hông′ kông′), 1 British crown colony on the SE coast of China. *Capital:* Victoria. 4,090,000 pop.; 391 sq. mi. 2 island in this colony. 32 sq. mi.

hon ied (hun′ēd), *v.* a pt. and a pp. of **honey.** *—adj.* honeyed.

honk (hongk, hôngk), *n.* 1 the cry of a wild goose. 2 any similar sound: *the honk of an automobile horn.* *—v.i., v.t.* make or cause to make a honking sound. [imitative] **—honk′er,** *n.*

honk y-tonk (hong′kē tongk′, hông′kē-tôngk′), *n.* U.S. SLANG. a cheap, low-class nightclub or dance hall.

Hon o lu lu (hon′ə lü′lü), *n.* seaport and capital of Hawaii, on S Oahu. 325,000.

hon or (on′ər), *n.* 1 credit for acting well; glory, fame, or reputation; good name: *It was greatly to her honor that she was awarded a grant to study abroad.* 2 source of credit; person or thing that reflects honor; cause of honor. 3 a nice sense of what is right or proper; nobility of mind; integrity: *a man of honor.* 4 great respect; high regard: *held in honor.* See synonym study below. 5 thing given or done to show honor; decoration. 6 **Honor,** title of respect used in speaking to or of a judge, mayor, etc. 7 act that shows respect or high regard: *The queen was received with honor.* 8 high rank or position; dignity; distinction: *Knighthood is an honor.* 9 a special privilege or favor: *have the honor of being presented at court.* 10 chastity; virtue. 11 (in golf) the privilege of teeing off first, awarded to the player or side winning the previous hole. 12 **honors,** *pl.* **a** special favors or courtesies. **b** special mention, grade, or credit given to a student by a school, college, or university for unusually excellent work. **c** course of study or series of examinations given in many universities of a higher or more specialized character than is required for an ordinary degree. **d** (in bridge) the ace, king, queen, jack, and ten of trumps, or the four aces in no-trump. 13 **do honor to, a** show honor to; treat with great respect. **b** cause honor to; bring honor to. 14 **do the honors,** act as host or hostess. 15 **on one's honor,** pledged to speak the truth and to do what is right.

—v.t. 1 respect highly; think highly of. 2 show respect to; treat with honor. 3 give an honor to; favor: *be honored by a royal visit.* 4 accept and pay (a check, note, etc.) when due. Also, BRITISH **honour.**

[< Old French < Latin *honos, honor*]

Syn. *n.* 4 **Honor, deference, homage** mean respect shown to someone. **Honor** means respect felt or shown in acknowledgment or appreciation of a person's high character, position, or achievement: *We pay*

hat, āge, fär; let, ēqual, tėrm;
it, īce; hot, ōpen, ôrder;
oil, out; cup, pu̇t, rüle;
ch, child; ng, long; sh, she;
th, thin; ᴛʜ, then; zh, measure;

ə represents *a* in about, *e* in taken, *i* in pencil, *o* in lemon, *u* in circus.

< = from, derived from, taken from.

honor to heroes. **Deference** means respect shown a person by putting his wishes or opinions before one's own: *In deference to his parents' wishes, he stopped smoking.* **Homage** implies honor paid with reverence or deference: *He bowed in homage to the Unknown Soldier.*

hon or a ble (on′ər ə bəl), *adj.* 1 having or showing a sense of what is right and proper; honest; upright: *It is not honorable to cheat.* 2 causing honor; bringing honor to the one that has it. 3 accompanied by honor or honors: *an honorable discharge.* 4 worthy of honor; noble: *perform honorable deeds.* 5 showing honor or respect: *honorable burial.* 6 having a title, rank, or position of honor. 7 **Honorable,** title of respect or distinction before the names of certain officials and (in England) the children of certain nobles: *the Honorable Nelson Rockefeller.* **—hon′or a ble ness,** *n.* **—hon′or a bly,** *adv.*

hon o rar i um (on′ə rer′ē əm, on′ə rar′ē əm), *n., pl.* **-rar i ums, -rar i a** (-rer′ē ə, -rar′ē ə). fee for professional services on which no fixed price is set; honorary payment. [< Latin]

hon o rar y (on′ə rer′ē), *adj.* 1 given or done as an honor: *an honorary degree.* 2 as an honor only; without pay or regular duties: *an honorary secretary.* **—hon′o rar′i ly,** *adv.*

honor guard, group of soldiers, etc., assigned to welcome officially someone important or to accompany the coffin at a funeral; guard of honor.

hon o rif ic (on′ə rif′ik), *adj.* 1 doing or giving honor. 2 showing respect or deference. *—n.* an honorific phrase or word.

ho no ris cau sa (ho nôr′is kô′zə; ho nōr′is kô′zə), LATIN. as an honor; honorary: *Doctor of Laws honoris causa.*

honor roll, 1 list of students who have achieved the highest grades during the school term or year. 2 a commemorative list of local citizens who served in the armed forces.

honors of war, special favors or courtesies shown to a brave but defeated enemy that allow them to retain their military dignity.

honor system, system of trusting people in schools and other institutions to obey the rules and do their work without being watched or forced.

hon our (on′ər), *n., v.t.* BRITISH. honor.

Hon shu (hon′shü), *n.* the largest and most important island of Japan. 76,758,000 pop.; 88,900 sq. mi. Also, **Hondo.**

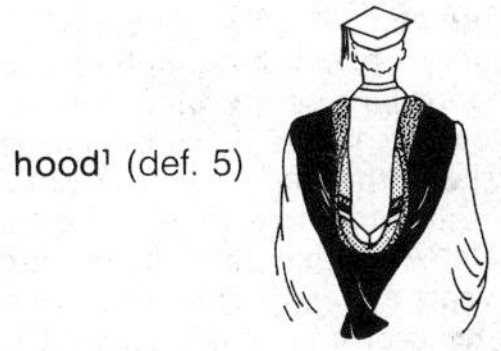

hood¹ (def. 5)

hood¹ (hu̇d), *n.* 1 a soft covering for the head and neck, either separate or as part of a coat. 2 any of various things used for covering, capping, or protection, or resembling a hood in shape or use. 3 something that serves as a covering for machinery. 4 the movable metal covering over the engine of an automobile. 5 fold of cloth, banded with distinguishing colors to show what degrees are held, that hangs down over the gown worn by graduates of universities and colleges. 6 crest or other part on a bird's or animal's head that suggests a hood in shape, color, etc. *—v.t.* cover with a hood; furnish with a hood. [Old English *hōd*] **—hood′less,** *adj.* **—hood′like′,** *adj.*

hood² (hu̇d, hüd), *n.* U.S. SLANG. hoodlum.

Hood (hu̇d), *n.* 1 **Mount,** mountain in N Oregon. 11,245 ft. 2 **Robin.** See **Robin Hood.** 3 **Thomas,** 1799-1845, English poet and humorist.

-hood, *suffix added to nouns to form other nouns.* 1 state or condition of being: *Boyhood = state of being a boy.* 2 character or nature of: *Sainthood = the character of a saint.* 3 group or body of: *Priesthood = the body or group of priests.* 4 a concrete instance of: *Falsehood = a concrete instance of falsity.* [Old English *-hād* < *hād* state]

hood ed (hu̇d′id), *adj.* 1 having a hood. 2 shaped like a hood.

hood lum (hüd′ləm), *n.* INFORMAL. 1 criminal or gangster. 2 a young rowdy; street ruffian. [origin uncertain]

hoo doo (hü′dü), *n., pl.* **-doos,** *v.* *—n.* 1 INFORMAL. person or thing that brings bad luck. 2 INFORMAL. bad luck. 3 voodoo. *—v.t.* INFORMAL. bring or cause bad luck to. [variant of *voodoo*]

hood wink (hu̇d′wingk), *v.t.* 1 mislead by a trick; deceive. 2 blindfold. **—hood′wink er,** *n.*

hoo ey (hü′ē), *n.* U.S. SLANG. nonsense.

hoof (hu̇f, hüf), *n., pl.* **hoofs** or **hooves,** *v.* *—n.* 1 a hard, horny covering on the feet of horses, cattle, sheep, pigs, and some other animals. 2 the whole foot of such animals. 3 SLANG. the human foot. 4 **on the hoof,** not killed and butchered; alive. *—v.i.* INFORMAL. walk or dance. [Old English *hōf*] **—hoof′less,** *adj.* **—hoof′like′,** *adj.*

hoof-and-mouth disease (hu̇f′ən mouth′, hüf′ən mouth′), foot-and-mouth disease.

hoof beat (hu̇f′bēt′, hüf′bēt′), *n.* sound made by an animal's hoof.

hoofed (hu̇ft, hüft), *adj.* having hoofs.

hoof er (hu̇f′ər, hü′fər), *n.* SLANG. a professional dancer, especially a tap-dancer.

hook (hu̇k), *n.* 1 piece of metal, wood, or other stiff material, curved or having a sharp angle, for catching hold of something or for hanging things on. 2 a curved piece of wire, usually with a barb at the end, for catching fish; fishhook. 3 anything curved or bent like a hook. 4 a large, curved knife for cutting down grass or grain. 5 a sharp bend. 6 a curved point of land. 7 act of hooking. 8 a curving throw in baseball. 9 a golf ball's path of flight curving to the left away from a right-handed player. 10 (in boxing) a short, swinging blow with the elbow bent and rigid. 11 line on the stem of certain musical notes; flag. 12 **by hook or by crook,** in any way at all; by fair means or foul. 13 **off the hook,** INFORMAL. free of responsibility; out of a predicament. 14 **on one's own hook,** INFORMAL. independently.
—v.t. 1 fasten with a hook or hooks. 2 catch or take hold of with a hook. 3 join or fit like a hook. 4 catch (fish) with a hook. 5 catch by a trick. 6 INFORMAL. steal. 7 give the form of a hook to. 8 throw or hit (a baseball) so that it curves. 9 hit (a golf ball) widely to the left. 10 (in boxing) hit (an opponent) with a short, swinging blow. 11 make (rugs, etc.) by pulling loops of yarn or strips of cloth through a piece of canvas, burlap, etc., with a hook. 12 **hook up, a** attach or fasten with a hook or hooks. **b** arrange and connect the parts of (a radio set, telephone, etc.). *—v.i.* 1 be fastened with a hook or hooks. 2 be curved or bent like a hook.
[Old English *hōc*] **—hook′like′,** *adj.*

hook ah or **hook a** (hu̇k′ə, hü′kə), *n.* a tobacco pipe with a long, flexible tube by which the smoke is drawn through water and cooled. Hookahs are used in the Orient. [< Arabic *huqqa* vase, pipe]

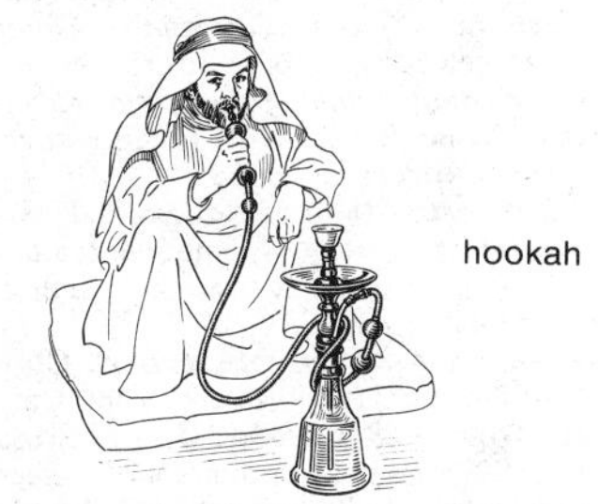

hookah

hook and eye, fastener for garments, etc., consisting of a hook and an eye or loop into which the hook fits.

hooked (hu̇kt), *adj.* 1 curved or bent like a hook. 2 having hooks. 3 made with a hook or by hooking: *a hooked rug.* 4 INFORMAL. slavishly dependent; addicted, especially to narcotics.

hook er (hu̇k′ər), *n.* 1 a small fishing boat. 2 an old-fashioned or clumsy ship. [< Dutch *hoeker* < *hoek* hook, fishhook]

hook up (hu̇k′up′), *n.* 1 arrangement and connection of the parts of a radio set, a telephone, radio-broadcasting facilities, etc. 2 INFORMAL. connection or combination: *a hookup of the Great Lakes with the Atlantic Ocean via the St. Lawrence River.*

hook worm (hu̇k′wėrm′), *n.* 1 any of several small nematodes that have strong cutting plates or teeth. Hookworms enter the body through the skin and fasten themselves on the walls of the small intestine. 2 Also, **hookworm disease,** disease caused by hookworms sucking blood from the small intestine, characterized by weakness, apparent laziness, and severe anemia.

hook y (hu̇k′ē), *n.* **play hooky,** INFORMAL. stay away from school without permission.

hoo li gan (hü′lə gən), *n.* INFORMAL. one of a gang of street ruffians; hoodlum. [< *Hooligan,* the name of a family in bad repute in London around 1900]

hoo li gan ism (hü′lə gə niz′əm), *n.* rough, noisy, or lawless behavior.

hoop (hu̇p, hüp), *n.* 1 ring or round, flat band: *a hoop for holding together the staves of a barrel.* 2 a large wooden, iron, or plastic ring used as a toy, especially for rolling along the ground. 3 a circular frame formerly used to hold out a woman's skirt. 4 the wicket used in croquet. 5 anything shaped like a hoop.

—*v.t.* bind or fasten together with a hoop or hoops. [Old English *hōp*] **—hoop′er,** *n.* **—hoop′like′,** *adj.*

hoop la (hü′plä, hůp′lä), *n.* INFORMAL. 1 excitement; hullabaloo. 2 sensational publicity; ballyhoo.

hoop skirt, a woman's skirt worn over a frame of flexible hoops to hold out or expand the skirt; crinoline.

hoo ray (hů rā′), *interj., n., v.i.* hurrah.

hoose gow (hüs′gou), *n.* U.S. SLANG. jail. [< Spanish *juzgado* court, tribunal (in Mexico, jail)]

Hoo sier (hü′zhər), *n.* U.S. native or inhabitant of Indiana.

hoot (hüt), *n.* 1 sound that an owl makes. 2 shout to show disapproval or scorn. 3 INFORMAL. the smallest thought; trifle. —*v.i.* 1 make the sound that an owl makes or one like it. 2 make a shout to show disapproval or scorn. —*v.t.* 1 show disapproval of or scorn for by hooting: *The audience hooted the speaker's plan.* 2 force or drive by hooting: *They hooted him off the platform.* 3 say or show by hooting. [Middle English *huten* to hoot] **—hoot′er,** *n.*

hoot e nan ny (hüt′n an′ē), *n., pl.* **-nies.** U.S. an informal party or jamboree featuring folk singing, especially one in which the audience participates.

Hoo ver (hü′vər), *n.* 1 **Herbert Clark,** 1874-1964, the 31st president of the United States, from 1929 to 1933. 2 **J(ohn) Edgar,** 1895-1972, American criminologist, director of the Federal Bureau of Investigation, 1924-1972.

Hoover Dam, dam on the Colorado River between Arizona and Nevada. Former name, **Boulder Dam.**

hooves (hůvz, hüvz), *n.* a pl. of **hoof.**

hop[1] (hop), *v.,* **hopped, hop ping,** *n.* —*v.i.* 1 spring, or move by springing, on one foot. 2 spring, or move by springing, with both or all feet at once: *Many birds hop.* 3 INFORMAL. fly in an airplane. 4 INFORMAL. dance. 5 **hop off,** rise from the ground in an airplane. —*v.t.* 1 jump over: *hop a ditch.* 2 INFORMAL. jump on (a train, car, etc.). —*n.* 1 a hopping; spring. 2 INFORMAL. flight in an airplane. 3 INFORMAL. **a** a dancing party, especially an informal one. **b** dance. 4 a short trip. [Old English *hoppian*]

hop[2] (hop), *n., v.,* **hopped, hop ping.** —*n.* 1 vine of the same family as the mulberry, having flower clusters that look like small pine cones. 2 **hops,** *pl.* the dried, ripe flower clusters of the hop vine, used to give a bitter flavor to beer and other malt drinks. —*v.t.* flavor with hops. —*v.i.* pick hops; gather hops. [< Middle Dutch *hoppe*]

hope (hōp), *n., v.,* **hoped, hop ing.** —*n.* 1 a feeling that what one desires will happen: *His promise gave me hope.* 2 thing hoped for. 3 person or thing that gives hope to others or that others have hope in: *She is the hope of the family.* 4 ground for expecting something desired; promise: *There is no hope for his recovery.* —*v.t.* 1 wish and expect: *I hope to do well in school this year.* 2 desire very much. 3 trust: *I hope I know what I am talking about.* 4 **hope against hope,** keep on hoping even though there is no good reason to have hope. —*v.i.* look with expectation: *We hope for brighter days.* [Old English *hopa*]

hope chest, chest in which a young unmarried woman collects articles of linen, tableware, etc., to be able to help furnish a home of her own after she marries.

hope ful (hōp′fəl), *adj.* 1 feeling or showing hope; expecting to receive what one desires: *a hopeful attitude.* 2 giving hope; likely to succeed. —*n.* 1 boy or girl thought likely to succeed: *a young hopeful.* 2 person who hopes to obtain or achieve something. **—hope′ful ness,** *n.*

hope ful ly (hōp′fə lē), *adv.* 1 in a hopeful manner. 2 it is hoped that: *Hopefully business will improve soon.*

Ho peh or **Ho pei** (hō′pā′), *n.* province in NE China.

hope less (hōp′lis), *adj.* 1 feeling or having no hope; without hope. See synonym study below. 2 giving no hope; causing no hope. 3 certain to fail or get worse: *a hopeless illness.* **—hope′less ly,** *adv.* **—hope′less ness,** *n.*

Syn. 1 **Hopeless, desperate, despairing** mean without hope. **Hopeless** suggests giving up so completely that one is willing to take passively whatever comes: *He was disappointed so often that he became hopeless.* **Desperate** suggests despair that leads to rash and daring risks to improve the situation: *People were so desperate they jumped from the burning building.* **Despairing** means completely hopeless because unable to think of anything else to do or anywhere else to look for help: *Despairing of saving his business, he declared bankruptcy.*

Ho pi (hō′pē), *n., pl.* **-pis** or **-pi** for 1. 1 member of a tribe of Pueblo Indians living in adobe-built villages in northern Arizona. 2 their language.

Hop kins (hop′kinz), *n.* 1 **Gerard Manley,** 1844-1889, English poet. 2 **Mark,** 1802-1887, American educator.

hop lite (hop′līt), *n.* a heavily armed foot soldier of ancient Greece. [< Greek *hoplitēs* < *hopla* arms]

hop per (hop′ər), *n.* 1 person or thing that hops. 2 any hopping insect or insect larva, such as a grasshopper or locust or a leafhopper. 3 container having a narrow opening at the bottom, used to receive and hold coal, grain, or other material before feeding it into a machine, storage bin, etc.; the receiver in various machines. 4 U.S. receptacle into which members of a lawmaking body drop bills proposed for enactment.

hop scotch (hop′skoch′), *n.* a children's game in which the players hop over the lines of a figure drawn on the ground and pick up an object thrown or kicked into one of the numbered squares of the figure.

ho ra (hôr′ə, hōr′ə), *n.* a lively Israeli folk dance performed by couples moving around to the left or right in a circle. [< Hebrew *hōrāh* < Romanian *horă*]

Ho race (hôr′is, hor′is), *n.* 65-8 B.C., Roman poet and satirist.

Ho rae (hôr′ē, hōr′ē), *n.pl.* (in Greek and Roman myths) the Hours, goddesses of the seasons and hours, and also of order and justice.

Ho ra tian (hə rā′shən), *adj.* of, like, or having to do with Horace or his poetry.

Ho ra tius (hə rā′shəs), *n.* (in Roman legends) a Roman hero who held back the Etruscan army until a bridge behind him was destroyed by the Romans, and then swam to safety.

horde (hôrd, hōrd), *n.* 1 a great company or number; multitude; swarm: *hordes of grasshoppers.* 2 a wandering tribe or troop: *Hordes of Mongols and Turks invaded Europe in the Middle Ages.* [< Polish *horda* < Turkic *orda* camp]

Ho reb (hôr′eb, hōr′eb), *n.* Mount Sinai.

hore hound (hôr′hound′, hōr′hound′), *n.* 1 plant of the mint family having woolly, whitish leaves and clusters of small, whitish flowers. 2 a bitter extract made from the leaves of this plant. 3 candy or cough medicine flavored with it. Also, **hoarhound.** [Old English *hārhūne* < *hār* hoar + *hūne,* name of a plant]

ho ri zon (hə rī′zn), *n.* 1 line where the earth and sky seem to meet. One cannot see beyond the horizon. 2 limit or range of one's thinking, experience, interest, or outlook. 3 (in geology) a stratum or series of strata differing in fossils, etc., from the deposits above or below. [< Greek *horizōn (kyklos)* bounding (circle) < *horos* boundary, limit]

ho ri zon tal (hôr′ə zon′tl, hor′ə zon′tl), *adj.* 1 parallel to the horizon; at right angles to a vertical line: *a horizontal surface.* 2 flat; level. 3 measured or contained in a plane of the horizon: *a horizontal distance.* 4 placed, acting, or working wholly or mainly in a horizontal direction. 5 of or having to do with the horizon; on, at, or near the horizon. 6 so organized as to include only one stage in production or one group of people or crafts: *Carpenters and plumbers belong to horizontal unions.* —*n.* a horizontal line, plane, direction, position, etc. **—ho′ri zon′tal ly,** *adv.*

hor mo nal (hôr mō′nl), *adj.* of, having to do with, or like a hormone.

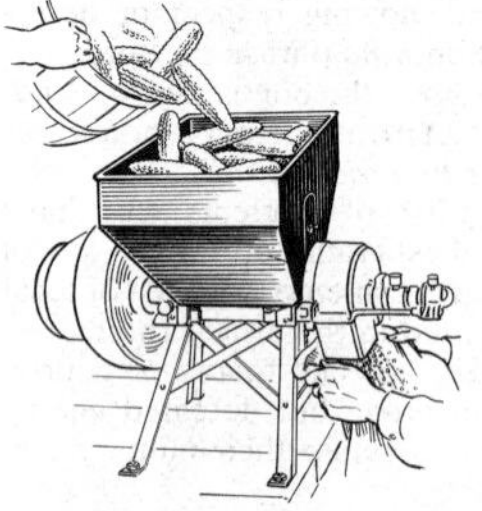

hopper (def. 3)

hor mone (hôr′mōn), *n.* 1 substance formed chiefly in the endocrine glands which enters the bloodstream and affects or controls the activity of some organ or tissue; internal secretion. Adrenaline and insulin are hormones. 2 a similar substance in the protoplasm of plants. Auxins and gibberellins are hormones. [< Greek *hormōn* setting in motion, ultimately < *hormē* impulse]

horn (hôrn), *n.* 1 a hard, hollow, permanent growth, usually curved and pointed and in pairs, on the heads of cattle, sheep, goats, and certain other animals. 2 one of a pair of solid, branching growths on the head of a deer, elk, etc., that fall off and grow back every year; antler. 3 anything that sticks up on the head of an animal: *a snail's horns, an insect's horns.* 4 the hard, durable, and partly transparent substance, principally keratin, of which true horns consist. A person's fingernails, the beaks of birds, the hoofs of horses, and tortoise shells are all made of horn. 5 thing made, or formerly made, of horn, such as a thimble or shoehorn. 6 container made by hollowing out a horn. It was used to drink out of or to carry gunpowder in. 7 a wind instrument, once made of horn but now made of brass or other metal. A French horn and a hunting horn are different

types of horns. 8 device sounded as a warning signal: *an automobile horn.* 9 anything that projects like a horn or is shaped like a horn: *a saddle horn, the horn of a bay.* 10 either pointed tip of a new or old moon, or of a crescent. 11 **draw in one's horns** or **pull in one's horns, a** restrain oneself. **b** back down; withdraw. 12 **horns of a dilemma,** two unpleasant choices, one of which must be taken.
—*adj.* made of horn.
—*v.t.* hit or wound with horns; gore. —*v.i.* **horn in,** U.S. SLANG. meddle or intrude.
[Old English] —**horn′less,** *adj.* —**horn′like′,** *adj.*

Horn (hôrn), *n.* **Cape.** cape which forms the S tip of South America. See **Antarctica** for map.

horn beam (hôrn′bēm′), *n.* any of a genus of trees of the same family as the birch, with very hard, heavy, white wood and hanging clusters of nuts.

horn bill (hôrn′bil′), *n.* any of a family of large birds having very large downturned bills with a horn or horny lump on them.

horn blende (hôrn′blend′), *n.* a group of common black, dark-green, or brown silicate minerals containing aluminum and varying proportions of several other elements. Hornblende is a variety of amphibole which is found in many igneous and metamorphic rocks. [< German *Hornblende*]

horn book (hôrn′bu̇k′), *n.* 1 page with the alphabet, figures, etc., on it, covered with a sheet of transparent horn and fastened in a frame with a handle, formerly used in teaching children to read, figure, spell, etc. 2 a primer.

horned (hôrnd), *adj.* having a horn, horns, or a hornlike growth.

horned owl, any of various owls with hornlike tufts of feathers on the head.

horned pout, hornpout.

horned toad, a small, harmless lizard with a broad, flat body, short tail, and many hornlike spines, common in the arid regions of western North America.

hor net (hôr′nit), *n.* any of various large social wasps, usually living in paperlike nests, that can give a very painful sting. [Old English *hyrnetu*]

horn of plenty, cornucopia.

horn pipe (hôrn′pīp′), *n.* 1 a lively dance done by one person, formerly popular among sailors. 2 music for it. 3 a wind instrument of former times, consisting of a wooden pipe with a bell-shaped end made of horn.

horn pout (hôrn′pout′), *n.* the common brown bullhead.

horn y (hôr′nē), *adj.,* **horn i er, horn i est.** 1 made of horn or a substance like it. 2 hard like a horn; calloused. 3 having a horn or horns; horned.

ho ro loge (hôr′ə lōj, hôr′ə loj; hor′ə lōj, hor′ə loj), *n.* any device which indicates the time, such as a clock, sundial, hourglass, etc. [< Greek *hōrologion* < *hōra* hour + *-logos* telling]

ho rol o ger (hô rol′ə jər, hō rol′ə jər), *n.* an expert in horology.

ho ro log ic (hôr′ə loj′ik, hor′ə loj′ik), *adj.* of or having to do with a horologe or horology.

ho ro log i cal (hôr′ə loj′ə kəl, hor′ə loj′ə-kəl), *adj.* horologic.

ho rol o gist (hô rol′ə jist, hō rol′ə jist), *n.* horologer.

ho rol o gy (hô rol′ə jē, hō rol′ə jē), *n.* 1 science of measuring time. 2 art of designing or making timepieces.

ho ro scope (hôr′ə skōp, hor′ə skōp), *n.* 1 the relative position of the planets at a particular time, especially at the hour of a person's birth, regarded as influencing his life. 2 diagram of the twelve signs of the zodiac, showing the arrangement of the heavens at a particular time. A horoscope is used in telling fortunes by the planets and the stars. 3 a fortune told by this means. 4 **cast a horoscope,** discover the influence that the stars and planets are supposed to have upon a person's life. [< Greek *hōroskopos* < *hōra* hour + *skopos* watcher]

hor ren dous (hô ren′dəs, ho ren′dəs), *adj.* causing horror; horrible. —**hor ren′dous ly,** *adv.*

hor ri ble (hôr′ə bəl, hor′ə bəl), *adj.* 1 causing horror; extremely repulsive to the senses or feelings; terrible; dreadful: *a horrible crime, a horrible disease.* 2 INFORMAL. extremely unpleasant; excessive: *a horrible noise.* —**hor′ri ble ness,** *n.* —**hor′ri bly,** *adv.*

hor rid (hôr′id, hor′id), *adj.* 1 causing great fear; terrible; frightful. 2 INFORMAL. very unpleasant; offensive; disagreeable. —**hor′rid ly,** *adv.* —**hor′rid ness,** *n.*

hor rif ic (hô rif′ik, ho rif′ik), *adj.* causing horror; horrifying.

hor ri fy (hôr′ə fī, hor′ə fī), *v.t.,* **-fied, -fy ing.** 1 cause to feel horror. 2 INFORMAL. shock very much.

hor ror (hôr′ər, hor′ər), *n.* 1 a shivering, shaking terror caused by something frightful or shocking; dread. 2 a very strong dislike or disgust; intense aversion; loathing. 3 quality of causing horror. 4 thing that causes horror. 5 INFORMAL. something very bad, unpleasant, or unattractive. 6 **the horrors,** INFORMAL. **a** fit of horror. **b** extreme depression. [< Latin < *horrere* to bristle]

Hor sa (hôr′sə), *n.* died A.D. 455, a chief of the Jutes and brother of Hengist.

hors de com bat (ôr də kôN bä′), FRENCH. out of the fight; disabled.

hors d'oeu vre (ôr′ dėrv′; *French* ôr dœ′vrə), *pl.* **hors d'oeu vres** (ôr′ dėrvz′). relish, light food, or dainty sandwich served as an appetizer before the regular courses of a meal. Olives, celery, anchovies, etc., are used as hors d'oeuvres. [< French, literally, apart from (the main) work]

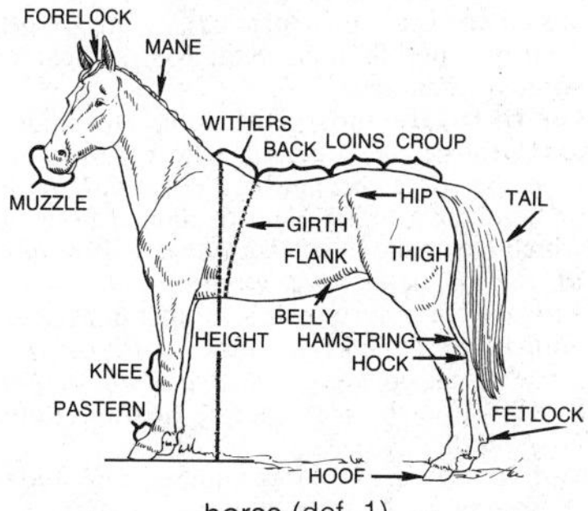

horse (def. 1)

horse (hôrs), *n., pl.* **hors es** or **horse,** *v.,* **horsed, hors ing,** *adj.* —*n.* 1 a large, four-legged, herbivorous mammal with solid hoofs and a mane and tail of long, coarse hair. Horses have been used from very early times for riding and for carrying and pulling loads. 2 a full-grown male horse; stallion or gelding. 3 piece of gymnasium apparatus to jump or vault over. 4 a supporting frame with legs. 5 cavalry. 6 SLANG. heroin. 7 **from the horse's mouth,** from the original source; from a well-informed source. 8 **horse of a different color** or **horse of another color,** something different.
—*v.t.* 1 provide with a horse or horses. 2 put on horseback. 3 set or carry on a person's back; carry on one's own back. —*v.i.* 1 go on horseback. 2 **horse around,** SLANG. fool around; get into mischief. —*adj.* 1 having to do with horses. 2 on horses. [Old English *hors*]

hat, āge, fär; let, ēqual, tėrm;
it, īce; hot, ōpen, ôrder;
oil, out; cup, pu̇t, rüle;
ch, child; ng, long; sh, she;
th, thin; ᴛʜ, then; zh, measure;

ə represents *a* in about, *e* in taken, *i* in pencil, *o* in lemon, *u* in circus.

< = from, derived from, taken from.

horse (def. 3)

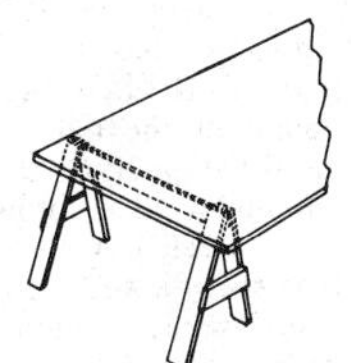
horse (def. 4)

horse-and-bug gy (hôrs′ən bug′ē), *adj.* out-of-date; old-fashioned: *horse-and-buggy approaches to modern problems.*

horse back (hôrs′bak′), *n.* the back of a horse. —*adv.* on the back of a horse.

horse car (hôrs′kär′), *n.* U.S. 1 streetcar or railroad car pulled by a horse or horses. 2 car used for transporting horses.

horse chestnut, 1 a large shade tree with spreading branches, large leaves, clusters of showy white flowers, and glossy brown nuts. 2 its nut.

horse flesh (hôrs′flesh′), *n.* 1 horses for riding, driving, and racing. 2 meat from horses.

horse fly (hôrs′flī′), *n., pl.* **-flies.** any of a family of large flies with two wings, the females of which bite animals, especially horses.

horse hair (hôrs′her′, hôrs′har′), *n.* 1 hair from the mane or tail of a horse. 2 a stiff fabric made of this hair. —*adj.* made of horsehair; stuffed with horsehair: *a horsehair cushion.*

horse hide (hôrs′hīd′), *n.* 1 hide of a horse. 2 leather made from this hide.

horse latitudes, either of two regions characterized by high pressure and winds which are usually calm or very light. They extend around the earth at about 30 degrees north and 30 degrees south of the equator.

horse laugh (hôrs′laf′), *n.* a loud, boisterous laugh.

horse less (hôrs′lis), *adj.* 1 without a horse. 2 not requiring a horse; self-propelled: *Automobiles used to be called horseless carriages.*

horse mackerel, any of several large fishes, especially the tuna[1].

horse man (hôrs′mən), *n., pl.* **-men.** 1 man

who rides on horseback. 2 man skilled in riding, managing, or breeding horses.

horse man ship (hôrs′mən ship), *n.* skill in riding or managing horses.

horse opera, SLANG. western.

horse pistol, a large pistol that used to be carried by horsemen.

horse play (hôrs′plā′), *n.* rough, boisterous fun.

horse pow er (hôrs′pou′ər), *n.* unit for measuring the power of engines, motors, etc. One horsepower is 746 watts or the power to lift 550 pounds one foot in one second.

horse rad ish (hôrs′rad′ish), *n.* 1 a tall plant of the mustard family, with a white, hot-tasting root. 2 its root, which is ground up and used as a relish with meat, fish, salads, etc. 3 relish made of this root.

horse sense, INFORMAL. plain, practical good sense; common sense.

horse shoe (hôrs′shü′, hôrsh′shü′), *n., v.,* **-shoed, -shoe ing.** —*n.* 1 a U-shaped metal plate nailed to a horse's hoof to protect it. 2 thing shaped like a horseshoe. 3 **horseshoes,** *pl.* game in which the players try to throw horseshoes or pieces of metal shaped like horseshoes over or near a stake 40 feet away. —*v.t.* put a horseshoe or horseshoes on. **—horse′sho′er,** *n.*

horseshoe crab, any of an order of crablike sea animals of the same class as spiders, with horseshoe-shaped shells and long, spiny tails; king crab.

horseshoe magnet, a steel magnet in the shape of a horseshoe.

horse tail (hôrs′tāl′), *n.* 1 a horse's tail. 2 equisetum.

horse trade, INFORMAL. a shrewd bargain or compromise.

horse-trade (hôrs′trād′), *v.i., v.t.,* **-trad ed, -trad ing.** INFORMAL. trade or barter shrewdly.

horse trader, a person who trades or barters shrewdly.

horse whip (hôrs′hwip′), *n., v.,* **-whipped, -whip ping.** —*n.* whip for driving or controlling horses. —*v.t.* beat with a horsewhip.

horse wom an (hôrs′wům′ən), *n., pl.* **-wom en.** 1 woman who rides on horseback. 2 woman skilled in riding, managing, or breeding horses.

hors y or **hors ey** (hôr′sē), *adj.,* **hors i er, hors i est.** 1 like a horse or horses. 2 having to do with horses. 3 fond of horses or horse racing. 4 dressing or talking like people who spend much time with horses. **—hors′i-ness,** *n.*

hort., 1 horticultural. 2 horticulture.

hor ta tive (hôr′tə tiv), *adj.* hortatory. **—hor′ta tive ly,** *adv.*

hor ta to ry (hôr′tə tôr′ē, hôr′tə tōr′ē), *adj.* serving to urge or encourage; giving advice; exhorting. [< Late Latin *hortatorius* < Latin *hortari* exhort]

hor ti cul tur al (hôr′tə kul′chər əl), *adj.* having to do with horticulture. **—hor′ti-cul′tur al ly,** *adv.*

hor ti cul ture (hôr′tə kul′chər), *n.* 1 science or art of growing flowers, fruits, vegetables, and plants. 2 cultivation of a garden. [< Latin *hortus* garden + English *culture*]

hor ti cul tur ist (hôr′tə kul′chər ist), *n.* an expert in horticulture.

Ho rus (hôr′əs, hōr′əs), *n.* a sun god of ancient Egypt, son of Osiris and Isis. Horus was represented as having the head of a hawk.

Hos., Hosea.

ho san na (hō zan′ə), *interj., n.* 1 a shout of praise to God. 2 any shout of praise or approval. [< Greek *hōsanna* < Hebrew *hōshīʿāhnnā* save, we pray]

hose (hōz), *n., pl.* **hos es** for 1, **hose** for 2 and 3, *v.,* **hosed, hos ing.** —*n.* 1 tube of rubber, canvas, plastic, or other flexible material, used for carrying water or other liquids for short distances. 2 stockings. 3 long, tight breeches formerly worn by men. —*v.t.* 1 put or spray water or other liquid on with a hose: *hose a garden.* 2 wash or drench with water or other liquid from a hose: *hose the walls of a building clean, hose down the crowd at a fire.* [Old English *hosa* stocking]

Ho se a (hō zē′ə, hō zā′ə), *n.* 1 book of the Old Testament. 2 its author, a Hebrew prophet who lived in the 700's B.C.

ho sier y (hō′zhər ē), *n.* hose; stockings.

hosp., hospital.

hos pice (hos′pis), *n.* house where travelers can stop and rest, especially one kept by monks. [< French < Latin *hospitium* < *hospitem* guest, host[1]]

hos pi ta ble (hos′pi tə bəl, ho spit′ə bəl), *adj.* 1 giving or liking to give a welcome, food and shelter, and friendly treatment to guests or strangers: *a hospitable family.* 2 with the mind open or receptive: *a person hospitable to new ideas.* [< Middle French < Latin *hospitari* stay as a guest < *hospitem* guest, host[1]] **—hos′pi ta bly,** *adv.*

hos pi tal (hos′pi təl), *n.* 1 place where sick or injured people are given medical or surgical treatment. 2 a similar place for animals. 3 a repair shop for usually small items, such as dolls and fountain pens. [< Old French < Medieval Latin *hospitale* inn, ultimately < Latin *hospitem* guest, host[1]. Doublet of HOSTEL, HOTEL.]

Hos pi tal er (hos′pi tə lər), *n.* member of an order of military monks, founded during the first Crusade at Jerusalem. Also, **Hospitaller.**

hos pi tal i ty (hos′pə tal′ə tē), *n., pl.* **-ties.** friendly reception; generous treatment of guests or strangers.

hos pi tal i za tion (hos′pi tə lə zā′shən), *n.* 1 act of being hospitalized. 2 period of being hospitalized. 3 insurance to cover or help cover hospital expenses.

hos pi tal ize (hos′pi tə līz), *v.t.,* **-ized, -iz ing.** put in a hospital for medical or surgical treatment.

Hos pi tal ler (hos′pi tə lər), *n.* Hospitaler.

host[1] (hōst), *n.* 1 person who receives another person as his guest. 2 keeper of an inn or hotel. 3 a living plant or animal in or on which a parasite lives: *The oak tree is the host of the mistletoe that grows on it.* —*v.t.* 1 receive or entertain at as a host does: *host dinner guests, host a party.* 2 INFORMAL. serve as an emcee of: *host a TV program.* [< Old French *hoste* guest, host < Latin *hospitem*]

host[2] (hōst), *n.* 1 a large number; multitude: *As it grew dark, a few stars appeared, then a host of them.* 2 army of soldiers. [< Old French < Late Latin *hostis* army < Latin, enemy]

Host (hōst), *n.* Often, **host.** bread or wafer used in the Mass of the Roman Catholic Church and at Holy Communion in some other Churches. [< Old French *hoiste* < Latin *hostia* sacrifice, animal sacrificed]

hos tage (hos′tij), *n.* 1 person given up to another or held by an enemy as a pledge that certain promises, agreements, etc., will be carried out. 2 pledge; security. [< Old French, lodging, status of a guest, hostage < *hoste* guest. See HOST[1].]

hos tel (hos′tl), *n.* 1 a lodging place, especially a supervised lodging place for young people on bicycle trips, hikes, etc. 2 hostelry. [< Old French < Medieval Latin *hospitale* inn. Doublet of HOSPITAL, HOTEL.]

hos tel er (hos′tl ər), *n.* 1 guest at a hostel. 2 ARCHAIC. innkeeper.

hos tel ry (hos′tl rē), *n., pl.* **-ries.** inn or hotel.

host ess (hō′stis), *n.* 1 woman who receives another person as her guest. 2 woman who keeps an inn or hotel, or helps her husband to do so. 3 woman hired to greet and attend to guests in a hotel, restaurant, etc. 4 an airline stewardess.

hos tile (hos′tl; *sometimes* hos′tīl), *adj.* 1 of an enemy or enemies: *the hostile army.* 2 opposed; unfriendly; unfavorable. See synonym study below. —*n.* a hostile person; enemy. [< Latin *hostilis* < *hostis* enemy] **—hos′tile ly,** *adv.*

Syn. 2 **Hostile, unfriendly, inimical** mean unfriendly and unfavorable. **Hostile** suggests whatever is characteristic of an enemy: *Their hostile looks showed that I was unwelcome.* **Unfriendly** suggests not being agreeable, kindly, helpful, or encouraging in any way: *A cold, damp climate is unfriendly to people who suffer from arthritis.* **Inimical,** a formal word, particularly suggests the harmful effects resulting from a hostile disposition: *Censorship is inimical to the idea of freedom of the press.*

hos til i ty (ho stil′ə tē), *n., pl.* **-ties.** 1 the feeling that an enemy has; being an enemy; unfriendliness. 2 state of being at war. 3 **hostilities,** *pl.* acts of war; warfare; fighting. 4 opposition; resistance.

hos tler (os′lər, hos′lər), *n.* person who takes care of horses at an inn or stable. Also, **ostler.** [Middle English < Old French *hostelier* < *hostel.* See HOSTEL.]

hot (hot), *adj.,* **hot ter, hot test,** *v.,* **hot ted, hot ting,** *adv.* —*adj.* 1 having or giving off much heat; very warm: *Fire is hot.* 2 having a relatively high temperature: *The food is too hot to eat.* 3 having the feeling of high bodily heat: *That long run has made me hot.* 4 having a sharp, burning taste: *Pepper and mustard are hot.* 5 fiery; violent: *a hot temper, hot with rage.* 6 dangerous: *a hot situation.* 7 full of great interest or enthusiasm; very eager. 8 new; fresh: *a hot scent, a hot trail.* 9 following closely: *hot in the pursuit of robbers.* 10 (in games, treasure hunts, etc.) very near or approaching what one is searching for. 11 radioactive: *the hot debris left by an atomic explosion.* 12 electrically charged. 13 (of swing music or jazz) played with exciting rhythms and variations from the score. 14 SLANG. obtained illegally; stolen: *hot diamonds.* 15 SLANG. fashionable because exciting. 16 SLANG. likely to win or succeed; difficult to beat, stop, or hinder: *a hot team.* 17 SLANG. good. 18 SLANG. unbelievable. 19 **make it hot for,** INFORMAL. make trouble for. —*v.i.* **hot up,** INFORMAL. become hot, intense, or enthusiastic: *as the situation hots up.* —*v.t.* **hot up,** INFORMAL. make hot or enthusiastic; intensify: *hot up the dramatic force of the play.* —*adv.* in a hot manner.

[Old English *hāt*] **—hot′ly,** *adv.* **—hot′ness,** *n.*

hot air, SLANG. empty, showy talk or writing.

hot bed (hot′bed′), *n.* 1 bed of earth covered with glass and heated especially by fermenting manure, for growing or forcing plants. 2 place where anything grows and develops rapidly: *Dirty, crowded cities are hotbeds of disease and crime.*

hot-blood ed (hot′blud′id), *adj.* 1 easily excited or angered. 2 passionate.

hot box (hot′boks′), *n.* a bearing on a shaft or axle, overheated by friction.

hot cake, 1 pancake. 2 **go like hot cakes** or **sell like hot cakes,** sell well and rapidly; be in great demand.

hotch potch (hoch′poch′), *n.* hodgepodge.

hot cross bun, bun marked with a cross, usually eaten during Lent or on Good Friday.

hot dog, INFORMAL. 1 sandwich made with a hot frankfurter enclosed in a split roll, often served with mustard, relish, etc. 2 frankfurter.

ho tel (hō tel′), *n.* house or large building that provides lodging, food, etc., for pay to travelers and others. [< French *hôtel* < Old French *hostel.* Doublet of HOSPITAL, HOSTEL.]

hot foot (hot′fu̇t′), *v., adv., n., pl.* **-foots.** *—v.i.* Also, **hotfoot it.** INFORMAL. go in great haste; hurry. *—adv.* INFORMAL. in great haste. *—n.* prank in which a match is inserted in the welt of an unsuspecting person's shoe and then lighted.

hot head (hot′hed′), *n.* a hotheaded person.

hot head ed (hot′hed′id), *adj.* 1 having a fiery temper; easily angered. 2 impetuous; rash. **—hot′head′ed ly,** *adv.* **—hot′-head′ed ness,** *n.*

hot house (hot′hous′), *n., pl.* **-hous es** (-hou′ziz), *adj. —n.* greenhouse. *—adj.* from or of a hothouse.

hot line, a direct telephone or telegraph line providing instantaneous communication in a crisis or emergency: *the hot line between the White House and the Kremlin.*

hot pants, short shorts worn by women.

hot plate, a small, portable electric stove with one or two burners, for cooking or heating food, beverages, etc.

hot rod, U.S. automobile, especially an older one, modified or rebuilt for faster acceleration and higher speeds.

hot-rod der (hot′rod′ər), *n.* U.S. person who drives a hot rod.

hot shot (hot′shot′), *n.* SLANG. person having more than ordinary skill at something and often showing some conceit.

hot-shot (hot′shot′), *adj.* SLANG. of or characteristic of a hotshot.

hot spring, a spring producing warm water, usually at a temperature above that of the human body.

Hot Springs, city in central Arkansas, near Hot Springs National Park. 36,000.

Hot Springs National Park, national park in central Arkansas, with many natural hot springs.

hot spur (hot′spėr′), *n.* an impetuous or reckless person.

Hot ten tot (hot′n tot), *n.* 1 member of a people related to the Bushmen, living mainly in southwestern Africa. 2 their language. *—adj.* of the Hottentots or their language.

hot war, war involving actual fighting.

hot water, INFORMAL. trouble or difficulty: *His lies got him into hot water.*

hou dah (hou′də), *n.* howdah.

hotbed (def. 1)

Hou di ni (hü dē′nē), *n.* **Harry,** 1874-1926, American magician.

hound (hound), *n.* 1 dog of any of various breeds, most of which hunt by scent and have large, drooping ears and short hair. 2 **follow the hounds** or **ride to hounds,** go hunting on horseback with hounds. 3 any dog. 4 a contemptible person. 5 SLANG. person who is very fond of something: *a bridge hound.* *—v.t.* 1 keep on chasing or driving. 2 urge on. [Old English *hund*]

hour (our), *n.* 1 one of the twelve equal periods of time between noon and midnight, or between midnight and noon, as marked on a timepiece. 2 one of the twenty-four equal periods of time between midnight and midnight; 60 minutes; $^1/_{24}$ of a day. 3 the time of day or night: *This clock strikes the hours and the half-hours.* 4 a particular or fixed time: *Our breakfast hour is at seven o'clock.* 5 **hours,** *pl.* **a** time for work, study, etc. **b** the usual time for going to bed and getting up. 6 a short or limited space of time: *After her hour of glory, she was soon forgotten.* 7 period for which a class meets, often less than a full hour. 8 distance which can be traveled in an hour. 9 the present time: *the man of the hour.* 10 **hours,** *pl.* **a** seven special times of the day set aside for prayer and worship. **b** prayers or services for these times. 11 **Hours,** *pl.* Horae. [< Old French *hore, ore* < Latin *hora* < Greek *hōra* season, time, hour]

➤ **hours.** In consecutive writing, especially if it is formal, hours are usually written in words: *four o'clock.* In much informal writing, figures are used, especially if several times are mentioned: *at 4 p.m., from 10 to 12.*

hourglass

hour glass (our′glas′), *n.* device for measuring time, made up of two glass bulbs connected by a narrow neck through which sand or mercury slowly runs down. It takes just an hour for the sand or mercury to pass from the top bulb to the bottom one.

hour hand, the shorter hand on a clock or watch that indicates hours. It moves around the whole dial once in twelve hours.

hour i (hu̇r′ē, hou′rē), *n.* one of the young, eternally beautiful girls of the Moslem paradise. [< Persian *hūrī* < Arabic *hūr* black-eyed]

hour ly (our′lē), *adj.* 1 done, happening, or counted every hour. 2 coming very often; frequent. 3 paid by the hour: *an hourly employee.* *—adv.* 1 every hour; hour by hour. 2 very often; frequently.

house (*n.* hous; *v.* houz), *n., pl.* **hous es** (hou′ziz), *v.,* **housed, hous ing.** *—n.* 1 building in which people live, especially a building that is the ordinary dwelling place of a family. 2 place in which an animal lives or into which it retires, as the nest of a bird or the den of a bear. 3 people living in a house; household. 4 Often, **House.** family regarded as consisting of ancestors, descendants, and kindred, especially a noble or royal family: *He was a prince of the house of David.* 5 building for any purpose: *an engine house.* 6 place of business or a business firm. 7 Often, **House. a** assembly for making laws and considering questions of government; lawmaking body. In the United States, the House of Representatives is the lower house of Congress; the Senate is the upper house. **b** building in which such an assembly meets. 8 place of entertainment; theater. 9 audience: *The singer sang to a large house.* 10 residence in a school or the students living in it. 11 residence of a religious order. 12 in astrology: **a** a twelfth part of the heavens as divided by great circles through the north and south points of the horizon. **b** sign of the zodiac considered as the seat of the greatest influence of a particular planet.

bring down the house, INFORMAL. be loudly applauded.

clean house, a clean a house and its furnishings. **b** get rid of bad conditions.

keep house, manage a home and its affairs; do housework.

on the house, paid for by the owner of the business; free.

—v.t. 1 receive or put into a house; provide with a house. 2 give shelter to; lodge. 3 place in a secure or protected position. *—v.i.* take shelter.

[Old English *hūs*] **—house′less,** *adj.* **—house′like′,** *adj.* ➤ See **home** for usage note.

house boat (hous′bōt′), *n.* boat fitted out for use as a place to live in, especially one having a flat bottom and a houselike structure built on the deck.

house boy (hous′boi′), *n.* boy or man employed as a servant in a house.

house break (hous′brāk′), *v.t.,* **-broke** (-brōk′), **-bro ken, -break ing.** train (a dog, cat, etc.) where to urinate and defecate; make housebroken.

house break er (hous′brā′kər), *n.* person who breaks into a house to steal or commit some other crime.

house break ing (hous′brā′king), *n.* act of breaking into a house to steal or commit some other crime.

house bro ken (hous′brō′kən), *adj.* (of a dog, cat, etc.) trained as to where to urinate and defecate, so that it may live indoors.

house call, visit by a nurse, therapist, etc., to the home of a patient to give care or treatment. Some doctors still make house calls.

house clean ing (hous′klē′ning), *n.* 1 the cleaning of a house and its furnishings. 2 act

hat, āge, fär; let, ēqual, tėrm;
it, īce; hot, ōpen, ôrder;
oil, out; cup, pu̇t, rüle;
ch, child; ng, long; sh, she;
th, thin; ᴛʜ, then; zh, measure;

ə represents *a* in about, *e* in taken, *i* in pencil, *o* in lemon, *u* in circus.

< = from, derived from, taken from.

or process of getting rid of bad conditions.

house coat (hous′kōt′), *n.* a loose, flowing outer garment worn indoors by women and girls.

house fly (hous′flī′), *n., pl.* **-flies.** any of a family of two-winged flies that live around and in houses in all parts of the world, especially a common disease-carrying species which feeds on food, garbage, and filth. Housefly larvae or maggots develop in decaying organic matter.

house guest (hous′gest′), *n.* guest who stays at one's house overnight or longer.

house hold (hous′hōld), *n.* 1 all the people living in a house; family; family and servants. 2 a home and its affairs. *—adj.* 1 of a household; having to do with a household; domestic: *household expenses.* 2 familiar or common: *a household name.*

house hold er (hous′hōl′dər), *n.* 1 person who owns or lives in a house. 2 head of a family.

household word, a very familiar word or phrase.

house keep (hous′kēp′), *v.i.,* **-kept** (-kept′), **-keep ing.** keep house.

house keep er (hous′kē′pər), *n.* 1 woman who manages a household; woman who does housework. 2 woman who is hired to direct the servants that do the housework in a home, hotel, etc.

house keep ing (hous′kē′ping), *n.* 1 management of a household; doing the housework. 2 management of a business or other concern.

house leek (hous′lēk′), *n.* any of a genus of plants of the same family as the sedum, especially a species having thick, juicy stems and leaves, and pink flowers. It commonly grows on the walls and roofs of houses.

house maid (hous′mād′), *n.* a woman servant who does housework.

housemaid's knee, inflammation on the kneecap, usually caused by kneeling.

house man (hous′mən), *n., pl.* **-men.** manservant employed to do general work about a house, hotel, etc.

house moth er (hous′muᴛʜ′ər), *n.* woman who supervises and takes care of a group of young people living together like a family.

House of Burgesses, the lower house of the colonial legislature in Virginia or Maryland.

house of cards, anything that can be easily knocked down; flimsy structure.

House of Commons, the lower, elective house of the Parliament of Great Britain or of Canada; the Commons.

house of correction, place of confinement and reform for persons convicted of minor offenses and not regarded as confirmed criminals.

House of Delegates, the lower branch of the legislature in Maryland, Virginia, and West Virginia.

House of Lords, the upper, nonelective house of the Parliament of Great Britain, composed of nobles and clergymen of high rank; the Lords.

House of Representatives, 1 the lower house of Congress or of the legislature of certain states of the United States. 2 the lower house of the Parliament of Australia. 3 the Parliament of New Zealand.

house organ, magazine published by a business concern for circulation among its employees or patrons.

house party, entertainment of guests in a home or at a college for a few days.

house plant, a plant in a pot or box, kept inside the house. Ferns are often used as house plants.

house-proud (hous′proud′), *adj.* taking pride in one's house and the way it is maintained.

house-rais ing (hous′rā′zing), *n.* U.S. a gathering of neighbors in a rural region to help a person raise the frame of his house.

house sparrow, English sparrow.

house top (hous′top′), *n.* top of a house; roof.

house warm ing (hous′wôr′ming), *n.* party given when a family moves into a home for the first time.

house wife (hous′wīf′ *for 1 and 2;* huz′if *for 3*), *n., pl.* **-wives** (-wīvz *for 1 and 2;* -ifs *for 3*). 1 woman who manages a household for her family. 2 woman who is the head of a household. 3 a small case for needles, thread, etc.

house wife ly (hous′wīf′lē), *adj.* of or like a housewife; skilled in household affairs. **—house′wife′li ness,** *n.*

house wif er y (hous′wī′fər ē), *n.* work of a housewife; housekeeping.

house work (hous′wėrk′), *n.* work to be done in housekeeping, such as washing, ironing, cleaning, and cooking.

hous ing[1] (hou′zing), *n.* 1 act of sheltering; providing houses as homes. 2 houses to live in; dwellings: *There is not enough housing in that city for the number of people living there.* 3 shelter or lodging. 4 frame or plate to hold part of a machine in place. [< *house*]

hous ing[2] (hou′zing), *n.* an ornamental covering on an animal's back, especially the back of a horse. [< earlier *house* covering < Old French *houce*]

Hous man (hous′mən), *n.* **A(lfred) E(dward),** 1859-1936, English poet.

Hous ton (hyü′stən), *n.* 1 **Sam(uel),** 1793-1863, American general and statesman who was twice president of Texas before it became a state in 1845. 2 city in SE Texas. 1,233,000.

hove (hōv), *v.* a pt. and a pp. of **heave.**

hov el (huv′əl, hov′əl), *n.* 1 house that is small, crude, and unpleasant to live in. 2 an open shed for sheltering cattle, tools, etc. [Middle English]

hov er (huv′ər, hov′ər), *v.i.* 1 hang fluttering or suspended in air: *The two birds hovered over their nest.* 2 stay in or near one place; wait nearby: *The dogs hovered around the kitchen door at mealtime.* 3 be in an uncertain condition: *The patient hovered between life and death.* [Middle English *hoveren*] **—hov′er er,** *n.*

Hov er craft (huv′ər kraft′, hov′ər kraft′), *n.* trademark for a vehicle that travels a few feet above the surface of land or water on a cushion of air provided by jets or fans blowing downward; cushioncraft; air cushion vehicle; ground effect machine.

how (hou), *adv.* 1 in what way; by what means: *Tell me how to do it.* 2 to what degree, amount, extent, etc.: *How tall are you?* 3 at what price: *How do you sell these apples?* 4 in what state or condition: *How are you?* 5 for what reason; why: *How is it you don't like candy?* 6 to what effect; with what meaning: *How do you mean?* 7 by what name: *How do you call yourself?* 8 **and how,** INFORMAL. certainly. 9 **any old how,** INFORMAL. carelessly. 10 **how about,** INFORMAL. what do you say to; would you consider: *How about coming over tonight?* 11 **how come,** INFORMAL. why: *How come you didn't call me last night?*
—conj. 1 in what way; by what means: *I don't know how I overlooked that detail.* 2 to what degree, amount, extent, etc.: *Please tell us how far it is to Atlanta.* 3 in what state or condition: *Let me know how she is.*
—n. way or manner of doing: *She considered all the hows and wherefores.*
[Old English *hū*]

how be it (hou bē′it), *adv.* ARCHAIC. nevertheless. *—conj.* though.

howdah

how dah (hou′də), *n.* seat to hold two or more persons, usually fitted with a railing and canopy, placed on the back of an elephant or camel. Also, **houdah.** [< Hindustani *haudah* < Arabic *haudaj*]

Howe (hou), *n.* 1 **Elias,** 1819-1867, American inventor of the sewing machine. 2 **Julia Ward,** 1819-1910, American writer and social reformer. 3 **William,** 1729-1814, commander in chief of the British army in the Revolutionary War.

how e'er (hou er′, hou ar′), *conj., adv.* however.

How ells (hou′əlz), *n.* **William Dean,** 1837-1920, American novelist and editor.

how ev er (hou ev′ər), *adv.* 1 in spite of that; nevertheless; yet: *It is hers; however, you may borrow it.* See **but** for synonym study. 2 to whatever extent, degree, or amount; no matter how: *I'll come, however busy I am.* 3 in whatever way; by whatever means: *However did you get so dirty?*

how it zer (hou′it sər), *n.* a short cannon for firing shells in a high curve. [< Dutch *houwitser* < German *Haubitze* < Czech *houfnice* catapult]

howl (houl), *v.i.* 1 give a long, loud, mournful cry: *Dogs and wolves howl.* 2 give a long, loud cry of pain or rage. 3 yell or shout: *It was so funny that we howled with laughter.* *—v.t.* 1 force or drive by howling: *The angry mob howled the speaker off the platform.* 2 **howl down,** drown out the words of by howling. *—n.* 1 a long, loud, mournful cry. 2 a long, loud cry of pain or rage. 3 a yell or shout: *howls of laughter.* [Middle English *houlen*]

howl er (hou′lər), *n.* 1 person or thing that howls. 2 any of a genus of monkeys of tropical America with long, prehensile tails. The call of the male is a powerful howl. 3 INFORMAL. a ridiculous mistake; stupid blunder.

howl ing (hou′ling), *adj.* INFORMAL. very great: *a howling success.* **—howl′ing ly,** *adv.*

How rah (hou′rə), *n.* city in NE India. 590,000.

how so ev er (hou′sō ev′ər), *adv.* 1 to whatever extent, degree, or amount. 2 in whatever way; by whatever means.

hat, āge, fär; let, ēqual, tėrm;
it, īce; hot, ōpen, ôrder;
oil, out; cup, pu̇t, rüle;
ch, child; ng, long; sh, she;
th, thin; ᴛʜ, then; zh, measure;

ə represents *a* in about, *e* in taken, *i* in pencil, *o* in lemon, *u* in circus.

< = from, derived from, taken from.

hoy den (hoid′n), *n.* a boisterous, romping girl; tomboy. [origin uncertain]

hoy den ish (hoid′n ish), *adj.* of or like a hoyden; boisterous; romping.

Hoyle (hoil), *n.* **according to Hoyle,** according to the rules; in a fair or correct manner. [< Edmond *Hoyle,* 1672-1769, English writer of a book of rules for games]

hp., h.p., HP, or **H.P.,** 1 high pressure. 2 horsepower.

h.q. or **H.Q.,** headquarters.

hr., *pl.* **hrs.** hour or hours.

H.R., House of Representatives.

H.R.H., 1 Her Royal Highness. 2 His Royal Highness.

ht., height.

HUAC, House Un-American Activities Committee (former, but still widely used, name of the Committee on Internal Security, a standing committee of the United States House of Representatives since 1945, charged with investigating subversion, anti-American propaganda, etc.).

hua ra che (hə rä′chē), *n.* a heavy leather sandal with a flat sole, common in Mexico. [< Mexican Spanish]

Huas ca rán (wä skə rän′), *n.* mountain in central Peru. 22,000 ft.

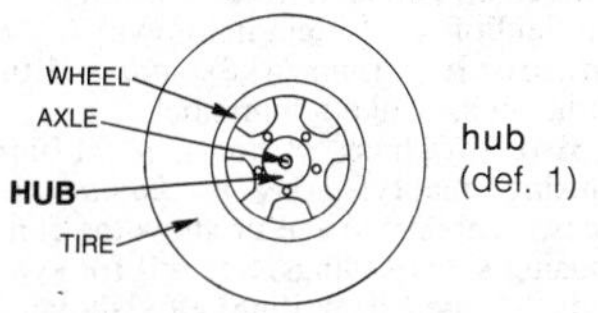

hub (def. 1)

hub (hub), *n.* 1 the central part of a wheel. 2 center of interest, activity, etc.: *London is the hub of English life.* [variant of *hob*[1]] **—hub′like′,** *adj.*

hub bub (hub′ub), *n.* loud, confused noise; uproar. [origin uncertain]

hub by (hub′ē), *n., pl.* **-bies.** INFORMAL. husband.

hub cap (hub′kap′), *n.* a removable, dish-shaped metal piece which covers the center of the outer side of a wheel.

hu bris (hyü′bris), *n.* insolent pride; arrogance. [< Greek *hybris*]

huck a back (huk′ə bak), *n.* a heavy, coarse, linen or cotton cloth with a rough surface, used especially for towels. [origin uncertain]

huck le ber ry (huk′əl ber′ē), *n., pl.* **-ries.** 1 a small berry like a blueberry, but darker and with larger seeds. 2 shrub of the heath family that it grows on.

huck ster (huk′stər), *n.* 1 peddler. 2 person who sells small articles. 3 person willing to profit in a small, mean way. 4 SLANG. person who is in the advertising business. *—v.i., v.t.* peddle or sell, especially in a petty way or in small quantities. [< Middle Dutch *hoekster.* Related to HAWKER[1].]

HUD, Housing and Urban Development (a department of the U.S. government).

hud dle (hud′l), *v.,* **-dled, -dling,** *n.* *—v.i.* 1 crowd close together: *The sheep huddled in a corner.* 2 nestle in a heap: *She huddled close to the fire on the hearth.* 3 INFORMAL. confer secretly. 4 (of football players) group together behind the line of scrimmage to receive signals, plan the next play, etc. *—v.t.* 1 put close; crowd together: *The animals huddled themselves in the lee of a hill out of the wind.* 2 nestle up: *The cat huddled itself on the cushion.* 3 put on (clothes) with careless haste. *—n.* 1 a confused heap, mass, or crowd. 2 slovenly hurry; confusion. 3 INFORMAL. a secret consultation: *After the meeting, the lawyer went into a huddle with his partner.* 4 a grouping of football players behind the line of scrimmage to receive signals, plan the next play, etc. [origin uncertain] **—hud′dler,** *n.*

Hud son (hud′sən), *n.* 1 **Henry,** died 1611, English navigator and explorer in America. Hudson River and Hudson Bay were named for him. 2 **William Henry,** 1841-1922, English naturalist and writer. 3 **Hudson River,** river in E New York State. New York City is at its mouth. 315 mi.

Hudson Bay, large bay in NE Canada, an extension of the Atlantic Ocean. 850 mi. long; 400,000 sq. mi.

Hudson's Bay Company, a British trading company chartered in 1670 to carry on the fur trade with the Indians of North America.

Hudson seal, a muskrat fur that is dyed and plucked to look like seal.

Hudson Strait, strait connecting Hudson Bay with the Atlantic. 450 mi. long.

hue (hyü), *n.* 1 that property of color by which it can be distinguished as red, yellow, blue, and other regions of the spectrum; color: *all the hues of the rainbow.* See **color** for synonym study. 2 a variety of a color; shade or tint: *silk of a pinkish hue.* 3 aspect or type: *politicians of every hue.* [Old English *hīw*]

Hue or **Hué** (hwā), *n.* seaport in NE South Vietnam. 157,000.

hue and cry, shouts of alarm or protest; outcry. [*hue* < Old French *hu* a hunting cry]

huff (huf), *n.* fit of anger or peevishness. *—v.t.* make angry; offend. *—v.i.* puff; blow. [imitative]

huff y (huf′ē), *adj.,* **huff i er, huff i est.** 1 in a huff; offended. 2 easily offended; touchy. **—huff′i ly,** *adv.* **—huff′i ness,** *n.*

hug (hug), *v.,* **hugged, hug ging,** *n.* *—v.t.* 1 put the arms around and hold close, especially to show love or friendship. 2 squeeze tightly with the arms, as a bear does. 3 cling firmly or fondly to: *hug an opinion.* 4 keep close to: *The boat hugged the shore.* *—n.* 1 a tight clasp with the arms; warm embrace. 2 a tight squeeze with the arms; grip in wrestling. [perhaps < Scandinavian (Old Icelandic) *hugga* to comfort]

huge (hyüj), *adj.,* **hug er, hug est.** 1 very big; unusually large or great: *a huge amount of money.* See synonym study below. 2 unusually great in extent, scope, degree, or capacity: *a huge undertaking.* [< Old French *ahuge*] **—huge′ly,** *adv.* **—huge′ness,** *n.*

Syn. 1 **Huge, enormous, immense** mean unusually large. **Huge** suggests massiveness or bulkiness: *A St. Bernard is a huge dog.* **Enormous** means abnormally or excessively large: *I have an enormous appetite.* **Immense** means so large or great in any way as to be impossible to measure by ordinary standards of measurement: *The national debt is immense.*

hug ger mug ger (hug′ər mug′ər), *n.* a confused condition; disorder. *—adj.* confused; disorderly.

Hugh Capet. See **Capet.**

Hughes (hyüz), *n.* 1 **Charles Evans,** 1862-1948, American statesman, chief justice of the United States Supreme Court from 1930 to 1941. 2 **Langston,** 1902-1967, American poet, novelist, and playwright.

Hu go (hyü′gō), *n.* **Victor,** 1802-1885, French poet, novelist, and dramatist.

Hu gue not (hyü′gə not), *n.* a French Protestant of the 1500's and 1600's. [< French *huguenot*]

huh (hu), *interj.* sound made to express surprise, contempt, etc., or to ask a question.

hu la (hü′lə), *n.* a native Hawaiian dance that tells a story in pantomime. [< Hawaiian]

Hula-Hoop (hü′lə hu̇p′, hü′lə hüp′), *n.* trademark for a hoop, usually made of plastic, that is rotated around the body by swinging the hips. Hula-Hoops are whirled for exercise and especially by children in play.

hu la-hu la (hü′lə hü′lə), *n.* hula.

hulk (hulk), *n.* 1 body of an old or worn-out ship. 2 Often, **hulks,** *pl.* ship used as a prison. 3 a big, clumsy ship. 4 a big, clumsy person or thing. *—v.i.* be bulky or unwieldy; loom bulkily. [Old English *hulc*]

hulk ing (hul′king), *adj.* big and clumsy.

hull (hul), *n.* 1 body or frame of a ship. Masts, sails, and rigging are not part of the hull. 2 the main body or frame of a seaplane, airship, etc. 3 the outer covering of a seed or fruit. 4 calyx of some fruits, such as the green leaves at the stem of a strawberry. 5 any outer covering. *—v.t.* remove the hull or hulls from. [Old English *hulu*] **—hull′er,** *n.*

Hull (hul), *n.* 1 **Cordell,** 1871-1955, American statesman, secretary of state from 1933 to 1944. 2 seaport in E England, on the Humber. 290,000.

hul la ba loo (hul′ə bə lü′), *n., pl.* **-loos.** a loud noise or disturbance; uproar.

hum (hum), *v.,* **hummed, hum ming,** *n., interj.* *—v.i.* 1 make a continuous murmuring sound like that of a bee or of a spinning top: *The sewing machine hummed busily.* 2 make a low sound like *mm* or *hm* in hesitation, embarrassment, dissatisfaction, etc. 3 sing with closed lips, not sounding words. 4 give forth an indistinct sound of mingled voices or noises; buzz: *The theater audience hummed with excitement.* 5 INFORMAL. be busy and active: *The new coach made things hum.* *—v.t.* 1 sing with closed lips, not sounding words: *hum a tune.* 2 put or bring by humming: *The mother hummed her baby to sleep.* *—n.* 1 a continuous murmuring sound: *the hum of the bees.* 2 an indistinct sound of mingled voices or noises: *the hum of a city street.* 3 a singing with closed lips, not sounding words. *—interj.* a low sound like *mm* or *hm* made in hesitation, embarrassment, etc. [imitative] **—hum′mer,** *n.*

hu man (hyü′mən), *adj.* 1 of persons; that people have: *Kindness is a human trait. To know what will happen in the future is beyond human power.* 2 being a person or persons; having the form or qualities of people: *Men, women, and children are human beings.* 3 having or showing qualities natural to people: *Their spontaneous offer of help to the stranded motorist was a very human reaction.* See synonym study below. 4 having to do with people; belonging to mankind: *human affairs.* —*n.* a human being; person. [< Old French *humain* < Latin *humanus*] **—hu′man ness,** *n.*

Syn. *adj.* 3 **Human, humane** mean having or showing qualities belonging to man. **Human** describes or suggests any quality, good or bad, characterizing man, but particularly suggests his feelings or faults: *He is a very human person, warm and understanding but not perfect.* **Humane** chiefly suggests man's tender and compassionate feelings and actions toward people or animals that are helpless, troubled, or suffering: *We believe in humane treatment of prisoners.*

hu mane (hyü mān′), *adj.* 1 not cruel or brutal; kind; merciful. See **human** for synonym study. 2 tending to humanize and refine: *humane studies.* [variant of *human*] **—hu mane′ly,** *adv.* **—hu mane′ness,** *n.*

hu man ism (hyü′mə niz′əm), *n.* 1 any system of thought or action concerned with human interests and values. 2 study of the humanities; literary culture. Humanism spread throughout Europe in the Middle Ages when scholars began to study Latin and Greek culture. As a result there was the great revival of art and learning called the Renaissance.

hu man ist (hyü′mə nist), *n.* 1 follower of humanism. 2 student of the humanities.

hu man is tic (hyü′mə nis′tik), *adj.* of humanism or humanists.

hu man i tar i an (hyü man′ə ter′ē ən), *adj.* helpful to humanity; philanthropic. —*n.* person who is devoted to the welfare of all human beings.

hu man i tar i an ism (hyü man′ə ter′ē ə niz′əm), *n.* humanitarian principles or practices.

hu man i ty (hyü man′ə tē), *n., pl.* **-ties.** 1 human beings; people; mankind: *Advances in science help all humanity.* 2 a being human; human nature. 3 a being humane; humane treatment; kindness; mercy: *Treat animals with humanity.* 4 **the humanities, a** the Latin and Greek classics. **b** cultural studies as opposed to the sciences, including languages, literature, philosophy, art, etc. **c** branches of learning concerned with man.

hu man ize (hyü′mə nīz), *v.t., v.i.,* **-ized, -iz ing.** 1 make or become human. 2 make or become humane. **—hu′man i za′tion,** *n.* **—hu′man iz′er,** *n.*

hu man kind (hyü′mən kīnd′), *n.* human beings; people; mankind.

hu man ly (hyü′mən lē), *adv.* 1 by human means: *We will do all that is humanly possible.* 2 according to the feelings, knowledge, or experience of human beings. 3 in a human manner.

hu man oid (hyü′mə noid), *adj.* of human form; manlike. —*n.* a humanoid being: *The Neanderthal man and Cro-Magnon man were humanoids.* Also, **hominoid.**

Hum ber (hum′bər), *n.* estuary of the Trent and Ouse rivers in E England. 37 mi. long.

hum ble (hum′bəl), *adj.,* **-bler, -blest,** *v.,* **-bled, -bling.** —*adj.* 1 low in position or condition; not important or grand: *They lived in a humble, one-room cottage.* 2 not proud; modest. See synonym study below. 3 deeply or courteously respectful: *in my humble opinion.* —*v.t.* make humble; make lower in position, condition, or pride: *humble oneself before God, humbled by defeat.* [< Old French < Latin *humilis* low < *humus* earth] **—hum′ble ness,** *n.* **—hum′bler,** *n.* **—hum′bly,** *adv.*

Syn. *adj.* 2 **Humble, lowly, meek** mean not proud in spirit or behavior. **Humble** suggests feeling inferior and belittling oneself: *Defeat and failure make people humble.* **Lowly,** though interchangeable with *humble,* is more literary and seldom used to describe people: *The beggar had a lowly manner.* **Meek** suggests being without proper pride and submitting tamely to abuse: *The boy was meek when the other boys made fun of him.*

hum ble bee (hum′bəl bē′), *n.* bumblebee. [Middle English *humbylbee,* ultimately < *hum* + *bee*]

humble pie, 1 an inferior pie made of certain of the inward parts of an animal. 2 **eat humble pie,** be forced to do something very disagreeable and humiliating.

Hum boldt (hum′bōlt), *n.* Baron **Alexander von,** 1769–1859, German scientist and explorer.

Humboldt Current, Peru Current.

hum bug (hum′bug′), *n., v.,* **-bugged, -bug ging.** —*n.* 1 person who pretends to be what he is not; fraud; impostor. 2 cheat; sham. 3 nonsense or pretense. —*v.t.* deceive with a sham; cheat. [origin unknown]

hum bug ger y (hum′bug′ər ē), *n., pl.* **-ger ies.** false pretense; humbugging.

hum ding er (hum ding′ər), *n.* SLANG. person or thing remarkable for its kind. [probably a coined word]

hum drum (hum′drum′), *adj.* without variety; commonplace; dull. —*n.* person or thing that is humdrum. [< *hum,* verb]

Hume (hyüm), *n.* **David,** 1711–1776, Scottish philosopher and historian.

hu mec tant (hyü mek′tənt), *n.* a moistening agent used in tobacco, cosmetics, textiles, etc. [< Latin *humectantem* moistening]

hu mer al (hyü′mər əl), *adj.* 1 of or near the humerus. 2 of or near the shoulder.

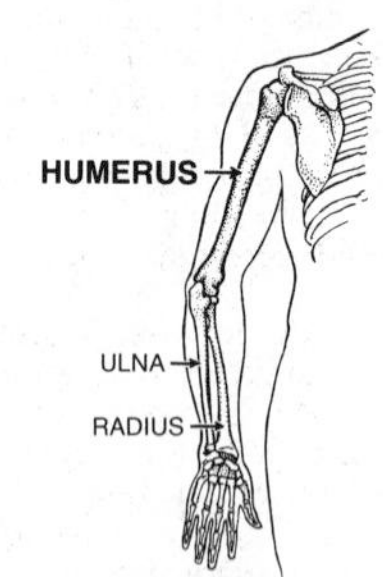

hu mer us (hyü′mər əs), *n., pl.* **-mer i** (-mə rī′). the long bone in the upper part of the arm, from the shoulder to the elbow. [< Latin, shoulder]

hu mid (hyü′mid), *adj.* slightly wet; moist; damp: *The air is very humid near the sea.* See **damp** for synonym study. [< Latin *humidus* < *humere* be moist] **—hu′mid ly,** *adv.* **—hu′mid ness,** *n.*

hu mid i fi ca tion (hyü mid′ə fə kā′shən), *n.* a humidifying.

hu mid i fi er (hyü mid′ə fī′ər), *n.* device for keeping air moist.

hu mid i fy (hyü mid′ə fī), *v.t.,* **-fied, -fy ing.** make moist or damp.

hu mid i ty (hyü mid′ə tē), *n.* 1 a being humid; moistness; dampness. 2 amount of moisture in the air.

hu mi dor (hyü′mə dôr), *n.* 1 box, jar, etc., fitted with the means for keeping tobacco properly moist. 2 any similar device.

hu mil i ate (hyü mil′ē āt), *v.t.,* **-at ed, -at ing.** lower the pride, dignity, or self-respect of; make ashamed: *Do not humiliate him by referring to his failures.* [< Latin *humiliare* < *humilis* low. See HUMBLE.] **—hu mil′i at′ing ly,** *adv.*

hu mil i a ted (hyü mil′ē āt id), *adj.* made to feel ashamed. See **ashamed** for synonym study.

hu mil i a tion (hyü mil′ē ā′shən), *n.* 1 a lowering of pride, dignity, or self-respect. 2 state or feeling of being humiliated.

hu mil i ty (hyü mil′ə tē), *n., pl.* **-ties.** humbleness of mind; lack of pride; meekness.

hum ma ble (hum′ə bəl), *adj.* easy to hum; likely to be hummed: *a hummable tune.*

hum ming bird (hum′ing bėrd′), *n.* any of a family of very small, brightly colored American birds with long, narrow bills and narrow wings that move so rapidly they make a humming sound.

hum mock (hum′ək), *n.* 1 a very small, rounded hill; knoll; hillock. 2 a bump or ridge in a field of ice. [origin unknown]

hum mock y (hum′ə kē), *adj.* 1 full of hummocks. 2 like a hummock.

hu mor (hyü′mər, yü′mər), *n.* 1 funny or amusing quality: *I see no humor in your tricks.* 2 ability to see or show the funny or amusing side of things. See **wit** for synonym study. 3 speech, writing, etc., showing this ability. 4 state of mind; disposition; temper: *in good humor.* See **mood** for synonym study. 5 fancy; whim. 6 any of four body fluids formerly supposed to determine a person's health and disposition. The four humors were blood, phlegm, yellow bile, and black bile. 7 **out of humor,** in a bad mood; angry or displeased; cross. —*v.t.* 1 give in to the fancies or whims of (a person); indulge. See synonym study below. 2 adapt oneself to; act so as to agree with. Also, BRITISH **humour.** [< Old French < Latin, fluid]

Syn. *v.t.* 1 **Humor, indulge, gratify** mean to give someone what he wants. **Humor** means to comply with another's whims, changing moods, or unreasonable demands, in order to quiet or comfort him: *humor a sick child.* **Indulge** often suggests yielding too often and too readily to someone's wishes, especially wishes that should not be granted, in order to please: *They indulged their child's every wish.* **Gratify** means to please by satisfying wishes or likings: *Praise gratifies most people.*

hu mor al (hyü′mər əl, yü′mər əl), *adj.* having to do with or caused by the bodily humors.

hu mor esque (hyü′mə resk′), *n.* a light, playful, or humorous piece of music. [< German *Humoreske*]

hu mor ist (hyü′mər ist, yü′mər ist), *n.* a humorous talker or writer; person who tells or writes jokes and funny stories.

hu mor less (hyü′mər lis, yü′mər lis), *adj.* without humor. **—hu′mor less ly,** *adv.* **—hu′mor less ness,** *n.*

hu mor ous (hyü′mər əs, yü′mər əs), *adj.* full of humor; funny; amusing. **—hu′mor ous ly,** *adv.* **—hu′mor ous ness,** *n.*

hu mour (hyü′mər, yü′mər), *n., v.t.* BRITISH. humor.

hump (hump), *n.* 1 a rounded lump that

hat, āge, fär; let, ēqual, tėrm;
it, īce; hot, ōpen, ôrder;
oil, out; cup, pu̇t, rüle;
ch, child; ng, long; sh, she;
th, thin; ᴛʜ, then; zh, measure;

ə represents *a* in about, *e* in taken, *i* in pencil, *o* in lemon, *u* in circus.

< = from, derived from, taken from.

sticks out: *Some camels have two humps on their backs.* 2 mound. 3 **over the hump,** INFORMAL. past a difficult period or crucial test. *—v.t.* 1 raise or bend up into a hump: *The cat humped her back when she saw the dog.* 2 U.S. SLANG. exert (oneself) in great effort. *—v.i.* 1 rise in a hump. 2 SLANG. exert oneself; make an effort. [origin uncertain] **—hump′like′,** *adj.*

hump back (hump′bak′), *n.* 1 hunchback. 2 a back having a hump on it. 3 a large whale that has a humplike dorsal fin.

hump backed (hump′bakt′), *adj.* hunchbacked.

humph (humpf), *interj., n.* exclamation expressing doubt, disgust, contempt, etc. [imitative]

Hum phrey (hum′frē), *n.* **Hubert Horatio,** born 1911, vice-president of the United States from 1965 to 1969.

hump y (hum′pē), *adj.,* **hump i er, hump i est.** 1 full of humps. 2 humplike.

hu mus (hyü′məs), *n.* a dark-brown or black part of soil formed from decayed leaves and other vegetable matter, containing valuable plant foods. [< Latin, earth]

Hun (hun), *n.* 1 member of a warlike Asian people who invaded Europe under the leadership of Attila in the A.D. 300's and 400's. 2 a barbarous, destructive person.

Hu nan (hü′nän′), *n.* province in SE China.

hunch (hunch), *n.* 1 a hump. 2 INFORMAL. a vague feeling or suspicion: *Having a hunch that it would rain, he took along an umbrella.* 3 a thick slice or piece; chunk. *—v.t.* 1 hump: *hunch one's shoulders.* 2 draw, bend, or form into a hump: *She sat hunched up with her chin on her knees.* 3 INFORMAL. have a vague feeling; suspect: *They hunched that he would win the election.* *—v.i.* 1 move, push, or shove by jerks. 2 draw, bend, or form oneself into a hump: *We hunched over the table.* [origin unknown]

hunch back (hunch′bak′), *n.* 1 person with a hump on his back; humpback. 2 back having a hump on it. *—adj.* hunchbacked.

hunch backed (hunch′bakt′), *adj.* having a hump on the back; humpbacked.

hun dred (hun′drəd), *n., pl.* **-dreds** or (as after a numeral) **-dred,** *adj.* *—n.* 1 ten times ten; 100. 2 a large number: *hundreds of uses.* 3 division of an English county. 4 a similar division in Delaware. *—adj.* being ten times ten. [Old English]

hun dred fold (hun′drəd fōld′), *adj., adv., n.* a hundred times, or being a hundred times, as much or as many.

hun dredth (hun′drədth), *adj., n.* 1 next after the 99th; last in a series of 100. 2 one, or being one, of 100 equal parts.

hun dred weight (hun′drəd wāt′), *n., pl.* **-weights** or (as after a numeral) **-weight.** measure of weight, equal to 100 pounds in the United States and Canada, and 112 pounds in Great Britain.

Hundred Years' War, series of wars between England and France from 1337 to 1453.

hung (hung), *v.* a pt. and a pp. of **hang.** ➔ See **hang** for usage note.

Hung., 1 Hungarian. 2 Hungary.

Hun gar i an (hung ger′ē ən), *adj.* of Hungary, its people, or their language. *—n.* 1 native or inhabitant of Hungary; Magyar. 2 the Finno-Ugric language of Hungary; Magyar.

Hun gar y (hung′gər ē), *n.* country in central Europe, formerly a part of the empire of Austria-Hungary. 10,314,000 pop.; 35,900 sq. mi. *Capital:* Budapest. See **Austria** for map.

hun ger (hung′gər), *n.* 1 an uncomfortable or painful feeling, especially in the stomach, or a weak condition caused by having had nothing to eat. 2 desire or need for food. 3 a strong desire; craving; longing: *a hunger for affection.* *—v.i.* 1 feel hunger; be hungry. 2 have a strong desire; long. *—v.t.* subject to hunger; starve. [Old English *hungor*]

hunger strike, refusal to eat, especially on the part of a prisoner, until certain demands are granted or as a protest against certain conditions.

hung jury, jury that cannot come to a unanimous verdict and is therefore dismissed.

hun gry (hung′grē), *adj.,* **-gri er, -gri est.** 1 feeling a desire or need for food. 2 showing hunger: *a hungry look.* 3 having a strong desire or craving; eager: *hungry for knowledge.* 4 not rich or fertile: *hungry soil.* [Old English *hungrig*] **—hun′gri ly,** *adv.* **—hun′gri ness,** *n.*

hunk (hungk), *n.* INFORMAL. a big lump or piece: *a hunk of cheese.* [< Flemish *hunke*]

hunk er (hung′kər), *v.i.* squat on one's haunches, or with the haunches brought near the heels: *hunker down in front of the TV.* *—n.* **on one's hunkers,** in a squatting position; on one's haunches. [origin uncertain]

hunk y-do ry (hung′kē dôr′ē, hung′kē dōr′ē), *adj.* SLANG. safe and sound; O.K.

hunt (hunt), *v.t.* 1 go after (wild animals, game birds, etc.) to catch or kill them for food or sport. 2 search through (a region) in pursuit of game. 3 use (horses or dogs) in the chase. 4 drive; chase; pursue. 5 try to find: *hunt a clue.* 6 **hunt down, a** hunt for until caught or killed. **b** look for until found. 7 **hunt up, a** look carefully for. **b** find by search. *—v.i.* 1 go after wild animals or game. 2 look thoroughly; search carefully: *hunt through drawers, hunt for a lost book.* *—n.* 1 act of hunting. 2 group of persons hunting together. 3 an attempt to find something; search. [Old English *huntian*]

hunt er (hun′tər), *n.* 1 person who hunts. 2 horse or dog trained for hunting. 3 person who searches eagerly for something: *a fortune hunter.*

hunt ing (hun′ting), *n.* act or sport of chasing game.

Hunt ing don shire (hun′ting dən shir, hun′ting dən shər), *n.* county in E England.

hunting ground, place or region for hunting.

Hunt ing ton (hun′ting tən), *n.* city in W West Virginia, on the Ohio River. 74,000.

Huntington Beach, city in SW California. 116,000.

hunt ress (hun′tris), *n.* woman who hunts.

hunts man (hunts′mən), *n., pl.* **-men.** 1 hunter. 2 manager of a hunt.

Hunts ville (hunts′vil), *n.* city in N Alabama. 138,000.

Hu peh or **Hu pei** (hü′pā′), *n.* province in E central China.

hur dle (hėr′dl), *n., v.,* **-dled, -dling.** *—n.* 1 barrier for people or horses to jump over in a race. 2 **hurdles,** *pl.* race in which the runners jump over hurdles. 3 obstacle, difficulty, etc. 4 frame made of sticks, used as a temporary fence, sheep pen, etc. *—v.t.* 1 jump over: *The horse hurdled both the fence and the ditch.* 2 overcome (an obstacle, difficulty, etc.). 3 enclose with a frame of sticks. *—v.i.* jump over a hurdle or other barrier. [Old English *hyrdel*] **—hur′dler,** *n.*

hur dy-gur dy (hėr′dē gėr′dē), *n., pl.* **-dies.** hand organ or street piano. [probably imitative]

hurl (hėrl), *v.t.* 1 throw with much force; fling: *The man hurled his spear at one bear, and the dogs hurled themselves at the other.* 2 throw forth (words, cries, etc.) violently; utter with vehemence: *He hurled insults at me.* *—n.* a forcible or violent throw. [Middle English *hurlen*] **—hurl′er,** *n.*

hur ly-bur ly (hėr′lē bėr′lē), *n., pl.* **-lies.** disorder and noise; commotion; tumult.

Hur on (hyu̇r′ən), *n.* 1 **Lake,** one of the five Great Lakes. 23,010 sq. mi. 2 member of a tribe of Iroquoian Indians formerly living between Lake Huron and Lake Ontario.

hur rah (hə rä′, hə rô′), *interj., n.* shout of joy, approval, etc. *—v.i.* shout hurrahs; cheer. *—v.t.* receive or encourage with shouts; cheer. Also, **hooray.**

hur ray (hə rā′), *interj., n., v.i., v.t.* hurrah.

hur ri cane (hėr′ə kān), *n.* 1 (in meteorology) a wind having a velocity of more than 75 miles per hour. 2 a tropical cyclone originating in the West Indies, usually accompanied by violent thunderstorms. 3 a sudden, violent outburst: *a hurricane of cheers.* [< Spanish *huracán* < Arawak *hurakán*]

hurricane deck, the upper deck on a riverboat, etc.

hur ried (hėr′ēd), *adj.* 1 done or made in a hurry; hasty. 2 forced to hurry. **—hur′ried ly,** *adv.*

hur ry (hėr′ē), *v.,* **-ried, -ry ing,** *n., pl.* **-ries.** *—v.t.* 1 drive, carry, send, or move quickly: *They hurried the sick child to the doctor.* 2 urge to act soon or too soon. 3 urge to great speed or to too great speed. 4 make go on or occur more quickly; hasten. *—v.i.* move or act with more than an easy or natural speed: *If you hurry, your work may be poor.* *—n.* 1 a hurried movement or action. See synonym study below. 2 need to hurry; eagerness to have quickly or do quickly. [origin uncertain]

Syn. *n.* 1 **Hurry, haste, speed** mean quickness or swiftness in action or movement. **Hurry** suggests urgency, rushing, or bustling: *In her hurry she dropped the eggs.* **Haste** suggests eager or necessary swiftness, but without really effective results: *All this haste was of no use.* **Speed** suggests calm and effective swiftness: *They did the work with speed.*

hurdle (def. 1) racers jumping hurdles

hur ry-scur ry or **hur ry-skur ry** (hėr′ē skėr′ē), *n., pl.* **-ries,** *adj., adv.* —*n.* a hurrying and confusion. —*adj.* hurried and confused. —*adv.* with hurry and confusion.

hurt (hėrt), *v.,* **hurt, hurt ing,** *n.* —*v.t.* 1 cause pain to; wound; injure: *The stone hurt her foot badly.* 2 have a bad effect on; do damage or harm to. See **injure** for synonym study. 3 give mental pain to; distress: *He hurt my feelings.* —*v.i.* 1 cause pain, harm, or damage. 2 suffer pain, harm, or damage. —*n.* 1 cut, bruise, or fracture; any wound or injury. 2 a bad effect; damage; harm. [apparently < Old French *hurter* to strike] **—hurt′er,** *n.*

hurt ful (hėrt′fəl), *adj.* causing hurt, harm, or damage; injurious. **—hurt′ful ly,** *adv.* **—hurt′ful ness,** *n.*

hur tle (hėr′tl), *v.,* **-tled, -tling,** *n.* —*v.i.* 1 dash or drive violently; rush violently; come with a crash: *The car hurtled across the road into a fence.* 2 move with a clatter; rush noisily: *The old subway train hurtled past.* —*v.t.* dash or drive violently; fling: *The impact of the crash hurtled the driver against the windshield of the car.* —*n.* act or fact of hurtling; clash. [Middle English *hurtelen* < *hurten* to hurt, in early sense "dash against"]

hus band (huz′bənd), *n.* man who has a wife; a married man. —*v.t.* 1 manage carefully; be saving of: *husband one's strength.* 2 marry. [Old English *hūsbōnda* < Scandinavian (Old Icelandic) *hūsbōndi* < *hūs* house + *bōndi* freeholder]

hus band ly (huz′bənd lē), *adj.* of, like, or befitting a husband.

hus band man (huz′bənd mən), *n., pl.* **-men.** farmer.

hus band ry (huz′bən drē), *n.* 1 farming. 2 management of one's affairs or resources. 3 careful management; thrift.

hush (hush), *v.i.* stop making a noise; become silent or quiet: *The wind has hushed.* —*v.t.* 1 make still; silence; quiet: *Hush your dog.* 2 soothe; calm.

hush up, a keep from being told; stop discussion of. b INFORMAL. be silent; hush.

—*n.* a stopping of noise; silence; quiet; stillness.

—*interj.* stop the noise! be silent! keep quiet! [Middle English *hussht* silent, originally interjection, silence!]

hush-hush (hush′hush′), *adj.* INFORMAL. secret: *a hush-hush meeting.*

hush money, money paid to keep a person from telling something.

husk (husk), *n.* 1 the dry outer covering of certain seeds or fruits. An ear of corn has a husk. 2 the dry or worthless outer covering of anything. —*v.t.* remove the husk from. [Middle English *huske*] **—husk′er,** *n.*

husk ing (hus′king), *n.* husking bee.

husking bee, U.S. a gathering of neighbors and friends to husk corn.

husk y[1] (hus′kē), *adj.,* **husk i er, husk i est,** *n., pl.* **husk ies.** —*adj.* 1 big and strong. 2 dry in the throat; hoarse; rough of voice: *a husky cough.* 3 of, like, or having husks. —*n.* INFORMAL. a big, strong person. [< *husk,* noun] **—husk′i ly,** *adv.* **—husk′i ness,** *n.*

hus ky[2] or **Hus ky** (hus′kē), *n., pl.* **-kies.** 1 Siberian husky. 2 Eskimo dog. [origin uncertain]

Huss (hus), *n.* **John,** 1369?-1415, Bohemian religious reformer and martyr.

hus sar (hù zär′), *n.* a light-armed cavalry soldier in various European armies. [< Hungarian *huszár,* originally, pirate < Old Serbian *husar* < Italian *corsaro* runner < Medieval Latin *cursarius.* Doublet of CORSAIR.]

Hus sein I (hü sān′), born 1935, king of Jordan since 1952.

Huss ite (hus′īt), *n.* follower of John Huss. —*adj.* of or having to do with John Huss or his teachings.

hus sy (huz′ē, hus′ē), *n., pl.* **-sies.** 1 a bad-mannered or pert girl. 2 a woman who flaunts her immorality. [Middle English *huswif* housewife]

hus tings (hus′tingz), *n.pl. or sing.* 1 platform or place from which speeches are made in a political campaign. 2 proceedings at an election. [< Scandinavian (Old Icelandic) *hūsthing* council < *hūs* house + *thing* assembly]

hus tle (hus′əl), *v.,* **-tled, -tling,** *n.* —*v.t.* 1 carry, send, or move quickly; hurry; bustle: *Mother hustled the baby to bed.* 2 push or shove roughly; jostle rudely: *The crowd hustled her along the street.* 3 force hurriedly or roughly: *We hustled the intruder out the door.* 4 INFORMAL. get or sell in a hurried, rough, or illegal manner: *hustle used cars, hustle stolen goods.* —*v.i.* 1 hurry; bustle. 2 rush roughly; push one's way. 3 INFORMAL go or work quickly or with tireless energy. 4 INFORMAL. get money, business, etc., in a hurried, rough, or illegal manner: *hustle on the streets to pay for drugs.* —*n.* 1 INFORMAL. tireless energy. 2 a bustling; hurry. 3 a rough pushing or shoving; rude jostling. 4 INFORMAL. business or activity, often one that is illegal; job: *make a living in the hustle of selling wigs.* 5 INFORMAL. sale, often one that is illegal: *arrested for a hustle of narcotics.* [< Dutch *hutselen* to shake] **—hus′tler,** *n.*

hut (hut), *n.* a small, roughly made house; small cabin. [< Middle French *hutte* < Middle High German *hütte*] **—hut′like′,** *adj.*

hutch (huch), *n.* 1 box or pen for small animals, such as rabbits. 2 hut. 3 box, chest, or bin. 4 cupboard with open shelves on the upper part for holding dishes, etc. [< Old French *huche* < Medieval Latin *hutica* chest]

Hutch in son (huch′in sən), *n.* **Anne,** 1591–1643, religious reformer in colonial America, born in England.

hut ment (hut′mənt), *n.* 1 hut, especially for troops. 2 accommodation in huts. 3 camp of huts.

Hut ter ite (hut′ə rīt′), *n.* member of a religious sect of Canada, Montana, and South Dakota. Hutterites practice common ownership of goods. [< Jacob *Hutter,* Austrian who founded the sect in 1528]

Hux ley (huk′slē), *n.* 1 **Aldous (Leonard),** 1894–1963, English novelist and essayist. 2 Sir **Julian Sorell,** born 1887, English biologist. 3 their grandfather, **Thomas Henry,** 1825–1895, English biologist.

Huy gens (hī′gənz), *n.* **Christian,** 1629-1695, Dutch physicist, mathematician, and astronomer.

huz za or **huz zah** (hə zä′), *interj., n., v.i., v.t.* hurrah.

Hwang ho (hwäng′hō′), *n.* Hwang Ho.

Hwang Ho (hwäng′ hō′), river in China flowing from N central China into the Yellow Sea; Yellow River. 2700 mi.

hwy., highway.

hy a cinth (hī′ə sinth), *n.* 1 plant of the lily family that grows from a bulb and has a spike of small, fragrant, bell-shaped flowers. 2 its flower. 3 a brownish or reddish-orange zircon, used as a gem; jacinth. [< Latin *hyacinthus* < Greek *hyakinthos* kind of flower or gem. Doublet of JACINTH.]

hy a cin thine (hī′ə sin′thən, hī′ə sin′thīn), *adj.* of or like the hyacinth.

Hy a des (hī′ə dēz′), *n.pl.* cluster of stars in the shape of a V in the head of the constellation Taurus. They were supposed by the ancients to be a sign of rain when they rose with the sun.

hy ae na (hī ē′nə), *n.* hyena.

hy a line (hī′ə lən, hī′ə līn), *adj.* glassy or transparent. —*n.* something glassy or transparent. [< Greek *hyalinos* < *hyalos* glass]

hyaline cartilage, a translucent bluish cartilage which forms most of the fetal skeleton and is present in joints, the nose, the trachea, etc., in adults.

hy a lite (hī′ə līt), *n.* a clear, colorless variety of opal. [< Greek *hyalos* glass]

hy a lu ron i dase (hī′ə lù ron′ə dās), *n.* enzyme that increases tissue permeability.

hy brid (hī′brid), *n.* 1 offspring of two animals or plants of different varieties, species, races, etc. The loganberry is a hybrid because it is a cross between a dewberry and the red raspberry. The mule is a hybrid of a female horse and a male donkey. 2 (in genetics) offspring of two individuals that differ in at least one gene. 3 anything of mixed origin. A word formed of parts from different languages is a hybrid. —*adj.* 1 bred from two different species, varieties, etc. A mule is a hybrid animal. 2 of mixed origin. [< Latin *hybrida*]

hy brid ism (hī′brə diz′əm), *n.* 1 production of hybrids. 2 hybrid character, nature, or condition.

hy brid i ty (hī brid′ə tē), *n.* hybrid character or condition.

hy brid ize (hī′brə dīz), *v.,* **-ized, -iz ing.** —*v.t.* cause to produce hybrids: *Botanists hybridize different kinds of plants to get new varieties.* —*v.i.* produce hybrids. **—hy′brid i za′tion,** *n.* **—hy′brid iz′er,** *n.*

hybrid vigor, heterosis.

hy da tid (hī′də tid), *n.* 1 cyst containing a clear, watery fluid, produced in man and animals by a tapeworm in the larval state. 2 the larva of a tapeworm in its encysted state. [< Greek *hydatidos* watery vesicle]

Hyde (hīd), *n.* 1 Edward. See **Clarendon.** 2 **Mr.,** the evil side of Dr. Jekyll's personality in Robert Louis Stevenson's story, *Dr. Jekyll and Mr. Hyde.*

Hyde Park, 1 park in London, England, containing fashionable drives and walks. 2 village in SE New York State, birthplace of Franklin D. Roosevelt. 3000.

Hy der a bad (hī′dər ə bad′, hī′dər ə bäd′), *n.* 1 city in S India. 1,295,000. 2 city in S Pakistan, on the Indus River. 435,000.

hydr-, *combining form.* form of **hydro-** before vowels, as in *hydrant.*

hy dra (hī′drə), *n., pl.* **-dras, -drae** (-drē). 1 any of a genus of freshwater polyps with stinging tentacles. When a hydra's body is cut into pieces, each piece forms a new individual. 2 **Hydra,** (in Greek myths) a monster with many snakelike heads, each of which was replaced by two or three heads after it was cut off. The Hydra was slain by Hercules. 3 any persistent evil. 4 **Hydra,** a southern constellation that stretches nearly one third of the way around the southern sky, seen by ancient astronomers as having the rough outline of a serpent. [< Latin < Greek, water serpent < *hydōr* water]

hy dran gea (hī drān′jə), *n.* 1 any of a genus of shrubs of the same family as the saxifrage, with large, showy clusters of small white, pink, or blue flowers. 2 the flower of any of these shrubs. [< New Latin < Greek *hydōr* water + *angeion* vessel, capsule]

hy drant (hī′drənt), *n.* a large, upright cylinder with a valve for drawing water directly from a water main; hose connection on a street, road, etc.; fireplug. Hydrants are used to get water to put out fires, wash the streets, etc.

hy drate (hī′drāt), *n., v.,* **-drat ed, -drat ing.** —*n.* any chemical compound produced when certain substances chemically unite with water in a definite weight ratio, represented in formulas as containing molecules of water. Washing soda ($Na_2CO_3 \cdot 10H_2O$) is a hydrate. —*v.i., v.t.* become or cause to become a hydrate; combine with water to form a hydrate. Blue vitriol is hydrated copper sulfate. —**hy dra′tion,** *n.*

hy drau lic (hī drô′lik), *adj.* 1 having to do with water or other liquids at rest or in motion. 2 operated by the pressure of water or other liquids in motion, especially when forced through an opening or openings: *a hydraulic press.* 3 hardening under water: *hydraulic cement.* 4 having to do with hydraulics: *hydraulic engineering, hydraulic mining.* [< Latin *hydraulicus,* ultimately < Greek *hydōr* water + *aulos* pipe] —**hy drau′li cal ly,** *adv.*

hydraulic brake, brake in which fluid under pressure operates the mechanical parts.

hy drau lics (hī drô′liks), *n.* science dealing with water and other liquids at rest or in motion, their uses in engineering, and the laws of their actions.

hy dra zine (hī′drə zēn′, hī′drə zən), *n.* a colorless, fuming, highly poisonous liquid used in organic synthesis and as a fuel for rockets. *Formula:* N_2H_4

hy dride (hī′drīd, hī′drid), *n.* compound of hydrogen with another element or radical.

hy dri od ic acid (hī′drē od′ik), a colorless, corrosive solution of hydrogen iodide in water, used as a disinfectant. *Formula:* HI

hy dro (hī′drō), *adj.* CANADIAN. hydroelectric.

hydro-, *combining form.* 1 of or having to do with water: *Hydrodynamic = having to do with the force of water.* 2 containing hydrogen: *Hydrochloric = containing hydrogen and chlorine.* Also, **hydr-,** before vowels. [< Greek < *hydōr* water]

hy dro bro mic acid (hī′drō brō′mik), a colorless, corrosive solution of hydrogen bromide in water, used in making organic compounds. *Formula:* HBr

hy dro car bon (hī′drō kär′bən), *n.* any of a class of compounds containing only hydrogen and carbon. Methane, benzene, and acetylene are hydrocarbons. Gasoline is a mixture of hydrocarbons.

hy dro ceph a lus (hī′drō sef′ə ləs), *n.* accumulation of cerebrospinal fluid within the cranium, especially in infancy, often causing great enlargement of the head.

hy dro ceph a ly (hī′drō sef′ə lē), *n.* hydrocephalus.

hy dro chlo ric acid (hī′drə klôr′ik, hī′drə klōr′ik), a clear, colorless solution of hydrogen chloride in water, that has a strong, sharp odor and is highly corrosive; muriatic acid. It is used in cleaning metals, in food processing, and in many industrial processes. *Formula:* HCl

hy dro chlo ride (hī′drə klôr′īd, hī′drə klôr′id; hī′drə klōr′īd, hī′drə klōr′id), *n.* compound of hydrochloric acid with an organic base.

hy dro cor ti sone (hī′drō kôr′tə sōn, hī′drō kôr′tə zōn), *n.* an adrenal hormone derived from cortisone, used in treating arthritis; cortisol. *Formula:* $C_{21}H_{30}O_5$

hy dro cy an ic acid (hī′drō sī an′ik), a colorless, volatile, poisonous liquid with an odor like that of bitter almonds, used in making plastics, dyes, etc.; prussic acid. *Formula:* HCN

hy dro dy nam ic (hī′drō dī nam′ik), *adj.* having to do with the force or motion of liquids, or with hydrodynamics.

hy dro dy nam ics (hī′drō dī nam′iks), *n.* branch of physics dealing with the forces that water and other liquids in motion exert.

hy dro e lec tric (hī′drō i lek′trik), *adj.* of or having to do with the generation of electricity by water power.

hy dro e lec tric i ty (hī′drō i lek′tris′ə tē), *n.* electricity produced from water power.

hy dro flu or ic acid (hī′drō flü ôr′ik, hī′drō flü or′ik), a colorless, corrosive, volatile solution of hydrogen fluoride in water, used for etching glass, as a cleaning agent, etc. *Formula:* HF

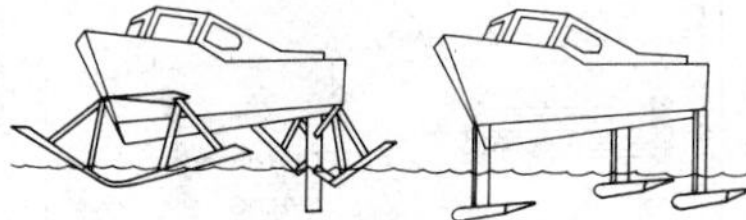

hydrofoil (defs. 1 and 2)
two types of hydrofoils

hy dro foil (hī′drə foil), *n.* 1 fin just below the water line of a boat that raises the hull out of the water at high speeds, decreasing friction and increasing the speed of the boat. 2 boat with hydrofoils.

hy dro gen (hī′drə jən), *n.* a colorless, odorless, gaseous element that burns easily and weighs less than any other element. It combines with oxygen to form water and is present in most organic compounds. *Symbol:* H; *atomic number* 1. See pages 326 and 327 for table. [< French *hydrogène* < *hydro-* + *-gène* -gen]

hy dro gen ate (hī′drə jə nāt, hī droj′ə nāt), *v.t.,* **-at ed, -at ing.** combine or treat with hydrogen. When vegetable oils are hydrogenated, they become solid fats. —**hy′dro gen a′tion,** *n.*

hydrogen bomb, bomb that uses the fusion of atoms to cause an explosion of tremendous force; H-bomb; fusion bomb. It is many times more powerful than the atomic bomb.

hydrogen bromide, a colorless, corrosive gas with a sharp odor. *Formula:* HBr

hydrogen chloride, a fuming, poisonous, colorless gas with a strong, sharp odor. *Formula:* HCl

hydrogen fluoride, a colorless, corrosive, poisonous gas which can cause severe burns. *Formula:* HF

hydrogen iodide, a colorless, corrosive gas with a suffocating odor. *Formula:* HI

hydrogen ion, a positively charged ion of hydrogen found in all acids in the hydrated form.

hat, āge, fär; let, ēqual, tėrm;
it, īce; hot, ōpen, ôrder;
oil, out; cup, pu̇t, rüle;
ch, child; ng, long; sh, she;
th, thin; ᴛʜ, then; zh, measure;

ə represents *a* in about, *e* in taken,
i in pencil, *o* in lemon, *u* in circus.

< = from, derived from, taken from.

hy drog e nous (hī droj′ə nəs), *adj.* of or containing hydrogen.

hydrogen peroxide, a colorless compound of hydrogen and oxygen; peroxide. It is used in dilute solution as an antiseptic, bleaching agent, etc. *Formula:* H_2O_2

hydrogen sulfide, a flammable, poisonous gas with an odor like that of rotten eggs, often found in mineral waters. *Formula:* H_2S

hy drog ra pher (hī drog′rə fər), *n.* an expert in hydrography.

hy dro graph ic (hī′drə graf′ik), *adj.* of or having to do with hydrography.

hy drog ra phy (hī drog′rə fē), *n.* science of the measurement and description of seas, lakes, rivers, etc., used especially in navigation and commerce.

hy droid (hī′droid), *n.* 1 the polyp form of a coelenterate as distinguished from a jellyfish. 2 any hydrozoan. —*adj.* of, having to do with, or like the hydrozoans.

hy dro log ic (hī′drə loj′ik), *adj.* of or having to do with hydrology.

hy drol o gist (hī drol′ə jist), *n.* an expert in hydrology.

hy drol o gy (hī drol′ə jē), *n.* science that deals with water and its properties, laws, geographical distribution, etc.

hy drol y sis (hī drol′ə sis), *n., pl.* **-ses** (-sēz′). chemical decomposition in which a compound is broken down and changed into other compounds by taking up the elements of water.

hy dro lyt ic (hī′drə lit′ik), *adj.* of or producing hydrolysis.

hy dro lyze (hī′drə līz), *v.t., v.i.,* **-lyzed, -lyz ing.** decompose by hydrolysis.

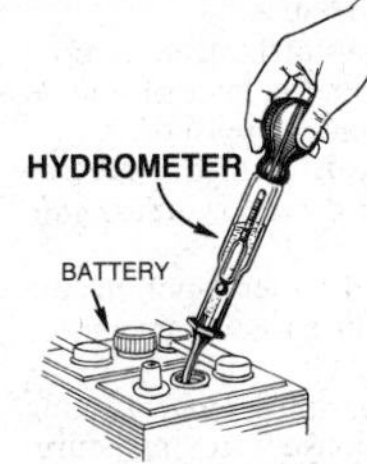

hydrometer being used to test an automobile battery. The amount that the weighted inner glass tube sinks in the liquid indicates the concentration of acid in the battery.

hy drom e ter (hī drom′ə tər), *n.* a graduated instrument for finding the specific gravities of liquids. A hydrometer is used to test the battery of an automobile.

hy dro met ric (hī′drə met′rik), *adj.* 1 of or having to do with hydrometry. 2 of or having to do with a hydrometer.

hy drom e try (hī drom′ə trē), *n.* determination of specific gravity, purity, etc., by means of a hydrometer.

hy dro ni um (hī drō′nē əm), *n.* a hydrogen ion combined with a molecule of water.

hy dro path ic (hī′drə path′ik), *adj.* of or using hydropathy.

hy drop a thy (hī drop′ə thē), *n.* the use of water in the treatment of disease; water cure.

hy dro phil ic (hī′drə fil′ik), *adj.* that readily absorbs or dissolves in water, as a gelatin.

hy dro pho bi a (hī′drə fō′bē ə), *n.* 1 rabies. 2 an abnormal fear of water.

hy dro pho bic (hī′drə fō′bik), *adj.* 1 of or having to do with hydrophobia. 2 suffering from hydrophobia. 3 having little or no ability to combine with or dissolve in water.

hy dro phone (hī′drə fōn), *n.* instrument used to detect sound under water and to determine its source and position.

hy dro phyte (hī′drə fīt), *n.* any plant that can grow only in water or very wet soil. Most algae are hydrophytes.

hy dro phyt ic (hī′drə fit′ik), *adj.* of or like a hydrophyte.

hy dro plane (hī′drə plān), *n., v.,* **-planed, -plan ing.** —*n.* 1 motorboat that glides on the surface of water. 2 seaplane. —*v.i.* 1 glide on the surface of water. 2 use or ride in a hydroplane. 3 (of a vehicle) undergo hydroplaning.

hy dro plan ing (hī′drə plā′ning), *n.* (of a vehicle) the floating or sliding of tires at certain speeds on a wet pavement, causing loss of traction for steering and braking.

hy dro pon ic (hī′drə pon′ik), *adj.* of hydroponics; produced or grown by hydroponics.

hy dro pon ics (hī′drə pon′iks), *n.* the growing of plants without soil by the use of water containing the necessary nutrients. [< *hydro-* + Greek *ponein* to labor]

hy dro qui none (hī′drō kwi nōn′, hī′drō-kwin′ōn), *n.* a white, sweetish, crystalline compound used in photographic developers and in medicine. *Formula:* $C_6H_4(OH)_2$

hy dro skim mer (hī′drō skim′ər), *n.* Hovercraft for traveling over water, with a fin along each side for piercing the water's surface.

hy dro sphere (hī′drə sfir), *n.* 1 the water portion of the earth as opposed to the lithosphere and the atmosphere. 2 the water vapor in the atmosphere and the water on the surface of the earth.

hy dro stat ic (hī′drə stat′ik), *adj.* of or having to do with hydrostatics.

hy dro stat ics (hī′drə stat′iks), *n.* branch of physics that deals with the laws of liquids at rest, and of liquids under pressure.

hy dro sul fur ous acid (hī′drō sul′fər-əs, hī′drō sul′fyər əs, hī′drō sul fyůr′əs), *adj.* hyposulfurous acid.

hy dro ther a py (hī′drō ther′ə pē), *n.* the medical treatment of disease by means of water; water cure.

hy dro trop ic (hī′drə trop′ik), *adj.* turning or bending in response to moisture. [< *hydro-* + Greek *tropos* a turning]

hy drot ro pism (hī drot′rə piz′əm), *n.* tendency of plants to turn or bend in response to moisture. Hydrotropism causes roots to grow toward water.

hy drous (hī′drəs), *adj.* containing water, usually in combination.

hy drox ide (hī drok′sīd), *n.* any compound consisting of an element or radical combined with one or more hydroxyl radicals. Hydroxides of metals are bases; those of nonmetals are acids.

hydroxide ion, a negatively charged ion found in all basic solutions.

hy drox yl (hī drok′səl), *n.* a univalent radical, —OH. It is in all hydroxides.

hydroxyl ion, hydroxide ion.

hy dro zo an (hī′drə zō′ən), *n.* any of a class of marine coelenterates including hydras and Portuguese men-of-war. —*adj.* of or belonging to this class.

hy e na (hī ē′nə), *n.* any of three species of wild, carnivorous, wolflike mammals of Africa and Asia, which feed at night, usually on carrion. Hyenas avoid contact with other animals and are noted for their terrifying yells. Also, **hyaena.** [< Latin *hyaena* < Greek *hyaina* < *hys* pig]

Hy ge ia (hī jē′ə), *n.* (in Greek myths) the goddess of health.

hy giene (hī′jēn′), *n.* science that deals with the maintenance of health; system of principles or rules for preserving or promoting health. [< French *hygiène,* ultimately < Greek *hygies* healthy]

hy gien ic (hī jē′nik, hī jen′ik, hī′jē en′ik), *adj.* 1 favorable to health; healthful; sanitary. 2 having to do with health or hygiene. —**hy gien′i cal ly,** *adv.*

hy gien ist (hī jē′nist, hī jen′ist, hī′jē nist, hī′jē ə nist), *n.* an expert in hygiene.

hygro-, *combining form.* moisture: *Hygrometer = instrument for measuring moisture.* [< Greek < *hygros* wet]

hy gro graph (hī′grə graf), *n.* instrument for recording the amount of moisture or humidity in the air.

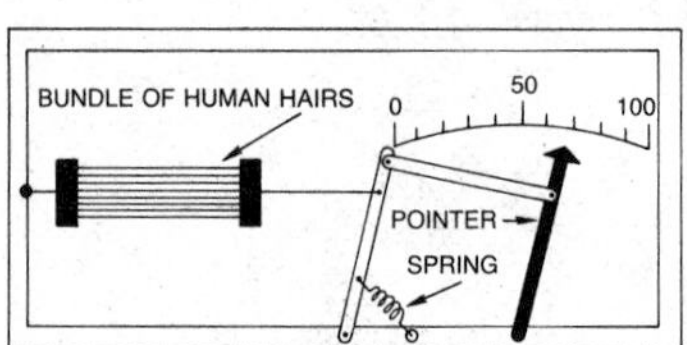

hair hygrometer—Moisture increases the length of the hairs, allowing the pointer to move to the right.

hy grom e ter (hī grom′ə tər), *n.* instrument for measuring the amount of moisture or humidity in the air.

hy gro met ric (hī′grə met′rik), *adj.* of or having to do with the measurement of moisture in the air.

hy gro scope (hī′grə skōp), *n.* instrument that shows the variations in the amount of moisture or humidity in the air.

hy gro scop ic (hī′grə skop′ik), *adj.* 1 having to do with or perceptible by the hygroscope. 2 absorbing or attracting moisture from the air.

hy ing (hī′ing), *v.* a ppr. of **hie.**

Hyk sos (hik′sos, hik′sōs), *n.pl.* the foreign rulers of Egypt from about 1750 B.C. to about 1600 B.C.

hy la (hī′lə), *n.* tree toad. [< New Latin < Greek *hylē* woods]

hy men (hī′mən), *n.* a fold of mucous membrane extending partly across the opening of the vagina, often ruptured by exercise or sexual intercourse. [< Late Latin < Greek *hymēn*]

Hy men (hī′mən), *n.* (in Greek myths) the god of marriage.

hy me ne al (hī′mə nē′əl), *adj.* having to do with marriage. —*n.* a wedding song.

hy me nop ter an (hī′mə nop′tər ən), *n.* any of an order of insects having, when winged, four membranous wings and the ovipositor of the female modified to form a stinger, and including all the social insects except the termites, noted for the complex organization of the groups or communities and caste system set up within each group. Ants, wasps, and bees belong to this order.

hy me nop te ron (hī′mə nop′tə ron′), *n., pl.* **-te ra** (-tər ə). hymenopteran.

hy me nop ter ous (hī′mə nop′tər əs), *adj.* of or belonging to the hymenopterans. [< Greek *hymenopteros* having membranous wings < *hymēn* membrane + *pteron* wing]

Hy met tus (hī met′əs), *n.* mountain in SE Greece, just E of Athens. 3370 ft.

hymn (him), *n.* 1 song in praise or honor of God. 2 any song of praise. —*v.t.* 1 praise or honor with a hymn. 2 praise or extol: *hymn the newly elected administration.* —*v.i.* sing hymns. [< Latin *hymnus* < Greek *hymnos*] —**hymn′like′,** *adj.*

hym nal (him′nəl), *n.* book of hymns.

hymn book (him′bůk′), *n.* hymnal.

hym nol o gy (him nol′ə jē), *n.* 1 study of hymns, their history, classification, etc. 2 hymns collectively.

hy oid (hī′oid), *n.* 1 the U-shaped bone at the root of the tongue in human beings. 2 a corresponding bone or series of bones in animals. —*adj.* of or having to do with this bone. [< Greek *hyoeidēs* U-shaped < *hy* upsilon (υ) + *eidos* form]

hyp., 1 hypotenuse. 2 hypothesis.

hype (hīp), *v.t.,* **hyped, hyp ing,** *n.* SLANG. —*v.t.* stimulate artificially; publicize or promote: *hype up the presidential campaign, hype a movie or a new book.* —*n.* 1 a drug addict. 2 publicity; advertisement: *The performers had lots of hype behind them.* 3 exaggeration; deception: *rely on hype to make money.* [alteration of *hypo*[2]]

hyper-, *prefix.* over; above; exceedingly; more than is normal; excessive: *Hypersensitive = exceedingly sensitive.* [< Greek]

hy per a cid i ty (hī′pər ə sid′ə tē), *n.* excessive acidity.

hy per ac tive (hī′pər ak′tiv), *adj.* overactive: *hyperactive children.*

hy per bar ic (hī′pər bar′ik), *adj.* of, at, or utilizing pressures greater than normal atmospheric pressure: *hyperbaric oxygen treatment.* [< *hyper-* + Greek *baros* weight]

hyperbaric chamber, an airtight compartment in which oxygen under pressure is forced into the tissues of a person undergoing open-heart surgery, etc.

hy per bo la (hī pėr′bə lə), *n.* a plane curve formed when a right circular cone is cut by a plane making a larger angle with the base than the side of the cone makes. See **conic section** for diagram. [< New Latin < Greek *hyperbolē* < *hyper-* + *ballein* to throw]

hy per bo le (hī pėr′bə lē), *n.* an exaggerated statement used especially as a figure of speech for rhetorical effect. EXAMPLE: Waves high as mountains broke over the reef. [< Latin < Greek *hyperbolē.* See HYPERBOLA.]

hy per bol ic (hī′pər bol′ik), *adj.* 1 of, like, or using hyperbole; exaggerated; exaggerating. 2 of, like, or having to do with hyperbolas. —**hy′per bol′i cal ly,** *adv.*

Hy per bo re an (hī′pər bôr′ē ən, hī′pər-bōr′ē ən), *n.* 1 (in Greek legends) one of a group of people living in a land of perpetual sunshine and plenty beyond the north wind. 2 **hyperborean,** inhabitant of the far north. —*adj.* **hyperborean,** of the far north; arctic; frigid.

hy per crit i cal (hī′pər krit′ə kəl), *adj.* too critical. —**hy′per crit′i cal ly,** *adv.*

Hy per i on (hī pir′ē ən), *n.* in Greek myths:

hat, āge, fär; let, ēqual, tėrm;
it, īce; hot, ōpen, ôrder;
oil, out; cup, pu̇t, rüle;
ch, child; ng, long; sh, she;
th, thin; ᴛʜ, then; zh, measure;

ə represents *a* in about, *e* in taken,
i in pencil, *o* in lemon, *u* in circus.

< = from, derived from, taken from.

1 a Titan, son of Uranus and Gaea and father of Helios. 2 Helios. 3 Apollo.

hy per me tro pi a (hī′pər mə trō′pē ə), *n.* far-sightedness; hyperopia.

hy per me trop ic (hī′pər mə trop′ik), *adj.* far-sighted; hyperopic.

hy per met ro py (hī′pər met′rə pē), *n.* hypermetropia.

hy per on (hī′pər on), *n.* a highly unstable elementary particle having a mass greater than the proton. [< *hyper-* + *(prot)on*]

hy per o pi a (hī′pər ō′pē ə), *n.* far-sightedness. [< New Latin < Greek *hyper-* + *ōps* eye]

hy per op ic (hī′pər op′ik), *adj.* far-sighted.

hy per par a site (hī′pər par′ə sīt), *n.* organism parasitic upon a parasite.

hy per sen si tive (hī′pər sen′sə tiv), *adj.* extremely sensitive. **—hy′per sen′si tive ness,** *n.*

hy per sen si tiv i ty (hī′pər sen′sə tiv′ə tē), *n.* extreme sensitiveness.

hy per son ic (hī′pər son′ik), *adj.* that moves or is able to move at a speed which is five or more times faster than the speed of sound in a given medium. In air, hypersonic speed is at least 5435 feet per second.

hy per ten sion (hī′pər ten′shən), *n.* arterial blood pressure that is abnormally high; high blood pressure.

hy per ten sive (hī′pər ten′siv), *adj.* having to do with or affected with hypertension. *—n.* person who has hypertension.

hy per thy roid (hī′pər thī′roid), *n.* 1 an excessively active thyroid gland. 2 person having such a gland. *—adj.* having to do with hyperthyroidism.

hy per thy roid ism (hī′pər thī′roi diz′əm), *n.* 1 excessive activity of the thyroid gland. 2 the abnormal condition resulting from this, characterized by a high metabolic rate, nervousness, and often an enlargement of the thyroid gland.

hy per troph ic (hī′pər trof′ik), *adj.* producing or affected with hypertrophy.

hy per tro phy (hī pėr′trə fē), *n., pl.* **-phies,** *v.,* **-phied, -phy ing.** *—n.* enlargement of a part or organ due to a diseased condition or overuse. *—v.t., v.i.* grow too big. [< Greek *hyper-* + *trophē* nourishment]

hy pha (hī′fə), *n., pl.* **-phae** (-fē). one of the long, slender, usually branched filaments which are the structural elements of the plant body of fungi. A mass of branching hyphae constitutes the mycelium. [< New Latin < Greek *hyphē* web]

hy phal (hī′fəl), *adj.* of or having to do with the hypha of a fungus.

hy phen (hī′fən), *n.* mark (-) used to join the parts of a compound word, or the parts of a word divided at the end of a line, etc. *—v.t.* hyphenate. [< Late Latin < Greek, in one, hyphen < *hypo-* under + *hen* one]

hy phen ate (hī′fə nāt), *v.t.,* **-at ed, -at ing.** join by a hyphen; write or print with a hyphen. **—hy′phen a′tion,** *n.*

hyp no sis (hip nō′sis), *n., pl.* **-ses** (-sēz′). condition resembling deep sleep, but more active, in which a person has little will of his own, and acts according to the suggestions of the person who brought about the condition. [< New Latin < Greek *hypnoun* put to sleep < *hypnos* sleep]

hyp no ther a py (hip′nə ther′ə pē), *n.* the use of hypnosis in the treatment of physical or mental disorders, as a substitute for anesthetics, etc.

hyp not ic (hip not′ik), *adj.* 1 of or having to do with hypnosis or hypnotism. 2 easily hypnotized. 3 causing sleep. *—n.* 1 drug or other means of causing sleep. 2 person who is hypnotized or easily hypnotized. **—hyp not′i cal ly,** *adv.*

hyp no tism (hip′nə tiz′əm), *n.* 1 a putting into a hypnotic state; a hypnotizing. 2 science dealing with hypnosis.

hyp no tist (hip′nə tist), *n.* person who hypnotizes.

hyp no tize (hip′nə tīz), *v.t.,* **-tized, -tiz ing.** 1 put into a hypnotic state; cause hypnosis in. 2 dominate or control by suggestion; cast a spell over. **—hyp′no tiz′a ble,** *adj.* **—hyp′no tiz′er,** *n.*

hy po[1] (hī′pō), *n.* a colorless or white crystalline salt used to treat photographic negatives and prints to keep them from fading; sodium thiosulfate. *Formula:* $Na_2S_2O_3 \cdot 5H_2O$ [short for *hyposulfite*]

hy po[2] (hī′pō), *n., v.t.* INFORMAL. *—n.* 1 hypodermic. 2 stimulus: *claiming that more inflation was the hypo to cure everything.* *—v.t.* 1 inject (a drug) by hypodermic syringe. 2 stimulate, often artificially; increase or promote: *hypo the sales of foreign cars in the U.S.A.*

hypo-, *prefix.* 1 under; beneath; below: *Hypodermic = under the skin.* 2 less than or deficient: *Hypothyroid = deficient thyroid gland.* 3 (in chemistry) indicating a compound which is less oxidized than the corresponding compound without the prefix: *Hypochlorous acid = less oxidized than chlorous acid.* [< Greek]

hy po chlo rite (hī′pə klôr′īt, hī′pə klōr′īt), *n.* salt or ester of hypochlorous acid.

hy po chlo rous acid (hī′pə klôr′əs, hī′pə klōr′əs), an unstable, weak acid existing as a yellow solution with an irritating odor, used as a bleach, disinfectant, etc. *Formula:* HClO

hy po chon dri a (hī′pə kon′drē ə), *n.* abnormal anxiety or depression over one's health, often involving imaginary illnesses accompanied by actual pains. [< Late Latin, abdomen (the supposed seat of melancholy) < Greek < *hypo-* under + *chondros* cartilage (of the breastbone)]

hy po chon dri ac (hī′pə kon′drē ak), *n.* person affected by hypochondria. *—adj.* affected by hypochondria.

hy po chon dri a cal (hī′pə kon drī′ə kəl), *adj.* hypochondriac. **—hy′po chon dri′a cal ly,** *adv.*

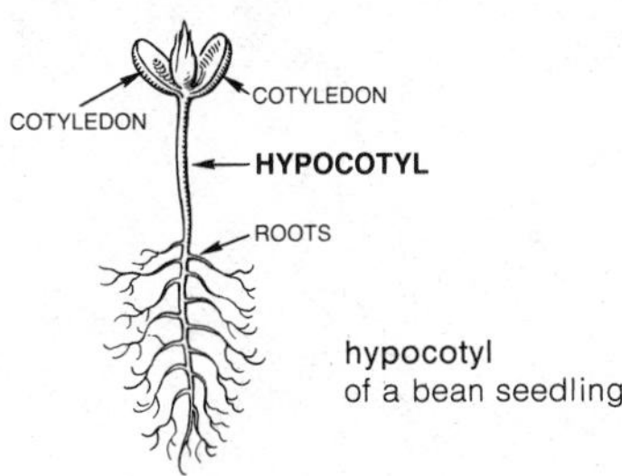

hypocotyl of a bean seedling

hy po cot yl (hī′pə kot′l), *n.* part of a plant embryo below the cotyledons, between the stem and the roots.

hy poc ri sy (hi pok′rə sē), *n., pl.* **-sies.** 1 a pretending to be very good or religious. 2 a pretending to be what one is not; pretense.

hyp o crite (hip′ə krit), *n.* 1 person who pretends to be very good or religious. 2 person who pretends to be what he is not; pretender. [< Greek *hypokritēs* actor < *hypo-* under + *kritēs* a judge]

hyp o crit i cal (hip′ə krit′ə kəl), *adj.* of or like a hypocrite; insincere. **—hyp′o crit′i cal ly,** *adv.*

hy po der mic (hī′pə dėr′mik), *adj.* 1 under the skin. 2 injected or used to inject under the skin: *The doctor used a hypodermic needle.* *—n.* 1 dose of medicine injected under the skin: *The doctor gave her a hypodermic to make her sleep.* 2 hypodermic syringe. [< Greek *hypo-* under + *derma* skin]

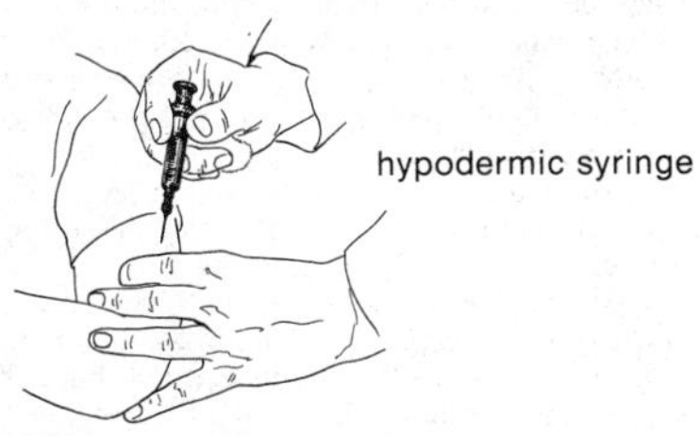
hypodermic syringe

hypodermic syringe, syringe fitted with a hollow needle, used to inject a dose of medicine under the skin.

hy po der mis (hī′pə dėr′mis), *n.* 1 layer of tissue lying under and secreting the integument of certain insects, crustaceans, and worms. 2 (in botany) the layer of cells just beneath the epidermis.

hy po gly ce mi a (hī′pō glī sē′mē ə), *n.* condition caused by an acute deficiency in the amount of glucose in the blood, usually caused by an excess of insulin.

hy po gly ce mic (hī′pō glī sē′mik), *adj.* causing or caused by a reduction of sugar content in the blood: *a hypoglycemic agent, hypoglycemic shock.*

hy po phos phite (hī′pō fos′fīt), *n.* salt of hypophosphorous acid, used in medicine as a tonic.

hy po phos pho ric acid (hī′pō fo sfôr′ik, hī′pō fo sfor′ik), a crystalline acid produced by the slow oxidation of phosphorus in moist air. *Formula:* $H_4P_2O_6$

hy po phos phor ous acid (hī′pō fos′fər əs), a colorless acid used as a reducing agent, and formerly as a nerve tonic. *Formula:* H_3PO_2

hy po phys e al (hī′pə fiz′ē əl, hī pof′ə sē′əl), *adj.* of or having to do with the hypophysis.

hy poph y sis (hī pof′ə sis), *n., pl.* **-ses** (-sēz′). pituitary gland. [< Greek, attachment underneath < *hypo-* under + *physis* a growing]

hy po pla sia (hī′pō plā′zhə), *n.* the defective or incomplete growth of an organ or tissue.

hy po plas tic (hī′pō plas′tik), *adj.* of or characterized by hypoplasia.

hy po sen si tize (hī′pō sen′sə tīz), *v.t.,*

-tized, -tiz ing. desensitize. —hy′po sen′si ti za′tion, *n.*

hy po sul fite (hī′pō sul′fīt), *n.* salt of hyposulfurous acid.

hy po sul fur ous acid (hī′pō sul′fər əs, hī′pō sul′fyər əs, hī′pō sul fyůr′əs), acid found only in solution or as salts, used as a reducing and bleaching agent; hydrosulfurous acid. *Formula:* $H_2S_2O_4$

hy po ten sion (hī′pō ten′shən), *n.* arterial blood pressure that is abnormally low; low blood pressure.

hy po ten sive (hī′pō ten′siv), *adj.* having to do with or affected with hypotension. —*n.* person who has hypotension.

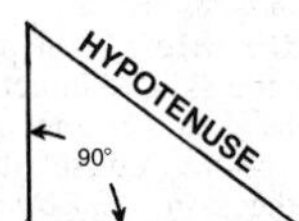

hy pot e nuse (hī pot′n üs, hī pot′n yüs), *n.* the side of a right triangle opposite the right angle. Also, **hypothenuse.** [< Latin *hypotenusa* < Greek *hypoteinousa,* present participle of *hypoteinein* subtend < *hypo-* under + *teinein* to stretch]

hy po tha lam ic (hī′pō thə lam′ik), *adj.* of or having to do with the hypothalamus.

hy po thal a mus (hī′pō thal′ə məs), *n., pl.* **-mi** (-mī). the region of the brain under the thalamus, controlling temperature, hunger, thirst, the pituitary gland, etc.

hy poth e cate[1] (hī poth′ə kāt, hi poth′ə kāt), *v.t.,* **-cat ed, -cat ing.** pledge (property, stock, etc.) to a creditor as security for a loan or debt; mortgage. [< Late Latin *hypotheca* a pledge < Greek *hypothēkē* < *hypo-* under + *tithenai* to place] **—hy poth′e ca′tion,** *n.* **—hy poth′e ca′tor,** *n.*

hy poth e cate[2] (hī poth′ə kāt, hi poth′ə kāt), *v.t.,* **-cat ed, -cat ing.** hypothesize.

hy poth e nuse (hī pot′n üs, hī pot′n yüs; hī poth′ə nüs, hī poth′ə nyüs), *n.* hypotenuse.

hy poth e sis (hī poth′ə sis), *n., pl.* **-ses** (-sēz′). 1 something assumed because it seems likely to be a true explanation. See **theory** for synonym study. 2 proposition assumed as a basis for reasoning. [< Greek < *hypo-* under + *thesis* a placing]

hy poth e size (hī poth′ə sīz), *v.,* **-sized, -siz ing.** —*v.i.* make a hypothesis. —*v.t.* assume; suppose.

hy po thet ic (hī′pə thet′ik), *adj.* hypothetical.

hy po thet i cal (hī′pə thet′ə kəl), *adj.* of or based on a hypothesis; assumed; supposed. **—hy′po thet′i cal ly,** *adv.*

hy po thy roid (hī′pō thī′roid), *n.* 1 an insufficiently active thyroid gland. 2 person having such a gland. —*adj.* having or having to do with hypothyroidism.

hy po thy roid ism (hī′pō thī′roi diz′əm), *n.* 1 abnormally decreased activity of the thyroid gland. 2 the abnormal condition resulting from this, characterized by a low metabolic rate and sluggishness, and sometimes producing cretinism in childhood.

hyp som e ter (hip som′ə tər), *n.* instrument for measuring altitudes of points on the earth's surface by determining atmospheric pressure from the boiling point of liquids. [< Greek *hypsos* height + English *-meter*]

hy rax (hī′raks), *n., pl.* **-rax es, -ra ces** (-rə sēz′). any of an order of small, timid, rabbitlike mammals of Africa and Asia; cony. [< Greek, shrew]

hys sop (his′əp), *n.* 1 a fragrant, bushy plant of the mint family, used for medicine, flavoring, etc. 2 (in the Bible) a plant whose twigs were used in certain religious ceremonies. [< Latin *hyssopus* < Greek *hyssōpos;* of Semitic origin]

hys te rec to my (his′tə rek′tə mē), *n., pl.* **-mies.** surgical removal of the uterus. [< Greek *hystera* uterus]

hys te re sis (his′tə rē′sis), *n.* a lagging of an effect behind its cause, as when a magnetic body is subjected to a varying force, or when an electric substance is subjected to a changing intensity. [< Greek *hysterein* to lag, come late < *hysteros* later]

hys ter i a (hi stir′ē ə, hi ster′ē ə), *n.* 1 unrestrained excitement or emotion. 2 a mental disorder, or neurosis, characterized by a physical disability such as paralysis, blindness, digestive upsets, etc., resulting from anxiety. [< New Latin < Greek *hystera* uterus; because originally women were thought to be the only ones affected]

hys ter ic (hi ster′ik), *adj.* hysterical. —*n.* person who is hysterical.

hys ter i cal (hi ster′ə kəl), *adj.* 1 excited or emotional. 2 showing an unnatural lack of self-control; unable to stop laughing, crying, etc. 3 of, having to do with, or affected by hysteria. 4 INFORMAL. very funny: *Isn't that picture hysterical!* **—hys ter′i cal ly,** *adv.*

hys ter ics (hi ster′iks), *n.pl.* a fit of hysterical laughing and crying.

I i

I[1] or **i** (ī), *n., pl.* **I's** or **i's.** 1 the ninth letter of the English alphabet. 2 the Roman numeral for 1.

I[2] (ī), *pron., nominative* **I,** *possessive* **my** or **mine,** *objective* **me;** *pl. nominative* **we,** *possessive* **ours** or **our,** *objective* **us;** *n., pl.* **I's.** the person who is speaking or writing. [Old English *ic*]

➤ The pronoun *I* is written with a capital letter because in the old handwritten manuscripts a small *i* was likely to be lost or to get attached to a neighboring word, and a capital letter helped keep it a distinct word.

I, iodine.

i., 1 intransitive. 2 island.

I., 1 Island. 2 Isle.

i-, *prefix.* the form of **in-**[1] before *gn,* as in *ignore.*

Ia., Iowa.

I a go (ē ä′gō), *n.* the villain in Shakespeare's play *Othello,* who deludes Othello into killing his innocent wife.

-ial, *suffix.* a form of **-al**[1], as in *adverbial, facial.*

i amb (ī′amb), *n.* an iambic foot or measure. [< Greek *iambos*]

i am bic (ī am′bik), *n.* foot of verse having two syllables, an unaccented followed by an accented. *—adj.* of or consisting of iambic feet. Much English poetry is iambic.

EXAMPLE:
"The sún | that bríef | De cém | ber dáy
Rose chéer | less ó | ver hílls | of gráy."

i am bus (ī am′bəs), *n., pl.* **-bi** (-bī), **-bus es.** iamb.

-ian, *suffix.* a form of **-an,** as in *mammalian, Italian.* [< Latin *-ianus*]

Iaşi (yäsh, yä′shē), *n.* Jassy.

ib., ibidem.

I ba dan (ē bä′dän), *n.* city in SW Nigeria. 800,000.

I ber i a (ī bir′ē ə), *n.* peninsula in SW Europe, containing Spain and Portugal.

I ber i an (ī bir′ē ən), *adj.* 1 of or having to do with Iberia or its people. 2 having to do with the Iberian race. *—n.* 1 native or inhabitant of Iberia. 2 member of a race once inhabiting a great part of southern Europe and parts of northern Africa.

ibex
about 2½ ft. high at the shoulder

i bex (ī′beks), *n., pl.* **i bex es, ib i ces** (ib′ə sēz′, ī′bə sēz′), or **i bex.** any of a genus of wild goats of mountainous regions of Europe, Asia, and Africa. The male has very large horns which curve backward. [< Latin]

ibid., ibidem.

➤ **Ibid.** is used in a footnote to refer to the work mentioned in the immediately preceding footnote.

i bi dem (i bī′dem), *adv.* LATIN. in the same place; in the same book, chapter, page, passage, etc.

i bis (ī′bis), *n., pl.* **i bis es** or **i bis.** any of various large, long-legged wading birds of warm regions having long, downward-curving bills. The ancient Egyptians regarded the ibis as sacred. [< Latin < Greek, of Egyptian origin]

ibis
about 3½ ft. long

-ible, *suffix added to verbs to form adjectives.* that can be ____ed: *Reducible = that can be reduced.* [< Old French < Latin *-ibilis*]

ibn-Sa ud (ib′ən sä üd′), *n.* **Abdul-Aziz,** 1880-1953, king of Saudi Arabia from 1932 to 1953.

I bo (ē′bō), *n., pl.* **-bo** or **-bos.** member of a west African people forming a large part of the population of Nigeria.

Ib sen (ib′sən), *n.* **Henrik,** 1828-1906, Norwegian dramatist.

iceberg

-ic, *suffix added to nouns to form adjectives.* 1 of or having to do with: *Atmospheric = of the atmosphere.* 2 having the nature of: *Heroic = having the nature of a hero.* 3 constituting or being: *Bombastic = constituting bombast.* 4 containing; made up of: *Alcoholic = containing alcohol.* 5 made by; caused by: *Volcanic = made by a volcano.* 6 like; like that of; characteristic of: *Meteoric = like a meteor.* 7 (in chemistry) indicating the presence in compounds or ions of the designated element in a higher valence than indicated by the suffix *-ous,* as in *boric, chloric, ferric.* [< French *-ique* or Latin *-icus* or Greek *-ikos*]

-ical, *suffix.* 1 *-ic,* as in *geometrical, parasitical, hysterical.* 2 *-ic* + *-al* or *-ics* + *-al,* as in *critical, musical, ethical, statistical.* [< Latin *-icalem* < *-icus* -ic + *-alem* -al[1]]

-ically, *suffix. -ic* + *-ly.* Instead of *artistic-ly* we write *artistically.* In speaking, the suffix is ordinarily pronounced in two syllables (-ik lē).

I car i an (i ker′ē ən, ī ker′ē ən), *adj.* rash; carelessly bold.

Ic ar us (ik′ər əs, ī′kər əs), *n.* (in Greek legends) the son of Daedalus. While escaping from Crete on wings that Daedalus had made, Icarus flew so high that the sun melted the wax by which his wings were attached, and he drowned in the sea.

ICBM, Intercontinental Ballistic Missile.

hat, āge, fär; let, ēqual, tėrm;
it, īce; hot, ōpen, ôrder;
oil, out; cup, pu̇t, rüle;
ch, child; ng, long; sh, she;
th, thin; TH, then; zh, measure;

ə represents *a* in about, *e* in taken, *i* in pencil, *o* in lemon, *u* in circus.

< = from, derived from, taken from.

ICC or **I.C.C.,** Interstate Commerce Commission.

ice (īs), *n., adj., v.,* **iced, ic ing.** *—n.* 1 water made solid by cold; frozen water. 2 layer or surface of ice. 3 something that looks or feels like ice. 4 U.S. a frozen dessert, usually one made of sweetened fruit juice: *raspberry ice.* 5 frosting. 6 SLANG. diamonds.

break the ice, a make a beginning; start something dangerous or difficult. **b** overcome first difficulties in talking or getting acquainted.

cut no ice, INFORMAL. have little or no effect.

on ice, a in reserve. **b** safely assured: *Our team had the game on ice.*

on thin ice, in a dangerous or difficult position.

—adj. of ice; having to do with ice.

—v.t. 1 make cool with ice; put ice in or around. 2 cover with ice. 3 turn to ice; freeze. 4 cover (cake) with frosting. *—v.i.* freeze.

[Old English *īs*] **—ice′less,** *adj.* **—ice′like′,** *adj.*

ice age, 1 glacial epoch. 2 Usually, **Ice Age.** Pleistocene.

ice bag, a waterproof bag filled with ice and applied to some part of the body.

ice berg (īs′bėrg′), *n.* a large mass of ice, detached from a glacier and floating in the sea; berg. About 90 per cent of its mass is below the surface of the water. [< Dutch *ijsberg,* literally, ice mountain]

ice boat (īs′bōt′), *n.* 1 a triangular frame on runners, fitted with sails or an engine for sailing on ice. 2 icebreaker.

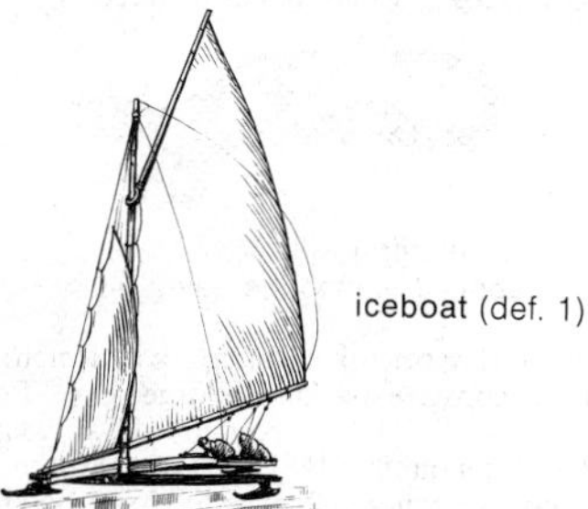

iceboat (def. 1)

ice bound (īs′bound′), *adj.* 1 held fast by ice; frozen in. 2 shut in or obstructed by ice.

ice box (īs′boks′), *n.* 1 refrigerator. 2 an insulated box in which food is kept cool with ice.

ice break er (īs′brā′kər), *n.* 1 a strong boat used to break a channel through ice; iceboat. 2 anything that helps overcome first difficulties in talking or getting acquainted.

ice cap (īs′kap′), *n.* 1 a permanent covering

I

of ice over large areas of land in the polar regions, sloping down on all sides from an elevated center. 2 glacier, usually one covering a large area, that flows in all directions from its center.

ice-cold (īs′kōld′), *adj.* cold as ice.

ice cream, a frozen dessert made of cream or custard sweetened and flavored.

ice cube, a small, usually square piece of ice used for keeping drinks cool.

iced (īst), *adj.* 1 cooled with ice. 2 covered with ice. 3 covered with icing.

ice field, a large sheet of ice floating in the sea.

ice floe, a large sheet of floating ice.

ice hockey, hockey (def. 1).

ice house (īs′hous′), *n., pl.* **-hous es** (-hou′ziz). building where ice is stored and kept from melting.

Ice land (īs′lənd), *n.* island country in the N Atlantic between Greenland and Norway, formerly a Danish possession. Iceland has been independent since 1944. 210,000 pop.; 39,800 sq. mi. *Capital:* Reykjavik.

Ice land er (īs′lan′dər, īs′lən dər), *n.* native or inhabitant of Iceland.

Ice lan dic (īs lan′dik), *adj.* of or having to do with Iceland, its people, or their language. —*n.* the Scandinavian language of Iceland.

Iceland moss, lichen of arctic regions, used as a food, in medicine, etc.

Iceland spar, a transparent variety of calcite, used extensively for optical purposes.

ice man (īs′man′), *n., pl.* **-men.** man who sells, delivers, or handles ice.

ice pack, 1 a large area of masses of ice floating in the sea. 2 bag containing ice for application to the body.

ice pick, a sharp-pointed hand tool for breaking up ice.

ice sheet, a broad, thick sheet of ice covering a very large area for a long time.

ice skate, a metal runner attached to a shoe for skating on ice.

ice-skate (īs′skāt′), *v.i.,* **-skat ed, -skat ing.** skate on ice.

ice skater, person who ice-skates.

ice water, water cooled with ice.

ichneumon (def. 1)
about 3 ft. long including the tail

ich neu mon (ik nü′mən, ik nyü′mən), *n.* 1 mongoose, especially a large, gray, Egyptian species that resembles a weasel. 2 ichneumon fly. [< Greek *ichneumōn,* literally, searcher (supposedly for crocodile's eggs), ultimately < *ichnos* track]

ichneumon fly, any of a family of wasplike insects that do not sting and whose larvae are internal parasites of caterpillars and other insects.

i chor (ī′kôr, ī′kər), *n.* (in Greek myths) the fluid supposed to flow like blood in the veins of the gods. [< Greek *ichōr*]

ich thy o log i cal (ik′thē ə loj′ə kəl), *adj.* of or having to do with ichthyology.

ich thy ol o gist (ik′thē ol′ə jist), *n.* an expert in ichthyology.

ich thy ol o gy (ik′thē ol′ə jē), *n.* branch of zoology dealing with fishes. [< Greek *ichthys* fish + English *-logy*]

ich thy or nis (ik′thē ôr′nis), *n.* any of a genus of extinct gull-like birds with vertebrae resembling those of fishes. [< Greek *ichthys* fish + *ornis* bird]

ichthyosaur—from 4 to 40 ft. long

ich thy o saur (ik′thē ə sôr), *n.* any of an order of extinct fishlike marine reptiles with a long beak, paddlelike flippers, and a tail with a large fin. [< Greek *ichthys* fish + *sauros* lizard]

i ci cle (ī′si kəl), *n.* a pointed, hanging stick of ice formed by the freezing of dripping water. [Middle English *isykle* < Old English *īs* ice + *gicel* icicle]

ic ing (ī′sing), *n.* frosting.

ICJ or **I.C.J.,** International Court of Justice.

i con (ī′kon), *n., pl.* **i cons, i co nes** (ī′kə nēz′). 1 picture or image of Christ, an angel, or a saint, usually painted on wood or ivory, and venerated as sacred in the Eastern Church. 2 picture; image. Also, **ikon, eikon.** [< Latin < Greek *eikōn*]

i con ic (ī kon′ik), *adj.* of or having to do with an icon; like an icon.

i con o clasm (ī kon′ə klaz′əm), *n.* belief or practice of iconoclasts.

i con o clast (ī kon′ə klast), *n.* 1 person who attacks cherished beliefs or institutions which he thinks are wrong or foolish. 2 person who is opposed to worshiping images or who breaks or destroys them. [< Medieval Greek *eikonoklastēs* < Greek *eikōn* image + *klan* to break]

i con o clas tic (ī kon′ə klas′tik), *adj.* of or having to do with iconoclasts or iconoclasm. —**i con′o clas′ti cal ly,** *adv.*

i con o scope (ī kon′ə skōp), *n.* an early kind of cathode-ray tube used in television cameras. It made television transmission possible.

i co sa he dron (ī′kō sə hē′drən), *n., pl.* **-drons, -dra** (-drə). a solid figure having twenty faces. [< Greek *eikosaedron* < *eikosi* twenty + *hedra* seat, base]

-ics, *suffix.* 1 body of facts or principles; science or field of study, as in *optics, aesthetics, metaphysics, genetics.* 2 system or method of action; art or practice, as in *tactics, gymnastics, ceramics.* [originally plural of *-ic*]

ic ter us (ik′tər əs), *n.* jaundice. [< Latin]

ic tus (ik′təs), *n., pl.* **-tus es** or **-tus.** rhythmical or metrical stress. [< Latin < *icere* to hit]

i cy (ī′sē), *adj.,* **i ci er, i ci est.** 1 like ice; very cold or slippery. 2 having much ice; covered with ice. 3 of ice. 4 without warm feeling; cold and unfriendly. —**i′ci ly,** *adv.* —**i′ci ness,** *n.*

id (id), *n.* (in psychoanalysis) the source of energy of the unconscious, associated with primitive, instinctual drives for pleasure and gratification. [< Latin, it]

I'd (īd), 1 I should. 2 I would. 3 I had.

-id, *suffix.* variant of **-ide.**

id., idem.

Id., Idaho.

I da (ī′də), *n.* **Mount,** 1 mountain in NW Asia Minor, overlooking the site of Troy and the Aegean Sea. 5750 ft. 2 an ancient name of Mount Psiloriti.

Ida., Idaho.

I da ho (ī′də hō), *n.* one of the western states of the United States. 713,000 pop.; 83,600 sq. mi. *Capital:* Boise. *Abbrev.:* Id. or Ida. —**I′da ho′an,** *n., adj.*

I.D. card, identity card.

-ide, *suffix.* compound of, as in *oxide, chloride, sulfide.* Also, **-id.** [< French]

i de a (ī dē′ə), *n.* 1 picture or belief in the mind; mental image: *a child's idea of happiness.* See synonym study below. 2 thought, fancy, or opinion: *I had no idea that work at high school was so hard.* 3 point or purpose: *The idea of a vacation is to get a rest.* 4 notion of something to be done; plan of action; intention: *It's a good idea, if you can carry it out.* [< Greek < *idein* to see] —**i de′a less,** *adj.*

Syn. 1 **Idea, notion, thought** mean something understood or formed in the mind. **Idea,** the general word, applies to something existing in the mind as the result of understanding, thinking, imagining, etc.: *Learn to express your ideas clearly.* **Notion** applies to an idea not clearly or completely formed or understood: *I have only a notion of what you mean.* **Thought** applies to an idea formed by reflection or reasoning, rather than by the imagination: *Tell me your thoughts on this proposal.*

➤ **idea.** With a dependent verb, the idiom is *idea of* plus a gerund: *They got the happy idea of climbing Sugarloaf Hill.* Not: *They got the happy idea to climb Sugarloaf Hill.*

i de al (ī dē′əl), *n.* 1 a perfect type; model to be imitated; what one would wish to be: *Religion holds up high ideals for us to follow.* 2 an ideal end; goal. —*adj.* 1 just as one would wish; perfect: *A warm, sunny day is ideal for a picnic.* 2 existing only in thought; imaginary: *A point without length, breadth, or thickness is an ideal object.* —**i de′al less,** *adj.*

ideal gas, a hypothetical gas which conforms exactly to the laws that apply to real gases.

i de al ism (ī dē′ə liz′əm), *n.* 1 an acting according to one's ideals of what ought to be, regardless of circumstances or of the approval or disapproval of others; a cherishing of fine ideals. 2 a neglecting practical matters in following ideals; not being practical. 3 (in philosophy) the belief that all our knowledge is a knowledge of ideas and that it is impossible to know whether or not there really is a world of objects on which our ideas are based. Idealism is opposed to materialism. 4 (in art or literature) the representation of imagined types rather than of exact likenesses of people, instances, or situations.

i de al ist (ī dē′ə list), *n.* 1 person who has high ideals and acts according to them. 2 person who neglects practical matters in following ideals. 3 adherent of idealism in philosophy, art, or literature.

i de al is tic (ī′dē ə lis′tik, ī dē′ə lis′tik), *adj.* 1 having high ideals and acting according to them. 2 forgetting or neglecting practical matters in trying to follow one's ideals; impractical. 3 of idealism or idealists. —**i de′al is′ti cal ly,** *adv.*

i de al ize (ī dē′ə līz), *v.,* **-ized, -iz ing.** —*v.t.* make ideal; think of or represent as perfect rather than as is actually true: *She idealized her older sister and thought that everything she did was right.* —*v.i.* imagine or

hat, āge, fär; let, ēqual, tėrm;
it, īce; hot, ōpen, ôrder;
oil, out; cup, pu̇t, rüle;
ch, child; ng, long; sh, she;
th, thin; ᴛʜ, then; zh, measure;

ə represents *a* in about, *e* in taken, *i* in pencil, *o* in lemon, *u* in circus.

< = from, derived from, taken from.

form an ideal or ideals. **—i de′al i za′tion,** *n.* **—i de′al iz′er,** *n.*

i de al ly (ī dē′ə lē), *adv.* 1 according to an ideal; perfectly. 2 only as an idea or theory; not really.

i de ate (ī dē′āt), *v.,* **-at ed, -at ing.** *—v.t.* form the idea of; imagine; conceive. *—v.i.* form ideas; think. **i′de a′tion,** *n.*

i de a tion al (ī′dē ā′shə nəl), *adj.* having to do with the formation of ideas.

i dée fixe (ē dā′fēks′), *pl.* ***i dées fixes*** (ē-dā′fēks′). FRENCH. a fixed idea; obsession.

i dem (ī′dem, id′em), *pron., adj.* LATIN. the same as previously given or mentioned.

i den ti cal (ī den′tə kəl), *adj.* 1 the same: *Both events happened on the identical day.* See **same** for synonym study. 2 exactly alike: *The two new pennies were identical.* [< Medieval Latin *identicus* < Latin *idem* same] **—i den′ti cal ly,** *adv.* **—i den′ti-cal ness,** *n.*

identical equation, identity.

identical twins, twins of the same sex and physical appearance coming from a single fertilized egg cell rather than from two egg cells.

i den ti fi ca tion (ī den′tə fə kā′shən), *n.* 1 an identifying. 2 a being identified. 3 something used to identify a person or thing: *She offered her driver's license as identification.*

i den ti fy (ī den′tə fī), *v.t.,* **-fied, -fy ing.** 1 recognize as being, or show to be, a particular person or thing; prove to be the same: *He identified the wallet as his by telling what it contained.* 2 make the same; treat as the same: *The good king identified his people's well-being with his own.* 3 connect closely; link; associate: *She identified herself with the movement for peace.* **—i den′ti fi′a ble,** *adj.* **—i den′ti fi′a bly,** *adv.* **—i den′ti fi′er,** *n.*

i den ti ty (ī den′tə tē), *n., pl.* **-ties.** 1 a being oneself or itself, and not another; who or what one is; individuality: *The writer concealed her identity by signing her stories with a pen name.* 2 a being identical; exact likeness; sameness: *The identity of the two crimes led the police to think that the same person committed them.* 3 state or fact of being the same one: *The museum established the identity of the painting with one described in an old document.* 4 identity element. 5 (in algebra) an equation that is satisfied by any number that replaces the letter for which the equation is defined; identical equation. [< Late Latin *identitatem,* ultimately < Latin *idem* same]

identity card, card issued to a person to prove his identity.

identity element, (in mathematics) an element that does not change any other element on which it operates; identity. The identity element for addition is 0. EXAMPLE: 28 + 0 = 28. The identity element for multiplication is 1. EXAMPLE: 28 × 1 = 28.

id e o gram (id′ē ə gram, ī′dē ə gram), *n.* ideograph.

id e o graph (id′ē ə graf, ī′dē ə graf), *n.* a graphic symbol that represents a thing or an idea directly, without representing the sounds of the word for the thing or idea. Most Egyptian hieroglyphics and some Chinese characters are ideographs.

id e o graph ic (id′ē ə graf′ik, ī′dē ə-graf′ik), *adj.* of, having to do with, or like an ideograph.

i de o log i cal (ī′dē ə loj′ə kəl, id′ē ə loj′ə-kəl), *adj.* having to do with ideology. **—i′de o log′i cal ly,** *adv.*

i de ol o gist (ī′dē ol′ə jist, id′ē ol′ə jist), *n.* 1 an expert in ideology. 2 person occupied with ideas. 3 visionary; theorist.

i de o logue (ī dē′ə lôg, ī dē′ə log), *n.* person occupied with ideas.

i de ol o gy (ī′dē ol′ə jē, id′ē ol′ə jē), *n., pl,* **-gies.** 1 set of doctrines or body of opinions of a person, class, or group. 2 the combined doctrines, assertions, and intentions of a social or political movement: *Communist ideology.* 3 abstract speculation, especially theorizing or speculation of a visionary or unpractical nature. 4 science of the origin and nature of ideas.

ides (īdz), *n. pl. or sing.* (in the ancient Roman calendar) the 15th day of March, May, July, and October, and the 13th day of the other months. [< Latin *Idus*]

id i o cy (id′ē ə sē), *n., pl.* **-cies.** 1 a being an idiot. 2 great stupidity. 3 a very stupid or foolish action, remark, etc.

id i om (id′ē əm), *n.* 1 phrase or expression whose meaning cannot be understood from the ordinary meanings of the words in it: *"Give in" is an English idiom meaning "yield."* 2 the language or dialect of a particular area or group: *the idiom of the French Canadians.* 3 a people's way of expressing themselves: *It is often hard to translate English into the French idiom.* See **language** for synonym study. 4 individual manner of expression in music, art, etc. [< Greek *idiōma* one's own manner of speaking < *idios* one's own]

id i o mat ic (id′ē ə mat′ik), *adj.* 1 containing an idiom; having or using idioms. 2 showing the individual character of a language; characteristic of a particular language. **—id′i o mat′i cal ly,** *adv.*

id i o syn cra sy (id′ē ō sing′krə sē), *n., pl.* **-sies.** 1 a personal peculiarity of taste, behavior, opinion, etc. 2 (in medicine) a constitutional peculiarity that causes an unusual reaction to a drug, treatment, etc. [< Greek *idiosynkrasia* < *idios* one's own + *synkrasis* temperament]

id i o syn crat ic (id′ē ō sin krat′ik), *adj.* of, having to do with, or caused by idiosyncrasy. **—id′i o syn crat′i cal ly,** *adv.*

id i ot (id′ē ət), *n.* 1 person born with such slight mental capacities that he can never learn to read or count; person who does not develop beyond a mental age of three years. 2 a very stupid or foolish person. *—adj.* idiotic. [< Latin *idiota* < Greek *idiōtēs* ignoramus, layman, (originally) private person, individual < *idios* one's own]

id i ot ic (id′ē ot′ik), *adj.* of or like an idiot; very stupid or foolish. **—id′i ot′i cal ly,** *adv.*

i dle (ī′dl), *adj.,* **i dler, i dlest,** *v.,* **i dled, i dling.** *—adj.* 1 doing nothing; not busy; not working: *idle hands.* 2 fond of doing nothing; not willing to work; lazy. See synonym study below. 3 useless; worthless: *He wasted his time in idle pleasures.* 4 without any good reason, cause, or foundation: *idle fears, idle rumors.* *—v.i.* 1 be idle; do nothing. 2 move or saunter idly. 3 run without transmitting power. The motor of a car idles when out of gear and running slowly. *—v.t.* 1 spend or waste (time). 2 cause (a person or thing) to be idle; take out of work or use. [Old English *īdel*] **—i′dle ness,** *n.* **—i′dly,** *adv.*

Syn. *adj.* 2 **Idle, lazy, indolent** mean not active or working: **Idle** means not willing to work at the moment, and often implies no blame: *They like to be idle on Sundays.* **Lazy** regularly implies blame, for it means not liking to work, and not industrious when at work: *Lazy people are seldom successful.* **Indolent** means by nature or habit fond of ease and opposed to work or activity: *Too much idleness sometimes makes one indolent.*

i dler (ī′dlər), *n.* 1 a lazy person. 2 device allowing a motor to idle.

idol (def. 1) Mayan idol

i dol (ī′dl), *n.* 1 image or other object worshiped as a god. 2 (in the Bible) a false god. 3 person or thing worshiped or loved very much; object of extreme devotion. [< Latin *idolum* < Greek *eidōlon* image < *eidos* form]

i dol a ter (ī dol′ə tər), *n.* 1 person who worships idols. 2 admirer; adorer.

i dol a tress (ī dol′ə tris), *n.* a woman idolater.

i dol a trous (ī dol′ə trəs), *adj.* 1 worshiping idols. 2 having to do with idolatry. 3 blindly adoring. **—i dol′a trous ly,** *adv.* **—i dol′a trous ness,** *n.*

i dol a try (ī dol′ə trē), *n., pl.* **-tries.** 1 worship of idols. 2 worship of a person or thing; extreme devotion. [< Old French *idolatrie* < Greek *eidōlolatreia* < *eidōlon* image + *latreia* worship]

i dol ize (ī′dl īz), *v.t.,* **-ized, -iz ing.** 1 love or admire very much; be extremely or excessively devoted to. 2 worship as an idol; make an idol of. **—i′dol i za′tion,** *n.* **—i′dol-iz′er,** *n.*

Id u mae a or **Id u me a** (id′yü mē′ə, ī′dyü mē′ə), *n.* Edom.

i dyll or **i dyl** (ī′dl), *n.* 1 a short poem or piece of prose describing some simple and charming scene or event, especially one connected with country life. 2 a simple and charming scene, event, or experience: *Idylls of the King.* [< Latin *idyllium* < Greek *eidyllion,* diminutive of *eidos* form]

i dyl lic (ī dil′ik), *adj.* suitable for an idyll; simple and charming. **—i dyl′li cal ly,** *adv.*

-ie, *suffix.* 1 little: *Dearie = little dear. Birdie = little bird.* 2 used to show kind feeling or intimacy, as in *auntie, Annie.* [variant of *-y*[2]]

i.e., that is; that is to say; namely. [for Latin *id est*]

➤ **i.e.** is seldom used except in reference works. Ordinarily *that is* is used instead.

-ier, *suffix.* person occupied or concerned with: *Financier = person occupied or con-*

cerned with finance. [< French < Latin *-arius*]

if (if), *conj.* 1 supposing that; on condition that; in case: *Come if you can.* 2 whether: *I wonder if he will go.* 3 although; even though: *It was a welcome if unexpected holiday.* —*n.* condition or supposition. [Old English *gif*]

if fy (if′ē), *adj.,* **-fi er, -fi est.** INFORMAL. conditional; questionable; doubtful. [< *if* + *-y*[1]]

If ni (ēf′nē), *n.* former Spanish province in NW Africa, now part of Morocco.

igloo

ig loo (ig′lü), *n., pl.* **-loos.** a dome-shaped hut used by Eskimos, often built of blocks of hard snow. [< Eskimo *igdlu* house]

Ig na tius Loyola (ig nā′shəs). See **Loyola.**

ig ne ous (ig′nē əs), *adj.* 1 of or having to do with fire. 2 produced by solidification from a molten state. Granite is an igneous rock. [< Latin *igneus* < *ignis* fire]

ig nis fat u us (ig′nis fach′ü əs), *pl.* **ig nes fat u i** (ig′nēz fach′ü ī). will-o'-the-wisp. [< New Latin, literally, foolish fire]

ig nite (ig nīt′), *v.,* **-nit ed, -nit ing.** —*v.t.* 1 set on fire: *She ignited the heap of rubbish.* See **kindle** for synonym study. 2 make intensely hot; cause to glow with heat. —*v.i.* take fire; begin to burn: *Gasoline ignites easily.* [< Latin *ignitum* fired, kindled < *ignis* fire] —**ig nit′er,** *n.*

ig ni tion (ig nish′ən), *n.* 1 a setting on fire. 2 a catching on fire. 3 apparatus for igniting the fuel vapor in the cylinders of an internal-combustion engine. 4 any chemical or mechanical device used to ignite a rocket propellant or a fuel mixture in a jet engine.

ignition coil, a device for converting low voltage into high voltage electricity; transformer.

ig no ble (ig nō′bəl), *adj.* 1 without honor; disgraceful; base: *To betray a friend is ignoble.* 2 not of noble birth or position; humble. [< Latin *ignobilis* < *in-* not + *nobilis* noble] —**ig no′ble ness,** *n.* —**ig no′bly,** *adv.*

ig no min i ous (ig′nə min′ē əs), *adj.* 1 shameful; disgraceful; dishonorable: *an ignominious defeat in warfare.* 2 contemptible. 3 lowering one's dignity; humiliating. —**ig′no min′i ous ly,** *adv.* —**ig′no min′i ous ness,** *n.*

ig no min y (ig′nə min′ē), *n., pl.* **-min ies.** 1 public shame and disgrace; dishonor. See **disgrace** for synonym study. 2 shameful action or conduct. [< Latin *ignominia* < *in-* not + *nominis* name]

ig no ra mus (ig′nə rā′məs, ig′nə ram′əs), *n.* an ignorant person. [< Latin, we do not know]

ig nor ance (ig′nər əns), *n.* a being ignorant; lack of knowledge.

ig nor ant (ig′nər ənt), *adj.* 1 knowing little or nothing; without knowledge. See synonym study below. 2 caused by or showing lack of knowledge: *Saying that the earth is flat is an ignorant remark.* 3 uninformed; unaware: *He was ignorant of the fact that his house had been burned.* —**ig′nor ant ly,** *adv.*

Syn. 1 **Ignorant, illiterate, uneducated** mean without knowledge. **Ignorant** means without general knowledge, or without knowledge of some subject: *People who live in the city are often ignorant of farm life.* **Illiterate** means unable to read and write: *There are many illiterate people in some underdeveloped countries.* **Uneducated** means without systematic training or learning, in schools or from books: *He was an uneducated but intelligent man.*

ig nore (ig nôr′, ig nōr′), *v.t.,* **-nored, -nor ing.** pay no attention to; disregard. [< Latin *ignorare* not know < *ignarus* unaware < *in-* not + *gnarus* aware] —**ig nor′er,** *n.*

I gua çú River (ē′gwä sü′), Iguassú River.

i gua na (i gwä′nə), *n.* any of a genus of large tropical American lizards having spiny crests along their backs. [< Spanish < Arawak]

I guas sú River (ē′gwä sü′), river flowing across S Brazil into the Paraná River. 380 mi. Also, **Iguaçú River.**

IGY, International Geophysical Year.

IHS, abbreviation or monogram for the name of Jesus. It is a Latin rendering of the first three letters of the name of Jesus in Greek.

IJs sel meer (ī′səl mār′), *n.* lake in NW Netherlands, formed by extensive diking of the Zuider Zee. 465 sq. mi.

i kon (ī′kon), *n.* icon.

il-[1], *prefix.* the form of **in-**[1] before *l,* as in *illegal, illegible,* etc.

il-[2], *prefix.* the form of **in-**[2] before *l,* as in *illuminate.*

il e i tis (il′ē ī′tis), *n.* inflammation of the ileum.

il e um (il′ē əm), *n.* the lowest part of the small intestine. [< Latin, groin]

i lex (ī′leks), *n.* 1 holly. 2 holm. [< Latin]

il i ac (il′ē ak), *adj.* 1 of, having to do with, or near the ilium. 2 of or having to do with the ileum.

Il i ad (il′ē əd), *n.* a Greek epic poem about the siege of Troy, attributed to Homer.

Il i on (il′ē ən), *n.* Ilium.

il i um (il′ē əm), *n., pl.* **il i a** (il′ē ə). the broad upper portion of the hipbone. [< Latin, groin]

Il i um (il′ē əm), *n.* ancient Troy.

ilk (ilk), *n.* class; kind; sort: *gamblers and other men of that ilk.* [Old English *ilca* same]

ill (il), *adj.,* **worse, worst,** *n., adv.* —*adj.* 1 in poor health; having some disease; not well; sick: *ill with a fever.* 2 bad; evil; harmful: *do a person an ill deed.* 3 unfavorable; unfortunate: *an ill wind.* 4 unkind; harsh; cruel. 5 not good; defective; imperfect; faulty: *ill manners.* 6 **ill at ease,** uncomfortable.

—*n.* 1 sickness; disease. 2 evil; harm; trouble: *Poverty is an ill.* 3 something unfavorable or unkind: *I can think no ill of her.* —*adv.* 1 badly; harmfully: *His strength was ill used in bullying other children.* 2 unfavorably; unfortunately: *fare ill.* 3 in an unkind manner; harshly; cruelly: *He speaks ill of his former friend.* 4 with trouble or difficulty; scarcely: *You can ill afford to waste your money.* 5 improperly; unskillfully.

[< Scandinavian (Old Icelandic) *illr*]

I'll (īl), 1 I shall. 2 I will.

ill., 1 illustrated. 2 illustration.

Ill., Illinois.

ill-ad vised (il′əd vīzd′), *adj.* acting or done without enough thought; unwise.

ill-ad vis ed ly (il′əd vī′zid lē), *adv.* in an ill-advised manner; unwisely.

Il lam pu (ē yäm′pü), *n.* mountain of the Andes, in W Bolivia. 21,275 ft.

ill-bred (il′bred′), *adj.* badly brought up; impolite; rude.

ill-con sid ered (il′kən sid′ərd), *adj.* not well considered; unwise; unsuitable.

ill-dis posed (il′dis pōzd′), *adj.* unfriendly; unfavorable.

il le gal (i lē′gəl), *adj.* not lawful; against the law; forbidden by law. —**il le′gal ly,** *adv.*

iguana
about 5 ft. long

il le gal i ty (il′ē gal′ə tē), *n., pl.* **-ties.** 1 a being illegal; unlawfulness. 2 an illegal act.

il leg i bil i ty (i lej′ə bil′ə tē), *n.* illegible quality or condition.

il leg i ble (i lej′ə bəl), *adj.* very hard or impossible to read; not plain enough to read: *illegible handwriting.* —**il leg′i ble ness,** *n.* —**il leg′i bly,** *adv.*

il le git i ma cy (il′i jit′ə mə sē), *n., pl.* **-cies.** fact or condition of being illegitimate.

il le git i mate (il′i jit′ə mit), *adj.* 1 not according to the law or the rules. 2 born of parents who are not married to each other; bastard. 3 not logical; not according to good usage; improper. —**il′le git′i mate ly,** *adv.*

ill-fat ed (il′fā′tid), *adj.* 1 sure to have a bad fate or end. 2 bringing bad luck; unlucky.

ill-fa vored (il′fā′vərd), *adj.* 1 not pleasant to look at; ugly. 2 unpleasant; offensive.

ill feeling, suspicious dislike; mistrust.

ill-found ed (il′foun′did), *adj.* without a good reason or sound basis: *an ill-founded argument.*

ill-got ten (il′got′n), *adj.* acquired by evil or unfair means; dishonestly obtained.

ill-hu mored (il′hyü′mərd, il′yü′mərd), *adj.* cross; unpleasant; sullen. —**ill′-hu′mored ly,** *adv.*

il lib er al (i lib′ər əl), *adj.* 1 not liberal; narrow-minded; prejudiced. 2 stingy; miserly. —**il lib′er al ly,** *adv.*

il lib e ral i ty (i lib′ə ral′ə tē), *n.* a being illiberal.

il lic it (i lis′it), *adj.* not permitted by law; forbidden. —**il lic′it ly,** *adv.* —**il lic′it ness,** *n.* ➤ See **elicit** for usage note.

il lim it a bil i ty (i lim′ə tə bil′ə tē), *n.* a being illimitable.

il lim it a ble (i lim′ə tə bəl), *adj.* without limit; boundless; infinite. —**il lim′it a ble ness,** *n.* —**il lim′it a bly,** *adv.*

Il li nois (il′ə noi′, il′ə noiz′), *n.* 1 one of the north central states of the United States. 11,114,000 pop.; 56,400 sq. mi. *Capital:* Springfield. *Abbrev.:* Ill. 2 member of an American Indian tribe formerly living between the Mississippi and Wabash rivers, and in parts of Iowa and Missouri. —**Il′li nois′an,** *n., adj.*

il lit er a cy (i lit′ər ə sē), *n., pl.* **-cies.** 1 inability to read and write. 2 lack of education; lack of cultural knowledge. 3 error in speaking or writing, caused by a lack of education or knowledge.

hat, āge, fär; let, ēqual, tėrm;
it, īce; hot, ōpen, ôrder;
oil, out; cup, pu̇t, rüle;
ch, child; ng, long; sh, she;
th, thin; ᴛʜ, then; zh, measure;

ə represents *a* in about, *e* in taken, *i* in pencil, *o* in lemon, *u* in circus.

< = from, derived from, taken from.

il lit er ate (i lit′ər it), *adj.* 1 unable to read and write: *People who have never gone to school are usually illiterate.* See **ignorant** for synonym study. 2 showing a lack of education; not cultured: *He writes in a very illiterate way.* —*n.* 1 person who is unable to read and write. 2 an uneducated person. **—il lit′er ate ly,** *adv.* **—il lit′er ate ness,** *n.*

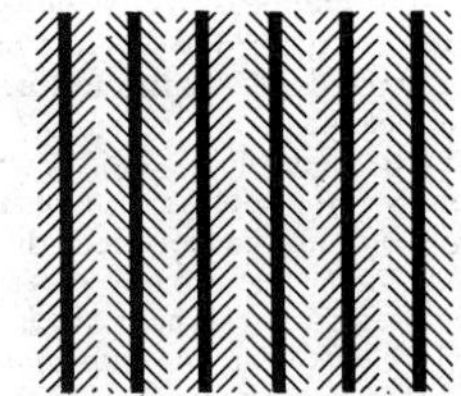
illusion (def. 2)—an optical illusion. The parallel vertical lines appear to go apart and come together because of the slanted lines.

ill-man nered (il′man′ərd), *adj.* having or showing bad manners; impolite; rude. **—ill′-man′nered ly,** *adv.*

ill-na tured (il′nā′chərd), *adj.* cross; disagreeable. **—ill′-na′tured ly,** *adv.*

ill ness (il′nis), *n.* an abnormal, unhealthy condition; disease; sickness.

il log i cal (i loj′ə kəl), *adj.* 1 contrary to the principles of sound reasoning; not logical. 2 not reasonable; foolish: *an illogical fear.* **—il log′i cal ly,** *adv.* **—il log′i cal ness,** *n.*

ill-spent (il′spent′), *adj.* spent badly; wasted; misspent.

ill-starred (il′stärd′), *adj.* unlucky; unfortunate.

ill-suit ed (il′sü′tid), *adj.* poorly suited; unsuitable.

ill-tem pered (il′tem′pərd), *adj.* having or showing a bad temper; cross. **—ill′-tem′pered ly,** *adv.*

ill-timed (il′tīmd′), *adj.* coming at a bad time; inappropriate.

ill-treat (il′trēt′), *v.t.* treat badly or cruelly; do harm to; abuse.

ill-treatment (il′trēt′mənt), *n.* bad or cruel treatment.

il lume (i lüm′), *v.t.,* **-lumed, -lum ing.** illuminate.

il lu mi nance (i lü′mə nəns), *n.* illumination (def. 2).

il lu mi nant (i lü′mə nənt), *n.* something that gives light, such as a lamp.

il lu mi nate (i lü′mə nāt), *v.t.,* **-nat ed, -nat ing.** 1 light up; make bright: *The room was illuminated by four large lamps.* 2 make clear; explain: *Our teacher could illuminate almost any subject we studied.* 3 decorate with lights: *The streets were illuminated for the celebration.* 4 decorate with gold, colors, pictures, and designs. The letters and pages in some old books and manuscripts were illuminated. 5 enlighten; inform; instruct. [< Latin *illuminatum* lit up < *in-* in + *lumen* light] **—il lu′mi na′tor,** *n.*

il lu mi na tion (i lü′mə nā′shən), *n.* 1 an illuminating; a lighting up; a making bright. 2 amount of light per unit area of a surface, measured in lumens; illuminance. 3 a making clear; explanation. 4 decoration with many lights. 5 decoration of letters and pages in books and manuscripts with gold, colors, pictures, and designs. 6 enlightenment.

il lu mi na tive (i lü′mə nā′tiv), *adj.* illuminating; tending to illuminate.

il lu mine (i lü′mən), *v.t.,* **-mined, -min ing.** make bright; illuminate.

illus., 1 illustrated. 2 illustration.

ill-us age (il′yü′sij, il′yü′zij), *n.* bad, cruel, or unfair treatment.

ill-use (*v.* il′yüz′; *n.* il′yüs′), *v.,* **-used, -us ing,** *n.* —*v.t.* treat badly, cruelly, or unfairly. —*n.* bad, cruel, or unfair treatment.

il lu sion (i lü′zhən), *n.* 1 appearance or feeling that misleads because it is not real; thing that deceives by giving a false idea. See synonym study below. 2 a false impression or perception: *an optical illusion.* 3 a false notion or belief: *Many people have the illusion that wealth is the chief cause of happiness.* 4 a delicate silk net or gauze, often used for veils and over wedding gowns. [< Latin *illusionem* < *illudere* mock < *in-* at + *ludere* play]

Syn. 1 Illusion, delusion mean something mistakenly or falsely believed to be true or real. **Illusion** applies to something appearing to be real or true, but actually not existing or being quite different from what it seems: *Good motion pictures create an illusion of reality.* **Delusion** applies to a false and often harmful belief about something that does exist: *The old woman had the delusion that the butcher was always trying to cheat her.*

➤ **Illusion, allusion** are sometimes confused. An *illusion* is a misleading appearance: *an illusion of wealth.* An *allusion* is an indirect reference or slight mention: *She made allusions to several recent novels.*

il lu sion ar y (i lü′zhə ner′ē), *adj.* characterized by or like an illusion.

il lu sion ist (i lü′zhə nist), *n.* person who produces illusions; conjurer.

il lu sive (i lü′siv), *adj.* illusory. **—il lu′sive ly,** *adv.* **—il lu′sive ness,** *n.*

il lu sor y (i lü′sər ē), *adj.* due to an illusion; misleading; deceptive. **—il lu′sor i ly,** *adv.* **—il lu′sor i ness,** *n.*

illust., 1 illustrated. 2 illustration.

il lus trate (il′ə strāt, i lus′trāt), *v.t.,* **-trat ed, -trat ing.** 1 make clear or explain by stories, examples, comparisons, etc.: *A model of a pump may be used to illustrate the action of the heart in sending blood around the body.* 2 provide with pictures, diagrams, maps, etc., that explain or decorate: *This book is well illustrated.* [< Latin *illustratum* illuminated < *in-* in + *lustrare* to light]

il lus tra tion (il′ə strā′shən), *n.* 1 picture, diagram, map, etc., used to explain or decorate something. 2 story, example, comparison, etc., used to make clear or explain something: *An apple cut into four equal pieces is a good illustration of what 1/4 means.* 3 act or process of illustrating.

il lus tra tive (i lus′trə tiv, il′ə strā′tiv), *adj.* illustrating; used to illustrate; helping to explain: *A good teacher uses many illustrative examples.* **—il lus′tra tive ly,** *adv.*

il lus tra tor (il′ə strā′tər), *n.* 1 artist who makes pictures to be used as illustrations. 2 person or thing that illustrates.

illumination (def. 5) illuminated letter P from a manuscript of the 1300's

il lus tri ous (i lus′trē əs), *adj.* 1 very famous; great; outstanding. 2 bringing or conferring glory; glorious. [< Latin *illustris* lighted up, bright < *in-* in + *lustrum* lighting] **—il lus′tri ous ly,** *adv.* **—il lus′tri ous ness,** *n.*

ill will, unkind or unfriendly feeling; dislike; spite.

ill-wish er (il′wish′ər), *n.* person who wishes ill to another.

il ly (il′ē, il′lē), *adv.* badly; ill.

Il lyr i a (i lir′ē ə), *n.* ancient country in the region east of the Adriatic. **—Il lyr′i an,** *adj., n.*

il men ite (il′mə nīt), *n.* a luminous black mineral consisting of iron, titanium, and oxygen. *Formula:* $FeTiO_3$ [< *Ilmen* Mountains in the Urals, where it was first discovered]

ILS, instrument landing system.

I'm (īm), I am.

im-[1], *prefix.* the form of **in-**[1] before *b, m, p,* as in *imbalance, immoral, impatient.*

im-[2], *prefix.* the form of **in-**[2] before *b, m, p,* as in *imbibe, immure, impart.*

im age (im′ij), *n., v.,* **-aged, -ag ing.** —*n.* 1 likeness or copy: *I saw my image in the mirror. She is almost the exact image of her mother.* 2 likeness made of stone, wood, or some other material; statue: *The ancient Greeks and Romans worshiped images of their gods.* 3 picture in the mind; idea. 4 a comparison, description, or figure of speech that helps the mind to form forceful or beautiful pictures. Poetry often contains images. 5 impression that a person, group, or organization presents to the public. 6 the optical reproduction of an object produced by reflection in a mirror, or refraction through a lens or small hole, etc. 7 a television picture. —*v.t.* 1 make or form an image of. 2 reflect as a mirror does. 3 picture in one's mind; imagine. 4 describe with images. 5 symbolize; typify. [< Old French < Latin *imago*]

im age ry (im′ij rē), *n., pl.* **-ries.** 1 pictures formed in the mind; things imagined. 2 comparisons, descriptions, and figures of speech that help the mind to form forceful or beautiful pictures. 3 images; statues.

i mag i na ble (i maj′ə nə bəl), *adj.* that can be imagined; possible. **—i mag′i na bly,** *adv.*

i mag i nar y (i maj′ə ner′ē), *adj., n., pl.* **-nar ies.** —*adj.* 1 existing only in the imagination; not real: *Ghosts are imaginary. The equator is an imaginary circle around the earth.* 2 of or having to do with the even root of a negative number or any expression involving such a root. $\sqrt{-1}$, $3 + \sqrt{-15}$, $\sqrt{-4} = 2\sqrt{-1}$ are imaginary numbers or expressions. —*n.* an imaginary number or expression. **—i mag′i nar′i ly,** *adv.* **—i mag′i nar′i ness,** *n.*

i mag i na tion (i maj′ə nā′shən), *n.*

1 power of forming pictures or images in the mind of things not present to the senses. 2 ability to create new things or ideas or to combine old ones in new forms. See synonym study below. 3 thing imagined; creation of the mind; fancy.

Syn. 2 **Imagination, fancy** mean the ability to form new pictures of things in the mind. **Imagination** applies to the ability to create believable or realistic pictures of things that never existed or happened: *His fascinating characters are the product of a fertile imagination.* **Fancy** applies to the ability to make unbelievable or fantastic pictures, by inventing them or by putting together in unrealistic ways things from reality: *Many comic strips are products of fancy.*

i mag i na tive (i maj′ə nə tiv, i maj′ə-nā′tiv), *adj.* 1 full of imagination; showing imagination: *Fairy tales are imaginative.* 2 having a good imagination; able to imagine well; fond of imagining. 3 of imagination. **—i mag′i na tive ly,** *adv.* **—i mag′i na-tive ness,** *n.*

i mag ine (i maj′ən), *v.t.,* **-ined, -in ing.** 1 picture in one's mind; form an image or idea of. See synonym study below. 2 suppose; guess: *I cannot imagine what you mean.* 3 think; believe: *I imagined someone was watching me.* [< Latin *imaginari* < *imago* image]

Syn. 1 **Imagine, conceive** mean to form an idea of something in the mind. **Imagine** means to form a clear and definite picture of something: *The girl likes to imagine herself a doctor.* **Conceive** means to bring an idea into existence and give it an outline, pattern, or shape: *The Wright brothers conceived the design of the first successful motor-powered airplane.*

im ag ism (im′ə jiz′əm), *n.* movement in poetry of the early 1900's which advocated the use of clear and precise imagery and opposed symbolism and conventional metrical rhythm.

im ag ist (im′ə jist), *n.* poet who practices imagism. Most imagists use free verse. *—adj.* having to do with imagists or imagism.

im ag is tic (im′ə jis′tik), *adj.* imagist.

i ma go (i mā′gō), *n., pl.* **i ma gos, i mag i-nes** (i maj′ə nēz′). insect in the final adult, especially winged, stage. [< Latin, image]

i mam (i mäm′), *n.* 1 a Moslem priest. 2 a Moslem leader, chief, etc. [< Arabic *imām*]

im bal ance (im bal′əns), *n.* lack of balance.

im be cile (im′bə səl), *n.* 1 person born with such limited mental capacities that he can be trained to do only very simple tasks and will probably never learn to read; person who does not develop beyond a mental age of three to eight years. 2 a very stupid or foolish person. *—adj.* 1 weak in the mind; lacking normal intelligence. 2 very stupid or foolish. [< Latin *imbecillus* weak < *in-* without + *bacillus* staff] **—im′be cile ly,** *adv.*

im be cil ic (im′bə sil′ik), *adj.* imbecile.

im be cil i ty (im′bə sil′ə tē), *n., pl.* **-ties.** 1 a being an imbecile. 2 great stupidity. 3 a very stupid or foolish action, remark, etc.

im bed (im bed′), *v.t.,* **-bed ded, -bed ding.** embed.

im bibe (im bīb′), *v.,* **-bibed, -bib ing.** *—v.t.* 1 drink in; drink. See **drink** for synonym study. 2 absorb: *The roots of a plant imbibe moisture from the earth.* 3 take into one's mind: *A child often imbibes superstitions that last all his life.* *—v.i.* drink. [< Latin *imbibere* < *in-* in + *bibere* to drink] **—im bib′er,** *n.*

im bi bi tion (im′bə bish′ən), *n.* act of imbibing; absorption.

im bri cate (*v.* im′brə kāt; *adj.* im′brə kit, im′brə kāt), *v.,* **-cat ed, -cat ing,** *adj.* *—v.t., v.i.,* overlap as tiles or shingles do. *—adj.* like the pattern of overlapping tiles. [< Latin *imbricatum* covered with tiles < *imbrex* hollow tile] **—im′bri cate ly,** *adv.* **—im′bri-ca′tion,** *n.*

im bro glio (im brō′lyō), *n., pl.* **-glios.** 1 a complicated or difficult situation. 2 a complicated misunderstanding or disagreement. 3 a confused heap. [< Italian]

im brue (im brü′), *v.t.,* **-brued, -bru ing.** wet; stain: *His sword was imbrued with blood.* [< Old French *embreuver* give to drink]

im bue (im byü′), *v.t.,* **-bued, -bu ing.** 1 fill the mind of; inspire: *The parents imbued their children with the ambition to succeed.* 2 fill with moisture or color; saturate or dye. [< Latin *imbuere*]

imit., 1 imitation. 2 imitative.

im i ta ble (im′ə tə bəl), *adj.* that can be imitated.

im i tate (im′ə tāt), *v.t.,* **-tat ed, -tat ing.** 1 try to be like or act like; follow the example of: *The little boy imitated his older brother.* 2 make or do something like; copy: *A parrot imitates the sounds it hears.* 3 act like: *She amused the class by imitating a baby, an old woman, and a bear.* 4 be like; look like; resemble: *wood painted to imitate stone.* [< Latin *imitatum* imitated, related to *imago* image]

im i ta tion (im′ə tā′shən), *n.* 1 an imitating: *We learn many things by imitation.* 2 thing that imitates something else; likeness; copy: *Give as good an imitation as you can of a rooster crowing.* 3 **in imitation of,** imitating; in order to be like or look like. *—adj.* made to look like something better; not real: *imitation pearls.*

im i ta tive (im′ə tā′tiv), *adj.* 1 fond of imitating; likely to imitate others: *Monkeys are imitative.* 2 reproducing more or less closely the appearance, character, sound, etc., of something: *"Bang" and "whiz" are imitative words.* 3 not real; counterfeit. **—im′i-ta′tive ly,** *adv.* **—im′i ta′tive ness,** *n.*

im i ta tor (im′ə tā′tər), *n.* person who imitates.

im mac u late (i mak′yə lit), *adj.* 1 without a spot or stain; absolutely clean. 2 without fault or errors. 3 without sin; pure. [< Latin *immaculatus* < *in-* not + *macula* spot] **—im mac′u late ly,** *adv.* **—im mac′u-late ness,** *n.*

Immaculate Conception, doctrine of the Roman Catholic Church that the Virgin Mary was conceived free of original sin.

im ma nence (im′ə nəns), *n.* condition of being immanent.

im ma nen cy (im′ə nən sē), *n.* immanence.

im ma nent (im′ə nənt), *adj.* 1 remaining within; inherent. 2 in the mind; subjective. [< Latin *immanentem* < *in-* in + *manere* to stay] **—im′ma nent ly,** *adv.*

Im man u el (i man′yü əl), *n.* Christ. Also, **Emmanuel.**

im ma ter i al (im′ə tir′ē əl), *adj.* 1 not important; insignificant. 2 not material; spiritual rather than physical. **—im′ma ter′i al-ly,** *adv.* **—im′ma ter′i al ness,** *n.*

im ma ture (im′ə chůr′, im′ə tůr′, im′ə-tyůr′), *adj.* not mature; undeveloped. **—im′ma ture′ly,** *adv.* **—im′ma ture′-ness,** *n.*

im ma tu ri ty (im′ə chůr′ə tē, im′ə tůr′ə-tē, im′ə tyůr′ə tē), *n.* immature condition or quality.

im meas ur a ble (i mezh′ər ə bəl, i mā′-zhər ə bəl), *adj.* too vast to be measured; very great; boundless. **—im meas′ur a ble-ness,** *n.* **—im meas′ur a bly,** *adv.*

im me di a cy (i mē′dē ə sē), *n., pl.* **-cies.** 1 a being immediate. 2 **immediacies,** *pl.* immediate needs.

im me di ate (i mē′dē it), *adj.* 1 coming at once; done without delay: *an immediate reply.* 2 with nothing in between; direct: *immediate contact.* See **direct** for synonym study. 3 closest; nearest; next: *my immediate neighbor.* 4 close; near: *the immediate future.* 5 having to do with the present; current: *our immediate plans.* [< Late Latin *immediatus* < Latin *in-* not + *medius* in the middle] **—im me′di ate ness,** *n.*

immediate constituent, any of the two or three largest components of a sentence, phrase, or word. EXAMPLE: the immediate constituents of *ungentlemanly* are *un-* and *gentlemanly* (not *ungentle* and *manly,* nor *ungentleman* and *-ly*).

im me di ate ly (i mē′dē it lē), *adv.* 1 at once; without delay: *I answered her letter immediately.* See synonym study below. 2 with nothing in between; directly.

Syn. 1 **Immediately, instantly, presently** mean with little or no delay. **Immediately** implies little delay: *My biology class comes immediately after my English class.* **Instantly** implies no delay: *The driver was killed instantly.* **Presently** implies some delay: *I will do the dishes presently, but I want to finish this story first.*

im med i ca ble (i med′ə kə bəl), *adj.* that cannot be healed; incurable.

im me mo ri al (im′ə môr′ē əl, im′ə mōr′ē-əl), *adj.* extending back beyond the bounds of memory; ancient beyond record or knowledge; extremely old. **—im′me mo′ri al ly,** *adv.*

im mense (i mens′), *adj.* 1 extremely large; huge; vast: *An ocean is an immense body of water.* See **huge** for synonym study. 2 INFORMAL. very good; fine; excellent. [< Latin *immensum* < *in-* not + *mensum* measured] **—im mense′ness,** *n.*

im mense ly (i mens′lē), *adv.* INFORMAL. very greatly; hugely.

im men si ty (i men′sə tē), *n., pl.* **-ties.** 1 very great size or extent; vastness. 2 infinite space or existence; infinity. 3 something which is immense.

im men sur a ble (i men′shər ə bəl), *adj.* immeasurable.

im merge (i mėrj′), *v.,* **-merged, -merg ing.** *—v.t.* immerse. *—v.i.* plunge or dip oneself into a liquid; sink.

im merse (i mėrs′), *v.t.,* **-mersed, -mers ing.** 1 dip or lower into a liquid until covered by it. See **dip** for synonym study. 2 baptize by dipping (a person) completely under water. 3 involve deeply; absorb: *immersed in business, immersed in debts.* [< Latin *immersum* plunged in < *in-* in + *mergere* to plunge]

im mer sion (i mėr′zhən, i mėr′shən), *n.* 1 an immersing. 2 a being immersed. 3 baptism by dipping a person completely under water.

im mi grant (im′ə grənt), *n.* person who comes into a foreign country or region to live there: *Canada has many immigrants from Europe.* —*adj.* immigrating.

im mi grate (im′ə grāt), *v.i.*, **-grat ed, -grat ing.** come into a foreign country or region to live there. ➤ See **emigrate** for usage note.

im mi gra tion (im′ə grā′shən), *n.* 1 a coming into a foreign country or region to live there: *There has been immigration to America from all the countries of Europe.* 2 the persons who immigrate; immigrants: *The immigration of 1956 included many people from Hungary.*

im mi nence (im′ə nəns), *n.* 1 a being imminent. 2 thing that is imminent, especially some evil or danger.

im mi nen cy (im′ə nən sē), *n.* imminence.

im mi nent (im′ə nənt), *adj.* likely to happen soon; about to occur: *The black clouds showed that a storm was imminent.* See synonym study below. [< Latin *imminentem* overhanging, threatening] **—im′mi nent ly,** *adv.*

Syn. Imminent, impending mean likely to happen soon. **Imminent** suggests being likely to happen any minute without further warning: *Lyndon Johnson was unaware that his succession to the Presidency was imminent.* **Impending** suggests hanging over one, often indefinitely, and keeping one in suspense: *For weeks I have had a feeling of impending disaster.* ➤ See **eminent** for usage note.

im mis ci bil i ty (i mis′ə bil′ə tē), *n.* quality of being immiscible.

im mis ci ble (i mis′ə bəl), *adj.* incapable of being mixed: *Water and oil are immiscible.* **—im mis′ci bly,** *adv.*

im mit i ga ble (i mit′ə gə bəl), *adj.* that cannot be softened or mitigated. **—im mit′i ga ble ness,** *n.* **—im mit′i ga bly,** *adv.*

im mo bile (i mō′bəl, i mō′bēl), *adj.* 1 not movable; firmly fixed. 2 not moving; not changing; motionless.

im mo bil i ty (im′ō bil′ə tē), *n.* a being immobile.

im mo bi lize (i mō′bə līz), *v.t.*, **-lized, -liz ing.** make immobile. **—im mo′bi li za′tion,** *n.*

im mod er a cy (i mod′ər ə sē), *n.*, *pl.* **-cies.** lack of moderation; excess.

im mod er ate (i mod′ər it), *adj.* not moderate; extreme or excessive: *loud and immoderate laughter.* **—im mod′er ate ly,** *adv.* **—im mod′er ate ness,** *n.* **—im mod′e ra′tion,** *n.*

im mod est (i mod′ist), *adj.* 1 not modest; bold and rude. 2 indecent; improper. **—im mod′est ly,** *adv.*

im mod es ty (i mod′ə stē), *n.* 1 lack of modesty; boldness and rudeness. 2 lack of decency; improper behavior.

im mo late (im′ə lāt), *v.t.*, **-lat ed, -lat ing.** 1 kill as a sacrifice. 2 offer in sacrifice; sacrifice. [< Latin *immolatum* sacrificed, (originally) sprinkled with sacrificial meal < *in-* on + *mola* sacrificial meal] **—im′mo la′tion,** *n.* **—im′mo la′tor,** *n.*

im mo ral (i môr′əl, i mor′əl), *adj.* 1 morally wrong; wicked: *Stealing is immoral.* 2 lewd; unchaste. **—im mo′ral ly,** *adv.*

im mo ral ist (i môr′ə list, i mor′ə list), *n.* person who advocates or accepts immorality.

im mo ral i ty (im′ə ral′ə tē), *n.*, *pl.* **-ties.** 1 wickedness; wrongdoing; vice. 2 lewdness; unchastity. 3 an immoral act or practice.

im mor tal (i môr′tl), *adj.* 1 living forever; never dying; everlasting. 2 of or having to do with immortal beings or immortality; divine. 3 remembered or famous forever. —*n.* 1 an immortal being. 2 **immortals,** *pl.* the gods of ancient Greece and Rome. 3 person remembered or famous forever. **—im mor′tal ly,** *adv.*

im mor tal i ty (im′ôr tal′ə tē), *n.* 1 life without death; a living forever. 2 fame that lasts forever.

im mor tal ize (i môr′tl īz), *v.t.*, **-ized, -iz ing.** 1 make immortal. 2 cause to be remembered or famous forever. **—im mor′tal i za′tion,** *n.* **—im mor′tal iz′er,** *n.*

im mor telle (im′ôr tel′), *n.* everlasting (def. 2). [< French, literally, immortal]

im mov a bil i ty (i mü′və bil′ə tē), *n.* a being immovable.

im mov a ble (i mü′və bəl), *adj.* 1 that cannot be moved; firmly fixed: *immovable mountains.* 2 not moving or changing; motionless. 3 firm; steadfast; unyielding: *an immovable purpose.* 4 unfeeling; impassive. —*n.* **immovables,** *pl.* land, buildings, and other property that cannot be carried from one place to another. **—im mov′a ble ness,** *n.* **—im mov′a bly,** *adv.*

im mune (i myün′), *adj.* 1 protected from disease, poison, etc.; having immunity: *Vaccination makes a person practically immune to polio.* 2 free from; exempt: *Nobody is immune from criticism.* —*n.* an immune person or animal. [< Latin *immunis,* originally, free from obligation < *in-* not + *munia* duties, services]

immune serum, serum in which antibodies to a particular disease are present.

im mu ni ty (i myü′nə tē), *n.*, *pl.* **-ties.** 1 resistance to disease, poison, etc.: *One attack of measles usually gives a person immunity to that disease.* 2 freedom; exemption: *The law gives schools and churches immunity from taxation.* See **exemption** for synonym study.

im mu nize (im′yə nīz), *v.t.*, **-nized, -niz ing.** give immunity to; make immune: *Vaccination immunizes people against smallpox.* **—im′mu ni za′tion,** *n.*

im mu no log ic (i myü′nə loj′ik), *adj.* immunological.

im mu no log i cal (i myü′nə loj′ə kəl), *adj.* of or having to do with immunology.

im mu nol o gist (im′yə nol′ə jist), *n.* an expert in immunology.

im mu nol o gy (im′yə nol′ə jē), *n.* science dealing with the nature and causes of immunity from diseases.

im mu no sup pres sive (i myü′nō sə pres′iv), *adj.* suppressing immunity: *an immunosuppressive drug.*

im mure (i myůr′), *v.t.*, **-mured, -mur ing.** 1 shut up within walls; put into prison; confine. 2 build up or entomb in a wall. [< Medieval Latin *immurare* < Latin *in-* in + *murus* wall] **—im mure′ment,** *n.*

im mu ta bil i ty (i myü′tə bil′ə tē), *n.* a being immutable.

im mu ta ble (i myü′tə bəl), *adj.* never changing; unchangeable. **—im mu′ta ble ness,** *n.* **—im mu′ta bly,** *adv.*

imp (imp), *n.* 1 a young or small devil; little demon. 2 a mischievous child. [Old English *impe* a shoot, graft]

imp., 1 imperative. 2 imperfect. 3 imperial. 4 import. 5 imprimatur.

im pact (im′pakt), *n.* 1 a striking (of one thing against another); collision. 2 a forceful or dramatic effect: *the impact of automation on society.* —*v.t.* 1 drive or press closely or firmly into something; pack in. 2 come upon; hit; reach: *The capsule impacted the moon.* [< Latin *impactum* struck against < *in-* on + *pangere* to strike] **—im pac′tion,** *n.*

hat, āge, fär; let, ēqual, tėrm;
it, īce; hot, ōpen, ôrder;
oil, out; cup, pu̇t, rüle;
ch, child; ng, long; sh, she;
th, thin; ᴛʜ, then; zh, measure;

ə represents *a* in about, *e* in taken, *i* in pencil, *o* in lemon, *u* in circus.

< = from, derived from, taken from.

im pact ed (im pak′tid), *adj.* 1 firmly wedged in place. 2 (of a tooth) wedged between the jawbone and another tooth.

im pair (im per′, im par′), *v.t.* make worse; damage; harm; weaken: *Poor food impaired her health.* See **injure** for synonym study. [< Old French *empeirer,* ultimately < Latin *in-* + *pejor* worse] **—im pair′er,** *n.* **—im pair′ment,** *n.*

im pale (im pāl′), *v.t.*, **-paled, -pal ing.** 1 pierce through with something pointed; fasten upon something pointed: *The dead butterflies were impaled on pins stuck in a sheet of cork.* 2 torture or punish by thrusting upon a pointed stake. [< Medieval Latin *impalare* < Latin *in-* on + *palus* stake] **—im pale′ment,** *n.*

im pal pa bil i ty (im pal′pə bil′ə tē), *n.* a being impalpable.

im pal pa ble (im pal′pə bəl), *adj.* 1 that cannot be felt by touching; intangible: *Sunbeams and shadows are impalpable.* 2 very hard to understand; that cannot be grasped by the mind: *impalpable distinctions.* **—im pal′pa bly,** *adv.*

im pan el (im pan′l), *v.t.*, **-eled, -el ing** or **-elled, -el ling.** 1 put on a list for duty on a jury. 2 select (a jury) from such a list. Also, **empanel.**

im par a dise (im par′ə dīs), *v.t.*, **-dised, -dis ing.** put in or as if in paradise; make supremely happy.

im part (im pärt′), *v.t.* 1 give a part or share of; give: *The furnishings imparted an air of newness to the old house.* 2 communicate; tell: *I will impart a secret to you.* See **communicate** for synonym study. [< Latin *impartire* < *in-* in + *partem* part] **—im part′ment,** *n.*

im par tial (im pär′shəl), *adj.* showing no more favor to one side than to the other; fair; just. See **fair**[1] for synonym study. **—im par′tial ly,** *adv.*

im par ti al i ty (im′pär shē al′ə tē), *n.* fairness; justice.

im pass a bil i ty (im pas′ə bil′ə tē), *n.* a being impassable.

im pass a ble (im pas′ə bəl), *adj.* not passable; so that one cannot go through, across, or along: *Snow and ice made the road impassable.* **—im pass′a ble ness,** *n.* **—im pass′a bly,** *adv.*

im passe (im pas′, im′pas), *n.* 1 position from which there is no escape; deadlock. 2 road or way closed at one end. [< French]

im pas si bil i ty (im pas′ə bil′ə tē), *n.* a being impassible.

im pas si ble (im pas′ə bəl), *adj.* 1 unable to suffer or feel pain. 2 that cannot be harmed. 3 without feeling or emotion; impassive. [< Latin *impassibilis,* ultimately

< *in-* not + *pati* suffer] **—im pas′si bly,** *adv.*

im pas sioned (im pash′ənd), *adj.* full of strong feeling; stirring; rousing: *The candidate made an impassioned speech.*

im pas sive (im pas′iv), *adj.* 1 without feeling or emotion; unmoved: *The Indians trained themselves to endure pain with impassive faces.* 2 not feeling pain or injury; insensible. **—im pas′sive ly,** *adv.* **—im pas′sive ness,** *n.*

im pas siv i ty (im′pa siv′ə tē), *n.* a being impassive.

im pas to (im pä′stō), *n., pl.* **-tos.** 1 technique in painting in which the paint is thickly applied, often with a palette knife. 2 paint thus applied. [< Italian]

im pa tience (im pā′shəns), *n.* 1 lack of patience; being impatient. 2 uneasiness and eagerness; restlessness.

im pa ti ens (im pā′shē enz), *n.* any of a genus of annual or perennial plants, which includes the balsam, with pods that burst open and eject the seeds, and irregular flowers in which the calyx and corolla are colored alike; jewelweed; touch-me-not. [< New Latin *Impatiens,* the genus name < Latin *impatiens* impatient]

im pa tient (im pā′shənt), *adj.* 1 not patient; not willing to put up with delay, opposition, pain, bother, etc.: *She is impatient with her little sister.* 2 uneasy and eager; restless: *The horses are impatient to start the race.* 3 showing lack of patience; cross: *an impatient answer.* 4 **impatient of,** unwilling to endure; not liking or wanting. **—im pa′tient ly,** *adv.* **—im pa′tient ness,** *n.*

im peach (im pēch′), *v.t.* 1 accuse (a public official) of wrong conduct during office before a competent tribunal: *The judge was impeached for taking a bribe.* 2 charge with wrongdoing; accuse. 3 cast doubt on; call in question: *impeach a person's honor.* [< Old French *empechier* hinder < Late Latin *impedicare* < Latin *in-* on + *pedica* shackle] **—im peach′a ble,** *adj.* **—im peach′ment,** *n.*

im pearl (im pėrl′), *v.t.* 1 form into pearllike drops. 2 adorn with pearls or pearllike drops.

im pec ca bil i ty (im pek′ə bil′ə tē), *n.* impeccable quality; faultlessness.

im pec ca ble (im pek′ə bəl), *adj.* 1 free from fault; irreproachable: *impeccable manners, an impeccable appearance.* 2 not capable of or liable to sin. [< Latin *impeccabilis* < *in-* not + *peccare* to sin] **—im pec′ca bly,** *adv.*

im pe cu ni os i ty (im′pi kyü′nē os′ə tē), *n.* lack of money; poverty.

im pe cu ni ous (im′pi kyü′nē əs), *adj.* having little or no money; poor. [< *im-*[1] not + Latin *pecunia* money, property] **—im′pe cu′ni ous ly,** *adv.* **—im′pe cu′ni ous ness,** *n.*

im ped ance (im pēd′ns), *n.* the apparent resistance in an alternating-current circuit, made up of two components, reactance and true or ohmic resistance.

im pede (im pēd′), *v.t.,* **-ped ed, -ped ing.** stand in the way of; hinder; obstruct: *Our progress was impeded by the deep snow.* See **prevent** for synonym study. [< Latin *impedire* < *in-* on + *pedem* foot] **—im ped′er,** *n.*

im ped i ment (im ped′ə mənt), *n.* 1 hindrance; obstruction. 2 some physical defect, especially a defect in speech.

im ped i men ta (im ped′ə men′tə), *n.pl.* 1 traveling equipment; baggage. 2 the military supplies carried along with an army. [< Latin]

im pel (im pel′), *v.t.,* **-pelled, -pel ling.** 1 drive or force; cause: *The cold impelled her to go indoors.* See **compel** for synonym study. 2 cause to move; drive forward; push along: *The wind and tide impelled the boat toward the shore.* [< Latin *impellere* < *in-* on + *pellere* to push] **—im pel′ler,** *n.*

im pend (im pend′), *v.i.* 1 be likely to happen soon; be about to happen: *Black clouds are signs that a storm impends.* 2 hang threateningly; hang. [< Latin *impendere* < *in-* over + *pendere* to hang]

im pend ing (im pen′ding), *adj.* 1 likely to happen soon; threatening; about to occur: *an impending storm.* See **imminent** for synonym study. 2 overhanging.

im pen e tra bil i ty (im pen′ə trə bil′ə tē), *n.* 1 a being impenetrable. 2 (in physics) the property of matter that prevents two bodies from occupying the same space at the same time.

im pen e tra ble (im pen′ə trə bəl), *adj.* 1 that cannot be penetrated, pierced, or passed: *A thick sheet of steel is impenetrable by an ordinary bullet.* 2 impossible to explain or understand; inscrutable: *an impenetrable mystery.* 3 not open to ideas, influences, etc.: *an impenetrable mind.* **—im pen′e tra ble ness,** *n.* **—im pen′e tra bly,** *adv.*

im pen i tence (im pen′ə təns), *n.* lack of any sorrow or regret for doing wrong.

im pen i tent (im pen′ə tənt), *adj.* not penitent; feeling no sorrow or regret for having done wrong. **—im pen′i tent ly,** *adv.*

im per a tive (im per′ə tiv), *adj.* 1 not to be avoided; that must be done; urgent: *It is imperative that this very sick child should stay in bed.* 2 expressing a command or request: *an imperative statement.* 3 (in grammar) having to do with a verb form which expresses a command, request, or advice. "Go!" and "Stop, look, listen!" are in the imperative mood. *—n.* 1 something imperative; command: *The great imperative is "Love thy neighbor as thyself."* 2 a verb form in the imperative mood. 3 the imperative mood. [< Latin *imperativus* < *imperare* to command] **—im per′a tive ly,** *adv.* **—im per′a tive ness,** *n.*

im pe ra tor (im′pə rā′tər), *n.* emperor, especially the Roman emperor. [< Latin]

im per cep ti bil i ty (im′pər sep′tə bil′ə tē), *n.* a being imperceptible.

im per cep ti ble (im′pər sep′tə bəl), *adj.* that cannot be perceived or felt; very slight, gradual, subtle, or indistinct. **—im′per cep′ti bly,** *adv.*

im per cep tive (im′pər sep′tiv), *adj.* not perceptive; lacking perception. **—im′per cep′tive ness,** *n.*

imperf., imperfect.

im per fect (im pėr′fikt), *adj.* 1 not perfect; having some defect or fault. 2 not complete; lacking some part. 3 (in grammar) expressing incompleted, continued, or customary action in the past. *—n.* 1 the imperfect tense. English has no imperfect, but such constructions as *was studying* and *used to study* are like the imperfect in other languages. 2 verb form in the imperfect tense. **—im per′fect ly,** *adv.* **—im per′fect ness,** *n.*

im per fec tion (im′pər fek′shən), *n.* 1 lack of perfection; imperfect condition or character. 2 fault; defect.

im per for ate (im pėr′fər it, im pėr′fə rāt′), *adj.* 1 not pierced through with holes. 2 (of stamps) not separated from other stamps by perforations; having the margins whole. *—n.* an imperforate stamp.

im per i al (im pir′ē əl), *adj.* 1 of or having to do with an empire, emperor, or empress. 2 of or having to do with the rule or authority of one country over other countries and colonies. 3 having the rank of an emperor. 4 supreme; majestic; magnificent. 5 of larger size or better quality. 6 according to the British standard of weights and measures. *—n.* 1 a small, pointed beard growing beneath the lower lip. 2 size of paper, 23 by 31 inches (in England 22 by 30 inches). [< Latin *imperialis* < *imperium* empire] **—im per′i al ly,** *adv.*

imperial (def. 1)

imperial gallon, the British gallon, equal to 160 fluid ounces or about 1-1/5 United States gallons.

im per i al ism (im pir′ē ə liz′əm), *n.* 1 policy of extending the rule or authority of one country over other countries and colonies. 2 an imperial system of government. 3 the dominating of another nation's economic, political, and even military structure without actually taking governmental control. 4 support of imperial interests.

im per i al ist (im pir′ē ə list), *n.* person who favors imperialism. *—adj.* imperialistic.

im per i al is tic (im pir′ē ə lis′tik), *adj.* 1 of imperialism or imperialists. 2 favoring imperialism. **—im per′i al is′ti cal ly,** *adv.*

Imperial Valley, flat, irrigated region in S California.

im per il (im per′əl), *v.t.,* **-iled, -il ing** or **-illed, -il ling.** put in danger; endanger; jeopardize.

im per i ous (im pir′ē əs), *adj.* 1 haughty or arrogant; domineering; overbearing. 2 not to be avoided; necessary; urgent. **—im per′i ous ly,** *adv.* **—im per′i ous ness,** *n.*

im per ish a bil i ty (im per′i shə bil′ə tē), *n.* a being imperishable.

im per ish a ble (im per′i shə bəl), *adj.* not perishable; unable to be destroyed; lasting forever; enduring. **—im per′ish a ble ness,** *n.* **—im per′ish a bly,** *adv.*

im per i um (im pir′ē əm), *n., pl.* **-per i a** (-pir′ē ə). 1 command; supreme power; empire. 2 (in law) the right to use the force of the state to enforce the law. [< Latin]

im per ma nence (im pėr′mə nəns), *n.* a being impermanent.

im per ma nent (im pėr′mə nənt), *adj.* not permanent; temporary. **—im per′ma nent ly,** *adv.*

im per me a bil i ty (im pėr′mē ə bil′ə tē), *n.* a being impermeable.

im per me a ble (im pėr′mē ə bəl), *adj.* 1 that cannot be permeated; impassable. 2 not allowing the passage of fluid through the pores, interstices, etc. **—in per′me a ble ness,** *n.* **—im per′me a bly,** *adv.*

im per mis si ble (im′pər mis′ə bəl), *adj.* not permissible or allowable.

impers., impersonal.

im per son al (im pėr′sə nəl), *adj.* 1 not referring to any one person in particular; not personal: *impersonal criticism. History is usually written from an impersonal point of view.* 2 having no existence as a person: *Electricity is an impersonal force.* 3 (of a verb) not requiring a subject or having indefinite *it* for a subject. EXAMPLE: *rained* in "It rained yesterday." **—im per′son al ly,** *adv.*

im per son al i ty (im pėr′sə nal′ə tē), *n., pl.* **-ties.** 1 impersonal character; absence of personal quality. 2 an impersonal thing, force, etc.

im per son ate (im pėr′sə nāt), *v.t.,* **-at ed, -at ing.** 1 play the part of: *impersonate Hamlet on the stage.* 2 pretend to be; mimic the voice, appearance, and manners of: *impersonate a well-known singer.* 3 represent in personal form; personify; typify. **—im per′son a′tion,** *n.*

im per son a tor (im pėr′sə nā′tər), *n.* 1 person who pretends to be someone else. 2 actor who impersonates particular persons or types; professional mimic.

im per ti nence (im pėrt′n əns), *n.* 1 a being impertinent; impudence; insolence. 2 an impertinent act or speech. 3 lack of pertinence; irrelevance.

im per ti nen cy (im pėrt′n ən sē), *n., pl.* **-cies.** impertinence.

im per ti nent (im pėrt′n ənt), *adj.* 1 rudely bold; impudent; insolent. See synonym study below. 2 not pertinent; not to the point; out of place. **—im per′ti nent ly,** *adv.*

Syn. 1 **Impertinent, impudent, saucy** mean showing rudeness or disrespect. **Impertinent** suggests a disrespectful attitude shown by rudely meddling in what is not one's business or by taking too many liberties with others: *Talking back to older people is impertinent.* **Impudent** adds the idea of shamelessness and defiance: *The impudent boy made faces at the teacher.* **Saucy** suggests a disrespectful attitude shown by light and flippant manner or speech: *The saucy girl laughed when her father scolded her.*

im per turb a bil i ty (im′pər tėr′bə bil′ə tē), *n.* a being imperturbable.

im per turb a ble (im′pər tėr′bə bəl), *adj.* not easily excited or disturbed; calm. **—im′per turb′a bly,** *adv.*

im per vi ous (im pėr′vē əs), *adj.* 1 allowing no passage; impermeable: *A coat made of rubber is impervious to rain.* 2 not open to argument, suggestions, etc.: *She is impervious to the gossip about her.* **—im per′vi ous ly,** *adv.* **—im per′vi ous ness,** *n.*

im pe ti go (im′pə tī′gō), *n.* an infectious skin disease characterized by pimples filled with pus. [< Latin < *impetere* to attach. See IMPETUS.]

im pet u os i ty (im pech′ü os′ə tē), *n., pl.* **-ties.** 1 sudden or rash energy; hastiness. 2 rushing force or violence. 3 an impetuous action.

im pet u ous (im pech′ü əs), *adj.* 1 acting or done with sudden or rash energy; hasty: *Children are more impetuous than adults.* 2 rushing with force and violence: *The dam broke and an impetuous torrent of water swept away the town.* **—im pet′u ous ly,** *adv.* **—im pet′u ous ness,** *n.*

im pe tus (im′pə təs), *n.* 1 the force with which a moving body tends to maintain its velocity and overcome resistance: *the impetus of a moving automobile.* 2 a driving force; cause of action or effort; incentive: *Ambition is an impetus to work for success.* [< Latin, an attack < *impetere* to attack < *in-* + *petere* aim for]

im pi e ty (im pī′ə tē), *n., pl.* **-ties.** 1 lack of piety or reverence for God; wickedness. 2 lack of dutifulness or respect. 3 an impious act.

im pinge (im pinj′), *v.i.,* **-pinged, -ping ing.** 1 hit; strike: *Rays of light impinge on the eye.* 2 encroach; infringe. [< Latin *impingere* < *in-* on + *pangere* to strike] **—im pinge′ment,** *n.*

im pi ous (im′pē əs, im pī′əs), *adj.* not pious; not having or not showing reverence for God; wicked; profane. **—im′pi ous ly,** *adv.* **—im′pi ous ness,** *n.*

imp ish (im′pish), *adj.* 1 of an imp; like an imp. 2 mischievous. **—imp′ish ly,** *adv.* **—imp′ish ness,** *n.*

im pla ca bil i ty (im plā′kə bil′ə tē, im plak′ə bil′ə tē), *n.* a being implacable.

im pla ca ble (im plā′kə bəl, im plak′ə bəl), *adj.* unable to be appeased; refusing to be reconciled; unyielding: *implacable enemies.* **—im pla′ca ble ness,** *n.* **—im pla′ca bly,** *adv.*

im plant (im plant′), *v.t.* 1 instill; fix deeply: *A good teacher implants high ideals in children.* 2 insert: *a steel tube implanted in a socket.* 3 set in the ground; plant. 4 graft or set (a piece of skin, bone, etc.) into the body. **—im′plan ta′tion,** *n.* **—im plant′er,** *n.*

im plau si bil i ty (im plô′zə bil′ə tē), *n.* a being implausible.

im plau si ble (im plô′zə bəl), *adj.* not plausible; not having the appearance of truth or reason. **—im plau′si bly,** *adv.*

im ple ment (*n.* im′plə mənt; *v.* im′plə ment), *n.* a useful article of equipment; tool; instrument; utensil. A plow, an ax, a shovel, and a broom are implements. See **tool** for synonym study. *—v.t.* 1 provide with implements or other means. 2 provide the power and authority necessary to accomplish or put (something) into effect: *implement an order.* 3 carry out; get done: *Do not undertake a project unless you can implement it.* [< Late Latin *implementum* that which fills a need < Latin *implere* to fill < *in-* in + *plere* to fill] **—im′ple men ta′tion,** *n.*

im pli cate (im′plə kāt), *v.t.,* **-cat ed, -cat ing.** 1 show to have a part or to be connected; involve: *The thief's confession implicated two other men.* See **involve** for synonym study. 2 imply. [< Latin *implicatum* involved, enfolded < *in-* in + *plicare* to fold. Doublet of EMPLOY, IMPLY.]

im pli ca tion (im′plə kā′shən), *n.* 1 an implying. 2 a being implied. 3 something implied; indirect suggestion; hint: *There was no implication of dishonesty in his failure in business.* 4 an implicating. 5 a being implicated.

im pli ca tive (im′plə kā′tiv), *adj.* tending to implicate or imply. **—im′pli ca′tive ly,** *adv.*

im plic it (im plis′it), *adj.* 1 meant, but not clearly expressed or distinctly stated; implied: *implicit consent.* 2 without doubting, hesitating, or asking questions; absolute: *implicit obedience, implicit confidence.* 3 involved as a necessary part or condition. [< Latin *implicitum* implied, enfolded < *in-* in + *plicare* to fold] **—im plic′it ness,** *n.*

im plic it ly (im plis′it lē), *adv.* 1 unquestioningly. 2 by implication.

im plied-con sent law (im plīd′kən sent′), law providing that when a person is granted a driver's license he must agree to take a chemical test for intoxication whenever asked to by proper authority or give up his driver's license.

hat, āge, fär; let, ēqual, tėrm;
it, īce; hot, ōpen, ôrder;
oil, out; cup, pu̇t, rüle;
ch, child; ng, long; sh, she;
th, thin; ᴛʜ, then; zh, measure;

ə represents *a* in about, *e* in taken, *i* in pencil, *o* in lemon, *u* in circus.

< = from, derived from, taken from.

im pli ed ly (im plī′id lē), *adv.* by implication.

im plode (im plōd′), *v.i.,* **-plod ed, -plod ing.** burst inward. [< *im-*[2] in + *-plode,* as in *explode*]

im plore (im plôr′, im plōr′), *v.t.,* **-plored, -plor ing.** 1 beg or pray earnestly for. 2 beg (a person) to do something. See **beg** for synonym study. [< Latin *implorare* < *in-* toward + *plorare* cry] **—im plor′er,** *n.* **—im plor′ing ly,** *adv.*

im plo sion (im plō′zhən), *n.* an imploding; a bursting inward.

im plo sive (im plō′siv), *adj.* of or involving implosion.

im ply (im plī′), *v.t.,* **-plied, -ply ing.** 1 mean without saying so; express indirectly; suggest: *Her smile implied that she had forgiven us.* 2 involve as a necessary part or condition: *Speech implies a speaker.* 3 signify; mean. [< Old French *emplier* involve, put (in) < Latin *implicare* < *in-* in + *plicare* to fold. Doublet of EMPLOY, IMPLICATE.] ➤ See **infer** for usage note.

im po lite (im′pə līt′), *adj.* not polite; having or showing bad manners; rude; discourteous. **—im′po lite′ly,** *adv.* **—im′po lite′ness,** *n.*

im pol i tic (im pol′ə tik), *adj.* not politic; not expedient; not judicious; unwise: *It is impolitic to offend people who can help you.* **—im pol′i tic ly,** *adv.*

im pon der a bil i ty (im pon′dər ə bil′ə tē), *n.* a being imponderable.

im pon der a ble (im pon′dər ə bəl), *adj.* without weight that can be felt or measured: *Faith and love are imponderable forces.* *—n.* something imponderable. **—im pon′der a ble ness,** *n.* **—im pon′der a bly,** *adv.*

im port (*v.* im pôrt′, im pōrt′; im′pôrt, im′pōrt; *n.* im′pôrt, im′pōrt), *v.t.* 1 bring in from a foreign country for sale or use: *The United States imports coffee from Brazil.* 2 mean; signify: *Tell me what your remark imports.* *—v.i.* be of importance or consequence. *—n.* 1 article imported: *Rubber is a useful import.* 2 act or fact of importing; importation: *The import of diseased animals is forbidden.* 3 meaning; significance: *What is the import of your remark?* 4 importance; consequence. [< Latin *importare* < *in-* in + *portare* carry] **—im port′a ble,** *adj.*

im por tance (im pôrt′ns), *n.* a being important; consequence; value; significance.

Syn. Importance, consequence mean the quality of having value, meaning, influence, etc. **Importance** is the general word: *Anybody can see the importance of good health.* **Consequence** applies particularly to that which is important for its results or effects: *The discovery of insulin was an event of great consequence for diabetics.*

im por tant (im pôrt′nt), *adj.* 1 meaning

much; carrying with it great or serious consequences; significant: *important business, an important occasion.* 2 having social position or influence. 3 having an air of importance; pompous or pretentious: *An important busybody rushed around giving orders.* **—im por′tant ly,** *adv.*

im por ta tion (im′pôr tā′shən, im′pōr tā′shən), *n.* 1 an importing. 2 thing imported; import.

im port er (im pôr′tər, im pōr′tər; im′pôr tər, im′pōr tər), *n.* person or company whose business is importing goods.

im por tu nate (im pôr′chə nit), *adj.* asking repeatedly; annoyingly persistent; urgent. **—im por′tu nate ly,** *adv.* **—im por′tu nate ness,** *n.*

im por tune (im′pôr tün′, im′pôr tyün′, im pôr′chən), *v.,* **-tuned, -tun ing,** *adj.* *—v.t.* ask urgently or repeatedly; annoy with pressing demands. *—adj.* importunate. [< Latin *importunus* inconvenient] **—im′por tune′ly,** *adv.* **—im′por tun′er,** *n.*

im por tu ni ty (im′pôr tü′nə tē, im′pôr tyü′nə tē), *n., pl.* **-ties.** persistence in asking; act of demanding again and again.

im pose (im pōz′), *v.,* **-posed, -pos ing.** *—v.t.* 1 put (a burden, tax, or punishment) on: *The judge imposed a fine of $500 on the guilty man.* 2 force or thrust (oneself or one's company) on another or others; obtrude; presume. 3 palm off (something upon a person) to deceive. 4 arrange (pages of type) for printing. 5 **impose on** or **impose upon, a** take advantage of; use for selfish purposes. **b** deceive; cheat; trick. *—v.i.* force or thrust one's authority or influence on another or others. [< Middle French *imposer* < *in-* on + *poser* put, place] **—im pos′er,** *n.*

im pos ing (im pō′zing), *adj.* impressive because of size, appearance, dignity, etc.: *The Capitol at Washington, D.C., is an imposing building.* **—im pos′ing ly,** *adv.*

im po si tion (im′pə zish′ən), *n.* 1 act of putting a burden, tax, or punishment on. 2 something imposed; burden, task, or punishment. 3 an unfair burden, task, or punishment. 4 an imposing upon a person by taking advantage of his good nature: *Would it be an imposition to ask you to mail this parcel?* 5 deception; fraud; trick.

im pos si bil i ty (im pos′ə bil′ə tē, im′pos ə bil′ə tē), *n., pl.* **-ties.** 1 quality or condition of being impossible. 2 something impossible.

im pos si ble (im pos′ə bəl), *adj.* 1 that cannot be or happen: *an accident that had seemed impossible.* 2 not possible to use; not to be done: *Few things are impossible.* 3 that cannot be true: *an impossible rumor.* 4 not possible to endure, tolerate, etc.: *an impossible situation.* 5 extremely undesirable, unsuitable, etc.; very objectionable: *an impossible person.* **—im pos′si bly,** *adv.*

im post[1] (im′pōst), *n.* tax or duty, especially on goods brought into a country. [< Middle French, ultimately < Latin *in-* on + *ponere* place, put]

im post[2] (im′pōst), *n.* the uppermost part of a column, etc., on which the end of an arch rests. [< Italian *imposta,* ultimately < Latin *in-* on + *ponere* place, put]

im pos tor or **im pos ter** (im pos′tər), *n.* 1 person who pretends to be someone else in order to deceive or defraud others. 2 deceiver; cheat. [< Late Latin < Latin *imponere* impose]

im pos ture (im pos′chər), *n.* deception; fraud.

im po tence (im′pə təns), *n.* condition or quality of being impotent.

im po ten cy (im′pə tən sē), *n.* impotence.

im po tent (im′pə tənt), *adj.* 1 not having power; helpless: *We were impotent against the force of the tornado.* 2 (of males) incapable of having sexual intercourse. **—im′po tent ly,** *adv.*

im pound (im pound′), *v.t.* 1 shut up in a pen or pound: *impound stray animals.* 2 enclose or confine within limits: *A dam impounds water.* 3 seize and put in the custody of a court of law: *The court impounded the documents to use as evidence.* **—im pound′er,** *n.*

im pound ment (im pound′mənt), *n.* 1 water that is impounded by a dam or other enclosure. 2 an impounding.

im pov er ish (im pov′ər ish), *v.t.* 1 make very poor: *A long war had impoverished the nation's treasury.* 2 exhaust the strength, richness, or resources of: *impoverish the soil, impoverish the mind.* [< Old French *empoveriss-,* a form of *poverir* make poor < *em-* em-[1] + *povre* poor] **—im pov′er ish er,** *n.* **—im pov′er ish ment,** *n.*

im pov er ished (im pov′ər isht), *adj.* very poor. See **poor** for synonym study.

im prac ti ca bil i ty (im prak′tə kə bil′ə tē), *n., pl.* **-ties.** 1 a being impracticable. 2 something impracticable.

im prac ti ca ble (im prak′tə kə bəl), *adj.* 1 impossible to put into practice; not practicable: *impracticable suggestions.* 2 not usable; unfit for use: *an impracticable road.* 3 very hard to manage or deal with: *an impracticable horse, an impracticable person.* **—im prac′ti ca bly,** *adv.* ➤ See **impractical** for usage note.

im prac ti cal (im prak′tə kəl), *adj.* 1 not practical; having to do with theory rather than actual practice; not useful. 2 not having good sense. **—im prac′ti cal ly,** *adv.*

➤ **Impractical, impracticable.** *Impractical* is applied to things that are useless or to people who are unrealistic or show little common sense in what they do: *Buying worthless things because they are on sale is impractical. Impracticable* is applied to things that have been proved unusable in actual practice or would be impossible to put into practice: *Most schemes to put an end to poverty have been impracticable.*

im prac ti cal i ty (im prak′tə kal′ə tē), *n., pl.* **-ties.** 1 a being impractical. 2 an impractical thing.

im pre cate (im′prə kāt), *v.,* **-cat ed, -cat ing.** *—v.t.* call down (curses, evil, etc.): *imprecate ruin on one's enemies.* *—v.i.* curse. [< Latin *imprecatum* prayed for < *in-* on + *prex* prayer] **—im′pre ca′tor,** *n.*

im pre ca tion (im′prə kā′shən), *n.* 1 an imprecating; cursing. 2 curse.

im pre ca to ry (im′prə kə tôr′ē, im′prə kə tōr′ē), *adj.* invoking curses.

im pre cise (im′pri sis′), *adj.* not precise; lacking precision; inaccurate; inexact. **—im′pre cise′ly,** *adv.*

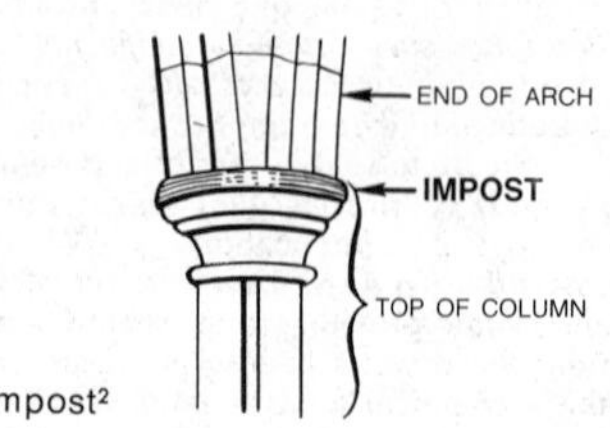

impost[2]

im pre ci sion (im′pri sizh′ən), *n.* lack of precision; inexactness.

im preg na bil i ty (im preg′nə bil′ə tē), *n.* a being impregnable.

im preg na ble (im preg′nə bəl), *adj.* able to resist attack; not yielding to force, persuasion, etc.: *an impregnable fortress, an impregnable argument.* **—im preg′na bly,** *adv.*

im preg nate (im preg′nāt), *v.t.,* **-nat ed, -nat ing.** 1 make pregnant. 2 spread through the whole of; fill; saturate: *Sea water is impregnated with salt.* 3 fill the mind of; inspire: *The captain impregnated the crew with his own courage.* [< Late Latin *impraegnatum* made pregnant < Latin *in-* + *praegnas* pregnant] **—im′preg na′tion,** *n.* **—im preg′na tor,** *n.*

im pre sa ri o (im′prə sär′ē ō), *n., pl.* **-ri os.** the organizer, director, or manager of a concert tour, an opera or ballet company, or other, especially musical, entertainment. [< Italian < *impresa* undertaking]

im pre scrip ti ble (im′pri skrip′tə bəl), *adj.* existing independently of law or custom; not justly to be taken away or violated: *imprescriptible rights.*

im press[1] (*v.* im pres′; *n.* im′pres), *v.t.* 1 have a strong effect on the mind or feelings of; influence deeply: *A hero impresses us with his courage.* 2 fix firmly in the mind: *She repeated the words to impress them in her memory.* 3 make marks on by pressing or stamping: *impress wax with a seal.* 4 produce by pressure; imprint; stamp. 5 produce or generate (an electromotive force or potential difference) in a conductor from some outside source, as a battery, dynamo, etc. *—v.i.* make an impression, especially a favorable one. *—n.* 1 mark or indentation made by pressure, especially one produced by a stamp or seal. 2 characteristic or distinctive mark or quality: *An author leaves the impress of his personality on what he writes.* 3 impression on the mind or feelings. 4 act of impressing. [< Latin *impressum* pressed in < *in-* in + *premere* to press] **—im press′er,** *n.*

im press[2] (im pres′), *v.t.* 1 take or seize by authority for public use: *The police impressed our car in order to pursue the escaping robbers.* 2 force (men) to serve in the armed forces. 3 bring in and use; press (a thing) into service by argument, etc. *—n.* impressment. [< *in-*[2] + *press*[2]]

im press i bil i ty (im pres′ə bil′ə tē), *n.* impressionability.

im press i ble (im pres′ə bəl), *adj.* impressionable. **—im press′i bly,** *adv.*

im pres sion (im presh′ən), *n.* 1 effect produced on the senses or mind: *Punishment seemed to make little impression on the stubborn child.* 2 effect produced by any operation or activity: *The rain left its impression on the dry fields.* 3 idea; notion: *I have a vague impression that I left the front door unlocked.* 4 mark made by pressing or stamping: *The thief's shoe had left an impression in the soft dirt of the garden.* 5 act of impressing. 6 condition of being impressed. 7 the total number of copies of a book made at one time. 8 a printed copy. 9 the process or result of printing paper from type, plates, etc.

im pres sion a bil i ty (im presh′ə nə bil′ə tē), *n.* impressionable quality or condition.

im pres sion a ble (im presh′ə nə bəl), *adj.* sensitive to impressions; easily impressed or influenced: *Children are more impressionable than adults.* **—im pres′sion a ble ness,** *n.* **—im pres′sion a bly,** *adv.*

im pres sion ism (im presh′ə niz′əm), *n.* 1 style of painting developed by French painters of the late 1800's, characterized by the use of strong, bright colors applied in dabs to convey the impression of light striking and reflecting from a surface, rather than a photographic reproduction of the surface. 2 style of literature characterized by the creation of general impressions and moods rather than realistic detail. 3 style of music characterized by the use of unusual and rich harmonies, tonal qualities, etc., to suggest the composer's impressions of a scene, an emotion, etc.

im pres sion ist (im presh′ə nist), *n.* artist, writer, or composer who practices impressionism.

im pres sion is tic (im presh′ə nis′tik), *adj.* 1 of or characteristic of impressionism or impressionists. 2 giving only a general or hasty impression. **—im pres′sion is′ti cal ly,** *adv.*

im pres sive (im pres′iv), *adj.* able to impress the mind, feelings, conscience, etc.; able to excite deep feeling: *an impressive sermon, an impressive storm, an impressive ceremony.* **—im pres′sive ly,** *adv.* **—im pres′sive ness,** *n.*

im press ment (im pres′mənt), *n.* an impressing of property for public use or of men to serve in the armed forces.

im pri ma tur (im′pri mā′tər), *n.* 1 an official license to print or publish a book, etc., now usually used to refer to works sanctioned by the Roman Catholic Church. 2 sanction; approval. [< New Latin, let it be printed]

im print (*n.* im′print; *v.* im print′), *n.* 1 mark made by pressure; print: *the imprint of a foot in the sand.* 2 a special mark or stamp; impression: *Suffering left its imprint on her face.* 3 the printer's or publisher's name, with the place and date of publication, on the title page or at the end of a book. *—v.t.* 1 mark by pressing or stamping: *imprint a postmark on an envelope, imprint a letter with a postmark.* 2 put by pressing: *imprint a kiss on someone's cheek.* 3 fix firmly in the mind: *My childhood home is imprinted in my memory.*

im pris on (im priz′n), *v.t.* 1 put in prison; keep in prison. 2 confine closely; restrain. **—im pris′on ment,** *n.*

im prob a bil i ty (im prob′ə bil′ə tē), *n., pl.* **-ties.** 1 a being improbable; unlikelihood. 2 something improbable.

im prob a ble (im prob′ə bəl), *adj.* not probable; not likely to happen; not likely to be true; unlikely. **—im prob′a ble ness,** *n.*

im prob a bly (im prob′ə blē), *adv.* in an improbable manner.

im pro bi ty (im prō′bə tē), *n.* lack of integrity; dishonesty.

im promp tu (im promp′tü, im promp′tyü), *adv.* without previous thought or preparation; offhand: *a speech made impromptu.* *—adj.* made or done without previous thought or preparation: *an impromptu speech, an impromptu party.* *—n.* something made or done without previous thought or preparation; improvisation. [< French < Latin *in promptu* in readiness]

im prop er (im prop′ər), *adj.* 1 not in accordance with accepted standards; not correct; wrong: *"You is" is an improper usage.* 2 not suitable; inappropriate: *A bright dress is improper for a funeral.* 3 showing bad judgment. See synonym study below. **—im prop′er ly,** *adv.* **—im prop′er ness,** *n.*

Syn. 3 **Improper, indecent** mean not right or fitting. **Improper** emphasizes bad judgment as to what is right or wrong: *It is an improper use of authority for a policeman to break one law to enforce another.* **Indecent** emphasizes bad taste as to what is acceptable or proper: *Leaving a dinner party without thanking one's host is indecent.*

improper fraction, fraction that is equal to or greater than 1. EXAMPLES: $^{3}/_{2}$, $^{4}/_{3}$, $^{27}/_{4}$, $^{8}/_{5}$, $^{21}/_{12}$, $^{4}/_{4}$, $^{12}/_{12}$.

im pro pri e ty (im′prə prī′ə tē), *n., pl.* **-ties.** 1 lack of propriety; quality of being improper. 2 improper conduct. 3 an improper act, expression, etc.: *Using "learn" to mean "teach" is an impropriety.*

im prove (im prüv′), *v.,* **-proved, -prov ing.** *—v.t.* 1 make better: *You could improve your handwriting if you tried.* 2 increase the value of: *Land is improved by using it for a farm or putting up a building on it.* 3 use well; make good use of: *We had two hours to wait and improved the time by seeing the city.* 4 **improve on** or **improve upon,** make better than; do better than: *improve on one's earlier work.* *—v.i.* become better: *His health is improving.* [< Anglo-French *emprouer* < Old French *en-* in + *prou* profit] **—im prov′a ble,** *adj.* **—im prov′er,** *n.*

im prove ment (im prüv′mənt), *n.* 1 a making better. 2 a becoming better. 3 increase in value. 4 change or addition that increases value: *The improvements in our house cost over a thousand dollars.* 5 a better condition; thing that is better than another; gain; advance.

im prov i dence (im prov′ə dəns), *n.* a being improvident; lack of foresight.

im prov i dent (im prov′ə dənt), *adj.* lacking foresight; not looking ahead; not careful in providing for the future; not thrifty. **—im prov′i dent ly,** *adv.*

im pro vi sa tion (im′prə vī zā′shən, im′prov ə zā′shən), *n.* 1 an improvising. 2 something improvised.

im pro vi sa tion al (im′prə vī zā′shə nəl, im′prov ə zā′shə nəl), *adj.* of or characterized by improvisation.

im pro vi sa tor (im′prə vī zā′tər, im-prov′ə zā′tər), *n.* person who improvises; improviser.

im pro vise (im′prə vīz), *v.,* **-vised, -vis ing.** *—v.t.* 1 make up (music, poetry, etc.) on the spur of the moment; sing, recite, speak, etc., without preparation. 2 provide offhand; make for the occasion: *The stranded motorists improvised a tent out of two blankets and some long poles.* *—v.i.* compose, utter, or do anything without preparation or on the spur of the moment. [< French *improviser,* ultimately < Latin *in-* not + *pro-* beforehand + *videre* see] **—im′pro vis′er,** *n.*

im pru dence (im prüd′ns), *n.* lack of prudence; imprudent behavior.

im pru dent (im prüd′nt), *adj.* not prudent; rash; unwise. **—im pru′dent ly,** *adv.*

im pu dence (im′pyə dəns), *n.* 1 a being impudent; shameless boldness; great rudeness; insolence. 2 impudent conduct or language.

im pu dent (im′pyə dənt), *adj.* shamelessly bold; very rude and insolent. See **impertinent** for synonym study. [< Latin *impudentem* < *in-* not + *pudere* be modest] **—im′pu dent ly,** *adv.*

im pugn (im pyün′), *v.t.* call in question; attack by words or arguments; challenge as false, worthless, etc.: *Do not impugn the umpire's fairness.* [< Latin *impugnare* to assault < *in-* against + *pugnare* to fight] **—im pugn′a ble,** *adj.* **—im pugn′er,** *n.*

hat, āge, fär; let, ēqual, tėrm;
it, īce; hot, ōpen, ôrder;
oil, out; cup, pu̇t, rüle;
ch, child; ng, long; sh, she;
th, thin; ꟻH, then; zh, measure;

ə represents *a* in about, *e* in taken, *i* in pencil, *o* in lemon, *u* in circus.

< = from, derived from, taken from.

im pulse (im′puls), *n.* 1 a sudden, driving force or influence; thrust; push: *the impulse of a wave, the impulse of hunger, the impulse of curiosity.* 2 the effect of a sudden, driving force or influence. 3 a sudden inclination or tendency to act: *The angry crowd was influenced more by impulse than by reason.* 4 stimulus that is transmitted, especially by nerve cells, and influences action in the muscle, gland, or other nerve cells that it reaches. 5 surge of electrical current in one direction. [< Latin *impulsus* < *impellere.* See IMPEL.]

im pul sion (im pul′shən), *n.* 1 an impelling; driving force. 2 impulse. 3 impetus.

im pul sive (im pul′siv), *adj.* 1 acting or done upon impulse; with a sudden inclination or tendency to act: *The impulsive child gave all his money to the beggar.* 2 driving with sudden force; able to impel; impelling. **—im pul′sive ly,** *adv.* **—im pul′sive ness,** *n.*

im pu ni ty (im pyü′nə tē), *n.* freedom from punishment, injury, or other bad consequences: *If laws are not enforced, crimes are committed with impunity.* [< Latin *impunitatem,* ultimately < *in-* without + *poena* punishment]

im pure (im pyůr′), *adj.* 1 not pure; dirty; unclean: *The air in cities is often impure.* 2 mixed with something of lower value; adulterated: *The salt we use is slightly impure.* 3 bad; corrupt: *to avoid impure talk, thoughts, acts, and people.* 4 not of one color, style, etc.; mixed. 5 forbidden by religion as unclean. 6 containing foreign idioms or grammatical errors. **—im pure′ly,** *adv.* **—im pure′ness,** *n.*

im pur i ty (im pyůr′ə tē), *n., pl.* **-ties.** 1 lack of purity; being impure. 2 impure thing; thing that makes something else impure: *Filtering the water removed some of the impurities from it.*

im pu ta tion (im′pyə tā′shən), *n.* 1 an imputing. 2 a charge or hint of wrongdoing.

im put a tive (im pyü′tə tiv), *adj.* 1 that imputes. 2 belonging or existing by imputation; imputed. **—im put′a tive ly,** *adv.*

im pute (im pyüt′), *v.t.,* **-put ed, -put ing.** consider as belonging; attribute; charge to a person or a cause; blame: *I impute his failure to laziness.* [< Latin *imputare* < *in-* in + *putare* reckon] **—im put′a ble,** *adj.* **—im put′a bly,** *adv.*

in (in), *prep.* *In* expresses inclusion, situation, presence, existence, position, and action within limits of space, time, state, circumstances, etc. 1 inside; within: *in the box. We live in the city.* 2 at, during, or after: *in the present time. I'll be back in an hour.* 3 into: *Go in the house.* 4 with; having; by: *cover a letter in an envelope.* 5 of; made of; using: *a*

dress in silk, a painting in oils. 6 surrounded by; in the midst of: *in the dust, in cold water.* 7 from among; out of: *one in a hundred.* 8 because of; for: *act in self-defense. The party is in honor of her birthday.* 9 about; concerning: *a book in American history.* 10 while; when: *in crossing the street.* 11 **in that,** because.
—*adv.* 1 in or into some place, position, condition, etc.; on the inside: *come in. Lock the dog in. A sheepskin coat has the woolly side in.* 2 present, especially in one's home or office: *The doctor is not in today.* 3 **in for,** unable to avoid; sure to get or have: *We are in for a storm.* 4 **in with, a** friendly with. **b** partners with.
—*adj.* 1 having power or influence: *The in party has won another election.* 2 coming or leading in: *The train is on the in track.* 3 INFORMAL. in style; fashionable: *an in outfit, in boots.*
—*n.* 1 position of familiarity or influence: *have an in with the company president.* 2 **ins,** *pl.* people in office; political party in power. 3 **ins and outs, a** turns and twists; nooks and corners. **b** different parts; details. [Old English]
➤ **in, into.** *In* generally shows location (literal or figurative); *into* generally shows direction: *He was in the house. She came into the house. He was in a stupor. She fell into a deep sleep.* ➤ See **at** for another usage note.

In, indium.

in-[1], *prefix.* not; the opposite of; the absence of: *Inexpensive = not expensive. Inattention = the absence of attention.* See also **i-, il-, im-,** and **ir-.** [< Latin]

in-[2], *prefix.* in; into; on; upon: *Incase = (put) into a case. Intrust = (give) in trust.* See also **il-, im-, ir-.** [< Latin < *in,* preposition]

in-[3], *prefix.* in; within; into; toward: *Indoors = within doors. Inland = toward land.* [Old English]

-in, *suffix.* variant of **-ine**[2], usually denoting neutral substances such as fats and proteins, as in *albumin, stearin.*

in., inch or inches.

in a bil i ty (in′ə bil′ə tē), *n.* lack of ability, power, or means; being unable.

in ab sen tia (in ab sen′shə), LATIN. while absent.

in ac ces si bil i ty (in′ək ses′ə bil′ə tē), *n.* a being inaccessible.

in ac ces si ble (in′ək ses′ə bəl), *adj.* 1 hard to get at; hard to reach or enter: *The house on top of the steep hill is inaccessible.* 2 not accessible; that cannot be reached or entered at all. **—in′ac ces′si bly,** *adv.*

in ac cur a cy (in ak′yər ə sē), *n., pl.* **-cies.** 1 lack of accuracy; being inaccurate. 2 error; mistake.

in ac cur ate (in ak′yər it), *adj.* not accurate; not exact; containing mistakes. **—in-ac′cur ate ly,** *adv.*

in ac tion (in ak′shən), *n.* absence of action; idleness.

in ac ti vate (in ak′tə vāt), *v.t.,* **-vat ed, -vat ing.** make inactive; destroy the action of: *inactivate a bomb, inactivate a virus.* **—in ac′ti va′tion,** *n.*

in ac tive (in ak′tiv), *adj.* 1 not active. See synonym study below. 2 idle; slow. 3 (in chemistry) showing little tendency to combine with other elements, as rare gases. 4 (in military use) not on active duty. **—in-ac′tive ly,** *adv.*
Syn. 1 **Inactive, inert, dormant** mean not in action or not showing activity. **Inactive** suggests inability or unwillingness to act: *He is an inactive member of the club.* **Inert** suggests being difficult or impossible to set in action or motion: *I dragged the inert, unconscious body from the water.* **Dormant** suggests a condition of sleep, sluggishness, or stupor: *Some animals and plants are dormant during the winter.*

in ac tiv i ty (in′ak tiv′ə tē), *n.* absence of activity; idleness; slowness.

in ad e qua cy (in ad′ə kwə sē), *n., pl.* **-cies.** 1 a being inadequate. 2 something that is inadequate.

in ad e quate (in ad′ə kwit), *adj.* not adequate; not enough; not as much as is needed: *inadequate preparation for an examination.* **—in ad′e quate ly,** *adv.* **—in ad′e quate-ness,** *n.*

in ad mis si bil i ty (in′əd mis′ə bil′ə tē), *n.* a being inadmissible.

in ad mis si ble (in′əd mis′ə bəl), *adj.* 1 not to be permitted; not allowable. 2 not to be admitted or considered as evidence or proof. **—in′ad mis′si bly,** *adv.*

in ad vert ence (in′əd vėrt′ns), *n.* 1 lack of attention; carelessness. 2 an inadvertent act; oversight; mistake.

in ad vert en cy (in′əd vėrt′n sē), *n., pl.* **-cies.** inadvertence.

in ad vert ent (in′əd vėrt′nt), *adj.* 1 not attentive; careless; negligent. 2 not done on purpose; caused by oversight. **—in′ad-vert′ent ly,** *adv.*

in ad vis a bil i ty (in′əd vī′zə bil′ə tē), *n.* a being inadvisable.

in ad vis a ble (in′əd vī′zə bəl), *adj.* not advisable; unwise; not prudent. **—in′ad-vis′a bly,** *adv.*

in al ien a bil i ty (in ā′lyə nə bil′ə tē, in-ā′lē ə nə bil′ə tē), *n.* a being inalienable.

in al ien a ble (in ā′lyə nə bəl, in ā′lē ə nə-bəl), *adj.* that cannot be given or taken away; that cannot be transferred to another: *an inalienable right.* Also, **unalienable. —in-al′ien a bly,** *adv.*

in al ter a bil i ty (in ôl′tər ə bil′ə tē), *n.* unchangeableness.

in al ter a ble (in ôl′tər ə bəl), *adj.* not alterable; unchangeable. **—in al′ter a bly,** *adv.*

in am o ra ta (in am′ə rä′tə), *n.* girl or woman with whom one is in love; sweetheart. [< Italian *innamorata,* ultimately < Latin *in-* in + *amor* love]

in ane (in ān′), *adj.* 1 without sense or ideas; silly; senseless: *inane questions.* 2 empty; void. [< Latin *inanis*] **—in ane′ly,** *adv.* **—in ane′ness,** *n.*

in an i mate (in an′ə mit), *adj.* 1 not living or alive; lifeless: *Stones are inanimate objects.* 2 without liveliness or spirit; dull. **—in an′i mate ly,** *adv.* **—in an′i mate-ness,** *n.*

in a ni tion (in′ə nish′ən), *n.* 1 weakness from lack of food. 2 emptiness. [< Late Latin *inanitionem* < Latin *inanire* to empty < *inanis* empty]

in an i ty (in an′ə tē), *n., pl.* **-ties.** 1 lack of sense or ideas; silliness. 2 a silly or senseless act, practice, remark, etc. 3 emptiness; void.

in ap par ent (in′ə par′ənt), *adj.* not apparent; not noticeable.

in ap pli ca bil i ty (in ap′lə kə bil′ə tē, in′ə plik′ə bil′ə tē), *n.* a being inapplicable.

in ap pli ca ble (in ap′lə kə bəl, in′ə plik′ə-bəl), *adj.* not applicable; unsuitable. **—in-ap′pli ca bly,** *adv.*

in ap po site (in ap′ə zit), *adj.* not pertinent; not suitable; inappropriate. **—in-ap′po site ly,** *adv.*

in ap pre ci a ble (in′ə prē′shē ə bəl, in′ə prē′shə bəl), *adj.* too small to be noticed or felt; very slight. **—in′ap pre′ci a bly,** *adv.*

in ap pre ci a tive (in′ə prē′shē ā′tiv, in′ə prē′shə tiv), *adj.* not appreciative; lacking in appreciation. **—in′ap pre′ci a′tive-ly,** *adv.* **—in′ap pre′ci a′tive ness,** *n.*

in ap pro pri ate (in′ə prō′prē it), *adj.* not appropriate; not fitting; unsuitable. **—in′ap-pro′pri ate ly,** *adv.* **—in′ap pro′pri ate-ness,** *n.*

in apt (in apt′), *adj.* 1 not apt; not suitable; unfit. 2 unskillful; awkward. **—in apt′ly,** *adv.* **—in apt′ness,** *n.*

in ap ti tude (in ap′tə tüd, in ap′tə tyüd), *n.* 1 unfitness. 2 lack of skill.

in ar tic u late (in′är tik′yə lit), *adj.* 1 not uttered in distinct syllables or words: *an inarticulate mutter.* 2 unable to speak in words; dumb: *Cats and dogs are inarticulate.* 3 not able to put one's thoughts or feelings into words easily and clearly. 4 not jointed: *A jellyfish's body is inarticulate.* **—in′ar-tic′u late ly,** *adv.* **—in′ar tic′u late-ness,** *n.*

in ar tis tic (in′är tis′tik), *adj.* not artistic; lacking good taste. **—in′ar tis′ti cal ly,** *adv.*

in as much as (in′əz much′), 1 because; since. 2 insofar as.

in at ten tion (in′ə ten′shən), *n.* lack of attention; carelessness; negligence.

in at ten tive (in′ə ten′tiv), *adj.* not attentive; careless; negligent. **—in′at ten′tive-ly,** *adv.* **—in′at ten′tive ness,** *n.*

in au di bil i ty (in ô′də bil′ə tē), *n.* a being inaudible.

in au di ble (in ô′də bəl), *adj.* that cannot be heard. **—in au′di bly,** *adv.*

in au gur al (in ô′gyər əl), *adj.* 1 of, for, or having to do with an inauguration: *an inaugural address.* 2 beginning; first. —*n.* the address or speech made by a person when formally admitted to office.

in au gu rate (in ô′gyə rāt′), *v.t.,* **-rat ed, -rat ing.** 1 install in office with formal ceremonies: *A President of the United States is inaugurated every four years.* 2 make a formal beginning of; begin: *The invention of the airplane inaugurated a new era in transportation.* 3 open for public use with a formal ceremony or celebration. [< Latin *inauguratum* consecrated by augury < *in-* for + *augurare* act as an augur, predict < *augur* taker of omens, augur] **—in au′gu ra′-tor,** *n.*

in au gu ra tion (in ô′gyə rā′shən), *n.* 1 act or ceremony of installing a person in office. 2 a formal beginning; beginning. 3 an opening for public use with a formal ceremony or celebration.

in aus pi cious (in′ô spish′əs), *adj.* with signs of failure; unfavorable; unlucky. **—in′aus pi′cious ly,** *adv.* **—in′aus-pi′cious ness,** *n.*

in board (in′bôrd′, in′bōrd′), *adv., adj.* 1 inside the hull of a ship or boat: *an inboard motor.* 2 in or toward the middle of a ship or boat. 3 in or toward the central axis of an aircraft or spacecraft.

in born (in′bôrn′), *adj.* born in a person; instinctive; natural.

in bound (in′bound′), *adj.* inward bound: *an inbound flight.*

in bred (in′bred′), *adj.* 1 inborn; natural: *an*

hat, āge, fär; let, ēqual, tėrm;
it, īce; hot, ōpen, ôrder;
oil, out; cup, pu̇t, rüle;
ch, child; ng, long; sh, she;
th, thin; ᴛʜ, then; zh, measure;

ə represents *a* in about, *e* in taken, *i* in pencil, *o* in lemon, *u* in circus.

< = from, derived from, taken from.

inbred courtesy. 2 produced by breeding between closely related ancestors: *an inbred strain of horses.* —*v.* pt. and pp. of **inbreed.**

in breed (in′brēd′, in brēd′), *v.t.,* **-bred, -breed ing.** 1 breed from closely related animals or plants. 2 produce or develop within.

in breed ing (in′brē′ding), *n.* breeding from closely related animals or plants so as to preserve desired or eliminate undesired characteristics.

inc., 1 including. 2 incorporated.

In ca (ing′kə), *n., pl.* **-cas** or **-ca.** 1 member of a highly civilized group of South American Indians who ruled a large empire in Peru and other parts of South America before the Spanish conquest in the 1500's. 2 ruler or member of the royal family of this group. **—In′can,** *n., adj.*

in cal cu la bil i ty (in kal′kyə lə bil′ə tē), *n.* a being incalculable.

in cal cu la ble (in kal′kyə lə bəl), *adj.* 1 too great in number to be counted; innumerable. 2 impossible to foretell or reckon beforehand. 3 that cannot be relied on; uncertain. **—in cal′cu la bly,** *adv.*

in can desce (in′kən des′), *v.i., v.t.,* **-desced, -desc ing.** glow or cause to glow with heat. [< Latin *incandescere* begin to glow < *in-* (intensive) + *candescere* become white-hot]

in can des cence (in′kən des′ns), *n.* a being incandescent.

in can des cent (in′kən des′nt), *adj.* 1 heated to such a high temperature that it gives out light; glowing with heat; red-hot or white-hot. 2 shining brightly; brilliant. 3 having to do with or containing a material that gives light by incandescence. **—in′can des′cent ly,** *adv.*

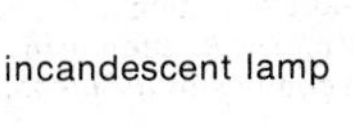
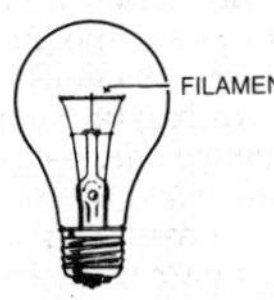

incandescent lamp

incandescent lamp, an electric lamp with a filament of very fine wire that becomes white-hot and gives off light when current flows through it; light bulb.

in can ta tion (in′kan tā′shən), *n.* 1 set of words spoken as a magic charm or to cast a magic spell. 2 the use of such words. [< Latin *incantationem* < *incantare* enchant < *in-* against + *cantare* to chant]

in can ta tion al (in′kan tā′shə nəl), *adj.* incantatory.

in can ta to ry (in kan′tə tôr′ē, in kan′tə tōr′ē), *adj.* of or like an incantation.

in ca pa bil i ty (in′kā pə bil′ə tē), *n.* a being incapable; incapacity.

in ca pa ble (in kā′pə bəl), *adj.* 1 without ordinary ability; not efficient; not competent: *An employer cannot afford to hire incapable workers.* 2 **incapable of,** a without the ability, power, or fitness for: *His honesty made him incapable of lying.* b not legally qualified for: *A foreigner is incapable of becoming President of the United States.* c not susceptible to; not open or ready for: *incapable of exact measurement.* **—in ca′pa ble ness,** *n.* **—in ca′pa bly,** *adv.*

in ca pac i tate (in′kə pas′ə tāt), *v.t.,* **-tat ed, -tat ing.** 1 deprive of ability, power, or fitness; disable: *Her injury incapacitated her for working.* 2 legally disqualify. **—in′ca pac′i ta′tion,** *n.*

in ca pac i ty (in′kə pas′ə tē), *n., pl.* **-ties.** 1 lack of ability, power, or fitness; disability. 2 legal disqualification.

in car ce rate (in kär′sə rāt′), *v.t.,* **-rat ed, -rat ing.** imprison. [< Late Latin *incarceratum* imprisoned < Latin *in-* + *carcer* prison] **—in car′ce ra′tion,** *n.*

in car na dine (in kär′nə dən, in kär′nə dīn, in kär′nə dēn′), *adj., v.,* **-dined, -din ing.** —*adj.* 1 blood-red. 2 flesh-colored. —*v.t.* make blood-red or flesh-colored. [ultimately < Latin *in-* + *carnem* flesh]

in car nate (*adj.* in kär′nit, in kär′nāt; *v.* in kär′nāt), *adj., v.,* **-nat ed, -nat ing.** —*adj.* embodied in flesh, especially in human form; personified; typified: *the Devil incarnate, evil incarnate.* —*v.t.* 1 make or be incarnate; embody: *Lancelot incarnated the spirit of chivalry.* 2 put into or represent in concrete form; realize: *The sculptor incarnated his vision in a beautiful statue.* [< Latin *incarnatum* < *in-* + *carnem* flesh]

in car na tion (in′kär nā′shən), *n.* 1 a taking on of human form by a divine being. 2 **the Incarnation,** (in Christian theology) the union of divine nature and human nature in the person of Jesus; assumption of human form by the son of God. 3 embodiment.

in case (in kās′), *v.t.,* **-cased, -cas ing.** encase. **—in case′ment,** *n.*

in cau tious (in kô′shəs), *adj.* not cautious; reckless; rash. **—in cau′tious ly,** *adv.* **—in cau′tious ness,** *n.*

in cen di a rism (in sen′dē ə riz′əm), *n.* 1 crime of setting property on fire intentionally. 2 the deliberate stirring up of strife, violence, or rebellion.

in cen di ar y (in sen′dē er′ē), *adj., n., pl.* **-ar ies.** —*adj.* 1 having to do with the crime of setting property on fire intentionally. 2 causing fires; used to start a fire: *an incendiary bomb.* 3 deliberately stirring up strife, violence, or rebellion: *incendiary speeches.* —*n.* 1 person who intentionally sets fire to property. 2 person who deliberately stirs up strife, violence, or rebellion. 3 shell or bomb containing chemical agents that cause fire. [< Latin *incendiarius* causing fire < *incendium* fire < *incendere* to set on fire]

in cense^1 (in′sens), *n.* 1 substance giving off a sweet smell when burned. 2 the perfume or smoke from it. 3 something sweet like incense: *the incense of flowers, the incense of flattery.* [< Old French *encens* < Late Latin *incensum* < Latin *incendere* to set on fire, burn]

in cense^2 (in sens′), *v.t.,* **-censed, -cens ing.** make very angry; fill with rage. [< Latin *incensum* inflamed, enraged, set on fire < *in-* (intensive) + *candere* glow white]

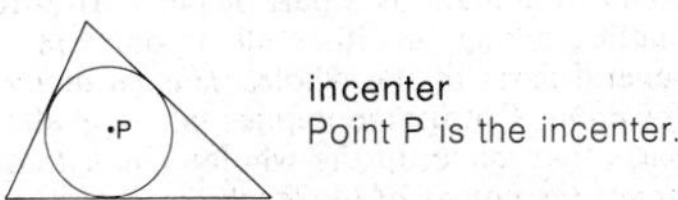

incenter
Point P is the incenter.

in cen ter (in′sen′tər), *n.* (in mathematics) the center of the inscribed circle of a triangle.

in cen tive (in sen′tiv), *n.* thing that urges a person on; cause of action or effort; motive; stimulus. —*adj.* inciting; encouraging. [< Latin *incentivum* < *incinere* cause to sound < *in-* on + *canere* sing]

in cep tion (in sep′shən), *n.* a beginning or originating; commencement: *the inception of* a plan. [< Latin *inceptionem* < *in-* on + *capere* take]

in cep tive (in sep′tiv), *adj.* 1 beginning; initial. 2 (in grammar) expressing the beginning of an action. —*n.* an inceptive verb.

in cer ti tude (in sėr′tə tüd, in sėr′tə tyüd), *n.* uncertainty; doubt.

in ces sant (in ses′nt), *adj.* never stopping; continued or repeated without interruption; continual: *the incessant noise from the factory.* [< Late Latin *incessantem* < Latin *in-* not + *cessare* cease] **—in ces′sant ly,** *adv.*

in cest (in′sest), *n.* sexual intercourse between persons so closely related that their marriage is prohibited by law or custom, as between brother and sister or parent and child. [< Latin *incestum* < *in-* not + *castus* chaste]

in ces tu ous (in ses′chü əs), *adj.* 1 of or involving incest. 2 guilty of incest. **—in ces′tu ous ly,** *adv.* **—in ces′tu ous ness,** *n.*

inch (inch), *n.* 1 unit of length, $^1/_{12}$ of a foot. See **measure** for table. 2 amount of rainfall, snowfall, etc., that would cover a surface to a depth of one inch. 3 the smallest part, amount, degree, measure, or distance; a very little bit: *Neither debater would yield an inch.*
by inches, by slow degrees; gradually.
every inch, in every way; completely.
inch by inch, little by little; slowly.
within an inch of, very near; close to.
—*v.i.* move slowly or little by little.
[< Old English *ynce* < Latin *uncia,* originally, a twelfth. Doublet of OUNCE^1.]

inch meal (inch′mēl′), *adv.* little by little; slowly.

in cho ate (in kō′it), *adj.* just begun; in an early stage; incomplete; undeveloped. [< Latin *inchoatum, incohatum,* originally, harnessed < *in-* on + *cohum* yoke fastener] **—in cho′ate ly,** *adv.* **—in cho′ate ness,** *n.*

in cho a tive (in kō′ə tiv), *adj.* 1 inchoate. 2 (in grammar) inceptive. —*n.* an inceptive verb.

In chon (in′chon′), *n.* seaport in W South Korea, on the Yellow Sea. 529,000.

inch worm (inch′wėrm′), *n.* measuring worm.

in ci dence (in′sə dəns), *n.* 1 range of occurrence or influence; extent of effects: *the incidence of a disease.* 2 a falling on or affecting. 3 the falling or striking of a projectile, ray of light, etc., on a surface. 4 angle of incidence.

in ci dent (in′sə dənt), *n.* 1 a happening or event viewed as a separate circumstance; occurrence. See **event** for synonym study. 2 something that occurs by chance in connection with something else; subordinate event. —*adj.* 1 liable to happen; belonging: *hardships incident to the life of a pioneer.* 2 falling or striking (upon): *rays of light incident upon a mirror.* 3 connected with or dependent on something else. [< Latin *incidentem* happening, befalling < *in-* on + *cadere* to fall]

in ci den tal (in′sə den′tl), *adj.* 1 happening or likely to happen along with something else more important: *Certain discomforts are incidental to camping out.* 2 occurring by chance: *an incidental meeting of an old friend on the street.* —*n.* 1 an incidental circumstance, event, etc. 2 **incidentals,** *pl.* secondary or minor charges or expenses.

in ci den tal ly (in′sə den′tl ē), *adv.* 1 in an incidental manner. 2 by the way.

incidental music, music played during a motion picture, play, etc., to help bring about a desired emotional response from the audience.

in cin e rate (in sin′ə rāt′), *v.t.,* **-rat ed, -rat ing.** burn to ashes. [< Medieval Latin *incineratum* burnt to ashes < Latin *in-* into + *cinis* ashes] —**in cin′e ra′tion,** *n.*

in cin e ra tor (in sin′ə rā′tər), *n.* furnace or other device for burning trash and other things to ashes.

in cip i ence (in sip′ē əns), *n.* the very beginning; early stage.

in cip i en cy (in sip′ē ən sē), *n.* incipience.

in cip i ent (in sip′ē ənt), *adj.* just beginning; in an early stage; commencing. [< Latin *incipientem* < *in-* on + *capere* take] —**in cip′i ent ly,** *adv.*

in cise (in sīz′), *v.t.,* **-cised, -cis ing.** 1 cut into. 2 carve; engrave. [< Latin *incisum* carved < *in-* into + *caedere* to cut]

in cised (in sīzd′), *adj.* 1 cut into. 2 produced by cutting; carved; engraved. 3 having the margin deeply notched.

in ci sion (in sizh′ən), *n.* 1 cut made in something; gash: *The doctor made a tiny incision to take out the splinter in my hand.* 2 act of incising. 3 incisive quality.

in ci sive (in sī′siv), *adj.* 1 sharp or keen; penetrating; acute: *incisive criticism.* 2 incising; cutting. —**in ci′sive ly,** *adv.* —**in ci′sive ness,** *n.*

in ci sor (in sī′zər), *n.* tooth having a sharp edge adapted for cutting; one of the front teeth in mammals between the canine teeth in either jaw. Human beings have eight incisors.

in ci ta tion (in′sī tā′shən, in′sə tā′shən), *n.* act of inciting.

in cite (in sīt′), *v.t.,* **-cit ed, -cit ing.** stimulate to action; urge on; stir up; rouse. [< Latin *incitare* < *in-* on + *citare* arouse] —**in cit′er,** *n.*

Syn. Incite, instigate mean to stir up or urge on to action. **Incite** means to stir up or stimulate to action, whether good or bad: *incite men to fight bravely, incite a riot.* **Instigate** means to stir up to do something bad: *instigate a rebellion.*

in cite ment (in sīt′mənt), *n.* 1 thing that urges on or rouses to action. 2 act of inciting.

in ci vil i ty (in′sə vil′ə tē), *n., pl.* **-ties.** 1 lack of courtesy; impoliteness; rudeness. 2 a rude or impolite act.

incl., 1 including. 2 inclusive.

in clem en cy (in klem′ən sē), *n., pl.* **-cies.** inclement condition or quality; severity; harshness.

in clem ent (in klem′ənt), *adj.* 1 rough or stormy. 2 not merciful or kindly; severe; harsh: *an inclement ruler.* —**in clem′ent ly,** *adv.*

in clin a ble (in klī′nə bəl), *adj.* 1 inclined; disposed. 2 favorably disposed: *inclinable to a plan.*

in cli na tion (in′klə nā′shən), *n.* 1 a tending toward a certain character or condition; natural bent; tendency: *an inclination toward fatness.* 2 preference; liking: *have a strong inclination for sports.* 3 an inclining toward something; leaning, bending, or bowing: *an inclination of the head.* 4 deviation from a normal position; slope; slant: *roof with a sharp inclination.* 5 an inclined surface; incline. 6 difference of direction of two lines or planes, especially as measured by the angle between them.

in cli na tion al (in′klə nā′shə nəl), *adj.* 1 relating to a slope or inclination to the horizon. 2 of or having to do with mental inclination or disposition.

in cline (*v.* in klīn′; *n.* in′klīn, in klīn′), *v.,* **-clined, -clin ing,** *n.* —*v.i.* 1 be favorable or willing; tend: *Dogs incline to eat meat as a food.* 2 slope; slant. 3 lean, bend, or bow. —*v.t.* 1 make favorable or willing; influence. 2 lean, bend, or bow: *incline one's head in prayer.* 3 cause to slope or slant; tilt. —*n.* 1 a slope; slant. 2 an inclined plane or surface. [< Latin *inclinare* < *in-* in + *clinare* to bend]

in clined (in klīnd′), *adj.* 1 favorable or willing; tending. 2 sloping; slanting. 3 (in mathematics) forming an angle with something else.

inclined plane, plank or other plane surface set at an acute angle to a horizontal surface. It is a simple machine.

in cli nom e ter (in′klə nom′ə tər), *n.* 1 instrument for measuring the angle that an aircraft makes with the horizontal. 2 instrument for measuring the angle that the earth's magnetic field makes with the horizontal.

in close (in klōz′), *v.t.,* **-closed, -clos ing.** enclose.

in clo sure (in klō′zhər), *n.* enclosure.

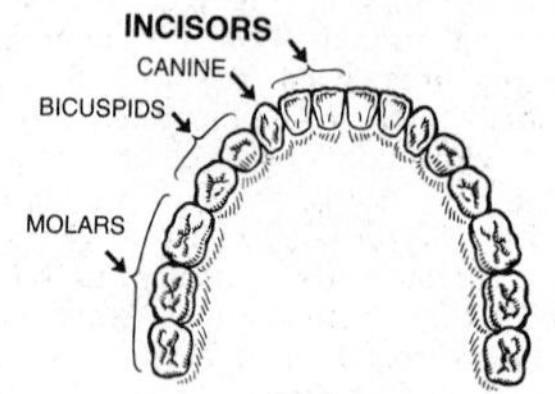

incisor—incisors of a human being

in clude (in klüd′), *v.t.,* **-clud ed, -clud ing.** 1 have within itself; contain; comprise: *Their farm includes 160 acres.* See synonym study below. 2 put in a total, a class, or the like; reckon in a count: *The price includes the land, house, and furniture.* 3 put, hold, or enclose within limits. [< Latin *includere* < *in-* in + *claudere* to shut] —**in clud′a ble, in clud′i ble,** *adj.*

Syn. 1 Include, comprise, comprehend mean to contain as a part or parts. **Include** implies taking in either all or only one or several parts of the whole: *The list includes my name.* **Comprise** implies taking in all the parts that make up the whole: *The list comprises the names of those who passed.* **Comprehend** implies that the parts are held or fall within the limits or scope of the whole: *The examination comprehended the whole course.*

in clu sion (in klü′zhən), *n.* 1 an including. 2 a being included. 3 thing included.

in clu sive (in klü′siv), *adj.* 1 including in consideration; including; comprising: *"Read pages 10 to 20 inclusive" means "Begin with page 10 and read through to the very end of page 20."* 2 including much; including everything concerned: *Make an inclusive list of your expenses.* 3 **inclusive of,** including; taking in; counting. —**in clu′sive ly,** *adv.* —**in clu′sive ness,** *n.*

incog., incognito.

in cog ni to (in kog′nə tō, in′kog nē′tō), *adj., adv., n., pl.* **-tos.** —*adj., adv.* with one's real name, character, rank, etc., concealed: *The prince traveled incognito to avoid crowds and ceremonies.* —*n.* 1 person who is incognito. 2 a disguised condition. [< Italian < Latin *incognitus* unknown < *in-* not + *cognitus* known < *co-* (intensive) + *gnoscere* know]

in co her ence (in′kō hir′əns), *n.* 1 disconnected thought or speech. 2 lack of logical connection. 3 failure to stick together; looseness.

in co her ent (in′kō hir′ənt), *adj.* 1 having or showing no logical connection of ideas; not coherent; disconnected; confused. 2 not sticking together; loose. —**in′co her′ent ly,** *adv.*

in com bus ti bil i ty (in′kəm bus′tə bil′ə tē), *n.* a being incombustible.

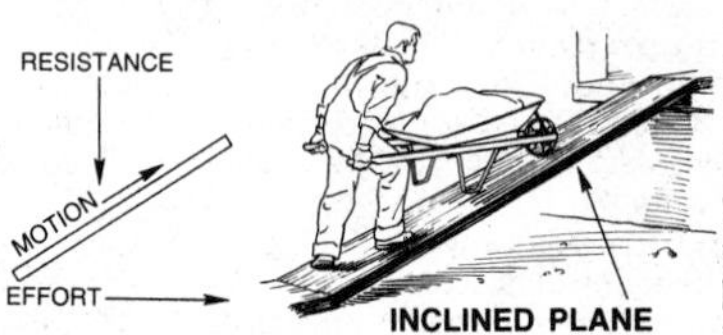

in com bus ti ble (in′kəm bus′tə bəl), *adj.* that cannot be burned; fireproof.

in come (in′kum), *n.* what comes in from property, business, work, etc.; money that comes in; receipts; returns.

income tax, a government tax on a person's or a corporation's income, usually with certain deductions and exemptions.

in com ing (in′kum′ing), *adj.* coming in: *the incoming tide.* —*n.* a coming in: *the incoming of the tide.*

in com men sur a bil i ty (in′kə men′shər ə bil′ə tē, in′kə men′sər ə bil′ə tē), *n.* a being incommensurable.

in com men sur a ble (in′kə men′shər ə bəl, in′kə men′sər ə bəl), *adj.* 1 that cannot be compared because not measurable in the same units or by the same scale: *Money and human life are incommensurable.* 2 (of lengths or numbers) having no common measure or number of which all the given lengths or numbers are integral multiples. $\sqrt{2}$ and 3 are incommensurable numbers because there is no third number which divides both of them evenly. A foot and a meter are incommensurable since the ratio between them must be expressed as an irrational number. —*n.* something that is incommensurable. —**in′com men′sur a bly,** *adv.*

in com men sur ate (in′kə men′shər it, in′kə men′sər it), *adj.* 1 not in proportion; not adequate: *strength incommensurate to a task.* 2 that cannot be compared; incommensurable. —**in′com men′sur ate ly,** *adv.*

in com mode (in′kə mōd′), *v.t.,* **-mod ed, -mod ing.** cause trouble, difficulty, etc., to; inconvenience. [< Latin *incommodare* < *incommodus* inconvenient < *in-* not + *commodus* convenient]

in com mo di ous (in′kə mō′dē əs), *adj.* 1 not roomy enough. 2 inconvenient; uncomfortable. —**in′com mo′di ous ly,** *adv.* —**in′com mo′di ous ness,** *n.*

in com mu ni ca bil i ty (in′kə myü′nə kə bil′ə tē), *n.* a being incommunicable.

in com mu ni ca ble (in′kə myü′nə kə bəl), *adj.* that cannot be communicated or told.

in com mu ni ca do (in′kə myü′nə kä′dō), *adj., adv.* without any way of communicating with others: *The prisoner was being held incommunicado.* [< Spanish *incomunicado*]

in com mu ni ca tive (in′kə myü′nə kā′tiv), *adj.* not communicative; reserved.

in com par a bil i ty (in′kom pər ə bil′ə tē), *n.* a being incomparable.

in com par a ble (in kom′pər ə bəl, in kom′prə bəl), *adj.* 1 without equal; matchless: *incomparable beauty.* 2 not able to be compared; unsuitable for comparison. **—in com′par a bly,** *adv.*

in com pat i bil i ty (in′kəm pat′ə bil′ə tē), *n., pl.* **-ties.** 1 quality of being incompatible; lack of harmony. 2 an incompatible thing, quality, etc.

in com pat i ble (in′kəm pat′ə bəl), *adj.* 1 not able to live or act together peaceably; opposed in character: *My cat and dog are incompatible.* 2 incapable of existing together; inconsistent: *Bad eating habits are incompatible with good health.* 3 of or designating drugs, blood types, etc., that cannot be combined or used together because of undesirable chemical or physiological reactions. *—n.* Usually, **incompatibles,** *pl.* incompatible persons or things. **—in′com pat′i bly,** *adv.*

in com pe tence (in kom′pə təns), *n.* 1 lack of ability, power, or fitness. 2 lack of legal qualification.

in com pe ten cy (in kom′pə tən sē), *n.* incompetence.

in com pe tent (in kom′pə tənt), *adj.* 1 not competent; lacking ability, power, or fitness. 2 not legally qualified. *—n.* an incompetent person. **—in com′pe tent ly,** *adv.*

in com plete (in′kəm plēt′), *adj.* not complete; lacking some part; unfinished. **—in′com plete′ly,** *adv.* **—in′com plete′ness,** *n.*

in com ple tion (in′kəm plē′shən), *n.* unfinished condition; incompleteness.

in com pre hen si bil i ty (in′kom pri hen′sə bil′ə tē), *n.* a being incomprehensible.

in com pre hen si ble (in′kom pri hen′sə bəl), *adj.* impossible to understand. **—in′com pre hen′si ble ness,** *n.* **—in′com pre hen′si bly,** *adv.*

in com pre hen sion (in′kom pri hen′shən), *n.* lack of comprehension or understanding.

in com press i bil i ty (in′kəm pres′ə bil′ə tē), *n.* a being incompressible.

in com press i ble (in′kəm pres′ə bəl), *adj.* that cannot be squeezed into a smaller size.

in con ceiv a bil i ty (in′kən sē′və bil′ə tē), *n.* a being inconceivable.

in con ceiv a ble (in′kən sē′və bəl), *adj.* 1 impossible to imagine: *A circle without a center is inconceivable.* 2 hard to believe; incredible. **—in′con ceiv′a ble ness,** *n.* **—in′con ceiv′a bly,** *adv.*

in con clu sive (in′kən klü′siv), *adj.* not convincing; not settling or deciding something doubtful; not effective: *The jury found the evidence against the defendant inconclusive and acquitted him.* **—in′con clu′sive ly,** *adv.* **—in′con clu′sive ness,** *n.*

in con gru ence (in kong′grü əns), *n.* lack of agreement; incongruity.

in con gru ent (in kong′grü ənt), *adj.* incongruous. **—in con′gru ent ly,** *adv.*

in con gru i ty (in′kən grü′ə tē), *n., pl.* **-ties.** 1 a being out of place; unfitness; inappropriateness. 2 lack of agreement or harmony; inconsistency. 3 something that is incongruous.

in con gru ous (in kong′grü əs), *adj.* 1 out of keeping; not appropriate; out of place: *A fur coat is incongruous with a bathing suit.* 2 lacking in agreement or harmony; not consistent. **—in con′gru ous ly,** *adv.* **—in con′gru ous ness,** *n.*

in con se quence (in kon′sə kwens, in kon′sə kwəns), *n.* a being inconsequent.

in con se quent (in kon′sə kwent, in kon′sə kwənt), *adj.* 1 not logical; not logically connected: *an inconsequent argument.* 2 not to the point; irrelevant: *an inconsequent remark.* 3 apt to think or talk without logical connection. **—in con′se quent ly,** *adv.*

in con se quen tial (in′kon sə kwen′shəl), *adj.* 1 unimportant; trifling. 2 inconsequent. **—in con′se quen′tial ly,** *adv.*

in con se quen ti al i ty (in kon′sə kwen′shē al′ə tē), *n.* a being inconsequential.

in con sid er a ble (in′kən sid′ər ə bəl), *adj.* not worth consideration; not important; insignificant. **—in′con sid′er a ble ness,** *n.* **—in′con sid′er a bly,** *adv.*

in con sid er ate (in′kən sid′ər it), *adj.* not thoughtful of others and their feelings; thoughtless. **—in′con sid′er ate ly,** *adv.* **—in′con sid′er ate ness,** *n.*

in con sist en cy (in′kən sis′tən sē), *n., pl.* **-cies.** 1 a being inconsistent. 2 thing, act, etc., that is inconsistent.

in con sist ent (in′kən sis′tənt), *adj.* 1 lacking in agreement or harmony; at variance: *The policeman's failure to arrest the thief was inconsistent with his duty.* 2 failing to keep to the same principles, course of action, etc.; changeable. 3 lacking harmony between its different parts; not uniform. 4 (in mathematics) having no common solution, as of two or more equations or inequalities. **—in′con sist′ent ly,** *adv.*

in con sol a bil i ty (in′kən sō′lə bil′ə tē), *n.* condition of being inconsolable.

in con sol a ble (in′kən sō′lə bəl), *adj.* not to be comforted; broken-hearted. **—in′con sol′a ble ness,** *n.* **—in′con sol′a bly,** *adv.*

in con so nance (in kon′sə nəns), *n.* lack of harmony; disagreement.

in con so nant (in kon′sə nənt), *adj.* not harmonious; not in agreement or accord. **—in con′so nant ly,** *adv.*

in con spic u ous (in′kən spik′yü əs), *adj.* not conspicuous; attracting little or no attention. **—in′con spic′u ous ly,** *adv.* **—in′con spic′u ous ness,** *n.*

in con stan cy (in kon′stən sē), *n.* lack of constancy; changeableness; fickleness.

in con stant (in kon′stənt), *adj.* not constant; changeable; fickle. **—in con′stant ly,** *adv.*

in con sum a ble (in′kən sü′mə bəl), *adj.* that cannot be consumed.

in con test a bil i ty (in′kən tes′tə bil′ə tē), *n.* a being incontestable.

in con test a ble (in′kən tes′tə bəl), *adj.* beyond dispute or doubt; unquestionable. **—in′con test′a bly,** *adv.*

in con ti nence (in kon′tə nəns), *n.* 1 lack of self-control. 2 lack of chastity.

in con ti nent (in kon′tə nənt), *adj.* 1 without self-control. 2 not chaste; licentious. **—in con′ti nent ly,** *adv.*

hat, āge, fär; let, ēqual, tėrm;
it, īce; hot, ōpen, ôrder;
oil, out; cup, pu̇t, rüle;
ch, child; ng, long; sh, she;
th, thin; ᴛʜ, then; zh, measure;

ə represents *a* in about, *e* in taken, *i* in pencil, *o* in lemon, *u* in circus.

< = from, derived from, taken from.

in con trol la ble (in′kən trō′lə bəl), *adj.* uncontrollable.

in con tro vert i ble (in′kon trə vėr′tə bəl), *adj.* that cannot be disputed or denied; too clear or certain to be argued about; unquestionable. **—in′con tro vert′i bly,** *adv.*

in con ven ience (in′kən vē′nyəns), *n., v.,* **-ienced, -ienc ing.** *—n.* 1 lack of convenience or ease; trouble; bother. 2 something inconvenient; cause of trouble, difficulty, or bother. *—v.t.* cause trouble, difficulty, or bother to.

in con ven ient (in′kən vē′nyənt), *adj.* not convenient; causing trouble, difficulty, or bother; troublesome. **—in′con ven′ient ly,** *adv.*

in con vert i bil i ty (in′kən vėr′tə bil′ə tē), *n.* a being inconvertible.

in con vert i ble (in′kən vėr′tə bəl), *adj.* not convertible; incapable of being converted or exchanged. Paper money is inconvertible when it cannot be exchanged for gold or silver. **—in′con vert′i bly,** *adv.*

in con vin ci ble (in′kən vin′sə bəl), *adj.* that cannot be convinced.

in co or di nate (in′kō ôrd′n it), *adj.* not coordinate.

in cor po rate (*v.* in kôr′pə rāt′; *adj.* in kôr′pər it) *v.,* **-rat ed, -rat ing,** *adj.* *—v.t.* 1 make (something) a part of something else; join or combine (something) with something else: *We will incorporate your suggestion in this new plan.* 2 make into a corporation: *When the business became large, the owners incorporated it.* 3 embody; give material form to: *incorporate one's thoughts in an article.* *—v.i.* 1 form a corporation. 2 unite or combine so as to form one body; merge. *—adj.* united; combined; incorporated. [< Latin *incorporatum* formed into a body < *in-* into + *corpus* body]

in cor po rat ed (in kôr′pə rā′tid), *adj.* made into a corporation; chartered as a corporation.

in cor po ra tion (in kôr′pə rā′shən), *n.* 1 an incorporating: *The new design reflected the incorporation of many revisions.* 2 a being incorporated: *Incorporation gives a company the power to act as one person.*

in cor po ra tive (in kôr′pə rā′tiv), *adj.* characterized by or tending to incorporate.

in cor po ra tor (in kôr′pə rā′tər), *n.* 1 person who incorporates. 2 one of the original members of a corporation.

in cor po re al (in′kôr pôr′ē əl, in′kôr pōr′ē əl), *adj.* not made of any material substance; spiritual. **—in′cor po′re al ly,** *adv.*

in cor rect (in′kə rekt′), *adj.* 1 containing errors or mistakes; wrong; faulty. 2 not agreeing with a good standard of taste; improper. **—in′cor rect′ly,** *adv.* **—in′cor rect′ness,** *n.*

in cor ri gi bil i ty (in kôr′ə jə bil′ə tē, in-kor′ə jə bil′ə tē), *n.* a being incorrigible.

in cor ri gi ble (in kôr′ə jə bəl, in kor′ə jə-bəl), *adj.* 1 too firmly fixed in bad ways, an annoying habit, etc., to be reformed or changed: *an incorrigible liar.* 2 so fixed that it cannot be changed or cured: *an incorrigible habit of giggling.* —*n.* an incorrigible person. —**in cor′ri gi ble ness,** *n.* —**in cor′ri gi-bly,** *adv.*

in cor rupt (in kə rupt′), *adj.* 1 not corruptible; honest. 2 free from decay; sound. 3 not marred by errors, alterations, etc.

in cor rupt i bil i ty (in′kə rup′tə bil′ə tē), *n.* a being incorruptible.

in cor rupt i ble (in′kə rup′tə bəl), *adj.* 1 not to be corrupted; honest: *The incorruptible judge could not be bribed.* 2 not subject to decay; lasting forever: *Diamonds are incorruptible.* —**in′cor rupt′i bly,** *adv.*

in crease (*v.* in krēs′; *n.* in′krēs), *v.,* **-creased, -creas ing,** *n.* —*v.t.* make greater, more numerous, more powerful, etc.; add to: *increase the speed of a car, increase taxes, increase one's possessions.* See synonym study below. —*v.i.* 1 become greater; advance in quality, power, etc.: *increase in wisdom. The danger increases.* 2 grow in numbers, especially by propagation; become more numerous; multiply: *These flowers will increase every year.* —*n.* 1 a gain in size, numbers, etc.; growth. 2 result of increasing; amount increased; addition. 3 **on the increase,** becoming greater or more frequent; increasing. 4 offspring. [< Old French *encreiss-,* a form of *encreistre* < Latin *increscere* < *in-* + *crescere* grow] —**in creas′a-ble,** *adj.* —**in creas′er,** *n.*

Syn. *v.t.* **Increase, enlarge, augment** mean to make greater. **Increase** means to make greater in amount, number, wealth, power, etc.: *increase sales.* **Enlarge** means to make greater in size, extent, or capacity: *They enlarged the school auditorium.* **Augment** means to increase by adding amounts or sums: *Many teachers do outside work to augment their salaries.*

in creas ing ly (in krē′sing lē), *adv.* to a greater degree; more and more.

in cre ate (in′krē āt′, in′krē āt), *adj.* not created; existing without having been created.

in cred i bil i ty (in kred′ə bil′ə tē), *n.* a being incredible.

in cred i ble (in kred′ə bəl), *adj.* hard to believe; seeming too extraordinary to be possible; unbelievable: *incredible bravery. Many old superstitions seem incredible to us.* —**in-cred′i bly,** *adv.*

in cre du li ty (in′krə dü′lə tē, in′krə-dyü′lə tē), *n.* lack of belief; doubt.

in cred u lous (in krej′ə ləs), *adj.* 1 not ready to believe; doubting; skeptical: *If they look incredulous show them the evidence.* 2 showing a lack of belief: *an incredulous smile.* —**in cred′u lous ly,** *adv.*

in cre ment (in′krə mənt, ing′krə mənt), *n.* 1 an increasing or becoming greater; increase; growth. 2 amount or portion added to a thing so as to increase it; addition. 3 (in mathematics) a positive or negative change, usually small, in the value of a variable. [< Latin *incrementum* < *increscere.* See INCREASE.]

in cre men tal (in′krə men′tl, ing′krə-men′tl), *adj.* of, having to do with, or like an increment.

in cres cent (in kres′nt), *adj.* increasing.

in crim i nate (in krim′ə nāt), *v.t.,* **-nat ed, -nat ing.** accuse of a crime; show to be guilty: *In his confession the thief incriminated two others.* [< Late Latin *incriminatum* charged with a crime < Latin *in-* against + *crimen* a charge] —**in crim′i na′tion,** *n.*

in crim i na to ry (in krim′ə nə tôr′ē, in-krim′ə nə tōr′ē), *adj.* tending to incriminate.

in crust (in krust′), *v.t., v.i.* encrust.

in crus ta tion (in′kru stā′shən), *n.* 1 an encrusting. 2 a being encrusted. 3 crust or hard coating. 4 a decorative layer of costly material. Also, **encrustation.**

in cu bate (ing′kyə bāt, in′kyə bāt), *v.,* **-bat ed, -bat ing.** —*v.t.* 1 sit on (eggs) in order to hatch them; brood. 2 maintain (premature babies, eggs, cultures of microorganisms, etc.) at a temperature, humidity, and oxygen level suitable for development. —*v.i.* 1 sit on eggs; brood. 2 (of a disease) undergo incubation. [< Latin *incubatum* incubated < *in-* on + *cubare* lie]

in cu ba tion (ing′kyə bā′shən, in′kyə-bā′shən), *n.* 1 act of incubating. 2 condition of being incubated. 3 stage of a disease from the time of infection until the first symptoms appear.

in cu ba tion al (ing′kyə bā′shə nəl, in′-kyə bā′shə nəl), *adj.* incubative.

in cu ba tive (ing′kyə bā′tiv, in′kyə bā′tiv), *adj.* of or having to do with incubation.

in cu ba tor (ing′kyə bā′tər, in′kyə bā′tər), *n.* 1 box or chamber for hatching eggs by keeping them warm and properly supplied with moisture and oxygen. 2 any similar box or chamber. Very small babies and premature babies are sometimes kept for a time in incubators. 3 apparatus in which cultures of microorganisms are developed.

in cu bus (ing′kyə bəs, in′kyə bəs), *n., pl.* **-bi** (-bī), **-bus es.** 1 an evil spirit supposed to descend upon sleeping persons. 2 nightmare. 3 an oppressive or burdensome thing. [< Late Latin < Latin *incubare* lie on < *in-* on + *cubare* lie]

in cu des (in kyü′dēz), *n.* pl. of **incus.**

in cul cate (in kul′kāt, in′kul kāt), *v.t.,* **-cat ed, -cat ing.** impress (ideas, opinions, etc.) on the mind of another by frequent repetition; teach persistently. [< Latin *inculcatum* impressed upon, originally, trampled in < *in-* in + *calcem* heel] —**in′cul ca′tion,** *n.* —**in cul′ca tor,** *n.*

in cul pa ble (in kul′pə bəl), *adj.* blameless.

in cul pate (in kul′pāt, in′kul pāt), *v.t.,* **-pat ed, -pat ing.** involve in responsibility for wrongdoing; incriminate. [< Late Latin *inculpatum* accused, blamed < Latin *in-* in + *culpa* blame] —**in′cul pa′tion,** *n.*

in cum ben cy (in kum′bən sē), *n., pl.* **-cies.** 1 term of office: *During his incumbency as governor the state prospered.* 2 a being incumbent.

in cum bent (in kum′bənt), *adj.* 1 lying, leaning, or pressing on something. 2 resting on a person as a duty or obligation: *She felt it incumbent upon her to answer the letter at once.* 3 currently holding an office, position, etc.: *the incumbent governor.* —*n.* person holding an office, position, etc. [< Latin *incumbentem* < *in-* on + *-cumbere* lie down]

in cum ber (in kum′bər), *v.t.* encumber.

in cum brance (in kum′brəns), *n.* encumbrance.

in cu nab u la (in′kyə nab′yə lə), *n.pl.* of **in cu nab u lum** (in′kyə nab′yə ləm). 1 the earliest stages or first traces in the development of anything; beginnings. 2 books printed before 1501. [< Latin, cradle < *in-* in + *cunae* cradle]

in cur (in kėr′), *v.t.,* **-curred, -cur ring.** run or fall into (something unpleasant or inconvenient); bring on oneself: *incur many expenses.* [< Latin *incurrere* < *in-* upon + *currere* to run]

in cur a bil i ty (in kyur′ə bil′ə tē), *n.* a being incurable.

in cur a ble (in kyůr′ə bəl), *adj.* not capable of being cured or healed: *an incurable invalid.* —*n.* person having an incurable disease. —**in cur′a ble ness,** *n.* —**in cur′a-bly,** *adv.*

in cur i ous (in kyůr′ē əs), *adj.* lacking curiosity; uninquiring; indifferent. —**in cur′i-ous ly,** *adv.*

in cur rence (in kėr′əns), *n.* act or fact of incurring.

in cur sion (in kėr′zhən, in kėr′shən), *n.* 1 a sudden attack; invasion; raid. 2 a running or flowing in: *Dikes protected the lowland from incursions of the sea.* [< Latin *incursionem* < *incurrere.* See INCUR.]

in cur sive (in kėr′siv), *adj.* making incursions.

in curve (in′kėrv′), *n., v.,* **-curved, -curv ing.** —*n.* an inward curve. —*v.t., v.i.* curve inward.

in cus (ing′kəs), *n., pl.* **in cu des.** the middle one of the three small bones of the middle ear of mammals, shaped somewhat like an anvil. [< Latin, anvil]

Ind (ind), *n.* 1 ARCHAIC. India. 2 OBSOLETE. the East or West Indies.

ind., 1 independent. 2 index. 3 indicative. 4 industrial.

Ind., 1 India. 2 Indian. 3 Indiana.

in debt ed (in det′id), *adj.* owing money, gratitude, etc.; in debt; obliged.

in debt ed ness (in det′id nis), *n.* 1 condition of being in debt. 2 amount owed; debts.

in de cen cy (in dē′sn sē), *n., pl.* **-cies.** 1 lack of decency; being indecent. 2 an indecent act or word.

in de cent (in dē′snt), *adj.* 1 not decent; in very bad taste; improper: *an indecent lack of gratitude. They left the party with indecent haste.* See **improper** for synonym study. 2 not modest; morally bad; disgusting; obscene. —**in de′cent ly,** *adv.*

in de ci pher a bil i ty (in′di sī′fər ə-bil′ə tē), *n.* quality or condition of being indecipherable.

in de ci pher a ble (in′di sī′fər ə bəl), *adj.* incapable of being deciphered; illegible.

in de ci sion (in′di sizh′ən), *n.* lack of decision; tendency to delay or to hesitate.

in de ci sive (in′di sī′siv), *adj.* 1 having the habit of hesitating and putting off decisions: *an indecisive person.* 2 not deciding or settling the matter; inconclusive: *an indecisive battle.* —**in′de ci′sive ly,** *adv.* —**in′de-ci′sive ness,** *n.*

in de clin a ble (in′di klī′nə bəl), *adj.* having the same form in all grammatical constructions. *None* is an indeclinable pronoun.

in dec or ous (in dek′ər əs, in′di kôr′əs, in′di kōr′əs), *adj.* not in accordance with proper behavior; in poor taste; improper. —**in dec′or ous ly,** *adv.* —**in dec′or ous-ness,** *n.*

in de co rum (in′di kôr′əm, in′di kōr′əm), *n.* 1 lack of decorum. 2 improper behavior, speech, dress, etc.

in deed (in dēd′), *adv.* 1 in fact; in truth; really; surely. 2 without doubt; admittedly:

It is indeed poor work. —*interj.* expression of surprise, doubt, contempt, etc.
indef., indefinite.
in de fat i ga bil i ty (in′di fat′ə gə bil′ə tē), *n.* a being indefatigable.
in de fat i ga ble (in′di fat′ə gə bəl), *adj.* never getting tired or giving up; tireless. [< Latin *indefatigabilis* < *in-* not + *defatigare* tire out < *de-* completely + *fatigare* to tire] **—in′de fat′i ga ble ness,** *n.* **—in′de fat′i ga bly,** *adv.*
in de fea si bil i ty (in′di fē′zə bil′ə tē), *n.* a being indefeasible.
in de fea si ble (in′di fē′zə bəl), *adj.* not capable of being annulled, made void, or done away with: *Kings were once believed to have an indefeasible right to rule.* [< *in-*[1] + Anglo-French *defaisible* that may be annulled < Old French *desfaire* undo < *des-* dis- + *faire* do] **—in′de fea′si bly,** *adv.*
in de fec ti bil i ty (in′di fek′tə bil′ə tē), *n.* quality of being indefectible.
in de fec ti ble (in′di fek′tə bəl), *adj.* 1 not liable to defect, failure, or decay; unfailing. 2 without blemish or flaw; faultless. **—in′de fec′ti bly,** *adv.*
in de fen si bil i ty (in′di fen′sə bil′ə tē), *n.* a being indefensible.
in de fen si ble (in′di fen′sə bəl), *adj.* 1 that cannot be defended: *an indefensible island.* 2 not justifiable; inexcusable: *an indefensible lie.* **—in′de fen′si bly,** *adv.*
in de fin a bil i ty (in′di fī′nə bil′ə tē), *n.* a being indefinable.
in de fin a ble (in′di fī′nə bəl), *adj.* that cannot be defined or described exactly. **—in′de fin′a ble ness,** *n.* **—in′de fin′a bly,** *adv.*
in def i nite (in def′ə nit), *adj.* 1 not clearly defined; not precise; vague: *"Maybe" is a very indefinite answer.* 2 not limited or fixed: *We have an indefinite time to finish this work.* 3 not specifying precisely; not identifying a specific person, thing, time, etc. *Some, many,* and *few* are often indefinite pronouns. **—in def′i nite ly,** *adv.* **—in def′i nite ness,** *n.*
indefinite article, the articles *a* or *an.*
in de his cence (in′di his′ns), *n.* a being indehiscent.
in de his cent (in′di his′nt), *adj.* (in botany) not splitting open at maturity. Acorns are indehiscent fruits.
in del i bil i ty (in del′ə bil′ə tē), *n.* a being indelible.
in del i ble (in del′ə bəl), *adj.* 1 that cannot be erased or removed; permanent: *indelible ink, an indelible impression.* 2 capable of making an indelible mark: *an indelible pencil.* [< Latin *indelebilis* < *in-* not + *delebilis* able to be destroyed < *delere* destroy] **—in del′i bly,** *adv.*
in del i ca cy (in del′ə kə sē), *n., pl.* **-cies.** 1 lack of delicacy; being indelicate. 2 an indelicate act, remark, etc.
in del i cate (in del′ə kit), *adj.* 1 not delicate; coarse; crude. 2 improper; immodest. **—in del′i cate ly,** *adv.* **—in del′i cate ness,** *n.*
in dem ni fi ca tion (in dem′nə fə kā′shən), *n.* 1 an indemnifying. 2 a being indemnified. 3 compensation.
in dem ni fy (in dem′nə fī), *v.t.,* **-fied, -fy ing.** 1 compensate for damage, loss, or hardship; make good; repay: *The railroad indemnified him for his injuries.* 2 secure or protect against damage or loss; insure. [< Latin *indemnis* unhurt (< *in-* not + *damnum* damage) + English *-fy*]
in dem ni ty (in dem′nə tē), *n., pl.* **-ties.** 1 payment for damage, loss, or hardship. Money demanded by a victorious nation at the end of a war as a condition of peace is an indemnity. 2 security or protection against damage or loss; insurance. [< Late Latin *indemnitatem* < Latin *indemnis* unhurt. See INDEMNIFY.]

indent[1] (def. 1) indented molding

in dent[1] (*v.* in dent′; *n.* in′dent, in dent′), *v.t.* 1 make notches or jags in (an edge, line, border, etc.): *an indented coastline.* 2 begin (a line) farther from the left margin than the other lines: *The first line of a paragraph is usually indented.* —*v.i.* form a notch or recess. —*n.* a notch; indentation. [< Old French *endenter* < Late Latin *indentare* to crunch on < Latin *in-* in + *dentem* tooth]
in dent[2] (in dent′), *v.t.* 1 make a dent in; mark with a dent. 2 press in; stamp. [< *in-*[2] + *dent*]
in den ta tion (in′den tā′shən), *n.* 1 an indenting. 2 a being indented. 3 a dent, notch, or cut.
in den tion (in den′shən), *n.* 1 a beginning of a line farther from the left margin than the other lines. 2 the blank space left by this. 3 indentation.
in den ture (in den′chər), *n., v.,* **-tured, -tur ing.** —*n.* 1 a written agreement, such as a contract or deed. 2 Also, **indentures,** *pl.* contract by which a servant or apprentice is bound to serve or work for someone else. 3 indentation. —*v.t.* bind by a contract to serve or work for someone else: *Many settlers came to the American colonies indentured for several years.* [< Old French *endenteüre* an indented document, indentation < *endenter.* See INDENT[1].]
in de pend ence (in′di pen′dəns), *n.* 1 condition of being independent; freedom from the control, influence, support, or help of others: *The American colonies won independence from England.* 2 ARCHAIC. enough income to live on.
In de pend ence (in′di pen′dəns), *n.* city in W Missouri, one of the terminals of the Santa Fe Trail. 112,000.
Independence Day, holiday in honor of the adoption of the Declaration of Independence on July 4, 1776; Fourth of July.
in de pend en cy (in′di pen′dən sē), *n., pl.* **-cies.** 1 independence. 2 an independent country.
in de pend ent (in′di pen′dənt), *adj.* 1 needing, wishing, or getting no help from others: *independent work, independent thinking.* 2 acting, working, or, especially, voting by one's own ideas, not as the crowd does. 3 guiding, ruling, or governing itself; not under another's rule: *an independent country.* 4 not depending on others: *independent income.* 5 not resulting from another thing; not controlled or influenced by something else; separate; distinct: *an independent plan.* 6 **independent of,** apart from; without regard to: *independent of the feelings of others.* 7 in mathematics: **a** (of a variable) that can be assigned any value. **b** indicating an equation which, when compared to one or more other equations, does not have as a solution at least one solution that satisfies the other equations. —*n.* 1 person or thing that is independent. 2 person who votes without regard to party. **—in′de pend′ent ly,** *adv.*

hat, āge, fär; let, ēqual, tėrm;
it, īce; hot, ōpen, ôrder;
oil, out; cup, pu̇t, rüle;
ch, child; ng, long; sh, she;
th, thin; ᴛʜ, then; zh, measure;

ə represents *a* in about, *e* in taken, *i* in pencil, *o* in lemon, *u* in circus.

< = from, derived from, taken from.

independent clause, main clause.
in-depth (in′depth′), *adj.* thorough; detailed.
in de scrib a ble (in′di skrī′bə bəl), *adj.* that cannot be described; beyond description. **—in′de scrib′a ble ness,** *n.* **—in′de scrib′a bly,** *adv.*
in de struct i bil i ty (in′di struk′tə bil′ə tē), *n.* indestructible quality or condition.
in de struct i ble (in′di struk′tə bəl), *adj.* that cannot be destroyed. **—in′de struct′i ble ness,** *n.* **—in′de struct′i bly,** *adv.*
in de ter mi na ble (in′di tėr′mə nə bəl), *adj.* not capable of being settled, decided, or determined exactly. **—in′de ter′mi na bly,** *adv.*
in de ter mi na cy (in′di tėr′mə nə sē), *n.* a being indeterminate.
in de ter mi nate (in′di tėr′mə nit), *adj.* 1 not determined; not definite or fixed; indefinite; vague. 2 having flowers which arise from axillary buds so that the tip continues to grow forming new bracts and flowers; racemose. **—in′de ter′mi nate ly,** *adv.* **—in′de ter′mi nate ness,** *n.*
in de ter mi na tion (in′di tėr′mə nā′shən), *n.* 1 lack of determination. 2 an unsettled state.
in dex (in′deks), *n., pl.* **-dex es** or **-di ces,** *v.* —*n.* 1 list of what is in a book, indicating on what pages to find topics, names, etc., usually put at the end of the book and arranged in alphabetical order. 2 thing that points out or shows; sign: *A person's face is often an index of his mood.* 3 index finger. 4 pointer or indicator on a dial or scale. 5 (in printing) a sign (☞) used to point out a particular note, paragraph, etc.; fist. 6 number or formula expressing some property, relationship, ratio, etc., in science. 7 index number. 8 in mathematics: **a** an exponent. **b** the number indicating the root: *In* $\sqrt[3]{764}$ *the index is 3.* 9 **Index,** list of books or passages in books that the Roman Catholic Church forbids its members to read without special permission. —*v.t.* 1 provide with an index; make an index of. 2 enter in an index. 3 serve as an index of; indicate. [< Latin, forefinger, originally, that which points out < *indicare* point out, indicate < *in-* in, to + *dicare* make known, proclaim] **—in′dex er,** *n.*
index finger, forefinger.
index fossil, any abundant and widely distributed fossil that is used to identify or date the rock in which it is found.
in dex i cal (in dek′sə kəl), *adj.* having to do with or like an index.
index number, (in statistics) a number indicating the relative level of prices, sales, credit, etc., at any given time with reference to the level of some predetermined time.
index of refraction, the ratio of the velocity of light in one medium, usually a vacuum or air, to its velocity in another; refractive index.

In di a (in′dē ə), *n.* 1 country in S Asia, a member of the Commonwealth of Nations. 547,000,000 pop.; 1,261,600 sq. mi. *Capital:* New Delhi. *Official name:* **Bharat.** 2 region and former country in S Asia. Until 1947 most of India was under British rule. It is now chiefly divided into the countries of India, Pakistan, and Bangladesh.

India ink, 1 a black pigment consisting of lampblack mixed with a binding material. 2 a liquid ink prepared from this pigment.

In di a man (in′dē ə mən), *n., pl.* **-men.** ship formerly used in trade with India.

In di an (in′dē ən), *n.* 1 American Indian. 2 any one of the languages of the American Indians. 3 native or inhabitant of India or the East Indies. *—adj.* 1 of or having to do with American Indians. 2 made of Indian corn. 3 of, living in, or belonging to India or the East Indies.

In di an a (in′dē an′ə), *n.* one of the north central states of the United States. 5,194,000 pop.; 36,300 sq. mi. *Capital:* Indianapolis. *Abbrev.:* Ind. **—In′di an′an, —In′di-an′i an,** *adj.*

In di a nap o lis (in′dē ə nap′ə lis, in′dē ə-nap′lis), *n.* capital of Indiana, in the central part. 745,000.

Indian club

Indian club, a bottle-shaped wooden club swung for exercise.

Indian corn, 1 species of cereal grass first raised by American Indians; maize. 2 grain or ears of this plant.

Indian Empire, parts of India formerly under British control.

Indian file, single file.

Indian giver, person who takes back a gift after having bestowed it.

Indian meal, corn meal.

Indian Ocean, ocean south of Asia, east of Africa, and west of Australia. 28,350,000 sq. mi.

Indian paintbrush, 1 any of a genus of plants of western North America of the same family as the figwort, with showy crimson, yellow, or pink bracts; paintbrush. 2 a hawkweed with reddish-orange flowers, that grows as a weed in much of North America.

Indian pipe, a waxy, leafless, white plant with a solitary bell-shaped flower that looks like a tobacco pipe.

Indian pudding, a baked pudding made with corn meal, molasses, milk, and suet.

Indian summer, time of mild, dry, hazy weather in late October or early November, after the first frosts of autumn.

Indian Territory, a former territory of the United States, now part of Oklahoma.

Indian tobacco, a North American weed, a species of lobelia, with small blue flowers and swollen capsules, used in medicine.

Indian turnip, jack-in-the-pulpit.

India paper, 1 a thin, tough paper, used chiefly for Bibles, prayer books, etc. 2 a thin, soft paper, used for the first and finest impressions of engravings, etc.

india rubber or **India rubber,** rubber.

In dic (in′dik), *adj.* 1 of or having to do with

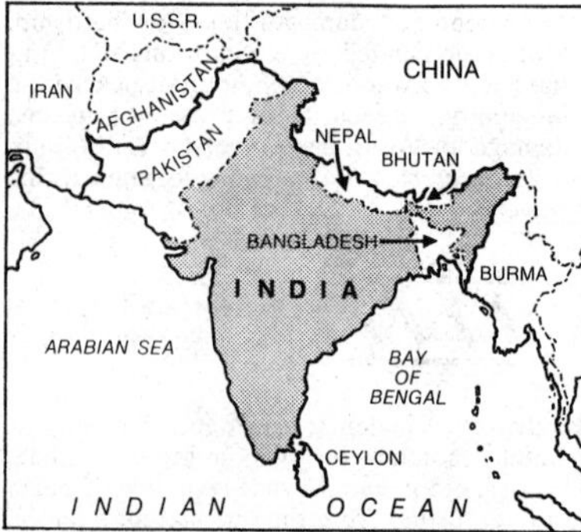

India
(def. 1, the shaded area; def. 2, the area within the heavy boundary line)

India; Indian. 2 designating or having to do with the Indian branch of the Indo-Iranian languages, which includes Hindi, Urdu, Sanskrit, etc.

indic., indicative.

in di cate (in′də kāt), *v.t.,* **-cat ed, -cat ing.** 1 point out; point to: *The arrow on the sign indicates the right way to go.* 2 make known; show: *A thermometer indicates temperature.* 3 be a sign or hint of: *Fever indicates illness.* 4 give a sign or hint of: *indicate one's views.* 5 show to be needed as a remedy or treatment: *In this case surgery is indicated.* [< Latin *indicatum* pointed out, shown < *in-* in, to + *dicare* make known, proclaim]

in di ca tion (in′də kā′shən), *n.* 1 act of indicating. 2 thing that indicates; sign. 3 amount or degree indicated: *The speedometer indication was 45 miles.*

in dic a tive (in dik′ə tiv), *adj.* 1 pointing out; showing; being a sign; suggestive: *A headache is sometimes indicative of eyestrain.* 2 (in grammar) having to do with a verb form which expresses or denotes a state, act, or happening as actual, or which asks a simple question of fact. *—n.* 1 a verb form in the indicative mood. In "I go" and "Did you win?" *go* and *did win* are indicatives. 2 the indicative mood. **—in dic′a-tive ly,** *adv.*

in di ca tor (in′də kā′tər), *n.* 1 person or thing that indicates. 2 pointer on the dial of an instrument that shows the amount of heat, pressure, speed, etc. 3 a measuring or recording instrument. 4 substance which, by changing color or some other property, indicates the concentration, presence or absence of a substance, or the endpoint of a chemical reaction. Litmus is an indicator.

in di ces (in′də sēz′), *n.* a pl. of **index.**

in dict (in dīt′), *v.t.* 1 charge with an offense or crime; accuse. 2 (of a grand jury) find enough evidence against (an accused person) to charge formally with a crime. [< Anglo-French *enditer,* in Old French, indite, dictate < Latin *in-* in + *dictare* declare, dictate < *dicere* say, speak] **—in dict′a ble,** *adj.* **—in dict′er, in dict′or,** *n.*

in dict ment (in dīt′mənt), *n.* 1 a formal written accusation, especially one presented by a grand jury. 2 accusation.

In dies (in′dēz), *n.pl.* 1 the East Indies. 2 the West Indies.

in dif fer ence (in dif′ər əns), *n.* 1 lack of interest or attention. See synonym study below. 2 lack of importance: *Where we ate was a matter of indifference.*

Syn. 1 **Indifference, unconcern, apathy** mean absence of feeling or lack of interest. **Indifference** suggests not caring one way or the other: *A lazy, careless person treats his work with indifference.* **Unconcern** implies indifference arising out of selfishness, callousness, etc., to something one should care about: *Nobody understands the unconcern of her parents.* **Apathy** suggests listless indifference to everything except one's own troubles, sorrow, or pain: *Her apathy since her husband's death worries her children.*

in dif fer ent (in dif′ər ənt), *adj.* 1 having or showing no interest or attention: *indifferent to an admirer.* 2 not inclined to prefer one person or thing to another; impartial; neutral; fair: *an indifferent decision.* 3 not mattering much; unimportant: *The time for starting is indifferent to me.* 4 neither good nor bad; just fair; mediocre. 5 rather bad; poor. 6 neutral in chemical, electrical, or magnetic quality. **—in dif′fer ent ly,** *adv.*

in di gence (in′də jəns), *n.* extreme need; poverty.

in dig e nous (in dij′ə nəs), *adj.* 1 originating or produced in a particular country; growing or living naturally in a certain region, soil, climate, etc.; native: *Lions are indigenous to Africa.* 2 born in a person; innate; inherent. [< Latin *indigena* a native, ultimately < *indu* in + *gignere* beget, bear] **—in dig′e nous ly,** *adv.*

in di gent (in′də jənt), *adj.* lacking the necessities of life; poor or needy. [< Latin *indigentem* < *indu* in + *egere* be in need]

in di gest i bil i ty (in′də jes′tə bil′ə tē, in′dī jes′tə bil′ə tē), *n.* indigestible nature or quality.

in di gest i ble (in′də jes′tə bəl, in′dī-jes′tə bəl), *adj.* that cannot be digested; hard to digest.

in di ges tion (in′də jes′chən, in′dī-jes′chən), *n.* inability to digest food; difficulty in digesting food; dyspepsia.

in dig nant (in dig′nənt), *adj.* angry at something unworthy, unjust, unfair, or mean. [< Latin *indignantem* < *indignus* unworthy < *in-* not + *dignus* worthy] **—in dig′nant-ly,** *adv.*

in dig na tion (in′dig nā′shən), *n.* anger at something unworthy, unjust, unfair, or mean; anger mixed with scorn; righteous anger: *Cruelty to animals aroused his indignation.* See **anger** for synonym study.

in dig ni ty (in dig′nə tē), *n., pl.* **-ties.** 1 an injury to one's dignity; lack of respect or proper treatment; insult. See **insult** for synonym study.

in di go (in′də gō), *n., pl.* **-gos** or **-goes,** *adj.* *—n.* 1 a blue dye formerly obtained from various plants, but now usually made artificially. 2 any of various plants of the pea family from which indigo was made. 3 a deep violet-blue. *—adj.* deep violet-blue. [< Spanish < Latin *indicum* < Greek *indikon,* originally adjective, Indian]

indigo bunting, a small American finch,

indigo bunting
about 5 in. long

the male of which is a deep violet-blue with blackish wings and tail. The female is brown.

indigo snake, gopher snake.

in di rect (in′də rekt′, in′dī rekt′), *adj.* 1 not going straight to the point; roundabout: *an indirect answer.* 2 not immediately resulting from an action or cause; secondary: *Happiness is an indirect result of doing one's work well.* 3 not direct; not straight: *an indirect route.* 4 not straightforward and honest; deceitful: *indirect methods.* **—in′di rect′ly,** *adv.* **—in′di rect′ness,** *n.*

indirect discourse, repetition of the substance of a person's speech without directly quoting it. EXAMPLE: "He said that he would come," instead of "He said, 'I will come.' "

in di rec tion (in′də rek′shən, in′dī rek′shən), *n.* 1 a roundabout act, course, or method. 2 deceitful or crooked dealing.

indirect lighting, artificial lighting that is diffused or reflected to illuminate without glare.

indirect object (in grammar) a word or group of words that usually comes before the direct object and denotes the person or thing to which or for which something is done. In "I gave John a book," *John* is the indirect object and *book* is the direct object.

indirect tax, tax paid indirectly by the consumer and included in the price of the article.

in dis cern i ble (in′də zėr′nə bəl, in′də sėr′nə bəl), *adj.* not discernible; imperceptible.

in dis ci pline (in dis′ə plən), *n.* lack of discipline.

in dis cov er a ble (in′dis kuv′ər ə bəl), *adj.* not discoverable.

in dis creet (in′dis krēt′), *adj.* not discreet; not wise and judicious; imprudent. **—in′dis creet′ly,** *adv.* **—in′dis creet′ness,** *n.*

in dis crete (in′dis krēt′, in dis′krēt), *adj.* not discrete; not consisting of distinct parts.

in dis cre tion (in′dis kresh′ən), *n.* 1 a being indiscreet; lack of good judgment; unwiseness; imprudence. 2 an indiscreet act.

in dis crim i nate (in′dis krim′ə nit), *adj.* 1 mixed up; confused: *She tipped everything out of her suitcase in an indiscriminate pile.* 2 without discrimination; not distinguishing carefully between persons, things, etc.: *an indiscriminate reader.* See **miscellaneous** for synonym study. **—in′dis crim′i nate ly,** *adv.* **—in′dis crim′i nate ness,** *n.*

in dis crim i na tion (in′dis krim′ə nā′shən), *n.* lack of discrimination.

in dis pen sa bil i ty (in′dis pen′sə bil′ə tē), *n.* a being indispensable.

in dis pen sa ble (in′dis pen′sə bəl), *adj.* absolutely necessary: *Air is indispensable to life.* See **necessary** for synonym study. *—n.* person or thing that is indispensable. **—in′dis pen′sa ble ness,** *n.* **—in′dis pen′sa bly,** *adv.*

in dis pose (in′dis pōz′), *v.t.,* **-posed, -pos ing.** 1 make unwilling; make not inclined: *Hot weather indisposes a person to work hard.* 2 make unfit or unable; disqualify. 3 make slightly ill.

in dis posed (in′dis pōzd′), *adj.* 1 slightly ill. 2 unwilling.

in dis po si tion (in′dis pə zish′ən), *n.* 1 a slight illness. 2 unwillingness.

in dis put a bil i ty (in′dis pyü′tə bil′ə tē, in dis′pyə tə bil′ə tē), *n.* a being indisputable.

in dis put a ble (in′dis pyü′tə bəl, in dis′pyə tə bəl), *adj.* too evident to be disputed; undoubted; certain; unquestionable. **—in′dis put′a ble ness,** *n.* **—in′dis put′a bly,** *adv.*

in dis sol u bil i ty (in′di sol′yə bil′ə tē), *n.* a being indissoluble.

in dis sol u ble (in′di sol′yə bəl), *adj.* that cannot be dissolved, undone, or destroyed; lasting; firm. **—in′dis sol′u ble ness,** *n.* **—in′dis sol′u bly,** *adv.*

in dis tinct (in′dis tingkt′), *adj.* not distinct; not clear to the eye, ear, or mind; confused: *an indistinct voice. He had an indistinct memory of the accident.* **—in′dis tinct′ly,** *adv.* **—in′dis tinct′ness,** *n.*

in dis tinc tive (in′dis tingk′tiv), *adj.* not distinctive; without distinctive character or features. **—in′dis tinc′tive ly,** *adv.* **—in′dis tinc′tive ness,** *n.*

in dis tin guish a bil i ty (in′dis ting′gwi shə bil′ə tē), *n.* quality or condition of being indistinguishable.

in dis tin guish a ble (in′dis ting′gwi shə bəl), *adj.* that cannot be distinguished. **—in′dis tin′guish a ble ness,** *n.* **—in′dis tin′guish a bly,** *adv.*

in dite (in dīt′), *v.t.,* **-dit ed, -dit ing.** put in words or writing; compose: *indite a letter.* [< Old French *enditer.* See INDICT.]

in di um (in′dē əm), *n.* a very soft, silvery metallic element found only in combination with other elements. It is resistant to abrasion and is used as a coating on metal parts. *Symbol:* In; *atomic number* 49. See pages 326 and 327 for table. [< New Latin < Latin *indicum.* See INDIGO.]

in di vert i ble (in′də vėr′tə bəl, in′dī vėr′tə bəl), *adj.* not divertible; not to be turned aside. **—in′di vert′i bly,** *adv.*

in di vid u al (in′də vij′ü əl), *n.* 1 person. See **person** for synonym study. 2 one person, animal, or thing. *—adj.* 1 single; particular; separate: *an individual question.* 2 for one only: *individual saltcellars.* 3 having to do with or peculiar to one person or thing: *individual tastes.* 4 marking off one person or thing specially: *She has an individual style of writing.* [< Medieval Latin *individualis* < Latin *individuus* indivisible < *in-* not + *dividuus* divisible] **—in′di vid′u al ly,** *adv.*

in di vid u al ism (in′də vij′ü ə liz′əm), *n.* 1 theory that individual freedom is as important as the welfare of the community or group as a whole. 2 any ethical, economic, or political theory that emphasizes the importance of individuals. 3 the pursuit of one's own ends or ideas as a mode or principle of life. 4 individuality.

in di vid u al ist (in′də vij′ü ə list), *n.* 1 person characterized by individualism. 2 supporter of a theory of individualism.

in di vid u al is tic (in′də vij′ü ə lis′tik), *adj.* of individualism or individualists. **—in′di vid′u a lis′ti cal ly,** *adv.*

in di vid u al i ty (in′də vij′ü al′ə tē), *n., pl.* **-ties.** 1 individual character; sum of the qualities which distinguish one person or thing from others. See **character** for synonym study. 2 condition of being individual; existence as an individual. 3 an individual person or thing.

in di vid u al ize (in′də vij′ü ə līz), *v.t.,* **-ized, -iz ing.** 1 make different for each individual; give a distinctive character to. 2 consider as individuals; list one by one; specify. **—in′di vid′u al i za′tion,** *n.*

in di vid u ate (in′də vij′ü āt), *v.,* **-at ed, -at ing.** *—v.t.* make individual; individualize. *—v.i.* become individual. **—in′di vid′u a′tion,** *n.*

hat, āge, fär; let, ēqual, tėrm;
it, īce; hot, ōpen, ôrder;
oil, out; cup, pu̇t, rüle;
ch, child; ng, long; sh, she;
th, thin; ᴛʜ, then; zh, measure;

ə represents *a* in about, *e* in taken,
i in pencil, *o* in lemon, *u* in circus.

< = from, derived from, taken from.

in di vis i bil i ty (in′də viz′ə bil′ə tē), *n.* a being indivisible.

in di vis i ble (in′də viz′ə bəl), *adj.* 1 that cannot be divided. 2 that cannot be divided without a remainder. **—in′di vis′i ble ness,** *n.* **—in′di vis′i bly,** *adv.*

Indo-, *combining form.* Indian and ___: *Indo-European* = *Indian and European.* [< Greek *Indos* the Indus River]

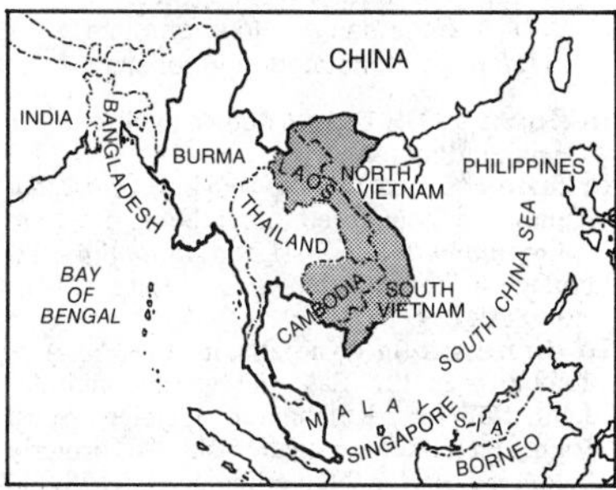

Indochina
(def. 1, the area within the heavy boundary line; def. 2, the shaded area)

In do chi na or **In do-Chi na** (in′dō chī′nə), *n.* 1 peninsula in SE Asia comprising Burma, Cambodia, Laos, Malaya, Singapore, Thailand, North Vietnam, and South Vietnam. 2 countries in the E part of this peninsula formerly comprising French Indochina.

In do chi nese or **In do-Chi nese** (in′dō chī nēz′), *adj., n., pl.* **-nese.** *—adj.* of or having to do with Indochina, the Mongoloid peoples living there, or their languages. *—n.* native or inhabitant of Indochina.

in doc ile (in dos′əl), *adj.* unteachable; intractable.

in do cil i ty (in′dō sil′ə tē), *n.* unteachableness; intractableness.

in doc tri nate (in dok′trə nāt), *v.t.,* **-nat ed, -nat ing.** 1 teach a doctrine, belief, or principle to. 2 teach; instruct. [ultimately < Latin *in-* in + *doctrina* doctrine] **—in doc′tri na′tion,** *n.*

In do-Eu ro pe an (in′dō yu̇r′ə pē′ən), *adj.* of or having to do with a group of related languages spoken in India, western Asia, and Europe; Aryan, English, German, Latin, Greek, Persian, and Sanskrit are Indo-European languages. *—n.* 1 this group of languages. 2 member of a people speaking an Indo-European language.

In do-I ra ni an (in′dō i rā′nē ən, in′dō ī rā′nē ən), *adj.* of or having to do with a division of Indo-European that comprises the Indic and Iranian branches.

in dole a ce tic acid (in′dōl ə sē′tik, in′dōl ə set′ik), a plant hormone, the principal auxin, which regulates growth and development. It is synthesized in the protoplasm of the young and active parts of plants.

in do lence (in′dl əns), *n.* dislike of work; laziness; idleness.

in do lent (in′dl ənt), *adj.* disliking work; lazy; idle. See **idle** for synonym study. **—in′do lent ly,** *adv.*

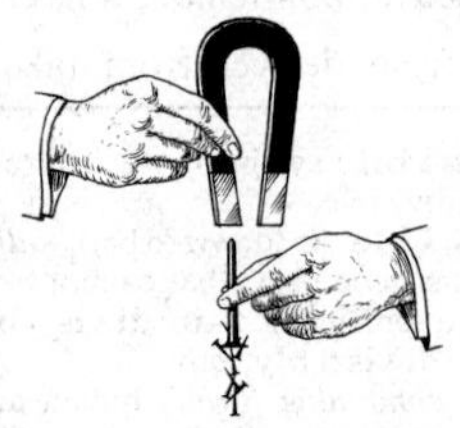

induction (def. 1)
Magnetic induction—the tacks stick to the nail and to each other because of induced magnetism.

in dom i ta bil i ty (in dom′ə tə bil′ə tē), *n.* a being indomitable.

in dom i ta ble (in dom′ə tə bəl), *adj.* that cannot be conquered; unyielding. [< Late Latin *indomitabilis* < Latin *indomitus* untamed < *in-* not + *domare* to tame] **—in dom′i ta bly,** *adv.*

In do ne sia (in′də nē′zhə, in′də nē′shə), *n.* 1 country in the East Indies that includes Java, Sumatra, Kalimantan, Celebes, West Irian, and numerous smaller islands, formerly belonging to the Netherlands. 121,198,000 pop.; 735,300 sq. mi. *Capital:* Djakarta. See **Australia** for map. 2 Malay Archipelago.

In do ne sian (in′də nē′zhən, in′də nē′shən), *adj.* of or having to do with Indonesia or its people. *—n.* 1 native or inhabitant of Indonesia. 2 the official language of Indonesia, based on Malay.

in door (in′dôr′, in′dōr′), *adj.* done, used, played, etc., in a house or building: *indoor tennis.*

in doors (in′dôrz′, in′dōrz′), *adv.* in or into a house or building: *Go indoors.*

In dore (in dōr′), *n.* city in central India. 448,000.

in dorse (in dôrs′), *v.t.,* **-dorsed, -dors ing.** endorse. **—in dorse′ment,** *n.* **—in dors′er,** *n.*

in drawn (in′drôn′), *adj.* 1 drawn in. 2 preoccupied; introspective.

in du bi ta ble (in dü′bə tə bəl, in dyü′bə tə bəl), *adj.* too evident to be doubted; certain; unquestionable. **—in du′bi ta ble ness,** *n.* **—in du′bi ta bly,** *adv.*

in duce (in düs′, in dyüs′), *v.t.,* **-duced, -duc ing.** 1 lead on; influence; persuade: *Advertisements induce people to buy.* 2 bring about; cause: *Some drugs induce sleep.* 3 produce (an electric current, electric charge, or magnetic change) by induction. 4 infer by reasoning from particular facts to general truths or principles. [< Latin *inducere* < *in-* in + *ducere* to lead] **—in duc′er,** *n.*

in duce ment (in düs′mənt, in dyüs′mənt), *n.* 1 something that influences or persuades; incentive. 2 act of influencing or persuading.

in duc i ble (in dü′sə bəl, in dyü′sə bəl), *adj.* that can be induced.

in duct (in dukt′), *v.t.* 1 put formally in possession (of an office, etc.); install. 2 bring in; introduce (into a place, seat, position, etc.). 3 enroll in military service. 4 initiate. [< Latin *inductum* led in < *in-* in + *ducere* to lead]

in duct ance (in duk′təns), *n.* property of an electric circuit by which an electromotive force is induced in it or in a nearby circuit by a change of current in either circuit. The tuner of a radio varies the inductance of its coils.

in duc tee (in duk′tē′), *n.* person who has been or soon will be inducted, especially into military service.

in duc tile (in duk′təl), *adj.* not ductile; not pliable; unyielding.

in duc til i ty (in′duk til′ə tē), *n.* quality of being inductile.

in duc tion (in duk′shən), *n.* 1 process by which an object having electrical or magnetic properties produces similar properties in a nearby object, without direct contact. 2 a reasoning from particular facts to general truths or principles. 3 a conclusion reached in this way. 4 act of inducting; act or ceremony of installing a person in office. 5 enrollment in military service. 6 act of bringing into existence or operation; causing; inducing.

induction coil, device in which an interrupted direct current of low voltage, in a coil consisting of a few turns of wire, induces an alternating current of high voltage in a surrounding coil consisting of a larger number of turns of wire.

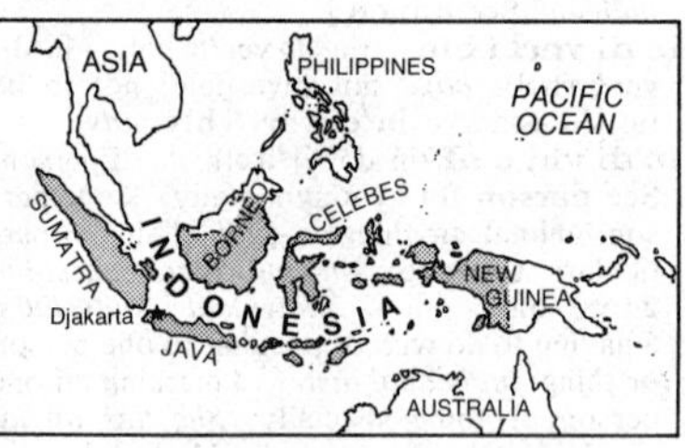

Indonesia (def. 1)

induction heating, process of heating metals by causing, through electromagnetic induction, an electric current to flow through them.

in duc tive (in duk′tiv), *adj.* 1 of or using induction; reasoning by induction. 2 having to do with or caused by electric or magnetic induction. **—in duc′tive ly,** *adv.* **—in duc′tive ness,** *n.*

in duc tiv i ty (in′duk tiv′ə tē), *n., pl.* **-ties.** inductive property; capacity for induction.

in duc tor (in duk′tər), *n.* 1 person who inducts another into office. 2 any part of an electrical apparatus that works or is worked by induction.

in due (in dü′, in dyü′), *v.t.,* **-dued, -du ing.** endue.

in dulge (in dulj′), *v.,* **-dulged, -dulg ing.** *—v.i.* give in to one's pleasure; let oneself have, use, or do what one wants: *A smoker indulges in tobacco.* *—v.t.* 1 give in to; let oneself have, use, or do: *She indulged her fondness for candy by eating a whole box.* 2 give in to the wishes or whims of; humor: *We often indulge a sick person.* See **humor** for synonym study. [< Latin *indulgere*] **—in dulg′er,** *n.*

in dul gence (in dul′jəns), *n.* 1 act of indulging. 2 condition of being indulgent. 3 something indulged in. 4 favor; privilege. 5 (in the Roman Catholic Church) a freeing from the punishment still due for sin after the guilt has been forgiven.

in dul gent (in dul′jənt), *adj.* 1 giving in to another's wishes or whims; too kind or agreeable. 2 making allowances; not critical; lenient. **—in dul′gent ly,** *adv.*

in dult (in dult′), *n.* license from the Pope granting some privilege not authorized by the common law of the Roman Catholic Church. [< Late Latin *indultum* < Latin *indulgere* indulge]

in du rate (*v.* in′dů rāt′, in′dyů rāt′; *adj.* in′důr it, in′dyůr it), *v.,* **-rat ed, -rat ing,** *adj.* *—v.t.* 1 make (a substance) hard; harden. 2 make hardy; inure. 3 make unfeeling. *—v.i.* 1 become hard. 2 become unfeeling. *—adj.* 1 hardened. 2 unfeeling. [< Latin *induratum* hardened < *in-* + *durus* hard] **—in′du ra′tion,** *n.*

in du ra tive (in′dů rā′tiv, in důr′ə tiv), *adj.* hardening.

In dus River (in′dəs), river flowing from W Tibet through Kashmir and Pakistan into the Arabian Sea. 2000 mi.

in dus tri al (in dus′trē əl), *adj.* 1 of or resulting from industry or productive labor: *industrial products.* 2 having many industries: *industrial nations.* 3 engaged in or connected with an industry or industries: *industrial workers. An industrial school teaches trades.* 4 of or having to do with the workers in industries: *industrial insurance.* 5 for use in industry: *industrial machines.* **—in dus′tri al ly,** *adv.*

industrial arts, 1 practical arts employed in industry. 2 these arts as taught in schools.

in dus tri al ism (in dus′trē ə liz′əm), *n.* system of social and economic organization in which large industries are important and industrial activities or interests prevail.

in dus tri al ist (in dus′trē ə list), *n.* person who manages or owns an industrial enterprise.

in dus tri al ize (in dus′trē ə līz), *v.t., v.i.,* **-ized, -iz ing.** 1 make or become industrial; develop large industries in (a country or economic system). **—in dus′tri al i za′tion,** *n.*

Industrial Revolution, the change from an agricultural to an industrial society and from home manufacturing to factory production, especially the one that took place in England from about 1750 to about 1850.

industrial union, a labor union of all persons in the same industry without regard to the various crafts or jobs.

in dus tri ous (in dus′trē əs), *adj.* working hard and steadily; diligent. See **busy** for synonym study. **—in dus′tri ous ly,** *adv.* **—in dus′tri ous ness,** *n.*

in dus try (in′də strē), *n., pl.* **-tries.** 1 any branch of business, trade, or manufacture: *the automobile industry.* 2 all such enterprises taken collectively: *Canadian industry is expanding.* 3 systematic work or labor; continual employment in some useful work. 4 steady effort; busy application. [< Latin *industria*]

in dwell (in dwel′), *v.,* **-dwelt** (-dwelt′) or **-dwelled, -dwell ing.** *—v.t.* dwell in; inhabit. *—v.i.* have one's abode; dwell. **—in′dwell′er,** *n.*

-ine[1], *suffix forming adjectives from nouns.* of; like; like that of: *Crystalline = of crystal. Elephantine = like an elephant.* [< Latin *-inus* < Greek *-inos*]

-ine[2], *suffix forming nouns.* (in chemistry) denoting the names of basic substances and the halogen elements, as in *aniline, fluorine.* See also **-in.** [< French < Latin *-ina,* feminine of *-inus* -ine[1]]

in e bri ate (*v.* in ē′brē āt; *n., adj.* in ē′brē it), *v.,* **-at ed, -at ing,** *n., adj.* —*v.t.* make drunk; intoxicate. —*n.* a drunken person. —*adj.* intoxicated; drunk. [< Latin *inebriatum* made drunk < *in-* + *ebrius* drunk] **—in e′bri a′tion,** *n.*

in e bri e ty (in′i brī′ə tē), *n.* drunkenness.

in ed i bil i ty (in′ed ə bil′ə tē, in ed′ə bil′ə tē), *n.* quality or condition of being inedible.

in ed i ble (in ed′ə bəl), *adj.* not edible; not fit to eat.

in ed u ca ble (in ej′ə kə bəl), *adj.* incapable of being educated.

in ef fa bil i ty (in ef′ə bil′ə tē), *n.* a being ineffable.

in ef fa ble (in ef′ə bəl), *adj.* not to be expressed in words; too great to be described in words. [< Latin *ineffabilis* < *in-* not + *effari* express in words < *ex-* out + *fari* speak] **—in ef′fa ble ness,** *n.* **—in ef′fa bly,** *adv.*

in ef face a bil i ty (in′ə fā′sə bil′ə tē), *n.* a being ineffaceable.

in ef face a ble (in′ə fā′sə bəl), *adj.* that cannot be rubbed out or wiped out; indelible. **—in′ef face′a bly,** *adv.*

in ef fec tive (in′ə fek′tiv), *adj.* 1 not producing the desired effect; of little use; ineffectual: *An ineffective medicine fails to cure a disease or relieve pain.* 2 unfit for work; incapable: *The doctor said I would be ineffective in my job until after a convalescence of several weeks.* **—in′ef fec′tive ly,** *adv.* **—in′ef fec′tive ness,** *n.*

in ef fec tu al (in′ə fek′chü əl), *adj.* 1 without effect; useless. See **useless** for synonym study. 2 not able to produce the effect wanted; powerless. **—in′ef fec′tu al ly,** *adv.* **—in′ef fec′tu al ness,** *n.*

in ef fi ca cious (in′ef ə kā′shəs), *adj.* not efficacious; not able to produce the effect wanted. **—in′ef fi ca′cious ly,** *adv.* **—in′ef fi ca′cious ness,** *n.*

in ef fi ca cy (in ef′ə kə sē), *n.* lack of efficacy; inability to produce the effect wanted.

in ef fi cien cy (in′ə fish′ən sē), *n.* 1 lack of efficiency; wastefulness. 2 inability to get things done.

in ef fi cient (in′ə fish′ənt), *adj.* 1 not able to produce an effect without waste of time or energy; wasteful: *A machine that uses too much fuel is inefficient.* 2 not able to get things done; incapable: *An inefficient housekeeper has an untidy house.* **—in′ef fi′cient ly,** *adv.*

in e las tic (in′i las′tik), *adj.* not elastic; stiff; inflexible; unyielding.

in e las tic i ty (in′i las tis′ə tē), *n.* lack of elasticity.

in el e gance (in el′ə gəns), *n.* lack of elegance.

in el e gant (in el′ə gənt), *adj.* not elegant; in poor taste; crude; vulgar. **—in el′e gant ly,** *adv.*

in el i gi bil i ty (in el′ə jə bil′ə tē), *n.* a being ineligible.

in el i gi ble (in el′ə jə bəl), *adj.* not eligible; not suitable or qualified; unfit to be chosen. —*n.* person who is not suitable or not qualified. **—in el′i gi bly,** *adv.*

in e luc ta bil i ty (in′i luk′tə bil′ə tē), *n.* a being ineluctable.

in e luc ta ble (in′i luk′tə bəl), *adj.* that cannot be escaped or avoided; inevitable. [< Latin *ineluctabilis* < *in-* not + *eluctari* to escape] **—in′e luc′ta bly,** *adv.*

in ept (in ept′), *adj.* 1 not suitable; out of place; inappropriate. 2 awkward; clumsy. 3 lacking in reason or judgment; foolish; absurd. [< Latin *ineptus* < *in-* not + *aptus* apt] **—in ept′ly,** *adv.* **—in ept′ness,** *n.*

in ept i tude (in ep′tə tüd, in ep′tə tyüd), *n.* 1 inept quality; unfitness; foolishness. 2 a silly or inappropriate act or remark.

in e qual i ty (in′i kwol′ə tē), *n., pl.* **-ties.** 1 lack of equality; a being unequal in amount, size, value, rank, etc. 2 lack of evenness, regularity, or uniformity. 3 an instance of this; an irregularity or variation. 4 a mathematical expression showing that two quantities are unequal. EXAMPLE: $a > b$ means a is greater than b; $a < b$ means a is less than b; $a \neq b$ means a and b are unequal.

in eq ui ta ble (in ek′wə tə bəl), *adj.* not equitable; unfair; unjust. **—in eq′ui ta bly,** *adv.*

in eq ui ty (in ek′wə tē), *n., pl.* **-ties.** 1 lack of equity; unfairness; injustice. 2 an unfair or unjust act.

in e rad i ca ble (in′i rad′ə kə bəl), *adj.* that cannot be rooted out or got rid of. **—in′e rad′i ca bly,** *adv.*

in ert (in ėrt′), *adj.* 1 having no power to move or act; lifeless: *A stone is an inert mass of matter.* 2 inactive; slow; sluggish. See **inactive** for synonym study. 3 with few or no active chemical, physiological, or other properties: *Helium and neon are inert gases.* [< Latin *inertem* idle, unskilled < *in-* without + *artem* art, skill] **—in ert′ly,** *adv.* **—in ert′ness,** *n.*

in er tia (in ėr′shə), *n.* 1 tendency to remain in the state one is in, and not start changes. 2 tendency of all objects and matter in the universe to stay still if still, or if moving, to go on moving in the same direction, unless acted on by some outside force. [< Latin, inactivity < *inertem* idle. See INERT.]

in er tial (in ėr′shəl), *adj.* having to do with or of the nature of inertia.

inertial guidance, method of guiding a missile, aircraft, or ship along a given course by means of gyroscopes and electronic equipment that react to inertial force, automatically adjusting the course.

in es cap a ble (in′ə skā′pə bəl), *adj.* that cannot be escaped or avoided; inevitable. **—in′es cap′a bly,** *adv.*

in es sen tial (in′ə sen′shəl), *adj.* 1 not essential; not necessary. 2 unsubstantial; immaterial.

in es ti ma ble (in es′tə mə bəl), *adj.* 1 not capable of being estimated; incalculable. 2 too precious to be estimated; priceless; invaluable. **—in es′ti ma bly,** *adv.*

in ev i ta bil i ty (in ev′ə tə bil′ə tē), *n.* a being inevitable.

in ev i ta ble (in ev′ə tə bəl), *adj.* not to be avoided; sure to happen; certain to come: *Death is inevitable.* [< Latin *inevitabilis* < *in-* not + *evitare* avoid < *ex-* out + *vitare* shun] **—in ev′i ta ble ness,** *n.* **—in ev′i ta bly,** *adv.*

in ex act (in′ig zakt′), *adj.* not exact; not accurate. **—in′ex act′ly,** *adv.* **—in′ex act′ness,** *n.*

in ex act i tude (in′ig zak′tə tüd, in′ig zak′tə tyüd), *n.* lack of accuracy or precision.

in ex cus a bil i ty (in′ik skyü′zə bil′ə tē), *n.* a being inexcusable.

in ex cus a ble (in′ik skyü′zə bəl), *adj.* that ought not to be excused; that cannot be justified; unpardonable. **—in′ex cus′a ble ness,** *n.* **—in′ex cus′a bly,** *adv.*

hat, āge, fär; let, ēqual, tėrm;
it, īce; hot, ōpen, ôrder;
oil, out; cup, pu̇t, rüle;
ch, child; ng, long; sh, she;
th, thin; ᴛʜ, then; zh, measure;

ə represents *a* in about, *e* in taken, *i* in pencil, *o* in lemon, *u* in circus.

< = from, derived from, taken from.

in ex haust i bil i ty (in′ig zô′stə bil′ə tē), *n.* a being inexhaustible.

in ex haust i ble (in′ig zô′stə bəl), *adj.* 1 that cannot be exhausted; very abundant. 2 that cannot be wearied; tireless. **—in′ex haust′i bly,** *adv.*

in ex ist ence (in′ig zis′təns), *n.* absence of existence; nonexistence.

in ex ist ent (in′ig zis′tənt), *adj.* not existing; having no existence.

in ex or a bil i ty (in ek′sər ə bil′ə tē), *n.* a being inexorable.

in ex or a ble (in ek′sər ə bəl), *adj.* not influenced by pleading or entreaties; relentless; unyielding: *The forces of nature are inexorable.* See **inflexible** for synonym study. [< Latin *inexorabilis* < *in-* not + *exorare* prevail upon, pray earnestly < *ex-* out + *orare* pray, entreat] **—in ex′or a ble ness,** *n.* **—in ex′or a bly,** *adv.*

in ex pe di en cy (in′ik spē′dē ən sē), *n.* lack of expediency.

in ex pe di ent (in′ik spē′dē ənt), *adj.* not expedient; not practicable, suitable, or wise. **—in′ex pe′di ent ly,** *adv.*

in ex pen sive (in′ik spen′siv), *adj.* not expensive; cheap; low-priced. See **cheap** for synonym study. **—in′ex pen′sive ly,** *adv.* **—in′ex pen′sive ness,** *n.*

in ex per i ence (in′ik spir′ē əns), *n.* lack of experience; lack of practice; lack of skill or wisdom gained from experience.

in ex per i enced (in′ik spir′ē ənst), *adj.* not experienced; lacking experience.

in ex pert (in′ik spėrt′, in ek′spėrt′), *adj.* not expert; unskilled. **—in′ex pert′ly,** *adv.* **—in′ex pert′ness,** *n.*

in ex pi a ble (in ek′spē ə bəl), *adj.* that cannot be atoned for: *Murder is an inexpiable crime.*

in ex plain a ble (in′ik splā′nə bəl), *adj.* that cannot be explained; inexplicable.

in ex plic a bil i ty (in′ik splik′ə bil′ə tē, in ek′splə kə bil′ə tē), *n.* a being inexplicable.

in ex plic a ble (in′ik splik′ə bəl, in ek′splə kə bəl), *adj.* that cannot be explained, understood, or accounted for; mysterious. **—in′ex plic′a ble ness,** *n.* **—in′ex plic′a bly,** *adv.*

in ex plic it (in′ik splis′it), *adj.* not explicit; not clearly expressed.

in ex press i bil i ty (in′ik spres′ə bil′ə tē), *n.* a being inexpressible.

in ex press i ble (in′ik spres′ə bəl), *adj.* that cannot be expressed; beyond expression; indescribable. **—in′ex press′i ble ness,** *n.* **—in′ex press′i bly,** *adv.*

in ex pres sive (in′ik spres′iv), *adj.* not expressive; lacking in expression. **—in′ex pres′sive ly,** *adv.* **—in′ex pres′sive ness,** *n.*

in ex ten si ble (in′ik sten′sə bəl), *adj.*

that cannot be extended; not extensible.

in ex ten so (in ik sten′sō), LATIN. at full length; in full.

in ex tin guish a ble (in′ik sting′gwi shə bəl), *adj.* that cannot be put out or stopped; unquenchable. **—in′ex tin′guish a bly,** *adv.*

in ex tre mis (in ik strē′mis), LATIN. at the point of death.

in ex tri ca bil i ty (in ek′strə kə bil′ə tē), *n.* quality or condition of being inextricable.

in ex tri ca ble (in ek′strə kə bəl), *adj.* 1 that one cannot get out of. 2 that cannot be disentangled or solved. **—in ex′tri ca bly,** *adv.*

in fal li bil i ty (in fal′ə bil′ə tē), *n.* 1 freedom from error; inability to be mistaken. 2 absolute reliability; sureness.

in fal li ble (in fal′ə bəl), *adj.* 1 free from error; that cannot be mistaken: *an infallible rule.* 2 absolutely reliable; sure: *infallible obedience, an infallible remedy.* 3 (in the Roman Catholic Church) incapable of error in the exposition of doctrine on faith and morals (said of the Pope as head of the Church). **—in fal′li bly,** *adv.*

in fa mous (in′fə məs), *adj.* 1 deserving or causing a very bad reputation; shamefully bad; disgraceful: *an infamous deed.* 2 having a very bad reputation; in public disgrace: *an infamous traitor.* [< Medieval Latin *infamosus,* Latin *infamis.* See INFAMY.] **—in′fa mous ly,** *adv.*

in fa my (in′fə mē), *n., pl.* **-mies.** 1 a very bad reputation; public disgrace: *Traitors are held in infamy.* 2 shameful badness; extreme wickedness. 3 an infamous or disgraceful act. [< Latin *infamia* < *infamis* of ill fame < *in-* without + *fama* fame, reputation]

in fan cy (in′fən sē), *n., pl.* **-cies.** 1 condition or time of being an infant; babyhood; early childhood. 2 an early stage; very beginning of development: *Space travel is still in its infancy.* 3 condition of being under the legal age of responsibility.

in fant (in′fənt), *n.* 1 a very young child; baby. 2 person under the legal age of responsibility; minor. *—adj.* 1 of or for an infant. 2 in an early stage; just beginning to develop. [< Latin *infantem,* originally, not speaking < *in-* not + *fari* speak]

in fan ta (in fan′tə), *n.* a royal princess of Spain or Portugal. [< Spanish and Portuguese]

in fan te (in fan′tā), *n.* a royal prince of Spain or Portugal, but not the heir to the throne. [< Spanish and Portuguese]

in fan ti cide (in fan′tə sīd), *n.* 1 the killing of a baby. 2 person who kills a baby.

in fan tile (in′fən tīl, in′fən təl), *adj.* 1 of an infant or infants; having to do with infants. 2 like an infant; babyish; childish. 3 in an early stage; just beginning to develop.

infantile paralysis, polio.

in fan ti lism (in fan′tl iz′əm), *n.* an abnormal persistence of a childish state in adults, often characterized by mental retardation and physical underdevelopment, especially of the sexual organs.

in fan til i ty (in′fən til′ə tē), *n.* infantile quality or condition.

in fan tine (in′fən tīn, in′fən tən), *adj.* infantile; babyish; childish.

in fan try (in′fən trē), *n., pl.* **-tries.** 1 troops trained, equipped, and organized to fight on foot. 2 branch of an army consisting of such troops. [< Middle French *infanterie* < Italian *infanteria* < *infante, fante* foot soldier, originally, a youth < Latin *infantem.* See INFANT.]

in fan try man (in′fən trē mən), *n., pl.* **-men.** soldier who fights on foot; foot soldier.

in farct (in färkt′), *n.* portion of dying or dead tissue, caused by the obstruction of the blood supply by an embolus, thrombus, etc. [< Latin *infarctum* stopped up < *in-* in + *farcire* to stuff]

in farc tion (in färk′shən), *n.* 1 formation of an infarct. 2 infarct.

in fat u ate (in fach′ü āt), *v.t.,* **-at ed, -at ing.** 1 inspire with a foolish or extreme passion. 2 make foolish. [< Latin *infatuatum* made foolish < *in-* + *fatuus* foolish]

in fat u at ed (in fach′ü ā′tid), *adj.* having an exaggerated fondness or passion; foolishly in love.

in fat u a tion (in fach′ü ā′shən), *n.* exaggerated fondness or passion; foolish love.

in fea si ble (in fē′zə bəl), *adj.* not feasible; inpracticable.

in fect (in fekt′), *v.t.* 1 cause disease or an unhealthy condition in by introducing disease-producing microorganisms: *Dirt infects an open cut.* 2 exert a bad influence upon; deprave. 3 influence by spreading from one to another: *Her enthusiasm infected everyone who worked with her.* [< Latin *infectum* dyed, originally, put in < *in-* in + *facere* make] **—in fec′tor,** *n.*

in fec tion (in fek′shən), *n.* 1 introduction of disease-producing microorganisms into the tissues of people, animals, or plants. 2 disease caused in this way. 3 an influence, feeling, or idea spreading from one to another. 4 fact or condition of being infected.

in fec tious (in fek′shəs), *adj.* 1 spread by infection: *Measles is an infectious disease.* 2 causing infection. 3 apt to spread from one to another: *an infectious laugh.* **—in fec′tious ly,** *adv.* **—in fec′tious ness,** *n.*

in fec tive (in fek′tiv), *adj.* causing infection; infectious.

in fec tiv i ty (in′fek tiv′ə tē), *n.* infective quality or condition.

in fe lic i tous (in′fə lis′ə təs), *adj.* 1 not appropriate; unsuitable. 2 unfortunate; unhappy. **—in′fe lic′i tous ly,** *adv.*

in fe lic i ty (in′fə lis′ə tē), *n., pl.* **-ties.** 1 unsuitability; inappropriateness. 2 something unsuitable; inappropriate word, remark, etc. 3 misfortune; unhappiness.

in fer (in fėr′), *v.,* **-ferred, -fer ring.** *—v.t.* 1 find out by a process of reasoning from something known or assumed; conclude: *People inferred that so able a governor would make a good President.* See **conclude** for synonym study. 2 be a sign or hint of; suggest indirectly; imply: *Ragged clothing infers poverty.* *—v.i.* draw inferences. [< Latin *inferre* introduce, bring in < *in-* in + *ferre* bring] **—in fer′a ble,** *adj.* **—in fer′rer,** *n.*

➔ **infer, imply.** Strictly, a writer or speaker *implies* something in his words or manner; a reader or listener *infers* something from what he reads, sees, or hears: *She implied by her smile that she did intend to keep the appointment. We inferred from the principal's announcement that he already knew who had broken his window. Infer* has been used so much with the meaning of *imply* that that is given as a secondary sense of the word in dictionaries.

in fer ence (in′fər əns), *n.* 1 process of inferring. 2 that which is inferred; conclusion: *What inference do you draw from smelling smoke?*

in fe ren tial (in′fə ren′shəl), *adj.* having to do with or depending on inference. **—in′fe ren′tial ly,** *adv.*

in fer i or (in fir′ē ər), *adj.* 1 below most others; low in quality; below the average: *an inferior mind, an inferior grade of coffee.* 2 not so good or so great; lower in quality; worse: *This cloth is inferior to real silk.* 3 lower in position, rank, importance, etc.; lesser; subordinate: *A lieutenant is inferior to a captain.* *—n.* 1 person who is lower in rank or station. 2 something that is below average. [< Latin, comparative of *inferus,* adjective, situated below]

in fer i or i ty (in fir′ē ôr′ə tē, in fir′ē or′ə tē), *n.* inferior condition or quality.

inferiority complex, an abnormal feeling of being inferior to other people, sometimes compensated for by overly aggressive behavior.

in fer nal (in fėr′nl), *adj.* 1 of or having to do with hell. 2 of the lower world which the ancient Greeks and Romans thought of as the abode of the dead. 3 fit to have come from hell; hellish; diabolical: *infernal cruelty.* 4 INFORMAL. abominable; outrageous. [< Late Latin *infernalis* < *infernus* hell < Latin, lower < *inferus* situated below] **—in fer′nal ly,** *adv.*

infernal machine, a disguised bomb or other explosive apparatus intended for the malicious destruction of life and property.

in fer no (in fėr′nō), *n., pl.* **-nos.** 1 hell. 2 place of torment like hell: *a roaring inferno of flames.* [< Italian]

in fer tile (in fėr′tl), *adj.* not fertile; sterile; barren.

in fer til i ty (in′fər til′ə tē), *n.* lack of fertility; being infertile.

in fest (in fest′), *v.t.* trouble or disturb frequently or in large numbers: *a swamp infested with mosquitoes. The national park was infested with tourists.* [< Latin *infestare* to attack < *infestus* hostile] **—in′fes ta′tion,** *n.* **—in fest′er,** *n.*

in fi del (in′fə dəl), *n.* 1 person who does not believe in religion. 2 person who does not accept a particular faith. During the Crusades, Moslems called Christians infidels. 3 person who does not accept Christianity. *—adj.* not believing in religion. [< Latin *infidelis* unfaithful < *in-* not < *fides* faith]

in fi del i ty (in′fə del′ə tē), *n., pl.* **-ties.** 1 lack of religious faith. 2 unbelief in Christianity. 3 unfaithfulness, especially to husband or wife; disloyalty. 4 an unfaithful or disloyal act.

in field (in′fēld′), *n.* 1 the part of a baseball field roughly bounded by the bases; diamond. 2 the first, second, and third basemen and shortstop of a baseball team.

in field er (in′fēl′dər), *n.* player in the infield.

in fight er (in′fī′tər), *n.* 1 person who is or becomes involved in conflict with his associates: *a tough political infighter.* 2 boxer who tends to fight at close quarters.

in fight ing (in′fī′ting), *n.* 1 internal dissension or conflict. 2 (in boxing) a fighting at close quarters.

in fil trate (in fil′trāt), *v.t., v.i.,* **-trat ed, -trat ing.** 1 pass into or through (a substance) by filtering. 2 penetrate or slip through (an enemy's lines) individually or in small groups. 3 penetrate (an organization)

hat, āge, fär; let, ēqual, tėrm;
it, īce; hot, ōpen, ôrder;
oil, out; cup, pu̇t, rüle;
ch, child; ng, long; sh, she;
th, thin; ᴛʜ, then; zh, measure;

ə represents *a* in about, *e* in taken, *i* in pencil, *o* in lemon, *u* in circus.

< = from, derived from, taken from.

for the purpose of spying, sabotage, or the like. 4 filter into or through; permeate. **—in′fil tra′tor,** *n.*

in fil tra tion (in′fil trā′shən), *n.* 1 an infiltrating. 2 a being infiltrated. 3 thing that infiltrates. 4 method of attack in which small groups of men penetrate the enemy's lines at various weak points to fire on the enemy from the side or the rear. 5 action of a person infiltrating for the purpose of spying, sabotage, or the like.

in fi nite (in′fə nit), *adj.* 1 without limits or bounds; endless: *the infinite reaches of outer space.* 2 extremely great; vast: *Teaching little children sometimes takes infinite patience.* 3 (in mathematics) greater than any assignable quantity or magnitude of the sort in question. *—n.* 1 that which is infinite. 2 **the Infinite,** God. [< Latin *infinitus* < *in-* not + *finis* limit, border] **—in′fi nite ly,** *adv.* **—in′fi nite ness,** *n.*

in fi ni tes i mal (in′fi nə tes′ə məl), *adj.* so small as to be almost nothing; extremely minute or insignificant. *—n.* an infinitesimal amount. **—in′fi ni tes′i mal ly,** *adv.*

in fin i tive (in fin′ə tiv), *n.* (in grammar) a form of a verb not limited by person and number. EXAMPLES: Let him *go.* We want *to go* now. *—adj.* of the infinitive.

➤ **infinitive.** The present infinitive is the simple form of the verb, with or without *to: I want* to buy *a hat. Let them* leave *if they want* to leave. Infinitives are used as: **a** nouns: To swim *across the English Channel is her ambition.* **b** adjectives: *They had money* to burn. **c** adverbs: *I went home* to rest. **d** part of verb phrases: *He will* do *most of the work.*

in fin i tude (in fin′ə tüd), in fin′ə tyüd), *n.* 1 condition of being infinite. 2 an infinite extent, amount, or number.

in fin i ty (in fin′ə tē), *n., pl.* **-ties.** 1 condition of being infinite. 2 an infinite distance, space, time, or quantity. 3 an infinite extent, amount, or number: *the infinity of God's mercy.* 4 (in mathematics) an infinite quantity.

in firm (in fėrm′), *adj.* 1 lacking strength or health; physically weak or feeble, especially through age. 2 without a firm purpose; not steadfast; faltering. 3 not firm, solid, or strong. **—in firm′ly,** *adv.* **—in firm′ness,** *n.*

in fir mar y (in fėr′mər ē), *n., pl.* **-mar ies.** 1 place for the care of the infirm, sick, or injured; hospital or dispensary in a school or institution. 2 any hospital.

in fir mi ty (in fėr′mə tē), *n., pl.* **-ties.** 1 weakness; feebleness. 2 sickness; illness. 3 weakness, flaw, or defect in a person's character.

in fix (in fiks′), *v.t.* 1 fix or fasten (one thing) in (another); implant. 2 fix (a fact, etc.) in the mind or memory; impress.

in fla gran te de lic to (in flə gran′tē di lik′tō), (in law) in the very act of committing the crime; in the performance of the deed; red-handed. [< Latin, literally, in blazing crime]

in flame (in flām′), *v.,* **-flamed, -flam ing.** *—v.t.* 1 make more violent; excite: *The stirring speech inflamed the crowd.* 2 make unnaturally hot, red, sore, or swollen: *The smoke had inflamed my eyes.* *—v.i.* 1 become excited with intense feeling. 2 become unnaturally hot, red, sore, or swollen. [< Latin *inflammare* < *in-* in + *flamma* flame]

in flam ma bil i ty (in flam′ə bil′ə tē), *n.* a being inflammable.

in flam ma ble (in flam′ə bəl), *adj.* 1 flammable. 2 easily excited or aroused; excitable: *an inflammable temper.* *—n.* something inflammable. **—in flam′ma ble ness,** *n.* **—in flam′ma bly,** *adv.*

in flam ma tion (in′flə mā′shən), *n.* 1 a diseased condition of some part of the body, marked by heat, redness, swelling, and pain: *A boil is an inflammation of the skin.* 2 an inflaming. 3 a being inflamed.

in flam ma to ry (in flam′ə tôr′ē, in flam′ə tōr′ē), *adj.* 1 tending to excite or arouse: *an inflammatory speech.* 2 of, causing, or accompanied by inflammation: *an inflammatory condition of the tonsils.*

in flate (in flāt′), *v.,* **-flat ed, -flat ing.** *—v.t.* 1 force air or gas into (a balloon, tire, ball, etc.) causing it to swell. 2 puff up with pride, self-importance, etc.; elate. 3 increase (prices or amount of currency) beyond the normal amount. *—v.i.* swell or puff out: *inflated with pride.* [< Latin *inflatum* swollen, blown up < *in-* into + *flare* to blow] **—in flat′a ble,** *adj.* **—in flat′er, in fla′tor,** *n.*

in fla tion (in flā′shən), *n.* 1 a swelling (with air, gas, pride, etc.). 2 a puffing up with pride, self-importance, etc.; elation. 3 a swollen state; too great expansion. 4 increase of the currency of a country by issuing much paper money. 5 a sharp increase in prices resulting from too great an expansion in paper money or bank credit.

in fla tion ar y (in flā′shə ner′ē), *adj.* of or having to do with inflation; tending to inflate.

in flect (in flekt′), *v.t.* 1 change the tone or pitch of (the voice). 2 (in grammar) vary the form of (a word) to show case, number, gender, person, tense, mood, voice, or comparison. By inflecting *who* we have *whose* and *whom.* 3 bend; curve. [< Latin *inflectere* < *in-* in + *flectere* to bend]

in flec tion (in flek′shən), *n.* 1 a change in the tone or pitch of the voice: *We usually end questions with a rising inflection.* 2 variation in the form of a word to show case, number, gender, person, tense, mood, voice, or comparison. 3 suffix or ending used for this: *-est and -ed are common inflections in English.* 4 a bending; curving. 5 a bend; curve. Also, BRITISH **inflexion.**

in flec tion al (in flek′shə nəl), *adj.* of, having to do with, or showing grammatical inflection. **—in flec′tion al ly,** *adv.*

in flec tive (in flek′tiv), *adj.* 1 (in grammar) having to do with or characterized by inflection. 2 tending to bend.

in flex i bil i ty (in flek′sə bil′ə tē), *n.* lack of flexibility.

in flex i ble (in flek′sə bəl), *adj.* 1 not to be turned from a purpose by persuasion or argument; not yielding; firm; steadfast. See synonym study below. 2 that cannot be changed; unalterable. 3 not easily bent; stiff; rigid. **—in flex′i bly,** *adv.*

Syn. 1 Inflexible, inexorable, unrelenting mean unyielding in character or purpose. **Inflexible** emphasizes holding fast or doggedly to what one intends, thinks, or believes: *She remained still inflexible, either to threats or promises.* **Inexorable** emphasizes remaining coldly determined and unaffected by begging or pleading: *The conquerors made inexorable demands for tribute.* **Unrelenting** emphasizes not softening and showing pity, or lessening in force, harshness, or cruelty: *He was unrelenting in his hatred.*

in flex ion (in flek′shən), *n.* BRITISH. inflection.

in flict (in flikt′), *v.t.* 1 cause to have or suffer; give (pain, a stroke, blow, or wound). 2 cause to be suffered or borne; impose (suffering, punishment, something unwelcome, etc.): *The king inflicted harsh sentences on the traitors.* [< Latin *inflictum* struck < *in-* on + *fligere* to strike, dash]

in flic tion (in flik′shən), *n.* 1 act of inflicting. 2 something inflicted.

in flic tive (in flik′tiv), *adj.* tending to inflict.

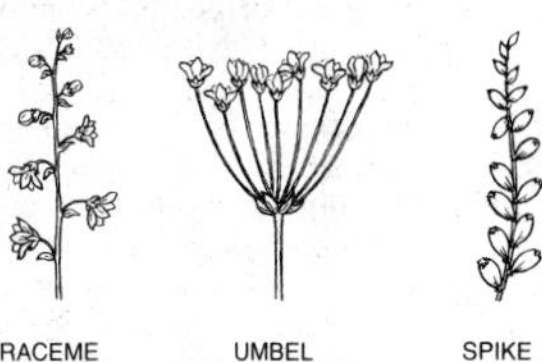

inflorescence (def. 1)—common types

in flo res cence (in′flô res′ns, in′flō res′ns), *n.* 1 arrangement of flowers on the stem or axis in relation to each other. 2 a flower cluster. 3 a beginning to blossom; flowering stage. [< New Latin *inflorescentia* < Latin *in-* in + *florescere* begin to bloom < *florem* flower]

in flo res cent (in′flô res′nt, in′flō res′nt), *adj.* showing inflorescence; flowering.

in flow (in′flō′), *n.* 1 a flowing in or into. 2 that which flows in.

in flu ence (in′flü əns), *n., v.,* **-enced, -enc ing.** *—n.* 1 power of persons or things to act on others, seen only in its effects: *the influence of the moon on the tides.* 2 power to produce an effect without using force or authority: *Use your influence to persuade your friends to join our club.* See **authority** for synonym study. 3 person or thing that has such power. *—v.t.* 1 have an influence on: *The moon influences the tides.* 2 use influence on: *Dishonest people tried to influence the judge by offering him money.* [< Medieval Latin *influentia* emanation from the stars believed to affect human destiny, originally, a flowing in < Latin *in-* in + *fluere* to flow] **—in′flu enc er,** *n.*

in flu en tial (in′flü en′shəl), *adj.* 1 having much influence: *Influential friends helped her to get a job.* 2 using influence; producing results. **—in′flu en′tial ly,** *adv.*

in flu en za (in′flü en′zə), *n.* an acute contagious disease caused by a virus, and occasionally resembling a very bad cold in some of its symptoms, but much more dangerous and exhausting; flu; grippe. [< Italian, originally, visitation, influence of the stars < Medieval Latin *influentia.* See INFLUENCE.]

in flu en zal (in′flü en′zəl), *adj.* of, having to do with, or characterized by influenza: *influenzal pneumonia.*

in flux (in′ fluks), *n.* a flowing in; steady flow;

inflow: *the influx of immigrants into a country.* [< Late Latin *influxus* < Latin *influere* to flow in < *in-* in + *fluere* to flow]

in fold (in fōld′), *v.t.* enfold.

in form (in fôrm′), *v.t.* 1 give knowledge, facts, or news to; tell. See synonym study below. 2 animate or inspire. *—v.i.* make an accusation or complaint; accuse: *The thief who was caught informed against the others.* [< Latin *informare* give form to, instruct < *in-* into + *forma* form]

Syn. *v.t.* 1 **Inform, acquaint, notify** mean to tell or let someone know something. **Inform** emphasizes telling or passing along directly to a person facts or knowledge of any kind: *Her letter informed us how and when she expected to arrive.* **Acquaint** implies making someone familiar with facts or knowledge that he has not known before: *He acquainted us with his plans.* **Notify** means to inform someone officially and formally of something he should or needs to know: *The college notified him that he was awarded a scholarship.*

in for mal (in fôr′məl), *adj.* 1 not formal; not in the regular or prescribed manner: *informal proceedings.* 2 without ceremony or formality; casual: *an informal party, informal clothes.* 3 used in everyday, common speech, but not used in formal speech or writing; colloquial. Expressions such as *ad* for *advertisement, funny* for *strange,* and *fire* for *dismiss* are informal. **—in for′mal ly,** *adv.*

in for mal i ty (in′fôr mal′ə tē), *n., pl.* **-ties.** 1 a being informal; lack of ceremony. 2 an informal act.

in form ant (in fôr′mənt), *n.* person who gives information to another.

in for ma tion (in′fər mā′shən), *n.* 1 knowledge given or received concerning some fact or circumstance; news: *We have just received information of the astronauts' safe landing.* See **knowledge** for synonym study. 2 things known; facts; data: *A dictionary contains much information about words.* 3 an informing: *A guidebook is for the information of travelers.* 4 person or office whose duty is to answer questions. 5 accusation or complaint against a person. 6 any message or part of a message in coded form assembled by or fed to a computer.

in for ma tion al (in′fər mā′shə nəl), *adj.* having to do with or giving information.

information theory, theory dealing with the measurement of factors which might prevent a message from being interpreted as it was intended. Static on a radio and improper coding for a computer are examples of such factors.

in form a tive (in fôr′mə tiv), *adj.* giving information; instructive. **—in form′a tive ly,** *adv.* **—in form′a tive ness,** *n.*

in form a to ry (in fôr′mə tôr′ē, in fôr′mə tōr′ē), *adj.* instructive.

in formed (in fôrmd′), *adj.* having knowledge or information; educated.

in form er (in fôr′mər), *n.* 1 person who makes an accusation or complaint against others. 2 informant.

infra-, *prefix.* below; beneath, as in *infrahuman, infrasonic.* [< Latin *infra* under]

in fract (in frakt′), *v.t.* break (a law or obligation); violate. **—in frac′tor,** *n.*

in frac tion (in frak′shən), *n.* a breaking of a law or obligation; violation: *Reckless driving is an infraction of the law.* [< Latin *infractionem* < *infringere.* See INFRINGE.]

in fra dig (in′frə dig′), INFORMAL. undignified. [abbreviation of Latin *infra dignitatem* beneath (one's) dignity]

in fra hu man (in′frə hyü′mən), *adj.* (of animals) beneath man in evolutionary development.

in fran gi bil i ty (in fran′jə bil′ə tē), *n.* quality of being infrangible.

in fran gi ble (in fran′jə bəl), *adj.* 1 that cannot be broken or separated into parts; unbreakable. 2 that cannot be infringed; inviolable. **—in fran′gi ble ness,** *n.* **—in fran′gi bly,** *adv.*

in fra red (in′frə red′), *adj.* of the invisible part of the spectrum whose rays have wavelengths longer than those of the red end of the visible spectrum and shorter than those of the microwaves. Most of the heat from sunlight, incandescent lamps, carbon arcs, resistance wires, etc., is from infrared rays. See **radiation** for table. *—n.* the infrared part of the spectrum.

in fra son ic (in′frə son′ik), *adj.* (of sound waves) having a frequency below the audible range.

in fra struc ture (in′frə struk′chər), *n.* the essential, underlying elements forming the basis of any system or structure.

in fre quence (in frē′kwəns), *n.* infrequency.

in fre quen cy (in frē′kwən sē), *n.* a being infrequent; scarcity; rarity.

in fre quent (in frē′kwənt), *adj.* occurring seldom or far apart; not frequent; scarce; rare: *words of infrequent occurrence, an infrequent visitor.* **—in fre′quent ly,** *adv.*

in fringe (in frinj′), *v.,* **-fringed, -fring ing.** *—v.t.* act contrary to or violate (a law, obligation, right, etc.); transgress: *A confusing label may infringe the food and drug law.* *—v.i.* go beyond the proper or usual limits; trespass; encroach: *infringe upon the rights of another.* [< Latin *infringere* < *in-* in + *frangere* to break] **—in fringe′ment,** *n.* **—in fring′er,** *n.*

in fur i ate (in fyůr′ē āt), *v.t.,* **-at ed, -at ing.** fill with wild, fierce anger; make furious; enrage. **—in fur′i at′ing ly,** *adv.* **—in fur′i a′tion,** *n.*

in fuse (in fyüz′), *v.t.,* **-fused, -fus ing.** 1 introduce as by pouring; put in; instill: *The captain infused his own courage into his soldiers.* 2 inspire: *The soldiers were infused with his courage.* 3 steep or soak (a plant, leaves, etc.) in a liquid to get something out. [< Latin *infusum* poured in < *in-* in + *fundere* pour] **—in fus′er,** *n.*

in fu si bil i ty (in fyü′zə bil′ə tē), *n.* a being infusible.

in fu si ble (in fyü′zə bəl), *adj.* that cannot be fused or melted. **—in fu′si ble ness,** *n.*

in fu sion (in fyü′zhən), *n.* 1 act or process of infusing. 2 a liquid extract obtained by steeping or soaking: *Tea is an infusion of tea leaves in hot water.* 3 something infused.

in fu so ri al (in′fyə sôr′ē əl, in′fyə sōr′ē əl), *adj.* of, having to do with, or containing infusorians: *infusorial strata.*

in fu so ri an (in′fyə sôr′ē ən, in′fyə sōr′ē ən), *n.* any of a group of one-celled animals that move by vibrating filaments. The paramecium is an infusorian. *—adj.* of or belonging to this group.

-ing[1], *suffix forming nouns chiefly from verbs.* 1 act of a person or thing that ____s: *Painting = act of one that paints.* 2 product or result of such an act, as *a drawing, a painting.* 3 thing that ____s: *Lining = thing that lines.* [Middle English *-ing,* Old English *-ing, -ung*]

-ing[2], 1 *suffix forming the present participle of verbs,* as in *raining, staying, talking.* 2 *suffix forming adjectives from verbs:* that ____s: *Lasting happiness = happiness that lasts.* [Middle English, variant of *-ind, -end,* Old English *-ende*]

in gath er ing (in gaᴛʜ′ər ing), *n.* 1 a gathering in. 2 harvest.

in gen ious (in jē′nyəs), *adj.* 1 skillful in making; good at inventing. See **clever** for synonym study. 2 cleverly planned or made: *This mousetrap is an ingenious device.* [< Latin *ingeniosus* < *ingenium* natural talent < *in-* in + *gignere* beget, be born] **—in gen′ious ly,** *adv.* **—in gen′ious ness,** *n.*

➤ **ingenious, ingenuous.** *Ingenious* means clever or skillful; *ingenuous* means frank or sincere: *My sister is so ingenious that she is sure to think of a way to do this work more easily. The ingenuous child had never thought of being suspicious of what others told her.*

in ge nue or **in gé nue** (an′zhə nü, an′zhə nyü; *French* ᴀɴ zhā ɴʏ′), *n.* 1 a simple, innocent girl or young woman. 2 actress who plays the part of such a girl or young woman. [< French *ingénue,* originally feminine adjective, ingenuous]

in ge nu i ty (in′jə nü′ə tē, in′jə nyü′ə tē), *n., pl.* **-ties.** 1 skill in planning or making something; cleverness. 2 skillfulness of contrivance or design: *the ingenuity of a puzzle.* 3 an ingenious device or contrivance. [< Latin *ingenuitatem* frankness < *ingenuus* ingenuous; influenced by *ingenious*]

in gen u ous (in jen′yü əs), *adj.* 1 free from restraint or reserve; frank and open; sincere. 2 simple and natural; innocent; naïve. [< Latin *ingenuus,* originally, native < *in-* in + *gignere* beget] **—in gen′u ous ly,** *adv.* **—in gen′u ous ness,** *n.* ➤ See **ingenious** for usage note.

in gest (in jest′), *v.t.* take (food, etc.) into the body for digestion. [< Latin *ingestum* carried in < *in-* in + *gerere* carry]

in ges tive (in jes′tiv), *adj.* of or having to do with ingestion.

in gle (ing′gəl), *n.* 1 fireplace. 2 fire burning on the hearth. [< Scottish Gaelic *aingeal* fire]

in gle nook (ing′gəl nůk′), *n.* nook or corner beside a fireplace.

In gle wood (ing′gəl wůd), *n.* city in SW California, a suburb of Los Angeles. 90,000.

in glo ri ous (in glôr′ē əs, in glōr′ē əs), *adj.* 1 bringing no glory; shameful; disgraceful. 2 having no glory; not famous; obscure. **—in glo′ri ous ly,** *adv.* **—in glo′ri ous ness,** *n.*

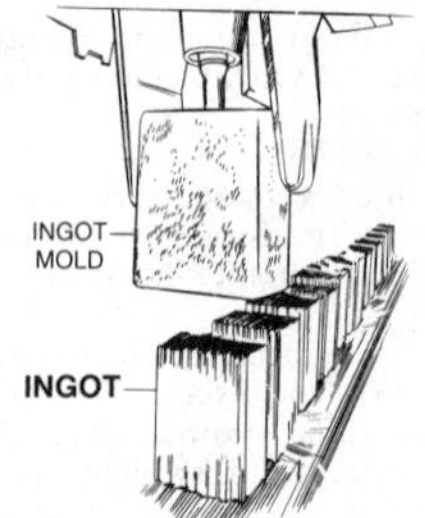

ingots
steel ingots just removed from molds by huge tongs suspended from a crane

in got (ing′gət), *n.* mass of metal, such as gold, silver, or steel, cast into a block or bar to be recast, rolled, or forged at a later time. [Middle English]

in graft (in graft′), *v.t.* engraft.

in grain (*v.* in grān′; *adj., n.* in′grān′), *v.t.* 1 dye through the fiber or yarn before manufacture. 2 fix deeply and firmly: *A habit becomes ingrained in us.* —*adj.* 1 dyed before manufacture. 2 made of yarn dyed before weaving: *an ingrain rug.* —*n.* yarn, wool, etc., dyed before manufacture.

in grained (in grānd′), *adj.* deeply and firmly fixed; thoroughly imbued: *ingrained honesty.*

in grate (in′grāt), *n.* an ungrateful person. [< Latin *ingratus* ungrateful < *in-* not + *gratus* grateful]

in gra ti ate (in grā′shē āt), *v.t.,* **-at ed, -at ing.** bring (oneself) into favor; make (oneself) acceptable: *He tried to ingratiate himself with the teacher by giving her presents.* [ultimately < Latin *in gratiam* into favor] **—in gra′ti at′ing ly,** *adv.* **—in gra′ti a′tion,** *n.*

in grat i tude (in grat′ə tüd, in grat′ə tyüd), *n.* lack of gratitude or thankfulness; being ungrateful.

in gre di ent (in grē′dē ənt), *n.* one of the parts of a mixture or combination: *the ingredients of a cake. Honesty is an important ingredient of character.* See **element** for synonym study. [< Latin *ingredientem* going into < *in-* in + *gradi* go]

In gres (aɴ′grə), *n.* **Jean Auguste Dominique,** 1780-1867, French painter.

in gress (in′gres), *n.* 1 a going in or entering: *A high fence prevented ingress to the field.* 2 way of going in; entrance. 3 right to go in: *have free ingress to the public library.* [< Latin *ingressus* < *ingredi* go into < *in-* in + *gradi* go]

in-group (in′grüp′), *n.* group of persons united by a common cause, interest, etc., and from which outsiders are often excluded.

in grow ing (in′grō′ing), *adj.* 1 growing within; growing inward. 2 growing into the flesh.

in grown (in′grōn′), *adj.* 1 grown within; natural; native: *ingrown ability.* 2 grown into the flesh: *an ingrown toenail.*

in gui nal (ing′gwə nəl), *adj.* of or in the region of the groin. [< Latin *inguinalis* < *inguen* groin]

in hab it (in hab′it), *v.t.* live in (a place, region, house, cave, tree, etc.): *Fish inhabit the sea. Thoughts inhabit the mind.* [< Latin *inhabitare* < *in-* in + *habitare* dwell] **—in hab′i ta′tion,** *n.* **—in hab′it er,** *n.*

in hab it a bil i ty (in hab′ə tə bil′ə tē), *n.* quality of being inhabitable.

in hab it a ble (in hab′ə tə bəl), *adj.* 1 capable of being inhabited. 2 fit to live in; habitable.

in hab it ant (in hab′ə tənt), *n.* person or animal that lives in a place; permanent resident; dweller.

in hab it ed (in hab′ə tid), *adj.* lived in: *an inhabited house.*

in hal ant (in hā′lənt), *n.* medicine to be inhaled. —*adj.* used for inhaling.

in ha la tion (in′hə lā′shən), *n.* 1 an inhaling. 2 medicine to be inhaled.

in ha la tion al (in′hə lā′shə nəl), *adj.* of or promoting inhalation.

in ha la tor (in′hə lā′tər), *n.* apparatus for inhaling medicine, gas, anesthetic, etc.; inhaler.

in hale (in hāl′), *v.,* **-haled, -hal ing.** —*v.t.* draw into the lungs; breathe in. —*v.i.* draw air, tobacco smoke, etc., into the lungs. [< Latin *inhalare* < *in-* in + *halare* breathe]

in hal er (in hā′lər), *n.* 1 inhalator. 2 person who inhales.

in har mon ic (in′här mon′ik), *adj.* not harmonic; not in harmony; dissonant.

in har mo ni ous (in′här mō′nē əs), *adj.* not harmonious; conflicting; discordant. **—in′har mo′ni ous ly,** *adv.* **—in′har mo′ni ous ness,** *n.*

in here (in hir′), *v.i.,* **-hered, -her ing.** belong as a quality or attribute; be inherent; exist: *The need to be loved inheres in human nature. Power to legislate laws for the United States inheres in Congress.* [< Latin *inhaerere* < *in-* in + *haerere* to stick]

in her ence (in hir′əns, in her′əns), *n.* a being inherent.

in her ent (in hir′ənt, in her′ənt), *adj.* belonging to a person or thing as a permanent and essential quality or attribute; intrinsic: *inherent honesty, the inherent sweetness of sugar.* **—in her′ent ly,** *adv.*

in her it (in her′it), *v.t.* 1 receive as an heir: *After his death his wife and children will inherit his property.* 2 receive from one's parents or ancestors through heredity: *inherit blue eyes.* 3 receive (anything) by succession from one who came before: *The new government inherited a financial crisis.* —*v.i.* succeed as an heir. [< Old French *enheriter* < Late Latin *inhereditare* < Latin *in-* + *heres* heir]

in her it a ble (in her′ə tə bəl), *adj.* 1 capable of being inherited. 2 capable of inheriting; qualified to inherit. **—in her′it a ble ness,** *n.*

in her it ance (in her′ə təns), *n.* 1 act or right of inheriting. 2 anything inherited.

inheritance tax, tax on inherited property.

in her i tor (in her′ə tər), *n.* person who inherits; heir.

in her i tress (in her′ə tris), *n.* heiress.

in her i trix (in her′ə triks), *n.* heiress.

in hib it (in hib′it), *v.t.* 1 hold back; hinder or restrain; check: *Some drugs can inhibit normal bodily activity.* 2 prohibit; forbid. [< Latin *inhibitum* held in < *in-* in + *habere* to hold] **—in hib′it er,** *n.*

in hi bi tion (in′ə bish′ən, in′hi bish′ən), *n.* 1 an inhibiting. 2 a being inhibited. 3 idea, emotion, attitude, habit, or other inner force holding back or checking one's impulses, desires, etc. 4 prohibition; forbidding.

in hib i tive (in hib′ə tiv), *adj.* inhibitory.

in hib i tor (in hib′ə tər), *n.* 1 person or thing that inhibits. 2 (in chemistry) anything that checks or interferes with a chemical reaction.

in hib i to ry (in hib′ə tôr′ē, in hib′ə tōr′ē), *adj.* inhibiting; tending to inhibit.

in hos pit a ble (in′ho spit′ə bəl, in hos′pi tə bəl), *adj.* 1 not hospitable; not making visitors comfortable. 2 providing no shelter; barren: *The Pilgrims landed on a rocky, inhospitable shore.* **—in′hos pit′a ble ness,** *n.* **—in′hos pit′a bly,** *adv.*

in hos pi tal i ty (in hos′pə tal′ə tē), *n.* lack of hospitality.

in hu man (in hyü′mən), *adj.* 1 without kindness, mercy, or tenderness; brutal; cruel. 2 not human; not having the qualities natural to a human being: *inhuman powers of endurance.* **—in hu′man ly,** *adv.*

in hu mane (in′hyü mān′), *adj.* not humane; lacking in kindness, mercy, or tenderness. **—in′hu mane′ly,** *adv.*

in hu man i ty (in′hyü man′ə tē), *n., pl.* **-ties.** 1 inhuman quality; lack of feeling; cruelty; brutality. 2 an inhuman, cruel, or brutal act.

hat, āge, fär; let, ēqual, tėrm;
it, īce; hot, ōpen, ôrder;
oil, out; cup, pu̇t, rüle;
ch, child; ng, long; sh, she;
th, thin; ᴛʜ, then; zh, measure;

ə represents *a* in about, *e* in taken, *i* in pencil, *o* in lemon, *u* in circus.

< = from, derived from, taken from.

in hu ma tion (in′hyə mā′shən), *n.* burial; interment.

in hume (in hyüm′), *v.t.,* **-humed, -hum ing.** bury or inter (a corpse). [< Latin *inhumare* < *in-* (intensive) + *humus* ground, earth]

in im i cal (in im′ə kəl), *adj.* 1 showing dislike or enmity; unfriendly; hostile. See **hostile** for synonym study. 2 unfavorable; harmful: *Lack of ambition is inimical to success.* [< Late Latin *inimicalis* < Latin *inimicus* hostile, an enemy < *in-* not + *amicus* friendly, a friend] **—in im′i cal ly,** *adv.*

in im i ta bil i ty (in im′ə tə bil′ə tē), *n.* a being inimitable.

in im i ta ble (in im′ə tə bəl), *adj.* impossible to imitate or copy; matchless. **—in im′i ta ble ness,** *n.* **—in im′i ta bly,** *adv.*

in iq ui tous (in ik′wə təs), *adj.* grossly unjust; wicked. **—in iq′ui tous ly,** *adv.* **—in iq′ui tous ness,** *n.*

in iq ui ty (in ik′wə tē), *n., pl.* **-ties.** 1 gross injustice or unrighteousness; wickedness; sin. 2 a wicked or unjust act. [< Latin *iniquitatem* < *iniquus* unjust < *in-* not + *aequus* just]

i ni tial (i nish′əl), *adj., n., v.,* **-tialed, -tial ing** or **-tialled, -tial ling.** —*adj.* 1 of, having to do with, or occurring at the beginning; first; earliest: *My initial effort at skating was a failure.* 2 standing at the beginning: *the initial letter of a word.* —*n.* 1 the first letter of a word or name. 2 an extra large letter, often decorated, at the beginning of a chapter or other division of a book or illuminated manuscript. —*v.t.* mark or sign with initials: *John Allen Smith initialed the note J.A.S.* [< Latin *initialis* < *initium* beginning < *inire* begin < *in-* in + *ire* go] **—i ni′tial ly,** *adv.*

i ni ti ate (*v.* i nish′ē āt; *n., adj.* i nish′ē it, i nish′ē āt), *v.,* **-at ed, -at ing,** *n., adj.* —*v.t.* 1 be the first one to start; set going; begin. 2 admit (a person) with formal ceremonies into a group or society. 3 help to get a first understanding; introduce into the knowledge of some art or subject: *initiate a person into modern business methods.* —*n.* person who is initiated. —*adj.* initiated. [< Latin *initiatum* begun < *initium* beginning < *inire* begin. See INITIAL.] **—i ni′ti a′tor,** *n.*

i ni ti a tion (i nish′ē ā′shən), *n.* 1 act or process of initiating; beginning. 2 fact of being initiated. 3 formal admission into a group or society. 4 ceremonies by which one is admitted to a group or society.

i ni ti a tive (i nish′ē ə tiv, i nish′ē ā′tiv), *n.* 1 active part in taking the first steps in any undertaking; lead: *A shy person is not likely to take the initiative in making acquaintances.* 2 readiness and ability to be the one to start something; enterprise: *A good leader must have initiative.* 3 right to be the first to act, legislate, etc. 4 right of citizens outside the legislature to introduce or enact a new law by vote, especially by petition. 5 procedure for doing this.

i ni ti a to ry (i nish′ē ə tôr′ē, i nish′ē ə-tōr′ē), *adj.* 1 first; beginning; introductory. 2 serving to initiate into some society or some special knowledge or study.

in ject (in jekt′), *v.t.* 1 force (liquid, medicine, etc.) into a chamber, passage, cavity, or tissue: *inject penicillin into a muscle, inject fuel into an engine.* 2 fill (a cavity, etc.) with liquid forced in: *The dentist injected the boy's gums with Novocaine.* 3 throw in; insert; interject: *inject a remark into a conversation.* [< Latin *injectum* thrown in < *in-* in + *jacere* to throw] **—in jec′tor,** *n.*

in jec tion (in jek′shən), *n.* 1 act or process of injecting: *Drugs are often given by injection.* 2 liquid injected: *an injection of penicillin.*

in ju di cious (in′jü dish′əs), *adj.* showing bad judgment; not judicious; unwise. **—in′ju di′cious ly,** *adv.* **—in′ju-di′cious ness,** *n.*

in junc tion (in jungk′shən), *n.* 1 an authoritative or emphatic order; command: *Injunctions of secrecy did not prevent the news from leaking out.* 2 a formal order from a court of law ordering a person or group to do, or refrain from doing, something. 3 act of commanding or authoritatively directing. [< Late Latin *injunctionem* < Latin *injungere* enjoin < *in-* in + *jungere* join]

in junc tive (in jungk′tiv), *adj.* serving to command.

in jure (in′jər), *v.t.*, **-jured, -jur ing.** 1 do damage to; harm; hurt: *Do not break or injure the bushes in the park.* See synonym study below. 2 be unfair to; do injustice or wrong to.

Syn. 1 **Injure, hurt, impair** mean to harm or damage. **Injure** implies any sort of damage, large or small: *Dishonesty injures a business.* **Hurt** particularly means to cause physical injury or bodily or mental pain to a person or animal: *He hurt my hand by twisting it.* **Impair** means to injure by weakening strength or value gradually in ways that cannot by remedied: *Poor eating habits impair health.*

in jur i ous (in ju̇r′ē əs), *adj.* 1 causing injury; harmful: *Hail is injurious to crops.* 2 unfair; unjust; wrongful. [< Latin *injuriosus*] **—in jur′i ous ly,** *adv.* **—in jur′i-ous ness,** *n.*

in jur y (in′jər ē), *n., pl.* **-jur ies.** 1 hurt or loss caused to or endured by a person or thing; harm; damage. 2 unfairness; injustice; wrong. [< Latin *injuria* unfairness, wrong < *in-* not + *jus, juris* right]

in jus tice (in jus′tis), *n.* 1 lack of justice; being unjust. 2 an unjust act.

ink (ingk), *n.* 1 a colored or black liquid used for writing, printing, or drawing. 2 a dark liquid thrown out for protection by cuttlefish, squids, etc. *—v.t.* put ink on; mark or stain with ink. [< Old French *enque* < Late Latin *encaustum* < Greek *enkauston* < *enkaiein* burn in < *en-* in + *kaiein* to burn] **—ink′er,** *n.* **—ink′like′,** *adj.*

ink blot (ingk′blot′), *n.* 1 blot made with ink. 2 one of the designs or patterns used in the Rorschach test.

ink horn (ingk′hôrn′), *n.* a small, portable container, often made of horn, formerly used to hold ink. *—adj.* learned or bookish; pedantic: *inkhorn terms.*

ink ling (ingk′ling), *n.* a vague notion; slight suspicion; hint. [Middle English < *inclen* to whisper, hint < Old English *inca* doubt]

ink stand (ingk′stand′), *n.* 1 stand to hold ink and pens. 2 container used to hold ink.

ink well (ingk′wel′), *n.* container used to hold ink on a desk or table.

ink y (ing′kē), *adj.,* **ink i er, ink i est.** 1 like ink; dark; black: *inky shadows.* 2 covered with ink; marked or stained with ink. 3 of ink; using ink. **—ink′i ness,** *n.*

in laid (in′lād′), *adj.* 1 set in the surface as a decoration or design: *The top of the desk had an inlaid design of light wood in dark.* 2 decorated with a design or material set in the surface: *The box had an inlaid cover.* *—v.* pt. and pp. of **inlay.**

in land (*adj.* in′lənd; *n., adv.* in′lənd, in′-land′), *adj.* 1 of or situated in the interior part of a country or region: *Illinois is an inland state.* 2 domestic; not foreign: *inland trade.* *—n.* interior of a country; land away from the border or the coast. *—adv.* in or toward the interior.

in land er (in′lən dər), *n.* person who lives in the interior of a country.

Inland Passage, coastal waterway connecting Seattle, Washington, with the coastal cities of British Columbia and Alaska.

Inland Sea, sea or strait formed by the three large islands of W Japan. 240 mi. long.

in-law (in′lô′), *n.* INFORMAL. person related by marriage.

in lay (in′lā′), *v.,* **-laid, -lay ing,** *n.* *—v.t.* 1 to set in the surface as a decoration or design: *inlay strips of gold.* 2 decorate with a design set in the surface: *inlay a wooden box with gold.* *—n.* 1 an inlaid decoration, design, or material. 2 a shaped piece of gold, porcelain, etc., cemented in a tooth as a filling. **—in′lay′er,** *n.*

in let (in′let), *n.* 1 a narrow strip of water running from a larger body of water into the land or between islands. 2 way of entering; entrance.

in lo co pa ren tis (in lō′kō pə ren′tis), LATIN. in the place of a parent; as a parent.

in ly (in′lē), *adv.* 1 inwardly; within. 2 thoroughly; deeply.

in mate (in′māt), *n.* 1 person confined in a prison, asylum, hospital, etc. 2 person who lives in the same building with another; occupant; inhabitant.

in me di as res (in mā′dē äs rās′; in-mē′dē as rēz′), LATIN. in or into the midst of things; beginning in the middle of the action or story, rather than at the beginning.

in me mo ri am (in mə môr′ē əm; in mə-mōr′ē əm), LATIN. in memory (of); to the memory (of).

in most (in′mōst), *adj.* 1 farthest in; deepest: *the inmost depths of the mine.* 2 most inward; most private, secret, or hidden: *one's inmost thoughts.*

inn (in), *n.* 1 a public house for lodging and caring for travelers. Hotels have largely taken the place of the old inn. 2 restaurant or tavern. [Old English < *inne* in]

in nards (in′ərdz), *n.pl.* INFORMAL. 1 the internal organs of the body; viscera. 2 the internal workings or parts of any complex mechanism, structure, etc. [variant of *inwards*]

in nate (i nāt′, in′āt), *adj.* 1 existing in a person from birth; natural; inborn; native. 2 existing naturally in anything; inherent. [< Latin *innatum* < *in-* in + *nasci* be born] **—in nate′ly,** *adv.* **—in nate′ness,** *n.*

in ner (in′ər), *adj.* 1 situated more within; farther in; inside. 2 more intimate; more private, secret, or hidden: *She kept her inner thoughts to herself.* 3 of the mind or soul; mental or spiritual. [Old English *innera,* comparative of *inne* within] **—in′ner ly,** *adv.* **—in′ner ness,** *n.*

inner city, U.S. 1 the central part of a large city or metropolitan area; the heart or core of a city. 2 this part characterized by congestion, poverty, dirt, etc.; the city slums.

inner ear, the innermost part of the ear, behind the middle ear. In man it contains the semicircular canals, the cochlea, and the sensory ends of the auditory nerve. See **ear**[1] for diagram.

Inner Light, (in the belief of Quakers) the light of Christ in the soul, acting as a spiritual guide.

Inner Mongolia, region in N China, south and east of the Mongolian People's Republic.

in ner most (in′ər mōst), *adj.* farthest in; inmost.

in ner sole (in′ər sōl′), *n.* insole.

inner space, 1 space beneath the surface of the sea. 2 region of the mind beyond the surface.

inlay (def. 1) several inlays on a portion of an inlaid table

inner tube, a flexible, inflatable rubber tube used inside the outer casings of some tires.

In ness (in′is), *n.* **George,** 1825-1894, American painter.

in ning (in′ing), *n.* 1 division of a baseball game during which each team has a turn at bat. 2 the turn one team or group has to play and score in a game. 3 Usually, **innings,** *pl.* the time a person or party is in power; chance for action: *When our party lost the election, the other side had its innings.* [Old English *innung* a taking in < *in* in]

in nings (in′ingz), *n.* (in cricket) an inning.

inn keep er (in′kē′pər), *n.* person who owns, manages, or keeps an inn.

in no cence (in′ə səns), *n.* 1 freedom from sin, wrong, or guilt: *The accused man proved his innocence with an alibi.* 2 simplicity; lack of cunning; naïveness: *the innocence of a little child.* 3 the common bluet.

in no cent (in′ə sənt), *adj.* 1 doing no wrong or evil; free from sin or wrong; not guilty. See synonym study below. 2 without knowledge of evil: *A baby is innocent.* 3 having or showing the simplicity and trusting nature of a child; guileless; naïve. 4 doing no harm; harmless: *innocent amusements.* —*n.* 1 an innocent person. 2 idiot; fool. [< Latin *innocentem* < *in-* not + *nocere* to harm] **—in′no cent ly,** *adv.*

Syn. *adj.* 1 **Innocent, blameless, guiltless** mean free from fault or wrong. **Innocent** implies having intended or consciously done no wrong, and therefore not deserving punishment for a particular offense: *The truck driver was proved innocent of manslaughter.* **Blameless** means neither at fault nor deserving blame, whether or not wrong has actually been done: *He was held blameless in the accident.* **Guiltless** is close in meaning to *innocent,* but emphasizes freedom from guilt or a feeling of guilt: *The other driver was not guiltless.*

In no cent II (in′ə sənt), died 1143, pope from 1130 to 1143.

Innocent III, 1161?-1216, pope from 1198 to 1216.

Innocent IV, died 1254, pope from 1243 to 1254.

Innocent XI, 1611-1689, pope from 1676 to 1689.

in noc u ous (i nok′yü əs), *adj.* not hurtful or injurious; harmless. [< Latin *innocuus* < *in-* not + *nocuus* hurtful < *nocere* to harm] **—in noc′u ous ly,** *adv.* **—in noc′u ous ness,** *n.*

in nom i nate bone (i nom′ə nit), hipbone.

in no vate (in′ə vāt), *v.,* **-vat ed, -vat ing.** —*v.i.* make changes; bring in something new or new ways of doing things. —*v.t.* introduce (something); bring in for the first time. [< Latin *innovatum* made new < *in-* (intensive) + *novus* new] **—in′no va′tor,** *n.*

in no va tion (in′ə vā′shən), *n.* 1 change made in the established way of doing things. 2 a making changes; bringing in new things or new ways of doing things.

in no va tion al (in′ə vā′shə nəl), *adj.* of or having to do with innovation.

in no va tive (in′ə vā′tiv), *adj.* tending to innovate.

Inns bruck (inz′brůk), *n.* city in W Austria. 110,000.

in nu en do (in′yü en′dō), *n., pl.* **-does.** 1 an indirect hint or reference; insinuation. 2 an indirect suggestion meant to discredit a person: *spread scandal by innuendo.* [< Latin, literally, by nodding to < *innuere* nod to, hint < *in-* + *-nuere* to nod]

in nu mer a ble (i nü′mər ə bəl, i nyü′mər ə bəl), *adj.* too many to count; very many; countless. See **many** for synonym study. **—in nu′mer a ble ness,** *n.* **—in nu′mer a bly,** *adv.*

in nu mer ous (i nü′mər əs, i nyü′mər əs), *adj.* ARCHAIC. innumerable.

in ob serv ance (in′əb zėr′vəns), *n.* 1 inattention. 2 nonobservance.

in ob serv ant (in′əb zėr′vənt), *adj.* 1 inattentive. 2 not observant.

in oc u lant (in ok′yə lənt), *n.* substance used in inoculating.

in oc u late (in ok′yə lāt), *v.,* **-lat ed, -lat ing.** —*v.t.* 1 infect (a person or animal) with killed or weakened germs or viruses that will cause a mild form of a disease so that thereafter the individual will not contract that disease or will suffer only a very mild form of it. 2 introduce (microorganisms) into surroundings suited to their growth. 3 treat (soil, seeds, etc.) with bacteria that will promote nitrogen fixation. 4 fill (a person's mind) with ideas, opinions, etc. —*v.i.* use disease germs to prevent diseases. [< Latin *inoculatum* engrafted < *in-* in + *oculus* bud, eye] **—in oc′u la′tor,** *n.*

in oc u la tion (in ok′yə lā′shən), *n.* 1 act or process of inoculating. 2 microorganisms used in inoculating. 3 a filling the mind with opinions or ideas.

in oc u la tive (in ok′yə lā′tiv), *adj.* of or having to do with inoculation.

in of fen sive (in′ə fen′siv), *adj.* not offensive or objectionable; not arousing objections; harmless: *an inoffensive odor, a mild, inoffensive man.* **—in′of fen′sive ly,** *adv.* **—in′of fen′sive ness,** *n.*

in op er a bil i ty (in op′ər ə bil′ə tē), *n.* condition of being inoperable.

in op er a ble (in op′ər ə bəl), *adj.* 1 unfit for a surgical operation; unable to be cured by surgery. 2 not operable; unworkable.

in op er a tive (in op′ər ə tiv, in op′ə rā′-tiv), *adj.* not operative; not working; without effect. **—in op′er a tive ness,** *n.*

in op por tune (in op′ər tün′, in op′ər-tyün′), *adj.* not opportune; coming at a bad time; unsuitable: *An inopportune telephone call delayed us.* **—in op′por tune′ly,** *adv.* **—in op′por tune′ness,** *n.*

in or di nate (in ôrd′n it), *adj.* much too great; not kept within proper limits; excessive: *inordinate demands.* See **excessive** for synonym study. [< Latin *inordinatus* not ordered, disarranged < *in-* not + *ordo* order] **—in or′di nate ly,** *adv.* **—in or′di nate ness,** *n.*

in or gan ic (in′ôr gan′ik), *adj.* 1 not organic; neither animal nor vegetable; not having the organized physical structure characteristic of animals and plants. Water and minerals are inorganic substances. 2 (in chemistry) of or having to do with substances not containing carbon. **—in′or gan′i cal ly,** *adv.*

inorganic chemistry, branch of chemistry dealing with inorganic compounds and elements.

in pa tient (in′pā′shənt), *n.* patient who is lodged and fed in a hospital while undergoing treatment.

in pet to (in pet′tō), ITALIAN. 1 secretly; not announced; undisclosed. 2 (literally) in the breast.

in put (in′půt′), *n.* 1 what is put in or taken in. 2 power supplied to a machine. 3 coded information fed into a computer. 4 point of putting in or taking in information, power, etc.

in quest (in′kwest), *n.* 1 a legal inquiry, especially before a jury, held to determine the cause of a death not clearly due to natural causes. 2 jury appointed to hold such an inquiry. 3 the finding in such an inquiry. [< Old French *enqueste,* ultimately < Latin *inquirere.* See INQUIRE.]

in qui e tude (in kwī′ə tüd, in kwī′ə tyüd), *n.* uneasy feeling; restlessness.

in quire (in kwīr′), *v.,* **-quired, -quir ing.** —*v.i.* 1 try to find out by questions; ask. See **ask** for synonym study. 2 make a search for information, knowledge, or truth; make an examination of facts or principles. —*v.t.* ask about; try to find out by questions: *inquire the way.* See **ask** for synonym study. Also, **enquire.** [< Latin *inquirere* < *in-* into + *quaerere* ask] **—in quir′er,** *n.* **—in quir′ing ly,** *adv.*

in quir y (in kwī′rē, in′kwər ē), *n., pl.* **-quir ies.** 1 act of inquiring; asking. 2 a search for information, knowledge, or truth.

hat, āge, fär; let, ēqual, tėrm;
it, īce; hot, ōpen, ôrder;
oil, out; cup, půt, rüle;
ch, child; ng, long; sh, she;
th, thin; ᴛʜ, then; zh, measure;

ə represents *a* in about, *e* in taken, *i* in pencil, *o* in lemon, *u* in circus.

< = from, derived from, taken from.

See **investigation** for synonym study. 3 question. Also, **enquiry.**

in qui si tion (in′kwə zish′ən), *n.* 1 a thorough investigation; searching inquiry. 2 an official investigation; judicial inquiry. 3 **the Inquisition,** court appointed by the Roman Catholic Church in the 1200's to discover and suppress heresy. It was abolished in the 1800's. [< Latin *inquisitionem* < *inquirere.* See INQUIRE.]

in qui si tion al (in′kwə zish′ə nəl), *adj.* 1 inquisitorial. 2 of or having to do with the Inquisition.

in quis i tive (in kwiz′ə tiv), *adj.* 1 asking many questions; curious. 2 prying into other people's affairs; too curious. See **curious** for synonym study. **—in quis′i tive ly,** *adv.* **—in quis′i tive ness,** *n.*

in quis i tor (in kwiz′ə tər), *n.* 1 person who makes an inquisition; official investigator; judicial inquirer. 2 **Inquisitor,** member of the Inquisition.

in quis i to ri al (in kwiz′ə tôr′ē əl, in-kwiz′ə tōr′ē əl), *adj.* 1 of an inquisitor or inquisition. 2 unduly curious; prying. **—in quis′i to′ri al ly,** *adv.*

in re (in rē′; in rā′), LATIN. in the matter of; concerning.

I.N.R.I., Jesus of Nazareth, King of the Jews. [for Latin *Iesus Nazarenus, Rex Iudaeorum*]

in road (in′rōd′), *n.* 1 an attack or raid; incursion. 2 encroachment by force: *The expenses of her trip made inroads upon the money that she had saved.*

in rush (in′rush′), *n.* a rushing in; inflow.

ins., 1 inches. 2 insulated. 3 insurance.

in sa lu bri ous (in′sə lü′brē əs), *adj.* unhealthful; unwholesome: *insalubrious living conditions.*

in sane (in sān′), *adj.* 1 not sane; mentally ill; crazy. See **crazy** for synonym study. 2 characteristic of one who is mentally ill: *an insane laugh.* 3 for insane people: *an insane asylum.* 4 extremely foolish; completely lacking in common sense. **—in sane′ly,** *adv.* **—in sane′ness,** *n.*

in san i tar y (in san′ə ter′ē), *adj.* not sanitary; not healthful. **—in san′i tar′i ness,** *n.*

in san i ty (in san′ə tē), *n., pl.* **-ties.** 1 state of being insane; madness; mental illness. 2 (in law) mental unsoundness, either temporary or permanent, in which a person is not held responsible for his actions. 3 complete lack of common sense; extreme folly. 4 an instance of this.

in sa tia bil i ty (in sā′shə bil′ə tē), *n.* insatiable quality.

in sa tia ble (in sā′shə bəl), *adj.* that cannot be satisfied; extremely greedy: *an insatiable appetite.* **—in sa′tia ble ness,** *n.* **—in sa′tia bly,** *adv.*

in sa ti ate (in sā′shē it), *adj.* never satisfied: *an insatiate desire for praise.* **—in sa′ti ate ly,** *adv.* **—in sa′ti ate ness,** *n.*

in scribe (in skrīb′), *v.t.*, **-scribed, -scrib ing.** 1 write or engrave (words, names, letters, etc.) on stone, paper, metal, etc. 2 mark or engrave (a surface, monument, etc.) with words, names, letters, etc.: *His tombstone was inscribed with his name and the date of his death.* 3 address or dedicate (a book, picture, etc.) informally to a person. 4 impress deeply: *My father's words are inscribed in my memory.* 5 put in a list; enroll. 6 (in geometry) draw (one figure) within another figure so that the inner touches the outer at as many points as possible. [< Latin *inscribere* < *in-* on + *scribere* write] **—in scrib′er,** *n.*

in scrip tion (in skrip′shən), *n.* 1 something inscribed; words, names, letters, etc., written or engraved on stone, metal, paper, etc. A monument or a coin has an inscription on it. 2 an informal dedication in a book, on a picture, etc. 3 act of writing upon or in something. [< Latin *inscriptionem* < *inscribere.* See INSCRIBE.]

in scrip tion al (in skrip′shə nəl), *adj.* inscriptive.

in scrip tive (in skrip′tiv), *adj.* of or having to do with inscription; used in inscriptions.

in scru ta bil i ty (in skrü′tə bil′ə tē), *n.* 1 a being inscrutable. 2 something inscrutable.

in scru ta ble (in skrü′tə bəl), *adj.* that cannot be understood; so mysterious or obscure that one cannot make out its meaning; incomprehensible. See **mysterious** for synonym study. [< Late Latin *inscrutabilis* < Latin *in-* not + *scrutari* examine, ransack < *scruta* trash] **—in scru′ta ble ness,** *n.* **—in scru′ta bly,** *adv.*

in seam (in′sēm′), *n.* the inner seam of a trouser leg, sleeve, shoe, etc.

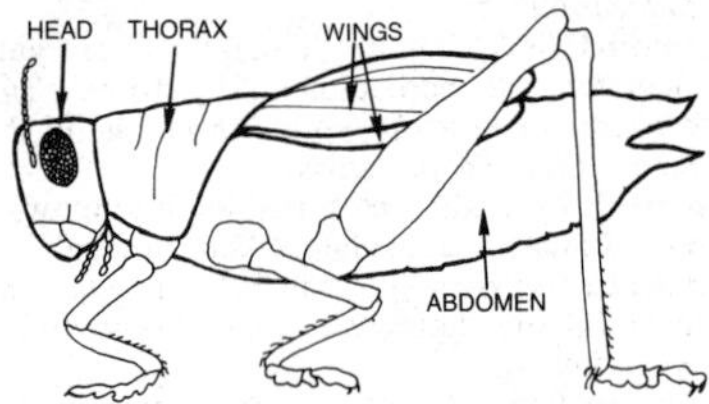

insect (def. 1)—a grasshopper

in sect (in′sekt), *n.* 1 any of a class of small arthropods with the body divided into three sections, the head, thorax, and abdomen, and having three pairs of legs and one or two pairs of wings. Flies, mosquitoes, butterflies, bees, grasshoppers, and beetles are insects. 2 any of certain similar arthropods, especially any of the wingless forms having four pairs of legs. Spiders, centipedes, mites, and ticks are often called insects. [< Latin *(animal) insectum,* literally, divided (animal) < *insecare* cut into, divide < *in-* into + *secare* to cut]

in sec tar y (in′sek ter′ē), *n., pl.* **-tar ies.** place for keeping, observing, or breeding insects.

in sec ti ci dal (in sek′tə sī′dl), *adj.* having to do with the killing of insects.

in sec ti cide (in sek′tə sīd), *n.* substance for killing insects.

in sec ti vore (in sek′tə vôr, in sek′tə vōr), *n.* 1 any animal or plant that feeds mainly on insects, such as a praying mantis. 2 any of an order of small mammals including moles, shrews, and hedgehogs that feed chiefly on insects.

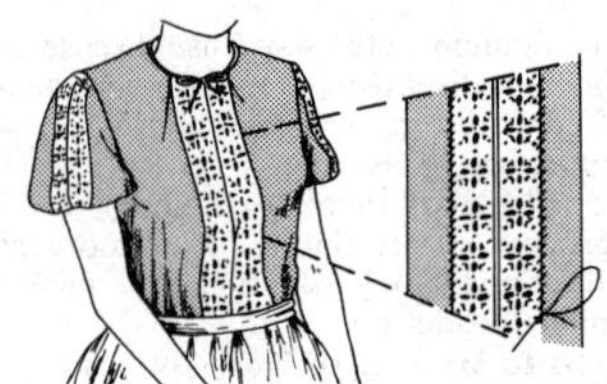
insertion (def. 3)

in sec tiv or ous (in′sek tiv′ər əs), *adj.* insect-eating; feeding mainly on insects. [< Latin *insectum* insect + *vorare* devour]

in se cure (in′si kyůr′), *adj.* 1 exposed to danger, loss, attack, etc.; not secure; unsafe: *a region where life is insecure.* See **uncertain** for synonym study. 2 liable to give way; not firm: *an insecure support, an insecure lock.* 3 lacking confidence; not sure of oneself; fearful; timid: *an insecure person.* **—in′se cure′ly,** *adv.* **—in′se cure′ness,** *n.*

in se cur i ty (in′si kyůr′ə tē), *n., pl.* **-ties.** 1 lack of security; being insecure. 2 something insecure.

in sem i nate (in sem′ə nāt′), *v.t.,* **-nat ed, -nat ing.** 1 inject semen into; fertilize; impregnate. 2 sow (seeds); implant. [ultimately < Latin *in-* in + *seminis* semen, seed] **—in sem′i na′tion,** *n.*

in sen sate (in sen′sāt, in sen′sit), *adj.* 1 without sensation; lifeless; inanimate: *insensate stones.* 2 unfeeling; brutal: *insensate cruelty.* 3 senseless; stupid: *insensate folly.* **—in sen′sate ly,** *adv.* **—in sen′sate ness,** *n.*

in sen si bil i ty (in sen′sə bil′ə tē), *n., pl.* **-ties.** 1 lack of feeling; unawareness. 2 lack of consciousness; senselessness.

in sen si ble (in sen′sə bəl), *adj.* 1 not sensitive; not able to feel or notice: *insensible to cold.* 2 not aware; unmoved; indifferent: *A lifetime as a soldier had not made him insensible to the suffering and sorrow of war.* 3 not able to feel anything; unconscious; senseless. 4 not easily felt; too slow to be noticed: *The room grew cold by insensible degrees as the sun went down.* **—in sen′si bly,** *adv.*

in sen si tive (in sen′sə tiv), *adj.* 1 not sensitive; not able to feel or notice. 2 slow to feel or notice. **—in sen′si tive ly,** *adv.* **—in sen′si tive ness,** *n.*

in sen si tiv i ty (in sen′sə tiv′ə tē), *n.* insensitive condition or quality.

in sen ti ence (in sen′shē əns, in sen′shəns), *n.* 1 lack of sensation. 2 inanimateness.

in sen ti ent (in sen′shē ənt, in sen′shənt), *adj.* unable to feel; lifeless.

in sep ar a bil i ty (in sep′ər ə bil′ə tē), *n.* a being inseparable.

in sep ar a ble (in sep′ər ə bəl), *adj.* 1 impossible to separate. 2 constantly together: *inseparable companions.* —*n.* **inseparables,** *pl.* inseparable persons or things. **—in sep′ar a ble ness,** *n.* **—in sep′ar a bly,** *adv.*

in sert (*v.* in sėrt′; *n.* in′sėrt′), *v.t.* put in; set in; introduce: *insert a key into a lock.* —*n.* something inserted: *The newspaper had an insert of several pages of pictures.* [< Latin *insertum* put or joined in < *in-* in + *serere* join, entwine] **—in sert′er,** *n.*

in ser tion (in sėr′shən), *n.* 1 act of inserting. 2 something inserted. 3 band of lace or embroidery to be sewed at each edge between parts of other material.

in-serv ice (in′sėr′vis), *adj.* taking place or acquired on the job: *an in-service training program.*

in ses so ri al (in′se sôr′ē əl, in′se sōr′ē əl), *adj.* 1 habitually perching. 2 adapted for perching: *insessorial feet.* [< Latin *insessor* occupant < *insidere* sit on < *in-* on + *sedere* sit]

in set (*v.* in set′, in′set′; *n.* in′set′), *v.,* **-set, -set ting,** *n.* —*v.t.* set in; insert. —*n.* 1 something inserted. 2 a small map, picture, etc., set within the border of a larger one. 3 piece of cloth inserted into a garment.

in shore (in′shôr′, in′shōr′), *adj.* near or toward the shore: *inshore fishing.* —*adv.* in toward the shore: *The boat was driven inshore by the winds.*

in side (*n., adj.* in′sīd′; *adv., prep.* in′sīd′), *n.* 1 the part within; the inner surface: *The inside of the box was lined with paper.* 2 the contents: *The inside of the book was more interesting than the cover.* —*adj.* 1 being on the inside: *an inside seat.* 2 done or known by those inside; secret: *The informer had inside information of the gang's plans.* 3 SLANG. working within a group or company as an emissary or spy: *an inside man.* 4 indoor. —*adv.* 1 on or to the inside; within; in the inner part. 2 indoors. 3 **inside out,** a so that what should be inside is outside; with the inside showing: *He turned his pockets inside out.* b completely; thoroughly: *She learned her lesson inside out.* —*prep.* 1 inside of; within the limits of; in: *The nut is inside the shell.* 2 INFORMAL. **inside of,** in; within the limits of: *They should be back inside of an hour.*

in sid er (in′sī′dər), *n.* 1 person who belongs to a certain group, club, society, political party, etc. 2 person who has private or secret information about something not known to most others.

in sides (in′sīdz′), *n.pl.* INFORMAL. parts inside the body, especially the stomach and bowels.

inside track, 1 the lane nearest the inside of the curve on a race track. 2 INFORMAL. an advantageous position or situation.

in sid i ous (in sid′ē əs), *adj.* 1 seeking to entrap or ensnare; wily or sly; crafty; tricky. 2 working secretly or subtly; developing without attracting attention: *an insidious disease.* [< Latin *insidiosus* < *insidiae* ambush < *insidere* sit in < *in-* in + *sedere* sit] **—in sid′i ous ly,** *adv.* **—in sid′i ous ness,** *n.*

in sight (in′sīt′), *n.* 1 a viewing of the inside with understanding. 2 wisdom and understanding in dealing with people or with facts. See synonym study below.

Syn. 2 **Insight, discernment, penetration** mean ability to understand people or things. **Insight** implies both the power to see deeply and sympathetic understanding: *Good teachers have insight into the problems of students.* **Discernment** emphasizes the power to make accurate judgments: *In selecting employees he shows discernment.* **Penetration** emphasizes the ability to go deeply into things and to see fine distinctions and relations: *Solving the mystery required penetration.*

in sig ne (in sig′nē), *n., pl.* **-ni a.** insignia.

in sig ni a (in sig′nē ə), *n., pl.* **-ni a** or **-ni as.** 1 medal, badge, or other distinguishing mark

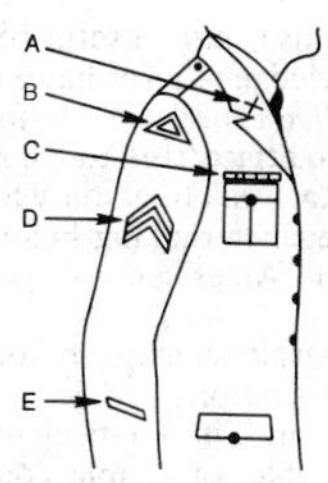

insignia (def. 1) of U.S. Army
A, branch of service
B, army or service
C, decorations
D, enlisted man's rank
E, three years service

of a position, honor, military rank, etc.: *The crown, scepter, and orb are the insignia of kings.* 2 pl. of **insigne.** [< Latin, plural of *insigne* badge < *in-* on + *signum* mark. Doublet of ENSIGN.]

in sig nif i cance (in′sig nif′ə kəns), *n.* a being insignificant; unimportance; uselessness; meaninglessness.

in sig nif i cant (in′sig nif′ə kənt), *adj.* 1 of no consequence, influence, or distinction: *an insignificant position, an insignificant person.* 2 too small to be important; unimportant; trivial; petty: *an insignificant detail, an insignificant amount of money.* 3 having little or no meaning; meaningless: *an insignificant gesture.* **—in′sig nif′i cant ly,** *adv.*

in sin cere (in′sin sir′), *adj.* not sincere; not honest or candid; deceitful. **—in′sin cere′ly,** *adv.*

in sin cer i ty (in′sin ser′ə tē), *n., pl.* **-ties.** lack of sincerity; being insincere; hypocrisy.

in sin u ate (in sin′yü āt), *v.,* **-at ed, -at ing.** —*v.t.* 1 suggest in an indirect way; hint: *To say "That man can't do it; no coward can" is to insinuate that the man is a coward.* See **hint** for synonym study. 2 push in or get in by an indirect, subtle way: *The stray cat insinuated itself into our kitchen. The spy insinuated himself into the confidence of important army officers.* —*v.i.* make insinuations. [< Latin *insinuatum* wound or twisted into < *in-* in + *sinus* a curve, winding] **—in sin′u at′ing ly,** *adv.* **—in sin′u a′tor,** *n.*

in sin u a tion (in sin′yü ā′shən), *n.* 1 an insinuating. 2 an indirect suggestion meant to discredit someone. 3 hint; suggestion. 4 act or speech to gain favor in an indirect, subtle way.

in sin u a tive (in sin′yü ā′tiv), *adj.* 1 insinuating; ingratiating. 2 subtly suggesting or hinting.

in sip id (in sip′id), *adj.* 1 without any particular flavor; tasteless: *A mixture of milk and water is an insipid drink.* 2 lacking interest or spirit; dull, colorless, or weak: *an insipid conversation.* [< Late Latin *insipidus* < Latin *in-* not + *sapidus* tasty] **—in sip′id ly,** *adv.* **—in sip′id ness,** *n.*

in si pid i ty (in′sə pid′ə tē), *n., pl.* **-ties.** 1 lack of flavor; lack of interest. 2 something insipid.

in sist (in sist′), *v.i.* keep firmly to some demand, statement, or position; take a stand and refuse to give in: *insist on one's innocence.* —*v.t.* maintain or demand persistently: *insist that something is true, insist that something should be done.* [< Latin *insistere* < *in-* on + *sistere* take a stand]

in sist ence (in sis′təns), *n.* 1 act of insisting. 2 quality of being insistent.

in sist en cy (in sis′tən sē), *n., pl.* **-cies.** insistence.

in sist ent (in sis′tənt), *adj.* 1 continuing to make a strong, firm demand or statement; insisting: *In spite of the rain she was insistent on going out.* 2 compelling attention or notice; pressing; urgent: *an insistent knocking on the door.* **—in sist′ent ly,** *adv.*

in si tu (in sī′tü; in sī′tyü), LATIN. in its original place; in position.

in snare (in sner′, in snar′), *v.t.,* **-snared, -snar ing.** ensnare.

in so bri e ty (in′sə brī′ə tē), *n.* intemperance; drunkenness.

in so cia ble (in sō′shə bəl), *adj.* not sociable; unsociable. **—in so′cia bly,** *adv.*

in so far as (in′sō fär′), to such an extent or degree as.

insol., insoluble.

in so la tion (in′sō lā′shən), *n.* 1 exposure to the sun's rays for drying, bleaching, etc. 2 amount of solar radiation per unit of horizontal surface in a given time. [ultimately < Latin *in-* in + *sol* sun]

in sole (in′sōl′), *n.* 1 the inner sole of a shoe or boot. 2 layer of warm or waterproof material put on the sole inside a shoe or boot.

in so lence (in′sə ləns), *n.* bold rudeness; insulting behavior or speech.

in so lent (in′sə lənt), *adj.* boldly rude; intentionally disregarding the feelings of others; insulting. [< Latin *insolentem* < *in-* not + *solere* be accustomed] **—in′so lent ly,** *adv.*

in sol u bil i ty (in sol′yə bil′ə tē), *n.* insoluble condition or quality.

in sol u ble (in sol′yə bəl), *adj.* 1 that cannot be dissolved; not soluble: *Fats are insoluble in water.* 2 that cannot be solved; unsolvable. **—in sol′u ble ness,** *n.* **—in sol′u bly,** *adv.*

in solv a ble (in sol′və bəl), *adj.* that cannot be solved. **—in solv′a bly,** *adv.*

in sol ven cy (in sol′vən sē), *n., pl.* **-cies.** condition of not being able to pay one's debts; bankruptcy.

in sol vent (in sol′vənt), *adj.* unable to pay one's debts; bankrupt. —*n.* an insolvent person.

in som ni a (in som′nē ə), *n.* inability to sleep, especially when chronic; sleeplessness. [< Latin < *in-* not + *somnus* sleep]

in som ni ac (in som′nē ak), *n.* person who has insomnia.

in so much (in′sō much′), *adv.* 1 in such a way; to such an extent or degree; so. 2 **insomuch as,** inasmuch as; since.

in sou ci ance (in sü′sē əns), *n.* freedom from care or anxiety; carefree feeling; unconcern.

in sou ci ant (in sü′sē ənt), *adj.* free from care or anxiety; carefree. [< French] **—in sou′ci ant ly,** *adv.*

in spect (in spekt′), *v.t.* 1 look over carefully; examine: *A dentist inspects my teeth twice a year.* 2 examine formally; look over officially: *All mines are inspected by government officials.* [< Latin *inspectum* looked over < *in-* + *specere* to look]

in spec tion (in spek′shən), *n.* 1 an inspecting; examination: *An inspection of the roof showed no leaks.* 2 a formal or official examination: *The soldiers lined up for their daily inspection by their officers.*

in spec tor (in spek′tər), *n.* 1 person who inspects. 2 officer or official appointed to inspect: *a milk inspector.* 3 a police officer, usually ranking next below a superintendent.

in spec tor ate (in spek′tər it), *n.* 1 office or function of an inspector. 2 group of inspectors.

in spec tor ship (in spek′tər ship), *n.* office of an inspector.

hat, āge, fär; let, ēqual, tėrm;
it, īce; hot, ōpen, ôrder;
oil, out; cup, pu̇t, rüle;
ch, child; ng, long; sh, she;
th, thin; ᴛʜ, then; zh, measure;

ə represents *a* in about, *e* in taken, *i* in pencil, *o* in lemon, *u* in circus.

< = from, derived from, taken from.

in spi ra tion (in′spə rā′shən), *n.* 1 influence of thought and strong feelings on actions, especially on good actions: *Some people get inspiration from sermons, some from poetry.* 2 any influence that arouses effort to do well: *The teacher was an inspiration to her students.* 3 idea that is inspired; sudden, brilliant idea. 4 divine influence. Inspiration helped men to write the Bible. 5 a breathing in; a drawing of air into the lungs; inhalation.

in spi ra tion al (in′spə rā′shə nəl), *adj.* 1 tending to inspire; inspiring. 2 under the influence of inspiration; inspired. 3 of or having to do with inspiration. **—in′spi ra′tion al ly,** *adv.*

in spir a to ry (in spī′rə tôr′ē, in spī′rə tōr′ē), *adj.* of or having to do with inspiration.

in spire (in spīr′), *v.,* **-spired, -spir ing.** —*v.t.* 1 fill with a thought or feeling; influence: *A chance to try again inspired him with hope.* 2 cause (thought or feeling): *The leader's courage inspired confidence in the others.* 3 put thought, feeling, life, force, etc., into: *The speaker inspired the crowd.* 4 cause to be told or written: *His enemies inspired false stories about him.* 5 arouse or influence by a divine force. 6 breathe in; inhale. —*v.i.* breathe in air. [< Latin *inspirare* < *in-* in + *spirare* breathe] **—in spir′er,** *n.* **—in spir′ing ly,** *adv.*

in spir it (in spir′it), *v.t.* put spirit into; encourage; hearten; cheer.

in spis sate (in spis′āt), *v.t., v.i.,* **-sat ed, -sat ing.** thicken, as by evaporation; condense. [ultimately < Latin *in-* + *spissus* thick]

inst., 1 instant (*adj.* def. 4). "The 10th inst." means "the tenth day of the present month." 2 institute. 3 institution.

in sta bil i ty (in′stə bil′ə tē), *n.* lack of firmness; being unstable; unsteadiness.

in sta ble (in stā′bəl), *adj.* unstable.

in stall or **in stal** (in stôl′), *v.t.,* **-stalled, -stall ing.** 1 put (a person) in office with ceremonies: *The new judge was installed without delay.* 2 put in a place or position; settle: *The cat installed itself in a chair.* 3 put in place for use: *install a telephone.* [< Medieval Latin *installare* < *in-* in + *stallum* stall[1]] **—in stall′er,** *n.*

in stal la tion (in′stə lā′shən), *n.* 1 an installing. 2 a being installed. 3 something installed, especially machinery placed in position for use. 4 a military base or camp, including personnel, equipment, buildings, etc.

in stall ment[1] or **in stal ment**[1] (in stôl′mənt), *n.* 1 part of a sum of money or of a debt to be paid at certain stated times: *The table cost $100; we paid for it in installments of $10 a month for ten months.* 2 one of several parts issued at different times as part of a series: *This magazine has a serial story* *in six installments.* [alteration of earlier *(e)stallment* < *stall* agree to the payment of a debt by installments < Old French *estaler* fix, place < *estal* position; of Germanic origin]

in stall ment² or **in stal ment**² (in-stôl′mənt), *n.* 1 an installing. 2 a being installed. [< *install*]

installment plan, system of paying for goods in installments.

in stance (in′stəns), *n., v.,* **-stanced, -stanc ing.** —*n.* 1 person or thing serving as an example; illustration; case: *Television is an instance of improved communication facilities.* See **case**¹ for synonym study. 2 stage or step in an action; occasion: *I went in the first instance because I was asked to go.* 3 request, suggestion, or urging: *They came at our instance.* 4 **for instance,** as an example. —*v.t.* 1 give as an example; cite. 2 exemplify. [< Old French < Latin *instantia* a being near or present < *instantem* standing near. See INSTANT.]

in stant (in′stənt), *n.* 1 particular moment: *Stop talking this instant!* 2 moment of time: *She paused for an instant.* See **minute** for synonym study. —*adj.* 1 coming at once; without delay; immediate: *The medicine gave instant relief from pain.* 2 pressing; urgent: *When there is a fire, there is an instant need for action.* 3 prepared beforehand and requiring little or no cooking, mixing, or additional ingredients: *instant coffee, instant pudding.* 4 of the present month; present. [< Latin *instantem* standing near, urgent, insistent < *in-* in + *stare* to stand]

in stan ta ne ous (in′stən tā′nē əs), *adj.* coming or done in an instant; happening or made in an instant: *instantaneous applause.* —**in′stan ta′ne ous ly,** *adv.* —**in′stan-ta′ne ous ness,** *n.*

in stan ter (in stan′tər), *adv.* at once; immediately. [< Late Latin < Latin *instantem.* See INSTANT.]

in stant ly (in′stənt lē), *adv.* 1 in an instant; at once; immediately. See **immediately** for synonym study. 2 ARCHAIC. urgently; persistently.

in star (in′stär), *n.* the particular stage of an insect or other arthropod between moltings. [< New Latin < Latin, likeness, form]

in state (in stāt′), *v.t.,* **-stat ed, -stat ing.** put into a certain state, position, or office; install.

in sta tu quo (in stā′tyü kwō′; in stā′chü kwō′; in stach′ü kwō′), LATIN. in the same situation, condition, or state.

in stead (in sted′), *adv.* 1 in another's place; as a substitute: *If you cannot go, let him go instead.* 2 **instead of,** in place of; as a substitute for: *Instead of studying, she watched television.*

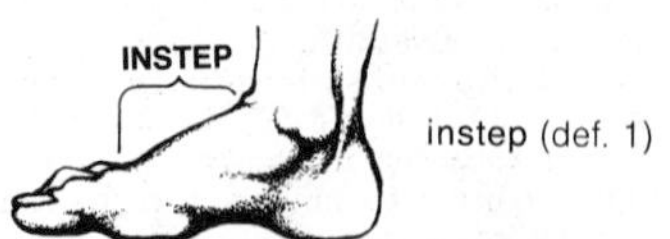

instep (def. 1)

in step (in′step), *n.* 1 the upper surface of the arch of the human foot between the toes and the ankle. 2 the part of a shoe, stocking, etc., over the instep.

in sti gate (in′stə gāt), *v.t.,* **-gat ed, -gat ing.** urge on; stir up: *instigate a quarrel.* See **incite** for synonym study. [< Latin *instigatum* incited, urged on] —**in′sti-ga′tion,** *n.* —**in′sti ga′tor,** *n.*

in sti ga tive (in′stə gā′tiv), *adj.* tending to instigate; stimulative.

in still or **in stil** (in stil′), *v.t.,* **-stilled, -still ing.** 1 put in little by little; cause to enter the mind, heart, etc., gradually: *Reading good books instills a love for really fine literature.* 2 put in drop by drop. [< Latin *instillare* < *in-* + *stilla* a drop] —**in′stil-la′tion,** *n.* —**in still′er,** *n.* —**in still′-ment,** *n.*

in stinct (*n.* in′stingkt; *adj.* in stingkt′), *n.* 1 a chain of unlearned, coordinated acts characteristic of a particular species or group of animals; inborn tendency to act in a certain way: *Birds do not learn to build nests but build them by instinct.* 2 a natural tendency or ability; talent. —*adj.* charged or filled with something: *The picture is instinct with life and beauty.* [< Latin *instinctus* impulse < *instinguere* incite, impel]

in stinc tive (in stingk′tiv), *adj.* of or having to do with instinct; caused or done by instinct; born in an animal or person, not learned: *The spinning of webs is instinctive in spiders.* —**in stinc′tive ly,** *adv.*

in stinc tu al (in stingk′chü əl), *adj.* of or having to do with instinct.

in sti tute (in′stə tüt, in′stə tyüt), *n., v.,* **-tut ed, -tut ing.** —*n.* 1 organization or society for some special purpose, usually educational, literary, scientific, artistic, or the like: *an art institute.* 2 building used by such an organization or society. 3 school that teaches technical subjects. 4 a short program of instruction for a particular group: *a teachers' institute.* 5 something instituted; institution. 6 an elementary principle or element of instruction. 7 **institutes,** *pl.* digest of the elements of a subject. —*v.t.* set up; establish; begin; start: *institute an inquiry into the cause of an accident. The Pilgrims instituted Thanksgiving.* [< Latin *institutum* established < *in-* in + *statuere* establish < *status* position] —**in′sti tut′er, in′sti tu′tor,** *n.*

in sti tu tion (in′stə tü′shən, in′stə-tyü′shən), *n.* 1 organization or society established for some public or social purpose, such as a church, school, university, hospital, asylum, or prison. 2 building used for the work of an institution. 3 an established law or custom: *Marriage is an institution among most of the peoples of the earth.* 4 a setting up; establishing; beginning; starting. 5 INFORMAL. a familiar person or thing.

in sti tu tion al (in′stə tü′shə nəl, in′stə-tyü′shə nəl), *adj.* 1 of or like an institution. 2 promoting reputation and establishing good will for a business rather than aiming at immediate sales: *institutional advertising.* —**in′sti tu′tion al ly,** *adv.*

in sti tu tion al ize (in′stə tü′shə nə līz, in′stə tyü′shə nə līz), *v.t.,* **-ized, -iz ing.** 1 make into an institution. 2 put into an institution.

instr., 1 instructor. 2 instrument.

in struct (in strukt′), *v.t.* 1 give knowledge to; show how to do; teach; train; educate. 2 give directions to; order: *The owner of the house instructed his agent to sell it.* 3 inform; tell. [< Latin *instructum* prepared, built < *in-* on + *struere* to pile, build]

in struc tion (in struk′shən), *n.* 1 a teaching or educating. 2 knowledge or teaching given; lesson. 3 **instructions,** *pl.* directions; orders.

in struc tion al (in struk′shə nəl), *adj.* of or for instruction; educational.

in struc tive (in struk′tiv), *adj.* useful for instruction; giving knowledge or information; instructing: *an instructive experience.* —**in-struc′tive ly,** *adv.* —**in struc′tive ness,** *n.*

in struc tor (in struk′tər), *n.* 1 person who instructs; teacher. 2 teacher ranking below an assistant professor in American colleges and universities.

in struc tor ship (in struk′tər ship), *n.* office or position of an instructor.

in stru ment (in′strə mənt), *n.* 1 a mechanical device that is portable, of simple construction, and usually operated by hand; tool: *a dentist's instruments.* 2 device for producing musical sounds: *wind instruments, stringed instruments.* 3 device for measuring, recording, or controlling. A compass and sextant are instruments of navigation. 4 thing with or by which something is done; person made use of by another; means: *The alderman proved to be merely an instrument of the mayor.* 5 a formal legal document, such as a contract, deed, or grant. —*v.t.* equip with instruments, especially for recording scientific data: *a fully instrumented missile.* [< Latin *instrumentum* < *instruere* prepare, equip, build < *in-* on + *struere* to pile, build]

in stru men tal (in′strə men′tl), *adj.* 1 acting or serving as a means; useful; helpful: *My uncle was instrumental in getting me a job.* 2 played on or written for musical instruments: *The singer was accompanied by instrumental music.* 3 of an instrument; made by a device or tool. —**in′stru-men′tal ly,** *adv.*

in stru men tal ist (in′strə men′tl ist), *n.* person who plays on a musical instrument.

in stru men tal i ty (in′strə men tal′ə tē), *n., pl.* **-ties.** quality or condition of being instrumental; helpfulness; agency; means.

in stru men ta tion (in′strə men tā′shən), *n.* 1 arrangement or composition of music for instruments. 2 use of instruments; work done with instruments. 3 the mechanized use of instruments, especially for scientific or technical purposes.

instrument board, instrument panel.

instrument flying, the directing of an aircraft by instruments only.

instrument landing, an approach and landing made by an aircraft with the aid of a system of electronic devices in the aircraft that are coordinated with radio beacons, radar equipment, and transmitters on the ground.

instrument panel, panel with various instruments showing how the parts of a machine, engine, or other device are functioning; instrument board.

in sub or di nate (in′sə bôrd′n it), *adj.* not submitting to authority; refusing to obey; disobedient; rebellious. —**in′sub or′di-nate ly,** *adv.*

in sub or di na tion (in′sə bôrd′n ā′shən), *n.* resistance to authority; refusal to obey; disobedience; rebellion.

in sub stan tial (in′səb stan′shəl), *adj.* 1 frail; flimsy: *A cobweb is very insubstantial.* 2 unreal; not actual; imaginary: *Dreams and ghosts are insubstantial.* —**in′sub-stan′tial ly,** *adv.*

in sub stan ti al i ty (in′səb stan′shē al′ə-tē), *n.* a being insubstantial.

in suf fer a ble (in suf′ər ə bəl), *adj.* intolerable; unbearable: *insufferable rudeness.* —**in suf′fer a ble ness,** *n.* —**in suf′fer a-bly,** *adv.*

in suf fi cien cy (in′sə fish′ən sē), *n., pl.*

hat, āge, fär; let, ēqual, tėrm;
it, īce; hot, ōpen, ôrder;
oil, out; cup, pu̇t, rüle;
ch, child; ng, long; sh, she;
th, thin; ᴛʜ, then; zh, measure;

ə represents *a* in about, *e* in taken,
i in pencil, *o* in lemon, *u* in circus.

< = from, derived from, taken from.

-cies. 1 an insufficient amount; too small a supply; lack; deficiency; inadequacy. 2 something deficient, inadequate, or unfit.

in suf fi cient (in′sə fish′ənt), *adj.* not sufficient; lacking in what is needed; inadequate. **—in′suf fi′cient ly,** *adv.*

in su lar (in′sə lər), *adj.* 1 of or having to do with islands or islanders. 2 living or situated on an island. 3 standing alone like an island; isolated: *an insular position in world affairs.* 4 narrow-minded; prejudiced. [< Late Latin *insularis* < Latin *insula* island]

in su lar ism (in′sə lə riz′əm), *n.* narrowness of ideas or opinions.

in su lar i ty (in′sə lar′ə tē), *n.* 1 condition of being an island or of living on an island. 2 narrow-mindedness; prejudice.

in su late (in′sə lāt), *v.t.,* **-lat ed, -lat ing.** 1 keep from losing or transferring electricity, heat, sound, etc., especially by covering, packing, or surrounding with a nonconducting material. 2 set apart; separate from others; isolate. [< Latin *insula* island]

in su la tion (in′sə lā′shən), *n.* 1 an insulating. 2 a being insulated. 3 material used in insulating.

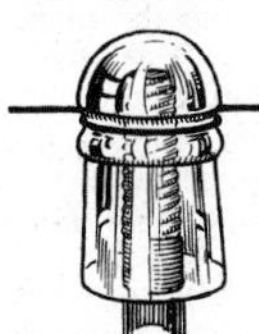
insulator
glass insulator for electric wires. With these, wires can be fastened to poles without any loss of current.

in su la tor (in′sə lā′tər), *n.* that which insulates; something that prevents the passage of electricity, heat, or sound; nonconductor.

in su lin (in′sə lən), *n.* 1 a protein hormone secreted by the islets of Langerhans in the pancreas that enables the body to use sugar and other carbohydrates by regulating the sugar metabolism of the body. 2 drug containing this hormone, obtained from the pancreas of slaughtered animals and used in treating diabetes. [< Latin *insula* island (in reference to the islets of Langerhans)]

in sult (*v.* in sult′; *n.* in′sult), *v.t.* say or do something very scornful, rude, or harsh to: *The man insulted me by calling me a liar.* *—n.* an insulting speech or action. See synonym study below. [< Latin *insultare* < *insilire* leap at or upon < *in-* on, at + *salire* to leap] **—in sult′er,** *n.*

Syn. *n.* **Insult, affront, indignity** mean something said or done to offend someone or something. **Insult** applies to an insolent and contemptuous statement or act intended to humiliate: *Stamping on the flag is an insult.* **Affront** applies to a deliberate and open show of disrespect: *Leaving during her song was an affront to my sister.* **Indignity** applies to an act or statement that hurts one's dignity: *Spanking is an indignity to a teenager.*

in sult ing (in sul′ting), *adj.* that insults; derogatory; abusive. **—in sult′ing ly,** *adv.*

in su per a ble (in sü′pər ə bəl), *adj.* that cannot be passed over or overcome; insurmountable: *an insuperable barrier.* **—in su′per a bly,** *adv.*

in sup port a ble (in′sə pôr′tə bəl, in′sə-pōr′tə bəl), *adj.* not endurable; unbearable; intolerable. **—in′sup port′a ble ness,** *n.* **—in′sup port′a bly,** *adv.*

in sup press i ble (in′sə pres′ə bəl), *adj.* not able to be suppressed. **—in′sup press′i bly,** *adv.*

in sur a bil i ty (in shu̇r′ə bil′ə tē), *n.* a being insurable.

in sur a ble (in shu̇r′ə bəl), *adj.* capable of being insured; fit to be insured.

in sur ance (in shu̇r′əns), *n.* 1 an insuring of property, person, or life. Fire insurance, burglary insurance, accident insurance, life insurance, and health insurance are some of the many kinds. 2 the business of insuring property, life, etc. 3 contract made between insurer and insured; policy. 4 amount of money for which a person or thing is insured: *His wife will receive $10,000 insurance if he dies before she does.* 5 amount of money paid for insurance; premium: *His fire insurance is $300 a year.* 6 any means of insuring or protecting.

in sure (in shu̇r′), *v.,* **-sured, -sur ing.** *—v.t.* 1 arrange for money payment in case of loss of (property, profit, etc.) or accident or death to (a person). An insurance company will insure your property, person, or life if you pay a certain amount of money at intervals. 2 make safe from financial loss by paying money to an insurance company: *insure a car against accident, theft, and fire.* 3 make sure or certain: *Check your work to insure its accuracy.* 4 make safe; protect: *More care will insure you against making so many mistakes.* *—v.i.* give or buy insurance. [variant of *ensure* < Anglo-French *enseurer* < *en-* in + Old French *seür* sure] **—in sur′er,** *n.* ➤ See **ensure** for usage note.

in sured (in shu̇rd′), *n.* person who is insured.

in sur gence (in sėr′jəns), *n.* a rising in revolt; rebellion.

in sur gen cy (in sėr′jən sē), *n., pl.* **-cies.** 1 insurgence. 2 (in international law) a minor revolt against a government, not recognized as belligerency.

in sur gent (in sėr′jənt), *n.* person who rises in revolt; rebel. *—adj.* rising in revolt; rebellious. [< Latin *insurgentem* rising up against < *in-* against + *surgere* to rise]

in sur mount a ble (in′sər moun′tə bəl), *adj.* that cannot be overcome. **—in′sur mount′a bly,** *adv.*

in sur rec tion (in′sə rek′shən), *n.* a rising against established authority; revolt; rebellion; uprising. See **revolt** for synonym study. [< Late Latin *insurrectionem* < Latin *insurgere* rise up against < *in-* against + *surgere* to rise]

in sur rec tion al (in′sə rek′shə nəl), *adj.* having to do with insurrection.

in sur rec tion ar y (in′sə rek′shə ner′ē), *adj., n., pl.* **-ar ies.** *—adj.* 1 having a tendency to revolt. 2 having to do with revolt. *—n.* insurrectionist.

in sur rec tion ist (in′sə rek′shə nist), *n.* person who takes part in or favors an insurrection; rebel.

in sus cep ti bil i ty (in′sə sep′tə bil′ə tē), *n.* a being insusceptible.

in sus cep ti ble (in′sə sep′tə bəl), *adj.* not susceptible; not easily affected or influenced.

int., 1 interest. 2 interior. 3 internal. 4 international.

in tact (in takt′), *adj.* with no part missing, as if untouched; whole; uninjured: *dishes still intact after being dropped.* [< Latin *intactus* < *in-* not + *tactum* touched] **—in tact′ness,** *n.*

in tagl io (in tal′yō, in tä′lyō), *n., pl.* **-tagl ios.** 1 process of engraving or carving by making cuts in the surface. 2 figure or design engraved in this way. 3 gem ornamented in this way. 4 method of printing in which paper is pressed into inked lines below the surface of the plate or cylinder. [< Italian < *intagliare* engrave < *in-* into + *tagliare* to cut]

in take (in′tāk′), *n.* 1 place where water, air, gas, etc., enters a channel, pipe, or other narrow opening. 2 act or process of taking in. 3 amount or thing taken in.

in tan gi bil i ty (in tan′jə bil′ə tē), *n.* a being intangible.

in tan gi ble (in tan′jə bəl), *adj.* 1 not capable of being touched or felt: *Sound and light are intangible.* 2 not easily grasped by the mind; vague: *The very popular girl had that intangible quality called charm.* *—n.* something intangible. **—in tan′gi ble ness,** *n.* **—in tan′gi bly,** *adv.*

in te ger (in′tə jər), *n.* 1 any positive or negative whole number, or zero. 2 thing complete in itself; something whole. [< Latin, whole < *in-* not + *tangere* to touch. Doublet of ENTIRE.]

in te gral (in′tə grəl), *adj.* 1 necessary to make something complete; essential: *Steel is an integral part of a modern skyscraper.* 2 entire; complete. 3 formed of parts that together constitute a whole. 4 in mathematics: **a** having to do with an integer; not fractional. **b** of or involving integrals. *—n.* 1 a whole; a whole number. 2 any function whose derivative is a given function. **—in′te gral ly,** *adv.*

integral calculus, branch of mathematics that investigates integrals, methods of finding integrals, and their applications in area, volume, etc.

in te gral i ty (in′tə gral′ə tē), *n.* integral condition or character.

in te grate (in′tə grāt), *v.,* **-grat ed, -grat ing.** *—v.t.* 1 make into a whole; complete. 2 put or bring together (parts) into a whole. 3 make (schools, parks, etc.) available to people of all races on an equal basis: *integrate a neighborhood.* 4 find the mathematical integral of (a given function or equation). *—v.i.* become integrated. [< Latin *integratum* made whole < *integer* whole. See INTEGER.] **—in′te gra′tor,** *n.*

in te gra tion (in′tə grā′shən), *n.* 1 act or process of integrating. 2 inclusion of people of all races on an equal basis in schools, parks, neighborhoods, etc.

in te gra tion ist (in′tə grā′shə nist), *n.* person who believes in or practices racial integration.

in te gra tive (in′tə grā′tiv), *adj.* tending to integrate.

intaglio (def. 2)
intaglio ring

in teg ri ty (in teg′rə tē), *n.* 1 honesty or sincerity; uprightness. See **honesty** for synonym study. 2 wholeness; completeness. 3 perfect condition; soundness: *the integrity of a text.*

in teg u ment (in teg′yə mənt), *n.* 1 a natural outer covering; skin, shell, rind, etc.; tegument. 2 any covering or coating. [< Latin *integumentum* < *integere* enclose < *in-* on + *tegere* to cover]

in teg u men tar y (in teg′yə men′tər ē), *adj.* of, having to do with, or of the nature of an integument.

in tel lect (in′tə lekt), *n.* 1 power of knowing; understanding; mind. 2 great intelligence; high mental ability: *Isaac Newton was a man of intellect.* 3 person of high mental ability. [< Latin *intellectus* < *intelligere* perceive, understand < *inter-* between + *legere* choose]

in tel lec tion (in′tə lek′shən), *n.* 1 act or process of reasoning or understanding. 2 a particular act of the intellect. 3 conception or idea.

in tel lec tive (in′tə lek′tiv), *adj.* 1 having the power to reason or understand. 2 having to do with the intellect. **—in′tel lec′tive ly,** *adv.*

in tel lec tu al (in′tə lek′chü əl), *adj.* 1 needing or using intelligence: *Teaching is an intellectual occupation.* 2 of the intellect: *Thinking is an intellectual process.* 3 having or showing intelligence: *an intellectual person.* 4 directed or inclined toward things that involve the intellect: *intellectual tastes.* *—n.* person who is intellectual. **—in′tel lec′tu al ly,** *adv.*

in tel lec tu al ism (in′tə lek′chü ə liz′əm), *n.* 1 exercise of the intellect. 2 devotion to intellectual pursuits.

in tel lec tu al ist (in′tə lek′chü ə list), *n.* person devoted to intellectual pursuits.

in tel lec tu al is tic (in′tə lek′chü ə lis′tik), *adj.* of or having to do with intellectualism.

in tel lec tu al i ty (in′tə lek′chü al′ə tē), *n., pl.* **-ties.** a being intellectual; intellectual nature or power.

in tel lec tu al ize (in′tə lek′chü ə līz), *v.t.,* **-ized, -iz ing.** make intellectual; give an intellectual quality to.

in tel li gence (in tel′ə jəns), *n.* 1 ability to learn and know; quickness of understanding; mind: *A dog has more intelligence than a worm.* 2 knowledge, news, or information: *intelligence of a person's whereabouts.* 3 a getting or distributing of information, especially secret information. 4 group engaged in obtaining secret information.

intelligence quotient, number that shows the rating of a person's intelligence. It is found by dividing the mental age shown in tests by the actual age (16 is the largest age used) and multiplying by 100.

intelligence test, any test used to measure mental development.

in tel li gent (in tel′ə jənt), *adj.* having or showing intelligence; able to learn and know; quick to understand: *an intelligent student, an intelligent remark.* [< Latin *intelligentem* < *inter-* between + *legere* choose] **—in tel′li gent ly,** *adv.*

in tel li gent si a (in tel′ə jent′sē ə, in tel′ə gent′sē ə), *n.pl.* persons representing, or claiming to represent, the superior intelligence or enlightened opinion of a country; the intellectuals. [< Russian *intelligentsiya* < Latin *intelligentia* < *intelligentem* intelligent]

in tel li gi bil i ty (in tel′ə jə bil′ə tē), *n.* a being intelligible.

in tel li gi ble (in tel′ə jə bəl), *adj.* capable of being understood; clear; comprehensible. [< Latin *intelligibilis* < *intelligere.* See INTELLECT.] **—in tel′li gi bly,** *adv.*

in tem per ance (in tem′pər əns), *n.* 1 lack of moderation or self-control; excess. 2 excessive drinking of intoxicating liquor.

in tem per ate (in tem′pər it), *adj.* 1 not moderate; lacking in self-control; excessive: *an intemperate appetite.* 2 drinking too much intoxicating liquor. 3 not temperate; extreme in temperature; severe: *an intemperate winter.* **—in tem′per ate ly,** *adv.* **—in tem′per ate ness,** *n.*

in tend (in tend′), *v.t.* 1 have in mind as a purpose; plan: *We intend to go home soon.* See synonym study below. 2 mean for a particular purpose or use: *That gift was intended for you.* [< Latin *intendere* to stretch, strain, attend to < *in-* toward + *tendere* to stretch]

Syn. 1 **Intend, mean** signify having in mind as a purpose. **Intend** implies having something firmly in mind as a definite purpose or plan: *I intend to finish this work before I go to bed.* **Mean** suggests less certainty about carrying it out: *I meant to get up early, but forgot to set the alarm.*

in tend an cy (in ten′dən sē), *n., pl.* **-cies.** 1 position or work of an intendant. 2 intendants. 3 district in South America under an intendant.

in tend ant (in ten′dənt), *n.* 1 person in charge; superintendent. 2 official who governs an intendancy in South America. [< French, ultimately < Latin *intendere* attend to. See INTEND.]

in tend ed (in ten′did), *adj.* 1 meant; planned: *an intended surprise.* 2 prospective: *a woman's intended husband.* *—n.* INFORMAL. a prospective husband or wife.

in tense (in tens′), *adj.* 1 very much; very great; very strong; extreme: *intense happiness, intense pain, intense light.* 2 full of vigorous activity, strong feelings, etc.: *An intense life is crowded with action, interests, etc.* 3 having or showing strong feeling: *an intense person, an intense face.* [< Latin *intensum* strained, stretched < *in-* toward + *tendere* to stretch] **—in tense′ly,** *adv.* **—in tense′ness,** *n.*

in ten si fi er (in ten′sə fī′ər), *n.* 1 (in grammar) an intensive. 2 person or thing that intensifies.

in ten si fy (in ten′sə fī), *v.t., v.i.,* **-fied, -fy ing.** make or become intense or more intense; strengthen; increase. **—in ten′si fi ca′tion,** *n.*

in ten si ty (in ten′sə tē), *n., pl.* **-ties.** 1 quality of being intense; great strength: *the intensity of sunlight.* 2 extreme degree; great vigor; violence: *intensity of thought, intensity of feeling.* 3 amount or degree of strength of electricity, heat, light, sound, etc., per unit of area, volume, etc.

in ten sive (in ten′siv), *adj.* 1 deep and thorough: *An intensive study of a few books is more valuable than a superficial reading of many.* 2 having to do with a system of farming in which more money and work are spent on a given area to produce additional crops. 3 (in grammar) giving force or emphasis; expressing intensity. In "He himself said it," *himself* is an intensive pronoun. *—n.* 1 something that makes intense. 2 an intensive word, prefix, etc. In "It's terribly late," *terribly* is an intensive. **—in ten′sive ly,** *adv.* **—in ten′sive ness,** *n.*

in tent (in tent′), *n.* 1 that which is intended; purpose; intention: *I'm sorry I hurt you; that wasn't my intent.* 2 meaning; significance: *What is the intent of that remark?* 3 **to all intents and purposes,** in almost every way; practically. *—adj.* 1 very attentive; having the eyes or thoughts earnestly fixed on something; earnest: *an intent look.* 2 earnestly engaged; much interested: *intent on making money.* [< Latin *intentum* strained, intense, variant of *intensum.* See INTENSE.] **—in tent′ly,** *adv.* **—in tent′ness,** *n.*

in ten tion (in ten′shən), *n.* 1 an intending; purpose; design: *hurt someone's feelings without intention.* See synonym study below. 2 meaning; significance: *The intention of the poem was clear.* 3 **intentions,** *pl.* INFORMAL. purposes with respect to marrying.

Syn. 1 **Intention, purpose, design** indicate what a person means or plans to get or do. **Intention** often suggests lack of determination in carrying out the plan: *My intention was to arrive early.* **Purpose** suggests determination but not necessarily success in carrying it out: *My purpose was to avoid the crowd.* **Design** suggests careful preliminary planning or preparation: *I arrived early by design.*

in ten tion al (in ten′shə nəl), *adj.* done on purpose; intended: *His insult was intentional; he wanted to hurt her feelings.* See **deliberate** for synonym study. **—in ten′tion al ly,** *adv.*

in ter (in tėr′), *v.t.,* **-terred, -ter ring.** put (a dead body) into a grave or tomb; bury. [< Medieval Latin *interrare* < Latin *in-* in + *terra* earth]

inter-, *prefix.* 1 one with the other; together: *Intercommunicate = communicate with each other.* 2 between: *Interpose = put between.* 3 between or among a group: *International = between or among nations.* [< Latin < *inter* among, between, during. Related to UNDER.]

in ter act (in′tər akt′), *v.i.* act on each other.

in ter ac tion (in′tər ak′shən), *n.* action on each other.

in ter a li a (in′tər ā′lē ə), LATIN. among other things.

in ter-A mer i can (in′tər ə mer′ə kən), *adj.* between or among countries of North, South, or Central America.

in ter a tom ic (in′tər ə tom′ik), *adj.* between atoms: *interatomic bonds, interatomic distance.*

in ter breed (in′tər brēd′), *v.t., v.i.,* **-bred** (-bred′), **-breed ing.** 1 (in botany) breed by the mating of different varieties or species of plants. 2 breed by the mating of different varieties or, rarely, species of animals.

in ter ca lar y (in tėr′kə ler′ē), *adj.* 1 inserted in the calendar to make the calendar year agree with the solar year. February 29 is an intercalary day. 2 put in between; interpolated.

in ter ca late (in tėr′kə lāt), *v.t.,* **-lat ed, -lat ing.** 1 put (an additional day or month) into the calendar. 2 put in between; interpolate. [< Latin *intercalatum* interposed, proclaimed between < *inter-* between + *calare* proclaim] **—in ter′ca la′tion,** *n.*

in ter cede (in′tər sēd′), *v.i.,* **-ced ed, -ced ing.** 1 plead for another; ask a favor from one person for another: *Friends of the condemned man interceded with the governor*

hat, āge, fär; let, ēqual, tėrm;
it, īce; hot, ōpen, ôrder;
oil, out; cup, pu̇t, rüle;
ch, child; ng, long; sh, she;
th, thin; ᴛʜ, then; zh, measure;

ə represents *a* in about, *e* in taken, *i* in pencil, *o* in lemon, *u* in circus.

< = from, derived from, taken from.

for a pardon. 2 act as an intermediary in order to bring about an agreement; mediate. [< Latin *intercedere* go between < *inter-* between + *cedere* go] **—in′ter ced′er,** *n.*

in ter cel lu lar (in′tər sel′yə lər), *adj.* situated between or among cells.

in ter cept (in′tər sept′), *v.t.* 1 take or seize on the way from one place to another: *intercept a letter, intercept a messenger.* 2 cut off (light, water, etc.). 3 check; stop: *intercept the flight of an escaped criminal.* 4 (in mathematics) cut off or bound a part of a line, plane, surface, or solid. —*n.* in mathematics: 1 an intercepted part. 2 distance from the origin to the point where a line, curve, or surface intercepts a coordinate axis. [< Latin *interceptum* caught between, interrupted < *inter-* between + *capere* to take, catch] **—in′ter cep′tion,** *n.*

in ter cep tor or **in ter cept er** (in′tər-sep′tər), *n.* 1 person or thing that intercepts. 2 airplane designed to intercept enemy aircraft.

in ter ces sion (in′tər sesh′ən), *n.* 1 act or fact of interceding. 2 prayer pleading for others. [< Latin *intercessionem* < *intercedere.* See INTERCEDE.]

in ter ces sion al (in′tər sesh′ə nəl), *adj.* of or containing an intercession.

in ter ces sor (in′tər ses′ər, in′tər ses′ər), *n.* person who intercedes.

in ter ces sor y (in′tər ses′ər ē), *adj.* interceding.

in ter change (*v.* in′tər chānj′; *n.* in′tər-chānj′), *v.*, **-changed, -chang ing,** *n.* —*v.t.* 1 put each of (two or more persons or things) in the other's place: *interchange two drawers in a dresser.* 2 give and take; exchange: *interchange gifts.* 3 cause to happen by turns; alternate: *interchange severity with indulgence.* —*v.i.* change places; alternate. —*n.* 1 a putting each of two or more persons or things in the other's place: *The word "team" becomes "meat" by the interchange of the first and last letters.* 2 a giving and taking; exchanging. 3 point at which a highway, especially an expressway highway, connects with another road without the streams of traffic interfering with each other. **—in′ter chang′er,** *n.*

in ter change a bil i ty (in′tər chān′jə-bil′ə tē), *n.* a being interchangeable.

in ter change a ble (in′tər chān′jə bəl), *adj.* 1 capable of being used or put in place of each other. 2 able to change places. **—in′ter change′a ble ness,** *n.* **—in′ter-change′a bly,** *adv.*

in ter cit y (in′tər sit′ē), *adj.* between cities: *intercity traffic.*

in ter col le giate (in′tər kə lē′jit, in′tər-kə lē′jē it), *adj.* between colleges or universities.

in ter com (in′tər kom′), *n.* any apparatus, usually using microphones and loudspeakers, with which members of an office staff, the crew of an airplane, tank, ship, etc., can talk to each other; intercommunication system.

in ter com mu ni cate (in′tər kə myü′nə-kāt), *v.t., v.i.,* **-cat ed, -cat ing.** communicate with each other. **—in′ter com mu′ni-ca′tion,** *n.*

intercommunication system, intercom.

in ter com mun ion (in′tər kə myü′nyən), *n.* fellowship between churches of different denominations or communions.

in ter con nect (in′tər kə nekt′), *v.t.* connect with each other. **—in′ter con-nec′tion,** *n.*

in ter con ti nen tal (in′tər kon′tə nen′tl), *adj.* between continents; involving two or more continents: *an intercontinental railroad, intercontinental warfare.*

Intercontinental Ballistic Missile, a ballistic missile with a range of over 5000 miles.

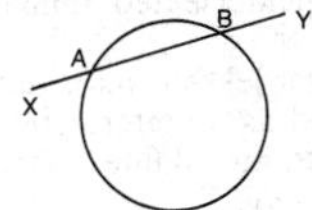

intercept (def. 4) Line XY intercepts arc AB of the circle.

in ter con vert (in′tər kən vėrt′), *v.t.* interchange.

in ter con vert i ble (in′tər kən vėr′tə-bəl), *adj.* interchangeable.

in ter cos tal (in′tər kos′tl, in′tər kôs′tl), *adj.* between the ribs: *an intercostal muscle.* —*n.* part situated between the ribs. [< *inter-* + Latin *costa* rib] **—in′ter cos′tal ly,** *adv.*

in ter course (in′tər kôrs, in′tər kōrs), *n.* 1 dealings between people; exchange of thoughts, services, feelings, etc.; communication. 2 sexual union. [< Latin *intercursus* a running between, ultimately < *inter-* between + *currere* to run]

in ter cul tur al (in′tər kul′chər əl), *adj.* between different groups or cultures: *intercultural understanding.*

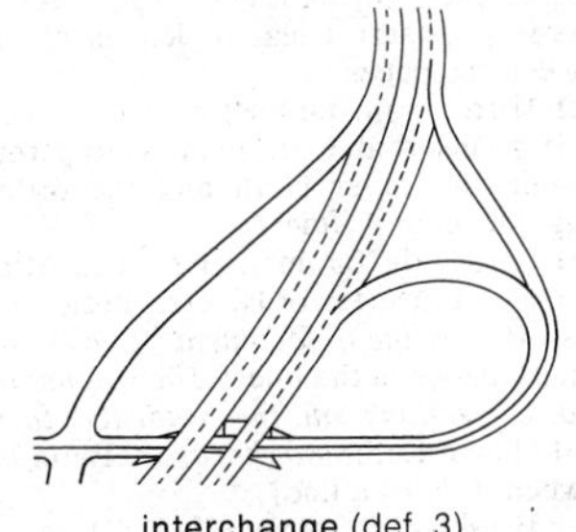
interchange (def. 3)

in ter de nom i na tion al (in′tər di-nom′ə nā′shə nəl), *adj.* between or involving different religious denominations.

in ter de nom i na tion al ism (in′tər di-nom′ə nā′shə nə liz′əm), *n.* interdenominational principles.

in ter de part men tal (in′tər dē′pärt-men′tl), *adj.* between departments. **—in′ter de′part men′tal ly,** *adv.*

in ter de pend (in′tər di pend′), *v.i.* be interdependent.

in ter de pend ence (in′tər di pen′dəns), *n.* dependence upon each other.

in ter de pend en cy (in′tər di pen′dən-sē), *n.* interdependence.

in ter de pend ent (in′tər di pen′dənt), *adj.* dependent upon each other; mutually dependent. **—in′ter de pend′ent ly,** *adv.*

in ter dict (*v.* in′tər dikt′; *n.* in′tər dikt), *v.t.* 1 prohibit or forbid; restrain. 2 (in the Roman Catholic Church) cut off from certain church functions and privileges. —*n.* 1 prohibition based on authority; formal order forbidding something. 2 (in the Roman Catholic Church) a cutting off from certain church functions and privileges. [< Latin *interdictum* prohibition < *interdicere* prohibit < *inter-* between + *dicere* speak] **—in′ter-dic′tion,** *n.* **—in′ter dic′tor,** *n.*

in ter dic tor y (in′tər dik′tər ē), *adj.* that serves to interdict; prohibitory.

in ter dig i tate (in′tər dij′ə tāt), *v.i.,* **-tat ed, -tat ing.** be inserted between each other like the fingers of both hands when clasped. **—in′ter dig′i ta′tion,** *n.*

in ter dis ci pli nar y (in′tər dis′ə plə-ner′ē), *adj.* between different fields of study: *interdisciplinary collaboration in research.*

in ter est (in′tər ist), *n.* 1 a feeling of wanting to know, see, do, own, share in, or take part in: *an interest in sports.* 2 power of arousing such a feeling: *A dull book lacks interest.* 3 a share or part in property and actions: *He bought a half interest in the farm.* 4 thing in which a person has a share or part. Any business, activity, or pastime can be an interest. 5 group of people having the same business, activity, etc.: *the business interests of the town.* 6 advantage; benefit; profit: *Each person should look after his own interest.* 7 **in the interest of,** for; to help. 8 money paid for the use of money, usually a percentage of the amount invested, borrowed, or loaned: *The interest on the loan was six per cent a year.* 9 something extra given in return: *She returned our favor with interest.* —*v.t.* 1 make curious and hold the attention of: *An exciting story interests us.* 2 cause (a person) to take a share or part in something; arouse the concern, curiosity, or attention of: *The agent tried to interest us in buying a car.* [< Latin, it is of importance, it makes a difference, 3rd person singular present of *interesse* be between < *inter-* between + *esse* be]

in ter est ed (in′tər ə stid, in′tə res′tid), *adj.* 1 feeling or showing interest. 2 having an interest or share. 3 influenced by personal considerations; prejudiced. **—in′ter est ed-ly,** *adv.* **—in′ter est ed ness,** *n.*

in ter est ing (in′tər ə sting, in′tə res′ting), *adj.* arousing interest; holding one's attention. **—in′ter est ing ly,** *adv.*

in ter face (in′tər fās′), *n.* surface lying between two bodies or spaces, and forming their common boundary.

in ter fa cial (in′tər fā′shəl), *adj.* 1 included between two faces of a solid. 2 of or having to do with an interface.

in ter faith (in′tər fāth′), *adj.* 1 for more than one faith or religion. 2 of different faiths or religions.

in ter fere (in′tər fir′), *v.i.,* **-fered, -fer ing.** 1 get in the way of each other; come into opposition; clash: *The two plans interfere; one must be changed.* 2 mix in the affairs of others; meddle: *interfere in other people's affairs. Don't interfere with your brother when he's busy.* See **meddle** for synonym study. 3 take part for a purpose: *The police interfered to stop the riot.* 4 (in football, baseball, hockey, and other sports) obstruct an opposing player illegally. 5 (in physics) to cause interference. [< Old French *entreferir* strike each other < *entre-* between + *ferir* to strike] **—in′ter fer′er,** *n.*

in ter fer ence (in′tər fir′əns), *n.* 1 act or

fact of interfering. 2 something that interferes. 3 (in physics) the reciprocal action of waves by which they reinforce or diminish one another. 4 in radio or television: **a** the interruption of a desired signal by other signals. **b** signals thus interfering. 5 (in football) the protecting of the player who has the ball by blocking opposing players. 6 (in football, baseball, hockey, and other sports) the illegal obstruction of an opposing player.

in ter fe rom e ter (in′tər fə rom′ə tər), *n.* instrument for measuring small lengths or distances by means of the interference of two rays of light.

in ter fer o met ric (in′tər fer′ə met′rik), *adj.* of or having to do with an interferometer or interferometry.

in ter fer on (in′tər fir′on), *n.* protein produced within vertebrate cells infected by a virus to protect similar types of cells for several days from infection by the same or other viruses.

in ter fold (in′tər fōld′), *v.t.* fold one with another; fold together.

in ter fuse (in′tər fyüz′), *v.t., v.i.,* **-fused, -fus ing.** 1 spread through; be diffused through; permeate. 2 fuse together; blend; mix. [< Latin *interfusum* poured between < *inter-* between + *fundere* pour] **—in′ter-fu′sion,** *n.*

in ter ga lac tic (in′tər gə lak′tik), *adj.* situated or taking place between galaxies: *intergalactic space.*

in ter gla cial (in′tər glā′shəl), *adj.* of or occurring in the period between two glacial epochs.

in ter gra da tion (in′tər grā dā′shən), *n.* act or process of intergrading.

in ter grade (*n.* in′tər grād′, *v.* in′tər-grād′), *n., v.,* **-grad ed, -grad ing.** *—n.* an intermediate grade or stage. *—v.i.* become alike through a continuous series of intermediate forms, as one population of animals or plants with another.

in ter im (in′tər im), *n.* time between; the meantime. *—adj.* for the meantime; temporary. [< Latin, in the meantime < *inter* between]

in ter i or (in tir′ē ər), *n.* 1 inner surface or part; inside: *The interior of the house was beautifully decorated and furnished.* 2 part of a region or country away from the coast or border. 3 affairs within a country, regarded as separate from foreign affairs: *The United States has a Department of the Interior.* 4 inner nature or character. *—adj.* 1 on the inside; inner. 2 away from the coast or border; inland. 3 having to do with affairs within a country; domestic. 4 private; secret. [< Latin, inner, comparative of *inter* between]

interior angle, 1 any of the four angles formed inside two lines intersected by a straight line. 2 an angle formed inside a polygon by two adjacent sides.

interior decoration, art or profession of an interior decorator.

interior decorator, person whose work is planning and arranging the furnishings, decorations, etc., of the interior of houses, offices, or public buildings.

in ter is land (in′tər ī′lənd), *adj.* operating or existing between islands.

interj., interjection (def. 1).

in ter ject (in′tər jekt′), *v.t.* throw in between other things; insert abruptly: *Every now and then the speaker interjected some witty remark.* [< Latin *interjectum* thrown between < *inter-* between + *jacere* to throw]

in ter jec tion (in′tər jek′shən), *n.* 1 an exclamation regarded as a part of speech. *Oh! ah! alas!* and *hurrah!* are interjections. 2 an interjecting. 3 something interjected; remark thrown in; exclamation.

in ter jec tion al (in′tər jek′shə nəl), *adj.* 1 of an interjection; used as an interjection. 2 containing an interjection. 3 interjected. **—in′ter jec′tion al ly,** *adv.*

in ter jec tor y (in′tər jek′tər ē), *adj.* interjectional.

in ter lace (in′tər lās′), *v.,* **-laced, -lac ing.** *—v.t.* 1 arrange (threads, strips, or branches) so that they go over and under each other; weave together; intertwine: *Baskets are made by interlacing reeds or fibers.* 2 give variety to; intersperse. *—v.i.* cross each other over and under; mingle together in an intricate manner: *interlacing roads and streams.*

in ter lard (in′tər lärd′), *v.t.* give variety to; mix; intersperse.

in ter lay er (in′tər lā′ər), *n.* layer between two or more layers.

in ter leaf (in′tər lēf′), *n., pl.* **-leaves.** leaf of paper put between other leaves of a book, for notes or the like.

in ter leave (in′tər lēv′), *v.t.,* **-leaved, -leav ing.** insert a leaf or leaves of paper between the pages of.

in ter line[1] (in′tər līn′), *v.t.,* **-lined, -lin ing.** insert an extra lining in (a garment) between the outer cloth and the ordinary lining. [< *inter-* + *line*[2]]

in ter line[2] (in′tər līn′), *v.t., v.i.,* **-lined, -lin ing.** 1 insert words, etc., between the lines of: *interline a document.* 2 write, print, or mark between the lines: *The teacher interlined corrections on the students' themes.* [< Medieval Latin *interlineare* < Latin *inter-* between + *linea* a line]

in ter lin e ar (in′tər lin′ē ər), *adj.* 1 inserted between the lines. 2 containing two different languages or versions in alternate lines. **—in′ter lin′e ar ly,** *adv.*

in ter lin ing (in′tər lī′ning), *n.* an extra lining inserted between the outer cloth and the ordinary lining of a garment.

in ter link (in′tər lingk′), *v.t., v.i.* link together.

in ter lock (in′tər lok′), *v.t., v.i.* join or fit tightly together; lock together: *The two stags interlocked their antlers. The different pieces of a jigsaw puzzle interlock.* *—n.* condition of being interlocked. **—in′ter lock′er,** *n.*

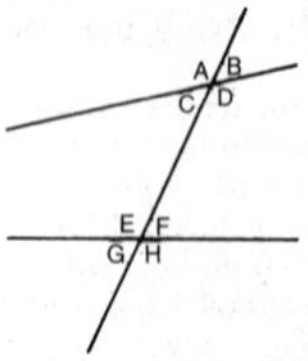

A B C D E F G H

interior angle (def. 1) Angles C, D, E, and F are interior angles. Angles A, B, G, and H are exterior angles.

interlocking directorate, directorate of a company, some of whose members are also on the directorates of other companies, thus extending their control over several companies.

in ter loc u tor (in′tər lok′yə tər), *n.* 1 person who takes part in a conversation or dialogue. 2 man in a minstrel show who asks the end man questions. [< Latin *interlocutum* engaged in conversation < *inter-* between + *loqui* speak]

in ter loc u to ry (in′tər lok′yə tôr′ē, in′-tər lok′yə tōr′ē), *adj.* 1 of or in conversation or dialogue. 2 made during a lawsuit or other action; not final: *an interlocutory decree.*

in ter lop er (in′tər lō′pər), *n.* person who thrusts himself in where he is not wanted or has no right; intruder.

in ter lude (in′tər lüd), *n.* 1 anything thought of as filling the time between two things; interval: *an interlude of sunshine between two showers.* 2 piece of music played between the parts of a song, church service, play, etc. 3 entertainment between the acts of a play. [< Medieval Latin *interludium* < Latin *inter-* between + *ludus* a play]

in ter lu nar (in′tər lü′nər), *adj.* having to do with the time when the moon is not seen at night, between the old moon and the new moon.

in ter mar riage (in′tər mar′ij), *n.* marriage between members of different families, tribes, religions, or racial groups.

in ter mar ry (in′tər mar′ē), *v.i.,* **-ried, -ry ing.** become connected by intermarriage.

in ter med dle (in′tər med′l), *v.i.,* **-dled, -dling.** meddle; interfere.

in ter me di ar y (in′tər mē′dē er′ē), *n., pl.* **-ar ies,** *adj.* *—n.* person who acts between others to bring about an agreement; person who acts for another; go-between. *—adj.* 1 acting between others; mediating. 2 being between; intermediate: *A cocoon is an intermediary stage between caterpillar and butterfly.*

in ter me di ate (in′tər mē′dē it), *adj.* being or occurring between; middle: *Gray is intermediate between black and white.* *—n.* 1 something in between. 2 person who acts between others to bring about an agreement; mediator. [< Latin *intermedius* < *inter-* between + *medius* in the middle] **—in′ter-me′di ate ly,** *adv.* **—in′ter me′di ate-ness,** *n.*

Intermediate Range Ballistic Missile, a ballistic missile with a range of over 200 but less than 1500 miles.

in ter med in (in′tər med′n), *n.* hormone of the pituitary gland that controls pigmentation, causing changes in body color.

in ter ment (in tėr′mənt), *n.* act of interring; burial.

in ter me tal lic (in′tər mə tal′ik), *adj.* (of a compound) formed by the union of two or more metallic elements. Intermetallic compounds are stronger and more heat resistant than ordinary metals.

in ter mez zo (in′tər met′sō, in′tər-med′zō), *n., pl.* **-mez zos, -mez zi** (-met′sē, -med′zē). 1 a short musical composition played between the main divisions of an opera, symphony, or other long musical work. 2 a short dramatic, musical, or other entertainment of light character between the acts of a drama or opera. 3 an independent musical composition of similar character. [< Italian < Latin *intermedius* intermediate]

in ter mi na ble (in tėr′mə nə bəl), *adj.* 1 never stopping; unceasing; endless. 2 so long as to seem endless; very long and tiring. **—in ter′mi na bly,** *adv.*

in ter min gle (in′tər ming′gəl), *v.t., v.i.,* **-gled, -gling.** mix together; mingle.

in ter mis sion (in′tər mish′ən), *n.* 1 a time between periods of activity; pause: *The band played from eight to twelve with a short intermission at ten.* 2 a stopping for a time;

hat, āge, fär; let, ēqual, tėrm;
it, īce; hot, ōpen, ôrder;
oil, out; cup, pu̇t, rüle;
ch, child; ng, long; sh, she;
th, thin; ᴛʜ, then; zh, measure;

ə represents *a* in about, *e* in taken, *i* in pencil, *o* in lemon, *u* in circus.

< = from, derived from, taken from.

interrupting: *The rain continued all day without intermission.* [< Latin *intermissionem* < *intermittere.* See INTERMIT.]

in ter mit (in′tər mit′), *v.t., v.i.,* **-mit ted, -mit ting.** stop for a time; discontinue; suspend. [< Latin *intermittere* < *inter-* between + *mittere* to leave]

in ter mit tence (in′tər mit′ns), *n.* condition of being intermittent.

in ter mit tent (in′tər mit′nt), *adj.* stopping for a time and beginning again; pausing at intervals. **—in′ter mit′tent ly,** *adv.*

in ter mix (in′tər miks′), *v.t., v.i.* mix or become mixed together; blend.

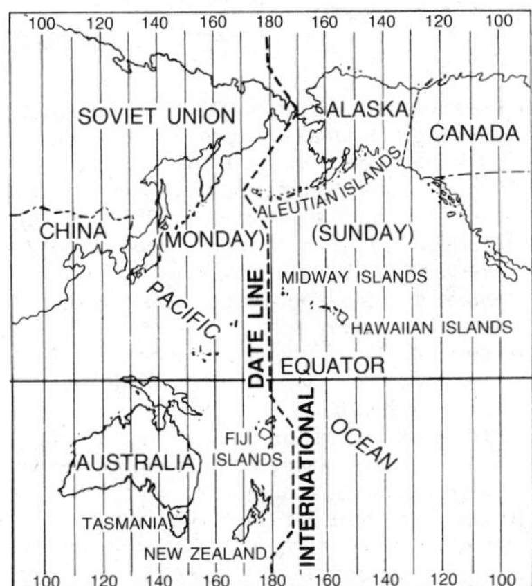

in ter mix ture (in′tər miks′chər), *n.* 1 a mixing together; blending. 2 mass of ingredients mixed together; blend.

in ter mo lec u lar (in′tər mə lek′yə lər), *adj.* being or occurring between molecules. **—in′ter mo lec′u lar ly,** *adv.*

in tern[1] (in tėrn′), *v.t.* confine within a country or place; force to stay in a certain place, especially during wartime. [< French *interner* < *interne* inner, internal < Latin *internus* < *in* in]

in tern[2] (in′tėrn′), *n.* 1 doctor acting as an assistant and undergoing training in a hospital. 2 student in a professional field who receives in-service training under experienced supervision. Also, **interne.** *—v.i.* be an intern. [< French *interne* < *interne* inner, internal. See INTERN[1].]

in ter nal (in tėr′nl), *adj.* 1 on the inside; inner: *internal injuries.* 2 to be taken inside the body: *internal remedies.* 3 belonging to a thing or subject in itself; entirely inside; coming from within; intrinsic: *Internal evidence of the date of a book may sometimes be obtained from the statements made in the book itself.* 4 having to do with affairs within a country; domestic: *internal politics.* 5 of the mind or soul; subjective. [< New Latin *internalis* < Latin *internus* within < *in* in]

in ter nal-com bus tion engine (in tėr′nl kəm bus′chən), engine in which power is produced by the combustion of a mixture of fuel and air inside the engine itself, usually inside cylinders. Gasoline engines and diesel engines are internal-combustion engines.

in ter nal ly (in tėr′nl ē), *adv.* 1 inside. 2 inside the body.

internal respiration, the absorption of oxygen and elimination of carbon dioxide by cells.

internal revenue, revenue derived from taxes on domestic goods and services.

internal rhyme, rhyme of a word within a line of verse with a word at the end of the line. EXAMPLE: *that orbed* maiden, *with fire* laden.

internal secretion, hormone.

in ter na tion al (in′tər nash′ə nəl), *adj.* 1 between or among nations: *A treaty is an international agreement.* 2 having to do with the relations between nations. *—n.* **International,** one of several international socialist organizations. **—in′ter na′tion al ly,** *adv.*

international candle, unit for measuring the strength or intensity of light, equivalent to the light from 5 square millimeters of platinum when heated to its melting point of 1773 degrees centigrade; candle. It was replaced by the candela in the United States in 1948.

International Court of Justice, World Court.

International Date Line, an imaginary line agreed upon as the place where each new calendar day begins; date line. It runs north and south through the Pacific, mostly along the 180th meridian. When it is Sunday just east of the International Date Line, it is Monday just west of it.

International Geophysical Year, period of time set aside for prolonged international study and investigation of the physical nature of the earth and its surroundings.

in ter na tion al ism (in′tər nash′ə nə liz′əm), *n.* principle of international cooperation for the good of all nations.

in ter na tion al ist (in′tər nash′ə nə list), *n.* person who favors internationalism.

in ter na tion al i ty (in′tər nash′ə nal′ə tē), *n.* international quality, condition, or character.

in ter na tion al ize (in′tər nash′ə nə līz), *v.t.,* **-ized, -iz ing.** make international; bring under the control of several nations or of an international body. **—in′ter na′tion al i za′tion,** *n.*

international law, system or rules regarding peace, war, and neutrality which nations consider binding in their relations with each other.

in terne (in′tėrn′), *n.* intern[2].

in ter ne cine (in′tər nē′sn, in′tər nē′sīn), *adj.* 1 destructive to both sides within a group: *internecine struggle for control of a party.* 2 deadly; destructive. [< Latin *internecinus* < *internecare* to kill, destroy < *inter-* between + *necare* kill]

in tern ee (in′tėr′nē′), *n.* person who is interned, such as a prisoner of war, enemy alien, etc.

in ter neur on (in′tər nu̇r′on, in′tər nyu̇r′on), *n.* a nerve cell that connects afferent and efferent nerve cells.

in tern ist (in tėr′nist), *n.* doctor who treats internal organs or diseases.

in tern ment (in tėrn′mənt), *n.* 1 an interning. 2 a being interned.

in ter node (in′tər nōd′), *n.* 1 (in botany) that part of a stem or branch between two of the nodes from which leaves arise. 2 (in anatomy) any part between two nodes or joints.

in tern ship (in′tėrn′ship), *n.* position or service as an intern.

in ter nun cial (in′tər nun′shəl), *adj.* 1 serving to connect nerve fibers or their paths of transmission: *internuncial neurons.* 2 of or having to do with an internuncio. **—in′ter nun′cial ly,** *adv.*

in ter nun ci o (in′tər nun′sē ō), *n., pl.* **-ci os.** ambassador of the Pope ranking next below a nuncio. [< Latin *internuntius* < *inter-* between + *nuntius* messenger]

in ter of fice (in′tər ô′fis, in′tər of′is), *adj.* between offices of an organization: *an interoffice memo.*

in ter pen e trate (in′tər pen′ə trāt), *v.,* **-trat ed, -trat ing.** *—v.t.* penetrate thoroughly or between the parts of; permeate. *—v.i.* penetrate each other; unite or mingle by mutual penetration. **—in′ter pen′e tra′tion,** *n.*

in ter phase (in′tər fāz), *n.* (in biology) period of time between the end of one cell division and the beginning of the next.

in ter plan e tar y (in′tər plan′ə ter′ē), *adj.* situated or taking place between the planets; in the region of the planets: *interplanetary travel.*

in ter play (in′tər plā′), *n.* action or influence on each other: *the interplay of light and shadow.* *—v.i.* exert mutual action or influence.

In ter pol (in′tər pōl′), *n.* International Criminal Police Commission, organized to assist police of its member nations in international crime investigations.

in ter po late (in tėr′pə lāt), *v.,* **-lat ed, -lat ing.** *—v.t.* 1 alter (a book, passage, etc.) by putting in new words or groups of words, especially without authorization or deceptively. 2 put in (new words, passages, etc.). 3 (in mathematics) find or insert a value between two known values by some method. 4 insert or introduce (something additional or different) between other things or in a series. *—v.i.* make insertions or interpolations. [< Latin *interpolatum* freshened up < *inter-* between + *polire* smooth] **—in ter′po la′tion,** *n.* **—in ter′po la′tor,** *n.*

in ter pose (in′tər pōz′), *v.,* **-posed, -pos ing.** *—v.t.* 1 put between; insert. 2 put forward; break in with: *She interposed an objection at this point.* *—v.i.* 1 come or be between other things. 2 interrupt. 3 interfere in order to help; intervene; intercede. [< Middle French *interposer* < *inter-* between + *poser* to place] **—in′ter pos′er,** *n.*

in ter po si tion (in′tər pə zish′ən), *n.* 1 an interposing. 2 something interposed.

in ter pret (in tėr′prit), *v.t.* 1 explain the meaning of: *interpret a difficult passage in a book, interpret a dream.* See **explain** for synonym study. 2 bring out the meaning of (a dramatic work, a character, music, etc.): *interpret a part in a play.* 3 understand or construe in a particular way: *We interpreted your silence as consent.* *—v.i.* serve as an interpreter; translate. [< Latin *interpretari* < *interpres* agent, interpreter] **—in ter′pret a ble,** *adj.*

in ter pre ta tion (in tėr′prə tā′shən), *n.* 1 an interpreting; explanation: *different interpretations of the same facts.* 2 a bringing out the meaning of a dramatic work, a character, music, etc.: *an actor's interpretation of Hamlet.* 3 work of an interpreter; translation.

in ter pre ta tive (in tėr′prə tā′tiv), *adj.* used for interpreting; explanatory. **—in ter′pre ta′tive ly,** *adv.*

in ter pret er (in tėr′prə tər), *n.* 1 person who interprets. 2 person whose business is translating, especially orally, from a foreign language.

in ter pre tive (in tėr′prə tiv), *adj.* interpretative. **—in ter′pre tive ly,** *adv.*

in ter ra cial (in′tər rā′shəl), *adj.* between or involving different racial groups.

in ter reg num (in′tər reg′nəm), *n., pl.* **-nums, -na** (-nə). 1 time between the end of one ruler's reign and the beginning of his successor's reign. 2 any time during which a nation is without its usual ruler. 3 period of inactivity; pause. [< Latin < *inter-* between + *regnum* reign]

in ter re late (in′tər ri lāt′), *v.t.,* **-lat ed, -lat ing.** bring into relation to each other.

in ter re lat ed (in′tər ri lā′tid), *adj.* mutually related.

in ter re la tion (in′tər ri lā′shən), *n.* mutual relationship.

in ter re la tion ship (in′tər ri lā′shən-ship), *n.* interrelation.

interrog., interrogative.

in ter ro gate (in ter′ə gāt), *v.,* **-gat ed, -gat ing.** *—v.t.* ask questions of; examine or get information from by asking questions; question thoroughly or in a formal manner: *The lawyer took two hours to interrogate the witness.* See **question** for synonym study. *—v.i.* ask a series of questions. [< Latin *interrogatum* interrogated < *inter-* between + *rogare* ask] **—in ter′ro ga′tor,** *n.*

in ter ro ga tion (in ter′ə gā′shən), *n.* 1 an interrogating; a questioning. The formal examination of a witness by asking questions is an interrogation. 2 a question.

interrogation mark or **interrogation point,** question mark; the mark (?).

in ter rog a tive (in′tə rog′ə tiv), *adj.* 1 asking a question; having the form or force of a question: *an interrogative look, an interrogative tone of voice.* 2 (in grammar) used in asking a question. *Where, when,* and *why* are interrogative adverbs. *Who* and *what* are interrogative pronouns. *—n.* (in grammar) a word used in asking a question. *Who, why,* and *what* are interrogatives. **—in′ter rog′a tive ly,** *adv.*

in ter rog a to ry (in′tə rog′ə tôr′ē, in′tə-rog′ə tōr′ē), *adj.* conveying or suggesting a question; questioning; interrogative: *an interrogatory manner.*

in ter rupt (in′tə rupt′), *v.t.* 1 break in upon (talk, work, rest, a person speaking, etc.); keep from going on; stop for a time; hinder: *A fire drill interrupted the lesson.* 2 make a break in: *A building interrupts the view from our window.* *—v.i.* cause a break; break in: *interrupt when someone is talking.* [< Latin *interruptum* broken off, interrupted < *inter-* between + *rumpere* to break] **—in′ter-rupt′er,** *n.*

in ter rup tion (in′tə rup′shən), *n.* 1 an interrupting. 2 a being interrupted. 3 something that interrupts. 4 intermission.

in ter rup tive (in′tə rup′tiv), *adj.* tending to interrupt.

in ter scho las tic (in′tər skə las′tik), *adj.* between schools: *interscholastic competition.*

in ter school (in′tər skül′), *adj.* interscholastic.

in ter se (in′tər sē′), LATIN. between or among themselves.

in ter sect (in′tər sekt′), *v.t.* cut or divide by passing through or crossing: *A path intersects the field.* *—v.i.* cross each other: *Streets usually intersect at right angles.* [< Latin *intersectum* divided, cut asunder < *inter-* between + *secare* to cut]

in ter sec tion (in′tər sek′shən), *n.* 1 act, fact, or process of intersecting. 2 point, line, or place where one thing crosses another. 3 (in mathematics) the set that contains only those elements shared by two or more sets. EXAMPLE: If set A = {1, 2, 3, 4} and set B = {3, 4, 5, 6}, then the intersection of the two sets is {3, 4}.

in ter sex (in′tər seks′), *n.* (in biology) an intersexual organism.

in ter sex u al (in′tər sek′shü əl), *adj.* 1 existing between the sexes. 2 (in biology) having sexual characteristics that are intermediate between those of the typical female and the typical male.

in ter sex u al i ty (in′tər sek′shü al′ə tē), *n.* a being intersexual.

in ter space (*n.* in′tər spās′; *v.* in′tər-spās′), *n., v.,* **-spaced, -spac ing.** *—n.* space between two things; interval. *—v.t.* put a space between.

in ter spe cies (in′tər spē′shēz), *adj.* interspecific.

in ter spe cif ic (in′tər spi sif′ik), *adj.* occurring or arising between species: *an interspecific hybrid.*

in ter sperse (in′tər spėrs′), *v.t.,* **-spersed, -spers ing.** 1 vary with something put here and there: *The grass was interspersed with beds of flowers.* 2 scatter or place here and there among other things: *Bushes were interspersed among the trees.* [< Latin *intersper-sum* scattered < *inter-* between + *spargere* to scatter]

in ter sper sion (in′tər spėr′zhən), *n.* 1 act of interspersing. 2 condition of being interspersed.

in ter stage (in′tər stāj′), *n.* section that connects two stages of a rocket.

in ter state (in′tər stāt′), *adj.* between persons or organizations in different states; between states, especially of the United States: *an interstate highway. The federal government regulates interstate commerce.*

in ter stel lar (in′tər stel′ər), *adj.* situated or taking place between the stars; in the region of the stars: *interstellar space, interstellar travel.*

in ter stice (in tėr′stis), *n., pl.* **-sti ces** (-stə-sēz′). a small or narrow space between things or parts; narrow chink, crack, or opening. [< Late Latin *interstitium* < Latin *inter-* between + *stare* to stand]

in ter sti tial (in′tər stish′əl), *adj.* 1 of or forming interstices. 2 occupying interstices of tissue: *interstitial cells.* **—in′ter sti′tial-ly,** *adv.*

in ter tid al (in′tər tī′dl), *adj.* living or located between the high-water mark and the low-water mark.

in ter trib al (in′tər trī′bəl), *adj.* between tribes.

in ter twine (in′tər twīn′), *v.t., v.i.,* **-twined, -twin ing.** twine, one with another; interlace. **—in′ter twine′ment,** *n.*

in ter twist (in′tər twist′), *v.t., v.i.* twist, one with another.

in ter ur ban (in′tər ėr′bən), *adj.* between different cities or towns.

in ter val (in′tər vəl), *n.* 1 period of time between; pause: *an interval of a week, intervals of freedom from worry.* 2 space between things; intervening space: *an interval of ten feet between trees.* 3 **at intervals, a** now and then. **b** here and there. 4 (in music) the difference in pitch between two tones. [< Latin *intervallum,* originally, space between palisades < *inter-* + *vallum* wall]

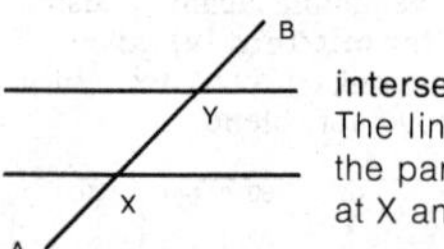

intersection (def. 2)
The line AB intersects the parallel lines at X and Y.

in ter vene (in′tər vēn′), *v.i.,* **-vened, -ven ing.** 1 come between; be between: *A week intervenes between Christmas and New Year's Day.* 2 come between persons or groups to help settle a dispute; act as an intermediary: *The President was asked to intervene in the coal strike.* [< Latin *intervenire* < *inter-* between + *venire* come] **—in′ter ven′er,** *n.*

in ter ven tion (in′tər ven′shən), *n.* 1 an intervening. 2 interference, especially by one nation in the affairs of another.

in ter ven tion ism (in′tər ven′shə niz′-əm), *n.* the favoring of intervention, especially in international affairs.

in ter ven tion ist (in′tər ven′shə nist), *n.* person who supports intervention in the affairs of another country. *—adj.* 1 favoring intervention. 2 of or having to do with intervention or interventionists.

in ter ver te bral disk or **interverte-bral disc** (in′tər vėr′tə brəl), the mass of fibrous cartilage lying between the bodies of adjacent vertebrae.

in ter view (in′tər vyü), *n.* 1 a meeting, generally of persons face to face, to talk over something special. 2 a meeting between a reporter, writer, radio or television commentator, etc., and a person from whom information is sought for publication or broadcast. 3 newspaper or magazine article, or broadcast containing the information given at such a meeting. *—v.t.* have an interview with; meet and talk with, especially to obtain information. [< Middle French *entrevue* < *entrevoir* to glimpse < *entre-* between + *voir* to see] **—in′ter view′er,** *n.*

in ter vo cal ic (in′tər vō kal′ik), *adj.* between vowels: *an intervocalic consonant.*

in ter weave (in′tər wēv′), *v.t., v.i.,* **-wove** (-wōv′) or **-weaved, -wo ven** or **-wove** (-wōv′) or **-weaved, -weav ing.** 1 weave together. 2 mix together; blend; intermingle.

in ter wo ven (in′tər wō′vən), *adj.* 1 woven together. 2 mixed together; blended. *—v.* a pp. of **interweave.**

in ter zon al (in′tər zō′nl), *adj.* between zones: *interzonal trade.*

in tes ta cy (in tes′tə sē), *n.* a being intestate at death.

in tes tate (in tes′tāt, in tes′tit), *adj.* 1 having made no will: *die intestate.* 2 not disposed of by a will. *—n.* person who has died without making a will. [< Latin *intestatus* < *in-* not + *testari* make a will]

in tes ti nal (in tes′tə nəl), *adj.* of, in, or affecting the intestines. **—in tes′ti nal ly,** *adv.*

intestinal fortitude, U.S. pluck; courage; tenacity.

in tes tine (in tes′tən), *n.* part of the alimentary canal extending from the stomach to the anus; small intestine and large intestine. —*adj.* within a country; internal. [< Latin *intestinum* < *intus* within < *in* in]

in ti ma cy (in′tə mə sē), *n., pl.* **-cies.** 1 a being intimate; close acquaintance; closeness. 2 a familiar or intimate act.

in ti mate[1] (in′tə mit), *adj.* 1 very familiar; known very well; closely acquainted: *intimate friends.* See **familiar** for synonym study. 2 resulting from close familiarity; close: *an intimate connection, intimate knowledge of a matter.* 3 personal; private: *A diary is a very intimate book.* 4 far within; deepest; inmost: *the intimate recesses of the heart.* —*n.* a close friend. [earlier *intime* < French < Latin *intimus* inmost. See INTIMATE[2].] **—in′ti mate ly,** *adv.* **—in′ti mate ness,** *n.*

in ti mate[2] (in′tə māt), *v.t.,* **-mat ed, -mat ing.** 1 suggest indirectly; hint. See **hint** for synonym study. 2 make known; announce; notify. [< Latin *intimatum* made known, brought in < *intimus* inmost, superlative of *in* in] **—in′ti mat′er,** *n.*

in ti ma tion (in′tə mā′shən), *n.* 1 an indirect suggestion; hint. 2 announcement; notice.

in tim i date (in tim′ə dāt), *v.t.,* **-dat ed, -dat ing.** 1 make afraid; frighten: *intimidate one's opponents with threats.* 2 influence or force by fear: *intimidate a witness.* [< Medieval Latin *intimidatum* frightened < Latin *in-* + *timidus* fearful] **—in tim′i da′tion,** *n.* **—in tim′i da′tor,** *n.*

in to (in′tü; *before consonants often* in′tə), *prep.* 1 to the inside of; toward the inside; within: *Come into the house.* 2 to the condition of; to the form of: *come into contact with someone, water turned into ice.* 3 (in mathematics) a word implying or expressing division. EXAMPLE: *5 into 30 is 6.* [Old English *intō* < *in,* adverb + *tō* to] ➤ See **in** for usage note.

in tol er a bil i ty (in tol′ər ə bil′ə tē), *n.* a being intolerable.

in tol er a ble (in tol′ər ə bəl), *adj.* too much to be endured; unbearable: *intolerable pain.* **—in tol′er a ble ness,** *n.* **—in tol′er a bly,** *adv.*

in tol er ance (in tol′ər əns), *n.* 1 lack of tolerance for difference of opinion or practice, especially in religious matters; denial of the right of others to differ. 2 inability to tolerate or endure some particular thing: *an intolerance to penicillin.*

in tol er ant (in tol′ər ənt), *adj.* 1 not tolerant; unwilling to let others do and think as they choose, especially in matters of religion; bigoted. 2 **intolerant of,** not able to endure; unwilling to endure. **—in tol′er ant ly,** *adv.*

in to na tion (in′tō nā′shən, in′tə nā′shən), *n.* 1 act of intoning. 2 something intoned. 3 manner of producing musical notes, especially with regard to pitch. 4 the rise and fall in the tone of voice during speech.

in tone (in tōn′), *v.,* **-toned, -ton ing.** —*v.t.* 1 read or recite (a psalm, prayer, etc.) in a singing voice; chant. 2 utter with a particular tone. —*v.i.* recite in a singing voice, especially in monotone. [< Medieval Latin *intonare* < Latin *in-* in + *tonus* tone] **—in ton′er,** *n.*

in to to (in tō′tō), LATIN. as a whole; completely.

in tox i cant (in tok′sə kənt), *n.* 1 an alcoholic liquor. 2 anything that intoxicates. —*adj.* intoxicating.

in tox i cate (in tok′sə kāt), *v.t.,* **-cat ed, -cat ing.** 1 make drunk: *Too much wine intoxicates people.* 2 excite greatly; exhilarate: *The team was intoxicated by its victory.* 3 (in medicine) to poison. [< Medieval Latin *intoxicatum* dipped in poison < Latin *in-* in + *toxicum* poison. See TOXIC.]

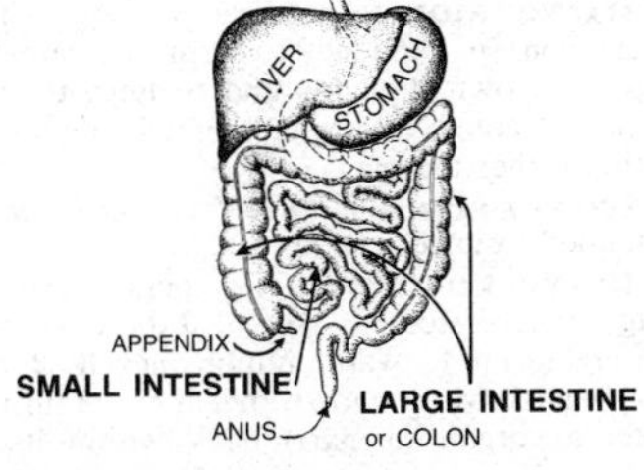

in tox i cat ed (in tok′sə kā′tid), *adj.* 1 drunk. 2 greatly excited.

in tox i ca tion (in tok′sə kā′shən), *n.* 1 drunkenness. 2 great excitement. 3 (in medicine) poisoning.

intra-, *prefix.* within; inside; on the inside, as in *intramural, intrastate.* [< Latin < *intra* inside of]

in tra cel lu lar (in′trə sel′yə lər), *adj.* occurring within a cell or cells: *intracellular circulation.* **—in′tra cel′lu lar ly,** *adv.*

in tra coast al (in′trə kō′stl), *adj.* within a coastal area: *intracoastal waterways.*

in trac ta bil i ty (in trak′tə bil′ə tē), *n.* a being intractable; stubbornness.

in trac ta ble (in trak′tə bəl), *adj.* 1 hard to manage; stubborn. 2 not easily treated: *an intractable disease.* **—in trac′ta ble ness,** *n.* **—in trac′ta bly,** *adv.*

in tra day (in′trə dā′), *adj.* occurring in the course of the day.

in tra dos (in trā′dos), *n., pl.* **-dos** (-dōz), **-dos es** (-dəs əz). the interior curve or surface of an arch or vault. [< French < *intra-* within + *dos* back]

in tra fa mil ial (in′trə fə mil′yəl), *adj.* within a family.

in tra mo lec u lar (in′trə mə lek′yə lər), *adj.* occurring or acting within a molecule or molecules. **—in′tra mo lec′u lar ly,** *adv.*

in tra mur al (in′trə myůr′əl), *adj.* 1 within the walls; inside. 2 carried on by members of the same school, college, etc.: *intramural games.* **—in′tra mur′al ly,** *adv.*

in tra mus cu lar (in′trə mus′kyə lər), *adj.* within or into a muscle: *intramuscular injection.* **—in′tra mus′cu lar ly,** *adv.*

in tran si gence (in tran′sə jəns), *n.* a being intransigent.

in tran si gent (in tran′sə jənt), *adj.* unwilling to agree or compromise; uncompromising. —*n.* person who is intransigent. [< Spanish *(los) intransigentes* (the) ones unwilling to transact, a name for various extreme political parties] **—in tran′si gent ly,** *adv.*

in tran si tive (in tran′sə tiv), *adj.* not taking a direct object. The verbs *belong, go,* and *seem* are intransitive. —*n.* an intransitive verb. **—in tran′si tive ly,** *adv.* **—in tran′si tive ness,** *n.*

in tra oc u lar (in′trə ok′yə lər), *adj.* within the eyeball.

in tra par ty (in′trə pär′tē), *adj.* occurring within a political party.

in tra per i to ne al (in′trə per′ə tə nē′əl), *adj.* within the peritoneum. **—in′tra per′i to ne′al ly,** *adv.*

in tra re gion al (in′trə rē′jə nəl), *adj.* within a region.

hat, āge, fär; let, ēqual, tėrm;
it, īce; hot, ōpen, ôrder;
oil, out; cup, pů t, rüle;
ch, child; ng, long; sh, she;
th, thin; ᴛʜ, then; zh, measure;

ə represents *a* in about, *e* in taken, *i* in pencil, *o* in lemon, *u* in circus.

< = from, derived from, taken from.

in tra spe cies (in′trə spē′shēz), *adj.* intraspecific.

in tra spe cif ic (in′trə spi sif′ik), *adj.* within a species; involving members of the same species.

in tra state (in′trə stāt′), *adj.* within a state, especially within a state of the United States: *intrastate commerce.*

in tra u ter ine (in′trə yü′tər ən, in′trə yü′tə rīn′), *adj.* within the uterus.

in tra ve nous (in′trə vē′nəs), *adj.* 1 within a vein or the veins. 2 into a vein or veins. **—in′tra ve′nous ly,** *adv.*

in tra vi res (in′trə vī′rēz), LATIN. 1 within the powers granted by authority or by law. 2 (literally) within the power.

in treat (in trēt′), *v.t.* entreat.

in trench (in trench′), *v.t.* entrench. **—in trench′ment,** *n.*

in trep id (in trep′id), *adj.* very brave; fearless; dauntless; courageous. [< Latin *intrepidus* < *in-* not + *trepidus* alarmed] **—in trep′id ly,** *adv.*

in tre pid i ty (in′trə pid′ə tē), *n.* great bravery; dauntless courage; fearlessness.

in tri ca cy (in′trə kə sē), *n., pl.* **-cies.** 1 intricate nature or condition; complexity: *The intricacy of the plan made it hard to understand.* 2 an intricate thing or event; complication: *The laws are full of intricacies.*

in tri cate (in′trə kit), *adj.* 1 with many twists and turns; puzzling, entangled, or complicated: *an intricate knot, an intricate plot.* 2 very hard to understand: *intricate directions.* [< Latin *intricatum* entangled < *in-* in + *tricae* hindrances] **—in′tri cate ly,** *adv.* **—in′tri cate ness,** *n.*

in trigue (*n.* in trēg′, in′trēg′; *v.* in trēg′), *n., v.,* **-trigued, -tri guing.** —*n.* 1 secret scheming; underhand planning to accomplish some purpose; plotting. 2 a crafty plot; secret scheme. 3 a secret love affair. —*v.i.* 1 form and carry out plots; plan in a secret or underhand way. 2 have a secret love affair. —*v.t.* excite the curiosity and interest of: *The book's unusual title intrigued me.* [< French < Italian *intrigo* < *intrigare* entangle < Latin *intricare*] **—in tri′guer,** *n.*

in tri guing (in trē′ging), *adj.* exciting the curiosity and interest: *an intriguing title.* **—in tri′guing ly,** *adv.*

in trin sic (in trin′sik), *adj.* 1 belonging to a thing by its very nature; essential; inherent: *The intrinsic value of a dollar bill is the cost of the paper it is printed on.* 2 originating or being inside the part on which it acts: *the intrinsic muscles of the larynx.* [< Late Latin *intrinsecus* internal < Latin, inwardly] **—in trin′si cal ly,** *adv.*

in trin si cal (in trin′sə kəl), *adj.* intrinsic. **—in trin′si cal ness,** *n.*

intro-, *prefix.* inwardly; within, as an *introvert.* [< Latin < *intro* within]

intro. or **introd.,** 1 introduction. 2 introductory.

in tro duce (in′trə düs′, in′trə dyüs′), *v.t.*, **-duced, -duc ing.** 1 bring in: *introduce a new subject into the conversation.* 2 put in; insert: *The doctor introduced a tube into the sick man's throat.* 3 bring into use, notice, knowledge, etc.: *introduce a reform, introduce a new word.* 4 bring into acquaintance with; make known: *The chairman introduced the speaker to the audience.* See synonym study below. 5 bring forward for consideration: *introduce a question for debate.* 6 begin; start: *Relative pronouns introduce adjective clauses.* [< Latin *introducere* < *intro-* in + *ducere* to lead] **—in′tro duc′er,** *n.*

Syn. 4 **Introduce, present** mean to make someone known to another or others. **Introduce** especially means to make two people acquainted with each other: *Mrs. Brown, may I introduce Mr. Smith?* **Present** means to introduce a person or group with some ceremony to someone regarded as a superior: *Freshmen are presented to the president of a college.*

in tro duc tion (in′trə duk′shən), *n.* 1 an introducing: *The introduction of steel made tall buildings easier to build.* 2 a being introduced: *She was enthusiastic at her introduction to so many new people.* 3 thing that introduces; first part of a book, speech, piece of music, etc., leading up to the main part. See synonym study below. 4 book intended as a manual for beginners, or as an explanation of elementary principles of a subject: *An Introduction to English Grammar.* 5 thing introduced; thing brought into use: *Television is a later introduction than radio.*

Syn. 3 **Introduction, preface, foreword** mean a section at the beginning of a book, etc. **Introduction** applies to an actual part of the book, article, play, etc., that leads into or gives what is necessary for understanding the main part: *The symbols used in the pronunciation key are explained in the introduction to this book.* **Preface** applies to a preliminary statement, often signed by the author, explaining his purpose in writing, his obligation to others, etc. **Foreword** is merely a short, simple preface: *The foreword was no more than a statement thanking those who had helped the author with his book.*

in tro duc tor y (in′trə duk′tər ē), *adj.* used to introduce; serving as an introduction; preliminary. **—in′tro duc′tor i ly,** *adv.*

in tro it (in trō′it), *n.* 1 Also, **Introit.** (in the Roman Catholic Church) a hymn or responsive anthem recited by the priest at the beginning of Mass or sung by the choir at High Mass. 2 (in the Anglican Church) a psalm, hymn, etc., at the beginning of the Communion service. [< Latin *introitus* entrance < *introire* enter < *intro-* in + *ire* go]

in trorse (in trôrs′), *adj.* (in botany) turned or facing inward, toward the axis. A violet has introrse stamens. [< Latin *introrsum* < *intro-* inward + *versum* turned]

in tro spect (in′trə spekt′), *v.i.* look inward; be introspective. [< Latin *introspectum* looked into < *intro-* + *specere* to look]

in tro spec tion (in′trə spek′shən), *n.* examination of one's own thoughts and feelings.

in tro spec tive (in′trə spek′tiv), *adj.* characterized by introspection. **—in′tro spec′tive ly,** *adv.*

in tro ver sion (in′trə vėr′zhən, in′trə vėr′shən), *n.* tendency to be more interested in one's own thoughts and feelings than in what is going on around one; tendency to think rather than act.

in tro ver sive (in′trə vėr′siv), *adj.* of or inclined to introversion.

in tro vert (in′trə vėrt′), *n.* person exhibiting introversion. *—v.t.* 1 direct (one's thoughts, etc.) inward or upon oneself. 2 turn or bend inward: *introverted toes.* 3 turn (a tubular organ or part) back within itself. [< *intro-* + Latin *vertere* to turn]

in tro vert ed (in′trə vėr′tid), *adj.* characterized by introversion.

in trude (in trüd′), *v.*, **-trud ed, -trud ing.** *—v.i.* 1 force oneself in; come unasked and unwanted: *If you are busy, I will not intrude.* See synonym study below. 2 (in geology) force (molten rock) into fissures or between strata. *—v.t.* give unasked and unwanted; force in: *intrude one's opinions upon others.* [< Latin *intrudere* < *in-* in + *trudere* to thrust] **—in trud′er,** *n.*

Syn. *v.i.* 1 **Intrude, trespass, encroach** mean to invade the rights or property of another. **Intrude** means to thrust oneself in without permission or invitation and often suggests rudeness and invasion of privacy: *I was unwilling to intrude upon them so late at night.* **Trespass** means to intrude unlawfully or in an offensive manner: *The hunters trespassed upon the farmer's land. She often unthinkingly trespasses upon my time.* **Encroach** means to trespass secretly and gradually upon the property or rights of another: *Our neighbor's irrigation system is encroaching on our land.*

in tru sion (in trü′zhən), *n.* 1 act of intruding; coming unasked and unwanted. 2 in geology: **a** the forcing of molten rock into fissures or between strata. **b** the molten rock forced in and solidified in place.

in tru sive (in trü′siv), *adj.* 1 intruding; coming unasked and unwanted. 2 (in geology) forced into fissures or between strata while molten. **—in tru′sive ly,** *adv.*

in trust (in trust′), *v.t.* entrust.

in tu it (in tü′it, in tyü′it; in′tü it, in′tyü it), *v.t., v.i.* know or learn by intuition.

in tu i tion (in′tü ish′ən, in′tyü ish′ən), *n.* 1 immediate perception or understanding of truths, facts, etc., without reasoning: *By experience with many kinds of people the doctor had developed great powers of intuition.* 2 truth, fact, etc., so perceived or understood. [< Late Latin *intuitionem* a gazing at < Latin *intueri* consider, look upon < *in-* + *tueri* to look]

in tu i tion al (in′tü ish′ə nəl, in′tyü ish′ə nəl), *adj.* of, having to do with, or characterized by intuition.

in tu i tive (in tü′ə tiv, in tyü′ə tiv), *adj.* 1 perceiving or understanding by intuition: *an intuitive mind.* 2 acquired by intuition; instinctive; natural: *an artist's intuitive understanding of color.* **—in tu′i tive ly,** *adv.*

in tu mesce (in′tü mes′, in′tyü mes′), *v.i.*, **-mesced, -mesc ing.** swell up; bubble up. [< Latin *intumescere* < *in-* in + *tumescere* swell up < *tumere* be swollen]

in turned (in′tėrnd′), *adj.* 1 turned inward. 2 self-centered; introverted.

in un date (in′un dāt, in un′dāt), *v.t.*, **-dat ed, -dat ing.** 1 overspread with a flow of water; flood. 2 overspread as if with a flood: *Requests for free tickets inundated the studio.* [< Latin *inundatum* flooded < *in-* onto + *undare* to flow < *unda* wave] **—in′un da′tor,** *n.*

in un da tion (in′un dā′shən), *n.* an inundating; flood. See **flood** for synonym study.

in un da to ry (in un′də tôr′ē, in un′də tōr′ē), *adj.* inundating.

in ure (in yůr′), *v.*, **-ured, -ur ing.** *—v.t.* toughen or harden; accustom; habituate: *Poverty had inured the beggar to hardships.* *—v.i.* have effect; be useful: *The agreement inures to the benefit of the employees.* [< *in* + obsolete *ure* use, noun < Anglo-French < Latin *opera* work] **—in ure′ment,** *n.*

inv., 1 invented. 2 inventor. 3 invoice.

in va cu o (in vak′yü ō), LATIN. in a vacuum.

in vade (in vād′), *v.*, **-vad ed, -vad ing.** *—v.t.* 1 enter with force or as an enemy for conquest or spoils: *Soldiers invaded the country.* 2 enter as if to take possession: *Tourists invaded the city.* 3 interfere with; encroach upon; violate: *The law punishes people who invade the rights of others.* *—v.i.* make an invasion. [< Latin *invadere* < *in-* in + *vadere* go, walk] **—in vad′er,** *n.*

in va lid[1] (in′və lid), *n.* person who is weak because of sickness or injury; infirm or sickly person. *—adj.* 1 weak and sick; not well. 2 for the use of invalids: *an invalid chair.* *—v.t.* 1 make weak or sick; disable. 2 remove from active service because of sickness or injury: *The wounded soldier was invalided and sent home.* [< French *invalide* < *Latin invalidus* not strong. See INVALID[2].]

in val id[2] (in val′id), *adj.* not valid; without force or effect; worthless: *Unless a check is signed, it is invalid.* [< Latin *invalidus* < *in-* not + *validus* strong] **—in val′id ly,** *adv.*

in val i date (in val′ə dāt), *v.t.*, **-dat ed, -dat ing.** make valueless; deprive of force or effect: *A contract is invalidated if only one party signs it.* **—in val′i da′tion,** *n.* **—in val′i da′tor,** *n.*

in va lid ism (in′və lə diz′əm), *n.* prolonged ill health.

in va lid i ty (in′və lid′ə tē), *n.* lack of validity; worthlessness.

in val u a ble (in val′yü ə bəl, in val′yə bəl), *adj.* valuable beyond measure; very precious; priceless. **—in val′u a ble ness,** *n.* **—in val′u a bly,** *adv.*

in var i a bil i ty (in ver′ē ə bil′ə tē, in var′ē ə bil′ə tē), *n.* lack of variability; being invariable.

in var i a ble (in ver′ē ə bəl, in var′ē ə bəl), *adj.* always the same; unchanging; unchangeable; constant: *an invariable habit.* *—n.* something invariable; a constant. **—in var′i a ble ness,** *n.* **—in var′i a bly,** *adv.*

in var i ant (in ver′ē ənt, in var′ē ənt), *adj.* unvarying; constant. *—n.* (in mathematics) an invariant quantity.

in va sion (in vā′zhən), *n.* 1 an invading; entering by force or as an enemy. 2 interference; encroachment; violation. [< Late Latin *invasionem* < *invadere.* See INVADE.]

in va sive (in vā′siv), *adj.* 1 tending to invade; invading. 2 characterized by or involving invasion.

in vec tive (in vek′tiv), *n.* a violent attack in words; railing speech, writing, or expression; abusive language. [< Late Latin *invectivus* abusive < Latin *invehi.* See INVEIGH.]

in veigh (in vā′), *v.i.* make a violent attack in words. [< Latin *invehi* launch an attack < *in-* against + *vehere* carry] **—in veigh′er,** *n.*

hat, āge, fär; let, ēqual, tėrm;
it, īce; hot, ōpen, ôrder;
oil, out; cup, pu̇t, rüle;
ch, child; ng, long; sh, she;
th, thin; ᴛʜ, then; zh, measure;

ə represents *a* in about, *e* in taken, *i* in pencil, *o* in lemon, *u* in circus.

< = from, derived from, taken from.

in vei gle (in vē′gəl, in vā′gəl), *v.t.*, **-gled, -gling.** 1 mislead by trickery; entice; lure: *The saleswoman inveigled me into buying four magazine subscriptions.* 2 obtain by trickery: *inveigle a promise.* [apparently alteration of Old French *aveugler* make blind < *aveugle* blind < Popular Latin *aboculus* < Latin *ab-* without + *oculus* eye] **—in vei′gle ment,** *n.* **—in vei′gler,** *n.*

in vent (in vent′), *v.t.* 1 make up for the first time; think out (something new): *Alexander Graham Bell invented the telephone.* See **discover** for synonym study. 2 make up; think up: *invent an excuse.* [< Latin *inventum* found out, have come upon < *in-* in + *venire* come]

in ven tion (in ven′shən), *n.* 1 the original making of something new; inventing: *the invention of gunpowder.* 2 thing invented: *Television is a modern invention.* 3 power of inventing: *An author must have invention to think up new ideas for stories.* 4 a made-up story; false statement.

in ven tive (in ven′tiv), *adj.* 1 good at inventing; quick to invent things. 2 of invention. 3 showing power of inventing. **—in ven′tive ly,** *adv.* **—in ven′tive ness,** *n.*

in ven tor (in ven′tər), *n.* person who invents: *Edison was a great inventor.*

in ven to ry (in′vən tôr′ē, in′vən tōr′ē), *n.*, *pl.* **-ries,** *v.*, **-ried, -ry ing.** *—n.* 1 a complete and detailed list of articles with their estimated value. 2 all the articles listed or to be listed; stock: *The storekeeper had a sale to reduce his inventory.* *—v.t.* make a complete and detailed list of; enter in a list: *Some stores inventory their stock once a month.*

inverness cape (def. 2)

In ver ness (in′vər nes′), *n.* 1 seaport in N Scotland, on the North Sea. 32,000. 2 **inverness,** overcoat with a long removable cape.

in verse (in vėrs′, in′vėrs′), *adj.* exactly opposite; reversed in position, direction, or tendency; inverted: *DCBA is the inverse order of ABCD.* *—n.* 1 something reversed: *The inverse of ¾ is ⁴⁄₃.* 2 direct opposite: *Evil is the inverse of good.* 3 in mathematics: **a** any operation which annuls a given operation. Subtraction is the inverse of addition. **b** one of a pair of elements in a set whose result under the operation of the set is the identity element. [< Latin *inversum* turned over, inverted] **—in verse′ly,** *adv.*

in ver sion (in vėr′zhən, in vėr′shən), *n.* 1 an inverting. 2 a being inverted. 3 something inverted. 4 reversal of the usual or natural order of words. 5 (in meteorology) an increase of air temperature with elevation instead of the usual decrease.

in ver sive (in vėr′siv), *adj.* characterized by inversion.

in vert (in vėrt′), *v.t.* 1 turn upside down: *invert a glass.* See **reverse** for synonym study. 2 turn the other way; reverse in position, direction, order, etc.: *If you invert "I can," you have "Can I?"* 3 (in music) change by making the lower or lowest note an octave higher or the higher or highest note an octave lower. 4 turn inside out or outside in. [< Latin *invertere* < *in-* over, around + *vertere* to turn] **—in vert′er,** *n.*

in vert ase (in vėr′tās), *n.* enzyme which acts as a catalyst to convert sucrose into glucose and fructose; sucrase.

in ver te brate (in vėr′tə brit, in vėr′tə brāt), *adj.* 1 without a backbone. 2 of or having to do with invertebrates. *—n.* animal without a backbone. Worms and insects are invertebrates.

in vest (in vest′), *v.t.* 1 lay out or use (money) for something that is expected to produce a profit in the form of interest, benefit, income, etc.: *She invested her money in stocks, bonds, and land.* 2 spend or put in (time, energy, etc.) for later benefit. 3 clothe; cover; surround: *Darkness invests the earth at night. The castle was invested with mystery.* 4 give power, authority, or right to: *I invested my lawyer with complete power to act for me.* 5 install in office with a ceremony: *A king is invested by being crowned.* 6 surround with soldiers or ships; besiege: *The enemy invested the city and cut it off from our army.* *—v.i.* invest money; make an investment: *Learn to invest wisely.* [< Latin *investire* clothe, cover < *in-* in + *vestis* clothing]

in ves ti gate (in ves′tə gāt), *v.*, **-gat ed, -gat ing.** *—v.t.* look into thoroughly; search into carefully; examine closely: *investigate a complaint.* *—v.i.* search; make investigation. [< Latin *investigatum* traced, searched out < *in-* in + *vestigare* to track, trace < *vestigium* footstep, vestige] **—in ves′ti ga′tor,** *n.*

in ves ti ga tion (in ves′tə gā′shən), *n.* a careful search; detailed or careful examination.

Syn. Investigation, examination, inquiry mean a search for information or truth. **Investigation** emphasizes a careful and systematic search for facts, especially one carried out by officials: *An investigation of the accident by the police put the blame on the drivers of both cars.* **Examination** emphasizes a search for facts by inspection: *The doctor gave her a physical examination.* **Inquiry** especially suggests a search for facts made by asking questions: *Advertisers began an inquiry into the buying habits of consumers.*

in ves ti ga tive (in ves′tə gā′tiv), *adj.* of or having to do with investigation: *investigative powers.*

in ves ti ga to ry (in ves′tə gə tôr′ē, in ves′tə gə tōr′ē), *adj.* investigative.

in ves ti ture (in ves′tə chu̇r, in ves′tə chər), *n.* 1 a formal investing of a person with an office, dignity, power, right, etc. 2 clothing; apparel.

in vest ment (in vest′mənt), *n.* 1 an investing; a laying out of money for something that is expected to produce a profit or benefit: *Getting an education is a wise investment of time and money.* 2 amount of money invested: *investments amounting to thousands of dollars.* 3 something that is expected to yield money as income or profit or both: *I consider United States bonds a safe investment.* 4 a surrounding with soldiers or ships; siege. 5 investiture.

in ves tor (in ves′tər), *n.* person who invests money.

in vet er a cy (in vet′ər ə sē), *n.* settled, fixed condition; habitualness.

in vet er ate (in vet′ər it), *adj.* 1 confirmed in a habit, practice, feeling, etc.; habitual: *an inveterate smoker.* 2 long and firmly established; deeply rooted: *Cats have an inveterate dislike of dogs.* [< Latin *inveteratum* grown old, long established < *in-* in + *vetus, veteris* old] **—in vet′er ate ly,** *adv.*

in vi a bil i ty (in vī′ə bil′ə tē), *n.* lacking viability.

in vi a ble (in vī′ə bəl), *adj.* unable to survive; not viable.

in vid i ous (in vid′ē əs), *adj.* likely to cause ill will or resentment; giving offense because unfair or unjust: *invidious comparisons.* [< Latin *invidiosus* < *invidia* envy. See ENVY.] **—in vid′i ous ly,** *adv.* **—in vid′i ous ness,** *n.*

in vig o rate (in vig′ə rāt′), *v.t.*, **-rat ed, -rat ing.** give vigor to; fill with life and energy. **—in vig′o rat′ing ly,** *adv.* **—in vig′o ra′tion,** *n.*

in vin ci bil i ty (in vin′sə bil′ə tē), *n.* a being invincible.

in vin ci ble (in vin′sə bəl), *adj.* unable to be conquered; impossible to overcome; unconquerable: *invincible courage, an invincible fighter.* [< Latin *invincibilis* < *in-* not + *vincere* conquer] **—in vin′ci ble ness,** *n.* **—in vin′ci bly,** *adv.*

in vi o la bil i ty (in vī′ə lə bil′ə tē), *n.* a being inviolable.

in vi o la ble (in vī′ə lə bəl), *adj.* 1 that must not be violated or injured; sacred: *an inviolable vow, an inviolable sanctuary.* 2 that cannot be violated or injured: *The gods are inviolable.* **—in vi′o la bly,** *adv.*

in vi o late (in vī′ə lit, in vī′ə lāt), *adj.* not violated; uninjured; unbroken: *an inviolate promise.* **—in vi′o late ly,** *adv.* **—in vi′o late ness,** *n.*

in vis i bil i ty (in viz′ə bil′ə tē), *n.* a being invisible.

in vis i ble (in viz′ə bəl), *adj.* 1 not visible; not capable of being seen: *Thought is invisible. The queen kept herself invisible in the palace. Germs are invisible to the naked eye.* 2 not listed in the regular financial statements: *an invisible asset.* *—n.* an invisible being or thing. **—in vis′i ble ness,** *n.* **—in vis′i bly,** *adv.*

in vi ta tion (in′və tā′shən), *n.* 1 a polite request to come to some place or to do something. Formal invitations are written or printed. 2 act of inviting.

in vi ta tion al (in′və tā′shə nəl), *adj.* restricted to invited guests, participants, etc.: *an invitational tennis match.*

in vite (*v.* in vīt′; *n.* in′vīt), *v.*, **-vit ed, -vit ing,** *n.* *—v.t.* 1 ask (someone) politely to come to some place or to do something: *We invited her to join our club.* See **call** for synonym study. 2 make a polite request for: *She invited our opinion of her story.* 3 give a chance for; tend to cause: *Carelessness invites trouble.* 4 attract; tempt; encourage: *The cool water invited us to swim.* —*n.* INFORMAL. invitation. [< Latin *invitare*] —**in vit′er,** *n.*

involute (def. 3)
A, involute leaf;
B, cross section of an involute leaf

in vi tee (in vī′tē′, in′vī tē′), *n.* person who is invited; guest.

in vit ing (in vī′ting), *adj.* attractive; tempting: *The cool water looks inviting.* —**in vit′ing ly,** *adv.*

in vi tro (in vī′trō; in vit′rō), in an artificial environment, such as a test tube; not in the living animal or plant. [< New Latin, in glass]

in vi vo (in vī′vō), in a living organism; inside an animal or plant. [< New Latin, in the living thing]

in vo ca ble (in vō′kə bəl, in′və kə bəl), *adj.* capable of being invoked.

in vo ca tion (in′və kā′shən), *n.* 1 a calling upon in prayer; appeal for help or protection: *A church service often begins with an invocation to God.* 2 a calling forth of spirits with magic words or charms. 3 set of magic words used to call forth spirits; incantation. [< Latin *invocationem* < *invocare.* See INVOKE.]

in voc a to ry (in vok′ə tôr′ē, in vok′ə-tōr′ē), *adj.* of the nature of, characterized by, or used in invocation.

in voice (in′vois), *n., v.,* **-voiced, -voic ing.** —*n.* 1 list of goods sent to a purchaser showing prices, amounts, shipping charges, etc. 2 shipment of invoiced goods. —*v.t.* make an invoice of; enter on an invoice. [earlier *invoyes,* plural of *invoy, envoy* < Old French *envoy* message < *envoier* send. See ENVOY[2].]

in voke (in vōk′), *v.t.,* **-voked, -vok ing.** 1 call on in prayer; appeal to for help or protection. 2 appeal to for confirmation or judgment: *invoke an authority.* 3 ask earnestly for; beg for: *The condemned criminal invoked the judge's mercy.* 4 call forth with magic words or charms. [< Latin *invocare* < *in-* on + *vocare* to call] —**in vok′er,** *n.*

in vo lu cral (in′və lü′krəl), *adj.* of or having to do with an involucre.

in vo lu cre (in′və lü′kər), *n.* circle of small leaves or bracts at the base of a flower or flower cluster. [< Latin *involucrum* a cover, envelope < *involvere* roll up. See INVOLVE.]

in vol un tar y (in vol′ən ter′ē), *adj.* 1 not voluntary; not done of one's own free will; unwilling: *involuntary consent.* 2 not done on purpose; not intended: *an involuntary injury.* See **automatic** for synonym study. 3 not controlled by the will: *Breathing is mainly involuntary.* —**in vol′un tar′i ly,** *adv.* —**in vol′un tar′i ness,** *n.*

involuntary muscle, smooth muscle.

in vo lute (in′və lüt), *adj.* 1 involved; intricate. 2 rolled up on itself; curved spirally. 3 (in botany) rolled inward from the edge: *an involute leaf.* 4 (of shells) having the whorls closely wound. —*n.* (in geometry) the curve traced by any point of a string when the string is unwound from a given curve under tension. [< Latin *involutum* rolled up, enveloped < *in-* in + *volvere* to roll]

in vo lu tion (in′və lü′shən), *n.* 1 an involving. 2 a being involved; entanglement; complexity. 3 something involved; complication. 4 (in mathematics) the raising of a quantity to any power. 5 (in biology) degeneration; retrograde change.

in vo lu tion al (in′və lü′shə nəl), *adj.* of or having to do with involution.

in volve (in volv′), *v.t.,* **-volved, -volv ing.** 1 have as a necessary part, condition, or result; take in; include: *Housework involves cooking, washing dishes, sweeping, and cleaning.* 2 have an effect on; affect: *These changes in the business involve the interests of all the owners.* 3 bring into difficulty, danger, etc.: *One foolish mistake can involve you in a good deal of trouble.* See synonym study below. 4 entangle; complicate: *an argument that is involved and hard to follow.* 5 take up the attention of; occupy: *She was involved in working out a puzzle.* 6 wrap; enfold; envelop: *The outcome of the war is involved in doubt.* [< Latin *involvere* roll up, enfold, involve < *in-* in + *volvere* to roll] —**in volve′ment,** *n.* —**in volv′er,** *n.*

Syn. 3 **Involve, implicate** mean to draw someone or something into a situation hard to get out of. **Involve** means entanglement in a situation that is unpleasant, embarrassing or hard to settle, but not a disgraceful one: *Buying an expensive car involved me in debt.* **Implicate** means to involve someone with something disgraceful: *Having the stolen goods in his possession implicated him in the robbery.*

in volved (in volvd′), *adj.* intricate; complicated: *an involved sentence.*

in vul ner a bil i ty (in vul′nər ə bil′ə tē), *n.* a being invulnerable.

in vul ner a ble (in vul′nər ə bəl), *adj.* 1 that cannot be wounded or hurt; safe from attack: *Achilles was invulnerable except for his heel.* 2 proof against attack; not easily assailable: *an invulnerable argument.* —**in vul′ner a ble ness,** *n.* —**in vul′ner a bly,** *adv.*

in ward (in′wərd), *adv.* 1 toward the inside or interior: *a passage leading inward.* 2 into the mind or soul: *Turn your thoughts inward.* —*adj.* 1 placed within; internal: *the inward parts of the body.* 2 directed toward the inside: *an inward slant of the eyes.* 3 in mind or soul: *inward peace.* —*n.* the inward or internal part; inside. [Old English *inweard*]

in ward ly (in′wərd lē), *adv.* 1 on the inside; within. 2 toward the inside: *The line curved inwardly.* 3 in the mind or soul: *suffer inwardly.* 4 not aloud or openly: *She laughed inwardly.*

in ward ness (in′wərd nis), *n.* 1 inner nature or meaning. 2 spirituality.

in wards (*adv.* in′wərdz; *n.* in′wərdz, in′ərdz), *adv.* inward. —*n.pl.* INFORMAL. parts inside the body, especially the stomach and intestines.

in weave (in wēv′), *v.t.,* **-wove** (-wōv) or **-weaved, -wo ven** (-wō′vən) or **-wove** (-wōv) or **-weaved, -weav ing.** weave in; weave together; interweave.

in wrought (in rôt′), *adj.* 1 having a decoration worked in. 2 worked in. 3 mixed together; closely blended.

Io, ionium.

i o date (ī′ə dāt), *v.t.,* **-dat ed, -dat ing.** combine, impregnate, or treat with iodine.

i od ic acid (ī od′ik), a colorless or white crystalline acid, used as an astringent and disinfectant. *Formula:* HIO_3

i o dide (ī′ə dīd, ī′ə did), *n.* compound of iodine with another element or radical.

i o din (ī′ə dən), *n.* iodine.

i o dine (ī′ə dīn, ī′ə dən, ī′ə dēn′), *n.* 1 a nonmetallic element in the form of grayish-black crystals which give off when heated a dense, violet vapor with an irritating odor resembling that of chlorine. Iodine occurs naturally only in combination with other elements and is used in medicine, in making dyes, in photography, etc. *Symbol:* I; *atomic number* 53. See pages 326 and 327 for table. 2 a brown liquid containing iodine dissolved in alcohol, used as an antiseptic. [< French *iode* iodine < Greek *ioeidēs* violet in color < *ion* violet + *eidos* form]

iodine 131, a radioactive isotope of iodine that is a product of the fission of uranium and present in fallout; radioiodine. *Symbol:* I^{131}; *atomic number* 53; *mass number* 131.

i o dize (ī′ə dīz), *v.t.,* **-dized, -diz ing.** treat or impregnate with iodine or an iodide, as in photography or medicine.

iodized salt, table salt containing small quantities of potassium iodide or other iodide as a supplement to the diet.

i o do form (ī ō′də fôrm, ī od′ə fôrm), *n.* a yellowish, crystalline compound of iodine, used as an antiseptic, especially in surgical dressings. *Formula:* CHI_3

i o dop sin (ī ə dop′sən), *n.* a violet pigment that is sensitive to light, found in the cones of the retina of the eye. [< Greek *ioeidēs* violet in color + *ōps, ōpos* eye]

i o moth (ī′ō), a large yellowish moth of North American forests with an eyelike spot on each hind wing.

ion (ī′ən, ī′on), *n.* atom or group of atoms having a negative or positive electric charge as a result of having lost or gained one or more electrons. When an acid, base, or salt dissolves in solution, some of its molecules separate into positive and negative ions. Each molecule forms two or more ions whose electric charges neutralize each other when recombined into a molecule. Cations are positive ions formed by the loss of electrons; anions are negative ions formed by the gain of electrons. [< Greek, neuter present participle of *ienai* go]

-ion, *suffix forming nouns chiefly from verbs.* 1 act of ___ing: *Attraction = act of attracting.* 2 condition of being ___ed: *Adoption = condition of being adopted.* 3 result of ___ing: *Abbreviation = result of abbreviating.* [< Old French < Latin *-ionem,* or directly < Latin]

ion exchange, process in which an insoluble substance, commonly a resin or zeolite, exchanges ions with the solution it is in, thereby removing a substance from the solution.

I o ni a (ī ō′nē ə), *n.* ancient region on the W coast of Asia Minor, with nearby islands, colonized by the Greeks in the 1000's B.C.

I o ni an (ī ō′nē ən), *adj.* 1 of or having to do with Ionia or its people. 2 having to do with one of the main branches of the ancient Greek race. The Athenians were of Ionian descent. —*n.* Greek of this branch.

Ionian Islands, islands along the W coast of Greece. 213,000 pop.; 890 sq. mi.

Ionian Sea, part of the Mediterranean Sea between Greece and S Italy.

i on ic (ī on′ik), *adj.* of, having to do with, or present as ions.

I on ic (ī on′ik), *adj.* 1 of or having to do with the order of ancient Greek architecture having scrolls in the capitals of the columns. 2 of Ionia or its people.

Ionic (def. 1)
Ionic temple

i o ni um (ī ō′nē əm), *n.* a radioactive isotope of thorium, formed from disintegrating uranium. *Symbol:* Io; *atomic number* 90; *mass number* 230. [< *ion*]

i on i za tion (ī′ə nə zā′shən), *n.* separation or conversion into ions; formation of ions.

ionization chamber, a closed, gas-filled chamber or tube containing a positive and a negative electrode. Cosmic rays or other forms of radiation passing through it are measured according to the degree of ionization they cause in the gas. The electroscope is a simple ionization chamber.

i on ize (ī′ə nīz), *v.,* **-ized, -iz ing.** —*v.i.* separate into ions. Acids, bases, and salts ionize when dissolved in a solution. —*v.t.* cause to separate or change into ions; produce ions in. —**i′on iz′er,** *n.*

i on o gram (ī on′ə gram), *n.* record or graph of data transmitted by an ionosonde.

i on o sonde (ī on′ə sond), *n.* instrument for studying the ionosphere. [< *iono(sphere)* + *(radio)sonde*]

i on o sphere (ī on′ə sfir), *n.* region of the atmosphere between the mesosphere and the exosphere. The ionosphere is composed of layers of atmosphere ionized by solar ultraviolet radiation which facilitate the transmission of certain radio waves over long distances on earth by reflection. See **atmosphere** for diagram.

i on o spher ic (ī on′ə sfir′ik, ī on′ə-sfer′ik), *adj.* in or having to do with the ionosphere.

i o ta (ī ō′tə), *n.* 1 a very small part or quantity; bit: *There is not an iota of truth in the story.* 2 the ninth letter of the Greek alphabet (Ι, ι). [< Latin < Greek *iōta.* Doublet of JOT.]

I O U or **I.O.U.** (ī′ō′yü′), 1 I owe you. 2 an informal note showing a debt: *Write me your IOU for ten dollars.*

I o wa (ī′ə wə), *n.* 1 one of the midwestern states of the United States. 2,824,000 pop.; 56,300 sq. mi. *Capital:* Des Moines. *Abbrev.:* Ia. 2 **Iowa River,** river flowing from N Iowa into the Mississippi. 291 mi. —**I′o wan,** *adj., n.*

IPA or **I.P.A.,** International Phonetic Alphabet.

ip e cac (ip′ə kak), *n.* 1 medicine made from

Ionia—about 1000 B.C. (the shaded area)

the dried roots and rhizomes of a South American shrub, used chiefly as an emetic or expectorant. 2 the dried roots and rhizomes. 3 the shrub, of the same family as the madder. [< Portuguese *ipecacuanha* < Tupi]

ip e cac u an ha (ip′ə kak′yü an′ə), *n.* ipecac.

Iph i ge ni a (if′ə jə nī′ə), *n.* (in Greek legends) the daughter of Agamemnon and Clytemnestra. Her father intended to sacrifice Iphigenia to Artemis to obtain favorable winds for the Greek ships sailing to Troy, but Artemis saved her and carried her off to become a priestess.

ip se dix it (ip′sē dik′sit), a dogmatic assertion; opinion based merely on someone's authority. [< Latin, he himself said (it)]

ip si lat er al (ip′sə lat′ər əl), *adj.* that is on the same side. [< Latin *ipse* self + English *lateral*]

ip so fac to (ip′sō fak′tō), by that very fact; by the fact itself. [< Latin]

IQ or **I.Q.,** intelligence quotient.

Ir, iridium.

ir-[1], *prefix.* the form of **in-**[1] before *r,* as in *irrational, irregular.*

ir-[2], *prefix.* the form of **in-**[2] before *r,* as in *irrigate.*

IRA or **I.R.A.,** Irish Republican Army (an association of outlawed Irish nationalists operating secretly by sabotage and other means for a united Irish republic).

I ran (i ran′, i rän′, ī ran′), *n.* country in SW Asia, south of the Caspian Sea. 28,662,000 pop.; 628,000 sq. mi. *Capital:* Teheran. Former name, **Persia.**

I ra ni an (i rā′nē ən, ī rā′nē ən), *adj.* of or having to do with Iran, its people, or their language. —*n.* 1 native or inhabitant of Iran. 2 language of Iran; Persian. 3 branch of Indo-European that includes Persian and Avestan.

I raq (i rak′, i räk′), *n.* country in SW Asia, west of Iran. 9,440,000 pop.; 170,000 sq. mi. *Capital:* Baghdad. See **Iran** for map.

hat, āge, fär; let, ēqual, tėrm;
it, īce; hot, ōpen, ôrder;
oil, out; cup, pu̇t, rüle;
ch, child; ng, long; sh, she;
th, thin; ᴛʜ, then; zh, measure;
ə represents *a* in about, *e* in taken, *i* in pencil, *o* in lemon, *u* in circus.
< = from, derived from, taken from.

I raq i (i rak′ē, i räk′ē), *adj.* of or having to do with Iraq, its people, or their language. —*n.* 1 native or inhabitant of Iraq. 2 the form of Arabic spoken in Iraq.

i ras ci bil i ty (i ras′ə bil′ə tē), *n.* quickness of temper; irritability.

i ras ci ble (i ras′ə bəl), *adj.* 1 easily made angry; with a quick temper; irritable. See **irritable** for synonym study. 2 showing anger. [< Late Latin *irascibilis* < Latin *irasci* grow angry < *ira* anger] —**i ras′ci ble ness,** *n.* —**i ras′ci bly,** *adv.*

i rate (ī′rāt, ī rāt′), *adj.* angry; enraged. —**i′rate ly,** *adv.*

IRBM, Intermediate Range Ballistic Missile.

ire (īr), *n.* anger; wrath. [< Old French < Latin *ira*]

Ire., Ireland.

ire ful (īr′fəl), *adj.* angry; wrathful. —**ire′ful ly,** *adv.*

Ire land (īr′lənd), *n.* 1 one of the British Isles, divided into the Republic of Ireland and Northern Ireland. 4,468,000 pop.; 32,500 sq. mi. See **British Isles** for map. 2 **Republic of,** country in NW, central, and S Ireland; Irish Republic; Eire. 2,944,000 pop.; 27,100 sq. mi. *Capital:* Dublin.

ir i des cence (ir′ə des′ns), *n.* display of changing colors; change of color when moved or turned: *the iridescence of mother-of-pearl.*

ir i des cent (ir′ə des′nt), *adj.* displaying changing colors; changing color when moved or turned. [< Latin *iris, iridis* rainbow] —**ir′i des′cent ly,** *adv.*

i rid i um (i rid′ē əm), *n.* a silver-white, hard, brittle metallic element which occurs in platinum ores and is twice as heavy as lead, used as an alloy with platinum for jewelry and the points of fountain pens. *Symbol:* Ir; *atomic number* 77. See pages 326 and 327 for table. [< New Latin < Latin *iris, iridis* rainbow; with reference to its iridescence in solution]

i ris (ī′ris), *n.* 1 any of a genus of plants with sword-shaped leaves and large, showy flowers most of which have three upright parts and three drooping parts; fleur-de-lis. 2 the flower of any of these plants. 3 the colored part around the pupil of the eye. It is a contractile disk between the cornea and the lens. The iris controls the amount of light entering the eye. See **eye** for diagram. 4 **Iris,** (in Greek myths) the goddess of the rainbow and messenger of the gods. 5 rainbow. [< Latin, rainbow < Greek]

I rish (ī′rish), *adj.* of or having to do with Ireland, its people, or their language. —*n.* 1 *pl. in use.* the people of Ireland or their descendants in other countries. 2 Irish Gaelic. 3 English as spoken by the Irish.

Irish Gaelic, the Celtic language of Ireland; Erse.

I rish man (ī′rish mən), *n., pl.* **-men.** man of Irish birth or descent.

Irish moss, a purplish or reddish-brown edible seaweed of the North Atlantic coasts; carrageen. When dried and bleached, it is used in making soups, blancmange, etc., and in ointments.

Irish potato, the common white potato.

Irish Republic, Republic of Ireland.

Irish Sea, part of the Atlantic between Ireland and England.

Irish setter
about 26 in. high
at the shoulder

Irish setter, a hunting dog with long, silky, reddish-brown hair.

Irish terrier, a small dog with reddish-brown, wiry hair, somewhat like a small Airedale.

Irish wolfhound, a very large and powerful dog, formerly used in hunting wolves and elk.

Irish wolfhound
about 31 in. high
at the shoulder

I rish wom an (ī′rish wu̇m′ən), *n., pl.* **-wom en.** woman of Irish birth or descent.

i ri tis (ī rī′tis), *n.* inflammation of the iris of the eye.

irk (ėrk), *v.t.* cause to feel disgusted, annoyed, or troubled; weary by being tedious or disagreeable: *It irks us to wait for people who are late.* [< Middle English *irken*]

irk some (ėrk′səm), *adj.* tiresome; tedious; annoying: *an irksome task.* **—irk′some ly,** *adv.* **—irk′some ness,** *n.*

Ir kutsk (ir kütsk′), *n.* city in SE Soviet Union. 451,000.

i ron (ī′ərn), *n.* 1 a very hard, strongly magnetic, silver-gray, heavy metallic element that is the commonest and most useful metal, from which steel is made. It is noted for its malleability and ductility when pure and for becoming oxidized in moist air. Iron occurs in the hemoglobin of the red blood cells where it serves to carry oxygen to all parts of the body. *Symbol:* Fe; *atomic number* 26. See pages 326 and 327 for table. 2 tool, instrument, or weapon made from this metal. 3 great hardness and strength; firmness: *men of iron.* 4 flatiron. 5 golf club with an iron or steel head. 6 branding iron. 7 **irons,** *pl.* chains or bands of iron; handcuffs; shackles. 8 **have too many irons in the fire,** try to do too many things at once. 9 **strike while the iron is hot,** act while conditions are favorable.
—*adj.* 1 made of iron: *an iron fence.* 2 having to do with iron. 3 like iron; hard and strong; unyielding: *an iron will.* 4 harsh or cruel: *the iron hand of fate.*
—*v.t.* 1 smooth or press (cloth, etc.) with a heated flatiron. 2 furnish or cover with iron. 3 **iron out,** smooth away or overcome (difficulties, differences, inconsistencies, etc.). —*v.i.* press clothes, etc., with a heated flatiron.
[Old English *īren, isern*]

Iron Age, period of human culture when iron began to be worked and used, It followed the Stone Age and the Bronze Age. In southern Europe the Iron Age started about 1000 B.C.

i ron bound (ī′ərn bound′), *adj.* 1 bound with iron. 2 hard; firm; rigid; unyielding. 3 rocky; craggy.

i ron clad (ī′ərn klad′), *n.* warship protected with iron plates. *—adj.* 1 protected with iron plates. 2 very hard to change or get out of: *an ironclad agreement.*

Iron Curtain, 1 an imaginary wall or dividing line separating the Soviet Union and the countries under Soviet control or influence from the non-Communist nations after World War II. Strict censorship and secrecy are enforced behind it. 2 **iron curtain,** any similar imaginary wall or dividing line.

i ron er (ī′ər nər), *n.* 1 person or thing that irons. 2 machine used to iron clothes, etc.

iron horse, INFORMAL. 1 an early steam locomotive. 2 bicycle or tricycle.

i ron ic (ī ron′ik), *adj.* ironical.

i ron i cal (ī ron′ə kəl), *adj.* 1 expressing one thing and meaning the opposite: *"Speedy" was the ironical name of our turtle.* 2 contrary to what would naturally be expected: *It was ironical that the man was run over by his own automobile.* 3 using or given to using irony. **—i ron′i cal ly,** *adv.*

ironing board, a padded board usually with folding legs and covered with a smooth cloth, used for ironing clothes, etc.

i ro nist (ī′rə nist), *n.* person, especially a writer, who takes an ironical view of life and things.

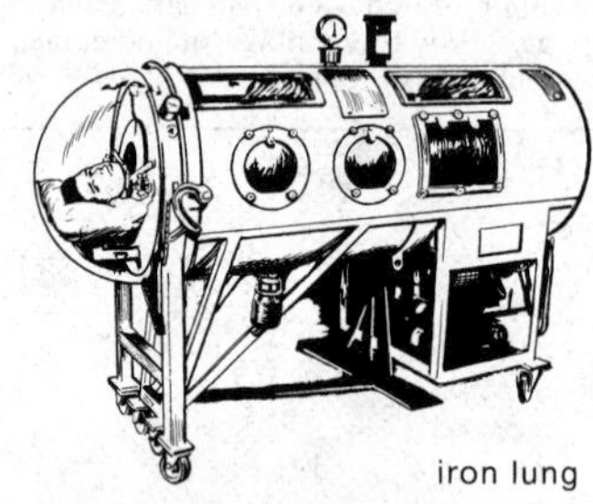

iron lung

iron lung, device which applies periodic pressure on the chest wall in order to force air in and out of the lungs, used to furnish artificial respiration to people whose chest muscles are paralyzed.

i ron mon ger (ī′ərn mung′gər, ī′ərn-mong′gər), *n.* BRITISH. dealer in ironware or hardware.

i ron mon ger y (ī′ərn mung′gər ē, ī′ərn-mong′gər ē), *n., pl.* **-ger ies.** BRITISH. shop or business of an ironmonger.

iron oxide, ferric oxide.

iron pyrites, pyrite.

I ron sides (ī′ərn sīdz′), *n.pl.* 1 regiment led by Oliver Cromwell. 2 his entire army. 3 **ironsides,** *pl. in form, sing. in use.* an armor-clad warship.

i ron stone (ī′ərn stōn′), *n.* 1 any clay, silica, or other type of rock that contains iron; iron ore. 2 type of very hard white pottery.

i ron ware (ī′ərn wer′, ī′ərn war′), *n.* articles made of iron, such as pots, kettles, tools, etc.; hardware.

i ron wood (ī′ərn wu̇d′), *n.* 1 any of various trees or shrubs with hard, heavy wood. 2 the wood itself.

i ron work (ī′ərn wėrk′), *n.* things made of iron; work in iron.

i ron work er (ī′ərn wėr′kər), *n.* 1 person whose work is making iron or iron articles. 2 person whose work is building the steel framework of bridges, skyscrapers, etc.

i ron works (ī′ərn wėrks′), *n. pl. or sing.* place where iron is made or worked into iron articles.

i ro ny (ī′rə nē), *n., pl.* **-nies.** 1 method of expression in which the ordinary meaning of the words is the opposite of the thought in the speaker's mind: *The boys called the very tall boy "Shorty" in irony.* 2 event or outcome which is the opposite of what would naturally be expected: *By the irony of fate farmers had rain when they needed sun.* 3 an ironical statement or expression; ironical quality. [< Latin *ironia* < Greek *eirōneia* dissimulation < *eirōn* dissembler]

➤ **Irony, sarcasm, satire** are often confused although they are not synonyms. *Irony* is the deliberate use of language in a sense opposite to that which the words ordinarily have; the hearer or reader must grasp the true meaning as well as the surface meaning: *that noble and loyal patriot, Benedict Arnold. Sarcasm* is the use of language to hurt, wound, or ridicule: *When a boy refers to another boy as "mama's little darling," he is using sarcasm. Satire* uses irony and sarcasm to expose and attack vices or follies: *In "Gulliver's Travels" Jonathan Swift makes notable use of satire.*

Ir o quoi an (ir′ə kwoi′ən), *n.* 1 family of North American Indian languages, including Huron, Mohawk, Oneida, Onondaga, Cayuga, Seneca, Tuscarora, and Cherokee. 2 Indian belonging to an Iroquoian tribe; Iroquois. *—adj.* of or having to do with the Iroquoian languages or the Iroquois.

Ir o quois (ir′ə kwoi, ir′ə kwoiz), *n., pl.* **-quois.** member of a powerful confederacy of American Indian tribes called the Five Nations (later, the Six Nations), formerly living mostly in what is now Quebec, Ontario, and New York State.

ir ra di ance (i rā′dē əns), *n.* radiance; shine.

ir ra di an cy (i rā′dē ən sē), *n.* irradiance.

ir ra di ant (i rā′dē ənt), *adj.* irradiating; radiant; shining.

ir ra di ate (i rā′dē āt), *v.,* **-at ed, -at ing.** —*v.t.* 1 shine upon; make bright; illuminate. 2 throw light upon intellectually; brighten spiritually. 3 radiate; give out. 4 treat with electromagnetic rays. —*v.i.* emit luminous rays; shine. **—ir ra′di a′tion,** *n.* **—ir ra′di a′tor,** *n.*

ir ra di a tive (i rā′dē ā′tiv), *adj.* serving to irradiate.

ir ra tion al (i rash′ə nəl), *adj.* 1 not rational; contrary to reason; unreasonable: *It is irrational to be afraid of the number 13.* 2 unable to think and reason clearly: *become irrational with rage.* 3 in mathematics: **a** (of an equation or expression) involving radicals or fractional exponents. **b** of or relating to an irrational number. **—ir ra′tion al ly,** *adv.*

ir ra tion al i ty (i rash′ə nal′ə tē), *n., pl.* **-ties.** 1 a being irrational. 2 something irrational; absurdity.

irrational number, any real number that

cannot be expressed as an integer or as a ratio between two integers. $\sqrt{2}$ and π are irrational numbers.

Ir ra wad dy River (ir′ə wod′ē), river flowing from E Tibet through Burma into the Bay of Bengal. 1300 mi.

ir re al i ty (ir′ē al′ə tē), *n.* lack of reality; unreality.

ir re claim a ble (ir′i klā′mə bəl), *adj.* that cannot be reclaimed. **—ir′re claim′a bly,** *adv.*

ir rec on cil a bil i ty (i rek′ən sī′lə bil′ə tē), *n.* a being irreconcilable.

ir rec on cil a ble (i rek′ən sī′lə bəl, i rek′ən sī′lə bəl), *adj.* that cannot be reconciled; that cannot be made to agree; opposed: *irreconcilable enemies.* —*n.* person who persists in opposing. **—ir rec′on cil′a ble ness,** *n.* **—ir rec′on cil′a bly,** *adv.*

ir re cov er a ble (ir′i kuv′ər ə bəl), *adj.* 1 that cannot be regained or got back: *Wasted time is irrecoverable.* 2 that cannot be remedied: *irrecoverable sorrow.* **—ir′re cov′er a ble ness,** *n.* **—ir′re cov′er a bly,** *adv.*

ir re deem a ble (ir′i dē′mə bəl), *adj.* 1 that cannot be redeemed or bought back. 2 that cannot be exchanged for coin: *irredeemable paper money.* 3 impossible to change; beyond remedy; hopeless: *an irredeemable mistake.* **—ir′re deem′a bly,** *adv.*

ir re den tism (ir′i den′tiz′əm), *n.* the system or political program of irredentists.

ir re den tist (ir′i den′tist), *n.* member of a party in any country advocating the taking over of some region in another country by reason of racial, cultural, or other ties with it. —*adj.* of irredentists; having to do with advocating irredentism. [< Italian *irredentista* < *(Italia) irredenta* unredeemed (Italy)]

ir re duc i bil i ty (ir′i dü′sə bil′ə tē, ir′i dyü′sə bil′ə tē), *n.* a being irreducible.

ir re duc i ble (ir′i dü′sə bəl, ir′i dyü′sə bəl), *adj.* 1 impossible to make less, smaller, simpler, etc. 2 unable to be changed or brought into a desired condition. 3 impossible to conquer or overcome.

ir ref ra ga bil i ty (i ref′rə gə bil′ə tē), *n.* a being irrefragable.

ir ref ra ga ble (i ref′rə gə bəl), *adj.* that cannot be refuted; unanswerable; undeniable. [< Late Latin *irrefragabilis* < Latin *in-* not + *refragari* oppose] **—ir ref′ra ga bly,** *adv.*

ir ref u ta bil i ty (i ref′yə tə bil′ə tē, ir′i fyü′tə bil′ə tē), *n.* a being irrefutable.

ir ref u ta ble (i ref′yə tə bəl, ir′i fyü′tə bəl), *adj.* that cannot be refuted or disproved; undeniable; unanswerable. **—ir ref′u ta bly,** *adv.*

ir re gard less (ir′i gärd′lis), *adj.* INFORMAL. regardless (not considered good usage).

ir reg u lar (i reg′yə lər), *adj.* 1 not regular; not according to rule; out of the usual order or natural way. 2 not according to law or morals: *irregular behavior.* See synonym study below. 3 not even; not smooth or straight; broken and rough; without symmetry: *New England has a very irregular coastline.* 4 not in the regular army: *irregular troops.* 5 (in grammar) not inflected in the usual way. *Be* is an irregular verb. —*n.* soldier not in the regular army. **—ir reg′u lar ly,** *adv.*

Syn. *adj.* 1, 2 **Irregular, abnormal** mean out of the usual or natural order or pattern. **Irregular** means not according to the accepted standard: *She has irregular habits.* **Abnormal** means a deviation from what is regarded as normal, average, or typical for the class: *Seven feet is an abnormal height for a man.*

ir reg u lar i ty (i reg′yə lar′ə tē), *n., pl.* **-ties.** 1 lack of regularity; being irregular. 2 something irregular.

ir rel a tive (i rel′ə tiv), *adj.* not relative; unrelated. **—ir rel′a tive ly,** *adv.*

ir rel e vance (i rel′ə vəns), *n.* 1 a being irrelevant. 2 something irrelevant.

ir rel e van cy (i rel′ə vən sē), *n., pl.* **-cies.** irrelevance.

ir rel e vant (i rel′ə vənt), *adj.* not to the point; off the subject: *an irrelevant question.* **—ir rel′e vant ly,** *adv.*

ir re li gion (ir′i lij′ən), *n.* 1 lack of religion. 2 hostility to religion; disregard of religion.

ir re li gious (ir′i lij′əs), *adj.* 1 not religious; indifferent to religion. 2 contrary to religious principles; impious. **—ir′re li′gious ly,** *adv.*

ir re me di a ble (ir′i mē′dē ə bəl), *adj.* that cannot be corrected or remedied; incurable. **—ir′re me′di a ble ness,** *n.* **—ir′re me′di a bly,** *adv.*

ir re mov a ble (ir′i mü′və bəl), *adj.* that cannot be removed. **—ir′re mov′a bly,** *adv.*

ir rep ar a ble (i rep′ər ə bəl), *adj.* that cannot be repaired, put right, or made good: *Losing a leg is an irreparable injury.* **—ir rep′ar a ble ness,** *n.* **—ir rep′ar a bly,** *adv.*

ir re place a ble (ir′i plā′sə bəl), *adj.* not replaceable; impossible to replace with another.

ir re press i bil i ty (ir′i pres′ə bil′ə tē), *n.* a being irrepressible.

ir re press i ble (ir′i pres′ə bəl), *adj.* that cannot be repressed or restrained; uncontrollable: *irrepressible laughter.* **—ir′re press′i ble ness,** *n.* **—ir′re press′i bly,** *adv.*

ir re proach a ble (ir′i prō′chə bəl), *adj.* free from blame; faultless. **—ir′re proach′a ble ness,** *n.* **—ir′re proach′a bly,** *adv.*

ir re sist i bil i ty (ir′i zis′tə bil′ə tē), *n.* a being irresistible.

ir re sist i ble (ir′i zis′tə bəl), *adj.* that cannot be resisted; too great to be withstood; overwhelming: *an irresistible desire to succeed.* **—ir′re sist′i ble ness,** *n.* **—ir′re sist′i bly,** *adv.*

ir res o lute (i rez′ə lüt), *adj.* not resolute; unable to make up one's mind; not sure of what one wants; hesitating; vacillating. **—ir res′o lute ly,** *adv.* **—ir res′o lute ness,** *n.*

ir res o lu tion (i rez′ə lü′shən), *n.* a being irresolute; lack of firm decision; hesitation.

ir re spec tive (ir′i spek′tiv), *adj.* without regard to particular persons, circumstances or conditions; regardless *(of): All students, irrespective of age, may join the club.* **—ir′re spec′tive ly,** *adv.*

ir re spon si bil i ty (ir′i spon′sə bil′ə tē), *n.* lack of responsibility; being irresponsible.

ir re spon si ble (ir′i spon′sə bəl), *adj.* 1 not responsible; that cannot be called to account. 2 without a sense of responsibility; untrustworthy; unreliable. **—ir′re spon′si bly,** *adv.*

ir re spon sive (ir′i spon′siv), *adj.* not responsive; not responding readily to speech, action, or feeling. **—ir′re spon′sive ness,** *n.*

ir re triev a ble (ir′i trē′və bəl), *adj.* that cannot be retrieved or recovered; impossible

hat, āge, fär; let, ēqual, tėrm;
it, īce; hot, ōpen, ôrder;
oil, out; cup, pu̇t, rüle;
ch, child; ng, long; sh, she;
th, thin; ᴛʜ, then; zh, measure;

ə represents *a* in about, *e* in taken, *i* in pencil, *o* in lemon, *u* in circus.

< = from, derived from, taken from.

to recall or restore to its former condition: *an irretrievable loss.* **—ir′re triev′a ble ness,** *n.* **—ir′re triev′a bly,** *adv.*

ir rev er ence (i rev′ər əns), *n.* 1 lack of reverence; disrespect. 2 instance of this; an irreverent act or utterance.

ir rev er ent (i rev′ər ənt), *adj.* not reverent; disrespectful. **—ir rev′er ent ly,** *adv.*

ir re vers i bil i ty (ir′i vėr′sə bil′ə tē), *n.* a being irreversible.

ir re vers i ble (ir′i vėr′sə bəl), *adj.* 1 not capable of being turned the other way. 2 unable to be changed or repealed; unalterable. **—ir′re vers′i bly,** *adv.*

ir rev o ca bil i ty (i rev′ə kə bil′ə tē), *n.* a being irrevocable.

ir rev o ca ble (i rev′ə kə bəl), *adj.* 1 not able to be revoked; final: *an irrevocable decision.* 2 impossible to call or bring back: *the irrevocable past.* **—ir rev′o ca bly,** *adv.*

ir ri ga ble (ir′ə gə bəl), *adj.* that can be irrigated.

ir ri gate (ir′ə gāt), *v.,* **-gat ed, -gat ing.** —*v.t.* 1 supply (land) with water by using ditches, by sprinkling, etc. 2 supply (a wound, cavity in the body, etc.) with a continuous flow of some liquid: *She irrigated her throat with warm water.* 3 refresh or make fruitful as if with a supply of moisture. —*v.i.* supply land, wounds, etc., with water or other liquid. [< Latin *irrigatum* watered, irrigated < *in-* + *rigare* to water, wet] **—ir′ri ga′tor,** *n.*

ir ri ga tion (ir′ə gā′shən), *n.* 1 an irrigating. 2 a being irrigated.

ir ri ta bil i ty (ir′ə tə bil′ə tē), *n., pl.* **-ties.** 1 a being irritable; impatience. 2 an unnatural sensitiveness of an organ or part of the body. 3 (in biology) the property that living plant or animal tissue has of responding to a stimulus.

ir ri ta ble (ir′ə tə bəl), *adj.* 1 easily made angry; impatient. See synonym study below. 2 unnaturally sensitive or sore: *irritable skin.* 3 (in biology) able to respond to stimuli. **—ir′ri ta ble ness,** *n.* **—ir′ri ta bly,** *adv.*

Syn. 1 **Irritable, irascible** mean easily made angry. **Irritable** means easily annoyed, either because of one's disposition or because of some temporary condition: *Ill health made him irritable.* **Irascible** implies a quick temper and a tendency to become angry at trifles: *an irascible old tyrant.*

ir ri tant (ir′ə tənt), *n.* thing that causes irritation: *Chlorine in swimming pools can be an irritant to the eyes.* —*adj.* causing irritation.

ir ri tate (ir′ə tāt), *v.t.,* **-tat ed, -tat ing.** 1 make impatient or angry; annoy; provoke; vex: *The boy's foolish questions irritated his father. Flies irritate horses.* 2 make unnaturally sensitive or sore: *Sunburn irritates the skin.* 3 (in biology) stimulate (an organ, muscle, tissue, etc.) to respond: *A muscle contracts when it is irritated by an electric* *shock.* [< Latin *irritatum* enraged, provoked] **—ir′ri tat′ing ly,** *adv.*

ir ri ta tion (ir′ə tā′shən), *n.* 1 act or process of irritating; annoyance; vexation. 2 irritated condition. 3 something that irritates.

ir ri ta tive (ir′ə tā′tiv), *adj.* serving or tending to irritate; annoying.

ir rupt (i rupt′), *v.i.* 1 break or burst in violently. 2 (of animals) to increase suddenly in population. [< Latin *irruptum* burst in < *in-* in + *rumpere* to break] **—ir rup′tion,** *n.*

ir rup tive (i rup′tiv), *adj.* bursting in; rushing in or upon anything.

IRS or **I.R.S.,** Internal Revenue Service.

Ir tysh River or **Ir tish River** (ir tish′), river flowing from NW China through S central Soviet Union to the Ob River. 1850 mi.

Ir ving (ėr′ving), *n.* 1 **Washington,** 1783-1859, American writer. 2 city in NE Texas. 97,000.

is (iz), *v.* 1 third person singular, present indicative of **be.** 2 **as is,** as it is now; in its present condition. [Old English]

is., 1 island or islands. 2 isle or isles.

Is. or **Isa.,** Isaiah.

I saac (ī′zək), *n.* (in the Bible) the son of Abraham and Sarah, and father of Jacob and Esau.

Is a bel la I (iz′ə bel′ə), 1451-1504, queen of Castile and León. She and her husband Ferdinand V were patrons of Christopher Columbus.

I sai ah (ī zā′ə, ī zī′ə), *n.* 1 Hebrew prophet of the late 700's B.C. 2 book of the Old Testament containing his prophecies.

I sai as (ī zā′əs, ī zī′əs), *n.* (in the Douay Bible) Isaiah.

Is car i ot (i skar′ē ət), *n.* 1 surname of Judas, the disciple who betrayed Jesus for thirty pieces of silver. 2 traitor.

is che mi a (i skē′mē ə), *n.* local anemia caused by an obstruction of the supply of arterial blood. [< New Latin *ischaemia* < Greek *ischaimos* that stops bleeding < *ischein* to hold, check + *haima* blood]

is che mic (i skē′mik, i skem′ik), *adj.* having to do with or affected with ischemia.

is chi al (is′kē əl), *adj.* having to do with the ischium.

is chi um (is′kē əm), *n., pl.* **-chi a** (-kē ə). the lowest bone of the three bones forming either half of the pelvis. [< New Latin < Greek *ischion*]

-ise, *suffix.* variant of **-ize.** ➤ See **-ize** for usage note.

I seult (i sült′), *n.* (in Arthurian legends) an Irish princess and wife of King Mark of Cornwall, loved by Tristan. Also, **Isolde.**

Is fa han (is′fə hän′), *n.* city in W Iran. In the 1800's Isfahan was the capital of Persia. 575,000.

-ish, *suffix forming adjectives from other adjectives and from nouns.* 1 somewhat ____: *Sweetish = somewhat sweet.* 2 like a ____: *Childish = like a child.* 3 like that of a ____: *Girlish = like that of a girl.* 4 of or having to do with ____: *English = of or having to do with England.* 5 inclined to be a ____: *Thievish = inclined to be a thief.* 6 near, but usually somewhat past ____: *Fortyish = near forty.* [< Old English *-isc*]

Ish ma el (ish′mē əl), *n.* 1 (in the Bible) the son of Abraham and Hagar, driven into the desert because of the jealousy of Sarah. 2 outcast.

Ish ma el ite (ish′mē ə līt), *n.* 1 descendant of Ishmael. 2 outcast.

Ish tar (ish′tär), *n.* (in Assyrian and Babylonian myths) the goddess of love, fertility, and war.

i sin glass (ī′zn glas′), *n.* 1 kind of gelatin obtained from the air bladders of sturgeon, hake, and similar fishes, used for making glue, clearing liquors, etc. 2 mica, especially in thin semitransparent layers. [alteration of Middle Dutch *huysenblas* sturgeon bladder]

I sis (ī′sis), *n.* (in Egyptian myths) the chief goddess of ancient Egypt, sister and wife of Osiris. She represented fertility.

isl., 1 island. 2 isle.

Is lam (is′ləm, i släm′), *n.* 1 the Moslem religion, based on the teachings of Mohammed as they appear in the Koran. It holds that there is only one God, Allah, and that Mohammed is his prophet. 2 Moslems as a group. 3 the countries inhabited by Moslems or under Moslem rule. [< Arabic *islām* submission (to the will of God)]

Is lam a bad (iz lä′mə bad), *n.* capital of Pakistan, in NE Pakistan. 50,000.

Is lam ic (i slam′ik, i släm′ik), *adj.* Moslem.

Is lam ism (is′lə miz′əm), *n.* the Moslem religion.

Is lam ite (is′lə mīt), *n., adj.* Moslem.

is land (ī′lənd), *n.* 1 body of land smaller than a continent and completely surrounded by water. 2 something resembling this. Platforms in the middle of busy streets are called traffic islands. 3 superstructure of an aircraft carrier. *—v.t.* make into an island or something resembling an island; isolate. [Old English *īgland* < *īg* island + *land* land; spelling influenced by *isle*] **—is′land like′,** *adj.*

is land er (ī′lən dər), *n.* native or inhabitant of an island.

islands of Lang er hans (läng′ər häns), islets of Langerhans.

island universe, (in astronomy) a galaxy.

isle (īl), *n.* 1 a small island. 2 island. [< Old French < Latin *insula*]

Isle of Man. See **Man, Isle of.**

Isle of Wight. See **Wight, Isle of.**

is let (ī′lit), *n.* a small island.

islets of Lang er hans (läng′ər häns), the small, scattered endocrine glands in the pancreas that secrete insulin. Also, **islands of Langerhans.** [< Paul *Langerhans,* 1847-1888, German physician and anatomist]

ism (iz′əm), *n.* INFORMAL. a distinctive doctrine, theory, system, or practice: *Communism and Fascism are well-known isms.* [< *-ism*]

-ism, *suffix forming nouns from other nouns and from adjectives and verbs.* 1 act or practice of ____ing: *Baptism = act or practice of baptizing.* 2 quality or condition of being a ____: *Heroism = quality of being a hero.* 3 illustration or instance of being ____: *Witticism = instance of being witty.* 4 an unhealthy condition caused by ____: *Alcoholism = an unhealthy condition caused by alcohol.* 5 doctrine, theory, system, or practice of ____: *Darwinism = theory of Charles Darwin.* [< Greek *-ismos, -isma*]

is n't (iz′nt), is not.

iso-, *combining form.* equal; alike: *Isometric = metrically equal.* [< Greek < *isos* equal]

i so bar (ī′sə bär), *n.* 1 line on a weather map connecting places having the same average atmospheric pressure. Isobars show the distribution of atmospheric pressure at a particular time, and are used in making forecasts of the weather. 2 one of two or more kinds of atoms that have the same atomic weight, but in most cases different atomic numbers. [< Greek *isobarēs* of equal weight < *iso-* + *baros* weight]

i so bar ic (ī′sə bar′ik), *adj.* 1 having or indicating equal atmospheric pressure. 2 having to do with isobars.

i so bath (ī′sə bath), *n.* line on a map connecting points that have the same depth below the surface of a body of water. [< *iso-* + Greek *bathos* depth]

i soch ro nous (ī sok′rə nəs), *adj.* 1 equal or uniform in time. 2 performed or happening in equal periods of time. 3 characterized by motions or vibrations of equal duration. **—i soch′ro nous ly,** *adv.*

i so cline (ī′sə klīn), *n.* (in geology) a fold of strata so tightly compressed that the parts on each side of the axis dip in the same direction.

i so e lec tric (ī′sō i lek′trik), *adj.* having equal electric potential.

i so en zyme (ī′sō en′zīm), *n.* one of the forms of an enzyme, differing chemically but not functionally, found in a single species of an organism; isozyme.

i so ga mete (ī′sō gə mēt′, ī′sō gam′ēt), *n.* either of two gametes, not differing in character or behavior, which can unite with the other to form a zygote. The gametes of certain algae are isogametes.

i sog a mous (ī sog′ə məs), *adj.* having isogametes; reproducing by the fusion of two similar gametes.

i sog a my (ī sog′ə mē), *n.* fusion of two similar gametes, as in certain algae.

i so gloss (ī′sə glôs, ī′sə glos), *n.* line on a map separating areas that differ in a given feature of language (pronunciation, syntax, etc.). [< *iso-* + Greek *glossa* tongue, word]

i so gon ic (ī′sə gon′ik), *adj.* having equal angles; having to do with equal angles. [< Greek *isogōnios* < *iso-* + *gōnia* angle]

isogonic line, line on a map connecting points on the earth's surface where the magnetic declination is the same.

i so late (ī′sə lāt, is′ə lāt), *v.t.,* **-lat ed, -lat ing.** 1 set apart; separate from others; keep alone: *People with contagious diseases should be isolated.* 2 obtain (a substance) in a pure or uncombined state: *A chemist can isolate the oxygen from the hydrogen in water.* [< French *isolé* < Italian *isolato* < Latin *insulatum* made into an island < *insula* island]

i so la tion (ī′sə lā′shən, is′ə lā′shən), *n.* 1 an isolating. 2 a being isolated.

i so la tion ism (ī′sə lā′shə niz′əm, is′ə-

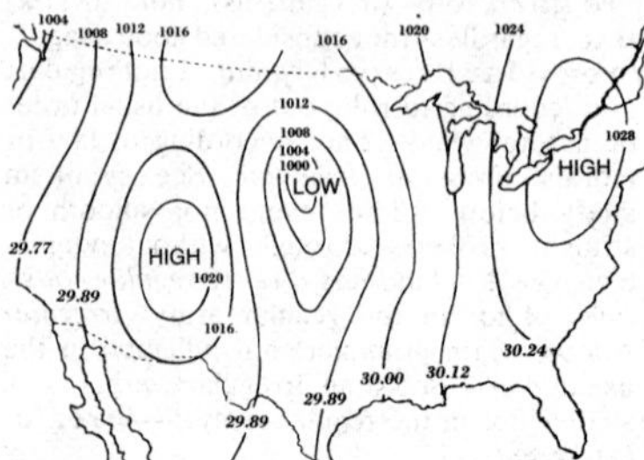

isobar (def. 1)
isobars with pressure given in inches at the bottom and millibars at the top

hat, āge, fär; let, ēqual, tėrm;
it, īce; hot, ōpen, ôrder;
oil, out; cup, pu̇t, rüle;
ch, child; ng, long; sh, she;
th, thin; ᴛʜ, then; zh, measure;

ə represents *a* in about, *e* in taken,
i in pencil, *o* in lemon, *u* in circus.

< = from, derived from, taken from.

lā′shə niz′əm), *n.* principle or policy of avoiding political and economic relations with other nations.

i so la tion ist (ī′sə lā′shə nist, is′ə lā′shə-nist), *n.* person who believes in or favors isolationism. *—adj.* of or having to do with isolationists or isolationism: *isolationist policies.*

I sol de (i sōl′də, i sōld′, i zôl′də), *n.* Iseult.

i so leu cine (ī′sə lü′sēn′, ī′sə lü′sən), *n.* an amino acid present in casein, body tissue, etc., that is essential to the diet of man and animals. *Formula:* $C_6H_{13}NO_2$

i so mer (ī′sə mər), *n.* an isomeric compound, ion, atom, etc. [< Greek *isomeres* sharing equally < *iso-* + *meros* part]

i so mer ic (ī′sə mer′ik), *adj.* 1 composed of the same chemical elements in the same proportions by weight, and having the same molecular weight, but differing in at least one physical or chemical property because of the difference in arrangement of atoms. 2 (of the nuclei of atoms) differing in energy and behavior, but having the same atomic number and mass number.

i som er ism (ī som′ə riz′əm), *n.* property or condition of being isomeric.

i som er ize (ī som′ə rīz′), *v.t., v.i.,* **-ized, -iz ing.** change into an isomer. **—i som′er-i za′tion,** *n.*

i som er ous (ī som′ər əs), *adj.* 1 having an equal number of parts, markings, etc. 2 (of a flower) having an equal number of members in each whorl.

i so met ric (ī′sə met′rik), *adj.* 1 having to do with equality of measure; having equality of measure. 2 having three equal axes at right angles to one another: *an isometric crystal.* 3 of isometrics. **—i′so met′ri cal-ly,** *adv.*

i so met rics (ī′sə met′riks), *n.pl.* physical exercises done without athletic activity, as by pressing one part of the body against another or against an object.

i so morph (ī′sə môrf′), *n.* an isomorphic organism or substance. [< *iso-* + Greek *morphē* form]

i so mor phic (ī′sə môr′fik), *adj.* 1 (in biology) having similar appearance or structure, but belonging to different species or races. 2 isomorphous.

i so mor phism (ī′sə môr′fiz′əm), *n.* property of being isomorphic or isomorphous.

i so mor phous (ī′sə môr′fəs), *adj.* crystallizing in the same form or related forms (used especially of substances of analogous chemical composition); isomorphic.

i so ni a zid (ī′sō nī′ə zid), *n.* drug chemically related to an isomer of nicotinic acid, used in the treatment of tuberculosis. *Formula:* $C_6H_7N_3O$

i so pod (ī′sə pod), *n.* any of an order of crustaceans having flat oval bodies, short abdomens, and, usually, seven pairs of similar legs. [< Greek *iso-* + *pous, podos* foot]

i so prene (ī′sə prēn′), *n.* a colorless, volatile, liquid hydrocarbon used in making synthetic rubber. *Formula:* C_5H_8

i so pro pyl alcohol (ī′sə prō′pəl), a colorless, flammable liquid used to make acetone, and as a solvent, rocket fuel, etc. *Formula:* $CH_3CHOHCH_3$

i sop ter an (ī sop′tər ən), *n.* any of the order of insects comprising the termites; termite. *—adj.* of or belonging to this order. [< *iso-* + Greek *pteron* wing]

i sop ter ous (ī sop′tər əs), *adj.* of or belonging to the isopterans.

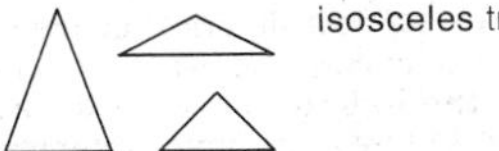

isosceles triangles

i sos ce les (ī sos′ə lēz′), *adj.* (of a triangle) having two sides equal. [< Late Latin < Greek *isoskelēs* < *iso-* + *skelos* leg]

i sos ta sy (ī sos′tə sē), *n.* 1 equilibrium of the earth's crust, believed to be due to the movement of rock material below the surface. 2 equilibrium or stability caused by equality of pressure. [< *iso-* + Greek *stasis* a stopping]

i so stat ic (ī′sə stat′ik), *adj.* having to do with or characterized by isostasy. **—i′so-stat′i cal ly,** *adv.*

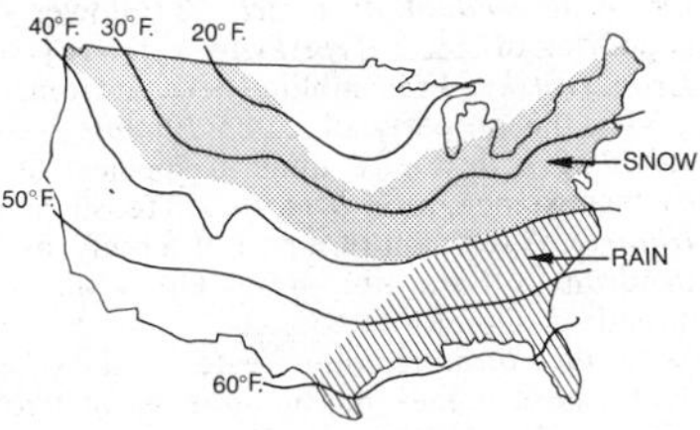

isotherm
isotherms on a map of the United States

i so therm (ī′sə thėrm′), *n.* line on a weather map connecting places having the same average temperature. [< *iso-* + Greek *therme* heat]

i so ther mal (ī′sə thėr′məl), *adj.* 1 having or indicating equal temperatures. 2 having to do with isotherms.

i so ton ic (ī′sə ton′ik), *adj.* having the same osmotic pressure. A solvent isotonic with a solution will not pass through a semipermeable membrane and mix with the solution.

i so tope (ī′sə tōp), *n.* any of two or more forms of a chemical element that have the same chemical properties and the same atomic number, but different atomic weights and slightly different physical properties. Chlorine, whose atomic weight is about 35.5, is a formation of two isotopes, one having an atomic weight of 37, the other, 35. Hydrogen and heavy hydrogen are isotopes. [< *iso-* + Greek *topos* place]

i so top ic (ī′sə top′ik), *adj.* of or having to do with an isotope or isotopes; like an isotope. **—i′so top′i cal ly,** *adv.*

i sot o py (ī sot′ə pē), *n.* occurrence or existence of isotopes.

i so trop ic (ī′sə trop′ik), *adj.* (in physics) having the same properties, such as elasticity or conduction, in all directions.

i so zyme (ī′sə zīm), *n.* isoenzyme.

Is ra el (iz′rē əl), *n.* 1 country in SW Asia, on the Mediterranean, including the major part of Palestine. It was the ancient land and kingdom of the Jews. 2,999,000 pop.; 8000 sq. mi. *Capital:* Jerusalem. See **Iran** for map. 2 kingdom in N Palestine formed when the original kingdom of Israel divided after the death of Solomon. See **Judah** for map. 3 (in the Bible) a name given to Jacob after he had wrestled with the angel. 4 name given to his descendants; the Jews; the Hebrews.

Is rae li (iz rā′lē), *n.* native or inhabitant of modern Israel. *—adj.* of or having to do with modern Israel.

Is ra el ite (iz′rē ə līt), *n.* Jew; Hebrew; descendant of Israel. *—adj.* of or having to do with Israel or the Jews.

Is sei (ēs′sā′), *n., pl.* **-sei.** a Japanese immigrant living in the United States or Canada. [< Japanese *issei* first generation]

is su ance (ish′ü əns), *n.* an issuing; issue.

is sue (ish′ü), *v.,* **-sued, -su ing,** *n.* *—v.t.* 1 send out; put forth: *The government issues money and stamps.* 2 put into public circulation; put out for sale or distribution; publish: *issue a new edition of a book.* 3 distribute officially to a person or persons: *Each soldier was issued a rifle.* 4 send forth; discharge; emit: *The chimney issues smoke from the fireplace.* *—v.i.* 1 come out; go out; proceed: *Smoke issues from the chimney.* See synonym study below. 2 be published. 3 emerge. 4 result or end *(in).* 5 result *(from).* 6 be born; be descended; be derived.

—n. 1 something sent out; quantity (of bonds, stamps, copies of a magazine, etc.) sent out at one time: *The last issue of our weekly paper consisted of 1000 copies.* 2 a sending out; a putting forth. 3 a coming forth; a flowing out; a discharge: *an issue of blood from the nose.* 4 way out; outlet; exit. 5 that which comes out. 6 profit; production. 7 result; outcome: *the issue of a battle.* 8 point to be debated; matter of dispute or discussion; problem: *political issues.* 9 child or children; offspring. **10 at issue, a** in question; to be considered or decided. **b** in disagreement. **11 join issue,** take opposite sides in an argument. **12 take issue,** disagree.

[< Old French < *issir, eissir* go out < Latin *exire* < *ex-* out + *ire* go] **—is′su a ble,** *adj.* **—is′su er,** *n.*

Syn. *v.i.* 1 **Issue, emerge, emanate** mean to come out. **Issue** is applied chiefly to what can be thought of as flowing out in a mass from a confined space through an opening: *Pus issued from the wound.* **Emerge** is applied to what can be thought of as coming into sight from a place where it has been hidden or covered up: *The train emerged from the tunnel.* **Emanate** means to flow out from a source: *The story emanated from the mayor's office.*

-ist, *suffix forming nouns chiefly from other nouns.* 1 person who does or makes: *Tourist = a person who tours.* 2 an expert in an art or science: *Botanist = an expert in botany.* 3 person who plays a musical instrument: *Organist = person who plays the organ.* 4 person engaged in or working with: *Journalist = a person engaged in journalism.* 5 person who believes in: *Socialist = a person who believes in socialism.* [< Greek *-istēs* < *-izein* -ize]

Is tan bul (is′tän bül′, is′tan bül′), *n.* city in NW Turkey, on the Bosporus. 2,248,000. Former name, **Constantinople.**

isth mi an (is′mē ən), *adj.* 1 of, having to do with, situated in, or forming an isthmus. 2 **Isthmian, a** of or having to do with the Isthmus of Panama. **b** of or having to do with the Isthmus of Corinth in Greece. *—n.* native or inhabitant of an isthmus.

Isthmian games, a national festival of ancient Greece, celebrated every two years on the Isthmus of Corinth.

isth mus (is′məs), *n.* a narrow strip of land with water on both sides, connecting two larger bodies of land. [< Latin < Greek *isthmos*]

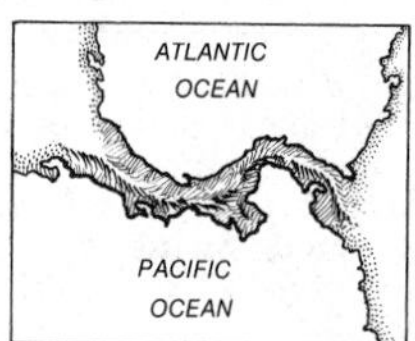

isthmus
isthmus
of Panama

ist le (ist′lē), *n.* fiber obtained from the leaves of certain tropical American agaves, used in making bags, carpets, cordage, nets, etc. [< Mexican Spanish *ixtle* < Nahuatl *ichtli*]

Is tri a (is′trē ə), *n.* peninsula in NW Yugoslavia, extending south into the Adriatic. **—Is′tri an,** *adj., n.*

it (it), *pron., nominative* **it,** *possessive* **its** or (OBSOLETE or DIALECT) **it,** *objective* **it;** *pl. nominative* **they,** *possessive* **their** or **theirs,** *objective* **them.** 1 the thing, part, animal, or person spoken about. 2 subject of an impersonal verb: *It snows in winter. It is cold.* 3 an apparent subject of a clause when the logical subject comes later: *It is hard to believe that she is dead.* 4 antecedent to any relative pronoun when separated by the predicate: *It was a blue car that passed.* 5 object without definite force or reference: *They lorded it over us.* *—n.* (in games) the player who must catch, find, guess, etc. [Old English *hit*]

It., 1 Italian. 2 Italy.

i.t.a. or **ITA,** Initial Teaching Alphabet (a system in teaching reading representing the speech sounds of English by means of 44 characters instead of 26).

ital., italic or italics.

Ital., 1 Italian. 2 Italy.

I tal ian (i tal′yən), *adj.* of Italy, its people, or their language. *—n.* 1 native or inhabitant of Italy. 2 the Romance language of Italy.

Italian So ma li land (sə mä′lē land′), former Italian colony in E Africa, now part of Somalia.

i tal ic (i tal′ik, ī tal′ik), *adj.* 1 of or in type whose letters slant to the right: *These words are in italic type.* 2 **Italic,** of ancient Italy, its people, or their Indo-European languages. *—n.* 1 an italic type, letter, or number. 2 **italics,** *pl.* type whose letters slant to the right. 3 **Italic,** branch of Indo-European including Latin and other ancient dialects of Italy.

➛ *italics.* In manuscript, both longhand and typewritten, italics are shown by single underlining.

i tal i cize (i tal′ə sīz), *v.,* **-cized, -ciz ing.** *—v.t.* 1 print in type in which the letters slant to the right. 2 underline with a single line to indicate italics. *—v.i.* use italics.

It a ly (it′l ē), *n.* country in S Europe on the Mediterranean. 53,670,000 pop.; 116,200 sq. mi. *Capital:* Rome.

I tas ca (ī tas′kə), *n.* **Lake,** lake in N Minnesota, a source of the Mississippi River. 2 sq. mi.

itch (ich), *n.* 1 a ticklish, prickling feeling in the skin that makes one want to scratch. 2 Usually, **the itch.** a contagious disease of the skin caused by a tiny mite, accompanied by this feeling. 3 a restless, uneasy feeling, longing, or desire for anything: *an itch to get away and explore.* *—v.i.* 1 cause an itching feeling: *Mosquito bites itch.* 2 have an itching feeling: *My nose itches.* 3 have an uneasy desire: *I itched to find out their secret.* *—v.t.* cause to itch: *This wool shirt itches my back.* [Old English *giccan* to itch]

itch y (ich′ē), *adj.,* **itch i er, itch i est.** itching; like the itch. **—itch′i ness,** *n.*

-ite[1], *suffix forming nouns.* 1 native or inhabitant of ___: *Canaanite = native or inhabitant of Canaan.* 2 descendant of ___: *Israelite = descendant of Israel.* 3 follower or supporter of ___: *Trotskyite = follower of Leon Trotsky.* 4 resembling, derived from, or having the property of ___: *Ebonite = resembling ebony.* 5 a mineral species, or a rock substance, as in *hematite.* 6 fossil, as in *trilobite.* 7 segment of a part of a body, as in *dendrite.* [< Latin *-ita, -ites* < Greek *-itēs,* or directly < Greek]

-ite[2], *suffix forming nouns.* ester or salt of an acid whose name ends in *-ous,* as in *phosphite, sulfite, nitrite.* [< French *-ite,* arbitrarily created variant of *-ate*[2]]

i tem (ī′təm), *n.* 1 a separate thing or article: *The list contains twelve items.* See synonym study below. 2 piece of news; bit of information: *There were several interesting items in today's paper.* *—adv.* also; likewise (in introducing each item of an enumeration). [< Latin adverb, likewise < *ita* thus]

Syn. *n.* 1 **Item, detail, particular** mean a separate thing that is part of a whole. **Item** applies to a separate thing included in a list, account, or total, or to an article listed: *An itemized account should list every item.* **Detail** applies to a separate thing that is part of a design, plan, structure, or the like: *Her report gave all the details.* **Particular** applies to a detail, item, etc., that is very small or insignificant: *Nobody wants to hear all the particulars of your troubles.*

i tem ize (ī′tə mīz), *v.t.,* **-ized, -iz ing.** give each item of; list by items: *itemize a bill.* **—i′tem i za′tion,** *n.*

item veto, (in the United States) veto of only part of a bill passed by a legislature and not of the entire bill. In some states, the governor may use this veto, but the Constitution does not grant it to the President.

it e rate (it′ə rāt′), *v.t.,* **-rat ed, -rat ing.** say again or repeatedly; repeat. [< Latin *iteratum* repeated < *iterum* again] **—it′e ra′tion,** *n.*

it e ra tive (it′ə rā′tiv, it′ər ə tiv), *adj.* repeating; full of repetitions.

Ith a ca (ith′ə kə), *n.* small island west of Greece, the legendary home of Ulysses. 5000 pop.; 37 sq. mi.

i tin er a cy (ī tin′ər ə sē, i tin′ər ə sē), *n.* itinerancy.

i tin er an cy (ī tin′ər ən sē, i tin′ər ən sē), *n.* 1 a traveling from place to place. 2 official work requiring much travel from place to place or frequent changes of residence.

i tin er ant (ī tin′ər ənt, i tin′ər ənt), *adj.* traveling from place to place, especially in connection with some employment or vocation. *—n.* person who travels from place to place. [< Late Latin *itinerantem* < Latin *iter* journey < *ire* go] **—i tin′er ant ly,** *adv.*

i tin e rar y (ī tin′ə rer′ē, i tin′ə rer′ē), *n., pl.* **-rar ies,** *adj.* *—n.* 1 route of travel; plan of travel. 2 record of travel. 3 guidebook for travelers. *—adj.* 1 of traveling or routes of travel. 2 itinerant.

i tin e rate (ī tin′ə rāt′, i tin′ə rāt′), *v.i.,* **-rat ed, -rat ing.** travel from place to place, especially in connection with some employment or vocation.

-itious, *combining form.* of or having the nature of ___: *Fictitious = having the nature of fiction.* [< Latin *-itius*]

-itis, *suffix forming nouns.* 1 inflammation of; inflammatory disease of, as in *appendicitis, bronchitis.* 2 state of mind or tendency fancifully regarded as a disease, as in the made-up word *telephonitis.* [< Greek, feminine of *-itēs* -ite[1]]

it'll (it′l), 1 it will. 2 it shall.

its (its), *adj.* possessive form of **it.** of it; belonging to it: *The dog wagged its tail.*

it's (its), 1 it is. 2 it has.

it self (it self′), *pron.* 1 emphatic form of **it.** *The land itself is worth the money, without the house.* 2 reflexive form of **it.** *The horse tripped and hurt itself.* 3 its normal or usual self.

-ity, *suffix forming nouns from adjectives.* quality, condition, or fact of being ___: *Sincerity = quality or condition of being sincere.* Also, **-ty.** [< Old French *-ité* < Latin *-itatem*]

I van III (ī′vən, i vän′), 1440-1505, grand duke of Muscovy from 1462 to 1505.

Ivan IV, 1530-1584, grand duke of Muscovy from 1533 to 1547, and czar of Russia from 1547 to 1584.

Ivan the Great, Ivan III.

Ivan the Terrible, Ivan IV.

I've (īv), I have.

-ive, *suffix forming adjectives from nouns.* 1 of or having to do with, as in *interrogative, inductive.* 2 tending to; likely to, as in *active, appreciative.* [< French *-ive* (feminine of *-if* < Latin *-ivus*) or directly < Latin]

Ives (īvz), *n.* **Charles Edward,** 1874-1954, American composer.

i vied (ī′vēd), *adj.* covered or overgrown with ivy.

i vor y (ī′vər ē), *n., pl.* **i vor ies,** *adj.* *—n.* 1 a hard, white substance composing the tusks of elephants, walruses, etc. Ivory is a form of dentine and is used for piano keys, billiard balls, combs, ornaments, etc. 2 substance like ivory. 3 a creamy white. 4 **ivories,** *pl.* SLANG. **a** piano keys. **b** dice. **c** teeth. *—adj.* 1 made of ivory. 2 of or like ivory. 3 creamy-white. [< Anglo-French *ivorie* < Latin *eboreus* of ivory < *ebur* ivory < Egyptian *āb* elephant]

Ivory Coast, country in W Africa, on the Atlantic. 4,310,000 pop.; 124,500 sq. mi. *Capital:* Abidjan.

ivory tower, place or condition of withdrawal from the world of practical affairs into a world of ideas and dreams.

i vy (ī′vē), *n., pl.* **i vies.** 1 a climbing plant of the same family as the ginseng, with smooth,

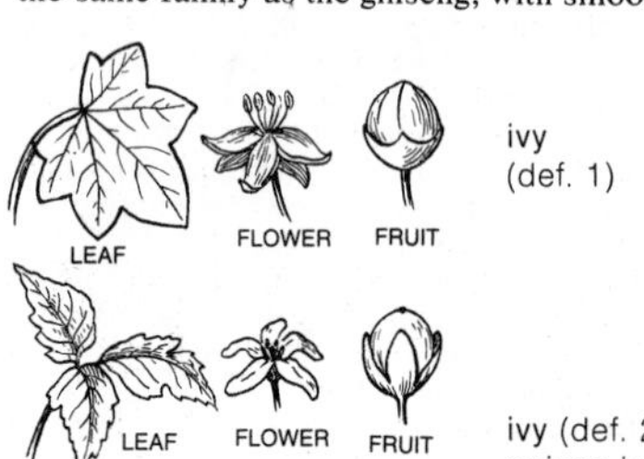

ivy (def. 1)

ivy (def. 2) poison ivy

shiny, evergreen leaves. It is native to Europe and parts of Asia, and bears clusters of greenish-yellow flowers, followed by dark berries. 2 any of various other climbing plants, such as poison ivy. [Old English *ifig*]

Ivy League, 1 group of eight old and prestigious universities of the northeastern United States, including Harvard, Yale, and Princeton. 2 of, having to do with, or characteristic of the Ivy League; marked by conservatism, restraint, breeding, etc.

i wis (i wis′), *adv.* ARCHAIC. certainly; indeed. [Old English *gewis*]

I wo Ji ma (ē′wō jē′mə), small island in the N Pacific belonging to Japan, site of a United States victory over Japanese forces in 1945. 8 sq. mi.

IWW or **I.W.W.,** Industrial Workers of the World.

Ix i on (ik sī′ən), *n.* (in Greek myths) the father of the centaurs, who made love to Hera and was punished by Zeus by being bound to an eternally revolving fiery wheel in Hades.

-ize, *suffix forming verbs from adjectives and nouns.* 1 make ___: *Legalize = make legal.* 2 become ___: *Crystallize = become crystal.* 3 engage in or use ___: *Criticize = engage in criticism.* 4 treat or combine with ___: *Oxidize = combine with oxygen.* 5 other meanings, as in *alphabetize, colonize, memorize.* Also, **-ise.** [< French *-iser* or Latin *-izare* < Greek *-izein,* or directly < Greek]

➤ **-ize, -ise.** American usage favors the spelling *-ize* for the suffix in words like *apologize, characterize, realize, revolutionize, visualize,* where British usage calls for *-ise.* A number of words which end in the sound of (-īz), however, do not include the suffix and do not have variant spellings. For instance, *chastise, devise, exercise, supervise,* and *surmise* are spelled only one way in American and British spelling.

Iz mir (iz′mir, iz mir′), *n.* seaport in W Turkey, on the Aegean Sea. 521,000. Former name, **Smyrna.**

iz zard (iz′ərd), *n.* ARCHAIC or DIALECT. the letter Z. [apparently variant of *zed* Z]

J or **j** (jā), *n., pl.* **J's** or **j's.** the tenth letter of the English alphabet.

J, joule.

j., joule.

J., 1 Judge. 2 Justice.

Ja., January.

jab (jab), *v.,* **jabbed, jab bing,** *n.* —*v.i., v.t.* 1 thrust with something pointed; poke: *jab a fork into a potato.* 2 (in boxing) to hit with a jab. —*n.* 1 a thrust with something pointed; poke. 2 (in boxing) a blow in which the arm is extended straight from the shoulder. [variant of Middle English *jobben*]

jab ber (jab′ər), *v.i., v.t.* talk or speak rapidly and indistinctly; chatter. —*n.* very fast, confused, or senseless talk; chatter. [probably imitative] **—jab′ber er,** *n.*

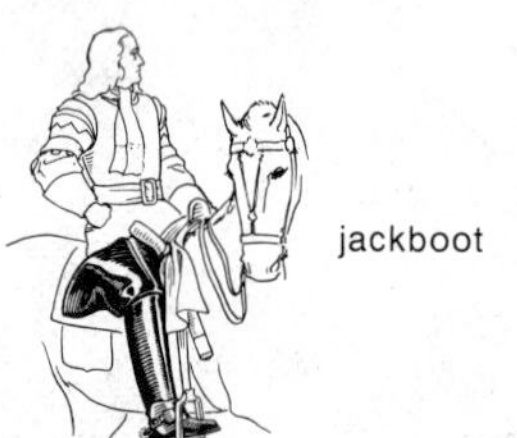

jackboot

jab ber wock y (jab′ər wok′ē), *n.* nonsensical talk or writing. [< *Jabberwocky,* a nonsense poem in Lewis Carroll's *Through the Looking-Glass*]

jab i ru (jab′ə rü′), *n.* a large, white stork of tropical America, with long legs and bill and a naked head and neck. [< Spanish or Portuguese *jabirú*]

ja bot (zha bō′, zhab′ō, jab′ō), *n.* ruffle or frill of lace, worn at the throat or down the front of a dress, shirt, or blouse. [< French]

jac a ran da (jak′ə ran′də), *n.* any of a genus of tropical American trees and shrubs of the same family as the bignonia, grown for their showy, tubular blue flowers and fragrant, ornamental wood. [< Portuguese *jacarandá* < Tupi (Brazil)]

ja cinth (jā′sinth, jas′inth), *n.* hyacinth. [< Old French *jacinte* < Latin *hyacinthus* hyacinth. Doublet of HYACINTH.]

jack (jak), *n.* 1 a portable tool or machine for lifting or pushing up heavy weights a short distance. 2 U.S. a playing card with a picture of a servant or soldier on it; knave. 3 pebble or small six-pointed metal piece used in the game of jacks; jackstone. 4 **jacks,** *pl.* a children's game in which jacks are tossed up and caught in various ways or are picked up while bouncing a ball; jackstones. 5 a small ball for players to aim at in lawn bowling. 6 a small flag used on a ship to show nationality or as a signal. 7 device for turning a spit in roasting meat. 8 a male donkey. 9 jack rabbit. 10 man or fellow. 11 Also, **Jack.** sailor. 12 an electrical device which can receive a plug to make a connection in a circuit. 13 SLANG. money.
—*v.t.* 1 lift or push up with a jack: *jack up a car.* 2 **jack up,** INFORMAL. raise (prices, wages, etc.). —*v.i.* hunt or fish with a jacklight.
[< *Jack,* proper name]

jackal (def. 1) about 15 in. high at the shoulder

jack al (jak′ôl, jak′əl), *n.* 1 any of several species of wild dogs of Asia, Africa, and eastern Europe, which hunt in packs at night and feed on small animals and carrion left by large animals. 2 person who does menial work for another. [< Turkish *çakāl* < Persian *shaghāl*]

jack a napes (jak′ə nāps), *n.* 1 an impertinent, forward person. 2 ARCHAIC. monkey or ape. [Middle English *Jack Napes,* name applied to William, Duke of Suffolk, 1396-1450, whose badge was a clog and chain, such as was used for tame apes]

jack ass (jak′as′), *n.* 1 a male donkey. 2 a very stupid or foolish person.

jack boot (jak′büt′), *n.* a heavy military boot reaching above the knee.

jack daw (jak′dô′), *n.* a small European crow; daw.

jack et (jak′it), *n.* 1 a short coat. 2 the outer, paper cover for a book; dust jacket. 3 the casing around a steam pipe. 4 the metal covering on a bullet. 5 the skin of a potato, etc. 6 any outer covering. —*v.t.* put a jacket on; cover with a jacket. [< Middle French *jaquet,* diminutive of *jaque* tunic < Spanish *jaco*]

Jack Frost, frost or freezing weather thought of as a person.

jack-in-the-box (jak′in ᴛʜə boks′), *n.* toy consisting of a box from which a figure springs up when the lid is unfastened.

jack-in-the-pul pit (jak′in ᴛʜə pu̇l′pit), *n.* a North American plant, a species of arum, with a greenish, petallike sheath arched over the flower stalk; Indian turnip; wake-robin.

jack knife (jak′nīf′), *n., pl.* **-knives,** *v.,* **-knifed, -knif ing.** —*n.* 1 a large, strong pocketknife. 2 kind of dive in which the diver touches his feet with his hands in midair, and straightens out before entering the water. —*v.t., v.i.* double up like a jackknife.

jack light (jak′līt′), *n.* U.S. light for hunting or fishing at night, especially one that attracts fish or game.

jack of all trades, person who can do many different kinds of work fairly well.

jack-o'-lan tern (jak′ə lan′tərn), *n.* 1 pumpkin hollowed out and cut to look like a face, used as a lantern at Halloween. 2 will-o'-the-wisp (def. 1).

jack pine, a slender pine tree growing in barren or rocky soil in the northeastern and midwestern United States and in Canada.

jack pot (jak′pot′), *n.* 1 stakes that accumulate in a poker game until some player wins with a pair of jacks or something better. 2 the accumulated stakes or the big prize of any game. 3 **hit the jackpot, a** get the big prize. **b** have a stroke of very good luck.

jack rabbit, a large hare of western North America, having very long hind legs and long ears.

jack screw (jak′skrü′), *n.* tool or machine for lifting heavy weights short distances, operated by a screw.

Jack son (jak′sən), *n.* 1 **Andrew,** 1767-1845, the seventh president of the United States, from 1829 to 1837. He was also a general in the War of 1812. 2 **Helen Hunt,** 1830-1885, American novelist who worked for American Indian rights. 3 **Jesse Louis,** born 1941, American civil rights leader. 4 **Thomas Jonathan,** 1824-1863, Confederate general. He was called "Stonewall" Jackson. 5 capital of Mississippi, in the central part. 154,000.

Jack so ni an (jak sō′nē ən), *adj.* of or like Andrew Jackson or his principles. —*n.* follower of Andrew Jackson.

Jack son ville (jak′sən vil), *n.* city in NE Florida. 529,000.

jack stone (jak′stōn′), *n.* 1 piece used in the game of jacks; jack. 2 **jackstones,** *pl.* the game of jacks.

jack straw (jak′strô′), *n.* 1 straw, strip of wood, bone, etc., used in the game of jackstraws. 2 **jackstraws,** *pl.* a children's game played with a set of jackstraws thrown down in a pile and picked up one at a time without moving any of the rest of the pile.

jack tar or **Jack Tar,** sailor.

Ja cob (jā′kəb), *n.* (in the Bible) the son of Isaac and Rebecca, and younger twin brother of Esau. The 12 tribes of Israel traced their descent from Jacob's 12 sons.

Jac o be an (jak′ə bē′ən), *adj.* 1 of King James I of England. 2 of the period of his reign, from 1603 to 1625. —*n.* statesman or writer of the time of James I. [< Late Latin *Jacobus* James]

Jac o bin (jak′ə bən), *n.* 1 member of a radical political club organized in 1789 during the French Revolution. 2 an extreme radical in politics. [< Old French < Medieval Latin *Jacobinus* of James; because the Jacobins' club was founded in a convent situated near the church of St. James in Paris]

Jac o bin ism (jak′ə bə niz′əm), *n.* 1 principles of the French Jacobins. 2 extreme radicalism in politics.

Jac o bite (jak′ə bīt), *n.* supporter of James II and his descendants (the Stuarts) in their claims to the English throne after the revolution in 1688. [< Late Latin *Jacobus* James]

Jac o bit ism (jak′ə bī′tiz′əm), *n.* the principles of the Jacobites; adherence to or sympathy with the cause of the Stuarts.

Jacob's ladder, 1 (in the Bible) a ladder to heaven that Jacob saw in a dream. 2 a rope ladder with wooden or metal rings, used on ships.

Ja cob's-lad der (jā′kəbz lad′ər), *n.* a common garden plant of the same family as the phlox, having ladderlike leaves.

jac o net (jak′ə net), *n.* a soft, light cotton cloth with a smooth finish. [alteration of *Jagannath,* India, where it was made]

jac quard (jə kärd′), *n.* fabric with a figured weave. [< Joseph *Jacquard,* 1752-1834, French weaver and inventor]

jade[1] (jād), *n.* 1 a hard stone used for jewels and ornaments. Most jade is green, but some is whitish. 2 a light green. —*adj.* light-green. [< French < Spanish *(piedra de) ijada* (stone of) colic (jade being supposed to cure this)] **—jade′like′,** *adj.*

jade[2] (jād), *n., v.,* **jad ed, jad ing.** —*n.* 1 an inferior or worn-out horse. 2 a disreputable, shrewish woman. —*v.t.* wear out; tire; weary. —*v.i.* become tired or weary; grow dull. [origin uncertain]

jad ed (jā′did), *adj.* 1 worn out; tired;

weary. 2 dulled from continual use; surfeited; satiated: *a jaded appetite.* **—jad′ed ly,** *adv.* **—jad′ed ness,** *n.*

jae ger (yā′gər, jā′gər), *n.* any of a genus of hawklike sea birds that pursue weaker birds and make them disgorge their prey. [< German *Jäger* hunter]

Jaf fa (jaf′ə), *n.* ancient seaport in W Israel, now a section of Tel Aviv. Ancient name, **Joppa.**

jag[1] (jag), *n., v.,* **jagged, jag ging.** *—n.* a sharp point sticking out; pointed projection: *a jag of rock.* *—v.t.* 1 cut or tear unevenly. 2 make notches in. [Middle English *jagge*]

jag[2] (jag), *n.* SLANG. 1 a period of unrestrained activity: *a crying jag.* 2 a drinking bout or spree. 3 DIALECT. a small load of hay, wood, etc. [origin unknown]

jag ged (jag′id), *adj.* with sharp points sticking out; unevenly cut or torn. **—jag′ged ly,** *adv.* **—jag′ged ness,** *n.*

jaguar—6 to 8 ft. long including tail

jag uar (jag′wär, jag′yü är), *n.* a large, fierce cat of the same genus as the lion, tiger, and leopard; panther. Jaguars resemble leopards but are more heavily built and live in forests in tropical America. [< Portuguese < Tupi *jaguara*]

ja gua run di (jä′gwə run′dē), *n.* a slender, short-legged, gray or reddish-brown wildcat, found from southwestern United States south to Argentina. [< Portuguese < Tupi]

Jah ve or **Jah veh** (yä′vā), *n.* Yahweh.

jai a lai (hī′ ä lī′), game similar to handball, played on a walled court with a hard ball, popular in Spain and Latin America; pelota. The ball is caught and thrown with a kind of curved wicker basket fastened to the arm. [< Spanish < Basque < *jai* festival + *alai* merry]

jail (jāl), *n.* prison, especially one for persons awaiting trial or being punished for minor offenses. *—v.t.* put in jail; keep in jail; imprison. Also, BRITISH **gaol.** [< Old French *jaiole,* ultimately < Latin *cavea* coop] **—jail′like′,** *adj.*

jail bird (jāl′bėrd′), *n.* INFORMAL. 1 prisoner in jail. 2 person who has been in jail many times.

jail break (jāl′brāk′), *n.* an escape from jail or prison.

jail er or **jail or** (jā′lər), *n.* keeper of a jail. Also, BRITISH **gaoler.**

Jain ism (jī′niz′əm), *n.* a religious system of southeast Asia established in the 500's B.C., stressing transmigration of the soul, nonviolence, and asceticism.

Jai pur (jī′pür), *n.* city in N India. 475,000.

Ja kar ta (jə kär′tə), *n.* Djakarta.

jal ap (jal′əp), *n.* 1 a yellow, sweet powder made from the dried roots of a Mexican vine of the same family as the morning-glory, used as a purgative. 2 the plant itself. [< Spanish *jalapa* < *Jalapa,* city in Mexico]

Ja lis co (hä lē′skō), *n.* state in W Mexico.

ja lop y (jə lop′ē), *n., pl.* **-lop ies.** INFORMAL. an old automobile or airplane in bad condition. [origin uncertain]

jal ou sie (jal′ə sē, zhal′ü zē′), *n.* 1 shade or shutter made of horizontal slats which may be tilted to let in light and air but keep out sun and rain. 2 window having a similar function, made of adjustable horizontal glass louvers set at an angle. [< French, literally, jealousy; because such shades prevent passers-by from looking in at the women of a household]

jam[1] (jam), *v.,* **jammed, jam ming,** *n.* *—v.t.* 1 press or squeeze tightly between two surfaces; wedge: *The ship was jammed between two rocks.* 2 crush by squeezing; bruise: *I jammed my fingers in the door.* 3 press or squeeze (things or persons) tightly together: *They jammed us all into one bus.* 4 fill or block up (the way, etc.) by crowding: *The river was jammed with logs.* 5 cause to stick or catch so that it cannot be worked: *The key broke off and jammed the lock.* 6 push or thrust (a thing) hard (into a place); shove: *jam one more book into the bookcase.* 7 make (radio signals, etc.) unintelligible by sending out others of approximately the same frequency. *—v.i.* 1 press or squeeze things or persons tightly together: *A crowd jammed into the bus.* 2 stick or catch so that it cannot be worked: *The window has jammed; I can't open it.* *—n.* 1 mass of people or things crowded together so that they cannot move freely: *a traffic jam.* 2 a jamming. 3 a being jammed. 4 INFORMAL. a difficulty or tight spot. [perhaps imitative]

jam[2] (jam), *n.* preserve made by boiling fruit with sugar until thick. [perhaps special use of *jam*[1]] **—jam′like′,** *adj.*

Jam., Jamaica.

Ja mai ca (jə mā′kə), *n.* island country in the West Indies, south of Cuba, a member of the Commonwealth of Nations. 2,000,000 pop.; 4400 sq. mi. *Capital:* Kingston. **—Ja mai′can,** *adj., n.*

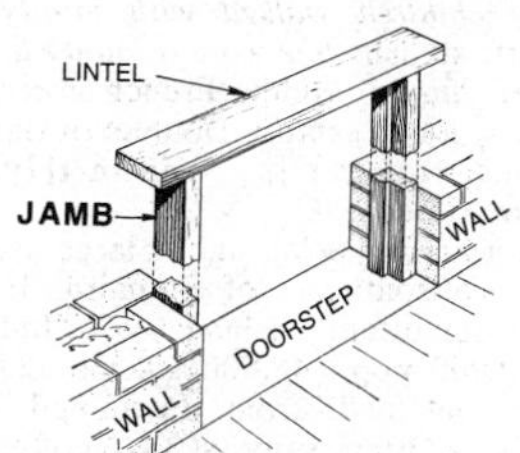

jamb (jam), *n.* an upright piece forming the side of a doorway, window, or fireplace. [< Old French *jambe,* originally, leg < Late Latin *gamba* hock < Greek *kampē* a bending]

jam ba lay a (jam′bə lī′ə), *n.* a Creole dish, usually consisting of ham or shrimp, rice, tomatoes, and spices. [probably < Haitian Creole < Provençal *jambalaia* stew made up of rice and fowl]

jam bo ree (jam′bə rē′), *n.* 1 a large rally or gathering of Boy Scouts. 2 INFORMAL. a noisy party; lively entertainment. [origin unknown]

James (jāmz), *n.* 1 in the Bible: **a** one of the apostles of Christ, sometimes called **James the Greater** (or **the Elder**). **b** another of the twelve apostles, sometimes called **James the Less** (or **the Younger**). **c** a brother of Jesus. 2 book of the New Testament. 3 **Henry,** 1843-1916, American novelist who lived in England. 4 **Jesse,** 1847-1882, American bandit and outlaw. 5 **William,** 1842-1910, American psychologist and philosopher, brother of Henry James. 6 **James River, a** river flowing from W Virginia into Chesapeake Bay. 340 mi. **b** river flowing from central North Dakota south through E South Dakota into the Missouri. 710 mi.

hat, āge, fär; let, ēqual, tėrm;
it, īce; hot, ōpen, ôrder;
oil, out; cup, pu̇t, rüle;
ch, child; ng, long; sh, she;
th, thin; ᴛʜ, then; zh, measure;
ə represents *a* in about, *e* in taken, *i* in pencil, *o* in lemon, *u* in circus.
< = from, derived from, taken from.

James I, 1566-1625, the first Stuart king of England, from 1603 to 1625. As James VI, he was king of Scotland from 1567 to 1625. The King James version of the Bible was written during his reign.

James II, 1633-1701, king of England from 1685 to 1688. He was deposed by Parliament.

James VI. See **James I.**

James Bay, the S part of Hudson Bay, in SE Canada. 350 mi. long.

James town (jāmz′toun), *n.* restored village in SE Virginia. The first successful English settlement in North America was made there in 1607.

jam mer (jam′ər), *n.* 1 device to jam radio signals. 2 person using such a device.

Jam mu and Kashmir (jum′ü), the official name of **Kashmir.**

jam-packed (jam′pakt′), *adj.* filled to absolute capacity; packed tightly.

jam session, gathering at which musicians play popular compositions with lively improvisations.

Jan., January.

Ja ná ček (yän′ə chek′), *n.* **Leoš,** 1854-1928, Czech composer.

jan gle (jang′gəl), *v.,* **-gled, -gling,** *n.* *—v.i.* 1 sound harshly; make a loud, clashing noise: *The pots and pans jangled in the kitchen.* 2 talk or argue in an angry or quarrelsome manner. *—v.t.* 1 cause to make a harsh, clashing sound: *The children jangled the cowbells.* 2 utter or give forth in an angry, quarrelsome manner. *—n.* 1 a harsh sound; clashing noise or ring. 2 a quarrel; dispute. [< Old French *jangler*] **—jan′gler,** *n.*

Jan is sar y or **jan is sar y** (jan′ə ser′ē), *n., pl.* **-sar ies.** Janizary.

jan i tor (jan′ə tər), *n.* 1 person hired to take care of an apartment house, school, office building, etc.; caretaker. 2 doorkeeper. [< Latin, doorkeeper < *janua* door < *janus* arched passageway; Janus]

jan i to ri al (jan′ə tôr′ē əl, jan′ə tōr′ē əl), *adj.* of or having to do with a janitor.

jan i tress (jan′ə tris), *n.* a woman janitor.

Jan i zar y or **jan i zar y** (jan′ə zer′ē), *n., pl.* **-zar ies.** 1 a Turkish soldier in the Sultan's guard, which existed from the 1300's until 1826. Janizaries formed the main fighting force of the Turkish army. 2 any Turkish soldier. Also, **Janissary, janissary.** [< Middle French *janissaire* < Italian *giannizzero* < Turkish *yeniçeri*]

Jan u ar y (jan′yü er′ē), *n., pl.* **-ar ies.** the first month of the year. It has 31 days. [< Latin *Januarius* < *Janus* Janus]

Ja nus (jā′nəs), *n.* (in Roman myths) the god

of gates and doors, and of beginnings and endings, represented with two faces, one looking forward and the other backward.

Jap., 1 Japan. 2 Japanese.

ja pan (jə pan′), *n., v.,* **-panned, -pan ning.** —*n.* 1 a hard, glossy varnish. Black japan is used on wood or metal. 2 articles varnished and ornamented in the Japanese manner. —*v.t.* varnish with japan or any similar substance. [< *Japan*]

Ja pan (jə pan′), *n.* 1 country made up of four large islands and many smaller ones, in the W Pacific east of the Asian mainland. 104,650,000 pop.; 142,700 sq. mi. *Capital:* Tokyo. See **China** for map. Also, JAPANESE **Nippon.** 2 **Sea of,** part of the Pacific between Japan and the Asian mainland. 405,000 sq. mi.

Japan Current, a strong, warm current that begins near the Philippines and flows northeastward, past Japan, across the Pacific Ocean.

Jap a nese (jap′ə nēz′), *adj., n., pl.* **-nese.** —*adj.* of Japan, its people, or their language. —*n.* 1 native or inhabitant of Japan. 2 language of Japan. Also, **Nipponese.**

Japanese beetle, a small green-and-brown beetle that eats fruits, leaves, and grasses. It was accidentally brought from Japan to the United States, where it has done much damage to crops.

Japanese ivy, a fast-growing woody vine, of the same genus as the Virginia creeper, much used to ornament walls; Boston ivy.

Japanese quince, japonica.

jape (jāp), *n., v.,* **japed, jap ing.** —*n.* 1 joke or gibe. 2 trick. —*v.t.* 1 mock; insult. 2 trick; deceive. —*v.i.* joke or jeer. [Middle English] **—jap′er,** *n.*

jap er y (jā′pər ē), *n., pl.* **-er ies.** jest; gibe.

ja pon i ca (jə pon′ə kə), *n.* 1 camellia. 2 an Asiatic shrub of the rose family, with showy red, pink, or white flowers; Japanese quince. [< New Latin, literally, Japanese]

jar[1] (jär), *n.* 1 a deep container made of glass, earthenware, or stone, with a wide mouth. 2 amount that it holds; jarful. [< Middle French *jarre* earthen vessel, ultimately < Arabic *jarrah*]

jar[2] (jär), *v.,* **jarred, jar ring,** *n.* —*v.t.* 1 cause to shake or rattle; vibrate: *Your heavy footsteps jar my table.* 2 have a harsh, unpleasant effect on; send a shock through (the ears, nerves, feelings, etc.): *The children's screams jarred my nerves.* —*v.i.* 1 make a harsh, grating noise. 2 shake; rattle: *The windows jarred when the wind blew.* 3 clash; quarrel; conflict: *Our opinions jar.* —*n.* 1 a shake; rattle. 2 a harsh, grating noise. 3 a slight shock to the ears, nerves, feelings, etc.; harsh, unpleasant effect. 4 a clash; quarrel. [probably imitative]

jar di niere (järd′n ir′), *n.* an ornamental pot or stand for flowers or plants. [< French *jardinière* < *jardin* garden]

jar ful (jär′fůl), *n., pl.* **-fuls.** as much as a jar will hold.

jar gon (jär′gən, jär′gon), *n.* 1 confused, meaningless talk or writing. 2 language that is not understood. 3 language or dialect composed of a mixture of two or more languages, such as pidgin English. 4 language of a special group, profession, etc. Doctors, actors, and sailors have jargons. —*v.i.* talk jargon. [< Old French]

jas mine or **jas min** (jas′mən, jaz′mən), *n.* 1 any of a genus of shrubs or vines of the olive family, with clusters of fragrant yellow, white, or reddish flowers. 2 any of several plants of other families bearing fragrant flowers. Also, **jessamine.** [< French *jasmin* < Arabic *yāsmīn* < Persian]

Ja son (jā′sn), *n.* (in Greek legends) the Greek hero who led the expedition of the Argonauts and secured the Golden Fleece.

jas per (jas′pər), *n.* an opaque, colored, granular quartz, usually red, yellow, or brown. [< Old French *jaspre* < Latin *iaspis* < Greek < Phoenician]

Jas per Park (jas′pər), national park in SW Canada, in the Rocky Mountains, in W Alberta. 4200 sq. mi.

Jas sy (yä′sē), *n.* city in NE Romania. 184,000. Also, **Iaşi.**

ja to (jā′tō), *n.* unit consisting of one or more rocket engines, used to provide auxiliary jet propulsion for speeding up the take-off of an airplane or for helping it to take off with heavy loads. [< *j(et)* + *a(ssisted)* + *t(ake)-o(ff)*]

jaun dice (jôn′dis, jän′dis), *n., v.,* **-diced, -dic ing.** —*n.* 1 an unhealthy bodily condition characterized by yellowness of the skin, eyes, and body fluids, caused by too much bile pigment in the blood; icterus. It is a symptom of some diseases and ailments, such as hepatitis. 2 a disturbed or unnaturally sour mental outlook, due to envy, discontent, jealousy, etc. —*v.t.* 1 cause jaundice in. 2 prejudice the mind and judgment of, by envy, discontent, jealousy, etc.; sour the temper of. [< Old French *jaunice* < *jaune* yellow < Latin *galbinus* greenish-yellow]

jaunt (jônt, jänt), *n.* a short journey or excursion, especially for pleasure. —*v.i.* take such a journey or excursion. [origin uncertain]

jaun ty (jôn′tē, jän′tē), *adj.,* **-ti er, -ti est.** 1 easy and lively; sprightly; carefree: *The happy children walked with jaunty steps.* 2 smart; stylish: *She wore a jaunty little hat.* [earlier *janty* < Middle French *gentil* noble, gentle < Latin *gentilis.* Doublet of GENTEEL, GENTILE, GENTLE.] **—jaun′ti ly,** *adv.* **—jaun′ti ness,** *n.*

Ja va (jä′və, jav′ə), *n.* 1 large island in Indonesia southeast of Sumatra. It is the most important island of Indonesia. 74,000,000 pop.; 48,800 sq. mi. 2 kind of coffee obtained from Java and nearby islands. 3 Often, **java.** SLANG. coffee.

Java man, a prehistoric man of the Pleistocene period, known from fossil remains found in Java; Pithecanthropus.

Jav a nese (jav′ə nēz′, jä′və nēz′), *adj., n., pl.* **-nese.** —*adj.* of Java, its people, or their language. —*n.* 1 native or inhabitant of Java. 2 language of Java.

jave lin (jav′lən), *n.* 1 a light spear thrown by hand. 2 a wooden or metal spear, thrown for distance in athletic contests. [< Middle French *javeline*]

jaw (jô), *n.* 1 the lower part of the face. 2 the upper or lower bone, or set of bones, that together form the framework of the mouth. The lower jaw is movable. 3 Usually, **jaws,** *pl.* mouth with its jawbones and teeth. 4 **jaws,** *pl.* **a** a narrow entrance to a valley, mountain pass, channel, etc. **b** the parts in a tool or machine that grip and hold. A vise has jaws. 5 SLANG. talk; gossip. —*v.i.* SLANG. 1 go on talking at great length, in a boring way. 2 find fault; scold. —*v.t.* SLANG. scold or lecture (a person). [Middle English *jowe*]

jaw bone (jô′bōn′), *n.* one of the bones in which the teeth are set, especially the lower jaw.

jaw break er (jô′brā′kər), *n.* 1 INFORMAL. word that is hard to pronounce. 2 a large, hard piece of candy, usually in the shape of a ball.

jaw less (jô′lis), *adj.* 1 having no jaws. 2 having no lower jaw, as a lamprey or hagfish.

jay (jā), *n.* any of various crested birds of Europe and North America which are of the same family as the crow, such as the blue jay. [< Old French]

Jay (jā), *n.* **John,** 1745-1829, American statesman, the first chief justice of the United States Supreme Court, from 1789 to 1795.

Jay cee (jā′sē′), *n.* INFORMAL. 1 a junior chamber of commerce. 2 one of its members. [< *J(unior) C(hamber of Commerce)*]

Jay hawk er (jā′hô′kər), *n.* native or inhabitant of Kansas.

jay vee (jā′vē′), *n.* INFORMAL. 1 a junior varsity team. 2 one of its members. [< *j(unior) v(arsity)*]

jay walk (jā′wôk′), *v.i.* INFORMAL. walk across a street without paying attention to traffic rules. [< *jay* a stupid person + *walk*] **—jay′walk′er,** *n.*

jazz (jaz), *n.* 1 class of music in which melody is subordinate to syncopated rhythms, characterized by improvisation, the use of dissonances, sliding from tone to tone, and the imitation of vocal effects by the instruments. Jazz is native to the United States. 2 dance music in the style of jazz. 3 SLANG. liveliness. 4 SLANG. worthless nonsense. —*adj.* of or like jazz: *a jazz band.* —*v.t.* 1 play (music) as jazz. 2 **jazz up,** SLANG. make lively; add flavor or interest to. —*v.i.* play jazz music or dance to jazz music. [of American Negro origin]

jazz man (jaz′man′, jaz′mən), *n., pl.* **-men.** man who plays jazz; jazz musician.

jazz y (jaz′ē), *adj.,* **jazz i er, jazz i est.** 1 having to do with or suggestive of jazz music. 2 SLANG. wildly active or lively. 3 SLANG. too fancy; ornate; flashy. **—jazz′i ly,** *adv.* **—jazz′i ness,** *n.*

J.C.C., Junior Chamber of Commerce.

JCS, Joint Chiefs of Staff.

jct., junction.

Je., June.

jeal ous (jel′əs), *adj.* 1 fearful that a person one loves may love or prefer someone else. 2 full of envy; envious: *He is jealous of his brother's good grades.* 3 requiring complete loyalty or faithfulness: *"The Lord thy God is a jealous God."* 4 watchful in keeping or guarding something; careful: *Our city is jealous of its rights within the State.* 5 close; watchful; suspicious: *The dog was a jealous guardian of the child.* [< Old French *gelos* < Late Latin *zelosus* < Latin *zelus* zeal < Greek *zēlos.* Doublet of ZEALOUS.] **—jeal′ous ly,** *adv.* **—jeal′ous ness,** *n.*

jeal ous y (jel′ ə sē), *n., pl.* **-ous ies.** dislike or fear of rivals; jealous condition or feeling; envy.

jean (jēn), *n.* 1 a strong, twilled cotton cloth, used for overalls, etc. 2 **jeans,** *pl.* trousers made of this cloth. [probably < French *Gênes* Genoa]

Jeanne d'Arc (zhän′ därk′), French name of **Joan of Arc.**

Jeans (jēnz), *n.* Sir **James H.,** 1877-1946, English mathematician, physicist, and astronomer.

Jeb el Mu sa (jeb′əl mü′sä), mountain in N Morocco, opposite Gibraltar. 2800 ft.

hat, āge, fär; let, ēqual, tėrm;
it, īce; hot, ōpen, ôrder;
oil, out; cup, pu̇t, rüle;
ch, child; ng, long; sh, she;
th, thin; ᴛʜ, then; zh, measure;

ə represents *a* in about, *e* in taken, *i* in pencil, *o* in lemon, *u* in circus.

< = from, derived from, taken from.

Jed da (jed′ə), *n.* Jidda.

jeep (jēp), *n.* a small, powerful general-purpose automobile with four-wheel drive, used by soldiers, farmers, builders, etc. It was originally designed for use by the United States Army. 2 **Jeep,** trademark for an automobile of similar design, for civilian use.

jeer (jir), *v.i.* make fun rudely or unkindly; mock; scoff. See **scoff** for synonym study. *—v.t.* speak to or treat with scornful derision. *—n.* a mocking or insulting remark; rude, sarcastic comment. [origin uncertain] **—jeer′er,** *n.* **—jeer′ing ly,** *adv.*

Jef fer son (jef′ər sən), *n.* **Thomas,** 1743-1826, American statesman, third president of the United States, from 1801 to 1809. He drafted the Declaration of Independence.

Jefferson City, capital of Missouri, in the central part. 32,000.

Jef fer so ni an (jef′ər sō′nē ən), *adj.* of or like Thomas Jefferson or his political principles. *—n.* follower of Thomas Jefferson.

Je hosh a phat (ji hosh′ə fat, ji hos′ə fat), *n.* a king of Judah from 873? to 848? B.C.

Je ho vah (ji hō′və), *n.* one of the names of God in the Old Testament. [modern representation of Hebrew *Yahweh,* originally written without vowels as JHVH]

Jehovah's Witness, member of a Christian sect founded in the 1870's, which maintains that governments and organized religions are evil, that personal religious conviction is beyond civil authority, and that the end of the world is near.

je hu (jē′hyü), *n.* INFORMAL. 1 a fast driver. 2 coachman. [< *Jehu,* with reference to his furious driving (II Kings 9:20)]

Je hu (jē′hyü), *n.* died 815 B.C., king of Israel from 842 to 815 B.C.

je june (ji jün′), *adj.* 1 flat and uninteresting. 2 lacking nourishing qualities. 3 immature; juvenile. [< Latin *jejunus,* originally, hungry] **—je june′ly,** *adv.* **—je june′ness,** *n.*

je ju num (ji jü′nəm), *n.* the middle portion of the small intestine, between the duodenum and the ileum. [< New Latin < Latin, neuter, empty]

Jek yll (jek′əl, jē′kəl), *n.* **Dr.,** a good, kind doctor in Robert Louis Stevenson's story *Dr. Jekyll and Mr. Hyde,* who discovered a drug that would change him into a brutal character called Mr. Hyde and another that would change him back to himself.

jell (jel), *v.i.* 1 become jelly; thicken or congeal. 2 INFORMAL. take definite form; become fixed: *His hunch soon jelled into a plan.* *—v.t.* cause to jell. *—n.* jelly.

Jel li coe (jel′ə kō), *n.* **John,** Earl, 1859-1935, English admiral.

jel lied (jel′ēd), *adj.* 1 turned into jelly; having the consistency of jelly. 2 spread with jelly.

jel ly (jel′ē), *n., pl.* **-lies,** *v.,* **-lied, -ly ing.** *—n.* 1 a food, liquid when hot, but somewhat firm and partly transparent when cold. Jelly can be made by boiling fruit juice and sugar together, by cooking bones and meat in water, or by using some thickening agent like gelatin. 2 a jellylike substance. *—v.i.* become jelly or like jelly; turn into jelly; thicken; congeal. *—v.t.* 1 make into jelly. 2 spread with jelly. [< Old French *gelee,* originally past participle of *geler* congeal < Latin *gelare*] **—jel′ly like′,** *adj.*

jel ly bean (jel′ē bēn′), *n.* a small candy made of jellied sugar, often shaped like a bean.

jel ly fish (jel′ē fish′), *n., pl.* **-fish es** or **-fish.** 1 any of a class of invertebrate sea animals with dome-shaped bodies formed of a mass of almost transparent jellylike tissue; scyphozoan; medusa. Most jellyfish have long, trailing tentacles that may bear stinging cells. 2 any similar animal, such as the free-swimming form of a hydrozoan; medusa.

jel ly roll (jel′ē rōl′), *n.* layer of sponge cake spread with jelly, rolled up, and often sprinkled with sugar.

Je na (yā′nä), *n.* city in S East Germany. Napoleon Bonaparte defeated the Prussians near there in 1806. 85,000.

Jen ghis Khan (jeng′gis kän′), Genghis Khan.

Jen ner (jen′ər), *n.* **Edward,** 1749-1823, English physician who discovered vaccination.

jen net (jen′it), *n.* 1 a small Spanish horse. 2 a female donkey. Also, **genet.** [< Middle French *genet* < Spanish *jinete* mounted soldier < Arabic *Zenāta,* name of a Berber tribe noted for its cavalry]

jen ny (jen′ē), *n., pl.* **-nies.** 1 spinning jenny. 2 female of certain animals and birds. [< *Jenny,* proper name]

jeop ar dize (jep′ər dīz), *v.t.,* **-dized, -diz ing.** put in danger; risk; endanger; imperil: *jeopardize one's fortune by making bad investments.*

jeop ar dy (jep′ər dē), *n.* 1 risk; danger; peril: *The woodman's life was in jeopardy as the tree suddenly fell.* 2 (in law) the danger of being convicted and punished when tried for a crime. [< Old French *jeu parti* an even or divided game]

Jeph thah (jef′thə), *n.* (in the Bible) a judge of Israel who sacrificed his only daughter to fulfill a rash vow.

Jer., 1 Jeremiah. 2 Jersey.

jerboa
15 in. long
including tail

jer bo a (jər bō′ə), *n.* any of a family of small, nocturnal, mouselike mammals inhabiting arid regions of Asia and northern Africa, having a long tail and long hind legs used for jumping. [< New Latin < Arabic *yarbū'*]

jer e mi ad (jer′ə mī′ad), *n.* a mournful complaint; lamentation. [< French *jérémiade* < *Jérémie* Jeremiah (reputed author of *Lamentations* in the Bible)]

Jer e mi ah (jer′ə mī′ə), *n.* 1 650?-586? B.C., Hebrew prophet. 2 book of the Old Testament containing his prophecies.

Jer e mi as (jer′ə mī′əs), *n.* (in the Douay Bible) Jeremiah.

Je rez (he reth′, he res′), *n.* Jerez de la Frontera.

Jerez de la Fron ter a (də lä frun ter′ə), city in SW Spain. 150,000.

Jer i cho (jer′ə kō), *n.* city in ancient Palestine, on a site now in W Jordan, north of the Dead Sea. According to the Bible, its walls fell down at the noise made by the trumpets of Joshua's attacking army.

jerk[1] (jėrk), *n.* 1 a sudden, sharp pull, twist, or start. 2 a pull or twist of the muscles that one cannot control; twitch. 3 SLANG. a stupid or simple-minded person. *—v.t.* 1 pull or twist suddenly. See **pull** for synonym study. 2 throw with a movement that stops suddenly. 3 speak or say abruptly. 4 INFORMAL. make (ice-cream sodas, etc.) behind a soda fountain. *—v.i.* move with a jerk: *The old wagon jerked along.* [probably imitative] **—jerk′er,** *n.*

jerk[2] (jėrk), *v.t.* preserve (meat) by cutting into long thin slices and drying in the sun. The early settlers in America used to jerk beef. [< American Spanish *charquear* < *charqui* jerked meat < Quechua]

jer kin (jėr′kən), *n.* a short, close-fitting coat or jacket without sleeves, such as men commonly wore in the 1500's and 1600's. [origin uncertain]

jerk wa ter (jėrk′wô′tər, jėrk′wot′ər), INFORMAL. *—n.* train on a branch railway. *—adj.* insignificant; unimportant.

jerk y[1] (jėr′kē), *adj.,* **jerk i er, jerk i est.** with sudden starts and stops; with jerks. [< *jerk*[1] + *-y*[1]] **—jerk′i ly,** *adv.* **—jerk′i ness,** *n.*

jerk y[2] (jėr′kē), *n.* strips of dried meat, usually beef. [< American Spanish *charqui* jerked meat]

Jer o bo am (jer′ə bō′əm), *n.* 1 the first king of the northern kingdom of Israel, from about 933 B.C. to 910 B.C., leader of the northern tribes against Judah. 2 **jeroboam,** a champagne bottle that holds 104 ounces.

Je rome (jə rōm′; *British* jer′əm), *n.* **Saint,** A.D. 340?-420, monk and scholar, author of the Latin translation of the Bible known as the Vulgate.

jer ry-built (jer′ē bilt′), *adj.* built in a cheap, unsubstantial, or shoddy way. [origin uncertain]

jer sey (jėr′zē), *n., pl.* **-seys.** 1 a machine-knitted cloth with a tight weave, of wool, cotton, rayon, nylon, silk, etc. 2 a close-fitting, pullover sweater made of this cloth. [< *Jersey* (def. 1), where worsted knitting was an industry]

Jer sey (jėr′zē), *n., pl.* **-seys** for 2. 1 one of the Channel Islands. 72,000 pop.; 45 sq. mi. 2 one of a breed of small, usually fawn-colored cattle that came from this island. Jerseys give very rich milk. 3 INFORMAL. New Jersey.

Jersey City, seaport in NE New Jersey, across the Hudson River from New York City. 261,000.

Je ru sa lem (jə rü′sə ləm), *n.* capital of Israel, in the E part. Formerly the capital of Palestine, Jerusalem was divided between Israel and Jordan in 1948 and reunited by Israel during the Arab-Israeli war of 1967. It is a holy city to Jews, Christians, and Moslems. 283,000.

Jerusalem artichoke, 1 kind of sunflower native to North America, whose root is edible. 2 its root.

Jerusalem cherry, an ornamental species of nightshade having poisonous orange or scarlet berries.

jess (jes), *n.* a short strap fastened around a

falcon's leg, to which a leash can be attached. —*v.t.* put jesses on. [< Old French *ges,* ultimately < Latin *jacere* to throw]

jes sa mine (jes′ə mən), *n.* jasmine.

Jes se (jes′ē), *n.* (in the Bible) the father of David.

Jes sel ton (jes′əl tən), *n.* former name of **Kota Kinabalu.**

jest (jest), *n.* 1 something said to cause laughter; joke. 2 act of poking fun at; mockery. 3 thing to be mocked or laughed at. 4 **in jest,** in fun; not seriously. —*v.i.* 1 to joke. 2 poke fun; make fun. [< Old French *geste,* originally, story, exploit < Latin *gesta* deeds, exploits < *gerere* accomplish] —**jest′ing ly,** *adv.*

jest er (jes′tər), *n.* 1 person who jests. 2 (in the Middle Ages) a clown kept by a king or lord to amuse people; fool.

Je su (jē′zü, jē′sü), *n.* Jesus.

Jes u it (jezh′ü it, jez′yü it), *n.* member of the Society of Jesus, a Roman Catholic religious order of men founded by Saint Ignatius of Loyola in 1534. Some of the first explorers of North America were Jesuits.

Jes u it ic (jezh′ü it′ik, jez′yü it′ik), *adj.* of or having to do with the Jesuits. —**Jes′u it′i cal ly,** *adv.*

Jes u it i cal (jezh′ü it′ə kəl, jez′yü it′ə kəl), *adj.* Jesuitic.

Je sus (jē′zəs), *n.* 6 B.C.?-A.D. 29?, founder of the Christian religion. The name means "God is salvation."

Jesus Christ, Jesus.

jet[1] (jet), *n., v.,* **jet ted, jet ting.** —*n.* 1 stream of water, steam, gas, or any liquid, sent with force, especially from a small opening: *A fountain sends up a jet of water.* 2 spout or nozzle for sending out a jet. 3 jet plane. 4 jet engine. —*v.i.* 1 shoot forth in a jet or forceful stream; gush out. 2 fly by jet plane. —*v.t.* send forth in a stream; shoot out. [< Middle French *giet* a throwing < Late Latin *jectus,* ultimately < Latin *jacere* to throw]

jet[2] (jet), *n.* 1 a hard, black mineral, glossy when polished, used for making beads, buttons, and ornaments. It is a kind of lignite. 2 a deep, glossy black. —*adj.* 1 made of jet. 2 deep, glossy black. [< Old French *jaiet* < Greek *gagatēs* of *Gagas,* town in Lycia, Asia Minor]

jet airplane, jet plane.

jet-black (jet′blak′), *adj.* very black.

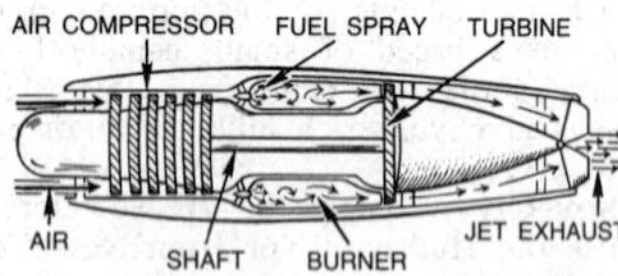

jet engine—Air is sucked in the front of the engine, compressed, and mixed with fuel. This mixture is burned in the burners, giving off gas which passes out in a powerful jet through the rear of the engine, producing thrust.

jet engine, engine using jet propulsion; jet.

jet lin er (jet′lī′nər), *n.* a large, jet-propelled plane for carrying many passengers; superjet.

jet pilot, person who operates a jet plane.

jet plane, airplane that is driven by jet propulsion; jet.

jet port (jet′pôrt′), *n.* airport designed for use by jet planes.

jet-pro pelled (jet′prə peld′), *adj.* driven by jet propulsion.

jet propulsion, propulsion produced by the forward reaction of a body to a jet of air, gas, etc., being ejected backward into space. Jet engines such as the ramjet, turbojet, and turboprop take in air which is compressed and used as an oxidizer to burn fuel, and eject hot gases backward causing a reaction which drives the engines forward.

jet sam (jet′səm), *n.* goods which are thrown overboard to lighten a ship in distress and often afterwards washed ashore. [variant of *jettison*]

jet set, the social set of fashionable people who travel a great deal by jet.

jet stream, 1 current of air traveling at very high speed from west to east at altitudes of six to eight miles. The jet stream is often used by airplane pilots to gain extra speed when traveling in an eastward direction. 2 the exhaust from a jet engine.

jet ti son (jet′ə sən, jet′ə zən), *v.t.* 1 throw (goods) overboard to lighten a ship or aircraft in distress. 2 throw away; discard. —*n.* 1 act of throwing goods overboard to lighten a ship or aircraft in distress. 2 goods thrown overboard; jetsam. [< Old French *getaison* < Latin *jactationem* < *jactare* toss < *jacere* to throw]

jet ty (jet′ē), *n., pl.* **-ties.** 1 structure of stones or wooden piles projecting out from the shore to break the force of a current or waves; breakwater. 2 a landing place; pier. [< Old French *jetee* < *jeter* to throw, ultimately < Latin *jactare.* See JETTISON.]

jeu d'es prit (zhœ des prē′), FRENCH. 1 a witty remark or piece of writing; witticism. 2 (literally) play of wit.

Jew (jü), *n.* 1 person descended from the Semitic people led by Moses, who settled in Palestine and now live in Israel and many other countries; Hebrew; Israelite. 2 person whose religion is Judaism. 3 (originally) a member of the tribe or kingdom of Judah. [< Old French *giu, jueu* < Latin *Judaeus* < Greek *Ioudaios* < Hebrew *Yehūdī* belonging to the tribe of Judah]

jew el (jü′əl), *n., v.,* **-eled, -el ing** or **-elled, -el ling.** —*n.* 1 a precious stone; gem. 2 a valuable ornament to be worn, set with precious stones. 3 person or thing that is very precious. 4 gem or hard material used as a bearing in a watch. —*v.t.* set or adorn with jewels or with things like jewels: *a jeweled comb, a sky jeweled with stars.* [< Old French *juel,* ultimately < Latin *jocus* joke, game] —**jew′el like′,** *adj.*

jew el er or **jew el ler** (jü′ə lər), *n.* person who makes, sells, or repairs jewelry and watches.

jew el ry or **jew el ler y** (jü′əl rē), *n.* 1 jewels and ornaments set with gems. 2 ring, bracelet, necklace, or other ornament to be worn, usually set with imitation gems or made of silver, gold-colored metal, etc.

jew el weed (jü′əl wēd′), *n.* impatiens.

Jew ett (jü′ət), *n.* **Sarah Orne,** 1849-1909, American writer.

jew fish (jü′fish′), *n., pl.* **-fish es** or **-fish.** 1 a giant sea bass. 2 any of various other large fishes of warm seas.

Jew ish (jü′ish), *adj.* of the Jews; belonging to the Jews; characteristic of the Jews. —*n.* INFORMAL. Yiddish. —**Jew′ish ly,** *adv.* —**Jew′ish ness,** *n.*

Jewish calendar, calendar used by the Jews, which dates the Creation at 3761 B.C.; Hebrew calendar.

Jew ry (jü′rē), *n., pl.* **-ries.** 1 Jews as a group; Jewish people. 2 ARCHAIC. district where Jews live; ghetto.

jews'-harp or **jew's-harp** (jüz′härp′), *n.* a simple musical instrument, held between the teeth and played by striking the free end of a flexible piece of metal with a finger.

Jez e bel (jez′ə bəl, jez′ə bel), *n.* 1 (in the Bible) the wicked wife of Ahab, king of Israel. 2 a shameless, immoral woman.

jg or **j.g.,** junior grade (in the U.S. Navy).

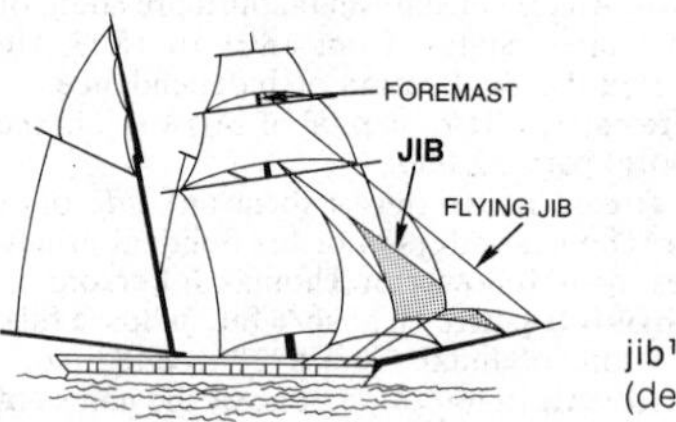

jib[1] (def. 1)

jib[1] (jib), *n.* 1 a triangular sail in front of the foremast. 2 **cut of one's jib,** INFORMAL. one's outward appearance. [earlier *gibb,* perhaps related to *gibbet*]

jib[2] (jib), *v.i., v.t.,* **jibbed, jib bing.** jibe[3].

jib[3] (jib), *v.i.,* **jibbed, jib bing.** move sideways or backward instead of forward; refuse to go ahead. [origin uncertain]

jib[4] (jib), *n.* the projecting arm of a crane or derrick. [probably < *gibbet*]

jib boom, spar extending out from a ship's bowsprit.

jibe[1] (jīb), *v.t., v.i.,* **jibed, jib ing,** *n.* gibe. —**jib′er,** *n.*

jibe[2] (jīb), *v.i.,* **jibed, jib ing.** INFORMAL. be in harmony; agree: *This doesn't jibe with what you said before.* [origin uncertain]

jibe[3] (jīb), *v.,* **jibed, jib ing.** —*v.i.* 1 shift a sail or boom from one side of a ship to the other when sailing before the wind. 2 shift itself in this way. 3 change the course of a ship so that the sails shift in this way. —*v.t.* cause (a sail or boom) to shift from one side of a ship to another when sailing before the wind. Also, **jib.** [perhaps < Dutch *gijben*]

Ji bu ti (ji bü′tē), *n.* Djibouti.

Jid da (jid′ə), *n.* city in W Saudi Arabia, in Hejaz, on the Red Sea. 300,000. Also, **Jedda.**

jiff (jif), *n.* INFORMAL. jiffy.

jif fy (jif′ē), *n., pl.* **-fies.** INFORMAL. a very short time; moment. [origin unknown]

jig[1] (jig), *n., v.,* **jigged, jig ging.** —*n.* 1 a lively dance, often in triple time. 2 music for it. 3 **the jig is up,** it's all over; there's no more chance. —*v.i.* 1 dance a jig. 2 move jerkily; jerk up and down or back and forth. [< Middle French *giguer* to dance < *gigue* fiddle]

jig[2] (jig), *n.* 1 a fishing lure consisting of a fishhook or a set of fishhooks weighted with a spoon-shaped piece of bright metal. It is bobbed up and down or pulled through the water. 2 any of various devices used to hold a piece of work and guide a drill, file, saw, etc., toward it. [origin uncertain]

jig ger[1] (jig′ər), *n.* 1 a small set of ropes and pulleys used on a ship. 2 a small sail. 3 jigger mast. 4 machine that operates with a jerky motion. 5 INFORMAL. some device, article, or part that one cannot name more precisely; gadget; contraption. 6 jig used in fishing. 7 U.S. a small glass or container that usually

hat, āge, fär; let, ēqual, tėrm;
it, īce; hot, ōpen, ôrder;
oil, out; cup, pu̇t, rüle;
ch, child; ng, long; sh, she;
th, thin; ᴛʜ, then; zh, measure;

ə represents *a* in about, *e* in taken, *i* in pencil, *o* in lemon, *u* in circus.

< = from, derived from, taken from.

holds $1\frac{1}{2}$ ounces, used to measure liquor. [< *jig*[2]]

jig ger[2] (jig′ər), *n.* 1 chigoe. 2 chigger. [alteration of *chigoe*]

jigger mast, mast in the stern of a ship.

jig gle (jig′əl), *v.,* **-gled, -gling,** *n.* —*v.t., v.i.* shake or jerk slightly. —*n.* a slight shake; light jerk. [< *jig*[1]]

jig saw (jig′sô′), *n.* saw with a narrow blade mounted in a frame and worked with an up-and-down motion, used to cut curves or irregular lines.

jigsaw puzzle, picture sawed into irregular pieces that can be fitted together again.

jilt (jilt), *v.t.* cast off (a lover or sweetheart) after giving encouragement. —*n.* woman who casts off a lover after encouraging him. [origin uncertain] **—jilt′er,** *n.*

Jim Crow (jim′ krō′), U.S. discrimination against Negroes. [originally (about 1835) a name in a Negro minstrel song]

Jim Crow ism (jim′ krō′iz′əm), U.S. practice of discriminating against Negroes.

jim-dan dy (jim′dan′dē), *n., pl.* **-dies,** *adj.* U.S. SLANG. —*n.* an excellent person. —*adj.* excellent; first-rate.

jim my (jim′ē), *n., pl.* **-mies,** *v.,* **-mied, -my ing.** —*n.* a short crowbar used especially by burglars to force open windows, doors, or other things. —*v.t.* force open with a jimmy. [< *Jimmy,* nickname for *James*]

jim son weed or **jim son-weed** (jim′-sən wēd′), *n.* a tall, coarse, bad-smelling weed of the nightshade family, with large white or violet funnel-shaped flowers and poisonous, narcotic leaves; stramonium; thorn apple. [< *jimson,* alteration of *Jamestown* (Virginia), where it was first found]

jim son weed or **Jim son weed** (jim′-sən), jimsonweed.

jin gle (jing′gəl), *n., v.,* **-gled, -gling.** —*n.* 1 a sound like that of little bells, or of coins or keys striking together. 2 verse or song that has repetition of similar sounds, or a catchy rhyme. "Higgledy, piggledy, my black hen" is a jingle. —*v.i.* 1 make a jingling sound: *The sleigh bells jingle as we ride.* 2 make jingling verses. 3 be full of simple repetitions or catchy rhymes. —*v.t.* cause to jingle: *jingle one's money.* [imitative]

jin gly (jing′glē), *adj.* like a jingle.

jin go (jing′gō), *n., pl.* **-goes,** *adj.* —*n.* 1 person who favors an aggressive foreign policy that might lead to war with other nations. 2 **by jingo!** INFORMAL. exclamation used chiefly for emphasis. —*adj.* jingoistic. [origin uncertain]

jin go ism (jing′gō iz′əm), *n.* attitude of mind, policy, or practices of jingoes.

jin go ist (jing′gō ist), *n.* jingo.

jin go is tic (jing′gō is′tik), *adj.* of jingoes; like that of jingoes. **—jin′go is′ti cal ly,** *adv.*

jinn (jin), *n. pl. or sing.* (in Moslem myths) spirits or spirit that can appear in human or animal form and do both good and evil. [< Arabic]

jin ni or **jin nee** (ji nē′), *n., pl.* **jinn.** one of the jinn; genie.

jin rik i sha or **jin rick sha** (jin rik′shə, jin rik′shô), *n.* a small, two-wheeled, hooded carriage pulled by one man, formerly used in the Orient. Also, **rickshaw, ricksha.** [< Japanese *jinrikisha* < *jin* man + *riki* strength + *sha* cart]

jinx (jingks), INFORMAL. —*n.* person or thing that brings bad luck. —*v.t.* bring bad luck to. [< Latin *iynx* bird used in charms < Greek]

jit ney (jit′nē), *n., pl.* **-neys.** SLANG. 1 automobile that carries passengers for a small fare. It usually travels along a regular route. 2 a five-cent piece; nickel. [origin uncertain]

jit ter bug (jit′ər bug′), *n., v.,* **-bugged, -bug ging.** —*n.* 1 a lively dance for couples, featuring rapid twirling movements and acrobatic maneuvers, usually done to swing music. It was especially popular in the 1940's. 2 person who dances the jitterbug. —*v.i.* dance the jitterbug. [< *jitters* + *bug*]

jit ters (jit′ərz), *n.pl.* INFORMAL. extreme nervousness. [< *jitter* be nervous, apparently variant of dialectal English *chitter* shiver, tremble, variant of *chatter*]

jit ter y (jit′ər ē), *adj.* INFORMAL. nervous.

jiu jit su or **jiu jut su** (jü jit′sü), *n.* jujitsu.

jive (jīv), *n., v.,* **jived, jiv ing.** SLANG. —*n.* 1 swing music. 2 dancing to swing music. 3 the talk of swing enthusiasts. 4 the latest slang. 5 misleading or tiresome talk. —*v.i.* dance to or perform swing music. [origin uncertain]

jo (jō), *n., pl.* **joes.** SCOTTISH. sweetheart. [variant of *joy*]

Joan of Arc (jōn′ əv ärk′), 1412-1431, French heroine who led armies against the invading English and saved the city of Orléans. She was condemned as a witch and burned to death. In 1920 she was made a saint. Also, FRENCH **Jeanne d'Arc.**

job (job), *n., adj., v.,* **jobbed, job bing.** —*n.* 1 piece of work: *We had the job of painting the boat.* 2 a definite piece of work undertaken for a fixed price: *If you want your house painted, they will do the job for $500.* 3 work done for pay; employment: *She is hunting for a job.* See **position** for synonym study. 4 anything a person has to do: *I'm not going to wash the dishes; that's your job.* 5 INFORMAL. affair; matter. 6 **on the job,** SLANG. tending to one's work or duty. 7 piece of public or official business managed dishonestly for private gain. —*adj.* done by the job; hired for a particular piece of work. —*v.t.* 1 buy (goods) from manufacturers in large quantities and sell to dealers in smaller lots. 2 let out (work) to different contractors, workmen, etc. 3 manage (a public job) for private gain in a dishonest way. —*v.i.* work at odd jobs. [origin uncertain]

Job (jōb), *n.* 1 (in the Bible) a very patient man who kept his faith in God in spite of many troubles. 2 book of the Old Testament that tells about him.

job ber (job′ər), *n.* 1 person who buys goods from manufacturers in large quantities and sells them to retail dealers in small quantities. 2 person who manages public business dishonestly for private gain. 3 person who works by the job; pieceworker.

job ber y (job′ər ē), *n.* the dishonest management of public business for private gain.

Job Corps (job), agency of the United States Government, established in 1964, which provides training and work for unemployed youths between the ages of 16 and 21.

job hold er (job′hōl′dər), *n.* 1 person regularly employed. 2 a government employee.

job less (job′lis), *adj.* having no job; unemployed. **—job′less ness,** *n.*

job lot, quantity of goods bought or sold together, often containing several different kinds of things.

Job's-tears (jōbz′tirz′), *n.* 1 the hard, grayish-white seeds of an Asiatic grass, used as beads. 2 the grass itself.

Jo cas ta (jō kas′tə), *n.* (in Greek legends) the mother of Oedipus, who married him without knowing who he was and killed herself when she learned the truth.

jock ey (jok′ē), *n., pl.* **-eys,** *v.* —*n.* person whose occupation is riding horses in races. —*v.t.* 1 ride (a horse) in a race. 2 trick; cheat: *Swindlers jockeyed them into buying some worthless land.* 3 maneuver so as to get advantage: *The crews were jockeying their boats to get into the best position for the race.* —*v.i.* 1 ride as a jockey. 2 aim at an advantage by skillful maneuvering. 3 act in a tricky way; trick; cheat. [originally proper name, diminutive of *Jock,* Scottish variant of *Jack*]

jock ey ship (jok′ē ship), *n.* skill or quality of a jockey.

jo cose (jō kōs′), *adj.* full of jokes; given to joking; jesting; humorous. [< Latin *jocosus* < *jocus* jest] **—jo cose′ly,** *adv.* **—jo cose′ness,** *n.*

jo cos i ty (jō kos′ə tē), *n., pl.* **-ties.** 1 jocose quality. 2 a joking. 3 joke.

joc u lar (jok′yə lər), *adj.* speaking or acting in jest; said or done in jest; funny; joking. [< Latin *jocularis* < *joculus,* diminutive of *jocus* jest] **—joc′u lar ly,** *adv.*

joc u lar i ty (jok′yə lar′ə tē), *n., pl.* **-ties.** 1 jocular quality. 2 jocular talk or behavior. 3 a jocular remark or act.

joc und (jok′ənd, jō′kənd), *adj.* feeling, expressing, or communicating mirth or cheer; cheerful; merry; gay. [< Latin *jocundus, jucundus* pleasant < *juvare* please] **—joc′und ly,** *adv.*

jo cun di ty (jō kun′də tē), *n.* cheerfulness; merriment; gaiety.

Jodh pur (jod′pər), *n.* city in NW India. 253,000.

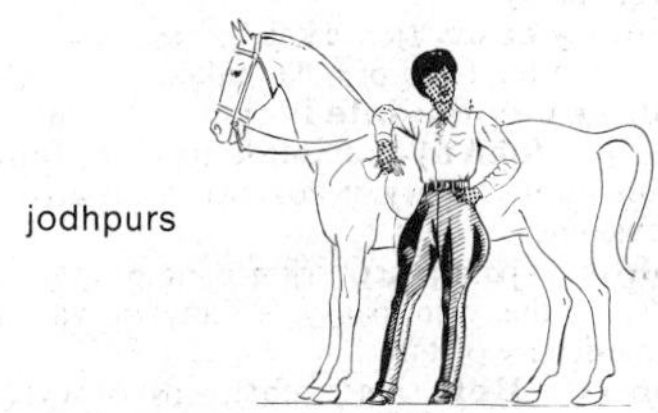

jodhpurs

jodh purs (jod′pərz), *n.pl.* breeches for horseback riding, loose above the knees and close-fitting below the knees. [< *Jodhpur,* India]

Jo el (jō′əl), *n.* 1 Hebrew prophet of the 400's B.C. 2 book of the Old Testament containing his prophecies.

Jof fre (zhôf′rə), *n.* **Joseph Jacques Césaire,** 1852-1931, French marshal in World War I.

jog[1] (jog), *v.,* **jogged, jog ging,** *n.* —*v.t.* 1 shake with a push or jerk: *She jogged my elbow to get my attention.* 2 stir up with a hint or reminder: *jog one's memory.* 3 move up and down with a jerk or a shaking motion: *The old horse jogged me on his back.* —*v.i.* 1 move up and down with a jerk or a shaking motion: *The old horse jogged along.* 2 run slowly; trot: *He jogs for exercise.* —*n.* 1 a shake, push, or nudge. 2 a hint or reminder: *give one's memory a jog.* 3 a slow run; trot. [Middle English *joggen* to prick or spur] —**jog′ger,** *n.*

jog² (jog), *n.* part that sticks out or in; unevenness in a line or a surface: *a jog in a wall.* [variant of *jag¹*]

jog gle¹ (jog′əl), *v.*, **-gled, -gling,** *n.* —*v.t., v.i.* shake slightly. —*n.* a slight shake. [< *jog¹*]

jog gle² (jog′əl), *n., v.*, **-gled, -gling.** —*n.* 1 projection on one of two joining surfaces, or notch on the other, to prevent slipping. 2 joint made in this way. —*v.t.* join or fasten with a joggle or joggles. [perhaps < *jog²*]

jog trot, 1 a slow, regular trot, as of a horse. 2 a routine or humdrum way of doing things.

Jo han nes burg (jō han′is bėrg′, yō-hän′is bėrg′), *n.* city in NE Republic of South Africa, noted for its gold mines. 1,365,000.

John (jon), *n.* 1 (in the Bible) one of Christ's twelve apostles. According to tradition, he wrote the Gospel of Saint John, the three epistles of John, and Revelation. 2 the fourth book of the New Testament, attributed to John. 3 John the Baptist. 4 1167?-1216, king of England from 1199 to 1216. He signed the Magna Charta in 1215.

John XXIII, 1881-1963, pope from 1958 to 1963.

john boat (jon′bōt′), *n.* U.S. a small, light rowboat with a flat bottom and square ends.

John Bull, 1 the typical Englishman. 2 the English nation; Englishmen.

John Doe, a fictitious name used in legal forms or proceedings for the name of an unknown person.

John Do ry (dôr′ē, dōr′ē), *pl.* **John Do rys.** either of two edible sea fishes that have high, flat bodies, spiny fins, and a large, black, yellow-ringed spot on each side.

John Hancock, U.S. a person's signature. [< *John Hancock,* because his signature on the Declaration of Independence is bold and prominent]

john ny cake (jon′ē kāk′), *n.* U.S. corn bread in the form of a flat cake.

John ny-come-late ly (jon′ē kum′lāt′lē), *n., pl.* **John ny-come-late lies** or **John-nies-come-late ly.** INFORMAL. a late arrival; newcomer.

John ny-jump-up (jon′ē jump′up′), *n.* U.S. 1 the wild pansy. 2 any of various American violets.

John ny Reb (jon′ē reb′), INFORMAL. a Confederate soldier in the Civil War. [< *Reb(el)*]

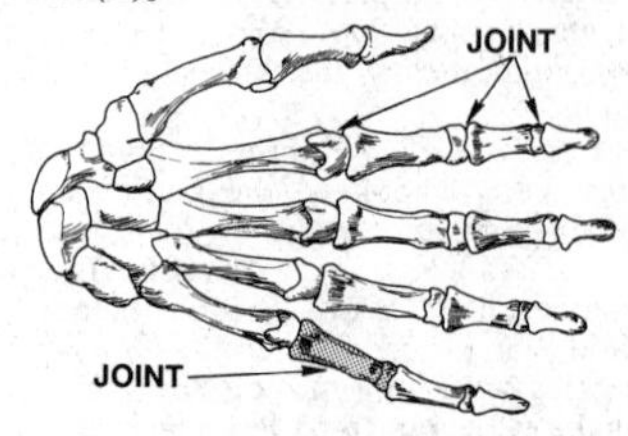

joint (def. 3, above; def. 4, below)

John of Gaunt. See **Gaunt.**

John son (jon′sən), *n.* 1 **Andrew,** 1808-1875, the 17th president of the United States, from 1865 to 1869. 2 **James Weldon,** 1871-1938, American poet. 3 **Lyndon Baines,** 1908-1973, the 36th president of the United States, from 1963 to 1969. 4 **Samuel,** 1709-1784, English author, lexicographer, and literary leader.

John so ni an (jon sō′nē ən), *adj.* 1 of Samuel Johnson or his writings. 2 having a literary style like that of Samuel Johnson; pompous and ponderous.

John ston (jon′stən), *n.* 1 **Albert Sidney,** 1803-1862, Confederate general. 2 **Joseph Eggleston,** 1807-1891, Confederate general.

John the Baptist, died A.D. 29?, Hebrew prophet who foretold the coming of Christ and baptized Him.

Jo hore (jō hôr′, jō hōr′), *n.* state at the S end of the Malay Peninsula, part of the Federation of Malaysia.

joie de vi vre (zhwä də vē′vrə), FRENCH. joy of living; enjoyment of life.

join (join), *v.t.* 1 bring or put together; connect, fasten, or clasp together: *join hands, join an island to the mainland by a bridge.* 2 meet and unite with: *The brook joins the river.* 3 make one; combine; unite. See synonym study below. 4 become a member of: *join a church.* 5 come into the company of: *Go now, and I'll join you later.* 6 take or return to one's place in: *After a few days on shore the sailor joined his ship.* 7 be next to; adjoin: *Their farm joins ours.* —*v.i.* 1 come together; meet: *The two roads join here.* 2 become one; combine; unite: *join in marriage.* See synonym study below. 3 take part with others: *join in a song.* —*n.* point or line where things are joined; seam. [< Old French *joindre* < Latin *jungere*]

Syn. *v.t.* 3, *v.i.* 2 **Join, combine, unite** mean to put or come together to form one thing. **Join** emphasizes bringing or coming together, but does not suggest how firm or lasting the association may be: *The two armies joined forces.* **Combine** emphasizes mixing or blending into one, for a common purpose: *combine the ingredients of a medicine.* **Unite** emphasizes the oneness of the result and the loss of separate or divided purposes, interests, etc.: *His family united to help him.*

➤ **join together.** The *together* is unnecessary, for *join* means bring or put together: *These ends must be joined before we go further.* Not: *These ends must be joined together before we go further.*

join er (joi′nər), *n.* 1 person or thing that joins. 2 carpenter who makes doors, windows, molding, and other inside woodwork. 3 INFORMAL. person who joins many clubs, societies, etc.

join er y (joi′nər ē), *n.* 1 skill or trade of a joiner. 2 woodwork or furniture made by a joiner.

joint (joint), *n.* 1 the place at which two things or parts are joined. A pocketknife has a joint to fold the blade inside the handle. 2 the way parts are joined: *a perfect joint.* 3 part in an animal where two bones join, allowing motion, and the immediately surrounding area. 4 one of the parts of which a jointed thing is made up: *the middle joint of the finger.* 5 **out of joint, a** out of place at the joint. **b** out of order; in bad condition. 6 part of the stem of a plant from which a leaf or branch grows. 7 a large piece of meat cut for roasting, usually with a bone in it. 8 SLANG. **a** a cheap, disreputable restaurant, bar, hotel, etc. **b** any place, building, etc. —*v.t.* 1 connect by a joint or joints. 2 divide at the joints: *Please ask the butcher to joint the chicken.*
—*adj.* 1 shared or done by two or more persons: *By our joint efforts we managed to push the car back on the road.* 2 joined with another or others; sharing: *The two of us are joint owners of this boat.*
[< Old French *jointe,* past participle of *joindre.* See JOIN.] —**joint′er,** *n.* —**joint′less,** *adj.*

Joint Chiefs of Staff, the principal military advisory board to the President of the United States and the Secretary of Defense, consisting of the chiefs of staff of the army and air force, the chief of naval operations, and the commandant of the Marine Corps, and headed by its chairman.

joint ed (join′tid), *adj.* having a joint or joints: *the jointed body of a crayfish.*

joint ly (joint′lē), *adv.* together; as partners: *The two of them owned the boat jointly.*

joint stock, stock or capital contributed and owned by a number of persons jointly. It is divided into shares and serves as a common fund.

joint-stock company (joint′stok′), company or firm whose capital is owned in shares by stockholders, any of whom can sell some or all of his shares without the consent of the others.

join ture (join′chər), *n.* property given to a woman at the time of her marriage. [< Old French < Latin *junctura* a joining < *jungere* to join. Doublet of JUNCTURE.]

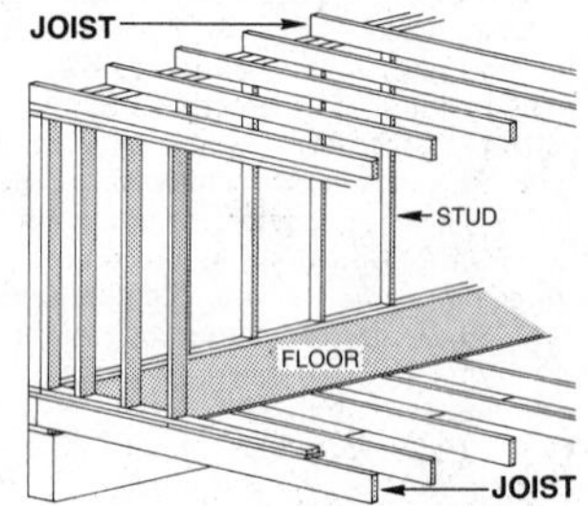

joist (joist), *n.* one of the parallel beams of timber or steel which supports the boards of a floor or ceiling. [< Old French *giste* < *gesir* to lie < Latin *jacere*]

joke (jōk), *n., v.,* **joked, jok ing.** —*n.* 1 something said or done to cause laughter or amusement; remark or act that is clever and funny; something funny; jest. 2 person or thing laughed at. 3 something that is not in earnest or actually meant. 4 **no joke,** a serious matter. —*v.i.* make jokes; say or do something as a joke; jest. —*v.t.* laugh at; make fun of; tease. [< Latin *jocus*] —**jok′ing ly,** *adv.*

jok er (jō′kər), *n.* 1 person who jokes. 2 an extra playing card used in some games. 3 U.S. phrase or sentence hidden away in a legislative bill, or contract, etc. to defeat its apparent purpose. 4 trick for getting the better of someone.

joke ster (jōk′stər), *n.* INFORMAL. humorist.

Jo li et (jō′lē et, jō′lē et′), *n.* 1 **Louis,** 1645-1700, French Canadian explorer of the Mississippi River. 2 city in NE Illinois. 80,000.

hat, āge, fär; let, ēqual, tėrm;
it, īce; hot, ōpen, ôrder;
oil, out; cup, pu̇t, rüle;
ch, child; ng, long; sh, she;
th, thin; ᴛʜ, then; zh, measure;

ə represents *a* in about, *e* in taken,
i in pencil, *o* in lemon, *u* in circus.

< = from, derived from, taken from.

jol li fi ca tion (jol′ə fə kā′shən), *n.* gay entertainment; merrymaking.

jol li ty (jol′ə tē), *n., pl.* **-ties.** fun; merriment; gaiety.

jol ly (jol′ē), *adj.,* **-li er, -li est,** *adv., v.,* **-lied, -ly ing.** —*adj.* 1 full of fun; very cheerful; merry. 2 BRITISH INFORMAL. pleasant or delightful. —*adv.* BRITISH INFORMAL. extremely; very. —*v.t.* 1 INFORMAL. flatter (a person) to make him feel good or agreeable. 2 tease playfully; banter. —*v.i.* jolly someone; banter. [< Old French *joli*] **—jol′li ly,** *adv.* **—jol′li ness,** *n.*

jolly boat, a small boat carried on a ship.

Jolly Rog er (roj′ər), a pirates' black flag with a white skull and crossbones on it; black flag; blackjack.

jolt (jōlt), *v.t.* 1 shake up; jar: *The wagon jolted us when the wheel went over a rock.* 2 shock or surprise suddenly. —*v.i.* move with a shock or jerk: *The car jolted across the rough ground.* —*n.* 1 a jar, shock, or jerk: *I put the brakes on suddenly and the car stopped with a jolt.* 2 a sudden surprise or shock. [origin uncertain] **—jolt′er,** *n.* **—jolt′ing ly,** *adv.*

jolt y (jōl′tē), *adj.* jolting.

Jo nah (jō′nə), *n.* 1 (in the Bible) a Hebrew prophet who was thrown overboard during a storm because he disobeyed God. He was swallowed by a large fish, and cast up on land alive after three days. 2 book of the Old Testament that tells about him. 3 person whose presence is supposed to bring bad luck.

Jo nas (jō′nəs), *n.* (in the Douay Bible) Jonah.

Jon a than (jon′ə thən), *n.* (in the Bible) a son of Saul, and devoted friend of David.

Jones (jōnz), *n.* **John Paul,** 1747-1792, American naval commander in the Revolutionary War, born in Scotland.

jon gleur (jong′glər; *French* zhôɴ glœr′), *n.* a wandering minstrel or entertainer in the Middle Ages. [< French < Old French *jogleor*]

jon quil (jong′kwəl), *n.* 1 plant with yellow or white flowers and long, slender leaves. It is a species of narcissus that is much like a daffodil. 2 its flower. [< French *jonquille* < Spanish *junquillo,* diminutive of *junco* reed < Latin *juncus*]

Jon son (jon′sən), *n.* **Ben,** 1573?-1637, English dramatist and poet.

Jop lin (jop′lən), *n.* **Scott,** 1869-1917, American composer, known for his use of ragtime.

Jop pa (jop′ə), *n.* ancient name of **Jaffa.**

Jor dan (jôrd′n), *n.* 1 **Jordan River,** river flowing from SW Syria through Israel and Jordan into the Dead Sea. 200 mi. 2 country in SW Asia, east of Israel. Part of Palestine was added to it in 1950. 2,320,000 pop.; 37,700 sq. mi. *Capital:* Amman. Formerly, **Transjordan.** See **Iran** for map. **—Jor da′ni an,** *adj., n.*

Jordan almond, a fine variety of almond, now coming chiefly from southern Spain.

Jo seph (jō′zəf), *n.* 1 in the Bible: **a** the favorite son of Jacob. His jealous brothers sold him into slavery in Egypt, where he finally became governor. **b** the husband of Mary, mother of Jesus. 2 **Chief Joseph,** 1840?-1904, a chief of the Nez Percé Indians. 3 **joseph,** a long riding cloak with a cape, worn by women in the 1700's.

Jo se phine (jō′zə fēn′), *n.* **de Beauharnais,** 1763-1814, first wife of Napoleon Bonaparte.

Joseph of Ar i ma the a (ar′ə mə thē′ə), (in the Bible) a rich man who put the body of Jesus in his own tomb.

Jo se phus (jō sē′fəs), *n.* **Flavius,** A.D. 37?-95?, Jewish historian who wrote in Greek.

josh (josh), *v.t.* INFORMAL. make goodnatured fun of; tease playfully; banter. —*v.i.* tease playfully; banter. [perhaps < *Josh,* nickname for *Joshua*] **—josh′er,** *n.*

Josh., Joshua.

Josh u a (josh′ü ə), *n.* 1 (in the Bible) the successor of Moses, who led the Israelites into the Promised Land. 2 book of the Old Testament.

Joshua tree, a small yucca tree that grows in dry or desert regions of the southwestern United States.

Jo si ah (jō sī′ə), *n.* died 608? B.C., king of Judah from about 639 to 608 B.C.

joss (jos), *n.* image of a Chinese god; Chinese idol. [pidgin English form of Portuguese *deos* god < Latin *deus*]

joss house, a Chinese temple.

joss stick, a slender stick of dried fragrant paste, burned as incense.

jos tle (jos′əl), *v.,* **-tled, -tling,** *n.* —*v.t.* shove, push, or crowd against; elbow roughly: *We were jostled by the big crowd at the entrance to the circus.* —*v.i.* crowd, strike, or push. —*n.* a jostling; push; knock. Also, **justle.** [< *joust*] **—jos′tler,** *n.*

Jos u e (jos′yü ē), *n.* (in the Douay Bible) Joshua.

jot (jot), *v.,* **jot ted, jot ting,** *n.* —*v.t.* write briefly or in haste: *The clerk jotted down the order.* —*n.* a little bit; very small amount: *I do not care a jot.* [< Latin *iota* iota, smallest letter in the Greek alphabet. Doublet of IOTA.]

jot ting (jot′ing), *n.* something jotted down; brief note; memorandum.

joule (joul, jül), *n.* (in physics) a unit of work or energy, equal to ten million ergs or about 0.7375 foot-pounds. [< James P. *Joule*]

Joule (joul), *n.* **James P.,** 1818-1889, British physicist.

jounce (jouns), *v.,* **jounced, jounc ing,** *n.* —*v.t., v.i.* shake up and down; bounce; bump; jolt: *The car jounced along on the rough road.* —*n.* a bump or jolt. [origin uncertain]

jour., 1 journal. 2 journeyman.

jour nal (jėr′nl), *n.* 1 a daily record of events or occurrences. 2 record or account of what a person thinks, feels, notices, etc., such as a diary. 3 a ship's log. 4 record of the daily proceedings of a legislative or other public body. 5 newspaper, magazine, or other periodical. 6 (in bookkeeping) a book in which every item of business is written down, so that the item can be entered under the proper account. 7 the part of a shaft or axle that turns in a bearing. [< Old French < Late Latin *diurnalis.* Doublet of DIURNAL.]

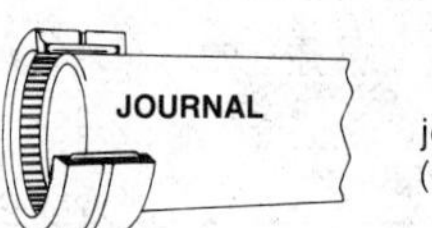

journal (def. 7)

jour nal ese (jėr′nl ēz′), *n.* style of writing typical of newspapers and magazines.

jour nal ism (jėr′nl iz′əm), *n.* 1 work of writing for, editing, managing, or publishing a newspaper or magazine. 2 newspapers, magazines, and press or wire services as a group.

jour nal ist (jėr′nl ist), *n.* person whose work is writing for, editing, managing, or publishing a newspaper or magazine. Editors and reporters are journalists.

jour nal is tic (jėr′nl is′tik), *adj.* of or like journalism or journalists. **—jour′nal is′ti cal ly,** *adv.*

jour nal ize (jėr′nl īz), *v.,* **-ized, -iz ing.** —*v.t.* enter or record in a journal. —*v.i.* keep or make entries in a journal. **—jour′nal iz′er,** *n.*

jour ney (jėr′nē), *n., pl.* **-neys,** *v.* —*n.* 1 a traveling from one place to another; trip: *a journey around the world.* See **trip** for synonym study. 2 distance traveled: *a week's journey.* —*v.i.* take a trip; travel. [< Old French *journee* day's travel, ultimately < Latin *diurnus* of one day < *dies* day] **—jour′ney er,** *n.*

jour ney man (jėr′nē mən), *n., pl.* **-men.** 1 workman who knows his trade. 2 workman who has served his apprenticeship and is qualified to practice his trade, but has not become an employer or master workman.

joust (just, joust, jüst), *n.* 1 combat between two knights on horseback, armed with lances, especially as part of a tournament. 2 **jousts,** *pl.* a tournament. —*v.i.* fight with lances on horseback. Knights used to joust with each other for sport. Also, **just.** [< Old French *jouste* < *jouster* to joust < Popular Latin *juxtare* be next to < Latin *juxta* beside] **—joust′er,** *n.*

Jove (jōv), *n.* 1 (in Roman myths) Jupiter. 2 **by Jove,** exclamation of surprise, pleasure, etc.

jo vi al (jō′vē əl), *adj.* good-hearted and full of fun; good-humored and merry. [< Latin *Jovialis* of the planet Jupiter (those born under the planet's sign being supposedly cheerful) < *Jovis* Jove] **—jo′vi al ly,** *adv.* **—jo′vi al ness,** *n.*

jo vi al i ty (jō′vē al′ə tē), *n.* jollity; merriment.

Jo vi an (jō′vē ən), *adj.* of or like the god Jove.

jowl[1] (joul, jōl), *n.* 1 jaw, especially the part under the jaw. 2 cheek. [Old English *ceafl*]

jowl[2] (joul, jōl), *n.* fold of flesh hanging from the jaw. [perhaps related to Old English *ceole* throat]

jowl y (jou′lē), *adj.,* **jowl i er, jowl i est.** having large or prominent jowls; having a double chin.

joy (joi), *n.* 1 a strong feeling of pleasure arising from a sense of well-being or satisfaction; gladness; happiness. See **pleasure** for synonym study. 2 something that causes gladness or happiness: *On a hot day, a cool swim is a joy.* 3 expression of happiness; outward rejoicing. —*v.i.* be joyful. [< Old French *joie* < Latin *gaudia,* plural of *gaudium* joy < *gaudere* rejoice]

joy ance (joi′əns), *n.* ARCHAIC. joy; gladness; gaiety.

Joyce (jois), *n.* **James,** 1882-1941, Irish novelist, short-story writer, and poet.

joy ful (joi′fəl), *adj.* 1 glad; happy: *a joyful heart.* 2 causing joy: *joyful news.* 3 showing joy: *a joyful look.* **—joy′ful ly,** *adv.* **—joy′ful ness,** *n.*

joy less (joi′lis), *adj.* 1 without joy; sad; dismal. 2 not causing joy: *a joyless prospect.* **—joy′less ly,** *adv.* **—joy′less ness,** *n.*

joy ous (joi′əs), *adj.* joyful; glad; gay. **—joy′ous ly,** *adv.* **—joy′ous ness,** *n.*

joy ride, INFORMAL. a ride in an automobile for pleasure, especially when the car is driven recklessly or without the owner's permission.

joy-ride (joi′rīd′), *v.i.,* **-rode** (-rōd′), **-rid den** (-rid′n), **-rid ing.** INFORMAL. take a joy ride. **—joy′-rid′er,** *n.*

J.P., Justice of the Peace.

jr. or **Jr.,** Junior.

jt., joint.

Juan Car los (hwän kär′lôs), **Prince,** born 1938, heir to the Spanish throne.

Juan de Fu ca Strait (hwän′ də fü′kä), strait between Vancouver Island and NW Washington. 100 mi. long.

Ju an Fer nán dez (jü′ən fər nan′dēz; *Spanish* hwän′ fer nän′des), group of three volcanic islands in the S Pacific, 400 miles west of Valparaiso and belonging to Chile. 1000 pop.; 70 sq. mi.

Juá rez (hwär′es), *n.* **Benito (Pablo),** 1806-1872, president of Mexico from 1858 to 1863 and from 1867 to 1872.

ju bi lance (jü′bə ləns), *n.* a rejoicing; great joy.

ju bi lant (jü′bə lənt), *adj.* expressing or showing joy; rejoicing. [< Latin *jubilantem* < *jubilum* wild shout] **—ju′bi lant ly,** *adv.*

Ju bi la te (jü′bə lā′tē, jü′bə lä′tē), *n.* the 100th Psalm in the Authorized Version and the 99th Psalm in the Douay Version of the Bible. [< Latin, rejoice (the first word of the Psalm)]

ju bi la tion (jü′bə lā′shən), *n.* 1 a rejoicing. 2 a joyful celebration.

ju bi lee (jü′bə lē), *n.* 1 an anniversary thought of as a time of rejoicing. 2 time of rejoicing or great joy. 3 a rejoicing; great joy. 4 a 25th or 50th anniversary. 5 (in the Roman Catholic Church) a year in which punishment for sin is remitted, after repentance and the performance of certain acts. Since the 1400's, jubilees have been proclaimed every 25 years. 6 (in Judaism) a year of emancipation observed every 50th year by not working the fields, by setting slaves free, and by restoring lands to their original owners. [< Old French *jubile* < Late Latin *jubilaeus* < Greek *iōbēlaios* < Hebrew *yōbēl,* originally, trumpet, ram('s horn)]

Ju dae a (jü dē′ə), *n.* Judea.

Ju dae an (jü dē′ən), *adj., n.* Judean.

Ju dah (jü′də), *n.* 1 in the Bible: **a** a son of Jacob and ancestor of the tribe of Judah. **b** the most powerful of the twelve tribes of Israel. 2 ancient Hebrew kingdom in S Palestine, consisting of the tribes of Judah and Benjamin.

Ju da ic (jü dā′ik), *adj.* of or having to do with the Jews or Judaism.

Ju da i cal (jü dā′ə kəl), *adj.* Judaic.

Ju da ism (jü′dē iz′əm), *n.* 1 religion of the Jews, based on the teachings of Moses and the prophets as found in the Bible, and on the interpretations of the rabbis. Judaism teaches belief in one God. 2 observance of this religion or of Jewish rules, customs, and traditions. 3 culture, religion, history, language, and civilization of the Jewish people. 4 Jews as a group.

Ju da ist (jü′dē ist), *n.* adherent of Judaism or of Jewish rites.

Ju da is tic (jü′dē is′tik), *adj.* of or having to do with Judaism or Judaists.

Ju da ize (jü′dē īz), *v.i., v.t.,* **-ized, -iz ing.** conform or cause to conform to Jewish usages or ideas. **—Ju′da i za′tion,** *n.* **—Ju′da iz′er,** *n.*

Ju das (jü′dəs), *n.* 1 (in the Bible) Judas Iscariot, the disciple who betrayed Jesus for money. 2 an utter traitor; person treacherous enough to betray a friend. 3 (in the Bible) Jude.

Judas Maccabaeus. See **Maccabaeus.**

Judas tree, shrub or small tree of the pea family that has red, pink, or purplish flowers before the leaves come out. [< *Judas* Iscariot, believed to have hanged himself on such a tree]

Jude (jüd), *n.* 1 (in the Bible) one of Christ's twelve apostles. 2 book of the New Testament.

Ju de a (jü dē′ə), *n.* the S part of Palestine when it was a province of the Roman Empire. See **Galilee** for map. Also, **Judaea.**

Ju de an (jü dē′ən), *adj.* 1 of Judea. 2 of the Jews. —*n.* a Jew. Also, **Judaean.**

Judg., Judges.

judge (juj), *n., v.,* **judged, judg ing.** —*n.* 1 a public official appointed or elected to hear and decide cases in a court of law. 2 person chosen to settle a dispute or decide who wins a race, contest, etc. 3 person qualified to form an opinion or estimate and decide how good a thing is: *a good judge of dogs, a poor judge of poetry.* 4 ruler in ancient Israel before the time of the kings. —*v.t.* 1 hear and decide (a case) in a court of law. 2 settle (a dispute); decide who wins (a race, contest, etc.). 3 form an opinion or estimate about: *judge the merits of a book.* 4 think; suppose; consider: *I judged that you had forgotten to come.* 5 consider and blame; criticize; condemn: *Who can judge another?* —*v.i.* 1 act as a judge. 2 form an opinion or estimate. [< Old French *juge* < Latin *judicem* < *jus* law + *dicere* say] **—judg′er,** *n.*

judge advocate, officer who acts as a prosecutor at a court-martial.

judge ment (juj′mənt), *n.* judgment.

Judg es (juj′iz), *n.* book of the Old Testament dealing with the period in Jewish history between the death of Joshua and Saul's accession to the throne.

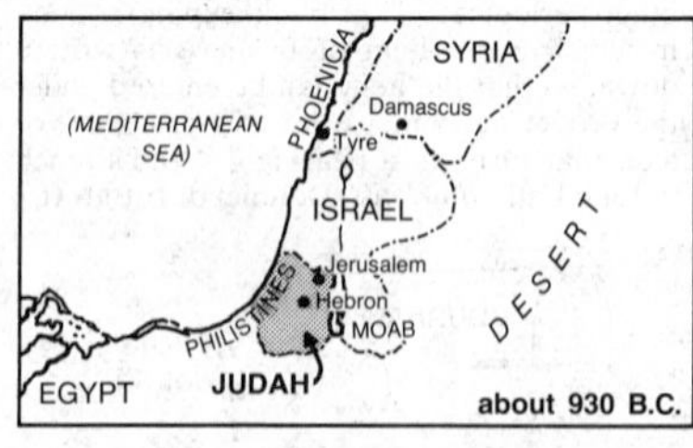

Judah (def. 2)

judge ship (juj′ship), *n.* position, duties, or term of office of a judge.

judg ment (juj′mənt), *n.* 1 result of judging; opinion or estimate: *It was a bad plan in our judgment.* 2 ability to form sound opinions; power to judge well; good sense. 3 act of judging. 4 decision, decree, or sentence given by a judge in a court of law. 5 debt arising from the decision of a judge or court. 6 decision made by anyone who judges. 7 criticism; condemnation: *pass judgment on one's neighbors.* 8 misfortune thought of as a punishment from God. 9 **the Judgment,** Judgment Day. Also, **judgement.**

judg men tal (juj men′tl), *adj.* having to do with judgment.

Judgment Day, day of God's final judgment of mankind at the end of the world; doomsday. Also, **Day of Judgment.**

ju di ca to ry (jü′də kə tôr′ē, jü′də kə-tōr′ē), *adj., n., pl.* **-ries.** —*adj.* of the administration of justice. —*n.* 1 administration of justice. 2 court where justice is administered.

ju di ca ture (jü′də kə chür, jü′də kə chər), *n.* 1 administration of justice. 2 position, duties, or authority of a judge. 3 extent of jurisdiction of a judge or court. 4 group of judges. 5 court where justice is administered.

ju di cial (jü dish′əl), *adj.* 1 of or by judges; having to do with courts or the administration of justice. 2 of or suitable for a judge; impartial; fair: *a judicial mind.* 3 ordered, permitted, or enforced by a judge or a court. 4 forming or expressing a judgment. [< Latin *judicialis* < *judicium* judgment < *judicem* judge] **—ju di′cial ly,** *adv.*

ju di ci ar y (jü dish′ē er′ē), *n., pl.* **-ar ies,** *adj.* —*n.* 1 branch of government that administers justice; system of courts of law of a country. 2 judges of a country, state, or city. —*adj.* of or having to do with courts, judges, or the administration of justice.

ju di cious (jü dish′əs), *adj.* having, using, or showing good judgment; wise; sensible: *A judicious historian selects and weighs facts carefully and critically.* **—ju di′cious ly,** *adv.* **—ju di′cious ness,** *n.*

Ju dith (jü′dith), *n.* in the Apocrypha and Douay Bible: 1 a Jewish widow who saved her countrymen by killing a Babylonian general. 2 book that relates her story.

ju do (jü′dō), *n.* 1 jujitsu. 2 a modern form of jujitsu practiced as a sport or a means of self-defense. [< Japanese *jūdō*]

Ju dy (jü′dē), *n.* wife of Punch in the puppet show *Punch and Judy.*

jug (jug), *n., v.,* **jugged, jug ging.** —*n.* 1 container for liquids. A jug usually has a short, narrow neck and a handle. 2 contents of a jug; jugful. 3 SLANG. jail. —*v.t.* SLANG. put in jail. [probably originally proper name, alteration of *Joan*]

jug ful (jug′fu̇l), *n., pl.* **-fuls.** as much as a jug can hold.

Jug ger naut (jug′ər nôt), *n.* 1 idol of the Hindu god Krishna, pulled around on a huge car. Devotees of the god are said to have thrown themselves under the wheels to be crushed to death. 2 Also, **juggernaut. a** something to which a person blindly devotes himself or is cruelly sacrificed. **b** a frightening, invisible machine, force, etc., that destroys anything in its path. [< Hindustani *Jagannāth* < Sanskrit *Jagannātha* lord of the world]

jug gle (jug′əl), *v.,* **-gled, -gling,** *n.* —*v.i.* do tricks that require skill of hand. —*v.t.* 1 do such tricks with: *He can juggle three balls, keeping them all in the air at one time.* 2 change by trickery: *The dishonest cashier juggled the store's accounts to hide his thefts.* 3 deceive; cheat. —*n.* 1 a juggling. 2 trick;

deception; fraud. [< Old French *jogler* < Latin *joculari* to joke < *joculus,* diminutive of *jocus* jest]

jug gler (jug′lər), *n.* 1 person who can do juggling tricks. 2 person who uses tricks, deception, or fraud.

jug gler y (jug′lər ē), *n., pl.* **-gler ies.** 1 skill or tricks of a juggler; sleight of hand. 2 trickery; deception; fraud.

Ju go slav (yü′gō släv′, yü′gō slav′), *n., adj.* Yugoslav.

Ju go sla vi a (yü′gō slä′vē ə), *n.* Yugoslavia. **—Ju′go sla′vi an,** *adj., n.*

Ju go slav ic (yü′gō slä′vik, yü′gō slav′ik), *adj.* Yugoslavic.

jug u lar (jug′yə lər, jü′gyə lər), *adj.* 1 of the neck or throat. 2 of the jugular vein. *—n.* jugular vein. [< New Latin *jugularis* < Latin *jugulum* collarbone, diminutive of *jugum* yoke]

jugular vein, one of the two large veins in each side of the neck and head that return blood from the head and neck to the heart.

juice (jüs), *n., v.,* **juiced, juic ing.** *—n.* 1 the liquid part of fruits, vegetables, and meats. 2 fluid in the body. The gastric juices of the stomach help to digest food. 3 SLANG. electricity. 4 SLANG. gasoline. *—v.t.,* **juice up,** SLANG. 1 brighten up; enliven: *The new tape cassettes juiced up the party.* 2 refuel: *Jet tankers juiced up the new transport plane on its long flight to Australia.* [< Old French *jus* < Latin, broth] **—juice′less,** *adj.*

juic er (jü′sər), *n.* a kitchen appliance used to extract juice from fruits and vegetables.

juic y (jü′sē), *adj.,* **juic i er, juic i est.** 1 full of juice; having much juice: *a juicy orange.* 2 INFORMAL. full of interest; lively. **—juic′i ly,** *adv.* **—juic′i ness,** *n.*

ju jit su (jü jit′sü), *n.* a Japanese method of wrestling or of fighting without weapons that uses the strength and weight of an opponent to his disadvantage; judo. Also, **jujutsu, jiujitsu, jiujutsu.** [< Japanese *jūjutsu* < *jū* soft + *jutsu* art]

ju jube (jü′jüb; *also* jü′jü bē *for 1*), *n.* 1 lozenge or small tablet of gummy candy. 2 an edible, datelike fruit of a shrub or tree of the same family as the buckthorn, used to flavor this candy. [< Middle French, ultimately < Greek *zizyphon*]

ju jut su (jü jit′sü), *n.* jujitsu.

juke box (jük′boks′), *n.* an automatic phonograph operated by inserting a coin in a slot. The records to be played are selected by pushing a button. [< Gullah *juke* disorderly + English *box*]

juke joint (jük), SLANG. tavern, roadhouse, etc., where music is furnished by a jukebox.

Jul., July.

ju lep (jü′ləp), *n.* drink made of bourbon, sugar, crushed ice, and fresh mint. [< Old French < Persian *gulāb,* originally, rose water]

Jul ian (jü′lyən), *adj.* of Julius Caesar.

Ju li an a (jü′lē an′ə, jü′lē ä′nə), *n.* born 1909, queen of the Netherlands since 1948.

Julian calendar, calendar in which the average length of a year was $365\frac{1}{4}$ days, with a leap year of 366 days every fourth year. It was introduced by Julius Caesar in 46 B.C. and used until 1582, when it was replaced by the Gregorian calendar. A year in the Julian calendar was about 11 minutes and 14 seconds longer than a solar year.

Julian the Apostate, A.D. 331-363, Roman emperor from A.D. 361 to 363 who renounced Christianity for paganism.

ju li enne (jü′lē en′), *adj.* cut in thin strips or small pieces: *julienne potatoes.* *—n.* a clear soup containing vegetables cut into thin strips or small pieces. [< French]

Ju li et (jü′lē et, jü′lyət), *n.* heroine of Shakespeare's play *Romeo and Juliet.*

Jul ius Caesar (jü′lyəs). See **Caesar.**

Ju ly (jù lī′), *n., pl.* **-lies.** the seventh month of the year. It has 31 days. [< Latin *Julius,* after *Julius* Caesar, who was born in this month]

jum ble (jum′bəl), *v.,* **-bled, -bling,** *n.* *—v.t.* mix or confuse: *She jumbled up everything in her drawer when she was hunting for her white gloves.* *—n.* a mixed-up mess; state of confusion; muddle. [perhaps imitative]

jum bo (jum′bō), *n., pl.* **-bos,** *adj.* INFORMAL. *—n.* a big, clumsy person, animal, or thing; something unusually large of its kind. *—adj.* very big. [< *Jumbo,* name of a large elephant exhibited by P. T. Barnum]

Jum na River (jum′nə), river flowing from N India into the Ganges River. 860 mi.

jump (jump), *v.i.* 1 spring from the ground; leap; bound: *jump up and down.* See synonym study below. 2 give a sudden start or jerk: *You made me jump.* 3 rise suddenly: *Prices jumped.* 4 (in checkers) pass over and capture an opponent's piece. 5 come (to) too quickly; arrive (at) too soon: *jump to conclusions.* 6 (in bridge) make a bid higher than necessary to raise or overcall a previous bid. *—v.t.* 1 leap over: *jump a stream.* 2 cause to jump: *jump a horse over a fence.* 3 pounce upon; attack. 4 SLANG. evade by running away: *jump bail.* 5 SLANG. get on by jumping: *jump a train.* 6 go around; by-pass, as an electric circuit. 7 skip or pass over. 8 (in checkers) pass over and capture (an opponent's piece). 9 (in bridge) raise a partner's bid by more than one trick. 10 (of a train, subway, etc.) leave (rails or tracks): *Three cars of the morning express jumped the tracks.*
jump at, accept eagerly and quickly.
jump off, a start out. **b** U.S. leave.
jump on, SLANG. blame; scold; criticize.
—n. 1 a spring from the ground; leap; bound. 2 thing to be jumped over. 3 distance jumped. 4 contest in jumping for height or distance. 5 a sudden nervous start or jerk. 6 a sudden rise. 7 move in the game of checkers made to capture an opponent's piece. 8 **get the jump on** or **have the jump on,** SLANG. get or have an advantage over. 9 **on the jump,** INFORMAL. rushing around; always busy.
[probably imitative]
Syn. *v.i.* 1 **Jump, leap** mean to spring into or through the air. **Jump** emphasizes the sudden and springing movement of the feet: *jump from the stair landing, jump across a puddle.* **Leap** emphasizes springing high into or through the air, or to a point, and suggests more grace, lightness, or liveliness than *jump: I love to watch a ballet dancer leap. The deer leaped lightly to the opposite bank of the stream.*

jump cables, electric cables which, when used to link a live battery of the same voltage to a dead battery, will transmit current and help start the engine.

jump er[1] (jum′pər), *n.* 1 person or thing that jumps. 2 tool or device that works with a jumping motion, as a drill to bore holes in rock. 3 wire used to cut out an instrument or part of a circuit or to close temporarily a break in a circuit.

jump er[2] (jum′pər), *n.* 1 a sleeveless dress to wear over a blouse. 2 a loose jacket.

hat, āge, fär; let, ēqual, tėrm;
it, īce; hot, ōpen, ôrder;
oil, out; cup, pu̇t, rüle;
ch, child; ng, long; sh, she;
th, thin; ᴛʜ, then; zh, measure;
ə represents *a* in about, *e* in taken, *i* in pencil, *o* in lemon, *u* in circus.
< = from, derived from, taken from.

Jumpers are worn by workmen to protect their clothes and by sailors as part of their uniform. 3 **jumpers,** *pl.* rompers. [< Middle French *juppe* skirt]

jumper cables, jump cables.

jumping bean, seed of a Mexican plant containing a moth larva whose movements cause the seed to jump.

jumping jack, a toy man or animal that can be made to jump by pulling a string.

jumping mouse, any of a family of mice with long hind legs and very long tail, which they use for jumping.

jump mas ter (jump′mas′tər), *n.* officer who controls the dropping of parachute troops and their equipment from an aircraft.

jump-off (jump′ôf′, jump′of′), *adj.* of or for starting or taking off: *a jump-off point for interplanetary travel.*

jump pass, (in football and basketball) a pass made by a player while jumping.

jump seat, 1 a collapsible seat hinged to the floor of an automobile directly behind the front seat and in front of the back seat. 2 any similar seat hinged to the floor or wall, especially in an airplane, elevator, or the like.

jump shot, (in basketball) shot made while jumping, especially at the highest point of the jump.

jump suit, 1 a one-piece suit worn by parachutists. 2 a woman's one-piece suit of slacks for informal wear.

jump y (jum′pē), *adj.,* **jump i er, jump i est.** 1 moving by jumps; making sudden, sharp jerks. 2 easily excited or frightened; nervous. **—jump′i ness,** *n.*

Jun., 1 June. 2 Junior.

Junc. or **junc.,** junction.

jun co (jung′kō), *n., pl.* **-cos** or **-coes.** any of a genus of small North American finches; snowbird. One kind is often seen in flocks during the winter. [< Spanish, reed < Latin *juncus*]

junc tion (jungk′shən), *n.* 1 a joining: *the junction of two rivers.* 2 a being joined. 3 place of joining or meeting. A railroad junction is a place where railroad lines meet or cross. [< Latin *junctionem* < *jungere* to join]

junc tur al (jungk′chər əl), *adj.* of or having to do with phonetic juncture.

junc ture (jungk′chər), *n.* 1 point or line where two things join; joint. 2 point of time. 3 state of affairs. 4 a critical state of affairs; crisis. 5 a joining. 6 a being joined. 7 the way in which sounds and sound sequences are joined: *There is a difference in juncture between "night rate* (nīt′ rāt′)*" and "nitrate* (nī′trāt).*"* 8 **at this juncture,** when affairs are in this state; at this moment. [< Latin *junctura* a joining < *jungere* to join. Doublet of JOINTURE.]

June (jün), *n.* the sixth month of the year. It has 30 days. [< Latin *Junius,* originally a Roman gens name]

Ju neau (jü′nō), *n.* capital of Alaska, in the SE part. 6000.
June beetle, June bug.
June bug, 1 any of a genus of large brown beetles of North America that appear in June. 2 a large green beetle of the southern United States, very destructive to fruit.
Jung (yůng), *n.* **Carl Gustav,** 1875-1961, Swiss psychologist and psychiatrist.
Jung frau (yůng′frou′), *n.* mountain in the Alps of S central Switzerland. 13,642 ft.
jun gle (jung′gəl), *n.* 1 wild land thickly overgrown with bushes, vines, trees, etc. Jungles are hot and humid regions with many kinds of plants and wild animals. 2 a tangled mass. 3 place or situation in which it is difficult to survive because of intense competition, violence, etc.: *the jungle of a city slum.* 4 SLANG. camp for tramps. [< Hindustani *jangal* < Sanskrit *jaṅgala* desert] **—jun′gle-like′,** *adj.*
jungle fowl, any of several wild birds of southern Asia and the East Indies that are much like domestic fowl and from which the domestic chicken is probably descended.
jungle gym, framework of steel bars for children to climb or swing on as a pastime.
jun gly (jung′glē), *adj.* of or like a jungle.
jun ior (jü′nyər), *adj.* 1 the younger (used especially of a son having the same name as his father): *John Parker, Junior, is the son of John Parker, Senior.* 2 of or for younger people: *a junior choir.* 3 of lower rank or shorter service: *a junior officer, a junior partner.* 4 of or having to do with students in the third year of high school or college. 5 of later date. *—n.* 1 a younger person. 2 person of lower rank or shorter service. 3 student in the third year of high school or college. [< Latin, comparative of *juvenis* young]
junior college, school giving the first two years of a standard four-year college course, or various training, subprofessional, or adult-education courses.
junior high school, school consisting of grades 7, 8, and sometimes 9, attended after elementary school and followed by high school.
junior varsity, a high school or college athletic team that competes on the level next below the varsity.
ju ni per (jü′nə pər), *n.* any of a genus of evergreen shrubs or trees of the same family as the cypress, with small berrylike cones. The cones of one kind of juniper contain an oil used in flavoring gin and in medicines. [< Latin *juniperus*]
junk¹ (jungk), *n.* 1 any old or discarded material, as metal, paper, rags, etc. 2 INFORMAL. anything regarded as worthless or mere trash. 3 hard salted meat eaten by sailors. 4 old rope used for making mats, oakum, etc. 5 SLANG. narcotics, especially heroin. *—v.t.* INFORMAL. throw away or discard as junk. [Middle English *jonk* old cable or cordage]
junk² (jungk), *n.* a Chinese sailing ship with a flat bottom, high stern, low bow, and lug or lateen sails of bamboo matting. [< Portuguese *junco,* ultimately < Javanese *jong*]
Jun ker or **jun ker** (yůng′kər), *n.* member of the former aristocratic class in Prussia. [< German *Junker*]
jun ket (jung′kit), *n.* 1 curdled milk, sweetened and flavored. 2 a feast or picnic. 3 a pleasure trip, especially one taken by an official at the expense of the government. *—v.i.* 1 hold a feast; join in a picnic. 2 go on a pleasure trip, especially at the expense of the government. [probably < dialectal Old French *jonquette* basket < *jonc* reed < Latin *juncus*] **—jun′ket er,** *n.*
jun ket eer (jung′kə tir′), *n.* person who goes on a junket. *—v.i.* go on a junket.
junk ie (jung′kē), *n.* SLANG. person who uses narcotics; drug addict. Also, **junky.**
junk man (jungk′man′), *n., pl.* **-men.** man who buys and sells old metal, paper, rags, etc.
junk y (jung′kē), *adj.,* **junk i er, junk i est,** *n., pl.* **junk ies.** *—adj.* of poor quality; like junk. *—n.* SLANG. junkie.
Ju no (jü′nō), *n., pl.* **-nos** for 2. 1 (in Roman myths) the wife of Jupiter and queen of the gods, identified with the Greek goddess Hera. She was the goddess of women and marriage. 2 a stately, majestic woman.
Ju no esque (jü′nō esk′), *adj.* like Juno; stately and majestic.
jun ta (jun′tə, hůn′tə), *n.* 1 a political or military group holding power after a revolution. 2 an assembly or council for deliberation or administration, especially in Spain and Latin America. 3 junto. [< Spanish, ultimately < Latin *jungere* to join]
jun to (jun′tō), *n., pl.* **-tos.** group of plotters, partisans, etc.; faction; clique. [alteration of *junta*]
Ju pi ter (jü′pə tər), *n.* 1 (in Roman myths) the chief god, ruler of gods and men, identified with the Greek god Zeus; Jove. 2 the largest planet in the solar system. It is the fifth in distance from the sun. See **solar system** for diagram.
Jur a Mountains (jůr′ə), mountain range in France and Switzerland. The highest peak is 5654 ft.
Ju ras sic (jů ras′ik), *n.* 1 the middle geological period of the Mesozoic era, after the Triassic and before the Cretaceous, when dinosaurs dominated the earth and birds first appeared. See chart under **geology.** 2 rocks formed in this period. *—adj.* of or having to do with this period or its rocks. [< French *jurassique* < the *Jura* Mountains]
ju rid i cal (jů rid′ə kəl), *adj.* 1 having to do with the administration of justice. 2 of law; legal. [< Latin *juridicus* < *jus, juris* law + *dicere* say] **—ju rid′i cal ly,** *adv.*
jur is dic tion (jůr′is dik′shən), *n.* 1 right, power, or authority to administer justice or exercise judicial functions. 2 authority; power; control. 3 extent of authority: *The judge ruled that the case was not within his jurisdiction.* 4 the things over which authority extends. 5 territory over which authority extends. [< Latin *jurisdictionem* < *jus, juris* law + *dicere* say]

junk²

jur is dic tion al (jůr′is dik′shə nəl), *adj.* of or having to do with jurisdiction. **—jur′is dic′tion al ly,** *adv.*
jur is pru dence (jůr′i sprüd′ns), *n.* 1 science or philosophy of law. 2 system of laws. 3 branch of law. Medical jurisprudence deals with the application of medical knowledge to certain questions of law. [< Latin *jurisprudentia* < *jus, juris* law + *prudentia* knowledge, prudence]
jur is pru den tial (jůr′i sprü den′shəl), *adj.* having to do with jurisprudence.
jur ist (jůr′ist), *n.* 1 an expert in law. 2 a learned writer on law. [< Medieval Latin *jurista* < Latin *jus, juris* law]
ju ris tic (jů ris′tik), *adj.* of or having to do with jurists or jurisprudence; relating to law. **—ju ris′ti cal ly,** *adv.*
jur or (jůr′ər), *n.* member of a jury.
jur y¹ (jůr′ē), *n., pl.* **jur ies.** 1 group of persons selected to hear evidence in a court of law and sworn to give a decision in accordance with the evidence presented to them. 2 group of persons chosen to give a judgment or to decide who is the winner in a contest and award prizes. [< Anglo-French *jurie* < Old French *jurer* swear < Latin *jurare* < *jus, juris* law]
jur y² (jůr′ē), *adj.* for temporary use on a ship; makeshift. [probably < Old French *ajurie* help < Latin *adjutare* to help]
jur y man (jůr′ē mən), *n., pl.* **-men.** juror.
just¹ (just), *adv.* 1 no more than; only; merely: *We are just an ordinary family, neither rich nor poor.* 2 barely: *The shot just missed the mark.* 3 INFORMAL. quite; truly; positively: *The weather is just glorious.* 4 exactly: *just a pound.* 5 almost exactly: *See the picture just above.* 6 a very little while ago: *She has just gone.* 7 **just now,** only a very short time ago: *I saw him just now.*
—adj. 1 in accordance with what is right and honest; fair: *a just price.* See **fair** for synonym study. 2 deserved; merited; due: *a just reward.* 3 having good grounds; well-founded: *just anger.* 4 true; correct; exact: *a just description.* 5 in accordance with standards or requirements; proper: *just proportions.* 6 righteous; upright: *a just life.* 7 lawful: *a just claim.*
[< Old French *juste* < Latin *justus* upright < *jus, juris* right, law] **—just′ness,** *n.*
➤ **just.** In formal English the limiting word *just* is placed immediately before the word, phrase, or clause it modifies to prevent ambiguity: *The teacher assigned just one chapter for tomorrow.*
just² (just), *n., v.i.* joust.
jus tice (jus′tis), *n.* 1 just conduct; fair dealing: *have a sense of justice.* 2 a being just; fairness; rightness: *the justice of a claim, uphold the justice of our cause.* 3 well-founded reason; rightfulness; lawfulness: *They complained with justice of the bad treatment they had received.* 4 just treatment; deserved reward or punishment. 5 administration of law; trial and judgment by process of law. 6 exercise of power and authority to maintain what is just and right. 7 a judge. The Supreme Court of the United States consists of nine justices. 8 justice of the peace. 9 **do justice to, a** treat fairly. **b** see the good points of; show proper appreciation for. 10 **do oneself justice,** do as well as one really can do. [< Old French < Latin *justitia* < *justus* upright. See JUST¹.]
justice of the peace, a local magistrate who tries minor cases, administers oaths, performs civil marriages, etc.; justice.
jus ti fi a bil i ty (jus′tə fī′ə bil′ə tē), *n.* a being justifiable.
jus ti fi a ble (jus′tə fī′ə bəl), *adj.* capable of being justified; that can be shown to be

just, right, or proper; defensible. **—jus′ti fi′a bly,** *adv.*

jus ti fi ca tion (jus′tə fə kā′shən), *n.* 1 a justifying. 2 a being justified. 3 fact or circumstance that justifies; good reason or excuse. 4 (in theology) a freeing or a being freed from the guilt or penalty of sin.

jus ti fy (jus′tə fī), *v.t.,* **-fied, -fy ing.** 1 show to be just or right; give a good reason for; defend: *The fine quality of the cloth justifies its high price.* 2 show to be just or right. 3 (in theology) clear of blame or guilt; exonerate. 4 make (lines of type) the right length by proper spacing. [< Old French *justifier* < Late Latin *justificare* < Latin *justus* just + *facere* make] **—jus′ti fi′er,** *n.*

Jus tin i an (ju stin′ē ən), *n.* A.D. 483-565, emperor of the Eastern Roman Empire from A.D. 527 to 565. During his reign a famous code of laws was compiled.

jus tle (jus′əl), *v.t., v.i.,* **-tled, -tling,** *n.* jostle.

just ly (just′lē), *adv.* 1 in a just manner. 2 rightly.

jut (jut), *v.,* **jut ted, jut ting,** *n.* —*v.i.* stick out; stand out; project: *The pier juts out from the shore into the water.* —*n.* part that sticks out; projection. [variant of *jet*[1]]

jute (jüt), *n.* 1 a strong fiber used for making coarse fabrics, rope, etc. Jute is obtained from two tropical plants of the same family as the linden. 2 either of these plants. [< Bengali *jhōto* < Sanskrit *jūta* mat of hair]

Jute (jüt), *n.* member of a Germanic tribe that, with the Angles and Saxons, conquered England in the A.D. 400's and 500's.

Jut ish (jü′tish), *adj.* of or having to do with the Jutes.

Jut land Peninsula (jut′lənd), peninsula on which most of Denmark and part of West Germany are located. The British and German navies fought near there in May 1916.

juv., juvenile.

Ju ve nal (jü′və nəl), *n.* A.D. 60?-140?, Roman satirical poet.

ju ve nile (jü′və nəl, jü′və nīl), *adj.* 1 young; youthful; immature. See **young** for synonym study. 2 of or for young people: *juvenile books.* —*n.* 1 a young person. 2 book for young people. 3 actor who plays youthful parts. [< Latin *juvenilis* < *juvenis* young] **—ju′ve nile ly,** *adv.*

juvenile court, court of law where cases involving boys and girls are heard.

juvenile delinquent, boy or girl usually under 18 years of age who has committed a legal offense.

hat, āge, fär; let, ēqual, tėrm;
it, īce; hot, ōpen, ôrder;
oil, out; cup, pu̇t, rüle;
ch, child; ng, long; sh, she;
th, thin; ᴛʜ, then; zh, measure;

ə represents *a* in about, *e* in taken, *i* in pencil, *o* in lemon, *u* in circus.

< = from, derived from, taken from.

ju ve nil i ty (jü′və nil′ə tē), *n.* juvenile quality, condition, or manner.

jux ta pose (juk′stə pōz′), *v.t.,* **-posed, -pos ing.** put close together; place side by side. [< French *juxtaposer* < Latin *juxta* beside + French *poser* to place]

jux ta po si tion (juk′stə pə zish′ən), *n.* 1 a putting close together; a placing side by side. 2 position close together or side by side.

j.v., junior varsity.

Jy., July.

K k

K or **k** (kā), *n., pl.* **K's** or **k's.** the 11th letter of the English alphabet.

K, 1 (in chess) king. 2 potassium [for New Latin *Kalium*]. 3 Kelvin.

k., 1 karat. 2 kilogram or kilograms. 3 kopeck.

Kaa ba (kä′bə), *n.* the most sacred shrine of the Moslems, a small structure, containing a black stone, in the courtyard of the great mosque at Mecca. It is the point toward which Moslems face when praying and the goal of the hajj or pilgrimage. [< Arabic *ka'ba,* literally, square building < *ka'b* cube]

ka bob (kə bob′), *n.* meat cut in small pieces, seasoned with various spices, and roasted on a skewer. Also, **kebab.** [< Hindustani *kabāb* < Arabic]

Ka bu ki (kä bü′kē), *n.* a form of Japanese drama with song and dance, a flamboyant style of acting, and rich décor and costuming. It dates from the 1600's. [< Japanese]

Ka bul (kä′bu̇l), *n.* capital of Afghanistan, in the E part. 435,000.

Kad dish or **kad dish** (kä′dish), *n.* a Hebrew prayer recited in the synagogue as part of daily service and by a person mourning for a deceased parent, brother, sister, etc. [< Aramaic *qaddish* holy]

Kae song (kā′sông′, ka′sung′), *n.* city in SW North Korea, the site of negotiations in the Korean War in 1951. 140,000.

kaf fee klatsch or **Kaf fee klatsch** (kôf′ē kluch′, kä′fā kläch′), *n.* an informal gathering or party at which coffee and pastry are served. [< German *Kaffeeklatsch* < *Kaffee* coffee + *Klatsch* gossip]

Kaf fir (kaf′ər), *n., pl.* **Kaf firs** or **Kaf fir.** 1 member of a Bantu race in South Africa. 2 their language. 3 **kaffir,** kaffir corn. Also, **Kafir.**

kaffir corn, species of sorghum with a stout, short-jointed, leafy stalk, grown for grain and forage in dry regions. Also, **kafir corn.**

Kaf ir (kaf′ər), *n., pl.* **Kaf irs** or **Kaf ir.** Kaffir.

kafir corn, kaffir corn.

Kaf ka (käf′kä), *n.* **Franz,** 1883-1924, Austrian novelist.

kaf tan (kaf′tən, käf tän′), *n.* caftan.

kai ak (kī′ak), *n.* kayak.

Kai feng (kī′feng′), *n.* city in E China. 300,000.

kai ser or **Kai ser** (kī′zər), *n.* 1 title of the rulers of Germany from 1871 to 1918. 2 title of the rulers of Austria from 1804 to 1918. 3 title of the emperors of the Holy Roman Empire from A.D. 962 to 1806. 4 **kaiser,** emperor. [< German *Kaiser* < Latin *Caesar*]

ka ka (kä′kə), *n.* an olive-brown parrot of New Zealand, about the size of a crow, marked with red on various parts of the body and wings. [< Maori]

Ka la ha ri Desert (kä′lä här′ē), large desert and plateau region in S Africa. 350,000 sq. mi.

Kal a ma zoo (kal′ə mə zü′), *n.* city in SW Michigan. 86,000.

kal an cho e (kal′an kō′ē), *n.* any of a genus of tropical, chiefly African plants of the same family as the stonecrop, with thick, fleshy leaves and stems and bright yellow, purple, or scarlet blossoms. [apparently < the Chinese name]

Kalb (kalb), *n.* **Johann.** See **De Kalb.**

kale (kāl), *n.* 1 species of cole having loose, curled leaves. Kale looks somewhat like spinach. 2 its leaves, eaten as a vegetable. [variant of *cole*]

ka lei do scope (kə lī′də skōp), *n.* 1 tube containing bits of colored glass and two mirrors. As it is turned, it reflects continually changing patterns. 2 a continually changing pattern or object. [< Greek *kalos* pretty + *eidos* shape + English *-scope*]

ka lei do scop ic (kə lī′də skop′ik), *adj.* of or like a kaleidoscope; continually changing. **—ka lei′do scop′i cal ly,** *adv.*

kal ends (kal′əndz), *n.pl.* calends.

Ka li man tan (kä′lē män′tän), *n.* part of Indonesia comprising the greater part of Borneo. 4,101,000 pop.; 208,300 sq. mi. Former name, **Dutch Borneo.**

Ka li nin (kə lē′nən), *n.* 1 **Mikhail Ivanovich,** 1875-1946, Soviet political leader, president of the Soviet Union from 1923 to 1946. 2 city in W central Soviet Union in Europe. 345,000.

Ka li nin grad (kə lē′nən grad, kə lē′nən-gräd), *n.* city in W Soviet Union, formerly in East Prussia. 297,000. Also, GERMAN **Königsberg.**

kal mi a (kal′mē ə), *n.* any of a genus of evergreen shrubs of the heath family, especially the mountain laurel, having clusters of cup-shaped rose, purple, or white flowers. [< Peter *Kalm,* 1715-1779, Swedish botanist]

Kal muck or **Kal muk** (kal′muk), *n.* 1 member of a group of Mongol tribes living in western China and the southeastern Soviet Union. Most of the Kalmucks are Buddhists. 2 their Mongolian language.

kal so mine (kal′sə mīn, kal′sə mən), *n., v.t.,* **-mined, -min ing.** calcimine.

ka ma a i na (kä mä′ä ē′nä, kä′mä ī′nä), *n.* HAWAIIAN. a native-born or old resident of Hawaii.

Kam chat ka Peninsula (kam chat′kə), peninsula of NE Asia between the Sea of Okhotsk and the Bering Sea. 750 mi. long; 104,260 sq. mi.

kame (kām), *n.* a hill or ridge of glacial detritus. [special use of *comb*[1]]

ka mi ka ze (kä′mē kä′zē), *n.* 1 a Japanese suicide pilot in World War II, often assigned to dive an airplane loaded with explosives, into a target, usually a naval vessel. 2 the airplane itself. 3 person or thing that acts like or resembles a kamikaze: *run for election as a political kamikaze, dodge the Roman kamikazes.* —*adj.* of, like, or acting in the manner of a kamikaze: *a kamikaze cab driver, kamikaze bugs.* [< Japanese, literally, divine wind]

Kam pa la (käm pä′lä), *n.* capital of Uganda, in the S part. 80,000.

kam pong (käm pong′, käm′pong), *n.* a Malay village. [< Malay]

Kan., Kansas.

Ka nak a (kə nak′ə, kan′ə kə), *n.* 1 native of Hawaii. 2 a South Sea islander. [< Hawaiian, man]

Kan chen jun ga (kän′chən jün′gə), *n.* mountain in the Himalayas, the third highest mountain in the world. 28,168 ft. Also, **Kinchinjunga.**

Kan din sky (kan din′skē), *n.* **Wassily,** 1866-1944, Russian painter.

Kan dy (kän′dē), *n.* city in central Ceylon, famous for its Buddhist temples. 68,000.

kan ga roo[1] (kang′gə rü′), *n., pl.* **-roos** or **-roo.** any of a family of herbivorous marsupial mammals of Australia, New Guinea, Tasmania, and nearby islands, having a small head, large ears, small forelegs, powerful hind legs which give them great leaping power, and a heavy tail for balance and support. [probably < native Austrialian name] **—kan′ga roo′like′,** *adj.*

kangaroo[1]
about 8 ft. long, including the tail

kan ga roo[2] (kang′gə rü′), *adj.* of or having to do with a kangaroo court; unauthorized or irregular; mock: *a kangaroo trial, kangaroo procedures, kangaroo justice.*

kangaroo court, an unauthorized, self-appointed court, such as a mock court by prisoners in a jail.

kangaroo rat, any of a genus of small, burrowing rodents of arid and semiarid regions of North America. Kangaroo rats have cheek pouches and long hind legs and tail.

Kan pur (kän′pu̇r), *n.* city in N India, on the Ganges River. 1,164,000. Also, **Cawnpore.**

Kans., Kansas.

Kan sas (kan′zəs), *n.* 1 one of the midwestern states of the United States. 2,249,000 pop.; 82,300 sq. mi. *Capital:* Topeka. *Abbrev.:* Kans. or Kan. 2 **Kansas River,** river flowing from NE Kansas into the Missouri River. 169 mi. **—Kan′san,** *adj., n.*

Kansas City, 1 city in W Missouri, on the Missouri River. 507,000. 2 city in NE Kansas adjoining it. 168,000.

Kan su (kan′sü′), *n.* province in N central China.

Kant (kant; *German* känt), *n.* **Immanuel,** 1724-1804, German philosopher.

Kant i an (kan′tē ən), *adj.* of or having to do with Kant or his system of philosophy.

ka o lin or **ka o line** (kā′ə lən), *n.* a fine white clay that is used chiefly as a filler in paper and, when mixed with ground feldspar and quartz, is used in making ceramics. [< French *kaolin* < *Kao-ling,* mountain in northern China]

ka on (kā′on), *n.* K meson.

ka pok (kā′pok), *n.* the silky fibers around the seeds of a tropical silk-cotton tree, used for stuffing pillows, mattresses, and life preservers, for insulation, etc.; silk cotton. [< Malay]

kap pa (kap′ə), *n.* the tenth letter of the Greek alphabet (Κ, κ).

ka put (kə pu̇t′), *adj.* INFORMAL. 1 finished; destroyed: *politically kaput. Their romance is kaput.* 2 **go kaput,** be unsuccessful; fail: *During the recession our business went kaput.* 3 out of style; outmoded: *Are westerns now kaput?* [< German *kaputt*]

Ka ra chi (kə rä′chē), *n.* city in S Pakistan, formerly the capital. 3,060,000.

kar a kul (kar′ə kəl), *n.* caracul.

Ka ra Sea, (kär′ə), arm of the Arctic

hat, āge, fär; let, ēqual, tėrm;
it, īce; hot, ōpen, ôrder;
oil, out; cup, pu̇t, rüle;
ch, child; ng, long; sh, she;
th, thin; ᴛʜ, then; zh, measure;
ə represents *a* in about, *e* in taken, *i* in pencil, *o* in lemon, *u* in circus.
< = from, derived from, taken from.

Ocean, off the N coast of Siberia. 300 mi. long; 200 mi. wide.

kar at (kar′ət), *n.* 1/24 part of gold by weight in an alloy. A gold ring of 18 karats is 18 parts pure gold and six parts alloy. Also, **carat.** [variant of *carat*]

ka ra te (kä rä′tē), *n.* a Japanese method of fighting without weapons by striking with the hands, elbows, knees, and feet at certain vulnerable parts of the opponent's body. [< Japanese]

kayak (def. 1)

Ka re li a (kə rē′lē ə, kə rē′lyə), *n.* region and self-governing republic in NW Soviet Union in Europe, next to Finland. 714,000 pop.; 69,700 sq. mi. **—Ka re′li an,** *adj., n.*

Kar lo vy Va ry (kär′lō vē vä′rē), health resort in NW Czechoslovakia. 46,000. Also, GERMAN **Karlsbad, Carlsbad.**

Karls bad (kärlz′bad; *German* kärls′bät), *n.* German name of **Karlovy Vary.** Also, **Carlsbad.**

Karls ruh e (kärlz′rü′ə), *n.* city in S West Germany. 257,000.

kar ma (kär′mə), *n.* (in Buddhism and Hinduism) all the acts, words, and thoughts of one life, supposed to determine a person's fate in his next stage of existence. [< Sanskrit, deed]

kar mic (kär′mik), *adj.* of, having to do with, or determined by karma.

Kar nak (kär′nak), *n.* village in Egypt on the Nile. The N part of ancient Thebes was located there.

Kar roo or **Ka roo** (kə rü′), *n.* 1 extensive plateau region in the Republic of South Africa, in Cape of Good Hope province. 2 **karroo** or **karoo,** a barren, elevated plateau with clayey soil in southern Africa.

kar y o ki ne sis (kar′ē ō ki nē′sis), *n.* (in biology) the division of the cell nucleus, especially in mitosis. [< Greek *karyon* nut, kernel + *kinēsis* motion]

kar y o ki net ic (kar′ē ō ki net′ik), *adj.* having to do with karyokinesis.

kar y o type (kar′ē ō tīp), *n.* the character of a set of chromosomes as defined by their arrangement, number, size, and shape.

Kash mir (kash mir′, kash′mir), *n.* large, mountainous area north of India, claimed by both India and Pakistan. 4,600,000 pop.; 82,300 sq. mi.

Kash mir i (kash mir′ē), *n.* the Indic language of Kashmir.

kash ruth (käsh rüt′), *n.* 1 the Jewish dietary laws. 2 a being kosher.

Ka tah din (kə täd′n), *n.* **Mount,** the highest mountain in Maine. 5268 ft.

Ka tan ga (kə täng′gə, kə tang′gə), *n.* province in SE Zaïre, noted for its richness in minerals. **—Ka tan′gan,** *adj., n.*

Kat man du (kät′män dü′), *n.* capital of Nepal, in the central part. 195,000.

Kat te gat (kat′ə gat), *n.* arm of the North Sea between Denmark and Sweden. 150 mi. long; 40-70 mi. wide.

ka ty did (kā′tē did), *n.* any of various large, green, long-horned grasshoppers. The male makes a shrill noise by rubbing its front wings together. [imitative of its call]

Kau ai (kou ī′), *n.* the fourth largest island of Hawaii. 30,000 pop.; 551 sq. mi.

Kau nas (kou′näs), *n.* city in W Soviet Union. 306,000. Also, RUSSIAN **Kovno.**

kau ri (kou′rē), *n.* 1 a tall evergreen tree that grows in New Zealand. 2 its wood. 3 resin obtained from this tree, used in making varnish. [< Maori]

Kay (kā), *n.* (in Arthurian legends) a rude, boastful knight of the Round Table, foster brother of King Arthur.

kay ak (kī′ak), *n.* 1 an Eskimo canoe made of skins stretched over a light frame of wood or bone with an opening in the middle for a person. 2 a similar small craft made of canvas or other material. Also, **kaiak.** [< Eskimo]

ka yo (kā′ō′), *v.t., n., pl.* **-yos.** SLANG. KO.

Ka zakh S.S.R. (kə zäk′), one of the constituent republics of the U.S.S.R., in the S central part. 12,900,000 pop.; 1,063,200 sq. mi. *Capital:* Alma-Ata.

Ka zan (kä zän′), *n.* city in NW Soviet Union, on the Volga River. 869,000.

ka zoo (kə zü′), *n., pl.* **-zoos.** a toy musical instrument made of a tube sealed off at one end with a membrane, that produces a buzzing or vibration when the tube is hummed into. [imitative]

kc., kilocycle or kilocycles.

K.C., 1 King's Counsel. 2 Knights of Columbus.

kcal., kilocalorie or kilocalories.

ke a (kē′ə, kā′ə), *n.* a large, green parrot of New Zealand with a powerful, hooked bill which it uses to dig out insects. It occasionally kills sheep by tearing at their backs to eat the fat around the kidneys. [< Maori]

Keats (kēts), *n.* **John,** 1795-1821, English poet.

ke bab (kə bob′), *n.* kabob.

kedge (kej), *v.,* **kedged, kedg ing,** *n.* *—v.t.* move (a ship, etc.) by pulling on a rope attached to an anchor that has been dropped some distance away. *—v.i.* use such a method of moving. *—n.* a small anchor used in kedging a boat, etc. [origin uncertain]

keel (kēl), *n.* 1 the main timber or steel piece that extends the whole length of the bottom of a ship or boat. The whole ship is built up on the keel. 2 ARCHAIC. ship. 3 something that resembles a ship's keel in any way, such as the bottom of an airship or airplane. 4 (in biology) a longitudinal ridge, as on the breastbone of a bird, or the two fused lower petals of the flowers of many plants of the pea family. 5 **on an even keel, a** horizontal. **b** calm; steady. *—v.t.* turn upside down; upset. *—v.i.* 1 turn over. 2 **keel over, a** turn over or upside down; upset. **b** fall over suddenly. **c** INFORMAL. faint. [< Scandinavian (Old Icelandic) *kjölr*]

keel boat (kēl′bōt′), *n.* U.S. a large, shallow barge, with a keel and covered deck, formerly used on the Missouri and other western rivers.

keel haul (kēl′hôl′), *v.t.* 1 haul (a person) under the keel of a ship for punishment. 2 scold severely; rebuke.

keel son (kel′sən, kēl′sən), *n.* beam or line of timbers or iron plates fastened along the top of a ship's keel to strengthen it. Also, **kelson.** [< *keel*]

keen[1] (kēn), *adj.* 1 so shaped as to cut well: *a keen blade.* 2 sharp; piercing; cutting: *a keen wind, keen hunger, keen wit, keen pain.* 3 strong; vivid: *keen competition.* 4 highly sensitive; able to perceive well; acute: *a keen mind, a keen sense of smell.* See **sharp** for synonym study. 5 full of enthusiasm; eager: *be keen about sailing.* See **eager** for synonym study. [Old English *cēne*] **—keen′ly,** *adv.* **—keen′ness,** *n.*

keen[2] (kēn), *n.* a wailing lament for the dead. *—v.i.* wail; lament. [< Irish *caoine*] **—keen′er,** *n.*

keep (kēp), *v.,* **kept, keep ing,** *n.* *—v.t.* 1 have for a long time or forever: *You may keep this book.* 2 have and not let go: *keep a secret.* See synonym study below. 3 have and take care of: *She keeps chickens.* 4 take care of and protect; guard: *The bank keeps money for people.* 5 have; hold: *Keep this in mind.* 6 hold back; prevent: *What is keeping her from coming?* 7 maintain in good condition; preserve: *A refrigerator keeps food fresh.* 8 cause to continue in some stated place, condition, etc.; cause to stay the same: *Keep the fire burning.* 9 celebrate; observe: *keep Thanksgiving Day as a holiday.* 10 be faithful to: *keep a promise.* 11 provide for; support: *He is not able to keep himself, much less a family.* 12 have habitually for sale: *That store keeps canned goods.* 13 make regular entries or records in: *keep a diary.* 14 have in one's service; employ: *keep a servant.* *—v.i.* 1 restrain oneself; refrain: *I could hardly keep from smiling.* 2 stay in good condition: *Milk does not keep long in hot weather.* 3 stay the same; continue: *Keep along this road for two miles.*

keep in with, INFORMAL. keep acquaintance or friendship with.

keep on, continue; go on.

keep to oneself, a avoid associating with others. **b** keep something a secret.

keep up, a prevent from ending; continue. **b** maintain in good condition. **c** not fall behind.

keep up with, not fall behind; go or move as fast as.

—n. 1 food and a place to sleep: *work for one's keep.* 2 the strongest part of a castle or fort. 3 **for keeps, a** for the winner to keep his winnings. **b** INFORMAL. forever. [Old English *cēpan* observe]

keep (def. 2)

Syn. *v.t.* 2 **Keep, retain, withhold** mean to hold in one's possession. **Keep** means to have and not let go from one's possession, control, or care: *They were kept in prison.* **Retain** emphasizes continuing to keep, especially against efforts to take away or make one let go: *Our team retained a commanding lead.* **Withhold** means to keep back or refuse to let go: *withhold part of one's salary.*

keep er (kē′pər), *n.* one that keeps: *a keeper of secrets.* 2 guard; watchman. 3 custodian; guardian: *Am I my brother's keeper?* 4 person who owns or carries on some establishment or business: *the keeper of an inn.*

keep ing (kē′ping), *n.* 1 care; charge; maintenance: *The children were left in their uncle's keeping.* 2 celebration; observance: *the keeping of Thanksgiving Day.* 3 agreement; harmony: *actions in keeping with one's promises.* 4 a being kept for future use; preservation.

keep sake (kēp′sāk′), *n.* thing kept in memory of the giver; remembrance; memento: *Before my friend went away, he gave me his picture as a keepsake.*

Kee wa tin (kē wät′n), *n.* district of the Northwest Territories, north of Manitoba. 228,200 sq. mi.

keg (keg), *n.* 1 a small barrel, usually holding less than 10 gallons. 2 as much as a keg can hold. 3 unit of weight for nails, equal to 100 pounds. [< Scandinavian (Old Icelandic) *kaggi*]

keg ler (keg′lər), *n.* INFORMAL. person who bowls; bowler.

Kel ler (kel′ər), *n.* **Helen** (Adams), 1880-1968, American writer and lecturer who was deaf, dumb, and blind from infancy, but was taught to read and speak.

Kel logg (kel′og), *n.* **Frank Billings,** 1856-1937, American statesman.

kelp (kelp), *n.* 1 any of various large, tough, brown seaweeds. 2 ashes of seaweed, used as a source of iodine. [Middle English *culpe*]

kel pie or **kel py** (kel′pē), *n., pl.* **-pies.** 1 (in Scottish folklore) a water spirit, usually in the form of a horse, supposed to drown people or warn them of drowning. 2 any of a breed of Australian sheep dogs. [origin uncertain]

kel son (kel′sən), *n.* keelson.

Kelt (kelt), *n.* Celt.

kel ter (kel′tər), *n.* DIALECT. kilter.

Kelt ic (kel′tik), *adj., n.* Celtic.

Kel vin (kel′vən), *adj.* of, based on, or according to a scale for measuring temperature on which 273 degrees marks the freezing point of water, 373 degrees marks the boiling point, and 0 degrees marks absolute zero. [< William Thomson, Lord *Kelvin,* 1824-1907, British physicist and mathematician]

Ke mal A ta türk (kə mäl′ ä′tä tyrk′, kə-mäl′ at′ə tėrk′), **Mustafa,** 1881-1938, first president of Turkey, from 1923 to 1938.

Kem pis (kem′pis), *n.* **Thomas à,** 1380?-1471, German churchman and religious writer.

kempt (kempt), *adj.* tidy and neat; well-groomed: *kempt clothing, a kempt hair style.* [back-formation from *unkempt*]

ken (ken), *n., v.,* **kenned** or **kent** (kent), **ken ning.** —*n.* 1 range of sight. 2 range of knowledge: *What happens on Mars is no longer beyond our ken.* —*v.t.* SCOTTISH. know. —*v.i.* SCOTTISH. have knowledge. [Old English *cennan* make declaration < *cann* know, can[1]]

Ken., Kentucky.

ke naf (kə naf′), *n.* 1 fiber of an Asian plant, used as a substitute for hemp or jute. 2 the plant itself, a species of hibiscus. [< Persian]

ken do (ken′dō), *n.* a Japanese form of fencing in which bamboo or wooden sticks are used for swords. [< Japanese]

Ken ne bec River (ken′ə bek), river flowing from W Maine into the Atlantic. 164 mi.

Ken ne dy (ken′ə dē), *n.* 1 **Cape,** cape in E Florida projecting into the Atlantic, from which the United States launches missiles and rockets. Former name, **Cape Canaveral.** 2 **John F(itzgerald),** 1917-1963, the 35th president of the United States, from 1961 to 1963.

Kennedy International Airport, a major international and domestic airport, in the borough of Queens in New York City.

ken nel (ken′l), *n., v.,* **-neled, -nel ing** or **-nelled, -nel ling.** —*n.* 1 house for a dog or dogs. 2 Often, **kennels,** *pl.* place where dogs are bred or boarded. 3 pack of hounds or dogs of any kind. —*v.t.* put or keep in a kennel. —*v.i.* take shelter or lodge in a kennel. [< unrecorded Old French *kenil,* ultimately < Latin *canis* dog]

ken ning (ken′ing), *n.* a descriptive poetical expression used instead of the simple name of a person or thing, especially in Old English or Old Norse poetry. EXAMPLES: "storm of swords" for "battle" and "wave-traveler" for "boat." [< Scandinavian (Old Icelandic) < *kenna vith* to name after]

ke no (kē′nō), *n.* a gambling game somewhat like lotto in which the players cover numbers on their cards. [origin uncertain]

Ke no sha (kə nō′shə), *n.* city in SW Wisconsin, on Lake Michigan. 79,000.

Kent (kent), *n.* 1 county in SE England. 2 ancient kingdom in SE England. See **Mercia** for map.

Kent ish (ken′tish), *adj.* of Kent or its people. —*n.* an Anglo-Saxon dialect spoken in the kingdom of Kent.

Ken tuck y (kən tuk′ē), *n.* 1 one of the south central states of the United States. 3,219,000 pop.; 40,400 sq. mi. *Capital:* Frankfort. *Abbrev.:* Ky. or Ken. 2 **Kentucky River,** river flowing from E Kentucky into the Ohio River. 259 mi. —**Ken tuck′i an,** *adj., n.*

Ken ya (ken′yə, kē′nyə), *n.* country in E Africa, a member of the Commonwealth of Nations. 10,943,000 pop.; 225,000 sq. mi. *Capital:* Nairobi. —**Ken′yan,** *adj., n.*

Ken yat ta (ken yä′tə), *n.* **Jomo,** born 1893, Kenyan political leader, president of Kenya since 1964.

kepi

kep i (kep′ē), *n.* a military cap with a round, flat top and a visor, worn by French soldiers. [< French *képi*]

Kep ler (kep′lər), *n.* **Johann,** 1571-1630, German astronomer.

kept (kept), *v.* pt. and pp. of **keep.**

Ke ra la (kär′ə lə), *n.* state in SW India.

ker a tin (ker′ə tən), *n.* a complex, insoluble protein, the chief structural constituent of horn, nails, hair, feathers, etc. [< Greek *keratos* horn]

ke rat i nous (kə rat′n əs), *adj.* horny.

kerb (kėrb), *n.* BRITISH. curb (def. 1).

ker chief (kėr′chif), *n.* 1 piece of cloth worn over the head or around the neck. 2 handkerchief. [< Old French *couvrechief* < *couvrir* to cover + *chief* head]

kerchief (def. 1)

Ke ren sky (kə ren′skē), *n.* **Alexander,** 1881-1970, Russian revolutionary leader and premier, active in the Russian Revolution of March 1917.

kerf (kėrf), *n.* cut made by an ax, saw, etc. [Old English *cyrf* < *ceorfan* carve]

Ker gue len Islands (kėr′gə len), archipelago in the S Indian Ocean, a territory of France. 2700 sq. mi.

ker mes (kėr′mēz), *n.* a red dyestuff made from the dried bodies of female scale insects, formerly used in medicine. [< French *kermès* < Arabic *qirmiz* < Sanskrit *kṛmis* worm, insect]

ker mess (kėr′mis), *n.* kermis.

ker mis (kėr′mis), *n.* 1 fair with games and merrymaking, held in the Netherlands, Belgium, and adjacent regions. 2 any fair or entertainment, usually to raise money for charity. Also, **kirmess.** [< Dutch < *kerk* church + *mis* Mass]

kern[1] (kėrn), *n.* 1 ARCHAIC. an Irish or Scottish foot soldier carrying light weapons. 2 an Irish peasant. Also, **kerne.** [< Irish *ceithern* troop of soldiers]

kern[2] (kėrn), *n.* the part of a letter or type face that projects above the body, as in *h,* or below, as in *p.* [< Old North French *carne* edge < Latin *cardinem* hinge]

kerne (kėrn), *n.* kern[1].

ker nel (kėr′nl), *n.* 1 the softer part inside the hard shell of a nut or inside the stone of a fruit. 2 the body of a seed within its coating. 3 grain or seed of wheat, corn, or other cereal plant. 4 the central or most important part of anything; core. [Old English *cyrnel* < *corn* seed, grain]

kern ite (kėr′nīt), *n.* a colorless or white crystalline mineral, an important ore of boron compounds. *Formula:* $Na_2B_4O_7 \cdot 4H_2O$ [< *Kern,* county in California, where it is found]

ker o sene or **ker o sine** (ker′ə sēn′, ker′ə sēn′), *n.* a thin, oily mixture of hydrocarbons distilled from petroleum; coal oil. It is used as fuel in lamps, stoves, some types of engines, etc. [< Greek *kēros* wax]

Ker ry (ker′ē), *n., pl.* **-ries** for 2. 1 county in the SW part of the Republic of Ireland. 2 one of a breed of small, black dairy cattle that originated there.

Kerry blue terrier, any of a breed of terriers originating in Ireland, having a short body and long legs and a soft, bluish-gray coat.

ker sey (kėr′zē), *n., pl.* **-seys.** a coarse, ribbed, woolen cloth with a cotton warp.

hat, āge, fär; let, ēqual, tėrm;
it, īce; hot, ōpen, ôrder;
oil, out; cup, pu̇t, rüle;
ch, child; ng, long; sh, she;
th, thin; ᴛʜ, then; zh, measure;

ə represents *a* in about, *e* in taken, *i* in pencil, *o* in lemon, *u* in circus.

< = from, derived from, taken from.

[probably < *Kersey,* village in Suffolk, England]

kes trel (kes′trəl), *n.* 1 a small European falcon, noted for its habit of hovering in the air facing into the wind. 2 any of several similar falcons. [probably < Old French *cresserelle*]

ketch (kech), *n.* a small fore-and-aft-rigged sailing ship with a large mainmast toward the bow and a smaller mast toward the stern. [probably < *catch,* noun, in sense of "pursuit, chase"]

ketch up (kech′əp), *n.* catsup.

ke to gen ic (kē′tə jen′ik), *adj.* 1 producing ketones. 2 that can be converted into ketones.

ke tone (kē′tōn), *n.* any of a group of organic compounds consisting of a carbonyl (-CO) radical attached to two univalent hydrocarbon radicals, or to derivatives of either of these, as acetone. [< German *Keton* < French *acétone* acetone]

ketone bodies, group of ketones resulting from incomplete oxidation of fatty acids. Their presence in urine is a symptom of diabetes.

ke ton ic (ki ton′ik), *adj.* of or having to do with ketones.

ke to ster oid (kē′tō ster′oid), *n.* any of a group of steroid hormones which originate in the adrenal glands and testes. Their presence in urine is used to determine the functioning conditions of these organs.

ket tle (ket′l), *n.* 1 any metal container for boiling liquids, cooking fruit, etc. 2 teakettle. 3 **kettle of fish,** awkward state of affairs; mess; muddle. [Old English *cetel* < Latin *catillus,* diminutive of *catinus* vessel]

kettledrum
two kettledrums

ket tle drum (ket′l drum′), *n.* drum consisting of a hollow brass or copper hemisphere and a parchment top that can be tuned to a definite pitch by adjusting the tension; timbal.

key¹ (kē), *n., pl.* **keys,** *adj., v.* —*n.* 1 a small metal instrument for locking and unlocking the lock of a door, a padlock, etc. 2 anything shaped or used like it: *a key to open a tin can.* 3 the answer to a puzzle or problem. 4 sheet or book of answers: *a key to a test.* 5 a systematic explanation of abbreviations and symbols used in a dictionary, map, etc. The pronunciation key in this dictionary lists all the symbols of the sounds in English that are used in the pronunciations, and also gives examples of words that contain these sounds. 6 place that commands or gives control of a sea, a district, etc., because of its position: *Gibraltar is the key to the Mediterranean.* 7 an important or essential person, thing, etc. 8 pin, bolt, wedge, or other piece put in a hole or space to hold parts together. 9 one of a set of levers pressed down by the fingers in playing some musical instruments, such as a piano, and in operating a typewriter or other instrument. 10 a mechanical device for opening and closing an electric circuit, as in a telegraph. 11 scale or system of related tones in music which are based on a keynote: *a song written in the key of C.* 12 device to turn a bolt or nut. Watches used to be wound with keys. 13 tone of voice; style of thought or expression: *The poet wrote in a melancholy key.* 14 key fruit; samara. 15 a guide to the identification of a group of plants or animals, having the outstanding determining characteristics arranged in a systematic way.
—*adj.* controlling; very important: *the key industries of a nation.*
—*v.t.* 1 fasten or adjust with a key. 2 regulate the pitch of; tune: *key a musical instrument in preparation for a concert.* 3 adjust (a speech, etc.) as if to a particular key: *key a letter to a tone of defiance.* 4 lock. 5 **key up,** raise the courage or nerve of: *The coach keyed up the team for the big game.*
[Old English *cǣg*] —**key′less,** *adj.*

key² (kē), *n., pl.* **keys.** a low island or reef, as in the West Indies or south of Florida; cay. [< Spanish *càyo* shoal, rock]

Key (kē), *n.* **Francis Scott,** 1779-1843, American lawyer, author of "The Star-Spangled Banner."

key board (kē′bôrd′, kē′bōrd′), *n.* the set of keys in a piano, organ, typewriter, etc.

keyed (kēd), *adj.* 1 having keys: *a keyed flute.* 2 set or pitched in a particular key. 3 fastened or strengthened with a key. 4 constructed with a keystone.

key fruit, samara.

key hole (kē′hōl′), *n.* the opening in a lock through which a key is inserted.

Keynes (kānz), *n.* **John Maynard,** first Baron, 1883-1946, British economist.

key note (kē′nōt′), *n., v.,* **-not ed, -not ing.** —*n.* 1 (in music) a tone on which a scale or system of tones is based; tonic. 2 main idea; guiding principle: *World peace was the keynote of the speech.* —*v.t.* 1 give the keynote address of (a conference, political campaign, etc.). 2 (in music) give the keynote of. —**key′not′er,** *n.*

keynote address or **keynote speech,** speech, usually at a political gathering, that presents the principal issues in which those present are interested.

key punch, machine having a keyboard similar to that of a typewriter, used to record and code information by punching patterns of holes in cards or tapes.

key signature, sharps or flats placed after the clef at the beginning of a staff of music to indicate the key.

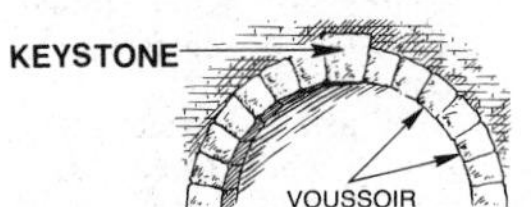

keystone (def. 1)

key stone (kē′stōn′), *n.* 1 the middle stone at the top of an arch, holding the other stones or pieces in place. 2 part on which other related parts depend; essential principle.

key way (kē′wā′), *n.* 1 groove or slot in a shaft in which a pin, bolt, wedge, etc., fits. 2 slit in a lock for a flat key. 3 keyhole for a peg or key.

Key West, 1 island off the coast of SW Florida. 2 seaport on this island, the southernmost city of the continental United States. 29,000.

key word, word, such as a headword or entry word, that serves as a guide to find other words, articles, topics, etc., in a list.

kg., 1 keg or kegs. 2 kilogram or kilograms.

K.G., Knight of the Garter.

Kha cha tu ri an (kach′ə tür′ē ən), *n.* **Aram,** born 1903, Russian composer.

khak i (kak′ē, kä′kē), *n.* 1 a dull yellowish brown. 2 a heavy twilled wool or cotton cloth of this color, much used for soldiers' uniforms. 3 **khakis,** *pl.* uniform made of this cloth. —*adj.* dull yellowish-brown. [< Hindi *khākī,* originally, dusty < Persian *khāk* dust]

kha lif (kā′lif, kal′if), *n.* caliph.

Khal kha (kal′kə), *n., pl.* **-kha** or **-khas** for 1. 1 member of a Mongolian people constituting the largest population group of the Mongolian People's Republic. 2 language of this people. It is the official language of their country.

khan¹ (kän, kan), *n.* 1 (formerly) a title of a ruler among Tartar or Mongol tribes. 2 title of respect in Iran, Afghanistan, India, etc. [< Turkish *khān*]

khan² (kän, kan), *n.* (in Turkey and nearby countries) an inn for travelers; caravansary. [< Persian *khān*]

khan ate (kä′nāt, kan′āt), *n.* 1 territory ruled by a khan. 2 position or authority of a khan.

Khar kov (kär′kôf), *n.* city in SW Soviet Union. 1,223,000.

Khar toum or **Khar tum** (kär tüm′), *n.* capital of Sudan, on the Nile. 194,000.

khe dive (kə dēv′), *n.* title of the Turkish viceroys who ruled Egypt between 1867 and 1914. [< Turkish *hidiv* < Persian *khidīv* ruler]

Khmer (kmer), *n., pl.* **Khmer** or **Khmers** for 1. 1 member of the dominant people of Cambodia. 2 language of Cambodia.

Khmer Republic, official name of **Cambodia.**

Khru shchev (krüsh chôf′, krüsh′chef), *n.* **Nikita S.,** 1894-1971, Russian statesman, premier of the Soviet Union from 1958 to 1964.

Khu fu (kü′fü), *n.* See **Cheops.**

Khy ber Pass (kī′bər), important mountain pass between N Pakistan and E Afghanistan. 33 mi. long; 3500 ft. high.

Kiang si (kyäng′sē′), *n.* province in SE China.

Kiang su (kyäng′sü′), *n.* province in E China.

kib butz (ki büts′), *n., pl.* **-butz im** (-bü tsēm′), an Israeli communal settlement, especially a farm cooperative. [< Hebrew *qibbūṣ* a gathering, collectivity]

kibe (kīb), *n.* a chapped or ulcerated sore, inflammation, or swelling, especially on the heel, caused by exposure to cold. [Middle English]

kib itz (kib′its), *v.i.* INFORMAL. look on as an outsider and offer unwanted advice. [< *kibitzer*]

kib itz er (kib′it sər), *n.* INFORMAL. 1 person who gives unwanted advice; meddler.

2 person watching a card game, especially one who gives unwanted advice to the players. [< Yiddish *kibitser* < German *Kiebitz* busybody, pewit]

ki bosh (kī′bosh, ki bosh′), *n.* SLANG. 1 nonsense; humbug. 2 **put the kibosh on,** finish off; squelch. [origin uncertain]

kick (kik), *v.i.* 1 strike out with the foot: *That horse kicks when anyone comes near him.* 2 spring back when fired; recoil: *This shotgun kicks.* 3 INFORMAL. find fault; complain; object; grumble. —*v.t.* 1 strike with the foot: *kick a ball.* 2 drive, force, or move by kicking: *kick off one's shoes.* 3 make (a score) by a kick: *kick a field goal in football.* 4 SLANG. get rid of: *kick the habit of smoking.*
kick around, INFORMAL. **a** treat roughly; abuse. **b** go about aimlessly. **c** consider or discuss (a plan, topic, proposal, etc.)
kick back, **a** INFORMAL. spring back suddenly and unexpectedly. **b** SLANG. return (a stolen item) to its owner. **c** SLANG. return a portion of money received as a fee.
kick in, SLANG. pay what is due or expected.
kick off, **a** put a football in play with a kick at the beginning of each half and after a field goal or conversion attempt has been made. **b** SLANG. begin. **c** SLANG. die.
kick out, INFORMAL. expel or turn out in a humiliating or disgraceful way: *be kicked out of school.*
kick up, SLANG. start; cause.
—*n.* 1 a blow with the foot. 2 recoil or backward motion of a gun when it is fired. 3 SLANG. cause for complaint; complaint; objection. 4 SLANG. excitement; thrill. 5 SLANG. the intoxicating effect of alcohol, a drug, etc.
[Middle English *kiken*] **—kick′er,** *n.*

kick back (kik′bak′), *n.* 1 SLANG. amount or portion of a fee returned, especially as a bribe for having received a contract: *The dishonest builder offered to pay a kickback to the mayor if the city would award business to his firm.* 2 SLANG. a returning of stolen goods. 3 a sudden violent or vigorous reaction, usually unexpected.

kick off (kik′ôf′, kik′of′), *n.* 1 kick that puts a football in play at the beginning of each half and after a field goal or conversion attempt has been made. 2 INFORMAL. any move, etc., made to begin.

kick shaw (kik′shô′), *n.* 1 a fancy article of food; delicacy. 2 trifle; trinket. [alteration of French *quelque chose* something]

kid[1] (kid), *n.* 1 a young goat. 2 its flesh, used as food. 3 its skin, used as fur. 4 leather made from its skin, used for gloves and shoes. 5 INFORMAL. child. [< Scandinavian (Old Icelandic) *kith*]

kid[2] (kid), *v.,* **kid ded, kid ding.** SLANG. —*v.t.* 1 tease playfully. 2 deceive; fool. —*v.i.* talk jokingly; banter. [perhaps < *kid*[1] in sense of "treat as a child"] **—kid′der,** *n.*

Kidd (kid), *n.* **William,** 1645?-1701, Scottish privateer and pirate, known as "Captain Kidd."

kid dush (kid′əsh), *n.* a Hebrew prayer said over a cup of wine or over bread in consecration of the Sabbath or a holiday. [< Hebrew *kiddūsh* sanctification]

kid-gloved (kid′gluvd′), *adj.* INFORMAL. careful; considerate.

kid gloves, 1 gloves made of soft kidskin. 2 **handle with kid gloves,** treat with great care; treat with consideration and delicacy.

kid nap (kid′nap), *v.t.,* **-naped, -nap ing** or **-napped, -nap ping.** steal or carry off (a person, especially a child) by force; seize and hold (a person) against his will by force or by fraud; abduct. [< *kid*[1] child + *nap* snatch away, variant of *nab*] **—kid′nap er, kid′nap per,** *n.*

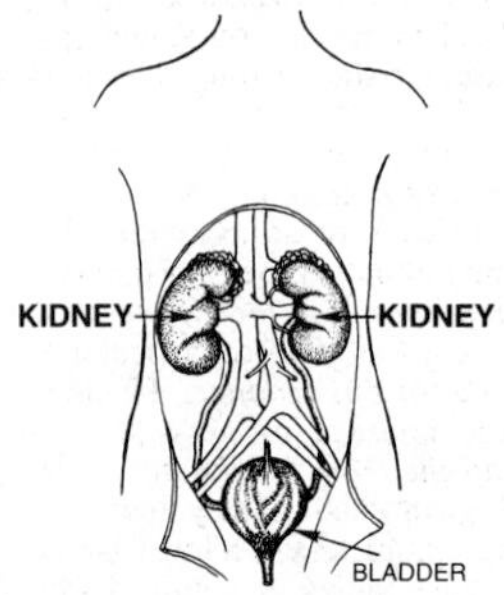

kidney (def. 1)—kidneys of a human being

kid ney (kid′nē), *n., pl.* **-neys.** 1 one of the pair of organs in the bodies of mammals, birds, and reptiles that separate waste matter from the blood and pass it off through the bladder as urine. In human beings, the kidneys are elongated ovals about four inches long, indented on one side. They are located on either side of the backbone at waist level and above. 2 kidney or kidneys of an animal, cooked for food. 3 nature; disposition. 4 kind; sort. [Middle English] **—kid′ney-like′,** *adj.*

kidney bean, 1 a large, red bean, shaped like a kidney and used as a vegetable. 2 the plant it grows on. 3 the seed of the scarlet runner.

kidney stone, a calculus or concretion forming in the kidney.

kid skin (kid′skin′), *n.* leather made from the skin of young goats, used for gloves and shoes.

Kiel (kēl), *n.* seaport in N West Germany, on the Baltic Sea. 269,000.

Kiel Canal, ship canal in N West Germany, from the North Sea to the Baltic Sea. 61 mi. long.

Kier ke gaard (kir′kə gärd; *Danish* kir′kə-gôr), *n.* **Sören (Aabye),** 1813-1855, Danish philosopher and theologian.

kie sel guhr (kē′zəl gůr), *n.* diatomite. [< German *Kieselguhr* < *Kiesel* gravel + *Guhr* earthy sediment]

Kie sing er (kē′zing ər), *n.* **Kurt Georg,** born 1904, German statesman, chancellor of West Germany from 1966 to 1969.

Ki ev (kē′ef), *n.* city in SW Soviet Union, capital of the Ukrainian S.S.R. 1,632,000.

Ki ga li (ki gä′lē), *n.* capital of Rwanda, in the central part. 7000.

Ki ku yu (ki kü′yü, kik′ə yü), *n., pl.* **-yus** or **-yu** for 1. 1 member of one of the principal Negro tribes in Kenya. 2 the Bantu language of this tribe.

Ki lau e a (kē′lou ä′ə), *n.* crater on the volcano Mauna Loa, in Hawaii. 4040 ft. high.

Kil dare (kil der′, kil dar′), *n.* county in E Republic of Ireland, in Leinster.

Kil i man ja ro (kil′ə mən jä′rō), *n.* **Mount,** the highest mountain in Africa, in NE Tanzania. 19,340 ft.

Kil ken ny (kil ken′ē), *n.* county in SE Republic of Ireland.

kill[1] (kil), *v.t.* 1 put to death; cause the death of. See synonym study below. 2 put an end to; get rid of; destroy: *kill odors, kill faith.* 3 cancel (a word, paragraph, item, etc.); delete. 4 defeat or veto (a legislative bill). 5 destroy or neutralize the active qualities of: *kill land in farming.* 6 spoil the effect of: *One color may kill another near it.* 7 use up (time). 8 INFORMAL. cause great pain or discomfort to: *My sore foot is killing me.* 9 INFORMAL. overcome completely: *His jokes really kill me.* 10 (in tennis, etc.) hit (a ball) so hard that it cannot be returned. —*v.i.* cause death: *"Thou shalt not kill."*
—*n.* 1 act of killing. 2 animal or animals killed, especially by sportsmen or beasts of prey. 3 the shooting down or destruction of an enemy missile or aircraft. 4 the missile, etc., so destroyed.
[Middle English *kyllen, cullen;* probably related to *quell*]
Syn. *v.t.* 1 **Kill, murder, slay** mean to cause death. **Kill** is the general word meaning to put to death a person, animal, or plant in any way: *Overwork killed him. Lack of water kills flowers.* **Murder** means to kill a person unlawfully, especially with premeditation: *He murdered his rich uncle.* **Slay,** chiefly literary or journalistic, means to kill a person or animal with violence, in battle, or by murdering: *The dragon was slain by Saint George.*

kill[2] (kil), *n.* U.S. DIALECT. stream, creek, or river. [< Dutch *kil*]

Kil lar ney (kə lär′nē), *n.* 1 town in SW Republic of Ireland. 7000. 2 **Lakes of,** three lakes near there.

kill deer (kil′dir′), *n., pl.* **-deers** or **-deer.** a North American bird of the same family as the plovers which has two black bands across its breast. It has a loud, shrill cry. [imitative of its call]

killed (kild), *adj.* (of a vaccine or virus) made powerless to produce disease; inactivated.

kill er (kil′ər), *n.* 1 person, animal, or thing that kills. 2 killer whale.

killer whale, a large mammal, of the same family as the dolphin, that travels in schools and kills and eats large fish, seals, and even other whales; grampus.

kill ing (kil′ing), *adj.* 1 deadly; destructive; fatal: *a killing frost.* 2 overpowering; exhausting: *work at a killing pace.* 3 INFORMAL. extremely funny. —*n.* INFORMAL. a sudden great financial success: *make a killing in stocks.*

kill joy (kil′joi′), *n.* person who spoils other people's fun.

Kil mer (kil′mər), *n.* **(Alfred) Joyce,** 1886-1918, American poet.

kiln (kil, kiln), *n.* furnace or oven for burning, baking, or drying something. Limestone is burned in a kiln to make lime. Bricks are baked in a kiln. —*v.t.* burn, bake, or dry in a kiln. [Old English *cyln, cylen* < Latin *culina* kitchen]

ki lo (kē′lō, kil′ō), *n., pl.* **-los.** 1 kilogram. 2 kilometer. [< French]

kilo-, *prefix.* one thousand: *Kilogram = one thousand grams.* [< French < Greek *chilioi*]

kil o cal or ie (kil′ə kal′ər ē), *n.* calorie (def. 1b).

kil o cy cle (kil′ə sī′kəl), *n.* 1 1000 cycles. 2 1000 cycles per second, used formerly to express the frequency of radio waves, now expressed in kilohertz.

kil o gram (kil′ə gram), *n.* unit of mass equal to 1000 grams. See **measure** for table.

kil o gramme (kil′ə gram), *n.* BRITISH. kilogram.

kil o gram-me ter (kil′ə gram mē′tər), *n.* unit used in measuring work, equal to 7.2334 foot-pounds. It is the amount of work done in lifting one kilogram one meter.

kil o hertz (kil′ə herts′), *n.* 1000 hertz, used to express the frequency of radio waves.

kil o li ter (kil′ə lē′tər), *n.* unit of volume equal to 1000 liters. See **measure** for table.

kil o li tre (kil′ə lē′tər), *n.* BRITISH. kiloliter.

kil o me ter (kə lom′ə tər, kil′ə mē′tər), *n.* unit of length equal to 1000 meters. See **measure** for table.

kil o me tre (kil′ə mē′tər), *n.* BRITISH. kilometer.

kil o met ric (kil′ə met′rik), *adj.* 1 of a kilometer. 2 measured in kilometers.

kil o ton (kil′ə tun′), *n.* 1 unit of weight equal to 1000 tons. 2 unit of atomic power equivalent to the energy released by one thousand tons of TNT.

kil o volt (kil′ə vōlt′), *n.* unit of electromotive force equivalent to 1000 volts.

kil o watt (kil′ə wot′), *n.* unit of electrical power equal to 1000 watts.

kil o watt-hour (kil′ə wot′our′), *n.* unit of electrical energy equal to the work done by one kilowatt acting for one hour.

kilt (kilt), *n.* 1 a pleated skirt reaching to the knees, usually of tartan cloth, worn especially by men in the Scottish Highlands. 2 any similar skirt. —*v.t.* SCOTTISH. tuck up; fasten up. [probably < Scandinavian (Danish) *kilte (op)* tuck up]

kilt ed (kil′tid), *adj.* 1 wearing a kilt. 2 pleated like a kilt.

kil ter (kil′tər), *n.* **out of kilter,** INFORMAL. out of working order; not in good condition: *Our radio is out of kilter.* Also, DIALECT **kelter.** [origin uncertain]

Kim ber ley (kim′bər lē), *n.* city in central Republic of South Africa. The world's largest diamond mines are near it. 96,000.

ki mo no (kə mō′nə), *n., pl.* **-nos.** 1 a loose outer garment held in place by a wide sash, worn by Japanese men and women. 2 a woman's loose dressing gown. [< Japanese]

kin (kin), *n.* 1 a person's family or relatives; kindred. 2 family relationship; connection by birth or marriage: *What kin is she to you?* 3 **next of kin,** nearest living relative. 4 **of kin,** related. —*adj.* related [Old English *cynn*]

-kin, *suffix.* little: *Lambkin = a little lamb.* [Middle English < Middle Dutch *-kijn, -ken*]

Kin chin jun ga (kin′chin jůn′gə), *n.* Kanchenjunga.

kind[1] (kīnd), *adj.* 1 doing good rather than harm; friendly: *a kind girl.* See synonym study below. 2 gentle: *Be kind to animals.* 3 showing or characterized by kindness: *kind words.* [Old English *(ge)cynde* natural < *(ge)cynd* nature, kind[2]]

Syn. 1 **Kind, kindly, gracious** mean having or showing a generous, sympathetic, considerate attitude toward others. **Kind** implies that the attitude is genuine, natural, and sincere: *The kind old man helped the young man get a job.* **Kindly** is a milder term and suggests a sympathetic manner or appearance: *The teacher's kindly manner encouraged me to ask for help.* **Gracious** means kindly and courteous in manner, especially toward younger people or those of lower position: *The famous singer is a gracious lady.*

kind[2] (kīnd), *n.* 1 group of individuals or objects having characteristics in common; class; sort; variety: *many kinds of candy.* See synonym study below. 2 natural group; race: *Snakes belong to the serpent kind.* 3 **in kind, a** in goods or produce, not in money. **b** in something of the same sort. **c** in characteristic quality: *difference in kind, not merely in degree.* 4 **kind of,** INFORMAL. nearly; almost; somewhat; rather: *kind of skinny.* 5 **of a kind, a** of the same sort; alike. **b** of a poor or mediocre quality: *Two boxes and a plank make a table of a kind.* [Old English *(ge)cynd*]

Syn. 1 **Kind, sort** mean a group of individuals or things alike in some way. **Kind** applies particularly to a group of the same nature or character, having enough closely similar essential qualities in their makeup to put them together as a class or division in some system of classification: *What kind of cake do you like best?* **Sort,** often interchangeable with *kind,* is usually vaguer, and sometimes means only of the same general description: *That sort of action disgusts me.*

➤ **kind, sort.** *Kind* and *sort* are both singular nouns in form. In formal English, demonstrative adjectives used to modify them agree with them in number: *This kind of apple is likely to be wormy. That sort of behavior is out of place here.* A plural adjective is used only when *kind* or *sort* is plural: *Those kinds of fish are caught with special tackle.* In informal spoken English the plural idea implied in these words often results in constructions like *those kind of books* and *these sort of ideas,* but it is wise to avoid such constructions in writing.

kin der gar ten (kin′dər gärt′n), *n.* school or class for children from four to six years old that educates them by games, toys, exercises, and pleasant occupations. [< German *Kindergarten* < *Kinder* children + *Garten* garden]

kin der gart ner or **kin der gar ten er** (kin′dər gärt′nər), *n.* 1 child who goes to kindergarten. 2 teacher in a kindergarten.

kind heart ed (kīnd′här′tid), *adj.* having or showing a kind heart; kindly; sympathetic. **—kind′heart′ed ly,** *adv.* **—kind′heart′ed ness,** *n.*

kin dle (kin′dl), *v.,* **-dled, -dling.** —*v.t.* 1 set on fire; light. See synonym study below. 2 stir up; arouse: *kindle enthusiasm. His cruelty kindled our anger.* 3 light up; brighten: *Pleasure kindled the boy's face.* —*v.i.* 1 catch fire; begin to burn: *This damp wood will never kindle.* 2 become stirred up or aroused. 3 light up; brighten: *The girl's face kindled as she told about the airplane ride.* [probably ultimately < Scandinavian (Old Icelandic) *kynda*] **—kin′dler,** *n.*

Syn. *v.t.* 1 **Kindle, ignite** mean to set on fire. **Kindle** means to cause something like wood to burn by setting fire to it, and usually suggests some work in getting a fire going: *kindle a fire in the fireplace.* **Ignite** suggests causing something highly flammable, like very dry wood and grass, cleaning fluids, gas, oil, etc., to burst into flame by putting a spark, tiny flame, or great heat to or near it: *Firemen tried to keep flying sparks from igniting the shingles of the house.*

kind li ness (kīnd′lē nis), *n.* 1 kindly feeling or quality. 2 a kindly act.

kin dling (kind′ling), *n.* small pieces of wood, etc., that ignite easily for setting fire to larger pieces and other fuel.

hat, āge, fär; let, ēqual, tėrm;
it, īce; hot, ōpen, ôrder;
oil, out; cup, pu̇t, rüle;
ch, child; ng, long; sh, she;
th, thin; ᴛʜ, then; zh, measure;
ə represents *a* in about, *e* in taken, *i* in pencil, *o* in lemon, *u* in circus.
< = from, derived from, taken from.

kind ly (kīnd′lē), *adj.* **-li er, -li est,** *adv.* —*adj.* 1 kind; friendly: *kindly faces.* See **kind**[1] for synonym study. 2 pleasant; agreeable: *a kindly shower.* —*adv.* 1 in a kind or friendly way. 2 pleasantly; agreeably: *He does not take kindly to criticism.* [Old English *(ge)cyndelīc*]

kind ness (kīnd′nis), *n.* 1 quality of being kind; kind nature. 2 kind treatment. 3 a kind act: *They showed me many kindnesses during my visit.*

kin dred (kin′drid), *adj.* 1 related in character or properties; like; similar: *We are studying about dew, frost, and kindred facts of nature.* 2 related by birth or descent: *kindred tribes.* —*n.* 1 a person's family or relatives. 2 family relationship; kinship. 3 a being alike; resemblance. [Middle English *kynrede* < *kyn* family (Old English *cynn*) + *-rede,* Old English *rǣden* condition]

kine (kīn), *n.pl.* ARCHAIC or DIALECT. cows or cattle. [earlier *kyen* (formed after pattern of *oxen*) < Old English *cȳ,* plural of *cū* cow]

kin e mat ic (kin′ə mat′ik), *adj.* having to do with pure motion or with kinematics.

kin e mat ics (kin′ə mat′iks), *n.* branch of physics that deals with the characteristics of different kinds of pure motion, that is, without reference to mass or to the causes of the motion. [< Greek *kinēmatos* motion < *kinein* to move]

kin e scope (kin′ə skōp), *n., v.,* **-scoped, -scop ing.** —*n.* 1 record on film of a television show or other entertainment that may be rebroadcast. 2 (in television) a cathode-ray tube that has a screen at one end on which images are reproduced; picture tube. —*v.t.* record on a kinescope.

ki ne si ol o gy (ki nē′sē ol′ə jē), *n.* science which investigates and analyzes human motion. [< Greek *kinēsis* motion + English *-logy*]

kin es the sia (kin′əs thē′zhə), *n.* the sensation of movement in the muscles, joints, and tendons. [< Greek *kinein* to move + *aisthēsis* perception]

kin es the sis (kin′əs thē′sis), *n.* kinesthesia.

kin es thet ic (kin′əs thet′ik), *adj.* having to do with sensations of motion from the muscles, joints, and tendons. **—kin′es thet′i cal ly,** *adv.*

ki net ic (ki net′ik), *adj.* 1 of motion. 2 caused by motion. [< Greek *kinētikos* < *kinein* to move]

kinetic energy, energy which a body has because it is in motion. It is equal to one half the product of the mass of a body and the square of its velocity.

ki net ics (ki net′iks), *n.* branch of physics that deals with the effects of forces in causing or changing the motion of objects.

kin folk (kin′fōk′), *n.pl.* kinsfolk.

king (king), *n.* 1 the male ruler of a nation; male sovereign, usually with a hereditary position and with either absolute or limited power. 2 **King,** God or Christ. 3 man supreme in a certain sphere: *a baseball king, a steel king.* 4 something best in its class. 5 the chief piece in chess, moving one square in any direction. 6 piece that has moved entirely across the board in checkers. It has the power of moving forward or backward and is usually marked by putting one checker on top of another. 7 a playing card bearing a picture of a king. [Old English *cyning*] **—king′less,** *adj.* **—king′like′,** *adj.*

King (king), *n.* 1 **Ernest Joseph,** 1878-1956, American admiral, chief of naval operations during World War II. 2 **(William Lyon) Mackenzie,** 1874-1950, Canadian statesman, prime minister of Canada from 1921 to 1926, 1926 to 1930, and 1935 to 1948. 3 **Martin Luther, Jr.,** 1929-1968, American minister who led a nonviolent movement to end racial discrimination in the United States.

king bird (king′bėrd′), *n.* any of several American flycatchers, especially a bold, black-and-white flycatcher of the eastern United States.

king bolt (king′bōlt′), *n.* a vertical bolt connecting the body of a wagon, etc., with the front axle, or the body of a railroad car with a set of wheels; kingpin.

king cobra, a large, very poisonous cobra found throughout southeastern Asia.

king crab, 1 horseshoe crab. 2 a large, edible crab found along the shores of the northern Pacific.

king dom (king′dəm), *n.* 1 nation that is governed by a king or a queen; land or territory ruled by one king. 2 realm, domain, or province in which a condition or quality, or a person, prevails: *The mind is the kingdom of thought.* 3 one of the three divisions of the natural world; the animal kingdom, the vegetable kingdom, or the mineral kingdom. See **classification** for chart. 4 Often, **Kingdom.** the spiritual sovereignty of God; domain over which God rules in heaven and on earth. [Old English *cyningdōm*]

kinkajou
about 2½ ft. long
including the tail

king fish (king′fish′), *n., pl.* **-fish es** or **-fish.** any of several large food fishes of the Atlantic or Pacific coast.

king fish er (king′fish′ər), *n.* any of numerous crested, bright-colored birds with large heads and strong beaks. Kingfishers eat fish and insects, and are found in most parts of the world.

King James Version, an English translation of the Bible prepared under James I and published in 1611, still widely used by English-speaking Protestants; Authorized Version.

king let (king′lit), *n.* 1 a petty king; king ruling over a small country. 2 any of various small, greenish songbirds similar to the warblers.

king ly (king′lē), *adj.,* **-li er, -li est,** *adv.* *—adj.* 1 of a king or kings; of royal rank. See **royal** for synonym study. 2 fit for a king: *a kingly crown.* 3 like a king; royal; noble. *—adv.* as a king does. **—king′li ness,** *n.*

king of beasts, lion.

king pin (king′pin′), *n.* 1 pin in front or in the center in bowling games. 2 INFORMAL. the most important person in a company, enterprise, organization, etc. 3 kingbolt.

king post, a vertical post between the apex of a triangular roof truss and a tie beam.

Kings (kingz), *n.* 1 (in the Protestant Old Testament) either of two books (I Kings or II Kings) containing the history of the reigns of the Hebrew kings after David. 2 (in the Douay Bible) any of the four books that correspond to I and II Samuel and I and II Kings in the Protestant Bible.

king's English, correct or accepted English usage in speech and writing.

king's evil, scrofula. [so named because it was formerly supposed to be cured by the touch of a king]

king ship (king′ship), *n.* 1 position, rank, or dignity of a king. 2 rule of a king; government by a king. 3 kingly nature or quality.

king-size (king′sīz′), *adj.* INFORMAL. large or long for its kind: *a king-size cigarette.*

king-sized (king′sīzd′), *adj.* INFORMAL. king-size.

Kings ley (kingz′lē), *n.* **Charles,** 1819-1875, English novelist and poet.

king snake, any of various large, harmless North American snakes that eat mice, rats, and other snakes and are constrictors of the same genus as the milk snakes.

king's ransom, a very large amount of money.

Kings ton (king′stən), *n.* 1 capital and chief seaport of Jamaica, in the SE part. 123,000. 2 city in SE Ontario, Canada, at the E end of Lake Ontario. 59,000.

Kings ton-up on-Hull (king′stən ə pon′-hul′), *n.* official name of **Hull.**

Kings town (kingz′toun), *n.* capital of St. Vincent. 20,000.

kink (kingk), *n.* 1 a twist or curl in thread, rope, hair, etc. 2 pain or stiffness in the muscles of the neck, back, etc.; crick. 3 INFORMAL. a mental twist; odd notion; eccentricity; whim. 4 hindrance; difficulty; obstruction. *—v.i.* form a kink or kinks. *—v.t.* make kinks in [probably < Dutch, a twist]

kin ka jou (king′kə jü), *n.* a yellowish-brown mammal of Central and South America, of the same family as and resembling the raccoon, but having a long prehensile tail. It lives in trees and hunts at night. [< French *quincajou*]

kink y (king′kē), *adj.,* **kink i er, kink i est.** full of kinks; twisted; curly. **—kink′i ness,** *n.*

kins folk (kinz′fōk′), *n.pl.* a person's family or relatives; kin. Also, **kinfolk.**

Kin sha sa (kēn shä′sä), *n.* capital of Zaïre, in the W part. 1,226,000. Former name, **Leopoldville.**

kin ship (kin′ship), *n.* 1 a being kin; family relationship. 2 relationship. 3 resemblance.

kins man (kinz′mən), *n., pl.* **-men.** a male relative.

kins wom an (kinz′wu̇m′ən), *n., pl.* **-wom en.** a female relative.

ki osk (kē osk′, kī′osk *for 1;* kē osk′ *for 2*), *n.* 1 a small building with one or more sides open, used as a newsstand, a bandstand, an opening to a subway, etc. 2 a light, open summerhouse in Turkey and other Eastern countries. [< French *kiosque* < Turkish *köshk* pavilion]

kip (kip), *n.* the untanned hide of a young or undersized animal. [origin uncertain]

Kip ling (kip′ling), *n.* **Rudyard,** 1865-1936, English writer of stories, novels, and poems, born in India.

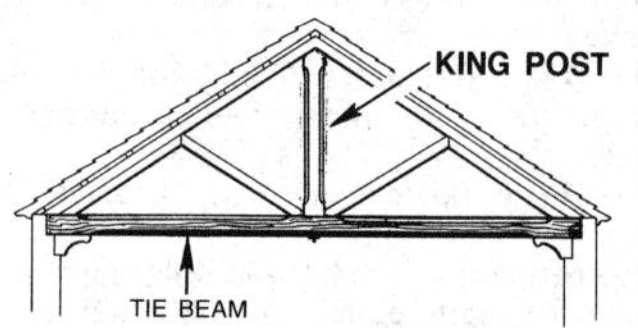

kip per (kip′ər), *v.t.* salt and dry or smoke (herring, salmon, etc.). *—n.* 1 herring, salmon, etc., that has been kippered. 2 the male salmon or sea trout during or after the spawning season. [Old English *cypera* male salmon]

Kir ghiz (kir gēz′), *n., pl.* **-ghiz** or **-ghiz es** for 1. 1 member of a Mongoloid people widely scattered over the western part of central Asia. 2 their Turkic language.

Kirghiz S.S.R., one of the constituent republics of the U.S.S.R., in the S part. 2,900,000 pop.; 77,000 sq. mi. *Capital:* Frunze.

Ki rin (kīr′in′), *n.* province in NE China.

kirk (kėrk), *n.* 1 SCOTTISH. church. 2 **the Kirk,** the national church of Scotland; the Scottish Presbyterian Church as distinguished from the Church of England or the Scottish Episcopal Church. [probably < Scandinavian (Old Icelandic) *kirkja*]

kir mess (kėr′mis), *n.* kermis.

kir tle (kėr′tl), *n.* ARCHAIC. 1 a woman's dress, skirt, or outer petticoat. 2 a man's short coat. [Old English *cyrtel,* probably < Latin *curtus* short]

Kish i nev (kish′ə nef), *n.* city in SW Soviet Union, capital of Moldavian S.S.R. 357,000.

kis met (kiz′met, kis′met), *n.* fate; destiny. [< Turkish *kısmet* < Arabic *qismah* portion, lot]

kiss (kis), *v.t.* 1 touch with the lips as a sign of love, greeting, or respect. 2 touch gently: *A soft wind kissed the treetops.* 3 put, bring, take, etc., by kissing: *kiss away tears.* *—v.i.* give a caress with the lips: *The two sisters kissed.* *—n.* 1 a touch with the lips as a sign of love, greeting, or respect. 2 a gentle touch. 3 a small piece of candy, usually of chocolate. 4 a small, fancy cake made of white of egg and powdered sugar. [Old English *cyssan*] **—kiss′a ble,** *adj.*

kiss er (kis′ər), *n.* 1 person who kisses. 2 SLANG. face or mouth.

Kis sing er (kis′in jər; *German* kis′ing ər), *n.* **Henry A(lfred),** born 1923, American diplomat and adviser on foreign policy, born in Germany.

kit[1] (kit), *n.* 1 the parts of anything to be put together by the buyer: *a radio kit, a model airplane kit.* 2 a person's equipment packed for traveling: *a soldier's kit.* 3 outfit of tools or supplies: *a plumber's kit, a first-aid kit.* 4 bag, case, knapsack, etc., for carrying such equipment or such an outfit. 5 INFORMAL. lot; set; collection. [probably < Middle Dutch *kitte* jug]

kit[2] (kit), *n.* a small pocket violin. [origin uncertain]

Ki ta kyu shu (kē′tə kyü′shü), *n.* seaport in N Kyushu, Japan. 1,094,000.

kitch en (kich′ən), *n.* 1 room or part of the house where food is cooked. 2 the cooking department. 3 outfit for cooking. [Old English *cycene* < Latin *coquina* < *coquere* to cook]

kitchen cabinet, 1 article of furniture for the kitchen containing shelves, drawers, etc. 2 group of advisers consulted by a President in addition to or rather than his cabinet.

Kitch en er (kich′ə nər), *n.* **Horatio Herbert,** Earl, 1850-1916, British field marshal.

kiwi—up to 24 in. long

kitch en ette or **kitch en et** (kich′ə net′), *n.* 1 a very small, compactly arranged kitchen. 2 part of a room fitted up as a kitchen.

kitchen garden, garden where vegetables and fruit for a family are grown.

kitchen midden, mound of shells, bones, and other refuse at a place where prehistoric people lived.

kitchen police, 1 a military duty of helping the cook prepare and serve food, wash dishes, and clean up the kitchen. 2 soldiers assigned to this duty.

kitch en ware (kich′ən wer′, kich′ən war′), *n.* kitchen utensils, such as pots, kettles, and pans.

kite (kīt), *n., v.,* **kit ed, kit ing.** —*n.* 1 a light wooden frame covered with paper, cloth, or plastic. Kites are flown in the air on the end of a long string. 2 any of various falconlike hawks usually having long, pointed wings and a long notched or forked tail. 3 any of the very high and light sails of a ship. —*v.i.* INFORMAL. fly like a kite; move rapidly and easily. [Old English *cȳta*]

kith (kith), *n.* 1 friends; acquaintances. 2 **kith and kin,** friends and relatives. [Old English *cȳthth* < *cunnan* know]

kitsch or **Kitsch** (kich), *n.* a shallow, pretentious, sentimental artistic production. [< German *Kitsch* trash]

kit ten (kit′n), *n.* 1 a young cat. 2 the young of certain other small animals, as rabbits. [< variant of Old French *cheton* < *chat* cat < Late Latin *cattus* cat]

kit ten ish (kit′n ish), *adj.* 1 like a kitten. 2 coquettish. —**kit′ten ish ly,** *adv.* —**kit′ten ish ness,** *n.*

kit ti wake (kit′ē wāk), *n.* either of two sea gulls of the North Atlantic and Arctic Oceans, with black or red legs and solid black wing tips. [imitative of its call]

kit ty[1] (kit′ē), *n., pl.* **-ties.** 1 kitten. 2 a pet name for a cat.

kit ty[2] (kit′ē), *n., pl.* **-ties.** 1 stakes in a poker game. 2 money pooled by the players in other games for some special purpose. 3 a fund of money. [origin uncertain]

kit ty-cor ner (kit′ē kôr′nər), *adj.* cater-cornered.

kit ty-cor nered (kit′ē kôr′nərd), *adj.* cater-cornered.

Kitty Hawk, village in NE North Carolina where Wilbur and Orville Wright made the first successful airplane flight in 1903.

ki va (kē′və), *n.* a large chamber, often wholly or partly underground, in a Pueblo Indian village, used for religious ceremonies and for other purposes. [< Hopi]

Ki wa ni an (ki wä′nē ən), *n.* member of a Kiwanis club. —*adj.* of or having to do with Kiwanis clubs.

Ki wa nis (ki wä′nis), *n.* an international group of clubs of business and professional men, organized for civic service and higher ideals in business and professional life. The first Kiwanis club was founded at Detroit in 1915.

ki wi (kē′wē), *n.* any of a genus of flightless birds of New Zealand having stocky bodies covered with shaggy, dull brown feathers, and long, flexible bills; apteryx. [< Maori]

KKK or **K.K.K.,** Ku Klux Klan.

kl., kiloliter or kiloliters.

Klan (klan), *n.* Ku Klux Klan.

Klans man (klanz′mən), *n., pl.* **-men.** member of the Ku Klux Klan.

Klee (klā), *n.* **Paul,** 1879-1940, Swiss painter.

Klee nex (klē′neks), *n.* trademark for a disposable paper tissue used as a handkerchief, etc.

klep to ma ni a (klep′tə mā′nē ə), *n.* an abnormal, irresistible desire to steal, especially things which one does not need or cannot use. [< Greek *kleptēs* thief + *mania* madness]

klep to ma ni ac (klep′tə mā′nē ak), *n.* person who has kleptomania.

klieg light (klēg), a bright, hot arc light used in taking motion pictures. [*klieg* < Anton *Kliegl,* 1872-1927, and his brother John, 1869-1959, who invented it]

Klon dike (klon′dīk), *n.* region in NW Canada, along the Yukon River, famous for its gold fields.

km., kilometer or kilometers.

K meson, meson having a mass about 967 times that of an electron; kaon.

knack (nak), *n.* 1 special skill; power to do something easily; aptitude. 2 trick or habit. [Middle English *knak*]

knack er (nak′ər), *n.* person who buys and slaughters useless horses and sells the hides, hoofs, and meat.

knapsack

knap sack (nap′sak′), *n.* a canvas or leather bag with two shoulder straps, used by soldiers, hikers, etc., for carrying clothes, equipment, and other articles on the back; rucksack. [< Low German < *knappen* eat + *sack* sack]

knap weed (nap′wēd′), *n.* a perennial weed of the same genus as the bachelor's-button, that has light-purple flowers. [Middle English *knopweed* < *knop* knob + *weed* weed]

knave (nāv), *n.* 1 a tricky, dishonest man; rogue; rascal. 2 jack (def. 2). 3 ARCHAIC. a male servant or any man of humble birth or position. [Old English *cnafa* boy]

knav er y (nā′vər ē), *n., pl.* **-er ies.** 1 behavior of a knave or rascal; trickery; dishonesty. 2 a tricky, dishonest act.

knav ish (nā′vish), *adj.* tricky; dishonest. —**knav′ish ly,** *adv.* —**knav′ish ness,** *n.*

knead (nēd), *v.t.* 1 work over or work up (moist flour or clay) usually by pressing with the hands into dough or paste: *A baker kneads dough.* 2 make or shape by kneading. 3 press and squeeze with the hands; massage: *Kneading the muscles in a stiff shoulder will take away the stiffness.* [Old English *cnedan*] —**knead′er,** *n.*

hat, āge, fär; let, ēqual, tėrm;
it, īce; hot, ōpen, ôrder;
oil, out; cup, pu̇t, rüle;
ch, child; ng, long; sh, she;
th, thin; ᴛʜ, then; zh, measure;

ə represents *a* in about, *e* in taken, *i* in pencil, *o* in lemon, *u* in circus.

< = from, derived from, taken from.

knee (nē), *n., v.* **kneed, knee ing.** —*n.* 1 the joint between the thigh and the lower leg, formed by the joining of the thighbone and shinbone. It is covered in front by the kneecap. 2 any joint in a four-footed animal corresponding to the human knee or elbow, as in the hind leg of a horse. 3 anything like a bent knee in shape or position. 4 part of a garment covering the knee. 5 **bring to one's knees,** force to yield. —*v.t.* strike or touch with the knee. [Old English *cnēo*]

knee cap (nē′kap′), *n.* the flat, movable bone at the front of the knee; patella.

knee-deep (nē′dēp′), *adj.* so deep as to reach the knees.

knee hole (nē′hōl′), *n.* hole or space between the lower drawers of a desk, to make room for the knees.

knee jerk, a sudden, involuntary kick produced by striking the tendon below the kneecap.

knee-jerk (nē′jėrk′), *adj.* INFORMAL. without thought; automatic: *knee-jerk responses.*

kneel (nēl), *v.i.,* **knelt** or **kneeled, kneel ing.** 1 go down on one's knee or knees: *She knelt down to pull a weed from the flower bed.* 2 remain in this position: *They knelt in prayer for half an hour.* [Old English *cnēowlian* < *cnēo* knee] —**kneel′er,** *n.*

knee pad (nē′pad′), *n.* pad worn around the knee for protection.

knell (nel), *n.* 1 sound of a bell rung slowly after a death or at a funeral. 2 a warning sign of death, failure, etc.: *Their refusal rang the knell of our hopes.* 3 a mournful sound. —*v.i.* 1 (of a bell) ring slowly, especially for a death or at a funeral; toll. 2 give a warning sign of death, failure, etc. 3 make a mournful sound. [Old English *cnyllan* to knell]

knelt (nelt), *v.* a pt. and a pp. of **kneel.**

Knes set (knes′et), *n.* the Israeli parliament.

knew (nü, nyü), *v.* pt. of **know.**

Knick er bock er (nik′ər bok′ər), *n.* 1 person descended from the early Dutch settlers of New York. 2 person living in New York.

knick er bock ers (nik′ər bok′ərz), *n.pl.* knickers.

knick ers (nik′ərz), *n.pl.* short, loose-fitting trousers gathered in at, or just below, the knee. [short for *knickerbockers* < *Knickerbocker*]

knick knack (nik′nak′), *n.* a pleasing trifle; ornament; trinket. Also, **nick nack.**

knife (nīf), *n., pl.* **knives,** *v.,* **knifed, knif ing.** —*n.* 1 a thin, flat, metal blade fastened in a handle so that it can be used to cut or spread. 2 any weapon having a short blade with a sharp edge and point, as a dagger. 3 a sharp blade forming part of a tool or machine: *the knives of a lawn mower.* —*v.t.* 1 cut or stab with a knife. 2 SLANG. try to defeat in an underhand way. —*v.i.* move or pass through as if with a knife: *The submarine knifed through the cold arctic waters.* [Old English *cnīf*] —**knife′like′,** *adj.*

knife edge, 1 edge of a knife. 2 anything very sharp. 3 wedge on the fine edge of which a scale, beam, pendulum, etc., is hung.

knight (nīt), *n.* 1 (in the Middle Ages) a man raised to an honorable military rank and pledged to do good deeds. After serving as a page and squire, a man was made a knight by the king or a lord. 2 (in modern times) a man raised to an honorable rank because of great achievement or service. A British knight ranks just below a baronet and uses the title *Sir* before his name. EXAMPLE: Sir John Smith or Sir John. 3 man devoted to the service or protection of a lady. 4 person in ancient history, mythology, etc., considered to hold a position similar to that of a medieval knight. 5 member or holder of a rank or degree in any order or society that bears the official title of *Knights.* 6 piece in the game of chess, usually having the figure of a horse's head. It moves two squares horizontally and one square vertically or two squares vertically and one square horizontally from the square it occupies, whether or not any of the intervening squares is occupied. —*v.t.* raise to the rank of knight. [Old English *cniht* boy]

knight bachelor, *pl.* **knights bachelors** or **knights bachelor.** an English knight of the lowest but most ancient order of knights.

knight-er rant (nīt′er′ənt), *n., pl.* **knights-er rant.** knight traveling in search of adventure, especially to exhibit military skill, bravery, and chivalry.

knight-er rant ry (nīt′er′ən trē), *n., pl.* **knight-er rant ries.** 1 conduct or action characteristic of a knight-errant. 2 quixotic conduct or action.

knight hood (nīt′hủd), *n.* 1 rank or dignity of a knight. 2 profession or occupation of a knight. 3 character or qualities of a knight; chivalrousness. 4 knights as a group or class.

knight ly (nīt′lē), *adj.* 1 of a knight; brave, generous, and courteous; chivalrous. 2 consisting or composed of knights. —*adv.* as a knight should do; bravely, generously, and courteously. —**knight′li ness,** *n.*

Knights of Columbus, a fraternal society of Roman Catholic men to increase the religious and civic usefulness of its members and to encourage benevolence. It was founded in 1882.

Knight Templar, *pl.* **Knights Templars** for 1; **Knights Templar** for 2. 1 Templar (def. 1). 2 Templar (def. 2).

knish (knish), *n.* pastry made of dough, wrapped around a stuffing of potato, cheese, etc. [< Yiddish]

knit (nit), *v.,* **knit ted** or **knit, knit ting.** —*v.t.* 1 make (cloth or an article of clothing) by looping yarn or thread together with long needles, or by machinery which forms loops instead of weaving: *Jersey is knitted cloth.* 2 join closely and firmly together. 3 draw (the brows) together in wrinkles. —*v.i.* 1 make cloth or an article of clothing by looping yarn or thread together with long needles, or by machinery which forms loops instead of weaving: *She knit a scarf.* 2 grow together; be joined closely and firmly: *A broken bone knits.* [Old English *cnyttan* < *cnotta* knot[1]] —**knit′ter,** *n.*

knit ting (nit′ing), *n.* 1 knitted work. 2 act or occupation of a person who knits.

knit wear (nit′wer′, nit′war′), *n.* clothing made of knitted fabric.

knives (nīvz), *n.* pl. of **knife.**

knob (nob), *n.* 1 a rounded lump or protuberance. 2 handle on a door, drawer, etc. 3 a rounded hill or mountain. [Middle English *knobbe*] —**knob′like′,** *adj.*

knobbed (nobd), *adj.* having a knob or knobs.

knob by (nob′ē), *adj.,* **-bi er, -bi est.** 1 covered with knobs. 2 rounded like a knob. —**knob′bi ness,** *n.*

knock (nok), *v.t.* 1 give a hard blow or blows to with the fist, knuckles, or anything hard; hit: *He knocked him on the head.* 2 hit and cause to fall: *The car crashed into a sign and knocked it down.* 3 SLANG. find fault with; criticize: *The critics knocked the new book.* —*v.i.* 1 hit with a noise, as with the fist, knuckles, or something hard: *knock on a door. My knees knocked together from fright.* 2 make a noise, especially a rattling or pounding noise caused by faulty operation: *The engine is knocking.*

knock about, INFORMAL. wander from place to place.

knock down, a take apart. b sell (an article) to the highest bidder at an auction.

knock off, INFORMAL. a take off; deduct: *knock 50 cents off the bill, knock off 10 cents from the price.* b stop work. c stop; quit (doing something): *Knock off that noise!* d accomplish hastily; do quickly. e defeat; overcome. f kill.

knock out, a make helpless, unconscious, etc.; defeat. b (in boxing) defeat (an opponent) by hitting him so that he falls to the canvas for ten seconds or more.

knock together, make or put together hastily.

—*n.* 1 a hit. 2 a hit with a noise. 3 act of knocking. 4 sound of knocking: *She did not hear the knock at the door.* 5 sound in an internal-combustion engine caused by loose parts or improper burning of fuel: *a knock in the engine.*

[Old English *cnocian*]

knock a bout (nok′ə bout′), *n.* 1 a small, easily handled sailboat having one mast, a mainsail, and a jib, but no bowsprit. 2 something suitable for rough use, as a car: *He drives an old knockabout.* —*adj.* 1 suitable for rough use. 2 noisy; boisterous.

knock down (nok′doun′), *adj.* 1 irresistible; overwhelming: *a knockdown bargain.* 2 constructed in separate parts, so as to be easily knocked down or taken apart for storage, etc. —*n.* 1 a knockdown piece of furniture. 2 the act of knocking down. 3 blow that knocks down; overwhelming blow.

knock er (nok′ər), *n.* 1 person or thing that knocks. 2 a hinged knob, ring, or the like, usually of iron or brass, fastened on a door for use in knocking.

knock-knee (nok′nē′), *n.* an inward bending of the legs, so that the knees knock together in walking.

knock-kneed (nok′nēd′), *adj.* having legs bent inward at the knees.

knock out (nok′out′), *n.* 1 act of knocking out. 2 condition of being knocked out. 3 blow that knocks out. 4 SLANG. a very attractive person; overwhelming or striking thing. —*adj.* SLANG. 1 that knocks out: *a knockout blow.* 2 outstanding: *a knockout performance.*

knoll (nōl), *n.* a small, rounded hill; mound. [Old English *cnoll*]

Knos sos (nos′əs), *n.* the capital of ancient Crete. Also, **Cnossus.**

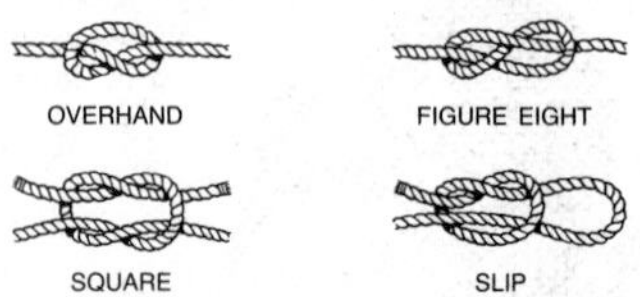

knot[1] (def. 1)—four common types of knots

knot[1] (not), *n., v.,* **knot ted, knot ting.** —*n.* 1 a fastening made by tying or twining together pieces of one or more ropes, cords, strings, etc. 2 bow of ribbon, etc., worn as an ornament. 3 group; cluster: *A knot of students stood talking outside the classroom.* 4 the hard mass of wood formed where a branch grows out from a tree, which shows as a roundish, cross-grained piece in lumber or a board. 5 a hard lump, such as a swelling in a muscle, nerve, etc. 6 joint where leaves grow out on the stem of a plant. 7 unit of speed used on ships, equal to one nautical mile per hour: *The ship averaged 12 knots.* 8 nautical mile: 6076.11549 feet. 9 difficulty or problem. 10 thing that unites closely or intricately; bond.

—*v.t.* 1 tie or twine together in a knot. 2 tangle in knots. 3 unite closely in a way that is hard to undo. —*v.i.* 1 tangle in knots; be or become tied or twisted into a knot. 2 form into a hard lump.

[Old English *cnotta*] —**knot′less,** *adj.*

knot[2] (not), *n.* a small, shore bird, of the same family as the sandpipers, which breeds in the Arctic and migrates southward in the winter. [origin uncertain]

knot grass (not′gras′), *n.* weed of the same family as the buckwheat, whose stems have large joints.

knot hole (not′hōl′), *n.* hole in a board where a knot has fallen out.

knot ted (not′id), *adj.* 1 having a knot or knots; knotty. 2 formed or decorated with knots or the like.

knot ty (not′ē), *adj.,* **-ti er, -ti est.** 1 full of knots: *knotty wood.* 2 difficult; puzzling: *a knotty problem.* —**knot′ti ness,** *n.*

knout (nout), *n.* whip formerly used in Russia to inflict punishment. —*v.t.* flog with a knout. [< French < Russian *knut* < Scandinavian (Swedish, Danish)]

know (nō), *v.,* **knew, known, know ing,** *n.* —*v.t.* 1 be sure of; have true information about: *He knows the facts of the case.* See synonym study below. 2 have firmly in the mind or memory: *know a lesson.* 3 have an understanding of through instruction, study, or practice; have experience with; be skilled in: *She knows American literature. I know how to cook.* 4 be aware of; have seen or heard; have information about: *know a person's name.* 5 be acquainted with; be familiar with: *I know her.* 6 recognize; identify: *You would hardly know him since his illness.* 7 tell apart from others; distinguish: *You will know our house by the red roof.* 8 **know what's what,** INFORMAL. be well informed. 9 **let know,** tell; inform: *I'll let him know that we are coming.* —*v.i.* have the facts and be sure they are true: *The doctor does not guess; he knows.* —*n.* **in the know,** INFORMAL. having inside information. [Old English *cnāwan*] —**know′er,** *n.*

Syn. *v.t.* 1 **Know, understand** mean to have a clear understanding of the meaning of something. **Know** is the common and general word for being well acquainted with a subject: *She knows more about Mexico than anyone else at this school.* **Understand** emphasizes having a thorough grasp of both facts and meaning, seeing clearly and fully not only the nature of a fact or idea but also its implications: *understand the relationship between mathematics and physics.*

know a ble (nō′ə bəl), *adj.* capable of being known.

know-how (nō′hou′), *n.* INFORMAL. ability to do something, especially something more or less complicated.

know ing (nō′ing), *adj.* 1 having knowledge; well-informed. 2 clever; shrewd. 3 suggesting shrewd or secret understanding of matters: *His only answer was a knowing look.*

know ing ly (nō′ing lē), *adv.* 1 in a knowing way. 2 on purpose; with knowledge.

koala
about 2 ft. long

knowl edge (nol′ij), *n.* 1 what one knows. See synonym study below. 2 all that is known or can be learned; the sum of what is known: *Science is a branch of knowledge.* 3 fact of knowing: *The knowledge of our victory caused great joy.* 4 act of knowing; familiarity with a thing, person, subject, etc.: *a knowledge of the surrounding countryside.* 5 clear and certain mental perception; understanding. 6 **to one's knowledge,** as far as one knows. [Middle English *knowleche* < *knowen* know (Old English *cnāwan*)]

Syn. 1 **Knowledge, information** mean what a person knows. **Knowledge** applies to the understanding of an organized body of facts and principles: *scientific knowledge. His knowledge of the subject is limited.* **Information** applies to what one has learned from books, through observation, or through being told by people, and often suggests isolated or unrelated facts: *She has acquired much information, but has little real knowledge.*

knowl edge a ble (nol′i jə bəl), *adj.* INFORMAL. well-informed, especially about a particular subject. —**knowl′edge a ble ness,** *n.* —**knowl′edge a bly,** *adv.*

known (nōn), *v.* pp. of **know.**

know-noth ing (nō′nuth′ing), *n.* 1 an ignorant person. 2 **Know-Nothing, a** an American political party prominent from 1853 to 1856 which wanted to keep control of the government in the hands of native-born citizens. **b** member of this party.

known quantity, an algebraic quantity of a given value, often designated by one of the first letters of the alphabet, as *a, b,* or *c.*

Knox (noks), *n.* **John,** 1505?-1572, Scottish religious and political leader and writer.

Knox ville (noks′vil), *n.* city in E Tennessee, on the Tennessee River. 175,000.

knuck le (nuk′əl), *n., v.,* **-led, -ling.** —*n.* 1 joint in a finger, especially one of the joints between a finger and the rest of the hand. 2 the rounded protuberance formed when a joint is bent. 3 knee or hock joint of an animal used as food: *boiled pigs' knuckles.* 4 **knuckles,** *pl.* brass knuckles. —*v.i.* 1 put the knuckles on the ground in playing marbles. 2 **knuckle down, a** INFORMAL. work hard; apply oneself earnestly. **b** submit; yield. 3 **knuckle under,** submit; yield. [Middle English *knokel*]

knuck le bone (nuk′əl bōn′), *n.* 1 bone of a finger which forms part of a knuckle. 2 bone corresponding to a bone of the hand or foot in human beings, as of a sheep.

knur (nėr), *n.* a knot or hardened excrescence on the trunk of a tree. [Middle English *knorre* lump]

knurl (nėrl), *n.* 1 a small projection or protuberance; knot, knob, or lump. 2 a small ridge, such as on the edge of a coin or thumbscrew. [apparently diminutive of *knur*]

knurled (nėrld), *adj.* 1 having knurls or knots; gnarled. 2 having small ridges on the edge or surface; milled.

knurl y (nėr′lē), *adj.,* **knurl i er, knurl i est.** gnarled.

K O (kā′ō′), *v.,* **K O'd, K O'ing,** *n., pl.* **K O's.** SLANG. —*v.t.* knock out. —*n.* knockout. Also, **kayo.**

K.O. or **k.o.,** knockout.

ko a la (kō ä′lə), *n.* a gray, furry, marsupial mammal of Australia having large ears and no tail and looking like a small bear. It lives in trees and eats eucalyptus leaves. [< native Australian name]

Ko be (kō′bē, kō′bā), *n.* seaport in W Japan. 1,217,000.

Ko blenz (kō′blents), *n.* city in W West Germany. 106,000.

ko bold (kō′bold, kō′bōld), *n.* in German folklore: 1 a mischievous sprite or goblin. 2 gnome that lives in mines or caves. [< German *Kobold*]

Koch (kôH), *n.* **Robert,** 1843-1910, German bacteriologist and physician.

Ko dak (kō′dak), *n.* trademark for a small camera with rolls of film on which photographs are taken.

Ko di ak (kō′dē ak), *n.* island off the S coast of Alaska. 100 mi. long. 9000 pop.; 3500 sq. mi.

Kodiak bear, a large brown bear living along the southern coast of Alaska and on nearby islands.

Koh i noor (kō′ə nůr), *n.* a very large and famous Indian diamond, now one of the British crown jewels. [< Persian *kōh-i-nūr,* literally, mountain of light]

kohl (kōl), *n.* powder used in the Orient to darken the eyelids and lashes, usually consisting of finely powdered antimony. [< Arabic *kuḥl* metallic powder]

kohl ra bi (kōl′rä′bē), *n., pl.* **-bies.** 1 plant related to the cabbage, a species of cole, that has a turnip-shaped stem. 2 its stem, which is eaten as a vegetable. [< German *Kohlrabi* < Italian *cavoli rape,* plural < *cavolo* cole, cabbage, *rapa* rape, turnip]

Ko hou tek (kə hō′tek), *n.* comet discovered in 1973. It will come within sight of earth again in about 75 thousand years. [< Luboš *Kohoutek,* born 1935, Czechoslovakian astronomer who discovered it]

kok-sa ghyz or **kok-sa gyz** (kōk′sə-gēz′), *n.* a Russian composite plant of the same genus as the dandelion, grown for its latex, from which rubber is made. [< Russian *kok-sagyz* < Turkic *kök* root + *sagïz* rubber]

ko la (kō′lə), *n.* 1 kola nut. 2 stimulant or tonic made from kola nuts. [< a West African language]

hat, āge, fär; let, ēqual, tėrm;
it, īce; hot, ōpen, ôrder;
oil, out; cup, pu̇t, rüle;
ch, child; ng, long; sh, she;
th, thin; ᴛʜ, then; zh, measure;

ə represents *a* in about, *e* in taken,
i in pencil, *o* in lemon, *u* in circus.

< = from, derived from, taken from.

kola nut, a bitter brownish nut of a tropical evergreen tree of the same family as the cacao. It contains about three per cent of caffeine and is used in soft drinks.

Ko la Peninsula (kō′lə), peninsula in NW Soviet Union in Europe.

ko lin sky (kə lin′skē), *n., pl.* **-skies.** 1 an Asian variety of mink. 2 its tawny fur. [< Russian *kolinskij* of the *Kola* Peninsula]

kol khoz (kol koz′), *n., pl.* **-khoz es, -khoz y** (-kô′zē). a Soviet collective farm. [< Russian]

Köln (kœln), *n.* German name of **Cologne.**

Kol Nid re (kōl nid′rə), a Jewish prayer of atonement, chanted in the synogogue on the eve of Yom Kippur. [< Aramaic *kol nidre* all vows (the prayer's opening phrase)]

Kom so mol (kom′sə mol), *n.* 1 the Young Communist League, a Soviet organization for youth between 15 and 28. 2 member of it. [< Russian]

Ko na kri (kon′ə krē), *n.* Conakry.

Kö nigs berg (kœ′nigs berg), *n.* German name of **Kaliningrad.**

koo doo (kü′dü), *n., pl.* **-doos.** kudu.

kook (kük), *n.* SLANG. a kooky person; an odd or crazy individual.

kook a bur ra (ku̇k′ə bėr′ə), *n.* a large kingfisher of Australia that has a harsh, cackling voice; laughing jackass. [< native Australian name]

kook y (kü′kē), *adj.,* **kook i er, kook i est.** SLANG. crazy; odd; silly. —**kook′i ness,** *n.*

ko peck or **ko pek** (kō′pek), *n.* unit of money in the Soviet Union, a coin worth 1/100 of a ruble. Also, **copeck.** [< Russian *kopeika*]

Ko ran (kô rän′, kô ran′; kō rän′, kō ran′), *n.* the sacred book of the Moslems. It consists of revelations of Allah to Mohammed and is the standard by which Moslems live. [< Arabic *qur'ān* a reading]

Ko ran ic (kô ran′ik, kō ran′ik), *adj.* of or having to do with the Koran.

Ko re a (kô rē′ə, kō rē′ə), *n.* former country on a peninsula in E Asia, divided into North Korea and South Korea after World War II. See **China** for map. Also, JAPANESE **Chosen.**

Ko re an (kô rē′ən, kō rē′ən), *adj.* of Korea, its people, or their language. —*n.* 1 native or inhabitant of Korea. 2 language of Korea.

Korean War, war between South Korea, aided by the United Nations, and North Korea, aided by communist China. The war lasted from June 1950 to July 1953.

Korea Strait, strait between Korea and Japan, joining the Sea of Japan to the Yellow Sea.

Kos ci us ko (kos′ē us′kō), *n.* 1 **Mount,** mountain peak in SE New South Wales, Australia, the highest point in Australia. 7328 ft. 2 **Thaddeus,** 1746-1817, Polish general who served in the American army during the Revolutionary War.

ko sher (kō′shər), *adj.* 1 right or clean according to Jewish ritual law: *kosher meat.* 2 dealing in products that meet the requirements of Jewish ritual law: *a kosher butcher.* 3 SLANG. all right; fine; legitimate: *It's not kosher to change the rules once the game has started.* —*v.t.* make kosher; prepare (food), clean (utensils), etc., according to the Jewish ritual law. [< Hebrew *kāshēr* proper]

Kos suth (kos′üth), *n.* **Louis** or **Lajos,** 1802-1894, Hungarian patriot.

Ko sy gin (kə sē′gin), *n.* **Aleksei N.,** born 1904, Russian statesman, premier of the Soviet Union since 1964.

Ko ta Kin a ba lu (kō′tə kin′ə bə lü′), seaport and capital of Sabah, Malaysia, in the W part. 33,000. Former name, **Jesselton.**

kou mis or **kou miss** (kü′mis), *n.* kumiss.

Kov no (kôv′nō), *n.* Russian name of **Kaunas.**

Kow loon (kou′lün′), *n.* 1 **Kowloon Peninsula,** peninsula in the colony of Hong Kong, located on the Chinese mainland opposite Hong Kong island. 3 sq. mi. 2 city on this peninsula. 853,000.

kow tow (kou′tou′), *v.i.* 1 kneel and touch the ground with the forehead to show deep respect, submission, or worship. 2 show slavish respect or obedience. —*n.* act of kowtowing. [< Chinese *k'o-t'ou,* literally, knock (the) head] —**kow′tow′er,** *n.*

K.P., kitchen police.

Kr, krypton.

kraal (kräl), *n.* 1 village of South African natives, protected by a fence or stockade. 2 pen for cattle or sheep in South Africa. [< Afrikaans < Portuguese *curral* corral]

kraft (kraft), *n.* a strong, smooth, brown wrapping paper obtained by boiling wood chips in an alkaline solution. [< German *Kraft* strength]

krait (krīt), *n.* any of a genus of very venomous snakes of the same family as the cobra, found in India and adjacent parts of Asia. [< Hindi *karait*]

Kra ka to a (krak′ə tō′ə), *n.* small volcanic island in Indonesia, between Java and Sumatra.

Krak ów (krak′ou, krā′kō), *n.* Polish name of **Cracow.**

Kras no dar (kräs′nō där), *n.* city in SW Soviet Union, near the Black Sea. 465,000.

K ration, U.S. an emergency army field ration used during World War II.

Krebs cycle (krebz), cycle of intracellular chemical reactions by means of which organisms convert food chemicals into physical energy. [< Hans A. *Krebs,* born 1900, English biochemist who discovered it]

Krei sler (krī′slər), *n.* **Fritz,** 1875-1962, American violinist and composer, born in Austria.

Krem lin (krem′lən), *n.* 1 citadel of Moscow, where the chief offices of the Soviet government are located. 2 the Soviet government. 3 **kremlin,** the citadel of any Russian city.

Krem lin ol o gist (krem′lə nol′ə jist), *n.* an expert in Kremlinology.

Krem lin ol o gy (krem′lə nol′ə jē), *n.* study of the policies and practices of the Soviet government.

kreut zer or **kreu zer** (kroit′sər), *n.* a former German or Austrian copper coin, worth about half a cent. [< German *Kreuzer*]

krill (kril), *n., pl.* **krill.** any of a genus of small, shrimplike crustaceans that feed on plankton and are in turn the staple diet of whales and certain other sea animals. [< Norwegian *kril*]

krim mer (krim′ər), *n.* a gray fur from lambs of the Crimean region, resembling Persian lamb. [< German *Krimmer* < *Krim* Crimea]

kris (krēs), *n.* creese.

Krish na (krish′nə), *n.* one of the most important Hindu gods, an incarnation of Vishnu.

Kriss Krin gle (kris′ kring′gəl), Santa Claus. [< German dialect *Christkindl* Christ child]

kro na (krō′nə), *n., pl.* **-nor** (-nôr). 1 the monetary unit of Sweden, a silver coin equal to 100 öre and worth about 21 cents. 2 the monetary unit of Iceland, a silver coin worth about one cent. [< Swedish, Icelandic *krona* crown]

kro ne[1] (krō′nə), *n., pl.* **-ner** (-nər). the monetary unit of Denmark and Norway, a silver coin equal to 100 öre and worth about 15 cents. [< Danish, Norwegian *krone* crown]

kro ne[2] (krō′nə), *n., pl.* **-nen** (-nən). 1 a former German gold coin, worth about $2.38. 2 a former Austrian silver coin, worth about 21 cents. [< German *Krone* crown]

Kru ger (krü′gər), *n.* **Paul,** 1825-1904, Boer statesman, president of Transvaal from 1883 to 1900.

Krupp (krup; *German* krüp), *n.* **Alfred,** 1812-1887, German manufacturer of artillery, munitions, etc.

kryp ton (krip′ton), *n.* a colorless, inert, gaseous element that forms a very small part of the air. Krypton is used to fill some fluorescent lamps. *Symbol:* Kr; *atomic number* 36. See pages 326 and 327 for table. [< Greek, neuter of *kryptos* hidden]

kt., 1 karat (carat). 2 kiloton.

Kua la Lum pur (kwä′lə lům′půr′), capital of Malaysia, in W Malaya. 593,000.

Ku blai Khan (kü′blī kän′), 1216?-1294, Mongol emperor from 1259 to 1294. He was the first of the Mongol rulers of China.

Ku ching (kü ching′), *n.* capital of Sarawak, Malaysia. 70,000.

ku dos (kyü′dos, kü′dos), *n., pl.* **-dos.** praise; glory; fame; renown. [< Greek *kydos*]

ku du (kü′dü), *n.* a large, grayish-brown African antelope with white stripes. Also, **koodoo.** [< Bantu *iqudu*]

kud zu (kůd′zü), *n.* a perennial vine of the pea family native to Japan and China. It is cultivated for its edible roots, as a hay and ensilage feed, and to curb soil erosion. [< Japanese *kuzu*]

Kui by shev (kwē′bə shef), *n.* city in NW Soviet Union, on the Volga River. 1,047,000. Former name, **Samara.**

Ku Klux Klan (kü′ kluks′ klan′, kyü′ kluks′ klan′), 1 a secret society of white people formed in the southern United States after the Civil War to suppress certain minority groups and maintain white supremacy. 2 a secret society founded in 1915 in the United States, violently opposed to Negroes, Jews, Catholics, and foreigners.

ku lak (kü läk′), *n.* (formerly in Russia) a well-to-do peasant, farmer, or trader who opposed Soviet collectivization. [< Russian, literally, fist]

Kul tur (kůl tür′), *n.* GERMAN. culture.

ku miss (kü′mis), *n.* 1 fermented mare's or camel's milk, used as a drink by Asiatic nomads. 2 a similar drink made from cow's milk, used in special diets. Also, **koumis, koumiss.** [< Russian *kumys* < Tatar *kumyz*]

küm mel (kim′əl), *n.* liqueur flavored with caraway seeds, anise, etc. [< German *Kümmel*]

kum quat (kum′kwot), *n.* 1 any of several yellow or orange fruits somewhat like a small orange, having a sour pulp and a sweet rind. Kumquats are used in preserves and candy. 2 any of a genus of trees of the same family as the rue that bear these fruits. Also, **cumquat.** [< Chinese (Canton) *kam* golden + *kwat* orange]

Kun lun Mountains (kůn′lůn′), mountain range extending from central Asia to the W border of China. Highest peak, 25,340 ft.

Kun ming (kůn′ming′), *n.* city in S China. 900,000.

Kuo min tang (kwō′min tang′, kwō′min-täng′), *n.* a Chinese nationalist party organized by Sun Yat-sen in 1912 and now the dominant party of the Chinese Nationalists.

Kurd (kėrd, kůrd), *n.* member of a nomadic and warlike Moslem people living chiefly in Kurdistan.

Kurd ish (kėr′dish, kůr′dish), *adj.* of or having to do with the Kurds or their language. —*n.* the Iranian language of the Kurds.

Kur di stan (kėr′də stan, kůr′di stän′), *n.* extensive plateau and mountainous region in SW Asia now divided among Turkey, Iran, and Iraq.

Ku re (kür′ā), *n.* seaport in W Japan. 225,000.

Ku rile Islands or **Ku ril Islands** (kür′-əl, kü rēl′), chain of more than 30 large islands and several smaller ones north of Japan, belonging to the Soviet Union. 15,000 pop.; 6200 sq. mi.

ku ruş (kə rüsh′), *n., pl.* **-ruş.** unit of money in Turkey, a coin worth $^1/_{100}$ of a lira.

Ku tu zov (kə tü′zof), *n.* **Mikhail I.,** 1745-1813, Russian field marshal.

Ku wait (kü wāt′, kü wīt′), *n.* 1 country in E Arabia, on the Persian Gulf. 733,000 pop.: 6200 sq. mi. 2 its capital. 100,000.

kudu
about 4½ ft. high at the shoulder

Ku wai ti (kü wä′tē), *adj.* of or having to do with Kuwait. —*n.* native or inhabitant of Kuwait.

Kuz netsk Basin (küz nyetsk′), rich coal basin in S Soviet Union in Asia. 10,000 sq. mi.

kw., kilowatt or kilowatts.

Kwang chow (kwäng′jō′), *n.* city in SE China. 3,000,000. Former name, **Canton.**

Kwang si (kwäng′sē′), *n.* former province in S China.

Kwang tung (kwäng′tůng′), *n.* province in S China.

kwa shi or kor (kwä′shē ôr′kôr), *n.* an

often fatal condition especially of infants and young children, caused by a protein deficiency in the diet. [< a West African language]

Kwei chow (kwā′chou′), *n.* province in S China.

K.W.H., kilowatt-hour or kilowatt-hours.

kwhr., kilowatt-hour or kilowatt-hours.

Ky., Kentucky.

kyat (kyät), *n.* the monetary unit of Burma, worth about 20 cents. [< Burmese]

ky mo graph (kī′mə graf), *n.* 1 instrument by which variations of motion or fluid pressure, such as muscle twitches or the pulse, can be measured and graphically recorded. 2 instrument which measures variations in the angle made by an airplane in flight in relation to fixed axes in space. [< Greek *kyma* wave + English *-graph*]

Kyo to (kyō′tō), *n.* city in central Japan. It was formerly the capital. 1,365,000.

ky pho sis (kī fō′sis), *n.* an excessive outward curvature of the spine; hunchback. [< Greek *kyphōsis* < *kyphos* hunchbacked, curved]

ky phot ic (kī fot′ik), *adj.* hunchbacked.

Kyr i e (kir′ē ā, kir′ē ē), *n.* Kyrie eleison.

Kyrie e le i son (ə lā′ə sən, ə lā′ə son), 1 "Lord have mercy," a prayer in various offices of the Eastern and Roman churches. 2 a musical setting for this prayer. [< Greek *Kyrie eleēson*]

Kyu shu (kyü′shü), *n.* large island at the SW end of Japan. 12,370,000 pop.; 14,100 sq. mi.

hat, āge, fär; let, ēqual, tėrm;
it, īce; hot, ōpen, ôrder;
oil, out; cup, pu̇t, rüle;
ch, child; ng, long; sh, she;
th, thin; ᴛʜ, then; zh, measure;

ə represents *a* in about, *e* in taken, *i* in pencil, *o* in lemon, *u* in circus.

< = from, derived from, taken from.

L l

L or **l** (el), *n., pl.* **L's** or **l's.** 1 the 12th letter of the English alphabet. 2 the Roman numeral for 50.

L (el), *n., pl.* **L's.** anything shaped like the letter L, as an extension to a building at right angles with the main part; ell[2].

l or **l.,** 1 book [for Latin *liber*]. 2 left. 3 length. 4 line. 5 lira or lire. 6 liter or liters.

L, 1 large. 2 Latin. 3 length. 4 longitude.

L., 1 lake. 2 Latin.

£, pound or pounds sterling [for Latin *libra*].

la (lä), *n.* the sixth tone of the diatonic scale. [< Medieval Latin]

La, lanthanum.

La., Louisiana.

L.A., Los Angeles.

lab (lab), *n.* INFORMAL. laboratory.

Lab., Labrador.

la bel (lā′bəl), *n., v.,* **-beled, -bel ing** or **-belled, -bel ling.** —*n.* 1 slip of paper or other material attached to anything and marked to show what or whose it is, or where it is to go. 2 word or short phrase used to describe some person, thing, or idea. —*v.t.* 1 put or write a label on: *The bottle is labeled "Poison."* 2 put in a class; call; name: *label someone a liar.* 3 infuse or treat (a substance) with a radioactive or other isotope so that its course or activity can be noted. [< Old French] **—la′bel er, la′bel ler,** *n.*

la bel lum (lə bel′əm), *n., pl.* **-bel la** (-bel′ə). the middle petal of an orchid, usually different in shape and color from the other two and suggestive of a lip. [< Latin, diminutive of *labium* lip]

la bi al (lā′bē əl), *adj.* 1 of the lips. 2 (in phonetics) made by closing, nearly closing, or rounding the lips. —*n.* (in phonetics) a labial sound. *B, p,* and *m* are labials. [< Medieval Latin *labialis* < Latin *labium* lip] **—la′bi al ly,** *adv.*

la bi ate (lā′bē āt, lā′bē it), *adj.* having one or more liplike parts. —*n.* a labiate plant.

la bile (lā′bəl), *adj.* 1 changing easily; plastic; adaptable. 2 apt to lapse or change; unstable. [< Latin *labilis* < *labi* to slip]

la bil i ty (lə bil′ə tē), *n., pl.* **-ties.** instability of form or character.

labio-, *combining form.* made with the lips and ____: *Labiodental = made with the lips and teeth.* [< Latin *labium* lip]

la bi o den tal (lā′bē ō den′tl), in phonetics: —*adj.* made with the lower lip and upper teeth; made with the lips and teeth. —*n.* a labiodental sound. *F* and *v* are labiodentals.

la bi um (lā′bē əm), *n., pl.* **-bi a** (-bē ə). a lip or liplike part, such as a portion of the corolla of certain flowers, or the organ that constitutes the lower lip of an insect. [< Latin]

la bor (lā′bər), *n.* 1 effort in doing or making something; work; toil. See **work** for synonym study. 2 piece of work to be done; task: *the twelve labors of Hercules.* 3 work, especially manual work, done by skilled and unskilled workers for wages. 4 skilled and unskilled workers as a group: *Labor favors a shorter workday.* 5 the physical exertions of childbirth prior to delivery: *She was in labor for two hours.* —*v.i.* 1 do work, especially hard work; toil. 2 move slowly and heavily: *The ship labored in the high waves.* 3 be burdened, troubled, or distressed: *labor under a mistake.* 4 be in childbirth. —*v.t.* elaborate with effort or in detail: *The speaker labored the point so that we lost interest.* Also, BRITISH **labour.** [< Latin]

lab o ra to ry (lab′rə tôr′ē, lab′rə tōr′ē), *n., pl.* **-ries.** 1 place where scientific work is done; room or building fitted with apparatus for conducting scientific investigations, experiments, tests, etc. 2 place for manufacturing drugs, chemicals, medicines, explosives, etc.

Labor Day, the first Monday in September, a legal holiday in the United States in honor of labor and laborers.

la bored (lā′bərd), *adj.* done with much effort; not easy or natural; forced: *labored breathing.* See **elaborate** for synonym study.

la bor er (lā′bər ər), *n.* 1 person who does work requiring much physical labor. 2 worker.

la bo ri ous (lə bôr′ē əs, lə bōr′ē əs), *adj.* 1 requiring much work; requiring hard work: *Climbing a mountain is laborious.* 2 showing signs of effort; not easy; labored: *laborious excuses for being late.* 3 hard-working; industrious: *Bees and ants are laborious insects.* **—la bo′ri ous ly,** *adv.*

La bor ite (lā′bə rīt′), *n.* member of a Labor Party.

Labor Party, any political party organized to protect and promote the interests of workers.

la bor-sav ing (lā′bər sā′ving), *adj.* that takes the place of or lessens labor.

labor union, association of workers to protect and promote their common interests by dealing collectively with their employers; union.

la bour (lā′bər), *n., v.i., v.t.,* BRITISH. labor.

La bour ite (lā′bə rīt′), *n.* member of the British Labour Party.

Labour Party, a political party in Great Britain that claims especially to protect and advance the interests of working people.

Lab ra dor (lab′rə dôr), *n.* 1 **Labrador Peninsula,** peninsula in NE North America, between Hudson Bay and the Atlantic. 2 the E part of this peninsula, part of the Canadian province of Newfoundland. 21,000 pop.; 112,800 sq. mi.

Labrador Current, a current of cold water that rises in the Arctic Ocean and flows along the coast of Labrador past Newfoundland, where it meets the Gulf Stream.

lab ra do rite (lab′rə dô rīt′, lab′rə dôr′īt), *n.* kind of feldspar that shows a brilliant variety of color when turned in the light. It is used as an ornamental stone. [< *Labrador,* where it is found]

la brum (lā′brəm), *n.* the upper lip of insects and certain other arthropods. [< Latin]

la bur num (lə bėr′nəm), *n.* any of a genus of small trees or shrubs of the pea family, having hanging clusters of bright-yellow flowers. [< Latin]

lab y rinth (lab′ə rinth′), *n.* 1 number of connecting passages so arranged that it is hard to find one's way from point to point; maze. 2 **Labyrinth** (in Greek legends) the maze built by Daedalus for King Minos of Crete to imprison the Minotaur. 3 any confusing, complicated arrangement: *a labyrinth of dark and narrow streets.* 4 a confusing, complicated state of affairs. 5 the inner ear. [< Greek *labyrinthos*]

lab y rin thine (lab′ə rin′thən, lab′ə rin′thēn′), *adj.* 1 of a labyrinth; forming a labyrinth. 2 confusing and complicated; intricate.

lac (lak), *n.* a resinous substance deposited on various trees in southern Asia by scale insects, used in making sealing wax, varnish, red dye, etc. [< Hindustani *lākh* < Sanskrit *lākṣā*]

lac co lith (lak′ə lith), *n.* a large mass of igneous rock that has spread on rising from below, causing the overlying strata to bulge upward in a domelike formation. See **volcano** for diagram. [< Greek *lakkos* pond + English *-lith*]

lace (lās), *n., v.,* **laced, lac ing.** —*n.* 1 an open weaving or net of fine thread in an ornamental pattern. 2 cord, string, leather strip, etc., passed through holes to pull or hold together the opposite edges of a shoe, garment, etc. 3 gold or silver braid used for trimming. Some uniforms have lace on them. —*v.t.* 1 trim with lace. 2 put laces through; pull or hold together with a lace or laces. 3 adorn or trim with narrow braid: *Our band uniforms are laced with gold.* 4 interlace; intertwine. 5 mark with streaks; streak: *a white petunia laced with purple.* 6 INFORMAL. lash; beat; thrash. 7 add a dash of whiskey, brandy, etc., to a beverage, especially coffee. 8 squeeze in the waist of (a person) by a tight corset. 9 **lace into, a** attack. **b** criticize severely. —*v.i.* be laced: *These shoes lace easily.* [< Old French *laz* < Latin *laqueus* noose. Doublet of LASSO.] **—lace′like′,** *adj.*

Lac e dae mon (las′ə dē′mən), *n.* Sparta.

Lac e dae mo ni an (las′ə di mō′nē ən), *adj., n.* Spartan.

lace mak ing (lās′mā′king), *n.* art or process of making lace.

lac e rate (*v.* las′ə rāt′; *adj.* las′ər it), *v.,* **-rat ed, -rat ing,** *adj.* —*v.t.* 1 tear roughly; mangle: *The bear's claws lacerated the hunter's arm.* 2 wound; hurt (the feelings, etc.). —*adj.* deeply or irregularly indented as if torn: *lacerate leaves.* [< Latin *laceratum* torn, mangled]

lac e ra tion (las′ə rā′shən), *n.* 1 a lacerating. 2 a rough tear; mangled place.

lac er til i an (las′ər til′ē ən), *adj.* of, like, or belonging to the lizards. —*n.* a lizard or lizardlike reptile. [< Latin *lacerta* lizard]

lace wing (lās′wing′), *n.* any of various insects with four delicate, lacelike wings, of the same order as the ant lions.

lace work (lās′wėrk′), *n.* 1 lace. 2 openwork like lace.

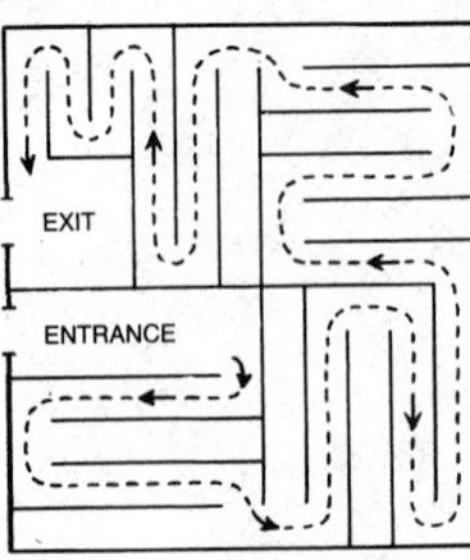

labyrinth (def. 1)

lach es (lach′iz), *n.* (in law) failure to do a thing at the right time; inexcusable negligence. [< Old French *laschesse* < *lasche* negligent < Latin *laxus* loose]

Lach e sis (lak′ə sis), *n.* (in Greek and Roman myths) one of the three Fates.

hat, āge, fär; let, ēqual, tėrm;
it, īce; hot, ōpen, ôrder;
oil, out; cup, pu̇t, rüle;
ch, child; ng, long; sh, she;
th, thin; ᴛʜ, then; zh, measure;

ə represents *a* in about, *e* in taken, *i* in pencil, *o* in lemon, *u* in circus.

< = from, derived from, taken from.

Lachesis measures off the thread of human life.

lach ry mal (lak′rə məl), *adj.* 1 of tears; producing tears. 2 for tears. *—n.* **lachrymals,** *pl.* lachrymal glands. Also, **lacrimal.** [< Medieval Latin *lachrymalis* < Latin *lacrima* tear]

lachrymal gland, either of the two glands, one above each eye, that produce tears.

lach ry ma to ry (lak′rə mə tôr′ē, lak′rə mə tōr′ē), *adj., n., pl.* **-ries.** *—adj.* of tears; producing tears. *—n.* a small vase with a narrow neck found in ancient Roman tombs, once believed to be used to hold the tears of mourners.

lach ry mose (lak′rə mōs), *adj.* 1 given to shedding tears; tearful. 2 suggestive of or tending to cause tears; mournful: *lachrymose poetry.* **—lach′ry mose ly,** *adv.*

lac ing (lā′sing), *n.* 1 cord, string, etc., for pulling or holding something together. 2 gold or silver braid used for trimming. 3 INFORMAL. lashing; beating.

lack (lak), *v.t.* 1 be without; have no: *A homeless person lacks a home.* See synonym study below. 2 have not enough: *A desert lacks water.* *—v.i.* be absent or missing. *—n.* 1 fact or condition of being without: *Lack of a fire made us cold.* 2 not having enough; shortage: *Lack of rest made her tired.* 3 thing needed: *The campers' main lack was fuel for a fire.* [apparently < Middle Dutch *lac* deficiency]

Syn. *v.t.* 1 **Lack, want, need** mean to be without something. **Lack** means to be completely without or without enough of something, good or bad: *A coward lacks courage.* **Want** means to lack something worth having, desired, or, especially, necessary for completeness: *That dress wants a belt.* **Need** means to lack something required for a purpose or that cannot be done without: *He does not have the tools he needs. She needs more sleep.*

lack a dai si cal (lak′ə dā′zə kəl), *adj.* lacking interest or enthusiasm; languid; listless; dreamy. [< *lackaday* alas, variant of *alack a day!*] **—lack′a dai′si cal ly,** *adv.*

lack ey (lak′ē), *n., pl.* **-eys,** *v.* *—n.* 1 a male servant; footman. 2 a slavish follower; toady. *—v.t.* 1 wait on. 2 be slavish to. [< Middle French *laquais* < Spanish *lacayo* foot soldier]

lack ing (lak′ing), *adj.* 1 not having enough; deficient: *A weak person is lacking in strength.* 2 absent; not here: *Water is lacking because the pipe is broken.* *—prep.* without; not having: *Lacking anything better, use what you have.*

lack lus ter or **lack lus tre** (lak′lus′tər), *adj.* lacking brightness; dull and drab.

La co ni a (lə kō′nē ə), *n.* ancient country in S Greece. Sparta was its capital. See **Peloponnesus** for map. **—La co′ni an,** *adj., n.*

la con ic (lə kon′ik), *adj.* using few words; brief in speech or expression; concise; terse. [< Latin *Laconicus* Spartan < Greek *Lakōnikos;* Spartans were noted for pithy speech] **—la con′i cal ly,** *adv.*

lac quer (lak′ər), *n.* 1 varnish consisting of shellac dissolved in alcohol or some other solvent, sometimes tinged with coloring matter, used for coating metals, wood, etc. 2 any of various kinds of varnish made from the resin of a sumac tree of southeast Asia. It gives a very high polish on wood. 3 wooden articles coated with such varnish. *—v.t.* coat with lacquer. [< Middle French *lacre* < Portuguese, sealing wax, ultimately < Hindustani *lākh.* See LAC.] **—lac′quer er,** *n.*

lac ri mal (lak′rə məl), *adj., n.* lachrymal.

la crosse (lə krôs′, lə kros′), *n.* game played on a field with a ball and long-handled, loosely-strung rackets by two teams, usually of 10 players each. The players carry the ball in the rackets, trying to send it into the other team's goal. [< French *la crosse,* the racket, literally, the crosier]

lact-, *combining form.* the form of **lacto-** before vowels, as in *lactase.*

lac tase (lak′tās), *n.* enzyme present in certain yeasts and in the body, capable of decomposing lactose into glucose and galactose.

lac tate (lak′tāt), *n., v.,* **-tat ed, -tat ing.** *—n.* salt or ester of lactic acid. *—v.i.* secrete milk.

lac ta tion (lak tā′shən), *n.* 1 secretion or formation of milk. 2 time during which a mother gives milk.

lac te al (lak′tē əl), *adj.* 1 of milk; like milk; milky. 2 carrying chyle, a milky liquid formed from digested food. *—n.* any of the tiny lymphatic vessels that carry chyle from the small intestine to be mixed with the blood.

lac tic (lak′tik), *adj.* of milk; from milk.

lactic acid, a colorless, odorless acid formed in sour milk, the fermentation of vegetable juices, etc. *Formula:* $CH_3CHOHCOOH$

lacto-, *combining form.* 1 milk, as in *lactometer.* 2 lactic acid, as in *lactobacillus.* See also **lact-.** [< Latin *lac, lactis* milk]

lac to ba cil lus (lak′tō bə sil′əs), *n., pl.* **-cil li** (-sil′ī). any of a genus of aerobic bacteria that produce lactic acid.

lac to fla vin (lak′tō flā′vən), *n.* riboflavin.

lac to gen ic (lak′tə jen′ik), *adj.* that stimulates the secretion and flow of milk.

lac tose (lak′tōs), *n.* a crystalline sugar present in milk; milk sugar. *Formula:* $C_{12}H_{22}O_{11}$

la cu na (lə kyü′nə), *n., pl.* **-nas, -nae** (-nē). 1 an empty space; gap; blank: *There were several lacunas in her letter where words had been erased.* 2 a space, cavity, depression, etc., in the anatomical structure of an animal or plant, such as a cavity in bones or tissues, or a depression in the surface of lichens. [< Latin, hole < *lacus* cistern, pond, lake. Doublet of LAGOON.]

la cu nal (lə kyü′nl), *adj.* 1 of or having to do with a lacuna. 2 having lacunas.

la cus trine (lə kus′trən), *adj.* 1 of lakes. 2 living or growing in lakes.

lac y (lā′sē), *adj.,* **lac i er, lac i est.** 1 of lace. 2 like lace; having an open, delicate pattern. **—lac′i ness,** *n.*

lad (lad), *n.* 1 boy; youth. 2 INFORMAL. man. [Middle English *ladde*]

lad der (lad′ər), *n.* 1 set of rungs or steps fastened to two long sidepieces for use in climbing. 2 means of climbing higher. 3 anything resembling or suggesting a ladder. [Old English *hlǣder*] **—lad′der like′,** *adj.*

lad die (lad′ē), *n.* SCOTTISH. lad.

lade (lād), *v.,* **lad ed, lad en** or **lad ed, lad ing.** *—v.t.* 1 put a burden on; load. 2 put cargo on board (a ship). 3 take up (liquid) with a ladle, scoop, etc.; dip. *—v.i.* 1 take on cargo. 2 dip a liquid. [Old English *hladan*]

lad en (lād′n), *adj.* loaded; burdened. *—v.* a pp. of **lade.**

la-di-da (lä′dē dä′), *adj.* SLANG. languidly genteel in speech or manner; affected.

lad ing (lā′ding), *n.* 1 act of loading. 2 load; freight; cargo.

la di no (lə dē′nō), *n., pl.* **-nos.** 1 (in Spanish America, especially Guatemala) a mestizo. 2 a large, white variety of clover valuable as a forage crop. [< Spanish < Latin *Latinus* Latin]

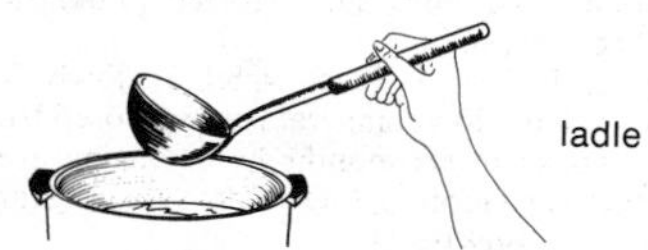

la dle (lā′dl), *n., v.,* **-dled, -dling.** *—n.* a large cup-shaped spoon with a long handle, for dipping out liquids. *—v.t.* 1 dip out. 2 carry in a ladle. [Old English *hlædel* < *hladan* lade] **—la′dler,** *n.*

La do ga (lä′dō gə), *n.* **Lake,** lake in NW Soviet Union. It is the largest lake in Europe. 7000 sq. mi.

La drone Islands (lə drōn′), Mariana Islands.

la dy (lā′dē), *n., pl.* **-dies.** 1 woman of good family and high social position. 2 a well-bred woman. 3 any woman. See **woman** for synonym study. 4 woman who has the rights or authority of a lord. 5 noblewoman. 6 **Lady,** title given to women of certain ranks in Great Britain. 7 woman whom a man loves or is devoted to. 8 wife. [Old English *hlæfdīge,* literally, loaf-kneader < *hlāf* loaf + *-dīge* kneader (of dough)]

lady beetle, ladybug.

la dy bird (lā′dē bėrd′), *n.* ladybug.

la dy bug (lā′dē bug′), *n.* any of a family of small beetles, with rounded backs and often with black or colored spots, that eat harmful insects.

Lady Day, Annunciation Day.

la dy fin ger (lā′dē fing′gər), *n.* a small sponge cake shaped somewhat like a finger.

la dy-in-wait ing (lā′dē in wā′ting), *n., pl.* **la dies-in-wait ing.** lady who is an attendant of a queen or princess.

la dy-kill er (lā′dē kil′ər), *n.* SLANG. man supposed to be fascinating to women.

la dy like (lā′dē līk′), *adj.* like a lady; suitable for a lady; well-bred; polite.

la dy love (lā′dē luv′), *n.* woman who is loved by a man; sweetheart.

la dy ship (lā′dē ship), *n.* 1 rank or position of a lady. 2 **Ladyship,** title used in speaking to or of a lady: *your Ladyship.*

la dy-slip per (lā′dē slip′ər), *n.* lady's-slipper.

la dy's-slip per (lā′dēz slip′ər), *n.* any of a genus of terrestrial wild orchids whose flowers look somewhat like slippers.

La Farge (lə färj′; lə färzh′), **John,** 1835-1910, American painter and designer of stained glass windows.

La fa yette (lä′fē et′, laf′ē et′), *n.* **Mar-**

quis de, 1757-1834, French general and statesman who served in the American army during the Revolutionary War.

La Fol lette (lə fol′it), **Robert Marion,** 1855-1925, American statesman and political leader.

La Fon taine (lä fon tān′; *French* lä fôN-ten′), **Jean de,** 1621-1695, French poet and writer of fables.

LAFTA, Latin American Free Trade Association.

lag (lag), *v.,* **lagged, lag ging,** *n.* —*v.i.* 1 move too slowly; fall behind: *The children lagged because they were tired.* See **linger** for synonym study. 2 toss a marble at a line on the ground. 3 become weaker; flag: *Interest lagged as the speaker droned on.* —*v.t.* cause to lag. —*n.* 1 a lagging. 2 amount by which a person or thing lags. [origin unknown] —**lag′ger,** *n.*

la ger (lä′gər), *n.* beer which is slowly fermented at a low temperature and stored from six weeks to six months before being used. [short for German *Lagerbier* < *Lager* storehouse + *Bier* beer]

La ger löf (lä′gər ləv), *n.* **Selma,** 1858-1940, Swedish novelist and poet.

lag gard (lag′ərd), *n.* person who moves too slowly or falls behind; backward person. —*adj.* falling behind; backward. —**lag′gard ly,** *adv.* —**lag′gard ness,** *n.*

la gniappe or **la gnappe** (lan yap′, lan′yap), *n.* something given to a customer with a purchase. [< Louisiana French < Spanish *la ñapa, la yapa* the gift < Quechua *yapa* an extra something]

lag o morph (lag′ə môrf), *n.* any of an order of mammals similar to rodents, but having two pairs of upper incisors and short tails, including the rabbits, hares, and pikas. [< Greek *lagōs* hare < *morphē* form]

la goon (lə gün′), *n.* 1 pond or small lake connected with a larger body of water. 2 shallow water separated from the sea by low sandbanks. 3 water within an atoll. Also, **lagune.** [< Italian *laguna* < Latin *lacuna* pond, hole. Doublet of LACUNA.]

La gos (lä′gōs, lā′gos), *n.* capital of Nigeria, a seaport in the SW part. 842,000.

La grange (lə grānj′; *French* lä gräNzh), *n.* **Joseph Louis,** 1736-1813, French mathematician.

la gune (lə gün′), *n.* lagoon.

La Ha ba na (lä ä vä′nä), Spanish name of **Havana.** Also, **Habana.**

La hore (lə hôr′, lə hōr′), *n.* city in E Pakistan. 849,000.

la ic (lā′ik), *adj.* of the laity; lay; secular. —*n.* layman. [< Latin *laicus* < Greek *laikos* < *laos* people. Doublet of LAY[3].] —**la′i cal ly,** *adv.*

la i cism (lā′ə siz′əm), *n.* power or influence of the laity.

la i cize (lā′ə sīz), *v.t.,* **-cized, -ciz ing.** secularize. —**la′i ci za′tion,** *n.*

laid (lād), *v.* pt. and pp. of **lay**[1].

lain (lān), *v.* pp. of **lie**[2].

lair (ler, lar), *n.* 1 den or resting place of a wild animal. 2 secret or secluded retreat; hideaway: *a pirate's lair.* [Old English *leger* < *licgan* lie[2]]

laird (lerd, lard), *n.* SCOTTISH. owner of land. [variant of *lord*]

lais sez faire or **lais ser faire** (les′ā fer′; les′ā far′), 1 principle that trade, business, industry, etc., should operate with a minimum or complete absence of regulation and interference by government. 2 principle of letting people do as they please. [< French *laissez faire* allow to do]

lais sez-faire (les′ā fer′, les′ā far′), *adj.* of or based on laissez faire.

la i ty (lā′ə tē), *n., pl.* **-ties.** 1 the people who are not members of the clergy or of a professional class; laymen collectively. [< *lay*[3]]

La ius (lā′əs), *n.* (in Greek legends) the king of Thebes and father of Oedipus.

lake[1] (lāk), *n.* 1 a large body of water entirely or nearly surrounded by land. 2 a wide place in a river. 3 pool of liquid, such as oil, tar, etc. [< Old French *lac* < Latin *lacus*]

lake[2] (lāk), *n.* 1 a deep-red or purplish-red coloring matter. 2 an insoluble colored compound formed from animal, vegetable, or coal tar coloring matter and metallic oxides. [variant of *lac*]

Lake Charles, city in SW Louisiana. 78,000.

Lake District or **Lake Country,** region of beautiful mountains and lakes in NW England, associated with Wordsworth, Coleridge, and other English poets.

lake dweller, inhabitant of a lake dwelling.

lake dwelling, house on piles, built over a lake, especially in prehistoric times.

lake herring, cisco.

lake shore (lāk′shôr′), *n.* lakeside.

lake side (lāk′sīd′), *n.* the margin or shore of a lake.

lake trout, a large, dark trout with gray or yellowish spots, found in lakes of the northern United States and Canada.

Lake wood (lāk′wu̇d), *n.* 1 city in SW California, near Los Angeles. 83,000. 2 city in central Colorado. 93,000.

lam (lam), *n.* SLANG. **on the lam,** a escaping. b in hiding. [origin unknown]

Lam., Lamentations.

la ma (lä′mə), *n.* a Buddhist priest or monk in Tibet and Mongolia. [< Tibetan *blama*]

La ma ism (lä′mə iz′əm), *n.* the religious system of the lamas in Tibet and Mongolia, a form of Mahayana Buddhism. It possesses a widespread monastic system and a hierarchal organization headed by the Dalai Lama.

La ma ist (lä′mə ist), *n.* believer in Lamaism. —*adj.* Lamaistic.

La ma is tic (lä′mə is′tik), *adj.* 1 characteristic of a Lamaist. 2 of or having to do with Lamaism.

La marck (lə märk′), *n.* **Jean de,** 1744-1829, French biologist and botanist.

La marck i an (lə mär′kē ən), *adj.* of Lamarck or Lamarckism. —*n.* person who supports Lamarckism.

La marck ism (lə mär′kiz′əm), *n.* theory of organic evolution proposed by Lamarck, which maintains that characteristics acquired by parents tend to be inherited by their descendants.

La mar tine (lä mär tēn′), *n.* **Alphonse de,** 1790-1869, French poet, historian, and statesman.

la ma ser y (lä′mə ser′ē), *n., pl.* **-ser ies.** a monastery of lamas in Tibet and Mongolia.

lamb (lam), *n.* 1 a young sheep. 2 meat from a lamb. 3 lambskin. 4 **the Lamb,** Christ. 5 a young, dear, or innocent person. 6 **like a lamb,** a meekly; timidly. b easily fooled. —*v.i.* give birth to a lamb or lambs. —*v.t.* attend (ewes) which are lambing. [Old English] —**lamb′like′,** *adj.*

Lamb (lam), *n.* **Charles,** 1775-1834, English writer. His pen name was Elia.

lam bast (lam bast′), *v.t.* lambaste.

lam baste (lam bāst′), *v.t.,* **-bast ed, -bast ing.** INFORMAL. 1 strike again and again; beat severely; thrash. 2 scold roughly; denounce violently. [probably < *lam* beat, thrash + *baste*[3]]

lamb da (lam′də), *n.* the 11th letter of the Greek alphabet (Λ, λ).

lambda particle, a heavy elementary particle, a form of hyperon, having a neutral charge and decaying very rapidly.

lam ben cy (lam′bən sē), *n.* lambent quality or condition.

lam bent (lam′bənt), *adj.* 1 moving lightly over a surface: *a lambent flame.* 2 playing lightly and brilliantly over a subject: *a lambent wit.* 3 softly bright: *lambent eyes.* [< Latin *lambentem* licking. Related to LAP[3].] —**lam′bent ly,** *adv.*

lam bert (lam′bərt), *n.* unit of brightness, equivalent to the brightness of a perfectly diffusing surface that emits or reflects one lumen per square centimeter. [< Johann H. *Lambert,* 1728-1777, German physicist]

Lam beth (lam′bəth), *n.* borough of London, England.

Lambeth Palace, the London residence of the Archbishop of Canterbury.

lamb kin (lam′kən), *n.* 1 a little lamb. 2 a young or dear person.

Lamb of God, Christ.

lam bre quin (lam′brə kən, lam′bər kən), *n.* drapery covering the top of a window or door, or hanging from a shelf. [< French]

lamb skin (lam′skin′), *n.* 1 skin of a lamb, especially with the wool on it. 2 leather made from the skin of a lamb. 3 parchment.

lamb's-quar ters (lamz′kwôr′tərz), *n., pl.* **-ters.** a species of pigweed which is sometimes cultivated and used as a potherb and in salad.

lame (lām), *adj.,* **lam er, lam est,** *v.,* **lamed, lam ing.** —*adj.* 1 not able to walk properly; having an injured leg or foot; crippled; disabled. 2 stiff and sore: *My arm is lame from playing ball.* 3 poor; weak; unsatisfactory: *Sleeping too long is a lame excuse for being late.* —*v.t.* make lame; cripple; disable: *The accident lamed him for life.* —*v.i.* become lame; go lame. [Old English *lama*] —**lame′ly,** *adv.* —**lame′ness,** *n.*

la mé (la mā′, lä mā′), *n.* a rich fabric made wholly or partly of metal threads. [< French, literally, laminated]

lame duck, 1 a public official, especially a Congressman, who has been defeated for reelection and is serving the last part of his term. 2 a disabled or helpless person or thing.

la mel la (lə mel′ə), *n., pl.* **-mel lae** (-mel′ē), **-mel las.** a thin plate, scale, or layer, especially of flesh or bone. [< Latin, diminutive of *lamina*]

la mel lar (lə mel′ər, lam′ə lər), *adj.* consisting of or arranged in lamellae.

lam el late (lam′ə lāt, lam′ə lit; lə mel′āt, lə-mel′it), *adj.* lamellar.

la mel li branch (lə mel′ə brangk), *n.* pelecypod.

la ment (lə ment′), *v.t.* 1 express grief for; mourn for: *lament the dead.* 2 regret: *We lamented his absence.* —*v.i.* express grief; mourn; weep: *Why does she lament?* —*n.* 1 expression of grief or sorrow; wail. 2 poem, song, or tune that expresses grief. [< Latin *lamentari* < *lamentum* a wailing] —**la ment′er,** *n.* —**la ment′ing ly,** *adv.*

lam en ta ble (lam′ən tə bəl), *adj.* 1 to be regretted or pitied; deplorable: *a lamentable* *accident.* 2 inferior; pitiful: *a lamentable fake.* 3 ARCHAIC. sorrowful; mournful. **—lam′en ta bly,** *adv.*

lam en ta tion (lam′ən tā′shən), *n.* 1 loud grief; cries of sorrow; mourning; wailing. 2 **Lamentations,** book of the Old Testament. According to tradition it was written by Jeremiah.

lam i na (lam′ə nə), *n., pl.* **-nae** (-nē′), **-nas.** 1 a thin plate, scale, or layer. 2 the flat, wide part of a leaf; blade. [< Latin]

lam i nar (lam′ə nər), *adj.* consisting of or arranged in laminae.

laminar flow, a steady flow of a fluid near a solid body, such as the flow of air over or about an airfoil.

lam i nate (*v.* lam′ə nāt; *adj., n.* lam′ə nāt, lam′ə nit), *v.,* **-nat ed, -nat ing,** *adj., n.* —*v.t.* 1 make (plywood, plastics, glass, etc.) by fastening together layer on layer of one or more materials. 2 beat or roll (metal) into a thin plate. 3 split into thin layers. 4 cover with thin plates. —*v.i.* split into thin layers. —*adj.* laminated; laminar. —*n.* a laminated plastic.

lam i nat ed (lam′ə nā′tid), *adj.* 1 consisting of or arranged in laminae. 2 formed or manufactured in a succession of layers of material.

lam i na tion (lam′ə nā′shən), *n.* 1 a laminating. 2 a being laminated. 3 a laminated structure; arrangement in thin layers. 4 a thin layer.

Lam mas (lam′əs), *n.* August 1. A harvest festival was formerly held in England on this day. [Old English *hlāfmæsse* < *hlāf* loaf + *mæsse* Mass; the year's first loaves were consecrated on Lammas]

lam mer gei er or **lam mer gey er** (lam′ər gī′ər), *n.* the largest European bird of prey, with a wingspread of 9 to 10 feet. [< German *Lämmergeier* < *Lämmer,* plural of *Lamm* lamb + *Geier* vulture]

lamp (lamp), *n.* 1 device that gives light, especially by gas or electricity or from a wick soaked in oil or alcohol: *a street lamp, a floor lamp.* 2 a similar device that gives heat: *a spirit lamp.* 3 something that suggests the light of a lamp: *the lamp of learning.* [< Greek *lampas* < *lampein* to shine]

lamp black (lamp′blak′), *n.* a fine black soot consisting of almost pure carbon that is deposited when oil, gas, etc., burn incompletely. Lampblack is used as a coloring matter in paint, ink, cement, etc.

lamp light (lamp′līt′), *n.* light from a lamp.

lamp light er (lamp′lī′tər), *n.* 1 person who lights lamps, especially a person formerly employed to light gas-burning street lamps. 2 torch, twisted paper, etc., used to light lamps.

lam poon (lam pün′), *n.* piece of writing that attacks and ridicules a person in a malicious or abusive way. —*v.t.* attack in a lampoon. [< earlier French *lampon* drinking song < *lampons* let us drink] **—lam poon′er,** *n.*

lam poon er y (lam pü′nər ē), *n., pl.* **-er ies.** 1 practice of writing lampoons. 2 lampooning quality or spirit.

lam poon ist (lam pü′nist), *n.* person who writes lampoons.

lamp post (lamp′pōst′), *n.* post used to support a street lamp.

lam prey (lam′prē), *n., pl.* **-preys.** any of an order of marine and freshwater vertebrate animals having a body like an eel, gill slits like a fish, no jaws, and a large, round mouth. Some species attach themselves to fishes with their mouths, sucking the body fluids. [< Old French *lampreie* < Medieval Latin *lampreda.* Doublet of LIMPET.]

lamp shade (lamp′shād′), *n.* shade over a lamp to soften or direct the light.

la nai (lä nī′), *n.* a porch or veranda. [< Hawaiian]

La nai (lä nī′), *n.* island in Hawaii, in the central Hawaiian Islands, west of Maui. 2000 pop.; 141 sq. mi.

Lan ark (lan′ərk), *n.* county in S Scotland.

Lan ca shire (lang′kə shər, lang′kə shir), *n.* county in NW England.

Lan cas ter (lang′kə stər *for 1 and 2;* lang′kə stər, lang′kas′tər *for 3*), *n.* 1 the royal house of England from 1399 to 1461. Its emblem was a red rose. 2 Lancashire. 3 city in SE Pennsylvania. 61,000.

Lan cas tri an (lang kas′trē ən), *n.* supporter or member of the royal house of Lancaster. —*adj.* of or having to do with the royal house of Lancaster.

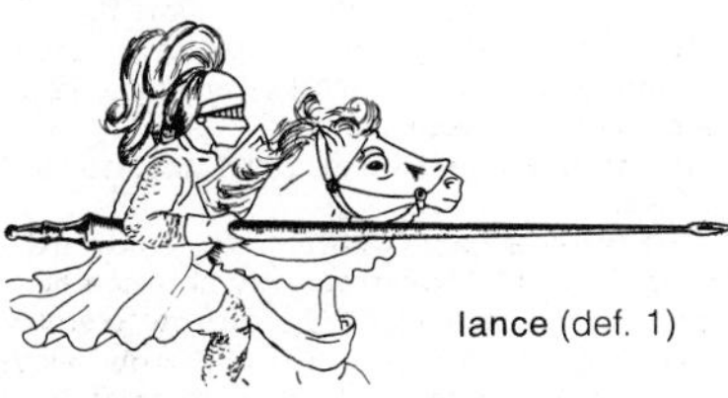

lance (def. 1)

lance (lans), *n., v.,* **lanced, lanc ing.** —*n.* 1 a long wooden spear with a sharp iron or steel head. Knights and cavalry troops carried lances. 2 lancer. 3 any instrument like a soldier's lance. 4 lancet. —*v.t.* 1 pierce with a lance: *lance a fish.* 2 cut open with a lancet: *The dentist lanced the gum so that the new tooth could come through.* [< Old French < Latin *lancea* light Spanish spear]

lance corporal, 1 (in the United States Marine Corps) an enlisted man ranking next below a corporal and next above a private first class. 2 (in the British army) a private acting temporarily as a corporal without increase of pay.

lance let (lans′lit), *n.* any of a subphylum of small, limbless, often translucent, fishlike marine chordates, which exhibit the most simplified chordate characteristics; cephalochordate.

Lan ce lot (lan′sə lot), *n.* (in Arthurian legends) the bravest of the knights of the Round Table and the lover of Queen Guinevere.

lan ce o late (lan′sē ə lāt, lan′sē ə lit), *adj.* shaped like the head of a lance; tapering from a rounded base toward the apex: *a lanceolate leaf.* [< Latin *lanceola,* diminutive of *lancea* lance]

lanc er (lan′sər), *n.* a mounted soldier armed with a lance; lance.

lanc ers (lan′sərz), *n.pl.* 1 form of square dance or quadrille popular in the 1800's, having figures imitating military drill. 2 music for it.

lance sergeant, (in the British army) a corporal appointed to act temporarily as sergeant without increase of pay.

lan cet (lan′sit), *n.* a small, pointed surgical knife, usually having two sharp edges; lance. Doctors use lancets for opening boils, abscesses, etc.

lance wood (lans′wu̇d′), *n.* 1 a tough, straight-grained, springy wood, used for fishing rods, carriage shafts, cabinetwork, etc. 2 any of various American trees that yield this wood.

hat, āge, fär; let, ēqual, tėrm;
it, īce; hot, ōpen, ôrder;
oil, out; cup, pu̇t, rüle;
ch, child; ng, long; sh, she;
th, thin; ᴛʜ, then; zh, measure;

ə represents *a* in about, *e* in taken, *i* in pencil, *o* in lemon, *u* in circus.

< = from, derived from, taken from.

Lan chow (län′chou′), *n.* city in N China. 700,000.

land (land), *n.* 1 the solid part of the earth's surface: *dry land.* 2 ground, soil: *This is good land for a garden.* 3 landed property; real estate. 4 country; region: *mountainous land.* 5 people of a country; nation. 6 realm; domain: *the land of the living.* 7 **how the land lies,** what the state of affairs is.
—*v.i.* 1 come to land: *The ship landed at the pier.* 2 go ashore: *The passengers landed.* 3 arrive: *The thief landed in jail.* —*v.t.* 1 bring to land: *The pilot landed the airplane at Seattle.* 2 cause to arrive in any place, position, or condition: *A combination of circumstances landed the company in bankruptcy.* 3 INFORMAL. catch; get: *land a job, land a fish.* 4 INFORMAL. strike (a blow) home: *I landed one on his chin.* [Old English]

Land[1] (länt), *n., pl.* ***Län der*** or ***Laen der*** (len′dər). GERMAN. state; province.

Land[2] (land), *n.* **Edwin Herbert,** born 1909, American inventor of photographic and optical equipment.

landau (def. 1)

lan dau (lan′dou, lan′dô), *n.* 1 a four-wheeled carriage with two inside seats and a top made in two parts that can be folded back. 2 automobile with a similar top or one that imitates such a top. [< *Landau,* German town where it was first made]

land breeze, breeze blowing from the land toward the sea.

land bridge, neck of land connecting two land masses.

land ed (lan′did), *adj.* 1 owning land: *landed nobles.* 2 consisting of land. Landed property is real estate.

land fall (land′fôl′), *n.* 1 a sighting of land. 2 the land sighted or reached. 3 approach to land; landing.

land form (land′fôrm′), *n.* the physical characteristics of land; irregularities of land.

land grant, grant of land; gift of land by the government for colleges, railroads, roads, etc.

land grave (land′grāv′), *n.* 1 (in the Middle Ages) a German count having authority over a considerable territory or over other counts. 2 title of certain German princes. [< German *Landgraf* < *Land* land + *Graf* count]

land hold er (land′hōl′dər), *n.* person who owns or occupies land.

land hold ing (land′hōl′ding), *adj.* that owns or occupies land. —*n.* an owning or occupying of land.

land ing (lan′ding), *n.* 1 a coming to land: *the landing of the Pilgrims at Plymouth.* 2 place where persons or goods are landed from a ship, helicopter, etc.: *the steamboat landing.* 3 platform between flights of stairs, or the floor at the top or bottom of a staircase.

landing craft, any of various kinds of boats or ships used for landing troops or equipment on a shore, especially during an assault.

landing field, field large enough and smooth enough for airplanes to land on and take off from safely.

landing gear, wheels, pontoons, etc., under an aircraft; undercarriage. When on land or water an aircraft rests on its landing gear.

landing net, a small net to take fish from the water after they are caught.

landing strip, airstrip.

land la dy (land′lā′dē), *n., pl.* **-dies.** 1 woman who owns buildings or land that she rents to others. 2 woman who runs an inn or rooming house.

land less (land′lis), *adj.* without land; owning no land.

land line (land′līn′), *n.* a communication cable that runs on or under the land.

land locked (land′lokt′), *adj.* 1 shut in, or nearly shut in, by land: *a landlocked harbor.* 2 living in waters shut off from the sea: *landlocked salmon.*

land lord (land′lôrd′), *n.* 1 person who owns buildings or land that he rents to others. 2 person who runs an inn or rooming house.

land lub ber (land′lub′ər), *n.* person not used to being on ships; inexperienced person who is awkward on board ship.

land lub ber ly (land′lub′ər lē), *adj.* confined to or used on land rather than the sea: *landlubberly sports.*

land mark (land′märk′), *n.* 1 something familiar or easily seen, used as a guide. 2 an important fact or event; happening that stands out above others: *The invention of the radio was a landmark in the history of communications.* 3 stone or other object that marks the boundary of a piece of land.

land mass (land′mas′), *n.* a large, unbroken area of land.

land mine, container filled with explosives or chemicals, placed either on the ground or slightly below the surface. It is usually set off by the weight of vehicles or troops passing over it.

land office, a government office that takes care of the business connected with public lands, and records sales, transfers, etc.

land-of fice business (land′ô′fis, land′of′is), INFORMAL. exceedingly active or rapid business.

Lan dor (lan′dər), *n.* **Walter Savage,** 1775-1864, English author.

land own er (land′ō′nər), *n.* person who owns land.

land own er ship (land′ō′nər ship), *n.* condition of being a landowner.

land own ing (land′ō′ning), *adj.* holding or possessing landed estates: *the landowning class.*

land-poor (land′pu̇r′), *adj.* 1 owning much land but needing ready money. 2 poor because of taxes, etc., on one's land.

land reform, 1 the breaking up and redistribution of large land holdings, often among the hands that worked them. 2 any social or economic measure that will benefit farmers.

land scape (land′skāp), *n., v.,* **-scaped, -scap ing.** —*n.* 1 view of scenery on land. 2 picture showing a land scene. —*v.t.* make (land) more pleasant to look at by arranging trees, shrubs, flowers, etc.: *The park is landscaped.* [< Dutch *landschap* < *land* land + *-schap* -ship] **—land′scap er,** *n.*

landscape gardening, arrangement of trees, shrubs, flowers, etc., to give a pleasing appearance to grounds, parks, etc. **—landscape gardener.**

land scap ist (land′skā pist), *n.* painter of landscapes.

Land's End, the SW tip of England.

land slide (land′slīd′), *n.* 1 a sliding down of a mass of soil or rock on a steep slope. 2 the mass that slides down. 3 an overwhelming majority of votes for one political party or candidate.

land slip (land′slip′), *n.* BRITISH. landslide (defs. 1 and 2).

lands man (landz′mən), *n., pl.* **-men.** 1 man who lives or works on land. 2 an inexperienced seaman.

land ward (land′wərd), *adv., adj.* toward the land.

land wards (land′wərdz), *adv.* landward.

lane (lān), *n.* 1 a narrow way between hedges, walls, or fences. 2 a narrow country road or city street. 3 any narrow way. 4 course or route used by ships or aircraft going in the same direction. 5 a single division of a highway marked for a line of traffic. 6 alley between buildings. 7 bowling alley. [Old English]

lang., language.

Lang land (lang′lənd), *n.* **William,** 1330?-1400?, English poet.

Lang ley (lang′lē), *n.* 1 **Edmund,** 1341-1402, Duke of York, son of Edward III of England. He founded the royal house of York. 2 **Samuel Pierpont,** 1834-1906, American astronomer and physicist, a pioneer in aeronautics.

Lang muir (lang′myu̇r), *n.* **Irving,** 1881-1957, American chemist.

lan gouste (läN güst′), *n.* FRENCH. lobster or crayfish.

lang syne (lang′ sīn′), SCOTTISH. long since; long ago.

lan guage (lang′gwij), *n.* 1 human speech, spoken or written. See diagram on page 577. 2 speech of one nation, tribe, or other similar group of people: *the Navaho language.* See synonym study below. 3 form, style, or kind of language; manner of expression: *bad language, Shakespeare's language.* 4 wording or words: *in the language of the Lord's Prayer.* 5 the special terms used by a science, art, or profession, or by a class of persons: *the language of chemistry.* 6 any means of expressing thoughts and feelings otherwise than by words: *sign language.* 7 the study of language or languages; linguistics. [< Old French *langage* < *langue* tongue < Latin *lingua*]

Syn. 2 **Language, dialect, idiom** mean the form and pattern of speech of a particular group of people. **Language** applies to the body of words, forms, and patterns of sounds and structure making up the speech of a people, nation, or group of peoples: *The language of the Romans was Latin.* **Dialect** applies to a form of speech peculiar either to one locality or to one class of people using a language: *The dialect of the English language spoken in Boston sounds strange to a Westerner.* **Idiom** applies to a particular language's characteristic manner of using words in phrases and sentences: *The use of prepositions is a striking feature of English idiom.*

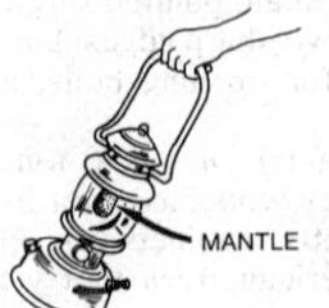

lantern (def. 1) of the type which burns gasoline and has a single mantle

language laboratory, schoolroom equipped with tape recorders and similar apparatus to enable students to practice hearing and speaking a language they are studying.

Langue doc (läNg dôk′), *n.* former province in S France.

langue d'oc (läNg dôk′), FRENCH. dialect spoken in southern France in the Middle Ages. It became modern Provençal.

langue d'o ïl (läNg dô ēl′), FRENCH. dialect spoken in northern France in the Middle Ages. It became modern French.

lan guid (lang′gwid), *adj.* 1 without energy; drooping; weak; weary: *A hot, sticky day makes a person feel languid.* 2 without interest or enthusiasm; indifferent; listless. 3 not brisk or lively; sluggish; dull. [< Latin *languidus* < *languere* be faint] **—lan′guid ly,** *adv.* **—lan′guid ness,** *n.*

lan guish (lang′gwish), *v.i.* 1 become weak or weary; lose energy; droop: *The flowers languished from lack of water.* 2 suffer under any unfavorable conditions: *He languished in prison for twenty years.* 3 grow dull, slack, or less intense: *His vigilance never languished.* 4 long or pine *(for): She languished for home.* 5 assume a soft, tender look for effect. [< Old French *languiss-*, a form of *languir* < Latin *languere*] **—lan′guish er,** *n.* **—lan′guish ment,** *n.*

lan guish ing (lang′gwi shing), *adj.* 1 drooping, as with longing. 2 tender; sentimental; loving. 3 lasting; lingering. **—lan′guish ing ly,** *adv.*

lan guor (lang′gər), *n.* 1 lack of energy; weakness; weariness: *A long illness causes languor.* 2 lack of interest or enthusiasm; indifference. 3 softness or tenderness of mood. 4 quietness; stillness: *the languor of a summer afternoon.* 5 lack of activity; sluggishness. [< Latin < *languere* be faint]

lan guor ous (lang′gər əs), *adj.* 1 languid. 2 causing languor. **—lan′guor ous ly,** *adv.*

lan gur (lung gu̇r′), *n.* any of several genera of large, long-tailed, slender monkeys of southern Asia. [< Hindustani *langūr*]

lan iard (lan′yərd), *n.* lanyard.

La nier (lə nir′), *n.* **Sidney,** 1842-1881, American poet.

lank (langk), *adj.* 1 long and thin; slender; lean: *a lank boy.* 2 straight and flat; not curly or wavy: *lank locks of hair.* [Old English *hlanc*] **—lank′ly,** *adv.* **—lank′ness,** *n.*

lank y (lang′kē), *adj.,* **lank i er, lank i est.** awkwardly long and thin; tall and ungraceful: *a lanky boy.* **—lank′i ly,** *adv.* **—lank′i ness,** *n.*

lan o lin (lan′l ən), *n.* fatty substance obtained from the natural coating on wool fibers, used in cosmetics, ointments, shoe polish, etc. [< Latin *lana* wool + *oleum* oil]

lan o line (lan′l ən, lan′l ēn′), *n.* lanolin.

Lan sing (lan′sing), *n.* capital of Michigan, in the S part. 132,000.

lan tern (lan′tərn), *n.* 1 case to protect a light from wind, rain, etc. It has sides of glass

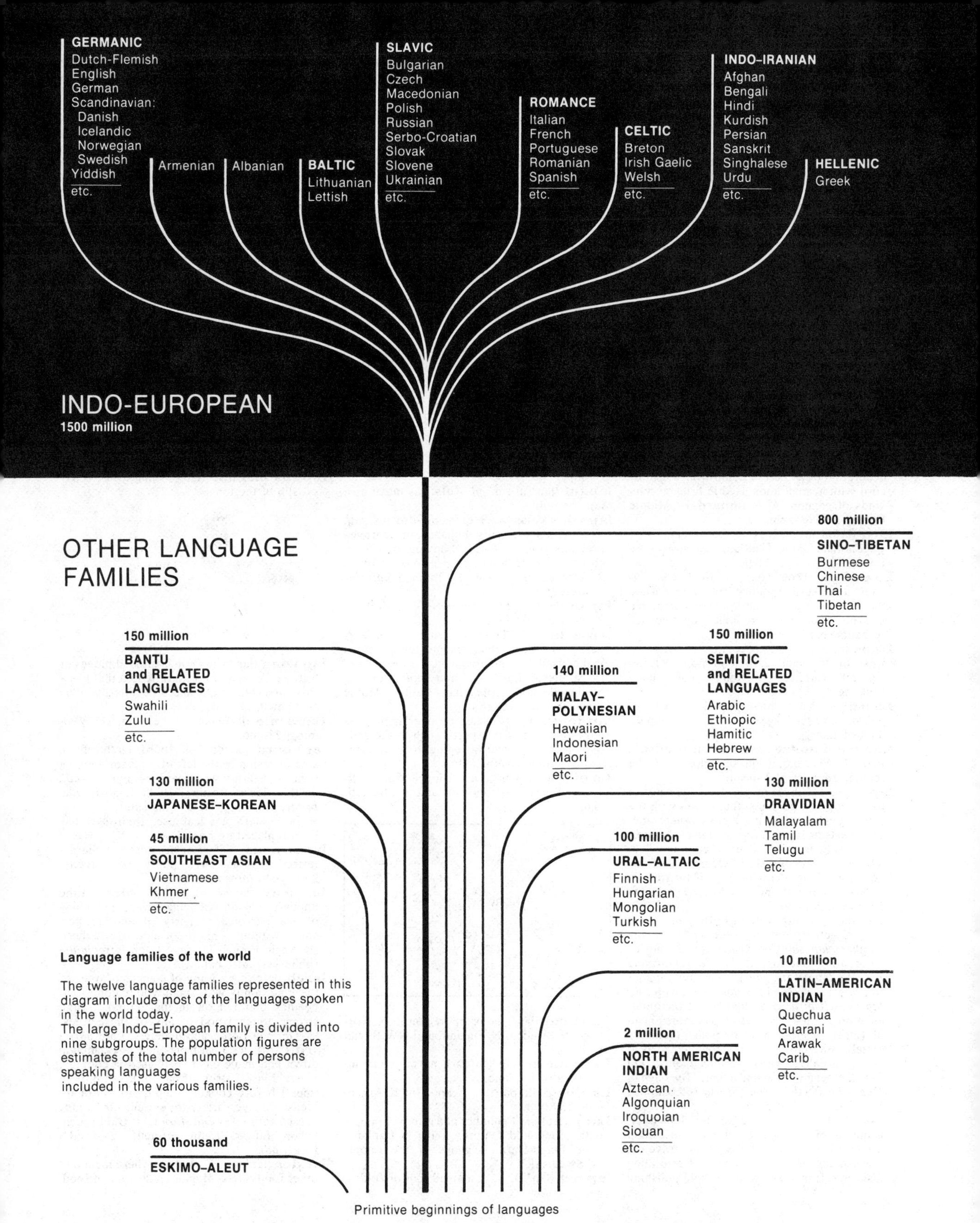

GERMANIC
Dutch-Flemish
English
German
Scandinavian:
Danish
Icelandic
Norwegian
Swedish
Yiddish
etc.

Armenian

Albanian

BALTIC
Lithuanian
Lettish

SLAVIC
Bulgarian
Czech
Macedonian
Polish
Russian
Serbo-Croatian
Slovak
Slovene
Ukrainian
etc.

ROMANCE
Italian
French
Portuguese
Romanian
Spanish
etc.

CELTIC
Breton
Irish Gaelic
Welsh
etc.

INDO-IRANIAN
Afghan
Bengali
Hindi
Kurdish
Persian
Sanskrit
Singhalese
Urdu
etc.

HELLENIC
Greek

INDO-EUROPEAN
1500 million

OTHER LANGUAGE FAMILIES

800 million
SINO-TIBETAN
Burmese
Chinese
Thai
Tibetan
etc.

150 million
BANTU and RELATED LANGUAGES
Swahili
Zulu
etc.

150 million
SEMITIC and RELATED LANGUAGES
Arabic
Ethiopic
Hamitic
Hebrew
etc.

140 million
MALAY-POLYNESIAN
Hawaiian
Indonesian
Maori
etc.

130 million
JAPANESE-KOREAN

130 million
DRAVIDIAN
Malayalam
Tamil
Telugu
etc.

45 million
SOUTHEAST ASIAN
Vietnamese
Khmer
etc.

100 million
URAL-ALTAIC
Finnish
Hungarian
Mongolian
Turkish
etc.

10 million
LATIN-AMERICAN INDIAN
Quechua
Guarani
Arawak
Carib
etc.

2 million
NORTH AMERICAN INDIAN
Aztecan
Algonquian
Iroquoian
Siouan
etc.

60 thousand
ESKIMO-ALEUT

Primitive beginnings of languages

Language families of the world

The twelve language families represented in this diagram include most of the languages spoken in the world today.
The large Indo-European family is divided into nine subgroups. The population figures are estimates of the total number of persons speaking languages included in the various families.

or some other material through which the light can shine. 2 room at the top of a lighthouse where the light is. 3 an upright structure on a roof or dome, for letting in light and air or for decoration. 4 magic lantern. [< Latin *lanterna* < Greek *lamptēr* torch < *lampein* to shine]

lan tern-jawed (lan′tərn jôd′), *adj.* having long, thin jaws and hollow cheeks.

lantern slide, a small, thin sheet of glass with a picture on it that is shown on a screen by a projector.

lan tha nide series (lan′thə nīd), the rare-earth elements.

lan tha num (lan′thə nəm), *n.* a soft, malleable, ductile, rare-earth metallic element which occurs in various minerals. It is used in making alloys. *Symbol:* La; atomic number 57. See pages 326 and 327 for table. [< New Latin < Greek *lanthanein* lie hidden]

lan yard (lan′yərd), *n.* 1 a short rope or cord used on ships to fasten rigging. 2 a loose cord around the neck on which to hang a knife, whistle, etc. 3 an ornamented or braided cord worn as a symbol of a military decoration or as part of a uniform. 4 a short cord with a small hook used in firing certain kinds of cannon. Also, **laniard.** [< Middle French *laniere* thong]

La o (lä′ō), *n., pl.* **La o** or **La os,** *adj.* —*n.* 1 a Laotian. 2 the Thai language spoken by Laotians. —*adj.* Laotian.

La oc o ön (lā ok′ō on), *n.* (in Greek legends) a priest of Apollo at Troy who warned the Trojans against the wooden horse. He and his two sons were killed by two sea serpents sent by Athena.

La os (lā′os, lä′ōs), *n.* country in SE Asia, west of Vietnam. 2,962,000 pop.; 91,400 sq. mi. *Capitals:* Vientiane and Luang Prabang.

La o tian (lā ō′shən), *adj.* of Laos, its people, or their language. —*n.* native or inhabitant of Laos.

Lao-tse, Lao-tze, or **Lao-tzu** (lou′tse′), *n.* 604?-531? B.C., Chinese philosopher, the reputed founder of Taoism.

lap[1] (lap), *n.* 1 the front part from the waist to the knees of a person sitting down, with the clothing that covers it. 2 place where anything rests or is cared for: *the lap of the gods.* 3 a loosely hanging edge of clothing; flap. 4 the front part of a skirt held up to catch or hold something. **5 in the lap of luxury,** in luxurious circumstances. [Old English *læppa* edge of a garment]

lap[2] (lap), *v.,* **lapped, lap ping,** *n.* —*v.t.* 1 lay together, one partly over or beside another: *lap shingles on a roof.* 2 wind or wrap; fold: *She lapped the blanket around her. We lapped the canvas over our supplies to protect them from the rain.* 3 wrap up *(in): lap oneself in a warm blanket.* 4 surround; envelop. 5 (in a race) get a lap or more ahead of (other racers). 6 cut or polish (gems or metal) with a lap. —*v.i.* 1 lie together so as to cover partially; overlap: *Shingles on a roof lap.* 2 extend out beyond a limit: *The reign of Queen Elizabeth I (from 1558 to 1603) lapped over into the 17th century.*
—*n.* 1 a lapping over. 2 part that laps over. 3 amount of lapping over. 4 one time around a race track. 5 part of any course traveled: *the last lap of an all-day hike.* 6 a rotating disk of soft metal or wood to hold polishing powder for cutting or polishing gems or metal.
[< *lap*[1]]

lap[3] (lap), *v.,* **lapped, lap ping,** *n.* —*v.t.* 1 drink by lifting up with the tongue: *Cats and dogs lap water.* 2 move or beat gently against with a lapping sound. **3 lap up,** take in eagerly or greedily; devour. —*v.i.* move or beat gently with a lapping sound; splash gently: *Little waves lapped against the boat.* —*n.* 1 act of lapping. 2 sound of lapping. [Old English *lapian* to lick] —**lap′per,** *n.*

La Paz (lä päs′), one of the two capitals (Sucre is the other) of Bolivia, in the W part. 525,000.

lap board (lap′bôrd′, lap′bōrd′), *n.* a thin flat board held on the lap and used as a table.

lap dog, a small pet dog.

la pel (lə pel′), *n.* the part of the front of a coat folded back just below the collar. [< *lap*[1]]

lap ful (lap′fu̇l), *n., pl.* **-fuls.** as much as a lap can hold.

lap i dar y (lap′ə der′ē), *n., pl.* **-dar ies,** *adj.* —*n.* person who cuts, polishes, or engraves precious stones. —*adj.* 1 having to do with cutting or engraving precious stones. 2 engraved on stone. [< Latin *lapidarius* < *lapis* stone]

lap in (lap′ən; *French* là paN′), *n.* 1 rabbit. 2 rabbit fur. [< French]

lap is laz u li (lap′is laz′yə lī; lap′is laz′yə lē), 1 a deep blue, opaque semiprecious stone used for an ornament. 2 deep blue. [< Medieval Latin < Latin *lapis* stone + Medieval Latin *lazulum* lapis lazuli < Arabic *lāzuward.* See AZURE.]

lap joint, joint formed by overlapping the edges or ends of two parts, such as the ends of two timbers, and fastening them together as by bolting, riveting, etc.

La place (lä pläs′), *n.* **Pierre de,** 1749-1827, French astronomer and mathematician.

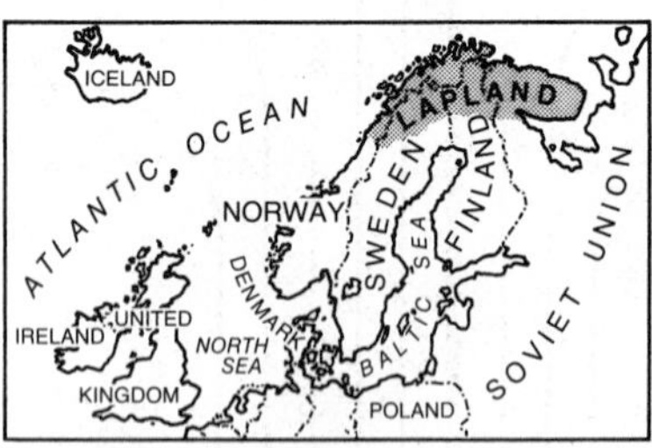

Lap land (lap′land′), *n.* region in N Norway, N Sweden, N Finland, and NW Soviet Union.

Lap land er (lap′lan′dər), *n.* native or inhabitant of Lapland.

La Pla ta (lä plä′tə), seaport in E Argentina. 337,000.

Lapp (lap), *n.* 1 member of a group of people with Mongoloid features living in Lapland. 2 the Finno-Ugric language of the Lapps. [< Swedish]

lap pet (lap′it), *n.* 1 a small flap or fold: *a lappet on a dress.* 2 a loose fold of flesh or membrane, such as the lobe of the ear or a bird's wattle. [< *lap*[1]]

lapse (laps), *n., v.,* **lapsed, laps ing.** —*n.* 1 a slight mistake or error. A slip of the tongue, pen, or memory is a lapse. 2 a slipping or falling away from what is right: *a moral lapse.* 3 a slipping by; a passing away: *A minute is a short lapse of time.* 4 a slipping back; sinking down; slipping into a lower condition: *a lapse into savage ways.* 5 a falling or passing into any state: *a lapse into silence.* 6 the ending of a right or privilege because it was not renewed, not used, or otherwise neglected. 7 a falling into disuse: *the lapse of a custom.*
—*v.i.* 1 make a slight mistake or error. 2 slip or fall away from what is right. 3 slip by; pass away: *Our interest in the dull story soon lapsed.* 4 slip back; sink down: *The house lapsed into ruin.* 5 fall or pass into any state: *lapse into silence.* 6 (of a privilege) end because it was not renewed, not used, etc. If a legal claim is not enforced, it lapses after a certain number of years. 7 fall into disuse. [< Latin *lapsus* fall < *labi* to slip] —**laps′er,** *n.*

lapse rate, rate of decrease of atmospheric temperature with increase in altitude.

lap sus lin guae (lap′səs ling′gwē), LATIN. slip of the tongue.

lapwing
about 1 ft. long

lap wing (lap′wing′), *n.* a crested plover of Europe, Asia, and northern Africa that has a slow, irregular flight and a peculiar, wailing cry; pewit.

Lar a mie (lar′ə mē), *n.* city in SE Wyoming. 23,000.

lar board (lär′bərd, lär′bôrd, lär′bōrd), *n.* side of a ship to the left of a person looking from the stern toward the bow; port. —*adj.* on this side of a ship. [Middle English *ladeborde,* originally, the loading side]
➤ In modern nautical use, **larboard** has been replaced by *port.*

lar ce nous (lär′sə nəs), *adj.* 1 characterized by larceny; guilty of larceny. 2 thievish: *larcenous habits.*

lar ce ny (lär′sə nē), *n., pl.* **-nies.** 1 the unlawful taking, carrying away, and using of the personal property of another person without his consent. 2 theft. [< Anglo-French *larcin* < Latin *latrocinium* robbery < *latro* bandit]

larch (lärch), *n.* 1 any of a genus of trees of the pine family with small woody cones and needles that fall off in the autumn. 2 the strong, tough wood of any of these trees. [< German *Lärche,* ultimately < Latin *larix*]

lard (lärd), *n.* fat of pigs and hogs, melted down and made clear. It is used in cooking. —*v.t.* 1 insert strips of bacon or salt pork in (meat) before cooking. 2 put lard on or in; grease. 3 give variety to; enrich: *lard a long speech with jokes and stories.* [< Old French, bacon fat < Latin *lardum*] —**lard′like′,** *adj.*

lar der (lär′dər), *n.* 1 place where meat and other foods are kept; pantry. 2 stock of food.

Lard ner (lärd′nər), *n.* **Ring(gold),** 1885-1933, American short story writer and journalist.

lard y (lär′dē), *adj.,* **lard i er, lard i est.** full of, containing, or like lard.

La re do (lə rā′dō), *n.* city in S Texas. 69,000.

lar es and pe na tes (ler′ēz ən pə-nā′tēz), 1 the household gods of the ancient Romans. The lares were believed to protect the home from outside damage, the penates protecting the interior. 2 the cherished possessions of a family or household.

large (lärj), *adj.,* **larg er, larg est,** *n.* —*adj.* 1 of great size, amount, or number; big: *a large crowd, a large sum of money, a large animal.* See **great** for synonym study. 2 of great scope or range; extensive; broad: *a person of large experience.* 3 on a great scale: *a large employer of labor.* —*n.* **1 at large, a** at liberty; free. **b** as a whole; altogether. **c** representing the whole of a state or district, not merely one division of it: *a congressman at large.* **d** fully; in detail. **2 in large** or **in the large,** on a big scale. [< Old French < Latin *largus* copious] —**large′ness,** *n.*

large-heart ed (lärj′här′tid), *adj.* generous; liberal.

large intestine, the wide, lower part of the intestines, between the small intestine and the anus, where water is absorbed and wastes are eliminated. The human large intestine is about five feet long and consists of the cecum, colon, and rectum.

large ly (lärj′lē), *adv.* 1 to a great extent; mainly: *This region consists largely of desert.* 2 in great quantity; much.

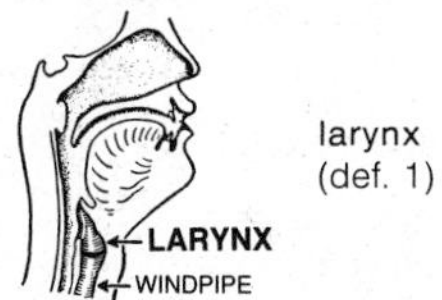

larynx (def. 1)

large-scale (lärj′skāl′), *adj.* 1 involving many persons or things; extensive: *a large-scale disaster.* 2 made or drawn to a large scale: *a large-scale map.*

lar gess or **lar gesse** (lär′jis), *n.* 1 a generous giving. 2 a generous gift or gifts. [< Old French *largesse* < *large*]

lar ghet to (lär get′ō), *adj., adv., n., pl.* **-tos.** in music: —*adj.* rather slow; not so slow as largo, but usually slower than andante. —*adv.* in larghetto tempo; rather slowly. —*n.* passage or piece of music in rather slow time. [< Italian, diminutive of *largo*]

larg ish (lär′jish), *adj.* rather large.

lar go (lär′gō), *adj., adv., n., pl.* **-gos.** in music: —*adj.* slow and dignified; stately. —*adv.* in largo tempo. —*n.* a slow, stately passage or piece of music. [< Italian < Latin *largus* large]

lar i at (lar′ē ət), *n.* 1 rope for fastening horses, mules, etc., to a stake while they are grazing. 2 lasso. [< Spanish *la reata* the rope]

lark[1] (lärk), *n.* 1 any of a family of small songbirds of Europe, Asia, America, and northern Africa with brown feathers and long hind claws, such as the skylark. Larks often sing while soaring in the air. 2 any of several similar songbirds in America, such as the meadowlark and titlark. [Old English *lāwerce*]

lark[2] (lärk), INFORMAL. —*n.* a merry adventure; frolic; prank. —*v.i.* have fun; play pranks; frolic. [origin uncertain]

lark spur (lärk′spėr′), *n.* any of a genus of plants of the same family as the buttercup, whose flowers have a petallike sepal shaped like a spur; delphinium. Most larkspurs have clusters of blue, pink, or white flowers on tall stalks.

La Roche fou cauld (lä rôsh fü kō′), **François de,** 1613-1680, French writer of maxims.

lar rup (lar′əp), *v.t.* INFORMAL. beat; thrash. [origin uncertain] —**lar′rup er,** *n.*

lar va (lär′və), *n., pl.* **-vae.** 1 the wormlike early form of an insect that undergoes metamorphosis, from the time it hatches from the egg until it becomes a pupa. A caterpillar is the larva of a butterfly or moth. A grub is the larva of a beetle. Maggots are the larvae of flies. 2 an immature form of certain animals that is different in structure from the adult form and must undergo a change or metamorphosis to become like the parent. A tadpole is the larva of a frog or toad. [< New Latin < Latin, ghost, mask]

lar vae (lär′vē), *n.* pl. of **larva.**

lar val (lär′vəl), *adj.* 1 of or having to do with larvae. 2 in the form of a larva. 3 characteristic of larvae.

lar vi cide (lär′və sīd), *n.* substance which kills larvae of mosquitoes, etc.

la ryn ge al (lə rin′jē əl), *adj.* 1 of, having to do with, or in the larynx. 2 used on the larynx. —*n.* a part of the larynx.

lar yn gi tis (lar′ən jī′tis), *n.* inflammation of the larynx, usually accompanied by hoarseness.

la ryn go scope (lə ring′gō skōp), *n.* instrument with mirrors for examining the larynx.

lar ynx (lar′ingks), *n., pl.* **la ryn ges** (lə-rin′jēz), **lar ynx es.** 1 the upper end of the human windpipe, containing the vocal cords and acting as an organ of voice; voice box. 2 a similar organ in other mammals, or the corresponding structure in other animals. 3 (in birds) either of two modifications of the trachea, one at the top and one at the bottom. [< Greek *larynx, laryngos*]

la sa gna (lə zä′nyə), *n.* dish consisting of chopped meat, cheese, and tomato sauce, baked with layers of wide noodles. [< Italian]

La Salle (lə sal′), **Robert Cavelier, Sieur de,** 1643-1687, Frenchman who explored the Mississippi and Ohio rivers.

las car (las′kər), *n.* a native sailor, artilleryman, or army servant of the East Indies. [< Portuguese *laschar,* probably < Hindustani *lashkarī* soldier]

las civ i ous (lə siv′ē əs), *adj.* 1 feeling lust. 2 showing lust. 3 causing lust. [< Late Latin *lasciviosus* < Latin *lascivia* playfulness < *lascivus* playful] —**las civ′i ous ly,** *adv.* —**las civ′i ous ness,** *n.*

lase (lāz), *v.i.,* **lased, las ing.** act as a laser. [< *laser*]

la ser (lā′zər), *n.* device which generates and amplifies light waves in a narrow and extremely intense beam of light of only one wavelength going in only one direction; optical maser. Laser beams are used to cut or melt hard materials, remove diseased body tissues, transmit television signals, etc. —*v.i.* act as a laser; lase. [< *l(ight) a(mplification by) s(timulated) e(mission of) r(adiation)*]

lash[1] (lash), *n.* 1 the usually flexible part of a whip beyond the handle. 2 stroke or blow with a whip, thong, etc. 3 a sudden, swift movement. 4 anything that hurts as a blow from a whip does. 5 eyelash. —*v.t.* 1 beat or drive with a whip, etc.; flog. 2 wave or beat back and forth: *The lion lashed his tail. The wind lashes the sails.* 3 strike violently; hit: *The rain lashed against the windows.* 4 attack severely in words; hurt severely. **5 lash out, a** hit; attack; strike. **b** attack severely in words; scold vigorously. **c** break forth into violent action, excess, or extravagance. [Middle English *lasshe*] —**lash′er,** *n.*

hat, āge, fär; let, ēqual, tėrm;
it, īce; hot, ōpen, ôrder;
oil, out; cup, pu̇t, rüle;
ch, child; ng, long; sh, she;
th, thin; ᴛʜ, then; zh, measure;

ə represents *a* in about, *e* in taken, *i* in pencil, *o* in lemon, *u* in circus.

< = from, derived from, taken from.

lash[2] (lash), *v.t.* tie or fasten with a rope, cord, etc. [< Middle French *lachier, lacier* < *lache* lace]

lash ing (lash′ing), *n.* rope, cord, etc., to tie or fasten.

Las Pal mas (läs päl′mäs), the largest city in the Canary Islands. 263,000.

La Spe zia (lə spāt′syä), seaport in NW Italy. 129,000.

lass (las), *n.* 1 girl or young woman. 2 sweetheart. [Middle English *lasse*]

Las sen Peak (las′n), volcano in N California. 10,466 ft. high.

las sie (las′ē), *n.* girl; lass.

las si tude (las′ə tüd, las′ə tyüd), *n.* lack of energy; weariness; languor. [< Latin *lassitudo* < *lassus* tired]

las so (las′ō, las′ü, la sü′), *n., pl.* **-sos** or **-soes,** *v.* —*n.* a long rope with a running noose at one end, used especially by cowboys to catch cattle, horses, etc.; lariat. —*v.t.* catch with a lasso. [< Spanish *lazo* < Latin *laqueus* noose. Doublet of LACE.]

last[1] (last), *adj.* 1 coming after all others; being at the end; final: *the last page of the book.* See synonym study below. 2 belonging to the end or final stage. 3 latest; most recent: *I saw her last week.* 4 most unlikely; least suitable: *That is the last thing one would expect.* 5 very great; extreme: *a paper of last importance.* 6 that remains: *my last dollar.*
—*adv.* 1 after all others; at the end; finally: *We arrived last.* 2 on the latest or most recent occasion: *When did you last see your missing glove?* 3 in conclusion; finally.
—*n.* 1 person or thing that is last: *the last in the row.* 2 end: *faithful to the last. You have not heard the last of this.* **3 at last,** at the end; after a long time; finally. **4 breathe one's last,** die. **5 see the last of,** not see again.
[Old English *latost, lætest,* superlative of *læt* late]

Syn. *adj.* 1 **Last, final, ultimate** mean coming after all others. **Last** applies to that which comes after all others in a series but that is not necessarily the end of the series: *The last person to leave should turn off the light.* **Final** emphasizes the definite end of a series: *The last day of school each year is the final one for graduating seniors.* **Ultimate** emphasizes the last that can ever be reached or found: *The ultimate cause of some diseases is unknown.*

➜ **last, latest.** *Last* refers to the final item of a series; *latest,* to the most recent in time of a series that may or may not be continued: *the scholar's latest (we hope it won't be his last) biography.*

last² (last), *v.i.* 1 go on; hold out; continue to be; endure: *The storm lasted three days.* See **continue** for synonym study. 2 continue in good condition, force, etc.: *I hope these shoes last a year.* 3 be enough: *How long will our money last?* —*v.t.* be enough for (a person): *This money won't last me a whole week.* [Old English *lǣstan* < *lǣst* track]

last³ (last), *n.* 1 block of wood or metal shaped like a person's foot, on which shoes and boots are formed or repaired. 2 **stick to one's last,** pay attention to one's own work; mind one's own business. —*v.t.* form (shoes and boots) on a last. [Old English *lǣste* footprint < *lǣst* track] **—last′er,** *n.*

last-ditch (last′dich′), *adj.* 1 of or serving as a last line of defense; used as a last resort: *a last-ditch weapon.* 2 refusing to give in: *last-ditch supporters.*

Las tex (las′teks), *n.* trademark for an elastic yarn.

last ing (las′ting), *adj.* that lasts a long time; that lasts or will last; permanent; durable. **—last′ing ly,** *adv.* **—last′ing ness,** *n.*

Syn. Lasting, enduring, permanent mean existing or continuing for a long time or forever. **Lasting** emphasizes going on and on indefinitely, long past what would be normal or expected: *The experience had a lasting effect on her.* **Enduring** emphasizes the idea of being able to withstand the attacks of time and circumstance: *All the world hoped for enduring peace.* **Permanent** emphasizes continuing in the same state or position, without changing or being likely to change: *What is your permanent address?*

Last Judgment, God's final judgment of all mankind at the end of the world.

last ly (last′lē), *adv.* in the last place; in conclusion; finally.

last-min ute (last′min′it), *adj.* at the latest possible time; just before it is too late: *last-minute shoppers.*

last quarter, 1 period between the second half moon and the new moon. 2 phase of the moon represented by the half moon after full moon.

last rites, religious rites performed for a dying person or at a funeral.

last sleep, death.

last straw, last of a series of troublesome things that finally causes a collapse, outburst, etc. [short variation of "the *straw* that broke the camel's back," in the fable]

lateen sail—ship with lateen sails

Last Supper, supper of Jesus and His disciples on the evening before He was crucified; Lord's Supper.

last word, 1 last thing said. 2 authority to make the final decision. 3 INFORMAL. the latest thing; most up-to-date style. 4 INFORMAL. thing that cannot be improved.

Las Ve gas (läs vā′gəs), city in SE Nevada. 126,000.

lat., latitude.

Lat., Latin.

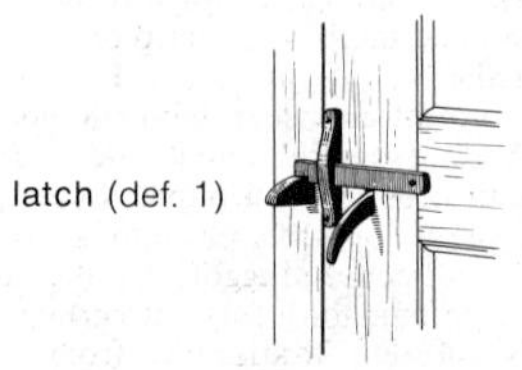

latch (def. 1)

latch (lach), *n.* 1 a movable tongue or bar of metal or wood for fastening a door, gate, or window. It fits into an opening, notch, etc., in the frame or wall adjoining and often does not need a key. 2 **on the latch,** not locked, but fastened only with a latch. —*v.i., v.t.* 1 fasten or secure with a latch. 2 **latch on to,** INFORMAL. get as one's own; catch and hold. [Old English *læccan* to grasp]

latch et (lach′it), *n.* strap or lace for fastening a shoe or sandal. [< Old French *lachet,* ultimately < *laz* lace. See LACE.]

latch key (lach′kē′), *n., pl.* **-keys.** key used to draw back or unfasten the latch of a door.

latch string (lach′string′), *n.* string passed through a hole in a door, for raising the latch from the outside.

late (lāt), *adj.,* **lat er** or **lat ter, lat est** or **last,** *adv.,* **lat er, lat est** or **last.** —*adj.* 1 happening, coming, etc., after the usual or proper time: *We had a late dinner last night.* See synonym study below. 2 happening, coming, etc., at an advanced time: *success late in life.* 3 not long past; recent: *The late storm did much harm.* 4 recently dead or retired from office: *The late president is still active.* 5 **of late,** lately; a short time ago; recently. —*adv.* 1 after the usual or proper time: *She worked late.* 2 at an advanced time: *It rained late in the afternoon.* 3 in recent times; recently. 4 recently but no longer: *John Smith, late of Boston.* [Old English *læt*] **—late′ness,** *n.*

Syn. *adj.* 1 **Late, tardy** mean happening or coming after the usual or proper time. **Late** applies whether the delay is avoidable or not: *Because my car broke down, I was late for school.* **Tardy** applies particularly when the delay is due to mere carelessness: *He was tardy again this morning.* ➜ See **last¹** for usage note.

late com er (lāt′kum′ər), *n.* person, group, etc., that has arrived late or recently.

la teen (la tēn′), *adj.* having a lateen sail. [< French *(voile) latine* Latin (sail)]

la teen-rigged (la tēn′rigd′), *adj.* having a lateen sail.

lateen sail, a triangular sail held up by a long yard on a short mast.

Late Greek, the Greek language from about A.D. 300 to 700.

Late Latin, the Latin language from about A.D. 300 to 700.

late ly (lāt′lē), *adv.* a short time ago; recently: *He is looking well lately.*

la ten cy (lāt′n sē), *n.* latent condition or quality.

la tent (lāt′nt), *adj.* present but not active; hidden; concealed: *latent germs of disease, latent ability.* [< Latin *latentem* lying hidden] **—la′tent ly,** *adv.*

Syn. Latent, potential mean existing as a possibility or fact, but not now showing itself plainly. **Latent** means actually existing as a fact, but lying hidden, not active or plainly to be seen at the present time: *A grain of wheat has the latent power to grow into a plant.* **Potential** means existing as a possibility and capable of coming into actual existence or activity if nothing happens to stop development: *You have great potential ability in science.*

latent heat, the heat required to change a solid to a liquid or a vapor, or to change a liquid to a vapor, without a change of temperature. It is also the heat released in the reverse processes.

lat er al (lat′ər əl), *adj.* of the side; at the side; from the side; toward the side. A lateral branch of a family is a branch not in the direct line of descent. —*n.* 1 a lateral part or outgrowth. 2 lateral pass. [< Latin *lateralis* < *latus* side] **—lat′er al ly,** *adv.*

lateral line, the row of connected sensory pores on the heads and sides of fishes, cyclostomes, and certain amphibians by which they detect changes in water pressure or current.

lateral pass, a throwing of a football in a direction either parallel to or backward toward one's goal line.

Lat er an (lat′ər ən), *n.* 1 church of Saint John Lateran, the cathedral church in Rome. The Lateran is the official church of the Pope. 2 palace next to it, once the residence of the Popes and now a museum.

lat e rite (lat′ə rīt′), *n.* a reddish soil rich in iron or aluminum and formed especially under tropical conditions by the decomposition of rock.

lat e rit ic (lat′ə rit′ik), *adj.* of or containing laterite: *lateritic ore.*

la tex (lā′teks), *n., pl.* **lat i ces** (lat′ə sēz′), **la tex es.** 1 a usually milky liquid found in many plants, including milkweeds, poppies, and plants yielding rubber. It hardens in the air, and the latex from some plants is used to make chicle, rubber, and other products. 2 an emulsion of rubber or plastic suspended in water, used mainly in paints. [< Latin, liquid]

lath (lath), *n., pl.* **laths** (laᴛʜz, laths), *v.* —*n.* 1 one of the thin, narrow strips of wood used to form a support for plaster or to make a lattice. 2 a wire cloth or sheet metal with holes in it, used in place of laths. 3 lining or support made of laths; laths. The walls of a frame house may be built with lath and plaster. —*v.t.* cover or line with laths. [Old English *lætt*]

lathe (lāᴛʜ), *n.* machine for holding pieces of wood, metal, etc., and turning them rapidly against a cutting tool which shapes them. [origin uncertain]

lath er¹ (laᴛʜ′ər), *n.* 1 foam made from soap and water. 2 foam formed in sweating: *the lather on a horse after a race.* 3 SLANG. a state of great agitation or excitement: *She worked herself into a lather over the final exam.* —*v.t.* 1 put lather on. 2 INFORMAL. beat; flog. —*v.i.* 1 form a lather: *This soap lathers well.* 2 become covered with the foam formed in sweating. [Old English *lēathor*] **—lath′er er,** *n.*

lath er² (lath′ər), *n.* workman who puts laths on walls, ceilings, etc. [< *lath*]

lath er y (laᴛʜ′ər ē), *adj.* consisting of or covered with lather.

lath ing (lath′ing), *n.* laths collectively.

lath work (lath′wėrk′), *n.* lathing.

Lat i mer (lat′ə mər), *n.* **Hugh,** 1485-1555, English bishop and religious reformer. He was burned at the stake.

Lat in (lat′n), *n.* 1 the Italic language of the ancient Romans, considered classical in the form acquired during the 200's and 100's B.C., used in written form by scholars through the Middle Ages, and still used in official documents of the Roman Catholic Church. 2 member of any of the peoples whose languages came from Latin. The Italians, French, Spanish, Portuguese, and Romanians are Latins. 3 native or inhabitant of Latium or of ancient Rome. 4 a Roman Catholic. 5 a Latin American. *—adj.* 1 of Latin; in Latin. 2 of the Latin peoples or their languages. 3 of Latium or its people; ancient Roman. 4 Roman Catholic. 5 Latin-American. [< Latin *Latinus* of Latium]

Latin America, South America, Central America, Mexico, and most of the West Indies. The lands get this name from the predominance of Latin languages there.

Lat in-A mer i can (lat′n ə mer′ə kən), *adj.* of or having to do with Latin America.

Latin American, native or inhabitant of Latin America.

Lat in ate (lat′n āt), *adj.* of, having to do with, or coming from Latin.

Latin Church, that part of the Catholic Church which follows the Latin Rite.

Latin cross, cross with the top and side arms equal and a longer shaft extending downward. See **cross** for picture.

Lat in ism (lat′n iz′əm), *n.* 1 a Latin idiom or expression. 2 conformity to Latin models.

Lat in ist (lat′n ist), *n.* person with much knowledge of the Latin language; Latin scholar.

La tin i ty (lə tin′ə tē), *n.* use of Latin idioms or expressions.

Lat in ize (lat′n īz), *v.t.,* **-ized, -iz ing.** 1 translate into Latin. 2 make like Latin. **—Lat′in i za′tion,** *n.*

Latin Quarter, district in Paris, south of the Seine River. Many students and artists live there.

Latin Rite, church ceremonies as used in the Diocese of Rome.

lat ish (lā′tish), *adj., adv.* rather late.

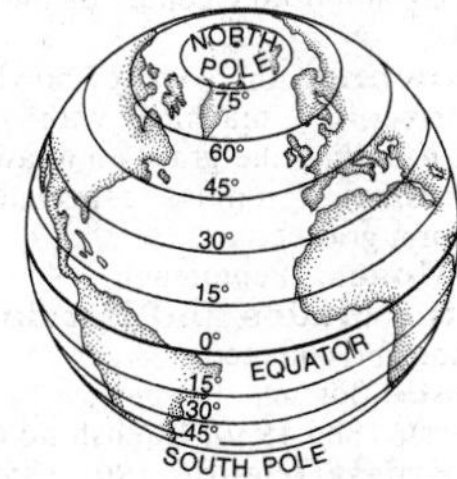

latitude (def. 1)—circles of latitude

lat i tude (lat′ə tüd, lat′ə tyüd), *n.* 1 distance north or south of the equator, measured in degrees. A degree of latitude is about 69 miles. 2 place or region having a certain latitude: *Polar bears live in the cold latitudes.* 3 room to act or think; freedom from narrow rules; scope: *An artist is allowed more latitude in his work than an architect.* 4 celestial latitude. [< Latin *latitudo* < *latus* wide]

lat i tu di nal (lat′ə tüd′n əl, lat′ə tyüd′n-əl), *adj.* of or relating to latitude. **—lat′i-tu′di nal ly,** *adv.*

lat i tu di nar i an (lat′ə tüd′n er′ē ən, lat′ə tyüd′n er′ē ən), *adj.* allowing others their own beliefs; not insisting on strict adherence to established principles, especially in religious views. *—n.* person who cares little about creeds, forms of worship, or methods of church government.

lat i tu di nar i an ism (lat′ə tüd′n er′ē ə-niz′əm, lat′ə tyüd′n er′ē ə niz′əm), *n.* the opinions, principles, or practices of latitudinarians.

La ti um (lā′shē əm), *n.* ancient country in Italy, southeast of Rome.

la trine (lə trēn′), *n.* toilet or privy, especially in a camp, barracks, factory, etc. [< French < Latin *latrina,* originally, washroom < *lavare* to wash]

lat ter (lat′ər), *adj., a comparative of* **late.** 1 second of two: *Canada and the United States are in North America; the former lies north of the latter.* 2 more recent; nearer the end; later: *Friday comes in the latter part of the week.* [Old English *lætra* later]

lat ter-day (lat′ər dā′), *adj.* belonging to recent times; modern: *latter-day problems, latter-day poets.*

Latter-day Saint, Mormon.

lat ter ly (lat′ər lē), *adv.* lately; recently.

lat tice (lat′is), *n., v.,* **-ticed, -tic ing.** *—n.* 1 structure of crossed wooden or metal strips with open spaces between them. 2 window, gate, etc., having a lattice. 3 the geometrical pattern of molecules, atoms, or ions in a crystal. *—v.t.* 1 form into a lattice; make like a lattice. 2 furnish with a lattice. [< Old French *lattis* < *latte* lath] **—lat′tice-like′,** *adj.*

lat tice work (lat′is wėrk′), *n.* 1 lattice. 2 lattices.

Lat vi a (lat′vē ə), *n.* Latvian S.S.R. **—Lat′vi an,** *adj., n.*

Latvian S.S.R., one of the constituent republics of the U.S.S.R., in the W part, on the Baltic Sea. 2,400,000 pop.; 25,600 sq. mi. *Capital:* Riga.

laud (lôd), *v.t.* praise; extol. *—n.* 1 praise. 2 song or hymn of praise. 3 **lauds** or **Lauds,** *pl.* **a** a morning church service with psalms of praise to God. **b** (in Roman Catholic use) a prescribed devotional service for priests and religious, forming, with matins, the first of the seven canonical hours. [< Latin *laudare* < *laudem* praise]

Laud (lôd), *n.* **William,** 1573-1645, archbishop of Canterbury who was executed for treason.

laud a bil i ty (lô′də bil′ə tē), *n.* praiseworthiness.

laud a ble (lô′də bəl), *adj.* worthy of praise; commendable: *Unselfishness is laudable.* **—laud′a bly,** *adv.* **—laud′a ble ness,** *n.*

lau da num (lôd′n əm), *n.* 1 solution of opium in alcohol, used to lessen pain. 2 (formerly) any of various preparations in which opium was the main ingredient. [< New Latin]

lau da tion (lô dā′shən), *n.* 1 act of praising. 2 praise.

laud a to ry (lô′də tôr′ē, lô′də tōr′ē), *adj.* expressing praise; extolling.

laugh (laf), *v.t.* 1 make the sounds and movements of the face and body that show mirth, amusement, scorn, etc. 2 suggest the feeling of joy; be lively. 3 **laugh at,** make fun of; ridicule. 4 **laugh off,** pass off or dismiss with a laugh; get out of by laughing.

hat, āge, fär; let, ēqual, tėrm;
it, īce; hot, ōpen, ôrder;
oil, out; cup, pu̇t, rüle;
ch, child; ng, long; sh, she;
th, thin; ᴛʜ, then; zh, measure;

ə represents *a* in about, *e* in taken, *i* in pencil, *o* in lemon, *u* in circus.

< = from, derived from, taken from.

—v.i. 1 express with laughter: *laugh a reply.* 2 drive, put, bring, etc., by or with laughing: *laugh one's tears away.* *—n.* 1 act or sound of laughing. 2 a cause for laughter. 3 **have the last laugh,** get the better of (someone) after appearing to lose. [Old English *hliehhan*] **—laugh′er,** *n.*

laugh a ble (laf′ə bəl), *adj.* such as to cause laughter; amusing; humorous. See **funny** for synonym study. **—laugh′a ble ness,** *n.* **—laugh′a bly,** *adv.*

laugh ing (laf′ing), *adj.* 1 that laughs or seems to laugh: *the laughing brook.* 2 accompanied by laughter. 3 **no laughing matter,** matter that is serious. *—n.* laughter. **—laugh′ing ly,** *adv.*

laughing gas, nitrous oxide.

laughing jackass, kookaburra.

laugh ing stock (laf′ing stok′), *n.* object of ridicule; person or thing that is made fun of.

laugh ter (laf′tər), *n.* 1 sound of laughing. 2 action of laughing.

launch[1] (lônch, länch), *v.t.* 1 cause to slide into the water; set afloat: *A new ship is launched from the supports on which it was built.* 2 push out or put forth into the air: *launch a plane from an aircraft carrier.* 3 set going; set out; start: *Our friends launched us in business by lending us money.* 4 send out; throw; hurl: *An angry person launches threats against enemies. A bow launches arrows into the air.* *—v.i.* 1 set out; start: *We used the money to launch into a new business.* 2 burst; plunge: *The rebels launched into a violent attack on the government.* 3 **launch out,** begin; start. *—n.* 1 act of launching a rocket, missile, aircraft, ship, etc. 2 movement of a boat or ship from the land into the water. [< Old French *lanchier, lancer* throw a lance < *lance* lance < Latin *lancea*] **—launch′a ble,** *adj.* **—launch′-er,** *n.*

launch[2] (lônch, länch), *n.* 1 an open motorboat used for pleasure trips, ferrying passengers, etc. 2 the largest boat carried by a warship. [< Spanish and Portuguese *lancha* kind of long boat < Malay *lancharān* < *lanchār* fast]

launching pad, surface or platform on which a rocket or missile is prepared for launching and from which it is launched.

launching site, place at which a rocket or missile is launched.

laun der (lôn′dər, län′dər), *v.t.* wash and iron (clothes, tablecloths, towels, etc.). *—v.i.* 1 be able to be washed; stand washing: *Cotton fabrics usually launder well.* 2 wash and iron clothes, etc. [Middle English *lander* one who washes < Old French *lavandier,* ultimately < Latin *lavare* to wash] **—laun′der-er,** *n.*

laun dress (lôn′dris, län′dris), *n.* woman whose work is washing and ironing clothes, etc.

Laun dro mat (lôn′drə mat, län′drə mat), *n.* trademark for a self-service laundry consisting of coin-operated washing machines and dryers.

laun dry (lôn′drē, län′drē), *n., pl.* **-dries.** 1 room or building where clothes, etc., are washed and ironed. 2 clothes, etc., washed or to be washed. 3 the washing and ironing of clothes.

laun dry man (lôn′drē mən, län′drē mən), *n., pl.* **-men.** 1 man who works in a laundry. 2 man who collects and delivers laundry.

laun dry wom an (lôn′drē wu̇m′ən, län′drē wu̇m′ən), *n., pl.* **-wom en.** laundress.

lau re ate (lôr′ē it), *adj.* 1 crowned with a laurel wreath as a mark of honor. 2 honored; distinguished. —*n.* 1 poet laureate. 2 person who is honored or receives a prize for outstanding achievement in a particular field.

lau re ate ship (lôr′ē it ship), *n.* 1 position of poet laureate. 2 time during which a poet is poet laureate.

lau rel (lôr′əl, lor′əl), *n.* 1 a small evergreen tree of southern Europe, with smooth, shiny leaves; bay; sweet bay. 2 its leaves. The ancient Greeks and Romans crowned victors with wreaths of laurel. 3 any tree or shrub of the same family as the laurel. 4 mountain laurel. 5 **laurels,** *pl.* **a** high honor; fame. **b** victory. 6 **look to one's laurels,** guard one's reputation or record from rivals. 7 **rest on one's laurels,** be satisfied with the honors that one has already won or the achievements one has already attained. [< Old French *lorier, laurier* < *lor* laurel < Latin *laurus*]

lau reled or **lau relled** (lôr′əld, lor′əld), *adj.* 1 crowned with a laurel wreath. 2 honored.

Lau ren cin (lô räN saN′), *n.* **Marie,** 1885-1956, French painter.

Lau ren tian Highlands (lô ren′shən), Canadian Shield.

Laurentian Mountains, range of low mountains or high hills in E Canada, between Hudson Bay and the St. Lawrence River. Highest peak, 3150 ft.

Lau ri er (lôr′ē ā), *n.* Sir **Wilfrid,** 1841-1919, Canadian statesman, premier of Canada from 1896 to 1911.

Lau sanne (lō zan′), *n.* city in W Switzerland, on Lake Geneva. 139,000.

la va (lä′və, lav′ə), *n.* 1 the molten rock flowing from a volcano or fissure in the earth. 2 rock formed by the cooling of this molten rock. Some lavas are hard and glassy; others are light and porous. [< Italian < Latin *labes* a fall, falling down < *labi* to slide, fall]

lava bed, layer or surface of lava.

la va bo or **La va bo** (lə vä′bō, lə vā′bō), *n., pl.* **-boes.** in the Roman Catholic church: 1 the ritual washing of the celebrant's hands during the Mass, before the consecration. 2 the portion of Psalm 25 said during this rite. [< Latin, I will wash, the first word of Psalm 25:6 in the Douay version]

lava field, a large area of cooled lava.

lav age (lav′ij), *n.* a laving or washing, especially in medicine.

lav a liere, lav a lier, or **lav al lière** (lav′ə lir′), *n.* ornament hanging from a chain, worn around the neck by women. [< French *lavallière*]

lav a to ry (lav′ə tôr′ē, lav′ə tōr′ē), *n., pl.* **-ries.** 1 room where a person can wash his hands and face. 2 bowl or basin to wash in. 3 bathroom; toilet. [< Late Latin *lavatorium* < Latin *lavare* to wash. Doublet of LAVER¹.]

lave (lāv), *v.,* **laved, lav ing.** —*v.t.* 1 wash; bathe. 2 wash or flow against: *The stream laves its banks.* —*v.i.* ARCHAIC. bathe. [Old English *lafian* < Latin *lavare*]

lav en der (lav′ən dər), *adj.* pale-purple. —*n.* 1 a pale purple. 2 any of a genus of plants of the mint family, especially a small shrub native to the Mediterranean region, having spikes of fragrant pale-purple flowers which yield an oil much used in perfumes. 3 its dried flowers, leaves, and stalks, used to perfume or preserve linens, clothes, etc. [< Anglo-French *lavendre* < Medieval Latin *lavendula*]

la ver¹ (lā′vər), *n.* 1 ARCHAIC. bowl or basin to wash in. 2 (in the Bible) a large brazen vessel for the ablutions of the Hebrew priests and the washing of the sacrifices. [< Old French *laveoir* < Late Latin *lavatorium* a place for washing < Latin *lavare* to wash. Doublet of LAVATORY.]

la ver² (lā′vər), *n.* any of various large, edible seaweeds. [< Latin]

lav ish (lav′ish), *adj.* 1 very free or too free in giving or spending; extravagant; prodigal: *A very rich person can be lavish with money.* 2 very abundant; more than enough; given or spent very freely or too freely: *lavish gifts.* —*v.t.* give or spend very freely or too freely: *It is a mistake to lavish kindness on ungrateful people.* [< Old French *lavasse* flood < *laver* to wash < Latin *lavare*] **—lav′ish er,** *n.* **—lav′ish ly,** *adv.* **—lav′ish ness,** *n.*

La voi sier (lä vwä zyā′), *n.* **Antoine Laurent,** 1743-1794, French chemist who discovered oxygen.

law (lô), *n.* 1 rule or regulation recognized by a state or a community as binding on its members: *There is a law against slavery in our country.* See synonym study below. 2 system of such rules formed to protect society: *English law is different from French law.* 3 the controlling influence of these rules, or the condition of society brought about by their observance: *maintain law and order.* 4 law as a system: *courts of law.* 5 department of knowledge or study concerned with these rules; jurisprudence: *study law.* 6 body of such rules concerned with a particular subject or derived from a particular source: *commercial law, criminal law.* 7 legal profession: *enter the law.* 8 legal action. 9 any act passed upon by the highest legislative body of a state or nation: *a congressional law.* 10 any rule or principle that must be obeyed: *the laws of hospitality.* 11 statement of a relation or sequence of phenomena invariable under the same conditions: *the law of gravitation, Ohm's law, the laws of nature.* 12 a divine rule or commandment. 13 **the Law, a** the first five books of the Old Testament, containing the Mosaic law. **b** the Old Testament. 14 a mathematical rule on which the construction of a curve, a series, etc., depends.

go to law, appeal to courts of law; take legal action.

lay down the law, a give orders that must be obeyed. **b** give a scolding.

read law, study to be a lawyer.

take the law into one's own hands, protect one's rights or punish a crime without appealing to courts of law.

[Old English *lagu;* of Scandinavian origin]

Syn. 1 Law, statute mean a rule or regulation recognized by a state or community as governing the action or procedure of its members. **Law** is the general word applying to any such rule or regulation, written or unwritten. **Statute** applies to a formally written law passed by a legislative body.

law-a bid ing (lô′ə bī′ding), *adj.* obedient to the law; peaceful and orderly.

law break er (lô′brā′kər), *n.* person who breaks the law.

law break ing (lô′brā′king), *n.* a breaking of the law. —*adj.* breaking the law.

law court, court of law.

law ful (lô′fəl), *adj.* 1 according to law; done as the law directs: *lawful arrest.* See synonym study below. 2 allowed by law; rightful: *lawful demands.* **—law′ful ly,** *adv.* **—law′ful ness,** *n.*

Syn. 1 Lawful, legal, legitimate mean according to law. **Lawful** means in agreement with or not against the laws of the state or community, the laws of a church, or moral law: *It is lawful for a citizen to make an arrest.* **Legal** means authorized by or according to the actual terms of the legislative acts and other laws of a state or community enforced by the courts: *Divorce is legal in the United States.* **Legitimate** means rightful according to law, recognized authority, or established standards: *Sickness is a legitimate reason for a child's being absent from school.*

law giv er (lô′giv′ər), *n.* person who prepares and puts into effect a system of laws for a people.

law less (lô′lis), *adj.* 1 paying no attention to the law; breaking the law: *a lawless life.* 2 having no laws: *a lawless wilderness.* 3 hard to control; disorderly; unruly: *long and lawless hair.* **—law′less ly,** *adv.* **—law′less ness,** *n.*

law mak er (lô′mā′kər), *n.* person who helps make the laws of a country; member of a legislature; legislator.

law mak ing (lô′mā′king), *adj.* having the duty and power of making laws; legislative. —*n.* the making of laws; legislation.

law man (lô′mən), *n., pl.* **-men.** a law enforcement officer.

lawn¹ (lôn), *n.* land covered with grass kept closely cut, especially near or around a house. [< Old French *launde* wooded ground]

lawn² (lôn), *n.* kind of thin, sheer linen or cotton cloth. [probably < *Laon,* town in France, an important center of linen manufacture]

lawn bowling, the game of bowls.

lawn mower, machine with revolving blades for cutting the grass on a lawn.

lawn tennis, tennis, especially when played on a grass court.

law of Moses, Pentateuch.

law of the Medes and Persians, law that cannot be changed.

Law rence (lôr′əns, lor′əns), *n.* 1 **D(avid) H(erbert),** 1885-1930, English novelist and poet. 2 **Ernest Orlando,** 1901-1958, American atomic physicist. 3 Sir **Thomas,** 1769-1830, English portrait painter. 4 **T(homas) E(dward),** 1888-1935, British soldier, writer, and archaeologist, known as "Lawrence of Arabia."

law ren ci um (lô ren′sē əm), *n.* a short-lived, radioactive, artificial element of the actinide series produced by bombarding californium with boron ions. *Symbol:* Lw; *atomic number* 103. See pages 326 and 327 for table. [< Ernest Orlando *Lawrence*]

law suit (lô′süt′), *n.* case in a court of law

started by one person to claim something from another; application to a court started by one person to compel another to do him justice.

law yer (lô′yər), *n.* person whose profession is giving advice about the laws or acting for others in a court of law.

lax (laks), *adj.* 1 not firm or tight; loose; slack. 2 not strict; careless; remiss. 3 loose in morals. 4 not exact; vague. 5 (of tissue, soils, etc.) loose in texture; loosely cohering. 6 (in botany) loose or open; not compacted. 7 (in phonetics) pronounced with the muscles of the articulating organs relatively relaxed: *lax vowels.* [< Latin *laxus*] **—lax′ly,** *adv.* **—lax′ness,** *n.*

lax a tive (lak′sə tiv), *n.* medicine that stimulates the bowels to move. *—adj.* making the bowels move. **—lax′a tive ly,** *adv.* **—lax′a tive ness,** *n.*

lax i ty (lak′sə tē), *n.* lax condition or quality: *moral laxity.*

lay[1] (lā), *v.,* **laid, lay ing,** *n.* *—v.t.* 1 place in a certain position; put down: *Lay your hat on the table.* 2 bring down; beat down: *A storm laid the crops low. A shower has laid the dust.* 3 smooth down: *lay the nap of cloth.* 4 place in a lying-down position or a position of rest: *Lay the baby down gently.* 5 place or set: *She lays great emphasis on good manners. The scene of the story is laid in New York.* 6 put: *Lay aside that book for me. The horse laid his ears back.* 7 place in proper position or in orderly fashion: *lay bricks.* 8 put into a certain state or condition: *lay a wound open.* 9 put over a surface as a layer: *lay paint.* 10 devise; arrange: *lay plans.* 11 put down as a bet; wager: *I lay five dollars that they will not come.* 12 make quiet or make disappear: *lay a ghost.* 13 impose a burden, penalty, etc.: *lay a tax on tea.* 14 present; bring forward: *lay claim to an estate.* 15 impute; attribute: *The theft was laid to him.* 16 produce (an egg or eggs): *Birds, fish, and reptiles lay eggs.* *—v.i.* 1 lay eggs. 2 wager; bet. 3 apply oneself vigorously: *The men laid to their oars.*

lay about, hit out on all sides.

lay aside, lay away, or **lay by,** put away for future use; save.

lay down, **a** declare; state. **b** give; sacrifice. **c** SLANG. quit; resign. **d** store away for future use. **e** bet.

lay for, INFORMAL. stay hidden ready to attack.

lay hold of or **lay hold on,** seize; grasp.

lay in, put aside for the future; provide; save.

lay into, **a** beat; thrash. **b** SLANG. scold.

lay off, **a** put aside. **b** put out of work for a time. **c** mark off. **d** INFORMAL. stop teasing or interfering with: *Let's lay off the new girl and give her a chance.* **e** SLANG. stop for a time; stop; desist. **f** take a rest; stop working.

lay on, **a** apply. **b** supply. **c** strike; inflict. **d** make an attack.

lay oneself out, INFORMAL. make a big effort; take great pains.

lay open, **a** make bare; expose. **b** make an opening in; wound.

lay out, **a** spread out. **b** arrange; plan. **c** pay out; spend. **d** prepare (a dead body) for burial. **e** SLANG. knock unconscious.

lay over, **a** break a journey; stay for a time. **b** SLANG. be better than; surpass; excel.

lay to, **a** blame on. **b** head into the wind and stand still.

lay up, **a** put away for future use. **b** cause to stay in bed or indoors because of illness or injury. **c** put (a ship) in dock. *—n.* way or position in which a thing is laid or lies: *the lay of the ground.*

[Old English *lecgān* cause to lie < *licgan* lie[2]]

➤ **lay, lie.** In uneducated English and sometimes in the spoken English of the educated the work of these two verbs is generally done by one *(lay, lay* or *laid, laid).* In modern standard writing and most educated speech they are kept distinct: *lie* (to recline, intransitive), *lay, lain; lay* (to place, transitive), *laid, laid.* You *lie* down for a rest or *lie* down on the job. A farm *lies* in a valley. You *lay* a floor, *lay* a book on the table, *lay* a bet, *lay* out clothes.

lay[2] (lā), *v.* pt. of **lie**[2].

lay[3] (lā), *adj.* 1 of the people of a church not belonging to the clergy. A lay sermon is one preached by a person who is not a clergyman. 2 of the people who do not belong to a particular profession: *Doctors feel that the lay mind understands little of the causes of diseases.* [< Old French *lai* < Latin *laicus.* Doublet of LAIC.]

lay[4] (lā), *n.* 1 a short lyric or narrative poem to be sung. 2 song; tune. [< Old French *lai*]

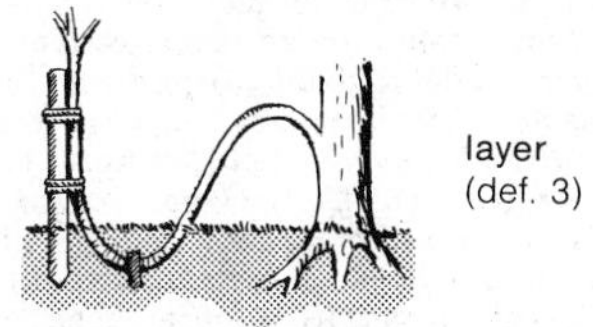

layer (def. 3)

lay er (lā′ər), *n.* 1 one thickness or fold: *the layer of clothing next to the skin, a layer of clay between two layers of sand.* 2 one that lays. 3 branch of a plant bent down and covered with earth so that it will take root and form a new plant. *—v.i.* spread by layers. *—v.t.* form (new plants) by layers; produce or develop by the method of layering.

layer cake, cake made in layers put together with filling and often covered with frosting.

lay er ing (lā′ə ring), *n.* method of forming new plants by placing a shoot or twig of a plant in the ground so that it will take root while still attached to the parent stock.

lay ette (lā et′), *n.* a complete set of clothes, bedding, etc., for a newborn baby. [< French]

lay figure, 1 a jointed model of a human body. Lay figures are used by artists and in shop windows. 2 an unimportant, weak, or stupid person; puppet. [earlier *layman* < Dutch *leeman, ledeman* < *lee, lede* limb + *man* man]

lay man (lā′mən), *n., pl.* **-men.** person outside of a particular profession, especially one not belonging to the clergy.

lay off (lā′ôf′, lā′of′), *n.* 1 a dismissing of workmen temporarily. 2 time during which the workmen are out of work.

lay of the land, 1 way in which the land lies. 2 condition of things; state of affairs.

lay out (lā′out′), *n.* 1 arrangement; plan: *the layout of a scout camp.* 2 plan or design for an advertisement, book, etc. 3 thing laid or spread out; display. 4 act of laying out. 5 outfit; supply; set.

lay o ver (lā′ō′vər), *n.* a stopping for a time in a place.

lay reader, 1 (in the Church of England) a layman appointed by the bishop to read from the Book of Common Prayer and otherwise assist at services. 2 (in the Roman Catholic Church) a layman, usually a volunteer, who reads from the scripture during church services; lector.

hat, āge, fär; let, ēqual, tėrm;
it, īce; hot, ōpen, ôrder;
oil, out; cup, pu̇t, rüle;
ch, child; ng, long; sh, she;
th, thin; ᴛʜ, then; zh, measure;

ə represents *a* in about, *e* in taken,
i in pencil, *o* in lemon, *u* in circus.

< = from, derived from, taken from.

lay-up (lā′up′), *n.* 1 (in basketball) a shot from close under the basket. 2 the laying up or storage of a ship for repair, cleaning, etc.

lay wom an (lā′wu̇m′ən), *n., pl.* **-wom en.** woman outside the clergy or a particular profession.

laz ar (laz′ər, lā′zər), *n.* ARCHAIC. a poor and diseased person, especially a leper. [< Medieval Latin *lazarus* < *Lazarus,* the beggar]

laz a ret or **laz a rette** (laz′ə ret′), *n.* lazaretto.

laz a ret to (laz′ə ret′ō), *n., pl.* **-tos.** 1 hospital for people having contagious or loathsome diseases; pesthouse. 2 building or ship used for quarantine purposes. 3 place in some merchant ships, near the stern, in which supplies are kept. [< Italian *lazzaretto*]

Laz ar us (laz′ər əs), *n.* 1 in the Bible: **a** the brother of Mary and Martha, whom Jesus raised from the dead. **b** a beggar in one of the parables who suffered on earth but went to heaven. 2 **Emma,** 1849-1887, American poet and philanthropist.

laze (lāz), *v.i.,* **lazed, laz ing.** be lazy or idle.

la zi ness (lā′zē nis), *n.* dislike of work; unwillingness to work or be active; being lazy.

la zy (lā′zē), *adj.,* **-zi er, -zi est.** 1 not willing to work or be active. See **idle** for synonym study. 2 moving slowly; not very active: *a lazy stream.* [perhaps < Middle Low German *lasich* weak, feeble] **—la′zi ly,** *adv.*

la zy bones (lā′zē bōnz′), *n.* INFORMAL. a very lazy person.

lazy Susan, a large revolving tray containing different foods arranged in individual compartments to make them easily accessible for serving.

lb., *pl.* **lb.** or **lbs.** pound. [for Latin *libra* pound]

l.c., 1 letter of credit. 2 lower case. 3 in the place cited [for Latin *loco citato*].

L.C., Library of Congress.

l.c.d. or **L.C.D.,** least common denominator; lowest common denominator.

l.c.m. or **L.C.M.,** least common multiple; lowest common multiple.

Ld., 1 limited. 2 lord.

LD, lethal dose.

lea (lē), *n.* a grassy field; meadow; pasture. [Old English *lēah*]

leach (lēch), *v.t.* 1 run (water or some other liquid) through slowly; filter. 2 dissolve out soluble parts from (ashes, ores, etc.) by running water or other liquid through slowly. 3 dissolve out by running water or other liquid through slowly: *Potash is leached from wood ashes.* *—v.i.* lose soluble parts when water or other liquid passes through. [Old English *leccan* to wet]

lead[1] (lēd), *v.,* **led, lead ing,** *n., adj.* *—v.t.*

1 show the way by going along with or in front of; guide; conduct: *The usher will lead you to your seats.* See **guide** for synonym study. 2 serve to guide: *His cries for help led us to him.* 3 conduct by a hand, rope, etc.: *lead a horse to water.* 4 conduct or bring (water, steam, a rope, a wire, etc.) in a particular channel or course; convey. 5 be first among; be at the top or head of: *She leads the class in spelling. The elephants led the parade.* 6 guide or direct in action, policy, opinion, etc.; influence; persuade: *Such actions lead us to distrust him.* 7 pass or spend (time, life, etc.) in some special way: *lead a quiet life in the country.* 8 be chief of; command; direct: *lead an orchestra. A general leads an army.* 9 begin or open: *She led the dance.* 10 (in card playing) begin a trick or round by playing (a card or suit named). 11 (in boxing) direct (a blow) at an opponent. *—v.i.* 1 act as guide; show the way: *Lead, I will follow.* 2 provide a way to a certain condition; be a means of proceeding to or effecting a certain result: *Hard work leads to success. The frequent outbreaks of violence led to civil war.* 3 form a channel or route: *The drain led into a common sewer.* 4 afford passage or way: *Broad steps lead down into the garden.* 5 be led; submit to being led: *This horse leads easily.* 6 be chief; direct; act as leader. 7 go first; have the first place: *lead in a race.* 8 make the first play at cards.

lead off, **a** begin; start. **b** (in baseball) be the first player in the batting order or the first to bat in an inning.

lead on, persuade or entice to follow an unwise course of action; mislead.

lead up to, **a** prepare the way for. **b** approach (a subject, etc.) in an evasive or gradual manner.

—n. 1 guidance or direction; leadership. 2 first or foremost place; position in advance: *take the lead.* 3 in card playing: **a** the right or fact of playing first. **b** the card or suit so played. 4 the principal part in a play. 5 the person who plays this part. 6 extent of advance; amount that one is ahead: *He had a lead of 3 yards in the race.* 7 something that leads. 8 string, strap, etc., for leading a dog or other animal; leash. 9 a guiding indication: *a good lead.* 10 an insulated conductor conveying electricity. 11 (in boxing) a blow directed at an opponent. 12 the opening paragraph in a newspaper or magazine article, usually summarizing the information in the body of the article. 13 (in baseball) a position assumed by a base runner, a short distance off the base in the direction of the next base.

—adj. that leads; leading: *the lead violin.* [Old English *lǣdan*]

lead² (led), *n.* 1 a soft, heavy, malleable, bluish-gray metallic element which occurs in galena and is used to make pipes and machinery, radiation shields, as a solder, in alloys, etc. *Symbol:* Pb; *atomic number* 82. See pages 326 and 327 for table. 2 something made of lead or one of its alloys. 3 bullets; shot. 4 a long, thin piece of graphite used in pencils. 5 weight on a line used to find out the depth of water; plumb. 6 thin metal stripping for widening the space between lines in printing. 7 **leads,** *pl.* frames of lead in which panes of glass are set. 8 white lead. *—adj.* made of lead: *a lead pipe.* *—v.t.* 1 cover, frame, or weight with lead. 2 insert leads between the lines of (print). 3 mix or impregnate with lead or a compound containing lead: *to lead gasoline.* 4 set (window glass) within leads. [Old English *lēad*]

lead acetate (led), a colorless or white, poisonous, crystalline compound used as a reagent, in dyeing, etc.; sugar of lead. *Formula:* $Pb(C_2H_3O_2)_2 \cdot 3H_2O$

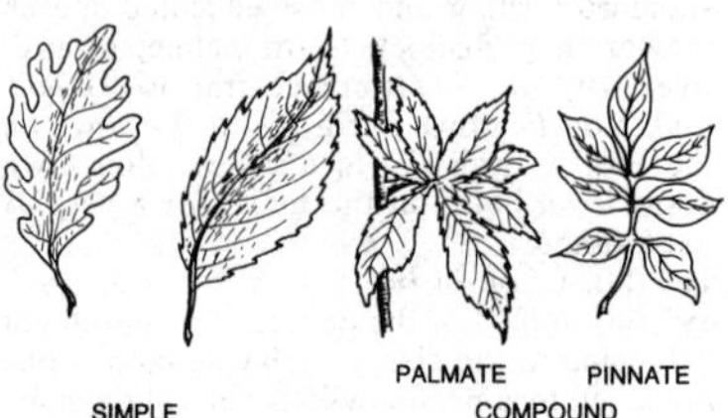

leaf (def. 1)—several types of leaves

lead arsenate (led), a poisonous, white, crystalline compound used as an insecticide; arsenate of lead. *Formula:* $Pb_3(AsO_4)_2$

lead en (led′n), *adj.* 1 made of lead: *a leaden coffin.* 2 hard to lift or move; heavy: *leaden arms tired from working.* 3 oppressive: *leaden air.* 4 dull; gloomy; spiritless: *leaden thoughts.* 5 bluish-gray: *leaden clouds.* **—lead′en ly,** *adv.* **—lead′en ness,** *n.*

lead er (lē′dər), *n.* 1 person or thing that leads: *an orchestra leader.* 2 person who is well fitted to lead: *a born leader.* 3 horse harnessed at the front of a team. 4 an important or leading article or editorial in a newspaper. 5 a short length of transparent material attaching the lure or hook to a fish line. 6 article offered at a low price to attract customers. 7 **leaders,** *pl.* row of dots or dashes to guide the eye across a printed page. 8 pipe for carrying or draining water, oil, etc. **—lead′er less,** *adj.*

lead er ship (lē′dər ship), *n.* 1 condition of being a leader. 2 ability to lead. 3 guidance or direction.

lead-in (lēd′in′), *n.* 1 wire leading from one apparatus or conductor to another, such as the wire that connects a television antenna with a television set. 2 a leading into; introduction: *a lead-in to a television commercial.*

lead ing¹ (lē′ding), *adj.* 1 showing the way; guiding; directing: *a leading light.* 2 most important; chief; principal: *the town's leading citizen, the leading man and leading lady in a play.* 3 having the front place; featured prominently: *a leading article.* *—n.* act of one who or that which leads; guidance; direction. [< *lead¹*]

lead ing² (led′ing), *n.* 1 covering or frame of lead. 2 (in printing) the spacing out of lines of type by putting leads between them. [< *lead²*]

lead ing edge (lē′ding), (in aeronautics) the forward edge of an airfoil or propeller blade.

lead ing question (lē′ding), question so worded that it suggests the answer desired.

lead monoxide (led), litharge.

lead off (lēd′ôf′, lēd′of′), *n.* 1 act of beginning or starting something. 2 (in baseball) the first player of the batting order or the first to come to bat in any inning. *—adj.* that begins or leads off.

lead pencil (led), pencil having a graphite lead, usually enclosed in wood; ordinary pencil.

lead poisoning (led), a diseased condition caused by ingesting lead, or paints and other mixtures containing lead, characterized by abdominal pain, paralysis, and convulsions; plumbism.

lead time (lēd), the time that elapses between the design of or request for a product and its completion or delivery.

leaf (lēf), *n., pl.* **leaves,** *v.* *—n.* 1 one of the thin, usually flat, green parts of a tree or other plant, that grow on the stem or up from the roots. Leaves are essential organs of most plants and use the carbon dioxide of the air or water in which they live and the light from the sun to carry on photosynthesis. 2 the foliage of a plant or tree; leafage; leaves. 3 petal of a flower: *a rose leaf.* 4 sheet of paper. Each side of a leaf is called a page. 5 a very thin sheet of metal, especially gold or silver. 6 a flat, movable piece in the top of a table. 7 the sliding, hinged, or movable part of a door, shutter, gate, etc. 8 **turn over a new leaf,** start all over again; try to do or be better in the future. *—v.i.* put forth leaves: *The trees leaf out in the spring.* *—v.t.* turn the pages of (a book, magazine, etc.). [Old English *lēaf*] **—leaf′less,** *adj.* **—leaf′like′,** *adj.*

leaf age (lē′fij), *n.* leaves; foliage.

leaf bud, a bud producing a stem with leaves only.

leaf hop per (lēf′hop′ər), *n.* any of various small, leaping homopterous insects which feed on plant juices.

leaf let (lēf′lit), *n.* 1 a small, flat or folded sheet of printed matter, or several sheets folded together: *advertising leaflets.* 2 a small or young leaf. 3 one of the separate blades or divisions of a compound leaf.

leaf miner, any of various insects which, in the larval stage, live and feed between the top and bottom surfaces of a leaf.

leaf mold, the partially decomposed leaves which form a surface layer in wooded areas.

leaf spring, spring, as for an automobile, made of layers of curved metal strips.

leaf stalk (lēf′stôk′), *n.* petiole.

leaf y (lē′fē), *adj.,* **leaf i er, leaf i est.** 1 having many leaves; covered with leaves. 2 resembling a leaf. 3 made of leaves. **—leaf′i ness,** *n.*

league¹ (lēg), *n., v.,* **leagued, lea guing.** *—n.* 1 a union of persons, parties, or countries formed to help one another. 2 association of sports clubs or teams: *a baseball league.* 3 INFORMAL. class; category: *The high school chess champion was out of his league in the professional tournament.* 4 **in league,** associated by agreement; allied. *—v.t., v.i.* unite in a league; form a league. [< Middle French *ligue* < Italian *liga* < Latin *ligare* to bind]

league² (lēg), *n.* measure of distance, varying at different periods and in different countries, usually about 3 miles. [< Late Latin *leuga* < Celtic]

League of Nations, association of many countries, established in 1920 to promote peace and cooperation among nations. It was dissolved on April 18, 1946, and the United Nations assumed some of its functions.

League of Women Voters, a nonpartisan women's political organization founded in 1920.

lea guer (lē′gər), *n.* member of a league.

Le ah (lē′ə), *n.* (in the Bible) Jacob's first wife, Rachel's older sister.

Lea hy (lā′hē), *n.* **William Daniel,** 1875-1959, American admiral, chief of staff, and diplomat.

hat, āge, fär; let, ēqual, tėrm;
it, īce; hot, ōpen, ôrder;
oil, out; cup, pu̇t, rüle;
ch, child; ng, long; sh, she;
th, thin; ᴛʜ, then; zh, measure;
ə represents *a* in about, *e* in taken, *i* in pencil, *o* in lemon, *u* in circus.
< = from, derived from, taken from.

leak (lēk), *n.* 1 hole or crack not meant to be there that lets something in or out: *a leak in the roof.* 2 act of leaking; leakage. 3 means of escape, loss, etc.: *a leak in the treasury.* —*v.i.* 1 go in or out through a hole or crack not meant to be there: *The gas leaked out of the pipe.* 2 go in or out through ways suggesting a hole or crack: *Spies leaked into the city.* 3 let something in or out which is meant to stay where it is: *My boat leaks and lets water in.* 4 become known gradually or indirectly: *The secret leaked out.* —*v.t.* 1 let (something) pass in or out: *That pipe leaks gas.* 2 make known stealthily or indirectly: *Someone had leaked the company's secret plans to its competitors.* [< Scandinavian (Old Icelandic) *leka* to leak]

leak age (lē′kij), *n.* 1 a leaking; entrance or escape by a leak. 2 that which leaks in or out. 3 amount of leaking.

Lea key (lē′kē), *n.* **Louis,** 1903-1972, British anthropologist and paleontologist, born in Kenya.

leak proof (lēk′prüf′), *adj.* that will not leak; free of leaks.

leak y (lē′kē), *adj.,* **leak i er, leak i est.** having a leak or leaks; leaking. **—leak′i ness,** *n.*

leal (lēl), *adj.* SCOTTISH. loyal. [< Old French *leial* < Latin *legalis* legal. Doublet of LEGAL, LOYAL.]

lean[1] (lēn), *v.,* **leaned** or **leant, lean ing,** *n.* —*v.i.* 1 bend or incline from an upright position or in a particular direction; slant; slope: *A small tree leans over in the wind.* 2 rest the body sloping or slanting against something for support: *Lean against me.* 3 depend; rely: *lean on a friend's advice.* 4 incline or tend in thought, affection, or conduct; bend or turn a little: *lean toward mercy.* —*v.t.* set or put in a leaning position: *Lean the ladder against the wall.* —*n.* act of leaning; inclination. [Old English *hleonian*]

lean[2] (lēn), *adj.* 1 not plump or fat; thin; spare: *a lean face, lean cattle.* See **thin** for synonym study. 2 containing little or no fat: *lean meat.* 3 producing little; scant; meager: *a lean harvest, a lean year for business.* —*n.* meat having little fat. [Old English *hlǣne*] **—lean′ness,** *n.*

Le an der (lē an′dər), *n.* (in Greek legends) a lover who swam the Hellespont nightly to visit his sweetheart, Hero.

lean ing (lē′ning), *n.* tendency; inclination.

leant (lent), *v.* a pt. and a pp. of **lean**[1].

lean-to (def. 1)

lean-to (lēn′tü′), *n., pl.* **-tos,** *adj.* —*n.* 1 a small building attached to another, with a roof sloping downward from the side of the larger building. 2 a crude shelter built against a tree or post. It is usually open on one side. —*adj.* having a roof sloping downward from the side of a larger building: *a lean-to shed.*

leap (lēp), *n., v.,* **leaped** or **leapt, leap ing.** —*n.* 1 a jump or spring; bound. 2 thing to be jumped. 3 distance covered by a jump. 4 **by leaps and bounds,** very fast and very much; swiftly. —*v.i.* 1 spring or bound; jump: *That frog leaps very high.* See **jump** for synonym study. 2 pass, come, rise, etc., as if with a leap or bound: *An idea leaped to his mind.* —*v.t.* 1 jump over: *leap a fence.* 2 cause to leap: *She leaped her horse over the hurdle.* [Old English *hlȳp,* noun, *hlēapan,* verb] **—leap′er,** *n.*

leap frog (lēp′frog′, lēp′frôg′), *n., v.,* **-frogged, -frog ging.** —*n.* game in which players take turns jumping over another player who is bending over. —*v.i., v.t.* leap or jump (over) as in this game.

leapt (lept, lēpt), *v.* a pt. and a pp. of **leap.**

leap year, year having 366 days. The extra day is February 29. A year is a leap year if its number can be divided exactly by four, except years at the end of a century, which must be exactly divisible by 400. The years 1968 and 2000 are leap years; 1969 and 1900 are not.

Lear (lir), *n.* the chief character in Shakespeare's play *King Lear,* an aged king who has three daughters, two of them very ungrateful.

learn (lėrn), *v.,* **learned** or **learnt, learn ing.** —*v.i.* 1 acquire knowledge or skill as a result of study, instruction, or experience: *Some children learn slowly.* 2 become informed; hear: *learn of an occurrence.* —*v.t.* 1 acquire knowledge of (a subject) or skill in (an art, trade, etc.) by study, instruction, or experience: *learn French, learn a new game.* 2 become able by study or practice: *learn to fly an airplane.* 3 memorize: *learn a poem by heart.* 4 find out; come to know: *We learned that* $^1/_4 + {}^1/_4 = {}^1/_2$. [Old English *leornian*] **—learn′a ble,** *adj.*

➤ **learn, teach.** Substandard English often uses *learn* in the sense of *teach: He learned me how to play chess.* Educated usage keeps the distinction: *I learned how to play chess from him. He taught me how to play chess.*

learn ed (lėr′nid), *adj.* having, showing, or requiring much knowledge; scholarly; erudite. **—learn′ed ly,** *adv.*

learn er (lėr′nər), *n.* 1 person who is learning. 2 beginner.

learn ing (lėr′ning), *n.* 1 the gaining of knowledge or skill. 2 possession of knowledge gained by study; scholarship. 3 knowledge.

learnt (lėrnt), *v.* a pt. and a pp. of **learn.**

lease (lēs), *n., v.,* **leased, leas ing.** —*n.* 1 the right to use real estate or other property for a certain length of time, usually by paying rent for it. 2 a written statement saying for how long a certain property is rented and how much money shall be paid for it. 3 property held by a lease. 4 length of time for which a lease is made. 5 **new lease on life,** chance to live longer, better, or happier. —*v.t.* 1 give a lease on. 2 take a lease on; rent: *lease an apartment for a year.* [< Anglo-French *les* < *lesser* let, let go < Latin *laxare* loosen < *laxus* loose]

lease hold (lēs′hōld′), *n.* 1 a holding by a lease. 2 real estate held by a lease.

leash (lēsh), *n.* 1 strap, chain, etc., for holding a dog or other animal in check. 2 group of three animals; three hounds, foxes, hares, etc. 3 **hold in leash,** control. —*v.t.* fasten or hold in with a leash; control. [< Old French *laisse* < Latin *laxa,* feminine of *laxus* loose]

least (lēst), *adj.* less than any other; smallest; slightest: *The least bit of dirt in a watch may make it stop.* —*n.* 1 the smallest thing, amount, or degree: *The least you can do is thank her.* 2 **at least** or **at the least, a** at the lowest estimate. **b** at any rate; in any case. 3 **not in the least,** not at all. —*adv.* to the smallest extent, amount, or degree: *I liked that book least of all.* [Old English *lǣst*]

least common denominator, the least common multiple of the denominators of a group of fractions: *30 is the least common denominator of* $^2/_3$, $^4/_5$, *and* $^1/_6$. Also, **lowest common denominator.**

least common multiple, the smallest quantity that is divisible by two or more given quantities without a remainder. 12 is the least common multiple of 3 and 4 and 6. Also, **lowest common multiple.**

least ways (lēst′wāz′), *adv.* INFORMAL. leastwise.

least wise (lēst′wīz′), *adv.* INFORMAL. at least; at any rate.

leath er (leᴛʜ′ər), *n.* 1 material made from the skin of animals by removing the hair and flesh, tanning, and usually dressing it. 2 article made of leather. —*adj.* made of leather: *leather gloves.* —*v.t.* 1 furnish or cover with leather. 2 INFORMAL. beat with a strap; thrash. [Old English *lether-*]

leath er back (leᴛʜ′ər bak′), *n.* a sea turtle of tropical waters, having a flexible, leathery shell studded with small bony plates. It is the largest living turtle, often weighing over 1000 pounds.

Leath er ette (leᴛʜ′ə ret′), *n.* trademark for imitation leather, made of paper or cloth.

leath ern (leᴛʜ′ərn), *adj.* 1 made of leather. 2 like leather; leathery.

leath er neck (leᴛʜ′ər nek′), *n.* SLANG. a United States marine.

leath er y (leᴛʜ′ər ē), *adj.* resembling leather in appearance or texture; tough.

leave[1] (lēv), *v.,* **left, leav ing.** —*v.i.* go away; depart: *We leave tonight.* See **go** for synonym study. —*v.t.* 1 go away from; depart from: *She left the house.* 2 stop living in, belonging to, or working at or for: *leave the country, leave a club, leave one's job.* 3 go without taking; let remain: *I left a book on the table.* 4 let remain in a particular condition: *leave a window open, leave a job undone.* 5 let (a person, etc.) alone to do something; let be: *Leave me to settle the matter.* 6 give when one dies; bequeath: *He left a large fortune to his children.* 7 let remain for someone to do: *Leave the matter to me. I left the cooking to my sister.* 8 not attend to: *I shall leave my homework until tomorrow.* 9 let remain uneaten, unused, unremoved, etc.: *There is some coal left.* 10 yield as a remainder after subtraction: *4 from 10 leaves 6.* 11 **leave off,** stop. 12 **leave out,** not do, say, or put in; omit. [Old English *lǣfan*]

➤ **leave, let.** A common substandard idiom is the use of *leave* in the sense of "allow," where formal and informal English use *let.* EXAMPLES: *Leave us go. Leave him be. Leave us not fight. Let* should be used in each of these sentences.

leave[2] (lēv), *n.* 1 permission asked for or granted; consent: *They gave him leave to go.* 2 Also, **leave of absence. a** an official permission to be absent from work, school, or military duty. **b** length of time that this lasts. 3 act of parting. 4 **on leave,** absent from duty with permission. 5 **take leave of,** say good-by to. [Old English *lēaf*]

leave³ (lēv), *v.i.,* **leaved, leav ing,** put forth leaves; leaf: *Trees leave in the spring.* [Middle English *levien* < *leef* leaf]

leaved (lēvd), *adj.* having leaves or foliage; in leaf.

leav en (lev′ən), *n.* 1 any substance, such as yeast, that will cause fermentation and raise dough. 2 a small amount of fermenting dough kept for this purpose. 3 influence which, spreading silently and strongly, changes conditions or opinions: *The leaven of reform was working.* —*v.t.* 1 raise with a leaven; make (dough) light or lighter. 2 spread through and transform. [< Old French *levain* < Latin *levamen* a lifting < *levare* to raise]

leav en ing (lev′ə ning), *n.* thing that leavens; leaven.

leaves (lēvz), *n.* pl. of **leaf.**

leave-tak ing (lēv′tā′king), *n.* act of taking leave; saying good-by.

leav ings (lē′vingz), *n.pl.* things left; leftovers; remnants.

Leb a nese (leb′ə nēz′), *adj., n., pl.* **-nese.** —*adj.* of or having to do with Lebanon or its inhabitants. —*n.* native or inhabitant of Lebanon.

Leb a non (leb′ə nən), *n.* country in the Middle East, at the E end of the Mediterranean, north of Israel. 2,790,000 pop.; 4000 sq. mi. *Capital:* Beirut.

Lebanon Mountains, mountain range running almost the length of Lebanon parallel to the Mediterranean near the coast. Highest peak, 10,050 ft.

Le bens raum (lā′bəns roum′), *n.* (in Nazi theory) the additional territory that a nation must control in order to expand economically. [< German, literally, living space]

lech er (lech′ər), *n.* man who indulges in lechery. [< Old French *lecheor* licker < *lechier* to lick, of Germanic origin]

lech er ous (lech′ər əs), *adj.* lewd; lustful. **—lech′er ous ly,** *adv.* **—lech′er ous ness,** *n.*

lech er y (lech′ər ē), *n.* gross indulgence of lust; lewdness.

lec i thin (les′ə thən), *n.* any of a group of nitrogenous fatty substances containing phosphorus, present in all plant and animal tissues but found especially in nerve cells and brain tissue. [< Greek *lekithos* egg yolk]

Le Cor bu sier (lə kôr′byü zyā′), 1887-1965, Swiss architect. His real name was Charles Édouard Jeanneret.

lec tern (lek′tərn), *n.* 1 a reading desk in a church, especially the desk from which the lessons are read at daily prayer. 2 a reading desk or stand. [< Medieval Latin *lectrum* < Latin *legere* to read]

lec tor (lek′tər, lek′tôr), *n.* 1 person in minor orders who reads passages in a church service. 2 lay reader. [< Latin, reader < *legere* to read]

lec ture (lek′chər), *n., v.,* **-tured, -tur ing.** —*n.* 1 a planned speech or talk on a chosen subject given before an audience, usually for the purpose of instruction. 2 such a speech or talk written down or printed. 3 a scolding. —*v.i.* give a lecture or lectures. —*v.t.* 1 instruct or entertain by a lecture. 2 scold; reprove. [< Late Latin *lectura* < Latin *legere* to read]

lec tur er (lek′chər ər), *n.* person who gives a lecture or lectures.

led (led), *v.* pt. and pp. of **lead¹.**

Le da (lē′də), *n.* (in Greek and Roman myths and legends) the mother of Castor and Pollux, Clytemnestra, and Helen of Troy.

le der ho sen (lā′dər hō′zn), *n.pl.* Tyrolean leather breeches, worn with suspenders. [< German *Lederhosen* leather trousers]

ledge (lej), *n.* 1 a narrow shelf: *a window ledge.* 2 shelf or ridge of rock, especially one near the shore beneath the surface of the sea. 3 (in mining) lode; vein. [Middle English *legge* crossbar on a door]

ledg er (lej′ər), *n.* book of accounts in which a business keeps a final record of all transactions, showing the debits and credits of the various accounts. [Middle English *legger,* probably < *leggen* to lay]

ledger line, a short line added above or below the musical staff for notes that are too high or too low to be put on the staff.

lee (lē), *n.* 1 shelter; protection. 2 side or part sheltered or away from the wind: *the lee of a ship.* —*adj.* sheltered or away from the wind: *the lee side of a ship.* [Old English *hlēo*]

Lee (lē), *n.* 1 **Ann,** 1736-1784, English religious leader, who founded the first Shaker colony in America. 2 **Harper,** born 1926, American novelist. 3 **Henry,** 1756-1818, American general in the Revolutionary War, known as "Light-Horse Harry." He was the father of Robert E. Lee. 4 his son, **Robert E.,** 1807-1870, Confederate general in the Civil War. 5 **Tsung Dao,** born 1926, American physicist, born in China.

leech¹ (lēch), *n.* 1 any of a class of bloodsucking or carnivorous annelid worms usually having a sucker at each end of the body and living chiefly in freshwater ponds and streams. Doctors formerly used leeches to draw blood from sick people. 2 person who tries persistently to get what he can from others, without doing anything to earn it; parasite. 3 ARCHAIC. doctor. [Old English *lǣce*]

leech² (lēch), *n.* 1 either of the vertical edges of a square sail. 2 the after edge of a fore-and-aft sail. [Middle English *lyche*]

Leeds (lēdz), *n.* city in N England. 506,000.

leek (lēk), *n.* vegetable of the same genus as and resembling the onion, but having flatter and broader leaves, a smaller bulb shaped like a cylinder, and a milder flavor; scallion. [Old English *lēac*]

lectern (def. 1)

leer (lir), *n.* a sly, sidelong look; evil glance. —*v.i.* give a sly, sidelong look; glance evilly. [probably < obsolete *leer* cheek, Old English *hlēor*]

leer y (lir′ē), *adj.,* **leer i er, leer i est.** INFORMAL. suspicious; wary: *We are leery of his advice.*

lees (lēz), *n.pl.* 1 the most worthless part of anything; dregs. 2 sediment deposited in the container by wine and some other liquids. [< Old French *lias,* plural of *lie,* probably < Late Latin *lia*]

lee shore, shore toward which the wind is blowing.

Leeu wen hoek (lā′vən hu̇k), *n.* **Anton van,** 1632-1723, Dutch scientist who was the first to study blood cells and microorganisms through magnifying lenses.

lee ward (lē′wərd, lü′ərd), *adj., adv.* 1 on the side away from the wind. 2 in the direction toward which the wind is blowing. —*n.* side away from the wind; lee.

Lee ward Islands (lē′wərd), the N part of the Lesser Antilles in the West Indies.

lee way (lē′wā′), *n.* 1 the sideways movement or drift of a ship or aircraft to leeward, out of its course. 2 extra space at the side; time, money, etc., more than is needed; margin of safety: *If you bring $60 on a trip that will cost $50, you are allowing yourself a leeway of $10.* 3 convenient room or scope for action.

left¹ (left), *adj.* 1 belonging to the side of the less used hand (in most people); of the side that is turned west when the main side is turned north; opposite of right. 2 on this side when viewed from the front: *Make a left turn at the next light.* 3 having liberal or radical ideas in politics. —*adv.* on or to the left side: *turn left.* —*n.* 1 the left side or what is on the left side. 2 Often, **Left. a** the part of a lawmaking body consisting of the more liberal or radical groups. In some European legislative assemblies this group sits on the left side of the chamber. **b** persons, parties, etc., that advocate or favor social or economic reform; liberals or radicals collectively. **c** a liberal or radical position or view. [Old English *lyft* weak]

left² (left), *v.* pt. and pp. of **leave¹.**

left field, (in baseball) the section of the outfield beyond third base.

left fielder, a baseball player whose position is in left field.

left-hand (left′hand′), *adj.* 1 on or to the left. 2 of, for, or with the left hand; left-handed.

left-hand ed (left′han′did), *adj.* 1 using the left hand more easily and readily than the right. 2 done with the left hand. 3 made to be used with the left hand. 4 turning from right to left: *a left-handed screw.* 5 clumsy; awkward. 6 ambiguous, doubtful, or insincere: *a left-handed compliment.* —*adv.* toward the left; with the left hand. **—left′-hand′ed ly,** *adv.* **—left′-hand′ed ness,** *n.*

left-hand er (left′han′dər), *n.* 1 a left-handed person. 2 (in baseball) a left-handed pitcher; southpaw.

left ist (lef′tist), *n.* 1 person who has liberal or radical ideas in politics. 2 member of a liberal or radical political organization. —*adj.* having liberal or radical ideas.

left o ver (left′ō′vər), *n.* thing that is left. Scraps of food from a meal are leftovers. —*adj.* that is left; remaining: *leftover meat.*

left ward (left′wərd), *adj., adv.* on or toward the left.

left wards (left′wərdz), *adv.* leftward.

left wing, 1 the liberal or radical members, especially of a political party. 2 persons or parties holding liberal or radical views.

left-wing (left′wing′), *adj.* belonging to or like the left wing.

left-wing er (left′wing′ər), *n.* a left-wing member of a political party or a supporter of left-wing political views.

hat, āge, fär; let, ēqual, tėrm;
it, īce; hot, ōpen, ôrder;
oil, out; cup, pu̇t, rüle;
ch, child; ng, long; sh, she;
th, thin; ᴛʜ, then; zh, measure;

ə represents *a* in about, *e* in taken, *i* in pencil, *o* in lemon, *u* in circus.

< = from, derived from, taken from.

left y (lef′tē), *n., pl.* **left ies.** SLANG. a left-handed person.

leg (leg), *n., v.,* **legged, leg ging.** —*n.* 1 one of the limbs on which people and animals support themselves and walk, especially the part of the limb between the knee and the ankle. 2 the part of a garment that covers a leg: *The legs of your trousers are wrinkled.* 3 anything shaped or used like a leg; any support that is much longer than it is wide: *a table leg. One leg of a compass holds the pencil.* 4 one of the distinct portions or stages of any course: *the last leg of a trip, the first leg of a relay race.* 5 either of two sides of a right triangle that is not the hypotenuse. 6 course or run made on one tack by a sailing vessel.
a leg up, a assistance in climbing or getting over an obstacle, as mounting a horse. **b** encouragement; support.
have not a leg to stand on, INFORMAL. to have no defense or reason.
on one's last legs, about to fail, collapse, die, etc.; at the end of one's resources.
pull one's leg, INFORMAL. fool, trick, or make fun of one.
—*v.t.* **leg it,** INFORMAL. walk or run: *We could not get a ride, so we had to leg it.*
[< Scandinavian (Old Icelandic) *leggr*]

leg., 1 legal. 2 legislative. 3 legislature.

leg a cy (leg′ə sē), *n., pl.* **-cies.** 1 money or other property left to a person by the will of someone who has died; bequest. 2 something that has been handed down from an ancestor or predecessor: *the legacy of freedom.* [< Medieval Latin *legatia* < Latin *legatum* bequest < *legare* bequeath. See LEGATE.]

le gal (lē′gəl), *adj.* 1 of law: *legal knowledge.* 2 of a lawyer or lawyers: *legal advice.* 3 according to law; permitted by law; lawful: *a legal precedent.* See **lawful** for synonym study. 4 recognized by law rather than by equity. [< Latin *legalis* < *lex, legis* law. Doublet of LEAL, LOYAL.]

legal age, age at which a person attains full legal rights and responsibilities; majority.

legal holiday, day set by law or statute as exempt from normal labor or business activities.

le gal ism (lē′gə liz′əm), *n.* strict adherence to law or prescription, especially to the letter of the law rather than the spirit.

le gal ist (lē′gə list), *n.* 1 person who adheres strictly to laws or rules. 2 an expert in law.

le gal is tic (lē′gə lis′tik), *adj.* adhering strictly to law or prescription. **—le′gal is′ti cal ly,** *adv.*

le gal i ty (li gal′ə tē), *n., pl.* **-ties.** condition or quality of being legal; accordance with law; lawfulness.

le gal ize (lē′gə līz), *v.t.,* **-ized, -iz ing.** make legal; authorize by law; sanction. **—le′gal i za′tion,** *n.*

le gal ly (lē′gə lē), *adv.* 1 in a legal manner. 2 according to law.

legal tender, currency or money that must, by law, be accepted if offered in payment of a debt.

leg ate (leg′it), *n.* ambassador or representative, especially a representative of the Pope. [< Latin *legatus* < *legare* to delegate, originally, provide with a contract < *lex, legis* contract, law]

leg a tee (leg′ə tē′), *n.* person to whom a legacy is left.

le ga tion (li gā′shən), *n.* 1 the diplomatic representative of a country and his staff of assistants. A legation ranks next below an embassy and is now usually headed by a minister. 2 the official residence, offices, etc., of such a representative in a foreign country. 3 office, position, or dignity of a legate.

le ga to (li gä′tō), *adj., adv.* (in music) smooth and connected; without breaks between successive tones. [< Italian, bound < Latin *ligatum*]

leg end (lej′ənd), *n.* 1 story coming down from the past, which many people have believed: *The stories about King Arthur and his knights of the Round Table are legends.* 2 such stories as a group: *Irish legend.* 3 inscription on a coin or medal. 4 words accompanying a picture, as the explanation of symbols on a map or diagram or the title under an illustration. [< Medieval Latin *legenda* < Latin, (things) to be read < *legere* to read]

➤ **legend, myth.** *Legend* applies particularly to a story associated with some period in the history of a people or nation, often containing an element of fact but sometimes wholly untrue. Legends are intended to glorify a hero, saint, object, etc., and tell marvelous deeds he or it supposedly performed. *Myth* applies particularly to a story connected with the religion or beliefs of a primitive civilization. Myths are told about gods or superhuman beings and are invented to explain beliefs or rituals or something in nature.

leg end ar y (lej′ən der′ē), *adj.* 1 of a legend or legends; like a legend; not historical. 2 celebrated or described in legend: *legendary heroes.*

leg end ry (lej′ən drē), *n., pl.* **-ries.** legends collectively.

leg er de main (lej′ər də mān′), *n.* 1 sleight of hand; conjuring tricks; jugglery: *A common trick of legerdemain is to take rabbits from an apparently empty hat.* 2 trickery; deception. [< French *léger de main* quick of hand]

-legged, *combining form.* having ____ legs: *long-legged = having long legs.*

leg gings (leg′ingz), *n.pl.* extra outer coverings of cloth or leather for the legs, for use out of doors.

leg gy (leg′ē), *adj.,* **-gi er, -gi est.** 1 having long legs. 2 having awkwardly long legs. 3 INFORMAL. having shapely legs.

Leg horn (leg′hôrn *for 1;* leg′hôrn, leg′ərn *for 2,3*), *n.* 1 seaport in W Italy. 174,000. Also, ITALIAN **Livorno.** 2 **leghorn, a** hat made of fine, smooth, plaited yellow straw. **b** this straw. 3 a rather small kind of domestic fowl which produces large numbers of eggs.

leg i bil i ty (lej′ə bil′ə tē), *n.* legible condition or quality; clearness of print or writing.

leg i ble (lej′ə bəl), *adj.* 1 that can be read. 2 easy to read; plain and clear. [< Late Latin *legibilis* < Latin *legere* to read] **—leg′i bly,** *adv.*

le gion (lē′jən), *n.* 1 body of soldiers in the ancient Roman army consisting of 3000 to 6000 foot soldiers and 300 to 700 cavalrymen. 2 a large body of soldiers; army. 3 a great many; very large number; multitude. 4 Often, **Legion.** any of various military or honorary groups or societies, especially a national organization of former servicemen: *the Royal Canadian Legion.* [< Latin *legionem* < *legere* choose, collect]

le gion ar y (lē′jə ner′ē), *adj., n., pl.* **-ar ies.** —*adj.* of, having to do with, or belonging to a legion. —*n.* member of a legion.

le gion naire (lē′jə ner′, lē′jə nar′), *n.* 1 member of the American Legion or any other group using the title of Legion. 2 soldier of a legion. [< French *légionnaire*]

Legion of Honor, an honorary society founded by Napoleon in 1802. Membership is given as a reward for great services to France.

Legion of Merit, U.S. a military award conferred by the President on Americans and people of allied nations for exceptional services.

leg is late (lej′ə slāt), *v.,* **-lat ed, -lat ing.** —*v.i.* make or enact laws: *Congress legislates for the United States.* —*v.t.* force by legislation; bring about by legislation. [< *legislator*]

leg is la tion (lej′ə slā′shən), *n.* 1 the making of laws; enactment of laws. 2 the laws made by a legislature or legislator.

leg is la tive (lej′ə slā′tiv), *adj.* 1 having to do with making laws: *legislative reforms.* 2 having the duty and power of making laws: *The British Parliament is a legislative body.* 3 ordered by law; enacted by legislation: *a legislative decree.* **—leg′is la′tive ly,** *adv.*

leggings

leg is la tor (lej′ə slā′tər), *n.* person who makes laws; member of a legislative body; lawmaker. [< Latin *legis lator* proposer of a law]

leg is la ture (lej′ə slā′chər), *n.* group of persons that has the duty and power of making laws for a state or country.

le git (lə jit′), *adj.* SLANG. legitimate.

le git i ma cy (lə jit′ə mə sē), *n.* a being legitimate or lawful; being recognized as lawful or proper.

le git i mate (*adj.* lə jit′ə mit; *v.* lə jit′ə māt), *adj., v.,* **-mat ed, -mat ing.** —*adj.* 1 allowed or admitted by law; rightful; lawful: *a legitimate claim.* See **lawful** for synonym study. 2 valid; logical; acceptable: *Sickness is a legitimate reason for absence from work.* 3 born of parents who are married: *a legitimate child.* 4 conforming to accepted standards; normal; regular. 5 resting on, or ruling by, the principle of hereditary right: *a legitimate sovereign.* —*v.t.* make or declare lawful or legal. [< Medieval Latin *legitimatum* made lawful < Latin *legitimus* lawful < *lex, legis* law] **—le git′i mate ly,** *adv.* **—le git′i ma′tion,** *n.*

legitimate theater, drama acted on the stage as opposed to motion pictures, vaudeville, musical comedy, etc.

le git i ma tize (lə jit′ə mə tīz), *v.t.*, **-tized, -tiz ing.** legitimize.

le git i mize (lə jit′ə mīz), *v.t.*, **-mized, -miz ing.** make or declare to be legitimate. **—le git′i mi za′tion,** *n.*

leg less (leg′lis), *adj.* having no legs; without legs.

leg man (leg′man′), *n., pl.* **-men.** 1 a newspaper reporter who gathers information by going to the scene of the news. 2 person who delivers messages, gathers information, or does other legwork.

leg-of-mut ton (leg′ə mut′n), *adj.* having the shape of a leg of mutton; wide at one end and narrow at the other: *a leg-of-mutton sleeve.*

leg ume (leg′yüm, li gyüm′), *n.* 1 any plant of the pea family; any of the group of dicotyledonous plants which bear pods containing a number of seeds, such as beans, peas, etc. Legumes can absorb nitrogen from the air and convert it into nitrates by means of bacteria present in nodules on the roots of the plants. 2 the pod of such a plant. 3 **legumes,** *pl.* vegetables used for food. [< French *légume* < Latin *legumen* < *legere* choose, collect]

le gu mi nous (li gyü′mə nəs), *adj.* 1 of or bearing legumes. 2 of or belonging to the pea family.

leg work (leg′wėrk′), *n.* work which involves much moving about or traveling, usually in pursuit of information.

Le Ha vre (lə hä′vrə), seaport in N France. 200,000. Also, **Havre.**

le hu a (lā hü′ä), *n.* 1 a showy tree of the myrtle family, found in Hawaii, Samoa, and other Pacific islands, having a hard wood and clusters of bright-red flowers. 2 its flower. [< Hawaiian]

lei of flowers

lei (lā), *n.* wreath of flowers, leaves, etc., worn as an ornament around the neck or on the head. [< Hawaiian]

Leib nitz or **Leib niz** (līb′nits), *n.* Baron **Gottfried Wilhelm von,** 1646-1716, German philosopher and mathematician.

Leices ter (les′tər), *n.* 1 **Earl of,** 1532?-1588, Robert Dudley, English statesman, favorite of Queen Elizabeth I. 2 city in central England. 277,000. 3 Leicestershire.

Leices ter shire (les′tər shər, les′tər shir), *n.* county in central England.

Lei den (līd′n), *n.* city in SW Netherlands. 101,000. Also, **Leyden.**

Lein ster (len′stər), *n.* district in E Republic of Ireland.

Leip zig (līp′sig; *German* līp′tsiн), *n.* city in S East Germany. 586,000.

lei sure (lē′zhər, lezh′ər), *n.* 1 time free from required work in which a person may rest, amuse himself, and do the things he likes to do. 2 condition of having time free from required work. 3 **at leisure,** a free; not busy. b without hurry; taking plenty of time. 4 **at one's leisure,** when one has leisure; at one's convenience. *—adj.* 1 free; not busy: *leisure hours.* 2 leisured: *the leisure class.* [< Old French *leisir* < Latin *licere* be allowed]

lei sured (lē′zhərd, lezh′ərd), *adj.* 1 having ample leisure. 2 leisurely.

lei sure ly (lē′zhər lē, lezh′ər lē), *adj., adv.* without hurry; taking plenty of time. See **slow** for synonym study. **—lei′sure li ness,** *n.*

leit mo tif or **leit mo tiv** (līt′mō tēf′), *n.* 1 a short passage in a musical composition, associated throughout the work with a certain person, situation, or idea. 2 any recurrent theme. [< German *Leitmotiv,* literally, leading motive]

lek (lek), *n.* the monetary unit of Albania, worth about 20 cents. [< Albanian]

LEM (lem), *n.* lunar excursion module.

lem an (lem′ən), *n.* ARCHAIC. 1 sweetheart; lover. 2 an unlawful lover or mistress. [Middle English *leofman,* literally, dear man]

Le man (lē′mən), *n.* **Lake.** See **Geneva, Lake.**

Lem berg (lem′bėrg′), *n.* German name of **Lvov.**

lemming—about 6 in. long

lem ming (lem′ing), *n.* any of several genera of small, mouselike, arctic rodents, having a short tail and furry feet. When food is scarce, some species of lemmings migrate in great masses. Some eventually reach the sea, where they swim until exhausted and drown. [< Norwegian]

lem on (lem′ən), *n.* 1 a sour, light-yellow citrus fruit growing in warm climates. The juice, used chiefly for flavoring and making beverages, yields citric acid; the rind yields oil or essence of lemons, used in cookery and perfumery. 2 the thorny tree that this fruit grows on. 3 a pale-yellow color like that of the rind of a ripe lemon. 4 SLANG. something or someone that is disagreeable, unpleasant, or worthless. *—adj.* 1 pale yellow. 2 flavored with lemon. [< Old French *limon* < Arabic *laimūn* < Persian *līmūn*]

lem on ade (lem′ə nād′), *n.* drink made of lemon juice, sugar, and water.

lem pir a (lem pir′ä), *n.* the monetary unit of Honduras, a note or coin equal to 100 centavos and worth about 50 cents. [< American Spanish]

le mur (lē′mər), *n.* any of several genera of small primates having large eyes, a foxlike face, and woolly fur. Lemurs are found mainly in Madagascar. They live in trees and are active chiefly at night. [< Latin *lemures,* plural, specters, ghosts]

Le na River (lē′nə), river in E Soviet Union, flowing into the Arctic Ocean. 2800 mi.

lend (lend), *v.,* **lent, lend ing.** *—v.t.* 1 let another have or use (something) with the understanding that it or its equivalent will be returned: *Will you lend me your bicycle for an hour?* 2 give the use of (money) for a fixed or specified amount of payment: *Banks lend money and charge interest.* 3 give for a time; give: *The Salvation Army is quick to lend aid in time of disaster.* 4 **lend itself to** or **lend oneself to,** help or be suitable for: *This subject lends itself admirably to dramatic treatment.* *—v.i.* make a loan or loans. [Old English *lǣnan* < *lǣn* loan] **—lend′a ble,** *adj.* **—lend′er,** *n.* ➤ See **loan** for usage note.

lend-lease (lend′lēs′), *n., v.,* **-leased, -leas ing.** *—n.* policy of making a loan to an allied country of certain equipment in which the lender is superior, and of receiving some service or material in return. *—v.t.* send as a loan under such a policy.

length (lengkth, length), *n.* 1 how long a thing is; what a thing measures from end to end; the longest way a thing can be measured: *the length of one's arm.* 2 how long something lasts; extent in time; duration: *the length of a performance.* 3 distance a thing extends. 4 a long stretch or extent. 5 piece or portion of a given length: *a length of rope.* 6 the distance from end to end of a boat, horse, etc., as a unit of measurement in racing: *The gray horse finished the race two lengths ahead of the brown one.* 7 quality or fact of being long: *a book noted for its length.* 8 (in prosody) the force with which a syllable or vowel is spoken, or the way it is pronounced. 9 (in phonetics) duration of sounds; quantity.

at full length, with the body stretched out flat.

at length, a at last; finally. b with all the details; in full.

go to any length, do everything possible.

keep at arm's length, discourage from becoming friendly.

[Old English *lengthu* < *lang* long[1]]

length en (lengk′thən, leng′thən), *v.t.* make longer. See synonym study below. *—v.i.* become or grow longer.

Syn. *v.t.* **Lengthen, extend, prolong** mean to increase in length. **Lengthen** means to make longer in space or time: *There is no way to lengthen a day.* **Extend** often applies to measurements in addition to length (*The ranch extends beyond the horizon*) and is frequently used figuratively (*Reading can extend one's knowledge*). **Prolong** means to lengthen in time beyond the usual or expected limit: *She prolonged her visit.*

length ways (lengkth′wāz′, length′wāz′), *adv., adj.* lengthwise.

lemur—about 3 ft. long with tail

length wise (lengkth′wīz′, length′wīz′), *adv., adj.* in the direction of the length.

length y (lengk′thē, leng′thē), *adj.,* **length i er, length i est.** 1 having unusually great length; long. 2 (of speeches, a speaker, a writer, etc.) too long; long-winded; tedious.

—length′i ly, *adv.* **—length′i ness,** *n.*

len ience (lē′nyəns, lē′nē əns), *n.* leniency.

len ien cy (lē′nyən sē, lē′nē ən sē), *n.* lenient quality; mildness; gentleness; mercy.

len ient (lē′nyənt, lē′nē ənt), *adj.* mild or gentle; not harsh or stern; merciful: *a lenient judge, a lenient punishment.* [< Latin *lenientem* < *lenis* mild] **—len′ient ly,** *adv.*

Len in (len′ən), *n.* **Nikolai,** 1870-1924, Russian Communist leader, the founder of the Soviet government and its first premier, from 1918 to 1924. His real name was Vladimir Ilich Ulyanov.

Len in ism (len′ə niz′əm), *n.* the political and economic principles of Nikolai Lenin, developed from Marxism and forming the basis of the communist policies and practices of the Soviet Union.

Len in ist (len′ə nist), *n.* advocate or supporter of Leninism. *—adj.* advocating or supporting Leninism.

Len in grad (len′ən grad, len′ən gräd), *n.* seaport in NW Soviet Union, on the Gulf of Finland. 3,950,000. Formerly called **St. Petersburg** and later **Petrograd.**

len i tive (len′ə tiv), *adj.* softening; soothing; mitigating. *—n.* anything that soothes or softens; palliative.

len i ty (len′ə tē), *n.* leniency. [< Latin *lenitatem* < *lenis* mild]

lens (lenz), *n., pl.* **lens es.** 1 piece of glass or other transparent material which focuses or spreads apart the rays of light passing through it to form an image. Lenses have two opposite surfaces, either both plane or one plane and one curved, and are used alone or in combination in optical instruments. 2 combination of two or more of these pieces, as used in a camera, microscope, telescope, etc. 3 a transparent oval body in the eye directly behind the iris, that focuses light rays upon the retina. See **eye** for diagram. 4 device to focus radiations other than those of light. [< Latin *lens, lentis* lentil (which has a biconvex shape)]

lent (lent), *v.* pt. and pp. of **lend.**

Lent (lent), *n.* the forty weekdays between Ash Wednesday and Easter, observed in many Christian churches as a time for fasting and repenting of sins. [Old English *lengten* spring < *lang* long[1]]

lent en or **Lent en** (len′tən), *adj.* 1 of, during, or suitable for Lent. 2 meager; plain.

len ti cel (len′tə sel′), *n.* a usually lenticular body of cells formed in the corky layer of bark, which serves as a pore for the exchange of gases between the plant and the atmosphere. [< New Latin *lenticella* < Latin *lens, lentis* lentil]

len tic u lar (len tik′yə lər), *adj.* having the form of a lens, especially a biconvex lens.

len til (len′tl), *n.* 1 an annual plant of the pea family having pods which contain small, flat seeds. Lentils are grown mostly in southern Europe, Egypt, and Asia. 2 its seed, which is used as a vegetable. Lentils are cooked like peas and are often eaten in soup. [< Old French *lentille* < Latin *lenticula,* diminutive of *lens, lentis* lentil]

len to (len′tō), in music: *—adj.* slow. *—adv.* slowly. [< Italian, slow]

l'en voi or **l'en voy** (len′voi, len voi′), *n.* envoy[2]. [< Middle French *l'envoi*]

Le o (lē′ō), *n.* 1 a northern constellation between Cancer and Virgo, seen by ancient astronomers as having the rough outline of a lion. 2 the fifth sign of the zodiac; Lion. The sun enters Leo about July 22.

Leo I, Saint, A.D. 390?-461, pope from A.D. 440 to 461. He was called "Leo the Great."

Leo III, Saint, A.D. 750?-816, pope from A.D. 795 to 816.

Leo X, 1475-1521, pope from 1513 to 1521.

Leo XIII, 1810-1903, pope from 1878 to 1903.

Le ón (lā ōn′), *n.* 1 former kingdom in NW Spain. 2 province in NW Spain, including part of this kingdom. 3 city in central Mexico, NW of Mexico City. 454,000.

Le o nar do da Vin ci (lā′ə när′dō də vin′chē). See **da Vinci.**

Le on ca val lo (lā ōn′kə vä′lō), *n.* **Ruggiero,** 1858-1919, Italian composer of operas.

le o ne (lē ō′nē), *n.* the monetary unit of Sierra Leone, a note equal to 100 Sierra Leone cents and worth about U.S. $1.20.

Le o nid (lē′ə nid), *n., pl.* **Le o nids, Le on i des** (lē on′ə dēz′). one of a shower of meteors occurring about November 15. The Leonids seem to come from the constellation Leo.

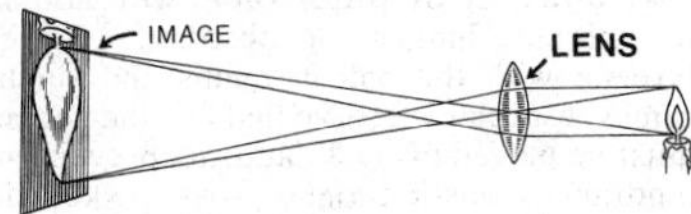

lens (def. 1)—The double convex lens shown above bends light rays to produce a magnified image.

Le on i das (lē on′ə dəs), *n.* died 480 B.C., king of Sparta from 491? to 480 B.C. He was killed at the battle of Thermopylae.

le o nine (lē′ə nīn), *adj.* of or like a lion. [< Latin *leoninus* < *leo* lion]

leopard (def. 1)—a pair of leopards; about 8 ft. long with the tail

leop ard (lep′ərd), *n.* 1 a large, fierce cat of Africa and Asia belonging to the same genus as the lion, tiger, and jaguar. Leopards usually have dull-yellowish fur spotted with black and are somewhat smaller than lions and tigers. Some leopards are black and may be called panthers. 2 any of various animals related to the leopard, as the jaguar. [< Greek *leopardos* < *leōn* lion + *pardos* leopard]

leop ard ess (lep′ər dis), *n.* a female leopard.

leopard frog, a spotted frog common in North America and found as far south as Panama.

Le o pold I (lē′ə pōld), 1790-1865, king of Belgium from 1831 to 1865.

Leopold II, 1835-1909, king of Belgium from 1865 to 1909.

Leopold III, born 1901, king of Belgium from 1934 to 1951.

Lé o pold ville (lē′ə pōld vil′), *n.* former name of **Kinshasa.**

le o tard (lē′ə tärd), *n.* Usually, **leotards,** *pl.* a tight-fitting one-piece garment, with or without sleeves, worn by dancers, acrobats, etc. [< French *léotard* < Jules *Léotard,* French aerialist of the 1800's]

hat, āge, fär; let, ēqual, tėrm;
it, īce; hot, ōpen, ôrder;
oil, out; cup, pu̇t, rüle;
ch, child; ng, long; sh, she;
th, thin; ᴛʜ, then; zh, measure;
ə represents *a* in about, *e* in taken, *i* in pencil, *o* in lemon, *u* in circus.
< = from, derived from, taken from.

lep er (lep′ər), *n.* person who has leprosy.

lep i dop ter an (lep′ə dop′tər ən), *n.* any of an order of insects having coiled, sucking mouth parts, four membranous wings covered with tiny, sometimes colorful, overlapping scales, and wormlike larvae called caterpillars. Butterflies and moths belong to this order. *—adj.* of or belonging to this order. [< New Latin *Lepidoptera,* the order < Greek *lepidos* scale + *pteron* wing]

lep i dop ter ist (lep′ə dop′tər ist), *n.* collector of butterflies.

lep i dop ter ous (lep′ə dop′tər əs), *adj.* of or belonging to the lepidopterans.

lep re chaun (lep′rə kôn, lep′rə kon), *n.* (in Irish legends) an elf resembling a little old man, believed to possess hidden gold. [< Irish *lupracan*]

lep ro sar i um (lep′rə ser′ē əm), *n., pl.* **-sar i ums, -sar i a** (-ser′ē ə). hospital or institution for the care and treatment of lepers.

lep ro sy (lep′rə sē), *n.* a chronic, infectious disease caused by certain rod-shaped bacteria that attack the skin and nerves, causing lumps or spots which may become ulcers; Hansen's disease. If not treated, the injury to the nerves results in numbness, paralysis, and deformity. [< Late Latin *leprosus* leprous < Greek *lepra* leprosy < *lepein* to peel]

lep rous (lep′rəs), *adj.* 1 having leprosy. 2 of or like leprosy. **—lep′rous ly,** *adv.*

lep ton (lep′ton), *n., pl.* **-tons** for 1, **-ta** (-tə) for 2. 1 any of a class of light elementary particles that includes the neutrino, electron, and positron. 2 unit of money in modern Greece, a coin worth 1/100 of a drachma. [< Greek, neuter of *leptos* thin, small]

les bi an or **Les bi an** (lez′bē ən), *n.* a homosexual female. *—adj.* having to do with homosexuality in females. [< *Lesbos*]

les bi an ism (lez′bē ə niz′əm), *n.* homosexual relations between females.

Les bos (lez′bos), *n.* Mytilene.

lèse-ma jes té (lez′mȧ zhes tā′), *n.* FRENCH. lese majesty.

lese maj es ty (lēz′ maj′ə stē), crime or offense against the sovereign power in a state; treason. [< Middle French *lèse-majesté* < Latin *laesa majestas* insulted sovereignty]

le sion (lē′zhən), *n.* 1 an injury; hurt. 2 an abnormal change in the structure of an organ or body tissue, caused by disease or injury. [< Latin *laesionem* injury < *laedere* to strike]

Le so tho (lə sō′tō), *n.* country in S Africa, a member of the Commonwealth of Nations. It was formerly the British protectorate of Basutoland. 1,040,000 pop.; 11,700 sq. mi. *Capital:* Maseru. See **South Africa** for map.

les pe de za (les′pə dē′zə), *n.* any of a genus of plants of the pea family grown for forage and ornament. [< New Latin *Lespedeza,* the genus name, alteration of *Zespedes,* a former Spanish governor of Florida]

less (les), *adj.* 1 smaller in size, degree, etc.; slighter: *of less width, less importance.* 2 not so much; not so much of: *less rain, less butter, less money.* 3 lower in age, rank, or importance: *no less a person than the President.* —*n.* a smaller amount or quantity: *I could do no less. She refused to take less than $5.* —*adv.* to a smaller extent or degree; not so; not so well: *less known, less important.* —*prep.* with (something) taken away; without; minus; lacking: *a year less two days, a coat less one sleeve.* [Old English *lǣssa*]

➔ **less, lesser.** Both are used as comparatives (of *little*), *less* more usually referring to size or quantity: *less time, less food; lesser,* a formal word, referring to value or importance: *a lesser writer.* ➔ See **few** for another usage note.

-less, *suffix forming adjectives from verbs and nouns.* 1 without a ____; that has no ____: *Homeless = without a home.* 2 that does not ____: *Ceaseless = that does not cease.* 3 that cannot be ____ed: *Countless = that cannot be counted.* [Old English *-lēas* < *lēas* without]

les see (le sē′), *n.* person to whom a lease is granted; tenant under a lease.

less en (les′n), *v.i.* grow less; diminish. —*v.t.* 1 make less; decrease. 2 represent as less; minimize; belittle.

less er (les′ər), *adj.* 1 less; smaller. 2 less important of two: *promote a policy of adopting the lesser of two evils.* ➔ See **less** for usage note.

Lesser Antilles, chain of small islands in the West Indies, southeast of Puerto Rico. It consists of the Leeward Islands, the Windward Islands, and the islands north of Venezuela.

lesser panda, panda (def. 2).

Les sing (les′ing), *n.* **Gotthold,** 1729-1781, German critic and dramatist.

les son (les′n), *n.* 1 anything learned or taught, especially a part of a book, an exercise, etc., assigned to a pupil for study; piece of instruction given or received: *classroom lessons.* 2 unit of learning or teaching; what is to be studied, taught, or practiced at one time: *a music lesson, a French lesson.* 3 an instructive experience or example, serving to encourage or warn. 4 a selection from the Bible or other sacred writing, read as part of a church service. 5 rebuke or punishment intended to prevent repetition of an offense. —*v.t.* 1 give a lesson or lessons to; instruct; teach. 2 rebuke; admonish. [< Old French *leçon* < Latin *lectionem* a reading < *legere* to read]

les sor (les′ôr, le sôr′), *n.* person who grants a lease.

lest (lest), *conj.* 1 for fear that: *Be careful lest you fall from that tree.* 2 that (after words meaning fear, danger, etc.): *I was afraid lest they should come too late to save us.* [Old English *(thȳ) lǣs the* (whereby) less that]

let[1] (let), *v.,* **let, let ting.** —*v.t.* 1 not stop from doing or having something; allow; permit: *Let the dog have a bone.* 2 allow to pass, go, or come: *let a person on board a ship.* 3 allow to run out: *Doctors used to let blood from people to lessen a fever.* 4 hire out; rent: *let a boat by the hour.* 5 assign or give out (a job) for contract by performance. 6 *Let* is used in giving suggestions or giving commands. *"Let's go home" means "I suggest that we go home." Let everyone do his duty.* 7 suppose; assume: *Let the two lines be parallel.* —*v.i.* be rented: *This room lets for $80 a month.*

let down, **a** lower. **b** slow up. **c** fail in supporting, aiding, or justifying (a person, etc.); disappoint.

let in, permit to enter; admit.

let in for, open the way to; cause (trouble, unpleasantness, etc.).

let off, **a** allow to go free; excuse from punishment, service, etc. **b** discharge; allow to get off.

let on, INFORMAL. **a** allow to be known; reveal one's knowledge of. **b** make believe; pretend.

let out, **a** permit to go out or escape; set free; release. **b** make larger or longer. **c** rent. **d** INFORMAL. dismiss or be dismissed. **e** make known; disclose; divulge.

let up, INFORMAL. stop; pause.

[Old English *lǣtan*] ➔ See *leave*[1] for usage note.

let[2] (let), *n., v.,* **let ted** or **let, let ting.** —*n.* 1 **without let or hindrance,** with nothing to prevent, hinder, or obstruct. 2 interference with the ball in tennis and similar games, especially a serve that hits the net and must be played over. 3 ARCHAIC. prevention; hindrance; obstruction. —*v.t.* ARCHAIC. prevent; hinder; obstruct. [Old English *lettan* hinder < *læt* late]

-let, *suffix added to nouns to form other nouns.* 1 little ____: *Booklet = a little book.* 2 band worn around the ____: *Anklet = band worn around the ankle.* [< Old French *-elet*]

let down (let′doun′), *n.* 1 a slowing up. 2 disappointment: *Losing the contest was a big letdown.*

le thal (lē′thəl), *adj.* causing death; deadly: *lethal weapons, a lethal dose.* [< Latin *lethalis* < *letum* death] —**le′thal ly,** *adv.*

le thal i ty (li thal′ə tē), *n.* quality of being lethal; deadliness.

le thar gic (lə thär′jik), *adj.* 1 affected with lethargy; unnaturally drowsy; sluggish; dull: *A hot, humid day makes most people feel lethargic.* 2 producing lethargy. —**le thar′gi cal ly,** *adv.*

leth ar gy (leth′ər jē), *n., pl.* **-gies.** 1 drowsy dullness; lack of energy; sluggish inactivity. 2 (in medicine) a state of prolonged unconsciousness resembling deep sleep, from which the person can be roused but immediately loses consciousness again. [< Greek *lēthargia* < *lēthē* forgetfulness + *argos* lazy < *a-* not + *ergon* work]

Le the (lē′thē), *n.* 1 (in Greek myths) a river in Hades. Drinking its water caused forgetfulness of the past. 2 forgetfulness; oblivion.

Le the an (li thē′ən), *adj.* 1 having to do with Lethe or its water. 2 causing forgetfulness.

Le to (lē′tō), *n.* (in Greek myths) the mother of Apollo and Artemis by Zeus.

let's (lets), let us.

Lett (let), *n.* member of a group of people living in Latvia, Lithuania, Estonia, and Germany, related to the Lithuanians.

let ter (let′ər), *n.* 1 mark or sign representing any of the speech sounds used in forming words; one of the symbols or characters that compose the alphabet. 2 a written or printed message addressed to a person or body of persons. 3 the exact wording; actual terms; literal meaning: *He kept the letter of the law but not the spirit.* 4 a block of type bearing a letter, used in printing. 5 a particular style of type. 6 the initial of a school, college, or other institution, given as an award or trophy to members of a sports team, etc. 7 **letters,** *pl. or sing.* **a** literature; belles-lettres. **b** knowledge of literature; literary culture; learning. **c** profession of an author. 8 **to the letter,** very exactly; just as one has been told. —*v.t.* 1 mark with letters. 2 inscribe (something) in letters. —*v.i.* to make letters. [< Old French *lettre* < Latin *littera*] —**let′ter er,** *n.*

letter carrier, person who collects or delivers mail; mailman; postman.

let tered (let′ərd), *adj.* 1 marked with letters. 2 able to read and write; literate. 3 having or characterized by learning or literary culture; learned.

let ter head (let′ər hed′), *n.* 1 words printed at the top of a sheet of paper, usually a name and address. 2 sheet or sheets of paper printed with such a heading.

let ter ing (let′ər ing), *n.* 1 letters drawn, painted, or stamped. 2 act of making letters.

letter of credit, document issued by a bank, allowing the person named in it to draw money up to a certain amount from other specified banks.

let ter-per fect (let′ər pėr′fikt), *adj.* 1 knowing one's part or lesson perfectly. 2 correct in every detail.

let ter press (let′ər pres′), *n.* 1 printed words, as distinguished from illustrations, etc. 2 printing from type or relief plates, as distinguished from offset, lithography, photogravure, etc.

letters of marque, an official document giving a person permission from a government to capture the merchant ships of an enemy; marque.

letters pat ent (pat′nt), an official document giving a person authority from a government to do some act or to have some right.

Let tish (let′ish), *adj.* of or having to do with the Letts or their language. —*n.* the Baltic language of the Letts.

let tre de ca chet (let′rə də kä shā′), *pl.* **let tres de ca chet** (let′rəz də kä shā′). letter under the seal of the king of France, especially one ordering the imprisonment or exile of someone without a trial or hearing. [< French]

let tuce (let′is), *n.* 1 any of a genus of garden plants of the composite family, having large, crisp, green leaves. 2 the leaves of any of these plants, much used in salad. [< Old French *laitues,* plural of *laitue* < Latin *lactuca* lettuce < *lac* milk; with reference to the milky juice of the plant]

let up (let′up′), *n.* INFORMAL. a stop or pause.

le u (le′ü), *n., pl.* **lei** (lā), the monetary unit of Romania, a coin or note worth about 17 cents. [< Romanian, literally, lion]

leu cine (lü′sēn′, lü′sn), *n.* a white, crystalline amino acid essential in nutrition, produced especially by the digestion of proteins by the pancreatic enzymes. *Formula:* $C_6H_{13}NO_2$

leu co cyte (lü′kə sīt), *n.* white blood cell. Also, **leukocyte.** [< Greek *leukos* white + English *-cyte*]

leu co cyt ic (lü′kə sit′ik), *adj.* of or having to do with leucocytes. Also, **leukocytic.**

leu co plast (lü′kə plast), *n.* one of the colorless plastids in the cytoplasm of plant cells that functions in the formation and storage of starch.

leu ke mi a (lü kē′mē ə, lü kē′myə), *n.* a cancerous, usually fatal, disease characterized by an excessive production of white blood cells in the blood. [< New Latin < Greek *leukos* white + *haima* blood]

leu ke mic (lü kē′mik), *adj.* of or having to do with leukemia.

leu ko cyte (lü′kə sīt), *n.* leucocyte.

leu ko cyt ic (lü′kə sit′ik), *adj.* leucocytic.

lev (lef), *n., pl.* **le va** (lev′ə). the monetary unit of Bulgaria, a coin worth about 86 cents. [< Bulgarian, literally, lion]

Le vant (lə vant′), *n.* region about the E Mediterranean from Greece to Egypt, especially Syria, Lebanon, and Israel.

Le van tine (lə van′tən, lev′ən tīn, lev′ən tēn′), *adj.* of the Levant. *—n.* person or ship of the Levant.

le va tor (lə vā′tər, lə vā′tôr), *n., pl.* **le va tor es** (lev′ə tôr′ēz, lev′ə tōr′ēz). muscle that raises some part of the body, such as the one that opens the eye. [< New Latin < Latin *levare* to raise]

lev ee¹ (lev′ē), *n.* 1 bank built to keep a river from overflowing. 2 a landing place for boats, such as a quay or pier. [< French *levée* < *lever* to raise < Latin *levare* < *levis* light]

lev ee² (lev′ē, lə vē′), *n.* 1 a formal reception: *The President held a levee on New Year's Day.* 2 reception held while rising. French kings used to hold levees in the morning while they were getting up and dressing. [< French *levé, lever* < *lever* to raise. See LEVEE¹.]

lev el (lev′əl), *adj., n., v.,* **-eled, -el ing** or **-elled, -el ling.** *—adj.* 1 having the same height everywhere; having a flat or even surface; flat; even: *a level floor.* See synonym study below. 2 lying in or reaching the same horizontal plane; of equal height: *The table is level with the sill of the window.* 3 of equal importance, rank, etc.: *Those five students are about level in ability.* 4 uniform; steady: *a calm and level tone, level colors.* 5 well-balanced; sensible: *a level head.* **6 one's level best,** INFORMAL. one's very best; as well as one can do.
—n. 1 something that is level; an even or flat surface, tract of land, etc. 2 one of the floors within a building. 3 instrument, such as a spirit level, for showing whether a surface is level: *a mason's level.* 4 level position or condition. 5 height: *The flood rose to a level of 60 feet.* 6 position or standard from a social, moral, or intellectual point of view: *His work is not up to a professional level.* **7 on the level,** INFORMAL. fair and straightforward; honest; legitimate.
—v.t. 1 make level; put on the same level. 2 bring to a level. 3 lay low; bring to the level of the ground: *The tornado leveled every house in the valley.* 4 raise and hold level for shooting; aim. 5 aim or direct (words, intentions, glances, etc.). 6 remove or reduce (differences, etc.); make uniform. **level off, a** come to an equilibrium; even off; steady. **b** return (an airplane) to a horizontal position in landing, or after a climb or dive.
[< Old French *livel* < Popular Latin *libellum* < Latin *libella,* diminutive of *libra* balance] **—lev′el er, lev′el ler,** *n.* **—lev′el ly,** *adv.* **—lev′el ness,** *n.*

Syn. *adj.* **1 Level, even, smooth** mean flat or having a flat surface. **Level** means not sloping and having no noticeably high or low places on the surface: *We built our house on level ground.* **Even** means having a uniformly flat, but not necessarily level, surface, with no irregular places: *The top of that card table is not even.* **Smooth** means perfectly even, without a trace of roughness to be seen or felt: *We sandpapered the shelves until they were smooth.*

level crossing, BRITISH. grade crossing.

lev el head ed (lev′əl hed′id), *adj.* having good common sense or good judgment; sensible. **—lev′el head′ed ness,** *n.*

first class lever—
fulcrum between effort and resistance; motion in direction opposite effort

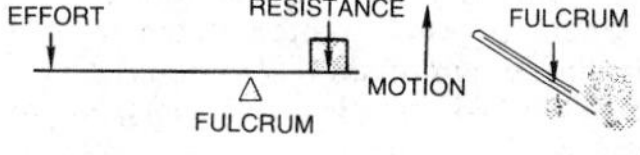

second class lever—
resistance between effort and fulcrum; motion in same direction as effort

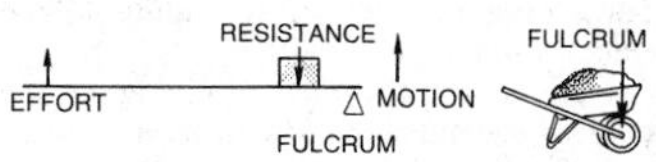

third class lever—
effort between resistance and fulcrum; motion in same direction as effort

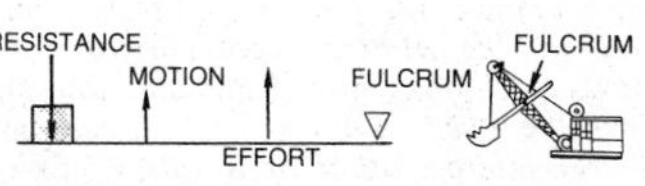

lever (def. 1)—the three classes

lev er (lev′ər, lē′vər), *n.* 1 bar which turns on a fixed support called a fulcrum and is used to transmit effort and motion. It is a simple machine. With a lever, a weight can be raised or moved at one end by pushing down at the other end. 2 any bar working on an axis for support, such as a crowbar, or the gearshift lever in an automobile. 3 any means of exerting control or achieving a purpose: *use the threat of a strike as a lever to obtain better wages from a company.* *—v.t.* move, lift, push, etc., with a lever. *—v.i.* use a lever. [< Old French *leveor* < *lever* to raise < Latin *levare* < *levis* light]

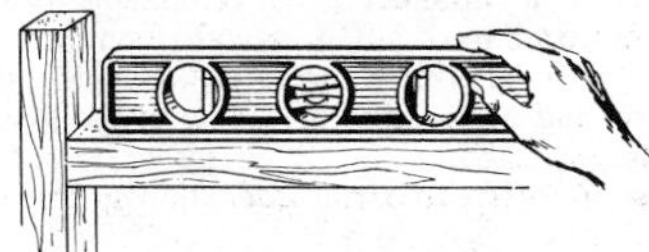

level (def. 3)—If the surface is level, an air bubble stays at the center of a glass tube containing liquid (as in the middle tube above). If the surface is not level, the bubble moves to one side.

lev er age (lev′ər ij, lē′vər ij), *n.* 1 action of a lever. 2 power of a lever; mechanical advantage gained by the use of a lever. 3 increased power of action; advantage for accomplishing a purpose.

lev er et (lev′ər it), *n.* a young hare, especially one in its first year. [< Old French *levrete,* diminutive of *levre* hare < Latin *leporem*]

hat, āge, fär; let, ēqual, tėrm;
it, īce; hot, ōpen, ôrder;
oil, out; cup, pu̇t, rüle;
ch, child; ng, long; sh, she;
th, thin; ᴛʜ, then; zh, measure;

ə represents *a* in about, *e* in taken, *i* in pencil, *o* in lemon, *u* in circus.

< = from, derived from, taken from.

Le vi (lē′vī), *n.* 1 (in the Bible) a son of Jacob and ancestor of the Levites. 2 the tribe that claimed to be descended from him, from which the priests and Levites were drawn.

le vi a than (lə vī′ə thən), *n.* 1 (in the Bible) a huge sea animal. 2 a whale or other large marine animal. 3 a huge ship. 4 any great and powerful person or thing. [< Late Latin < Hebrew *liwyāthān*]

lev i er (lev′ē ər), *n.* person who levies.

Le vi's (lē′vīz), *n.pl.* trademark for tight-fitting, heavy blue denim trousers reinforced at strain points with copper rivets or extra stitching.

lev i tate (lev′ə tāt), *v.,* **-tat ed, -tat ing.** *—v.i.* rise or float in the air. *—v.t.* cause to rise or float in the air. [< *levit(y)* + *-ate¹*] **—lev′i ta′tion,** *n.*

Le vite (lē′vīt), *n.* member of the tribe of Levi, from which assistants to the Jewish priests were chosen.

Le vit i cal (lə vit′ə kəl), *adj.* 1 of or having to do with the Levites. 2 of or having to do with Leviticus or the law contained in it.

Le vit i cus (lə vit′ə kəs), *n.* the third book of the Old Testament, containing the laws for the priests and Levites and the ritual for Jewish rites and ceremonies.

lev i ty (lev′ə tē), *n., pl.* **-ties.** lightness of mind, character, or behavior; lack of proper seriousness or earnestness; flippancy; frivolity. [< Latin *levitatem* < *levis* light]

levo-, *combining form.* toward the left: *Levorotatory = rotatory toward the left.* [< Latin *laevus* left]

le vo ro ta to ry (lē′vō rō′tə tôr′ē, lē′vō rō′tə tōr′ē), *adj.* 1 turning or causing to turn toward the left or in a counterclockwise direction. 2 (in physics and chemistry) characterized by turning the plane of polarization of light to the left, as a crystal, lens, or compound in solution.

lev u lose (lev′yə lōs), *n.* fructose.

lev y (lev′ē), *v.,* **lev ied, lev y ing,** *n., pl.* **lev ies.** *—v.t.* 1 order to be paid: *The government levies taxes to pay its expenses.* 2 draft or enlist (men) for an army: *levy troops in time of war.* 3 undertake or begin; wage: *levy war against the enemy.* 4 seize by law for unpaid debts. *—n.* 1 money collected by authority or force. 2 men drafted or enlisted for an army. 3 act of buying. [< Middle French *levée* < *lever* to raise. See LEVEE¹.]

lewd (lüd), *adj.* not decent; lustful; obscene; lascivious. [Old English *lǣwede* laic, unlearned] **—lewd′ly,** *adv.* **—lewd′ness,** *n.*

Lew is (lü′is), *n.* **1 John L(ewellyn),** 1880-1969, American labor leader. **2 Meriwether,** 1774-1809, American explorer in the Lewis and Clark expedition to Oregon. **3 Sinclair,** 1885-1951, American novelist.

lex (leks), *n., pl.* **le ges** (lē′jēz), LATIN. law.

lex i cog ra pher (lek′sə kog′rə fər), *n.* writer or maker of a dictionary.

lex i co graph ic (lek′sə kə graf′ik), *adj.* lexicographical.

lex i co graph i cal (lek′sə kə graf′ə kəl), *adj.* of or having to do with lexicography. **—lex′i co graph′i cal ly,** *adv.*

lex i cog ra phy (lek′sə kog′rə fē), *n.* the writing or making of dictionaries.

lex i con (lek′sə kən, lek′sə kon), *n.* 1 dictionary, especially of Greek, Latin, or Hebrew. 2 the vocabulary of a language or of a certain subject, group, or activity. [< Greek *lexikon (biblion)* wordbook < *lexis* word < *legein* to say]

Lex ing ton (lek′sing tən), *n.* 1 town in E Massachusetts where the first battle of the Revolutionary War was fought on April 19, 1775. 32,000. 2 city in N Kentucky. 108,000.

Ley den (līd′n), *n.* Leiden.

Leyden jar, an electrical condenser consisting of a glass jar coated inside and outside, for most of its height, with tin or aluminum foil, and sealed with a stopper containing a metal rod which is connected to the internal coating. [< *Leiden,* the Netherlands, where it was invented]

Ley te (lā′tē; *Spanish* lā′tā), *n.* island in the E central Philippines. 1,975,000 pop.; 2800 sq. mi.

LF, L.F., or **l.f.,** low frequency.

l.f., 1 left field. 2 left fielder.

LH, luteinizing hormone.

l.h., (in music) left hand.

Lha sa (lä′sə), *n.* capital of Tibet, in the S part. 70,000.

Li, lithium.

L.I., Long Island.

li a bil i ty (lī′ə bil′ə tē), *n., pl.* **-ties.** 1 state of being susceptible: *liability to disease.* 2 state of being under obligation: *liability for a debt.* 3 **liabilities,** *pl.* debts or other financial obligations of a business. 4 something that is to one's disadvantage: *Poor handwriting is a liability for a teacher.*

li a ble (lī′ə bəl), *adj.* 1 subject to the possibility; likely or possible, especially unpleasantly likely: *That glass is liable to break.* 2 exposed to or in danger of something likely or possible; susceptible: *We are all liable to diseases.* See **likely** for synonym study. 3 responsible; bound by law to pay: *The Postal Service is not liable for damage to a parcel sent by mail unless it is insured.* 4 under obligation; subject: *Citizens are liable to jury duty.* [< Old French *lier* to bind < Latin *ligare*]

li aise (lē āz′), *v.i.,* **-aised, -ais ing.** form a liaison; make a connection. [< *liaison*]

li ai son (lē′ā zon′, lē ā′zon, lē′ə zon), *n.* 1 connection between parts of an army, branches of a service, etc., to secure proper cooperation. 2 similar connection or communication between civilian bodies, such as government departments, companies, or schools. 3 illicit intimacy between a man and a woman. 4 (in French and other languages) the pronunciation of a usually silent final consonant when the next word begins with a vowel or mute *h* and there is no pause between the words. [< French < Latin *ligationem* a binding < *ligare* to bind]

liaison officer, a military officer whose duty is to secure proper cooperation between parts of an army or between allied armies.

li a na (lē ä′nə, lē an′ə), *n.* a climbing plant or vine, especially one of those having woody stems that twine around the trunk of trees of tropical forests. [< French *liane*]

li ane (lē än′), *n.* liana.

li ar (lī′ər), *n.* person who tells lies.

lib., 1 book [for Latin *liber*]. 2 librarian. 3 library.

li ba tion (lī bā′shən), *n.* 1 a pouring out of wine, water, etc., as an offering to a god. 2 the wine, water, etc., offered in this way. 3 INFORMAL. liquid poured out to be drunk; drink. [< Latin *libationem* < *libare* pour out]

Lib by (lib′ē), *n.* **Willard Frank,** born 1908, American chemist, discoverer of carbon 14 and originator of carbon dating.

li bel (lī′bəl), *n., v.,* **-beled, -bel ing** or **-belled, -bel ling.** *—n.* 1 a written or published statement, picture, etc., tending to damage a person's reputation or hold him up to public ridicule and disgrace. 2 crime of writing or publishing a libel. 3 any false or damaging statement about a person. *—v.t.* 1 write or publish a libel about. 2 make false or damaging statements about. [< Old French, a formal written statement < Latin *libellus,* diminutive of *liber* book]

li bel er or **li bel ler** (lī′bə lər), *n.* person who libels another.

li bel ous or **li bel lous** (lī′bə ləs), *adj.* 1 containing a libel. 2 spreading libels: *a libelous tongue.*

lib er al (lib′ər əl), *adj.* 1 giving or given freely; generous: *a liberal contributor to charity, a liberal donation.* 2 plentiful; abundant; ample: *We put in a liberal supply of coal for the winter.* 3 not narrow in one's views and ideas; broad-minded; tolerant: *a liberal thinker.* 4 not strict; not rigorous: *a liberal interpretation of a rule.* 5 favoring progress and reforms: *a liberal political program.* 6 Often, **Liberal.** of or belonging to a political party that favors progress and reforms, especially the Liberal Party of Great Britain or Canada. 7 giving the general thought; not a word-for-word rendering: *a liberal translation.* 8 of or having to do with the liberal arts or a liberal education. *—n.* 1 person who holds liberal principles and views; person favorable to progress and reforms. 2 **Liberal,** member of a Liberal Party. [< Latin *liberalis* befitting free men, honorable, generous < *liber* free] **—lib′er al ly,** *adv.* **—lib′er al ness,** *n.*

liberal arts, subjects in a college or university curriculum studied for general knowledge and intellectual development rather than for immediate practical, technical, or professional use. Literature, languages, history, and philosophy are some of the liberal arts.

liberal education, education in the liberal arts.

lib er al ism (lib′ər ə liz′əm), *n.* 1 liberal principles and ideas; belief in progress and reforms. 2 Also, **Liberalism,** the principles and practices of liberal political parties. 3 movement in Protestantism stressing the ethical nature of religion.

lib er al ist (lib′ər ə list), *n.* person who holds liberal principles and ideas; believer in progress and reforms.

lib e ral i ty (lib′ə ral′ə tē), *n., pl.* **-ties.** 1 liberal act or behavior; generosity. 2 a liberal gift. 3 tolerant and progressive nature; broad-mindedness.

lib er al ize (lib′ər ə līz), *v.t., v.i.,* **-ized, -iz ing.** make or become liberal. **—lib′er al i za′tion,** *n.* **—lib′er al iz′er,** *n.*

Liberal Party, 1 any political party that favors progress and reforms. 2 a political party in Great Britain formed about 1830. 3 one of the principal political parties of Canada.

lib e rate (lib′ə rāt′), *v.t.,* **-rat ed, -rat ing.** 1 set free; free or release from slavery, prison, confinement, etc. 2 (in chemistry) set free from combination: *liberate a gas.* [< Latin *liberatum* freed < *liber* free] **—lib′e ra′tor,** *n.*

lib e ra tion (lib′ə rā′shən), *n.* 1 a setting free. 2 a being set free.

Li ber i a (lī bir′ē ə), *n.* country in W Africa, first settled by freed American Negro slaves in 1822. 1,170,000 pop.; 43,000 sq. mi. *Capital:* Monrovia. **—Li ber′i an,** *adj., n.*

lib er tar i an (lib′ər ter′ē ən), *n.* 1 person who advocates liberty, especially in thought or conduct. 2 person who maintains the doctrine of the freedom of the will. *—adj.* of or having to do with liberty or libertarians.

lib er tar i an ism (lib′ər ter′ē ə niz′əm), *n.* the principles or doctrines of libertarians.

lib er tine (lib′ər tēn′), *n.* person without moral restraints; immoral or licentious person. *—adj.* without moral restraints; dissolute; licentious. [< Latin *libertinus* freedman < *libertus* made free < *liber* free]

lib er tin ism (lib′ər tēn′iz′əm, lib′ər tə niz′əm), *n.* libertine practices or habits of life.

lib er ty (lib′ər tē), *n., pl.* **-ties.** 1 condition of being free; freedom from captivity, imprisonment, or slavery; independence. 2 right or power to do as one pleases; power or opportunity to do something: *liberty of speech, liberty of action.* See **freedom** for synonym study. 3 official permission granted to a sailor to be absent from his ship or station, usually for not more than 48 hours. 4 right of being in, using, etc.: *We give our dog the liberty of the yard.* 5 too great freedom; excessive or undue familiarity, license, etc.: *The author took liberties with the facts to make the story more interesting.* 6 **at liberty,** **a** not in captivity or confinement; free: *set prisoners at liberty.* **b** allowed; permitted: *You are at liberty to make any choice you please.* **c** not busy: *The principal will see us as soon as she is at liberty.* [< Old French *liberte* < Latin *libertatem* < *liber* free]

Liberty Bell, bell that was rung at Philadelphia on July 8, 1776, when the Continental Congress passed the Declaration of Independence.

liberty cap, a cone-shaped cap used as a symbol of liberty. It was given to freed slaves in ancient Rome, and was used by the opponents of the monarchy at the start of the French Revolution.

Liberty Island, small island in New York Bay, where the Statue of Liberty is located. Former name, **Bedloe's Island.**

Liberty Party, the first American political party to oppose the extension of slavery into the territories. It existed from 1840 to 1848.

Liberty ship, a cargo ship of about 10,000 gross tons, built in large numbers by the United States during World War II.

li bid i nal (lə bid′n əl), *adj.* of or having to do with the libido.

li bid i nous (lə bid′n əs), *adj.* lustful; lewd; lascivious. [< Latin *libidinosus* < *libido.* See LIBIDO.] **—li bid′i nous ly,** *adv.*

li bi do (lə bē′dō), *n.* 1 sexual energy or desire. 2 the energy associated with instincts generally; vital impulse. [< Latin, desire < *libere* be pleasing]

hat, āge, fär; let, ēqual, tėrm;
it, īce; hot, ōpen, ôrder;
oil, out; cup, pu̇t, rüle;
ch, child; ng, long; sh, she;
th, thin; ᴛʜ, then; zh, measure;

ə represents *a* in about, *e* in taken,
i in pencil, *o* in lemon, *u* in circus.

< = from, derived from, taken from.

Li bra (lī′brə, lē′brə), *n.* 1 a southern constellation between Virgo and Scorpio, seen by ancient astronomers as having the rough outline of a pair of scales. 2 the seventh sign of the zodiac; Scales. The sun enters Libra about September 23. [< Latin *libra* balance, weight]

li brar i an (lī brer′ē ən), *n.* 1 person in charge of a library or part of a library. 2 person trained for work in a library.

li brar y (lī′brer′ē, lī′brər ē), *n., pl.* **-brar ies.** 1 a collection of books, periodicals, manuscripts, films, tapes, etc., either public or private: *a large reference library.* 2 room or building where such a collection is kept for public reading and borrowing. 3 any classified group of objects, collected for use or study: *a film library, a library of classical records.* [< Latin *librarium* bookcase < *liber* book]

li bra tion (lī brā′shən), *n.* (in astronomy) a real or apparent oscillatory motion of a planet or satellite in its orbit. [< Latin *libra* balance]

li bret tist (lə bret′ist), *n.* writer of a libretto.

li bret to (lə bret′ō), *n., pl.* **-bret tos, -bret ti** (-bret′ē). 1 the words of an opera or other long musical composition. 2 book containing the words. [< Italian, diminutive of *libro* book < Latin *liber*]

Li bre ville (lē′brə vil), *n.* capital of Gabon, in the NW part. 73,000.

Lib y a (lib′ē ə), *n.* 1 country in N Africa, west of Egypt. 1,900,000 pop.; 679,400 sq. mi. *Capitals:* Tripoli and Benghazi. 2 an ancient Greek and Roman name for that part of N Africa west of Egypt. **—Lib′y an,** *adj., n.*

Libyan Desert, part of the Sahara west of the Nile.

lice (līs), *n.* pl. of **louse.**

li cence (lī′sns), *n., v.,* **-cenced, -cenc ing.** license.

li cense (lī′sns), *n., v.,* **-censed, -cens ing.** *—n.* 1 permission given by law to do something, as to marry, carry on some business or profession, etc.: *a license to drive an automobile.* 2 paper, card, plate, etc., showing such permission. 3 fact or condition of being permitted to do something. 4 freedom of action, speech, thought, etc., that is permitted or conceded. Poetic license is the freedom from rules that is permitted in poetry and other arts. 5 too much liberty; disregard of what is right and proper; abuse of liberty. *—v.t.* give a license to; permit by law: *A doctor is licensed to practice medicine.* [< Old French *licence* < Latin *licentia* < *licere* be allowed] **—li′cens a ble,** *adj.* **—li′cens er,** *n.*

li cen see (lī′sn sē′), *n.* person to whom a license is given.

li cen ti ate (lī sen′shē it, lī sen′shē āt), *n.* person who has a license or permit to practice an art or a profession: *An attorney is a licentiate in law.*

li cen tious (lī sen′shəs), *adj.* 1 not restrained by morality; loose in sexual activities; immoral. 2 disregarding commonly accepted rules or principles; lawless. [< Latin *licentiosus* < *licentia.* See LICENSE.] **—li cen′tious ly,** *adv.* **—li cen′tious ness,** *n.*

li chee (lē′chē), *n.* litchi.

li chen (lī′kən), *n.* any of a large group of flowerless plants that look somewhat like moss and grow in patches on trees, rocks, etc. Lichens consist of a fungus and an alga growing together, the alga providing the food, and the fungus usually providing the water and protection. [< Latin < Greek *leichēn*]

li chen ous (lī′kə nəs), *adj.* of, like, or abounding in lichens.

lich gate (lich), a roofed gate to a churchyard. Also, **lych gate.** [*lich,* Old English *līc* body, corpse]

lic it (lis′it), *adj.* lawful; permitted. [< Latin *licitus* < *licere* be allowed] **—lic′it ly,** *adv.*

lick (lik), *v.t.* 1 pass the tongue over: *lick a stamp.* 2 lap up with the tongue. 3 make or bring by using the tongue: *The cat licked the plate clean.* 4 pass about or play over like a tongue: *The flames were licking the roof of the burning house.* 5 INFORMAL. beat or thrash. 6 INFORMAL. defeat in a fight, etc.; conquer. *—n.* 1 stroke of the tongue over something. 2 place where natural salt is found and where animals go to lick it up. 3 INFORMAL. a blow. 4 a small quantity: *She didn't do a lick of work.* 5 INFORMAL. a brief stroke of activity or effort. [Old English *liccian*]

lick e ty-split (lik′ə tē split′), *adv.* INFORMAL. at full speed; headlong; rapidly.

lick spit tle (lik′spit′l), *n.* a contemptible flatterer; parasite; toady.

lic or ice (lik′ər is, lik′ər ish), *n.* 1 the sweet-tasting, dried root of a European and Asiatic plant. 2 the plant itself, a perennial herb of the pea family. 3 a sweet, black, gummy extract obtained from the root, used in making candy, in medicine, in brewing, etc. 4 candy flavored with this extract. Also, **liquorice.** [< Anglo-French *lycorys* < Late Latin *liquiritia,* alteration of Greek *glykyrrhiza* < *glykys* sweet + *rhiza* root]

lic tor (lik′tər), *n.* (in ancient Rome) an officer who was an attendant to a magistrate and whose duties included carrying the fasces and executing sentences at the magistrate's orders. [< Latin, related to *ligare* to bind]

lid (lid), *n.* 1 a movable cover; top: *the lid of a box.* 2 eyelid. 3 SLANG. hat or cap. [Old English *hlid*] **—lid′less,** *adj.*

lid ded (lid′id), *adj.* having a lid; covered with or as if with a lid.

lie[1] (lī), *n., v.,* **lied, ly ing.** *—n.* 1 a false statement known to be false by the person who makes it. See synonym study below. 2 something that gives or is intended to give a false impression. 3 **give the lie to, a** call a liar; accuse of lying. **b** show to be false. *—v.i.* 1 speak falsely; tell a lie or lies. 2 give a false impression; mislead. *—v.t.* get, bring, put, etc., by lying: *lie oneself out of a difficulty.* [Old English *lyge*]

Syn. *n.* 1 **Lie, falsehood, fib** mean an untruthful statement. **Lie** applies to an untruthful statement deliberately made with knowledge that it is untruthful and with the purpose of deceiving: *Saying the other boy stole the money was a lie.* **Falsehood** can apply to an untruthful statement made when the truth would be undesirable: *Since he did not want to hurt his sister's feelings, he told a falsehood and said he didn't know.* **Fib** means a lie or excusable falsehood about something unimportant: *Many children tell fibs.*

lie[2] (lī), *v.,* **lay, lain, ly ing,** *n.* *—v.i.* 1 have one's body in a flat position along the ground or other surface; recline: *lie on the grass, lie in bed.* 2 assume such a position: *lie down on the couch.* 3 rest (on a surface): *The book was lying on the table.* 4 be kept or stay in a given state, position, etc.: *lie idle, lie hidden, lie unused.* 5 be; be placed: *The lake lies to the south of us.* 6 exist; have its place; belong: *The cure for ignorance lies in education.* 7 be in the grave; be buried: *His body lies in Plymouth.* 8 ARCHAIC. spend the night; lodge.

lie in, be confined in childbirth.

lie off, (of a ship, etc.) stay not far from.

lie over, be left waiting until a later time.

lie to, (of a ship, etc.) come almost to a stop, facing the wind.

take lying down, yield to; not stand up to.

—n. 1 manner, position, or direction in which something lies: *the lie of the land.* 2 place where an animal is accustomed to lie or lurk.

[Old English *licgan*] ➤ See **lay[1]** for usage note.

Lie (lē), *n.* **Trygve Haldane,** 1896-1968, Norwegian statesman, secretary-general of the United Nations from 1946 to 1953.

Liech ten stein (lik′tən stīn; *German* lēʜ′tən shtīn), *n.* country between W Austria and E Switzerland. 28,000 pop.; 62 sq. mi. *Capital:* Vaduz.

lied[1] (līd), *v.* pt. and pp. of **lie[1].**

lied[2] (lēd; *German* lēt), *n., pl.* **lie der** (lē′dər). a German song or ballad, especially one of the songs of Franz Schubert or Robert Schumann or one of similar character. [< German *Lied*]

lie detector, device that records the physical reaction of an emotion, used especially to determine whether a person is lying; polygraph.

lief (lēf), *adv.* willingly. *—adj.* ARCHAIC. beloved; dear; precious. [Old English *lēof* dear]

liege (lēj), *n.* in the Middle Ages: 1 lord having a right to the homage and loyal service of his vassals; liege lord. 2 vassal obliged to give homage and loyal service to his lord; liegeman. *—adj.* 1 having a right to the homage and loyal service of vassals. 2 obliged to give homage and loyal service to a lord. [< Old French, ultimately of Germanic origin]

Li ège (lē ezh′), *n.* city in E Belgium. 149,000.

liege lord, a feudal lord.

liege man (lēj′mən), *n., pl.* **-men.** 1 vassal. 2 a faithful follower.

lien (lēn), *n.* a legal claim which one has on the property of another for payment of a debt: *The garage owner has a lien upon my automobile until I pay his bill.* [< Old French < Latin *ligamen* bond < *ligare* to bind]

lieu (lü), *n.* 1 place; stead. 2 **in lieu of,** in place of; instead of. [< Old French < Latin *locus*]

Lieut., Lieutenant.

lieu ten an cy (lü ten′ən sē; *British, except in the navy,* lef ten′ən sē), *n., pl.* **-cies.** rank, commission, or authority of a lieutenant.

lieu ten ant (lü ten′ənt; *British, except in the navy,* lef ten′ənt), *n.* 1 person, usually a civil or military officer, who acts in the place of someone above him in authority. 2 (in the army, air force, and marines) a first lieutenant or a second lieutenant. 3 (in the navy) a commissioned officer ranking next below a lieutenant commander and next above a lieutenant junior grade. 4 a police or fire department officer, usually ranking next below a captain and next above a sergeant. [< Middle French < *lieu* a place + *tenant* holding]

lieutenant colonel, (in the army, air force, or marines) a commissioned officer ranking next below a colonel and next above a major.

lieutenant commander, (in the navy) a commissioned officer ranking next below a commander and next above a lieutenant.

lieutenant general, (in the army, air force, or marines) a commissioned officer ranking next below a general and next above a major general.

lieutenant governor, 1 (in the United States) a public official next in rank to the governor of a state. In case of the governor's absence or death, the lieutenant governor takes his place. 2 (in Canada) the official head of a provincial government, appointed by the governor general as the representative of the crown in a province.

lieutenant junior grade, (in the navy) a commissioned officer ranking next below a lieutenant and next above an ensign.

life (līf), *n., pl.* **lives,** *adj.* —*n.* 1 quality or condition of living or being alive; the form of existence that people, animals, and plants have and that rocks, dirt, and metals lack; animate existence, characterized by growth, reproduction, metabolism, and response to stimuli. 2 time of being alive; existence as an individual: *a long life.* 3 time of existence or action of inanimate things: *a machine's life, the life of a lease.* 4 a living being; person: *Five lives were lost.* 5 living beings considered together: *The desert island had almost no animal or vegetable life.* 6 way of living: *a dull life, a country life.* 7 account of a person's life; biography: *a life of Lincoln.* 8 spirit; vigor: *Put more life into your work.* 9 source of activity or liveliness: *the life of the party.* 10 existence in the world of affairs or society: *young people on the threshold of life.*

as big as life, a as big as the living person or thing. **b** in person.

bring to life, a revive; restore to consciousness. **b** cause to live; give life to. **c** make vivid or lively.

come to life, a be revived; be restored to consciousness. **b** be or become vivid.

for dear life, to save one's life.

for the life of me, INFORMAL. if my life depended on it.

from life, using a living model.

see life, get experience, especially of the exciting features of human activities.

to the life, like the model; exactly; perfectly.

—*adj.* 1 for a lifetime: *a life member, a life sentence.* 2 of or having to do with life or one's life: *life span.* 3 painted, etc., from life: *a life portrait.*

[Old English *līf*]

life belt, life preserver made like a belt.

life blood (līf′blud′), *n.* 1 blood necessary to life. 2 source of strength and energy; the vital part or vitalizing influence.

life boat (līf′bōt′), *n.* a strong boat especially built for saving lives at sea or along the coast.

life raft

life buoy, a cork or plastic ring, belt, or jacket used as a buoy.

life cycle, (in biology) the successive stages of development that a living thing passes through from a particular stage in one generation to the same stage in the next.

life expectancy, the average number of remaining years that a person at a given age can expect to live.

life guard (līf′gärd′), *n.* person trained in lifesaving who is employed on a beach or at a swimming pool to help in case of accident or danger to swimmers.

Life Guards, two British cavalry regiments whose duty is to guard the king and queen of England.

life history, 1 (in biology) the successive stages of development of an organism from its inception to death. 2 one series of such stages, often equivalent to a life cycle. 3 biography.

life insurance, 1 contract by which a person pays a regular premium in order to have a designated sum paid to his family or heirs at his death. 2 sum paid by the insurance company at death.

life jacket

life jacket, a sleeveless jacket filled with a light material, such as cork or kapok, or with compressed air, worn as a life preserver.

life less (līf′lis), *adj.* 1 without life: *a lifeless planet.* 2 dead: *The lifeless body floated ashore.* See **dead** for synonym study. 3 dull: *a lifeless performance.* —**life′less ly,** *adv.* —**life′less ness,** *n.*

life like (līf′līk′), *adj.* like life; exactly like something in real life: *a lifelike portrait.* —**life′like′ness,** *n.*

life line (līf′līn′), *n.* 1 rope for saving life, such as one thrown to a person in the water or a line fired across a ship to haul aboard a breeches buoy. 2 a diver's signaling line. 3 anything that maintains or helps to maintain something that cannot exist by itself, as a remote military position, etc.

life long (līf′lông′, līf′long′), *adj.* lasting or continuing for a lifetime: *a lifelong friendship.*

life net, a strong net or sheet of canvas, used to catch people jumping from burning buildings.

life preserver, 1 a wide belt, jacket, circular tube, etc., usually filled with cork, kapok, or compressed air to keep a person afloat in the water until he is rescued. 2 BRITISH. a short stick with a heavy head or a blackjack, used for self-defense.

lif er (lī′fər), *n.* SLANG. person sentenced to prison for life.

life raft, raft for saving lives in a shipwreck or an aircraft crash at sea.

life sav er (līf′sā′vər), *n.* 1 person who saves people from drowning. 2 any lifesaving person or thing. 3 INFORMAL. one that saves someone from trouble, discomfort, embarrassment, etc.

life sav ing (līf′sā′ving), *n.* a saving of people's lives; keeping people from drowning. —*adj.* designed or used for lifesaving: *lifesaving apparatus.*

life sciences, botany, zoology, biochemistry, microbiology, and other sciences dealing with living matter.

life-size (līf′sīz′), *adj.* as big as the living person, animal, etc.; equal in size to the original: *a life-size statue.*

life-sized (līf′sīzd′), *adj.* life-size.

life-style (līf′stīl′), *n.* a person's or group's characteristic manner of living; one's style of life.

life-sup port system (līf′sə pôrt′), equipment necessary to maintain human life where a normal environment is lacking. A spacecraft's life-support system enables the crew to live outside the earth's atmosphere.

life time (līf′tīm′), *n.* time of being alive; period during which a life lasts. —*adj.* for life.

life work (līf′wėrk′), *n.* work that takes or lasts a whole lifetime; main work in life.

life zone, region that supports or is capable of supporting life.

lift (lift), *v.t.* 1 bring up to a higher position or place; take up; pick up; raise: *lift a chair.* See **raise** for synonym study. 2 raise in rank, condition, estimation, spirits, etc.; elevate; exalt. 3 send up loudly: *lift a cry, lift one's voice.* 4 INFORMAL. pick or take up; steal. 5 INFORMAL. plagiarize. 6 tighten the skin and erase the wrinkles of (a person's face) through surgery. —*v.i.* 1 rise and go; go away: *The fog lifted at dawn.* 2 go up; be raised: *This window will not lift.* 3 rise.

—*n.* 1 an elevating influence or effect: *The promotion gave him a lift.* 2 act of lifting, raising, or rising. 3 distance through which a thing is lifted or moved. 4 a helping hand; assistance: *Give me a lift with this job.* 5 a ride in a vehicle given to a traveler on foot; free ride: *Can I give you a lift to town?* 6 BRITISH. elevator. 7 one of the layers of leather in the heel of a shoe or boot. 8 a rise in position, condition, etc.; promotion; advancement. 9 elevated carriage (of the head, neck, eyes, etc.): *a haughty lift of the chin.* 10 quantity or weight that can be lifted at one time: *A lift of fifty pounds was all the boy could manage.* 11 cable or rope with seats or attachments for holding on to raise a skier to the top of a slope. 12 (in aeronautics) the upward reaction of an aircraft to the flow of air being forced downward by an airfoil.

[< Scandinavian (Old Icelandic) *lypta* < *lopt* air] —**lift′er,** *n.*

lift off (lift′ôf′, lift′of′), *n.* the firing or launching of a rocket.

lift pump, any pump that lifts a liquid without forcing it out under pressure.

lig a ment (lig′ə mənt), *n.* 1 band of strong, flexible, white tissue which connects bones or holds organs of the body in place. 2 a connecting tie; bond of union or attachment. [< Latin *ligamentum* < *ligare* to bind]

hat, āge, fär; let, ēqual, tėrm;
it, īce; hot, ōpen, ôrder;
oil, out; cup, pu̇t, rüle;
ch, child; ng, long; sh, she;
th, thin; ᴛʜ, then; zh, measure;

ə represents *a* in about, *e* in taken, *i* in pencil, *o* in lemon, *u* in circus.

< = from, derived from, taken from.

li gate (lī′gāt), *v.t.,* **-gat ed, -gat ing.** tie up or bind with a ligature.

lig a ture (lig′ə chu̇r, lig′ə chər), *n., v.,* **-tured, -tur ing.** *—n.* 1 anything used to bind or tie up; band, bandage, cord, etc. 2 thread, wire, string, etc., used by surgeons to tie up a bleeding artery or vein, remove a tumor by strangulation, etc. 3 a binding or tying up. 4 (in music) a slur or a group of notes connected by a slur. 5 two or three letters joined in printing to form one character. *Æ* and *ffl* are ligatures. *—v.t.* bind or tie up with a ligature. [< Late Latin *ligatura* < Latin *ligare* to bind]

ligature (def. 4)

li ger (lī′gər), *n.* a hybrid animal, the offspring of a lion and a tigress. [blend of *lion* and *tiger*]

light[1] (līt), *n., adj., v.,* **light ed** or **lit, light ing.** *—n.* 1 that by which we see; form of radiant energy that acts on the retina of the eye. Light consists of electromagnetic waves that travel at about 186,282 miles per second. 2 a similar form of radiant energy which does not affect the retina, such as ultraviolet rays or infrared rays. 3 anything that gives light, as the sun, the moon, a lamp, a burning candle, or a lighthouse. 4 supply of light: *A tall building cuts off our light.* 5 brightness; clearness; illumination; particular case of this: *a strong or dim light.* 6 a bright part: *light and shade in a painting.* 7 time of daylight; daytime. 8 dawn; daybreak. 9 window or other means of letting in light. 10 thing with which to start something burning, as a match. 11 mental or spiritual illumination; understanding; enlightenment: *We need more light on this subject.* 12 public knowledge; open view: *The reporter brought to light graft in the city government.* 13 aspect in which a thing is viewed: *The principal put the matter in the right light.* 14 a gleam or sparkle in the eye, expressing lively feeling. 15 person conspicuous for virtue, intelligence, or other merit; luminary: *one of the leading lights of modern science.* 16 a traffic light. 17 **in the light of,** because of; considering. 18 **see the light** or **see the light of day, a** be born. **b** be made public. **c** get the right idea. 19 **shed light on** or **throw light on,** make clear; explain.
—adj. 1 having light: *the lightest room in the house.* 2 bright; clear: *It is as light as day.* 3 pale in color; whitish: *light hair, light blue.*
—v.t. 1 cause to give light: *She lighted the lamp.* 2 give light to; provide with light: *The room is lighted by six windows.* 3 make bright or clear: *Her face was lighted by a smile.* 4 show the way by means of a light: *Here is a candle to light you to bed.* 5 set fire to; kindle; ignite: *She lighted the candles.* *—v.i.* 1 become light: *The sky lights up at dawn.* 2 take fire; become ignited. 3 become bright with animation, eagerness, or happiness: *Her face lit up with satisfaction.*
[Old English *lēoht*]

light[2] (līt), *adj.* 1 of little weight; easy to carry; not heavy: *a light load.* 2 of little weight for its size; of low specific gravity: *a light metal. Feathers are light.* 3 of less than usual or normal weight: *light summer clothing.* 4 less than usual in amount, force, etc.: *a light sleep, a light rain, a light meal.* 5 easy to do or bear; not hard or severe: *light punishment, a light task.* 6 not looking heavy; graceful; delicate: *a light bridge, light carving.* 7 moving easily; nimble; agile: *light on one's feet, a light step.* 8 free from care or sorrow; happy; gay; cheerful: *a light laugh, light spirits.* 9 not serious enough; changing easily; fickle: *a light mind, light of purpose.* 10 aiming to entertain; not serious: *light reading, light opera.* 11 not important: *light losses.* 12 careless in morals. 13 not dense or abundant: *a light fog, a light snow.* 14 porous; sandy: *a light soil.* 15 containing little alcohol: *a light wine.* 16 that has risen properly; not soggy: *light dough.* 17 lightly armed or equipped: *light cavalry, in light marching order.* 18 **light in the head, a** dizzy. **b** silly; foolish. **c** crazy. 19 **make light of,** treat as of little importance.
—adv. in a light manner; lightly: *travel light.*
[Old English *lēoht, līht*]

light[3] (līt), *v.i.,* **light ed** or **lit, light ing.** 1 come down to the ground: *He lighted from his horse.* 2 come down from flight: *A bird lighted on the branch.* 3 come by chance: *My eye lighted upon a coin in the road.* 4 fall suddenly: *The blow lighted on his head.* 5 **light into,** SLANG. **a** attack. **b** scold. 6 **light out,** SLANG. leave suddenly; go away quickly. [Old English *līhtan* < *līht* light[2]]

light bulb, incandescent lamp.

light en[1] (līt′n), *v.t.* 1 make light; make brighter; brighten: *Dawn lightens the sky.* 2 make lighter in color. *—v.i.* 1 become light; become brighter; brighten: *Her face lightened.* 2 become lighter in color. 3 flash with lightning. [Middle English < *light*[1]]

light en[2] (līt′n), *v.t.* 1 reduce the load of; make lighter: *lighten a ship, lighten the burden of his work.* 2 make more cheerful: *The good news lightened our hearts.* *—v.i.* 1 have the load reduced; become lighter. 2 become more cheerful. [Middle English < *light*[2]]

light er[1] (lī′tər), *n.* 1 thing used to set something else on fire: *a cigarette lighter.* 2 person who lights or kindles. [< *light*[1]]

light er[2] (lī′tər), *n.* a flat-bottomed barge used for loading and unloading ships or for carrying cargo over a short route. *—v.t.* carry (goods) in such a barge. [< *light*[3]]

light er age (lī′tər ij), *n.* 1 the loading, unloading, or carrying of goods in a lighter. 2 price paid for this.

light er-than-air (lī′tər ᴛʜən er′, lī′tər ᴛʜən ar′), *adj.* having less weight than air and depending for support on the buoyancy of the air around it, as gas-filled balloons or airships.

light face (līt′fās′), *n.* printing type that has thin, light lines. This sentence is in lightface.

light-fin gered (līt′fing′gərd), *adj.* 1 skillful at picking pockets; thievish. 2 having light and nimble fingers.

light-foot ed (līt′fu̇t′id), *adj.* stepping lightly.

light-hand ed (līt′han′did), *adj.* having a light hand or touch; dexterous.

light-head ed (līt′hed′id), *adj.* 1 dizzy; giddy; out of one's head. 2 empty-headed; silly; thoughtless; frivolous. **—light′-head′ed ly,** *adv.* **—light′-head′ed ness,** *n.*

light heart ed (līt′här′tid), *adj.* without worry; carefree; cheerful; gay. **—light′heart′ed ly,** *adv.* **—light′heart′ed ness,** *n.*

light heavyweight, boxer who weighs more than 160 and less than 175 pounds.

light house (līt′hous′), *n., pl.* **-hous es** (-hou′ziz). tower or framework with a bright light that usually revolves or flashes as it shines far over the water. It is often located at a dangerous place to warn and guide ships.

light industry, industry that manufactures products, such as shoes or food, for use by consumers.

light ing (lī′ting), *n.* 1 a giving of light or providing with light; illumination. 2 way in which lights are arranged. 3 a starting to burn; kindling; ignition.

light ly (līt′lē), *adv.* 1 with little weight, force, etc.; gently: *The seagull rested lightly on the waves. Cares rested lightly on the little girl.* 2 to a small degree or extent; to no great amount: *lightly clad.* 3 in an airy way: *flags floating lightly.* 4 quickly; easily; nimbly: *jump lightly aside.* 5 cheerfully; gaily: *take bad news lightly.* 6 indifferently or slightingly: *speak lightly of a person.* 7 thoughtlessly; carelessly; frivolously: *behave lightly.*

light meter, instrument for measuring the intensity of light, such as a photometer.

light-mind ed (līt′mīn′did), *adj.* empty-headed; thoughtless; frivolous. **—light′-mind′ed ly,** *adv.*

light ness[1] (līt′nis), *n.* 1 a condition or state of being lighted; brightness; clearness; illumination. 2 light color; paleness; whitishness. 3 amount of light: *The lightness of the sky showed that the rain was really over.* [Old English *līhtnes* < *lēoht* light[1]]

light ness[2] (līt′nis), *n.* 1 a being light in weight; not being heavy. 2 not being hard or severe. 3 gracefulness; delicacy. 4 agility; nimbleness; swiftness. 5 a being gay or cheerful: *lightness of spirits.* 6 lack of proper seriousness; fickleness; frivolity: *Lightness of conduct is not permitted here.* [< *light*[2]]

light ning (līt′ning), *n.* flash of light in the sky caused by a discharge of electricity between clouds, or between one part of a cloud and another part, or between a cloud and the earth's surface. *—adj.* quick as lightning; very rapid.

lightning arrester, device that protects electrical apparatus from damage by lightning by carrying to the ground the excess voltage produced by lightning discharges.

lightning bug, firefly.

lightning rod, a metal rod fixed to the

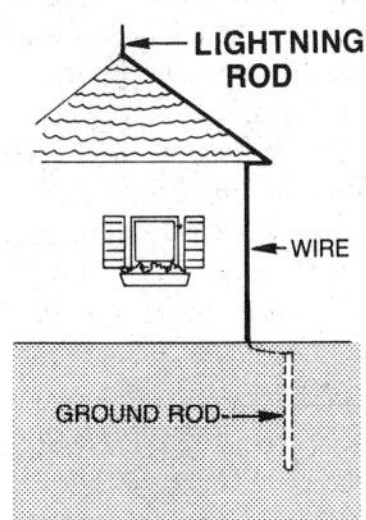

lightning rod
Lightning which strikes the rod is conducted down a heavy wire and grounded through a metal rod.

highest point or other exposed place on a building or ship to conduct lightning into the earth or water.

lights (līts), *n.pl.* the lungs of animals, especially sheep, pigs, etc., used as food. [so called because of their light weight]

light ship (līt′ship′), *n.* ship with a bright light that shines far over the water, anchored at a dangerous place to warn and guide ships.

light some (līt′səm), *adj.* 1 nimble; lively: *lightsome feet.* 2 happy; gay; cheerful. 3 frivolous. **—light′some ly,** *adv.* **—light′some ness,** *n.*

light weight (līt′wāt′), *n.* 1 person or thing of less than average weight. 2 boxer who weighs more than 126 and less than 135 pounds. 3 INFORMAL. person who has little intelligence, importance, or influence. *—adj.* 1 light in weight. 2 unimportant; insignificant.

light-year (līt′yir′), *n.* distance that light travels in one year, about six trillion (6,000,000,000,000) miles, used to measure astronomical distances.

lig ne ous (lig′nē əs), *adj.* of or like wood; woody. [< Latin *ligneus* < *lignum* wood]

lig nin (lig′nən), *n.* (in botany) an organic substance which, together with cellulose, forms the essential part of woody tissue, making up the greater part of the weight of dry wood.

lig nite (lig′nīt), *n.* a brownish-black coal in which decomposition of vegetable matter has proceeded farther than in peat but not so far as in bituminous coal. Lignite usually has the original form of the wood clearly visible; brown coal.

lig num vi tae (lig′nəm vī′tē), 1 an extremely heavy and hard wood, used for making pulleys, rulers, etc. 2 the trees of tropical America from which it comes. 3 any of several other trees having similar wood. [< Latin, wood of life]

lig ule (lig′yül), *n.* (in botany) any of several strap-shaped organs or parts, as the flattened corolla in the ray florets of composites or the projection from the top of the leaf sheath in many grasses. [< Latin *ligula* strap, tonguelike part]

Li gur i a (li gyůr′ē ə), *n.* district in NW Italy. **—Li gur′i an,** *adj., n.*

Ligurian Sea, the part of the Mediterranean between the NW coast of Italy and the island of Corsica.

lik a ble (lī′kə bəl), *adj.* having qualities that win good will or friendship; popular; pleasing; agreeable. Also, **likeable. —lik′a bleness,** *n.*

like[1] (līk), *prep.* 1 resembling something or each other; similar to: *Our house is like theirs.* 2 in the same way as; as well as: *sing like a bird, work like a beaver.* 3 such as one would expect of; characteristic of: *Isn't that just like him to be late?* 4 in the right state or frame of mind for: *I feel like working.* 5 giving promise or indication of: *It looks like rain.* 6 INFORMAL. such as: *On our trip we will visit cities like Paris, London, and Rome.*

—adj. 1 of the same form, kind, amount, etc.; the same or almost the same; similar: *a like sum. She enjoys drawing, painting, and like arts.* 2 ARCHAIC. likely. 3 DIALECT. about: *He seemed like to choke.*

—adv. 1 INFORMAL. probably: *Like enough it will rain.* 2 DIALECT. to a certain extent or degree; somewhat.

—n. 1 person or thing like another; match; counterpart or equal: *We shall not see his like again.* 2 **and the like, a** and so forth. **b** and other like things.

—conj. INFORMAL. 1 as if: *He acted like he was afraid.* 2 in the same way as; as.

[Old English *(ge)līc*]

➤ **like, as.** In written English *as* and *as if* are used to introduce clauses of comparison: *He writes as he used to when he was a child. Act as if you were accustomed to being here.* In spoken or informal English *like* is often used instead of *as* and *as if: He writes like he used to. Act like you know what you are doing.* Although historically both *like* and *as* are justified, custom has made *as* the preferred form in introducing clauses in written English.

like[2] (līk), *v.,* **liked, lik ing,** *n.* *—v.t.* 1 be pleased with; be satisfied with; enjoy: *My cat likes milk.* 2 regard with favor; have a kindly or friendly feeling for: *to like a person.* 3 wish for; wish to have: *I'd like more time to finish this.* *—v.i.* feel inclined; wish: *Come whenever you like.* *—n.* **likes,** *pl.* likings; preferences: *Mother knows all my likes and dislikes.* [Old English *līcian* please]

-like, *suffix added to nouns to form adjectives.* 1 like: *Wolflike = like a wolf.* 2 like that of; characteristic of: *Childlike = like that of a child.* 3 suited to; fit or proper for: *Businesslike = suited to business.* [< *like*[1]]

like a ble (lī′kə bəl), *adj.* likable. **—like′able ness,** *n.*

like li hood (līk′lē hůd), *n.* probability: *Is there any great likelihood of rain today?*

like ly (līk′lē), *adj.,* **-li er, -li est,** *adv.* *—adj.* 1 probable: *One likely result of this heavy rain is the rising of the river.* 2 to be expected: *It is likely to be hot in August.* See synonym study below. 3 appearing to be true; believable: *a likely story.* 4 suitable: *Is this a likely place to fish?* 5 promising: *a likely boy.* *—adv.* probably: *I shall very likely be at home all day.*

Syn. *adj.* 1,2 **Likely, apt, liable** indicate possibility but not in the same way. *Likely* implies probability: *It is likely to rain tonight. Apt* implies natural or habitual tendency: *Children are apt to be noisy at play. Liable* implies risk or danger: *Because he doesn't study, he is liable to fail.*

like-mind ed (līk′mīn′did), *adj.* 1 in agreement or accord. 2 that thinks along the same lines.

lik en (lī′kən), *v.t.* represent as like; compare.

like ness (līk′nis), *n.* 1 quality or fact of being like; resemblance: *a boy's likeness to his father.* 2 something that is like; copy; picture: *have one's likeness painted.* 3 appearance; shape: *assume the likeness of a swan.*

like wise (līk′wīz′), *adv.* 1 the same: *Watch what I do. Now you do likewise.* 2 as well; also; moreover; too: *I must go home now, and she likewise.*

lik ing (lī′king), *n.* 1 kindly feeling; preference; fondness: *a liking for apples, a liking for children.* 2 taste; pleasure: *food to your liking.*

li lac (lī′lək, lī′lak), *n.* 1 any of a genus of shrubs or small trees of the olive family, especially a common garden plant with clusters of tiny, fragrant, pale pinkish-purple or white blossoms. 2 a cluster of these blossoms. 3 a pale pinkish purple. *—adj.* pale pinkish-purple. [< obsolete French < Spanish < Arabic *līlak* < Persian *nīlak* < *nīl* indigo < Sanskrit *nīla* dark blue]

lil i a ceous (lil′ē ā′shəs), *adj.* 1 of or characteristic of lilies. 2 belonging to the lily family.

Lille (lēl), *n.* city in N France. 191,000.

Lil li put (lil′ə put), *n.* an imaginary island in Swift's *Gulliver's Travels.* Its tiny people are represented as being about six inches tall.

Lil li pu tian (lil′ə pyü′shən), *adj.* 1 of or suitable for Lilliput or its inhabitants. 2 very small; tiny; petty. *—n.* 1 inhabitant of Lilliput. 2 a very small person.

lilt (lilt), *v.i.* sing or play (a tune) in a light, tripping manner. *—v.i.* 1 sing or play in a light, tripping manner. 2 move in a light, springing manner. *—n.* 1 a lively song or tune with a swing. 2 a rhythmical cadence or swing. 3 a lively, springing movement. [Middle English *lilten*] **—lilt′ing ly,** *adv.*

lil y (lil′ē), *n., pl.* **lil ies,** *adj.* *—n.* 1 any of a genus of plants of the lily family that grow from a bulb. Lilies have tall, slender stems and large, showy, usually bell-shaped flowers, often divided into six parts. 2 the flower of any of these plants. The white lily is a symbol of purity. 3 any of various other plants of the lily family or similar plants of other families, such as the calla lily or water lily. 4 (in heraldry) the fleur-de-lis. 5 **gild the lily,** ornament or overstate something that is already good or pleasing. *—adj.* like a white lily; pure and lovely. [Old English *lilie* < Latin *lilium*] **—lil′y like′,** *adj.*

lily family, group of monocotyledonous herbs, shrubs, and trees that usually have flowers with six parts, grow from fleshy rhizomes or bulbs, and have stemless leaves, including the lily, tulip, hyacinth, and asparagus.

lil y-liv ered (lil′ē liv′ərd), *adj.* cowardly.

lily of the valley, *pl.* **lilies of the valley.** 1 a low, perennial herb of the lily family, having tiny, fragrant, bell-shaped, white flowers arranged up and down a single flower stem. 2 its flowers.

lily pad, the broad, flat floating leaf of a water lily.

lil y-white (lil′ē hwīt′), *adj.* 1 clean; free of stigma. 2 white as a lily. 3 U.S. excluding or seeking to exclude Negroes: *a lily-white country club.*

Li ma (lē′mə), *n.* capital of Peru, in the W part. 1,884,000.

li ma bean (lī′mə), 1 a broad, flat, pale-green bean, used as a vegetable. 2 the plant it grows on. [< *Lima*]

limb[1] (lim), *n.* 1 leg, arm, wing, or other member of an animal body distinct from the head or trunk. 2 a large or main branch of a tree. See **branch** for synonym study. 3 part that projects: *the four limbs of a cross.* 4 person or thing thought of as a branch or offshoot: *The housing committee is a limb of the city council.* 5 **limb from limb,** completely apart; entirely to pieces. 6 **out on a limb,** in a dangerous or vulnerable position. *—v.t.* pull limb from limb; dismember. [Old English *lim*]

limb[2] (lim), *n.* 1 the graduated edge of a quadrant or similar instrument. 2 the edge of the disk of a heavenly body. [< Latin *limbus* border, edge]

lim ber[1] (lim′bər), *adj.* bending or moving easily; flexible; supple: *A piano player should have limber fingers.* See **flexible** for synonym study. *—v.t.* make limber. *—v.i.* become limber: *He is stiff when he begins to skate, but limbers up quickly.* [perhaps < *limb*[1]] **—lim′ber ly,** *adv.* **—lim′berness,** *n.*

lim ber[2] (lim′bər), *n.* the detachable front part of the carriage of a field gun. [Middle English *lymor*]

limb less (lim′lis), *adj.* having no limbs.

lim bo (lim′bō), *n.* 1 Often, **Limbo.** (in Roman Catholic theology) a place for those who have not received the grace of Christ while living, and yet have not deserved the punishment of willful and impenitent sinners. 2 place for persons and things forgotten, cast aside, or out of date: *The belief that the earth is flat belongs to the limbo of outworn ideas.* 3 prison; jail; confinement. [< Latin *(in) limbo* (on) the edge]

Lim burg er (lim′bėr′gər), *n.* a soft white cheese with a strong smell. [< *Limburg,* province in Belgium]

lime[1] (līm), *n., v.,* **limed, lim ing.** —*n.* 1 a solid, white compound of calcium and oxygen obtained by burning limestone, shells, bones, or other forms of calcium carbonate; calcium oxide; quicklime. Lime is used in making mortar and on fields to improve the soil. *Formula:* CaO 2 any of various other compounds containing calcium. 3 birdlime. —*v.t.* treat with lime; put lime on. [Old English *līm*]

lime[2] (līm), *n.* 1 a juicy, greenish-yellow citrus fruit which is smaller and sourer than a lemon. Its juice is used for flavoring and as a source of vitamin C. 2 the small tropical tree it grows on. [< French < Spanish *lima* < Arabic *līmah*]

lime[3] (līm), *n.* the linden tree of Europe. [earlier *line,* Old English *lind*]

lime ade (līm′ād′, līm′ād′), *n.* drink made of lime juice, sugar, and water.

lime kiln (līm′kil′, līm′kiln′), *n.* furnace or kiln for making lime by burning limestone, shells, bones, etc.

lime light (līm′līt′), *n.* 1 an intense white light produced by heating a piece of lime in a flame, formerly used in a theater to light up certain persons or objects on the stage and draw attention to them. 2 fixture that produced this light. 3 center of public attention and interest.

lim er ick (lim′ər ik), *n.* a form of humorous nonsense verse of five lines. EXAMPLE:

"There was a young lady from Lynn
Who was so exceedingly thin
That when she essayed
To drink lemonade
She slid down the straw and fell in."

[apparently < a song about the county or city of *Limerick*]

Lim er ick (lim′ər ik), *n.* 1 county in SW Republic of Ireland. 2 seaport city in this county. 56,000.

lime stone (līm′stōn′), *n.* rock consisting mostly of calcium carbonate, much used for building. Limestone yields lime when heated. Marble is a kind of limestone.

lime wa ter (līm′wô′tər, līm′wot′ər), *n.* solution of slaked lime in water, used as an antacid.

lim ey (lī′mē), *n., pl.* **-eys.** SLANG. any Englishman, especially a sailor or soldier. [< the use of *lime juice* on British vessels to control scurvy]

lim it (lim′it), *n.* 1 farthest edge or boundary; point where something ends or must end: *the limit of one's vision, the limit of a person's authority.* 2 **limits,** *pl.* boundary; bounds: *Keep within the limits of the school grounds.* 3 (in mathematics) a value toward which terms of a sequence or values of a function approach indefinitely near. 4 an established maximum amount: *catch the legal limit of five fish per day.* 5 **the limit,** SLANG. as much as, or more than, one can stand. —*v.t.* set a limit to; restrict: *limit the expense to $10.* [< Latin *limitem* boundary] **—lim′it a ble,** *adj.* **—lim′it er,** *n.*

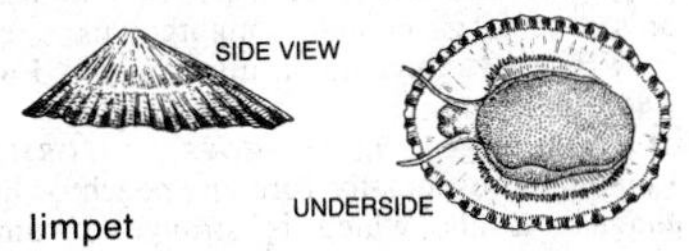

limpet

lim i ta tion (lim′ə tā′shən), *n.* 1 a limiting. 2 limited condition. 3 thing that limits; limiting rule or circumstance; restriction.

lim i ta tive (lim′ə tā′tiv), *adj.* tending to limit; limiting; restrictive.

lim it ed (lim′ə tid), *adj.* 1 kept within limits; restricted. 2 traveling fast and making only a few stops: *a limited train.* —*n.* train, bus, etc., that travels fast and makes only a few stops. **—lim′it ed ly,** *adv.* **—lim′it ed ness,** *n.*

limited monarchy, monarchy in which the ruler's powers are limited by the laws of the nation.

limited war, war confined to a limited area, usually of strategic importance.

lim it ing (lim′ə ting), *adj.* 1 that limits. 2 (of an adjective, etc.) serving to restrict the meaning of the word modified.

lim it less (lim′it lis), *adj.* without limits; boundless; infinite. **—lim′it less ly,** *adv.* **—lim′it less ness,** *n.*

limn (lim), *v.t.* 1 paint (a picture or portrait). 2 portray or depict (a subject) in a painting, drawing, etc. 3 portray in words; describe. [Middle English *lymnen,* variant of *luminen* < Old French *luminer* < Latin *luminare* light up, make bright] **—lim′ner,** *n.*

lim no log i cal (lim′nə loj′ə kəl), *adj.* of or having to do with limnology.

lim nol o gist (lim nol′ə jist), *n.* an expert in limnology.

lim nol o gy (lim nol′ə jē), *n.* the scientific study of inland bodies of fresh water, such as lakes and ponds. [< Greek *limnē* lake + English *-logy*]

Li moges (li mōzh′), *n.* 1 city in central France. 133,000. 2 porcelain made at Limoges.

li mo nite (lī′mə nīt), *n.* mineral, a hydrated ferric oxide, found in lakes and marshes. [< German *Limonit* < Greek *leimōn* meadow]

lim ou sine (lim′ə zēn′, lim′ə zēn′), *n.* a usually closed automobile, seating from three to five passengers, with a driver's seat separated from the passengers by a partition. [< French < *Limousin,* former French province]

limp[1] (limp), *n.* a lame step or walk. —*v.i.* 1 walk with a limp. 2 proceed slowly and with difficulty: *The plane limped toward the airfield.* [perhaps related to Old English *lempheali* lame] **—limp′er,** *n.*

limp[2] (limp), *adj.* 1 lacking stiffness; ready to bend or droop: *limp flowers, a limp body.* See synonym study below. 2 lacking firmness, force, energy, etc. [perhaps related to *limp*[1]] **—limp′ly,** *adv.* **—limp′ness,** *n.*

Syn. 1 **Limp, flabby** mean lacking firmness. **Limp** suggests drooping or hanging loosely: *My clothes hung limp in the humid weather.* **Flabby** suggests being soft and weak, flapping or shaking easily: *She is so fat her flesh is flabby.*

lim pet (lim′pit), *n.* a small marine mollusk of the same class as snails, with a conical shell that clings to rocks, etc. Limpets are used for bait and sometimes for food. [Old English *lempedu* < Medieval Latin *lampreda* lamprey. Doublet of LAMPREY.]

hat, āge, fär; let, ēqual, tėrm;
it, īce; hot, ōpen, ôrder;
oil, out; cup, pu̇t, rüle;
ch, child; ng, long; sh, she;
th, thin; ᴛʜ, then; zh, measure;

ə represents *a* in about, *e* in taken, *i* in pencil, *o* in lemon, *u* in circus.

< = from, derived from, taken from.

lim pid (lim′pid), *adj.* 1 clear or transparent: *limpid water, limpid eyes.* 2 free from obscurity; lucid. [< Latin *limpidus,* related to *lympha* clear water] **—lim′pid ly,** *adv.* **—lim′pid ness,** *n.*

lim pid i ty (lim pid′ə tē), *n.* limpid quality or condition.

Lim po po River (lim pō′pō), river in SE Africa. 1000 mi.

lim y (lī′mē), *adj.,* **lim i er, lim i est.** 1 of, containing, or resembling lime. 2 smeared with birdlime.

lin., 1 lineal. 2 linear.

lin age (lī′nij), *n.* 1 alignment. 2 quantity of printed or written matter estimated in number of lines. 3 the charge or rate of charge for a line. Also, **lineage.**

linch pin (linch′pin′), *n.* pin inserted through a hole in the end of an axle to keep the wheel on. [< *linch-* (Old English *lynis* linchpin) + *pin*]

Lin coln (ling′kən), *n.* 1 **Abraham,** 1809-1865, the 16th president of the United States, from 1861 to 1865. 2 capital of Nebraska, in the SE part. 150,000. 3 city in E England. 75,000. 4 Lincolnshire.

Lin coln esque (ling′kə nesk′), *adj.* characteristic of Abraham Lincoln.

Lincoln's Birthday, February 12, the anniversary of Abraham Lincoln's birthday, a legal holiday in some states of the United States.

Lin coln shire (ling′kən shər, ling′kən-shir), *n.* county in E England.

Lind (lind), *n.* **Jenny,** 1820-1887, Swedish soprano. She was called "the Swedish Nightingale."

lin dane (lin′dān), *n.* a benzene compound used as an insecticide. *Formula:* $C_6H_6Cl_6$

Lind bergh (lind′bėrg′), *n.* **Charles Augustus,** born 1902, American aviator who made the first solo flight across the Atlantic, in 1927.

lin den (lin′dən), *n.* 1 any of a genus of shade trees with heart-shaped leaves and clusters of small, fragrant, yellowish flowers. 2 the light, white wood of any of these trees. 3 basswood. [Old English, of linden wood]

Lind say (lind′zē), *n.* **Vachel,** 1879-1931, American poet.

line[1] (līn), *n., v.,* **lined, lin ing.** —*n.* 1 piece of rope, cord, string, thread, or wire: *hang washing on a line. An angler fishes with a hook and line.* 2 cord for measuring, making level or straight, etc. 3 a long narrow mark: *Draw two lines along the margin.* 4 anything like such a mark: *the lines in your face.* 5 a straight line. 6 **the line,** the equator. 7 circle of the terrestrial or celestial sphere: *the equinoctial line.* 8 (in mathematics) the path traced by a moving point. It has length, but no thickness. 9 the use of lines in drawing: *clearness of line in an artist's work.* 10 **lines,** *pl.* **a** outline; contour: *a ship of fine lines.* **b** plan of construction: *two books written along the same lines.* 11 edge or boundary: *the line between Texas and Mexico.* 12 row of persons or things: *a line of trees.* 13 row of words on a page or in a column: *a column of 40 lines.* 14 a short letter; note: *Drop me a line.* 15 a connected set or series of persons or things following one another in time: *The Stuarts were a line of English kings.* 16 family or lineage: *of noble line.* 17 course, track, or direction: *the line of march of an army.* 18 a course of action, conduct, or thought: *a line of policy, the Communist Party line.* 19 (in warfare) a front row of trenches or other defenses: *a line extending along a five-mile front.* 20 **lines,** *pl.* **a** double row (front and rear rank) of soldiers. **b** troops or ships arranged abreast. 21 the arrangement of an army or fleet for battle. 22 **the line, a** the regular army or navy; the soldiers or ships that do all the fighting. **b** the group of officers in charge of such forces. 23 wires connecting points or stations in a telegraph system, telephone system, radar warning operation, or the like. 24 the system itself. 25 pipe, hose, or other tube running from one point to another: *a steam line.* 26 a single track of railroad. 27 one branch of a system of transportation: *the main line of a railroad.* 28 a whole system of transportation or conveyance: *the municipal bus line.* 29 branch of business; kind of activity: *the dry-goods line.* 30 kind or branch of goods: *a good line of hardware.* 31 the portion of a metrical composition which is usually written in one line; verse. 32 **lines,** *pl.* **a** poetry; verses. **b** words that an actor speaks in a play: *forget one's lines.* 33 talk, usually intended to deceive or confuse: *The burglar tried to hand the police a line.* 34 (in music) one of the horizontal lines that make a staff. 35 in football: **a** line of scrimmage. **b** the players along the line of scrimmage at the start of a play. 36 (in bowling) a complete game of ten frames. 37 (in television) a single scanning line. 38 **lines,** *pl.* **a** one's fate; one's lot in life. **b** U.S. reins. **c** INFORMAL. a marriage certificate.

all along the line, at every point; everywhere.

bring into line, cause to agree or conform.

come into line, agree; conform.

down the line, the whole way; as far as possible; to the end.

draw a line or **draw the line,** set a limit.

get a line on or **have a line on,** INFORMAL. get or have information about.

in line, a in alignment. **b** in agreement. **c** ready: *in line for action.*

on a line, even; level.

on the line, in between; neither one thing nor the other.

out of line, in disagreement.

read between the lines, get more from the words than they say; find a hidden meaning.

toe the line, conform to a certain standard of duty, conduct, etc.

—*v.t.* 1 mark with lines on paper, etc. 2 cover with lines: *a face lined with age.* 3 arrange in line; bring into a line or row; align. 4 arrange a line along; form a line along: *Cars lined the road for a mile.* 5 measure or test with a line. 6 (in baseball) hit (a line drive). —*v.i.* 1 form a line; take a position in a line; range. 2 (in baseball) line out.

line out, a (in baseball) hit a line drive which is caught. **b** draw a line or lines to indicate an outline.

line up, a form a line; form into a line: *The horses lined up for the start of the race.* **b** make available or accessible.

[fusion of Old English *līne* line, rope, and Old French *ligne* line, both ultimately < Latin *linea* line, linen thread < *linum* flax]

line[2] (līn), *v.*, **lined, lin ing.** 1 put a layer inside of; cover the inner side of with something: *line a coat with sheepskin.* 2 fill: *line one's pockets with money.* 3 serve as a lining for. [Old English *līn* flax, linen thread or cloth < Latin *linum*]

lin e age (lin′ē ij), *n.* 1 descent in a direct line from a common ancestor. 2 the descendants of a common ancestor. 3 family or race. 4 linage.

lin e al (lin′ē əl), *adj.* 1 in the direct line of descent: *A grandson is a lineal descendant of his grandfather.* 2 having to do with such descent; hereditary. 3 linear. **—lin′e al ly,** *adv.*

lin e a ment (lin′ē ə mənt), *n.* part or feature, especially a part or feature of a face with attention to its outline.

lin e ar (lin′ē ər), *adj.* 1 of, in, or like a line, especially a straight line. 2 made of lines; making use of lines. 3 of length. 4 long and narrow, as a leaf. **—lin′e ar ly,** *adv.*

linear accelerator, device for accelerating charged particles in a straight line through a vacuum tube or series of tubes by means of alternating negative and positive impulses from electric fields.

linear equation, (in mathematics) an equation whose terms involving variables are of the first degree.

lin e ar i ty (lin′ē ar′ə tē), *n.* linear state or form.

linear measure, 1 measure of length. 2 system of units, such as foot and mile, used for measuring length. See **measure** for table.

linear programming, method of solving operational problems by stating a number of variables simultaneously in the form of linear equations and calculating the optimal solution within the given limitations.

line back er (līn′bak′ər), *n.* (in football) a defensive player whose position is directly behind the line.

line-breed (līn′brēd′), *v.i., v.t.,* **-bred** (-bred), **-breed ing.** breed within one line or strain of stock in order to develop certain favorable characteristics.

line drawing, drawing done completely in lines, including the shading, often made especially to be engraved.

line drive, baseball hit so that it goes in almost a straight line, usually close to the ground; liner.

line graph, graph in which points representing quantities are plotted and then connected by a series of short straight lines.

line man (līn′mən), *n., pl.* **-men.** 1 man who sets up or repairs telegraph, telephone, or electric wires; linesman. 2 (in football) a player in the line; a center, guard, tackle, or end. 3 man who inspects railroad tracks. 4 man who carries the line in surveying.

lin en (lin′ən), *n.* 1 cloth, thread, or yarn woven from flax. 2 household articles or clothing made of linen or some substitute. 3 linen paper. —*adj.* made of linen. [Old English *līnen* of flax < *līn* flax]

linen paper, writing paper of very fine quality. It was formerly made from linen rags.

line of battle, soldiers or ships in battle formation.

line of duty, performance of duty or service, especially military duty.

line of fire, path of a bullet, shell, etc.

line of force, line in a field of electrical or magnetic force that indicates the direction in which the force is acting.

line of scrimmage, (in football) an imaginary line running across the field at any point where the ball is placed; scrimmage line.

line of sight, 1 the straight line from the eye to the object it is looking at, such as a target in shooting or bombing. 2 the straight line of the beam from a radar antenna. **—line′-of-sight′,** *adj.*

lin er[1] (lī′nər), *n.* 1 ship or airplane belonging to a transportation system. 2 one who makes or draws lines. 3 instrument, tool, or device that makes lines or stripes. 4 line drive. [< *line*[1]]

lin er[2] (lī′nər), *n.* 1 person who lines or fits a lining to anything. 2 something that serves as a lining. 3 a short passage usually on the cover of a phonograph record giving information about the record. [< *line*[2]]

line segment, any finite section between two points on a line; segment.

lines man (līnz′mən), *n., pl.* **-men.** 1 lineman. 2 (in sports) an official who watches the lines that mark out the court, rink, field, etc., and assists the umpire or referee.

line-up or **line up** (līn′up′), *n.* 1 formation of persons or things into a line. 2 in sports: **a** a list of the players who will take part or are taking part in a game. **b** the players themselves. 3 any alignment of persons or groups for a common purpose.

ling (ling), *n., pl.* **ling** or **lings.** any of various food fishes of the North Atlantic of the same family as the cod. [Middle English *lenge*]

-ling, *suffix forming nouns.* 1 little; unimportant: *Duckling = a little duck.* 2 one that is: *Underling = one that is under.* 3 one belonging to or concerned with: *Earthling = one belonging to the earth.* [Old English]

lin ger (ling′gər), *v.i.* 1 stay on; go slowly, as if unwilling to leave. See synonym study below. 2 be slow to pass away or disappear: *Daylight lingers long in the summertime.* 3 be slow or late in doing or beginning anything; delay; dawdle. [Middle English *lengeren,* frequentative of *lengen* to delay, Old English *lengan* < *lang* long] **—lin′ger er,** *n.* **—lin′ger ing ly,** *adv.*

Syn. 1 **Linger, loiter, lag** mean to delay in starting or along the way. **Linger** emphasizes delay in starting, and suggests reluctance to leave: *She lingered long after the others had left.* **Loiter** emphasizes delaying along the way, and suggests moving slowly and aimlessly: *She loitered downtown, looking into all the shop windows.* **Lag** emphasizes falling behind others and suggests failing to keep up the necessary speed or pace: *The child lagged because he was tired.*

lin ge rie (lan′zhə rē′, län′zhə rā′), *n.* women's undergarments, nightgowns, etc. [< French < *linge* linen, ultimately < Latin *linum* flax]

lin go (ling′gō), *n., pl.* **-goes.** INFORMAL. 1 language, especially foreign speech or language. 2 talk which is strange or unintelligible. 3 language of a special trade, field of knowledge, a particular class, etc.: *baseball lingo.* [< Provençal *lengo* < Latin *lingua* tongue]

lin gua fran ca (ling′gwə frang′kə), *pl.* **lin gua fran cas.** 1 a hybrid language, consisting of Italian mixed with French, Spanish, Greek, Arabic, and Turkish, used especially by traders in the eastern Mediterranean. 2 any language, especially a hybrid language, used as a trade or communication medium by people speaking different languages. [< Italian, literally, Frankish language]

lin gual (ling′gwəl), *adj.* 1 of or having to do with the tongue. 2 (in phonetics) formed with the aid of the tongue, particularly the tip. *D* and *t* are lingual sounds. —*n.* (in phonetics) a lingual sound. [< Medieval Latin *lingualis* < Latin *lingua* tongue]

lin guist (ling′gwist), *n.* 1 an expert in languages or linguistics. 2 person skilled in a number of languages.

lin guis tic (ling gwis′tik), *adj.* having to do with language or linguistics. —**lin guis′ti cal ly,** *adv.*

lin guis tics (ling gwis′tiks), *n.* the science of language, including the study of speech sounds, language structures, and the history and historical relationship of languages and linguistic forms.

lin i ment (lin′ə mənt), *n.* a soothing liquid which is rubbed on the skin to relieve the pain of sore muscles, sprains, and bruises, or to act as a counterirritant. [< Late Latin *linimentum* < Latin *linere* anoint]

lin ing (lī′ning), *n.* layer of material covering the inner surface of something: *the lining of a coat.*

link[1] (lingk), *n.* 1 any ring or loop of a chain. 2 anything that joins as a link joins. 3 part or parts so joined: *links of sausage.* 4 fact or thought that connects others: *a link in a chain of evidence.* 5 the hundredth part of a surveyor's chain, equal to 7.92 inches. 6 rod, bar, or similar piece connected at its ends to two parts of a machine and transmitting motion from one to the other. 7 cuff link. 8 (in chemistry) a bond. —*v.t., v.i.* join as a link does; unite or connect: *link arms.* [apparently < Scandinavian (Swedish) *länk*]

link[2] (lingk), *n.* torch, especially one made of tow and pitch, formerly used to light people's way along the streets. [origin uncertain]

link age (ling′kij), *n.* 1 a linking. 2 a being linked. 3 arrangement or system of links. 4 (in biology) the association of two or more genes or their characteristics on the same chromosome so that they are transmitted together. 5 any of various devices consisting of a number of bars linked or pivoted together, used to produce a desired motion in a machine part, for tracing lines, etc.

linking verb, verb with little or no meaning of its own, used to connect a subject with a predicate adjective or predicate noun; copula. ➤ See **copula** for usage note.

links (lingks), *n., pl. in form, sing. or pl. in use.* a golf course. [Old English *hlinc* rising ground]

link-up (lingk′up′), *n.* connection; affiliation; tie.

Lin nae an (lə nē′ən), *adj.* Linnean.

Lin nae us (lə nē′əs), *n.* **Carolus,** 1707-1778, Swedish naturalist who established the binomial system of classifying animals and plants.

Lin ne an (lə nē′ən), *adj.* of or having to do with Linnaeus or his system of classification. Also, **Linnaean.**

lin net (lin′it), *n.* a small finch of Europe, Asia, and Africa, having brown or gray plumage, the color changing at different ages and seasons. [< Middle French *linette*]

lin o le ic acid (lin′ə lē′ik, lə nō′lē ik), an unsaturated fatty acid essential to the human diet, found as a glyceride in linseed and other oils, and used as a drying agent in paint and varnish. *Formula:* $C_{18}H_{32}O_2$

li no le um (lə nō′lē əm), *n.* 1 a floor covering made by putting a hard surface of ground cork mixed with oxidized linseed oil on a canvas or burlap back. 2 any similar floor covering. [< Latin *linum* flax + *oleum* oil]

Li no type (lī′nə tīp), *n.* trademark for a typesetting machine that is operated by a keyboard and that casts each line of type in one piece.

lin seed (lin′sēd′), *n.* flaxseed. [Old English *līnsǣd*]

linseed oil, a yellowish oil obtained by pressing flaxseed, used in making paints, printing inks, and linoleum.

lin sey-wool sey (lin′zē wu̇l′zē), *n., pl.* **-wool seys.** a strong, coarse fabric made of linen and wool or of cotton and wool.

lint (lint), *n.* 1 the soft down or fleecy material obtained by scraping linen. Lint was formerly much used as a dressing for wounds. 2 tiny bits of thread or fluff of any material. 3 raw cotton that has been ginned and is ready for baling. [Middle English]

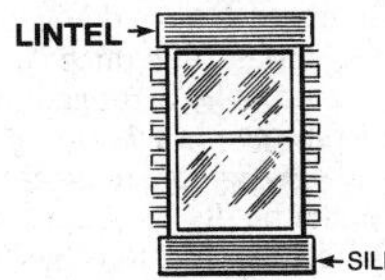

lin tel (lin′tl), *n.* a horizontal beam or stone over a door, window, etc., to support the structure above it. [< Old French, threshold, ultimately < Latin *limitem* limit]

lint er (lin′tər), *n.* U.S. 1 machine for stripping off the short cotton fibers remaining on the cottonseed after ginning. 2 **linters,** *pl.* the cotton fibers so removed.

lint y (lin′tē), *adj.,* **lint i er, lint i est.** 1 full of or marked with lint. 2 like lint.

lion (def. 1)—a pair of lions; about 3 ft. high at the shoulder; male lion above, lioness below

li on (lī′ən), *n.* 1 a large, strong, tawny, mammal of the cat family, found in Africa and southern Asia, belonging to the same genus as the tiger, jaguar, and leopard. The male has a full, flowing mane of coarse hair. 2 any of various related animals, especially the puma. 3 a very brave or strong person. 4 a famous or important person. 5 **Lion,** Leo. [< Old French < Latin *leonem* < Greek *leōn*] —**li′on like′,** *adj.*

hat, āge, fär; let, ēqual, tėrm;
it, īce; hot, ōpen, ôrder;
oil, out; cup, pu̇t, rüle;
ch, child; ng, long; sh, she;
th, thin; ᴛʜ, then; zh, measure;

ə represents *a* in about, *e* in taken, *i* in pencil, *o* in lemon, *u* in circus.

< = from, derived from, taken from.

li on ess (lī′ə nis), *n.* a female lion.

li on heart ed (lī′ən här′tid), *adj.* brave; courageous.

li on ize (lī′ə nīz), *v.t.,* **-ized, -iz ing.** treat (a person) as very important. —**li′on i za′tion,** *n.*

lion's share, the biggest or best part.

lip (lip), *n., adj., v.,* **lipped, lip ping.** —*n.* 1 either of the two fleshy movable edges of the mouth. 2 **lips,** *pl.* mouth. 3 a folding or bent-out edge of any opening: *the lip of a bell, the lip of a pitcher, the lip of a crater, one of the lips of a wound.* 4 in music: **a** the mouthpiece of a musical instrument. **b** the manner of shaping the mouth to play a wind instrument; embouchure. **c** the edges above and below the mouth of a flue pipe of an organ. 5 SLANG. impudent talk. 6 in botany: **a** either of the two parts (upper and lower) into which the corolla or calyx of certain plants is divided. **b** (in an orchid) the labellum. 7 (in zoology) a labium. 8 **hang on the lips of,** listen to with great attention or admiration. 9 **keep a stiff upper lip,** be brave or firm; show no fear or discouragement.
—*adj.* 1 not heartfelt or deep, but just on the surface; insincere: *lip worship.* 2 of a lip or lips. 3 (in phonetics) formed or produced by the lips; labial.
—*v.t.* 1 touch with the lips. 2 pronounce with the lips only; murmur softly. 3 kiss.
—*v.i.* use the lips in playing a wind instrument.
[Old English *lippa*] —**lip′like′,** *adj.*

li pase (lī′pās, lip′ās), *n.* any of a class of enzymes occurring in pancreatic and gastric juices, certain seeds, etc., that can change fats into fatty acids and glycerin. [< Greek *lipos* fat]

lip id (lip′id, lī′pid), *n.* any of a group of organic compounds including the fats, oils, waxes, and sterols. They are characterized by an oily feeling, solubility in fat solvents such as chloroform, benzene, or ether, and insolubility in water.

lip ide (lip′īd, lip′id; lī′pīd, lī′pid), *n.* lipid.

lip less (lip′lis), *adj.* having no lips.

lip oid (lip′oid, lī′poid), *adj.* like fat or oil. —*n.* any of a group of nitrogenous fatlike substances, as the lecithins.

lip o pro tein (lip′ə prō′tēn′, lip′ə prō′tē ən), *n.* any of a class of proteins, one of the components of which is a lipid.

Lip pi (lip′ē), *n.* **Fra Filippo,** 1406?-1469, Italian painter.

lip py (lip′ē), *adj.* SLANG. impertinent.

lip-read (lip′rēd′), *v.i., v.t.,* **-read** (-red′), **-read ing.** understand speech by watching the movements of the speaker's lips. —**lip′-read′er,** *n.*

lip reading, the understanding of speech by watching the movements of the speaker's lips.

lip service, service with the lip or words

only; insincere profession of devotion or good will.

lip stick (lip′stik′), *n.* a small stick of a waxlike cosmetic, used for coloring the lips.

liq., 1 liquid. 2 liquor.

liq ue fac tion (lik′wə fak′shən), *n.* 1 act or process of liquefying. 2 liquefied condition.

liq ue fy (lik′wə fī), *v.t., v.i.,* **-fied, -fy ing.** change into a liquid; make or become liquid: *Liquefied air is extremely cold.* **—liq′ue fi′a ble,** *adj.* **—liq′ue fi′er,** *n.*

li ques cence (li kwes′ns), *n.* liquescent condition.

li ques cent (li kwes′nt), *adj.* 1 becoming liquid. 2 apt to become liquid.

li queur (li kėr′, li kyůr′), *n.* a strong, sweet, highly flavored alcoholic liquor, often served after dinner. [< French < Latin *liquor* liquid. Doublet of LIQUOR.]

liq uid (lik′wid), *n.* 1 substance that is neither a solid nor a gas and flows like water; substance composed of molecules that move freely over each other so that a mass has the shape of its container, like a gas, but, unlike a gas, it seeks its own level. See synonym study below. 2 (in phonetics) the sound of *l* or *r.* —*adj.* 1 in the form of a liquid; melted: *liquid soap.* 2 flowing or capable of flowing like water. 3 clear and bright like water. 4 clear and smooth-flowing in sound: *the liquid notes of a bird.* 5 (in phonetics) having the nature of a liquid. 6 smooth and easy in movement; graceful. 7 capable of being easily converted into cash: *liquid assets.* [< Latin *liquidus* < *liquere* be fluid] **—liq′uid ly,** *adv.* **—liq′uid ness,** *n.*

Syn. *n.* 1 **Liquid, fluid** mean a substance that flows. **Liquid** applies only to a substance that is neither a solid nor a gas: *Milk and oil are liquids; oxygen is not a liquid.* **Fluid** applies to anything that flows in any way, either a liquid or a gas: *Milk, water, and oxygen are fluids.*

liquid air, an intensely cold liquid formed by putting air under very great pressure and then cooling it. It is used as a refrigerant.

liq ui date (lik′wə dāt), *v.,* **-dat ed, -dat ing.** —*v.t.* 1 clear off or pay (a debt or obligation): *liquidate a mortgage.* 2 settle the accounts of (a business, etc.) by distributing the assets; clear up the affairs of (a bankrupt). 3 get rid of (an undesirable person or thing). 4 kill ruthlessly; exterminate. —*v.i.* liquidate debts, etc. [< Medieval Latin *liquidatum* made clear < Latin *liquidus.* See LIQUID.] **—liq′ui da′tion,** *n.* **—liq′ui da′tor,** *n.*

li quid i ty (li kwid′ə tē), *n.* liquid condition or quality.

liquid measure, 1 measurement of liquids. 2 system of units, such as pint and gallon, used for measuring the volume of liquids. See **measure** for table.

liquid oxygen, an intensely cold, transparent liquid formed by putting oxygen under very great pressure and then cooling it; lox. It is used as a rocket fuel.

liq uor (lik′ər), *n.* 1 an alcoholic drink, especially brandy, gin, rum, and whiskey. 2 any liquid, especially a liquid in which food is packaged, canned, or cooked: *Pickles are put up in a salty liquor.* [< Latin < *liquere* be fluid. Doublet of LIQUEUR.]

liq uor ice (lik′ər is, lik′ər ish), *n.* licorice.

lir a (lir′ə), *n., pl.* **lir e** (lir′ā), **lir as.** 1 the monetary unit of Italy, a coin or note equal to 100 centesimi and worth about one-fifth of a cent. 2 the Turkish pound, a coin or note equal to 100 kurus and worth about 6⅔ cents. [< Italian < Latin *libra* pound]

Lis bon (liz′bən), *n.* capital of Portugal, in the SW part. 828,000.

lisle (līl), *n.* a fine, strong, twisted, linen or cotton thread, used for making stockings, gloves, shirts, etc. —*adj.* made of lisle. [< *Lisle,* former name of *Lille*]

lisp (lisp), *v.i.* 1 pronounce the sounds of *s* and *z* imperfectly as *th* in *thin* and *then: A person who lisps might say, "Thing a thong" for "Sing a song."* 2 speak imperfectly or by lisping. —*v.t.* say in a lisping manner. —*n.* 1 act or habit of lisping. 2 sound of lisping, or a sound resembling this. [Old English *-wlispian*] **—lisp′er,** *n.*

lis some or **lis som** (lis′əm), *adj.* 1 bending easily; limber; supple. 2 nimble, active. [variant of *lithesome*] **—lis′some ly,** *adv.* **—lis′some ness,** *n.*

list[1] (list), *n.* series of names, numbers, words, phrases, etc.: *a long list of figures, a shopping list.* See synonym study below. —*v.t.* 1 make a list of; enter in a list: *A dictionary lists words in alphabetical order.* 2 enter (a stock, etc.) on the list of those traded on a stock exchange. —*v.i.* be listed. [< French *liste* < Italian *lista;* of Germanic origin]

Syn. *n.* **List, catalog, roll** mean a series of names or items. **List** is the general word applying to a series of names, figures, etc., whether systematically arranged or not: *This is the list of the people who are going to the picnic.* **Catalog** applies to a complete list arranged alphabetically or according to some other system, often with short descriptions of the items: *Has the new mail-order catalog come?* **Roll** applies to a list of the names of all members of a group: *His name is on the honor roll.*

list[2] (list), *n.* 1 the woven edge of cloth, where the material is a little different; selvage. 2 any strip of fabric. 3 a narrow strip of wood cut from the edge of a plank. [Old English *līste* border]

list[3] (list), *n.* a tipping to one side; tilt: *the list of a ship.* —*v.i.* tip to one side; tilt. —*v.t.* cause a tipping or list in (a ship). [perhaps extended use of *list*[4] in sense of "being inclined to"]

list[4] (list), ARCHAIC. —*v.t.* be pleasing to; please. —*v.i.* like; wish. —*n.* desire; longing; inclination. [Old English *lystan* < *lust* pleasure]

list[5] (list), ARCHAIC. —*v.i.* listen. —*v.t.* listen to; hear. [Old English *hlystan.* Related to LISTEN.]

lis ten (lis′n), *v.i.* 1 try to hear; attend closely with the ears so as to hear: *listen to the radio.* See **hear** for synonym study. 2 give heed (to advice, temptation, etc.); pay attention. 3 **listen in,** a listen to others talking on a telephone. b listen to the radio. [Old English *hlysnan*] **—lis′ten er,** *n.*

list er (lis′tər), *n.* plow with a double moldboard that throws the dirt to both sides of the furrow. [< *list*[2]]

Lis ter (lis′tər), *n.* **Joseph,** 1827-1912, English surgeon. He was the first to use antiseptic methods in performing operations.

list less (list′lis), *adj.* seeming too tired to care about anything; not interested in things; not caring to be active; languid. [< *list*[4]] **—list′less ly,** *adv.* **—list′less ness,** *n.*

list price, price of an article published in a catalog, advertisement, or list. Discounts are figured from it.

lists (lists), *n.pl.* 1 place where knights fought in tournaments or tilts. 2 any place or scene of combat. 3 **enter the lists,** join in a contest; take part in a fight, argument, etc. [< *list*[2]]

Liszt (list), *n.* **Franz,** 1811-1886, Hungarian composer and pianist.

lit[1] (lit), *v.* a pt. and a pp. of **light**[1].

lit[2] (lit), *v.* a pt. and a pp. of **light**[3].

lit., 1 liter or liters. 2 literal. 3 literally. 4 literature.

lit a ny (lit′n ē), *n., pl.* **-nies.** 1 prayer consisting of a series of supplications said by the minister and responses said by the congregation. 2 a repeated series. [< Greek *litaneia* litany, entreaty < *litesthai* entreat]

li tchi (lē′chē), *n.* 1 the small nut-shaped fruit of a Chinese tree. It consists of a thin, brittle, rough red shell enclosing a sweet, white jellylike pulp which contains a single brown seed. 2 the tree it grows on. Also, **lichee.** [< Chinese]

Lit. D., Doctor of Letters; Doctor of Literature [for Latin *Literarum Doctor*].

-lite, *combining form.* stone; rock; mineral, as in *chrysolite.* [< French < Greek *lithos* stone]

li ter (lē′tər), *n.* the basic unit of volume in the metric system, equal to the volume of 1000 cubic centimeters. See **measure** for table. Also, BRITISH **litre.** [< French *litre* < Medieval Latin *litra* < Greek, pound]

lit er a cy (lit′ər ə sē), *n.* a being literate; ability to read and write.

lit er al (lit′ər əl), *adj.* 1 following the exact words of the original: *a literal translation.* 2 taking words in their usual meaning, without exaggeration or imagination; matter-of-fact: *the literal meaning of a phrase, a literal type of mind.* 3 true to fact: *a literal account.* 4 of the letters of the alphabet; expressed by letters. [< Late Latin *lit(t)eralis* < Latin *lit(t)era* letter] **—lit′er al ness,** *n.*

lit er al ism (lit′ər ə liz′əm), *n.* 1 a keeping to the literal meaning in translation or interpretation. 2 (in the fine arts) the faithful representation of things, without any idealization.

lit er al ist (lit′ər ə list), *n.* 1 person who adheres to the exact literal meaning. 2 person who represents or portrays without idealizing.

lit er al ly (lit′ər ə lē), *adv.* 1 word for word; without exaggeration or imagination: *translate literally.* 2 actually: *He is literally without fear.* 3 INFORMAL. in effect, though not actually; virtually: *The champion runner literally flew around the track.*

lit e rar y (lit′ə rer′ē), *adj.* 1 having to do with literature. 2 knowing much about literature. 3 engaged in literature as a profession.

lit er ate (lit′ər it), *adj.* 1 able to read and write. 2 acquainted with literature; educated. —*n.* 1 person who can read and write. 2 an educated person.

lit e ra ti (lit′ə rä′tē, lit′ə rā′tī), *n.pl.* men of letters; scholarly or literary people. [< Latin]

lit e ra tim (lit′ə rā′tim), *adv.* letter for letter; exactly as written. [< Medieval Latin < Latin *lit(t)era* letter]

lit er a ture (lit′ər ə chůr, lit′ər ə chər), *n.* 1 the body of writings of a period, language, or country, especially those kept alive by their beauty or effectiveness of style or thought: *English literature.* 2 all the books and articles on a subject: *the literature of stamp collecting.* 3 profession of a writer.

4 the study of literature: *I shall take literature and mathematics this spring.* 5 INFORMAL. printed matter of any kind: *election campaign literature.* [< French *littérature* < Latin *lit(t)eratura* writing < *lit(t)era* letter]

-lith, *combining form.* stone, as in *megalith, monolith.* [< Greek *lithos*]

lith arge (lith′ärj, li thärj′), *n.* a yellow or reddish oxide of lead, used in making glass, glazes for pottery, and driers for paints and varnish; lead monoxide. *Formula:* PbO [< Old French *litarge* < Greek *lithargyros* < *lithos* stone + *argyros* silver]

lithe (līᴛʜ), *adj.* bending easily; supple: *lithe of body, a lithe willow.* [Old English *līthe* mild] **—lithe′ly,** *adv.* **—lithe′ness,** *n.*

lithe some (līᴛʜ′səm), *adj.* lissome.

lith i a (lith′ē ə), *n.* a white oxide of lithium, soluble in water, and forming an acrid and caustic solution. *Formula:* Li_2O [< New Latin]

lith ic (lith′ik), *adj.* 1 of or having to do with stone. 2 of or having to do with lithium. [< Greek *lithos* stone]

lith i fi ca tion (lith′ə fə kā′shən), *n.* process by which rocks are formed from sediment.

lith i um (lith′ē əm), *n.* a soft, silver-white metallic element which occurs in small quantities in various minerals. Lithium is the lightest of all metals and is used in lubricants, ceramics, and chemical processes. *Symbol:* Li; *atomic number* 3. See pages 326 and 327 for table. [< New Latin < Greek *lithos* stone]

litho-, *combining form.* stone, as in *lithography, lithology.* [< Greek *lithos*]

lith o graph (lith′ə graf), *n.* print made by lithography. *—v.t.* print, reproduce, etc., by lithography.

litter (def. 7)

li thog ra pher (li thog′rə fər), *n.* person who makes lithographs.

lith o graph ic (lith′ə graf′ik), *adj.* 1 of a lithograph. 2 of or made by lithography. **—lith′o graph′i cal ly,** *adv.*

li thog ra phy (li thog′rə fē), *n.* art or process of printing from a smooth, flat stone or metal plate on which the picture, design, etc., is made with a greasy material that will hold printing ink, the rest of the surface being made ink-repellent with water.

lith o log ic (lith′ə loj′ik), *adj.* of or having to do with lithology.

li thol o gy (li thol′ə jē), *n.* science of rocks and their composition.

lith o pone (lith′ə pōn), *n.* a dry, white pigment used in paints, made from a mixture of zinc sulfide, barium sulfate, and zinc oxide. [< *litho-* + Greek *ponos* work]

lith o sphere (lith′ə sfir), *n.* the solid portion of the earth as opposed to the atmosphere and the hydrosphere; geosphere.

Lith u a ni a (lith′ü ā′nē ə, lith′ü ā′nyə), *n.* Lithuanian S.S.R. **—Lith′u a′ni an,** *adj., n.*

Lithuanian S.S.R. one of the constituent republics of the U.S.S.R. in the W part, on the Baltic Sea. 3,100,000 pop.; 25,200 sq. mi. *Capital:* Vilnius.

lit i ga ble (lit′ə gə bəl), *adj.* capable of being litigated.

lit i gant (lit′ə gənt), *n.* person engaged in a lawsuit.

lit i gate (lit′ə gāt), *v.,* **-gat ed, -gat ing.** *—v.i.* engage in a lawsuit. *—v.t.* contest in a lawsuit; make the subject of a lawsuit. [< Latin *litigatum* brought to law < *litem* lawsuit + *agere* to drive] **—lit′i ga′tor,** *n.*

lit i ga tion (lit′ə gā′shən), *n.* 1 a carrying on a lawsuit. 2 a going to law. 3 a lawsuit or legal proceeding.

li ti gious (lə tij′əs), *adj.* 1 having the habit of going to law. 2 that can be disputed in a court of law. 3 of or having to do with litigation.

lit mus (lit′məs), *n.* a blue dye obtained from lichens, used in litmus paper as a chemical indicator. [< Scandinavian (Old Icelandic) *litmosi* dyer's herbs < *litr* color + *mosi* moss]

litmus paper, paper treated with litmus. Blue litmus paper turns red when put into acid; red litmus paper turns blue when put into alkali.

li to tes (lī′tə tēz′, lit′ə tēz′), *n.* figure of speech that makes an assertion by denying its opposite. EXAMPLE: "This was no small storm" means that the storm was quite violent. [< Greek *litotēs* < *litos* small, plain, simple]

li tre (lē′tər), *n.* BRITISH. liter.

Litt. D., Doctor of Letters; Doctor of Literature [for Latin *Litterarum Doctor*].

lit ter (lit′ər), *n.* 1 things scattered about or left in disorder; scattered rubbish. 2 state of disorder or untidiness. 3 the whole number of young brought forth at one birth by an animal. 4 straw, hay, etc., used as bedding for animals, or for other purposes, as the protection of plants. 5 the surface layer of a forest floor, consisting of slightly decayed organic matter. 6 stretcher for carrying a sick, injured, or wounded person. 7 framework supported on long poles and carried on men's shoulders or by beasts of burden, with a couch usually enclosed by curtains. *—v.t.* 1 leave (odds and ends) lying around; scatter (things) about. 2 make disordered or untidy: *She littered her room with books and papers.* 3 give birth to (young animals). 4 make a bed for (an animal) with straw, hay, etc. [< Anglo-French *litere* < Medieval Latin *lectaria* < Latin *lectus* bed]

lit tér a teur or **lit ter a teur** (lit′ər-ə tėr′), *n.* a literary man; writer or critic of literature. [< French *littérateur*]

lit ter bug (lit′ər bug′), *n.* U.S. person who throws down trash along a highway, sidewalk, in a park, etc.

lit tle (lit′l), *adj.,* **less** or **less er, least;** or **lit tler, lit tlest;** *adv.,* **less, least,** *n.* *—adj.* 1 not great or big; of small size: *a little boy, a little bird.* See synonym study below. 2 short; brief: *Wait a little while.* 3 not much; small in number, amount, degree, or importance: *a little army, little money, little hope.* 4 mean; narrow-minded: *little thoughts.*

—adv. 1 in a small amount or degree; slightly: *a little known book.* 2 not at all: *He little knows what will happen.*

—n. 1 a small amount, quantity, or degree: *Add a little* 2 a short time or distance: *Move a little to the left.*

hat, āge, fär; let, ēqual, tėrm;
it, īce; hot, ōpen, ôrder;
oil, out; cup, pu̇t, rüle;
ch, child; ng, long; sh, she;
th, thin; ᴛʜ, then; zh, measure;
ə represents *a* in about, *e* in taken,
i in pencil, *o* in lemon, *u* in circus.
< = from, derived from, taken from.

in little, on a small scale; in miniature: *paint in little.*

little by little, by a small amount at a time; slowly; gradually.

make little of, treat or represent as of little importance: *They made little of the incident.*

not a little, much; very: *We were not a little upset by the news.*

think little of, a not value much; consider as unimportant or worthless. **b** not hesitate about.

[Old English *lȳtel*] **—lit′tle ness,** *n.*

Syn. *adj.* 1 **Little, small, diminutive** mean not big or large. **Little** sometimes suggests affection or sympathy for what it describes: *a cozy little cottage.* **Small,** often used interchangeably with *little,* means relatively not large or great, and often suggests being below average: *He is small for his age.* **Diminutive** means very small in size: *His feet are diminutive.*

Little America, camp near the South Pole established by Admiral Richard E. Byrd in 1929. See **Antarctica** for map.

Little Bear, Ursa Minor.

Little Dipper, group of seven bright stars in the constellation Ursa Minor shaped like a dipper with the North Star at the dipper's handle.

Little Rock, capital of Arkansas, in the central part. 132,000.

Little Russia, region in SW Soviet Union in Europe that includes the Ukrainian S.S.R. and adjoining regions.

little theater, a small theater that presents experimental or amateur plays.

lit tor al (lit′ər əl), *adj.* 1 of a shore. 2 on or near the shore. *—n.* region along the shore. [< Latin *litoralis* < *litus* shore]

li tur gic (lə tėr′jik), *adj.* liturgical.

li tur gi cal (lə tėr′jə kəl), *adj.* 1 of liturgies. 2 used in liturgies. 3 of or having to do with the Communion or Eucharistic service. **—li tur′gi cal ly,** *adv.*

lit ur gy (lit′ər jē), *n., pl.* **-gies.** 1 an appointed form for the rites and ceremonies of public worship, especially in the Christian church. 2 **the Liturgy** or **the liturgy, a** (in the Episcopal Church) the Book of Common Prayer. **b** (in the Eastern Church) the Eucharist. [< Greek *leitourgia* < *laos* people + *ergon* work]

liv a bil i ty (liv′ə bil′ə tē), *n.* 1 condition of being fit to live in; livable state. 2 ability to survive various conditions and diseases.

liv a ble (liv′ə bəl), *adj.* 1 fit to live in. 2 easy to live with. 3 worth living; endurable. Also, liveable. **—liv′a ble ness,** *n.*

live[1] (liv), *v.,* **lived** (livd), **liv ing.** *—v.i.* 1 have life; be alive; exist: *All creatures have a right to live.* 2 remain alive; continue in life: *live long.* 3 (of things) last; endure. 4 keep up life; maintain life; *live by one's wits.* 5 feed or subsist: *Lions live upon other animals.* 6 pass life in a particular manner:

live in peace, live extravagantly. 7 dwell; reside: *live in the country.* 8 have a rich and full life. —*v.t.* 1 pass (life): *live a life of ease.* 2 carry out or show in life: *live one's ideals.* 3 **live down,** live in such a manner that some fault or sin of the past is overlooked or forgotten. 4 **live out,** stay alive or hold out through; last through. 5 **live up to,** act according to; do (what is expected or promised). [Old English *lifian, libban*]

live² (līv), *adj.* 1 having life; alive; living: *live animals.* 2 burning or glowing: *live coals, a live quarrel.* 3 full of energy or activity: *a live person.* 4 up-to-date: *live ideas.* 5 U.S. of present interest or importance: *a live question.* 6 still in use or to be used; still having power: *live steam.* 7 being in play: *a live football.* 8 charged with or carrying an electric current: *The electrician checked to see whether the wire was live.* 9 loaded with explosives; not fired or exploded: *a live cartridge.* 10 lit: *a live cigar.* 11 not shown or aired on tape or film, but broadcast during the actual performance: *a live television show.* 12 made up of actual people: *a live audience.* 13 moving or imparting motion or power: *live wheels, a live axle.* 14 in the native or pure state; not mined or quarried: *live metal, live rocks.* 15 bright; vivid: *a live color.*
—*adv.* with the actual performance or event shown; as it takes place: *The game will be telecast live.*
[variant of *alive*] **—live′ness,** *n.*

live a ble (liv′ə bəl), *adj.* livable.

live li hood (līv′lē hůd), *n.* means of keeping alive; a living: *write for a livelihood.* See **living** for synonym study.

live long (liv′lông′, liv′long′), *adj.* whole length of; whole; entire: *She is busy the livelong day.*

live ly (līv′lē), *adj.,* **-li er, -li est,** *adv.* —*adj.* 1 full of life and spirit; active; vigorous. 2 exciting: *a lively time.* 3 bright; vivid: *lively colors.* 4 cheerful; gay: *a lively conversation.* 5 bouncing well and quickly: *a lively baseball.* —*adv.* in a lively manner. **—live′li ness,** *n.*

liv en (lī′vən), *v.t.* put life into; cheer up. —*v.i.* become more lively; brighten.

live oak (līv), 1 an evergreen oak of the southern United States. 2 its wood, formerly used in shipbuilding, etc. 3 any of various other evergreen oaks.

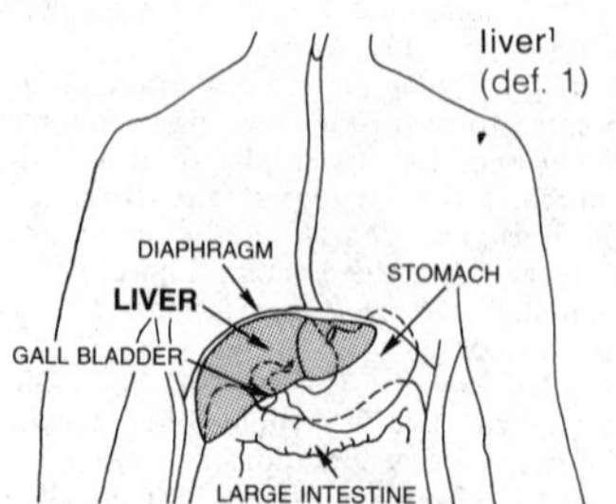

liv er¹ (liv′ər), *n.* 1 the large, reddish-brown organ in vertebrate animals that secretes bile and is active in the absorption and storage of vitamins, minerals, and sugar (which it changes into glycogen). The liver frees the blood of its waste matter and manufactures blood proteins. 2 a large gland in some invertebrates that secretes into the digestive tract. 3 the liver of an animal used as food. [Old English *lifer*]

liv er² (liv′ər), *n.* 1 person who lives a certain way: *an evil liver, long liver.* 2 inhabitant; dweller. [< *live¹*]

liver fluke, any of certain leaf-shaped flukes infesting the liver of various mammals.

liv er ied (liv′ər ēd), *adj.* clothed in livery.

liv er ish (liv′ər ish), *adj.* INFORMAL. having the symptoms of a disordered liver, especially a disagreeable disposition; testy; cross.

Liv er pool (liv′ər pül), *n.* seaport in W England. 667,000.

Liv er pud li an (liv′ər pud′lē ən), *adj.* of or belonging to Liverpool. —*n.* native or inhabitant of Liverpool.

liv er wort (liv′ər wėrt′), *n.* 1 any of a class of bryophytic plants related to and somewhat resembling the mosses, growing mostly on damp ground, the trunks of trees, etc. 2 hepatica.

liv er wurst (liv′ər wėrst′, liv′ər wůrst′), *n.* sausage consisting largely of liver. [< German *Leberwurst*]

liv er y (liv′ər ē), *n., pl.* **-er ies.** 1 any special uniform provided for the servants of a household, or adopted by any group or profession. 2 any characteristic dress, garb, or outward appearance. 3 the feeding, stabling, and care of horses for pay. 4 the hiring out of horses and carriages. 5 the keeping of cars, boats, bicycles, etc., for hire. 6 livery stable. [< Old French *livree* provisions dispensed to servants < *livrer* dispense < Latin *liberare* liberate]

liv er y man (liv′ər ē mən), *n., pl.* **-men.** person who works in or keeps a livery stable.

livery stable, stable where horses are cared for for pay or hired out.

lives (līvz), *n.* pl. of **life.**

live stock (līv′stok′), *n.* domestic animals kept or raised on a farm for use or profit, such as cattle, pigs, or sheep.

live wire (līv), 1 INFORMAL. an energetic, wide-awake person. 2 wire in which an electric current is flowing.

liv id (liv′id), *adj.* 1 having a dull-bluish or grayish color. 2 discolored by a bruise; black-and-blue. 3 very pale: *livid with rage.* [< Latin *lividus* < *livere* be bluish] **—liv′id ly,** *adv.* **—liv′id ness,** *n.*

li vid i ty (li vid′ə tē), *n.* condition of being livid.

liv ing (liv′ing), *adj.* 1 having life; being alive: *a living plant.* 2 full of life; vigorous; strong; active: *a living faith.* 3 in actual existence; still in use: *a living language.* 4 true to life; vivid; lifelike: *a living picture.* 5 for living in: *living quarters, poor living conditions.* 6 of or having to do with human beings: *within living memory.* —*n.* 1 condition of being alive: *tired of living.* 2 means of obtaining what is needed to keep alive; livelihood. See synonym study below. 3 manner of life: *plain living.* 4 (in Great Britain) position in the church with the income attached; benefice. **—liv′ing ly,** *adv.* **—liv′ing ness,** *n.*

Syn. *n.* 2 **Living, livelihood, support** mean a person's means of providing shelter, food, etc., for himself. **Living,** the general word, applies to what he earns and how he does so: *earn a bare living, work hard for one's living.* **Livelihood** applies particularly to the kind of work he does: *Painting, once merely a hobby, became her livelihood.* **Support** applies particularly to what is provided for another's living: *depend on one's parents for support.*

living room, room for general family use, usually during leisure hours and for entertaining; sitting room.

Liv ing stone (liv′ing stən), *n.* **David,** 1813-1873, Scottish missionary and explorer in Africa.

living wage, wage sufficient to provide a worker and his or her dependents with the necessities and comforts required for their well-being.

Li vo ni a (li vō′nē ə), *n.* 1 former Russian province on the Gulf of Riga, now divided between the Estonian S.S.R. and the Latvian S.S.R. 2 city in SE Michigan, near Detroit. 110,000.

Li vor no (li vôr′nō), *n.* Italian name of **Leghorn.**

Liv y (liv′ē), *n.* 59 B.C.-A.D. 17, Roman historian.

liz ard (liz′ərd), *n.* any of a large suborder of reptiles with a dry, scaly skin, a long body and tail, movable eyelids, and usually four legs. Some lizards have no legs and look much like snakes. The chameleon, horned toad, and iguana are lizards. [< Old French *lesard* < Latin *lacertus*] **—liz′ard-like′,** *adj.*

ll., lines.

llama—two llamas
about 4 ft. high at the shoulder

lla ma (lä′mə), *n., pl.* **-mas** or **-ma.** a woolly-haired South American ruminant, of the same family as the camel but smaller and without a hump. Llamas are used as beasts of burden. [< Spanish < Quechua]

lla no (lä′nō), *n., pl.* **-nos.** (in Spanish America and the southwestern United States) a broad, grassy, treeless plain. [< Spanish < Latin *planum* level]

LL. D., Doctor of Laws. [for Latin *Legum Doctor*]

Lloyd George (loid′ jôrj′), **David,** 1863-1945, British statesman, prime minister from 1916 to 1922.

lo (lō), *interj.* look! see! behold! [Old English *lā*]

loach (lōch), *n.* any of a family of small European freshwater fishes. [< Old French *loche*]

load (lōd), *n.* 1 that which is placed on a person, animal, or vehicle to be carried; burden: *The cart has a load of hay.* See synonym study below. 2 the quantity that can be or usually is carried. 3 such quantity taken as a unit of measure or weight: *Send us four loads of sand.* 4 **loads,** *pl.* INFORMAL. a great quantity or number. 5 something that weighs down, oppresses, or impedes: *a load of debt, a load of anxiety.* 6 (in mechanics) the weight or force supported by a structure or any part of it. 7 the external resistance overcome by an engine, dynamo, or the like, under a given condition, measured by the power required. 8 the total amount of power

hat, āge, fär; let, ēqual, tėrm;
it, īce; hot, ōpen, ôrder;
oil, out; cup, pu̇t, rüle;
ch, child; ng, long; sh, she;
th, thin; ᴛʜ, then; zh, measure;

ə represents *a* in about, *e* in taken, *i* in pencil, *o* in lemon, *u* in circus.

< = from, derived from, taken from.

supplied by a dynamo, generator, or other source of electricity in a given time. 9 amount of work that a person, business, or machine is expected to perform. 10 one charge of powder and shot for a gun. 11 **get a load of,** SLANG. take note of; notice; observe.
—*v.t.* 1 place on or in something for conveyance: *load grain.* 2 put a load in or on: *load a car, load a ship, load a camera with film.* 3 weigh down; burden; oppress: *load the mind with worries.* 4 add weight to: *load dice fraudulently so as to regulate the fall after a roll.* 5 supply amply or in excess: *load a person with gifts.* 6 put a charge in (a gun).
—*v.i.* 1 take on a load or cargo: *The ship loaded in five days.* 2 provide a gun with a charge, bullet, shell, etc.
[Old English *lād* way, course, a carrying. Doublet of LODE.] **—load′er,** *n.*

Syn. *n.* 1 **Load, burden** mean what one is carrying. **Load,** the common word, applies literally to whatever is carried by a person, animal, or vehicle, and figuratively to something that weighs heavily on the mind or spirit: *That is a heavy load of groceries. That's a load off my mind.* **Burden** means something borne, and now, except in a few phrases, is used only figuratively, applying to sorrow, care, duty, or work: *She had too heavy a burden and became sick.*

load ed (lō′did), *adj.* 1 INFORMAL. full of hidden meanings and implications: *a loaded question.* 2 SLANG. drunk. 3 SLANG. having plenty of money; rich.

load star (lōd′stär′), *n.* lodestar.

load stone (lōd′stōn′), *n.* 1 piece of magnetite that attracts iron and steel. 2 something that attracts: *Gold was the loadstone that drew men to Alaska.* Also, **lodestone.**

loaf[1] (lōf), *n., pl.* **loaves.** 1 bread shaped and baked as one piece. 2 a rather large cake, often baked in the shape of a loaf of bread. 3 anything like a loaf in shape, especially food. Meat loaf is meat chopped and mixed with other ingredients and then baked. 4 a cone-shaped mass of sugar. [Old English *hlāf*]

loaf[2] (lōf), *v.i.* spend time idly; do nothing: *I can loaf all day Saturday.* —*v.t.* idle (away): *loaf one's life away.* [origin uncertain]

lobate (def. 1) foot of a bird

loaf er (lō′fər), *n.* 1 person who loafs; idler. 2 **Loafer,** trademark for a shoe resembling a moccasin, but with sole and heel stitched to the upper.

loam (lōm), *n.* 1 rich, fertile earth in which much humus is mixed with clay and sand. 2 mixture of clay, sand, and straw used to make molds for large metal castings, and also to plaster walls, stop up holes, etc. —*v.t.* cover or fill with loam. [Old English *lām*]

loam y (lō′mē), *adj.* of or like loam.

loan (lōn), *n.* 1 a lending. 2 anything lent, especially a sum of money lent at interest. —*v.t.* make a loan of; lend (money, etc.). —*v.i.* make a loan. [< Scandinavian (Old Icelandic) *lān*] **—loan′a ble,** *adj.* **—loan′er,** *n.*

➔ **loan, lend.** In standard British English *loan* is a noun and *lend* a verb. But in American English *loan* and *lend* are verbs, and *loan* is both a verb and a noun: *I loaned (or lent) him my tuxedo. He asked me for a small loan.*

loan shark, INFORMAL. person who lends money at an extremely high or unlawful rate of interest.

loan word (lōn′wėrd′), *n.* word borrowed from another language, especially a foreign word that has become naturalized.

loath (lōth, lōᴛʜ), *adj.* unwilling or reluctant; averse: *The little girl was loath to leave her mother. They were loath to admit that their son had run away.* See **reluctant** for synonym study. Also, **loth.** [Old English *lāth* hostile]

loathe (lōᴛʜ), *v.t.,* **loathed, loath ing.** feel strong dislike and disgust for; abhor; hate; detest: *loathe cockroaches.* [Old English *lāthian* to hate < *lāth* hostile]

loath ing (lō′ᴛʜing), *n.* strong dislike and disgust; intense aversion.

loath ly[1] (lōth′lē, lōᴛʜ′lē), *adj.* loathsome.

loath ly[2] (lōth′lē, lōᴛʜ′lē), *adv.* unwillingly; reluctantly.

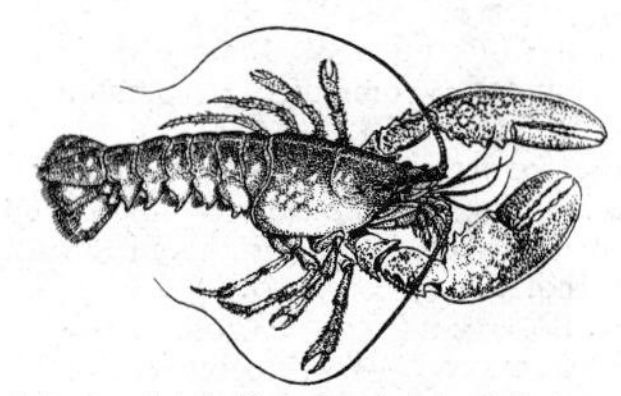
lobster (def. 1)—about 1 to 2 ft. long

loath some (lōᴛʜ′səm), *adj.* making one feel sick; disgusting. **—loath′some ly,** *adv.* **—loath′some ness,** *n.*

loaves (lōvz), *n.* pl. of **loaf**[1].

lob (lob), *n., v.,* **lobbed, lob bing.** —*n.* 1 a tennis ball hit in a high arc, usually to the back of the opponent's court. 2 a slow underhand throw in cricket. —*v.t.* 1 hit (a tennis ball) in a high arc, usually to the back of the opponent's court. 2 throw (a cricket ball) with a slow underhand movement. [earlier verb, move clumsily]

Lo ba chev sky (lō′bə chef′skē), *n.* **Nikolai,** 1793-1856, Russian mathematician.

lo bar (lō′bər, lō′bär′), *adj.* of, having to do with, or affecting a lobe or lobes: *lobar pneumonia.*

lo bate (lō′bāt), *adj.* 1 having a lobe or lobes. 2 having the form of a lobe.

lo bat ed (lō′bā tid), *adj.* lobate.

lo ba tion (lō bā′shən), *n.* 1 lobate formation or state. 2 lobe.

lob by (lob′ē), *n., pl.* **-bies,** *v.,* **-bied, -by ing.** —*n.* 1 an entrance hall connected with one or more rooms in a building, used as a passageway or anteroom: *the lobby of a theater, a hotel lobby.* 2 room or hall outside a legislative chamber: *the lobby of the House of Commons.* 3 person or group that tries to influence legislators; body of lobbyists. —*v.i.* try to influence legislators in their votes. —*v.t.* 1 get or try to get (a bill) passed by lobbying. 2 influence (legislators) in their votes. [< Medieval Latin *lobium, lobia* a covered walk; of Germanic origin]

lob by ist (lob′ē ist), *n.* person who tries to influence legislators.

lobe (lōb), *n.* a rounded projecting part. The brain, liver, etc., are divided into lobes. The lobe of the ear is the lower rounded end. [< Greek *lobos*]

lobed (lōbd), *adj.* having a lobe or lobes.

lo bel ia (lō bē′lyə), *n.* any of a genus of plants, both wild and cultivated, with small blue, red, yellow, purple, or white flowers. [< New Latin < Matthias de *Lobel,* 1538-1616, Flemish botanist]

lob lol ly (lob′lol′ē), *n., pl.* **-lies.** 1 a pine tree growing in swampy soils in the southern United States, having thick bark, long needles, and cones with spiny tips. 2 its coarse, inferior wood. [origin uncertain]

lo bot o my (lō bot′ə mē), *n., pl.* **-mies.** surgical incision into a lobe of the brain, especially to cut nerve fibers in the treatment of mental disorders.

lob ster (lob′stər), *n.* 1 any of a genus of large marine crustaceans, having compound eyes on thick stalks and five pairs of legs, with large claws on the front pair. Their shells turn bright red when boiled. 2 the flesh of a lobster, used as food. 3 any of various related crustaceans that lack an enlarged pair of claws. [Old English *loppestre,* probably < Latin *locusta* locust, lobster]

lobster pot, trap to catch lobsters.

lob ule (lob′yül), *n.* 1 a small lobe. 2 part of a lobe.

lo cal (lō′kəl), *adj.* 1 of a place; having to do with a certain place or places: *the local doctor, local self-government, local news.* 2 of just one part of the body: *a local pain, local disease, local application of a remedy.* 3 making all, or almost all, stops: *a local train.* 4 of or having to do with position in space. —*n.* 1 train, bus, etc., that stops at all, or almost all, of the stations on its route. 2 branch or chapter of a labor union, fraternity, etc. 3 a newspaper item of interest to a particular place. [< Latin *localis* < *locus* place] **—lo′cal ly,** *adv.*

local color, distinctive customs, peculiarities, etc., of a certain place or period, used in stories and plays to add realism.

lo cale (lō kal′), *n.* a place, especially with reference to events or circumstances connected with it: *The locale of "Don Quixote" is Spain in the 1600's.*

lo cal ism (lō′kə liz′əm), *n.* 1 a local expression, practice, custom, etc. 2 sectionalism. 3 attachment to a certain place.

lo cal i ty (lō kal′ə tē), *n., pl.* **-ties.** one place and the places near it; region, district, or neighborhood.

lo cal ize (lō′kə līz), *v.,* **-ized, -iz ing.** —*v.t.* make local; fix in, assign, or limit to a particular place or locality: *The infection seemed to be localized in the foot.* —*v.i.* become localized. **—lo′cal i za′tion,** *n.*

local option, right granted by the legislature of a country or state to the inhabitants of a political district to decide by vote certain matters, especially whether the sale of liquor shall be permitted within the district.

lo cate (lō′kāt, lō kāt′), *v.,* **-cat ed, -cat ing.** —*v.t.* 1 establish in a place: *They located their new store on Main Street.* 2 find out the exact position of: *We followed the stream* *until we located its source.* 3 state or show the position of: *locate Paris on the map.* 4 establish the boundaries or rights of: *locate a claim.* —*v.i.* 1 establish oneself in a place: *Early settlers located where there was water.* 2 **be located,** be situated; lie. [< Latin *locatum* placed < *locus* place] **—lo′cat er, lo′ca tor,** *n.*

lo ca tion (lō kā′shən), *n.* 1 a locating. 2 a being located. See **place** for synonym study. 3 position or place. 4 plot of ground marked out by boundaries; lot: *a mining location.* 5 place outside a studio, used in making all or part of a motion picture: *shoot a film on location.*

lo ca tion al (lō kā′shə nəl), *adj.* of or having to do with location. **—lo ca′tion al ly,** *adv.*

loc a tive (lok′ə tiv), in grammar: —*adj.* indicating place where. —*n.* 1 the locative case. 2 word in this case.

loc. cit., in the place cited [for Latin *loco citato*].

loch (lok, loH), *n.* SCOTTISH. 1 lake. 2 arm of the sea, especially when narrow or partially landlocked.

Loch Lomond. See **Lomond.**

lo ci (lō′sī), *n.* pl. of **locus.**

lock[1] (lok), *n.* 1 means of fastening doors, boxes, etc., consisting of a bolt and usually needing a key of special shape to open it. 2 an enclosed section of a canal, dock, etc., in which the level of the water can be changed by letting water in or out to raise or lower ships. 3 gunlock. 4 device to keep a wheel from turning. A lock is used when a vehicle is going downhill. 5 airlock. 6 a kind of hold in wrestling: *an arm lock.* 7 **lock, stock, and barrel,** INFORMAL. completely; entirely.
—*v.t.* 1 fasten with a lock. 2 shut (something in or out or up): *lock up jewels in a safe.* 3 hold fast: *The ship was locked in ice. The secret was locked in her heart.* 4 join, fit, jam, or link together: *The girls locked arms.* 5 make or set fast; fasten. 6 fasten (a wheel) to keep from turning. 7 embrace closely. 8 grapple in combat. 9 move (a ship) by means of a lock. 10 **lock out,** refuse to give work to (employees) until they accept the employer's terms. 11 **lock the wheels** or **lock the brakes,** (of a vehicle) apply the brakes hard enough to prevent the wheels from turning at all. —*v.i.* 1 be locked. 2 become locked: *This gear has locked.* 3 go or pass by means of a lock.
[Old English *loc*]

lock[2] (lok), *n.* 1 curl of hair. 2 portion of hair, wool, flax, cotton, etc. 3 **locks,** *pl.* the hair of the head. [Old English *locc*]

lock age (lok′ij), *n.* 1 construction, use, or operation of locks in canals or streams. 2 the passing of ships through a lock or series of locks. 3 walls, gates, etc., forming a lock or locks.

Locke (lok), *n.* **John,** 1632-1704, English philosopher.

lock er (lok′ər), *n.* 1 chest, small closet, cupboard, or other compartment that can be locked. Ships have lockers for storing equipment or supplies. 2 a refrigerated compartment for storing frozen foods. 3 person or thing that locks.

locker room, room with lockers near a gymnasium, in a clubhouse, etc., for dressing and storing sports equipment.

lock et (lok′it), *n.* a small ornamental case, often hinged, of gold, silver, etc., for holding a picture of someone or a lock of hair. It is usually worn around the neck on a chain or necklace. [< Middle French *loquet* latch; of Germanic origin]

lock jaw (lok′jô′), *n.* a form of tetanus in which the jaws become firmly closed.

lock nut (lok′nut′), *n.* 1 nut that can be screwed down on another to keep it securely in place. 2 nut that locks in place when tightly screwed.

lock out (lok′out′), *n.* refusal of an employer to furnish work to employees, used as a means of making them accept his terms; shutout.

lock smith (lok′smith′), *n.* person who makes or repairs locks.

lock step, way of marching in step very close together, with the legs of each man nearly touching those of the men in front and back.

lock stitch, a sewing-machine stitch in which two threads are fastened together at short intervals.

lock up (lok′up′), *n.* 1 house or room for the temporary detention of persons under arrest. 2 any jail.

Lock wood (lok′wu̇d), *n.* **Belva,** 1830-1917, American reformer, who worked for woman's rights and the rights of the American Indian.

lo co (lō′kō), *adj., n., pl.* **-cos,** *v.* U.S. —*adj.* SLANG. crazy. —*n.* 1 locoweed. 2 disease caused by eating this weed. —*v.t.* poison with locoweed. [< Spanish, crazy]

lo co mo tion (lō′kə mō′shən), *n.* act or power of moving from place to place. Walking, swimming, and flying are common forms of locomotion. [< Latin *loco* from a place + English *motion*]

lo co mo tive (lō′kə mō′tiv), *n.* engine that moves from place to place on its own power, used to pull railroad trains. —*adj.* 1 moving from place to place; having the power of locomotion: *locomotive bacteria.* 2 of or having to do with the power to move from place to place. 3 of or designating locomotion by means of a vehicle, engine, etc.

lo co mo tor (lō′kə mō′tər), *n.* person, animal, or thing that is capable of locomotion. —*adj.* of or having to do with locomotion.

locomotor ataxia, a degenerative disease of the spinal cord caused by syphilis and marked by loss of control over walking and certain other movements.

lo co weed (lō′kō wēd′), *n.* any of several herbs of the pea family, growing in western North America, which cause a disease affecting the brain in horses, sheep, etc., that eat it.

lo cum te nens (lō′kəm tē′nənz), *pl.* **lo cum te nen tes** (tə nen′tēz′). person temporarily holding the place or office of another; deputy or substitute. [< Medieval Latin]

lo cus (lō′kəs), *n., pl.* **lo ci.** 1 place or locality. 2 (in mathematics) the set of all the points, and only those points, that satisfy a given condition. The locus of all the points which are equidistant from a given point is the surface of a sphere. [< Latin]

lo cust (lō′kəst), *n.* 1 any of various grasshoppers which migrate in great swarms, destroying the crops along the way. 2 cicada. 3 any of a genus of American trees of the pea family, with small rounded leaflets and clusters of sweet-smelling white or rose-colored flowers. 4 the hard wood of any of these trees. [< Latin *locusta*]

lo cu tion (lō kyü′shən), *n.* 1 style of speech; manner of expression. 2 a form of expression or phraseology. [< Latin *locutionem* < *loqui* speak]

lode (lōd), *n.* 1 a vein of metal ore: *The miners struck a rich lode of copper.* 2 any mineral deposit filling a fissure in a rock. [Old English *lād* course, a carrying. Doublet of LOAD.]

lode star (lōd′stär′), *n.* 1 star that shows the way. 2 the North Star. 3 guiding principle or center of attraction. Also, **loadstar.** [*lode* (Old English *lād* course) + *star*]

lode stone (lōd′stōn′), *n.* loadstone.

lodge (loj), *v.,* **lodged, lodg ing,** *n.* —*v.i.* 1 live in a place, especially temporarily: *lodge at a motel.* 2 live in a rented room in another's house. 3 get caught or stay in a place without falling or going farther: *The kite lodged in the top of a tree.* —*v.t.* 1 provide with a place to live in or sleep in, especially temporarily. 2 rent a room or rooms to. 3 put or send into a place: *The hunter lodged a bullet in the lion's heart.* 4 put for safekeeping. 5 lay before a court or proper authority: *We lodged a complaint with the police.* 6 put (power, authority, etc.) in a person or thing. 7 beat down or lay flat, as crops by rain or wind.
—*n.* 1 place to live in. 2 a small or temporary house, as used during the hunting season or in summer. 3 cottage on an estate or the like, as for a caretaker, gardener, etc. 4 **a** one of the branches of a secret or fraternal society. **b** the place where it meets. 5 den of an animal, especially the large structure built near or in the water by beavers. 6 U.S. **a** a wigwam, tepee, or other dwelling of a North American Indian. **b** the number of Indians living in one dwelling.
[< Old French *logier* < *loge* arbor, covered walk; of Germanic origin]

Lodge (loj), *n.* 1 **Henry Cabot,** 1850-1924, United States senator and writer on history and politics. 2 Sir **Oliver,** 1851-1940, English physicist.

lodge ment (loj′mənt), *n.* lodgment.

lodg er (loj′ər), *n.* person who lives in a rented room or rooms in another's house; roomer.

lodg ing (loj′ing), *n.* 1 place where one is living only for a time: *a lodging for the night.* 2 **lodgings,** *pl.* a rented room or rooms in a house, not in a hotel.

lodging house, house in which rooms are rented.

lodg ment (loj′mənt), *n.* 1 act of lodging. 2 condition of being lodged. 3 something lodged or deposited. 4 position gained; foothold. 5 entrenchment built temporarily on a position gained from the enemy. Also, **lodgement.**

Łódź (lüj), *n.* city in central Poland. 751,000.

lo ess (lō′is, les), *n.* a yellowish-brown loam, usually deposited by the wind. [< German *Löss*]

lo ess i al (lō es′ē əl), *adj.* of or having to do with loess.

Lo fo ten (lō fōt′n), *n.* group of islands northwest of, and belonging to, Norway. 30,000 pop.; 484 sq. mi.

loft (lôft, loft), *n.* 1 space just below the roof in a cabin; attic. 2 room under the roof of a barn: *This loft is full of hay.* 3 gallery in a church or hall: *a choir loft.* 4 an upper floor of a business building or warehouse. 5 the backward slope of the face of a golf club. 6 stroke that drives a golf ball upward. 7 act of driving a golf ball upward. —*v.t.* hit (a golf ball) high up. [< Scandinavian (Old Icelandic) *lopt* air, sky, loft]

loft y (lôf′tē, lof′tē), *adj.*, **loft i er, loft i est.** 1 very high; towering: *lofty mountains.* See **high** for synonym study. 2 exalted or dignified; grand: *lofty aims, lofty thoughts.* 3 proud; haughty: *a lofty sneer.* **—loft′i ly,** *adv.* **—loft′i ness,** *n.*

log (def. 5)—A sailor throws the log into the water behind the ship. By noting the length of line which runs off the reel in a given time he obtains a rough estimate of the ship's speed.

log (lôg, log), *n.*, *v.*, **logged, log ging,** *adj.* —*n.* 1 section of the trunk of a tree that has not been shaped or made into boards; a length of wood just as it comes from the tree. 2 the daily record of a ship's voyage. 3 a similar record of an airplane trip. 4 record of the operation or performance of an engine, etc. 5 float for measuring the speed of a ship. —*v.i.* cut down trees, saw them into logs, and move them out of the forest. —*v.t.* 1 cut (trees) into logs. 2 cut down trees on (land). 3 enter in the log of a ship or airplane. 4 travel (a distance), especially as indicated by the rate of speed registered by a log. —*adj.* made of logs: *a log house.* [Middle English *logge*] **—log′like′,** *adj.*

log, logarithm.

Lo gan (lō′gən), *n.* **Mount,** mountain in SW Yukon Territory, Canada, the second highest mountain in North America. 19,850 ft.

lo gan ber ry (lō′gən ber′ē), *n., pl.* **-ries.** 1 a large, purplish-red fruit of a bramble developed from a cross between a dewberry and the red raspberry. 2 the plant it grows on. [< J. H. *Logan,* 1841-1928, American horticulturist who developed it]

lo ga rithm (lô′gə riᴛʜ′əm, log′ə riᴛʜ′əm), *n.* 1 exponent of the power to which a fixed number or base (usually 10) must be raised in order to produce a given number. If the fixed number or base is 10, the logarithm of 1000 is 3; the logarithm of 10,000 is 4; the logarithm of 100,000 is 5. 2 one of a system of such exponents used to shorten calculations in mathematics. [< New Latin *logarithmus* < Greek *logos* proportion + *arithmos* number]

lo ga rith mic (lô′gə riᴛʜ′mik, log′ə-riᴛʜ′mik), *adj.* of or having to do with a logarithm or logarithms.

lo ga rith mi cal (lô′gə riᴛʜ′mə kəl, log′ə-riᴛʜ′mə kəl), *adj.* logarithmic.

log book (lôg′bu̇k′, log′bu̇k′), *n.* 1 book in which a daily record of a ship's voyage is kept. 2 book for records of an airplane's trip. 3 journal of travel.

loge (lōzh), *n.* 1 box in a theater or opera house. 2 booth or stall, as at a fair. [< French]

log ger (lô′gər, log′ər), *n.* 1 person whose work is logging; lumberjack. 2 machine for loading or hauling logs.

log ger head (lô′gər hed′, log′ər hed′), *n.* 1 a stupid person; blockhead. 2 any of a genus of large marine turtles, especially a carnivorous species of tropical Atlantic waters. 3 **at loggerheads,** at enmity; disputing.

log gia (loj′ə; *Italian* lôd′jä), *n., pl.* **log gias,** ɪᴛᴀʟɪᴀɴ **log gie** (lôd′jā). gallery or arcade open to the air on at least one side. [< Italian]

log ging (lô′ging, log′ing), *n.* work of cutting down trees, sawing them into logs, and moving the logs from the forest.

log ic (loj′ik), *n.* 1 the principles of reasoning and inference; science of reasoning or the science of proof. 2 a particular system or theory of logic. 3 use of argument; reasoning. 4 sound sense; reason: *There is much logic in what you say.* 5 logical outcome or effect; inevitable result: *The logic of events proved them wrong.* [< Greek *logikē (technē)* reasoning (art) < *logos* word < *legein* speak]

log i cal (loj′ə kəl), *adj.* 1 having to do with logic; according to the principles of logic. 2 reasonably expected; reasonable. 3 reasoning correctly. **—log′i cal ly,** *adv.* **—log′i cal ness,** *n.*

lo gi cian (lō jish′ən), *n.* an expert in logic.

lo gis tic (lō jis′tik), *adj.* of or having to do with logistics. **—lo gis′ti cal ly,** *adv.*

lo gis ti cal (lō jis′tə kəl), *adj.* logistic.

lo gis tics (lō jis′tiks), *n.* the planning and carrying out of any complex or large-scale operation, especially one of military movement, evacuation, and supply. [< French *logistique*]

log jam (lôg′jam′, log′jam′), *n.* 1 a blocking of the downstream movement of logs, causing a jumbled overcrowding of the timber in the river. 2 a deadlock or standstill.

lo gor rhe a (lô′gə rē′ə, log′ə rē′ə), *n.* 1 habit of talking too much. 2 a great flow of words. [< Greek *logos* word + *rhein* to flow]

log roll (lôg′rōl′, log′rōl′), ɪɴꜰᴏʀᴍᴀʟ. —*v.t.* get (a bill) passed by logrolling. —*v.i.* take part in logrolling. **—log′roll′er,** *n.*

log roll ing (lôg′rō′ling, log′rō′ling), *n.* 1 a giving of political aid in return for a like favor, as by pledging to vote for another's bill if he will vote for yours. 2 act of rolling logs, especially by treading on them. 3 sport including various maneuvers on logs, especially a contest in which two men standing on a floating log try to upset each other by spinning the log with their feet.

log wood (lôg′wu̇d′, log′wu̇d′), *n.* 1 the heavy, hard, brownish-red wood of a Central American tree of the pea family, used in dyeing. 2 the tree.

lo gy (lō′gē), *adj.*, **-gi er, -gi est.** heavy, sluggish, or dull; lethargic. [related to Dutch *log*]

-logy, *combining form.* 1 doctrine, study, or science of: *Biology = the science of life.* 2 speech or discussion: *Tautology = the same speech.* [< Greek *-logia* < *logos* word, discourse]

Lo hen grin (lō′ən grin), *n.* (in German legends) a knight of the Holy Grail and son of Parsifal.

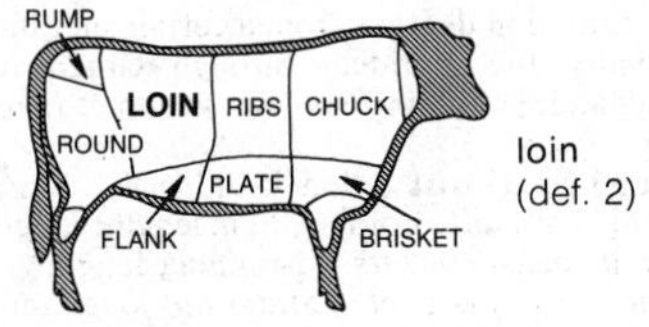

loin (def. 2)

loin (loin), *n.* 1 Usually, **loins,** *pl.* the part of the body of an animal or man between the ribs and the hipbones. The loins are on both sides of the spinal column and nearer to it than the flanks. 2 piece of meat from this part of an animal: *a loin of pork.* 3 **loins,** *pl.* the genitals or the genital region. 4 **gird up one's loins,** get ready for action. [< Old French *loigne,* ultimately < Latin *lumbus*]

hat, āge, fär; let, ēqual, tėrm;
it, īce; hot, ōpen, ôrder;
oil, out; cup, pu̇t, rüle;
ch, child; ng, long; sh, she;
th, thin; ᴛʜ, then; zh, measure;

ə represents *a* in about, *e* in taken,
i in pencil, *o* in lemon, *u* in circus.

< = from, derived from, taken from.

loin cloth (loin′klôth′, loin′kloth′), *n., pl.* **-cloths** (-klôᴛʜz′, -klôths′; -kloᴛʜz′, -kloths′). piece of cloth worn around the hips and between the thighs by natives of warm countries, commonly as the only garment.

Loire River (lwär), river flowing from S France into the Bay of Biscay, the longest river in France. 625 mi.

loi ter (loi′tər), *v.i.* 1 linger idly or aimlessly on one's way; move or go in a slow or lagging manner. See **linger** for synonym study. 2 waste time in idleness; idle; loaf. —*v.t.* spend (time) idly: *loiter the hours away.* [< Middle Dutch *loteren* be loose] **—loi′ter er,** *n.*

Lo ki (lō′kē), *n.* (in Scandinavian myths) the god of destruction.

loll (lol), *v.i.* 1 recline or lean in a lazy manner: *loll on a sofa.* 2 hang loosely or droop; dangle: *A dog's tongue lolls out in hot weather.* —*v.t.* allow to hang or droop. —*n.* a lolling. [Middle English *lollen*]

Lol lard (lol′ərd), *n.* one of the followers of John Wycliffe. The Lollards advocated certain religious, political, and economic reforms, and were persecuted as heretics. [< Middle Dutch *lollaerd* mumbler < *lollen* to mumble]

lol li pop or **lol ly pop** (lol′ē pop), *n.* piece of hard candy, usually on the end of a small stick. [origin uncertain]

Lom bard (lom′bärd, lom′bərd; lum′bärd, lum′bərd), *n.* 1 member of a Germanic tribe which in the ᴀ.ᴅ. 500's conquered the part of northern Italy since known as Lombardy. 2 native or inhabitant of Lombardy. Also, **Longobard.**

Lom bard y (lom′bər dē, lum′bər dē), *n.* region in N Italy.

Lo mé (lô mā′), *n.* capital of Togo, a seaport in the SW part. 135,000.

Lo mond (lō′mənd), *n.* **Loch,** lake in S central Scotland. 23 mi. long; 27 sq. mi.

lon., longitude.

Lon don (lun′dən), *n.* 1 capital of the United Kingdom of Great Britain and Northern Ireland, in SE England, on the Thames. City with suburbs, 7,612,000. 2 county in SE England that includes this city. 3 **City of,** ancient center of the administrative county of London. 11,000 pop.; 675 acres. 4 city in SW Ontario, Canada. 194,000. 5 **Jack,** 1876-1916, American writer of novels and short stories.

Lon don der ry (lun′dən der′ē), *n.* seaport in NW Northern Ireland. 55,000.

Lon don er (lun′də nər), *n.* native or inhabitant of London, England.

lone (lōn), *adj.* 1 without others; alone; solitary; single: *a lone traveler, the lone survivor.* 2 lonesome; lonely: *a lone life.* 3 standing apart; isolated: *a lone house.* [variant of *alone*]

lone ly (lōn′lē), *adj.,* **-li er, -li est,** *n.* —*adj.* 1 dejected because of want of company or friends; sad at the thought that one is alone. 2 without many people: *a lonely road.* 3 alone; isolated: *a lonely tree.* —*n.* 1 a lonely person. 2 loner. **—lone′li ness,** *n.*

lon er (lō′nər), *n.* person who is, lives, or works alone, especially by choice: *the loners who like to listen to music in solitude, a professional loner.*

lone some (lōn′səm), *adj.,* **-som er, -som est.** 1 feeling lonely. 2 making one feel lonely. 3 unfrequented; desolate. 4 solitary. **—lone′some ly,** *adv.* **—lone′some ness,** *n.*

long[1] (lông, long), *adj.,* **long er** (lông′gər, long′gər), **long est** (lông′gist, long′gist), *adv., n.* —*adj.* 1 measuring much, or more than usual, from end to end in space or time: *a long distance, a long speech.* 2 having a specified length in space or time or in a series: *five feet long, two hours long.* 3 having a long, narrow shape: *a long board.* 4 extending to a great distance in space or time; far-reaching: *a long memory, a long look ahead.* 5 involving considerable risk, liability to error, etc.: *a long chance.* 6 (of vowels or syllables) taking a comparatively long time to speak. The vowels are long in *late, be, note.* 7 well supplied (with some commodity): *long in salt.* 8 depending on a rise in prices for profit.
—*adv.* 1 throughout the whole length of: *all night long.* 2 for a long time: *a reform long advocated. I can't stay long.* 3 at a point of time far distant from the time indicated: *long since. It happened long before you were born.* 4 **as long as** or **so long as,** provided that.
—*n.* 1 a long time: *Summer will come before long.* 2 a long sound or syllable. 3 a size of garment for men who are taller than average. 4 **the long and the short of it,** the sum total (of something); substance; upshot.
[Old English *lang*]

long[2] (lông, long), *v.i.* have a strong desire; wish very much; yearn. [Old English *langian* < *lang* long[1]]

long., longitude.

Long Beach, seaside resort in SW California, near Los Angeles. 359,000.

long boat (lông′bōt′, long′bōt′), *n.* the largest boat carried by a sailing ship.

long bow (lông′bō′, long′bō′), *n.* a large bow drawn by hand, for shooting a long, feathered arrow.

long distance, operator or exchange that takes care of long-distance calls.

long-dis tance (lông′dis′təns, long′dis′təns), *adj., adv., v.,* **-tanced, -tanc ing.** —*adj.* 1 of or having to do with telephone service between distant places. 2 from or covering a great distance: *long-distance trucking, a long-distance yacht race.* —*adv.* 1 by long-distance telephone. 2 over a great distance: *ship the cars long-distance by freight.* —*v.t.* call by long distance: *As soon as he reached the hotel, he long-distanced his wife.*

long division, method of dividing numbers in which each step of the division is written out. It is used to divide large numbers.

long-drawn (lông′drôn′, long′drôn′), *adj.* lasting a long time; prolonged to great length.

lon gev i ty (lon jev′ə tē), *n.* 1 long life. 2 length or duration of life. [< Late Latin *longaevitatem* < *longaevus* long-lived < *longus* long + *aevum* age]

Long fel low (lông′fel′ō, long′fel′ō), *n.* **Henry Wadsworth,** 1807-1882, American poet.

long hair (lông′her′, lông′har′; long′her′, long′har′), *n.* INFORMAL. 1 person who enjoys, performs, or composes classical music. 2 an intellectual. 3 hippie.

long-hair (lông′her′, lông′har′; long′her′, long′har′), *adj.* INFORMAL. 1 enjoying, performing, or composing classical music. 2 intellectual. 3 classical: *long-hair music.*

long-haired (lông′herd′, lông′hard′; long′herd′, long′hard′), *adj.* long-hair.

long hand (lông′hand′, long′hand′), *n.* ordinary writing, not shorthand or typewriting.

long head ed (lông′hed′id, long′hed′id), *adj.* 1 having a long head; dolichocephalic. 2 shrewd; far-sighted. **—long′head′ed ness,** *n.*

long horn (lông′hôrn′, long′hôrn′), *n.* one of a breed of cattle with very long horns, formerly common in the southwestern United States and Mexico and descended from Spanish stock.

long house, a large, usually rectangular communal dwelling of the Iroquois and certain other American Indians, and various tribal societies in southeastern Asia, Borneo, New Guinea, and elsewhere.

long ing (lông′ing, long′ing), *n.* earnest desire: *a longing for home.* See **desire** for synonym study. —*adj.* having or showing earnest desire. **—long′ing ly,** *adv.*

long ish (lông′ish, long′ish), *adj.* somewhat long.

Long Island, island south of Connecticut. It is part of New York State. 118 mi. long; 1700 sq. mi.

Long Island Sound, long, narrow strip of water between Connecticut and Long Island. It is an inlet of the Atlantic. 110 mi. long.

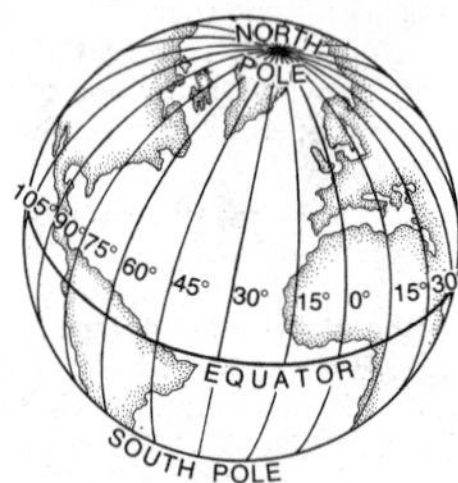

longitude—circles of longitude

lon gi tude (lon′jə tüd, lon′jə tyüd), *n.* distance east or west on the earth's surface, measured in degrees from a certain meridian, usually the meridian through Greenwich, England. [< Latin *longitudo* length < *longus* long]

lon gi tu di nal (lon′jə tüd′n əl, lon′jə tyüd′n əl), *adj.* 1 of length; in length: *longitudinal measurements.* 2 running lengthwise: *The flag of the United States has longitudinal stripes.* 3 of or having to do with longitude. **—lon′gi tu′di nal ly,** *adv.*

long jump, BRITISH. broad jump.

long-lived (lông′līvd′, lông′livd′; long′līvd′, long′livd′), *adj.* living or lasting a long time. **—long′-lived′ness,** *n.*

Lon go bard (long′gə bärd), *n.* Lombard.

long-play ing record (lông′plā′ing, long′plā′ing), a phonograph record playing at $33^1/_3$ revolutions per minute.

long-range (lông′rānj′, long′rānj′), *adj.* 1 looking ahead; future: *long-range plans.* 2 of or for a long period: *a long-range trend toward inflation.* 3 having a long range; covering a great distance: *a long-range ballistic missile.*

Long shanks (lông′shanks′), *n.* **Edward.** See **Edward I.**

long shore man (lông′shôr′mən, lông′shōr′mən; long′shôr′mən, long′shōr′mən), *n., pl.* **-men.** man employed on the wharves of a port to load and unload ships; stevedore. [< *longshore* (short for *alongshore*) + *man*]

long shot, INFORMAL. 1 an attempt at something difficult. 2 a venture, racehorse, etc., unlikely to succeed but rewarding if it should: *bet on a long shot. The whole idea seemed a long shot.* 3 **not by a long shot,** not at all.

long-sight ed (lông′sī′tid, long′sī′tid), *adj.* 1 far-sighted. 2 having foresight; wise. **—long′-sight′ed ness,** *n.*

long stand ing (lông′stan′ding, long′stan′ding), *adj.* having lasted for a long time: *a longstanding feud.*

Long street (lông′strēt, long′strēt), *n.* **James,** 1821-1904, Confederate general in the Civil War.

long-suf fer ing (lông′suf′ər ing, long′suf′ər ing), *adj.* enduring trouble, pain, or injury long and patiently. —*n.* long and patient endurance of trouble, pain, or injury.

long suit, 1 (in card games) the suit in which one has most cards. 2 a strong point: *Patience is his long suit.*

long-term (lông′tėrm′, long′tėrm′), *adj.* 1 of or for a long period of time. 2 falling due after a long time: *a long-term loan.*

long ton, the British ton, 2240 pounds.

lon gueur (lông gėr′), *n.* a long or tedious passage in a book, play, piece of music, etc. [< French, length]

long ways (lông′wāz′, long′wāz′), *adv.* longwise.

long-wind ed (lông′win′did, long′win′did), *adj.* 1 talking or writing at tedious length; tiresome: *a long-winded speaker, a long-winded magazine article.* 2 capable of long-continued action or effort without getting out of breath: *A long-distance runner must be long-winded.* **—long′-wind′ed ly,** *adv.* **—long′-wind′ed ness,** *n.*

long wise (lông′wīz′, long′wīz′), *adv.* lengthwise.

long yi (long′yē), *n.* sarong worn in Burma. [< Burmese]

loo (lü), *n.* 1 card game in which players who fail to take a trick pay forfeits into a pool. 2 the forfeit paid. [short for *lanterloo,* originally a nonsense refrain of a French song]

look (lu̇k), *v.i.* 1 direct the eyes; try to see: *He looked this way.* 2 glance or gaze in a certain way: *look questioningly at a person.* 3 search: *I looked through the drawer for my keys.* 4 have a view; face: *The house looks upon a garden. These windows look to the north.* 5 expect; anticipate: *I look to hear from you soon.* 6 seem; appear: *She looks pale.* —*v.t.* 1 direct a look at: *look one in the eyes.* 2 express or suggest by looks: *She said nothing but looked her disappointment.* 3 appear as benefits or accords with (one's character, condition, etc.): *look one's age.*

look after, attend to; take care of.

look alive, hurry up! be quick!

look at, pay attention or regard to; examine: *You must look at all the facts.*

hat, āge, fär; let, ēqual, tėrm;
it, īce; hot, ōpen, ôrder;
oil, out; cup, pu̇t, rüle;
ch, child; ng, long; sh, she;
th, thin; ᴛʜ, then; zh, measure;

ə represents *a* in about, *e* in taken, *i* in pencil, *o* in lemon, *u* in circus.

< = from, derived from, taken from.

look back, think about the past; recollect.
look down on, despise; scorn.
look for, expect; anticipate.
look forward to, expect with pleasure; be eager for.
look in, make a short visit.
look into, examine; inspect; investigate.
look on, **a** watch without taking part. **b** regard; consider.
look oneself, seem like oneself; seem well.
look out, be careful; watch out.
look over, examine; inspect.
look to, **a** attend to; take care of. **b** turn to for help. **c** look forward to; expect.
look up, **a** search for; refer to. **b** INFORMAL. call on; visit. **c** INFORMAL. get better; improve.
look upon, regard; consider.
look up to, respect; admire.
—n. 1 act of looking; glance or gaze. 2 search; examination. 3 appearance; aspect. 4 **looks,** *pl.* personal appearance: *good looks.* [Old English *lōcian*] **—look′er,** *n.*

look er-on (lu̇k′ər ôn′, lu̇k′ər on′), *n., pl.* **look ers-on.** onlooker.

looking glass, mirror.

look out (lu̇k′out′), *n.* 1 a careful watch, as for someone to appear, something to happen, land to be sighted from a ship, etc. 2 station, building, or place from which a lookout can be kept, as a high point of land, a tower, a crow's nest, etc. 3 the person or group that has the duty of keeping a lookout. 4 what one sees ahead; outlook; prospect. 5 INFORMAL. thing to be cared for or worried about.

Lookout Mountain, range of low mountains in Georgia, Tennessee, and Alabama. Highest peak, 2126 ft.

look-see (lu̇k′sē′), *n.* SLANG. a quick look or inspection.

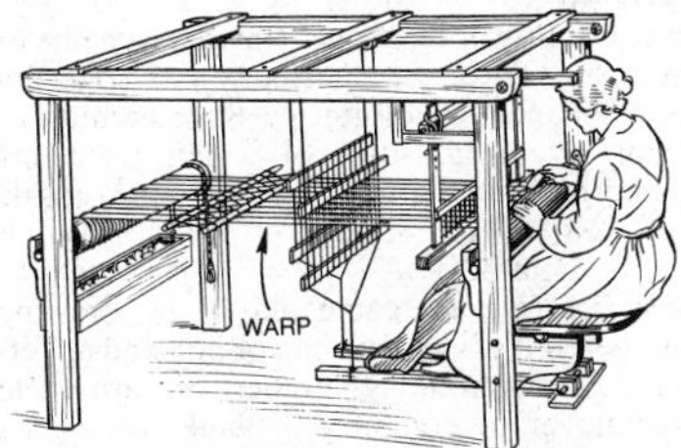

loom[1]—To make cloth the weaver passes the shuttle carrying the thread of the woof through the threads of the warp. Foot pedals raise and lower alternate warp threads.

loom[1] (lüm), *n.* frame or machine for weaving yarn or thread into cloth. [Old English *(ge)lōma* implement]

loom[2] (lüm), *v.i.* appear dimly or vaguely as a large, threatening shape: *A large iceberg loomed through the thick, gray fog. War loomed ahead.* [origin uncertain]

loon[1] (lün), *n.* any of a genus of large, fish-eating, web-footed diving birds that have a loud, wild cry and live in northern regions. [earlier *loom* < Scandinavian (Old Icelandic) *lōmr*]

loon[2] (lün), *n.* a contemptible, lazy, or stupid person. [origin uncertain]

loon y or **loon ey** (lü′nē), *adj.,* **loon i er, loon i est,** *n., pl.* **loon ies.** SLANG. *—adj.* crazy, foolish, or silly. *—n.* a crazy person; lunatic. [variant of *luny* < *lunatic*]

loop (lüp), *n.* 1 the shape of a curved string, ribbon, bent wire, etc., that crosses itself. 2 thing, bend, course, or motion shaped like this: *The road makes a wide loop around the lake.* 3 a fastening or ornament formed of cord, etc., bent and crossed. 4 a complete vertical turn or revolution, such as that made by an airplane. 5 in physics: **a** the portion of a vibrating string, column of air in an organ pipe, etc., between two nodes. **b** the middle point of such a part. 6 a complete or closed electric circuit. 7 **knock for a loop,** SLANG. overwhelm with confusion, embarrassment, etc. 8 **loop the loop,** turn over and over; make a loop in the air.
—v.t. 1 make a loop of. 2 make loops in. 3 fasten with a loop. 4 encircle with a loop. 5 cause (an airplane) to fly in a loop or loops.
—v.i. 1 form a loop or loops. 2 perform a loop, as an airplane.
[Middle English *loupe*] **—loop′er,** *n.*

loop hole (lüp′hōl′), *n.* 1 a small opening in a wall for observation, ventilation, etc., especially one in a parapet through which weapons may be fired. 2 means of escape or evasion: *The clever lawyer found a loophole in the law to save his client.*

loose (lüs), *adj.,* **loos er, loos est,** *v.,* **loosed, loos ing,** *adv. —adj.* 1 not fastened or attached; untied: *a loose thread.* 2 not tight; slack: *loose clothing, loose reins.* 3 not firmly set or fixed in place: *a loose tooth, loose planks on a bridge.* 4 not bound together: *loose papers.* 5 not put in a box, can, or other container: *loose coffee.* 6 not shut in or up; free: *The dog has been loose all night.* 7 not pressed close together; having spaces between the parts; open: *cloth with a loose weave.* 8 not strict, exact, or precise; vague; indefinite: *a loose account of the accident, a loose translation from another language.* 9 moving too freely: *a loose tongue.* 10 careless about morals or conduct; immoral: *a loose character.* 11 INFORMAL. not tense; relaxed.
break loose, run away; free oneself.
cast loose, unfasten; separate.
cut loose, **a** separate from anything; break a connection or relation. **b** run away; free oneself.
let loose, set loose, or **turn loose,** set free; let go; release.
on the loose, INFORMAL. **a** without restraint; free. **b** on a spree.
—v.t. 1 set free; let go. 2 shoot (an arrow, gun, etc.). 3 make loose; untie; unfasten: *loose a knot.* 4 make less tight; relax; slacken.
—adv. in a loose manner; loosely.
[< Scandinavian (Old Icelandic) *lauss*] **—loose′ly,** *adv.* **—loose′ness,** *n.*

loon[1] about 32 in. long

loose-joint ed (lüs′join′tid), *adj.* 1 able to move very freely. 2 having loose joints; loosely built.

loose-leaf (lüs′lēf′), *adj.* having pages or sheets that can be taken out and replaced: *a loose-leaf notebook, a loose-leaf manual.*

loos en (lü′sn), *v.t., v.i.* make or become loose or looser. **—loos′en er,** *n.*

loose strife (lüs′strīf′), *n.* any of a genus of erect or creeping herbs of the same family as the primrose, including a common species with clusters of yellow flowers and a tall, downy weed with spikes of purple flowers.

loot (lüt), *n.* 1 goods taken from an enemy, a captured city, etc., in time of war. 2 anything taken illegally, especially by force or with violence: *burglar's loot.* See **plunder** for synonym study. *—v.t.* 1 plunder, rob, or sack (a city, building, store, etc.). 2 carry off as loot or booty. *—v.i.* plunder; rob. [< Hindustani *lūṭ*] **—loot′er,** *n.*

lop[1] (lop), *v.t.,* **lopped, lop ping.** 1 cut off; cut. 2 cut branches, twigs, etc., from. 3 remove parts as if by cutting. [Middle English *loppe* smaller branches and twigs] **—lop′per,** *n.*

lop[2] (lop), *v.,* **lopped, lop ping,** *adj. —v.i.* 1 hang loosely or limply; droop. 2 flop. *—adj.* hanging loosely; drooping. [origin uncertain]

lope (lōp), *v.,* **loped, lop ing,** *n. —v.i.* run with a long, easy stride. *—n.* a long, easy stride. [< Scandinavian (Old Icelandic) *hlaupa* to leap] **—lop′er,** *n.*

lop-eared (lop′ird′), *adj.* having ears that hang loosely or droop.

lop py (lop′ē), *adj.* hanging loosely; drooping; limp.

lop sid ed (lop′sī′did), *adj.* larger or heavier on one side than the other; unevenly balanced; leaning to one side. **—lop′sid′ed ly,** *adv.* **—lop′sid′ed ness,** *n.*

lo qua cious (lō kwā′shəs), *adj.* talking much; fond of talking. See **talkative** for synonym study. **—lo qua′cious ly,** *adv.* **—lo qua′cious ness,** *n.*

lo quac i ty (lō kwas′ə tē), *n.* inclination to talk a great deal; talkativeness. [< Latin *loquacitatem* < *loquax* talkative < *loqui* to talk]

lo quat (lō′kwot, lō′kwat), *n.* 1 a small evergreen tree of the rose family with small, orange-yellow, edible, plumlike fruit, native to Asia, but grown in North America since the 1700's. 2 its fruit. [< Chinese (Canton) *lō-kwat*]

Lo rain (lə rān′), *n.* city in N Ohio. 78,000.

lo ran (lôr′ən, lōr′ən), *n.* system of navigation by which an airplane or ship can determine its position by plotting two or more fixed radio signals that are part of a radio beacon system. [< *lo(ng) ra(nge) n(avigation)*]

lord (lôrd), *n.* 1 one who has power over others or to whom service and obedience are due; master, ruler, or chief. 2 a feudal superior; proprietor of a manor, fief, etc. 3 **the Lord,** **a** God. **b** Christ. 4 (in Great Britain) a man of rank; peer of the realm; person entitled by courtesy to the title of lord.

5 **Lord,** in Great Britain: **a** a titled nobleman or peer of the realm belonging to the House of Lords. **b** title used in writing or speaking about noblemen of certain ranks: *Lord Tennyson.* **c** title given by courtesy to men holding certain positions: *the Lord Chief Justice.* 6 **the Lords,** House of Lords. 7 ARCHAIC. husband. —*v.i.* rule proudly or absolutely. —*v.t.* 1 raise to the rank of lord; ennoble. 2 **lord it over,** domineer over. [Old English *hlāford* < *hlāf* loaf + *weard* keeper, ward]

Lord Chancellor or **Lord High Chancellor,** the highest judicial official of the United Kingdom.

lord ling (lôrd′ling), *n.* a little or unimportant lord.

lord ly (lôrd′lē), *adj.,* **-li er, -li est,** *adv.* —*adj.* 1 like a lord; suitable for a lord; grand; magnificent. 2 haughty; insolent; scornful. —*adv.* in a lordly manner. **—lord′li ness,** *n.*

lor do sis (lôr dō′sis), *n.* a forward curvature of the spine that appears to bend the upper body slightly backward. [< Greek *lordos* bent backward]

Lord's Day, Sunday.

lord ship (lôrd′ship), *n.* 1 rank or position of a lord. 2 Often, **Lordship.** title used in speaking to or of a man having the rank of Lord: *your Lordship, his Lordship.* 3 rule; authority; power.

Lord's Prayer, (in the Bible) the prayer given by Jesus to His disciples which begins with the words "Our Father Who art in Heaven."

Lord's Supper, 1 Last Supper. 2 Holy Communion.

lore (lôr, lōr), *n.* 1 the body of knowledge on a particular subject, especially traditional facts, anecdotes, or beliefs: *bird lore, Irish lore.* 2 learning; knowledge. 3 ARCHAIC. teaching or something taught. [Old English *lār.* Related to LEARN.]

Lo re lei (lôr′ə lī, lor′ə lī), *n.* (in German legends) a siren of the Rhine whose beauty and singing distracted sailors and caused them to wreck their ships.

lor gnette (lôr nyet′), *n.* eyeglasses or opera glasses mounted on a handle. [< French < *lorgner* look sidelong at]

lo ris (lôr′is, lōr′is), *n., pl.* **-ris.** either of two small, slow-moving nocturnal lemurs of southern Asia. [< French]

lorn (lôrn), *adj.* forsaken; forlorn. [Old English *-loren,* lost. Related to FORLORN.]

Lor rain (lə rān′; *French* lô raN′), *n.* **Claude,** 1600-1682, French landscape painter.

Lor raine (lə rān′), *n.* region in NE France, formerly part of Alsace-Lorraine.

lor ry (lôr′ē, lor′ē), *n., pl.* **-ries.** 1 BRITISH. a motor truck. 2 a long, flat, horse-drawn wagon without sides, set on four low wheels. [probably < dialectal *lurry* to pull, lug]

lo ry (lôr′ē, lōr′ē), *n., pl.* **-ries.** any of various small, bright-colored parrots with a bristled tongue adapted to their diet of nectar, found in Australia and nearby islands. [< Malay *luri*]

Los Al a mos (lôs al′ə mōs; lōs al′ə mōs), town in N New Mexico, a center for atomic research. 11,000.

Los An ge les (lôs an′jə ləs; lôs an′jə lēz′; lôs ang′gə ləs), city in SW California, the third largest in the United States. 2,810,000.

lose (lüz), *v.,* **lost, los ing.** —*v.t.* 1 not have any longer; have taken away from one by accident, carelessness, parting, death, etc.: *lose a finger, lose a friend, lose one's life.* 2 be unable to find: *lose a book.* 3 fail to keep, preserve, or maintain: *lose patience, lose one's balance.* 4 fail to follow with eye, hearing, mind, etc.: *lose a face in a crowd, lose words here and there in a speech.* 5 fail to have, get, catch, etc.: *lose a sale, lose a train.* 6 fail to win: *lose the prize, lose a bet, lose a game.* 7 bring to destruction or ruin: *The ship and its crew were lost.* 8 let pass without any use or profit; waste: *lose an opportunity, lose time waiting. The hint was not lost on me.* 9 cause the loss of: *Delay lost the battle.* 10 cause to lose: *That one act of misconduct lost him his job.* 11 **lose oneself, a** let oneself go astray; become bewildered. **b** become absorbed or engrossed. —*v.i.* 1 be defeated: *Our team lost.* 2 suffer loss: *lose on a contract. The gambler lost heavily at poker.* 3 **lose out,** U.S. be unsuccessful; fail: *He lost out in the election.* [Old English *losian* be lost < *los* destruction, loss] **—los′er,** *n.*

los ing (lü′zing), *adj.* that cannot win or be won: *a losing game.* —*n.* **losings,** *pl.* losses, especially in gambling.

loss (lôs, los), *n.* 1 a losing. 2 a being lost. 3 person, thing, or amount lost. 4 harm or disadvantage caused by losing something. 5 **losses,** *pl.* **a** the number of soldiers dead, wounded, or captured. **b** the excess of money spent or invested over money gained. 6 **at a loss,** uncertain; puzzled; in difficulty: *at a loss how to proceed, at a loss for words.* 7 **at a loss to,** unable to: *at a loss to understand.* [Old English *los*]

loss leader, article of trade sold below cost to attract customers.

lost (lôst, lost), *v.* pt. and pp. of **lose.** —*adj.* 1 no longer possessed or retained: *lost friends.* 2 no longer to be found; missing: *lost articles.* 3 attended with defeat; not won: *a lost battle.* 4 not used to good purpose; spent in vain; wasted: *lost time.* 5 having gone astray: *a lost child.* 6 hopeless: *a lost cause.* 7 destroyed or ruined: *a lost soul.* 8 bewildered: *a lost expression.* 9 **be lost on** or **be lost upon,** have no effect on; fail to influence. 10 **lost in, a** completely absorbed or interested in: *lost in contemplation.* **b** hidden or obscured in: *outlines lost in the fog.* 11 **lost to, a** no longer possible or open to. **b** no longer belonging to. **c** insensible to. **—lost′ness,** *n.*

lorry (def. 2)

lot (lot), *n., v.,* **lot ted, lot ting,** *adv.* —*n.* 1 one of a set of objects, such as bits of paper, wood, etc., used to decide something by chance. 2 such a method of deciding: *divide property by lot.* 3 choice made in this way: *The lot fell to me.* 4 what one gets by lot; one's share or portion. 5 fate; fortune: *a happy lot.* 6 plot of land: *an empty lot.* 7 a motion-picture studio and its grounds. 8 a distinct portion or parcel of anything, such as merchandise. 9 number of persons or things considered as a group; collection; set: *a fine lot of boys. This lot of sweaters will go on sale tomorrow.* 10 **a lot of** or, often, **lots of,** INFORMAL. a great many; much: *a lot of books, lots of money.* 11 INFORMAL. a person of a certain kind: *He is a bad lot.* 12 **cast in one's lot with** or **throw in one's lot with,** share the fate of; become a partner with. 13 **cast lots** or **draw lots,** use lots to decide something: *We drew lots to determine who should be captain.*
—*v.t., v.i.* cast lots; divide into lots.
—*adv.* **a lot** or, often, **lots,** INFORMAL. a great deal; much: *I feel a lot better.*
[Old English *hlot*]

➤ **a lot, a lot of, lots, lots of.** The meaning "a great many; a good deal" is Informal and, particularly in the plural, tends to be avoided in Formal English. The same idea may be expressed in a number of ways, ranging from very informal to formal: *He tried lots of different ways to improve his writing. He tried a lot of different ways to improve his writing. He tried a great many different ways to improve his writing. He tried a variety of ways to improve his writing.*

Lot (lot), *n.* (in the Bible) Abraham's nephew, who was allowed to escape from Sodom before God destroyed it. His wife looked back and was changed into a pillar of salt.

loth (lōth), *adj.* loath.

Lo thar i o (lō ther′ē ō, lō thar′ē ō), *n., pl.* **-thar i os.** man who makes love to many women; libertine. [< the name of a character in *The Fair Penitent,* a play by Nicholas Rowe, 1674-1718, English dramatist]

lo tion (lō′shən), *n.* a liquid medicine or cosmetic which is applied to the skin. Lotions are used to relieve pain or to heal, cleanse, or beautify the skin. [< Latin *lotionem* a washing, ultimately < *lavere* to wash]

lo tos (lō′təs), *n.* lotus.

lot ter y (lot′ər ē), *n., pl.* **-ter ies.** scheme or arrangement for the distribution of prizes by lot or chance. In a lottery a large number of tickets are sold, some of which, as determined by drawing lots after the sale, entitle the holders to prizes. [< Middle Dutch *loterije* < *lot* lot]

lot to (lot′ō), *n.* game played by drawing numbered disks from a bag or box and covering the corresponding numbers on cards. The first player to complete a blank row is the winner. [< Italian, lot < French *lot;* of Germanic origin]

lo tus (lō′təs), *n.* 1 any of various water lilies having large, often floating leaves and showy flowers, commonly represented in the decorative art of the Hindus and the Egyptians. 2 any of a genus of shrubby plants of the pea family, bearing red, pink, or white flowers. 3 in Greek legends: **a** a plant whose fruit was supposed to cause a dreamy and contented forgetfulness in those who ate it, and make them lose all desire to return home. **b** the fruit itself. Also, **lotos.** [< Latin < Greek *lōtos*]

lo tus-eat er (lō′təs ē′tər), *n.* 1 person who leads a life of dreamy, indolent ease. 2 (in Greek legends) person who lived on the fruit of the lotus, and became content and indolent, having no desire to return home.

loud (loud), *adj.* 1 making a strong sound or noise; not quiet or soft: *a loud bang, a loud voice.* 2 noisy; resounding: *loud music, a loud place to study.* See synonym study below. 3 clamorous; insistent: *be loud in demands.* 4 INFORMAL. showy; flashy, especially in dress or manner: *loud clothes.*

hat, āge, fär; let, ēqual, tėrm;
it, īce; hot, ōpen, ôrder;
oil, out; cup, pu̇t, rüle;
ch, child; ng, long; sh, she;
th, thin; ꟈH, then; zh, measure;

ə represents *a* in about, *e* in taken, *i* in pencil, *o* in lemon, *u* in circus.

< = from, derived from, taken from.

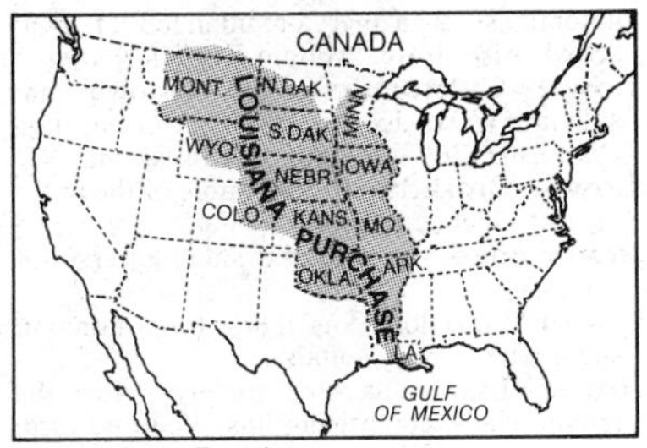

Louisiana Purchase shown by shaded area on a modern map

5 INFORMAL. obtrusive; somewhat vulgar: *a loud person.* —*adv.* in a loud manner; with a loud noise or voice; aloud; loudly: *He called long and loud.* [Old English *hlūd*] —**loud′ly,** *adv.* —**loud′ness,** *n.*

Syn. *adj.* 2 **Loud, noisy** mean making much or intense sound. **Loud** suggests strength or intensity of sound, but not necessarily disagreeableness: *They speaker's voice was loud, clear, and pleasing.* **Noisy** always suggests disagreeable loudness and sometimes implies that it is constant or habitual: *The people next door are noisy.*

loud mouth (loud′mouth′), *n., pl.* **-mouths** (-mouꟈHz′). SLANG. a loudmouthed person.

loud mouthed (loud′mouꟈHd′, loud′moutht′), *adj.* 1 talking loudly; irritatingly or offensively noisy. 2 talking too much; not discreet.

loud speak er (loud′spē′kər), *n.* device for converting electrical impulses into sounds and amplifying them, as in a radio, phonograph, or public address system.

Lou is II of Bourbon (lü′ē, lü′is), 1621-1686, Prince de Condé, French general.

Louis IX, 1214-1270, king of France from 1226 to 1270. He is called "Saint Louis."

Louis XI, 1423-1483, king of France from 1461 to 1483.

Louis XII, 1462-1515, king of France from 1498 to 1515.

Louis XIII, 1601-1643, king of France from 1610 to 1643.

Louis XIV, 1638-1715, king of France from 1643 to 1715. He was called "Louis the Great."

Louis XV, 1710-1774, king of France from 1715 to 1774.

Louis XVI, 1754-1793, king of France from 1774 to 1792. He was guillotined in the French Revolution.

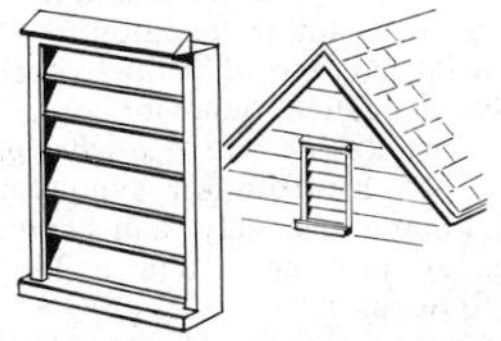
louver (def. 1, left)—wooden louvers across a window; (def. 2, right)

Louis XVII, 1785-1795, son of Louis XVI, king of France in name only from 1793 to 1795.

Louis XVIII, 1755-1824, king of France from 1814 to 1824, the successor of Napoleon I.

lou is d'or (lü′ē dôr′), 1 an old French gold coin, issued from 1640 to 1795, worth from about $4 to about $4.60. 2 a later French gold coin worth 20 francs. [< French, gold Louis (Louis XIII)]

Lou ise (lü ēz′), *n.* **Lake,** lake in the Canadian Rockies. 5670 ft. above sea level.

Lou i si an a (lu̇ ē′zē an′ə, lü′ē zē an′ə), *n.* one of the south central states of the United States. 3,643,000 pop.; 48,500 sq. mi. *Capital:* Baton Rouge. *Abbrev.:* La. —**Lou i′si an′i an, Lou i′si an′an,** *adj., n.*

Louisiana Purchase, large region that the United States bought from France in 1803. It extended from the Mississippi River to the Rocky Mountains and from Canada to the Gulf of Mexico.

Lou is Na po le on (lü′ē nə pō′lē ən; lü′ē nə pō′lyən), See **Napoleon III.**

Lou is Phi lippe (lü′ē fə lēp′), 1773-1850, king of France from 1830 to 1848.

Lou is ville (lü′ē vil), *n.* city in N Kentucky, on the Ohio River. 362,000.

lounge (lounj), *v.,* **lounged, loung ing,** *n.* —*v.i.* 1 stand, stroll, sit, or lie at ease and lazily: *I lounged on the beach.* 2 pass time lazily or at one's ease. —*v.t.* pass (time, etc.) lounging: *She lounged away the weekend.* —*n.* 1 a comfortable and informal room in which one can lounge and be at ease: *a theater lounge.* 2 couch or sofa. 3 act or state of lounging. [origin uncertain] —**loung′er,** *n.*

lour (lour), *v.i., n.* lower².

Lourdes (lu̇rd), *n.* town in SW France where there is a famous Catholic shrine. 16,000.

Lou ren ço Mar ques (lō ren′sō mär′kəs), capital of Mozambique, in the S part. 79,000.

louse (lous), *n., pl.* **lice,** *v.,* **loused, lous ing.** —*n.* 1 any of an order of certain small, wingless insects that have flat bodies and suck blood, infesting the hair or skin of people and animals, causing great irritation. 2 any of an order of similar insects with biting mouth parts, that are parasitic on birds and a few other animals. 3 any of certain other superficially similar arthropods, as the wood louse. 4 SLANG. a mean, contemptible person. —*v.t.* **louse up,** SLANG. spoil; get (something) all confused or in a mess: *louse up a deal.* [Old English *lūs*]

lous y (lou′zē), *adj.,* **lous i er, lous i est.** 1 infested with lice. 2 SLANG. bad; poor; of low quality. 3 SLANG. well supplied: *lousy with money.* —**lous′i ly,** *adv.* —**lous′i ness,** *n.*

lout (lout), *n.* an awkward, stupid fellow; boor. [probably < Scandinavian (Old Icelandic) *lūtr* stooping]

lout ish (lou′tish), *adj.* awkward and stupid; boorish.

Lou vain (lü vān′), *n.* city in central Belgium. 32,000.

lou ver (lü′vər), *n.* 1 any of several overlapping horizontal strips of wood, glass, etc., set across a window or other opening, so as to keep out rain but provide ventilation and light. 2 window or other opening covered with these boards. 3 a ventilating slit, especially one for the escape of heat, as in the bulkhead of a ship. Also, **louvre.** [< Old French *lover*]

lou vered (lü′vərd), *adj.* 1 provided with a louver or louvers. 2 arranged like louvers.

lou vre (lü′vər), *n.* louver.

Lou vre (lü′vrə), *n.* a famous museum in Paris, formerly a palace of the kings of France.

lov a ble (luv′ə bəl), *adj.* worthy of being loved; endearing. Also, **loveable.** —**lov′a ble ness,** *n.* —**lov′a bly,** *adv.*

love (luv), *n., v.,* **loved, lov ing.** —*n.* 1 a warm and tender liking; deep feeling of fondness and friendship; great affection or devotion: *love of one's family, love for a friend.* See synonym study below. 2 a strong or passionate affection for a person one desires sexually. 3 instance of such feeling; a being in love. 4 this feeling as a subject for books or as a personified influence. 5 **Love, a** Venus. **b** Cupid. 6 a strong liking for or devotion to (something): *a love of books.* 7 person who is loved, especially a sweetheart. 8 the kindly feeling or benevolence of God for His creatures, or the reverent devotion due from them to God, or the kindly affection they should have for each other. 9 (in tennis and certain other games) a score of zero for a player or side.

fall in love, begin to love; come to feel love.

for the love of, for the sake of; because of.

in love, feeling love.

make love, a caress, kiss, etc., as lovers do; pay amorous attention (to); woo. **b** have sexual intercourse (with).

—*v.t.* 1 have a warm liking or deep feeling for; hold dear. 2 have a lover's strong or passionate affection for; be in love with. 3 like very much; take great pleasure in: *I love music.* 4 embrace affectionately. —*v.i.* 1 be in love; fall in love. 2 have affection: *He can hate but cannot love.*

[Old English *lufian*]

Syn. *n.* 1 **Love, affection** mean a feeling of warm liking and tender attachment. **Love** applies to a strong attachment that suggests tenderness, as for a child or parent, and devotion and loyalty, as to friends or family: *Every person needs to give and receive love.* **Affection** applies to a less strong feeling, suggesting warm fondness: *I like my teacher, but feel no affection for her.*

love a ble (luv′ə bəl), *adj.* lovable.

love apple, ARCHAIC. tomato.

love bird (luv′bėrd′), *n.* any of various small parrots that show great affection for their mates.

love feast, 1 meal eaten together by the early Christians as a symbol of brotherly love. 2 a religious ceremony imitating this. 3 banquet or other gathering to promote good feeling.

love knot, an ornamental knot or bow of ribbons as a symbol or token of love.

Love lace (luv′lās), *n.* **Richard,** 1618-1658, English poet.

love less (luv′lis), *adj.* 1 without love; feeling no love; unloving: *a loveless heart.* 2 receiving no love; unloved: *a loveless child.* —**love′less ly,** *adv.* —**love′less ness,** *n.*

love-lies-bleed ing (luv′līz blē′ding), *n.* amaranth with long spikes of crimson flowers that often droop on the ground.

love li ness (luv′lē nis), *n.* beauty.

love lorn (luv′lôrn′), *adj.* suffering because of love; forsaken by the person whom one loves. **—love′lorn′ness,** *n.*

love ly (luv′lē), *adj.,* **-li er, -li est,** *n., pl.* **-lies.** *—adj.* 1 beautiful or endearing in appearance or character; lovable. See **beautiful** for synonym study. 2 INFORMAL. very pleasing; delightful. *—n.* INFORMAL. a pretty girl.

love mak ing (luv′mā′king), *n.* 1 attentions or caresses between lovers; wooing; courtship. 2 sexual intercourse.

lov er (luv′ər), *n.* 1 person who loves. 2 man who is in love with a woman. 3 **lovers,** *pl.* man and a woman who are in love with each other. 4 man who loves illicitly; paramour. 5 person having a strong liking: *a lover of music, a lover of books.* **—lov′er like′,** *adj.*

lowboy

lov er ly (luv′ər lē), *adj.* like a lover. *—adv.* in the manner of a lover.

love seat, seat or small sofa for two persons.

love sick (luv′sik′), *adj.* 1 languishing for or with love. 2 expressing a languishing caused by love: *a lovesick song.* **—love′sick′-ness,** *n.*

lov ing (luv′ing), *adj.* feeling or showing love; affectionate; fond: *loving glances.* **—lov′ing ly,** *adv.*

loving cup, 1 a large cup with two or more handles, passed around for all to drink from, as at the close of a banquet. 2 such a cup awarded as a trophy.

lov ing-kind ness (luv′ing kīnd′nis), *n.* kindness coming from love: *the loving-kindness of God's mercies.*

low[1] (lō), *adj.* 1 not high or tall; short: *low walls, a low hedge.* 2 in a low place; near the ground, floor, or other base: *a low shelf.* 3 rising but slightly from a surface or background: *low relief.* 4 of less than ordinary height, depth, or quantity: *The well is getting low.* 5 lying or being below the general level, as the regions of a country lying near the sea: *low ground.* 6 small in amount, degree, force, value, etc.; moderate: *a low price, a low diet of few calories.* 7 of humble rank; lowly: *a low position.* 8 unfavorable; poor: *I have a low opinion of his abilities.* 9 not advanced in organization; inferior: *Bacteria are low organisms.* 10 mean or base; coarse; vulgar; degraded: *low company.* See **base**[2] for synonym study. 11 lacking in strength; weak; feeble: *a low state of health.* 12 not loud; soft: *a low whisper.* 13 lacking in dignity or elevation: *low thoughts.* 14 depressed or dejected: *low in spirit.* 15 near the horizon: *the low evening sun.* 16 near the equator: *low latitudes.* 17 prostrate or dead. 18 deep: *a low bow.* 19 (of a dress, etc.) cut low; low-necked. 20 not high in the musical scale: *a low pitch, a low note.* 21 (in phonetics) pronounced with the tongue far from the palate. The *a* in *fat* and the *o* in *got* are low vowels. 22 designating an arrangement of gears that gives the lowest speed and the greatest power.
—adv. 1 in, at, or to a low portion, point, degree, condition, price, etc.: *Supplies are running low.* 2 near the ground, floor, or base: *fly low.* 3 softly; quietly; not loudly. 4 at a low pitch on the musical scale. 5 meanly; humbly: *You value yourself too low.* 6 near the horizon: *The sun sank low.* 7 near the equator. 8 **lay low,** a knock down. b kill. 9 **lie low,** stay hidden; keep still.
—n. 1 arrangement of gears to give the lowest speed and the greatest power, as in an automobile and similar machines. 2 area of comparatively low barometric pressure. 3 a low point, level, position, etc.: *Many stocks fell to new lows after the news was received.* [< Scandinavian (Old Icelandic) *lāgr*] **—low′ness,** *n.*

low[2] (lō), *v.i., v.t.* make the sound of a cow; moo. *—n.* the sound a cow makes; mooing. [Old English *hlōwan*]

low blood pressure, hypotension.

low born (lō′bôrn′), *adj.* of humble birth.

low boy (lō′boi′), *n.* a low chest of drawers, usually with legs.

low bred (lō′bred′), *adj.* coarse; vulgar.

low brow (lō′brou′), INFORMAL. *—n.* person lacking in appreciation of intellectual or artistic things. *—adj.* of or suitable for a lowbrow.

Low-Church (lō′chėrch′), *adj.* of or having to do with a party in the Anglican communion that lays little stress on church authority and ceremonies, emphasizing the evangelical rather than the priestly or Catholic character of the church.

Low-Church man (lō′chėrch′mən), *n., pl.* **-men.** person who favors Low-Church practices.

low comedy, comedy of a broad rather than a subtle nature, relying more on boisterous physical action and ludicrous situations than on witty dialogue.

Low Countries, the Netherlands, Belgium, and Luxembourg.

low-coun try (lō′kun′trē), *adj.* of the Low Countries.

low down (lō′doun′), *n.* SLANG. actual facts or truth.

low-down (lō′doun′), *adj.* INFORMAL. low; mean; contemptible: *a low-down trick.*

Low ell (lō′əl), *n.* 1 **Amy,** 1874-1925, American poet and critic. 2 **James Russell,** 1819-1891, American poet, essayist, and diplomat. 3 **Robert,** born 1917, American poet. 4 city in NE Massachusetts. 94,000.

low er[1] (lō′ər), *v.t.* 1 let down or haul down: *lower the flag.* 2 make more low in height or level: *lower the water in a canal.* 3 reduce in amount, degree, force, etc.: *lower the volume of a radio, lower the price of a car.* 4 bring down in rank, station, or estimation; degrade; dishonor. *—v.i.* become lower; sink; descend: *The sun lowered slowly.* *—adj., comparative of* **low**[1]. 1 consisting of representatives usually elected by popular vote: *the lower branch of a legislature.* 2 below others on a comparative scale: *lower organisms, lower prices.* 3 Usually, **Lower.** (in geology) being or relating to an earlier division of a period, system, or the like: *Lower Cretaceous.* *—adv.* comparative of **low**[1]. [< *low*[1]]

low er[2] (lou′ər), *v.i.* 1 (of the sky, weather, etc.) look dark and threatening. 2 look angry or sullen; frown; scowl. *—n.* 1 (of the sky, weather, etc.) a dark and threatening look; gloominess. 2 an angry or sullen look; frown; scowl. Also, **lour.** [Middle English *louren*]

Low er California (lō′ər), narrow peninsula in NW Mexico, south of California; Baja California. 760 mi. long; 55,654 sq. mi.

Lower Canada, former name of the province of Quebec.

lower case, (in printing) small letters, not capitals.

low er-case (lō′ər kās′), *adj.* (in printing) in small letters, not capitals.

lower class, class of society below the middle class, comprising unskilled and farm laborers, unemployed people, and (sometimes) the working class.

low er-class (lō′ər klas′), *adj.* 1 of or having to do with the lower class. 2 (in schools and colleges) of or having to do with the freshman and sophomore classes.

low er class man (lō′ər klas′mən), *n., pl.* **-men.** freshman or sophomore.

lower house or **Lower House,** the larger or more representative branch of a legislature that has two branches, such as the House of Representatives or the House of Commons.

low er ing (lou′ər ing), *adj.* 1 (of the sky, weather, etc.) dark and threatening. 2 frowning; scowling. **—low′er ing ly,** *adv.*

low er most (lō′ər mōst), *adj.* lowest.

lower regions, hell; Hades.

lower world, 1 hell; Hades. 2 earth.

lowest common denominator, least common denominator.

lowest common multiple, least common multiple.

low frequency, (in electronics) a frequency ranging from 30 to 300 kilocycles per second.

low-fre quen cy (lō′frē′kwən sē), *adj.* having low frequency.

Low German, 1 the Germanic speech of the Low Countries (Dutch, Flemish, etc.). 2 the German dialect of northern Germany.

low-grade (lō′grād′), *adj.* of poor quality; inferior: *low-grade ores.*

low-key (lō′kē′), *adj.* understated; played down.

low-keyed (lō′kēd′), *adj.* low-key.

low land (lō′lənd), *n.* 1 country or region that is lower and flatter than the neighboring country. 2 **Lowlands,** *pl.* a low, flat region in S and E Scotland. *—adj.* of or in such a country or region.

low land er (lō′lən dər), *n.* 1 native or inhabitant of a lowland. 2 **Lowlander,** native or inhabitant of the Lowlands of Scotland.

low ly (lō′lē), *adj.,* **-li er, -li est,** *adv.* *—adj.* 1 low in rank, station, position, or development: *a lowly corporal, a lowly occupation.* 2 modest in feeling, behavior, or condition; humble; meek: *He held a lowly opinion of himself.* See **humble** for synonym study. *—adv.* 1 humbly; meekly. 2 in a low manner, degree, or position. 3 in a low voice. **—low′li ness,** *n.*

Low Mass, a simplified form of High Mass, conducted by one priest assisted by altar boys. There is no chanting in Low Mass.

low-mind ed (lō′mīn′did), *adj.* having or showing a coarse or low mind; mean; vulgar. **—low′-mind′ed ly,** *adv.* **—low′-mind′ed-ness,** *n.*

low-necked (lō′nekt′), *adj.* (of a dress, etc.) cut low so as to show the neck, part of the bosom, and the shoulders or back; décolleté.

low-pitched (lō′picht′), *adj.* 1 of low tone or sound; deep. 2 having little slope.

low-pres sure (lō′presh′ər), *adj.* 1 having or using less than the usual pressure. 2 having a low barometric pressure. 3 using easygoing methods; not pressuring: *a low-pressure salesman.*

low relief, bas-relief.

low-spir it ed (lō′spir′ə tid), *adj.* sad; depressed. **—low′-spir′it ed ly,** *adv.* **—low′-spir′it ed ness,** *n.*

low spirits, sadness; depression.

low-ten sion (lō′ten′shən), *adj.* having or using a low voltage.

low tide, 1 the lowest level of the tide. 2 time when the tide is lowest. 3 the lowest point.

low-wa ter mark (lō′wô′tər, lō′wot′ər), 1 the lowest level reached by a body of water. 2 any lowest point.

lox[1] (loks), *n.* kind of smoked salmon. [< Yiddish *laks*]

lox[2] (loks), *n.* liquid oxygen. [< *l(iquid) ox(ygen)*]

loy al (loi′əl), *adj.* 1 true and faithful to love, promise, duty, or other obligations. See **faithful** for synonym study. 2 faithful to one's king, government, or country. [< Middle French < Latin *legalis* legal. Doublet of LEAL, LEGAL.] **—loy′al ly,** *adv.*

loy al ist (loi′ə list), *n.* 1 person who supports his king or the existing government, especially in time of revolt. 2 **Loyalist, a** an American colonist who opposed independence for the American colonies at the time of the Revolutionary War; Tory. **b** person loyal to the Spanish republic and opposed to Franco and the Falangists during the civil war in Spain from 1936 to 1939.

loy al ty (loi′əl tē), *n., pl.* **-ties.** loyal feeling or behavior; faithfulness.

Loy o la (loi ō′lə), *n.* **Ignatius of,** 1491-1556, Spanish soldier, priest, and saint, founder of the Jesuit order.

loz enge (loz′inj), *n.* 1 design or figure having four equal sides, two acute angles, and two obtuse angles; diamond; rhombus. 2 a small tablet of any shape used as medicine or candy. Cough drops are sometimes called lozenges. [< Old French *losenge*]

LP, trademark for a long-playing microgroove phonograph record, usually played at 33⅓ revolutions per minute.

L.S., place of seal [for Latin *locus sigilli*].

LSD, drug that produces hallucinations and temporary symptoms somewhat like those of schizophrenia. It is a derivative of an acid obtained from ergot. [< *l(y)s(ergic acid) d(iethylamide)*]

L.S.D. or **l.s.d.,** pounds, shillings, and pence [for Latin *librae, solidi, denarii*].

Lt., Lieutenant.

Ltd. or **ltd.,** limited.

Lu, lutetium.

Lu an da (lü än′də), *n.* capital of Angola, on the Atlantic. 142,000.

Lu ang Pra bang (lü äng′ prä bäng′), royal capital of Laos, in the N part. 60,000.

lu au (lü′ou), *n.* a Hawaiian feast, generally held outdoors, with roast pig as the main dish. [< Hawaiian *lū′au*]

lub ber (lub′ər), *n.* 1 a big, clumsy, stupid fellow. 2 a clumsy sailor. [Middle English *lober*]

lub ber ly (lub′ər lē), *adj.* 1 loutish; clumsy; stupid. 2 awkward in the work of a sailor. *—adv.* in a lubberly manner. **—lub′ber li ness,** *n.*

Lub bock (lub′ək), *n.* city in NW Texas. 149,000.

lube (lüb), *n.* INFORMAL. lubricant.

Lü beck (ly′bek), *n.* seaport in NE West Germany. 242,000.

Lu blin (lü′blən), *n.* city in E Poland. 238,000.

lu bri cant (lü′brə kənt), *n.* oil, grease, etc., for putting on parts of machines that slide or move against one another, to make them work smoothly and easily. *—adj.* lubricating.

lu bri cate (lü′brə kāt), *v.,* **-cat ed, -cat ing.** *—v.t.* 1 apply oil, grease, or other substance to (a machine, etc.) to make it run smoothly and easily. 2 make slippery or smooth; expedite. *—v.i.* act as a lubricant. [< Latin *lubricatum* made slippery < *lubricus* slippery] **—lu′bri ca′tion,** *n.* **—lu′bri ca′tor,** *n.*

lu bri cious (lü brish′əs), *adj.* 1 slippery; smooth; slimy. 2 shifty; unstable; elusive. 3 wanton; lewd.

lu bric i ty (lü bris′ə tē), *n., pl.* **-ties.** 1 oily smoothness; slipperiness. 2 shiftiness; unsteadiness. 3 lasciviousness; lewdness.

lu cent (lü′snt), *adj.* 1 bright or shining; luminous. 2 letting light through; translucent; lucid; clear. [< Latin *lucentem* < *lux, lucis* light] **—lu′cent ly,** *adv.*

lu cerne (lü sėrn′), *n.* alfalfa. [< French *luzerne* < Provençal *luzerno*]

Lu cerne (lü sėrn′), *n.* 1 city in central Switzerland. 73,000. 2 **Lake of,** lake in central Switzerland. 24 mi. long; 44 sq. mi.

Lu cian (lü′shən), *n.* A.D. 120?-200?, Greek writer of satires.

lu cid (lü′sid), *adj.* 1 marked by clearness of reasoning, expression, or arrangement; easy to follow or understand: *a lucid explanation.* 2 clear in intellect; rational; sane: *An insane person sometimes has lucid intervals.* 3 translucent; clear: *a lucid stream.* 4 shining; bright; luminous. [< Latin *lucidus* < *lux, lucis* light] **—lu′cid ly,** *adv.* **—lu′cid ness,** *n.*

lu cid i ty (lü sid′ə tē), *n.* lucid quality or condition.

Lu ci fer (lü′sə fər), *n.* the chief rebel angel who was cast out of heaven; Satan; the Devil.

Lu cite (lü′sīt), *n.* trademark for a clear plastic compound, an acrylic resin, used instead of glass for airplane windows, lenses, etc.

luck (luk), *n.* 1 that which seems to happen or come to one by chance; fortune; chance: *Luck favored me, and I won.* 2 good fortune; success, prosperity, or advantage coming by chance: *wish one luck, have luck in fishing.*
down on one's luck, INFORMAL. having bad luck; unlucky.
in luck, having good luck; lucky.
out of luck, having bad luck; unlucky.
try one's luck, see what one can do.
[< Middle Dutch *(ghe)luc*]

luck i ly (luk′ə lē), *adv.* by good luck; fortunately.

luck less (luk′lis), *adj.* having or bringing bad luck; unlucky. **—luck′less ly,** *adv.* **—luck′less ness,** *n.*

Luck now (luk′nou), *n.* city in N India. 764,000.

luck y (luk′ē), *adj.,* **luck i er, luck i est.** 1 having good luck: *a lucky person.* See **fortunate** for synonym study. 2 bringing good luck: *a lucky charm, a lucky meeting.* **—luck′i ness,** *n.*

lu cra tive (lü′krə tiv), *adj.* yielding gain or profit; profitable. [< Latin *lucrativus* < *lucrum* gain] **—lu′cra tive ly,** *adv.* **—lu′cra tive ness,** *n.*

lu cre (lü′kər), *n.* money considered bad or degrading. [< Latin *lucrum* gain]

hat, āge, fär; let, ēqual, tėrm;
it, īce; hot, ōpen, ôrder;
oil, out; cup, pu̇t, rüle;
ch, child; ng, long; sh, she;
th, thin; ᴛʜ, then; zh, measure;

ə represents *a* in about, *e* in taken, *i* in pencil, *o* in lemon, *u* in circus.

< = from, derived from, taken from.

Lu cre tius (lü krē′shəs), *n.* 99?-55 B.C., Roman poet and philosopher.

lu cu bra tion (lü′kyə brā′shən), *n.* 1 laborious study. 2 a learned or carefully written production, especially one that is labored and dull. 3 study carried on late at night. [< Latin *lucubrationem* < *lucubrare* work at night]

Lu den dorff (lüd′n dôrf), *n.* **Erich Friedrich Wilhelm von,** 1865-1937, German general.

lu di crous (lü′də krəs), *adj.* causing derisive laughter; amusingly absurd; ridiculous. [< Latin *ludicrus* < *ludus* sport] **—lu′di crous ly,** *adv.* **—lu′di crous ness,** *n.*

luff (luf), *v.i.* turn the bow of a ship toward the wind; sail into the wind. *—n.* 1 act of turning the bow of a ship toward the wind. 2 the forward edge of a fore-and-aft sail. [< Dutch *loef*]

Luft waf fe (lu̇ft′vä′fə), *n.* the German air force, especially in World War II.

lug[1] (lug), *v.,* **lugged, lug ging.** *—v.t.* 1 pull along or carry with effort; drag. 2 introduce irrelevantly or without appropriateness. *—v.i.* pull; tug. [perhaps < Scandinavian (Swedish) *lugga* pull by the hair]

lug[2] (lug), *n.* 1 a projecting part used to hold or grip something, such as a handle on a pitcher. 2 SLANG. a clumsy or stupid person. [origin uncertain]

lug[3] (lug), *n.* lugsail. [origin uncertain]

lug gage (lug′ij), *n.* baggage, especially of a traveler or passenger; suitcases and the like. [< *lug*[1]]

lugger

lug ger (lug′ər), *n.* boat rigged with lugsails.

lug sail (lug′sāl′; *Nautical* lug′səl), *n.* a four-cornered sail held by a yard that slants across the mast.

lu gu bri ous (lü gü′brē əs, lü gyü′brē əs), *adj.* too sad; overly mournful: *the lugubrious howl of a dog.* [< Latin *lugubris* < *lugere* mourn] **—lu gu′bri ous ly,** *adv.* **—lu gu′bri ous ness,** *n.*

lug worm (lug′wėrm′), *n.* any of a genus of large annelid worms with a row of gills in pairs along the back. Lugworms burrow in sand along the seashore and are much used for bait.

Luke (lük), *n.* 1 (in the Bible) a physician who was the companion of the apostle Paul and is traditionally believed to have written the third Gospel and the Acts of the Apostles. 2 the third book of the New Testament.

luke warm (lük′wôrm′), *adj.* 1 neither hot nor cold; moderately warm; tepid. 2 showing little enthusiasm; half-hearted; indifferent: *a lukewarm greeting.* [Middle English *luke,* perhaps < Old English *(ge)hleow* warm] **—luke′warm′ly,** *adv.* **—luke′warm′ness,** *n.*

lull (lul), *v.t.* 1 soothe with sounds or caresses; hush to sleep: *The mother lulled the crying baby.* 2 make peaceful or tranquil; quiet: *lull one's suspicions.* *—v.i.* become calm or more nearly calm. *—n.* 1 period of less noise or violence; brief calm: *a lull in a storm.* 2 period of reduced activity: *a lull in trade.* [Middle English *lullen*]

lul la by (lul′ə bī), *n., pl.* **-bies.** song for singing to a child in a cradle; soft song to lull a baby to sleep.

lu lu (lü′lü), *n.* SLANG. an unusual person or thing: *The thunderstorm was a lulu.*

lum ba go (lum bā′gō), *n.* form of rheumatism characterized by pain in the muscles of the small of the back and in the loins. [< Late Latin < Latin *lumbus* loin]

lum bar (lum′bər), *adj.* of the loin or loins: *the lumbar region.* *—n.* a lumbar vertebra, artery, nerve, etc. [< Latin *lumbus* loin]

lum ber[1] (lum′bər), *n.* 1 timber that has been roughly cut into boards, planks, etc., and prepared for use. 2 household articles no longer in use; old furniture and other useless things that take up room. *—v.i.* cut and prepare lumber. *—v.t.* 1 fill up or obstruct with odds and ends; burden uselessly; encumber. 2 heap together in disorder. [original meaning "useless goods," perhaps < an early variant of *lombard* pawnshop] **—lum′ber er,** *n.*

lum ber[2] (lum′bər), *v.i.* 1 move along heavily and noisily; roll along with difficulty. 2 make a rumbling noise. [Middle English *lomeren*]

lum ber ing[1] (lum′bər ing), *n.* business of cutting and preparing timber for use. [< *lumber*[1]]

lum ber ing[2] (lum′bər ing), *adj.* ponderous in movement; inconveniently bulky. [< *lumber*[2]]

lum ber jack (lum′bər jak′), *n.* person whose work is cutting down trees and sending the logs to the sawmill; woodsman; logger.

lum ber man (lum′bər mən), *n., pl.* **-men.** 1 lumberjack. 2 man who prepares lumber or buys and sells lumber.

lum ber yard (lum′ber yärd′), *n.* place where lumber is stored and sold.

lu men (lü′mən), *n., pl.* **-min a** (-mə nə), **-mens.** 1 (in physics) the unit of luminous flux, equal to the amount of light given out through a solid angle by a source of one candela radiating equally in all directions. 2 (in anatomy) the space within a tubular organ, such as a blood vessel. [< Latin, light, opening in a tube]

lu mi naire (lü mə ner′, lü mə nar′), *n.* a lighting fixture complete with all its necessary parts and accessories, including reflector, socket, etc. [< French]

Lu mi nal (lü′mə nəl, lü′mə nal), *n.* trademark for phenobarbital.

lu mi nance (lü′mə nəns), *n.* the intensity of light in relation to the area of its source.

lu mi nar y (lü′mə ner′ē), *n., pl.* **-nar ies,** *adj.* *—n.* 1 a heavenly body that gives or reflects light. 2 anything that gives light. 3 a famous person. *—adj.* having to do with light. [< Late Latin *luminarium* < Latin *lumen* light]

lu mi nesce (lü′mə nes′), *v.i.,* **-nesced, -nesc ing.** exhibit luminescence.

lu mi nes cence (lü′mə nes′ns), *n.* emission of light occurring at a temperature below that of incandescent bodies. Luminescence includes phosphorescence and fluorescence.

lu mi nes cent (lü′mə nes′nt), *adj.* 1 giving out light without much heat. 2 having to do with luminescence.

lu mi nif er ous (lü′mə nif′er əs), *adj.* producing or transmitting light.

lu mi nos i ty (lü′mə nos′ə tē), *n., pl.* **-ties.** 1 luminous quality or condition. 2 something luminous.

lu mi nous (lü′mə nəs), *adj.* 1 shining by its own light: *The sun and stars are luminous bodies.* 2 full of light; shining; bright. 3 easily understood; clear; enlightening. **—lu′mi nous ly,** *adv.* **—lu′mi nous ness,** *n.*

luminous flux, the rate at which light is transmitted. Its unit is the lumen.

lum mox (lum′əks), *n.* INFORMAL. an awkward, stupid person. [origin uncertain]

lump[1] (lump), *n.* 1 a small, solid mass of no particular shape: *a lump of coal.* 2 protuberance or swelling; bump: *a lump on the head.* 3 lot; mass; heap: *a lump of money.* 4 INFORMAL. **a** a stupid person. **b** a big, sturdy person. 5 **lumps,** *pl.* INFORMAL. a beating; punishment. 6 **a lump in the throat,** feeling of inability to swallow, caused by pity, sorrow, or other strong emotion. 7 **in the lump,** in the mass; as a whole. *—v.i.* 1 form into a lump or lumps. 2 move heavily. *—v.t.* 1 make lumps of, on, or in. 2 put together; deal with in a mass or as a whole: *We will lump all our expenses.*
—adj. 1 in lumps; in a lump: *lump coal, lump sugar.* 2 including a number of items: *a lump sum.*
[Middle English *lumpe,* perhaps < Middle Dutch *lompe* mass, chunk]

lump[2] (lump), *v.t.* INFORMAL. put up with; endure: *If you don't like it, you can lump it.* [origin uncertain]

lump ish (lum′pish), *adj.* 1 like a lump; heavy and clumsy. 2 dull; stupid. **—lump′ish ly,** *adv.* **—lump′ish ness,** *n.*

lump y (lum′pē), *adj.,* **lump i er, lump i est.** 1 full of lumps: *lumpy gravy.* 2 covered with lumps: *lumpy ground.* 3 heavy and clumsy: *a lumpy animal.* 4 (of water) rough, with the surface cut up by the wind into small waves. **—lump′i ly,** *adv.* **—lump′i ness,** *n.*

Lu na (lü′nə), *n.* (in Roman myths) the goddess of the moon, identified with the Greek goddess Selene.

lu na cy (lü′nə sē), *n., pl.* **-cies.** 1 insanity. 2 extreme folly. [< *lunatic*]

luna moth or **Luna moth,** a large North American moth having light-green wings with crescent-shaped spots and a long tail on each hind wing.

lu nar (lü′nər), *adj.* 1 of the moon. 2 like the moon. 3 measured by the moon's revolutions: *a lunar year.* [< Latin *luna* moon]

lunar excursion module, module used to land on the moon after separating from a spacecraft near the lunar surface.

lunar month, the period of one complete revolution of the moon around the earth; the interval between one new moon and the next; about 29½ days.

lu nate (lü′nāt), *adj.* crescent-shaped.

lu na tic (lü′nə tik), *n.* 1 an insane person. 2 an extremely foolish person. *—adj.* 1 insane. 2 for insane people: *a lunatic asylum.* 3 extremely foolish or mad. [< Late Latin *lunaticus* < Latin *luna* moon; because it was once thought that insanity was brought about by the changes of the moon]

lunatic fringe, those whose zeal in some cause, movement, etc., goes beyond reasonable limits.

lunch (lunch), *n.* 1 a light meal between breakfast and dinner. 2 a light meal. 3 food for a lunch. *—v.i.* eat lunch. *—v.t.* provide with a lunch. [origin unknown] **—lunch′er,** *n.*

lunch eon (lun′chən), *n.* 1 lunch. 2 a formal lunch. *—v.i.* eat lunch.

lunch eon ette (lun′chə net′), *n.* restaurant in which light meals are served.

lunch room (lunch′rüm′, lunch′rům′), *n.* 1 restaurant in which light meals are served. 2 room in a school, factory, etc., where lunch is eaten.

lunch time (lunch′tīm′), *n.* time at which lunch is eaten or served.

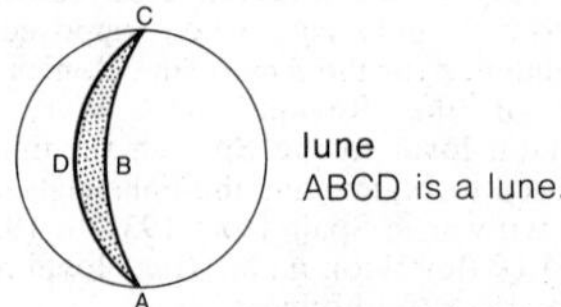

lune (lün), *n.* a crescent-shaped figure on a plane or a sphere bounded by two arcs of circles. [< French < Latin *luna* moon]

lu nette (lü net′), *n.* 1 a crescent-shaped opening or space in a vaulted ceiling, dome, wall, etc. 2 an arched or rounded opening, window, etc. [< French, diminutive of *lune* moon]

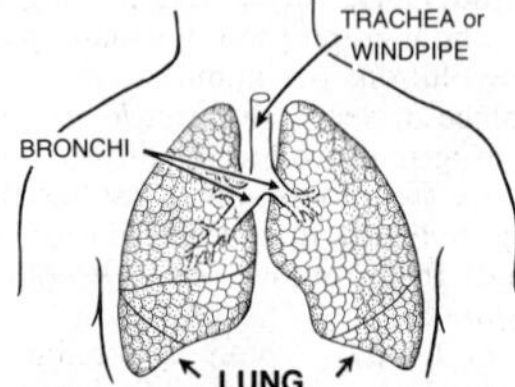

lung (def. 1)—lungs of a human being

lung (lung), *n.* 1 either one of a pair of saclike, spongy organs by means of which the blood receives oxygen and is rid of carbon dioxide in vertebrates that breathe air. 2 a similar organ in certain invertebrates, such as snails and spiders. 3 a mechanical device for aiding respiration. [Old English *lungen*] **—lung′like′,** *adj.*

lunge (lunj), *n., v.,* **lunged, lung ing.** *—n.* any sudden forward movement, such as a thrust with a sword or other weapon. *—v.i.* move with a lunge; make a sudden forward movement; thrust. [< French *allonger,* originally, to lengthen] **—lung′er,** *n.*

lung fish (lung′fish′), *n., pl.* **-fish es** or **-fish.** any of various freshwater fishes having a lunglike air bladder in addition to gills, enabling them to obtain oxygen both in and out of water. Lungfishes are found in Australia, Africa, and South America.

lung wort (lung′wėrt′), *n.* any of a genus of perennial plants of the same family as the borage, especially a European herb with small purple flowers and leaves spotted with white that was once a popular remedy for lung disease.

Lu per ca li a (lü′pər kā′lē ə), *n.pl.* an ancient Roman fertility festival held annually on February 15. [< Latin]

lu pine[1] or **lu pin** (lü′pən), *n.* any of a large genus of plants of the pea family, having long spikes of flowers, radiating clusters of grayish, hairy leaflets, and flat pods with bean-shaped seeds. It is grown for its showy flowers, its edible seeds, for fodder, and as a cover crop. [< Latin *lupinum* < *lupus* wolf]

lu pine[2] (lü′pīn), *adj.* 1 of or like a wolf; ravenous; fierce. 2 related to the wolf. [< Latin *lupinus* < *lupus* wolf]

lu pus (lü′pəs), *n.* any of several skin diseases, especially one caused by the tuberculosis bacillus. [< Latin, wolf]

lurch[1] (lėrch), *n.* 1 a sudden leaning or roll to one side, like that of a ship, a car, or a staggering person. 2 a swaying motion or gait; stagger. —*v.i.* lean or roll suddenly to one side; make a lurch; stagger: *The injured man lurched forward.* [origin uncertain]

lurch[2] (lėrch), *n.* 1 (in cribbage and other games) a condition in which one player scores nothing or less than half his winning opponent's score, or is badly beaten. 2 **leave in the lurch,** leave in a helpless condition or difficult situation. [< French *lourche*]

lurch er (lėr′chər), *n.* a kind of crossbred hunting dog much used by poachers.

lure (lůr), *n., v.,* **lured, lur ing.** —*n.* 1 power of attracting or fascinating; charm; allure; attraction: *the lure of the sea.* 2 something that allures, entices, or tempts. 3 a decoy or bait, especially an artificial bait used in fishing. —*v.t.* 1 lead away or into something by arousing desire; allure; entice; tempt. See synonym study below. 2 attract with a bait. [< Old French *leurre,* of Germanic origin] **—lur′er,** *n.*

Syn. *v.t.* 1 **Lure, allure, entice** mean to attract or tempt. **Lure,** commonly in a bad sense, means to tempt by rousing desire and usually to lead into something bad or not to one's advantage: *The hope of high profits lured him into questionable dealings.* **Allure,** seldom in a bad sense, means to tempt by appealing to the senses and feelings and by offering pleasure or advantage: *Hawaii allures many tourists.* **Entice,** in a good or bad sense, means to tempt by appealing to hopes and desires and by using persuasion: *We enticed the kitten from the tree.*

lur id (lůr′id), *adj.* 1 lighted up with a red or fiery glare: *The sky was lurid with the flames of the burning city.* 2 glaring in brightness or color: *a lurid red.* 3 shockingly terrible, repulsive, etc.; sensational; startling: *lurid crimes.* 4 pale and dismal in color; wan and sallow. [< Latin *luridus* pale yellow, ghastly] **—lur′id ly,** *adv.* **—lur′id ness,** *n.*

lurk (lėrk), *v.i.* 1 stay about without arousing attention; wait out of sight. 2 be hidden; be unsuspected or latent. 3 move about in a secret and sly manner. See synonym study below. [Middle English *lurken,* apparently < *louren* lower[2]] **—lurk′er,** *n.*

Syn. 3 **Lurk, skulk** mean to move in a secret or furtive way. **Lurk** often but not always suggests an evil purpose: *A stray dog was seen lurking about the house.* **Skulk,** implying sneakiness, cowardice, or shame, always suggests an evil purpose: *The cattle thieves skulked in the woods until the posse had passed.*

Lu sa ka (lü sä′kə), *n.* capital of Zambia, in the central part. 161,000.

lus cious (lush′əs), *adj.* 1 highly pleasant to the taste or smell; richly sweet; delicious: *a luscious peach.* See **delicious** for synonym study. 2 very pleasing to the eye, ear, or mind: *a luscious view of a garden.* [Middle English, perhaps variant of *delicious*] **—lus′cious ly,** *adv.* **—lus′cious ness,** *n.*

lute[1]

lush[1] (lush), *adj.* 1 tender and juicy; growing thick and green: *Lush grass grows along the river banks.* 2 characterized by abundant growth; producing abundantly. 3 luxurious. 4 rich in ornament; flowery. [Middle English *lache*] **—lush′ly,** *adv.* **—lush′ness,** *n.*

lush[2] (lush), *n.* SLANG. 1 alcoholic liquor; drink. 2 person who drinks too much; an alcoholic. [origin unknown]

Lü shun (lü′shůn′), *n.* former seaport in NE China, now part of Lüta. Former name, **Port Arthur.**

Lu si ta ni a (lü′sə tā′nē ə), *n.* ancient name for Portugal.

lust (lust), *n.* 1 strong desire. 2 desire for indulgence of sex; excessive sexual desire. —*v.i.* 1 have a strong desire. 2 have excessive sexual desire. [Old English, pleasure]

lus ter (lus′tər), *n.* 1 a bright shine on the surface; sheen: *the luster of pearls.* See **polish** for synonym study. 2 brightness; radiance: *Her eyes lost their luster.* 3 fame; glory; brilliance: *The deeds of heroes add luster to a nation's history.* 4 a shiny, metallic, often iridescent surface on pottery or china. 5 lusterware. 6 the appearance of the surface of a mineral due to the reflection of light. Also, **lustre.** [< Middle French *lustre,* ultimately < Latin *lustrare* brighten] **—lus′ter less,** *adj.*

lus ter ware (lus′tər wer′, lus′tər war′), *n.* pottery that has a lustrous, metallic, often iridescent surface.

lust ful (lust′fəl), *adj.* full of lust or desire; sensual; lewd. **—lust′ful ly,** *adv.* **—lust′ful ness,** *n.*

lus tral (lus′trəl), *adj.* of or used in ceremonial purification.

lus trate (lus′trāt), *v.t.,* **-trat ed, -trat ing.** purify by offering a sacrifice or by any ceremonial method. **—lus tra′tion,** *n.*

lus tre (lus′tər), *n.* luster.

lus trous (lus′trəs), *adj.* 1 having luster; shining; glossy: *lustrous satin.* 2 brilliant; splendid. **—lus′trous ly,** *adv.* **—lus′trous ness,** *n.*

lus trum (lus′trəm), *n., pl.* **-trums, -tra** (-trə). 1 a ceremonial purification of the ancient Romans, performed every five years after the census had been taken. 2 the ancient Roman census. 3 a period of five years. [< Latin]

hat, āge, fär; let, ēqual, tėrm;
it, īce; hot, ōpen, ôrder;
oil, out; cup, půt, rüle;
ch, child; ng, long; sh, she;
th, thin; ᴛʜ, then; zh, measure;

ə represents *a* in about, *e* in taken, *i* in pencil, *o* in lemon, *u* in circus.

< = from, derived from, taken from.

lust y (lus′tē), *adj.,* **lust i er, lust i est.** strong and healthy; full of vigor; robust: *a lusty boy.* **—lust′i ly,** *adv.* **—lust′i ness,** *n.*

Lü ta (lü′tä′), *n.* seaport in NE China, on the Yellow Sea, consisting of Talien and Lüshun. 3,600,000.

lu ta nist (lüt′n ist), *n.* lutist.

lute[1] (lüt), *n.* a musical instrument much used in the 1500's and 1600's, having a pear-shaped body and usually six pairs of strings. It is played by plucking the strings with the fingers of one hand or with a plectrum. [< Old French *lut* < Old Provençal *laut* < Arabic *al-'ūd* the lute]

lute[2] (lüt), *n., v.,* **lut ed, lut ing.** —*n.* 1 a sealing compound of clay used around joints in pipes, on walls, etc., to prevent leakage or seepage by gas or water. 2 U.S. tool used to scrape excess clay from a brick mold. —*v.t.* seal (a pipe, wall, etc.) with lute. [< Medieval Latin *lutum* < Latin, mud]

lu te al (lü′tē əl), *adj.* of or having to do with the corpus luteum.

lu te ci um (lü tē′shē əm), *n.* lutetium.

lu te in ize (lü′tē ə nīz), *v.i.,* **-ized, -iz ing.** stimulate the production of the corpus luteum.

luteinizing hormone, the pituitary hormone which fosters the development of the corpus luteum.

lu te nist (lüt′n ist), *n.* lutist.

lu te ous (lü′tē əs), *adj.* golden-yellow; orange-yellow. [< Latin *luteus*]

lu te ti um (lü tē′shē əm), *n.* a rare-earth metallic element which usually occurs in nature with ytterbium. *Symbol:* Lu; *atomic number* 71. See pages 326 and 327 for table. Also, **lutecium.** [< New Latin < *Lutetia,* ancient Latin name for Paris (because a French scientist discovered it)]

Lu ther (lü′thər), *n.* **Martin,** 1483-1546, leader of the Protestant Reformation in Germany.

Lu ther an (lü′thər ən), *adj.* having to do with Luther, Lutheranism, or the Lutheran Church. —*n.* member of the Lutheran Church.

Lu ther an ism (lü′thər ə niz′əm), *n.* doctrine, organization, and manner of worship of the Lutheran Church, characterized by a belief in justification by faith alone, denial of the material presence of Christ in the Eucharist, and lack of an organized hierarchy.

Lu thu li (lü tü′lē), *n.* **Albert John,** 1898-1967, South African political leader, a former Zulu chief who worked to end racial segregation in South Africa.

lut ing (lü′ting), *n.* 1 a seal of lute. 2 the material used; lute.

lut ist (lü′tist), *n.* a lute player. Also, **lutanist, lutenist.**

lux (luks), *n., pl.* **lux es, lu ces** (lü′sēz′). the

international unit of illumination, equal to one lumen per square meter. [< Latin, light]

Lux em bourg or **Lux em burg** (luk′səm bėrg′), *n.* 1 country in W Europe, bordered by West Germany, France, and Belgium. 339,000 pop.; 999 sq. mi. 2 its capital. 77,000.

Lux or (luk′sôr), *n.* town in E Egypt on the site of part of ancient Thebes. 40,000.

lux ur i ance (lug zhůr′ē əns, luk shůr′ē əns), *n.* luxuriant growth or productiveness; rich abundance.

lux ur i ant (lug zhůr′ē ənt, luk shůr′ē ənt), *adj.* 1 growing thick and green; lush: *luxuriant jungle growth.* 2 producing abundantly; fertile. 3 richly abundant; profuse. 4 rich in ornament; florid. **—lux ur′i ant ly,** *adv.*

lux ur i ate (lug zhůr′ē āt, luk shůr′ē āt), *v.i.,* **-at ed, -at ing.** 1 indulge in luxury. 2 take great delight; revel: *luxuriate in a hot bath.* 3 grow very abundantly.

lux ur i ous (lug zhůr′ē əs, luk shůr′ē əs), *adj.* 1 fond of luxury; tending toward luxury; self-indulgent. 2 giving or characterized by luxury; very comfortable and beautiful: *a luxurious apartment.* **—lux ur′i ous ly,** *adv.* **—lux ur′i ous ness,** *n.*

lux ur y (luk′shər ē, lug′zhər ē), *n., pl.* **-ur ies,** *adj.* —*n.* 1 comforts and beauties of life beyond what is really necessary. 2 use of the best and most costly food, clothes, houses, furniture, and amusements: *The movie star was accustomed to luxury.* 3 thing that one enjoys, usually something choice and costly: *luxuries such as fine paintings.* 4 thing that is pleasant but not necessary: *Candy is a luxury.* —*adj.* providing lavish comfort and enjoyment; luxurious: *a luxury hotel.* [< Latin *luxuria* < *luxus* excess]

Lu zon (lü zon′), *n.* chief island of the Philippines, in the N part. 11,800,000 pop.; 41,800 sq. mi.

Lvov (lə vôf′), *n.* city in SW Soviet Union, formerly in Poland. 553,000. Also, GERMAN **Lemberg,** POLISH **Lwów.**

Lw, lawrencium.

Lwów (lə vüf′), *n.* Polish name of **Lvov.**

-ly[1], *suffix forming adverbs from adjectives.* 1 in a ____ manner: *Cheerfully = in a cheerful manner.* 2 in ____ ways or respects: *Financially = in financial respects.* 3 to a ____ degree or extent: *Greatly = to a great degree.* 4 in, to, or from a ____ direction: *Northwardly = to or from the north.* 5 in a ____ place: *Thirdly = in the third place.* 6 at a ____ time: *Recently = at a recent time.* [Old English *-līce* < *-līc* -ly[2]]

-ly[2], *suffix forming adjectives from nouns.* 1 like a ____: *Ghostly = like a ghost.* 2 like that of a ____; characteristic of a ____: *Brotherly = like that of a brother.* 3 suited to a ____; fit or proper for a ____: *Womanly = suited to a woman.* 4 of each or every ____; occurring once per ____: *Daily = of every day.* 5 being a ____; that is a ____: *Heavenly = that is a heaven.* [Old English *-līc* < *līc* body, form]

ly cée (lē sā′), *n.* a French secondary school maintained by the government. [< French < Latin *Lyceum*]

ly ce um (lī sē′əm, lī′sē əm), *n.* 1 lecture hall; building or room where popular lectures are given. 2 association for instruction and entertainment through lectures, debates, and concerts. 3 **Lyceum,** an ancient outdoor grove and gymnasium near Athens, where Aristotle taught. 4 lycée. [< Latin *Lyceum* < Greek *Lykeion* (def. 3), named after the nearby temple of Apollo, called *Lykeios*]

lych gate (lich), lich gate.

Ly ci a (lish′ē ə), *n.* ancient district in Asia Minor.

ly co pod (lī′kə pod), *n.* club moss.

ly co po di um (lī′kə pō′dē əm), *n.* 1 club moss. 2 a fine, yellow, inflammable powder made from the spores of certain club mosses, used in fireworks, in surgery, etc. [< New Latin < Greek *lykos* wolf + *pous, podos* foot (because of the shape of the roots)]

lynx—about 3 ft. long with the tail

Ly cur gus (lī kėr′gəs), *n.* Spartan lawgiver who lived in or near the 800's B.C.

Lyd i a (lid′ē ə), *n.* ancient country in W Asia Minor, famous for its wealth and luxury. See **Persia** for map. **—Lyd′i an,** *adj., n.*

lye (lī), *n.* 1 a strong alkaline solution of sodium hydroxide or potassium hydroxide. Lye is used in making soap and in cleaning. 2 an alkaline solution made by leaching wood or other vegetable ashes. [Old English *lēag*]

ly ing[1] (lī′ing), *n.* a telling a lie; the habit of telling lies. —*adj.* false; untruthful. —*v.* ppr. of **lie**[1].

ly ing[2] (lī′ing), *v.* ppr. of **lie**[2].

ly ing-in (lī′ing in′), *n.* confinement in childbirth; giving birth to a child. —*adj.* of or having to do with childbirth: *a lying-in hospital.*

lymph (limf), *n.* a nearly colorless liquid in the tissues of the body, derived from parts of the blood which have filtered through blood capillary walls. Lymph is conveyed back to the blood stream by the lymphatic vessels. It has a slightly alkaline quality and serves to bathe and nourish the tissues. [< Latin *lympha* clear water]

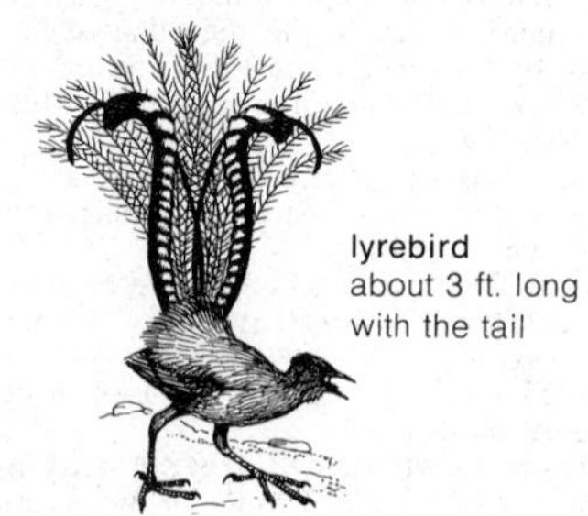

lyrebird about 3 ft. long with the tail

lym phat ic (lim fat′ik), *adj.* 1 of, carrying, or relating to lymph: *the lymphatic system.* 2 sluggish; pale; lacking energy. —*n.* a lymphatic vessel. **—lym phat′i cal ly,** *adv.*

lymphatic vessel, tube or canal through which lymph is carried from different parts of the body.

lymph node or **lymph gland,** any of the small oval bodies occurring along the paths of the lymphatic vessels, active in filtering out harmful microorganisms from the lymph and as a source of lymphocytes.

lymph o cyte (lim′fə sīt), *n.* a type of white blood cell, produced by lymph tissues.

lymph o cyt ic (lim′fə sit′ik), *adj.* of or having to do with a lymphocyte or lymphocytes.

lymph oid (lim′foid), *adj.* of or having to do with lymph, lymphocytes, or lymph tissue.

lynch (linch), *v.t.* put (an accused person) to death, usually by hanging, without a lawful trial. [apparently < Charles *Lynch,* 1736-1796, a planter of Virginia who drew up a vigilante compact with his neighbors] **—lynch′er,** *n.*

lynch law, a putting an accused person to death without a lawful trial.

Lynn (lin), *n.* city in E Massachusetts. 90,000.

lynx (lingks), *n., pl.* **lynx es** or **lynx.** any of a genus of wildcats with short tails, rather long legs, and tufts of hair at the end of their ears, especially a large, shaggy species of Canada and the northern United States. [< Latin < Greek] **—lynx′like′,** *adj.*

lynx-eyed (lingks′īd′), *adj.* having sharp eyes; sharp-sighted.

Ly on (lyôɴ), *n.* French name of **Lyons.**

ly on naise (lī′ə nāz′), *adj.* fried with pieces of onions: *lyonnaise potatoes.* [< French, literally, of Lyons]

Ly ons (lī′ənz, lē ôn′; *French* lyôɴ′), *n.* city in E central France, on the Rhone River. 528,000. Also, FRENCH **Lyon.**

Ly ra (lī′rə), *n.* a small northern constellation that was seen by ancient astronomers as having the rough outline of the lyre of Mercury or Orpheus. It contains the star Vega. Also, **Lyre.**

ly rate (lī′rāt), *adj.* shaped like a lyre, as the tail of certain birds.

lyre (def. 1)

lyre (līr), *n.* 1 an ancient stringed musical instrument somewhat like a small harp. 2 **Lyre,** Lyra. [< Latin *lyra* < Greek]

lyre bird (līr′bėrd′), *n.* either of two Australian perching birds, the male of which has a long tail that resembles the shape of a lyre when spread during courtship.

lyr ic (lir′ik), *n.* 1 a short poem expressing personal emotion. A love poem, a patriotic song, a lament, and a hymn might all be lyrics. 2 Usually, **lyrics,** *pl.* the words for a song, especially a popular song. —*adj.* 1 having to do with lyric poems: *a lyric poet.* 2 characterized by a spontaneous expression of feeling. 3 of or suitable for singing. 4 (of a singing voice) light in volume and tender in character, and often used in the higher register. 5 of or for the lyre. [< Latin *lyricus* < Greek *lyrikos* of a lyre]

lyr i cal (lir′ə kəl), *adj.* 1 having the qualities or characteristics of lyric poetry; emotional; poetic. 2 lyric. **—lyr′i cal ly,** *adv.*

lyr i cism (lir′ə siz′əm), *n.* 1 lyric character or style. 2 a lyric form or expression. 3 lyric outpouring of feeling.

hat, āge, fär; let, ēqual, tėrm;
it, īce; hot, ōpen, ôrder;
oil, out; cup, pu̇t, rüle;
ch, child; ng, long; sh, she;
th, thin; ᴛʜ, then; zh, measure;

ə represents *a* in about, *e* in taken, *i* in pencil, *o* in lemon, *u* in circus.

< = from, derived from, taken from.

lyr i cist (lir′ə sist), *n.* 1 person who writes lyrics, especially for popular songs. 2 a lyric poet.

lyr ist (lir′ist *for 1;* lī′rist, lir′ist *for 2*), *n.* 1 a lyric poet. 2 person who plays on the lyre.

Ly san der (lī san′dər), *n.* died 395 B.C., Spartan naval commander and statesman.

ly ser gic acid di eth yl am ide (lī-sėr′jik; dī eth′ə lam′īd), LSD.

ly sin (lī′sn), *n.* any of a class of antibodies which are developed in blood serum, and which are capable of causing the dissolution or destruction of bacteria, red blood cells, and other cellular elements. [< Greek *lysis* dissolution]

ly sine (lī′sēn′, lī′sn), *n.* a basic amino acid essential for growth, formed by the hydrolysis of various proteins. *Formula:* $C_6H_{14}N_2O_2$

ly sis (lī′sis), *n., pl.* **ly ses** (lī′sēz′). 1 the destruction of a cell by dissolution of the cell membrane, as by a lysin. 2 the gradual ending of an acute disease. [< Greek, a loosening < *lyyen* to loosen]

ly so some (lī′sə sōm), *n.* particle in the cytoplasm of most cells that contains enzymes which form the digestive system of the cell.

ly so zyme (lī′sə zīm, lī′sə zim), *n.* an enzymelike substance that is capable of destroying many kinds of bacteria. It is found in human tears, saliva, and most body fluids. [< Greek *lysis* dissolution + English *(en)zyme*]

lyt ic (lit′ik), *adj.* 1 having to do with or producing lysis. 2 of or having to do with a lysin.

Lyt ton (lit′n), *n.* **Baron.** See **Bulwer-Lytton.**

M m

M or **m** (em), *n., pl.* **M's** or **m's.** 1 the 13th letter of the English alphabet. 2 the Roman numeral for 1000.
M, 1 Mach. 2 medium.
m., 1 male. 2 married. 3 masculine. 4 meter or meters. 5 midnight. 6 mile. 7 minute. 8 month. 9 noon [for Latin *meridies*].
M., 1 Monday. 2 Monsieur.
ma (mä), *n.* INFORMAL. mamma; mother.
M.A., Master of Arts. Also, **A.M.**
ma'am (mam), *n.* INFORMAL. madam.
mac (mak), *n.* BRITISH INFORMAL. mackintosh.
ma ca bre (mə kä′brə, mə kä′bər), *adj.* causing horror; gruesome; horrible; ghastly. [< French] **—ma ca′bre ly,** *adv.*
ma cad am (mə kad′əm), *n.* 1 small, broken stones. Layers of macadam are rolled until solid and smooth to make roads. 2 road or pavement made of this. [< John L. *McAdam,* 1756-1836, Scottish engineer who invented this kind of road]
mac a da mi a (mak′ə dā′mē ə), *n.* 1 any of a small genus of trees or tall shrubs native to eastern Australia, especially a species cultivated for its nut. 2 its nut. [< New Latin < John *Macadam,* 1827-1865, Australian scientist]
ma cad am ize (mə kad′ə mīz), *v.t.,* **-ized, -iz ing.** make or cover (a road) with macadam.
Ma cao (mə kou′), *n.* 1 seaport on a peninsula on the S coast of China. 169,000. 2 Portuguese colony that includes this peninsula and two small islands nearby. 260,000 pop.; 6 sq. mi.
ma caque (mə käk′), *n.* any of a genus of short-tailed monkeys of Asia, the East Indies, and North Africa, that include the Barbary ape and the rhesus. [< French < Portuguese *macaco*]

macaque—two macaques about 2 ft. long with the tail

mac a ro ni (mak′ə rō′nē), *n., pl.* **-nis** or **-nies.** 1 flour paste that has been dried, usually in the form of tubes, to be cooked for food. 2 an English dandy of the 1700's who affected the manners and dress of European society. [< earlier Italian *maccaroni,* plural]
mac a roon (mak′ə rün′), *n.* a very sweet cookie made of whites of eggs, sugar, and ground almonds or coconut. [< French *macaron* < Italian *maccarone*]
Mac Ar thur (mək är′thər), *n.* **Douglas,** 1880-1964, American general in World War II and the Korean War.
Ma cau lay (mə kô′lē), *n.* **Thomas Babington,** Baron, 1800-1859, English essayist, historian, poet, and statesman.
ma caw (mə kô′), *n.* any of several large parrots of South and Central America, characterized by long tails, brilliant feathers, and harsh voices. [< Portuguese *macao*]
Mac beth (mək beth′, mak beth′), *n.* 1 play by Shakespeare. 2 its principal character, who murders his king with the aid of Lady Macbeth.
Mac ca bae us (mak′ə bē′əs), *n.* **Judas,** died 160 B.C., leader of a successful Jewish revolt in 166 B.C. against Syrian rule of Palestine.
Mac ca be an (mak′ə bē′ən), *adj.* of or having to do with Judas Maccabaeus or the Maccabees.
Mac ca bees (mak′ə bēz′), *n.pl.* 1 the supporters or successors of Judas Maccabaeus, especially the members of his family who ruled Palestine as a dynasty from about 141 B.C. to 37 B.C. 2 two books of the Old Testament Apocrypha dealing with the Maccabees.
Mac don ald (mək don′ld), *n.* Sir **John Alexander,** 1815-1891, first prime minister of Canada, from 1867 to 1873, and from 1878 to 1891. He was born in Scotland.
Mac Don ald (mək don′ld), *n.* **James Ramsay,** 1866-1937, British labor leader and statesman, prime minister in 1924 and from 1929 to 1935.
Mac Dow ell (mək dou′əl), *n.* **Edward A.,** 1861-1908, American composer and pianist.

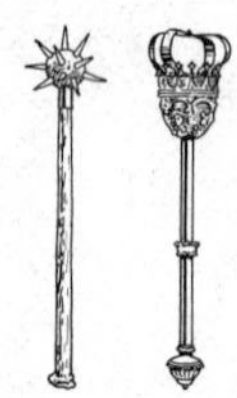

mace[1] (def. 1, left; def. 2, right)

mace[1] (mās), *n.* 1 a club with a heavy metal head, often spiked, used as a weapon in the Middle Ages to smash armor. 2 staff carried by or before an official as a symbol of his authority. [< Old French < Popular Latin *mattea* < Latin *matteola* a digging tool]
mace[2] (mās), *n.* spice made from the dried outer covering of nutmegs. [< Old French *macis* < Latin *macir* a fragrant resin < Greek *makir*]
Mac e don (mas′ə don), *n.* Macedonia.
Mac e do ni a (mas′ə dō′nē ə), *n.* ancient country in SE Europe, north of Greece. Macedonia now forms parts of Yugoslavia, Bulgaria, and Greece. **—Mac′e do′ni an,** *adj., n.*
mac e rate (mas′ə rāt′), *v.,* **-rat ed, -rat ing.** *—v.t.* 1 soften or separate the parts of a substance by soaking for some time. Flowers are macerated to extract their perfume. 2 cause to grow thin. *—v.i.* become thin; waste away. [< Latin *maceratum* softened] **—mac′e ra′tion,** *n.*
Mach (mäk), *n.* Mach number.
mach., 1 machine. 2 machinery.
ma chet e (mə shet′ē, mə chet′ē; *Spanish* mä chā′tā), *n.* a large, heavy knife, used in Latin America as a tool for cutting brush, sugar cane, etc., and as a weapon. [< Spanish]
Mach i a vel li (mak′ē ə vel′ē), *n.* **Niccolò,** 1469-1527, Italian statesman and writer who advised that rulers use craft and deceit to maintain their authority.
Mach i a vel li an (mak′ē ə vel′ē ən), *adj.* 1 of Machiavelli or his political theory. 2 characterized by subtle or unscrupulous cunning; crafty. *—n.* follower of the political theory of Machiavelli.
Mach i a vel li an ism (mak′ē ə vel′ē ə niz′əm), *n.* the principles and practices of Machiavelli or his followers; unscrupulous political cunning.
ma chic o lat ed (mə chik′ə lā′tid), *adj.* having machicolations.

machicolation (defs. 1 and 2)

ma chic o la tion (mə chik′ə lā′shən), *n.* 1 an opening in the floor of a projecting gallery or parapet, or in the roof of an entrance, through which missiles, hot liquids, etc., might be cast upon attackers. Machicolations were much used in medieval fortified structures. 2 a projecting gallery or parapet with such openings. [< Medieval Latin *machicolationem,* ultimately < Old French *macher* to crush + *couler* to flow]
ma chin a bil i ty (mə shē′nə bil′ə tē), *n.* ease of operation by machine.
ma chin a ble (mə shē′nə bəl), *adj.* that can be worked or tooled by machine.
mach i nate (mak′ə nāt), *v.i., v.t.,* **-nat ed, -nat ing.** contrive or devise artfully or with evil purpose; plot; intrigue. **—mach′i na′tor,** *n.*
mach i na tion (mak′ə nā′shən, mash′ə nā′shən), *n.* 1 evil or artful plotting; scheming against authority. 2 Usually, **machinations,** *pl.* an evil plot; secret or cunning scheme.
ma chine (mə shēn′), *n., adj., v.,* **-chined, -chin ing.** *—n.* 1 arrangement of fixed and moving parts for doing work, each part having some special function; mechanical apparatus or device: *a sewing machine.* 2 any device for applying or changing the direction of power, force, or motion, as a lever or pulley. 3 conveyance or vehicle, especially an automobile. 4 airplane. 5 person or group that acts without thinking; automaton. 6 group of people controlling a political party or other organization: *the boss of a state machine.* *—adj.* 1 of or having to do with a machine or machines: *the machine age.* 2 by or with a machine, not by hand: *machine printing.* *—v.t.* make or finish with a machine. [< Middle French < Latin *machina* < Greek *mēchanē* device] **—ma chine′like′,** *adj.*
machine gun, gun that fires small-arms ammunition automatically and can keep up a rapid fire of bullets.
ma chine-gun (mə shēn′gun′), *v.t.,* **-gunned, -gun ning.** fire at with a machine gun.
machine gunner, person who operates a machine gun, as a soldier or airman.
machine language, system of numbers or letters for processing information by a computer.
ma chine-made (mə shēn′mād′), *adj.* made by machinery, not by hand.

ma chin er y (mə shē′nər ē), *n., pl.* **-er ies.** 1 machines: *construction machinery.* 2 the parts or works of a machine; mechanism: *the machinery of a typewriter.* 3 any combination of persons or things by which something is kept going or something is done: *Judges and courts are part of the legal machinery.*

machine shop, workshop for making or repairing machines or parts of machines.

machine tool, an automatic power-driven tool or machine used to form metal into desired shapes by cutting, hammering, squeezing, etc.

machine translation, 1 translation from one language to another by a computer. 2 the result of this process.

ma chin ist (mə shē′nist), *n.* 1 worker skilled with machine tools. 2 person who runs a machine. 3 person who makes and repairs machinery.

ma chis mo (mä chēz′mō), *n.* manliness, especially when aggressive or assertive in nature; excessive concern over one's virility. [< Spanish < *macho* male]

Mach number, number expressing the ratio of the speed of an object to the speed of sound in the same medium. An aircraft traveling at the speed of sound is going at Mach 1. Also, **Mach.** [< Ernst *Mach,* 1838-1916, Austrian physicist]

mac in tosh (mak′ən tosh), *n.* mackintosh.

Mac ken zie (mə ken′zē), *n.* 1 **Mackenzie River,** river in NW Canada flowing into the Arctic Ocean. 1120 mi. long; with tributaries, 2635 mi. 2 district in the Northwest Territories, Canada. 19,000 pop.; 527,500 sq. mi. 3 **William Lyon,** 1795-1861, Canadian political leader.

mack er el (mak′ər əl), *n., pl.* **-el** or **-els.** 1 any of a family of saltwater fishes, especially a species of the northern Atlantic, much used for food. It is blue-green with dark bands on the back and silver below. 2 any of various related fishes. [< Old French *maquerel*]

mackerel sky, sky spotted with small, white, fleecy clouds.

Mack i nac (mak′ə nô), *n.* 1 **Straits of,** strait connecting Lake Michigan and Lake Huron. 4 mi. wide. 2 island in Lake Huron, near this strait. 3 mi. long.

mack i naw (mak′ə nô), *n.* 1 kind of short coat made of heavy woolen cloth, often in a plaid pattern. 2 kind of thick woolen blanket, often with bars of color, used in the northern and western United States by Indians, lumbermen, etc. 3 a large, heavy, flat-bottomed boat with a sharp prow and square stern, formerly used on the Great Lakes. [< *Mackinaw* City, town in northern Michigan]

mack in tosh (mak′ən tosh), *n.* 1 a waterproof raincoat. 2 waterproof cloth. Also, **macintosh.** [< Charles *Macintosh,* 1766-1843, Scottish inventor]

Mac Leish (mək lēsh′), *n.* **Archibald,** born 1892, American poet and dramatist.

Mac mil lan (mək mil′ən), *n.* **Harold,** born 1894, British statesman, prime minister from 1957 to 1963.

Mac Mil lan (mək mil′ən), *n.* **Donald Baxter,** 1874-1970, American arctic explorer.

Ma con (mā′kən), *n.* city in central Georgia. 122,000.

mac ra mé (mak′rə mā), *n.* a coarse lace or fringe made by knotting thread or cord in patterns. [< French < Italian *macramè* < Turkish *makrama* napkin]

macro-, *combining form.* 1 large or long: *Macromolecule = large molecule.* 2 abnormally large: *Macrocephalic = having an abnormally large head.* [< Greek *makro-* < *makros* long, large]

mac ro ce phal ic (mak′rō sə fal′ik), *adj.* having an abnormally large head or skull.

mac ro ceph a lous (mak′rō sef′ə ləs), *adj.* macrocephalic.

mac ro ceph a ly (mak′rō sef′ə lē), *n.* condition in which the head or skull is abnormally large.

mac ro cosm (mak′rə koz′əm), *n.* the whole universe; cosmos. [< Medieval Latin *macrocosmus* < Greek *makros* great + *kosmos* world]

mac ro cos mic (mak′rə koz′mik), *adj.* of or having to do with the macrocosm; immense; comprehensive.

mac ro e co nom ic (mak′rō ē′kə nom′ik, mak′rō ek′ə nom′ik), *adj.* of or having to do with macroeconomics.

mac ro e co nom ics (mak′rō ē′kə-nom′iks, mak′rō ek′ə nom′iks), *n.* economics dealing with the controlling factors in the economy as a whole.

mac ro ev o lu tion (mak′rō ev′ə lü′shən), *n.* evolution of animals and plants on a large scale, resulting in new classifications at the species level or in large groupings.

mac ro ga mete (mak′rō gə mēt′, mak′rō-gam′ēt), *n.* the larger, usually the female, of two conjugating gametes of an organism which reproduces by the union of unlike gametes; megagamete.

mac ro mo lec u lar (mak′rō mə lek′yə-lər), *adj.* of or having to do with macromolecules.

mac ro mol e cule (mak′rō mol′ə kyül), *n.* a large and complex molecule made up of many smaller molecules linked together, as in a resin or polymer.

ma cron (mā′kron, mak′ron), *n.* a straight, horizontal line (¯) placed over a vowel to show that it is pronounced as a long vowel. EXAMPLES: cāme, bē. [< Greek *makron* long]

mac ro nu cle us (mak′rō nü′klē əs, mak′rō nyü′klē əs), *n., pl.* **-cle i** (-klē ī), **-cle us es.** the larger of two types of nuclei present in various ciliate protozoans, which controls metabolic functions within the cell.

mac ro nu tri ent (mak′rō nü′trē ənt, mak′rō nyü′trē ənt), *n.* a nutrient element of which relatively large amounts are necessary for plant growth, such as calcium, phosphorus, sulfur, and potassium.

mac ro phage (mak′rō fāj), *n.* any large or abnormally large phagocyte.

mac ro scop ic (mak′rō skop′ik), *adj.* visible to the naked eye.

mac u la (mak′yə lə), *n., pl.* **-lae** (-lē′). 1 spot on the skin which is unlike the surrounding tissues. 2 macule. 3 sunspot. [< Latin]

mac ule (mak′yül), *n.* 1 spot, stain, or blotch on the skin which is not raised above the surface. 2 macula (def. 1).

mad (mad), *adj.,* **mad der, mad dest,** *n.* —*adj.* 1 out of one's mind; crazy; insane. See **crazy** for synonym study. 2 INFORMAL. very angry; furious: *The insult made me mad.* 3 much excited; wild; frantic: *The dog made mad efforts to catch up with the automobile.* 4 foolish; unwise: *a mad undertaking.* 5 blindly and unreasonably fond: *mad about skiing.* 6 wildly gay or merry. 7 having rabies: *a mad dog.* 8 **like mad,** INFORMAL. furiously; very hard, fast, etc.: *I ran like mad to catch the train.*

hat, āge, fär; let, ēqual, tėrm;
it, īce; hot, ōpen, ôrder;
oil, out; cup, pu̇t, rüle;
ch, child; ng, long; sh, she;
th, thin; ᴛʜ, then; zh, measure;

ə represents *a* in about, *e* in taken, *i* in pencil, *o* in lemon, *u* in circus.

< = from, derived from, taken from.

—*n.* 1 anger; rage. 2 fit of bad temper; sullen mood: *have a mad on.* [Old English *(ge)mǣded* rendered insane]

Mad a gas can (mad′ə gas′kən), *n., adj.* Malagasy.

Mad a gas car (mad′ə gas′kər), *n.* large island country in the Indian Ocean, east of S Africa. Its official name is **Malagasy Republic.**

mad am (mad′əm), *n., pl.* **mad ams, mes dames** (mā däm′). a polite title used in writing or speaking to any woman. [< Old French *ma dame* my lady]

ma dame (mä däm′; *Anglicized* mad′əm), *n., pl.* ***mes dames*** (mā däm′). FRENCH. title for a married woman; Mrs.

mad cap (mad′kap′), *n.* a very impulsive person. —*adj.* wild; hasty; impulsive.

mad den (mad′n), *v.t., v.i.* make or become mad: *The crowd was maddened by the umpire's decision.*

mad den ing (mad′n ing), *adj.* very annoying; irritating: *maddening delays.* —**mad′den ing ly,** *adv.*

mad der (mad′ər), *n.* 1 a European and Asian herbaceous vine with prickly leaves and small yellowish flowers. 2 its red root, used for making dyes. 3 a red dye made from these roots. 4 red; crimson. [Old English *mædere*]

mad ding (mad′ing), *adj.* 1 acting as if mad; mad: *"Far from the madding crowd's ignoble strife."* 2 making mad; maddening.

made (mād), *v.* pt. and pp. of **make.** —*adj.* 1 built; formed: *a strongly made swing.* 2 specially prepared: *made gravy, a made dish.* 3 artificially produced: *made land.* 4 invented; made-up: *a made word.* 5 certain of success; successful: *a made man.* 6 **have (got) it made,** INFORMAL. be assured of success.

Ma deir a (mə dir′ə), *n.* 1 group of Portuguese islands in the Atlantic, west of N Africa. 269,000 pop.; 308 sq. mi. 2 the most important island of this group. 3 Often, **madeira.** kind of wine made there, ranging from quite pale and dry to brownish and sweet. 4 **Madeira River,** a large river flowing from W Brazil into the Amazon. 2000 mi.

ma de moi selle (måd mwå zel′; *Anglicized* mad′ə mə zel′), *n., pl.* ***mes demoi selles*** (mād mwå zel′). FRENCH. title for an unmarried woman; Miss.

made-to-or der (mād′tü ôr′dər), *adj.* made according to the buyer's wishes.

made-up (mād′up′), *adj.* 1 not real; invented; imaginary: *a made-up story.* 2 painted, powdered, etc., with cosmetics: *made-up lips.* 3 put together.

mad house (mad′hous′), *n., pl.* **-hous es** (-hou′ziz). 1 asylum for the insane. 2 place of uproar and confusion.

Ma di net al-Shaab (mä dē′nət äl shäb′), capital of Southern Yemen, in the SW part. 1000.

Mad i son (mad′ə sən), *n.* 1 **James,** 1751-1836, the fourth president of the United States, from 1809 to 1817. He had an important part in drawing up the Constitution of the United States. 2 his wife, **Dolley** or **Dolly,** 1768-1849. 3 capital of Wisconsin, in the S part. 173,000.

Madison Avenue, 1 street in midtown New York City, the chief advertising center of the United States. 2 the advertising industry of the United States.

mad ly (mad′lē), *adv.* 1 insanely. 2 furiously. 3 foolishly.

mad man (mad′man′, mad′mən), *n., pl.* **-men.** 1 an insane man; crazy person. 2 person who behaves madly; wildly foolish person.

mad ness (mad′nis), *n.* 1 a being crazy; insane condition; loss of one's mind. 2 great anger; rage; fury. 3 folly. 4 rabies.

Ma don na (mə don′ə), *n.* 1 Mary, the mother of Jesus. 2 picture or statue of her. [< Italian *madonna* my lady]

Madonna lily, a common, early-blooming lily whose white blossom is a symbol of purity.

mad ras (mad′rəs, mə dras′), *n.* a closely woven cotton cloth with a design on a plain background, used for shirts, dresses, etc. [< *Madras*]

Ma dras (mə dras′, mə dräs′), *n.* 1 seaport in SE India. 2,048,000. 2 state in SE India.

mad re pore (mad′rə pôr, mad′rə pōr), *n.* any of an order of stony corals that often form reefs in tropical seas. [< Italian *madrepora*]

Ma drid (mə drid′), *n.* capital of Spain, in the central part. 3,031,000.

mad ri gal (mad′rə gəl), *n.* 1 a short poem, often about love, that can be set to music. 2 song with parts for several voices, usually sung without instrumental accompaniment. 3 any song. [< Italian *madrigale*]

ma dro ña (mə drō′nyə), *n.* an evergreen tree or shrub of the heath family, growing in western North America. It has a very hard wood and bears orange, edible berries. [< Spanish *madroño* arbutus]

Ma dur a (mə dur′ə), *n.* island off northeast Java, a part of Indonesia. 2,150,000 pop.; 2100 sq. mi.

mad wom an (mad′wum′ən), *n., pl.* **-wom en.** 1 woman who is insane. 2 a wildly foolish woman.

Mae ce nas (mi sē′nəs), *n.* 1 **Gaius,** 74?-8 B.C., Roman patron of literature, and friend of Vergil and Horace. 2 a generous patron, especially of literature or art.

mael strom (māl′strəm), *n.* 1 a great or turbulent whirlpool. 2 **Maelstrom,** a dangerous whirlpool off the NW coast of Norway. 3 a violent confusion of feelings, ideas, or conditions. [< earlier Dutch < *malen* to grind + *stroom* stream]

mae nad (mē′nad), *n.* 1 a woman attendant of Bacchus; bacchante. 2 woman who is extremely excited or in a frenzy. Also, **menad.** [< Latin *maenadem* < Greek *mainesthai* to rage, be mad]

mae nad ic (mi nad′ik), *adj.* of or like the maenads; frenzied. Also, **menadic.**

ma es to so (mä′es tō′sō), *adj., adv.* (in music) with majesty or dignity. [< Italian]

maes tro (mī′strō; *Italian* mä es′trō), *n., pl.* **-tros,** ITALIAN **ma es tri** (mä es′trē). 1 a great composer, teacher, or conductor of music. 2 master of any art. [< Italian < Latin *magister* master]

Mae ter linck (mā′tər lingk), *n.* **Maurice,** 1862-1949, Belgian poet, dramatist, and essayist.

Mae West (mā′ west′), an inflatable vest worn as a life preserver. [< *Mae West,* born 1892, American actress]

Ma fi a or **ma fi a** (mä′fē ə), *n.* 1 a secret organization of criminals supposed to control underworld activities in various parts of the world. 2 a secret Sicilian society hostile to the law and practicing terrorism. [< Italian *mafia*]

Ma fi o so or **ma fi o so** (mä′fē ō′sō), *n., pl.* **-si** (-sē). member of the Mafia. [< Italian *mafioso*]

mag., 1 magazine. 2 magnitude.

mag a zine (mag′ə zēn′, mag′ə zēn′), *n.* 1 publication issued regularly, especially weekly, semimonthly, or monthly, which contains stories, articles, etc., by various contributors. 2 room in a fort or warship for storing gunpowder and other explosives. 3 building for storing gunpowder, guns, food, or other military supplies. 4 chamber for cartridges in a repeating or automatic gun. 5 chamber for holding a roll or reel of film in a camera or projector. [< Old French *magazin,* ultimately < Arabic *makhzan* storehouse]

Mag da len (mag′də lən), *n.* Magdalene.

Mag da le na River (mäg′ᴛʜä lā′nä), river flowing from SW Colombia into the Caribbean Sea. 1060 mi.

Mag da lene (mag′də lēn′), *n.* 1 See **Mary Magdalene.** 2 **magdalene,** woman who has reformed from a sinful life; repentant prostitute.

Mag de burg (mag′də bėrg′), *n.* city in W East Germany, on the Elbe River. 270,000.

Ma gel lan (mə jel′ən), *n.* 1 **Ferdinand,** 1480?-1521, Portuguese navigator. His ship was the first to sail around the world. 2 **Strait of,** strait at the S tip of South America. 360 mi. long; 2½-17 mi. wide.

Mag el lan ic Clouds (maj′ə lan′ik), two faintly luminous patches in the heavens south of the Equator. They are the two galaxies nearest to our own.

ma gen ta (mə jen′tə), *n.* 1 a purplish-red dye. 2 a purplish red. *—adj.* purplish-red. [< Battle of *Magenta,* Italy, in 1859 (because discovered then)]

Mag gio re (mäd jō′rā), *n.* **Lake,** lake between Italy and Switzerland. 40 mi. long; 83 sq. mi.

mag got (mag′ət), *n.* the legless, wormlike larva of any of various kinds of two-winged flies, often living in decaying matter. [Middle English *magot*]

Magh reb (mä′greb), *n.* Arabic name for North Africa.

Ma gi (mā′jī, maj′ī), *n.pl.* of **Magus.** 1 (in the Bible) the Three Wise Men who followed the Star of Bethlehem and brought gifts to the infant Jesus. 2 priests of ancient Persia. [< Latin *magi,* plural of *magus* < Greek *magos.* See MAGIC.]

mag ic (maj′ik), *n.* 1 the pretended art of using secret charms, spirits, or occult forces in nature, to make unnatural things happen; sorcery. 2 something that produces results as if by magic; mysterious influence; unexplained power: *the magic of music.* 3 art or skill of creating illusions, especially by sleight of hand. *—adj.* 1 done by magic or as if by magic. 2 magical. [< Latin *magice* < Greek *magikē (technē)* (art) of the Magi of Persia < *magos* Persian priest or astrologer < Old Persian *magu* member of a priestly clan of Media]

mag i cal (maj′ə kəl), *adj.* 1 of magic; used in magic; done by magic. 2 like magic; mysterious; unexplained. **—mag′i cal ly,** *adv.*

ma gi cian (mə jish′ən), *n.* 1 person skilled in the use of magic; sorcerer. 2 person skilled in sleight of hand.

magic lantern, an early type of projector for showing photographic slides on a screen.

Ma gi not Line (mazh′ə nō), an elaborate system of defensive structures built by France along the border with Germany after World War I. The German army outflanked it in 1940. [< André *Maginot,* 1877-1932, French minister of war]

mag is ter i al (maj′ə stir′ē əl), *adj.* 1 of a magistrate; suited to a magistrate: *A judge has magisterial rank.* 2 showing authority; authoritative: *The captain spoke with a magisterial voice.* 3 imperious; domineering; overbearing. **—mag′is ter′i al ly,** *adv.*

mag is tra cy (maj′ə strə sē), *n., pl.* **-cies.** 1 position, rank, or duties of a magistrate. 2 magistrates as a group. 3 district under a magistrate.

mag is trate (maj′ə strāt, maj′ə strit), *n.* 1 a government official who has power to apply the law and put it in force. The President is the chief magistrate of the United States. 2 judge in a minor court. A justice of the peace is a magistrate. [< Latin *magistratus,* ultimately < *magister* master < *magnus* great]

mag ma (mag′mə), *n.* the molten material beneath the earth's crust from which igneous rock is formed. [< Greek, unguent, ultimately < *massein* to knead, mold]

mag mat ic (mag mat′ik), *adj.* of or having to do with magma.

Mag na Char ta or **Mag na Car ta** (mag′nə kär′tə), 1 the great charter which the English barons forcibly secured from King John at Runnymede on June 15, 1215. The Magna Charta provided a basis for guaranteeing the personal and political liberties of the people of England, and placed the king under the rule of the law. 2 any fundamental constitution guaranteeing civil and political rights. [< Medieval Latin *magna carta* great charter]

mag na cum lau de (mag′nə kum lou′də; mag′nə kum lô′dē), with great distinction (added to the diploma of a student who has done superior academic work): *graduate magna cum laude.* [< Latin, with great praise]

mag nal i um (mag nā′lē əm), *n.* a strong, hard alloy of aluminum and magnesium, used for airplane parts.

mag na nim i ty (mag′nə nim′ə tē), *n., pl.* **-ties.** 1 magnanimous nature or quality; nobility of soul or mind; generosity. 2 a magnanimous act.

mag nan i mous (mag nan′ə məs), *adj.* 1 noble in soul or mind; generous in forgiving; free from mean or petty feelings or acts; unselfish. 2 showing or arising from a generous spirit: *a magnanimous attitude toward a conquered enemy.* [< Latin *magnanimus* < *magnus* great + *animus* spirit] **—mag nan′i mous ly,** *adv.* **—mag nan′i mous ness,** *n.*

mag nate (mag′nāt), *n.* an important, powerful, or prominent person: *a railroad magnate.* [< Late Latin *magnatem* < Latin *magnus* great]

M

hat, āge, fär; let, ēqual, tėrm;
it, īce; hot, ōpen, ôrder;
oil, out; cup, pu̇t, rüle;
ch, child; ng, long; sh, she;
th, thin; ᴛʜ, then; zh, measure;

ə represents *a* in about, *e* in taken, *i* in pencil, *o* in lemon, *u* in circus.

< = from, derived from, taken from.

mag ne sia (mag nē′zhə, mag nē′shə), *n.* a white, tasteless, alkaline powder, used in medicine as an antacid and a laxative, and in industry in making fertilizers and heat-resistant building materials; magnesium oxide. *Formula:* MgO [< Medieval Latin < Greek *Magnēsia (lithos)* (stone) from *Magnēsia.* See MAGNET.]

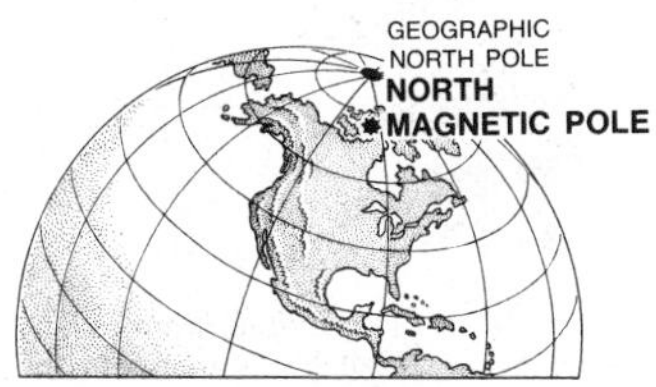

Magnetic Pole (def. 2)

mag ne site (mag′nə sīt), *n.* mineral composed of carbonate of magnesium, used in making steel. *Formula:* $MgCO_3$

mag ne si um (mag nē′zhē əm, mag nē′shē əm), *n.* a light, silver-white metallic element that is very ductile and malleable and burns with a dazzling white light. Magnesium is used in photography, fireworks, and metal alloys. *Symbol:* Mg; *atomic number* 12. See pages 326 and 327 for table. [< New Latin < *magnesia*]

magnesium carbonate, a white, odorless compound, found in mineral water. *Formula:* $MgCO_3$

magnesium chloride, a colorless, crystalline, deliquescent salt found in salt water, used as a source of magnesium. *Formula:* $MgCl_2$

magnesium hydroxide, a white, odorless powder which, when suspended in water, is milk of magnesia. *Formula:* $Mg(OH)_2$

magnesium oxide, magnesia.

magnesium sulfate, a colorless crystalline salt used in matches, explosives, etc., and in the hydrated form is Epsom salts. *Formula:* $MgSO_4$

mag net (mag′nit), *n.* 1 stone or piece of metal that has the property, either natural or induced, of attracting iron or steel. A loadstone is a natural magnet. 2 anything that attracts: *The rabbits in our backyard were a magnet that attracted all the children in the neighborhood.* [< Latin *magnes, magnetis* < Greek *Magnēs (lithos)* (stone) from *Magnēsia,* ancient region in Thessaly]

mag net ic (mag net′ik), *adj.* 1 having the properties of a magnet. 2 of or having to do with a magnet or magnetism; producing magnetism: *a magnetic circuit.* 3 of or having to do with the earth's magnetism: *the magnetic meridian.* 4 capable of being magnetized or of being attracted by a magnet. 5 very attractive: *a magnetic personality.* **—mag net′i cal ly,** *adv.*

magnetic bottle, (in nuclear physics) any arrangement of magnetic fields for confining or constricting charged particles in a controlled thermonuclear reaction.

magnetic compass, compass (def. 1).

magnetic field, space around a magnet or electric current in which magnetic force is felt.

magnetic flux, the total number of magnetic lines of force passing through a specified area.

magnetic induction, 1 amount of magnetic flux in a unit area taken perpendicular to the direction of the magnetic flux. 2 process by which a substance (iron, steel, etc.) becomes magnetized by a magnetic field.

magnetic mine, an underwater mine exploded by metal parts of an approaching ship.

magnetic needle, a slender bar of magnetized steel used as a compass. When mounted so that it turns easily, it points approximately north and south toward the earth's Magnetic Poles.

magnetic north, the direction shown by the magnetic needle of a compass.

magnetic pole, 1 one of the two poles of a magnet. 2 **Magnetic Pole,** one of the two variable points on the earth's surface toward which a compass needle points. The **North Magnetic Pole** is in the Arctic, about 75.5 degrees North latitude and 100 degrees West longitude. The **South Magnetic Pole** is in Antarctica, about 66.5 degrees South latitude and 140.5 degrees East longitude.

magnetic storm, a marked disturbance or variation of the earth's magnetic field, associated with solar flares.

magnetic tape, plastic or paper tape, coated with iron oxide, on which sounds or images can be recorded.

mag net ism (mag′nə tiz′əm), *n.* 1 properties or qualities of a magnet; manifestation of magnetic properties. 2 branch of physics dealing with magnets and magnetic properties. 3 power to attract or influence; personal charm.

mag net ite (mag′nə tīt), *n.* an important iron ore that is strongly attracted by a magnet. Magnetite that possesses polarity is called loadstone. *Formula:* Fe_3O_4

mag net ize (mag′nə tīz), *v.t.,* **-ized, -iz ing.** 1 give the properties of a magnet to. An electric coil around a bar of iron can magnetize the bar. 2 attract or influence (a person). **—mag′net iz′a ble,** *adj.* **—mag′net i za′tion,** *n.* **—mag′net iz′er,** *n.*

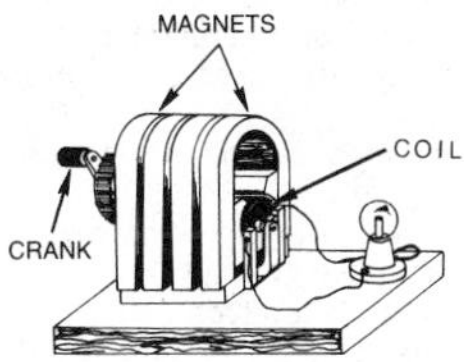

magneto
The coil is turned rapidly by means of the crank. Electricity is produced in the coil as it moves through the magnetic field of a series of magnets.

mag ne to (mag nē′tō), *n., pl.* **-tos.** a small electric generator which uses a magnetic field to produce an electric current. In some internal-combustion engines, a magneto supplies an electric spark to ignite the gasoline vapor. [short for *magnetoelectric machine*]

mag ne to e lec tric (mag nē′tō i lek′trik), *adj.* of electricity produced by magnets.

mag ne to hy dro dy nam ic (mag nē′tō hī′drō dī nam′ik), *adj.* of or having to do with magnetohydrodynamics.

mag ne to hy dro dy nam ics (mag nē′tō hī′drō dī nam′iks), *n.* the study of the interaction of magnetic fields and electrically conducting liquids and gases.

mag ne tom e ter (mag′nə tom′ə tər), *n.* instrument for measuring the intensity and direction of magnetic forces.

mag ne to mo tive force (mag nē′tō mō′tiv), force producing a magnetic flux. It is equal to the work necessary to move a magnetic pole of unit strength around a closed path of magnetic flux.

mag ne to sphere (mag nē′tō sfir), *n.* region in which the earth's magnetic field dominates the movement of ionized plasma. See **atmosphere** for diagram.

mag ne to stric tion (mag nē′tō strik′shən), *n.* change in the dimensions of a ferromagnetic substance when subjected to a magnetic field.

mag ne to stric tive (mag nē′tō strik′tiv), *adj.* of, having to do with, or utilizing magnetostriction.

mag ne tron (mag′nə tron), *n.* vacuum tube in which the flow of electrons is regulated by an external magnetic field.

Mag nif i cat (mag nif′ə kat, mag nif′ə kät), *n.* 1 hymn of the Virgin Mary beginning "My soul doth magnify the Lord." 2 music for this hymn. [< Latin, it magnifies]

mag ni fi ca tion (mag′nə fə kā′shən), *n.* 1 act of magnifying. 2 magnified condition. 3 power to magnify. 4 a magnified copy, model, or picture.

mag nif i cence (mag nif′ə səns), *n.* richness of material, color, and ornament; grand beauty; splendor. [< Old French < Latin *magnificentia* < *magnificus* noble < *magnus* great + *facere* to make]

mag nif i cent (mag nif′ə sənt), *adj.* 1 richly colored or decorated; splendid; grand; stately. See synonym study below. 2 noble; exalted: *magnificent words.* **—mag nif′i cent ly,** *adv.*

Syn. 1 **Magnificent, splendid, superb** mean impressive in beauty, brilliance, or excellence. **Magnificent** emphasizes impressive beauty and costly richness or stateliness of things: *The palace at Versailles is magnificent.* **Splendid** emphasizes impressive brilliance or shining brightness in appearance: *The queen wore a splendid gown glittering with jewels.* **Superb** means of the highest possible excellence, magnificence, splendor, richness, etc.: *We have a superb view of the ocean.*

mag nif i co (mag nif′ə kō), *n., pl.* **-coes.** 1 a Venetian nobleman. 2 person in an exalted position or of great importance. [< Italian]

mag ni fi er (mag′nə fī′ər), *n.* 1 one that magnifies. 2 magnifying glass.

mag ni fy (mag′nə fī), *v.,* **-fied, -fy ing.** —*v.t.* 1 cause to look larger than the real size; enlarge. 2 make too much of; go beyond the truth in telling; exaggerate. 3 ARCHAIC. praise highly. —*v.i.* increase the apparent size of an object. [< Latin *magnificare* esteem greatly < *magnificus* noble. See MAGNIFICENCE.]

magnifying glass, lens or combination of lenses that causes things to look larger than they really are.

mag nil o quence (mag nil′ə kwəns), *n.* 1 high-flown, lofty style of speaking or writing; use of big and unusual words, elaborate phrases, etc. 2 boastfulness. [< Latin *magniloquentia* < *magnus* great + *loqui* speak]

mag nil o quent (mag nil′ə kwənt), *adj.* 1 using big and unusual words; expressed in high-flown language. 2 boastful. **—mag-nil′o quent ly,** *adv.*

Mag ni to gorsk (mag nē′tō gôrsk), *n.* city in W central Soviet Union, important as an iron and steel center. 364,000.

mag ni tude (mag′nə tüd, mag′nə tyüd), *n.* 1 greatness of size. 2 great importance, effect, or consequence. 3 size, whether great or small. 4 degree of brightness of a star. The brightest stars are of the first magnitude. Those just visible to the naked eye are of the sixth magnitude. Each degree is 2.512 times brighter than the next degree. 5 number expressing this. 6 (in mathematics) a number given to a quantity so that it may be compared with similar quantities. [< Latin *magnitudo* < *magnus* large]

mag nol ia (mag nō′lyə), *n.* 1 any of a genus of trees or shrubs of North America and Asia, having large white, yellow, pink, or purplish flowers. 2 its flower. [< Pierre *Magnol,* 1638-1715, French botanist]

mag num (mag′nəm), *n.* 1 bottle that holds two quarts of wine or alcoholic liquor. 2 amount that it holds. [< Latin, great]

mag num o pus (mag′nəm ō′pəs), 1 a large or important work of literature or art. 2 person's greatest work; masterpiece. [< Latin, great work]

mag pie (mag′pī), *n.* 1 any of a genus of black and white birds with a long tail and short wings, of the same family as the jays and noted for their noisy chatter. 2 person who chatters. [< *Mag,* nickname for *Margaret* + *pie*[2]]

mag uey (mag′wā), *n.* 1 any of various agaves with fleshy leaves, found especially in Mexico. 2 any of various similar plants of another genus of the same family, from which a fiber is obtained. 3 fiber obtained from any of these plants. [< Spanish < Arawak]

Ma gus (mā′gəs), *n., pl.* **Ma gi.** one of the Magi.

Mag yar (mag′yär; *Hungarian* mod′yor), *n.* 1 member of the chief group of people living in Hungary. 2 their language; Hungarian. *—adj.* of the Magyars or their language.

ma ha ra ja or **ma ha ra jah** (mä′hə-rä′jə, mä′hə rä′zhə), *n.* a former ruling prince in India, especially one who ruled a state. [< Sanskrit *mahārājā* < *mahā* great + *rājan* rajah]

ma ha ra nee or **ma ha ra ni** (mä′hə-rä′nē), *n.* 1 wife of a maharaja. 2 a former ruling princess in India, especially one who ruled a state. [< Hindustani *mahārānī* < Sanskrit *mahā* great + *rājñī* queen]

ma hat ma (mə hät′mə, mə hat′mə), *n.* (in India) a wise and holy person. [< Sanskrit *mahātman* < *mahā* great + *ātman* soul]

Ma ha ya na (mä′hə yä′nə), *n.* form of Buddhism, now predominant in Japan, China, Korea, Tibet, and Mongolia, which worships Buddha as a divine being. [< Sanskrit *mahāyāna* < *mahā* great + *yāna* vehicle, way]

Mah di (mä′dē), *n.* 1 leader expected by Moslems to come and establish a reign of righteousness. 2 person claiming to be this leader. [< Arabic *mahdīy* one who is rightly guided]

Ma hi can (mə hē′kən), *n.* Mohican.

mah-jongg or **mah-jong** (mä′jong′, mä′zhong′), *n.* game of Chinese origin played by four people with 144 oblong tiles. Each player tries to form winning combinations by drawing or discarding. [< dialectal Chinese *ma chiang,* literally, sparrows (from a design on the pieces)]

Mah ler (mä′lər), *n.* **Gustav,** 1860-1911, Austrian composer.

ma hog a ny (mə hog′ə nē), *n., pl.* **-nies,** *adj.* *—n.* 1 any of a genus of large tropical American trees which yield a hard, durable, reddish-brown wood. 2 its wood, used in making furniture. 3 any of various related or similar trees of the same family or their woods. 4 a dark reddish brown. *—adj.* 1 made of mahogany. 2 dark reddish-brown. [< obsolete Spanish *mahogani*]

Ma hom et (mə hom′it), *n.* Mohammed.

Ma hom et an (mə hom′ə tən), *adj., n.* Mohammedan.

ma hout (mə hout′), *n.* (in the East Indies) the keeper and driver of an elephant. [< Hindustani *mahāut*]

maid (mād), *n.* 1 a young unmarried woman; girl. 2 an unmarried woman. 3 a woman servant. [Middle English *maide,* short for *maiden*]

maid en (mād′n), *n.* 1 a young unmarried woman; maid; girl. 2 ARCHAIC. virgin. *—adj.* 1 of a maiden. 2 unmarried: *a maiden aunt.* 3 new; fresh; untried; unused: *maiden ground.* 4 first: *a ship's maiden voyage.* [Old English *mægden*]

maid en hair (mād′n her′, mād′n har′), *n.* fern with very slender stalks and delicate, finely divided fronds.

maidenhair fern, maidenhair.

maidenhair tree, ginkgo.

maid en hood (mād′n hůd), *n.* 1 condition of being a maiden. 2 time when one is a maiden.

maid en ly (mād′n lē), *adj.* 1 of a maiden. 2 like a maiden; gentle; modest. 3 suited to a maiden: *maidenly reserve.* **—maid′en li-ness,** *n.*

maiden name, a woman's surname before her marriage.

maid-in-wait ing (mād′in wā′ting), *n., pl.* **maids-in-wait ing.** an unmarried noble lady who attends a queen or princess.

maid of honor, 1 an unmarried woman who is the chief attendant of the bride at a wedding. 2 an unmarried lady, usually of noble birth, who attends a queen or princess.

Maid of Orléans, Joan of Arc.

maid serv ant (mād′sėr′vənt), *n.* a woman servant.

mail[1] (māl), *n.* 1 letters, postcards, papers, parcels, etc., to be sent by post. 2 system by which such mail is sent; post: *You can pay most bills by mail.* 3 all that comes by one post or delivery: *the morning mail.* 4 train, boat, etc., that carries mail. *—v.t.* send by mail; put in a mailbox; post. *—adj.* of or for mail. [< Old French *male* wallet, bag; of Germanic origin] **—mail′a ble,** *adj.*

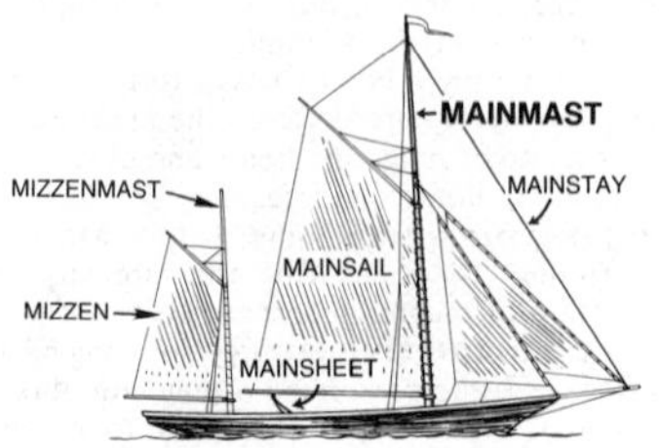

mail[2] (def. 1) mail of the 1000's made of leather with small metal scales sewn to it

mail[2] (māl), *n.* 1 a flexible armor made of metal rings or small loops of chain linked together, or of overlapping plates, for protecting the body against arrows, spears, etc. 2 protective covering. [< Old French *maille* < Latin *macula* a mesh in network]

mail box (māl′boks′), *n.* 1 a public box from which mail is collected. 2 a private box to which mail is delivered.

mail carrier, mailman.

mailed (māld), *adj.* covered, armed, or protected with mail: *the mailed fist.*

mail er (mā′lər), *n.* 1 person who mails. 2 machine for addressing and stamping mail. 3 container in which to mail maps, photographs, etc.

Mail er (mā′lər), *n.* **Norman,** born 1923, American writer.

Mail lol (mä yôl′), *n.* **Aristide,** 1861-1944, French sculptor.

mail man (māl′man′), *n., pl.* **-men.** man who carries or delivers mail; postman.

mail order, order for goods sent by mail.

mail-or der (māl′ôr′dər), *adj.* of or having to do with mail orders or a mail-order house.

mail-order house, business firm that receives orders and ships goods by mail.

maim (mām), *v.t.* cut off or make useless an arm, leg, ear, etc., of; cripple; disable. [Middle English *maimen* < Old French *mahaignier.* Related to MAYHEM.] **—maim′er,** *n.*

main[1] (mān), *adj.* 1 most important; chief or principal; largest: *the main office of a company, the main street of town.* 2 exerted to the utmost; full; sheer: *by main strength.* *—n.* 1 a large pipe for water, gas, sewage, electricity, etc. 2 the open sea; ocean. 3 (in nautical use) mainmast or mainsail. 4 ARCHAIC. mainland. 5 **in the main,** for the most part; chiefly; mostly. 6 **with might and main,** with all one's force. [Old English *mægen* power]

main[2] (mān), *n.* match between gamecocks. [origin uncertain]

main clause, (in grammar) a clause in a complex sentence that can act by itself as a sentence; independent clause.

main drag, SLANG. main stem.

Maine (mān), *n.* one of the northeastern states of the United States. 992,000 pop.; 33,200 sq. mi. *Capital:* Augusta. *Abbrev.:* Me.

main land (mān′land′, mān′lənd), *n.* the main part of a continent or landmass, apart from outlying islands and peninsulas.

main land er (mān′lən dər, mān′lan′dər), *n.* person who lives on the mainland.

main line (mān′līn′), *v.t., v.i.,* **-lined, -lin-ing.** SLANG. inject a narcotic, especially heroin, directly into a vein. **—main′lin′er,** *n.*

main ly (mān′lē), *adv.* for the most part; chiefly; mostly.

main mast (mān′mast′; *Nautical* mān′məst), *n.* the principal mast of a ship.

Main River (mān; *German* mīn), river flowing through West Germany into the Rhine. 305 mi.

main sail (mān′sāl′; *Nautical* mān′səl), *n.* the largest sail on the mainmast. See **mainmast** for picture.

main sheet (mān′shēt′), *n.* rope or tackle that controls the angle at which the mainsail is set. See **mainmast** for picture.

main spring (mān′spring′), *n.* 1 the principal spring in the mechanism of a clock, watch, etc. 2 the main cause, motive, or influence.

main stay (mān′stā′), *n.* 1 rope or wire securing the head of the mainmast. See **mainmast** for picture. 2 main support: *Loyal friends are a person's mainstay in time of trouble.*

main stem, SLANG. the busiest or chief street of a city or town.

main stream (mān′strēm′), *n.* a main course or direction in the development of an idea, institution, country, etc.

Main Street, 1 the chief street in a small town. 2 the typical behavior, point of view, and opinions found in a small town.

main tain (mān tān′), *v.t.* 1 keep in existence or continuance; carry on; keep up: *maintain a business, maintain a family.* 2 support, uphold, or defend: *maintain an opinion.* See **support** for synonym study. 3 declare to be true: *He maintained that he was innocent.* 4 assert against opposition; affirm: *He maintains his innocence.* 5 keep supplied, equipped, or in repair: *This apartment house is maintained very well.* [< Old French *maintenir* < Latin *manu tenere* hold by the hand] **—main tain′a ble,** *adj.* **—main tain′er,** *n.*

main te nance (mān′tə nəns), *n.* 1 a maintaining: *maintenance of quiet.* 2 a being maintained; support: *A government collects taxes to pay for its maintenance.* 3 a keeping in good repair: *the maintenance of roads.* 4 enough to support life; means of living; subsistence: *His small farm provides a maintenance, but not much more.*

main top (mān′top′), *n.* platform at the head of the mainmast.

main top mast (mān′top′mast′; *Nautical* mān′top′məst), *n.* the second section of the mainmast above the deck.

main top sail (mān′top′sāl′; *Nautical* mān′top′səl), *n.* sail above the mainsail.

main yard, beam or pole fastened across the mainmast, used to support the mainsail.

Mainz (mīnts), *n.* city in W West Germany. 177,000.

mai son ette (mā′zn et′), *n.* 1 house divided into apartments. 2 apartment, especially a duplex. [< French *maisonnette,* diminutive of *maison* house]

maî tre d' (mā′trə dē′; mā′tər dē′), INFORMAL. maître d'hôtel (def. 1).

maî tre d'hô tel (me′trə dō tel′), *pl.* **maî tres d'hô tel** (me′trə dō tel′). 1 headwaiter. 2 butler or steward; major-domo. 3 a hotel manager. [< French, literally, master of the house]

maize (māz), *n.* 1 corn; Indian corn. 2 the color of ripe corn; yellow. [< Spanish *maíz* < Arawak *mahiz*]

Maj., Major.

ma jes tic (mə jes′tik), *adj.* of or having majesty; grand; noble; dignified; stately. **—ma jes′ti cal ly,** *adv.*

ma jes ti cal (mə jes′tə kəl), *adj.* majestic.

maj es ty (maj′ə stē), *n., pl.* **-ties.** 1 royal dignity; stately appearance; nobility: *the majesty of the starry heavens.* 2 supreme power or authority: *the majesty of the law.* 3 **Majesty,** title used in speaking to or of a king, queen, emperor, empress, etc.: *Your Majesty, His Majesty, Her Majesty.* [< Old French *majeste* < Latin *majestatem* < *major.* See MAJOR.]

ma jol i ca (mə jol′ə kə, mə yol′ə kə), *n.* 1 kind of enameled Italian pottery richly decorated in colors. 2 any similar pottery made elsewhere. [< Italian *maiolica* Majorca]

ma jor (mā′jər), *adj.* 1 more important; larger; greater: *Take the major share of the profits.* 2 of the first rank or order: *a major poet, a major American port.* 3 of the legal age of responsibility (18 or 21 years). 4 in music: **a** greater by a half step than the corresponding minor interval: *a major chord.* **b** denoting a scale, key, or mode having half steps after the third and seventh tones: *the C major scale.* 5 of, having to do with, or designating a student's principal subject or course of study. *—n.* 1 officer of the army, air force, or marines, ranking next below a lieutenant colonel and next above a captain. 2 person of the legal age of responsibility. 3 (in music) a major scale, key, chord, interval, etc. 4 subject or course of study to which a student gives most of his time and attention. 5 student engaged in such a course of study: *She is a classics major.* *—v.i.* have or take as a major subject of study: *major in mathematics.* [< Latin, comparative of *magnus* great. Doublet of MAYOR.]

Ma jor ca (mə jôr′kə), *n.* Spanish island in the W Mediterranean Sea. It is the largest of the Balearic Islands. 363,000 pop.; 1400 sq. mi. Also, SPANISH **Mallorca.** **—Ma jor′can,** *adj., n.*

ma jor-do mo (mā′jər dō′mō), *n., pl.* **-mos.** 1 man in charge of a royal or noble household. 2 butler or steward. [< Spanish *mayordomo* or Italian *maggiordomo* < Medieval Latin *major domus* chief of the household]

ma jor ette (mā′jə ret′), *n.* drum majorette.

major general, officer in the army, air force, or marines ranking next below a lieutenant general and next above a brigadier general.

ma jor i ty (mə jôr′ə tē, mə jor′ə tē), *n., pl.* **-ties.** 1 the largest number; greater part; more than half the whole number. 2 the number by which the votes on one side are more than all the rest. If Smith received 12,000 votes, Adams 7000, and White 3000, Smith had a majority of 2000 and a plurality of 5000. 3 the legal age of responsibility. Under the varying laws of the states of the United States, a person may reach his majority at the age of 18 or 21. 4 rank or position of an army major. 5 party or group having the larger number of votes.

major league, either of the two highest ranking leagues in American professional baseball.

major premise, the more inclusive or general premise of a syllogism.

major scale, a musical scale having eight notes with half steps instead of whole steps after the third and seventh notes.

major suit, spades or hearts in bridge.

ma jus cu lar (mə jus′kyə lər), *adj.* of or like a majuscule; large.

ma jus cule (mə jus′kyül), *n.* a large letter in medieval writing, whether capital or uncial. *—adj.* 1 (of a letter) large. 2 written in majuscules. [< French < Latin *majusculus* somewhat larger < *major.* See MAJOR.]

make (māk), *v.,* **made, mak ing,** *n.* *—v.t.* 1 bring into being; put together; build; form; shape: *make a new dress, make a boat.* See synonym study below. 2 have the qualities needed for: *Wood makes a good fire.* 3 bring about; cause: *make trouble, make peace, make a noise, make a bargain. Haste makes waste.* 4 cause to; force to: *He made me go.* 5 cause to be or become; cause oneself to be: *make a room warm, make a fool of oneself.* 6 turn out to be; become: *She will make a good teacher.* 7 get ready for use; arrange: *make a bed.* 8 get; obtain; acquire; earn: *make a fortune, make one's living.* 9 do; perform: *make an attempt, make a mistake. Don't make a move.* 10 put forth; deliver: *make a speech.* 11 amount to; add up to; count as: *Two and two make four.* 12 think of as; figure to be: *I make the distance across the room 15 feet.* 13 reach; arrive at: *The ship made port.* 14 go; travel: *Some airplanes can make more than 600 miles an hour.* 15 cause the success of: *One big deal made the young businessman.* 16 draw up (a legal document): *make a will.* 17 INFORMAL. get on; get a place on: *He made the football team.* 18 in card games: **a** win (a trick). **b** state (the trump or bid). 19 close (an electric circuit). 20 (in sports and games) score; have a score of. *—v.i.* 1 cause something to be in a certain condition: *make sure, make ready.* 2 behave or act in a certain way: *make merry.*

make after, follow; chase; pursue.

make as if or **make as though,** pretend that; act as if.

make away with, **a** get rid of. **b** kill. **c** steal.

make believe, pretend.

make do, get along; manage.

make fast, attach firmly.

make for, **a** go toward. **b** rush at; attack. **c** help bring about; favor.

make it, INFORMAL. succeed.

make like, INFORMAL. imitate.

make off, run away; leave suddenly.

make off with, steal.

make out, **a** write out: *make out an order.* **b** show to be; prove: *make out a strong case.* **c** try to prove: *They aren't as rich as they make out.* **d** understand: *make out what someone says.* **e** see with difficulty: *make out a figure in the distance.* **f** complete; fill out: *We need two more eggs to make out a dozen.* **g** INFORMAL. get along; manage; succeed.

make over, **a** alter; make different. **b** hand over; transfer ownership of.

make up, **a** put together: *make up a prescription.* **b** invent: *make up a story.* **c** settle (a dispute, etc.); reconcile: *make up one's differences.* **d** give or do in place of: *make up for lost time.* **e** pay for; compensate: *make up a loss.* **f** become friends again after a quarrel: *The two friends made up.* **g** put rouge, lipstick, powder, etc., on the face. **h** arrange (type, pictures, etc.) in the pages of a book,

hat, āge, fär; let, ēqual, tėrm;
it, īce; hot, ōpen, ôrder;
oil, out; cup, pu̇t, rüle;
ch, child; ng, long; sh, she;
th, thin; ᴛʜ, then; zh, measure;
ə represents *a* in about, *e* in taken, *i* in pencil, *o* in lemon, *u* in circus.
< = from, derived from, taken from.

paper, or magazine. **i** decide: *make up one's mind.* **j** compose; constitute: *Girls made up the audience.*

make up to, try to get the friendship of; flatter.

—*n.* 1 way in which a thing is made; build; style: *the make of a coat.* 2 kind; brand: *What make of car is this?* 3 nature; character. 4 act or process of making. 5 amount made; output. 6 the closing of an electric circuit. 7 **on the make,** INFORMAL. trying for success, profit, etc.

[Old English *macian*]

Syn. *v.t.* 1 **Make, construct, fashion** mean to put together or give form to something. **Make** is the general word meaning to bring something into existence by forming or shaping it or putting it together: *She made a cake.* **Construct** means to put parts together in proper order, and suggests a plan or design: *They constructed a bridge.* **Fashion** means to give a definite form, shape, or figure to something and usually suggests that the maker is inventive or resourceful: *fashion beautiful bowls out of myrtle wood.*

make-be lieve (māk′bi lēv′), *n.* 1 pretense: *His friendships with important people are all make-believe.* 2 person who pretends; pretender. —*adj.* pretended; imaginary: *a make-believe playmate.*

mak er (mā′kər), *n.* 1 person or thing that makes; manufacturer. 2 (in law) person who signs a promissory note, etc. 3 **Maker,** God.

make-read y (māk′red′ē), *n.* in printing: 1 the preparation of a form for the press by leveling and adjusting type, plates, etc. 2 material used for this.

make shift (māk′shift′), *n.* something used for a time instead of the right thing; temporary substitute. —*adj.* used for a time instead of the right thing.

make-up or **make up** (māk′up′), *n.* 1 way in which something is put together. 2 nature; disposition: *a nervous make-up.* 3 way in which an actor is dressed and painted to look his part. 4 clothes, cosmetics, wigs, etc., used by an actor. 5 rouge, lipstick, powder, etc., put on the face; cosmetics. 6 arrangement of type, pictures, etc., in a book, paper, or magazine.

make-work (māk′wėrk′), *n.* U.S. the contriving of unnecessary activity. —*adj.* of or used for unnecessary work.

mak ing (mā′king), *n.* 1 cause of a person's success; means of advancement: *Early hardships were the making of him.* 2 Often, **makings,** *pl.* material needed. 3 qualities needed: *I see in him the making of a hero.* 4 something made. 5 amount made at one time. 6 **in the making,** in the process of being made; not fully developed: *Our plans are still in the making.*

mal-, *combining form.* bad or badly; poor or poorly: *Malodorous = smelling bad. Maladjusted = poorly adjusted.* [< Middle French < Latin *male* badly < *malus* bad]

Mal a bar Coast (mal′ə bär), region along the SW coast of India.

Ma lac ca (mə lak′ə), *n.* 1 former British territory on the Malay Peninsula, now part of Malaysia. 2 **Strait of,** strait between the Malay Peninsula and Sumatra. 35-185 mi. wide.

Malacca cane, a light walking stick made of the stem of an East Indian rattan palm.

Mal a chi (mal′ə kī), *n.* 1 Hebrew prophet who lived about 450 B.C. 2 the last book of the Old Testament.

Mal a chi as (mal′ə kī′əs), *n.* (in the Douay Bible) Malachi.

mal a chite (mal′ə kīt), *n.* a green mineral that is an ore of copper and is used for ornamental articles. *Formula:* $Cu_2CO_3(OH)_2$ [< French < Greek *malache* mallow (from the similar color)]

mal a cos tra can (mal′ə kos′trə kən), *n.* any of a subclass of crustaceans usually having many appendages on the thorax and abdomen. Lobsters, crabs, and shrimps belong to this subclass. [< Greek *malakos* soft + *ostrakon* shell]

mal ad just ed (mal′ə jus′tid), *adj.* 1 badly adjusted; not in a healthy relation with one's environment.

mal ad just ment (mal′ə just′mənt), *n.* a poor or unsatisfactory adjustment.

mal ad min is ter (mal′əd min′ə stər), *v.t.* administer badly; manage inefficiently or dishonestly.

mal ad min is tra tion (mal′əd min′e-strā′shən), *n.* bad administration; inefficient or dishonest management.

mal a droit (mal′ə droit′), *adj.* unskillful; awkward; clumsy. **—mal′a droit′ly,** *adv.* **—mal′a droit′ness,** *n.*

mal a dy (mal′ə dē), *n., pl.* **-dies.** 1 any bodily disorder or disease, especially one that is chronic or deep-seated. 2 any unwholesome or disordered condition. [< Old French *maladie* < *malade* ill < Latin *male habitus* doing badly]

Mál a ga (mal′ə gə), *n.* 1 province in S Spain. 2 seaport in S Spain. 351,000.

Mal a ga (mal′ə gə), *n.* 1 kind of large, oval, firm, white grape. 2 kind of white wine. [< *Málaga*]

Mal a gas y (mal′ə gas′ē), *n., pl.* **-gas y** or **-gas ies** for 1, *adj.* —*n.* 1 native or inhabitant of Madagascar. 2 the Indonesian language of Madagascar. —*adj.* of or having to do with Madagascar, its people, or their language.

Malagasy Republic, official name of Madagascar. It is a member of the French Community. 6,750,000 pop.; 226,700 sq. mi. *Capital:* Tananarive. See **South Africa** for map.

ma laise (ma lāz′), *n.* 1 an uneasy, disturbed, or disordered condition. 2 vague bodily discomfort. [< French < *mal-* imperfect + *aise* ease]

mal a mute (mal′ə myüt, mal′ə müt), *n.* Alaskan malamute. Also, **malemute.**

mal a pert (mal′ə pėrt′), *adj.* ARCHAIC. too bold; pert; saucy. [< Middle French < *mal* badly + *apert* adroit]

mal ap por tion ment (mal′ə pôr′shən-mənt, mal′ə pōr′shən mənt), *n.* U.S. wrong or unfair assignment of representation in a legislature.

mal a prop ism (mal′ə prop′iz′əm), *n.* 1 a ridiculous misuse of words, especially a confusion of two words somewhat similar in sound but different in meaning, as a musical *progeny* for a musical *prodigy.* Malapropisms are often used for humorous effect. 2 instance of this; a misused word. [< Mrs. *Malaprop,* character in Richard Sheridan's play *The Rivals,* noted for her absurd misuse of words < *malapropos*]

mal ap ro pos (mal′ap′rə pō′), *adv., adj.* at the wrong time or place. [< French *mal à propos* badly for the purpose]

ma lar (mā′lər), *adj.* of or having to do with the cheekbone or cheek. [< Latin *mala* jaw, cheek]

ma lar i a (mə ler′ē ə, mə lar′ē ə), *n.* disease characterized by periodic chills, fever, and sweating. Malaria is caused by parasitic protozoans in the red blood cells, and is transmitted by the bite of an anopheles mosquito which has bitten an infected person. [< Italian < *mala aria* bad air]

ma lar i al (mə ler′ē əl, mə lar′ē əl), *adj.* 1 having malaria. 2 of or like malaria.

ma lar i ous (mə ler′ē əs, mə lar′ē əs), *adj.* malarial.

ma lar key or **ma lar ky** (mə lär′kē), *n.* SLANG. nonsense. [origin uncertain]

Ma la wi (mə lä′wē), *n.* country in SE Africa, a member of the Commonwealth of Nations. 4,530,000 pop.; 45,500 sq. mi. *Capital:* Zomba. Former name, **Nyasaland.** See **South Africa** for map. **—Ma la′wi an,** *adj., n.*

Ma lay (mā′lā, mə lā′), *n.* 1 member of the native people of the Malay Peninsula and nearby islands. 2 their language. —*adj.* of the Malays, their country, or their language.

Ma lay a (mə lā′ə), *n.* 1 Malay Peninsula. 2 former country of the Malay Peninsula, now part of Malaysia.

Mal a ya lam (mal′ə yä′ləm), *n.* a Dravidian language spoken on the southwestern coast of India.

Ma lay an (mə lā′ən), *n., adj.* Malay.

Malay Archipelago, group of islands between SE Asia and Australia; East Indies; Indonesia. See **East Indies** for map.

Malay Peninsula, peninsula in SE Asia, north of Sumatra; Malaya.

Ma lay sia (mə lā′zhə), *n.* 1 **Federation of,** federation consisting of Sabah, Sarawak, Malaya, and many small islands of the Malay Archipelago, a member of the Commonwealth of Nations. 10,790,000 pop.; 128,400 sq. mi. *Capital:* Kuala Lumpur. 2 Malay Archipelago. **—Ma lay′sian,** *adj., n.*

Mal colm X (mal′kəm eks′), 1925-1965, American black nationalist leader. His real name was Malcolm Little.

mal con tent (mal′kən tent′), *adj.* discontented; rebellious. —*n.* a discontented, rebellious person.

mal de mer (mål də mer′), FRENCH. seasickness.

Mal dive Islands (mal′dīv), country consisting of a group of atolls in the Indian Ocean southwest of Ceylon. 114,000 pop.; 115 sq. mi. *Capital:* Male.

male (māl), *n.* 1 person of the sex that, when mature, produces sperm; man or boy. 2 any animal of corresponding sex. 3 in botany: **a** flower having a stamen or stamens and no pistils. **b** plant bearing only flowers with stamens. —*adj.* 1 of, or having to do with, or belonging to the sex that, when mature, produces sperm. See synonym study below. 2 composed or consisting of men or boys: *a male chorus.* 3 (in botany) having flowers which contain stamens but not pistils; staminate. 4 designating the projecting part of a connection, machine, etc., which fits inside a corresponding part: *a male plug.* [< Old French *male, masle* < Latin *masculus,* diminutive of *mas* male] **—male′ness,** *n.*

Syn. *adj.* 1 **Male, masculine, manly** mean having to do with men or the sex to which they belong. **Male** suggests only the sex: *We have a male kitten.* **Masculine** is applied to characteristics (especially strength, vigor, etc.) more commonly associated with men and boys than with women or girls: *She had a brisk, masculine stride.* **Manly** suggests admirable characteristics such as courage and honor more likely to be found in a mature man than in a boy: *The boy fought back with manly courage.*

Ma le (mä′lā), *n.* capital of the Maldive Islands. 12,000.

mal e dic tion (mal′ə dik′shən), *n.* invocation of evil upon someone; curse. [< Latin *maledictionem* < *maledicere* speak evil < *male* badly + *dicere* speak. Doublet of MALISON.]

mal e dic tor y (mal′ə dik′tər ē), *adj.* characterized by or like malediction.

mal e fac tion (mal′ə fak′shən), *n.* an evil deed; crime.

mal e fac tor (mal′ə fak′tər), *n.* criminal; evildoer. [< Latin < *malefacere* do evil < *male* badly + *facere* do]

mal e fac tress (mal′ə fak′tris), *n.* a woman malefactor.

ma lef ic (mə lef′ik), *adj.* producing evil or harm; baleful.

ma lef i cence (mə lef′ə səns), *n.* the doing of evil or harm; harm; evil.

ma lef i cent (mə lef′ə sənt), *adj.* doing evil or harm; harmful; evil.

ma le ic hy dra zide(mə lē′ik hī′drə zīd), compound that affects the growth of plants, used to retard leaf or flower development or the sprouting of stored potatoes, onions, etc. *Formula:* $C_4H_4N_2O_2$

mal e mute (mal′ə myüt, mal′ə müt), *n.* Alaskan malamute.

ma lev o lence (mə lev′ə ləns), *n.* the wish that evil may happen to others; ill will; spite.

ma lev o lent (mə lev′ə lənt), *adj.* wishing evil to happen to others; showing ill will; spiteful. [< Latin *malevolentem* < *male* badly + *velle* to wish] **—ma lev′o lent ly,** *adv.*

mal fea sance (mal fē′zns), *n.* official misconduct; violation of a public trust or duty: *A judge who accepts a bribe is guilty of malfeasance.* [< French *malfaisance* < *mal-* badly + *faire* do]

mal for ma tion (mal′fôr mā′shən), *n.* faulty, irregular, abnormal, or distorted formation or structure of parts.

mal formed (mal fôrmd′), *adj.* badly shaped; marked by malformation.

mal func tion (mal′fungk′shən), *n.* an improper functioning; failure to work or perform. *—v.i.* function badly; work or perform improperly.

Ma li (mä′lē), *n.* country in W Africa south of Algeria, the former French Sudan. 5,022,000 pop.; 464,000 sq. mi. *Capital:* Bamako. See **Algeria** for map. **—Ma′li an,** *adj., n.*

mal ic acid (mal′ik, mā′lik), acid found in apples and numerous other fruits. *Formula:* $C_4H_6O_5$ [< French *malique (acide)* < Latin *malum* apple]

mal ice (mal′is), *n.* 1 active ill will; wish to hurt or make suffer; rancor. See **spite** for synonym study. 2 (in law) intent to commit an act which will result in harm to another person without justification. [< Old French < Latin *malitia* < *malus* bad, evil]

ma li cious (mə lish′əs), *adj.* 1 showing active ill will; wishing to hurt or make suffer; spiteful. 2 proceeding from malice: *malicious mischief.* **—ma li′cious ly,** *adv.* **—ma li′cious ness,** *n.*

ma lign (mə līn′), *v.t.* speak evil of; slander: *You malign a generous person when you call him stingy.* *—adj.* 1 evil; injurious: *Gambling often has a malign influence.* 2 hateful; malicious. [< Late Latin *malignare* < Latin *malignus* disposed to evil < *malus* evil + *-gnus* born] **—ma lign′er,** *n.* **—ma lign′ly,** *adv.*

ma lig nance (mə lig′nəns), *n.* malignancy.

ma lig nan cy (me lig′nən sē), *n., pl.* **-cies.** 1 malignant quality or tendency. 2 (in medicine) something malignant, as a tumor.

ma lig nant (mə lig′nənt), *adj.* 1 very evil, hateful, or malicious. 2 having an evil influence; very harmful. 3 very dangerous; causing or threatening to cause death: *A cancer is a malignant growth.* 4 ARCHAIC. disaffected; malcontent. **—ma lig′nant ly,** *adv.*

ma lig ni ty (mə lig′nə tē), *n., pl.* **-ties.** 1 great malice; extreme hate or ill will. 2 great harmfulness; dangerous quality; deadliness. 3 a malignant feeling or act.

ma li hi ni (mä′lē hē′nē), *n.* (in Hawaii) a new arrival; stranger or foreigner. [< Hawaiian]

ma lines or **ma line** (mə lēn′), *n.* 1 Mechlin lace. 2 a thin, stiff, silk net used in dressmaking. [< French *malines* < *Malines* (or Mechlin), Belgium]

ma lin ger (mə ling′gər), *v.i.* pretend to be sick, injured, etc., in order to escape work or duty; shirk. [< French *malingre* sickly] **—ma lin′ger er,** *n.*

mal i son (mal′ə zən, mal′ə sən), *n.* ARCHAIC. malediction; curse. [< Old French *maleiçon* < Latin *maledictionem.* Doublet of MALEDICTION.]

mall[1] (môl, mal), *n.* 1 a shaded walk; public walk or promenade. 2 a central walk in a shopping center. [< Old French *mail, maul* mallet (used in a game played in a mall)]

mall[2] (môl), *n., v.t.* maul.

mal lard (mal′ərd), *n., pl.* **-lards** or **-lard.** a wild duck of Europe, northern Asia, and North America, from which the domestic duck has descended. The male has a greenish-black head and a white band around his neck. [< Old French *mallart*]

mal le a bil i ty (mal′ē ə bil′ə tē), *n.* malleable quality or condition.

mal le a ble (mal′ē ə bəl), *adj.* 1 that can be hammered, rolled, or extended into various shapes without being broken. Gold, silver, copper, and tin are malleable; they can be beaten into thin sheets. 2 adaptable; yielding. [< Old French < Latin *malleus* hammer]

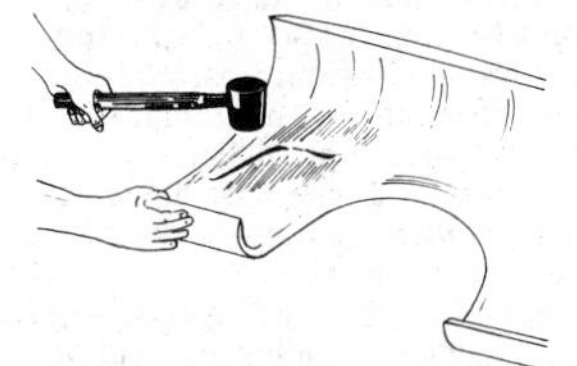

mallet with a rubber head used to pound out a dent in an automobile fender

mal let (mal′it), *n.* kind of hammer, usually with a wooden head. Mallets are used for driving a chisel, for playing croquet, and for playing polo. [< Old French *maillet,* diminutive of *mail* < Latin *malleus* hammer]

mal le us (mal′ē əs), *n., pl.* **mal le i** (mal′ē ī). the outermost of three small bones in the middle ear of mammals, shaped like a hammer; hammer. [< Latin, hammer]

Mal lor ca (mä lyôr′kä, mä yôr′kä), *n.* Spanish name of **Majorca.**

hat, āge, fär; let, ēqual, tėrm;
it, īce; hot, ōpen, ôrder;
oil, out; cup, pu̇t, rüle;
ch, child; ng, long; sh, she;
th, thin; ꟆH, then; zh, measure;

ə represents *a* in about, *e* in taken, *i* in pencil, *o* in lemon, *u* in circus.

< = from, derived from, taken from.

mal low (mal′ō), *n.* any of a genus of ornamental plants of the mallow family, with purple, pink, or white, five-petaled flowers, and hairy leaves and stems. [Old English *mealwe* < Latin *malva.* Doublet of MAUVE.]

mallow family, group of dicotyledonous plants, most of which have sticky, gummy juice, and flowers shaped like those of the hollyhock. Mallows, hollyhock, cotton, okra, etc., belong to the mallow family.

Mal mö (mal′mō; *Swedish* mälm′œ′), *n.* seaport in S Sweden. 258,000.

malm sey (mäm′zē), *n.* kind of strong, sweet wine, originally made in Greece. [< Medieval Latin *malmasia,* alteration of *Monembasia,* a Greek seaport]

mal nour ished (mal nėr′isht), *adj.* improperly nourished.

mal nu tri tion (mal′nü trish′ən, mal′nyü-trish′ən), *n.* a malnourished condition. Improper food can cause malnutrition.

mal oc clu sion (mal′ə klü′zhən), *n.* (in dentistry) failure of the upper and lower teeth to meet or close properly.

mal o dor ous (mal ō′dər əs), *adj.* smelling bad; unsavory; fetid. **—mal o′dor ous ly,** *adv.* **—mal o′dor ous ness,** *n.*

Mal or y (mal′ər ē), *n.* Sir **Thomas,** English writer who lived about 1470. He collected legends about King Arthur and his knights.

Mal pigh i an body or **Malpighian corpuscle** (mal pig′ē ən), a minute, rounded structure in the kidney consisting of a glomerulus and its surrounding capsule. [< Marcello *Malpighi,* 1628-1694, Italian anatomist]

Malpighian tubule, any of the slender tubules connected to the alimentary canal of various arthropods, serving as excretory organs.

mal prac tice (mal prak′tis), *n.* 1 criminal neglect or wrong treatment of a patient by a doctor. 2 misconduct in any official or professional position.

mal prac ti tion er (mal′prak tish′ə nər), *n.* person guilty of malpractice.

Mal raux (mal rō′), *n.* **André,** born 1901, French author and statesman.

malt (môlt), *n.* 1 barley or other grain soaked in water until it sprouts, and then dried and aged. Malt has a sweet taste and is used in brewing and distilling alcoholic liquors. 2 beer or ale. *—v.t.* 1 make or change (grain) into malt. 2 prepare or treat with malt or an extract of malt. *—v.i.* be changed into malt. [Old English *mealt*]

Mal ta (môl′tə), *n.* 1 island in the Mediterranean, south of Sicily. 285,000 pop.; 95 sq. mi. 2 country including Malta and smaller islands nearby, a member of the Commonwealth of Nations. 326,000 pop.; 122 sq. mi. *Capital:* Valletta.

malt ase (môl′tās), *n.* enzyme that changes maltose to dextrose, present in intestinal secretion, yeast, etc.

malt ed milk (môl′tid), 1 a soluble powder made of dried milk, malted barley, and wheat flour. 2 drink prepared by mixing this powder with milk, flavoring, and often ice cream.

Mal tese (môl tēz′), *n., pl.* **-tese,** *adj.* *—n.* 1 native or inhabitant of Malta. 2 the native language of Malta. It is a form of Arabic with many Italian words. *—adj.* of Malta, its people, or their language.

Maltese cat, a short-haired domestic cat with a bluish-gray coat.

Maltese cross, a cross with four equal arms resembling arrowheads pointed toward the center. See **cross** for picture.

malt extract, a sugary substance obtained by soaking malt in water.

Mal thus (mal′thəs), *n.* **Thomas R.,** 1766-1834, English clergyman and economist.

Mal thu sian (mal thü′zhən, mal thü′zē ən), *adj.* of Malthus, or his theory that population tends to increase faster than the food supply, unless checked by war, famine, or other means. *—n.* believer in this theory.

Mal thu sian ism (mal thü′zhə niz′əm, mal thü′zē ə niz′əm), *n.* the theories of Malthus and his followers.

mal tose (môl′tōs), *n.* a white crystalline sugar made by the action of various enzymes on starch; malt sugar. It is used in brewing and distilling alcoholic liquors. *Formula:* $C_{12}H_{22}O_{11} \cdot H_2O$

mal treat (mal trēt′), *v.t.* treat roughly or cruelly; abuse: *maltreat animals.* **—mal-treat′ment,** *n.*

malt ster (môlt′stər), *n.* person who makes or sells malt.

malt sugar, maltose.

malt y (môl′tē), *adj.,* **malt i er, malt i est.** of, like, or containing malt.

ma ma (mä′mə; *British* mə mä′), *n.* mother.

mam ba (mam′bə), *n.* any of a genus of poisonous snakes of Africa of the same family as the cobras but hoodless. [< Kaffir *imamba*]

mam bo (mäm′bō), *n., pl.* **-bos,** *v.* *—n.* 1 a ballroom dance of Caribbean origin, similar to the rumba. 2 music for this dance. *—v.i.* dance the mambo. [< Haitian Creole]

Mam e luke (mam′ə lük), *n.* member of a military group that ruled Egypt from about 1250 to 1517 and had great power until 1811. The Mamelukes were originally slaves.

mam ma[1] (mä′mə; *British* mə mä′), *n.* mother.

mam ma[2] (mam′ə), *n., pl.* **mam mae** (mam′ē′). mammary gland. [< Latin, breast]

mam mal (mam′əl), *n.* any of a class of warm-blooded, vertebrate animals usually having hair, the females of which secrete milk from mammary glands to nourish their young. Human beings, horses, dogs, lions, bats, and whales are all mammals. [< New Latin *Mammalia,* ultimately < Latin *mamma* breast]

Mam ma li a (ma mā′lē ə, ma mā′lyə), *n.pl.* class of vertebrates comprising the mammals.

mam ma li an (ma mā′lē ən, ma mā′lyən), *adj.* of or belonging to the mammals. *—n.* mammal.

mam mal o gist (ma mal′ə jist), *n.* an expert in mammalogy.

mam mal o gy (ma mal′ə jē), *n.* branch of zoology that deals with the study of mammals.

mam mar y gland (mam′ər ē), gland in the breast of mammals, enlarged in females and capable of producing milk which issues through the nipple; mamma.

mam mon or **Mam mon** (mam′ən), *n.* riches thought of as an evil; greed for wealth. [< Latin *mammona* < Greek *mamonas* < Aramaic *māmōnā* riches]

mam moth (mam′əth), *n.* any of a genus of large, extinct Pleistocene elephants, having a hairy skin and long, curved tusks. *—adj.* huge; gigantic: *a mammoth undertaking.* [< earlier Russian *mamot*]

Mammoth Cave, a huge limestone cave in central Kentucky.

mam my (mam′ē), *n., pl.* **-mies.** mother; mamma.

man (man), *n., pl.* **men,** *v.,* **manned, man ning.** *—n.* 1 an adult male person. 2 a human being; person; individual: *No man can be sure of the future. All men are created equal.* 3 all human beings; the human race; mankind: *Man has existed for thousands of years.* 4 (in zoology) human being classified as belonging to the genus *Homo,* of which there is now only one species, *Homo sapiens,* characterized by high mental development. 5 a male follower, servant, or employee: *Robin Hood and his merry men.* 6 husband. 7 a male lover; suitor. 8 one of the pieces used in games such as chess and checkers. 9 person characterized by manly qualities: *He was every inch a man.*

act the man, be courageous.

as one man, with complete agreement.

be one's own man, a be free to do as one pleases. **b** have complete control of oneself.

to a man, without exception; all.

—v.t. 1 supply with men: *Sailors man a ship.* 2 serve or operate; get ready to operate: *Man the guns.* 3 make courageous or strong; brace: *The captive manned himself to endure torture.*

[Old English *mann* human being]

Man (man), *n.* **Isle of,** small island in the British Isles west of N England in the Irish Sea. 50,000 pop.; 227 sq. mi. See **British Isles** for map.

Man., Manitoba.

ma na (mä′nä), *n.* supernatural or magical power or influence, attached to certain objects, making them sacred or taboo, or giving authority and prestige. [< Maori]

man-a bout-town (man′ə bout toun′), *n., pl.* **men-a bout-town.** man who spends much of his time in clubs, theaters, etc.

man a cle (man′ə kəl), *n., v.,* **-cled, -cling.** *—n.* 1 Usually, **manacles,** *pl.* fetter for the hands; handcuff. 2 anything that fetters; restraint. *—v.t.* 1 put manacles on: *manacle a prisoner.* 2 restrain; hamper. [< Old French *manicle* < Latin *manicula,* diminutive of *manus* hand]

man age (man′ij), *v.,* **-aged, -ag ing,** *n.* *—v.t.* 1 guide or handle with skill or authority; control; direct: *manage a business, manage a horse.* See synonym study below. 2 succeed in accomplishing; contrive; arrange: *I shall manage to keep warm with this blanket.* 3 make use of: *manage tools well.* 4 get one's way with (a person) by craft or by flattering. *—v.i.* 1 conduct affairs. 2 get along: *manage on one's income.* *—n.* manège: *the manage of horses.* [earlier *manege* < Italian *maneggiare* handle or train (horses) < *mano* hand < Latin *manus*]

Syn. *v.t.* 1 **Manage, conduct, direct** mean to guide or handle with authority. **Manage** implies skillful handling of people and details so as to get results: *He manages a large department store.* **Conduct** implies supervising the action of a group working together for something: *The teacher conducted the class on a tour of the museum.* **Direct** implies guiding the affairs or actions of a group by giving advice and instructions to be followed: *An ornithologist directed our bird conservation program.*

man age a bil i ty (man′ə jə bil′ə tē), *n.* a being manageable.

man age a ble (man′ə jə bəl), *adj.* that can be managed. **—man′age a ble ness,** *n.* **—man′age a bly,** *adv.*

man age ment (man′ij mənt), *n.* 1 a managing or handling; control; direction: *Bad management caused the bank's failure.* 2 persons that manage a business or an institution: *The management of the company decided to spend more money on advertising.*

man ag er (man′ə jər), *n.* 1 person who manages, especially one who manages a business; director; administrator: *a bank manager, a baseball manager.* 2 person skilled in managing (affairs, time, money, etc.): *She is a good manager and always saves part of her salary.*

man a ger i al (man′ə jir′ē əl), *adj.* of a manager; having to do with management. **—man′a ger′i al ly,** *adv.*

man ag er ship (man′ə jər ship), *n.* position or control of a manager.

Ma na gua (mə nä′gwə), *n.* capital of Nicaragua, in the W part. 300,000.

Ma na ma (mə nä′mə), *n.* capital of Bahrein. 79,000.

ma ña na (mä nyä′nä), *n., adv.* tomorrow; some time. [< Spanish]

man-ape (man′āp′), *n.* a fossil man of the early Pleistocene, having both human and subhuman characteristics.

Ma nas sas (mə nas′əs), *n.* town in NE Virginia where the two battles of Bull Run were fought in the Civil War.

Ma nas seh (mə nas′ə), *n.* in the Bible: 1 the older son of Joseph. 2 tribe of Israel descended from him.

man-at-arms (man′ət ärmz′), *n., pl.* **men-at-arms.** 1 soldier. 2 a heavily armed soldier on horseback.

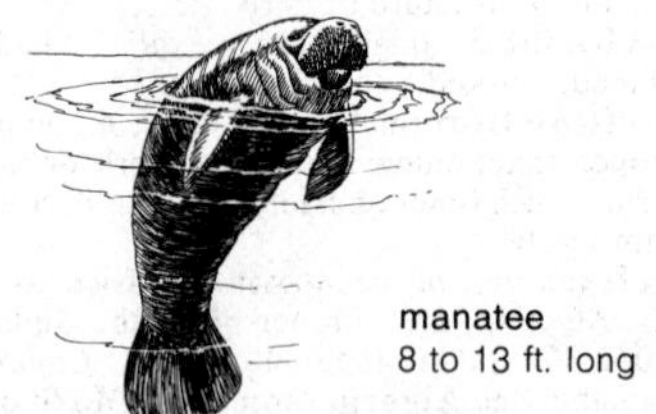

manatee
8 to 13 ft. long

man a tee (man′ə tē′), *n.* a large, herbivorous sea mammal having two flippers and a flat, oval tail, living in warm, shallow water near coasts; sea cow. It is of the same order as the dugong. [< Spanish *manatí*]

Man ches ter (man′ches′tər, man′chəstər), *n.* 1 important textile-manufacturing city in W England. 603,000 2 city in S New Hampshire. 88,000.

Man chou kuo (man′chü′kwō′), *n.* Manchukuo.

Man chu (man′chü), *n.* 1 member of a Mongoloid people of Manchuria who conquered China in 1644 and ruled it until 1912. 2 their Altaic language. *—adj.* of the Manchus, their country, or their language.

Man chu kuo (man′chü′kwō′), *n.* former Japanese state (1931-1945) in E Asia, north of China, now a part of China. Also, **Manchoukuo.**

Man chur i a (man chůr′ē ə), *n.* region in NE China, including several provinces of China. **—Man chur′i an,** *adj., n.*

man ci ple (man′sə pəl), *n.* a purchasing agent for a college or other institution; steward. [< Old French < Latin *mancipium* purchase < *manu capere* take in hand]

Man da lay (man′də lā′, man′də lā), *n.* city in central Burma. 360,000.

man da mus (man dā′məs), *n.* a written order from a higher court to a lower court, an official, a city, a corporation, etc., directing that a certain thing be done. [< Latin, we order]

Man dan (man′dan), *n., pl.* **-dan** or **-dans.** a western plains tribe of North American Indians, famous as traders.

man dar in (man′dər ən), *n.* 1 an official of any of nine ranks under the Chinese empire. 2 **Mandarin,** a the dialect of Chinese spoken by officials and educated people under the Manchu dynasty. b the chief Chinese dialect, spoken in northern China, especially the dialect of Peking. 3 kind of small, sweet, spicy citrus fruit with a thin, orange-colored, very loose peel and segments that separate easily. 4 tree it grows on. [< Portuguese *mandarim* < Malay *mantrī* < Sanskrit *mantrin* advisor]

man da tar y (man′də ter′ē), *n., pl.* **-tar ies.** nation to which a mandate over another country has been given.

man date (*n.* man′dāt, man′dit; *v.* man′dāt), *n., v.,* **-dat ed, -dat ing.** *—n.* 1 an order or command: *a royal mandate.* 2 order from a higher court or official to a lower one. 3 the will of voters expressed to their representative. 4 commission given to one nation by a group of nations to administer the government and affairs of a territory, colony, etc. After World War I a system of mandates was established by the League of Nations. 5 a mandated territory, etc. *—v.t.* put (a territory, etc.) under the administration of another nation. [< Latin *mandatum* < *mandare* to order]

man da to ry (man′də tôr′ē, man′də tōr′ē), *adj., n., pl.* **-ries.** *—adj.* 1 of or like a mandate; giving a command or order. 2 required by a command or order: *a mandatory sentence for manslaughter.* 3 of, having to do with, or having received a mandate, as a nation commissioned to take care of a dependent territory. *—n.* mandatary. **—man′da to′ri ly,** *adv.*

man-day (man′dā′), *n.* one day of one man's work, used as a unit in figuring cost, time, etc., of production.

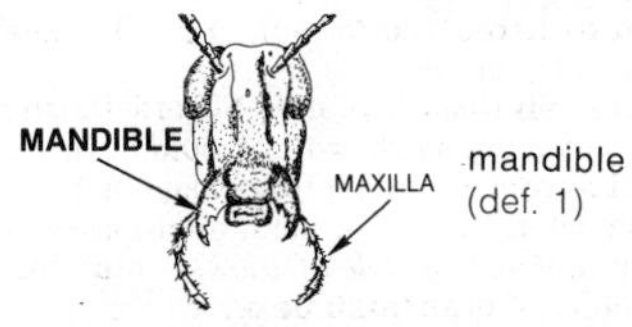

mandible (def. 1)

man di ble (man′də bəl), *n.* 1 (in arthropods) one of a pair of mouth parts used for seizing, biting, etc. 2 the upper or lower part of a bird's beak. 3 jaw or jawbone, especially the lower one. [< Late Latin *mandibula* < Latin *mandere* to chew]

man dib u lar (man dib′yə lər), *adj.* of, having to do with, or like a mandible.

man do lin (man′də lin′, man′dl ən), *n.* a musical instrument with a pear-shaped body, like that of the lute, having four to six pairs of metal strings and a fretted neck, played with a plectrum. [< French *mandoline* < Italian *mandolino*]

man drag or a (man drag′ər ə), *n.* mandrake. [< Latin < Greek *mandragoras*]

man drake (man′drāk), *n.* 1 any of a genus of poisonous herbs of the nightshade family, having very short stems and thick, often forked roots thought to resemble the human form. Mandrake roots were formerly used in medicine. 2 U.S. the May apple. [Middle English *mandragge,* short for *mandragora*]

man drel or **man dril** (man′drəl), *n.* 1 spindle or bar of a lathe that supports the material being turned. 2 rod or core around which metal or other material is shaped. [< French *mandrin*]

mandrill
3 ft. long

man drill (man′drəl), *n.* a large, fierce baboon of western Africa. The face of the male mandrill is marked with blue and scarlet. [< *man* + *drill* baboon]

mane (mān), *n.* 1 the long, heavy hair growing on the back of or around the neck of a horse, lion, etc. 2 a person's hair when long and thick. [Old English *manu*]

man-eat er (man′ē′tər), *n.* 1 cannibal. 2 lion, tiger, shark, etc., that attacks or is supposed to attack human beings and devour them.

man-eat ing (man′ē′ting), *adj.* eating or devouring human beings.

maned (mānd), *adj.* having a mane.

ma nège (mə nezh′, mə nāzh′), *n.* 1 art of training or riding horses; horsemanship. 2 movements of a trained horse. 3 a riding school. [< French]

ma nes or **Ma nes** (mā′nēz′), *n.pl.* 1 (in ancient Roman belief) the deified souls of dead ancestors, together with the gods of the lower world. 2 the spirit or shade of a particular dead person. [< Latin]

Ma net (mȧ nā′), *n.* **Édouard,** 1832-1883, French painter.

ma neu ver (mə nü′vər), *n.* 1 a planned movement of troops, ships, etc., especially for tactical purposes. 2 **maneuvers,** *pl.* a training exercise between two or more military or naval units, simulating combat situations. 3 a skillful plan; clever trick: *a series of political maneuvers to get votes.* 4 an agile or skillful movement made to elude or deceive. *—v.i.* 1 perform maneuvers. 2 plan skillfully; use clever tricks; scheme: *maneuver for some advantage.* *—v.t.* 1 cause to perform maneuvers. 2 force by skillful plans; get by clever tricks: *She maneuvered her lazy brother out of bed.* 3 move or manipulate skillfully: *maneuver scenery on a stage.* Also, **manoeuvre.** [< French *manœuvre,* ultimately < Latin *manu operare* to work by hand. Doublet of MANURE.] **—ma neu′ver a ble,** *adj.*

ma neu ver a bil i ty (mə nü′vər ə bil′ə tē), *n.* quality or power of being maneuverable.

man Friday, a faithful servant or indispensable assistant. [< *Friday,* Robinson Crusoe's manservant, whom he called "my *man Friday*"]

hat, āge, fär; let, ēqual, tėrm;
it, īce; hot, ōpen, ôrder;
oil, out; cup, pu̇t, rüle;
ch, child; ng, long; sh, she;
th, thin; ᴛʜ, then; zh, measure;

ə represents *a* in about, *e* in taken, *i* in pencil, *o* in lemon, *u* in circus.

< = from, derived from, taken from.

man ful (man′fəl), *adj.* characterized by manliness; brave; resolute. **—man′ful ly,** *adv.* **—man′ful ness,** *n.*

man ga nese (mang′gə nēz′), *n.* a hard, brittle, grayish-white or reddish-gray metallic element that resembles iron but is not magnetic and is softer. It is used chiefly in making alloys of steel, fertilizers, paints and industrial chemicals. *Symbol:* Mn; *atomic number* 25. See pages 326 and 327 for table. [< Italian, alteration of Medieval Latin *magnesia.* See MAGNESIA.]

manganese dioxide, a black crystal, or brownish-black powder, used in making dyes, dry-cell batteries, as an oxidizing agent, etc. *Formula:* MnO_2

mange (mānj), *n.* a skin disease of animals, caused by any of several parasitic mites, some of which also attack man, and marked by scabs, itching, and loss of hair. [< Old French *manjüe* itch < *mangier* eat < Latin *manducare* to chew]

man gel-wur zel (mang′gəl wėr′zəl), *n.* a large, coarse variety of beet grown as food for cattle. [< German *Mangelwurzel,* variant of *Mangoldwurzel* beet root]

man ger (mān′jər), *n.* box or trough in which hay or other food can be placed for horses or cows to eat. [< Old French *mangeoire* < *mangier* eat < Latin *manducare* to chew]

man gle[1] (mang′gəl), *v.t.,* **-gled, -gling.** 1 cut or tear (the flesh) roughly; lacerate. 2 spoil; ruin. [< Anglo-French *mangler* < Old French *mahaignier* to maim] **—man′gler,** *n.*

man gle[2] (mang′gəl), *n., v.,* **-gled, -gling.** *—n.* machine with rollers for pressing and smoothing sheets, towels, and other flat things after washing. *—v.t.* press or make smooth in a mangle. [< Dutch *mangel,* ultimately < Late Latin *manganum* < Greek *manganon* contrivance]

man go (mang′gō), *n., pl.* **-goes** or **-gos.** 1 a slightly sour, juicy, oval fruit with a thick, yellowish-red rind. Mangoes are eaten ripe or are pickled for eating when green. 2 the tropical evergreen tree of the same family as the cashew, that it grows on. [< Portuguese *manga* < Tamil *mānkāy*]

man go steen (mang′gə stēn′), *n.* 1 a juicy edible fruit with a thick reddish-brown rind. 2 tree of the East Indies that it grows on. [< Malay *mangustan*]

man grove (mang′grōv), *n.* any of a genus of tropical trees or shrubs having branches that send down many roots which look like additional trunks. Mangroves grow in swamps along the banks of rivers. [< Spanish *mangle;* spelling influenced by English *grove*]

mang y (mān′jē), *adj.,* **mang i er,**

mang i est. 1 having, caused by, or like mange; with the hair falling out. 2 shabby and dirty. 3 INFORMAL. mean; contemptible. —**mang′i ness,** *n.*

man han dle (man′han′dl), *v.t.,* **-dled, -dling.** 1 treat roughly; pull or push about. 2 move by human force alone.

Man hat tan (man hat′n), *n.* 1 island on which the chief business section of New York City is located. It is a borough of New York City. 1,525,000 pop.; 31 sq. mi. 2 cocktail consisting of rye whiskey, Italian vermouth, and usually bitters.

Manhattan Project, the project organized by the United States government in 1942 to produce the first atomic bomb.

man hole (man′hōl′), *n.* hole through which a workman can enter a sewer, steam boiler, etc., to inspect or repair it.

man hood (man′hu̇d), *n.* 1 condition or time of being a man. 2 character or qualities of a man. 3 men as a group: *American manhood.*

man-hour (man′our′), *n.* one hour of one man's work, used as a unit in industry in figuring cost, time, etc., of production.

man hunt (man′hunt′), *n.* an organized hunt for a criminal, escaped convict, etc.

ma ni a (mā′nē ə), *n.* 1 kind of mental disorder characterized by great excitement, elation, and uncontrolled, often violent, activity. It is a recurring state in manic-depressive psychosis. 2 unusual or unreasonable fondness; craze. [< Latin < Greek < *mainesthai* to rage]

ma ni ac (mā′nē ak), *n.* an insane person; raving lunatic. —*adj.* insane; raving.

ma ni a cal (mə nī′ə kəl), *adj.* insane; raving. —**ma ni′a cal ly,** *adv.*

ma nic (man′ik, mā′nik), *adj.* 1 of or like mania. 2 suffering from mania.

man ic-de pres sive (man′ik di pres′iv), *adj.* having alternating attacks of mania and depression. —*n.* a manic-depressive person.

man i cure (man′ə kyu̇r), *v.,* **-cured, -cur ing,** *n.* —*v.t., v.i.* 1 care for (the fingernails and hands); trim, clean, and polish (the fingernails). 2 trim (a hedge, grounds, etc.) carefully. —*n.* 1 the care of the hands; trimming, cleaning, and polishing of fingernails. 2 manicurist. [< French < Latin *manus* hand + *cura* care]

man i cur ist (man′ə kyu̇r′ist), *n.* person whose work is manicuring.

man i fest (man′ə fest), *adj.* apparent to the eye or to the mind; plain; clear: *a manifest error.* —*v.t.* 1 show plainly; reveal; display. 2 put beyond doubt; prove. —*n.* list of cargo of a ship or aircraft. [< Latin *manifestus* palpable < *manus* hand + *-festus* (able to be) seized] —**man′i fest′ly,** *adv.*

man i fes ta tion (man′ə fə stā′shən), *n.* 1 a showing; making manifest. 2 a being manifested. 3 thing that manifests. 4 a public demonstration by a government, political party, etc., intended as a display of its power and determination to enforce some demand.

manifest destiny, U.S. the belief in the 1840's in the inevitable territorial expansion of the United States.

man i fes to (man′ə fes′tō), *n., pl.* **-toes** or **-tos.** a public declaration of intentions, purposes, or motives by an important person or group; proclamation. [< Italian]

man i fold (man′ə fōld), *adj.* 1 of many kinds; many and various: *manifold duties.* 2 having many parts or forms. 3 doing many things at the same time. —*n.* 1 pipe with several openings for connection with other pipes. 2 one of many copies. —*v.t.* make many copies of. [Old English *manigfeald*] —**man′i fold′ly,** *adv.* —**man′i fold′ness,** *n.* ➤ See **manyfold** for usage note.

man i kin (man′ə kən), *n.* 1 a little man; dwarf. 2 mannequin. Also, **mannikin.** [< Dutch *manneken,* diminutive of *man* man]

ma nil a (mə nil′ə), *n.* 1 abaca. 2 Manila paper. Also, **manilla.**

Ma nil a (mə nil′ə), *n.* largest city and former capital of the Philippines, on Luzon. 1,582,000.

Manila Bay, large bay at Manila. The American fleet under Admiral George Dewey defeated the Spanish fleet there in 1898.

Manila hemp, abaca.

Manila paper, a strong brown or brownish-yellow paper, originally made from abaca, used for wrapping, sketching, etc.

Manila rope, a strong rope made from abaca.

ma nil la (mə nil′ə), *n.* manila.

man in the street, the average person, especially as typifying public opinion.

man i oc (man′ē ok, mā′nē ok), *n.* cassava. [< French < Tupi *manioca*]

man i ple (man′ə pəl), *n.* 1 subdivision of the ancient Roman legion, containing 120 or 60 men. 2 an ornamental band or strip of cloth worn on the left arm near the wrist as a eucharistic vestment. [< Latin *manipulus* handful. See MANIPULATE.]

ma nip u late (mə nip′yə lāt), *v.t.,* **-lat ed, -lat ing.** 1 handle or treat, especially skillfully: *manipulate the controls of an airplane.* 2 manage cleverly, sometimes using personal influence, especially unfair influence: *He so manipulated the ball team that he was elected captain.* 3 change for one's own purpose or advantage; treat unfairly or dishonestly: *manipulate a company's accounts to conceal embezzlement.* [< Latin *manipulus* handful < *manus* hand + root of *plere* to fill] —**ma nip′u la′tor,** *n.*

ma nip u la tion (mə nip′yə lā′shən), *n.* 1 skillful handling or treatment. 2 clever use of influence. 3 change made for one's own purpose or advantage.

ma nip u la tive (mə nip′yə lā′tiv), *adj.* 1 of or having to do with manipulation. 2 done by manipulation.

man i to (man′ə tō), *n., pl.* **-tos.** spirit worshiped by Algonquian Indians as a force of nature with supernatural powers. Also, **manitou, manitu.** [< Algonquian]

Man i to ba (man′ə tō′bə), *n.* 1 province in S central Canada. 985,000 pop.; 251,000 sq. mi. *Capital:* Winnipeg. *Abbrev.:* Man. 2 **Lake,** lake in S Manitoba. 120 mi. long; 1817 sq. mi. —**Man′i to′ban,** *adj., n.*

man i tou or **man i tu** (man′ə tü), *n.* manito.

man kind (man′kīnd′ *for 1;* man′kīnd′ *for 2*), *n.* 1 the human race; all human beings. 2 the male sex; men.

man like (man′līk′), *adj.* 1 like a man. 2 suitable for a man.

man ly (man′lē), *adj.,* **-li er, -li est.** 1 like a man; as a man should be; strong, frank, brave, noble, independent, and honorable. See **male** for synonym study. 2 suitable for a man; masculine: *a manly sport.* —**man′li ness,** *n.*

man-made (man′mād′), *adj.* made by man; not natural; artificial or synthetic: *a man-made satellite.*

Mann (man *for 1;* män *for 2*), *n.* 1 **Horace,** 1796-1859, American educator, who established the first teacher-training school in the United States. 2 **Thomas,** 1875-1955, German novelist and essayist, in the United States after 1938.

man na (man′ə), *n.* 1 (in the Bible) the food miraculously supplied to the Israelites in the wilderness. 2 food for the soul or mind. 3 any necessity unexpectedly supplied. [Old English < Late Latin < Greek < Hebrew *mān*]

manned (mand), *adj.* occupied or controlled by one or more persons: *a manned space vehicle.*

man ne quin (man′ə kən), *n.* 1 woman who models new clothes for potential customers. 2 model or figure of a person used by tailors, artists, stores, etc. Also, **manikin, mannikin.** [< French < Dutch *manneken.* See MANIKIN.]

man ner (man′ər), *n.* 1 way of doing, being done, or happening; fashion: *The trouble arose in this manner.* See **way** for synonym study. 2 way of acting or behaving: *a kind manner, an arrogant manner.* 3 **manners,** *pl.* **a** ways of behaving: *good manners, bad manners.* **b** polite ways of behaving: *a person of manners.* **c** customs; ways of living: *a comedy of manners.* 4 kind or kinds: *all manner of birds.* 5 characteristic or customary way; mode; fashion: *a house decorated in the Italian manner.* 6 a distinguished or fashionable air. 7 personal style in art, music, etc.: *an operatic manner of singing.*

by all manner of means, most certainly.

by no manner of means, not at all; under no circumstances.

in a manner of speaking, as one might say; so to speak.

to the manner born, accustomed since birth to some way or condition.

[< Old French *maniere* way of handling < Latin *manuarius* belonging to the hand < *manus* hand]

man nered (man′ərd), *adj.* affected; artificial; having many mannerisms: *a mannered style of writing.*

man ner ism (man′ə riz′əm), *n.* 1 too much use of some manner in speaking, writing or behaving; affectation. 2 an odd little trick; queer habit; a peculiar way of acting.

man ner less (man′ər lis), *adj.* without good manners.

man ner ly (man′ər lē), *adj.* having or showing good manners; polite; well-behaved. —*adv.* politely. —**man′ner li ness,** *n.*

Mann heim (män′hīm), *n.* city in SW West Germany, on the Rhine. 331,000.

man ni kin (man′ə kən), *n.* 1 manikin. 2 mannequin.

man nish (man′ish), *adj.* 1 characteristic of a man: *a mannish way of holding a baby.* 2 (of a woman) resembling a man; masculine. 3 similar to that of a man; appropriate to a man: *a mannish style of dress.* —**man′nish ly,** *adv.* —**man′nish ness,** *n.*

ma noeu vre (mə nü′vər), *n., v.i., v.t.,* **-vred, -vring.** maneuver.

man of letters, 1 writer. 2 person who has a wide knowledge of literature.

man of the world, man who knows people and customs, and is tolerant of both.

man-of-war (man′əv wôr′), *n., pl.* **men-of-war.** warship of a type used in former times.

man-of-war bird, frigate bird.

hat, āge, fär; let, ēqual, tėrm;
it, īce; hot, ōpen, ôrder;
oil, out; cup, pu̇t, rüle;
ch, child; ng, long; sh, she;
th, thin; ᴛʜ, then; zh, measure;

ə represents *a* in about, *e* in taken, *i* in pencil, *o* in lemon, *u* in circus.

< = from, derived from, taken from.

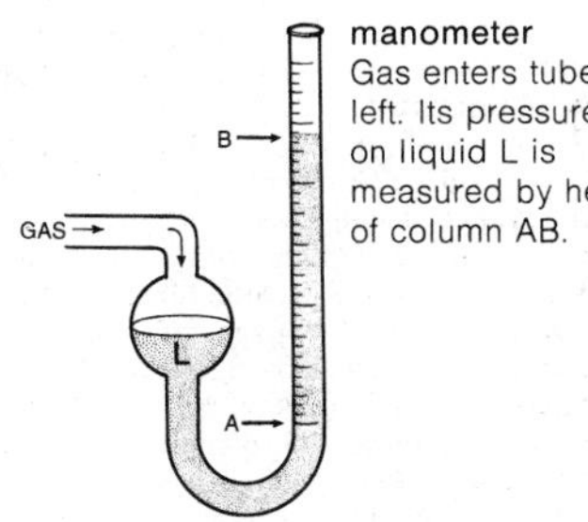

manometer
Gas enters tube at left. Its pressure on liquid L is measured by height of column AB.

ma nom e ter (mə nom′ə tər), *n.* instrument for measuring the pressure of gases or vapors. [< Greek *manos* thin, loose + English *-meter*]

man or (man′ər), *n.* 1 (in the Middle Ages) a feudal estate, part of which was set aside for the lord and the rest divided among his peasants, who paid the owner rent in goods, services, or money. If the lord sold his manor, the peasants or serfs were sold with it. 2 a large estate. 3 the main house or mansion of an estate. [< Old French *manoir* a dwelling < *maneir* dwell < Latin *manere* to stay]

manor house, house of the owner of a manor.

ma no ri al (mə nôr′ē əl, mə nōr′ē əl), *adj.* 1 of a manor. 2 forming a manor.

man-o'-war bird (man′ə wôr), frigate bird.

man pow er (man′pou′ər), *n.* 1 power supplied by the physical work of men. 2 strength thought of in terms of the number of men needed or available.

man qué (mäɴ kā′), *adj.* FRENCH. defective or abortive; unfulfilled, unrealized, or frustrated: *an artist manqué, an adventure manqué.*

mansard (def. 1)

man sard (man′särd), *n.* 1 roof with two slopes on each side. 2 the story under such a roof. [< François *Mansard,* 1598-1666, French architect]

manse (mans), *n.* parsonage, especially in Scotland. [< Medieval Latin *mansa* a dwelling < Latin *manere* to stay]

man serv ant (man′sėr′vənt), *n., pl.* **men serv ants.** a male servant.

Mans field (manz′fēld′), *n.* **Katherine,** 1888-1923, British writer, born in New Zealand.

man sion (man′shən), *n.* a large house; stately residence. [< Latin *mansionem* place to stay in < *manere* to stay]

man-size (man′sīz′), *adj.* man-sized.

man-sized (man′sīzd′), *adj.* 1 suitable for a full-grown man; large: *man-sized portions.* 2 INFORMAL. requiring a grown man's strength or judgment: *man-sized responsibilities.*

man slaugh ter (man′slô′tər), *n.* 1 the killing of a human being. 2 (in law) the killing of a person unlawfully but without deliberate intent.

man ta (man′tə), *n.* 1 cloak or wrap worn by women in Spain and Latin America. 2 Also, **manta ray.** devilfish. [< Spanish]

man teau (man′tō), *n., pl.* **-teaus, -teaux** (-tōz). mantle or cloak. [< French]

Man te gna (män tā′nyä), *n.* **Andrea,** 1431-1506, Italian painter and engraver.

man tel (man′tl), *n.* 1 the shelf, beam, or arch above a fireplace with its vertical supports. 2 shelf above a fireplace; mantelpiece. 3 the decorative framework around a fireplace. [variant of *mantle*]

man tel et (man′tl et), *n.* a short mantle or cape.

man tel piece (man′tl pēs′), *n.* mantel (def. 2); chimney piece.

man til la (man til′ə, man tē′yə), *n.* 1 veil or scarf, often of lace, covering the hair and falling down over the shoulders. Spanish and Mexican women often wear mantillas. 2 a short mantle or cape. [< Spanish, diminutive of *manta* cloak]

man tis (man′tis), *n., pl.* **-tis es, -tes** (-tēz). any of an order of large insects having forelegs modified for capturing other insects and often lifted as if in prayer; praying mantis. [< Greek, prophet (from its posture)]

man tis sa (man tis′ə), *n.* the decimal part of a logarithm. In the logarithm 2.95424, the characteristic is 2 and the mantissa is .95424. [< Latin, an addition < Etruscan]

mantle (def. 1)

man tle (man′tl), *n., v.,* **-tled, -tling.** —*n.* 1 a loose cloak without sleeves. 2 anything that covers like a mantle: *The ground had a mantle of snow.* 3 a lacelike tube around a gas flame that gets so hot it glows and gives light. See **lantern** for picture. 4 fold of the body wall of a mollusk that lines the shell and secretes the material of which the shell is formed. 5 a pair of similar folds of a brachiopod. 6 (in geology) the layer of the earth, lying between its crust and its core. —*v.t.* 1 cover with a mantle. 2 cover or conceal; obscure; cloak: *Clouds mantled the moon.* —*v.i.* 1 redden: *Her face mantled with shame.* 2 be or become covered with a coating or scum: *The pond has mantled.* [partly Old English *maentel,* partly < Old French *mantel;* both < Latin *mantellum*]

mantle rock, regolith.

Man toux test (man′tü), test for tuberculosis in which diluted tuberculin is injected between the layers of the skin. [< Charles *Mantoux,* 1877-1947, French physician, who developed it]

man tra (man′trə), *n.* (in Hinduism) a prayer or invocation, sometimes held to have magical power. [< Sanskrit]

man-trap (man′trap′), *n.* 1 trap for catching trespassers in private grounds. 2 any trap for catching men.

man tu a (man′chu̇ ə), *n.* 1 a loose gown or cloak, worn by women in the 1600's and 1700's. 2 mantle. [< French *manteau;* spelling influenced by *Mantua*]

Man tu a (man′chu̇ ə), *n.* city in N Italy. Vergil was born there. 62,000. **—Man′tu an,** *adj., n.*

man u al (man′yü əl), *adj.* of or having to do with the hands; done with the hands: *manual labor.* —*n.* 1 a small book that helps its readers to understand or use something; handbook. 2 a prescribed drill in handling a rifle or other weapons, especially at formal military ceremonies. 3 an organ keyboard played with the hands. [< Latin *manualis* < *manus* hand] **—man′u al ly,** *adv.*

manual alphabet, finger alphabet.

manual training, training in work done with the hands; practice in various arts and crafts, especially in making things out of wood or metal.

manuf., manufacturer.

man u fac tor y (man′yə fak′tər ē), *n., pl.* **-tor ies.** factory.

man u fac ture (man′yə fak′chər), *v.,* **-tured, -tur ing,** *n.* —*v.t.* 1 make by hand or by machine; produce by human labor, especially in large quantities with the help of machines and division of labor: *manufacture steel, manufacture furniture.* 2 make into something useful. 3 make up; invent: *manufacture excuses.* —*n.* 1 act or process of manufacturing. 2 thing manufactured. 3 action or process of making by hand. [< Middle French < Medieval Latin *manufactura* < Latin *manu facere* make by hand]

man u fac tur er (man′yə fak′chər ər), *n.* person or company whose business is manufacturing; owner of a factory.

man u mis sion (man′yə mish′ən), *n.* 1 a freeing from slavery. 2 a being freed from slavery.

man u mit (man′yə mit′), *v.t.,* **-mit ted, -mit ting.** release from slavery; set free from bondage. [< Latin *manumittere* < *manus* hand + *mittere* send, release]

ma nure (mə nu̇r′, mə nyu̇r′), *n., v.,* **-nured, -nur ing.** —*n.* substance put in or on the soil as fertilizer, such as dung or refuse from stables —*v.t.* put manure in or on. [< Old French *manouvrer* to till, work by hand < Latin *manu operare.* Doublet of MANEUVER.]

man u script (man′yə skript), *n.* book or paper written by hand or with a typewriter. Before printing was invented, all books and papers were handwritten manuscripts. —*adj.* written by hand or with a typewriter. [< Latin *manu scriptus* written by hand]

Manx (mangks), *adj.* of the Isle of Man, its people, or their language. —*n.* 1 *pl. in use.* people of the Isle of Man. 2 their Celtic language.

Manx cat, a short-haired domestic cat that has no tail or only the stump of a tail.

Manx man (mangks′mən), *n., pl.* **-men.** native or inhabitant of the Isle of Man.

man y (men′ē), *adj.,* **more, most,** *n. adj.* 1 consisting of a great, indefinite number; numerous: *many people, many years ago.* See synonym study below. 2 **how many,** what number of: *How many days until Christmas?*

—*n.* 1 a great, indefinite number: *many of us.* 2 many people or things: *There were many at the dance.* 3 **a good many,** a fairly large number. 4 **a great many,** a very large number. 5 **one too many for,** more than a match for: *We were one too many for the enemy.* [Old English *manig*]

Syn. *adj.* 1 **Many, innumerable** mean consisting of a large number. **Many** is the general word: *Were many people there?* **Innumerable** means more than can be counted, or so many that counting would be very hard: *He has given innumerable excuses for being late.*

man-year (man′yir′), *n.* one year of one man's work, used as a unit in figuring cost, time, output, etc., of production.

man y fold (men′ē fōld′), *adv.* many times; to a great extent.

➔ **Manyfold, manifold.** *Manyfold* is a compound recently formed on the analogy of such compounds as *twofold* and *threefold,* which denote the number of times an action recurs: *The population of our city has increased manyfold. Manifold* is an adjective expressing kind and variety, never time and duration: *His responsibilities are manifold.*

man y plies (men′ē plīz′), *n.* the third stomach of a cow or other ruminant; omasum. [< *many* + *plies,* plural of *ply,* noun]

man y-sid ed (men′ē sī′did), *adj.* 1 having many sides. 2 having many interests or abilities. 3 having many aspects, possibilities, etc.: *a many-sided problem.*

man za ni ta (man′zə nē′tə), *n.* any of various evergreen shrubs or small trees of the heath family that grow in western North America. [< Spanish, diminutive of *manzana* apple]

Ma o ism (mä′ō iz′əm, mou′iz′əm), *n.* principles and practices of Mao Tse-tung, characterized by rigid adherence to Marxian doctrines.

Ma o ist (mä′ō ist, mou′ist), *adj.* of or having to do with Maoism. —*n.* supporter of Maoism.

Ma o ri (mä′ōr ē, mou′rē), *n.* 1 member of the native Polynesian people of New Zealand. 2 their language. —*adj.* of the Maoris or their language.

Ma o Tse-tung (mä′ō dzü′dúng′; mou′ tse′túng′), born 1893, Chinese Communist leader, chairman of the Chinese Communist Party since 1945.

map (map), *n., v.,* **mapped, map ping.** —*n.* 1 drawing representing the earth's surface or part of it, usually showing countries, cities, rivers, seas, lakes, and mountains. See synonym study below. 2 drawing representing the sky or part of it, showing the position of the stars, etc. 3 **put on the map,** make well-known. —*v.t.* 1 make a map of; show on a map. 2 arrange in detail; plan: *map out the week's work.* 3 (in mathematics) to cause an element in (one set) to correspond to an element in the same or another set. [< Medieval Latin *mappa* < Latin, napkin, cloth (on which maps were once drawn)] **—map′like′,** *adj.* **—map′per,** *n.*

Syn. *n.* 1 **Map, chart** mean a drawing representing a surface or area. **Map** applies particularly to a representation of some part of the earth's surface showing relative geographical positions, shape, size, etc.: *A map of a city shows streets and parks.* **Chart** applies particularly to a map used in navigation, showing deep and shallow places, islands, channels, etc., in a body of water, or altitudes, radio beacons, air currents, airlanes, etc., for flying: *The reef that the ship struck is on the chart.*

ma ple (mā′pəl), *n.* 1 any of a family of trees growing in north temperate regions, valued for their shade, their wood, and their sap. All maples have dry fruits with two wings and opposite leaves without stipules. 2 the hard, fine-grained, light-colored wood of any of these trees. 3 flavor of maple sugar or maple syrup. [Old English *mapeltrēow* maple tree] **—ma′ple like′,** *adj.*

maple leaf, 1 leaf of the maple tree. 2 this leaf as the national emblem of Canada.

maple sugar, a pale-brown sugar made by boiling maple syrup.

maple syrup, syrup made by boiling the sap of various maples, especially the sugar maple.

map mak er (map′mā′kər), *n.* cartographer.

ma quette (ma ket′), *n.* a preliminary sketch or model of a painting, monument, building, etc. [< French]

ma quil lage (ma kē yäzh′), *n.* cosmetics; make-up. [< French]

Ma quis (mä kē′), *n., pl.* **Ma quis** (mä kēz′). 1 the French underground resistance movement against the Germans in World War II. 2 member of this movement. [< French < *maquis* bushy land < Italian *macchia* thicket, as cover for bandits]

Ma qui sard (mä kē zärd′), *n.* member of the Maquis.

mar (mär), *v.t.,* **marred, mar ring.** spoil the beauty of; damage; injure; ruin. [Old English *merran* to waste]

mar., 1 marine. 2 maritime. 3 married.

Mar., March.

mar a bou or **mar a bout**[1] (mar′ə bü), *n.* 1 any of several varieties of large, white-bodied storks of Africa and Asia. 2 a furlike trimming made from its soft, white, downy feathers. 3 **a** a silk that is nearly pure-white in the raw state. **b** a delicate cloth made from it. [< *marabout*[2] (because the bird appears reflective)]

mar a bout[2] (mar′ə büt), *n.* a Moslem holy man or ascetic of northern Africa. [< French < Arabic *murābiṭ* hermit]

ma ra ca (mə rä′kə), *n.* a percussion instrument consisting of seeds, pebbles, etc., enclosed in a dry gourd and shaken like a rattle, usually in pairs. [< Portuguese]

Mar a cai bo (mar′ə kī′bō), *n.* 1 seaport in NW Venezuela. 625,000. 2 **Lake,** lake in NW Venezuela. 130 mi. long; 60 mi. wide.

mar a schi no (mar′ə skē′nō, mar′ə shē′nō), *n.* a strong, sweet liqueur made from the fermented juice of a kind of small, bitter black cherry. [< Italian < *marasca, amarasca* a sour cherry]

maraschino cherry, cherry preserved in a sweet syrup. It is used to decorate and add flavor to drinks, desserts, etc.

Ma rat (mȧ rȧ′), *n.* **Jean Paul,** 1743-1793, leader in the French Revolution.

mar a thon (mar′ə thon), *n.* 1 a foot race of 26 miles, 385 yards. 2 any race over a long distance. 3 any activity that calls for endurance. 4 **Marathon,** plain in Greece about 25 miles northeast of Athens. After the Athenians defeated the Persians there in 490 B.C., a runner ran all the way to Athens with the news of the victory.

ma raud (mə rôd′), *v.i.* go about in search of plunder. —*v.t.* plunder. [< French *marauder*] **—ma raud′er,** *n.*

mar ble (mär′bəl), *n., adj., v.,* **-bled, -bling.** —*n.* 1 a hard, metamorphic rock formed from limestone, usually white or variegated, capable of taking a high polish, and long valued in sculpture and architecture. 2 piece, block, or slab of marble, especially one that has been cut or shaped by man. 3 a small, usually colored ball of clay, glass, marble, etc., used in games. 4 **marbles,** *pl.* a children's game played with these balls, in which the player flips a marble with his thumb to knock his opponents' marbles outside of a ring. —*adj.* 1 made of marble. 2 like marble; white, hard, cold, or unfeeling. —*v.t.* color in imitation of the patterns in marble: *marble the edges of a book.* [< Old French *marbre* < Latin *marmor* < Greek *marmaros*] **—mar′ble like′,** *adj.*

mar ble ize (mar′bə līz), *v.t.,* **-ized, -iz ing.** make like marble in pattern, grain, etc.

mar bling (mär′bling), *n.* a coloring, graining, etc., that suggests marble: *beefsteak with a marbling of fat.*

mar bly (mär′blē), *adj.,* **-bli er, -bli est.** like marble.

mar ca site (mär′kə sīt), *n.* a whitish-yellow mineral with a metallic luster, of the same composition as and similar in appearance to pyrite; white iron pyrites. *Formula:* FeS_2 [< Medieval Latin *marcasita* < Arabic *marqashīṭā*]

mar cel (mär sel′), *n., v.,* **-celled, -cel ling.** —*n.* series of regular waves put in the hair. —*v.t.* set (the hair) with such waves. [< *Marcel Grateau,* 1852-1936, French hairdresser who originated the style]

march[1] (märch), *v.i.* 1 walk as soldiers do, in time and with steps of the same length: *march in a parade. The minister marched to the altar.* 2 proceed steadily; advance: *History marches on.* —*v.t.* cause to march or go: *March the regiment to the barracks.* —*n.* 1 act or fact of marching. 2 music for marching. 3 distance marched: *The camp is a day's march away.* 4 a long, hard walk. 5 advance; progress: *History records the march of events.* 6 **steal a march,** gain an advantage without being noticed. [< Middle French *marcher* to march, trample; probably of Germanic origin] **—march′er,** *n.*

march[2] (märch), *n.* 1 land along the border of a country; frontier; border. 2 **the Marches,** the districts along the border between England and Scotland, or between England and Wales. —*v.i.* border (on). [< Old French *marche;* of Germanic origin]

March (märch), *n.* the third month of the year. It has 31 days. [< Old French *marche* < Latin *Martius (mensis)* (month) of Mars]

mar chio ness (mär′shə nis), *n.* marquise. [< Medieval Latin *marchionissa* < *marchionem* marquis < *marcha* march[2]; of Germanic origin]

march pane (märch′pān′), *n.* marzipan.

march-past (märch′past′), *n.* march or parade, especially by troops, past a reviewing stand.

Mar co ni (mär kō′nē), *n.* **Guglielmo,** 1874-1937, Italian inventor who perfected the wireless telegraph.

Mar co Po lo (mär′kō pō′lō), 1254?-1324?, Italian merchant who wrote about his travels in Asia.

Mar cus Au re li us An to ni nus (mär′kəs ô rē′lē əs an′tə nī′nəs), A.D.

hat, āge, fär; let, ēqual, tėrm;
it, īce; hot, ōpen, ôrder;
oil, out; cup, pu̇t, rüle;
ch, child; ng, long; sh, she;
th, thin; ᴛʜ, then; zh, measure;

ə represents *a* in about, *e* in taken, *i* in pencil, *o* in lemon, *u* in circus.

< = from, derived from, taken from.

121-180, Roman emperor from A.D. 161 to 180 and Stoic philosopher.

Mar di gras (mär′dē grä′), the last day before Lent; Shrove Tuesday. It is celebrated with parades and festivities. [< French *mardi gras* fat (that is, meat-eating) Tuesday]

mare[1] (mer, mar), *n.* a female horse, donkey, etc., especially when mature. [Old English *mere*]

ma re[2] (mär′ē), *n., pl.* **ma ri a.** 1 any of certain dark regions on the surface of the moon. 2 a similar dark region on any planet. [< Latin, sea]

ma re nos trum (mär′ē nos′trəm), LATIN. our sea (applied to the Mediterranean by the ancient Romans).

mare's-nest (merz′nest′, marz′nest′), *n.* 1 a supposedly great discovery that turns out to be a mistake or hoax. 2 condition of great disorder or confusion.

mare's-tail (merz′tāl′, marz′tāl′), *n.* a long, feathery cirrus cloud, shaped somewhat like a horse's tail.

Mar gar et of Navarre (mär′gər it), 1492-1549, queen of Navarre, a poet and author.

mar gar in (mär′jər ən), *n.* margarine.

mar gar ine (mär′jər ən, mär′jə rēn′), *n.* substitute for butter consisting mainly of vegetable fat usually derived from cottonseed and soybean oils and sometimes corn and peanut oils; oleomargarine. [< French, ultimately < Greek *margaron* pearl]

mar gay (mär′gā), *n.* a small, long-tailed, spotted cat of the same genus as and similar to the ocelot, found from Texas south to Argentina. [< French < Tupi *mbaracaïa*]

marge (märj), *n.* ARCHAIC. margin.

marimba—The pipes underneath give a rich quality to the tones.

mar gin (mär′jən), *n.* 1 edge or border: *the margin of a lake.* 2 the blank space around the writing or printing on a page. 3 an extra amount; amount beyond what is necessary; difference: *We allow a margin of 15 minutes in catching a train.* 4 difference between the cost and selling price of stocks, etc. 5 money or security deposited with a broker to protect him from loss on contracts undertaken for the real buyer or seller. —*v.t.* provide with a margin. [< Latin *marginem* edge]

mar gin al (mär′jə nəl), *adj.* 1 written or printed in a margin: *a marginal comment.* 2 of a margin. 3 on or near the margin. 4 barely capable of producing goods, crops, etc., at a profitable rate: *marginal land.* 5 of, having to do with, or obtained from goods that are so produced and marketed: *marginal income.* **—mar′gin al ly,** *adv.*

mar gi na li a (mär′jə nā′lē ə), *n.pl.* marginal notes. [< New Latin]

mar gin al i ty (mär′jə nal′ə tē), *n.* quality or condition of being marginal.

mar grave (mär′grāv), *n.* 1 title of certain princes of Germany. 2 (formerly) the military governor of a German border province. [< Middle Dutch *markgrave* count of the marches]

mar gra vine (mär′grə vēn′), *n.* wife or widow of a margrave.

Mar gre the II (mär grā′tə), born 1940, queen of Denmark since 1972.

mar gue rite (mär′gə rēt′), *n.* 1 any of various species of chrysanthemums with daisy-like flowers, especially a species having flowers with white petals and a yellow center. 2 any of several other similar plants of the composite family. [< French]

ma ri a (mär′ē ə), *n.* pl. of **mare**[2].

ma ri a chi (mär′ē ä′chē), *n.* member of a Mexican band of strolling singers and musicians. [< Mexican Spanish]

Mar i an (mer′ē ən, mar′ē ən), *adj.* 1 of or having to do with the Virgin Mary. 2 of or having to do with some other Mary, such as Mary, Queen of Scots.

Mar i an a Islands (mar′ē an′ə), group of 15 small islands in the Pacific, east of the Philippines; Ladrone Islands. The largest island, Guam, belongs to the United States; the others are under United States trusteeship. 136,000 pop.; 451 sq. mi.

Ma ri a The re sa (mə rē′ə tə rē′sə), 1717-1780, archduchess of Austria, queen of Hungary and Bohemia from 1740 to 1780. She was the mother of Marie Antoinette.

Ma rie An toi nette (mə rē′ an′twə net′), 1755-1793, wife of Louis XVI and queen of France from 1774 to 1792. She was guillotined during the French Revolution.

Ma rie Lou ise (mə rē′ lü ēz′), 1791-1847, Austrian princess who was the second wife of Napoleon I.

mar i gold (mar′ə gōld), *n.* 1 any of a genus of plants of the composite family having showy yellow, orange, brownish, or red flowers. 2 any calendula, especially the pot marigold. 3 flower of any of these plants. [< (the Virgin) *Mary* + *gold*]

mar i jua na or **mar i hua na** (mar′ə wä′nə, mar′ə hwä′nə), *n.* 1 kind of hemp. 2 its dried leaves and flowers, smoked in cigarettes for narcotic effect; cannabis. [< Mexican Spanish *marihuana*]

ma rim ba (mə rim′bə), *n.* a musical instrument somewhat like a xylophone. [< Bantu]

ma ri na (mə rē′nə), *n.* dock or basin where moorings, supplies, etc., are available for small boats. [< Italian or Spanish, seashore]

mar i nade (mar′ə nād′; mar′ə nād), *n., v.,* **-nad ed, -nad ing.** —*n.* 1 a spiced vinegar or wine used to pickle meat or fish. 2 meat or fish pickled in this. —*v.t.* marinate. [< French < *mariner* to marinate < *marin* marine]

mar i nate (mar′ə nāt), *v.t.,* **-nat ed, -nat ing.** 1 soak in brine or marinade. 2 soak in oil and vinegar.

ma rine (mə rēn′), *adj.* 1 of the sea; found in the sea; produced by the sea: *Whales are marine animals.* 2 of shipping or commerce at sea; maritime: *marine law.* 3 of the navy; naval: *marine power.* 4 for use at sea, on a ship, etc.: *marine supplies.* 5 of or having to do with a marine or marines. —*n.* 1 shipping; fleet. 2 soldier formerly serving only at sea, now also participating in land and air action. 3 Also, **Marine.** person serving in the Marine Corps. 4 **marines,** *pl.* Marine Corps. [< Old French *marin* < Latin *marinus* of the sea < *mare* sea]

Marine Corps, branch of the armed forces of the United States, whose members are trained especially for landing operations. The Marine Corps has its own sea, air, and land units.

mar i ner (mar′ə nər), *n.* person who navigates or assists in navigating a ship; sailor; seaman.

Mar i ol o gy (mer′ē ol′ə jē), *n.* the body of theory or doctrine concerning the Virgin Mary.

Mar i on (mar′ē ən), *n.* **Francis,** 1732-1795, American general in the Revolutionary War, called "the Swamp Fox."

mar i o nette (mar′ē ə net′), *n.* doll or puppet made to imitate persons or animals and moved by strings or the hands, often on a miniature stage. [< French *marionnette,* ultimately < *Marie* Mary]

Mar i po sa lily (mar′ə pō′sə, mar′ə pō′zə), 1 any of a genus of plants of the lily family with tulip-like yellow, white, blue, or lilac flowers, growing in the western United States and in Mexico. 2 the flower of any of these plants. [< Spanish *mariposa* butterfly]

mar i tal (mar′ə təl), *adj.* 1 of or having to do with marriage; matrimonial: *A man and woman take marital vows when they marry.* 2 ARCHAIC. of a husband. [< *maritalis* < *maritus* married man] **—mar′i tal ly,** *adv.*

mar i time (mar′ə tīm), *adj.* 1 of the sea; having to do with shipping and sailing; nautical: *maritime law.* 2 on or near the sea: *Boston is a maritime city.* 3 living near the sea: *Many maritime peoples are fishermen.* [< Latin *maritimus* < *mare* sea]

Maritime Alps, part of the Alps in SE France and NW Italy.

Maritime Provinces, provinces of Canada along the Atlantic coast; New Brunswick, Newfoundland, Nova Scotia, and Prince Edward Island.

Mar i us (mer′ē əs, mar′ē əs), *n.* **Gaius,** 155?-86 B.C., Roman general and consul.

mar jor am (mär′jər əm), *n.* any of a genus of fragrant herbs of the mint family. **Sweet marjoram** is used as flavoring in cooking. [< Old French *majorane* < Medieval Latin *majorana*]

mark[1] (märk), *n.* 1 trace or impression, such as a line, dot, spot, stain, or scar, made by some object on the surface of another. 2 line, dot, etc., to show position. The line where a race starts is the mark. 3 something indicating the presence of something else; sign; indication: *Courtesy is a mark of good breeding.* See Synonym study below. 4 something that shows what or whose a thing is: *A simple mark served as the brand for his cattle.* 5 a written or printed stroke or sign: *a punctuation mark.* 6 grade or rating. 7 cross or other sign made by a person who cannot write his name. 8 something aimed at; target; goal. 9 what is usual, proper, or expected; standard: *A tired person does not feel up to the mark.* 10 influence; impression: *A great man leaves his mark on whatever he does.* 11 tag with a mark on it. 12 piece of bunting, bit of leather, knot, etc., used to mark depths on a lead line. 13 SLANG. person easily deceived or duped; sucker. 14 ARCHAIC. border or frontier.

beside the mark, a not hitting the thing aimed at. **b** not to the point; not relevant.

hit the mark, a succeed in doing what one tried to do. **b** be exactly right.

make one's mark, become famous; succeed.

miss the mark, a fail to do what one tried to do. **b** be not exactly right.

of mark, important; famous: *He was a man of mark.*

—*v.t.* 1 give grades to; rate: *mark examination papers.* 2 put a mark or marks on: *Be careful not to mark the table.* 3 trace or form by marks or as if by marks. 4 show by a mark or marks. 5 designate by or as if by a mark or marks: *mark a man for death.* 6 show clearly; indicate; manifest: *A frown marked her disapproval.* 7 distinguish; set off: *Many important discoveries mark the last 150 years.* 8 pay attention to; notice; observe: *Mark well my words.* 9 keep (the score); record. 10 put a price mark on; tag. —*v.i.* 1 make a mark or marks. 2 pay attention; take notice; consider. 3 keep the score in a game.

mark down, a write down; note. **b** to mark for sale at a lower price.

mark off or **mark out,** make lines, etc., to show the position of or to separate: *We marked out a tennis court.*

mark out for, single out for; select for.

mark up, a deface or disfigure. **b** to mark for sale at a higher price.

[Old English *mearc* boundary, limit]

Syn. *n.* 3 **Mark, sign, token** mean an indication of something not visible or readily apparent. **Mark** implies an indication of the character of something: *Generosity is a mark of greatness.* **Sign** is the general word, applying to any mental or physical state: *We could see no signs of life.* **Token** implies something that stands as a reminder or promise of something else, as of a feeling or an event: *This gift is a token of my love.*

mark[2] (märk), *n.* 1 the monetary unit of Germany, a coin or note equal to 100 pfennigs; Deutsche mark. The mark of West Germany is worth about 31 cents; the mark of East Germany is worth about 45 cents. 2 coin or paper note equal to the mark. 3 markka. [< German *Mark*]

Mark (märk), *n.* 1 (in the Bible) one of Christ's twelve apostles. He was one of the four Evangelists and a fellow worker with Paul and Peter. 2 the second book of the New Testament, attributed to him. 3 **King,** (in Arthurian legends) a king of Cornwall, the uncle of Tristan and husband of Iseult.

Mark Antony. See **Antony.**

mark down (märk′doun′), *n.* 1 decrease in the price of an article. 2 amount of this decrease.

marked (märkt), *adj.* 1 having a mark or marks: *a marked table, marked money.* 2 very noticeable; very plain; easily recognized: *There are marked differences between apples and oranges.* 3 distinguished or singled out as if by a mark: *marked for success.*

mark ed ly (mär′kid lē), *adv.* in a marked manner or degree; noticeably; plainly.

marked man, person watched as an object of suspicion, hatred, or vengeance.

mark er (mär′kər), *n.* 1 person or thing that marks, especially one who keeps the score in a game. 2 bookmark.

mar ket (mär′kit), *n.* 1 a meeting of people for buying and selling. 2 the people so gathered. 3 space or public building in which provisions, cattle, etc., are shown for sale. 4 store for the sale of provisions: *a fish market.* 5 trade or traders, especially as regards a particular article: *the cotton market, the grain market.* 6 opportunity to sell or buy: *lose one's market.* 7 demand for something; price offered: *a good market.* 8 region where goods can be sold: *South America is a market for American automobiles.* 9 **be in the market for,** be a possible buyer of. 10 **play the market,** speculate on the stock exchange. —*v.i.* buy or sell in a market. —*v.t.* 1 sell: *He cannot market the goods he makes.* 2 carry or send to market. [< Old French *market, marchiet* < Latin *mercatus* trade, ultimately < *mercem* merchandise] —**mar′ket er,** *n.*

mar ket a bil i ty (mär′kə tə bil′ə tē), *n.* quality of being marketable.

mar ket a ble (mär′kə tə bəl), *adj.* that can be sold; salable.

market garden, a truck farm. —**market gardener.**

mar ket place (mär′kət plās′), *n.* 1 place where a market is held, usually an open space or a square in a town. 2 the world of commerce.

market price, price that an article brings when sold; the current price.

market value, value of a given commodity, stock, etc., established as an average of the market prices over a certain period of time.

marmoset about 16 in. long with the tail

Mark ham (mär′kəm), *n.* **Edwin,** 1852-1940, American poet.

mark ing (mär′king), *n.* 1 mark or marks. 2 pattern or arrangement of marks.

mark ka (märk′kä), *n., pl.* **-kaa** (-kä). the monetary unit of Finland, a coin worth about 24½ cents; mark. [< Finnish]

marks man (märks′mən), *n., pl.* **—men.** 1 person who shoots well. 2 person who shoots.

marks man ship (märks′mən ship), *n.* skill in shooting.

Mark Twain. See **Twain.**

mark up (märk′up′), *n.* 1 increase in the price of an article. 2 amount of this increase. 3 percentage or amount added to the cost of an article to determine the selling price.

marl (märl), *n.* 1 a loose, crumbly soil or earthy deposit containing clay and calcium carbonate, used as a fertilizer. 2 ARCHAIC. earth. —*v.t.* fertilize with marl. [< Old French *marle* < Medieval Latin *margila* < Latin *marga*]

Marl bor ough (märl′bėr′ō), *n.* **Duke of,** 1650-1722, John Churchill, English general who defeated the French at Blenheim in 1704.

mar lin[1] (mär′lən), *n.* any of a genus of large marine game fishes of the same family as sailfishes. [short for *marlinespike* (which the marlin's long snout resembles)]

mar line or **mar lin**[2] (mär′lən), *n.* a small cord of two loosely twisted strands which sailors wind around the ends of a rope to keep it from fraying. [< Dutch *marlijn* < *marren* to tie + *lijn* line]

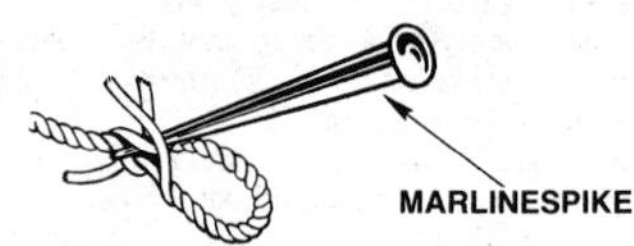

mar line spike or **mar lin spike** (mär′lən spīk′), *n.* a pointed iron implement used by sailors to separate strands of rope in splicing, etc.

Mar lowe (mär′lō), *n.* **Christopher,** 1564-1593, English dramatist and poet.

marl y (mär′lē), *adj.,* **marl i er, marl i est.** of, like, or full of marl.

mar ma lade (mär′mə lād), *n.* preserve similar to jam, made of oranges or of other fruit. The peel is usually sliced and boiled with the fruit. [< Portuguese *marmelada,* ultimately < Greek *meli* honey + *mēlon* apple]

Mar mar a or **Mar mor a** (mär′mər ə), *n.* **Sea of,** small sea between Europe and Asia Minor. It is connected with the Aegean Sea by the Dardanelles and with the Black Sea by the Bosporus. 170 mi. long; 50 mi. wide; 4300 sq. mi.

mar mo re al (mär môr′ē əl, mär mōr′ē əl), *adj.* 1 of marble. 2 like marble; cold, smooth, or white. [< Latin *marmoreus* < *marmor* marble]

mar mo re an (mär môr′ē ən, mär mōr′ē ən), *adj.* marmoreal.

mar mo set (mär′mə set, mär′mə zet), *n.* any of various very small South or Central American monkeys, having soft, thick fur and a long, bushy tail. [< Old French *marmouset* grotesque figurine]

mar mot (mär′mət), *n.* any of a genus of burrowing rodents of the same family as the squirrel, having a thick body and bushy tail. Woodchucks are marmots. [< French *marmotte*]

Marne River (märn), river flowing from NE France into the Seine River. 325 mi.

ma roon[1] (mə rün′), *adj.* very dark brownish-red. —*n.* a very dark brownish red. [< Middle French *marron* < Italian *marrone* chestnut]

ma roon[2] (mə rün′), *v.t.* 1 put (a person) ashore in a desolate place and leave him there: *Pirates used to maroon people on desert islands.* 2 leave in a lonely, helpless position. —*n.* descendant of escaped Negro slaves living in the West Indies and Surinam. [< French *marron* an escaped slave < American Spanish *cimarrón* wild, hiding in the bushes]

mar plot (mär′plot′), *n.* person who spoils a plan by meddling or blundering.

marque (märk), *n.* letters of marque. [< French]

marquee (def. 1) of a theater

mar quee (mär kē′), *n.* 1 a rooflike shelter over an entrance, especially of a theater or hotel. 2 a large tent, often one put up for some outdoor entertainment or exhibition. [< French *marquise*]

Mar que sas Islands (mär kā′zəz, mär-kā′səs), group of eleven French islands in the S Pacific, northwest of Tahiti. 5000 pop.; 480 sq. mi. —**Mar que′san,** *adj., n.*

mar quess (mär′kwis), *n.* BRITISH. marquis.

mar que try (mär′kə trē), *n., pl.* **-tries.** decoration made with thin pieces of wood, ivory, metal, tortoise shell, etc., fitted together to form a design on furniture. [< Middle French *marqueterie* < *marqueter* to inlay < *marque* mark[1]]

Mar quette (mär ket′), *n.* **Father Jacques,** 1637-1675, French Jesuit missionary who explored part of the Mississippi River and its valley.

mar quis (mär′kwis, mär kē′), *n., pl.* **mar quis es, mar quis** (mär kē′). nobleman ranking below a duke and above an earl or count. Also, BRITISH **marquess.** [< Old French < *marche* march[2]]

mar quise (mär kēz′), *n.* 1 wife or widow of a marquis. 2 woman equal in rank to a marquis. [< French]

mar qui sette (mär′kə zet′, mär′kwə zet′), *n.* a very thin, sheer fabric with square meshes, made of cotton, silk, rayon, nylon, etc., and often used for window draperies, dresses, etc. [< French, diminutive of *marquise* marquee]

Mar ra kech or **Mar ra kesh** (mä rä′-kesh, mar′ə kesh′), *n.* city in W Morocco. 295,000

mar riage (mar′ij), *n.* 1 a living together as husband and wife; married life; wedlock. 2 condition of being a husband or wife. 3 act or ceremony of being married; a marrying. See synonym study below. 4 a close union. [< Old French *mariage* < *marier.* See MARRY[1].]

Syn. 3 **Marriage, matrimony, wedding** mean the act of marrying. **Marriage** emphasizes the legal union of a man and woman: *The marriage took place on June 26, 1970.* **Matrimony** applies especially to the spiritual or religious bond established by the union: *They were wedded in holy matrimony.* **Wedding** is the common word for the ceremony or celebration: *It was a beautiful wedding.*

mar riage a bil i ty (mar′i jə bil′ə tē), *n.* a being marriageable.

mar riage a ble (mar′i jə bəl), *adj.* fit for marriage; old enough to marry.

mar ried (mar′ēd), *adj.* 1 living together as husband and wife. 2 having a husband or wife. 3 of marriage; of husbands and wives. 4 closely united. —*n.* **marrieds,** *pl.* a married couple: *newly marrieds.*

mar ron (mar′ən; *French* mȧ rôN′), *n.* a large, sweet European chestnut, often used in cooking, or candied or preserved in syrup. [< French]

mar row (mar′ō), *n.* 1 the soft, vascular tissue that fills the cavities of most bones and is the source of red blood cells and many white blood cells. 2 the inmost or essential part. [< Old English *mearg*]

mar row bone (mar′ō bōn′), *n.* 1 bone containing edible marrow. 2 **marrowbones,** *pl.* knees.

mar row fat (mar′ō fat′), *n.* kind of pea that has a large seed.

mar row y (mar′ō ē), *adj.* of, like, or full of marrow.

mar ry[1] (mar′ē), *v.,* **-ried, -ry ing.** —*v.t.* 1 join as husband and wife according to the laws and customs of a state, people, or religious group: *The minister married them.* 2 take as husband or wife: *He is going to marry my sister.* 3 give in marriage: *She has married off all her daughters.* 4 bring together in any close union. —*v.i.* take a husband or wife; become married: *She married late in life.* [< Old French *marier* < Latin *maritare* < *maritus* husband]

mar ry[2] (mar′ē), *interj.* ARCHAIC. exclamation showing surprise, indignation, etc. [< (the Virgin) *Mary*]

Mars (märz), *n.* 1 (in Roman myths) the god of war, identified with the Greek god Ares. 2 planet nearest the earth. It is the seventh largest planet in the solar system and the fourth in distance from the sun. See **solar system** for diagram.

Mar seil laise (mär′sə lāz′; *French* mȧr se-yez′), *n.* the French national anthem, written in 1792 during the French Revolution.

Mar seille (mȧr sā′), *n.* French name of **Marseilles.**

mar seilles (mär sālz′), *n.* a thick, stiff cotton cloth. [< *Marseilles*]

Mar seilles (mär sā′, mär sālz′), *n.* seaport in SE France, on the Mediterranean. 889,000.

marsh (märsh), *n.* low land covered at times by water; soft wet land. Such plants as reeds, rushes, and sedges grow in marshes. [< Old English *mersc* < *mere* lake]

mar shal (mär′shəl), *n., v.,* **-shaled, -shal ing** or **-shalled, -shal ling.** —*n.* 1 officer of various kinds, especially a police officer. A United States marshal is an officer of a federal court whose duties are like those of a sheriff. 2 chief of police or head of the fire department in some cities. 3 officer of the highest rank in certain foreign armies. 4 person who arranges the order of march in a parade. 5 person in charge of events or ceremonies. 6 one of the highest officials of a royal household or court. —*v.t.* 1 arrange in proper order: *He marshaled his facts well.* 2 conduct with ceremony: *We were marshaled before the queen.* [< Old French *mareschal;* of Germanic origin]

mar shal cy (mär′shəl sē), *n., pl.* **-cies.** office, rank, or position of a marshal.

Mar shall (mär′shəl), *n.* 1 **George Catlett,** 1880-1959, American general and statesman, author of the Marshall Plan. 2 **John,** 1755-1835, chief justice of the United States Supreme Court from 1801 to 1835. 3 **Thurgood,** born 1908, American civil rights leader and jurist, an associate justice of the United States Supreme Court since 1967.

Marshall Islands, group of islands in the N Pacific, near the equator, under United States trusteeship. 19,000 pop.; 160 sq. mi. See **Melanesia** for map.

Marshall Plan, plan adopted by the United States for giving financial aid to European nations after World War II. [< George Catlett *Marshall,* who proposed it]

hat, āge, fär; let, ēqual, tėrm;
it, īce; hot, ōpen, ôrder;
oil, out; cup, pu̇t, rüle;
ch, child; ng, long; sh, she;
th, thin; ᴛʜ, then; zh, measure;

ə represents *a* in about, *e* in taken, *i* in pencil, *o* in lemon, *u* in circus.

< = from, derived from, taken from.

mar shal ship (mär′shəl ship), *n.* marshalcy.

marsh gas, methane.

marsh hawk, the only harrier in North America, living in open and marshy regions and feeding on frogs, snakes, etc.

marsh land (märsh′land′), *n.* marshy land.

marsh mal low (märsh′mal′ō, märsh′-mel′ō), *n.* a soft, white, spongy candy, covered with powdered sugar, made from corn syrup, sugar, starch, and gelatin. It was originally made from the root of marsh mallow. [< Old English *merscmealwe* marsh mallow]

marsh mallow, a shrubby herb of the mallow family that grows in marshy places. It has pink flowers and a root that is used in medicine to soothe or protect irritated mucous tissues.

marsh marigold, plant with bright yellow flowers, of the same family as the buttercup, that grows in moist meadows and swamps; cowslip.

marsh y (mär′shē), *adj.,* **marsh i er, marsh i est.** 1 soft and wet like a marsh. 2 having many marshes. 3 of marshes. —**marsh′i ness,** *n.*

mar su pi al (mär sü′pē əl), *n.* any of an order of mammals having a pouch covering the mammary glands on the abdomen, in which the female nurses and carries her incompletely developed young. Kangaroos, opossums, and wombats belong to this order. —*adj.* 1 of marsupials. 2 having a pouch for carrying the young.

mar su pi um (mär sü′pē əm), *n., pl.* **-pi a** (-pē ə). pouch or fold of skin on the abdomen of a female marsupial for carrying its young. [< Latin < Greek *marsipos* pouch]

mart (märt), *n.* center of trade; market. [< Dutch *markt* market]

Mar tel (mär tel′), *n.* **Charles,** A.D. 690?-741, Frankish ruler who defeated the Moslems and stopped their invasion of Europe near Tours in A.D. 732.

marten (def. 1)—2½ ft. long with the tail

mar ten (märt′n), *n., pl.* **-tens** or **-ten.** 1 any of various slender carnivorous mammals of the same family as and resembling the weasel, but larger. Several species are valued for their brown fur. 2 their fur. [< Old French *martrine;* ultimately, of Germanic origin]

Mar tha (mär′thə), *n.* (in the Bible) the sister of Lazarus and Mary.

Martha's Vineyard, island south of Cape

Cod. It is a part of Massachusetts. 20 mi. long; 9½ mi. wide.

Mar tí (mär tē′), *n.* **José Julián,** 1853-1895, Cuban patriot, poet, and national hero.

mar tial (mär′shəl), *adj.* 1 of war; suitable for war: *martial music.* See **military** for synonym study. 2 such as war requires; brave; valiant: *a martial spirit.* 3 given to fighting; warlike: *a martial nation.* 4 of or having to do with the army and navy. [< Latin *Martialis* of Mars < *Mars* Mars] **—mar′tial ly,** *adv.*

Mar tial (mär′shəl), *n.* A.D. 40?-102? Roman poet, famous for witty epigrams.

martial law, rule by the army or militia with special military courts instead of the usual civil authorities. Martial law is declared during a time of trouble or war.

Mar tian (mär′shən), *adj.* of the planet Mars. —*n.* a supposed inhabitant of the planet Mars. [< Latin *Martius* of Mars]

mar tin (märt′n), *n.* any of several swallows with long, pointed wings and a forked or square tail. The **purple martin** is a large, blue and black martin of North America. [< the name *Martin*]

Mar tin (märt′n), *n.* **Saint,** A.D. 316?-400?, French bishop of Tours, a patron saint of France, who divided his cloak with a beggar.

mar ti net (märt′n et′), *n.* person who upholds and enforces very strict discipline. [< J. *Martinet,* died 1672, French general and drillmaster]

Mar ti nez (mär tē′nez), *n.* **Maria,** born 1875, American ceramic artist.

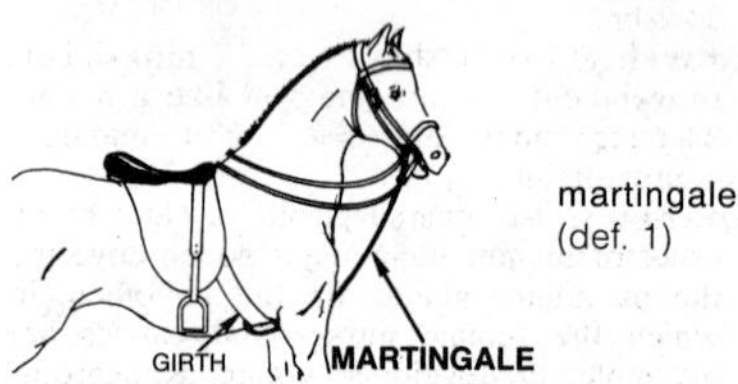

martingale (def. 1)

mar tin gale (märt′n gāl), *n.* 1 strap of a horse's harness that prevents the horse from rearing or throwing back its head. 2 rope or spar that steadies the jib boom on a ship. [< French]

mar ti ni (mär tē′nē), *n.* cocktail consisting of gin or vodka and dry vermouth. [< *Martini* and Rossi, wine makers]

Mar ti nique (märt′n ēk′), *n.* island in the West Indies, since 1946 an overseas department of France. 320,000 pop.; 385 sq. mi. *Capital:* Fort-de-France.

Mar tin mas (märt′n məs), *n.* November 11, a church festival in honor of Saint Martin; St. Martin's Day.

mar tyr (mär′tər), *n.* 1 person who chooses to die or suffer rather than renounce his religious faith. Many of the early Christians were martyrs. 2 person who is put to death or made to suffer greatly because of a belief, cause, or principle. 3 person who suffers great pain or anguish. —*v.t.* 1 put (a person) to death or torture because of his religion or other beliefs. 2 cause to suffer greatly; torture. [Old English < Latin < Greek, witness] **—mar′tyr like′,** *adj.*

mar tyr dom (mär′tər dəm), *n.* 1 death or suffering of a martyr. 2 great suffering; torment.

mar tyr ize (mär′tə rīz′), *v.t.,* **-ized, -iz ing.** 1 make a martyr of. 2 torment. **—mar′tyr i za′tion,** *n.*

mar vel (mär′vəl), *n., v.,* **-veled, -vel ing** or **-velled, -vel ling.** —*n.* something wonderful; astonishing thing: *the marvels of science.* —*v.i.* be filled with wonder; be astonished: *I marvel at your boldness.* —*v.t.* express wonder at: *We marveled that no one had been injured in the accident.* [< Old French *merveille* < Latin *mirabilia* wonders, ultimately < *mirus* strange]

mar vel ous or **mar vel lous** (mär′və ləs), *adj.* 1 causing wonder or astonishment; extraordinary. 2 improbable. 3 INFORMAL. excellent; splendid; fine. **—mar′vel ous ly, mar′vel lous ly,** *adv.* **—mar′vel ous ness, mar′vel lous ness,** *n.*

Marx (märks), *n.* **Karl,** 1818-1883, German political philosopher, writer on economics, and advocate of socialism.

Marx i an (märk′sē ən), *adj.* of Marx or his theories. —*n.* Marxist.

Marx ism (märk′siz′əm), *n.* the theories of Karl Marx and Friedrich Engels, who interpreted history as a continuing struggle between the interests of conflicting economic groups, resulting in a classless society and communal ownership of all property.

Marx ist (märk′sist), *n.* follower of Marx; believer in Marxism. *adj.* Marxian.

Mar y (mer′ē, mar′ē), *n.* in the Bible: 1 the mother of Jesus. 2 the sister of Lazarus and Martha. 3 Mary Magdalene.

Mary I, 1516-1558, queen of England from 1553 to 1558 and wife of Philip II of Spain. She was called "Bloody Mary." Also, **Mary Tudor.**

Mary II, 1662-1694, queen of England from 1689 to 1694. She was ruler of England with her husband William III.

Mar y land (mer′ə lənd), *n.* one of the southeastern states of the United States. 3,922,000 pop.; 10,600 sq. mi. *Capital:* Annapolis. *Abbrev.:* Md.

Mary Magdalene, (in the Bible) a woman from whom Jesus cast out seven devils. She is commonly supposed to be the repentant sinner forgiven by Jesus.

Mary, Queen of Scots or **Mary Stuart,** 1542-1587, queen of Scotland from 1542 to 1567. She was beheaded by order of her cousin, Queen Elizabeth I.

Mary Tudor, Mary I.

mar zi pan (mär′zə pan, märt′sə pän), *n.* confection made of ground almonds and sugar, molded into various forms. Also, **marchpane.** [< German *Marzipan* < Italian *marzapane*]

Ma sai (mä sī′), *n., pl.* **-sai** or **-sais.** member of a tribe of tall natives of East Africa, noted as hunters and as cattle raisers.

Mas a ryk (mas′ə rik′), *n.* **Thomas G(arrigue),** 1850-1937, the first president of Czechoslovakia, from 1918 to 1935.

masc., masculine.

Mas ca gni (mä skä′nyē), *n.* **Pietro,** 1863-1945, Italian composer of operas.

mas car a (ma skar′ə), *n.* preparation used for coloring the eyelashes and eyebrows. [< Spanish *máscara* mask]

mas cot (mas′kot, mas′kət), *n.* animal, person, or thing supposed to bring good luck. [< French *mascotte*]

mas cu line (mas′kyə lin), *adj.* 1 of men or boys. 2 like a man; manly; virile: *masculine courage.* 3 (of a woman) mannish. See **male** for synonym study. 4 (in grammar) of the gender to which nouns, adjectives, and other forms usually referring to males belong. *Actor, king, ram,* and *bull* are masculine nouns. —*n.* 1 the masculine gender. 2 word or form in the masculine gender. [< Latin *masculinus* < *masculus* a male, diminutive of *mas* male] **—mas′cu line ly,** *adv.* **—mas′cu line ness,** *n.*

masculine rhyme, rhyme in which the final syllables are stressed, as in *disdain* and *complain.*

mas cu lin i ty (mas′kyə lin′ə tē), *n.* masculine quality or condition.

Mase field (mās′fēld, māz′fēld), *n.* **John,** 1878-1967, English poet.

ma ser (mā′zər), *n.* device which amplifies or generates electromagnetic waves. Masers are used in long-distance radar and radio astronomy. [< *m(icrowave) a(mplification* by*) s(timulated) e(mission* of*) r(adiation)*]

Mas e ru (maz′ə rü′), *n.* capital of Lesotho, in the NW part. 14,000.

mash (mash), *n.* 1 a soft mixture; pulpy mass. 2 a warm mixture of bran or meal and water for horses and other animals. 3 crushed malt or meal soaked in hot water to form wort, used in making beer. —*v.t.* 1 beat into a soft mass; crush to a uniform mass. 2 mix (crushed malt or meal) with hot water in brewing. [Old English *māsc-*] **—mash′er,** *n.*

mash ie (mash′ē), *n., pl.* **mash ies.** a golf club with a short, sloping steel face. [perhaps < French *massue* club]

mashie niblick, a golf club with a face that slopes more than a mashie, but less than a niblick.

mask (mask), *n.* 1 a covering to hide or protect the face. 2 a false face worn for amusement. 3 a masked person. 4 clay, wax, or plaster likeness of a person's face. 5 thing that hides or disguises: *hide one's dislike under a mask of friendship.* 6 piece of fine gauze worn over the mouth and nose of surgeons, nurses, etc., during operations, etc. 7 any similar covering, such as one used to aid in breathing. —*v.t.* 1 cover (the face) with a mask. 2 hide or disguise: *A smile masked his disappointment.* —*v.i.* put on or wear a mask. [< Middle French *masque* < Italian *maschera* < Arabic *maskhara* laughingstock < *sakhira* to ridicule]

masked ball, dance at which masks are worn.

masking tape, a gummed tape used to mask or protect surfaces not to be treated, painted, sprayed, etc.

mas och ism (mas′ə kiz′əm), *n.* abnormal pleasure derived from being dominated or physically abused. [< Leopold von Sacher-*Masoch,* 1836-1895, Austrian novelist, who described it in his stories]

mas och ist (mas′ə kist), *n.* person who derives pleasure from being dominated or physically abused; person who enjoys suffering.

mas och is tic (mas′ə kis′tik), *adj.* of or having to do with masochists or masochism. **—mas′och is′ti cal ly,** *adv.*

ma son (mā′sn), *n.* 1 person whose work is building with stone or brick. 2 **Mason,** Freemason. [< Old French *maçon* < Late Latin *machionem*]

Ma son-Dix on line (mā′sn dik′sən), boundary between Pennsylvania and Maryland, formerly thought of as separating the free states of the North and the slave states of the South.

ma son ic or **Ma son ic** (mə son′ik), *adj.* of Masons or Masonry; having to do with the Freemasons or Freemasonry.

hat, āge, fär; let, ēqual, tėrm;
it, īce; hot, ōpen, ôrder;
oil, out; cup, pu̇t, rüle;
ch, child; ng, long; sh, she;
th, thin; ᴛʜ, then; zh, measure;

ə represents *a* in about, *e* in taken, *i* in pencil, *o* in lemon, *u* in circus.

< = from, derived from, taken from.

Ma son ite (mā′sn īt), *n.* trademark for a type of fiberboard.

Mason jar, a glass jar used in home canning. [< John *Mason,* American inventor, who patented it in 1858]

ma son ry (mā′sn rē), *n., pl.* **-ries.** 1 wall, foundation, or part of a building built by a mason; stonework or brickwork. 2 trade or skill of a mason. 3 **Masonry.** Freemasonry.

masque (mask), *n.* 1 an amateur dramatic entertainment in which fine costumes, scenery, music, and dancing are more important than the story. Masques were frequently given in England in the 1500's and 1600's, at court and at the homes of nobles. 2 play written for such an entertainment. 3 a masked ball; masquerade. [< Middle French. See MASK.]

mas que rade (mas′kə rād′), *v.,* **-rad ed, -rad ing,** *n.* —*v.i.* 1 disguise oneself; go about under false pretenses: *The king masqueraded as a beggar to find out if his people really liked him.* 2 take part in a masquerade. —*n.* 1 party or dance at which masks and fancy costumes are worn. 2 costume and mask worn at such a party or dance. 3 false outward show; disguise; pretense. **—mas′que rad′er,** *n.*

mass[1] (mas), *n.* 1 piece or amount of anything without any clear shape or size; lump: *a mass of dough.* 2 a large quantity together: *a mass of treasure.* 3 the greater part; majority: *the mass of mankind.* 4 bulk or size: *the sheer mass of an iceberg.* 5 measure of the quantity of matter a body contains; the property of a physical body which gives the body inertia. Mass is a constant not dependent on gravity and is obtained by either dividing the weight of the body by the acceleration of gravity or comparing an unknown mass with a known mass, as on a balance. 6 **in the mass,** as a whole; without distinguishing parts or individuals. 7 **the masses,** the common people; the working classes; the lower classes of society. —*v.t., v.i.* form or collect into a mass; assemble. —*adj.* 1 of or by many people: *a mass protest, mass culture.* 2 on a large scale: *mass buying.* [< Middle French *masse* < Latin *massa* kneaded dough, lump < Greek *maza* barley bread, related to *massein* to knead]

Mass or **mass**[2] (mas), *n.* 1 the central service of worship in the Roman Catholic Church and in some other churches; the Eucharist as a sacrament. The ritual of the Mass consists of various prayers and ceremonies. 2 a particular celebration of the Eucharist. 3 music written for certain parts of it. [Old English *mæsse* < Late Latin *missa* < Latin *mittere* send away]

Mass., Massachusetts.

Mas sa chu set (mas′ə chü′sit), *n., pl.* **-set** or **-sets** for 1. 1 member of a tribe of Algonquian Indians who formerly lived near Massachusetts Bay. 2 their language.

Mas sa chu setts (mas′ə chü′sits, mas′ə-chü′zits), *n.* one of the northeastern states of the United States. 5,689,000 pop.; 8300 sq. mi. *Capital:* Boston. *Abbrev.:* Mass.

Massachusetts Bay, bay off the Massachusetts coast.

Massachusetts Bay Colony, a small settlement established at Salem, Massachusetts in 1628 by a group of Puritans.

mas sa cre (mas′ə kər), *n., v.,* **-cred, -cring.** —*n.* the wholesale, pitiless slaughter of people or animals. —*v.t.* kill (many people or animals) needlessly or cruelly; slaughter in large numbers. [< Middle French, in Old French *macecle* shambles] **—mas sa crer** (mas′ə krər), *n.*

mas sage (mə säzh′), *n., v.,* **-saged, -sag ing.** —*n.* a rubbing and kneading of the muscles and joints to increase the circulation of blood; rubdown. A thorough massage relaxes tired muscles. —*v.t.* give a massage to. [< French < *masser* to massage < Arabic *massa* to touch, handle] **—mas sag′er,** *n.*

Mas sa soit (mas′ə soit), *n.* 1580?-1661, American Indian chief who was friendly to the Pilgrims.

Mas sé na (mə sā′nə; *French* mȧ sā nȧ′), *n.* **André,** 1758-1817, French marshal under Napoleon I.

mass-en er gy equation (mas′en′ər jē), Einstein equation.

Mas se net (mas′ə nā′; *French* mȧs nā′), *n.* **Jules,** 1842-1912, French composer of operas.

mas seur (mə sėr′; *French* mȧ sœr′), *n.* man whose work is massaging people. [< French]

mas seuse (mə süs′, mə süz′; *French* mȧ-sœz′), *n.* woman whose work is massaging people. [< French]

mas sif (mas′if; *French* mȧ sēf′), *n.* the main part of a mountain range, surrounded by valleys. [< French]

mas sive (mas′iv), *adj.* 1 forming a large mass; bulky and heavy; huge: *a massive rock.* 2 giving the impression of being large and broad: *a massive forehead.* 3 imposing; impressive. 4 in or by great numbers; extensive: *a massive assault.* 5 affecting a large area of bodily tissue: *a massive hemorrhage.* 6 (of minerals) not definitely crystalline. **—mas′sive ly,** *adv.* **—mas′sive ness,** *n.*

mass media, the forms of communication, such as the press, television, and radio, which reach large numbers of people.

mass meeting, a large public assembly to hear or discuss some matter of common interest.

mass number, number that indicates the atomic weight of an isotope rounded off to the nearest integer. It is equal to the sum of the protons and neutrons in the nucleus.

mass-pro duce (mas′prə düs′, mas′prə-dyüs′), *v.t.,* **-duced, -duc ing.** make (any product) in large quantities, especially by machinery.

mass production, the making of goods in large quantities, especially by machinery.

mass ratio, the ratio of the weight of a rocket with fuel to its weight after its fuel is consumed.

mass spectrograph, apparatus for determining the mass numbers of isotopes by passing streams of ions through electric and magnetic fields which separate ions of different masses. The results are recorded on a photographic plate.

mass spectrometer, mass spectrograph.

mass y (mas′ē), *adj.,* **mass i er, mass i est.** bulky and heavy; massive. **—mass′i-ness,** *n.*

mast[1] (mast), *n.* 1 a long pole or spar of wood or metal rising from the keel of a vessel set upright on a ship to support the yards, sails, rigging, etc. 2 **before the mast,** serving as a common sailor. 3 any tall, upright pole: *the mast of a derrick.* —*v.t.* equip or rig with a mast or masts. [Old English *mæst*] **—mast′less,** *adj.* **—mast′like′,** *adj.*

mast[2] (mast), *n.* acorns, chestnuts, beechnuts, etc., on the ground; fruit of certain forest trees, especially as food for swine. [Old English *mæst*]

mas ter (mas′tər), *n.* 1 person who has power, authority, or control. 2 the man at the head of a household: *the master of the house.* 3 the captain or officer in charge of a merchant ship. 4 employer. 5 a male teacher in private schools. 6 title of respect for a boy not old enough to be called *Mr.* 7 artist, musician, or author of the highest rank. 8 ARCHAIC. picture, painting, or sculpture by a great artist. 9 person who has thorough knowledge of a subject or is highly skilled in something; expert: *a master of the violin.* 10 workman qualified by training and experience to teach apprentices and carry on his trade independently. 11 Also, **Master.** person who has taken a certain advanced degree above bachelor and below doctor. 12 victor. 13 **the Master,** Jesus Christ. 14 an initial copy or original, as of a recording or tape, used as a source for duplication: *make thousands of long-playing records from a master, prepare masters of the semester exams.*
—*adj.* 1 being master; of a master: *a master printer.* 2 main; controlling: *a master plan, a master switch.* 3 serving as the source for duplication: *a master tape, a master test.*
—*v.t.* 1 become master of; conquer; control: *She learned to master her anger.* 2 become expert in; become skillful at; learn: *master algebra, master the violin.*
[fusion of Old English *mægester* and Old French *maistre,* both < Latin *magister* < *magnus* great]

mas ter-at-arms (mas′tər ət ärmz′), *n., pl.* **mas ters-at-arms.** a petty officer on a ship who has charge of discipline, the custody of prisoners, etc.

mas ter ful (mas′tər fəl), *adj.* 1 fond of power or authority; domineering. 2 expert or skillful; masterly. **—mas′ter ful ly,** *adv.* **—mas′ter ful ness,** *n.*

master key, 1 key that opens all the different locks of a set. 2 key that will open many different locks of a similar type.

mas ter ly (mas′tər lē), *adj.* very skillful; expert: *a masterly piece of work.* —*adv.* expertly; skillfully. **—mas′ter li ness,** *n.*

mas ter mind (mas′tər mīnd′), *n.* person who plans and supervises a scheme or opera-

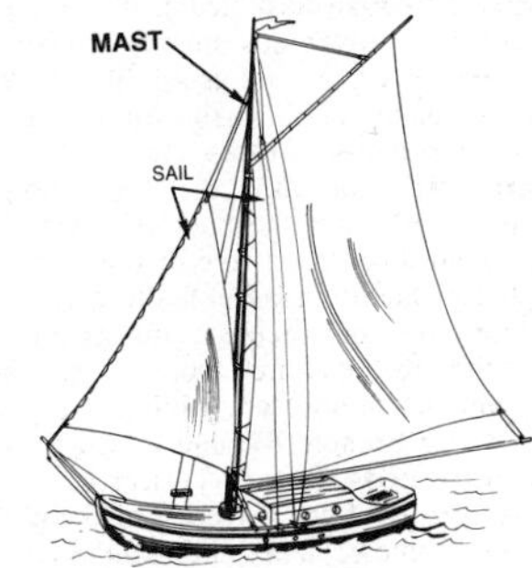

mast[1] (def. 1)

tion, usually behind the scenes. —*v.t.* devise and conduct (a plan of action), usually behind the scenes.

Master of Arts, 1 degree given by a college or university to a person who has completed a graduate course of study in the liberal arts or humanities. 2 person who has this degree.

master of ceremonies, 1 person in charge of a program or entertainment who makes sure all parts of it take place in the proper order and who introduces speakers or performers. 2 person appointed to plan and supervise a formal, usually public ceremony.

Master of Science, 1 degree given by a college or university to a person who has completed a graduate course of study in science. 2 person who has this degree.

mas ter piece (mas′tər pēs′), *n.* 1 anything done or made with wonderful skill; perfect piece of art or workmanship. 2 a person's greatest piece of work.

master race, 1 a racial or other group that considers itself superior to others. 2 (in Nazi use) the German Aryans.

mas ter's (mas′tərz), *n.* a master's degree given by a college or university.

Mas ters (mas′tərz), *n.* **Edgar Lee,** 1869-1950, American poet.

master sergeant, a noncommissioned officer in the United States Army, Air Force, or Marine Corps having the highest rank but no command responsibility.

mas ter ship (mas′tər ship), *n.* 1 position of a master. 2 power or authority of a master. 3 expert knowledge.

mas ter stroke (mas′tər strōk′), *n.* a very skillful act or achievement.

mas ter work (mas′tər wėrk′), *n.* masterpiece.

mas ter y (mas′tər ē), *n., pl.* **-ter ies.** 1 power or authority of a master; rule; control. 2 the upper hand; victory. 3 great skill or expert knowledge; command or grasp: *a mastery over musical instruments.*

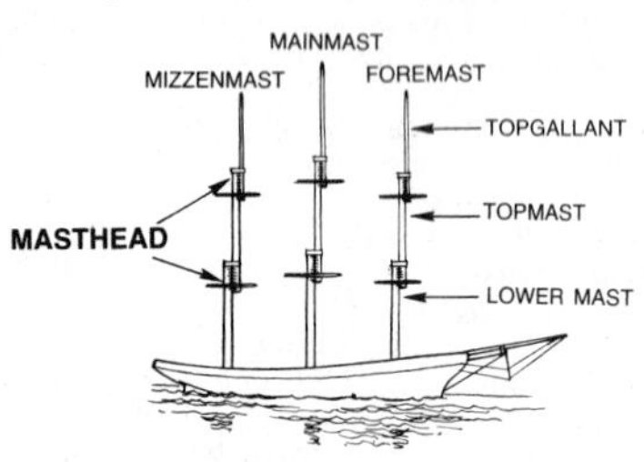

masthead (def. 1)

mast head (mast′hed′), *n.* 1 top of a ship's mast. A crow's-nest near the masthead of the lower mast is used as a lookout. 2 part of a newspaper or magazine that gives the title, owner, address, rates, etc.

mas tic (mas′tik), *n.* 1 a yellowish resin obtained from the bark of a small Mediterranean evergreen tree of the same family as the pistachio, used in making varnish, chewing gum, and incense, and as an astringent. 2 the tree it comes from. 3 any of various cements or mortars having a pasty texture. [< Old French. Related to MASTICATE.]

mas ti cate (mas′tə kāt), *v.t., v.i.,* **-cat ed, -cat ing.** 1 grind (food) to a pulp with the teeth; chew. 2 crush or knead (rubber, etc.) to a pulp. [< Late Latin *masticatum* chewed < Greek *mastichan* gnash the teeth] **—mas′ti ca′tion,** *n.* **—mas′ti ca′tor,** *n.*

mas ti ca to ry (mas′tə kə tôr′ē, mas′tə kə-tōr′ē), *adj., n., pl.* **-ries.** —*adj.* of, having to do with, or used in chewing. —*n.* substance chewed to increase the flow of saliva.

mas tiff (mas′tif), *n.* any of a breed of large, powerful dogs having a short, thick coat, drooping ears, and hanging lips. [< Old French *mastin;* influenced by Old French *mestif* mongrel]

mas ti tis (ma stī′tis), *n.* inflammation of the mammary glands or the udder.

mas to don (mas′tə don), *n.* any of various large extinct mammals somewhat resembling mammoths and present-day elephants. [< New Latin < Greek *mastos* breast + *odon* tooth (from the nipple-shaped projections on its teeth)]

mas toid (mas′toid), *n.* projection of bone behind the ear of many mammals. —*adj.* of, having to do with, or near the mastoid. [< Greek *mastoeides* breast-shaped < *mastos* breast + *eidos* shape, form]

mas toid i tis (mas′toi dī′tis), *n.* inflammation of the mastoid.

mas tur bate (mas′tər bāt), *v.i., v.t.,* **-bat ed, -bat ing.** engage in masturbation. [< Latin *masturbatum* engaged in masturbation]

mas tur ba tion (mas′tər bā′shən), *n.* stimulation of sexual organs by practices other than sexual intercourse, especially manual self-stimulation.

ma sur i um (mə sůr′ē əm), *n.* former name of the element technetium. [< *Masuria,* region in Poland]

mat[1] (mat), *n., v.,* **mat ted, mat ting.** —*n.* 1 piece of coarse fabric like a small rug, made of woven rushes, fiber, straw, rope, etc., used for floor covering, for wiping mud from the shoes, etc. 2 piece of material to put under a dish, vase, lamp, etc. 3 anything growing thickly packed or tangled together: *a mat of weeds.* 4 a large, thick pad covering part of a floor to protect wrestlers or gymnasts. —*v.t.* 1 cover with mats or matting. 2 pack or tangle thickly (together): *The swimmer's wet hair was matted together.* —*v.i.* pack or tangle thickly together. [Old English *matt, meatt* < Late Latin *matta*]

mat[2] (mat), *n., v.,* **mat ted, mat ting.** —*n.* border or background for a picture, used as a frame or placed between the picture and its frame. —*v.t.* put a mat around or under: *mat a picture.* [< French, originally adjective, dull, dead, perhaps < Latin *mattus* sodden]

mat[3] (mat), *adj., n., v.,* **mat ted, mat ting.** —*adj.* not shiny; dull. —*n.* a dull surface or finish. —*v.t.* give a dull surface or finish to. Also, **matte.** [< French]

mat a dor (mat′ə dôr), *n.* the chief performer in a bullfight, whose duty it is finally to kill the bull with his sword. [< Spanish, literally, killer]

match[1] (mach), *n.* 1 a short, slender piece of wood, pasteboard, etc., tipped with a mixture that takes fire when rubbed on a rough or specially prepared surface. 2 wick or cord prepared to burn at a uniform rate, formerly used for firing guns and cannon. [< Middle French *meiche,* probably ultimately < Greek *myxa* lamp wick]

match[2] (mach), *n.* 1 person able to contend or compete with another as an equal: *meet one's match.* 2 person or thing like another in some respect: *a period without its match in history.* 3 two persons or things that are alike or go well together: *Those two horses make a good match.* 4 game, contest, or competition: *a tennis match.* 5 marriage. 6 person considered as a possible husband or wife.
—*v.t.* 1 be equal to; be a match for: *No one could match the unknown archer.* 2 be the same as: *The color of the skirt does not match that of the coat.* 3 find or produce an equal or one exactly alike. 4 make like; fit together. 5 arrange a match for; marry. 6 put in opposition; oppose: *He matched his strength against his friend's.* —*v.i.* 1 be alike; go well together: *The rugs and the wallpaper match.* 2 marry.
[Old English *mæcca* < *(ge)mæcca* companion] **—match′er,** *n.*

match book (mach′bůk′), *n.* folder of safety matches with a surface for striking at the bottom.

match less (mach′lis), *adj.* so great or wonderful that it cannot be equaled. **—match′less ly,** *adv.* **—match′less-ness,** *n.*

match lock (mach′lok′), *n.* 1 an old form of musket fired by lighting the powder with a wick or cord. 2 its gunlock.

match mak er[1] (mach′mā′kər), *n.* person who makes matches for burning.

match mak er[2] (mach′mā′kər), *n.* 1 person who arranges, or tries to arrange, marriages for others. 2 person who arranges contests, prize fights, races, etc.

match mak ing[1] (mach′mā′king), *n.* business of making matches for burning. —*adj.* of matchmakers or matchmaking.

match mak ing[2] (mach′mā′king), *n.* practice of trying to arrange marriages. —*adj.* of matchmakers or matchmaking.

match play, (in golf) a form of competition in which the game is won by the winner of the greatest number of holes, regardless of total strokes.

match point, (in tennis, etc.) the final point needed to win a match.

match wood (mach′wůd′), *n.* 1 wood for making matches. 2 splinters.

mate[1] (māt), *n., v.,* **mat ed, mat ing.** —*n.* 1 one of a pair: *Where is the mate to this glove?* 2 husband or wife; spouse. 3 a deck officer of a merchant ship, ranking next below the captain. 4 assistant: *a carpenter's mate.* 5 a petty officer who assists a warrant officer in the United States Navy. 6 companion or fellow worker. 7 one of a pair of animals that are mated. —*v.t., v.i.* 1 join in a pair. 2 join as husband and wife; marry. 3 (of animals) to pair; breed. [apparently < Middle Low German, messmate. Related to MEAT.]

mate[2] (māt), *n., v.,* **mat ed, mat ing.** —*n.* checkmate. —*v.t.* checkmate.

ma té or **ma te**[3] (mä′tā, mat′ā), *n.* 1 an aromatic tea made from the dried leaves and twigs of a South American holly, popular in Argentina and Uruguay. 2 the plant. 3 its leaves. [< American Spanish *mate* < Quechua *mati* calabash dish]

ma ter (mā′tər), *n.* BRITISH INFORMAL. mother. [< Latin]

ma ter i al (mə tir′ē əl), *n.* 1 what a thing is made from; matter from which anything is manufactured or built: *building material, dress material.* See **substance** for synonym study. 2 **materials,** *pl.* tools or apparatus necessary for making or doing something: *writing materials, teaching materials.* —*adj.* 1 having to do with whatever occupies space; of matter or things; physical: *the material world.* 2 of the body: *Food and shelter are* *material comforts.* 3 caring too much for the things of this world and neglecting spiritual needs; worldly. 4 that matters; important: *Hard work is a material factor in success.* [< Latin *materialis* of matter < *materia* timber, matter, trunk (of a tree) < *mater* mother]

ma ter i al ism (mə tir′ē ə liz′əm), *n.* 1 the philosophical theory that all action, thought, and feeling can be explained by the movements and changes of matter. 2 tendency to care too much for the things of this world and to neglect spiritual needs. 3 the ethical doctrine that material self-interest should and does determine conduct.

ma ter i al ist (mə tir′ē ə list), *n.* 1 believer in materialism. 2 person who cares too much for the things of this world and neglects spiritual needs. —*adj.* materialistic.

ma ter i al is tic (mə tir′ē ə lis′tik), *adj.* of materialism or materialists. **—ma ter′i al is′ti cal ly,** *adv.*

ma ter i al ize (mə tir′ē ə līz), *v.,* **-ized, -iz ing.** —*v.i.* 1 become an actual fact; be realized: *Our plans did not materialize.* 2 appear in material or bodily form: *A spirit materialized from the smoke of the magician's fire.* —*v.t.* 1 give material form to: *The inventor materialized his ideas by building a model.* 2 cause to appear in material or bodily form. **—ma ter′i al i za′tion,** *n.*

ma ter i al ly (mə tir′ē ə lē), *adv.* 1 with regard to material things; physically. 2 considerably; greatly; substantially. 3 in matter or substance; not in form.

ma ter i a med i ca (mə tir′ē ə med′ə kə), 1 drugs or other substances used in medicine. 2 branch of medical science dealing with these drugs and substances. [< New Latin, healing matter]

ma ter i el or **ma tér i el** (mə tir′ē el′), *n.* everything used by an army, organization, undertaking, etc.; equipment. [< French *matériel* material]

ma ter nal (mə tėr′nl), *adj.* 1 of or like a mother; motherly. 2 related on the mother's side of the family: *a maternal uncle, maternal grandparents.* 3 received or inherited from one's mother: *His blue eyes were a maternal inheritance.* [< Middle French *maternel* < Latin *maternus* < *mater* mother] **—ma ter′nal ly,** *adv.*

ma ter ni ty (mə tėr′nə tē), *n.* 1 a being a mother; motherhood. 2 qualities of a mother; motherliness. —*adj.* 1 for a woman soon to have a baby: *maternity clothes.* 2 for women in or after childbirth: *maternity ward.*

mat ey (mā′tē), *adj., n., pl.* **-eys.** BRITISH INFORMAL. —*adj.* friendly. —*n.* mate. **—mat′ey ness,** *n.*

math (math), *n.* INFORMAL. mathematics.

math., 1 mathematical. 2 mathematics.

math e mat i cal (math′ə mat′ə kəl, math mat′ə kəl), *adj.* 1 of or having to do with mathematics. 2 exact; accurate. [< Latin *mathematicus* < Greek *mathēmatikos,* ultimately < *manthanein* learn] **—math′e mat′i cal ly,** *adv.*

math e ma ti cian (math′ə mə tish′ən, math′mə tish′ən), *n.* expert in mathematics.

math e mat ics (math′ə mat′iks, math mat′iks), *n.* science dealing with the measurement, properties, and relationships of quantities, as expressed in numbers or symbols. Mathematics includes arithmetic, algebra, geometry, calculus, etc.

Math er (maᴛʜ′ər), *n.* 1 **Cotton,** 1663-1728, American clergyman and author. 2 his father, **Increase,** 1639-1723, American clergyman.

maths (maths), *n.* BRITISH INFORMAL. mathematics.

mat i nee or **mat i née** (mat′n ā′), *n.* a dramatic or musical performance held in the afternoon. [< French *matinée* < Old French *matin* morning]

mat ins (mat′nz), *n.pl.* 1 first of the seven canonical hours in the breviary of the Roman Catholic Church. 2 service for this hour, often joined to lauds. 3 morning prayer in the Church of England and other churches of the Anglican communion. 4 a morning song. Also, **mattins** for 2. [< Old French *matines* < Latin *matutinus* of or in the morning]

Ma tisse (mà tēs′), *n.* **Henri,** 1869-1954, French painter.

ma tri arch (mā′trē ärk), *n.* 1 mother who is the ruler of a family or tribe. 2 a venerable old woman, especially one who dominates the group of which she is a member: *Mrs. Astor was the matriarch of New York society for many years.* [< Latin *mater, matris* mother + English *(patri)arch*]

ma tri ar chal (mā′trē är′kəl), *adj.* 1 of a matriarch or matriarchy. 2 suitable for a matriarch.

ma tri ar chate (mā′trē är′kit), *n.* 1 family or community governed by a matriarch. 2 a matriarchal system.

ma tri ar chy (mā′trē är′kē), *n., pl.* **-chies.** 1 form of social organization in which the mother is the ruler of a family or tribe, descent being traced through the mother. 2 government by women; matriarchate.

ma tri ces (mā′trə sēz′, mat′rə sēz′), *n.* a pl. of **matrix.**

ma tri cid al (mā′trə sī′dl, mat′rə sī′dl), *adj.* of or having to do with matricide.

ma tri cide (mā′trə sīd, mat′rə sīd), *n.* 1 act of killing one's mother. 2 person who kills his mother.

ma tric u late (mə trik′yə lāt), *v.t., v.i.,* **-lat ed, -lat ing.** enroll, especially in a college or university, as a candidate for a degree. [< Medieval Latin *matriculatum* enrolled < Latin *matricula* a register, diminutive of Latin *matrix*] **—ma tric′u la′tion,** *n.*

mat ri lin e al (mat′rə lin′ē əl), *adj.* having or maintaining relationship through the female line of a family, tribe, etc. **—mat′ri lin′e al ly,** *adv.*

mat ri mo ni al (mat′rə mō′nē əl), *adj.* of or having to do with marriage. **—mat′ri mo′ni al ly,** *adv.*

mat ri mo ny (mat′rə mō′nē), *n., pl.* **-nies.** 1 married life. 2 act of marrying; rite or ceremony of marriage. See **marriage** for synonym study. 3 relation between married persons; wedlock. [< Latin *matrimonium* < *mater* mother]

ma trix (mā′triks, mat′riks), *n., pl.* **-tri ces** or **-trix es.** 1 that which gives origin or form to something enclosed within it, such as the mold for a casting or the rock in which gems, fossils, etc., are embedded. 2 womb. 3 the formative part of a tooth or fingernail. 4 the intercellular nonliving substance of a tissue. 5 (in mathematics) a set of quantities in a rectangular array, subject to operations such as multiplication or inversion according to specified rules. [< Latin, womb < *mater* mother]

ma tron (mā′trən), *n.* 1 wife or widow, especially one who is mature in age, character, or bearing. 2 woman who manages the household affairs of a school, hospital, dormitory, or other institution. A police matron has charge of the women in a jail. [< Latin *matrona* < *mater* mother]

hat, āge, fär; let, ēqual, tėrm;
it, īce; hot, ōpen, ôrder;
oil, out; cup, pu̇t, rüle;
ch, child; ng, long; sh, she;
th, thin; ᴛʜ, then; zh, measure;

ə represents *a* in about, *e* in taken,
i in pencil, *o* in lemon, *u* in circus.

< = from, derived from, taken from.

ma tron ly (mā′trən lē), *adj.* like a matron; suitable for a matron; dignified. **—ma′tron li ness,** *n.*

matron of honor, a married woman who is the chief attendant of the bride at a wedding.

Mat su (mat′sü), *n.* island in Formosa Strait belonging to Taiwan.

Matt., Matthew.

matte (mat), *adj., n., v.t.* mat[3].

mat ted[1] (mat′id), *adj.* 1 formed into a mat; entangled in a thick mass. 2 covered with mats or matting. [< *mat*[1]]

mat ted[2] (mat′id), *adj.* having a dull finish. [< *mat*[3]]

mat ter (mat′ər), *n.* 1 what things are made of; material; substance. Matter occupies space, has weight, and can exist in solid, liquid, or gaseous form. See **substance** for synonym study. 2 the substance of the material world; the opposite of mind or spirit. 3 a specific substance or body: *foreign matter, coloring matter.* 4 thing to do; concern; activity, etc.; affair: *business matters, a matter of life and death.* 5 what is said or written, thought of apart from the way in which it appears. 6 reason or cause; grounds; basis: *You have no matter for complaint.* 7 an instance or case; thing or things: *a matter of record, a matter of accident.* 8 things written or printed: *reading matter.* 9 mail: *Second-class matter requires less postage than first-class matter.* 10 amount; quantity: *a matter of two days, a matter of 20 miles.* 11 importance; significance: *an event of little matter.* 12 pus.

as a matter of course, as something that is to be expected.

as a matter of fact, in truth; in reality; actually.

for that matter, so far as that is concerned.

no matter, a it is not important. b regardless of.

What is the matter? What is the trouble?

—*v.i.* 1 be of importance. 2 form pus; discharge pus.

[< Old French *matiere* < Latin *materia.* See MATERIAL.]

Mat ter horn (mat′ər hôrn), *n.* mountain peak in the Alps, between Switzerland and Italy. 14,685 ft.

mat ter-of-course (mat′ər əv kôrs′, mat′ər əv kōrs′), *adj.* to be expected; normal.

mat ter-of-fact (mat′ər əv fakt′), *adj.* dealing with or adhering to facts; not imaginative or fanciful. **—mat′ter-of-fact′ly,** *adv.* **—mat′ter-of-fact′ness,** *n.*

Mat thew (math′yü), *n.* 1 (in the Bible) one of Christ's twelve apostles. He was a tax collector who became one of the four Evangelists. 2 the first book of the New Testament, attributed to him.

mat ting (mat′ing), *n.* 1 fabric of grass, straw, hemp, or other fiber, for mats, floor

covering, wrapping material, etc. 2 mats.

mat tins (mat′nz), *n.pl.* BRITISH. matins.

mat tock (mat′ək), *n.* a large tool with a steel head like a pickax, but having a flat blade on one side or flat blades on both sides, used for loosening soil and cutting roots. [Old English *mattuc*]

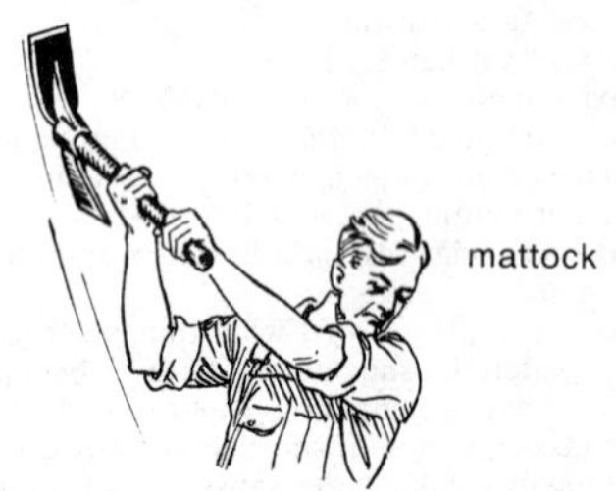

mat tress (mat′ris), *n.* 1 a covering of strong cloth stuffed with hair, cotton, straw, foam rubber, etc., used on a bed or as a bed. A spring mattress contains wire springs. 2 air mattress. [< Old French *materas* < Italian *materasso* < Arabic *al-matrah* the cushion]

mat u rate (mach′ü rāt′), *v.i.*, **-rat ed, -rat ing.** 1 mature. 2 discharge pus.

mat u ra tion (mach′ü rā′shən), *n.* 1 a ripening or a maturing. 2 (in biology) the final stages in the preparation of germ cells for fertilization, including meiosis. 3 formation of pus.

ma ture (mə chůr′, mə tůr′, mə tyůr′), *adj.*, *v.*, **-tured, -tur ing.** —*adj.* 1 ripe or full-grown: *Fifty is a mature age.* 2 brought by time, treatment, etc., to excellence: *mature wine, mature cheese.* 3 characteristic of full development: *a mature appearance, mature wisdom.* 4 fully worked out; carefully thought out; fully developed: *mature plans.* 5 due; payable: *a mature savings bond.* —*v.i.* 1 come to full growth; ripen. 2 fall due: *This note to the bank matured yesterday.* —*v.t.* 1 bring to full growth or development. 2 work out carefully. [< Latin *maturus* ripe] **—ma ture′ly,** *adv.* **—ma ture′ness,** *n.*

ma tur i ty (mə chůr′ə tē, mə tůr′ə tē, mə-tyůr′ə tē), *n.* 1 full development; ripeness. 2 a being completed or ready. 3 a falling due; time a note or debt is payable.

ma tu ti nal (mə tüt′n əl, mə tyüt′n əl), *adj.* having to do with or occurring in the morning; early in the day. [< Late Latin *matutinalis* < Latin *matutinus* of or in the morning] **—ma tu′ti nal ly,** *adv.*

mat zo (mät′sə, mät′sō′), *n., pl.* **mat zoth** (mät′sōt′), **mat zos** (mät′səz). a thin piece of unleavened bread, eaten especially during the Jewish holiday of Passover. [< Hebrew *maṣṣāh*]

maud lin (môd′lən), *adj.* 1 sentimental in a weak, silly way: *We saw a maudlin movie about a boy who lost his dog.* 2 tearfully silly because of drunkenness or excitement. [alteration of Mary *Magdalene,* often painted as weeping]

Maugham (môm), *n.* **(William) Somerset,** 1874-1965, English writer of novels, plays, and short stories.

mau gre (mô′gər), *prep.* ARCHAIC. in spite of. [< Old French]

Mau i (mou′ē), *n.* the second largest island of Hawaii. 46,000 pop.; 728 sq. mi.

maul (môl), *n.* a very heavy hammer or mallet for driving stakes, piles, or wedges. —*v.t.* beat and pull about; handle roughly: *The lion mauled its keeper badly.* [variant of *mall*] **—maul′er,** *n.*

Mau Mau (mou′ mou′), a secret society of African tribesmen, active during the 1950's, sworn to expel Europeans from Kenya by violent means.

Mau na Ke a (mou′nə kē′ə), extinct volcano on the island of Hawaii, the highest peak in the Pacific Ocean. 13,796 ft.

Mau na Lo a (mou′nə lō′ə), active volcano on the island of Hawaii. 13,675 ft.

maun der (môn′dər), *v.i.* 1 talk in a rambling, foolish way. 2 move or act in an aimless, confused manner. [origin uncertain] **—maun′der er,** *n.*

Maun dy Thursday (môn′dē), Holy Thursday. [*Maundy* < Old French *mande* < Latin *mandatum* a command)

Mau pas sant (mō′pə sänt; *French* mō pä-sän′), *n.* **Guy de,** 1850-1893, French writer of short stories and novels.

Mau re ta ni a (môr′ə tā′nē ə, môr′ə-tā′nyə), *n.* ancient kingdom in NW Africa, south of Spain.

Mau ri ta ni a (môr′ə tā′nē ə, môr′ə-tā′nyə), *n.* country in W Africa on the Atlantic. 1,100,000 pop.; 419,000 sq. mi. *Capital:* Nouakchott. See **Algeria** for map. **—Mau′ri ta′ni an,** *adj., n.*

Mau ri tius (mô rish′əs), *n.* island country in the Indian Ocean, east of Madagascar, a member of the Commonwealth of Nations. 870,000 pop.; 720 sq. mi. *Capital:* Port Louis. **—Mau ri′tian,** *adj., n.*

Mau ser (mou′zər), *n.* trademark for a kind of powerful repeating rifle or pistol.

mau so le um (mô′sə lē′əm, mô′zə lē′əm), *n., pl.* **-le ums, -le a** (-lē′ə) for 1. 1 a large, magnificent tomb, especially one above ground. 2 **Mausoleum,** a magnificent tomb built at Halicarnassus, in Asia Minor. It was one of the Seven Wonders of the World. [< Latin *Mausoleum* < Greek *Mausōleion* < *Mausōlus,* a king of the 300's B.C. in whose honor the Mausoleum at Halicarnassus was built]

mauve (mōv), *adj.* delicate, pale purple. —*n.* a delicate, pale purple. [< French < Latin *malva* mallow. Doublet of MALLOW.]

mav er ick (mav′ər ik), *n.* U.S. 1 calf or other animal not marked with an owner's brand. 2 INFORMAL. person who refuses to affiliate with a regular political party. [< Samuel *Maverick,* 1803-1870, cattle owner of Texas who did not brand the calves of one of his herds]

ma vis (mā′vis), *n.* the European song thrush. [< Old French *mauvis*]

ma vour neen or **ma vour nin** (mə-vůr′nēn′), *n.* IRISH. my darling. [< Irish *mo mhuirnīn*]

maw (mô), *n.* 1 mouth, throat, or gullet, especially of a meat-eating animal. 2 stomach. 3 crop of a bird. [Old English *maga*]

mawk ish (mô′kish), *adj.* 1 sickening; nauseating. 2 sickly sentimental; weakly emotional [originally, maggoty < Middle English *mawke* maggot < Scandinavian (Old Icelandic) *mathkr*] **—mawk′ish ly,** *adv.* **—mawk′ish ness,** *n.*

max., maximum.

max i (mak′sē), *adj.* reaching to the ankle (usually in compounds such as *maxicoat, maxi-length*). —*n.* dress, coat, etc., reaching to the ankle. [< *maxi(mum)*]

max il la (mak sil′ə), *n., pl.* **max il lae** (mak sil′ē), **max il las.** 1 jaw or jawbone, especially the upper jawbone in mammals and most vertebrates. 2 either of a pair of appendages just behind the mandibles of insects, crabs, etc. See **mandible** for picture. [< Latin, jaw]

max il lar y (mak′sə ler′ē), *adj., n., pl.* **-lar ies.** —*adj.* of or having to do with the jaw or jawbone, especially the upper jawbone. —*n.* maxilla.

max im (mak′səm), *n.* 1 a short rule of conduct expressed as a proverb: *"Look before you leap" is a maxim.* 2 statement expressing some general truth. [< Late Latin *maxima (propositio)* axiom, literally, greatest proposition]

max i ma (mak′sə mə), *n.* a pl. of **maximum.**

max i mal (mak′sə məl), *adj.* of or being a maximum; greatest possible; highest: *maximal loyalty.* **—max′i mal ly,** *adv.*

Max i mil ian (mak′sə mil′yən), *n.* 1832-1867, archduke of Austria, emperor of Mexico from 1864 to 1867.

Maximilian I, 1459-1519, emperor of the Holy Roman Empire from 1493 to 1519.

Maximilian II, 1527-1576, emperor of the Holy Roman Empire from 1564 to 1576.

max i mize (mak′sə mīz), *v.t.*, **-mized, -miz ing.** increase or magnify to the highest possible amount or degree: *maximize sales.* **—max′i miz′er,** *n.*

max i mum (mak′sə məm), *n., pl.* **-mums** or **-ma,** *adj.* —*n.* 1 the largest or highest amount; greatest possible amount; highest point or degree: *Sixteen miles in a day was the maximum that any of our club walked last summer. The speed limit is 40 miles an hour; drivers must not exceed this maximum.* 2 (in mathematics) a value of a function greater than any values close to it. —*adj.* largest or highest; greatest possible: *The maximum score on the test is 100.* [< Latin, neuter of *maximus* greatest, superlative of *magnus* great]

max well (mak′swel), *n.* unit of magnetic flux in the centimeter-gram-second system. [< James Clerk *Maxwell*]

Max well (mak′swəl), *n.* **James Clerk,** 1831-1879, Scottish physicist.

may (mā), *auxiliary v., present sing.* and *pl.* **may,** *past* **might.** 1 be permitted or allowed to: *May I go now?* 2 be possible that it will: *It may rain tomorrow.* 3 it is hoped that: *May you have a pleasant trip.* 4 *May* is used to express contingency, concession, purpose, result, etc.: *I write that you may know my plans.* [Old English *mæg*] ➤ See **can**[1] for usage note.

May (mā), *n.* the fifth month of the year. It has 31 days. [< Latin *Maius*]

Ma ya (mī′ə, mä′yə), *n., pl.* **-yas** or **-ya** for 1. 1 member of an ancient American Indian people who lived in Central America and Mexico. The Mayas had a high degree of civilization from about A.D. 350 to about A.D. 800. 2 their language. **—Ma′yan,** *adj., n.*

May apple, 1 a North American perennial plant of the same family as the barberry with a large, white flower and poisonous leaves and roots; mandrake. 2 its yellowish, slightly acid fruit, sometimes eaten.

may be (mā′bē), *adv.* it may be; possibly; perhaps.

➤ **maybe, may be.** *Maybe* is an adverb; *may be* is a verb form: *Maybe you'll have better luck next time. He may be the next mayor.*

May day (mā′dā′), *n.* the international radiotelephone call for help. [< French *m'aidez* help me!]

May Day, May 1, often celebrated by crowning a girl honored as the May queen, dancing around the maypole, etc. In some parts of the world, labor parades and meetings are held on May Day.

May er (mā′ər), *n.* **Maria Goeppert,** 1906-1972, American physicist, born in Germany.

may est (mā′əst), *v.* ARCHAIC. may. "Thou mayest" means "You may." Also, **mayst.**

may flow er (mā′flou′ər), *n.* any of several plants whose flowers blossom in May, as the trailing arbutus (in the United States), and the hawthorn or cowslip (in England).

May flow er (mā′flou′ər), *n.* ship on which the Pilgrims came to America in 1620.

Mayflower Compact, the written agreement signed by the Pilgrims on the Mayflower, providing for a form of self-government under majority rule to be set up in the New World.

may fly (mā′flī′), *n., pl.* **-flies.** any of an order of slender insects, having lacy forewings which are much larger than the hind wings; ephemerid. Mayflies die soon after reaching the adult stage.

may hap (mā′hap, mā′hap′), *adv.* ARCHAIC. perhaps. [for *it may hap*]

may hem (mā′hem), *n.* 1 crime of intentionally maiming a person or injuring him so that he is less able to defend himself. 2 any crime of violence which causes permanent physical injury. [< Anglo-French *mahem* < Old French *mahaignier* to maim]

May ing (mā′ing), *n.* celebration of May Day; taking part in May festivities.

may n't (mā′ənt), may not.

May o (mā′ō), *n.* 1 **Charles H.,** 1865-1939, American surgeon. 2 his brother, **William J.,** 1861-1939, American surgeon.

may on naise (mā′ə nāz′), *n.* dressing made of egg yolks, vegetable oil, vinegar or lemon juice, and seasoning, beaten together until thick, used on salads, fish, vegetables, etc. [< French, ultimately < *Mahón,* seaport in Minorca]

may or (mā′ər, mer), *n.* person at the head of a city or town government; chief official, usually elected, of a city, borough, or town. [< Old French *maire, maor* < Latin *major.* Doublet of MAJOR.]

may or al (mā′ər əl, mer′əl), *adj.* of or having to do with a mayor.

may or al ty (mā′ər əl tē, mer′əl tē), *n., pl.* **-ties.** 1 position of mayor. 2 mayor's term of office.

may pole or **May pole** (mā′pōl′), *n.* a high pole decorated with flowers or ribbons, around which merrymakers dance on May Day.

may pop (mā′pop′), *n.* 1 the small, edible, yellow fruit of a passionflower growing in the southern United States. 2 the plant itself.

May queen, girl crowned with flowers and honored as queen on May Day.

mayst (māst), *v.* ARCHAIC. mayest.

May tide (mā′tīd′), *n.* Maytime.

May time (mā′tīm′), *n.* month of May.

Maz ar in (maz′ər ən; *French* mȧ zȧ raN′), *n.* **Jules,** 1602-1661, French cardinal and statesman, born in Italy.

maze (māz), *n.* 1 network of paths through which it is hard to find one's way; labyrinth. 2 state of confusion; muddled condition. [variant of *amaze*]

ma zur ka or **ma zour ka** (mə zėr′kə, mə zůr′kə), *n.* 1 a lively Polish folk dance in moderately quick triple rhythm. 2 music for it. [< Polish *mazurka,* originally, woman of *Mazovia* in Poland]

maz y (mā′zē), *adj.,* **maz i er, maz i est.** like a maze; intricate.

maz zard (maz′ərd), *n.* a wild sweet cherry used as a rootstock for propagating varieties of sweet and of sour cherries. [origin uncertain]

Maz zi ni (mät sē′nē), *n.* **Giuseppe,** 1805-1872, leader in the movement for uniting Italy.

mb., millibar or millibars.

M ba bane (əm bä bän′, əm bä bä′nä), *n.* capital of Swaziland, in the NW part. 14,000.

mc., megacycle or megacycles.

M.C., 1 Master of Ceremonies. 2 Member of Congress.

Mc Car thy (mə kär′thē), *n.* **Mary,** born 1912, American writer of novels, short stories, and criticism.

meadowlark
about 10 in. long

Mc Car thy ism (mə kär′thē iz′əm), *n.* policy or practice of publicly accusing suspected individuals or groups of political disloyalty and subversion. [< Senator Joseph R. *McCarthy,* 1909-1957, chairman of the United States Senate Permanent Investigations Committee]

Mc Clel lan (mə klel′ən), *n.* **George B.,** 1826-1885, Union general in the Civil War.

Mc Cor mick (mə kôr′mik), *n.* **Cyrus Hall,** 1809-1884, American inventor of harvesting machinery.

Mc Coy (mə koi′), *n.* **the real McCoy,** SLANG. the genuine person or thing.

Mc Cul lers (mə kul′ərz), *n.* **Carson,** 1917-1967, American novelist.

Mc Gin ley (mə gin′lē), *n.* **Phyllis,** born 1905, American poet.

Mc Kin ley (mə kin′lē), *n.* 1 **William,** 1843-1901, the 25th president of the United States, from 1897 to 1901. 2 **Mount,** mountain in central Alaska, the highest peak in North America. 20,300 ft.

Md, mendelevium.

Md., Maryland.

M.D., Doctor of Medicine [for Latin *Medicinae Doctor*].

mdse., merchandise.

me (mē; *unstressed* mi), *pron.* objective case of **I:** *Give me a pencil.* [Old English *mē*]

Me., Maine.

M.E., 1 Mechanical Engineer. 2 Methodist Episcopal. 3 Mining Engineer. 4 Middle English.

hat, āge, fär; let, ēqual, tėrm;
it, īce; hot, ōpen, ôrder;
oil, out; cup, pu̇t, rüle;
ch, child; ng, long; sh, she;
th, thin; ᴛʜ, then; zh, measure;

ə represents *a* in about, *e* in taken, *i* in pencil, *o* in lemon, *u* in circus.

< = from, derived from, taken from.

me a cul pa (mē′ə kul′pə; mā′ə kul′pə), 1 plea or confession of guilt. 2 apology. 3 recantation, especially of a political ideology. [< Latin, (it is) my fault]

mead[1] (mēd), *n.* ARCHAIC. meadow. [Old English *mæd*]

mead[2] (mēd), *n.* an alcoholic drink made from fermented honey and water. [Old English *medu*]

Mead (mēd), *n.* 1 **Lake,** lake formed by Hoover Dam in the Colorado River, between Arizona and Nevada. 115 mi. long; 227 sq. mi. 2 **Margaret,** born 1901, American anthropologist.

Meade (mēd), *n.* **George Gordon,** 1815-1872, Union general in the Civil War.

mead ow (med′ō), *n.* 1 piece of grassy land; field when hay is grown. 2 low, grassy land near a stream. [Old English *mǣdwe,* oblique case of *mǣd* mead[1]]

mead ow lark (med′ō lärk′), *n.* any of a genus of North American songbirds, having thick bodies, short tails, and yellow breasts marked with a black crescent.

mead ow sweet (med′ō swēt′), *n.* 1 shrub, a species of spiraea, with dense clusters of small, fragrant pink or white flowers. 2 any of a genus of tall herbs of the rose family, having many small white, pink, or purple flowers.

mead ow y (med′ō ē), *adj.* 1 like a meadow. 2 of meadows.

mea ger or **mea gre** (mē′gər), *adj.* 1 lacking fullness or richness; poor or scanty; sparse: *a meager meal.* See **scanty** for synonym study. 2 thin; lean: *a meager face.* [< Old French *maigre* < Latin *macer*] **—mea′ger ly, mea′gre ly,** *adv.* **—mea′ger ness, mea′gre ness,** *n.*

meal[1] (mēl), *n.* 1 breakfast, lunch, dinner, supper, or tea. 2 food served or eaten at any one time. [Old English *mǣl* appointed time, meal]

meal[2] (mēl), *n.* 1 coarsely ground grain, especially corn meal. 2 anything ground to a powder. [Old English *melu*]

meal ie (mē′lē), *n.* in South Africa: **a** an ear of corn. **b mealies,** *pl.* corn: *a sack of mealies.* [< Afrikaans *milje*]

meal time (mēl′tīm′), *n.* the usual time for eating a meal.

meal worm (mēl′wėrm′), *n.* a beetle larva that feeds on flour and meal and is raised as food for caged animals, such as birds.

meal y (mē′lē), *adj.,* **meal i er, meal i est.** 1 like meal; dry and powdery. 2 of or containing meal. 3 covered with meal. 4 pale. 5 mealy-mouthed. 6 flecked as if with meal; spotty. **—meal′i ness,** *n.*

meal y bug (mē′lē bug′), *n.* any of a family of small scale insects covered with a whitish secretion. Mealybugs cause damage to citrus trees and other plants.

meal y-mouthed (mē′lē mouŦHd′, mē′lē-moutht′), *adj.* unwilling to tell the full truth in plain words; using soft words insincerely.

mean[1] (mēn), *v.,* **meant, mean ing.** *—v.t.* 1 have as its thought; signify; import; denote: *What does this word mean?* 2 intend to express or indicate: *"Keep out; that means you."* 3 have as a purpose; have in mind; intend: *I do not mean to go.* See **intend** for synonym study. 4 design for a definite purpose; destine: *meant for each other.* 5 **mean well by,** have kindly feelings toward. *—v.i.* have intentions of some kind; be minded or disposed: *She means well.* [Old English *mǣnan* to mean, tell, say]

mean[2] (mēn), *adj.* 1 of a petty, unkind, small-minded nature: *mean thoughts.* 2 low in quality or grade; poor: *the meanest of gifts.* 3 **no mean,** very good: *He is no mean scholar.* 4 low in social position or rank; humble. 5 of little importance or value: *the meanest flower.* 6 of poor appearance; shabby: *a mean hut.* 7 stingy or selfish: *mean about money.* 8 INFORMAL. humiliated; ashamed: *feel mean.* 9 INFORMAL. hard to manage; troublesome; bad-tempered: *a mean horse.* 10 INFORMAL. in poor physical condition; unwell: *I feel mean today.* [Old English *(ge)mǣne* common] **—mean′ly,** *adv.* **—mean′ness,** *n.*

mean[3] (mēn), *adj.* 1 halfway between two extremes: *the mean annual air temperature.* 2 intermediate in kind, quality, or degree; average. 3 (in mathematics) having a value intermediate between the values of other quantities: *a mean diameter.*

—n. 1 condition, quality, or course of action halfway between two extremes. 2 in mathematics: **a** a quantity having a value intermediate between the values of other quantities, especially the average obtained by dividing the sum of all the quantities by the total number of quantities. **b** either the second or third term of a proportion of four terms. 3 **means,** *pl.* agency, method, etc., used to attain an end: *He won by fair means.* 4 **means,** *pl.* **a** financial resources; worth: *live beyond one's means.* **b** wealth: *a man of means.*

by all means, certainly; without fail.

by any means, at all; in any possible way; at any cost.

by means of, by the use of; through; with.

by no means, certainly not; not at all; under no circumstances.

means to an end, way of getting or doing something.

[< Old French *meien* < Latin *medianus* of the middle < *medius* middle of. Doublet of MEDIAN.]

me an der (mē an′dər), *v.i.* 1 follow a winding course: *A brook meanders through the meadow.* 2 wander aimlessly: *We meandered through the park.* *—n.* 1 a winding course. 2 aimless wandering. 3 a looplike turn in a river or stream. [< Latin *maeander* a winding course < Greek *Maiandros* (now, *Menderes*) a winding river in Asia Minor]

mean ing (mē′ning), *n.* 1 that which is meant or intended; significance: *misunderstand the meaning of a statement.* See synonym study below. 2 ARCHAIC. intention or purpose. *—adj.* that means something; expressive; significant: *a meaning look.* **—mean′ing ly,** *adv.*

Syn. *n.* 1 **Meaning, sense, purport** mean what one intends to express or communicate to another or others. **Meaning** is the general word, applying to anything that is subject to explanation or interpretation, such as a word, a statement, a gesture, an action, a painting, etc.: *The meaning of the sentence is clear.* **Sense** applies especially to a particular meaning of a word: *He used the word "lady" in the special sense of "a British noblewoman."* **Purport,** formal, applies to the main idea or general drift of a longer statement: *That was the purport of the president's address.*

mean ing ful (mē′ning fəl), *adj.* full of meaning; having much meaning; significant. **—mean′ing ful ly,** *adv.* **—mean′ing fulness,** *n.*

measure (def. 11)—four measures

mean ing less (mē′ning lis), *adj.* not making sense; without meaning; not significant. **—mean′ing less ly,** *adv.* **—mean′ingless ness,** *n.*

mean proportional, (in mathematics) the means in a proportion when they are equal. EXAMPLE: In a:b = b:c, b is the mean proportional.

meant (ment), *v.* pt. and pp. of **mean**[1].

mean time (mēn′tīm′), *n.* time between. *—adv.* 1 in the intervening time; in the time between. 2 at the same time.

mean while (mēn′hwīl′), *n., adv.* meantime.

meas., 1 measurable. 2 measure.

mea sles (mē′zəlz), *n. sing. or pl.* 1 an acute, contagious virus disease, usually attacking children, characterized by the symptoms of a bad cold, fever, and a breaking out of small red spots on the skin; rubeola. 2 any of various similar but milder diseases, such as German measles. [Middle English *maseles*]

mea sly (mē′zlē), *adj.,* **-sli er, -sli est.** 1 of or like measles. 2 infected with measles. 3 SLANG. scanty; meager.

meas ur a bil i ty (mezh′ər ə bil′ə tē, mā′zhər ə bil′ə tē), *n.* quality or condition of being measurable.

meas ur a ble (mezh′ər ə bəl, mā′zhər ə-bəl), *adj.* capable of being measured. **—meas′ur a ble ness,** *n.* **—meas′ur a-bly,** *adv.*

meas ure (mezh′ər, mā′zhər), *v.,* **-ured, -ur ing,** *n.* *—v.t.* 1 find out the extent, size, quantity, capacity, etc., of (something); estimate by some standard: *measure a room.* 2 get, take, or set apart by measuring: *measure out a bushel of potatoes, measure off 2 yards of cloth.* 3 serve as a measure of. 4 compare or judge: *measure one's abilities against those of another.* 5 adjust; suit: *measure one's behavior by the company one is in.* 6 ARCHAIC. travel over; traverse. *—v.i.* 1 be of specified measure: *Buy some paper that measures 8 by 10 inches.* 2 take measurements; find out sizes or amounts. 3 **measure up,** have the necessary qualifications: *The composer's new piano score doesn't measure up.* 4 **measure up to,** meet the standard of, be in accord with or be equal to: *The party did not measure up to our expectations.*

—n. 1 act or process of finding the extent, size, quantity, capacity, etc., of something, especially by comparison with a standard. 2 the size, dimensions, quantity, etc., thus obtained: *a waist measure of 32 inches.* **Short measure** means less than it should be; **full measure** means all that it should be. 3 instrument for measuring. A foot rule, a yardstick, a pint measure, a quart dipper, and a bushel basket are common measures. 4 system of measuring. 5 unit or standard of measuring. Inch, acre, mile, quart, pound, gallon, peck, and hour are common measures. 6 any standard of comparison, estimation, or judgment, etc.; criterion. 7 quantity or degree that should not be exceeded; reasonable limit. 8 quantity, degree, or proportion: *a measure of relief. Sickness is in great measure preventable.* 9 rhythmical movement or arrangement in poetry or music. 10 a metrical unit; foot of verse. 11 bar of music. 12 dance, especially a slow, stately dance. 13 a definite course of action; procedure: *adopt measures to relieve poverty.* 14 a legislative bill; law: *This measure has passed the Senate.* 15 (in mathematics) a factor. 16 a definite quantity measured out: *drink a measure.*

beyond measure, very greatly; exceedingly.

for good measure, as something extra.

in a measure, to some degree; partly.

take measures, do something; act.

take one's measure, judge one's character.

tread a measure, dance.

[< Old French *mesurer* < Late Latin *mensurare* < Latin *mensura* a measure < *metiri* to measure] **—meas′ur er,** *n.*

meas ured (mezh′ərd, mā′zhərd), *adj.* 1 regular; uniform: *measured portions of food.* 2 rhythmical. 3 written in poetry, not in prose; metrical. 4 deliberate and restrained: *measured speech.*

meas ure less (mezh′ər lis, mā′zhər lis), *adj.* without measure; unlimited.

meas ure ment (mezh′ər mənt, mā′zhər-mənt), *n.* 1 way of measuring; way of finding the size, quantity, or amount; gauge: *Clocks give us a measurement of time.* 2 act or fact of measuring: *The measurement of length by a yardstick is easy.* 3 size, quantity, or amount found by measuring. 4 system of measuring or of measures.

measuring worm, larva of any geometrid moth; inchworm. It moves by bringing the rear end of its body forward, forming a loop, and then advancing the front end.

meat (mēt), *n.* 1 animal flesh, especially mammal flesh, used as food. Fish and poultry are not usually called meat. 2 food, especially solid food: *meat and drink.* 3 the edible part of anything: *meat of a nut.* 4 ARCHAIC. meal, especially the principal meal. 5 the essential part or parts; food for thought; substance. [Old English *mete*] **—meat′less,** *adj.*

meat ball (mēt′bôl′), *n.* ball of chopped or ground meat, cooked and usually served in gravy or sauce, especially with spaghetti.

me a tus (mē ā′təs), *n., pl.* **-tus es** or **-tus.** passage, duct, or opening in the body, as in the ear. [< Latin, path < *meare* to pass]

meat y (mē′tē), *adj.,* **meat i er, meat i est.** 1 of meat; having the flavor of meat. 2 like meat. 3 full of meat. 4 full of substance; giving food for thought; solid and nourishing: *The speech was very meaty; it contained many valuable ideas.* **—meat′i ly,** *adv.* **—meat′i ness,** *n.*

Measures and Weights

Most of the world uses the metric system. In the United States, the metric system is used commonly only in science, and most measurements are made in an older, less regular system. In the table below, metric and United States measures and weights are at the left. United States and metric equivalents are at the right.

METRIC SYSTEM

linear measure

1/1000 meter	= 1 millimeter
1/100 meter	= 1 centimeter
1/10 meter	= 1 decimeter
10 meters	= 1 decameter
100 meters	= 1 hectometer
1000 meters	= 1 kilometer

square measure

1 square meter	= 1 centiare
100 centiares	= 1 are
100 ares	= 1 hectare
10,000 ares	= 1 square kilometer

cubic measure

10 decisteres	= 1 stere
1 stere	= 1 cubic meter
10 steres	= 1 decastere
1000 cubic centimeters	= 1 cubic decimeter
1000 cubic decimeters	= 1 cubic meter

liquid and dry measure

1/1000 liter	= 1 milliliter
1/100 liter	= 1 centiliter
1/10 liter	= 1 deciliter
10 liters	= 1 decaliter
100 liters	= 1 hectoliter
1000 liters	= 1 kiloliter

weight

1/1000 gram	= 1 milligram
1/100 gram	= 1 centigram
1/10 gram	= 1 decigram
10 grams	= 1 decagram
100 grams	= 1 hectogram
1000 grams	= 1 kilogram
1000 kilograms	= 1 metric ton

UNITED STATES SYSTEM

linear measure

12 inches	= 1 foot
3 feet	= 1 yard
$5^1/_2$ yards	= 1 rod
40 rods	= 1 furlong
8 furlongs	= 1 mile
1760 yards	= 1 mile
5280 feet	= 1 mile

square measure

144 square inches	= 1 square foot
9 square feet	= 1 square yard
$30^1/_4$ square yards	= 1 square rod
160 square rods	= 1 acre
640 acres	= 1 square mile

cubic measure

1728 cubic inches	= 1 cubic foot
27 cubic feet	= 1 cubic yard

apothecaries' measure

60 minims	= 1 fluid dram
8 fluid drams	= 1 fluid ounce
16 fluid ounces	= 1 pint
8 pints	= 1 gallon

liquid measure

4 gills	= 1 pint
2 pints	= 1 quart
4 quarts	= 1 gallon

dry measure

2 pints	= 1 quart
8 quarts	= 1 peck
4 pecks	= 1 bushel

avoirdupois weight

$27^{11}/_{32}$ grains	= 1 dram
16 drams	= 1 ounce
16 ounces	= 1 pound
2000 pounds	= 1 short ton
2240 pounds	= 1 long ton

troy weight

24 grains	= 1 pennyweight
20 pennyweights	= 1 ounce
12 ounces	= 1 pound

apothecaries' weight

20 grains	= 1 scruple
3 scruples	= 1 dram
8 drams	= 1 ounce
12 ounces	= 1 pound

UNITED STATES AND METRIC EQUIVALENTS

linear measure

1 inch	= 2.54 centimeters
1 yard	= 0.914 meter
1 mile	= 1.609 kilometers
0.394 inch	= 1 centimeter
1.0936 yards	= 1 meter
0.62 mile	= 1 kilometer

square measure

1 square inch	= 6.45 square centimeters
1 square foot	= 0.093 square meter
1 square yard	= 0.836 square meter
1 square mile	= 2.59 square kilometers
0.155 square inch	= 1 square centimeter
10.76 square feet	= 1 square meter
0.386 square mile	= 1 square kilometer

cubic measure

1 cubic inch	= 16.387 cubic centimeters
1 cubic foot	= 0.028 cubic meter
1 cubic yard	= 0.765 cubic meter
0.061 cubic inch	= 1 cubic centimeter
1.31 cubic yards	= 1 cubic meter

liquid measure

1 fluid ounce	= 29.57 milliliters
1 quart	= 0.946 liter
1 gallon	= 3.785 liters
0.338 fluid ounce	= 1 centiliter
1.057 quarts	= 1 liter

dry measure

1 quart	= 1.101 liters
1 peck	= 8.810 liters
1 bushel	= 35.24 liters
0.908 quart	= 1 liter

weight

1 grain, avoirdupois, apothecaries', troy	= 0.0648 gram
1 ounce, avoirdupois	= 28.35 grams
1 ounce, apothecaries' and troy	= 31.10 grams
1 pound, avoirdupois	= 0.4536 kilogram
1 pound, apothecaries' and troy	= 0.3732 kilogram
1 short ton	= 907.18 kilograms
1 long ton	= 1016.05 kilograms
2.2046 pounds, avoirdupois	= 1 kilogram
0.0353 ounce, avoirdupois	= 1 gram

Mec ca (mek′ə), *n.* 1 the religious capital of Saudi Arabia, in the W part. Because Mohammed was born there, Moslems turn toward Mecca when praying and go there on pilgrimages. 250,000. Also, **Mekka.** 2 Also, **mecca.** **a** place that many people visit. **b** place that a person longs to visit. **c** goal of one's desires or ambitions.

mech., 1 mechanical. 2 mechanics.

me chan ic (mə kan′ik), *n.* 1 worker skilled with tools, especially one who makes repairs, or uses machinery. 2 ARCHAIC. person who works with his hands; artisan. *—adj.* mechanical. [< Latin *mechanicus* < Greek *mēchanikos* < *mēchanē* machine]

me chan i cal (mə kan′ə kəl), *adj.* 1 of or having to do with a machine, mechanism, or machinery. 2 made or worked by machinery. 3 like a machine; like that of a machine; without feeling or expression; automatic: *Her reading is very mechanical.* 4 of, having to do with, or in accordance with the science of mechanics. 5 ARCHAIC. of or having to do with artisans. **—me chan′i cal ly,** *adv.*

mechanical advantage, the ratio of resistance or load to the force or effort that is applied in a machine. Mechanical advantage is shown by the number of times a machine increases the force exerted on it.

mechanical drawing, drawing of machines, tools, etc., done to exact scale with rulers, squares, compasses, etc.

mech a ni cian (mek′ə nish′ən), *n.* mechanic.

me chan ics (mə kan′iks), *n.* 1 *pl. in form, sing. in use.* branch of physics dealing with the action of forces on solids, liquids, and gases at rest or in motion. 2 *pl. in form, sing. in use.* knowledge dealing with machinery. 3 *pl. in form and use.* mechanical part; technique: *the mechanics of playing the piano.*

mech a nism (mek′ə niz′əm), *n.* 1 means or way by which something is done; machinery. 2 machine or its working parts. 3 system of parts working together as the parts of a machine do: *The bones and muscles are parts of the mechanism of the body.* 4 mechanical part; technique. 5 theory that everything in the universe is produced and can be explained by mechanical or material forces.

mech a nist (mek′ə nist), *n.* 1 person who believes that all the changes in the universe are the effects of physical and chemical forces. 2 ARCHAIC. mechanic.

mech a nis tic (mek′ə nis′tik), *adj.* 1 of or having to do with mechanics or mechanical theories. 2 of or having to do with the theory of mechanism. **—mech′a nis′ti cal ly,** *adv.*

mech a ni za tion (mek′ə nə zā′shən), *n.* 1 a mechanizing. 2 a being mechanized.

mech a nize (mek′ə nīz), *v.t.,* **-nized, -niz ing.** 1 make mechanical. 2 do by machinery, rather than by hand: *Much housework can be mechanized.* 3 replace men or animals by machinery in (a business, etc.). 4 equip (a military unit) with armored vehicles, tanks, and other machines.

Meck len burg (mek′lən bėrg′), *n.* former state in NE Germany, now a region in N East Germany.

med al (med′l), *n.* piece of metal usually like a coin, with a figure or inscription commemorating a person or event stamped on it. Medals are often given as awards for achievement. Some medals are worn to invoke the favor of a saint. [< Middle French *medaille* < Italian *medaglia,* perhaps ultimately < Latin *metallum* metal]

med al ist (med′l ist), *n.* 1 person who designs or makes medals. 2 person who has won a medal. Also, **medallist.**

me dal lion (mə dal′yən), *n.* 1 a large medal. 2 design, ornament, etc., shaped like a medal. A design on a book or a pattern in lace may be called a medallion.

med al list (med′l ist), *n.* medalist.

Medal of Honor, the highest military decoration of the United States, given by Congress to members of the armed forces for bravery in combat at the risk of their lives and beyond the call of duty.

medal play, (in golf) a form of competition in which the game is won by the player or side that scores the lowest number of strokes.

med dle (med′l), *v.i.,* **-dled, -dling.** busy oneself with or in other people's things or affairs without being asked or needed. [< Old French *medler,* ultimately < Latin *miscere* to mix] **—med′dler,** *n.*

Syn. Meddle, tamper, interfere mean to concern oneself unnecessarily or unduly with someone or something. **Meddle** implies busying oneself, without right or permission, with something not one's own affair: *That old busybody is always meddling in someone's business.* **Tamper** suggests meddling in order to alter or experiment with a thing or improperly influence a person: *Don't tamper with electrical appliances.* **Interfere** suggests meddling in a way that disturbs or hinders: *She interferes when we scold the children.*

med dle some (med′l səm), *adj.* fond of meddling in other people's affairs; meddling; interfering. **—med′dle some ness,** *n.*

Mede (mēd), *n.* native or inhabitant of Media.

Me de a (mi dē′ə), *n.* (in Greek legends) an enchantress who helped Jason win the Golden Fleece and returned to Greece with him. Later he deserted her.

Me del lín (med′l ēn′, med′l ən; *Spanish* mā′ᴛʜā yēn′), *n.* city in W Colombia. 1,089,000.

Med fly (med′flī′), *n., pl.* **-flies.** Mediterranean fruit fly.

me di a (mē′dē ə), *n.* 1 a pl. of **medium** (defs. 2, 3, and 4). 2 medium (def. 2). 3 mass media.

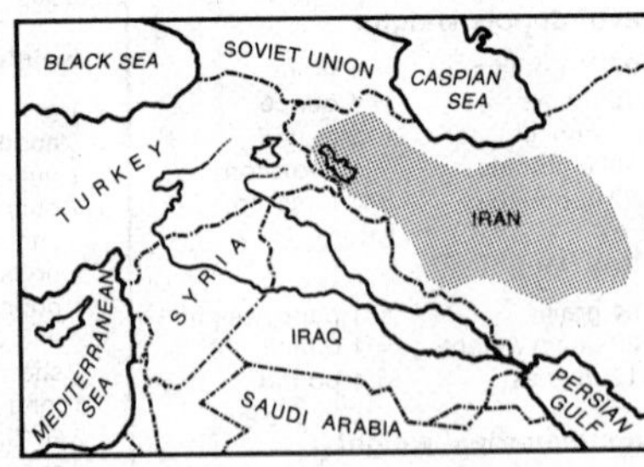

Media—The shaded area indicates Media in about 600 B.C.

Me di a (mē′dē ə), *n.* ancient country in SW Asia, south of the Caspian Sea. **—Me′di an,** *adj., n.*

me di ae val (mē′dē ē′vəl, med′ē ē′vəl), *adj.* medieval.

me di al (mē′dē əl), *adj.* 1 in the middle. 2 average; ordinary. 3 (in phonetics) occurring in the middle of or within a word: *In "dairy" the "i" is in medial position.* [< Late Latin *medialis* < Latin *medius* middle] **—me′di al ly,** *adv.*

me di an (mē′dē ən), *adj.* 1 of, having to do with, or situated in the middle; middle. 2 of a median; having as many above as below a certain number: *The median age of the population was found to be 21 (that is, there were as many persons above 21 as below it), while the average age was found to be 25.* *—n.* 1 the middle number of a sequence having an odd number of values. If the sequence has an even number of values, the median is the average of the two middle values. EXAMPLES: The median of 1, 3, 4, 8, 9 is 4. The median of 1, 3, 4, 8, 9, 10 is 6. 2 (of a triangle) a line from a vertex to the midpoint of the opposite side. 3 (of a trapezoid) the line joining the midpoints of the nonparallel sides. 4 median strip. [< Latin *medianus* < *medius* middle. Doublet of MEAN[3].] **—me′di an ly,** *adv.*

median strip, strip of land, usually grass-covered or landscaped, between the lanes for traffic going in opposite directions on some highways and expressways.

me di ant (mē′dē ənt), *n.* the third note or tone of a diatonic musical scale, halfway from the keynote to the dominant.

me di ate (*v.* mē′dē āt; *adj.* mē′dē it), *v.,* **-at ed, -at ing,** *adj.* *—v.i.* come in to help settle a dispute; be a go-between; act in order to bring about an agreement between persons or sides. *—v.t.* 1 effect by intervening; settle by intervening: *mediate an agreement, mediate a strike.* 2 be a connecting link between. 3 be the medium for effecting (a result), for conveying (a gift), or for communicating (knowledge). *—adj.* 1 connected, but not directly; involving or dependent on some intermediate agency. 2 intermediate. [< Late Latin *mediatum* situated in the middle < Latin *medius* middle] **—me′di ate ly,** *adv.*

me di a tion (mē′dē ā′shən), *n.* a mediating; effecting an agreement; friendly intervention.

me di a tor (mē′dē ā′tər), *n.* person or group that intervenes between others for the purpose of effecting reconciliation; one who mediates.

me di a to ry (mē′dē ə tôr′ē, mē′dē ə-tōr′ē), *adj.* of or having to do with mediation; mediating.

med ic[1] (med′ik), *n.* INFORMAL. 1 physician. 2 a medical student. 3 member of a medical corps of the armed forces. [< Latin *medicus* physician]

med ic[2] (med′ik), *n.* any of a genus of herbs of the pea family, having purple or yellow flowers. Alfalfa is a kind of medic. [< Latin *medica* < Greek *(poa) Mēdikē* Median (herb)]

med i ca ble (med′ə kə bəl), *adj.* that can be cured or relieved by medical treatment; curable.

Med i caid (med′ə kād′), *n.* U.S. program sponsored by the federal, state, and local governments providing medical benefits for needy or disabled persons not covered by social security. [< *medic(al) aid*]

med i cal (med′ə kəl), *adj.* of or having to do with healing or with the science or practice of medicine. **—med′i cal ly,** *adv.*

medical examiner, physician appointed by a local government to determine the cause of any unnatural death.

me dic a ment (mə dik′ə mənt, med′ə kə-mənt), *n.* substance used to cure or heal; medicine.

Med i care (med′ə ker′, med′ə kar′), *n.* U.S. a federal government-sponsored program providing medical care and hospital services under social security for persons over sixty-five years old. [< *medi(cal) care*]

med i cate (med′ə kāt), *v.t.,* **-cat ed, -cat ing.** 1 treat with medicine: *medicate an infection.* 2 put medicine on or in: *medicated gauze.*

med i ca tion (med′ə kā′shən), *n.* 1 treatment with medicine. 2 a putting medicine on or in. 3 medicine.

Med i ci (med′ə chē′), *n.* any member of a rich and powerful family of Florence, Italy, from the 1400's to the 1600's, especially: **a Catherine de',** 1519-1589, queen of Henry II of France from 1547 to 1559. **b Cosmo de',** 1389-1464, banker, statesman, and patron of art and literature. **c Cosmo de',** 1519-1574, duke of Florence and first grand duke of Tuscany. **d Giulio de',** Clement VII. **e Lorenzo de',** 1449-1492, ruler of Florence, statesman, poet and patron of art and literature. **f Marie de',** 1573-1642, queen of Henry IV of France, and regent of France after his death.

me dic i nal (mə dis′n əl), *adj.* having value as medicine; healing; helping; relieving. **—me dic′i nal ly,** *adv.*

med i cine (med′ə sən), *n.* 1 substance, such as a drug, used to treat, prevent, or cure disease; medication. 2 **take one's medicine,** do what one must; do something one dislikes to do. 3 science of treating, preventing, or curing disease; study or practice of maintaining and improving health. 4 the field of medicine, as distinguished from surgery, obstetrics, etc. 5 any object or ceremony that certain primitive peoples believe has magic power over disease, evil spirits, etc. this power. [< Latin *medicina* < *medicus* physician]

medicine ball, a large, heavy, stuffed leather ball tossed from one person to another for exercise.

medicine man, man supposed by North American Indians and certain primitive peoples to have magic power over diseases, evil spirits, and other things.

medicine show, U.S. a traveling show at which patent medicines, remedies, etc., were formerly advertised and sold.

med i co (med′ə kō), *n., pl.* **-cos.** INFORMAL. 1 physician. 2 a medical student. [< Italian]

me di e val (mē′dē ē′vəl, med′ē ē′vəl), *adj.* 1 of, having to do with, or belonging to the Middle Ages (the years from about A.D. 500 to about 1450). 2 like that of the Middle Ages, Also, **mediaeval.** [< Latin *medium* middle + *aevum* age] **—me′di e′val ly,** *adv.*

Medieval Greek, the Greek language from about A.D. 700 to about 1500.

me di e val ism (mē′dē ē′və liz′əm, med′ē ē′və liz′əm), *n.* 1 spirit, ideals, and customs of the Middle Ages; medieval thought, religion, and art. 2 devotion to medieval ideals or customs. 3 a medieval belief or custom.

me di e val ist (mē′dē ē′və list, med′ē-ē′və list), *n.* 1 an expert on the Middle Ages. 2 sympathizer with medieval ideas or customs.

Medieval Latin, the Latin language from about A.D. 700 to about 1500.

Me di na (mə dē′nə), *n.* city in W Saudi Arabia, the site of Mohammed's tomb. 60,000.

me di o cre (mē′dē ō′kər, mē′dē ō′kər), *adj.* neither good nor bad; of average quality; ordinary. [< Latin *mediocris,* originally, halfway up < *medius* middle + *ocris* jagged mountain]

me di oc ri ty (mē′dē ok′rə tē), *n., pl.* **-ties.** 1 mediocre quality. 2 mediocre ability or accomplishment. 3 a mediocre person.

med i tate (med′ə tāt), *v.,* **-tat ed, -tat ing.** *—v.i.* engage in deep and serious thought; think quietly; reflect: *In some religious orders monks and nuns meditate on holy things for hours at a time.* See **think** for synonym study. *—v.t.* think about; consider; plan; intend. [< Latin *meditatum* considered]

med i ta tion (med′ə tā′shən), *n.* quiet thought; reflection, especially on sacred or solemn subjects; contemplation.

med i ta tive (med′ə tā′tiv), *adj.* 1 fond of or given to meditating; thoughtful. 2 expressing meditation. **—med′i ta′tive ly,** *adv.*

Med i ter ra ne an (med′ə tə rā′nē ən, med′ə tə rā′nyən), *adj.* of the Mediterranean Sea or the lands around it.

Mediterranean fruit fly, a very destructive fly whose larvae attack fruits and vegetables; Medfly. It is found in warm regions of the world.

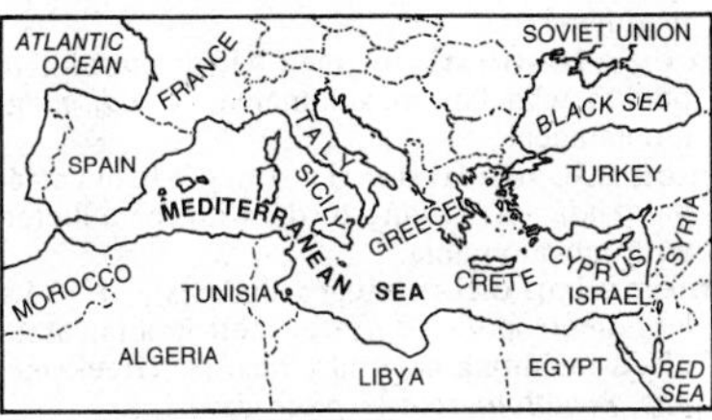

Mediterranean Sea, large sea bordered by Europe, Asia, and Africa. 2330 mi. long; 1,145,000 sq. mi.

me di um (mē′dē əm), *adj., n., pl.* **-di ums** or (also for 2, 3, 4) **-di a.** *—adj.* having a middle position, quality, or condition; moderate: *of medium height.* *—n.* 1 something that is in the middle in nature or degree; neither one extreme nor the other; middle condition. 2 substance or agent through which anything acts; a means: *Television and radio are media of communication. Money is a medium of exchange in trading.* 3 substance in which something can live; environment: *Water is the natural medium of fish.* 4 a nutritive substance in or upon which microorganisms are grown for study. 5 liquid with which paints are mixed. 6 person through whom messages from the spirits of the dead are supposedly sent to the living. [< Latin, neuter of *medius* middle]

medium frequency, (in electronics) a frequency ranging from 300 to 3000 kilocycles per second.

med lar (med′lər), *n.* 1 fruit resembling a crab apple. It is picked after frost and usually preserved. 2 the small, bushy tree of the rose family that it grows on. [< Old French *medler*]

med ley (med′lē), *n., pl.* **-leys,** *adj.* *—n.* 1 mixture of things that ordinarily do not belong together. 2 piece of music made up of parts from other pieces. *—adj.* made up of parts that are not alike; mixed. [< Old French *medlee, meslee* < *mesler* to mix, ultimately < Latin *miscere.* Doublet of MELEE.]

me dul la (mi dul′ə), *n., pl.* **-dul las** or (especially for 1, 2) **-dul lae** (-dul′ē). 1 medulla oblongata. 2 marrow of bones. 3 the inner part or tissue of an organ or structure. 4 the pith of plants. [< Latin, marrow]

hat, āge, fär; let, ēqual, tėrm;
it, īce; hot, ōpen, ôrder;
oil, out; cup, pu̇t, rüle;
ch, child; ng, long; sh, she;
th, thin; ᴛʜ, then; zh, measure;

ə represents *a* in about, *e* in taken, *i* in pencil, *o* in lemon, *u* in circus.

< = from, derived from, taken from.

medulla ob lon ga ta (ob′long gä′tə), the part of the brain that controls breathing and other involuntary functions. It consists of nerve fibers and nerve centers and is located at the top end of the spinal cord. See **brain** for diagram. [< New Latin, prolonged medulla]

med ul lar y (med′ə ler′ē, mi dul′ər ē), *adj.* of, having to do with, or like medulla or the medulla oblongata.

medullary ray, one of the radiating vertical bands of woody tissue which divide the vascular bundles and connect the pith with the bark in the stems of exogenous plants.

me du sa (mə dü′sə, mə dyü′sə), *n., pl.* **-sas, -sae** (-sē′). jellyfish. [< *Medusa*]

Me du sa (mə dü′sə, mə dyü′sə), *n.* (in Greek legends) one of the three Gorgons or horrible monsters with snakes for hair. Anyone who looked upon her was turned to stone. She was slain by Perseus. **—Me du′sa like′,** *adj.*

me du san (mə dü′sn, mə dyü′sn), *adj.* of or having to do with jellyfish. *—n.* jellyfish.

me du soid (mə dü′soid, mə dyü′soid), *adj.* of or like a jellyfish. *—n.* jellyfish.

meed (mēd), *n.* ARCHAIC. what one deserves or has earned; reward. [Old English *mēd*]

meek (mēk), *adj.* 1 not easily angered; mild; patient. See **gentle** for synonym study. 2 submitting tamely when ordered about or injured by others; submissive; yielding: *The boy was meek as a lamb when he was reproved.* See **humble** for synonym study. [< Scandinavian (Old Icelandic) *mjūkr* soft] **—meek′ly,** *adv.* **—meek′ness,** *n.*

meer schaum (mir′shəm, mir′shôm), *n.* 1 a soft, light, white, clayey mineral used especially to make tobacco pipes. *Formula:* $H_4Mg_2Si_3O_{10}$ 2 a tobacco pipe with a bowl made of this substance. [< German *Meerschaum,* literally, sea foam]

meet[1] (mēt), *v.,* **met, meet ing,** *n.* *—v.t.* 1 come face to face with: *Our car met another car on a narrow road.* 2 come together with; come into contact or connection with: *Sword met sword in battle.* 3 join; intersect: *The accident occurred where Oak Street meets Main Street.* 4 keep an appointment with: *Meet me at one o'clock.* 5 be introduced to; become acquainted with: *Have you met my sister?* 6 receive on arrival; be present at the arrival of: *meet a plane.* 7 come into company with; be together: *an appointment to meet someone for dinner.* 8 be perceived by; be visible or audible to: *There is more to this matter than meets the eye.* 9 satisfy; fulfill: *meet one's needs, meet obligations.* 10 pay when due; settle: *meet bills, meet debts.* 11 fight with; deal with; oppose: *meet an enemy in battle, meet threats with defiance.* 12 face directly: *He met her*

glance with a smile. 13 experience: *He met open scorn before he won fame.* 14 **meet with,** **a** come across; light upon: *We met with bad weather.* **b** have; get: *The plan met with approval.* —*v.i.* 1 come face to face: *Their cars met on the narrow road.* 2 assemble: *Congress will meet next month.* 3 come into contact; come together; join: *where the two streets meet.* 4 be united; join in harmony: *His is a nature in which courage and caution meet.*
—*n.* 1 a meeting; gathering: *an athletic meet.* 2 the people at a meeting. 3 the place of meeting.
[Old English *mētan* < *mōt* meeting]

megalith—megaliths at Stonehenge

meet² (mēt), *adj.* ARCHAIC. 1 fitting; becoming. 2 suitable; proper. [Old English *(ge)mǣte*]

meet ing (mē′ting), *n.* 1 a coming together: *a meeting of minds, a chance meeting with an old friend.* 2 an assembly of people for religious worship: *a Quaker meeting.* 3 a gathering or assembly of people for any of various purposes. See synonym study below. 4 place where things meet; junction: *a meeting of roads.*
Syn. 3 **Meeting, assembly, gathering** mean a coming together of a group of people. **Meeting** applies especially when the purpose is to discuss or arrange business or action: *The club held a meeting.* **Assembly** often applies when the purpose is less explicit but suggests that the occasion is rather formal: *The principal called an assembly.* **Gathering** suggests that the occasion is less formal or organized and that it may be for social pleasure: *There was a large gathering at her house.*

meet ing house (mē′ting hous′), *n., pl.* **-hous es** (-hou′ziz). 1 building used for worship in the Quaker fashion. 2 any place of worship; church.

meet ly (mēt′lē), *adv.* in a meet manner; suitably; properly.

mega-, *combining form.* 1 large: *Megaspore = large spore.* 2 one million: *Megacycle = one million cycles.* [< Greek *megas, megalou* great]

meg a cy cle (meg′ə sī′kəl), *n.* 1 one million cycles in radio. 2 one million cycles per second, used formerly to express the frequency of radio waves, now expressed in megahertz.

meg a death (meg′ə deth′), *n.* the death of one million persons, such as could result from nuclear warfare.

meg a gam ete (meg′ə gam′ēt, meg′ə gə-mēt′), *n.* macrogamete.

meg a hertz (meg′ə hėrts′), *n.* unit of frequency equal to one million hertz, used to express the frequency of radio waves.

meg a lith (meg′ə lith), *n.* stone of great size, especially in ancient constructive work or in monuments left by people of prehistoric times.

meg a lo ma ni a (meg′ə lō mā′nē ə), *n.* a mental disorder marked by delusions of great personal power, importance, wealth, etc. [< Greek *megas, megalou* great + *mania* madness]

meg a lo ma ni ac (meg′ə lō mā′nē ak), *n.* person who has megalomania. —*adj.* megalomaniacal.

meg a lo ma ni a cal (meg′ə lō mə nī′ə-kəl), *adj.* of, having to do with, or afflicted with megalomania.

meg a lop o lis (meg′ə lop′ə lis), *n.* 1 a large metropolis. 2 a large metropolitan area, often including several cities. [< Greek *megas, megalou* great + *polis* city]

meg a phone (meg′ə fōn), *n.* a large, funnel-shaped horn or similar device, used to increase the loudness of the voice or the distance at which it can be heard.

meg a spore (meg′ə spôr, meg′ə spōr), *n.* an asexually produced spore of comparatively large size from which the female gametophyte develops in certain ferns.

meg a ton (meg′ə tun′), *n.* 1 unit of weight equal to one million tons. 2 unit of atomic power equivalent to the energy released by one million tons of TNT.

Me gid do (mə gid′ō), *n.* city in ancient Palestine. Armageddon in the Bible probably refers to Megiddo.

meg ohm (meg′ōm′), *n.* unit of electrical resistance equal to one million ohms.

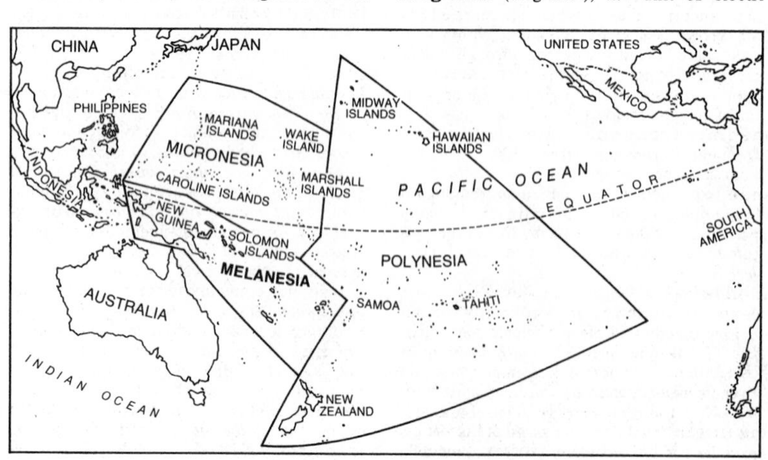

me grim (mē′grim), *n.* 1 migraine. 2 a passing fancy; whim. 3 **megrims,** *pl.* morbid low spirits. [variant of *migraine;* influenced by *grim*]

mei o sis (mī ō′sis), *n., pl.* **-ses** (-sēz′). (in biology) the process by which the number of chromosomes in reproductive cells of sexually reproducing organisms is reduced to half the original number, resulting in the production of gametes or spores; reduction division. [< Greek *meiōsis* a lessening < *meioun* lessen < *meion* less]

mei ot ic (mī ot′ik), *adj.* of or having to do with meiosis.

Me ir (me ir′), *n.* **Golda,** born 1898, prime minister of Israel since 1969.

Meit ner (mīt′nər), *n.* **Lise,** 1878-1968, Austrian nuclear physicist.

Meis ter sing er (mī′stər sing′ər; *German* mī′stər zing′ər), *n.* member of one of the guilds, chiefly of workingmen, established in the principal German cities during the 1300's, 1400's, and 1500's for the cultivation of poetry and music. [< German, literally, master singer]

Mé ji co (me′hē kō), *n.* Spanish name of **Mexico.**

Mek ka (mek′ə), *n.* Mecca.

Me kong River (mā′kong′), river flowing from E Tibet through S China and Indochina. 2600 mi.

mel a mine (mel′ə mēn′, mel′ə mən), *n.* a white, crystalline substance that reacts with formaldehyde to form a group of resins which are used for coatings, insulators, plastics, etc. *Formula:* $C_3N_3(NH_2)_3$

mel an cho li a (mel′ən kō′lē ə), *n.* a mental disorder characterized by great depression of spirits and activity, and gloomy thoughts and fears often accompanied by vivid delusions.

mel an chol ic (mel′ən kol′ik), *adj.* 1 emotionally depressed; melancholy; gloomy. 2 having to do with, like, or suffering from melancholia. **—mel′an chol′i cal ly,** *adv.*

mel an chol y (mel′ən kol′ē), *n., pl.* **-chol ies,** *adj.* —*n.* 1 condition of sadness and low spirits; gloominess; dejection. 2 sober thoughtfulness; pensiveness. —*adj.* 1 depressed in spirits; sad; gloomy. 2 causing sadness; depressing: *a melancholy scene.* 3 lamentable; deplorable: *a melancholy fact.* 4 soberly thoughtful; pensive. [< Greek *melancholia* < *melanos* black + *cholē* bile (see HUMOR, 6)]

Me lanch thon (mə langk′thən), *n.* **Philipp,** 1497-1560, German theologian, religious reformer, and educator.

Mel a ne sia (mel′ə nē′zhə, mel′ə nē′shə), *n.* group of islands in the Pacific, northeast of Australia. **—Mel′a ne′sian,** *adj., n.*

mé lange (mā länzh′; *Anglicized* mā länj′), *n.* FRENCH. a heterogeneous mixture; medley.

mel a nin (mel′ə nən), *n.* any of a class of dark-brown or black pigments occurring in the skin, hair, or retina of human beings and many animals. [< Greek *melanos* black]

mel a nism (mel′ə niz′əm), *n.* darkness of color resulting from an abnormal development of melanin in the skin, hair, and eyes of a human being, or in the skin, coat, plumage, etc., of an animal.

mel a no ma (mel′ə nō′mə), *n., pl.* **-mas, -ma ta** (-mə tə). a dark-colored or blackish tumor arising in the skin or in the pigmented layers of the eye.

Mel ba toast (mel′bə), a very thin, crisp toast. [< Dame Nellie *Melba,* 1861-1931, Australian soprano]

Mel bourne (mel′bərn), *n.* seaport in SE Australia. 2,372,700.

meld (meld), *v.t., v.i.* announce and show (cards for a score) in rummy, canasta, pinochle, etc. *—n.* 1 act of melding. 2 any grouping of cards which can be melded. [< German *melden* announce]

Mel e a ger (mel′ē ā′jər), *n.* (in Greek legends) the hero who killed the Calydonian boar. He was one of the Argonauts.

me lee or **mê lée** (mā′lā, mā lā′), *n.* a confused fight; hand-to-hand fight among a number of fighters. [< French *mêlée* (in Old French *meslee*). Doublet of MEDLEY.]

mel io rate (mē′lyə rāt′, mē′lē ə rāt′), *v.t., v.i.,* **-rat ed, -rat ing.** improve; ameliorate. [< Latin *melior* better] **—mel′io ra′tion,** *n.* **—mel′io ra′tor,** *n.*

mel io ra tive (mē′lyə rā′tiv, mē′lē ə rā′-tiv), *adj.* improving.

mel lif lu ence (mə lif′lü əns), *n.* sweet sound; smooth flow.

mel lif lu ent (mə lif′lü ənt), *adj.* mellifluous. **—mel lif′lu ent ly,** *adv.*

mel lif lu ous (mə lif′lü əs), *adj.* sweetly or smoothly flowing: *a mellifluous speech.* [< Late Latin *mellifluus* < Latin *mel* honey + *fluere* to flow] **—mel lif′lu ous ly,** *adv.* **—mel lif′lu ous ness,** *n.*

mel low (mel′ō), *adj.* 1 soft and full-flavored from ripeness; sweet and juicy: *a mellow apple.* 2 fully matured: *mellow wine.* 3 soft and rich; full and pure without harshness: *a violin with a mellow tone, a mellow color.* 4 soft, rich, and loamy: *mellow soil.* 5 softened and made wise by age or experience. *—v.t., v.i.* make or become mellow. [Middle English *melwe*] **—mel′low ly,** *adv.* **—mel′low ness,** *n.*

me lo de on (mə lō′dē ən), *n.* a small reed organ in which air is sucked inward by a bellows.

me lod ic (mə lod′ik), *adj.* 1 having to do with melody. 2 melodious. **—me lod′i cal ly,** *adv.*

me lo di ous (mə lō′dē əs), *adj.* 1 sweet-sounding; pleasing to the ear; musical; melodic; harmonious: *melodious verse.* 2 producing melody; singing sweetly: *melodious birds.* 3 having a melody; having to do with or of the nature of melody. **—me lo′di ous ly,** *adv.* **—me lo′di ous ness,** *n.*

mel o dist (mel′ə dist), *n.* composer or singer of melodies.

mel o dra ma (mel′ə drä′mə, mel′ə-dram′ə), *n.* 1 a sensational drama with exaggerated appeal to the emotions and, usually, a happy ending. 2 any sensational writing, speech, or action with exaggerated appeal to the emotions. [< French *mélodrame* < Greek *melos* music + *drama* drama]

mel o dra mat ic (mel′ə drə mat′ik), *adj.* of, like, or suitable for melodrama; sensational and exaggerated. See **dramatic** for synonym study. *—n.* **melodramatics,** *pl.* melodramatic actions. **—mel′o dra mat′i cal ly,** *adv.*

mel o dy (mel′ə dē), *n., pl.* **-dies.** 1 musical sounds in agreeable succession or arrangement; sweet music; any sweet sound. 2 succession of single tones in musical composition, as distinguished from harmony and rhythm; tune. 3 the main tune in harmonized music; air; theme. [< Late Latin *melodia* < Greek *meloidia,* ultimately < *melos* song, melody + *ōidē* song]

mel on (mel′ən), *n.* the large, juicy fruit of any of several vines of the gourd family. Watermelons, canteloupes, muskmelons, and honeydew melons are different kinds. [< Late Latin *melonem,* short for Latin *melopeponem* < Greek *mēlopepōn* < *mēlon* apple + *pepōn* gourd] **—mel′on like′,** *adj.*

Mel pom e ne (mel pom′ə nē), *n.* (in Greek myths) the Muse of tragedy.

melt (melt), *v.,* **melt ed, melt ed** or **mol ten, melt ing,** *n. —v.t.* 1 change from solid to liquid by the application of heat: *Great heat melts iron.* 2 dissolve: *melt sugar in water.* See synonym study below. 3 cause to disappear gradually; disperse: *The noon sun will melt away the fog.* 4 change very gradually; blend; merge: *Dusk melted the colors of the hill into a soft gray.* 5 make tender or gentle; soften: *Pity melted her heart. —v.i.* 1 be changed from solid to liquid by the application of heat. 2 dissolve: *Sugar melts in water.* 3 disappear gradually: *The clouds melted away, and the sun came out. The crowd melted away.* 4 blend; merge: *In the rainbow, the green melts into blue, the blue into violet.* 5 be made gentle; soften. *—n.* 1 a melted metal. 2 a quantity of metal melted at one operation or over a specified period. [Old English *meltan*] **—melt′a ble,** *adj.* **—melt′er,** *n.*

Syn. *v.t.* 1, 2 **Melt, dissolve, thaw, fuse** mean to change from a solid state. **Melt** either suggests a gradual change caused by heat, by which a solid softens, loses shape, and finally becomes liquid *(The warm air melted the butter)* or the change of a solid going into solution in a liquid composed of another substance and becoming a part of it *(The lump of sugar melted in the cup of coffee).* **Dissolve** also has both these meanings, although the second is far more frequent: *The candle dissolved into a pool of wax as it burned. Dissolve some salt in a glass of water.* **Thaw,** used only of frozen things, means to change to the unfrozen state, either liquid or less hard and stiff: *thaw frozen fruit.* **Fuse** means to reduce a solid substance to a fluid state by subjecting it to a high temperature and is used especially of the blending together of metals into a combination which persists when they again solidify: *fuse copper and tin.*

melt a bil i ty (mel′tə bil′ə tē), *n.* capacity of being melted.

melting point, temperature at which a solid substance melts.

melting pot, 1 country or city thought of as a place in which various races or sorts of people are assimilated. America has often been called a melting pot. 2 pot in which metals, etc., are melted.

mel ton (melt′n), *n.* a smooth, heavy woolen cloth, used especially for overcoats. [< *Melton* Mowbray, town in central England]

Mel ville (mel′vil), *n.* **Herman,** 1819-1891, American novelist.

mem ber (mem′bər), *n.* 1 person, animal, or thing belonging to a group: *a member of Congress, a member of the cat family.* 2 a constituent part of a whole; component. 3 part or organ of an animal, human body, or plant, especially a leg, arm, wing, or branch. 4 in mathematics: **a** a quantity that belongs to a set; element of a set. **b** expression on either side of an equation. [< Latin *membrum*]

mem ber ship (mem′bər ship), *n.* 1 fact or state of being a member. 2 members as a group. 3 number of members in a particular body.

hat, āge, fär; let, ēqual, tėrm;
it, īce; hot, ōpen, ôrder;
oil, out; cup, pu̇t, rüle;
ch, child; ng, long; sh, she;
th, thin; ᴛʜ, then; zh, measure;

ə represents *a* in about, *e* in taken, *i* in pencil, *o* in lemon, *u* in circus.

< = from, derived from, taken from.

mem brane (mem′brān), *n.* 1 a thin, soft, pliable sheet or layer of animal tissue lining, covering, separating, or connecting some part of the body. 2 a similar layer of vegetable tissue. [< Latin *membrana* < *membrum* member]

mem bra nous (mem′brə nəs, mem brā′-nəs), *adj.* 1 of or like membrane. 2 characterized by the formation of a membrane or a layer like a membrane. In **membranous croup,** a deposit similar to a membrane forms in the throat and hinders breathing.

Me mel (mā′məl), *n.* seaport in NW Soviet Union, on the Baltic Sea. 115,000.

me men to (mə men′tō), *n., pl.* **-tos** or **-toes.** something serving as a reminder of what is past or gone; souvenir: *These post cards are mementos of our trip abroad.* [< Latin, remember!]

me men to mo ri (mə men′tō môr′ī, mə-men′tō mōr′ī), object such as a skull, used as a reminder of death or mortality. [< Latin, remember that you must die]

mem o (mem′ō), *n., pl.* **mem os.** INFORMAL. memorandum.

mem oir (mem′wär, mem′wôr), *n.* 1 biography or biographical note. 2 report of a scientific or scholarly study made to a learned society. 3 **memoirs,** *pl.* **a** record of facts and events written from personal knowledge or special information. **b** record of a person's own life and experiences; autobiography. [< French *mémoire* < Latin *memoria.* Doublet of MEMORY.]

mem or a bil i a (mem′ər ə bil′ē ə), *n.pl.* 1 things or events worth remembering. 2 account of such things. [< Latin, plural of *memorabilis* memorable]

mem or a ble (mem′ər ə bəl), *adj.* worth remembering; not to be forgotten; notable. **—mem′or a ble ness,** *n.* **—mem′or a bly,** *adv.*

mem o ran dum (mem′ə ran′dəm), *n., pl.* **-dums, -da** (-də). 1 a short written statement for future use; note to aid one's memory. 2 an informal letter, note, or report. 3 (in law) a writing containing the terms of a transaction. [< Latin, (thing) to be remembered]

me mo ri al (mə môr′ē əl, mə mōr′ē əl), *n.* 1 something that is a reminder of some event or person, such as a statue, an arch or column, a book, or a holiday. 2 statement sent to a government or person in authority, usually giving facts and asking that some wrong be corrected. *—adj.* helping people to remember some person, thing, or event; commemorative: *memorial services.*

Memorial Day, day for honoring the American servicemen who have died for their country, observed by decorating their graves and memorials; Decoration Day. It is a legal holiday, observed in most states on the last Monday in May.

me mo ri al ize (mə môr′ē ə līz, mə mōr′ē-ə līz), *v.t.*, **-ized, -iz ing.** 1 preserve the memory of; commemorate. 2 submit a memorial to; petition.

mem o rize (mem′ə rīz′), *v.t.*, **-rized, -riz ing.** commit to memory; learn by heart. **—mem′or i za′tion,** *n.* **—mem′o riz′-er,** *n.*

mem or y (mem′ər ē), *n., pl.* **-or ies.** 1 ability to remember; capacity to retain or recall that which is learned, experienced, etc. 2 act or fact of remembering; remembrance; recollection: *the memory of things past.* See synonym study below. 3 person, thing, or event that is remembered: *His childhood is now only a vague memory.* 4 all that a person remembers; what can be recalled to mind: *examine one's memory carefully.* 5 the length of time during which the past is remembered: *This has been the hottest summer within my memory.* 6 system of storing information in a computer on magnetic tape, etc. 7 **in memory of,** to help in remembering; as a reminder of. [< Old French *memorie,* < Latin *memoria* < *memor* mindful. Doublet of MEMOIR.]

Syn. 2 **Memory, recollection** mean the act or fact of remembering. **Memory** emphasizes keeping in mind something once learned or experienced: *Her memory of the incident is still fresh.* **Recollection** emphasizes calling back to mind, often with effort, something not thought of for a long time: *I have little recollection of my childhood.*

Mem phis (mem′fis), *n.* 1 city in SW Tennessee, on the Mississippi. 624,000. 2 city in ancient Egypt.

mem sa hib (mem′sä′ib, mem′sä′hib), *n.* (in colonial India) a term of respect for a European woman, used by native servants. [< Hindustani *mem-sāhib* < *mem* (< English *ma'am*) + *sāhib* master]

men (men), *n.* 1 pl. of **man.** 2 human beings; people in general.

men ace (men′is), *n., v.,* **-aced, -ac ing.** —*n.* something that threatens; threat: *In dry weather forests fires are a menace.* —*v.t.* offer a menace to; threaten: *Floods menaced the valley with destruction.* See **threaten** for synonym study. —*v.i.* be threatening. [< Middle French < Latin *minaciae* (plural), ultimately < *minae* projecting points, threats] **—men′ac ing ly,** *adv.*

me nad (mē′nad), *n.* maenad.

mé nage or **me nage** (mā näzh′), *n.* 1 a domestic establishment; household. 2 management of a household. [< French]

me nag er ie (mə naj′ər ē, mə nazh′ər ē), *n.* 1 collection of wild or strange animals kept in cages or enclosures, especially for exhibition, as in a zoo or a circus. 2 place where such animals are kept. [< French *ménagerie,* literally, management of a household]

Men ci us (men′shē əs), *n.* 372?-289 B.C., Chinese philosopher.

Menck en (meng′kən), *n.* **H(enry) L(ouis),** 1880-1956, American critic and editor.

mend (mend), *v.t.* 1 put in good condition again; make whole or serviceable; repair (something broken, worn, or otherwise damaged): *mend a road, mend clothes.* See synonym study below. 2 remove or correct faults in; set right; improve: *He should mend his manners.* —*v.i.* 1 get back one's health; recover from illness, injury, etc. 2 become better; improve: *There is no prospect of matters mending.* —*n.* 1 place that has been mended. 2 a mending; improvement. 3 **on the mend, a** improving. **b** getting well. [Middle English *menden,* variant of *amenden* amend] **—mend′er,** *n.*

Syn. *v.t.* 1 **Mend, repair, patch** mean to put in good or usable condition again. **Mend** means to restore something that has been broken, torn, or worn, but is now seldom used of large things: *She mended the broken cup with cement.* **Repair** means to correct something damaged, run down, decayed, or weakened: *He repaired the old barn.* **Patch** means to mend by putting a piece (or amount) of material on or in a hole, tear, or worn place: *His mother patched his torn trousers.*

men da cious (men dā′shəs), *adj.* 1 given to telling lies; lying; untruthful. 2 false; untrue. [< Latin *mendacem* lying] **—men-da′cious ly,** *adv.* **—men da′cious ness,** *n.*

men dac i ty (men das′ə tē), *n., pl.* **-ties.** 1 habit of telling lies; untruthfulness. 2 a lie; falsehood.

Men del (men′dl), *n.* **Gregor Johann,** 1822-1884, Austrian botanist and monk, whose investigations of heredity laid the foundations for the science of genetics.

Men de le ev (men′dl ā′ef), *n.* **Dmitri Ivanovich,** 1834-1907, Russian chemist who devised the periodic table.

men de le vi um (men′dl ē′vē əm), *n.* a rare, radioactive, metallic element, produced artificially from einsteinium. *Symbol:* Mv or Md; *atomic number* 101. See pages 326 and 327 for table. [< D.I. *Mendeleev*]

Men de li an (men dē′lē ən), *adj.* 1 of or having to do with Mendel. 2 inherited in accordance with Mendel's laws. —*n.* follower of Mendel or supporter of his theories.

Mendel's laws, laws governing the inheritance of certain characteristics by plants and animals, formulated by Mendel. They state that each characteristic is inherited independently, that characteristics show dominant and recessive forms, and that successive generations of crossbred offspring exhibit inherited characteristics in different combinations, each combination in a specific proportion of individuals.

Men dels sohn (men′dl sən, men′dl sōn), *n.* **Felix,** 1809-1847, German composer.

men di can cy (men′də kən sē), *n.* 1 act of begging. 2 state of being a beggar.

men di cant (men′də kənt), *adj.* begging. Mendicant friars ask alms for charity. —*n.* 1 beggar. 2 member of a mendicant religious order. [< Latin *mendicantem* < *mendicus* beggar]

men dic i ty (men dis′ə tē), *n.* mendicancy.

Men e la us (men′ə lā′əs), *n.* (in Greek legends) a king of Sparta, husband of Helen, and brother of Agamemnon.

men folk (men′fōk′), *n.pl.* 1 men. 2 the male members of a family or other group.

men folks (men′fōks′), *n.pl.* menfolk.

men ha den (men hād′n), *n., pl.* **-den.** a marine fish of the same family as the herring, common along the eastern coast of the United States, used for making oil and fertilizer; pogy. [< Algonquian]

me ni al (mē′nē əl, mē′nyəl), *adj.* suited to or belonging to a servant; low; mean; servile. —*n.* servant who does the humblest and most unpleasant tasks. [< Anglo-French < *meinée,* variant of Old French *meisniee* household] **—me′ni al ly,** *adv.*

me nin ge al (mə nin′jē əl), *adj.* of or having to do with the meninges.

me nin ges (mə nin′jēz), *n.* pl. of **meninx** (mē′ningks). the three protective membranes that surround the brain and spinal cord. [< New Latin < Greek *mēningos* membrane]

men in gi tis (men′in jī′tis), *n.* inflammation of the meninges, usually caused by a bacterium or virus, resulting in acute, sometimes fatal, illness.

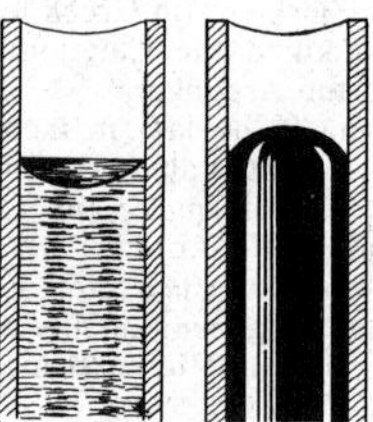

meniscus (def. 1) left, concave right, convex

me nis cus (mə nis′kəs), *n., pl.* **-nis cus es, -nis ci** (-nis′ī). 1 the curved upper surface of a column of liquid. It is concave when the walls of the container are moistened, convex when they are dry. 2 lens that is convex on one side and concave on the other. 3 a crescent or crescent-shaped body. [< New Latin < Greek *mēniskos,* diminutive of *mēnē* moon]

Men non ite (men′ə nīt), *n.* member of a Christian church opposed to infant baptism, taking oaths, holding public office, and military service. The Mennonites often wear very plain clothes and live simply. [< *Menno* Simons of Friesland, 1492-1559, leader of the original church]

men-of-war (men′əv wôr′), *n.* pl. of **man-of-war.**

Me nom i nee (mə nom′ə nē), *n., pl.* **-nees** or **-nee** for 1. 1 member of a tribe of Indians living in Wisconsin and northern Illinois, of Algonquian stock. 2 language of this tribe.

men o pause (men′ə pôz), *n.* the final cessation of the menses, occurring normally between the ages of 45 and 50; change of life. [< Greek *mēnos* month + *pausis* pause]

menorah—The center candle is used to light one candle on each of the eight days of Hanukkah.

me no rah (mə nôr′ə, mə nōr′ə), *n.* candlestick with eight branches used during the Jewish festival of Hanukkah. [< Hebrew *menōrāh*]

Me nor ca (mā nôr′kä), *n.* Spanish name of **Minorca.**

Me not ti (mə not′ē; *Italian* mə nôt′tē), *n.* **Gian Carlo,** born 1911, American composer of operas, born in Italy.

men serv ants (men′sėr′vənts), *n.* pl. of **manservant.**

men ses (men′sēz′), *n.pl.* discharge of bloody fluid from the uterus that normally occurs approximately every four weeks between puberty and the menopause. [< Latin, plural of *mensis* month]

Men she vik (men′shə vik), *n., pl.* **Men she viks, Men she vi ki** (men′shə vē′kē). member of the less radical wing of the Russian Social Democratic Party, opposed to the Bolsheviks from 1903 to 1917. [< Russian *men'shevik* < *men'shij* lesser; with reference to their temporary minority within the party in 1903]

Men she vism (men′shə viz′əm), *n.* doctrines or principles of the Mensheviks.

Men she vist (men′shə vist), *n.* a Menshevik. *—adj.* of the Mensheviks or Menshevism.

men stru al (men′strü əl), *adj.* 1 of or having to do with the menses. 2 monthly. [< Latin *menstruus* < *mensis* month]

men stru ate (men′strü āt), *v.i.,* **-at ed, -at ing.** have a discharge of bloody fluid from the uterus, normally at intervals of approximately four weeks.

men stru a tion (men′strü ā′shən), *n.* act or period of menstruating.

men stru um (men′strü əm), *n., pl.* **-stru ums, -stru a** (-strü ə). ARCHAIC. any liquid substance that dissolves a solid; solvent. [< Medieval Latin]

men sur a bil i ty (men′shər ə bil′ə tē), *n.* property of being mensurable.

men sur a ble (men′shər ə bəl), *adj.* measurable.

men su ra tion (men′shə rā′shən), *n.* 1 act, art, or process of measuring. 2 branch of mathematics that deals with finding measurements, as lengths, areas, and volumes. [< Late Latin *mensurationem,* ultimately < Latin *mensura.* See MEASURE.]

-ment, *suffix added to verbs to form nouns.* 1 act, process, or fact of ___ing: *Enjoyment = act of enjoying.* 2 condition of being ___ed: *Amazement = condition of being amazed.* 3 product or result of ___ing: *Pavement = product of paving.* 4 means of or instrument for ___ing: *Inducement = means of inducing.* [< French < Latin *-mentum* result of]

men tal (men′tl), *adj.* 1 of the mind: *a mental test, a mental disease.* 2 for the mind: *a mental reminder.* 3 done by or existing in the mind: *mental arithmetic.* 4 having a mental disease or weakness: *a mental patient.* 5 for people having mental disease: *a mental hospital.* [< Late Latin *mentalis* < Latin *mentem,* mind]

mental age, a measure of the level of a person's mental development (as determined by intelligence tests) stated as the chronological age at which this level is most common.

men tal i ty (men tal′ə tē), *n., pl.* **-ties.** 1 mental capacity; intellectual ability; mind: *An idiot has a very low mentality.* 2 attitude or outlook: *a childish mentality.*

men tal ly (men′tl ē), *adv.* 1 in or with the mind. 2 with regard to the mind: *mentally unbalanced.*

men thol (men′thôl, men′thol), *n.* a white, crystalline substance used in medicine and obtained from oil of peppermint or by synthesis. *Formula:* $C_{10}H_{19}OH$ [< German *Menthol* < Latin *menta* mint + *oleum* oil]

men tho lat ed (men′thə lā′tid), *adj.* 1 containing menthol. 2 treated with menthol.

men tion (men′shən), *v.t.* 1 speak about; refer to. **2 not to mention,** not even considering; besides. *—n.* 1 a short statement about something; reference; mentioning. **2 make mention of,** speak of; refer to. [< Old French < Latin *mentionem* < *mentem* mind] **—men′tion a ble,** *adj.* **—men′tion er,** *n.*

Men tor (men′tər), *n.* 1 (in Greek legends) a faithful friend of Ulysses. He was the teacher and adviser of Ulysses' son Telemachus until Ulysses returned from the Trojan War. **2 mentor,** a wise and trusted adviser.

men u (men′yü, mā′nyü), *n.* 1 list of the food served at a meal; bill of fare. 2 the food served. [< French, small, detailed < Latin *minutum* made small. Doublet of MINUTE[2].]

me ow (mē ou′), *n.* sound made by a cat or kitten. *—v.i.* make this sound. Also, **miaow, miaou.** [imitative]

Meph is to phe le an (mef′ə stə fē′lē ən), *adj.* Mephistophelian.

Meph i stoph e les (mef′ə stof′ə lēz′), *n.* 1 one of the chief evil spirits of medieval European demonology, especially the devil of the Faust legend. 2 a powerful evil spirit; crafty devil.

Meph is to phe li an (mef′ə stə fē′lē ən), *adj.* 1 like Mephistopheles; wicked and crafty; sardonic; scoffing. 2 of or having to do with Mephistopheles.

me phit ic (mi fit′ik), *adj.* 1 having a nasty smell. 2 noxious; poisonous; pestilential. [< Latin *mephitis* stench]

me pro ba mate (mə prō′bə māt), *n.* a synthetic drug widely used as a tranquilizer. *Formula:* $C_9H_{18}N_2O_4$

mer., meridian.

mer can tile (mėr′kən til, mėr′kən tīl), *adj.* 1 of or having to do with merchants or trade; commercial: *a mercantile firm, mercantile law.* 2 of or having to do with mercantilism. [< French < Italian < *mercante* merchant, ultimately < Latin *merx, mercis* wares]

mer can til ism (mėr′kən ti liz′əm, mėr′kən tī liz′əm), *n.* the economic system of Europe in the 1500's and 1600's, which favored a balance of exports of commodities over imports and regulated a nation's agriculture, industry, and trade with that end in view.

mer can til ist (mėr′kən ti list, mėr′kən tī list), *n.* person who favors mercantilism.

mer can ti lis tic (mėr′kən ti lis′tik, mėr′kən tī lis′tik), *adj.* of or having to do with mercantilism or mercantilists.

Mer ca tor (mər kā′tər), *n.* **Gerhardus,** 1512-1594, Flemish cartographer.

Mercator projection, method of drawing maps with parallel straight lines instead of curved lines for latitude and longitude. The latitudes increase in distance from each other as they approach the poles. [< *Mercator*]

mer ce nar y (mėr′sə ner′ē), *adj., n., pl.* **-nar ies.** *—adj.* 1 working for money only; acting with money as the motive; hireling. 2 done for money or gain. *—n.* 1 soldier serving for pay in a foreign army. 2 person who works merely for pay. [< Latin *mercenarius* < *merces* wages < *merx, mercis* wares] **—mer′ce nar′i ly,** *adv.* **—mer′ce nar′i ness,** *n.*

mer cer (mėr′sər), *n.* dealer in textile fabrics. [< Old French *mercier,* ultimately < Latin *merx, mercis* wares]

mer cer ize (mėr′sə rīz′), *v.t.,* **-ized, -iz ing.** treat (cotton thread or cloth) with a chemical solution that strengthens the cotton, makes it hold dyes better, and gives it a silky luster. [< John *Mercer,* 1791-1866, English calico printer who patented the process]

mer chan dise (mėr′chən dīz), *n., v.,* **-dised, -dis ing.** *—n.* goods for sale; articles bought and sold; wares. *—v.t., v.i.* 1 buy and sell; trade. 2 further the sales of (goods and services) by advertising and other methods. **—mer′chan dis′er,** *n.*

hat, āge, fär; let, ēqual, tėrm;
it, īce; hot, ōpen, ôrder;
oil, out; cup, pu̇t, rüle;
ch, child; ng, long; sh, she;
th, thin; ᴛʜ, then; zh, measure;

ə represents *a* in about, *e* in taken, *i* in pencil, *o* in lemon, *u* in circus.

< = from, derived from, taken from.

mer chant (mėr′chənt), *n.* 1 person who buys and sells commodities for profit, now especially on a relatively large scale. 2 storekeeper; retail shopkeeper. *—adj.* 1 of or having to do with the merchant marine: *a merchant seaman.* 2 of or having to do with trade; trading; commercial: *merchant ships.* [< Old French *marchëant,* ultimately < Latin *merx, mercis* wares]

mer chant a ble (mėr′chən tə bəl), *adj.* marketable; salable.

mer chant man (mėr′chənt mən), *n., pl.* **-men.** ship used in commerce.

merchant marine, 1 the trading vessels of a nation; ships used in commerce. 2 body of officers and sailors who serve on such ships.

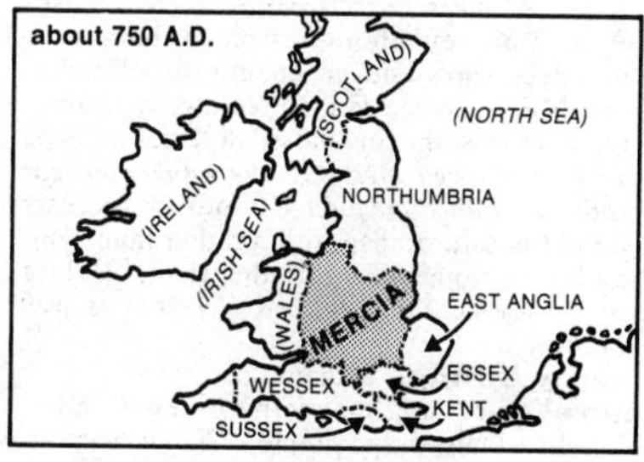

Mer cia (mėr′shə, mėr′shē ə), *n.* ancient Anglo-Saxon kingdom in central England. **—Mer′cian,** *adj., n.*

Mer cier (mer syā′), *n.* **Désiré Joseph,** 1851-1926, Belgian cardinal and patriot.

mer ci ful (mėr′si fəl), *adj.* having, showing, or feeling mercy; full of mercy; compassionate; clement. **—mer′ci ful ly,** *adv.* **—mer′ci ful ness,** *n.*

mer ci less (mėr′si lis), *adj.* without mercy; having or showing no mercy; pitiless; ruthless. **—mer′ci less ly,** *adv.* **mer′ci less ness,** *n.*

mer cur i al (mər kyu̇r′ē əl), *adj.* 1 sprightly and animated; quick. 2 changeable; fickle. 3 caused by the use of mercury: *mercurial poisoning.* 4 containing mercury. *—n.* drug containing mercury. **—mer cur′i al ly,** *adv.* **—mer cur′i al ness,** *n.*

mer cur ic (mər kyu̇r′ik), *adj.* 1 of mercury. 2 (of compounds) containing mercury, especially with a valence of two.

mercuric chloride, an extremely poisonous white substance, used in taxidermy and in metallurgy, and formerly used in solution as an oral medication; corrosive sublimate; bichloride of mercury. *Formula:* $HgCl_2$

Mer cur o chrome (mər kyu̇r′ə krōm′), *n.* trademark for a red solution containing a compound of mercury, used externally as an antiseptic.

mer cur ous (mər kyůr′əs, mėr′kyůr əs), *adj.* 1 of mercury. 2 (of compounds) containing mercury, especially with a valence of one.

mercurous chloride, calomel.

mer cur y (mėr′kyər ē), *n., pl.* **-cur ies.** 1 a heavy, silver-white metallic element that is liquid at ordinary temperatures; quicksilver. It occurs naturally in the mineral cinnabar and combines with most other metals to form amalgams. *Symbol:* Hg; *atomic number* 80. See pages 326 and 327 for table. 2 column of mercury in a thermometer or barometer. 3 **Mercury,** (in Roman myths) the messenger of the gods, the god of commerce, of skill of hands, quickness of wit, eloquence, and thievery, indentified with the Greek god Hermes. 4 **Mercury,** the smallest planet in the solar system and the one nearest to the sun. See **solar system** for diagram. [< Latin *Mercurius* (definition 3)]

mer cy (mėr′sē), *n., pl.* **-cies.** 1 more kindness than justice requires; kindness beyond what can be claimed or expected. See synonym study below. 2 kindly treatment; pity: *deeds of mercy.* 3 something to be thankful for; blessing: *It's a mercy that you weren't injured in the accident.* 4 **at the mercy of,** in the power of: *at the mercy of the elements.* [< Old French *merci* < Latin *merces* reward, wages < *merx, mercis* wares, merchandise]

Syn. 1 **Mercy, clemency** mean kindness or mildness shown to an enemy, an offender, etc. **Mercy** suggests kind feeling, sympathy, or compassion for those in trouble: *The women showed mercy to the hungry beggar and gave him some food.* **Clemency** suggests a mild nature or disposition rather than sympathy in someone with the right or duty to be severe: *That judge's clemency is well known.*

mercy killing, euthanasia.

mere[1] (mir), *adj., superlative* **mer est.** nothing else than; only; simple: *The cut was the merest scratch.* [< Latin *merus* pure, unmixed]

mere[2] (mir), *n.* ARCHAIC. lake or pond. [Old English, body of water]

-mere, *combining form.* part; division; segment, as in *metamere.* [< Greek *meres*]

Mer e dith (mer′ə dith), *n.* **George,** 1828-1909, English novelist and poet.

mere ly (mir′lē), *adv.* and nothing more; and that is all; simply; only.

mer e tri cious (mer′ə trish′əs), *adj.* attractive in a showy way; alluring by false charms: *meretricious advertising.* [< Latin *meretricius* < *meretrix* prostitute < *mereri* earn] **—mer′e tri′cious ly,** *adv.* **—mer′e-tri′cious ness,** *n.*

mer gan ser (mər gan′sər), *n., pl.* **-sers** or **-ser.** any of several kinds of large, fish-eating ducks with long, slender bills which are hooked at the tip; sheldrake. They often have crested heads. [< Latin *mergus* diver + *anser* goose]

merge (mėrj), *v.,* **merged, merg ing.** *—v.t.* cause to be swallowed up or absorbed so as to lose its own character or identity; combine or consolidate: *The steel trusts merged various small businesses.* *—v.i.* become swallowed up or absorbed so as to lose its own character or identity: *The twilight merges into darkness.* [< Latin *mergere* to dip]

merg er (mėr′jər), *n.* a merging or a being merged; absorption; combination; consolidation: *One big company was formed by the merger of four small ones.*

Mé ri da (mā′rē dä), *n.* city in SE Mexico. 254,000.

meridian (def. 2) meridians of longitude

me rid i an (mə rid′ē ən), *n.* 1 an imaginary great circle passing through any place on the earth's surface and through the North and South Poles. 2 the half of such a circle from pole to pole. All the places on the same meridian have the same longitude. 3 the highest point or period of highest development or perfection; culmination. *—adj.* highest; greatest. [< Latin *meridianus* of noon < *meridies* noon, south < *medius* middle + *dies* day]

me rid i o nal (mə rid′ē ə nəl), *adj.* 1 having to do with or characteristic of the south or people living there, especially of southern France. 2 situated in the south; southern. 3 of or having to do with a meridian. *—n.* inhabitant of the south, especially the south of France. **—me rid′i o-nal ly,** *adv.*

me ringue (mə rang′), *n.* 1 mixture made of egg whites and sugar, beaten stiff. Meringue is often spread on pies, puddings, etc., and lightly browned in the oven. 2 a small shell, cake, etc., made of this mixture and filled with fruit, whipped cream, etc. [< French]

me ri no (mə rē′nō), *n., pl.* **-nos,** *adj.* *—n.* 1 Often, **Merino.** any of a breed of sheep having long, fine wool. 2 wool of this sheep. 3 a soft, woolen yarn made from it. 4 a thin, soft, woolen fabric made from this yarn. 5 a similar fabric of a fine wool mixed with cotton. *—adj.* made of this wool, yarn, or fabric. [< Spanish]

mer i stem (mer′ə stem), *n.* (in botany) the undifferentiated, growing cellular tissue of the younger parts of plants. [< Greek *meristos* divisible, divided < *merizein* divide < *meros* part]

mer it (mer′it), *n.* 1 worth or value; goodness: *You will be marked according to the merit of your work.* 2 something that deserves praise or reward; commendable quality. 3 Usually, **merits,** *pl.* actual facts or qualities, whether good or bad: *The judge will consider the case on its merits.* *—v.t.* be worthy of; deserve: *merit praise.* [< Old French *merite* < Latin *meritum* earned < *mereri* earn]

mer i to ri ous (mer′ə tôr′ē əs, mer′ə-tōr′ē əs), *adj.* deserving reward or praise; having merit; worthy; commendable. **—mer′i to′ri ous ly,** *adv.* **—mer′i to′ri-ous ness,** *n.*

merit system, system in which appointments and promotions in the civil service are made on the basis of merit or good performance rather than on allegiance to a political party.

merle or **merl** (mėrl), *n.* the blackbird of Europe. [< Old French *merle* < Latin *merula*]

mer lin (mėr′lən), *n.* 1 a kind of small falcon, one of the smallest European birds of prey. 2 pigeon hawk. [< Anglo-French *merilun* < Old French *esmeril*]

Mer lin (mėr′lən), *n.* (in Arthurian legends) a seer and magician who helped King Arthur.

mer maid (mėr′mād′), *n.* 1 an imaginary sea maiden having the form of a fish from the waist down. 2 an expert woman swimmer. [< *mere*[2] + *maid*]

mer man (mėr′man′), *n., pl.* **-men.** 1 an imaginary man of the sea having the form of a fish from the waist down. 2 an expert male swimmer.

Mer o vin gi an (mer′ə vin′jē ən), *adj.* of or having to do with the first Frankish dynasty, which ruled in France from about A.D. 486 to 751. *—n.* member of the Merovingian dynasty.

Mer ri mac (mer′ə mak), *n.* a United States frigate rebuilt with iron armor by the Confederates during the Civil War and renamed the **Virginia.** The Merrimac was the first armored warship.

Mer ri mack River (mer′ə mak), river flowing from central New Hampshire through NE Massachusetts into the Atlantic. 110 mi.

mer ri ment (mer′ē mənt), *n.* laughter and gaiety; merry enjoyment; fun; mirth.

mer ry (mer′ē), *adj.,* **-ri er, -ri est.** 1 laughing and gay; full of fun; jolly; jovial. 2 characterized by festivity and rejoicing; joyful: *a merry holiday.* 3 ARCHAIC. pleasant or delightful. 4 **make merry,** laugh and be gay; have fun. [Old English *myrge*] **—mer′ri ly,** *adv.* **—mer′ri ness,** *n.*

mer ry-an drew (mer′ē an′drü), *n.* clown or buffoon.

mer ry-go-round (mer′ē gō round′), *n.* 1 set of animal figures and seats on a circular platform that is driven round and round by machinery and that children ride for fun; carrousel. 2 any whirl or rapid round: *The holidays were a merry-go-round of parties.*

mer ry mak er (mer′ē mā′kər), *n.* person engaged in merrymaking.

mer ry mak ing (mer′ē mā′king), *n.* 1 laughter and gaiety; fun. 2 a gay festival; merry entertainment. *—adj.* gay and full of fun; engaged in merrymaking.

Mer sey River (mėr′zē), river in NW England flowing west into the Irish Sea at Liverpool. 70 mi.

mes-, *combining form.* form of **meso-** before vowels, as in *mesencephalon.*

mesa

me sa (mā′sə), *n.* a small, isolated, high plateau with a flat top and steep sides, common in dry regions of the western and southwestern United States. [< Spanish < Latin *mensa* table]

Me sa bi Range (mə sä′bē), large ore-mining range in NE Minnesota.

mé sal li ance (mā zȧ lyäɴs′), *n.* FRENCH. marriage with a person of lower social position.

Mesa Verde National Park (vėrd′), national park in SW Colorado containing large Indian cliff dwellings. 80 sq. mi.

mes cal (mes kal′), *n.* 1 an alcoholic drink of Mexico made from the fermented juice of certain agaves, especially the maguey. 2 any of the plants yielding this. 3 a small cactus of northern Mexico and the southwestern

hat, āge, fär; let, ēqual, tėrm;
it, īce; hot, ōpen, ôrder;
oil, out; cup, pu̇t, rüle;
ch, child; ng, long; sh, she;
th, thin; ᴛʜ, then; zh, measure;

ə represents *a* in about, *e* in taken, *i* in pencil, *o* in lemon, *u* in circus.

< = from, derived from, taken from.

United States, whose buttonlike tops are dried and chewed as a stimulant and hallucinogen, especially by some tribes of Indians during religious ceremonies. [Mexican Spanish < Nahuatl *mexcalli*]

mes cal ine (mes′kə lēn), *n.* peyote.

mes dames (mā däm′), *n.* 1 a pl. of **madam.** 2 FRENCH. pl. of **madame.**

mes de moi selles (mād mwä zel′), *n.* FRENCH. pl. of **mademoiselle.**

me seems (mi sēmz′), *v., pt.* **me seemed.** ARCHAIC. it seems to me.

mes en ce phal ic (mes′en sə fal′ik), *adj.* of or having to do with the midbrain.

mes en ceph a lon (mes′en sef′ə lon), *n.* midbrain.

mes en ter ic (mes′n ter′ik), *adj.* of or having to do with a mesentery.

mes en ter y (mes′n ter′ē), *n., pl.* **-ter ies.** membrane that enfolds and supports an internal organ, attaching it to the body wall or to another organ. [< Greek *mesenterion* < *mesos* middle + *enteron* intestine]

mesh (mesh), *n.* 1 one of the open spaces of a net, sieve, or screen: *This net has half-inch meshes.* 2 cord, wire, etc., used in a net, screen, etc. 3 the engagement or fitting together of gear teeth. 4 **in mesh,** in gear; fitted together. 5 **meshes,** *pl.* **a** network; net. **b** snares: *The conspirators were entangled in the meshes of their own plot.* —*v.t., v.i.* 1 catch or be caught in a net. 2 engage or become engaged. The teeth of a small gear mesh with the teeth of a larger one. 3 bring closely together; fit together; blend; integrate. [probably from earlier Dutch *maesche*]

mesh work (mesh′wėrk′), *n.* structure consisting of meshes; network.

mes mer ic (mez mer′ik, me smer′ik), *adj.* hypnotic.

mes mer ism (mez′mə riz′əm, mes′mə riz′əm), *n.* hypnotism.

mes mer ist (mez′mər ist, mes′mər ist), *n.* hypnotist.

mes mer ize (mez′mə rīz′, mes′mə rīz′), *v.t., v.i.,* **-ized, -iz ing.** hypnotize. [< Franz A. *Mesmer,* 1734-1815, Austrian physician who made hypnotism popular] **—mes′mer iz′er,** *n.*

meso-, *combining form.* middle; halfway; midway; intermediate: *Mesoderm = middle layer of cells.* Also, **mes-** before vowels. [< Greek *mesos*]

mes o carp (mes′ə kärp), *n.* the middle layer of the pericarp of a fruit, such as the fleshy part of a peach or plum. See **pericarp** for diagram. [< *meso-* + Greek *karpos* fruit]

mes o derm (mes′ə dėrm′), *n.* 1 the middle layer of cells formed during the development of the embryos of animals. 2 tissues, derived from this layer of cells, such as the muscles, bones, circulatory system, connective tissue, etc. [< *meso-* + Greek *derma* skin]

mes o der mal (mes′ə dėr′məl), *adj.* of or having to do with the mesoderm.

Mes o lith ic (mes′ə lith′ik), *adj.* of or having to do with the middle part of the Stone Age, transitional between the Paleolithic and the Neolithic periods.

mes o morph (mes′ə môrf), *n.* person with a relatively strong, muscular body build developed from the mesodermal layer of the embryo. [< *meso-* + Greek *morphē* form]

mes o mor phic (mes′ə môr′fik), *adj.* of, like, or having to do with a mesomorph; designating the muscular type of body build. **—mes′o mor′phi cal ly,** *adv.*

mes on (mes′on), *n.* an elementary particle having a mass greater than that of an electron and less than that of a proton and a positive, negative, or neutral charge. It is a highly unstable particle in the nucleus. [< Greek *mesos* middle]

mes o pause (mes′ə pôz′), *n.* area of atmospheric demarcation between the mesosphere and the ionosphere.

mes o phyll or **mes o phyl** (mes′ə fil), *n.* the inner green tissue of a leaf, lying between the upper and lower layers of epidermis. [< *meso-* + Greek *phyllon* leaf]

mes o phyte (mes′ə fīt), *n.* plant that grows under conditions in which moisture is neither scarce nor abundant.

Mes o po ta mi a (mes′ə pə tā′mē ə, mes′ə pə tā′myə), *n.* ancient country in SW Asia, between the Tigris and Euphrates rivers. **—Mes′o po ta′mi an,** *adj., n.*

mes o sphere (mes′ə sfir), *n.* region of the atmosphere between the stratosphere and the ionosphere. Most of the ozone in the atmosphere is created in the mesosphere and there is almost no variation in the temperature. See **atmosphere** for diagram.

Mes o zo ic (mes′ə zō′ik), *n.* 1 the geological era before the present era, characterized by the development of mammals, flying reptiles, birds, flowering plants, and the appearance and death of dinosaurs. See chart under **geology.** 2 the rocks formed in this era. —*adj.* of or having to do with this era or its rocks. [< *meso-* + Greek *zōē* life]

me squite (me skēt′), *n.* a deep-rooted tree or shrub of the pea family, common in the southwestern United States and in Mexico, that often grows in dense clumps or thickets and bears pods that are used as livestock fodder. [< Mexican Spanish *mezquite* < Nahuatl *mizquitl*]

mess (mes), *n.* 1 a dirty or untidy mass or group of things; dirty or untidy condition: *The children kept the house in a mess.* 2 confusion or difficulty: *His business affairs are in a mess.* 3 an unpleasant or unsuccessful affair or state of affairs: *make a mess of a final examination.* 4 group of people who take meals together regularly, especially such a group in the armed forces. 5 meal of such a group: *The officers are at mess now.* 6 portion of food, especially a portion of soft food: *a mess of oatmeal.* —*v.t.* 1 make dirty or untidy: *mess up a room.* 2 make a failure of; confuse or spoil. 3 supply with meals, as soldiers or sailors. —*v.i.* 1 take one's meals *(with): The passengers messed with the officers.* 2 **mess about** or **mess around,** be busy without really accomplishing anything; putter around. [< Old French *mes* < Late Latin *missus* a course at dinner, (literally) thing put (that is, on the table) < Latin *mittere* send]

mes sage (mes′ij), *n.* 1 words sent from one person, group, etc., to another; communication. 2 an official speech or writing: *the President's message to Congress.* 3 lesson or moral contained in a story, play, speech, etc. 4 inspired words: *the message of a prophet.* 5 the business entrusted to a messenger; mission; errand. [< Old French < Medieval Latin *missaticum,* ultimately < Latin *mittere* send]

mes sa line (mes′ə lēn′), *n.* a thin, soft silk cloth with a surface like satin. [< French]

mes sen ger (mes′n jər), *n.* 1 person who carries a message or goes on an errand. 2 anything thought of as carrying a message: *Each bullet was a messenger of death.* 3 sign that something is coming; forerunner; herald: *Dawn is the messenger of day.*

messenger RNA, form of ribonucleic acid which controls protein synthesis.

Mes se ni a (mə sē′nē ə), *n.* region in ancient Greece, in the Peloponnesus. See **Peloponnesus** for map.

mess hall, place where a group of people eat together regularly, especially such a group on a military post.

Mes si ah (mə sī′ə), *n.* 1 the expected leader and deliverer of the Jewish people. 2 (in Christian use) Jesus. 3 Often, **messiah.** any person hailed as or thought of as a savior. Also, **Messias.** [< Greek *Messias* < Hebrew *māshīaḥ* anointed]

Mes si an ic (mes′ē an′ik), *adj.* 1 of the Messiah. 2 Often, **messianic.** of or characteristic of a messiah or savior.

Mes si an ism (mə sī′ə niz′əm), *n.* 1 belief in a Messiah. 2 Also, **messianism.** a visionary outlook; utopianism.

Mes si as (mə sī′əs), *n.* Messiah.

mes sieurs (mā syœ′; *Anglicized* mes′ərz); *n.* FRENCH. pl. of **monsieur.**

Mes si na (mə sē′nə), *n.* 1 seaport in NE Sicily. 272,000. 2 **Strait of,** a narrow, dangerous strait between Italy and Sicily. 2½ to 12 mi. wide.

mess jacket, a man's short jacket, open in front and reaching to the waist, worn as part of a dress uniform.

mess kit, a shallow, metal container that includes a fork, spoon, knife, and metal cup, for use by a soldier in the field, a camper, etc.

mess mate (mes′māt′), *n.* one of a group of people who eat together regularly.

Messrs., messieurs.

➤**Messrs.** is used as the plural of *Mr. (Messrs. Harrison and Smith)* and sometimes, though rarely now in American usage, in addressing firms *(Messrs. Brown, Hubbell and Company).*

mess y (mes′ē), *adj.,* **mess i er, mess i est.** in a mess; like a mess; untidy; in disorder; dirty. **—mess′i ly,** *adv.* **—mess′i ness,** *n.*

mes ti za (mə stē′zə), *n.* a female mestizo.

mes ti zo (mə stē′zō), *n., pl.* **-zos** or **-zoes.** person of mixed descent, especially the child of a Spaniard and an American Indian. [< Spanish, ultimately < Latin *mixtum* mixed. Doublet of MÉTIS.]

met (met), *v.* pt. and pp. of **meet**[1].

meta-, *prefix.* 1 between; among, as in *metacarpus.* 2 change of place or state, as in *metathesis.* 3 behind; after, as in *metagalaxy.* [< Greek *meta* with, after]

met a bol ic (met′ə bol′ik), *adj.* of or having to do with metabolism. **—met′a bol′i cal ly,** *adv.*

me tab o lism (mə tab′ə liz′əm), *n.* the sum of the physiological processes by which an organism maintains life. In metabolism protoplasm is broken down to produce energy, which is then used by the body to build up new cells and tissues, provide heat, and engage in physical activity. Growth and action depend on metabolism. [< Greek *metabolē* change < *meta-* after + *bolē* a throwing]

me ta bo lite (mə tab′ə līt), *n.* substance produced by metabolism.

me tab o lize (mə tab′ə līz), *v.,* **-lized, -liz ing.** —*v.t.* alter by or subject to metabolism. —*v.i.* function in or undergo metabolism.

met a car pal (met′ə kär′pəl), *adj.* of or having to do with the metacarpus. —*n.* bone of the metacarpus.

met a car pus (met′ə kär′pəs), *n., pl.* **-pi** (-pī). 1 part of the hand, especially the bones, between the wrist and the fingers. 2 the corresponding part of a forefoot of a quadruped, between the carpus and the phalanges.

met a gal ax y (met′ə gal′ək sē), *n., pl.* **-ax ies.** the universe outside the Milky Way, including the whole system of external galaxies.

met al (met′l), *n., adj., v.,* **-aled, -al ing** or **-alled, -al ling.** —*n.* 1 any of a class of elements, such as iron, gold, sodium, copper, lead, magnesium, tin, and aluminum, which usually have a shiny surface, are good conductors of heat and electricity, and can be melted or fused, hammered into thin sheets, or drawn into wires. Metals form alloys with each other and react with nonmetals to form salts by losing electrons. 2 any alloy of these, such as steel, bronze, and brass. 3 anything made out of metal. 4 broken stone, cinders, etc., used for roads and roadbeds. 5 the melted material that becomes glass or pottery. 6 basic stuff; material; substance: *Cowards are not made of the same metal as heroes.* 7 mettle. —*adj.* made of metal. —*v.t.* furnish, cover, or fit with metal. [< Greek *metallon,* originally, mine]

me tal lic (mə tal′ik), *adj.* 1 of or containing metal. 2 like metal; characteristic of metal; that suggests metal: *a metallic luster.* 3 resembling the sound produced when metal is struck: *a metallic voice.*

met al lif er ous (met′l if′ər əs), *adj.* containing or yielding metal: *metalliferous rocks.*

met al log ra pher (met′l og′rə fər), *n.* an expert in metallography.

met al log ra phy (met′l og′rə fē), *n.* the study of metals and alloys, chiefly with the aid of a microscope.

met al loid (met′l oid), *n.* an element having properties of both a metal and a nonmetal, as arsenic, antimony, or silicon.

met al lur gic (met′l ėr′jik), *adj.* metallurgical.

met al lur gi cal (met′l ėr′jə kəl), *adj.* of or having to do with metallurgy.

met al lur gist (met′l ėr′jist), *n.* person who is trained in metallurgy.

met al lur gy (met′l ėr′jē), *n.* science or art of working with metals, including the study of their properties and structure, the separation and refining of metals from their ores, and the production of alloys. [< New Latin *metallurgia,* ultimately < Greek *metallon* metal + *ergon* work]

met al ware (met′l wer′, met′l war′), *n.* articles or utensils made of metal.

met al work (met′l wėrk′), *n.* 1 things, especially artistic things, made out of metal. 2 a making things out of metal.

met al work er (met′l wėr′kər), *n.* person who makes things out of metal.

met al work ing (met′l wėr′king), *n.* act or process of making things out of metal.

met a mere (met′ə mir), *n.* any of a longitudinal series of more or less similar parts or segments composing the body of various animals, as the earthworm; somite. [< *meta-* + Greek *meros* part]

met a mor phic (met′ə môr′fik), *adj.* 1 characterized by metamorphosis; having to do with change of form. 2 changed in structure by heat, moisture, and pressure. Slate is a metamorphic rock that is formed from shale, a sedimentary rock.

met a mor phism (met′ə môr′fiz′əm), *n.* 1 change of form; metamorphosis. 2 change in the structure of a rock caused by pressure, heat, and moisture, especially when the rock becomes harder and more crystalline.

met a mor phose (met′ə môr′fōz), *v.,* **-phosed, -phos ing.** —*v.t.* 1 change in form, structure, or substance by or as if by witchcraft; transform. 2 change the form or structure of by metamorphosis or metamorphism. —*v.i.* undergo metamorphosis or metamorphism.

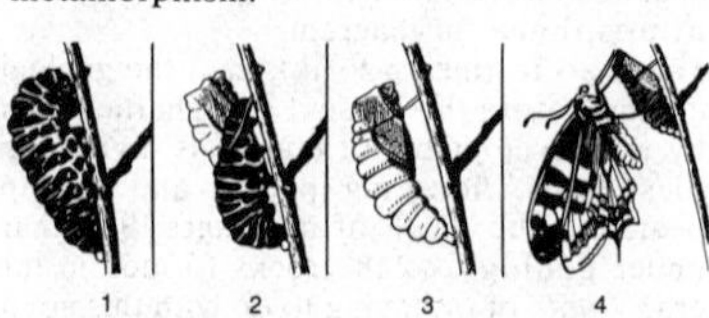

metamorphosis (def. 1) of a butterfly
1 Caterpillar prepares to change form.
2 It sheds skin, exposing chrysalis.
3 Chrysalis is entirely exposed.
4 Adult emerges from the chrysalis.

met a mor pho sis (met′ə môr′fə sis), *n., pl.* **-ses** (-sēz′). 1 a marked change in the form, and usually the habits, of an animal in its development after the embryonic stage. Tadpoles become frogs by metamorphosis; they lose their tails and grow legs. 2 change of form, structure, or substance by or as if by witchcraft; transformation. 3 form, shape, substance, etc., resulting from any such change. 4 a noticeable or complete change of character, appearance, circumstances, etc. [< Greek, ultimately < *meta-* after + *morphē* form]

met a phase (met′ə fāz), *n.* (in biology) the second stage in mitosis, characterized by the arrangement of the chromosomes along the middle of the spindle.

met a phor (met′ə fôr, met′ə fər), *n.* 1 an implied comparison between two different things; figure of speech in which a word or phrase that ordinarily means one thing is applied to another thing in order to suggest a likeness between the two: *"A copper sky" and "a heart of stone" are metaphors.* **2 mix metaphors,** confuse two or more metaphors in the same expression. [< Greek *metaphora* transfer, ultimately < *meta-* after + *pherein* to carry]

➤ **Metaphors** and **similes** both make comparisons, but in a *metaphor* the comparison is implied and in a *simile* it is indicated by *like* or *as.* "The sea of life" is a metaphor. "Life is like a sea" is a simile.

met a phor i cal (met′ə fôr′ə kəl, met′ə-for′ə kəl), *adj.* using metaphors; figurative. **—met′a phor′i cal ly,** *adv.*

met a phys i cal (met′ə fiz′ə kəl), *adj.* 1 of or having to do with metaphysics. 2 highly abstract; hard to understand; abstruse. 3 of or having to do with a group of English poets of the 1600's whose verse is characterized by hard-to-understand metaphors and fanciful, elaborate imagery. 4 ARCHAIC. supernatural. **—met′a phys′i cal ly,** *adv.*

met a phy si cian (met′ə fə zish′ən), *n.* person skilled in or familiar with metaphysics.

met a phys ics (met′ə fiz′iks), *n.* 1 branch of philosophy that tries to discover and explain reality and knowledge; the philosophical study of the real nature or basic principles of the universe. 2 the more abstruse or speculative divisions of philosophy. [< Medieval Latin *metaphysica* < Medieval Greek *(ta) metaphysika* for Greek *ta meta ta physika* the (works) after the *Physics;* with reference to philosophical works of Aristotle]

met a sta ble (met′ə stā′bəl), *adj.* relatively stable; intermediate between stable and unstable: *a metastable compound.*

me tas ta sis (mə tas′tə sis), *n., pl.* **-ses** (-sēz′). 1 the transfer of a function, pain, or disease from one organ or part to another, especially such a transfer of cancerous cells. 2 a cancerous growth or tumor that has been so transferred. [< Greek, removal, ultimately < *meta-* after + *histanai* to place]

me tas ta size (mə tas′tə sīz), *v.i.,* **-sized, -siz ing.** spread by or undergo metastasis.

met a tar sal (met′ə tär′səl), *adj.* of or having to do with the metatarsus. —*n.* a bone of the metatarsus.

met a tar sus (met′ə tär′səs), *n., pl.* **-si** (-sī). 1 part of the foot, especially the bones, between the ankle and the toes. 2 the corresponding part of a hind foot of a quadruped, between the tarsus and the phalanges.

me tath e sis (mə tath′ə sis), *n., pl.* **-ses** (-sēz′). 1 transposition of two sounds, syllables, or letters in a word, as in English *bird,* Old English *bridd.* 2 interchange of radicals between two compounds in a chemical reaction. 3 change or reversal of condition; transposition.

Met a zo a (met′ə zō′ə), *n.pl.* metazoans.

met a zo an (met′ə zō′ən), *n.* any of a large subkingdom of animals, comprising all animals except the protozoans, having the body made up of many cells arranged in tissues, developing from a single cell. —*adj.* of or belonging to the metazoans.

met a zo on (met′ə zō′on, met′ə zō′ən), *n., pl.* **-zo a.** metazoan.

mete (mēt), *v.t.,* **met ed, met ing.** 1 give to each his share or what is due him; distribute; allot: *The judge will mete out praise and blame.* 2 ARCHAIC. measure. [Old English *metan*]

met em psy cho sis (met′əm sī kō′sis, mə temp′sə kō′sis), *n., pl.* **-ses** (-sēz′). the passing of the soul at death from one body into another body. Some Oriental philosophies teach that by metempsychosis a person's soul lives again in an animal's body. [< Greek < *meta-* after + *en* in + *psychē* soul]

met en ceph a lon (met′en sef′ə lon), *n.* the anterior part of the hindbrain, which comprises the cerebellum and pons.

me te or (mē′tē ər), *n.* mass of rock or metal that enters the earth's atmosphere from outer space with enormous speed; falling star; shooting star. Friction with air molecules in the atmosphere causes meteors to become so hot that they glow and usually burn up before reaching the earth's surface. [< Greek *meteoron* (thing) in the air < *meta-* after + *aeirein* to lift]

me te or ic (mē′tē ôr′ik, mē′tē or′ik), *adj.*

1 of, having to do with, or consisting of a meteor or meteors: *a meteoric shower.* 2 brilliant, swift, and soon ended; transiently dazzling: *a meteoric rise to fame.* 3 of the atmosphere: *Wind and rain are meteoric phenomena.* **—me′te or′i cal ly,** *adv.*

me te o rite (mē′tē ə rīt′), *n.* meteor that has reached the earth without burning up.

me te o roid (mē′tē ə roid′), *n.* any of the many bodies that travel through space and become meteors when they enter the earth's atmosphere.

me te or o log ic (mē′tē ər ə loj′ik), *adj.* meteorological.

me te or o log i cal (mē′tē ər ə loj′ə kəl), *adj.* 1 of or having to do with the atmosphere, atmospheric phenomena, or weather. 2 of or having to do with meteorology. **—me′te or o log′i cal ly,** *adv.*

me te or ol o gist (mē′tē ə rol′ə jist), *n.* an expert in meteorology.

me te or ol o gy (mē′tē ə rol′ə jē), *n.* science dealing with the atmosphere and atmospheric conditions or phenomena, especially as they relate to weather.

me ter[1] (mē′tər), *n.* 1 any kind of poetic rhythm; the arrangement of beats or accents in a line of poetry. 2 musical rhythm; the arrangement of beats in music as divided into parts or measures of a uniform length of time. Three-fourths meter is waltz time. Also, BRITISH **metre.** [< Old French *mètre* < Latin *metrum* measure < Greek *metron*]

me ter[2] (mē′tər), *n.* the basic unit of length in the metric system, approximately equal to 39.37 inches. See **measure** for table. Also, BRITISH **metre.** [< French *mètre.* See METER[1].]

me ter[3] (mē′tər), *n.* 1 device for measuring. 2 device that measures and records the amount of gas, water, electricity, etc., used. *—v.t., v.i.* measure or record with a meter. [< *mete*]

-meter, *combining form.* 1 device for measuring ___: *Speedometer = device for measuring speed.* 2 meter; 39.37 inches: *Millimeter = one thousandth of a meter.* 3 having ___ metrical feet: *Tetrameter = having four metrical feet.* [< New Latin *-metrum* < Greek *metron* measure]

me ter-kil o gram-sec ond (mē′tər-kil′ə gram sek′ənd), *adj.* of or having to do with a system of measurement in which the meter is the unit of length, the kilogram is the unit of mass, and the second is the unit of time.

meter maid, U.S. woman assigned to issue tickets for violations of parking regulations.

Meth., Methodist.

meth a done (meth′ə dōn), *n.* a synthetic narcotic used to relieve pain and to aid in curing heroin addiction. *Formula:* $C_{21}H_{27}NO$

meth ane (meth′ān), *n.* a colorless, odorless, flammable gas, the simplest of the hydrocarbons; marsh gas. Methane is formed naturally by the decomposition of plant or other organic matter, as in marshes, petroleum wells, volcanoes, and coal mines. It is obtained commercially from natural gas. *Formula:* CH_4 [< *methyl*]

meth a nol (meth′ə nôl, meth′ə nol), *n.* wood alcohol.

me thinks (mi thingks′), *v., pt.* **methought.** ARCHAIC. it seems to me.

meth od (meth′əd), *n.* 1 way of doing something, especially according to a defined plan; mode; manner. See **way** for synonym study. 2 habit of acting according to plan; order or system in getting things done or in thinking. 3 orderly arrangement of ideas and topics in thinking or writing. 4 **method in one's madness,** system and sense in apparent folly. [< Greek *methodos,* originally, pursuit < *meta-* after + *hodos* a traveling]

me thod ic (mə thod′ik), *adj.* methodical.

me thod i cal (mə thod′ə kəl), *adj.* 1 done according to a method; systematic; orderly. See **orderly** for synonym study. 2 acting with method or order: *a methodical person.* **—me thod′i cal ly,** *adv.* **—me thod′i cal ness,** *n.*

Meth od ism (meth′ə diz′əm), *n.* doctrine, organization, and manner of worship of the Methodist Church.

Meth od ist (meth′ə dist), *n.* member of a church that had its origin in the teachings and work of John Wesley; Wesleyan. *—adj.* of or having to do with the Methodists or Methodism.

meth od ize (meth′ə dīz), *v.t.,* **-ized, -iz ing.** reduce to a method; arrange with method.

meth od o log i cal (meth′ə də loj′ə kəl), *adj.* of or having to do with methodology.

meth od ol o gy (meth′ə dol′ə jē), *n.* 1 system of methods or procedures used in any field. 2 branch of logic dealing with the application of its principles in any field of knowledge.

me thought (mi thôt′), *v.* ARCHAIC. pt. of **methinks.**

Me thu se lah (mə thü′zə lə), *n.* 1 (in the Bible) a man who lived 969 years. 2 a very old man.

meth yl (meth′əl), *n.* a univalent radical that occurs in many organic compounds. *Formula:* CH_3— [< French *méthyle,* ultimately < Greek *methy* wine + *hylē* wood]

methyl alcohol, wood alcohol.

meth yl at ed spirit (meth′ə lā′tid), ordinary alcohol mixed with wood alcohol to render it unfit for drinking.

me tic u los i ty (mə tik′yə los′ə tē), *n., pl.* **-ties.** quality of being meticulous.

me tic u lous (mə tik′yə ləs), *adj.* extremely or excessively careful about small details. [< Latin *meticulosus* fearful, timid < *metus* fear] **—me tic′u lous ly,** *adv.*

mé tier (mā tyā′), *n.* 1 trade; profession. 2 kind or field of work for which a person has special ability. [< French]

mé tis (mā tēs′), *n., pl.* **-tis.** 1 person of mixed descent. 2 U.S. octoroon. 3 (in Canada) a person of white (especially French) and American Indian descent. [< French, ultimately < Latin *mixtum* mixed. Doublet of MESTIZO.]

me ton y my (mə ton′ə mē), *n.* figure of speech that consists in substituting for the name of a thing the name of an attribute of it or something which it naturally suggests. EXAMPLE: The pen (power of literature) is mightier than the sword (force). [< Greek *metōnymia* < *meta-* after + *onyma* name]

met o pe (met′ə pē, met′ōp), *n.* one of the square spaces, either decorated or plain, between triglyphs in a Doric frieze. [< Greek *metopē* < *meta* between + *opē* an opening]

me tre (mē′tər), *n.* BRITISH. meter[1], meter[2].

met ric (met′rik), *adj.* 1 of or having to do with the meter or the metric system. 2 metrical.

met ri cal (met′rə kəl), *adj.* 1 of meter; having a regular arrangement of accents; written in verse, not in prose: *a metrical translation of Homer.* 2 of, having to do with, or used in measurement; metric. **—met′ri cal ly,** *adv.*

hat, āge, fär; let, ēqual, tėrm;
it, īce; hot, ōpen, ôrder;
oil, out; cup, pu̇t, rüle;
ch, child; ng, long; sh, she;
th, thin; ᴛʜ, then; zh, measure;

ə represents *a* in about, *e* in taken, *i* in pencil, *o* in lemon, *u* in circus.

< = from, derived from, taken from.

met rics (met′riks), *n.* science or art of meter; art of metrical composition.

metric system, a decimal system of measurement based on the meter as its unit of length, the gram as its unit of mass, and the liter as its unit of volume. See **measure** for table.

metric ton, unit of weight equal to 1000 kilograms or about 2204.62 avoirdupois pounds. See **measure** for table.

met ro or **Met ro** (met′rō), *n., pl.* **-ros.** U.S. and CANADA. form of municipal government whose powers extend over a metropolitan area and usually encompass a group of smaller municipalities. [< *metro(politan) area*]

mét ro or **Mét ro** (met′rō), *n., pl.* **-ros.** (in Paris and certain other European cities) the subway system; subway. [< French, short for *(chemin de fer) métropolitain* metropolitan (railroad)]

me trol o gy (mi trol′ə jē), *n.* science of measures and weights.

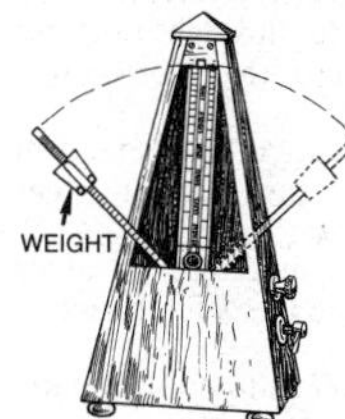

metronome
Moving the weight up or down changes the speed of the ticking. If weight is near top, it ticks more slowly. Moving it down increases the speed.

met ro nome (met′rə nōm), *n.* device that can be adjusted to make loud ticking sounds at different speeds. Metronomes are used especially to mark time for persons practicing on musical instruments. [< Greek *metron* measure + *-nomos* regulating < *nemein* regulate]

met ro nom ic (met′rə nom′ik), *adj.* of, having to do with, or like a metronome.

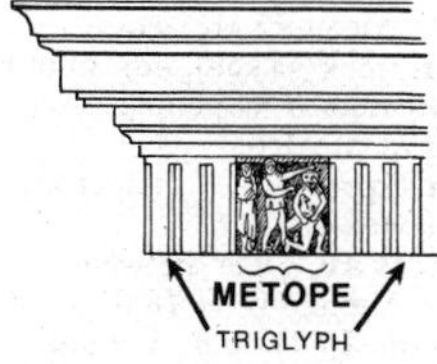

me trop o lis (mə trop′ə lis), *n.* 1 the most important city of a country or region: *New York is the metropolis of the United States.* 2 a large city; important center, especially the center of some activity: *a financial metropolis. Chicago is a busy metropolis.* 3 the chief diocese of a church province. 4 the mother city or parent state of a colony, especially of an ancient Greek colony.

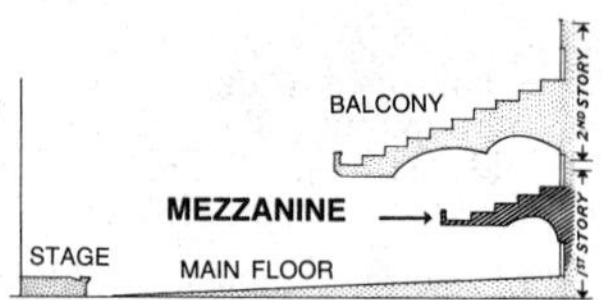

[< Greek *mētropolis* < *mētēr* mother + *polis* city]

met ro pol i tan (met′rə pol′ə tən), *adj.* 1 of a metropolis; belonging to a large city or cities: *metropolitan newspapers.* 2 of or having to do with a metropolitan of the church, or his see or province. —*n.* 1 person who lives in a large city and has metropolitan ideas or manners. 2 archbishop presiding over an ecclesiastical province.

metropolitan area, area or region including a large city and its suburbs.

-metry, *combining form.* process or art of measuring ____: *Biometry = process or art of measuring life.* [< Greek *-metria* < *metron* measure]

Met ter nich (met′ər nik), *n.* Prince **Klemens von,** 1773-1859, Austrian diplomat and statesman.

met tle (met′l), *n.* 1 quality of disposition or temperament. 2 spirit; courage. 3 **on one's mettle,** ready to do one's best. [variant of *metal*]

met tle some (met′l səm), *adj.* full of mettle; spirited; courageous.

Metz (mets), *n.* city in NE France. 108,000.

Meuse River (myüz; *French* mœz), river flowing from NE France through Belgium and the Netherlands into the North Sea. 575 mi.

Mev or **MeV** (mev), *n.* a million electron volts, used as a unit for measuring in nuclear physics.

mew¹ (myü), *n.* sound made by a cat or kitten; meow. —*v.i.* make this sound; meow. [probably imitative]

mew² (myü), *n.* gull, especially the common European gull. [Old English *mǣw*]

mew³ (myü), *n.* cage for hawks, especially molting hawks. —*v.t.* shut up in or as if in a cage; conceal; confine. [< Old French *müe* < *muer* to molt < Latin *mutare* to change]

mewl (myül), *v.i., v.t.* cry like a baby; make a feeble, whining noise; whimper. —*n.* cry of a baby. [imitative]

mews (myüz), *n. sing. or pl.* 1 group of stables built around a court or alley. 2 street or alley that was formerly part of a mews. [originally plural of *mew³*]

Mex., 1 Mexican. 2 Mexico.

Mex i can (mek′sə kən), *adj.* of or having to do with Mexico or its people. —*n.* native or inhabitant of Mexico.

Mexican Spanish, dialect of Spanish spoken in Mexico.

Mexican War, war between the United States and Mexico from 1846 to 1848.

Mex i co (mek′sə kō), *n.* 1 country in North America, just south of W United States. 48,313,000 pop.; 761,600 sq. mi. *Capital:* Mexico City. Also, SPANISH **Méjico.** 2 **Gulf of,** gulf of the Atlantic, south of the United States and east of Mexico. 716,000 sq. mi.

Mexico City, capital of Mexico, in the central part. 7,006,000.

Mey er beer (mī′ər bir; *German* mī′ər bār), *n.* **Giacomo,** 1791-1864, German composer of operas.

me zuz ah or **me zuz a** (me zu̇z′ə), *n.* a small container holding a parchment scroll inscribed with certain Biblical passages and God's name on the outside, attached by Jews to the right-hand doorposts of their homes as a symbol of their religion. [< Hebrew *mezūzāh* doorpost]

mez za nine (mez′n ēn′), *n.* a low story, usually extending above a part of the main floor to form a balcony. In a theater the lowest balcony is often called a mezzanine. In a hotel the upper part of the lobby is often surrounded by a mezzanine. [< Italian *mezzanino* < *mezzano* middle < Latin *medianus* median]

mez zo (met′sō, mez′ō), *adj., n., pl.* **-zos.** in music: —*adj.* middle; medium; half. —*n.* mezzo-soprano.

mez zo for te (met′sō fôr′tā; mez′ō fôr′tā), (in music) half as loud as forte; moderately loud. [< Italian]

mez zo-so pran o (met′sō sə pran′ō), *n., pl.* **-pran os.** 1 voice between soprano and contralto. 2 singer having such a voice. [< Italian, middle soprano]

mez zo tint (met′sō tint′, mez′ō tint′), *n.* 1 engraving on copper or steel made by polishing and scraping away parts of a roughened surface, so as to produce the effect of light and shade. 2 this method of engraving pictures. —*v.t.* engrave in mezzotint. [< Italian *mezzotinto* half-tint]

mf., 1 mezzo forte. 2 microfarad.

mfd., 1 manufactured. 2 microfarad.

mfg., manufacturing.

mfr., manufacturer.

Mg, magnesium.

mg., milligram or milligrams.

Mgr., 1 Manager. 2 Monseigneur. 3 Monsignor.

mho (mō), *n., pl.* **mhos.** unit of electrical conductance, equivalent to the conductance of a body through which one ampere of current flows when the difference of potential is one volt. It is the reciprocal of the ohm. [reversed spelling of *ohm*]

mi (mē), *n.* (in music) the third tone of the diatonic scale. [< Medieval Latin]

mi., mile or miles.

Mi am i (mī am′ē, mī am′ə), *n.* city in SE Florida. 335,000.

Miami Beach, city in SE Florida, a winter resort. 87,000.

mi aow or **mi aou** (mē ou′), *n., v.i.* meow.

mi as ma (mī az′mə, mē az′mə), *n., pl.* **-mas, -ma ta** (-mə tə). 1 a bad-smelling vapor rising from decaying matter on the earth. The miasma of swamps was formerly thought to cause disease. 2 anything considered to resemble this in its ability to spread and poison: *a miasma of fear.* [< Greek, pollution < *miainein* pollute]

mi ca (mī′kə), *n.* any of a group of minerals containing silicon that divide readily into thin, partly transparent, and usually flexible layers; isinglass. Mica is highly resistant to heat and is used in electric fuses, lanterns, etc. [< Latin, grain, crumb]

Mi cah (mī′kə), *n.* 1 Hebrew prophet of the 700's B.C. 2 book of the Old Testament.

Mi caw ber (mə kô′bər), *n.* **Wilkins,** character in Dickens's novel *David Copperfield* who is seldom able to pay his bills but is always hoping "something will turn up."

mice (mīs), *n.* pl. of **mouse.**

Mich., 1 Michaelmas. 2 Michigan.

Mi chael (mī′kəl), *n.* **Saint,** (in the Bible) the archangel who led the loyal angels in defeating the revolt of Lucifer.

Michael I, born 1921, king of Romania from 1927 to 1930 and from 1940 to 1947.

Mich ael mas (mik′əl məs), *n.* September 29, a church festival in honor of the archangel Michael.

Mi chel an ge lo (mī′kə lan′jə lō), *n.* 1475-1564, Italian sculptor, painter, architect, and poet.

Mi chel son (mī′kəl sən), *n.* **Albert A.,** 1852-1931, American physicist, born in Germany.

Mich i gan (mish′ə gən), *n.* 1 one of the north central states of the United States. 8,875,000 pop.; 58,200 sq. mi. *Capital:* Lansing. *Abbrev.:* Mich. 2 **Lake,** one of the five Great Lakes, the only one entirely in the United States. 22,400 sq. mi.

Mich i gan der (mish′ə gan′dər), *n.* native or inhabitant of Michigan.

Mich i gan ite (mish′ə gə nīt), *n.* Michigander.

mick ey finn or **Mick ey Finn** (mik′ē fin′), SLANG. an alcoholic drink containing a drug.

mick le (mik′əl), *adj., adv., n.* ARCHAIC or DIALECT. much. [Old English *micel*]

micro-, *combining form.* 1 small; very small; microscopic: *Microorganism = a microscopic organism.* 2 done with, or involving the use of, a microscope: *Microbiology = biology involving the use of a microscope.* 3 one millionth of a ____: *Microfarad = one millionth of a farad.* 4 that magnifies small ____: *Microphone = instrument that magnifies small sounds.* [< Greek *mikros* small]

mi cro bal ance (mī′krō bal′əns), *n.* a very sensitive scale used to weigh minute quantities (one milligram or less) of chemicals or other substances.

mi crobe (mī′krōb), *n.* 1 germ; microorganism. 2 bacterium, especially one causing diseases or fermentation. [< French < Greek *mikros* small + *bios* life]

mi cro bi al (mī krō′bē əl), *adj.* of or caused by microbes.

mi cro bic (mī krō′bik), *adj.* microbial.

mi cro bi o log i cal (mī′krō bī′ə loj′ə kəl), *adj.* 1 of or having to do with microbiology. 2 of or having to do with microorganisms. —**mi′cro bi′o log′i cal ly,** *adv.*

mi cro bi ol o gist (mī′krō bī ol′ə jist), *n.* an expert in microbiology.

mi cro bi ol o gy (mī′krō bī ol′ə jē), *n.* branch of biology dealing with microorganisms.

mi cro chem is try (mī′krō kem′ə strē), *n.* branch of chemistry dealing with very small amounts or samples.

mi cro cli mate (mī′krō klī′mit), *n.* the climate of a very small, specific area such as a glacier, valley bottom, cornfield, or animal burrow.

mi cro coc cus (mī′krō kok′əs), *n., pl.* **-coc ci** (-kok′sī). any of a genus of spherical or egg-shaped bacteria. Certain micrococci cause disease; others produce fermentation.

mi cro cop y (mī′krō kop′ē), *n., pl.* **-cop ies;** *v.,* **-cop ied, -cop y ing.** —*n.* copy of a book or other printed work made on microfilm. —*v.t.* make a copy of on microfilm.

mi cro cosm (mī′krō koz′əm), *n.* 1 community, etc., regarded as an epitome of the world; a little world; universe in miniature. 2 man thought of as a miniature representation of the universe. [< Late Greek *mikros kosmos* little world]

mi cro cos mic (mī′krə koz′mik), *adj.* of or having to do with a microcosm.

mi cro ev o lu tion (mī′krō ev′ə lü′shən), *n.* the evolution of animals and plants on the level of subspecies due to a succession of small genetic variations.
mi cro far ad (mī′krō far′əd, mī′krō-far′ad), *n.* unit of electrical capacity, equal to one millionth of a farad.
mi cro fiche (mī′krō fēsh′), *n., pl.* **-fich es, -fiche** (-fēsh′). a card-sized sheet of microfilm showing entire pages of books, etc. [< *micro-* + French *fiche* card]
mi cro film (mī′krō film′), *n.* film for making very small photographs of pages of a book, newspapers, records, etc., to preserve them in a very small space. —*v.t., v.i.* photograph on microfilm.
mi cro ga mete (mī′krō gə mēt′, mī′krō-gam′ēt), *n.* the smaller, typically the male, of two gametes of an organism that reproduces by the union of unlike gametes.
mi cro gram (mī′krō gram), *n.* unit of mass equal to one millionth of a gram.
mi cro graph (mī′krə graf), *n.* photomicrograph.
mi cro groove (mī′krō grüv′), *n.* a very narrow groove on long-playing phonograph records.
mi cro me te or ite (mī′krō mē′tē ə rīt′), *n.* a tiny particle of meteoric dust, so small that it does not burn as it falls to the earth from outer space.
mi crom e ter (mī krom′ə tər), *n.* 1 instrument for measuring very small distances, angles, objects, etc. Certain kinds are used with a microscope or telescope. 2 micrometer caliper.

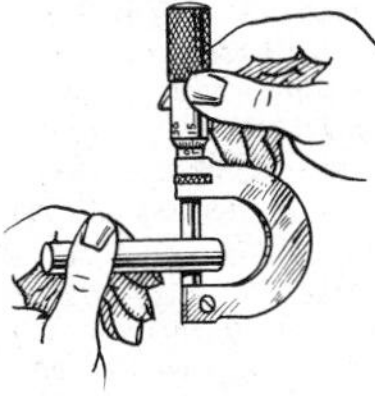
micrometer caliper

micrometer caliper, caliper having a screw with a very fine thread, used for very accurate measurement.
mi cron (mī′kron), *n., pl.* **-crons, -cra** (-krə). unit of length equal to one millionth of a meter. *Symbol:* μ [< Greek, small]
Mi cro ne sia (mī′krō nē′zhə, mī′krō-nē′shə), *n.* group of small islands in the Pacific, east of the Philippines. See **Melanesia** for map. —**Mi′cro ne′sian,** *adj., n.*
mi cro nu cle us (mī′krō nü′klē əs, mī′-krō nyü′klē əs), *n., pl.* **-cle i** (-klē ī), **-cle us es.** the smaller of two kinds of nuclei of ciliate protozoans, containing chromatin materials necessary for reproduction.
mi cro or gan ism (mī′krō ôr′gə niz′əm), *n.* a microscopic or ultramicroscopic animal or vegetable organism; microbe. Bacteria are microorganisms.
mi cro phone (mī′krə fōn), *n.* instrument for magnifying or transmitting sounds by changing sound waves into an electric current. Microphones are used in broadcasting, telephony, etc.
mi cro pho to graph (mī′krō fō′tə graf), *n.* 1 photograph of microscopic size that has to be enlarged for viewing. 2 photomicrograph.
mi cro print (mī′krə print′), *n.* a microphotograph of newspapers, records, etc.
mi cro pro jec tor (mī′krō prə jek′tər), *n.* apparatus consisting of a microscope lens system and an illuminator, used to project enlarged images of minute objects on a screen.
mi cro scope (mī′krə skōp), *n.* an optical instrument consisting of a lens or combination of lenses for magnifying things that are invisible or indistinct to the naked eye.

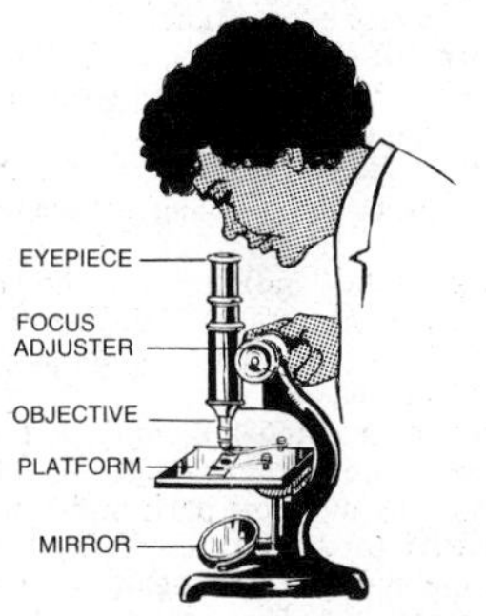

microscope—There are magnifying lenses in the eyepiece and objective. The mirror reflects light up through the platform, which has an opening in it or is made of glass.

mi cro scop ic (mī′krə skop′ik), *adj.* 1 so small as to be invisible or indistinct without the use of a microscope; tiny. 2 like that of a microscope; suggesting the use of a microscope: *a microscopic eye for mistakes.* 3 of or having to do with a microscope; made or effected by a microscope: *a microscopic examination.*
mi cro scop i cal (mī′krə skop′ə kəl), *adj.* microscopic. —**mi′cro scop′i cal ly,** *adv.*
mi cros co pist (mī kros′kə pist, mī′krə-skō′pist), *n.* an expert in microscopy.
mi cros co py (mī kros′kə pē, mī′krə-skō′pē), *n.* use of a microscope; microscopic investigation.
mi cro sec ond (mī′krō sek′ənd), *n.* unit of time equal to one millionth of a second.
mi cro spore (mī′krə spôr′, mī′krə spōr′), *n.* an asexually produced spore of comparatively small size from which a male gametophyte develops in certain ferns.
mi cro tome (mī′krə tōm), *n.* instrument for cutting extremely thin sections of tissues for microscopic examination. [< *micro-* + Greek *-tomos* cutting]
mi cro wave (mī′krō wāv′), *n.* an electromagnetic wave having a very short wave length, usually ranging from one millimeter to fifty centimeters.
mic tu rate (mik′chə rāt′), *v.i.,* **-rat ed, -rat ing.** urinate. [< Latin *micturire* + English *-ate*[1]]
mic tu ri tion (mik′chə rish′ən), *n.* act of urinating.
mid[1] (mid), *adj.* 1 in the middle of; middle. 2 (in phonetics) articulated with the tongue midway between high and low position, as English *e* in *bet, u* in *but.* [Old English *midd*]
mid[2] or **'mid** (mid), *prep.* ARCHAIC. amid. [variant of *amid*]
mid-, *prefix.* 1 the middle point or part of ___: *Midcontinent = the middle part of a continent.* 2 of, in, or near the middle of ___: *Midsummer = in the middle of summer.* [< *mid*[1]]
mid air (mid′er′, mid′ar′), *n.* air above the ground: *The acrobat made a somersault in midair.*
Mi das (mī′dəs), *n.* (in Greek myths) a king of Phrygia who had the power to turn everything he touched into gold. —**Mi′das like′,** *adj.*

hat, āge, fär; let, ēqual, tėrm;
it, īce; hot, ōpen, ôrder;
oil, out; cup, pu̇t, rüle;
ch, child; ng, long; sh, she;
th, thin; ᴛʜ, then; zh, measure;
ə represents *a* in about, *e* in taken, *i* in pencil, *o* in lemon, *u* in circus.
< = from, derived from, taken from.

mid brain (mid′brān′), *n.* the middle section of the brain; mesencephalon.
mid day (mid′dā′), *n.* middle of the day; noon. —*adj.* of midday.
mid den (mid′n), *n.* 1 kitchen midden. 2 DIALECT. dunghill; refuse heap. [apparently < Scandinavian (Danish) *mödding,* alteration of *mög dynge* muck heap]
mid dle (mid′l), *adj.* 1 halfway between; in the center; at the same distance from either end or side: *the middle point of a line.* 2 in between; intermediate; medium: *a man of middle size, take a middle view in a matter.* 3 **Middle,** of or having to do with an intermediate part or division of a language, period, etc.: *Middle Irish, Middle Cambrian.* —*n.* 1 point or part that is the same distance from each end or side or other limit; the center: *the middle of the road.* See synonym study below. 2 the middle part of a person's body; waist. [Old English *middel*]
Syn. *n.* 1 **Middle, center** mean a point or part halfway between certain limits. **Middle** means the part more or less the same distance from each end, side, or other limit: *the middle of the room, in the middle of the day.* **Center** applies to the point in the exact middle: *the center of a circle.*
middle age, time of life between youth and old age, between about 40 and 65.
mid dle-aged (mid′l ājd′), *adj.* between youth and old age; being of middle age.
Middle Ages, period of European history between ancient and modern times, from about A.D. 500 to about 1450.
Middle America, area between the United States and South America. It includes Mexico, Central America, and usually the islands of the West Indies. —**Middle American.**
mid dle brow (mid′l brou′), INFORMAL. —*n.* person who is somewhat interested in education and culture, and is therefore about midway between a highbrow and a lowbrow. —*adj.* of or suitable for a middlebrow.
middle C, the musical note on the first added line below the treble staff and the first above the bass staff. See **clef** for diagram.
middle class, class of people who are socially and economically between the very wealthy class and the class of unskilled laborers and unemployed people. The middle class includes businessmen, professional people, office workers, and many skilled workers.
mid dle-class (mid′l klas′), *adj.* of, having to do with, or characteristic of the middle class; bourgeois.
Middle Dutch, the Dutch language from about 1100 to about 1500.
middle ear, the hollow space between the eardrum and the inner ear; tympanum. In

man it contains three small bones which transmit sound waves from the eardrum to the inner ear. See **ear**[1] for diagram.

Middle East, region extending from Sudan, Egypt, and Turkey in the west to Iran in the east, and including the countries of SW Asia. Iraq, Israel, Jordan, Syria, and Saudi Arabia are among the countries in the Middle East. Also, **Mideast. —Middle Eastern.**

Middle English, 1 period in the development of the English language between Old English and Modern English, lasting from about 1100 to about 1500. 2 language of this period. Chaucer wrote in Middle English.

Middle French, the French language from 1400 to 1600.

Middle High German, the High German language from 1100 to 1450.

Middle Low German, the Low German language from 1100 to 1450.

mid dle man (mid′l man′), *n., pl.* **-men.** 1 trader or merchant who buys goods from the producer and sells them to a retailer or directly to the consumer. 2 person who acts as a go-between for two persons or groups concerned in some matter of business.

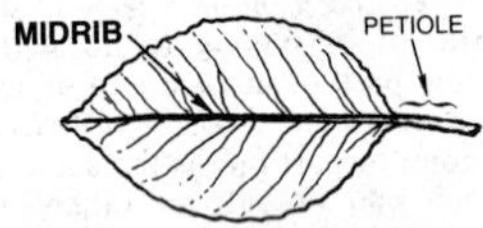

mid dle most (mid′l mōst), *adj.* midmost.

mid dle-of-the-road (mid′l əv ᴛʜə rōd′), *adj.* moderate, especially in politics; shunning extremes.

mid dle-of-the-road er (mid′l əv ᴛʜə-rō′dər), *n.* a moderate, especially in politics.

Mid dle sex (mid′l seks), *n.* county in SE England.

middle term, term in the major and minor premises of a syllogism but not in the conclusion.

mid dle weight (mid′l wāt′), *n.* 1 person of average weight. 2 boxer or wrestler who weighs more than 147 pounds and less than 160 pounds.

Middle West, the part of the United States west of the Appalachian Mountains, east of the Rocky Mountains, and north of the Ohio River and the S boundaries of Missouri and Kansas. Also, **Midwest. —Middle Western. —Middle Westerner.**

mid dling (mid′ling), *adj.* medium in size, quality, grade, etc.; ordinary; average. *—adv.* INFORMAL or DIALECT. moderately; fairly. *—n.* **middlings,** *pl.* **a** products of medium size, quality, grade, or price. **b** coarse particles of ground wheat mixed with bran, used in making a very nutritious flour. [< *mid-* + Old English *-ling* condition]

mid dy (mid′ē), *n., pl.* **-dies.** 1 INFORMAL. midshipman. 2 middy blouse.

middy blouse, a loose blouse having a collar with a broad flap at the back, worn by sailors, children, and girls.

Mid east (mid′ēst′), *n.* Middle East.

Mid east ern (mid′ē′stərn), *adj.* Middle Eastern.

midge (mij), *n.* 1 any of various very small two-winged flies. 2 a very small person, as a child. [Old English *mycg*]

midg et (mij′it), *n.* 1 person very much smaller than normal; tiny person. See **dwarf** for synonym study. 2 anything much smaller than the usual size for its type or kind. *—adj.* very small; miniature; diminutive. [< *midge*]

mid i (mid′ē), *adj.* reaching to the calf (usually in compounds such as *midi-skirt, midi-length*). *—n.* dress, coat, etc., reaching to the calf. [< *mid*[1]; patterned after *mini*]

Mi di (mē dē′), *n.* the south, especially the south of France. [< French]

Mid i an ite (mid′ē ə nīt), *n.* (in the Bible) a member of a wandering tribe of Arabs that fought against the Israelites.

mid i ron (mid′ī′ərn), *n.* a golf club with a steel or iron head having a face of small slope.

mid land (mid′lənd), *n.* 1 the middle part of a country; the interior. 2 **Midlands,** *pl.* the central part of England. *—adj.* in or of the midland; inland.

mid most (mid′mōst′), *adj.* in the exact middle; nearest the middle; middlemost. *—adv.* in the midmost part; in the midst.

mid night (mid′nīt′), *n.* twelve o'clock at night; the middle of the night. *—adj.* 1 of or at midnight. 2 dark as midnight.

midnight sun, sun seen throughout the day and night in the arctic and antarctic regions during their summers.

mid point (mid′point′), *n.* the middle part of anything; midway point: *the midpoint of a journey.*

mid rib (mid′rib′), *n.* the central vein of a leaf.

mid riff (mid′rif), *n.* 1 diaphragm separating the chest cavity from the abdomen. 2 the middle portion of the human body. [Old English *midhrif* < *midd* mid + *hrif* belly]

mid ship (mid′ship′), *adj.* in, of, or belonging to the middle part of a ship.

mid ship man (mid′ship′mən), *n., pl.* **-men.** 1 student at the United States Naval Academy at Annapolis. 2 graduate of the British naval schools until he is made sublieutenant; officer of the same rank as such a graduate. 3 (in former times) a boy or young man who assisted the officers of a ship.

mid ships (mid′ships′), *adv.* amidships.

midst[1] (midst), *n.* 1 the middle point or part; center; middle. 2 **in our midst,** among us. 3 **in the midst of, a** in the middle of; surrounded by; among. **b** during. [Middle English *in middes* in the middle]

midst[2] or **'midst** (midst), *prep.* amidst; amid. [short for *amidst*]

mid stream (mid′strēm′), *n.* middle of a stream.

mid sum mer (mid′sum′ər), *n.* 1 middle of summer. 2 time of the summer solstice, about June 21. *—adj.* in the middle of summer.

mid town (mid′toun′), *n.* section of a city or town between downtown and uptown. *—adj.* of or situated in midtown.

mid way (mid′wā′), *adv., adj.* in the middle; halfway. *—n.* 1 a middle way or course. 2 place for games, rides, side shows, and other amusements at a fair, exposition, etc.

Midway Islands, group of small islands in the Pacific, belonging to the United States, about halfway between the United States and the Philippines. 2400 pop.; 2 sq. mi.

mid week (mid′wēk′), *n.* 1 the middle of the week. 2 **Midweek,** Wednesday. It is so called by the Quakers. *—adj.* in the middle of the week.

mid week ly (mid′wēk′lē), *adv., adj.* in the middle of the week.

Mid west (mid′west′), *n.* Middle West.

Mid west ern (mid′wes′tərn), *adj.* Middle Western.

Mid west ern er (mid′wes′tər nər), *n.* Middle Westerner.

mid wife (mid′wīf′), *n., pl.* **-wives.** woman who helps women in childbirth. [Old English *mid* with + *wīf* woman]

mid wi fer y (mid′wī′fər ē), *n.* art or practice of helping women in childbirth.

mid win ter (mid′win′tər), *n.* 1 middle of winter. 2 time of the winter solstice, about December 21. *—adj.* in the middle of winter.

mid year (mid′yir′), *adj.* happening in the middle of the year. *—n.* **midyears,** *pl.* INFORMAL. **a** midyear examinations. **b** period during which these examinations are held.

mien (mēn), *n.* manner of holding the head and body; way of acting and looking; bearing; demeanor: *He had the mien of a judge.* [probably < *demean*[2]]

miff (mif), INFORMAL. *—n.* a peevish fit; petty quarrel. *—v.i.* be offended; have a petty quarrel. *—v.t.* offend: *She was miffed at the idea that she could be mistaken.* [origin uncertain]

MIG or **Mig** (mig), *n.* any of various Russian-designed jet fighter planes.

might[1] (mīt), *v.* pt. of **may.** [Old English *mihte*] ➔ See **could** for usage note.

might[2] (mīt), *n.* 1 great power; strength: *Work with all your might.* 2 **with might and main,** with all one's strength. [Old English *miht*]

might i ly (mī′tə lē), *adv.* 1 in a mighty manner; powerfully; vigorously. 2 very much; greatly.

might i ness (mī′tē nis), *n.* power; strength.

might y (mī′tē), *adj.,* **might i er, might i est,** *adv.* *—adj.* 1 having or showing strength or power; powerful; strong: *a mighty ruler, mighty force.* See synonym study below. 2 very great: *a mighty famine.* *—adv.* INFORMAL. very: *a mighty long time.*

Syn. *adj.* 1 **Mighty, powerful** mean strong. **Mighty** suggests great strength and size but not necessarily effective force: *The mighty battleship was so badly damaged that it had to be scuttled.* **Powerful** suggests the strength, energy, or authority to exert great force: *The battleship was a powerful weapon.*

mi gnon ette (min′yə net′), *n.* any of a genus of herbs, especially a common garden plant having long, pointed clusters of small, fragrant, greenish-white flowers. [< French]

mi graine (mī′grān), *n.* a severe headache, usually recurrent, on one side of the head only, and accompanied by nausea; sick headache; megrim. [< French < Late Latin *hemicrania* < Greek *hemikrania* < *hemi-* half + *kranion* skull]

mi grant (mī′grənt), *adj.* migrating; roving: *a migrant worker.* *—n.* person, animal, bird, or plant that migrates.

mi grate (mī′grāt), *v.i.,* **-grat ed, -grat ing.** 1 move from one place to settle in another. 2 go from one region to another with the change in the seasons. Most birds migrate to warmer countries in the winter. [< Latin *migratum* moved]

mi gra tion (mī grā′shən), *n.* 1 a migrating. 2 number of people or animals migrating together.

mi gra to ry (mī′grə tôr′ē, mī′grə tōr′ē), *adj.* 1 moving from one place to another; migrating. 2 of or having to do with migration. 3 wandering: *a migratory pain.*

mi ka do or **Mi ka do** (mə kä′dō), *n., pl.* **-dos.** a former title of the emperor of Japan. [< Japanese]

mike (mīk), *n.* INFORMAL. microphone.

mil (mil), *n.* unit of length equal to .001 of an inch, used in measuring the diameter of wires. [< Latin *mille* thousand]

mil., 1 military. 2 militia.

mi la dy or **mi la di** (mi lā′dē), *n., pl.* **-dies.** 1 my lady (applied by continental Europeans, especially formerly, to any English-speaking woman of fashion). 2 an English lady or noblewoman.

Mi lan (mi lan′), *n.* city in N Italy. 1,702,000.

Mil a nese (mil′ə nēz′), *adj., n., pl.* **-nese.** —*adj.* of or having to do with Milan or its people. —*n.* native or inhabitant of Milan.

milch (milch), *adj.* giving milk; kept for the milk it gives: *a milch cow.* [Old English *-milce* < *mioluc* milk]

mild (mīld), *adj.* 1 having a gentle disposition; behaving kindly; kind: *a mild old gentleman.* See **gentle** for synonym study. 2 calm; warm; temperate; moderate; not harsh or severe: *a mild climate, a mild winter.* 3 soft or sweet to the senses; not sharp, sour, bitter, or strong in taste: *mild cheese, a mild cigar.* [Old English *milde*] **—mild′ly,** *adv.* **—mild′ness,** *n.*

mil dew (mil′dü, mil′dyü), *n.* 1 any of numerous, minute, parasitic fungi producing a whitish coating or a discoloration on plants or on paper, clothes, leather, etc., during damp weather. 2 the coating or discoloration, or the diseased condition, produced by such fungi. —*v.t., v.i.* cover or become covered with mildew. [Old English *mildēaw* honeydew]

mil dew y (mil′dü ē, mil′dyü ē), *adj.* of, like, or affected with mildew.

mile (mīl), *n.* 1 unit of distance equal to 5280 feet; statute mile. See **measure** for table. 2 nautical mile. [Old English *mīl* < Latin *milia (passuum),* plural of *mille (passus)* a thousand (paces)]

mile age (mī′lij), *n.* 1 miles covered or traveled: *Our car's mileage last year was 10,000 miles.* 2 miles traveled per gallon of gasoline: *Do you get good mileage with your car?* 3 length, extent, or distance in miles. The mileage of a railroad is its total number of miles of roadbed. 4 allowance for traveling expenses at so much a mile: *Congressmen are given mileage between their homes and Washington, D.C.* 5 rate charged per mile, as on a toll highway or for a rental car. 6 INFORMAL. benefit; use; gain.

mile post (mīl′pōst′), *n.* post or stake set up to show the distance in miles to a certain place or the distance covered.

mil er (mī′lər), *n.* person, horse, etc., competing in or trained for a mile race.

mile stone (mīl′stōn′), *n.* 1 stone set up to show the distance in miles to a certain place. 2 an important event: *The invention of printing was a milestone in progress.*

mil foil (mil′foil), *n.* yarrow. [< Old French < Latin *millefolium* < *mille* thousand + *folium* leaf]

Mil haud (mē yō′), *n.* **Darius,** born 1892, French composer.

mi lieu (mē lyœ′), *n.* surroundings; environment. [< French]

mil i tan cy (mil′ə tən sē), *n.* warlike behavior or tendency; militant spirit or policy.

mil i tant (mil′ə tənt), *adj.* 1 very aggressive; fighting; warlike. 2 engaged in warfare; warring. 3 active in serving a cause or in spreading a belief: *a militant churchman.* —*n.* a militant person. **—mil′i tant ly,** *adv.*

mil i ta rism (mil′ə tə riz′əm), *n.* 1 policy of making military organization and power very strong. 2 the political condition in which the military interest is predominant in government or administration. 3 military spirit and ideals.

mil i tar ist (mil′ə tər ist), *n.* 1 person who believes in a very powerful military organization or the predominance of military interests. 2 expert in warfare and military matters.

mil i ta ris tic (mil′ə tə ris′tik), *adj.* of or having to do with militarists or militarism. **—mil′i ta ris′ti cal ly,** *adv.*

mil i ta rize (mil′ə tə rīz′), *v.t.,* **-rized, -riz ing.** 1 make the military organization of (a country) very powerful. 2 fill with military spirit and ideals. **—mil′i tar i za′tion,** *n.*

mil i tar y (mil′ə ter′ē), *adj.* 1 of or for soldiers; done by soldiers: *a military uniform, military discipline, military maneuvers.* 2 befitting a soldier; suitable for war: *military valor.* 3 backed up by armed force: *a military government.* 4 of or having to do with the army, the armed forces, affairs of war, or a state of war: *military history, military personnel.* See synonym study below. —*n.* **the military, a** the army; soldiers. **b** the armed forces. [< Latin *militaris* < *militem* soldier] **—mil′i tar′i ly,** *adv.*

Syn. *adj.* 4 **Military, martial, warlike** mean having to do with war. **Military** applies to warfare as carried on by trained forces and to the activities and attitudes of fighting men: *military strength, military bearing.* **Martial** emphasizes the glory and pomp or the gallantry of fighting men: *martial music.* **Warlike** is applied particularly to aggressive acts or to sentiments that lead to war: *a warlike demonstration.*

military police, soldiers or marines who act as police for the Army or Marine Corps.

mil i tate (mil′ə tāt), *v.i.,* **-tat ed, -tat ing.** have or exert force; act; work; operate (against or in favor of): *Bad weather militated against the success of the picnic.* [< Latin *militatum* soldiered < *militem* soldier]

mi li tia (mə lish′ə), *n.* a military force consisting especially of citizens trained for war, emergency duty, or the national defense. Every state of the United States has a militia called the National Guard. [< Latin]

mi li tia man (mə lish′ə mən), *n., pl.* **-men.** member of the militia.

milk (milk), *n.* 1 the whitish liquid secreted by the mammary glands of female mammals for the nourishment of their young. 2 any liquid resembling this in appearance, taste, etc., as the juice of the coconut or the latex of certain plants. 3 **cry over spilt milk,** to waste sorrow or regret on what has happened and cannot be remedied. —*v.t.* 1 draw milk, by hand or by means of a machine, from (a cow, goat, ewe, etc.). 2 drain contents, strength, information, wealth, etc., from: *milk a company of its resources.* —*v.i.* yield or produce milk. [Old English *mioluc, milc*]

milk er (mil′kər), *n.* 1 person who milks. 2 machine that milks. 3 any animal that gives milk, especially a cow.

milk maid (milk′mād′), *n.* 1 woman who milks cows. 2 woman who works in a dairy; dairymaid.

milk man (milk′man′), *n., pl.* **-men.** man who sells or delivers milk to customers.

milk of magnesia, a milk-white medicine consisting of magnesium hydroxide, suspended in water, used as a laxative and antacid. *Formula:* $Mg(OH)_2$

milk run, SLANG. a routine flight, especially a short reconnaissance mission in wartime.

hat, āge, fär; let, ēqual, tėrm;
it, īce; hot, ōpen, ôrder;
oil, out; cup, pu̇t, rüle;
ch, child; ng, long; sh, she;
th, thin; ᴛʜ, then; zh, measure;

ə represents *a* in about, *e* in taken,
i in pencil, *o* in lemon, *u* in circus.

< = from, derived from, taken from.

milk shake, a drink consisting of milk, flavoring, and often ice cream, shaken or beaten until frothy.

milk snake, any of several harmless, tricolored, blotched or ringed snakes of North America which are constrictors of the same genus as the king snakes.

milk sop (milk′sop′), *n.* an unmanly fellow; coward.

milk sugar, lactose.

milk tooth, one of the first set of temporary teeth of a mammal, of which children have twenty.

milk weed (milk′wēd′), *n.* any of a genus of herbs, especially a common species having juice that looks like milk, and seed pods tufted with long, silky hairs.

milk-white (milk′hwīt′), *adj.* white as milk.

milk y (mil′kē), *adj.,* **milk i er, milk i est.** 1 like milk; white as milk; whitish. 2 of or yielding milk. 3 mild; weak; timid. **—milk′i ness,** *n.*

Milky Way, 1 a broad band of faint light that stretches across the sky at night. It is made up of countless stars too far away to be seen separately without a telescope. 2 the galaxy in which these countless stars are found; Galaxy. The sun, earth, and the other planets around the sun are part of the Milky Way.

mill[1] (mil), *n.* 1 machine for grinding grain into flour or meal. 2 building specially designed and fitted with machinery for the grinding of grain into flour. 3 any machine or apparatus for crushing or grinding: *a pepper mill.* 4 building where manufacturing is done: *a cotton mill.* 5 any of various other machines for performing certain operations upon material in the process of manufacture. 6 **go through the mill,** INFORMAL. **a** get a thorough training or experience. **b** learn by hard or painful experience. 7 **put through the mill,** INFORMAL. **a** test; examine; try out. **b** teach by hard or painful experience. —*v.t.* 1 grind (grain) into flour or meal. 2 grind into powder or pulp. 3 manufacture. 4 cut a series of fine notches or ridges in the edge of (a coin): *A dime is milled.* —*v.i.* move (around) in confusion: *The frightened cattle began to mill around.* [Old English *mylen* < Late Latin *molina, molinum* < Latin *mola* millstone, mill]

mill[2] (mil), *n.* \$.001, or $^1/_{10}$ of a cent. Mills are used in figuring, but not as coins. [short for Latin *millesimus* one thousandth < *mille* thousand]

Mill (mil), *n.* **John Stuart,** 1806-1873, English economist and philosopher.

Mil lay (mə lā′), *n.* **Edna St. Vincent,** 1892-1950, American poet.

mill dam (mil′dam′), *n.* 1 dam built across a stream to supply water power for a mill. 2 pond made by such a dam; millpond.

mil len ni al (mə len′ē əl), *adj.* 1 of a thousand years. 2 like that of the millennium; fit for the millennium.

mil len ni um (mə len′ē əm), *n., pl.* **-len ni ums, -len ni a** (-len′ē ə). 1 period of a thousand years: *The world is many millenniums old.* 2 a thousandth anniversary. 3 (in the Bible) the period of a thousand years during which Christ is expected to reign on earth. 4 period of righteousness and happiness, of just government, of peace and prosperity, etc. [< New Latin < Latin *mille* thousand + *annus* year]

mil le pede (mil′ə pēd′), *n.* millipede.

mill er (mil′ər), *n.* 1 person who owns or runs a mill, especially a flour mill. 2 any of certain moths whose wings are covered with a whitish powder resembling flour.

Mill er (mil′ər), *n.* **Arthur,** born 1915, American playwright.

mil let (mil′it), *n.* 1 an annual cereal grass bearing a large crop of very small, nutritious seeds, cultivated as a food grain in Europe, Asia, and Africa, and as fodder in the United States. 2 any of various other grasses grown for their seeds or for forage. 3 grain or seed of any of these plants. [< Middle French < Latin *milium*]

Mil let (mə lā′), *n.* **Jean François,** 1814-1875, French painter.

milli-, *combining form.* one thousandth of a ____: *Millimeter = one thousandth of a meter.* [< Latin *mille*]

mil li am pere (mil′ē am′pir), *n.* unit for measuring electric current equal to $^1/_{1000}$ of an ampere.

mil liard (mil′yərd, mil′yärd), *n.* BRITISH. a thousand millions; billion; 1,000,000,000.

mil li bar (mil′ə bär), *n.* unit of atmospheric or barometric pressure equal to 1000 dynes per square centimeter. Standard atmospheric pressure at sea level is about 1013 millibars or 14.69 pounds per square inch. An inch of mercury equals about 34 millibars.

mil li gram (mil′ə gram), *n.* unit of mass equal to $^1/_{1000}$ of a gram. See **measure** for table.

mil li gramme (mil′ə gram), *n.* BRITISH. milligram.

Mil li kan (mil′ə kən), *n.* **Robert A.,** 1868-1953, American physicist.

mil li li ter (mil′ə lē′tər), *n.* unit of volume equal to $^1/_{1000}$ of a liter. See **measure** for table.

mil li li tre (mil′ə lē′tər), *n.* BRITISH. milliliter.

mil li me ter (mil′ə mē′tər), *n.* unit of length equal to $^1/_{1000}$ of a meter. See **measure** for table.

mil li me tre (mil′ə mē′tər), *n.* BRITISH. millimeter.

mil li mi cron (mil′ə mī′kron), *n.* unit of length equal to $^1/_{1000}$ of a micron.

mil li ner (mil′ə nər), *n.* person who makes, trims, or sells women's hats. [variant of *Milaner,* dealer in goods from *Milan,* Italy, famous for its straw work]

mil li ner y (mil′ə ner′ē, mil′ə nər ē), *n., pl.* **-ner ies.** 1 women's hats. 2 business of making, trimming, or selling women's hats.

mill ing (mil′ing), *n.* 1 business of grinding grain in a mill. 2 manufacturing. 3 act or process of cutting notches or ridges on the edge of a coin. 4 such notches or ridges.

milling machine, a machine tool with rotary cutters for working metal.

mil lion (mil′yən), *n., adj.* 1 one thousand thousand; 1,000,000. 2 a very large number; very many: *millions of fish.* [< Old French < Italian *milione* < *mille* thousand < Latin]

mil lion aire (mil′yə ner′, mil′yə nar′), *n.* 1 person whose wealth amounts to a million or more dollars, pounds, francs, etc. 2 a very wealthy person.

mil lion fold (mil′yən fōld′), *adv., adj.* a million times as much or as many.

mil lionth (mil′yənth), *adj., n.* 1 last in a series of a million. 2 one, or being one, of a million equal parts.

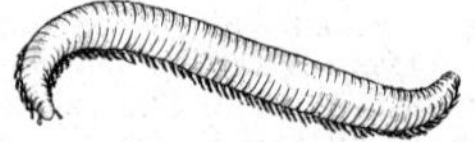

millipede—about 1 in. long

mil li pede (mil′ə pēd′), *n.* any of a class of small, wormlike arthropods having a body consisting of many segments, most of which bear two pairs of legs; diplopod. Also, **millepede.** [< Latin *millepeda* < *mille* thousand + *pedem* foot]

mill pond (mil′pond′), *n.* pond supplying water to drive a mill, especially such a pond formed by a milldam.

mill race (mil′rās′), *n.* 1 current of water that drives a mill wheel. 2 channel in which it flows to the mill; sluice.

mill stone (mil′stōn′), *n.* 1 either of a pair of round, flat stones for grinding corn, wheat, etc. 2 a heavy burden. 3 anything that grinds or crushes.

mill stream (mil′strēm′), *n.* the stream in a millrace.

mill wheel, wheel that supplies power for a mill, especially a water wheel.

mill work (mil′wėrk′), *n.* 1 doors, windows, moldings, and other things made in a planing mill. 2 work done in a mill.

mill wright (mil′rīt′), *n.* 1 person who designs, builds, or sets up mills or machinery for mills. 2 mechanic who sets up and takes care of the machinery in a factory, etc.

Milne (miln), *n.* **A. A.** 1882-1956, English writer of children's verses and stories and of plays.

mi lord (mi lôrd′), *n.* 1 my lord (applied by continental Europeans, especially formerly, to an English gentleman). 2 an English lord or nobleman.

milque toast (milk′tōst′), *n.* an extremely timid person. [< Caspar *Milquetoast,* a comic strip character]

milt (milt), *n.* 1 the sperm cells of male fishes with the milky fluid containing them. 2 the reproductive gland in male fishes when containing this fluid. [perhaps < Middle Dutch *milte* milt of fish, spleen]

Mil ti a des (mil ti′ə dēz′), *n.* 540?-488? B.C., Athenian general who defeated the Persians at Marathon.

Mil ton (milt′n), *n.* **John,** 1608-1674, English poet who wrote *Paradise Lost.*

Mil to ni an (mil tō′nē ən), *adj.* Miltonic.

Mil ton ic (mil ton′ik), *adj.* 1 of or having to do with Milton. 2 resembling Milton's literary style; solemn and majestic.

Mil wau kee (mil wô′kē), *n.* city in SE Wisconsin, on Lake Michigan. 717,000.

mime (mīm), *n., v.,* **mimed, mim ing.** —*n.* 1 a mimic, jester, or clown. 2 among the ancient Greeks and Romans: **a** a coarse farce using funny or ludicrous actions and gestures. **b** actor in such a farce. 3 pantomime. 4 actor, especially in a pantomime. —*v.t.* 1 imitate; mimic. 2 act or play (a part), usually without words. —*v.i.* act in a pantomime; act without using words. [< Greek *mimos*] **—mim′er,** *n.*

mim e o graph (mim′ē ə graf), *n.* machine for making copies of written or typewritten material by means of stencils. —*v.t.* make (copies) with a mimeograph. [< Greek *mimeisthai* imitate < *mimos* mime]

mi met ic (mi met′ik, mī met′ik), *adj.* 1 imitative: *mimetic gestures.* 2 make-believe. 3 having to do with or exhibiting mimicry. **—mi met′i cal ly,** *adv.*

mim ic (mim′ik), *v.,* **-icked, -ick ing,** *n., adj.* —*v.t.* 1 make fun of by imitating. 2 copy closely; imitate; ape: *A parrot can mimic a person's voice.* 3 represent imitatively; simulate. 4 resemble closely in form, color, etc.: *Some insects mimic leaves.* —*n.* person or thing that mimics. —*adj.* 1 not real, but imitated or pretended for some purpose: *a mimic battle.* 2 imitative: *mimic gestures.*

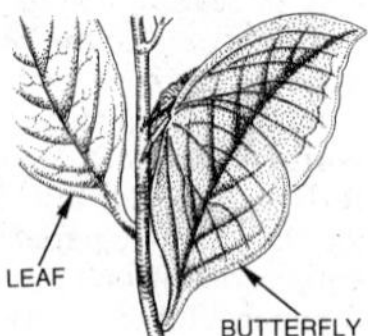

mimicry (def. 3)

mim ic ry (mim′ik rē), *n., pl.* **-ries.** 1 act or practice of mimicking. 2 an instance, performance, or result of mimicking. 3 the close outward resemblance of an animal to some different animal or to its environment, especially for protection or concealment.

mi mo sa (mi mō′sə), *n.* 1 any of a genus of trees, shrubs, and herbs of the pea family, growing in tropical or warm regions and usually having fernlike leaves and heads or spikes of small flowers. The sensitive plant is a mimosa. 2 acacia. [< Greek *mimos* mime]

min., 1 minimum. 2 minute or minutes.

mi na (mī′nə), *n., pl.* **mi nae** (mī′nē), **mi nas.** unit of weight and value used by the ancient Greeks, Egyptians, and others, equal to $^1/_{60}$ of a talent. [< Latin < Greek *mna,* of Semitic origin]

min a ret (min′ə ret′), *n.* a slender, high tower of a Moslem mosque with one or more projecting balconies, from which a muezzin, or crier, calls the people to prayer. [< French or Spanish < Arabic *manārah* lighthouse]

min a to ry (min′ə tôr′ē, min′ə tōr′ē), *adj.* menacing; threatening. [< Late Latin *minatorius* < Latin *minari* threaten]

mince (mins), *v.,* **minced, minc ing,** *n.* —*v.t.* 1 chop up into very small pieces; shred; hash. 2 speak or do in an affectedly polite or elegant manner. 3 **not to mince matters** or **not to mince words,** speak plainly and frankly. —*v.i.* walk with short, affectedly dainty steps. —*n.* 1 anything cut up into very small pieces. 2 mincemeat. [< Old French *mincier,* ultimately < Latin *minutum* small] **—minc′er,** *n.*

mince meat (mins′mēt′), *n.* 1 mixture of chopped apples, suet, raisins, currants, spices, etc., and sometimes meat, used as a filling for pies. 2 meat cut up into very small pieces.

mince pie, pie filled with mincemeat.

minc ing (min′sing), *adj.* 1 putting on a dainty and refined manner: *a mincing voice.* 2 walking with short steps. **—minc′ing ly,** *adv.*

mind (mīnd), *n.* 1 the part of an individual that knows, thinks, feels, reasons, wills, etc.

hat, āge, fär; let, ēqual, tėrm;
it, īce; hot, ōpen, ôrder;
oil, out; cup, pu̇t, rüle;
ch, child; ng, long; sh, she;
th, thin; ᴛʜ, then; zh, measure;

ə represents *a* in about, *e* in taken, *i* in pencil, *o* in lemon, *u* in circus.

< = from, derived from, taken from.

2 mental ability; intellect or understanding; intelligence: *a good mind.* 3 person who has intelligence: *the greatest minds of the period.* 4 reason; sanity: *be out of one's mind, lose one's mind.* 5 way of thinking and feeling; opinion; view: *change one's mind.* 6 desire, purpose, intention, or will. 7 attention; thought; mental effort: *Keep your mind on your work.* 8 remembrance or recollection; memory: *This brings to mind a story.*
bear in mind or **keep in mind,** remember.
be of one mind, agree.
cross one's mind, occur to one; come into one's thoughts suddenly.
have a mind to, intend to; think of favorably.
have in mind, 1 remember. 2 take into account; consider. 3 intend; plan.
make up one's mind, decide; resolve.
on one's mind, in one's thoughts; troubling one.
put in mind, remind.
set one's mind on, want very much.
speak one's mind, give one's frank opinion; speak plainly or freely.
to one's mind, in one's opinion; to one's way of thinking.
—*v.t.* 1 bear in mind; give heed to: *Mind my words!* 2 be careful concerning: *Mind the step.* 3 look after; take care of; tend: *Mind the baby.* 4 obey: *Mind your father.* 5 object to; feel concern about: *Do you mind closing the door for me?* 6 turn one's attention to; apply oneself to. 7 **never mind,** don't let it trouble you; it does not matter. 8 DIALECT. remember. 9 DIALECT. remind. 10 DIALECT. intend; contemplate. —*v.i.* 1 take notice; observe. 2 be obedient: *train a dog to mind.* 3 be careful. 4 feel concern; care; object: *They don't mind if I'm late.* 5 DIALECT. remember.
[Old English *(ge)mynd* memory, thinking] —**mind′er,** *n.*

Min da na o (min′də nä′ō), *n.* second largest island in the Philippines, in the S part. 2,703,000 pop.; 36,500 sq. mi.

mind ed (mīn′did), *adj.* 1 having a certain kind of mind (usually in compounds such as *high-minded, strong-minded*). 2 inclined; disposed: *Come a little early, if you are so minded.*

mind ful (mīnd′fəl), *adj.* 1 having in mind; aware; heedful: *Mindful of your advice, I went slowly.* 2 taking thought; careful: *We had to be mindful of every step we took on the slippery sidewalk.* —**mind′ful ly,** *adv.* —**mind′ful ness,** *n.*

mind less (mīnd′lis), *adj.* 1 without mind or intelligence; stupid. 2 not taking thought; careless. —**mind′less ly,** *adv.* —**mind′less ness,** *n.*

Min do ro (min dôr′ō, min dōr′ō), *n.* island in the central Philippines. 168,000 pop.; 3800 sq. mi.

mind reader, person who can guess the thoughts of others. —**mind reading.**

mind's eye, mental view or vision; imagination.

mine^{1} (mīn), possessive form of **I.** *pron.* 1 the one or ones belonging to me: *Please lend me your pen; I have lost mine.* 2 **of mine,** belonging to me. —*adj.* ARCHAIC. my (used only before a vowel or *h*, or after a noun): *mine own, sister mine.* [Old English *mīn*]

mine^{2} (mīn), *n., v.,* **mined, min ing.** —*n.* 1 a large hole or pit dug in the earth for the purpose of taking out metals or metallic ores, or certain other minerals, as coal, salt, and precious stones. 2 deposit of mineral or ore, either under the ground or at its surface. 3 a rich or plentiful source: *The book proved to be a mine of information about radio.* 4 an underground passage in which an explosive is placed to blow up the enemy's entrenchment, forts, etc. 5 container holding an explosive charge that is put under water and exploded by propeller vibrations, changes in water pressure, or magnetic attraction, or that is laid on the ground or shallowly buried and exploded by contact with a vehicle, etc.
—*v.t., v.i.* 1 dig into the earth to take out ores, coal, etc. 2 get ores, coal, etc., from a mine. 3 work in a mine. 4 make a passage, hole, space, etc., below the surface of the earth. 5 lay explosive mines in or under: *mine the mouth of a harbor.* [< Old French]

mine field (mīn′fēld′), *n.* area throughout which explosive mines have been laid.

mine lay er (mīn′lā′ər), *n.* a surface vessel or submarine designed or equipped for laying underwater mines.

min er (mī′nər), *n.* 1 person who works in a mine. 2 soldier who lays explosive mines. 3 machine used for mining.

min er al (min′ər əl), *n.* 1 any natural substance obtained by mining or quarrying, such as coal, ore, salt, and stone. Gold, silver, and iron are metallic minerals; quartz, feldspar, and calcite are nonmetallic minerals. 2 any substance that is neither plant nor animal. —*adj.* 1 of minerals. 2 like a mineral. 3 containing minerals. 4 neither animal nor vegetable; inorganic. [< Medieval Latin *minerale* < *minera* a mine < Old French *minere* < *mine* mine^{2}]

min er al ize (min′ər ə līz), *v.t.,* **-ized, -iz ing.** 1 convert into mineral substance; transform (metal) into an ore. 2 impregnate or supply with mineral substances. —*v.i.* search for minerals. —**min′er al i za′tion,** *n.*

min er a log i cal (min′ər ə loj′ə kəl), *adj.* of or having to do with mineralogy. —**min′er a log′i cal ly,** *adv.*

min e ral o gist (min′ə rol′ə jist, min′ə ral′ə jist), *n.* an expert in mineralogy.

min e ral o gy (min′ə rol′ə jē, min′ə ral′ə jē), *n.* science of minerals.

mineral oil, 1 any oil derived from minerals, as petroleum. 2 a colorless, odorless, tasteless oil obtained from petroleum, used as a laxative.

mineral water, water containing mineral salts or gases. People drink various mineral waters for their health.

mineral wool, a woollike material made from melted slag, used as insulation against heat and cold.

Mi ner va (mə nėr′və), *n.* (in Roman myths) the goddess of wisdom, the arts, and defensive war, identified with the Greek goddess Athena.

min e stro ne (min′ə strō′nē), *n.* a thick soup containing vegetables, vermicelli, etc. [< Italian]

mine sweep er (mīn′swē′pər), *n.* ship used for dragging a harbor, the sea, etc., to remove, disarm, or harmlessly explode mines laid by an enemy.

Ming (ming), *n.* 1 the ruling Chinese dynasty from 1368 to 1644, known for the exquisitely decorated ceramics, paintings, etc., produced under it. 2 piece of fine porcelain made in China during this dynasty.

min gle (ming′gəl), *v.,* **-gled, -gling.** —*v.t.* combine in a mixture; mix; blend: *Two rivers that join mingle their waters.* —*v.i.* 1 be or become mingled; mix; blend. 2 associate: *mingle with important people.* [Middle English *mengelen* < Old English *mengan* to mix] —**min′gler,** *n.*

Min ho (min′hō′), *n.* Foochow.

min i (min′ē), *adj., n., pl.* **min is.** —*adj.* small or short for its kind (usually in compounds such as *minibus, minidress*). —*n.* miniskirt. [< *mini(ature)*]

min i a ture (min′ē ə chu̇r, min′ə chər), *n.* 1 anything represented on a very small scale; a reduced image or likeness: *In the museum there is a miniature of the ship "Mayflower."* 2 **in miniature,** on a very small scale; reduced in size. 3 a very small painting, usually a portrait on ivory or vellum. 4 art of painting these. 5 a picture in an illuminated manuscript. —*adj.* done or made on a very small scale; tiny; diminutive: *miniature furniture for a dollhouse.* [< Italian *miniatura* picture in an illuminated manuscript < Medieval Latin *miniare* illuminate (a manuscript) in red < Latin *miniare* paint red < *minium* red lead]

min i a tur ize (min′ē ə chə rīz′, min′ə chə rīz′), *v.t.,* **-ized, -iz ing.** reduce to a very small size: *miniaturized electronic devices.* —**min′i a tur i za′tion,** *n.*

min im (min′əm), *n.* 1 the smallest unit of liquid measure, equal to one sixtieth of a dram, or about a drop. See **measure** for table. 2 BRITISH. a half note in music. 3 something very small or insignificant. 4 a single stroke made vertically downward in writing by hand. [< Latin *minimus* smallest. See MINIMUM.]

min i mal (min′ə məl), *adj.* least possible; very small; having to do with a minimum. —**min′i mal ly,** *adv.*

min i mize (min′ə mīz), *v.t.,* **-mized, -miz ing.** 1 reduce to the least possible amount or degree: *The polar explorers took every precaution to minimize the dangers of their trip.* 2 state or represent at the lowest possible estimate; belittle: *An ungrateful person minimizes the help others have given him.* —**min′i mi za′tion,** *n.* —**min′i miz′er,** *n.*

min i mum (min′ə məm), *n., pl.* **-mums, -ma** (-mə), *adj.* —*n.* 1 the least possible amount; lowest amount: *Eight hours' sleep is the minimum I need a night.* 2 the lowest amount of variation attained or recorded. 3 (in mathematics) a value of a function less than any values close to it. —*adj.* least possible; lowest: *Eighteen is the minimum age for voting.* [< Latin, neuter of *minimus* smallest, superlative of *minor* smaller, lesser]

minimum wage, 1 the wage agreed upon or fixed by law as the lowest payable to certain employees. 2 a living wage.

min ing (mī′ning), *n.* 1 the working of mines for ores, coal, etc. 2 business of digging coal or ores from mines. 3 the laying of explosive mines.

min ion (min′yən), *n.* 1 servant or follower willing to do whatever he is ordered; servile or obsequious person. 2 a darling; favorite. 3 size of printing type; 7 point. This sentence is set in minion. [< Middle French *mignon* petite, dainty]

min is cule (min′ə skyül), *adj., n.* minuscule.

min i skirt (min′ē skėrt′), *n.* a short skirt, several inches above the knee.

min is ter (min′ə stər), *n.* 1 clergyman serving a church, especially a Protestant church; spiritual guide; pastor. 2 person who is given charge of a department of the government: *the French Minister of Justice.* 3 diplomat sent to a foreign country to represent his own government, especially a diplomat ranking below an ambassador: *the United States Minister to Switzerland.* 4 person or thing employed in carrying out a purpose, the will, etc., of another; agent. *—v.i.* be of service or aid; be helpful: *minister to a sick person.* [< Latin, servant < *minus* less]

min is ter i al (min′ə stir′ē əl), *adj.* 1 of a minister. 2 of a ministry. 3 suited to a clergyman. 4 executive; administrative: *a ministerial act.* 5 concerned as an agent or instrument; instrumental. **—min′is ter′i al ly,** *adv.*

minister plenipotentiary, *pl.* **ministers plenipotentiary.** plenipotentiary.

min is trant (min′ə strənt), *adj.* ministering. *—n.* person who ministers.

min is tra tion (min′ə strā′shən), *n.* 1 service as a minister of a church. 2 help; aid: *ministration to the poor.*

min is try (min′ə strē), *n., pl.* **-tries.** 1 office, duties, or time of service of a minister. 2 the body of ministers of a church; clergy. 3 the ministers of a government, especially of the British or a European government. Ministers of a government are often equivalent to cabinet members in the United States. 4 in Great Britain and Europe: **a** a government department under a minister. **b** the offices of such a department. 5 a ministering or serving. 6 agency; instrumentality.

min i track (min′ə trak′), *n.* an electronic system for tracking satellites and rockets by means of radio signals. [< *mini(mum weight) track(ing)*]

min i ver (min′ə vər), *n.* 1 a white, spotted, or gray and white fur, formerly much used for lining and trimming garments, especially ceremonial costumes. 2 any pure white fur, especially ermine. [< Old French *menu vair* small vair]

mink (def. 1)—2 ft. long with the tail

mink (mingk), *n., pl.* **minks** or **mink.** 1 a small mammal of North America that resembles and is of the same genus as the weasel and lives in water part of the time. 2 its soft, valuable fur, commonly a deep brown. [apparently < Scandinavian (Swedish) *mänk*] **—mink′like′,** *adj.*

Minn., Minnesota.

Min ne ap o lis (min′ē ap′ə lis), *n.* city in SE Minnesota, on the Mississippi. 434,000.

min ne sing er or **Min ne sing er** (min′ə sing′ər), *n.* one of a class of German lyrical poets and singers of the 1100's to the 1300's. [< German *Minnesinger* singer of love]

Min ne so ta (min′ə sō′tə), *n.* one of the midwestern states of the United States. 3,805,000 pop.; 84,100 sq. mi. *Capital:* St. Paul. *Abbrev.:* Minn. **—Min′ne so′tan,** *adj., n.*

min now (min′ō), *n., pl.* **-nows** or **-now.** 1 any of various very small, freshwater fish belonging to the same family as the carp. 2 any very tiny fish. [Middle English *minwe*]

Mi no an (mi nō′ən), *adj.* of or having to do with the civilization of Crete from about 3500 to 1400 B.C. *—n.* native or inhabitant of Minoan Crete. [< *Minos*]

mi nor (mī′nər), *adj.* 1 less important; smaller; lesser: *a minor fault, a minor gain.* 2 of a lower rank or order: *a minor poet, a minor political party.* 3 under the legal age of responsibility (18 or 21 years). 4 in music: **a** less by a half step than the corresponding major interval: *a minor chord.* **b** denoting a scale, key, or mode whose third tone is minor in relation to the main tone: *the C minor scale.* 5 of, having to do with, or designating a minor in education: *a minor subject.* *—n.* 1 person under the legal age of responsibility. 2 (in music) a minor key, scale, chord, interval, etc. 3 subject or course of study to which a student gives less time and attention than to his major subject. *—v.i.* have or take as a minor subject of study: *minor in French.* [< Latin, smaller, lesser]

Mi nor ca (mə nôr′kə), *n.* one of the Balearic Islands in the W Mediterranean, belonging to Spain. 43,000 pop.; 271 sq. mi. Also, SPANISH **Menorca. —Mi nor′can,** *adj., n.*

mi nor i ty (mə nôr′ə tē, mə nor′ə tē; mī-nôr′ə tē, mī nor′ə tē), *n., pl.* **-ties.** 1 the smaller number or part; less than half. 2 a smaller party or group opposed to a majority, as in voting or other action. 3 group within a country, state, etc., that differs in race, religion, or national origin from the larger part of the population. 4 condition or time of being under the legal age of responsibility.

minor league, any professional sports league or association, especially in baseball, other than the major leagues.

minor premise, the premise that refers to a particular case in a syllogism.

minor scale, a musical scale having eight notes with half steps instead of whole steps after the second and fifth notes.

minor suit, diamonds or clubs in bridge.

Mi nos (mī′nəs, mī′nos), *n.* in Greek legends: **a** a king and lawgiver of Crete, the son of Zeus and Europa, who became a judge in Hades. **b** his grandson, who built the Labyrinth at Crete.

Min o taur (min′ə tôr), *n.* (in Greek legends) a monster with a bull's head and a man's body, kept in the Labyrinth at Crete, where every year it devoured seven Athenian youths and seven maidens offered in tribute until Theseus killed it.

Minsk (minsk), *n.* city in W Soviet Union, capital of the Byelorussian S.S.R. 916,000.

min ster (min′stər), *n.* 1 church of a monastery. 2 a large or important church; cathedral. [Old English *mynster* < Late Latin *monasterium.* Doublet of MONASTERY.]

min strel (min′strəl), *n.* 1 (in the Middle Ages) a singer or musician who entertained in the household of a lord or went about and sang or recited poems, often of his own making, to the accompaniment of a harp or other instrument. 2 member of a minstrel show. 3 musician, singer, or poet. [< Old French *menestrel,* ultimately < Latin *minister* servant, minister]

minstrel show, show or entertainment in which the performers blackened their faces and hands with burnt cork and played music, sang songs, and told jokes. Minstrel shows were very popular until the end of the 1800's.

min strel sy (min′strəl sē), *n., pl.* **-sies.** 1 art or practice of a minstrel. 2 collection of songs and ballads. 3 company of minstrels.

mint[1] (mint), *n.* 1 any of a genus of sweet-smelling herbs of the mint family, often used for flavoring, as the peppermint and spearmint. 2 any other plant of the mint family. 3 piece of candy flavored with mint, often eaten after a meal. [Old English *minte* < Latin *menta*]

mint[2] (mint), *n.* 1 place where money is coined by government authority. 2 a large amount: *A billion dollars is a mint of money.* 3 place where anything is made or fabricated. *—v.t.* 1 coin (money). 2 make or fabricate; originate: *mint words, mint phrases.* *—adj.* without a blemish; as good as new: *a car in mint condition.* [Old English *mynet* coin < Latin *moneta* mint, money. Doublet of MONEY.] **—mint′er,** *n.*

mint age (min′tij), *n.* 1 a minting; coinage. 2 product of minting; output of a mint. 3 charge for coining; cost of coining. 4 stamp or character impressed in minting.

mint family, a large group of dicotyledonous herbs and shrubs having square stems and opposite or whorled aromatic leaves which usually contain a volatile, aromatic oil. The family includes many herbs used in preparing food, as the mints, sage, thyme, and basil.

min u end (min′yü end), *n.* number or quantity from which another is to be subtracted. EXAMPLE: In 100 − 23 = 77, the minuend is 100. [< Latin *minuendus* to be made smaller < *minus* less]

minuet (def. 1)
couple dancing the minuet

min u et (min′yü et′), *n.* 1 a slow, stately dance with complex figures, fashionable in the 1600's and 1700's. 2 music for it. [< French *menuet,* diminutive of *menu* small. See MENU.]

mi nus (mī′nəs), *prep.* 1 decreased by; less: *5 minus 2 leaves 3.* 2 INFORMAL. without; lacking: *a book minus its cover.* *—adj.* 1 less than: *a mark of B minus.* 2 less than zero; negative in quantity. *—n.* 1 minus sign. 2 a negative quantity. 3 any deficiency or shortcoming; lack. [< Latin, less, neuter of *minor* lesser]

mi nus cu lar (mi nus′kyə lər), *adj.* of or like a minuscule; small.

mi nus cule (mi nus′kyül), *adj.* 1 extremely small: *a minuscule person.* 2 **a** (of a letter) small. **b** written in minuscules. *—n.* a small letter in medieval writing, neither capital nor uncial. Also, **miniscule.** [< French < Latin *minusculus* < *minus* less]

minus sign, the sign (−), indicating that the quantity following is to be subtracted, or is a negative quantity.

min ute[1] (min′it), *n., v.,* **-ut ed, -ut ing.** —*n.* 1 one sixtieth of an hour; sixty seconds. 2 a short time; instant: *I'll be there in a minute.* See synonym study below. 3 an exact point of time: *The minute you see him, tell me.* 4 one sixtieth of a degree (often indicated by the symbol ′). **5 minutes,** *pl.* **a** an official record of proceedings at a meeting of a society, board, committee, etc. **b** a rough draft or written summary; note; memorandum. **6 up to the minute,** up to date. —*v.t.* 1 record in the minutes (of a meeting, etc.). 2 draft (a document, etc.); summarize in a memorandum. [< Old French < Late Latin *minuta* minute, small part < Latin, feminine of *minutum* made small. See MINUTE[2].]

Syn. *n.* 2 **Minute, moment, instant** mean a point or extremely short period of time. When **minute** is less definite in meaning than "sixty seconds," it is interchangeable with **moment,** both suggesting a brief time of noticeable duration: *May I rest a minute? I'll be with you in a moment.* **Instant** suggests a point of time too brief to be noticed: *I recognized him the instant I saw him.*

mi nute[2] (mī nüt′, mī nyüt′), *adj.* 1 very small; tiny: *a minute speck of dust.* 2 going into or concerned with very small details: *minute instructions.* 3 of minor importance; trifling; petty. [< Latin *minutum* made small < *minus* less. Doublet of MENU.] —**mi nute′ly,** *adv.* —**mi nute′ness,** *n.*

min ute hand (min′it), hand on a clock or watch that indicates minutes. It moves around the dial once an hour.

min ute man (min′it man′), *n., pl.* **-men.** member of the American militia just before and during the Revolutionary War. The minutemen kept themselves ready for military service at a minute's notice.

mi nu ti ae (mi nü′shē ē, mi nyü′shē ē), *n.pl.* very small matters; trifling details. [< Latin, trifles, plural of *minutia* smallness < *minutum.* See MINUTE[2].]

minx (mingks), *n.* a pert girl. [origin uncertain]

Mi o cene (mī′ə sēn′), *n.* 1 the fourth epoch of the Tertiary period, after the Oligocene and before the Pliocene, during which grasses developed and grazing mammals flourished. 2 the rocks formed in this epoch. —*adj.* of or having to do with this epoch or its rocks. See chart under **geology.** [< Greek *meiōn* less + *kainos* recent]

mir (mir), *n.* a self-governing agricultural community in Russia in the middle 1800's. [< Russian]

Mir a beau (mir′ə bō), *n.* **Comte de,** 1749-1791, Honoré Gabriel Victor Riqueti, French statesman and orator.

mir a cle (mir′ə kəl), *n.* 1 a wonderful happening that is contrary to or independent of the known laws of nature, and is therefore ascribed to God or some supernatural being or power. 2 something marvelous; a wonder: *It was a miracle you weren't hurt in that accident.* 3 a remarkable example: *a miracle of patience, an engineering miracle.* [< Latin *miraculum,* ultimately < *mirus* wonderful]

miracle play, play based on Bible stories, especially on the life of Christ, or on the legends of the saints, produced during the Middle Ages.

mi rac u lous (mə rak′yə ləs), *adj.* 1 constituting a miracle; contrary to or independent of the known laws of nature; supernatural. 2 marvelous; wonderful: *miraculous good fortune.* 3 producing miracles; having the power to work miracles. —**mi rac′u lous ly,** *adv.* —**mi rac′u lous ness,** *n.*

mi rage (mə räzh′), *n.* 1 an optical illusion, usually in the desert, at sea, or over a hot paved road, in which some distant scene appears to be much closer than it actually is. It is caused by the refraction of light rays from the distant scene by air layers of different temperatures. Often what is reflected is seen inverted or as something other than it is. Travelers on the desert may see a mirage of palm trees and water. 2 anything that does not exist; illusion. [< French < *mirer* look at]

mire (mīr), *n., v.,* **mired, mir ing.** —*n.* 1 soft, deep mud; slush. 2 wet, swampy ground; bog. —*v.t.* 1 cause to be stuck in mire. 2 soil with mud or mire. 3 involve in difficulties; entangle. —*v.i.* stick in mire; be bogged. [< Scandinavian (Old Icelandic) *mȳrr*]

Mir i am (mir′ē əm), *n.* (in the Bible) the sister of Moses and Aaron.

mirk (mėrk), *n.* murk.

mirk y (mėr′kē), *adj.,* **mirk i er, mirk i est.** murky.

Mi ró (mi rō′), *n.* **Joan,** born 1893, Spanish painter.

mir ror (mir′ər), *n.* 1 piece of glass that reflects images; looking glass. It is coated on one side with silver or aluminum. 2 any surface that reflects light. 3 whatever reflects or gives a true description: *This book is a mirror of the life of the pioneers.* 4 something to be imitated; model; pattern: *That knight was a mirror of chivalry.* —*v.t.* reflect as a mirror does: *the still water mirrored the trees along the bank.* [< Old French *mirour* < *mirer* look at < Latin *mirari* wonder, admire] —**mir′ror like′,** *adj.*

mirror image, an image in reverse; reflection.

mirth (mėrth), *n.* merry fun; being joyous or gay; merriment. [Old English *myrgth* < *myrge* merry]

mirth ful (mėrth′fəl), *adj.* full of or expressing mirth; merry; gay. —**mirth′ful ly,** *adv.* —**mirth′ful ness,** *n.*

mirth less (mėrth′lis), *adj.* without mirth; joyless; gloomy. —**mirth′less ly,** *adv.* —**mirth′less ness,** *n.*

MIRV (mėrv), *n.* Multiple Independently Targeted Reentry Vehicle.

mir y (mī′rē), *adj.,* **mir i er, mir i est.** 1 muddy; slushy. 2 swampy; boggy; marshy. 3 dirty; filthy. —**mir′i ness,** *n.*

mis-, *prefix.* 1 bad: *Misgovernment = bad government.* 2 badly: *Misbehave = behave badly.* 3 wrong: *Mispronunciation = wrong pronunciation.* 4 wrongly: *Misapply = apply wrongly.* [Old English or < Old French *mes-*]

mis ad ven ture (mis′əd ven′chər), *n.* an unfortunate accident; bad luck; mishap.

mis al li ance (mis′ə lī′əns), *n.* an unsuitable alliance or association, especially in marriage.

mis an thrope (mis′ən thrōp), *n.* person who dislikes or distrusts people in general; hater of mankind. [< Greek *misanthrōpos* < *misein* to hate + *anthrōpos* man]

mis an throp ic (mis′ən throp′ik), *adj.* of or like a misanthrope. —**mis′an throp′i cal ly,** *adv.*

hat, āge, fär; let, ēqual, tėrm;
it, īce; hot, ōpen, ôrder;
oil, out; cup, pu̇t, rüle;
ch, child; ng, long; sh, she;
th, thin; ᴛʜ, then; zh, measure;

ə represents *a* in about, *e* in taken,
i in pencil, *o* in lemon, *u* in circus.

< = from, derived from, taken from.

mis an thro pist (mis an′thrə pist), *n.* misanthrope.

mis an thro py (mis an′thrə pē), *n.* hatred, dislike, or distrust of people in general.

mis ap pli ca tion (mis′ap′lə kā′shən), *n.* a misapplying or a being misapplied; wrong application.

mis ap ply (mis′ə plī′), *v.t.,* **-plied, -ply ing.** apply wrongly; make a wrong application or use of.

mis ap pre hend (mis′ap′ri hend′), *v.t.* misunderstand.

mis ap pre hen sion (mis′ap′ri hen′shən), *n.* a misunderstanding.

mis ap pro pri ate (mis′ə prō′prē āt), *v.t.,* **-at ed, -at ing.** 1 use dishonestly as one's own: *The treasurer misappropriated the club's funds.* 2 put to a wrong use. —**mis′ap pro′pri a′tion,** *n.*

mis be come (mis′bi kum′), *v.t.,* **-came** (-kām′), **-come, -com ing.** be unbecoming to; be unfit for.

mis be got ten (mis′bi got′n), *adj.* unlawfully or improperly begotten; illegitimate.

mis be have (mis′bi hāv′), *v.i., v.t.,* **-haved, -hav ing.** behave badly.

mis be hav ior (mis′bi hā′vyər), *n.* bad behavior.

mis be lief (mis′bi lēf′), *n.* a wrong or erroneous belief.

mis be liev er (mis′bi lē′vər), *n.* person who holds a wrong or erroneous belief.

mis brand (mis brand′), *v.t.* 1 brand or mark incorrectly. 2 label improperly or falsely.

misc., 1 miscellaneous. 2 miscellany.

mis cal cu late (mis kal′kyə lāt), *v.t., v.i.,* **-lat ed, -lat ing.** calculate wrongly or incorrectly. —**mis′cal′cu la′tion,** *n.*

mis call (mis kôl′), *v.t.* call by a wrong name.

mis car riage (mis kar′ij), *n.* 1 failure, especially to achieve the proper result: *Because the judge was unfair, that trial resulted in a miscarriage of justice.* 2 failure to arrive or deliver: *the miscarriage of a letter, a miscarriage of freight.* 3 expulsion from the uterus of a fetus or embryo before it can live.

mis car ry (mis kar′ē), *v.i.,* **-ried, -ry ing.** 1 go wrong; be unsuccessful: *My plans miscarried, and I could not go on vacation.* 2 fail to arrive. 3 have a miscarriage; give birth so prematurely that the fetus or embryo cannot live.

mis cast (mis kast′), *v.t.,* **-cast, -cast ing.** put in a role for which one is not suited.

mis ce ge na tion (mis′ə jə nā′shən), *n.* intermarriage or interbreeding between supposedly different races of people, especially between whites and blacks. [< Latin *miscere* to mix + *genus* race]

mis cel la ne ous (mis′ə lā′nē əs), *adj.* 1 not all of one kind or nature; of mixed composition or character: *miscellaneous expenses.* See synonym study below. 2 dealing with various subjects; many-sided: *a miscellaneous writer.* [< Latin *miscellaneus* < *miscellus* mixed < *miscere* to mix] **—mis′cel la′ne ous ly,** *adv.* **—mis′cel la′ne ous ness,** *n.*

Syn. 1 **Miscellaneous, indiscriminate** mean including various things or kinds, without plan or order in selection. **Miscellaneous** emphasizes the varied or mixed nature of the things gathered together: *The boy had a miscellaneous collection of stones, butterflies, birds' nests, etc.* **Indiscriminate** emphasizes the lack of judgment or taste in selection and always suggests disapproval: *Indiscriminate buying is wasteful.*

mis cel la ny (mis′ə lā′nē), *n., pl.* **-nies.** 1 a miscellaneous collection; mixture. 2 Also, **miscellanies,** *pl.* a collection of miscellaneous articles in one book.

mis chance (mis chans′), *n.* 1 bad luck; misfortune. 2 piece of bad luck; unlucky accident.

mis chief (mis′chif), *n.* 1 conduct that causes harm or trouble, often unintentionally. 2 harm or injury, usually done by some person. 3 person who does harm or causes annoyance, often just in fun. 4 merry teasing: *Her eyes were full of mischief.* [< Old French *meschief* < *meschever* come to grief < *mes-* wrongly, mis- + *chever* come to an end < *chief* head]

mis chie vous (mis′chə vəs), *adj.* 1 causing mischief; naughty: *mischievous behavior.* 2 harmful: *mischievous gossip.* 3 full of pranks and teasing fun: *mischievous children.* **—mis′chie vous ly,** *adv.* **—mis′chie vous ness,** *n.*

mis ci bil i ty (mis′ə bil′ə tē), *n.* quality or condition of being miscible.

mis ci ble (mis′ə bəl), *adj.* capable of being mixed: *Water is not miscible with oil.* [< Latin *miscere* to mix]

mis con ceive (mis′kən sēv′), *v.t.,* **-ceived, -ceiv ing.** have wrong ideas about; misunderstand. **—mis′con ceiv′er,** *n.*

mis con cep tion (mis′kən sep′shən), *n.* a mistaken idea or notion; wrong conception.

mis con duct (*n.* mis kon′dukt; *v.* mis′kən dukt′), *n.* 1 bad behavior; improper conduct. 2 bad management; mismanagement. *—v.i.* behave badly. *—v.t.* manage badly; mismanage.

mis con struc tion (mis′kən struk′shən), *n.* wrong or mistaken meaning; misunderstanding; misinterpretation.

mis con strue (mis′kən strü′), *v.t.,* **-strued, -stru ing.** take in a wrong or mistaken sense; misunderstand; misinterpret.

mis count (*v.* mis kount′; *n.* mis′kount′), *v.t., v.i.* count wrongly or incorrectly. *—n.* a wrong or incorrect count.

mis cre ant (mis′krē ənt), *adj.* having very bad morals; wicked; base. *—n.* a base or wicked person; villain. [< Old French *mescreant* < *mes-* wrongly, mis- + *creire* believe]

mis cue (mis kyü′), *n., v.,* **-cued, -cu ing.** *—n.* 1 (in billiards, pool, etc.) a stroke in which the cue slips, causing it to miss the cue ball or strike it improperly. 2 INFORMAL. error; mistake. *—v.i.* 1 (in billiards, pool, etc.) make a miscue. 2 (in the theater) miss one's cue; respond to a wrong cue.

mis date (mis dat′), *v.,* **-dat ed, -dat ing,** *n.* *—v.t.* date wrongly or incorrectly. *—n.* a wrong or incorrect date.

mis deal (*v.* mis dēl′; *n.* mis′dēl′), *v.,* **-dealt** (-delt′), **-deal ing,** *n.* *—v.i.* deal wrongly at cards. *—n.* a wrong deal at cards.

mis deed (mis dēd′, mis′dēd′), *n.* a bad act; wicked deed.

mis de mean or (mis′di mē′nər), *n.* 1 a breaking of the law, not so serious as a felony. Disturbing the peace and breaking traffic laws are misdemeanors. 2 misdeed. 3 misbehavior.

mis di rect (mis′də rekt′, mis′dī rekt′), *v.t.* direct wrongly; give wrong directions to. **—mis′di rec′tion,** *n.*

mis do er (mis dü′ər), *n.* wrongdoer.

mis do ing (mis dü′ing), *n.* 1 wrongdoing. 2 misdeed.

mis doubt (mis dout′), *v.t.* 1 have doubts about; be distrustful of; suspect; distrust. 2 fear. *—n.* 1 suspicion; distrust; doubt. 2 fear.

mise en scène (mē′ zäN sen′), FRENCH. 1 the setting for a play. 2 the placing of scenery and actors in a scene. 3 setting; surroundings.

mis em ploy (mis′em ploi′), *v.t.* use wrongly or improperly; misuse. **—mis′em ploy′ment,** *n.*

mi ser (mī′zər), *n.* person who loves money for its own sake; one who lives poorly in order to save money and keep it. [< Latin, wretched]

mis er a ble (miz′ər ə bəl), *adj.* 1 very unhappy or unfortunate; wretched: *A sick child is often miserable.* 2 causing trouble or unhappiness: *a miserable cold.* 3 poor; mean; pitiful: *They live in miserable surroundings.* *—n.* person who is in misery or great want. [< Latin *miserabilis* < *miserari* to lament < *miser* wretched] **—mis′er a ble ness,** *n.* **—mis′er a bly,** *adv.*

Mis e rer e (miz′ə rer′ē, miz′ə rir′ē), *n.* 1 the 51st Psalm in the Revised and Authorized versions of the Bible; the 50th Psalm in the Douay Bible. 2 a musical setting for this psalm. [< Latin *miserere* have pity, the first word of this psalm in the Vulgate]

mi ser ly (mī′zər lē), *adj.* of, like, or suited to a miser; stingy: *miserly habits.* **—mi′ser li ness,** *n.*

mis er y (miz′ər ē), *n., pl.* **-er ies.** 1 a miserable, unhappy state of mind. 2 poor, mean, miserable circumstances: *a life of misery.* 3 a miserable condition; cause or source of wretchedness. [< Latin *miseria* < *miser* wretched]

mis fea sance (mis fē′zns), *n.* the wrongful performance of a lawful act; wrongful and injurious exercise of lawful authority. [< Old French *mesfaisance* < *mes-* wrong, mis- + *faire* do]

mis file (mis fīl′), *v.t.,* **-filed, -fil ing.** file incorrectly: *a misfiled memorandum.*

mis fire (mis fīr′), *v.,* **-fired, -fir ing,** *n.* *—v.i.* 1 fail to be fired or exploded properly, as when the fuel vapor does not ignite in the cylinders of an internal-combustion engine at the correct time, or a gun fails to shoot when the trigger is pulled. 2 go wrong; fail. *—n.* act or instance of misfiring.

mis fit (*n.* mis′fit′; *v.* mis fit′), *n., v.,* **-fit ted, -fit ting.** *—n.* 1 person who does not fit in a job, a group, etc.; maladjusted person. 2 a bad fit. *—v.t., v.i.* fit badly.

mis for tune (mis fôr′chən), *n.* 1 bad or adverse fortune; bad luck. 2 piece of bad luck; unlucky accident. See synonym study below.

Syn. 2 **Misfortune, adversity, mishap** mean something unlucky. **Misfortune** applies to an unfortunate condition that is not one's own fault: *She had the misfortune of being born lame.* **Adversity** applies chiefly to misfortune marked by a series of accidents or hardships: *Displaced persons have experienced adversity.* **Mishap** applies to a minor accident or unlucky incident: *By some mishap the letter went astray.*

mis give (mis giv′), *v.,* **-gave** (-gāv′), **-giv en** (-giv′ən), **-giv ing.** *—v.t.* cause to feel doubt, suspicion, or anxiety. *—v.i.* have misgivings.

mis giv ing (mis giv′ing), *n.* a feeling of doubt, suspicion, or anxiety: *We started off through the storm with some misgivings.*

mis gov ern (mis guv′ərn), *v.t.* govern or manage badly. **—mis gov′ern ment,** *n.*

mis guid ance (mis gīd′ns), *n.* bad or wrong guidance; misdirection.

mis guide (mis gīd′), *v.t.,* **-guid ed, -guid ing.** lead into mistakes or wrongdoing; mislead; misdirect.

mis guid ed (mis gī′did), *adj.* led into mistakes or wrongdoing; misled: *The misguided boy joined a gang of thieves.* **—mis guid′ed ly,** *adv.*

mis han dle (mis han′dl), *v.t.,* **-dled, -dling.** 1 handle or treat badly; maltreat. 2 manage badly; mismanage.

mis hap (mis′hap, mis hap′), *n.* an unlucky accident. See **misfortune** for synonym study.

mish mash (mish′mash′), *n.* a confused mixture; hodgepodge; jumble. [probably reduplication of *mash*]

Mish na or **Mish nah** (mish′nə), *n.* collection of Jewish laws and traditions based on Mosaic law, codified in A.D. 210. The Mishna forms the basic part of the Talmud. [< Hebrew *mishnāh* instruction]

mis in form (mis′in fôrm′), *v.t.* give wrong or misleading information to. **—mis′in for ma′tion,** *n.*

mis in ter pret (mis′in tėr′prit), *v.t.* interpret or explain wrongly; misunderstand. **—mis′in ter′pre ta′tion,** *n.*

mis judge (mis juj′), *v.t.,* **-judged, -judg ing.** judge wrongly or unjustly. **—mis judg′ment, mis judge′ment,** *n.*

mis lay (mis lā′), *v.t.,* **-laid** (-lād′), **-lay ing.** 1 put in a place and then forget where it is; lose temporarily. 2 put in an incorrect place.

mis lead (mis lēd′), *v.t.,* **-led, -lead ing.** 1 cause to go in the wrong direction; lead astray: *Our guide misled us in the woods, and we got lost.* 2 cause to do wrong; lead into wrongdoing: *He is a good boy, but bad companions misled him.* 3 lead to think what is not so; deceive: *His lies misled me.*

mis lead ing (mis lē′ding), *adj.* 1 leading to wrong conclusions; deceiving. 2 causing error or wrongdoing.

mis led (mis led′), *v.* pt. and pp. of **mislead.**

mis man age (mis man′ij), *v.t.,* **-aged, -ag ing.** manage badly or improperly. **—mis man′age ment,** *n.*

mis match (mis mach′), *v.t.* match badly or unsuitably, especially in marriage. *—n.* a bad or unsuitable match.

mis mate (mis māt′), *v.t., v.i.,* **-mat ed, -mat ing.** mate unsuitably.

mis name (mis nām′), *v.t.,* **-named, -nam ing.** call by a wrong name; miscall.

mis no mer (mis nō′mər), *n.* 1 name that describes wrongly: *"Lightning" is a misnomer for that slow, old horse.* 2 error in naming. [< Middle French *mesnommer* < *mes-* wrongly, mis- + *nommer* to name]

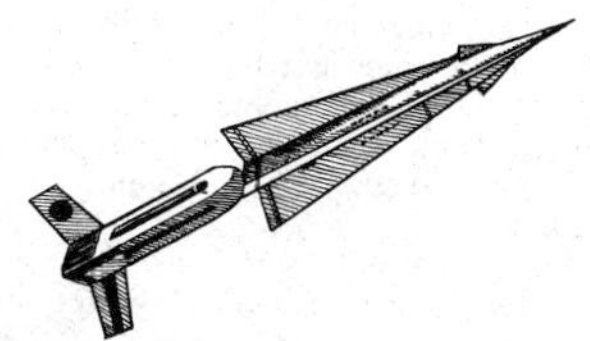

missile (def. 2)
of the type guided by radar to destroy enemy aircraft or missiles in midair

mi sog a mist (mi sog′ə mist), *n.* person who hates marriage.

mi sog a my (mi sog′ə mē), *n.* hatred of marriage. [< Greek *misos* hatred + *gamos* marriage]

mi sog y nist (mi soj′ə nist), *n.* hater of women.

mi sog y nous (mi soj′ə nəs), *adj.* hating women.

mi sog y ny (mi soj′ə nē), *n.* hatred of women. [< Greek *misogynia* < *misos* hatred + *gynē* woman]

mis place (mis plās′), *v.t.,* **-placed, -plac ing.** 1 put in the wrong place. 2 INFORMAL. put in a place and then forget where it is; mislay: *I have misplaced my pencil.* 3 give (one's love or trust) to the wrong person. **—mis place′ment,** *n.*

mis play (mis plā′), *n.* a wrong play. *—v.t., v.i.* play wrongly.

mis print (*n.* mis′print′; *v.* mis print′), *n.* mistake in printing. *—v.t.* print wrongly.

mis prize (mis prīz′), *v.t.,* **-prized, -priz ing.** 1 value too little; undervalue; slight. 2 despise; scorn.

mis pro nounce (mis′prə nouns′), *v.t., v.i.,* **-nounced, -nounc ing.** pronounce incorrectly. **—mis′pro nun′ci a′tion,** *n.*

mis quote (mis kwōt′), *v.t., v.i.,* **-quot ed, -quot ing.** quote incorrectly. **—mis′quo ta′tion,** *n.*

mis read (mis rēd′), *v.t.,* **-read** (-red′), **-read ing.** 1 read wrongly. 2 interpret wrongly; misunderstand.

mis rep re sent (mis′rep′ri zent′), *v.t.* represent falsely; give a wrong idea of. **—mis′rep re sen ta′tion,** *n.*

mis rule (mis rül′), *n., v.,* **-ruled, -rul ing.** *—n.* 1 bad or unwise rule; misgovernment. 2 condition of disorder, anarchy, or rebellion. *—v.t.* rule or govern badly; misgovern.

miss (mis), *v.t.* 1 fail to hit or strike: *miss a target in shooting.* 2 fail to find, get, or meet: *I set out to meet my father, but in the dark I missed him.* 3 let slip by; not seize: *I missed the chance of a ride to town.* 4 fail to catch: *miss the train.* 5 leave out: *miss a word in reading.* 6 fail to understand or grasp: *miss the point of a remark.* 7 fail to keep, do, or be present at: *miss school.* 8 escape or avoid: *barely miss being hit.* 9 notice the absence or loss of; feel keenly the absence of: *I missed my friend when she went away.* *—v.i.* fail to hit: *He fired twice, but both shots missed.* *—n.* 1 a failure to hit, attain, get, find, etc. 2 **a miss is as good as a mile,** a failure is a failure however near one may have been to success. [Old English *missan*]

Miss (mis), *n.* 1 title put before a girl's or unmarried woman's name. 2 **miss,** a young unmarried woman; girl. [short for *mistress*]
➤ **Miss.** Of the two plural forms used in referring to unmarried women of the same family, *the Misses Thorne* is more formal than the *Miss Thornes.*

Miss., Mississippi.

mis sal (mis′əl), *n.* book containing the prayers, etc., for celebrating Mass throughout the year. [< Medieval Latin *missale* < Late Latin *missa* Mass]

mis shape (mis shāp′), *v.t.,* **-shaped, -shaped** or **-shap en, -shap ing.** shape badly; deform.

mis shap en (mis shā′pən), *adj.* badly shaped; deformed.

mis sile (mis′əl), *n.* 1 object or weapon that is thrown, hurled, or shot, such as a stone, bullet, arrow, or lance. 2 a self-propelled rocket or bomb, such as a guided missile. [< Latin *missilis* that can be thrown, ultimately < *mittere* send]

mis sile man (mis′əl mən), *n., pl.* **-men.** person who works with missiles, either in construction or in use and maintenance.

mis sile ry or **mis sil ry** (mis′əl rē), *n.* 1 science or art having to do with the design, manufacture, and operation of missiles. 2 missiles collectively.

miss ing (mis′ing), *adj.* not found when looked for; lacking; absent; lost: *One book is missing from the set.*

missing link, 1 a hypothetical creature assumed to have been the connecting link between man and the anthropoid apes. 2 something lacking from a series.

mis sion (mish′ən), *n.* 1 a sending or being sent on some special work or service; errand. 2 group of persons sent on some special business, as by their government, to a foreign country to conduct negotiations. 3 a permanent diplomatic establishment, embassy, or legation. 4 task or function assigned to a military or naval unit, especially combat operation by one or more aircraft. 5 group of persons sent by a religious organization into other parts of the world to spread its beliefs. 6 **missions,** *pl.* an organized effort by a religious group to set up churches, schools, hospitals, etc. 7 the business on which a mission is sent. 8 station or headquarters of a religious mission, as the center of missionary effort in a particular area. 9 a special series of religious services to revive, stimulate, or create religious feeling. 10 business or purpose in life, especially what one seems (or feels himself) destined to do; calling: *It seemed to be her mission to care for her brother's children.* [< Latin *missionem* < *mittere* to send]

mis sion ar y (mish′ə ner′ē), *n., pl.* **-ar ies,** *adj.* *—n.* 1 person sent on a religious mission. 2 person who works to advance some cause or idea. *—adj.* 1 of religious missions or missionaries. 2 sent on a mission; engaged in missionary work.

Mis sis sip pi (mis′ə sip′ē), *n.* one of the south central states of the United States. 2,217,000 pop.; 47,700 sq. mi. *Capital:* Jackson. *Abbrev.:* Miss.

hat, āge, fär; let, ēqual, tėrm;
it, īce; hot, ōpen, ôrder;
oil, out; cup, pu̇t, rüle;
ch, child; ng, long; sh, she;
th, thin; ᴛʜ, then; zh, measure;

ə represents *a* in about, *e* in taken, *i* in pencil, *o* in lemon, *u* in circus.

< = from, derived from, taken from.

Mis sis sip pi an (mis′ə sip′ē ən), *n.* 1 native or inhabitant of Mississippi. 2 the earlier of the two periods into which the Carboniferous period is divided, after the Devonian and before the Pennsylvanian, characterized by the appearance of conifer, fern, and lichen forests. See chart under **geology.** 3 the rocks formed during this period. *—adj.* 1 of or having to do with Mississippi or the Mississippi River. 2 of or having to do with the Mississippian or its rocks.

Mississippi River, river in North America, flowing south through the United States from N Minnesota to the Gulf of Mexico. 2470 mi.

mis sive (mis′iv), *n.* a written message; letter. [< Medieval Latin *missivus,* ultimately < Latin *mittere* send]

Mis sour i (mə zu̇r′ē, mə zu̇r′ə), *n.* one of the midwestern states of the United States. 4,677,000 pop.; 69,700 sq. mi. *Capital:* Jefferson City. *Abbrev.:* Mo. **—Mis sour′i an,** *adj., n.*

Missouri River, river in the N part of the United States, flowing from SW Montana into the Mississippi. 2475 mi.

mis speak (mis spēk′), *v.t., v.i.,* **-spoke** (-spōk′), **-spo ken** (-spō′kən), **-speak ing.** speak, utter, or pronounce wrongly or incorrectly.

mis spell (mis spel′), *v.t., v.i.,* **-spelled** or **-spelt** (-spelt′), **-spell ing.** spell incorrectly.

mis spell ing (mis spel′ing), *n.* an incorrect spelling.

mis spent (mis spent′), *adj.* spent foolishly or wrongly; wasted: *a misspent fortune, a misspent life.*

mis state (mis stāt′), *v.t.,* **-stat ed, -stat ing.** state wrongly or incorrectly. **—mis state′ment,** *n.*

mis step (mis step′, mis′step′), *n.* 1 a wrong step. 2 error or slip in conduct.

miss y (mis′ē), *n., pl.* **miss ies.** INFORMAL. little miss; miss.

mist (mist), *n.* 1 suspension of very fine water droplets in the air above the ground; haze. 2 cloud of very fine drops of any liquid in the air. 3 anything that dims, blurs, or obscures: *A mist of prejudice spoiled his judgment.* *—v.i.* 1 come down in mist; rain in very fine drops; drizzle. 2 be covered with mist; become dim. *—v.t.* cover with a mist; put a mist before; make dim: *Tears misted her eyes.* [Old English] **—mist′like′,** *adj.*

mis tak a ble (mə stā′kə bəl), *adj.* that may be mistaken or misunderstood.

mis take (mə stāk′), *n., v.,* **-took, -tak en, -tak ing.** *—n.* 1 error in action, thought, or judgment: *It was a mistake to leave before the snow stopped.* 2 misunderstanding: *a mistake in interpretation.* *—v.t.* 1 misunderstand (what is seen or heard); take in a wrong sense. 2 take wrongly; take (to be some other person or thing): *I mistook him for his brother.* 3 estimate wrongly: *mistake one's own* *strength.* [< Scandinavian (Old Icelandic) *mistaka*] **—mis tak′er,** *n.*

mis tak en (mə stā′kən), *adj.* 1 wrong in opinion. 2 wrongly judged; wrong; erroneous: *a mistaken opinion.* —*v.* pp. of **mistake. —mis tak′en ly,** *adv.*

Mis ter (mis′tər), *n.* 1 Mr., a title put before a man's name or the name of his office or occupation: *Mr. Smith, Mr. President.* 2 **mister,** INFORMAL. sir. [variant of *master*]

mis time (mis tīm′), *v.t.,* **-timed, -tim ing.** 1 say or do at the wrong time. 2 miscalculate or misstate the time of.

mis tle toe (mis′əl tō), *n.* 1 a woody shrub with small, waxy, white berries and yellow flowers. Mistletoe is partly parasitic. It attaches itself to the branches and trunks of various trees, but produces some chlorophyll and is capable of photosynthesis. 2 sprig of mistletoe, often used as a Christmas decoration. [Old English *misteltān* < *mistel* mistletoe + *tān* twig]

mis took (mə stu̇k′), *v.* pt. of **mistake.**

mis tral (mis′trəl, mis träl′), *n.* a strong, cold, dry, northerly wind common in the Mediterranean provinces of France and neighboring regions. [< French < Provençal, originally, dominant < Latin *magistralis* < *magister* master]

Mis tral (mē sträl′), *n.* **Gabriela,** 1889-1957, Chilean poet and educator.

mis trans late (mis′tran slāt′, mis′tranz-lāt′; mis tran′slāt, mis tranz′lāt), *v.t., v.i.,* **-lat ed, -lat ing.** translate incorrectly. **—mis′trans la′tion,** *n.*

mis treat (mis trēt′), *v.t.* treat badly or wrongly; abuse. **—mis treat′ment,** *n.*

mis tress (mis′tris), *n.* 1 woman who is at the head of a household. 2 woman or country that is in control or can rule. 3 a woman owner or possessor. 4 woman who has a thorough knowledge or mastery: *She is a complete mistress of the art of cookery.* 5 woman teaching in a school, or at the head of a school, or giving lessons in a special subject. *the dancing mistress.* 6 ARCHAIC. woman loved and courted by a man. 7 woman who has a more or less permanent sexual relationship with a man to whom she is not married. 8 **Mistress,** ARCHAIC. Mrs., Madam, or Miss. [< Old French *maistresse,* feminine of *maistre* master. See MASTER.]

mis tri al (mis trī′əl), *n.* 1 trial in which the jury fails to agree on a verdict. 2 trial of no effect in law because of some error in the proceedings.

mis trust (mis trust′), *v.t.* feel no trust or confidence in; distrust; doubt: *She mistrusted her ability to learn to swim.* —*n.* lack of trust or confidence; suspicion.

mis trust ful (mis trust′fəl), *adj.* lacking confidence; distrustful; doubting; suspicious. **—mis trust′ful ly,** *adv.* **—mis trust′ful ness,** *n.*

mist y (mis′tē), *adj.,* **mist i er, mist i est.** 1 of or consisting of mist. 2 characterized by mist; full of or covered with mist: *misty hills.* 3 not clearly seen or outlined: *a misty figure.* 4 as if seen through a mist; vague; indistinct: *a misty notion.* [Old English *mistig*] **—mist′i ly,** *adv.* **—mist′i ness,** *n.*

mis un der stand (mis′un′dər stand′), *v.t., v.i.,* **-stood, -stand ing.** 1 understand wrongly. 2 take in a wrong sense; give the wrong meaning to.

mis un der stand ing (mis′un′dər-stan′ding), *n.* 1 wrong understanding; failure to understand; mistake as to meaning. 2 disagreement; quarrel.

mis un der stood (mis′un′dər stu̇d′), *v.* pt. and pp. of **misunderstand.**

mis us age (mis yü′sij, mis yü′zij), *n.* 1 a wrong or improper usage; misuse. 2 bad treatment; ill-usage.

mis use (*v.* mis yüz′; *n.* mis yüs′), *v.,* **-used, -us ing,** *n.* —*v.t.* 1 use for the wrong purpose; misapply. 2 mistreat; abuse. —*n.* a wrong or improper use; misapplication: *I noticed a misuse of the word "who" in your letter.*

Mitch ell (mich′əl), *n.* 1 **Margaret,** 1900-1949, American novelist. 2 **Maria,** 1818-1889, American astronomer. 3 **Mount,** peak in W North Carolina, the highest of the Appalachian Mountains. 6684 ft.

mite[1]
about 1/16 in. long

mite[1] (mīt), *n.* any of various tiny arachnids of the same order as ticks, usually living in stored foods or as parasites on plants or animals, but sometimes found as free-living scavengers in soil or water. [Old English *mīte*]

mite[2] (mīt), *n.* 1 anything very small; little bit. 2 coin of very small value. 3 a very small sum of money. 4 a very small child. [< Middle Dutch]

miter (def. 1)

mi ter (mī′tər), *n.* 1 a tall, pointed, folded cap worn as the official headdress of bishops, abbots, and other ecclesiastics. 2 miter joint. 3 the bevel on either of the pieces in a miter joint. —*v.t.* 1 bestow a miter on; raise to a rank of bishop. 2 join with a miter joint. 3 prepare (ends of wood) for joining in a miter joint. Also, **mitre.** [< Greek *mitra* headband]

miter joint, kind of joint or corner where two pieces of wood are fitted together at right angles with the ends cut slanting.

Mith ra ism (mith′rā iz′əm), *n.* religion of the worshipers of Mithras.

Mith ras (mith′ras), *n.* a Persian and Aryan god of light, truth, and justice, the subject of an extensive cult during the late Roman Empire.

Mith ri da tes VI (mith′rə dā′tēz), 131?-63 B.C., king of Pontus from 120? to 63 B.C. and enemy of Rome.

mit i gate (mit′ə gāt), *v.t., v.i.,* **-gat ed, -gat ing.** make or become mild or milder; make or become less harsh; soften. Anger, grief, pain, punishments, heat, cold, and many other conditions may be mitigated. [< Latin *mitigatum* made gentle < *mitis* gentle]

mit i ga tion (mit′ə gā′shən), *n.* 1 a mitigating. 2 a being mitigated. 3 something that mitigates.

mit i ga tive (mit′ə gā′tiv), *adj.* tending to mitigate. —*n.* something that mitigates.

mi to chon dri a (mī′tə kon′drē ə), *n.* pl. of **mi to chon dri on** (mī′tə kon′drē ən). minute sausage-shaped structures in the cytoplasm of cells, containing many enzymes important for cell metabolism. [< Greek *mitos* thread + *chondros* lump]

mi to chon dri al (mī′tə kon′drē əl), *adj.* of or having to do with mitochondria.

mi to sis (mī tō′sis, mi tō′sis), *n.* a continuous process in four stages by which a plant or animal cell divides to form two new cells, each containing the same number of chromosomes as the original cell; cell division. [< New Latin < Greek *mitos* thread]

mi tot ic (mī tot′ik, mi tot′ik), *adj.* of mitosis.

mi tral (mī′trəl), *adj.* 1 of or like a miter. 2 of the mitral valve.

mitral valve, the valve of the heart between the left auricle and left ventricle, which prevents the blood from flowing back into the auricle.

mi tre (mī′tər), *n., v.t.,* **mi tred, mi tring.** miter.

mitt (mit), *n.* 1 kind of long glove without fingers, or with very short fingers. 2 a baseball glove, especially one with a big pad over the palm and fingers: *a catcher's mitt.* 3 mitten. 4 SLANG. a hand. [short for *mitten*]

mit ten (mit′n), *n.* kind of winter glove covering the four fingers together and the thumb separately. [< French *mitaine*]

mitz vah (mits′və), *n., pl.* **-voth** (-vōth), **-vahs.** in Judaism: 1 a religious obligation or commandment. 2 act fulfilling a religious or ethical duty; good deed; kind act. [< Hebrew *miṣwah* commandment]

mix (miks), *v.,* **mixed** or **mixt, mix ing,** *n.* —*v.t.* 1 put together in one mass; combine and stir well together: *mix ingredients to make a cake.* See synonym study below. 2 prepare by putting different things together: *mix a cake, mix cement.* 3 carry on at the same time; join: *mix business and pleasure.* 4 **mix up, a** confuse. **b** involve; concern. 5 cross in breeding. —*v.i.* 1 be mixed: *Oil and water will not mix.* 2 associate together; get along together: *mix well in almost any group of people.* 3 be crossed in breeding. —*n.* 1 a mixture. 2 the ingredients, especially dry ingredients, for a cake, pudding, etc., packaged and sold together. 3 INFORMAL. a mixed or muddled condition; mess. [< earlier *mixt* mixed < Middle French *mixte* < Latin *mixtum* < *miscere* to mix]

Syn. *v.t.* 1 **Mix, blend** mean to put two or more ingredients together. **Mix** applies particularly when the ingredients retain all or some of their distinct identities: *Mix gravel and cement.* **Blend** implies a thorough mixing so that the ingredients lose their identities and the resulting whole has the qualities of both or all elements: *blend teas. Blend the flour into the melted butter.*

mixed (mikst), *adj.* 1 put together or formed by mixing; composed of different parts or elements; of different kinds combined: *mixed candies, mixed emotions.* 2 of different classes, kinds, status, character, etc.; not exclusive: *a mixed society.* 3 of or for persons of both sexes: *a mixed chorus.* 4 (of stock prices) some rising and some falling from previous levels.

mixed bag, mixture; medley: *a mixed bag of characters, a mixed bag of explanations.*

mixed metaphor, an incongruous combination of metaphors. EXAMPLE: "He set forth early on the stream of public life where he climbed to the peak of success."

mixed number, number consisting of a positive or negative integer and a fraction. EXAMPLES: $1^1/_2$, $16^2/_3$, $-25^9/_{10}$.

mix er (mik′sər), *n.* 1 thing that mixes: *a bread mixer, an electric mixer.* 2 one who mixes. A person who gets along well with others is called a good mixer.

mix ture (miks′chər), *n.* 1 a mixing. 2 a being mixed; mixed condition: *a mixture of relief and disappointment.* 3 what has been mixed; product of mixing: *Orange is a mixture of yellow and red.* 4 two or more substances mixed together but not chemically combined. [< Latin *mixtura* < *miscere* to mix]

mix-up (miks′up′), *n.* 1 confusion; mess. 2 INFORMAL. a confused fight.

miz zen or **miz en** (miz′n), *n.* 1 a fore-and-aft sail on the mizzenmast. See **mainmast** for picture. 2 mizzenmast. *—adj.* of or on the mizzenmast. [< Middle French *misaine* < Italian *mezzana* < Latin *medianus* in the middle < *medius* middle]

miz zen mast (miz′n mast′; *Nautical* miz′n məst), *n.* mast nearest the stern in a two-masted or three-masted ship. See **masthead** for picture.

mks or **MKS,** meter-kilogram-second.

ml., milliliter or milliliters.

Mlle., *pl.* **Mlles.** Mademoiselle.

mm., millimeter or millimeters.

MM., Messieurs.

Mme., *pl.* **Mmes.** Madame.

mmf or **m.m.f.,** magnetomotive force.

Mn, manganese.

mne mon ic (ni mon′ik), *adj.* 1 aiding the memory. 2 intended to aid the memory. 3 of or having to do with the memory. [< Greek *mnēmonikos* < *mnasthai* remember] **—mne mon′i cal ly,** *adv.*

Mne mos y ne (ni mos′n ē), *n.* (in Greek myths) the goddess of memory, and mother of the Muses by Zeus.

Mo, molybdenum.

mo., month or months.

Mo., Missouri.

M.O., 1 money order. 2 mail order.

moa
10 to 14 ft. tall

mo a (mō′ə), *n.* any of various recently extinct, flightless birds of New Zealand, somewhat like an ostrich. [< Maori]

Mo ab (mō′ab), *n.* ancient kingdom east of the Dead Sea and lower Jordan River, in what is now Jordan. See **Judah** for map.

Mo ab ite (mō′ə bīt), *n.* native or inhabitant of Moab. *—adj.* of Moab or its people.

moan (mōn), *n.* 1 a long, low sound of suffering. 2 any similar sound: *the moan of the winter wind.* *—v.i.* 1 make moans. 2 complain; lament; grieve. *—v.t.* 1 utter with a moan. 2 complain about; grieve for: *moan one's fate.* [Middle English *mone*] **—moan′ing ly,** *adv.*

moat (mōt), *n.* a deep, wide ditch dug around a castle, town, etc., as a protection against enemies. Moats were usually kept filled with water. [< Old French *mote* mound]

mob (mob), *n., v.,* **mobbed, mob bing.** *—n.* 1 a disorderly and riotous crowd, easily moved to acts of lawlessness. 2 a large number of people; crowd. 3 Also, **the mob,** the common mass of people, thought of as lacking taste, culture, etc.; the masses. 4 INFORMAL. group of criminals who work together; gang. *—v.t.* 1 crowd around in curiosity, anger, etc. 2 attack with violence, as a mob does. [shortened form of Latin *mobile vulgus* fickle common people]

mo bile (*adj.* mō′bəl, mō′bēl; *n.* mō′bēl′), *adj.* 1 easy to move; movable: *a mobile hospital unit.* 2 moving easily; changing easily: *a mobile mind, a face with mobile features.* *—n.* decoration suspended on wires or threads to shift in currents of air. [< Latin *mobilis* movable < *movere* to move]

Mo bile (mō bēl′), *n.* seaport in SW Alabama, on Mobile Bay. 190,000.

Mo bile Bay (mō′bēl), part of the Gulf of Mexico that extends into SW Alabama. 30 mi. long; 8–18 mi. wide.

mobile home, a house trailer, especially a large one set on a more or less permanent site.

mo bil i ty (mō bil′ə tē), *n.* a being mobile; ability or readiness to move or be moved.

mo bi li za tion (mō′bə lə zā′shən), *n.* 1 act of mobilizing. 2 condition of being mobilized.

mo bi lize (mō′bə līz), *v.,* **-lized, -liz ing.** *—v.t.* 1 call (troops, ships, etc.) into active military service; organize for war. 2 organize or call to take part, usually during an emergency: *mobilize Red Cross units for rescue work in a flood.* 3 put into motion or active use: *mobilize the wealth of a country.* *—v.i.* 1 assemble and prepare for war: *The troops mobilized quickly.* 2 organize or assemble in an emergency. [< French *mobiliser* < *mobile* mobile]

mob ster (mob′stər), *n.* gangster.

moc ca sin (mok′ə sən), *n.* 1 a soft leather shoe or sandal originally worn by American Indians, typically without heels and having the sole and the sides stitched to upper or vamp with rawhide. 2 water moccasin. [< Algonquian]

moccasin flower, a pink or white North American lady's-slipper.

mo cha (mō′kə), *n.* a choice variety of coffee originally coming from Arabia. *—adj.* flavored with coffee, or with chocolate and coffee. [< *Mocha*]

Mo cha (mō′kə), *n.* seaport in SW Yemen, near the mouth of the Red Sea. 5000.

mock (mok), *v.t.* 1 laugh at scornfully; make fun of; ridicule. See **ridicule** for synonym study. 2 make fun of by copying or imitating; mimic. 3 imitate; copy. 4 make light of; pay no attention to; disregard. 5 deceive or disappoint. *—v.i.* scoff; jeer. *—adj.* not real; copying; sham; imitation: *a mock battle, mock modesty.* *—adv.* in a feigned or false manner; feignedly; falsely (usually in compounds such as *a mock-modest person, a mock-pompous statement*). *—n.* 1 action or speech that mocks. 2 person or thing scorned or deserving scorn. 3 imitation; counterfeit; copy. 4 derision; mockery. [< Middle French *mocquer*] **—mock′er,** *n.* **—mock′ing ly,** *adv.*

hat, āge, fär; let, ēqual, tėrm;
it, īce; hot, ōpen, ôrder;
oil, out; cup, pu̇t, rüle;
ch, child; ng, long; sh, she;
th, thin; ᴛʜ, then; zh, measure;

ə represents *a* in about, *e* in taken, *i* in pencil, *o* in lemon, *u* in circus.

< = from, derived from, taken from.

mock er y (mok′ər ē), *n., pl.* **-er ies.** 1 a making scornful fun; ridicule; derision. 2 person, thing, or action to be made fun of. 3 a bad copy or imitation. 4 a disregarding; a setting at naught: *The unfair trial was a mockery of justice.*

mock-he ro ic (mok′hi rō′ik), *adj.* imitating or burlesquing the heroic style or character: *Alexander Pope's "Rape of the Lock" is a mock-heroic poem.*

mock ing bird (mok′ing bėrd′), *n.* a grayish songbird of the southern United States, of the same family as the catbird, that imitates the calls of other birds.

mock orange, syringa.

mock turtle soup, an imitation of the soup made from the green turtle.

mock-up (mok′up′), *n.* a full-sized model of an airplane, machine, etc., used for teaching purposes or for testing.

mod (mod), *adj.* very stylish or up-to-date; extremely modern: *mod fashions, mod music.* [< *mod(ern)*]

mod., 1 moderate. 2 moderato. 3 modern.

mo dal (mō′dəl), *adj.* 1 of or having to do with mode, manner, or form as contrasted with substance. 2 (in grammar) of or having to do with the mood of a verb. **—mo′dal ly,** *adv.*

modal auxiliary, one of a set of auxiliary verbs in English, including words like *may, can, must, would,* and *should,* that indicates the mood of the verb with which it is used.

mo dal i ty (mō dal′ə tē), *n., pl.* **-ties.** quality or fact of being modal.

mode[1] (mōd), *n.* 1 manner or way in which a thing is done; method: *Riding a donkey is a slow mode of travel.* 2 manner or state of existence of a thing: *Heat is a mode of motion.* 3 (in grammar) mood. 4 in music: **a** any of various arrangements of the tones of an octave. **b** either of the two classes (major and minor) of keys. **c** any of the various scales used in ancient Greek and medieval music, having the intervals differently arranged. 5 (in statistics) the value of the variable with the highest frequency in a set of data. [< Latin *modus* measure, manner]

mode[2] (mōd), *n.* style, fashion, or custom that prevails; the way most people are behaving, talking, dressing, etc. [< French < Latin *modus* mode[1]]

mod el (mod′l), *n., v.,* **-eled, -el ing** or **-elled, -el ling,** *adj.* *—n.* 1 a small copy of something: *a model of a ship.* 2 object or figure made in clay, wax, or the like, that is to be copied in marble, bronze, etc.: *a model for a statue.* 3 way in which a thing is made;

design; style: *a plane of an advanced model.* 4 thing or person to be copied or imitated: *a model of courage.* See synonym study below. 5 person who poses for artists, photographers, etc. 6 woman in a clothing store who wears garments that are for sale in order to show customers how they look. —*v.t.* 1 make, shape, or fashion; design; plan: *model a horse in clay.* 2 follow as a model; form (something) after a particular model: *Model yourself on your father.* 3 wear as a model: *model a dress.* —*v.i.* 1 make models; design. 2 be a model; pose: *She models for an illustrator.* —*adj.* 1 just right or perfect, especially in conduct; exemplary: *a model child.* 2 serving as a model: *a model house.* [< French *modèle* < Italian *modello,* diminutive of *modo* mode[1] < Latin *modus* measure, manner] **—mod′el er, mod′el ler,** *n.*

Syn. *n.* 4 **Model, example, pattern** mean someone or something to be copied or followed. **Model** implies especially a quality of conduct or character worth copying or imitating: *The saint was a model of unselfishness.* **Example** implies especially action or conduct, good or bad, that one is likely to follow or copy: *Children follow the example set by their parents.* **Pattern** applies particularly to any example or model that is followed or copied very closely: *The family's pattern of living has not changed in generations.*

mod el ing or **mod el ling** (mod′l ing), *n.* 1 act or art of a person who models. 2 the production of designs in clay or wax for reproduction in marble, bronze, etc. 3 the representation of solid form, as in sculpture.

mod er ate (*adj., n.* mod′ər it; *v.* mod′ə rāt′), *adj., n., v.,* **-at ed, -at ing.** —*adj.* 1 kept or keeping within proper bounds; not extreme: *moderate expenses, moderate styles.* See synonym study below. 2 not violent, severe, or intense; calm: *moderate in speech.* 3 not very large or good; fair; medium: *a moderate profit.* —*n.* person who holds moderate opinions, especially in politics. —*v.t.* 1 make less violent, severe, or intense. 2 act in as moderator; preside over. —*v.i.* 1 become less extreme or violent. 2 act as moderator; preside. [< Latin *moderatum* regulated < *modus* measure] **—mod′er ate ly,** *adv.* **—mod′er ate ness,** *n.*

Syn. *adj.* 1 **Moderate, temperate** mean not extreme in any way. **Moderate** emphasizes freedom from excess: *a moderate eater, moderate speed.* **Temperate** emphasizes deliberate restraint, especially with regard to the feelings or appetites: *a temperate reply to an angry attack.*

mod e ra tion (mod′ə rā′shən), *n.* 1 a moderating. 2 a being moderate; freedom from excess; proper restraint; temperance: *eat and drink in moderation.*

mod e ra to (mod′ə rä′tō), *adj., adv.* (in music) in moderate time. [< Italian]

mod e ra tor (mod′ə rā′tər), *n.* 1 a presiding officer; chairman: *the moderator of a town meeting, the moderator of a church assembly.* 2 arbitrator; mediator. 3 material, as graphite, used in a reactor to reduce the speed of neutrons, making them more efficient in splitting atomic nuclei.

mod ern (mod′ərn), *adj.* 1 of present or recent time; of or in the current age or period: *Color television is a modern invention.* See **new** for synonym study. 2 up-to-date; not old-fashioned: *modern views.* —*n.* 1 person who has modern ideas and tastes. 2 person who lives in or belongs to the present time. [< Late Latin *modernus* < Latin *modo* just now, ablative of *modus* measure, manner] **—mod′ern ly,** *adv.* **—mod′ern ness,** *n.*

Modern English, 1 period in the development of the English language from about 1500 through the present. 2 the English language of this period.

modern history, history from about 1450 to the present time.

mod ern ism (mod′ər niz′əm), *n.* 1 modern attitudes or methods; sympathy with what is modern. 2 a modern word, phrase, or usage. 3 **Modernism,** tendency in religion to interpret the teachings of the Bible or the church in accordance with modern scientific theories.

mod ern ist (mod′ər nist), *n.* 1 person who holds modern views or uses modern methods. 2 person who interprets religious teachings in a modern way.

mod ern is tic (mod′ər nis′tik), *adj.* 1 modern. 2 having to do with modernism or modernists.

mo der ni ty (mə dėr′nə tē, mō dėr′nə tē), *n., pl.* **-ties.** 1 a being modern. 2 something modern.

mod ern ize (mod′ər nīz), *v.,* **-ized, -iz ing.** —*v.t.* make modern; bring up to present ways or standards. —*v.i.* become modern. **—mod′ern i za′tion,** *n.* **—mod′ern iz′er,** *n.*

mod est (mod′ist), *adj.* 1 having or showing a moderate estimate of one's merits, importance, achievements, etc.; not vain; humble: *In spite of the honors he received, the scientist remained a modest man.* 2 held back by a sense of what is fit and proper; not bold or forward. See synonym study below. 3 having or showing decency of actions, thoughts, clothing, etc. 4 not excessive; moderate: *a modest request.* 5 not conspicuous or gaudy; humble in appearance; quiet: *a modest little house.* [< Latin *modestus* in due measure, moderate < *modus* measure] **—mod′est ly,** *adv.*

Syn. 2 **Modest, demure** mean not bold or forward. **Modest** emphasizes a sense of fit and proper behavior that holds a person back from calling attention to himself: *He is a modest boy, not bashful, but not loud either.* **Demure,** which is used only with reference to girls and young women, often suggests undue modesty or pretended shyness thought to be attractive and put on for effect: *She sipped her soda and looked demure.*

mod est y (mod′ə stē), *n., pl.* **-est ies.** 1 freedom from vanity; being modest or humble. 2 shyness; bashfulness. 3 a being decent.

mod i cum (mod′ə kəm), *n.* a small or moderate quantity. [< Latin, moderate < *modus* measure]

mod i fi ca tion (mod′ə fə kā′shən), *n.* 1 partial alteration or change: *With these modifications your essay will do for the school paper.* 2 a making less severe, strong, etc.; a toning down: *The modification of his anger made him able to think clearly again.* 3 limitation of meaning; qualification. 4 a modified form; variety. 5 a change in an organism resulting from external influences.

mod i fi er (mod′ə fī′ər), *n.* 1 word or group of words that limits the meaning of another word or group of words. In "a very tight coat," the adjective *tight* is a modifier of *coat,* and the adverb *very* is a modifier of *tight.* 2 person or thing that modifies.

mod i fy (mod′ə fī), *v.t.,* **-fied, -fy ing.** 1 make partial changes in; change somewhat; alter: *modify the design of an automobile, modify the terms of a lease.* 2 make less; tone down; make less severe or strong: *modify one's demands.* 3 limit the meaning of; qualify. Adverbs modify verbs, adjectives, and other adverbs. [< Latin *modificare* to limit < *modus* measure + *facere* to make] **—mod′i fi′a ble,** *adj.*

Mo di glia ni (mō′dē lyä′nē), *n.* **Amedeo,** 1884-1920, Italian painter.

mod ish (mō′dish), *adj.* fashionable; stylish. **—mod′ish ly,** *adv.* **—mod′ish ness,** *n.*

mo diste (mō dēst′), *n.* person who makes or sells fashionable women's dresses, hats, etc. [< French < *mode* mode[2]]

Mo dred (mō′drəd), *n.* (in Arthurian legends) King Arthur's nephew, and one of the knights of the Round Table, who led a rebellion against Arthur.

mod u lar (moj′ə lər), *adj.* of or having to do with a module or a modulus.

mod u late (moj′ə lāt), *v.,* **-lat ed, -lat ing.** —*v.t.* 1 regulate or adjust so as to tone down; soften. 2 alter (the voice) in pitch, tone, or volume for expression. 3 in music: **a** attune (sounds, etc.) to a certain pitch or key. **b** cause to change from one key to another. 4 (in electronics) to vary the amplitude, frequency, or phase of (the carrier wave) in accordance with the sound wave or other signal being sent. —*v.i.* undergo modulation. [< Latin *modulatum* regulated, ultimately < *modus* measure] **—mod′u la′tor,** *n.*

mod u la tion (moj′ə lā′shən), *n.* 1 a modulating. 2 a being modulated. 3 the change from one key to another in the course of a piece of music. 4 (in electronics) variation of the amplitude, frequency, or phase of the carrier wave in accordance with the sound wave or other signal being sent.

mod ule (moj′ül), *n.* 1 a standard or basic unit for measuring. 2 (in architecture) the size of some part taken as a unit of measure for other parts. 3 a standard piece or component. 4 a self-contained unit or system within a larger system, designed for a particular function: *the lunar module of a spacecraft.* [< Latin *modulus,* diminutive of *modus* measure. Doublet of MOLD[1].]

mod u lo (moj′ə lō), *adv.* (in mathematics) with respect to a (specified) modulus. EXAMPLE: 54 is congruent to 66 modulo 12. [< Latin, ablative of *modulus*]

mod u lus (moj′ə ləs), *n., pl.* **-li** (-lī). 1 (in physics) a number or quantity expressing the measure of some function, property, etc. 2 (in mathematics) a number by which two different numbers can be divided to leave the same remainders. The modulus of 54 and 66 is 12 because both 54 and 66 leave a remainder of 6 when divided by 12.

mo dus o pe ran di (mō′dəs op′ə ran′dī), LATIN. method or manner of working.

mo dus vi ven di (mō′dəs vi ven′dī), LATIN. way of getting along; temporary arrangement while waiting for a final settlement.

Mog a di scio (mog′ə dē′shō), *n.* capital of Somalia, a seaport in the SE part. 173,000.

Mog a di shu (mog′ə dē′shü), *n.* Mogadiscio.

Mo gul or **Mo ghul** (mō′gul, mō gul′), *n.* 1 a Mongol or Mongolian. 2 one of the Mongol conquerors of India in the 1500's or one of their descendants. 3 **mogul,** an important or powerful person. [< Persian *Mughul* < the native name *Mongol*]

mo hair (mō′her, mō′har), *n.* 1 cloth made from the long, silky hair of the Angora goat; angora. 2 a similar cloth made of wool and cotton, used for upholstery and clothing. 3 hair of the Angora goat. [ultimately < Arabic *mukhayyar*]

Mo ham med (mō ham′id), *n.* A.D. 570?-632, Arab prophet, founder of Islam, a religion widely accepted in Asia and Africa. Also, **Mahomet, Muhammad.**

Mo ham med an (mō ham′ə dən), *adj.* 1 of Mohammed. 2 Moslem. —*n.* a Moslem. Also, **Mahometan, Muhammadan.**

Mo ham med an ism (mō ham′ə də niz′əm), *n.* Islam, the religion of the Moslems. Also, **Muhammadanism.**

Mohammed Ri za Pah le vi (ri zä′ pä′lə vē), born 1919, shah of Iran since 1941.

Mo ha ve (mō hä′vē), *n.* 1 member of a tribe of American Indians dwelling chiefly on the eastern side of the Colorado River. 2 Mojave.

Mo hawk (mō′hôk), *n., pl.* **-hawks** or **-hawk** for 1. 1 member of a tribe of Iroquois Indians formerly living in central New York State. 2 **Mohawk River,** river flowing from central New York State into the Hudson. 148 mi.

Mo he gan (mō hē′gən), *n., pl.* **-gans** or **-gan.** member of a tribe of American Indians related to the Mohicans, formerly living in western Connecticut.

Mo hi can (mō hē′kən), *n., pl.* **-cans** or **-can.** member of either of two tribes of American Indians formerly living in the upper Hudson valley and in Connecticut. Also, **Mahican.**

Mo ho (mō′hō), *n.* the Mohorovicic discontinuity.

Mo hole (mō′hōl), *n.* a proposed experimental drilling project to bore into the earth's mantle. [blend of *Moho* and *hole*]

Mo ho ro vic ic discontinuity (mō′-hō rō vē′chēch), the boundary between the earth's crust and mantle, the depth of which varies from approximately 6 to 8 miles under ocean basins to 20 to 22 miles under the continents. [< Andrija *Mohorovičić,* 1857-1936, Yugoslav geophysicist, who discovered it]

Mohs' scale (mōz), a scale for classifying the relative hardness of minerals, as follows: talc 1; gypsum 2; calcite 3; fluorite 4; apatite 5; orthoclase 6; quartz 7; topaz 8; corundum 9; diamond 10. [< Friedrich *Mohs,* 1773-1839, German mineralogist, who invented it]

moi e ty (moi′ə tē), *n., pl.* **-ties.** 1 half. 2 part: *Only a small moiety of college students win scholarships.* [< Middle French *moité* < Latin *medietatem* half < *medius* middle]

moil (moil), *v.i.* work hard; drudge. —*n.* 1 hard work; drudgery. 2 confusion, turmoil, or trouble. [< Old French *moillier* moisten < Latin *mollis* soft] **—moil′er,** *n.*

moire (mwär, mwä rā′, mô rā′, mō rā′), *n.* fabric, usually silk or rayon, having a wavelike pattern; watered fabric. [< French *moire* < English *mohair*]

moi ré (mwä rā′, mô rā′, mō rā′), *n.* moire. —*adj.* having a wavelike pattern or clouded appearance; watered: *moiré silk.* [< French, variant of *moire* moire]

moist (moist), *adj.* 1 slightly wet; not dry; damp. See **damp** for synonym study. 2 (of the eyes) wet with tears; tearful. [< Old French *moiste* < Popular Latin *muscidus* moldy < Latin *mucidus,* and *musteus* musty] **—moist′ly,** *adv.* **—moist′ness,** *n.*

mois ten (moi′sn), *v.t.* make moist; dampen. —*v.i.* become moist. **—mois′ten er,** *n.*

mois ture (mois′chər), *n.* slight wetness; water or other liquid suspended in very small drops in the air or spread on a surface. Dew is moisture that collects at night on the grass.

Mo ja ve (mō hä′vē), *n.* 1 **Mojave Desert,** desert in S California. 15,000 sq. mi. 2 Mohave.

mol (mōl), *n.* mole⁴.

mo lal (mō′ləl), *adj.* 1 of or having to do with a mole or gram molecule. 2 (of a solution) having one mole of solute in 1000 grams of solvent. [< *mole*⁴]

mo lal i ty (mō lal′ə tē), *n.* the molal concentration of a solution. It is expressed as the number of moles of solute in 1000 grams of solvent.

mo lar¹ (mō′lər), *n.* tooth with a broad surface for grinding, having somewhat flattened points; grinder. The twelve permanent back teeth in man are molars. See **incisor** for diagram. —*adj.* 1 adapted for grinding. 2 of the molar teeth. [< Latin *molaris* < *mola* mill]

mo lar² (mō′lər), *adj.* 1 (in physics) of mass or a body as a whole. 2 (in chemistry) having one mole of solute in a liter of solution. [< Latin *moles* mass]

mo lar i ty (mō lar′ə tē), *n.* the molar concentration of a solution. It is expressed as the number of moles of solute in a liter of solution.

mo las ses (mə las′iz), *n.* a sweet, brown syrup obtained in the process of making sugar from sugar cane, or from raw sugar, sorghum, etc. [< Portuguese *melaço* < Late Latin *mellaceum* must² < Latin *mel, mellis* honey]

mold¹ (mōld), *n.* 1 a hollow shape in which anything is formed, cast, or solidified, such as the mold into which melted metal is poured to harden into shape or the mold in which gelatin is left to stiffen. 2 the shape or form which is given by a mold. 3 the model according to which anything is shaped: *He is cast in his father's mold.* 4 something shaped in a mold: *a mold of pudding.* 5 nature; character: *a man of base mold.* 6 the shape or frame on or about which something is made: *a basket mold.* —*v.t.* 1 form; shape: *mold figures out of clay.* 2 make or form into shape: *mold dough into loaves, mold character.* Also, **mould.** [< Old French *modle* < Latin *modulus.* Doublet of MODULE.] **—mold′a ble,** *adj.* **—mold′er,** *n.*

mold² (mōld), *n.* 1 a woolly or furry fungous growth, often greenish-blue or whitish in color, that appears on the surface of food and other animal or vegetable substances when they are left too long in a warm, moist place or when they are decaying. 2 fungus producing such a growth. —*v.i.* become covered with mold. Also, **mould.** [Middle English *moul;* probably influenced by *mold*³]

mold³ (mōld), *n.* loose, broken, or crumbly earth, especially fine, soft soil rich in decayed leaves, manure, or other organic matter, suitable for the cultivation of plants. Also, **mould.** [Old English *molde*]

Mol da vi a (mol dā′vē ə), *n.* 1 Moldavian S.S.R. 2 region in NE Romania. **—Mol da′vi an,** *adj., n.*

Moldavian S.S.R., one of the constituent republics of the U.S.S.R., in the SW part.

hat, āge, fär; let, ēqual, tėrm;
it, īce; hot, ōpen, ôrder;
oil, out; cup, pu̇t, rüle;
ch, child; ng, long; sh, she;
th, thin; ꟻH, then; zh, measure;

ə represents *a* in about, *e* in taken, *i* in pencil, *o* in lemon, *u* in circus.

< = from, derived from, taken from.

3,600,000 pop.; 13,700 sq. mi. *Capital:* Kishinev.

mold board (mōld′bôrd′, mōld′bōrd′), *n.* the curved metal plate of a plowshare, that lifts and turns over the earth from the furrow. See **plowshare** for picture. [< *mold*³]

mold er (mōl′dər), *v.i.* turn into dust by natural decay; waste away; crumble. Also, **moulder.** [probably < *mold*³]

mold ing (mōl′ding), *n.* 1 act of shaping in or by means of a mold or molds: *the molding of dishes from clay.* 2 something molded. 3 strip, usually of wood, around the upper walls of a room, used to support pictures, to cover electric wires, for decoration, etc. 4 a decorative variety of contour or outline given to cornices, jambs, strips of woodwork, etc. Also, **moulding.**

mold y (mōl′dē), *adj.,* **mold i er, mold i est.** 1 covered with mold. 2 musty, as from decay or age: *a moldy smell.* 3 stale: *a moldy joke.* 4 of or like mold. Also, **mouldy.** **—mold′i ness,** *n.*

mole¹ (mōl), *n.* a congenital spot or slight protrusion on the skin, usually brown. [Old English *māl*]

mole²—about 7 in. long with the tail

mole² (mōl), *n.* any of a family of small mammals that live underground most of the time and feed on insects, worms, etc. Moles have dark, velvety fur, very small eyes that cannot see well, and forelimbs adapted for digging. [Middle English *molle*] **—mole′-like′,** *adj.*

mole³ (mōl), *n.* 1 a massive structure of stone or earth serving as a pier or breakwater. 2 harbor formed by it. [< Latin *moles* mass]

mole⁴ (mōl), *n.* gram molecule. Also, **mol.** [< *mole(cule)*]

mo lec u lar (mə lek′yə lər), *adj.* having to do with, caused by, or consisting of molecules.

molecular formula, a chemical formula that shows the number and kinds of atoms in a molecule without indicating how the atoms are arranged.

molecular weight, sum of the atomic weights of all the atoms in a molecule.

mol e cule (mol′ə kyül), *n.* 1 the smallest particle into which an element or compound can be divided without changing its chemical and physical properties. A molecule of an element consists of one or more like atoms. A molecule of a compound consists of two or more different atoms. 2 a very small particle.

[< New Latin *molecula,* diminutive of Latin *moles* mass]

mole hill (mōl′hil′), *n.* 1 a small mound or ridge of earth raised up by moles burrowing under the ground. 2 something insignificant.

mole skin (mōl′skin′), *n.* 1 skin of the mole used as fur. 2 a strong, thick cotton fabric used for sportsmen's and laborers' clothing. 3 **moleskins,** *pl.* garments, especially trousers, made of this fabric.

mo lest (mə lest′), *v.t.* 1 meddle with and injure or trouble; disturb; annoy. 2 interfere with improperly or indecently, especially by making sexual advances. [< Latin *molestare* < *molestus* troublesome < *moles* burden, mass] **mo′les′ta′tion,** *n.* **—mo lest′er,** *n.*

Mol ière (mō lyer′, mō lyar′), *n.* 1622-1673, French writer of comedies. His real name was Jean Baptiste Poquelin.

moll (mol), *n.* SLANG. the female companion of a gangster, gunman, or other criminal. [short for *Molly,* female name]

mol li fy (mol′ə fī), *v.t.,* **-fied, -fy ing.** soften in temper; calm, pacify, or appease; mitigate. [< Late Latin *mollificare* < *mollis* soft + *facere* to make] **—mol′li fi ca′tion,** *n.*

mol lusc (mol′əsk), *n.* mollusk.

Mol lus ca (mə lus′kə), *n.pl.* phylum of invertebrates comprising the mollusks.

mol lus can (mə lus′kən), *adj.* of or having to do with mollusks. *—n.* a mollusk.

mol lusk (mol′əsk), *n.* any of a large phylum of invertebrate animals having a soft, unsegmented body, usually covered with a hard shell secreted by a covering mantle, and a muscular foot. Snails, mussels, oysters, clams, and octopuses belong to this phylum. [< Latin *molluscus* soft < *mollis* soft]

mol ly cod dle (mol′ē kod′l), *n., v.,* **-dled, -dling.** *—n.* person, especially a boy or man, accustomed to being fussed over and pampered. *—v.t.* coddle; pamper. [< *Molly,* female name + *coddle*] **—mol′ly cod′dler,** *n.*

Mo loch (mō′lok), *n.* 1 an ancient Semitic deity worshiped through the sacrifice of children as burnt offerings by their parents. 2 anything requiring frightful sacrifice: *War is a Moloch.*

Mo lo kai (mō′lō kī′), *n.* the fifth largest island of Hawaii. 5000 pop.; 260 sq. mi.

Mo lo tov (mô′lə tôf, mol′ə tôf), *n.* 1 **Vyacheslav Mikhailovich,** born 1890, Soviet foreign minister from 1939 to 1949 and from 1953 to 1956. 2 former name of **Perm.**

Molotov cocktail, a crude type of hand grenade, consisting of a bottle filled with gasoline, and having a rag as a wick. [< Vyacheslav *Molotov*]

molt (mōlt), *v.i.* shed the feathers, skin, hair, shell, antlers, etc., before a new growth. Birds, snakes, insects, etc., molt. *—v.t.* shed (feathers, skin, etc.): *We saw the snake molt its skin.* *—n.* act or process of molting. Also, **moult.** [Middle English *mouten* < Old English *mūtian* (as in *bemūtian* exchange for) < Latin *mutare* to change] **—molt′er,** *n.*

mol ten (mōlt′n), *adj.* 1 made liquid by heat; melted: *molten steel.* 2 made by melting and casting: *a molten image.* *—v.* a pp. of **melt.**

Molt ke (môlt′kə), *n.* Count **Helmut Karl Bernhard von,** 1800-1891, Prussian field marshal.

mol to (mōl′tō), *adv.* (in music) much; very (used with other directions): *molto allegro.* [< Italian < Latin *multum*]

Mo luc cas (mə luk′əz, mō luk′əz), *n.pl.* group of islands in Indonesia, between Celebes and New Guinea; Spice Islands. 700,000 pop.; 32,300 sq. mi. **—Mo luc′can,** *adj., n.*

mo ly (mō′lē), *n., pl.* **mo lies.** (in Greek legends) an herb with a milk-white flower and a black root, having magic properties. [< Greek *mōly*]

mo lyb de nite (mə lib′də nīt), *n.* a soft, native sulfide of molybdenum that resembles graphite. It is the chief ore of molybdenum. *Formula:* MoS_2

mo lyb de num (mə lib′də nəm), *n.* a heavy, hard, grayish or silver-white metallic element, much used to strengthen and harden steel. *Symbol:* Mo; *atomic number* 42. See pages 326 and 327 for table. [< New Latin < Greek *molybdaina* ore of lead < *molybdos* lead]

mom (mom), *n.* INFORMAL. mother.

Mom ba sa (mom bä′sə), *n.* seaport in Kenya on an island off the E coast of Africa. 246,000.

mo ment (mō′mənt), *n.* 1 a very short space of time; instant: *In a moment the house was in flames.* See **minute**[1] for synonym study. 2 a particular point of time: *We both arrived at the same moment.* 3 importance; weight; consequence: *a matter of moment.* 4 a definite stage, period, or turning point in a course of events. 5 tendency to cause rotation around a point or axis. 6 the product of a (specified) physical quantity and the length of the perpendicular from a point or axis. [< Latin *momentum* movement < *movere* to move]

mo men tar i ly (mō′mən ter′ə lē, mō′mən ter′ə lē), *adv.* 1 for a moment: *hesitate momentarily.* 2 at every moment; from moment to moment: *The danger was increasing momentarily.* 3 at any moment: *We were expecting the postman momentarily.*

mo men tar y (mō′mən ter′ē), *adj.* lasting only a moment; fleeting; transitory. **—mo′men tar′i ness,** *n.*

mo ment ly (mō′mənt lē), *adv.* momentarily.

mo men tous (mō men′təs), *adj.* very important; of great consequence; weighty: *Choosing between peace and war is a momentous decision.* **—mo men′tous ly,** *adv.* **—mo men′tous ness,** *n.*

mo men tum (mō men′təm), *n., pl.* **-tums, -ta** (-tə). 1 quantity of motion of a moving body, equal to the product of its mass and velocity; force with which a body moves: *A falling object gains momentum as it falls.* 2 impetus resulting from movement: *The runner's momentum carried him far beyond the finish line.* [< Latin, movement < *movere* to move]

Momm sen (mom′sən), *n.* **Theodor,** 1817-1903, German historian and scholar.

mom my (mom′ē), *n., pl.* **-mies.** INFORMAL. mother.

mon-, *prefix.* the form of **mono-** before vowels, as in *monatomic, monism.*

Mon., Monday.

Mon a co (mon′ə kō, mə nä′kō), *n.* 1 country on the SE coast of France, on the Mediterranean. 23,000 pop.; ½ sq. mi. 2 its capital. 2000. **—Mon′a can,** *adj., n.*

mon ad (mon′ad, mō′nad), *n.* 1 a very simple single-celled animal or plant. 2 an atom, element, or radical having a valence of one. [< Greek *monados* unit < *monos* alone]

mo nan drous (mə nan′drəs), *adj.* 1 having only one husband at a time. 2 (of a flower) having only one stamen. 3 (of a plant) having such flowers. [< Greek *monandros* < *monos* single + *andros* husband]

mon arch (mon′ərk), *n.* 1 king, queen, emperor, empress, etc.; ruler. 2 person or thing like a monarch: *A tall, solitary pine was monarch of the forest.* 3 a large, orange-and-black butterfly whose larvae feed on milkweed. The butterfly migrates south each fall. [< Greek *monarchos* < *monos* alone + *archein* to rule]

mo nar chal (mə när′kəl), *adj.* of or having to do with a monarch.

mo nar chi al (mə när′kē əl), *adj.* monarchal.

mo nar chic (mə när′kik), *adj.* monarchical.

mo nar chi cal (mə när′kə kəl), *adj.* 1 of, having to do with, or having the characteristics of a monarch or monarchy. 2 favoring monarchy or monarchism.

mon ar chism (mon′ər kiz′əm), *n.* 1 principles of monarchy. 2 advocacy of monarchical principles.

mon ar chist (mon′ər kist), *n.* person who supports or favors government by a monarch.

mon ar chy (mon′ər kē), *n., pl.* **-chies.** 1 government by a monarch. In a monarchy supreme power is formally vested in a single person. 2 nation governed by a monarch.

mon as ter i al (mon′ə stir′ē əl), *adj.* 1 of a monastery. 2 characteristic of a monastery.

mon as ter y (mon′ə ster′ē), *n., pl.* **-ter ies.** building or buildings where a community of persons, especially monks, lives a contemplative life according to fixed rules and under religious vows. [< Late Latin *monasterium* < Greek *monasterion* < *monazein* live alone < *monos* alone. Doublet of MINSTER.]

mo nas tic (mə nas′tik), *adj.* 1 of monks or nuns: *the monastic vows of chastity, poverty, and obedience.* 2 of monasteries: *monastic architecture.* 3 like that of monks or nuns; ascetic. *—n.* monk. **—mo nas′ti cal ly,** *adv.*

mo nas ti cal (mə nas′tə kəl), *adj.* monastic.

mo nas ti cism (mə nas′tə siz′əm), *n.* system or condition of living a monastic life.

mon a tom ic (mon′ə tom′ik), *adj.* 1 having one atom in the molecule. 2 having one replaceable atom or group of atoms. 3 univalent.

mon au ral (mon ôr′əl), *adj.* 1 monophonic: *monaural recordings.* 2 of, with, or for one ear: *a monaural hearing aid.* **—mon au′ral ly,** *adv.*

mon ax i al (mon ak′sē əl), *adj.* 1 having but one axis. 2 (in botany) having flowers growing directly from the main axis.

Mon day (mun′dē, mun′dā), *n.* the second day of the week; day after Sunday. [Old English *mōn(an)dæg* the moon's day]

Mon dri an (môn′drē än), *n.* **Piet,** 1872-1944, Dutch painter.

mo ne cious (mə nē′shəs), *adj.* monoecious.

Mo nel metal (mō nel′), trademark for a corrosion-resistant alloy consisting mainly of nickel and copper.

Mo net (mō nā′), *n.* **Claude,** 1840-1926, French painter.

mon e tar y (mon′ə ter′ē, mun′ə ter′ē), *adj.* 1 of or having to do with coinage or currency. 2 of money; pecuniary: *a monetary reward.* See **financial** for synonym study. [< Late Latin *monetarius* < *moneta.* See MONEY.]

monetary unit, the unit of a currency taken as the standard of comparative value for that currency, as the dollar in the United States and Canada, and the pound in Great Britain.

mon e tize (mon′ə tīz, mun′ə tīz), *v.t.,* **-tized, -tiz ing.** 1 legalize as money; assign a specified value to (silver, gold, etc.) in the currency of a country. 2 coin into money. **—mon′e ti za′tion,** *n.*

mon ey (mun′ē), *n., pl.* **-eys** or **-ies.** 1 any medium of exchange issued by a government or authorized public authority in the form of coins of gold, silver, or other metal, or paper notes which represent these metals. 2 a particular form or denomination of money. 3 any object or material used for buying and selling, such as checks drawn on a bank, or nuggets or the dust of a precious metal. 4 wealth: *a man of money.* 5 **in the money,** in a winning position in a race or contest, especially in first, second, or third place in a horse race. 6 **make money, a** get money. **b** become rich. [< Old French *moneie* < Latin *moneta* mint, money < *(Juno) Moneta* (Juno) the protectress, in whose temple money was coined. Doublet of MINT[2].]
➔ **money.** Exact sums of money are usually written in figures: 72¢; $4.98; $5; $168.75; $42,810. Round sums are more likely to be written in words: *two hundred dollars, a million and a half dollars.*

mon ey bag (mun′ē bag′), *n.* 1 bag for money. 2 **moneybags,** *pl. in form, sing. in use.* INFORMAL. a wealthy or avaricious person.

mon ey chang er (mun′ē chān′jər), *n.* person whose business is to exchange money, usually that of one country for that of another.

mon eyed (mun′ēd), *adj.* 1 having money; wealthy. 2 consisting of or representing money: *moneyed resources.* Also, **monied.**

mon ey lend er (mun′ē len′dər), *n.* person whose business is lending money at interest.

mon ey mak er (mun′ē mā′kər), *n.* 1 person skilled in earning money or building a fortune. 2 thing which yields pecuniary profit.

mon ey mak ing (mun′ē mā′king), *n.* acquisition of money. *—adj.* 1 occupied in gaining wealth. 2 yielding money; lucrative.

money of account, a monetary denomination used in reckoning, especially one not issued as a coin. In the United States, the mill is a money of account but not a coin.

mongoose—about 2 ft. long with the tail

money order, order for the payment of a certain sum of money to a specified person. A money order can be bought at a post office, bank, telegraph office, etc., and sent to a person in another city, who can collect the money at such a place there.

-monger, *combining form.* 1 dealer in ____; person who sells ____: *Fishmonger = dealer in fish.* 2 person who traffics in, spreads, or busies himself with ____: *Scandalmonger = person who spreads scandal.* [Old English *mangere* dealer < Latin *mangonem* trader]

Mon gol (mong′gəl, mong′gol, *or* mong′gōl), *n.* 1 member of an Asian people now inhabiting Mongolia and nearby parts of China and Siberia. 2 Mongoloid. 3 language of the Mongols; Mongolian. *—adj.* of this people.

Mongol Empire, former empire of the Mongols, which encompassed most of Asia and part of E Europe during the late 1200's.

Mongol Empire—Shaded area shows the Empire at its greatest extent in 1294.

Mon go li a (mong gō′lē ə), *n.* vast region in Asia, south of Siberia. Mongolia includes part of N China and the Mongolian People's Republic.

Mon go li an (mong gō′lē ən), *adj.* 1 of Mongolia, the Mongols, or their languages. 2 Mongoloid. *—n.* 1 the Altaic language of the Mongols or Mongolia. 2 native or inhabitant of Mongolia; Mongol. 3 Mongoloid.

Mongolian People's Republic, country in central Asia, north of China and south of the Soviet Union. 1,200,000 pop.; 604,000 sq. mi. *Capital:* Ulan Bator. Also, **Outer Mongolia.**

monitor (def. 6)—about 4 ft. long with the tail

Mon gol ism (mong′gə liz′əm), *n.* form of congenital idiocy characterized by abnormal body characteristics, including slanting eyes and a small, round head, flat at the back.

Mon gol oid (mong′gə loid), *adj.* 1 of or resembling the Mongols. The Chinese, Japanese, Tartars, and Eskimos are Mongoloid peoples. 2 having characteristics of Mongolism: *a Mongoloid child.* *—n.* 1 member of the Mongoloid race. 2 person affected with Mongolism.

mon goose or **mon goos** (mong′güs), *n., pl.* **-goos es.** any of several genera of slender, carnivorous mammals of Asia and Africa, especially a species native to India, belonging to the same family as the civet and resembling a ferret. The Indian species has been introduced elsewhere to destroy rats and is noted for its ability to kill cobras and certain other poisonous snakes. [< Marathi (a language of western India) *mangūs*]

mon grel (mung′grəl, mong′grəl), *n.* 1 animal or plant of mixed breed, especially a dog. 2 person of mixed breed (used in an unfriendly way). 3 anything of a haphazardly mixed nature. *—adj.* of mixed breed, origin, nature, etc. [probably related to Old English *(ge)mang* mixture]

mon grel ize (mung′grə līz, mong′grə līz), *v.t.,* **-ized, -iz ing.** to mix various elements, especially characteristics of racial groups, supposedly to the injury of a dominant group (used in an unfriendly way). **—mon′grel i za′tion,** *n.*

hat, āge, fär; let, ēqual, tėrm;
it, īce; hot, ōpen, ôrder;
oil, out; cup, pu̇t, rüle;
ch, child; ng, long; sh, she;
th, thin; ᴛʜ, then; zh, measure;

ə represents *a* in about, *e* in taken, *i* in pencil, *o* in lemon, *u* in circus.

< = from, derived from, taken from.

mon ick er (mon′ə kər), *n.* moniker.

mon ied (mun′ēd), *adj.* moneyed.

mon ies (mun′ēz), *n.* a pl. of **money.**

mon i ker (mon′ə kər), *n.* INFORMAL. 1 a person's name or signature. 2 a nickname. [origin unknown]

mon ism (mon′iz′əm, mō′niz′əm), *n.* 1 doctrine that the universe can be explained by one substance or principle. 2 doctrine that reality is an indivisible, universal organism.

mon ist (mon′ist, mō′nist), *n.* person who believes in monism.

mo nis tic (mō nis′tik), *adj.* of or having to do with monism.

mo ni tion (mō nish′ən), *n.* 1 admonition; warning. 2 an official or legal notice.

mon i tor (mon′ə tər), *n.* 1 pupil in school with special duties, such as helping to keep order and taking attendance. 2 person who gives advice or warning. 3 something that reminds or gives warning. 4 a low, armored warship, chiefly of the late 1800's, having a low freeboard and one or more revolving turrets, each with one or two heavy guns. 5 **Monitor,** the first warship of this type designed for the Union Navy in the Civil War. It engaged in a famous battle with the Merrimac on July 9, 1862. 6 any of a family of large, carnivorous lizards of Africa, southern Asia, Australia, and the East Indies. 7 receiver or other device used for checking and listening to radio or television transmissions, telephone messages, etc., as they are being recorded or broadcast. *—v.t., v.i.* 1 check the quality, wave frequency, etc., of (radio or television transmissions, telephone messages, etc.) by means of a monitor. 2 listen to (broadcasts, telephone messages, etc.) for censorship, military significance, etc. 3 (in physics) test the intensity of radiations, especially of radiations produced by radioactivity. 4 check in order to control something. [< Latin, admonisher < *monere* admonish, warn]

mon i to ri al (mon′ə tôr′ē əl, mon′ə tōr′ē əl), *adj.* 1 of or having to do with a monitor. 2 using monitors. 3 serving to admonish or warn.

mon i tor ship (mon′ə tər ship), *n.* office, work, or period of service of a monitor.

mon i to ry (mon′ə tôr′ē, mon′ə tōr′ē), *adj.* serving to admonish; warning.

monk (mungk), *n.* man who gives up all worldly things and enters a monastery to live a life devoted to religious duties and contemplation. Monks live either in solitude as hermits or as members of a religious order and are bound by the vows of poverty, celibacy, and obedience to a superior. [Old English *munuc* < Late Latin *monachus* < Late

monocle

Greek *monachos* < Greek *monos* alone] ➤ Though the terms **monk** and **friar** are often used as synonyms, a *monk* specifically is a member of an order living a cloistered life; a *friar* properly is a member of a mendicant order.

mon key (mung′kē), *n., pl.* **-keys,** *v.* —*n.* 1 any animal of the highest order of mammals, most closely allied to and resembling man and ranging from the anthropoid apes to the marmosets, but excluding man and, usually, the lemurs. 2 any of the smaller mammals in this group, usually having a long tail, as distinguished from a chimpanzee, gorilla, or other large ape. 3 person, especially a child, who is full of mischief. 4 **make a monkey out of** or **make a monkey of,** INFORMAL. make (a person) look foolish; make a fool of. —*v.i.* INFORMAL. play in a mischievous way; fool; trifle: *Don't monkey with the television.* [probably < Middle Low German *Moneke,* name of an ape in the story of Reynard the Fox] —**mon′key like′,** *adj.*

mon key ish (mung′kē ish), *adj.* like a monkey, especially in imitativeness or mischievousness.

mon key shine (mung′kē shīn′), *n.* SLANG. a mischievous trick; clownish joke.

monkey wrench, 1 a wrench with a movable jaw that can be adjusted to fit different sizes of nuts. 2 **throw a monkey wrench into,** INFORMAL. interfere with; subvert; destroy.

monk ish (mung′kish), *adj.* 1 of a monk; having to do with monks or monasticism. 2 like a monk; characteristic of a monk. 3 like monks or their way of life. —**monk′ish ly,** *adv.* —**monk′ish ness,** *n.*

monks hood (mungks′hu̇d′), *n.* species of aconite grown for its purple or white hooded flowers. Its roots are the source of the drug aconite.

Mon mouth (mon′məth), *n.* 1 **Duke of,** 1649-1685, James Scott, supposed son of Charles II of England, who led a rebellion against James II. 2 Monmouthshire.

monogram

Mon mouth shire (mon′məth shər, mon′məth shir), *n.* county in W England.

mono-, *prefix.* 1 having one ____: *Monosyllabic = having one syllable.* 2 a single ____; one ____: *Monorail = a single rail.* 3 containing one atom, etc., of the substance specified, as in *monoxide.* Also, **mon-** before vowels. [< Greek < *monos* single]

mon o ba sic (mon′ō bā′sik), *adj.* (of an acid) having only one atom of hydrogen that can be replaced by an atom or radical of a base in forming salts.

mon o chro mat ic (mon′ə krō mat′ik), *adj.* 1 having or showing one color only. 2 (of light) consisting of one wavelength. 3 producing such light.

mon o chrome (mon′ə krōm), *n.* a painting, drawing, print, etc., in a single color or shades of a single color.

mon o cle (mon′ə kəl), *n.* eyeglass for one eye. [< French < Late Latin *monoculus* one-eyed < Greek *monos* single + Latin *oculus* eye]

mon o cled (mon′ə kəld), *adj.* wearing a monocle.

mon o clin ic (mon′ō klin′ik), *adj.* (of crystals or crystallization) having the three axes unequal with one oblique intersection.

mon o cot (mon′ə kot), *n.* monocotyledon.

mon o cot y le don (mon′ə kot′l ēd′n), *n.* any of a class of flowering plants of the angiosperm subdivision, having a single cotyledon in the embryo. Monocotyledons have leaves with parallel veins and flower parts in threes. They include the grasses, palms, lilies, irises, etc.

mon o cot y le don ous (mon′ə kot′l-ēd′n əs), *adj.* having only one cotyledon.

mo noc u lar (mə nok′yə lər), *adj.* 1 having to do with or intended for use by one eye only. 2 having only one eye. —*n.* any monocular instrument.

mo nod ic (mə nod′ik), *adj.* of, having to do with, or like a monody.

mon o dist (mon′ə dist), *n.* person who composes or sings a monody.

mon o dy (mon′ə dē), *n., pl.* **-dies.** 1 a mournful song; lament; dirge. 2 a plaintive poem in which a mourner laments death. 3 style of musical composition in which one part or melody predominates. 4 composition written in this style. [< Greek *monōidia* < *mono-* + *ōidē* song]

monkey wrench (def. 1)

mo noe cious (mə nē′shəs), *adj.* having the stamens and the pistils in separate flowers on the same plant. Also, **monecious.** [< Greek *mono-* + *oikos* house]

mo nog a mist (mə nog′ə mist), *n.* person who practices or advocates monogamy.

mo nog a mous (mə nog′ə məs), *adj.* 1 practicing or advocating monogamy. 2 of or having to do with monogamy. —**mo nog′a mous ly,** *adv.*

mo nog a my (mə nog′ə mē), *n.* 1 practice or condition of being married to only one person at a time. 2 the condition of having only one mate during a lifetime.

mon o gram (mon′ə gram), *n.* a person's initials combined in one design. Monograms are used on note paper, table linen, clothing, jewelry, etc.

mon o grammed (mon′ə gramd), *adj.* bearing a monogram.

mon o graph (mon′ə graf), *n.* book or article, especially a scholarly one, about a particular subject.

mon o lay er (mon′ə lā′ər), *n.* a monomolecular layer.

mon o lin gual (mon′ə ling′gwəl), *adj.* limited to or using only one language: *a monolingual dictionary.*

mon o lith (mon′l ith), *n.* 1 a single large block of stone. 2 monument, column, statue, etc., formed of a single large block of stone. 3 nation, political party, etc., that in its rigid and unyielding attitudes and policies suggests a massive block of stone. [< Greek *monolithos* < *mono-* + *lithos* stone]

mon o lith ic (mon′l ith′ik), *adj.* of a monolith; being a monolith.

mon o log (mon′l ôg, mon′l og), *n.* monologue.

mon o log ist (mon′l ôg′ist, mon′l og′ist, mə nol′ə jist), *n.* 1 person who talks or acts in monologue, or delivers monologues. 2 person who monopolizes conversation.

mon o logue (mon′l ôg, mon′l og), *n.* 1 a long speech by one person in a group; speech that monopolizes conversation. 2 entertainment by a single speaker. 3 a play for a single actor. 4 part of a play in which a single actor speaks alone. 5 poem or other literary composition in the form of a soliloquy. Also, **monolog.** [< French < *mono-* + *(dia)logue*]

mon o logu ist (mon′l ôg′ist, mon′l og′ist, mə nol′ə jist), *n.* monologist.

mon o ma ni a (mon′ə mā′nē ə), *n.* 1 a mental disorder in which a person's behavior is controlled by a single idea or subject. 2 interest or tendency so dominant or obsessive as to seem almost insane.

mon o ma ni ac (mon′ə mā′nē ak), *n.* person characterized by monomania.

mon o mer (mon′ə mər), *n.* a single molecule that can combine with others to form a polymer. [< *mono-* + Greek *meros* part]

mon o mer ic (mon′ə mer′ik), *adj.* of or like a monomer.

mon o me tal lic (mon′ō mə tal′ik), *adj.* 1 using one metal only. 2 having to do with monometallism.

mon o met al lism (mon′ō met′l iz′əm), *n.* use of one metal only, such as gold or silver, as the standard of money values.

mo no mi al (mō nō′mē əl), *n.* 1 expression in algebra consisting of a single term. The expressions $2x^2$, $3ax$, and $\frac{3a}{b}$ are monomials. 2 a scientific name of a plant or animal consisting of a single term. —*adj.* consisting of a single word or term. [< *mono-* + *(bi)-nomial*]

mon o mo lec u lar (mon′ō mə lek′yə lər), *adj.* that is one molecule in thickness: *a monomolecular layer.* —**mon′o mo lec′u-lar ly,** *adv.*

Mo non ga he la River (mə non′gə hē′lə, mə nong′gə hē′lə), river flowing from N West Virginia which, with the Allegheny River, forms the Ohio River at Pittsburgh. 128 mi.

mon o nu cle ar (mon′ə nü′klē ər, mon′ə-nyü′klē ər), *adj.* having only a single nucleus.

mon o nu cle o sis (mon′ə nü′klē ō′sis, mon′ə nyü′klē ō′sis), *n.* an infectious disease characterized by fever, a sore throat, swelling of the lymph glands, and an abnormal increase in the number of mononuclear leucocytes in the blood.

mon o phon ic (mon′ə fon′ik), *adj.* 1 sung or played in unison without accompaniment. 2 of or having to do with the transmission or reproduction of sound by means of a single channel; monaural.

mon oph thong (mon′əf thông, mon′əf-thong), *n.* a single, simple vowel sound showing little or no change in quality throughout its duration. EXAMPLE: *i* in *pin.* [< Greek *mono-* + *phthongos* sound]

mon o plane (mon′ə plān), *n.* airplane with only one pair of wings. Most modern airplanes are monoplanes.

mon o ploid (mon′ə ploid), *adj.* having a single set of chromosomes in the germ cell or gamete; haploid. —*n.* a monoploid organism or cell; haploid.

mo nop o list (mə nop′ə list), *n.* 1 person who has a monopoly. 2 person who favors monopoly.

mo nop o lis tic (mə nop′ə lis′tik), *adj.* 1 that monopolizes. 2 having to do with monopolies or monopolists. **—mo nop′o lis′ti cal ly,** *adv.*

mo nop o lize (mə nop′ə līz), *v.t.,* **-lized, -liz ing.** 1 have or get exclusive possession or control of. 2 occupy wholly; keep entirely to oneself. **—mo nop′o li za′tion,** *n.* **—mo nop′o liz′er,** *n.*

mo nop o ly (mə nop′ə lē), *n., pl.* **-lies.** 1 the exclusive control of a commodity or service: *The only milk company in town has a monopoly on milk delivery.* 2 such control granted by a government: *An inventor has a monopoly on his invention for a certain number of years.* 3 control that, though not exclusive, enables the person or company to fix prices. 4 a commercial product or service that is exclusively controlled or nearly so. 5 person or company that has a monopoly on some commodity or service. 6 the exclusive possession or control of something: *a monopoly of a person's time.* [< Greek *monopōlion* < *mono-* + *pōlein* to sell]

mon o rail (mon′ə rāl′), *n.* 1 a single rail serving as a complete track. 2 railway in which cars run on a single rail, either balanced on it or suspended from it.

mon o sac cha ride (mon′ə sak′ə rīd′), *n.* any of a class of sugars, such as glucose and fructose, that cannot be decomposed by hydrolysis; simple sugar.

mon o syl lab ic (mon′ə sə lab′ik), *adj.* 1 having only one syllable. 2 consisting of a word or words of one syllable. **—mon′o syl lab′i cal ly,** *adv.*

mon o syl la ble (mon′ə sil′ə bəl), *n.* word of one syllable. *Yes, no,* and *grand* are monosyllables.

mon o the ism (mon′ə thē′iz′əm), *n.* doctrine or belief that there is only one God.

mon o the ist (mon′ə thē′ist), *n.* believer in only one God.

mon o the is tic (mon′ə thē is′tik), *adj.* 1 believing in only one God. 2 having to do with belief in only one God.

mon o tone (mon′ə tōn), *n.* 1 sameness of tone, style of writing, color, etc. 2 manner of speaking, singing, etc., without change of pitch; unvaried sound or repetition of sounds: *Don't speak in a monotone; use expression.* 3 in music: **a** a single tone without change of pitch. **b** recitative singing, especially of liturgy, in such a tone. 4 person who sings or speaks in a monotone. —*adj.* continuing on one tone; of one tone, style, color, etc.; monotonous.

mo not o nous (mə not′n əs), *adj.* 1 continuing in the same tone or pitch: *a monotonous voice.* 2 not varying; without change; uniform. 3 wearying because of its sameness; tedious: *monotonous work.* **—mo not′o nous ly,** *adv.* **—mo not′o nous ness,** *n.*

mo not o ny (mə not′n ē), *n.* 1 sameness of tone or pitch. 2 lack of variety. 3 wearisome sameness.

mon o treme (mon′ə trēm), *n.* any of an order of mammals which lay eggs and have a common opening for the genital and urinary organs and the digestive tract. Duckbilled platypuses and echidnas are monotremes. [< *mono-* + Greek *trema* hole]

Mon o type (mon′ə tīp), *n., v.,* **-typed, -typ ing.** —*n.* 1 trademark for a machine that sets and casts type in separate letters. 2 **monotype,** type set and cast on a Monotype. —*v.t.* **monotype,** set (type) with a Monotype.

mon o typ ic (mon′ə tip′ik), *adj.* in biology: 1 being the sole representative of its group: *a monotypic form.* 2 (of a genus) having only one species.

mon o va lent (mon′ə vā′lənt), *adj.* having a valence of one; univalent.

mon ox ide (mo nok′sīd, mo nok′sid), *n.* oxide containing one oxygen atom in each molecule.

Mon roe (mən rō′), *n.* **James,** 1758-1831, the fifth president of the United States, from 1817 to 1825.

Monroe Doctrine, doctrine that European nations should not interfere with American nations or try to acquire more territory in the Western Hemisphere. The Monroe Doctrine was derived from President Monroe's message to Congress on December 2, 1823, and became a part of United States foreign policy.

Mon ro vi a (mon rō′vē ə), *n.* capital of Liberia, a seaport in the NW part. 100,000.

mon sei gneur or ***Mon sei gneur*** (môɴ se nyœr′), *n., pl.* ***mes sei gneurs*** or ***Mes sei gneurs*** (mā se nyœr′). FRENCH. 1 title of honor given to princes, bishops, and other persons of importance. 2 person having this title. 3 (literally) my lord.

mon sieur (mə syœ′), *n., pl.* ***mes sieurs.*** FRENCH. Mr.; sir.

mon si gnor or **Mon si gnor** (mon sē′nyər; *Italian* mōn′sē nyôr′), *n., pl.* **mon si gnors** or **Mon si gnors; mon si gno ri** or **Mon si gno ri** (mōn′sē nyō′rē). 1 title given to prelates and certain dignitaries in the Roman Catholic Church. 2 person having this title. [< Italian *monsignore* < French *monseigneur* monseigneur]

mon soon (mon sün′), *n.* 1 a seasonal wind of the Indian Ocean and southern Asia, blowing from the southwest from April to October and from the northeast during the rest of the year. 2 the rainy season during which this wind blows from the southwest. [< earlier Dutch *monssoen* < Portuguese *monçao* < Arabic *mausim* season]

mon ster (mon′stər), *n.* 1 any animal or plant that is very unlike those usually found in nature. A cow with two heads is a monster. 2 an imaginary creature composed of parts of different animals, as a centaur, sphinx, or griffin. 3 an imaginary animal of strange and horrible appearance. 4 person too wicked to be considered human. 5 a huge creature or thing. —*adj.* enormous; huge. [< Old French *monstre* < Latin *monstrum* portent, divine warning]

mon strance (mon′strəns), *n.* (in the Roman Catholic Church) a receptacle in which the consecrated Host is shown for adoration or is carried in procession. [< Medieval Latin *monstrantia* < Latin *monstrare* to show]

mon stros i ty (mon stros′ə tē), *n., pl.* **-ties.** 1 monster. 2 condition or character of being monstrous.

mon strous (mon′strəs), *adj.* 1 of extremely large size; huge; enormous. 2 wrongly or abnormally formed or shaped; like a monster. 3 having the nature or appearance of a monster of fable or legend. 4 outrageously wrong or absurd. 5 shocking; horrible; dreadful. **—mon′strous ly,** *adv.* **—mon′strous ness,** *n.*

hat, āge, fär; let, ēqual, tėrm;
it, īce; hot, ōpen, ôrder;
oil, out; cup, pu̇t, rüle;
ch, child; ng, long; sh, she;
th, thin; ᴛʜ, then; zh, measure;

ə represents *a* in about, *e* in taken,
i in pencil, *o* in lemon, *u* in circus.

< = from, derived from, taken from.

Mont., Montana.

mon tage (mon täzh′), *n.* 1 (in photography) the combination of several distinct pictures to make a composite picture. 2 a composite picture so made. 3 (in motion pictures, television, etc.) any combining or blending of pictures or their elements, at once or in succession. [< French < *monter* to mount]

mon ta gnard or **Mon ta gnard** (mon tə nyärd′), *n.* one of a large group of dark-skinned, aboriginal tribesmen living in the mountainous regions of Vietnam. [< French, literally, mountaineer]

Mon taigne (mon tān′), *n.* **Michel de,** 1533-1592, French essayist and philosopher.

Mon tan a (mon tan′ə), *n.* one of the western states of the United States. 694,000 pop.; 147,100 sq. mi. *Capital:* Helena. *Abbrev.:* Mont. **—Mon tan′an,** *adj., n.*

Mont Blanc (môɴ bläɴ′), the highest mountain in the Alps, between France and Italy. 15,781 ft.

Mont calm (mont käm′, mont kälm′), *n.* **Louis Joseph, Marquis de,** 1712-1759, French general defeated by the English at Quebec.

Mon te Car lo (mon′tə kär′lō), town in Monaco, noted as a gambling resort. 10,000.

Mon te ne grin (mon′tə nē′grən), *adj.* of or having to do with Montenegro or its people. —*n.* native or inhabitant of Montenegro.

Mon te ne gro (mon′tə nē′grō), *n.* former country in S Europe, on the Adriatic Sea. After World War I it became a part of Yugoslavia.

Mon te rey (mon′tə rā′), *n.* town in W California. It was the capital of California until 1849. 26,000.

Mon ter rey (mon′tə rā′), *n.* city in NE Mexico. 830,000.

Mon tes quieu (mon′tə skyü), *n.* Baron **de La Brède et de,** 1689-1755, French philosopher and writer. His real name was Charles de Secondat.

Mon tes so ri (mon′tə sôr′ē, mon′tə sōr′ē), *n.* **Maria,** 1870-1952, Italian educator.

Mon te ver di (mon′tə ver′dē), *n.* **Claudio,** 1567-1643, Italian composer.

Mon te vi de o (mon′tə vi dā′ō), *n.* capital of Uruguay, a seaport on the Plata River. 1,200,000.

Mon te zu ma II (mon′tə zü′mə), 1480?-1520, Aztec emperor of Mexico, from 1502 to 1520, defeated by Cortés.

Mont gom er y (mont gum′ər ē), *n.* 1 capital of Alabama, in the central part. 133,000. 2 Sir **Bernard Law,** first Viscount Montgomery of Alamein, born 1887, British field marshal.

month (munth), *n.* 1 one of the 12 parts into which the year is divided. 2 time from any day of one month to the corresponding day of the next month. 3 lunar month. [Old English *mōnath.* Related to MOON.]

➛ **months.** In technical and informal writing, the names of months with more than four letters are abbreviated in dates: *Jan. 21, 1969; Aug. 16, 1968.* But: *May 1, 1967; July 4, 1969.* When only the month or month and year are given, abbreviations are rarely used: *January 1970. He held office from September to February.* In formal writing, the names of the months are not abbreviated.

month ly (munth′lē), *adj., adv., n., pl.* **-lies.** —*adj.* 1 of a month; for a month; lasting a month. 2 done, happening, payable, etc., once a month. —*adv.* once a month; every month. —*n.* 1 periodical published once a month. 2 **monthlies,** *pl.* menses.

Mon ti cel lo (mon′tə sel′ō, mon′tə chel′ō), *n.* home of Thomas Jefferson, near Charlottesville, Virginia.

Mont mar tre (mônN mär′trə), *n.* section in the N part of Paris, noted for its night life.

Mont pel ier (mont pē′lyər), *n.* capital of Vermont, in the central part. 9000.

Mon tre al (mon′trē ôl′), *n.* large seaport in Quebec, Canada, on the St. Lawrence River. 1,222,000.

Mont St. Mi chel (mônN saN mē shel′), small island off the NW coast of France, famous for its abbey.

mon u ment (mon′yə mənt), *n.* 1 object or structure set up to commemorate a notable person, action, or event. A monument may be a building, pillar, arch, statue, tomb, or stone. 2 anything that keeps alive the memory of a person, civilization, period, or event. 3 an enduring or prominent instance: *a monument of learning.* 4 any permanent object, natural or artificial, serving to mark a boundary. 5 any area or site officially designated by a government as having special historical or natural significance. [< Latin *monumentum* < *monere* remind]

mon u men tal (mon′yə men′tl), *adj.* 1 of a monument. 2 serving as a monument. 3 like a monument. 4 weighty and lasting; important: *a monumental decision.* 5 very great; colossal: *monumental ignorance.* —**mon′u men′tal ly,** *adv.*

moo (mü), *n., pl.* **moos,** *v.* —*n.* sound made by a cow. —*v.i.* make the sound of a cow.

mooch (müch), SLANG. —*v.t.* get from another by begging or sponging. —*v.i.* sponge or beg shamelessly. [probably < Old French *muchier* hide, skulk] —**mooch′er,** *n.*

mood[1] (müd), *n.* 1 state of mind or feeling. See synonym study below. 2 **moods,** *pl.* fits of depression or bad temper. [Old English *mōd* mind]

Syn. 1 **Mood, humor** mean a person's state of mind or feeling at a particular time. **Mood** applies to a state of mind determined by some emotion or desire that affects everything a person says or does: *I am not in the mood to study just now; I want to watch television.* **Humor** applies to a state of mind determined by a person's natural disposition or physical condition, and suggests the likelihood of changing suddenly or without apparent reason: *He is in a good humor today.*

mood[2] (müd), *n.* form of a verb which shows whether the act or state it expresses is thought of as a fact, condition, command, etc. In *"I am hungry," am* is in the indicative mood. In *"I demand that she answer," answer* is in the subjunctive mood. Also, **mode.** [alteration of *mode*[1]; influenced by *mood*[1]]

mood y (mü′dē), *adj.,* **mood i er, mood i est.** 1 likely to have changes of mood. 2 often having gloomy moods. 3 sunk in sadness; gloomy; sullen: *She sat in moody silence.* 4 expressive of a mood, especially a bad mood: *a moody remark.* —**mood′i ly,** *adv.* —**mood′i ness,** *n.*

moon (def. 1)

moon (mün), *n.* 1 a heavenly body that revolves around the earth once in approximately $29^1/_2$ days at a mean distance of 238,855 miles. It is a natural satellite of the earth and is held in orbit by the earth's gravity. The moon's diameter is about 2160 miles, and its volume is about $^1/_{50}$ that of the earth. The force of the moon's gravity on the earth causes tides in the ocean. 2 the moon as it looks at a certain period of time in its cycle: *a new moon, a full moon.* 3 one lunar month; about $29^1/_2$ days. The Indians counted time by moons. 4 moonlight. 5 something shaped like the moon in any of its appearances. 6 satellite of any planet: *the moons of Jupiter.* 7 an artificial earth satellite. —*v.i.* wander about or gaze idly or dreamily. —*v.t.* spend (time) idly. [Old English *mōna*] —**moon′less,** *adj.* —**moon′like′,** *adj.*

moon beam (mün′bēm′), *n.* ray of moonlight.

moon calf (mün′kaf′), *n.* 1 a congenital idiot. 2 a foolish person; fool; dolt.

moon craft (mün′kraft′), *n., pl.* **-craft.** a space vehicle designed for flight to the moon.

moon flow er (mün′flou′ər), *n.* 1 a tropical plant of the same family as the morning-glory, having large, fragrant white flowers that open in the evening. 2 any of various related plants.

moon light (mün′līt′), *n.* light of the moon. —*adj.* 1 having the light of the moon. 2 while the moon is shining; by night. —*v.i.* INFORMAL. work at a second job, often at night, in order to supplement the wages earned at a regular job. —**moon′light′er,** *n.*

moon lit (mün′lit′), *adj.* lighted by the moon: *moonlit woods.*

moon scape (mün′skāp′), *n.* 1 view of the surface of the moon. 2 the surface viewed.

moon shine (mün′shīn′), *n.* 1 moonlight. 2 empty talk; foolish talk or ideas; nonsense. 3 INFORMAL. intoxicating liquor made unlawfully or smuggled into the country.

moon shin er (mün′shī′nər), *n.* INFORMAL. person who distills intoxicating liquor, especially corn whiskey, contrary to law.

moon stone (mün′stōn′), *n.* a whitish, translucent gem with a pearly luster. Moonstone is a variety of feldspar.

moon struck (mün′struk′), *adj.* dazed, crazed, or confused.

moon y (mü′nē), *adj.,* **moon i er, moon i est.** 1 of the moon. 2 like the moon. 3 dreamy.

moor[1] (mür), *v.t.* 1 put or keep (a ship, etc.) in place by means of ropes or chains fastened to the shore or to anchors. 2 fix firmly; secure. —*v.i.* 1 moor a ship. 2 be made secure by ropes, anchors, etc. [Middle English *moren*]

moor[2] (mür), *n.* open, waste land, especially if heather grows on it. [Old English *mōr*]

Moor (mür), *n.* member of a Moslem people of mixed Arab and Berber ancestry, living in northwestern Africa. In the A.D. 700's the Moors invaded and conquered Spain. They were finally driven out in 1492.

moor age (mür′ij), *n.* 1 a mooring. 2 a being moored. 3 place for mooring. 4 fee charged for its use.

moor cock, the male red grouse.

Moore (mür, môr, mōr), *n.* 1 **Douglas,** 1893-1969, American composer. 2 **George,** 1852-1933, Irish author. 3 **Henry,** born 1898, British sculptor. 4 **Marianne,** 1887-1972, American poet. 5 **Thomas,** 1779-1852, Irish poet.

moor fowl (mür′foul′), *n.* the red grouse.

moor hen (mür′hen′), *n.* 1 the female red grouse. 2 BRITISH. gallinule.

moor ing (mür′ing), *n.* 1 act of tying up or securing a ship, etc. 2 Also, **moorings,** *pl.* place where a ship is or may be tied up. 3 **moorings,** *pl.* ropes, cables, anchors, etc., by which a ship is made fast. 4 Also, **moorings,** *pl.* anything to which a person or thing is attached or fastened.

Moor ish (mür′ish), *adj.* 1 of the Moors. 2 in the style of the Moors.

moor land (mür′lənd, mür′land′), *n.* land covered with heather; moor.

moose (def. 1)
about 6 ft. high at the shoulder

moose (müs), *n., pl.* **moose.** 1 a large ruminant mammal of the same family as the deer, found in wooded areas of Canada and the northern United States. The male has a heavy build, large head, and broad antlers. 2 the European elk. [of Algonquian origin]

moot (müt), *adj.* that can be argued; debatable; doubtful: *a moot point.* —*v.i.* 1 bring forward (a point, subject, case, etc.) for discussion. 2 ARCHAIC. argue, discuss, or debate (a point, subject, case, etc.). [Old English *mōtian* to argue, discuss < *(ge)mōt* meeting]

moot court, mock court held in a law school to give students practice.

mop[1] (mop), *n., v.,* **mopped, mop ping.** —*n.* 1 bundle of coarse yarn, rags, cloth, etc., or a sponge fastened at the end of a stick, for cleaning floors, etc. 2 a thick, tangled, or unruly mass, as of hair. 3 any of various small instruments resembling a mop, especially one used in surgery to apply medicated fluids or to remove infected matter.

—*v.t.* 1 wash or wipe up; clean with a mop: *mop the floor.* 2 wipe sweat or tears from: *mop one's brow with a handkerchief.* —*v.i.* use a mop.

mop up, a clean up with a mop. b INFORMAL. finish. c clear out or rid (an area, town, etc.) of scattered or remaining enemy troops.

[Middle English *mappe*]

mop² (mop), *v.,* **mopped, mop ping,** *n.* —*v.i.* make a wry face; grimace. —*n.* grimace. [perhaps related to Dutch *moppen* to pout]

mope (mōp), *v.,* **moped, mop ing,** *n.* —*v.i.* be dull, silent, and sad. —*n.* 1 person who is dull, silent, and sad. 2 **the mopes,** low spirits; the blues. [perhaps related to MOP²] —**mop′er,** *n.*

mop pet (mop′it), *n.* a little child. [< obsolete *mop* doll]

mop-up (mop′up′), *n.* INFORMAL. 1 a cleaning up; a wiping out. 2 the clearing out of scattered or remaining enemy troops in an area after a battle.

mo rain al (mə rā′nl), *adj.* of or having to do with a moraine.

mo raine (mə rān′), *n.* mass or ridge of rocks, dirt, etc., deposited at the sides or end of a glacier. The material is scraped up by the glacier as it moves along. [< French]

mo rain ic (mə rā′nik), *adj.* morainal.

mo ral (môr′əl, mor′əl), *adj.* 1 good in character or conduct; virtuous according to civilized standards of right and wrong; right; just: *a moral act, a moral man.* See synonym study below. 2 capable of understanding right and wrong: *A little baby is not a moral being.* 3 having to do with character or with the difference between right and wrong: *a moral question, a moral responsibility.* 4 teaching a good lesson; having a good influence: *a moral book.* 5 that raises one's morale; inspiring confidence: *give moral support to a candidate.* 6 practical: *a moral certainty.* —*n.* 1 lesson, inner meaning, or teaching of a fable, a story, or an event: *The moral of the story was "Look before you leap."* 2 **morals,** *pl.* a principles in regard to conduct. b character or behavior in matters of right and wrong. [< Latin *moralis* < *mores* manners]

Syn. *adj.* 1 **Moral, ethical** mean in agreement with a standard of what is right and good in character or conduct. **Moral** implies conformity to the customary rules and accepted standards of society: *He leads a moral life.* **Ethical** implies conformity to principles of right conduct expressed in a formal system or code, as of a profession or business: *It is not considered ethical for doctors to advertise.*

➔ **moral, morale.** A common error is writing *moral* (concerning right conduct) when *morale* (mental condition as regards courage, confidence, enthusiasm, etc.) is the word intended.

mo rale (mə ral′), *n.* moral or mental condition or attitude of a person or group as regards courage, confidence, enthusiasm, etc.: *the morale of troops, the morale of a team.* [< French, feminine of *moral* moral] ➔ See **moral** for usage note.

mo ral ist (môr′ə list, mor′ə list), *n.* 1 person who leads a moral life. 2 person who teaches, studies, or writes about morals. 3 person who believes in regulating the morals of others.

mo ral is tic (môr′ə lis′tik, mor′ə lis′tik), *adj.* 1 moralizing; teaching the difference between right and wrong. 2 of or having to do with a moralist or moral teaching. 3 narrow-minded or self-righteous in moral judgment or beliefs. —**mo′ral is′ti cally,** *adv.*

mo ral i ty (mə ral′ə tē), *n., pl.* **-ties.** 1 right or wrong of an action. 2 doing right; virtue. 3 system of morals; set of rules or principles of conduct. 4 moral instruction; moral lesson or precept.

morality play, type of drama popular during the 1400's and 1500's, in which the characters were personifications of abstract qualities, such as vice, virtue, wealth, poverty, knowledge, or ignorance.

mo ral ize (môr′ə līz, mor′ə līz), *v.,* **-ized, -iz ing.** —*v.i.* think, talk, or write about questions of right and wrong. —*v.t.* 1 point out the lesson or inner meaning of. 2 improve the morals of. —**mo′ral i za′tion,** *n.* —**mo′ral iz′er,** *n.*

mo ral ly (môr′ə lē, mor′ə lē), *adv.* 1 in a moral manner. 2 in morals; as to morals. 3 from a moral point of view; ethically. 4 practically.

moral victory, defeat that has the effect on the mind that a victory would have.

mo rass (mə ras′), *n.* 1 piece of low, soft, wet ground; swamp; marsh. 2 a difficult situation; puzzling mess. [< Dutch *moeras*]

mo ra to ri um (môr′ə tôr′ē əm, môr′ə tōr′ē əm; mor′ə tôr′ē əm, mor′ə tōr′ē əm), *n., pl.* **-ri ums, -ri a** (-rē ə). 1 a legal authorization to delay payments of money due, as during an emergency. 2 period during which such authorization is in effect. 3 a voluntary or negotiated temporary cessation of action on any issue. [< New Latin < Latin *morari* to delay < *mora* a delay]

Mo ra vi a (mô rā′vē ə, mō rā′vē ə), *n.* region in central Czechoslovakia.

Mo ra vi an (mô rā′vē ən, mō rā′vē ən), *adj.* 1 having to do with Moravia, its Slavic inhabitants, or their language. 2 of or having to do with the Protestant church organized in Moravia and Bohemia and based on the teachings of John Huss. —*n.* 1 native or inhabitant of Moravia. 2 the Slavic language of Moravia, a dialect of Czech. 3 member of the Moravian church.

mo ray (môr′ā, mōr′ā; mô rā′, mō rā′), *n.* any of various fierce, often brilliantly colored eels of tropical seas. [< Portuguese *moreia* < Latin *murena, muraena* < Greek *myraina*]

mor bid (môr′bid), *adj.* 1 not wholesome; unhealthy: *A liking for horrors is morbid.* 2 caused by disease; characteristic of disease; diseased: *Cancer is a morbid growth.* 3 having to do with diseased parts: *morbid anatomy.* 4 horrible; gruesome; grisly: *the morbid details of a murder.* [< Latin *morbidus* < *morbus* disease] —**mor′bid ly,** *adv.* —**mor′bid ness,** *n.*

mor bid i ty (môr bid′ə tē), *n.* 1 morbid condition or quality. 2 degree of prevalence of a disease in a certain group or locality.

mor dan cy (môrd′n sē), *n.* mordant quality.

mor dant (môrd′nt), *adj.* 1 biting; cutting; sarcastic: *mordant criticism, a mordant sense of humor.* 2 that fixes colors in dyeing. —*n.* 1 substance that fixes colors by combining in a chemical reaction with a dye to form an insoluble compound that will not wash from the fibers of cloth, leather, etc. 2 acid that eats into metal, used in etching. —*v.t.* treat with a mordant. [< Old French, present participle of *mordre* to bite < Latin *mordere*] —**mor′dant ly,** *adv.*

hat, āge, fär; let, ēqual, tėrm;
it, īce; hot, ōpen, ôrder;
oil, out; cup, pu̇t, rüle;
ch, child; ng, long; sh, she;
th, thin; ᴛʜ, then; zh, measure;

ə represents *a* in about, *e* in taken, *i* in pencil, *o* in lemon, *u* in circus.

< = from, derived from, taken from.

Mor de cai (môr′də kī), *n.* (in the Bible) the cousin of Esther, who helped her save the Jews from being destroyed by Haman.

mor dent (môrd′nt), *n.* (in music) a grace note or embellishment consisting of the rapid alternation of a tone with another tone usually a half step below it. [< Italian *mordente*]

more (môr, mōr), *adj., comparative of* **much** *and* **many;** *n., adv., comparative of* **much.** —*adj.* 1 greater in amount, degree, or number: *more men, more help. A foot is more than an inch.* 2 further; additional: *This plant needs more sun.* 3 greater: *The more fool you, to believe such a tale.* —*n.* 1 a greater amount, degree, or number: *The more they have, the more they want.* 2 an additional amount: *Tell me more.* —*adv.* 1 in or to a greater extent or degree: *That hurts more.* 2 in addition; further; longer; again: *Sing once more.* 3 **more or less,** a somewhat: *Most people are more or less selfish.* b nearly; approximately: *five miles more or less.* [Old English *māra*]

More (môr, mōr), *n.* Sir **Thomas,** 1478-1535, English statesman and author, canonized in 1935.

Mo re a (mô rē′ə, mō rē′ə), *n.* Peloponnesus.

mo rel (mə rel′), *n.* any of various small, edible mushrooms with brown, spongy, pitted caps. [< French *morille*]

more o ver (môr ō′vər, mōr ō′vər), *adv.* in addition to that; also; besides: *The proposal was not well thought out; moreover, it would have been very expensive.*

mo res (môr′āz, mōr′āz; môr′ēz, mōr′ēz), *n.pl.* traditional rules and customs of a group of people or a society. They are accepted as right and morally binding. [< Latin, customs]

Mor gan (môr′gən), *n.* 1 Sir **Henry,** 1635?-1688, British buccaneer. 2 **J(ohn) P(ierpont),** 1837-1913, American financier and art collector. 3 any of an American breed of sturdy, relatively light horses that originated in Vermont, used as trotting horses and for work on farms.

mor ga nat ic (môr′gə nat′ik), *adj.* of or having to do with a form of marriage in which a man of noble or royal rank marries a woman of lower rank, especially a commoner, with an agreement that neither she nor her children shall have any claim to his rank or property. [< New Latin *morganaticus* < Medieval Latin *(matrimonium ad) morganaticam* (marriage with) morning gift; the gift to the bride on the day after the wedding was her only share in her husband's goods and rights]

Mor gan le Fay (môr′gən lə fā′), (in Arthurian legends) King Arthur's half sister, a fairy, usually represented as harming him whenever she could.

morgue (môrg), *n.* 1 place in which the bodies of persons unidentified or killed by accident or violence are temporarily held, for identification and claim or for investigation. 2 the reference library of a newspaper, magazine, etc., in which clippings and other materials are kept. [< French]

mo ri bund (môr′ə bund, mor′ə bund), *adj.* at the point of death or extinction; dying. [< Latin *moribundus* < *mori* die]

mo ri bun di ty (môr′ə bun′də tē, mor′ə-bun′də tē), *n.* moribund condition.

morion

mo ri on (môr′ē on, mōr′ē on), *n.* helmet without a visor, shaped like a hat, with a comb-shaped crest and an upturned rim forming a peak in front. [< French]

Mor mon (môr′mən), *n.* member of the Church of Jesus Christ of Latter-day Saints, founded in 1830 by Joseph Smith. —*adj.* of or having to do with the Mormons or their religion.

Mor mon ism (môr′mə niz′əm), *n.* the religious system of the Mormons.

morn (môrn), *n.* ARCHAIC. morning. [Old English *morgen*]

morn ing (môr′ning), *n.* 1 the early part of the day, from midnight to noon, or from sunrise to noon. 2 the first or early part of anything: *the morning of life.* 3 dawn; daybreak. —*adj.* of or in the morning. [Middle English *morwening* < *morwen* morn (Old English *morgen*) + *-ing*[1]; patterned on *evening*]

morn ing-glo ry (môr′ning glôr′ē, môr′-ning glōr′ē), *n., pl.* **-ries.** 1 any of a genus of vines, shrubs, and small trees, especially a vine with heart-shaped leaves and funnel-shaped flowers of varying colors. 2 the flower of any of these plants, which blooms early in the day.

morning star, a bright planet, especially Venus, seen in the eastern sky before sunrise; daystar.

Mo ro (môr′ō, mōr′ō), *n., pl.* **-ros.** member of any of various tribes of Moslem Malays in Mindanao and other islands of the southern Philippines. —*adj.* of or having to do with these people.

mo roc co (mə rok′ō), *n., pl.* **-cos.** 1 a fine leather made from goatskin tanned with vegetable extracts, used in binding books. 2 leather imitating this. [< *Morocco*]

Mo roc co (mə rok′ō), *n.* country in NW Africa, most of which was formerly under French and Spanish control. 15,030,000 pop.; 172,100 sq. mi. *Capital:* Rabat. See **Algeria** for map. —**Mo roc′can,** *adj., n.*

mo ron (môr′on, mōr′on), *n.* 1 person born with such limited mental capacities that he can be trained to do only routine tasks but probably can learn to read; person who does not develop beyond a mental age of 8 to 12 years. 2 INFORMAL. a very stupid or foolish person. [< Greek *mōron,* neuter of *mōros* foolish, dull]

mo ron ic (mə ron′ik), *adj.* of or like a moron. —**mo ron′i cal ly,** *adv.*

mo rose (mə rōs′), *adj.* gloomy; sullen; ill-humored: *a morose scowl, a morose person.* [< Latin *morosus,* originally, set in one's ways < *morem* custom, habit] —**mo rose′ly,** *adv.* —**mo rose′ness,** *n.*

mor pheme (môr′fēm), *n.* (in linguistics) the smallest meaningful unit in the grammar or structure of a language. A morpheme can be an affix, a combining form, a word, and even an intonation. The word *unclearly* consists of the morphemes *un-, clear,* and *-ly.* [< French *morphème* < Greek *morphē* form]

mor phe mic (môr fē′mik), *adj.* of, having to do with, or characteristic of a morpheme.

Mor phe us (môr′fē əs, môr′fyüs), *n.* the Greek god of dreams, a name first used by Ovid and common in literary references.

mor phi a (môr′fē ə), *n.* morphine.

mor phine (môr′fēn′), *n.* a bitter, white, crystalline narcotic drug obtained from opium, used in the form of its salts to relieve pain and induce sleep. *Formula:* $C_{17}H_{19}NO_3 \cdot H_2O$ [< French < *Morpheus* Morpheus]

mor pho log ic (môr′fə loj′ik), *adj.* morphological.

mor pho log i cal (môr′fə loj′ə kəl), *adj.* of or having to do with morphology; relating to form; structural. —**mor′pho log′i cal ly,** *adv.*

mor phol o gist (môr fol′ə jist), *n.* an expert in morphology.

mor phol o gy (môr fol′ə jē), *n.* 1 branch of biology that deals with the form and structure of animals and plants without regard to function. 2 form and structure of an organism or one of its parts. 3 branch of grammar or linguistics dealing with the forms of words and their formation by inflection, derivation, etc. 4 study of forms in any science, as in geology. [< Greek *morphē* form + English *-logy*]

mor ris (môr′is, mor′is), *n.* morris dance.

Mor ris (môr′is, mor′is), *n.* 1 **Gouverneur,** 1752-1816, American statesman. 2 **Robert,** 1734-1806, American patriot and financier, born in England. 3 **William,** 1834-1896, English poet, artist, and socialist writer.

morris chair or **Morris chair,** armchair with removable cushions and an adjustable back. [< William *Morris,* who designed it]

morris dance, an old English folk dance performed chiefly on May Day by persons, especially men, in fancy costumes. [*morris,* earlier *morys* Moorish]

mor row (môr′ō, mor′ō), *n.* 1 the following day or time. 2 ARCHAIC. morning. [Middle English *morwe, morwen* morn, Old English *morgen*]

Morse (môrs), *n.* **Samuel F. B.,** 1791-1872, American painter and inventor who developed the first successful telegraph instrument.

Morse code, system by which letters, numbers, etc., are represented by dots, dashes, and spaces or by long and short sounds or flashes of light. Morse code is now used mainly in signaling, and in some telegraphy. [< Samuel F. B. *Morse*]

mor sel (môr′səl), *n.* 1 a small portion of food; bite. 2 a small piece, quantity, or amount of anything; fragment; bit. [< Old French, diminutive of *mors* a bite, ultimately < Latin *mordere* to bite]

mor tal (môr′tl), *adj.* 1 sure to die sometime; destined to undergo death. 2 of man; of mortals; human: *Mortal flesh has many pains and diseases.* 3 of death. 4 causing death; lethal; fatal: *a mortal wound, a mortal illness.* See **fatal** for synonym study. 5 to the death; implacable; relentless: *a mortal enemy, a mortal battle.* 6 very great; deadly: *mortal terror.* 7 (in the Roman Catholic Church) causing death of the soul: *a mortal sin.* 8 INFORMAL. long and tedious. —*n.* 1 a being that is sure to die sometime. All living creatures are mortals. 2 man; human being. [< Latin *mortalis* < *mortem* death]

mor tal i ty (môr tal′ə tē), *n.* 1 mortal nature; condition of being sure to die sometime. 2 loss of life on a large scale: *The mortality from automobile accidents is very serious.* 3 death rate; number of deaths in proportion to population or to a specified part of a population. 4 the human race; humanity.

mor tal ly (môr′tl ē), *adv.* 1 fatally; so as to cause death: *mortally wounded.* 2 very greatly; bitterly; grievously: *mortally offended.*

mor tar[1] (môr′tər), *n.* mixture of lime, cement, sand, and water, placed between bricks or stones to hold them together when it has dried and hardened. —*v.t.* plaster with mortar; fix with mortar. [< Old French *mortier* < Latin *mortarium* mortar[2]]

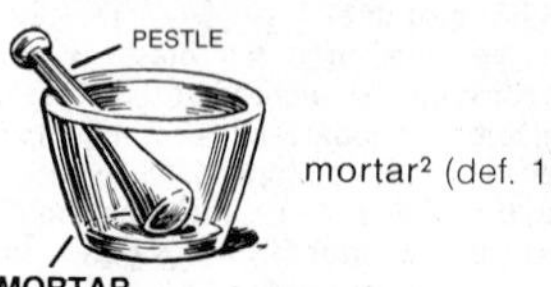

mortar[2] (def. 1)

mor tar[2] (môr′tər), *n.* 1 bowl of porcelain, glass, or other very hard material, in which substances may be pounded to a powder with a pestle. 2 a very short cannon with a wide, unrifled barrel, used to fire shells at high angles over a short range. [Old English *mortere* < Latin *mortarium*]

mortarboard (def. 2)

mor tar board (môr′tər bôrd′, môr′tər-bōrd′), *n.* 1 a flat, square board used by masons to hold mortar while working with it. 2 cap with a close-fitting crown topped by a stiff, flat, cloth-covered square piece from which usually a tassel hangs, worn at graduation exercises and on other academic occasions.

mort gage (môr′gij), *n., v.,* **-gaged, -gag ing.** —*n.* 1 a legal right or claim to a piece of property, given as security to a person, bank, or firm that has loaned money in case the money is not repaid when due. 2 a formal document that gives such a claim. —*v.t.* 1 give a lender a claim to (one's property) in case a debt is not paid when due: *mortgage a house.* 2 put under some obligation; pledge: *Faust mortgaged his soul to the Devil.* [< Old French < *mort* dead + *gage* pledge]

mort gag ee (môr′gi jē′), *n.* person to whom property is mortgaged.

mort ga gor or **mort gag er** (môr′gi-jər), *n.* person who mortgages his property.

mor tice (môr′tis), *n., v.,* **-ticed, -tic ing.** mortise.

mor ti cian (môr tish′ən), *n.* undertaker. [< *mort(uary)* + *-ician,* as in *physician*]

mor ti fi ca tion (môr′tə fə kā′shən), *n.* 1 a feeling of shame; humiliation: *mortification at having spilled food on the table.* 2 cause or source of shame or humiliation. 3 a mortifying. 4 a being mortified. 5 gangrene; necrosis.

mor ti fy (môr′tə fī), *v.*, **-fied, -fy ing.** —*v.t.* 1 wound the feelings of; make feel humbled and ashamed; humiliate: *He mortified his parents with his bad behavior.* See **ashamed** for synonym study. 2 overcome (bodily desires and feelings) by pain and self-denial: *The saint mortified his body.* —*v.i.* become gangrenous; die or decay: *The injured foot has mortified and must be amputated.* [< Old French *mortifier* < Latin *mortificare* to kill < *mortem* death + *facere* to make] —**mor′ti fi′er,** *n.*

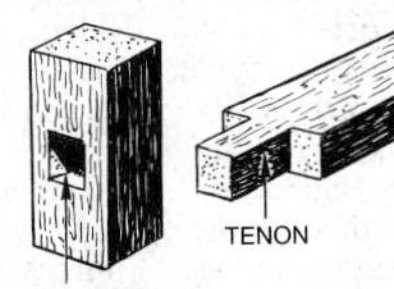

mor tise (môr′tis), *n.*, *v.*, **-tised, -tis ing.** —*n.* hole cut in or through one piece of wood to receive the tenon on another piece so as to form a joint. —*v.t.* 1 fasten or join by a mortise and tenon: *Good furniture is mortised together, not nailed.* 2 cut a mortise in; provide with a mortise. Also, **mortice.** [< Old French *mortaise*]

mort main (môrt′mān), *n.* (in law) the condition of lands or tenements held without right to sell them or give them away; inalienable possession. [< Old French *mortemain*]

mor tu ar y (môr′chü er′ē), *n.*, *pl.* **-ar ies,** *adj.* —*n.* building or room where dead bodies are kept until burial or cremation. —*adj.* of or having to do with death or burial. [< Medieval Latin *mortuarium* < Latin *mortuus* dead]

mos., months.

mo sa ic (mō zā′ik), *n.* 1 decoration made of small pieces of stone, glass, wood, etc., of different colors inlaid to form a picture or design. 2 such a picture or design. Mosaics are used in the floors, walls, or ceilings of some fine buildings. 3 art or process of making such a picture or design. 4 anything like a mosaic: *Her music is a mosaic of folk melodies.* 5 mosaic disease. —*adj.* formed by, having to do with, or resembling a mosaic. [< Medieval Latin *mosaicus, musaicus* of the Muses, artistic]

Mo sa ic (mō zā′ik), *adj.* of Moses or of writings ascribed to him.

mosaic disease, any of various virus diseases of tobacco and other plants in which the leaves become spotted or mottled.

mo sa i cist (mō zā′ə sist), *n.* maker or seller of mosaics.

Mosaic law, the ancient law of the Hebrews, ascribed to Moses and contained chiefly in the Pentateuch or the Torah.

Mos cow (mos′kou, mos′kō), *n.* capital of the Soviet Union and of the Russian Soviet Federated Socialist Republic, in the W part of the Soviet Union. 7,061,000. Also, RUSSIAN **Moskva.**

Mo sel (mō′zəl), *n.* German name of **Moselle.**

Mo selle (mō zel′), *n.* 1 **Moselle River,** river flowing from NE France into the Rhine in West Germany. 320 mi. 2 a light, dry, white wine produced along the Moselle River in Germany. Also, GERMAN **Mosel.**

Mo ses (mō′ziz), *n.* 1 (in the Bible) the great leader and lawgiver of the Israelites, who led them out of Egypt. 2 **Anna Mary,** 1860-1961, American painter, known as "Grandma" Moses.

mo sey (mō′zē), *v.i.* INFORMAL. 1 shuffle along. 2 saunter; amble. [origin uncertain]

Mos kva (mosk vä′), *n.* Russian name of **Moscow.**

Mos lem (moz′ləm), *n.*, *pl.* **-lems** or **-lem,** *adj.* —*n.* follower of Mohammed; believer in the religion founded by him; a Mohammedan; Mussulman. —*adj.* of Mohammed, his followers, or the religion founded by him; Mohammedan. Also, **Muslim, Muslem.** [< Arabic *muslim* one who submits. Related to ISLAM, SALAAM.]

mosque (mosk), *n.* a Moslem place of worship. [< Middle French *mosquée* < Italian *moschea* < Arabic *masjid*]

mo squi to (mə skē′tō), *n.*, *pl.* **-toes** or **-tos.** any of a family of small, slender insects with two wings. The females have mouthparts that can pierce the skin of humans and animals and draw blood, causing itching. One kind of mosquito transmits malaria; another transmits yellow fever. [< Spanish, diminutive of *mosca* fly < Latin *musca*]

mosquito boat, PT boat.

mosquito net, a thin, light net that can be hung on a frame over a bed, chair, etc., to keep off mosquitoes.

moss (môs, mos), *n.* 1 any of a class of very small, soft, green or brown bryophytic plants that grow close together in clumps or like a carpet on the ground, on rocks, on trees, etc. Mosses have small stems and numerous, generally narrow leaves. 2 any of various other plants which grow close together like mosses, such as some lichens, club mosses, and liverworts. [Old English *mos* bog] —**moss′like′,** *adj.*

moss back (môs′bak′, mos′bak′), *n.* SLANG. person whose ideas are out of date; fogy.

moss y (mô′sē, mos′ē), *adj.*, **moss i er, moss i est.** 1 covered with moss or a mosslike substance: *a mossy bank, the mossy antlers of a deer.* 2 like moss: *mossy green.* —**moss′i ness,** *n.*

most (mōst), *adj.*, *superlative of* **much** *and* **many;** *n.*, *adv.*, *superlative of* **much.** —*adj.* 1 greatest in amount, degree, or number: *The winner gets the most money.* 2 almost all: *Most children like candy.* 3 **for the most part,** mainly; usually. —*n.* 1 the greatest amount, degree, or number: *He does most of his work at night. Most of my books are old.* 2 the greatest number of persons; the majority: *He has a better appetite than most.* 3 **at most** or **at the most,** at the utmost extent; at furthest; at the outside. 4 **make the most of,** use to the best advantage: *making the most of an opportunity.* —*adv.* 1 in or to the greatest extent or degree: *This tooth hurts most.* 2 INFORMAL. almost; nearly: *A drop in prices will appeal to most everybody.* [Old English *māst*]

-most, *suffix forming superlatives of adjectives and adverbs.* greatest in amount, degree, or number, as in *foremost, inmost, topmost, uttermost.* [Old English *-mest;* influenced by *most*]

most ly (mōst′lē), *adv.* almost all; for the most part; mainly; chiefly.

Mo sul (mō sül′), *n.* city in N Iraq. 264,000.

mot (mō), *n.* a clever or witty remark. [< French, word < Latin *muttum* grunt, word. Doublet of MOTTO.]

hat, āge, fär; let, ēqual, tėrm;
it, īce; hot, ōpen, ôrder;
oil, out; cup, pu̇t, rüle;
ch, child; ng, long; sh, she;
th, thin; ᴛʜ, then; zh, measure;

ə represents *a* in about, *e* in taken, *i* in pencil, *o* in lemon, *u* in circus.

< = from, derived from, taken from.

mosque

mote (mōt), *n.* 1 speck of dust. 2 any very small thing. [Old English *mot*]

mo tel (mō tel′), *n.* a roadside hotel or group of furnished cottages or cabins providing overnight lodging for motorists; motor court. Most motels have units that can be entered directly from an outdoor court where cars are parked. [blend of *motor* and *hotel*]

mo tet (mō tet′), *n.* (in music) a vocal composition in polyphonic style, on a Biblical or similar prose text, for use in a church service. [< Old French, diminutive of *mot* word]

moth (môth, moth), *n.*, *pl.* **moths** (môᴛʜz, môths; moᴛʜz, moths). any of various broad-winged insects of the same order as and resembling the butterfly, but lacking knobs at the ends of the antennae, having less brightly colored wings, and flying mostly at night. The larvae of many moths are very destructive to plants, woolen goods, etc. Some larvae, such as the silkworm, are useful to man. [Old English *moththe*]

moth ball (môth′bôl′, moth′bôl′), *n.* 1 a small ball of camphor or naphthalene, used to keep moths away from clothing, blankets, silk, fur, etc. 2 **in mothballs** or **into mothballs,** in or into storage to protect against deterioration or damage.

moth-eat en (môth′ēt′n, moth′ēt′n), *adj.* 1 eaten by moths; having holes made by moths. 2 looking as if eaten into by moths; worn-out; out-of-date.

moth er[1] (muᴛʜ′ər), *n.* 1 a female parent. 2 cause or source of anything. 3 mother superior. 4 woman exercising control and responsibility like that of a mother. 5 a familiar name for an old woman. —*v.t.* 1 be mother of; act as mother to: *She mothers her baby sister.* 2 give birth to; bring forth as a mother. —*adj.* 1 that is a mother: *the mother church.* 2 like a mother. 3 of a mother. 4 native: *one's mother country.* [Old English *mōdor*] —**moth′er less,** *adj.*

moth er[2] (muᴛʜ′ər), *n.* a stringy, sticky, bacterial ferment that forms on the surface of alcoholic liquids that are turning to vinegar, or is added to them to cause them to turn to vinegar; mother of vinegar. [probably special use of *mother*[1]]

Mother Car ey's chicken (ker′ēz,

kar/ēz), 1 storm petrel. 2 any of various other petrels.

Mother Goose, the imaginary author of certain old fairy tales and nursery rhymes.

moth er hood (muᴛʜ/ər hu̇d), *n.* 1 condition of being a mother. 2 qualities of a mother. 3 mothers collectively.

Mother Hub bard (hub/ərd), 1 a full, loose garment worn by women. 2 the old woman who is the subject of a well-known Mother Goose nursery rhyme.

moth er-in-law (muᴛʜ/ər in lô/), *n., pl.* **moth ers-in-law.** mother of one's husband or wife.

moth er land (muᴛʜ/ər land/), *n.* 1 one's native country. 2 land of one's ancestors.

mother lode, a rich or main vein of ore in a mine.

moth er ly (muᴛʜ/ər lē), *adj.* 1 like a mother; like a mother's; kindly. 2 of a mother. **—moth/er li ness,** *n.*

moth er-of-pearl (muᴛʜ/ər əv pėrl/), *n.* the hard, smooth, glossy lining of certain mollusk shells, as of the pearl oyster, mussel, and abalone; nacre. It changes colors as the light changes and is used to make ornaments, buttons, etc.

mother of vinegar, mother[2].

Mother's Day, the second Sunday in May, set apart in the United States and Canada in honor of mothers.

mother superior, woman who is the head of a convent of nuns; mother.

mother tongue, 1 one's native language. 2 an original language to which other languages owe their origin.

mother wit, natural intelligence; common sense.

moth y (mô/thē, moth/ē), *adj.,* **moth i er, moth i est.** infested by moths; moth-eaten.

mo tif (mō tēf/), *n.* 1 a subject for development or treatment in art, literature, etc.; a principal idea or feature; motive; theme: *This opera contains a love motif.* 2 a distinctive figure in a design, painting, etc. 3 (in music) a motive. [< French]

mo tile (mō/tl), *adj.* (in biology) moving or able to move by itself. [< Latin *motum* moved]

mo til i ty (mō til/ə tē), *n.* motile quality.

mo tion (mō/shən), *n.* 1 change of position or place; movement; moving: *the motion of a ship, the motion of one's hand in writing.* See synonym study below. 2 a formal suggestion made in a meeting, legislative body, court of law, etc., to be voted or acted upon: *The motion to adjourn was carried.* —*v.i.* make a movement, as of the hand or head, to show one's meaning: *He motioned to show us the way.* —*v.t.* show (a person) what to do by such a motion: *He motioned me out.* [< Latin *motionem* < *movere* to move]

Syn. *n.* 1 **Motion, movement** mean change of place or position. **Motion** emphasizes the state of not being at rest or the process of moving, especially as thought of apart from any particular thing or definite action: *We study the laws of motion.* **Movement** emphasizes a definite moving in a particular direction and regular way: *the movement of the earth.*

mo tion less (mō/shən lis), *adj.* not moving. **—mo/tion less ly,** *adv.* **—mo/tion less ness,** *n.*

motion picture, 1 series of pictures projected on a screen in rapid succession giving the viewer the impression that the persons and objects pictured are moving; moving picture; movie. 2 story or drama told by this means. **—mo/tion-pic/ture,** *adj.*

motion sickness, condition of nausea and dizziness, caused by the motion of a train, plane, bus, ship, etc.

motorcycle

mo ti vate (mō/tə vāt), *v.t.,* **-vat ed, -vat ing.** provide with a motive or incentive; induce to act.

mo ti va tion (mō/tə vā/shən), *n.* act or process of furnishing with an incentive or inducement to action.

mo ti va tion al (mō/tə vā/shə nəl), *adj.* of or having to do with motivation.

mo tive (mō/tiv), *n.* 1 thought or feeling that makes one act; moving consideration or reason; incentive: *My motive in going away was a wish to travel.* See **reason** for synonym study. 2 motif in art, literature, etc. 3 (in music) the briefest intelligible melodic or rhythmic fragment of a theme or subject; motif. —*adj.* that makes something move. [< Late Latin *motivus* moving, impelling < Latin *movere* to move] **—mo/tive less,** *adj.*

motive power, power used to impart motion; source of mechanical energy.

mot juste (mō zhʏst/), FRENCH. word or phrase that exactly fits the case.

mot ley (mot/lē), *adj., n., pl.* **-leys.** —*adj.* 1 made up of parts or kinds that are different or varied: *a motley crowd, a motley collection of butterflies, shells, and stamps.* 2 of different colors like a clown's suit. —*n.* 1 mixture of things that are different. 2 suit of more than one color worn by clowns: *Medieval jesters and fools wore motley.* 3 jester; fool. 4 a woolen fabric of mixed colors used for clothing in the 1300's to 1600's, especially in England. [Middle English *motteley*]

Mot ley (mot/lē), *n.* **John Lothrop,** 1814-1877, American historian and diplomat.

Mo ton (mō/tən), *n.* **Robert Russa,** 1867-1940, American educator.

mo tor (mō/tər), *n.* 1 engine that makes a machine go: *an electric motor.* 2 apparatus that converts electrical into mechanical energy. 3 an internal-combustion engine. 4 automobile. —*adj.* 1 run by a motor: *a motor vehicle.* 2 of, having to do with, or by means of automobiles: *a motor tour.* 3 causing or having to do with motion or action. 4 (of nerves or nerve fibers) conveying or imparting an impulse from the central nervous system to a muscle or organ which results in motion or activity. 5 (of muscles, impulses, centers, etc.) concerned with or involving motion or activity. 6 of, having to do with, or involving muscular or glandular activity: *a motor response.* —*v.i.* travel by automobile; ride in an automobile. [< Latin, mover < *movere* to move]

mo tor bike (mō/tər bīk/), *n.* INFORMAL. 1 bicycle with an auxiliary motor. 2 motorcycle.

mo tor boat (mō/tər bōt/), *n.* boat propelled by a motor.

mo tor bus (mō/tər bus/), *n.* bus powered by a motor.

mo tor cade (mō/tər kād), *n.* procession or long line of automobiles. [< *motor* + *(caval)cade*]

mo tor car (mō/tər kär/), *n.* automobile.

mo tor coach (mō/tər kōch/), *n.* motorbus.

motor court, motel.

mo tor cy cle (mō/tər sī/kəl), *n., v.,* **-cled, -cling.** —*n.* a two-wheeled vehicle powered by an internal-combustion engine, resembling a bicycle but heavier and larger, and usually having one or two seats. Some motorcycles have a sidecar attached with a third wheel to support it. —*v.i.* travel by motorcycle.

mo tor cy clist (mō/tər sī/klist), *n.* person who rides a motorcycle.

mo tor ist (mō/tər ist), *n.* person who drives or travels in an automobile.

mo tor ize (mō/tə rīz/), *v.t.,* **-ized, -iz ing.** 1 furnish with a motor. 2 supply with motor-driven vehicles in place of horses and horse-drawn vehicles. **—mo/tor i za/tion,** *n.*

mo tor man (mō/tər mən), *n., pl.* **-men.** 1 man who runs an electric train or streetcar. 2 man who runs a motor.

motor scooter

motor scooter, a motor-driven vehicle similar to a child's scooter but having a driver's seat.

motor truck, truck with an engine and chassis made for carrying heavy loads.

Mott (mot), *n.* **Lucretia Coffin,** 1793-1880, American reformer, leader in the woman's rights and antislavery movements.

mot tle (mot/l), *v.,* **-tled, -tling,** *n.* —*v.t.* mark with spots or streaks of different colors or shades. —*n.* 1 a mottled coloring or pattern. 2 spot, blotch, streak, etc., on a mottled surface. [related to MOTLEY]

mot to (mot/ō), *n., pl.* **-toes** or **-tos.** 1 a brief sentence adopted as a rule of conduct: *"Think before you speak" is a good motto.* 2 word, sentence, or phrase written or engraved on some object. [< Italian < Latin *muttum* grunt, word. Doublet of MOT.]

moue (mü), *n.* a grimace; pout. [< French]

mouf lon or **mouf flon** (müf/lon), *n.* 1 a wild sheep of the mountainous regions of Sardinia, Corsica, etc., the male of which has large, curving horns. 2 its wool, used for fur. 3 any of various similar wild sheep. [< French *mouflon*]

mou jik (mü zhik/, mü/zhik), *n.* muzhik.

Mouk den (mu̇k/den/, mük/den/), *n.* Mukden.

mould (mōld), *n., v.t., v.i.* mold.

mould er (mōl/dər), *v.i.* molder.

mould ing (mōl/ding), *n.* molding.

mould y (mōl/dē), *adj.,* **mould i er, mould i est.** moldy. **—mould/i ness,** *n.*

moult (mōlt), *v.i., v.t., n.* molt.

mound (mound), *n.* 1 bank or heap, as of

earth or stones: *a mound of hay.* 2 a small hill. 3 the slightly elevated ground from which a baseball pitcher pitches. —*v.t.* 1 heap up: *mound earth.* 2 enclose with a mound or embankment. [origin uncertain]

Mound Builders, prehistoric Indians that lived in central and eastern North America, especially in the valleys of the Mississippi and Ohio Rivers and the Great Lakes region. They built mounds of earth to bury their dead, to use as temples, or for defense.

mount[1] (mount), *v.t.* 1 go up on or climb up; ascend: *mount a hill, mount a ladder, mount stairs.* See **climb** for synonym study. 2 get up on: *mount a horse, mount a platform.* 3 put on a horse, etc.; furnish with a horse or other animal for riding: *Some policemen in this city are mounted.* 4 put or fix in proper position or order for use: *mount specimens on a slide.* 5 fix in a setting, backing, support, etc.: *mount gems in gold, mount a picture on cardboard.* 6 carry or place (guns) in position for use, as a fortress or ship. 7 provide (a play) with scenery, costumes, properties, etc. 8 assign (a guard) as a sentry or watch. —*v.i.* 1 move or proceed upward. 2 rise in amount; increase; rise: *The cost of living mounts steadily.* 3 get on a horse, etc.; get up on something: *mount and ride away.* —*n.* 1 horse, bicycle, etc., provided for riding. 2 something in or on which anything is mounted; setting; backing; support: *a mount for microscopic examination.* [< Old French *monter* < Latin *montare* < *montem* mountain] **—mount′a ble,** *adj.* **—mount′er,** *n.*

mount[2] (mount), *n.* a high hill; mountain. *Mount* is often used before the names of mountains. *Mount Rainier, Mount Everest, Mount Olympus.* [Old English *munt* < Latin *montem*]

moun tain (moun′tən), *n.* 1 a very high hill; a natural elevation of the earth's surface rising high above the surrounding level. 2 a very large heap or pile of anything: *a mountain of rubbish.* 3 a huge amount: *a mountain of difficulties.* 4 **the Mountain,** an extreme revolutionary party led by Danton and Robespierre in the legislatures of the French Revolution. 5 **make a mountain out of a molehill,** give great importance to something which is really insignificant. [< Old French *montaigne,* ultimately < Latin *montem*]

mountain ash, any of a genus of trees and shrubs of the rose family with pinnate leaves, white flowers, and bright-red berries.

moun tain eer (moun′tə nir′), *n.* 1 person who lives in the mountains. 2 person skilled in mountain climbing. —*v.i.* climb mountains.

mountain goat
3 ft. high
at the shoulder

mountain goat, a goatlike antelope of the Rocky Mountains, with slender, backward-curving black horns and long, white hair.

mountain laurel, an evergreen shrub or tree of the heath family, with glossy leaves and pale-pink or white flowers, found in eastern North America.

mountain lion, puma.

moun tain ous (moun′tə nəs), *adj.* 1 covered with mountain ranges: *mountainous country.* 2 like a mountain; large and high; huge: *a mountainous wave.* **—moun′tain ous ly,** *adv.*

mountain range, row of connected mountains; large group of mountains.

mountain sheep, 1 bighorn. 2 any of several other wild sheep inhabiting mountains.

moun tain side (moun′tən sīd′), *n.* the slope of a mountain below the summit.

Mountain Standard Time, the standard time in the Rocky Mountain regions of the United States and Canada. It is seven hours behind Greenwich Time.

moun tain top (moun′tən top′), *n.* top or summit of a mountain.

moun te bank (moun′tə bangk), *n.* 1 person who sells quack medicines in public, appealing to his audience by tricks, stories, jokes, etc. 2 anybody who tries to deceive people by tricks, stories, etc.; charlatan. [< Italian *montambanco* < *montare in banco* mount on a bench]

mount ed (moun′tid), *adj.* 1 on a horse, mule, bicycle, etc. 2 serving on horseback: *mounted police.* 3 in a position for use: *a mounted gun.* 4 on a support; in a setting: *a mounted diamond.*

Mount ie (moun′tē), *n.* INFORMAL. member of the Royal Canadian Mounted Police, a force maintained by the government of Canada.

mount ing (moun′ting), *n.* support, setting, etc. The mounting of a photograph is the paper or cardboard on which it is pasted.

Mount Ver non (vėr′nən), home of George Washington in Virginia, on the Potomac River near Washington, D.C.

mourn (môrn, mōrn), *v.i.* feel or express sorrow or grief; grieve. —*v.t.* feel or show grief over: *mourn a person's death.* [Old English *murnan*]

mourn er (môr′nər, mōr′nər), *n.* person who mourns, especially at a funeral.

mourn ful (môrn′fəl, mōrn′fəl), *adj.* 1 full of grief; sad; sorrowful: *a mournful voice.* 2 causing sorrow or mourning: *a mournful death.* 3 gloomy; dreary; somber: *a mournful scene.* **—mourn′ful ly,** *adv.* **—mourn′ful ness,** *n.*

mourn ing (môr′ning, mōr′ning), *n.* 1 the wearing of black or some other color to show sorrow for a person's death. 2 a draping of buildings, flying flags at half-mast, etc., as an outward sign of sorrow for death. 3 clothes or decorations to show sorrow for death. 4 act of a person who mourns; sorrowing; lamentation. 5 period of time during which one mourns. —*adj.* of mourning; used in mourning. **—mourn′ing ly,** *adv.*

mourning dove, a wild dove of North America that has a low, mournful call.

mouse (*n.* mous; *v.* mouz, mous), *n., pl.* **mice,** *v.,* **moused, mous ing.** —*n.* 1 any of numerous small, gnawing rodents found throughout the world. Mice have soft fur, usually brown, gray, or white, a pointed snout, round black eyes, rounded ears, and a thin tail. 2 a shy, timid person. 3 SLANG. a black eye. —*v.i.* 1 hunt for mice; catch mice for food. 2 search as a cat does; move about as if searching; prowl. —*v.t.* hunt for by patient and careful search. [Old English *mūs*] **—mouse′like′,** *adj.*

mous er (mou′zər, mou′sər), *n.* animal that catches mice, such as a cat.

hat, āge, fär; let, ēqual, tėrm;
it, īce; hot, ōpen, ôrder;
oil, out; cup, pu̇t, rüle;
ch, child; ng, long; sh, she;
th, thin; ŦH, then; zh, measure;

ə represents *a* in about, *e* in taken,
i in pencil, *o* in lemon, *u* in circus.

< = from, derived from, taken from.

mouse trap (mous′trap′), *n.* trap for catching mice.

mous ey (mou′sē), *adj.,* **mous i er, mous i est.** mousy.

mous sa ka (mü′sä kä′), *n.* a Greek baked dish consisting of layers of ground meat with eggplant or zucchini between them, olive oil, and a topping of cheese and dough. [< Greek]

mousse (müs), *n.* 1 dessert made with whipped cream or gelatin, frozen without stirring: *chocolate mousse.* 2 a meat or fish purée lightened with gelatin or whipped cream or both. [< French]

Mous sorg sky (mu̇ sôrg′skē), *n.* **Modest,** 1839-1881, Russian composer. Also, **Mussorgsky.**

mous tache (mus′tash, mə stash′), *n.* mustache.

mous y (mou′sē), *adj.,* **mous i er, mous i est.** 1 resembling or suggesting a mouse in color, odor, behavior, etc.: *mousy hair.* 2 quiet as a mouse. 3 infested with mice. Also, **mousey.**

mouth (*n.* mouth; *v.* mouŦH), *n., pl.* **mouths** (mouŦHz), *v.* —*n.* 1 the opening through which a person or animal takes in food; cavity containing the tongue and teeth. 2 an opening suggesting a mouth: *the mouth of a cave, the mouth of a bottle.* 3 a part of a river or the like where its waters are emptied into some other body of water: *the mouth of the Ohio River.* 4 grimace. 5 **down in the mouth.** INFORMAL. in low spirits; discouraged. —*v.t.* 1 utter (words) in an affected or pompous way: *I dislike actors who mouth their speeches.* 2 seize or rub with the mouth. —*v.i.* 1 speak oratorically. 2 make grimaces. [Old English *mūth*] **—mouth′like′,** *adj.*

mouth er (mou′ŦHər), *n.* person who mouths; long-winded talker.

mouth ful (mouth′fu̇l), *n., pl.* **-fuls.** 1 the amount the mouth can easily hold. 2 what is taken into the mouth at one time. 3 a small amount. 4 INFORMAL. word or phrase that is very long or difficult to pronounce. 5 SLANG. a statement notable for its truth or appropriateness: *You said a mouthful.*

mouth less (mouth′lis), *adj.* having no mouth or opening.

mouth organ, harmonica.

mouth parts (mouth′pärts′), *n.pl.* the parts of the mouth of insects, crustaceans, etc.

mouth piece (mouth′pēs′), *n.* 1 the part of a musical instrument, telephone, pipe, etc., that is placed in, against, or near a person's mouth. 2 piece placed at the mouth of something or forming its mouth, as of a receptacle or tube. 3 person or medium of communication that expresses the sentiments, opinions, etc., of another or others; spokesman. 4 SLANG. lawyer, especially a criminal lawyer.

mouth-to-mouth (mouth′tə mouth′), *adj.* of or designating a method of artificial respiration in which air is breathed directly into the victim's mouth and nose to inflate the lungs, with intervals to allow the lungs to empty.

mouth wash (mouth′wosh′, mouth′-wôsh′), *n.* a mildly antiseptic liquid to cleanse the mouth and teeth.

mouth y (mou′ᴛʜē, mou′thē), *adj.*, **mouth i er, mouth i est.** loud-mouthed; ranting; bombastic.

mou ton (mü′ton), *n.* fur made from a sheep's pelt by shearing it to medium length and processing and dyeing it, commonly to resemble that of beaver. [< French, sheep. See MUTTON.]

mov a ble (mü′və bəl), *adj.* 1 that can be moved; not fixed in one place or position: *Our fingers are movable.* 2 that can be carried from place to place as personal belongings can. 3 changing from one date to another in different years: *Thanksgiving is a movable holiday.* —*n.* 1 a piece of furniture that is not a fixture but can be moved to another house or building. 2 **movables,** *pl.* (in law) personal property. Also, **moveable.** —**mov′a ble ness,** *n.* —**mov′a bly,** *adv.*

move (müv), *v.*, **moved, mov ing,** *n.* —*v.t.* 1 change the place or position of; shift: *Do not move your hand.* 2 put or keep in motion; shake, stir, or disturb: *The wind moves the leaves.* 3 cause (someone) to do something; impel; rouse: *What moved you to do this?* See synonym study below. 4 affect with emotion; excite to tender feelings: *The sad story moved her to tears.* 5 (in games) change the position of (a piece): *move a pawn in chess.* 6 bring forward formally; propose: *Mr. Chairman, I move that we adjourn.* 7 find buyers for; sell: *That store cannot move these dresses.* 8 cause (the intestines) to empty. —*v.i.* 1 change place or position: *The child moved in his sleep. The earth moves around the sun.* 2 change one's place of living: *We have moved to the country.* 3 make progress; proceed; go: *How fast is the train moving?* 4 act: *God moves in a mysterious way.* 5 make a formal request, application, or proposal: *move for a new trial.* 6 in games: **a** (of a player) change the position of a piece. **b** (of a piece) be changed in position. 7 change hands or be sold: *These pink dresses are moving slowly.* 8 be active; exist: *move in artistic circles.* 9 turn; swing; operate: *Most doors move on a hinge.* 10 carry oneself: *move with dignity and grace.* 11 INFORMAL. start off; depart: *It's time to be moving. When the ambulance had left, the crowd moved on.* 12 **move in,** move oneself, one's family, one's belongings, etc., into a new place to live. 13 (of the intestines) be emptied.
—*n.* 1 act of moving; movement: *an impatient move of her head.* 2 action taken to bring about some result; step: *a move to disconcert one's opponents.* 3 a player's turn to move in a game. 4 the moving of a piece in chess and other games: *That was a good move.* 5 a change of a place to live. 6 **on the move,** moving about; traveling.
[< Anglo-French *mover* < Latin *movere*]
Syn. *v.t.* 3 **Move, actuate, prompt** mean to cause a person to act in a certain way. **Move** does not suggest whether the cause is an outside force or an inner urge: *Something moved him to change his mind.* **Actuate,** always implies a powerful inner force: *He was actuated by desire for praise.* **Prompt** is used chiefly when the cause of action is thought of as comparatively minor: *My conversation with her prompted me to write you.*

move a ble (mü′və bəl), *adj., n.* movable.

move ment (müv′mənt), *n.* 1 act or fact of moving: *We run by movements of the legs.* See **motion** for synonym study. 2 a change in the placing of troops, ships, etc., especially as part of a tactical maneuver. 3 the moving parts of a machine or mechanism; special group of parts that move on each other, as in a watch or clock. 4 in music: **a** the kind of rhythm and tempo a piece has: *the movement of a waltz.* **b** a principal division of a symphony, sonata, concerto, or other long work, distinguished from the other divisions by tempo and by melodic and rhythmical structure. 5 (in poetry) rhythmical or accentual structure or character. 6 abundance of incidents; action. 7 the efforts and results of a group of people working together to bring about some one thing: *the movement for a safe Fourth of July.* 8 a notable change in the price of something. 9 activity in the market for some commodity, stock, etc.: *The movement in coffee is insignificant.* 10 an emptying of the bowels. 11 the waste matter emptied from the intestines.

mov er (mü′vər), *n.* 1 person or thing that moves. 2 person or company whose business is moving furniture, etc., from one house or place to another.

mov ie (mü′vē), *n.* 1 motion picture. 2 theater showing motion pictures: *a neighborhood movie.* 3 **the movies,** a showing of motion pictures: *go to the movies.* 4 **movies,** *pl.* the motion-picture industry. —*adj.* of or having to do with motion pictures: *a movie actress.*

mov ing (mü′ving), *adj.* 1 that moves: *a moving car.* 2 causing or producing motion; having motion. 3 causing action; actuating. 4 touching; pathetic: *a moving story.* —**mov′ing ly,** *adv.*

moving picture, motion picture.

moving staircase or **moving stairway,** escalator.

mow[1] (mō), *v.*, **mowed, mowed** or **mown, mow ing.** —*v.t.* 1 cut down with a machine or a scythe: *mow grass.* 2 cut down the grass or grain from: *mow a field.* 3 destroy at a sweep or in large numbers, as if by mowing: *The enemy fire mowed down a platoon of soldiers.* —*v.i.* cut down grass, etc. [Old English *māwan*] —**mow′er,** *n.*

mow[2] (mou), *n.* 1 the place in a barn where hay, grain, or the like is piled or stored. 2 pile or stack of hay, grain, etc., in a barn. [Old English *mūga, mūwa*]

mowing machine, 1 machine with cutting blades attached to a metal arm, used to cut down tall grass, standing hay, grain, etc. 2 any machine used to mow.

mown (mōn), *v.* a pp. of **mow**[1].

mox ie (mok′sē), *n.* SLANG. 1 courage; bravery. 2 know-how; skill; experience.

Mo zam bique (mō′zam bēk′), *n.* Portuguese colony in SE Africa; Portuguese East Africa. 7,376,000 pop.; 297,700 sq. mi. *Capital:* Lourenço Marques.

Mo zart (mōt′särt), *n.* **Wolfgang Amadeus,** 1756-1791, Austrian composer.

moz za rel la (moz′ə rel′ə, mot′sə rel′ə), *n.* a soft, white, mild Italian cheese. [< Italian]

m.p., melting point.

MP or **M.P.,** 1 Member of Parliament. 2 Metropolitan Police. 3 Military Police. 4 Mounted Police.

mph or **m.p.h.,** miles per hour.

Mr. or **Mr** (mis′tər), *pl.* **Messrs.** Mister, a title put in front of a man's name or the name of his position: *Mr.Jackson, Mr. President.*
➛ **Mr.** is written out only when it represents informal usage and when it is used without a name: *"Watch where you're going, mister."*

Mrs. or **Mrs** (mis′iz), *pl.* **Mmes.** a title put in front of a married woman's name: *Mrs. Jackson.*
➛ **Mrs.** is written out only in representing informal usage and is then spelled *missus* (or *missis*): *Mrs. Dorothy Adams. "Where's the missus?"*

ms., Ms., or **MS.,** *pl.* **mss., Mss.,** or **MSS.** manuscript.

Ms. (miz), *pl.* **Mses.** a title put in front of a woman's name.

M.S. or **M.Sc.,** Master of Science.

Msgr., Monsignor.

M.S.T., Mountain Standard Time.

mt., *pl.* **mts.** mountain.

Mt., Mount: *Mt. Everest, Mt. Whitney.*

M.T., metric ton.

mtg. or **mtge.,** mortgage.

mtn., mountain.

mu (myü), *n.* the 12th letter of the Greek alphabet (M, μ).

much (much), *adj.,* **more, most,** *adv.,* **more, most,** *n.* —*adj.* great in amount, degree, or number: *much money, much time, much rain.* —*n.* 1 a great amount, degree, or number: *Much of this is not true. I did not hear much of the talk.* 2 a great, important, or notable thing or matter: *The rain did not amount to much. The house is not much to look at.* 3 **make much of,** treat, represent, or consider as of great importance. 4 **not much of a,** not very good: *Thirty dollars a week is not much of a salary.* 5 **too much for,** more than a match for. —*adv.* 1 in or to a great extent or degree: *much higher.* 2 nearly; about: *This is much the same as the others.* [Middle English *muche,* short for *muchel,* Old English *micel*] —**much′ness,** *n.*

mu ci lage (myü′sə lij), *n.* 1 a sticky substance, especially a solution of gum, glue, etc., in water, used as an adhesive. 2 any of various sticky, gelatinous secretions present in various plants such as seaweeds. [< Late Latin *mucilago* musty juice < Latin *mucus* mucus]

mu ci lag i nous (myü′sə laj′ə nəs), *adj.* 1 like mucilage; sticky; gummy. 2 containing or secreting mucilage.

mu cin (myü′sn), *n.* any of various proteins forming the chief constituents of mucous secretions. [< *mucus*]

muck (muk), *n.* 1 unclean matter; dirt or filth. 2 moist farmyard manure, used as a fertilizer. 3 a heavy, moist, dark soil made up chiefly of decayed plants. 4 INFORMAL. an untidy condition; mess. —*v.t.* 1 soil or make dirty. 2 put muck on. [< Scandinavian (Old Icelandic) *myki* cow dung]

muck rake (muk′rāk′), *v.i.,* **-raked, -rak ing.** hunt for and expose real or alleged corruption in government, big business, etc.

muck rak er (muk′rā′kər), *n.* person who muckrakes, especially one of a group of American journalists and novelists of the early 1900's noted for exposing social and political evils.

muck y (muk′ē), *adj.,* **muck i er, muck i est.** 1 of muck. 2 filthy; dirty.

mu co sa (myü kō′sə), *n., pl.* **-sae** (-sē).

mucous membrane. [< New Latin *(membrana) mucosa* mucous (membrane)]

mu cous (myü′kəs), *adj.* 1 of or like mucus. 2 containing or secreting mucus.

mucous membrane, tissue containing glands that secrete mucus; mucosa. It lines the nose, throat, digestive tract, and other passages and cavities of the body that open to the air.

mu cus (myü′kəs), *n.* a viscid, slimy substance, consisting chiefly of mucin, that is secreted by and moistens and protects the mucous membranes. [< Latin]

mud (mud), *n.* soft, sticky, wet earth. [Middle English *mudde*]

mud dle (mud′l), *v.,* **-dled, -dling,** *n.* —*v.t.* 1 mix up; bring (things) into a mess: *muddle a piece of work.* 2 make confused or stupid. —*v.i.* think or act in a confused, blundering way. —*n.* mess; disorder; confusion. [< *mud*] —**mud′dler,** *n.*

mud dle head ed (mud′l hed′id), *adj.* stupid; confused.

mud dy (mud′ē), *adj.,* **-di er, -di est,** *v.,* **-died, -dy ing.** —*adj.* 1 of or like mud. 2 having much mud; covered with mud. 3 clouded with mud or any other sediment; turbid; cloudy: *muddy water, muddy coffee.* 4 not clear, pure, or bright; dull: *a muddy color.* 5 not clear in mind; confused; muddled: *muddy thinking.* 6 obscure; vague: *muddy writing.* —*v.t.* 1 make muddy; cover or soil with mud. 2 make turbid or cloudy. 3 make confused or obscure. —*v.i.* become muddy. —**mud′di ly,** *adv.* —**mud′di ness,** *n.*

mud guard (mud′gärd′), *n.* guard or shield so placed as to protect riders or passengers from the mud thrown up by the moving wheels of a carriage, bicycle, or motor vehicle.

mud puppy, 1 either of two large aquatic salamanders of the same genus, that live in the eastern part of the United States. 2 any of various other salamanders, especially the hellbender.

mud sling er (mud′sling′ər), *n.* person given to mudslinging.

mud sling ing (mud′sling′ing), *n.* the use of offensive charges and misleading or slanderous accusations, especially against an opponent in a political campaign.

mud turtle, any of a genus of freshwater turtles of North America.

mu ez zin (myü ez′n), *n.* crier who calls Moslems to prayer at five stated times daily. [< Arabic *mu'adhdhin*]

muff (muf), *n.* 1 a covering of fur or other material for keeping both hands warm. One hand is put in at each end. 2 a failure to catch a ball that comes into one's hands. 3 awkward handling; bungling. —*v.t.* 1 fail to catch (a ball) when it comes into one's hands. 2 handle awkwardly; bungle. [< Dutch *mof* < French *moufle* mitten]

muf fin (muf′ən), *n.* a small, round cake made of wheat flour, corn meal, or the like, often without sugar. Muffins are usually served hot and eaten with butter. [origin uncertain]

muf fle (muf′əl), *v.,* **-fled, -fling,** *n.* —*v.t.* 1 wrap or cover up in order to keep warm and dry: *She muffled her throat in a warm scarf.* 2 wrap in something in order to soften or stop the sound: *muffle oars, muffle a drum.* 3 dull or deaden (a sound): *The wind muffled their voices.* —*n.* 1 a muffled sound. 2 thing that muffles. [< Old French *mofler* to stuff < *moufle* thick glove. Related to MUFF.]

muf fler (muf′lər), *n.* 1 wrap or scarf worn around the neck for warmth. 2 anything used to deaden sound. An automobile muffler, attached to the exhaust pipe, deadens the sound of the engine's exhaust.

muf ti (muf′tē), *n.* 1 ordinary clothes, not a military or other uniform, especially when worn by someone who usually wears a uniform. 2 a Moslem official who assists a judge by formal exposition of the religious law. [< Arabic *muftī*]

mug (mug), *n., v.,* **mugged, mug ging.** —*n.* 1 a heavy drinking cup with a handle, usually of earthenware or metal and cylindrical in shape. 2 amount a mug holds. 3 SLANG. face or mouth. 4 SLANG. hoodlum; ruffian; criminal. —*v.t.* SLANG. 1 attack (a person) from behind, usually to rob. 2 make a photograph of (a person's face) for police purposes. —*v.i.* SLANG. exaggerate one's facial expressions, as in acting. [probably related to Scandinavian (Norwegian) *mugge* mug]

mug ger[1] (mug′ər), *n.* SLANG. person who mugs.

mug ger[2] (mug′ər), *n.* a large, freshwater crocodile of India and Ceylon, having a broad snout. [< Hindi *magar* < Sanskrit *makara* sea monster]

mug gy (mug′ē), *adj.,* **-gi er, -gi est.** warm and humid; damp and close: *muggy weather.* [< Scottish *mug* drizzle < Scandinavian (Old Icelandic) *mugga*] —**mug′gi ly,** *adv.* —**mug′gi ness,** *n.*

mug wump (mug′wump′), *n.* U.S. 1 person who is independent in politics. 2 Republican who refused to support the party candidate, James G. Blaine, for President in 1884. [< Algonquian *mukquomp* chief]

Mu ham mad (mu̇ ham′əd), *n.* 1 Mohammed. 2 **Elijah,** born 1897, American leader of the Nation of Islam. His original name was Elijah Poole.

Mu ham mad an (mu̇ ham′ə dən), *adj., n.* Mohammedan.

Mu ham mad an ism (mu̇ ham′ə də niz′əm), *n.* Mohammedanism.

Muir (myu̇r), *n.* **John,** 1838-1914, American naturalist and writer, born in Scotland.

mu jik (mü zhik′, mü′zhik), *n.* muzhik.

Muk den (mu̇k′den′, mük′den′), *n.* former name of **Shenyang.** Also, **Moukden.**

mukh tar (mu̇k′tär, mu̇ᴴ′tär), *n.* the elected headman of an Arab or Turkish town or village. [< Arabic *mukhtār*]

muk luk (muk′luk), *n.* a high, waterproof boot, often made of sealskin, worn by Eskimos and others in arctic regions. [< Eskimo *muklok* large seal]

mu lat to (mə lat′ō, myu̇ lat′ō), *n., pl.* **-toes.** 1 person having one white and one Negro parent. 2 any person of mixed white and Negro descent. [< Spanish and Portuguese *mulato* < *mulo* mule < Latin *mulus;* because of its hybrid origin]

mul ber ry (mul′ber′ē, mul′bər ē), *n., pl.* **-ries.** 1 any of a genus of trees with small, edible, berrylike fruit. The leaves of some species are used for feeding silkworms. 2 its sweet, usually dark purple fruit. 3 a dark purplish red. [Old English *mōrberie* < Latin *morum* mulberry + Old English *berie* berry]

mulch (mulch), *n.* a loose material, such as straw, leaves, manure, grass, sawdust, etc., spread on the ground around trees or plants to protect the roots from cold or heat, to prevent evaporation of moisture from the soil, to check weed growth, to decay and enrich the soil through decay, or to keep the fruit clean. —*v.t.* cover with straw, leaves,

hat, āge, fär; let, ēqual, tėrm;
it, īce; hot, ōpen, ôrder;
oil, out; cup, pu̇t, rüle;
ch, child; ng, long; sh, she;
th, thin; ᴛʜ, then; zh, measure;

ə represents *a* in about, *e* in taken, *i* in pencil, *o* in lemon, *u* in circus.

< = from, derived from, taken from.

etc.; spread mulch under or around. [probably Old English *melsc* mellow, sweet]

mulct (mulkt), *v.t.* 1 deprive of something by cunning or deceit; defraud: *He was mulcted of his money by a shrewd trick.* 2 punish (a person) by a fine. —*n.* fine; penalty. [< Latin *mulctare, multare* < *multa* a fine]

mule[1] (def. 1)
4 to 5 ft. high at the shoulder

mule[1] (myül), *n.* 1 the hybrid offspring of a donkey and a horse, especially of a male donkey and a mare. It has the form and size of a horse, and the large ears, small hoofs, and tufted tail of a donkey, and is usually sterile. 2 any hybrid animal or plant, especially one that is sterile. 3 INFORMAL. a stubborn person. 4 kind of spinning machine for drawing and twisting cotton, wool, or other fibers into yarn and winding it on spindles. [partly Old English *mūl,* partly < Old French *mule;* both < Latin *mulus*]

mule[2] (myül), *n.* kind of woman's slipper that leaves the heel uncovered. [< Middle French < Dutch *muil* < Latin *mulleus* red leather (shoe)]

mule deer, deer of western North America having long ears and a white tail with a black tip.

mule skinner, INFORMAL. muleteer.

mu le teer (myü′lə tir′), *n.* driver of mules. [< French *muletier*]

mul ga (mul′gə), *n.* any of various small acacias of Australia that yield a hard, durable wood much used for carving ornaments. [< a native name in Australia]

Mul house (mʏ lüz′), *n.* city in E France. 116,000.

mul ish (myü′lish), *adj.* like a mule; stubborn; obstinate. —**mul′ish ly,** *adv.* —**mul′ish ness,** *n.*

mull[1] (mul), *v.t., v.i.* think (about) without making much progress; ponder: *mull over a problem.* [origin uncertain]

mull[2] (mul), *v.t.* make (wine, beer, cider, etc.) into a warm drink, adding sugar, spices, etc. [origin uncertain]

mul lah (mul′ə, mu̇l′ə), *n.* (in Moslem countries) a title of respect for one who is learned in or teaches the sacred law. [< Hindustani *mullā* < Arabic *mawlā*]

mul lein or **mul len** (mul′ən), *n.* any of a genus of plants, many of which are weeds, that belong to the same family as the figwort and have coarse, woolly leaves and spikes of yellow flowers. [< Anglo-French *moleine*]

mul let (mul′it), *n., pl.* **-lets** or **-let.** any of various edible marine or freshwater fishes with small mouths and weak teeth, living in warm waters and belonging to either of two families, **red mullet** or **gray mullet.** [< Old French *mulet* < Latin *mullus* red mullet < Greek *myllos*]

mul li gan (mul′ə gən), *n.* SLANG. stew of meat or, sometimes, fish and vegetables. [origin uncertain]

mul li ga taw ny (mul′ə gə tô′nē), *n., pl.* **-nies.** soup made from a chicken or meat stock flavored with curry, originally made in India. [< Tamil *milagu-taṇṇi* pepper water]

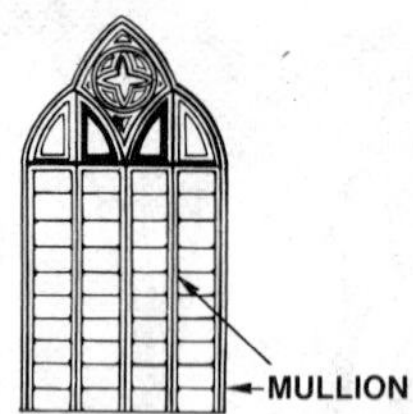

mul lion (mul′yən), *n.* a vertical bar between the panes of a window, the panels in the wall of a room, etc. —*v.t.* divide or provide with mullions. [alteration of Middle English *muniall, monial* < Old French *moienel, meienel* < *meien* in the middle < Latin *medianus*]

multi-, *combining form.* 1 many; having many or much: *Multiform = having many forms.* 2 many times: *Multimillionaire = a millionaire many times over.* [< Latin < *multus* much, many]

mul ti cel lu lar (mul′ti sel′yə lər), *adj.* having or consisting of many cells.

mul ti col ored (mul′ti kul′ərd), *adj.* having many colors.

mul ti far i ous (mul′tə fer′ē əs, mul′tə-far′ē əs), *adj.* 1 having many different parts, elements, forms, etc. 2 many and varied. [< Latin *multifarius*] **—mul′ti far′i ous ly,** *adv.* **—mul′ti far′i ous ness,** *n.*

mul ti fold (mul′tə fōld), *adj.* manifold.

mul ti form (mul′tə fôrm), *adj.* having many different shapes, forms, or kinds.

mul ti fu el (mul′ti fyü′əl), *adj.* capable of running without adjustments on various types of fuels: *a multifuel engine.*

Mul ti graph (mul′tə graf), *n.* trademark for a machine for printing circulars, letters, etc., with type similar to that of a typewriter. —*v.t.* **multigraph,** make copies (of) by a Multigraph.

mul ti lat er al (mul′ti lat′ər əl), *adj.* 1 having many sides; many-sided. 2 involving three or more nations: *a multilateral treaty.* **—mul′ti lat′er al ly,** *adv.*

mul ti mil lion aire (mul′ti mil′yə ner′, mul′ti mil′yə nar′), *n.* person who owns property worth several millions (of dollars, pounds, francs, etc.); millionaire many times over.

mul ti nu cle ate (mul′ti nü′klē it, mul′ti-nyü′klē it), *adj.* having two or more nuclei.

mul tip ar ous (mul tip′ər əs), *adj.* 1 producing two or more at a birth. 2 of or having to do with a woman who has borne more than one child. [< New Latin *multiparus* < Latin *multus* much, many + *parere* bring forth]

mul ti par tite (mul′ti pär′tīt), *adj.* 1 divided into many parts. 2 multilateral.

mul ti ple (mul′tə pəl), *adj.* of, having, or involving many parts, elements, relations, etc.; manifold: *a man of multiple interests.* —*n.* a number into which another number can be divided an integral number of times without a remainder: *12 is a multiple of 3.* [< French < Late Latin *multiplus* manifold]

mul ti ple-choice (mul′tə pəl chois′), *adj.* containing two or more suggested answers from which the correct or best one must be chosen: *a multiple-choice test.*

Multiple Independently Targeted Reentry Vehicle, a guided missile with multiple nuclear warheads to be aimed at several targets at a time; MIRV.

multiple sclerosis, disorder of the nervous system, attacking the brain and the spinal cord, and characterized by the degeneration and scarring of patches of nerve tissue, followed by paralysis, muscle spasms, disorders of speech, tremors of the hand, etc.

mul ti plex (mul′tə pleks), *adj.* 1 manifold; multiple. 2 (in telegraphy and telephony) of or designating a system for sending two or more messages in each direction over the same wire or circuit at the same time. 3 (in radio and television) of or designating the transmission of two or more signals on one carrier wave at the same time. [< Latin]

mul ti pli cand (mul′tə plə kand′), *n.* number to be multiplied by another: *In 497 multiplied by 5, the multiplicand is 497.* [< Latin *multiplicandum* < *multiplicare.* See MULTIPLY.]

mul ti pli ca tion (mul′tə plə kā′shən), *n.* 1 a multiplying. 2 a being multiplied. 3 operation of multiplying one number by another.

mul ti pli ca tive (mul′tə plə kā′tiv), *adj.* tending or able to multiply.

mul ti plic i ty (mul′tə plis′ə tē), *n., pl.* **-ties.** 1 manifold variety; diversity. 2 a great many; great number: *a multiplicity of gifts.*

mul ti pli er (mul′tə plī′ər), *n.* 1 number by which another number is to be multiplied: *In 83 multiplied by 5, the multiplier is 5.* 2 person or thing that multiplies. 3 (in physics) an instrument or device used for intensifying by repetition intensity of a force, current, etc.

mul ti ply (mul′tə plī), *v.,* **-plied, -ply ing.** —*v.t.* 1 add (a number) a given number of times: *To multiply 16 by 3 means to add 16 three times, making 48.* 2 increase the number, amount, etc., of: *Fear multiplies the difficulties of life.* —*v.i.* 1 grow in number, amount, etc.; increase: *The difficulties of the pioneers multiplied when winter came.* 2 increase in number by natural generation or procreation. 3 perform the process of multiplication. [< Old French *multiplier* < Latin *multiplicare* < *multiplex* manifold < *multus* many + *-plex* -fold]

mul ti ra cial (mul′ti rā′shəl), *adj.* consisting of or having to do with a number of races.

mul ti stage (mul′ti stāj), *adj.* 1 having a number of stages in going through a complete process: *a multistage automatic washer.* 2 (of a rocket or missile) having two or more propulsive sections, each operating after the preceding stage has burned out and separated.

mul ti tude (mul′tə tüd, mul′tə tyüd), *n.* 1 a great many; crowd; host: *a multitude of difficulties, a multitude of enemies.* 2 **the multitude,** the common people. [< Latin *multitudo* < *multus* much]

mul ti tu di nous (mul′tə tüd′n əs, mul′tə-tyüd′n əs), *adj.* 1 forming a multitude; very numerous; existing or occurring in great numbers. 2 including many parts, elements, items, or features. **—mul′ti tu′di nous ly,** *adv.* **—mul′ti tu′di nous ness,** *n.*

mul ti va lence (mul′ti vā′ləns, mul tiv′ə-ləns), *n.* multivalent quality.

mul ti va lent (mul′ti vā′lənt, mul tiv′ə-lənt), *adj.* 1 having a valence of three or more. 2 having more than one valence.

mul ti vol ume (mul′ti vol′yəm), *adj.* 1 filling many volumes. 2 containing many volumes.

mum[1] (mum), *adj.* saying nothing; silent: *keep mum about this.* —*interj.* be silent! say nothing! —*n.* **mum's the word,** be silent; say nothing. [Middle English]

mum[2] (mum), *n.* INFORMAL. chrysanthemum.

mum ble (mum′bəl), *v.,* **-bled, -bling,** *n.* —*v.i.* 1 speak indistinctly, as a person does when his lips are partly closed; speak in low tones; mutter. See **murmur** for synonym study. 2 chew as a person does who has no teeth. —*v.t.* 1 say indistinctly, as a person does when his lips are partly closed: *mumble one's words.* 2 chew as a person does who has no teeth: *The old dog mumbled the crust.* —*n.* a mumbling. [Middle English *momelen*] **—mum′bler,** *n.* **—mum′bling ly,** *adv.*

mum ble ty-peg (mum′bəl tē peg′), *n.* game in which the players in turn flip a knife from various positions, trying to make it stick in the ground. [earlier *mumble-the-peg*]

mum bo jum bo (mum′bō jum′bō), 1 foolish or meaningless incantation; ritualistic or ceremonial nonsense. 2 object foolishly worshiped or feared; bugaboo; bogy. [origin unknown]

mu meson, meson having a mass about 207 times that of the electron; muon. Mu mesons decay to form high-energy electrons.

Mum ford (mum′fərd), *n.* **Lewis,** born 1895, American writer and philosopher.

mum mer (mum′ər), *n.* 1 person who wears a mask, fancy costume, or disguise for fun, such as at Christmas time or at a Mardi Gras. 2 actor. [< Old French *momeur* < *momer* mask oneself]

mum mer y (mum′ər ē), *n., pl.* **-mer ies.** 1 performance of mummers. 2 any useless or silly show or ceremony.

mum mi fy (mum′ə fī), *v.,* **-fied, -fy ing.** —*v.t.* 1 make (a dead body) into a mummy by embalming and drying. 2 make like a mummy. —*v.i.* dry or shrivel up. **—mum′mi fi ca′tion,** *n.*

mum my (mum′ē), *n., pl.* **-mies.** 1 a dead body of a human being or animal embalmed according to the ancient Egyptian or some similar method as a preparation for burial. 2 a dead body dried and preserved by nature. [< Medieval Latin *mumia* < Arabic *mūmiya* < Persian *mūm* wax]

mumps (mumps), *n.* a contagious disease caused by a virus, characterized by inflammation and swelling of the parotid and often other salivary glands, and by difficulty in swallowing. [plural of obsolete *mump* grimace]

mun., municipal.

munch (munch), *v.t., v.i.* chew vigorously and steadily; chew noisily: *A horse munches its oats.* [apparently imitative] **—munch′er,** *n.*

Mun chau sen (mun′chô zən, mun′chou-zən), *n.* **Baron,** 1720-1797, supposed author of incredible tales.

Mün chen (MYN′Hən), *n.* German name of **Munich.**

mun dane (mun′dān), *adj.* 1 of this world, not of heaven; earthly; worldly: *mundane matters of business.* 2 of the universe; cosmic. [< Latin *mundanus* < *mundus* world] **—mun′dane ly,** *adv.*

Mu nich (myü′nik), *n.* city in S West Germany, the capital of Bavaria. 1,326,000. Also, GERMAN **München.**

Munich Pact, agreement signed in Munich September 30, 1938, by Germany, France, Great Britain, and Italy, by which the Sudetenland, a part of Czechoslovakia, was given over to Germany.

mu nic i pal (myü nis′ə pəl), *adj.* 1 of or having to do with the affairs of a city, town, or other municipality. 2 run by a city, town, or other municipality: *a municipal hospital.* 3 having local self-government: *a municipal township.* [< Latin *municipalis,* ultimately < *munia* official duties + *capere* take on] **—mu nic′i pal ly,** *adv.*

mu nic i pal i ty (myü nis′ə pal′ə tē), *n., pl.* **-ties.** city, town, or other district having local self-government, especially an incorporated one.

mu nif i cence (myü nif′ə səns), *n.* very great generosity. [< Latin *munificentia,* ultimately < *munus* gift + *facere* to make]

mu nif i cent (myü nif′ə sənt), *adj.* extremely generous; bountiful; bounteous. **—mu nif′i cent ly,** *adv.*

mu ni tion (myü nish′ən), *n.* Usually, **munitions,** *pl.* material used in war. Munitions are military supplies, such as guns, ammunition, or bombs. *—adj.* having to do with military supplies: *A munition plant is a factory for making munitions.* *—v.t.* provide with military supplies: *munition a fort.* [< Latin *munitionem* < *munire* fortify < *moenia* walls]

Mu ñoz Ma rín (mü nyōs′ mä rēn′), **Luis,** born 1898, Puerto Rican political leader.

Mun ster (mun′stər), *n.* district in the SW Republic of Ireland.

Mün ster (MYN′stər), *n.* city in NW West Germany. 205,000.

mu on (myü′on), *n.* mu meson.

mur al (myůr′əl), *adj.* 1 placed, fixed, or executed on a wall: *A mural painting is painted on a wall of a building.* 2 of a wall; having to do with walls; like a wall. *—n.* picture or decoration, usually of extensive size, painted or placed on a wall. [< Latin *muralis* < *murus* wall]

mur al ist (myůr′ə list), *n.* painter or designer of murals.

Mu rat (MY rä′), *n.* **Joachim,** 1767-1815, French marshal, brother-in-law of Napoleon I, and king of Naples from 1808 to 1815.

mur der (mėr′dər), *n.* 1 the unlawful and intentional killing of a human being. 2 an instance of such a crime: *The detective solved the murder.* 3 SLANG. anything exceedingly difficult or unpleasant: *That job was murder.* *—v.t.* 1 kill a human being unlawfully and intentionally. See **kill**[1] for synonym study. 2 do very badly; spoil or ruin: *She murdered the song she sang.* [Old English *morthor*]

mur der er (mėr′dər ər), *n.* person who is guilty of murder.

mur der ess (mėr′dər is), *n.* woman who is guilty of murder.

mur der ous (mėr′dər əs), *adj.* 1 able to inflict great harm or to kill: *a murderous blow.* 2 ready to murder; guilty or capable of murder: *a murderous villain.* 3 causing murder: *a murderous plot, a murderous hate.* 4 characterized by or involving murder, death, or bloodshed; bloody: *a murderous riot.* **—mur′der ous ly,** *adv.* **—mur′der ous ness,** *n.*

mur i at ic acid (myůr′ē at′ik), hydrochloric acid. [< Latin *muria* brine]

Mu ril lo (myů ril′ō), *n.* **Bartolomé Esteban,** 1617-1682, Spanish painter.

mur ine (myůr′īn, myůr′ən), *adj.* of or having to do with the family of rodents that includes many mice and rats. [< Latin *murinus* < *mus, muris* mouse]

murk (mėrk), *n.* 1 darkness; gloom. 2 thick or murky air or vapor. Also, **mirk.** [< Scandinavian (Old Icelandic) *myrkr*]

murk y (mėr′kē), *adj.,* **murk i er, murk i est.** 1 dark; gloomy: *a murky prison.* 2 very thick and dark; misty; hazy: *murky smoke.* 3 hard to understand; obscure: *a murky argument. Also,* **mirky. —murk′i ly,** *adv.* **—murk′i ness,** *n.*

Mur mansk (mėr′mansk′), *n.* seaport and railroad terminus in NW Soviet Union. 309,000.

mur mur (mėr′mər), *n.* 1 a soft, low, indistinct sound that rises and falls a little and goes on without breaks: *the murmur of a stream, the murmur of voices.* 2 a sound in the heart or lungs, especially an abnormal sound caused by a leaky valve in the heart. 3 a softly spoken word or speech. 4 complaint made under the breath, not aloud. *—v.i.* 1 make a soft, low, indistinct sound. 2 speak softly and indistinctly. See synonym study below. 3 complain under the breath; grumble. *—v.t.* utter in a murmur. [< Latin] **—mur′mur er,** *n.* **—mur′mur ing ly,** *adv.*

Syn. *v.i.* 2 **Murmur, mumble, mutter** mean to speak indistinctly. **Murmur** means to speak too softly to be clearly heard or plainly understood: *He murmured his thanks.* **Mumble** means to speak with the lips partly closed, either habitually or from embarrassment: *She mumbled an apology.* **Mutter** means to mumble in a low voice, as if not wanting to be heard, and especially suggests complaining or anger: *He muttered some rude remarks.*

mur mur ous (mėr′mər əs), *adj.* characterized by murmurs; murmuring. **—mur′mur ous ly,** *adv.*

mur rain (mėr′ən), *n.* 1 any of various diseases of cattle, such as anthrax. 2 ARCHAIC. pestilence; plague. [< Old French *morine* < Medieval Latin *morina* plague < Latin *mori* to die]

Mur ray River (mėr′ē), river in SE Australia. 1150 mi.

mus., 1 museum. 2 music.

mus ca dine (mus′kə dən, mus′kə dīn), *n.* species of grape growing in the southern United States.

mus cat (mus′kat, mus′kət), *n.* 1 any of several light-colored varieties of grape with the flavor or odor of musk. 2 muscatel wine. [< Provençal, having the fragrance of musk < *musc* musk < Late Latin *muscus.* See MUSK.]

Mus cat (mus′kat), *n.* capital of Oman, a seaport in the N part. 6000.

Muscat and Oman, former name of **Oman.**

hat, āge, fär; let, ēqual, tėrm;
it, īce; hot, ōpen, ôrder;
oil, out; cup, půt, rüle;
ch, child; ng, long; sh, she;
th, thin; ᴛʜ, then; zh, measure;

ə represents *a* in about, *e* in taken,
i in pencil, *o* in lemon, *u* in circus.

< = from, derived from, taken from.

mus ca tel (mus′kə tel′), *n.* 1 a strong, sweet wine made from muscat grapes. 2 the muscat grape.

mus cle (mus′əl), *n., v.,* **-cled, -cling.** *—n.* 1 a body tissue composed of fibers, each of which is a long cell. The fibers contract in groups in response to nerve stimuli in order to produce movement. 2 organ consisting of a special bundle of such tissue which moves some particular bone, part, or substance. The biceps muscle bends the arm. The heart muscle pumps blood. 3 strength or power, especially muscular strength. *—v.t.* **muscle in,** INFORMAL. force oneself into a situation where one is not wanted. [< French < Latin *musculus,* diminutive of *mus* mouse; from the appearance of certain muscles]

mus cle-bound (mus′əl bound′), *adj.* having some of the muscles abnormally enlarged or tight, and lacking normal elasticity, usually as a result of too much physical exercise.

Mus cle Shoals (mus′əl shōlz′), rapids of the Tennessee River in NW Alabama. Wilson Dam and other dams were built there to improve navigation, control floods, and produce electricity.

Mus co vite (mus′kə vīt), *n.* 1 Russian. 2 native or inhabitant of the principality of Muscovy. 3 native or inhabitant of Moscow. 4 **muscovite,** a common, light-colored variety of mica. *—adj.* 1 Russian. 2 of or having to do with the principality of Muscovy. 3 of or having to do with Moscow.

Mus co vy (mus′kə vē), *n.* 1 ARCHAIC. Russia. 2 an ancient principality around the city of Moscow.

Muscovy duck—about 2½ ft. long

Muscovy duck, a large duck, originally native to tropical America, and now widely domesticated.

mus cu lar (mus′kyə lər), *adj.* 1 of the muscles; influencing the muscles: *muscular structure, muscular contraction.* 2 having well-developed muscles; strong: *a muscular arm.* 3 consisting of muscle. **—mus′cu lar ly,** *adv.*

muscular dystrophy, a hereditary disease characterized by muscle degeneration, leading to progressive weakness and sometimes complete wasting away of the muscles.

mus cu lar i ty (mus′kyə lar′ə tē), *n.* muscular development or strength.

mus cu la ture (mus′kyə lə chůr, mus′kyə-lə chər), *n.* system or arrangement of muscles.

muse (myüz), *v.,* **mused, mus ing.** —*v.i.* 1 be completely absorbed in thought; ponder; meditate. 2 look thoughtfully. —*v.t.* say thoughtfully. [< Old French *muser,* apparently (originally) put one's nose in the air < *muse* muzzle]

Muse (myüz), *n.* 1 (in Greek myths) one of the nine goddesses of the fine arts and sciences. 2 Sometimes, **muse.** spirit that inspires a poet, composer, writer, etc.; source of inspiration.

mu sette bag (myü zet′), a small canvas or leather bag carried suspended from a shoulder, used by soldiers, hikers, etc., to carry toilet articles, food, etc. [*musette* < French, kind of bagpipe]

mu se um (myü zē′əm), *n.* building or rooms where a collection of objects illustrating science, art, history, or other subjects is kept and displayed. [< Latin < Greek *mouseion* seat of the Muses < *Mousa* Muse]

mush[1] (mush), *n.* 1 U.S. corn meal boiled in water. 2 anything soft, thick, and pulpy like mush. 3 INFORMAL. weak or maudlin sentiment; silly talk. [variant of *mash*]

mush[2] (mush), *n.* journey on foot through snow, driving a dog sled. —*v.i.* travel in this way. —*interj.* a shout to a team of sled dogs to start or to speed up. [perhaps used for *mush on,* alteration of French *marchons!* let us advance] —**mush′er,** *n.*

mushroom (def. 1)

mush room (mush′rüm, mush′rům), *n.* 1 any of various fleshy fungi that grow very fast and are shaped like an umbrella, ball, or other thickened mass. Some mushrooms are good to eat; some, such as toadstools, are poisonous. 2 anything shaped or growing like a mushroom, as the mushroom-shaped cloud that rises from the explosion of a nuclear bomb. —*adj.* 1 of or like a mushroom. 2 of very rapid growth: *a mushroom town.* —*v.i.* 1 grow very fast: *The little town mushroomed into a city.* 2 become flattened at one end: *A bullet sometimes mushrooms when it hits a very hard object.* [< Old French *mousseron*]

mush y (mush′ē), *adj.,* **mush i er, mush i est.** 1 like mush; pulpy. 2 INFORMAL. weakly or foolishly sentimental. —**mush′i ly,** *adv.* —**mush′i ness,** *n.*

mu sic (myü′zik), *n.* 1 art of combining tones or sounds to achieve beautiful, pleasing, or interesting arrangements. The study of music deals with the principles of melody, harmony, rhythm, etc. 2 beautiful, pleasing, or interesting arrangements of tones or sounds, especially as produced by the voice or instruments. 3 written or printed signs for tones; a score or scores: *Can you read music?* 4 a pleasant sound; something delightful to hear: *the music of a bubbling brook.* 5 **face the music,** INFORMAL. meet trouble boldly or bravely. 6 **set to music,** provide (the words of a song, etc.) with music. [< Old French *musique* < Latin *musica* < Greek *mousikē technē* art of the Muses < *Mousa* Muse]

mu si cal (myü′zə kəl), *adj.* 1 of or having to do with music: *a musical composer.* 2 beautiful or pleasing to hear; melodious; harmonious: *a musical voice.* 3 set to music; accompanied by music. 4 fond of music. 5 skilled in music. —*n.* musical comedy. —**mu′si cal ly,** *adv.*

musical comedy, play or motion picture consisting of a story spoken in dialogue form, with songs, choruses, dances, and incidental music.

mu si cale (myü′zə kal′), *n.* a social gathering to enjoy music. [< French, short for *soirée musicale* musical evening]

musical instrument, instrument for producing music, such as a piano, violin, trumpet, etc.

music box, box or case containing apparatus for producing music mechanically.

music hall, 1 hall for musical entertainments. 2 theater for vaudeville.

mu si cian (myü zish′ən), *n.* 1 person skilled in music. 2 person who sings or who plays on a musical instrument, especially as a profession or business. 3 composer of music.

mu si cian ly (myü zish′ən lē), *adj.* of or suited to a musician.

mu si cian ship (myü zish′ən ship), *n.* skill in playing, conducting, or composing music; musical ability.

mu si col o gist (myü′zə kol′ə jist), *n.* an expert in musicology.

mu si col o gy (myü′zə kol′ə jē), *n.* the systematic study of music, especially its literature, history, forms, methods, and principles.

mus ing (myü′zing), *adj.* meditative. —*n.* meditation. —**mus′ing ly,** *adv.*

musk (musk), *n.* 1 substance with a strong and lasting odor, used in making perfumes. Musk is found in a gland in the abdomen of the male musk deer. 2 a similar substance found in the glands of other animals, such as the mink and muskrat. 3 odor of musk. 4 any plant whose leaves or flowers smell like musk. [< Late Latin *muscus* < Late Greek *moschos* < Persian *mushk* < Sanskrit *muṣka* testicle, diminutive of *mūs* mouse]

musk deer, a small, hornless deer of central and northeastern Asia, the male of which has a gland containing musk.

mus keg (mus′keg), *n.* bog or marsh filled with sphagnum moss, chiefly in the tundra or forest regions of Canada, Alaska, and northern Europe. [< Algonquian]

mus kel lunge (mus′kə lunj), *n., pl.* **-lunge.** a very large North American pike, valued as a food and game fish, but difficult to catch. [< Algonquian]

mus ket (mus′kit), *n.* gun introduced in the 1500's and widely used before rifles were invented. [< Middle French *mousquet* < Italian *moschetto,* originally, a kind of hawk < *mosca* fly < Latin *musca*]

mus ket eer (mus′kə tir′), *n.* soldier armed with a musket.

mus ket ry (mus′kə trē), *n.* 1 muskets. 2 art of shooting with muskets or rifles. 3 the fire of muskets, rifles, etc.; small-arms fire.

musk mel on (musk′mel′ən), *n.* 1 a small, round or oval melon with sweet, juicy, light-green or orange flesh, a hard, thick rind with a ribbed or netlike pattern, and a smell like that of musk. The cantaloupe and honeydew melon are muskmelons. 2 the plant of the gourd family it grows on.

Mus ko gee (mus kō′gē), *n., pl.* **-gee** or **-gees** for 1. 1 member of a tribe of Indians of Georgia and Alabama that formed part of the Creek confederacy of tribes. 2 language of this tribe.

musk ox, a large arctic mammal of the same family as the ox, having a hump and dense, extremely long hair, and sometimes giving off a musky smell. It is found especially in the tundra regions of northern North America and Greenland.

musk ox—to 5 ft. high at the shoulder

musk rat (musk′rat′), *n., pl.* **-rats** or **-rat.** 1 a water rodent of North America, like a rat, but larger, having webbed hind feet, a glossy coat, and a musky smell; water rat. 2 its valuable dark-brown fur.

musk y (mus′kē), *adj.,* **musk i er, musk i est.** of or like musk; like that of musk: *a musky odor.* —**musk′i ness,** *n.*

Mus lim or **Mus lem** (muz′ləm), *n., adj.* Moslem.

mus lin (muz′lən), *n.* 1 a thin, fine cotton cloth, used for dresses, curtains, etc. 2 a heavier cotton cloth, used for sheets, undergarments, etc. —*adj.* made of muslin: *white muslin curtains.* [< French *mousseline* < Italian *mussolina* of the city of Mosul < *Mussolo* Mosul]

muss (mus), *v.t.* put into disorder; rumple: *The child's dress was mussed.* —*n.* INFORMAL. untidy state; disorder; mess. [variant of *mess*]

mus sel (mus′əl), *n.* any of various bivalve mollusks resembling clams, found in both fresh and salt water. Sea mussels have dark-blue shells and are edible. The shells of freshwater mussels are an important source of mother-of-pearl, used in the manufacture of buttons, etc. [Old English *muscle, musle* < Latin *musculus* mussel, muscle. See MUSCLE.]

Mus set (mY sā′), *n.* **Alfred de,** 1810-1857, French writer of poetry, plays, and stories.

Mus so li ni (mů′sə lē′nē, mü′sə lē′nē), *n.* **Benito,** 1883-1945, leader of the Italian Fascists and prime minister of Italy from 1922 to 1943.

Mus sorg sky (mů sôrg′skē), *n.* Moussorgsky.

Mus sul man (mus′əl mən), *n., pl.* **-mans.** Moslem.

muss y (mus′ē), *adj.,* **muss i er, muss i est.** INFORMAL. untidy; messy; rumpled. —**muss′i ly,** *adv.* —**muss′i ness,** *n.*

must[1] (must; *unstressed* məst), *auxiliary v., past* **must,** *n., adj.* —*auxiliary v.* 1 be obliged to; be forced to: *Man must eat to live.* 2 ought to; should: *I must go home soon. I must keep my promise.* 3 be certain to (be, do, etc.): *I must seem very rude.* 4 be supposed or expected to: *You must have that book.* 5 *Must* is sometimes used with its verb omitted. *We must to horse. We must away.* —*n.* something necessary; obligation: *This rule is a must.* —*adj.* INFORMAL. demanding

hat, āge, fär; let, ēqual, tėrm; it, īce; hot, ōpen, ôrder; oil, out; cup, pu̇t, rüle; ch, child; ng, long; sh, she; th, thin; ᴛʜ, then; zh, measure;

ə represents *a* in about, *e* in taken, *i* in pencil, *o* in lemon, *u* in circus.

< = from, derived from, taken from.

attention or doing; necessary: *a must item, must legislation.* [Old English *mōste,* past tense of *mōtan* might, may]

must[2] (must), *n.* the expressed, unfermented or partially unfermented juice of the grape or other fruit. [Old English < Latin *(vinum) mustum* fresh (wine)]

must[3] (must), *n.* musty condition; mold. [< *musty*]

mus tache (mus′tash, mə stash′), *n.* 1 hair growing on a man's upper lip. 2 hairs or bristles growing near the mouth of an animal. Also, **moustache.** [< French *moustache* < Italian *mostacchio* < Medieval Latin *mustacia* < Greek *mystax* upper lip, mustache]

mus tached (mus′tasht, mə stasht′), *adj.* having a mustache.

mus ta chio (mə stä′shō), *n., pl.* **-chios.** mustache.

mus ta chioed (mə stä′shōd), *adj.* mustached.

Mus ta fa Ke mal (mu̇s′tä fä kə mäl′), former name of **Kemal Ataturk.**

mus tang (mus′tang), *n.* a small, wiry, wild or half-wild horse of the North American plains, descended from domesticated Spanish stock. [< Spanish *mestengo* untamed]

mus tard (mus′tərd), *n.* 1 any of various species of cole, whose seeds have a sharp, hot taste. 2 a yellow powder or paste made from its seeds. It is used as seasoning to give a pungent taste to meats, etc., or medicinally in a mustard plaster. 3 a dark yellow color. [< Old French *moustarde,* ultimately < Latin *mustum* must[2]]

mustard family, group of dicotyledonous herbs with cross-shaped flowers and bearing a two-valved capsule as the fruit, including the mustard, cress, cabbage, cauliflower, broccoli, etc.

mustard gas, a colorless or brown oily liquid which evaporates slowly to a poison gas that causes burns, blindness, and death. *Formula:* $C_4H_8Cl_2S$

mustard plaster, poultice made of mustard and water, or of mustard, flour, and water, used as a counterirritant.

mus ter (mus′tər), *v.t.* 1 gather together; assemble; collect: *muster financial resources, muster soldiers.* 2 summon: *muster up courage.* 3 number; comprise: *The garrison musters eighty men.* 4 **muster in,** enlist. 5 **muster out,** discharge. —*v.i.* come together; gather; assemble. —*n.* 1 assembly; collection. 2 a bringing together of men or troops for review, service, roll call, etc. 3 list of those assembled; roll. 4 the number assembled. 5 **pass muster,** be inspected and approved; come up to the required standards. [< Old French *mostrer* < Latin *monstrare* to show < *monstrum* portent]

must n't (mus′nt), must not.

mus ty (mus′tē), *adj.,* **-ti er, -ti est.** 1 having a smell or taste suggesting mold, damp, poor ventilation, decay, etc.; moldy: *a musty room, musty crackers.* 2 stale; out-of-date: *musty laws about witches.* [perhaps < *moisty* < *moist* + *-y*[1]] **—mus′ti ly,** *adv.* **—mus′ti ness,** *n.*

mu ta bil i ty (myü′tə bil′ə tē), *n.* 1 ability or tendency to change. 2 fickleness.

mu ta ble (myü′tə bəl), *adj.* 1 capable of or liable to change; changeable: *mutable customs.* 2 fickle: *a mutable person.* **—mu′ta ble ness,** *n.* **—mu′ta bly,** *adv.*

mu ta gen (myü′tə jən), *n.* agent that causes mutation in an organism.

mu ta gen ic (myü′tə jen′ik), *adj.* of or having to do with a mutagen.

mu tant (myüt′nt), *n.* a new variety of plant or animal resulting from mutation. —*adj.* that is the result of mutation: *a mutant species.*

mu tate (myü′tāt), *v.t., v.i.,* **-tat ed, -tat ing.** 1 change. 2 undergo or produce mutation.

mu ta tion (myü tā′shən), *n.* 1 act or process of changing; change; alteration. 2 change within a gene or chromosome of animals or plants resulting in the appearance of a new, inheritable feature or character. 3 a new genetic character or new variety of plant or animal formed in this way; mutant. [< Latin *mutationem* < *mutare* to change]

mu ta tis mu tan dis (myü tā′tis myü-tan′dis), LATIN. with the necessary changes.

mute (myüt), *adj., n., v.,* **mut ed, mut ing.** —*adj.* 1 not making any sound; silent: *The little girl stood mute with embarrassment.* 2 unable to speak; dumb. 3 not pronounced; silent: *The "e" in "mute" is mute.* 4 without speech or sound: *a mute refusal of an offer, mute astonishment.* —*n.* 1 person who cannot speak, usually because of deafness, loss of or damage to the tongue, etc. 2 clip, pad, or other device, used to soften, deaden, or muffle the sound of a musical instrument. 3 a silent letter. 4 (in phonetics) a stop. —*v.t.* deaden or soften the sound of (a tone, voice, a musical instrument, etc.) with or as if with a mute: *He played the violin with muted strings.* [< Latin *mutus*] **—mute′ly,** *adv.* **—mute′-ness,** *n.*

mu ti late (myü′tl āt), *v.t.,* **-lat ed, -lat ing.** 1 cut, tear, or break off a limb or other important part of; injure seriously by cutting, tearing, or breaking off some part; maim. 2 make (a book, story, song, etc.) imperfect by removing parts. [< Latin *mutilatum* maimed] **—mu′ti la′tor,** *n.*

mu ti la tion (myü′tl ā′shən), *n.* 1 a mutilating. 2 a being mutilated.

mu ti neer (myüt′n ir′), *n.* person who takes part in a mutiny.

mu ti nous (myüt′n əs), *adj.* 1 given to or engaged in mutiny; rebellious: *a mutinous crew.* 2 like or involving mutiny; characterized by mutiny: *a mutinous look.* 3 not controllable; unruly: *mutinous passions.* **—mu′ti nous ly,** *adv.* **—mu′ti nous-ness,** *n.*

mu ti ny (myüt′n ē), *n., pl.* **-nies,** *v.,* **-nied, -ny ing.** —*n.* open rebellion against lawful authority, especially by sailors or soldiers against their officers. —*v.i.* take part in a mutiny; rebel. [< obsolete *mutine* to revolt < Old French *mutiner* < *mutin* rebellious, ultimately < Latin *movere* to move]

mut ism (myü′tiz′əm), *n.* condition of being mute; muteness.

Mut su hi to (müt′sü hē′tō), *n.* 1852-1912, emperor of Japan from 1867 to 1912.

mutt (mut), *n.* SLANG. dog, especially a mongrel. [origin uncertain]

mut ter (mut′ər), *v.t.* speak (words) low and indistinctly with the lips partly closed. —*v.i.* 1 speak indistinctly and in a low voice, with the lips partly closed; mumble. See **murmur** for synonym study. 2 complain; grumble. —*n.* 1 act of muttering. 2 muttered words: *a mutter of discontent.* [Middle English *muteren*] **—mut′ter er,** *n.*

mut ton (mut′n), *n.* the flesh of a sheep used as food, especially of a mature sheep as distinguished from a lamb. [< Old French *mouton* < Medieval Latin *multonem* ram]

mut ton chops (mut′n chops′), *n. pl.* Also, **muttonchop whiskers.** sideburns narrow at the temples and broad near the chin.

mu tu al (myü′chü əl), *adj.* 1 done, said, felt, etc., by each toward the other; given and received: *mutual promises, mutual dislike.* 2 each to the other: *mutual enemies.* 3 belonging to each of several: *our mutual friend.* [< Latin *mutuus* reciprocal] **—mu′tu al ly,** *adv.*

mutual fund, a financial organization that invests the pooled capital of its members in diversified securities.

mu tu al ism (myü′chü ə liz′əm), *n.* relationship between two organisms in which they benefit each other.

mu tu al i ty (myü′chü al′ə tē), *n.* the state or quality of being mutual.

muu muu (mü′mü′), *n.* a long, loose-fitting cotton dress, originally worn by Polynesian women. [< Hawaiian]

mu zhik or **mu zjik** (mü zhik′, mü′zhik), *n.* a Russian peasant. Also, **moujik, mujik.** [< Russian]

muz zle (muz′əl), *n., v.,* **-zled, -zling.** —*n.* 1 the projecting part of the head of an animal, including the nose, mouth, and jaws; snout. 2 cover or cage of straps or wires to put over an animal's head or mouth to keep it from biting or eating. 3 the open front end of the barrel of a gun, pistol, etc. —*v.t.* 1 put a muzzle on. 2 compel to keep silent about something; prevent from expressing views: *The government muzzled the newspapers during the rebellion.* [< Old French *musel* < *muse* muzzle] **—muz′zler,** *n.*

muz zle load er (muz′əl lō′dər), *n.* a muzzleloading gun.

muz zle load ing (muz′əl lō′ding), *adj.* (of a gun) loaded by putting gunpowder in through the open front end of the barrel and ramming it down.

Mv, mendelevium.

my (mī), *adj.* possessive form of **I.** of or belonging to me; that I have, hold, or possess: *my house, in my opinion.* —*interj.* INFORMAL. an exclamation of surprise: *My! How pleasant to see you!* [Old English *mīn*]

my as the ni a (mī′əs thē′nē ə), *n.* extreme muscular weakness. [< New Latin < Greek *myos* muscle + *astheneia* weakness]

my as then ic (mī′əs then′ik), *adj.* affected with myasthenia.

my ce li al (mī sē′lē əl), *adj.* of or having to do with the mycelium.

my ce li um (mī sē′lē əm), *n., pl.* **-li a** (-lē ə). the vegetative part of a fungus, consisting of one or more white, interwoven filaments or hyphae. [< New Latin < Greek *mykēs* mushroom]

My ce nae (mī sē′nē), *n.* city in the S part of ancient Greece.

My ce nae an (mī′sn ē′ən), *adj.* of or having to do with Mycenae or the civilization, culture, or art that flourished there from about 1500 B.C. to about 1100 B.C.

my col o gist (mī kol′ə jist), *n.* an expert in mycology.

my col o gy (mī kol′ə jē), *n.* 1 branch of botany that deals with fungi. 2 the fungi of a particular region or country. [< Greek *mykēs* fungus + English *-logy*]

my co sis (mī kō′sis), *n., pl.* **-ses** (-sēz). 1 the presence of parasitic fungi in or on any part of the body. 2 disease caused by such fungi.

my e len ceph a lon (mī′ə len sef′ə lon), *n.* the posterior part of the hindbrain, which comprises the medulla oblongata.

my e lin (mī′ə lən), *n.* a soft, whitish, fatty substance that forms a sheath about the core of certain nerve fibers. [< German *Myelin* < Greek *myelos* marrow]

my e li tis (mī′ə lī′tis), *n.* inflammation of the spinal cord or of the bone marrow.

my na or **my nah** (mī′nə), *n.* any of several starlings that can imitate human speech, found in India and certain other countries of Asia. [< Hindustani *mainā*]

Myn heer (mīn her′, mīn hir′), *n.* DUTCH. Sir; Mr.

my o car di al (mī′ə kär′dē əl), *adj.* of or having to do with the myocardium.

my o car di um (mī′ə kär′dē əm), *n.* the muscle tissue of the heart. [< New Latin < Greek *myos* muscle + *kardia* heart]

my o pi a (mī ō′pē ə), *n.* 1 near-sightedness. 2 short-sightedness: *intellectual myopia.* [< Greek *myōpia* < *myein* to shut + *ōps* eye]

my op ic (mī op′ik), *adj.* near-sighted. **—my op′i cal ly,** *adv.*

my o sin (mī′ə sən), *n.* one of two protein components of muscle cells important in the elasticity and contraction of muscles. The other is actin.

myr i ad (mir′ē əd), *n.* 1 ten thousand. 2 a very great number: *There are myriads of stars.* —*adj.* 1 ten thousand. 2 countless; innumerable. [< Greek *myriados* ten thousand, countless]

myr i a pod (mir′ē ə pod′), *n.* any of an obsolete classification of arthropods, now considered to be four classes, the two largest being the centipedes and millipedes. [< Greek *myriados* myriad + *podos* foot]

Myr mi don (mėr′mə don), *n.* 1 (in Greek legends) a member of a warlike people of ancient Thessaly who accompanied Achilles, their king, to the Trojan War. 2 **myrmidon,** an obedient and unquestioning follower, especially one who unscrupulously carries out his master's orders.

myrrh (mėr), *n.* a fragrant gum resin with a bitter taste, used in medicine as an astringent tonic, in perfumes, and in incense. It is obtained from certain small trees, of the same family as frankincense, that grow in southern Arabia and eastern Africa. [Old English *myrre* < Latin *myrrha* < Greek; of Semitic origin]

myr tle (mėr′tl), *n.* 1 any of a genus of shrubs of the myrtle family, especially an evergreen shrub of southern Europe with shiny leaves, fragrant white flowers, and black berries. 2 periwinkle. [< Old French *mirtile* < Latin *myrtus* < Greek *myrtos*]

myrtle family, group of dicotyledonous woody plants, natives of warm climates, usually having a fragrant, volatile oil, and including the clove, guava, and eucalyptus.

my self (mī self′), *pron., pl* **ourselves.** 1 the emphatic form of **me** or **I.** *I did it myself. I myself will go.* 2 the reflexive form of **me.** *I hurt myself. I can cook for myself.* 3 my real self; my normal self: *I am not myself today.*

➤ In informal English, **myself** is sometimes substituted for *I* or *me* in a compound subject or object: *Mrs. Johnson and myself are both very grateful.* This use is not regarded as standard.

My si a (mish′ē ə), *n.* ancient country in Asia Minor.

My sore (mī sôr′, mī sōr′), *n.* 1 city in SW India. 260,000 2 state in SW India.

mys ter i ous (mi stir′ē əs), *adj.* 1 full of mystery; hard to explain or understand; secret; hidden. See synonym study below. 2 suggesting mystery; enigmatical: *a mysterious look.* **—mys ter′i ous ly,** *adv.* **—mys ter′i ous ness,** *n.*

Syn. 1 **Mysterious, inscrutable** mean hard to explain or understand. **Mysterious** describes whatever arouses curiosity or wonder by being unexplainable or puzzling: *She had a mysterious telephone call.* **Inscrutable** describes whatever baffles and defeats all attempts to interpret it: *His mother began to cry, but his father's face was inscrutable.*

mys ter y (mis′tər ē), *n., pl.* **-ter ies.** 1 something that is hidden, inexplicable, or unknown; secret; enigma: *the mysteries of the universe, the mystery of love.* 2 condition or property of being secret or secretive; secrecy; obscurity: *an atmosphere of mystery, a man of mystery.* 3 something that is not explained or understood: *It is a mystery to me how they survived the accident.* 4 novel, story, etc., about a mysterious event or events which are not explained until the end, so as to keep the reader in suspense. 5 a religious conception or doctrine that human reason cannot understand. 6 Often, **mysteries,** *pl.* a secret religious rite to which only initiated persons are admitted. 7 a sacramental rite of the Christian religion. 8 the Eucharist or Mass. 9 Often, **mysteries,** *pl.* the elements of the Eucharist. 10 an incident in the life of Jesus or one of the saints, regarded as of special significance. 11 mystery play. [< Latin *mysterium* < Greek *mystērion* < *mystēs* an initiate < *myein* to close (the lips or eyes)]

mystery play, a medieval religious play based on the Bible.

mys tic (mis′tik), *adj.* 1 mystical. 2 having to do with the ancient religious mysteries or other occult rites: *mystic arts.* 3 of or having to do with mystics or mysticism. 4 of hidden meaning or nature; enigmatical; mysterious. —*n.* 1 person who believes that union with God or knowledge of truths inaccessible to the ordinary powers of the mind can be attained through faith, spiritual insight, intuition, or exaltation of feeling. 2 person who has the mental tendencies or habits of thought and feeling characteristic of a mystic. [< Latin *mysticus* < Greek *mystikos* < *mystēs* an initiate. See MYSTERY.]

mys ti cal (mis′tə kəl), *adj.* 1 having some secret meaning; beyond human understanding; mysterious. 2 spiritually symbolic: *The lamb and the dove are mystical symbols of the Christian religion.* 3 of, having to do with, or characteristic of mystics or mysticism. 4 of or having to do with secret rites open only to the initiated. **—mys′ti cal ly,** *adv.* **—mys′ti cal ness,** *n.*

mys ti cism (mis′tə siz′əm), *n.* 1 beliefs or mode of thought of mystics. 2 vague or fuzzy thinking; dreamy speculation.

mys ti fi ca tion (mis′tə fə kā′shən), *n.* 1 a mystifying or a being mystified; bewilderment; perplexity. 2 something that mystifies or is designed to mystify.

mys ti fy (mis′tə fī), *v.t.,* **-fied, -fy ing.** 1 bewilder purposely; puzzle; perplex: *The magician's tricks mystified the audience.* 2 make mysterious; involve in mystery.

mys tique (mi stēk′), *n.* 1 atmosphere of mystery about someone or something; mystic quality or air. 2 a mystical or peculiar way of interpreting reality, especially one associated with a cult or doctrine and acting as a guide to action. [< French]

myth (mith), *n.* 1 a traditional story, often involving supernatural beings, and usually attempting to explain a phenomenon of nature. Most myths express a religious belief of a people and are of unknown origin. *The myth of Persephone is the ancient Greek explanation of summer and winter.* 2 such stories as a group. 3 any invented story. 4 an imaginary or fictitious person, thing, or event: *Her wealthy uncle was a myth invented to impress the other girls.* 5 belief, opinion, or theory that is not based on fact or reality. [< Greek *mythos* word, story] ➤ See **legend** for usage note.

myth., mythology.

myth ic (mith′ik), *adj.* mythical.

myth i cal (mith′ə kəl), *adj.* 1 of a myth; like a myth; in myths: *a mythical interpretation of nature, mythical monsters, mythical places.* 2 not real; made-up; imaginary; fictitious. **—myth′i cal ly,** *adv.*

myth o log i cal (mith′ə loj′ə kəl), *adj.* of mythology: *The phoenix is a mythological bird.* **—myth′o log′i cal ly,** *adv.*

my thol o gist (mi thol′ə jist), *n.* 1 writer of myths. 2 person who knows much about mythology.

my thol o gy (mi thol′ə jē), *n., pl.* **-gies.** 1 group of myths relating to a particular country or person: *Greek mythology.* 2 study of myths.

Myt i le ne (mit′l ē′nē), *n.* Greek island in the Aegean Sea. 140,000 pop.; 630 sq. mi. Also, **Lesbos.**

myx o vi rus (mik′sə vī′rəs), *n.* any of a group of viruses that agglutinate red blood cells, including the viruses which cause influenza and mumps. [< Greek *myxa* mucus + English *virus*]

N n

hat, āge, fär; let, ēqual, tėrm;
it, īce; hot, ōpen, ôrder;
oil, out; cup, pu̇t, rüle;
ch, child; ng, long; sh, she;
th, thin; ᴛʜ, then; zh, measure;

ə represents *a* in about, *e* in taken, *i* in pencil, *o* in lemon, *u* in circus.

< = from, derived from, taken from.

N or **n** (en), *n., pl.* **N's** or **n's.** the 14th letter of the English alphabet.

n, (in algebra) an indefinite number.

N, 1 (in chess) knight. 2 nitrogen. 3 North. 4 Northern.

n., 1 neuter. 2 new. 3 nominative. 4 north. 5 northern. 6 noun. 7 number.

N., 1 New. 2 Noon. 3 North. 4 Northern.

Na, sodium [for Latin *natrium*].

N.A., North America.

N.A.A.C.P. or **NAACP,** National Association for the Advancement of Colored People.

nab (nab), *v.t.,* **nabbed, nab bing.** SLANG. 1 catch or seize suddenly; grab. 2 arrest. [earlier *nap,* probably < Scandinavian (Swedish) *nappa* catch, snatch]

na bob (nā′bob), *n.* 1 nawab (def. 1). 2 a very rich or important man; nawab. [< Hindustani *nabāb,nawwāb.* See NAWAB.]

na celle (nə sel′), *n.* an enclosed part of an aircraft for holding an engine and sometimes passengers or cargo. [< French < Late Latin *navicella* small boat, diminutive of Latin *navis* ship]

na cre (nā′kər), *n.* mother-of-pearl. [< Middle French < Italian *nacchera,* ultimately < Arabic *naqqārah* drum]

na cre ous (nā′krē əs), *adj.* of or like nacre.

Na der (nā′dər), *n.* **Ralph,** born 1934, American lawyer, known for his work in promoting safe business practices and protecting the rights of consumers.

na dir (nā′dər, nā′dir), *n.* 1 the point in the celestial sphere directly beneath the observer or a given place; the point opposite the zenith. See **zenith** for diagram. 2 the lowest point: *Efforts to achieve agreement reached their nadir.* [< Old French < Arabic *naẓīr* opposite (i.e., to the zenith)]

nae (nā), *adj., adv.* SCOTTISH. no.

nag[1] (nag), *v.,* **nagged, nag ging,** *n.* —*v.i.* irritate or annoy by peevish complaints. —*v.t.* find fault with (a person) all the time; scold. —*n.* person given to nagging. [probably < Scandinavian (Icelandic) *nagga* grumble] —**nag′ger,** *n.*

nag[2] (nag), *n.* 1 INFORMAL. a horse. 2 an old or inferior horse. [Middle English *nagge* pony]

Na ga sa ki (nä′gə sä′kē), *n.* seaport in SW Japan, the target of the second atomic bomb to be used in war, on August 9, 1945. 471,000.

Na go ya (nä gô′yə), *n.* city in central Japan. 2,021,000.

Nag pur (näg′pu̇r, nag′pu̇r), *n.* city in central India. 876,000.

Na hua tl (nä′wä təl), *n.* language of the Aztecs, Toltecs, and other Amerian Indian tribes of central Mexico and parts of Central America. —*adj.* of or having to do with this language.

Na hua tlan (nä′wä tlən), *n., adj.* Nahuatl.

Na hum (nā′əm, nā′həm), *n.* 1 Hebrew prophet of about 600 B.C. 2 book of the Old Testament containing his prophecies.

nai ad (nā′ad, nī′ad), *n., pl.* **-ads, -a des** (-ə dēz′). 1 Also, **Naiad.** (in Greek and Roman myths) a nymph guarding a river, stream, or spring. 2 a girl swimmer. 3 an immature insect in one of a series of aquatic stages of development characteristic of dragonflies, mayflies, etc. Naiads somewhat resemble the adult form, but have gills.

na ïf (nä ēf′), *adj.* naïve. [< French]

nail (nāl), *n.* 1 a slender piece of metal to be hammered into or through wood, etc., to hold separate pieces together or to serve as a peg. 2 **hit the nail on the head,** guess or understand correctly; say or do something just right. 3 the thin, horny plate on the upper side of the end of a finger or toe. 4 a claw or talon. —*v.t.* 1 fasten with a nail or nails. 2 hold or keep fixed: *nail one's eyes on a painting. Nail them down to what they promised.* 3 **nail down,** find out definitely; make certain; settle finally: *The buyer of a house should nail down the terms of the sale.* 4 INFORMAL. catch; seize. 5 INFORMAL. detect and expose (a lie, etc.). [Old English *nægel*] —**nail′er,** *n.*

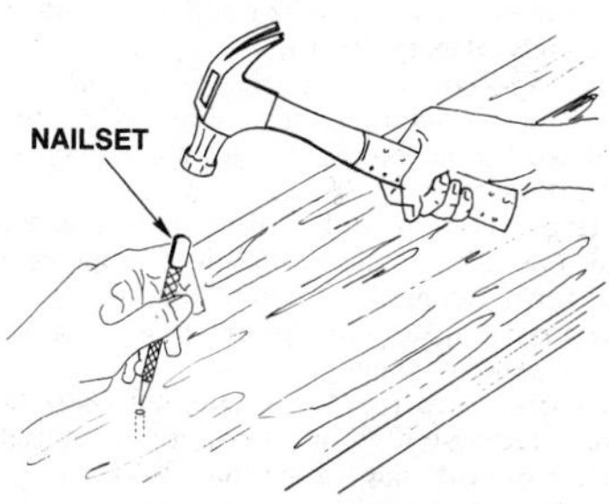

nail set (nāl′set′), *n.* tool for driving nails beneath the surface.

nain sook (nān′su̇k), *n.* a soft, light cotton fabric. [< Hindustani *nainsukh* < *nain* eye + *sukh* pleasure]

Nai ro bi (nī rō′bē), *n.* capital of Kenya, in the SW part. 509,000.

na ïve or **na ive** (nä ēv′), *adj.* simple in nature; like a child; not sophisticated; artless. Also, **naïf.** [< French *naïve,* feminine of *naïf* < Latin *nativus.* Doublet of NATIVE.] —**na-ïve′ly, na ive′ly,** *adv.* —**na ïve′ness, na-ive′ness,** *n.*

na ï ve té or **na i ve te** (nä ē′və tā′), *n.* 1 quality of being naïve: unspoiled freshness: artlessness. 2 a naïve action, remark, etc. [< French *naïveté*]

na ive ty (nä ēv′tē), *n., pl.* **-ties.** naïveté.

na ked (nā′kid), *adj.* 1 with no clothes on; bare; nude. See **bare** for synonym study. 2 not covered; stripped: *naked fields.* 3 not protected; exposed: *a naked sword.* 4 without addition of anything else; plain; unadorned: *the naked truth.* [Old English *nacod*] —**na′ked ly,** *adv.* —**na′ked ness,** *n.*

naked eye, the eye unaided by any glass, telescope, or microscope.

NAM or **N.A.M.,** National Association of Manufacturers.

nam a ble (nā′mə bəl), *adj.* that can be named. Also, **nameable.**

nam by-pam by (nam′bē pam′bē), *adj., n., pl.* **-bies.** —*adj.* weakly simple, silly, or sentimental; insipid: *Valentines are often namby-pamby.* —*n.* a namby-pamby person. [< *Namby Pamby,* nickname used for *Ambrose* Philips, 1674-1749, an English poet, to ridicule his verses addressed to babies]

name (nām), *n., adj., v.,* **named, nam ing.** —*n.* 1 word or words by which a person, animal, place, or thing is called or known. 2 word or words applied descriptively; appellation, title, or epithet. See synonym study below. 3 a title or term as distinguished from fact. 4 persons grouped under one name; family; clan; tribe: *hostile to the name of Campbell.* 5 reputation; fame: *get a bad name, make a name for oneself.* 6 a famous or well-known person: *the great names in medicine.*

call names, call bad names; swear at; curse.

in name only, supposed to be, but not really so: *a king in name only.*

in the name of, a for the sake of. b acting for.

know only by name, know only by hearing about.

to one's name, belonging to one.

—*adj.* well-known: *a name brand.*

—*v.t.* 1 give a name or names to: *name a newborn baby.* 2 call by name; mention by name: *Three persons were named in the report.* 3 give the right name for: *Can you name these flowers?* 4 speak of; mention; state: *name several reasons.* 5 specify or fix; settle on: *name a price.* 6 choose for some duty or office; nominate; appoint: *I was named for class president.*

[Old English *nama*] —**nam′er,** *n.*

Syn. *n.* 2 **Name, title** mean what someone or something is called. **Name** is used of any descriptive or characterizing term applied to a person or thing: *"The Corn State" is a name for Iowa.* **Title** is used of a distinguishing name given to a book, song, play, etc., or to a person as a sign of honor, rank, office, or occupation: *His title is Secretary.*

name a ble (nā′mə bəl), *adj.* namable.

name day, day sacred to the saint whose name a person bears.

name less (nām′lis), *adj.* 1 having no name: *a nameless stranger.* 2 not marked with a name: *a nameless grave.* 3 that cannot be named or described: *a strange, nameless longing.* 4 not fit to be mentioned: *nameless crimes.* 5 not named: *a former convict, who shall remain nameless.* 6 unknown to fame; obscure: *a nameless author.* —**name′less-ly,** *adv.* —**name′less ness,** *n.*

name ly (nām′lē), *adv.* that is to say: *The railroad connects two cities—namely, New York and Chicago.*

name sake (nām′sāk′), *n.* one having the same name as another, especially one named after another: *Theodore, namesake of President Theodore Roosevelt.*

Nan cy (nan′sē; *French* näɴ sē′), *n.* city in NE France. 123,000.

nan keen or **nan kin** (nan kēn′), *n.* 1 a firm, yellow or buff fabric made from a yellow variety of cotton. 2 **nankeens,** *pl.* trousers made of nankeen. [< *Nanking,* where it was first made]

Nan king (nan′king′), *n.* city in E China, on the Yangtze River. It was the capital of China from 1928 to 1937 and from 1946 to 1949. 1,419,000.

nan ny (nan′ē), *n., pl.* **-nies.** BRITISH. a child's nurse. [< *Nanny,* a feminine name]

nanny goat, a female goat.

nano- *combining form.* billionth of: *Nanosecond = a billionth of a second.* [< Greek *nanos* dwarf]

na no sec ond (nā′nō sek′ənd, nan′ō-sek′ənd), *n.* billionth of a second.

Nan sen (nän′sən), *n.* **Fridtjof,** 1861-1930, Norwegian arctic explorer, scientist, author, and diplomat.

Nantes (nants; *French* näNt), *n.* 1 seaport in W France, on the Loire River. 259,000. 2 **Edict of,** edict granting religious toleration to Huguenots, signed in 1598 by Henry IV and revoked in 1685.

Nan tuck et (nan tuk′it), *n.* island in the Atlantic Ocean south of Cape Cod. It is part of Massachusetts. 15 mi. long.

Na o mi (nā ō′mē, nā′ō mē), *n.* (in the Bible) Ruth's mother-in-law.

nap[1] (nap), *n., v.,* **napped, nap ping.** —*n.* a short sleep; doze. —*v.i.* 1 take a short sleep; doze. 2 be off guard; be unprepared: *The test caught me napping.* [Old English *hnappian* to doze]

nap[2] (nap), *n., v.,* **napped, nap ping.** —*n.* the soft, short, woolly threads or hairs on the surface of cloth. —*v.t.* raise a nap on (a fabric). [< Middle Dutch *noppe*] **—nap′-less,** *adj.*

na palm (nā′päm′, nā′pälm′), *n.* 1 a chemical substance used to thicken gasoline. 2 the thickened or jellied gasoline, used for making incendiary bombs and in flame throwers. [< *na(phthenic)* and *palm(itic)* acids (the salts of these acids are used in its manufacture)]

nape (nāp, nap), *n.* back of the neck. [Middle English]

na per y (nā′pər ē), *n.* tablecloths, napkins, and doilies. [< Old French *naperie* < *nape* cloth. See NAPKIN.]

Naph ta li (naf′tə lī), *n.* in the Bible: 1 a son of Jacob. 2 the tribe of Israel descended from him.

naph tha (naf′thə, nap′thə), *n.* any of several highly volatile and flammable liquid mixtures of hydrocarbons distilled from petroleum, coal tar, etc., and used as fuel, as solvents (especially in dry cleaning), and in making varnishes. [< Greek, originally, a flammable liquid issuing from the earth; of Iranian origin]

naph tha lene (naf′thə lēn′, nap′thə lēn′), *n.* a white, crystalline hydrocarbon distilled from coal tar or petroleum, used in making moth balls, dyes, lubricants, disinfectants, etc. *Formula:* $C_{10}H_8$

naph tha lin (naf′thə lən, nap′thə lən), *n.* naphthalene.

naph the nic acid (naf thē′nik, naf-then′ik; nap thē′nik, nap then′ik), any of various oily liquids obtained from petroleum, used in certain soaps, paint driers, and fungicides.

naph thol (naf′thōl, naf′thol; nap′thōl, nap′thol), *n.* either of two isomeric compounds obtained from naphthalene, used in making dyes, as an antiseptic, etc. *Formula:* $C_{10}H_7OH$

nap kin (nap′kin), *n.* 1 piece of soft cloth or absorbent paper used at meals for protecting the clothing or for wiping the lips or fingers. 2 any similar piece, such as a baby's diaper or a small towel. [Middle English *napekyn,* diminutive of Old French *nape* cloth < Latin *mappa*]

Na ples (nā′pəlz), *n.* 1 seaport in SW Italy, on the Bay of Naples. 1,277,000. Also, ITALIAN **Napoli.** 2 **Bay of,** arm of the Mediterranean on the SW coast of Italy, noted for its beauty.

na po le on (nə pō′lē ən, nə pō′lyən), *n.* 1 a former French gold coin worth 20 francs, or about $3.86. 2 kind of pastry with a custard, cream, or jam filling. [< *Napoleon I*]

Na po le on I (nə pō′lē ən, nə pō′lyən), 1769-1821, Napoleon Bonaparte, French general, born in Corsica, who made himself emperor of France in 1804. He conquered a large part of Europe, but was defeated at Waterloo in 1815, and exiled to the island of St. Helena.

Napoleon II, 1811-1832, son of Napoleon I and Marie Louise. He never ruled France.

Napoleon III, 1808-1873, Louis Napoleon, president of France from 1848 to 1852 and emperor from 1852 to 1870. He was the nephew of Napoleon I.

Na po le on ic (nə pō′lē on′ik), *adj.* of, having to do with, or resembling Napoleon I.

Na po li (nä′pô lē), *n.* Italian name of **Naples.**

nappe (nap), *n.* either of the two equal parts of a conical surface which join at the vertex to form a cone. [< French, sheet]

nap py (nap′ē), *adj.,* **-pi er, -pi est.** having a nap; downy; shaggy.

nar cis sism (när′sə siz′əm, när sis′iz′əm), *n.* excessive love or admiration of oneself.

nar cis sist (när′sə sist, när sis′ist), *n.* person characterized by narcissism. —*adj.* narcissistic.

nar cis sis tic (när′sə sis′tik), *adj.* of or characterized by narcissism.

nar cis sus (när sis′əs), *n., pl.* **-cis sus es, -cis sus, -cis si** (-sis′ī). 1 any of a genus of spring plants of the amaryllis family which grow from bulbs and have yellow or white flowers and long, slender leaves. Jonquils and daffodils are narcissuses. 2 the flower of any of these plants. [< Latin]

Nar cis sus (när sis′əs), *n.* (in Greek myths) a beautiful youth who fell in love with his reflection in a spring. He pined away and was changed into the flower narcissus.

nar co sis (när kō′sis), *n.* condition of profound stupor and insensibility caused by the action or effect of narcotics or other chemicals.

nar cot ic (när kot′ik), *n.* 1 any drug that produces drowsiness, sleep, dullness, or an insensible condition, and lessens pain by dulling the nerves. Taken in excess narcotics, such as opium, cause systemic poisoning, delirium, paralysis, or even death. 2 anything that numbs, soothes, or dulls. —*adj.* 1 having the properties and effects of a narcotic. 2 of or having to do with narcotics or their use. [< Greek *narkōtikos* benumbing < *narkoun* benumb < *narkē* numbness] **—nar cot′i cal ly,** *adv.*

nar co tize (när′kə tīz), *v.t.,* **-tized, -tiz ing.** 1 subject to the action of a narcotic; stupefy. 2 to dull; deaden.

nard (närd), *n.* spikenard. [< Greek *nardos,* ultimately < Sanskrit *naladā*]

nar es (ner′ēz, nar′ēz), *n.pl.* of **naris.** nostrils. [< Latin]

nar ghi le or **nar gi le** (när′gə lē), *n.* an Oriental tobacco pipe in which the smoke is drawn through water. [ultimately < Persian *nārgīleh*]

nar is (ner′is, nar′is), *n.* sing. of **nares.**

nark (närk), BRITISH SLANG. —*n.* a police spy; informer. —*v.i.* turn spy or informer. [perhaps < Romany *nāk* nose]

Nar ra gan sett (nar′ə gan′sit), *n.* member of an American Indian tribe formerly living near Narragansett Bay.

Narragansett Bay, bay of the Atlantic, in E Rhode Island. 28 mi. long; 3½ mi. wide.

nar rate (nar′āt, na rāt′), *v.,* **-rat ed, -rat ing.** —*v.t.* give an account of; tell (a story, etc.) of; relate; recount: *narrate an incident.* —*v.i.* tell stories, etc. [< Latin *narratum* made known, told] **—nar′ra-tor,** *n.*

nar ra tion (na rā′shən), *n.* 1 act of telling. 2 the form of composition that relates an event or a story. Novels, short stories, histories, and biographies are forms of narration. 3 story or account. See **narrative** for synonym study.

nar ra tive (nar′ə tiv), *n.* 1 story or account; tale. See synonym study below. 2 narration; storytelling. —*adj.* that narrates: *a narrative poem.* **—nar′ra tive ly,** *adv.*

Syn. *n.* 1 **Narrative, narration** mean something told as a story or account. **Narrative** chiefly applies to what is told, emphasizing the events or experiences told like a story: *His trip through the Near East made an interesting narrative.* **Narration** chiefly applies to the act of narrating and emphasizes the way in which the story or account is put together and presented: *His narration of his trip was interesting.*

nar row (nar′ō), *adj.* 1 not wide; having little width; of less than the specified, understood, or usual width: *a narrow path.* 2 limited or small in extent, amount, range, scope, opportunity, etc.; restricted: *a narrow circle of friends.* 3 with little margin; close: *a narrow escape.* 4 lacking breadth of view or sympathy; not liberal; prejudiced: *a narrow point of view.* 5 careful; minute; detailed: *a narrow scrutiny.* 6 with barely enough to live on: *live in narrow circumstances.* 7 (in phonetics) tense. —*n.* 1 a narrow part, place, or thing. 2 **narrows,** *pl.* the narrow part of a river, strait, sound, valley, pass, etc. —*v.t., v.i.* make or become narrower; decrease in breadth, extent, etc.; limit. [Old English *nearu*] **—nar′row ly,** *adv.* **—nar′row-ness,** *n.*

nar row-gauge (nar′ō gāj′), *adj.* having railroad tracks less than 56½ inches apart.

nar row-mind ed (nar′ō mīn′did), *adj.* lacking breadth of view or sympathy; prejudiced. **—nar′row-mind′ed ly,** *adv.* **—nar′row-mind′ed ness,** *n.*

nar thex (när′theks), *n.* 1 portico of some early Christian churches. 2 a church vestibule that opens onto the nave. [< Late Greek *narthēx* < Greek, cane, small box, plant with a hollow stalk]

nar whal (när′hwəl, när′wəl), *n.* a large, spotted whale of the arctic seas. The male

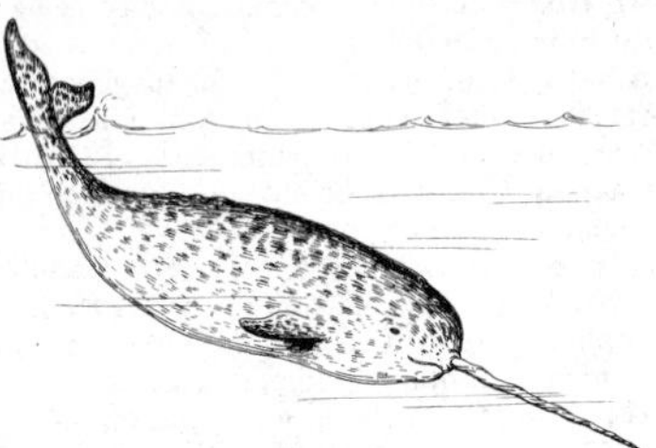

narwhal—up to 16 ft. long without tusk

hat, āge, fär; let, ēqual, tėrm;
it, īce; hot, ōpen, ôrder;
oil, out; cup, pu̇t, rüle;
ch, child; ng, long; sh, she;
th, thin; ᴛʜ, then; zh, measure;

ə represents *a* in about, *e* in taken, *i* in pencil, *o* in lemon, *u* in circus.

< = from, derived from, taken from.

has a long, slender, twisted tusk that extends forward and that developed from a tooth in the upper jaw. [< Scandinavian (Danish) *narhval* < *nār* corpse + *hval* whale]

nar y (ner′ē, nar′ē), *adv.* DIALECT. not: *nary a one.* [< *ne'er a*]

NAS A (nas′ə), *n.* National Aeronautics and Space Administration (an agency of the United States government established to direct and aid civilian research and development in aeronautics and aerospace technology).

na sal (nā′zəl), *adj.* 1 of, in, or from the nose: *nasal bones, a nasal voice.* 2 (in phonetics) requiring the nose passage to be open; spoken through the nose. *M, n,* and *ng* represent nasal sounds. —*n.* 1 a nasal bone or part. 2 (in phonetics) a nasal sound. [< Latin *nasus* nose] **—na′sal ly,** *adv.*

na sal i ty (nā zal′ə tē), *n.* nasal quality.

na sal ize (nā′zə līz), *v.t., v.i.,* **-ized, -iz ing.** utter or speak with a nasal sound. **—na′sal i za′tion,** *n.*

nas cence (nas′ns, nā′sns), *n.* a being nascent; birth; origin.

nas cen cy (nas′n sē, nā′sn sē), *n.* nascence.

nas cent (nas′nt, nā′snt), *adj.* in the process of coming into existence; just beginning to exist, grow, or develop. [< Latin *nascentem* being born]

Nash (nash), *n.* **Ogden,** 1902–1971, American poet.

Nash ville (nash′vil), *n.* capital of Tennessee, in the central part. 448,000.

na so pha ryn ge al (nā′zō fə rin′jē əl), *adj.* of or having to do with the part of the pharynx above the soft palate which is continuous with the nasal passages.

Nas sau (nas′ô), *n.* capital of the Bahama Islands, a seaport on New Providence island. 81,000.

Nas ser (nä′sər, nas′ər), *n.* **Gamal Abdel,** 1918–1970, Egyptian political leader, president of the United Arab Republic from 1958 to 1970.

na stur tium (nə stėr′shəm), *n.* 1 any of a genus of garden plants with yellow, orange, or red flowers, and sharp-tasting seeds and leaves. 2 the flower of any of these plants. [< Latin]

nas ty (nas′tē), *adj.,* **-ti er, -ti est.** 1 disgustingly dirty; foul; filthy: *a nasty room.* 2 morally filthy; indecent; vile: *a nasty mind.* 3 very unpleasant; disagreeable: *nasty weather, a nasty remark.* 4 rather serious; bad: *a nasty problem.* [Middle English] **—nas′ti ly,** *adv.* **—nas′ti ness.** *n.*

nat., 1 national. 2 native. 3 natural.

na tal (nā′tl), *adj.* 1 of or having to do with one's birth: *one's natal day. The horoscope was based on my natal hour.* 2 native: *one's natal land.* [< Latin *natalis,* ultimately < *nasci* be born. Doublet of NOEL.]

Na tal (nə tal′, nə täl′), *n.* province of the Republic of South Africa, on the E coast.

na tal i ty (nā tal′ə tē), *n.* birth rate.

na ta tion (nā tā′shən), *n.* act or art of swimming. [< Latin *natationem* < *natare* to swim]

na ta to ri al (nā′tə tôr′ē əl, nā′tə tōr′ē əl) *adj.* 1 having to do with swimming; adapted for swimming. 2 characterized by swimming.

na ta to ri um (nā′tə tôr′ē əm, nā′tə tōr′ē-əm), *n., pl.* **-to ri ums, -to ri a** (-tôr′ē ə, -tōr′ē ə). a swimming pool, especially one in a gymnasium or other building.

na ta to ry (nā′tə tôr′ē, nā′tə tōr′ē), *adj.* natatorial.

nathe less (nāth′lis, nath′lis), *adv.* ARCHAIC. nevertheless. [Old English *nā thȳ lǣs* not the less]

na tion (nā′shən), *n.* 1 a people occupying the same country, under the same government, and usually speaking the same language. See **people** for synonym study. 2 a sovereign state; country: *the nations of the West.* 3 a people, race, or tribe; those having the same descent, language, and history: *the Scottish nation, the Jewish nation.* 4 a North American Indian tribe, especially one belonging to a confederacy: *the Sioux nation.* [< Latin *nationem* stock, race, ultimately < *nasci* be born]

Na tion (nā′shən), *n.* **Carry Amelia,** 1846–1911, American reformer, active in the temperance movement.

na tion al (nash′ə nəl), *adj.* of a nation; belonging to a whole nation. —*n.* 1 citizen of a nation. 2 person who owes allegiance to a nation.

national anthem, the official patriotic song or hymn of a nation, sung or played on public occasions.

national bank, bank that has a charter from the national government. In the United States, the national banks are members of the Federal Reserve System.

National Guard, the reserve militia of each state of the United States, supported in part by the federal government. The National Guard may be ordered to serve either the state or the federal government in time of emergency.

national income, the total net income of a country for a year, computed as the total of money received as income or taxable revenue by individuals, business organizations, and publicly-owned undertakings in the country.

na tion al ism (nash′ə nə liz′əm), *n.* 1 patriotic feelings or efforts. 2 desire and plans for national independence.

na tion al ist (nash′ə nə list), *n.* person who believes in nationalism; upholder of nationalism. —*adj.* 1 nationalistic. 2 **Nationalist,** of or having to do with Nationalist China.

Nationalist China, the non-Communist Republic of China.

na tion al is tic (nash′ə nə lis′tik), *adj.* of nationalism or nationalists. **—na′tion-al is′ti cal ly,** *adv.*

na tion al i ty (nash′ə nal′ə tē), *n., pl.* **-ties.** 1 nation (def. 1). 2 condition of belonging to a nation, especially as a citizen through birth or naturalization; status as a national: *Her nationality is French.* 3 condition of being a nation. 4 national quality or character.

na tion al ize (nash′ə nə līz), *v.t.,* **-ized, -iz ing.** 1 make national. 2 bring (land, industries, railroads, etc.) under the control or ownership of a nation. 3 make into a nation. **—na′tion al i za′tion,** *n.* **—na′tion-al iz′er,** *n.*

na tion al ly (nash′ə nə lē), *adv.* 1 in a national manner; as a nation. 2 throughout the nation.

national park, land kept by the national government for people to enjoy because of its beautiful scenery, historical interest, etc.

National Security Council, U.S. board of advisers to the President on military, economic, and diplomatic affairs.

National Socialism, Nazism.

National Socialist, Nazi.

National Socialist Party, a fascist political party that controlled Germany from 1933 to 1945 under the leadership of Adolf Hitler; the Nazi party.

na tion hood (nā′shən hu̇d), *n.* condition of being a nation.

Nation of Islam, an American Negro organization that follows Moslem teachings and advocates complete segregation between Negroes and whites.

na tion wide (nā′shən wīd′), *adj.* extending throughout the nation: *a nationwide election.*

na tive (nā′tiv), *n.* 1 person born in a certain place or country. 2 person who lives in a place, as opposed to visitors or foreigners. 3 one of the original inhabitants of a place or country as contrasted with conquerors, settlers, etc. 4 member of a less civilized people. 5 animal or plant that originated in a place.
—*adj.* 1 born in a certain place or country: *native Texans.* 2 belonging to one because of his birth: *my native land.* 3 belonging to one because of his country or the nation to which he belongs: *French is her native language.* 4 born in a person; natural: *native ability, native courtesy.* See synonym study below. 5 of or having to do with the original inhabitants of a place, especially those of a less civilized people: *native customs, native huts.* 6 **go native,** live as the less civilized natives do. 7 originating, grown, or produced in a certain place: *Tobacco is native to America.* 8 found pure in nature: *native copper.* 9 found in nature; not produced: *Native salt is refined for use.*
[< Latin *nativus* innate, ultimately < *nasci* be born. Doublet of NAÏVE.] **—na′tive ly,** *adv.* **—na′tive ness,** *n.*

Syn. *adj.* 4 **Native, natural** mean belonging to someone or something by nature. **Native** emphasizes the idea of being born in a person, as contrasted with being acquired: *He has native artistic talent.* **Natural** emphasizes being part of the nature or essential character of a person, animal, or thing: *Monkeys have natural agility.*

na tive-born (nā′tiv bôrn′), *adj.* born in the place or country indicated: *a native-born American.*

na tiv ism (nā′tə viz′əm), *n.* 1 a feeling or attitude of superiority shown by the natives of a country toward foreigners. 2 the policy of advancing the interests of native inhabitants rather than those of immigrants.

na tiv i ty (nə tiv′ə tē, nā tiv′ə tē), *n., pl.* **-ties.** 1 a being born; birth. 2 a person's horoscope at the time of birth. 3 **the Nativity, a** the birth of Christ. **b** a picture of this, usually with the animals grouped about the manger. **c** Christmas.

natl., national.

NA TO (nā′tō), *n.* North Atlantic Treaty Organization (an alliance of fourteen Western nations providing for joint military cooperation, formed in 1949).

nat ter (nat′ər), *v.i.* 1 grumble; fret. 2 chatter; prate. —*n.* idle chatter or prating. [origin uncertain]

nat ty (nat′ē), *adj.*, **-ti er, -ti est.** neatly smart in dress or appearance; trim and tidy. [origin uncertain] **—nat′ti ly,** *adv.* **—nat′ti ness,** *n.*

nat ur al (nach′ər əl), *adj.* 1 produced by nature; based on some state of things in nature: *the natural beauty of flowers.* 2 not artificial: *the natural color of hair. Coal and oil are natural products.* 3 born in one; instinctive; inborn: *natural intelligence.* See **native** for synonym study. 4 coming in the ordinary course of events; normal: *die a natural death.* 5 in accordance with the nature of things or the circumstances of the case: *a natural response.* 6 instinctively felt to be right and fair: *natural rights.* 7 like nature; true to nature: *The picture looked natural.* 8 free from affectation or restraint; easy: *a natural manner.* 9 of, having to do with, or based on nature: *natural religion.* 10 by birth merely, and not legally recognized; illegitimate: *a natural son.* 11 in music: **a** neither sharp nor flat; without sharps and flats. **b** neither sharped nor flatted: *C natural.* **c** having the pitch affected by the natural sign.
—*n.* 1 that which is natural. 2 in music: **a** a natural note or tone. **b** sign (♮) used to cancel the effect of a preceding sharp or flat. **c** a white key on a piano. 3 a half-witted person. 4 INFORMAL. an expert by nature: *a natural on the saxophone.* 5 INFORMAL. a sure success. **—nat′ur al ness,** *n.*

nat ur al-born (nach′ər əl bôrn′), *adj.* 1 that is so by nature; born so: *a natural-born boxer, a natural-born fool.* 2 native in a country; not alien: *a natural-born citizen.*

natural gas, a combustible gas formed naturally in the earth, consisting primarily of methane. It is used as a fuel.

natural history, the study of animals, plants, minerals, and other things in nature.

nat ur al ism (nach′ər ə liz′əm), *n.* 1 (in art and literature) close adherence to nature and reality. 2 principles and methods of a group of writers of the late 1800's and early 1900's whose realism includes all the details however repulsive. 3 action, thought, or belief based on natural instincts. 4 (in philosophy) a view of the world that takes account only of natural elements and forces, excluding the supernatural or spiritual. 5 doctrine that all religious truth is derived from the study of nature.

nat ur al ist (nach′ər ə list), *n.* 1 person who makes a study of animals and plants, especially in their native habitats; zoologist, botanist, etc. 2 writer or artist who practices or advocates naturalism.

nat ur al is tic (nach′ər ə lis′tik), *adj.* 1 of natural history or naturalists. 2 of naturalism, especially in art or literature. 3 of or in accordance with nature. **—nat′ur al is′ti cal ly,** *adv.*

nat ur al ize (nach′ər ə līz), *v.*, **-ized, -iz ing.** —*v.t.* 1 admit (a foreigner) to citizenship. 2 adopt (a foreign word, custom, etc.): *"Chauffeur" is a French word that has been naturalized in English.* 3 (of animals or plants) introduce and make at home in another country: *The English oak has been naturalized in parts of Massachusetts.* 4 make natural; free from conventional characteristics. 5 regard or explain as natural rather than supernatural. —*v.i.* 1 become like a native. 2 become a citizen of another country. **—nat′ur al i za′tion,** *n.*

natural law, law based upon nature or the natural tendency of human beings to exercise right reason in dealings with others.

natural logarithm, logarithm which has as a base the irrational number *e*, whose value is approximately equal to 2.71828.

nat ur al ly (nach′ər ə lē), *adv.* 1 in a natural way: *speak naturally.* 2 without special teaching or training; by nature: *a naturally obedient child.* 3 as might be expected; of course: *She offered me some candy; naturally, I took it.*

natural number, a positive integer. The natural numbers are 1, 2, 3, 4, etc.

natural philosophy, 1 physics. 2 natural science.

natural resources, materials supplied by nature. Minerals, timber, land, and water power are natural resources.

natural science, science dealing with the objects, phenomena, or laws of nature. Biology, geology, physics, and chemistry are natural sciences.

natural selection, process in nature by which animals and plants best adapted to their environment tend to survive.

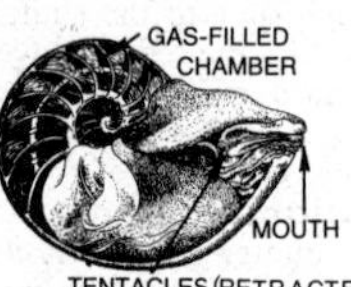

pearly (or chambered) nautilus
shell to 6 in. in diameter

na ture (nā′chər), *n.* 1 all things except those made by man; the world: *the wonders of nature.* 2 the sum total of the forces at work throughout the universe: *the laws of nature.* 3 **Nature,** the personification of all natural facts and forces: *Who can paint like Nature?* 4 the instincts or inherent tendencies directing conduct; temperament: *It is against a mother's nature to hurt her child.* 5 reality: *true to nature.* 6 a primitive, wild condition; condition of human beings before social organization: *The hermit lived in a state of nature.* 7 what a thing really is; quality; character: *It is the nature of robins to fly and build nests.* 8 a particular sort; kind: *books of a scientific nature.* 9 physical being; vital powers: *food sufficient to sustain nature.* 10 person of a particular character: *She is a gentle nature.* 11 a natural desire or function, as that of sex or elimination: *the demands of nature.* 12 **by nature,** because of the essential character of the person or thing: *She was liberal by nature.* 13 **of the nature of** or **in the nature of,** having the nature of; being a kind of; being. [< Latin *natura* birth, character, ultimately < *nasci* be born. See NATIVE.]

nature study, study of animals, plants, and other things and events in nature.

naught (nôt), *n.* 1 nothing. 2 zero; 0. Also, **nought.** [Old English *nāwiht* < *nā* no + *wiht* thing]

naugh ty (nô′tē), *adj.*, **-ti er, -ti est.** 1 not obedient; bad. 2 somewhat improper. [Middle English < *naught*] **—naugh′ti ly,** *adv.* **—naugh′ti ness,** *n.*

nau pli us (nô′plē əs), *n.*, *pl.* **-pli i** (-plē ī). the first stage in development of certain crustaceans, as the shrimp, after leaving the egg; a larval form with an unsegmented body, three pairs of appendages, and a single median eye. [< Latin, kind of shellfish]

Na u ru (nä ü′rü), *n.* island country in the S Pacific, northeast of the Solomon Islands; a member of the Commonwealth of Nations. 7000 pop.; 8 sq. mi.

nau se a (nô′zē ə, nô′shə, nô′zhə), *n.* 1 the feeling a person has when about to vomit. 2 seasickness. 3 extreme disgust; loathing. [< Greek *nausia* seasickness < *naus* ship. Doublet of NOISE.]

nau se ate (nô′zē āt, nô′shē āt, nô′zhē āt), *v.*, **-at ed, -at ing.** —*v.t.* 1 cause nausea in; make sick. 2 cause to feel loathing. —*v.i.* feel nausea; become sick. **—nau′se at′ing ly,** *adv.*

nau seous (nô′shəs, nô′zē əs, nô′zhəs), *adj.* 1 causing nausea; sickening. 2 disgusting; loathsome. 3 feeling nausea; nauseated. **—nau′seous ly,** *adv.* **—nau′seous ness,** *n.*

naut., nautical

nautch (nôch), *n.* (in India) an entertainment consisting of dancing by professional dancing girls. [< Hindustani *nāch*]

nau ti cal (nô′tə kəl), *adj.* of or having to do with ships, sailors, or navigation; maritime. [< Greek *nautikos* < *nautes* sailor < *naus* ship] **—nau′ti cal ly,** *adv.*

nautical mile, unit of distance equal to 6076.11549 feet; geographical mile; sea mile.

nau ti lus (nô′tl əs), *n.*, *pl.* **-lus es, -li** (-lī). either of two kinds of cephalopod. The **pearly nautilus** or **chambered nautilus** has a spiral shell divided into many compartments which have a pearly lining. The **paper nautilus** resembles the octopus and has a thin shell. [< Greek *nautilos,* originally, sailor < *naus* ship]

nav., 1 naval. 2 navigation.

Nav a ho (nav′ə hō), *n.*, *pl.* **-ho, -hos,** or **-hoes** for 1. 1 member of a tribe of American Indians living in New Mexico, Arizona, and Utah. The Navahos are noted for their skill in weaving blankets and rugs with bright patterns. 2 language of this tribe.

Nav a jo (nav′ə hō), *n.*, *pl.* **-jo, -jos,** or **-joes.** Navaho.

na val (nā′vəl), *adj.* 1 of or for warships or the navy: *a naval officer, naval supplies.* 2 having a navy: *the naval powers.* **—na′val ly,** *adv.*

naval stores, rosin, turpentine, etc., as used in building and repairing wooden ships.

Na varre (nə vär′), *n.* former kingdom including parts of SW France and N Spain.

nave[1] (nāv), *n.* the main part of a church or cathedral between the side aisles. The nave extends from the main entrance to the transepts. See **apse** for diagram. [< Medieval Latin *navis* < Latin, ship]

nave[2] (nāv), *n.* hub or central part of a wheel. [Old English *nafu*]

na vel (nā′vəl), *n.* 1 the mark or scar in the middle of the surface of the abdomen, where the umbilical cord was attached before birth; umbilicus. 2 center; middle. [Old English *nafela*]

navel orange, a seedless orange with a small growth at one end shaped somewhat like a navel and enclosing a small secondary fruit.

nav i ga bil i ty (nav′ə gə bil′ə tē), *n.* condition of being navigable.

nav i ga ble (nav′ə gə bəl), *adj.* 1 that ships can travel on or through. 2 seaworthy. 3 that can be steered. **—nav′i ga ble ness,** *n.* **—nav′i ga bly,** *adv.*

hat, āge, fär; let, ēqual, tėrm;
it, īce; hot, ōpen, ôrder;
oil, out; cup, pu̇t, rüle;
ch, child; ng, long; sh, she;
th, thin; ꟻH, then; zh, measure;

ə represents *a* in about, *e* in taken, *i* in pencil, *o* in lemon, *u* in circus.

< = from, derived from, taken from.

nav i gate (nav′ə gāt), *v.*; **-gat ed, -gat ing.** —*v.t.* 1 sail, manage, or steer (a ship, airplane, etc.). 2 sail on or over (a sea or river). 3 convey (goods) by water. 4 sail through (the air) in an aircraft, etc. 5 manage to get up, over, past, or through; negotiate: *navigate ramps in a garage, navigate a curving flight of stairs.* 6 guide, steer, or make (one's way). —*v.i.* 1 travel by water; sail. 2 manage a ship or aircraft. 3 move, walk, or swim about: *I can scarcely navigate today. Turtles can navigate from one part of the ocean to another.* 4 guide, steer, or make one's way. [< Latin *navigatum* navigated < *navis* ship + *agere* to drive]

nav i ga tion (nav′ə gā′shən), *n.* 1 act or process of navigating. 2 art or science of finding a ship's or aircraft's position and course.

nav i ga tion al (nav′ə gā′shə nəl), *adj.* of, having to do with, or used in navigation.

nav i ga tor (nav′ə gā′tər), *n.* 1 person who sails the seas. 2 person who has charge of the navigating of a ship or aircraft or who is skilled in navigating. 3 explorer of the seas.

nav vy (nav′ē), *n., pl.* **-vies.** BRITISH. an unskilled laborer who works on canals, railways, etc. [short for *navigator* navvy]

na vy (nā′vē), *n., pl.* **-vies.** 1 Often, **Navy.** the branch of a nation's armed forces which includes its ships of war, the officers and men who man them, and the department that manages them. 2 officers and men of the navy. 3 fleet of ships. 4 a dark blue; navy blue. [< Old French *navie,* ultimately < Latin *navis* ship]

navy bean, a small, common, white bean, dried for use as food.

navy blue, a dark blue.

navy yard, a government dockyard where naval vessels are built, repaired, and fitted out.

na wab (nə wôb′), *n.* 1 a native ruler in India under the Mogul empire; nabob. 2 a princely title formerly given to important Moslems in India. 3 nabob (def. 2). [< Hindustani *nawwāb* < Arabic *nuwwāb,* plural of *nā'ib* deputy]

nay (nā), *adv.* 1 ARCHAIC. no. 2 not only that, but also: *We are willing, nay, eager to go.* —*n.* 1 a denial or refusal; no. 2 a negative vote or voter. [< Scandinavian (Old Icelandic) *nei* < *ne* not + *ei* ever]

nay say (nā′sā′), *v.t., v.i.* say nay (to); deny; oppose; vote in the negative. **—nay′-say′er,** *n.*

Naz a rene (naz′ə rēn′, naz′ə rēn′), *n.* 1 native or inhabitant of Nazareth. 2 **the Nazarene,** Jesus. 3 an early Christian. 4 member of the Church of the Nazarene, a protestant denomination following the early teachings of Methodism. —*adj.* of or having to do with the Nazarenes or with Nazareth.

Naz ar eth (naz′ər əth), *n.* ancient town in N Israel. Jesus lived there during His early youth. 29,000.

Naz a rite (naz′ə rīt′), *n.* (among the ancient Hebrews) a Jew who had taken certain strict religious vows.

Na zi (nä′tsē, nat′sē), *n.* 1 member or supporter of the National Socialist Party in Germany led by Adolf Hitler; an advocate of Nazism; a German fascist. 2 Often, **nazi.** any fascist. —*adj.* of or having to do with the Nazis. [< German, short for *Na(tional-so)zi(alist)* National Socialist]

na zi fy or **Na zi fy** (nä′tsə fī, nat′sə fī), *v.t.,* **-fied, -fy ing.** 1 place under control of the Nazis. 2 indoctrinate with Nazi views. **—na′zi fi ca′tion, Na′zi fi ca′tion,** *n.*

Na zi ism (nä′tsē iz′əm, nat′sē iz′əm), *n.* Nazism.

Na zism (nä′tsiz′əm, nat′siz′əm), *n.* the doctrines and practices of the Nazis, including totalitarian government, state control of industry, opposition to communism, and anti-Semitism.

Nb, niobium.

N.B., 1 New Brunswick. 2 Also, **n.b.** note well; observe carefully [for Latin *nota bene*].

NBC, National Broadcasting Company.

NBS, National Bureau of Standards.

N.C., North Carolina.

NCO or **N.C.O.,** noncommissioned officer.

Nd, neodymium.

n.d., no date; not dated.

N. Dak. or **N.D.,** North Dakota.

Ne, neon.

NE, N.E., or **n.e.** 1 northeast. 2 northeastern.

N.E., New England.

N.E.A., National Education Association.

Ne an der thal (nē an′dər täl, nē an′dər-thôl), *adj.* 1 of, having to do with, or belonging to a prehistoric people that lived in caves in Europe, North Africa, and western and central Asia in the early Stone Age. The **Neanderthal man** had a large, heavy skull and low forehead, a broad, flat nose, and a heavy lower jaw with teeth intermediate in shape between those of modern man and the apes. 2 like the Neanderthal man. 3 Often, **neanderthal.** reactionary, especially in politics: *the Neanderthal wing of the Republican Party.* —*n.* Often, **neanderthal.** a reactionary: *a political Neanderthal.* [< *Neanderthal,* the Neander Gorge in West Germany, where the fossils of Neanderthal man were first found]

Ne an der thal er (nē an′dər tä′lər, nē-an′dər thô′lər), *n.* a Neanderthal man.

neap (nēp), *adj.* of, having to do with, or being a neap tide. —*n.* neap tide. [Old English *nēp*]

Ne a pol i tan (nē′ə pol′ə tən), *adj.* 1 of or having to do with Naples. 2 having layers of different colors and flavors: *Neapolitan ice cream.* —*n.* native or inhabitant of Naples.

neap tide, tide that occurs when the difference in height between high and low tide is least; lowest level of high tide. Neap tide comes twice a month, in the first and third quarters of the moon.

near (nir), *adv.* 1 to, at, or within a short distance; not far; close: *The holiday season is drawing near.* 2 close in relation; closely: *tribes near allied.* 3 INFORMAL. all but; almost; nearly: *The war lasted near a year.* 4 **come near doing,** almost do. 5 **near at hand, a** within easy reach. **b** not far in the future.

—*adj.* 1 close by; not distant; less distant: *The post office is quite near.* 2 close in feeling; intimate; familiar: *a near friend.* 3 closely related: *a near relative.* 4 resembling closely: *near silk.* 5 approximating an original: *a near translation.* 6 left: *The near horse and the off horse make a team.* 7 short; direct: *Go by the nearest route.* 8 stingy. 9 by a close margin; narrow: *a near escape.*

—*prep.* close to in space, time, condition, etc.: *Our house is near the river.*

—*v.t., v.i.* come or draw near to; approach: *The ship neared the land.*

[Old English *nēar* nearer, comparative of *nēah* nigh, near] **—near′ness,** *n.*

near by (nir′bī′), *adj., adv.* close at hand, near.

Near East, the countries of SW Asia, sometimes including the Balkan States and Egypt. **—Near Eastern.**

near ly (nir′lē), *adv.* 1 almost: *I nearly missed the train.* 2 closely: *It will cost too much as nearly as I can figure it.*

near sight ed (nir′sī′tid), *adj.* seeing distinctly at a short distance only, because the parallel light rays entering the eye come to a focus in front of, rather than on, the retina; not able to see far; myopic. **—near′sight′-ed ly,** *adv.* **—near′sight′ed ness,** *n.*

neat[1] (nēt), *adj.* 1 clean and in order: *a neat desk.* See synonym study below. 2 able and willing to keep things in order: *a neat child.* 3 well-formed; in proportion: *a neat design.* 4 skillful; clever: *a neat trick.* 5 without anything mixed in it; straight: *He drinks his brandy neat.* 6 SLANG. very pleasing; fine: *a neat party.* 7 clear; net: *a neat profit.* [< Middle French *net* < Latin *nitidus* gleaming < *nitere* to shine] **—neat′ly,** *adv.* **—neat′ness,** *n.*

Syn. 1 **Neat, tidy, trim** mean in good order. **Neat** suggests cleanness or the absence of anything messy: *Her clothes are always neat.* **Tidy** suggests orderliness: *She keeps her room tidy.* **Trim** suggests proportion, pleasing compactness, and clean lines: *That is a trim sailboat.*

neat[2] (nēt), *n. pl. or sing.* ARCHAIC. 1 cattle; oxen. 2 ox, cow, or heifer. [Old English *nēat*]

neat en (nēt′n), *v.t.* put in order; clean; tidy up.

neath or **'neath** (nēth, nēꟻH), *prep.* ARCHAIC. beneath.

neat herd (nēt′hėrd′), *n.* ARCHAIC. cowherd.

neat's-foot oil (nēts′fu̇t′), an oil obtained by boiling the feet and shinbones of cattle, used to soften leather.

neb (neb), *n.* SCOTTISH. 1 bill; beak. 2 a person's mouth or nose. 3 an animal's snout. 4 tip of anything; nib. [Old English *nebb*]

Ne bo (nē′bō), *n.* **Mount,** (in the Bible) the mountain near the Dead Sea from which Moses looked down upon Canaan, the Promised Land.

Nebr. or **Neb.,** Nebraska.

Ne bras ka (nə bras′kə), *n.* one of the midwestern states of the United States. 1,483,000 pop.; 77,200 sq. mi. *Capital:* Lincoln. *Abbrev.:* Nebr. or Neb. **—Ne-bras′kan,** *adj., n.*

Neb u chad nez zar II (neb′yə kəd-nez′ər, neb′ə kəd nez′ər), died 562 B.C., king of Babylon from 605 to 562 B.C. He twice captured Jerusalem and destroyed it in 586 B.C.

neb u la (neb′yə lə), *n., pl.* **-lae** (-lē′), **-las.** a cloudlike cluster of stars or a hazy mass of dust particles and gases which occurs in interstellar space and which may be either dark or illuminated by surrounding stars. **Galactic nebulae** are clouds of gas and dust particles within our galaxy. **Extragalactic nebulae** are galaxies outside the Milky Way. [< Latin, mist, cloud]

neb u lar (neb′yə lər), *adj.* of or having to do with a nebula or nebulae.

nebular hypothesis, (in astronomy) a theory that the solar system developed from the cooling and contracting of a hot, rotating nebula.

neb u los i ty (neb′yə los′ə tē), *n., pl.* **-ties.** 1 nebulous quality or condition. 2 cloudlike matter; nebula.

neb u lous (neb′yə ləs), *adj.* 1 hazy; vague; confused. 2 cloudlike. 3 of or like a nebula or nebulae. **—neb′u lous ly,** *adv.* **—neb′u lous ness,** *n.*

nec es sar i ly (nes′ə ser′ə lē), *adv.* 1 because of necessity. 2 as a necessary result; inevitably.

nec es sar y (nes′ə ser′ē), *adj., n., pl.* **-sar ies.** *—adj.* 1 that cannot be done without; indispensable; essential: *I prepared all things necessary for my journey.* See synonym study below. 2 that must be, be had, or be done; inevitable; required; indispensable: *Death is a necessary end.* 3 compelled by another or others; compulsory. 4 (in logic) that cannot be denied or avoided: *a necessary truth, a necessary inference.* *—n.* thing impossible to do without; essential; necessity: *Food, clothing, and shelter are necessaries of human life.* [< Latin *necessarius* < *necesse* unavoidable, probably < *ne-* not + *cedere* withdraw]

Syn. *adj.* 1 **Necessary, indispensable, essential** mean needed or required. **Necessary** applies to whatever is needed but not absolutely required: *Work is a necessary part of life.* **Indispensable** implies that, without it, the intended result or purpose cannot be achieved: *Studying is an indispensable part of education.* **Essential** implies that the existence or proper functioning of something depends upon it: *Food is essential to survival.*

ne ces si tate (nə ses′ə tāt), *v.t.,* **-tat ed, -tat ing.** 1 make necessary; require; demand: *His broken leg necessitated an operation.* 2 compel, oblige, or force: *What necessitated you to take this action?* **—ne ces′si ta′tion,** *n.*

ne ces si tous (nə ses′ə təs), *adj.* very poor; needy: *a necessitous family.* **—ne ces′si tous ly,** *adv.* **—ne ces′si tous ness,** *n.*

ne ces si ty (nə ses′ə tē), *n., pl.* **-ties.** 1 fact of being necessary; extreme need: *the necessity of eating.* See **need** for synonym study. 2 quality or condition of being necessary. 3 that which cannot be done without; indispensable thing: *Water is a necessity.* 4 that which forces one to act in a certain way: *Necessity sometimes drives people to do disagreeable things.* 5 **of necessity,** because it must be. 6 that which is inevitable: *Night follows day as a necessity.* 7 need; poverty: *a family in great necessity.*

➔ **Necessity.** The idiom is *necessity of* or *for* doing something and, less formally, *to* do something: *Most athletes can see the necessity of* (or *for*) *keeping in top physical condition. Most musicians can see the necessity to practice daily.*

neck (nek), *n.* 1 the part of the body that connects the head with the shoulders. 2 the part of a garment that fits the neck: *the neck of a shirt.* 3 any narrow part like a neck. 4 a narrow strip of land. 5 the slender part of a bottle, flask, retort, or other container. 6 the lowest part of the capital of a column. 7 part of a tooth between the crown and the root. 8 (in horse racing) the length of the neck of a horse or other animal as a measure.

neck and neck, a abreast. **b** running equal or even in a race or contest.

risk one's neck, put oneself in a dangerous position.

stick one's neck out, INFORMAL. put oneself in a dangerous or vulnerable position by foolish or zealous action.

up to one's neck, INFORMAL. thoroughly involved.

—v.i. SLANG. kiss and caress; embrace; hug. [Old English *hnecca*]

neck band (nek′band′), *n.* 1 band worn around the neck. 2 part of a shirt to which the collar is attached.

neck er chief (nek′ər chif), *n.* cloth worn round the neck.

neck lace (nek′lis), *n.* string of jewels, gold, silver, beads, etc., worn around the neck as an ornament.

neck line (nek′līn′), *n.* the line around the neck where a garment ends.

neck piece (nek′pēs′), *n.* a fur scarf.

neck tie (nek′tī′), *n.* a narrow band or a tie worn around the neck and tied in front.

neck wear (nek′wer′, nek′war′), *n.* collars, ties, and other articles that are worn around the neck.

nec ro log i cal (nek′rə loj′ə kəl), *adj.* having to do with necrology.

ne crol o gist (ne krol′ə jist), *n.* person who writes or prepares obituaries.

ne crol o gy (ne krol′ə jē), *n., pl.* **-gies.** 1 list of persons who have died. 2 notice of a person's death; obituary. [< Greek *nekros* dead body + English *-logy*]

nec ro man cer (nek′rə man′sər), *n.* 1 person who is supposed to foretell the future by communicating with the dead. 2 magician; sorcerer.

nec ro man cy (nek′rə man′sē), *n.* 1 a foretelling of the future by communicating with the dead. 2 magic; sorcery. [< Greek *nekromanteia* < *nekros* dead body + *manteia* divination]

nec ro man tic (nek′rə man′tik), *adj.* of or having to do with necromancy.

ne crop o lis (ne krop′ə lis), *n.* cemetery, usually a large one. [< Greek *nekropolis* < *nekros* dead body + *polis* city]

nec rop sy (nek′rop sē), *n., pl.* **-sies.** autopsy.

ne cro sis (ne krō′sis), *n., pl.* **-ses** (-sēz′). death (of a part of an animal or plant) from injury or disease; mortification; gangrene.

ne crot ic (ne krot′ik), *adj.* of, characterized by, or showing necrosis.

nec tar (nek′tər), *n.* 1 (in Greek and Roman myths) the drink of the gods. 2 any delicious drink. 3 a sweet liquid found in many flowers. Bees gather nectar and make it into honey. [< Latin < Greek *nektar*] **—nec′tar like′,** *adj.*

nec tar e ous (nek ter′ē əs, nek tar′ē əs), *adj.* nectarous.

nec ta rine (nek′tə rēn′, nek′tə rēn′), *n.* 1 kind of peach having no down on its skin. 2 tree it grows on.

nec tar ous (nek′tər əs), *adj.* of or like nectar; delicious; nectareous.

nec tar y (nek′tər ē), *n., pl.* **-tar ies.** the gland of a flower or plant that secretes nectar.

NED or **N.E.D.,** New English Dictionary (Oxford English Dictionary).

nee or **née** (nā, nē), *adj.* born. [< French *née*]

➔ **Nee** is placed after the name of a married woman to show her maiden name: *Mrs. Smith, nee Adams.* It is sometimes italicized.

need (nēd), *v.t.* be in want of; be unable to do without; require; lack: *He needs money. I need a new hat. Plants need water.* See **lack** for synonym study. *—v.i.* 1 be in want: *Give to those that need.* 2 be necessary: *The rope cuts his hands more than needs.* 3 have to; ought to; must; should: *You need not go.* *—n.* 1 lack of a useful or desired thing; want: *His writing showed need of grammar.* See synonym study below. 2 a useful or desired thing that is lacking: *In the jungle their need was fresh water.* 3 necessity; requirement: *There is no real need to hurry.* 4 situation or time of difficulty: *a friend in need.* 5 extreme poverty. 6 **have need to,** must; should; have to. 7 **if need be,** if it has to be; if necessary. [Old English *nēd, nīed* a need]

Syn. *n.* 1 **Need, necessity** mean lack of something required or desired. **Need** suggests a lack of something required for one's welfare or success or of something useful or satisfying: *She is in need of a rest.* **Necessity** suggests an urgent need, but implies a more objective attitude and has less emotional appeal than *need* sometimes does: *She realizes the necessity of getting enough sleep.*

need ful (nēd′fəl), *adj.* needed; necessary. **—need′ful ly,** *adv.* **—need′ful ness,** *n.*

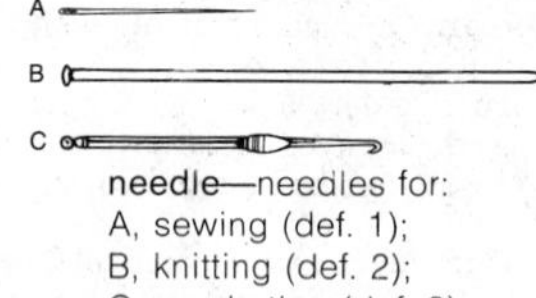

needle—needles for:
A, sewing (def. 1);
B, knitting (def. 2);
C, crocheting (def. 3)

nee dle (nē′dl), *n., v.,* **-dled, -dling.** *—n.* 1 a very slender tool, pointed at one end and with a hole or eye to pass a thread through, used in sewing. 2 a slender rod used in knitting. 3 rod with a hook at one end used in crocheting, etc. 4 a thin steel pointer on a compass, electrical machinery, or some gauges, such as a speedometer, altimeter, etc. 5 end of a syringe or tube, used for injecting something below the skin, withdrawing blood, etc. 6 INFORMAL. injection, as of a drug. 7 instrument somewhat like a needle, used in etching and engraving. 8 the small, pointed piece of metal, sapphire, diamond, etc., in a phonograph which receives and transmits the vibrations from the record. 9 the needle-shaped leaf of a fir tree, pine tree, etc. 10 any of various small, slender objects resembling a needle in sharpness: *needles of broken glass.* 11 a slender needle-shaped rod that controls the opening of a valve. 12 pillar; obelisk: *Cleopatra's needle.* 13 INFORMAL. vexation; prod or goad. 14 **a needle in a haystack,** something extremely difficult or impossible to find or reach. 15 **on the needle,** INFORMAL. addicted to or using drugs: *criminals on the needle. Two days later he was back on the needle.*

—v.t. 1 INFORMAL. vex by repeated sharp prods, gibes, etc.; goad, incite, or annoy. 2 sew or pierce with a needle. 3 INFORMAL. give an injection, as of a drug, to.

[Old English *nǣdl*] **—nee′dle like′,** *adj.* **—nee′dler,** *n.*

nee dle point (nē′dl point′), *n.* 1 embroidery made on a canvas cloth, usually with woolen yarn, used to cover chairs, footstools, etc. 2 lace made entirely with a needle instead of a bobbin. *—adj.* of or having to do with needlepoint.

need less (nēd′lis), *adj.* not needed; unnecessary. **—need′less ly,** *adv.* **—need′less ness,** *n.*

needle valve, valve whose very small opening is controlled by a slender, needle-shaped rod.

nee dle wom an (nē′dl wu̇m′ən), *n., pl.* **-wom en.** 1 woman who is a skillful sewer. 2 woman who earns her living by sewing; seamstress.

nee dle work (nē′dl wėrk′), *n.* work done with a needle; sewing; embroidery.

need n't (nēd′nt), need not.

needs (nēdz), *adv.* because of necessity; necessarily: *A soldier needs must go where duty calls.* [Old English *nēdes,* originally genitive of *nēd* need]

need y (nē′dē), *adj.,* **need i er, need i est.** not having enough to live on; very poor. **—need′i ness,** *n.*

ne'er (ner), *adv.* ARCHAIC. never.

ne'er-do-well (ner′dü wel′), *n.* a worthless fellow; good-for-nothing person. *—adj.* worthless; good-for-nothing.

ne far i ous (ni fer′ē əs, ni far′ē əs), *adj.* very wicked; villainous. [< Latin *nefarius* < *nefas* wickedness < *ne-* not + *fas* right] **—ne far′i ous ly,** *adv.* **—ne far′i ous ness,** *n.*

neg., 1 negative. 2 negatively.

ne gate (ni gāt′, nē′gāt), *v.t.,* **-gat ed, -gat ing.** 1 destroy, nullify, or make ineffective. 2 declare not to exist; deny. [< Latin *negatum* denied, related to *nec* not]

ne ga tion (ni gā′shən), *n.* 1 a denying; denial: *Shaking the head is a sign of negation.* 2 absence or opposite of some positive thing or quality: *Darkness is the negation of light.* 3 a negative statement, doctrine, etc.

neg a tive (neg′ə tiv), *adj., n., v.,* **-tived, -tiv ing.** *—adj.* 1 stating that something is not so; answering no to a question put or implied. 2 arguing against a question being formally debated: *the negative side.* 3 not positive: *negative suggestions.* 4 in mathematics: **a** less than zero; minus: *−5 is a negative number.* **b** lying on the side of a point, line, or plane opposite to that considered positive. 5 in physics and chemistry: **a** of the kind of electricity produced on rubber when it is rubbed with silk, or that is present in a charged body which has an excess of electrons: *Protons are positive; electrons are negative.* **b** having a tendency to gain electrons. **c** of the part to which the current flows into the wire in an electric cell: *a negative electrode.* 6 (in photography) showing the lights and shadows reversed: *the negative image on a photographic plate.* 7 showing the absence of the germs, symptoms, etc., of a specific disease or condition. 8 (in biology) moving or turning away from light, the earth, or any other stimulus.
—n. 1 word or statement that denies or negates. 2 **the negative,** the side opposing the affirmative in an argument or debate. 3 negative quality or characteristic. 4 a minus quantity, sign, symbol, etc. 5 the kind of electricity produced on rubber when it is rubbed with silk. 6 the negative element in an electric cell. 7 a photographic image in which the lights and shadows are reversed. Positive prints are made from it. 8 **in the negative,** expressing disagreement by saying no; denying.
—v.t. 1 negate or deny. 2 vote against or veto. 3 show to be false; disprove. 4 make useless; counteract; neutralize.
—neg′a tive ly, *adv.* **—neg′a tive ness,** *n.*

neg a tiv ism (neg′ə tə viz′əm), *n.* tendency to say or do the opposite of what is suggested.

neg a tiv ist (neg′ə tə vist), *n.* a negativistic person. *—adj.* negativistic.

neg a tiv is tic (neg′ə tə vis′tik), *adj.* given to or characterized by negativism.

neg a tiv i ty (neg′ə tiv′ə tē), *n.* negative quality or condition.

ne ga tor (ni gā′tər), *n.* person who denies.

Neg ev (neg′ev), *n.* desert region in S Israel.

ne glect (ni glekt′), *v.t.* 1 give too little care or attention to; slight: *neglect one's health.* See **slight** for synonym study. 2 leave undone; not attend to: *The maid neglected her work.* 3 omit; fail: *Don't neglect to water the plants before you leave.* *—n.* 1 act or fact of neglecting; disregard. See synonym study below. 2 want of attention to what should be done. 3 a being neglected. [< Latin *neglectum* disregarded < *nec* not + *legere* pick up] **—ne glect′er,** *n.*

Syn. *n.* 1 **Neglect, negligence** mean lack of proper care or attention. **Neglect** implies habitual inattention due to carelessness or laziness: *He has shown a persistent neglect of duty.* **Negligence** implies inattentiveness to work or duty or carelessness in doing it: *Many accidents in industry are caused by the negligence of the workers.*

ne glect ful (ni glekt′fəl), *adj.* careless; negligent; heedless. **—ne glect′ful ly,** *adv.* **—ne glect′ful ness,** *n.*

né gli gé (nā glē zhā′), *n.* FRENCH. negligee.

neg li gee (neg′lə zhā′, neg′lə zhā), *n.* 1 a woman's loose dressing gown made of a light fabric. 2 any easy, informal dress or attire. [alteration of French *négligé,* influenced by French *négligée* (feminine) neglected, careless]

neg li gence (neg′lə jəns), *n.* 1 lack of proper care or attention; neglect: *Negligence was the cause of the accident.* See **neglect** for synonym study. 2 a careless or indifferent act. 3 carelessness; indifference. [< Latin *negligentia* < *negligere* to disregard, neglect < *nec* not + *legere* pick up]

neg li gent (neg′lə jənt), *adj.* 1 given to or showing neglect; neglectful. 2 careless; indifferent. **—neg′li gent ly,** *adv.*

neg li gi bil i ty (neg′lə jə bil′ə tē), *n.* a being negligible.

neg li gi ble (neg′lə jə bəl), *adj.* that can be disregarded; unimportant; insignificant. **—neg′li gi bly,** *adv.*

ne go tia bil i ty (ni gō′shə bil′ə tē, ni gō′shē ə bil′ə tē), *n.* condition of being negotiable.

ne go tia ble (ni gō′shə bəl, ni gō′shē ə bəl), *adj.* 1 capable of being negotiated: *negotiable securities, negotiable demands.* 2 that can be got past or over: *a negotiable path.*

ne go ti ate (ni gō′shē āt), *v.,* **-at ed, -at ing.** *—v.i.* talk over and arrange terms; confer; consult: *The colonists negotiated for peace with the Indians.* *—v.t.* 1 arrange for: *They finally negotiated a peace treaty.* 2 INFORMAL. get past or over: *The car negotiated the sharp curve by slowing down.* 3 sell. 4 transfer or assign (a bill, stock, etc.) to another in return for some equivalent in value: *A broker negotiated the stocks and bonds for us.* [< Latin *negotiatum* engaged in business < *negotium* business < *neg-* not + *otium* ease] **—ne go′ti a′tor,** *n.*

hat, āge, fär; let, ēqual, tėrm;
it, īce; hot, ōpen, ôrder;
oil, out; cup, pu̇t, rüle;
ch, child; ng, long; sh, she;
th, thin; ᴛʜ, then; zh, measure;

ə represents *a* in about, *e* in taken, *i* in pencil, *o* in lemon, *u* in circus.

< = from, derived from, taken from.

ne go ti a tion (ni gō′shē ā′shən), *n.* a negotiating; arrangement.

Ne gril lo (ni gril′ō), *n., pl.* **-los.** a Negrito, especially of Africa; Bushman or Pygmy.

Ne gri to (ni grē′tō), *n., pl.* **-tos** or **-toes.** member of certain dwarfish Negroid peoples of southeastern Asia and of Africa, especially of the Philippine Islands and East Indies.

ne gri tude (nē′grə tüd, nē′grə tyüd), *n.* Often, **Negritude.** a being a Negro; Negro distinctiveness.

Ne gro (nē′grō), *n., pl.* **-groes,** *adj.* *—n.* 1 member of the so-called black race. The chief peoples of Africa south of the Sahara are Negroes. 2 any person having black ancestry. *—adj.* of, having to do with, or resembling Negroes. [< Spanish *negro* black < Latin *niger*]

Ne groid (nē′groid), *adj.* of, resembling, or related to the Negro race. *—n.* person belonging to a Negroid people.

Ne gros (nā′grōs), *n.* island in the central Philippines, one of the Visayan Islands. 1,482,000 pop.; 4900 sq. mi.

ne gus (nē′gəs), *n.* drink made of wine, hot water, sugar, lemon, and nutmeg. [< Colonel Francis *Negus,* died 1732, its inventor]

Neh., Nehemiah.

Ne he mi ah (nē′ə mī′ə), *n.* 1 Hebrew leader of the 400's B.C. who rebuilt the walls of Jerusalem about 444 B.C. 2 book of the Old Testament describing his achievements.

Ne he mi as (nē′ə mī′əs), *n.* (in the Douay Bible) Nehemiah.

Neh ru (nā′rü), *n.* **Jawaharlal,** 1889-1964, prime minister of India from 1947 to 1964.

neigh (nā), *n.* a prolonged, loud, quavering sound that a horse makes. *—v.i.* make this sound. [Old English *hnǣgan*]

neigh bor (nā′bər), *n.* 1 one who lives near another. 2 person or thing that is near another. 3 a fellow human being. *—v.i.* 1 live or be near *(to).* 2 be friendly *(with).* *—v.t.* touch or border on; adjoin: *The United States neighbors Canada to the north and Mexico to the south.* *—adj.* living or situated near to another: *two neighbor farms.* [Old English *nēahgebūr* < *nēah* nigh + *gebūr* dweller, countryman] **—neigh′bor less,** *adj.*

neigh bor hood (nā′bər hu̇d), *n.* 1 region near some place or thing; vicinity. 2 place; district: *Is North Street a good neighborhood?* 3 people living near one another; people of a place: *The whole neighborhood came to the big party.* 4 nearness. 5 **in the neighborhood of,** INFORMAL. somewhere near; about. *—adj.* of or having to do with a neighborhood.

neigh bor ing (nā′bər ing, nā′bring), *adj.* living or being near; bordering; adjoining; near.

neigh bor ly (nā′bər lē), *adj.* characteristic of or befitting a good neighbor; kindly, friendly, or sociable. **—neigh′bor li ness,** *n.*

neigh bour (nā′bər), *n., v.i., v.t., adj.* BRITISH. neighbor.

nei ther (nē′ᴛʜər, nī′ᴛʜər), *conj.* 1 not either: *Neither you nor I will go.* 2 nor yet; nor: *"They toil not, neither do they spin."* —*adj.* not either: *Neither statement is true.* —*pron.* not either: *Neither of the statements is true.* [Old English *nāhwæther* < *nā* not + *hwæther* which of two]

Nejd (nejd), *n.* former country in central Arabia, since 1932 part of Saudi Arabia.

nek ton (nek′ton), *n.* the relatively large organisms, such as fish, that possess the power to swim freely in oceans and lakes, independent of water movements, in contrast to plankton. [< Greek *nēkton* neuter of *nēktos* swimming < *nēchein* to swim]

Nel son (nel′sən), *n.* Viscount **Horatio,** 1758-1805, British admiral, noted for victories over the navy of Napoleon I.

nem a to cide (nem′ə tə sīd, nə mat′ə sīd), *n.* substance used to kill nematodes.

nem a to cyst (nem′ə tə sist, nə mat′ə sist), *n.* a coiled, threadlike stinging process of coelenterates, discharged to capture prey and for defense. [< Greek *nēma, nēmatos* thread + English *cyst*]

Nem a to da (nem′ə tō′də), *n.pl.* phylum of invertebrates comprising the nematodes.

nem a tode (nem′ə tōd), *n.* any of a phylum of slender, unsegmented, cylindrical worms, often tapered near the ends; roundworm. Parasitic forms, such as the hookworm, pinworm, and trichina, belong to this phylum. —*adj.* of or belonging to this phylum. [< Greek *nēma, nēmatos* thread < *nēn* to spin]

Nem bu tal (nem′byə tôl, nem′byə tal), *n.* trademark for pentobarbital sodium.

ne mer te an (ni mėr′tē ən), *n.* any of a phylum of long, flat, unsegmented marine worms with a complete digestive system, mouth, and anus; ribbon worm. [< Greek *Nēmertēs* Nemertes, a sea nymph]

Nem e sis (nem′ə sis), *n., pl.* **-ses** (-sēz′). 1 (in Greek myths) the goddess of vengeance. 2 **nemesis,** a just punishment; retribution. b person who punishes; agent of retribution, especially one who cannot be eluded. [< Greek < *nemein* give what is due]

neo-, *combining form.* new; recent, as in *neocolonialism.* [< Greek *neos*]

ne o clas sic (nē′ō klas′ik), *adj.* of or having to do with the revival of classical principles or practices in art, music, and literature.

ne o clas si cal (nē′ō klas′ə kəl), *adj.* neoclassic.

ne o clas si cism (nē′ō klas′ə siz′əm), *n.* movement in art, music, and literature to revive or restore classical principles or practices.

ne o co lo ni al ism (nē′ō kə lō′nē ə liz′-əm), *n.* policy or practice of a large nation dominating smaller nations, especially former colonies, politically or economically.

ne o co lo ni al ist (nē′ō kə lō′nē ə list), *n.* advocate or supporter of neocolonialism. —*adj.* of or having to do with neocolonialism.

ne o dym i um (nē′ō dim′ē əm), *n.* a yellowish, rare-earth metallic element found in various rare minerals. The rose-colored salts of neodymium are used to color glass. *Symbol:* Nd; *atomic number* 60. See pages 326 and 327 for table. [< *neo-* + *(di)dymium*]

Ne o lith ic (nē′ə lith′ik), *adj.* of, designating, or belonging to the latest part of the Stone Age, marked by the beginning of agriculture and the use of polished stone weapons and tools. [< *neo-* + Greek *lithos* stone]

ne ol o gism (nē ol′ə jiz′əm), *n.* 1 use of new words or of old words with new meanings. 2 a new word or expression, or a new meaning for an old word. [< Greek *neos* new + *logos* word]

ne ol o gist (nē ol′ə jist), *n.* person who introduces or uses neologisms.

ne ol o gis tic (nē ol′ə jis′tik), *adj.* of or having to do with neologism or neologists.

ne o my cin (nē′ō mī′sn), *n.* antibiotic similar to streptomycin, obtained from a related soil actinomycete. [< *neo-* + Greek *mykēs* fungus]

ne on (nē′on), *n.* 1 a colorless, odorless, inert gaseous element, forming a very small part of the air. It is used in neon lamps. *Symbol:* Ne; *atomic number* 10. See pages 326 and 327 for table. 2 neon lamp. 3 a sign for advertising made up of neon lamps. [< Greek, neuter of *neos* new]

ne o na tal (nē′ō nā′tl), *adj.* of or having to do with newborn babies: *neonatal disease, neonatal mortality.*

ne o nate (nē′ə nāt), *n.* a newborn baby.

neon lamp or **neon light,** a glass tube containing neon gas and two electrodes instead of a filament. When voltage is applied to the electrodes, an electric discharge occurs and the gas glows.

ne o phyte (nē′ə fīt), *n.* 1 a new convert; one recently admitted to a religious body. 2 beginner; novice. [< Greek *neophytos* < *neos* new + *phyein* to plant]

ne o plasm (nē′ə plaz′əm), *n.* a new, abnormal growth of tissue, as a tumor. [< *neo-* + Greek *plasma* something formed]

ne o plas tic (nē′ə plas′tik), *adj.* having to do with a neoplasm.

ne o prene (nē′ə prēn′), *n.* a synthetic rubber derived from acetylene, used in products where resistance to oil, heat, and weather is desirable.

Nep or **NEP** (nep), *n.* New Economic Policy, a policy of the Soviet government in effect from 1921 to 1928 that allowed some businesses to be privately owned. [< Russian *N(ovaja) E(konomičeskaja) P(olitika)* New Economic Policy]

Ne pal (nə pôl′), *n.* country between India and Tibet in the Himalayas. 11,000,000 pop.; 54,600 sq. mi. *Capital:* Katmandu.

Nep a lese (nep′ə lēz′), *n., pl.* **-lese,** *adj.* —*n.* native or inhabitant of Nepal. —*adj.* of or having to do with Nepal or its people.

Ne pa li (ne pä′lē), *n., adj.* Nepalese.

ne pen the (ni pen′thē), *n.* 1 a drink or drug supposed to bring forgetfulness of sorrow or trouble, according to old legend. 2 anything that does this. [< Greek *nēpenthēs* dispelling grief < *nē-* not + *penthos* grief]

ne pen the an (ni pen′thē ən), *adj.* of, having to do with, or induced by nepenthe.

neph a nal y sis (nef′ə nal′ə sis), *n., pl.* **-ses** (-sēz′). 1 analysis of the cloud formations over a large area, using weather charts drawn especially from photographs taken by weather satellites. 2 chart of such cloud formations. [< Greek *nephos* cloud + English *analysis*]

neph ew (nef′yü), *n.* son of one's brother or sister; son of one's brother-in-law or sister-in-law. [< Old French *neveu* < Latin *nepotem* grandson, nephew]

neph o scope (nef′ə skōp), *n.* instrument used to determine the altitude of clouds and the velocity and direction of their motion. [< Greek *nephos* cloud]

neph ric (nef′rik), *adj.* renal.

ne phrid i um (ni frid′ē əm), *n., pl.* **-i a** (-ē ə). a primitive excretory organ in some invertebrates such as the annelids, analogous in function to the kidneys of higher animals. [< New Latin < Greek *nephros* kidney]

ne phrit ic (ni frit′ik), *adj.* of or having to do with nephritis.

ne phri tis (ni frī′tis), *n.* inflammation of the kidneys, especially Bright's disease. [< Greek < *nephros* kidney]

neph ron (nef′ron), *n.* any of the numerous functional units of the kidney, serving to filter waste matter from the blood. A human kidney has more than one million nephrons.

ne plus ultra (nē plus ul′trə), highest or furthest point attainable; height of excellence or achievement; culmination. [< Latin, no more beyond]

nep man (nep′mən), *n., pl.* **-men.** tradesman allowed under the Nep to engage in private business in the Soviet Union during the 1920's.

nep o tism (nep′ə tiz′əm), *n.* the showing of too much favor by one in power to his relatives, especially by giving them desirable positions. [< Italian *nepotismo* < *nepote* nephew < Latin *nepotem* grandson, nephew]

Nep tune (nep′tün, nep′tyün), *n.* 1 (in Roman myths) the god of the sea, identified with the Greek god Poseidon. 2 the fourth largest planet in the solar system and the eighth in distance from the sun, visible only through a telescope. See **solar system** for diagram.

Nep tu ni an (nep tü′nē ən, nep tyü′nē ən), *adj.* of or having to do with Neptune.

nep tu ni um (nep tü′nē əm, nep tyü′nē-əm), *n.* a radioactive metallic element which occurs in minute amounts in uranium ore and is obtained by bombardment of an isotope of uranium with neutrons. It is used in certain types of atomic bombs. *Symbol:* Np; *atomic number* 93. See pages 326 and 327 for table. [< *Neptune,* planet whose orbit lies beyond Uranus; similarly, neptunium comes after uranium in the periodic table]

Ner e id (nir′ē id), *n.* (in Greek myths) any of the fifty daughters of Nereus. The Nereids were sea nymphs who attended Poseidon.

Ner eus (nir′üs, nir′ē əs), *n.* (in Greek myths) a sea god who was the father of the Nereids.

Ner o (nir′ō), *n.* A.D. 37-68, Roman emperor from A.D. 54 to 68. He was noted for his vices, cruelty, and tyranny.

ner va tion (nėr vā′shən), *n.* venation.

nerve (nėrv), *n., v.,* **nerved, nerv ing.** —*n.* 1 fiber or bundle of fibers through which impulses, especially of sensation and motion, pass between the brain or spinal cord and the eyes, ears, muscles, glands, etc. 2 mental strength; courage: *nerves of iron.* 3 bodily strength; vigor; energy. 4 SLANG. rude boldness; impudence. 5 vein of a leaf. 6 rib of an insect's wing. 7 pulp of a tooth. 8 **get on one's nerves,** annoy or irritate one. 9 **nerves,** *pl.* a nervousness. b attack of nervousness. 10 **strain every nerve,** exert oneself to the utmost. —*v.t.* arouse strength or courage in: *The soldiers nerved themselves for battle.* [< Latin *nervus* sinew, tendon]

nerve cell, 1 neuron. 2 the cell body of a neuron, excluding its fibers.

nerve center, 1 group of nerve cells closely connected with one another and acting together in the performance of some function. 2 any place that is the center of activity or source of direction.

nerve fiber, any of the long, threadlike processes or fibers of a neuron; an axon or a dendrite.

nerve gas, any of various poison gases containing phosphorus that may be absorbed through the skin as well as by breathing, and that attack the central nervous system to cause extreme weakness or death. Nerve gas is used in warfare.

nerve less (nėrv′lis), *adj.* 1 without strength or vigor; feeble; weak. 2 without courage or firmness. 3 without nervousness; controlled; calm. 4 without nerves. **—nerve′less ly,** *adv.* **—nerve′less-ness,** *n.*

nerve-rack ing or **nerve-wrack ing** (nėrv′rak′ing), *adj.* extremely irritating; causing great annoyance; very trying.

nerv ous (nėr′vəs), *adj.* 1 of or proceeding from the nerves: *a nervous disorder, nervous energy.* 2 having easily excited nerves; jumpy: *a nervous driver.* 3 restless, uneasy, or timid: *She is nervous about staying alone at night.* 4 vigorous; spirited; energetic: *a nervous style of writing, paint with quick, nervous strokes.* **—nerv′ous ly,** *adv.* **—nerv′ous ness,** *n.*

nervous breakdown, neurasthenia.

nervous system, system of nerve fibers, nerve cells, and nerve centers in the body, whose function is to carry and interpret impulses. The central nervous system of vertebrates includes the brain and spinal cord. The peripheral nervous system consists of the cranial nerves, spinal nerves, ganglia, etc.

ner vure (nėr′vyůr), *n.* 1 vein of a leaf. 2 rib of an insect's wing. [< French]

nerv y (nėr′vē), *adj.,* **nerv i er, nerv i est.** 1 SLANG. rude and bold; impudent. 2 requiring courage or firmness: *a nervy undertaking.* 3 nervous. **—nerv′i ly,** *adv.* **—nerv′i ness,** *n.*

nes cience (nesh′əns, nesh′ē əns), *n.* ignorance. [< Late Latin *nescientia,* ultimately < Latin *ne-* not + *scire* know]

nes cient (nesh′ənt, nesh′ē ənt), *adj.* ignorant.

-ness, *suffix added to adjectives to form nouns.* 1 quality or condition of being ___: *Preparedness = condition of being prepared.* 2 ___ action; ___ behavior: *Carefulness = careful action; careful behavior.* [Old English *-ness, -niss*]

Nes sus (nes′əs), *n.* (in Greek myths) a centaur shot by Hercules with a poisoned arrow. Hercules was himself fatally poisoned by a shirt steeped in the blood of Nessus.

nest (nest), *n.* 1 structure or place built by birds out of twigs, straw, etc., as a place for laying eggs and rearing young. 2 structure or place used by insects, fishes, turtles, rabbits, or the like, for depositing eggs or young. 3 a snug abode, retreat, or resting place. 4 place that swarms (usually with something bad): *a nest of thieves.* 5 the birds, animals, etc., living in a nest. 6 set or series (often from large to small) such that each fits within another: *a nest of drinking cups.* —*v.i.* build or have a nest: *The bluebirds are nesting here again.* —*v.t.* settle or place in, or as if in, a nest. [Old English]

nest egg, 1 a natural or artificial egg left in a nest to induce a hen to continue laying eggs there. 2 something, usually a sum of money, saved up as the beginning of a fund or as a reserve.

nest er (nes′tər), *n.* 1 U.S. a farmer, homesteader, or squatter seeking to settle on land used as a cattle range. 2 animal that makes or lives in a nest.

nes tle (nes′əl), *v.,* **-tled, -tling.** —*v.i.* 1 settle oneself comfortably or cozily: *She nestled down into the big chair.* 2 be settled comfortably or cozily; be sheltered: *The little house nestled among the trees.* 3 press close in affection or for comfort: *nestle up to one's mother.* —*v.t.* press close; cuddle: *nestle a baby in one's arms.* [Old English *nestlian* < *nest* nest] **—nes′tler,** *n.*

nest ling (nest′ling), *n.* bird too young to leave the nest.

Nes tor (nes′tər), *n.* 1 (in Greek legends) the oldest and wisest of the Greeks at the siege of Troy. 2 a wise old man.

net[1] (net), *n., v.,* **net ted, net ting.** —*n.* 1 an open fabric made of string, cord, thread, or hair, knotted together in such a way as to leave holes regularly arranged. 2 anything made of net. Nets are used to catch butterflies, birds, and fish, to keep a woman's hair in place, to separate opposing players in a game such as tennis, etc. 3 anything like net; set of things that cross each other. 4 lacelike cloth often used as a veil: *cotton net.* 5 a trap or snare: *The guilty man was caught in the net of his own lies.* 6 a ball, shuttlecock, etc., that hits the net in tennis, badminton, and other games played with a net, causing the loss of a point. —*v.t.* 1 catch in a net; take with nets: *net a fish.* 2 cover, confine, or protect with a net. 3 make into net: *net cord.* 4 catch or capture as if with a net. 5 hit (a ball, shuttlecock, etc.) into the net in tennis, badminton, etc., thus losing a point. [Old English *nett*] **—net′like′,** *adj.* **—net′ter,** *n.*

net[2] (net), *adj., n., v.,* **net ted, net ting.** —*adj.* remaining after deductions; free from deductions. A net gain or profit is the actual gain after all working expenses have been paid. The net weight of a glass jar of candy is the weight of the candy itself. The net price of a book is the real price from which no discount can be made. —*n.* the net profit, weight, price, etc. —*v.t.* gain or yield as clear profit: *The sale netted him a thousand dollars.* [< Middle French, neat. See NEAT[1].]

neth er (neᴛʜ′ər), *adj.* 1 lower; under. 2 lying or conceived as lying beneath the surface of the earth: *nether regions.* [Old English *neothera*]

Neth er land er (neᴛʜ′ər lan′dər), *n.* native or inhabitant of the Netherlands.

Neth er lands (neᴛʜ′ər ləndz), *n.* **the,** country in NW Europe, west of Germany and north of Belgium; Holland. 12,958,000 pop.; 15,800 sq. mi. *Capital:* The Hague (actual), Amsterdam (official).

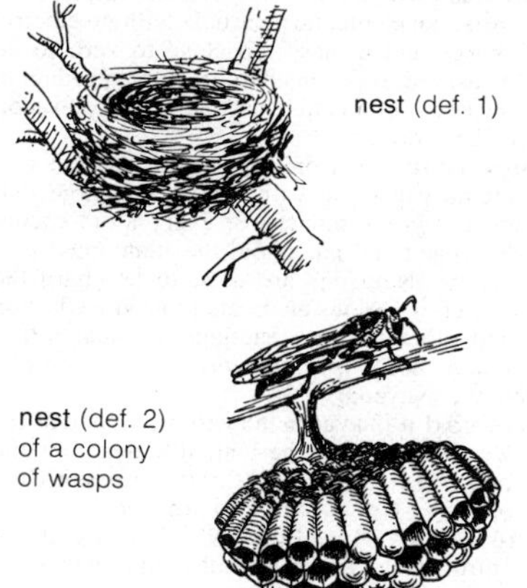

nest (def. 1)

nest (def. 2) of a colony of wasps

hat, āge, fär; let, ēqual, tėrm;
it, īce; hot, ōpen, ôrder;
oil, out; cup, pu̇t, rüle;
ch, child; ng, long; sh, she;
th, thin; ᴛʜ, then; zh, measure;

ə represents *a* in about, *e* in taken, *i* in pencil, *o* in lemon, *u* in circus.

< = from, derived from, taken from.

net[1] (def. 2)—top, tennis net; left, fish net; right, mosquito net

Netherlands Antilles, the, overseas territory of the Netherlands consisting of six islands in the S Caribbean, including Curaçao and Aruba. 216,000 pop.; 400 sq. mi. *Capital:* Willemstad (Curaçao). Also, **Dutch West Indies, Netherlands West Indies.**

Netherlands East Indies, Dutch East Indies.

Netherlands West Indies, the Netherlands Antilles.

neth er most (neᴛʜ′ər mōst), *adj.* lowest.

nether world, 1 Hades. 2 hell.

net ting (net′ing), *n.* 1 a netted or meshed material. 2 process of making a net. 3 act or right of fishing with a net or nets.

net tle (net′l), *n., v.,* **-tled, -tling.** —*n.* any of a genus of herbs having sharp hairs on the leaves and stems that sting the skin when touched. —*v.t.* sting the mind of; irritate; provoke; vex: *I was very much nettled by their refusal to help.* [Old English *netele*] **—net′tle like′,** *adj.*

net tle some (net′l səm), *adj.* 1 easily nettled; irritable. 2 irritating.

net work (net′wėrk′), *n.* 1 a netting; net. 2 any system of lines that cross: *a network of vines, a network of railroads.* 3 group of radio or television stations so connected that the same programs may be broadcast by all.

neur al (nůr′əl, nyůr′əl), *adj.* of or having to do with a nerve, neuron, or nervous system. [< Greek *neuron* nerve]

neu ral gia (nů ral′jə, nyů ral′jə), *n.* 1 pain, usually sharp, along the course of a nerve. 2 condition characterized by such pain.

neu ral gic (nů ral′jik, nyů ral′jik), *adj.* of or having to do with neuralgia.

neur as the ni a (nůr′əs thē′nē ə, nyůr′əs-thē′nē ə), *n.* a neurosis with feelings of mental and physical exhaustion, often accompanied by varying aches and pains with no discernible organic cause; nervous breakdown.

neur as then ic (nůr′əs then′ik, nyůr′əs-then′ik), *adj.* of or having to do with neurasthenia. —*n.* person who has neurasthenia. —**neur′as then′i cal ly,** *adv.*

neur i lem ma (nůr′ə lem′ə, nyůr′ə lem′ə), *n.* the membranous outer sheath of a nerve fiber. [< *neuro-* + Greek *eilēma* a covering]

neu ri tis (nů rī′tis, nyů rī′tis), *n.* inflammation of a nerve or nerves, causing pain, loss of reflexes, paralysis, and the wasting of muscles controlled by those nerves.

neuro-, *combining form.* nerve; nerve tissue; nervous system: *Neurology = study of the nervous system.* [< Greek *neuron*]

neur o gen ic (nůr′ə jen′ik, nyůr′ə jen′ik), *adj.* originating in the nerves or nervous system.

neu rog li a (nů rog′lē ə, nyů rog′lē ə), *n.* the delicate connective tissue forming a supporting network for the conducting elements of nervous tissue in the brain and the spinal cord. [< *neuro-* + Late Greek *glia* glue]

neur o hor mone (nůr′ō hôr′mōn, nyůr′ō-hôr′mōn), *n.* hormone that stimulates nerve cells or the nervous system.

neur o hu mor (nůr′ō hyü′mər, nyůr′ō-hyü′mər), *n.* substance secreted by the endings of a nerve cell and capable of activating a muscle or another nerve cell.

neur o log i cal (nůr′ə loj′ə kəl, nyůr′ə-loj′ə kəl), *adj.* of or having to do with neurology.

neu rol o gist (nů rol′ə jist, nyů rol′ə jist), *n.* an expert in neurology.

neu rol o gy (nů rol′ə jē, nyů rol′ə jē), *n.* study of the nervous system and its diseases.

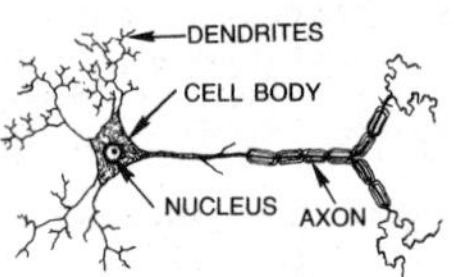

neuron—A nerve impulse is received by the dendrites and carried to the cell body. The axon carries the impulse away from the cell body to another cell. In this way, the nerve impulse is passed from one neuron to another.

neur on (nůr′on, nyůr′on), *n.* one of the impulse-conducting cells of which the brain, spinal cord, and nerves are composed; nerve cell. A neuron consists of a cell body containing the nucleus, and usually several dendrites and a single axon. [< Greek, nerve]

neur on al (nůr′ə nəl, nyůr′ə nəl; nů rō′nəl, nyů rō′nəl), *adj.* neuronic.

neur one (nůr′ōn, nyůr′ōn), *n.* neuron.

neu ron ic (nů ron′ik, nyů ron′ik), *adj.* of or having to do with a neuron.

neu rop ter an (nů rop′tər ən, nyů rop′tər-ən), *n.* any of an order of carnivorous insects having four large delicate wings and mouthparts adapted for chewing. Lacewings and ant lions belong to this order. —*adj.* of or belonging to this order. [< Greek *neuron* nerve + *pteron* wing]

neu ro sis (nů rō′sis, nyů rō′sis), *n., pl.* **-ses** (-sēz′). any of various mental or emotional disorders, less severe than a psychosis, characterized by depression, anxiety, abnormal fears, compulsive behavior, etc.; psychoneurosis.

neu rot ic (nů rot′ik, nyů rot′ik), *adj.* 1 having or appearing to have a neurosis. 2 of or having to do with a neurosis or neuroses. —*n.* a neurotic person. —**neu-rot′i cal ly,** *adv.*

neut., neuter.

neu ter (nü′tər, nyü′tər), *adj.* 1 (in grammar) neither masculine nor feminine. *It* is a neuter pronoun. 2 without sex organs or with sex organs that are not fully developed. Worker bees are neuter. 3 being on neither side; neutral. —*n.* 1 a neuter word or form. 2 the neuter gender. 3 animal, plant, or insect that is neuter. 4 a neutral. —*v.t.* 1 castrate. 2 counteract or neutralize. [< Latin < *ne-* not + *uter* either]

neu tral (nü′trəl, nyü′trəl), *adj.* 1 on neither side in a quarrel or war. 2 of or belonging to a neutral country or neutral zone: *a neutral port.* 3 neither one thing nor the other; indefinite. 4 having little or no color; grayish. 5 neither acid nor alkaline. 6 (of electricity) neither positive nor negative. —*n.* 1 a neutral person or country; one not taking part in a war. 2 position of gears when they do not transmit motion from the engine to the wheels or other working parts. 3 the position of a gearshift lever when gears are in neutral. 4 a color that is neutral. [< Latin *neutralis* of neuter gender < *neuter.* See NEUTER.] —**neu′tral ly,** *adv.*

neu tral ism (nü′trə liz′əm, nyü′trə-liz′əm), *n.* practice of maintaining a position as a neutral, especially in international affairs.

neu tral ist (nü′trə list, nyü′trə list), *n.* person who practices or advocates neutrality, especially in international affairs. —*adj.* practicing or advocating neutrality.

neu tral i ty (nü tral′ə tē, nyü tral′ə tē), *n.* 1 quality or condition of being neutral; neutral character or status. 2 the attitude or policy of a nation that does not take part directly or indirectly in a war between other nations.

neu tral ize (nü′trə līz, nyü′trə līz), *v.t.,* **-ized, -iz ing.** 1 make chemically or electrically neutral: *Bases neutralize acids.* 2 keep war out of; keep neutral: *Switzerland was neutralized in 1815.* 3 make of no effect by some opposite force; counterbalance: *She neutralized the bright colors in the room by using a tan rug.* —**neu′tral i za′tion,** *n.* —**neu′tral iz′er,** *n.*

neutral vowel, schwa.

neu tri no (nü trē′nō, nyü trē′nō), *n., pl.* **-nos.** an elementary particle with no electric charge and a mass too close to zero to be measured. It is considered a stable product in the decay of unstable particles, as in emission of beta rays.

neu tron (nü′tron, nyü′tron), *n.* an elementary particle with a neutral charge that occurs in the nucleus of every atom except hydrogen and has about the same mass as a proton. Neutrons are used to bombard the nuclei of various elements to produce fission and other nuclear reactions. [< *neutr(al)* + *-on,* as in *electron, proton*]

Nev., Nevada.

Ne vad a (nə vad′ə, nə vä′də), *n.* one of the western states of the United States. 489,000 pop.; 110,500 sq. mi. *Capital:* Carson City. *Abbrev.:* Nev. —**Ne vad′an,** *adj., n.*

né vé (nā vā′), *n.* 1 the crystalline or granular snow on the upper part of a glacier that has not yet been compressed into ice. 2 field of such snow. [< French, ultimately < Latin *nivis* snow]

nev er (nev′ər), *adv.* 1 not ever; at no time: *He never has seen a more perfect copy.* 2 in no case; not at all; to no extent or degree: *never the wiser.* 3 **never so,** **a** not even so. **b** no matter how. [Old English *nǣfre* < *ne* not + *ǣfre* ever]

nev er more (nev′ər môr′, nev′ər mōr′), *adv.* never again.

nev er-nev er land (nev′ər nev′ər), an imaginary place or unrealistic condition.

nev er the less (nev′ər ᴛʜə les′), *adv.* however; nonetheless; for all that; in spite of it: *She was very tired; nevertheless she kept on working.*

Nev ille (nev′əl), *n.* **Richard.** See **Warwick.**

ne vus (nē′vəs), *n., pl.* **-vi** (-vī). birthmark. [< Latin *naevus* mole, wart]

new (nü, nyü), *adj.* 1 never having existed before; now first made, thought out, known or heard of, felt, or discovered: *a new invention, a new idea.* See synonym study below. 2 lately grown, come, or made; not old: *a new bud, a new make of car.* 3 now first used; not worn or used up; fresh: *a new path.* 4 beginning again: *a new attempt.* 5 changed or renewed; different: *A night's sleep will make a new man of you.* 6 not familiar; strange: *a new country to me.* 7 not yet accustomed: *new to the work.* 8 later or latest; modern; recent: *new dances.* 9 just come; having just reached the position: *a new arrival, a new president.* 10 further; additional; more: *He sought new information on the subject.* 11 being the later or latest of two or more things of the same kind: *New England, New Testament.* 12 **New,** (of a language) in use in modern times, usually contrasted with *Old* and *Medieval* or *Middle: New Hebrew.* —*adv.* 1 recently or lately; newly; freshly: *a new-found friend.* 2 again; anew; afresh. [Old English *nīwe*] —**new′ness,** *n.*

Syn. *adj.* 1 **New, novel, modern** mean having only now or recently come into existence or knowledge. **New** describes something now existing, made, seen, or known for the first time: *They own a new house.* **Novel** adds and emphasizes the idea of being unusual, strikingly different, or strange: *The house has a novel dining room.* **Modern** describes people and things belonging to or characteristic of the present time, or recent times, and sometimes suggests being up-to-date, not old-fashioned: *The architecture is modern.*

New Amsterdam, name of New York City when it was a Dutch colonial town, the capital of New Netherland, from 1625 to 1664.

New ark (nü′ərk, nyü′ərk), *n.* city in NE New Jersey, near New York City. 382,000.

New Bed ford (bed′fərd), seaport in SE Massachusetts, formerly an important whaling port. 102,000.

new born (nü′bôrn′, nyü′bôrn′), *adj.* 1 recently or only just born. 2 ready to start a new life; born again.

New Britain, 1 city in central Connecticut. 83,000. 2 largest island of the Bismarck Archipelago, in the East Indies. 154,000 pop.; 15,000 sq. mi.

New Bruns wick (brunz′wik), province in SE Canada. 617,000 pop.; 28,000 sq. mi. *Capital:* Fredericton.

New burgh (nü′bėrg′, nyü′bėrg′), *n.* city in SE New York State, on the Hudson River. 26,000.

New Cal e do ni a (kal′ə dō′nē ə, kal′ə-

hat, āge, fär; let, ēqual, tėrm;
it, īce; hot, ōpen, ôrder;
oil, out; cup, pu̇t, rüle;
ch, child; ng, long; sh, she;
th, thin; ᴛʜ, then; zh, measure;

ə represents *a* in about, *e* in taken, *i* in pencil, *o* in lemon, *u* in circus.

< = from, derived from, taken from.

dō′nyə), 1 French island in the S Pacific, east of Australia. 101,000 pop.; 7400 sq. mi. 2 overseas territory of France in the S Pacific comprising the island of New Caledonia and other nearby islands. 116,000 pop.; 8500 sq. mi. *Capital:* Nouméa.

New cas tle (nü′kas′əl, nyü′kas′əl), *n.* 1 city in NE England on the Tyne River, important as a coal-mining and shipbuilding center. 237,000. **2 carry coals to Newcastle,** waste one's time, effort, etc.

Newcastle-upon-Tyne (tīn), *n.* Newcastle.

new com er (nü′kum′ər, nyü′kum′ər), *n.* 1 person who has just come or who came not long ago. 2 a novice.

New Deal, 1 the policies and measures advocated by President Franklin D. Roosevelt as a means of improving the economic and social welfare of the United States. 2 the Roosevelt administration.

New Dealer, supporter or advocate of the New Deal.

New Delhi, capital of India, in the N part, just south of Delhi. 324,000.

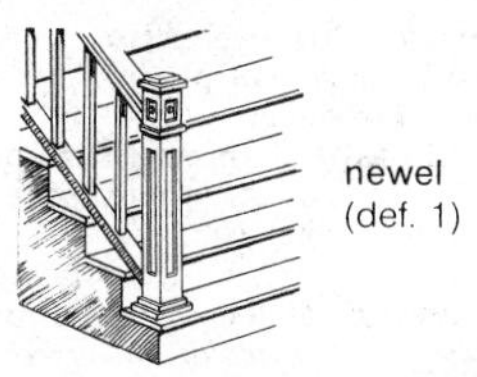

newel (def. 1)

new el (nü′əl, nyü′əl), *n.* 1 the post at the top or bottom of a stairway that supports the railing. 2 the central post of a winding stairway. [< Old French *nouel* newel, kernel < Late Latin *nucalis* nutlike < Latin *nux* nut]

New England, the NE part of the United States; Maine, New Hampshire, Vermont, Massachusetts, Rhode Island, and Connecticut.

New Englander, native or inhabitant of New England.

new fan gled (nü′fang′gəld, nyü′fang′gəld), *adj.* 1 lately come into fashion; of a new kind; novel. 2 fond of novelty. [Middle English *newefangle* < *newe* new + *fangen* to take]

new-fash ioned (nü′fash′ənd, nyü′fash′ənd), *adj.* of a new fashion; lately come into style.

New found land (nü′fənd lənd, nü found′lənd; nyü′fənd lənd, nyü found′lənd), *n.* 1 large island in the Atlantic northeast of Nova Scotia. 472,000 pop.; 42,700 sq. mi. 2 province in E Canada that includes Newfoundland and Labrador. 517,000 pop.; 156,200 sq. mi. *Capital:* St. John's. *Abbrev.:* Nfld. 3 one of a breed of shaggy, very large, intelligent dogs, usually black, developed in Newfoundland.

Newfoundland (def. 3)
26 to 28 in. high at the shoulder

New found land er (nü′fənd lən dər, nü found′lən dər; nyü′fənd lən dər, nyü found′lən dər), *n.* native or inhabitant of Newfoundland.

New France, name of the territory in North America belonging to France from 1609 to 1763.

New Greek, the Greek language as used in modern times, especially after 1500.

New Guin ea (gin′ē), 1 large island north of Australia; Papua. The west part of New Guinea (West Irian) belongs to Indonesia, the east part to Australia. 2,909,000 pop.; 312,000 sq. mi. 2 Territory of, a United Nations trust territory including NE New Guinea, the Bismarck Archipelago, and the N part of the Solomon Islands. It is administered with the Territory of Papua by Australia. 1,663,000 pop.; 92,200 sq. mi.

New Hamp shire (hamp′shər, hamp′shir), one of the northeastern states of the United States. 738,000 pop.; 9300 sq. mi. *Capital:* Concord. *Abbrev.:* N.H.

New Hamp shi rite (hamp′shə rīt′, hamp′shi rīt′), native or inhabitant of New Hampshire.

New Ha ven (hā′vən), city in S Connecticut. 134,000.

New Hebrides, group of islands east of Australia, under joint rule of Great Britain and France. 85,000 pop.; 5700 sq. mi.

new ish (nü′ish, nyü′ish), *adj.* rather new.

New Jersey, one of the northeastern states of the United States. 7,168,000 pop.; 7800 sq. mi. *Capital:* Trenton. *Abbrev.:* N.J.

New Jer sey ite (jėr′zē īt), native or inhabitant of New Jersey.

New Jerusalem, heaven.

New Latin, the Latin language after 1500. It contains words formed from Greek and Latin elements.

New Left, U.S. a political movement developed in the 1960's chiefly by college and university students seeking radical changes in American foreign policy, civil rights, and the academic establishment.

new ly (nü′lē, nyü′lē), *adv.* 1 lately; recently: *newly arrived.* 2 again; freshly: *a newly revived scandal.* 3 in a new way.

new ly wed (nü′lē wed′, nyü′lē wed′), *n.* person who has recently become married.

New man (nü′mən, nyü′mən), *n.* **John Henry,** 1801-1890, English theologian and author who became a Roman Catholic and was made a cardinal.

New Mexico, one of the southwestern states of the United States. 1,016,000 pop.; 121,700 sq. mi. *Capital:* Santa Fe. *Abbrev.:* N.M. **—New Mexican.**

new moon, 1 the moon when seen as a thin crescent with the hollow side on the left. 2 the moon when its dark side is toward the earth, appearing almost invisible.

New Neth er land (neᴛʜ′ər lənd), former Dutch colony in America, from 1613 to 1664, along the Hudson River and later along the Delaware River. England took possession of it in 1664 and divided it into the colonies of New York and New Jersey.

New Or le ans (ôr′lē ənz, ôr lēnz′, ôr′lənz), seaport in SE Louisiana, near the mouth of the Mississippi River. 593,000.

New port (nü′pôrt, nü′pōrt; nyü′pôrt, nyü′pōrt), *n.* city in SE Rhode Island, on Narragansett Bay. 35,000.

Newport News, Seaport in SE Virginia, at the mouth of the James River. 138,000.

New Providence, one of the Bahama Islands, in the central part. 81,000 pop.; 58 sq. mi.

New Ro chelle (rō shel′, rə shel′), city in SE New York State, near New York City. 75,000.

news (nüz, nyüz), *n.* 1 report or information on recent happenings; tidings: *The news that she was leaving made us sad.* 2 report of a current event or events in a newspaper, on television, radio, etc. 3 news important enough to report. 4 **break the news,** make something known; tell something.

news agency, agency that gathers and distributes news to newspapers, magazines, and radio and television stations subscribing to its service.

news boy (nüz′boi′, nyüz′boi′), *n.* boy who sells or delivers newspapers; paperboy.

news cast (nüz′kast′, nyüz′kast′), *n.* a radio or television program devoted to news bulletins, current events, etc.

news cast er (nüz′kas′tər, nyüz′kas′tər), *n.* 1 person who gives the news on a newscast. 2 commentator on the news.

news deal er (nüz′dē′lər, nyüz′dē′lər), *n.* seller of newspapers and magazines.

news let ter (nüz′let′ər, nyüz′let′ər), *n.* letter or report presenting an informal or confidential coverage of news, as one distributed by an organization to its members or subscribers.

news man (nüz′man′, nyüz′man′), *n., pl.* **-men.** 1 man who sells or delivers newspapers. 2 newspaperman or newscaster.

news mon ger (nüz′mung′gər, nüz′mong′gər; nyüz′mung′gər, nyüz′mong′gər), *n.* person who spreads news or gossip.

New South Wales, a state in SE Australia. 4,567,000 pop; 309,400 sq. mi. *Capital:* Sydney.

news pa per (nüz′pā′pər, nyüz′pā′pər), *n.* a daily or weekly publication printed on large sheets of paper, containing the news, carrying advertisements, and often having feature articles and editorials, stories, pictures, and useful information.

news pa per man (nüz′pā′pər man′, nyüz′pā′pər man′), *n., pl.* **-men.** reporter, editor, or other person working for a newspaper.

news print (nüz′print′, nyüz′print′), *n.* soft, cheap paper, made chiefly from wood pulp and unsized, on which newspapers are usually printed.

news reel (nüz′rēl′, nyüz′rēl′), *n.* a motion picture showing current news or events.

news stand (nüz′stand′, nyüz′stand′), *n.* place where newspapers and magazines are sold.

New Style, method of reckoning time according to the Gregorian calendar.

news wor thy (nüz′wėr′ᴛʜē, nyüz′wėr′ᴛʜē), *adj.,* **-thi er, -thi est.** having enough public interest to be printed in a newspaper.

news y (nü′zē, nyü′zē), *adj.,* **news i er, news i est.** INFORMAL. full of news: *a newsy letter.*

newt (nüt, nyüt), *n.* any of various small salamanders that live in water part of the time. [Old English *efete* eft; Middle English *an ewt* taken as *a newt*]

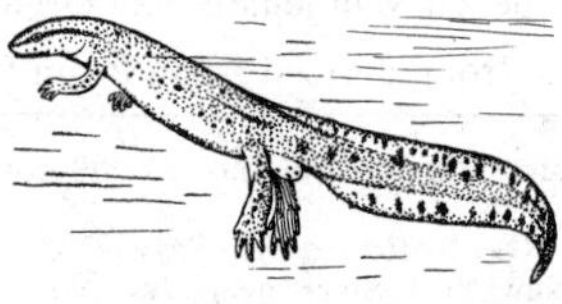

newt—3 to 4 in. long

New Testament, the second of the two principal divisions of the Bible, which contains the life and teachings of Christ recorded by His followers, together with their own experiences and teachings.

new ton (nüt′n, nyüt′n), *n.* unit of force in the meter-kilogram-second system equal to 100,000 dynes. It is the force required to give an acceleration of one meter per second per second to a mass of one kilogram. [< Sir Isaac *Newton*]

New ton (nüt′n, nyüt′n), *n.* 1 Sir **Isaac,** 1642-1727, English mathematician, physicist, and philosopher, who discovered the law of gravitation. 2 city in E Massachusetts. 91,000.

New to ni an (nü tō′nē ən, nyü tō′nē ən), *adj.* of or by Sir Isaac Newton.

New World, the Western Hemisphere; North America and South America.

new-world or **New-World** (nü′wėrld′, nyü′wėrld′), *adj.* of or having to do with the Western Hemisphere; not of the Old World: *new-world monkeys.*

new year, 1 year approaching or newly begun. 2 **New Year** or **New Year's, a** the first day or days of the year. **b** New Year's Day. 3 **New Year,** Rosh Hashanah.

New Year's Day, January 1, usually observed as a legal holiday.

New York, 1 Often, **New York State.** one of the northeastern states of the United States. 18,237,000 pop.; 49,600 sq. mi. *Capital:* Albany. *Abbrev.:* N.Y. 2 Often, **New York City.** seaport in SE New York State, at the mouth of the Hudson River. It is the largest city in the United States. 7,896,000.

New York Bay, bay south of Manhattan Island, at the mouth of the Hudson River.

New York er (yôr′kər), native or inhabitant of New York City or New York State.

New Zea land (zē′lənd), country in the S Pacific, consisting of two main islands and various small ones. It is a member of the Commonwealth of Nations. 2,821,000 pop.; 103,700 sq. mi. *Capital:* Wellington.

New Zea land er (zē′lən dər), native or inhabitant of New Zealand.

next (nekst), *adj.* following at once; nearest: *the next train, the next room.* —*adv.* 1 the first time after this: *When you next come, bring it.* 2 in the place, time, or position that is nearest: *Your name comes next.* 3 **next to, a** nearest to. **b** almost; nearly. —*prep.* nearest to: *the house next the church.* [Old English *nēhst* nearest, superlative of *nēah* near, nigh]

next door, 1 in or at the next house, apartment, etc. 2 very close.

next-door (nekst′dôr′, nekst′dōr′; neks′dôr′, neks′dōr′), *adj.* in or at the next house, apartment, etc.

next of kin, the nearest blood relative or relatives.

nex us (nek′səs), *n., pl.* **nex us** or **nex us es.** 1 connection; link. 2 a connected series. [< Latin < *nectere* to bind]

Ney (nā), *n.* **Michel,** 1769-1815, French marshal who fought under Napoleon I.

Nez Percé (nez′ pėrs′; *French* nā per sā′), *n.* member of an American Indian tribe that formerly lived in Idaho, Oregon, and Washington.

N.F., Newfoundland.

Nfld., Newfoundland.

n.g., no good.

N.G., 1 National Guard. 2 no good.

N.H., New Hampshire.

Ni, nickel.

N.I., Northern Ireland.

ni a cin (nī′ə sən), *n.* nicotinic acid. [< *ni(cotinic) ac(id)* + *-in*]

Ni ag ar a (nī ag′rə), *n.* 1 **Niagara River,** river flowing from Lake Erie into Lake Ontario over Niagara Falls, forming part of the border between the United States and Canada. 34 mi. 2 Niagara Falls. 3 cataract; torrent; deluge. 4 something resembling a cataract in amount or force.

Niagara Falls, 1 a great waterfall of the Niagara River, on the boundary between the United States and Canada. 167 ft. high on the American side, 158 ft. on the Canadian side. 2 city in NW New York State, on the Niagara River at Niagara Falls. 86,000.

Nia mey (nyä′mā), *n.* capital of Niger, in the SW part. 79,000.

nib (nib), *n.* 1 point of a pen. 2 either of its parts. 3 tip; point. 4 a bird's bill or beak. [variant of *neb*]

nib ble (nib′əl), *v.,* **-bled, -bling,** *n.* —*v.t.* eat away with quick, small bites, as a rabbit or a mouse does. —*v.i.* bite gently or lightly: *A fish nibbles at the bait.* —*n.* a nibbling; small bite. [origin uncertain] —**nib′bler,** *n.*

Ni be lung (nē′bə lůng), *n.* (in German legends) any of a northern race of dwarfs who owned a golden treasure, captured by Siegfried and his followers.

Ni be lung en lied (nē′bə lůng′ən lēt′), *n.* a German epic given its present form by an unknown author in southern Germany during the first half of the 1200's.

nib lick (nib′lik), *n.* a golf club with an iron or steel head having a sharply sloping face, used especially for high, short shots. [origin uncertain]

nibs (nibz), *n.* INFORMAL. a humorous title of respect for a person, as if in recognition of importance: *How is his nibs?* [origin uncertain]

Ni cae a (nī sē′ə), *n.* city in ancient Asia Minor, site of important church councils in A.D. 325 and 787.

Nic a ra gua (nik′ə rä′gwə), *n.* 1 country in Central America, north of Costa Rica. 1,984,000 pop.; 57,100 sq. mi. *Capital:* Managua. 2 **Lake,** lake in S Nicaragua. 100 mi. long; 45 mi. wide; 2970 sq. mi. —**Nic′a ra′guan,** *adj., n.*

nice (nīs), *adj.,* **nic er, nic est.** 1 that is good or pleasing; agreeable; satisfactory: *a nice face.* 2 thoughtful; kind: *They were nice to us.* 3 very fine; minute; subtle: *a nice distinction.* 4 able to make very fine distinctions; exact; precise; discriminating: *a nice ear for music.* 5 delicately skillful; requiring care, skill, or tact: *a nice problem.* 6 hard to please; exacting; particular; fastidious; dainty: *nice in his eating.* 7 refined; cultured: *a nice accent.* 8 proper; suitable: *nice clothes for a party.* 9 demanding a high standard of conduct; scrupulous: *those of the nicest virtue.* 10 ARCHAIC. affectedly modest; coyly reserved. [Middle English, simple-minded < Old French, silly < Latin *nescius* ignorant < *ne-* not + *scire* know] —**nice′ly,** *adv.* —**nice′ness,** *n.*

Nice (nēs), *n.* seaside resort in SE France. 244,000.

Ni cene (nī sēn′, nī′sēn′), *adj.* of or having to do with Nicaea.

Nicene Council, either of two general ecclesiastical councils that met at Nicaea, the first in A.D. 325 to deal with the Arian heresy, the second in A.D. 787 to consider the question of images.

Nicene Creed, a formal statement of the chief tenets of Christian belief, based on that adopted by the first Nicene Council, and generally accepted throughout western Christendom.

nice Nelly or **nice Nellie,** *pl.* **nice Nellies,** person who is overly modest or prudish.

nice-Nel ly or **nice-Nel lie** (nīs′nel′ē), *adj.* overly modest or prudish: *a nice-Nelly reaction to the movie.*

nice-Nel ly ism (nīs′nel′ē iz′əm), *n.* 1 extreme modesty or prudishness. 2 circumlocution; euphemism.

ni ce ty (nī′sə tē), *n., pl.* **-ties.** 1 carefulness and delicacy in handling; exactness; accuracy: *Television sets require nicety of adjustment.* 2 a fine point; small distinction; detail: *the niceties of law.* 3 quality of being very particular; daintiness; refinement. 4 something dainty or refined: *clean linen and other niceties of apparel.* 5 **to a nicety,** just right: *cookies browned to a nicety.*

niche (nich), *n., v.,* **niched, nich ing.** —*n.* 1 recess or hollow in a wall for a statue, vase, etc.; nook. 2 a suitable place or position; place for which a person is suited. —*v.t.* place in a niche or similar recess. [< Middle French, ultimately < Latin *nidus* nest]

Nich o las (nik′ə ləs), *n.* **Saint,** 1 the patron saint of Russia, and of young people, sailors, travelers, and merchants. He was a bishop in Asia Minor in the A.D. 300's. 2 Santa Claus.

Nicholas I, 1 **Saint,** died A.D. 867, pope from A.D. 858 to 867. 2 1796-1855, czar of Russia from 1825 to 1855.

Nicholas II, 1868-1918, the last czar of Russia, from 1894 to 1917, executed during the Russian Revolution.

nick (nik), *n.* 1 place where a small bit has been cut or broken out; notch; groove: *He cut nicks in a stick to keep count of his score.* 2 **in the nick of time,** just at the right moment. —*v.t.* 1 make a nick or nicks in. 2 cut into or through: *nick a wire.* 3 hit, guess, catch, etc., exactly. 4 SLANG. cheat; defraud. [origin uncertain]

nick el (nik′əl), *n., v.,* **-eled, -el ing** or **-elled, -el ling.** —*n.* 1 a hard, silvery-white metallic element found in igneous rocks, much used as an alloy and in electroplating. *Symbol:* Ni; *atomic number* 28. See pages 326 and 327 for table. 2 coin containing a mixture of nickel and copper; a United States or Canadian five-cent piece. —*v.t.* cover or coat with nickel. [< Swedish < German *Kupfernickel,* literally, copper devil (because the ore resembles copper but yields none)]

nick el o de on (nik′ə lō′dē ən), *n.* U.S. 1 (formerly) place of amusement with motion-picture exhibitions, etc., to which the price of admission was only five cents. 2 jukebox. [< *nickel* the coin + *-odeon,* perhaps patterned on *melodeon*]

nickel plate, a thin coating of nickel deposited on a metal object, usually by electroplating, to prevent rust, improve the appearance, etc.

nick el-plate (nik′əl plāte′), *v.t.,* **-plat ed, -plat ing.** coat with nickel, usually by electroplating.

nickel silver, a silver-white alloy of copper, zinc, and nickel, used for ornaments, utensils, wire, etc.; German silver.

nick er (nik′ər), *v.i.* 1 to neigh. 2 laugh loudly or shrilly. *—n.* 1 a neigh. 2 a loud laugh. [apparently imitative]

nick nack (nik′nak′), *n.* knickknack.

nick name (nik′nām′), *n., v.,* **-named, -nam ing.** *—n.* name added to a person's real name or used instead of it often humorously or in allusion to some special characteristic. *—v.t.* give a nickname to: *They nicknamed the short boy "Shorty."* [Middle English *ekename* < *eke* an addition (Old English *ēaca*) + *name* name; *an ekename* taken as *a nekename*]

Nic o bar Islands (nik′ə bär′, nik′ə bär′), group of small islands in the Bay of Bengal. Together with the Andaman Islands it forms a territory of India. 15,000 pop.; 635 sq. mi.

Nic o si a (nik′ə sē′ə), *n.* capital of Cyprus, in the N central part. 114,000.

nic o tine (nik′ə tēn′), *n.* a poisonous alkaloid contained in the leaves, roots, and seeds of tobacco. It is used as an insecticide, and sometimes in medicine. *Formula:* $C_{10}H_{14}N_2$ [< French < Jacques *Nicot,* about 1530-1600, French ambassador to Portugal, who introduced tobacco into France about 1560]

nic o tin ic acid (nik′ə tin′ik), one of a group of vitamins of the vitamin B complex, found in meat, liver, wheat germ, milk, eggs, and yeast; niacin. It is used to treat and prevent pellagra. *Formula:* C_5H_4NCOOH

nic ti tate (nik′tə tāt), *v.i.,* **-tat ed, -tat ing.** to wink. [alteration of Latin *nictatum* winked, blinked] **—nic′ti ta′tion,** *n.*

nictitating membrane, a transparent inner eyelid present in birds and certain other animals that can draw over the eye to protect and moisten it.

Nie buhr (nē′bu̇r), *n.* **Reinhold,** 1892-1971, American theologian.

niece (nēs), *n.* daughter of one's brother or sister; daughter of one's brother-in-law or sister-in-law. [< Old French, ultimately < Latin *neptis* granddaughter, niece]

Nie tzsche (nē′chə), *n.* **Friedrich Wilhelm,** 1844-1900, German philosopher and writer.

nif ty (nif′tē), *adj.,* **-ti er, -ti est,** *n., pl.* **-ties.** INFORMAL. *—adj.* 1 attractive or stylish; smart. 2 fine; splendid. *—n.* something nifty, especially a clever remark or act. [origin uncertain]

Ni ger (nī′jər), *n.* 1 country in W Africa north of Nigeria. 4,016,000 pop.; 489,100 sq. mi. See **Algeria** for map. *Capital:* Niamey. 2 **Niger River,** river flowing from W Africa into the Gulf of Guinea. 2600 mi.

Ni ger i a (nī jir′ē ə), *n.* country in W Africa north of the Gulf of Guinea, a member of the Commonwealth of Nations. 66,174,000 pop.; 356,700 sq. mi. *Capital:* Lagos. See **Upper Volta** for map. **—Ni ger′i an,** *adj., n.*

nig gard (nig′ərd), *n.* a stingy person; miser. *—adj.* stingy. [< Scandinavian (Old Icelandic) *hnöggr* stingy]

nig gard ly (nig′ərd lē), *adj.* 1 stingy; miserly. 2 meanly small or scanty: *a niggardly gift.* *—adj.* stingily; grudgingly. **—nig′gard li ness,** *n.*

nig gling (nig′ling), *adj.* trifling; mean; petty. *—n.* niggling work or activity. **—nig′gling ly,** *adv.*

nigh (nī), *adv.* 1 near (in position, time, relationship, etc.). 2 nearly; almost. *—adj.* 1 near; close. 2 (of one of a team of horses) left; near. *—prep.* near. *—v.t., v.i.* draw near. [Old English *nēah*]

night (nīt), *n.* 1 the time between evening and morning; the time from sunset to sunrise, especially when it is dark. 2 the darkness of night; the dark. 3 the darkness of ignorance, sin, sorrow, old age, death, etc. 4 evening; nightfall. 5 **make a night of it,** celebrate until very late at night. *—adj.* of night. [Old English *niht*]

night-blind (nīt′blīnd′), *adj.* affected with night blindness.

night blindness, condition of the eyes in which the sight is abnormally poor or wholly gone at night or in a dim light.

night-bloom ing cereus (nīt′blü′ming), any of a genus of climbing American cactuses whose large, fragrant, white flowers open at night.

night cap (nīt′kap′), *n.* 1 cap to be worn in bed. 2 INFORMAL. **a** a drink, especially an alcoholic drink, taken just before going to bed. **b** the last event in a sports program, especially the second baseball game of a double-header.

night clothes, clothes to be worn in bed, as for sleeping.

night club (nīt′klub′), *n.* place for dancing, eating, and entertainment, open only at night.

night crawler, any large earthworm that comes to the surface of the ground at night; nightwalker.

night dress (nīt′dres′), *n.* nightgown.

night fall (nīt′fôl′), *n.* the coming of night; dusk.

night gown (nīt′goun′), *n.* a long, loose garment worn by a woman or child in bed.

night hawk (nīt′hôk′), *n.* 1 goatsucker, a bird similar to the whippoorwill but with white wing patches. Nighthawks fly about at dusk in search of insects. 2 INFORMAL. person who stays up late at night.

night ie (nī′tē), *n.* INFORMAL. nightgown or nightshirt. Also, **nighty.**

nightingale
6 to 7 in. long

night in gale (nīt′n gāl), *n.* a small, reddish-brown thrush of Europe. The male sings sweetly at night as well as in the day. [Old English *nihtegale* < *niht* night + *galan* sing]

Night in gale (nīt′n gāl), *n.* **Florence,** 1820-1910, English nurse, who worked to bring about improvements in nursing and hospital sanitation.

night jar (nīt′jär′), *n.* goatsucker.

night latch, latch or lock, opened by a key from the outside or by a knob from the inside.

night letter, telegram sent at night at a reduced rate and usually delivered the following morning.

hat, āge, fär; let, ēqual, tėrm;
it, īce; hot, ōpen, ôrder;
oil, out; cup, pu̇t, rüle;
ch, child; ng, long; sh, she;
th, thin; ᴛʜ, then; zh, measure;

ə represents *a* in about, *e* in taken, *i* in pencil, *o* in lemon, *u* in circus.

< = from, derived from, taken from.

night light, a small light to be kept burning all night.

night long (nīt′lông′, nīt′long′), *adj.* lasting all night. *—adv.* through the whole night.

night ly (nīt′lē), *adj.* 1 done, happening, or appearing every night. 2 done, happening, or appearing at night. *—adv.* 1 every night. 2 at night; by night.

night mare (nīt′mer′, nīt′mar′), *n.* 1 a very distressing dream; dream causing great fear or anxiety. 2 a very distressing experience. [Old English *niht* night + *mare* incubus]

night mar ish (nīt′mer′ish, nīt′mar′ish), *adj.* like a nightmare; causing fear or anxiety; very distressing.

night owl, INFORMAL. person who often stays up late at night.

night rid er (nīt′rī′dər), *n.* U.S. one of a band of mounted men in the South who rode masked at night bent on intimidation and violence.

night robe, a nightgown.

night school, school held in the evening for persons who work during the day.

night shade (nīt′shād′), *n.* 1 any of a large genus of plants of the nightshade family, including the potato, Jerusalem cherry, and eggplant. 2 belladonna; deadly nightshade.

nightshade family, group of dicotyledonous herbs, shrubs, or small trees, many of which contain narcotic or poisonous alkaloids. The family includes the potato, tobacco, belladonna, jimson weed, mandrake, tomato, bittersweet, and petunia.

night shirt (nīt′shėrt′), *n.* a long, loose shirt, usually reaching the knees, worn by a man or boy in bed.

night stick (nīt′stik′), *n.* U.S. a policeman's club.

night time (nīt′tīm′), *n.* time between evening and morning.

night walk er (nīt′wô′kər), *n.* 1 person who goes around at night, especially for a bad purpose. 2 night crawler.

night watch, 1 watch or guard kept during the night. 2 person or persons keeping such a watch. 3 period or division of the night.

night y (nī′tē), *n., pl.* **night ies.** nightie.

ni hil ism (nī′ə liz′əm), *n.* 1 entire rejection of the established beliefs in religion, morals, government, laws, etc. 2 (in philosophy) the denial of all existence. 3 Also, **Nihilism.** the beliefs and practices of a revolutionary party in Russia in the middle 1800's, which advocated destruction of the old order by violence and terrorism to make way for reform. 4 use of violent methods against a government. [< Latin *nihil* nothing]

ni hil ist (nī′ə list), *n.* 1 person who believes in some form of nihilism. 2 terrorist. *—adj.* nihilistic.

ni hil is tic (nī′ə lis′tik), *adj.* of nihilists or nihilism.

ni hil ob stat (nī′hil ob′stat), 1 (in the Roman Catholic Church) a phrase on the title page of a book, preceding the name of the official censor and indicating his approval. 2 official or authoritative approval. [< Latin, nothing hinders]

Ni jin sky (nə jin′skē), *n.* **Vaslav,** 1890-1950, Russian ballet dancer.

Ni ke (nī′kē, nē′kā), *n.* (in Greek myths) the goddess of victory, usually represented with wings.

nil (nil), *n.* nothing. [< Latin, short for *nihil*]

Nile green (nīl), a pale bluish green.

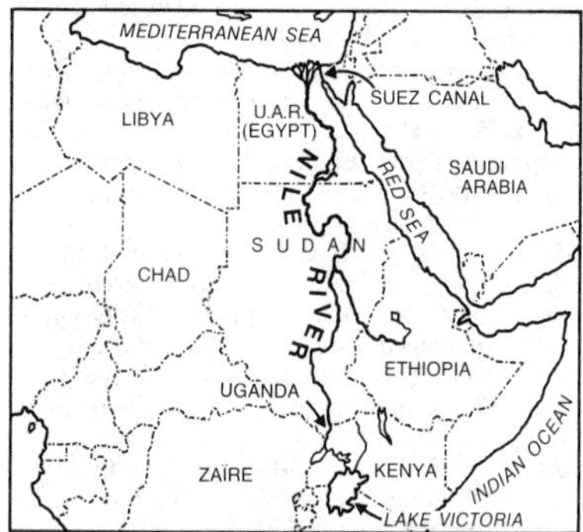

Nile River, river in E Africa flowing north from its headstream near Lake Victoria through Uganda, Sudan, and Egypt into the Mediterranean. It is the longest river in the world. 4150 mi.

Ni lot ic (nī lot′ik), *adj.* of or having to do with the Nile or the inhabitants of the Nile valley.

nim ble (nim′bəl), *adj.,* **-bler, -blest.** 1 active and sure-footed; light and quick; agile: *Goats are nimble in climbing among the rocks.* 2 quick to understand and to reply; clever: *a nimble mind.* [Old English *numol* quick to grasp] **—nim′ble ness,** *n.* **—nim′bly,** *adv.*

nim bo stra tus (nim′bō strā′təs), *n., pl.* **-ti** (-tī). cloud formation consisting of a dark-gray layer of clouds and occurring at heights under 6500 feet; nimbus. These clouds usually produce prolonged rain or snow.

nim bus (nim′bəs), *n., pl.* **-bus es, -bi** (-bī). 1 halo. 2 a bright cloud surrounding a god, person, or thing. 3 nimbostratus. [< Latin, cloud]

Nim itz (nim′its), *n.* **Chester W.,** 1885-1966, American admiral.

Nim rod (nim′rod), *n.* 1 (in the Bible) a descendant of Noah who was a great hunter. 2 hunter.

nin com poop (nin′kəm püp), *n.* fool; simpleton. [origin unknown]

nine (nīn), *n.* 1 one more than eight; 9. 2 set of nine persons or things. 3 team of nine players: *a baseball nine.* 4 **the Nine,** the Muses. 5 **dressed to the nines,** elaborately dressed. *—adj.* being one more than eight. [Old English *nigon*]

nine fold (nīn′fōld′), *adj.* 1 nine times as much or as great. 2 having nine parts. *—adv.* nine times as much or as great.

nine pence (nīn′pəns), *n.* 1 nine British pennies. 2 a former British coin having this value.

nine pins (nīn′pinz′), *n.* game in which nine large wooden pins are set up to be bowled over with a ball.

nine teen (nīn′tēn′), *n., adj.* nine more than ten; 19.

nine teenth (nīn′tēnth′), *adj.* next after the 18th; last in a series of 19. *—n.* 1 next after the 18th; last in a series of 19. 2 one of 19 equal parts.

nine ti eth (nīn′tē ith), *adj.* next after the 89th; last in a series of 90. *—n.* 1 next after the 89th; last in a series of 90. 2 one of 90 equal parts.

nine ty (nīn′tē), *n., pl.* **-ties,** *adj.* nine times ten; 90.

Nin e veh (nin′ə və), *n.* capital of ancient Assyria. Its ruins are on the Tigris River, opposite Mosul in N Iraq.

Ning po (ning′pō′), *n.* port in E China, formerly a treaty port. 238,000.

nin ny (nin′ē), *n., pl.* **-nies.** fool. [origin uncertain]

ninth (nīnth), *adj.* next after the eighth; last in a series of nine. *—n.* 1 next after the eighth; last in a series of nine. 2 one of nine equal parts. 3 in music: **a** a tone distant from another by an octave and a second. **b** interval between such tones. **c** combination of such tones.

Ni o be (nī′ō bē′), *n.* (in Greek myths) the daughter of Tantalus whose fourteen beautiful children were slain because she boasted about them. Turned by Zeus into a stone fountain, she weeps forever for her children.

ni o bi um (nī ō′bē əm), *n.* a soft, ductile metallic element of steel-gray color and brilliant luster, found in nature with tantalum, which it resembles in chemical properties. It is used in making stainless steel and in alloys. *Symbol:* Nb; *atomic number* 41. See pages 326 and 327 for table. [< New Latin < *Niobe,* daughter of Tantalus (for whom tantalum was named)]

nip[1] (nip), *v.,* **nipped, nip ping,** *n.* *—v.t.* 1 squeeze tightly and suddenly; pinch; bite: *The crab nipped my toe.* 2 take off by biting or pinching; cut off by snipping: *nip twigs from a bush.* 3 blight; injure: *Some of our tomato plants were nipped by frost.* 4 have a sharp, biting effect on: *Cold winds nip your ears and nose.* 5 SLANG. steal. 6 DIALECT. take suddenly or quickly; snatch. *—v.i.* BRITISH INFORMAL. move rapidly or nimbly. *—n.* 1 a tight squeeze; pinch; sudden bite. 2 injury caused by frost. 3 sharp cold; chill: *There is a nip in the air on a frosty morning.* 4 a small portion; bit. 5 a sharp flavor: *cheese with a real nip.* 6 **nip and tuck,** so evenly matched in a race or contest that the result remains in doubt till the end. [Middle English *nyppen*]

nip[2] (nip), *n., v.,* **nipped, nip ping.** *—n.* a small drink, especially of alcoholic liquor. *—v.i.* take nips of alcoholic liquor. [origin uncertain]

nip per (nip′ər), *n.* 1 person or thing that nips. 2 one of the large claws of a lobster or crab. 3 **nippers,** *pl.* pincers, forceps, pliers, or any tool that nips. 4 a cutting tooth of a horse. 5 BRITISH. a small boy; lad.

nip ple (nip′əl), *n.* 1 the small projection on a breast or udder through which an infant or a baby animal gets its mother's milk; teat. 2 the rubber cap or mouthpiece of a baby's bottle. 3 anything shaped or used like a nipple. [origin uncertain]

Nip pon (ni pon′, nip′on), *n.* Japanese name for **Japan.**

Nip pon ese (nip′ə nēz′), *adj., n., pl.* **-ese.** Japanese.

nip py (nip′ē), *adj.,* **-pi er, -pi est.** biting; sharp.

nir va na or **Nir va na** (nir vä′nə), *n.* 1 the Buddhist idea of heavenly peace; condition in which the soul is free from all desire and pain. 2 any condition like this; blessed oblivion. [< Sanskrit *nirvāṇa* extinction]

Ni sei (nē′sā′), *n., pl.* **-sei.** a native-born United States or Canadian citizen whose parents were Japanese immigrants. [< Japanese *nisei* second generation]

Nis sen hut (nis′n), Quonset hut. [< Peter N. *Nissen,* 1871-1930, who designed it]

nit (nit), *n.* 1 egg of a louse or similar parasitic insect. 2 a very young louse or similar insect. [Old English *hnitu*]

ni ter (nī′tər), *n.* 1 potassium nitrate, especially when it occurs naturally as a white salt in the soil and encrusted on rocks; saltpeter. It is used in making gunpowder. 2 sodium nitrate, especially as it occurs in natural deposits. It is used as a fertilizer. Also, **nitre.** [< Old French *nitre* sodium carbonate < Latin *nitrum* < Greek *nitron,* of Semitic origin]

nit-pick (nit′pik′), *v.t., v.i.* INFORMAL. pick at something in a petty or niggling manner; search for petty faults. **—nit′-pick′er,** *n.*

ni trate (nī′trāt), *n., v.,* **-trat ed, -trat ing.** *—n.* 1 salt or ester of nitric acid. 2 potassium nitrate or sodium nitrate when used as fertilizers. *—v.t.* combine or treat with nitric acid or a nitrate. **—ni tra′tion,** *n.*

ni tre (nī′tər), *n.* niter.

ni tric (nī′trik), *adj.* of or containing nitrogen, especially with a valence of five.

nitric acid, a clear, colorless, fuming liquid that eats into flesh, clothing, metal, and other substances. It is used in etching and metallurgy and in making dyes and explosives. *Formula:* HNO_3

ni tride (nī′trīd, nī′trid), *n.* compound of nitrogen with a more electropositive element or radical, such as phosphorus, boron, or a metal.

ni tri fy (nī′trə fī), *v.t.,* **-fied, -fy ing.** 1 oxidize (ammonia compounds, etc.) to nitrites or nitrates, especially by bacterial action. 2 impregnate (soil, etc.) with nitrates. 3 combine or treat with nitrogen or one of its compounds. **—ni′tri fi ca′tion,** *n.* **—ni′tri fi′er,** *n.*

ni trite (nī′trīt), *n.* salt or ester of nitrous acid.

ni tro (nī′trō), *adj.* containing the univalent radical $—NO_2$. *—n.* INFORMAL. nitroglycerin.

ni tro bac ter i a (nī′trō bak tir′ē ə), *n.pl.* any of various bacteria living in soil that oxidize ammonium compounds into nitrites or nitrites into nitrates.

ni tro ben zene (nī′trō ben′zēn′, nī′trō ben zēn′), *n.* a poisonous yellowish liquid obtained from benzene by the action of nitric acid, used in making aniline, as a reagent, etc. *Formula:* $C_6H_5NO_2$

ni tro cel lu lose (nī′trō sel′yə lōs), *n.* substance used to make various plastics, obtained by treating cellulose with nitric acid and sulfuric acid; cellulose nitrate.

ni tro gen (nī′trə jən), *n.* a colorless, odorless, tasteless gaseous element that forms about four fifths of the atmosphere and is a necessary part of all animal and vegetable tissues. *Symbol:* N; *atomic number* 7. See pages 326 and 327 for table. [< French *nitrogène* < *nitre* niter + *gène* -gen]

nitrogen cycle, the circulation of nitrogen and its compounds by living organisms in

hat, āge, fär; let, ēqual, tėrm;
it, īce; hot, ōpen, ôrder;
oil, out; cup, pu̇t, rüle;
ch, child; ng, long; sh, she;
th, thin; ꟌH, then; zh, measure;

ə represents *a* in about, *e* in taken, *i* in pencil, *o* in lemon, *u* in circus.

< = from, derived from, taken from.

nature. Nitrogen in the air passes into the soil, where it is changed to nitrates by bacteria and used by green plants and then in turn by animals. Decaying plants and animals, and animal waste products, are in turn acted on by bacteria and the nitrogen in them is again made available for circulation.

nitrogen fixation, 1 the conversion of atmospheric nitrogen into nitrates by bacteria found in the soil and in nodules on the roots of various leguminous plants. 2 the combination of free atmospheric nitrogen with other substances, as in making explosives and fertilizers.

ni tro gen-fix ing (nī′trə jən fik′sing), *adj.* converting atmospheric nitrogen into nitrates: *nitrogen-fixing bacteria.*

ni tro gen ize (nī′trə jə nīz), *v.t.*, **-ized, -iz ing.** combine with nitrogen or one of its compounds.

nitrogen mustard, any of a class of compounds similar to mustard gas but containing nitrogen instead of sulfur, used in medicine.

ni trog e nous (nī troj′ə nəs), *adj.* of or containing nitrogen.

ni tro glyc er in (nī′trə glis′ər ən), *n.* an oily, pale yellow, explosive liquid made by treating glycerin with nitric and sulfuric acids. Nitroglycerin is used in making dynamite and in medicine to dilate blood vessels. *Formula:* $C_3H_5(NO_3)_3$

ni tro glyc er ine (nī′trə glis′ər ən, nī′trə-glis′ə rēn′), *n.* nitroglycerin.

ni tro so (nī trō′sō), *adj.* indicating the presence of the univalent radical —NO.

ni trous (nī′trəs), *adj.* 1 of or containing nitrogen, especially with a valence of 3. 2 of or containing niter.

nitrous oxide, a colorless, sweet-tasting gas that causes laughing and dulls pain; laughing gas. It is sometimes used as an anesthetic in surgery and dentistry. *Formula:* N_2O

nit wit (nit′wit′), *n.* a very stupid person.

nix[1] (niks), SLANG. *—interj.* no! stop! *—n.* nothing; nobody. *—v.t.* refuse; deny. *—adv.* no. [< German]

nix[2] (niks), *n.* (in German legends) a water fairy.

nix ie (nik′sē), *n.* (in German legends) a female water fairy.

Nix on (nik′sən), *n.* **Richard Milhous,** born 1913, the 37th president of the United States, since 1969, vice-president from 1953 to 1961.

Ni zam (ni zäm′, ni zam′), *n.* title after 1713 of the former native rulers of Hyderabad, India. [< Hindustani *nizām* governor]

Nizh ni Nov go rod (nizh′nē nôv′gə-rod′), former name of **Gorki.**

N.J., New Jersey.

N kru mah (en krü′mə, nə krü′mə), *n.* **Kwame,** 1909-1972, prime minister of Ghana from 1957 to 1960, president from 1960 to 1966.

N. lat., north latitude.

NLF or **N.L.F.,** National Liberation Front (political arm of the Vietcong).

NLRB, National Labor Relations Board.

N.M. or **N. Mex.,** New Mexico.

NNE or **N.N.E.,** north-northeast.

NNW or **N.N.W.,** north-northwest.

no[1] (nō), *adv., n., pl.* **noes,** *adj.* *—adv.* 1 word used to deny, refuse, or disagree: *Will you come? No.* 2 not in any degree; not at all: *He is no better.* 3 not, chiefly in phrases like *whether or no.* *—n.* 1 denial; refusal. 2 a negative vote or voter: *The noes have it.* *—adj.* not any; not a: *They have no friends.* [Old English *nā* < *ne* not + *ā* ever] ➤ See **yes** for usage note.

no[2] (nō), *n., pl.* **no** or **nos.** type of Japanese classical drama with formalized dancing and chanting by actors wearing symbolic masks. [< Japanese *nō*]

No, nobelium.

no., *pl.* **nos.** number [for Latin *numero* by number].

➤ The abbreviation **no.** or **No.** for *number* is appropriate chiefly in business and technical English. In the United States it is not written with street numbers.

No., 1 north. 2 northern. 3 *pl.* **Nos.** number [for Latin *numero* by number].

No ah (nō′ə), *n.* (in the Bible) a man whom God told to make an ark to save himself, his family, and a pair of each kind of animal from the Flood.

nob (nob), *n.* SLANG. 1 head. 2 BRITISH. person of wealth or social importance. [perhaps variant of *knob*]

nob by (nob′ē), *adj.*, **-bi er, -bi est.** SLANG. 1 smart; fashionable; elegant. 2 first-rate.

No bel (nō bel′), *n.* **Alfred Bernhard,** 1833-1896, Swedish inventor of dynamite and manufacturer of explosives, founder of the Nobel prizes.

No bel ist (nō bel′ist), *n.* recipient of a Nobel prize.

no be li um (nō bē′lē əm), *n,* a very heavy radioactive chemical element produced artificially by bombarding curium with carbon ions. *Symbol:* No; *atomic number* 102. See pages 326 and 327 for table. [< New Latin < Alfred B. *Nobel*]

Nobel prize, any of five money prizes established by Alfred B. Nobel to be given annually to those persons or organizations who have done outstanding work in physics, chemistry, medicine or physiology, literature, and the promotion of peace. A sixth category, economics, was added in 1969.

no bil i ty (nō bil′ə tē), *n., pl.* **-ties.** 1 people of noble rank, title, or birth; peerage. Earls, marquises, and counts belong to the nobility. 2 noble birth; noble rank. 3 noble character.

no ble (nō′bəl), *adj.*, **-bler, -blest,** *n.* *—adj.* 1 high and great by birth, rank, or title; aristocratic: *a noble family, noble blood.* 2 high and great in character; showing greatness of mind; good; worthy: *a noble knight, a noble deed.* 3 having excellent qualities; fine: *a noble poem, a noble animal.* 4 grand in appearance; splendid; magnificent: *a noble sight.* See **grand** for synonym study. 5 chemically inert. Helium, neon, argon, krypton, xenon, and radon are the noble gases. *—n.* 1 person high and great by birth, rank, or title. 2 an English gold coin of the late Middle Ages. It was worth 6 shillings and 8 pence. [< Old French < Latin *nobilis* renowned, well-known < *gnoscere* to know] **—no′ble ness,** *n.*

no ble man (nō′bəl mən), *n., pl.* **-men.** man of noble rank, title, or birth.

no blesse o blige (nô bles′ ô blēzh′), FRENCH. 1 persons of noble rank should behave nobly. 2 (literally) nobility obligates.

no ble wom an (nō′bəl wu̇m′ən), *n., pl.* **-wom en.** woman of noble birth or rank.

no bly (nō′blē), *adv.* in a noble manner.

no bod y (nō′bod′ē, nō′bə dē), *pron., n., pl.* **-bod ies.** *—pron.* no one; no person. *—n.* person of no importance.

nock (nok), *n.* notch on a bow or arrow for the bowstring. *—v.t.* 1 furnish (a bow or arrow) with a nock. 2 fit (an arrow) to the bowstring ready for shooting. [Middle English *nocke*]

noc tur nal (nok tėr′nl), *adj.* 1 of the night: *Stars are a nocturnal sight.* 2 in the night: *a nocturnal visitor.* 3 active in the night: *The owl is a nocturnal bird.* 4 closed by day, open by night: *a nocturnal flower.* [< Latin *nocturnus* of the night < *noctem* night] **—noc tur′nal ly,** *adv.*

noc turne (nok′tėrn′), *n.* 1 a dreamy or pensive musical piece. 2 a painting of a night scene. [< French, nocturnal]

nod (nod), *v.*, **nod ded, nod ding,** *n.* *—v.t.* 1 bow (the head) slightly and raise it again quickly. 2 express by nodding: *nod consent.* *—v.i.* 1 indicate approval by nodding. 2 let the head fall forward and bob about when sleepy or falling asleep. 3 be sleepy; become careless and dull. 4 droop, bend, or sway back and forth: *Trees nod in the wind.* *—n.* a nodding of the head. [Middle English *nodden*] **—nod′der,** *n.*

nod al (nō′dl), *adj.* having to do with or like a node or nodes.

nod dle (nod′l), *n.* INFORMAL. the head. [Middle English *nodel, nodul*]

nod dy (nod′ē), *n., pl.* **-dies.** 1 fool. 2 any of various terns common in the West Indies and Florida Keys.

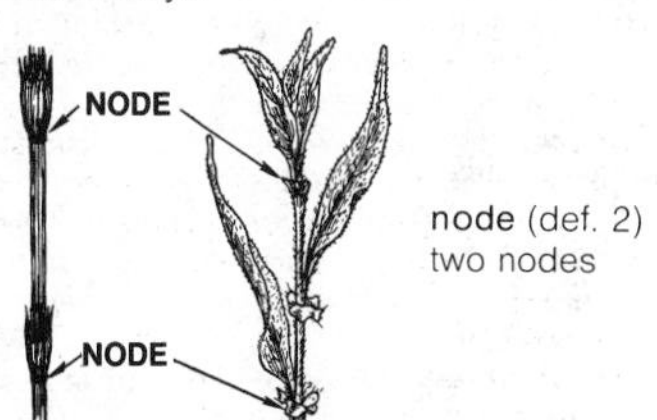

node (def. 2)
two nodes

node (nōd), *n.* 1 knot, knob, or swelling. 2 (in botany) a joint on a stem where leaves grow out; part of a stem that normally bears a leaf or leaves. 3 (in physics) a point, line, or plane in a vibrating body at which there is comparatively no vibration. 4 (in astronomy) either of the two points at which the orbit of a heavenly body intersects the path of the sun or the orbit of another heavenly body. [< Latin *nodus* knot]

nod u lar (noj′ə lər), *adj.* having nodules.

nod ule (noj′ül), *n.* 1 a small knot, knob, or swelling. 2 a small, rounded mass or lump: *nodules of pure gold.* 3 a small swelling on the root of a leguminous plant that contains nitrogen-fixing bacteria.

nod u lose (noj′ə lōs, noj′ə lōs′), *adj.* having little knots or knobs.

nod u lous (noj′ə ləs), *adj.* nodulose.

No el or **No ël** (nō el′), *n.* 1 Christmas. 2 **noel** or **noël,** a Christmas song; carol. [< French *Noël* < Latin *natalis* natal (i.e. the natal day of Christ). Doublet of NATAL.]

nog (nog), *n.* 1 eggnog or the like made with

alcoholic liquor. 2 BRITISH. a strong ale or beer.

nog gin (nog′ən), *n.* 1 a small cup or mug. 2 a small drink, usually equal to 1/4 pint. 3 INFORMAL. a person's head. [origin uncertain]

no-good (nō′gůd′), INFORMAL. —*n.* a worthless person or thing. —*adj.* good-for-nothing; worthless.

no-hit ter (nō′hit′ər), *n.* U.S. a baseball game in which a pitcher gives up no base hits to the opposing team.

no how (nō′hou′), *adv.* INFORMAL. in no way; not at all.

noise (noiz), *n., v.,* **noised, nois ing.** —*n.* 1 sound that is not musical or pleasant; loud or harsh sound. See synonym study below. 2 any sound. 3 din of voices and movements; loud shouting; outcry; clamor. 4 disturbance in a radio or television signal. —*v.t.* spread the news of; report; tell: *It was noised about that the company was going out of business.* [< Old French, uproar, brawl < Latin *nausea.* Doublet of NAUSEA.]

Syn. *n.* 1 **Noise, din, uproar** mean loud, confused sound. **Noise** applies to any disagreeably unmusical or loud sound: *The noise on the street kept me awake.* **Din** applies to a prolonged and deafening confusion or clanging or piercing noises: *The din of machines and factory whistles hurt my ears.* **Uproar** applies especially to the shouting and loud noises of a crowd and the wild excitement that causes such noise: *You should have heard the uproar when officials called back the touchdown.*

noise less (noiz′lis), *adj.* making little or no noise: *a noiseless typewriter.* —**noise′less ly,** *adv.* —**noise′less ness,** *n.*

noise mak er (noiz′mā′kər), *n.* 1 person who makes too much noise. 2 thing that makes noise, especially a horn, rattle, etc., used to make noise at a party.

noi some (noi′səm), *adj.* 1 that disgusts; offensive, especially to the smell: *a noisome odor.* 2 harmful; injurious: *a noisome pestilence.* [Middle English *noy,* variant of *annoy* + *-some*[1]] —**noi′some ly,** *adv.* —**noi′some ness,** *n.*

nois y (noi′zē), *adj.,* **nois i er, nois i est.** 1 making much noise: *a noisy crowd.* See **loud** for synonym study. 2 full of noise: *a noisy street.* 3 having much noise with it: *a noisy quarrel.* —**nois′i ly,** *adv.* —**nois′i ness,** *n.*

nol le pros e qui (nol′ē pros′ə kwī), (in law) an entry made upon the records of a court by the plaintiff or prosecutor that he will proceed no further in a suit. [< Latin, be unwilling to pursue]

no lo con ten de re (nō′lō kən ten′də rē′), (in law) a defendant's plea that he will accept conviction but not admit his guilt. [< Latin, I do not wish to contend]

nol pros (nol′pros′), *v.t.,* **-prossed, -pros sing.** (in law) to abandon (a lawsuit or indictment) by entering a nolle prosequi. [short for *nolle prosequi*]

nol. pros., nolle prosequi.

nom., nominative.

no mad (nō′mad, nom′ad), *n.* 1 member of a tribe that moves from place to place to have food or pasture for its cattle. 2 wanderer. —*adj.* 1 wandering from place to place to find pasture. 2 wandering. [< Greek *nomados,* ultimately < *nemein* to pasture]

no mad ic (nō mad′ik), *adj.* of nomads or their life; wandering; roving. —**no mad′i cal ly,** *adv.*

no mad ism (nō′ma diz′əm, nom′a diz′əm), *n.* the way that nomads live.

no man's land, 1 (in war) the land between opposing lines of trenches. 2 tract of land to which no one has a recognized or established claim. 3 scope of activity over which no jurisdiction or authority exists.

nom de guerre (nôN də ger′), FRENCH. 1 pseudonym. 2 (literally) war name.

nom de plume (nom′ də plüm′), pen name. [formed in English from French *nom* name, *de* of, *plume* pen]

Nome (nōm), *n.* seaport and mining town in W Alaska, on the Bering Sea. 3000.

no men (nō′men), *n., pl.* **nom i na** (nom′ə nə). (in ancient Rome) the second name of a person, indicating his clan or gens. *Julius* in *Gaius Julius Caesar* was Caesar's nomen, indicating membership in the Julian gens. [< Latin, literally, name]

no men cla ture (nō′mən klā′chər, nō men′klə chər), *n.* set or system of names or terms: *the nomenclature of music.* [< Latin *nomenclatura* < *nomen* name + *calare* to call]

nom i nal (nom′ə nəl), *adj.* 1 existing in name only; not real: *The president is the nominal head of the club, but the secretary really runs its affairs.* 2 too small to be considered; unimportant compared with the real value: *We paid our friend a nominal rent for the cottage each summer—$5 a month.* 3 giving the name or names: *a nominal list of the students in our room.* 4 (in grammar) of, as, or like a name or a noun. *Day* is the nominal root of *daily, daybreak,* and *Sunday.* [< Latin *nominalis* < *nomen* name]

nom i nal ly (nom′ə nə lē), *adv.* 1 in name; as a matter of form; in a nominal way only. 2 by name.

nom i nate (nom′ə nāt), *v.t.,* **-nat ed, -nat ing.** 1 name as candidate for an office: *William Jennings Bryan was nominated for President three times, but he was never elected.* 2 appoint for an office or duty: *President Woodrow Wilson nominated William Jennings Bryan as Secretary of State.* —**nom′i na tor,** *n.*

nom i na tion (nom′ə nā′shən), *n.* 1 a naming as a candidate for office. 2 selection for office or duty; appointment to office or duty. 3 a being nominated.

nom i na tive (nom′ə nə tiv, nom′ə nā′tiv), *adj.* showing the subject of a verb or the words agreeing with the subject. *I, he, she, we,* and *they* are in the nominative case. —*n.* 1 the nominative case. 2 word in that case. *Who* and *I* are nominatives.

nom i nee (nom′ə nē′), *n.* person who is nominated.

non-, *prefix.* not; not a; opposite of; lack of; failure of: *Nonessential = not essential. Nonresident = not a resident. Nonconformity = lack of conformity.* [< Latin < *non* not]

If an adjective formed with *non-* is not defined in this dictionary, its meaning will be clear if *not* is put in place of the *non.* If a noun formed with *non-* is not defined, its meaning will be clear if *not, not a, the opposite of,* or *the absence of* is put in place of the *non. Non-* is a living prefix and may be used with any noun, adjective, or adverb; but if there is a commonly used word of the same meaning formed with *un-, in-,* or *dis-,* that word is usually preferable. Most of the words that have *non-* as the preferred usage, or as a respectable rival of *un-,* are listed below, or as regular entries.

non′ab sorb′ent
non ac′a dem′ic
non′ad dic′tive
non′ad her′ence
non′ad he′sive
non′ad ja′cent
non′ad min′is tra′tive
non′ad mis′sion
non′ag gres′sive
non′a gree′ment
non ag′ri cul′tur al
non′ap pear′ance
non′a quat′ic
non′as sess′a ble
non′as sim′i la′tion
non′ath let′ic
non′at tend′ance
non′au thor′i ta′tive
non ba′sic
non be′ing
non′be liev′er
non′bel lig′er ent
non break′a ble
non cak′ing
non′cal car′e ous
non′ca non′i cal
non-Cath′o lic
non cel′lu lar
non charge′a ble
non-Chris′tian
non cit′i zen
non civ′i lized
non cler′i cal
non clin′i cal
non clot′ting
non′col laps′i ble
non′col lect′i ble
non′col le′giate
non com′bat
non′com bus′ti ble
non′com mer′cial
non′com mu′ni ca ble
non com′mu nist
non′com pet′ing
non′com pet′i tive
non′com press′i ble
non′com pul′sion
non′con form′ing
non′con sec′u tive
non′con sti tu′tion al
non′con ta′gious
non′con tem′po rar′y
non′con tin′u ous
non con′tra band
non′con tra dic′tor y
non′con tro ver′sial
non′con vert′i ble
non′co op′e ra′tive
non′cor ro′sive
non′cre a′tive
non crim′i nal
non crit′i cal
non crys′tal line
non cu′mu la tive
non′de cep′tive
non′de duct′i ble
non′dem o crat′ic
non′de struc′tive
non dir′i gi ble
non′dis crim′i na′tion
non′dis pos′al
non′dis tinc′tive
non′di ver′gent
non′di vis′i ble
non′dog mat′ic
non′dra mat′ic
non earn′ing
non ed′i ble
non ed′u ca ble
non′ed u ca′tion al
non′e las′tic
non′e mo′tion al
non′en force′ment
non-Eng′lish
non′e quiv′a lent
non eth′i cal
non′-Eu clid′e an
non′ex change′a ble
non′ex clu′sive
non′ex ist′ing
non′ex plo′sive
non′ex port′a ble
non′ex tend′ed
non fac′tu al
non fad′ing
non fed′er al
non fed′e rat′ed
non fer′rous
non fes′tive
non fis′cal
non fis′sion a ble
non flow′er ing
non freez′ing
non func′tion al
non gas′e ous
non′gov ern men′tal
non hab′it a ble
non′he red′i tar′y
non her′it a ble
non′his to′ric
non hu′man
non hu′mor ous
non′i den′ti cal
non′i den′ti ty
non′id i o mat′ic
non′im mu′ni ty
non′im por ta′tion
non′im preg′nat ed
non′in clu′sive
non′in dict′a ble
non′in dict′ment
non′in dus′tri al
non′in fec′tion
non′in fec′tious
non′in flam′ma ble
non′in flect′ed
non′in form′a tive
non′in her′it a ble
non′in sti tu′tion al
non in′te grat′ed
non in′ter course
non′in ter fer′ence
non′in ter sect′ing
non′in tox′i cant
non′in tox′i cat′ing
non ir′ri tant
non ir′ri tat′ing
non le′gal
non lit′e rar′y
non mar′ry ing
non mar′tial
non′me chan′i cal
non mem′ber
non mi′gra to′ry
non mil′i tant
non mil′i tar′y
non min′er al
non mo′tile
non nav′i ga ble
non′ne go′tia ble

non neu′tral
non nu′cle ar
non′nu tri′tious
non′o be′di ence
non′o blig′a to′ry
non′ob serv′ance
non′oc cur′rence
non o′dor ous
non′of fi′cial
non op′e rat′ing
non′op e ra′tion al
non or′tho dox
non par′al lel
non′par a sit′ic
non′pa rish′ion er
non′par lia men′tar y
non′pa ro′chi al
non′par tic′i pa′tion
non pas′ser ine
non pay′ing
non per′ma nent
non per′me a ble
non′per pen dic′u lar
non′per sist′ence
non′phil o soph′i cal
non′po et′ic
non poi′son ous
non′po lit′i cal
non po′rous
non pred′a to′ry
non′pre dict′a ble
non′pre hen′sile
non′pre scrip′tive
non′pro fes′sion al
non′prof it eer′ing
non′pro gres′sive
non′pro pri′e tar′y
non′pro tec′tive
non ra′cial
non′re al′i ty
non′re cip′ro cal
non′rec og ni′tion
non′re cur′rent
non′re fill′a ble
non′re fu′el ing
non reg′i ment′ed
non′re li′gious
non′re mu′ne ra′tive
non′re new′a ble
non′res i den′tial
non′re strict′ed
non′re turn′a ble
non′re vers′i ble
non rhyth′mic
non rig′id
non rur′al
non-Rus′sian
non sal′a ble
non sal′ar ied
non′sci en tif′ic
non sea′son al
non′se lec′tive
non sen′si tive
non shar′ing
non shrink′a ble
non sink′a ble
non smok′ing
non so′cial
non spe′cial ized
non′spe cif′ic
non spir′i tu al
non stain′a ble
non stan′dard ized
non strik′er
non strik′ing
non stu′dent
non′sub mis′sive
non′sub scrib′er
non′suc ces′sive
non′sup port′er
non′sup port′ing
non′sus tain′ing
non swim′mer
non′sym met′ri cal
non sym′pa thiz′er
non′sys tem at′ic
non tax′a ble
non teach′a ble
non tech′ni cal
non′ter ri to′ri al
non tox′ic
non′trans fer′a ble
non trib′u tar′y
non typ′i cal
non ur′ban
non us′er
non vet′er an
non′vi o la′tion
non vis′u al
non′vo cal′ic
non′vo ca′tion al
non vol′a tile
non vol′un tar′y
non vot′ing
non white′
non work′er
non work′ing
non yield′ing

non ac cept ance (non′ak sep′təns), *n.* failure or refusal to accept.

non age (non′ij, nō′nij), *n.* 1 a being under the legal age of responsibility; minority. 2 an early stage; period before maturity. [< Anglo-French *nonnage* < *non-* not + *age* age]

non a ge nar i an (non′ə jə ner′ē ən, nō′nə jə ner′ē ən), *n.* person who is 90 years old or between 90 and 100 years old. *—adj.* 90 years old or between 90 and 100 years old. [< Latin *nonagenarius* containing ninety]

non ag gres sion (non′ə gresh′ən), *n.* a refraining from aggression.

non a gon (non′ə gon), *n.* a plane figure having nine angles and nine sides. [< Latin *nonus* ninth + Greek *gōnia* angle]

non al co hol ic (non′al kə hô′lik, non′al-kə hol′ik), *adj.* containing no alcohol.

non a ligned (non′ə līnd′), *adj.* not aligned politically; neutral. Also, **unaligned.**

non a lign ment (non′ə līn′mənt), *n.* condition of being nonaligned.

nonce (nons), *n.* 1 the one or particular occasion or purpose. 2 **for the nonce,** for the present time or occasion. [Middle English *(for then) ones* (for the) once, taken as *(for the) nones*]

nonce word, word formed and used for a single occasion.

non cha lance (non′shə ləns, non′shə-läns′), *n.* cool unconcern; indifference.

non cha lant (non′shə lənt, non′shə länt′), *adj.* without enthusiasm; coolly unconcerned; indifferent: *It was hard to remain nonchalant during all the excitement.* [< French < *non-* not + *chaloir* care about] **—non′cha lant ly,** *adv.*

non com (non′kom′), *n.* INFORMAL. a noncommissioned officer.

noncom., noncommissioned officer.

non com bat ant (non′kəm bat′nt, non-kom′bə tənt), *n.* 1 member of the armed forces who takes no part in combat, such as a surgeon, nurse, or chaplain. 2 person having civilian status in wartime. *—adj.* not taking part in combat; having civilian status.

non com mis sioned (non′kə mish′ənd), *adj.* without a commission; not commissioned.

noncommissioned officer, officer in the armed forces who does not hold a commission or a warrant, especially an enlisted man with the rank of corporal, sergeant, petty officer, or airman first class.

non com mit tal (non′kə mit′l), *adj.* not committing oneself; not saying yes or no: *"I will think it over" is a noncommittal answer.* **—non′com mit′tal ly,** *adv.*

non com pli ance (non′kəm plī′əns), *n.* fact of not complying; failure to comply.

non com pos men tis (non′ kom′pəs men′tis), LATIN. mentally unable to manage one's affairs; insane.

non con duct ing (non′kən duk′ting), *adj.* not conducting; that is a nonconductor. Asbestos is a nonconducting material used in heat insulation.

non con duc tor (non′kən duk′tər), *n.* substance that does not readily conduct heat, electricity, sound, etc. Rubber is a nonconductor of electricity.

non con form ance (non′kən fôr′məns), *n.* fact of not conforming; failure to conform.

non con form ist (non′kən fôr′mist), *n.* 1 person who refuses to conform to an established church or social group. 2 Usually, **Nonconformist.** Protestant who is not a member of the Church of England.

non con form i ty (non′kən fôr′mə tē), *n.* 1 lack of conformity; failure or refusal to conform. 2 failure or refusal to conform to an established church. 3 Usually, **Nonconformity.** **a** principles or practices of English Protestants who do not belong to the Church of England. **b** Nonconformists as a group.

non co op e ra tion (non′kō op′ə rā′shən), *n.* 1 failure or refusal to cooperate. 2 refusal to cooperate with a government for political reasons.

non de liv er y (non′di liv′ər ē), *n.* failure to deliver.

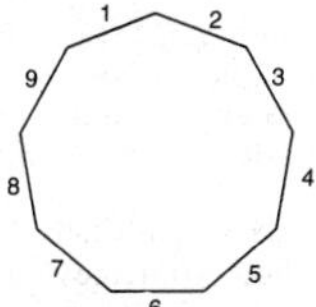

regular nonagon

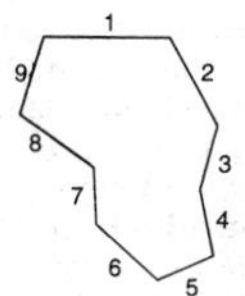

irregular nonagon

hat, āge, fär; let, ēqual, tėrm;
it, īce; hot, ōpen, ôrder;
oil, out; cup, pu̇t, rüle;
ch, child; ng, long; sh, she;
th, thin; ᴛʜ, then; zh, measure;

ə represents *a* in about, *e* in taken, *i* in pencil, *o* in lemon, *u* in circus.

< = from, derived from, taken from.

non de script (non′də skript), *adj.* not easily classified; not of any one particular kind: *She had nondescript eyes, neither brown, blue, nor gray.* *—n.* a nondescript person or thing. [< *non-* + Latin *descriptum* (to be) described]

non dur a ble (non du̇r′ə bəl, non dyu̇r′ə-bəl), *adj.* that will not last long; that can be used up or worn out quickly; perishable: *Tomatoes are nondurable.* *—n.* something that is nondurable.

none[1] (nun), *pron.* 1 not any: *We have none of that paper left.* 2 no one; not one: *None of these is a typical case.* 3 no persons or things: *None have arrived.* 4 no part; nothing: *The teacher said she would have none of our nonsense.* *—adv.* to no extent; in no way; not at all: *Our supply is none too great.* [Old English *nān* < *ne* not + *ān* one]

➔ **none, no one.** *None* is a single word, but *no one* is often used instead of *none* for emphasis. *None* may be either singular or plural, but *no one* is always singular: *As only ten jurors have been chosen so far, none of the witnesses were called* (or *was called*). *I read three books on the subject, no one of which was helpful.*

none[2] (nōn), *n.* singular of **nones**[2].

non e lec tro lyte (non′i lek′trə līt), *n.* substance which in water solution does not conduct an electric current. Sugar is a nonelectrolyte.

non en ti ty (non en′tə tē), *n., pl.* **-ties.** 1 person or thing of little or no importance. 2 something that does not exist or that exists only in the imagination.

nones[1] (nōnz), *n.pl.* (in the ancient Roman calendar) the ninth day before the ides, counting both days; the 7th of March, May, July, and October, and the 5th of the other months. [< Latin *nonae* < *nonus* ninth]

nones[2] (nōnz), *n., pl.* of **none**[2]. 1 the fifth of the seven canonical hours. 2 service or services for it. [Old English *nōn* ninth hour, 3 p.m. Doublet of NOON.]

non es sen tial (non′ə sen′shəl), *adj.* not essential; not necessary. *—n.* person or thing not essential.

none such (nun′such′), *n.* person or thing without equal or parallel; paragon. Also, **nonsuch.**

none the less (nun′ᴛʜə les′), *adv.* nevertheless.

non ex ist ence (non′ig zis′təns), *n.* 1 condition of not existing. 2 thing that has no existence.

non ex ist ent (non′ig zis′tənt), *adj.* having no existence.

non fea sance (non fē′zns), *n.* (in law) the failure to perform some act which ought to have been performed. [< *non-* + Anglo-French *fesance* < French *faire* do]

non fic tion (non fik′shən), *n.* writing that is not fiction; prose literature that deals with real people and events rather than imaginary ones. Biographies and histories are nonfiction.

non fic tion al (non fik′shə nəl), *adj.* not fictional.

non flam ma ble (non flam′ə bəl), *adj.* that will not catch fire.

non ful fill ment (non′fu̇l fil′mənt), *n.* failure to fulfill or to be fulfilled.

no nil lion (nō nil′yən), *n.* 1 (in the United States and France) an octillion multiplied by 1000, equal to 1 followed by 30 zeros. 2 (in Great Britain and Germany) a million to the ninth power, equal to 1 followed by 54 zeros. [< Latin *nonus* ninth + English *(m)illion*]

non in ter ven tion (non′in tər ven′shən), *n.* 1 failure or refusal to intervene. 2 systematic avoidance of any interference by a nation in the affairs of other nations or of its own states, etc.

non in ter ven tion ist (non′in tər ven′shə nist), *n.* person who favors or advocates nonintervention. —*adj.* that favors or advocates nonintervention.

non ju ror (non ju̇r′ər), *n.* one who refuses to take a required oath.

non lin e ar (non lin′ē ər), *adj.* not linear; not containing or contained in a line: *a nonlinear set of points.*

non liv ing (non liv′ing), *adj.* not living.

non mag net ic (non′mag net′ik), *adj.* not having the properties of a magnet; that cannot be attracted by a magnet.

non met al (non met′l), *n.* a chemical element lacking the physical and chemical properties of a metal; nonmetallic element.

non me tal lic (non′mə tal′ik), *adj.* not metallic; lacking the physical and chemical properties of a metal. Carbon, oxygen, sulfur, and nitrogen are nonmetallic elements.

non mo ral (non môr′əl, non mor′əl), *adj.* having no relation to morality; neither moral nor immoral.

non ob jec tive (non′əb jek′tiv), *adj.* nonrepresentational.

non pa reil (non′pə rel′), *adj.* having no equal. —*n.* 1 person or thing having no equal. 2 painted bunting. 3 (in printing) size of type; 6-point. This sentence is in nonpareil. 4 a small chocolate drop covered with tiny white pellets of sugar. [< Middle French < *non-* not + *pareil* equal]

non par ti san or **non par ti zan** (non-pär′tə zən), *adj.* not partisan; not supporting, or controlled by, any of the regular political parties: *a nonpartisan voter.*

non pay ment (non pā′mənt), *n.* failure to pay or condition of not being paid.

non per form ance (non′pər fôr′məns), *n.* fact of not performing; failure to perform.

non plus (non plus′, non′plus), *v.*, **-plused, -plus ing** or **-plussed, -plus sing,** *n.* —*v.t.* puzzle completely; make unable to say or do anything; perplex. —*n.* state of being nonplused; quandary. [< Latin *non plus* no further]

non pro duc tive (non′prə duk′tiv), *adj.* 1 not productive. 2 not directly connected with production. **—non′pro duc′tive-ness,** *n.*

non prof it (non prof′it), *adj.* not for profit; without profit: *The Salvation Army is a nonprofit organization.*

non pro lif e ra tion (non′prō lif′ə rā′shən), *n.* the regulation of the spread of nuclear weapons among nations, especially by means of an agreement.

non rep re sen ta tion al (non′rep ri zen-tā′shə nəl), *adj.* not representing or resembling natural objects; abstract: *nonrepresentational art.*

non res i dence (non rez′ə dəns), *n.* a being nonresident.

non res i dent (non rez′ə dənt), *adj.* 1 living elsewhere; not living in a particular place. 2 not residing where official duties require one to reside. —*n.* a nonresident person.

non re sist ance (non′ri zis′təns), *n.* fact or condition of not resisting; lack of resistance; passive obedience of or submission to authority or force.

non re sist ant (non′ri zis′tənt), *adj.* not resisting; passively obedient or submissive to authority or force. —*n.* a nonresistant person.

non re stric tive (non′ri strik′tiv), *adj.* not restricting or limiting.

nonrestrictive clause, (in grammar) any clause which adds descriptive detail but is not an essential part of the sentence in which it appears. EXAMPLE: My bicycle, *which had a flat tire,* was stolen today.

non sched uled (non skej′u̇ld), *adj.* not operating according to regular schedule: *a nonscheduled flight.*

non sec tar i an (non′sek ter′ē ən), *adj.* not connected with any religious denomination.

non sense (non′sens), *n.* 1 words, ideas, or acts without meaning; foolish talk or doings; a plan or suggestion that is foolish. 2 worthless stuff; junk: *a drawer full of useless gadgets and other nonsense.*

non sen si cal (non sen′sə kəl), *adj.* foolish or absurd. **—non sen′si cal ly,** *adv.* **—non sen′si cal ness,** *n.*

non seq., non sequitur.

non se qui tur (non sek′wə tər), inference or conclusion that does not follow from the premises. [< Latin, it does not follow]

non sked (non′sked′), *n.* INFORMAL. a nonscheduled airline.

non skid (non′skid′), *adj.* made to prevent or resist skidding.

non stand ard (non stan′dərd), *adj.* 1 not conforming to the existing or prescribed standard. 2 (of pronunciation, grammar, vocabulary, etc.) not conforming to the usage characteristic of cultivated native speakers and writers of the language.

non stop (*adj.* non′stop′; *adv.* non′stop′), *adj., adv.* without stopping: *a nonstop flight (adj.). We flew nonstop from New York to Los Angeles (adv.).*

non such (nun′such′), *n.* nonesuch.

non suit (non′süt′), *n.* (in law) a judgment terminating a lawsuit when the plaintiff neglects to prosecute, fails to show a legal case, or fails to bring sufficient evidence. —*v.t.* stop (a plaintiff) by a nonsuit.

non sup port (non′sə pôrt′, non′sə pōrt′), *n.* 1 lack of support. 2 (in law) failure to provide for someone for whom one is legally responsible.

non trop po (nōn trō′pō), (in music) not too much. [< Italian]

non un ion (non yü′nyən), *adj.* 1 not belonging to a trade union: *a nonunion worker.* 2 not following trade-union rules. 3 not recognizing or favoring trade unions: *a nonunion company.*

non vi o lence (non vī′ə ləns), *n.* belief in the use of peaceful methods to achieve any goal; opposition to any form of violence.

non vi o lent (non vī′ə lənt), *adj.* not violent; opposing violence: *nonviolent protest.*

non vot er (non vō′tər), *n.* person who does not vote or is not eligible to vote.

non zer o (non zir′ō), *adj.* not zero; not being equal to zero: *nonzero integers.*

noo dle¹ (nü′dl), *n.* a mixture of flour and water, or flour and eggs, like macaroni, but made in flat strips. [< German *Nudel*]

noo dle² (nü′dl), *n.* 1 a very stupid person; fool. 2 SLANG. head. [origin uncertain]

nook (nu̇k), *n.* 1 a cozy little corner: *a nook facing the fire.* 2 a hidden spot; sheltered place: *I found a wonderful nook in the woods behind my house.* [Middle English *noke*]

noon (nün), *n.* twelve o'clock in the daytime; middle of the day. —*adj.* of noon. [Old English *nōn* < Latin *nona (hora)* ninth (hour), 3 p.m.; the meaning shifted with a change in time of church service. Doublet of NONES².]

noon day (nün′dā′), *n., adj.* noon.

no one, no person; nobody. ➤ See **none¹** for usage note.

no-one (nō′wun), *pron.* no one.

noon ing (nü′ning), *n.* DIALECT. 1 rest or time for rest at noon. 2 meal at noon. 3 noon.

noon tide (nün′tīd′), *n.* 1 noon. 2 the highest, finest, or brightest point.

noon time (nün′tīm′), *n.* noon.

noose (nüs), *n., v.,* **noosed, noos ing.** —*n.* 1 loop with a slip knot that tightens as the string or rope is pulled. Nooses are used especially in lassos and snares. 2 snare or bond. 3 **the noose,** death by hanging. —*v.t.* 1 make a noose with; tie a noose in. 2 catch with a noose; snare. [probably < Old French *nos* < Provençal *nous* < Latin *nodus* knot]

no-par (nō′pär′), *adj.* without any face value; issued without a par: *no-par stock.*

nor (nôr; *unstressed* nər), *conj.* and not; or not; neither; and not either. *Nor* is used: 1 with a preceding *neither* or negative: *Not a boy nor girl stirred.* 2 ARCHAIC. with preceding *neither* or *not* left out: *"Great brother, thou nor I have made the world."* 3 ARCHAIC. instead of *neither* as correlative to following nor: *Nor silver nor gold will buy it.* [reduction of Old English *nāhwæther* < *ne* not + *āhwæther* either]

NOR AD (nôr′ad, nor′ad), *n.* North American Air Defense Command.

nor ad ren a lin (nôr′ə dren′l ən), *n.* hormone, similar to adrenaline, secreted by the adrenal medulla; norepinephrine. It stimulates the contraction of small blood vessels and is used in the treatment of hypotension and shock.

Nor dic (nôr′dik), *adj.* belonging to or characteristic of the Germanic people of Scandinavia and certain other parts of northern Europe, characterized by tall stature, blond hair, blue eyes, and long heads. —*n.* 1 a northern European. Scandinavians are Nordics. 2 any person of the Nordic type. [< French *nordique* < *nord* north < Old English *north*]

nor ep i neph rine (nôr ep′ə nef′rən, nôr-ep′ə nef′rēn′), *n.* noradrenalin.

Nor folk (nôr′fək), *n.* 1 seaport in SE Virginia, near the mouth of Chesapeake Bay. 308,000. 2 county in E England.

Norfolk jacket, a loose-fitting, single-breasted jacket with a belt and box pleats in front and back.

norm (nôrm), *n.* 1 standard for a certain group; type, model, or pattern: *determine the norm for a test.* 2 average; mean: *sales above the norm for the year.* [< Latin *norma* rule]

hat, āge, fär; let, ēqual, tėrm;
it, īce; hot, ōpen, ôrder;
oil, out; cup, pu̇t, rüle;
ch, child; ng, long; sh, she;
th, thin; ᴛʜ, then; zh, measure;

ə represents *a* in about, *e* in taken, *i* in pencil, *o* in lemon, *u* in circus.

< = from, derived from, taken from.

nor mal (nôr′məl), *adj.* 1 of the usual standard; regular; usual: *The normal temperature of the human body is 98.6 degrees.* 2 in psychology: **a** not mentally ill; sane. **b** of average intelligence, emotional stability, etc. 3 not diseased; well; healthy. 4 in chemistry: **a** (of a solution) containing the equivalent of one gram of hydrogen ions per liter. **b** (of hydrocarbons) consisting of a straight unbranched chain of carbon atoms. 5 (in geometry) being at right angles. —*n.* 1 the usual state or level: *two pounds above normal.* 2 (in geometry) a line or plane that is at right angles to another. **—nor′mal ly,** *adv.*

nor mal cy (nôr′məl sē), *n.* normal condition.

normal distribution, (in statistics) a frequency distribution represented by a bell-shaped curve.

nor mal i ty (nôr mal′ə tē), *n.* 1 normal condition. 2 the normal concentration of a solution. It is expressed as the number of equivalents of one gram of hydrogen ions in a liter of solution.

nor mal ize (nôr′mə līz), *v.t.,* **-ized, -iz ing.** make normal: *normalize the relations between two countries.* **—nor′mal i za′tion,** *n.* **—nor′mal iz′er,** *n.*

normal school, school where people are trained to be teachers, especially a separate institution for teacher education offering a two-year course and a certificate. Normal schools were common in the United States during the early part of this century.

Nor man (nôr′mən), *n.* 1 native or inhabitant of Normandy. 2 member of the people descended from the Scandinavians who settled in Normandy in the A.D. 900's and the French who lived there; Anglo-Norman. They conquered England in 1066. 3 one of the Scandinavian ancestors of these people; Northman. 4 Anglo-French. —*adj.* 1 of the Normans or Normandy. 2 Norman-French.

Norman Conquest, the conquest of England by the Normans in 1066, under the leadership of William I.

Nor man dy (nôr′mən dē), *n.* region in NW France, at one time a duchy, later a province. The invasion of Europe in World War II began there on June 6, 1944.

Nor man-French (nôr′mən french′), *n.* Anglo-French. —*adj.* of or having to do with Anglo-French or those who spoke it.

nor ma tive (nôr′mə tiv), *adj.* 1 establishing or setting up a norm or standard. 2 based on or prescribing standards of usage: *normative grammar.*

Norn (nôrn), *n.* (in Scandinavian myths) any one of the three goddesses of fate **(the Norns).**

Norse (nôrs), *adj.* 1 of or having to do with ancient Scandinavia, its people, or their language. 2 of or having to do with Norway or its people. —*n.* 1 *pl. in use.* the people of ancient Scandinavia; Norsemen; Northmen. 2 *pl. in use.* Norwegians. 3 Old Norse. 4 language of Norway; Norwegian.

Norse man (nôrs′mən), *n., pl.* **-men.** one of the Nordic people of ancient Scandinavia, noted as great sailors and sea fighters; Northman. The Vikings were Norsemen.

north (nôrth), *n.* 1 direction to which a compass needle points; direction to the right as one faces the setting sun. 2 Also, **North,** the part of any country toward the north. 3 **the North,** the northern part of the United States; the states north of Maryland, the Ohio River, and Missouri, making up most of the states that formed the Union side in the Civil War. —*adj.* 1 toward the north; farther toward the north. 2 coming from the north. 3 in the north. 4 **north of,** further north than. —*adv.* toward the north. [Old English]

North (nôrth), *n.* Lord **Frederick,** 1732-1792, British statesman, prime minister of England from 1770 to 1782.

North Africa, region in the N part of the continent of Africa, especially the countries bordering on or north of the Sahara. **—North African.**

North America, the northern continent of the Western Hemisphere. The United States, Mexico, and Canada are the three largest countries in North America. 289,184,000 pop.; 8,436,800 sq. mi. **—North American.**

north bound (nôrth′bound′), *adj.* bound northward; going north.

North Cape, 1 point of land in the Arctic Ocean at the N tip of Norway. 2 the N end of New Zealand.

North Car o li na (kar′ə lī′nə), one of the southeastern states of the United States. 5,082,000 pop.; 52,600 sq. mi. *Capital:* Raleigh. *Abbrev.:* N.C. **—North Carolinian.**

North Da ko ta (də kō′tə), one of the midwestern states of the United States. 618,000 pop.; 70,700 sq. mi. *Capital:* Bismarck. *Abbrev.:* N. Dak., N.D. **—North Dakotan.**

north east (nôrth′ēst′), *adj.* 1 halfway between north and east. 2 lying toward or situated in the northeast. 3 coming from the northeast: *a northeast wind.* 4 directed toward the northeast. —*n.* 1 a northeast direction. 2 place that is in the northeast part or direction. 3 **the Northeast,** New England and nearby states. —*adv.* 1 toward the northeast. 2 from the northeast. 3 in the northeast.

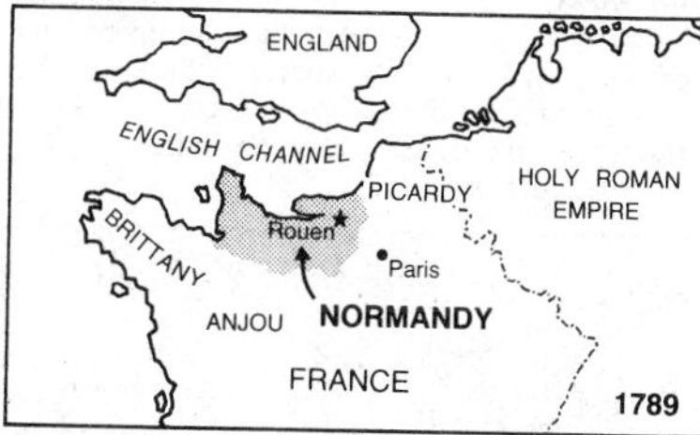

north east er (nôrth′ē′stər), *n.* wind or storm from the northeast.

north east er ly (nôrth′ē′stər lē), *adj., adv.* 1 toward the northeast. 2 from the northeast.

north east ern (nôrth′ē′stərn), *adj.* 1 toward the northeast. 2 from the northeast. 3 of the northeast; having to do with the northeast. 4 **Northeastern,** of, having to do with, or in the Northeast.

North east ern er (nôrth′ē′stər nər), *n.* native or inhabitant of the Northeast.

north east ward (nôrth′ēst′wərd), *adv., adj.* 1 toward the northeast. 2 northeast. —*n.* northeast.

north east ward ly (nôrth′ēst′wərd lē), *adj.* 1 toward the northeast. 2 (of winds) from the northeast. —*adv.* toward the northeast.

north east wards (nôrth′ēst′wərdz), *adv.* northeastward.

north er (nôr′ᴛʜər), *n.* wind or storm from the north.

north er ly (nôr′ᴛʜər lē), *adj., adv., n., pl.* **-lies.** —*adj., adv.* 1 toward the north. 2 from the north: *a northerly wind.* —*n.* norther.

north ern (nôr′ᴛʜərn), *adj.* 1 toward the north. 2 from the north. 3 of or in the north. 4 **Northern,** of or in the northern part of the United States. —*n.* person living in a northern region.

Northern Cross, cross of six stars in the northern constellation Cygnus.

north ern er (nôr′ᴛʜər nər), *n.* 1 native or inhabitant of the north. 2 **Northerner,** native or inhabitant of the North of the United States.

Northern Hemisphere, the half of the earth that is north of the equator.

Northern Ireland, self-governing district in NE Ireland that refused to join the Republic of Ireland and is a part of the United Kingdom of Great Britain and Northern Ireland. 1,524,000 pop.; 5500 sq. mi. *Capital:* Belfast. See **United Kingdom** for map.

northern lights, aurora borealis.

north ern most (nôr′ᴛʜərn mōst), *adj.* farthest north.

Northern Rhodesia, former British protectorate in SE Africa, now the country of Zambia.

Northern Territory, territory in N central Australia. 71,000 pop.; 523,600 sq. mi.

North Island, the northernmost of the two main islands of New Zealand. 2,018,000 pop.; 44,300 sq. mi.

North Korea, country on the Korean peninsula north of the 38th parallel. It is under Communist control. 13,900,000 pop.; 46,800 sq. mi. *Capital:* Pyongyang. **—North Korean.**

north land (nôrth′lənd), *n.* 1 land in the north; the northern part of a country. 2 **Northland, a** the northern regions of the world. **b** peninsula containing Norway and Sweden.

north land er (nôrth′lən dər), *n.* inhabitant of the northland.

North man (nôrth′mən), *n., pl.* **-men.** Norseman.

north-north east (nôrth′nôrth ēst′; *Nautical* nôr′nôr ēst′), *n.* the point of the compass or the direction midway between north and northeast, two points or 22 degrees 30 minutes to the east of north.

north-north west (nôrth′nôrth west′; *Nautical* nôr′nôr west′), *n.* the point of the compass or the direction midway between north and northwest, two points or 22 degrees 30 minutes to the west of north.

North Pole, 1 the northern end of the earth's axis. See **arctic circle** for map. 2 **north pole,** the pole of a magnet that points north.

North River, mouth of the Hudson River, between New York City and New Jersey.

North Sea, sea that is a part of the Atlantic Ocean, east of Great Britain, west of Denmark, and south of Norway. 600 mi. long; 400 mi. wide.

North Star, the bright star almost directly

above the North Pole, formerly much used as a guide by sailors; Polaris; polestar; lodestar.

North um ber land (nôr thum′bər lənd), *n.* county in NE England. **—North um′bri-an,** *adj., n.*

North um bri a (nôr thum′brē ə), *n.* ancient kingdom in N England. See **Mercia** for map. **—North um′bri an,** *adj., n.*

North Vietnam, country in SE Asia, north of the 17th parallel. It is under Communist control. 21,150,000 pop.; 61,300 sq. mi. *Capital:* Hanoi. **—North Vietnamese.**

north ward (nôrth′wərd), *adv., adj.* toward the north. *—n.* a northward part, direction, or point.

north ward ly (nôrth′wərd lē), *adj., adv.* 1 toward the north. 2 from the north.

north wards (nôrth′wərdz), *adv.* northward.

north west (nôrth′west′), *adj.* 1 halfway between north and west. 2 lying toward or situated in the northwest. 3 coming from the northwest: *a northwest wind.* 4 directed toward the northwest. *—n.* 1 a northwest direction. 2 place that is in the northwest part or direction. 3 **the Northwest, a** Washington, Oregon, and Idaho. **b** Northwest Territory. *—adv.* 1 toward the northwest. 2 from the northwest. 3 in the northwest.

north west er (nôrth′wes′tər), *n.* wind or storm from the northwest.

north west er ly (nôrth′wes′tər lē), *adj., adv.* 1 toward the northwest. 2 from the northwest.

north west ern (nôrth′wes′tərn), *adj.* 1 toward the northwest. 2 from the northwest. 3 of or in the northwest; having to do with the northwest. 4 **Northwestern,** of, having to do with, or in the Northwest.

North west ern er (nôrth′wes′tər nər), *n.* native or inhabitant of the Northwest.

Northwest Passage, sea route from the Atlantic to the Pacific along the N coast of North America.

Northwest Territories, division of N Canada east of the Yukon territory and including the arctic islands and the islands of Hudson Bay. 26,000 pop.; 1,305,000 sq. mi.

Northwest Territory, former region north of the Ohio River and east of the Mississippi, organized by Congress in 1787, now forming Ohio, Indiana, Illinois, Michigan, Wisconsin, and the NE part of Minnesota.

north west ward (nôrth′west′wərd), *adj., adv.* 1 toward the northwest. 2 northwest. *—n.* northwest.

north west ward ly (nôrth′west′wərd lē), *adj., adv.* 1 toward the northwest. 2 from the northwest.

north west wards (nôrth′west′wərdz), *adv.* northwestward.

Nor walk (nôr′wôk), *n.* 1 city in SW California, near Los Angeles. 92,000. 2 city in W Connecticut. 79,000.

Nor way (nôr′wā), *n.* mountainous country in N Europe, west and north of Sweden. 3,866,000 pop.; 125,200 sq. mi. *Capital:* Oslo.

Nor we gian (nôr wē′jən), *adj.* of Norway, its people, or their language. *—n.* 1 native or inhabitant of Norway. 2 the Scandinavian language of Norway.

nor'west er (nôr wes′tər), *n.* a heavy, waterproof, oilskin coat worn by seamen.

Nor wich (nôr′ij, nôr′ich; nor′ij, nor′ich), *n.* city in E England, the site of a famous cathedral. 120,000.

nos. or **Nos.,** numbers.

nose (nōz), *n., v.,* **nosed, nos ing.** *—n.* 1 the part of the face or head just above the mouth which contains the nostrils and serves as the organ of smell. 2 the sense of smell: *a dog with a good nose.* 3 faculty for perceiving or detecting: *a reporter with a nose for news.* 4 part that stands out, especially at the front of anything: *the nose of a ship.*

count noses, find out how many people are present.

follow one's nose, go straight ahead.

lead by the nose, have complete control over.

look down one's nose at, treat with contempt or scorn.

on the nose, SLANG. **a** exactly. **b** solidly.

pay through the nose, pay a great deal too much.

poke one's nose into, pry into in a nosy way; meddle in.

put one's nose out of joint, a displace or supplant one. **b** put in a bad humor.

turn up one's nose at, treat with contempt or scorn.

under one's nose, in plain sight; very easy to notice.

win by a nose, a win a horse race by no more than the length of a horse's nose. **b** win by a small margin.

—v.t. 1 discover by smell; smell out; scent. 2 examine with the nose; smell. 3 rub with the nose; nuzzle. 4 push with the nose or forward end: *The bulldozer nosed the rock off the road.* *—v.i.* 1 sniff. 2 push forward or move, especially slowly, cautiously, or hesitantly: *The little boat nosed carefully between the rocks.* 3 search; pry: *Don't nose into my affairs.* 4 **nose around,** look about quietly or secretly. 5 **nose out, a** find out by looking around quietly or secretly: *nose out the truth.* **b** defeat by a small margin. [Old English *nosu*]

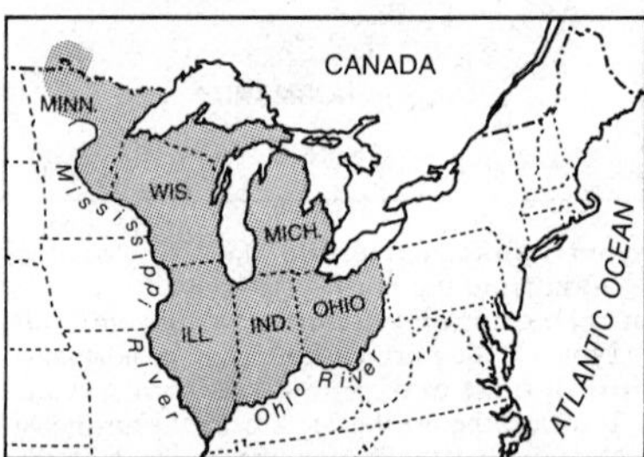

Northwest Territory—the shaded area

nose band (nōz′band′), *n.* part of a bridle that goes over the animal's nose.

nose bleed (nōz′blēd′), *n.* a bleeding from the nose.

nose cone, the cone-shaped front section of a missile or rocket, covered by a heat shield and designed to separate from the main structure of the missile or rocket. A nose cone may carry a bomb to a target or instruments or passengers into space.

nose dive, 1 a swift plunge straight downward by an aircraft. 2 a sudden, sharp drop.

nose-dive (nōz′dīv′), *v.i.,* **-dived, -div ing.** take a nose dive.

nose gay (nōz′gā′), *n.* bunch of flowers; bouquet. [< *nose* + obsolete *gay* something gay or pretty]

nose piece (nōz′pēs′), *n.* 1 part of a helmet that covers and protects the nose. 2 part of a microscope to which the objective is attached.

nos ey (nō′zē), *adj.* nosy.

no-show (nō′shō′), *n.* U.S. person who reserves a seat or other space, especially on an airplane, and fails either to cancel it or to use it.

no sol o gy (nō sol′ə jē), *n.* 1 the classification of diseases. 2 branch of medicine dealing with the classification of diseases. [< Greek *nosos* disease + English *-logy*]

nos tal gia (no stal′jə), *n.* a painful or wistful yearning for one's home, country, city, or for anything far removed in space or time. [< New Latin < Greek *nostos* homecoming + *algos* pain]

nos tal gic (no stal′jik), *adj.* feeling or showing nostalgia. **—nos tal′gi cal ly,** *adv.*

nos tril (nos′trəl), *n.* either of the two openings in the nose. Air is breathed into the lungs, and smells come into the sensitive parts of the nose, through the nostrils. [Old English *nosthyrl* < *nosu* nose + *thyrel* hole]

nos trum (nos′trəm), *n.* 1 medicine made by the person who is selling it; quack remedy; patent medicine. 2 a pet scheme for producing wonderful results; cure-all. [< Latin, neuter of *noster* ours < *nos* we]

nos y (nō′zē), *adj.,* **nos i er, nos i est.** INFORMAL. prying or inquisitive. Also, **nosey. —nos′i ly,** *adv.* **—nos′i ness,** *n.*

not (not), *adv.* word that says no; a negative: *That is not true. Is it true or not?* [unstressed variant of *nought*]

no ta be ne (nō′tə bē′nē), LATIN. note well; observe what follows; take notice.

no ta bil i ty (nō′tə bil′ə tē), *n., pl.* **-ties.** 1 quality or condition of being notable; distinction. 2 a prominent person.

no ta ble (nō′tə bəl), *adj.* worthy of notice; striking; remarkable: *a notable event, a notable book.* *—n.* person who is notable: *Many notables came to the President's reception.* [< Latin *notabilis* < *notare* to note < *nota* note] **—no′ta ble ness,** *n.*

no ta bly (nō′tə blē), *adv.* in a notable manner; to a notable degree.

no tar i al (nō ter′ē əl, nō tar′ē əl), *adj.* 1 of or having to do with a notary public. 2 made or done by a notary public. **—no tar′i al-ly,** *adv.*

no ta rize (nō′tə rīz′), *v.t.,* **-rized, -riz ing.** certify (a contract, deed, will, etc.) as a notary public does; give legal authenticity to.

no tar y (nō′tər ē), *n., pl.* **-tar ies.** notary public. [< Latin *notarius* clerk < *nota* note]

notary public, *pl.* **notaries public** or **notary publics.** a public officer authorized to certify deeds and contracts, to record the fact that a certain person swears that something is true, and to attend to other legal matters.

no ta tion (nō tā′shən), *n.* 1 set of signs or symbols used to represent numbers, quanti-

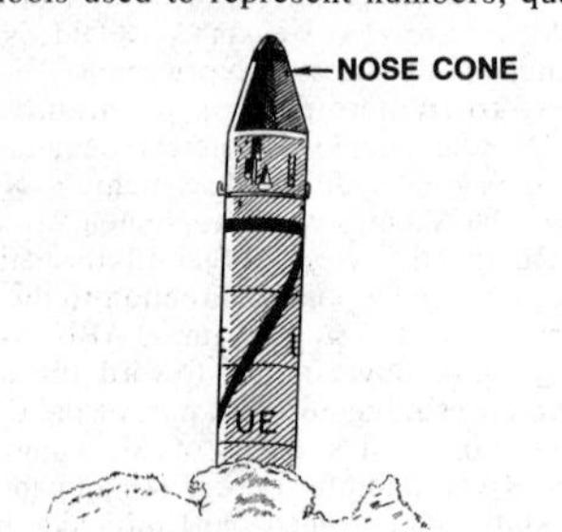

ties, or other values: *In arithmetic we use the Arabic notation (1, 2, 3, 4, etc.).* 2 the representing of numbers, quantities, or other values by symbols or signs: *Music has a special system of notation.* 3 note to assist the memory; record; jotting: *make a notation in the margin of a book.* 4 act of noting.

no ta tion al (nō tā′shə nəl), *adj.* of or having to do with notation.

notch (noch), *n.* 1 a V-shaped nick or cut made in an edge or on a curving surface: *The Indians cut notches on a stick to keep count.* 2 U.S. a deep, narrow pass or gap between mountains. 3 INFORMAL. grade; step; degree. —*v.t.* 1 make a notch or notches in. 2 record by notches; score; tally. [< Middle French *oche; an och* taken as *a noch*]

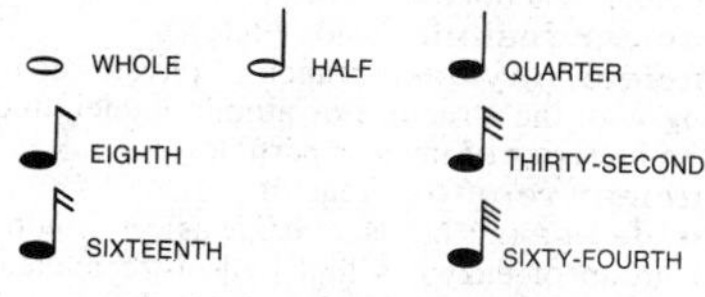

note (def. 6a)
seven notes of differing duration

note (nōt), *n.*, *v.*, **not ed, not ing.** —*n.* 1 words written down to remind one of something: *Her notes helped her remember what the speaker said.* 2 notice; heed; observation: *Give careful note to his words.* 3 piece of information; comment; remark: *Her chemistry book has many helpful notes at the back.* 4 a very short letter, written instruction, list, etc.: *a note to the milkman, a note of thanks.* 5 a formal letter from one government to another; diplomatic or official communication in writing. 6 in music: **a** any of various characters used in writing music to indicate the pitch and duration of a sound. Pitch is indicated by the position of a character on a staff and duration by its appearance. **b** a single sound of definite pitch made by a musical instrument or voice. 7 any one of the black or white keys of a piano or other instrument. 8 a bird's song or call: *the robin's cheerful note.* 9 a significant tone, sound, or way of expression: *There was a note of anxiety in her voice.* 10 sign, token, or proof of genuineness; characteristic or distinguishing feature: *His writing displays the note of scholarship.* 11 true importance; distinction; consequence; significance: *a person of note.* 12 promissory note. 13 bank note. 14 a piece of paper money.

compare notes, exchange ideas or opinions.

strike the right note, say or do something suitable.

take note of, take notice of; give attention to; observe.

take notes, write down things to be remembered.

—*v.t.* 1 record in writing; make a memorandum or written record of. 2 observe carefully; give attention to. 3 mention especially; emphasize. 4 indicate; signify.

[< Old French < Latin *nota* a mark, note] **—note′less,** *adj.* **—not′er,** *n.*

note book (nōt′bu̇k′), *n.* book in which to write notes of things to be learned or remembered.

not ed (nō′tid), *adj.* especially noticed or well-known; celebrated; famous: *Samson was noted for strength. Kipling was a noted author.* See **famous** for synonym study. **—not′ed ly,** *adv.* **—not′ed ness,** *n.*

note wor thy (nōt′wėr′ᴛʜē), *adj.* worthy of notice; remarkable: *a noteworthy achievement.* **—note′wor′thi ly,** *adv.* **—note′wor′thi ness,** *n.*

noth ing (nuth′ing), *n.* 1 not anything; no thing: *Nothing arrived by mail.* 2 thing that does not exist: *create a world out of nothing.* 3 thing or person of no importance or value: *Don't worry, it's nothing. He was so ashamed he felt like a nothing.* 4 zero; naught.

for nothing, a without paying; free. **b** in vain; uselessly.

nothing doing, INFORMAL. certainly not; by no means.

nothing less than, just the same as.

think nothing of, a consider as easy to do. **b** treat as unimportant or worthless.

—*adv.* not at all; in no way: *She is nothing like her sister in looks.*

[Old English *nān* no + *thing* thing]

noth ing ness (nuth′ing nis), *n.* 1 a being nothing; nonexistence. 2 a being of no value; worthlessness. 3 unconsciousness.

no tice (nō′tis), *n.*, *v.*, **-ticed, -tic ing.** —*n.* 1 attention or heed; observation; awareness: *escape one's notice.* 2 announcement or warning: *The bell gave notice that the class was over.* 3 a written or printed sign; paper posted in a public place. 4 a warning that one will end an agreement with another at a certain time: *It is customary to give a month's notice before leaving to take another job.* 5 a written or printed account, usually brief: *a notice in the newspaper about the wedding. The new book got a favorable notice.* 6 **serve notice,** give warning; inform; announce. 7 **take notice of,** give attention; observe; see. —*v.t.* 1 take notice of; give attention to; observe; perceive: *I noticed a big difference at once.* 2 mention; refer to: *notice a matter in a speech or book.* [< Middle French < Latin *notitia* cognizance < *noscere* know]

no tice a ble (nō′ti sə bəl), *adj.* 1 easily seen or noticed: *The class has made noticeable improvement.* 2 worth noticing; deserving notice. **—no′tice a bly,** *adv.*

no ti fi ca tion (nō′tə fə kā′shən), *n.* 1 a notifying or making known. 2 notice: *Have you received a notification of the meeting?*

no ti fy (nō′tə fī), *v.t.*, **-fied, -fy ing.** 1 give notice to; let know; inform; announce to: *I was notified of the unpaid bill.* See **inform** for synonym study. 2 to make (something) known; proclaim. **—no′ti fi′er,** *n.*

no tion (nō′shən), *n.* 1 idea; understanding: *He has no notion of what I mean.* See **idea** for synonym study. 2 opinion; view; belief: *modern notions about raising children.* 3 intention: *He has no notion of risking his money.* 4 inclination or desire; whim; fancy: *a sudden notion to take a trip.* 5 a foolish idea or opinion. 6 **notions,** *pl.* U.S. small, useful articles; pins, needles, thread, tape, etc. [< Latin *notionem* < *noscere* know]

no tion al (nō′shə nəl), *adj.* 1 in one's imagination or thought only; not real. 2 U.S. full of notions; having strange notions.

no to chord (nō′tə kôrd), *n.* 1 a flexible, rodlike structure of cells running lengthwise in the back of the lowest vertebrates. It forms the main supporting structure of the body. 2 a similar structure in the embryos of higher vertebrates. [< Greek *nōton* back + English *chord*[2]]

no to ri e ty (nō′tə rī′ə tē), *n.*, *pl.* **-ties.** 1 a being famous for something bad; ill fame: *The scandal brought much notoriety to those involved in it.* 2 a being widely known. 3 a well-known person.

hat, āge, fär; let, ēqual, tėrm;
it, īce; hot, ōpen, ôrder;
oil, out; cup, pu̇t, rüle;
ch, child; ng, long; sh, she;
th, thin; ᴛʜ, then; zh, measure;

ə represents *a* in about, *e* in taken, *i* in pencil, *o* in lemon, *u* in circus.

< = from, derived from, taken from.

no to ri ous (nō tôr′ē əs, nō tōr′ē əs), *adj.* 1 well-known, especially because of something bad; having a bad reputation: *a notorious gambler.* 2 well-known; celebrated: *a notorious court case.* [< Medieval Latin *notorius* < Latin *notus* known] **—no to′ri ous ly,** *adv.* **—no to′ri ous ness,** *n.*

➤ **Notorious** usually means well-known for unsavory reasons: *a notorious cheat.* **Famous** means well-known for accomplishment or excellence: *a famous writer.*

no-trump (nō′trump′), *adj.* without any trumps. —*n.* 1 declaration in bridge to play with no suit as trumps. 2 hand in bridge that is so played.

Not ting ham (not′ing əm), *n.* 1 Nottinghamshire. 2 city in this county. Many of Robin Hood's adventures took place in Nottingham. 301,000.

Not ting ham shire (not′ing əm shər, not′ing əm shir), *n.* county in central England.

not with stand ing (not′wiᴛʜ stan′ding, not′with stan′ding), *prep.* in spite of: *I bought it notwithstanding the high price.* —*conj.* in spite of the fact that: *Notwithstanding there was need for haste, he still delayed.* —*adv.* in spite of it; nevertheless: *It is raining; but I shall go, notwithstanding.*

Nouak chott (nwäk shôt′), *n.* capital of Mauritania, in the W part. 20,000.

nou gat (nü′gət, nü′gä), *n.* a kind of soft candy containing nuts. [< French < Provençal *noga,* ultimately < Latin *nux* nut]

nought (nôt), *n.* naught.

noun (noun), *n.* any of a class of words used as the names of persons, places, things, qualities, events, etc. A noun can take a plural or possessive ending and is usually the subject or object in a sentence or phrase. Words like *John, table, school, kindness, skill,* and *party* are nouns. —*adj.* 1 of a noun. 2 used as a noun. [< Anglo-French, variant of Old French *nom* name < Latin *nomen*]

➤ **forms of nouns.** Nouns may be single words or compound words written solid, as two words, or hyphened: *ceremony, bookcase, high school, go-getter.* Most nouns change their form to make the plural, usually adding *-s* or *-es: boys, kindnesses, manufacturers.* Nouns change their form for case only in the genitive or possessive, typically by adding *'s: boy's, Harriet's.* A very few nouns in English may have different forms for male and female sex: *executor—executrix, actor—actress.*

nour ish (nėr′ish), *v.t.* 1 make grow, or keep alive and well, with food; feed; nurture: *Milk nourishes a baby.* 2 maintain, foster, or support: *nourish a hope.* [< Old French *noriss-,* a form of *norir* to feed < Latin *nutrire*] **—nour′ish er,** *n.* **—nour′ish ing ly,** *adv.*

nour ish ment (nėr′ish mənt), *n.* 1 food. 2 a nourishing. 3 a being nourished.

nou veau riche (nü vō rēsh′), *pl.* **nou-**

veaux riches (nü vō rēsh′), FRENCH. one who has recently become rich.

Nov., November.

no va (nō′və), *n., pl.* **-vae** (-vē′), **-vas.** star that suddenly becomes brighter and then gradually fades, returning over a period of several weeks, months, or sometimes years to its normal brightness. [< Latin, feminine of *novus* new]

No va Sco tia (nō′və skō′shə), province in SE Canada consisting chiefly of a peninsula that extends into the Atlantic. 767,000 pop.; 21,400 sq. mi. *Capital:* Halifax. *Abbrev.:* N.S.

No va ya Zem lya (nô′və yə zim lyä′), two large islands in the Arctic Ocean belonging to the Soviet Union, used for nuclear bomb tests. 35,000 sq. mi.

nov el (nov′əl), *adj.* of a new kind or nature; strange; new; unfamiliar: *a novel idea, a novel sensation.* See **new** for synonym study. —*n.* story with characters and a plot, long enough to fill one or more volumes. See synonym study below. [< Latin *novellus,* diminutive of *novus* new]

Syn. *n.* **Novel, romance** mean a long fictitious story. **Novel** applies particularly to a long work of prose fiction dealing with characters, situations, and scenes that represent those of real life. **Romance** applies especially to a story, often a novel in form, presenting characters and situations not likely to be found in real life and emphasizing exciting or romantic adventures, usually set in distant or unfamiliar times or places.

nov el ette (nov′ə let′), *n.* a short novel.

nov el ist (nov′ə list), *n.* writer of novels.

nov el is tic (nov′ə lis′tik), *adj.* of or like novels.

nov el ize (nov′ə līz), *v.t.,* **-ized, -iz ing.** put into the form of a novel; make a novel from. **—nov′el i za′tion,** *n.*

no vel la (nō vel′ə; *Italian* nō vel′lä), *n., pl.* **no vel las,** ITALIAN **no vel le** (nō vel′lā). a short story with a simple plot. [< Italian]

nov el ty (nov′əl tē), *n., pl.* **-ties.** 1 novel character; newness: *After the novelty of washing dishes wore off, she did not want to do it any more.* 2 a new or unusual thing: *Staying up late was a novelty to the children.* 3 **novelties,** *pl.* small, unusual articles, such as toys, cheap jewelry, etc.

No vem ber (nō vem′bər), *n.* the 11th month of the year. It has 30 days. [< Latin < *novem* nine; from the order of the early Roman calendar]

no ve na (nō vē′nə), *n., pl.* **-nas, -nae** (-nē). (in the Roman Catholic Church) a devotion for some special purpose, consisting of prayers or services on nine successive days: *a novena of nine first Fridays.* [< Medieval Latin, ultimately < Latin *novem* nine]

Nov go rod (nôv′gə rot′), *n.* city in NW Soviet Union. 107,000.

nov ice (nov′is), *n.* 1 one who is new to what he is doing; beginner. 2 person in the period of preparation before becoming a monk or a nun. [< Latin *novicius* < *novus* new]

no vi ti ate or **no vi ci ate** (nō vish′ē it, nō vish′ē āt), *n.* 1 period of trial and preparation in a religious order. 2 novice. 3 house or rooms occupied by religious novices. 4 state or period of being a beginner in anything.

No vo caine (nō′və kān), *n.* trademark for procaine hydrochloride.

now (nou), *adv.* 1 at the present time; at this moment: *He is here now. Most people do not believe in ghosts now.* 2 by this time: *She must have reached the city now.* 3 at once: *Do it now!* 4 then; next: *If passed, the bill now goes to the President.* 5 at the time referred to: *The clock now struck three.* 6 a little while ago: *I just now saw what you're looking for.* 7 under the present circumstances; as things are; as it is: *I would believe almost anything now.* 8 *Now* is also used to introduce or emphasize. *Now what do you mean? Oh, come now! Now you knew that was wrong.* 9 **now and again** or **now and then,** from time to time; once in a while. —*n.* the present; this very time, moment, hour, etc.: *by now, until now, from now on.* —*conj.* seeing that; since; inasmuch as: *Now you are older, you should know better.* —*interj.* be careful! please! [Old English *nū*]

NOW (nou), *n.* National Organization for Women.

now a days (nou′ə dāz′), *adv.* at the present day; in these times. —*n.* the present day; these times.

no way (nō′wā), *adv.* nowise.

no ways (nō′wāz), *adv.* nowise.

no where (nō′hwer, nō′hwar), *adv.* 1 in no place; at no place; to no place. 2 **nowhere near,** INFORMAL. not nearly; not by a long way. —*n.* a nonexistent place.

no wise (nō′wīz), *adv.* in no way; not at all.

nox ious (nok′shəs), *adj.* 1 very harmful to life or health; pernicious; poisonous: *Fumes from the exhaust of an automobile are noxious.* 2 morally hurtful; corrupting. [< Latin *noxius* < *noxa* hurt < *nocere* to hurt] **—nox′ious ly,** *adv.* **—nox′ious ness,** *n.*

Noyes (noiz), *n.* **Alfred,** 1880-1958, English poet.

noz zle (noz′əl), *n.* tip put on a hose, pipe, etc., forming an outlet. [diminutive of *nose*]

Np, neptunium.

N.P., Notary Public.

NROTC or **N.R.O.T.C.,** Naval Reserve Officer Training Corps.

N.S., Nova Scotia.

N.S.W., New South Wales.

N.T., 1 New Testament. 2 Northern Territory.

nth (enth), *adj.* 1 last in the sequence 1, 2, 3, 4 . . . n; being of the indefinitely large or small amount denoted by *n.* 2 **to the nth degree,** to the utmost.

nt. wt., net weight.

nu (nü, nyü), *n.* the 13th letter (N,ν) of the Greek alphabet.

nu ance (nü äns′, nü′äns; nyü äns′, nyü′äns), *n.* 1 shade of expression, meaning, feeling, etc. 2 shade of color or tone. [< French < *nuer* to shade < *nue* cloud < Latin *nubes*]

nub (nub), *n.* 1 knob or protuberance. 2 lump or small piece. 3 INFORMAL. point or gist of anything. [apparently variant of *knob*]

nub bin (nub′ən), *n.* 1 a small or imperfect ear of corn. 2 an undeveloped fruit. 3 a small lump or piece.

nub ble (nub′əl), *n.* nub or nubbin.

nub bly (nub′lē), *adj.,* **-bli er, -bli est.** knobby or lumpy.

nub by (nub′ē), *adj.,* **-bi er, -bi est.** nubbly.

Nu bi a (nü′bē ə, nyü′bē ə), *n.* region in NE Africa between the Red Sea and the Nile River, including parts of SE Egypt and NE Sudan. **—Nu′bi an,** *adj., n.*

Nubian Desert, large desert south of Egypt in NE Sudan between the Nile River and the Red Sea.

nu bile (nü′bəl, nyü′bəl), *adj.* (of girls) old enough to be married; marriageable. [< Latin *nubilis* < *nubere* take a husband]

nu bil i ty (nü bil′ə tē, nyü bil′ə tē), *n.* condition of being nubile.

nu cel lus (nü sel′əs, nyü sel′əs), *n., pl.* **-cel li** (-sel′ī). (in botany) the central mass of cells within the integument of the ovule containing the embryo sac. [< New Latin < Latin *nux, nucis* nut]

nu cle ar (nü′klē ər, nyü′klē ər), *adj.* 1 of or having to do with nuclei or a nucleus, especially the nucleus of an atom: *nuclear particles.* 2 of or having to do with atoms or atomic energy; atomic: *the nuclear age.*

nuclear energy, atomic energy.

nuclear fission, fission (def. 3).

nuclear fuel, substance which will sustain a chain reaction.

nuclear fusion, fusion (def. 4).

nuclear physics, branch of physics dealing with the structure of atomic nuclei, and the behavior of nuclear particles.

nuclear reactor, reactor.

nu cle ase (nü′klē ās, nyü′klē ās), *n.* any of a group of enzymes that hydrolyze nucleic acids.

nu cle ate (*v.* nü′klē āt, nyü′klē āt; *adj.* nü′klē it, nyü′klē it; nü′klē āt, nyü′klē āt), *v.,* **-at ed, -at ing,** *adj.* —*v.t., v.i.* form into a nucleus or around a nucleus. —*adj.* having a nucleus. **—nu′cle a′tion,** *n.*

nu cle i (nü′klē ī, nyü′klē ī), *n.* a pl. of **nucleus.**

nu cle ic acid (nü klē′ik, nyü klē′ik), any of a group of compounds occurring chiefly in combination with proteins in living cells and viruses, consisting of linked nucleotides.

nu cle o lus (nü klē′ə ləs, nyü klē′ə ləs), *n., pl.* **-li** (-lī). a small structure, usually round, found within the nucleus of a cell, containing a high concentration of ribonucleic acid.

nu cle on (nü′klē on, nyü′klē on), *n.* a proton or neutron, especially as a component of an atomic nucleus.

nu cle on ics (nü′klē on′iks, nyü′klē-on′iks), *n.* study of the behavior and characteristics of atomic nuclei.

nu cle o plasm (nü′klē ə plaz′əm, nyü′klē-ə plaz′əm), *n.* the protoplasm in the nucleus of a cell.

nu cle o pro tein (nü′klē ō prō′tēn′, nü′-klē ō prō′tē ən; nyü′klē ō prō′tēn′, nyü′-klē ō prō′tē ən), *n.* any of a group of substances present in the nuclei of cells and viruses, consisting of proteins in combination with nucleic acids.

nu cle o side (nü′klē ə sīd, nyü′klē ə sīd), *n.* any of a group of compounds of a nitrogen base (purine or pyrimidine) and a sugar (pentose), similar to a nucleotide but lacking phosphoric acid.

nu cle o tide (nü′klē ə tīd, nyü′klē ə tīd), *n.* any of a group of compounds consisting of a sugar, phosphoric acid, and a nitrogen base. Nucleotides are the constituents of nucleic acid and determine the structure of genes.

nu cle us (nü′klē əs, nyü′klē əs), *n., pl.* **-cle i** or **-cle us es.** 1 a central part or thing around which other parts or things are collected. 2 a beginning to which additions are to be made. 3 the central part of an atom, consisting of a proton or protons, neutrons, and other particles. The nucleus carries a positive charge and forms a core containing most of the mass of an atom around which electrons orbit. 4 the fundamental, stable arrangement of atoms in a particular compound. 5 (in biology) a mass of specialized protoplasm found in most plant and animal cells without which the cell cannot grow and divide. See **cell** for diagram. 6 (in astronomy) the dense central part of a comet's head. 7 a specialized mass of gray matter in the brain or spinal cord. [< Latin, kernel < *nux, nucis* nut]

nu clide (nü′klīd, nyü′klīd), *n.* a particular type of atom having a characteristic nucleus and a measurable life span.

nude (nüd, nyüd), *adj.* naked; unclothed; bare. See **bare** for synonym study. *—n.* 1 a naked figure in painting, sculpture, or photography. 2 **the nude, a** the naked figure. **b** a naked condition. [< Latin *nudus*] **—nude′ness,** *n.*

nudge (nuj), *v.,* **nudged, nudg ing,** *n. —v.t.* push slightly; jog with the elbow to attract attention, etc. *—v.i.* give a nudge or slight push. *—n.* a slight push or jog. [origin uncertain] **—nudg′er,** *n.*

nud ism (nü′diz′əm, nyü′diz′əm), *n.* practice of going naked for health or as a fad.

nud ist (nü′dist, nyü′dist), *n.* person who goes naked for health or as a fad. *—adj.* of nudism or nudists.

nu di ty (nü′də tē, nyü′də tē), *n., pl.* **-ties.** 1 nakedness. 2 something naked.

Nue vo Le ón (nwā′vō lā ōn′), state in NE Mexico, across the Rio Grande from Texas.

nu ga to ry (nü′gə tôr′ē, nü′gə tōr′ē; nyü′gə tôr′ē, nyü′gə tōr′ē), *adj.* 1 trifling; worthless. 2 ineffective; useless. [< Latin *nugatorius* < *nugari* to trifle < *nugae* trifles]

nug get (nug′it), *n.* 1 a valuable lump; lump: *nuggets of gold.* 2 anything valuable: *nuggets of wisdom.* [origin uncertain]

nui sance (nü′sns, nyü′sns), *n.* 1 thing or person that annoys, troubles, offends, or is disagreeable; annoyance: *Flies are a nuisance.* 2 (in law) anything annoying, harmful, or offensive to a community or a member of it, especially a property owner. [< Old French < *nuire* to harm < Latin *nocere*]

nuisance tax, tax that is annoying because it is collected in very small amounts from the consumer.

Nu ku a lo fa (nü′kü ä lō′fä), *n.* capital of Tonga, a seaport in the S part. 16,000.

null (nul), *adj.* 1 not binding; of no effect; as if not existing: *A promise obtained by force is legally null.* 2 unimportant; useless; meaningless; empty; valueless. 3 not any; zero. 4 **null and void,** without legal force or effect; worthless. [< Latin *nullus* not any < *ne-* not + *ullus* any]

nul li fi ca tion (nul′ə fə kā′shən), *n.* 1 a making null. 2 a being nullified. 3 Often, **Nullification.** U.S. action taken by a state to nullify or declare unconstitutional a federal law or judicial decision and prevent its enforcement within the state's boundaries.

nul li fi ca tion ist or **Nul li fi ca tion ist** (nul′ə fə kā′shə nist), *n.* U.S. supporter or advocate of the right of states to nullify federal laws.

nul li fi er (nul′ə fī′ər), *n.* 1 person who nullifies. 2 U.S. nullificationist.

nul li fy (nul′ə fī), *v.t.,* **-fied, -fy ing.** 1 make not binding; render void: *nullify a treaty.* 2 make of no effect; make unimportant, useless, or meaningless; destroy; cancel; wipe out: *The difficulties of the plan nullify its advantages.*

nul li ty (nul′ə tē), *n., pl.* **-ties.** 1 condition of being null; futility; nothingness. 2 a mere nothing. 3 something that is null, such as a nullified law or agreement.

null set, empty set.

Num., Numbers.

numb (num), *adj.* having lost the power of feeling or moving: *numb with cold. —v.t.* 1 make numb. 2 dull the feelings of: *numbed with grief.* [Old English *numen* taken, seized] **—numb′ly,** *adv.* **—numb′ness,** *n.*

num ber (num′bər), *n.* 1 the amount of units; sum; total. See synonym study below. 2 word that tells exactly how many. Two, fourteen, twenty-six are cardinal numbers; second, fourteenth, twenty-sixth are ordinal numbers. 3 figure or mark that stands for a number; numeral. 4 quantity, especially a rather large quantity: *a number of reasons. A large number cannot read.* 5 a collection or company: *the number of saints.* 6 one of a numbered series, often a particular numeral identifying a person or thing: *an apartment number, a license number.* 7 single part of a program, etc.: *She sang four musical numbers.* 8 a single issue of a periodical. 9 INFORMAL. thing or person viewed apart from a collection or company: *That hat is the most fashionable number in the store.* 10 in grammar: **a** the property or feature of a word that indicates whether it refers to one, or more than one, person or thing. *Boy, ox,* and *this* are in the singular number; *boys, oxen,* and *these* are in the plural number. **b** the form or group of forms indicating this. 11 **numbers,** *pl.* **a** arithmetic. **b** many: *Numbers were turned away.* **c** numerical preponderance: *win a war by force of numbers.* **d** poetry; lines of verse. **e** U.S. numbers game. 12 **beyond number,** too many to count. 13 **without number,** too many to be counted.

—v.t. 1 assign a number to; mark with a number; distinguish with a number: *The pages of this book are numbered.* 2 be able to show; have: *This city numbers a million inhabitants.* 3 amount to: *The candidate's plurality numbered 5000 votes.* 4 reckon as one of a class or collection; classify: *numbered among his followers.* 5 fix the number of; limit: *That old man's years are numbered.* 6 enumerate; count. *—v.i.* 1 make a count. 2 be numbered or included with.

[< Old French *nombre* < Latin *numerus*] **—num′ber er,** *n.*

Syn. *n.* 1 **Number, sum** mean total of two or more persons, things, or units taken together. **Number** applies to the total reached by counting the persons or things in a group or collection: *The number of students in our class is thirty.* **Sum** applies to the total reached by adding figures or things: *The sum of two and two is four.*

➤ **Number** is a collective noun, requiring a singular or plural verb according as the total or the individual units are meant: *A number of tickets have already been sold. The number of tickets sold is astonishing.* See **amount** for another usage note.

➤ **numbers.** In informal writing, figures are usually used for numbers over ten, words for smaller numbers. In formal writing, figures are usually used for numbers over 100 except when they can be written in two words: informal: *four, ten, 15, 92, 114, 200.* Formal: *four, ten, fifteen, ninety-two, 114, two hundred.* But practice is not consistent.

num ber less (num′bər lis), *adj.* 1 very numerous; too many to count: *There are numberless fish in the sea.* 2 without a number; not numbered.

number one, INFORMAL. oneself; one's own welfare: *look out for number one.*

Num bers (num′bərz), *n.* the fourth book of the Old Testament. It tells about the counting of the Israelites after they left Egypt.

hat, āge, fär; let, ēqual, tėrm;
it, īce; hot, ōpen, ôrder;
oil, out; cup, pu̇t, rüle;
ch, child; ng, long; sh, she;
th, thin; ᴛʜ, then; zh, measure;

ə represents *a* in about, *e* in taken,
i in pencil, *o* in lemon, *u* in circus.

< = from, derived from, taken from.

numbers game, U.S. a daily lottery in which bets are made on the appearance of any three digit numbers in a published statistic, such as the total amount bet at a race track.

numb ing (num′ing), *adj.* that numbs or induces numbness: *numbing cold or grief.* **—numb′ing ly,** *adv.*

numb skull (num′skul′), *n.* numskull.

nu mer a ble (nü′mər ə bəl, nyü′mər ə bəl), *adj.* that can be counted.

nu mer al (nü′mər əl, nyü′mər əl), *n.* 1 figure, letter, or word standing for a number; group of figures, letters, or words standing for a number. 1, 5, 10, 50, 100, 500, and 1000 are Arabic numerals. I, V, X, L, C, D, and M are Roman numerals. 2 **numerals,** *pl.* big cloth numbers given by a school for excellence in some sport. They state the year in which the person who wins them will graduate. *—adj.* of numbers; standing for a number. [< Late Latin *numeralis* < Latin *numerus* number]

nu me rate (nü′mə rāt′, nyü′mə rāt′), *v.t.,* **-rat ed, -rat ing.** number, count, or enumerate.

nu me ra tion (nü′mə rā′shən, nyü′mə rā′shən), *n.* 1 a numbering, counting, or enumerating. 2 the reading of numbers expressed in figures.

numeration system, any system of counting or naming numbers, such as the decimal system and the binary system.

nu me ra tor (nü′mə rā′tər, nyü′mə rā′tər), *n.* 1 number above the line in a fraction which shows how many parts are taken: *In $^3/_8$. 3 is the numerator and 8 is the denominator.* 2 person or thing that makes a count.

nu mer ic (nü mer′ik, nyü mer′ik), *adj.* numerical.

nu mer i cal (nü mer′ə kəl, nyü mer′ə kəl), *adj.* 1 of a number; having to do with numbers; in numbers; by numbers. 2 shown by numbers, not by letters: *10 is a numerical quantity; bx is an algebraic quantity.* **—nu mer′i cal ly,** *adv.*

nu me rol o gist (nü′mə rol′ə jist, nyü′mə rol′ə jist), *n.* person who practices numerology.

nu me rol o gy (nü′mə rol′ə jē, nyü′mə rol′ə jē), *n.* practice of foretelling the future by the study of supposedly meaningful numbers or combinations of numbers.

nu mer ous (nü′mər əs, nyü′mər əs), *adj.* 1 very many; several: *The child asked numerous questions.* 2 in great numbers: *He has a numerous acquaintance among politicians.* **—nu′mer ous ly,** *adv.* **—nu′mer ous ness,** *n.*

Nu mid i a (nü mid′ē ə, nyü mid′ē ə), *n.* ancient country in N Africa, corresponding generally to modern Algeria. **—Nu mid′i an,** *adj., n.*

nu mis mat ic (nü′miz mat′ik, nyü′miz-mat′ik), *adj.* 1 of numismatics or numismatists. 2 of coins and medals. **—nu′mis mat′i cal ly,** *adv.*

nu mis mat ics (nü′miz mat′iks, nyü′miz mat′iks), *n.* the study or collecting of coins and medals. [< French *numismatique* < Latin *numisma* coin < Greek *nomisma* < *nomizein* have in use]

nu mis ma tist (nü miz′mə tist, nyü miz′mə tist), *n.* an expert in numismatics.

num skull (num′skul′), *n.* a stupid person; blockhead. Also, **numbskull.**

nun (nun), *n.* woman who gives up all worldly things and enters a convent to live a life devoted to religion. Some nuns teach; some care for the poor and sick. [Old English *nunne* < Late Latin *nonna,* feminine of *nonnus* monk]

Nunc Di mit tis (nungk′ di mit′is), canticle of Simeon in Luke 2:29-32, beginning "Lord, now lettest thou thy servant depart in peace." [< Latin *Nunc dimittis,* the first words as given in the Vulgate]

nun ci o (nun′shē ō), *n., pl.* **-ci os.** ambassador from the Pope to a government. [< Italian < Latin *nuntius* messenger]

nun ner y (nun′ər ē), *n., pl.* **-ner ies.** building or buildings where nuns live; convent.

nup tial (nup′shəl), *adj.* of marriage or weddings. *—n.* **nuptials,** *pl.* a wedding or the wedding ceremony. [< Latin *nuptialis,* ultimately < *nubere* take a husband]

Nur em berg (nůr′əm bėrg′, nyůr′əm bėrg′), *n.* city in SE West Germany. 477,000.

nurse (nėrs), *n., v.,* **nursed, nurs ing.** *—n.* 1 person who is trained to take care of the sick, the injured, or the old, especially under a doctor's supervision. 2 woman who cares for and brings up the young children or babies of another person. 3 wet nurse. 4 one who feeds, protects, or gives any sort of aid or comfort. 5 worker in a colony of bees or ants that cares for the young.
—v.i. 1 be a nurse; act as a nurse; work as a nurse. 2 suck milk from a mother or nurse.
—v.t. 1 act as a nurse for; wait on or take care of (the sick); take care of (sick, injured, or old people). 2 cure or try to cure by care: *She nursed a bad cold by going to bed.* 3 have charge of or bring up (another's baby or young child). 4 nourish; protect; make grow: *nurse a plant, nurse a fire, nurse a grudge.* 5 use or treat with special care: *He nursed his sore arm by using it very little.* 6 hold closely; clasp fondly. 7 give milk to (a baby).
[< Old French *nurrice* < Latin *nutricia* < *nutrire* to feed] **—nurs′er,** *n.*

nurse ling (nėrs′ling), *n.* nursling.

nurse maid (nėrs′mād′), *n.* girl or woman employed to care for children.

nurs er y (nėr′sər ē), *n., pl.* **-er ies.** 1 room set apart for the use of the children of the household. 2 piece of ground or place where young trees and plants are raised for transplanting or sale. 3 place or condition that helps something to grow and develop: *Slums are often nurseries of disease.* 4 nursery school.

nurs er y maid (nėr′sər ē mād′), *n.* nursemaid.

nurs er y man (nėr′sər ē mən), *n., pl.* **-men.** man who grows or sells young trees and plants.

nursery rhyme, a short poem for children. "Sing a Song of Sixpence" is a famous nursery rhyme.

nursery school, school for children not old enough to go to kindergarten.

nurs ling (nėrs′ling), *n.* 1 baby that is being nursed. 2 any person or thing that is receiving tender care. Also, **nurseling.**

nur ture (nėr′chər), *v.,* **-tured, -tur ing,** *n.* *—v.t.* 1 bring up; care for; foster; rear; train: *They nurtured the child as if he had been their own.* 2 nourish. *—n.* 1 a bringing up; rearing; training; education: *The two sisters had received very different nurture.* 2 nourishment. [< Old French *nourture* < Late Latin *nutritura* a nursing, suckling < Latin *nutrire* to feed] **—nur′tur er,** *n.*

nut (def. 3)—above, five kinds of nuts; left, nut on a bolt

nut (nut), *n., v.,* **nut ted, nut ting.** *—n.* 1 a dry fruit or seed with a hard, woody or leathery shell and a kernel inside. 2 kernel of a nut, usually edible. 3 a small, usually metal block having a threaded hole, which screws on to a bolt to hold the bolt in place. 4 piece at the upper end of a violin, cello, etc., over which the strings pass. 5 SLANG. **a** a foolish or crazy person. **b** an enthusiast. **6 hard nut to crack,** a difficult question, problem, or undertaking. *—v.i.* gather nuts. [Old English *hnutu*] **—nut′like′,** *adj.*

nut crack er (nut′krak′ər), *n.* 1 instrument for cracking the shells of nuts. 2 any of several birds of the same family as the crow that feed especially on pine seeds.

nut hatch (nut′hach′), *n.* any of a family of small, sharp-beaked birds that feed on small nuts, seeds, and insects. [Middle English *notehache,* literally, nut hacker]

nut let (nut′lit), *n.* 1 a small nut or nutlike fruit. 2 stone of a drupe.

nut meat (nut′mēt′), *n.* kernel of a nut.

nut meg (nut′meg), *n.* 1 a hard, spicy seed about as big as a marble, obtained from the fruit of an East Indian evergreen tree or various other trees of the same genus. The seed is grated and used for flavoring. 2 the tree it grows on. [Middle English *notemuga*]

nut pick (nut′pik′), *n.* a sharp-pointed instrument for removing nuts from their shells.

nu tri a (nü′trē ə, nyü′trē ə), *n.* 1 coypu. 2 its valuable beaverlike fur. [< Spanish *nutria, lutria* otter]

nu tri ent (nü′trē ənt, nyü′trē ənt), *adj.* nourishing. *—n.* a nourishing substance.

nu tri ment (nü′trə mənt, nyü′trə mənt), *n.* that which is required by an organism for life and growth; nourishment; food.

nu tri tion (nü trish′ən, nyü trish′ən), *n.* 1 series of processes by which food is taken in and used by animals and plants for growth, energy, etc. 2 food; nourishment.

nu tri tion al (nü trish′ə nəl, nyü trish′ə nəl), *adj.* having to do with nutrition. **—nu tri′tion al ly,** *adv.*

nu tri tion ist (nü trish′ə nist, nyü trish′ə nist), *n.* an expert in the study of nutrition.

nu tri tious (nü trish′əs, nyü trish′əs), *adj.* valuable as food; nourishing. [< Latin *nutritius, nutricius* < *nutrix* nurse < *nutrire* nourish] **—nu tri′tious ly,** *adv.* **—nu tri′tious ness,** *n.*

nu tri tive (nü′trə tiv, nyü′trə tiv), *adj.* 1 having to do with foods and the use of foods. Digestion is part of the nutritive process. 2 nutritious. **—nu′tri tive ly,** *adv.* **—nu′tri tive ness,** *n.*

nuts (nuts), *adj.* SLANG. 1 crazy. **2 be nuts about,** be very fond of or delighted with (a person or thing).

nut shell (nut′shel′), *n.* 1 shell of a nut. **2 in a nutshell,** in very brief form; in a few words.

nut ting (nut′ing), *n.* a looking for nuts; gathering nuts.

nut ty (nut′ē), *adj.,* **-ti er, -ti est.** 1 containing many nuts: *nutty cake.* 2 like nuts; tasting like nuts. 3 SLANG. **a** crazy. **b** very interested or enthusiastic. **—nut′ti ness,** *n.*

nux vom i ca (nuks vom′ə kə), 1 the poisonous seed of a tree, growing in southern Asia and northern Australia, which is a source of strychnine. 2 the tree it grows on. [< Medieval Latin, vomiting nut]

nuz zle (nuz′əl), *v.,* **-zled, -zling.** *—v.t.* poke or rub with the nose; press the nose against: *The calf nuzzles his mother.* *—v.i.* nestle; snuggle; cuddle. [< *nose;* influenced by *nestle*]

NW, N.W., or **n.w.,** 1 northwest. 2 northwestern.

N.W.T., Northwest Territories.

N.Y., New York State.

Ny as a (nī as′ə, nē as′ə), *n.* **Lake,** large lake in SE Africa, bordered by Malawi, Mozambique, and Tanzania. 360 mi. long; 11,000 sq. mi.

Ny as a land (nī as′ə land′, nē as′ə land′), *n.* former British protectorate in SE Africa, now the country of Malawi.

N.Y.C., New York City.

ny lon (nī′lon), *n.* 1 any of a group of extremely strong, elastic, and durable synthetic substances, used to make clothing, stockings, bristles, etc. **2 nylons,** *pl.* stockings made of nylon. *—adj.* made of nylon. [< *Nylon,* a trademark]

nymph (nimf), *n.* 1 (in Greek and Roman myths) one of the lesser goddesses of nature, who lived in seas, rivers, fountains, springs, hills, woods, or trees. 2 a beautiful or graceful young woman. 3 any of certain insects in the stage of development between the egg and the adult form. It resembles the adult but has no wings. [< Greek *nymphē*] **—nymph′like′,** *adj.*

N.Z., New Zealand.

O o

O[1] or **o** (ō), *n., pl.* **O's** or **o's.** 1 the 15th letter of the English alphabet. 2 anything shaped like an O. 3 zero.
O[2] (ō), *interj.* oh!
o' (ə, ō), *prep.* 1 of: *man-o'-war.* 2 on.
o-, *prefix.* form of **ob-** before *m,* as in *omit.*
o, ohm.
O, 1 oxygen. 2 one of the four main blood groups.
O., Ohio.
oaf (ōf), *n.* 1 a very stupid child or man. 2 a deformed child. 3 a clumsy person. [< Scandinavian (Old Icelandic) *ālfr* elf]
oaf ish (ō′fish), *adj.* very stupid; clumsy. **—oaf′ish ly,** *adv.* **—oaf′ish ness,** *n.*
O a hu (ō ä′hü), *n.* the third largest island of Hawaii. Honolulu, the capital of Hawaii, is on Oahu. 629,000 pop.; 604 sq. mi.
oak (ōk), *n.* 1 any of a genus of trees or shrubs of the same family as the beech and found in most parts of the world, with strong, hard, durable wood and nuts called acorns. 2 the wood of any of these trees, used in building, for flooring, etc. 3 tree or shrub resembling or suggesting an oak. *—adj.* 1 of an oak: *oak leaves.* 2 made of oak wood; oaken: *an oak table.* [Old English *āc*] **—oak′like′,** *adj.*
oak apple, an apple-shaped gall on an oak leaf or stem caused by a gall wasp; oak gall.
oak en (ō′kən), *adj.* made of oak wood: *the old oaken bucket.*
oak gall, oak apple.
Oak land (ōk′lənd), *n.* city in W California, just east of San Francisco, on San Francisco Bay. 362,000.
Oak Ridge, city in E Tennessee, an atomic-energy research center. 28,000.
oa kum (ō′kəm), *n.* a loose fiber obtained by untwisting and picking apart old tarred hemp ropes, used for stopping up the seams or cracks in ships. [Old English *ācumba*]
oar (ôr, ōr), *n.* 1 a long pole with a flat blade at one end, used in rowing. Sometimes an oar is used to steer a boat. 2 person who rows; oarsman: *The fisherman is the best oar in the lifeboat crew.* 3 **put one's oar in,** meddle; interfere. 4 **rest on one's oars,** stop working or trying and take a rest. 5 **ship oars,** lift oars from the oarlocks and put them in the boat. *—v.t.* row (a boat). *—v.i.* row. [Old English *ār*]
oared (ôrd, ōrd), *adj.* furnished with oars; moved by oars.

oarlock

oar lock (ôr′lok′, ōr′lok′), *n.* a notch or U-shaped support for holding the oar in place while rowing; rowlock. [Old English *ārloc*]
oars man (ôrz′mən, ōrz′mən), *n., pl.* **-men.** 1 person, especially a man, who rows; rower. 2 an expert rower.

OAS, Organization of American States.
o a sis (ō ā′sis, ō′ə sis), *n., pl.* **-ses** (-sēz′). 1 a fertile spot in the desert where there is water and some vegetation. 2 any fertile spot in a barren land; any pleasant place in a desolate region. [< Late Latin < Greek]
oat (ōt), *n.* 1 Often, **oats,** *pl. or sing.* a tall cereal grass whose seed is used in making oatmeal and as a food for horses and other livestock. 2 **oats,** *pl. or sing.* seeds of the oat plant. 3 **feel one's oats,** INFORMAL. **a** be lively or frisky. **b** feel pleased or important and show it. 4 **sow one's wild oats,** indulge in youthful carefree, uninhibited pleasures and pursuits before settling down. [Old English *āte*]
oat cake (ōt′kāk′), *n.* a thin cake made of oatmeal.
oat en (ōt′n), *adj.* 1 made of oats or oatmeal. 2 made of oat straw. 3 of or having to do with the oat.
oath (ōth), *n., pl.* **oaths** (ōᴛʜz, ōths). 1 a solemn promise: *The oath bound him to secrecy.* 2 a statement that something is true, which God or some holy person or thing is called on to witness; vow. 3 name of God or some holy person or thing used as an exclamation to add force or to express anger. 4 a curse; swearword. 5 **take oath,** make an oath; promise or state solemnly. 6 **under oath,** sworn to tell the truth. [Old English *āth*]
oat meal (ōt′mēl′), *n.* 1 oats made into meal; rolled or ground oats. 2 a cooked cereal made from oatmeal.
Oa xa ca (wä hä′kä), *n.* 1 state in S Mexico. 2 its capital, in the central part. 117,000.
Ob (ōb, ôp), *n.* 1 **Ob River,** river flowing from SE Soviet Union into the Gulf of Ob. 2500 mi. 2 **Gulf of,** gulf of the Arctic Ocean, in NE Soviet Union. 550 mi. long.
ob-, *prefix.* 1 against; in the way; opposing; hindering, as in *obstruct.* 2 inversely; contrary to the usual position, as in *oblate.* 3 toward; to, as in *obvert.* 4 on; over, as in *obscure.* See also **o-, oc-, of-, op-,** and **os-.** [< Latin]
ob., died [for Latin *obiit*].
O ba di ah (ō′bə dī′ə), *n.* 1 Hebrew prophet of the 500's B.C. 2 book of the Old Testament containing his prophecies.
ob bli ga to (ob′lə gä′tō), *adj., n., pl.* **-tos.** in music: *—adj.* accompanying a solo, but having a distinct character and independent importance. *—n.* an obbligato part or accompaniment, especially an obbligato instrumental solo. Also, **obligato.** [< Italian, literally, obliged]
ob dur a cy (ob′dər ə sē, ob′dyər ə sē), *n.* a being obdurate.
ob dur ate (ob′dər it, ob′dyər it), *adj.* 1 stubborn or unyielding; obstinate: *an obdurate refusal.* 2 hardened in feelings or heart; not repentant: *an obdurate criminal.* [< Latin *obduratum* hardened < *ob-* against + *durare* harden] **—ob′dur ate ly,** *adv.* **—ob′dur ate ness,** *n.*
o be di ence (ō bē′dē əns), *n.* an obeying; doing what one is told; submission to authority or law: *Soldiers act in obedience to the orders of their officers.*
o be di ent (ō bē′dē ənt), *adj.* doing what one is told; willing to obey. See synonym study below. [< Latin *oboedientem* obeying] **—o be′di ent ly,** *adv.*
Syn. Obedient, compliant, docile mean acting as another asks or commands. **Obedient** emphasizes being willing to follow instructions and carry out orders of someone whose authority or control one acknowledges: *The obedient dog came at his master's whistle.* **Compliant** emphasizes bending easily, sometimes too easily, to another's will and being ready to do whatever he wishes or commands: *Compliant people are not good leaders.* **Docile** emphasizes having a submissive disposition and no desire to rebel against authority or control: *She always rides a docile horse.*

hat, āge, fär; let, ēqual, tėrm;
it, īce; hot, ōpen, ôrder;
oil, out; cup, pu̇t, rüle;
ch, child; ng, long; sh, she;
th, thin; ᴛʜ, then; zh, measure;
ə represents *a* in about, *e* in taken, *i* in pencil, *o* in lemon, *u* in circus.
< = from, derived from, taken from.

o bei sance (ō bā′sns, ō bē′sns), *n.* 1 movement of the body expressing deep respect or reverence; deep bow or curtsy. 2 deference; homage. [< Old French *obeissance* obedience < *obeir* obey]
o bei sant (ō bā′snt, ō bē′snt), *adj.* showing obeisance.

obelisk from ancient Egypt

ob e lisk (ob′ə lisk), *n.* a tapering, four-sided shaft of stone with a top shaped like a pyramid. [< Greek *obeliskos,* diminutive of *obelos* a spit]
O ber am mer gau (ō′bə rä′mər gou), *n.* village in S West Germany where a traditional passion play is performed every ten years. 5000.
O ber hau sen (ō′bər hou′zn), *n.* city in W West Germany. 250,000.
O be ron (ō′bə ron′), *n.* (in medieval legends) the king of the fairies and husband of Titania. He is a main character in Shakespeare's *A Midsummer Night's Dream.*
o bese (ō bēs′), *adj.* extremely fat. [< Latin *obesus* < *ob-* on + *edere* eat] **—o bese′ness,** *n.*
o bes i ty (ō bē′sə tē, ō bes′ə tē), *n.* extreme fatness.
o bey (ō bā′), *v.i.* do what one is told to do: *The dog obeyed and went home.* *—v.t.* 1 follow the orders of: *Obey your parents.* 2 act in accordance with; comply with: *A good citizen obeys the laws.* 3 yield to the control of: *A car obeys the driver.* [< Old French *obeir* < Latin *oboedire* < *ob-* to + *audire* listen, give ear] **—o bey′er,** *n.*
ob fus cate (ob fus′kāt, ob′fu skāt), *v.t.,* **-cat ed, -cat ing.** 1 confuse; bewilder; stupefy: *A person's mind may be obfuscated by liquor.* 2 darken; obscure. [< Latin *obfuscatum* darkened < *ob-* against + *fuscus* dark] **—ob′fus ca′tion,** *n.* **—ob fus′ca tor,** *n.*

ob fus ca to ry (ob fus′kə tôr′ē, ob fus′kə-tōr′ē), *adj.* that obfuscates; confusing.

o bi (ō′bē), *n.* a long, broad sash worn by Japanese around the waist of a kimono. [< Japanese]

o bit (ō′bit, ob′it), *n.* INFORMAL. an obituary.

ob i ter dic tum (ob′ə tər dik′təm; ō′bə-tər dik′təm), *pl.* **ob i ter dic ta** (dik′tə). 1 an incidental statement; passing remark. 2 an incidental opinion given by a judge. [< Latin, said by the way]

o bit u ar y (ō bich′ü er′ē), *n., pl.* **-ar ies,** *adj.* —*n.* a notice of death, often with a brief account of the person's life. —*adj.* of a death; recording a death or deaths. [< Medieval Latin *obituarius* < Latin *obitus* death < *obire (mortem)* meet (death) < *ob-* away + *ire* go]

obj., 1 object. 2 objection. 3 objective.

ob ject (*n.* ob′jikt, ob′jekt; *v.* əb jekt′), *n.* 1 something that can be seen or touched; thing: *The museum was full of interesting objects.* 2 person or thing toward which feeling, thought, or action is directed: *an object of charity.* 3 thing aimed at; end; purpose; goal: *The object of his campaign is to get elected.* 4 (in grammar) a word or group of words toward which the action of the verb is directed or to which a preposition expresses some relation. In "He threw the ball to his brother," *ball* is the object of *threw,* and *brother* is the object of *to.* —*v.i.* make an objection or objections; be opposed; feel dislike: *Many people object to loud noise.* —*v.t.* give as a reason against; bring forward in opposition; oppose: *Mother objected that the weather was too wet to play outdoors.* [< Medieval Latin *objectum* < Latin, thrown in the way of < *ob-* against + *jacere* to throw] —**ob jec′tor,** *n.*

object glass, the objective of a telescope, microscope, etc.

ob jec ti fy (əb jek′tə fī), *v.t.,* **-fied, -fy ing.** make objective. —**ob jec′ti fi ca′tion,** *n.*

ob jec tion (əb jek′shən), *n.* 1 something said or written in objecting; reason or argument against something: *An objection to the plan was its high cost.* 2 feeling of disapproval or dislike; opposition: *A lazy person has an objection to working.* 3 act of objecting.

ob jec tion a ble (əb jek′shə nə bəl), *adj.* 1 likely to be objected to: *an objectionable movie.* 2 unpleasant; disagreeable; offensive: *an objectionable odor.* —**ob jec′tion a bly,** *adv.*

ob jec tive (əb jek′tiv), *n.* 1 something aimed at; object; goal: *My objective this summer will be learning to play tennis better.* 2 something real and observable. 3 in grammar: **a** the objective case. **b** word in that case. *Whom* and *me* are objectives. 4 lens or combination of lenses in a telescope, microscope, etc., that first receives light rays from the object and forms the image viewed through the eyepiece; object glass. —*adj.* 1 being the object of endeavor. 2 existing outside the mind as something actual and not merely in the mind as an idea; real. Actions are objective; ideas are subjective. 3 dealing with outward things, not with the thoughts and feelings of the speaker, writer, painter, etc.; giving facts as they are without bias; impersonal: *A scientist must be objective in his experiments.* 4 (in grammar) showing the direct object of a verb or the object of a preposition. In "John hit me," *me* is in the objective case. —**ob jec′tive ly,** *adv.* —**ob jec′tive ness,** *n.*

objective complement, (in grammar) a noun, pronoun, or adjective used as a complement to a transitive verb to modify its direct object. In "I consider him *smart,*" *smart* is the objective complement of *consider.*

ob jec tiv i ty (ob′jek tiv′ə tē), *n.* condition or quality of being objective; intentness on objects external to the mind; external reality.

object lesson, a practical illustration of a principle: *Many accidents are object lessons in the dangers of carelessness.*

ob jet d'art (ôb zhe′ där′), *pl.* **ob jets d'art** (ôb zhe′ där′). FRENCH. 1 a small picture, vase, etc., of some artistic value. 2 (literally) object of art.

ob jur gate (ob′jər gāt, əb jėr′gāt), *v.t.,* **-gat ed, -gat ing.** reproach vehemently; upbraid violently; berate. [< Latin *objurgatum* scolded < *ob-* against + *jurgare* to scold] —**ob′jur ga′tion,** *n.* —**ob′jur ga′tor,** *n.*

ob jur ga to ry (əb jėr′gə tôr′ē, əb jėr′gə-tōr′ē), *adj.* vehemently reproachful; upbraiding; berating.

obl., 1 oblique. 2 oblong.

ob last (ob′ləst; *Russian* ô′bläst), *n., pl.* **-lasts, -las ti** (-lə stē). a regional subdivision of any of the constituent republics of the Soviet Union. [< Russian *oblast′*]

ob late¹ (ob′lāt, o blāt′), *adj.* flattened at the poles: *The earth is an oblate spheroid.* [< New Latin *oblatum* < Latin *ob-* inversely + *(pro)latum* prolate] —**ob′late ness,** *n.*

ob late² (ob′lāt, o blāt′), *n.* 1 person devoted to the service of a monastery as a lay brother. 2 a member of any of various secular societies in the Roman Catholic Church devoted to religious work. [< Latin *oblatum* offered < *ob-* up to + *latum* brought]

o bla tion (o blā′shən), *n.* 1 act of offering to God or a god. 2 the offering of bread and wine in the Communion service. 3 something offered to a god; sacrifice. 4 gift for religious uses.

ob li gate (*v.* ob′lə gāt; *adj.* ob′lə git, ob′lə-gāt), *v.,* **-gat ed, -gat ing,** *adj.* —*v.t.* bind morally or legally; pledge: *A witness in court is obligated to tell the truth.* —*adj.* 1 (in biology) restricted to a particular condition or way of life, as a parasite. 2 obligated.

ob li ga tion (ob′lə gā′shən), *n.* 1 duty under the law; duty due to a promise or contract; duty on account of social relationship or kindness received; responsibility: *an obligation to pay taxes. Parents have obligations to their children.* See **duty** for synonym study. 2 binding power (of a law, promise, sense of duty, etc.): *The one who did the damage is under obligation to pay for it.* 3 a binding legal agreement; bond; contract: *The firm was not able to meet its obligations.* 4 bond, note, bill, or certificate serving as security for payment of indebtedness. 5 a binding oneself or being bound by oath, promise, etc., to do something: *It was my obligation to return the favor.* 6 service; favor; benefit: *An independent person likes to repay all obligations.*

ob li ga to (ob′lə gä′tō), *adj., n., pl.* **-tos.** obbligato.

o blig a to ry (ə blig′ə tôr′ē, ə blig′ə tōr′ē; ob′lə gə tôr′ē, ob′lə gə tōr′ē), *adj.* binding morally or legally; compulsory; required: *Attendance in school is obligatory.* —**o blig′a-to′ri ly,** *adv.*

o blige (ə blīj′), *v.,* **o bliged, o blig ing.** —*v.t.* 1 bind by a promise, contract, duty, etc.; compel; force: *The law obliges parents to send their children to school.* 2 put under a debt of thanks for some favor or service: *We are obliged to you for your help.* —*v.i.* do a favor: *She obliged graciously by singing another song.* [< Old French *obliger* < Latin *obligare* < *ob-* to + *ligare* to bind] —**o blig′er,** *n.*

o blig ing (ə blī′jing), *adj.* willing to do favors; helpful. —**o blig′ing ly,** *adv.* —**o blig′ing ness,** *n.*

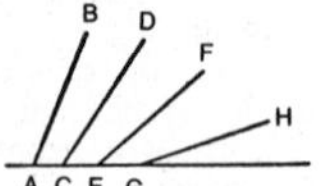

oblique (def. 1) AB, CD, EF, and GH are oblique lines

o blique (ə blēk′; *military* ə blīk′), *adj., v.,* **o bliqued, o bliqu ing.** —*adj.* 1 neither perpendicular to nor parallel with a given line or surface; not straight up and down or straight across; slanting. 2 not straightforward; indirect: *She made an oblique reference to her illness, but did not mention it directly.* —*v.i., v.t.* have or take an oblique direction; slant. [< Latin *obliquus*] —**o blique′ly,** *adv.* —**o blique′ness,** *n.*

oblique angle, any angle that is not a right angle or a multiple of a right angle. Acute angles and obtuse angles are oblique angles.

oblique case, any case of a noun or pronoun except the nominative and vocative.

o bliq ui ty (ə blik′wə tē), *n., pl.* **-ties.** 1 indirectness or crookedness of thought, speech, or behavior, especially conduct that is not upright and moral. 2 a being oblique. 3 inclination, or degree of inclination.

o blit e rate (ə blit′ə rāt′), *v.t.,* **-rat ed, -rat ing.** 1 remove all traces of; blot out; efface: *The heavy rain obliterated the footprints.* 2 blot out so as to leave no distinct traces; make unrecognizable. [< Latin *obliteratum* struck out < *ob literas (scribere)* (draw) across the letters, strike out] —**o blit′e ra′tion,** *n.* —**o blit′e ra′tor,** *n.*

o bliv i on (ə bliv′ē ən), *n.* 1 condition of being entirely forgotten: *Many ancient cities have long since passed into oblivion.* 2 fact of forgetting; forgetfulness. [< Latin *oblivionem* < *oblivisci* forget]

o bliv i ous (ə bliv′ē əs), *adj.* 1 not mindful; forgetful: *The book was so interesting that I was oblivious of my surroundings.* 2 bringing or causing forgetfulness. —**o bliv′i ous ly,** *adv.* —**o bliv′i ous ness,** *n.*

ob long (ob′lông, ob′long), *adj.* 1 longer than broad: *an oblong loaf of bread.* 2 (in geometry) having the opposite sides parallel and the adjacent sides at right angles but not

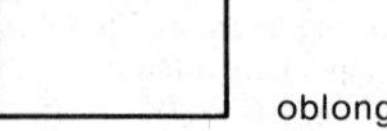

oblong

square. —*n.* rectangle that is not a square. [< Latin *oblongus* < *ob-* toward + *longus* long]

ob lo quy (ob′lə kwē), *n., pl.* **-quies.** 1 public reproach or condemnation; abuse; blame. 2 disgrace; shame. [< Late Latin *obloquium* < Latin *ob-* against + *loqui* speak]

ob nox ious (əb nok′shəs), *adj.* very disagreeable; offensive; hateful. See **hateful** for synonym study. [< Latin *obnoxius* < *ob-* toward + *noxa* injury] —**ob nox′ious ly,** *adv.* —**ob nox′ious ness,** *n.*

oboe

o boe (ō′bō), *n.* a woodwind instrument in which a thin, high-pitched tone is produced by a double reed; hautboy. [< Italian < French *hautbois* hautboy]

o bo ist (ō′bō ist), *n.* person who plays an oboe.

obs., obsolete.

ob scene (əb sēn′), *adj.* offending modesty or decency; impure; filthy; vile. [< Latin *obscenus*] —**ob scene′ly,** *adv.*

ob scen i ty (əb sen′ə tē, əb sē′nə tē), *n., pl.* **-ties.** 1 obscene quality or character. 2 obscene language or behavior; obscene word or act.

ob scur ant (əb skyůr′ənt), *adj.* 1 that obscures or darkens. 2 obscurantist.

ob scur ant ism (əb skyůr′ən tiz′əm), *n.* 1 opposition to progress and the spread of knowledge. 2 a being deliberately unclear or evasive.

ob scur ant ist (əb skyůr′ən tist), *n.* person who practices obscurantism. —*adj.* of obscurantists or obscurantism.

ob scure (əb skyůr′), *adj.,* **-scur er, -scur est,** *v.,* **-scured, -scur ing.** —*adj.* 1 not clearly expressed; hard to understand: *an obscure passage in a book.* See synonym study below. 2 not expressing meaning clearly: *an obscure style of writing.* 3 not well known; attracting no notice: *an obscure little village, an obscure poet, an obscure position in the government.* 4 not easily discovered; hidden: *an obscure path, an obscure meaning.* 5 not distinct; not clear: *an obscure form, obscure sounds, an obscure view.* 6 dark; dim: *an obscure corner.* 7 indefinite: *an obscure brown, an obscure vowel.* —*v.t.* 1 hide from view; make obscure; dim; darken: *Clouds obscure the sun.* 2 make dim or vague to the understanding. 3 (in phonetics) to make (a vowel) indefinite or neutral in quality. [< Latin *obscurus*] —**ob′scu ra′tion,** *n.* —**ob scure′ly,** *adv.* —**ob scure′ness,** *n.* —**ob scur′er,** *n.*

Syn. *adj.* 1 **Obscure, vague, ambiguous, equivocal** mean not clearly expressed or understood. **Obscure** suggests that the meaning of something is not clearly or plainly expressed or the reader or hearer lacks the knowledge necessary for understanding: *Much legal language is obscure.* **Vague** suggests that the meaning or statement is too general or not clearly and completely thought out: *No one can be sure what that vague statement means.* **Ambiguous** means so expressed that either of two meanings is possible: *"She kissed her when she left" is an ambiguous statement.* **Equivocal** suggests a conscious effort to confuse by allowing for conflicting interpretations: *The candidate was a master of the equivocal statement which tended to satisfy everyone.*

ob scur i ty (əb skyůr′ə tē), *n., pl.* **-ties.** 1 lack of clearness; difficulty in being understood: *The obscurity of the passage makes several interpretations possible.* 2 something obscure; thing hard to understand; point or passage not clearly expressed; doubtful or vague meaning. 3 condition of being unknown: *Lincoln rose from obscurity to fame.* 4 a little-known person or place. 5 lack of light; dimness.

ob se quies (ob′sə kwēz), *n.pl.* funeral rites or ceremonies; stately funeral. [< Medieval Latin *obsequiae,* used for Latin *exsequiae* funeral rites < *ex-* out + *sequi* follow]

ob se qui ous (əb sē′kwē əs), *adj.* polite or obedient from hope of gain or from fear; servile; fawning: *Obsequious courtiers greeted the king.* [< Latin *obsequiosus* < *obsequium* dutiful service < *ob-* after + *sequi* follow] —**ob se′qui ous ly,** *adv.* —**ob se′qui ous ness,** *n.*

ob serv a ble (əb zėr′və bəl), *adj.* 1 that can be or is noticed; noticeable; easily seen: *That distant star is observable on a dark night.* 2 that can be or is followed or practiced: *Lent is observable by some churches.* —**ob serv′a bly,** *adv.*

ob serv ance (əb zėr′vəns), *n.* 1 act of observing or keeping laws or customs: *the observance of the Sabbath.* 2 act performed as a sign of worship or respect; religious ceremony; rite. 3 rule or custom to be observed. 4 ARCHAIC. respectful attention or service. 5 observation; notice. ➤ See **observation** for usage note.

ob serv ant (əb zėr′vənt), *adj.* 1 quick to notice; watchful; observing: *If you are observant in the fields and woods, you will find many flowers that others fail to notice.* 2 careful in observing (a law, rule, custom, etc.); properly mindful: *observant of the traffic rules.* —**ob serv′ant ly,** *adv.*

ob ser va tion (ob′zər vā′shən), *n.* 1 act, habit, or power of seeing and noting: *By his trained observation the doctor knew that the unconscious man was not dead.* 2 fact or condition of being seen; notice: *The spy avoided observation.* 3 Often, **observations,** *pl.* something seen and noted; data or information secured by observing: *publish important observations in physics.* 4 act of watching for some special purpose; study: *The observation of nature is important in science.* 5 remark; comment.

➤ **Observation, observance** are sometimes confused because both are related to the verb *observe. Observation* means primarily the act of seeing and noting: *An observatory is for the observation of the stars. Observance* means primarily the act of keeping and following customs or laws: *You go to church for the observance of religious duties.*

ob ser va tion al (ob′zər vā′shə nəl), *adj.* of, having to do with, or based on observation.

ob serv a to ry (əb zėr′və tôr′ē, əb zėr′və tōr′ē), *n., pl.* **-ries.** 1 place or building from which astronomical observations are made, equipped with a telescope for observing the stars and other heavenly bodies. 2 place or building for observing facts or happenings of nature. 3 a high place or building giving a wide view.

hat, āge, fär; let, ēqual, tėrm;
it, īce; hot, ōpen, ôrder;
oil, out; cup, pu̇t, rüle;
ch, child; ng, long; sh, she;
th, thin; ᴛʜ, then; zh, measure;

ə represents *a* in about, *e* in taken, *i* in pencil, *o* in lemon, *u* in circus.

< = from, derived from, taken from.

ob serve (əb zėrv′), *v.t.,* **-served, -serv ing.** 1 see and note; notice; perceive: *I observed nothing strange in his behavior.* See **see** for synonym study. 2 watch carefully or examine for some special purpose; study: *An astronomer observes the stars.* 3 remark; comment: *"Bad weather," the captain observed.* 4 follow in practice; keep: *observe silence, observe a rule.* 5 show proper regard for; celebrate: *observe the Sabbath.* [< Latin *observare* < *ob-* over + *servare* to watch, keep] —**ob serv′er,** *n.*

ob serv ing (əb zėr′ving), *adj.* quick to notice; observant. —**ob serv′ing ly,** *adv.*

ob sess (əb ses′), *v.t.* fill the mind of; keep the attention of to an unreasonable or unhealthy extent; haunt: *Fear that someone might steal his money obsessed him.* [< Latin *obsessum* possessed < *ob-* on + *sedere* sit]

ob ses sion (əb sesh′ən), *n.* 1 an obsessing or a being obsessed; influence of a feeling, idea, or impulse to an unreasonable or unhealthy extent. 2 the feeling, idea, or impulse itself.

ob ses sive (əb ses′iv), *adj.* of, having to do with, or causing obsession. —**ob ses′sive ly,** *adv.*

ob sid i an (ob sid′ē ən), *n.* a hard, dark, glassy rock that is formed when lava cools. [< Latin *obsidianus (lapis)* (stone) of *Obsius,* Roman explorer supposed to have discovered it]

ob so les cence (ob′sə les′ns), *n.* a passing out of use; getting out of date; becoming obsolete.

ob so les cent (ob′sə les′nt), *adj.* passing out of use; tending to become out of date: *Horse-drawn vehicles are obsolescent.* —**ob′so les′cent ly,** *adv.*

ob so lete (ob′sə lēt, ob′sə lēt′), *adj.* 1 no longer in use; disused: *"Eft" (meaning again) is an obsolete word.* 2 not commonly used in the present; old-fashioned; out-of-date: *We still use this machine though it is obsolete.* 3 (in biology) imperfectly developed; vestigial. [< Latin *obsoletum* fallen into disuse < *ob-* away + *solere* be usual] —**ob′so lete ly,** *adv.* —**ob′so lete ness,** *n.*

ob sta cle (ob′stə kəl), *n.* something that

observatory (def. 1)

stands in the way or stops progress: *He overcame the obstacle of blindness and became a musician.* [< Latin *obstaculum* < *ob-* in the way of + *stare* to stand]
Syn. Obstacle, obstruction, hindrance mean something that gets in the way of action or progress. **Obstacle** applies to something that stands in the way and must be moved or overcome before one can continue toward a goal: *A fallen tree across the road was an obstacle to our car.* **Obstruction** applies especially to something that blocks a passage: *The enemy built obstructions in the road.* **Hindrance** applies to something that holds back or makes progress difficult: *Noise is a hindrance to studying.*

ob stet ric (ob stet′rik), *adj.* having to do with obstetrics or childbirth.

ob stet ri cal (ob stet′rə kəl), *adj.* obstetric.

ob ste tri cian (ob′stə trish′ən), *n.* doctor who specializes in obstetrics.

ob stet rics (ob stet′riks), *n.* branch of medicine concerned with caring for and treating women before, in, and after childbirth. [< Latin *obstetrica* < *obstetrix* midwife < *ob-* by + *stare* to stand]

ob sti na cy (ob′stə nə sē), *n., pl.* **-cies.** 1 a being obstinate; stubbornness. 2 an obstinate act.

ob sti nate (ob′stə nit), *adj.* 1 not giving in; stubborn. See synonym study below. 2 hard to control, treat, or remove; persistent: *an obstinate cough.* [< Latin *obstinatum* determined < *ob-* by + *stare* to stand] **—ob′stinate ly,** *adv.* **—ob′sti nate ness,** *n.*
Syn. 1 **Obstinate, stubborn** mean fixed in purpose or opinion. **Obstinate** suggests an unyielding persistence, often unreasonable or contrary, in doing things in one's own way: *The obstinate man refused to obey orders.* **Stubborn** suggests strong determination to withstand attempts to change one's way: *fight one's enemies with stubborn courage.*

ob strep er ous (əb strep′ər əs), *adj.* 1 loud or noisy; boisterous; clamorous. 2 unruly; disorderly. [< Latin *obstreperus* < *ob-* against + *strepere* make a noise] **—ob strep′er ous ly,** *adv.* **—ob strep′erous ness,** *n.*

ob struct (əb strukt′), *v.t.* 1 make hard to pass through; block or close up: *Fallen trees obstruct the road.* 2 be in the way of; block or close off: *Trees obstruct our view of the ocean.* 3 oppose the course of; hinder; impede: *obstruct justice.* [< Latin *obstructum* blocked, hindered < *ob-* in the way of + *struere* to pile] **—ob struc′tor,** *n.*

ob struc tion (əb struk′shən), *n.* 1 thing that obstructs; something in the way: *Ignorance is an obstruction to progress.* See **obstacle** for synonym study. 2 a blocking or hindering: *the obstruction of progress by prejudices.*

ob struc tion ism (əb struk′shə niz′əm), *n.* act or practice of hindering the progress of business in a meeting, legislature, etc.

ob struc tion ist (əb struk′shə nist), *n.* person who hinders (progress, legislation, reform, etc.).

ob struc tive (əb struk′tiv), *adj.* tending or serving to obstruct.

ob tain (əb tān′), *v.t.* get through diligence or effort; come to have; secure; gain: *obtain a prize, obtain knowledge through study.* See **get** for synonym study. *—v.i.* be in use; be customary; prevail: *Different rules obtain in different schools.* [< Middle French *obtenir* < Latin *obtinere* < *ob-* to + *tenere* to hold] **—ob tain′a ble,** *adj.* **—ob tain′er,** *n.* **—ob tain′ment,** *n.*

ob trude (əb trüd′), *v.,* **-trud ed, -trud ing.** *—v.t.* 1 put forward unasked and unwanted; force: *Don't obtrude your opinions on others.* 2 push out; thrust forward: *A turtle obtrudes its head from its shell.* *—v.i.* come unasked and unwanted; force oneself; intrude. [< Latin *obtrudere* < *ob-* toward + *trudere* to thrust] **—ob trud′er,** *n.*

ob tru sion (əb trü′zhən), *n.* 1 an obtruding. 2 something obtruded.

ob tru sive (əb trü′siv), *adj.* inclined to obtrude; intrusive. **—ob tru′sive ly,** *adv.* **—ob tru′sive ness,** *n.*

ob tuse (əb tüs′, əb tyüs′), *adj.* 1 not sharp or acute; blunt. 2 having an angle of more than 90 degrees but less than 180 degrees: *an obtuse triangle.* 3 slow in understanding; stupid: *too obtuse to take a hint.* 4 not sensitive; dull: *One's hearing often becomes obtuse in old age.* [< Latin *obtusum* blunted < *ob-* against + *tundere* to beat] **—obtuse′ly,** *adv.* **—ob tuse′ness,** *n.*

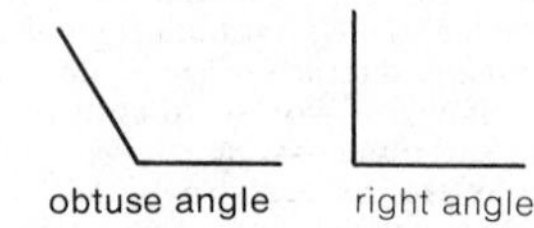

obtuse angle, angle larger than a right angle but less than 180 degrees.

ob verse (*n.* ob′vėrs′; *adj.* ob vėrs′, ob′vėrs′), *n.* 1 side of a coin, medal, etc., that has the principal design on it. 2 the face of anything that is meant to be turned toward the observer; front. 3 counterpart. *—adj.* 1 turned toward the observer. 2 being a counterpart to something else. 3 having the base narrower than the top or tip: *an obverse leaf.* [< Latin *obversum* turned toward < *ob-* toward + *vertere* to turn] **—ob verse′ly,** *adv.*

ob vi ate (ob′vē āt), *v.t.,* **-at ed, -at ing.** meet and dispose of; clear out of the way; remove: *obviate a difficulty, obviate danger, obviate objections.* [< Late Latin *obviatum* met in the way < Latin *obvius.* See OBVIOUS.] **—ob′vi a′tion,** *n.* **—ob′vi a′tor,** *n.*

ob vi ous (ob′vē əs), *adj.* easily seen or understood; clear to the eye or mind; not to be doubted; plain: *It is obvious that a blind man ought not to drive an automobile.* [< Latin *obvius* being in the way < *obviam* in the way < *ob* across + *via* way] **—ob′vious ly,** *adv.* **—ob′vi ous ness,** *n.*

oc-, *prefix.* form of **ob-** before *c,* as in *occasion.*

oc a ri na (ok′ə rē′nə), *n.* a small wind instrument, usually made of terra cotta or plastic, with finger holes and a protruding, whistlelike mouthpiece. It produces a soft sound. [< Italian, diminutive of *oca* goose (because of its shape)]

O'Ca sey (ō kā′sē), *n.* **Sean,** 1880-1964, Irish playwright.

oc ca sion (ə kā′zhən), *n.* 1 a particular time: *We have met them on several occasions.* 2 a special event; ceremony, celebration, etc.: *The jewels were worn only on great occasions.* 3 a good chance; opportunity. 4 cause; reason: *The dog that was the occasion of the quarrel had run away.* See **cause** for synonym study. 5 need; necessity: *A simple cold is no occasion for alarm.* 6 **occasions,** *pl.* affairs; business. 7 **improve the occasion,** take advantage of an opportunity. 8 **on occasion,** now and then; once in a while. *—v.t.* cause; bring about: *Her strange behavior occasioned talk.* [< Latin *occasionem* < *occidere* fall in the way < *ob-* in the way + *cadere* to fall]

oc ca sion al (ə kā′zhə nəl), *adj.* 1 happening or coming now and then, or once in a while: *an occasional thunderstorm.* 2 caused by or used for some special time or event: *occasional music.* 3 for use once in a while: *occasional chairs.* **—oc ca′sion al ly,** *adv.*

Oc ci dent (ok′sə dənt), *n.* 1 countries in Europe and America as distinguished from those in Asia; the West. 2 **occident,** the west. [< Latin *occidentem* falling toward, going down < *ob-* toward + *cadere* to fall (with reference to the setting sun)]

Oc ci den tal (ok′sə den′tl), *adj.* 1 Western; of the Occident. 2 **occidental,** western. *—n.* native of the West. Europeans and Americans are Occidentals.

oc cip i tal (ok sip′ə təl), *adj.* of or having to do with the occiput or the occipital bone. *—n.* occipital bone.

occipital bone, the compound bone forming the lower back part of the skull.

oc ci put (ok′sə pət), *n., pl.* **oc cip i ta** (ok-sip′ə tə). the back part of the head or skull. [< Latin < *ob-* behind + *caput* head]

oc clude (o klüd′), *v.,* **-clud ed, -clud ing.** *—v.t.* 1 stop up (a passage, pores, etc.); close. 2 shut in, out, or off. 3 (in chemistry) absorb and retain (gases and other substances): *Platinum occludes hydrogen.* *—v.i.* (in dentistry) meet closely in proper position: *The teeth in the upper jaw and those in the lower jaw should occlude.* [< Latin *occludere* < *ob-* up + *claudere* to close]

occluded front, (in meteorology) the front formed when a cold air mass overtakes a warm air mass and displaces it upward, usually bringing bad weather.

oc clu sion (ə klü′zhən), *n.* 1 an occluding. 2 a being occluded.

oc cult (ə kult′, ok′ult), *adj.* 1 beyond the bounds of ordinary knowledge; mysterious. 2 outside the laws of the natural world; magical: *Astrology and alchemy are occult sciences.* 3 not disclosed; secret; revealed only to the initiated. [< Latin *occultum* hidden < *ob-* up + *celare* to hide] **—oc cult′ly,** *adv.*

oc cul ta tion (ok′ul tā′shən), *n.* 1 a blocking off of the light of one heavenly body by another passing between it and the observer: *the occultation of a star by the moon.* 2 disappearance from view or notice; concealment; hiding.

oc cult ism (ə kul′tiz′əm, ok′ul tiz′əm), *n.* 1 belief in occult powers. 2 study or use of occult sciences.

oc cult ist (ə kul′tist, ok′ul tist), *n.* person who believes or is skilled in occultism.

oc cu pan cy (ok′yə pən sē), *n.* act or fact of occupying; holding (land, houses, a pew, etc.) by being in possession.

oc cu pant (ok′yə pənt), *n.* 1 person who occupies. 2 person in actual possession of a house, estate, office, etc.

oc cu pa tion (ok′yə pā′shən), *n.* 1 business; employment; trade. See synonym study below. 2 an occupying or a being occupied; possession: *the occupation of a town by the enemy.*

Syn. 1 **Occupation, business, employment** mean work a person does regularly or to earn his living. **Occupation** means work of any kind one does regularly or for which he is trained, whether or not he is working at the moment or is paid: *By occupation she is a housewife.* **Business** means work done for profit, often for oneself, especially in commerce, banking, merchandising, etc.: *My business is real estate.* **Employment** means work done for another, for which one is paid: *He has no employment at present.*

oc cu pa tion al (ok′yə pā′shə nəl), *adj.* of or having to do with a person's occupation, especially with trades, callings, etc. **—oc′cu pa′tion al ly,** *adv.*

occupational therapy, the treatment of persons having physical or mental disabilities through specific types of activities, work, etc., to promote recovery or rehabilitation.

oc cu py (ok′yə pī), *v.t.,* **-pied, -py ing.** 1 take up; fill: *The building occupies an entire block.* 2 keep busy; engage; employ: *Sports often occupy a boy's attention.* 3 take possession of, as by invasion: *The enemy occupied our fort.* 4 keep possession of; have; hold: *A judge occupies an important position.* 5 live in: *Two families occupy the duplex next door.* [< Old French *occuper* < Latin *occupare* seize < *ob-* into + *capere* to grasp] **—oc′cu pi′er,** *n.*

oc cur (ə kėr′), *v.i.,* **-curred, -cur ring.** 1 take place; happen: *Storms often occur in winter.* See **happen** for synonym study. 2 be found; appear; exist: *"E" occurs in print more than any other letter.* 3 come to mind; suggest itself: *Did it occur to you to close the window?* [< Latin *occurrere* < *ob-* in the way of + *currere* to run]

oc cur rence (ə kėr′əns), *n.* 1 an occurring: *The occurrence of storms delayed our trip.* 2 event; happening; incident: *an unexpected occurrence.* See **event** for synonym study.

o cean (ō′shən), *n.* 1 the great body of salt water that covers almost three fourths of the earth's surface; the sea. 2 any of its four main divisions; the Atlantic, Pacific, Indian, and Arctic oceans. The waters around the Antarctic continent are considered by some to form a separate ocean. 3 a vast expanse or quantity: *oceans of trouble.* [< Latin *oceanus* < Greek *ōkeanos*]

o cean aut (ō′shə nôt), *n.* an underwater explorer of an ocean or sea. [< *ocean* + *-naut,* as in *astronaut*]

O ce an i a (ō′shē an′ē ə), *n.* 1 islands of the central and south Pacific, north, northeast, and east of Australia. 2 these islands, together with Australasia and the Malay Archipelago.

o ce an ic (ō′shē an′ik), *adj.* 1 of or having to do with the ocean. 2 living in the ocean. 3 like the ocean; wide; vast.

o ce an ics (ō′shē an′iks), *n.* the group of sciences dealing with the exploration and study of the ocean.

o cean og ra pher (ō′shə nog′rə fər), *n.* an expert in oceanography.

o cean o graph ic (ō′shə nə graf′ik), *adj.* of or having to do with oceanography.

o cean og ra phy (ō′shə nog′rə fē), *n.* science that deals with the oceans and seas, including marine life.

O ce a nus (ō sē′ə nəs), *n.* (in Greek myths) the god of the great stream that was supposed to surround all the land.

oc el lat ed (os′ə lā′tid, ō sel′ā tid), *adj.* 1 having ocelli or eyelike spots. 2 eyelike: *ocellated spots.*

o cel lus (ō sel′əs), *n., pl.* **o cel li** (ō sel′ī). 1 one of the rudimentary, single-lens eyes found in certain invertebrates, especially one of the simple eyes situated between the compound eyes of insects. 2 an eyelike spot or marking. There are ocelli on peacock feathers. [< Latin, diminutive of *oculus* eye]

o ce lot (ō′sə lot, os′ə lot), *n.* a spotted cat somewhat like a leopard, but smaller, found from Texas through Mexico and into parts of South America. [< French < Nahuatl *ocelotl*]

o cher (ō′kər), *n.* 1 any of various yellow, brown, or red earthy mixtures containing clay and iron oxide, used as pigments. 2 a pale brownish yellow. [< Greek *ōchra* < *ōchros* pale yellow]

o cher ous (ō′kər əs), *adj.* of, like, or containing ocher.

o chre (ō′kər), *n.* ocher.

o chre ous (ō′kər əs, ō′krē əs), *adj.* ocherous.

o'clock (ə klok′), 1 of the clock; by the clock: *It is now five o'clock.* 2 as if on the dial of a clock. 12 o'clock in an airplane is the horizontal direction straight ahead, or the vertical position straight overhead.

O'Con nor (ō kon′ər), *n.* 1 **Flannery,** 1925-1964, American novelist and short-story writer. 2 **Frank,** 1903-1966, Irish short-story writer. His real name was Michael O'Donovan.

OCS, Officer Candidate School.

oct., octavo.

Oct., October.

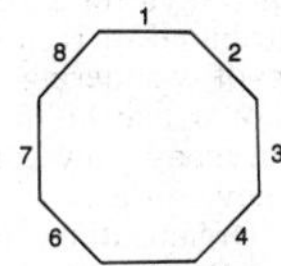

regular octagon

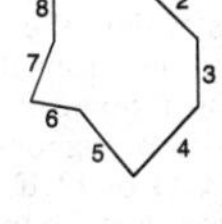

irregular octagon

oc ta gon (ok′tə gon, ok′tə gən), *n.* a plane figure having eight angles and eight sides. [< Greek *oktagōnos* < *okta* eight + *gōnia* angle]

oc tag o nal (ok tag′ə nəl), *adj.* having eight angles and eight sides. **—oc tag′o nal ly,** *adv.*

oc ta he dral (ok′tə hē′drəl), *adj.* having eight plane faces.

oc ta he dron (ok′tə hē′drən), *n., pl.* **-drons, -dra** (-drə). a solid figure having eight plane faces. [< Greek *oktaedron* < *okta* eight + *hedra* seat, base]

oc tane (ok′tān), *n.* any of various isomeric hydrocarbons that occur in petroleum. High quality gasoline contains more octane than the lower grades. *Formula:* C_8H_{18} [< Latin *octo* eight]

octane number or **octane rating,** number indicating the quality of a motor fuel, based on its antiknock properties.

oc tant (ok′tənt), *n.* 1 one eighth of a circle; a 45-degree angle or arc. 2 instrument having an arc of 45 degrees, used in navigation to measure the altitude of heavenly bodies in order to determine latitude and longitude. 3 position of a planet, the moon, or other heavenly body when 45 degrees distant from another.

hat, āge, fär; let, ēqual, tėrm;
it, īce; hot, ōpen, ôrder;
oil, out; cup, pu̇t, rüle;
ch, child; ng, long; sh, she;
th, thin; ᴛʜ, then; zh, measure;

ə represents *a* in about, *e* in taken, *i* in pencil, *o* in lemon, *u* in circus.

< = from, derived from, taken from.

oc tave (ok′tiv, ok′tāv), *n.* 1 interval between a musical tone and another tone having twice or half as many vibrations. From middle C to the C above it is an octave. 2 the eighth tone above or below a given tone, having twice or half as many vibrations per second. 3 series of tones, or of keys of an instrument, filling the interval between a tone and its octave. 4 the sounding together of a tone and its octave. 5 group of eight. 6 group of eight lines of poetry. 7 the first eight lines of a sonnet. 8 a church festival and the week after it. 9 the last day of such a week. [< Latin *octavus* eighth < *octo* eight]

Oc ta vi an (ok tā′vē ən), *n.* Augustus.

oc ta vo (ok tā′vō, ok tä′vō), *n., pl.* **-vos.** 1 the page size of a book in which each leaf is one eighth of a whole sheet of paper. 2 book having pages of this size, usually about 6 by 9 inches. [< Medieval Latin *in octavo* in an eighth]

oc tet or **oc tette** (ok tet′), *n.* 1 a musical composition for eight voices or instruments. 2 group of eight singers or players performing together. 3 octave (defs. 6 and 7). 4 group of eight electrons in the outer atomic shell. 5 any group of eight.

oc til lion (ok til′yən), *n.* 1 (in the United States and France) 1 followed by 27 zeros. 2 (in Great Britain and Germany) 1 followed by 48 zeros. [< French < Latin *octo* eight + French *million* million]

Oc to ber (ok tō′bər), *n.* the tenth month of the year. It has 31 days. [< Latin < *octo* eight; from the order of the Roman calendar]

oc to dec i mo (ok′tə des′ə mō), *n., pl.* **-mos.** 1 the page size of a book in which each leaf is one eighteenth of a whole sheet of paper; eighteenmo. 2 book having pages of this size, usually about 4 by $6\frac{1}{2}$ inches. [< New Latin *in octodecimo* in an eighteenth]

oc to ge nar i an (ok′tə jə ner′ē ən), *n.* person who is 80 years old or between 80 and 90 years old. *—adj.* 80 years old or between 80 and 90 years old. [< Latin *octogenarius* containing eighty]

oc to pod (ok′tə pod), *n.* any of an order of eight-armed cephalopods that includes the octopus. *—adj.* having eight arms.

oc to pus (ok′tə pəs), *n.* 1 a cephalopod sea mollusk having a soft body and eight arms

octopus (def. 1) from 6 in. to 20 ft. across

with suckers on them. 2 anything like an octopus. A powerful, grasping organization with far-reaching influence is often called an octopus. [< New Latin < Greek *oktōpous* < *oktō* eight + *pous* foot]

oc to roon (ok′tə rün′), *n.* person having one eighth Negro ancestry. [< Latin *octo* eight + *(quad)roon*]

oc u lar (ok′yə lər), *adj.* 1 of or having to do with the eye: *an ocular muscle.* 2 like an eye; eyelike. 3 received by actual sight; seen: *ocular proof.* —*n.* eyepiece of a telescope, microscope, etc. [< Latin *oculus* eye]

oc u list (ok′yə list), *n.* doctor who examines and treats defects and diseases of the eye; ophthalmologist.

O.D., 1 Officer of the Day. 2 olive drab.

odd (od), *adj.* 1 left over; extra: *Pay the bill with this money and keep the odd change.* 2 being one of a pair or set of which the rest is missing: *an odd stocking.* 3 occasional; casual: *odd jobs, odd moments, odd volumes of a magazine.* 4 with some extra: *six hundred-odd children in school.* 5 leaving a remainder of 1 when divided by 2: *Seven is an odd number.* 6 having an odd number: *the odd symphonies of Beethoven.* 7 strange; peculiar; unusual: *It is odd that I cannot remember your name.* See **strange** for synonym study. [< Scandinavian (Old Icelandic) *odda-*] —**odd′ly,** *adv.* —**odd′ness,** *n.*

odd ball (od′bôl′), *n.* SLANG. a very eccentric person.

odd i ty (od′ə tē), *n., pl.* **-ties.** 1 a being odd; strangeness; queerness; peculiarity. 2 a strange, queer, or peculiar person or thing.

odd ment (od′mənt), *n.* thing left over; extra bit; remnant.

odds (odz), *n. pl. or sing.* 1 difference in favor of one and against another; advantage. In betting, odds of 3 to 1 mean that 3 will be paid if the bet is lost for every 1 that is received if the bet is won. 2 (in games) an extra allowance given to the weaker player or side. 3 things that are odd, uneven, or unequal. 4 difference: *It makes no odds to me if you go or stay.* 5 **at odds,** quarreling; disagreeing. 6 **odds and ends,** things left over; extra bits; odd pieces; scraps; remnants. 7 **the odds are,** the chances are; the probability is.

odds-on (odz′ôn′, odz′on′), *adj.* having the odds in one's favor; having a good chance to win in a contest.

ode (ōd), *n.* a lyric poem, usually rhymed and sometimes in irregular meter, full of noble feeling expressed with dignity. It is often addressed to some person or thing. [< Late Latin < Greek *ōidē,* related to *aeidein* sing]

O der River (ō′dər), river flowing from Czechoslovakia through W Poland into the Baltic Sea. In its lower course it is the boundary between Poland and East Germany. 560 mi.

O des sa (ō des′ə), *n.* 1 seaport in SW Soviet Union, on the Black Sea. 822,000. 2 city in W Texas. 78,000.

O din (ōd′n), *n.* (in Scandinavian myths) the chief god; the god of wisdom, culture, war, and the dead. He is identified with the Anglo-Saxon god Woden.

o di ous (ō′dē əs), *adj.* very displeasing; hateful; offensive. See **hateful** for synonym study. [< Latin *odiosus* < *odium* odium] —**o′di ous ly,** *adv.* —**o′di ous ness,** *n.*

o di um (ō′dē əm), *n.* 1 hatred; great dislike. 2 reproach; blame: *bear the odium of having betrayed one's friend.* [< Latin < *odisse* to hate]

o dom e ter (ō dom′ə tər), *n.* device for measuring distance traveled by a vehicle by recording the number of revolutions of a wheel.

o do nate (ō′də nāt), *n.* any of an order of insects having chewing mouthparts, hind wings as large or larger than the forewings, and large compound eyes. Dragonflies and damselflies belong to this order. [< New Latin *Odonata* < Greek *odontos* tooth]

o don tol o gist (ō′don tol′ə jist), *n.* an expert in odontology.

o don tol o gy (ō′don tol′ə jē), *n.* branch of anatomy dealing with the structure, development, and diseases of the teeth. [< Greek *odontos* tooth]

o dor (ō′dər), *n.* 1 smell or scent. See **smell** for synonym study. 2 reputation; repute; standing: *be in bad odor.* 3 fragrance; perfume; aroma. 4 quality characteristic or suggestive of something: *an odor of impropriety.* Also, **odour.** [< Old French < Latin] —**o′dor less,** *adj.*

o dor if er ous (ō′də rif′ər əs), *adj.* 1 giving forth an odor, especially a pleasant odor; fragrant. 2 giving forth an unpleasant or foul odor. [< Latin *odorifer* < *odor* odor + *ferre* carry] —**o′dor if′er ous ly,** *adv.* —**o′dor if′er ous ness,** *n.*

o dor ous (ō′dər əs), *adj.* giving forth or having an odor, especially a pleasant odor; sweet-smelling; fragrant: *Spices are odorous.* —**o′dor ous ly,** *adv.* —**o′dor ous ness,** *n.*

o dour (ō′dər), *n.* odor.

O dys se us (ō dis′ē əs, ō dis′yüs), *n.* Ulysses.

Od ys sey (od′ə sē), *n., pl.* **-seys** for 2. 1 a long Greek epic poem attributed to Homer, describing the ten years of wandering of Ulysses after the Trojan War and his final return home. 2 Also, **odyssey.** any long series of wanderings and adventures.

OECD or **O.E.C.D.,** Organization for Economic Cooperation and Development.

oec u men i cal (ek′yə men′ə kəl), *adj.* ecumenical.

OED or **O.E.D.,** Oxford English Dictionary.

oed i pal or **Oed i pal** (ed′ə pəl, ē′də pəl), *adj.* having to do with or characteristic of Oedipus or the Oedipus complex.

Oed i pus (ed′ə pəs, ē′də pəs), *n.* (in Greek legends) a Greek king who unknowingly killed his father and married his mother. When he learned this, he blinded himself and passed the rest of his life wandering miserably.

Oedipus complex, (in psychoanalysis) a strong childhood attachment for the parent of the opposite sex, often accompanied by a feeling of rivalry, hostility, or fear toward the other parent.

Oe no ne (ē nō′nē), *n.* (in Greek legends) a nymph of Mt. Ida, who became the wife of Paris, but was deserted by him when he fell in love with Helen of Troy.

OEO or **O.E.O.,** Office of Economic Opportunity.

o'er (ôr, ōr), *prep., adv.* ARCHAIC. over.

oer sted (ėr′sted), *n.* the centimeter-gram-second unit of magnetic intensity, equivalent to the intensity of the force of one dyne acting in a vacuum on a magnetic pole of unit strength. [< Hans Christian *Oersted,* 1777-1851, Danish physicist]

oe soph a gus (ē sof′ə gəs), *n., pl.* **-gi** (-jī). esophagus.

of (ov, uv; *unstressed* əv), *prep.* 1 belonging to: *the children of a family.* 2 made from: *a house of bricks.* 3 that has; containing; with: *a house of six rooms.* 4 that has as a quality: *a word of encouragement.* 5 that is; named: *the city of Chicago.* 6 away from; from: *north of Boston.* 7 having to do with; in regard to; concerning; about: *think well of someone.* 8 that is used for or has as a purpose: *a house of prayer.* 9 by: *the writings of Shakespeare.* 10 as a result of having or using; through: *die of a disease.* 11 out of: *She came of a noble family.* 12 among: *a mind of the finest.* 13 during: *of late years.* 14 (in telling time) before: *ten minutes of six.* 15 *Of* connects nouns and adjectives having the meaning of a verb with what would be the object of a verb; indicating the object or goal (especially of a verbal noun): *the eating of fruit, the love of truth.* [Old English]

➤ **of, have.** In unstressed position *have* is pronounced (əv), as is *of.* Writers sometimes substitute *of* for *have* to suggest a greater departure from standard speech than they are actually recording.

➤ **of, off.** A redundant *of* (as in *off of, inside of,* etc.) is sometimes used in informal English, but the usage is not regarded as standard: *step off* (not *off of*) *a sidewalk.*

of-, *prefix.* form of **ob-** before *f,* as in *offer.*

off (ôf, of), *adv.* 1 from the usual, normal, or correct position, condition, etc.: *I took off my hat.* 2 away: *go off on a journey.* 3 distant in time or space: *Christmas is only five weeks off.* 4 so as to stop or lessen: *Turn the water off. The game was called off.* 5 without work: *an afternoon off.* 6 in full; wholly; entirely: *Clear off the table. They paid off the mortgage.* 7 on one's way: *Her friends saw her off at the station.* 8 **be off, a** go away; leave quickly: *I'm off now.* **b** have deteriorated in quality, etc. 9 **off and on,** at some times and not at others; now and then.

—*prep.* 1 from; away from: *miles off the main road. He will be off duty at four o'clock.* 2 subtracted from: *25 per cent off the marked price.* 3 not in the usual, normal, or correct position on; not on: *A button is off your coat.* 4 below the usual or normal standard of performance: *be off one's game.* 5 seaward from: *The ship anchored off Maine.* 6 leading out of: *an alley off 12th Street.*

—*adj.* 1 not connected; stopped: *The electricity is off.* 2 no longer contemplated; canceled: *The game is off.* 3 not at work: *pursue one's hobby during off hours.* 4 in a specified condition in regard to money, property, etc.: *How well off are your neighbors?* 5 not very good; not up to average: *an off season for fruit. We all have our off days.* 6 possible but not likely: *There is an off chance of rain.* 7 in error; wrong: *Your figures are way off.* 8 INFORMAL. not normal or stable; abnormal. 9 on the right-hand side; right: *The near horse and the off horse make a team.* 10 on one's way. 11 more distant; farther: *the off side of a wall.* 12 seaward.

—*interj.* 1 go away! stay away! 2 **off with, a** take off. **b** away with!

[Old English *of*] ➤ See **of** for usage note.

off., 1 office. 2 officer. 3 official.

of fal (ô′fəl, of′əl), *n.* 1 the waste parts of an animal killed for food. 2 garbage; refuse. 3 waste produced by any of various industrial processes as chips in milling wood, scraps of leather in trimming hides, etc. [< *off* + *fall*]

off beat (ôf′bēt′, of′bēt′), *n.* a musical beat

with little or no accent. *—adj.* out of the ordinary; unusual; unconventional: *offbeat drama.*

off-col or (ôf′kul′ər, of′kul′ər), *adj.* 1 not of the right or required color or shade; defective in color. 2 somewhat improper; risqué.

Of fen bach (ôf′ən bäk; *German* ôf′ən-bäH), *n.* **Jacques,** 1819-1880, French composer of light operas, born in Germany.

of fence (ə fens′), *n.* BRITISH. offense.

of fend (ə fend′), *v.t.* 1 hurt the feelings of; make angry; displease; pain. 2 affect in an unpleasant or disagreeable way. *—v.i.* sin or do wrong. [< Latin *offendere* < *ob-* against + *fendere* to strike]

of fend er (ə fen′dər), *n.* 1 person who offends. 2 person who does wrong or breaks a law.

of fense (ə fens′), *n.* 1 a breaking of the law; crime or sin. Offenses against the law are punished by fines or imprisonment. See **crime** for synonym study. 2 cause of wrongdoing. 3 condition of being offended; hurt feelings; anger or resentment: *Try not to cause offense.* 4 act of offending; hurting someone's feelings: *No offense was meant.* 5 something that offends or causes displeasure. 6 act of attacking; attack: *A gun is a weapon of offense.* 7 an attacking team or force. 8 **give offense,** offend. 9 **take offense,** be offended. Also, BRITISH **offence.** [< Latin *offensa* < *offendere* offend] **—of fense′less,** *adj.*

of fen sive (ə fen′siv), *adj.* 1 giving offense; irritating; annoying; insulting: *"Shut up" is an offensive remark.* 2 unpleasant; disagreeable; disgusting: *Bad eggs have an offensive odor.* 3 ready to attack; attacking; aggressive: *an offensive army.* 4 used for attack; having to do with attack: *offensive weapons.* 5 belonging to an attacking team or force: *offensive players.* *—n.* 1 position or attitude of attack: *The army took the offensive.* 2 attack; assault: *a major offensive, supported by air and artillery.* **—of fen′sive ly,** *adv.* **—of fen′sive ness,** *n.*

of fer (ô′fər, of′ər), *v.t.* 1 hold out to be taken or refused; present: *They offered us their help.* See synonym study below. 2 present for sale: *offer suits at reduced prices.* 3 bid as a price: *He offered twenty dollars for our old stove.* 4 be willing if another approves: *They offered to help us.* 5 propose; advance; suggest: *She offered a few ideas to improve the plan.* 6 present in worship: *offer prayers.* 7 give; show: *The enemy offered resistance to our soldiers' attack.* 8 give or show intention; attempt; try: *He did not offer to hit back.* 9 attempt to inflict, deal, or bring to bear (violence or injury of any kind). *—v.i.* present itself; occur: *I will come if the opportunity offers.* *—n.* 1 act of offering: *an offer of money, an offer to sing, an offer of marriage.* 2 thing that is offered. 3 an attempt or show of intention. [Old English *offrian* < Latin *offerre* < *ob-* to + *ferre* bring]

Syn. *v.t.* 1 **Offer, proffer, tender** mean to hold out something to someone to be accepted. **Offer** is the common word: *She offered him coffee.* **Proffer** is a literary word, usually suggesting offering with warmth, courtesy, or earnest sincerity: *He refused the proffered hospitality.* **Tender** is a formal word, and usually applies to an obligation or polite act rather than to an object: *I tendered my apologies.*

of fer ing (ô′fər ing, of′ər ing), *n.* 1 the giving of something as an act of worship. 2 contribution or gift, as to a church, for some special purpose. 3 act of one that offers.

of fer to ry (ô′fər tôr′ē, ô′fər tōr′ē; of′ər-tôr′ē, of′ər tōr′ē), *n., pl.* **-ries.** 1 collection of offerings, as of money, at a religious service. 2 verses said or the music sung or played while the offering is received. 3 Sometimes, **Offertory.** in the Roman Catholic Church: **a** the part of the Mass at which bread and wine are offered to God. **b** prayers said or sung at this time.

off hand (*adv.* ôf′hand′, of′hand′; *adj.* ôf′hand′, of′hand′), *adv.* without previous thought or preparation; at once: *The carpenter could not tell offhand how much the work would cost.* *—adj.* 1 done or made offhand; extemporaneous: *Her offhand remarks were sometimes very wise.* 2 free and easy; casual; informal. 3 without due courtesy; impolite.

off hand ed (ôf′han′did, of′han′did), *adj.* offhand. **—off′hand′ed ly,** *adv.* **—off′hand′ed ness,** *n.*

of fice (ô′fis, of′is), *n.* 1 place in which the work of a position is done; room or rooms in which to work. 2 position, especially in the public service; post: *The President holds the highest office in the United States.* 3 duty of one's position; task; job; work: *A teacher's office is teaching.* 4 person or staff of persons carrying on work in an office. 5 an administrative department of a governmental organization. 6 act of kindness or unkindness; attention; service: *Through the good offices of a friend, I was able to get a job.* 7 a religious ceremony or prayer: *the communion office, last offices.* [< Latin *officium* service < *opus* work + *facere* do]

office boy, boy whose work is doing odd jobs in an office.

of fice hold er (ô′fis hōl′dər, of′is hōl′-dər), *n.* person who holds a public office; government official.

of fi cer (ô′fə sər, of′ə sər), *n.* 1 (in the armed forces) person who commands others, especially a person who holds a commission, such as a major, a general, a captain, or an admiral. 2 captain or master of a merchant vessel, yacht, etc., or any of his chief assistants. 3 person who holds a public, church, or government office: *a health officer, a police officer.* 4 person appointed or elected to an administrative position in a club, society, etc. 5 member above the lowest rank in some honorary societies. *—v.t.* 1 provide with officers. 2 direct, conduct, or manage as an officer. **—of′fi cer less,** *adj.*

officer of the day, a military officer who has charge, for any given day, of the guards, prisoners, barracks, etc.

of fi cial (ə fish′əl), *n.* 1 person who holds a public position or who is in charge of some public work or duty: *The mayor is a government official.* 2 person holding office; officer: *bank officials.* *—adj.* 1 of or having to do with an office or officers: *Policemen wear an official uniform.* 2 having authority; authoritative: *An official record is kept of the proceedings of Congress.* 3 being an official: *Each state has its own official representatives in Congress.* 4 suitable for a person in office: *the official dignity of a judge.* 5 holding office: *an official body.* **—of fi′cial ly,** *adv.*

of fi cial dom (ə fish′əl dəm), *n.* 1 position or domain of officials. 2 officials or the official class.

of fi cial ism (ə fish′ə liz′əm), *n.* 1 official methods or system. 2 excessive attention to official routine.

hat, āge, fär; let, ēqual, tėrm;
it, īce; hot, ōpen, ôrder;
oil, out; cup, pu̇t, rüle;
ch, child; ng, long; sh, she;
th, thin; ᴛʜ, then; zh, measure;

ə represents *a* in about, *e* in taken, *i* in pencil, *o* in lemon, *u* in circus.

< = from, derived from, taken from.

of fi ci ant (ə fish′ē ənt), *n.* person who officiates at a religious service.

of fi ci ate (ə fish′ē āt), *v.i.,* **-at ed, -at ing.** 1 perform the duties of any office or position; serve or act in some official capacity: *The president officiates as chairman at all club meetings.* 2 perform the duties of a priest, minister, or rabbi: *The bishop officiated at the cathedral.*

of fic i nal (ə fis′n əl), *adj.* 1 kept in stock by druggists; not made by prescription: *officinal medicines.* 2 recognized by the pharmacopoeia. *—n.* drug or medicine that is kept in stock. [< Latin *officina* shop, storeroom, ultimately < *opus* work + *facere* do]

of fi cious (ə fish′əs), *adj.* too ready to offer services or advice; minding other people's business; meddlesome. [< Latin *officiosus* dutiful < *officium* service] **—of fi′cious ly,** *adv.* **—of fi′cious ness,** *n.*

off ing (ô′fing, of′ing), *n.* 1 the more distant part of the sea as seen from the shore. 2 position at a distance from the shore. 3 **in the offing, a** just visible from the shore. **b** in the making; impending: *trouble in the offing.*

off ish (ô′fish, of′ish), *adj.* INFORMAL. inclined to keep aloof; distant and reserved in manner; stand-offish. **—off′ish ness,** *n.*

off-key (ôf′kē′, of′kē′), *adj.* 1 not in the right musical key. 2 somewhat improper.

off scour ings (ôf′skou′ringz, of′skou′-ringz), *n.pl.* 1 low, contemptible, or depraved people. 2 filth; refuse.

off set (*v.* ôf′set′, of′set′; *n.* ôf′set′, of′-set′), *v.,* **-set, -set ting,** *n.* *—v.t.* 1 make up for; counterbalance; compensate for: *The better roads offset the greater distance.* 2 balance (one thing) by another as an equivalent: *We offset the greater distance by the better roads.* 3 set off or balance: *offset a trip to the mountains against a summer job.* 4 make offsets in (a wall, etc.). *—v.i.* form an offset or offsets. *—n.* 1 something which makes up for something else; compensation. 2 a short side shoot from the base of a main stem that can take root and grow into a new plant. 3 any offshoot. 4 in printing: **a** process in which the inked impression is first made on a rubber roller and transferred to the paper, instead of being printed directly on the paper. **b** the transfer or blotting of an impression onto another sheet because the ink is still wet. 5 a short distance measured perpendicularly from a main line in surveying. 6 ledge formed on a wall by lessening its thickness above. 7 an abrupt bend in a pipe or bar to carry it past something in the way.

off shoot (ôf′shüt′, of′shüt′), *n.* 1 shoot or branch growing out from the main stem of a plant, tree, etc. 2 anything coming, or thought of as coming, from a main part, stock, race, etc.; branch: *an offshoot of a mountain range.*

off shore (ôf′shôr′, ôf′shōr′; of′shôr′,

of′shôr′), *adj., adv.* of or away from the shore: *offshore fisheries, a wind blowing offshore.*

off side (ôf′sīd′, of′sīd′), *adj.* (in sports) not on the side permitted by the rules; illegally in advance of the ball, puck, etc.

off spring (ôf′spring′, of′spring′), *n.* 1 what is born from or grows out of something; the young of a person, animal, or plant; descendant; progeny. 2 result; effect. [Old English *ofspring*]

off stage (ôf′stāj′, of′stāj′), *adj.* away from the part of the stage that the audience can see; behind the scenes.

off-the-cuff (ôf′ŦHə kuf′, of′ŦHə kuf′), *adj.* INFORMAL. not prepared in advance; extemporaneous; impromptu.

off-the-record (ôf′ŦHə rek′ərd, of′ŦHə-rek′ərd), *adj.* not intended for publication; not to be repeated publicly or issued as news: *an off-the-record opinion.*

off-track (ôf′trak′, of′trak′), *adj.* away from the race track: *off-track betting.*

off-white (ôf′hwīt′, of′hwīt′), *n.* a very light shade of color, verging on white. *—adj.* that is nearly white: *an off-white ceiling.*

off-year (ôf′yir′, of′yir′), *n.* U.S. 1 year of unfavorable conditions or lower than average yield. 2 year in which elections are held for offices other than the presidency, governorship, or mayoralty.

oft (ôft, oft), *adv.* ARCHAIC. often. [Old English]

of ten (ô′fən, of′ən), *adv.,* **of ten er, of ten est.** in many cases or on numerous occasions; many times; frequently: *Blame is often misdirected. We come here often.* [Middle English, extension of *ofte* oft]

Syn. *adv.* **Often, frequently** mean many times or in many instances, and are often interchangeable. But **often** suggests only that something happens a number of times or in a considerable proportion of the total number of instances: *We often see them.* **Frequently** emphasizes happening again and again, regularly or at short intervals: *We saw them frequently last week.*

of ten times (ô′fən tīmz′, of′ən tīmz′), *adv.* often.

oft times (ôft′tīmz′, oft′tīmz′), *adv.* often.

Og den (og′dən), *n.* city in N Utah. 69,000.

o gee (ō jē′, ō′jē), *n.* 1 an S-shaped curve or line. 2 molding with such a curve. 3 ogee arch. [< French *ogive*]

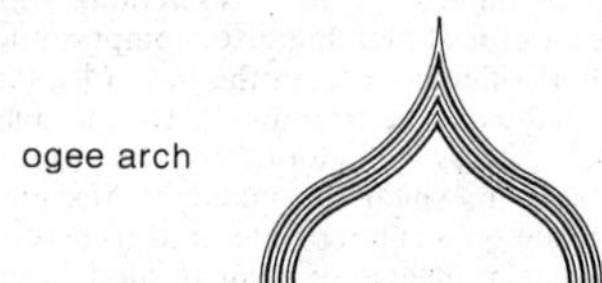

ogee arch

ogee arch, form of pointed arch, each side of which has the curve of an ogee.

o gle (ō′gəl), *v.,* **o gled, o gling,** *n.* *—v.t., v.i.* look at with desire; make eyes at. *—n.* an ogling look. [probably < Low German *oeglen* < *oegen* look at < *oog* eye] **—o′gler,** *n.*

O gle thorpe (ō′gəl thôrp), *n.* **James Edward,** 1696-1785, English general who founded the colony of Georgia.

o gre (ō′gər), *n.* 1 (in folklore and fairy tales) a man-eating giant or monster. 2 man like such a monster in appearance or character. [< French]

o gre ish (ō′gər ish), *adj.* like an ogre.

o gress (ō′gris), *n.* a female ogre.

oh or **Oh** (ō), *interj.* 1 word used before names in addressing persons: *Oh Mary, look!* 2 expression of surprise, joy, grief, pain, and other feelings. Also, **O.**

O'Hare Airport (ō her′, ō har′), major international and domestic airport in Chicago, Illinois.

O. Henry. See **Henry, O.**

O hi o (ō hī′ō), *n.* 1 one of the north central states of the United States. 10,652,000 pop. 41,200 sq. mi. *Capital:* Columbus. *Abbrev.:* O. 2 **Ohio River,** river in the N central United States, flowing SW from Pittsburgh into the Mississippi. 981 mi. **—O hi′o an,** *adj., n.*

ohm (ōm), *n.* unit of electrical resistance equal to the resistance of a conductor in which a potential difference of one volt produces a current of one ampere. [< Georg Simon *Ohm,* 1787-1854, German physicist]

ohm age (ō′mij), *n.* the electrical resistance of a conductor, expressed in ohms.

ohm ic (ō′mik), *adj.* of or having to do with the ohm.

ohm me ter (ōm′mē′tər), *n.* instrument for measuring the electrical resistance of a conductor in ohms.

Ohm's law, (in physics) a law that the current in amperes in an electrical circuit is directly proportional to the electromotive force in volts and inversely proportional to the resistance in ohms.

-oid, *suffix forming adjectives and nouns.* 1 like ____; like that of ____: *Amoeboid = like an amoeba.* 2 thing like a ____: *Spheroid = thing like a sphere (in form).* [< Greek *-oeidēs* < *eidos* form]

oil (oil), *n.* 1 any of several kinds of thick, fatty or greasy liquids that are lighter than water, burn easily, and are soluble in alcohol and ether but not in water. Mineral oils, such as kerosene, are used for fuel; animal and vegetable oils, such as olive oil, are used in cooking, medicine, and in many other ways. Essential oils, such as oil of peppermint, are distilled from plants, leaves, flowers, etc., and are thin and evaporate very quickly. 2 petroleum. 3 olive oil. 4 substance that resembles oil in some respect. Sulfuric acid is called oil of vitriol. 5 oil paint. 6 an oil painting. 7 **burn the midnight oil,** study or work late at night. 8 **pour oil on troubled waters,** make things calm and peaceful. 9 **strike oil,** a find oil by boring a hole in the earth. b find something very profitable.
—v.t. 1 put oil on or in; lubricate; grease. 2 INFORMAL. bribe. *—v.i.* become oil: *Butter oils when heated.*
—adj. of, having to do with, or for oil.
[< Old French *oile* < Latin *oleum* olive oil < Greek *elaion* < *elaia* olive]

oil burner, furnace, ship, etc., that uses oil for fuel.

oil cake, mass of linseed, cottonseed, etc., from which the oil has been pressed. Oil cakes are used as a food for cattle and sheep or as a fertilizer.

okapi
about 5 ft. high
at the shoulder

oil cloth (oil′klôth′, oil′kloth′), *n., pl.* **-cloths** (-klôŦHz, -klôths; -kloŦHz, -kloths). 1 cloth made waterproof by coating it with paint or oil, used to cover shelves, tables, etc. 2 piece of this cloth; oilskin.

oil color, 1 oil paint; oil. 2 pigment that is ground in oil to make oil paint. 3 oil painting.

oil er (oi′lər), *n.* 1 person or thing that oils. 2 can with a long spout used in oiling machinery.

oil field, area where significant deposits of petroleum have been found.

oil of turpentine, a colorless, flammable, volatile oil made from turpentine, used in mixing paints.

oil of vitriol, sulfuric acid.

oil paint, paint made by grinding or mixing a pigment with oil.

oil painting, 1 picture painted with oil paint. 2 action or art of painting with oil paint.

oil pa per (oil′pā′pər), *n.* paper treated with oil to make it transparent and waterproof.

oil skin (oil′skin′), *n.* 1 oilcloth. 2 Usually, **oilskins,** *pl.* coat and trousers made of this cloth.

oil slick, 1 a smooth place on the surface of water caused by the presence of oil. 2 the oil covering such an area.

oil stone (oil′stōn′), *n.* any fine-grained whetstone, the rubbing surface of which is oiled.

oil well, well drilled in the earth to gain access to a deposit of petroleum.

oil y (oi′lē), *adj.,* **oil i er, oil i est.** 1 of oil. 2 containing oil. 3 covered or soaked with oil. 4 like oil; smooth; slippery. 5 too smooth; suspiciously or disagreeably smooth; unctuous: *an oily smile.* **—oil′i ness,** *n.*

oint ment (oint′mənt), *n.* substance made from oil or fat, often containing medicine, used on the skin to heal, soothe, or beautify it. Cold cream and salve are ointments. [< Old French *oignement* < Popular Latin *unguimentum* < Latin *unguentum.* See UNGUENT.]

Oise River (wäz), river flowing from S Belgium into the Seine River near Paris. 186 mi.

O jib wa (ō jib′wā), *n., pl.* **-wa** or **-was.** member of a large tribe of American Indians formerly living in the region of Lake Superior; Chippewa.

O jib way (ō jib′wā), *n., pl.* **-way** or **-ways.** Ojibwa.

OK (ō′kā′), *adj., adv., interj., v.,* **OK'd, OK'ing,** *n., pl.* **OK's.** INFORMAL. *—adj., adv.* all right; correct; approved. *—interj.* all right. *—v.t.* endorse; approve. *—n.* approval. [probably < the initial letters of "oll korrect," a phonetic respelling of *all correct*]

O.K. (ō′kā′), *adj., adv., interj., v.,* **O.K.'d, O.K.'ing,** *n., pl.* **O.K.'s.** OK.

o ka pi (ō kä′pē), *n., pl.* **-pis** or **-pi.** an African mammal of the same family as and similar to the giraffe, but smaller, without spots, and with a much shorter neck. [< an African word]

o kay (ō′kā′), *adj., adv., interj., v., n.* INFORMAL. OK.

O kee cho bee (ō′kē chō′bē), *n.* **Lake,** lake just north of the Florida Everglades. 40 mi. long; 25 mi. wide.

O'Keeffe (ō kēf′), *n.* **Georgia,** born 1887, American painter.

O khotsk (ō kotsk′), *n.* **Sea of,** sea east of Siberia and north of Japan; part of the Pacific Ocean. 582,000 sq. mi.

O kie (ō′kē), *n.* INFORMAL. a migratory farm worker, originally one from Oklahoma.

O ki na wa (ō′kə nä′wə), *n.* largest of the Ryukyu Islands, belonging to Japan. It was administered by the United States from 1945 to 1972. 840,000 pop.; 454 sq. mi.

Okla., Oklahoma.

O kla ho ma (ō′klə hō′mə), *n.* one of the southwestern states of the United States. 2,559,000 pop.; 69,900 sq. mi. *Capital:* Oklahoma City. *Abbrev.:* Okla. **—O′kla-ho′man,** *adj., n.*

Oklahoma City, capital of Oklahoma, in the central part. 366,000.

o kra (ō′krə), *n.* 1 a tall plant of the mallow family, cultivated for its sticky pods, which are used in soups and as a vegetable; gumbo. 2 the pods. [< a West African word]

O laf (ō′läf), *n.* **Saint,** A.D. 995-1030, king of Norway from 1015 to 1028.

O lav V (ō′läf), born 1903, king of Norway since 1957.

old (ōld), *adj.,* **old er** or **eld er, old est** or **eld est,** *n.* *—adj.* 1 having existed for a long time; not young; aged: *an old man.* See synonym study below. 2 of age; in age: *The baby is one year old.* 3 not new or recent; made before or long ago; ancient: *an old excuse, and old tomb.* 4 much worn by age or use: *old clothes.* 5 looking or seeming old; mature: *That child is old for her years.* 6 having much experience: *be old in wrongdoing.* 7 former: *a teacher's old students.* 8 **Old,** earlier or earliest: *Old English, Old Testament.* 9 familiar; dear: *a good old fellow.* 10 INFORMAL. good; fine: *We had a high old time at the party.* —*n.* 1 the time long ago; earlier or ancient time; the past: *the heroes of old.* 2 **the old,** old people: *a home for the old.* [Old English *ald, eald*] **—old′ness,** *n.*

Syn. *adj.* 1 **Old, elderly, aged** mean having lived a long time. **Old** means advanced in years and near the end of life: *Grandmother is old, almost eighty, but she is hale and hearty.* **Elderly** means past middle age and getting old, and frequently suggests a certain dignity and stateliness: *Elderly people have little interest in participating in sports.* **Aged** means very old and has a strong connotation of infirmity or even senility: *An aged woman sat mumbling by the fire.* ➤ See **elder** for usage note.

old age, years of life from about 65 on.

Old Church Slavonic or **Old Church Slavic,** a Slavic language preserved in Russian religious texts of the A.D. 800's and 900's, and still used in some liturgies of the Eastern Church.

old country, country an emigrant comes from, especially a country of Europe.

old en (ōl′dən), *adj.* of old; old; ancient: *olden times.*

Old English, 1 period in the history of the English language and literature before 1100. 2 language of this period; Anglo-Saxon. 3 kind of black-letter type. **This is Old English.**

old-fash ioned (ōld′fash′ənd), *adj.* 1 of an old fashion; out of date in style, construction, etc.: *an old-fashioned dress.* 2 keeping to old ways, ideas, etc.: *an old-fashioned cook.*

old-fo gy or **old-fo gey** (ōld′fō′gē), *adj.* out-of-date; behind the times.

old-fo gy ish or **old-fo gey ish** (ōld′-fō′gē ish), *adj.* old-fogy.

Old French, the French language from about A.D. 800 to about 1400.

Old Glory, flag of the United States; Stars and Stripes.

Old Guard, 1 a very conservative section of the Republican Party of the United States. 2 the imperial guard of Napoleon I, which made the last French charge at Waterloo. 3 Also, **old guard,** the conservative members of a country, community, organization, etc.

Old ham (ōl′dəm), *n.* city in W England. 108,000.

old hand, a very skilled or experienced person; expert.

Old High German, form of the German language spoken in southern Germany from about A.D. 800 to 1100. Modern standard German is descended from Old High German.

Old Icelandic, the Icelandic language of the Middle Ages; Old Norse.

old ish (ōl′dish), *adj.* somewhat old.

Old Latin, the Latin language before the 100's B.C.

old-line (ōld′līn′), *adj.* 1 keeping to old ideas and ways; conservative. 2 having a long history; established: *an old-line company.*

old maid, 1 woman who has not married and seems unlikely to; spinster. 2 a prim, fussy person. 3 a simple card game in which players draw cards from each other's hands to make pairs. The player holding the extra queen at the end of the game loses.

old-maid ish (ōld′mā′dish), *adj.* like, suggesting, or befitting an old maid; prim; fussy.

old man, INFORMAL. 1 father or husband. 2 man in charge of anything, as the captain of a ship, commander of a military unit, etc.

old master, 1 any great painter who lived before 1700. 2 a painting by such a painter.

Old Nick, the Devil.

Old Norse, 1 the Scandinavian language from the Viking period to about 1300. 2 Old Icelandic.

Old North French, the dialects of northern France from the A.D. 800's to the 1500's, especially those of Normandy and Picardy.

Old Regime, ancien régime.

Old Saxon, the form of Low German spoken by the Saxons in northwestern Germany from about A.D. 800 to about 1100.

old school, group of people who have old-fashioned or conservative ideas.

old ster (ōld′stər), *n.* INFORMAL. an old or older person.

Old Style, method of reckoning time according to the Julian calendar, replaced by New Style in most European countries in 1582.

Old Testament, the earlier part of the Bible, which contains the religious and social laws of the Hebrews, a record of their history, their important literature, and writings of their prophets.

old-time (ōld′tīm′), *adj.* of former times; like that of old times.

old-tim er (ōld′tī′mər), *n.* INFORMAL. 1 person who has long been a resident, member, worker, etc. 2 person who favors old ideas and ways.

old wives' tale, a foolish story; silly or superstitious belief.

old-wom an ish (ōld′wu̇m′ə nish), *adj.* like, suggesting, or befitting an old woman; fussy.

Old World, the Eastern Hemisphere; Europe, Asia, and Africa.

hat, āge, fär; let, ēqual, tėrm;
it, īce; hot, ōpen, ôrder;
oil, out; cup, pu̇t, rüle;
ch, child; ng, long; sh, she;
th, thin; ᴛʜ, then; zh, measure;

ə represents *a* in about, *e* in taken, *i* in pencil, *o* in lemon, *u* in circus.

< = from, derived from, taken from.

old-world (ōld′wėrld′), *adj.* 1 Also, **Old-World.** of or having to do with the Eastern Hemisphere; not of the New World: *old-world monkeys.* 2 belonging to or characteristic of a former period: *old-world courtesy.* 3 of or having to do with the ancient world.

o le ag i nous (ō′lē aj′ə nəs), *adj.* 1 having the nature or properties of oil; oily; greasy. 2 unctuous. [< Latin *oleaginus* of the olive < *olea* olive] **—o′le ag′i nous ly,** *adv.*

o le an der (ō′lē an′dər), *n.* a poisonous evergreen shrub of the same family as the dogbane, with fragrant red, pink, white, or purple flowers. [< Medieval Latin]

o le ic acid (ō lē′ik, ō′lē ik), an oily, unsaturated acid obtained by hydrolyzing various animal and vegetable oils and fats, much used in making soaps. *Formula:* $C_{17}H_{33}COOH$

o le in (ō′lē ən), *n.* ester of oleic acid and glycerin, one of the most abundant natural fats. Lard, olive oil, and cottonseed oil are mostly olein.

o le o (ō′lē ō), *n.* oleomargarine. [< Latin *oleum* oil]

o le o mar gar in (ō′lē ō mär′jər ən), *n.* oleomargarine.

o le o mar gar ine (ō′lē ō mär′jər ən, ō′lē-ō mär′jə rēn′), *n.* a substitute for butter made from animal fats and oils or from pure vegetable oils; margarine.

o le o res in (ō′lē ō rez′n), *n.* a natural or prepared mixture of resin in oil, as that obtained from a plant by means of a volatile solvent.

ol fac tion (ol fak′shən), *n.* 1 act of smelling. 2 sense of smell.

ol fac tor y (ol fak′tər ē), *adj., n., pl.* **-tor ies.** *—adj.* having to do with smelling; of smell. The nose is an olfactory organ. [< Latin *olfactum* smelled < *olere* emit a smell + *facere* make]

ol i garch (ol′ə gärk), *n.* one of the rulers in an oligarchy.

ol i gar chic (ol′ə gär′kik), *adj.* of an oligarchy or oligarchs; having to do with rule by a few.

ol i gar chi cal (ol′ə gär′kə kəl), *adj.* oligarchic.

ol i gar chy (ol′ə gär′kē), *n., pl.* **-chies.** 1 form of government in which a few people have the ruling power. 2 country or state having such a government. Ancient Sparta was really an oligarchy, though it had two kings. 3 the ruling few. [< Greek *oligarchia* < *oligos* few + *archos* leader]

Ol i go cene (ol′ə gō sēn′), *n.* 1 the third epoch of the Tertiary period, after the Eocene and before the Miocene, during which the first apes appeared, and modern mammals became dominant. See chart under **geology.** 2 the series of rocks formed in this epoch. *—adj.* of or having to do with this epoch or its rocks. [< Greek *oligos* small, little + *kainos* recent]

ol i gop o ly (ol′ə gop′ə lē), *n., pl.* **-lies.** condition in a market in which so few producers supply a commodity or service that each of them can influence its price, with or without an agreement between them. [< Greek *oligos* few + English *(mono)poly*]

o li o (ō′lē ō), *n., pl.* **o li os.** 1 any mixture; jumble; hodgepodge. 2 miscellany; medley. [< Spanish *olla* stew, olla]

ol ive (ol′iv), *n.* 1 an evergreen tree with gray-green leaves, grown in southern Europe and other warm regions for its fruit and also for its wood. 2 fruit of this tree, with a hard stone and a bitter pulp. Olives are eaten green or ripe as a relish and are used to make olive oil. 3 wood of the olive tree. 4 olive branch. 5 a yellowish green. 6 a yellowish brown. *—adj.* 1 yellowish-green. 2 yellowish-brown. [< Latin *oliva* < Greek *elaia*]

olive branch, 1 branch of the olive tree as an emblem of peace. 2 anything offered as a sign of peace. 3 child.

olive drab, 1 a dark greenish-yellow color. 2 a dark greenish-yellow woolen cloth, formerly used by the United States Army for uniforms.

olive family, group of dicotyledonous trees and shrubs native to warm and temperate regions, including the olive, ash, jasmine, lilac, etc.

olive green, a dull, yellowish green; olive.

olive oil, oil pressed from olives, used in cooking, medicine, etc.

Ol i ver (ol′ə vər), *n.* one of Charlemagne's twelve peers and a friend of Roland.

Ol ives (ol′ivz), *n.* **Mount of,** a small ridge of hills, just east of Jerusalem, where Jesus talked with his disciples. 2680 ft.

Ol i vet (ol′ə vet), *n.* **Mount,** the Mount of Olives.

ol i vine (ol′ə vēn, ol′ə vēn′), *n.* a green or yellow semiprecious stone; chrysolite. It is a silicate of magnesium and iron.

ol la (ol′ə), *n.* 1 an earthen water jar or cooking pot. 2 a stew. [< Spanish]

Ol mec (ōl′mek), *n.* member of a highly civilized people who lived in southeastern Mexico before the Aztecs, from about 800 B.C. to A.D. 200.

ol o gy (ol′ə jē), *n., pl.* **-gies.** INFORMAL. any science or branch of knowledge. [< words ending in *-ology,* such as *geology*]

O lym pi a (ō lim′pē ə), *n.* 1 plain in ancient Greece where the Olympic games were held. 2 capital of Washington, in the W part. 23,000.

o lym pi ad or **O lym pi ad** (ō lim′pē ad), *n.* 1 period of four years reckoned from one celebration of the Olympic games to the next, by which Greeks computed time from 776 B.C. 2 celebration of the modern Olympic games.

O lym pi an (ō lim′pē ən), *adj.* 1 having to do with Olympia in ancient Greece or with Mount Olympus; Olympic. 2 like a god; heavenly. 3 polite and gracious, but in a rather lofty, aloof way: *Olympian calm, Olympian manners.* *—n.* 1 one of the major Greek gods who lived on Mount Olympus. 2 contender in the Olympic games.

O lym pic (ō lim′pik), *adj.* 1 of or having to do with Olympia in ancient Greece. 2 of or having to do with Mount Olympus. 3 of or having to do with the Olympic games. *—n.* **Olympics,** *pl.* Olympic games.

Olympic games, 1 contests in athletics, poetry, and music, held every four years by the ancient Greeks in honor of Zeus. 2 modern international athletic contests imitating the athletic contests of these games, held once every four years in a different country.

Olympic Mountains, part of the Coast Ranges in NW Washington. Highest peak, 7954 ft.

Olympic National Park, national park in NW Washington that includes the Olympic Mountains.

O lym pus (ō lim′pəs), *n.* 1 **Mount,** mountain in NE Greece, where the major Greek gods were supposed by the ancient Greeks to live. 9550 ft. 2 heaven.

O ma ha (ō′mə hô, ō′mə hä), *n.* 1 city in E Nebraska, on the Missouri River. 347,000. 2 member of a tribe of Siouan Indians now living in Nebraska.

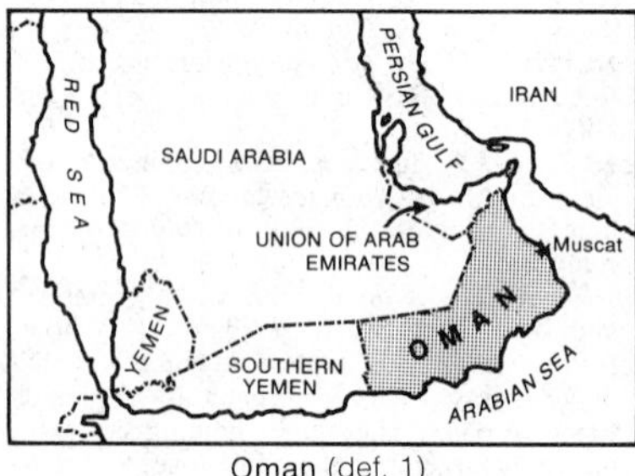

Oman (def. 1)

O man (ō män′), *n.* 1 country in SE Arabia. 750,000 pop.; 82,000 sq. mi. *Capital:* Muscat. Former name, **Muscat and Oman.** 2 **Gulf of,** gulf of the Arabian Sea, between Oman and S Iran. See **Iran** for map.

O man i (ō mä′nē), *adj.* of or having to do with Oman. *—n.* native or inhabitant of Oman.

O mar Khay yám (ō′mär kī yäm′, ō′mär kī′am), 1050?-1123?, Persian poet, astronomer, and mathematician who wrote *The Rubáiyát.*

o ma sum (ō mā′səm), *n., pl.* **-sa** (-sə). manyplies. [< Latin]

om buds man (om′budz man′), *n., pl.* **-men.** a government official appointed to receive and investigate grievances of citizens against the government. [< Swedish]

o meg a (ō meg′ə, ō mē′gə, ō mā′gə), *n.* 1 the 24th and last letter of the Greek alphabet (Ω or ω). 2 last of any series; end. [< Greek *ō mega* great "o"]

om e let or **om e lette** (om′lit, om′l it), *n.* eggs beaten up with milk or water, fried or baked, and then folded over. [< French *omelette*]

o men (ō′mən), *n.* 1 sign of what is to happen; object or event that is believed to mean good or bad fortune; augury; presage: *Spilling salt is said to be an omen of misfortune.* See **sign** for synonym study. 2 prophetic meaning; foreboding: *Some people consider a black cat a creature of ill omen.* *—v.t.* be a sign of; presage; forbode. [< Latin *omen, ominis*]

o men tum (ō men′təm), *n., pl.* **-ta** (-tə). a fold of the peritoneum connecting the stomach with certain of the other viscera. [< Latin]

om i cron (om′ə kron, ō′mə kron), *n.* the 15th letter of the Greek alphabet (*O* or *o*). [< Greek *ō mikron* small "o"]

om i nous (om′ə nəs), *adj.* of bad omen; unfavorable; threatening: *ominous clouds.* **—om′i nous ly,** *adv.* **—om′i nous ness,** *n.*

o mis si ble (ō mis′ə bəl), *adj.* that can be omitted.

o mis sion (ō mish′ən), *n.* 1 an omitting. 2 a being omitted. 3 thing omitted.

o mis sive (ō mis′iv), *adj.* characterized by omission; omitting.

o mit (ō mit′), *v.t.,* **o mit ted, o mit ting.** 1 leave out: *omit a letter in a word.* 2 fail to do; neglect: *She omitted making her bed.* [< Latin *omittere* < *ob-* by + *mittere* let go]

omni-, *combining form.* all; completely: *Omnipotent = all powerful.* [< Latin *omnis*]

om ni bus (om′nə bus), *n.* 1 bus (def. 1). 2 volume of works by a single author or of similar works by several authors. *—adj.* covering many things at once: *an omnibus law.* [< French *(voiture) omnibus* (vehicle) for all < Latin *omnibus*]

om ni di rec tion al (om′nə də rek′shə nəl, om′nə dī rek′shə nəl), *adj.* transmitting or receiving signals in every direction: *an omnidirectional radio beacon.*

om ni far i ous (om′nə fer′ē əs, om′nə far′ē əs), *adj.* of all forms, varieties, or kinds. [< Late Latin *omnifarius* < Latin *omnis* all + *fari* speak]

om nip o tence (om nip′ə təns), *n.* complete power; unlimited power.

om nip o tent (om nip′ə tənt), *adj.* 1 having all power; almighty. 2 having very great power or influence. *—n.* **the Omnipotent,** God. **—om nip′o tent ly,** *adv.*

om ni pres ence (om′nə prez′ns), *n.* presence everywhere at the same time: *God's omnipresence.*

om ni pres ent (om′nə prez′nt), *adj.* present everywhere at the same time.

om ni range (om′nə rānj′), *n.* a navigational system for aircraft, in which position is determined by picking up omnidirectional radio signals from a ground station.

om nis cience (om nish′əns), *n.* knowledge of everything; complete or infinite knowledge. [< Medieval Latin *omniscientia* < Latin *omnis* all + *scientia* knowledge]

om nis cient (om nish′ənt), *adj.* knowing everything; having complete or infinite knowledge. **—om nis′cient ly,** *adv.*

om ni um-gath er um (om′nē əm-gaᴛʜ′ər əm), *n.* a miscellaneous collection; confused mixture. [< Latin *omnium* of all + *gatherum,* a Latinization of English *gather*]

om niv or ous (om niv′ər əs), *adj.* 1 eating every kind of food. 2 eating both animal and vegetable food: *Man is an omnivorous animal.* 3 taking in everything; fond of all kinds: *An omnivorous reader reads all kinds of books.* [< Latin *omnivorus* < *omnis* all + *vorare* eat greedily] **—om niv′or ous ly,** *adv.* **—om niv′or ous ness,** *n.*

Omsk (omsk), *n.* city in central Soviet Union. 821,000.

on (ôn, on), *prep.* 1 above and supported by; above and in contact with; upon: *stand on one foot, ride on a train.* 2 touching so as to cover, be around, etc.: *shoes on one's feet, a ring on one's finger.* 3 close to; near: *a house on the shore.* 4 in the direction of; toward: *The workers marched on the capitol.* 5 against; upon: *the picture on the wall.* 6 by means of; by the use of: *talk on the telephone. This news is on good authority.* 7 in the condition of; in the process of; in the way of: *on fire, on purpose, on duty, on sale.* 8 at the time of; during: *They greeted us on our arrival.* 9 in relation to; in connection with; concerning: *a book on animals.* 10 for the

hat, āge, fär; let, ēqual, tėrm;
it, īce; hot, ōpen, ôrder;
oil, out; cup, pu̇t, rüle;
ch, child; ng, long; sh, she;
th, thin; ᴛʜ, then; zh, measure;

ə represents *a* in about, *e* in taken, *i* in pencil, *o* in lemon, *u* in circus.

< = from, derived from, taken from.

purpose of: *go on an errand.* 11 in addition to: *Defeat on defeat discouraged them.* 12 among: *on a committee.*
—*adv.* 1 on something or someone: *The walls are up, and the roof is on. Put on a clean shirt.* 2 to something: *Hold on, or you may fall.* 3 toward something: *Some played; the others looked on.* 4 farther: *March on.* 5 in or into a condition, process, manner, action, etc.: *Turn on the gas.* 6 from a time; forward: *later on, from that day on.* 7 **and so on,** and more of the same; et cetera. 8 **on and off,** now and then. 9 **on and on,** without stopping.
—*adj.* 1 taking place: *The race is on.* 2 in operation; operating: *The radio is on.*
[Old English]

once (wuns), *adv.* 1 one time: *once a day.* 2 at some one time in the past; formerly: *a once powerful nation.* 3 even a single time; ever: *if the facts once become known.*
once and again, repeatedly.
once and for all or **once for all,** finally or decisively.
once in a while, at one time or another; now and then.
once or twice, a few times.
once upon a time, long ago; once.
—*n.* 1 a single occasion: *Once is enough.* 2 **all at once,** suddenly. 3 **at once, a** immediately. **b** at one and the same time. 4 **for once,** for one time at least.
—*conj.* if ever; whenever: *Once you cross the river you are safe.*
—*adj.* former: *a once friend.*
[Old English *ānes* < *ān* one]

once-o ver (wuns′ō′vər), *n.* INFORMAL. a short, quick look, as for inspection, evaluation, etc.

on com ing (ôn′kum′ing, on′kum′ing), *adj.* approaching or advancing: *oncoming winter.* —*n.* approach or advance: *the oncoming of the storm.*

one (wun), *n.* 1 the first and lowest whole number; the number 1. 2 a single person or thing indicated: *I like the one in that box.*
at one, in agreement or harmony.
make one, a form or be one of a number, assembly, or party. **b** join together; unite in marriage.
one and all, everyone.
one by one, one after another.
one up on, INFORMAL. an advantage over.
one or two, a few.
—*adj.* 1 being a single unit or individual: *one apple, one dollar.* 2 some: *One day he will be sorry.* 3 of a single kind, nature, or character; the same: *They held one opinion. Graphite and diamond are chemically one substance.* 4 joined together; united: *They replied in one voice.* 5 a certain; particular: *One John Smith was elected.* 6 **all one, a** exactly the same. **b** making no difference; of no consequence.
—*pron.* 1 some person or thing: *Two may go, but one must stay.* 2 any person or thing: *One must work hard to achieve success.* 3 the same person or thing.
[Old English *ān*]

one another, one the other; each other: *They looked at one another. They were in one another's way.*

one-celled (wun′seld′), *adj.* having only one cell.

one-horse (wun′hôrs′), *adj.* 1 drawn or worked by a single horse: *a one-horse sleigh.* 2 using or having only a single horse: *a one-horse farmer.* 3 INFORMAL. of little scope, capacity, or importance; minor: *a one-horse town.*

O nei da (ō nī′də), *n., pl.* **-da** or **-das** for 1. 1 member of a tribe of Iroquois Indians formerly living in central New York State. 2 **Lake,** lake in central New York State, near Syracuse. 20 mi. long; 6 mi. wide.

O'Neill (ō nēl′), *n.* **Eugene (Gladstone),** 1888-1953, American playwright.

one ness (wun′nis), *n.* 1 quality of being one in number or kind; singleness. 2 sameness; identity. 3 fact of forming a whole; unity. 4 agreement; harmony.

on er ous (on′ər əs), *adj.* hard to take or carry; burdensome; oppressive: *Overtime work is well paid, but it is often onerous.* [< Latin *onerosus* < *onus* burden] —**on′er ous ly,** *adv.* —**on′er ous ness,** *n.*

one self (wun self′), *pron.* 1 one's own self: *One should not praise oneself.* 2 **be oneself, a** have full control of one's mind or body. **b** act naturally.

one-shot (wun′shot′), *adj.* INFORMAL. intended for use on only one occasion, and sometimes as a quick, temporary measure.

one-sid ed (wun′sī′did), *adj.* 1 seeing only one side of a question; partial; unfair; prejudiced: *The umpire seemed one-sided in his decisions.* 2 uneven; unequal: *If one team is much better than the other, a game is one-sided.* 3 having but one side. 4 on only one side. 5 having one side larger or more developed than the other. —**one′-sid′ed ly,** *adv.* —**one′-sid′ed ness,** *n.*

one-step (wun′step′), *n., v.,* **-stepped, -step ping.** —*n.* 1 a ballroom dance much like a quick walk. 2 music for it, in $^2/_4$ time. —*v.i.* dance the one-step.

one-time (wun′tīm′), *adj.* of the past; former.

one-to-one (wun′tə wun′), *adj.* (in mathematics) matching every element in a set with one and only one element in another set. EXAMPLE: {1, 2, 3, 4, 5} and {10, 20, 30, 40, 50} are two sets showing a one-to-one correspondence.

one-track (wun′trak′), *adj.* 1 having only one track. 2 INFORMAL. understanding or doing only one thing at a time; narrow: *a one-track mind.*

one-way (wun′wā′), *adj.* moving or allowing movement in only one direction: *a one-way street, a one-way ticket.*

on go ing (ôn′gō′ing, on′gō′ing), *adj.* continuous; uninterrupted.

on ion (un′yən), *n.* 1 bulb of a plant of the amaryllis family, having a sharp, strong smell and taste, and eaten raw or used in cooking. 2 plant it grows on. [< Old French *oignon* < Latin *unionem*] —**on′ion like′,** *adj.*

on ion skin (un′yən skin′), *n.* a thin, glossy, translucent paper.

on look er (ôn′lu̇k′ər, on′lu̇k′ər), *n.* person who watches without taking part; spectator; bystander; looker-on.

on look ing (ôn′lu̇k′ing, on′lu̇k′ing), *adj., n.* watching; seeing; noticing.

on ly (ōn′lē), *adj.* 1 by itself or themselves; sole, single, or few of the kind or class: *an only son, the only remnants of a great civilization.* See **single** for synonym study. 2 best; finest: *He is the only writer for my taste.* —*adv.* 1 merely; just: *I sold only two.* 2 and no one else; and nothing more; and that is all: *Only he remained. I did it only through friendship.* 3 **if only,** I wish: *If you would only say yes. If only wars would cease!* 4 **only too,** very: *She was only too glad to help us.* —*conj.* 1 except that; but: *I would have gone, only you objected.* 2 but then; it must be added that: *We camped right beside the stream, only the water was not fit to drink.* [Old English *ānlīc*]

on o mat o poe ia (on′ə mat′ə pē′ə), *n.* 1 formation of a name or word by imitating the sound associated with the thing designated, as in *buzz, hum, cuckoo, slap, splash.* 2 word or passage so formed. 3 adaptation of the sound to the sense for rhetorical effect, as in "the murmurous haunt of flies on summer eves." [< Greek *onomatopoiia* < *onoma* word, name + *poiein* make, do]

on o mat o poe ic (on′ə mat′ə pē′ik), *adj.* onomatopoetic.

on o mat o po et ic (on′ə mat′ə pō et′ik), *adj.* having to do with or like onomatopoeia; imitative in sound; echoic. —**on′o mat′o po et′i cal ly,** *adv.*

On on da ga (on′ən dô′gə, on′ən dä′gə), *n., pl.* **-ga** or **-gas.** member of a tribe of Iroquois Indians formerly living in central New York State.

on rush (ôn′rush′, on′rush′), *n.* a violent forward rush.

on set (ôn′set′, on′set′), *n.* 1 the beginning or start: *the onset of a disease.* 2 attack; assault: *The onset of the enemy took us by surprise.*

on shore (ôn′shôr′, ôn′shōr′; on′shôr′, on′shōr′), *adv., adj.* 1 toward the shore. 2 on the shore.

on side (ôn′sīd′, on′sīd′), *adj., adv.* (in sports) on the side permitted by the rules; not offside.

on slaught (ôn′slôt′, on′slôt′), *n.* a vigorous attack: *The pirates made an onslaught on the ship.* [probably < Dutch *aanslag* an attempt, stroke]

Ont., Ontario.

On tar i o (on ter′ē ō), *n.* 1 province in Canada, north of the Great Lakes. 7,795,000 pop.; 412,600 sq. mi. *Capital:* Toronto. *Abbrev.:* Ont. 2 **Lake,** the smallest of the five Great Lakes, between the United States and Canada. 193 mi. long; 7540 sq. mi. —**On tar′i an,** *adj., n.*

on to (ôn′tü, on′tü; *before consonants often* ôn′tə, on′tə), *prep.* 1 on to; to a position on or upon: *throw a ball onto the roof, get onto a horse, a boat driven onto the rocks.* 2 INFORMAL. familiar with; aware of: *It doesn't take long to get onto him and his alibis.*
➔ **onto, on to.** When *on* is clearly an adverb and *to* a preposition, the two words should of course be separated: *The rest of us drove on to the city.* When the two words make a definite preposition, they are usually written solid: *They looked out onto the park.*

on to ge net ic (on′tō jə net′ik), *adj.* of or having to do with ontogeny. —**on′to ge net′i cal ly,** *adv.*

on tog e ny (on toj′ə nē), *n.* the development of an individual organism, or the history of its development. [< Greek *ontos* being + *-geneia* origin]

o nus (ō′nəs), *n.* burden; responsibility; duty; obligation: *The onus of housekeeping fell upon the daughters.* [< Latin]

on ward (ôn′wərd, on′wərd), *adv.* toward the front; further on; on; forward: *The crowd around the store window began to move onward.* See **forward** for synonym study. —*adj.* toward the front; forward: *An onward movement began.*

on wards (ôn′wərdz, on′wərdz), *adv.* onward.

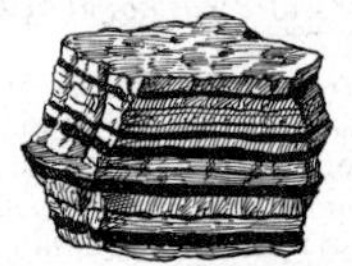

onyx before cutting and polishing

on yx (on′iks), *n.* a semiprecious variety of quartz having straight bands of different colors and shades. It is used in making cameos. [< Greek, nail, claw]

oo-, *combining form.* egg; ovum: *Oology = the study of eggs.* [< Greek *ōion* egg]

o o cyte (ō′ə sīt), *n.* ovum in the stage that precedes maturation.

oo dles (ü′dlz), *n.pl.* INFORMAL. large or unlimited quantities; heaps; loads: *oodles of money.* [origin uncertain]

o o gen e sis (ō′ə jen′ə sis), *n.* the formation and development of ova.

o o go ni um (ō′ə gō′nē əm), *n., pl.* **-ni a** (-nē ə), **-ni ums.** 1 a primitive germ cell that divides and gives rise to the oocytes. 2 the female reproductive organ in various thallophytes. [< New Latin < *oo-* + Greek *-gonos* producing]

o o lite (ō′ə līt), *n.* rock, usually limestone, composed of rounded concretions of calcium carbonate.

o o log i cal (ō′ə loj′ə kəl), *adj.* of or having to do with oology.

o ol o gy (ō ol′ə jē), *n.* branch of ornithology that deals with birds' eggs.

oo long (ü′lông, ü′long), *n.* a dark tea made by partially fermenting the leaves before drying them. [< Chinese *wu-lung* black dragon]

oo mi ak (ü′mē ak), *n.* umiak.

ooze[1] (üz), *v.,* **oozed, ooz ing,** *n.* —*v.i.* pass out slowly through small openings; leak out slowly and quietly: *Blood still oozed from the cut. My courage oozed away as I waited.* —*v.t.* give out slowly; exude: *The cut oozed blood.* —*n.* 1 an oozing; slow flow. 2 something that oozes. [Old English *wōs* juice]

ooze[2] (üz), *n.* 1 a soft mud or slime, especially at the bottom of a body of water. 2 piece of soft, boggy ground; marsh. [Old English *wāse* mud]

oo zy[1] (ü′zē), *adj.* oozing. [< *ooze[1]*] —**oo′zi ly,** *adv.*

oo zy[2] (ü′zē), *adj.,* **-zi er, -zi est.** containing ooze; muddy and soft; slimy. [< *ooze[2]*] —**oo′zi ly,** *adv.*

op-, *prefix.* form of *ob-* before *p,* as in *oppress.*

op., 1 opera. 2 operation. 3 opposite. 4 opus.

OPA, Office of Price Administration.

o pac i ty (ō pas′ə tē), *n., pl.* **-ties.** 1 a being opaque; being impervious to light; darkness. 2 a being impervious to sound, heat, etc. 3 obscurity of meaning. 4 something opaque. 5 denseness or stupidity. [< Latin *opacitatem* < *opacus* dark]

o pal (ō′pəl), *n.* a mineral, an amorphous form of hydrous silica, somewhat like quartz, found in many varieties and colors, certain of which reflect light with peculiar rainbow play of colors and are valued as gems. Black opals show brilliant colored lights against a black background; milk opals are milky white with rather pale lights. [< Latin *opalus* < Greek *opallios* < Sanskrit *upala* gem]

o pal esce (ō′pə les′), *v.i.,* **-esced, -esc ing.** exhibit a play of colors like that of the opal.

o pal es cence (ō′pə les′ns), *n.* a play of colors like that of an opal.

o pal es cent (ō′pə les′nt), *adj.* having a play of colors like that of an opal.

o pal ine (ō′pə līn, ō′pə lēn), *adj.* of or like opal; opalescent.

o paque (ō pāk′), *adj.* 1 not letting light through; not transparent or translucent. 2 not conducting heat, sound, electricity, etc. 3 not shining; dark; dull. 4 hard to understand; obscure. 5 stupid. —*n.* something opaque. [< Latin *opacus* dark, shady] —**o paque′ly,** *adv.* —**o paque′ness,** *n.*

op art (op), optical art.

op. cit., in the book, etc., referred to [for Latin *opere citato*].

ope (ōp), *v.t., v.i.,* **oped, op ing,** *adj.* ARCHAIC. open.

o pen (ō′pən), *adj.* 1 letting (anyone or anything) in or out; not shut; not closed: *an open window.* 2 not having its door, gate, lid, etc., closed; not closed up: *an open box, an open house.* 3 not closed in or confined: *the open sea, an open field.* 4 having spaces or holes: *open ranks, cloth of open texture.* 5 not taken; unfilled; free: *a position still open, have an hour open.* 6 that may be entered, used, shared, or competed for, etc., by all: *an open meeting, an open market.* 7 not covered or protected; exposed: *an open fire, an open wound, open to temptation.* 8 having no cover, roof, etc.; letting in air freely: *an open car, an open boat.* 9 exposed to general view, knowledge, etc.; not hidden or secret: *open disregard of rules.* 10 not obstructed: *an open view, an open harbor.* 11 not finally settled or determined; undecided; debatable: *an open question.* 12 ready to listen to new ideas and judge them fairly; not prejudiced: *an open mind.* 13 **open to,** ready to take; willing to consider: *open to suggestions.* 14 unreserved, candid, or frank; straightforward; sincere: *an open face. Please be open with me.* 15 that is spread out; unfolded; expanded: *an open flower, an open newspaper.* 16 with space between words; not solid or hyphenated: *"Open air" is an open compound.* 17 generous; liberal: *Give with an open hand.* 18 free from frost: *an open winter.* 19 free from ice; not frozen: *open water in arctic regions.* 20 INFORMAL. allowing saloons, gambling, etc.: *an open town.* 21 (of a vowel) pronounced with a relatively wide opening above the tongue, as (ä) in *calm;* low. 22 in music: **a** (of an organ pipe) not closed at the upper end. **b** (of a string) not stopped by the finger. **c** (of a note) produced by such a pipe or string, or without aid of slide, key, etc. 23 (of an electric circuit) not complete or closed.
—*n.* 1 **the open, a** the open country, air, sea, etc.: *sleep out in the open.* **b** public view or knowledge: *act in the open.* 2 an open or clear space; opening. 3 an open competition, tournament, etc.: *play in the golf open.*
—*v.t.* 1 move or turn away from a shut or closed position to allow passage; give access to: *open a door, open a bottle.* 2 cause to be open or more open; make accessible: *open a path through the woods, open a road.* 3 expand, extend, or spread out; make less compact: *open a newspaper.* 4 establish or set going: *open a new store.* 5 cut into: *open a wound.* 6 **open up,** make accessible. —*v.i.* 1 afford access (into, to, etc.); have an opening: *This door opens into the dining room.* 2 become open or more open; become accessible. 3 move apart; become less compact: *The ranks opened.* 4 begin; start: *Congress opens tomorrow. School opens soon.* 5 (of a theatrical company) begin a season or tour: *They opened in Boston.* 6 come apart, especially so as to allow passage or show the contents: *the wound opened. The clouds opened and the sun shone through.*
[Old English. Related to UP.] —**o′pen ly,** *adv.* —**o′pen ness,** *n.*

open air, outdoors.

o pen-air (ō′pən er′, ō′pən ar′), *adj.* outdoor: *an open-air concert.*

o pen-and-shut (ō′pən ən shut′), *adj.* INFORMAL. simple and direct; obvious; straightforward: *an open-and-shut case.*

open door, free and equal chance for all countries to do business in another country. —**o′pen-door′,** *adj.*

o pen-end (ō′pən end′), *adj.* of or having to do with investment trusts, such as mutual funds, that have no fixed capitalization and continually issue shares on request to old or new investors.

o pen-end ed (ō′pən en′did), *adj.* open to later consideration, revision, or adjustment: *an open-ended settlement.*

o pen er (ō′pə nər), *n.* 1 person or thing that opens. 2 the first game of a scheduled series.

o pen-eyed (ō′pən īd′), *adj.* 1 having eyes wide open as in wonder. 2 having the eyes open; watchful or vigilant; observant.

o pen-faced (ō′pən fāst′), *adj.* 1 having the face uncovered. 2 having a frank face.

o pen hand ed (ō′pən han′did), *adj.* generous; liberal. —**o′pen hand′ed ly,** *adv.* —**o′pen hand′ed ness,** *n.*

o pen heart ed (ō′pən här′tid), *adj.* 1 candid; frank; unreserved. 2 kindly; generous. —**o′pen heart′ed ly,** *adv.* —**o′pen-heart′ed ness,** *n.*

o pen-hearth (ō′pən härth′), *adj.* having an open hearth; using a furnace with an open hearth.

open-hearth process, process of making steel from pig iron in a furnace that reflects the heat from the roof onto the raw material.

open house, 1 party or other social event that is open to all who wish to come. 2 occasion when a school, university, factory, etc., is opened for inspection by the public.

o pen ing (ō′pə ning), *n.* 1 an open or clear space between portions of solid matter; gap, hole, or passage: *an opening in a roof, an opening in the forest.* 2 the first part; the beginning: *the opening of a lecture.* 3 a performance, display, etc., that formally begins an undertaking and introduces it to the public, especially the first performance of a play. 4 a place or position that is open or vacant: *an opening for a clerk.* 5 a favorable chance or opportunity: *seize every opening.* 6 (in chess) the beginning of a game, distinguished from the moves that follow. 7 a standard series of moves beginning a game. 8 act of making open. 9 fact of becoming open.

—*adj.* first; beginning: *an opening paragraph.*

open letter, letter of protest, criticism, or appeal addressed to the public or to a person or organization and published in a newspaper, magazine, etc.

o pen-mind ed (ō′pən mīn′did), *adj.* having or showing a mind open to new arguments or ideas; unprejudiced. **—o′pen-mind′edly,** *adv.* **—o′pen-mind′ed ness,** *n.*

o pen-mouthed (ō′pən mouᴛʜd′, ō′pənmoutht′), *adj.* 1 having the mouth open. 2 gaping with surprise or astonishment. 3 having a wide mouth.

open primary, U.S. primary in which any registered voter of the state, city, etc., may vote, whether or not he is an enrolled member of a political party.

open season, 1 any of various periods during which the hunting, trapping, or fishing of certain game is permitted. 2 time when complete freedom of action or expression prevails, especially in a matter usually subject to control.

open secret, a supposed secret that is actually generally known.

open sentence, (in mathematics) an equation or inequality containing one or more variables, which in its present form is neither true nor false. EXAMPLE: $x + 2 = 6$.

open ses a me (ses′ə mē), 1 the magic command that made the door of the robbers' cave fly open in the story of Ali Baba. 2 anything which removes the barriers to entering a restricted place or to reaching a certain goal.

open shop, factory or business that employs workers on equal terms, whether members of labor unions or not.

open syllable, syllable that ends in a vowel or diphthong. EXAMPLE: *clo-* in *clover.*

o pen work (ō′pən wėrk′), *n.* ornamental work that shows openings. —*adj.* resembling such ornamental work.

op er a[1] (op′ər ə), *n.* 1 play in which music is an essential and prominent part, featuring arias, choruses, etc., with orchestral accompaniment. *Faust, Lohengrin,* and *Carmen* are well-known operas. 2 branch of art represented by such plays. 3 performance of an opera. 4 opera house. [< Italian, literally, work < Latin, effort, originally, neuter plural of *opus* work]

op er a[2] (op′ər ə, ō′pər ə), *n.* a pl. of **opus.**

op er a ble (op′ər ə bəl), *adj.* 1 fit for, or admitting of, a surgical operation. 2 that can be operated; in a condition to be used.

o pé ra bouffe (op′ər ə büf′; *French* ô pā-rä büf′), a farcical comic opera. [< French]

opera glasses

opera glasses or **opera glass,** small binoculars for use at the opera and in theaters.

opera hat, a tall collapsible hat worn by a man with formal clothes.

opera house, theater where operas are performed.

op e rate (op′ə rāt′), *v.,* **-rat ed, -rat ing.** —*v.i.* 1 be at work; run; function: *The machinery operates night and day.* 2 produce an effect; work; act: *Several causes operated to bring on the war.* 3 produce a desired effect: *Some medicines operate more quickly than others.* 4 do something to the body, usually with instruments, to improve or restore health; perform surgery: *The doctor operated on the injured man.* 5 carry on military movements, duties, or functions. —*v.t.* 1 keep at work; drive; run: *operate an elevator.* 2 direct the working of as owner or manager; manage: *operate a factory.* [< Latin *operatum* worked < *opus* work]

op e rat ic (op′ə rat′ik), *adj.* of or like the opera: *operatic music.* **—op′e rat′i cal ly,** *adv.*

op e ra tion (op′ə rā′shən), *n.* 1 act or process of operating; keeping at work, in motion, etc.; working: *the operation of a railroad.* 2 the way a thing works: *the operation of a machine.* 3 a doing; action; activity: *the operation of binding a book.* 4 **in operation,** in action or in use. 5 something done to the body, usually with instruments, to improve or restore health: *A tonsillectomy is a common operation.* 6 movements of soldiers, ships, supplies, etc., especially for war purposes. 7 (in mathematics) something done to one or more numbers or quantities according to specific rules. Addition, subtraction, multiplication, and division are the four commonest operations in arithmetic.

op e ra tion al (op′ə rā′shə nəl), *adj.* 1 of or having to do with operations of any kind. 2 in condition to operate effectively.

op er a tive (op′ər ə tiv, op′ə rā′tiv), *adj.* 1 exerting force, energy, or influence; in operation; operating: *the laws operative in a community.* 2 producing the intended or proper effect; effective; efficacious: *an operative medicine.* 3 having to do with work or productiveness: *operative sections of a factory.* 4 of, concerned with, or consisting of surgical operations. —*n.* 1 worker, especially one who works with a machine or machines; skilled or semiskilled laborer. 2 detective. 3 a secret agent or spy. **—op′er a tive ly,** *adv.* **—op′er a tive ness,** *n.*

op e ra tor (op′ə rā′tər), *n.* 1 person who operates. 2 a skilled worker who operates a machine, telephone switchboard, telegraph, etc. 3 person who runs a factory, mine, etc. 4 INFORMAL. a shrewd individual who maneuvers people and events for his own purpose. 5 person who speculates in stocks or a commodity.

o per cu late (ō pėr′kyə lit, ō pėr′kyə lāt), *adj.* having an operculum.

o per cu lum (ō pėr′kyə ləm), *n., pl.* **-la** (-lə), **-lums.** (in biology) a lidlike part or organ; any flap covering an opening, as the lid of the spore case in mosses, the plate of some gastropods that closes the opening of the shell, or the gill cover of a fish. [< Latin < *operire* to cover]

op e ret ta (op′ə ret′ə), *n., pl.* **-tas.** a short, amusing opera with some spoken dialogue. [< Italian, diminutive of *opera*]

o phid i an (ō fid′ē ən), *n.* snake. —*adj.* 1 like a snake. 2 of or having to do with snakes. [< New Latin *Ophidia,* former name of an order of reptiles < Greek *ophidion* small serpent, diminutive of *ophis* serpent]

oph i u ran (of′ē yůr′ən, ō′fē yůr′ən), *n.* any of a class of echinoderms with five slender arms, greatly elongated and flexible, that are sharply marked off from the central disk; brittle star. [< Greek *ophis* snake + *oura* tail]

hat, āge, fär; let, ēqual, tėrm;
it, īce; hot, ōpen, ôrder;
oil, out; cup, půt, rüle;
ch, child; ng, long; sh, she;
th, thin; ᴛʜ, then; zh, measure;

ə represents *a* in about, *e* in taken, *i* in pencil, *o* in lemon, *u* in circus.

< = from, derived from, taken from.

oph thal mi a (of thal′mē ə, op thal′mē ə), *n.* an acute inflammation of the eye or the membrane around the eye, caused by infection or injury and sometimes causing blindness. [< Greek < *ophthalmos* eye]

oph thal mic (of thal′mik, op thal′mik), *adj.* 1 of or having to do with the eye; ocular. 2 having to do with or affected with ophthalmia.

oph thal mol o gist (of′thal mol′ə jist, op′thal mol′ə jist), *n.* doctor who specializes in ophthalmology; oculist.

oph thal mol o gy (of′thal mol′ə jē, op′-thal mol′ə jē), *n.* branch of medicine dealing with the structure, functions, and diseases of the eye.

oph thal mo scope (of thal′mə skōp, op-thal′mə skōp), *n.* instrument for examining the interior of the eye or the retina.

o pi ate (ō′pē it, ō′pē āt), *n.* 1 any medical preparation containing opium or a derivative of opium and used especially to dull pain or bring sleep. 2 anything that quiets, soothes, etc. —*adj.* 1 containing opium. 2 bringing sleep or ease.

o pine (ō pīn′), *v.t., v.i.,* **o pined, o pin ing.** hold or express an opinion; think. [< French *opiner* < Latin *opinari*]

o pin ion (ə pin′yən), *n.* 1 what one thinks; belief not so strong as knowledge; judgment. See synonym study below. 2 an impression or estimation of quality, character, or value; estimate: *What is your opinion of him as a candidate?* 3 a formal judgment by an expert; professional advice. 4 statement by a judge or jury of the reasons for the decision of the court. [< Latin *opinionem* < *opinari* opine]

Syn. 1 **Opinion, view** mean what a person thinks about something. **Opinion** suggests a carefully thought out conclusion based on facts, but without the certainty of knowledge: *I try to learn the facts and form my own opinions.* **View** suggests an opinion affected by personal leanings or feelings: *Her views are conservative.*

o pin ion at ed (ə pin′yə nā′tid), *adj.* obstinate or conceited with regard to one's opinions; dogmatic. **—o pin′ion at′ed ly,** *adv.*

o pin ion a tive (ə pin′yə nā′tiv), *adj.* 1 opinionated. 2 related to or consisting of opinion or belief.

o pi um (ō′pē əm), *n.* 1 a powerful narcotic drug containing morphine and other alkaloids, made by drying the milky juice from the unripened capsule of the opium poppy. Opium is valuable in medicine but it is dangerously habit-forming. 2 anything having the properties or effects of opium. —*adj.* of or having to do with opium. [< Latin < Greek *opion* poppy juice, opium]

opium poppy, a usually white poppy of Asia and Europe from which opium is derived. Its tiny seeds and oil are used as food.

O por to (ō pôr′tō, ō pōr′tō), *n.* seaport in

NW Portugal, noted for port wine. 324,000.

o pos sum (ə pos′əm), *n., pl.* **-sums** or **-sum.** any of a family of small, omnivorous, marsupial mammals that live mostly in trees and are active chiefly at night; possum. One kind, common in the southern and eastern United States, sometimes gives the appearance of being dead when it is frightened or caught. [of Algonquian origin]

opp., opposite.

Op pen hei mer (op′ən hī′mər), *n.* **J(ulius) Robert,** 1904-1967, American nuclear physicist, who directed the building of the first atomic bomb.

op po nent (ə pō′nənt), *n.* person who is on the other side in a fight, game, or discussion; person fighting, struggling, or speaking against another. See synonym study below. —*adj.* 1 being opposite; opposing. 2 of or having to do with opposable muscles, such as those of the hand by which the fingers and thumb may be placed against each other, so as to pick up or hold something. [< Latin *opponentem* setting against < *ob-* against + *ponere* to place]

Syn. *n.* **Opponent, antagonist, adversary** mean someone against a person or thing. **Opponent** applies to someone on the other side in an argument, game, or other contest, but does not suggest personal ill will: *He defeated his opponent in the election.* **Antagonist,** more formal, suggests active, personal, and unfriendly opposition, often in a fight for power or control: *Hamlet and his uncle were antagonists.* **Adversary** usually means a hostile antagonist actively blocking or openly fighting another: *Gamblers found a formidable adversary in the new district attorney.*

op por tune (op′ər tün′, op′ər tyün′), *adj.* meeting the requirements of the time or occasion; timely; suitable: *An opportune remark kept me from a disastrous investment. You have arrived at an opportune moment—just in time to help rearrange furniture.* [< Latin *opportunus* favorable (of wind) < *ob portum (veniens)* (coming) to port] **—op′por tune′ly,** *adv.* **—op′por tune′ness,** *n.*

op por tun ism (op′ər tü′niz′əm, op′ər tyü′niz′əm), *n.* policy or practice of using every opportunity to one's advantage without considering whether such an action is right or wrong in each particular circumstance.

op por tun ist (op′ər tü′nist, op′ər tyü′nist), *n.* person who uses every opportunity to his advantage, regardless of right or wrong.

op por tun is tic (op′ər tü nis′tik, op′ər tyü nis′tik), *adj.* of or given to opportunism.

op por tu ni ty (op′ər tü′nə tē, op′ər tyü′nə tē), *n., pl.* **-ties.** 1 a favorable time or condition; convenient occasion: *an opportunity to visit with friends.* 2 chance or prospect for advancing in position or attaining a goal: *good job opportunities.*

op pos a ble (ə pō′zə bəl), *adj.* 1 capable of being opposed. 2 capable of being opposite something else. The human thumb is opposable to the fingers.

op pose (ə pōz′), *v.,* **-posed, -pos ing.** —*v.t.* 1 be against; be in the way of; act, fight, or struggle against; try to hinder; resist: *Many people opposed the building of a new highway.* See synonym study below. 2 set up against; place in the way of: *Let us oppose good nature to anger.* 3 put in contrast: *Love is opposed to hate.* 4 put in front of; cause to face: *oppose one's finger to one's thumb.* —*v.i.* be or act in opposition. [< Old French *opposer* < *op-* against + *poser* put] **—op pos′er,** *n.*

opossum—about 33 in. long with tail

Syn. *v.t.* 1 **Oppose, resist, withstand** mean to act or be against someone or something. **Oppose** implies setting oneself against a person or thing but does not suggest the nature or effectiveness of the action or stand taken: *We opposed the plan because of the cost.* **Resist** implies making a stand and actively striving against an attack or force of some kind: *She resisted all our efforts to make her change her mind.* **Withstand** implies holding firm against attack: *The bridge withstood the flood.*

op po site (op′ə zit), *adj.* 1 placed against; as different in direction as can be; face to face; back to back: *The house straight across the street is opposite to ours.* 2 as different as can be; completely contrary: *Sour is opposite to sweet.* See synonym study below. 3 (in botany) placed in pairs at different heights along the sides of a stem; not alternate: *opposite leaves.* —*n.* thing or person that is opposite: *A brave person is the opposite of a coward.* —*prep.* opposite to: *opposite the church.* —*adv.* in an opposite position or direction; on opposite sides. [< Latin *oppositum* placed against < *ob-* against + *ponere* to place] **—op′po site ly,** *adv.* **—op′po site ness,** *n.*

Syn. *adj.* 2 **Opposite, contrary** mean completely different (from each other). **Opposite** particularly applies to two things so far apart in position, nature, meaning, etc., that they can never be made to agree: *"True" and "false" have opposite meanings.* **Contrary** particularly applies to two things going in opposite directions, or set against each other, often in strong disagreement or conflict: *Your statement is contrary to the facts.*

op po si tion (op′ə zish′ən), *n.* 1 action against; resistance: *There was some opposition to the workers' request for higher wages.* 2 a being opposed or adverse. 3 contrast. 4 Also, **Opposition.** a political party opposed to the party in power. 5 any party or body of opponents. 6 a placing opposite. 7 opposite direction or position. 8 position of two heavenly bodies when their longitude differs by 180 degrees, especially such a position of a heavenly body with respect to the sun.

op press (ə pres′), *v.t.* 1 govern harshly; keep down unjustly or by cruelty: *A good government will not oppress the poor.* 2 weigh down; lie heavily on; burden: *A sense of trouble ahead oppressed my spirits.* [< Medieval Latin *oppressare* < Latin *opprimere* press against < *ob-* against + *premere* to press]

op pres sion (ə presh′ən), *n.* 1 cruel or unjust treatment; tyranny; persecution; despotism: *Oppression of the poor often leads to revolution. Our camp rules were so strict we considered them unnecessary oppression.* 2 a heavy, weary feeling of the body or mind; depression.

op pres sive (ə pres′iv), *adj.* 1 hard to bear; burdensome: *The intense heat was oppressive.* 2 harsh; unjust; tyrannical: *Oppressive measures were taken to crush the rebellion.* **—op pres′sive ly,** *adv.* **—op pres′sive ness,** *n.*

op pres sor (ə pres′ər), *n.* person who is cruel or unjust to people under him.

op pro bri ous (ə prō′brē əs), *adj.* 1 expressing scorn, reproach, or abuse: *Coward, liar, and thief are opprobrious names.* 2 disgraceful; shameful; infamous. **—op pro′bri ous ly,** *adv.* **—op pro′bri ous ness,** *n.*

op pro bri um (ə prō′brē əm), *n.* 1 disgrace or reproach caused by shameful conduct; infamy; scorn; abuse. 2 cause or object of such reproach. [< Latin < *opprobare* to reproach < *ob-* at, against + *probrum* infamy, reproach]

op so nin (op′sə nən), *n.* substance in blood serum that weakens invading bacteria, cells, etc., so that the phagocytes can destroy them more easily. [< Latin *opsonium* a relish (especially meat, fish)]

opt (opt), *v.i.* choose or favor: *The class opted to go on a field trip.* [< French *opter* < Latin *optare*]

op ta tive (op′tə tiv), in grammar: —*adj.* expressing a wish. "Oh! that I had wings to fly!" is an optative expression. —*n.* 1 the optative mood. 2 verb in the optative mood. [< Latin *optativus* < *optare* to wish, choose] **—op′ta tive ly,** *adv.*

op tic (op′tik), *adj.* of the eye; of the sense of sight. [< Greek *optikos* < *op-* see]

op ti cal (op′tə kəl), *adj.* 1 of the eye or the sense of sight; visual: *an optical illusion. Nearsightedness is an optical defect.* 2 made to assist sight: *Telescopes and microscopes are optical instruments.* 3 of vision and light in relation to each other. 4 having to do with optics. **—op′ti cal ly,** *adv.*

optical art, form of abstract painting in which unusual optical illusions and effects are produced by means of complex geometrical designs; op art.

optical maser, laser.

op ti cian (op tish′ən), *n.* maker or seller of eyeglasses and other optical instruments.

optic nerve, the nerve of sight, which goes from the brain to the eyeball and terminates in the retina.

op tics (op′tiks), *n.* branch of physics dealing with the properties and phenomena of those electromagnetic waves with wavelengths greater than x-rays and smaller than microwaves. Optics includes the ultraviolet, visible, and infrared parts of the spectrum.

op ti mal (op′tə məl), *adj.* most favorable; best; optimum. **—op′ti mal ly,** *adv.*

op ti mism (op′tə miz′əm), *n.* 1 tendency to look on the bright side of things. 2 belief that everything will turn out for the best. 3 doctrine that the existing world is the best of all possible worlds. [< French *optimisme* < Latin *optimus* best]

op ti mist (op′tə mist), *n.* 1 person who looks on the bright side of things. 2 person who believes that everything in life will turn out for the best. 3 believer in the doctrine of optimism.

op ti mis tic (op′tə mis′tik), *adj.* 1 inclined to look on the bright side of things. 2 hoping for the best. 3 having to do with optimism. **—op′ti mis′ti cal ly,** *adv.*

op ti mum (op′tə məm), *n., pl.* **-mums, -ma** (-mə). the best or most favorable point, degree, amount, etc., for the purpose. *—adj.* best or most favorable. [< Latin]

op tion (op′shən), *n.* 1 right or freedom of choice: *Pupils in our school have the option of taking Spanish, French, or German.* 2 act of choosing: *Where to travel should be left to each person's option.* 3 thing that is or can be chosen. See **choice** for synonym study. 4 right to buy something at a certain price within a certain time: *We paid $500 for an option on the land.* 5 (in insurance) the right of an insured person to decide how he shall receive the money due him on a policy. [< Latin *optionem,* related to *optare* opt]

op tion al (op′shə nəl), *adj.* left to one's choice; not required; elective. **—op′tion al ly,** *adv.*

op to met ric (op′tə met′rik), *adj.* of or having to do with optometry. **—op′to met′ri cal ly,** *adv.*

op tom e trist (op tom′ə trist), *n.* person skilled in examining the eyes and prescribing eyeglasses, but not an M.D.

op tom e try (op tom′ə trē), *n.* measurement of the powers of sight; practice or occupation of testing eyes in order to fit them with glasses. [< Greek *optos* seen + English *-metry*]

op u lence (op′yə ləns), *n.* 1 much money or property; wealth; riches. 2 abundance; plenty.

op u lent (op′yə lənt), *adj.* 1 having wealth; rich. 2 showing wealth; costly and luxurious: *an opulent home.* 3 abundant; plentiful: *opulent hair.* [< Latin *opulentem* < *ops* power, resources] **—op′u lent ly,** *adv.*

o pus (ō′pəs), *n., pl.* **op er a** or **o pus es.** 1 a musical composition, especially one numbered among the works of a composer in order of publication. 2 any artistic or other work or composition. [< Latin, work]

or[1] (ôr; *unstressed* ər), *conj.* 1 word used to express a choice or a difference, or to connect words or groups of words of equal importance in the sentence. *You may go or stay. Is it sweet or sour?* 2 and if not; otherwise: *Either eat this or go hungry. Hurry, or you will be late.* 3 that is; being the same as: *an igloo or Eskimo snow house.* [Middle English *or,* reduction of *other* < Old English *oththe*]

or[2] (ôr), *prep., conj.* ARCHAIC. before; ere. [Old English *ār* early]

or[3] (ôr), *n.* (in heraldry) gold or yellow. [< Old French, gold < Latin *aurum*]

-or, *suffix forming nouns from verbs.* person or thing that ____s: *Governor = person who governs. Accelerator = thing that accelerates.* [< Latin]

➤ **-or, -our.** American spelling prefers *-or* in such words as *color, governor, honor.* When referring to Jesus, *Saviour* is frequently spelled with the *u* but in other senses without it. British usage prefers *-our* spellings, but not in certain derivatives. Thus words like *honorific, honorary,* and *humorous* are so spelled on both sides of the Atlantic.

o ra cle (ôr′ə kəl, or′ə kəl), *n.* 1 (in ancient Greece and Rome) an answer believed to be given by a god through a priest or priestess to some question. It often had a hidden meaning that was ambiguous or hard to understand. 2 place where the god was believed to give such answers. A famous oracle was at Delphi. 3 the priest, priestess, or other means by which the god's answer was believed to be given. 4 a very wise person. 5 something regarded as a very reliable and sure guide. 6 a very wise answer. [< Latin *oraculum* < *orare* speak formally]

o rac u lar (ô rak′yə lər, ō rak′yə lər), *adj.* 1 of or like an oracle. 2 with a hidden meaning that is ambiguous or difficult to make out. 3 very wise. **—o rac′u lar ly,** *adv.*

o ral (ôr′əl, ōr′əl), *adj.* 1 using speech; spoken: *an oral command.* 2 of the mouth: *oral hygiene. The oral opening in an earthworm is small.* 3 through or by the mouth: *an oral dose of penicillin.* [< Latin *os, oris* mouth] **—o′ral ly,** *adv.*

➤ **oral, verbal.** *Oral* means spoken, as distinguished from written: *She gave an oral report. Verbal* means in words, as distinguished from other means of expression: *This written report contains both a verbal description and a sketch of the building.*

O ran (ô ran′, ō ran′; ô rän′, ō rän′), *n.* city in NW Algeria, on the Mediterranean. 325,000.

o range (ôr′inj, or′inj), *n.* 1 a round, reddish-yellow, edible citrus fruit with a juicy, sweetish or slightly acid pulp enclosed in a soft rind. Oranges grow in warm climates. 2 any of the evergreen trees that bear this fruit. The orange has fragrant white blossoms and oval or elliptical leaves. 3 any of various fruits or trees that resemble an orange. 4 a reddish yellow. *—adj.* 1 of or like an orange. 2 reddish-yellow. [< Old French *orenge* < Spanish *naranja* < Arabic *nāranj* < Persian *nārang*] **—or′ange like′,** *adj.*

O range (ôr′inj, or′inj), *n.* 1 **Orange River,** river flowing from Lesotho across the Republic of South Africa into the Atlantic. 1300 mi. 2 former principality in W Europe, now a part of France. 3 a princely family of Europe that ruled the former principality of Orange. William III of England was of this family, and so is the present royal family of the Netherlands. 4 city in SW California, near Los Angeles. 77,000.

o range ade (ôr′inj ād′, or′inj ād′), *n.* drink made of orange juice, sugar, and water.

Orange Free State, central province of the Republic of South Africa. 1,387,000 pop.; 49,900 sq. mi. *Capital:* Bloemfontein.

O range man (ôr′inj mən, or′inj mən), *n., pl.* **-men.** 1 member of a secret society formed in the north of Ireland in 1795, to uphold the Protestant religion and Protestant control in Ireland. 2 any Irish Protestant, especially one living in Northern Ireland.

orange pekoe, a black tea from Ceylon or India, especially a superior one made from the youngest leaves at the tips of the branches.

o range wood (ôr′inj wu̇d′, or′inj wu̇d′), *n.* the hard, fine-grained wood of the orange tree, used as a cabinet wood, for small dental tools, and for manicuring the nails.

o rang-ou tang (ô rang′ü tang′), *n.* orangutan.

o rang u tan or **o rang-u tan** (ô rang′ü tan′), *n.* a large anthropoid ape of the forests of Borneo and Sumatra, that has very long arms and long, reddish-brown hair. It lives mostly in trees and eats fruits and leaves. [< Malay < *orang* man + *utan* of the woods]

o rate (ô rāt′, ō rāt′; ôr′āt, ōr′āt), *v.,* **o rat ed, o rat ing.** *—v.i.* make an oration; talk in a grand manner. *—v.t.* harangue. [< *oration*]

o ra tion (ô rā′shən, ō rā′shən), *n.* a formal public speech, especially one delivered on a special occasion: *the orations of Cicero.* See **speech** for synonym study. [< Latin *orationem* < *orare* speak formally, pray. Doublet of ORISON.]

hat, āge, fär; let, ēqual, tėrm;
it, īce; hot, ōpen, ôrder;
oil, out; cup, pu̇t, rüle;
ch, child; ng, long; sh, she;
th, thin; ᴛʜ, then; zh, measure;

ə represents *a* in about, *e* in taken, *i* in pencil, *o* in lemon, *u* in circus.

< = from, derived from, taken from.

o ra tor (ôr′ə tər, or′ə tər), *n.* 1 person who makes an oration. 2 person who can speak very well in public and often with great eloquence.

o ra tor i cal (ôr′ə tôr′ə kəl, or′ə tor′ə kəl), *adj.* 1 of oratory; having to do with orators or oratory: *an oratorical contest.* 2 characteristic of orators or oratory: *He has an oratorical manner even in conversation.* **—or′a tor′i cal ly,** *adv.*

o ra to ri o (ôr′ə tôr′ē ō, ôr′ə tōr′ē ō; or′ə tôr′ē ō, or′ə tōr′ē ō), *n., pl.* **-ri os.** an extended musical composition, usually based on a Biblical or mythological theme, sung by solo voices and a chorus to orchestral accompaniment, and dramatic in character but performed without action, costumes, or scenery. [< Italian, originally, place of prayer < Late Latin *oratorium.* Doublet of ORATORY[2].]

o ra to ry[1] (ôr′ə tôr′ē, ôr′ə tōr′ē; or′ə tôr′ē, or′ə tōr′ē), *n.* 1 skill in public speaking; eloquent speaking or language. 2 the art of public speaking. [< Latin *(ars) oratoria* oratorical (art) < *orare* speak formally, pray]

o ra to ry[2] (ôr′ə tôr′ē, ôr′ə tōr′ē; or′ə tôr′ē, or′ə tōr′ē), *n., pl.* **-ries.** a small chapel, room, or other place set apart for private prayer. [< Late Latin *oratorium* < Latin *orare* plead, pray. Doublet of ORATORIO.]

orb (ôrb), *n.* 1 anything round like a ball; sphere; globe. 2 sun, moon, planet, or star. 3 the eyeball or eye. 4 Also, **Orb.** globe surmounted by a cross, symbolizing royal sovereignty. *—v.t.* 1 form into a circle, disk, or sphere. 2 ARCHAIC. encircle; enclose. [< Latin *orbis* circle]

or bic u lar (ôr bik′yə lər), *adj.* like a circle or sphere; rounded; circular; spherical. **—or bic′u lar ly,** *adv.*

or bic u late (ôr bik′yə lit, ôr bik′yə lāt), *adj.* orbicular.

or bit (ôr′bit), *n.* 1 the curved, usually elliptical path of a heavenly body, planet, or satellite about another body in space: *the earth's orbit about the sun, the moon's orbit about the earth, the orbit of a weather satellite about the earth.* 2 the curved path of an electron

orangutan
about $4^1/_2$ ft. tall

about the nucleus of an atom. 3 regular course of life or experience; sphere of knowledge or activity. 4 the bony cavity or socket in which the eyeball is set. *—v.t.* 1 travel in an orbit around: *orbit the earth.* 2 put into an orbit: *orbit a satellite.* *—v.i.* 1 travel in an orbit. 2 (of a satellite, etc.) arrive in its orbit. [< Latin *orbita* wheel track < *orbis* wheel, circle]

or bit al (ôr′bə təl), *adj.* of an orbit.

or bit er (ôr′bə tər), *n.* something that orbits, especially an artificial satellite.

orch., orchestra.

or chard (ôr′chərd), *n.* 1 piece of ground on which fruit trees are grown. 2 trees in an orchard. [Old English *ortgeard* < *ort-* (< Latin *hortus* garden) + *geard* yard[1]]

or ches tra (ôr′kə strə), *n.* 1 group of musicians organized to play together on various instruments, especially violins and other stringed instruments. Orchestras usually play at concerts, operas, or plays. 2 the violins, cellos, clarinets, and other instruments played together by such a group. 3 the part of a theater just in front of the stage, where musicians sit to play. 4 the main floor of a theater, especially the part near the front. [< Greek *orchēstra* the space where the chorus of dancers performed < *orcheisthai* to dance]

or ches tral (ôr kes′trəl), *adj.* of an orchestra; composed for or performed by an orchestra. **—or ches′tral ly,** *adv.*

or ches trate (ôr′kə strāt), *v.t.,* **-trat ed, -trat ing.** compose or arrange (music) for performance by an orchestra. **—or′ches tra′tion,** *n.* **—or′ches tra′tor,** *n.*

or chid (ôr′kid), *n.* 1 any of a family of terrestrial or epiphytic perennial plants with beautiful flowers that are formed of three petallike sepals and three petals, one petal being much larger than the other two and of special color and shape. 2 its flower. 3 a light purple. *—adj.* light-purple. [< New Latin *Orchideae,* former name of the orchid family, ultimately < Greek *orchis* orchid, testicle]

or chis (ôr′kis), *n.* orchid, especially any of a genus of terrestrial orchids of temperate regions. A common North American species has a spike of pink-purple flowers with a white lip.

ord., 1 ordained. 2 order. 3 ordinal. 4 ordnance.

or dain (ôr dān′), *v.t.* 1 establish as a law; order; fix; decide; appoint. 2 appoint or consecrate officially as a clergyman. 3 appoint as part of the order of the universe or of nature; destine. [< Old French *ordener* < Latin *ordinare* < *ordinem* order] **—or dain′er,** *n.*

or deal (ôr dēl′, ôr′dēl), *n.* 1 a severe test or experience. 2 (in early times) an effort to decide the guilt or innocence of an accused person by making him do something dangerous like holding fire or taking poison. It was supposed that God would not let an innocent person be harmed by such danger. [Old English *ordāl* judgment]

or der (ôr′dər), *n.* 1 the way one thing follows another: *in order of size, in alphabetical order, the order of history.* 2 condition in which every part or piece is in its right place: *put a room in order.* 3 a regular, methodical, or harmonious arrangement: *the order of a fleet of ships.* 4 condition; state: *My affairs are in good order.* 5 way things or events happen: *the order of nature.* 6 condition of things in which the law is obeyed and there is no trouble; rule of law: *The police maintained order.* 7 the principles and rules by which a meeting is run: *rise to a point of order.* 8 a telling what to do; command: *On a ship the orders of the captain must be obeyed.* 9 a paper saying that money is to be given or paid, or something handed over: *a postal money order.* 10 a spoken or written request for goods that one wants to buy or receive: *a grocery order.* 11 the goods so requested. 12 kind or sort: *have ability of a high order.* 13 a primary group of related plants and animals ranking below a class and above a family. The rose family, the pea family, and several others belong to one order. See **classification** for chart. 14 a social rank, grade, or class: *all orders of society.* 15 rank or position in the church: *the order of bishops.* 16 Usually, **orders. a** ordination. **b** the rite of ordination; holy orders. 17 brotherhood of monks, friars, or knights: *the Benedictine Order.* 18 a sisterhood of nuns. 19 society to which one is admitted as an honor: *the Order of the Garter.* 20 a modern fraternal organization: *the Order of Masons.* 21 the badge worn by those belonging to an honorary order. 22 any of several styles of columns and architecture, having differences in proportion, decoration, etc.: *the Doric, Ionic, and Corinthian orders of Greek architecture.* 23 the regular form of worship for a given occasion. 24 portion or serving of food served in a restaurant, etc.

by order, according to an order given by the proper person.

call to order, ask to be quiet and start work: *call a meeting to order.*

in order, a in the right arrangement or condition. **b** working right. **c** allowed by the rules of a meeting, etc. **d** likely to be done; natural; logical.

in order that, so that; with the purpose that.

in order to, as a means to; to.

in short order, without delay; quickly.

on order, having been ordered but not yet received.

on the order of, somewhat like; similar to: *a house on the order of ours.*

out of order, a in the wrong arrangement or condition. **b** not working right. **c** against the rules of a meeting, etc.

take (holy) orders, become ordained as a Christian minister or priest.

to order, according to the buyer's wishes or requirements.

—v.t. 1 put in order; arrange: *order one's affairs.* 2 tell what to do; give an order to; command; bid: *order a person to leave.* See **command** for synonym study. 3 give (a store, etc.) an order for; direct (a thing) to be made or furnished: *order dinner, order a cab.* 4 decide; will; determine: *The authorities ordered it otherwise.* 5 **order about** or **order around,** send here and there; tell to do this and that. *—v.i.* give an order or orders, directions, etc.: *Please order for me.*

[< Old French *ordre* < Latin *ordinem* row, rank, series] **—or′der er,** *n.*

order arms, the command to bring a weapon to a prescribed position, especially to bring a rifle to an erect position at the side with the butt on the ground while one is standing at attention.

ordered pair, (in mathematics) any two numbers written in a meaningful order, so that one can be considered as the first and the other as the second of the pair.

or der ly (ôr′dər lē), *adj., n., pl.* **-lies.** *—adj.* 1 in order; with regular arrangement, method, or system: *an orderly arrangement of dishes on shelves, an orderly mind.* See synonym study below. 2 keeping order; well-behaved or regulated: *an orderly class.* *—n.* 1 soldier who attends a superior officer to carry orders, etc. 2 a male hospital attendant who keeps things clean and in order, often tends to patients, etc. *—adv.* in or with due order; methodically. **—or′der li ness,** *n.*

Syn. *adj.* 1 **Orderly, methodical, systematic** mean following a plan of arrangement or action. **Orderly** suggests lack of confusion and careful arrangement according to some rule or scheme: *The chairs are in orderly rows.* **Methodical** suggests following step by step a plan carefully worked out in advance or regularly followed: *The bookkeeper made a methodical check of the accounts for the error.* **Systematic** adds to *methodical* the idea of thoroughness and completeness: *The commission made a systematic investigation of the problem of air pollution.*

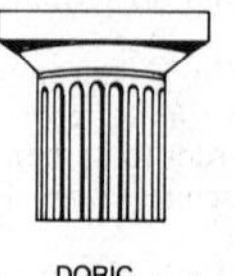

order (def. 22)
portions of columns illustrating three orders of Greek architecture

or di nal (ôrd′n əl), *adj.* 1 showing order or position in a series. 2 of or having to do with an order of animals or plants. *—n.* 1 an ordinal number. 2 **Ordinal,** book of special forms for certain church ceremonies, as the conferring of holy orders in the Church of England or the conducting of the daily office in the Roman Catholic Church. [< Late Latin *ordinalis* < Latin *ordinem* order]

ordinal number, number that shows order or position in a series. First, second, third, etc., are ordinal numbers; one, two, three, etc., are cardinal numbers.

➤ See **cardinal number** for usage note.

or di nance (ôrd′n əns), *n.* 1 rule or law made by authority, especially one adopted and enforced by a municipal or other local authority; decree: *a traffic ordinance.* 2 an established religious ceremony. [< Old French *ordenance* < Latin *ordinare* arrange, regulate < *ordinem* order]

or di nar i ly (ôrd′n er′ə lē), *adv.* 1 usually; regularly; normally. 2 to the usual extent.

or di nar y (ôrd′n er′ē), *adj., n., pl.* **-nar ies.** *—adj.* 1 according to habit or custom; usual; regular; normal: *an ordinary day's work.* 2 not special; common; everyday; average: *an ordinary situation.* See **common** for synonym study. 3 somewhat below the average; mediocre; inferior: *The speaker was ordinary and tiresome.* *—n.* 1 **out of the ordinary,** not regular or customary; unusual; extraordinary. 2 BRITISH. **a** meal served at a fixed price. **b** inn or dining room of an inn. 3 person who has authority in his own right, especially a bishop or a judge. 4 Also, **Ordinary.** the form for saying Mass. 5 **in ordinary,** in regular service: *physician in ordinary to the king.* [< Latin *ordinarius* < *ordinem* order] **—or′di nar′i ness,** *n.*

or di nate (ôrd′n it, ôrd′n āt), *n.* the distance of a point on a graph above or below the horizontal axis, measured on a line parallel to the vertical axis. The ordinate and the abscissa together are coordinates of the point. [< Latin *ordinatum* arranged < *ordinem* order]

or di na tion (ôrd′n ā′shən), *n.* 1 act or ceremony of ordaining as a clergyman. 2 condition of being ordained as a clergyman.

ord nance (ôrd′nəns), *n.* 1 cannon or artillery. 2 military apparatus or supplies of all kinds, such as weapons, vehicles, ammunition, etc. [variant of *ordinance*]

Or do vi cian (ôr′də vish′ən), *n.* 1 the geological period of the Paleozoic era after the Cambrian and before the Silurian, characterized by the first appearance of vertebrates. See chart under **geology.** 2 the rocks formed in this period. *—adj.* of or having to do with this period or its rocks. [< Latin *Ordovices* ancient Celtic tribe in Wales]

or dure (ôr′jər, ôr′dyůr), *n.* 1 dung; excrement. 2 anything morally filthy or defiling, especially vile language. [< Old French < *ord* filthy < Latin *horridus* horrid]

ore (ôr, ōr), *n.* mineral or rock containing a high enough concentration of one or more metals to make mining it profitable. The ore may be found in its natural state or as part of a compound. [Old English *ār* brass]

ö re (œ′rə), *n.* unit of money in Denmark, Norway, and Sweden, a bronze coin equal to $^1/_{100}$ of a krone or krona. [< Danish and Norwegian *øre,* Swedish *öre*]

Ore., Oregon.

o re ad or **O re ad** (ō′rē ad, ō′rē ad), *n.* (in Greek myths) a mountain nymph. [< Greek *oreiados* < *oros* mountain]

Oreg., Oregon.

o reg a no (ə reg′ə nō), *n., pl.* **-nos.** an aromatic herb, a species of marjoram, the leaves of which are used for seasoning food. [< Spanish *orégano*]

O re gon (ôr′ə gən, ôr′ə gon; or′ə gən, or′ə-gon), *n.* one of the Pacific states of the United States. 2,091,000 pop.; 97,000 sq. mi. *Capital:* Salem. *Abbrev.:* Oreg. or Ore. **—O re go ni an** (ôr′ə gō′nē ən, or′ə gō′-nē ən), *adj., n.*

Oregon grape, 1 an evergreen shrub of the western United States, belonging to the same family as the barberry and bearing clusters of yellow flowers and small blue-black berries. 2 its berry.

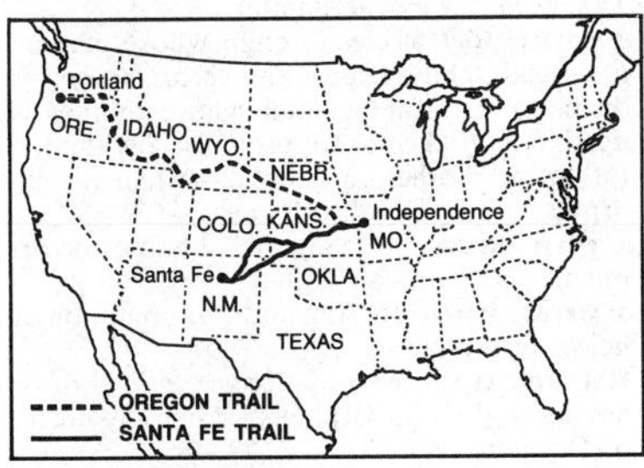

Oregon Trail, trail from Missouri northwest into Oregon, much used by early pioneers and settlers in the 1800's.

O res tes (ô res′tēz, ō res′tēz), *n.* (in Greek legends) the son of Agamemnon and Clytemnestra, who killed his mother and her lover to avenge the murder of his father. He was pursued by the Furies for this crime.

org., 1 organic. 2 organization. 3 organized.

ordinate
The ordinate of point P is the distance PM measured on the axis Y′Y.

or gan (ôr′gən), *n.* 1 a musical instrument consisting of one or more sets of pipes of different lengths, sounded by compressed air supplied by a bellows, and played by means of keys arranged in one or more keyboards; pipe organ. Organs are used especially in church. 2 any of certain similar instruments somewhat like the pipe organ but sounded by electronic devices. 3 any of various other musical instruments, such as a hand organ, reed organ, or mouth organ. 4 any part of an animal or plant that is composed of various tissues organized to perform some particular function. The eyes, stomach, heart, and lungs are organs of the body. Stamens and pistils are organs of flowers. 5 means of action; instrument: *A court is an organ of government.* 6 newspaper or magazine that speaks for and gives the views of a political party or some other group or organization. [< Latin *organum* < Greek *organon* instrument, related to *ergon* work]

or gan dy or **or gan die** (ôr′gən dē′), *n., pl.* **-dies.** a fine, thin, stiff, transparent muslin, used for dresses, curtains, etc. [< French *organdi*]

or gan elle (ôr′gə nel′), *n.* (in biology) a minute specialized part of a cell, such as a vacuole in protozoans, analogous in function to an organ of higher animals.

organ grinder, a wandering street musician who plays a hand organ by turning a crank.

or gan ic (ôr gan′ik), *adj.* 1 of the bodily organs; affecting an organ; vital: *an organic disease.* 2 of, having to do with, or obtained from plants or animals: *organic fertilizer.* 3 (in chemistry) of or having to do with compounds containing carbon; containing carbon. Starch is an organic compound. 4 having organs or an organized physical structure. 5 made up of related parts, but being a unit; coordinated; organized: *The United States is an organic whole made up of 50 states.* 6 that is part of the structure or constitution of a person or thing; fundamental: *The Constitution is the organic law of the United States.* **—or gan′i cal ly,** *adv.*

organic chemistry, branch of chemistry that deals with compounds of carbon, such as foods and fuels.

or gan ism (ôr′gə niz′əm), *n.* 1 a living body made up of separate parts, such as cells, tissues, and organs, which work together to carry on the various processes of life; an individual animal or plant. 2 any organized system similar to this; a whole made up of related parts that work together. Human society, or any community, may be spoken of as a social organism.

or gan ist (ôr′gə nist), *n.* person who plays an organ.

or gan i za tion (ôr′gə nə zā′shən), *n.* 1 group of persons united for some purpose. Churches, clubs, and political parties are organizations. 2 an organizing; grouping and arranging parts to form a whole: *The organization of a big picnic takes time and thought.* 3 the way in which a thing's parts are arranged to work together: *The organization of the human body is very complicated.* 4 thing made up of related parts, each having a special duty: *A tree is an organization of roots, trunk, branches, leaves, and fruit.* 5 people who manage a business, political party, etc.; management.

hat, āge, fär; let, ēqual, tėrm;
it, īce; hot, ōpen, ôrder;
oil, out; cup, pu̇t, rüle;
ch, child; ng, long; sh, she;
th, thin; ᴛʜ, then; zh, measure;

ə represents *a* in about, *e* in taken, *i* in pencil, *o* in lemon, *u* in circus.

< = from, derived from, taken from.

or gan i za tion al (ôr′gə nə zā′shə nəl), *adj.* of or having to do with organization.

organization man, man who submerges or loses his individuality in his complete dedication to the company which employs him.

Organization of American States, organization of 21 American republics formed to promote mutual cooperation and further the interests of peace. It was created by the Pan American Union in 1948.

or gan ize (ôr′gə nīz), *v.,* **-ized, -iz ing.** *—v.t.* 1 put into working order; get together and arrange: *The explorer organized an expedition to the North Pole.* 2 bring together into a labor union, as the workers of a particular industry: *organize the truckers.* 3 furnish with organs; provide with an organic structure; make organic. *—v.i.* 1 combine in a company, party, labor union, etc.; form an organization. 2 assume organic structure; become living tissue. **—or′gan iz′a ble,** *adj.* **—or′gan iz′er,** *n.*

or gan za (ôr gan′zə), *n.* a sheer cloth of rayon, silk, etc., resembling organdy, used especially for dresses. [origin uncertain]

or gasm (ôr′gaz′əm), *n.* the highest point of sexual excitement, accompanied by a release of sexual tension, and in the male by ejaculation of semen; climax. [< Greek *orgasmos* < *organ* become ripe]

or gi as tic (ôr′jē as′tik), *adj.* of, having to do with, or of the nature of orgies. **—or′gi-as′ti cal ly,** *adv.*

or gy (ôr′jē), *n., pl.* **-gies.** 1 a wild, drunken revel. 2 period of uncontrolled indulgence: *an orgy of eating.* 3 **orgies,** *pl.* secret rites or ceremonies in the worship of certain Greek and Roman gods, especially the god of wine, celebrated by drinking, wild dancing, and singing. [< Greek *orgia* secret rites]

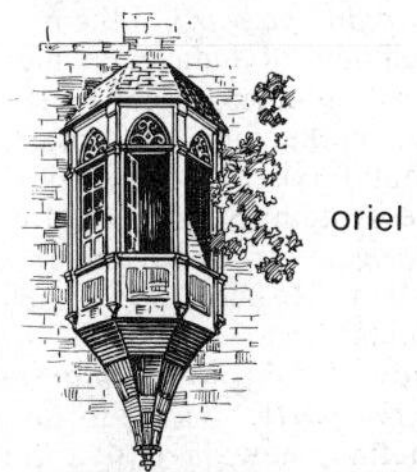
oriel

o ri el (ôr′ē əl, ōr′ē əl), *n.* a bay window projecting from the outer face of a wall, often supported by a bracket of stone, wood, etc. [< Old French *oriol* porch]

o ri ent (*n., adj.* ôr′ē ənt, ōr′ē ənt; *v.* ôr′ē-ent, ōr′ē ent), *n.* 1 the east. 2 **the Orient,** countries in Asia as distinguished from those in Europe and America; the East. —*adj.* 1 **Orient,** of the Orient; Oriental. 2 bright; shining: *an orient pearl.* 3 ARCHAIC. rising: *the orient sun.* —*v.t.* 1 put facing east. 2 place or build (a church) with the chief altar at the eastern end of its longer axis. 3 place so that it faces in any indicated direction: *The building is oriented north and south.* 4 find the direction or position of; determine the compass bearings of. 5 bring into the right relationship with surroundings; adjust to a new situation, condition of affairs, etc. [< Latin *orientem* the East, literally, rising (with reference to the rising sun)]

O ri en tal (ôr′ē en′tl, ōr′ē en′tl), *adj.* 1 Eastern; of the Orient. 2 **oriental,** eastern. —*n.* native of the East. Turks, Arabs, Iranians, Indians, and Chinese are Orientals.

o ri en tal ism or **O ri en tal ism** (ôr′ē-en′tl iz′əm, ōr′ē en′tl iz′əm), *n.* 1 Oriental character or characteristics; an Oriental mode of thought or expression. 2 knowledge or study of Oriental languages, literature, etc.

o ri en tal ist or **O ri en tal ist** (ôr′ē-en′tl ist, ōr′ē en′tl ist), *n.* an expert in Oriental languages, literature, history, etc.

Oriental rug, a handmade rug in one piece with a distinctive pattern, made especially in the Orient.

o ri en tate (ôr′ē en tāt, ōr′ē en tāt), *v.t.,* **-tat ed, -tat ing.** orient.

o ri en ta tion (ôr′ē en tā′shən, ōr′ē en-tā′shən), *n.* 1 an orienting. 2 a being oriented. 3 a finding out of the actual facts or conditions and putting oneself in the right relation to them.

o ri fice (ôr′ə fis, or′ə fis), *n.* an opening or hole; mouth: *the orifice of a tube.* [< Latin *orificium* < *os, oris* mouth + *facere* make]

o ri flamme (ôr′ə flam, or′ə flam), *n.* 1 the red banner carried as a military ensign by the early kings of France. 2 any banner used as an ensign or standard. 3 anything that serves as a rallying point in a struggle. [< Old French *orieflambe,* literally, golden flame]

orig., 1 origin. 2 original. 3 originally.

o ri ga mi (ôr′ə gä′mē), *n.* the Japanese art of folding paper to make decorative objects, such as figures of birds and flowers. [< Japanese]

o ri gin (ôr′ə jin, or′ə jin), *n.* 1 thing from which anything comes; starting point; source; beginning: *the origin of a quarrel, the origin of a disease.* 2 parentage, ancestry, or birth: *a person of humble origin.* 3 an originating; rise; derivation: *a certificate of origin, trace the origin of a word.* 4 the main or more fixed attachment of a muscle, which does not change position during the muscle's contraction. 5 (in mathematics) the intersection of the horizontal axis and the vertical axis in a coordinate system. See **x-axis** for diagram. [< Latin *originem* < *oriri* to rise]

o rig i nal (ə rij′ə nəl), *adj.* 1 belonging to the beginning; first; earliest: *the original settlers.* 2 new; fresh; novel: *plan an original game for the party.* 3 able to do, make, or think something new; inventive: *a very original writer.* 4 not copied, imitated, or translated from something else: *an original poem.* —*n.* 1 thing from which another is copied, imitated, or translated: *The original of this painting is in Rome.* 2 a new written work, picture, etc., that is not a copy or imitation. 3 the language in which a book was first written: *Our minister can read the Bible in the original.* 4 an unusual or peculiar person. 5 person who acts or thinks in an original way. 6 ARCHAIC. origin; source. —**o rig′i-nal ness,** *n.*

o rig i nal i ty (ə rij′ə nal′ə tē), *n.* 1 ability to do, make, or think up something new; inventiveness. 2 freshness; novelty. 3 a being original.

o rig i nal ly (ə rij′ə nə lē), *adv.* 1 by origin: *a plant originally African.* 2 at first; in the first place: *a house originally small.* 3 in an original manner: *decorate a room originally.*

original sin, (in Christian theology) a tendency to sin or do evil held to be innate in mankind and transmitted from Adam to the race in consequence of his sin.

o rig i nate (ə rij′ə nāt), *v.,* **-nat ed, -nat ing.** —*v.t.* cause to be; invent: *originate a new style of painting.* —*v.i.* come into being; begin; arise: *Where did that story originate?* —**o rig′i na′tion,** *n.* —**o rig′i-na′tor,** *n.*

o rig i na tive (ə rij′ə nā′tiv), *adj.* having originality; inventive; creative. —**o rig′i-na′tive ly,** *adv.*

O ri no co River (ôr′ə nō′kō, ōr′ə nō′kō), large river in South America, flowing from S Venezuela, between Venezuela and Colombia, into the Atlantic. 1500 mi.

o ri ole (ôr′ē ōl, ōr′ē ōl), *n.* 1 any of several American songbirds that build hanging nests and usually have yellow- or orange-and-black feathers. 2 any of several Old-World birds that build hanging nests and have rich yellow and black feathers. [< French *oriol* < Medieval Latin *oryolus, aureolus* < Latin *aureolus* golden, diminutive of *aureus* < *aurum* gold]

O ri on (ô rī′ən, ō rī′ən), *n.* constellation near the equator of the celestial sphere that contains the extremely bright star Betelgeuse. To ancient astronomers it appeared to have the rough outline of a man wearing a belt and a sword and holding a shield and a club.

o ri son (ôr′ə zən, or′ə zən; ôr′ə sən, or′ə-sən), *n.* ARCHAIC. prayer. [< Old French < Late Latin *orationem* < Latin, oration < *orare* pray. Doublet of ORATION.]

O ri za ba (ôr′ə zä′bə, ōr′ə zä′bə; *Spanish* ō′rē sä′vä), *n.* 1 volcano in SE Mexico. 18,700 ft. 2 city near it. 70,000.

Ork ney Islands (ôrk′nē), group of islands northeast of, and belonging to, Scotland. 18,000 pop.; 376 sq. mi. See **British Isles** for map.

Or lan do (ôr lan′dō), *n.* city in E Florida. 99,000.

Or lé ans (ôr′lē ənz; *French* ôr lā äN′), *n.* city in central France, on the Loire River. 96,000.

Or lon (ôr′lon), *n.* trademark for a lightweight synthetic fiber resistant to sun, rain, and acids. It is used for clothing, sails, awnings, etc.

Or ly (ôr′lē; *French* ôr lē′), *n.* town of N France, a suburb of Paris, site of a major international airport. 30,000.

Or mazd (ôr′mazd), *n.* (in the Zoroastrian religion) the spirit of good; Ahura Mazda. Ormazd is in ceaseless conflict with Ahriman, the spirit of evil.

or mo lu (ôr′mə lü), *n.* alloy of copper, zinc, and tin, used to imitate gold. Ormolu is used in decorating furniture, clocks, etc. [< French *or moulu,* literally, ground gold]

or na ment (*n.* ôr′nə mənt; *v.* ôr′nə ment), *n.* 1 something pretty or decorative; something to add beauty; adornment; decoration: *ornaments for a Christmas tree.* 2 use of ornaments. 3 person or act that adds beauty, grace, or honor. 4 (in music) an additional note or notes introduced as an embellishment but not essential to the harmony or melody. —*v.t.* add beauty to; make more pleasing or attractive; adorn; decorate. See **decorate** for synonym study. [< Latin *ornamentum* < *ornare* adorn]

or na men tal (ôr′nə men′tl), *adj.* 1 of or having to do with ornament. 2 for ornament; used as an ornament. 3 decorative. —*n.* something ornamental, especially a plant cultivated for decorative purposes. —**or′na-men′tal ly,** *adv.*

or na men ta tion (ôr′nə men tā′shən), *n.* 1 an ornamenting. 2 a being ornamented. 3 decorations; ornaments.

or nate (ôr nāt′), *adj.* 1 much adorned; much ornamented. 2 characterized by the use of elaborate figures of speech, flowery language, etc. [< Latin *ornatum*] —**or-nate′ly,** *adv.* —**or nate′ness,** *n.*

or ner y (ôr′nər ē), *adj.* INFORMAL. 1 mean or irritable in disposition. 2 of a mean kind: *an ornery remark.* [contraction of *ordinary*] —**or′ner i ness,** *n.*

or ni this chi an (ôr ni this′kē ən), *n.* any of an order of dinosaurs having a hip structure similar to that of modern birds, including the stegosaurus. —*adj.* of or belonging to this order. [< Greek *ornithos* bird + *ischion* hip]

or ni tho log i cal (ôr′nə thə loj′ə kəl), *adj.* dealing with birds. —**or′ni tho log′i cal ly,** *adv.*

or ni thol o gist (ôr′nə thol′ə jist), *n.* an expert in ornithology.

or ni thol o gy (ôr′nə thol′ə jē), *n.* branch of zoology dealing with the study of birds. [< Greek *ornithos* bird + English *-logy*]

o rog e ny (ô roj′ə nē, ō roj′ə nē), *n., pl.* **-nies.** the formation of mountains, as by the folding of the earth's crust. [< Greek *oros* mountain + English *-geny* production or formation of]

o ro tund (ôr′ə tund, ōr′ə tund), *adj.* 1 strong, full, rich, and clear in voice or speech. 2 pompous; bombastic. [alteration of Latin *ore rotundo,* literally, with round mouth]

o ro tun di ty (ôr′ə tun′də tē, ōr′ə tun′-də tē), *n.* quality of being orotund.

O roz co (ô rô′skô), *n.* **José Clemente,** 1883-1949, Mexican painter.

or phan (ôr′fən), *n.* 1 child whose parents are dead; child whose father or mother is dead. 2 an infant animal whose mother is dead. —*adj.* 1 of or for orphans. 2 without a father or mother or both. —*v.t.* make an orphan of. [< Greek *orphanos*]

or phan age (ôr′fə nij), *n.* 1 home for orphans. 2 a being an orphan.

or phan hood (ôr′fən hủd), *n.* condition of being an orphan.

Or phe an (ôr fē′ən, ôr′fē ən), *adj.* 1 of or having to do with Orpheus. 2 like the music of Orpheus.

Or phe us (ôr′fē əs, ôr′fyüs), *n.* (in Greek myths) a musician who played his lyre so sweetly that animals and even trees and rocks followed him.

Or phic (ôr′fik), *adj.* 1 of or having to do with Orpheus. 2 having to do with religious or philosophical cults ascribed to Orpheus as founder. 3 Also, **orphic.** having a hidden meaning; mystic; oracular. 4 like the music of Orpheus; melodious; entrancing.

hat, āge, fär; let, ēqual, tėrm;
it, īce; hot, ōpen, ôrder;
oil, out; cup, pu̇t, rüle;
ch, child; ng, long; sh, she;
th, thin; ᴛʜ, then; zh, measure;

ə represents *a* in about, *e* in taken, *i* in pencil, *o* in lemon, *u* in circus.

< = from, derived from, taken from.

or ris (ôr′is, or′is), *n.* 1 orrisroot. 2 plant that it grows on; any of certain European species of iris. [apparently alteration of *iris*]

or ris root (ôr′is rüt′, ôr′is ru̇t′; or′is rüt′, or′is ru̇t′), *n.* the fragrant rootstock of the orris plant used in making perfume, tooth-powder, etc.

ortho-, *combining form.* 1 straight; upright: *Orthoclase = straight cleavage.* 2 correct: *Orthography = correct spelling.* [< Greek *orthos* straight, correct]

or tho cen ter (ôr′thə sen′tər), *n.* point at which the altitudes of a triangle intersect.

or tho clase (ôr′thə klās, ôr′thə klāz), *n.* a common feld-spar, a silicate of aluminum and potassium, that often occurs in granite and is used in making glass, ceramics, and abrasives. *Formula:* $KAlSi_3O_8$ [< German *Orthoklas* < Greek *ortho-* + *klasis* cleavage]

or tho don tia (ôr′thə don′chə, ôr′thə-don′chē ə), *n.* orthodontics.

or tho don tic (ôr′thə don′tik), *adj.* of or having to do with orthodontics.

or tho don tics (ôr′thə don′tiks), *n.* branch of dentistry that deals with straightening and adjusting teeth. [< *ortho-* + Greek *odontos* tooth]

or tho don tist (ôr′thə don′tist), *n.* dentist who specializes in orthodontics.

or tho dox (ôr′thə doks), *adj.* 1 generally accepted, especially in religion. 2 having generally accepted views or opinions, especially in religion; adhering to established customs and traditions: *an orthodox Methodist.* 3 **Orthodox,** of or having to do with the Eastern Church or any of various national churches conforming to its doctrines. 4 **Orthodox,** of or having to do with the branch of Judaism adhering most closely to ancient ritual, customs, and traditions. 5 approved by convention; usual; customary: *the orthodox Thanksgiving dinner of turkey and pumpkin pie.* [< Greek *orthodoxos* < *orthos* correct + *doxa* opinion]

Orthodox Church, Eastern Church.

or tho dox y (ôr′thə dok′sē), *n., pl.* **-dox ies.** the holding of correct or generally accepted beliefs; orthodox practice, especially in religion; being orthodox.

or tho e pist (ôr thō′ə pist, ôr′thō ə pist), *n.* an expert in orthoepy.

or tho e py (ôr thō′ə pē, ôr′thō ə pē), *n.* 1 correct, accepted, or customary pronunciation. 2 part of grammar that deals with pronunciation; phonology. [< Greek *orthoepia* < *orthos* correct + *epos* utterance]

or tho gen e sis (ôr′thō jen′ə sis), *n.* theory that evolution of new species proceeds along lines predetermined by inherent tendencies and uninfluenced by external forces or natural selection.

or thog o nal (ôr thog′ə nəl), *adj.* having to do with or involving right angles; rectangular. [< Greek *orthogōnios* < *orthos* right + *gōnia* angle]

or tho graph ic (ôr′thə graf′ik), *adj.* 1 having to do with orthography. 2 correct in spelling. 3 orthogonal. **—or′tho graph′i cal ly,** *adv.*

or tho graph i cal (ôr′thə graf′ə kəl), *adj.* orthographic.

or thog ra phy (ôr thog′rə fē), *n., pl.* **-phies.** 1 correct spelling; spelling according to accepted usage. 2 art of spelling; study of spelling. 3 any system of spelling.

or tho pe dic or **or tho pae dic** (ôr′thə-pē′dik), *adj.* of or having to do with orthopedics. **—or′tho pe′di cal ly** or **or′tho pae′di cal ly,** *adv.*

or tho pe dics or **or tho pae dics** (or′-thə pē′diks), *n.* branch of surgery that deals with the deformities and diseases of bones and joints, especially in children. [< *ortho-* + Greek *paidos* child]

or tho pe dist or **or tho pae dist** (ôr′-thə pē′dist), *n.* surgeon who specializes in orthopedics.

or thop ter an (ôr thop′tər ən), *n.* any of an order of insects characterized by mouth-parts adapted for chewing, broad membranous hind wings that fold like a fan beneath hard, narrow forewings, and an incomplete metamorphosis. Crickets, grasshoppers, and cockroaches belong to this order. *—adj.* of or belonging to this order. [< *ortho-* + Greek *pteron* wing]

or thop ter ous (ôr thop′tər əs), *adj.* of or belonging to the orthopterans.

or tho rhom bic (ôr′thə rom′bik), *adj.* (of crystals and crystallization) having three unequal axes intersecting at right angles; rhombic (def. 2).

or to lan (ôr′tl ən), *n.* 1 a small bunting of Europe, northern Africa, or western Asia, the meat of which is regarded as a delicacy. 2 any of various small wild birds of North America, such as the bobolink. [< French]

Or well (ôr′wel), *n.* **George,** 1903-1950, English novelist and essayist, born in India.

Or well i an (ôr wel′ē ən), *adj.* of, having to do with, or suggestive of Orwell or his works: *an Orwellian view of society.*

-ory, *suffix forming adjectives and nouns.* 1 ___ing: *Contradictory = contradicting.* 2 of or having to do with ___ion; characterized by ___ion: *Illusory = of or having to do with illusion. Compulsory = characterized by compulsion.* 3 serving to ___: *Preparatory = serving to prepare.* 4 tending to ___; inclined to ___: *Conciliatory = inclined to conciliate.* 5 place or establishment for ___ing: *Depository = place for depositing.* [< Old French *-oir, -oire* < Latin *-orius, -oria, -orium*]

o ryx (ôr′iks, ōr′iks), *n., pl.* **o ryx es** or **o ryx.** an African antelope with long, nearly straight horns. [< Latin < Greek]

os[1] (os), *n., pl.* ***os sa*** (os′ə). LATIN. bone.

os[2] (os), *n., pl.* ***o ra*** (ôr′ə, ōr′ə). LATIN. mouth; opening.

os-, *prefix.* form of **ob-** in some instances before *c* and *t*, as in *oscine, ostensible.*

Os, osmium.

O.S., Old Style.

O sage (ō′sāj, ō sāj′), *n.* member of a tribe of American Indians, originally inhabiting the region of the Arkansas River and the Missouri River.

Osage orange, 1 an ornamental, spreading tree of the same family as the mulberry, with glossy leaves and hard, bright-orange wood. 2 its inedible, greenish fruit.

O sa ka (ō sä′kə), *n.* seaport in S Japan. 3,156,000.

Os can (os′kən), *n.* 1 one of the ancient inhabitants of Campania. 2 the ancient Italic dialect of Campania, closely related to Umbrian.

Os car (os′kər), *n.* a small golden statuette awarded annually by the Academy of Motion Picture Arts and Sciences for the best performances, production, photography, etc., during the year.

os cil late (os′l āt), *v.,* **-lat ed, -lat ing.** *—v.i.* 1 swing to and fro like a pendulum; move to and fro between two points. 2 vary between opinions, purposes, etc. 3 (in physics) have or produce oscillations. *—v.t.* cause to swing to and fro. [< Latin *oscillatum* swung, rocked < *oscillum* a swing]

os cil la tion (os′l ā′shən), *n.* 1 fact or process of oscillating. 2 a single swing of a vibrating body. 3 in physics: **a** the variation of a quantity from one limit to another, as the voltage of an alternating current. **b** a single swing from one limit to another.

os cil la tor (os′l ā′tər), *n.* 1 person or thing that oscillates. 2 device which converts direct current into an alternating current of a particular frequency. The oscillator in a radio transmitting apparatus is a vacuum tube which produces the carrier wave for a radio signal.

os cil la to ry (os′l ə tôr′ē, os′l ə tōr′ē), *adj.* oscillating.

os cil lo scope (ə sil′ə skōp), *n.* instrument for representing the oscillations of a varying voltage or current on the fluorescent screen of a cathode-ray tube.

oryx
about 5 ft. high at the shoulder

os cine (os′n, os′īn), *n.* any of a large suborder of perching birds that have well-developed vocal organs and usually sing. *—adj.* of or belonging to this group of birds. [< New Latin *Oscines,* suborder of perching birds < Latin *oscinem* songbird used especially for augury < *ob-* to + *canere* sing]

os cu late (os′kyə lāt), *v.t., v.i.,* **-lat ed, -lat ing.** kiss. [< Latin *osculatum* kissed < *osculum* a kiss]

os cu la tion (os′kyə lā′shən), *n.* 1 act of kissing. 2 a kiss.

os cu la to ry (os′kyə lə tôr′ē, os′kyə lə-tōr′ē), *adj.* of or having to do with kissing.

-ose[1], *suffix forming adjectives.* 1 full of; having much or many: *Verbose = having many words.* 2 inclined to; fond of: *Jocose = fond of jest.* 3 like: *Schistose = like schist.* [< Latin *-osum*]

-ose[2], *suffix forming nouns.* in chemistry: 1 type of sugar or other carbohydrate, as in *fructose, lactose.* 2 a primary protein derivative, as in *proteose.* [< French < *(gluc)ose*]

O see (ō′zē, ō′sē), *n.* (in the Douay Bible) Hosea.

o sier (ō′zhər), *n.* 1 any of various willows with tough, flexible branches or shoots.

2 one of these branches, used in weaving baskets or other wickerwork. 3 any of various shrubby dogwoods of North America. —*adj.* made of osiers. [< Middle French]

O si ris (ō sī′ris), *n.* (in Egyptian myths) one of the chief gods of ancient Egypt, ruler of the lower world and judge of the dead. He represented good and productivity and is identified with the Nile.

-osis, *pl.* **-oses.** *suffix.* 1 act or process of ——, as in *osmosis.* 2 abnormal condition, as in *mononucleosis, neurosis.* [< Latin < Greek *-ōsis*]

Os ler (ōs′lər, ōz′lər), *n.* Sir **William,** 1849-1919, Canadian physician, writer, and teacher of medicine.

Os lo (oz′lō, os′lō), *n.* capital of Norway, a seaport in the SE part. From 1624 to 1925 it was called Christiania. 487,000.

Os man (oz män′, os män′), *n.* 1259-1326, founder of the Ottoman Empire.

Os man li (oz man′lē, os man′lē), *n.* 1 Ottoman. 2 language of the Ottoman Turks. —*adj.* Ottoman.

os mi um (oz′mē əm), *n.* a hard, heavy, bluish-white metallic element which occurs with platinum and iridium. Osmium is the heaviest or densest known element and is used for electric-light filaments and phonograph needles. *Symbol:* Os; *atomic number* 76. See pages 326 and 327 for table. [< New Latin < Greek *osmē* odor]

os mose (oz mōs′, o smōs′), *v.,* **-mosed, -mos ing.** —*v.t.* to subject to osmosis. —*v.i.* pass by osmosis.

os mo sis (oz mō′sis, o smō′sis), *n.* 1 the tendency of two solutions with different concentrations of dissolved substances, separated by a semipermeable membrane, to become equally concentrated by diffusion of the solvent of the less concentrated solution through the membrane. Osmosis is the chief means by which nutrients dissolved in fluids pass in and out of plant and animal cells. 2 a gradual, often unconscious, absorbing or understanding of facts, theories, ideas, etc.: *try to learn French by osmosis.* [< New Latin < Greek *ōsmos* a thrust]

os mot ic (oz mot′ik, o smot′ik), *adj.* of or having to do with osmosis. **—os mot′i cal ly,** *adv.*

osmotic pressure, the force exerted by dissolved material in a solution on a semipermeable membrane separating the solution from another solution or from pure solute, such as water.

os prey (os′prē), *n., pl.* **-preys.** 1 a large hawk that feeds on fish; fish hawk. It has white underparts and a dark brown back and wings. 2 an ornamental feather, used for trimming hats, etc. [ultimately < Latin *ossifraga* < *os, ossis* bone + *frangere* to break]

Os sa (os′ə), *n.* **Mount,** mountain in NE Greece. 6490 ft. See **Pelion.**

os se ous (os′ē əs), *adj.* 1 bony. 2 containing bones. [< Latin *osseus*]

os si cle (os′ə kəl), *n.* 1 a small bone, especially of the ear. 2 a small bony or bonelike part.

os si fi ca tion (os′ə fə kā′shən), *n.* 1 process of changing into bone. 2 condition of being changed into bone. 3 a part that is ossified; bony formation. 4 a being or becoming fixed, hardhearted, or very conservative.

os si fy (os′ə fī), *v.t., v.i.,* **-fied, -fy ing.** 1 change into bone; become bone: *The soft parts of a baby's skull ossify as he grows older.* 2 harden like bone; make or become fixed, hardhearted, or very conservative.

Os si ning (os′ə ning), *n.* village in SE New York State. Sing Sing prison is located there. 22,000.

os su ar y (os′yü er′ē, osh′yü er′ē), *n., pl.* **-ar ies.** vault, urn, or the like for the bones of the dead.

os te ich thy an (os′tē ik′thē ən), *n.* any of a class of fishes having a bony skeleton, gills, scales, and fins. Perch, carp, and trout belong to this class. [< Greek *osteon* bone + *ichthys* fish]

Os te ich thy es (os′tē ik′thē ēz), *n.pl.* class of fishes comprising the osteichthyans.

Ost end (ost end′), *n.* seaport in NW Belgium, noted as a summer resort. 57,000.

os ten si ble (o sten′sə bəl), *adj.* according to appearances; declared as genuine; apparent; pretended; professed: *Her ostensible purpose was borrowing sugar, but she really wanted to see the new furniture.* [< Latin *ostensum* shown, ultimately < *ob-* toward + *tendere* to stretch] **—os ten′si bly,** *adv.*

os ten ta tion (os′ten tā′shən), *n.* a showing off; display intended to impress others: *the ostentation of a rich, vain man.* [< Latin *ostentationem,* ultimately < *ob-* toward + *tendere* to stretch]

os ten ta tious (os′ten tā′shəs), *adj.* 1 done for display; intended to attract notice. 2 showing off; liking to attract notice. **—os′ten ta′tious ly,** *adv.* **—os′ten ta′tious ness,** *n.*

os te ol o gy (os′tē ol′ə jē), *n.* branch of anatomy that deals with bones. [< Greek *osteon* bone + English *-logy*]

os te o my e li tis (os′tē ō mī′ə lī′tis), *n.* inflammation of the bone and bone marrow caused by infection with pus-forming microorganisms.

os te o path (os′tē ə path), *n.* person who specializes in osteopathy.

os te o path ic (os′tē ə path′ik), *adj.* of osteopathy or osteopaths.

os te op a thist (os′tē op′ə thist), *n.* osteopath.

os te op a thy (os′tē op′ə thē), *n.* treatment of disease chiefly by manipulating the bones and muscles but also including other types of medical and physical therapy.

ost ler (os′lər), *n.* hostler.

ost mark (ôst′märk′), *n.* unit of money in East Germany, worth about 45 cents. [< German *Ostmark* < *Ost* east + *Mark* mark[2]]

os tra cism (os′trə siz′əm), *n.* 1 banishment from one's native country. 2 (in ancient Greece) a method of temporary banishment practiced in Athens and other cities, determined by popular vote with ballots consisting of tablets of earthenware. 3 a being shut out from society, favor, privileges, or association with one's fellows.

os tra cize (os′trə sīz), *v.t.,* **-cized, -ciz ing.** 1 banish by ostracism. The ancient Greeks ostracized unpopular citizens considered dangerous to the state. 2 shut out from society, favor, privileges, etc. [< Greek *ostrakizein* < *ostrakon* tile, potsherd (because originally potsherds were used in balloting)]

os tra cod (os′trə kod), *n.* any of a subclass of very small, free-swimming, bivalve crustaceans living in fresh or salt water. [< Greek *ostrakōdēs* like a shell < *ostrakon* shell]

os trich (os′trich, ôs′trich), *n.* 1 a large African and Arabian bird that can run swiftly but cannot fly. Ostriches have two toes and are the largest of existing birds. Their large feathers or plumes are used for decorating hats, fans, etc. In former times it was believed that an ostrich buried its head in the sand to avoid oncoming dangers. 2 person who avoids facing reality or an approaching danger. [< Old French *ostrusce* < Popular Latin *avis struthio* < Latin *avis* bird + Late Latin *struthio* ostrich < Greek *strouthos*]

Os tro goth (os′trə goth), *n.* member of the eastern division of Goths that overran the Roman Empire and controlled Italy from A.D. 493 to 555.

Os we go tea (o swē′gō), a North American plant of the mint family, with showy, bright-red flowers. [< *Oswego* River, in central New York State]

O.T., Old Testament.

O thel lo (ə thel′ō), *n.* 1 play by Shakespeare. 2 the principal character in this play, a brave but jealous Moor who kills his wife after being falsely persuaded that she is not true to him. Later he kills himself when he discovers her innocence.

oth er (uᴛʜ′ər), *adj.* 1 remaining: *I am home, but the other members of the family are away now.* 2 additional or further: *They have no other place to go.* 3 not the same as one or more already mentioned: *Come some other day.* 4 different: *I would not have him other than he is.* 5 **every other,** every second; every alternate: *buy milk every other day.* 6 **the other day (night,** etc.), recently. —*pron.* 1 the other one; not the same ones: *Each praises the other.* 2 another person or thing: *There are others to be considered.* 3 **of all others,** more than all others. —*adv.* in any different way; otherwise: *I can't do other than to go.* [Old English *ōther*]

oth er wise (uᴛʜ′ər wīz′), *adv.* 1 in a different way; differently: *I could not do otherwise.* 2 in other ways: *an otherwise satisfactory piece of work.* 3 under other circumstances; in a different condition: *You reminded me of what I would otherwise have forgotten.* —*adj.* different: *It might have been otherwise.* —*conj.* or else; if not: *Come at once; otherwise you will be too late.* [Old English *on ōthre wīsan* in another way]

other world, the life to come; life after death.

oth er world ly (uᴛʜ′ər wėrld′lē), *adj.* 1 devoted to the world to come; preoccupied with life after death. 2 devoted to the world of mind or imagination. 3 of or having to do with a world or realm other than that of actual life. **—oth′er world′li ness,** *n.*

o ti ose (ō′shē ōs, ō′tē ōs), *adj.* 1 at leisure or rest; lazy; idle; inactive. 2 of no value; trifling. 3 having no practical function; superfluous; useless. [< Latin *otiosus* < *otium* leisure] **—o′ti ose′ly,** *adv.*

o ti tis (ō tī′tis), *n.* inflammation of the ear. [< Greek *ous, ōtos* ear + *-itis*]

o to lar yn gol o gy (ō′tō lar′ing gol′ə jē),

ostrich (def. 1) up to 8 ft. tall

n. branch of medicine that deals with diseases of the ear, nose, and throat.

o to lith (ō′tl ith), *n.* a calcareous body in the inner ear of lower vertebrates and some invertebrates, helpful in maintaining equilibrium.

O tran to (ō tran′tō, ō trän′tō), *n.* **Strait of,** strait between Italy and the Balkan Peninsula. It connects the Adriatic Sea with the Ionian Sea. 44 mi. wide.

ot ta va ri ma (ō tä′və rē′mə), stanza of eight lines with the lines according to the rhyme scheme *a b a b a b c c.* In Italian each line normally has eleven syllables; in English ten. [< Italian, octave rhyme]

Ot ta wa (ot′ə wə, ot′ə wä), *n., pl.* **-was** or **-wa** for 3. 1 capital of Canada, in SE Ontario. 291,000. 2 **Ottawa River,** river in SE Canada, flowing southeast into the St. Lawrence River at Montreal. 685 mi. 3 member of a tribe of Algonquian Indians who lived near Lake Superior and Lake Huron.

otter (def. 1)—up to 4 ft. long with the tail

ot ter (ot′ər), *n., pl.* **-ters** or **-ter.** 1 any of several aquatic, carnivorous mammals, of the same family as the minks and weasels, that have short legs with webbed toes and claws and are good swimmers. 2 its fur, usually dark brown. Otter is thick and glossy, somewhat like seal or beaver. [Old English *oter*]

Ot to (ot′ō), *n.* A.D. 912-973, king of Germany from A.D. 936 to 973 and emperor of the Holy Roman Empire from A.D. 962 to 973. He was called "Otto the Great."

ot to man (ot′ə mən), *n.* 1 a low, cushioned seat without back or arms. 2 a cushioned footstool. [< *Ottoman*]

Ot to man (ot′ə mən), *n., pl.* **-mans,** *adj.* —*n.* 1 Turk. 2 Turk descended from the tribe of Osman; Osmanli. —*adj.* 1 Turkish. 2 of the tribe of Osman or the Ottoman Empire; Osmanli.

Ottoman Empire, former empire of the Turks which occupied Asia Minor and parts of northern Africa, southeastern Europe, and southwestern Asia in the middle 1500's; Turkish Empire.

Oua ga dou gou (wä gə dü′gü), *n.* capital of Upper Volta, in the central part. 110,000.

ou bli ette (ü′blē et′), *n.* a secret dungeon with an opening only at the top. [< French < *oublier* forget]

ouch (ouch), *interj.* exclamation of sudden pain. [probably imitative]

oud (üd), *n.* an Arabian lute, usually having seven pairs of strings. [< Arabic *'ūd,* literally, wood]

ought[1] (ôt), *auxiliary v.* 1 have a duty; be obliged: *You ought to obey your parents.* 2 be right or suitable: *It ought to be allowed.* 3 be wise: *I ought to go before it rains.* 4 be expected: *At your age you ought to know better.* 5 be very likely: *It ought to be a fine day tomorrow.* [Old English *āhte,* past tense of *āgan* to owe, own]

ought[2] (ôt), *n., adv.* aught[1].

ought[3] (ôt), *n.* aught[2].

ought n't (ôt′nt), ought not.

ounce[1] (ouns), *n.* 1 unit of weight, $^1/_{16}$ of a pound in avoirdupois, and $^1/_{12}$ of a pound in troy weight. See **measure** for table. 2 unit of volume for liquids; fluid ounce. See **measure** for table. 3 a little bit; very small amount. [< Old French *unce* < Latin *uncia* twelfth part. Doublet of INCH.]

ounce[2] (ouns), *n.* a large, carnivorous cat having thick, heavy, whitish or brownish hair with irregular dark spots resembling those of a leopard; snow leopard. It is found in the mountains of central Asia. [< Old French *once, lonce* < Latin *lynx* lynx]

our (our, är), *adj.* possessive form of **we.** of us; belonging to us: *We need our coats now.* [Old English *ūre*]

Our Father, the Lord's Prayer.

Our Lady, the Virgin Mary.

ours (ourz, ärz), *pron.* possessive form of **we.** the one or ones belonging to us: *This garden is ours. Ours is a large house.*

our self (our self′, är self′), *pron.* myself. *Ourself* is used by an author, king, judge, etc.: *"We will ourself reward the victor," said the queen.*

our selves (our selvz′, är selvz′), *pron.pl.* 1 the emphatic form of **we** or **us:** *We ourselves will do the work.* 2 the reflexive form of **us:** *We cook for ourselves.* 3 our real or true selves: *We weren't ourselves when we said that.*

-ous, *suffix forming adjectives from nouns.* 1 full of; having much; having: *Joyous = full of joy.* 2 characterized by: *Zealous = characterized by zeal.* 3 having the nature of: *Idolatrous = having the nature of an idolater.* 4 of or having to do with: *Monogamous = having to do with monogamy.* 5 like: *Thunderous = like thunder.* 6 committing or practicing: *Bigamous = practicing bigamy.* 7 inclined to: *Blasphemous = inclined to blasphemy.* 8 (in chemistry) indicating the presence in a compound of the designated element in a lower valence than indicated by the suffix *-ic,* as in *stannous, ferrous, sulfurous.* [< Old French *-os, -us* < Latin *-osum*]

ou sel (ü′zəl), *n.* ouzel.

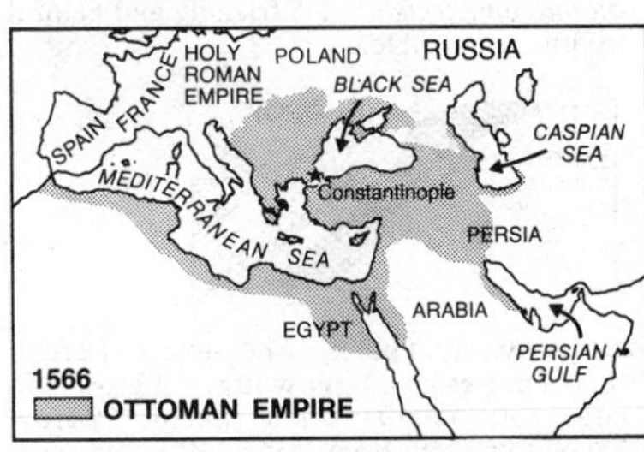

Ouse River (üz), 1 river in E England, flowing into the Wash. 160 mi. 2 river in N England. It flows south and joins the Trent River to form the Humber. 57 mi.

oust (oust), *v.t.* force out; drive out; expel. [< Anglo-French *ouster* < Old French *oster,* ultimately < Latin *ob-* against + *stare* to stand]

oust er (ou′stər), *n.* an ousting, especially an illegal forcing of a person out of his property.

out (out), *adv.* 1 away; forth: *rush out. Spread the rug out.* 2 not in or at a position, state, etc.: *The miners are going out on strike.* 3 not at home; away from one's office, work, etc. 4 into the open air: *Let's go out before it rains.* 5 from the usual place, condition, position, etc.: *Put the light out.* 6 not correct: *be out in one's calculations.* 7 from a state of composure, satisfaction, or harmony: *feel put out, fall out with a friend.* 8 at a money loss: *be out ten dollars.* 9 into the open; made public; made known; into being; so as to be seen: *Flowers came out.* 10 to an end; to completion or exhaustion: *play a game out, before the year runs out.* 11 aloud; loudly: *Speak out.* 12 completely; effectively: *fit out for an expedition.* 13 so as to project or extend: *stand out, stick out one's hand.* 14 to others: *Give out the books.* 15 from a number, stock, store, source, cause, material, etc.; from among others: *Pick out an apple for me. She picked out a new coat.* 16 (in baseball) so as to be retired from offensive play: *He flied out.* 17 into society: *She came out last year.* 18 **out and away,** beyond all others; by far: *She is out and away the best player.* 19 **out of, a** from within. **b** away from; beyond: *move out of hearing. The jet plane was soon out of sight. That style went out of fashion.* **c** not within: *out of town.* **d** not having; without: *We are out of coffee.* **e** so as to take away: *She was cheated out of her money.* **f** from: *a house made out of brick. My dress is made out of silk.* **g** from among: *choose one out of many.* **h** because of: *I only went out of curiosity.*

—*adj.* 1 not in possession or control: *The Republicans are out, the Democrats in.* 2 not in use, action, fashion, etc.: *The fire is out. Last year's fad is out this season.* 3 (in baseball) not succeeding in reaching base or advancing from one base to another: *The outfielder caught the fly and the batter was out.* 4 external; exterior; outer. 5 outlying: *an out island.* 6 not usual or normal: *an out size.* 7 for that which is outgoing; outgoing: *an out basket for mail. I took an out flight.* 8 **out for,** looking for; trying to get: *be out for a good time.* 9 **out to,** eagerly or determinedly trying to: *be out to show them up.*

—*n.* 1 **outs,** *pl.* people not in office; political party not in power. 2 something wrong. 3 that which is omitted. 4 in baseball: **a** a being out. **b** a putting out. 5 defense or excuse: *have an out for stealing.* 6 (in tennis) serve or return that lands outside the lines. 7 **at outs** or **on the outs,** quarreling; disagreeing: *be on the outs with a friend.*

—*prep.* 1 from out; forth from: *He went out the door.* 2 INFORMAL. out along: *Drive out Main Street.*

—*v.i.* go or come out; be disclosed: *The truth will out.*

[Old English *ūt*]

out-, *prefix.* 1 outward; forth; away: *Outbound = outward bound. Outburst = a bursting forth.* 2 at a distance; outside: *Outlying = lying outside.* 3 more than or longer than: *Outlive = live longer than.* 4 better than: *Outdo = do better than.* [< *out*]

hat, āge, fär; let, ēqual, tėrm;
it, īce; hot, ōpen, ôrder;
oil, out; cup, pu̇t, rüle;
ch, child; ng, long; sh, she;
th, thin; ᴛʜ, then; zh, measure;

ə represents *a* in about, *e* in taken, *i* in pencil, *o* in lemon, *u* in circus.

< = from, derived from, taken from.

out-and-out (out′n out′), *adj.* thorough; complete: *an out-and-out lie.*

out back (out′bak′), *n.* 1 the Australian hinterland or back country. 2 the hinterland of any country.

out bal ance (out bal′əns), *v.t.,* **-anced, -anc ing.** outweigh.

out bid (out bid′), *v.t.,* **-bid, -bid** or **-bid den** (-bid′n), **-bid ding.** bid higher than (someone else).

out board (out′bôrd′, out′bōrd′), *adj., adv.* 1 outside the hull of a ship or boat. 2 away from the center line of a ship, boat, or aircraft.

outboard motor

outboard motor, a gasoline motor, often portable, connected by a vertical driveshaft to a propeller and clamped to the outside of the stern of a small boat.

out bound (out′bound′), *adj.* outward bound: *an outbound ship, outbound flights.*

out brave (out brāv′), *v.t.,* **-braved, -brav ing.** 1 face bravely. 2 be braver than.

out break (out′brāk′), *n.* 1 a breaking out or forth: *the outbreak of war, an outbreak of smallpox.* 2 a violent public disturbance; riot; insurrection.

out breed (out′brēd), *v.t.,* **-bred** (-bred), **-breed ing.** breed from individuals or stocks that are not closely related.

out build ing (out′bil′ding), *n.* shed or building built near a main building: *Barns are outbuildings on a farm.*

out burst (out′bėrst′), *n.* a bursting out or forth; eruption: *an outburst of laughter.*

out cast (out′kast′), *n.* person or animal cast out from home and friends: *Criminals are outcasts of society.* —*adj.* being an outcast; homeless; friendless.

out class (out klas′), *v.t.* be of higher class than; be much better than.

out come (out′kum′), *n.* result; consequence: *the outcome of a race.*

out crop (*n.* out′krop′; *v.* out krop′), *n., v.,* **-cropped, -crop ping.** —*n.* 1 a coming (of a rock, stratum, etc.) to the surface of the earth: *the outcrop of a vein of coal.* 2 part that comes to the surface: *The outcrop that we found proved to be very rich in gold.* —*v.i.* come to the surface; appear.

out cry (out′krī′), *n., pl.* **-cries.** 1 a crying out; sudden cry or scream. 2 a great noise or clamor; uproar.

out dat ed (out dā′tid), *adj.* out-of-date; old-fashioned; obsolete.

out did (out did′), *v.* pt. of **outdo.**

out dis tance (out dis′təns), *v.t.,* **-tanced, -tanc ing.** leave behind; outstrip.

out do (out dü′), *v.t.,* **-did, -done, -do ing.** do more or better than; surpass. See **excel** for synonym study.

out done (out dun′), *v.* pp. of **outdo.**

out door (out′dôr′, out′dōr′), *adj.* 1 done, used, or living outdoors: *outdoor games, an outdoor meal.* 2 designed for the outdoors; open-air: *an outdoor theater.*

out doors (out′dôrz′, out′dōrz′), *adv.* out in the open air; not indoors or in the house. —*n.* the world outside of houses; the open air.

out er (out′ər), *adj.* 1 on the outside; external: *an outer garment.* 2 farther out from a center: *the sun's outer corona.*

outer ear, external ear.

Outer Mongolia, Mongolian People's Republic. —**Outer Mongolian.**

out er most (ou′tər mōst), *adj.* farthest out.

outer space, 1 space immediately beyond the earth's atmosphere. 2 space between the planets or between the stars.

out face (out fās′), *v.t.,* **-faced, -fac ing.** 1 face boldly; defy. 2 stare at (a person) until he stops staring back; browbeat; abash.

out field (out′fēld′), *n.* 1 the part of a baseball field beyond the diamond or infield. 2 the three players in the outfield.

out field er (out′fēl′dər), *n.* a baseball player stationed in the outfield.

out fight (out fīt′), *v.t.,* **-fought** (-fôt′), **-fight ing.** fight better than; surpass in a fight.

out fit (out′fit), *n., v.,* **-fit ted, -fit ting.** —*n.* 1 all the articles necessary for any undertaking or purpose: *a sailor's outfit, an outfit for a camping trip.* 2 group working together, such as a military unit, business organization, etc. —*v.t.* furnish with everything necessary for any purpose; equip: *We outfitted ourselves for camp.* —**out′fit′ter,** *n.*

out flank (out flangk′), *v.t.* 1 go or extend beyond the flank of (an opposing army, etc.); turn the flank of. 2 get the better of; circumvent.

out flow (out′flō′), *n.* 1 a flowing out: *the outflow from a waterpipe, an outflow of sympathy.* 2 that which flows out.

out fox (out foks′), *v.t.* outsmart.

out gen er al (out jen′ər əl), *v.t.,* **-aled, -al ing** or **-alled, -al ling.** be a better general than; get the better of by superior strategy.

out go (out′gō′), *n., pl.* **-goes.** what goes out; what is paid out; amount that is spent; outlay; expenditure.

out go ing (out′gō′ing), *n.* 1 a going out. 2 that which goes out. —*adj.* 1 outward bound; going out; departing: *an outgoing ship, the outgoing tide.* 2 retiring or defeated: *an outgoing legislator.* 3 friendly and helpful to others; sociable.

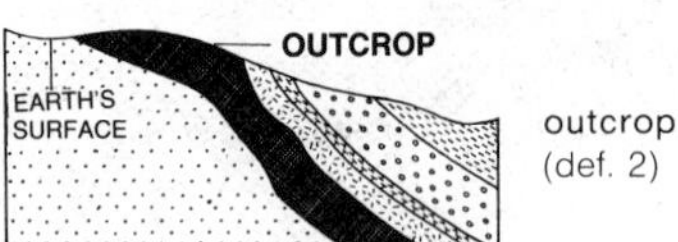

outcrop (def. 2)

out grow (out grō′), *v.t.,* **-grew** (-grü′), **-grown** (-grōn′), **-grow ing.** 1 grow too large for: *outgrow one's clothes.* 2 grow beyond or away from; get rid of by growing older: *outgrow early friends, outgrow a babyish habit.* 3 grow faster or taller than.

out growth (out′grōth′), *n.* 1 a natural development, product, or result: *This large store is an outgrowth of a little shop started ten years ago.* 2 something that has grown out; offshoot: *A corn is an outgrowth on a toe.* 3 a growing out or forth: *the outgrowth of new leaves in the spring.*

out guess (out ges′), *v.t.* be too clever for; get the better of; outwit.

out house (out′hous′), *n., pl.* **-hous es** (-hou′ziz). 1 a separate building used in connection with a main building; outbuilding. 2 an outdoor toilet.

out ing (ou′ting), *n.* a short pleasure trip; walk or airing; holiday spent outdoors away from home: *On Sunday the family went on an outing to the beach.*

out land er (out′lan′dər), *n.* 1 foreigner; alien. 2 INFORMAL. outsider; stranger.

out land ish (out lan′dish), *adj.* 1 not familiar; strange or ridiculous; odd: *an outlandish hat.* 2 looking or sounding as if it belonged to a foreign country: *their outlandish customs, an outlandish dialect.* 3 far removed from civilization; out-of-the-way; remote: *an outlandish place.* —**out-land′ish ly,** *adv.* —**out land′ish ness,** *n.*

out last (out last′), *v.t.* 1 last longer than. 2 outlive; survive.

out law (out′lô′), *n.* 1 a lawless person; criminal. 2 person outside the protection of the law; exile; outcast. —*v.t.* 1 make or declare (a person) an outlaw. 2 make or declare illegal: *A group of nations agreed to outlaw war.* 3 deprive of legal force. An outlawed debt is one that cannot be collected because it has been due too long. [Old English *ūtlaga* < Scandinavian (Old Icelandic) *ūtlagi* < *ūt* out + *lög* law]

out law ry (out′lô′rē), *n., pl.* **-ries.** 1 a being condemned as an outlaw; a being outlawed. Outlawry was formerly used as a punishment in England. 2 condition of being an outlaw.

out lay (*n.* out′lā′; *v.* out lā′), *n., v.,* **-laid** (-lād′), **-lay ing.** —*n.* 1 a laying out money; spending; expense: *a large outlay for clothing.* 2 the amount spent; expenditure. —*v.t.* expend.

out let (out′let), *n.* 1 means or place of letting out or getting out; way out; vent; opening: *the outlet of a lake, an outlet for one's energies.* 2 market for a product. 3 store selling the products of a particular manufacturer. 4 point in an electric circuit where an electric plug may be inserted to receive power, usually set in a wall.

out line (out′līn′), *n., v.,* **-lined, -lin ing.** —*n.* 1 line that shows the shape of an object; line that bounds a figure: *We saw the outlines of the mountains against the evening sky.* See synonym study below. 2 a drawing or style of drawing that gives only outer lines without shading. 3 a general plan, sketch, account, or report, giving only the main features: *an outline of a novel, an outline of the work planned during the term.* 4 **in outline, a** with only the outline shown. **b** with only the main features. —*v.t.* 1 draw the outer line of. 2 give a plan of; sketch: *She outlined their trip abroad.*

Syn. *n.* 1 **Outline, contour, profile** mean the line or lines showing the shape of something. **Outline** applies to the line marking the outer limits or edge of an object, figure, or shape: *We could see the outline of a man.* **Contour** emphasizes the shape shown by the outline: *The contours of his face are rugged.* **Profile** applies to the side view of something in outline, especially the face in a side view, seen against a background: *a sketch of a model's head in profile.*

out live (out liv′), *v.t.,* **-lived, -liv ing.** live or last longer than; survive; outlast: *The idea was good once, but it has outlived its usefulness.*

out look (out′lu̇k′), *n.* 1 what one sees on looking out; view: *The room has a pleasant outlook.* 2 what seems likely to happen; prospect: *The outlook for skiing is very good; it looks as if it will snow.* 3 way of thinking about things; attitude of mind; point of view:

hat, āge, fär; let, ēqual, tėrm;
it, īce; hot, ōpen, ôrder;
oil, out; cup, pu̇t, rüle;
ch, child; ng, long; sh, she;
th, thin; ᴛʜ, then; zh, measure;

ə represents *a* in about, *e* in taken, *i* in pencil, *o* in lemon, *u* in circus.

< = from, derived from, taken from.

a cheerful outlook on life. 4 tower or other place to watch from; lookout.

out ly ing (out′lī′ing), *adj.* lying outside the boundary; far from the center; remote: *outlying suburbs.*

out ma neu ver (out′mə nü′vər), *v.t.* outdo in maneuvering; get the better of by maneuvering.

out match (out mach′), *v.t.* surpass; outdo.

out mod ed (out mō′did), *adj.* out of fashion; not in present use; outdated: *an outmoded custom, outmoded machinery.*

out most (out′mōst), *adj.* farthest out; outermost.

out num ber (out num′bər), *v.t.* be more than; exceed in number: *They outnumbered us three to one.*

out-of-bounds (out′əv boundz′), *adj., adv.* outside the boundary line; out of play.

out-of-date (out′əv dāt′), *adj.* old-fashioned; not in present use; outmoded.

out-of-door (out′əv dôr′, out′əv dōr′), *adj.* outdoor.

out-of-doors (out′əv dôrz′, out′əv dōrz′), *adj.* outdoor. *—adv., n.* outdoors.

out-of-the-way (out′əv ᴛʜə wā′), *adj.* 1 seldom visited; remote; unfrequented; secluded: *an out-of-the-way cottage.* 2 seldom met with; unusual: *out-of-the-way bits of information.*

out pa tient (out′pā′shənt), *n.* patient receiving treatment at a hospital but not staying there.

out play (out plā′), *v.t.* play better than.

out point (out point′), *v.t.* 1 score more points than. 2 sail closer to the wind than.

out post (out′pōst′), *n.* 1 guard, or small number of soldiers, placed at some distance from an army or camp to prevent surprise attacks. 2 place where they are stationed. 3 a settlement or village in an outlying place: *a frontier outpost.*

out pour (*n.* out′pôr′, out′pōr′; *v.* out pôr′, out pōr′), *n.* 1 a pouring out. 2 that which is poured out. *—v.t.* pour out.

out pour ing (out′pôr′ing, out′pōr′ing), *n.* 1 anything that is poured out; outflow. 2 a pouring out. 3 an uncontrolled expression of thoughts or feelings: *an outpouring of grief.*

out put (out′pu̇t′), *n.* 1 what is put out; amount produced; product or yield: *the daily output of automobiles.* 2 a putting forth: *a sudden output of effort.* 3 power or energy produced by a machine, etc. 4 information put out by or delivered from the storage unit of a computer.

out rage (out′rāj), *n., v.,* **-raged, -rag ing.** *—n.* act showing no regard for the rights or feelings of others; an overturning of the rights of others by force; act of violence; offense; insult; injury. *—v.t.* 1 offend greatly; do violence to; insult; injure. 2 break (the law, a rule of morality, etc.) openly; treat as nothing at all. [< Old French, literally, a going beyond propriety < *outre* beyond < Latin *ultra*]

out ra geous (out rā′jəs), *adj.* very offensive or insulting; shocking. **—out ra′geous ly,** *adv.* **—out ra′geous ness,** *n.*

out ran (out ran′), *v.* pt. of **outrun.**

out rank (out rangk′), *v.t.* rank higher than.

ou tré (ü trā′), *adj.* passing the bounds of what is usual and considered proper; eccentric; bizarre. [< French]

out reach (out rēch′), *v.t.* 1 reach beyond. 2 reach out; stretch out; extend.

out ride (out rīd′), *v.t.,* **-rode, -rid den, -rid ing.** ride faster, better, or farther than.

out rid er (out′rī′dər), *n.* servant or attendant riding on a horse before or beside a carriage, wagon, etc.

out rig ger (out′rig′ər), *n.* 1 framework extending outward from the side of a light boat or canoe and ending in a float. It keeps the boat from turning over. 2 bracket extending outward from either side of a boat to hold an oarlock. 3 boat equipped with such brackets. 4 spar projecting outward from the rail of a ship on which a sail may be set. 5 a projecting frame or spar connecting extended parts of an aircraft, such as the tail unit, with the main structure.

outrigger (def. 1)

out right (out′rīt′), *adv.* 1 not gradually; altogether; entirely: *sell a thing outright.* 2 without restraint; openly: *I laughed outright.* 3 at once; on the spot: *She fainted outright.* *—adj.* 1 complete; thorough: *an outright loss.* 2 downright; straightforward; direct: *an outright refusal.* 3 entire; total.

out run (out run′), *v.t.,* **-ran, -run, -run ning.** 1 run faster than. 2 leave behind; run beyond; pass the limits of.

out sell (out sel′), *v.t.,* **-sold** (-sōld′), **-sell ing.** 1 outdo in selling; sell more than: *He outsold every salesman in the company last year.* 2 be sold in greater quantity than: *This brand outsells all other brands on the market.*

out set (out′set′), *n.* a setting out; start; beginning: *At the outset, it looked like a nice day.*

out shine (out shīn′), *v.t.,* **-shone** (-shōn′), **-shin ing.** 1 shine more brightly than. 2 be more brilliant or excellent than; surpass.

out shoot (out shüt′), *v.t.,* **-shot** (-shot′), **-shoot ing.** 1 shoot better or farther than. 2 shoot beyond.

out side (out′sīd′; *prep. also* out′sīd′), *n.* 1 side or surface that is out; outer part: *the outside of a house.* 2 external appearance. 3 space or position that is beyond or not inside. 4 **at the outside,** at the utmost limit: *I can do it in a week, at the outside.* *—adj.* 1 on the outside; of or nearer the outside: *the outside leaves.* 2 not belonging to a certain group, set, district, etc.: *Outside people tried to get control of the business.* 3 being, acting, done, or originating without or beyond a wall, boundary, etc.: *Outside noises disturbed the class.* 4 reaching the utmost limit; highest or largest; maximum: *an outside estimate of the cost.* 5 barely possible; very slight: *The team has an outside chance to win.* *—adv.* on or to the outside; outdoors: *Run outside and play.* *—prep.* 1 INFORMAL. with the exception of: *Outside my cousin, everyone there was a stranger to me.* 2 out of; beyond the limits of: *Stay outside the house. That is outside my plans.* 3 **outside of,** INFORMAL. **a** with the exception of: *Outside of tennis, she had no interest in sports.* **b** beyond the limits of: *act outside of the law. The relatives waited outside of the chapel.*

out sid er (out′sī′dər), *n.* person not belonging to a particular group, set, company, party, district, etc.

out size (out′sīz′), *adj.* larger than the usual size. *—n.* article of clothing, etc., larger than the usual size.

out sized (out′sīzd′), *adj.* outsize.

out skirts (out′skėrts′), *n.pl.* the outer parts or edges of a town, district, etc., or of a subject of discussion; outlying parts.

out smart (out smärt′), *v.t.* outdo in cleverness; outwit.

out soar (out sôr′, out sōr′), *v.t.* soar above or beyond.

out spo ken (out′spō′kən), *adj.* not reserved; frank: *an outspoken person, outspoken criticism.* See **frank**[1] for synonym study. **—out′spo′ken ly,** *adv.* **—out′spo′ken ness,** *n.*

out spread (*adj.* out′spred′; *v.* out spred′), *adj., v.,* **-spread, -spread ing.** *—adj.* spread out; extended: *an eagle with outspread wings.* *—v.t.* spread out; extend.

out stand ing (out stan′ding), *adj.* 1 standing out from others; prominent or conspicuous; well-known; important; eminent: *an outstanding work of fiction.* 2 unsettled or unpaid: *outstanding debts, an outstanding claim.* 3 projecting. **—out stand′ing ly,** *adv.*

out sta tion (out′stā′shən), *n.* an outlying military post, trading post, etc., in a sparsely settled region.

out stay (out stā′), *v.t.* 1 stay longer than: *outstay the other guests at a party, outstay one's welcome.* 2 outlast.

out stretched (out′strecht′), *adj.* stretched out; extended: *She welcomed her old friend with outstretched arms.*

out strip (out strip′), *v.t.,* **-stripped, -strip ping.** 1 go faster than; leave behind in a race: *A horse can outstrip a man.* 2 do better than; excel: *He can outstrip most boys in sports.*

out ward (out′wərd), *adj.* 1 going toward the outside; turned toward the outside: *an outward motion, an outward glance.* 2 outer; external: *to all outward appearances.* 3 that can be seen; plain to see: *the outward man, outward behavior.* *—adv.* 1 toward the outside; away: *A porch extends outward from the house.* 2 on the outside: *turn a coat with the lining outward.* **—out′ward ness,** *n.*

out ward ly (out′wərd lē), *adv.* 1 on the outside or outer surface; externally. 2 in appearance: *Though frightened she remained outwardly calm.*

out wards (out′wərdz), *adv.* outward.

out wear (out wer′, out war′), *v.t.,* **-wore** (-wôr′, -wōr′), **-worn, -wear ing.** 1 wear longer than: *Some plastics outwear leather.* 2 wear out. 3 outgrow.

out weigh (out wā′), *v.t.* 1 weigh more than. 2 exceed in value, importance, influence, etc.: *The advantages of the plan outweigh its disadvantages.*

out wit (out wit′), *v.t.*, **-wit ted, -wit ting.** get the better of by being more intelligent; be too clever for: *The prisoner outwitted his guards and escaped.*

out work (*n.* out′wėrk′; *v.* out wėrk′), *n.* a part of the fortifications of a place lying outside the main ones; a less important defense. —*v.t.* surpass in working; work harder or faster than.

out worn (*adj.* out′wôrn′, out′wōrn′; *v.* out wôrn′, out wōrn′), *adj.* 1 worn out: *outworn clothes.* 2 out-of-date; outgrown: *outworn habits.* —*v.* pp. of **outwear.**

ou zel (ü′zəl), *n.* 1 a black thrush of Europe. 2 water ouzel. Also, **ousel.** [Old English *ōsle*]

ou zo (ü′zō), *n., pl.* **-zos.** a licorice-flavored Greek liqueur. [< New Greek *ouzon*]

o va (ō′və), *n.* pl. of **ovum.**

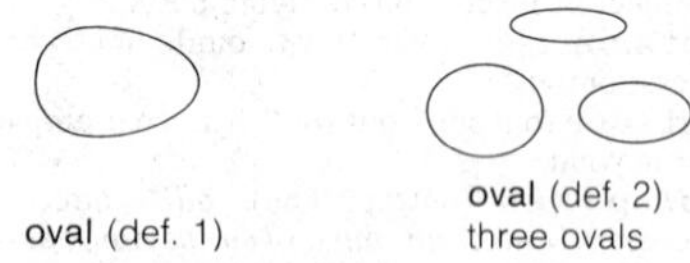

oval (def. 1)

oval (def. 2)
three ovals

o val (ō′vəl), *adj.* 1 egg-shaped. 2 shaped like an ellipse. —*n.* something having an oval shape. —**o′val ly,** *adv.*

o var i an (ō ver′ē ən, ō var′ē ən), *adj.* of or having to do with an ovary.

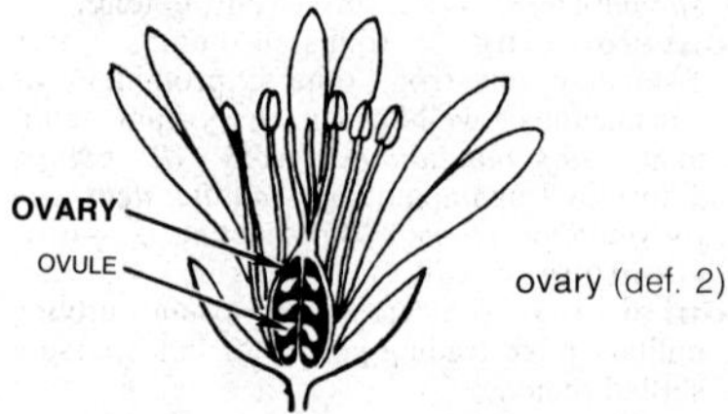

ovary (def. 2)

o var y (ō′vər ē), *n., pl.* **o var ies.** 1 the organ of a female animal in which eggs and sex hormones are produced. 2 the enlarged lower part of the pistil of a flowering plant, enclosing the ovules. [< Latin *ovum* egg]

o vate (ō′vāt), *adj.* egg-shaped: *an ovate leaf.*

o va tion (ō vā′shən), *n.* 1 an enthusiastic public welcome; burst of loud clapping or cheering: *The President received a great ovation.* 2 (in ancient Rome) a lesser celebration than a triumph, given to a victorious commander. [< Latin *ovationem* < *ovare* rejoice]

ov en (uv′ən), *n.* 1 an enclosed space, usually in a stove or near a fireplace, for baking food. 2 kiln. [Old English *ofen*]

ov en bird (uv′ən bėrd′), *n.* any of various birds that build nests with dome-shaped roofs, especially a North American warbler that nests on the ground.

o ver (ō′vər), *prep.* 1 directly above in place or position; higher up than: *the roof over one's head.* 2 above in authority, power, etc.: *We have a captain over us.* 3 above and to the other side of; across: *leap over a wall, climb over a hill.* 4 on the other side of: *lands over the sea.* 5 forward and down from: *The ball rolled over the edge of the cliff.* 6 on; upon: *a coat over one's shoulders, a blanket lying over a bed.* 7 at all or various places on: *A blush came over her face. Farms were scattered over the valley.* 8 here and there on or in; throughout: *We shall travel over Europe.* 9 through every part of; all through: *go over one's notes before a test.* 10 from end to end of; along: *We drove over the new thruway.* 11 during: *over a period of years.* 12 more than; beyond: *over sixty miles. I like golf over all other sports.* 13 in reference to; concerning; about: *worry over one's health.* 14 while engaged in or concerned with: *talk over dinner.* 15 until the end of: *stay over the weekend.* 16 by means of: *talk over the telephone.* 17 **over and above,** in addition to; besides.
—*adv.* 1 above; on high: *hang over.* 2 from side to side; across any intervening space; to the other side: *Come over to my house.* 3 from one to another: *Hand the money over.* 4 over and above the top of something: *boil over, climb over into the garden.* 5 forward and down: *push over, fall over.* 6 so as to cover the surface, or affect the whole surface: *paint a wall over. Spread the canvas over the new cement.* 7 on the other side; at some distance: *over in Europe, over by the hill.* 8 from beginning to end: *talk a matter over, read a newspaper over.* 9 in excess or addition: *receive the full sum and something over.* 10 so as to bring the upper side or end down or under: *turn over a page.* 11 through a region, area, etc.: *travel all over.* 12 again; once more; in repetition: *do a thing over.* 13 excessively; too: *I am not over well.* 14 throughout or beyond a period of time: *Please stay over until Monday.*
over again, once more.
over against, a opposite to; in front of. **b** so as to bring out a difference.
over and over, again and again; repeatedly.
over with, INFORMAL. done; finished.
—*adj.* 1 at an end; done; past: *The play is over.* 2 extra; surplus: *There was a copy of the bylaws for each club member and three copies over.* 3 upper; higher up: *the over eyelid.* 4 serving to cover something; outer: *an over drapery.*
—*n.* 1 amount in excess; extra. 2 (in military use) a shot which strikes beyond the target. [Old English *ofer*]

over-, *prefix.* 1 above: *Overhead* = *above the head.* 2 higher in rank: *Overlord* = *superior lord.* 3 across: *Overseas* = *across the seas.* 4 too; too much; too long, etc.: *Overcrowded* = *too crowded. Overburden* = *burden too much.* 5 above normal; extra: *Oversize* = *above normal size. Overtime* = *extra time.* 6 being above; worn as an outer covering: *Overcoat* = *coat worn as an outer covering.* [< *over*]

If an adjective beginning with *over* is not specially defined in this dictionary, its meaning may be learned by putting *too* in place of *over*. Some such words are:

o′ver a bun′dant
o′ver am bi′tious
o′ver anx′ious
o′ver bold′
o′ver care′ful
o′ver cau′tious
o′ver com pet′i tive
o′ver con′fi dent
o′ver con serv′a tive
o′ver crit′i cal
o′ver cur′i ous
o′ver dig′ni fied
o′ver ea′ger
o′ver e mo′tion al
o′ver en thu′si as′tic
o′ver ex cit′a ble
o′ver ex plic′it
o′ver ex u′ber ant
o′ver fa mil′iar
o′ver fond′
o′ver fre′quent
o′ver gen′er ous
o′ver greed′y
o′ver hast′y
o′ver jeal′ous
o′ver lib′er al
o′ver long′
o′ver mod′est
o′ver neg′li gent
o′ver nerv′ous
o′ver o be′di ent
o′ver op′ti mis′tic
o′ver pop′u lous
o′ver pub′li cized
o′ver pre cise′
o′ver pro tec′tive
o′ver proud′
o′ver rash′
o′ver right′eous
o′ver ripe′
o′ver scru′pu lous
o′ver sen′si tive
o′ver ser′i ous
o′ver skep′ti cal
o′ver strict′
o′ver stu′di ous
o′ver sub′tle
o′ver suf fi′cient
o′ver sus pi′cious
o′ver sweet′
o′ver talk′a tive
o′ver tech′ni cal
o′ver word′y
o′ver zeal′ous

If a noun beginning with *over* is not specially defined in this dictionary, its meaning may be learned by putting *too much* or *excessive* in place of *over*. Some such words are:

o′ver a bun′dance
o′ver ac tiv′i ty
o′ver anx i′e ty
o′ver cau′tion
o′ver con′fi dence
o′ver em′pha sis
o′ver ex′er cise
o′ver ex er′tion
o′ver ex pan′sion
o′ver in dul′gence
o′ver pay′ment
o′ver pop′u la′tion
o′ver praise′
o′ver sim′pli fi ca′tion
o′ver spe′cial i za′tion
o′ver spec′u la′tion
o′ver strain′
o′ver val′u a′tion

If a verb beginning with *over* is not specially defined in this dictionary, its meaning may be learned by putting ___ *too much* in place of *over* ___. Some such words are:

o′ver buy′
o′ver com′pli cate
o′ver cook′
o′ver e lab′or ate
o′ver ex′er cise
o′ver ex ert′
o′ver ex pand′
o′ver ex tend′
o′ver feed′
o′ver heat′
o′ver in dulge′
o′ver pay′
o′ver pop′u late
o′ver praise′
o′ver price′
o′ver prize′
o′ver pro duce′
o′ver pro tect′
o′ver pro vide′
o′ver sim′pli fy
o′ver spend′
o′ver stim′u late
o′ver strain′
o′ver stud′y
o′ver tire′
o′ver val′ue

o ver a chiev er (ō′vər ə chē′vər), *n.* pupil whose work is better than it might be expected from his intelligence tests.

o ver act (ō′vər akt′), *v.t., v.i.* act to excess; overdo in acting; act (a part) in an exaggerated manner.

o ver ac tive (ō′vər ak′tiv), *adj.* too active; active to excess; hyperactive. —**o′ver ac′tive ly,** *adv.*

o ver age[1] (ō′vər āj′), *adj.* past a certain age; past the age of greatest use, eligibility, etc. [< *over-* + *age*]

o ver age[2] (ō′vər ij), *n.* surplus of any commodity. [< *over* + *-age*]

o ver all (ō′vər ôl′), *adj.* 1 from one end to the other: *an overall measurement.* 2 including everything: *an overall estimate.* —*adv.* generally.

o ver alls (ō′vər ôlz′), *n.pl.* loose trousers, usually of denim and with a piece covering the chest, worn over clothes to keep them clean.

o ver arch (ō′vər ärch′), *v.t.* 1 arch over; span with or like an arch: *The street was overarched by elm trees.* 2 curve like an arch.

o ver arm (ō′vər ärm′), *adj.* with the arm raised above the shoulder; overhand.

o ver awe (ō′vər ô′), *v.t.*, **-awed, -aw ing.** overcome or restrain with awe: *Eclipses of the sun overawed primitive man.*

o ver bal ance (ō′vər bal′əns), *v.t.*, **-anced, -anc ing.** 1 be greater than in weight, importance, value, etc.: *The gains* *overbalanced the losses.* 2 cause to lose balance: *Don't lean over the side, your weight will overbalance the canoe and upset it.*

o ver bear (ō′vər ber′, ō′vər bar′), *v.*, **-bore** (-bôr′, -bōr′), **-borne** (-bôrn′, -bōrn′), **-bear ing.** —*v.t.* 1 overcome by weight or force; oppress; master: *They overbore all my objections.* 2 bear down by weight or force; overthrow; upset. —*v.i.* bear or produce too much or too many.

o ver bear ing (ō′vər ber′ing, ō′vər-bar′ing), *adj.* inclined to dictate; forcing others to one's own will; domineering. See **proud** for synonym study. —**o′ver-bear′ing ly,** *adv.*

o ver bid (*v.* ō′vər bid′; *n.* ō′vər bid′), *v.*, **-bid, -bid** or **-bid den** (-bid′n), **-bid ding,** *n.* —*v.t.* 1 bid more than the value of (a thing). 2 outbid. —*v.i.* bid too high. —*n.* an overbidding.

o ver blown (ō′vər blōn′), *adj.* 1 more than fullblown; between ripeness and decay: *an overblown flower.* 2 blown over, down, or away. 3 carried too far; exaggerated; overdone: *overblown interpretations of stories.*

o ver board (ō′vər bôrd′, ō′vər bōrd′), *adv.* 1 from a ship or boat into the water. 2 **go overboard,** INFORMAL. go too far in an effort because of extreme enthusiasm. 3 **throw overboard, a** throw into the water. **b** INFORMAL. get rid of; give up; abandon; discard.

o ver build (ō′vər bild′), *v.t.*, **-built** (-bilt′), **-build ing.** build too much or too elaborately.

o ver bur den (*v.* ō′vər bėrd′n; *n.* ō′vər-bėrd′n), *v.t.* load with too great a burden. —*n.* clay, rock, etc., which has to be removed to get at a deposit of ore.

o ver cap i tal ize (ō′vər kap′ə tə līz), *v.t.*, **-ized, -iz ing.** fix or estimate the capital of (a company, enterprise, etc.) at too high an amount. —**o′ver cap′i tal i za′tion,** *n.*

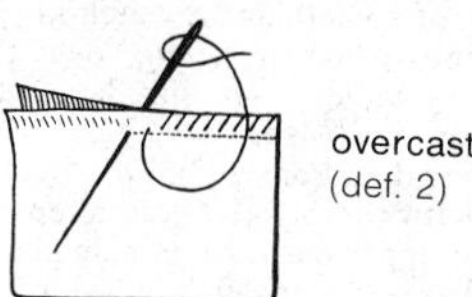

overcast (def. 2)

o ver cast (*adj., v.* ō′vər kast′, ō′vər kast′; *n.* ō′vər kast′), *adj., v.*, **-cast, -cast ing,** *n.* —*adj.* 1 cloudy or dark; gloomy: *The sky was overcast before the storm.* 2 sewed with overcast stitches. —*v.t.* 1 cover with clouds or darkness. 2 sew over and through (the edges of a seam) with long stitches to prevent raveling. —*v.i.* become dark or cloudy. —*n.* the clouds covering the sky.

o ver charge (*v.* ō′vər chärj′; *n.* ō′vər-chärj′), *v.*, **-charged, -charg ing,** *n.* —*v.t.* 1 charge too high a price: *The grocer overcharged you for the eggs.* 2 load too heavily; fill too full: *The overcharged musket burst.* 3 exaggerate. —*v.i.* charge too much. —*n.* 1 charge that is too great. 2 too heavy or too full a load.

o ver clothes (ō′vər klōz′, ō′vər klōᴛʜz′), *n.pl.* outer garments.

o ver cloud (ō′vər kloud′), *v.t., v.i.* 1 cloud over or become clouded over; darken. 2 make or become gloomy.

o ver coat (ō′vər kōt′), *n.* an outer coat worn over regular clothing for warmth in cold weather.

o ver come (ō′vər kum′), *v.t.*, **-came** (-kām′), **-come, -com ing.** 1 get the better of; win the victory over; conquer; defeat: *overcome an enemy, overcome one's faults, overcome all difficulties.* See **defeat** for synonym study. 2 make weak or helpless: *overcome by weariness.*

o ver com pen sa tion (ō′vər kom′pən-sā′shən), *n.* (in psychology) an excessive effort or attempt to make up for a shortcoming in one's personality.

o ver cooked (ō′vər kůkt′), *adj.* cooked too much or too long.

o ver crowd (ō′vər kroud′), *v.t., v.i.* crowd too much.

o ver de vel op (ō′vər di vel′əp), *v.t.* develop too much or too long. If a photograph is overdeveloped, it is too dark. —**o′ver de-vel′op ment,** *n.*

o ver do (ō′vər dü′), *v.*, **-did** (-did′), **-done** (-dun′), **-do ing.** —*v.t.* 1 do or attempt to do too much: *She overdoes exercise.* 2 exaggerate: *The funny scenes in the play were overdone.* 3 cook too much: *The meat is overdone.* 4 exhaust; tire. —*v.i.* do or attempt to do too much.

o ver dose (*n.* ō′vər dōs′; *v.* ō′vər dōs′), *n., v.*, **-dosed, -dos ing.** —*n.* too large a dose. —*v.t.* give too large a dose or too many doses to.

o ver draft (ō′vər draft′), *n.* 1 an overdrawing of an account, especially a bank account. 2 amount of the excess.

o ver draw (ō′vər drô′), *v.*, **-drew** (-drü′), **-drawn** (-drôn′), **-draw ing.** —*v.t.* 1 draw from (a bank account, allowance, etc.) more than the amount one has to his credit or at his disposal. 2 exaggerate: *The characters in the book were greatly overdrawn.* —*v.i.* 1 make an overdraft. 2 exaggerate.

o ver dress (*v.* ō′vər dres′; *n.* ō′vər dres′), *v.t., v.i.* dress too elaborately. —*n.* dress worn over the main dress.

o ver drive (ō′vər drīv′), *n.* an arrangement of gears in an automobile that produces greater speed while using less power than when the car is in high.

o ver due (ō′vər dü′, ō′vər dyü′), *adj.* more than due; due some time ago but not yet arrived, paid, etc.: *The train is overdue. This bill is overdue.*

o ver eat (ō′vər ēt′), *v.i.*, **-ate** (-āt′), **-eat en** (-ēt′n), **-eat ing.** eat too much.

o ver em pha size (ō′vər em′fə sīz), *v.t.*, **-sized, -siz ing.** give too much force or emphasis to; stress too much.

o ver es ti mate (*v.* ō′vər es′tə māt; *n.* ō′vər es′tə mit), *v.*, **-mat ed, -mat ing,** *n.* —*v.t., v.i.* estimate at too high a value, amount, rate, etc. —*n.* an estimate that is too high. —**o′ver es′ti ma′tion,** *n.*

o ver ex pose (ō′vər ek spōz′), *v.t.*, **-posed, -pos ing.** 1 expose too much. 2 (in photography) expose (a film or negative) too long to light.

o ver ex po sure (ō′vər ek spō′zhər), *n.* too much or too long an exposure.

o ver fill (ō′vər fil′), *v.t., v.i.* fill too full; fill to overflowing.

o ver flight (ō′vər flīt′), *n.* flight by aircraft over the territory of a country.

o ver flow (*v.* ō′vər flō′; *n.* ō′vər flō′), *v.*, **-flowed, -flown** (-flōn′), **-flow ing,** *n.* —*v.i.* 1 flow over the bounds: *Rivers often overflow in the spring.* 2 have the contents flowing over: *My cup is overflowing.* 3 be very abundant: *an overflowing harvest, overflowing kindness.* —*v.t.* 1 cover or flood: *The river overflowed my garden.* 2 flow over the top of: *The milk is overflowing the cup.* 3 extend out beyond; be too many for: *The crowd overflowed the little parlor and filled the hall.* —*n.* 1 an overflowing; excess. 2 something that flows or runs over. 3 outlet or container for overflowing liquid.

hat, āge, fär; let, ēqual, tėrm;
it, īce; hot, ōpen, ôrder;
oil, out; cup, půt, rüle;
ch, child; ng, long; sh, she;
th, thin; ᴛʜ, then; zh, measure;

ə represents *a* in about, *e* in taken, *i* in pencil, *o* in lemon, *u* in circus.

< = from, derived from, taken from.

o ver fly (ō′vər flī′), *v.t.*, **-flew** (-flü′), **-flown** (-flōn′), **-fly ing.** 1 make an overflight above. 2 fly over or past without stopping. 3 fly faster, farther, or higher than.

o ver graze (ō′vər grāz′), *v.t.*, **-grazed, -graz ing.** destroy (pasture land) by grazing so long and uninterruptedly as to reduce seriously the grass cover.

o ver grow (ō′vər grō′), *v.*, **-grew** (-grü′), **-grown, -grow ing.** —*v.t.* 1 grow over: *The wall is overgrown with vines.* 2 outgrow. —*v.i.* grow too fast; become too big.

o ver grown (ō′vər grōn′), *adj.* grown too big: *an overgrown boy.* —*v.* pp. of **overgrow.**

o ver growth (ō′vər grōth′), *n.* 1 too great or too rapid growth. 2 growth overspreading or covering something.

o ver hand (ō′vər hand′), *adj., adv.* 1 with the hand raised above the shoulder and the arm swung downward: *an overhand throw (adj.), pitch overhand (adv.).* 2 with the knuckles upward. 3 over and over; with stitches passing successively over an edge. —*n.* an overhand throw, stroke, etc. —*v.t.* sew with overhand stitches.

o ver hand ed (ō′vər han′did), *adj.* overhand.

overhand knot, a simple knot, used in beginning other knots.

o ver hang (*v.* ō′vər hang′; *n.* ō′vər hang′), *v.*, **-hung, -hang ing,** *n.* —*v.t.* 1 hang over; project over: *Trees overhang the street to form an arch of branches.* 2 hang over so as to darken, sadden, or threaten. —*n.* 1 a hanging over. 2 something that projects: *The overhang of the roof shaded the flower bed.*

o ver haul (*v.* ō′vər hôl′; *n.* ō′vər hôl′), *v.t.* 1 examine thoroughly so as to make any repairs or changes that are needed. 2 gain upon; overtake: *Our horse overhauled the favorite to win by a head.* —*n.* an overhauling.

o ver head (*adv.* ō′vər hed′; *adj., n.* ō′vər-hed′), *adv.* over the head; on high; above: *the stars overhead.* —*adj.* 1 being, working, or passing overhead: *overhead wires.* 2 of or having to do with general business expenses. —*n.* general expenses of running a business, such as rent, lighting, heating, taxes, and repairs.

o ver hear (ō′vər hir′), *v.t.*, **-heard** (-hėrd′), **-hear ing.** hear when one is not meant to hear.

o ver hung (*adj.* ō′vər hung′; *v.* ō′vər-hung′), *adj.* hung from above: *an overhung door.* —*v.* pt. and pp. of **overhang.**

o ver joy (ō′vər joi′), *v.t.* make extremely joyful.

o ver joyed (ō′vər joid′), *adj.* very joyful; filled with joy; delighted.

o ver kill (*v.* ō′vər kil′; *n.* ō′vər kil′), *v.t.* destroy with greater force or damage than necessary. —*n.* 1 act or process of overkilling. 2 capacity of a force or weapon to cause greater destruction than necessary.

o ver laid (ō′vər lād′), *v.* pt. and pp. of **overlay**[1].

o ver lain (ō′vər lān′), *v.* pp. of **overlie.**

o ver land (ō′vər land′, ō′vər lənd), *adv., adj.* on land; by land: *travel overland (adv.), an overland route (adj.).*

Overland Park, city in NE Kansas. 77,000.

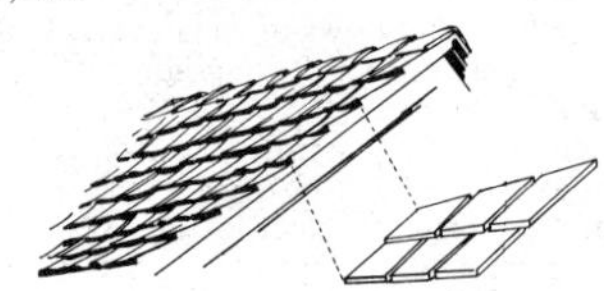

overlap (def. 1)—overlapping shingles

o ver lap (*v.* ō′vər lap′; *n.* ō′vər lap′), *v.,* **-lapped, -lap ping,** *n.* —*v.t.* 1 lap over; cover and extend beyond: *Shingles are laid to overlap each other.* 2 coincide partly with. —*v.i.* overlap another thing or each other: *The shingles overlap.* —*n.* 1 a lapping over. 2 part that overlaps.

o ver lay[1] (*v.* ō′vər lā′; *n.* ō′vər lā′), *v.,* **-laid, -lay ing,** *n.* —*v.t.* 1 lay or place (one thing) over or upon another. 2 cover, overspread, or surmount with something; finish with a layer or applied decoration of something: *wood overlaid with gold.* 3 weigh down. —*n.* something laid over something else; layer or decoration; covering.

o ver lay[2] (ō′vər lā′), *v.* pt. of **overlie.**

o ver leap (ō′vər lēp′), *v.t.,* **-leaped** or **-leapt** (-lept′), **-leap ing.** 1 leap over; pass beyond. 2 overreach (oneself) by leaping too far.

o ver lie (ō′vər lī′), *v.t.,* **-lay, -lain, -ly ing.** 1 lie over; lie upon. 2 smother by lying on.

o ver load (*v.* ō′vər lōd′; *n.* ō′vər lōd′), *v.t.* load too heavily. —*n.* too great a load.

o ver look (ō′vər luk′), *v.t.* 1 fail to see: *Here are the letters you overlooked.* See **slight** for synonym study. 2 pay no attention to; excuse: *I will overlook your bad behavior this time.* 3 have a view of from above; be higher than: *This high window overlooks half the city.* 4 look over; watch: *She did not know that she was being overlooked by the woman next door.* 5 oversee; manage.

o ver lord (ō′vər lôrd′), *n.* person who is lord over another lord or other lords: *The duke was the overlord of barons and knights who held land from him.*

o ver lord ship (ō′vər lôrd′ship), *n.* position or authority of an overlord.

o ver ly (ō′vər lē), *adv.* overmuch; excessively; too.

o ver man (ō′vər man′), *v.t.,* **-manned, -man ning.** supply with too many workers.

o ver mas ter (ō′vər mas′tər), *v.t.* overcome; overpower.

o ver match (ō′vər mach′), *v.t.* be more than a match for; surpass.

o ver much (ō′vər much′), *adj., adv., n.* too much.

o ver nice (ō′vər nīs′), *adj.* too fastidious.

o ver night (*adv.* ō′vər nīt′; *adj.* ō′vər nīt′), *adv.* 1 during the night: *stay overnight.* 2 on the night before: *Preparations were made overnight for an early start.* 3 at once; immediately; in a very short time: *Change will not come overnight.* —*adj.* 1 done, occurring, etc., during the night: *an overnight stop.* 2 for the night: *An overnight bag contains articles needed for one night's stay.* 3 of or having to do with the night before.

o ver pass (*n.* ō′vər pas′; *v.* ō′vər pas′), *n., v.,* **-passed** or **-past** (-past′), **-pass ing.** —*n.* bridge over a road, railroad, canal, etc. —*v.t.* 1 pass over (a region, bounds, etc.). 2 go beyond; exceed; surpass. 3 pass without notice; overlook; disregard.

o ver play (ō′vər plā′), *v.t.* 1 play (a part, etc.) in an exaggerated manner. 2 count too heavily on the power or advantage of: *The diplomat was careful not to overplay his hand during the negotiations.* 3 play better than; surpass.

o ver plus (ō′vər plus′), *n.* surplus.

o ver pow er (ō′vər pou′ər), *v.t.* 1 overcome or conquer; master; overwhelm: *overpower one's enemies.* 2 be much greater or stronger than: *Anger overpowered every other feeling.* **—o′ver pow′er ing ly,** *adv.*

o ver print (*v.* ō′vər print′; *n.* ō′vər print′), *v.t.* print or stamp over with additional marks or matter, as in making revisions, in color work, etc. —*n.* 1 any mark, design, or writing printed across a stamp to change its use, value, etc. 2 postage stamp printed with such a mark.

o ver pro duc tion (ō′vər prə duk′shən), *n.* production of more than is needed or more than can be sold.

o ver rate (ō′vər rāt′), *v.t.,* **-rat ed, -rat ing.** rate or estimate too highly.

o ver reach (ō′vər rēch′), *v.t.* 1 reach over or beyond. 2 get the better of by cunning: *overreach someone in a bargain.* 3 get the better of by trickery or fraud; cheat. 4 **overreach oneself, a** fail or miss by trying for too much. **b** fail by being too crafty or tricky. —*v.i.* 1 reach too far. 2 cheat. **—o′ver reach′er,** *n.*

o ver re act (ō′vər rē akt′), *v.i.* react with greater force, intensity, or emotion than is necessary or expected. **—o′ver re ac′tion,** *n.*

o ver ride (ō′vər rīd′), *v.t.,* **-rode** (-rōd′), **-rid den** (-rid′n), **-rid ing.** 1 act in spite of: *override objections.* 2 prevail over: *The new rule overrides all previous ones.* 3 ride over; trample on. 4 ride over (a region, place, etc.). 5 tire out by riding; ride too much. 6 pass or extend over; overlap.

o ver ripe (ō′vər rīp′), *adj.* too ripe; more than ripe.

o ver rule (ō′vər rül′), *v.t.,* **-ruled, -rul ing.** 1 rule or decide against (a plea, argument, objection, etc.); set aside: *The president overruled my plan.* 2 prevail over; be stronger than. **—o′ver rul′ing ly,** *adv.*

o ver run (*v.* ō′vər run′; *n.* ō′vər run′), *v.,* **-ran** (-ran′), **-run, -run ning,** *n.* —*v.t.* 1 spread over and spoil or harm in some way, as weeds, vermin, disease, or invading troops do. 2 spread over; cover pleasingly: *Vines had overrun the wall.* 3 run or go beyond: *The speaker overran the time set for him. He overran third base and was tagged out.* —*n.* 1 an overrunning. 2 amount overrunning or carried over.

o ver sea (*adv.* ō′vər sē′; *adj.* ō′vər sē′), *adv., adj.* overseas.

o ver seas (*adv.* ō′vər sēz′; *adj.* ō′vər sēz′), *adv.* across the sea; beyond the sea; abroad. —*adj.* 1 done, used, or serving overseas. 2 of countries across the sea; foreign.

o ver see (ō′vər sē′), *v.t.,* **-saw** (-sô′), **-seen** (-sēn′), **-see ing.** 1 look after and direct (work or workers); superintend; manage. 2 overlook as from a higher position; survey.

o ver se er (ō′vər sē′ər, ō′vər sir′), *n.* one who oversees others or their work.

o ver sell (ō′vər sel′), *v.t.,* **-sold** (-sōld′), **-sell ing.** 1 sell to excess; sell more of than can be delivered. 2 sell too much of.

o ver set (*v.* ō′vər set′; *n.* ō′vər set′), *v.,* **-set, -set ting,** *n.* —*v.t.* 1 upset; overturn. 2 overthrow. —*n.* overthrow.

o ver shad ow (ō′vər shad′ō), *v.t.* 1 be more important than; surpass: *He overshadowed his brother in school.* 2 cast a shadow over; make dark or gloomy.

o ver shoe (ō′vər shü′), *n.* a waterproof shoe or boot, often made of rubber, worn over another shoe to keep the foot dry and warm.

o ver shoot (ō′vər shüt′), *v.,* **-shot, -shoot ing.** —*v.t.* 1 shoot over, higher than, or beyond. 2 go over, higher than, or beyond. —*v.i.* go, run, or shoot too far.

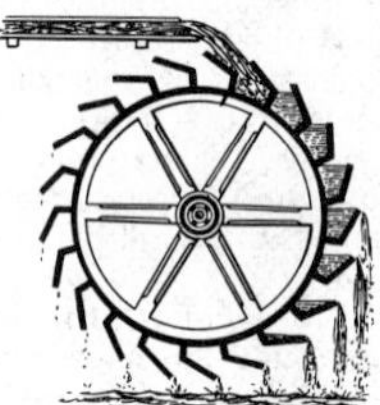

overshot (def. 2)—overshot water wheel

o ver shot (*adj.* ō′vər shot′; *v.* ō′vər shot′), *adj.* 1 having the upper jaw projecting beyond the lower. 2 driven by water flowing over from above. —*v.* pt. and pp. of **overshoot.**

o ver sight (ō′vər sīt′), *n.* 1 failure to notice or think of something. 2 watchful care.

o ver size (ō′vər sīz′), *adj.* over the usual size; very large. —*n.* size larger than the proper or usual size.

o ver sized (ō′vər sīzd′), *adj.* oversize.

o ver skirt (ō′vər skėrt′), *n.* a separate skirt over the upper part of the main skirt.

o ver sleep (ō′vər slēp′), *v.,* **-slept** (-slept′), **-sleep ing.** —*v.i.* sleep too long. —*v.t.* sleep beyond (a certain hour).

o ver spread (ō′vər spred′), *v.t.,* **-spread, -spread ing.** spread over: *A smile overspread his broad face.*

o ver state (ō′vər stāt′), *v.t.,* **-stat ed, -stat ing.** state too strongly; exaggerate. **—o′ver state′ment,** *n.*

o ver stay (ō′vər stā′), *v.t.* stay beyond the time or duration of.

o ver step (ō′vər step′), *v.t.,* **-stepped, -step ping.** go beyond; exceed.

o ver stock (*v.* ō′vər stok′; *n.* ō′vər stok′), *v.t.* supply with more than is needed. —*n.* too great a stock or supply.

o ver strung (ō′vər strung′), *adj.* too nervous or sensitive.

o ver stuff (ō′vər stuf′), *v.t.* 1 stuff too full. 2 make (upholstered furniture) soft and comfortable by thick padding.

o ver sub scribe (ō′vər səb skrīb′), *v.t., v.i.,* **-scribed, -scrib ing.** subscribe for in excess of what is available or required.

o ver sub scrip tion (ō′vər səb skrip′shən), *n.* an oversubscribing.

o ver sup ply (*v.* ō′vər sə plī′; *n.* ō′vər sə-plī′), *v.,* **-plied, -ply ing,** *n., pl.* **-plies.** —*v.t.* supply in excess. —*n.* an excessive supply.

o vert (ō′vėrt′, ō vėrt′), *adj.* open or public; evident; not hidden: *Hitting someone is an overt act.* [< Old French, past participle of *ovrir* to open < Latin *aperire.* Related to APERTURE.] **—o′vert ly,** *adv.*

o ver take (ō′vər tāk′), *v.t.,* **-took** (-tůk′), **-tak en** (-tā′kən), **-tak ing.** 1 come up with; catch up with. 2 catch up with and pass: *They soon overtook us and were at the picnic grounds before we arrived.* 3 come upon suddenly: *A storm overtook the children.*

o ver tax (ō′vər taks′), *v.t.* 1 tax too heavily. 2 put too heavy a burden on. **—o′ver-tax a′tion,** *n.*

o ver-the-count er (ō′vər ᴛʜə koun′tər), *adj.* 1 not bought or sold through a regular exchange; not listed on a stock exchange. 2 that may be dispensed without a doctor's prescription.

o ver throw (*v.* ō′vər thrō′; *n.* ō′vər thrō′), *v.,* **-threw** (-thrü′), **-thrown** (-thrōn′), **-throw ing,** *n.* —*v.t.* 1 take away the power of; defeat: *overthrow a monarch.* 2 put an end to; destroy: *overthrow slavery.* 3 overturn; upset; knock down. 4 throw (a ball) past the place for which it is intended. —*n.* a defeat; upset: *the overthrow of one's plans.*

o ver time (*n., adv., adj.* ō′vər tīm′; *v.* ō′vər tīm′), *n., adv., adj., v.,* **-timed, -tim ing.** —*n.* 1 extra time; time beyond the regular hours. 2 wages for this period: *pay overtime.* —*adv.* beyond the regular hours. —*adj.* 1 of or for overtime: *overtime work.* 2 beyond the allotted or permitted time: *overtime parking.* —*v.t.* give too much time to: *overtime a camera exposure.*

o ver tone (ō′vər tōn′), *n.* 1 a fainter and higher musical tone heard along with the main or fundamental tone; harmonic. 2 hint or suggestion of something felt, believed, etc.: *an overtone of anger.*

o ver top (ō′vər top′), *v.t.,* **-topped, -top ping.** 1 rise above; be higher than. 2 surpass; excel.

o ver train (ō′vər trān′), *v.t., v.i.* subject to or undergo so much athletic training that the condition is injured rather than improved; train to excess.

o ver trump (ō′vər trump′), *v.i., v.t.* play a higher trump (than one played earlier).

o ver ture (ō′vər chůr, ō′vər chər), *n.* 1 proposal or offer: *The enemy is making overtures for peace.* 2 a musical composition played by the orchestra as an introduction to an opera, oratorio, or other long musical composition. [< Old French < Latin *apertura* opening. Doublet of APERTURE.]

o ver turn (*v.* ō′vər tėrn′; *n.* ō′vər tėrn′), *v.t.* 1 turn upside down. See **upset** for synonym study. 2 make fall down; overthrow; destroy the power of: *The rebels overturned the government.* —*v.i.* upset; fall down; fall over: *The boat overturned.* —*n.* an overturning.

o ver use (*v.* ō′vər yüz′; *n.* ō′vər yüs′), *v.,* **-used, -us ing,** *n.* —*v.t.* 1 use too much. 2 use too hard or too often. —*n.* too much or too hard use.

o ver view (ō′vər vyü′), *n.* a broad view; survey; inspection.

o ver watch (ō′vər woch′, ō′vər wôch′), *v.t.* 1 watch over. 2 make weary by watching.

o ver ween ing (o′vər wē′ning), *adj.* 1 thinking too much of oneself; conceited; self-confident; presumptuous. 2 excessive; exaggerated. **—o′ver ween′ing ly,** *adv.* **—o′ver ween′ing ness,** *n.*

o ver weigh (ō′vər wā′), *v.t.* 1 be greater than in weight, importance, etc.; outweigh; overbalance. 2 weigh down; oppress.

o ver weight (*adj., n.* ō′vər wāt′; *v.* ō′vər-wāt′), *adj.* having too much weight: *overweight for one's height.* —*n.* 1 too much weight. 2 extra weight: *The butcher gave us overweight on this roast.* —*v.t.* 1 overburden. 2 weight too heavily; attach too much importance to.

o ver whelm (ō′vər hwelm′), *v.t.* 1 overcome completely; crush: *overwhelm with grief.* 2 cover completely as a flood would: *A great wave overwhelmed the boat.*

o ver whelm ing (ō′vər hwel′ming), *adj.* too many, too great, or too much to be resisted; overpowering: *an overwhelming majority.* **—o′ver whelm′ing ly,** *adv.*

o ver wind (ō′vər wīnd′), *v.t.,* **-wound** (-wound′), **-wind ing.** wind beyond the proper limit; wind too far.

o ver work (*n.* ō′vər wėrk′; *v.* ō′vər-wėrk′), *n., v.,* **-worked** or **-wrought, -work ing.** —*n.* 1 too much or too hard work. 2 extra work. —*v.i.* work too hard or too long. —*v.t.* 1 use to excess. 2 cause to work too hard or too long.

o ver write (ō′vər rīt′), *v.t., v.i.,* **-wrote** (-rōt′), **-writ ten** (-rit′n), **-writ ing.** 1 write too much (about a subject). 2 write ornately or pretentiously. 3 write on or over (other writing).

o ver wrought (ō′vər rôt′), *adj.* 1 wearied or exhausted by too much work or excitement; greatly excited: *overwrought nerves.* 2 too elaborate. —*v.* a pt. and a pp. of **overwork.**

Ov id (ov′id), *n.* 43 B.C.-A.D. 17?, Roman poet.

o vi duct (ō′və dukt), *n.* tube through which the ovum or egg passes from the ovary. [< Latin *ovum* egg + *ductus* duct]

O vie do (ō vyā′ᴛʜō), *n.* city in NW Spain. 143,000.

o vi form (ō′və fôrm), *adj.* egg-shaped.

o vip ar ous (ō vip′ər əs), *adj.* producing eggs that are hatched after leaving the body. Birds are oviparous. [< Latin *oviparus* < *ovum* egg + *parere* bring forth] **—o vip′ar ous ly,** *adv.* **—o vip′ar ous ness,** *n.*

o vi pos i tor (ō′və poz′ə tər), *n.* (in certain female insects) an organ at the end of the abdomen, by which eggs are deposited.

o void (ō′void), *adj.* egg-shaped; ovate. —*n.* an egg-shaped object.

o voi dal (ō voi′dl), *adj.* ovoid.

o vo vi vip ar ous (ō′vō vī vip′ər əs), *adj.* producing eggs that are hatched within the body of the parent, so that young are born alive but without placental attachment, as certain reptiles and fishes and many invertebrate animals. **—o′vo vi vip′ar ous-ly,** *adv.*

o vu lar (ō′vyə lər), *adj.* of an ovule; being an ovule.

o vu late (ō′vyə lāt), *v.i.,* **-lat ed, -lat ing.** 1 produce ova or ovules. 2 discharge ova from the ovary. **—o′vu la′tion,** *n.*

o vule (ō′vyül), *n.* 1 a small ovum, especially when immature or unfertilized. 2 part of a plant that develops into a seed. In higher plants the ovule contains the egg, which after fertilization develops into an embryo. See **ovary** for diagram. [< New Latin *ovulum,* diminutive of Latin *ovum* egg]

o vum (ō′vəm), *n., pl.* **o va.** a female germ cell, produced in the ovary; egg. After the ovum is fertilized, a new organism or embryo develops. [< Latin, egg]

hat, āge, fär; let, ēqual, tėrm;
it, īce; hot, ōpen, ôrder;
oil, out; cup, pu̇t, rüle;
ch, child; ng, long; sh, she;
th, thin; ᴛʜ, then; zh, measure;

ə represents *a* in about, *e* in taken, *i* in pencil, *o* in lemon, *u* in circus.

< = from, derived from, taken from.

owe (ō), *v.,* **owed, ow ing.** —*v.t.* 1 have to pay; be in debt for: *I owe the grocer $10.* 2 be obliged or indebted for: *We owe a great deal to our parents.* 3 bear toward another: *owe a grudge.* —*v.i.* be in debt: *He is always owing for something.* [Old English *āgan*]

Ow en (ō′ən), *n.* **Robert,** 1771-1858, British social reformer who organized the first cooperatives.

Ow ens (ō′ənz), *n.* **Jesse,** born 1913, American athlete, track star of the 1936 Olympic games.

ow ing (ō′ing), *adj.* 1 due; owed: *pay what is owing.* 2 **owing to,** on account of; because of; as a result of.

owl
about 2 ft. tall

owl (oul), *n.* any of an order of birds of prey with a large head, large eyes, short, hooked beak, and soft feathers that enable them to fly noiselessly. Owls hunt small animals and birds at night. Some kinds have tufts of feathers on their heads called "horns" or "ears." [Old English *ūle*] **—owl′like′,** *adj.*

owl et (ou′lit), *n.* 1 a young owl. 2 a small owl.

owl ish (ou′lish), *adj.* 1 like an owl; like an owl's. 2 trying to look wise. **—owl′ish ly,** *adv.* **—owl′ish ness,** *n.*

own (ōn), *v.t.* 1 have as property; possess: *I own many books.* See **have** for synonym study. 2 acknowledge; admit; confess: *own one's guilt. I own you are right.* 3 acknowledge as belonging to one: *His father will not own him.* —*v.i.* 1 confess: *She owns to many faults.* 2 **own up,** confess fully: *own up to a crime.* —*adj.* 1 of oneself or itself; belonging to oneself or itself: *This is my own book. We have our own troubles.* 2 in closest relationship. Own sisters have the same parents.
—*n.* the one or ones belonging to oneself or itself.
come into one's own, a get what belongs to one. **b** get the success or credit that one deserves.
hold one's own, a keep one's position against opposition; stand one's ground. **b** maintain one's strength or state of health.
of one's own, belonging to oneself.
on one's own, on one's own account, responsibility, resources, etc.; not ruled or directed by someone else; independent.
[Old English *āgen*]

own er (ō′nər), *n.* one who owns; possessor; proprietor. **—own′er less,** *adj.*
own er ship (ō′nər ship), *n.* condition of being an owner; the possessing (of something); right of possession.
ox (oks), *n., pl.* **ox en.** 1 the full-grown male of domestic cattle, that has been castrated and is used as a draft animal or for beef. 2 any of a genus of ruminant mammals with horns and cloven hoofs, including domestic cattle, buffaloes, bison, etc. [Old English *oxa*] **—ox′like′,** *adj.*
ox a late (ok′sə lāt), *n.* salt or ester of oxalic acid.
ox al ic acid (ok sal′ik), a poisonous organic acid that occurs in many plants. It is used for bleaching, removing stains, making dyes, etc. *Formula:* $C_2H_2O_4 \cdot 2H_2O$ [*oxalic* < French *oxalique* < Latin *oxalis* wood sorrel]
ox a lis (ok′sə lis), *n.* wood sorrel. [< Latin < Greek < *oxys* sour]
ox blood (oks′blud′), *n.* a deep red color.

oxbow (def. 1)—two oxbows

ox bow (oks′bō′), *n.* 1 a U-shaped piece of wood placed under and around the neck of an ox, with the upper ends inserted in the bar of the yoke. 2 a U-shaped bend in a river.
ox cart (oks′kärt′), *n.* cart drawn by oxen.
ox en (ok′sən), *n.* pl. of **ox.**
ox eye (oks′ī′), *n.* 1 the common American daisy. 2 any of several other composite plants like it.
ox-eyed (oks′īd′), *adj.* having large, full eyes like those of an ox.
ox ford (ok′sfərd), *n.* 1 kind of low shoe, laced over the instep. 2 kind of cotton or rayon cloth used for shirts, blouses, and other garments. 3 Oxford gray. [< *Oxford,* the city]
Ox ford (ok′sfərd), *n.* 1 city in S England. 110,000. 2 the very old and famous English university located there. 3 oxford.
Oxford gray, a very dark gray.
ox heart (oks′härt′), *n.* a large, heart-shaped, sweet cherry.
ox i dant (ok′sə dənt), *n.* oxidizer.
ox i dase (ok′sə dās, ok′sə dāz), *n.* any of a group of enzymes that cause oxidation.
ox i da tion (ok′sə dā′shən), *n.* 1 act or process of oxidizing. Burning is one kind of oxidation. 2 condition of being oxidized.
ox i da tion-re duc tion (ok′sə dā′shən-ri duk′shən), *n.* a chemical reaction involving the transfer of electrons from one atom or ion to another atom or ion by the processes of oxidation and reduction.
ox ide (ok′sīd, ok′sid), *n.* compound of oxygen with another element or radical.
ox i diz a ble (ok′sə dī′zə bəl), *adj.* that can be oxidized.
ox i dize (ok′sə dīz), *v.,* **-dized, -diz ing.** *—v.t.* 1 combine with oxygen. When a substance burns or rusts, it is oxidized. 2 cause to rust. 3 cause to lose hydrogen by the action of oxygen. 4 change (atoms or ions) to a higher valence by the loss of electrons. *—v.i.* become oxidized: *Iron oxidizes in water.*
ox i diz er (ok′sə dī′zər), *n.* 1 something that oxidizes; an oxidizing agent. 2 substance that supports the combustion of a fuel.
ox lip (oks′lip′), *n.* primrose that has clusters of pale-yellow flowers.
Ox o ni an (ok sō′nē ən), *adj.* of or having to do with Oxford University or Oxford. *—n.* 1 member or graduate of Oxford University. 2 native or inhabitant of Oxford. [< Medieval Latin *Oxonia* Oxford]
Ox us River (ok′səs), river in W Asia, flowing into the Aral Sea. 1500 mi.
ox y a cet y lene (ok′sē ə set′l ēn′), *adj.* of, having to do with, or using a mixture of oxygen and acetylene. An oxyacetylene torch is used for welding or cutting metals.
ox y gen (ok′sə jən), *n.* a colorless, odorless, tasteless gaseous element that forms about one fifth of the atmosphere by volume. Oxygen is present in a combined form in water, carbon dioxide, iron ore, and many other substances. Animals and plants cannot live, and fire will not burn, without oxygen. *Symbol:* O; *atomic number* 8. See pages 326 and 327 for table. [< French *oxygène* < Greek *oxys* sharp + *-genēs* born]
ox y gen ate (ok′sə jə nāt), *v.t.,* **-at ed, -at ing.** treat or combine with oxygen. **—ox′y gen a′tion,** *n.*

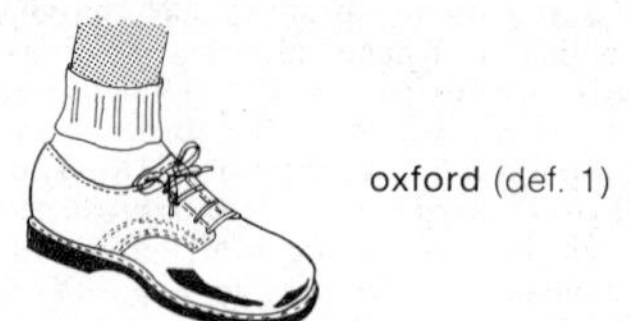
oxford (def. 1)

ox y gen ize (ok′sə jə nīz), *v.t.,* **-ized, -iz ing.** oxygenate. **—ox′y gen iz′a ble,** *adj.*
oxygen mask, device worn over the nose and mouth through which supplementary oxygen is supplied from an attached container. Oxygen masks are used at high altitudes or where the body is unable to take in enough oxygen by normal breathing.
oxygen tent, a small, usually transparent, tent which is supplied with a constant regulated flow of a mixture of oxygen and air . It is usually placed over the head and shoulders of a patient who has difficulty breathing.
ox y he mo glo bin (ok′si hē′mə glō′bən, ok′si hem′ə glō′bən), *n.* substance in arterial blood consisting of hemoglobin combined with oxygen. Oxyhemoglobin gives arterial blood its bright red color.
ox y hy dro gen (ok′si hī′drə jən), *adj.* of, having to do with, or using a mixture of oxygen and hydrogen. An oxyhydrogen torch is used for welding or cutting metals.
ox y mo ron (ok′si môr′on, ok′si mōr′on), *n., pl.* **-mo ra** (-môr′ə, -mōr′ə). figure of speech in which words of opposite meaning or suggestion are used together. EXAMPLES: *a wise fool, cruel kindness, make haste slowly.* [< Late Greek *oxymōron* < Greek *oxys* sharp + *mōros* stupid]
ox y to cin (ok′si tō′sn, ok′si tos′n), *n.* hormone of the pituitary gland effecting contraction of the uterus in childbirth and stimulating lactation. *Formula:* $C_{43}H_{66}N_{12}O_{12}S_2$ [< Greek *oxys* sharp + *tokos* birth]
o yez or **o yes** (ō′yes, ō′yez), *interj., n.* hear! attend! a cry uttered, usually three times, by a public or court crier to command silence and attention before a proclamation, etc., is made. [< Anglo-French *oyez* hear ye! < *oyer, oïr* hear < Latin *audire*]
oys ter (oi′stər), *n.* any of several kinds of mollusks much used as food, having rough, irregular shells in two halves. Oysters are found in shallow water along seacoasts. Some kinds yield pearls. [< Old French *oistre* < Latin *ostrea* < Greek *ostreon*]
oyster bed, place where oysters breed or are cultivated.
oyster cracker, a small, round or hexagonal, salted cracker eaten with oysters, soups, etc.
oyster farm, place where oysters are raised for the market.
oys ter man (oi′stər mən), *n., pl.* **-men.** man who gathers, sells, or raises oysters.
oyster plant, salsify.
oz., *pl.* **oz.** or **ozs.** ounce.
O zark Mountains (ō′zärk), low mountain range in S Missouri, N Arkansas, and E Oklahoma. 1500-2300 ft.
O zarks (ō′zärks), *n.pl.* the Ozark Mountains.
o zone (ō′zōn), *n.* 1 form of oxygen with a sharp, pungent odor, produced by electricity and present in the air, especially after a thunderstorm. It is a strong oxidizing agent and is produced commercially for use in bleaching, in sterilizing water, etc. *Formula:* O_3 2 INFORMAL. pure air that is refreshing. [< German *Ozon* < Greek *ozein* to smell]
o zon ic (ō zon′ik, ō zō′nik), *adj.* of, having to do with, or containing ozone.
o zo nif er ous (ō′zn if′ər əs), *adj.* containing ozone.
o zon o sphere (ō zon′ə sfir), *n.* region of concentrated ozone in the outer stratosphere and the mesosphere. It shields the earth from excessive ultraviolet radiation. See **atmosphere** for diagram.

P p

P or **p** (pē), *n., pl.* **P's** or **p's.** 1 the 16th letter of the English alphabet. 2 **mind one's P's and Q's,** be careful about what one says and does.

P, 1 (in chess) pawn. 2 phosphorus.

p., 1 page. 2 participle.

pa (pä), *n.* INFORMAL. papa; father.

Pa, protactinium.

Pa., Pennsylvania.

p.a., 1 participial adjective. 2 per annum.

PA or **P.A.,** public address system.

PABA, para-aminobenzoic acid.

pab u lum (pab′yə ləm), *n.* food; anything taken in by an animal or plant to maintain life and growth. [< Latin, fodder]

Pac., Pacific.

pace[1] (pās), *n., v.,* **paced, pac ing.** —*n.* 1 a step. 2 the length of a normal adult step in walking, used as a rough unit of measure; about $2\frac{1}{2}$ feet. 3 way of stepping; gait. The walk, trot, and gallop are some of the paces of a horse. 4 a particular gait of some horses in which the feet on the same side are lifted and put down together. 5 rate of movement; speed: *a fast pace in walking.* 6 **keep pace with,** keep up with; go as fast as. 7 **put one through his paces,** try one out; find out what one can do. 8 **set the pace, a** fix or regulate the speed. **b** be an example or model for others to follow. —*v.i.* 1 walk with slow or regular steps: *The tiger paced back and forth in his cage.* 2 (of a horse) move at a pace. —*v.t.* 1 walk over with slow or regular steps: *pace the floor.* 2 measure by pacing or in paces: *We paced off the distance and found it to be 69 paces.* 3 set the pace for: *A motorboat will pace the rowing crew.* [< Old French *pas* < Latin *passus* step < *pandere* to stretch. Doublet of PASS.]

pa ce[2] (pā′sē), *prep., adv.* with the indulgence of; by the leave of; with regrets for differing from. [< Latin]

pace mak er (pās′mā′kər), *n.* 1 person, animal, or thing that sets the pace. 2 area of specialized tissue in the heart, near the top of the wall of the right auricle, that sends out the rhythmic impulses which regulate the contractions of the heart muscles. 3 an electronic device implanted in the chest wall to maintain or restore the normal rhythm of the heartbeat.

pac er (pā′sər), *n.* 1 person or thing that paces, especially one bred and trained for racing.

pa cha (pə shä′, pash′ə, pä′shə), *n.* pasha.

pa chi si (pə chē′zē), *n.* game somewhat like backgammon, originally from India, played on a cross-shaped board. [< Hindustani *pachīsī*]

pach y derm (pak′ə dėrm′), *n.* 1 any of several thick-skinned mammals with hoofs, as the elephant, hippopotamus, and rhinoceros. 2 person who is not sensitive to criticism or ridicule; thick-skinned person. [< Greek *pachydermos* thick-skinned < *pachys* thick + *derma* skin]

pach y der ma tous (pak′ə dėr′mə təs), *adj.* of, like, or characteristic of pachyderms.

pa cif ic (pə sif′ik), *adj.* 1 tending to make peace; making peace; peaceable. 2 loving peace; not warlike. 3 peaceful; calm; quiet. —**pa cif′i cal ly,** *adv.*

Pa cif ic (pə sif′ik), *n.* **Pacific Ocean,** ocean west of North and South America, extending to Asia and Australia. 70,000,000 sq. mi. —*adj.* 1 of the Pacific Ocean. 2 on, in, over, or near the Pacific Ocean. 3 of or on the Pacific coast of the United States.

pac i fi ca tion (pas′ə fə kā′shən), *n.* 1 a pacifying. 2 a being pacified.

pa cif i ca to ry (pə sif′ə kə tôr′ē, pə sif′ə-kə tōr′ē), *adj.* tending to make peace; conciliatory.

Pacific Standard Time, the standard time in the westernmost parts of the continental United States and Canada, excluding most of Alaska. It is eight hours behind Greenwich Time.

pac i fi er (pas′ə fī′ər), *n.* 1 person or thing that pacifies. 2 a rubber or plastic nipple or ring given to a baby to suck.

pac i fism (pas′ə fiz′əm), *n.* principle or policy of establishing and maintaining universal peace; settlement of all differences between nations by peaceful means; opposition to war.

pac i fist (pas′ə fist), *n.* person who is opposed to war and favors settling all disputes between nations by peaceful means. —*adj.* pacifistic.

pac i fis tic (pas′ə fis′tik), *adj.* of pacifism or pacifists.

pac i fy (pas′ə fī), *v.t.,* **-fied, -fy ing.** 1 make calm; quiet down; give peace to: *Can't you pacify that screaming baby?* See **appease** for synonym study. 2 bring peace to: *pacify a rebellious region.* [< Latin *pacificare* < *pax, pacis* peace + *facere* to make] —**pac′i fi′a ble,** *adj.*

pack[1] (pak), *n.* 1 bundle of things wrapped up or tied together for carrying: *The hikers carried packs on their backs.* 2 the total quantity of any natural product, especially a food, canned, frozen, etc., in one year or season: *the annual pack of salmon.* 3 a set; lot; a number together: *a pack of thieves, a pack of nonsense.* 4 number of animals of the same kind hunting or living together: *a pack of wolves.* 5 group of dogs kept together for hunting. 6 a complete set of playing cards, usually 52; deck. 7 ice pack. 8 something put on the body or skin as a treatment. A cloth soaked in hot or cold water is often used as a pack. 9 the cloth, sheet, blanket, etc., so used. 10 a small, absorbent cotton pad that is applied to open wounds or body cavities in order to check the flow of blood. —*v.t.* 1 put together in a bundle, box, bale, etc.: *Pack your books in this box.* 2 fill with things; put one's things into: *pack a suitcase.* 3 press or crowd closely together: *A hundred people were packed into one small room.* 4 press together; make firm: *The heavy trucks packed the snow on the highway.* 5 fill (a space) with all that it will hold: *pack a small theater with a large audience.* 6 put into a container to be sold or stored: *Meat, fish, and vegetables are often packed in cans.* 7 make tight with something that water, steam, air, etc., cannot leak through: *The plumber packed a joint in the pipe.* 8 load (an animal) with a pack; burden. 9 INFORMAL. carry: *pack a gun.* 10 U.S. carry in a pack: *pack supplies up a mountain.* 11 cover, surround, or protect with closely applied materials; treat with a therapeutic pack: *The dentist packed my gum after he extracted my tooth.* 12 **pack off** or **pack away,** send away.

hat, āge, fär; let, ēqual, tėrm;
it, īce; hot, ōpen, ôrder;
oil, out; cup, pu̇t, rüle;
ch, child; ng, long; sh, she;
th, thin; ᴛʜ, then; zh, measure;

ə represents *a* in about, *e* in taken, *i* in pencil, *o* in lemon, *u* in circus.

< = from, derived from, taken from.

—*v.i.* 1 put things together in a bag, box, bundle, bale, etc.: *Are you ready to pack?* 2 fit together closely; admit of storing and shipping: *These small cans will pack well.* 3 become or be packed; crowd together: *The whole group packed into one small room.* 4 **send packing,** send away in a hurry. [probably < Middle Dutch *pac*]

pack[2] (pak), *v.t.* arrange unfairly. To pack a court, a jury, or a convention is to fill it unfairly with those who will favor one side. [perhaps special use of *pack*[1]]

pack age (pak′ij), *n., v.,* **-aged, -ag ing.** —*n.* 1 bundle of things packed or wrapped together; box or relatively small receptacle with things packed in it; parcel. 2 box, can, bottle, or other receptacle for packing goods, with its contents, as offered for sale: *a package of soap.* 3 group of related items or elements, as goods, services, laws, etc., offered, provided, sold, accepted, or rejected as a unit. —*v.t.* 1 put in a package. 2 make a package or packages out of. —**pack′ag er,** *n.*

package deal, offer or transaction involving a number of elements or items grouped as a unit.

package store, U.S. store selling alcoholic beverages in sealed containers which must be removed from the premises for consumption.

pack animal, animal used for carrying loads or packs.

pack er (pak′ər), *n.* 1 person or thing that packs, especially a person or company that packs meat, fruit, vegetables, etc., to be sold to wholesalers. 2 person who transports goods by means of pack animals.

pack et (pak′it), *n.* 1 a small package; parcel. 2 packet boat.

packet boat, boat that carries mail, passengers, and goods regularly on a fixed route.

pack horse (pak′hôrs′), *n.* horse used to carry loads or packs.

pack ing (pak′ing), *n.* 1 material used to keep water, steam, etc., from leaking through: *the packing around the valves of a radiator.* 2 material placed around goods to protect them from damage in shipment, storage, etc. 3 business of preparing and packing meat, fish, fruit, vegetables, etc., to be sold.

packing house or **packing plant,** place where meat, fruit, vegetables, etc., are prepared and packed to be sold.

pack mule, mule used for carrying loads.

pack rat, any of a genus of large North American rats, with bushy tails, that carry away bits of food, clothing, small tools, etc., and hide them in their nests; wood rat.

pack sack (pak′sak′), *n.* bag of strong material to hold equipment, carried on the back when traveling.

pack sad dle (pak′sad′l), *n.* saddle specially adapted for supporting the load on a pack animal.

pack thread (pak′thred′), *n.* a strong

thread or twine for sewing or tying up packages.

pack train (pak′trān′), *n.* line or group of animals carrying loads.

pact (pakt), *n.* agreement between persons or parties; compact; treaty. [< Latin *pactum* < *pacisci* make an agreement]

pad[1] (pad), *n., v.,* **pad ded, pad ding.** —*n.* 1 a soft mass used for comfort, protection, or stuffing; cushion. 2 a soft, stuffed saddle. 3 one of the cushionlike parts on the bottom side of the feet of dogs, foxes, and some other animals. 4 foot of a dog, fox, etc. 5 the large floating leaf of the water lily. 6 number of sheets of paper fastened together along one edge; tablet. 7 cloth or other absorbant material soaked with ink to use with a rubber stamp. 8 launching pad. 9 SLANG. room, house, or apartment. —*v.t.* 1 fill with something soft; stuff. 2 expand or lengthen (a written paper or speech) by using words just to fill space. [origin uncertain]

pad[2] (pad), *v.,* **pad ded, pad ding,** *n.* —*v.t.* walk along (a path, road, etc.); tramp; trudge. —*v.i.* 1 go on foot; tramp or trudge along; walk. 2 walk or trot softly. —*n.* 1 a dull sound, as of footsteps on the ground. 2 a slow horse for riding on a road. [probably < earlier Dutch, path]

pad ding (pad′ing), *n.* 1 material used to pad with, such as hair, cotton, or straw. 2 words used just to fill space in making a speech or a written paper longer.

paddle[1] (def. 1)

pad dle[1] (pad′l), *n., v.,* **-dled, -dling.** —*n.* 1 lightweight oar with a broad blade at one end or both ends, usually held with both hands without fixed supports, used in rowing a boat or canoe. 2 act of paddling; a turn at the paddle. 3 one of the broad boards fixed around a water wheel or a paddle wheel to push, or be pushed by, the water. 4 a broad piece of wood with a handle at one end, used for stirring, for mixing, for beating clothes in washing, etc. 5 a small, flat wooden racket, faced with sandpaper or rubber, used to hit the ball in table tennis. 6 flipper or similar limb, as of a turtle, whale, or penguin. —*v.t.* 1 row (a boat or canoe) with a paddle or paddles. 2 beat with a paddle; spank. —*v.i.* 1 use a paddle to move a canoe, etc. 2 row gently. [origin uncertain] **—pad′dler,** *n.*

pad dle[2] (pad′l), *v.i.,* **-dled, -dling.** 1 move the hands or feet about in water; dabble or play in shallow water. 2 walk with short, unsteady steps, like those of a young child; toddle. [apparently related to PAD[2]] **—pad′dle like′,** *adj.* **—pad′dler,** *n.*

pad dle fish (pad′l fish′), *n., pl.* **-fish es** or **-fish.** any of a family of large scaleless fishes with long, flat paddlelike snouts, especially one species occurring in the Mississippi River and its tributaries.

paddle wheel, wheel with paddles fixed around it for propelling a ship over the water.

pad dock (pad′ək), *n.* 1 a small, enclosed field near a stable or house, used for exercising animals or as a pasture. 2 pen at a race track where horses are saddled before a race. [variant of *parrock,* Old English *pearroc.* Related to PARK.]

pad dy (pad′ē), *n., pl.* **-dies.** 1 rice. 2 rice in the husk, uncut or gathered. 3 field of rice. Also, **padi.** [< Malay *padi*]

paddy wagon, SLANG. patrol wagon.

Pad e rew ski (pad′ə ref′skē), *n.* **Ignace Jan,** 1860-1941, Polish pianist, composer, and statesman.

pad i (pad′ē), *n.* paddy.

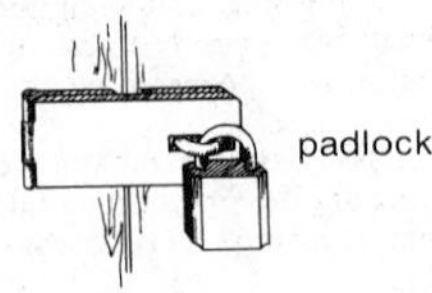
padlock

pad lock (pad′lok′), *n.* a detachable lock, designed to hang on the object fastened by a curved bar, hinged at one end and snapped shut at the other. —*v.t.* fasten with a padlock.

pa dre (pä′drā), *n.* 1 father. It is used as a name for a priest, especially in regions where Spanish, Portuguese, or Italian is spoken. 2 INFORMAL. chaplain in the armed forces. [< Italian, Spanish, or Portuguese < Latin *pater* father]

pa dro ne (pä drō′nā *for 1;* pə drō′nē *for 2*), *n.* 1 ITALIAN. **a** master; boss. **b** innkeeper. 2 person who provides Italian laborers on contract with an employer, as in America. [< Italian < Latin *patronus.* Doublet of PATRON, PATROON.]

Pad u a (paj′ü ə, pad′yü ə), *n.* city in NE Italy. 226,000.

pae an (pē′ən), *n.* song of praise, thanksgiving, joy, or triumph. Also, **pean.** [< Greek *paian* hymn to Apollo (called *Paian*)]

pa gan (pā′gən), *n.* 1 person who is not a Christian, Jew, or Moslem; one who worships many gods, or no gods; heathen. The ancient Greeks and Romans were pagans. See **heathen** for synonym study. 2 person who has no religion. —*adj.* 1 of or having to do with pagans; heathen. 2 not religious. [< Latin *paganus* rustic (at a time when Christianity was accepted by urban populations) < *pagus* village]

pa gan dom (pā′gən dəm), *n.* the pagan world; pagans collectively; all pagans.

Pag a ni ni (pag′ə nē′nē), *n.* **Nicolò,** 1782-1840, Italian violinist.

pa gan ism (pā′gə niz′əm), *n.* 1 pagan attitude toward religion or morality. 2 beliefs and practices of pagans. 3 condition of being a pagan.

pa gan ize (pā′gə nīz), *v.t., v.i.,* **-ized, -iz ing.** make or become pagan.

page[1] (pāj), *n., v.,* **paged, pag ing.** —*n.* 1 one side of a leaf or sheet of paper: *a page in this book.* 2 print or writing on one side of a leaf. 3 a record: *the pages of history.* 4 happening or time considered as part of history: *The settling of the West is an exciting page in the history of the United States.* —*v.t.* number the pages of. [< Middle French < Latin *pagina*]

page[2] (pāj), *n., v.,* **paged, pag ing.** —*n.* 1 person employed by a hotel, club, legislature, etc., to run errands, carry parcels, deliver messages, etc. 2 youth who attends a person of rank. 3 youth who was preparing to be a knight. —*v.t.* try to find (a person) at a hotel, club, etc., by having his name called out. —*v.i.* act as page; be a page. [< Old French, perhaps < Medieval Latin *pagius* a rustic]

pag eant (paj′ənt), *n.* 1 an elaborate spectacle; procession in costume; pomp; display; show: *The coronation of a new ruler is always a splendid pageant.* 2 a public entertainment that represents scenes from history, legend, or the like. 3 empty show, not reality. [Middle English *pagent, pagen,* probably < Late Latin *pagina* stage, plank < Latin, page[1]]

pag eant ry (paj′ən trē), *n., pl.* **-ries.** 1 a splendid show; gorgeous display; pomp. 2 mere show; empty display. 3 pageant, or pageants collectively.

page boy (pāj′boi′), *n.* a shoulder-length hair style for women in which the hair in the back is turned under at the ends in a soft roll.

pag i nate (paj′ə nāt), *v.t.,* **-nat ed, -nat ing.** mark the number of pages of; page (a book, etc.).

pag i na tion (paj′ə nā′shən), *n.* 1 act of numbering the pages of books, etc. 2 the figures with which pages are numbered. 3 number of pages or leaves in a book, etc.

pagoda in the Chinese style of architecture

pa go da (pə gō′də), *n.* temple or other sacred building having many stories, with a roof curving upward from each story, found in India, China, Japan, and other Asian countries. [< Portuguese *pagode* < Tamil *pagavadi* < Sanskrit *bhagavatī* goddess]

Pa go Pa go (päng′ō päng′ō; päng′gō päng′gō; pä′gō pä′gō), capital of American Samoa, on Tutuila, in the SW Pacific. 2000.

paid (pād), *adj.* 1 receiving money; hired. 2 no longer owed; settled. 3 cashed. —*v.* pt. and pp. of **pay**[1].

pail (pāl), *n.* 1 a round container with a handle, for carrying liquids, etc.; bucket. 2 amount a pail holds; pailful. [Old English *pægel* and < Old French *paielle,* both < Medieval Latin *pagella* a liquid measure]

pail ful (pāl′fu̇l), *n., pl.* **-fuls.** amount that fills a pail.

pain (pān), *n.* 1 a feeling of being hurt; suffering. 2 a single or localized feeling of hurt: *a sharp pain in one's back.* See synonym study below. 3 mental suffering; grief; sorrow. 4 **pains,** *pl.* sufferings of childbirth. 5 **on pain of** or **under pain of,** with the punishment or penalty of unless a certain thing is done. 6 **take pains,** be careful: *She took pains to do the job well.* —*v.t.* cause to suffer; give pain to; hurt. —*v.i.* cause suffering; give pain. [< Old French *peine* < Latin *poena* penalty < Greek *poinē*]

Syn. *n.* 1 **Pain, ache** mean a feeling of being hurt. **Pain** particularly suggests a sharp hurt, but of any degree from a sudden jab in one spot to a very severe and sometimes long-lasting hurt of the whole body: *I have a pain in my side.* **Ache** means a steady, usually dull hurt: *I have a headache from reading too long. I have a stomach ache.*

Paine (pān), *n.* **Thomas,** 1737-1809, American writer on politics and religion, born in England.

pained (pānd), *adj.* 1 hurt, distressed, grieved, etc. 2 expressing or showing pain: *a pained look.*

pain ful (pān′fəl), *adj.* 1 causing pain; unpleasant; hurting: *a painful illness, a painful duty.* 2 involving much trouble or labor; difficult. **—pain′ful ly,** *adv.* **—pain′ful ness,** *n.*

pain less (pān′lis), *adj.* without pain; causing no pain. **—pain′less ly,** *adv.* **—pain′less ness,** *n.*

pains tak ing (pānz′tā′king), *adj.* 1 very careful; particular; scrupulous. 2 marked or characterized by attentive care; carefully done. **—pains′tak′ing ly,** *adv.*

paint (pānt), *n.* 1 substance consisting of solid coloring matter or pigment mixed with a liquid, that can be spread on a surface to make a layer or film of white, black, or colored matter. 2 layer or film created by applying paint to a surface. 3 any cosmetic that colors or tints, especially one applied to the face, as rouge. —*v.t.* 1 cover or decorate with paint: *paint a house.* 2 represent (an object, etc.) in colors, usually on a prepared surface. 3 picture vividly in words. 4 put on like paint: *The doctor painted iodine on the cut.* —*v.i.* 1 use paint in covering, decorating, or coloring. 2 practice the art of painting; make pictures. [< Old French *peint,* past participle of *peindre* to paint < Latin *pingere*]

paint brush (pānt′brush′), *n.* 1 brush for putting on paint. 2 Indian paintbrush.

painted bunting, a small bright-colored finch of the southern United States, the male of which has a purple head, red breast, and green back; nonpareil.

paint er¹ (pān′tər), *n.* 1 person who paints pictures; artist. 2 person who paints houses, woodwork, etc. [< Old French *peinteur,* ultimately < Latin *pictorem* < *pingere* to paint]

paint er² (pān′tər), *n.* a rope, usually fastened to the bow of a boat, for tying it to a ship, pier, etc. [probably < Middle French *pentoir* hanging cordage < Latin *pendere* to hang]

paint er³ (pān′tər), *n.* puma. [variant of earlier *panter* panther]

paint er ly (pān′tər lē), *adj.* of, suitable to, or characteristic of a painter.

paint ing (pān′ting), *n.* 1 something painted; picture. 2 act of one who paints. 3 art of representation, decoration, and creating beauty with paints.

pair (per, par), *n., pl.* **pairs** or *(sometimes after a numeral)* **pair,** *v.* —*n.* 1 set of two; two that go or are used together: *a pair of shoes, a pair of horses.* See synonym study below. 2 a single thing consisting of two parts that cannot be used separately: *a pair of scissors, a pair of trousers.* 3 man and woman who are married or are engaged to be married. 4 two animals that are mated. 5 two members on opposite sides in a legislative body who arrange not to vote on a certain question or for a certain time, especially so that their absence may not affect the voting. 6 the arrangement thus made. 7 two cards of the same value in different suits, viewed as a unit in one's hand: *a pair of sixes, a pair of jacks.* —*v.t.* arrange as a pair or in pairs: *pair socks. Her gloves were neatly paired in a drawer.* —*v.i.* 1 be arranged as a pair or in pairs; match. 2 join in love and marriage. 3 mate.

palanquin

pair off, arrange in pairs; form into pairs. [< Old French *paire* < Latin *paria* equals, neuter plural of *par, paris* part, share]

Syn. *n.* 1 **Pair, couple** mean two things of the same kind. **Pair** applies to two things that belong together because they match or complement each other: *I bought a new pair of gloves.* **Couple** usually applies to any two of the same kind: *I bought a couple of shirts.*

pais ley (pāz′lē), *n., pl.* **-leys,** *adj.* —*n.* 1 a soft woolen cloth with a very elaborate and colorful pattern. 2 something made of paisley. —*adj.* made of paisley; having a pattern like paisley. [< *Paisley,* city in Scotland]

Pai ute (pī yüt′, pī üt′), *n., pl.* **-ute** or **-utes.** 1 member of a tribe of Indians living in Utah, Nevada, California, and Arizona. 2 language of this tribe.

pajama party, slumber party.

pa ja mas (pə jä′məz, pə jam′əz), *n.pl.* 1 sleeping or lounging garments consisting of a jacket or blouse and loose trousers fastened at the waist. 2 loose trousers worn by Moslem men and women. Also, **pyjamas.** [< Hindustani *pājāmā* < Persian *pāe* leg + *jāmah* garment]

Pak i stan (pak′ə stan, pä′kə stän), *n.* country in S Asia, west of India. 39,000,000 pop.; 310,000 sq. mi. *Capital:* Islamabad. See **Bangladesh** for map.

Pak i stan i (pak′ə stan′ē, pä′kə stä′nē), *n., pl.* **-stan is** or **-stan i,** *adj.* —*n.* native or inhabitant of Pakistan. —*adj.* of or having to do with Pakistan.

pal (pal), *n., v.,* **palled, pal ling.** —*n.* a close friend; comrade; partner. —*v.i.* associate as pals. [< Romany, variant of *pral* brother < Sanskrit *bhratr*]

pal ace (pal′is), *n.* 1 the official home of a king, queen, bishop, or some other exalted personage. 2 BRITISH. the official residence of an archbishop or bishop within his cathedral city. 3 a very fine house or building. 4 a more or less imposing or pretentious place of entertainment. 5 an official building, especially one of imposing size: *the palace of justice.* [< Old French *palais* < Latin *palatium* < *Palatium* Palatine Hill in Rome]

pal a din (pal′ə dən), *n.* 1 one of the twelve knights in attendance on Charlemagne. 2 a knightly defender; champion. [< French < Italian *paladino* < Latin *palatinus.* See PALATINE.]

palaeo-, *combining form.* a variant form of **paleo-.**

pa laes tra (pə les′trə), *n.* 1 a public place for physical exercise and training in ancient Greece. 2 a wrestling school. 3 any gymnasium. Also, **palestra.** [< Greek *palaistra* < *palaiein* to wrestle]

hat, āge, fär; let, ēqual, tėrm;
it, īce; hot, ōpen, ôrder;
oil, out; cup, pu̇t, rüle;
ch, child; ng, long; sh, she;
th, thin; ᴛʜ, then; zh, measure;

ə represents *a* in about, *e* in taken, *i* in pencil, *o* in lemon, *u* in circus.

< = from, derived from, taken from.

pal an quin or **pal an keen** (pal′ən kēn′), *n.* a covered litter enclosed at the sides, carried by poles resting on the shoulders of four or six men, formerly used in the Orient. [< Portuguese *palanquim* < Malay *palangki* couch]

pal at a bil i ty (pal′ə tə bil′ə tē), *n.* palatable quality or condition.

pal at a ble (pal′ə tə bəl), *adj.* 1 agreeable to the taste; pleasing. 2 agreeable to the mind or feelings; acceptable. **—pal′at a ble ness,** *n.* **—pal′at a bly,** *adv.*

pal a tal (pal′ə təl), *adj.* 1 of or having to do with the palate. 2 (of speech sounds) made with the front or middle of the tongue near or touching the hard palate. The *y* in *yet* is a palatal sound. —*n.* a palatal sound.

pal a tal ize (pal′ə tə līz), *v.t.,* **-ized, -iz ing.** make palatal; change into a palatal sound. **—pal′a tal i za′tion,** *n.*

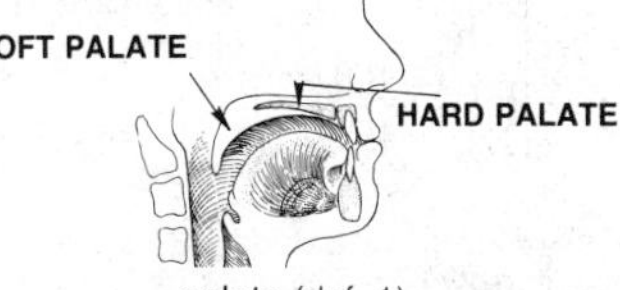

palate (def. 1)

pal ate (pal′it), *n.* 1 roof of the mouth. The bony part in front is the hard palate, and the fleshy part in back is the soft palate. 2 sense of taste: *The new flavor pleased his palate.* 3 a liking; relish: *have no palate for danger.* [< Latin *palatum*]

pa la tial (pə lā′shəl), *adj.* of, like, or fit for a palace; magnificent. **—pa la′tial ly,** *adv.*

Pa lat i nate (pə lat′n āt, pə lat′n it), *n.* 1 two regions in S West Germany, which together formed an independent state from the 1300's to 1620. 2 **palatinate,** region under the rule of a palatine.

pal a tine (pal′ə tīn, pal′ə tən), *adj.* 1 having royal rights in one's own territory. A count palatine was subject only to the emperor or king, especially the Holy Roman Emperor. 2 of a lord who has royal rights in his own territory. 3 palatial. 4 **Palatine,** of or having to do with the Palatinate. —*n.* 1 lord having royal rights in his own territory. 2 officer of an imperial palace. 3 **Palatine,** native or inhabitant of the Palatinate. [< Latin *palatinus* of the Palatium or Palatine Hill in Rome, where the emperor's palace was located]

Pa lau (pä lou′), *n.* group of about 100 islands in the W Pacific, a part of the Caroline Islands. 12,000 pop.; 185 sq. mi.

pa lav er (pə lav′ər), *n.* 1 parley or conference, especially between Europeans and peoples of other cultures, whose customs required the formal exchange of compliments, gifts, etc., before the bringing up of any matter of business. 2 unnecessary or idle words; mere talk. 3 smooth, persuading talk; fluent talk; flattery. —*v.i.* 1 talk, especially talk profusely or unnecessarily. 2 talk fluently and flatteringly. [< Portuguese *palavra* < Late Latin *parabola* speech. Doublet of PARABLE, PARABOLA, PARLEY, PAROLE.]

pa laz zo (pä lät′sō), *n., pl.* **-zi** (-sē). palace, mansion, or large town house in Italy. [< Italian]

pale¹ (pāl), *adj.,* **pal er, pal est,** *v.,* **paled, pal ing.** —*adj.* 1 without much color; whitish: *When you have been ill, your face is sometimes pale.* See synonym study below. 2 not bright; dim: *a pale blue.* —*v.i.* turn pale. —*v.t.* cause to become pale. [< Old French < Latin *pallidum* < *pallere* be pale. Doublet of PALLID.] **—pale′ly,** *adv.* **—pale′ness,** *n.*

Syn. *adj.* 1 **Pale, pallid, wan** mean with little or no color. **Pale** means without much natural or healthy color: *He is pale and tired-looking.* **Pallid** suggests having all color drained away, as by sickness or weakness: *Her pallid face shows her suffering.* **Wan** emphasizes the faintness and whiteness coming from a weakened or unhealthy condition: *The starved refugees were wan.*

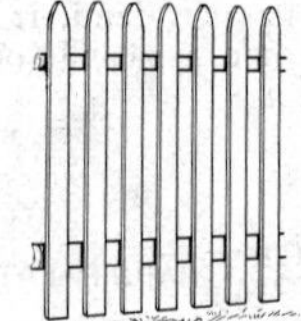

pale² (def. 1) fence made of pales

pale² (pāl), *n., v.,* **paled, pal ing.** —*n.* 1 a long, narrow board, pointed on top, used for fences; picket. 2 boundary; restriction: *outside the pale of civilized society.* 3 **beyond the pale,** socially unacceptable; improper: *His rude behavior at the party was beyond the pale.* 4 an enclosed place; enclosure. 5 district or territory within fixed bounds or subject to a particular jurisdiction. 6 a broad vertical stripe in the middle of an escutcheon. —*v.t.* enclose with pales or a fence. [< Old French *pal* < Latin *palus* stake. Doublet of POLE¹.]

pale face (pāl′fās′), *n.* a white person. The American Indians are said to have called white people palefaces.

paleo-, *combining form.* 1 old; ancient; prehistoric, as in *paleography.* 2 early or earliest, as in *Paleocene.* Also, **palaeo-.** [< Greek *palaio-* < *palaios* ancient]

pa le o bot a ny (pā′lē ō bot′n ē), *n.* branch of paleontology dealing with fossil plants.

Pa le o cene (pā′lē ə sēn′), *n.* 1 the earliest epoch of the Tertiary period, before the Eocene, during which shallow inland seas drained and the first primates appeared. See chart under **geology.** 2 the rocks formed in this epoch. —*adj.* of or having to do with this epoch or its rocks. [< *paleo-* + Greek *kainos* recent]

pa le og ra pher (pā′lē og′rə fər), *n.* an expert in paleography.

pa le o graph ic (pā′lē ə graf′ik), *adj.* of or having to do with paleography.

pa le og ra phy (pā′lē og′rə fē), *n.* 1 ancient writing or forms of writing. 2 study of ancient writings to determine the dates, origins, meaning, etc.

Pa le o-In di an (pā′lē ō in′dē ən), *n.* one of a prehistoric group of people believed to have migrated from Asia to the Americas during the late Ice Age. —*adj.* of or having to do with Paleo-Indians: *Paleo-Indian artifacts.*

Pa le o lith ic (pā′lē ə lith′ik), *adj.* of or having to do with the earliest part of the Stone Age. Paleolithic tools were crudely chipped out of stone.

pa le on to log i cal (pā′lē on′tl oj′ə kəl), *adj.* of or having to do with paleontology.

pa le on tol o gist (pā′lē on tol′ə jist), *n.* an expert in paleontology.

pa le on tol o gy (pā′lē on tol′ə jē), *n.* science of the forms of life existing in prehistoric time, as represented by fossil animals and plants. [< *paleo-* + Greek *on, ontos* a being]

Pa le o zo ic (pā′lē ə zō′ik), *n.* 1 the geological era after the Proterozoic and before the Mesozoic, characterized by the development of the first fishes, land plants, amphibians, reptiles, insects, and forests of fernlike trees. See chart under **geology.** 2 the rocks formed in this era. —*adj.* of or having to do with this era or its rocks.

pa le o zo ol o gy (pā′lē ō zō ol′ə jē), *n.* branch of paleontology dealing with fossil animals.

Pa ler mo (pə ler′mō, pə lėr′mō), *n.* seaport and capital of Sicily, in the NW part. 659,000.

Pal es tine (pal′ə stīn), *n.* region or country in SW Asia between the Mediterranean Sea and the Jordan River, sometimes including various other lands. The name has been applied since ancient times to the land of the Jews. Palestine is often called the Holy Land and in the Bible is called Canaan. It is now divided chiefly between Israel and Jordan. **—Pal′es tin′i an,** *adj., n.*

pa les tra (pə les′trə), *n.* palaestra.

Pal es tri na (pal′ə strē′nə), *n.* **Giovanni da,** 1526?-1594, Italian composer of church music.

palette (def. 1)

pal ette (pal′it), *n.* 1 a thin board, usually oval or oblong, with a thumb hole at one end, used by painters to lay and mix colors on. 2 set of colors on this board. [< French, diminutive of *pale* spade < Latin *pala*]

pal frey (pôl′frē), *n., pl.* **-freys.** ARCHAIC. a gentle riding horse, especially one used by ladies. [< Old French *palefrey* < Late Latin *paraveredus* horse for outlying districts]

Pa li (pä′lē), *n.* an Indic language, a later form of Sanskrit, used in the sacred writings of the Buddhists and still existing as a literary language in Ceylon, Burma, and Thailand.

pal imp sest (pal′imp sest), *n.* 1 parchment or other writing material from which one or more previous writings have been erased to make room for another. 2 manuscript with one text written over another. [< Greek *palimpsestos* scraped again < *palin* again + *psēn* rub]

pal in drome (pal′in drōm), *n.* word, verse, or sentence which reads the same backward or forward. The sentence "Madam, I'm Adam" is a palindrome that contains (in its first word) another palindrome. [< Greek *palindromos* a recurrence, a running back < *palin* again, back < *dromos* a running]

pal ing (pā′ling), *n.* 1 fence of pales. 2 pales collectively, as fencing material. 3 pale in a fence.

palisades (def. 3)

pal i sade (pal′ə sād′), *n., v.,* **-sad ed, -sad ing.** —*n.* 1 a long, strong wooden stake pointed at the top end. 2 a strong fence of such stakes set firmly and closely together in the ground to enclose or defend. 3 **palisades,** *pl.* line of high, steep cliffs. 4 palisade layer. —*v.t.* furnish or surround with a palisade. [< Middle French *palissade* < Provençal *palissada* < Latin *palus* stake]

palisade layer, layer of elongated cells between the upper and lower epidermis of leaves; palisade. The palisade layer has many chloroplasts and takes part in photosynthesis.

Pal i sades (pal′ə sādz′), *n.pl.* line of high, steep cliffs along the western bank of the Hudson River opposite New York City and Yonkers.

pall¹ (pôl), *n.* 1 a heavy, dark cloth, often made of velvet, spread over a coffin, a hearse, or a tomb. 2 a dark, gloomy covering: *A pall of smoke shut out the sun from the city.* 3 a linen cloth, or now usually a square piece of cardboard covered with linen, used to cover the chalice. [Old English *pæll* < Latin *pallium* cloak]

pall² (pôl), *v.i.* become distasteful or very tiresome because there has been too much of something. —*v.t.* cloy. [variant of *appall*]

pal la di um¹ (pə lā′dē əm), *n.* a light, silver-white metallic element which occurs in nature with platinum. Palladium is ductile and malleable and is used in making scientific instruments, in alloys with precious metals such as gold and silver, and as a catalyst. *Symbol:* Pd; *atomic number* 46. See pages 326 and 327 for table. [< New Latin < the asteroid *Pallas*]

pal la di um² (pə lā′dē əm), *n., pl.* **-di a** (-dē ə). 1 anything regarded as an important safeguard. 2 **Palladium,** statue of Pallas Athena in Troy. On the preservation of this statue, the safety of the city was supposed to depend. [< Latin < Greek *palladion,* diminutive of *Pallas*]

Pal las (pal′əs), *n.* 1 (in Greek myths) a name of Athena. 2 one of the asteroids.

Pallas Athena, Athena.

pall bear er (pôl′ber′ər, pôl′bar′ər), *n.*

hat, āge, fär; let, ēqual, tėrm;
it, īce; hot, ōpen, ôrder;
oil, out; cup, pu̇t, rüle;
ch, child; ng, long; sh, she;
th, thin; ᴛʜ, then; zh, measure;

ə represents *a* in about, *e* in taken, *i* in pencil, *o* in lemon, *u* in circus.

< = from, derived from, taken from.

one of the men who walk with or carry the coffin at a funeral.

pal let[1] (pal′it), *n.* bed of straw; small or poor bed. [< Old French *paillet* < *paille* straw < Latin *palea*]

pal let[2] (pal′it), *n.* 1 a flat blade used by potters and others for shaping their work. 2 a painter's palette. 3 projection on a pawl that engages with a ratchet wheel. 4 any of the projections in the escapement of a watch, clock, or other mechanism, that alternately catch and release the notches of the wheels. 5 a low, portable platform on which loads are stacked to keep them off the ground in storage and to make the entire stack, including the pallet, easy to pick up. [variant of *palette*]

pal let ize (pal′ə tīz), *v.t.,* **-ized, -iz ing.** 1 put (a load) on a pallet. 2 equip with pallets: *palletize machines.* **—pal′let i za′tion,** *n.*

pal li ate (pal′ē āt), *v.t.,* **-at ed, -at ing.** 1 lessen the severity of without curing; mitigate: *palliate a disease.* 2 make appear less serious; excuse: *palliate a fault.* [< Late Latin *palliatum* covered with a cloak < Latin *pallium* cloak] **—pal′li a′tion,** *n.* **—pal′li a′tor,** *n.*

pal li a tive (pal′ē ā′tiv), *adj.* useful to lessen or soften; mitigating; excusing. *—n.* something that lessens, softens, mitigates, or excuses. **—pal′li a′tive ly,** *adv.*

pal lid (pal′id), *adj.* lacking normal color; wan; pale: *a pallid complexion.* See **pale** for synonym study. [< Latin *pallidum.* Doublet of PALE[1].] **—pal′lid ly,** *adv.* **—pal′lid ness,** *n.*

pal lor (pal′ər), *n.* lack of normal color from fear, illness, death, etc.; paleness. [< Latin < *pallere* to pale]

palm[1] (päm, pälm), *n.* 1 the inside of the hand between the wrist and the fingers. 2 width of a hand as a rough unit of measure; 3 to 4 inches. 3 length of a hand as a rough unit of measure; 7 to 10 inches. 4 part of a glove covering the palm. 5 any relatively flat, widened part at the end of an armlike projection, as the blade of an oar or paddle or the inner side of the fluke of an anchor. **6 grease the palm of,** bribe. **7 have an itching palm,** be greedy for money. *—v.t.* 1 conceal in the hand. 2 pass or get accepted (something not good). **3 palm off,** pass off or get accepted by tricks, fraud, or false representation. [< Old French *paume* < Latin *palma*] **—palm′er,** *n.*

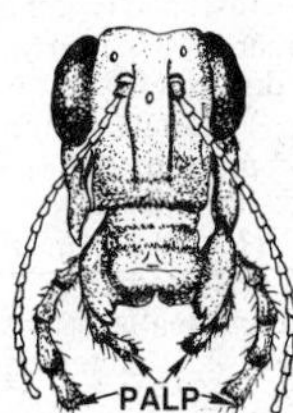

palp
palps of a grasshopper

palm[2] (päm, pälm), *n.* 1 any of a family of monocotyledonous trees or shrubs which grow in warm climates. Most palms have tall trunks, no branches, and many large pinnate or fan-shaped leaves at the top. 2 leaf or stalk of leaves of a palm tree, used as a symbol of victory or triumph. 3 victory; triumph. **4 bear off the palm** or **carry off the palm,** be the victor; win. **5 yield the palm to,** admit defeat by; defer to. [Old English *pælm* < Latin *palma* palm tree, palm[1] (perhaps because the shape of the leaves is somewhat like a hand)] **—palm′like′,** *adj.*

Pal ma (päl′mä), *n.* seaport in W Majorca, capital of the Balearic Islands. 208,000.

pal mar (pal′mər), *adj.* of or having to do with the palm of the hand.

pal mate (pal′māt), *adj.* 1 shaped like a hand with the fingers spread out: *a palmate leaf.* See **leaf** for picture. 2 having the front toes joined by a web; web-footed.

pal ma tion (pal mā′shən), *n.* 1 palmate formation or structure. 2 one division of a palmate structure.

Palm Beach, winter resort in SE Florida. 9000.

palm er (pä′mər, päl′mər), *n.* 1 pilgrim returning from the Holy Land bringing a palm branch as a token. 2 any pilgrim.

Palm er ston (pä′mər stən, päl′mər stən), *n.* **Viscount,** 1784-1865, Henry John Temple, British statesman, prime minister from 1855 to 1858 and from 1859 to 1865.

pal met to (pal met′ō), *n., pl.* **-tos** or **-toes.** any of a genus of relatively small palms with fan-shaped leaves, abundant on the southeastern coast of the United States. [< Spanish *palmito,* diminutive of *palma* palm]

palm ist (pä′mist, päl′mist), *n.* person who practices palmistry.

palm is try (pä′mə strē, päl′mə strē), *n.* the supposed art, or its practice, of telling a person's fortune, ascertaining his character, etc., from the lines and marks in the palm of his hand. [Middle English *pawmestry, palmestrie* < *paume, palme* palm]

pal mit ic acid (pal mit′ik), a white crystalline acid, solid at ordinary temperatures, contained as a glyceride in palm oil and in most solid fats. *Formula:* $C_{16}H_{32}O_2$

palm oil, a yellowish fat from the fruit of the palm, used to make soap and candles.

Palm Sunday, the Sunday before Easter Sunday, commemorating the triumphal entry of Christ into Jerusalem, when palm branches were strewn before Him.

palm y (pä′mē, päl′mē), *adj.,* **palm i er, palm i est.** 1 abounding in or shaded by palms. 2 flourishing; prosperous.

pal my ra (pal mī′rə), *n.* a tropical Asian palm with large, fan-shaped leaves, important for its great variety of uses, as the wood for timber, the leaves for thatch, baskets, and paper, the sap for a kind of sugar, and the fruit and young roots for food. [< Portuguese *palmeira* < Latin *palma* palm[2]]

pal o mi no (pal′ə mē′nō), *n., pl.* **-nos.** a cream-colored or golden-tan horse of Arabian stock, typically of slender, graceful build, and having a mane and tail usually lighter colored. [< Spanish, originally, young dove]

palp (palp), *n.* a sensory appendage of arthropods usually located near the mouth; palpus. [< French *palpe* < Latin *palpus* a pat, caress]

pal pa bil i ty (pal′pə bil′ə tē), *n.* quality of being palpable.

pal pa ble (pal′pə bəl), *adj.* 1 readily seen or heard and recognized; obvious: *a palpable error.* 2 that can be touched or felt; tangible. [< Late Latin *palpabilis* < Latin *palpare* to feel, pat]

pal pa bly (pal′pə blē), *adv.* 1 plainly; obviously. 2 to the touch.

pal pate (pal′pāt), *v.t.,* **-pat ed, -pat ing.** examine by touch, especially in medical diagnosis. **—pal pa′tion,** *n.*

pal pi (pal′pī), *n.* pl. of **palpus.**

pal pi tant (pal′pə tənt), *adj.* palpitating.

pal pi tate (pal′pə tāt), *v.i.,* **-tat ed, -tat ing.** 1 beat very rapidly, as from emotion, exercise, or disease; throb: *Your heart palpitates when you are excited.* 2 quiver; tremble: *palpitate with terror.* [< Latin *palpitare* to throb < *palpare* to pat]

pal pi ta tion (pal′pə tā′shən), *n.* 1 a very rapid beating of the heart; throb. 2 a quivering; trembling.

pal pus (pal′pəs), *n., pl.* **pal pi.** palp.

pal sied (pôl′zēd), *adj.* 1 having palsy; paralyzed. 2 shaking; trembling.

pal sy (pôl′zē), *n., pl.* **-sies,** *v.,* **-sied, -sy ing.** *—n.* paralysis, especially a form of paralysis occurring with Parkinson's disease. *—v.t.* afflict with palsy. [Middle English *palesie* < Old French *paralysie* < Latin *paralysis.* Doublet of PARALYSIS.]

pal ter (pôl′tər), *v.i.* 1 talk or act insincerely; trifle deceitfully. 2 act carelessly; trifle. 3 haggle. [origin unknown] **—pal′ter er,** *n.*

pal try (pôl′trē), *adj.,* **-tri er, -tri est.** 1 almost worthless; trifling; petty; mean. 2 of no worth; despicable; contemptible. [probably related to Low German *paltrig* ragged, torn] **—pal′tri ly,** *adv.* **—pal′tri ness,** *n.*

pal y nol o gy (pal′ə nol′ə jē), *n.* the study of plant spores and pollen, especially in fossil form. [< Greek *palynein* to strew + English *-logy*]

Pa mirs (pə mirz′), *n.pl.* high plateau and mountain range covering a large part of central Asia, in the Soviet Union, China, India, Pakistan and Afghanistan. Highest peak, 25,146 ft.

Pam li co Sound (pam′lə kō), narrow stretch of water in E North Carolina between the coast and a long chain of narrow islands. 80 mi. long.

pam pas (pam′pəz), *n.pl.* the vast, grassy, treeless plains of South America, especially in Argentina. [< Spanish < Quechua *pampa* a plain]

pam pe an (pam pē′ən, pam′pē ən), *adj.* of or having to do with the pampas.

pam per (pam′pər), *v.t.* indulge too much; allow too many privileges; spoil: *pamper a child, pamper one's appetite.* [Middle English *pamperen*] **—pam′per er,** *n.*

pam phlet (pam′flit), *n.* booklet in paper covers; brochure. It often deals with a question of current interest. [Middle English *pamflet* booklet < Old French *Pamphilet,* popular name for a Latin poem of the 1100's called "Pamphilus, seu de Amore" Pamphilus, or on Love]

pam phlet eer (pam′flə tir′), *n.* person who writes pamphlets, especially on controversial subjects. *—v.i.* write and issue pamphlets.

pan[1] (pan), *n., v.,* **panned, pan ning.** *—n.* 1 dish for cooking and other household uses, usually broad, shallow, and often with no cover. 2 anything like this. Gold and other metals are sometimes obtained by washing ore in pans. The dishes on a pair of scales are called pans. 3 (in old-fashioned guns) the hollow part of the lock that held a little gunpowder to set the gun off. 4 hardpan. 5 a hollow or depression in the ground, especially one in which water stands. —*v.t.* 1 cook in a pan. 2 wash in a pan: *pan gold.* 3 wash (gravel, sand, etc.) in a pan to separate the gold. 4 INFORMAL. criticize severely: *The drama critic panned the new play.* —*v.i.* 1 wash gold-bearing gravel, sand, etc., in a pan in order to separate the gold. 2 yield gold when washed in a pan. 3 **pan out,** INFORMAL. turn out; work out: *The scheme panned out well.* [Old English *panne*]

pan² (pan), *v.,* **panned, pan ning.** —*v.i.* (of a motion picture or television camera) move horizontally or vertically so as to take in a larger scene, or to follow a moving object: *The camera panned from the speaker to the audience.* —*v.t.* move (a camera) in this way. [shortened from *panorama*]

Pan (pan), *n.* (in Greek myths) the god of forests, pastures, flocks, and shepherds. Pan is described as a man with the legs, horns, and ears of a goat, who wandered through the woods playing on musical pipes.

pan-, *combining form.* all; of all; entirely: *Pan-American = of all Americans. Panchromatic = entirely chromatic.* [< Greek < *pan,* neuter of *pas* all]

Pan., Panama.

pan a ce a (pan′ə sē′ə), *n.* remedy for all diseases or ills; cure-all. [< Latin < Greek *panakeia* < *pan-* + *akos* cure]

pan a ce an (pan′ə sē′ən), *adj.* of the nature of a panacea.

pa nache (pə nash′), *n.* 1 tuft or plume of feathers used ornamentally, especially on a helmet. 2 a flamboyant manner or style; swagger; dash. [< Middle French *pennache* < Italian *pennacchio* < *penna* feather < Latin]

Pan a ma (pan′ə mä, pan′ə mä′), *n.* 1 **Isthmus of,** narrow neck of land which connects North America with South America. 420 mi. long; 31 mi. wide at the narrowest part. 2 country on the Isthmus of Panama, on either side of the Canal Zone. 1,415,000 pop.; 29,200 sq. mi. *Capital:* Panama. 3 its capital, a seaport on the Bay of Panama. 412,000. 4 **Bay of,** bay of the Pacific on the S coast of the Isthmus of Panama. 5 **panama,** a fine hat woven from the young leaves of a palmlike plant of Central and South America.

Panama Canal, canal cut across the Isthmus of Panama to connect the Atlantic and Pacific oceans, built and controlled by the United States. 40 mi. long; 100-300 ft. wide.

Panama Canal Zone, Canal Zone.

Pan a ma ni an (pan′ə mā′nē ən), *adj.* of or having to do with Panama. —*n.* native or inhabitant of Panama.

Pan-A mer i can (pan′ə mer′ə kən), *adj.* of all Americans or the Americas; including all the people or countries of North, Central, and South America.

Pan-A mer i can ism (pan′ə mer′ə kə-niz′əm), *n.* principle or policy that all the countries in South America, Central America, and North America should cooperate to promote cultural, commercial, and social progress.

Pan American Union, organization of 21 American republics formed in 1890 to promote mutual cooperation and peace. It created the Organization of American States in 1948.

pan a tel a (pan′ə tel′ə), *n.* a long, slender cigar pointed at the closed end. Also, **panetela, panetella.** [< Spanish *panetela*]

Pa nay (pä nī′), *n.* one of the central islands in the Philippines. 2,441,000 pop.; 4400 sq. mi.

pan cake (pan′kāk′), *n., v.,* **-caked, -cak ing.** —*n.* 1 a thin, flat cake of batter, fried or baked in a pan or on a griddle. 2 a quick, almost flat landing made by an aircraft, as a result of its leveling off and stalling several feet above the ground. —*v.i.* (of an aircraft) make a quick, almost flat landing.

Pan chen Lama (pän′chən), one of the two principal lamas of Tibet (the Dalai Lama is the other).

pan chro mat ic (pan′krō mat′ik), *adj.* sensitive to light of all colors: *a panchromatic photographic film.*

pan cre as (pan′krē əs), *n.* 1 a large gland in vertebrates near the stomach that secretes insulin into the blood and **pancreatic juice,** a digestive juice which contains various enzymes, into the small intestine. The pancreas of animals when used for food is called sweetbread. 2 a similar organ in certain invertebrates. [< Greek *pankreas* < *pan-* all + *kreas* flesh]

pan cre at ic (pan′krē at′ik), *adj.* of the pancreas: *pancreatic secretions.*

pan cre a tin (pan′krē ə tən, pang′krē ə-tən), *n.* 1 any of the enzymes of pancreatic juice. 2 preparation extracted from the pancreas of animals, used to aid digestion.

panda (def. 1)—about 5 ft. long

pan da (pan′də), *n.* 1 a bearlike mammal of Tibet and parts of southern and southwestern China, of the same family as the raccoon, mostly white with black legs; giant panda. 2 a reddish-brown mammal of the same family as and resembling the raccoon, that lives in the Himalayas; lesser panda. [origin uncertain]

pan da nus (pan dā′nəs), *n.* any of a genus of tropical shrubs and trees found chiefly in the Malay Archipelago and Pacific islands, having a palmlike or branched stem, long, narrow leaves, and strong aerial roots; screw pine. [< Malay *pandan*]

Pan dar us (pan′dər əs), *n.* (in medieval legends) the go-between in the love affair of Troilus and Cressida, portrayed by Boccaccio, Chaucer, and Shakespeare.

pan dem ic (pan dem′ik), *adj.* spread over an entire country, continent, or the whole world. An epidemic disease may be endemic or pandemic. —*n.* a pandemic disease. [< Greek *pandēmos* < *pan-* + *dēmos* people]

pan de mo ni um (pan′də mō′nē əm), *n.* 1 place of wild disorder or lawless confusion. 2 wild uproar or lawlessness. 3 **Pandemonium, a** abode of all the demons; hell. **b** hell's capital. In Milton's *Paradise Lost,* it is the palace built by Satan as the central part of hell. [< Greek *pan-* + *daimōn* demon]

pan der (pan′dər), *n.* 1 person who helps other people indulge low desires, passions, or vices. 2 man who procures prostitutes for others; pimp. 3 a go-between in illicit love affairs. —*v.i.* act as a pander. [earlier *pandar* < *Pandarus*] **—pan′der er,** *n.*

Pan do ra (pan dôr′ə, pan dōr′ə), *n.* (in Greek myths) the first woman, sent to earth by Zeus to punish mankind for having learned the use of fire. Curiosity led her to open a box (**Pandora's box**) and thus let out all sorts of ills into the world. Only Hope remained at the bottom.

pan dow dy (pan dou′dē), *n., pl.* **-dies.** U.S. a deep-dish apple pie or pudding with a crust on top only, often sweetened with brown sugar or molasses. [origin uncertain]

pane (pān), *n.* 1 a single sheet of glass in a division of a window, a door, or a sash. 2 (in philately) a portion of a full sheet containing a unit of stamps as distributed to post offices. 3 piece, portion, or side of anything. [< Old French *pan* < Latin *pannus* piece of cloth]

pan e gyr ic (pan′ə jir′ik), *n.* 1 speech or writing in praise of a person or thing; formal eulogy. 2 enthusiastic or extravagant praise. [< Greek *panēgyrikos* < *panēgyris* public assembly < *pan-* all + *agyris* assembly]

pan e gyr i cal (pan′ə jir′ə kəl), *adj.* of the nature of a panegyric; eulogistic. **—pan′e-gyr′i cal ly,** *adv.*

pan e gyr ist (pan′ə jir′ist, pan′ə jir′ist), *n.* person who praises enthusiastically or extravagantly; eulogist.

pan el (pan′l), *n., v.,* **-eled, -el ing** or **-elled, -el ling.** —*n.* 1 strip or surface that is different in some way from what is around it. A panel is often sunk below or raised above the rest, and used for a decoration. Panels may be in a door or other woodwork, on large pieces of furniture, or made as parts of a dress. 2 picture, photograph, or design much longer than wide. 3 list of persons called as jurors; the members of a jury. 4 a small group selected for a special purpose, such as holding a discussion, judging a contest, or participating in a quiz. 5 one section of a switchboard. 6 board containing the instruments, controls, or indicators used in operating an automobile, aircraft, computer, or other mechanism. 7 a thin wooden board used as a surface for oil painting, sometimes made of several pieces fastened together. 8 a painting on such a board. —*v.t.* arrange in panels; furnish or decorate with panels. [< Old French, piece < Popular Latin *pannellus* < Latin *pannus* piece of cloth]

panel discussion, the discussion of a particular issue by a selected group of people, usually before an audience.

panel heating, radiant heating.

pan el ing (pan′l ing), *n.* panels collectively.

pan el ist (pan′l ist), *n.* member of a panel formed for discussing, judging, etc.

panel truck, a small, fully enclosed truck, used for deliveries.

pan e tel a or **pan e tel la** (pan′ə tel′ə), *n.* panatela.

pan fish, an edible fish of a size that permits frying whole, as a perch, sunfish, etc.

pang (pang), *n.* a sudden, short, sharp pain or feeling: *the pangs of a toothache, a pang of pity.* [origin uncertain]

pan go lin (pang gō′lən), *n.* any of a genus of scaly, toothless, ant-eating mammals of tropical Asia and Africa. When in danger, a pangolin rolls itself into a ball. [< Malay *peng-giling* roller]

pan han dle (pan′han′dl), *n., v.,* **-dled, -dling.** —*n.* 1 handle of a pan. 2 a narrow strip of land projecting like a handle: *the Texas panhandle.* —*v.i., v.t.* INFORMAL. beg, especially in the streets. **—pan′han′dler,** *n.*

pan hel len ic or **Pan hel len ic** (pan′hə len′ik), *adj.* 1 of or having to do with all Greek people or all Greece. 2 of or having to do with all college fraternities and sororities.

pan ic (pan′ik), *n., adj., v.,* **-icked, -ick ing.** —*n.* 1 sudden unreasoning fear that causes an individual or entire group to lose self-control and take wild flight; demoralizing terror. 2 outbreak of widespread alarm, as in a community, over financial matters, leading to hasty, ill-advised measures to avoid loss: *When four banks failed in one day, there was a panic among businessmen.* —*adj.* caused by panic; showing panic; unreasoning. —*v.t.* 1 affect with panic. 2 SLANG. make laugh (an audience, etc.). —*v.i.* be affected with panic: *The audience panicked when the fire broke out.* [< Greek *Panikos* of the god *Pan* (who caused fear in herds and crowds)]

pan ick y (pan′ə kē), *adj.* 1 caused by panic. 2 showing panic. 3 like panic. 4 liable to lose self-control and have a panic.

pan i cle (pan′ə kəl), *n.* a loose, diversely branching flower cluster, produced when a raceme becomes irregularly compound: *a panicle of oats.* [< Latin *panicula,* diminutive of *panus* a swelling]

pan ic-strick en (pan′ik strik′ən), *adj.* frightened out of one's wits; demoralized by fear.

pa nic u late (pə nik′yə lāt), *adj.* growing in a panicle; arranged in panicles.

Pan ja bi (pun jä′bē), *n.* 1 a Punjabi. 2 the Indo-European language of the Punjab, related to Hindi; Punjabi.

pan jan drum (pan jan′drəm), *n.* a mock title for any pretentious personage or official. [coined by Samuel Foote, 1720-1777, English dramatist]

Pank hurst (pangk′herst′), *n.* **Emmeline,** 1858-1928, English social reformer, who worked to secure woman suffrage.

pannier (def. 1)—panniers on a donkey

pan ni er (pan′ē ər), *n.* 1 basket, especially one of a pair of considerable size to be slung across the shoulders or across the back of a beast of burden. 2 frame formerly used for stretching out the skirt of a woman's dress at the hips. 3 puffed drapery about the hips on a woman's skirt. [< Old French *panier* < Latin *panarium* bread basket < *panis* bread]

pan ni kin (pan′ə kən), *n.* 1 a small pan. 2 a metal cup or mug, usually shallow.

pa no cha (pə nō′chə), *n.* 1 a coarse grade of sugar made in Mexico. 2 penuche. [< Mexican Spanish < Latin *panicula.* See PANICLE.]

pa no che (pə nō′chē), *n.* panocha.

pan o plied (pan′ə plēd), *adj.* completely armed, equipped, covered, or arrayed.

pan o ply (pan′ə plē), *n., pl.* **-plies.** 1 a complete suit of armor. 2 complete equipment or covering. 3 any splendid array. [< Greek *panoplia* < *pan-* + *hopla* arms]

pan o ram a (pan′ə ram′ə), *n.* 1 a wide, unbroken view of a surrounding region. 2 a complete survey of some subject: *a panorama of history.* 3 picture of a landscape or other scene, often shown as if seen from a central point; picture unrolled a part at a time and made to pass continuously before the spectators. 4 a continuously passing or changing scene: *the panorama of city life.* [< *pan-* + Greek *horama* view < *horan* to see]

pan o ram ic (pan′ə ram′ik), *adj.* of or like a panorama: *a panoramic view.* **—pan′o ram′i cal ly,** *adv.*

panpipe

pan pipe (pan′pīp′), *n.* an early musical instrument made of reeds or tubes of different lengths, fastened together side by side, in order of their length. The reeds or tubes were closed at one end; the player blew across their open tops. [< *Pan* + *pipe*]

pan sy (pan′zē), *n., pl.* **-sies.** 1 variety of violet that has large flowers with flat, velvety petals usually of several colors. 2 its flower. [< French *pensée,* literally, thought]

pant (pant), *v.i.* 1 breathe hard and quickly as when out of breath; gasp. 2 speak with short, quick breaths. 3 long eagerly; yearn. 4 throb violently. 5 emit steam or the like in loud puffs. —*v.t.* breathe or utter gaspingly. —*n.* 1 a short, quick breath; gasp. 2 puff of an engine. 3 a throb. [< Old French *pantaisier* < Popular Latin *phantasiare* be oppressed with nightmare, ultimately < Greek *phantasia* image]

pan ta lets or **pan ta lettes** (pan′tl ets′), *n.pl.* long drawers with a frill or the like at the bottom of each leg, extending to the ankles and showing beneath the skirt, formerly worn by women and girls.

pan ta loon (pan′tl ün′), *n.* 1 clown. 2 **Pantaloon,** a lean, foolish old man wearing tight-fitting trousers and slippers who is a comic character in old Italian comedies. 3 **pantaloons,** *pl.* trousers. [< Italian *Pantalone*]

pan the ism (pan′thē iz′əm), *n.* 1 belief that God and the universe are identical; doctrine that God is an expression of the physical forces of nature. 2 worship of all the gods.

pan the ist (pan′thē ist), *n.* believer in pantheism.

pan the is tic (pan′thē is′tik), *adj.* of or having to do with pantheism or pantheists. **—pan′the is′ti cal ly,** *adv.*

Pan the on (pan′thē on, pan thē′ən), *n.*

hat, āge, fär; let, ēqual, tėrm;
it, īce; hot, ōpen, ôrder;
oil, out; cup, pu̇t, rüle;
ch, child; ng, long; sh, she;
th, thin; ᴛʜ, then; zh, measure;

ə represents *a* in about, *e* in taken,
i in pencil, *o* in lemon, *u* in circus.

< = from, derived from, taken from.

1 temple for all the gods, built at Rome about 27 B.C. and later used as a Christian church. 2 **pantheon,** temple dedicated to all the gods. 3 a public building in Paris containing tombs or memorials of famous French people. 4 **pantheon,** **a** a public building containing tombs or memorials of the illustrious dead of a nation. **b** all the deities of a people, country, culture, etc.

pan ther (pan′thər), *n., pl.* **-thers** or **-ther.** 1 leopard, especially a black leopard. 2 puma. 3 jaguar. [< Greek]

pan tie (pan′tē), *n.* Usually, **panties,** *pl.* undergarment with short legs, fitting around the waist and the lower torso, worn by women and children. Also, **panty.**

pan to graph (pan′tə graf), *n.* instrument for copying plans, drawings, etc., on any scale desired. [< French *pantographe* < Greek *pantos* all + *graphein* write]

pan to graph ic (pan′tə graf′ik), *adj.* of or produced by a pantograph.

pan to mime (pan′tə mīm), *n., v.,* **-mimed, -mim ing.** —*n.* 1 a play without words, in which the actors express themselves by gestures. 2 gestures without words; dumb show. 3 mime or mimic, especially in the ancient Roman theater. —*v.t.* express by gestures. [< Greek *pantomimos* < *pantos* all + *mimos* mimic]

pan to mim ic (pan′tə mim′ik), *adj.* of, in, or like pantomime.

pan to mim ist (pan′tə mī′mist), *n.* 1 actor in a pantomime. 2 person who writes or composes pantomimes.

pan to then ic acid (pan′tə then′ik), a yellow oily acid, a constituent of the vitamin B complex, found in plant and animal tissues, especially liver, yeast, bran, and molasses. *Formula:* $C_9H_{17}NO_5$ [< Greek *pantothen* from every side]

pan try (pan′trē), *n., pl.* **-tries.** a small room in which food, dishes, silverware, table linen, etc., are kept. [< Old French *paneterie* bread room, ultimately < Latin *panis* bread]

pants (pants), *n.pl.* 1 trousers. 2 underpants. [short for *pantaloons*]

pant suit (pant′süt′), *n.* a woman's or girl's suit consisting of a jacket and trousers.

pan ty (pan′tē), *n., pl.* **-ties.** pantie.

pan ty hose (pan′tē hōz′), *n.* undergarment that combines panty and hose.

pan ty waist (pan′tē wāst′), *n.* 1 a child's garment in two pieces, with short pants buttoning to the shirt at the waist. 2 SLANG. a sissy.

pan zer (pan′zər), *adj.* armored, or mechanized and armored. A panzer division consists largely of tanks. [< German *Panzer* armor]

pap[1] (pap), *n.* 1 soft food for infants or invalids. 2 political patronage. 3 ideas, facts, etc., watered down so as to make them palatable. [Middle English]

pap[2] (pap), *n.* DIALECT. 1 teat or nipple.

2 something resembling a teat or nipple. [Middle English *pappe*]

pa pa (pä′pə, pə pä′), *n.* father; daddy. [< French]

pa pa cy (pā′pə sē), *n., pl.* **-cies.** 1 position, rank, or authority of a pope. 2 time during which a pope rules. 3 all the popes. 4 government by a pope.

pa pal (pā′pəl), *adj.* 1 of or having to do with the pope; pontifical: *a papal letter.* 2 of the papacy. 3 of the Roman Catholic Church: *papal ritual.* [< Late Latin *papa* pope. See POPE.]

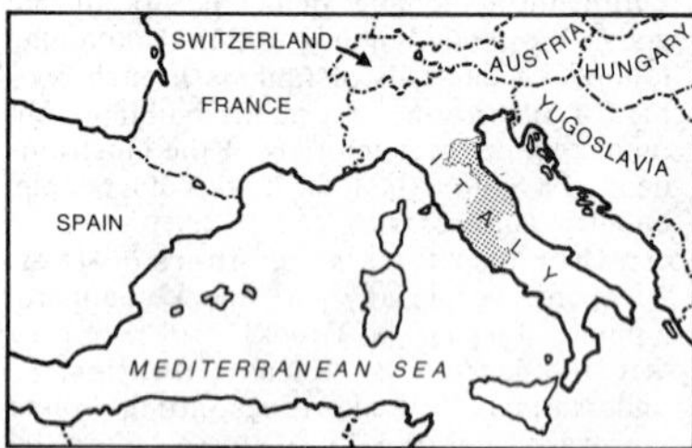

Papal States—The shaded area shows the Papal States about 1740.

Papal States, large district in central Italy ruled by popes from A.D. 755 to 1870. Most of it was annexed by Italy in 1860, the rest in 1870.

pa paw (pô′pô), *n.* 1 a small North American tree of the same genus as the custard apple, bearing oblong, yellowish, edible fruit with many beanlike seeds. 2 its fruit. 3 papaya. Also, **pawpaw.** [< Spanish *papaya*]

pa pa ya (pə pä′yə), *n.* 1 a tropical American tree having a straight, palmlike trunk with a tuft of large leaves at the top and edible, melonlike fruit with yellowish pulp. 2 its fruit. Also, **pawpaw.** [< Spanish, probably < Arawak]

Pa pe e te (pä′pē ā′tā), *n.* seaport and the capital of French Polynesia, on Tahiti. 22,000.

pa per (pā′pər), *n.* 1 material in thin sheets made from wood pulp, rags, or other fibrous substances, used for writing, printing, drawing, wrapping packages, covering walls, etc. 2 piece or sheet of paper. 3 piece of paper or sheet with writing or printing on it; document: *Important papers were stolen.* 4 **papers,** *pl.* documents telling who or what one is. 5 wrapper, container, or sheet of paper containing something: *a paper of pins.* 6 newspaper. 7 article; essay: *a paper on the teaching of English.* 8 a written promise to pay money or a note, bill of exchange, etc.: *commercial paper.* 9 paper money. 10 wallpaper. **11 on paper, a** in writing or print. **b** in theory.
—*adj.* 1 made of paper: *a paper napkin, a paper towel.* 2 like paper; thin or flimsy: *almonds with paper shells, paper walls.* 3 existing only on paper. 4 having to do with or used for paper: *a paper clip.*
—*v.t.* 1 cover or line with paper. 2 cover with wallpaper: *paper a room.* 3 **paper over,** smooth over or cover up (a difference, quarrel, disagreement, etc.).
[< Old French *papier* < Latin *papyrus* papyrus. Doublet of PAPYRUS.] **—pa′per er,** *n.* **—pa′per like′,** *adj.*

pa per back (pā′pər bak′), *n.* book with a flexible paper binding or cover, usually sold at a low price. *—adj.* 1 bound with a flexible paper binding or cover. 2 of or having to do with paperback books.

pa per board (pā′pər bôrd′, pā′pər bōrd′), *n.* pasteboard or cardboard.

pa per boy (pā′pər boi′), *n.* newsboy.

paper clip, a flat, looped piece of wire forming a clip for holding papers together.

pa per hang er (pā′pər hang′ər), *n.* person whose business is to cover walls with wallpaper.

paper knife, knife with a blade of metal, wood, ivory, etc., used to cut open letters and the pages of books.

paper money, money made of paper, not metal, as government and bank notes, which by law represents money. A dollar bill is paper money.

paper profits, profits existing on paper, but not yet realized.

paper tiger, person or thing that appears to be strong or threatening but is really weak or cowardly.

pa per weight (pā′pər wāt′), *n.* a small, heavy object put on papers to keep them from being scattered.

pa per work (pā′pər wėrk′), *n.* 1 work done on paper; writing. 2 office or clerical work, such as the writing, checking, and sorting of letters, reports, etc. 3 planning and theoretical work rather than a practical application, as mechanical drawing or drafting.

pa per y (pā′pər ē), *adj.* like paper; thin or flimsy.

pa pier-mâ ché (pā′pər mə shā′), *n.* a paper pulp mixed with some stiffener such as glue and molded when moist. It becomes hard and strong when dry. *—adj.* made of papier-mâché. [< French *papier mâché* chewed paper]

pa pil la (pə pil′ə), *n., pl.* **-pil lae** (-pil′ē). 1 a small, nipplelike projection. 2 a small vascular process at the root of a hair or feather. 3 one of certain small protuberances concerned with the senses of touch, taste, or smell: *the papillae on the tongue.* [< Latin, nipple]

pap il lar y (pap′ə ler′ē), *adj.* 1 of or like a papilla. 2 having papillae.

pa pil lo ma (pap′ə lō′mə), *n., pl.* **-mas, -ma ta** (-mə tə). a benign tumor formed by overgrown papillae, as a wart or corn. [< New Latin]

pap il lose (pap′ə lōs), *adj.* having many papillae.

pa pist (pā′pist), *n., adj.* UNFRIENDLY USE. Roman Catholic. [< Late Latin *papa* pope]

pa poose or **pap poose** (pa püs′), *n.* an American Indian baby. [< Algonquian *papoos* child]

pap pose (pap′ōs), *adj.* 1 having a pappus. 2 downy.

pap pous (pap′əs), *adj.* pappose.

pap pus (pap′əs), *n., pl.* **pap pi** (pap′ī). a fine feathery or bristlelike appendage to a seed which aids in the seed's dispersal in the wind. Dandelion and thistle seeds have pappi. [< Greek *pappos*]

pa pri ka (pa prē′kə, pap′rə kə), *n.* 1 the ground, dried fruit of certain mild red peppers, used as a seasoning in food. 2 plant that produces the fruit from which this is made. [< Hungarian < Serbo-Croatian < Greek *piperi* pepper]

Pap test (pap), test for diagnosing cancer in the uterine cervix, bladder, stomach, etc., by smearing a specimen of cells on a glass slide and staining it for microscopic examination. [< *Pap*, short for George N. *Papanicolaou*, 1883-1962, Greek-born American physician who developed it]

Pap u a (pap′yü ə, pä′pü ä), *n.* 1 New Guinea. 2 **Territory of,** the SE part of New Guinea, with nearby islands. It is a territory of Australia. 610,000 pop.; 86,100 sq. mi. *Capital:* Port Moresby. **—Pap′u an,** *adj., n.*

pap ule (pap′yül), *n.* pimple that does not form pus. [< Latin *papula*]

pa py rus (pə pī′rəs), *n., pl.* **-ri** (-rī). 1 a tall aquatic sedge, from which the ancient Egyptians, Greeks, and Romans made a kind of paper to write on. 2 a writing material made from the pith of the papyrus plant by laying thin strips of it side by side, the whole being then soaked, pressed, and dried. 3 an ancient record written on papyrus. [< Latin < Greek *papyros.* Doublet of PAPER.]

par (pär), *n.* 1 an equal level; equality: *The gains and losses are about on a par. He is on a par with his sister in intelligence.* 2 average or normal amount, degree, or condition: *A sick person feels below par.* 3 face value: *That stock is selling above par.* 4 the established normal value of the money of one country in terms of the money of another country. 5 (in golf) a score which is used as a standard for a particular hole or course and which represents the number of strokes that will be taken if the hole or course is played well. Par is based on the length and difficulty of the hole or course. *—adj.* 1 average; normal. 2 of or at par. [< Latin, equal. Doublet of PEER[1].]

par., 1 paragraph. 2 parallel. 3 parenthesis. 4 parish.

Pa rá (pä rä′), *n.* 1 **Pará River,** the S mouth of the Amazon River. 200 mi. long; 40 mi. wide. 2 Belém.

para-[1], *prefix.* 1 beside; near, as in *parathyroid.* 2 related or similar to, as in *parainfluenza, paramedical.* 3 disordered condition, as in *paranoia, paraplegia.* [< Greek < *para* beside, near]

para-[2], *combining form.* 1 defense against; protection from, as in *parachute, parasol.* 2 parachute, as in *paratrooper.* [< French < Italian < *parare* ward off]

par a-a mi no ben zo ic acid (par′ə ə-mē′nō ben zō′ik, par′ə am′ə nō ben zō′ik), a yellow, crystalline acid, a constituent of the vitamin B complex, present in yeast and in bran. It is used in the manufacture of local anesthetics and in the treatment of rheumatic fever and various skin conditions. *Formula:* $C_7H_7NO_2$

par a ble (par′ə bəl), *n.* a brief story used to teach some truth or moral lesson: *Jesus taught in parables.* [< Late Latin *parabola* speech, story, parable < Latin, comparison < Greek *parabolē* < *para-*[1] + *bolē* a throwing. Doublet of PALAVER, PARABOLA, PARLEY, PAROLE.]

pa rab o la (pə rab′ə lə), *n.* a plane curve formed by the intersection of a right circular cone with a plane parallel to a side of the cone. See **conic section** for diagram. [< Greek *parabolē* comparison, juxtaposition. Doublet of PALAVER, PARABLE, PARLEY, PAROLE.]

par a bol ic (par′ə bol′ik), *adj.* 1 having to do with or resembling a parabola. 2 having to do with or expressed in a parable. **—par′a-bol′i cal ly,** *adv.*

pa rab o loid (pə rab′ə loid), *n.* solid or surface generated by the revolution of a parabola about its axis.

hat, āge, fär; let, ēqual, tėrm;
it, īce; hot, ōpen, ôrder;
oil, out; cup, pu̇t, rüle;
ch, child; ng, long; sh, she;
th, thin; ᴛʜ, then; zh, measure;

ə represents *a* in about, *e* in taken, *i* in pencil, *o* in lemon, *u* in circus.

< = from, derived from, taken from.

Par a cel sus (par′ə sel′səs), *n.* 1493?-1541, Swiss alchemist and physician.

par a chute (par′ə shüt), *n., v.,* **-chut ed, -chut ing.** —*n.* 1 apparatus shaped like an umbrella and made of nylon or silk, used in descending gradually through the air from a great height. 2 any contrivance, natural or artificial, serving to check a fall through the air. —*v.i.* come down by, or as if by, a parachute. —*v.t.* convey to earth by a parachute. [< French < *para-*[2] + *chute* a fall]

par a chut ist (par′ə shü′tist), *n.* person who uses a parachute or is skilled in making descents with a parachute.

Par a clete (par′ə klēt), *n.* the Holy Ghost. [< Greek *paraklētos* comforter]

pa rade (pə rād′), *n., v.,* **-rad ed, -rad ing.** —*n.* 1 march for display; public procession: *The circus had a parade.* 2 group of people walking for display or pleasure. 3 BRITISH. place where people walk for display or pleasure; public promenade. 4 a great show or display: *The modest man did not make a parade of his wealth.* 5 a military display or review of troops. 6 the place used for the regular parade of troops. —*v.t.* 1 march through in procession or with display: *The circus performers and animals paraded the streets.* 2 make a great show of; flaunt: *parade one's wealth.* 3 assemble (troops) for review, ceremony, or inspection. —*v.i.* 1 march in procession; walk proudly as if in a parade. 2 come together in military order for review, ceremony, or inspection. [< French < Spanish *parada* < *parar* to check < Latin *parare* prepare] **—pa rad′er,** *n.*

par a digm (par′ə dim, par′ə dīm), *n.* 1 pattern; example. 2 example of a noun, verb, pronoun, etc., in all its inflections. [< Greek *paradeigma* pattern, ultimately < *para-*[1] + *deiknynai* to show]

par a dig mat ic (par′ə dig mat′ik), *adj.* of, having to do with, or consisting of a paradigm.

par a dise (par′ə dīs), *n.* 1 heaven. 2 place or condition of great happiness. 3 place of great beauty. 4 Also, **Paradise.** the garden of Eden. [< Greek *paradeisos* < Iranian (Avestan) *pairidaēza* enclosed park]

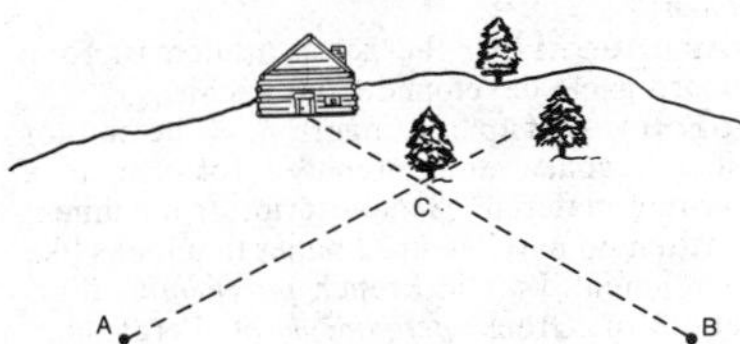

parallax—Viewed from A, C appears to be the middle tree in a group of three trees. From B, C appears to be a single tree in front of the cabin.

par a di si a cal (par′ə di sī′ə kəl), *adj.* of, having to do with, or belonging to paradise; like that of paradise. **—par′a di si′a cal ly,** *adv.*

par a dox (par′ə doks), *n.* 1 statement that may be true but seems to say two opposite things. EXAMPLES: "More haste, less speed." "The child is father to the man." See **epigram** for synonym study. 2 statement that is false because it says two opposite things. 3 person or thing that seems to be full of contradictions. [< Greek *paradoxos* contrary opinion < *para-*[1] + *doxa* opinion]

par a dox i cal (par′ə dok′sə kəl), *adj.* 1 of paradoxes; involving a paradox. 2 having the habit of using paradoxes. **—par′a dox′i cal ly,** *adv.*

par af fin (par′ə fin), *n.* 1 a white, tasteless, waxy substance, used for making candles, for sealing jars, etc. It is obtained chiefly from crude petroleum, being chemically a mixture of hydrocarbons. 2 (in chemistry) any of a family of hydrocarbons similar in structure to methane. Ethane, propane, and butane are paraffins. *Formula:* C_nH_{2n+2} 3 Also, **paraffin oil.** BRITISH. kerosene. —*v.t.* cover or treat with paraffin. [< German *Paraffin* < Latin *parum* not very + *affinis* related; because of small affinity for other substances]

par af fine (par′ə fin), *n., v.,* **-fined, -fin ing.** paraffin.

par a gon (par′ə gon), *n.* model of excellence or perfection. [< Middle French, comparison < Italian *paragone* touchstone < Greek *parakonan* to whet < *para-*[1] + *akonē* whetstone]

par a graph (par′ə graf), *n.* 1 group of sentences relating to the same idea or topic and forming a distinct part of a chapter, letter, or other piece of writing. It is customary to begin a paragraph on a new line and to indent this line. 2 a separate note or item of news in a newspaper. 3 sign (¶) used to show where a paragraph begins or should begin. It is used mostly in correcting written work. —*v.t.* 1 divide into paragraphs. 2 write paragraphs about. —*v.i.* write paragraphs. [< Greek *paragraphos* line (in the margin) marking a break in sense < *para-*[1] + *graphein* write] **—par′a graph′er,** *n.*

Par a guay (par′ə gwā, par′ə gwī), *n.* 1 country in central South America, bordered by Bolivia, Brazil, and Argentina. 2,396,000 pop.; 157,000 sq. mi. *Capital:* Asunción. 2 **Paraguay River,** river flowing south from W Brazil through Paraguay into the Paraná. 1500 mi. **—Par′a guay′an,** *adj., n.*

par a in flu en za (par′ə in flü en′zə), *n.* a respiratory illness similar to influenza, caused by any of various viruses that are associated with the common cold.

par a keet (par′ə kēt), *n.* any of various small parrots, most of which have slender bodies and long tails. Also, **parrakeet, paroquet.** [< Middle French *paroquet,* perhaps alteration of *Perrot,* diminutive of *Pierre* Peter]

par al lac tic (par′ə lak′tik), *adj.* of or having to do with a parallax.

par al lax (par′ə laks), *n.* the apparent change in the position of an object when it is seen or photographed from two different points which are not on a direct line with the object. Parallax is used in surveying, astronomy, etc., to determine distances of objects. [< Greek *parallaxis* alternation < *para-*[1] + *allassein* to change]

par al lel (par′ə lel), *adj., n., v.,* **-leled, -lel ing** or **-lelled, -lel ling.** —*adj.* 1 (of straight lines or planes) lying or extending alongside of one another, always equidistant: *the two parallel rails of a railroad track.* 2 (of curved lines, surfaces, etc.) always equidistant at corresponding points. 3 similar; corresponding; like: *parallel customs in different countries.*
—*n.* 1 a parallel line or surface. 2 in geography: **a** any of the imaginary circles around the earth parallel to the equator, marking degrees of latitude. **b** the markings on a map or globe that represent these circles. 3 thing like or similar to another; counterpart. 4 comparison to show likeness: *Draw a parallel between this winter and last winter.* 5 condition or relation of being parallel; parallelism. 6 arrangement of the wiring of batteries, lights, etc., in which all the positive poles or terminals are joined to one conductor, and all the negative to the other. 7 **parallels,** *pl.* (in printing) a reference mark consisting of a pair of vertical parallel lines (‖).
—*v.t.* 1 be at the same distance from throughout the length: *The street parallels the railroad.* 2 cause to be or run parallel to. 3 be like; be similar to; correspond or be equivalent to: *Your story closely parallels the one I heard earlier.* 4 compare in order to show likeness; bring into comparison; liken. 5 find a case that is similar or parallel to; furnish a match for: *Can you parallel that for friendliness?*
[< Greek *parallēlos* < *para allēlōs* beside one another]

parallel bars, pair of raised bars horizontal to the ground, used in gymnastics to develop the muscles of the arms, chest, etc.

par al lel e pi ped (par′ə lel′ə pī′pid), *n.* prism whose six faces are parallelograms. [< Greek *parallēlos* parallel + *epipedon* a plane surface]

par al lel ism (par′ə lel′iz′əm), *n.* 1 a being parallel. 2 likeness or similarity; correspondence. 3 parallel statements in writing, expressed in the same grammatical form. EXAMPLE: "He was advised to rise early, to work hard, and to eat heartily."

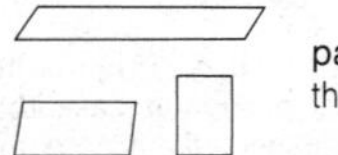

parallelogram
three parallelograms

par al lel o gram (par′ə lel′ə gram), *n.* a four-sided plane figure whose opposite sides are parallel and equal.

parallel parking, parking with the length of the car parallel to the curb.

par a lyse (par′ə līz), *v.t.,* **-lysed, -lys ing.** BRITISH. paralyze.

parallel (defs. 1 and 2)—parallel lines

pa ral y sis (pə ral′ə sis), *n., pl.* **-ses** (-sēz′). 1 a lessening or loss of the power of motion or sensation in any part of the body. 2 condition of powerlessness or helpless inactivity; crippling: *The war caused a paralysis of trade.* [< Greek < *paralyein* be loosened < *para-*[1] + *lyein* loosen. Doublet of PALSY.]

par a lyt ic (par′ə lit′ik), *adj.* of paralysis; having paralysis. —*n.* person who has paralysis.

parapet (def. 1)

par a lyze (par′ə līz), *v.t.*, **-lyzed, -lyz ing.** 1 affect with a lessening or loss of the power of motion or feeling: *His left arm was paralyzed.* 2 make powerless or helplessly inactive; cripple: *Fear paralyzed my mind.* Also, BRITISH **paralyse.** —**par′a lyz′er,** *n.*

par a mag net ic (par′ə mag net′ik), *adj.* having to do with a class of substances, such as liquid oxygen, whose capability for being magnetized is much less than that of iron. The magnetization of such a substance is parallel to the lines of force in a magnetic field and proportional to the intensity of the field.

par a mag net ism (par′ə mag′nə tiz′əm), *n.* the phenomena exhibited by paramagnetic substances.

Par a mar i bo (par′ə mar′ə bō), *n.* seaport and capital of Surinam, in the N part. 150,000.

par a me ci um (par′ə mē′shē əm, par′ə-mē′sē əm), *n., pl.* **-ci a** (-shē ə, -sē ə). any of a genus of protozoans, each shaped like a slender slipper and having a groove along one side leading into a gullet. Paramecia are free-swimming ciliates that live in almost all fresh water. [< New Latin < Greek *paramēkēs* oblong < *para-*[1] + *mēkos* length]

par a med i cal (par′ə med′ə kəl), *adj.* having to do with medicine in an auxiliary capacity; involving services, studies, etc., that are related to but not part of the medical profession.

pa ram e ter (pə ram′ə tər), *n.* 1 (in mathematics) a constant in a particular case that varies in other cases, especially a constant occurring in the equation of a curve or surface, by the variation of which the equation is made to represent a family of such curves or surfaces. 2 a constant factor: *the parameters of space and time.*

par a met ric amplifier (par′ə met′rik), a high-frequency amplifier of very low noise that amplifies a signal by varying the capacitance or inductance.

par a mil i tar y (par′ə mil′ə ter′ē), *adj.* organized militarily, but not part of or in cooperation with the official armed forces of a country.

par a mount (par′ə mount), *adj.* chief in importance; above others; supreme: *Truth is of paramount importance.* See **dominant** for synonym study. [< Anglo-French *paramont* above < Old French *par* by + *amont* up]

par a mour (par′ə mür), *n.* 1 person who takes the place of a husband or wife illegally. 2 ARCHAIC. lover. [< Old French < *par amour* by love]

Pa ra ná River (pä′rə nä′), river flowing south from central Brazil between Paraguay and Argentina into the Plata. 2450 mi.

par a noi a (par′ə noi′ə), *n.* 1 form of psychosis characterized by continuing, elaborate delusions of persecution or grandeur. 2 an irrational distrust of others; complex of persecution. [< Greek, mental derangement < *paranous* out of one's mind < *para-*[1] + *nous* mind]

par a noi ac (par′ə noi′ak), *n.* person who has paranoia. —*adj.* of or like paranoia.

par a noid (par′ə noid), *adj.* 1 resembling or tending toward paranoia. 2 having the characteristics of paranoia. —*n.* a paranoid person.

par a pet (par′ə pet, par′ə pit), *n.* 1 a low wall or mound of stone, earth, etc., in front of a walk or platform at the top of a fort, trench, etc., to protect soldiers; rampart. 2 a low wall or barrier at the edge of a balcony, roof, bridge, etc. [< Italian *parapetto* < *parare* defend + *petto* chest]

par a pher nal ia (par′ə fər nā′lyə), *n., pl. or sing.* 1 personal belongings. 2 equipment; outfit. [< Medieval Latin < Greek *parapherna* a woman's personal property besides her dowry < *para-*[1] + *phernē* dowry]

par a phrase (par′ə frāz), *v.*, **-phrased, -phras ing,** *n.* —*v.t.* state the meaning of (a passage) in other words. —*n.* expression of the meaning of a passage in other words.

par a ple gi a (par′ə plē′jē ə), *n.* paralysis of the legs and the lower part of the trunk. [< Greek *paraplēgia* < *paraplessein* strike at the side < *para-*[1] + *plessein* to strike]

par a ple gic (par′ə plē′jik, par′ə plej′ik), *n.* person afflicted with paraplegia. —*adj.* having to do with, or afflicted with, paraplegia.

par a po di um (par′ə pō′dē əm), *n., pl.* **-di a** (-dē ə). one of the paired, jointless processes or rudimentary limbs of certain annelids, that serve as organs of locomotion, and sometimes of sensation or respiration. [< New Latin < Greek *para-*[1] + *podos* foot]

par a psy chol o gy (par′ə sī kol′ə jē), *n.* branch of psychology dealing with psychic phenomena, such as extrasensory perception, telepathy, and clairvoyance.

par a site (par′ə sīt), *n.* 1 animal or plant that lives on or in another from which it gets its food, always at the expense of the host, which is often injured by the relationship. Lice and tapeworms are parasites. Mistletoe is a parasite on oak trees. 2 person who lives on others without making any useful and fitting return; hanger-on: *The lazy man was a parasite on his family.* [< Greek *parasitos* feeding beside < *para-*[1] + *sitos* food]

par a sit ic (par′ə sit′ik), *adj.* of or like a parasite; living on others. —**par′a sit′i cal ly,** *adv.*

par a sit i cal (par′ə sit′ə kəl), *adj.* parasitic.

par a sit ism (par′ə sī′tiz′əm), *n.* 1 relationship between two organisms in which one obtains benefits at the expense of the other, often injuring it. 2 parasitic infestation.

par a si tol o gist (par′ə sī tol′ə jist), *n.* an expert in parasitology.

par a si tol o gy (par′ə sī tol′ə jē), *n.* branch of biology or medicine dealing with parasites and parasitism.

par a sol (par′ə sôl, par′ə sol), *n.* a light umbrella used as a protection from the sun. [< Italian *parasole* < *para-*[2] + *sole* sun]

par a sym pa thet ic nervous system (par′ə sim′pə thet′ik), the part of the autonomic nervous system that produces such involuntary responses as dilating blood vessels, increasing the activity of digestive and reproductive organs and glands, contracting the pupils of the eyes, slowing down the heartbeat, and other responses opposed to the action of the sympathetic nervous system.

par a thy roid glands (par′ə thī′roid), several (usually four) small endocrine glands in or near the thyroid gland that secrete a vital hormone which enables the body to use calcium.

par a troop er (par′ə trü′pər), *n.* soldier trained to use a parachute for descent from an aircraft into a battle area.

par a troops (par′ə trüps′), *n.pl.* troops trained to use parachutes for descent from an aircraft into a battle area.

par a ty phoid (par′ə tī′foid), *adj.* of the nature of or having to do with paratyphoid fever. —*n.* paratyphoid fever.

paratyphoid fever, a bacterial disease caused by salmonella organisms, which resembles typhoid fever but is usually milder. It occurs in different varieties and with different effects in man and other animals.

par boil (pär′boil′), *v.t.* 1 boil till partly cooked. 2 overheat. —*v.i.* become overheated. [< Old French *parboillir* < Late Latin *perbullire* < Latin *per-* thoroughly + *bullire* to boil]

Par cae (pär′sē), *n.pl.* (in Roman myths) the three Fates.

par cel (pär′səl), *n., v.,* **-celed, -cel ing** or **-celled, -cel ling.** —*n.* 1 bundle of things wrapped or packed together; package. See **bundle** for synonym study. 2 container with things packed in it. 3 piece; tract: *a parcel of land.* 4 group of indefinite size; lot; pack: *a parcel of liars.* —*v.t.* make into a parcel; put up in parcels. —*v.i.* **parcel out,** divide into, or distribute in, portions. [< Old French *parcelle,* ultimately < Latin *particula* particle]

parcel post, branch of the postal service which carries parcels.

parch (pärch), *v.t.* 1 dry by heating; roast slightly: *Corn is sometimes parched.* 2 make hot and dry or thirsty: *The fever parched her.* —*v.i.* become dry, hot, or thirsty: *I am parched with the heat.* [Middle English *parchen*]

Par chee si (pär chē′zē), *n.* trademark for a board game developed from pachisi.

parch ment (pärch′mənt), *n.* 1 the skin of sheep, goats, etc., prepared for use as a writing material. 2 manuscript or document written on parchment. 3 paper that looks like parchment. [< Old French *parchemin,* alteration of Greek *pergamēnē* of Pergamum, where it came from]

pard[1] (pärd), *n.* ARCHAIC. leopard or panther. [< Old French *parde* < Latin *pardus* < Greek *pardos*]

pard[2] (pärd), *n.* DIALECT. partner; friend; companion. [short for *pardner*]

pard ner (pärd′nər), *n.* DIALECT. partner.

par don (pärd′n), *n.* 1 a passing over an offense without punishment; forgiveness. 2 excuse or toleration. 3 a setting free from punishment. 4 a legal document setting a person free from punishment. —*v.t.* 1 forgive or excuse: *It is hard to pardon such shameful behavior.* 2 set free from punishment. See **excuse** for synonym study. [< Old French < *pardonner* forgive < Late Latin *perdonare* < Latin *per-* thoroughly + *donare* to give] —**par′don a ble,** *adj.* —**par′don a bly,** *adv.*

par don er (pärd′n ər), *n.* 1 person who

pardons. 2 (in the Middle Ages) a church official charged with the granting of indulgences in return for offerings made to the church.

pare (per, par), *v.t.,* **pared, par ing.** 1 cut, trim, or shave off the outer part of; peel: *pare an apple.* 2 cut away (an outer layer, part, etc.): *pare a layer from a corn.* 3 cut away little by little: *pare down expenses.* [< Old French *parer* arrange, dispose < Latin *parare* make ready. Doublet of PARRY.]

par e go ric (par′ə gôr′ik, par′ə gor′ik), *n.* a soothing medicine containing camphor and a very little opium. *—adj.* soothing. [< Greek *parēgorikos* soothing < *parēgorein* speak soothingly to < *para-*[1] + *agora* assembly]

paren., parenthesis.

pa ren chy ma (pə reng′kə mə), *n.* 1 the fundamental tissue in higher plants, composed of living, unspecialized cells from which all other cells are formed. Most of the tissue in the softer parts of leaves, the pulp of fruits, the pith of stems, etc., is parenchyma. 2 the tissue of an animal organ or part special or essential to it, as distinguished from its connective or supporting tissue. [< Greek, anything poured in < *para-*[1] + *en-* in + *chyma* what is poured]

par en chym a tous (par′eng kim′ə təs), *adj.* having to do with or of the nature of parenchyma.

par ent (per′ənt, par′ənt), *n.* 1 father or mother. 2 any animal or plant that produces offspring. 3 that from which another thing springs or is derived; source; cause. *—adj.* parental. [< Old French < Latin *parentem* < *parere* bring forth]

par ent age (per′ən tij, par′ən tij), *n.* 1 descent from parents; family line; ancestry. 2 parenthood.

pa ren tal (pə ren′tl), *adj.* of or having to do with a parent or parents; like a parent's. **—pa ren′tal ly,** *adv.*

par en ter al (pə ren′tər əl), *adj.* not entering or passing through the alimentary canal; not intestinal. An intravenous injection provides parenteral nourishment. **—par en′ter al ly,** *adv.*

pa ren the sis (pə ren′thə sis), *n., pl.* **-ses** (-sēz′). 1 word, phrase, sentence, etc., inserted within a sentence to explain or qualify something. 2 either or both of two curved lines () used to set off such an expression. 3 interval or digression. [< Greek < *parentithenai* put in beside < *para-*[1] + *en-* in + *tithenai* to put, place]

pa ren the size (pə ren′thə sīz), *v.t.,* **-sized, -siz ing.** insert as or in a parenthesis; put between the marks of parenthesis.

par en thet ic (par′ən thet′ik), *adj.* 1 serving or helping to explain; qualifying; explanatory. 2 enclosed in parentheses. 3 using parentheses. **—par′en thet′i cal ly,** *adv.*

par en thet i cal (par′ən thet′ə kəl), *adj.* parenthetic.

par ent hood (per′ənt hu̇d, par′ənt hu̇d), *n.* condition of being a parent.

pa re sis (pə rē′sis, par′ə sis), *n.* 1 a slight or partial paralysis. 2 a progressive disease of the brain caused by syphilis that gradually results in general paralysis. [< Greek < *parienai* let go, fall < *para-*[1] + *hienai* let go]

pa ret ic (pə ret′ik, pə rē′tik), *adj.* of or having to do with paresis; caused by paresis. *—n.* person who has paresis.

par ex cel lence (pär ek sə läns′), FRENCH. beyond comparison; above all others of the same sort.

par fait (pär fā′, pär′fā), *n.* 1 ice cream with syrup or crushed fruit and whipped cream, served in a tall glass. 2 a rich ice cream containing eggs and whipped cream. [< French, literally, perfect]

par he li on (pär hē′lē ən, pär hē′lyən), *n., pl.* **-he li a** (-hē′lē ə, -hē′lyə). a bright spot of light, often showing the colors of the spectrum, that is sometimes seen on either side of the sun on a solar halo; sundog. Parhelia are caused by the refraction of sunlight through ice crystals suspended in the atmosphere. [< Greek *parēlion* < *para-*[1] + *hēlios* sun]

pa ri ah (pə rī′ə, pär′ē ə), *n.* 1 any person or animal generally despised; outcast. 2 Usually, **Pariah,** member of a low caste in southern India and Burma. [< Tamil *paṛaiyar,* plural of *paṛaiyan* drummer]

Par i an (per′ē ən, par′ē ən), *adj.* of or having to do with Paros.

pa ri e tal (pə rī′ə təl), *adj.* 1 of the wall of the body or of one of its cavities. 2 of or having to do with a parietal. *—n.* either of two bones that form part of the sides and top of the skull. [< Late Latin *parietalis* < Latin *paries* wall]

par i-mu tu el (par′i myü′chü əl), *n.* 1 system of betting on horse races in which those who have bet on the winning horses divide all the money bet, except for a part withheld by the management for costs, profits, taxes, etc. 2 machine for recording such bets. [< French, mutual wager]

par ing (per′ing, par′ing), *n.* 1 part pared off; skin; rind. 2 act of paring.

par i pas su (par′ē pas′ü), LATIN. at an equal pace or rate; in equal proportion.

Par is (par′is), *n.* 1 capital and largest city of France, in the N part, on the Seine River. 2,608,000. 2 (in Greek legends) a son of Hecuba and Priam, king of Troy. The kidnaping of Helen by Paris was the cause of the Trojan War.

Paris green, a poisonous, emerald-green powder containing copper and arsenic, used as a pigment and in making sprays for killing insects.

par ish (par′ish), *n.* 1 district that has its own church and clergyman. 2 people of a parish. 3 members of the congregation of a particular church. 4 (in Louisiana) a county. 5 (in Great Britain) a civil district. [< Old French *paroisse* < Late Latin *parochia* < Late Greek *paroikia,* ultimately < *para-*[1] + *oikos* dwelling]

pa rish ion er (pə rish′ə nər), *n.* inhabitant or member of a parish.

Pa ri sian (pə rizh′ən), *adj.* of or having to do with Paris or its people. *—n.* native or inhabitant of Paris.

par i ty (par′ə tē), *n.* 1 similarity or close correspondence with regard to state, position, condition, value, quality, degree, etc.; equality. 2 balance between the market prices for a farmer's commodities and his own gross expenditures. Parity is calculated to maintain the price of the farmer's product at a level equal in purchasing power to that of a base period. 3 equivalence in value in the currency of a foreign country. [< Latin *paritatem* < *par* equal]

park (pärk), *n.* 1 land set apart for the pleasure of the public. 2 land set apart for wild animals. 3 grounds around a fine house. 4 place to leave an automobile, etc., for a time. 5 space where army vehicles, supplies, artillery, etc., are put when an army camps. *—v.t.* 1 leave (an automobile, truck, or other vehicle) for a time in a certain place. 2 assemble and arrange (army vehicles, artillery, etc.) in a park. 3 INFORMAL. place, put, or leave: *park one's coat in a chair.* *—v.i.* park an automobile, truck, or other vehicle. [< Old French *parc* < Medieval Latin *parricus* enclosure] **—park′like′,** *adj.*

hat, āge, fär; let, ēqual, tėrm;
it, īce; hot, ōpen, ôrder;
oil, out; cup, pu̇t, rüle;
ch, child; ng, long; sh, she;
th, thin; ᴛʜ, then; zh, measure;

ə represents *a* in about, *e* in taken,
i in pencil, *o* in lemon, *u* in circus.

< = from, derived from, taken from.

par ka (pär′kə), *n.* 1 a fur jacket with a hood, worn in Alaska and in northeastern Asia. 2 jacket with a hood. [< Russian]

Par ker (pär′kər), *n.* **Dorothy,** 1893-1967, American writer of short stories and light verse.

parking lot, an open area used for parking automobiles and other vehicles, often for a fee.

parking meter, device containing a clock mechanism which is operated by the insertion of coins. It allows an automobile a specified amount of time in a parking area for each coin.

Par kin son's disease (pär′kin sənz), a chronic nervous disease, usually occurring late in life, characterized by muscular tremors, weakness, and paralysis; shaking palsy. [< James *Parkinson,* 1755-1824, English physician, who first described it]

Park man (pärk′mən), *n.* **Francis,** 1823-1893, American historian.

park way (pärk′wā′), *n.* a broad road with spaces planted with grass, trees, etc.

par lance (pär′ləns), *n.* way of speaking; talk; language: *legal parlance.* [< Old French < *parler* speak. See PARLEY.]

par lay (pär′lā, pär′lē), U.S. *—v.t., v.i.* risk (an original bet and its winnings) on another bet. *—n.* such a wager or a series of such wagers. [< French *paroli* < Italian, grand cast at dice]

par ley (pär′lē), *n., pl.* **-leys.** 1 conference or informal talk. 2 an informal discussion with an enemy during a truce about terms of surrender, exchange of prisoners, etc. *—v.i.* 1 discuss terms, especially with an enemy. 2 ARCHAIC. speak; talk. [< Old French *parlee,* past participle of *parler* speak < Late Latin *parabolare* < *parabola* speech, story. Doublet of PALAVER, PARABLE, PARABOLA, PAROLE.]

par lia ment (pär′lə mənt), *n.* 1 council or congress that is the highest lawmaking body in some countries. 2 the highest lawmaking body of any political unit. 3 **Parliament, a** the national lawmaking body of Great Britain, consisting of the House of Lords and the House of Commons. **b** the national lawmaking body of Canada, consisting of the Senate and the House of Commons. **c** the lawmaking body of a country or colony having the British system of government. 4 (in France, before the French Revolution) a high court of justice. [< Old French *parlement* < *parler* speak. See PARLEY.]

par lia men tar i an (pär′lə men tar′ē ən), *n.* 1 person skilled in parliamentary procedure or debate. 2 **Parliamentarian,**

person who supported Parliament against Charles I.

par lia men tar y (pär′lə men′tər ē), *adj.* 1 of a parliament. 2 done by a parliament. 3 according to the rules and customs of a parliament or other lawmaking body. 4 having a parliament.

par lor (pär′lər), *n.* 1 room for receiving or entertaining guests; sitting room. 2 room or suite of rooms used for various commercial purposes, requiring special or elaborate decoration, fittings, etc.: *a funeral parlor.* 3 a separate room in a hotel, club, etc., more private than the taproom. Also, BRITISH **parlour.** [< Old French *parleor* < *parler* speak. See PARLEY.]

parlor car, a railroad passenger car for day travel, with more comfortable seating than a coach, at a higher fare.

par lour (pär′lər), *n.* BRITISH. parlor.

par lous (pär′ləs), ARCHAIC. —*adj.* 1 full of peril; dangerous. 2 very clever; shrewd. —*adv.* extremely. [variant of *perilous*]

Par ma (pär′mə), *n.* 1 city in N Italy. 172,000. 2 city in NE Ohio. 100,000.

Par me san (pär′mē zan), *n.* a hard, dry Italian cheese made from skim milk. [< *Parma*]

Par nas sus (pär nas′əs), *n.* 1 **Mount,** mountain in central Greece. In ancient Greek times it was sacred to Apollo and the Muses. 8070 ft. 2 the fabled mountain of poets, whose summit is their goal. —**Par nas′si an,** *adj.*

Par nell (pär nel′, pär′nl), *n.* **Charles Stewart,** 1846-1891, Irish political leader.

pa ro chi al (pə rō′kē əl), *adj.* 1 of or in a parish: *a parochial church.* 2 narrow; limited: *a parochial viewpoint.* [< Late Latin *parochialis* < *parochia* parish. See PARISH.]

pa ro chi al ism (pə rō′kē ə liz′əm), *n.* parochial character, spirit, or tendency; narrowness of interests or views.

parochial school, school maintained by a church or a religious organization.

par o dist (par′ə dist), *n.* writer of parodies.

par o dy (par′ə dē), *n., pl.* **-dies,** *v.,* **-died, -dy ing.** —*n.* 1 a humorous imitation of a serious writing. A parody follows the form of the original, but often changes its sense to nonsense in order to ridicule the writer's characteristics. 2 a poor imitation. 3 a musical composition making fun of another. —*v.t.* 1 ridicule by imitating; make a parody on. 2 imitate poorly. [< Greek *parōidia* < *para-*[1] + *ōidē* song]

pa role (pə rōl′), *n., v.,* **-roled, -rol ing.** —*n.* 1 conditional release from prison or jail before the full term is served. 2 conditional freedom allowed in place of imprisonment. 3 word of honor, especially the promise of a prisoner of war not to escape if permitted a degree of freedom by his captors or not to take up arms against them if released. —*v.t.* give a conditional release from jail or prison before the full term is served. [< French, word, speech < Late Latin *parabola.* Doublet of PALAVER, PARABLE, PARABOLA, PARLEY.]

par o quet (par′ə ket), *n.* parakeet.

Par os (per′os, par′os), *n.* Greek island in the Aegean Sea, noted for its beautiful, white marble. 8000 pop.; 77 sq. mi.

pa rot id (pə rot′id), *adj.* near the ear. The **parotid glands,** one in front of each ear, supply saliva to the mouth through the **parotid ducts.** —*n.* parotid gland. [< Greek *parōtidos* < *para-*[1] + *ōtos* ear]

par ox ysm (par′ək siz′əm), *n.* 1 a sudden, severe attack of the symptoms of a disease, usually recurring periodically: *a paroxysm of coughing.* 2 a sudden outburst of emotion or activity: *a paroxysm of rage.* [< Greek *paroxysmos* < *para-*[1] + *oxynein* make sharp < *oxys* sharp]

par ox ys mal (par′ək siz′məl), *adj.* of, like, or having paroxysms.

par quet (pär kā′, pär ket′), *n., v.,* **-queted** (-kād′, -ket′id), **-quet ing** (-kā′ing, -ket′ing) or **-quet ted** (-ket′id), **-quet ting** (-ket′ing). —*n.* 1 an inlaid wooden flooring. 2 the main floor of a theater; orchestra. 3 part of the main floor of a theater from the orchestra pit to the parquet circle. —*v.t.* make or put down (an inlaid wooden floor). [< French, an enclosed portion, diminutive of *parc* park]

parquet circle, the part of the main floor of a theater that is under the balcony.

par quet ry (pär′kə trē), *n., pl.* **-ries.** mosaic of wood used for floors, wainscoting, etc.

parr (pär), *n., pl.* **parrs** or **parr.** a young salmon before it is old enough to go to sea. [origin uncertain]

par ra keet (par′ə kēt), *n.* parakeet.

par ri cid al (par′ə sī′dl), *adj.* of or having to do with parricide.

par ri cide (par′ə sīd), *n.* 1 act of killing one's parent or parents. 2 person who kills his parent or parents. [< Latin *parricidium, parricida*]

par rot (par′ət), *n.* 1 any bird of an order that includes parakeets, cockatoos, lovebirds, macaws, etc., with stout, hooked bills and often with bright-colored feathers. Some parrots can imitate sounds and repeat words and sentences. 2 person who repeats words or acts without understanding them. —*v.t.* repeat without understanding. [perhaps < French *Perrot,* diminutive of *Pierre* Peter] —**par′rot like′,** *adj.*

parrot fever or **parrot disease,** psittacosis.

parrot fish (par′ət fish), *n.* any of various, mainly tropical, marine fishes having a hard jaw resembling the bill of a parrot.

par ry (par′ē), *v.,* **-ried, -ry ing,** *n., pl.* **-ries.** —*v.t.* 1 ward off or block (a thrust, stroke, weapon, etc.) in fencing, boxing, etc. 2 meet and turn aside (an awkward question, a threat, etc.); avoid; evade. —*n.* act of parrying; avoiding. [< French *parez,* imperative of *parer* ward off < Italian *parare* < Latin, prepare. Doublet of PARE.]

parse (pärs), *v.t.,* **parsed, pars ing.** 1 analyze (a sentence) grammatically, telling its parts of speech and their uses in the sentence. 2 describe (a word) grammatically, telling what part of speech it is, its form, and its use in a sentence. [< Latin *pars (orationis)* part (of speech)]

par sec (pär′sek), *n.* unit of distance used in astronomy, equal to 3.26 light years, or 19.2 trillion miles. [< *par(allax of one) sec(ond)*]

Par see or **Par si** (pär′sē, pär sē′), *n.* member of a Zoroastrian sect in India, descended from Persians who first settled there in the early part of the A.D. 700's.

Par si fal (pär′sə fəl, pär′sə fäl), *n.* (in German legends) a knight corresponding to the Percival of Arthurian legend.

par si mo ni ous (pär′sə mō′nē əs), *adj.* too economical; stingy; miserly. —**par′si mo′ni ous ly,** *adv.* —**par′si mo′ni ous ness,** *n.*

par si mo ny (pär′sə mō′nē), *n.* extreme economy; stinginess. [< Latin *parsimonia* < *parcere* to spare]

par sley (pär′slē), *n., pl.* **-sleys.** a garden herb of the same family as the carrot, a native of the Mediterranean region, with finely divided, fragrant leaves, used to flavor food and to trim platters of meat, fish, etc. [Old English *petersilie* < Latin *petroselinum* < Greek *petrōselinon* < *petros* rock + *selinon* parsley]

par snip (pär′snip), *n.* 1 a biennial garden herb, a native of Europe and parts of Asia, having a long, tapering, whitish root. It is of the same family as the carrot. 2 its root, which is eaten as a vegetable. [< Old French *pasnaie* < Latin *pastinaca*]

par son (pär′sən), *n.* 1 minister in charge of a parish. 2 any clergyman; minister. [< Medieval Latin *persona* < Latin, person. Doublet of PERSON.]

par son age (pär′sə nij), *n.* house provided for a minister by a church.

part (pärt), *n.* 1 something less than the whole: *the western part of the country.* See synonym study below. 2 each of several equal quantities into which a whole may be divided; fraction: *A dime is a tenth part of a dollar.* 3 thing that helps to make up a whole: *A radio has many parts.* 4 portion of an organism; member, limb, or organ. Stamens and pistils are floral parts. 5 replacement for a worn or otherwise defective component of a machine, tool, etc.: *spare parts.* 6 share: *do one's part.* 7 side in a dispute or contest: *take one's friend's part.* 8 character in a play, motion picture, etc.; role: *the part of Hamlet.* 9 the words spoken by a character in a play: *study one's part.* 10 a dividing line left in combing one's hair. 11 one of the voices or instruments in a piece of music: *the tenor part, the violin part.* 12 the music for it. 13 **parts,** *pl.* **a** ability; talent: *a man of parts.* **b** regions; districts: *in foreign parts.*

for one's part, as far as one is concerned.

for the most part, mostly.

in good part, in a friendly or gracious way.

in part, in some measure or degree; to some extent; partly.

on the part of one or **on one's part, a** as far as one is concerned. **b** by one.

part and parcel, an essential part.

take part, have a share; be involved.

—*v.t.* 1 divide into two or more portions. 2 force apart; divide: *The policeman on horseback parted the crowd.* 3 keep apart; form a boundary between. 4 brush or comb (the hair) away from a dividing line. 5 dissolve or terminate (a connection, etc.) by separation of the parties concerned: *part company.* 6 **part from,** go away from; leave. 7 **part with,** give up; let go. —*v.i.* 1 go apart; separate: *The friends parted in anger.* 2 be divided into parts; come or go in pieces; break up; break.

—*adv.* in some measure or degree; partly.

[< Old French < Latin *partem* part]

Syn. *n.* 1 **Part, portion, piece** mean something less than the whole. **Part** is the general word, meaning an element or member of the whole considered apart from the rest: *Save part of the roast for tomorrow night.* **Portion** means a part thought of less in relation to the whole than as an amount or quantity making up a section or share: *Give a portion of each day to recreation.* **Piece** means a separate part, often thought of as complete in itself: *She ate a big piece of cake.*

part., 1 participle. 2 particular.

par take (pär tāk′), *v.i.*, **-took, -tak en, -tak ing.** 1 eat or drink some; take some: *We are eating lunch. Will you partake?* 2 take or have a share; participate. See **share**[1] for synonym study. 3 **partake of, a** take some; have a share in. **b** have to some extent the nature or character of: *Her graciousness partakes of condescension.* [< *partaker,* for *part-taker*] **—par tak′er,** *n.*

par tak en (pär tā′kən), *v.* pp. of **partake.**

part ed (pär′tid), *adj.* 1 divided into parts; severed; cloven. 2 (in botany) divided into distinct lobes by depressions extending from the margin nearly to the base, as a leaf.

par terre (pär ter′), *n.* 1 the part of the main floor of a theater under the balcony. 2 an ornamental arrangement of flower beds. [< French < *par terre* on the ground]

par the no gen e sis (pär′thə nō jen′ə sis), *n.* reproduction by means of unfertilized eggs, as in certain insects and lower plants. [< Greek *parthenos* virgin + English *genesis*]

par the no ge net ic (pär′thə nō jə net′ik), *adj.* having to do with or exhibiting parthenogenesis. **—par′the no ge net′i cal ly,** *adv.*

Par the non (pär′thə non), *n.* temple of Athena on the Acropolis in Athens, regarded as the finest example of Doric architecture.

Par thi a (pär′thē ə), *n.* ancient country in Asia southeast of the Caspian Sea, now a part of NE Iran. **—Par′thi an,** *adj., n.*

Parthian shot, a sharp parting remark or the like. [< the practice of the Parthian cavalry to launch a volley of arrows while retreating]

par tial (pär′shəl), *adj.* 1 not complete; not total: *a partial eclipse.* 2 inclined to favor one side more than another; favoring unfairly; biased: *A parent should not be partial to any one of his children.* 3 having a liking for; favorably inclined: *I am partial to sports.* [< Late Latin *partialis* < Latin *partem* part] **—par′tial ly,** *adv.*

par ti al i ty (pär′shē al′ə tē, pär shal′ə tē), *n., pl.* **-ties.** 1 the favoring of one more than another or others; favorable prejudice; being partial; bias. 2 a particular liking; fondness; preference: *Children often have a partiality for candy.*

par ti ci pant (pär tis′ə pənt), *n.* person who shares or participates. *—adj.* participating.

par tic i pate (pär tis′ə pāt), *v.i.*, **-pat ed, -pat ing.** have a share; take part: *The teacher participated in the children's games.* See **share**[1] for synonym study. [< Latin *participatum* taken part, ultimately < *partem* part + *capere* to take] **—par tic′i pa′tion,** *n.* **—par tic′i pa′tor,** *n.*

par ti cip i al (pär′tə sip′ē əl), *adj.* of, having to do with, or resembling a participle, as a **participial adjective** (a *masked* man, a *becoming* dress), a **participial noun** (in *cutting* ice, the fatigue of *marching*). **—par′ti cip′i al ly,** *adv.*

par ti ci ple (pär′tə sip′əl), *n.* a verb form that retains all the attributes of a verb, such as tense, voice, power to take an object, and modification by adverbs, but may be used as an adjective. EXAMPLES: the girl *writing* sentences at the blackboard, the *stolen* silver, the boy *having missed* the boat. In these phrases, *writing* is a present participle; *stolen* is a past participle; *having missed* is a perfect participle. [< Old French, variant of *participe* < Latin *participium* a sharing, ultimately < *partem* part + *capere* to take]

par ti cle (pär′tə kəl), *n.* 1 a very little bit: *I got a particle of dust in my eye.* 2 any of the extremely small units that make up matter, such as a molecule, atom, electron, proton, or neutron. 3 a derivational prefix or suffix. 4 a function word of indeterminate nature, useful in expressing certain relations and meanings, and including negatives, intensifiers, salutations, etc. A preposition, conjunction, article, or interjection is a particle. [< Latin *particula,* diminutive of *partem* part]

particle accelerator, any of several machines, such as the betatron and cyclotron, that greatly increase the speed and energy of protons, electrons, and other atomic particles and direct them in a steady stream at a target; accelerator. The accelerated particles are used to bombard the nuclei of atoms, causing the nuclei to release new particles.

par ti-col ored (pär′tē kul′ərd), *adj.* 1 colored differently in different parts. 2 diversified: *a parti-colored story.* [*parti-* < French *parti* divided]

par tic u lar (pər tik′yə lər), *adj.* 1 considered by itself or apart from others; taken separately; single: *That particular chair is already sold.* 2 belonging to some one person, thing, group, occasion, etc.: *A particular characteristic of a skunk is its smell.* See **special** for synonym study. 3 different from others; unusual; special: *a particular friend.* 4 hard to please; wanting everything to be just right; fastidious: *be particular about one's food.* 5 very careful; exact. 6 giving details; full of details: *a particular account of the game.* *—n.* 1 an individual part; item; point: *The work is complete in every particular.* See **item** for synonym study. 2 **in particular,** especially. [< Middle French *particuler* < Latin *particularis* < *particula* particle]

par tic u lar i ty (pər tik′yə lar′ə tē), *n., pl.* **-ties.** 1 detailed quality; minuteness. 2 special carefulness. 3 attentiveness to details. 4 a particular feature or trait. 5 quality of being hard to please. 6 quality or fact of being particular.

par tic u lar ize (pər tik′yə lə rīz′), *v.*, **-ized, -iz ing.** *—v.t.* mention particularly or individually; treat in detail; specify. *—v.i.* mention individuals; give details. **—par tic′u lar i za′tion,** *n.*

par tic u lar ly (pər tik′yə lər lē), *adv.* 1 in a high degree; especially. See **especially** for synonym study. 2 in a particular manner; in all its parts; in detail; minutely.

par tic u late (pär tik′yə lāt), *adj.* of, having to do with, or consisting of separate particles.

part ing (pär′ting), *n.* 1 a going away; taking leave; departure. 2 division; separation. 3 place of division or separation: *Her hair is arranged with a side parting.* *—adj.* 1 given, taken, done, etc., at parting: *a parting request.* 2 going away; departing. 3 dividing; separating.

par ti san (pär′tə zən), *n.* 1 a strong supporter of a person, party, or cause; one whose support is based on feeling rather than on reasoning. 2 member of light, irregular troops or armed civilians; guerrilla. *—adj.* of or like a partisan. Also, **partizan.** [< Middle French < Italian *partigiano* < *parte* part < Latin *partem*]

par ti san ship (pär′tə zən ship), *n.* 1 strong loyalty to a party or cause. 2 a taking sides. Also, **partizanship.**

par ti tion (pär tish′ən), *n.* 1 division into parts; apportionment: *the partition of a man's wealth when he dies.* 2 portion; part;

hat, āge, fär; let, ēqual, tėrm;
it, īce; hot, ōpen, ôrder;
oil, out; cup, pu̇t, rüle;
ch, child; ng, long; sh, she;
th, thin; ᴛʜ, then; zh, measure;

ə represents *a* in about, *e* in taken, *i* in pencil, *o* in lemon, *u* in circus.

< = from, derived from, taken from.

section. 3 wall between rooms, etc. *—v.t.* 1 divide into parts: *partition an empire among three brothers, partition a house into rooms.* 2 separate by a partition. **—par ti′tion er,** *n.*

par ti tive (pär′tə tiv), *n.* word or phrase meaning a part of a collective whole. *Some, few,* and *any* are partitives. *—adj.* expressing a part of a collective whole: *a partitive adjective.* **—par′ti tive ly,** *adv.*

par ti zan (pär′tə zən), *n., adj.* partisan.

par ti zan ship (pär′tə zən ship), *n.* partisanship.

part ly (pärt′lē), *adv.* in part; in some measure or degree.

part music, music for two or more parts, especially vocal music.

part ner (pärt′nər), *n.* 1 person who shares: *My sister was the partner of my walks.* 2 member of a company or firm who shares the risks and profits of the business. 3 wife or husband. 4 companion in a dance. 5 player on the same team or side in a game. *—v.t.* 1 associate as partners. 2 be the partner of. [Middle English variant of *parcener* < Old French *parçonier* < *parçon* partition < Latin *partitionem* < *partire* to part < *partem* part]

part ner ship (pärt′nər ship), *n.* 1 a being a partner; joint interest; association: *a business partnership, the partnership of marriage.* 2 company or firm with two or more members who share in the risks and profits of the business. 3 contract that creates such a relation.

part of speech, class of words grouped together on the basis of their distribution in sentences. The traditional parts of speech are the noun, pronoun, adjective, verb, adverb, preposition, conjunction, and interjection.

➤ **parts of speech.** One of the fundamental facts of English grammar is that a word may function as more than one part of speech: In *Iron rusts if left in the rain, rust* is a verb; in *Remove the rust with a wire brush, rust* is a noun; in *She wore a rust dress and brown shoes, rust* is an adjective.

par took (pär tu̇k′), *v.* pt. of **partake.**

par tridge (pär′trij), *n., pl.* **-tridg es** or **-tridge.** 1 any of several game birds of Europe, Asia, and Africa belonging to the same family as the quail and pheasant. 2 any of several similar birds of the United States, such as the ruffed grouse and the quail or bobwhite. [< Old French *perdriz* < Latin *perdix* < Greek]

par tridge ber ry (pär′trij ber′ē), *n., pl.* **-ries.** 1 a North American trailing plant of the same family as the madder, having evergreen leaves, fragrant white flowers, and edible but insipid scarlet berries; checkerberry. 2 its berry.

part song, song with parts in simple harmony for two or more voices, especially one meant to be sung without an accompaniment.

part-time (pärt′tīm′), *adj.* for part of the usual time.

par tur i ent (pär tůr′ē ənt, pär tyůr′ē ənt), *adj.* 1 bringing forth young; about to give birth to young. 2 having to do with childbirth.

par tu ri tion (pär′tů rish′ən, pär′tyů-rish′ən, pär′chů rish′ən), *n.* act of giving birth to young; childbirth. [< Latin *parturitionem* < *parturire* be in labor, ultimately < *parere* to bear]

par ty (pär′tē), *n., pl.* **-ties,** *adj.* —*n.* 1 a social gathering or entertainment: *give a party, a busy round of Christmas parties.* 2 group of people doing something together: *a hunting party.* See **company** for synonym study. 3 group of people organized to gain political influence and control, especially of the legislative or executive branches of a government. 4 person who takes part in, aids, or knows about: *party to a plot.* 5 each of the persons or sides in a contract, lawsuit, etc. 6 INFORMAL. a person: *Your party's on the telephone.* See **person** for synonym study. —*adj.* 1 of or having to do with a party of people. 2 of or belonging to a political party. [< Old French *partie* < *partir* to divide < Latin *partire* < *partem* part]

party line, 1 a telephone line by which two or more subscribers are connected with the exchange by one circuit. 2 a boundary line between adjoining premises. 3 the officially adopted policies of a political party. 4 policy advocated and followed by the Communist Party.

party liner, 1 person who follows the party line of a political party. 2 person who follows the policies of the Communist Party.

par value, face value.

par ve nu (pär′və nü, pär′və nyü), *n.* 1 person who has risen above his class, especially one who has risen through the acquisition of wealth, political power, etc. 2 person who has risen to a higher place than he is fit for; upstart. —*adj.* of or like a parvenu. [< French, past participle of *parvenir* arrive < Latin *pervenire* < *per-* through + *venire* come]

par ve nue (pär′və nü, pär′və nyü), *n.* a woman parvenu.

pas (pä), *n.* FRENCH. step or movement in dancing.

Pas a de na (pas′ə dē′nə), *n.* 1 city in SW California, near Los Angeles. 113,000. 2 city in SE Texas, near Houston. 89,000.

Pas cal (pas′kəl, pa skal′; *French* pä skäl′), *n.* **Blaise,** 1623-1662, French philosopher, mathematician, and physicist.

Pascal's law, (in physics) the law that pressure applied to a confined fluid is transmitted equally in all directions. [< Blaise *Pascal*]

Pasch (pask), *n.* 1 Passover. 2 Easter. [< Greek *pascha* < Hebrew *pesah*]

pas chal (pas′kəl), *adj.* 1 of or having to do with Passover. 2 of or having to do with Easter.

paschal lamb, 1 (in the Bible) a lamb killed and eaten at Passover. 2 **Paschal Lamb,** Christ or any representation of Him.

pas de deux (pä də dœ′), FRENCH. dance or figure in ballet for two persons.

pa sha (pə shä′, pash′ə, pä′shə), *n.* a former title used after the name of civil or military officials of high rank in Turkey. Also, **pacha.** [< Turkish *paşa*]

Pash to (push′tō), *n.* the Iranian language of Afghanistan and of the Pathans of Pakistan; Afghan. Also, **Pushtu.** [< Persian *pashtō* Afghan]

pasque flow er (pask′flou′ər), *n.* any of several anemones with purple or white flowers that bloom early in the spring. [*pasque* < Old French, Easter < Latin *pascha* < Greek. See PASCH.]

pas qui nade (pas′kwə nād′), *n., v.,* **-nad ed, -nad ing.** —*n.* a publicly posted satirical writing; lampoon. —*v.t.* attack by lampoons. [< French]

pass (pas), *v.,* **passed, passed** or **past, pass ing,** *n.* —*v.t.* 1 go by; move past; leave behind: *We passed the big truck. The car passed us.* 2 cause to go from one to another; hand around: *pass the butter.* 3 get through or by: *We passed the dangerous section of the road successfully.* 4 go across or over: *The horse passed the stream.* 5 make (a thing) go in any specific manner or direction: *pass a rope around a tree.* 6 cause to go, move onward, or proceed: *pass troops in review.* 7 discharge from the body. 8 be successful in (an examination, a course, etc.): *pass Latin.* 9 allow to go through an examination, a course, etc., successfully: *pass a student.* 10 cause or allow to go through something; sanction or approve: *pass accounts as correct.* 11 ratify or enact: *pass a bill, pass a law.* 12 be approved by (a lawmaking body, etc.): *The new law passed the city council.* 13 go beyond; exceed; surpass: *Such a strange story passes belief.* 14 use or spend: *We passed the days happily.* 15 cause to go about; circulate: *pass a counterfeit bill.* 16 cause to be accepted or received: *After examining the item, the inspector passed it.* 17 express; pronounce: *A judge passes sentence on guilty persons.* 18 let go without action or notice; leave unmentioned: *pass an insult.* 19 leave out; omit, especially payment of (a dividend, etc.) 20 throw (a football, basketball, etc.) or shoot (a hockey puck) from one player to another. 21 (in baseball) pitch four balls to (a batter), allowing him to walk to first base. 22 refuse (a hand, chance to bid, etc.) while playing cards. 23 promise: *pass one's word.* —*v.i.* 1 go on; move on; make one's way: *The parade passed.* 2 go from one to another: *His estate passed to his children.* 3 go away; depart: *The years pass rapidly.* 4 be successful in an examination, course, etc. 5 be discharged from the body. 6 be approved by a court, lawmaking body, etc.; be ratified: *The bill passed.* 7 come to an end; die: *Grandmother passed in peace. Dynasties pass.* 8 change: *When water freezes, it passes from a liquid to a solid state.* 9 be interchanged or transacted: *Friendly words passed between them.* 10 take place; happen: *Tell me all that has passed.* 11 be handed about; be in circulation: *Money passes from person to person.* 12 be accepted (*for* or *as*): *Use silk or a material that will pass for silk.* 13 give a judgment or opinion: *The judges passed on each contestant.* 14 go without notice: *He was rude, but let that pass.* 15 throw a football, basketball, etc., or shoot a hockey puck from one player to another. 16 (in card playing) refrain from bidding or playing a hand. 17 (in fencing) make a thrust.

bring to pass, cause to be; accomplish.

come to pass, take place; happen.

pass away or **pass on,** come to an end; die.

pass by, fail to notice; overlook; disregard.

pass off, a go away; disappear gradually. b take place; be done. c get accepted: *pass oneself off as a wealthy person.*

pass out, a give out; distribute. b SLANG. lose consciousness; faint. c SLANG. die.

pass over, fail to notice; overlook; disregard.

pass up, fail to take advantage of; give up; renounce.

—*n.* 1 act of passing; passage. 2 success in an examination, course, etc., especially without a distinctive grade or honors. 3 note, license, etc., permitting one to do something: *No one can get into the fort without a pass.* 4 a free ticket: *a pass to the circus.* 5 state; condition: *Things have come to a strange pass.* 6 motion of the hand or hands. 7 a sleight-of-hand motion; manipulation; trick. 8 a narrow road, path, way, channel, etc., especially through mountains. 9 throw of a football, basketball, etc., or a shooting of a hockey puck from one player to another. 10 (in baseball) the pitching of four balls to a batter, allowing him to walk to first base; a walk. 11 a thrust in fencing. 12 (in card playing) a refraining from bidding or playing a hand. 13 INFORMAL. a attempt to kiss or flirt. b a sexual overture.

[< Old French *passer* < Latin *passus* a step. Doublet of PACE[1].] —**pass′er,** *n.*

pass., 1 passenger. 2 passive.

pass a ble (pas′ə bəl), *adj.* 1 fairly good; moderate; tolerable: *a passable knowledge of geography.* 2 that can be passed: *a passable river.* 3 that may be circulated; current; valid: *passable coin.* —**pass′a bly,** *adv.*

pas sage (pas′ij), *n.* 1 hall or way through or between parts of a building; passageway; corridor. 2 means of passing; way through: *open a passage through a crowd.* 3 right, liberty, or leave to pass: *The guard refused us passage.* 4 a passing; a going or moving onward: *the passage of time.* 5 a passing from one place or state to another: *passage from sleep to wakefulness.* 6 a piece from a speech or writing: *a passage from the Bible.* 7 a phrase or other division of a piece of music. 8 a going across, especially across a sea or ocean; voyage: *a stormy passage across the Atlantic.* 9 ticket that entitles the holder to transportation, especially by boat: *obtain passage for Europe.* 10 a making into law by a favoring vote of a legislature: *the passage of a bill.* 11 what passes between persons. 12 exchange of blows or a dispute.

pas sage way (pas′ij wā′), *n.* way along which one can pass; passage. Halls and alleys are passageways.

Pas sa ma quod dy Bay (pas′ə mə-kwod′ē), inlet of the Bay of Fundy, between Maine and New Brunswick, Canada.

pass book (pas′bůk′), *n.* bankbook.

pas sé (pa sā′, pas′ā), *adj.* out of date; outmoded. [< French, passed]

passed ball, (in baseball) a pitched ball, not touched by the bat, on which a runner or runners advance to the next base or bases because of the catcher's failure to stop the ball.

pas sel (pas′əl), *n.* group of indeterminate number: *a passel of birds, a passel of TV commercials.* [variant of *parcel*]

pas sen ger (pas′n jər), *n.* traveler in an aircraft, bus, ship, train, etc., usually one that pays a fare. [< Old French *passagier* < *passage* passage]

passenger pigeon, a wild pigeon of North America, now extinct, that flew far in very large flocks.

passe-par tout (pas′pär tü′), *n.* 1 frame

for a picture consisting of strips of gummed paper that fasten the glass to the backing. 2 paper prepared for this purpose. 3 that which passes everywhere, or by means of which one can pass everywhere, such as a master key. [< French < *passe partout* pass everywhere]

pass er-by (pas′ər bī′), *n., pl.* **pass ers-by.** one that passes by.

pas ser ine (pas′ər ən, pas′ər īn), *adj.* of or belonging to the very large order of perching birds, including more than half of all birds, such as the warblers, sparrows, chickadees, wrens, thrushes, and swallows. *—n.* a perching bird. [< Latin *passerinus* of a sparrow < *passer* sparrow]

pas sim (pas′im), *adv.* LATIN. here and there; in various places.

➤ **Passim** is used in footnotes to indicate that a subject is discussed in various places in the work cited: "Jespersen, *Language, passim.*"

pass ing (pas′ing), *adj.* 1 that goes by or passes. 2 fleeting; transitory: *a passing smile.* 3 cursory; incidental: *passing mention.* 4 that is now happening: *the passing scene.* 5 allowing a person to pass an examination, course, etc.: *75 will be a passing mark.* *—n.* 1 act of one that passes; going by; departure. 2 **in passing,** in that connection; incidentally. 3 means or place of passing. 4 death. *—adv.* surpassingly; very. **—pass′ing ly,** *adv.*

pas sion (pash′ən), *n.* 1 a very strong or violent feeling or emotion, such as great hate and fear. See **feeling** for synonym study. 2 Often, **passions,** *pl.* strong feelings or emotions as an obstacle to civilized conduct or rational behavior. 3 fit or mood of some emotion, especially violent anger: *fly into a passion.* 4 a very strong love or sexual desire. 5 person who is the object of such love or desire. 6 a very strong liking: *She has a passion for music.* 7 object of such a passion: *Music is her passion.* 8 ARCHAIC. suffering. 9 Often, **the Passion. a** the sufferings of Jesus on the Cross or after the Last Supper. **b** the story of these sufferings in the Bible. [< Old French < Latin *passionem* < *pati* suffer] **—pas′sion less,** *adj.*

pas sion ate (pash′ə nit), *adj.* 1 having or showing strong feelings: *a passionate believer in human rights.* 2 easily moved to a fit or mood of some emotion, especially to violent anger. 3 resulting from strong feeling. 4 having or showing a very strong love or sexual desire. **—pas′sion ate ly,** *adv.* **—pas′sion ate ness,** *n.*

pas sion flow er (pash′ən flou′ər), *n.* 1 any of a genus of mostly American climbing herbs and shrubs grown for their edible, yellowish or purple fruits and their large, showy flowers. 2 the flower of any of these plants. [< the imagined likeness of parts of the flower to the crown of thorns, nails, and cross of Christ's crucifixion]

passion play or **Passion Play,** play representing the sufferings and death of Christ.

Passion Sunday, the second Sunday before Easter Sunday. It is the fifth Sunday in Lent.

Passion Week, the second week before Easter; fifth week in Lent, between Passion Sunday and Palm Sunday.

pas sive (pas′iv), *adj.* 1 being acted on without itself acting; not acting in return: *a passive mind, a passive disposition.* 2 not resisting; yielding or submitting to the will of another; submissive: *the passive obedience of a slave.* 3 (in grammar) of or having to do with the passive voice. *—n.* in grammar: 1 the passive voice. 2 a verb form in the passive voice. [< Latin *passivus* < *pati* suffer] **—pas′sive ly,** *adv.* **—pas′sive ness,** *n.*

passive immunity, immunity from a disease due to antibodies of a serum obtained from another organism.

passive resistance, peaceful refusal to comply with a law, injunction, etc., especially as a form of resistance to a government or other authority.

passive satellite, a communications satellite that reflects a signal but does not receive it and transmit it again.

passive voice, (in grammar) the form of the verb that shows the subject as acted upon, not acting. In "A letter was written by me," *was written* is in the passive voice.

pas siv i ty (pa siv′ə tē), *n.* a being passive; lack of action or resistance.

pass key (pas′kē′), *n., pl.* **-keys.** 1 key for opening several locks. 2 a private key.

Pass o ver (pas′ō′vər), *n.* an annual Jewish holiday commemorating the escape of the Hebrews from Egypt, where they had been slaves. It occurs in March or April and lasts eight days. [< the phrase *pass over* (translation of Hebrew *pesah*), in reference to the Biblical account of a destroying angel "passing over" the houses of the Hebrews when it killed the first-born child in every Egyptian house]

pass port (pas′pôrt, pas′pōrt), *n.* 1 an official document or booklet granting a citizen permission to travel abroad under the protection of his government and giving him the right to leave and reenter his native country. 2 anything that gives one admission or acceptance: *An interest in gardening was a passport to my aunt's favor.* [< Middle French *passeport* < *passer* to pass + *port* harbor]

pass word (pas′wėrd′), *n.* a secret word that allows a person speaking it to pass a guard.

past (past), *adj.* 1 gone by; ended; over: *Our troubles are past.* 2 just gone by: *the past year, the past century.* 3 having served a term or terms in office but not now in office: *a past president.* 4 (in grammar) of or expressing the past tense: *The past forms of "eat" and "smile" are "ate" and "smiled."*

—n. 1 the time gone by; time before: *Life began far back in the past.* 2 what has happened in the time gone by: *forget the past. History is a study of the past.* 3 a past life or history: *Our country has a glorious past.* 4 a person's past life, especially if hidden or unknown. 5 the past tense or a verb form in it.

—prep. 1 farther on than; beyond: *The arrow went past the mark.* 2 later than; after: *It is past noon.* 3 beyond in number, amount, age, or degree; more than: *He is past 60.* 4 beyond the ability, range, scope, etc., of: *absurd fancies that are past belief.*

—adv. so as to pass by or beyond; by: *The cars sped past.*

—v. a pp. of **pass.**

pas ta (pä′stə), *n.* any of various foods, as macaroni, spaghetti, etc., made of flour, water, salt, and sometimes milk or eggs, shaped in tubular or other forms and dried. [< Italian < Late Latin, dough. See PASTE.]

paste (pāst), *n., v.,* **past ed, past ing.** *—n.* 1 mixture, such as flour and water boiled together, that will stick paper together, stick it to a wall, etc. 2 dough for pastry, made with butter, lard, or other shortening. 3 pasta. 4 a preparation of fish, tomatoes, ground nuts, or some other article of food reduced to a smooth, soft mass: *shrimp paste, almond paste.* 5 a mixture of clay and water to make earthenware or porcelain. 6 a hard, brilliant, heavy glass material used in making imitations of precious stones. 7 any of various soft, jellylike confections. *—v.t.* 1 stick with paste: *paste a label on a box.* 2 cover by pasting: *paste a door over with notices.* 3 SLANG. hit with a hard, sharp blow. [< Old French < Late Latin *pasta* dough, pastry < Greek, porridge]

hat, āge, fär; let, ēqual, tėrm;
it, īce; hot, ōpen, ôrder;
oil, out; cup, pu̇t, rüle;
ch, child; ng, long; sh, she;
th, thin; TH, then; zh, measure;

ə represents *a* in about, *e* in taken, *i* in pencil, *o* in lemon, *u* in circus.

< = from, derived from, taken from.

paste board (pāst′bôrd′, pāst′bōrd′), *n.* a stiff material made of sheets of paper pasted together or of paper pulp pressed and dried.

pas tel (pa stel′, pas′tel), *n.* 1 kind of chalklike crayon used in drawing, made of a dry paste of ground pigments compounded with resin or gum. 2 this paste. 3 a drawing made with such crayons. 4 a soft, pale shade of some color. *—adj.* soft and pale: *pastel pink, pastel shades.* [< French]

past er (pā′stər), *n.* 1 a slip to paste on or over something. 2 person or thing that pastes.

pas tern (pas′tərn), *n.* 1 the part of a horse's foot between the fetlock and the hoof. See **horse** for picture. 2 the corresponding part in related animals, such as a donkey, mule, or cow. [< Old French *pasturon* < *pasture* tether for a horse, pasture]

Pas ter nak (pas′tər nak), *n.* **Boris,** 1890-1960, Russian poet and novelist.

Pas teur (pa stėr′), *n.* **Louis,** 1822-1895, French chemist who discovered the means of immunization against rabies and developed pasteurization.

pas teur i za tion (pas′chər ə zā′shən, pas′tər ə zā′shən), *n.* 1 process of pasteurizing. 2 fact or condition of being pasteurized.

pas teur ize (pas′chə rīz′, pas′tə rīz′), *v.t.,* **-ized, -iz ing.** heat (milk, wine, beer, etc.) to a high enough temperature and for a long enough time to destroy harmful bacteria and prevent or arrest fermentation. When milk is pasteurized, it is heated to about 145 degrees Fahrenheit for not less than 30 minutes, then chilled quickly to 50 degrees Fahrenheit or less. [< Louis *Pasteur*]

pas teur iz er (pas′chə rī′zər, pas′tə-rī′zər), *n.* apparatus for pasteurizing milk, wine, beer, etc.

pas tiche (pa stēsh′), *n.* an artistic, musical, or literary work made up of portions of various works; medley or potpourri. [< French < Italian *pasticcio,* originally, pasty[2]]

pas til (pas′til), *n.* pastille.

pas tille (pa stēl′), *n.* 1 a flavored or medicated lozenge; troche. 2 a small roll or cone of aromatic paste, burnt as a disinfectant, incense, etc. [< French < Latin *pastillus* roll, lozenge]

pas time (pas′tīm′), *n.* a pleasant way of passing time; amusement; recreation; diversion. Games and sports are pastimes.

past master, 1 person who has filled the office of master in a society, lodge, etc. 2 person who has much experience in any profession, art, etc.; expert.

pas tor (pas′tər), *n.* minister or clergyman having charge of a church or congregation; spiritual guide. [< Latin, shepherd < *pascere* to feed]

pas tor al (pas′tər əl), *adj.* 1 of shepherds or country life: *a pastoral occupation, a pastoral poem.* 2 simple or naturally beautiful like the country: *a pastoral scene.* See **rural** for synonym study. 3 of a pastor or his duties. —*n.* 1 a pastoral play, poem, or picture. 2 letter from a bishop to his clergy or to the people of his church district. **—pas′tor al ly,** *adv.*

pas tor ate (pas′tər it), *n.* 1 position or duties of a pastor. 2 term of service of a pastor. 3 pastors as a group.

past participle, the participle used in forming the English passive and perfect constructions and as an adjective, as *stolen* in *is stolen, has stolen,* and *stolen money.* For most verbs the past participle has the same form whether used as an adjective or in a verb phrase.

past perfect, 1 designating or belonging to a tense that indicates an action which was completed before a given past time. In "He had learned to read before he went to school," *had learned* is the past perfect of *learn. Past perfect* and *pluperfect* mean the same. 2 such a tense. 3 a verb form in such a tense.

pas tra mi (pə strä′mē), *n.* a smoked and well-seasoned cut of beef, especially a shoulder cut. [< Yiddish < Romanian *pastramă*]

pas try (pā′strē), *n., pl.* **-tries.** 1 pies, tarts, and other foods wholly or partly made of rich flour paste. 2 any food made of baked flour paste enriched with lard, butter, or a vegetable shortening. [< *paste*]

past tense, 1 tense expressing time gone by, or a former action or state. 2 a verb form in the past tense; preterit.

pas tur age (pas′chər ij), *n.* 1 the growing grass and other plants for cattle, sheep, or horses to feed on. 2 pasture land. 3 a pasturing.

pas ture (pas′chər), *n., v.,* **-tured, -tur ing.** —*n.* 1 a grassy field or hillside; grasslands on which cattle, sheep, or horses can feed. 2 grass and other growing plants. —*v.t.* 1 put (cattle, sheep, etc.) out to pasture. 2 feed on (growing grass, etc.). —*v.i.* (of cattle, sheep, etc.) to graze. [< Old French < Late Latin *pastura* < Latin *pascere* to feed]

past y[1] (pā′stē), *adj.,* **past i er, past i est.** 1 like paste. 2 pale. 3 flabby. [< *paste*] **—past′i ness,** *n.*

pas ty[2] (pas′tē, pās′tē), *n., pl.* **-ties.** pie filled with meat, fish, etc.: *a venison pasty.* [< Old French *pastee* < *paste* paste, dough < Late Latin *pasta.* See PASTE. Doublet of PATTY.]

pat (pat), *v.,* **pat ted, pat ting,** *n., adj., adv.* —*v.t.* 1 strike or tap lightly with the fingers, hand, or something flat, especially so as to flatten or smooth: *She patted the dough into a flat cake.* 2 tap with the hand as a sign of sympathy, approval, or affection: *pat a dog.* 3 **pat on the back,** praise; compliment. —*v.i.* 1 walk or run with a patting sound. 2 strike lightly or gently. —*n.* 1 a light stroke or tap with the hand or with something flat. 2 the sound made by patting. 3 a small mass, especially of butter. 4 **pat on the back,** a praise; compliment. —*adj.* to the point; suitable; apt: *a pat reply.* —*adv.* 1 aptly; exactly; suitably. 2 **have pat, have down pat,** or **know pat,** INFORMAL. have perfectly; know thoroughly. 3 **stand pat,** INFORMAL. hold to things as they are and refuse to change. [perhaps imitative] **—pat′ly,** *adv.* **—pat′ness,** *n.*

pat., 1 patent. 2 patented.

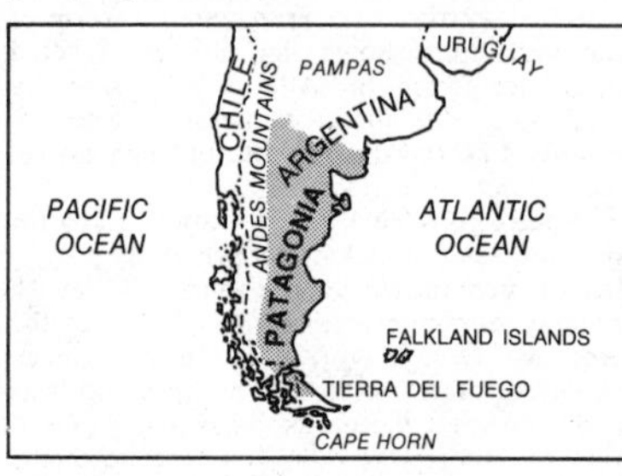

Pat a go ni a (pat′ə gō′nē ə), *n.* region in the extreme south of South America. The larger part of Patagonia is in Argentina; the rest is in Chile. **—Pat′a go′ni an,** *adj., n.*

patch (pach), *n.* 1 piece put on to cover a hole or a tear in something, or to strengthen a weak place. 2 piece of cloth, etc., put over a wound or a sore. 3 a pad over a hurt eye to protect it. 4 a small bit of black cloth that ladies used to wear on their faces, especially in the 1600's and 1700's, to show off their fair skin. 5 a small, uneven spot: *a patch of brown on the skin.* 6 piece of ground: *a garden patch.* 7 scrap or bit of cloth, etc., left over. 8 shoulder patch.

—*v.t.* 1 protect or adorn with a patch or patches; put patches on; mend: *patch clothes.* See **mend** for synonym study. 2 make by joining patches or pieces together: *patch a quilt.* 3 piece together; make hastily. 4 **patch up, a** put an end to; settle: *patch up a quarrel.* **b** make right hastily or for a time: *patch up a leaking faucet.* **c** put together hastily or poorly: *patch up a costume for a play.* —*v.i.* mend clothes with patches. [Middle English *pacche*] **—patch′er,** *n.*

patch ou li (pach′ů lē, pə chü′lē), *n.* 1 an East Indian plant of the mint family having an essential oil from which a fragrant and lasting perfume is obtained. 2 the perfume. [probably < Tamil *pacculi*]

patch ou ly (pach′ů le, pə chü′le), *n., pl.* **-lies.** patchouli.

patch pocket, a flat pocket attached to the outside of a garment.

patch test, test for allergy to a particular substance, made by applying the substance to a small area of unbroken skin, usually by means of pads.

patch work (pach′wėrk′), *n.* 1 pieces of cloth of various colors or shapes sewed together: *a cover of patchwork for a cushion.* 2 anything like this: *From the airplane, we saw a patchwork of fields and woods.* 3 a miscellaneous collection; jumble.

patch y (pach′ē), *adj.,* **patch i er, patch i est.** 1 abounding in or characterized by patches. 2 occurring in, forming, or resembling patches. **—patch′i ness,** *n.*

pate[1] (pāt), *n.* top of the head; head: *a bald pate.* [Middle English]

pa te[2] (pä tā′), *n.* pâté.

pâ té (pä tā′), *n.* FRENCH. 1 paste of finely chopped meat, liver, etc., with spices and herbs, often served chilled and sliced. 2 pastry case filled with chicken, oysters, etc.; patty.

pâ té de foie gras (pä tā′ də fwä grä′), FRENCH. patty or paste made with livers of specially fattened geese and usually finely chopped truffles.

pa tel la (pə tel′ə), *n., pl.* **-tel las, -tel lae** (-tel′ē). kneecap. See **fibula** for diagram. [< Latin, diminutive of *patina* pan. See PATEN.]

pa tel lar (pə tel′ər), *adj.* having to do with the kneecap.

pat en (pat′n), *n.* 1 plate on which the bread is placed at the celebration of the Eucharist or Mass. 2 plate or flat piece of metal. Also, **patina.** [< Latin *patena, patina* pan, dish < Greek *patanē* flat dish]

pa ten cy (pāt′n sē, pat′n sē), *n.* a being patent; obviousness.

pat ent (*n., adj. 1, 2, v.* pat′nt; *British* pāt′nt; *adj. 3, 4* pāt′nt, pat′nt), *n.* 1 a government grant which gives a person or company sole rights to make, use, or sell a new invention for a certain number of years. 2 invention that is patented. 3 an official document from a government giving a right, privilege, office, etc. 4 the instrument by which public land is granted to a person. 5 land so granted. —*adj.* 1 given or protected by a patent. 2 of or having to do with patents: *patent law.* 3 evident; plain: *It is patent that cats dislike dogs.* 4 open. —*v.t.* 1 get a patent for. 2 grant a patent to. 3 obtain a patent right to (land). [< Latin *patentem* lying open] **—pat′ent a ble,** *adj.*

pat ent ee (pat′n tē′), *n.* person to whom a patent is granted.

pat ent leather (pat′nt), leather with a very glossy, smooth surface, usually black.

pa tent ly (pāt′nt lē, pat′nt lē), *adv.* plainly or openly; clearly; obviously.

pat ent medicine (pat′nt), 1 any medicine that may be purchased without a doctor's prescription. 2 medicine sold by a company which has a patent on its manufacture and trade name.

Patent Office, government office that issues patents.

pat en tor (pat′n tər), *n.* person who grants a patent.

pa ter (pā′tər; *also* pat′ər, pät′ər *for 2*), *n.* 1 BRITISH INFORMAL. father. 2 paternoster. [< Latin]

Pa ter (pā′tər), *n.* **Walter Horatio,** 1839-1894, English critic and essayist.

pa ter fa mil i as (pā′tər fə mil′ē əs), *n.* father or head of a family. [< Latin < *pater* father + Old Latin *familias* of a family]

pa ter nal (pə tėr′nl), *adj.* 1 of or like a father; fatherly. 2 related on the father's side of the family: *a paternal aunt, paternal grandparents.* 3 received or inherited from one's father: *Her blue eyes are a paternal inheritance.* [< Latin *paternus* < *pater* father] **—pa ter′nal ly,** *adv.*

pa ter nal ism (pə tėr′nl iz′əm), *n.* principle or practice of managing the affairs of a country or group of people, such as the employees of a company, as a father manages the affairs of children.

pa ter nal ist (pə tėr′nl ist), *n.* person

who believes in or practices paternalism.

pa ter nal is tic (pə tėr′nl is′tik), *adj.* having to do with or characterized by paternalism.

pa ter ni ty (pə tėr′nə tē), *n.* 1 a being a father; fatherhood. 2 paternal origin.

pa ter nos ter or **Pat er nos ter** (pat′ər nos′tər, pät′ər nos′tər, pā′tər nos′tər), *n.* the Lord's Prayer, especially in Latin. [< Latin *pater noster* our father]

Pat er son (pat′ər sən), *n.* city in NE New Jersey. 145,000.

path (path), *n., pl.* **paths** (paᴛʜz, paths). 1 way made by people or animals walking, usually too narrow for automobiles or wagons. 2 way made to walk upon or to ride horses, bicycles, etc., upon: *a garden path.* 3 line along which a person or thing moves; route; track; course: *The moon has a regular path through the sky.* 4 way of acting or behaving; way of life: *paths of glory, paths of ease.* [Old English *pæth*] **—path′less,** *adj.*

path., 1 pathological. 2 pathology.

Pa than (pə tän′, pət hän′), *n.* 1 person of Afghan descent living in or near the borderland of Pakistan and Afghanistan. 2 an Afghan.

pa thet ic (pə thet′ik), *adj.* 1 arousing pity; pitiful; pitiable: *the pathetic sight of a crippled child.* 2 full of pathos: *pathetic music.* [< Greek *pathētikos,* ultimately < *paschein* suffer] **—pa thet′i cal ly,** *adv.*

Pa thet La o (pä′thət lä′ō), the communist-supported forces in Laos.

path find er (path′fīn′dər), *n.* one that finds a path or way, as through a wilderness, an unexplored area, etc.

path o gen (path′ə jən), *n.* any agent capable of producing disease, especially a living microorganism or virus. [< Greek *pathos* disease + English *-gen*]

path o gen e sis (path′ə jen′ə sis), *n.* the production or development of disease.

path o ge net ic (path′ə jə net′ik), *adj.* pathogenic.

path o gen ic (path′ə jen′ik), *adj.* having to do with pathogenesis; producing disease.

pa thog e ny (pa thoj′ə nē), *n.* pathogenesis.

path o log ic (path′ə loj′ik), *adj.* pathological.

path o log i cal (path′ə loj′ə kəl), *adj.* 1 of pathology; dealing or concerned with diseases: *pathological studies.* 2 due to or accompanying disease: *a pathological condition of the blood cells.* **—path′o log′i cal ly,** *adv.*

pa thol o gist (pa thol′ə jist), *n.* an expert in pathology.

pa thol o gy (pa thol′ə jē), *n., pl.* **-gies.** 1 study of the causes and nature of diseases, especially the structural and functional changes brought about by diseases. 2 unhealthy conditions and processes caused by a disease, especially changes in the tissues and organs of the body. [< Greek *pathos* disease + English *-logy*]

pa thos (pā′thos), *n.* 1 quality in speech, writing, music, events, or a scene that arouses a feeling of pity or sadness; power of evoking tender or melancholy emotion. 2 a pathetic expression or utterance. [< Greek, suffering, feeling < *path-,* stem of *paschein* suffer]

path way (path′wā′), *n.* path.

-pathy, *combining form.* 1 feeling; emotion: *Antipathy = a hostile feeling.* 2 disease: *Psychopathy = mental disease.* 3 treatment of disease: *Osteopathy = treatment of disease in bones.* [< Greek *-patheia* < *pathos.* See PATHOS.]

pa tience (pā′shəns), *n.* 1 willingness to put up with waiting, pain, trouble, etc., calm endurance without complaining or losing self-control. 2 long, hard work; steady effort. See synonym study below. 3 card game played by one person; solitaire.

Syn. 1, 2 Patience, forbearance, fortitude mean power to endure, without complaining, something unpleasant or painful. **Patience** implies calmness and self-control and applies whether one is enduring something unpleasant, merely waiting, or doing something requiring steady effort: *The teacher needed patience to handle the unruly student.* **Forbearance** implies uncommon self-control when greatly tried or provoked: *He endured the many attacks of his political opponents with admirable forbearance.* **Fortitude** implies strength of character and calm courage in facing danger or enduring suffering: *With fortitude, the disabled veteran learned a new trade.*

pa tient (pā′shənt), *adj.* 1 having or showing patience: *patient suffering.* 2 with steady effort or long, hard work; persistent; diligent: *patient research.* *—n.* person who is being treated by a doctor. [< Latin *patientem* suffering] **—pa′tient ly,** *adv.*

pat i na[1] (pat′n ə, pə tē′nə), *n.* 1 film or incrustation, usually green, formed by oxidation on the surface of old bronze or copper, and often regarded as ornamental on a statue or other object of art. 2 film or coloring produced in the course of time on wood or other substance. 3 a surface appearance added to or assumed by anything: *the patina of soft, supple leather, the patina of success.* [< Italian, perhaps < Latin, pan, patina[2] (because of the incrustation on ancient dishes)]

pat i na[2] (pat′n ə), *n., pl.* **pat i nae** (pat′n ē). 1 a broad, shallow dish or pan used by the ancient Romans. 2 paten. [< Latin, pan, dish. See PATEN.]

patio (def. 1)

pat i o (pat′ē ō), *n., pl.* **pat i os.** 1 an inner court or yard open to the sky, found especially in relatively large dwellings of Spanish or Spanish-American design. 2 terrace of cement or flat stones for outdoor eating, lounging, etc. [< Spanish]

Pat mos (pat′mos), *n.* Greek island in the Aegean Sea off the coast of Turkey. 3000 pop.; 22 sq. mi.

Pat na (pat′nə), *n.* city in E India, on the Ganges River. 449,000.

pat ois (pat′wä), *n., pl.* **pat ois** (pat′wäz). 1 dialect spoken by the common people of a district. 2 cant or jargon of a particular group. 3 a provincial dialect or form of speech. [< French]

pa tri arch (pā′trē ärk), *n.* 1 father and ruler of a family or tribe, especially one of the ancestral figures in the Bible, such as Abraham, Isaac, or Jacob. 2 person thought of as the father or founder of something. 3 a venerable old man, especially the elder of a village, community, etc. 4 bishop of the highest rank in the early Christian church, especially the bishop of Antioch, Alexandria, Rome, Constantinople, or Jerusalem. 5 bishop of the highest rank in the Eastern Church or the Roman Catholic Church. [< Latin *patriarcha* < Greek *patriarchēs* < *patria* family, clan + *archos* leader]

hat, āge, fär; let, ēqual, tėrm;
it, īce; hot, ōpen, ôrder;
oil, out; cup, pu̇t, rüle;
ch, child; ng, long; sh, she;
th, thin; ᴛʜ, then; zh, measure;

ə represents *a* in about, *e* in taken, *i* in pencil, *o* in lemon, *u* in circus.

< = from, derived from, taken from.

pa tri ar chal (pā′trē är′kəl), *adj.* 1 suitable to a patriarch; having to do with a patriarch. 2 under the rule of a patriarch: *a patriarchal church.*

pa tri ar chate (pā′trē är′kit), *n.* 1 position, dignity, or authority of a church patriarch. 2 church district under a patriarch's authority. 3 residence of a patriarch. 4 patriarchy.

pa tri ar chy (pā′trē är′kē), *n., pl.* **-chies.** 1 form of social organization in which the father is head of the family and in which descent is reckoned in the male line, the children belonging to the father's clan. 2 family, community, tribe, etc., having this form of organization.

pa tri cian (pə trish′ən), *n.* 1 member of the nobility of ancient Rome, composed of the families descended from the original body of Roman citizens. 2 person of noble birth; noble; aristocrat. *—adj.* 1 of the patricians. 2 of high social rank; aristocratic. 3 suitable for an aristocrat. [< Latin *patricius* of the *patres* (senators, literally, fathers) at Rome]

pat ri cid al (pat′rə sī′dl), *adj.* of or having to do with patricide.

pat ri cide (pat′rə sīd), *n.* 1 act of killing one's father. 2 person who kills his father.

Pat rick (pat′rik), *n.* **Saint,** A.D. 389?-461?, British missionary and bishop who converted Ireland to Christianity. He is the patron saint of Ireland.

pat ri lin e al (pat′rə lin′ē əl), *adj.* having or maintaining relationship through the male line of a family, tribe, etc. **—pat′ri lin′e al ly,** *adv.*

pat ri mo ni al (pat′rə mō′nē əl), *adj.* having to do with a patrimony; inherited from one's father or ancestors.

pat ri mo ny (pat′rə mō′nē), *n., pl.* **-nies.** 1 property inherited from one's father or ancestors. 2 property held as an endowment by a church, monastery, or convent. 3 any heritage. [< Latin *patrimonium* < *pater* father]

pa tri ot (pā′trē ət), *n.* person who loves and loyally supports his country. [< Greek *patriotēs* fellow countryman < *patris* fatherland < *patēr* father]

pa tri ot ic (pā′trē ot′ik), *adj.* 1 loving one's country. 2 showing love and loyal support of one's own country. **—pa′tri ot′i cal ly,** *adv.*

pa tri ot ism (pā′trē ə tiz′əm), *n.* love and loyal support of one's country.

Patriots' Day, U.S. April 19, the anniversary of the battles at Lexington and Concord in 1775, observed on the third Monday in April as a legal holiday in Maine and Massachusetts.

pa tris tic (pə tris′tik), *adj.* having to do with the early leaders, or fathers, of the Christian church or with their writings.

pa tris ti cal (pə tris′tə kəl), *adj.* patristic.

Pa tro clus (pə trō′kləs), *n.* (in Greek legends) a friend of Achilles, killed by Hector.

pa trol (pə trōl′), *v.,* **-trolled, -trol ling,** *n.* *—v.i.* go the rounds of a particular area, district, etc., watching, guarding, and checking irregularity or disorder so as to protect life and property. *—v.t.* go around (an area, district, etc.) to watch or guard. *—n.* 1 a going of the rounds to watch or guard. 2 person who patrols or persons who patrol: *a police patrol.* 3 group of soldiers, ships, or airplanes, sent toward, into, or over enemy lines to gain information, engage in a raid, warn and protect the main body, etc. 4 one of the subdivisions of a troop of boy scouts or girl scouts, usually consisting of eight members. [< French *patrouiller* to paddle in mud, ultimately < *patte* paw] **—pa trol′ler,** *n.*

patrol car, automobile used by policemen to patrol an area.

pa trol man (pə trōl′mən), *n., pl.* **-men.** 1 man who patrols. 2 policeman who patrols a certain district.

patrol wagon, a closed wagon or truck used by police for carrying prisoners.

pa tron (pā′trən), *n.* 1 person who buys regularly at a given store or goes regularly to a given restaurant, hotel, etc. 2 person who gives his approval and support to some person, art, cause, or undertaking: *a patron of artists.* 3 a guardian saint or god. *—adj.* guarding; protecting. [< Latin *patronus* protector, patron < *pater* father. Doublet of PADRONE, PATROON.]

pa tron age (pā′trə nij, pat′rə nij), *n.* 1 regular business given to a store, hotel, etc., by customers. 2 favor, encouragement, or support given by a patron. 3 condescending favor: *an air of patronage.* 4 power to give jobs or favors: *the patronage of a congressman.* 5 political jobs or favors.

pa tron ess (pā′trə nis, pat′rə nis), *n.* a woman patron.

pa tron ize (pā′trə nīz, pat′rə nīz), *v.t.,* **-ized, -iz ing.** 1 be a regular customer of; give regular business to: *We patronize our neighborhood stores.* 2 act as a patron toward; support or protect: *patronize the ballet.* 3 treat in a haughty, condescending way. **—pa′tron iz′ing ly,** *adv.*

patron saint, saint regarded as the special guardian of a person, church, city, etc.

pat ro nym ic (pat′rə nim′ik), *n.* name derived from the name of a father or paternal ancestor, especially by the addition of a prefix or suffix: *Williamson meaning "son of William" is a patronymic.* [< Greek *patrōnymikos* derived from the name of a father < *patēr* father + *onyma* name]

pa troon (pə trün′), *n.* 1 landowner who had certain privileges under the former Dutch governments of New York and New Jersey. A patroon usually owned a large amount of land. [< Dutch < Latin *patronus* patron. Doublet of PADRONE, PATRON.]

pat sy (pat′sē), *n., pl.* **-sies.** SLANG. an easy victim or scapegoat. [origin uncertain]

pat ten (pat′n), *n.* 1 a wooden overshoe with a thick sole. 2 kind of wooden sandal or overshoe mounted on an iron ring, to raise the foot above wet ground. [< Old French *patin* < *pate* paw]

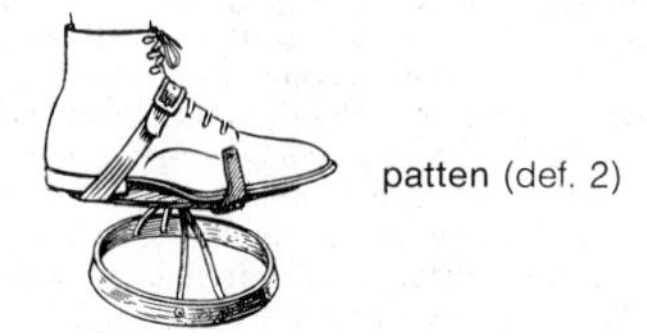
patten (def. 2)

pat ter¹ (pat′ər), *v.i.* 1 make rapid taps: *The rain patters on a windowpane.* 2 move with a rapid tapping sound: *patter across the room.* *—n.* series of quick taps or the sound they make: *the patter of little feet.* [< *pat*]

pat ter² (pat′ər), *n.* 1 rapid and easy talk: *a magician's patter, a salesman's patter.* 2 special vocabulary of a class or group; jargon: *the patter of thieves.* 3 rapid speech introduced into a song, usually for comic effect. *—v.t.* talk or say rapidly and easily, without much thought: *patter a prayer.* *—v.i.* talk rapidly, fluently, or glibly. [variant of *pater* in *paternoster* (because the prayer was said very rapidly)] **—pat′ter er,** *n.*

pat tern (pat′ərn), *n.* 1 arrangement of forms and colors; design: *the pattern of a wallpaper, a pattern of polka dots.* 2 model or guide for something to be made: *She used a paper pattern in cutting out her new dress.* 3 a fine example; model to be followed. See **model** for synonym study. 4 form; shape; configuration: *a large, deep cup with a bowl-like pattern.* 5 structure or design in a work of literature, music, etc.: *a novelistic pattern.* 6 configuration of qualities or traits characterizing a person or group: *cultural patterns, patterns of thought.* 7 a typical specimen; sample. 8 a model in wood or metal from which a mold is made for casting. *—v.t.* make according to a pattern: *She patterned herself after her mother.* [< Old French *patron* patron, pattern (from a person's copying his patron) < Latin *patronus.* See PATRON.]

Pat ton (pat′n), *n.* **George Smith,** 1885-1945, American general in World War II.

pat ty (pat′ē), *n., pl.* **-ties.** 1 a hollow form or case of pastry filled with chicken, sweetbreads, oysters, etc. 2 a small, round, flat piece of food or candy. [< French *pâté* < Old French *pastee.* Doublet of PASTY².]

pau ci ty (pô′sə tē), *n.* 1 small number; fewness. 2 a small amount; scarcity; lack. [< Latin *pauci* few]

Paul (pôl), *n.* **Saint,** died A.D. 67?, apostle who established Christian churches in many countries and wrote most of the epistles in the New Testament.

Paul I, 1 1754-1801, czar of Russia from 1796 to 1801, infamous for the cruelty of his reign. 2 1901-1964, king of Greece from 1947 to 1964.

Paul III, 1468-1549, pope from 1534 to 1549.

Paul V, 1552-1621, pope from 1605 to 1621.

Paul VI, born 1897, pope since 1963.

Paul Bunyan. See **Bunyan.**

Pau li (pô′lē), *n.* **Wolfgang,** 1900-1958, Austrian physicist.

Paul ine (pô′lən, pô′līn, pô′lēn), *adj.* of, having to do with, or written by the apostle Paul.

Pau ling (pô′ling), *n.* **Linus Carl,** born 1901, American chemist.

paunch (pônch, pänch), *n.* 1 belly; stomach. 2 a large, protruding belly; potbelly. 3 rumen. [< Old French *panche* < Latin *pantex*]

paunch y (pôn′chē, pän′chē), *adj.,* **paunch i er, paunch i est.** having a big paunch. **—paunch′i ness,** *n.*

pau per (pô′pər), *n.* 1 a very poor person. 2 person supported by charity or public welfare. [< Latin, poor. Doublet of POOR.]

pau per ism (pô′pə riz′əm), *n.* poverty.

pau per ize (pô′pə rīz′), *v.t.,* **-ized, -iz ing.** make a pauper of. **—pau′per i za′tion,** *n.*

pause (pôz), *v.,* **paused, paus ing,** *n.* *—v.i.* 1 stop for a time; wait. See **stop** for synonym study. 2 dwell; linger: *pause upon a word.* *—n.* 1 a brief or temporary stop or rest: *a pause for lunch. It rained all day without pause.* 2 **give pause,** cause to stop or hesitate. 3 a brief stop made, according to the sense, in speaking or reading. 4 a punctuation mark indicating such a stop. 5 a sign (⌒ or ◡) above or below a musical note or rest, meaning that it is to be held for a longer time. 6 an interval in a line of verse. [< Latin *pausa* a pause < Greek *pausis* < *pauein* to stop]

pav an (pav′ən), *n.* pavane.

pa vane (pə van′, pə vän′), *n.* 1 a slow, stately dance introduced into England in the 1500's, performed by couples. 2 the music for it. [< Middle French]

pave (pāv), *v.t.,* **paved, pav ing.** 1 cover (a street, sidewalk, etc.) with a pavement. 2 overlay as if with a pavement; cover in a mass or compactly. 3 make (the course of any undertaking) smooth or easy; prepare (the way): *The discovery of electricity paved the way for many inventions.* [< Old French *paver* < Latin *pavire* to beat, tread down] **—pav′er,** *n.*

pave ment (pāv′mənt), *n.* 1 a covering or surface for streets, sidewalks, etc., made of such material as asphalt, concrete, gravel, or stones. 2 a paved road, sidewalk, etc. 3 material used for paving.

pavilion (def. 1)

pa vil ion (pə vil′yən), *n.* 1 a light building, usually somewhat open, used for shelter, pleasure, etc.: *a dance pavilion, a bathing pavilion.* 2 a large tent with a floor raised on posts, and usually with a peaked top. 3 part of a building higher and more decorated than the rest. 4 one of a group of buildings forming a hospital. 5 any building that houses an exhibition at a fair. *—v.t.* furnish with a pavilion; enclose or shelter in a pavilion. [< Old French *pavillon* < Latin *papilionem* tent]

pav ing (pā′ving), *n.* 1 material for pavement. 2 pavement.

Pav lov (pav′lov, päv′lôf), *n.* **Ivan,** 1849-1936, Russian physiologist noted for his studies of the digestive glands and the conditioned reflex.

Pav lo va (päv′lō və, päv lō′və), *n.* **Anna,** 1885-1931, Russian ballerina.

Pav lov i an (pav lō′vē ən), *adj.* of or having to do with Ivan Pavlov or his experiments.

paw (pô), *n.* 1 foot of an animal, especially the foot of a four-footed animal with claws, such as a cat or dog. 2 INFORMAL. the hand, especially when clumsy, or awkwardly used. —*v.t.* 1 strike or scrape with the paws or feet: *The cat pawed the mouse. The horse pawed the ground, eager to be going again.* 2 INFORMAL. handle awkwardly, roughly, or in too familiar a manner. [< Old French *powe, poue*]

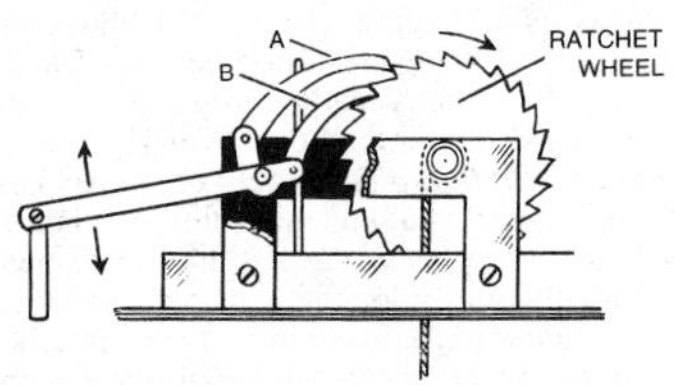

pawl—The ratchet wheel is moved in the direction of the arrow by pawl A when the lever is moved up, and by pawl B when the lever is moved down.

pawl (pôl), *n.* a pivoted bar arranged to catch in the teeth of a ratchet, etc., so as to prevent movement backward or to impart motion. [origin uncertain]

pawn[1] (pôn), *v.t.* leave (something) with another person as security that borrowed money will be repaid: *He pawned his watch to buy food until he could get work.* —*n.* 1 something left as security. 2 **in pawn,** in another's possession as security. 3 a pledge. [< Middle French *pan*] **—pawn′er,** *n.*

pawn[2] (pôn), *n.* 1 (in chess) one of the 16 pieces of lowest value. A pawn can move only one square forward at a time, except on its first move, when a player has the option of moving it either one or two squares. When capturing an enemy piece, it must move diagonally. 2 an unimportant person or thing used by someone to gain some advantage. [< Old French *peon,* originally, foot soldier < Late Latin *pedonem* < Latin *pedem* foot. Doublet of PEON.]

pawn bro ker (pôn′brō′kər), *n.* person who lends money at interest on articles that are left with him as security for the loan.

Paw nee (pô nē′), *n., pl.* **-nees** or **-nee.** member of an American Indian tribe that once lived in Nebraska and Kansas, and now lives in Oklahoma.

pawn shop (pôn′shop′), *n.* a pawnbroker's shop.

paw paw (pô′pô), *n.* 1 papaw. 2 papaya.

Paw tuck et (pô tuk′it), *n.* city in NE Rhode Island. 77,000.

pax vo bis cum (paks′ vō bis′kəm; poks′ wō bēs′kum), LATIN. peace be with you.

pay (pā), *v.,* **paid** (or **payed** for 10), **pay ing,** *n., adj.* —*v.t.* 1 give (a person, business firm, etc., money or its equivalent for things bought, work done, etc.: *pay a doctor for an operation.* See synonym study below. 2 give (money, etc.) that is due: *pay $50 for a coat.* 3 give money for: *Pay your fare.* 4 furnish or deliver the amount of (what is owed): *pay a debt, pay taxes.* 5 give or offer: *pay attention, pay compliments, pay a visit.* 6 be profitable or worthwhile to: *It pays me to keep that stock.* 7 yield as a return: *That stock pays me four per cent.* 8 return for favors or hurts; recompense or requite; reward or punish: *He paid them for their insults by causing them trouble.* 9 suffer; undergo: *The one who does wrong must pay the penalty.* 10 let out (a rope) by slackening. —*v.i.* 1 give money, etc.; give what is due: *He owes it and must pay.* 2 be profitable or advantageous: *It pays to be polite.*
pay back, **a** return borrowed money. **b** give the same treatment as received. **c** take revenge on: *I'll pay you back yet!*
pay off, **a** give all the money that is owed; pay in full. **b** get even with; get revenge on.
pay up, pay in full; pay.
—*n.* 1 money or the equivalent given for things, service, or work; wages; salary. 2 return for favors or hurts. 3 a source of payment. 4 act of paying. 5 payment, especially of wages: *rate of pay.* 6 condition of being paid, or receiving wages. 7 **in the pay of,** paid by and working for.
—*adj.* 1 containing a device for receiving money for use: *a pay telephone.* 2 containing enough metal, oil, etc., to be worth mining, drilling, etc.: *a pay lode.* 3 limited to paying subscribers: *pay television.*
[< Old French *paier* < Latin *pacare* pacify < *pax* peace]
Syn. *v.t.* 1 **Pay, compensate, remunerate** mean to give money or its equivalent in return for something. **Pay** is the common word meaning to give someone money due for goods, work, or services: *I paid the grocer for the things I bought.* **Compensate** suggests making up for time spent, things lost, service given, or the like: *We'll compensate him for his work as consultant.* **Remunerate** suggests giving a reward in return for services, trouble, etc., and is used especially, as *compensate* also is, as more polite than *pay* and not suggesting crudely that money is expected or due: *The club remunerated the lecturer.*

pay a ble (pā′ə bəl), *adj.* 1 required to be paid; falling due; due: *I must spend $100 soon on bills payable.* 2 that may be paid.

pay-as-you-go (pā′əz yü gō′), *n.* U.S. 1 the withholding of income tax at the time wages or salaries are paid. 2 the payment or discharge of obligations as they are incurred.

pay check (pā′chek′), *n.* check given in payment of wages or salary.

pay day (pā′dā′), *n.* day on which wages are paid.

pay dirt, 1 earth, ore, etc., containing enough metal to be worth mining. 2 INFORMAL. something that yields a profit or beneficial result.

pay ee (pā ē′), *n.* person to whom money is paid or is to be paid.

pay er (pā′ər), *n.* person who pays or is to pay.

pay load (pā′lōd′), *n.* 1 the load carried by an aircraft, train, truck, etc., which is capable of producing a revenue. 2 the cargo of a rocket, including passengers and instruments. 3 the warhead of a missile.

pay mas ter (pā′mas′tər), *n.* person whose job is to pay wages.

pay ment (pā′mənt), *n.* 1 a paying. 2 amount paid: *a monthly payment of $10.* 3 pay: *My child's good health is payment enough for me.* 4 reward or punishment.

pay nim or **Pay nim** (pā′nim), *n.* ARCHAIC. 1 pagan; heathen. 2 Moslem; Saracen. [< Old French *paienisme* heathendom < Late Latin *paganismus* paganism < Latin *paganus.* See PAGAN.]

hat, āge, fär; let, ēqual, tėrm;
it, īce; hot, ōpen, ôrder;
oil, out; cup, pu̇t, rüle;
ch, child; ng, long; sh, she;
th, thin; ᴛʜ, then; zh, measure;

ə represents *a* in about, *e* in taken, *i* in pencil, *o* in lemon, *u* in circus.

< = from, derived from, taken from.

pay off (pā′ôf′, pā′of′), *n.* 1 a paying of wages. 2 time of such payment. 3 returns from an enterprise, specific action, etc. 4 a dividing of the returns from some undertaking among those having an interest in it. 5 SLANG. climax (of a story, situation, etc.).

pay o la (pā ō′lə), *n.* SLANG. undercover payments made in return for favors, such as the promotion of a product.

pay roll (pā′rōl′), *n.* 1 list of persons to be paid and the amount that each one is to receive. 2 the total amount to be paid to them.

pay station, a public pay telephone.

payt., payment.

Pb, lead [for Latin *plumbum*].

pc., piece.

p.c., 1 per cent. 2 post card.

p/c, or **P/C,** 1 petty cash. 2 price or prices current.

Pd, palladium.

pd., paid.

p.d., 1 per diem. 2 potential difference.

P.D., 1 per diem. 2 Police Department.

P.E., Protestant Episcopal.

pea (pē), *n., pl.* **peas** or **pease.** 1 one of the round, smooth, or wrinkled seeds, used as a vegetable, that are contained in the long, green pod of an annual vine of the pea family. 2 the vine itself, having white flowers and pinnate leaves. 3 any seed or plant resembling or related to a pea. 4 **as like as two peas,** exactly alike. [< *pease,* originally singular, later taken as a plural < Old English *pise* < Late Latin *pisa* < Latin *pisum* < Greek *pison*] **—pea′like′,** *adj.*

peace (pēs), *n.* 1 freedom from strife of any kind; condition of quiet, order, and security: *peace in the family.* 2 freedom from war: *work for world peace.* 3 agreement between contending parties to end war: *sign the peace.* 4 quiet; calm; serenity: *peace of mind. We enjoy the peace of the country.* 5 **at peace,** **a** not in a state of war. **b** not quarreling. **c** in a state of quietness; quiet; peaceful. 6 **hold one's peace** or **keep one's peace,** be silent; keep still. [< Old French *pais* < Latin *pax*]

peace a ble (pē′sə bəl), *adj.* 1 liking peace; keeping peace. 2 peaceful: *a peaceable reign.* See **peaceful** for synonym study. **—peace′a ble ness,** *n.* **—peace′a bly,** *adv.*

Peace Corps, agency of the United States government, established in 1961, which sends trained volunteers to help improve conditions in underdeveloped countries.

Peace Corpsman, volunteer working for the Peace Corps.

peace ful (pēs′fəl), *adj.* 1 full of peace; quiet; calm: *a peaceful countryside.* 2 liking peace; keeping peace; peaceable: *peaceful* *neighbors.* See synonym study below. 3 free from trouble, disturbance, violence, or strife: *peaceful coexistence, settle a dispute by peaceful means.* **—peace′ful ly,** *adv.* **—peace′ful ness,** *n.*

Syn. 1 Peaceful, peaceable, placid, serene mean characterized by peace and quiet. **Peaceful** usually suggests a state of inner quiet, free from disturbance or strife: *She felt peaceful and contented after a hard day's work.* **Peaceable** usually suggests a disposition that avoids strife and seeks to maintain peace and order: *We have friendly, peaceable neighbors.* (In informal usage these two words are often interchangeable.) **Placid** suggests a disposition that stays undisturbed and undistracted: *Placid cows grazed beside the highway.* **Serene** suggests a disposition that remains quietly and graciously composed even in the midst of confusion: *She is always cool, gracious, and serene.*

peace keep ing (pēs′kē′ping), *adj.* maintaining, enforcing, or intervening to achieve a cessation of hostilities between opposing armies, countries, etc.: *a peacekeeping force.*

peace mak er (pēs′mā′kər), *n.* person who makes peace.

peace mak ing (pēs′mā′king), *n.* act of making or bringing about peace. *—adj.* that makes or brings about peace.

peace offering, an offering made to obtain peace, such as a gift or favor.

peace officer, policeman, sheriff, constable, or other civil officer in charge of preserving and enforcing the public peace.

peace pipe, calumet.

Peace River, river in W Canada, flowing northeast from British Columbia into the Slave River in NE Alberta. 1065 mi.

peace time (pēs′tīm′), *n.* a time of peace. *—adj.* of or having to do with a time of peace.

peach¹ (pēch), *n.* 1 a juicy, nearly round fruit of a yellowish-pink color, with downy skin, a sweet pulp, and a hard, rough stone or pit. Peaches are widely cultivated in many varieties in temperate climates. 2 the tree that it grows on, belonging to the rose family. 3 a yellowish pink. 4 SLANG. person or thing especially admired or liked. *—adj.* yellowish-pink. [< Old French *peche* < Late Latin *persica* < Latin *Persicum (malum)* Persian (apple)] **—peach′like′,** *adj.*

peach² (pēch), *v.i.* SLANG. give secret information; turn informer. [short for Middle English *apechen* impeach]

peach y (pē′chē), *adj.,* **peach i er, peach i est.** 1 SLANG. fine; wonderful. 2 like a peach; like that of a peach. **—peach′i ness,** *n.*

pea cock (pē′kok′), *n., pl.* **-cocks** or **-cock,** *v.* *—n.* 1 the male of the peafowl, distinguished by beautiful green, blue, and gold feathers. The tail feathers have spots like eyes on them and can be spread out and held upright like a fan. 2 any peafowl. 3 person who is vain and fond of showing off. *—v.i.* strut like a peacock; make a conceited display. [Middle English *pekok* < Old English *pēa, pāwa* peafowl (< Latin *pavo*) + *cocc,* *cock¹*]

peacock (def. 1)—20 in. long without tail

peacock blue, greenish blue.

pea family, a large group of dicotyledonous plants, including ornamentals such as the lupine and wisteria and many plants of great economic importance such as the pea, peanut, bean, indigo, clover, and licorice; the legumes.

pea fowl (pē′foul′), *n.* any of several large birds of the same family as the pheasant, found in India, Ceylon, southeast Asia, the East Indies, and Africa.

pea green, light green.

pea hen (pē′hen′), *n.* a female peafowl, smaller and less showy than the peacock.

pea jacket, a short, heavy, double-breasted coat of woolen cloth, worn especially by sailors.

peak (pēk), *n.* 1 the pointed top of a mountain or hill: *snowy peaks.* 2 a mountain or hill that stands alone: *Pikes Peak.* 3 any pointed end or top: *the peak of a roof, the peak of a beard.* 4 the highest point: *reach the peak of one's profession.* 5 the projecting front part or the brim of a cap. 6 the narrow part of a ship's hold at the bow or at the stern. 7 the upper rear corner of a sail that is extended by a gaff. 8 a promontory or point of land; headland. *—v.t.* 1 raise straight up; tilt up. 2 bring to a peak or head. *—v.i.* come to a peak or head. *—adj.* highest; maximum: *peak output.* [variant of *pick²*]

peaked¹ (pēkt, pē′kid), *adj.* having a peak; pointed: *a peaked hat.*

peak ed² (pē′kid), *adj.* sickly in appearance; wan; thin. [< earlier *peak* look sick; origin uncertain]

peal (pēl), *n.* 1 a loud, long sound: *a peal of thunder, peals of laughter.* 2 the loud ringing of bells. 3 set of bells tuned to each other, especially a set of seven tuned to the tones of the major scale for use in ringing changes. 4 a series of changes rung on a set of bells. *—v.t., v.i.* sound out in a peal; ring: *The bells pealed forth their message of Christmas joy.* [Middle English *pele*]

pe an (pē′ən), *n.* paean.

pea nut (pē′nut′), *n.* 1 the large nutlike seed of a plant of the pea family, roasted for use as food or pressed to obtain its oil for cooking. 2 pod of this plant, ripening underground and usually containing two of the seeds. 3 the plant itself, an annual, low-growing herb with small, yellow flowers, widely cultivated in warm climates. 4 SLANG. a small or unimportant person. 5 **peanuts,** *pl.* INFORMAL. **a** something of little or no value. **b** a relatively small amount of money.

peanut butter, a thick, pasty, brown food made of roasted peanuts ground until soft and smooth, used as a spread on bread, crackers, etc.

peanut oil, oil pressed from peanuts, used especially in cooking and in margarine.

pear (per, par), *n.* 1 a sweet, juicy, pomaceous fruit rounded at one end and smaller toward the stem end, grown in temperate climates. 2 the tree that it grows on, belonging to the rose family. [Old English *pere* < Latin *pirum*]

pearl (pėrl), *n.* 1 a hard, smooth, white or nearly white gem having a soft shine like satin, formed inside the shell of certain oysters or in other similar mollusks by secretions of calcium carbonate with layers of animal membrane around a grain of sand, parasitic worm, or other foreign matter. 2 something that looks like a pearl, such as a dewdrop or a tear. 3 a very fine one of its kind: *She is a pearl among women.* 4 a very pale, clear, bluish gray. 5 mother-of-pearl. 6 a size of printing type (5 point). This sentence is set in pearl. *—adj.* 1 very pale, clear bluish-gray. 2 formed into small, round pieces: *pearl tapioca.* *—v.i.* hunt or dive for pearls. *—v.t.* 1 adorn or set with pearls or with mother-of-pearl. 2 make pearly in color or luster. 3 make like pearls in form. [< Old French *perle* < Popular Latin *perla*] **—pearl′like′,** *adj.*

pearl gray, a soft, pale, bluish gray.

Pearl Harbor, United States naval base near Honolulu, on the S coast of Oahu, site of the attack by Japanese bombers on December 7, 1941, that was the immediate cause of American entry into World War II.

pearl y (pėr′lē), *adj.,* **pearl i er, pearl i est.** 1 like a pearl; having the color or luster of pearls: *pearly teeth.* 2 like mother-of-pearl, especially in color and luster; nacreous. 3 adorned with or containing many pearls.

Pear y (pir′ē, per′ē), *n.* **Robert Edwin,** 1856-1920, American naval officer and arctic explorer, discoverer of the North Pole in 1909.

peas ant (pez′nt), *n.* 1 farmer of the working class in Europe. 2 any farm laborer of low social status. 3 an uneducated, uncouth, or boorish person. *—adj.* of peasants: *peasant labor.* [< Old French *paysant* < *pays* country < Late Latin *pagensis* living in a rural district < Latin *pagus* rural district]

peas ant ry (pez′n trē), *n.* peasants as a group.

peas cod (pēz′kod′), *n.* peasecod.

pease (pēz), *n.* a pl. of **pea.**

pease cod (pēz′kod′), *n.* pod of a pea. Also, **peascod.**

pea-soup fog (pē′süp′), INFORMAL. a very thick and heavy fog.

peat (pēt), *n.* 1 kind of heavy turf made up of partly decomposed vegetable matter, such as a sphagnum moss, found in bogs and used as a fertilizer or as fuel, especially in Ireland and Great Britain. 2 piece of this, usually cut in the shape of a brick, and dried for use as fuel. [Middle English *pete* < Medieval Latin *peta*] **—peat′like′,** *adj.*

peat moss, kind of moss, such as sphagnum, from which peat has formed or may form.

peat y (pē′tē), *adj.,* **peat i er, peat i est.** of, like, or abounding in peat.

pea vey (pē′vē), *n., pl.* **-veys.** a cant hook tipped with an iron or steel point. Lumbermen use peaveys in managing logs.

peavey

[< Joseph *Peavey,* who invented it in the 1800's]

pea vy (pē′vē), *n., pl.* **-vies.** peavey.

peb ble (peb′əl), *n., v.,* **-bled, -bling.** —*n.* 1 a small stone, usually worn and rounded by being rolled about by water. 2 a rough, uneven surface on leather, paper, etc. —*v.t.* 1 pave with pebbles: *pebble a walk.* 2 prepare (leather) so that it has a rough, uneven surface. 3 pelt with pebbles. [Old English *papol(stānas)* pebble(stones)] —**peb′ble like′,** *adj.*

peb bly (peb′lē), *adj.,* **-bli er, -bli est.** having many pebbles; covered with pebbles: *a pebbly beach.*

pe can (pi kän′, pi kan′, pē′kan), *n.* 1 an olive-shaped, edible nut with a smooth, thin shell, that grows on a hickory tree common in the southern and central United States. 2 the tree that it grows on. [< Algonquian *pakan* hard-shelled nut]

pec ca dil lo (pek′ə dil′ō), *n., pl.* **-loes** or **-los.** a slight sin or fault. [< Spanish *pecadillo,* diminutive of *pecado* sin < Latin *peccatum*]

pec car y (pek′ər ē), *n., pl.* **-car ies** or **-car y.** either of two species of hoofed mammals resembling the pig, found in tropical America from Texas to Paraguay, usually living and traveling in groups in forests. [< Carib *pakira*]

peck[1] (pek), *v.t.* 1 strike and pick with the beak or a pointed tool. 2 make by striking with the beak or a pointed tool: *Woodpeckers peck holes in trees.* 3 strike at and pick up with the beak: *A hen pecks corn.* 4 INFORMAL. eat only a little, bit by bit. —*v.i.* 1 strike with or use the beak. 2 aim with a beak; make a pecking motion. 3 take food with the beak. 4 INFORMAL. eat very lightly and daintily. 5 **peck at,** a try to peck. b INFORMAL. eat only a little, bit by bit: *She just pecked at her food.* c keep criticizing. —*n.* 1 stroke made with the beak: *The hen gave me a peck.* 2 hole or mark made by pecking. 3 INFORMAL. a stiff, unwilling kiss: *a peck on the cheek.* [apparently variant of *pick*[1]]

peck[2] (pek), *n.* 1 unit of dry measure, 8 quarts or $^1/_4$ of a bushel. See **measure** for table. 2 container holding just a peck, to measure with. 3 a great deal: *a peck of trouble.* [Middle English *pek*]

peck er (pek′ər), *n.* 1 person or thing that pecks. 2 woodpecker. 3 BRITISH SLANG. courage.

pecking order or **peck order,** 1 order of dominance in bird flocks, prescribing which bird can peck another and which bird or birds can, in turn, peck it. The pecking order never changes once it is established at an early age among a flock. 2 order of precedence among the members of any group.

pec ten (pek′tən), *n., pl.* **-tens** or (esp. for 1) **-ti nes** (-tə nēz′). 1 (in zoology) a comblike part or projection. 2 any of a common genus of scallops. [< Latin, comb]

pec tin (pek′tən), *n.* any of a group of substances, soluble in water, that occur in most fruits and certain vegetables, especially apples and currants. A solution of pectin, on evaporating, yields a fine jelly which serves as the basis of fruit jellies and jams. [< Greek *pēktos* stiff, congealed < *pēgnynai* make stiff, congeal]

pec tor al (pek′tər əl), *adj.* of, in, or on the breast or chest. [< Latin *pectoralis* < *pectus* chest]

pectoral fin, either of a pair of fins in fishes, usually just behind and in line with the gills, corresponding to the forelimbs of higher vertebrates. See **fin** for picture.

pec u late (pek′yə lāt), *v.t.* **-lat ed, -lat ing.** embezzle. [< Latin *peculatum* embezzled < *peculium* private property. See PECULIAR.] —**pec′u la′tion,** *n.* —**pec′u la′tor,** *n.*

pe cul iar (pi kyü′lyər), *adj.* 1 out of the ordinary; strange; odd; unusual. See **strange** for synonym study. 2 belonging to one person or thing and not to another; special; particular; distinctive: *This old Bible has a peculiar value.* [< Latin *peculiaris* of one's own < *peculium* private property < *pecu* money, cattle] —**pe cul′iar ly,** *adv.*

pe cu li ar i ty (pi kyü′lē ar′ə tē), *n., pl.* **-ties.** 1 a being peculiar; strangeness; oddness; unusualness. 2 thing or feature that is strange or odd. 3 a peculiar or characteristic quality.

pe cu ni ar y (pi kyü′nē er′ē), *adj.* 1 of or having to do with money. 2 in the form of money: *a pecuniary gift.* [< Latin *pecuniarius* < *pecunia* money < *pecu* money, cattle]

pedestal (def. 1) supporting a bust

ped a gog (ped′ə gog, ped′ə gôg), *n.* pedagogue.

ped a gog ic (ped′ə goj′ik, ped′ə gō′jik), *adj.* of teachers or teaching; of pedagogy. —**ped′a gog′i cal ly,** *adv.*

ped a gog i cal (ped′ə goj′ə kəl, ped′ə-gō′jə kəl), *adj.* pedagogic.

ped a gogue (ped′ə gog, ped′ə gôg), *n.* 1 teacher of children; schoolmaster. 2 a dull, narrow-minded teacher; pedant. Also, **pedagog.** [< Greek *paidagōgos* < *pais, paidos* boy + *agōges* leader]

ped a go gy (ped′ə gō′jē, ped′ə goj′ē), *n.* 1 teaching. 2 science or art of teaching.

ped al (ped′l; *adj. also* pē′dl *for 2*), *n., v.,* **-aled, -al ing** or **-alled, -al ling,** *adj.* —*n.* lever worked by the foot to move any kind of machinery: *the pedals of a bicycle, the brake pedal of an automobile.* Organs and pianos have pedals for changing the tone. —*v.t.* work or use the pedals of; move by pedals: *pedal a bicycle up a hill.* —*v.i.* work pedals. —*adj.* 1 of or having to do with a pedal or pedals. 2 of or having to do with the foot or feet. [< Latin *pedalis* of the foot < *pedem* foot]

pedal pushers, close-fitting calf-length pants for women, originally for bicycle riding.

ped ant (ped′nt), *n.* 1 person who displays his knowledge in an unnecessary or tiresome way or who puts great stress on minor points of learning. 2 a dull, narrow-minded teacher or scholar. [< Italian *pedante*]

pe dan tic (pi dan′tik), *adj.* 1 displaying one's knowledge more than is necessary. 2 tediously learned; scholarly in a dull and narrow way. —**pe dan′ti cal ly,** *adv.*

ped ant ry (ped′n trē), *n., pl.* **-ries.** 1 an unnecessary or tiresome display of knowledge. 2 overemphasis on rules, details, etc., especially in learning. 3 a pedantic form or expression.

hat, āge, fär; let, ēqual, tėrm;
it, īce; hot, ōpen, ôrder;
oil, out; cup, pu̇t, rüle;
ch, child; ng, long; sh, she;
th, thin; ᴛʜ, then; zh, measure;

ə represents *a* in about, *e* in taken, *i* in pencil, *o* in lemon, *u* in circus.

< = from, derived from, taken from.

ped ate (ped′āt), *adj.* 1 having a foot or feet. 2 footlike. 3 (of a leaf) parted or divided in a palmate manner with the two lateral lobes divided into smaller segments. [< Latin *pedem* foot]

ped dle (ped′l), *v.,* **-dled, -dling.** —*v.t.* 1 carry from place to place and sell. 2 sell or deal out, especially in small quantities: *peddle gossip.* —*v.i.* travel about with things to sell. [< *peddler*]

ped dler (ped′lər), *n.* person who travels about selling things that he carries in a pack or in a truck, wagon, or cart. Also, **pedlar.** [Middle English *pedlere*]

ped es tal (ped′i stəl), *n.* 1 base on which a column or a statue stands. 2 base of a tall vase, lamp, etc. 3 any base; support; foundation. 4 **place on a pedestal,** accord a very high place to; idolize. [< Middle French *piedestall* < Italian *piedestallo* < *pie di stallo* foot of stall[1]]

pe des tri an (pə des′trē ən), *n.* person who goes on foot; walker. —*adj.* 1 going on foot; walking. 2 for or used by pedestrians. 3 without imagination; dull; slow; commonplace: *a pedestrian style of writing.* [< Latin *pedester* on foot < *pedem* foot]

pe des tri an ism (pə des′trē ə niz′əm), *n.* 1 practice of traveling on foot; walking. 2 commonplace quality or style.

pe di at ric (pē′dē at′rik, ped′ē at′rik), *adj.* of or having to do with pediatrics. [< Greek *paidos* child + *iatros* physician]

pe di a tri cian (pē′dē ə trish′ən, ped′ē ə-trish′ən), *n.* doctor who specializes in pediatrics.

pe di at rics (pē′dē at′riks, ped′ē at′riks), *n.* branch of medicine dealing with children's diseases and the care of babies and children.

ped i cab (ped′ə cab′), *n.* a three-wheeled vehicle with a hooded cab for one or two passengers, operated by pedals. It is used especially in the Orient. [< Latin *pedem* foot + English *(taxi)cab*]

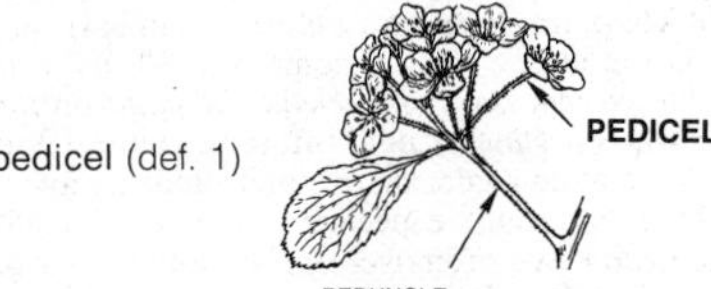

pedicel (def. 1)

ped i cel (ped′ə səl), *n.* 1 a small stalk or stalklike part in a plant, such as a secondary stalk that bears a single flower. 2 any small stalklike structure in an animal. [< New Latin *pedicellus* < Latin *pedem* foot]

ped i cure (ped′ə kyu̇r), *n.* 1 care or treatment of the feet and toenails. 2 podiatrist. [< French *pédicure* < Latin *pedem* foot + *cura* care]

ped i cur ist (ped′ə kyůr′ist), *n.* podiatrist.

ped i gree (ped′ə grē′), *n.* 1 list of ancestors of a person or animal. 2 line of descent; ancestry; lineage. 3 derivation, as from a source: *the pedigree of a word.* 4 distinguished or noble descent: *a man of pedigree.* [< Middle French *pie de grue* foot of crane (because a symbol resembling the toes of a bird was used in showing descent)]

ped i greed (ped′ə grēd′), *adj.* having a known pedigree: *a pedigreed dog.*

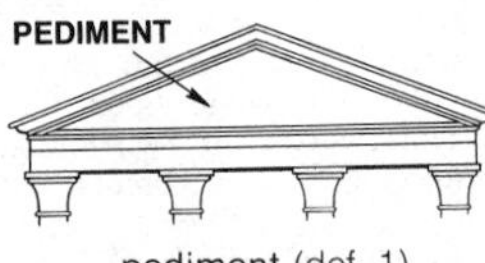

pediment (def. 1)

ped i ment (ped′ə mənt), *n.* 1 the low triangular part on the front of buildings in the Greek style. A pediment is like a gable. 2 any similar decorative part on a building, door, bookcase, etc. [earlier *periment, peremint,* perhaps alteration of *pyramid*]

ped i men tal (ped′ə men′tl), *adj.* of, on, or like a pediment.

ped lar (ped′lər), *n.* peddler.

pe dol o gy[1] (pi dol′ə jē), *n.* science dealing with the origin, classification, and utilization of soils. [< Greek *pedon* soil + English *-logy*]

pe dol o gy[2] (pi dol′ə jē, pē dol′ə jē), *n.* the scientific study of the nature of children. [< Greek *pais, paidos* child + English *-logy*]

pe dom e ter (pi dom′ə tər), *n.* instrument for recording the number of steps taken by the person who carries it and thus measuring the distance traveled in walking. [< French *pédomètre* < Latin *pedem* foot + Greek *metron* measure]

pe dun cle (pi dung′kəl), *n.* stalk; stem; stalklike part (of a flower, fruit cluster, or animal body). See **pedicel** for picture. [< New Latin *pedunculus,* diminutive of Latin *pedem* foot]

pe dun cu lar (pi dung′kyə lər), *adj.* of or having to do with a peduncle.

pe dun cu late (pi dung′kyə lit, pi dung′kyə lāt), *adj.* having a peduncle; growing on a peduncle.

peek (pēk), *v.i.* look quickly and slyly; peep. —*n.* a quick, sly look. [Middle English *piken*]

peel[1] (pēl), *n.* the rind or outer covering of certain fruits, especially citrus fruits. —*v.t.* 1 strip the skin, rind, or bark from: *peel an orange, peel a potato.* 2 strip: *The Indians peeled the bark from trees to make canoes.* 3 **keep one's eyes peeled,** INFORMAL. be on the alert. —*v.i.* 1 come off: *When I was sunburned, my skin peeled. The paint on the shed is peeling.* 2 **peel off,** (of an aircraft) to move at an angle, sharply and suddenly away from a group, especially to dive or land. 3 INFORMAL. remove one's clothes; strip. [< Old French *peler* to peel < Latin *pilare* to strip of hair < *pilus* hair] —**peel′er,** *n.*

peel[2] (pēl), *n.* a long-handled shovel used to put bread, pies, etc., into an oven or take them out. [< Old French *pele* < Latin *pala* spade]

Peel (pēl), *n.* Sir **Robert,** 1788-1850, British statesman, prime minister from 1834 to 1835 and from 1841 to 1846.

peel ing (pē′ling), *n.* part peeled off or pared off: *a potato peeling.*

peen (pēn), *n.* the part of the head of a hammer opposite to the face, when rounded, edged, etc., for any of various special uses. [< Scandinavian (Norwegian) *pen* or *pænn*]

peep[1] (pēp), *v.i.* 1 look through a small or narrow hole or crack. 2 look furtively, slyly, or pryingly. 3 look out as if peeping; come partly out. —*v.t.* cause to stick out a little; show slightly. —*n.* 1 a look through a hole or crack; little look; peek. 2 a secret look. 3 the first looking or coming out: *at the peep of day.* 4 a small hole or crack to look through; peephole. [perhaps variant of *peek*]

peep[2] (pēp), *n.* 1 the cry of a young bird or chicken; a sound like a chirp or squeak. 2 a slight word or sound, often of complaint: *without a peep out of anyone.* —*v.i.* 1 make such a sound; chirp. 2 speak in a thin, weak voice. [probably imitative]

peep er[1] (pē′pər), *n.* 1 person who peeps, especially a peeping tom. 2 INFORMAL. eye. [< *peep*[1]]

peep er[2] (pē′pər), *n.* 1 person or thing that peeps. 2 any of certain frogs that make peeping noises. [< *peep*[2]]

peep hole (pēp′hōl′) *n.* hole through which one may peep.

peeping tom, 1 a prying observer, especially a man who goes about looking through the windows of houses at the occupants without himself being observed. 2 **Peeping Tom,** a legendary tailor who peeped at Lady Godiva as she rode naked through Coventry and was struck blind for it.

peep show, exhibition of objects or pictures viewed through a small opening, usually fitted with a magnifying glass.

peer[1] (pir), *n.* 1 person of the same rank, ability, etc., as another; equal. 2 man belonging to the nobility, especially a British nobleman having the rank of duke, marquis, earl, count, viscount, or baron. [< Old French *per* < Latin *par* equal. Doublet of PAR.]

peer[2] (pir), *v.i.* 1 look closely to see clearly, as a nearsighted person does: *She peered at the tag to read the price.* 2 come out slightly; peep out: *The sun was peering from behind a cloud.* [perhaps variant of *appear*]

peer age (pir′ij), *n.* 1 rank or dignity of a peer. 2 peers of a country. 3 book giving a list of the peers of a country and their family histories.

peer ess (pir′is), *n.* 1 wife or widow of a peer. 2 woman having the rank of a peer in her own right.

peer group, group of people of about the same age or the same social background.

peer less (pir′lis), *adj.* without an equal; matchless. —**peer′less ly,** *adv.* —**peer′less ness,** *n.*

peeve (pēv), *v.,* **peeved, peev ing,** *n.* INFORMAL. —*v.t.* make peevish. —*n.* 1 thing that annoys or irritates. 2 a peevish mood or disposition.

peeved (pēvd), *adj.* annoyed; irritated: *seem quite peeved about the report.*

pee vish (pē′vish), *adj.* 1 feeling cross; fretful; complaining: *a peevish child.* 2 showing annoyance or irritation. [Middle English *pevysh*] —**pee′vish ly,** *adv.* —**pee′vish ness,** *n.*

pee wee (pē′wē), *n.* 1 a very small person or thing. 2 pewee. —*adj.* small; undersized: *a peewee fighter.*

peg (peg), *n., v.,* **pegged, peg ging.** —*n.* 1 pin or small bolt of wood, metal, etc., used to fasten parts together, hang things on, stop a hole, make fast a rope or string, mark the score in a game, etc. 2 a wooden or metal pin on a stringed instrument which is turned to adjust the pitch of a string. 3 step; degree: *Your plan is several pegs above all the others.* 4 INFORMAL. a hard throw of a ball, especially in baseball. 5 BRITISH. a small drink of alcoholic liquor. 6 **take down a peg,** lower the pride of; humble. —*v.t.* 1 fasten or hold with pegs: *peg down a tent.* 2 mark with pegs. 3 keep the price of (a commodity, stock, etc.) from going up or down: *peg wheat at $1.56 a bushel.* 4 INFORMAL. throw hard: *peg the ball to the shortstop.* 5 strike or pierce with a peg. —*v.i.* INFORMAL. work hard; keep on energetically and patiently: *peg away at a dull job.* [apparently < Middle Dutch *pegge*]

Pegasus (def. 1)

Peg a sus (peg′ə səs), *n.* 1 (in Greek myths) a horse with wings, the steed of the Muses. 2 poetic genius; the means by which poets soar in the realms of poetry. 3 constellation in the northern sky near Andromeda.

peg board (peg′bôrd′, peg′bōrd′), *n.* board containing evenly spaced holes in which pegs or hooks are inserted to hold tools, displays, memorandums, etc.

peg leg, 1 a wooden leg. 2 INFORMAL. person who has a wooden leg.

peg ma tite (peg′mə tīt), *n.* a coarse-grained igneous rock occurring in veins and dikes, and usually containing crystals of the common minerals found in granite, but sometimes containing rare minerals rich in such elements as lithium, uranium, and tantalum. [< Greek *pēgmatos* something joined]

peg top, 1 a wooden top with a metal peg on which it spins when a string wound around the top is rapidly uncoiled. 2 **peg tops,** *pl.* trousers wide at the hips and gradually narrowing to the ankles.

peg-top (peg′top′), *adj.* shaped like a peg top.

peg-top trousers, peg tops.

P.E.I., Prince Edward Island.

peign oir (pān wär′, pen wär′; pān′wär, pen′wär), *n.* a loose dressing gown or negligee for women. [< French < *peigner* to comb hair]

Pei ping (pā′ping′, bā′ping′), *n.* former name of Peking, from 1928 to 1949.

Pei rae us (pī rē′əs), *n.* Piraeus.

pe jo ra tive (pi jôr′ə tiv, pi jor′ə tiv, pē′jə rā′tiv), *adj.* tending to make worse; disparaging; depreciatory. [< Late Latin *pejoratum* made worse < Latin *pejor* worse] —**pe jo′ra tive ly,** *adv.*

Pe kin ese (pē′kə nēz′), *n., pl.* **-ese,** *adj.* Pekingese.

Pe king (pē′king′), *n.* capital of China, in the NE part. 7,000,000. Former name, **Peiping.**

Pe king ese (pē′kə nēz′, pē′king ēz′), *n., pl.* **-ese,** *adj.* —*n.* 1 any of a breed of small dogs, originally of China, with long silky hair and a broad, flat face. 2 native or inhabitant of Peking. 3 the form of the Chinese language used in Peking, the standard form of Mandarin. —*adj.* of or having to do with Peking or its people. Also, **Pekinese.**

Peking man, a prehistoric man of the Pleistocene period, identified from fossil bones found in caves near Peking in 1929; Sinanthropus.

pe koe (pē′kō), *n.* kind of black tea from Ceylon or India, made from leaves picked while very young. [< Chinese]

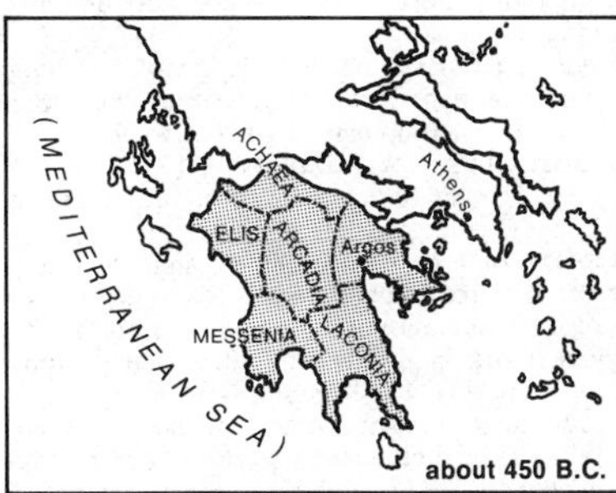

Peloponnesus—the shaded area

pel age (pel′ij), *n.* hair, fur, wool, or other soft covering of a mammal. [< French < Old French *peil* hair]

pe lag ic (pə laj′ik), *adj.* 1 of the ocean or the open sea; oceanic. 2 living on or near the surface of the open sea or ocean. [< Greek *pelagikos* < *pelagos* sea]

pel ar go ni um (pel′är gō′nē əm), *n.* any of a genus of plants of the same family as the geranium, with fragrant leaves and large clusters of showy flowers; geranium. The plants are often grown in pots and window boxes. [< Greek *pelargos* stork]

pe lec y pod (pə les′ə pod), *n.* any of a class of mollusks having a headless body enclosed in a hinged, two-part shell and a wedge-shaped foot; lamellibranch. Oysters, clams, and scallops belong to this class. [< Greek *pelekys* ax + *podos* foot]

pelf (pelf), *n.* money or riches, thought of as bad or degrading. [< Old French *pelfre* spoils]

pel i can (pel′ə kən), *n.* any of a family of very large web-footed water birds with a huge bill and a pouch on the underside of the bill for scooping up fish. [< Greek *pelekan*]

Pe li on (pē′lē ən), *n.* **Mount,** mountain in NE Greece. 5340 ft. According to Greek myths, when the giants made war on the gods, they piled Mount Pelion on Mount Ossa in an attempt to reach their foes on Mount Olympus.

pe lisse (pə lēs′), *n.* 1 a long cloak or coat lined or trimmed with fur. 2 a long cloak of silk, velvet, etc., worn by women. [< French, ultimately < Latin *pellis* skin]

pel lag ra (pə lag′rə, pə lā′grə), *n.* disease marked by inflammation and scaling of the skin, digestive disturbances, nervousness, and sometimes mental disorders. It is caused by an improper diet, especially one lacking sufficient nicotinic acid. [< Italian < Latin *pellis* skin]

pel lag rous (pə lag′rəs, pə lā′grəs), *adj.* of, having to do with, or affected with pellagra.

pel let (pel′it), *n.* 1 a little ball of mud, paper, food, medicine, etc.; pill. 2 bullet, especially a spherical bullet intended to be fired by a shotgun or other gun without a rifled barrel: *a pellet of bird shot.* 3 ball, usually of stone, used as a missile in the 1300's and 1400's. —*v.t.* 1 hit with pellets. 2 form into pellets. [< Old French *pelote* < Popular Latin *pilotta* < Latin *pila* ball]

pel li cle (pel′ə kəl), *n.* a very thin skin; membrane. [< Latin *pellicula,* diminutive of *pellis* skin]

pell-mell or **pell mell** (pel′mel′), *adv.* 1 in a rushing, tumbling mass or crowd. 2 in headlong haste. —*adj.* headlong; tumultuous. —*n.* violent disorder or confusion. [< French *pêle-mêle*]

pel lu cid (pə lü′sid), *adj.* 1 transparent; clear: *a pellucid stream.* 2 clearly expressed; easy to understand: *pellucid language.* [< Latin *pellucidus* < *per-* through + *lucere* to shine] —**pel lu′cid ly,** *adv.* —**pel lu′cid ness,** *n.*

pel lu cid i ty (pel′yə sid′ə tē), *n.* pellucid quality; pellucidness.

Pel o pon ne sus (pel′ə pə nē′səs), *n.* peninsula constituting the S part of Greece. In ancient times it was a center of Greek civilization and the site of important city-states such as Argos and Sparta. —**Pel′o pon ne′sian,** *adj., n.*

pe lo ta (pe lō′tə), *n.* 1 jai alai. 2 ball used in jai alai. [< Spanish < Old French *pelote* a little ball. See PELLET.]

pelt[1] (pelt), *v.t.* 1 hit with (objects, words, etc.) thrown one after another; attack or assail by throwing things at: *The children were pelting each other with snowballs. The attorney pelted the witness with angry questions.* 2 beat heavily or continuously upon: *Hail pelted the roof.* 3 throw; hurl: *The clouds pelted rain upon us.* —*v.i.* 1 beat heavily or continuously: *The rain came pelting down.* 2 go rapidly; hurry. —*n.* 1 a pelting. 2 speed: *The horse is coming at full pelt.* [origin uncertain] —**pelt′er,** *n.*

pelt[2] (pelt), *n.* skin of a sheep, goat, or small fur-bearing animal, before it is tanned. See **skin** for synonym study. [probably < *peltry*]

pelt ry (pel′trē), *n., pl.* **-ries.** 1 pelts; skins; furs. 2 a pelt. [< Old French *peleterie* < *pel* skin < Latin *pellis*]

pel vic (pel′vik), *adj.* of, having to do with, or in the region of the pelvis.

pelvic arch, pelvic girdle.

pelvic fin, either of a pair of fins in fishes, usually behind and below the pectoral fins, corresponding to the hind limbs of higher vertebrates. See **fin** for picture.

pelvic girdle, the bony or cartilaginous arch supporting the hind limbs of vertebrates; pelvic arch.

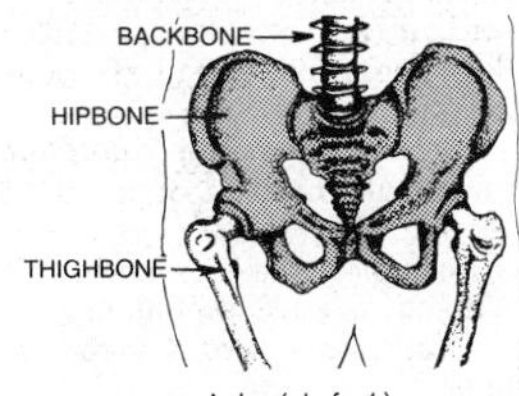

pelvis (def. 1)

pel vis (pel′vis), *n., pl.* **-vis es, -ves** (-vēz′). 1 the basin-shaped cavity in human beings formed by the hipbones and the end of the backbone. 2 the corresponding cavity of any vertebrate. 3 bones forming this cavity. 4 a basinlike cavity in the kidney which collects urine before its passage into the ureter. [< Latin, basin]

Pem ba (pem′bə), *n.* island off E Africa, a part of Tanzania. 164,000 pop.; 380 sq. mi.

pem mi can or **pem i can** (pem′ə kən), *n.* dried, lean meat pounded into a paste with melted fat and pressed into cakes. It was an important food among certain tribes of North American Indians. [< Algonquian *pimikan*]

hat, āge, fär; let, ēqual, tėrm;
it, īce; hot, ōpen, ôrder;
oil, out; cup, pu̇t, rüle;
ch, child; ng, long; sh, she;
th, thin; ᴛʜ, then; zh, measure;

ə represents *a* in about, *e* in taken,
i in pencil, *o* in lemon, *u* in circus.

< = from, derived from, taken from.

pen[1] (pen), *n., v.,* **penned, pen ning.** —*n.* 1 instrument used for writing or drawing with ink, such as a fountain pen, a ball-point pen, or a quill. 2 point of a pen; nib. 3 point of a pen together with its holder. 4 style of writing; writing: *an ironic pen.* 5 writer; author. 6 the internal, somewhat feather-shaped shell of various cephalopods, as the squids. 7 a female swan. —*v.t.* write: *I penned a short note to my aunt today.* [< Old French *penne* pinion, quill pen < Latin *penna* feather] —**pen′like′,** *adj.*

pen[2] (pen), *n., v.,* **penned** or **pent, pen ning.** —*n.* 1 a small, closed yard for cows, sheep, pigs, chickens, etc. 2 any of various enclosures for keeping something, as a portable playpen for a baby, or a place to keep a dog in a kennel. 3 the number of animals in a pen, or required to fill a pen. —*v.t.* 1 shut in a pen. 2 confine closely; shut in. [Old English *penn*] —**pen′like′,** *adj.*

pen[3] (pen), *n.* SLANG. penitentiary.

pen., peninsula.

pe nal (pē′nl), *adj.* 1 of, having to do with, or given as punishment: *penal laws, penal labor.* 2 liable to be punished: *Robbery is a penal offense.* [< Latin *poenalis* < *poena* punishment < Greek *poinē* penalty]

pe nal ize (pē′nl īz, pen′l īz), *v.t.,* **-ized, -iz ing.** 1 declare punishable by law or by rule; set a penalty for: *Speeding on city streets is penalized. Fouls are penalized in many sports and games.* 2 inflict a penalty on; punish: *The football team was penalized five yards.* 3 subject to a disadvantage; handicap: *His deafness penalizes him in public life.*

pen al ty (pen′l tē), *n., pl.* **-ties.** 1 punishment imposed by law: *The penalty for speeding is a fine of fifteen dollars.* 2 disadvantage imposed on a team or player for breaking the rules of a sport or game. 3 disadvantage attached to some act or condition: *the penalties of old age.* 4 something forfeited by a person if an obligation is not fulfilled.

pen ance (pen′əns), *n.* 1 punishment borne to show sorrow for sin, make up for a wrong done, and obtain pardon. 2 (in the Roman Catholic Church, Eastern Church, etc.) a sacrament that includes repentance, intention to amend, full confession of sin to a priest, voluntary submission to penalty, and absolution. 3 any act done to show that one is sorry or repents. [< Old French < Latin *paenitentia* penitence. Doublet of PENITENCE.]

Pe nang (pi nang′), *n.* 1 island just off the W coast of the Malay Peninsula. 288,000 pop.; 110 sq. mi. 2 division of the Federation of Malaysia, including the island of Penang and part of the Malay Peninsula. 779,000 pop.; 400 sq. mi. 3 Georgetown (def. 2).

pe na tes (pə nā′tēz), *n.pl.* household gods of the ancient Romans, worshiped together with the lares and believed to protect the home from interior damage. [< Latin < *penus* interior of the house]

pence (pens), *n.* a pl. of **penny** (def. 2).

pen chant (pen′chənt), *n.* a strong taste or liking; inclination: *a penchant for taking long walks.* [< French, present participle of *pencher* to incline]

pen cil (pen′səl), *n., v.,* **-ciled, -cil ing** or **-cilled, -cil ling.** *—n.* 1 instrument used for writing or drawing, made of a slender rod of graphite encased in wood or in a metal tube. 2 any object of like shape. 3 stick of coloring matter. 4 an artist's paintbrush. 5 the skill or style of an artist. 6 set of lines, light rays, or the like, coming to a point or extending in different directions from a point. *—v.t.* 1 mark or write with a pencil. 2 **pencil in,** include, list, or schedule, especially in haste: *pencil in an increase in the budget. An unknown actor was penciled in to play the leading role.* [< Old French *pincel* < Latin *penicillus* small brush or tail, diminutive of *penis* tail] **—pen′cil er, pen′cil ler,** *n.*

pend ant (pen′dənt), *n.* 1 a hanging ornament, such as a locket. 2 ornament hanging down from a ceiling or roof. *—adj.* pendent. [< Old French, present participle of *pendre* hang < Latin *pendere*]

pend ent (pen′dənt), *adj.* 1 hanging; suspended: *the pendent branches of a willow.* 2 overhanging: *a pendent cliff.* 3 pending. *—n.* pendant. [< Latin *pendentem*] **—pend′ent ly,** *adv.*

pend ing (pen′ding), *adj.* 1 waiting to be decided or settled: *while the agreement was pending.* 2 likely to happen soon; about to occur; threatening. *—prep.* 1 while waiting for; until: *Pending your return, we'll get everything ready.* 2 during: *pending the investigation.*

pen drag on (pen drag′ən), *n.* chief leader, ruler, or king among the ancient Britons. [< Welsh < *pen* chief + *dragon* war leader, dragon]

pen du lous (pen′jə ləs, pen′dyə ləs), *adj.* 1 hanging loosely: *The oriole builds a pendulous nest.* 2 swinging like a pendulum. [< Latin *pendulus* < *pendere* hang] **—pen′du lous ly,** *adv.* **—pen′du lous ness,** *n.*

pen du lum (pen′jə ləm, pen′dyə ləm), *n.* weight so hung from a fixed point that it is free to swing to and fro through a regular arc under the influence of gravity. The movement of the works of a tall clock is often timed by a pendulum. [< New Latin < Latin *pendulus* hanging loosely. See PENDULOUS.]

Pe nel o pe (pə nel′ə pē), *n.* (in Greek legends) the faithful wife of Odysseus (Ulysses) who waited twenty years for his return in spite of the entreaties of her many suitors.

pe ne plain or **pe ne plane** (pē′nə plān′, pen′ə plān′), *n.* a formerly mountainous or hilly area reduced nearly to a plain by erosion. [< Latin *paene* almost + English *plain* or *plane*]

pen e tra bil i ty (pen′ə trə bil′ə tē), *n.* capability of being penetrated.

pen e tra ble (pen′ə trə bəl), *adj.* that can be penetrated. **—pen′e tra bly,** *adv.*

pen e trate (pen′ə trāt), *v.,* **-trat ed, -trat ing.** *—v.t.* 1 enter into or pass through: *The bullet penetrated this wall and two inches into the one beyond.* See synonym study below. 2 pierce through: *Our eyes could not penetrate the darkness.* 3 soak or spread through; permeate: *The odor penetrated the whole house.* 4 see into or through; understand: *I could not penetrate the mystery.* 5 affect or impress very much. *—v.i.* pass through: *Even where the trees were thickest, the sunshine penetrated.* [< Latin *penetratum* gone through, pierced < *penitus* deep within]

Syn. *v.t.* 1 **Penetrate, pierce** mean to go into or through something. **Penetrate** implies going deeply into something and suggests both a driving force and resistance to it: *The arrow penetrated the board.* **Pierce** implies stabbing through the surface, or going into it and out the other side: *She had the lobes of her ears pierced for earrings.*

pen e trat ing (pen′ə trā′ting), *adj.* 1 sharp; piercing: *a penetrating scream, a penetrating odor.* 2 having or showing insight; acute; discerning: *a penetrating mind, penetrating criticism.* **—pen′e trat′ing ly,** *adv.*

pen e tra tion (pen′ə trā′shən), *n.* 1 the act or power of penetrating. 2 sharpness of intellect; insight. See **insight** for synonym study. 3 the depth to which a projectile will enter a material at a given range.

pen e tra tive (pen′ə trā′tiv), *adj.* penetrating; piercing; acute; keen.

pen guin (pen′gwin, peng′gwin), *n.* any of an order of web-footed, short-legged sea birds with black and white plumage, living in Antarctica and other cold regions of the Southern Hemisphere. Penguins cannot fly but use their short wings, which resemble flippers, for swimming and diving. [perhaps < Welsh *pen* head + *gwyn* white]

pen hold er (pen′hōl′dər), *n.* 1 handle by which a pen is held in writing. 2 rack for pens.

pen i cil lin (pen′ə sil′ən), *n.* antibiotic made from a penicillium mold, used to treat diseases caused by certain bacteria.

pen i cil li um (pen′ə sil′ē əm), *n., pl.* **-cil li ums, -cil li a** (-sil′ē ə), any of a genus of green or bluish-green fungi that grow as molds on citrus fruits, cheeses, etc. [< New Latin < Latin *penicillus* small brush or tail. See PENCIL.]

pe nin su la (pə nin′sə lə, pə nin′syə lə), *n.* piece of land almost surrounded by water, or extending far out into the water. Florida is a peninsula. [< Latin *paeninsula* < *paene* almost + *insula* island]

pe nin su lar (pə nin′sə lər, pə nin′syə lər), *adj.* 1 like a peninsula. 2 in or of a peninsula.

pe nis (pē′nis), *n., pl.* **-nis es, -nes** (-nēz). the male organ of copulation. In mammals it is also the male urinary organ. [< Latin, penis, tail]

pen i tence (pen′ə təns), *n.* sorrow for sinning or doing wrong; repentance. [< Old French < Latin *paenitentia* < *paenitere* repent. Doublet of PENANCE.]

pen i tent (pen′ə tənt), *adj.* sorry for sinning or doing wrong; repenting; repentant. *—n.* 1 person who is sorry for sin or wrongdoing. 2 person who confesses and does penance for his sins under the direction of a church. **—pen′i tent ly,** *adv.*

pen i ten tial (pen′ə ten′chəl), *adj.* 1 of, showing, or having to do with penitence: *The penitential psalms express remorse for sin.* 2 of or having to do with penance. **—pen′i ten′tial ly,** *adv.*

pen i ten tiar y (pen′ə ten′chər ē), *n., pl.* **-tiar ies,** *adj.* *—n.* prison for criminals, especially a state or federal prison. *—adj.* 1 making one liable to punishment in a prison: *a penitentiary offense.* 2 used for punishment, discipline, and reformation: *penitentiary measures.* 3 of penance; penitential.

pen knife (pen′nīf′), *n., pl.* **-knives** (-nīvz′). a small pocketknife.

pen man (pen′mən), *n., pl.* **-men.** 1 writer; author. 2 person whose handwriting is good. 3 person whose work is to copy documents, etc.

pen man ship (pen′mən ship), *n.* 1 writing with pen, pencil, etc.; handwriting. 2 manner or style of composing a written work.

Penn (pen), *n.* **William,** 1644-1718, English Quaker who founded the first settlement in Pennsylvania, at Philadelphia.

Penn. or **Penna.,** Pennsylvania.

pen name, name used by a writer instead of his real name; nom de plume; pseudonym.

pen nant (pen′ənt), *n.* 1 flag, usually long and tapering, used on ships for signaling or identification, as a school banner, etc. 2 flag taken as an emblem of superiority or success, especially in an athletic contest. [blend of *pennon* and *pendant*]

pen nate (pen′āt), *adj.* 1 having wings; having feathers. 2 pinnate. [< Latin *penna* feather, wing]

pen ni less (pen′ē lis), *adj.* without a cent of money; very poor. See **poor** for synonym study.

Pen nine Chain (pen′īn), chain of mountains in N England, especially rich in coal. Highest peak, 2930 ft.

pen non (pen′ən), *n.* 1 a long, narrow flag, triangular or swallow-tailed, originally carried on the lance of a knight. 2 any flag or banner. 3 pennant. 4 wing; pinion. [< Old French *penon,* ultimately < Latin *penna* feather]

Penn syl van ia (pen′səl vā′nyə, pen′səl vā′nē ə), *n.* one of the northeastern states of the United States. 11,794,000 pop.; 45,300 sq. mi. *Capital:* Harrisburg. *Abbrev.:* Pa., Penn., or Penna.

Pennsylvania Dutch, 1 the descendants of immigrants to southeastern Pennsylvania from southern Germany and Switzerland in the 1600's and 1700's. 2 dialect of German with English intermixed, spoken by them.

Penn syl van ian (pen′səl vā′nyən, pen′səl vā′nē ən), *n.* 1 native or inhabitant of Pennsylvania. 2 the later of the two periods into which the Carboniferous period is divided, after the Mississippian and before the Permian, characterized by coal-, oil-, and gas-bearing deposits. See chart under **geology.** 3 the rocks formed during this period. *—adj.* 1 of or having to do with Pennsylvania. 2 of or having to do with the Pennsylvanian or its rocks.

pen ny (pen′ē), *n., pl.* **pen nies** (or **pence** for 2). 1 cent. 100 pennies = 1 dollar. 2 a British coin equal to $^1/_{100}$ of a pound since February 1971. Formerly, equal to $^1/_{240}$ of a pound and to $^1/_{12}$ of a shilling. 3 sum of money. 4 **a pretty penny,** INFORMAL. a large sum of money. [Old English *pending*]

penny ante, poker in which the ante for each hand is set at one cent or some other trifling sum.

penny arcade, place of cheap amusements where the games of chance, pinball machines, etc., originally cost a penny a play.

penny pincher, INFORMAL. person who does not spend or use money freely; stingy person.

hat, āge, fär; let, ēqual, tėrm;
it, īce; hot, ōpen, ôrder;
oil, out; cup, pu̇t, rüle;
ch, child; ng, long; sh, she;
th, thin; ᴛʜ, then; zh, measure;

ə represents *a* in about, *e* in taken, *i* in pencil, *o* in lemon, *u* in circus.
< = from, derived from, taken from.

pen ny-pinch ing (pen′ē pin′ching), INFORMAL. —*n.* stinginess. —*adj.* stingy.

pen ny roy al (pen′ē roi′əl), *n.* 1 a perennial European herb of the mint family, having small aromatic leaves. 2 a similar American herb of the mint family that yields a pungent oil formerly much used as a mosquito repellent and medicinally. 3 a fragrant oil made from either species.

pen ny weight (pen′ē wāt′), *n.* 24 grains or 1/20 of an ounce in troy weight. See **measure** for table.

pen ny-wise (pen′ē wīz′), *adj.* 1 saving in regard to small sums. 2 **penny-wise and pound-foolish,** saving in small expenses and wasteful in big ones.

pen ny worth (pen′ē wėrth′), *n.* 1 as much as can be bought for a penny. 2 a small amount.

Pe nob scot (pə nob′skot), *n., pl.* **-scots** or **-scot** for 2. 1 **Penobscot River,** river flowing from NW Maine into the Atlantic. 350 mi. 2 member of an American Indian tribe formerly living near this river.

pe nol o gist (pē nol′ə jist), *n.* an expert in penology.

pe nol o gy (pē nol′ə jē), *n.* science of punishment of crime and management of prisons. [< Greek *poinē* penalty + English *-logy*]

pen pal, person with whom one corresponds regularly, often in another country and without ever having met.

Pen sa co la (pen′sə kō′lə), *n.* seaport in NW Florida, on the Gulf of Mexico. 60,000.

pen sile (pen′səl), *adj.* 1 hanging; pendent. 2 (of birds) building a hanging nest. [< Latin *pensilis* < *pendere* hang]

pen sion[1] (pen′shən), *n.* a fixed sum of money paid at regular intervals by the government, a company, etc., to a person or his dependents, especially a person who is retired because of old age or disability. —*v.t.* 1 give a pension to. 2 **pension off,** retire from service with a pension. [< Old French < Latin *pensionem* payment, rent < *pendere* weigh, pay]

pen sion[2] (päN syôN′), *n.* FRENCH. 1 boarding house. 2 payment for board and lodging.

pen sion er (pen′shə nər), *n.* 1 person who receives a pension. 2 a hireling; dependent.

pen sive (pen′siv), *adj.* 1 thoughtful in a serious or sad way. 2 melancholy. [< Old French *pensif* < *penser* think < Latin *pensare* ponder < *pendere* weigh] —**pen′sive ly,** *adv.* —**pen′sive ness,** *n.*

pen stock (pen′stok′), *n.* 1 channel or pipe for carrying water to a water wheel or turbine. 2 gate or sluice for controlling the flow of water, etc.

pent (pent), *adj.* closely confined; penned; shut: *pent in the house all winter.* —*v.* a pt. and a pp. of **pen**[2].

penta-, *combining form.* five, as in *pentameter.* Also, **pent-** before vowels. [< Greek < *pente* five]

pen ta gon (pen′tə gon), *n.* 1 a plane figure having five sides and five angles. 2 **the Pentagon,** a five-sided building in Arlington, Virginia, that is the headquarters of the Department of Defense of the United States. [< Greek *pentagōnon* < *penta-* + *gōnia* angle]

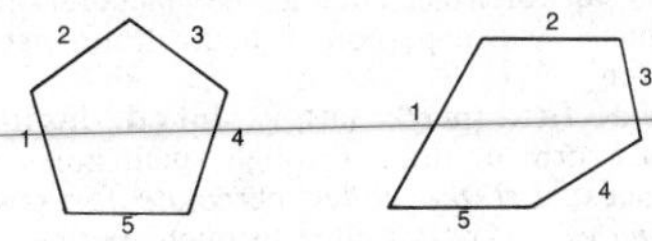

pentagon (def. 1)
left, regular; right, irregular

pen tag o nal (pen tag′ə nəl), *adj.* having five sides and five angles.

pen ta he dron (pen′tə hē′drən), *n., pl.* **-drons, -dra** (-drə). a solid figure having five faces. [< Greek *penta-* + *hedra* base, seat]

pen tam e ter (pen tam′ə tər), *n.* line of verse having five metrical feet. EXAMPLE: "A lit′|tle learn′|ing is′|a dan′|g'rous thing′."

pen tane (pen′tān), *n.* any of three colorless, flammable, isomeric hydrocarbons derived from petroleum and used as solvents. *Formula:* C_5H_{12}

Pen ta teuch (pen′tə tük, pen′tə tyük), *n.* the first five books of the Old Testament, consisting of Genesis, Exodus, Leviticus, Numbers, and Deuteronomy. [< Greek *pentateuchos* < *penta-* + *teuchos* vessel, book]

pen tath lon (pen tath′lən, pen tath′lon), *n.* an athletic contest consisting of five different events. The person having the highest total score wins. [< Greek < *penta-* + *athlon* contest]

Pen te cost (pen′tə kôst, pen′tə kost), *n.* 1 the seventh Sunday after Easter celebrated as a church festival in memory of the descent of the Holy Ghost upon the apostles; Whitsunday. 2 Shabuoth. [< Greek *pentēkostē (hēmera)* fiftieth (day)]

Pen te cos tal or **pen te cos tal** (pen′tə-kô′stl, pen′tə kos′tl), *adj.* 1 of or having to do with Pentecost. 2 of or having to do with any of various American Protestant groups, usually fundamentalist, that stress divine inspiration and believe in manifestations of the Holy Ghost.

pent house (pent′hous′), *n., pl.* **-hous es** (-hou′ziz). 1 apartment or house built on the top of a building. 2 a sloping roof projecting from a building. 3 shed with a sloping roof attached to a building. [Middle English *pentis* < Old French *apentis,* ultimately < Latin *appendere* append]

pen to bar bi tal sodium (pen′tō bär′-bə tôl), a white, bitter, crystalline powder used as a sedative and hypnotic. *Formula:* $C_{11}H_{17}N_2O_3Na$

pent ode (pen′tōd), *n.* a vacuum tube with five electrodes. It is the type most commonly used in radio and television sets.

pen tose (pen′tōs), *n.* any of a class of simple sugars that contain five atoms of carbon in each molecule, and are constituents of ribonucleic acid.

Pen to thal Sodium (pen′tə thôl, pen′tə-thol), trademark for thiopental sodium.

pent-up (pent′up′), *adj.* shut up; closely confined: *pent-up feelings.*

pe nu che (pə nü′chē), *n.* candy made from brown sugar, butter, milk, and nuts. Also, **panocha.** [variant of *panocha*]

pe nult (pē′nult, pi nult′), *n.* the next to the last syllable in a word. [< Latin *paene* almost + *ultimus* last]

pe nul ti mate (pi nul′tə mit), *adj.* 1 next to the last. 2 of or having to do with the penult. —*n.* penult.

pe num bra (pi num′brə), *n., pl.* **-brae** (-brē), **-bras.** 1 the partial shadow outside of the complete shadow formed by the sun, moon, etc., during an eclipse. See **eclipse** for diagram. 2 the grayish outer part of a sunspot. [< Latin *paene* almost + *umbra* shadow]

pe num bral (pi num′brəl), *adj.* having to do with or like a penumbra.

pe nur i ous (pi nu̇r′ē əs, pi nyu̇r′ē əs), *adj.* 1 mean about spending or giving money; stingy. 2 in a condition of penury; extremely poor. —**pe nur′i ous ly,** *adv.* —**pe nur′i-ous ness,** *n.*

pen ur y (pen′yər ē), *n.* great poverty; extreme want; destitution. [< Latin *penuria* want, need]

pe on (pē′on, pē′ən), *n.* 1 (in Spanish America) a person doing work that requires little skill. 2 (in the southwestern United States and Mexico) a worker held for service to work off a debt. 3 any unskilled worker; menial. [< Spanish *péon* < Late Latin *pedonem* foot soldier. Doublet of PAWN[2].]

pe on age (pē′ə nij), *n.* 1 condition or service of a peon. 2 practice of holding persons to work off debts.

pe o ny (pē′ə nē), *n., pl.* **-nies.** 1 any of a genus of perennial garden plants of the same family as the buttercup, with large, globular, showy flowers of various shades of red, pink, and white, often becoming double under cultivation. 2 the flower of any of these plants. [< Greek *paiōnia* < *Paiōn* Paeon, physician of the gods (because of the plant's use in medicine)]

peo ple (pē′pəl), *n., pl.* **-ple** (or **-ples** for 2); *v.,* **-pled, -pling.** —*n.* 1 men, women, and children; human beings; persons: *a street emptied of people. There were ten people present.* 2 body of persons composing a tribe, race, or nation: *the American people, the peoples of Asia.* See synonym study below. 3 the body of enfranchised citizens of a state; the electorate: *seek the support of the people.* 4 persons of a place, class, or group: *city people, the people of the South.* 5 the common people; lower classes: *The French nobles oppressed the people.* 6 persons in relation to a superior: *a pastor and his people. A king rules over his people.* 7 family; relatives: *He has many friends but he likes his own people best.* 8 ancestors: *Our people were Dutch.* 9 species or other group of animals: *the monkey people.* —*v.t.* 1 fill with people; populate: *Europe very largely peopled America.* 2 fill (with animals, inanimate objects, etc.); stock: *pools peopled with fish.* [< Old French *peuple* < Latin *populus*]

Syn. *n.* 2 **People, race, nation** mean a group of persons thought of as a unit larger than a family or community. **People** emphasizes cultural and social unity: *the peoples of Latin America.* **Race** emphasizes biological unity, having common descent and common physical characteristics: *The Japanese people belong to the Mongolian race.* **Nation** emphasizes political unity, applying to a group united under one government: *Americans are a people and a nation, not a race.*

People's Party, Populist Party.

Pe o ri a (pē ôr′ē ə, pē ōr′ē ə), *n.* city in central Illinois. 127,000.

pep (pep), *n., v.,* **pepped, pep ping.** —*n.* briskness of spirit and manner; energy; vim. —*v.t.* **pep up,** fill or inspire with energy, etc.; put new life into. [short for *pepper*]

pep lum (pep′ləm), *n., pl.* **-lums, -la** (-lə). kind of short overskirt attached about the waist, usually reaching around the hips, as on a coat, dress, etc. [< Latin, a woman's outer garment < Greek *peplos*]

pep per (pep′ər), *n.* 1 a seasoning with a hot, spicy taste, made from the berries of a tropical vine and used for soups, meats, vegetables, etc. Black pepper is made from whole berries; white pepper is made from husked berries. 2 plant bearing these berries, a climbing shrub native to the East Indies. 3 any of several hollow, mild or hot, green or red vegetables with many seeds. They are eaten raw, cooked, pickled, or dried and ground for use as seasoning in food. 4 any of a genus of shrublike plants belonging to the nightshade family, bearing such a vegetable. —*v.t.* 1 season or sprinkle with pepper. 2 sprinkle thickly: *a face peppered with freckles.* 3 hit with small objects sent thick and fast: *We peppered the enemy's lines with our shot.* [Old English *pipor* < Latin *piper* < Greek *piperi, peperi*]

pep per-and-salt (pep′ər ən sôlt′), *adj.* black and white finely mixed: *pepper-and-salt hair, a pepper-and-salt coat.*

pep per box (pep′ər boks′), *n.* container with holes in the top for sprinkling ground pepper on food.

pep per corn (pep′ər kôrn′), *n.* 1 a dried berry of the pepper vine ground up to make black pepper. 2 a small tribute or nominal token.

pep per mint (pep′ər mint), *n.* 1 a native European herb of the mint family, grown for its aromatic, pungent essential oil that is used in medicine and in candy. 2 this oil, or a preparation of it. 3 candy flavored with oil of peppermint.

pep per y (pep′ər ē), *adj.* 1 full of pepper; like pepper. 2 hot; sharp. 3 having a hot temper; easily made angry. 4 angry and sharp: *peppery words.* **—pep′per i ness,** *n.*

pep pill, INFORMAL. a stimulating drug, such as an amphetamine, in the form of a tablet or pill.

pep py (pep′ē), *adj.,* **-pi er, -pi est.** SLANG. full of pep; energetic; lively. **—pep′pi ness,** *n.*

pep sin (pep′sən), *n.* 1 enzyme in the gastric juice of the stomach that helps to digest meat, eggs, cheese, and other proteins. 2 preparation containing this enzyme, used as a medicine to help the digestion of protein. It is usually obtained from the stomach lining of pigs. [< Greek *pepsis* digestion]

pep sin o gen (pep sin′ə jən), *n.* substance present in the gastric glands from which pepsin is formed during digestion.

pep talk, INFORMAL. speech or short talk designed to fill or inspire with energy, enthusiasm, etc.: *a sales manager giving a pep talk to the sales force.*

pep tic (pep′tik), *adj.* 1 having to do with or promoting digestion; digestive. 2 able to digest. 3 of, having to do with, or secreting pepsin. 4 caused by the digestive action of gastric juice: *peptic ulcer.* —*n.* substance promoting digestion. [< Greek *peptikos* < *peptos* cooked, digested]

pep tide (pep′tīd, pep′tid), *n.* any compound of two or more amino acids in which the carboxyl group of one acid is joined with the amino group of another.

pep tone (pep′tōn), *n.* any of a class of diffusible and water soluble substances into which meat, eggs, cheese, and other proteins are changed by pepsin or trypsin. [< German *Pepton* < Greek *peptos* cooked, digested]

Pepys (pēps, peps, pep′is), *n.* **Samuel,** 1633-1703, English writer of a famous diary.

Pe quot (pē′kwot), *n., pl.* **-quots, -quot.** member of a tribe of Indians of Algonquian stock formerly living in southern New England.

per (pər; *stressed* pėr), *prep.* 1 for each; for every: *a pint of milk per child, ten cents per pound.* 2 by means of; by; through: *I send this per my son.* 3 according to: *per invoice.* [< Latin]

per-, *prefix.* 1 throughout; thoroughly; utterly; very: *Perfervid* = *very fervid. Peruse* = *use* (i.e., read) *thoroughly.* 2 in chemistry: **a** the maximum or a large amount of, as in *peroxide.* **b** having the indicated element in its highest or a high valence, as in perchloric acid. [< Latin, through, thoroughly, to the end, to destruction]

per., 1 period. 2 person.

per ad ven ture (pėr′əd ven′chər), *adv.* ARCHAIC. maybe; perhaps. —*n.* chance; doubt. [< Old French *par aventure* by chance]

per am bu late (pə ram′byə lāt), *v.,* **-lat ed, -lat ing.** —*v.t.* 1 walk through. 2 walk through and examine. —*v.i.* walk or travel about; stroll. [< Latin *perambulatum* walked through < *per-* through + *ambulare* to walk] **—per am′bu la′tion,** *n.*

per am bu la tor (pə ram′byə lā′tər), *n.* 1 BRITISH. a small carriage in which a baby is pushed about; pram. 2 person who perambulates.

per an num (pər an′əm), for each year; yearly: *Her salary was $10,000 per annum.* [< Latin]

per cale (pər kāl′, pər kal′), *n.* a closely woven cotton cloth with a smooth finish, used for dresses, sheets, etc. [< French < Persian *pargāla*]

per cap i ta (pər kap′ə tə), for each person: *$40 for eight men is $5 per capita.* [< Latin]

per ceive (pər sēv′), *v.t.,* **-ceived, -ceiv ing.** 1 be aware of through the senses; see, hear, taste, smell, or feel. See **see** for synonym study. 2 take in with the mind; observe; understand: *I soon perceived that I could not make him change his mind.* [< Old French *perceivre* < Latin *percipere* < *per-* thoroughly + *capere* to grasp] **—per ceiv′a ble,** *adj.* **—per ceiv′a bly,** *adv.*

per cent (pər sent′), *n.* per cent.

per cent, 1 parts in each hundred; hundredths. 5 per cent is 5 of each 100, or $\frac{5}{100}$ of the whole. 5 per cent (5%) of 40 is the same as $\frac{5}{100} \times 40$, or $.05 \times 40$. *Per cent* is used to express many proportions: *shrinkage of less than one per cent. Ten per cent of the employees were absent today.* 2 percentage: *A large per cent of the state's apple crop was ruined.* [< Medieval Latin *per centum* by the hundred]

per cent age (pər sen′tij), *n.* 1 rate or proportion of each hundred; part of each hundred; per cent: *What percentage of children were absent?* 2 part or proportion: *A large percentage of schoolbooks now have pictures.* 3 allowance, commission, discount, rate of interest, etc., figured by per cent. 4 INFORMAL. advantage or profit.

per cen tile (pər sen′tīl, pər sen′tl), *n.* 1 any value in a series of points on a scale arrived at by dividing a group into a hundred equal parts in order of magnitude. 2 one of these parts: *A student in the ninetieth percentile of his class on a particular test is in the top ten per cent.*

per centum, 1 by the hundred. 2 for or in every hundred.

per cept (pėr′sept), *n.* 1 that which is perceived. 2 understanding that is the result of perceiving.

per cep ti bil i ty (pər sep′tə bil′ə tē), *n.* a being perceptible.

per cep ti ble (pər sep′tə bəl), *adj.* that can be perceived: *a perceptible improvement.* **—per cep′ti bly,** *adv.*

per cep tion (pər sep′shən), *n.* 1 act of perceiving: *His perception of the change came in a flash.* 2 power of perceiving: *a keen perception.* 3 understanding that is the result of perceiving: *I now have a clear perception of what went wrong.* [< Latin *perceptionem* < *percipere* perceive. See PERCEIVE.]

per cep tive (pər sep′tiv), *adj.* 1 having to do with perception. 2 having the power of perceiving. 3 having keen perception; discerning; intelligent. **—per cep′tive ly,** *adv.*

per cep tu al (pər sep′chü əl), *adj.* of or having to do with perception. **—per cep′tu al ly,** *adv.*

perch[1] (pėrch), *n.* 1 bar, branch, or anything else on which a bird can come to rest. 2 a rather high seat or position. 3 measure of length equal to $5\frac{1}{2}$ yards; rod. 4 measure of area equal to $30\frac{1}{4}$ square yards; square rod. —*v.i.* 1 alight and rest; sit. 2 sit rather high: *He perched on a stool.* —*v.t.* place high up: *a village perched on a high hill.* [< Old French *perche* < Latin *pertica* pole] **—perch′er,** *n.*

perch[2] (pėrch), *n., pl.* **perch es** or **perch.** 1 any of a genus of small freshwater food fishes with a spiny fin. 2 any of various related freshwater or saltwater fish. [< Old French *perche* < Latin *perca* < Greek *perkē*]

per chance (pər chans′), *adv.* perhaps. [< Anglo-French *par chance* by chance]

Per che ron (pėr′chə ron′, pėr′shə ron′), *n.* one of a breed of large and strong draft horses. [< French]

per chlo ric acid (pər klôr′ik, pər klōr′ik), a colorless, syrupy acid used as an oxidizing agent, for plating metals, in explosives, etc. It is stable when diluted, but its concentrated form is highly explosive when in contact with oxidizable substances. *Formula:* $HClO_4$

per cip i ence (pər sip′ē əns), *n.* perception; discernment.

per cip i ent (pər sip′ē ənt), *adj.* 1 that perceives or is capable of perceiving; conscious. 2 having keen perception; discerning. —*n.* person or thing that perceives. [< Latin *percipientem* perceiving]

Per ci val or **Per ci vale** (pėr′sə vəl), *n.* (in Arthurian legends) one of King Arthur's knights who sought and finally saw the Holy Grail.

per coid (pėr′koid), *adj.* 1 resembling a perch. 2 of or belonging to a large suborder of spiny-finned fishes, including the freshwater perches, basses, and sunfishes, and certain saltwater fish, such as the mackerels and tunas. —*n.* a percoid fish. [< Latin *perca* perch]

per co late (pėr′kə lāt), *v.,* **-lat ed, -lat ing.** —*v.i.* drip or drain through small holes or spaces: *Let the coffee percolate for seven minutes.* —*v.t.* 1 filter through; permeate: *Water percolates sand.* 2 cause (a liquid or particles) to pass through; filter; sift. 3 make (coffee) in a percolator. [< Latin *percolatum* strained through < *per-* through + *colum* strainer] **—per′co la′tion,** *n.*

per co la tor (pėr′kə lā′tər), *n.* 1 coffeepot in which boiling water rises through a tube and then drains over and over again through an upper section containing ground coffee. 2 person or thing that percolates.

per cus sion (pər kush′ən), *n.* 1 the striking of one body against another with force; stroke; blow. 2 the striking of a percussion cap or similar device to set off the charge in a firearm. 3 shock made by the striking of one body against another with force; impact. 4 (in medicine) the tapping of a part of the body surface to determine by the quality of the sound the condition of the organs underneath. 5 in music: **a** the striking of percussion instruments to produce tones. **b** the percussion instruments of an orchestra. 6 the striking of sound upon the ear. [< Latin *percussionem* < *per-* thoroughly + *quatere* to strike, beat]

percussion cap, a small cap containing powder that explodes when struck by the hammer of the gun and sets off a larger charge.

percussion instrument, a musical instrument played by striking it, such as a drum, cymbal, or piano.

per cus sion ist (pər kush′ə nist), *n.* person who plays a percussion instrument.

per cus sive (pər kus′iv), *adj.* of, having to do with, or characterized by percussion. **—per cus′sive ly,** *adv.* **—per cus′sive ness,** *n.*

Per cy (pėr′sē), *n.* Sir **Henry,** 1364-1403, English military leader who was nicknamed "Hotspur."

per di em (pər dē′əm), 1 per day; for each day. 2 allowance of so much every day for living expenses, usually while traveling in connection with work. [< Medieval Latin]

per di tion (pər dish′ən), *n.* 1 loss of one's soul and the joys of heaven; damnation. 2 hell. 3 utter loss or destruction; complete ruin. [< Latin *perditionem* < *perdere* destroy < *per-* to destruction + *dare* to give]

père (per), *n.* FRENCH. father (often used after names to distinguish a father from his son): *Dumas père.*

per e gri nate (per′ə grə nāt), *v.*, **-nat ed, -nat ing.** *—v.i.* travel around. *—v.t.* travel over; traverse. **—per′e gri na′tion,** *n.* **—per′e gri na′tor,** *n.*

peregrine
18 in. long

per e grine (per′ə grən, per′ə grēn′), *n.* a large, swift, powerful falcon, the species preferred for falconry. *—adj.* 1 foreign or strange. 2 being upon a pilgrimage; traveling abroad. [< Latin *peregrinus* foreigner. Doublet of PILGRIM.]

pe remp tor y (pə remp′tər ē, per′əmp tôr′ē, per′əmp tōr′ē), *adj.* 1 leaving no choice; decisive; final; absolute: *a peremptory decree.* 2 allowing no denial or refusal: *a peremptory command.* 3 imperious; dictatorial: *a peremptory teacher.* [< Latin *peremptorius* that puts an end to, ultimately < *per-* to the end + *emere* to take] **—pe remp′tor i ly,** *adv.* **—pe remp′tor i ness,** *n.*

pe ren ni al (pə ren′ē əl), *adj.* 1 lasting through the whole year: *a perennial stream.* 2 lasting for a very long time; enduring: *the perennial beauty of the hills.* 3 (of a plant) lasting more than two years. *—n.* a perennial plant. [< Latin *perennis* < *per-* through + *annus* year] **—pe ren′ni al ly,** *adv.*

perf., 1 perfect. 2 perforated.

per fect (*adj., n.* pėr′fikt; *v.* pər fekt′), *adj.* 1 without defect; free from any flaw; faultless: *a perfect spelling paper.* 2 completely skilled; expert: *a perfect golfer.* 3 having all its parts; complete: *The set was perfect; nothing was missing or broken.* 4 exact; precise: *a perfect copy, a perfect circle.* 5 entire; total: *perfect quiet, a perfect stranger to us.* 6 utter; absolute: *a perfect fool, perfect nonsense.* 7 (in grammar) showing an action or event completed at the time of speaking or at the time spoken of. The three perfect tenses in English are the present perfect *(I have eaten),* past perfect *(I had eaten),* and future perfect *(I will have eaten).* 8 (in botany) having both stamens and pistils. 9 (in music) having to do with the intervals or original consonances of unison, a fourth, fifth, and octave.
—v.t. 1 make perfect; remove all faults from; bring to perfection: *perfect an invention.* 2 carry through; complete; finish. 3 make fully skilled: *perfect oneself in an art.*
—n. in grammar: 1 the perfect tense. 2 a verb form in the perfect tense.
[< Latin *perfectum* completed < *per-* thoroughly + *facere* make, do] **—per fect′er,** *n.* **—per′fect ness,** *n.*

per fect i bil i ty (pər fek′tə bil′ə tē), *n.* a being perfectible.

per fect i ble (pər fek′tə bəl), *adj.* capable of becoming, or being made, perfect; able to attain perfection.

per fec tion (pər fek′shən), *n.* 1 perfect condition; highest excellence; faultlessness. 2 a perfect person or thing. 3 a making complete or perfect: *Perfection of our plans will take another week.* 4 **to perfection,** perfectly: *She played the difficult violin concerto to perfection.*

per fec tion ist (pər fek′shə nist), *n.* person who is not content with anything that is not perfect or nearly perfect.

per fec tion is tic (pər fek′shə nis′tik), *adj.* seeking or demanding perfection, especially to an impractical degree; being a perfectionist.

per fect ly (pėr′fikt lē), *adv.* 1 in a perfect manner; faultlessly: *do a job perfectly.* 2 completely; fully: *perfectly clear. I am perfectly able to do it myself.*

perfect number, a positive integer which is equal to the sum of its factors (other than itself). 6, being the sum of its factors 1, 2, and 3, is a perfect number, as is 28 (1, 2, 4, 7, and 14).

per fec to (pər fek′tō), *n., pl.* **-tos.** a thick cigar that tapers nearly to a point at both ends. [< Spanish]

perfect participle, participle expressing action completed before the time of speaking or acting. In "Having written the letter, she mailed it," *having written* is a perfect participle.

perfect pitch, the sense of pitch that enables a person to identify a tone heard and name it as a note on a musical scale; absolute pitch.

hat, āge, fär; let, ēqual, tėrm;
it, īce; hot, ōpen, ôrder;
oil, out; cup, pu̇t, rüle;
ch, child; ng, long; sh, she;
th, thin; ᴛʜ, then; zh, measure;

ə represents *a* in about, *e* in taken, *i* in pencil, *o* in lemon, *u* in circus.

< = from, derived from, taken from.

per fer vid (pėr′fėr′vid), *adj.* very fervid.

per fid i ous (pər fid′ē əs), *adj.* deliberately faithless; treacherous. **—per fid′i ous ly,** *adv.* **—per fid′i ous ness,** *n.*

per fi dy (pėr′fə dē), *n., pl.* **-dies.** a breaking faith; base treachery; being false to a trust. [< Latin *perfidia* < *perfidus* faithless < *per-* + *fides* faith]

per fo rate (*v.* pėr′fə rāt′; *adj.* pėr′fər it, pėr′fə rāt′), *v.*, **-rat ed, -rat ing,** *adj. —v.t.* 1 make a hole or holes through; bore or punch through, as with a sharp instrument; pierce. 2 make a row or rows of holes through: *Sheets of postage stamps are perforated. —v.i.* make its way into or through something; make a perforation. *—adj.* pierced. [< Latin *perforatum* bored through < *per-* through + *forare* to bore] **—per′fo ra′tor,** *n.*

per fo ra tion (pėr′fə rā′shən), *n.* 1 hole bored or punched through or into something: *the perforations in the top of a salt shaker.* 2 a perforating. 3 a being perforated.

per force (pər fôrs′, pər fōrs′), *adv.* by necessity; necessarily. [< Old French *par force* by force]

per form (pər fôrm′), *v.t.* 1 go through and finish; accomplish; do: *Perform your duties well.* See **do**[1] for synonym study. 2 put into effect; carry out: *Perform your promise.* See synonym study below. 3 go through; render: *perform a piece of music. —v.i.* 1 act, play, sing, etc., in public. 2 act; work; behave: *perform well in a test.* [< Anglo-French *perfourmer,* variant of Old French *parfournir* < *par-* completely + *fournir* finish] **—per form′a ble,** *adj.*

Syn. *v.t.* 2 **Perform, execute, discharge** mean to carry out or put into effect. **Perform** suggests carrying out a process that is long or that requires effort, attention, or skill: *The surgeon performed an operation.* **Execute** suggests carrying out a plan or an order: *The nurse executed the doctor's orders.* **Discharge** suggests carrying out an obligation or duty: *She gave a large party to discharge all her social obligations.*

per form ance (pər fôr′məns), *n.* 1 a carrying out; doing; performing. 2 thing performed; act; deed. 3 act or manner of performing on a musical instrument, in a play, etc. 4 the giving of a play, concert, circus, or other show: *The evening performance is at 8 o'clock.* 5 power or ability to perform: *a machine's performance.*

per form er (pər fôr′mər), *n.* person who performs, especially one who performs for the entertainment of others.

per fume (*n.* pėr′fyüm, pər fyüm′; *v.* pər fyüm′), *n., v.,* **-fumed, -fum ing.** *—n.* 1 a sweet-smelling liquid made from natural or synthetic oils. 2 a sweet smell; fragrance.

—*v.t.* 1 put a sweet-smelling liquid on. 2 give a sweet smell to; fill with sweet odor: *Flowers perfumed the air.* [< Middle French *parfum,* ultimately < Latin *per-* through + *fumare* to smoke]

per fum er (pər fyü′mər), *n.* person who makes or sells perfumes.

per fum er y (pər fyü′mər ē), *n., pl.* **-er ies.** 1 a perfume. 2 perfumes collectively. 3 business of making or selling perfumes. 4 a perfumer's place of business.

per func tor y (pər fungk′tər ē), *adj.* 1 done merely for the sake of getting rid of the duty; done from force of habit; mechanical; indifferent: *The little boy gave his face a perfunctory washing.* 2 acting in a perfunctory way: *The new nurse was perfunctory; she did not really care about her work.* [< Late Latin *perfunctorius* < Latin *per-* through + *fungi* execute] **—per func′tor i ly,** *adv.* **—per func′tor i ness,** *n.*

per fuse (pər fyüz′), *v.t.,* **-fused, -fus ing.** 1 pass a substance through (an organ or other part of the body), especially by way of the bloodstream: *perfuse the heart with a stimulant.* 2 suffuse. 3 diffuse. [< Latin *perfusum* poured over < *per-* + *fundere* pour] **—per fu′sion,** *n.*

Per ga mum (pėr′gə məm), *n.* Greek city in ancient Asia Minor. In the 100's B.C. it was the capital of an empire including most of W and central Asia Minor.

per go la (pėr′gə lə), *n.* arbor made of a trellis supported by posts. [< Italian < Latin *pergula*]

per haps (pər haps′, pə raps′), *adv.* it may be; maybe; possibly. [Middle English *per happes* by chances]

per i (pir′ē), *n.* (in Persian myths) a beautiful fairy descended from fallen angels who is shut out from paradise until its penance is accomplished. [< Persian *perī*]

peri-, *prefix.* 1 around; surrounding, as in *perimeter, periscope.* 2 near, as in *perihelion.* [< Greek]

per i anth (per′ē anth), *n.* envelope of a flower, including the calyx and the corolla. [< Greek *peri-* + *anthos* flower]

per i car di al (per′ə kär′dē əl), *adj.* 1 around the heart. 2 of or having to do with the pericardium.

per i car di tis (per′ə kär dī′tis), *n.* inflammation of the pericardium.

per i car di um (per′ə kär′dē əm), *n., pl.* **-di a** (-dē ə). the membranous sac enclosing the heart. [< New Latin < Greek *peri-* + *kardia* heart]

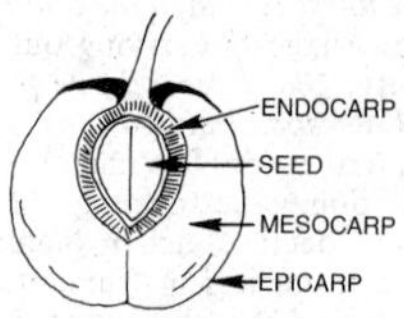

pericarp of a cherry

per i carp (per′ə kärp), *n.* walls of a ripened ovary or fruit of a flowering plant, sometimes consisting of three layers, the epicarp, mesocarp, and endocarp; seed vessel. [< *peri-* + Greek *karpos* fruit]

Per i cles (per′ə klēz′), *n.* 490?-429 B.C., Athenian statesman, orator, and military commander, under whose leadership ancient Athens reached its peak of culture and power.

per i cy cle (per′ə sī′kəl), *n.* the outer portion of the stele of a plant, lying between the vascular tissues internally and the innermost layer of the cortex externally, and consisting mainly of parenchyma cells.

per i gee (per′ə jē), *n.* point closest to the earth in the orbit of the moon or any other earth satellite. See **apogee** for diagram. [< *peri-* + Greek *gē* earth]

per i he li on (per′ə hē′lē ən, per′ə hē′lyən), *n., pl.* **-he li a** (-hē′lē ə, -hē′lyə). point closest to the sun in the orbit of a planet or comet. See **aphelion** for diagram. [< *peri-* + Greek *hēlios* sun]

per il (per′əl), *n., v.,* **-iled, -il ing** or **-illed, -il ling.** —*n.* 1 chance of harm or loss; exposure to danger: *a time of great peril.* See **danger** for synonym study. 2 cause of peril or danger: *Hidden rocks are a peril to ships.* —*v.t.* put in danger. [< Old French < Latin *periculum*]

per il ous (per′ə ləs), *adj.* full of peril; dangerous. **—per′il ous ly,** *adv.* **—per′il ous ness,** *n.*

pe rim e ter (pə rim′ə tər), *n.* 1 the outer boundary of a surface or figure: *the perimeter of a circle.* 2 distance around such a boundary. The perimeter of a square equals four times the length of one side. 3 the outer line or edge of an area or object.

pergola

per i ne al (per′ə nē′əl), *adj.* of or having to do with the perineum.

per i ne um (per′ə nē′əm), *n., pl.* **-ne a** (-nē′ə). 1 area of the body between the genitals and the anus. 2 region included in the opening of the pelvis, containing the roots of the genitals, the anal canal, the urethra, etc. [< Late Latin]

per i od (pir′ē əd), *n.* 1 portion of time: *They visited us for a short period.* 2 portion of time marked off by events that happen again and again; time after which the same things begin to happen again: *A month, from new moon to new moon, is a period.* 3 a certain series of years: *the period of World War II.* 4 a portion of a game during which there is actual play. 5 one of the portions of time into which a school day is divided. 6 the time needed for a disease to run its course. 7 end; termination; final stage. 8 the dot (.) marking the end of a declarative sentence or showing an abbreviation. EXAMPLES: Mr., Dec., U.S. 9 the pause at the end of a sentence. 10 a complete sentence: *The orator spoke in stately periods.* 11 periodic sentence. 12 one of the divisions of time into which a geological era is divided. A period is divided into epochs. 13 the time of menstruating; menstruation. 14 (in physics) the interval of time between the recurrence of like phases in a vibration or other periodic motion or phenomenon. 15 (in chemistry) a horizontal row of elements having consecutive atomic numbers in the periodic table. 16 (in mathematics) the smallest interval of the independent variable required for a function to begin to repeat itself. —*adj.* characteristic of a certain period of time: *period furniture, a period novel.* [< Greek *periodos* cycle, circuit < *peri-* around + *hodos* a going, a way]

per i od ic (pir′ē od′ik), *adj.* 1 occurring, appearing, or done again and again at regular intervals: *periodic attacks of malaria.* 2 happening every now and then: *a periodic fit of clearing up one's desk.* 3 of or having to do with a period.

per i od i cal (pir′ē od′ə kəl), *n.* magazine that appears regularly, but less often than daily. —*adj.* 1 of or having to do with periodicals. 2 published at regular intervals, less often than daily. 3 periodic.

per i od i cal ly (pir′ē od′ik lē), *adv.* 1 at regular intervals. 2 every now and then.

per i o dic i ty (pir′ē ə dis′ə tē), *n., pl.* **-ties.** 1 periodic character; tendency to happen at regular intervals. 2 (in electricity) frequency of alternation. 3 the tendency of elements having similar positions in the periodic table to have similar properties.

periodic law, law that the properties of chemical elements change at regular intervals when the elements are arranged in the order of their atomic numbers.

periodic sentence, (in grammar) a sentence not complete in meaning or grammatical structure without the final words. EXAMPLE: Delighted with the invitation to visit the farm, we prepared to go.

periodic table, table in which the chemical elements, arranged in the order of their atomic numbers, are shown in related groups. See pages 326 and 327 for table.

per i o don tal (per′ē ə don′tl), *adj.* encasing or surrounding a tooth: *a periodontal membrane.* [< *peri-* + Greek *odontos* tooth]

per i os te um (per′ē os′tē əm), *n., pl.* **-te a** (-tē ə). the dense fibrous membrane covering the surface of bones except at the joints. [< New Latin < *peri-* around + Greek *osteon* bone]

per i pa tet ic (per′ə pə tet′ik), *adj.* walking or riding about; traveling from place to place; itinerant. [< Greek *peripatetikos* < *peri-* around + *patein* to walk] **—per′i pa tet′i cal ly,** *adv.*

pe riph er al (pə rif′ər əl), *adj.* 1 having to do with, situated in, or forming an outside boundary. 2 of the surface or outer part of a body; external. 3 perceived or perceiving near the outer edges of the retina: *peripheral vision.* 4 of the peripheral nervous system. **—pe riph′er al ly,** *adv.*

peripheral nervous system, the part of the vertebrate nervous system that is made up of all the nerves outside the central nervous system.

pe riph er y (pə rif′ər ē), *n., pl.* **-er ies.** 1 an outside boundary. 2 in geometry: **a** the circumference of a circle or other closed curve. **b** the perimeter of a polygon. **c** the surface of a solid figure. [< Greek *peri-* around + *pherein* carry]

pe riph ra sis (pə rif′rə sis), *n., pl.* **-ses** (-sēz′). a roundabout way of speaking or writing; circumlocution.

per i phras tic (per′ə fras′tik), *adj.* 1 expressed in a roundabout way. 2 formed by using auxiliaries or particles rather than inflection. EXAMPLES: *of John* rather than *John's; did run* rather than *ran.* **—per′i phras′ti cal ly,** *adv.*

pe rique (pə rēk′), *n.* a strongly flavored dark tobacco grown in Louisiana. [< Creole French]

hat, āge, fär; let, ēqual, tėrm;
it, īce; hot, ōpen, ôrder;
oil, out; cup, pu̇t, rüle;
ch, child; ng, long; sh, she;
th, thin; ᴛʜ, then; zh, measure;

ə represents *a* in about, *e* in taken, *i* in pencil, *o* in lemon, *u* in circus.

< = from, derived from, taken from.

per i scope (per′ə skōp), *n.* an optical instrument consisting of an arrangement of prisms or mirrors that reflect light rays down a vertical tube, used in a submarine, trench, etc., to obtain a view of the surface. **—per′i-scope like′,** *adj.*

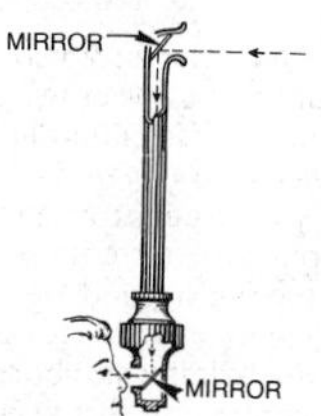

periscope on a submarine. It can be turned in any direction, and also be raised and lowered.

per i scop ic (per′ə skop′ik), *adj.* giving distinct vision obliquely as well as in a direct line.

per ish (per′ish), *v.i.* be destroyed; die: *Soldiers perish in battle. Flowers perish when frost comes.* See **die**[1] for synonym study. [< Old French *periss-*, a form of *perir* < Latin *perire* < *per-* to destruction + *ire* go]

per ish a bil i ty (per′i shə bil′ə tē), *n.* a being perishable.

per ish a ble (per′i shə bəl), *adj.* liable to spoil or decay: *Fruit is perishable.* —*n.* Usually, **perishables,** *pl.* something perishable. **—per′ish a ble ness,** *n.*

pe ris so dac tyl (pə ris′ō dak′tl), *n.* any of an order of hoofed mammals having an odd number of toes on each foot. Horses, tapirs, and rhinoceroses belong to this order. [< Greek *perissos* uneven + *daktylos* finger]

per i stal sis (per′ə stal′sis), *n., pl.* **-ses** (-sēz′). the wavelike contractions of the alimentary canal or other tubular organ by which its contents are moved onward. [New Latin < Greek *peri-* + *stellein* to wrap]

per i stal tic (per′ə stal′tik), *adj.* of or having to do with peristalsis.

per i style (per′ə stīl), *n.* 1 row of columns surrounding a building, court, or the like. 2 space or court so enclosed. [< Greek *peristylon* < *peri-* + *stylon* column]

per i to ne al (per′ə tə nē′əl), *adj.* of the peritoneum.

per i to ne um (per′ə tə nē′əm), *n., pl.* **-ne a** (-nē′ə). the thin, transparent, serous membrane that lines the walls of the abdomen and covers the organs in it. [< Late Latin, ultimately < Greek *peri-* + *teinein* to stretch]

per i to ni tis (per′ə tə nī′tis), *n.* inflammation of the peritoneum.

per i wig (per′ə wig), *n.* wig or peruke. [earlier *perewyke* < French *perruque.* See PERUKE.]

per i win kle[1] (per′ē wing′kəl), *n.* any of a genus of usually low, trailing evergreen plants with blue flowers, of the same family as the dogbane; myrtle. [Old English *pervince* < Latin *pervinca;* influenced by *periwinkle*[2]]

per i win kle[2] (per′ē wing′kəl), *n.* any of a genus of sea snails with thick, cone-shaped, spiral shells. Some species are used for food, chiefly in Europe. [Old English *pīnewincle*]

per jure (pėr′jər), *v.t.,* **-jured, -jur ing.** 1 make (oneself) guilty of perjury. 2 **perjure oneself,** swear falsely; lie under oath. [< Latin *perjurare* < *per-* to destruction + *jurare* swear]

per jured (pėr′jərd), *adj.* guilty of perjury.

per jur er (pėr′jər ər), *n.* person who commits perjury.

per jur y (pėr′jər ē), *n., pl.* **-jur ies.** act or crime of willfully giving false testimony or withholding evidence while under oath; a swearing falsely.

perk (pėrk), *v.t.* 1 raise smartly or briskly: *The sparrow perked up its tail.* 2 make trim or smart: *She is all perked out in her Sunday clothes.* —*v.i.* 1 move, lift the head, or act briskly or saucily. 2 **perk up,** brighten up; become lively and vigorous. [Middle English *perken*]

Per kins (pėr′kənz), *n.* **Frances,** 1882-1965, American social worker, who served as Secretary of Labor from 1933 to 1945.

perk y (pėr′kē), *adj.,* **perk i er, perk i est.** smart; brisk; saucy; pert. **—perk′i ly,** *adv.* **—perk′i ness,** *n.*

Perm (perm, pėrm), *n.* city in W Soviet Union. 850,000.

perm a frost (pėr′mə frôst′, pėr′mə-frost′), *n.* layer of permanently frozen subsoil, found throughout most of the arctic regions. [< *perma(nent)* + *frost*]

per ma nence (pėr′mə nəns), *n.* a being permanent; lasting quality or condition.

per ma nen cy (pėr′mə nən sē), *n., pl.* **-cies.** 1 permanence. 2 a permanent person, thing, or position.

per ma nent (pėr′mə nənt), *adj.* intended to last; not for a short time only; lasting: *a permanent filling in a tooth, a permanent job.* See **lasting** for synonym study. —*n.* INFORMAL. permanent wave. [< Latin *permanentem* staying to the end < *per-* through + *manere* to stay] **—per′ma nent ly,** *adv.*

permanent magnet, magnet that retains its magnetism after the magnetizing current or force is removed.

permanent wave, wave put in the hair by a special process, using chemical and mechanical means, so as to last several months; permanent.

per man ga nate (pər mang′gə nāt), *n.* salt of permanganic acid. A solution of potassium permanganate is used as an antiseptic.

per man gan ic acid (pėr′mang gan′ik), an unstable acid existing only in solution. *Formula:* $HMnO_4$

per me a bil i ty (pėr′mē ə bil′ə tē), *n.* 1 condition of being permeable. 2 (in physics) the ratio of magnetic induction to the intensity of the magnetic field.

per me a ble (pėr′mē ə bəl), *adj.* that can be permeated; allowing the passage or diffusion of liquids or gases through it: *permeable cell walls.*

per me ate (pėr′mē āt), *v.t.,* **-at ed, -at ing.** 1 spread through the whole of; pass through; pervade: *Smoke permeated the house.* 2 penetrate through pores or openings; soak through: *Water will easily permeate a cotton dress.* [< Latin *permeatum* passed through < *per-* through + *meare* to pass] **—per′me-a′tion,** *n.*

Per mi an (pėr′mē ən), *n.* 1 the last geological period of the Paleozoic era, when reptiles began to spread over the earth. See chart under **geology.** 2 rocks formed in this period. —*adj.* of or having to do with this period or its rocks. [< *Perm,* a former Russian province]

per mis si ble (pər mis′ə bəl), *adj.* that can be permitted; allowable. **—per mis′si bly,** *adv.*

per mis sion (pər mish′ən), *n.* a permitting; consent; leave: *I asked the teacher's permission to go early.* [< Latin *permissionem* < *permittere.* See PERMIT.]

per mis sive (pər mis′iv), *adj.* 1 not forbidding; tending to permit; allowing. 2 permitted; allowed. **—per mis′sive ly,** *adv.* **—per mis′sive ness,** *n.*

per mit (*v.* pər mit′; *n.* pėr′mit, pər mit′), *v.,* **-mit ted, -mit ting,** *n.* —*v.t.* 1 allow (a person, etc.) to do something: *Permit me to explain.* See synonym study below. 2 let (something) be done or occur; authorize: *The law does not permit smoking in this store.* —*v.i.* give leave or opportunity: *I will go on Monday if the weather permits.* —*n.* 1 a formal written order giving permission to do something: *a permit to fish or hunt.* 2 permission. [< Latin *permittere* < *per-* through + *mittere* let go, send] **—per-mit′ter,** *n.*

Syn. *v.t.* 1 **Permit, allow** mean to let someone or something do something. **Permit** implies willingness or consent: *His parents permitted him to enlist when he was seventeen.* **Allow** implies letting something happen without necessarily giving permission or approval: *That teacher allows too much noise in the room.*

per mu ta tion (pėr′myə tā′shən), *n.* 1 a change from one state, position, etc., to another; alteration. 2 in mathematics: **a** a changing of the order of a set of things; arranging in different orders. **b** such an arrangement or group. The permutations of *a, b,* and *c* are *abc, acb, bac, bca, cab, cba.* [< Latin *permutationem* < *permutare* to change through < *per-* through + *mutare* to change]

per mute (pər myüt′), *v.t.,* **-mut ed, -mut ing.** subject to permutation.

Per nam bu co (pėr′nəm byü′kō), *n.* former name of **Recife.**

per ni cious (pər nish′əs), *adj.* 1 that will destroy or ruin; causing great harm or damage; very injurious: *a pernicious habit.* 2 fatal; deadly. [< Latin *perniciosus,* ultimately < *per-* completely + *necis* death] **—per ni′cious ly,** *adv.* **—per ni′cious-ness,** *n.*

pernicious anemia, a very severe form of anemia in which the number of red corpuscles in the blood decreases.

per nick e ty (pər nik′ə tē), *adj.* persnickety.

per o rate (per′ə rāt′), *v.i.,* **-rat ed, -rat ing.** make a peroration.

per o ra tion (per′ə rā′shən), *n.* 1 the concluding part of an oration or discussion. It sums up what has been said. 2 a rhetorical speech or passage. [< Latin *perorationem* < *per-* to a finish + *orare* speak formally]

pe rox ide (pə rok′sīd), *n., v.,* **-id ed, -id ing.** —*n.* 1 oxide of an element or radical that contains the greatest possible, or an unusual, proportion of oxygen, especially one containing an oxygen atom joined to another oxygen atom. 2 hydrogen peroxide. —*v.t.* bleach (hair) by applying hydrogen peroxide.

perpendicular (def. 3)
perpendicular lines

per pen dic u lar (pėr′pən dik′yə lər), *adj.* 1 standing straight up; vertical; upright. 2 very steep; precipitous. 3 at right angles to a given line, plane, or surface. —*n.* 1 line or plane at right angles to another line, plane, or surface. 2 an upright or erect position. [< Latin *perpendicularis* < *perpendiculum* plumb line < *per-* thoroughly + *pendere* hang] **—per′pen dic′u lar ly,** *adv.*

per pen dic u lar i ty (pėr′pən dik′yə-lar′ə tē), *n.* perpendicular position or direction.

per pe trate (pėr′pə trāt), *v.t.,* **-trat ed, -trat ing.** do or commit (a crime, fraud, trick, or anything bad or foolish). [< Latin *perpetratum* perpetrated < *per-* thoroughly + *patrare* perform] **—per′pe tra′tion,** *n.* **—per′pe tra′tor,** *n.*

per pet u al (pər pech′ü əl), *adj.* 1 lasting forever; eternal: *the perpetual hills.* 2 lasting throughout life: *a perpetual income.* 3 never ceasing; continuous; constant: *a perpetual stream of visitors.* 4 being in bloom more or less continuously throughout the year or the season. [< Latin *perpetuus* continuous < *per-* to the end + *petere* go after] **—per-pet′u al ly,** *adv.*

perpetual motion, the motion of a hypothetical machine which being once started should go on forever by creating its own energy.

per pet u ate (pər pech′ü āt), *v.t.,* **-at ed, -at ing.** make perpetual; keep from being forgotten: *The Washington Monument was built to perpetuate the memory of a great man.* **—per pet′u a′tion,** *n.* **—per pet′u-a′tor,** *n.*

per pe tu i ty (pėr′pə tü′ə tē, pėr′pə tyü′ə-tē), *n., pl.* **-ties.** 1 a being perpetual; existence forever. 2 **in perpetuity,** forever.

per plex (pər pleks′), *v.t.* 1 trouble with doubt; puzzle; bewilder. See **puzzle** for synonym study. 2 make difficult to understand or settle; confuse. [< Latin *perplexus* confused < *per-* thoroughly + *plectere* intertwine] **—per plex′ed ly,** *adv.* **—per-plex′ing ly,** *adv.*

per plex i ty (pər plek′sə tē), *n., pl.* **-ties.** 1 a perplexed condition; being puzzled; confusion; bewilderment. 2 an entangled or confused state. 3 something that perplexes.

per qui site (pėr′kwə zit), *n.* 1 anything received for work besides the regular pay: *The minister had a parsonage as a perquisite.* 2 tip expected as a matter of course for doing one's job. [< Medieval Latin *perquisitum* (thing) gained < Latin, sought after, ultimately < *per-* + *quaerere* seek]

Per ry (per′ē), *n.* 1 **Matthew C.,** 1794-1858, American naval officer. He arranged a treaty between the United States and Japan which opened Japan to American trade. 2 his brother, **Oliver Hazard,** 1785-1819, American naval commander.

per se (pər sā′), by itself; in itself; intrinsically. [< Latin]

per se cute (pėr′sə kyüt), *v.t.,* **-cut ed, -cut ing.** 1 cause to suffer repeatedly; do harm to persistently; oppress. 2 oppress because of one's principles or beliefs. 3 annoy; harass: *persecuted by suitors.* **—per′se cu′tor,** *n.*

per se cu tion (pėr′sə kyü′shən), *n.* 1 a persecuting. 2 a being persecuted. 3 course or period of systematic punishment or oppression. [< Latin *persecutionem* < *per-* through + *sequi* follow]

Per seph o ne (pər sef′ə nē), *n.* (in Greek myths) the daughter of Zeus and Demeter, made queen of the lower world by Pluto, but allowed to spend part of each year on the earth. The Roman equivalent is Proserpina.

Per sep o lis (pər sep′ə lis), *n.* capital of ancient Persia, in the S part, near modern Shiraz.

Per se us (pėr′sē əs, pėr′syüs), *n.* 1 (in Greek legends) a hero, the son of Zeus, who slew Medusa and rescued Andromeda from a sea monster. 2 a northern constellation extending in a curving line southeastward from Cassiopeia nearly to the Pleiades.

per se ver ance (pėr′sə vir′əns), *n.* a sticking to a purpose or an aim; a persevering; tenacity. See **persistence** for synonym study.

per se vere (pėr′sə vir′), *v.i.,* **-vered, -ver ing.** continue steadily in doing something hard; persist. [< Latin *perseverare* < *per-* thoroughly + *severus* strict] **—per′se ver′ing ly,** *adv.*

Per shing (pėr′shing), *n.* **John Joseph,** 1860-1948, general in command of the United States Army during World War I.

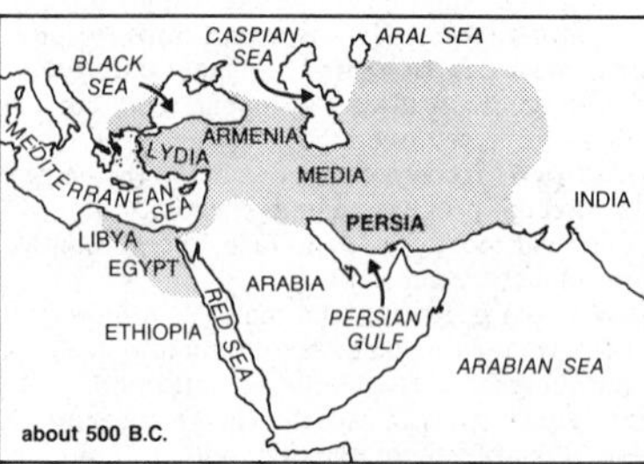

Persia (def. 2)—Shaded area indicates the empire at its greatest extent.

Per sia (pėr′zhə), *n.* 1 former country in SW Asia south of the Caspian Sea. Its name was officially changed to Iran in 1935. 2 ancient empire in W and SW Asia. Alexander the Great conquered the Persian Empire in 334-331 B.C.

Per sian (pėr′zhən), *adj.* of or having to do with ancient Persia or modern Iran, its people, or their language. —*n.* 1 native or inhabitant of ancient Persia or modern Iran. 2 language of ancient Persia or modern Iran.

Persian cat, a long-haired domestic cat originally from Iran and Afghanistan.

Persian Gulf, gulf of the Arabian Sea, between Iran and the peninsula of Arabia. 600 mi. long; about 97,000 sq. mi. See **Iran** for map.

Persian lamb, a very curly fur from caracul lambs of Iran and some parts of central Asia.

per si flage (pėr′sə fläzh), *n.* light, joking talk or writing. [< French < *persifler* to banter]

per sim mon (pər sim′ən), *n.* 1 any of various species of ebony, such as a North American tree with a yellowish-orange, plumlike fruit which contains one to ten seeds and is sweet and edible when very ripe. 2 fruit of any of these trees. [< Algonquian]

per sist (pər sist′, pər zist′), *v.i.* 1 continue firmly; refuse to stop or be changed; persevere. 2 remain in existence; last; stay: *On the tops of very high mountains snow persists throughout the year.* 3 say again and again; maintain. [< Latin *persistere* < *per-* to the end + *sistere* to stand]

per sist ence (pər sis′təns, pər zis′təns), *n.* 1 a persisting. See synonym study below. 2 a being persistent; doggedness. 3 a continuing existence: *the persistence of a cough.*

Syn. 1 **Persistence, perseverance** mean a holding fast to a purpose or course of action. **Persistence,** having a good or bad sense according to one's attitude toward what is done, emphasizes holding stubbornly to one's purpose and continuing firmly and often annoyingly against disapproval, opposition, advice, etc.: *By persistence many people won religious freedom.* **Perseverance,** always in a good sense, emphasizes refusing to be discouraged by obstacles or difficulties, but continuing steadily with courage and patience: *Perseverance led to his success.*

per sist en cy (pər sis′tən sē, pər zis′tən-sē), *n.* persistence.

per sist ent (pər sis′tənt, pər zis′tənt), *adj.* 1 not giving up, especially in the face of dislike, disapproval, or difficulties; persisting; persevering: *a persistent worker, a persistent beggar.* 2 going on; continuing; lasting: *a persistent headache that lasted for three days.* **—per sist′ent ly,** *adv.*

per snick e ty (pər snik′ə tē), *adj.* INFORMAL. 1 overly fastidious; fussy. 2 requiring precise and careful handling. Also, **pernickety.** [origin uncertain]

per son (pėr′sən), *n.* 1 man, woman, or child; human being. See synonym study below. 2 body of a human being: *The king's person was closely guarded.* 3 bodily appearance: *keep one's person neat and trim.* 4 in grammar: **a** change in a pronoun or verb to show the person speaking (first person), the person spoken to (second person), or the person or thing spoken of (third person). *I* and *we* are used for the first person; *you,* for the second person; *he, she, it,* and *they,* for the third person. **b** a form of a pronoun or verb giving such indication. *Comes* is the third person singular of *come.* 5 any of the three modes of being in the Trinity (Father, Son, and Holy Ghost). 6 (in law) a human being, or an entity such as a corporation or a partnership, recognized by the law as capable of having legal rights and duties. 7 **in person,** with or by one's own action or bodily presence; personally: *appear in person.* 8 **in the person of,** in the character or guise of. [< Latin *persona* person, (originally) character in a drama, actor, mask worn by an actor. Doublet of PARSON.]

Syn. 1 **Person, individual, party** mean a human being. **Person** is the common word: *She is a nice person.* **Individual** emphasizes the person's singleness and is slightly pretentious unless that emphasis is needed: *I speak as an individual.* Unless **party** means one who takes part in *(a party to the conspiracy),* it is restricted to legal or informal use: *the party of the first part. Who is the party that called?*

per so na (pər sō′nə), *n., pl.* **-nae** (-nē). 1 person. 2 the voice of the author or the author's creation in a literary work. [< Latin]

per son a ble (pėr′sə nə bəl), *adj.* having a pleasing appearance; good-looking; attractive. **—per′son a ble ness,** *n.*

hat, āge, fär; let, ēqual, tėrm;
it, īce; hot, ōpen, ôrder;
oil, out; cup, pu̇t, rüle;
ch, child; ng, long; sh, she;
th, thin; ᴛʜ, then; zh, measure;

ə represents *a* in about, *e* in taken, *i* in pencil, *o* in lemon, *u* in circus.

< = from, derived from, taken from.

per son age (pėr′sə nij), *n.* 1 person of high rank, distinction, or importance. 2 person. 3 character in a book or play.

per son al (pėr′sə nəl), *adj.* 1 of, having to do with, or belonging to a person; individual; private: *a personal letter.* 2 done in person; directly by oneself, not through others or by letter: *a personal visit.* 3 of the body or bodily appearance: *personal beauty.* 4 about or against a person or persons: *personal abuse, a personal question.* 5 inclined to make remarks or ask questions about the private affairs of others: *Don't be too personal.* 6 (in grammar) showing person. *I, we, you, he, she, it* and *they* are personal pronouns. 7 (in law) of or having to do with property that can be moved, such as furniture and clothing, as contrasted with real property, such as land or buildings. 8 having the nature of a person. —*n.* U.S. a short paragraph or advertisement in a newspaper written to or about a particular person or persons.

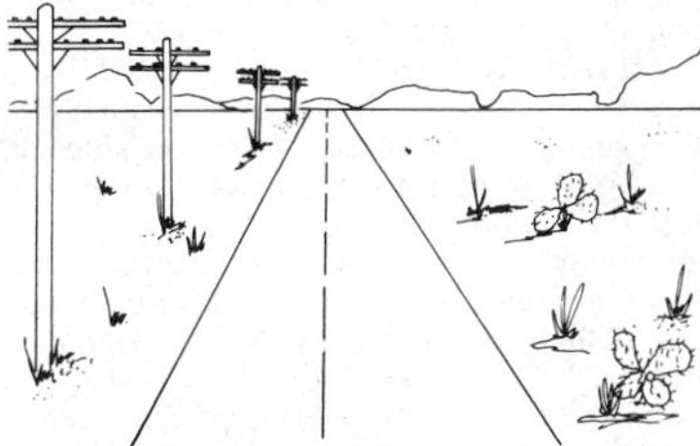

perspective (def. 1) illustrated by the convergence of the parallel lines of the road, the diminishing distance between the equally-spaced poles, and the decreasing size of the poles

personal equation, individual tendency for which allowance should be made.

per son al i ty (pėr′sə nal′ə tē), *n., pl.* **-ties.** 1 the personal or individual quality that makes one person be different and act differently from another. See **character** for synonym study. 2 pleasing or attractive qualities of a person: *He may be smart, but he has no personality.* 3 **personalities,** *pl.* personal remarks made about or against some person: *Please refrain from personalities and stick to the issues.* 4 person, especially a person of distinction; personage: *personalities of stage and screen.*

per son al ize (pėr′sə nə līz), *v.t.,* **-ized, -iz ing.** 1 make personal; cause to be distinctly one's own: *personalize stationery.* 2 personify.

per son al ly (pėr′sə nə lē), *adv.* 1 in person; not by the aid of others: *deal personally with one's customers.* 2 as far as oneself is concerned: *Personally, I like movies better than plays.* 3 as a person: *We like him personally, but dislike his way of living.* 4 as being meant for oneself: *I intended no insult to you; do not take what I said personally.*

personal property, property that is not land, buildings, mines, or forests; possessions that can be moved.

per son al ty (pėr′sə nəl tē), *n., pl.* **-ties.** personal property.

per so na non gra ta (pər sō′nə non grä′tə), *pl.* ***per so nae non gra tae*** (pər sō′nē non grä′tē). LATIN. person who is not acceptable, especially a diplomatic representative who is not acceptable to the government to which he is accredited.

per son ate (pėr′sə nāt), *v.t.,* **-at ed, -at ing.** 1 impersonate. 2 personify. 3 (in law) pretend to be (someone else). **—per′son a′tion,** *n.* **—per′son a′tor,** *n.*

per son i fi ca tion (pər son′ə fə kā′shən), *n.* 1 a striking example; embodiment; type: *A miser is the personification of greed.* 2 a representing as a person, such as speaking of the sun as *he* and the moon as *she.* 3 person or creature imagined as representing a thing or idea: *Satan is the personification of evil.* 4 figure of speech in which a lifeless thing or quality is spoken of as if alive.

per son i fy (pər son′ə fī), *v.t.,* **-fied, -fy ing.** 1 be a type of; embody: *Satan personifies evil.* 2 regard or represent as a person. We personify time and nature when we refer to *Father Time* and *Mother Nature.* **—per son′i fi′er,** *n.*

per son nel (pėr′sə nel′), *n.* persons employed in any work, business, or service. [< French]

per spec tive (pər spek′tiv), *n.* 1 art of picturing objects on a flat surface so as to give the appearance of distance or depth. 2 the effect of distance or depth on the appearance of objects: *Railroad tracks seem to meet at the horizon because of perspective.* 3 the effect of the distance of events upon the mind: *Perspective makes happenings of last year seem less important.* 4 view of things or facts in which they are in the right relations: *a lack of perspective.* 5 view in front; distant view: *a perspective of lakes and hills.* 6 a mental view, outlook, or prospect. —*adj.* 1 of perspective. 2 drawn so as to show the proper perspective: *a perspective drawing.* [< Medieval Latin *perspectiva (ars)* (science of) optics < Latin *perspicere* look through < *per-* through + *specere* to look] **—per spec′tive ly,** *adv.*

per spi ca cious (pėr′spə kā′shəs), *adj.* keen in observing and understanding; discerning; shrewd. [< Latin *perspicacem* sharp-sighted < *perspicere* look through. See PERSPECTIVE.] **—per′spi ca′cious ly,** *adv.*

per spi cac i ty (pėr′spə kas′ə tē), *n.* keen perception; wisdom and understanding in dealing with people or with facts; discernment.

per spi cu i ty (pėr′spə kyü′ə tē), *n.* ease in being understood; clearness in expression; lucidity.

per spic u ous (pər spik′yü əs), *adj.* easily understood; clear; lucid. [< Latin *perspicuus* < *perspicere* look through. See PERSPECTIVE.] **—per spic′u ous ly,** *adv.* **—per spic′u ous ness,** *n.*

per spi ra tion (pėr′spə rā′shən), *n.* 1 the salty fluid secreted by sweat glands through the pores of the skin; sweat. See **sweat** for synonym study. 2 act of perspiring.

per spire (pər spīr′), *v.i., v.t.,* **-spired, -spir ing.** give off perspiration; sweat. [< Latin *perspirare* < *per-* through + *spirare* breathe]

per suade (pər swād′), *v.t.,* **-suad ed, -suad ing.** win over to do or believe; make willing or sure by urging, arguing, etc.; convince. See synonym study below. [< Latin *persuadere* < *per-* thoroughly + *suadere* to urge] **—per suad′er,** *n.*

Syn. Persuade, convince mean to get someone to do or believe something. **Persuade** emphasizes winning a person over to a desired belief or action by strong urging, arguing, advising, and appealing to his feelings as well as to his mind: *I knew I should study, but he persuaded me to go to the movies.* **Convince** emphasizes overcoming a person's objections or disbelief by proof or arguments appealing to his reason and understanding: *I have convinced her that she needs a vacation, but cannot persuade her to take one.*

per sua si ble (pər swā′sə bəl), *adj.* that can be persuaded; open to persuasion.

per sua sion (pər swā′zhən), *n.* 1 a persuading: *All our persuasion was of no use; she would not come with us.* 2 power of persuading. 3 a firm belief; conviction. 4 a religious belief; creed: *All Christians are not of the same persuasion.* 5 a body of persons holding a particular religious belief; sect; denomination.

per sua sive (pər swā′siv, pər swā′ziv), *adj.* able, intended, or fitted to persuade: *a persuasive argument, a persuasive smile.* **—per sua′sive ly,** *adv.* **—per sua′sive ness,** *n.*

pert (pėrt), *adj.* 1 too forward or free in speech or action; saucy; bold; impudent. 2 stylish; jaunty: *a pert outfit for casual wear.* 3 INFORMAL. lively; in good health or spirits. [< Old French *apert* open < Latin *apertus*] **—pert′ly,** *adv.* **—pert′ness,** *n.*

per tain (pər tān′), *v.i.* 1 belong or be connected as a part, possession, etc.: *We own the house and the land pertaining to it.* 2 have to do with; be related; refer: *documents pertaining to the case.* 3 be appropriate: *We had turkey and everything else that pertains to Thanksgiving.* [< Old French *partenir* < Latin *pertinere* reach through, connect < *per-* through + *tenere* to hold]

Perth (pėrth), *n.* 1 city in central Scotland. 41,000. 2 city in SW Australia, the capital of Western Australia. City with suburbs, 626,000.

per ti na cious (pėrt′n ā′shəs), *adj.* 1 holding firmly to a purpose, action, or opinion; very persistent. 2 obstinately or persistently continuing. [< Latin *pertinacem* firm < *per-* + *tenacem* tenacious] **—per′ti na′cious ly,** *adv.*

per ti nac i ty (pėrt′n as′ə tē), *n.* great persistence; holding firmly to a purpose, action, or opinion.

per ti nence (pėrt′n əns), *n.* a being to the point; fitness; relevance: *The pertinence of the girl's replies showed that she was alert and intelligent.*

per ti nen cy (pėrt′n ən sē), *n.* pertinence.

per ti nent (pėrt′n ənt), *adj.* having to do with what is being considered; relating to the matter in hand; to the point. See synonym study below. [< Latin *pertinentem* pertaining] **—per′ti nent ly,** *adv.*

Syn. Pertinent, relevant mean relating to the matter in hand. **Pertinent** means relating directly to the point of the matter and helping to explain or clarify it: *A summary of the events leading up to this situation would be pertinent information.* **Relevant** means having some bearing on the matter or enough connection with it to have some meaning or importance: *Even incidents seeming unimportant in themselves might be relevant.*

per turb (pər tėrb′), *v.t.* 1 disturb greatly; make uneasy or troubled; distress: *Mother was much perturbed by my illness.* 2 cause disorder or irregularity in; agitate. [< Latin *perturbare* < *per-* thoroughly + *turbare* confuse]

per tur ba tion (pėr′tər bā′shən), *n.* 1 a perturbing. 2 a perturbed condition. 3 thing, act, or event that causes disturbance or agitation. 4 (in astronomy) a disturbance in the motion of a planet or other heavenly body in orbit caused by the attraction of a body or bodies other than its primary.

per tus sis (pər tus′əs), *n.* whooping cough. [< New Latin < Latin *per-* thorough + *tussis* cough]

Pe ru (pə rü′), *n.* mountainous country on the W coast of South America. 13,586,000 pop.; 496,200 sq. mi. *Capital:* Lima.

Peru Current, a cool ocean current of the Pacific which flows northward along the W coast of South America; Humboldt Current.

Per u gi no (per′ü jē′nō), *n.* 1446-1524, Italian painter.

peruke

pe ruke (pə rük′), *n.* wig, especially of the type worn by men in the 1600's and 1700's; periwig. [< Middle French *perruque* < Italian *perruca*]

pe rus al (pə rü′zəl), *n.* a perusing; reading: *the perusal of a letter.*

pe ruse (pə rüz′), *v.t.*, **-rused, -rus ing.** read, especially thoroughly and carefully. [originally, use up < *per-* + *use*] **—pe rus′er,** *n.*

Pe ru vi an (pə rü′vē ən), *adj.* of or having to do with Peru or its people. *—n.* native or inhabitant of Peru.

Peruvian bark, cinchona.

per vade (pər vād′), *v.t.*, **-vad ed, -vad ing.** go or spread throughout; be throughout: *The odor of pines pervades the air.* [< Latin *pervadere* < *per-* through + *vadere* go] **—per vad′er,** *n.*

per va sion (pər vā′zhən), *n.* 1 a pervading. 2 a being pervaded.

per va sive (pər vā′siv), *adj.* 1 tending to pervade. 2 having power to pervade. **—per va′sive ly,** *adv.* **—per va′sive ness,** *n.*

per verse (pər vėrs′), *adj.* 1 contrary and willful; obstinately opposing what is wanted, reasonable, or required. 2 persistent in wrong. 3 morally bad; perverted; depraved. 4 not correct; wrong: *perverse reasoning.* [< Latin *perversum* turned away, perverted] **—per verse′ly,** *adv.* **—per verse′ness,** *n.*

per ver sion (pər vėr′zhən, pər vėr′shən), *n.* 1 a turning or being turned to what is wrong; change to what is unnatural, abnormal, or wrong. 2 a perverted form. 3 deviation or abnormality in sexual behavior.

per ver si ty (pər vėr′sə tē), *n., pl.* **-ties.** 1 quality of being perverse. 2 perverse character or conduct. 3 a perverse act.

per vert (*v.* pər vėrt′; *n.* pėr′vėrt′), *v.t.* 1 lead or turn from what is true, desirable, good, or morally right; corrupt: *Reading silly stories perverted his taste for good books.* 2 give a wrong meaning to; distort: *His enemies perverted his friendly remark and made it into an insult.* 3 use for wrong purposes or in a wrong way: *A clever criminal perverts his talents.* 4 change from what is natural or normal. *—n.* a perverted person, especially one who practices sexual perversion. [< Latin *pervertere* < *per-* to destruction + *vertere* to turn] **—per vert′ed ly,** *adv.* **—per vert′er,** *n.*

per vi ous (pėr′vē əs), *adj.* 1 giving passage or entrance; permeable: *Sand is easily pervious to water.* 2 open to influence, argument, etc. [< Latin *pervius* < *per-* through + *via* way]

Pe sach (pā′säH), *n.* Passover. [< Hebrew *pesaḥ*]

Pes ca do res (pes′kə dôr′ēz, pes′kə dōr′ēz), *n.pl.* group of islands in Formosa Strait, belonging to Taiwan. 80,000 pop.; 49 sq. mi.

pe se ta (pə sā′tə), *n.* the monetary unit of Spain, a coin or note equal to 100 centimos and worth about $1^1/_2$ cents. [< Spanish, diminutive of *peso*]

pe se wa (pə sē′wə), *n.* unit of money in Ghana, equal to $^1/_{100}$ of a cedi.

Pe sha war (pe shä′wər), *n.* city in N Pakistan, near Khyber Pass. 219,000.

pes ky (pes′kē), *adj.*, **-ki er, -ki est.** INFORMAL. troublesome; annoying. [probably alteration of *pesty* < *pest*] **—pes′ki ly,** *adv.* **—pes′ki ness,** *n.*

pe so (pā′sō), *n., pl.* **-sos.** 1 the monetary unit in various countries of Latin America and in the Philippines, a coin or note usually equal to 100 centavos, its value varying from $8^1/_3$ cents in Bolivia to one dollar in Cuba. 2 coin or piece of paper money worth one peso. 3 a former gold or silver coin used in Spain and in the Spanish colonies, worth eight reals. [< Spanish, weight < Latin *pensum* < *pendere* weigh]

peso bo li via no (bō lē vyä′nō), the monetary unit of Bolivia, a coin or note equal to 100 centavos and worth about $8^1/_3$ cents.

pes si mism (pes′ə miz′əm), *n.* 1 tendency to look on the dark side of things or to see all the difficulties and disadvantages. 2 belief that things naturally tend to evil. 3 doctrine that the evil in life outweighs the good. [< Latin *pessimus* worst]

pes si mist (pes′ə mist), *n.* 1 person inclined to look on the dark side of things or to see all the difficulties and disadvantages. 2 person who believes that things naturally tend to evil. 3 believer in the doctrine of pessimism.

pes si mis tic (pes′ə mis′tik), *adj.* 1 having a tendency to look at the dark side of things or to see all the difficulties and disadvantages. See **cynical** for synonym study. 2 expecting the worst: *He is pessimistic about the outcome of the trial.* 3 having to do with pessimism. **—pes′si mis′ti cal ly,** *adv.*

pest (pest), *n.* 1 a destructive or harmful insect, animal, etc.: *garden pests.* 2 thing or person that is persistently annoying; nuisance: *That whining child is an awful pest.* 3 ARCHAIC. pestilence, especially an outbreak of the plague. [< Latin *pestis* plague]

Pes ta loz zi (pes′tə lot′sē), *n.* **Johann Heinrich,** 1746-1827, Swiss educator.

pes ter (pes′tər), *v.t.* trouble persistently; annoy; vex: *Don't pester me with foolish questions.* See **tease** for synonym study.

pest hole (pest′hōl′), *n.* place that breeds or is likely to have epidemic disease.

pest house (pest′hous′), *n., pl.* **-hous es** (-hou′ziz). hospital for persons ill with highly contagious diseases.

pes ti cide (pes′tə sīd), *n.* substance used to kill pests.

pes tif er ous (pe stif′ər əs), *adj.* 1 bringing disease or infection; pestilential. 2 bringing moral evil; pernicious. 3 INFORMAL. troublesome; annoying. **—pes tif′er ous ly,** *adv.*

pes ti lence (pes′tl əns), *n.* 1 any infectious or contagious epidemic disease that spreads rapidly, often causing many deaths. 2 the bubonic plague.

pes ti lent (pes′tl ənt), *adj.* 1 often causing death: *a pestilent disease.* 2 harmful to morals; destroying peace; pernicious: *a pestilent den of vice, the pestilent effects of war.* 3 troublesome; annoying. [< Latin *pestilentem* < *pestis* plague]

pes ti len tial (pes′tl en′shəl), *adj.* 1 like a pestilence; having to do with pestilences. 2 causing or likely to cause pestilence. 3 harmful; dangerous; pernicious. **—pes′ti len′tial ly,** *adv.*

pes tle (pes′əl, pes′tl), *n., v.,* **-tled, -tling.** *—n.* tool, usually club-shaped, for pounding or crushing substances into a powder in a mortar. See **mortar^2** for picture. *—v.t., v.i.* pound or crush with a pestle. [< Old French *pestel* < Latin *pistillum* < *pinsere* to pound. Doublet of PISTIL.]

pet^1 (pet), *n., adj., v.,* **pet ted, pet ting.** *—n.* 1 animal kept as a favorite and treated with affection. 2 a darling or favorite. *—adj.* 1 treated or kept as a pet. 2 darling or favorite. 3 showing affection: *a pet name.* *—v.t.* 1 treat as a pet; stroke or pat; touch lovingly and gently. 2 yield to the wishes of; indulge. *—v.i.* INFORMAL. make love by caressing and fondling. [perhaps shortened < *petty*]

pet^2 (pet), *n.* fit of being cross or peevish; fretful discontent. [origin uncertain]

Pé tain (pā taN′), *n.* **Henri Philippe,** 1856-1951, French marshal and World War I hero, who headed the Vichy government in France from 1940 to 1944.

pet al (pet′l), *n.* one of the parts of a flower that are usually colored; one of the leaves of a corolla. A daisy has many petals. [< Greek *petalon* leaf] **—pet′al like′,** *adj.*

pet aled or **pet alled** (pet′ld), *adj.* having petals: *six-petaled.*

pe tard (pi tärd′), *n.* 1 an explosive device formerly used in warfare to break doors or gates or to breach a wall. 2 **hoist with** (or **on**) **one's own petard,** injured or destroyed by one's own scheme for ruin of others. [< Middle French *pétard*]

pet cock (pet′kok′), *n.* a small faucet or valve in a pipe or cylinder, for reducing pressure or draining liquids.

pe ter (pē′tər), *v.i.* INFORMAL. **peter out,** gradually come to an end; fail; give out. [origin unknown]

Pe ter (pē′tər), *n.* 1 **Saint,** died A.D. 67?, fisherman who was one of Christ's twelve apostles, also called Simon or Simon Peter. 2 either of two books in the New Testament that bear his name.

Peter I, 1 1672-1725, czar of Russia from 1682 to 1725, called "Peter the Great." 2 1844-1921, king of Serbia from 1903 to 1921.

hat, āge, fär; let, ēqual, tėrm;
it, īce; hot, ōpen, ôrder;
oil, out; cup, pu̇t, rüle;
ch, child; ng, long; sh, she;
th, thin; ᴛʜ, then; zh, measure;

ə represents *a* in about, *e* in taken, *i* in pencil, *o* in lemon, *u* in circus.

< = from, derived from, taken from.

Peter II, 1923-1970, king of Yugoslavia from 1934 to 1945.

Peter Pan, 1 play by Sir James M. Barrie, produced in 1904. 2 hero of this play, a boy who refused to grow up.

Peter Pan collar, a small, round collar which can close at the front.

Peter the Hermit, 1050?-1115, French monk who urged the first of the Crusades.

pet i o late (pet′ē ə lāt), *adj.* having a petiole: *a petiolate leaf.*

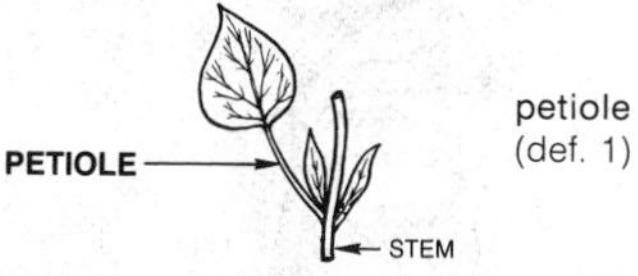

petiole (def. 1)

pet i ole (pet′ē ōl), *n.* 1 the slender stalk by which a leaf is attached to the stem; leafstalk. 2 (in zoology) a stalklike part. A petiole connects the thorax and abdomen of a wasp. [< Latin *petiolus*]

pet it (pet′ē), *adj.* (in law) small; petty; minor: *petit larceny.* [< Old French. Doublet of PETTY.]

pe tite (pə tēt′), *adj.* of small stature or size; little, especially with reference to a woman or girl. [< Old French, feminine of *petit*]

pet it four (pet′ē fôr′; pet′ē fōr′), *pl.* **pet its fours** (pet′ē fôrz′; pet′ē fōrz′). a small, fancy cake with decorative frosting. [< French, small oven]

pe ti tion (pə tish′ən), *n.* 1 a formal request to a superior or to one in authority for some privilege, right, benefit, etc.: *The people signed a petition asking the city council for a new sidewalk.* 2 (in law) a written application for an order of court or for some action by a judge. 3 prayer. 4 that which is requested or prayed for. *—v.t., v.i.* 1 ask earnestly; make a petition to: *They petitioned the mayor to use his influence with the city council.* 2 pray. [< Latin *petitionem* < *petere* seek] **—pe ti′tion er,** *n.*

pe ti tion ar y (pə tish′ə ner′ē), *adj.* of a petition.

pet it jury (pet′ē), group of 12 persons chosen to decide a case in court; trial jury. Also, **petty jury.**

pe tit mal (pə tē mal′), a mild form of epilepsy. [< French]

pe tit point (pet′ē point′), embroidery made on canvas by short, slanting parallel stitches suggesting tents; tent stitch. [< French]

Pe trarch (pē′trärk), *n.* 1304-1374, Italian poet, famous for his sonnets. **—Pe trar′chan,** *adj.*

pet rel (pet′rəl), *n.* any of various sea birds, especially the storm petrel. [perhaps diminutive of St. *Peter,* who walked on the sea]

Pe tri dish (pē′trē), a shallow, circular glass dish with a loose cover, used in the preparation of bacteriological cultures. [< Julius *Petri,* 1852-1922, German bacteriologist, who invented it]

pet ri fac tion (pet′rə fak′shən), *n.* 1 a petrifying. 2 a being petrified. 3 something petrified.

pet ri fi ca tion (pet′rə fə kā′shən), *n.* petrifaction.

Petrified Forest, ancient forest whose trees have turned to stone, in E Arizona. 40 sq. mi.

pet ri fy (pet′rə fī), *v.,* **-fied, -fy ing.** *—v.t.* 1 turn into stone; change (plant or animal matter) into a substance like stone. 2 make hard as stone; stiffen; deaden. 3 paralyze with fear, horror, or surprise: *The bird was petrified as the snake came near.* *—v.i.* 1 become stone or a substance like stone. 2 become rigid like stone; harden. [< French *pétrifier* < Latin *petra* stone]

Pe trine (pē′trīn, pē′trən), *adj.* of or having to do with the apostle Peter.

petro-, *combining form.* 1 rock; rocks, as in *petrology.* 2 petroleum, as in *petrochemical.* [< Greek *petra* rock]

pet ro chem i cal (pet′rō kem′ə kəl), *n.* chemical made or derived from petroleum or natural gas. *—adj.* of or having to do with petrochemicals.

Pet ro grad (pet′rə grad), *n.* former capital of Russia, now called **Leningrad.**

pet ro graph ic (pet′rə graf′ik), *adj.* of or having to do with petrography. **—pet′ro graph′i cal ly,** *adv.*

pet ro graph i cal (pet′rə graf′ə kəl), *adj.* petrographic.

pe trog ra phy (pi trog′rə fē), *n.* branch of geology that deals with the description and classification of rocks.

pet rol (pet′rəl), *n.* BRITISH. gasoline. [< French *(essence de) pétrole* (essence of, that is, refined) petroleum]

pet ro la tum (pet′rə lā′təm), *n.* 1 salve or ointment made from petroleum. 2 mineral oil.

pe tro le um (pə trō′lē əm), *n.* a dark, oily, flammable liquid found in the earth's crust, consisting mainly of a mixture of various hydrocarbons. Gasoline, kerosene, and paraffin are made from petroleum. [< Medieval Latin < Greek *petra* rock + Latin *oleum* oil]

pe trol o gy (pi trol′ə jē), *n.* science of rocks, including their origin, structure, changes, etc.

Pet ro za vodsk (pet′rə zə vôtsk′), *n.* city in the NW Soviet Union, capital of Karelia. 185,000.

pet ti coat (pet′ē kōt), *n.* 1 skirt worn beneath a dress or outer skirt by women and girls. 2 skirt, trimmed and sometimes stiffened. 3 INFORMAL. woman or girl. *—adj.* female or feminine: *petticoat government.* [originally, *petty coat* little coat]

pet ti fog ger (pet′ē fog′ər, pet′ē fôg′ər), *n.* 1 an inferior lawyer who uses petty, mean, cheating methods. 2 any person who habitually uses such methods.

pet ti fog ger y (pet′ē fog′ər ē, pet′ē fôg′ər ē), *n., pl.* **-ger ies.** act or practice of a pettifogger; trickery; chicanery.

pet ti fog ging (pet′ē fog′ing, pet′ē fôg′ing), *adj.* tricky, shifty, or quibbling. *—n.* pettifoggery.

pet tish (pet′ish), *adj.* peevish; cross: *a pettish reply, a pettish child.* [< *pet*[2]] **—pet′tish ly,** *adv.*

pet ty (pet′ē), *adj.,* **-ti er, -ti est.** 1 having little importance or value; small: *petty troubles.* 2 mean; narrow-minded. 3 lower in rank or importance; subordinate. [< Old French *petit* little, small. Doublet of PETIT.] **—pet′ti ly,** *adv.* **—pet′ti ness,** *n.*

petty cash, 1 small sums of money spent or received. 2 sum of money kept on hand to pay small expenses.

petty jury, petit jury.

petty larceny, theft in which the value of the property taken is less than a certain amount.

petty officer, (in the navy) an enlisted man of any of the four grades or classes above seaman.

pet u lance (pech′ə ləns), *n.* a being petulant; peevishness.

pet u lan cy (pech′ə lən sē), *n.* petulance.

pet u lant (pech′ə lənt), *adj.* likely to have little fits of bad temper; irritable over trifles; peevish. [< Latin *petulantem*] **—pet′u lant ly,** *adv.*

pe tun ia (pə tü′nyə, pə tü′nē ə; pə tyü′nyə, pə tyü′nē ə), *n.* 1 any of a genus of common garden plants of the nightshade family, with funnel-shaped flowers of white, pink, red, or various shades of purple. 2 the flower of any of these plants. [< New Latin < French *petun* tobacco < Guarani *petȳ*]

pew (pyü), *n.* bench in a church for people to sit on, fastened to the floor and provided with a back. In some churches the pews are separated by partitions and are set apart for the use of a certain family or group of people. [< Old French *puie* < Latin *podia,* plural of *podium* balcony]

pe wee (pē′wē), *n.* any of several small American flycatchers with an olive-colored or gray back. Also, **peewee.** [imitative]

pe wit (pē′wit, pyü′it), *n.* 1 lapwing. 2 a European black-headed gull. 3 pewee. [imitative]

pew ter (pyü′tər), *n.* 1 alloy of tin with lead, copper, or other metals. 2 dishes or other utensils made of this alloy. *—adj.* made of pewter. [< Old French *peautre* < Medieval Latin *peltrum*]

pe yo te (pā ō′tē), *n.* 1 the mescal or any of several other cacti. 2 a stimulating drug contained in the small buttonlike tops of the mescal; mescaline. It induces hallucinations and reactions associated with psychoses. [< Mexican Spanish < Nahuatl *peyotl*]

pf., 1 pfennig. 2 preferred.

Pfc., private first class.

pfd., preferred.

pfen nig (pfen′ig), *n., pl.* **pfen nigs, pfen ni ge** (pfen′i gə). unit of money in East and West Germany, a coin worth 1/100 of a Deutsche mark. [< German *Pfennig.* Related to PENNY.]

pfg., pfennig.

Pg., 1 Portugal. 2 Portuguese.

pH, symbol indicating the acidity or basicity of a solution in terms of the relative concentration of hydrogen ions in the solution. The pH scale commonly used ranges from 0 to 14, pH7 (the hydrogen-ion concentration in pure water) being taken as neutral, 6 to 0 increasingly acid, and 8 to 14 increasingly basic. Most soils are in the range between pH3 and pH10. [< *p(otential for) H(ydrogen)*]

Phae dra (fē′drə), *n.* (in Greek legends) the wife of Theseus, king of Athens. She loved her stepson, but caused his death by falsely accusing him.

Pha ë thon (fā′ə thon), *n.* (in Greek and Roman myths) the son of Helios who tried for one day to drive the sun, his father's chariot. He so nearly set the earth on fire that Zeus had to strike him dead with a thunderbolt.

pha e ton (fā′ə tən), *n.* 1 a light, four-wheeled carriage with or without a top, pulled by one or two horses. 2 an open automobile similar to a touring car. [< *Phaëthon*]

phage (fāj), *n.* bacteriophage.

-phage, *combining form.* that eats or devours ___: *Bacteriophage = that devours bacteria.* [< Greek *phagein* eat]

phag o cyte (fag′ə sīt), *n.* a cell, such as a white blood cell, occurring in body fluids or tissues and capable of absorbing and destroying waste or harmful material, such as disease-producing bacteria. [< Greek *phagein* eat + English *-cyte*]

phag o cyt ic (fag′ə sit′ik), *adj.* of or having to do with a phagocyte or phagocytes.

pha lan ger (fə lan′jər), *n.* any of several genera of small, tree-climbing marsupial mammals of Australia and New Guinea. [< New Latin]

pha lanx (fā′langks, fal′angks), *n., pl.* **pha lanx es** or (especially for 5) **pha lan ges** (fə lan′jēz). 1 (in ancient Greece) a special battle formation of infantry fighting in close ranks with their shields joined and long spears overlapping each other. 2 any body of troops in close array. 3 a compact or closely massed body of persons, animals, or things. 4 number of persons united for a common purpose. 5 any bone in the fingers or toes. [< Latin < Greek]

phal a rope (fal′ə rōp′), *n.* any of a family of small swimming and wading birds that breed in the Northern Hemisphere, resembling the sandpipers but with lobate toes. [< French < Greek *phalaris* coot + *pous* foot]

phal lic (fal′ik), *adj.* of or having to do with a phallus.

phal lus (fal′əs), *n., pl.* **phal li** (fal′ī), **phal lus es.** 1 penis. 2 image or model of the penis. [< Latin]

phan tasm (fan′taz′əm), *n.* 1 thing seen only in one's imagination; unreal fancy: *the phantasms of a dream.* 2 a supposed appearance of an absent person, living or dead. 3 a deceiving likeness (of something). 4 ARCHAIC. deceptive appearance; illusion. [< Greek *phantasma* image, ultimately < *phainein* to show. Doublet of PHANTOM.]

phan tas ma go ri a (fan taz′mə gôr′ē ə, fan taz′mə gōr′ē ə), *n.* 1 a shifting scene of real things, illusions, imaginary fancies, deceptions, and the like: *the phantasmagoria of a dream.* 2 show of optical illusions in which figures increase or decrease in size, fade away, and pass into each other.

phan tas ma go ric (fan taz′mə gôr′ik, fan taz′mə gor′ik), *adj.* of or like a phantasmagoria.

phan tas mal (fan taz′məl), *adj.* of a phantasm; unreal; imaginary.

phan ta sy (fan′tə sē, fan′tə zē), *n., pl.* **-sies.** fantasy.

phan tom (fan′təm), *n.* 1 image of the mind which seems to be real: *phantoms of a dream.* 2 thought or apprehension of anything that haunts the imagination. 3 a vague, dim, or shadowy appearance; ghost; apparition. 4 mere show; appearance without material substance: *a phantom of a government.* —*adj.* like a ghost; unreal: *a phantom ship.* [< Old French *fantome* < Greek *phantasma* image. Doublet of PHANTASM.]

phaeton (def. 1)

phar aoh or **Phar aoh** (fer′ō), *n.* any of the kings of ancient Egypt.

Phar i sa ic (far′ə sā′ik), *adj.* 1 of or having to do with the Pharisees. 2 **pharisaic, a** making an outward show of religion or morals without the real spirit. **b** thinking oneself more moral than others; self-righteous or hypocritical. **—phar′i sa′i cal ly,** *adv.*

phar i sa i cal (far′ə sā′ə kəl), *adj.* pharisaic.

Phar i sa ism (far′ə sā iz′əm), *n.* 1 doctrine and practice of the Pharisees. 2 **pharisaism, a** rigid observance of the external forms of religion without genuine piety. **b** self-righteousness or hypocrisy.

Phar i see (far′ə sē), *n.* 1 member of a Jewish sect at the time of Christ that was very strict in keeping to tradition and the laws of its religion. 2 **pharisee, a** person who makes a show of religion rather than following its spirit. **b** a self-righteous or hypocritical person. [< Greek *pharisaios* < Aramaic *p'rīshaiyā* separated]

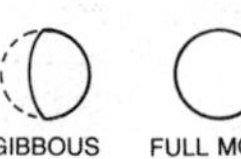

phase (def. 3)—four phases of the moon

phar i see ism (far′ə sē iz′əm), *n.* pharisaism.

pharm. or **Pharm.** 1 pharmaceutical. 2 pharmacy.

phar ma ceu tic (fär′mə sü′tik), *adj., n.* pharmaceutical.

phar ma ceu ti cal (fär′mə sü′tə kəl), *adj.* having to do with pharmacy. —*n.* a medicinal drug. **—phar′ma ceu′ti cal ly,** *adv.*

phar ma ceu tics (fär′mə sü′tiks), *n.* pharmacy (def. 2).

phar ma cist (fär′mə sist), *n.* person licensed to fill prescriptions; druggist.

phar ma co log i cal (fär′mə kə loj′ə kəl), *adj.* having to do with or relating to pharmacology. **—phar′ma co log′i cal ly,** *adv.*

phar ma col o gist (fär′mə kol′ə jist), *n.* an expert in pharmacology.

phar ma col o gy (fär′mə kol′ə jē), *n.* science of drugs, their properties, preparation, uses, and effects.

phar ma co poe ia (fär′mə kə pē′ə), *n.* 1 book containing an official list and description of drugs, chemicals, and medicines. 2 stock or collection of drugs. [< Greek *pharmakopoiia* < *pharmakon* drug + *poiein* to make]

phar ma cy (fär′mə sē), *n., pl.* **-cies.** 1 place where drugs and medicines are prepared or sold; drugstore. 2 preparation and dispensing of drugs and medicines; occupation of a druggist; pharmaceutics. 3 pharmacopoeia (def. 2). [< Late Latin *pharmacia* < Greek *pharmakeia* < *pharmakon* drug]

phar os (far′os), *n.* lighthouse, beacon, or other guiding light. [< Greek < *Pharos,* island near Alexandria, Egypt, famous for its huge lighthouse, which was one of the Seven Wonders of the World]

pha ryn ge al (fə rin′jē əl, far′in jē′əl), *adj.* having to do with or connected with the pharynx.

phar yn gi tis (far′in jī′tis), *n.* inflammation of the mucous membrane of the pharynx.

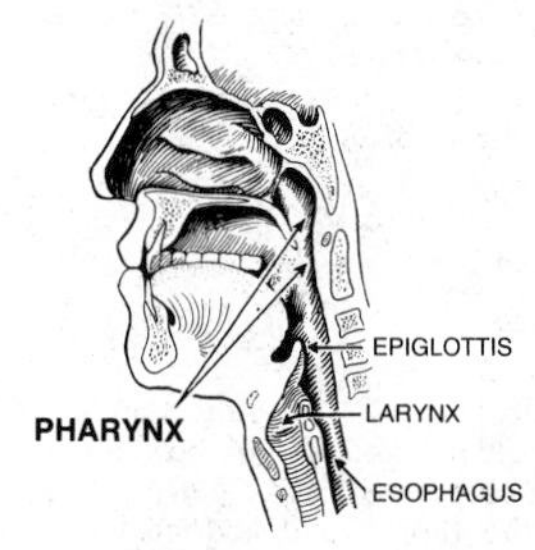

phar ynx (far′ingks), *n., pl.* **phar ynx es, pha ryn ges** (fə rin′jēz). tube or cavity that connects the mouth with the esophagus. In mammals, the pharynx contains the opening from the mouth, the opening of the esophagus, of the larynx, and of the passages from the nose. [< Greek *pharynx, pharyngos*]

phase (fāz), *n., v.,* **phased, phas ing.** —*n.* 1 one of the changing states or stages of development of a person or thing. 2 one side, part, or view (of a subject): *What phase of mathematics are you studying now?* 3 the apparent shape of the illuminated part of the disk of the moon or of a planet at a given time. The first quarter and last quarter are two phases of the moon. 4 (in physics) a particular stage or point in a recurring sequence of movements or changes, considered in relation to a starting point of normal position (used with reference to circular motion, simple harmonic motion, or an alternating current, sound vibration, etc.). 5 (in chemistry) a homogeneous part of a heterogeneous system, separated from other parts by definite boundaries, as ice in water. —*v.t.* 1 carry out or adjust by stages: *phase an army's withdrawal.* 2 put into operation in stages. 3 **phase in,** develop or integrate as a phase or in phases. 4 **phase out,** discontinue or eliminate as a phase or in phases. [< Greek *phasis* phase, appearance < *phainein* to show, appear]

phase-con trast microscope (fāz′-kon′trast), microscope which uses the differences in phase of light passing through or reflected by the object under examination, to form distinct and contrastive images of different parts of the object.

phase-out (fāz′out′), *n.* the discontinuation of an operation, production, program, etc., by stages.

Ph.B., Bachelor of Philosophy.

Ph.D., Doctor of Philosophy.

pheas ant (fez′nt), *n., pl.* **-ants** or **-ant.** any of a group of large game birds of the same family as the domestic fowl and the peacock, having brightly colored feathers in the male, and long, pointed tail feathers. Pheasants are native to Asia but now live in many parts of Europe and America. [< Anglo-French *fesant,* ultimately < Greek *phasianos,* literally, of the river *Phasis,* in Colchis]

phen-, *combining form.* a benzene derivative, as in *phenol, phenyl.* Also, **pheno-** before consonants. [< French *phén-* < Greek *phainein* show forth (because such early substances were by-products from the making of illuminating gas)]

Phe ni cia (fə nish′ə), *n.* Phoenicia.

phe nix (fē′niks), *n.* phoenix.

pheno-, *combining form.* the form of **phen-** before consonants, as in *phenobarbital.*

phe no bar bi tal (fē′nō bär′bə tôl), *n.* a white, crystalline powder, a barbiturate, used as a hypnotic or sedative. *Formula:* $C_{12}H_{12}N_2O_3$

phe nol (fē′nol, fē′nōl), *n.* 1 carbolic acid. 2 any of a series of aromatic hydroxyl derivatives of benzene, of which carbolic acid is the first member.

phe nol ic (fi nol′ik, fi nō′lik), *adj.* 1 of the nature of phenol. 2 belonging to phenol. —*n.* any of a group of synthetic resins obtained chiefly by the reaction of a phenol with an aldehyde, used for molding, in varnishes, etc.

phe nol phthal ein (fē′nōl thal′ēn, fē′nōl fthal′ēn), *n.* a white or pale-yellow powder whose solution is red when basic, colorless when acid, used in testing acidity, making dyes, as a laxative, etc. *Formula:* $C_{20}H_{14}O_4$

phe nom e na (fə nom′ə nə), *n.* a pl. of **phenomenon.**

phe nom e nal (fə nom′ə nəl), *adj.* 1 of or having to do with a phenomenon or phenomena. 2 having the nature of a phenomenon. 3 extraordinary; remarkable: *a phenomenal memory.* —**phe nom′e nal ly,** *adv.*

phe nom e non (fə nom′ə non), *n., pl.* **-na** (or **-nons** for 4). 1 fact, event, or circumstance that can be observed: *Lightning is an electrical phenomenon.* 2 any sign, symptom, or manifestation: *Fever and inflammation are phenomena of disease.* 3 any exceptional fact or occurrence: *historical phenomena.* 4 an extraordinary or remarkable person or thing. A genius or prodigy is sometimes called a phenomenon. [< Greek *phainomenon* < *phainesthai* appear]

phe no type (fē′nə tīp), *n.* 1 the physical appearance of an organism resulting from the interaction of its genotype and its environment. 2 group of organisms having one or more such characters in common.

phe no typ ic (fē′nə tip′ik), *adj.* of or having to do with phenotypes. —**phe′no typ′i cal ly,** *adv.*

phen yl (fen′l, fē′nl), *n.* a univalent radical ($—C_6H_5$), formed by removing one hydrogen atom from a benzene molecule.

phen yl al a nine (fen′l al′ə nēn′, fē′nl al′ə nēn′), *n.* amino acid which results from the hydrolysis of protein and is normally converted to tyrosine in the body. *Formula:* $C_9H_{11}NO_2$

phen yl ke to nur i a (fen′l kēt′n yůr′ē ə, fen′l kēt′n ůr′ē ə; fē′nl kēt′n yůr′ē ə, fē′nl kēt′n ůr′ē ə), *n.* a hereditary disease caused by an inability to metabolize phenylalanine properly in the body, resulting in mental deficiency and poor physical development if not treated by a special diet in infancy.

phew (fyü), *interj.* exclamation of disgust, impatience, etc.

phi (fī, fē), *n.* the 21st letter of the Greek alphabet (Φ, φ).

phi al (fī′əl), *n.* vial. [< Greek *phialē* a broad, flat vessel]

Phi Be ta Kap pa (fī′ bā′tə kap′ə; fī′ bē′tə kap′ə), an honorary society composed of American college students and graduates who have ranked high in scholarship. [< the initial letters of Greek *ph(ilosophia) b(iou) k(ybernetes)* philosophy, the guide of life]

Phid i as (fid′ē əs), *n.* 500?-432? B.C., Greek sculptor.

Phil., Philippians.

Phila., Philadelphia.

Phil a del phi a (fil′ə del′fē ə, fil′ə del′fyə), *n.* city in SE Pennsylvania, on the Delaware River. 1,950,000. —**Phil′a del′phi an,** *adj., n.*

phil a del phus (fil′ə del′fəs), *n.* syringa.

phi lan der (fə lan′dər), *v.i.* make love without serious intentions; flirt. [< Greek *philandros* loving man] —**phi lan′der er,** *n.*

phil an throp ic (fil′ən throp′ik), *adj.* 1 having to do with or characterized by philanthropy. 2 charitable; benevolent; kindly. —**phil′an throp′i cal ly,** *adv.*

phil an throp i cal (fil′ən throp′ə kəl), *adj.* philanthropic.

phi lan thro pist (fə lan′thrə pist), *n.* person who practices philanthropy, especially by giving sizable donations of money to worthy causes.

phi lan thro py (fə lan′thrə pē), *n., pl.* **-pies.** 1 love of mankind shown by practical kindness and helpfulness to humanity: *The Red Cross appeals to philanthropy.* 2 thing that benefits humanity; a philanthropic agency, gift, act, etc.: *A hospital is a useful philanthropy.* [< Greek *philanthrōpia* < *philos* loving + *anthrōpos* man]

phil a tel ic (fil′ə tel′ik), *adj.* of or having to do with philately.

phi lat e list (fə lat′l ist), *n.* collector of postage stamps, postmarks, etc.

phi lat e ly (fə lat′l ē), *n.* the collecting, arranging, and study of postage stamps, stamped envelopes, post cards, etc. [< French *philatélie* < Greek *philos* loving + *ateleia* exemption from tax; the stamp indicates the tax is paid]

-phile, *combining form.* lover or admirer of ____: *bibliophile = a lover of books.* [< French < Greek *philos* loving]

Phi le mon (fə lē′mən), *n.* book of the New Testament, a letter from Paul to a convert of his.

phil har mon ic (fil′här mon′ik, fil′ər mon′ik), *adj.* 1 devoted to music; loving music. A musical club is often called a philharmonic society. 2 given by a philharmonic society: *a philharmonic concert.* —*n.* a philharmonic society or concert. [ultimately < Greek *philos* loving + *harmonia* music]

Phil ip (fil′əp), *n.* 1 (in the Bible) one of Christ's twelve apostles. 2 died 1676, Indian chief in New England who led the Indians in a war against the colonists from 1675 to 1676. 3 **Prince,** born 1921, the Duke of Edinburgh, consort of Elizabeth II. He was born in Greece.

Philip II, 1 382-336 B.C., king of Macedonia from 359 to 336 B.C. and the father of Alexander the Great. 2 1165-1223, king of France from 1180 to 1223. He was also called "Philip Augustus." 3 1527-1598, king of Spain from 1556 to 1598 who married Mary I of England and later sent the Armada against England.

Phi lip pi (fə lip′ī), *n.* city in ancient Macedonia. In 42 B.C., Octavian and Mark Antony defeated Brutus and Cassius there. —**Phi lip′pi an,** *adj., n.*

Phi lip pi ans (fə lip′ē ənz), *n.* book of the New Testament, a letter from Paul to the early Christians of Philippi.

hat, āge, fär; let, ēqual, tėrm;
it, īce; hot, ōpen, ôrder;
oil, out; cup, pu̇t, rüle;
ch, child; ng, long; sh, she;
th, thin; ᴛʜ, then; zh, measure;

ə represents *a* in about, *e* in taken, *i* in pencil, *o* in lemon, *u* in circus.

< = from, derived from, taken from.

Phi lip pic (fə lip′ik), *n.* 1 any of several orations by Demosthenes denouncing Philip II of Macedonia and arousing the Athenians to resist Philip's growing power. 2 any of several orations by Cicero denouncing Mark Antony. 3 **philippic,** a bitter attack in words.

Phil ip pine (fil′ə pēn′), *adj.* of or having to do with the Philippines or its inhabitants. Also, **Filipino.**

Philippine Islands, Philippines.

Phil ip pines (fil′ə pēnz′), *n.pl.* country in the W Pacific, southeast of China and northeast of Borneo, consisting of over 7000 islands. The Philippines were governed by the United States from 1898 until 1946. 37,008,000 pop.; 115,700 sq. mi. *Capital:* Quezon City. See **Melanesia** for map.

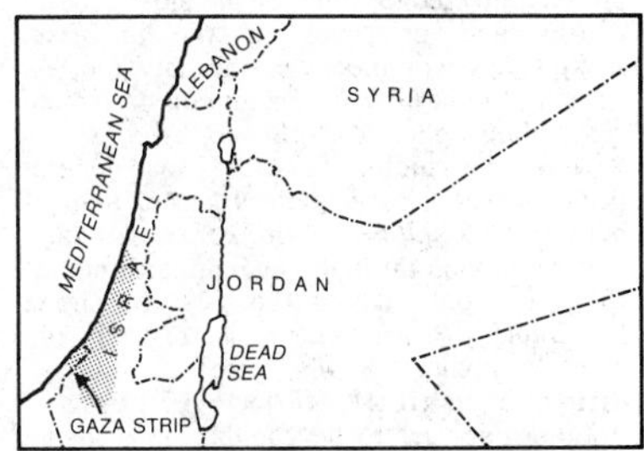

Philistia (def. 2)—The shaded area (on a modern map) shows Philistia about 700 B.C.

Phi lis ti a (fə lis′tē ə), *n.* 1 place where uncultured, commonplace people live. 2 land of the ancient Philistines.

Phil is tine (fil′ə stēn′, fə lis′tən), *n.* 1 (in the Bible) one of the warlike people in southwestern Palestine who fought the Israelites many times. 2 Also, **philistine.** person who is commonplace in ideas and tastes; one who is indifferent to or contemptuous of poetry, music, the fine arts, etc. —*adj.* 1 of the Philistines. 2 Also, **philistine.** lacking culture; commonplace.

Phil is tin ism or **phil is tin ism** (fil′ə stē niz′əm, fə lis′tə niz′əm), *n.* character or views of uncultured, commonplace persons.

phil o den dron (fil′ə den′drən), *n.* any of a genus of climbing evergreen arums with smooth, shiny leaves, native to tropical America and often grown as house plants. [< Greek < *philos* loving + *dendron* tree]

phil o log i cal (fil′ə loj′ə kəl), *adj.* having to do with philology. —**phil′o log′i cal ly,** *adv.*

phi lol o gist (fə lol′ə jist), *n.* an expert in philology.

phi lol o gy (fə lol′ə jē), *n.* 1 an older name for linguistics, especially comparative or historical linguistics. 2 the study of literary and other records. [< Greek *philologia* < *philos* loving + *logos* word, speech]

phil o mel (fil′ə mel), *n.* ARCHAIC. nightingale. [< Latin *philomela*]

philos., philosophy.

phi los o pher (fə los′ə fər), *n.* 1 student, teacher, or lover of philosophy. 2 author or founder of a system of philosophy. 3 person who is calm and reasonable under hard conditions, accepting life and making the best of it.

philosophers' stone, substance or preparation believed by alchemists to have the power to change baser metals into gold or silver.

phil o soph ic (fil′ə sof′ik), *adj.* philosophical.

phil o soph i cal (fil′ə sof′ə kəl), *adj.* 1 of philosophy or philosophers. 2 knowing much about philosophy. 3 devoted to philosophy. 4 wise; calm; reasonable. **—phil′o soph′i cal ly,** *adv.*

phi los o phize (fə los′ə fīz), *v.i.,* **-phized, -phiz ing.** think or reason as a philosopher does; try to understand and explain things: *philosophize about life and death.* **—phi los′o phiz′er,** *n.*

phi los o phy (fə los′ə fē), *n., pl.* **-phies.** 1 study of the truth or principles underlying all real knowledge; study of the most general causes and principles of the universe. 2 explanation or theory of the universe, especially the particular explanation or system of a philosopher: *the philosophy of Plato.* 3 system for guiding life. 4 the broad general principles of a particular subject or field of activity: *the philosophy of history.* 5 a calm and reasonable attitude; accepting things as they are and making the best of them. [< Greek *philosophia* love of wisdom < *philos* loving + *sophos* wise]

phil ter or **phil tre** (fil′tər), *n.* 1 drug or potion supposed to be capable of arousing sexual love. 2 drug or potion to produce some magical effect. [< Greek *philtron*]

phiz (fiz), *n.* SLANG. face; countenance. [short for *physiognomy*]

phle bi tis (fli bī′tis), *n.* inflammation of a vein. [< New Latin < Greek *phlebos* vein]

phle bot o mist (fli bot′ə mist), *n.* an expert in phlebotomy.

phle bot o my (fli bot′ə mē), *n., pl.* **-mies.** the opening of a vein to let blood; bleeding as a therapeutic device; venesection. [< Greek *phlebotomia* < *phlebos* vein + *-tomia* a cutting]

phlegm (flem), *n.* 1 the thick mucus discharged into the mouth and throat during a cold or other respiratory disease. 2 sluggish disposition or temperament; indifference. 3 coolness; calmness. [< Greek *phlegma* clammy humor (resulting from heat) < *phlegein* to burn]

phleg mat ic (fleg mat′ik), *adj.* 1 not easily aroused to feeling or action; sluggish; indifferent. 2 cool; calm: *He is phlegmatic; he never seems to get excited about anything.* **—phleg mat′i cal ly,** *adv.*

phleg mat i cal (fleg mat′ə kəl), *adj.* phlegmatic.

phlo em (flō′em), *n.* tissue in a vascular plant through which the sap containing dissolved food materials passes downward to the stems and roots; bast. [< German *Phloem* < Greek *phloos* bark]

phlo gis ton (flō jis′tən), *n.* a supposed element causing inflammability, once thought to exist in all things that burn. [< Greek < *phlegein* burn]

phlox (floks), *n.* 1 any of a genus of common garden plants with clusters of showy flowers in various colors. 2 the flower of any of these plants. [< Greek, a kind of plant, literally, flame < *phlegein* burn]

Phnom Penh (pə nôm′ pen′), capital of Cambodia, in the S part. 600,000. Also, **Pnompenh.**

-phobe, *combining form.* person who has fear, aversion, or hatred toward ___: *Anglophobe = a person who fears or hates England or the English.* [< French < Greek *phobos* fear]

pho bi a (fō′bē ə), *n.* a persistent, abnormal, or irrational fear of a certain thing or group of things. [< Greek *-phobia* < *phobos* fear]

pho co me li a (fo′kə mē′lē ə), *n.* a congenital absence or incomplete development of the arms or legs. [< Greek *phoke* seal + *melos* limb]

phoe be (fē′bē), *n.* any of various small flycatchers, especially one of eastern North America, having a grayish-brown back, a yellowish-white breast, and a low crest on the head. [imitative; spelling influenced by *Phoebe*]

Phoe be (fē′bē), *n.* 1 (in Greek myths) Artemis, the goddess of the moon. 2 the moon.

Phoe bus (fē′bəs), *n.* 1 (in Greek myths) Apollo, the god of the sun. 2 the sun.

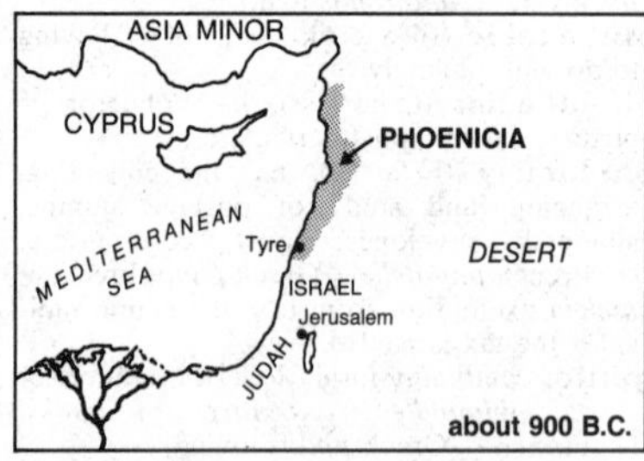

Phoe ni cia (fə nish′ə), *n.* ancient country on the Mediterranean Sea, in the region of Lebanon, W Syria, and N Israel. It was famous for its traders. Also, **Phenicia.**

Phoe ni cian (fə nish′ən), *adj.* of or having to do with Phoenicia, its people, or their language. —*n.* 1 native or inhabitant of Phoenicia. 2 the Semitic language of Phoenicia.

phoe nix (fē′niks), *n.* a mythical bird, the only one of its kind, said to live 500 or 600 years, to burn itself on a funeral pile, and to rise again from the ashes, fresh and beautiful, for another long life. Also, **phenix.** [Old English *fenix* < Latin *phoenix* < Greek *phoinix*]

Phoe nix (fē′niks), *n.* capital of Arizona, in the central part. 582,000.

phon (fon), *n.* unit for measuring the level of loudness of sound. [< Greek *phōnē* sound]

phon-, *combining form.* the form of **phono-** before vowels, as in *phonic.*

phon., phonetics.

pho nate (fō′nāt), *v.t., v.i.,* **-nat ed, -nat ing.** utter (speech sounds); sound vocally. **—pho na′tion,** *n.*

phone[1] (fōn), *n., v.t., v.i.,* **phoned, phon ing.** INFORMAL. telephone.

phone[2] (fōn), *n.* (in phonetics) a speech sound. [< Greek *phōnē* voice, sound]

pho neme (fō′nēm), *n.* (in linguistics) any one of a set of speech sounds by which the words of a language are distinguished one from another; the smallest significant unit of speech in a language. The words *cat* and *bat* are distinguished by their initial phonemes /k/ and /b/. A phoneme comprises several slightly different sounds (allophones) the differences between which are not meaningful. The *p* in *pit* and the *p* in *ship,* though differing slightly in pronunciation, belong to the one phoneme /p/. [< French *phonème* < Greek *phōnēma* a speech sound < *phōnein* to utter < *phōnē* voice, sound]

pho ne mic (fō nē′mik), *adj.* 1 of or having to do with phonemics: *phonemic analysis of speech sounds.* 2 having to do with or involving phonemes: *The difference between "p" and "b" is phonemic in English.* **—pho ne′mi cal ly,** *adv.*

pho ne mics (fō nē′miks), *n.* branch of linguistics dealing with phonemes.

pho net ic (fə net′ik), *adj.* 1 of or having to do with speech sounds: *phonetic laws.* 2 representing speech sounds; indicating pronunciation: *phonetic symbols, phonetic spelling.* 3 of or having to do with phonetics. [< Greek *phōnētikos,* ultimately < *phōnē* voice, sound] **—pho net′i cal ly,** *adv.*

phonetic alphabet, set of characters or symbols for transcribing speech sounds, in which each character or symbol represents one distinct sound.

pho ne ti cian (fō′nə tish′ən), *n.* an expert in phonetics.

pho net ics (fə net′iks), *n.* 1 *pl. in form, sing. in use.* science dealing with speech sounds and the art of pronunciation. 2 *pl. in form and use.* the speech sounds of any one language, dialect, etc.

pho ney (fō′nē), *adj.,* **-ni er, -ni est,** *n., pl.* **-neys.** INFORMAL. phony.

phon ic (fon′ik, fō′nik), *adj.* 1 of or having to do with sound. 2 of speech sounds; phonetic. 3 voiced.

phon ics (fon′iks, fō′niks), *n.* 1 *pl. in form and use.* simplified phonetics for teaching reading. 2 *pl. in form, sing. in use.* science of sound; acoustics.

phono-, *combining form.* sound; sounds: *Phonology = study of sounds.* Also, **phon-** before vowels. [< Greek *phōnē*]

pho no gram (fō′nə gram), *n.* character or symbol representing a single speech sound, syllable, or word.

pho no graph (fō′nə graf), *n.* instrument that reproduces the sounds transcribed on phonograph records; record player.

pho no graph ic (fō′nə graf′ik), *adj.* 1 of a phonograph. 2 of phonography. **—pho′no graph′i cal ly,** *adv.*

phonograph needle, needle (n. def. 8).

phonograph record, record (n. def. 4).

pho nog ra phy (fō nog′rə fē), *n.* writing or spelling according to pronunciation, especially in shorthand.

pho no log i cal (fō′nə loj′ə kəl), *adj.* of or having to do with phonology. **—pho′no log′i cal ly,** *adv.*

pho nol o gist (fō nol′ə jist), *n.* an expert in phonology.

pho nol o gy (fō nol′ə jē), *n., pl.* **-gies.** 1 system of sounds used in a language. 2 study of the sounds of a language, their history and changes.

pho ny (fō′nē), *adj.,* **-ni er, -ni est,** *n., pl.* **-nies.** INFORMAL. —*adj.* not genuine; counterfeit; fake. —*n.* fake; pretender. Also, **phoney.** [origin uncertain] **—pho′ni ly,** *adv.* **—pho′ni ness,** *n.*

hat, āge, fär; let, ēqual, tėrm;
it, īce; hot, ōpen, ôrder;
oil, out; cup, pu̇t, rüle;
ch, child; ng, long; sh, she;
th, thin; ᴛʜ, then; zh, measure;

ə represents *a* in about, *e* in taken, *i* in pencil, *o* in lemon, *u* in circus.

< = from, derived from, taken from.

phos gene (fos′jēn′), *n.* a colorless, poisonous liquid or gas with a suffocating odor, used in chemical warfare. *Formula:* $COCl_2$ [< Greek *phōs* light + *-genēs* born, produced]

phos phate (fos′fāt), *n.* 1 salt or ester of phosphoric acid. Bread contains phosphates. 2 fertilizer containing such salts. 3 drink of carbonated water flavored with fruit syrup, and containing a little phosphoric acid.

phos phat ic (fos fat′ik), *adj.* of or containing phosphoric acid or phosphates.

phos phide (fos′fīd, fos′fid), *n.* compound of phosphorus with a basic element or radical.

phos phite (fos′fīt), *n.* salt or ester of phosphorous acid.

phos phor (fos′fər), *n.* substance which gives off light when exposed to certain types of energy, such as ultraviolet rays or X rays, widely used in fluorescent lamps and television tubes.

Phos phor (fos′fər), *n.* the morning star; Venus (when appearing at or just before sunrise).

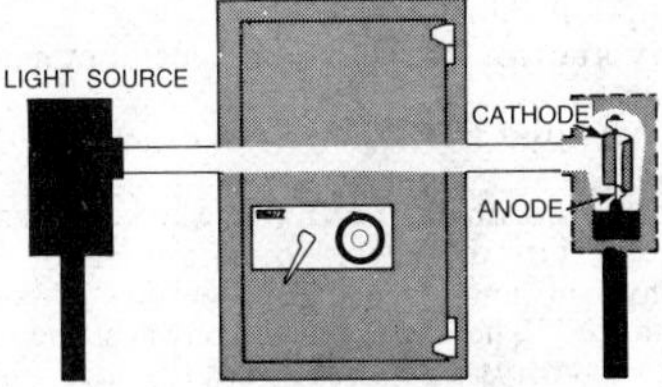

photoelectric cell in a burglar alarm. When light strikes the cathode of the photoelectric cell, it emits electrons which flow to the anode. Interrupting the light beam causes an interruption of this flow which triggers the alarm.

phosphor bronze, a hard, tough bronze containing less than one per cent of phosphorus, used especially in marine propellers, springs, fittings, etc.

phos pho resce (fos′fə res′), *v.i.,* **-resced, -resc ing.** be luminous without noticeable heat.

phos pho res cence (fos′fə res′ns), *n.* 1 act or process of giving out light without burning or by very slow burning without noticeable heat: *the phosphorescence of fireflies.* 2 light given out in this way. 3 (in physics) light given off by a substance as a result of the absorption of certain rays, as X rays or ultraviolet rays, and continuing for a period of time after the substance has ceased to be exposed to these rays.

phos pho res cent (fos′fə res′nt), *adj.* showing phosphorescence.

phos phor ic (fo sfôr′ik, fo sfor′ik), *adj.* having to do with or containing phosphorus, especially with a valence of five.

phosphoric acid, a colorless, odorless acid containing phosphorus, used in making fertilizers. *Formula:* H_3PO_4

phos phor ous (fos′fər əs, fo sfôr′əs, fo sfōr′əs), *adj.* having to do with or containing phosphorus, especially with a valence of three.

phosphorous acid, a colorless, unstable, crystalline acid. Its salts are phosphites. *Formula:* H_3PO_3

phos phor us (fos′fər əs), *n.* a nonmetallic element which exists in several allotropic forms. The two common forms are a yellow or white poisonous, waxy substance which burns slowly at ordinary temperatures and glows in the dark, and a reddish-brown powder, nonpoisonous, and less flammable. *Symbol:* P; *atomic number* 15. See pages 326 and 327 for table. [< Greek *phōsphoros* bringing light < *phōs* light + *pherein* bring]

pho to (fō′tō), *n., pl.* **-tos,** *v.t., v.i.* INFORMAL. photograph.

photo-, *combining form.* 1 light, as in *photochemical.* 2 photographic or photograph, as in *photoengraving.* [< Greek < *phōs, photos* light]

pho to cell (fō′tə sel′), *n.* photoelectric cell.

pho to chem i cal (fō′tō kem′ə kəl), *adj.* of or having to do with the chemical action of light.

pho to chem is try (fō′tō kem′ə strē), *n.* branch of chemistry dealing with the chemical action of light.

pho to con duc tion (fō′tō kən duk′shən), *n.* the ability of an electrical conductor to conduct electricity upon exposure to light.

pho to con duc tive (fō′tō kən duk′tiv), *adj.* of or having to do with photoconduction.

pho to cop y (fō′tō kop′ē), *n., pl.* **-cop ies,** *v.,* **-cop ied, -cop y ing.** —*n.* a photographic copy or reproduction of a document, print, etc. —*v.t.* produce a photocopy of.

pho to e lec tric (fō′tō i lek′trik), *adj.* having to do with the electricity or electrical effects produced by the action of light.

photoelectric cell, vacuum tube that varies the flow of electric current according to the amount of light reaching its sensitive element; electric eye; photocell. Variations or interruptions of the light can start machines to work that open doors, set off alarms, etc.

pho to e lec tron (fō′tō i lek′tron), *n.* electron emitted from a surface exposed to light.

pho to e mis sive (fō′tō i mis′iv), *adj.* emitting electrons when subjected to the action of light.

pho to en grav ing (fō′tō en grā′ving), *n.* 1 process by which plates to print from are produced with the aid of photography. 2 plate so produced. 3 picture printed from it.

photo finish, 1 (in racing) a finish so close that a photograph is required to decide the winner. 2 any contest decided by a narrow margin of victory.

pho to flash lamp (fō′tə flash′), (in photography) a flashbulb.

pho to flood lamp (fō′tə flud′), an electric lamp of high wattage that gives very bright, sustained light for taking photographs.

photog., 1 photographic. 2 photography.

pho to gen ic (fō′tə jen′ik), *adj.* 1 having characteristics that photograph very well, especially in motion pictures: *a photogenic face.* 2 phosphorescent, as certain bacteria. 3 produced or caused by light. **—pho′to-gen′i cal ly,** *adv.*

pho to gram me try (fō′tō gram′ə trē), *n.* art or science of making surveys or maps with the help of photographs, especially aerial photographs.

pho to graph (fō′tə graf), *n.* picture made with a camera by exposing film or plates to the action of light rays. —*v.t.* take a photograph of. —*v.i.* 1 take photographs. 2 look (clear, unnatural, etc.) in a photograph: *She does not photograph well.*

pho tog ra pher (fə tog′rə fər), *n.* 1 person who takes photographs. 2 person whose business is taking photographs.

pho to graph ic (fō′tə graf′ik), *adj.* 1 of or like photography: *photographic accuracy.* 2 used in or produced by photography: *photographic plates, a photographic record of a trip.* 3 reproducing images accurately; minutely accurate: *a photographic painting.* **—pho′to graph′i cal ly,** *adv.*

pho tog ra phy (fə tog′rə fē), *n.* process, art, or business of taking photographs.

pho to gra vure (fō′tə grə vyůr′, fō′tə-grā′vyůr), *n.* 1 photoengraving. 2 picture printed from a metal plate on which a photograph has been engraved.

pho to jour nal ism (fō′tō jėr′nl iz′əm), *n.* journalism which uses photographic rather than written material as the basis of a story.

pho tol y sis (fō tol′ə sis), *n.* chemical decomposition of a substance resulting from the action of light.

pho tom e ter (fō tom′ə tər), *n.* any of various instruments for measuring the intensity of light, light distribution, illumination, luminous flux, etc.

pho to met ric (fō′tə met′rik), *adj.* having to do with photometry or a photometer. **—pho′to met′ri cal ly,** *adv.*

pho tom e try (fō tom′ə trē), *n.* branch of physics dealing with measurements of the intensity of light, light distribution, illumination, luminous flux, etc.

pho to mi cro graph (fō′tō mī′krə graf), *n.* an enlarged photograph of a microscopic object, taken through a microscope; microphotograph; micrograph.

pho to mon tage (fō′tō mon täzh′, fō′tō-môn täzh′), *n.* 1 process of combining several photographs, or parts of them, into a single picture. 2 the resulting picture.

pho to mul ti pli er (fō′tō mul′tə plī′ər), *n.* vacuum tube having a series of supplementary electrodes between the cathode and the anode. When light strikes the photoemissive cathode a cascade of electrons is emitted and amplified at each supplementary electrode.

pho ton (fō′ton), *n.* a quantum of radiant energy, moving as a unit with the velocity of light. It is considered to be one of the elementary particles.

pho to-off set (fō′tō ôf′set, fō′tō of′set), *n.* process of printing in which a page of type, a picture, etc., is photographed and the image then transferred to a specially sensitized lithographic plate and printed by offset.

pho to per i od (fō′tō pir′ē əd), *n.* the length of time during which a plant or animal is exposed to light each day.

pho to per i od ic (fō′tō pir′ē od′ik), *adj.* of or having to do with a photoperiod or photoperiodism.

pho to per i od ism (fō′tō pir′ē ə diz′əm), *n.* the response of a plant or animal to the length of its daily exposure to light, especially as shown by changes in vital processes.

pho to play (fō′tə plā′), *n.* a motion-picture story or scenario.

pho to sen si tive (fō′tō sen′sə tiv), *adj.* readily stimulated to action by light or other radiant energy.

pho to sphere (fō′tə sfir), *n.* the visible, gaseous, and intensely bright layer surrounding the sun or other stars.

pho to stat (fō′tə stat), *n.* 1 photograph made with a special camera for making photocopies directly on specially prepared paper. 2 **Photostat,** trademark for a camera of this kind. —*v.t.* make a photostat of.

pho to stat ic (fō′tə stat′ik), *adj.* of, having to do with, or produced by a photostat.

pho to syn the sis (fō′tō sin′thə sis), *n.* 1 process by which plant cells make carbohydrates by combining carbon dioxide and water in the presence of chlorophyll and light, and release oxygen as a by-product. 2 process by which chemical compounds are synthesized by means of light or other forms of radiant energy.

pho to syn thet ic (fō′tō sin thet′ik), *adj.* of or having to do with photosynthesis. **—pho′to syn thet′i cal ly,** *adv.*

pho to te leg ra phy (fō′tō tə leg′rə fē), *n.* 1 telegraphy by means of light, as with a heliograph. 2 the electric transmission of facsimiles of photographs; telephotography.

pho to trop ic (fō′tō trop′ik), *adj.* 1 turning or bending in response to light: *Most plants are phototropic.* 2 sensitive to changes in amount of radiation: *phototropic glass.* **—pho′to trop′i cal ly,** *adv.*

pho tot ro pism (fō to′trə piz′əm), *n.* tendency of plants to turn in response to light.

pho to vol ta ic (fō′tō vol tā′ik), *adj.* generating an electric current when acted on by light or a similar form of radiant energy, as a photoelectric cell.

phras al (frā′zəl), *adj.* consisting of or like a phrase or phrases.

phrase (frāz), *n., v.,* **phrased, phras ing.** —*n.* 1 combination of words: *Speak in simple phrases so that we can understand you.* 2 expression often used: *"Call up" is the common phrase for "make a telephone call."* 3 a short, striking expression. EXAMPLES: A Fair Deal. A war to end wars. Liberty or death. 4 (in grammar) a group of words not containing a subject and predicate and functioning as a subject, object, verb, modifier, etc., within a sentence. 5 division of a piece of music, usually several measures in length, ending with a cadence. 6 manner or style of expression; diction; phraseology; language. —*v.t.* 1 express in a particular way: *She phrased her excuse politely.* 2 mark off or bring out the phrases of (a piece of music). [< Greek *phrasis* speech, way of speaking < *phrazein* to express, tell]

phra se ol o gy (frā′zē ol′ə jē), *n., pl.* **-gies.** selection and arrangement of words; particular way in which thoughts are expressed in language: *scientific phraseology.* See **diction** for synonym study.

phre net ic (fri net′ik), *adj.* frenetic.

phren ic (fren′ik), *adj.* (in anatomy) of or having to do with the diaphragm. [< Greek *phrēn* diaphragm]

phren o log i cal (fren′ə loj′ə kəl), *adj.* of or having to do with phrenology.

phre nol o gist (fri nol′ə jist), *n.* person who professes to tell a person's character from the shape of his skull.

phre nol o gy (fri nol′ə jē), *n.* 1 theory that the shape of the skull shows what sort of mind and character a person has. 2 practice of reading character from the shape of the skull. [< Greek *phren* mind + English *-logy*]

Phryg i a (frij′ē ə), *n.* ancient country in the central and NW part of Asia Minor. **—Phryg′i an,** *adj., n.*

phthal ic acid (thal′ik, fthal′ik), one of three isomeric acids formed from certain benzene derivatives, especially a colorless crystalline substance prepared from naphthalene and used in making dyes and various synthetics. *Formula:* $C_6H_4(COOH)_2$ [< *(na)phthal(ene)* + *-ic*]

phthis i cal (tiz′ə kəl), *adj.* having to do with, having the nature of, or affected by phthisis.

phthi sis (thī′sis), *n.* a wasting disease of the body or of some part of the body, especially tuberculosis of the lungs. [< Greek < *phthinein* waste away]

phy co my cete (fī′kō mī sēt′), *n.* any of a class of fungi whose members live as parasites or saprophytes and resemble algae. [< Greek *phykos* seaweed + *mykēs* fungus]

phy co my ce tous (fī′kō mī sē′təs), *adj.* of or belonging to the phycomycetes.

phy lac ter y (fə lak′tər ē), *n., pl.* **-ter ies.** 1 either of two small leather cases containing texts from the Jewish law, worn by Orthodox Jewish males during weekday morning prayers, to remind them to keep the law. One is strapped to the forehead, the other to the left arm. 2 reminder. 3 a charm worn as a protection; amulet. [< Greek *phylaktērion* safeguard, ultimately < *phylax* watchman]

phyl lo tax is (fil′ə tak′sis), *n.* the distribution or arrangement of leaves on a stem. [< Greek *phyllon* leaf + *taxis* arrangement]

phyl lo tax y (fil′ə tak′sē), *n.* phyllotaxis.

phyl lox er a (fil′ek sir′ə, fə lok′sər ə), *n.* plant louse that destroys grapevines. [< Greek *phyllon* leaf + *xēros* dry]

phy lo ge net ic (fī′lō jə net′ik), *adj.* of or having to do with phylogeny. **—phy′lo ge net′i cal ly,** *adv.*

phy lo gen ic (fī′lō jen′ik), *adj.* phylogenetic.

phy log e ny (fī loj′ə nē), *n., pl.* **-nies.** the origin and development of a species or higher grouping of animal or plant, or the history of its development. [< Greek *phylon* race + *-geneia* origin]

phy lum (fī′ləm), *n., pl.* **-la** (-lə). 1 (in zoology) a primary group of the animal or vegetable kingdom, ranking above a class. The animals in a phylum are thought to be related by descent from a common ancestral form. See **classification** for chart. 2 (in botany) division (def. 7). [< New Latin < Greek *phylon* race, stock]

phys., 1 physical. 2 physician. 3 physics.

phys ic (fiz′ik), *n., v.,* **-icked, -ick ing.** —*n.* 1 medicine, especially one that acts as a laxative. 2 ARCHAIC. art of healing; science and practice of medicine. —*v.t.* 1 give a laxative to. 2 give medicine to. 3 act like a medicine on; cure.

phys i cal (fiz′ə kəl), *adj.* 1 of the body; bodily: *physical exercise.* 2 of matter; material: *The tide is a physical force.* 3 according to the laws of nature; of or having to do with natural science: *It is a physical impossibility for the sun to rise in the west.* 4 of the science of physics. **—phys′i cal ly,** *adv.* [< Latin *physica* physic < Greek *physikē (epistēmē)* (knowledge) of nature < *physis* nature < *phyein* produce]

physical change, (in chemistry) a change in the size or form of a substance without any alteration in the composition of its molecules or without its producing or becoming a new substance.

physical chemistry, branch of chemistry that deals with the basic laws of the properties of substances as formulated by physics and their relations to chemical composition and changes.

physical education, instruction in how to exercise and take care of the body, especially as a course at a school or college.

physical geography, branch of geography that deals with the natural features of the earth's surface, such as landforms, climate, winds, and ocean currents; physiography.

physical science, 1 physics. 2 physics, chemistry, geology, astronomy, and other sciences dealing with inanimate matter.

physical therapy, treatment of diseases and defects by physical remedies, such as exercise and massage, rather than by drugs; physiotherapy.

phy si cian (fə zish′ən), *n.* doctor of medicine.

phys i cist (fiz′ə sist), *n.* an expert in physics.

phys i co chem i cal (fiz′ē kō kem′ə kəl), *adj.* 1 of or having to do with both the physical and chemical properties of substances. 2 having to do with physical chemistry. **—phys′i co chem′i cal ly,** *adv.*

phys ics (fiz′iks), *n.* science that deals with the properties and interrelationships of matter and energy, excluding chemical and biological change. Physics includes the study of mechanics, heat, light, sound, electricity, magnetism, and atomic energy.

physio-, *combining form.* physical, as in *physiology, physiography.* [< Greek *physis* nature]

phys i og nom ic (fiz′ē og nom′ik, fiz′ē ə-nom′ik), *adj.* of or having to do with physiognomy. **—phys′i og nom′i cal ly,** *adv.*

phys i og no my (fiz′ē og′nə mē, fiz′ē-on′ə mē), *n., pl.* **-mies.** 1 kind of features or type of face one has; one's face. 2 art of estimating character from the features of the face or the form of the body. 3 the general aspect or looks of a countryside, a situation, etc. [< Greek *physis* nature + *gnōmōn* judge < *gnōnai* recognize]

phys i og ra pher (fiz′ē og′rə fər), *n.* an expert in physiography.

phys i o graph ic (fiz′ē ə graf′ik), *adj.* having to do with physiography.

phys i og ra phy (fiz′ē og′rə fē), *n.* physical geography.

phys i o log i cal (fiz′ē ə loj′ə kəl), *adj.* 1 having to do with physiology: *Digestion is a physiological process.* 2 having to do with the normal or healthy functioning of an organism: *Food and sleep are physiological needs.* **—phys′i o log′i cal ly,** *adv.*

phys i ol o gist (fiz′ē ol′ə jist), *n.* an expert in physiology.

phys i ol o gy (fiz′ē ol′ə jē), *n.* 1 branch of biology dealing with the normal functions of living things or their parts: *animal physiology, plant physiology.* 2 all the functions and activities of a living thing or of one of its parts.

phys i o ther a py (fiz′ē ō ther′ə pē), *n.* physical therapy.

phy sique (fə zēk′), *n.* bodily structure,

organization, or development; physical appearance: *a strong physique.* [< French, physical]

-phyte, *combining form.* growth or plant, as in *epiphyte.* [< Greek *phyton*]

phyto-, *combining form.* plant or plants, as in *phytotoxic.* [< Greek *phyton*]

phy to chrome (fī′tō krōm), *n.* a bluish, light-sensitive pigment in plants which absorbs red or infrared rays and acts as an enzyme in controlling growth and other photoperiodic responses.

phy to ge og ra phy (fī′tō jē og′rə fē), *n.* science that deals with the geographical distribution of plants.

phy to plank ton (fī′tō plangk′tən), *n.* the part of the plankton of any body of water which consists of plants, usually algae.

phy to tox ic (fī′tō tok′sik), *adj.* toxic or injurious to plants.

pi¹ (pī), *n.* 1 the 16th letter of the Greek alphabet (Π, π). 2 this letter, used as a symbol for the ratio of the circumference of any circle to its diameter. 3 the ratio itself, equal to 3.141592+.

pi² (pī), *n.* 1 printing types all mixed up. 2 any confused mixture. —*v.t.* mix up (type). Also, **pie.** [origin uncertain]

P.I., Philippine Islands.

pi a ma ter (pī′ə mā′tər), the delicate, vascular membrane which is the innermost of three membranes enveloping the brain and spinal cord. [< Medieval Latin, thin or tender mother]

pi a nis si mo (pē′ə nis′ə mō), in music: —*adj.* very soft. —*adv.* very softly. [< Italian, superlative of *piano* soft]

pi an ist (pē an′ist, pē′ə nist), *n.* person who plays the piano.

pi an o¹ (pē an′ō), *n., pl.* **-an os.** a large percussion instrument whose tones come from many wires. The wires are sounded by felt-covered hammers that are worked by striking keys on a keyboard. [short for *pianoforte*]

pi an o² (pē an′ō, pē ä′nō), in music: —*adj.* soft. —*adv.* softly. [< Italian < Latin *planus* plain, flat. Doublet of PLAIN¹, PLAN, PLANE².]

pi an o for te (pē an′ə fôr′tē, pē an′ə-fôr′tē; pē an′ə fôrt, pē an′ə fōrt), *n.* piano¹. [< Italian < *piano* soft + *forte* loud]

pi as ter or **pi as tre** (pē as′tər), *n.* 1 unit of money in Egypt, Lebanon, Sudan and Syria, any of various coins worth 1/100 of a pound. 2 the former Spanish silver peso. [< French *piastre* < Italian *piastra* < Latin *emplastra* plaster]

piazza (def. 1)

pi az za (pē az′ə *for 1, 3;* pē ät′sə, pē az′ə *for 2*), *n.* 1 a large porch along one or more sides of a house; veranda. 2 an open public square in Italian towns. 3 BRITISH. an exterior covered walk with columns. [< Italian < Latin *platea* courtyard, broad street. Doublet of PLACE, PLAZA.]

pi broch (pē′brok), *n.* kind of musical piece performed on the bagpipe, usually of either a warlike or sad character. [< Scottish Gaelic *piobaireachd* pipe music]

pi ca (pī′kə), *n.* 1 size of type, 12 point.

This sentence is in pica.

2 this size used as a measure; about 1/6 inch. 3 size of typewriter type, larger than elite, having 10 characters to the inch.

pic a dor (pik′ə dôr), *n.* one of the horsemen who open a bullfight by irritating the bull with pricks of their lances. [< Spanish < *picar* pierce]

Pi car die (pē kȧr dē′; *Anglicized* pik′ər dē), *n.* French name of **Picardy.**

Pic ar dy (pik′ər dē), *n.* region and former province in N France. See **Normandy** for map.

pic a resque (pik′ə resk′), *adj.* dealing with rogues and their questionable adventures: *a picaresque novel.* [< Spanish *picaresco* < *pícaro* rogue]

pic a roon (pik′ə rün′), *n.* 1 rogue, thief, or brigand. 2 pirate. 3 a piratical or privateering ship. —*v.i.* act or cruise as a brigand or pirate. [< Spanish *picarón* < *pícaro* rogue]

Pi cas so (pi kä′sō), *n.* **Pablo,** 1881-1973, Spanish painter and sculptor.

pic a yune (pik′ə yün′), *adj.* small; petty; mean; paltry. —*n.* 1 an insignificant person or thing; trifle. 2 any coin of small value. 3 the Spanish half real, formerly used in Florida, Louisiana, etc. [< Creole *picaillon,* a coin worth 5 cents]

Pic ca dil ly (pik′ə dil′ē), *n.* one of the main business streets of London.

pic ca lil li (pik′ə lil′ē), *n.* relish made of chopped pickles, onions, tomatoes, etc., with hot spices. [origin uncertain]

pic co lo (pik′ə lō), *n., pl.* **-los.** a small, shrill flute, an octave higher in pitch than an ordinary flute. [< Italian < *(flauto) piccolo* small (flute)]

pick¹ (pik), *v.t.* 1 choose out of a number or quantity; select: *pick the right words. I picked a winning horse at the races.* 2 pull away with the fingers, beak, etc.; gather; pluck: *pick flowers.* 3 pierce, dig into the surface of, or break up with something pointed: *pick a road, pick ground.* 4 use something pointed to remove things from: *pick one's teeth.* 5 open with a pointed instrument, wire, etc., or by manipulation of the mechanism: *pick a lock, pick a safe.* 6 steal the contents of: *pick a pocket.* 7 prepare for use by removing feathers, waste parts, etc.: *pick a chicken.* 8 pull apart: *pick rags.* 9 U.S. pluck at with fingers or a plectrum: *play a banjo by picking its strings.* 10 seek and find occasion for; look for and hope to find: *pick a fight. He picks flaws in every offer I make.* 11 take up (seeds, small pieces of food, etc.) with the bill or teeth, as a bird or squirrel. 12 eat (food) in small pieces, slowly, or without appetite. —*v.i.* 1 use or work with a pick, pickax, etc. 2 eat with small bites slowly, or without appetite. 3 make a careful choice or selection. 4 gather fruit, etc. 5 pilfer.

pick at, a pull on with the fingers, etc. **b** eat only a little at a time. **c** INFORMAL. find fault with; nag.

pick off, a shoot one at a time. **b** (in baseball) catch (a runner) off base and throw him out.

pick on, a INFORMAL. find fault with; nag at. **b** INFORMAL. annoy; tease. **c** choose; select: *Why did he pick on you first?*

pick out, a choose with care; select. **b** distinguish from the surroundings. **c** select the notes of (a tune) one by one, especially laboriously, on a keyboard, etc., and so play it.

pick over, look over carefully in making a selection.

pick up, a take up: *pick up a stone.* **b** get by chance: *pick up a bargain.* **c** learn without being taught: *She picks up games easily.* **d** take into a vehicle or ship: *pick up passengers.* **e** INFORMAL. recover or improve: *He seemed to pick up quickly after his fever went down.* **f** take along with one: *pick up a coat at the cleaner's.* **g** find again; regain: *Here we picked up the trail.* **h** go faster; increase in speed. **i** succeed in seeing, hearing, etc.: *pick up a radio program from Paris.* **j** INFORMAL. meet casually (especially a person of the opposite sex) and take along with one. **k** U.S. tidy up; put in order: *pick up a room.*

—*n.* 1 act of choosing; choice; selection: *You may have the first pick this time.* 2 person or thing selected from among others: *That book is my first pick.* 3 the best or most desirable part: *We got a high price for the pick of our peaches.* 4 the total amount of a crop gathered at one time. 5 plectrum. [Middle English *picken,* perhaps < Scandinavian (Old Icelandic) *pikka*]

pick² (pik), *n.* 1 pickax. 2 any of various pointed or pronged tools or instruments. Ice is broken into pieces with a pick. [Middle English *pik,* variant of *pike²*]

pick a back (pik′ə bak′), *adv., adj.* piggyback.

pickax

pick ax or **pick axe** (pik′aks′), *n.* tool with a heavy metal bar pointed at one or both ends and attached through the center to a wooden handle, used for breaking up or loosening dirt, rocks, etc.; pick.

picked (pikt), *adj.* 1 specially selected for merit; choice: *a crew of picked men.* 2 with waste parts removed and ready for use.

pick er (pik′ər), *n.* 1 person who gathers, picks, or collects. 2 tool for picking anything.

pick er el (pik′ər əl), *n., pl.* **-els** or **-el.** 1 any of certain small species of pike of North America. 2 pike perch. [diminutive of *pike³*]

pick er el weed (pik′ər əl wēd′), *n.* any of a genus of North American herbs with spikes of blue flowers and heart-shaped leaves, growing in shallow, usually quiet, water.

pick et (pik′it), *n.* 1 a pointed stake or peg placed upright to make a fence, to tie a horse to, etc. 2 a small body of troops, or a single man, posted at some place to watch for the enemy and guard against surprise attacks. 3 person stationed by a labor union near a factory, store, etc., where there is a strike, to

hat, āge, fär; let, ēqual, tėrm;
it, īce; hot, ōpen, ôrder;
oil, out; cup, pu̇t, rüle;
ch, child; ng, long; sh, she;
th, thin; ᴛʜ, then; zh, measure;
ə represents *a* in about, *e* in taken, *i* in pencil, *o* in lemon, *u* in circus.
< = from, derived from, taken from.

try to prevent employees from working or customers from buying. 4 person who takes part in a public demonstration or boycott to support a cause. —*v.t.* 1 enclose with pickets; fence. 2 tie to a picket: *picket a horse.* 3 post as a picket; guard with or as if with a picket. 4 station pickets at or near: *picket a factory.* —*v.i.* act as a picket. [< French *piquet,* diminutive of *pic* a pick] —**pick/et er,** *n.*

picket fence

picket fence, fence made of pickets.

Pick ett (pik/it), *n.* **George Edward,** 1825-1875, Confederate general in the Civil War.

pick ings (pik/ingz), *n.pl.* 1 amount picked. 2 things left over; scraps. 3 profits; returns.

pick le (pik/əl), *n., v.,* **-led, -ling.** —*n.* 1 salt water, vinegar, or other liquid in which meats, fish, vegetables, etc., can be preserved. 2 cucumber preserved in pickle. 3 any other vegetable preserved in pickle. 4 INFORMAL. trouble; difficulty. 5 an acid bath or other chemical preparation for removing oxides or other corrosion from metals. —*v.t.* 1 preserve in pickle: *pickle beets.* 2 clean with an acid bath or other chemical preparation. [< Middle Dutch *pekel*]

pick lock (pik/lok/), *n.* 1 person who picks locks; thief; burglar. 2 instrument for picking locks.

pick pock et (pik/pok/it), *n.* person who steals from people's pockets.

pick up (pik/up/), *n.* 1 a picking up: *the daily pickup of mail.* 2 INFORMAL. a getting better; improvement: *a pickup in business.* 3 acceleration; going faster; increase in speed. 4 INFORMAL. a casual meeting or acquaintance, especially with a member of the opposite sex. 5 a catching of a ball after it has bounced on the ground. 6 device that transforms into electrical current the vibrations set up in a phonograph needle by variations in the grooves of a record. 7 reception of sounds or images in radio or television and their conversion into electric waves for broadcasting. 8 apparatus for such reception or the place where it occurs. 9 a small, light truck with an open back, used for light hauling.

pic nic (pik/nik), *n., v.,* **-nicked, -nick ing.** —*n.* 1 a pleasure trip with a meal in the open air. 2 any outdoor meal. 3 SLANG. a pleasant time or experience; very easy job. —*v.i.* 1 go on a picnic. 2 eat in picnic style. [< French *piquenique*]

pic nick er (pik/ni kər), *n.* person who picnics.

pi co far ad (pī/kō far/əd), *n.* one trillionth of a farad. [< Spanish *pico* tiny amount, bit + English *farad*]

pi cot (pē/kō), *n.* one of a number of fancy loops in embroidery, tatting, etc., or along the edge of lace, ribbon, etc. —*v.t., v.i.* trim with picots. [< French, diminutive of *pic* a pick]

pic ric acid (pik/rik), a very poisonous, yellow, crystalline acid used in explosives, in dyeing, and in medicine. Formula: $C_6H_2(NO_2)_3OH$ [< Greek *pikros* bitter]

Pict (pikt), *n.* member of an ancient people of uncertain ethnic origin formerly living in Great Britain, especially Scotland. They disappeared as a distinct group about A.D. 900.

Pict ish (pik/tish), *adj.* of or having to do with the Picts.

pic to graph (pik/tə graf), *n.* 1 picture used as a sign or symbol, especially in a system of picture writing. 2 writing or record in such symbols. 3 diagram or chart presenting statistical data by using pictures of different colors, sizes, or numbers.

pic to graph ic (pik/tə graf/ik), *adj.* of pictographs.

pic tog ra phy (pik tog/rə fē), *n.* the use of pictographs; picture writing.

pic to ri al (pik tôr/ē əl, pik tōr/ē əl), *adj.* 1 having to do with pictures; expressed in pictures. 2 making a picture for the mind; vivid. 3 illustrated by pictures: *a pictorial history.* 4 having to do with painters or painting. [< Latin *pictorius* < *pictor* painter] —**pic to/ri al ly,** *adv.*

pic ture (pik/chər), *n., v.,* **-tured, -tur ing.** —*n.* 1 a drawing, painting, portrait, or photograph, or a print of any of these. 2 a scene. 3 something beautiful. 4 an exact likeness; image: *He is the picture of his father.* 5 an example; embodiment: *She was the picture of happiness.* 6 a mental image; visualized conception; idea: *have a clear picture of the problem.* 7 a vivid description or account. 8 a motion picture. 9 a visible image of something formed by physical means, as by a lens: *a picture on a television screen.* 10 state of affairs; condition; situation: *the employment picture.* —*v.t.* 1 draw, paint, etc.; make into a picture. 2 form a picture of in the mind; imagine: *He was older than she had pictured him.* 3 depict in words; describe graphically and vividly. [< Latin *pictura* < *pingere* to paint]

picture hat, a woman's wide-brimmed hat, originally often black and trimmed with ostrich feathers.

pic tur esque (pik/chə resk/), *adj.* 1 quaint or interesting enough to be used as the subject of a picture: *a picturesque old mill.* 2 making a picture for the mind; vivid: *picturesque language.* —**pic/tur esque/ly,** *adv.* —**pic/tur esque/ness,** *n.*

picture tube, kinescope.

picture window, a large window designed to frame a wide view of the outside.

picture writing, 1 the recording of events or expressing of ideas by pictures that represent things and actions. 2 the pictures so used.

pid dle (pid/l), *v.i.,* **-dled, -dling.** do anything in a trifling or ineffective way. [origin uncertain] —**pid/dler,** *n.*

pid dling (pid/ling), *adj.* trifling; petty.

pidg in (pij/ən), *n.* 1 pidgin English. 2 any language spoken with a reduced grammar and vocabulary as a trade or communications jargon.

pidgin English, one of several forms of English, with simplified grammatical structure and often a mixed vocabulary, used in western Africa, Australia, Melanesia, and China as a language of trade or communication between natives and foreigners. [*pidgin,* Chinese alteration of *business*]

pie[1] (pī), *n.* 1 fruit, meat, vegetables, etc., enclosed partially or wholly by a crust of pastry and baked: *apple pie, chicken pie.* 2 a round layer cake with a filling of cream, custard, jelly, etc. [Middle English *pye*] —**pie/like/,** *adj.*

pie[2] (pī), *n.* magpie. [< Old French < Latin *pica*]

pie[3] (pī), *n., v.t.,* **pied, pie ing.** pi[2].

pictograph (def. 1)—six pictographs

pie bald (pī/bôld/), *adj.* spotted in two colors, especially black and white: *a piebald horse.* —*n.* a piebald animal, especially a horse. [< *pie*[2] + *bald*]

piece (pēs), *n., adj., v.,* **pieced, piec ing.** —*n.* 1 one of the parts into which a thing is divided or broken; bit: *a piece of wood. The cup broke into pieces.* 2 a small quantity; limited part; portion: *a piece of land, a piece of bread.* See **part** for synonym study. 3 a single thing of a set or class: *a piece of furniture, a piece of luggage.* 4 a single composition in an art: *a new piece at a theater, a piece of music.* 5 a coin: *A nickel is a five-cent piece.* 6 an example or instance of an action, function, quality, etc.: *a piece of nonsense, a piece of luck, a piece of news.* 7 a more or less definite quantity in which various industrial products are made, sold, or used: *cloth sold only by the piece.* 8 the amount of work done: *paid by the piece.* 9 gun or cannon. 10 any of the disks, cubes, figures, stones, etc., used in playing checkers, chess, and other games; man. 11 **go to pieces,** a break into fragments; break up. b break down physically or mentally; collapse. 12 **of a piece,** of the same kind or quality; in keeping; uniform. 13 **piece of one's mind,** INFORMAL. a scolding.
—*adj.* 1 composed of pieces. 2 having to do with piecework.
—*v.t.* 1 make or repair by adding or joining pieces; patch: *piece a quilt.* 2 join the pieces of; put together in one piece: *piece together a story.*
[< Old French < Popular Latin *pettia,* probably < Celtic] —**piec/er,** *n.*

pièce de ré sis tance (pyes də rā zēs täns/), FRENCH. 1 the chief dish of a meal. 2 the main or outstanding item in any collection.

piece goods, cloth cut to measure and sold by the yard from bolts.

piece meal (pēs/mēl/), *adv.* 1 piece by piece; a little at a time: *work done piecemeal.* 2 piece from piece; to pieces; into fragments. —*adj.* done piece by piece; gradual.

piece of eight, an old Spanish peso, worth 8 reals, used during the Spanish colonization of America.

piece work (pēs/wėrk/), *n.* work paid for by the amount done, not by the time it takes.

piece work er (pēs/wėr/kər), *n.* person who does piecework.

pie chart, graph in the form of a circle divided into sectors that resemble pieces of a pie, drawn to show the percentages into which any total sum is divided.

pie crust (pī/krust/), *n.* pastry used for the bottom or top of a pie.

pied (pīd), *adj.* 1 having patches of two or more colors; parti-colored. 2 wearing a costume of two or more colors. [< *pie*[2]]

pied-à-terre (pyā tä ter/), *n., pl.* ***pieds-à-terre*** (pyā tä ter/). FRENCH. 1 a temporary lodging. 2 foothold. 3 (literally) foot on the ground.

pied mont (pēd′mont), *n.* district lying along or near the foot of a mountain range. *—adj.* lying along or near the foot of a mountain range: *a piedmont glacier.* [< *Piedmont,* Italy]

Pied mont (pēd′mont), *n.* 1 plateau in the E United States between the Appalachian Mountains and the low land along the Atlantic coast. The Piedmont extends over parts of New Jersey, Pennsylvania, New York, Delaware, Maryland, Virginia, North Carolina, South Carolina, Georgia, and Alabama. 2 region in NW Italy.

pie plant (pī′plant′), *n.* U.S. rhubarb.

pier (pir), *n.* 1 structure supported on columns extending into the water, used as a walk or a landing place for ships. 2 breakwater. 3 one of the solid supports on which the arches of a bridge rest. 4 any solid support, especially of masonry. 5 the solid part of a wall between windows, doors, etc. [< Medieval Latin *pera*]

pierce (pirs), *v.,* **pierced, pierc ing.** *—v.t.* 1 make a hole in; bore into or through: *A nail pierced the tire of our car.* 2 go into; go through: *A tunnel pierces the mountain.* See **penetrate** for synonym study. 3 force a way through or into: *A sharp cry pierced the air.* 4 make a way through with the eye or mind: *pierce a disguise, pierce a mystery.* 5 affect sharply with some feeling: *a heart pierced with grief.* *—v.i.* force or make a way into or through something; penetrate. [< Old French *percier*]

Pierce (pirs), *n.* **Franklin,** 1804-1869, the 14th president of the United States, from 1853 to 1857.

pierc ing (pir′sing), *adj.* that pierces; penetrating; sharp; keen. **—pierc′ing ly,** *adv.*

pier glass, a tall mirror, originally designed to fill the space between two windows.

Pi er i an (pī ir′ē ən), *adj.* 1 of or having to do with the Muses or with poetry. 2 of or having to do with Pieria, a district in ancient Thessaly, the fabled home of the Muses.

Pierre (pir), *n.* capital of South Dakota, in the central part. 10,000.

Pi er rot (pē′ər ō; *French* pye rō′), *n.* clown who is a frequent character in French pantomimes. He has his face whitened and wears loose white pantaloons and usually a white jacket with big buttons. [< French, diminutive of *Pierre* Peter]

pie tà (pyā tä′), *n.* a representation of the Virgin Mary holding the body of the dead Christ on her lap or in her arms. [< Italian, pity]

pi e tism (pī′ə tiz′əm), *n.* 1 deep piety. 2 exaggerated or pretended piety. 3 **Pietism,** movement for reviving piety in the Lutheran Church beginning in the late 1600's in Germany.

pi e tist (pī′ə tist), *n.* 1 person conspicuous for pietism. 2 **Pietist,** adherent of Pietism.

pi e tis tic (pī′ə tis′tik), *adj.* conspicuous for pietism; very pious. **—pi′e tis′ti cal ly,** *adv.*

pi e ty (pī′ə tē), *n., pl.* **-ties.** 1 a being pious; reverence for God; devotion to religion; godliness; devoutness. 2 dutiful regard for one's parents. 3 a pious act, remark, belief, etc. [< Old French *piete* < Latin *pietatem* < *pius* pious. Doublet of PITY.]

pi e zo e lec tric (pī ē′zō i lek′trik), *adj.* of or having to do with piezoelectricity. **—pi e′zo e lec′tri cal ly,** *adv.*

pi e zo e lec tric i ty (pī ē′zō i lek′tris′ə tē, pī ē′zō ē′lek tris′ə tē), *n.* electricity or electric polarity induced by pressure on certain crystals, such as quartz. [< Greek *piezein* to press + English *electricity*]

pif fle (pif′əl), *n., v.,* **-fled, -fling.** INFORMAL. *—n.* silly talk or behavior; nonsense. *—v.i.* talk or act in a foolish, trifling, or ineffective manner. [probably imitative]

pig (pig), *n., v.,* **pigged, pig ging.** *—n.* 1 any of a family of four-footed mammals with stout, heavy bodies, cloven hoofs, and broad snouts; hog; swine. Domesticated pigs are raised for their meat. 2 any similar animal. 3 a young pig. 4 pork. 5 INFORMAL. person who seems or acts like a pig; one who is greedy, dirty, dull, sullen, or stubborn. 6 an oblong mass of metal, especially of iron or lead, obtained from the smelting furnace and poured into a mold while molten. *—v.i., v.t.* 1 bring forth pigs; farrow. 2 Also, **pig it,** herd, lodge, or sleep together like pigs. [Middle English *pigge*] **—pig′like′,** *adj.*

pig eon (pij′ən), *n.* 1 any of a family of birds with thick bodies, short tails, and usually short legs, comprising numerous species found throughout the world and including doves and many varieties of domestic pigeons. 2 SLANG. person who is easily tricked. [< Old French *pijon* < Late Latin *pipionem* squab < Latin *pipiare* to cheep]

pigeon breast, deformity of the chest due to a sharply protruded breastbone, often associated with rickets.

pigeon hawk, a small North American falcon; merlin.

pig eon-heart ed (pij′ən här′tid), *adj.* very timid or cowardly; chicken-hearted.

pig eon hole (pij′ən hōl′), *n., v.,* **-holed, -hol ing.** *—n.* 1 a small place built, usually as one of a series, for a pigeon to nest in. 2 one of a set of boxlike compartments for holding papers and other articles in a desk, a cabinet, etc. *—v.t.* 1 put in a pigeonhole; put away. 2 classify and lay aside in memory where one can refer to it. 3 put aside, especially with the idea of dismissing, forgetting, or neglecting.

pig eon-toed (pij′ən tōd′), *adj.* having the toes or feet turned inward.

pig ger y (pig′ər ē), *n., pl.* **-ger ies.** place where pigs are kept or raised.

pig gish (pig′ish), *adj.* of, having to do with, or like a pig; greedy; filthy. **—pig′gish ly,** *adv.* **—pig′gish ness,** *n.*

pig gy (pig′ē), *n., pl.* **-gies.** a little pig.

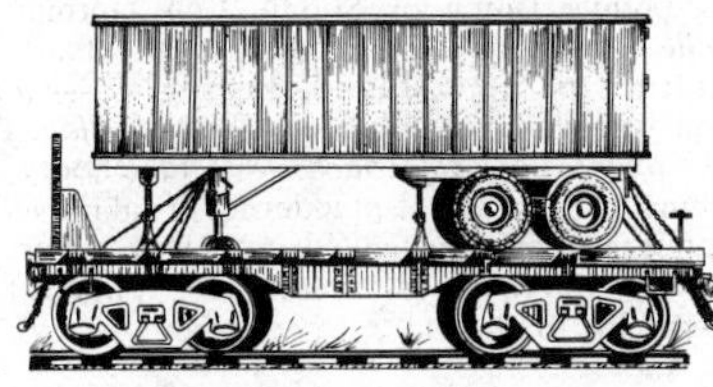

piggyback (def. 2)
trailer carried piggyback

pig gy back (pig′ē bak′), *adv., adj.* 1 on the back or shoulders. 2 on railroad flatcars: *Loaded truck trailers are often taken piggyback across the country.* Also, **pickaback.**

piggy bank, 1 a small container in the shape of a pig, with a slot in the top for coins. 2 any coin bank.

pig-head ed (pig′hed′id), *adj.* stupidly obstinate or stubborn.

pig iron, crude iron as it first comes from the blast furnace or smelter, used to make steel, cast iron, and wrought iron. Formerly, it was usually cast into oblong masses called pigs.

hat, āge, fär; let, ēqual, tėrm;
it, īce; hot, ōpen, ôrder;
oil, out; cup, pu̇t, rüle;
ch, child; ng, long; sh, she;
th, thin; ᴛʜ, then; zh, measure;
ə represents *a* in about, *e* in taken, *i* in pencil, *o* in lemon, *u* in circus.
< = from, derived from, taken from.

pig ment (pig′mənt), *n.* 1 a coloring matter, especially a powder or some easily pulverized dry substance that constitutes a paint or dye when mixed with oil, water, or some other liquid. 2 the natural substance occurring in and coloring the tissues of an animal or plant. *—v.t.* color with or as if with pigment. [< Latin *pigmentum* < *pingere* to paint. Doublet of PIMENTO.]

pig men tar y (pig′mən ter′ē), *adj.* of or containing pigment.

pig men ta tion (pig′mən tā′shən), *n.* deposit of pigment in the tissue of a living animal or plant, causing coloration or discoloration.

pig my (pig′mē), *n., pl.* **-mies,** *adj.* pygmy.

pig nut (pig′nut′), *n.* 1 the thin-shelled, oily, somewhat bitter nut of any of several species of hickory grown in North America. 2 any of the trees that bear these nuts.

pig pen (pig′pen′), *n.* 1 pen where pigs are kept. 2 a filthy place.

pig skin (pig′skin′), *n.* 1 skin of a pig. 2 leather made from it. 3 INFORMAL. **a** a football. **b** saddle.

pig sty (pig′stī′), *n., pl.* **-sties.** pigpen.

pig tail (pig′tāl′), *n.* 1 braid of hair hanging from the back of the head. 2 tobacco in a thin, twisted roll or rope.

pig tailed (pig′tāld′), *adj.* wearing a pigtail or pigtails.

pig weed (pig′wēd′), *n.* 1 any of a genus of goosefoots, especially a coarse weed with narrow, notched leaves sometimes used as a potherb and in salad. 2 any of certain weedy amaranths.

pike[1] (pīk), *n.* a long wooden shaft with a sharp-pointed metal head; spear. Foot soldiers used to carry pikes. [< Middle French *pique* < *piquer* pierce < *pic* pick]

pike[2] (pīk), *n.* a sharp point, pointed tip, or spike, such as the head of an arrow or spear. [Old English *pīc* pick]

pike[3] (pīk), *n., pl.* **pikes** or **pike.** 1 any of a family of large, slender, predatory, freshwater fishes of the Northern Hemisphere, having spiny fins and a long, pointed head, such as the muskellunge and pickerel. 2 any of certain similar fishes, such as the pike perch. [apparently short for *pikefish* < *pike[2]* + *fish*]

pike[4] (pīk), *n.* turnpike.

pike man (pīk′mən), *n., pl.* **-men.** soldier armed with a pike.

pike perch, any of several large varieties of North American perches that resemble a pike, especially the walleyed pike.

pik er (pī′kər), *n.* SLANG. 1 person who does things in a small or cheap way. 2 a stingy or niggardly person. [origin uncertain]

Pikes Peak (pīks), mountain in the Rocky Mountains, in central Colorado. 14,108 ft.

pike staff (pīk′staf′), *n., pl.* **-staves**

(-stāvz′). 1 staff or shaft of a pike or spear. 2 staff or walking stick with a metal point or spike at the lower end like an alpenstock.

pi laf or **pi laff** (pi läf′), *n.* an Oriental dish consisting of rice or cracked wheat boiled with mutton, fowl, or fish, and flavored with spices, raisins, etc. Also, **pilau, pilaw.** [< Persian *pilāw*]

pi las ter (pə las′tər), *n.* a shallow, rectangular pillar, forming part of a wall from which it projects somewhat, and serving as a support or decoration. [< Italian *pilastro* < Latin *pila* pillar]

Pi late (pī′lət), *n.* **Pontius,** Roman governor who ruled over Judea in Palestine from A.D. 26 to 36? During his rule Christ was crucified.

pi lau or **pi law** (pi lô′), *n.* pilaf.

pil chard (pil′chərd), *n.* 1 a small European marine food fish of the same family as the herring, but smaller and rounder. A sardine is a young pilchard. 2 any of certain similar fishes, as a variety found off the California coast. [origin uncertain]

pile[1] (pīl), *n., v.,* **piled, pil ing.** —*n.* 1 a number of things lying one upon another in a more or less orderly way; stack: *a pile of firewood.* 2 mass like a hill or mound: *a pile of dirt, a pile of snow.* 3 a large structure or mass of buildings. 4 Also, **piles,** *pl.* INFORMAL. a large amount: *I have a pile of work to do.* 5 INFORMAL. a very large amount of money; fortune: *make one's pile.* 6 heap of wood on which a dead body or sacrifice is burned. 7 (in nuclear physics) reactor. 8 in electricity: **a** a series of plates of different metals, arranged alternately with cloth or paper wet with acid between them, for producing an electric current. **b** any similar apparatus for producing an electric current; battery.
—*v.t.* 1 make into a pile; heap up; stack: *Pile the blankets in the corner.* 2 amass; accumulate: *pile up a fortune.* 3 cover with large amounts: *pile a plate with food.* —*v.i.* 1 gather or rise in piles: *Snow piled against the fence.* 2 go in a confused, rushing crowd: *pile out into the street.*
[< Middle French < Latin *pila* pillar] **—pil′er,** *n.*

pile[2] (pīl), *n., v.,* **piled, pil ing.** —*n.* a large, heavy beam or post of timber, steel, or concrete, driven or set upright into the earth, often under water, to help support a bridge, wharf, building, etc. —*v.t.* furnish, strengthen, or support with piles; drive piles into. [Old English *pīl* stake < Latin *pilum* javelin]

pile[3] (pīl), *n.* 1 a soft, thick layer of projecting threads on the surface of certain fabrics, as velvet or plush, and on various types of carpet. 2 a soft, fine hair or down. [< Latin *pilus* hair]

pi le ate (pī′lē it, pī′lē āt; pil′ē it, pil′ē āt), *adj.* 1 having a pileus. 2 having a crest.

pi le at ed (pī′lē ā′tid, pil′ē ā′tid), *adj.* pileate.

piled (pīld), *adj.* having a pile, as velvet and similar fabrics.

pile driver, machine for driving down piles or stakes, usually a tall framework in which a heavy weight is raised and then allowed to fall upon the pile.

piles (pīlz), *n.pl.* hemorrhoids. [Middle English *pyles*]

pile up (pīl′up′), *n.* 1 a piling up; accumulation. 2 a massive collision.

pi le us (pī′lē əs, pil′ē əs), *n., pl.* **pi le i** (pī′lē ī, pil′ē ī). the broad umbrellalike fruiting structure forming the top of certain fungi, such as mushrooms; cap. [< Latin, skullcap]

pil fer (pil′fər), *v.i., v.t.* steal in small quantities; commit petty theft. See **steal** for synonym study. [< Old French *pelfrer* rob < *pelfre* booty] **—pil′fer er,** *n.*

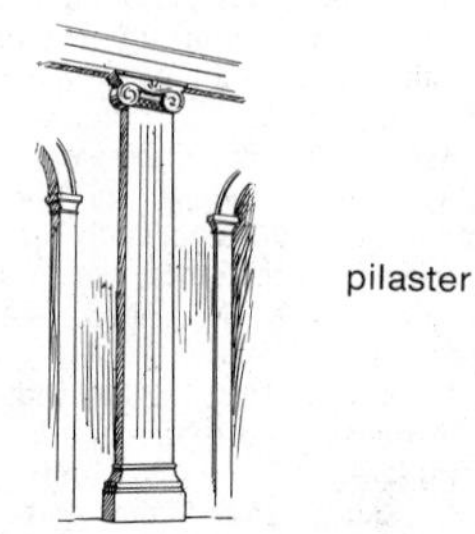
pilaster

pil fer age (pil′fər ij), *n.* act or practice of pilfering; petty theft.

pil grim (pil′grəm), *n.* 1 person who goes on a journey to a sacred or holy place, especially a distant shrine, as an act of religious devotion. 2 person on a journey; traveler; wanderer. 3 **Pilgrim,** one of the English Puritan settlers who founded the first permanent colony in New England, at Plymouth in 1620. [< Anglo-French (unrecorded) *pelegrim,* variant of Old French *pelerin* < Latin *peregrinus* foreigner < *per-* outside + *ager (Romanus)* the (Roman) territory. Doublet of PEREGRINE.]

pil grim age (pil′grə mij), *n.* 1 a pilgrim's journey; journey to some sacred place as an act of religious devotion. 2 a long journey.

Pilgrim's Progress, The, an allegorical story by John Bunyan telling of the difficulties and blessings of a Christian life.

pil ing (pī′ling), *n.* 1 piles or heavy beams driven into the ground, etc. 2 structure made of piles.

pill (pil), *n.* 1 medicine made up into a small pellet, tablet, or capsule to be swallowed whole. 2 **the pill,** any oral contraceptive taken by women. 3 a very small ball or mass of anything; pellet. 4 something disagreeable that has to be endured. 5 SLANG. an unpleasant, disagreeable, or boring person. [< Middle Dutch or Middle Low German *pille* < Latin *pilula,* diminutive of *pila* ball]

pil lage (pil′ij), *v.,* **-laged, -lag ing,** *n.* —*v.t.* rob with violence; plunder: *Pirates pillaged the towns along the coast.* —*v.i.* take booty; plunder. —*n.* act of plundering or taking as spoil; plunder, especially as practiced in war. [< Old French < *piller* to plunder] **—pil′lag er,** *n.*

pillar (def. 1)—pillars of a Doric temple

pil lar (pil′ər), *n.* 1 a slender, upright structure; column. Pillars are usually made of stone, wood, or metal and used as supports or ornaments for a building. Sometimes a pillar stands alone as a monument. 2 anything slender and upright like a pillar. 3 an important support or supporter: *a pillar of society, a pillar of the church.* 4 **from pillar to post,** from one thing or place to another without any definite purpose. [< Old French *piler,* ultimately < Latin *pila* pillar, pile[1]]

pil lared (pil′ərd), *adj.* 1 having pillars. 2 formed into pillars.

Pillars of Hercules, two high points of land at the E end of the Strait of Gibraltar, one on either side of the strait. The one on the European side is the Rock of Gibraltar; the one on the African side is Jebel Musa.

pill box (pil′boks′), *n.* 1 a small box, usually shallow and often round, for holding pills. 2 a small, low fortress with thick concrete walls and roof, having machine guns, antitank weapons, etc. 3 a woman's brimless hat of felt, straw, etc., fashioned like a shallow cylinder.

pil lion (pil′yən), *n.* 1 pad or cushion attached behind a saddle for a person to sit on. 2 seat behind the ordinary saddle of a motorcycle, on which a second person may ride. —*adv.* on a pillion: *ride pillion on a motorcycle.* [< Scottish Gaelic *pillin,* diminutive of *pell* cushion < Latin *pellis* skin]

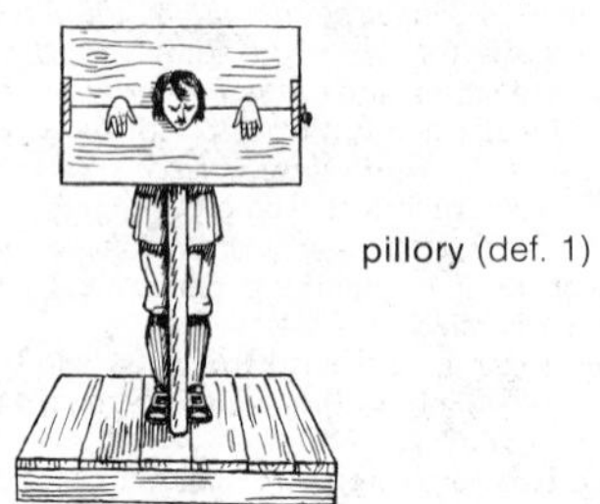
pillory (def. 1)

pil lor y (pil′ər ē), *n., pl.* **-lor ies,** *v.,* **-lor ied, -lor y ing.** —*n.* 1 frame of wood with holes through which a person's head and hands were put formerly in a public place as punishment for an offense. 2 any means of exposing to public ridicule, contempt, or abuse. —*v.t.* 1 put in the pillory. 2 expose to public ridicule, contempt, or abuse. [< Old French *pellori*]

pil low (pil′ō), *n.* bag or case filled with feathers, down, foam rubber, or some other soft material, usually used to support the head when resting or sleeping. —*v.t.* 1 rest on or as if on a pillow. 2 be a pillow for. —*v.i.* rest on or as if on a pillow. [Old English *pyle, pylu* < Latin *pulvinus*]

pil low case (pil′ō kās′), *n.* a cotton or linen cover pulled over a pillow.

pil low slip (pil′ō slip′), *n.* pillowcase.

pi lose (pī′lōs), *adj.* covered with soft hair; hairy. [< Latin *pilosus* < *pilus* hair]

pi los i ty (pī los′ə tē), *n.* hairiness.

pi lot (pī′lət), *n.* 1 person who steers a ship or boat; helmsman. 2 person trained and licensed to steer ships in or out of a harbor or through dangerous waters. 3 person who operates the controls of an aircraft in flight, especially one qualified and licensed to do this. 4 guide; leader. 5 device in a machine, motor, etc., that controls or activates a larger and more complex part. 6 U.S. the cowcatcher of a locomotive, streetcar, etc. —*v.t.* 1 act as the pilot of; steer or navigate: *pilot an airplane.* 2 guide; lead: *The manager piloted us through the big factory.* —*adj.* 1 that serves as a guide: *a pilot star.* 2 that serves as a model, sample, or trial version: *a pilot study, a pilot film for a new television series.* 3 that controls or activates the operation of a larger and more complex part: *a pilot switch.*

[< Middle French *pilote* < Italian *pilota*] **—pi′lot less,** *adj.*

pi lot age (pī′lə tij), *n.* 1 act or practice of piloting. 2 a pilot's art or duties. 3 fee paid for a pilot's service.

pilot balloon, a small balloon sent aloft to indicate the direction and speed of the wind to observers on the ground.

pilot biscuit or **pilot bread,** ship biscuit; hardtack.

pilot burner, pilot light.

pilot fish, a small fish, bluish with dark vertical bars, found in warm seas, often accompanying sharks.

pi lot house (pī′lət hous′), *n., pl.* **-hous es** (-hou′ziz). an enclosed place on the upper deck of a ship, sheltering the steering wheel and pilot; wheelhouse.

pilot lamp, a small electric light on a machine, appliance, etc., that lights up when the power is turned on or burns continuously to show the location of a switch, etc.

pilot light, 1 a small flame kept burning continuously, used to light the main burner of a gas stove, gas water heater, etc., whenever desired. 2 pilot lamp.

Pil sud ski (pil süt′skē), *n.* **Józef,** 1867-1935, Polish general and statesman.

Pilt down Man (pilt′doun′), an alleged prehistoric man identified from bones found at Piltdown, Sussex, England, in 1911, but proved in 1953 to be a hoax.

pi men to (pə men′tō), *n., pl.* **-tos.** 1 a fleshy, red variety of sweet pepper, used as a vegetable, relish, and stuffing for green olives; pimiento. 2 allspice. 3 the tropical American tree of the myrtle family which bears berries from which allspice is made. [< Spanish *pimiento* capsicum < Medieval Latin *pigmentum* spice < Latin, pigment. Doublet of PIGMENT.]

pi meson, meson having a mass from 264 to 273 times that of an electron; pion.

pi mien to (pi myen′tō), *n., pl.* **-tos.** pimento (def. 1). [< Spanish]

pimp (pimp), *n., v.i.* pander. [origin uncertain]

pim per nel (pim′pər nel), *n.* 1 any of a genus of small herbs of the same family as the primrose, with bright scarlet, purple, white, or blue flowers that close when cloudy or rainy weather approaches. 2 the flower of any of these plants. [< Old French *pimprenele* < Medieval Latin *pimpinella,* ultimately < Latin *pepinem* melon]

pim ple (pim′pəl), *n.* a small, inflamed swelling of the skin with or without pus; papule or pustule. [Middle English] **—pim′ple like′,** *adj.*

pim pled (pim′pəld), *adj.* having pimples.

pim ply (pim′plē), *adj.,* **-pli er, -pli est.** pimpled.

pin (pin), *n., v.,* **pinned, pin ning.** *—n.* 1 a short, slender piece of wire with a point at one end and a head at the other, for fastening things together. 2 any of various similar fastenings, such as a hairpin or safety pin. 3 badge with a pin or clasp, usually concealed at the back, to fasten it to the clothing: *She wore her class pin.* 4 brooch. 5 peg made of wood or metal, used to fasten things or parts together, hold something, hang things on, etc. 6 belaying pin. 7 peg in a stringed musical instrument around which the string is fastened at one end, and by turning which it is tuned. 8 one of a set of bottle-shaped wooden objects to be knocked down by a ball in bowling. 9 (in golf) a stick with a numbered flag at the top, placed in a hole to mark it. 10 something small or worthless: *not worth a pin, not to care a pin.* 11 **pins,** *pl.* INFORMAL. legs. 12 **on pins and needles,** very anxious or uneasy.

—v.t. 1 fasten with a pin or pins; put a pin through. 2 fasten or attach firmly to or on; tack; fasten as if with pins. 3 hold fast in one position: *When the tree fell, it pinned his shoulder to the ground.* 4 **pin down, a** hold or bind to an undertaking or pledge. **b** fix firmly; determine with accuracy; establish. 5 **pin on,** fix (blame, responsibility, etc.) on: *pin a crime on someone.*

[Old English *pinn* peg] **—pin′like′,** *adj.*

pin a fore (pin′ə fôr′, pin′ə fōr′), *n.* 1 a child's apron that covers most of the dress. 2 a light dress without sleeves. [< *pin,* verb + *afore*]

pi ña ta (pē nyä′tä), *n.* pot filled with candy, fruit, etc., hung at Christmas time in Mexico and other Latin-American countries above the heads of children who are blindfolded and given chances to break the pot to obtain its contents. [< Spanish]

pin ball (pin′bôl′), *n.* game played on a slanted board in which a ball is propelled by a spring so that it rolls up a groove, then down the board, striking bumpers, pins, or pegs, or rolling into numbered compartments or through alleys to score points.

pinball machine, a gambling device used for playing pinball.

pince-nez (pans′nā′, pins′nā′), *n., pl.* **pince-nez** (pans′nāz′, pins′nāz′). eyeglasses kept in place by a spring that clips onto the bridge of the nose. [< French, pinch-nose]

pincers (def. 1)

pin cers (pin′sərz), *n. pl. or sing.* 1 tool for gripping and holding tight, made like scissors but with jaws instead of blades. 2 Also, **pincer,** *sing.* organ or pair of organs resembling this tool, as the chela of a crab, lobster, etc. 3 a military operation in which the enemy is surrounded and crushed by the meeting of columns driven on each side of him. Also, **pinchers.** [Middle English *pynceours,* apparently < Old French *pincier* to pinch]

pinch (pinch), *v.t.* 1 squeeze between the thumb and forefinger, or with the teeth or claws, or with any instrument having two jaws or parts between which something may be grasped. 2 press so as to hurt; squeeze painfully: *These shoes pinch my feet.* 3 cause sharp discomfort or distress to, as cold, hunger, or want does. 4 cause to shrink or become thin: *a face pinched by hunger.* 5 limit closely; stint: *be pinched for time.* 6 SLANG. **a** arrest. **b** steal. *—v.i.* 1 exert a squeezing pressure or force: *Where does that shoe pinch?* 2 cause discomfort, distress, etc. 3 be sparing or stingy. 4 (of a vein or deposit of ore, etc.) become narrower or smaller; give out altogether.

—n. 1 act of pinching; a squeeze between two hard edges. 2 a sharp pressure that hurts; squeeze: *the pinch of tight shoes.* 3 sharp discomfort or distress: *the pinch of poverty.* 4 time or occasion of special need; emergency: *I will help you in a pinch.* 5 as much as can be taken up with the tip of the finger and thumb: *a pinch of salt.* 6 SLANG. **a** an arrest. **b** a stealing.

[< Old North French *pinchier,* variant of Old French *pincier*] **—pinch′er,** *n.*

hat, āge, fär; let, ēqual, tėrm;
it, īce; hot, ōpen, ôrder;
oil, out; cup, pu̇t, rüle;
ch, child; ng, long; sh, she;
th, thin; ᴛʜ, then; zh, measure;

ə represents *a* in about, *e* in taken, *i* in pencil, *o* in lemon, *u* in circus.

< = from, derived from, taken from.

pinch bar, crowbar or lever with a projection that serves as a fulcrum, used for moving heavy objects or loosening coal.

pinch beck (pinch′bek), *n.* 1 alloy of zinc and copper, used in imitation of gold in cheap jewelry, etc. 2 something not genuine; imitation. *—adj.* 1 made of pinchbeck. 2 not genuine; sham; spurious. [< Christopher *Pinchbeck,* about 1670-1732, English watchmaker]

pinch effect, (in physics) the constriction of plasma by the magnetic field of an electric current, used in controlling thermonuclear fusion.

pinch ers (pin′chərz), *n. pl. or sing.* pincers.

pinch-hit (pinch′hit′), *v.i.,* **-hit, -hit ting.** 1 (in baseball) bat for another player, especially when a hit is badly needed. 2 take another's place in an emergency. **—pinch hitter.**

pin curl, curl of hair kept in place by a hairpin or clip.

pin cush ion (pin′ku̇sh′ən), *n.* a small cushion to stick pins in until they are needed.

Pin dar (pin′dər), *n.* 522?-443? B.C., Greek lyric poet, famous for the eloquence and grandeur of his poetic style.

Pin dar ic (pin dar′ik), *adj.* of, having to do with, or in the style of Pindar.

Pin dus Mountains (pin′dəs), mountain chain in central Greece and SE Albania. Highest peak, 7665 ft.

pine[1] (pīn), *n.* 1 any of a genus of evergreen trees of the pine family that have woody cones, and clusters of needle-shaped leaves that grow out from temporary scalelike leaves. Pines are valuable for timber, turpentine, resin, tar, etc. 2 any of various similar trees which bear cones. 3 the wood of any of these trees. [Old English *pīn* < Latin *pinus*]

pine[2] (pīn), *v.i.,* **pined, pin ing.** 1 long eagerly; yearn: *pine for home.* 2 waste away with pain, hunger, grief, or desire: *pine with homesickness.* [Old English *pīnian* suffer < *pīn* torture, punishment < Latin *poena* penalty]

pin e al (pin′ē əl), *adj.* 1 resembling a pine cone in shape. 2 having to do with the pineal body.

pineal body or **pineal gland,** a small, somewhat conical structure of unknown function, present in the brain of all vertebrates having a cranium. It has been thought to be a vestigial sense organ or a ductless gland.

pine ap ple (pī′nap′əl), *n.* 1 a large, edible, juicy fruit somewhat like a large pine cone in appearance, developed from a conical spike of flowers and surmounted by a crown of small leaves. 2 the plant that it grows on, widely cultivated in tropical regions, with a short stem and slender, stiff leaves edged with spines.

pine family, a large group of coniferous, mostly evergreen trees and shrubs that have needle-shaped leaves and resinous sap, including the pine, fir, spruce, hemlock, and larch.

pine needle, the very slender leaf of a pine tree.

pine tar, tar obtained by destructive distillation of pine wood, used in making certain soaps and paints and in medicine for the treatment of certain skin diseases.

pine y (pī′nē), *adj.,* **pin i er, pin i est.** piny.

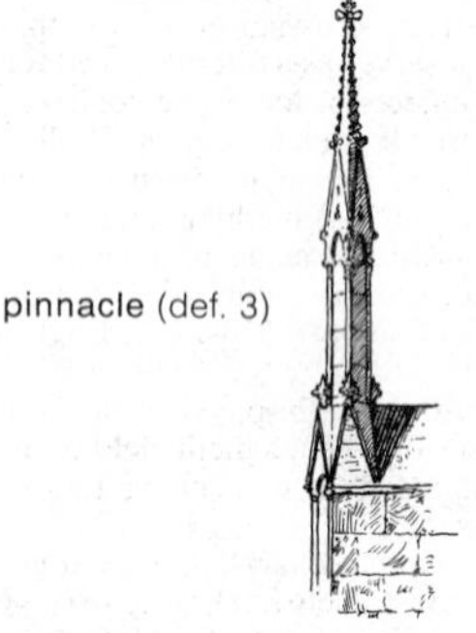

pinnacle (def. 3)

pin feath er (pin′feᴛʜ′ər), *n.* an undeveloped feather, especially one just breaking through the skin, that looks like a small stub.

ping (ping), *n.* sound like that of a rifle bullet whistling through the air or striking an object. —*v.i.* make such a sound; produce a ping. [imitative]

Ping-Pong (ping′pong′, ping′pông′), *n.* trademark for table tennis.

pin head (pin′hed′), *n.* 1 the head of a pin. 2 something very small or worthless. 3 SLANG. person of little intelligence; nitwit.

pin head ed (pin′hed′id), *adj.* SLANG. having little intelligence; stupid.

pin hole (pin′hōl′), *n.* 1 hole made by or as if by a pin. 2 hole for a pin or peg to go in.

pin ion¹ (pin′yən), *n.* 1 the last joint of a bird's wing. 2 wing. 3 any one of the stiff flying feathers of the wing; quill. —*v.t.* 1 cut off or tie the pinions of (a bird) to prevent flying. 2 bind; bind the arms of; bind (to something): *pinion a man's arms.* [< Middle French *pignon* < Popular Latin *pinnionem* < Latin *penna* feather and *pinna* wing]

pin ion² (pin′yən), *n.* 1 a small gear with teeth that fit into those of a larger gear or rack. 2 a spindle, arbor, or axle having teeth that engage with the teeth of a wheel. [< French *pignon*]

pink¹ (pingk), *n.* 1 color obtained by mixing red with white; a light or pale red, often with a slight purple tinge. 2 the highest degree or condition; height: *in the pink of health.* 3 any of a family of herbs widely grown for their showy, spicy-smelling flowers of various colors, mostly white, pink, and red, such as the carnation. 4 flower of any of these plants. 5 a scarlet coat worn by fox hunters. 6 Also, **Pink.** INFORMAL. person with moderately radical political opinions. —*adj.* 1 having the color pink; light-red or pale-red, often with a slight purple tinge. 2 INFORMAL. moderately radical. [origin uncertain] —**pink′ly,** *adv.* —**pink′ness,** *n.*

pink² (pingk), *v.t.* 1 prick or pierce with a sword, spear, or dagger. 2 cut the edge of (cloth) in small scallops or notches. 3 ornament (cloth, leather, etc.) with small, round holes. [Middle English *pynken*]

pink eye (pingk′ī′), *n.* an acute, very contagious form of conjunctivitis.

pink ie (ping′kē), *n.* the smallest finger. Also, **pinky.** [probably < Dutch *pink* little finger]

pinking shears, shears for pinking cloth.

pink ish (ping′kish), *adj.* somewhat pink.

pink y (ping′kē), *n., pl.* **pink ies.** pinkie.

pin money, 1 allowance of money made by a man to his wife for her own use. 2 a small amount of money used to buy extra things for one's own use.

pin na (pin′ə), *n., pl.* **pin nae** (pin′ē), **pin nas.** 1 feather, wing, or winglike part. 2 fin; flipper. 3 auricle of the ear; external ear. 4 one of the primary divisions of a pinnate leaf; leaflet. [< Latin]

pin nace (pin′is), *n.* 1 a ship's boat. 2 any light sailing vessel. [< Middle French *pinace*]

pin na cle (pin′ə kəl), *n.* 1 a high peak or point of rock. 2 the highest point: *at the pinnacle of one's fame.* 3 a slender turret or spire. [< Old French *pinacle* < Latin *pinnaculum,* diminutive of *pinna* wing, point]

pin nate (pin′āt, pin′it), *adj.* 1 like a feather. 2 (of a leaf) having a series of leaflets on each side of a stalk, the leaflets being usually opposite, sometimes alternate. See **leaf** for picture. Also, **pennate.** [< Latin *pinna* feather] —**pin′nate ly,** *adv.*

pi noch le or **pi noc le** (pē′nuk′əl, pē′nok′əl), *n.* 1 game played with a double deck of all cards from the nine to the ace, totaling 48. Points are scored according to the value of certain combinations of cards. 2 combination of the jack of diamonds and the queen of spades in this game. [origin uncertain]

piñ on (pin′yən, pē′nyōn), *n.* 1 any of various low pines, especially of the southern Rocky Mountain region, producing large, edible nutlike seeds. 2 its seed. [< Spanish]

pin point (pin′point′), *n.* the point of a pin. —*v.t.* aim at accurately; determine precisely: *pinpoint a target.* —*adj.* extremely accurate or precise: *pinpoint bombing.*

pin prick (pin′prik′), *n.* 1 a minute puncture such as that made by the point of a pin. 2 a petty annoyance; minute irritation.

Pin spot ter (pin′spot′ər), *n.* trademark for a machine that automatically sets up the pins in a bowling alley, removes downed pins, and returns the ball to the bowler.

pin stripe (pin′strīp′), *n.* 1 a fine stripe. 2 garment made of cloth having fine stripes.

pin striped (pin′strīpt′), *adj.* having pinstripes; marked with fine stripes.

pint (pīnt), *n.* 1 unit of measure equal to $^1/_2$ quart; 2 cups; 16 ounces. See **measure** for table. 2 container holding a pint. [< Old French *pinte*]

pin tail (pin′tāl′), *n.* any of various birds that have long feathers in the center of the tail, such as certain ducks and grouse.

Pin ter (pin′tər), *n.* **Harold,** born 1930, English playwright.

pin tle (pin′tl), *n.* pin or bolt, especially one upon which something turns, as in a hinge. [Old English *pintel*]

pin to (pin′tō), *adj., n., pl.* **-tos.** —*adj.* spotted in two or more colors; pied. —*n.* a pinto horse. [< Spanish, painted, ultimately < Popular Latin *pinctus* < Latin *pictus*]

pin up (pin′up′), *n.* 1 picture of a very attractive or famous person, pinned up on a wall. 2 person in such a picture. —*adj.* designed for hanging on a wall.

pin wheel (pin′hwēl′), *n.* 1 toy made of a paper wheel fastened to a stick by a pin so that it revolves in the wind. 2 kind of firework that revolves when lighted.

pin worm (pin′wėrm′), *n.* a small, threadlike, nematode worm infesting the large intestine, colon, and rectum, especially of children.

pin y (pī′nē), *adj.,* **pin i er, pin i est.** 1 abounding in or covered with pine trees: *piny mountains.* 2 having to do with or suggesting pine trees: *a piny odor.* Also, **piney.**

pi on (pī′on), *n.* pi meson.

pi o neer (pī′ə nir′), *n.* 1 person who settles in a part of the country that has not been occupied before except by primitive tribes. 2 person who goes first, or does something first, and so prepares a way for others. 3 one of a group of soldiers in a unit, especially of military engineers, who make roads, build bridges, dig trenches, etc. —*v.t.* 1 prepare, clear, or open up (a way, road, etc.). 2 prepare the way for. —*v.i.* act as pioneer; open or prepare the way as a pioneer. —*adj.* that goes ahead so that others may follow; exploratory: *pioneer research in nuclear physics.* [< Middle French *pionnier* < *peon* foot soldier < Medieval Latin *pedonem* < Latin *pedem* foot]

pi ous (pī′əs), *adj.* 1 active in worship or prayer; religious. See synonym study below. 2 done under pretense of religion or of serving a good cause: *a pious fraud.* 3 sacred rather than secular. [< Latin *pius*] —**pi′ous ly,** *adv.* —**pi′ous ness,** *n.*

Syn. 1 **Pious, devout** mean religious. **Pious** emphasizes careful observance of religious duties and practices: *She is a pious woman who goes to church every morning.* **Devout** emphasizes devotion and sincerity in carrying out religious practices: *He is a charitable, humble, and devout Christian.*

pip¹ (pip), *n.* 1 the seed of a fleshy fruit, as an apple or orange. 2 SLANG. person or thing that is very attractive, admirable, or extraordinary. [apparently short for *pippin*]

pip² (pip), *n.* 1 a contagious disease of poultry and other birds, characterized by the secretion of thick mucus in the mouth and throat and sometimes by white scale on the tongue. 2 the scale itself. 3 INFORMAL. a slight illness. [apparently < Middle Dutch *pippe* < Popular Latin *pippita* < Latin *pituita* phlegm]

pip³ (pip), *n.* 1 one of the spots or symbols on playing cards, dominoes, or dice. 2 the individual rhizome of various plants, especially the lily of the valley. 3 one of the diamond-shaped segments of a pineapple. 4 a luminous spot or irregularity on a radar screen. [origin uncertain]

pip⁴ (pip), *v.,* **pipped, pip ping,** *n.* —*v.i.* peep; chirp. —*v.t.* (of a young bird) break through (the shell) when hatching. —*n.* a brief, high-pitched sound, as in radio transmission. [probably variant of *peep*]

pi pal (pē′pəl), *n.* bo tree. [< Sanskrit *pippala*]

pipe (pīp), *n., v.,* **piped, pip ing.** —*n.* 1 tube through which a liquid or gas can flow. 2 tube with a bowl of clay, wood, or other material at one end, for smoking tobacco, opium, etc. 3 the quantity of tobacco, opium, etc., a pipe

will hold. 4 a musical wind instrument consisting of a single tube of reed, straw, etc., or especially wood, into which a player blows, as a flute, oboe, or clarinet. 5 **pipes,** *pl.* **a** set of musical tubes: *the pipes of Pan.* **b** bagpipe. 6 one of the wooden or metal tubes in an organ. 7 a shrill sound, voice, or song: *the pipe of a lark.* 8 a boatswain's whistle. 9 the signal or call made by blowing it. 10 cask, varying in size, for wine, etc. 11 as much as such a cask holds, now usually reckoned as four barrels or 126 (wine) gallons. 12 any of various tubular or cylindrical objects, contrivances, or parts.
—*v.t.* 1 convey (water, gas, oil, etc.) through or by means of a pipe or pipes. 2 furnish or supply with pipes: *Our street is being piped for gas.* 3 play (a tune, music) on a pipe. 4 utter in a loud, shrill or clear voice, as a bird, a singer, or a speaker. 5 give orders, signals, calls, etc., to with a boatswain's whistle. 6 lead or summon by the sound of a pipe: *Pipe all hands on deck.* 7 trim or ornament (a dress, etc.) with piping. 8 transmit (a recording, television program, conversation, etc.) by means of radiofrequency, telephone, or other types of transmission lines. —*v.i.* 1 play on a pipe. 2 speak or talk loudly and shrilly. 3 give orders, signals, etc., with or as with a boatswain's whistle.
pipe down, SLANG. be quiet; shut up.
pipe up, **a** begin to play or sing (music); strike up. **b** speak.
[Old English *pīpe* < Latin *pipare* to chirp] **—pipe′like′,** *adj.*

pipe dream, INFORMAL. an impractical, groundless, or fantastic idea, scheme, etc.

pipe fish (pīp′fish′), *n., pl.* **-fish es** or **-fish.** any of a family of marine fish commonly having a long snout and a long, slender, angular body covered with armorlike plates.

pipe ful (pīp′fu̇l), *n., pl.* **-fuls.** quantity of tobacco sufficient to fill the bowl of a pipe.

pipe line (pīp′līn′), *n.* 1 line of pipes for carrying oil, natural gas, water, etc. 2 source of information.

pipe organ, organ with pipes of different lengths sounded by air blown through them.

pip er (pī′pər), *n.* 1 person who plays on a pipe or bagpipe. 2 **pay the piper,** pay for one's pleasure; bear the consequences.

pipette
Uncovering the top of the tube allows the liquid to flow from the other end.

pi pette (pī pet′, pi pet′), *n.* a slender pipe or tube for transferring or measuring small quantities of a liquid or gas, especially a small glass tube into which liquid is sucked and retained by closing the top end. [< French, diminutive of *pipe* pipe]

pip ing (pī′ping), *n.* 1 a shrill sound: *the piping of frogs in the spring.* 2 pipes: *a house equipped with copper piping.* 3 material for pipes; a pipe: *three feet of piping.* 4 the music of pipes. 5 a narrow band of material, sometimes containing a cord, used for trimming along edges and seams, as of dresses, etc. —*adj.* 1 sounding shrilly; shrill: *a high, piping voice.* 2 so as to hiss; very hot; boiling: *The coffee is piping hot.*

pip it (pip′it), *n.* any of various small, brownish birds, similar to the lark, that sings while flying; titlark. [imitative]

pip kin (pip′kən), *n.* a small earthen or metal pot. [perhaps < *pipe* + *-kin*]

pip pin (pip′ən), *n.* 1 any of several kinds of apple that are yellowish-green in color and have firm flesh of excellent flavor. 2 SLANG. someone or something especially attractive. [< Old French *pepin*]

pip sis se wa (pip sis′ə wə), *n.* any of a genus of low, creeping evergreen plants whose leaves are used in medicine as a tonic, astringent, etc. [< Algonquian]

pip squeak (pip′skwēk′), *n.* SLANG. person who is small or unimportant; insignificant person.

pi quan cy (pē′kən sē), *n.* piquant quality.

pi quant (pē′kənt), *adj.* 1 stimulating to the mind, interest, etc.: *a piquant bit of news, a piquant face.* 2 pleasantly sharp; stimulating to the taste: *a piquant sauce.* [< French, pricking, stinging] **—pi′quant ly,** *adv.*

pique (pēk), *n., v.,* **piqued, pi quing.** —*n.* a feeling of anger at being slighted; wounded pride: *In a pique, she left the party.* —*v.t.* 1 cause a feeling of anger in; wound the pride of: *It piqued her that they should have a secret she did not share.* 2 arouse; stir up: *Our curiosity was piqued by the locked trunk.* 3 **pique oneself on,** feel proud about. [< French < *piquer* to prick, sting]

pi qué (pi kā′), *n.* fabric of cotton, rayon, or silk, with narrow ribs or raised stripes. [< French, literally, pricked, quilted]

pi quet (pi ket′), *n.* card game for two people, played with a deck of 32 cards. [< French]

pi ra cy (pī′rə sē), *n., pl.* **-cies.** 1 robbery on the sea. 2 act of publishing or using a book, play, invention, etc., without permission.

Pi rae us (pī rē′əs), *n.* city in SE Greece, the seaport of Athens. 184,000. Also, **Peiraeus.**

Pir an del lo (pir′ən del′ō), *n.* **Luigi,** 1867-1936, Italian playwright, poet, and novelist.

pi ra nha (pi rä′nyə), *n., pl.* **-nhas** or **-nha.** a small South American fish that attacks man and other large mammals; caribe. [< Portuguese < Tupi]

pi rate (pī′rit), *n., v.,* **-rat ed, -rat ing.** —*n.* 1 person who attacks and robs ships unlawfully; robber on the sea; buccaneer; freebooter. 2 ship used by pirates. —*v.i.* be a pirate. —*v.t.* 1 commit piracy upon; plunder; rob. 2 publish or use without the author's, inventor's, or owner's permission. [< Latin *pirata* < Greek *peiratēs* < *peiran* to attack] **—pi′rate like′,** *adj.*

pi rat i cal (pī rat′ə kəl), *adj.* of pirates; like pirates; like piracy. **—pi rat′i cal ly,** *adv.*

pi rogue (pə rōg′), *n.* 1 canoe hollowed from the trunk of a tree; dugout. 2 any canoe or other small boat resembling a canoe. [< French < Spanish *piragua*]

pir o plas mo sis (pir′ō plaz mō′sis), *n.* any of various infectious diseases of cattle, sheep, horses, etc., caused by a protozoan parasite and transmitted by ticks. [< Latin *pirum* pear + Greek *plasma* something molded + English *-osis*]

pir ou ette (pir′ü et′), *n., v.,* **-et ted, -et ting.** —*n.* a whirling about on one foot or on the toes, as in dancing. —*v.i.* whirl in this way. [< Middle French, spinning top]

Pi sa (pē′zə), *n.* city in NW Italy, famous for its leaning tower. 103,000.

hat, āge, fär; let, ēqual, tėrm;
it, īce; hot, ōpen, ôrder;
oil, out; cup, pu̇t, rüle;
ch, child; ng, long; sh, she;
th, thin; ᴛʜ, then; zh, measure;

ə represents *a* in about, *e* in taken,
i in pencil, *o* in lemon, *u* in circus.

< = from, derived from, taken from.

pis ca to ri al (pis′kə tôr′ē əl, pis′kə tōr′ē-əl), *adj.* of or having to do with fishermen or fishing. [< Latin *piscatorius,* ultimately < *piscis* fish] **—pis′ca to′ri al ly,** *adv.*

pis ca to ry (pis′kə tôr′ē, pis′kə tōr′ē), *adj.* piscatorial.

Pis ces (pī′sēz, pis′ēz′), *n.* 1 a northern constellation between Aquarius and Aries, seen by ancient astronomers as having the rough outline of a fish. 2 the 12th sign of the zodiac. The sun enters Pisces about February 19. 3 Also, **pisces.** any of a superclass of aquatic vertebrates having gills and fins, two pairs of which are used for movement. All fishes belong to this superclass. [< Latin, plural of *piscis* fish]

pis cine (pis′īn, pis′n), *adj.* of, having to do, or characteristic of a fish or fishes. [< Latin *piscis* fish]

Pi sis tra tus (pī sis′trə təs), *n.* 605?-527 B.C., Greek statesman and ruler of Athens.

pis mire (pis′mīr′), *n.* ant. [Middle English *pissemire* < *pisse* urine + *mire* ant (of Scandinavian origin); with reference to the strong smell of formic acid from ants]

Pis sar ro (pi sär′ō; *French* pē sȧ rō′), *n.* **Camille,** 1830-1903, French painter, born in the Virgin Islands.

pis ta chi o (pi stä′shē ō, pi stash′ē ō), *n., pl.* **-chi os.** 1 a greenish nut having a flavor that suggests almond. 2 a small tree that it grows on, belonging to the same family as the sumac. 3 the flavor of this nut. 4 a light green. —*adj.* light-green. [< Italian *pistacchio*]

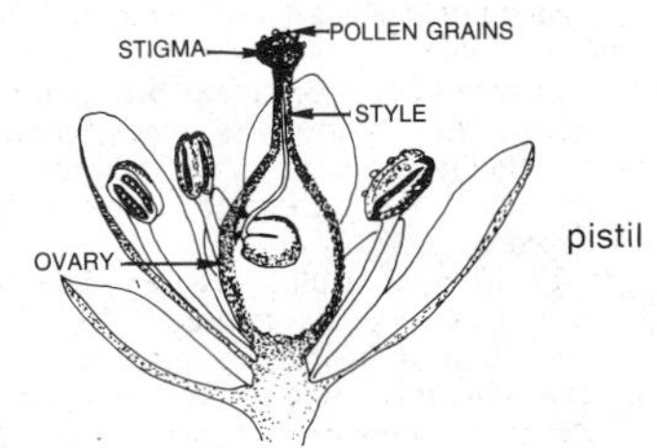

pistil

pis til (pis′tl), *n.* the part of a flower that produces seeds, consisting, when complete, of an ovary, a style, and a stigma. [< New Latin < Latin *pistillum* pestle. Doublet of PESTLE.]

pis til late (pis′tl āt, pis′tl it), *adj.* 1 having a pistil or pistils. 2 having a pistil or pistils but no stamens.

pis tol (pis′tl), *n.* a small, short gun held and fired with one hand; handgun. [< Middle French *pistole* < German *pistole* < Czech *pištala,* originally, pipe]

pis tole (pi stōl′), *n.* 1 a former Spanish gold coin worth $4.00. 2 any of various former European gold coins worth about the same amount. [< French]

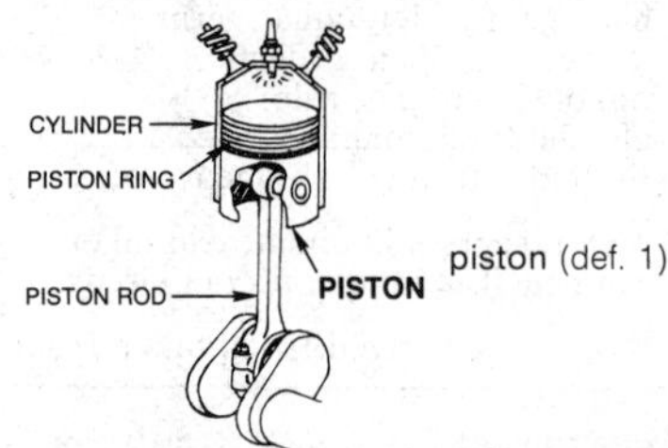

piston (def. 1)

pis ton (pis′tən), *n.* 1 a short cylinder, or a flat, round piece of wood or metal, fitting closely inside a tube or hollow cylinder in which it is moved back and forth by the force of vapor combustion or steam. Pistons are used in pumps, engines, compressors, etc. 2 a sliding valve in a brass wind instrument that lowers the pitch when pressed by the fingers. [< French < Italian *pistone* < *pistare* to pound]

piston ring, a metal ring, fitted in a groove around a piston, to insure a tight fit against the cylinder wall.

piston rod, rod by which a piston imparts motion, or by which motion is imparted to it.

pit[1] (pit), *n., v.,* **pit ted, pit ting.** —*n.* 1 hole or cavity in the ground, formed either by digging or by some natural process. 2 an open hole or excavation made in digging for some mineral deposit. 3 the shaft of a coal mine. 4 a hollow on the surface of anything; hole. 5 a natural hollow or depression in the body: *the pit of the stomach.* 6 a small depressed scar, as one left on the skin after smallpox. 7 a covered or otherwise hidden hole, used as a trap for wild animals; pitfall. 8 an unsuspected danger or trap. 9 an enclosure in which animals, as gamecocks or terriers, are set to fight. 10 BRITISH. **a** the rear part of the main floor of a theater, where the seats are cheaper. **b** the people who sit there. 11 the area in front of the stage in a theater where the musicians sit. 12 U.S. that portion of the floor of an exchange, especially a commodity exchange, devoted to trade in a particular item: *the wheat pit.* 13 a large grave for many bodies. 14 **the pit,** hell, or some part of it. 15 **the pits,** place for the repair, refueling, inspection, etc., of motor vehicles beside the track of an automobile racing course.
—*v.t.* 1 mark with small depressed scars or pits. 2 set (gamecocks, terriers, etc.) to fight for sport. 3 set to fight or compete; match: *The little man pitted his brains against the big man's strength.* 4 put or cast into a pit. —*v.i.* become marked with pits or small depressions.
[Old English *pytt,* ultimately < Latin *puteus* pit, well]

pit[2] (pit), *n., v.,* **pit ted, pit ting.** —*n.* the stone of a fruit, as of the cherry, peach, plum, date, etc. —*v.t.* remove the pit from (fruit). [< Dutch, kernel]

pit a pat (pit′ə pat′), *n., adv., v.i.,* **-pat ted, -pat ting.** pitter-patter.

Pit cairn (pit′kern, pit′karn), *n.* a small British island in the S Pacific. 80 pop.; 2 sq. mi.

pitch[1] (pich), *v.t.* 1 throw or fling; hurl; toss: *pitch a stone into a lake, pitch horseshoes.* 2 throw a baseball to a batter. 3 fix firmly; set up or erect (a tent, etc.). 4 set at a particular value, level, point, or degree: *pitch one's hopes too high.* 5 determine the musical key of (a tune, instrument, the voice, etc.). 6 SLANG. sell or try to sell (a product, service, etc.), often by high-pressure means. 7 **pitch into,** INFORMAL. attack. —*v.i.* 1 throw; toss; hurl: *He nearly always pitches too far.* 2 in baseball: **a** throw the ball to the batter. **b** act as pitcher for a team. 3 set up a tent, shelter, etc.; establish a camp; encamp. 4 take up a position; settle; alight. 5 plunge or fall forward; fall headlong. 6 plunge with the bow rising and then falling: *The ship pitched about in the storm.* 7 slope downward; incline; dip. 8 SLANG. sell or try to sell something, often by high-pressure means. 9 **pitch in,** INFORMAL. work or begin to work vigorously.
—*n.* 1 a throw or fling; hurl; toss. 2 something pitched. 3 in baseball: **a** delivery of the ball to the batter by the pitcher. **b** ball so delivered. **c** manner of pitching: *a fast pitch.* 4 a point or position on a scale; degree; level: *the lowest pitch of bad fortune.* 5 in music: **a** the highness or lowness of a tone or sound, which depends upon the frequency of the vibrations producing it. The slower the rate of vibrations per second the lower the pitch. **b** a particular standard of pitch for voices and instruments. 6 height, especially of an arch or roof. 7 the highest point or degree; acme. 8 INFORMAL. a talk, argument, offer, plan, etc., used to persuade, as in selling: *make a strong sales pitch.* 9 amount of slope: *Some roads in the Rocky Mountains have a very steep pitch.* 10 distance between the centers of two successive teeth of a cogwheel, etc. 11 distance between two successive lines or points, especially in screw threads, where it is measured parallel to the axis. 12 distance which an aircraft propeller moves forward in one revolution. 13 a plunge forward or headlong; lurch. 14 a downward plunging of the fore part of a ship in a rough sea.
[Middle English *picchen*]

pitch[2] (pich), *n.* 1 a thick, black, sticky substance made from tar or turpentine, used to fill the seams of wooden ships, to cover roofs, to make pavements, etc. 2 resin from certain evergreen trees. —*v.t.* cover, coat, or smear with pitch. [Old English *pic* < Latin *picem*] **—pitch′like′,** *adj.*

pitch-black (pich′blak′), *adj.* very black or dark.

pitch blende (pich′blend′), *n.* mineral consisting largely of an oxide of uranium, found usually in blackish, pitchlike masses. It is a source of radium, uranium, and actinium. [< German *Pechblende* < *Pech* pitch + *Blende* blende]

pitch-dark (pich′därk′), *adj.* pitch-black.

pitched battle, battle with troops properly arranged.

pitch er[1] (pich′ər), *n.* 1 container for holding and pouring liquids, with a lip on one side and a handle on the other. 2 amount that a pitcher holds. [< Old French *pichier*] **—pitch′er like′,** *adj.*

pitch er[2] (pich′ər), *n.* the player on a baseball team who throws the ball to the batter. [< *pitch*[1]]

pitch er ful (pich′ər fu̇l), *n., pl.* **-fuls.** quantity sufficient to fill a pitcher.

pitcher plant, any of a genus of plants with pitcher-shaped leaves that often contain a liquid secretion in which insects are captured and digested by the plant.

pitch fork (pich′fôrk′), *n.* a large fork with a long handle, for lifting and throwing hay, etc.; hayfork. —*v.t.* lift and throw with a pitchfork.

pitch man (pich′man′), *n., pl.* **-men.** INFORMAL. person who makes a sales pitch; salesman.

pitch out (pich′out′), *n.* 1 (in baseball) a wide pitch to prevent the batter from hitting the ball and give the catcher a chance to catch a runner off base. 2 (in football) a lateral pass behind the line of scrimmage.

pitch pipe, a small musical pipe having one or more notes, used to give the pitch for singing or for tuning an instrument.

pitch y (pich′ē), *adj.,* **pitch i er, pitch i est.** 1 full of pitch. 2 like pitch; sticky. 3 black.

pit e ous (pit′ē əs), *adj.* to be pitied; moving the heart; deserving pity. See **pitiful** for synonym study. **—pit′e ous ly,** *adv.* **—pit′e ous ness,** *n.*

pit fall (pit′fôl′), *n.* 1 a hidden pit to catch animals or men in. 2 any trap or hidden danger.

pith (pith), *n.* 1 the central column of spongy tissue in the stems of most herbaceous plants and of some trees. 2 a similar tissue occurring in other parts of plants, as that lining the skin of an orange. 3 the soft inner substance of a bone, feather, etc. 4 the important or essential part: *the pith of a speech.* 5 strength; energy. [Old English *pitha*]

Pith e can thro pus (pith′ə kan thrō′pəs, pith′ə kan′thrə pəs), *n., pl.* **-pi** (-pī). Java man. [< New Latin < Greek *pithēkos* ape + *anthrōpos* man]

pith y (pith′ē), *adj.,* **pith i er, pith i est.** 1 full of substance, meaning, force, or vigor: *pithy phrases, a pithy speaker.* 2 of or like pith. 3 having much pith: *a pithy orange.* **—pith′i ly,** *adv.* **—pith′i ness,** *n.*

pit i a ble (pit′ē ə bəl), *adj.* 1 to be pitied; moving the heart; deserving pity; lamentable. See **pitiful** for synonym study. 2 deserving contempt; mean; to be scorned. **—pit′i a ble ness,** *n.* **—pit′i a bly,** *adv.*

pit i ful (pit′i fəl), *adj.* 1 to be pitied; moving the heart; deserving pity. See synonym study below. 2 feeling or showing pity; feeling sorrow for the troubles of others. 3 deserving contempt; mean; to be scorned: *Driving away after hitting a dog is a pitiful act.* **—pit′i ful ly,** *adv.*

Syn. 1 **Pitiful, piteous, pitiable** mean arousing pity. **Pitiful** emphasizes the effect of pity aroused by someone or something felt to be touching or pathetic: *The deserted children were pitiful.* **Piteous** emphasizes the quality in the thing itself that makes it appeal for pity: *Their sad faces were piteous.* **Pitiable** emphasizes arousing sorrow or regret for what deserves or needs to be pitied: *Their clothes were in a pitiable condition.*

pit i less (pit′ē lis), *adj.* without pity or mercy. See **cruel** for synonym study. **—pit′i less ly,** *adv.* **—pit′i less ness,** *n.*

pitchfork

hat, āge, fär; let, ēqual, tėrm;
it, īce; hot, ōpen, ôrder;
oil, out; cup, pu̇t, rüle;
ch, child; ng, long; sh, she;
th, thin; ᴛʜ, then; zh, measure;

ə represents *a* in about, *e* in taken, *i* in pencil, *o* in lemon, *u* in circus.

< = from, derived from, taken from.

Pi tot tube (pē tō′), (in aeronautics) a bent tube with an open end pointed against the flow of a gas or liquid, used for determining the velocity of fluids. [< Henri *Pitot,* 1695-1771, French physicist]

Pitt (pit), *n.* 1 **William,** 1708-1778, the first Earl of Chatham, British statesman. 2 his son, **William,** 1759-1806, prime minister of England from 1783 to 1801 and from 1804 to 1806.

pit tance (pit′ns), *n.* 1 a small allowance of money. 2 a small amount or share. [< Old French *pitance* portion of food allotted a monk, piety, pity, ultimately < Latin *pietatem* piety]

pit ter-pat ter (pit′ər pat′ər), *n.* a rapid succession of light beats or taps: *the pitter-patter of rain.* —*adv.* with a rapid succession of beats or taps. —*v.i.* go pitter-patter. Also, **pitapat.**

Pitts burgh (pits′bėrg′), *n.* city in SW Pennsylvania, a center of the iron and steel industry. 520,000.

pi tu i tar y (pə tü′ə ter′ē, pə tyü′ə ter′ē), *n.* the pituitary gland. —*adj.* having to do with the pituitary gland. [< Latin *pituitarius* < *pituita* phlegm]

pituitary body, pituitary gland.

pituitary gland, a small, oval endocrine gland that is situated at the base of the brain in most vertebrates, and secretes hormones that promote growth, stimulate other glands, and regulate many other bodily functions; hypophysis.

pit viper, any of a family of venomous snakes having perforated fangs and a pit between the eye and nostril, including rattlesnakes, water moccasins, copperheads, fer-de-lances, and bushmasters.

pit y (pit′ē), *n., pl.* **pit ies,** *v.,* **pit ied, pit y ing.** —*n.* 1 sorrow for another's suffering or distress; feeling for the sorrows of others; compassion; sympathy. See synonym study below. 2 cause for pity or regret; thing to be sorry for: *It is a pity to be kept in the house in good weather.* 3 **have pity on** or **take pity on,** show pity for. —*v.t.* feel pity for. —*v.i.* feel pity. [< Old French *pite* < Latin *pietatem.* Doublet of PIETY.] —**pit′y ing ly,** *adv.*

Syn. *n.* 1 **Pity, compassion, sympathy** mean a feeling for the sorrows or suffering of others. **Pity** means a feeling of sorrow for someone who is suffering or in distress, and often felt to be weak or unfortunate: *The beggar's hungry look and ragged appearance aroused the stranger's pity.* **Compassion** adds the idea of tenderness and a strong desire to help or protect: *He felt compassion for the sobbing child.* **Sympathy** means a feeling with another in his sorrow and sharing and understanding it: *His friends expressed great sympathy for him when his mother died.*

Pi us IX (pī′əs), 1792-1878, pope from 1846 to 1878.

Pius X, 1835-1914, pope from 1903 to 1914.

Pius XI, 1857-1939, pope from 1922 to 1939.

Pius XII, 1876-1958, pope from 1939 to 1958.

piv ot (piv′ət), *n.* 1 shaft, pin, or point on which something turns. 2 a turn on a pivot. 3 that on which something turns, hinges, or depends; central point. —*v.t.* mount on, attach by, or provide with a pivot. —*v.i.* turn on or as if on a pivot. [< French]

piv ot al (piv′ə təl), *adj.* 1 of, having to do with, or serving as a pivot. 2 being that on which something turns, hinges, or depends; very important. —**piv′ot al ly,** *adv.*

pix y or **pix ie** (pik′sē), *n., pl.* **pix ies.** fairy or elf. [origin uncertain]

Pi zar ro (pi zär′ō), *n.* **Francisco,** 1471?-1541, Spanish explorer, who conquered Peru.

pi zazz (pə zaz′), *n.* SLANG. 1 liveliness; pep. 2 flashy style or quality; ornateness. Also, **pizzazz.** [origin unknown]

pizz., pizzicato.

piz za (pēt′sə), *n.* a spicy, pielike Italian dish made by baking a large flat layer of bread dough covered with cheese, tomato sauce, herbs, etc. [< Italian]

piz zazz (pə zaz′), *n.* SLANG. pizazz.

piz ze ri a (pēt′sə rē′ə), *n.* restaurant or bakery where pizzas are baked and sold. [< Italian]

piz zi ca to (pit′sə kä′tō), *adj., n., pl.* **-ti** (-tē). in music: —*adj.* played by plucking the strings of a musical instrument with the finger instead of using the bow. —*n.* note or passage so played. [< Italian, picked, pinched]

pk., 1 park. 2 peak. 3 peck.

pkg., package.

pkt., packet.

PKU, phenylketonuria.

pl., 1 place. 2 plate. 3 plural.

pla ca ble (plā′kə bəl, plak′ə bəl), *adj.* that may be placated; easily quieted, forgiving, or mild. —**pla′ca bly,** *adv.*

plac ard (*n.* plak′ärd; *v.* plə kärd′, plak′-ärd), *n.* notice to be posted in a public place; poster. —*v.t.* 1 put placards on or in: *The circus placarded the city with advertisements.* 2 give notice of with placards. [< Middle French < *plaquier* to stick, plaster]

pla cate (plā′kāt, plak′āt), *v.t.,* **-cat ed, -cat ing.** soothe or satisfy the anger of; make peaceful; appease: *placate a person one has offended.* [< Latin *placatum* soothed] —**pla ca′tion,** *n.*

pla ca to ry (plā′kə tôr′ē, plā′kə tōr′ē; plak′ə tôr′ē, plak′ə tōr′ē), *adj.* tending or calculated to placate.

place (plās), *n., v.,* **placed, plac ing.** —*n.* 1 the part of space occupied by a person or thing. 2 a particular portion of space; definite position in space; location. See synonym study below. 3 city, town, village, district, etc.: *What is the name of this place?* 4 building or spot used for a specified purpose: *a place of worship, a place of business.* 5 a house, house and grounds, etc.; dwelling: *have a place in the country.* 6 part or spot in something: *a sore place on one's foot, mark one's place in a book.* 7 a fitting or reasonable ground or occasion: *There is a time and place for everything.* 8 the proper or natural position or situation for a person or thing: *books in place on shelves.* 9 position; rank; standing: *a high place in society.* 10 position among the leaders at the finish of a race or competition. 11 position in time: *The performance went too slowly in several places.* 12 space or a seat for a person, as in a theater, train, coach, etc. 13 situation, job, post, or office: *get a place in a store.* 14 official position; political power. 15 official function; duty; business: *It's not the place of a newspaper to print rumors.* 16 a step or point in any order of proceeding: *In the first place, the room is too small; in the second place, it is too dirty.* 17 the position of a figure in a number or series, in decimal or any other notation. 18 a short street, court, etc.: *Waverley Place.* 19 space in general; extension in three dimensions.

give place or **make place, a** make room; step aside. **b** yield; give in.

go places, INFORMAL. advance rapidly toward success; achieve success.

in place, a in the proper or usual place; in the original place. **b** fitting, appropriate, or timely.

in place of, instead of.

know one's place, act according to one's position in life.

out of place, a not in the proper or usual place. **b** inappropriate or ill-timed; unsuitable.

take place, happen; occur.

—*v.t.* 1 put in a spot, position, condition, or relation; set: *place confidence in a person, place money in a bank. The orphan was placed in a good home.* See **put** for synonym study. 2 give the place, position, or condition of; identify: *I remember her name, but I cannot place her.* 3 appoint (a person) to a position or office; find a place or situation for. —*v.i.* 1 finish among the first three, or other stated number, in a race or competition. 2 finish second in a horse race.

[< Old French < Latin *platea* courtyard, broad street < Greek *plateia (hodos)* broad (way) < *platys* broad. Doublet of PLAZA, PIAZZA.]

Syn. *n.* 2 **Place, position, location** mean a particular portion of space, or of the earth's surface. **Place** is the general term: *a quiet place, a strange place for storing books.* **Position** is place with respect to another place or places or within a framework or reference: *We are in a good position to see the parade.* **Location** may be used for either *place* or *position,* but it stresses a little more than either of these the uniqueness or isolation of a place in relation to anything or everything outside it: *a good location for a housing project.*

place a ble (plā′sə bəl), *adj.* that can be placed.

pla ce bo (plə sē′bō), *n., pl.* **-bos** or **-boes.** pill, preparation, etc., containing no active ingredients but given as medicine for psychological effect to satisfy a patient, or used as a control in testing the effectiveness of new medicines. [< Latin, I shall please]

place hold er (plās′hōl′dər), *n.* (in mathematics) a symbol that holds the place for numerals that are being considered.

place kick, the kicking of a football placed or held nearly upright on the ground.

place-kick (plās′kik′), *v.i.* make a place kick.

place mat, mat of linen, plastic, paper, etc., put under a person's plate or table setting.

place ment (plās′mənt), *n.* 1 a placing or being placed; location; arrangement. 2 the finding of work or a job for a person. 3 a placing of a football on the ground for a place kick. 4 place kick.

pla cen ta (plə sen′tə), *n., pl.* **-tae** (-tē), **-tas.** 1 the spongy vascular organ in most mammals by which the fetus is attached to the wall of the uterus and nourished. 2 the tissue in the ovary of flowering plants to which the ovules are attached. [< New Latin < Latin, flat cake < Greek *plakounta* < *plakos* flat surface]

pla cen tal (plə sen′tl), *adj.* 1 of or having to do with the placenta. 2 having a placenta.

plac er (plas′ər), *n.* deposit of sand, gravel, or earth in the bed of a stream, containing particles of gold or other valuable minerals. [< Spanish]

placer mining, the washing of loose sand or gravel for gold or other minerals. **—placer miner.**

place value, the value which a digit has because of its place in a number. In 438.7, the place values of the digits are 4 × 100, 3 × 10, 8 × 1, and 7 × $^1/_{10}$.

plac id (plas′id), *adj.* pleasantly calm or peaceful; quiet: *a placid lake, a placid temper.* See **peaceful** for synonym study. [< Latin *placidus* < *placere* to please] **—plac′id ly,** *adv.* **—plac′id ness,** *n.*

pla cid i ty (plə sid′ə tē), *n.* calmness; peace.

plack et (plak′it), *n.* an opening or slit in a garment, especially at the top of a skirt, to make it easy to put on. [origin uncertain]

plac o derm (plak′ō dėrm′), *n.* any of a class of extinct fishes with primitive jaws, and hard, bony plates covering the body. [< Greek *plakos* flat surface + *derma* skin]

pla gia rism (plā′jə riz′əm), *n.* 1 act of plagiarizing. 2 something plagiarized. [< Latin *plagiarius* kidnaper, plunderer < *plagium* kidnaping < *plaga* net]

pla giar ist (plā′jər ist), *n.* person who plagiarizes.

pla gia rize (plā′jə rīz′), *v.t., v.i.,* **-rized, -riz ing.** take and use as one's own the thoughts, writings, etc., of another; take and use (a passage, plot, etc.) from the work of another writer and represent it as one's own. **—pla′gia riz′er,** *n.*

pla gi o clase (plā′jē ə klās), *n.* a triclinic feldspar containing either sodium or calcium and having its two prominent cleavage directions oblique to one another. [< Greek *plagios* oblique + *klasis* cleavage]

plague (plāg), *n., v.,* **plagued, pla guing.** *—n.* 1 highly contagious, epidemic, and often fatal bacterial disease that occurs in several forms, one of which is bubonic plague. The plague is common in Asia and has several times swept through Europe. 2 any epidemic disease; pestilence. 3 punishment thought to be sent from God. 4 thing or person that torments, annoys, troubles, or is disagreeable. *—v.t.* 1 cause to suffer from a plague. 2 vex; annoy; bother. See **tease** for synonym study. [< Late Latin *plaga* pestilence < Latin, blow, wound] **—pla′guer,** *n.*

pla guy or **pla guey** (plā′gē), *adj.* INFORMAL. troublesome; annoying. *—adv.* vexatiously. **—pla′gui ly,** *adv.*

plaice (plās), *n., pl.* **plaice** or **plaic es.** 1 a European flatfish important as a food fish. 2 any of various American flatfishes. [< Old French *plaïs* < Late Latin *platessa*]

plaid (plad), *n.* 1 a long piece of woolen cloth, usually having a pattern of checks or stripes in many colors, worn over one shoulder by the Scottish Highlanders. 2 any cloth with a pattern of checks or crisscross stripes. 3 a pattern of this kind; tartan. *—adj.* having a pattern of checks or crisscross stripes: *a plaid dress.* [< Scottish Gaelic *plaide*]

plaid ed (plad′id), *adj.* made of plaid; having a plaid pattern.

plain (plān), *adj.* 1 clear to the senses or mind; easily seen or heard; evident: *It was plain he was offended.* 2 without ornament, decoration, or bright color; simple: *a plain dress.* 3 without figured pattern, varied weave, or variegated colors: *a plain blue fabric.* 4 not rich or highly seasoned: *plain cake, a plain diet.* 5 simple in manner; common; ordinary: *a plain man of the people.* 6 not beautiful; homely. 7 not very hard; easy: *plain words.* 8 not artful or roundabout; frank; candid: *plain speech.* 9 flat; level; smooth: *plain ground.* 10 without obstructions; open; clear: *in plain sight.* *—adv.* in a plain manner; clearly. *—n.* 1 a flat stretch of land; tract of level or nearly level land; prairie. 2 a broad, level expanse, as a lunar sea. [< Old French < Latin *planus* flat, level. Doublet of PIANO[2], PLAN, PLANE[2].] **—plain′ly,** *adv.* **—plain′ness,** *n.*

plain clothes man (plān′klōz′mən, plān′klōᴛʜz′mən), *n., pl.* **-men.** policeman or detective wearing ordinary clothes, not a uniform, when on duty.

plain sailing, a simple or easy course of action; clear path or line of progress.

plains man (plānz′mən), *n., pl.* **-men.** man who lives on the plains.

plain song (plān′sông′), *n.* vocal music used in the Christian church from the earliest times, sung in unison and rhythmical, although the beats are not regular.

plain-spo ken (plān′spō′kən), *adj.* plain or frank in speech; candid: *a plain-spoken man, a plain-spoken rebuke.*

plaint (plānt), *n.* 1 complaint. 2 ARCHAIC. lament. [< Old French < Latin *planctus* lamentation < *plangere* to lament, beat the breast]

plain tiff (plān′tif), *n.* person who begins a lawsuit: *The plaintiff accused the defendant of fraud.* [< Old French *plaintif* complaining, plaintive]

plain tive (plān′tiv), *adj.* expressive of sorrow; mournful; sad. [< Old French *plaintif* < *plaint* plaint] **—plain′tive ly,** *adv.* **—plain′tive ness,** *n.*

plait (plāt, plat *for 1;* plāt, plēt *for 2*), *n., v.t.* 1 braid. 2 pleat. [< Old French *pleit,* ultimately < Latin *plicare* to fold]

plan (plan), *n., v.,* **planned, plan ning.** *—n.* 1 way of making or doing something that has been worked out beforehand; scheme of action: *Our summer plans were upset by mother's illness.* See synonym study below. 2 a drawing or diagram to show how a garden, a floor of a house, a park, etc,, is arranged. *—v.t.* 1 think out beforehand how (something) is to be made or done; design, scheme, or devise: *plan a trip.* 2 have in mind as a purpose; intend. 3 make a drawing or diagram of. *—v.i.* make plans. [< French, literally, a plane < Latin *planus;* with reference to a sketch on a flat surface. Doublet of PIANO[2], PLAIN, PLANE[2].]

Syn. *n.* 1 **Plan, design, project** mean a proposed way of doing or making something. **Plan** is the general term: *He has a plan for increasing production.* **Design** applies to a plan carefully contrived to achieve a given effect, purpose, or goal: *They have a design for a rich, full life.* **Project** applies to a plan proposed for trial or experiment, often on a large scale: *He introduced a project for slum clearance.*

pla nar (plā′nər), *adj.* of, having to do with, or situated in a plane.

pla nar i an (plə ner′ē ən), *n.* any of a family of freshwater flatworms that are bilaterally symmetrical and have cilia and an intestine divided into three main branches. *—adj.* of or belonging to the planarians. [ultimately < Latin *planus* flat]

pla na tion (plā nā′shən), *n.* (in geology) the process of erosion and deposition by which a stream produces a nearly level land surface.

Planck (plängk), *n.* **Max,** 1858-1947, German physicist who formulated the quantum theory in 1900.

plane[1] (plān), *n.* 1 any flat or level surface. 2 level; grade: *Try to keep your work on a high plane.* 3 a thin, flat or curved supporting surface of an airplane. 4 airplane. 5 surface such that if any two points on it are joined by a straight line, the line will be contained wholly in the surface. *—adj.* 1 not convex or concave; flat; level. 2 being wholly in a plane: *a plane figure.* 3 of or having to do with such figures. [< Latin *planum* level place]

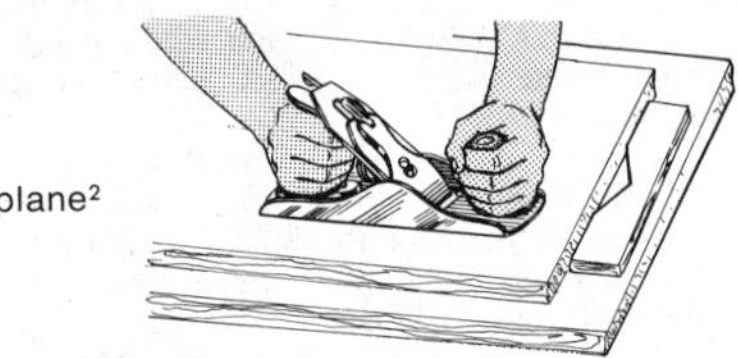

plane[2]

plane[2] (plān), *n., v.,* **planed, plan ing.** *—n.* a carpenter's tool with a blade for smoothing or shaping wood. *—v.t.* 1 smooth or level with a plane; use a plane on. 2 remove with a plane. [< Old French < Latin *plana* < *planare* make level < *planus* flat. Doublet of PIANO[2], PLAIN, PLAN.]

plane[3] (plān), *n.* plane tree. [< French < Latin *platanus* < Greek *platanos*]

plane geometry, branch of geometry that deals with figures lying in one plane.

plan er (plā′nər), *n.* person or thing that planes, especially a machine for planing wood or for finishing flat surfaces on metal.

plan et (plan′it), *n.* 1 one of the heavenly bodies (except comets and meteors) that move around the sun in nearly circular paths. The planets of our solar system include Mercury, Venus, the earth, Mars, Jupiter, Saturn, Uranus, Neptune, Pluto, and the asteroids between Mars and Jupiter. 2 any similar body revolving around a star other than the sun. 3 (in astrology) a heavenly body supposed to influence people's lives. [< Late Latin *planetes* < Greek *planētai (asteres)* wandering (stars) < *planasthai* wander] **—plan′et like′,** *adj.*

plan e tar i um (plan′ə ter′ē əm, plan′ə tar′ē əm), *n., pl.* **-tar i a** (-ter′ē ə, -tar′ē ə), **-tar i ums.** 1 apparatus that shows the movements of the sun, moon, planets, and stars by projecting lights on the inside of a dome shaped like a hemisphere. 2 room or building with such an apparatus. 3 any plan, model, or structure representing the planetary system.

plan e tar y (plan′ə ter′ē), *adj.* 1 of a planet; having to do with planets. 2 moving in an orbit. 3 terrestrial; global. 4 having to do with a form of transmission for varying the speed in automobiles.

plan e tes i mal (plan′ə tes′ə məl), *adj.* of or having to do with minute bodies in space which, according to a certain hypothesis, move in planetary orbits and gradually unite to form the planets of a given planetary system. *—n.* one of these minute bodies.

plan et oid (plan′ə toid), *n.* asteroid.

plane tree, the sycamore of North America. Also, **plane**[3].

plan gen cy (plan′jən sē), *n.* quality of being plangent.

plan gent (plan′jənt), *adj.* 1 making the noise of waves breaking or beating on the shore. 2 having a loud metallic or plaintive sound. [< Latin *plangentem* beating the breast, lamenting] **—plan′gent ly,** *adv.*

plank (plangk), *n.* 1 a long, flat piece of sawed timber thicker than a board, especially one more than two inches thick and four inches wide. 2 article or feature of the platform of a political party or other organization. 3 **walk the plank,** be put to death by being forced to walk off a plank extending from a ship's side over the water. Pirates used to make their prisoners do this. *—v.t.* 1 cover or furnish with planks. 2 cook or serve on a board, often with a decorative border of vegetables and potatoes: *planked steak.* 3 **plank down,** INFORMAL. put down or pay then and there: *plank down a package. She planked down her money.* [< Old North French < Latin *planca*]

plank ing (plang′king), *n.* 1 act of laying or covering with planks. 2 planks collectively.

plank ton (plangk′tən), *n.* the small animal and plant organisms that float or drift in water, especially at or near the surface. [< German *Plankton* < Greek, wandering, drifting < *plazesthai* wander, drift]

plank ton ic (plangk ton′ik), *adj.* of, having to do with, or characteristic of plankton.

plan ner (plan′ər), *n.* person who plans.

pla no-con cave (plā′nō kon′kāv), *adj.* flat on one side and concave on the other.

pla no-con vex (plā′nō kon′veks), *adj.* flat on one side and convex on the other.

plan og ra phy (pla nog′rə fē), *n.* printing done from plane surfaces, as in lithography and offset, in contrast to intaglio or relief work.

plant (plant), *n.* 1 any living organism that is not an animal and is distinguished from animals by its lack of a nervous system and sense organs, its inability to move about, and its ability to use chlorophyll to manufacture its own food; any member of the vegetable kingdom. 2 a living thing that has leaves, roots, and a soft stem and is small in contrast with a tree or a shrub: *a tomato plant, a house plant.* 3 a young growth ready for transplanting. 4 the fixtures, implements, machinery, apparatus, and often the buildings used in carrying on any industrial process, as manufacturing some article, producing power, etc.: *an aircraft plant.* 5 the complete apparatus used for a specific mechanical operation or process: *the heating plant on a ship.* 6 the buildings, equipment, etc., belonging to an institution: *a college plant.* 7 SLANG. scheme or plot to swindle or defraud a person.
—v.t. 1 put or set in the ground to take root and grow, as seeds, young trees, shoots, cuttings, etc. 2 furnish with plants; put seed in: *plant a garden.* 3 set or place firmly; put or fix in position: *The boy planted his feet far apart.* 4 establish or set up (a colony, city, etc.). 5 put in or instill (principles, doctrines, ideas, etc.). 6 deposit (young fish, spawn, oysters) in a river, tidal water, etc. 7 SLANG. **a** deliver (a blow, etc.) with a definite aim. **b** hide (something stolen, etc.). **c** place (a person or thing) as a plant, trap, or trick. [Old English *plante* < Latin *planta* sprout] **—plant′like′,** *adj.*

Plan tag e net (plan taj′ə nit), *n.* member of the royal family that ruled England from 1154 to 1485. The English kings from Henry II through Richard III were Plantagenets.

plan tain[1] (plan′tən), *n.* 1 a tropical plant of the same family as the banana. 2 its fruit, longer and more starchy than the banana, eaten cooked. It is one of the chief articles of food in tropical countries. [< Spanish *plátano*]

plan tain[2] (plan′tən), *n.* any of a genus of herbs, especially a common weed with broad, flat leaves spread out close to the ground, and long slender spikes carrying seeds and tiny, greenish flowers. [< Old French *plantain* < Popular Latin *plantanus* < Latin *plantaginem* < *planta* sole of the foot (because of its flat leaves)]

plan tar (plan′tər), *adj.* of or having to do with the sole of the foot. [< Latin *planta* sole of the foot]

plan ta tion (plan tā′shən), *n.* 1 a large farm or estate, especially in a tropical or semitropical country, on which cotton, tobacco, sugar cane, rubber trees, etc., are grown. The work on a plantation is done by laborers who live there. 2 a large group of trees or other plants that have been planted: *a rubber plantation.* 3 colony; settlement.

plant er (plan′tər), *n.* 1 person who owns or runs a plantation. 2 machine for planting: *a corn planter.* 3 person who plants. 4 an early settler; colonist. 5 box, stand, or other holder, usually decorative, for house plants.

plan ti grade (plan′tə grād), *adj.* walking on the sole of the foot with the heel touching the ground, as bears, raccoons, man, etc. [< Latin *planta* sole + *gradi* to step]

plant louse, aphid.

plaque (plak), *n.* 1 a thin, flat, ornamental plate or tablet of metal, porcelain, etc., usually intended to be hung up as a wall decoration. 2 a platelike brooch or ornament, especially one worn as the badge of an honorary order. [< Middle French < Middle Dutch *plak* flat board]

plash (plash), *v.t., v.i., n.* splash.

plasm (plaz′əm), *n.* plasma.

plas ma (plaz′mə), *n.* 1 the clear, almost colorless liquid part of blood or lymph, consisting of water, salts, proteins, and other substances, in which the corpuscles or blood cells float. 2 the watery part of milk, as distinguished from the globules of fat. 3 protoplasm. 4 a highly ionized gas consisting of almost equal numbers of free electrons and positive ions. [< Greek, something formed or molded < *plassein* to mold]

plasma membrane, cell membrane.

plas mo di um (plaz mō′dē əm), *n., pl.* **-di a** (-dē ə). 1 mass of protoplasm formed by the aggregation of amoebalike bodies. 2 any of a group of parasitic sporozoans, including the organisms which cause malaria. [< New Latin]

plas ter (plas′tər), *n.* 1 a soft, sticky mixture of lime, sand, and water that hardens on drying, used for covering walls, ceilings, etc. 2 plaster of Paris. 3 a medical preparation consisting of some substance spread on

hat, āge, fär; let, ēqual, tėrm;
it, īce; hot, ōpen, ôrder;
oil, out; cup, pu̇t, rüle;
ch, child; ng, long; sh, she;
th, thin; ᴛʜ, then; zh, measure;

ə represents *a* in about, *e* in taken, *i* in pencil, *o* in lemon, *u* in circus.

< = from, derived from, taken from.

cloth, that will stick to the body and protect cuts, relieve pain, etc. *—v.t.* 1 cover (walls, ceilings, etc.) with plaster. 2 spread with anything thickly: *Her shoes were plastered with mud.* 3 make smooth and flat: *He plastered his hair down.* 4 apply a plaster to. 5 apply like a plaster: *plaster posters on a wall.* [Old English < Latin *emplastrum* < Greek *emplastron* < *en-* on + *plassein* to mold] **—plas′ter er,** *n.* **—plas′ter like′,** *adj.*

plas ter board (plas′tər bôrd′, plas′tər-bōrd′), *n.* a thin board made of a layer of plaster between layers of pressed felt, covered with paper and used for walls, partitions, etc.

plaster cast, 1 mold, as of a piece of sculpture, made with plaster of Paris. 2 mold made from a bandage of gauze and plaster of Paris to hold a broken or dislocated bone in place.

plas ter ing (plas′tər ing), *n.* a covering of plaster on walls, etc.

plaster of Paris, a white, powdery substance which is made by heating gypsum and which, when mixed with water to form a paste, turns hard quickly. It is used for making molds, cheap statuary, casts, etc.

plas tic (plas′tik), *n.* any of a large group of synthetic organic compounds made from such basic raw materials as coal, water, and limestone, and molded by heat, pressure, etc., into various forms, such as sheets, fibers, and bottles. Nylon, vinyl, and many cellulose products are plastics. *—adj.* 1 made of plastic. 2 easily molded or shaped: *Clay, wax, and plaster are plastic substances.* 3 molding or giving shape to material. 4 having to do with or involving molding or modeling: *Sculpture is a plastic art.* 5 easily influenced; impressionable; pliable: *the plastic mind of a child.* 6 capable of forming, or being organized into, living tissue. 7 (of a substance) able to be deformed in any direction and to retain its deformed condition permanently without rupture. [< Latin *plasticus* able to be molded < Greek *plastikos* < *plassein* to form, mold] **—plas′ti cal ly,** *adv.*

Plas ti cine (plas′tə sēn′), *n.* trademark for a paste that remains plastic for a long time, used by children and sculptors instead of modeling clay.

plas tic i ty (pla stis′ə tē), *n.* plastic quality.

plas ti cize (plas′tə sīz), *v.t., v.i.* **-cized, -ciz ing.** make or become plastic.

plas ti ciz er (plas′tə sī′zər), *n.* chemical that causes a substance to become or remain soft, flexible, or viscous.

plastic surgery, surgery that restores or improves the outer appearance of the body by replacing or repairing lost, damaged, or deformed parts. **—plastic surgeon.**

plas tid (plas′tid), *n.* any of various small differentiated masses of protoplasm in the cytoplasm of a plant cell, such as a chloroplast. [< German *Plastid* < Greek *plassein* to form]

plas tron (plas′trən), *n.* 1 a metal breastplate worn under a coat of mail. 2 a leather guard worn over the chest of a fencer. 3 an ornamental, detachable front of a woman's bodice. 4 the ventral part of the shell of a turtle or tortoise. [< Middle French, ultimately < Latin *emplastrum* plaster. See PLASTER.]

plat (plat), *n., v.,* **plat ted, plat ting.** —*n.* 1 map, chart, or plan, especially of a town or other group of buildings proposed to be built. 2 a small piece of ground; plot. —*v.t.* map out in detail; chart; plan. [apparently variant of *plot*]

Pla ta (plä′tə), *n.* inlet of the Atlantic in SE South America between Argentina and Uruguay. The Uruguay and Paraná rivers empty into the Plata. 170 mi. Also, SPANISH **Río de la Plata.**

plate (plāt), *n., v.,* **plat ed, plat ing.** —*n.* 1 dish, usually round, that is almost flat. 2 contents of such a dish: *a plate of stew.* 3 something having the shape of a plate: *A plate is passed in church to receive the collection.* 4 a part of a meal, served on or in a separate dish; course. 5 dishes and food served to one person at a meal. 6 dishes or utensils of silver or gold. 7 dishes and utensils covered with a thin layer of silver or gold. 8 a thin, flat sheet or piece of metal. 9 one of the pieces of steel welded together or riveted to form the hull of a ship. 10 armor composed of thin pieces of iron or steel fastened together. 11 a platelike part, organ, or structure. Some reptiles and fishes have a covering of horny or bony plates. 12 a smooth or polished piece of metal, etc., for writing or engraving on, for printing from, etc. 13 such a piece when engraved. 14 a printed impression obtained from such an engraved piece of metal, especially a full-page illustration printed on special paper: *a color plate.* 15 any sheet of metal, plastic, etc., engraved or otherwise treated so as to be printed from. 16 a thin sheet of glass, metal, etc., coated with chemicals that are sensitive to light: *a photographic plate.* 17 (in baseball) home plate. 18 a piece of metal, plastic, or other firm material shaped to the mouth with false teeth set into it. 19 a thin cut of beef from the lower end of the ribs. See **beef** for diagram. 20 (in electronics) the electrode toward which the electrons flow in a vacuum tube. 21 beam that supports the ends of rafters, etc.
—*v.t.* 1 cover with a thin layer of gold, silver, or other metal by mechanical, electrical, or chemical means. 2 overlay with protective metal plates; cover with armor plate. 3 make a plate from (type) for printing.
[< Old French, feminine of *plat* flat < Popular Latin *plattus* < Greek *platys*] **—plate′like′,** *adj.*

pla teau (pla tō′), *n., pl.* **-teaus** or **-teaux** (-tōz′). 1 plain in the mountains or at a height considerably above sea level; large, high plain; tableland. 2 a level, especially the level at which something is stabilized for a period. [< French < Old French *platel,* diminutive of *plat* flat. See PLATE.]

plate ful (plāt′fu̇l), *n., pl.* **-fuls.** as much as a plate will hold.

plate glass, thick and very clear glass made in smooth, polished sheets and used for large windowpanes, mirrors, etc.

plate let (plāt′lit), *n.* 1 a small or minute plate. 2 blood platelet.

plat en (plat′n), *n.* 1 a flat metal plate in a printing press, that presses the paper against the inked type. 2 the roller against which the paper rests in a typewriter.

plat form (plat′fôrm), *n.* 1 a raised level surface. There usually is a platform beside the track at a railroad station. A hall usually has a platform for speakers. 2 plan of action or statement of principles of a person or group, especially one adopted by a political party at a nominating convention. 3 a thick outer sole on a woman's shoe. 4 Usually, **platform shoe,** a woman's shoe with a thick outer sole. [< Middle French *plateforme* flat form]

plat ing (plā′ting), *n.* 1 a thin layer of silver, gold, or other metal. 2 a covering of metal plates. 3 act of a person or thing that plates.

pla tin ic (plə tin′ik), *adj.* of or containing platinum, especially with a valence of four.

plat i nous (plat′n əs), *adj.* of or containing platinum, especially with a valence of two.

plat i num (plat′n əm), *n.* 1 a heavy, silver-white, precious metallic element with a very high melting point, that is ductile, malleable, resistant to acid, and does not tarnish easily. It is used as a catalyst, for chemical and industrial equipment, in jewelry, etc. *Symbol:* Pt; *atomic number* 78. See pages 326 and 327 for table. 2 a light-gray color. [< New Latin < Spanish *platina* < *plata* silver]

platinum blonde or **platinum blond,** 1 silvery blond hair. 2 woman or girl with such hair.

plat i tude (plat′ə tüd, plat′ə tyüd), *n.* 1 a dull or commonplace remark, especially one given out solemnly as if it were fresh and important: *"Better late than never" is a platitude.* 2 flatness; triteness; dullness. [< French < *plat* flat]

plat i tu di nous (plat′ə tüd′n əs, plat′ə-tyüd′n əs), *adj.* characterized by platitudes; using platitudes; being a platitude.

Pla to (plā′tō), *n.* 427?-347? B.C., Greek philosopher, the pupil of Socrates and teacher of Aristotle.

Pla ton ic (plə ton′ik), *adj.* 1 of or having to do with Plato or his philosophy. 2 Also, **platonic.** designating love or affection of a purely spiritual character, free from sensual desire. 3 idealistic; not practical: *The League of Nations seemed a Platonic scheme to many people.* **—pla ton′i cal ly,** *adv.*

Pla to nism (plāt′n iz′əm), *n.* philosophy or doctrines of Plato or his followers.

Pla to nist (plāt′n ist), *n.* follower of Plato; adherent of Platonism.

pla toon (plə tün′), *n.* 1 a military unit made up of two or more squads, usually commanded by a lieutenant. It is smaller than a company. 2 (in football) either of two divisions of a team, one of which specializes in offensive play and the other in defensive play. 3 a small group. [< French *peloton,* diminutive of *pelote* pellet]

plat ter (plat′ər), *n.* 1 a large, shallow dish for holding or serving food, especially meat and fish. 2 SLANG. a phonograph record. [< Anglo-French *plater* < Old French *plat* plate]

Platte River (plat), river flowing from central Nebraska into the Missouri River. 310 mi.

plat y hel minth (plat′ə hel′minth), *n.* any of a phylum of flat or cylindrical worms, having soft, bilaterally symmetrical bodies, a distinct head, and no body cavity; flatworm. Tapeworms, turbellarians, and flukes belong to this phylum. [< Greek *platys* flat + *helminthos* worm, helminth]

Plat y hel min thes (plat′ə hel min′thēz), *n.pl.* phylum of invertebrates comprising the platyhelminths.

plat y pus (plat′ə pəs), *n., pl.* **-pus es, -pi** (-pī). duckbilled platypus. [< Greek *platypous* < *platys* flat + *pous* foot]

plau dit (plô′dit), *n.* Usually, **plaudits,** *pl.* round of applause; enthusiastic expression of approval or praise. [alteration of Latin *plaudite* applaud!]

plau si bil i ty (plô′zə bil′ə tē), *n.* appearance of being true or reasonable; plausible quality.

plau si ble (plô′zə bəl), *adj.* 1 appearing true, reasonable, or fair. 2 apparently worthy of confidence but often not really so: *a plausible liar.* [< Latin *plausibilis* deserving applause, pleasing < *plaudere* applaud] **—plau′si bly,** *adv.*

Plau tus (plô′təs), *n.* 254?-184 B.C., Roman writer of comedies.

play (plā), *n.* 1 something done to amuse oneself; fun; sport; recreation: *children at play.* See synonym study below. 2 a turn, move, or act in a game: *a clever play at checkers. It is your play next.* 3 act of carrying on or playing a game: *Play was slow in the first half of the game.* 4 manner or style of carrying on or playing a game. 5 story written for or presented as a dramatic or theatrical performance; drama. 6 a dramatic or theatrical performance, as on the stage. 7 action or dealing of a specified kind: *fair play.* 8 activity; operation; working: *the lively play of fancy.* 9 light, quick movement or change: *the play of sunlight on leaves, the play of light in a diamond.* 10 freedom or opportunity for action; scope for activity: *give free play to one's faculties.* 11 free or unimpeded movement: *too much play in the steering wheel.* 12 the proper motion of a piece of mechanism or of a part of the living body: *the play of muscles.* 13 gambling: *lose vast sums at play.* 14 **in play, a** (of a ball, etc.) in actual use within bounds during a play in a game. **b** as a joke. 15 **out of play,** (of a ball, etc.) officially declared to be no longer in play.
—*v.t.* 1 engage in (a game or definite form of amusement): *play golf. Children play tag and ball.* 2 perform, do, or execute: *play a trick on someone.* 3 represent or imitate, especially for amusement: *play spacemen, play store.* 4 contend against in a game or as in a game: *New York played Boston for the championship.* 5 represent or act (a part) in a dramatic performance or in real life: *play one's part well.* 6 act or behave as or like: *play the host, play the fool.* 7 represent (a person or character) in a dramatic performance: *play Hamlet.* 8 perform or act (a drama, pageant, etc.) on the stage: *play a tragedy.* 9 give dramatic performances in: *play the best theaters, play the largest cities.* 10 perform (music or a piece of music) on an instrument: *play a symphony.* 11 perform on (a musical instrument): *play a piano.* 12 keep in continuous motion or exercise; operate; work (any instrument): *play a hose on a burning building.* 13 cause to move or pass lightly: *The ship played its light along the coast.* 14 stake or wager in a game: *play five dollars.* 15 lay a stake or wager on: *play the horses.* 16 put into action in a game: *play the king of hearts.*

17 allow (a hooked fish) to exhaust itself by pulling on the line. —*v.i.* 1 have fun; do something in sport; amuse or divert oneself: *The children played in the yard.* 2 do something which is not to be taken seriously, but merely as done in sport. 3 make believe; pretend in fun. 4 dally; trifle; toy: *play with a new idea, play with matches.* 5 engage or take part in a game: *play with skill.* 6 act, behave, or conduct oneself in some specified way: *play fair, play sick.* 7 perform on a musical instrument: *play in an orchestra.* 8 (of the instrument or the music) to sound: *The music began playing.* 9 act on or as on a stage; perform: *play in a tragedy.* 10 move briskly or lightly, especially with alternating or irregular motion: *A breeze played on the waters.* 11 change or alternate rapidly. 12 move or revolve freely: *The wheel plays in a track.* 13 operate with continued or repeated action: *A fountain played in the garden.* 14 gamble.

play back, replay (a phonograph or tape recording), especially just after it has been made.

play down, make light of; understate.

played out, a exhausted. b finished; done with.

play off, a play an additional game or match in order to decide (a draw or tie). b pit (one person or thing against another), especially for one's own advantage.

play on or **play upon,** take advantage of; make use of.

play out, perform to the end; bring to an end: *play out a tragedy.*

play up, U.S. make the most of; exploit.

play up to, SLANG. try to get into the favor of; flatter.

[Old English *plega*]

Syn. *n.* 1 **Play, sport, game** mean activity or exercise of mind or body engaged in for recreation or fun. **Play** is the general word: *Play is as necessary as work.* **Sport** applies to any form of athletics or an outdoor pastime, whether it requires much or little activity or is merely watched for pleasure: *Fencing, swimming, fishing, and horse racing are his favorite sports.* **Game** applies especially to an activity in the form of a contest, mental or physical, played by certain rules: *Tennis and chess are games.*

pla ya (plä′yə), *n.* 1 (in the southwestern United States) a plain of silt or mud, covered with water during the wet season. 2 (in geology) the basin floor of an undrained desert which contains water at irregular periods. [< Spanish, beach]

play a ble (plā′ə bəl), *adj.* 1 that can be played. 2 fit to be played on.

play act (plā′akt′), *v.i.* 1 perform in a dramatic production. 2 make believe; pretend.

play back (plā′bak′), *n.* the replaying of a tape recording, videotape, etc., especially just after it has been made.

play bill (plā′bil′), *n.* 1 handbill or placard announcing a play. 2 program of a play.

play boy (plā′boi′), *n.* man, usually wealthy, whose chief interest is in having a good time.

play-by-play (plā′bī plā′), *adj.* U.S. presenting a running commentary, especially on a sports event.

play er (plā′ər), *n.* 1 person who plays, especially in a game. 2 actor in a theater. 3 musician. 4 thing or device that plays, especially a mechanical device for playing a musical instrument or reproducing music: *a record player.*

player piano, piano played by machinery.

play fel low (plā′fel′ō), *n.* playmate.

play ful (plā′fəl), *adj.* 1 full of fun; fond of playing; sportive. 2 joking; not serious. **—play′ful ly,** *adv.* **—play′ful ness,** *n.*

play go er (plā′gō′ər), *n.* person who goes often to the theater.

play ground (plā′ground′), *n.* place for outdoor play, especially by children, often containing equipment for games and sports.

play house (plā′hous′), *n., pl.* **-hous es** (-hou′ziz). 1 a small house for a child to play in. 2 dollhouse. 3 theater.

playing card, card used in playing games like bridge, poker, and pinochle, usually being one of a set of 52 cards including 4 suits (spades, hearts, diamonds, and clubs) of 13 cards each.

play let (plā′lit), *n.* a short play.

play mate (plā′māt′), *n.* person who plays with another.

play-off (plā′ôf′, plā′of′), *n.* 1 game or series of games played after the regular season to decide a championship. 2 an extra game, round, etc., played to settle a tie.

play on words, pun.

play pen (plā′pen′), *n.* a small folding pen for a baby or young child to play in.

play room (plā′rüm′, plā′rům′), *n.* room for children to play in.

play thing (plā′thing′), *n.* thing to play with; toy.

play time (plā′tīm′), *n.* time for playing.

play wright (plā′rīt′), *n.* writer of plays; dramatist.

plaz a (plaz′ə, plä′zə), *n.* a public square in a city or town. [< Spanish < Latin *platea* broad street. Doublet of PLACE, PIAZZA.]

plea (plē), *n.* 1 request or appeal; an asking: *a plea for pity.* 2 excuse or defense: *The man's plea was that he did not see the signal.* 3 answer made by a defendant to a charge against him in a court of law. [< Old French *plaid* < Late Latin *placitum* (that) which pleases < Latin *placere* please]

plead (plēd), *v.,* **plead ed** or **pled, plead ing.** —*v.t.* 1 offer reasons for or against; argue. 2 offer as an excuse: *The woman who stole pleaded poverty.* 3 speak for or against in a court of law: *A good lawyer pleaded the case.* 4 answer to a charge in a court of law: *The defendant pleaded guilty.* —*v.i.* 1 ask earnestly; make an earnest appeal; beg; implore. 2 conduct a case in a court of law. [< Old French *plaidier* < *plaid* plea] **—plead′a ble,** *adj.* **—plead′ing ly,** *adv.*

plead er (plē′dər), *n.* person who pleads, especially in a court of law.

plead ing (plē′ding), *n.* 1 the advocating of a case in a court of law. 2 **pleadings,** *pl.* the formal charges or claims by the plaintiff and answers by the defendant in a lawsuit.

pleas ance (plez′ns), *n.* 1 a pleasant place, usually with trees, fountains, and flowers, and maintained as part of the grounds of a country estate. 2 ARCHAIC. pleasure.

pleas ant (plez′nt), *adj.* 1 that pleases; giving pleasure; agreeable: *a pleasant swim on a hot day.* See synonym study below. 2 easy to get along with; friendly. 3 fair; not stormy. **—pleas′ant ly,** *adv.* **—pleas′ant ness,** *n.*

Syn. 1 **Pleasant, pleasing, agreeable** mean giving pleasure or satisfaction to the mind, feelings, or senses. **Pleasant** applies to the person or thing that gives pleasure: *We spent a pleasant evening.* **Pleasing** focuses attention on the person who receives pleasure: *It was pleasing to me because I wanted to see them.* **Agreeable** suggests being to a person's own taste or liking: *I think this cough medicine has an agreeable flavor.*

hat, āge, fär; let, ēqual, tėrm;
it, īce; hot, ōpen, ôrder;
oil, out; cup, pu̇t, rüle;
ch, child; ng, long; sh, she;
th, thin; ᴛʜ, then; zh, measure;

ə represents *a* in about, *e* in taken, *i* in pencil, *o* in lemon, *u* in circus.

< = from, derived from, taken from.

pleas ant ry (plez′n trē), *n., pl.* **-ries.** 1 a good-natured joke; jesting action or witty remark. 2 fun; joking.

please (plēz), *v.,* **pleased, pleas ing.** —*v.t.* 1 be agreeable to: *Toys please children.* 2 be the will of: *May it please the court to show mercy.* —*v.i.* 1 be agreeable: *Such a fine meal cannot fail to please.* 2 wish; think fit: *Do what you please.* 3 may it please you (now used merely as a polite addition to requests or commands). 4 **be pleased,** a be moved to pleasure. b be disposed; like; choose. 5 **if you please,** if you like; with your permission. [< Old French *plaisir* < Latin *placere*]

pleas ing (plē′zing), *adj.* giving pleasure; pleasant. See **pleasant** for synonym study. **—pleas′ing ly,** *adv.* **—pleas′ing ness,** *n.*

pleas ur a ble (plezh′ər ə bəl, plā′zhər ə-bəl), *adj.* pleasant; agreeable. **—pleas′ur a-ble ness,** *n.* **—pleas′ur a bly,** *adv.*

pleas ure (plezh′ər, plā′zhər), *n.* 1 a feeling of being pleased; enjoyment; delight; joy. See synonym study below. 2 something that pleases; cause of joy or delight. 3 anything that amuses; sport; play. 4 one's will, desire, or choice: *What is your pleasure in this matter?* [< Old French *plaisir,* noun use of verb. See PLEASE.]

Syn. 1 **Pleasure, delight, joy** mean a feeling of satisfaction and happiness coming from having, experiencing, or expecting something good or to one's liking. **Pleasure** is the general word applying to the feeling whether or not it is shown in any way: *The compliment gave her pleasure.* **Delight** means great pleasure, usually shown or expressed in a lively way: *He expressed his delight with a warm handshake.* **Joy** applies to intense delight, expressing itself in cheer and high spirits: *The child clapped her hands with joy.*

pleat
pleats in a skirt

pleat (plēt), *n.* a flat, usually narrow, fold made in cloth by doubling it on itself. —*v.t.* fold or arrange in pleats: *a pleated skirt.* Also, **plait.** [variant of *plait*] **—pleat′er,** *n.*

plebe (plēb), *n.* member of the lowest class at a military or naval academy, especially the United States Military Academy, Naval Academy, or Air Force Academy. [short for *plebeian*]

ple be ian (pli bē′ən), *adj.* 1 belonging or having to do with the common people; common; vulgar. 2 belonging or having to do with the lower class of citizens in ancient Rome. *—n.* 1 one of the common people. 2 one of the common people of ancient Rome. [< Latin *plebeius* < *plebs* the common people]

ple be ian ism (pli bē′ə niz′əm), *n.* plebeian character or ways.

pleb i scite (pleb′ə sīt, pleb′ə sit), *n.* a direct vote by the qualified voters of a country, state, community, etc., on some important question. [< Latin *plebiscitum* < *plebs* the common people + *scitum* decree]

plebs (plebz), *n., pl.* **ple bes** (plē′bēz). 1 the common people of ancient Rome. 2 the common people; the populace. [< Latin]

plec trum (plek′trəm), *n., pl.* **-trums, -tra** (-trə). a small piece of ivory, horn, metal, etc., used for plucking the strings of a mandolin, lyre, zither, etc.; pick. [< Latin < Greek *plēktron* < *plēssein* to strike]

pled (pled), *v.* INFORMAL. a pt. and a pp. of **plead.**

pledge (plej), *n., v.,* **pledged, pledg ing.** *—n.* 1 solemn promise: *a pledge to support a candidate.* 2 something given to another as a guarantee of good faith, the performance of an action, etc.; security. 3 condition of being held as security: *put bonds in pledge for a loan.* 4 act of handing something over to another as security. 5 the drinking of a health or toast. 6 something given to show favor or love or as a promise of something to come; sign; token. 7 U.S. person who has promised to join an organization but is serving a probationary period before membership. 8 **take the pledge,** promise not to drink alcoholic liquor. *—v.t.* 1 undertake to give; promise solemnly: *pledge allegiance to the flag, pledge $100 to a charity.* 2 cause to promise solemnly; bind by a promise: *pledge hearers to secrecy.* 3 give as security: *pledge land for a loan.* 4 drink a health to; drink in honor of (someone) and wish (him) well; toast. [< Old French *plege* < Medieval Latin *plegium, plebium;* of Germanic origin] **—pledg′er, pledg′or,** *n.*

pledg ee (plej ē′), *n.* person with whom something is deposited as a pledge.

Ple iad (plē′ad, plī′ad), *n.* any of the Pleiades.

Ple ia des (plē′ə dēz′, plī′ə dēz′), *n.pl.* 1 cluster of several hundred stars in the shoulder of the constellation Taurus. Six of these stars can normally be seen with the naked eye. 2 (in Greek myths) seven of the daughters of Atlas, who were transformed by the gods into this group of stars.

Pleis to cene (plī′stə sēn′), *n.* 1 the geological epoch before the present period; ice age. See chart under **geology.** 2 deposits of gravel, etc., made in this epoch. *—adj.* of or having to do with this epoch or its deposits. [< Greek *pleistos* most + *kainos* recent]

ple nar y (plē′nər ē, plen′ər ē), *adj.* 1 not lacking in any way; full; complete; absolute: *an ambassador with plenary powers.* 2 attended by all of its qualified members: *a plenary session of a committee.* [< Late Latin *plenarius* < Latin *plenus* full]

plenary indulgence, (in the Roman Catholic Church) complete remission of temporal penalty for sin.

plen i po ten ti ar y (plen′ə pə ten′shē er′ē, plen′ə pə ten′shər ē), *n., pl.* **-ar ies,** *adj.* *—n.* a diplomatic agent having full power or authority. *—adj.* having or giving full power and authority. [< Medieval Latin *plenipotentiarius* < Latin *plenus* full + *potentem* powerful]

plen i tude (plen′ə tüd, plen′ə tyüd), *n.* fullness; completeness; abundance. [< Latin *plenitudo* < *plenus* full]

plen te ous (plen′tē əs), *adj.* 1 present or existing in full supply; abundant; plentiful. 2 bearing or yielding abundantly; prolific; fertile. **—plen′te ous ly,** *adv.* **—plen′te ous ness,** *n.*

plen ti ful (plen′ti fəl), *adj.* 1 more than enough; ample; abundant: *a plentiful supply of food.* 2 furnished with or yielding abundance. **—plen′ti ful ly,** *adv.* **—plen′ti ful ness,** *n.*

plen ty (plen′tē), *n., pl.* **-ties,** *adj., adv.* *—n.* 1 a full supply; all that one needs; large enough number or quantity: *There is plenty of time.* 2 quality or condition of being plentiful; abundance: *years of peace and plenty.* *—adj.* enough; plentiful; abundant: *Six potatoes will be plenty.* *—adv.* INFORMAL. quite; fully: *plenty good enough.* [< Latin *plenitatem* fullness < *plenus* full]

ple num (plē′nəm), *n., pl.* **-nums, -na** (-nə). 1 an enclosed quantity of air or other gas under greater pressure than the outside atmosphere. 2 a full assembly, as a joint assembly of the upper and lower houses of a legislature. [< Latin *plenum (spatium)* full (space)]

ple o nasm (plē′ə naz′əm), *n.* 1 use of more words than are necessary to express an idea; redundancy. "The two twins" is a pleonasm. 2 an instance of this. 3 the unnecessary word, phrase, or expression. [< Greek *pleonasmos,* ultimately < *pleōn* more]

ple o nas tic (plē′ə nas′tik), *adj.* using more words than are needed; superfluous; redundant. **—ple′o nas′ti cal ly,** *adv.*

ple si o saur (plē′sē ə sôr′), *n.* any of an order of large sea reptiles of the Mesozoic era, now extinct, that had a long neck and flippers instead of legs. [< Greek *plēsios* near + *sauros* lizard]

pleth or a (pleth′ər ə), *n.* 1 excessive fullness; superabundance; excess. 2 an abnormal condition characterized by an excess of blood in the body. [< Greek *plēthōrē* < *plēthein* be full]

ple thor ic (ple thôr′ik, ple thor′ik, pleth′ər ik), *adj.* 1 too full; inflated. 2 having too much blood; afflicted with plethora.

pleur a (plůr′ə), *n., pl.* **pleur ae** (plůr′ē). a thin membrane in the body of a mammal, covering each lung and folded back to make a lining for the thorax or chest cavity. [< Greek, rib]

pleur al (plůr′əl), *adj.* of the pleura.

pleur i sy (plůr′ə sē), *n.* inflammation of the pleura, often marked by fever, chest pains, and difficulty in breathing.

pleu rit ic (plů rit′ik), *adj.* 1 having pleurisy. 2 of pleurisy. 3 causing pleurisy.

pleur o pneu mo nia (plůr′ō nü mō′nyə, plůr′ō nü mō′nē ə; plůr′ō nyü mō′nyə, plůr′ō nyü mō′nē ə), *n.* pneumonia complicated with pleurisy.

Plex i glas (plek′sə glas′), *n.* trademark for a light, transparent thermoplastic, often used in place of glass.

plex us (plek′səs), *n., pl.* **-us es** or **-us.** 1 network of nerve fibers, blood vessels, etc. 2 any complicated network. [< Latin < *plectere* to twine]

pli a bil i ty (plī′ə bil′ə tē), *n.* pliable condition or quality.

pli a ble (plī′ə bəl), *adj.* 1 easily bent; flexible; supple: *Willow twigs are pliable.* 2 easily influenced; yielding: *He is too pliable to be a good leader.* [< French < *plier* to bend] **—pli′a ble ness,** *n.* **—pli′a bly,** *adv.*

pli an cy (plī′ən sē), *n.* pliant condition or quality.

pli ant (plī′ənt), *adj.* 1 bending easily; flexible; supple. 2 easily influenced; yielding: *a pliant nature.* See **flexible** for synonym study. 3 changing easily to fit different conditions; adaptable. **—pli′ant ly,** *adv.*

pli cate (plī′kāt), *adj.* 1 folded like a fan; pleated. 2 (of a leaf) folded along its ribs like a closed fan. [< Latin *plicatum* folded] **—pli′cate ly,** *adv.* **—pli′cate ness,** *n.*

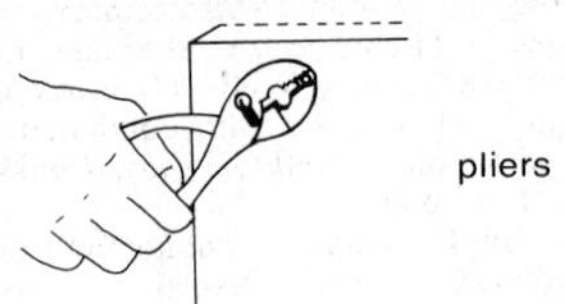
pliers

pli ers (plī′ərz), *n. pl. or sing.* small pincers with long jaws, for bending or cutting wire, holding small objects, etc. [< *ply*[1]]

plight[1] (plīt), *n.* condition or situation, usually bad: *in a sad plight.* See **predicament** for synonym study. [Middle English *plite,* originally, manner of folding < Old French *pleit* < Latin *plicare* to fold]

plight[2] (plīt), *v.t.* promise solemnly; pledge: *plight one's loyalty.* *—n.* a solemn promise; pledge. [Old English *plihtan* < *pliht,* originally, danger, risk]

Plim soll mark or **Plimsoll line** (plim′səl, plim′sol), one of a set of marks or lines on the hull of a ship that show how deep it may ride in the water, under varying conditions of water temperature and weather, after loading. [< Samuel *Plimsoll,* 1824-1898, British reformer of shipping practices]

plink (plingk), *v.t., v.i.* 1 produce a tinkling sound. 2 shoot or throw at a target, especially in a more or less casual way. [imitative]

plinth (plinth), *n.* 1 the lower, square part of the base of a column. 2 a square base of a pedestal, as for a statue, bust, or vase. [< Greek *plinthos*]

Plin y (plin′ē), *n.* 1 A.D. 23-79, Roman naturalist and writer, called "Pliny the Elder." 2 his nephew, A.D. 61?-113?, Roman orator, statesman, and writer, called "Pliny the Younger."

Pli o cene (plī′ə sēn′), *n.* 1 the latest geological epoch of the Tertiary period, during which the first manlike apes appeared. See chart under **geology.** 2 rocks formed in this epoch. *—adj.* of or having to do with this epoch or its rocks. [< Greek *pleiōn* more + *kainos* recent]

Pli o film (plī′ə film), *n.* trademark for a clear, flexible plastic used to make raincoats, protective bags, etc.

plod (plod), *v.,* **plod ded, plod ding.** *—v.i.* 1 walk heavily or slowly; trudge. See **walk** for synonym study. 2 proceed in a slow or dull way; work patiently with effort: *I plodded away at the lessons until I learned them.* *—v.t.* walk heavily or slowly along or through. *—n.* 1 act or course of plodding. 2 sound of heavy tread. [perhaps imitative] **—plod′der,** *n.* **—plod′ding ly,** *adv.*

plop (plop), *n., v.,* **plopped, plop ping.** *—n.* sound like that of a flat object striking water without a splash. *—v.i.* 1 make such a sound. 2 fall with such a sound. *—v.t.* cause (some-

hat, āge, fär; let, ēqual, tėrm;
it, īce; hot, ōpen, ôrder;
oil, out; cup, pu̇t, rüle;
ch, child; ng, long; sh, she;
th, thin; ᴛʜ, then; zh, measure;

ə represents *a* in about, *e* in taken, *i* in pencil, *o* in lemon, *u* in circus.

< = from, derived from, taken from.

thing) to plop, or fall with a plop. [imitative]

plot (plot), *n., v.,* **plot ted, plot ting.** *—n.* 1 a secret plan, especially to do something wrong; conspiracy: *Two men formed a plot to rob the bank.* 2 the plan or main story of a play, novel, poem, etc. 3 a small piece of ground: *a garden plot.* 4 a map, diagram, or chart. *—v.t.* 1 plan secretly with others; plan: *plot revenge.* 2 divide (land) into plots. 3 make a map, diagram, or chart of. 4 mark the position of (something) on a map, diagram, or chart. 5 in mathematics: **a** determine the location of (a point) by means of its coordinates. **b** form (a curve) by connecting points marked out on a graph. *—v.i.* 1 contrive a secret plot; conspire. See synonym study below. 2 devise a literary plot. [Old English, patch of ground] **—plot′less,** *adj.* **—plot′ter,** *n.*

Syn. *v.i.* 1 **Plot, conspire, scheme** mean to plan secretly. **Plot** implies forming secretly, alone or together with others, a carefully designed plan, usually harmful or treacherous, against a person, group, or country: *Enemy agents plotted to blow up the plant.* **Conspire** implies combining with others to carry out an illegal act, especially treachery or treason: *They conspired to overthrow the government.* **Scheme** implies careful planning, often in a crafty or underhand way, to gain one's own ends: *He schemed to become president.*

plough (plou), *n., v.t., v.i.* plow.

plough boy (plou′boi′), *n.* plowboy.

plough man (plou′mən), *n., pl.* **-men.** plowman.

plough share (plou′sher′, plou′shar′), *n.* plowshare.

plov er (pluv′ər, plō′vər), *n., pl.* **-ers** or **-er.** any of various small shore birds of the same family as the killdeer, with short tails and bills and long, pointed wings. [< Anglo-French, ultimately < Latin *pluvia* rain]

plow (plou), *n.* 1 a farm implement used for cutting and lifting the soil and turning it over. 2 snowplow. 3 any of various instruments, parts of machinery, etc., resembling a plow in shape or action. *—v.t.* 1 turn up the soil of with a plow; furrow: *plow a field.* 2 remove with a plow or as if with a plow: *plow snow, plow up old roots.* 3 move through as a plow does: *The ship plowed the waves.* 4 **plow back,** reinvest (the profits of a business) in the same business. 5 **plow under, a** plow into the ground to make manure. **b** INFORMAL. defeat or overwhelm. *—v.i.* 1 use a plow. 2 move as a plow does; advance slowly and with effort: *plow through a book.* Also, **plough.** [Old English *plōh*] **—plow′a ble,** *adj.* **—plow′er,** *n.*

plow boy (plou′boi′), *n.* boy who guides a plow or the horses drawing a plow. Also, **ploughboy.**

plow man (plou′mən), *n., pl.* **-men.** 1 man who guides a plow. 2 a farm worker. Also, **ploughman.**

plow share (plou′sher′, plou′shar′), *n.* blade of a plow; the part that cuts the soil. Also, **ploughshare.**

ploy (ploi), *n.* gambit or maneuver by which an advantage is or may be gained over another. [short for *employ*]

pluck (pluk), *v.t.* 1 pull off; pick: *pluck flowers in the garden.* 2 pull at; pull; tug; jerk: *pluck a person by the sleeve.* 3 pull on (the strings of a musical instrument). 4 pull off the feathers or hair from: *pluck a chicken.* 5 SLANG. rob; swindle; fleece. *—v.i.* 1 pull sharply or forcibly; tug (at): *She plucked at the loose threads of her coat.* 2 **pluck up,** get new courage; cheer up. *—n.* 1 act of picking or pulling. 2 courage; boldness; spirit. 3 heart, liver, and lungs of an animal killed for food. [Old English *pluccian*]

pluck y (pluk′ē), *adj.,* **pluck i er, pluck i est.** having or showing courage. **—pluck′i ly,** *adv.* **—pluck′i ness,** *n.*

plug (plug), *n., v.,* **plugged, plug ging.** *—n.* 1 a piece of wood, etc., used to stop up a hole which it tightly fits, to fill a gap, or to act as a wedge; stopper. 2 device to make an electrical connection. Some plugs screw into sockets; others have prongs. 3 hydrant. 4 a cake of pressed tobacco. 5 a piece of this cut off for chewing. 6 a spark plug. 7 INFORMAL. **a** an advertisement or recommendation, especially one put in a radio or television program. **b** a worn-out or inferior horse. 8 a fishing lure made of wood, metal, or plastic, and imitating the action or appearance of some natural food of a fish. 9 a cylindrical mass of igneous rock formed in the crater of an extinct volcano.
—v.t. 1 stop up or fill with a plug. 2 **plug in,** make an electrical connection by inserting a plug. 3 INFORMAL. recommend or advertise, especially on a radio or television program: *plug a new product.* 4 SLANG. put a bullet into; shoot. *—v.i.* INFORMAL. work steadily; plod: *She plugged away at the typewriter.*
[< Middle Dutch *plugge* a bung, stopper] **—plug′ger,** *n.*

plug hat, INFORMAL. a man's high silk hat.

plug-ug ly (plug′ug′lē), *n., pl.* **-lies.** SLANG. ruffian.

plum[1] (plum), *n.* 1 a roundish, juicy, edible fruit with a smooth skin of purple, blue, red, green, or yellow, and a stone or pit. 2 tree that it grows on, belonging to the rose family. 3 raisin in a pudding, cake, etc. 4 sugarplum. 5 something very good or desirable: *His new job is a fine plum.* 6 a dark purple varying from bluish to reddish. *—adj.* dark bluish-purple or reddish-purple. [Old English *plūme* < Latin *prunum* < Greek *proumnon.* Doublet of PRUNE.] **—plum′like′,** *adj.*

plum[2] (plum), *adj., adv.* plumb.

plum age (plü′mij), *n.* feathers of a bird: *A parrot has bright plumage.* [< Old French < *plume* plume]

plumb (plum), *n.* 1 a small weight used on the end of a line to find the depth of water or to see if a wall is vertical; plummet; lead. 2 **out of plumb** or **off plumb,** not vertical. *—adj.* 1 vertical. 2 INFORMAL. complete; thorough. Also, **plum.** *—adv.* 1 vertically. 2 INFORMAL. completely; thoroughly. Also, **plum.** *—v.t.* 1 test or adjust by a plumb line; sound: *Our line was not long enough to plumb the depths of the lake.* 2 get to the bottom of; fathom: *No one could plumb the mystery.* [< Latin *plumbum* lead]

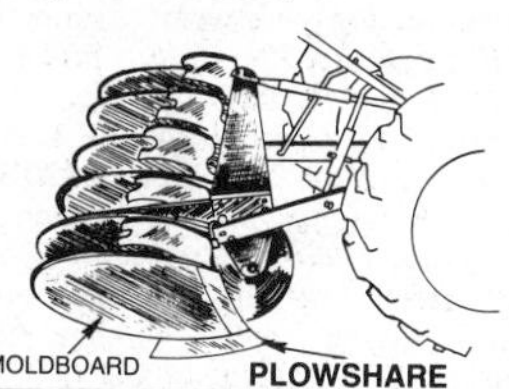

plum ba go (plum bā′gō), *n.* graphite. [< Latin, lead ore < *plumbum* lead]

plumb bob, weight at the end of a plumb line.

plumb er (plum′ər), *n.* person whose work is putting in and repairing water pipes and fixtures in buildings. [< Old French *plombier,* ultimately < Latin *plumbum* lead]

plumb ing (plum′ing), *n.* 1 work or trade of a plumber. 2 the water pipes and fixtures in a building: *bathroom plumbing.*

plum bism (plum′biz′əm), *n.* lead poisoning.

plumb line, line with a plumb at the end, used to find the depth of water or to test the straightness of a wall.

plume (plüm), *n., v.,* **plumed, plum ing.** *—n.* 1 feather, especially a large, long, or conspicuous feather. 2 feather or bunch of feathers, tuft of hair, etc., worn as an ornament on a hat, helmet, etc. 3 any feathered part or formation as of an insect, seed, leaf, etc. 4 ornament or token of distinction or honor. *—v.t.* 1 furnish with plumes. 2 smooth or arrange the feathers of; preen: *The eagle plumed its wing.* 3 show pride in (oneself): *She plumed herself on her skill in dancing.* [< Old French < Latin *pluma*]

plum met (plum′it), *n.* plumb. *—v.i.* plunge; drop. [< Old French *plommet* < *plomb* lead < Latin *plumbum*]

plu mose (plü′mōs), *adj.* 1 having feathers or plumes; feathered. 2 like a plume; feathery. **—plu′mose ly,** *adv.*

plump[1] (plump), *adj.* rounded out; attractively fat. *—v.t., v.i.* make or become plump. [origin uncertain] **—plump′ness,** *n.*

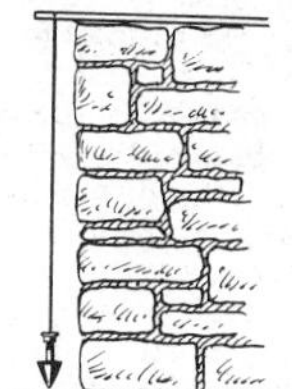

plumb (def. 1) used to test vertical line of a wall

plump[2] (plump), *v.i.* fall or drop heavily or suddenly: *All out of breath, she plumped down on a chair.* *—v.t.* 1 let fall or drop heavily or suddenly: *plump down one's bags at the station.* 2 **plump for,** give one's complete support to; champion vigorously. *—n.* INFORMAL. 1 a sudden plunge; heavy fall. 2 sound made by a plunge or fall. *—adv.* 1 heavily or suddenly: *He ran plump into me.* 2 directly; bluntly. *—adj.* direct; downright; blunt. [imitative]

plum pudding, a rich, boiled or steamed pudding containing raisins, currants, spices, etc.

plu mule (plü′myül), *n.* 1 a small soft feather. 2 the rudimentary terminal bud of the embryo of a seed. [< Latin *plumula,* diminutive of *pluma* feather]

plum y (plü′mē), *adj.* 1 having plumes or feathers. 2 adorned with a plume or plumes. 3 like a plume.

plun der (plun′dər), *v.t.* rob by force; rob: *The pirates entered the harbor and began to plunder the town.* —*n.* 1 things taken in plundering; booty; loot. See synonym study below. 2 act of robbing by force. [< German *plündern*] —**plun′der er,** *n.*

Syn. *n.* 1 **Plunder, booty, loot** mean things taken by force. **Plunder** applies especially to things carried off by invading soldiers during a war: *Much plunder from Europe reached Russia after World War II.* **Booty** applies particularly to things carried off and shared later by a band of robbers: *The bandits fought over their booty.* **Loot** applies particularly to things carried off from bodies and buildings in a city destroyed in war or the scene of a fire, wreck, etc., but is used also of anything taken by robbery or other crime: *Much loot was sold after the great riots.*

plunge (plunj), *v.,* **plunged, plung ing,** *n.* —*v.t.* throw or thrust with force into a liquid, place, or condition: *plunge one's hand into water, plunge the world into war.* See **dip** for synonym study. —*v.i.* 1 throw oneself (into water, danger, a fight, etc.): *plunge into debt, plunge feverishly into study.* 2 rush; dash: *The fullback plunged forward five yards.* 3 pitch suddenly and violently: *The ship plunged about in the storm.* 4 INFORMAL. gamble or speculate recklessly or heavily. —*n.* 1 act of plunging. 2 a jump or thrust; dive. [< Old French *plungier,* ultimately < Latin *plumbum* lead]

plung er (plun′jər), *n.* 1 person or thing that plunges. 2 part of a machine, such as a piston in a pump, that acts with a plunging motion. 3 a rubber suction cup on a long stick, used for unplugging stopped-up drains, toilets, etc. 4 INFORMAL. a reckless gambler or speculator.

plunk (plungk), *v.t.* 1 pluck (a banjo, guitar, etc.). 2 make a sudden twanging sound like the plucking of a stringed musical instrument; twang. 3 throw, push, put, drop, etc., heavily or suddenly. 4 **plunk for,** INFORMAL. plump for. —*v.i.* make a sharp, twanging sound. —*n.* INFORMAL. act or sound of plunking. [imitative]

plu per fect (plü′pėr′fikt, plü′pėr′fikt), *n., adj.* past perfect. [short for Latin *plus quam perfectum* more than perfect]

plur., plural.

plur al (plůr′əl), *adj.* 1 more than one: *plural citizenship.* 2 in grammar: **a** signifying or implying more than one person or thing: *the plural ending -s, the plural noun "fishes."* **b** more than one in number. *Book* is singular; *books* is plural. —*n.* 1 the plural number in grammar. 2 a word in the plural number. [< Latin *pluralis* < *plus* more]

plu ral i ty (plů ral′ə tē), *n., pl.* **-ties.** 1 difference between the number of votes received by the winner of an election and the number received by the next highest candidate. 2 the number of votes received by the winner of an election which is less than a majority of the total vote. 3 the greater number; the majority. 4 a large number; multitude. 5 state or fact of being plural.

plur al ize (plůr′ə līz), *v.t.,* **-ized, -iz ing.** make plural; express in the plural form. —**plur′al i za′tion,** *n.*

plur al ly (plůr′ə lē), *adv.* in the plural number; so as to express or imply more than one.

plus (plus), *prep.* 1 increased by; added to: *3 plus 2 equals 5.* 2 and also: *The work of an engineer requires intelligence plus experience.* —*adj.* 1 more than: *a mark of B plus.* 2 INFORMAL. additional; extra. 3 more than zero; positive in quantity. 4 positively electrified; positive. 5 **be plus,** INFORMAL. have in addition. —*n.* 1 plus sign. 2 a positive quantity. 3 an added quantity; something extra; gain. [< Latin, more]

plus fours, loose, baggy knickers that come down below the knee.

plush (plush), *n.* fabric like velvet but having a longer and softer pile. —*adj.* INFORMAL. luxurious; expensive; stylish: *a plush office.* [< French *pluche,* ultimately < Latin *pilus* hair]

plush y (plush′ē), *adj.,* **plush i er, plush i est.** of or like plush.

plus sign, the sign (+), indicating that the quantity following is to be added, or is a positive quantity.

Plu tarch (plü′tärk), *n.* A.D. 46?-120?, Greek biographer, who wrote about the lives of famous Greeks and Romans.

Plu to (plü′tō), *n.* 1 (in Greek and Roman myths) the god of the lower world. 2 the eighth largest planet in the solar system and the farthest from the sun. See **solar system** for diagram.

plu toc ra cy (plü tok′rə sē), *n., pl.* **-cies.** 1 government in which the rich rule. 2 a ruling class of wealthy people. [< Greek *ploutokratia* < *ploutos* wealth + *kratos* power]

plu to crat (plü′tə krat), *n.* 1 person who has power or influence because of his wealth. 2 a wealthy person.

plu to crat ic (plü′tə krat′ik), *adj.* having power and influence because of wealth; of or having to do with plutocrats or plutocracy. —**plu′to crat′i cal ly,** *adv.*

plu ton ic (plü ton′ik), *adj.* of or having to do with a class of igneous rocks that have solidified far below the earth's surface.

plu to ni um (plü tō′nē əm), *n.* a radioactive metallic element produced artificially from uranium and found in minute quantities in pitchblende and other uranium ores. It is used as a source of energy in nuclear reactors and bombs. *Symbol:* Pu; *atomic number* 94. See pages 326 and 327 for table. [< *Pluto,* the planet]

plu vi al (plü′vē əl), *adj.* 1 of or having to do with rain. 2 characterized by much rain; rainy. 3 caused by rain. [< Latin *pluvialis* < *pluvia* rain]

ply[1] (plī), *v.,* **plied, ply ing.** —*v.t.* 1 work with; use: *The dressmaker plies her needle.* 2 keep up work on; work away at or on: *ply one's trade. We plied the water with our oars.* 3 urge again and again: *She plied me with questions to make me tell her what was in the package.* 4 supply with in a pressing manner: *ply a person with food or drink.* —*v.i.* go back and forth regularly between certain places: *A bus plies between the station and the hotel.* [variant of *apply*]

ply[2] (plī), *n., pl.* **plies.** 1 thickness or layer of cloth, paper, etc. 2 strand or twist of cord, yarn, or thread. [< Middle French *plier* to fold < Latin *plicare*]

Plym outh (plim′əth), *n.* 1 seaport in SW England, on the English Channel. 257,000. 2 town in SE Massachusetts. 19,000.

Plymouth Colony, settlement established by the Pilgrims in 1620, on the site of Plymouth, Massachusetts.

Plymouth Rock, 1 rock at Plymouth, Massachusetts, on which the Pilgrims are said to have landed in 1620. 2 one of an American breed of medium-sized fowls kept for the production of meat and eggs.

ply wood (plī′wůd′), *n.* a strong, relatively light building material made of thin sheets of wood glued together, usually with the grain of each layer at right angles to the next.

Pm, promethium.

p.m., 1 the time from noon to midnight [for Latin *post meridiem*]. 2 post mortem. ➤ See **a.m.** for usage note.

P.M., 1 the time from noon to midnight [for Latin *post meridiem*]. 2 Postmaster. 3 Prime Minister. 4 Provost Marshal.

p.n. or **P/N,** promissory note.

pneu mat ic (nü mat′ik, nyü mat′ik), *adj.* 1 filled with air; containing air, especially compressed air: *a pneumatic tire.* 2 worked by air, especially compressed air: *a pneumatic drill.* 3 having to do with air and other gases. [< Greek *pneumatikos* < *pneuma* breath < *pnein* breathe] —**pneu mat′i cal ly,** *adv.*

pneu mat ics (nü mat′iks, nyü mat′iks), *n.* branch of physics that deals with the pressure, elasticity, weight, and other mechanical properties of air and other gases.

pneu mo coc cal (nü′mə kok′əl, nyü′mə kok′əl), *adj.* having to do with or caused by a pneumococcus.

pneu mo coc cus (nü′mə kok′əs, nyü′mə kok′əs), *n., pl.* **-coc ci** (-kok′sī). the bacterium that causes lobar pneumonia.

pneu mo nia (nü mō′nyə, nü mō′nē ə; nyü mō′nyə, nyü mō′nē ə), *n.* 1 a bacterial or viral disease in which the lung becomes inflamed, often accompanied by chills, a pain in the chest, a hard, dry cough, and a high fever. 2 inflammation of the lung from irritants, such as chemicals, foreign particles, etc. [< Greek < *pneumōn* lung]

pneu mon ic (nü mon′ik, nyü mon′ik), *adj.* 1 of or resembling pneumonia. 2 of or affecting the lungs; pulmonary.

Pnom penh (nom′pen′), *n.* Phnom Penh.

Po (pō), *n.* See **Po River.**

Po, polonium.

p.o. or **P.O.,** post office.

poach[1] (pōch), *v.t.* 1 trespass on (another's land), especially to hunt or fish. 2 take (game or fish) without any right. [< Middle French *pocher* poke out; of Germanic origin] —**poach′er,** *n.*

poach[2] (pōch), *v.t.* 1 cook (an egg) by breaking it into water that is simmering. 2 cook (any of various foods, especially fish) by simmering for a short time in a liquid. [< Middle French *pochier* < *poche* cooking spoon]

Po ca hon tas (pō′kə hon′təs), *n.* 1595?-1617, American Indian girl who is said to have saved the life of Captain John Smith.

pock (pok), *n.* pimple, mark, or pit on the skin, caused by smallpox and certain other diseases. —*v.t.* to pit, scar, or mark with or as if with pocks. [Old English *pocc*]

pock et (pok′it), *n.* 1 a small bag sewed into clothing for carrying money, small articles, etc. 2 a hollow place; enclosed place. 3 a small bag or pouch. 4 **be out of pocket,** spend or lose money. 5 bag at the corner or side of a pool or billiard table. 6 a hole in the earth containing gold or other ore: *The miner struck a pocket of silver.* 7 a single lump of ore; small mass of ore. 8 air pocket. 9 an isolated group or collection of things: *The candidate met with pockets of resistance within his own political party.*

—*v.t.* 1 put in one's pocket. 2 shut in; hem in. 3 hold back; suppress; hide: *Pocket your*

pride and say nothing. 4 take and endure, without doing anything about it: *pocket an insult.* 5 take secretly or dishonestly: *One partner pocketed all the profits.* 6 knock or drive into a pocket, as a pool ball.
—*adj.* 1 meant to be carried in a pocket: *a pocket handkerchief.* 2 small enough to go in a pocket: *a pocket camera.* 3 small for its kind.
[< Anglo-French *pokete* < Old North French *poke* bag, poke[2]] **—pock′et like′,** *adj.*

pocket battleship, warship smaller than a cruiser but carrying much larger guns.

pocket billiards, pool[2] (def. 1).

pock et book (pok′it bu̇k′), *n.* 1 a woman's purse; handbag. 2 a small, flat or folded case for carrying money, papers, etc., in a pocket; wallet. 3 supply of money; finances; funds. 4 Also, **pocket book,** a soft-covered or paper-bound book of such size that it is easily carried in the pocket.

pock et ful (pok′it fu̇l), *n., pl.* **-fuls.** as much as a pocket will hold.

pock et knife (pok′it nīf′), *n., pl.* **-knives.** a small knife with one or more blades that fold into the handle.

pock et-size (pok′it sīz′), *adj.* 1 small enough to go in a pocket: *a pocket-size radio.* 2 INFORMAL. small for its kind: *a pocket-size field.*

pocket veto, method of vetoing a bill that can be used by the President of the United States on a bill presented to him within ten days of the end of a session of Congress. If the President does not sign the bill before Congress adjourns, it does not become a law.

pock mark (pok′märk′), *n.* mark or pit on the skin; pock.

pock marked (pok′märkt′), *adj.* marked with pocks.

pock y (pok′ē), *adj.,* **pock i er, pock i est.** marked with pocks.

po co (pō′kō), *adv., adj.* (in music) little; somewhat (used in directions to qualify other expressions). [< Italian < Latin *paucus* little, few]

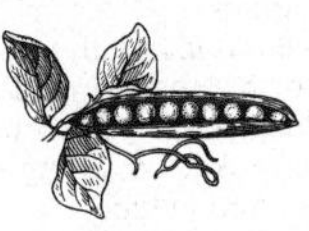

pod (def. 1) opened to show peas

pod (pod), *n., v.,* **pod ded, pod ding.** —*n.* 1 the bivalve shell or case in which plants like beans and peas grow their seeds. 2 a streamlined cover over anything carried externally, especially on the wings or fuselage of an aircraft. —*v.t.* produce pods. [origin uncertain]

p.o.d., pay on delivery.

Pod gor ny (pod gôr′nē), *n.* **Nikolai Viktorovich,** born 1903, Soviet political leader, president of the Soviet Union since 1965.

podg y (poj′ē), *adj.,* **podg i er, podg i est.** short and fat; pudgy. **—podg′i ness,** *n.*

po di a trist (pə dī′ə trist), *n.* person who treats ailments of the human foot; chiropodist.

po di a try (pə dī′ə trē), *n.* the study and treatment of ailments of the human foot; chiropody. [< Greek *podos* foot + *iatreia* a healing]

po di um (pō′dē əm), *n., pl.* **-di ums, -di a** (-dē ə). 1 a raised platform, especially one used by a public speaker or an orchestra conductor. 2 a raised platform surrounding the arena in an ancient amphitheater. 3 a continuous projecting base or pedestal. [< Latin < Greek *podion* < *podos* foot]

Po dunk (pō′dungk), *n.* U.S. a small or insignificant town or village. [< Algonquian *Potunk,* a place name]

Poe (pō), *n.* **Edgar Allan,** 1809-1849, American poet, critic, and writer of tales.

POE or **P.O.E.,** 1 port of embarkation. 2 port of entry.

po em (pō′əm), *n.* 1 arrangement of words in lines having rhythm or a regularly repeated accent and, often, rhyme; composition in verse, often highly imaginative or emotional, designed to express or convey deep feelings and thoughts. 2 composition of any kind showing beauty or nobility of language or thought. 3 something beautiful. [< Latin *poema* < Greek *poiēma* < *poiein* to make, compose]

po e sy (pō′ə sē, pō′ə zē), *n., pl.* **-sies.** ARCHAIC. poetry.

po et (pō′it), *n.* 1 person who writes poetry. 2 person who has great ability to feel and express beauty. [< Latin *poeta* < Greek *poiētēs* maker, author < *poiein* to make, compose]

po et as ter (pō′i tas′tər), *n.* writer of rather poor poetry. [< New Latin < Latin *poeta* + *-aster,* suffix denoting inferiority]

po et ess (pō′i tis), *n.* a woman poet.

po et ic (pō et′ik), *adj.* 1 having to do with poems or poets. 2 suitable for poems or poets. *Alas, o'er,* and *blithe* are poetic words. 3 showing beautiful or noble language, imagery, or thought. 4 consisting of verse or poems. **—po et′i cal ly,** *adv.*

po et i cal (pō et′ə kəl), *adj.* poetic.

poetic justice, ideal justice, with virtue being suitably rewarded and vice properly punished, as shown often in poetry, drama, and fiction.

poetic license, variation from regular usages and facts allowed in poetry.

po et ics (pō et′iks), *n.* 1 the part of literary criticism that deals with the nature and laws of poetry. 2 a formal or systematic study on poetry.

poet laureate, *pl.* **poets laureate.** 1 (in Great Britain) a poet appointed by the king or queen to write poems in celebration of court and national events. 2 any poet regarded as the best or most typical of his country or region. 3 any poet distinguished for excellence.

po et ry (pō′i trē), *n.* 1 the writings of a poet or poets; poems or verses as a form of literature: *a collection of poetry.* 2 art of writing poems: *Shakespeare and Milton were masters of English poetry.* 3 poetic quality; poetic spirit or feeling: *the poetry of nature.*

po go stick (pō′gō), toy consisting of a stick with a spring and footrests near the bottom and a handle at the top, used to hop from place to place by jumping up and down on the footrests while holding the handle. [originally a trademark]

po grom (pō grom′, pō′grəm), *n.* an organized massacre, especially of Jews. [< Russian, devastation]

po gy (pō′gē), *n., pl.* **-gies** or **-gy.** menhaden. [of Algonquian origin]

poi (poi), *n.* a Hawaiian food made of the root of the taro, baked, pounded, moistened, and fermented. [< Hawaiian]

poign an cy (poi′nyən sē), *n.* a being poignant; sharpness; piercing quality.

poign ant (poi′nyənt), *adj.* 1 very painful; piercing: *poignant suffering.* 2 stimulating to the mind, feelings, or passions; keen; intense: *a subject of poignant interest.* 3 sharp, pungent, or piquant to the taste or smell: *poignant sauces.* [< Old French, present participle of *poindre* to prick < Latin *pungere*] **—poign′ant ly,** *adv.*

hat, āge, fär; let, ēqual, tėrm;
it, īce; hot, ōpen, ôrder;
oil, out; cup, pu̇t, rüle;
ch, child; ng, long; sh, she;
th, thin; ᴛʜ, then; zh, measure;

ə represents *a* in about, *e* in taken, *i* in pencil, *o* in lemon, *u* in circus.

< = from, derived from, taken from.

poi ki lo therm (poi′kə lō thėrm′), *n.* a cold-blooded animal.

poi ki lo ther mal (poi′kə lō thėr′məl), *adj.* (in zoology) cold-blooded. [< Greek *poikilos* variegated + *thermē* heat]

poi ki lo ther mic (poi′kə lō thėr′mik), *adj.* poikilothermal.

Poin ca ré (pwaɴ kä rā′), *n.* **Raymond,** 1860-1934, French statesman, president of France from 1913 to 1920.

poin ci a na (poin′sē ā′nə), *n.* 1 any of a genus of tropical trees or shrubs of the pea family, having showy scarlet, orange, or yellow flowers. 2 a tropical tree of another genus of the pea family, having showy scarlet flowers and pods up to two feet long. [< New Latin < de *Poinci,* governor of the Antilles in the 1600's]

poin set ti a (poin set′ē ə, poin set′ə), *n.* plant having a small, greenish-yellow flower surrounded by large scarlet or white leaves that look like petals. The poinsettia is a perennial Mexican plant of the same family as the spurge. [< New Latin < Joel R. *Poinsett,* 1779-1851, American diplomat who discovered the plant]

point (point), *n.* 1 a sharp, tapering end; something having a sharp end: *the point of a needle, the point of a dagger.* 2 a tiny round mark; dot: *A period is a point. Use a point to set off decimals.* 3 a diacritical mark used in Semitic languages. 4 (in mathematics) something that has position but not extension. Two lines meet or cross at a point. 5 place; spot: *Stop at this point.* 6 any particular or definite position, condition, or time; degree; stage: *the boiling point.* 7 item; detail: *I answered the questions point by point.* 8 a distinguishing mark or quality: *Honesty is not her strong point.* 9 a physical characteristic or feature of an animal, as one used to judge excellence or purity of breed. 10 **points,** *pl.* the extremities of an animal; the feet, ears, tail, etc. 11 the main idea or purpose; important or essential thing: *miss the point of a joke.* 12 force; effectiveness: *He writes with point.* 13 a particular aim, end, or purpose: *carry one's point.* 14 each of the 32 positions indicating direction marked at the circumference of the card of a compass. 15 the interval between any two adjacent points of a compass; 11 degrees 15 minutes. 16 a piece of land with a sharp end sticking out into the water; cape. 17 a unit of credit, scoring, or measuring: *Our team won the game by ten points. The university credited her with five points for the semester's work. The price of that stock has gone up a point.* 18 (in printing) a unit for measuring type; about 1/72 inch. 19 INFORMAL. hint; suggestion: *get some points on farming.* 20 lace made with a needle; needlepoint. 21 BRITISH. a railroad switch. 22 the position of one of the players in cricket, lacrosse, etc. 23 the player in this position. 24 (in hunting) the attitude, usually with muzzle pointing and one foreleg raised, assumed by a pointer or setter on finding game. 25 one of the 24 long pointed spaces of a backgammon board. 26 one of two tungsten or platinum pieces, especially in the distributor of a gasoline engine, for making or breaking the flow of current. 27 a short, musical strain, especially one sounded as a signal. 28 ARCHAIC. a tagged lace or cord used in the Middle Ages to lace or fasten various parts of the clothes.

at the point of, in the act of; very near to: *at the point of leaving.*

beside the point, having nothing to do with the question; irrelevant.

in point, pertinent; apt: *a case in point.*

make a point of, insist upon.

on the point of, just about; on the verge of.

stretch a point, **a** exceed the reasonable limit. **b** make a special exception.

to the point, pertinent; apt.

—*v.t.* 1 sharpen: *point a pencil.* 2 mark with dots; punctuate. 3 indicate decimals. 4 mark points in (the writing of Semitic languages, shorthand, etc.). 5 give force to (speech, action, etc.): *point one's remarks.* 6 show with the finger; call attention to. 7 direct (a finger, weapon, etc.): *point a gun at a person.* 8 fill joints of (brickwork) with mortar or cement. 9 (of a dog) show (game) by standing rigid looking toward it. 10 **point off,** mark off with points or dots. 11 **point out,** show or call attention to: *Please point out my mistakes.* 12 **point up,** put emphasis on; call or give special attention to. —*v.i.* 1 indicate position or direction, or direct attention with, or as if with, the finger: *point at a house.* 2 tend; aim. 3 have a specified direction: *The signboard points north.* 4 (of a dog) show the presence of game by standing rigid and looking toward it. 5 (of an abscess) come to a head.

[< Old French, puncture, mark, sharp point, a small measure of space or time < Latin *punctum* < *pungere* to pierce]

point-blank (*adj.* point′blangk′; *adv.* point′blangk′), *adj.* 1 aimed straight at the mark: *a point-blank salvo.* 2 close enough for aim to be taken in this way: *point-blank range.* 3 plain and blunt; direct: *a point-blank question.* —*adv.* 1 straight at the mark. 2 plainly and bluntly; directly: *One boy gave excuses, but the other refused point-blank.*

point ed (poin′tid), *adj.* 1 having a point or points: *a pointed roof.* 2 sharp; piercing: *a pointed wit.* 3 directed; aimed: *a pointed remark.* 4 emphatic; marked: *He showed her pointed attention.* —**point′ed ly,** *adv.* —**point′ed ness,** *n.*

point er (poin′tər), *n.* 1 person or thing that points. 2 a long, tapering stick used in pointing things out on a map, blackboard, etc. 3 hand of a clock, meter, etc. 4 a short-haired hunting dog with a smooth coat, trained to find game by scent and show where it is by standing still and pointing toward it. 5 INFORMAL. hint; suggestion: *She gave him some pointers on improving his tennis.* 6 **Pointers,** *pl.* the two stars in the Big Dipper which point to the North Star in the Little Dipper.

poin til lism (pwan′tl iz′əm), *n.* method of painting by laying on the colors in points or dots of unmixed color that are blended by the eye. [< French *pointillisme*]

poin til list (pwan′tl ist), *n.* artist who uses pointillism. —*adj.* of, having to do with, or characteristic of pointillism.

point less (point′lis), *adj.* 1 without a point. 2 without force or meaning: *a pointless story.* —**point′less ly,** *adv.* —**point′less ness,** *n.*

point of honor, matter that affects a person's honor, principles, sense of duty, etc.

point of order, question raised as to whether proceedings are according to the rules.

point of view, 1 position from which one looks at something. 2 attitude of mind: *a stubborn point of view.*

poise[1] (poiz), *n., v.,* **poised, pois ing.** —*n.* 1 mental balance, composure, or self-possession: *She has perfect poise and never seems embarrassed.* 2 the way in which the body, head, etc., are held; carriage. 3 state of balance; equilibrium. —*v.t.* 1 balance: *poise yourself on your toes.* 2 hold or carry evenly or steadily: *The waiter poised the tray on his hand.* —*v.i.* 1 be balanced or held in equilibrium. 2 hang supported or suspended. 3 hover, as a bird in the air. [< Old French *pois, peis* < Popular Latin *pesum* < Latin *pensum* weight]

poise[2] (poiz), *n.* unit of measurement of viscosity in the centimeter-gram-second system. [apparently < Jean Marie *Poiseuille,* about 1797-1869, French physiologist]

poi son (poi′zn), *n.* 1 drug or other substance that destroys life or injures health by its action inside the body or on its surface. Strychnine and arsenic are poisons. 2 anything dangerous or deadly: *the poison of hate.* 3 substance that stops or weakens the action of a catalyst or enzyme. —*v.t.* 1 kill or harm by poison. 2 put poison in or on: *poison arrows.* 3 have a dangerous or harmful effect on. 4 stop or weaken the action of (a catalyst or enzyme). —*adj.* poisonous. [< Old French < Latin *potionem* potion. Doublet of POTION.] —**poi′son er,** *n.*

poison gas, a poisonous gas such as mustard gas or tear gas, used especially as a weapon in warfare.

poison ivy, any of various North American shrubs or climbing plants, varieties of a species of sumac, that resemble ivy and have white, berrylike fruit, glossy green compound leaves of three leaflets each, and a poisonous oil that irritates skin and causes a painful rash on most people if they touch the plant.

poison oak, 1 any of several poison ivies or other species of sumac that have poisonous oils and grow as shrubs. 2 poison sumac.

poi son ous (poi′zn əs), *adj.* 1 containing poison; very harmful to life and health; venomous. 2 having a dangerous or harmful effect. —**poi′son ous ly,** *adv.* —**poi′sonous ness,** *n.*

poison sumac, a tall North American shrub, a species of sumac, growing in swamps, with leaves composed of seven to thirteen leaflets, white berrylike fruit, and a poisonous oil like that in poison ivy which causes a severe rash on most people if they touch the plant.

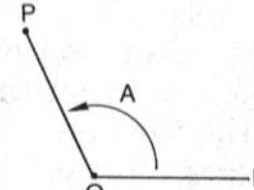

polar coordinate—O is the fixed point; OL is the fixed line. The position of the point P is determined by the length of OP and the size of angle A.

poke[1] (pōk), *v.,* **poked, pok ing,** *n.* —*v.t.* 1 push against with something pointed; prod: *She poked me in the ribs with her elbow.* 2 thrust; push: *He poked his head in the kitchen window.* 3 make by poking: *poke a hole through paper.* 4 INFORMAL. hit with the fist; punch. —*v.i.* 1 make a thrust with the arm, fist, a stick, or the like. 2 pry; search; grope. 3 go lazily; loiter; dawdle. —*n.* 1 a poking; thrust; push. 2 INFORMAL. a blow with the fist; punch. 3 a slow, lazy person. [Middle English *poken*]

poke[2] (pōk), *n.* DIALECT. bag; sack. [Middle English < Old North French]

poke[3] (defs. 1 and 2)

poke[3] (pōk), *n.* 1 bonnet or hat with a large brim in front. 2 the brim. [perhaps special use of *poke*[1]]

poke[4] (pōk), *n.* pokeweed. [of Algonquian origin]

poke ber ry (pōk′ber′ē), *n., pl.* **-ries.** 1 berry of the pokeweed. 2 pokeweed.

poke bonnet, bonnet with a projecting brim.

pok er[1] (pō′kər), *n.* 1 person or thing that pokes. 2 a metal rod for stirring a fire. [< *poke*[1]]

pok er[2] (pō′kər), *n.* a card game in which the players bet on the value of the cards that they hold in their hands to win a pool. [origin uncertain]

poker face, INFORMAL. face that does not show one's thoughts or feelings.

po ker-faced (pō′kər fāst′), *adj.* having a poker face; expressionless.

poke weed (pōk′wēd′), *n.* a tall, branching perennial herb of North America with greenish-white flowers, deep purple, juicy berries, and poisonous roots; poke. Its young shoots are sometimes boiled and eaten.

pok y or **pok ey** (pō′kē), *adj.,* **pok i er, pok i est.** 1 moving or acting slowly; puttering; slow; dull: *a poky old man.* 2 small and cramped; mean. 3 shabby; dowdy. [< *poke*[1]]

Pol., 1 Poland. 2 Polish.

Po land (pō′lənd), *n.* country in central Europe between East Germany and the Soviet Union. 32,670,000 pop.; 120,700 sq. mi. *Capital:* Warsaw.

po lar (pō′lər), *adj.* 1 of or near the North or South Pole: *the polar regions, a polar wind.* 2 having to do with a pole or poles. 3 of or having to do with the poles of a magnet, electric battery, etc. 4 opposite in character, like the poles of a magnet: *Love and hatred are polar feelings or attitudes.* 5 (in chemistry) ionizing when dissolved or fused. 6 serving to guide; guiding.

polar bear, a large, white bear of the arctic regions.

polar circle, the arctic circle or antarctic circle.

polar coordinate, (in mathematics) either one of the two coordinates for determining the position of a point in a plane. The two coordinates are the length of the line segment drawn to the point from a fixed point and the angle which this line segment makes with a fixed line or axis.

Po lar is (pō ler′is, pō lar′is), *n.* the North Star.

po lar i scope (pō lar′ə skōp), *n.* instrument for showing the polarization of light, or for examining substances in polarized light.

po lar i ty (pō lar′ə tē), *n., pl.* **-ties.** 1 the possession of two opposed poles. A magnet or battery has polarity. 2 a positive or negative polar condition, as in electricity. 3 possession or exhibition of two opposite or contrasted principles or tendencies.

po lar i za tion (pō′lər ə zā′shən), *n.* 1 a polarizing. 2 a being polarized. 3 production or acquisition of polarity. 4 process by which gases produced during electrolysis are deposited on electrodes of a cell, giving rise to a reverse electromotive force. 5 (in optics) a state, or the production of a state, in which rays of light exhibit different properties in different directions.

po lar ize (pō′lə rīz′), *v.,* **-ized, -iz ing.** —*v.t.* give polarity to; cause polarization in. —*v.i.* acquire polarity. **—po′lar iz′a ble,** *adj.* **—po′lar iz′er,** *n.*

Po la roid (pō′lə roid′), *n.* trademark for a thin, transparent material that polarizes light, used in lamps, eyeglasses, etc., to reduce glare.

pol der (pōl′dər), *n.* tract of lowland reclaimed from the sea or other body of water and protected by dikes. [< Dutch]

pole[1] (pōl), *n., v.,* **poled, pol ing.** —*n.* 1 a long, slender piece of wood, steel, etc.: *a telephone pole, a ski pole.* 2 measure of length; rod; 5½ yards. 3 measure of area; square rod; 30¼ square yards. —*v.t.* move (a boat, raft, etc.) with a pole. —*v.i.* pole a boat, raft, etc. [Old English *pāl* < Latin *palus* stake. Doublet of PALE[2].]

pole[2] (pōl), *n.* 1 either end of the earth's axis; North Pole or South Pole. 2 either end of the axis of any sphere. 3 each of the two terminal points of an electric cell, battery, or dynamo. 4 each of the two opposite points on a magnet at which the magnetic forces are manifested. 5 the origin or fixed point in a system of polar coordinates. 6 (in biology) each extremity of the main axis of an organism, nucleus, or cell, especially an egg cell. 7 each of two opposed or complementary principles. [< Latin *polus* < Greek *polos*]

Pole (pōl), *n.* person of Polish birth or descent.

pole ax or **pole axe** (pōl′aks′), *n.* 1 ax with a long handle and a hook or spike opposite the blade. 2 kind of battle-ax with a short handle. [Middle English *pollax* < *polle* head + *ax* ax]

pole cat (pōl′kat′), *n.* 1 a small, dark-brown, carnivorous European weasel which can emit a very disagreeable odor; fitch. The domesticated form is the ferret. 2 skunk. [Middle English < Old French *poule* fowl + Middle English *cat* cat]

po lem ic (pə lem′ik), *n.* 1 a disputing discussion; controversy; argument. 2 person who takes part in a controversy or argument. —*adj.* of controversy or disagreement; of dispute. [< Greek *polemikos* belligerent < *polemos* war] **—po lem′i cal ly,** *adv.*

po lem i cal (pə lem′ə kəl), *adj.* polemic.

po lem i cist (pə lem′ə sist), *n.* writer of polemics.

po lem ics (pə lem′iks), *n.* 1 art or practice of disputation or controversy, especially in theology. 2 branch of theology that deals with the history or conduct of ecclesiastical controversy.

pole star (pōl′stär′), *n.* 1 the North Star. 2 a guiding principle; guide. 3 center of attraction, interest, or attention.

pole vault, an athletic contest or event in which the contestants vault over a high crossbar by using a long pole.

pole vault

pole-vault (pōl′vôlt′), *v.i.* vault over a high crossbar with a long, flexible pole. **—pole′-vault′er,** *n.*

po lice (pə lēs′), *n., v.,* **-liced, -lic ing.** —*n.* 1 persons whose duty is keeping order and arresting people who break the law. 2 the department of a government that keeps order and arrests persons who break the law. 3 regulation and control of a community, especially with reference to matters of public order, safety, health, morals, etc.; public order. 4 the cleaning and keeping in order of a military camp, area, etc. 5 soldiers detailed to do this. —*v.t.* 1 keep order in: *police the streets.* 2 control, regulate, or administer (a law, operation, program, etc.) to discover or prevent the breaking of a law, rule, or agreement. 3 keep (a military camp, area, etc.) clean and in order. [< Middle French < Late Latin *politia* the state, settled order of government < Greek *politeia* citizenship < *politēs* citizen < *polis* city-state. Doublet of POLICY[1], POLITY.]

police court, court for settling minor charges brought by the police. It has the power to hold people charged with serious offenses for trial in higher courts.

police dog, 1 German shepherd. 2 any dog trained to work with policemen.

po lice man (pə lēs′mən), *n., pl.* **-men.** member of the police.

police state, state strictly policed by governmental authority, thus having only a minimum of social, economic, and political liberty.

police station, headquarters of the police for a particular precinct; station house.

po lice wom an (pə lēs′wu̇m′ən), *n., pl.* **-wom en.** woman who is a member of the police.

pol i clin ic (pol′i klin′ik), *n.* department of a hospital at which outpatients are treated. [< German *Poliklinik* < Greek *polis* city + German *Klinik* clinic]

pol i cy[1] (pol′ə sē), *n., pl.* **-cies.** 1 plan of action adopted as tactically or strategically best by a government, person, etc.; way of managing affairs so as to achieve some purpose: *It is a poor policy to promise more than you can do.* 2 practical wisdom; prudence. [< Old French *policie* < Late Latin *politia.* Doublet of POLICE, POLITY.]

pol i cy[2] (pol′ə sē), *n., pl.* **-cies.** 1 a written contract made between insurer and insured. 2 U.S. method of gambling by betting that a certain number will be drawn in a lottery or will appear in a published statistic. [< Middle French *police* < Italian *polizza,* ultimately < Latin *apodixis* proof < Greek *apodeixis*]

hat, āge, fär; let, ēqual, tėrm;
it, īce; hot, ōpen, ôrder;
oil, out; cup, pu̇t, rüle;
ch, child; ng, long; sh, she;
th, thin; ᴛʜ, then; zh, measure;

ə represents *a* in about, *e* in taken, *i* in pencil, *o* in lemon, *u* in circus.

< = from, derived from, taken from.

pol i cy hold er (pol′ə sē hōl′dər), *n.* person who holds an insurance policy.

po li o (pō′lē ō), *n.* an acute, infectious, virus disease that destroys nervous tissue in the spinal cord, causing fever, paralysis of various muscles, and sometimes death; infantile paralysis. [short for *poliomyelitis*]

po li o my e li tis (pō′lē ō mī′ə lī′tis, pol′ē ō mī′ə lī′tis), *n.* polio. [< New Latin < Greek *polios* gray + *myelos* marrow]

pol ish (pol′ish), *v.t.* 1 make smooth and shiny by rubbing, waxing, etc.: *polish shoes.* 2 put into a better condition; improve: *polish a manuscript.* 3 make elegant; refine: *polish one's manners.* 4 **polish off,** INFORMAL. get done with; finish. —*v.i.* become smooth and shiny; take on a polish. —*n.* 1 substance used to give smoothness or shine: *silver polish.* 2 polished condition; smoothness and shine: *The polish of the furniture reflected our faces like a mirror.* See synonym study below. 3 a polishing. 4 a being polished. 5 culture; elegance; refinement. [< Old French *poliss-,* a form of *polir* < Latin *polire*] **—pol′ish er,** *n.*

Syn. *n.* 2 **Polish, luster, sheen** mean the shine of a surface. **Polish** suggests the shine given a surface by rubbing: *Rain spoiled the car's bright polish.* **Luster** emphasizes shining by reflecting light, often of shifting colors: *Furniture that has been waxed has a luster.* **Sheen** suggests a more steady gleam or brilliance than either *polish* or *luster: Highly polished metal has a sheen.*

Pol ish (pō′lish), *adj.* of or having to do with Poland, its people, or their language. —*n.* the Slavic language of Poland.

polit., 1 political. 2 politics.

Po lit bur o (pə lit′byu̇r′ō), *n.* the Communist Party executive committee which examines and controls policy and matters of state in the Soviet Union. [< Russian *Politbjuro,* literally, political bureau]

po lite (pə līt′), *adj.* 1 having or showing good manners; characterized by courtesy and consideration; behaving properly. See synonym study below. 2 characterized by refined and civilized taste; elegant: *the customs of polite society.* [< Latin *politum* polished] **—po lite′ly,** *adv.* **—po lite′ness,** *n.*

Syn. 1 **Polite, civil, courteous** mean having the manners necessary in social relations. **Polite** means having and showing good manners at all times, and emphasizes following the rules for proper behavior: *That polite boy gave me his seat.* **Civil** means being just polite enough not to be rude: *Anyone should be able to give a civil answer.* **Courteous** adds to *polite* the idea of showing thoughtful attention to the feelings and wishes of others: *I go to that store because the clerks are courteous.*

pol i tesse (pol′ə tes′), *n.* politeness: *diplomatic politesse.* [< French]

pol i tic (pol′ə tik), *adj.* 1 wise in looking out for one's own interests; prudent; shrewd. 2 showing wisdom or shrewdness: *a politic answer.* 3 scheming; crafty. 4 political. [< Latin *politicus* < Greek *politikos* < *polis* city-state] **—pol′i tic ly,** *adv.*

po lit i cal (pə lit′ə kəl), *adj.* 1 of or concerned with politics: *political parties.* 2 having to do with citizens or government: *Treason is a political offense.* 3 of politicians or their methods: *a political slogan.* 4 of or having to do with government or a government; governmental: *political districts.* 5 having an organized system of government. **—po lit′i cal ly,** *adv.*

political economy, economics.

political science, science of the principles and conduct of government. **—political scientist.**

pol i ti cian (pol′ə tish′ən), *n.* 1 person who gives much time to political affairs; person who is experienced in politics. See synonym study below. 2 person active in politics chiefly for his own profit or that of his party. 3 person holding a political office.

Syn. 1 **Politician, statesman** mean someone active or skilled in political or governmental affairs. **Politician** especially suggests ability to deal with people and accomplish things for the good of the people and the country, but often is used slightingly or contemptuously to suggest a man without principles scheming for his own or his party's good: *All officeholders are politicians.* **Statesman,** always in a good sense, emphasizes sound judgment, farsightedness, and skill in dealing with and managing national and international affairs: *Winston Churchill was a statesman.*

pol i tick (pol′ə tik), *v.i.* practice politics; engage in political activity.

po lit i co (pə lit′ə kō), *n., pl.* **-cos.** a politician. [< Italian]

pol i tics (pol′ə tiks), *n. sing. or pl.* 1 management of political affairs; the science and art of government. 2 political principles or opinions: *present-day politics.* 3 political methods or maneuvers.

pol i ty (pol′ə tē), *n., pl.* **-ties.** 1 government. 2 a particular form or system of government. 3 community with a government; state. [< Late Latin *politia.* Doublet of POLICE, POLICY[1].]

Polk (pōk), *n.* **James Knox,** 1795-1849, the 11th president of the United States, from 1845 to 1849.

pol ka (pōl′kə, pō′kə), *n.* 1 a lively dance of Bohemian origin, in duple time and usually performed by couples, consisting of a pattern of three steps and a skip or hop. 2 music for it. *—v.i.* dance a polka. [< Czech]

pol ka dot (pō′kə), 1 dot or round spot repeated to form a pattern on cloth. 2 pattern or fabric with such dots.

poll (pōl), *n.* 1 a casting or registering of votes, as at an election. 2 number of votes cast: *a heavy poll.* 3 the results of these votes. 4 **polls,** *pl.* place where votes are cast and counted: *The polls will be open all day.* 5 list of persons, especially a list of voters. 6 a survey of public opinion concerning a particular subject. 7 the head, especially the part of it on which the hair grows. 8 the blunt end of a pick, hammer, or other tool. *—v.t.* 1 receive at an election: *She polled 25,000 votes.* 2 cast (a vote). 3 take or register the votes of: *poll a village.* 4 question or canvass in a poll of public opinion. 5 cut off or cut short the hair, wool, horns, branches, etc., of. *—v.i.* vote at a poll; give one's vote. [probably < Middle Dutch *polle* top of the head] **—poll′er,** *n.*

pol lack (pol′ək), *n., pl.* **-lacks** or **-lack.** a saltwater food fish of the same family as the haddock and the cod. Also, **pollock.** [origin uncertain]

pol len (pol′ən), *n.* a fine, yellowish powder consisting of grains or microspores, that are released from the anthers of flowers to fertilize the pistils. [< Latin, fine flour]

pollen count, a count of the number of grains of pollen to be found at a specified time and place in a cubic yard of air.

pol le no sis (pol′ə nō′sis), *n.* pollinosis.

pol li nate (pol′ə nāt), *v.t.,* **-nat ed, -nat ing.** transfer pollen from anthers to stigmas of; shed pollen on. **—pol′li na′tion,** *n.*

pol li na tor (pol′ə nā′tər), *n.* insect or other agent that pollinates plants.

pol li no sis (pol′ə nō′sis), *n.* hay fever. Also, **pollenosis.**

pol li wog (pol′ē wog), *n.* tadpole. Also, **pollywog.** [Middle English *polwigle*]

pol lock (pol′ək), *n., pl.* **-locks** or **-lock.** pollack.

Pol lock (pol′ək), *n.* **Jackson,** 1912-1956, American painter.

poll ster (pōl′stər), *n.* person who takes a poll of public opinion or evaluates the results of such a poll.

poll tax, a tax on every adult citizen, especially as a prerequisite to the right to vote in public elections.

pol lu tant (pə lüt′nt), *n.* a polluting agent or medium.

pol lute (pə lüt′), *v.t.,* **-lut ed, -lut ing.** make impure, foul, or dirty; contaminate: *The water at the bathing beach was polluted by refuse from the factory.* [< Latin *pollutum* soiled, defiled]

pol lu tion (pə lü′shən), *n.* a polluting; defiling; uncleanness.

Pol lux (pol′əks), *n.* 1 (in Greek and Roman myths) one of the twin sons of Zeus and Leda. Pollux was immortal; his brother, Castor, was mortal. 2 the brighter of the two brightest stars in the constellation Gemini.

Pol ly an na (pol′ē an′ə), *n.* person who is untiringly cheerful and optimistic about everything and everyone. [< *Pollyanna,* heroine of a novel by Eleanor Porter, 1868-1920, American writer]

pol ly wog (pol′ē wog), *n.* polliwog.

po lo (pō′lō), *n.* 1 game like hockey, played on horseback with long-handled mallets and a wooden ball. 2 water polo. [perhaps < Tibetan *pulu*]

Po lo (pō′lō), *n.* **Marco.** See **Marco Polo.**

po lo ist (pō′lō ist), *n.* person who plays polo.

pol o naise (pol′ə nāz′, pō′lə nāz′), *n.* 1 a slow, stately dance of Polish origin, in three-quarter time, consisting chiefly of a march or promenade of couples. 2 music for it. 3 a woman's overdress with a waist and an open skirt, popular especially in the 1700's and 1800's. [< French, literally, Polish]

po lo ni um (pə lō′nē əm), *n.* a rare, radioactive metallic element found in pitchblende or produced artificially from bismuth. It decays into an isotope of lead by the emission of alpha rays. *Symbol:* Po; *atomic number* 84. See pages 326 and 327 for table. [< *Polonia,* Latin name of Poland, homeland of Marie Curie, who discovered this element]

polo shirt, a close-fitting shirt of knitted cotton, jersey, etc., with short sleeves and with or without a collar, pulled on over the head.

pol ter geist (pōl′tər gīst), *n.* spirit or ghost that is supposed to make its presence known by tappings, the slamming of doors, or other sounds that cannot be explained. [< German *Poltergeist* < *poltern* to rap + *Geist* spirit]

pol troon (pol trün′), *n.* a wretched coward. *—adj.* base; cowardly; contemptible. [< Middle French *poltrôn* < Italian *poltrone* < *poltro* lazy]

pol troon er y (pol trü′nər ē), *n.* the behavior of a poltroon; cowardice.

poly-, *combining form.* 1 more than one or several; many; multi-, as in *polysyllable, polysyllabic.* 2 polymeric, as in *polyester, polystyrene.* [< Greek < *polys* much, many]

pol y an drous (pol′ē an′drəs), *adj.* 1 having more than one husband at one time. 2 (in botany) having numerous stamens.

pol y an dry (pol′ē an′drē), *n.* 1 practice or condition of having more than one husband at the same time. 2 (in botany) condition of being polyandrous. [< *poly-* + Greek *andros* man, husband]

pol y an thus (pol′ē an′thəs), *n.* 1 a narcissus bearing clusters of small, yellow or white flowers. 2 a hybrid primrose bearing flowers of many kinds in umbels. [< *poly-* + Greek *anthos* flower]

pol y a tom ic (pol′ē ə tom′ik), *adj.* containing more than two atoms: *a polyatomic molecule.*

pol y ba sic (pol′ē bā′sik), *adj.* (of an acid) having two or more hydrogen atoms that can be replaced by basic atoms or radicals.

pol y chro mat ic (pol′ē krō mat′ik), *adj.* polychrome.

pol y chrome (pol′ē krōm), *adj.* having many or various colors; decorated or executed in many colors. *—n.* 1 a work of art in several colors. 2 combination of many colors.

pol y clin ic (pol′ē klin′ik), *n.* clinic or hospital dealing with many different diseases.

pol y es ter (pol′ē es′tər), *n.* any of a large group of polymeric resins used in the manufacture of paints, synthetic fibers, films, and reinforced plastics for construction.

pol y eth y lene (pol′ē eth′ə lēn′), *n.* any of various very durable thermoplastics produced by the polymerization of ethylene, used for containers, insulation, tubing, etc.

po lyg a mist (pə lig′ə mist), *n.* person who practices or favors polygamy.

po lyg a mous (pə lig′ə məs), *adj.* 1 having more than one wife or more than one husband at the same time. 2 bearing both unisexual and hermaphrodite flowers on the same plant. 3 (of an animal) having several mates at the same time. **—po lyg′a mous ly,** *adv.*

po lyg a my (pə lig′ə mē), *n.* 1 practice or condition of being married to more than one person at the same time. 2 (in zoology) the practice of having several mates at the same time, usually one male with several females.

pol y glot (pol′ē glot), *adj.* 1 speaking or writing several languages. 2 written in several languages. *—n.* 1 person who speaks or writes several languages. 2 book written in several languages. [< *poly-* + Greek *glotta* tongue]

hat, āge, fär; let, ēqual, tėrm;
it, īce; hot, ōpen, ôrder;
oil, out; cup, pu̇t, rüle;
ch, child; ng, long; sh, she;
th, thin; ᴛʜ, then; zh, measure;

ə represents *a* in about, *e* in taken, *i* in pencil, *o* in lemon, *u* in circus.

< = from, derived from, taken from.

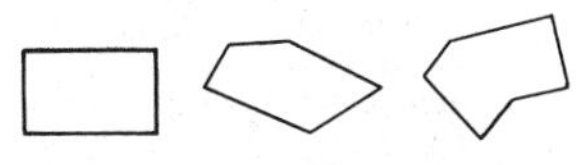

polygon—three polygons

pol y gon (pol′ē gon), *n.* a closed plane figure with three or more sides and angles. [< *poly-* + Greek *gōnia* angle]

po lyg o nal (pə lig′ə nəl), *adj.* of or having to do with a polygon.

pol y graph (pol′ə graf), *n.* 1 lie detector. 2 instrument for recording several pulsations, as of an artery, a vein, or the heart, all at once.

po lyg y nous (pə lij′ə nəs), *adj.* 1 having more than one wife at one time. 2 (in botany) having many pistils or styles.

po lyg y ny (pə lij′ə nē), *n.* 1 practice or condition of having more than one wife at the same time. The Moslem religion permits polygyny. 2 (in botany) condition of being polygynous. [< *poly-* + Greek *gynē* woman, wife]

pol y he dral (pol′ē hē′drəl), *adj.* 1 of or having to do with a polyhedron. 2 having many faces.

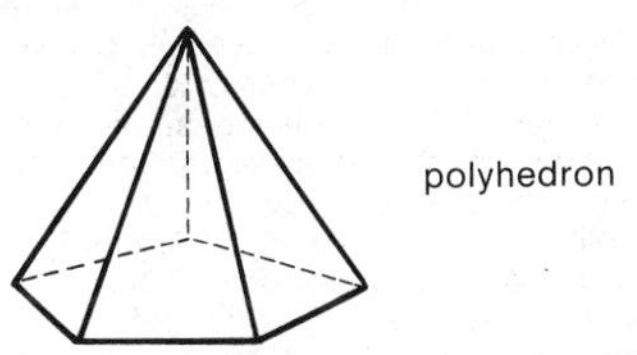

polyhedron

pol y he dron (pol′ē hē′drən), *n., pl.* **-drons, -dra** (-drə). a solid figure having four or more faces. [< *poly-* + Greek *hedra* seat, side]

Pol y hym ni a (pol′ē him′nē ə), *n.* (in Greek myths) the Muse of religious poetry.

pol y mer (pol′ə mər), *n.* a chemical compound formed by polymerization, such as nylon or cellulose.

pol y mer ase (pol′ə mə rās′), *n.* enzyme that polymerizes nucleotides to form nucleic acid.

pol y mer ic (pol′ē mer′ik), *adj.* having the same elements combined in the same proportions by weight, but differing in molecular weight and in chemical and physical properties. Acetylene, C_2H_2, and benzene, C_6H_6, are polymeric compounds. [< *poly-* + Greek *meros* part]

pol y mer i za tion (pol′ə mər ə zā′shən, pə lim′ər ə zā′shən), *n.* 1 a chemical reaction in which many small molecules unite to form a more complex molecule with a higher molecular weight and different chemical properties. 2 the conversion of one compound into another by such a process.

pol y mer ize (pol′i mə rīz′, pə lim′ə rīz′), *v.t., v.i.,* **-ized, -iz ing.** make or become polymeric; undergo or cause to undergo polymerization.

pol y morph (pol′ē môrf), *n.* a polymorphous organism.

pol y mor phic (pol′ē môr′fik), *adj.* polymorphous.

pol y mor phism (pol′ē môr′fiz′əm), *n.* polymorphous state or condition.

pol y mor phous (pol′ē môr′fəs), *adj.* having, assuming, or passing through many or various forms, stages, etc., as the honeybee.

Pol y ne sia (pol′ə nē′zhə, pol′ə nē′shə), *n.* group of many small islands in the Pacific, east of Micronesia and Melanesia. See **Melanesia** for map.

Pol y ne sian (pol′ə nē′zhən, pol′ə-nē′shən), *n.* 1 member of any of the brown peoples that live in Polynesia. 2 the languages of Polynesia, including Maori, Hawaiian, etc. —*adj.* of or having to do with Polynesia, its people, or their languages.

pol y no mi al (pol′ē nō′mē əl), *n.* an algebraic expression consisting of two or more terms. $ab + x^2y$ and $pq - p^2 + q$ are polynomials. —*adj.* consisting of two or more terms. [< *poly-* + *(bi)nomial*]

pol y o ma (pol′ē ō′mə), *n.* virus shown to produce cancerous tumors in several species of rodents. [< New Latin]

pol yp (pol′ip), *n.* 1 a small coelenterate attached at the base of its tubular body, with a mouth at the other end surrounded by fingerlike tentacles to gather in food, often growing in colonies, as hydras, corals, sea anemones, etc. 2 tumor or similar mass of enlarged tissue arising from a mucous or serous surface. [< Greek *polypous* < *poly-* + *pous* foot]

pol y pep tide (pol′ē pep′tīd, pol′ē-pep′tid), *n.* peptide containing many molecules of amino acids.

pol y phase (pol′ē fāz), *adj.* having more than one phase, as some systems of alternating current.

Pol y phe mus (pol′ə fē′məs), *n.* (in Greek legends) a Cyclops who captured Ulysses and his companions. Ulysses blinded him and escaped.

pol y phon ic (pol′ē fon′ik), *adj.* (in music) having two or more voices or parts, each with an independent melody, but all harmonizing; contrapuntal.

po lyph o ny (pə lif′ə nē), *n.* (in music) polyphonic composition; counterpoint. [< *poly-* + Greek *phōnē* voice]

pol y ploid (pol′ē ploid), *adj.* having three or more sets of chromosomes. —*n.* a polyploid organism or cell. [< *poly-* + *(ha)ploid*]

pol y sac cha ride (pol′ē sak′ə rīd′, pol′ē-sak′ər id), *n.* any of a class of carbohydrates that can be decomposed into two or more monosaccharides by hydrolysis.

pol y sty rene (pol′ē stī′rēn′), *n.* any of a group of colorless, transparent plastics used for insulation and in making household appliances, synthetic rubber, tile, implements, etc.

pol y syl lab ic (pol′ē sə lab′ik), *adj.* of more than three syllables. **—pol′y syl-lab′i cal ly,** *adv.*

pol y syl la ble (pol′ē sil′ə bəl), *n.* word of more than three syllables.

pol y tech nic (pol′ē tek′nik), *adj.* having to do with or dealing with many technical arts and sciences: *a polytechnic school.*

pol y the ism (pol′ē thē′iz′əm), *n.* belief in more than one god. The religion of the ancient Greeks was polytheism.

pol y the ist (pol′ē thē′ist), *n.* person who believes in more than one god.

pol y the is tic (pol′ē thē is′tik), *adj.* having to do with or characterized by belief in more than one god.

pol y to nal (pol′ē tō′nl), *adj.* (in music) having or using different harmonic keys simultaneously. **—pol′y to′nal ly,** *adv.*

pol y un sat u rate (pol′ē un sach′ə rāt′), *n.* a polyunsaturated substance.

pol y un sat u rat ed (pol′ē un sach′ə-rā′tid), *adj.* having many double or triple bonds and free valences, as a vegetable oil or fatty acid.

pol y va lence (pol′ē vā′ləns), *n.* multivalence.

pol y va lent (pol′ē vā′lənt), *adj.* 1 multivalent. 2 containing the proper antibodies or antigens to resist more than one species or strain of disease organisms.

pom ace (pum′is), *n.* 1 apple pulp or similar fruit pulp before or after the juice has been pressed out. 2 what is left after oil has been pressed out of something.

po ma ceous (pə mā′shəs), *adj.* 1 of, having to do with, or resembling pomes. 2 of or having to do with apples.

po made (pə mād′), *n., v.,* **-mad ed, -mad ing.** —*n.* a perfumed ointment for the scalp and hair. —*v.t.* dress (the scalp and hair) with pomade. [< Middle French *pommade,* ultimately < Latin *pomum* fruit]

po man der (pə man′dər, pō′man dər), *n.* ball of mixed aromatic substances formerly carried for perfume or as a guard against infection. [< Old French *pome d'ambre* apple of amber]

pome (pōm), *n.* fruit consisting of firm, juicy flesh surrounding a core that contains several seeds. Apples, pears, and quinces are pomes. [< Old French < Latin *pomum* fruit, apple]

pome gran ate (pom′gran′it, pom gran′it, pum′gran′it), *n.* 1 a reddish-yellow fruit with a thick skin and many seeds, each enveloped in a juicy red pulp which has a pleasant, slightly sour taste. 2 tree that it grows on, native to tropical Asia and Africa. [< Old French *pome grenate* apple with grains]

Pom e ra ni a (pom′ə rā′nē ə, pom′ə-rā′nyə), *n.* former German province on the Baltic Sea, now chiefly in Poland.

Pom e ra ni an (pom′ə rā′nē ən, pom′ə-rā′nyən), *adj.* of or having to do with Pomerania or its people. —*n.* 1 native or inhabitant of Pomerania. 2 one of a breed of small dogs with a sharp nose, pointed ears, and long, thick, silky hair, related to the chow and the spitz.

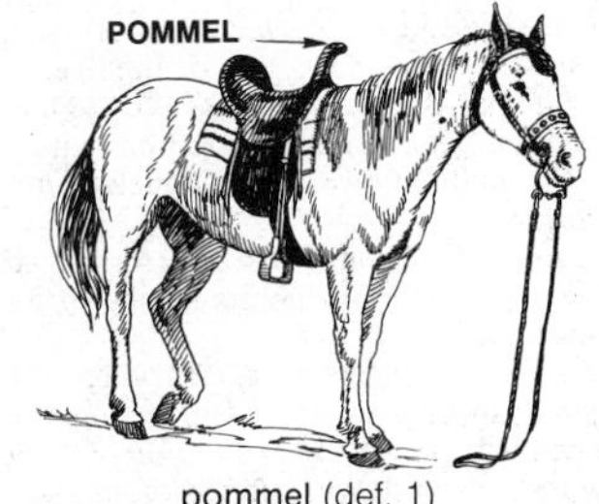

pommel (def. 1)

pom mel (pum′əl, pom′əl), *n., v.,* **-meled, -mel ing** or **-melled, -mel ling.** —*n.* 1 part of a saddle that sticks up at the front. 2 a rounded knob on the hilt of a sword, dagger, etc. —*v.t.* pummel. [< Old French *pomel*]

po mo log i cal (pō′mə loj′ə kəl), *adj.* of or having to do with pomology.

po mol o gist (pō mol′ə jist), *n.* an expert in pomology.

po mol o gy (pə mol′ə jē), *n.* branch of science that deals with fruits and fruit growing. [< Latin *pomum* fruit, apple]

Po mo na (pə mō′nə), *n.* 1 (in Roman myths) the goddess of fruits and fruit trees. 2 city in SW California. 87,000.

pomp (pomp), *n.* 1 a stately display; splendor; magnificence: *The king was crowned with great pomp.* 2 a showy display; boastful show. [< Greek *pompē* parade]

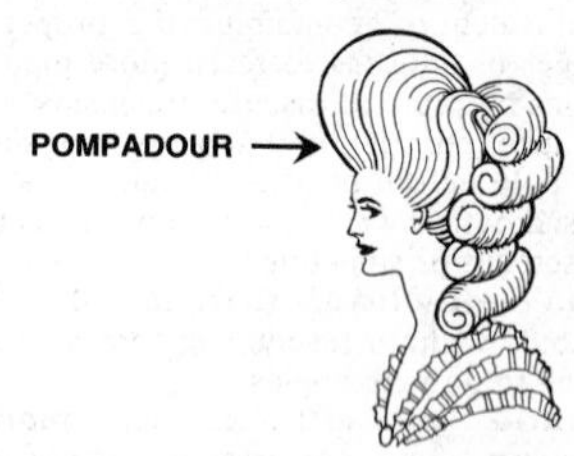

pompadour (defs. 1 and 2)

pom pa dour (pom′pə dôr, pom′pə dōr), *n.* 1 arrangement of a woman's hair in which it is puffed high over the forehead or brushed straight up and back from the forehead. 2 hair so arranged. [< the Marquise de *Pompadour*]

Pom pa dour (pom′pə dôr, pom′pə dōr, pom′pə dùr), *n.* **Marquise de,** 1721-1764, mistress of Louis XV of France. Her real name was Jeanne Antoinette Poisson.

pom pa no (pom′pə nō), *n., pl.* **-nos.** 1 any of several food fishes of the West Indies and the coasts of southern North America. 2 a similar fish of the California coast. [< American Spanish *pámpano*]

Pom peii (pom pā′, pom pā′ē), *n.* city in ancient Italy, buried by an eruption of Mount Vesuvius in A.D. 79. Its ruins have been partly laid bare by excavation. **—Pom pei′an,** *adj., n.*

Pom pey (pom′pē), *n.* 106-48 B.C., Roman general and statesman. He was called "Pompey the Great."

Pom pi dou (pom′pē dü; *French* pôN pē-dü′), *n.* **Georges,** born 1911, president of France since 1969.

pom-pom (pom′pom), *n.* an automatic anti-aircraft gun, used especially on shipboard. [imitative]

pom pon (pom′pon), *n.* 1 an ornamental tuft or ball of feathers, silk, or the like, worn on a hat or dress, on shoes, etc. 2 any of various chrysanthemums or dahlias with very small, rounded flowers. [< French < *pompe* pomp]

pom pos i ty (pom pos′ə tē), *n., pl.* **-ties.** 1 pompous quality. 2 pompous show of self-importance.

pom pous (pom′pəs), *adj.* 1 trying to seem magnificent or very important; vainglorious; self-important: *a pompous manner.* 2 overly flowery or high-flown; inflated: *pompous language.* 3 characterized by pomp; splendid; magnificent. **—pom′pous ly,** *adv.* **—pom′pous ness,** *n.*

Pon ce (pōn′sā), *n.* city in S Puerto Rico. 128,000.

Ponce de Le ón (pons′ də lē′ən; *Spanish* pôn′thā ᴛʜā lā ôn′), **Juan,** 1460?-1521, Spanish explorer and soldier, who discovered Florida.

pon cho (pon′chō), *n., pl.* **-chos.** a large piece of cloth, often waterproof, with a slit in the middle for the head to go through. Ponchos are worn in South America as cloaks. Waterproof ponchos are used in the armed forces and by hikers and campers. [< American Spanish]

pond (pond), *n.* body of still water, smaller than a lake. [originally variant of *pound*[3]]

pon der (pon′dər), *v.t.* consider carefully; think over. [< Latin *ponderare* weigh < *pondus* weight] **—pon′der er,** *n.*

pon der a ble (pon′dər ə bəl), *adj.* capable of being weighed; having perceptible weight; appreciable.

pon der ous (pon′dər əs), *adj.* 1 very heavy. 2 heavy and clumsy: *A hippopotamus is ponderous.* 3 dull; tiresome: *The speaker talked in a ponderous way.* **—pon′der ous ly,** *adv.* **—pon′der ous ness,** *n.*

Pon di cher ry (pon′də cher′ē, pon′də-sher′ē), *n.* city in SE India, former capital of French India. 60,000.

pond lily, water lily.

pond scum, 1 any free-floating, fresh-water alga that forms a green scum on stagnant water, as a spirogyra or related alga. 2 the green film formed by these algae.

pond weed (pond′wēd′), *n.* any of a large genus of water plants that grow in quiet water, usually having oval leaves on the surface of the water and grasslike leaves under water.

pone (pōn), *n.* U.S. 1 bread made of corn meal, popular in the southern United States. 2 loaf or cake of this bread. [< Algonquian]

pon gee (pon jē′), *n.* 1 a soft silk fabric whose thread is obtained from the cocoon of a silkworm native to China, usually left in natural brownish-yellow color. 2 a similar cloth of cotton or rayon, or of dyed silk. [< Chinese *pen-chi*]

pon iard (pon′yərd), *n.* a short, relatively slender dagger. *—v.t.* kill or wound by stabbing with a poniard. [< Middle French *poignard* < *poing* fist < Latin *pugnus*]

pons Va ro li i (ponz′ və rō′lē ī), band of nerve fibers in the brain, just above the medulla oblongata, consisting of transverse fibers connecting the two lobes of the cerebellum, and longitudinal fibers connecting the medulla with the cerebrum. See **brain** for diagram. [< New Latin, Varoli's bridge < Costanzo *Varoli,* 1543?-1575, Italian anatomist]

Pont char train (pon′chər trān), *n.* **Lake,** shallow lake in SE Louisiana, just north of New Orleans. 40 mi. long; 600 sq. mi.

Pon ti ac (pon′tē ak), *n.* 1 city in SE Michigan. 85,000. 2 1720?-1769, American Indian chief.

pon ti fex (pon′tə feks), *n., pl.* **pon tif i ces** (pon tif′ə sēz′). member of the principal college of priests in ancient Rome. [< Latin]

pon tiff (pon′tif), *n.* 1 the pope. 2 bishop. 3 high priest. 4 pontifex. [< French *pontif* < Latin *pontifex,* probably < *pons* bridge + *facere* to make]

pon tif i cal (pon tif′ə kəl), *adj.* 1 of or having to do with the pope; papal. 2 of or having to do with a bishop; episcopal. 3 characteristic of a pontiff; stately. *—n.* **1 pontificals,** *pl.* vestments and marks of dignity used by cardinals and bishops at certain ecclesiastical functions or ceremonies. 2 book containing the forms for sacraments and other rites to be performed by bishops. **—pon tif′i cal ly,** *adv.*

pon tif i cate (*n.* pon tif′ə kit, pon tif′ə kāt; *v.* pon tif′ə kāt), *n., v.,* **-cat ed, -cat ing.** *—n.* office or term of office of a pontiff. *—v.i.* 1 officiate as a pontiff. 2 behave or speak pompously.

Pon tine Marshes (pon′tīn), district southeast of Rome, Italy, on the Mediterranean Sea, formerly a marsh.

Pon tius Pilate (pon′shəs, pon′tē əs). See **Pilate.**

pontoon (def. 2)

pon toon (pon tün′), *n.* 1 a low, flat-bottomed boat. 2 such a boat, or some other floating structure, used as one of the supports of a temporary bridge. 3 either of two air-filled, watertight, boat-shaped parts of an aircraft for landing, floating on, or taking off from water; float. [< French *ponton* < Latin *pontonem* < *pons* bridge]

pontoon bridge, a temporary bridge supported by low, flat-bottomed boats or other floating structures.

Pon tus (pon′təs), *n.* 1 an ancient name of the Black Sea. 2 ancient country just south of the Black Sea in NE Asia Minor, later a Roman province.

po ny (pō′nē), *n., pl.* **-nies,** *v.,* **-nied, -ny ing.** *—n.* 1 horse of any of several small breeds, such as the Shetland pony, usually less than 14 hands high. 2 any small horse. 3 INFORMAL. **a** a translation of a work in a foreign language, which a pupil uses to avoid doing the work himself. **b** a small glass for alcoholic liquor. 4 amount such a glass will hold. *—v.t.* **pony up,** pay (money), especially in settlement of an account. [< French *poulenet,* ultimately < Latin *pullus* foal]

pony express, system of carrying letters and small packages in the western United States in 1860 and 1861 by relays of men riding fast ponies or horses.

po ny tail (pō′nē tāl′), *n.* a hair style for girls and women in which the hair is pulled back and bound, with the ends falling free from where the hair is gathered.

pooch (püch), *n.* SLANG. dog. [origin uncertain]

pood (püd), *n.* a Russian weight equal to 36.113 pounds [< Russian *pud* < Scandinavian (Norwegian) *pund* pound]

poo dle (pü′dl), *n.* one of a breed of intelligent dogs with thick, curly hair, usually black, brown, gray, or white, that is often clipped or shaved in an elaborate manner. [< German *Pudel*]

pooh (pü), *interj., n.* exclamation of contempt.

Pooh-Bah (pü′bä′), *n.* person holding many offices or positions, especially many small offices without much authority. [< *Pooh-Bah,* character in *The Mikado,* by Gilbert and Sullivan]

pooh-pooh (pü′pü′, pü′pü′), *v.t.* express contempt for; make light of. *—v.i.* pooh-pooh someone or something.

pool[1] (pül), *n.* 1 tank of water to swim or bathe in: *a swimming pool.* 2 a small body of still water; small pond. 3 a still, deep place in a stream. 4 puddle: *a pool of grease under a car.* [Old English *pōl*]

pool[2] (pül), *n.* 1 form of billiards played, usually with 15 object balls and a cue ball, on a rectangular table with six pockets; pocket billiards. 2 things or money put together by different persons for common advantage: *The hikers put all their food and money in a pool.* 3 group of people, usually having the same skills, who are drawn upon as needed: *the labor pool, a secretarial pool.* 4 arrangement between several companies, groups, etc., to prevent competition by controlling prices. 5 persons who form a pool. 6 fund raised by a group of persons for purposes of speculation, as in the stock market, commodities, etc. 7 stake played for in some gambling games. 8 the total amount of money bet on something, such as a horse race. —*v.t.* put (things or money) together for common advantage: *We plan to pool our savings for a year to buy a boat.* [< French *poule* booty, (originally) hen < Late Latin *pulla* chick < Latin *pullus*]

pool room (pül′rüm′, pül′rům′), *n.* 1 room or place in which the game of pool is played. 2 place where bets are taken on races, sporting events, etc.

Poo na (pü′nə), *n.* city in W India, southeast of Bombay. 718,000.

poop[1] (def. 1)

poop[1] (püp), *n.* 1 Also, **poop deck.** deck at the stern above the ordinary deck, often forming the roof of a cabin. 2 stern of a ship. —*v.t.* 1 (of a wave) break over the stern of (a ship). 2 (of a ship) receive (a wave) over the stern. [< Old French *poupe* < Italian *poppa* < Latin *puppis* stern]

poop[2] (püp), *v.t., v.i.* SLANG. make or become exhausted: *A set of tennis in the hot sun really poops me. After such exertion we were pooped out.* [origin unknown]

poor (pür), *adj.* 1 having few things or nothing; lacking money or property; needy. See synonym study below. 2 not good in quality; lacking something needed: *poor soil, a poor performance.* 3 scanty; insufficient; inadequate: *a poor crop.* 4 lacking ability; inefficient: *a poor cook.* 5 not satisfactory; frail: *poor health.* 6 needing pity; unfortunate: *This poor child has hurt himself.* 7 not favorable: *a poor chance for recovery.* 8 shabby or worn-out: *poor, threadbare clothing.* —*n.* **the poor,** persons who are needy. [< Old French *povre* < Latin *pauper.* Doublet of PAUPER.] —**poor′ness,** *n.*

Syn. *adj.* 1 **Poor, penniless, impoverished** mean with little or no money or property. **Poor** has a rather wide range of meaning, from being needy and dependent on charity for the necessities of life to not having enough money to buy comforts or luxuries: *She is a poor widow.* **Penniless** means without any money at all, but sometimes only temporarily: *She found herself penniless in a strange city.* **Impoverished** means reduced to poverty from comfortable circumstances, even wealth: *Many people became impoverished during the depression of the 1930's.*

poor house (pür′hous′), *n., pl.* **-hous es** (-hou′ziz). formerly, a house in which paupers lived at public expense.

poor ish (pür′ish), *adj.* somewhat poor; of rather poor quality.

poor law, law providing for the relief or support of the poor.

poor ly (pür′lē), *adv.* in a poor manner; not enough; badly; meanly. —*adj.* INFORMAL. in bad health.

poor-spir it ed (pür′spir′ə tid), *adj.* having or showing a poor, cowardly, or abject spirit.

pop[1] (pop), *v.,* **popped, pop ping,** *n., adv.* —*v.i.* 1 make a short, quick, explosive sound: *The firecrackers popped in bunches.* 2 burst open with a pop: *The chestnuts were popping in the fire.* 3 move, go, or come suddenly or unexpectedly: *Our neighbor popped in for a short call.* 4 INFORMAL. shoot. 5 bulge; protrude: *Surprise made her eyes pop out.* 6 (in baseball) hit a pop fly. 7 **pop off,** SLANG. **a** fall asleep. **b** die. **c** state loudly as a complaint. 8 **pop out** or **pop up,** (in baseball) hit a pop fly. —*n.* 1 a short, quick, explosive sound: *the pop of a cork.* 2 shot from a gun, etc. 3 a nonalcoholic carbonated drink: *strawberry pop.* 4 (in baseball) a pop fly. —*adv.* with a pop; suddenly. [imitative]

pop[2] (pop), *n.* INFORMAL. papa; father. [variant of *papa*]

pop[3] (pop), *adj.* INFORMAL. 1 popular: *pop songs.* 2 having to do with pop art: *pop paintings.*

pop., 1 popular. 2 population.

pop art, painting and sculpture based on the style of comic strips, advertising posters, etc.

pop corn (pop′kôrn′), *n.* 1 kind of Indian corn, the kernels of which burst open and puff out when heated. 2 the white, puffed-out kernels.

pope or **Pope** (pōp), *n.* the supreme head of the Roman Catholic Church. [Old English *pāpa* < Late Latin *papa* < Latin, bishop < Greek *pappas* father]

Pope (pōp), *n.* **Alexander,** 1688-1744, English poet.

pop er y (pō′pər ē), *n.* UNFRIENDLY USE. the doctrines, customs, and ceremonies of the Roman Catholic Church.

pop eyed (pop′īd′), *adj.* having bulging, prominent eyes.

pop fly, (in baseball) a short, high fly ball which can be caught easily.

pop gun (pop′gun′), *n.* a toy gun that shoots a pellet by compressed air, causing a popping sound.

pop in jay (pop′in jā), *n.* a vain, overly talkative person; conceited, silly person. [< Old French *papingay* parrot < Spanish *papagayo* < Arabic *babbaghā′*]

pop ish (pō′pish), *adj.* UNFRIENDLY USE. having to do with the Roman Catholic Church. —**pop′ish ly,** *adv.*

pop lar (pop′lər), *n.* 1 any of a genus of trees native to temperate regions and of the same family as the willow, that grow very rapidly and produce light, soft wood. The cottonwood and the aspen are poplars. 2 tree resembling these in some way, especially the tulip tree. 3 wood of any of these trees. [< Old French *poplier* < Latin *populus*]

pop lin (pop′lən), *n.* a ribbed dress fabric, made of silk, wool, cotton, or rayon. [< French *popeline*]

Po po cat e pet l (pō′pō kat′ə pet′l; *Spanish* pō po′kä tā′pet l), *n.* volcano in S central Mexico, near Mexico City. 17,876 ft. high.

pop o ver (pop′ō′vər), *n.* a very light and hollow muffin.

hat, āge, fär; let, ēqual, tėrm;
it, īce; hot, ōpen, ôrder;
oil, out; cup, pu̇t, rüle;
ch, child; ng, long; sh, she;
th, thin; ᴛʜ, then; zh, measure;

ə represents *a* in about, *e* in taken, *i* in pencil, *o* in lemon, *u* in circus.

< = from, derived from, taken from.

pop per (pop′ər), *n.* 1 person or thing that pops. 2 a wire basket or metal pan used for popping popcorn.

pop py (pop′ē), *n., pl.* **-pies.** 1 any of a family of herbs with milky juice, showy, delicate flowers of various colors, and roundish capsules containing many small seeds. The juice from the capsule of one variety is used to make opium. 2 flower of any of these plants. 3 a bright red. [Old English *popæg,* ultimately < Latin *papaver*]

pop py cock (pop′ē kok′), *n., interj.* INFORMAL. nonsense; bosh.

poppy seed, seed of the poppy, used in baking to flavor rolls, bread, cookies, etc.

pop u lace (pop′yə lis), *n.* the common people; the masses.

pop u lar (pop′yə lər), *adj.* 1 liked or admired by most people or by people generally: *a popular song.* 2 liked by acquaintances or associates: *Her ability and good nature make her the most popular girl in the class.* 3 of or by the people; representing the people: *The United States has a popular government.* 4 widespread among many people; common; prevalent: *a popular belief.* See **general** for synonym study. 5 suited to or intended for ordinary people: *popular prices, popular science.* [< Latin *popularis* < *populus* people] —**pop′u lar ly,** *adv.*

popular front, coalition of communist, socialist, and moderate political parties against fascism.

pop u lar i ty (pop′yə lar′ə tē), *n.* fact or condition of being popular.

pop u lar ize (pop′yə lə rīz′), *v.t.,* **-ized, -iz ing.** make popular. —**pop′u lar i za′tion,** *n.* —**pop′u lar iz′er,** *n.*

Popular Latin, the popular or commonly used form of Latin which was the main source of French, Spanish, Italian, Portuguese, and Romanian; Vulgar Latin.

popular sovereignty, U.S. doctrine advocated before the Civil War that the settlers of new territories had the right to decide in their own legislatures whether or not they wanted slavery; squatter sovereignty.

popular vote, the votes cast by the electorate, as opposed to the electoral vote.

pop u late (pop′yə lāt), *v.t.,* **-lat ed, -lat ing.** 1 live in; inhabit: *This city is densely populated.* 2 furnish with inhabitants; people: *Europeans populated much of America.*

pop u la tion (pop′yə lā′shən), *n.* 1 people of a city or a country. 2 the number of people. 3 part of the inhabitants distinguished in any way from the rest: *the urban population.* 4 act or process of furnishing with inhabitants. 5 (in statistics) the entire group of items or individuals from which the samples under consideration are presumed to come. 6 (in biology) the aggregate of organisms which inhabit a particular locality or region.

Pop u lism (pop′yə liz′əm), *n.* U.S. the

principles and policies of the Populists.

Pop u list (pop′yə list), *n.* U.S. member of the Populist Party.

Populist Party, an American political party formed in 1891, and active until 1896, which advocated government control of the railroads, limitation of private ownership of land, an increase in currency, an income tax, etc.; People's Party.

pop u lous (pop′yə ləs), *adj.* full of people; having many people per square mile. **—pop′u lous ly,** *adv.* **—pop′u lous-ness,** *n.*

por ce lain (pôr′sə lin, pōr′sə lin), *n.* 1 a very fine earthenware, usually having a translucent white body and a transparent glaze; china: *Teacups are often made of porcelain.* 2 dish or other object made of this material. [< Middle French *pourcelaine* < Italian *porcellana*]

porch (pôrch, pōrch), *n.* 1 a covered entrance to a building. 2 U.S. veranda. [< Old French *porche* < Latin *porticus* < *porta* gate. Doublet of PORTICO.]

por cine (pôr′sīn, pôr′sən), *adj.* 1 of pigs or hogs. 2 like or characteristic of pigs or hogs. [< Latin *porcinus* < *porcus* pig]

por cu pine (pôr′kyə pīn), *n.* any of various rodents covered with spines or quills growing in their coarse hair. [< Old French *porc-espin* spiny pig]

pore[1] (pôr, pōr), *v.i.*, **pored, por ing.** 1 gaze earnestly or steadily. 2 study long and steadily: *He would rather pore over a book than play.* 3 meditate or ponder intently: *pore over a problem.* [Middle English *pouren*]

pore[2] (pôr, pōr), *n.* a very small opening for perspiration, absorption, etc., especially in animal or vegetable tissue, such as the openings in the skin where the ducts of the sweat glands are. [< Old French < Latin *porus* < Greek *poros* passage]

por gy (pôr′gē), *n., pl.* **-gies** or **-gy.** any of various saltwater food fishes, such as the scup of the eastern coast of the United States and the sea bream of Mediterranean and Atlantic waters. [origin uncertain]

Po rif er a (pə rif′ər ə), *n.pl.* phylum comprising the poriferans.

po rif er an (pə rif′ər ən), *n.* any of a phylum of water animals with highly porous bodies, through which water passes continuously, that live attached to the sea bottom; sponge. [< Late Latin *porus* hole, passage + Latin *ferre* to bear]

Po River (pō), river flowing from NW Italy into the Adriatic Sea. 418 mi.

pork (pôrk, pōrk), *n.* meat of a pig or hog used for food. [< Old French *porc* < Latin *porcus* pig]

pork barrel, U.S. a government appropriation for a project that will benefit a particular body of constituents, although it may not fulfill a need. **—pork′-bar′rel,** *adj.*

pork er (pôr′kər, pōr′kər), *n.* pig, especially one fattened to eat.

pork pie (pôrk′pī′, pōrk′pī′), *n.* Also, **porkpie hat.** hat with a low, round crown and a flat top.

por nog ra pher (pôr nog′rə fər), *n.* person who writes, sells, or distributes pornography.

por no graph ic (pôr′nə graf′ik), *adj.* of or having to do with pornography. **—por′no graph′i cal ly,** *adv.*

por nog ra phy (pôr nog′rə fē), *n.* writings or pictures dealing with sexual matters in a manner intended to incite lust. [< Greek *pornē* harlot + *-graphos* writing about]

po ros i ty (pô ros′ə tē, pō ros′ə tē), *n., pl.* **-ties.** 1 porous quality or condition. 2 a porous part or structure.

po rous (pôr′əs, pōr′əs), *adj.* full of pores; permeable by water, air, etc.: *Cloth, blotting paper, and earthenware are porous.* **—po′rous ly,** *adv.* **—po′rous ness,** *n.*

por phyr y (pôr′fər ē), *n., pl.* **-phyr ies.** 1 a hard red or purplish Egyptian rock which contains crystals of feldspar. 2 any igneous rock in which coarse crystals are scattered through a groundmass of finer-grained minerals. [< Greek *porphyros* purple]

por poise (pôr′pəs), *n., pl.* **-pois es** or **-poise.** 1 a sea mammal with a blunt, rounded snout, of the same order as the whale but smaller, and living in groups in the northern Atlantic and Pacific. 2 any of several other small sea mammals, especially the dolphin. [< Old French *porpeis,* ultimately < Latin *porcus* pig + *piscis* fish]

porcupine—about 2½ ft. long with tail

por ridge (pôr′ij, por′ij), *n.* a soft food made of oatmeal or other cereal boiled in water or milk until it thickens. [variant of *pottage*]

por rin ger (pôr′ən jər, por′ən jər), *n.* 1 a small dish from which soup, porridge, bread and milk, etc., can be eaten. 2 a small bowl, mug, etc., especially one intended to be used by a child.

port[1] (pôrt, pōrt), *n.* 1 place where ships and boats can be sheltered from storms; harbor. See **harbor** for synonym study. 2 place where ships and boats can load and unload; city or town with a harbor. 3 port of entry. [Old English < Latin *portus*]

port[2] (pôrt, pōrt), *n.* 1 porthole. 2 cover for a porthole. 3 opening in a ship, wall, etc., through which to shoot. 4 opening in a cylinder or pipe for steam, air, water, etc., to pass through. [< Old French *porte* < Latin *porta* gate]

port[3] (pôrt, pōrt), *n.* the side of a ship or aircraft to the left of a person facing the bow or front. *—adj.* on the left side of a ship or aircraft. *—v.t., v.i.* turn or shift to the left side: *port the helm.* [origin uncertain]

port[4] (pôrt, pōrt), *n.* way of holding one's head and body; bearing. [< Old French < *porter* carry < Latin *portare*]

port[5] (pôrt, pōrt), *n.* a strong, sweet wine that is dark red or tawny. [< *Oporto,* from which it was shipped]

Port., 1 Portugal. 2 Portuguese.

port a ble (pôr′tə bəl, pōr′tə bəl), *adj.* capable of being carried; easily carried: *a portable typewriter.* [< Late Latin *portabilis* < Latin *portare* carry]

por tage (pôr′tij, pōr′tij), *n., v.,* **-taged, -tag ing.** *—n.* 1 a carrying of boats, provisions, etc., overland from one river, lake, etc., to another. 2 place over which this is done. 3 act of carrying. *—v.t., v.i.* 1 carry (boats, goods, etc.) over land between navigable waters. 2 make a portage over (a place) or around (rapids, a cataract, etc.).

por tal (pôr′tl, pōr′tl), *n.* door, gate, or entrance, usually an imposing one. *—adj.* of or having to do with the portal vein. [< Medieval Latin *portale* < Latin *porta* gate]

por tal-to-por tal pay (pôr′tl tə pôr′tl, pōr′tl tə pōr′tl), wages paid to an employee for the time he spends going to, and coming from, his actual place of work after having arrived on the grounds of the employer.

porpoise (def. 1)—4 to 8 ft. long

portal vein, the large vein carrying blood to the liver from the veins of the stomach, intestine, and spleen.

por ta men to (pôr′tə men′tō, pōr′tə-men′tō), *n., pl.* **-ti** (-tē). (in music) a gliding continuously without break from one pitch or note to another. [< Italian, literally, a carrying]

Port Arthur, former name of **Lüshun.**

Port-au-Prince (pôrt′ō prins′, pōrt′ō-prins′), *n.* seaport and capital of Haiti, in the S part. 350,000.

port cul lis (pôrt kul′is, pōrt kul′is), *n.* a strong gate or grating of iron sliding up and down in grooves, used to close the gateway of an ancient castle or fortress. [< Old French *porte coleice* sliding gate]

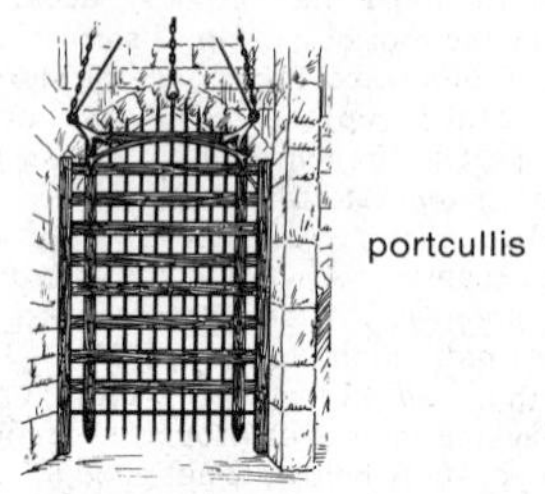

portcullis

porte-co chere or **porte-co chère** (pôrt′kō sher′, pōrt′kō sher′), *n.* 1 porch at the door of a building under which carriages and automobiles stop so that persons getting in or out are sheltered. 2 entrance for carriages, leading into a courtyard. [< French *porte-cochère* coach gate]

porte-cochere (def. 1)

porte-mon naie (pôrt′mun′ē, pōrt′mun′ē; *French* pôrt mô nā′), *n.* purse; pocketbook. [< French, literally, carry money]

por tend (pôr tend′, pōr tend′), *v.t.* indicate beforehand; be a portent of; bode: *Black clouds portend a storm.* [< Latin *portendere* < *por-* before + *tendere* extend]

por tent (pôr′tent, pōr′tent), *n.* 1 a warning of coming evil; sign; omen. 2 ominous significance. [< Latin *portentum* indicated beforehand]

por ten tous (pôr ten′təs, pōr ten′təs), *adj.* 1 indicating evil to come; ominous; threatening. 2 amazing; extraordinary. **—por ten′tous ly,** *adv.* **—por ten′tous ness,** *n.*

por ter[1] (pôr′tər, pōr′tər), *n.* 1 person employed to carry loads or baggage, especially at a hotel, railroad station, airport, etc. 2 attendant in a parlor car or sleeping car of a railroad train. [< Old French *porteur* < Late Latin *portator* < Latin *portare* carry]

por ter[2] (pôr′tər, pōr′tər), *n.* 1 doorman. 2 janitor. [< Old French *portier* < Late Latin *portarius* < Latin *porta* gate]

por ter[3] (pôr′tər, pōr′tər), *n.* a heavy, dark-brown beer. [short for *porter's ale,* apparently < *porter*[2] (who perhaps originally drank it)]

Por ter (pôr′tər, pōr′tər), *n.* 1 **Katherine Anne,** born 1890, American short-story writer and novelist. 2 **William Sydney,** the real name of **O. Henry.**

por ter house (pôr′tər hous′, pōr′tər-hous′), *n.* a choice beefsteak containing the tenderloin. [< *porter*[3] + *house*]

porterhouse steak, porterhouse.

port fo li o (pôrt fō′lē ō, pōrt fō′lē ō), *n., pl.* **-li os.** 1 a portable case for loose papers, drawings, etc.; briefcase. 2 position and duties of a cabinet member, diplomat, or minister of state: *The Secretary of Defense resigned his portfolio.* 3 holdings in the form of stocks, bonds, etc. [< Italian *portafoglio,* ultimately < Latin *portare* carry + *folium* sheet, leaf]

port hole (pôrt′hōl′, pōrt′hōl′), *n.* 1 opening in a ship's side to let in light and air. 2 opening in a ship, wall, etc., through which to shoot.

Por tia (pôr′shə, pōr′shə), *n.* heroine in Shakespeare's *The Merchant of Venice,* who acts as a lawyer.

portico

por ti co (pôr′tə kō, pōr′tə kō), *n., pl.* **-coes** or **-cos.** roof supported by columns, forming a porch or a covered walk. [< Italian < Latin *porticus.* Doublet of PORCH.]

por tiere or **por tière** (pôr tyer′, pōr-tyer′), *n.* curtain hung across a doorway. [< French *portière*]

por tion (pôr′shən, pōr′shən), *n.* 1 a part or share. See **part** for synonym study. 2 quantity of food served for one person. 3 the part of an estate that goes to an heir; property inherited. 4 dowry. 5 one's lot; fate. *—v.t.* 1 divide into parts or shares. 2 give (a thing to a person) as a share; give a portion, inheritance, dowry, etc., to. [< Old French < Latin *portionem*] **—por′tion less,** *adj.*

Port land (pôrt′lənd, pōrt′lənd), *n.* 1 seaport in SW Maine. 65,000. 2 seaport in NW Oregon. 381,000.

portland cement, cement made by burning in a kiln a mixture of limestone and clay, or a chemically similar substance, and then grinding this product to a very fine powder, used in making mortar and concrete. [< Isle of *Portland,* peninsula of southern England]

Port Lou is (lü′is, lü′ē), capital of Mauritius, a seaport in the NW part. 139,000.

port ly (pôrt′lē, pōrt′lē), *adj.,* **-li er, -li est.** 1 having a large body; stout; corpulent. See **fat** for synonym study. 2 stately; dignified. [< *port*[4]] **—port′li ness,** *n.*

port man teau (pôrt man′tō, pōrt man′tō), *n., pl.* **-teaus** or **-teaux** (-tōz). a stiff, oblong traveling bag with two compartments opening like a book. [< Middle French < *porter* carry + *manteau* mantle]

portmanteau word, word made by combining parts of two words; blend.

Port Mores by (môrz′bē), capital of the Territory of Papua, a seaport in the S part. 42,000.

Por to A le gre (pôr′tù ä lā′grə), seaport in S Brazil. 886,000.

port of call, port where ships usually stop to discharge and receive cargo and passengers, take on supplies, etc.

Portuguese man-of-war
Its tentacles may be up to 100 ft. long.

port of entry, place with a custom house, through which persons or merchandise may enter legally into a country.

Port of Spain, Port-of-Spain.

Port-of-Spain (pôrt′əv spān′, pōrt′əv-spān′), *n.* capital of Trinidad and Tobago, a seaport in NW Trinidad. 94,000.

Por to-No vo (pôr′tō nō′vō), *n.* capital of Dahomey, in the S part. 75,000.

Por to Ri co (pôr′tō rē′kō; pōr′tō rē′kō), former name of **Puerto Rico.**

por trait (pôr′trit, pôr′trāt; pōr′trit, pōr′trāt), *n.* 1 picture of a person, especially of the face, such as a painting, drawing, photograph, etc. 2 picture in words; description. [< Old French < *portraire* portray]

por trait ist (pôr′trā tist, pōr′trā tist), *n.* person who paints portraits.

por trai ture (pôr′trə chůr, pôr′trə chər; pōr′trə chůr, pōr′trə chər), *n.* 1 act of portraying. 2 portrait.

por tray (pôr trā′, pōr trā′), *v.t.* 1 make a likeness of in a drawing or painting; make a picture of: *portray a historical scene.* 2 picture in words; describe: *The book portrays life long ago.* 3 represent in a play or motion picture; impersonate; act. [< Old French *portraire* < Latin *protrahere* < *pro-* forth + *trahere* to draw] **—por tray′er,** *n.*

por tray al (pôr trā′əl, pōr trā′əl), *n.* 1 a portraying by drawing or in words. 2 picture or description.

Port Sa id (sä ēd′), seaport in NE Egypt, at the Mediterranean end of the Suez Canal. 283,000.

Ports mouth (pôrts′məth, pōrts′məth), *n.* 1 seaport in S England, on the English Channel. 212,000. 2 seaport in SE Virginia. 111,000.

hat, āge, fär; let, ēqual, tėrm;
it, īce; hot, ōpen, ôrder;
oil, out; cup, půt, rüle;
ch, child; ng, long; sh, she;
th, thin; ᴛʜ, then; zh, measure;

ə represents *a* in about, *e* in taken, *i* in pencil, *o* in lemon, *u* in circus.

< = from, derived from, taken from.

Por tu gal (pôr′chə gəl, pōr′chə gəl), *n.* country in SW Europe, west of Spain. 9,583,000 pop.; 35,400 sq. mi. *Capital:* Lisbon.

Por tu guese (pôr′chə gēz′, pōr′chə gēz′), *n., pl.* **-guese,** *adj.* *—n.* 1 native or inhabitant of Portugal. 2 the Romance language of Portugal. Portuguese is also the chief language of Brazil. *—adj.* of or having to do with Portugal, its people, or their language.

Portuguese East Africa, Mozambique.

Portuguese Guinea, Portuguese colony in NW Africa. 560,000 pop.; 13,900 sq. mi. *Capital:* Bissau.

Portuguese India, former Portuguese colony, now part of India, on the W coast of the Indian peninsula.

Portuguese man-of-war, *pl.,* **Portuguese men-of-war.** a large marine hydrozoan having a large air sac that acts as a float from which a number of polyps are suspended. It is noted for brilliant coloring and great power of stinging by long tentacles.

Portuguese Timor, Portuguese colony in the East Indies. 600,000 pop.; 7300 sq. mi. *Capital:* Dili.

Portuguese West Africa, Angola.

por tu lac a (pôr′chə lak′ə, pōr′chə lak′ə), *n.* a low, succulent herb related to the purslane, with thick, fleshy leaves and dainty white, yellow, red, or purple flowers. [< Latin, purslane]

pos., 1 positive. 2 possessive.

pose[1] (pōz), *n., v.,* **posed, pos ing.** *—n.* 1 position of the body; way of holding the body: *a natural pose, a pose taken in exercising.* 2 attitude assumed for effect; pretense; affectation: *Her interest in others is real, not just a pose.* *—v.t.* 1 hold a position: *pose for a portrait.* 2 put on an attitude for effect; make a false pretense: *He posed as a rich man though he owed more than he owned.* *—v.i.* 1 put in a certain position: *The photographer posed the family before taking the picture.* 2 put forward for discussion; state: *pose a question.* [< Old French *poser* to place < Late Latin *pausare* to stop, pause < Latin *pausa* a pause]

pose[2] (pōz), *v.,* **posed, pos ing.** puzzle completely. [variant of *oppose*]

Po sei don (pə sīd′n), *n.* (in Greek myths) the god of the sea, identified wih the Roman god Neptune.

pos er[1] (pō′zər), *n.* person who poses. [< *pose*[1]]

pos er[2] (pō′zər), *n.* a very puzzling problem or question. [< *pose*[2]]

po seur (pō zėr′; *French* pō zœr′), *n.* an affected person; one who poses to impress others. [< French < *poser* to pose]

posh (posh), *adj.* INFORMAL. elegant or fine in appearance; stylish; luxurious. [origin unknown]

pos i grade (poz′ə grād), *adj.* having positive acceleration; going or thrusting forward:

posigrade rockets. [< *posi(tive)* + *(retro)-grade*]

pos it (poz′it), *v.t.* lay down or assume as a fact or principle; affirm the existence of; postulate. [< Latin *positum* laid down, posited]

po si tion (pə zish′ən), *n.* 1 place where a thing or person is; place with respect to another place: *The flowers grew in a sheltered position behind the house.* See **place** for synonym study. 2 way of being placed: *Sit in a more comfortable position.* 3 proper place: *Each band member got into position to march in the parade.* 4 condition with reference to place or circumstances: *He maneuvered for position before shooting the basketball. Your careless remark put me in an awkward position.* 5 job. See synonym study below. 6 rank; standing, especially high standing: *He was raised to the position of captain.* 7 way of thinking; set of opinions: *What is your position on this question?* —*v.t.* place in a certain position. [< Latin *positionem* < *ponere* to put, set]

Syn. *n.* 5 **Position, job** mean employment. **Position** is somewhat formal and usually suggests white-collar work: *She has a position in a bank.* **Job** is the informal word for employment of any kind, but emphasizes the idea of work to do: *He has a job on a ranch this summer.*

po si tion al (pə zish′ə nəl), *adj.* of, having to do with, or depending on position.

pos i tive (poz′ə tiv), *adj.* 1 admitting of no question; without doubt: *positive proof.* 2 formally or arbitrarily laid down or imposed: *positive law.* 3 sure; confident: *Are you positive you can go?* 4 too sure; too confident: *Her positive manner annoys people.* 5 definite; emphatic: *"No. I will not," was his positive refusal.* 6 of the simple form of an adjective or adverb. 7 that can be thought of as real and present: *Light is a positive thing; darkness is only the absence of light.* 8 showing that a particular disease, condition, germ, etc., is present. 9 that definitely does something or adds something; practical: *Don't just make criticisms; give us some positive help.* 10 tending in the direction thought of as that of increase or progress: *Motion in the direction that the hands of the clock move is positive.* 11 counting up from zero; plus: *Five above zero is a positive quantity.* 12 of the kind of electricity produced on glass by rubbing it with silk; lacking electrons. 13 characterized by the presence or production of such electricity. 14 having a tendency to lose electrons, and thus to become charged with positive electricity, as a chemical element or radical. 15 (in photography) having the lines and shadows in the same position as in the original.
—*n.* 1 a positive degree or quantity. 2 the plate in a battery from which the current flows into the wire. 3 (in photography) a print made from a photographic film or plate. 4 the simple form of an adjective or adverb as distinct from the comparative and superlative. *Fast* is the positive; *faster* is the comparative; *fastest* is the superlative.
[< Latin *positivus,* ultimately < *ponere* to set] **—pos′i tive ly,** *adv.* **—pos′i tive-ness,** *n.*

pos i tiv ism (poz′ə tə viz′əm), *n.* a philosophical system founded by Auguste Comte, which deals only with positive facts and phenomena, rejecting abstract speculation.

pos i tron (poz′ə tron), *n.* an elementary particle having the same magnitude of mass and charge as an electron, but with a positive charge; antiparticle of an electron.

poss., possessive.

pos se (pos′ē), *n.* 1 group of men summoned by a sheriff to help him: *The posse pursued the thief.* 2 band, company, or assemblage: *a posse of spectators.* [< Medieval Latin *posse (comitatus),* literally, force (of the county)]

pos sess (pə zes′), *v.t.* 1 have as belonging to one; own: *The President possessed great force and knowledge.* 2 hold as property; hold; occupy. 3 control; influence strongly: *She was possessed by a desire to be rich.* 4 control by an evil spirit: *He fought like one possessed.* 5 ARCHAIC. take; win.

pos ses sion (pə zesh′ən), *n.* 1 a possessing; holding: *The soldiers fought hard for possession of the hilltop.* 2 ownership. 3 thing possessed; property. 4 territory under the rule of a country: *Guam is a possession of the United States.* 5 domination by a particular feeling, idea, evil spirit, etc. 6 self-control. [< Latin *possessionem* < *possidere* possess < *posse* be able + *sedere* to sit]

pos ses sive (pə zes′iv), *adj.* 1 of possession. 2 showing possession. *My, your, his,* and *our* are in the possessive case because they indicate who possesses or owns. 3 desirous of ownership: *a possessive nature.* 4 asserting or claiming ownership: *a possessive manner.* —*n.* 1 the possessive case. 2 word in this case. In "the boy's books," *boy's* is a possessive. **—pos ses′sive ly,** *adv.* **—pos ses′sive ness,** *n.*

possessive adjective, adjective that shows possession. It is formed from a personal pronoun. *My, your, his,* etc., are possessive adjectives.

possessive pronoun, pronoun that shows possession.

pos ses sor (pə zes′ər), *n.* person who possesses.

pos set (pos′it), *n.* a hot drink made of milk curdled by ale, wine, etc., and sweetened and spiced. [Middle English]

pos si bil i ty (pos′ə bil′ə tē), *n., pl.* **-ties.** 1 a being possible: *There is a possibility that the train may be late.* 2 a possible thing or person.

pos si ble (pos′ə bəl), *adj.* 1 that can be; that can be done; that can happen: *Come if possible.* See synonym study below. 2 that can be true or a fact: *It is possible that she went.* 3 that can be done, chosen, etc., properly: *the only possible action, the only possible candidate.* [< Latin *possibilis* < *posse* be able]

Syn. 1 **Possible, practicable, feasible** mean capable of happening or being done. **Possible** means that with suitable conditions and methods something may exist, happen, or be done: *It is possible to cure tuberculosis.* **Practicable** means that under present circumstances or by available means something can easily or effectively be carried out, done, or used: *The X ray is a practicable way of discovering unsuspected diseases.* **Feasible** suggests that which is likely to work satisfactorily: *No method of preventing cancer is yet feasible.*

pos si bly (pos′ə blē), *adv.* 1 by any possibility; no matter what happens: *I cannot possibly go.* 2 perhaps: *Possibly you are right.*

pos sum (pos′əm), *n., pl.* **-sums** or **-sum.** 1 opossum. 2 **play possum,** put on a false appearance; pretend. [variant of *opossum*]

post[1] (pōst), *n.* 1 piece of timber, metal, or the like, set upright, usually as a support: *the posts of a door, a hitching post.* 2 post, line, etc., where a race starts or ends. —*v.t.* 1 fasten (a notice) up in a place where it can easily be seen. 2 make known by, or as if by, a posted notice; make public: *post a reward.* 3 put in a list that is published or posted up: *post three ships as missing, post a train as on time.* 4 cover (a wall, etc.) with notices or bills. 5 put up notices warning people to keep out of: *That farmer posts his land.* [Old English < Latin *postis*]

post[2] (pōst), *n.* 1 place where a soldier, policeman, etc., is stationed; place where one is supposed to be when on duty. 2 place where soldiers are stationed; military station; fort. 3 U.S. a local branch of a veterans' organization. 4 job or position: *the post of secretary, a diplomatic post.* 5 a trading point. —*v.t.* 1 station at a post at a particular point: *We posted guards at the door.* 2 make a deposit of: *post bail.* [< Middle French *poste* < Italian *posto* < Latin *positum* stationed, placed]

post[3] (pōst), *n.* 1 an established system, especially a governmental system, for carrying letters, papers, packages, etc.; the mail: *send a package by post.* 2 a single delivery of mail; the letters, etc., thus delivered: *this morning's post.* 3 ARCHAIC. postman. 4 post office. 5 mailbox. 6 one of a series of fixed stations along a route that furnished relays of men and horses for carrying letters, etc., and supplying service to travelers by post horse, post chaise, etc. 7 courier; postrider.
—*v.t.* 1 send by post; mail: *post a letter.* 2 INFORMAL. supply with up-to-date information; inform: *be well posted on current events.* 3 in bookkeeping: **a** transfer (an entry) from journal to ledger. **b** enter (an item) in due place and form. **c** make all requisite entries in (a ledger, etc.). —*v.i.* 1 travel with post horses or by post chaise. 2 travel with speed; hasten. 3 rise and fall in the saddle in rhythm with the horse's trot.
—*adv.* by post; speedily.
[< Middle French *poste* < Italian *posta* < Latin *posita* placed]

Post (pōst), *n.* **Emily (Price),** 1873-1960, American writer, known as an authority on etiquette.

post-, *prefix.* 1 after in time; later: *Postwar* = *after a war.* 2 after in space; behind: *Postnasal* = *behind the nasal cavity.* [< Latin]

post age (pō′stij), *n.* amount paid on anything sent by mail.

postage meter, machine that stamps postage on a letter or package and postmarks it.

postage stamp, stamp (n. def. 1).

post al (pō′stəl), *adj.* having to do with mail and post offices.

postal card, post card.

Postal Service, an independent agency of the United States government that provides postal services, sells postage stamps, etc. It replaced the U.S. Post Office Department in 1971.

post au dit (pōst ô′dit), *n.* audit conducted after a transaction has been completed.

post boy (pōst′boi′), *n.* postilion.

post card (pōst′kärd′), *n.* post card.

post card, card, usually about $3^1/_2$ inches by $5^1/_2$ inches, for sending a message by mail. Some post cards have a government postage stamp printed on them; others have pictures on one side.

hat, āge, fär; let, ēqual, tėrm;
it, īce; hot, ōpen, ôrder;
oil, out; cup, pu̇t, rüle;
ch, child; ng, long; sh, she;
th, thin; ᴛʜ, then; zh, measure;
ə represents *a* in about, *e* in taken, *i* in pencil, *o* in lemon, *u* in circus.
< = from, derived from, taken from.

post chaise, a four-wheeled carriage used for carrying passengers and mail in the 1700's and early 1800's, usually having seats for two or four people.

post date (pōst′dāt′), *v.t.,* **-dat ed, -dat ing.** 1 give a later date than the true date to (a letter, check, etc.). 2 follow in time.

post doc tor al (pōst dok′tər əl), *adj.* having to do with advanced academic work after the doctorate.

post er (pō′stər), *n.* 1 a large printed sheet or notice put up in some public place. 2 person who posts notices, etc.

poste res tante (pōst′ re stänt′), 1 direction written on mail which is to remain at the post office till called for. 2 a post-office department in charge of such mail. [< French, remaining mail]

pos ter i or (po stir′ē ər), *adj.* 1 situated behind; back; rear; hind. 2 coming after; later; subsequent. —*n.* Often, **posteriors,** *pl.* the buttocks. [< Latin, comparative of *posterus* coming after, behind < *post* after] **—pos ter′i or ly,** *adv.*

pos ter i ty (po ster′ə tē), *n.* 1 generations of the future: *Posterity may travel to distant planets.* 2 all of a person's descendants. [< Latin *posteritatem* < *posterus* coming after]

pos tern (pō′stərn, pos′tərn), *n.* 1 a back door or gate. 2 any small or private entrance. —*adj.* rear; lesser: *The castle had a postern door.* [< Old French *posterne,* ultimately < Latin *posterus* behind. See POSTERIOR.]

post exchange or **Post Exchange,** store at a military post that sells merchandise and services to military personnel and their dependents.

post grad u ate (pōst graj′ü it), *n.* student who continues studying in college or at school after graduation. —*adj.* 1 taking a course of study after graduation. 2 of or for postgraduates.

post haste (pōst′hāst′), *adv.* very speedily; in great haste. [< *post*[3]]

post hoc, er go prop ter hoc (pōst′ hok ėr′gō prop′tər hok), LATIN. after this, therefore as a result of this (a phrase used to denote a common logical fallacy that what comes before an event must also be its cause).

post horse, horse used by persons riding post or hired by travelers.

post hu mous (pos′chə məs), *adj.* 1 happening after death: *posthumous fame.* 2 published after the death of the author: *a posthumous book.* 3 born after the death of the father: *a posthumous daughter.* [< Late Latin *posthumus,* variant of Latin *postumus* last born, originally superlative of *posterus* coming after] **—post′hu mous ly,** *adv.*

post hyp not ic (pōst′hip not′ik), *adj.* 1 after hypnosis: *a posthypnotic trance.* 2 (of a suggestion given during hypnosis) intended to be carried out after the subject has emerged from hypnosis. **—post′hyp not′i cal ly,** *adv.*

pos til ion or **pos til lion** (pō stil′yən, po-stil′yən), *n.* person who guides a team of horses drawing a carriage or post chaise by riding the left-hand horse when one pair is used, or the left-hand horse of the leading pair when two or more pairs are used. [< French *postillon*]

post im pres sion ism (pōst′im presh′ə-niz′əm), *n.* style of painting developed by a group of French artists at the end of the 1800's, which departed from impressionism by its freer use of color, form, design, and expression.

post lude (pōst′lüd), *n.* 1 a concluding musical piece or movement. 2 music played at the end of a church service. [< *post-* + *(pre)lude*]

post man (pōst′mən), *n., pl.* **-men.** mailman.

post mark (pōst′märk′), *n.* an official mark stamped on mail to cancel the postage stamp and record the place and date of mailing. —*v.t.* stamp with a postmark.

post mas ter (pōst′mas′tər), *n.* person in charge of a post office.

postmaster general, *pl.* **postmasters general.** 1 person at the head of the postal system of a country. 2 **Postmaster General,** the chief executive officer of the Postal Service.

post me rid i an (pōst′mə rid′ē ən), *adj.* occurring after noon.

post me rid i em (pōst mə rid′ē əm; post me rē′di em), LATIN. after noon. *Abbrev.:* p.m., P.M.

post mis tress (pōst′mis′tris), *n.* woman in charge of a post office.

post-mor tem or **post mor tem** (pōst′-môr′təm), *adj.* 1 after death: *A post-mortem examination showed that the man had been poisoned.* 2 of or having to do with a post-mortem examination or autopsy. 3 following, and concerned with, some event, often one that is difficult or unpleasant: *a post-mortem discussion.* —*n.* 1 autopsy. 2 a discussion following, and concerned with, some event, often one that is difficult or unpleasant, such as the loss of an election. [< Latin *post mortem* after death]

post na sal (pōst nā′zəl), *adj.* behind the nose or nasal cavity.

post na tal (pōst nā′tl), *adj.* 1 after childbirth: *postnatal care.* 2 occurring after birth: *postnatal diseases of children.* **—post-na′tal ly,** *adv.*

post office, 1 place where mail is handled and postage stamps are sold. 2 Often, **Post Office.** the former United States government department in charge of mail, replaced by the Postal Service in 1971.

post op e ra tive (pōst op′ər ə tiv, pōst-op′ə rā′tiv), *adj.* occurring after a surgical operation: *postoperative pains.* **—post-op′e ra tive ly,** *adv.*

post paid (pōst′pād′), *adj.* with the postage paid for.

post par tum (pōst pär′təm), *adj.* occurring after childbirth. [< Latin *post partum* after birth]

post pone (pōst pōn′), *v.t.,* **-poned, -pon ing.** put off till later or to a later time; delay; defer. See **delay** for synonym study. [< Latin *postponere* < *post-* + *ponere* put] **—post pon′er,** *n.*

post pone ment (pōst pōn′mənt), *n.* a putting off till later; a putting off to a later time; delay; deferment.

post pran di al (pōst pran′dē əl), *adj.* after-dinner: *postprandial speeches.* [< *post-* + Latin *prandium* lunch]

post road, 1 road or route over which mail is or was carried. 2 road with stations which furnish horses.

post script (pōst′skript), *n.* 1 addition to a letter, written after the writer's name has been signed. 2 a supplementary part added to any composition or literary work.

pos tu lant (pos′chə lənt), *n.* candidate, especially for admission to a religious order. [< Latin *postulantem* demanding, requesting]

pos tu late (*n.* pos′chə lit; *v.* pos′chə lāt), *n., v.,* **-lat ed, -lat ing.** —*n.* something taken for granted or assumed as a basis for reasoning; fundamental principle; necessary condition: *One postulate of plane geometry is that a straight line may be drawn between any two points.* —*v.t.* 1 assume as a postulate; take for granted. 2 require; demand; claim. [< Latin *postulatum* a demand < *postulare* to demand] **—pos′tu la′tion,** *n.*

pos tur al (pos′chər əl), *adj.* of or having to do with posture.

pos ture (pos′chər), *n., v.,* **-tured, -tur ing.** —*n.* 1 position of the body; way of holding the body: *Good posture is important for health.* 2 condition; situation; state: *In the present posture of public affairs it is difficult to predict what will happen.* 3 mental or spiritual attitude. —*v.i.* 1 take a certain posture: *The dancer postured before the mirror, bending and twisting her body.* 2 pose for effect. —*v.t.* put in a certain posture. [< French < Italian *postura* < Latin *positura* < *ponere* to place] **—pos′tur er,** *n.*

post vo cal ic (pōst′vō kal′ik), *adj.* following immediately after a vowel.

post war (pōst′wôr′), *adj., adv.* after a war.

po sy (pō′zē), *n., pl.* **-sies.** 1 flower. 2 bunch of flowers; bouquet. 3 motto or line of poetry engraved within a ring, etc. [variant of *poesy*]

pot (pot), *n., v.,* **pot ted, pot ting.** —*n.* 1 a round, relatively deep container made of metal or earthenware for cooking and other uses, especially domestic. 2 the amount a pot can hold; potful. 3 basket used as a trap to catch fish, lobsters, etc. 4 INFORMAL. a large sum of money. 5 INFORMAL. all the money bet at one time. 6 SLANG. marijuana. 7 **go to pot,** go to ruin. —*v.t.* 1 put into or grow in a pot: *pot young tomato plants.* 2 cook and preserve in a pot or can. 3 take a potshot at; shoot. —*v.i.* take a potshot; shoot. [Old English *pott*] **—pot′like′,** *adj.*

po ta ble (pō′tə bəl), *adj.* fit or suitable for drinking; drinkable. —*n.* Usually, **potables,** *pl.* anything drinkable. [< Late Latin *potabilis* < Latin *potare* to drink]

po tage (pô täzh′), *n.* FRENCH. soup.

pot ash (pot′ash′), *n.* 1 any of several substances made from various minerals, wood ashes, etc., used in making soap, fertilizers, and glass. It is mainly impure potassium carbonate. 2 potassium or any compound containing potassium. 3 potassium hydroxide. [< earlier *pot ashes*]

po tas si um (pə tas′ē əm), *n.* a soft, silver-white metallic element that occurs in nature only in compounds, is essential for the growth of plants, and oxidizes rapidly when exposed to the air. Potassium is one of the most abundant elements in the earth's crust. *Symbol:* K; *atomic number* 19. See pages 326 and 327 for table. [< New Latin < English *potash*]

po tas si um-ar gon dating (pə tas′ē əm är′gon), method of dating organic, geological, or archaeological specimens by measuring in the rock in which a specimen is found the amount of argon accumulated through the decay of radioactive potassium.

potassium bromide, a white, crystalline substance with a pungent, salty taste, used in medicine as a sedative, in photography, etc. *Formula:* KBr

potassium carbonate, a white, alkaline salt obtained from wood ashes, etc.; potash. *Formula:* K_2CO_3

potassium chlorate, a colorless, poisonous, crystalline substance used as an oxidizing agent in explosives, matches, etc. *Formula:* $KClO_3$

potassium cyanide, a very poisonous, white, crystalline compound used for removing gold from ore, electroplating, killing insects, etc. *Formula:* KCN

potassium dichromate, a poisonous, yellowish-red, crystalline salt used in dyeing, in photography, as an oxidizing agent, etc. *Formula:* $K_2Cr_2O_7$

potassium hydroxide, a white, solid substance which releases great heat when it dissolves in water; caustic potash. It is used as a reagent, in bleaching, in making liquid soaps, and in medicine. *Formula:* KOH

potassium iodide, a white or colorless crystalline compound, used in manufacturing photographic emulsions, as an additive in iodized salt, and in medicine as an expectorant. *Formula:* KI

potassium nitrate, a white or colorless crystalline salt produced from sodium nitrate and another potassium compound; niter; saltpeter. It is used as an oxidizing agent, in gunpowder, explosives, fertilizers, medicine, and meat preservatives. *Formula:* KNO_3

potassium permanganate, a dark purple crystalline compound used as an oxidizing agent, disinfectant, etc. *Formula:* $KMnO_4$

po ta tion (pō tā′shən), *n.* 1 act of drinking. 2 a drink, especially of alcoholic liquor. [< Latin *potationem* < *potare* to drink]

po ta to (pə tā′tō, pə tā′tə), *n., pl.* **-toes.** 1 a widely cultivated annual plant of the nightshade family, with a starchy tuber used as a vegetable. 2 this tuber, which is round or oval, hard, and has a very thin skin; white potato; Irish potato. The potato is one of the most widely used vegetables in Europe and America. 3 sweet potato. [< Spanish *patata* < Carib *batata* sweet potato]

potato beetle or **potato bug,** beetle with black and yellow stripes that devours the leaves of potato plants.

potato chip, a thin slice of potato fried crisp in deep fat and salted.

pot bel lied (pot′bel′ēd), *adj.* having a potbelly.

potbellied stove, potbelly stove.

pot bel ly (pot′bel′ē), *n., pl.* **-lies.** 1 a bulging or protuberant belly. 2 person who has such a belly. 3 a potbelly stove.

potbelly stove, a squat, bulging stove that burns wood or coal. Also, **potbellied stove.**

pot boil er (pot′boi′lər), *n.* INFORMAL. an inferior work of literature or art produced merely to make a living.

pot boy (pot′boi′), *n.* man or boy who works in a tavern, serving customers, washing glasses, etc.

po ten cy (pōt′n sē), *n., pl.* **-cies.** a being potent; power; strength.

po tent (pōt′nt), *adj.* 1 having great power; powerful; strong: *a potent ruler, potent reasons, a potent remedy for a disease.* 2 capable of having sexual intercourse. [< Latin *potentem* < *potis* having power, able] **—po′tent ly,** *adv.*

po ten tate (pōt′n tāt), *n.* 1 person having great power. 2 ruler; sovereign.

po ten tial (pə ten′shəl), *adj.* 1 possible as opposed to actual; capable of coming into being or action: *There is a potential danger of being bitten when one plays with a strange dog.* See **latent** for synonym study. 2 (in grammar) expressing possibility by the use of *may, might, can, could,* etc.: *the potential mood of a verb.* —*n.* 1 something potential; possibility. 2 (in grammar) the potential mood. 3 amount of electrification of a point with reference to some standard. A current of high potential is used in transmitting electric power over long distances. **—po ten′tial ly,** *adv.*

potential energy, energy which a body has because of its position or structure rather than as a result of its motion. A coiled spring or a raised weight has potential energy.

po ten ti al i ty (pə ten′shē al′ə tē), *n., pl.* **-ties.** 1 potential condition or quality; possible power. 2 something potential; possibility.

po ten ti ate (pə ten′shē āt), *v.t.,* **-at ed, -at ing.** give potency to; make more active; strengthen: *Certain narcotic drugs potentiate the effects of alcohol in the body.* **—po ten′ti a′tion,** *n.*

po ten ti om e ter (pə ten′shē om′ə tər), *n.* instrument for measuring electromotive force.

pot ful (pot′fůl), *n., pl.* **-fuls.** as much as a pot can hold.

poth er (poᴛʜ′ər), *n.* 1 confusion; disturbance; fuss. 2 a choking cloud of dust or smoke. 3 mental disturbance. —*v.t.* bother; worry. —*v.i.* fuss. [origin uncertain]

pot herb (pot′ėrb′, pot′hėrb′), *n.* 1 any plant whose leaves and stems are boiled for use as a vegetable, such as spinach. 2 plant used as seasoning in cooking, such as sage and parsley.

pot hold er (pot′hōl′dər), *n.* a thick pad of cloth or other material for handling hot pots, lids, etc.

pot hole (pot′hōl′), *n.* 1 a deep, round hole, especially one made in the rocky bed of a river by stones and gravel being spun around in the current. 2 depression or hollow part forming a defect in the surface of a street or road.

pot hook (pot′hůk′), *n.* 1 hook for hanging a pot or kettle over an open fire. 2 rod with a hook for lifting hot pots, etc. 3 an S-shaped stroke in writing, especially one made by children in learning to write.

pot hunt er (pot′hun′tər), *n.* person who hunts game for food or for profit, without regard for the rules of sport.

po tion (pō′shən), *n.* a drink, especially one that is used as a medicine or poison, or in magic. [< Latin *potionem.* Doublet of POISON.]

pot latch (pot′lach′), *n.* 1 a ceremonial festival among certain American Indians of the northern Pacific coast at which they gave away or destroyed valuable objects to display their wealth. 2 U.S. INFORMAL. feast at which presents are given and received. [< Chinook *patshatl* giving, gift]

pot luck (pot′luk′), *n.* whatever food happens to be ready or on hand for a meal.

pot marigold, a calendula whose flower heads are sometimes used for seasoning.

Po to mac River (pə tō′mək), river flowing from E West Virginia between Maryland and Virginia, into Chesapeake Bay. 450 mi.

pot pie (pot′pī′), *n.* 1 a baked meat pie. 2 stew, as of chicken or veal, with dumplings.

pot pour ri (pō′pů rē′, pot pür′ē), *n.* 1 medley or mixture: *a potpourri of Italian, French, and Austrian folk songs.* 2 a fragrant mixture of dried flower petals and spices. [earlier, a mixed stew < French *pot pourri* rotten pot]

pot roast, beef browned in a pot and cooked slowly with only a little water.

Pots dam (pots′dam), *n.* city in central East Germany. 111,000.

pot sherd (pot′shėrd′), *n.* a broken piece of earthenware.

pot shot (pot′shot′), *n.* 1 shot fired at game to get food, with little regard to the rules of sport. 2 a quick shot at something from close range without careful aim. 3 Often, **potshots,** *pl.* criticism, usually made in a careless manner: *counter medical potshots at tobacco products.* 4 **take potshots at, a** shoot at from close range without careful aim. **b** criticize, usually in a careless manner: *take potshots at the company executives.*

pot tage (pot′ij), *n.* a thick soup of vegetables or vegetables and meat. [< Old French *potage* < *pot* pot]

pot ted (pot′id), *adj.* SLANG. 1 shortened; condensed: *potted biography.* 2 recorded; canned: *potted music.*

pot ter¹ (pot′ər), *n.* person who makes pottery. [Old English *pottere* < *pott* pot]

pot ter² (pot′ər), *v.i., v.t.* putter. [apparently < earlier *pote* to poke, Old English *potian* to push] **—pot′ter er,** *n.*

potter's field, a public cemetery used for burying paupers, unidentified persons, and criminals.

potter's wheel operated by means of a treadle. The momentum of the heavy wheel at the bottom helps keep the upper wheel in motion. Some kinds are operated by electricity.

potter's wheel, a rotating horizontal disk upon which clay is molded into dishes, etc.

pot ter y (pot′ər ē), *n., pl.* **-ter ies.** 1 pots, dishes, vases, etc., made from clay hardened by heat. Porcelain and earthenware are two kinds of pottery. 2 art or business of making them. 3 place where they are made.

pot ty¹ (pot′ē), *adj.,* **-ti er, -ti est.** BRITISH INFORMAL. foolish; crazy. [origin uncertain]

pot ty² (pot′ē), *n., pl.* **-ties.** INFORMAL. a small chamber pot.

pouch (pouch), *n.* 1 bag, sack, etc., of a relatively small size: *a pouch of tobacco.*

2 bag for carrying mail or documents: *a diplomat's pouch.* 3 a natural receptacle resembling a bag or pocket, as the **cheek pouch** of certain rodents or the marsupium in which the kangaroo and other marsupial mammals carry their young. —*v.t.* put into a pouch. —*v.i.* form a pouch. [< Old French *pouche, poche;* of Germanic origin] —**pouch′like′,** *adj.*

pouched (poucht), *adj.* having a pouch.

pouch y (pou′chē), *adj.,* **pouch i er, pouch i est.** having pouches; like a pouch; baggy.

Pou lenc (pü läNk′), *n.* **Francis,** 1899-1963, French composer.

poul ter er (pōl′tər ər), *n.* dealer in poultry.

poul tice (pōl′tis), *n., v.,* **-ticed, -tic ing.** —*n.* a soft, moist mass of mustard, herbs, etc., applied to the body as a medicine. —*v.t.* put a poultice on. [< Latin *pultes,* plural of *puls* mush]

poul try (pōl′trē), *n.* birds such as chickens, turkeys, geese, ducks, etc., raised for their meat or eggs. [< Old French *pouleterie* < *poulet,* diminutive of *poule* hen < Latin *pullus* young fowl]

pounce[1] (pouns), *v.,* **pounced, pounc ing,** *n.* —*v.i.* 1 come down with a rush and seize something: *The cat pounced upon the mouse.* 2 dash, come, or jump suddenly. —*n.* a sudden swoop or pouncing. [Middle English, talon, claw]

pounce[2] (pouns), *n., v.,* **pounced, pounc ing.** —*n.* 1 a fine powder formerly used to prevent ink from spreading in writing, or to prepare parchment for writing. 2 a fine powder used for transferring a design through a stencil. —*v.t.* sprinkle, smooth, or prepare with pounce. [< French *ponce* < Latin *pumicem* pumice. Doublet of PUMICE.]

pound[1] (pound), *n., pl.* **pounds** or **pound.** 1 unit of weight equal to 16 ounces in avoirdupois and 12 ounces in troy weight. See **measure** for table. 2 pound sterling. 3 the monetary unit of certain countries in the Commonwealth of Nations. 4 the monetary unit of certain Middle Eastern countries, such as Egypt, Israel, Lebanon, and Syria. [Old English *pund* < Latin *pondo* by weight]

pound[2] (pound), *v.t.* 1 hit hard again and again; hit heavily: *He pounded the door with his fist.* See **beat** for synonym study. 2 make into a powder or pulp by pounding. 3 produce (sound) by pounding or as if by pounding: *pound out a tune on a piano.* —*v.i.* 1 beat hard; throb: *After running fast you can feel your heart pound.* 2 move with a pounding sound: *She pounded down the hill to catch the bus.* 3 produce sound by pounding or as if by pounding: *We could hear drums pounding in the distance.* —*n.* 1 act of pounding. 2 a heavy or forcible blow or its sound. [Old English *pūnian*]

pound[3] (pound), *n.* 1 an enclosed place in which to keep stray animals: *a dog pound.* 2 enclosure for keeping, confining, or trapping animals. 3 area of water enclosed by nets for catching fish, lobster, etc. [Old English *pund-*]

Pound (pound), *n.* **Ezra (Loomis),** 1885-1972, American poet.

pound al (poun′dl), *n.* unit of force equal to the force necessary to give a mass of one pound an acceleration of one foot per second per second.

pound cake, a rich, sweet cake, originally made with one pound each of flour, sugar, and butter, and many eggs.

pound er[1] (poun′dər), *n.* person or thing that pounds, pulverizes, or beats.

pound er[2] (poun′dər), *n.* 1 person or thing weighing a specified number of pounds. 2 gun firing a shell that weighs a specified number of pounds. 3 a bank note, etc., worth a specified number of pounds sterling.

pound-fool ish (pound′fü′lish), *adj.* foolish or careless in regard to large sums of money.

pound sterling, the monetary unit of Great Britain. Since February 1971, 1 pound = 100 pence. Formerly, 1 pound = 240 pence. The gold in one pound sterling is worth about $2.50.

powder horn

pour (pôr, pōr), *v.t.* 1 cause to flow in a steady stream: *I poured the milk from the bottle.* 2 make known freely or without reserve: *The melancholy poet poured forth his sorrow in a song.* —*v.i.* 1 flow in a steady stream: *The crowd poured out of the church.* 2 rain heavily. —*n.* 1 a pouring. 2 a heavy rain; downpour. [Middle English *pouren*] —**pour′er,** *n.*

pour boire (pür bwär′), *n.* FRENCH. 1 tip; gratuity. 2 (literally) for drinking.

pout[1] (pout), *v.i.* 1 thrust or push out the lips, as a displeased or sulky child does. 2 show displeasure. 3 swell out; protrude. —*v.t.* push out or protrude, especially the lips. —*n.* 1 a pushing out of the lips when one is displeased or sulky. 2 a fit of sullenness. [Middle English *pouten*]

pout[2] (pout), *n.* 1 any of various freshwater catfishes. 2 eelpout. [Old English *-pūte*]

pout er (pou′tər), *n.* 1 person who pouts. 2 one of a breed of domestic pigeons that puff out their crops.

pout y (pou′tē), *adj.,* **pout i er, pout i est.** INFORMAL. inclined to pout; sulky.

pov er ty (pov′ər tē), *n.* 1 condition of being poor. See synonym study below. 2 lack of what is needed; poor quality: *The poverty of the soil makes the crops small.* 3 a small amount; fewness: *A dull person's talk shows poverty of ideas.* [< Old French *pouerte* < Latin *paupertatem* < *pauper* poor]

Syn. 1 **Poverty, want, destitution** mean the condition of being poor. **Poverty** emphasizes, more strongly than *poorness* does, the condition of having little or no money or property: *Their tattered clothing and broken furniture indicated their poverty.* **Want** emphasizes great need or lack of enough to live on: *Welfare agencies help those in want.* **Destitution** emphasizes complete lack even of food and shelter, and often suggests having been deprived of possessions once had: *The Red Cross relieved the destitution following the floods.*

pov er ty-strick en (pov′ər tē strik′ən), *adj.* extremely poor; destitute.

POW, prisoner of war.

pow der (pou′dər), *n.* 1 a solid reduced to dust by pounding, crushing, or grinding. 2 some special kind of powder: *face powder, talcum powder, powders taken as medicine.* 3 gunpowder or any similar explosive. —*v.t.* 1 make into powder. 2 sprinkle or cover with powder. 3 sprinkle. 4 apply powder to (the face, etc.): *powder one's nose.* —*v.i.* become powder. [< Old French *poudre* < Latin *pulvis* dust] —**pow′der er,** *n.*

hat, āge, fär; let, ēqual, tėrm;
it, īce; hot, ōpen, ôrder;
oil, out; cup, pu̇t, rüle;
ch, child; ng, long; sh, she;
th, thin; ᴛʜ, then; zh, measure;

ə represents *a* in about, *e* in taken, *i* in pencil, *o* in lemon, *u* in circus.

< = from, derived from, taken from.

powder blue, a light blue.

powder flask, flask or case of horn, metal, or leather for carrying gunpowder.

powder horn, powder flask made of an animal's horn.

powder keg, 1 a small barrel for storing gunpowder. 2 something that threatens to explode suddenly or without warning.

powder puff, a soft puff or pad for applying powder to the skin.

powder room, lavatory for women, especially one with a dressing table.

pow der y (pou′dər ē), *adj.* 1 of powder. 2 like powder; in the form of powder; dusty. 3 easily made into powder. 4 sprinkled or covered with powder.

pow er (pou′ər), *n.* 1 strength or force; might: *great physical power.* 2 ability to do or act: *I will give you all the help in my power.* See synonym study below. 3 a particular ability: *He has great powers of concentration.* 4 control; authority; influence; right: *Congress has the power to declare war.* 5 person, thing, body, or nation having authority or influence: *Five powers held a peace conference.* 6 energy or force that can do work: *Running water produces power to run mills.* 7 the product of a number multiplied by itself a certain number of times: *16 is the 4th power of 2 (2 × 2 × 2 × 2 = 16).* 8 the capacity of an instrument to magnify. An object seen through a microscope with a power of ten looks ten times its actual size. 9 a simple machine. 10 the rate at which work is done, expressed in foot-pounds per minute, ergs per second, horsepower, watts, etc. 11 **in power,** having control or authority. 12 **the powers that be,** those who have control or authority.
—*v.t.* supply (something) with power.
—*adj.* operated by a motor; equipped with its own motor: *a power drill.*
[< Old French *poeir,* noun use of verb *poeir* be able < Popular Latin *potere* < Latin *potis* able]

Syn. *n.* 2 **Power, strength, force** mean ability to do something or capacity for something. **Power** is the general word applying to any physical, mental, or moral ability or capacity, whether used or not: *Every normal, healthy person has power to think.* **Strength** means a natural or innate power within the person or thing to do, bear, or resist much: *She had the strength of character to endure the death of her only child.* **Force** means active use of power or strength to get something done or overcome opposition: *The force of his argument convinced me.*

pow er boat (pou′ər bōt′), *n.* boat propelled by an engine on board; motorboat.

power brake, brake in a motor vehicle that uses the vacuum produced by the engine to force hydraulic fluid or compressed air to the brake shoes of the wheel, requiring very little pressure on the brake pedal to stop the vehicle.

power dive, dive made by an airplane at or nearly at peak power, especially as a maneuver in bombing or aerial fighting.

pow er ful (pou′ər fəl), *adj.* having great power or force; mighty; strong: *a powerful man, a powerful argument.* See **mighty** for synonym study. **—pow′er ful ly,** *adv.*

pow er house (pou′ər hous′), *n., pl.* **-hous es** (-hou′ziz). 1 a building containing boilers, engines, etc., for generating electric power. 2 INFORMAL. a powerful, energetic, or highly effective person or group.

pow er less (pou′ər lis), *adj.* without power; lacking ability to produce an effect; helpless. **—pow′er less ly,** *adv.* **—pow′er less ness,** *n.*

power loom, loom worked by steam, electricity, water power, etc., not by hand.

power of attorney, a written statement giving one person legal power to act for another.

power pack, assemblage of electrical units used to change the voltage of a power line or battery to the voltage needed for various electronic circuits.

power plant, 1 building with machinery for generating power. 2 motor; engine.

power politics, diplomacy in international affairs which uses the threat of superior military power.

power saw, saw worked by a motor, not by hand.

power shovel, machine for digging operated by an engine, especially a diesel or gasoline engine.

power steering, a steering mechanism in a motor vehicle that uses a mechanical, hydraulic, or pneumatic device to enable the wheels to be turned with very little effort.

Pow ha tan (pou′ə tan′), *n.* 1550?-1618, Indian chief in Virginia.

pow wow (pou′wou′), *n.* 1 an American Indian ceremony, usually accompanied by magic, feasting, and dancing, performed for the cure of disease, success in hunting, victory in war, etc. 2 council or conference of or with American Indians. 3 INFORMAL. any conference or meeting. 4 an American Indian priest or medicine man. *—v.i.* hold a powwow; confer. [of Algonquian origin]

pox (poks), *n.* 1 any disease characterized by eruption of pustules on the skin, such as chicken pox or smallpox. 2 syphilis. [variant of *pocks,* plural of *pock*]

Poz nań (pôz′nä′nyə, pōz′nan), *n.* city in W Poland. 462,000.

pp, pianissimo.

pp., 1 pages. 2 past participle.

p.p., 1 parcel post. 2 past participle. 3 postpaid.

P.P., Parcel Post.

ppd., 1 postpaid. 2 prepaid.

ppr. or **p.pr.,** present participle.

P.P.S. or **p.p.s.,** a second postscript [for Latin *post postscriptum*].

Pr, praseodymium.

pr., 1 pair. 2 price.

PR, 1 proportional representation. 2 public relations.

P.R., Puerto Rico.

prac ti ca bil i ty (prak′tə kə bil′ə tē), *n.* quality of being practicable.

prac ti ca ble (prak′tə kə bəl), *adj.* 1 that can be done; capable of being put into practice; feasible: *a practicable idea.* See **possible** for synonym study. 2 that can be used: *a practicable road.* **—prac′ti ca bly,** *adv.*

prac ti cal (prak′tə kəl), *adj.* 1 having to do with action or practice rather than thought or theory: *Earning a living is a practical matter.* 2 fit for actual practice: *a practical plan.* 3 useful. 4 having good sense: *A practical person does not spend money foolishly.* See **sensible** for synonym study. 5 inclined toward or fitted for action rather than thought or imagination: *a practical mind.* 6 engaged in actual practice or work: *Today's practical farmer has more use for tractors than horses.* 7 being such in effect; virtual: *So many of our soldiers were captured that our victory was a practical defeat.* **—prac′ti cal ness,** *n.*

prac ti cal i ty (prak′tə kal′ə tē), *n., pl.* **-ties.** 1 quality of being practical; practical usefulness; practical habit of mind. 2 a practical matter.

practical joke, trick played on a person to have a laugh at him. **—practical joker.**

prac ti cal ly (prak′tik lē), *adv.* 1 so far as the results will be; in effect; really. 2 INFORMAL. almost; nearly: *We are practically home.* 3 in a practical way; in a useful way. 4 by actual practice: *I learned the game practically rather than by watching others.*

practical nurse, person whose occupation is to care for the sick, but who lacks the hospital training or diploma of a registered nurse.

prac tice (prak′tis), *n., v.,* **-ticed, -tic ing.** *—n.* 1 action done many times over for the purpose, or with the result, of acquiring skill or proficiency: *Practice makes perfect.* See **exercise** for synonym study. 2 skill gained by experience or exercise: *He was out of practice at batting.* 3 action or process of doing or being something: *Your plan is good in theory, but not in actual practice.* 4 the usual way; custom: *It is the practice to blow a whistle at the factory at noon.* See **custom** for synonym study. 5 the working at or following of a profession or occupation: *engaged in the practice of law.* 6 business of a lawyer or doctor: *The old doctor sold his practice.* 7 (in law) the established method of conducting legal proceedings.
—v.t. 1 do (some act) again and again for the purpose, or with the result, of acquiring skill or proficiency: *practice playing the piano.* 2 follow, observe, or use day after day; make a custom of; do usually: *practice moderation. Practice what you preach.* 3 work at or follow as a profession, art, or occupation: *practice medicine.* 4 give training to; drill; train. *—v.i.* 1 do something again and again for the purpose, or with the result of, acquiring skill or proficiency: *practice on the piano.* 2 do something as a habit or practice: *practice as well as preach.* 3 practice a profession: *That young lawyer is just starting to practice.*
[< Old French *practiser* to practice < Late Latin *practicus* practical < Greek *praktikos* < *praessein* do, act] **—prac′tic er,** *n.*

prairie dog
about 15 in. long
with the tail

prac ticed (prak′tist), *adj.* 1 experienced; skilled; expert. 2 acquired through practice.

prac tise (prak′tis), *n., v.t., v.i.,* **-tised, -tis ing.** practice.

prac tised (prak′tist), *adj.* practiced.

prac ti tion er (prak tish′ə nər), *n.* person engaged in the practice of a profession: *a medical practitioner.*

prae no men (prē nō′mən), *n., pl.* **-no mens** or **-nom i na** (-nom′ə nə, -nō′mə-nə). the first or personal name of a Roman citizen. [< Latin < *prae-* pre- + *nomen* name]

prae tor (prē′tər, prē′tôr), *n.* (in ancient Rome) a magistrate or judge ranking next below a consul. [< Latin]

prae to ri an (prē tôr′ē ən, prē tōr′ē ən), *adj.* 1 of or having to do with a praetor. 2 Often, **Praetorian.** having to do with the bodyguard of a Roman commander or emperor. *—n.* Often, **Praetorian.** soldier of the bodyguard of a Roman commander or emperor.

prag mat ic (prag mat′ik), *adj.* 1 concerned with practical results or values; viewing things in a matter-of-fact way. 2 of or having to do with pragmatism: *a pragmatic philosophy.* [< Latin *pragmaticus* < Greek *pragmatikos* efficient, ultimately < *prassein* do] **—prag mat′i cal ly,** *adv.*

prag mat i cal (prag mat′ə kəl), *adj.* pragmatic.

pragmatic sanction, any of various imperial decrees issued as fundamental law by former European emperors or monarchs.

prag ma tism (prag′mə tiz′əm), *n.* 1 philosophy based on the belief that the truth, meaning, or value of ideas must be judged by their practical consequences. Pragmatism originated in America in the 1800's. 2 pragmatic quality or condition; concern with practical results or values.

prag ma tist (prag′mə tist), *n.* person who believes in pragmatism.

Prague (präg), *n.* capital and largest city of Czechoslovakia, in the W part. 1,034,000.

Pra ha (prä′hä), *n.* Czech name of **Prague.**

Pra ia (prä′yə), *n.* capital of Cape Verde Islands. 13,000.

prair ie (prer′ē), *n.* a large area of level or rolling land with grass but no trees or very few trees, especially such an area comprising much of central North America. [< French, ultimately < Latin *pratum* meadow]

prairie chicken
about 16 in. long

prairie chicken, either of two brown, black, and white grouse that live on the prairies of North America.

prairie dog, any of a genus of grayish-brown burrowing rodents like woodchucks but smaller, found on the Great Plains and in the Rocky Mountain region. Prairie dogs sometimes live in large colonies and have a shrill bark like that of a dog.

Prairie Provinces, provinces along the prairies of W Canada; Manitoba, Saskatchewan, and Alberta.

Prair ies (prer′ēz), *n.pl.* Prairie Provinces.

hat, āge, fär; let, ēqual, tėrm;
it, īce; hot, ōpen, ôrder;
oil, out; cup, pu̇t, rüle;
ch, child; ng, long; sh, she;
th, thin; ᴛʜ, then; zh, measure;

ə represents *a* in about, *e* in taken, *i* in pencil, *o* in lemon, *u* in circus.

< = from, derived from, taken from.

prairie schooner

prairie schooner, a large covered wagon used by emigrants in crossing the plains of North America before the railroads were built.

prairie wolf, coyote.

praise (prāz), *n., v.,* **praised, prais ing.** —*n.* 1 a saying that a thing or person is good; words that tell the worth or value of a thing or person; commendation. 2 words or song worshiping God. 3 **sing the praises of,** praise with enthusiasm. —*v.t.* 1 express approval or admiration of. See synonym study below. 2 worship in words or song: *praise God.* —*v.i.* give praise. [< Old French *preisier* to praise, value, prize < Late Latin *pretiare* to prize < Latin *pretium* price] —**prais′er,** *n.*

Syn. *v.t.* 1 **Praise, approve, commend** mean to think or speak well of. **Praise** means to express heartily a high opinion or admiration of someone or something: *The coach praised the team for its fine play.* **Approve** means to have or express a favorable opinion of: *Everyone approved her idea.* **Commend** suggests a formal expression of favorable opinion: *The mayor commended the boys for their quick thinking at the disaster.*

praise wor thy (prāz′wėr′ᴛʜē), *adj.* worthy of praise; deserving approval. —**praise′wor′thi ly,** *adv.* —**praise′wor′thi ness,** *n.*

Pra krit (prä′krit), *n.* any of the Indo-European vernacular languages or dialects of northern and central India, especially those of the ancient and medieval periods. [< Sanskrit *prākṛta* natural, common, vulgar]

pra line (prä′lēn′, prā′lēn′), *n.* a small cake of brown candy made of brown or maple sugar and nuts, usually pecans or almonds. [< French < Marshal Duplessis-*Praslin,* 1598-1675, whose cook invented it]

pram (pram), *n.* BRITISH INFORMAL. baby carriage; perambulator.

prance (prans), *v.,* **pranced, pranc ing,** *n.* —*v.i.* 1 spring about on the hind legs: *Horses prance when they feel lively.* 2 ride on a horse doing this. 3 move gaily or proudly; swagger. 4 caper; dance. —*n.* a prancing. [Middle English *prancen, prauncen*] —**pranc′er,** *n.* —**pranc′ing ly,** *adv.*

prank (prangk), *n.* piece of mischief; playful trick: *On April Fools' Day people often play pranks on each other.* —*v.t.* dress in a showy way; adorn. [origin uncertain]

prank ish (prang′kish), *adj.* 1 full of pranks; fond of pranks. 2 like a prank. —**prank′ish ly,** *adv.* —**prank′ish ness,** *n.*

prank ster (prangk′stər), *n.* person who plays pranks.

pra se o dym i um (prā′zē ō dim′ē əm), *n.* a yellowish-white rare-earth metallic element which occurs with neodymium. Its green salts are used to tint ceramics. *Symbol:* Pr; *atomic number* 59. See pages 326 and 327 for table. [< New Latin < Greek *prasios* bluish-green + New Latin *(di)dymium* didymium]

prat (prat), *n.* buttocks. [origin unknown]

prate (prāt), *v.,* **prat ed, prat ing,** *n.* —*v.i.* talk a great deal in a foolish way. —*v.t.* say in an empty or foolish way. —*n.* a prating; empty or foolish talk. [< Middle Dutch *praeten*] —**prat′er,** *n.* —**prat′ing ly,** *adv.*

prat fall (prat′fôl′), *n.* SLANG. a fall on the buttocks.

prat tle (prat′l), *v.,* **-tled, -tling,** *n.* —*v.i.* 1 talk as a child does; tell freely and carelessly. 2 talk or tell in a foolish way. 3 sound like baby talk; babble. —*v.t.* say in a foolish or childish way. —*n.* 1 childish or foolish talk. 2 sounds like baby talk; babble. [< *prate*] —**prat′tler,** *n.*

prau (prou), *n.* proa.

prawn (prôn), *n.* any of various edible shellfish related to and resembling the shrimp but larger. [Middle English *prane*]

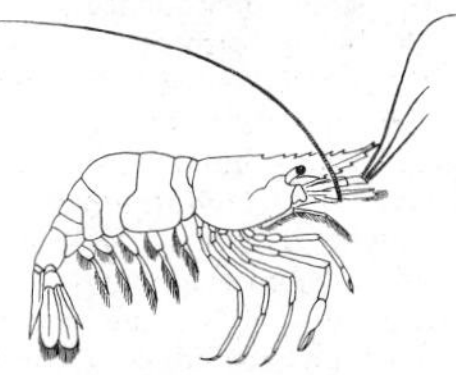
prawn—3 to 4 in. long

Prax it e les (prak sit′l ēz′), *n.* Greek sculptor who lived about 350 B.C.

pray (prā), *v.i.* 1 speak to God in worship; enter into spiritual communion with God; offer worship. 2 make earnest request to God or to any other object of worship: *pray for help, pray for one's family.* —*v.t.* 1 ask earnestly; implore; beseech: *pray God for help.* 2 ask earnestly for: *pray one's forgiveness.* 3 bring or get by praying. 4 please: *Pray come with me.* [< Old French *preier* < Latin *precari* < *precem* prayer] —**pray′er,** *n.*

prayer (prer, prar), *n.* 1 act of praying. 2 thing prayed for: *Our prayers were granted.* 3 form of words to be used in praying. 4 form of worship; religious service consisting mainly of prayers. 5 an earnest or humble request. [< Old French *preiere,* ultimately < Latin *precem* prayer]

prayer book, 1 book of prayers. 2 **Prayer Book,** Book of Common Prayer.

prayer ful (prer′fəl, prar′fəl), *adj.* having the habit of praying often; devout. —**prayer′ful ly,** *adv.* —**prayer′ful ness,** *n.*

prayer meeting, meeting for prayer and religious exercises, usually one at which several participants offer prayer.

praying mantis, mantis.

pre-, *prefix.* 1 before in time, rank, etc.: *Precambrian = before the Cambrian.* 2 before in position, space, etc.; in front of: *Premolar = in front of the molars.* [< Latin *prae-, pre-*]

preach (prēch), *v.i.* 1 speak publicly on a religious subject. 2 give earnest advice, especially in a meddling or tiresome way: *She is forever preaching about good table manners.* —*v.t.* 1 deliver (a sermon). 2 make known by preaching; proclaim: *preach the gospel.* 3 recommend strongly; urge: *The coach was always preaching exercise and fresh air.* [< Old French *prechier* < Latin *praedicare* declare, preach < *prae-* pre- + *dicare* make known. Doublet of PREDICATE.]

preach er (prē′chər), *n.* person who preaches; clergyman; minister; pastor.

preach i fy (prē′chə fī), *v.i.,* **-fied, -fy ing.** preach or moralize too much, or in a tedious or pompous way.

preach ing (prē′ching), *n.* what is preached; sermon.

preach ment (prēch′mənt), *n.* 1 a preaching. 2 a long, tiresome sermon or speech.

preach y (prē′chē), *adj.,* **preach i er, preach i est.** INFORMAL. 1 inclined to preach; didactic. 2 suggestive of preaching. —**preach′i ness,** *n.*

pre am ble (prē′am′bəl), *n.* 1 a preliminary statement; introduction to a speech or a writing. The reasons for a law and its general purpose are often stated in a preamble. 2 a preliminary or introductory fact or circumstance, especially one showing what is to follow. [< Medieval Latin *praeambulum* < Late Latin, walking before < Latin *prae-* pre- + *ambulare* to walk]

pre ar range (prē′ə rānj′), *v.t.,* **-ranged, -rang ing.** arrange beforehand. —**pre′ar range′ment,** *n.*

pre au dit (prē ô′dit), *n.* audit conducted before a transaction has been completed.

preb end (preb′ənd), *n.* 1 salary given to a clergyman connected with a cathedral or a collegiate church. 2 the particular property or church tax from which the money comes for this salary. 3 prebendary. [< Late Latin *praebenda*]

preb en dar y (preb′ən der′ē), *n., pl.* **-dar ies.** clergyman who has a prebend.

prec., preceding.

Pre cam bri an (prē′kam′brē ən), *n.* 1 the earliest geological era, including all the time before the Cambrian period; the Archeozoic and Proterozoic eras together. See chart under **geology.** 2 rocks formed in this era. —*adj.* of or having to do with this era or its rocks.

pre can cel (prē kan′səl), *v.t.,* **-celed, -cel ing** or **-celled, -cel ling.** put a mark of cancellation on (a postage stamp) before sale for use on bulk mail or parcel post.

pre car i ous (pri ker′ē əs, pri kar′ē əs), *adj.* 1 not safe or secure; uncertain; dangerous; risky: *Soldiers on the battlefield lead a precarious life.* 2 dependent on chance or circumstance. 3 poorly founded; doubtful. [< Latin *precarius* obtainable by prayer, uncertain < *precem* prayer] —**pre car′i ous ly,** *adv.* —**pre car′i ous ness,** *n.*

pre cau tion (pri kô′shən), *n.* 1 care taken beforehand; thing done beforehand to ward off evil or secure good results: *Locking doors is a precaution against thieves.* 2 a taking care beforehand; prudent foresight.

pre cau tion ar y (pri kô′shə ner′ē), *adj.* of or using precaution.

pre cede (prē sēd′), *v.,* **-ced ed, -ced ing.** —*v.t.* 1 go or come before in order, place, or time: *A precedes B in the alphabet. She preceded me into the room.* 2 be higher than in rank or importance: *A knight precedes a pawn in the game of chess.* 3 introduce by something preliminary; preface. —*v.i.* go or come before. [< Latin *praecedere* < *prae-* pre- + *cedere* go]

prec e dence (pres′ə dəns, pri sēd′ns), *n.* 1 act or fact of preceding. 2 higher position or rank; greater importance: *This work takes precedence over all other work.* 3 right to precede others in ceremonies or social affairs; social superiority: *A Senator takes precedence over a Representative.*

prec e den cy (pres′ə dən sē, pri sēd′n sē), *n., pl.* **-cies.** precedence.

prec e dent (*n.* pres′ə dənt; *adj.* pri sēd′nt, pres′ə dənt), *n.* 1 action that may serve as an example or reason for a later action. 2 (in law) a judicial decision, case, etc., that serves as a pattern in future situations that are similar or analogous. —*adj.* preceding.

pre ced ing (prē sē′ding), *adj.* going or coming before; previous. See **previous** for synonym study.

pre cen tor (pri sen′tər), *n.* person who leads and directs the singing of a church choir or congregation. [< Late Latin *praecentor,* ultimately < Latin *prae-* pre- + *canere* sing]

pre cept (prē′sept), *n.* rule of action or behavior; maxim: *"If at first you don't succeed, try, try again" is a familiar precept.* [< Latin *praeceptum* < *praecipere* instruct, anticipate < *prae-* pre- + *capere* to take]

pre cep tor (pri sep′tər, prē′sep tər), *n.* instructor; teacher; tutor.

pre cep to ri al (prē′sep tôr′ē əl, prē′sep-tōr′ē əl), *adj.* 1 of or like that of a preceptor. 2 using preceptors.

pre cep tress (pri sep′tris), *n.* a woman preceptor.

pre ces sion (prē sesh′ən), *n.* 1 act or fact of going first; precedence. 2 rotation of a spinning rigid body that has been tipped from its vertical axis by an external force acting on it. This phenomenon is illustrated by the wobble of a top and the gyration of the earth's axis. [< Late Latin *praecessionem* < Latin *praecedere* precede]

pre cinct (prē′singkt), *n.* 1 district within certain boundaries, for government, administrative, or other purposes: *an election precinct, a police precinct.* 2 Often, **precincts,** *pl.* **a** space within a boundary: *Do not leave the school precincts during school hours.* **b** the region immediately surrounding a place; environs: *a factory and its precincts.* 3 boundary; limit. [< Medieval Latin *praecinctum* < Latin *praecingere* enclose < *prae-* pre- + *cingere* gird]

pre ci os i ty (presh′ē os′ə tē), *n., pl.* **-ties.** too much refinement; affectation, especially in the use of language.

pre cious (presh′əs), *adj.* 1 worth much; valuable. Gold, platinum, and silver are often called the precious metals. Diamonds, rubies, and sapphires are precious stones. See **valuable** for synonym study. 2 much loved; dear: *a precious child.* 3 too nice; overrefined: *precious language.* 4 INFORMAL. very great: *What a precious mess!* —*adv.* INFORMAL. very: *precious little money.* [< Old French *precios* < Latin *pretiosus* < *pretium* price] **—pre′cious ly,** *adv.* **—pre′cious ness,** *n.*

prec i pice (pres′ə pis), *n.* 1 a very steep or almost vertical face of a rock, etc.; cliff, crag, or steep mountainside. 2 situation of great peril; critical position. [< Latin *praecipitium* < *praecipitem* steep, literally, headlong < *prae-* pre- + *caput* head]

pre cip i tance (pri sip′ə təns), *n.* headlong haste; rashness.

pre cip i tan cy (pri sip′ə tən sē), *n., pl.* **-cies.** precipitance.

pre cip i tant (pri sip′ə tənt), *adj.* falling or rushing headlong; acting in a hasty or rash manner; very sudden or abrupt. —*n.* substance that causes another substance to be separated out of a solution as a solid. **—pre-cip′i tant ly,** *adv.*

pre cip i tate (*v.* pri sip′ə tāt; *adj., n.* pri-sip′ə tit, pri sip′ə tāt), *v.,* **-tat ed, -tat ing,** *adj., n.* —*v.t.* 1 hasten the beginning of; bring about suddenly: *precipitate an argument.* 2 throw headlong; hurl: *precipitate a rock down a cliff, precipitate oneself into a struggle.* 3 separate (a substance) out from a solution as a solid. 4 condense (water vapor) from the air in the form of rain, dew, snow, etc. —*v.i.* 1 be deposited from solution as a solid. 2 be condensed as rain, dew, snow, etc. —*adj.* 1 very hurried; sudden: *A cool breeze caused a precipitate drop in the temperature.* 2 with great haste and force; plunging or rushing headlong; hasty; rash. —*n.* substance, usually crystalline, separated out from a solution as a solid. [< Latin *praecipitatum* thrown headlong < *praecipitem* headlong. See PRECIPICE.] **—pre cip′i tate ly,** *adv.* **—pre cip′i tate ness,** *n.* **—pre cip′i-ta′tor,** *n.*

pre cip i ta tion (pri sip′ə tā′shən), *n.* 1 act or state of precipitating; throwing down or falling headlong. 2 a hastening or hurrying. 3 a sudden bringing on: *the precipitation of war without warning.* 4 unwise or rash rapidity; sudden haste. 5 the separating out of a substance from a solution as a solid. 6 the depositing of moisture in the form of rain, dew, snow, etc. 7 something that is precipitated, such as rain, dew, or snow. 8 amount that is precipitated.

pre cip i tous (pri sip′ə təs), *adj.* 1 like a precipice; very steep: *precipitous cliffs.* See **steep**[1] for synonym study. 2 hasty; rash. 3 rushing headlong; very rapid. **—pre cip′i-tous ly,** *adv.* **—pre cip′i tous ness,** *n.*

pré cis (prā′sē, prā sē′), *n., pl.* **-cis** (-sēz). a concise or abridged statement; abstract; summary. [< French]

pre cise (pri sīs′), *adj.* 1 very definite or correct; exact; accurate: *a precise instrument. We were given precise directions. The precise sum was 34 cents.* 2 very careful: *precise handwriting. She is precise in her manners.* 3 strict: *We had precise orders to report back by eleven o'clock.* [< Latin *praecisum* abridged < *prae-* pre- + *caedere* to cut] **—pre cise′ly,** *adv.* **—pre cise′ness,** *n.*

pre ci sion (pri sizh′ən), *n.* fact or condition of being precise; accuracy; exactness: *the precision of a machine, speak with precision.* —*adj.* having to do with or characterized by precision: *precision instruments.*

pre ci sion ist (pri sizh′ə nist), *n.* person who insists on or affects precision, especially in language.

pre clude (pri klüd′), *v.t.,* **-clud ed, -clud ing.** shut out; make impossible; prevent: *The heavy thunderstorm precluded our going to the beach.* [< Latin *praecludere* < *prae-* pre- + *claudere* to shut]

pre clu sion (pri klü′zhən), *n.* 1 a precluding. 2 a being precluded.

pre clu sive (pri klü′siv), *adj.* tending or serving to preclude. **—pre clu′sive ly,** *adv.*

pre co cious (pri kō′shəs), *adj.* 1 developed earlier than usual in knowledge, skill, etc.: *This very precocious child could read well at the age of four.* 2 developed too early; occurring before the natural time. [< Latin *praecocem* < *praecoquere* to mature or ripen early < *prae-* pre- + *coquere* ripen] **—pre co′cious ly,** *adv.* **—pre-co′cious ness,** *n.*

pre coc i ty (pri kos′ə tē), *n.* precocious development; early maturity.

pre-Co lum bi an (prē′kə lum′bē ən), *adj.* of or belonging to the period before the arrival of Columbus in America; representative of American culture during or before the 1400's.

pre con ceive (prē′kən sēv′), *v.t.,* **-ceived, -ceiv ing.** form an idea or opinion of beforehand: *The beauty of the scenery surpassed all our preconceived notions.*

pre con cep tion (prē′kən sep′shən), *n.* idea or opinion formed beforehand.

pre con cert (prē′kən sėrt′), *v.t.* arrange beforehand: *At a preconcerted signal we sang "Happy Birthday."*

pre con di tion (prē′kən dish′ən), *n.* prerequisite. —*v.t.* condition beforehand.

pre con scious (prē kon′shəs), *adj.* not in the conscious mind but readily recalled: *preconscious memories.* —*n.* the part of the mind between the conscious and the subconscious.

pre cur sor (pri kėr′sər, prē′kər sər), *n.* 1 forerunner: *A severe cold may be the precursor of pneumonia.* 2 predecessor. [< Latin *praecursor* < *praecurrere* run before < *prae-* pre- + *currere* run]

pre cur sor y (pri kėr′sər ē), *adj.* indicative of something to follow; introductory.

pred., predicate.

pre da cious or **pre da ceous** (pri-dā′shəs), *adj.* living by prey; predatory. **—pre da′cious ness, pre da′ceous-ness,** *n.*

pre date (prē dāt′), *v.t.,* **-dat ed, -dat ing.** antedate.

pre da tion (prē dā′shən), *n.* 1 act or habit of preying on another animal or animals; predatory behavior. 2 act of plundering or pillaging; depredation.

pred a tor (pred′ə tər), *n.* animal or person that is predatory.

pred a to ry (pred′ə tôr′ē, pred′ə tōr′ē), *adj.* 1 living by preying upon other animals. Hawks and owls are predatory birds. 2 of or inclined to plundering or robbery: *Predatory pirates infested the seas.* [< Latin *praedatorius* < *praedari* prey upon, plunder < *praeda* prey] **—pred′a to′ri ly,** *adv.* **—pred′a to′ri ness,** *n.*

pre de cease (prē′di sēs′), *v.t.,* **-ceased, -ceas ing.** die before (someone): *Her husband predeceased her.*

pred e ces sor (pred′ə ses′ər), *n.* 1 person holding a position or office before another: *John Adams was Jefferson's predecessor as President.* 2 thing that came before another. 3 ARCHAIC. ancestor; forefather. [< Late Latin *praedecessor* < Latin *prae-* pre- + *decedere* retire < *de-* from + *cedere* go]

pre des ti nate (prē des′tə nāt), *v.t.,* **-nat ed, -nat ing.** 1 decree or ordain beforehand. 2 foreordain by divine purpose.

pre des ti na tion (prē des tə nā′shən), *n.* 1 an ordaining beforehand; destiny; fate. 2 action of God in deciding beforehand what shall happen; doctrine that by God's decree certain souls will be saved and others lost.

pre des tine (prē des′tən), *v.t.,* **-tined, -tin ing.** determine or settle beforehand; foreordain.

hat, āge, fär; let, ēqual, tėrm;
it, īce; hot, ōpen, ôrder;
oil, out; cup, pu̇t, rüle;
ch, child; ng, long; sh, she;
th, thin; ᴛʜ, then; zh, measure;

ə represents *a* in about, *e* in taken, *i* in pencil, *o* in lemon, *u* in circus.

< = from, derived from, taken from.

pre de ter mine (prē′di tėr′mən), *v.t.*, **-mined, -min ing.** 1 determine or decide beforehand: *We met at the predetermined time.* 2 direct or impel beforehand (to something). **—pre′de ter′mi na′tion,** *n.*

pred i ca ble (pred′ə kə bəl), *adj.* that can be predicated or affirmed.

pre dic a ment (pri dik′ə mənt), *n.* an unpleasant, difficult, or dangerous situation. See synonym study below. [< Late Latin *praedicamentum* quality, category < Latin *praedicare* to predicate]

Syn. Predicament, plight, dilemma mean a bad situation. **Predicament** implies that it is perplexing or difficult to get out of it: *The people inside the burning house were in a dangerous predicament.* **Plight** implies that it is unfortunate or even hopeless: *We are distressed by the plight of the refugees caught in the midst of the war.* **Dilemma** implies that it involves a choice between two things, both disagreeable: *She is faced with the dilemma of telling a lie or betraying her friend.*

pred i cate (*n., adj.* pred′ə kit; *v.* pred′ə kāt), *n., adj., v.,* **-cat ed, -cat ing.** *—n.* 1 word or words expressing what is said about the subject. EXAMPLES: Men *work.* The men *dug wells.* The men *are carpenters.* 2 (in logic) that which is said of the subject in a proposition; the second term in a proposition. EXAMPLES: No feathered animals are *elephants.* All birds are *feathered animals.* No birds are *elephants.* In the three propositions of this syllogism, *elephants, feathered animals,* and *elephants* are predicates. *—adj.* (in grammar) belonging to the predicate. In "Horses are strong," *strong* is a **predicate adjective.** In "The men are carpenters," *carpenters* is a **predicate noun** or predicate nominative. *—v.t.* 1 found or base (a statement, action, etc.) on something. 2 declare, assert, or affirm to be real or true: *Most religions predicate life after death.* 3 connote; imply. 4 declare to be an attribute or quality (of some person or thing): *We predicate goodness and mercy of God.* 5 (in logic) state or assert (something) about the subject of a proposition. [< Latin *praedicatum* proclaimed, preached, predicated < *prae-* pre- + *dicare* make known. Doublet of PREACH.]

➤ **predicate.** The predicate of a clause or sentence is the verb with its modifiers, object, complement, etc. It may be a simple verb of complete meaning (The big bell *tolled*), a verb and its modifier (The sun *sank quickly*), a transitive verb and its object (He *landed the big fish*), a linking verb and a predicate adjective (The girl *was healthy*), or a linking verb and a predicate noun (The man *was a carpenter*).

predicate nominative, a noun or pronoun complement that follows a linking verb.

pred i ca tion (pred′ə kā′shən), *n.* 1 a predicating. 2 something predicated.

pred i ca tive (pred′ə kā′tiv, pred′ə kə tiv), *adj.* 1 predicating; expressing predication. 2 acting as a predicate. **—pred′i ca′tive ly,** *adv.*

pre dict (pri dikt′), *v.t.* announce or tell beforehand; foretell; forecast: *The weather bureau predicts rain for tomorrow.* [< Latin *praedictum* told beforehand < *prae-* pre- + *dicere* say]

pre dict a bil i ty (pri dik′tə bil′ə tē), *n.* quality of being predictable.

pre dict a ble (pri dik′tə bəl), *adj.* that can be predicted. **—pre dict′a bly,** *adv.*

pre dic tion (pri dik′shən), *n.* 1 act of predicting. 2 thing predicted; prophecy.

pre dic tive (pri dik′tiv), *adj.* foretelling; prophetic. **—pre dic′tive ly,** *adv.*

pre di gest (prē′də jest′, prē′dī jest′), *v.t.* treat (food) by an artificial process, similar to digestion, in order to make it more easily digestible. **—pre′di ges′tion,** *n.*

pre di lec tion (prē′də lek′shən, pred′ə lek′shən), *n.* a liking; preference. [< Medieval Latin *praedilectum* preferred < Latin *prae-* pre- + *diligere* choose]

pre dis pose (prē′dis pōz′), *v.t.,* **-posed, -pos ing.** give an inclination or tendency to; make liable or susceptible: *A cold predisposes a person to other diseases.*

pre dis po si tion (prē′dis′pə zish′ən), *n.* previous inclination or tendency; liability or susceptibility.

pre dom i nance (pri dom′ə nəns), *n.* a being predominant; prevalence.

pre dom i nan cy (pri dom′ə nən sē), *n.* predominance.

pre dom i nant (pri dom′ə nənt), *adj.* 1 having more power, authority, or influence than others; superior. See **dominant** for synonym study. 2 most noticeable; prevailing: *Green was the predominant color in the forest.* **—pre dom′i nant ly,** *adv.*

pre dom i nate (*v.* pri dom′ə nāt; *adj.* pri dom′ə nət), *v.,* **-nat ed, -nat ing,** *adj. —v.i.* be greater in power, strength, influence, or numbers: *Sunny days predominate over rainy days in desert regions. —v.t.* dominate. *—adj.* predominant. **—pre dom′i nate ly,** *adv.*

pre dom i na tion (pri dom′ə nā′shən), *n.* act of predominating; superior power or influence; prevalence.

pree mie (prē′mē), *n.* INFORMAL. a premature baby. Also, **premie.**

pre em i nence or **pre-em i nence** (prē em′ə nəns), *n.* a being outstanding or preeminent; superiority.

pre em i nent or **pre-em i nent** (prē em′ə nənt), *adj.* standing out above all others; superior to others. **—pre em′i nent ly, pre-em′i nent ly,** *adv.*

pre empt or **pre-empt** (prē empt′), *v.t.* 1 secure before someone else can; acquire or take possession of beforehand: *The cat had preempted the comfortable chair.* 2 settle on (land) with the right to buy it before others. **—pre emp′tor, pre-emp′tor,** *n.*

pre emp tion or **pre-emp tion** (prē emp′shən), *n.* act or right of purchasing before others or in preference to others. [< *pre-* + Latin *emptionem* a buying + *emere* to buy]

pre emp tive or **pre-emp tive** (prē emp′tiv), *adj.* having to do with preemption; having preemption.

preen (prēn), *v.t.* 1 smooth or arrange (the feathers) with the beak, as a bird does. 2 dress (oneself) carefully; primp. 3 pride or please (oneself). *—v.i.* 1 dress oneself carefully; primp. 2 pride or please oneself. [Middle English *preynen*]

pre ex ist or **pre-ex ist** (prē′ig zist′), *v.i.* exist beforehand, or before something else. *—v.t.* exist before (something).

pre ex ist ence or **pre-ex ist ence** (prē′ig zis′təns), *n.* previous existence, especially of the soul before its union with the body.

pre ex ist ent or **pre-ex ist ent** (prē′ig zis′tənt), *adj.* existing previously.

pref., 1 preface. 2 preferred. 3 prefix.

pre fab (prē′fab′), *n.* something prefabricated, especially a house.

pre fab ri cate (prē fab′rə kāt), *v.t.,* **-cat ed, -cat ing.** 1 make all standardized parts of (a house, etc.) at a factory. The erection of a prefabricated house requires merely the assembling of the various sections. 2 prepare in advance. **—pre′fab ri ca′tion,** *n.*

pref ace (pref′is), *n., v.,* **-aced, -ac ing.** *—n.* 1 introduction to a book, writing, or speech. See **introduction** for synonym study. 2 something preliminary or introductory. *—v.t.* 1 introduce by written or spoken remarks; give a preface to. 2 be a preface to; begin. [< Old French < Latin *praefationem* < *praefari* speak beforehand < *prae-* pre- + *fari* speak]

pref a to ry (pref′ə tôr′ē, pref′ə tōr′ē), *adj.* of or like a preface; given as a preface; introductory; preliminary: *a prefatory note to the reader.* **—pref′a to′ri ly,** *adv.*

pre fect (prē′fekt), *n.* 1 title of various military and civil officers in ancient Rome and elsewhere. 2 the chief administrative official of a department of France. 3 a chief officer, chief magistrate, etc. 4 a student monitor in certain schools. 5 (in Jesuit schools, colleges, etc.) a dean. [< Latin *praefectus* < *praeficere* put in front < *prae-* pre- + *facere* to make]

pre fec tur al (pri fek′chər əl), *adj.* of or belonging to a prefecture.

pre fec ture (prē′fek chər), *n.* office, jurisdiction, territory, or official residence of a prefect.

pre fer (pri fėr′), *v.,* **-ferred, -fer ring.** *—v.t.* 1 like better; choose rather: *He prefers golf as a sport, but I prefer to swim than to golf. She prefers reading to sewing. My students preferred fiction over history. We would prefer that they draw their own conclusions.* 2 put forward; present: *prefer a claim to property. The policeman preferred charges of speeding against the driver.* 3 promote; advance. *—v.i.* have or express a preference: *I will come later, if you prefer.* [< Latin *praeferre* put before < *prae-* pre- + *ferre* carry] **—pre fer′rer,** *n.*

pref er a ble (pref′ər ə bəl), *adj.* to be preferred; more desirable. **—pref′er a ble ness,** *n.* **—pref′er a bly,** *adv.*

pref er ence (pref′ər əns), *n.* 1 act or attitude of liking better: *My preference is for beef rather than lamb.* 2 thing preferred; first choice: *Her preference in reading is a novel.* See **choice** for synonym study. 3 the favoring of one above another: *A teacher should not show preference for any one student.*

pref e ren tial (pref′ə ren′shəl), *adj.* 1 of, giving, or receiving preference: *preferential treatment.* 2 having import duties favoring particular countries: *a preferential tariff.* 3 (of votes, voting, etc.) indicating or permitting indication of the order of one's preference. 4 giving preference to union members in hiring, promotion, etc.: *a preferential shop.* **—pref′e ren′tial ly,** *adv.*

prehensile monkey with a prehensile tail

pre fer ment (pri fėr′mənt), *n.* 1 advancement; promotion: *seek preferment in one's job.* 2 position or office giving social or financial advancement, especially one in the church. 3 act of preferring.

preferred stock, stock on which dividends must be paid at a predetermined rate before any can be paid on common stock.

pre fig u ra tion (prē′fig yə rā′shən), *n.* 1 a prefiguring; representation beforehand by a figure or type. 2 that in which something is prefigured; prototype.

pre fig ure (prē fig′yər), *v.t.,* **-ured, -ur ing.** 1 represent beforehand by a figure or type: *In one painting of Christ, His shadow is that of a cross, prefiguring the Crucifixion.* 2 imagine or picture to oneself beforehand. **—pre fig′ure ment,** *n.*

pre fix (prē′fiks; *also* prē fiks′ *for v.*), *n.* a syllable, syllables, or word put at the beginning of a word to change its meaning or to form another word, as *pre-* in *prepaid, under-* in *underline, dis-* in *disappear, un-* in *unlike,* and *re-* in *redo.* —*v.t.* 1 **prefix to,** put (something) before: *We prefix "Mr." to a man's name.* 2 add as a prefix: *prefix a syllable to a word.* [< New Latin *praefixum* < Latin *praefigere* fix in front < *prae-* pre- + *figere* to fix]

pre fix al (prē′fik səl, prē fik′səl), *adj.* 1 of the nature of a prefix. 2 characterized by prefixes. **—pre′fix al ly,** *adv.*

pre flight (prē′flīt′), *adj.* preceding or occurring before flight, as of an aircraft, missile, or satellite: *a preflight inspection of a plane, preflight training.*

pre form (prē fôrm′), *v.t.* form or shape beforehand.

pre for ma tion (prē′fôr mā′shən), *n.* 1 a shaping beforehand. 2 an old theory of generation according to which the individual exists complete in the germ cell, further development being merely in size.

pre fron tal (prē frun′təl), *adj.* of or having to do with the anterior portion of the frontal part of the brain: *prefrontal lobotomy.*

preg na bil i ty (preg′nə bil′ə tē), *n.* a being pregnable; vulnerability.

preg na ble (preg′nə bəl), *adj.* open to attack; assailable; vulnerable. [< Old French *prenable* < *prendre* seize, take < Latin *prehendere*]

preg nan cy (preg′nən sē), *n., pl.* **-cies.** 1 pregnant quality or condition. 2 period of being pregnant.

preg nant (preg′nənt), *adj.* 1 having an embryo or embryos developing in the uterus; being with child or young. 2 filled; loaded. 3 fertile; rich; abounding: *a mind pregnant with ideas.* 4 filled with meaning; very significant: *a pregnant saying, pregnant years.* [< Latin *praegnantem* < *prae-* pre- + *gen-* to bear] **—preg′nant ly,** *adv.*

pre heat (prē hēt′), *v.t.* heat before using.

pre hen sile (pri hen′səl), *adj.* adapted for seizing, grasping, or holding on. Many monkeys have prehensile tails. [< French *préhensile,* ultimately < Latin *prehendere* to grasp]

pre hen sion (pri hen′shən), *n.* the act of taking hold; grasping; seizing.

pre his to ric (prē′hi stôr′ik, prē′hi-stor′ik), *adj.* of or belonging to periods before recorded history: *Some prehistoric people lived in caves.* **—pre′his to′ri cal ly,** *adv.*

pre his to ri cal (prē′hi stôr′ə kəl, prē′hi-stor′ə kəl), *adj.* prehistoric.

pre his tor y (prē his′tər ē), *n.* history before recorded history; prehistoric matters or times.

pre judge (prē juj′), *v.t.,* **-judged, -judg ing.** pass judgment on (a person, opinion, action, etc.) beforehand, especially without knowing all the facts. **—pre-judg′ment, pre judge′ment,** *n.*

prej u dice (prej′ə dis), *n., v.,* **-diced, -dic ing.** —*n.* 1 opinion formed without taking time and care to judge fairly: *a prejudice against doctors, a prejudice toward foreigners.* See synonym study below. 2 harm or injury as the consequence of some action or judgment: *I will do nothing to the prejudice of my cousin in this matter.* —*v.t.* 1 cause a prejudice in; fill with prejudice: *One unfortunate experience prejudiced him against all lawyers.* 2 harm or injure, as by some action that weakens (a right, claim, statement, etc.) [< Latin *praejudicium* prior judgment < *prae-* pre- + *judicium* judgment]

Syn. *n.* 1 **Prejudice, bias** mean an opinion, attitude, or tendency formed unfairly or unjustly. **Prejudice** applies especially to an opinion or judgment, usually unfavorable, formed beforehand because of personal feelings or a fixed idea: *She has a prejudice against modern furniture.* **Bias** applies to a strong leaning or propensity against or in favor of someone or something because of personal dislike, liking, or a fixed idea: *A judge is not supposed to have a bias to either party in a lawsuit.*

prej u di cial (prej′ə dish′əl), *adj.* causing prejudice or disadvantage; hurtful; detrimental: *acting in a manner prejudicial to others.* **—prej′u di′cial ly,** *adv.*

prel a cy (prel′ə sē), *n., pl.* **-cies.** 1 position or rank of a prelate. 2 prelates. 3 church government by prelates.

prel ate (prel′it), *n.* clergyman of high rank, such as a bishop. [< Medieval Latin *praelatus* < Latin, one preferred, literally, brought in front < *prae-* pre- + *latum* brought]

pre lim (prē′lim, pri lim′), *n., adj.* INFORMAL. preliminary.

prelim., preliminary.

pre lim i nar y (pri lim′ə ner′ē), *adj., n., pl.* **-nar ies.** —*adj.* coming before the main business; leading to something more important: *After the preliminary exercises of prayer and song, the speaker of the day gave an address.* —*n.* 1 a preliminary step; something preparatory. 2 a preliminary examination. 3 an athletic contest or match preceding the main event, especially in boxing or wrestling. [< New Latin *praeliminaris* < Latin *prae-* pre- + *limen* threshold] **—pre lim′i-nar′i ly,** *adv.*

prel ude (prel′yüd, prē′lüd, prā′lüd), *n., v.,* **-ud ed, -ud ing.** —*n.* 1 anything serving as an introduction; preliminary performance, action, event, condition, etc.: *The German invasion of Poland was a prelude to World War II.* 2 in music: **a** a composition, or part of it, that introduces another composition or part. **b** a short, independent instrumental composition of an imaginative, improvised nature. **c** a composition played at the beginning of a church service, especially an organ solo. —*v.t.* 1 be a prelude or introduction to. 2 introduce with a prelude. 3 (in music) play as a prelude. —*v.i.* give a prelude or introductory performance. [< Medieval Latin *praeludium* < Latin *praeludere* play before < *prae-* pre- + *ludere* to play]

prem., premium.

pre ma ture (prē′mə chůr′, prē′mə tůr′, prē′mə tyůr′), *adj.* before the proper time; too soon. A premature baby is one born more than two weeks early or weighing less than $5^1/_2$ pounds. **—pre′ma ture′ly,** *adv.* **—pre′ma ture′ness,** *n.*

pre ma tur i ty (prē′mə chůr′ə tē, prē′mə-tůr′ə tē, prē′mə tyůr′ə tē), *n.* quality or state of being premature.

pre med (prē′med′), INFORMAL. —*n.* a premedical student. —*adj.* premedical.

pre med i cal (prē med′ə kəl), *adj.* preparing for the study of medicine: *a premedical student, a premedical course.*

pre med i tate (prē med′ə tāt), *v.t.,* **-tat ed, -tat ing.** consider or plan beforehand: *The murder was premeditated.*

pre med i tat ed ly (prē med′ə tā′tid lē), *adv.* with premeditation; deliberately.

pre med i ta tion (prē′med ə tā′shən), *n.* previous deliberation or planning.

pre mie (prē′mē), *n.* preemie.

pre mier (*n.* pri mir′, prē′mē ər; *adj.* prē′mē ər, prem′yər), *n.* prime minister. —*adj.* 1 first in rank or importance; chief. 2 first in time; earliest. [< Old French, first < Latin *primarius* primary < *primus* first]

pre miere (pri mir′, prə myer′), *n., adj., v.,* **-miered, -mier ing.** —*n.* a first public performance: *the premiere of a new play.* —*adj.* premier. —*v.t.* give the first public performance or showing of (a play, movie, etc.). —*v.i.* 1 have the first public performance or showing: *The movie is premiering this month.* 2 perform publicly for the first time, especially as a star: *She premiered in London.* 3 appear for the first time: *The magazine is scheduled to premiere next fall.* [< French *première*]

pre mier ship (pri mir′ship, prē′mē ər-ship), *n.* office or rank of a prime minister.

prem ise (prem′is; *also* pri mīz′ *for v.*), *n., v.,* **pre mised, pre mis ing.** —*n.* 1 (in logic) a statement assumed to be true and used to draw a conclusion. EXAMPLE: Major premise: All men are mortal. Minor premise: He is a man. Conclusion: He is mortal. 2 **premises,** *pl.* **a** house or building with its grounds. **b** a piece or tract of land. **c** (in law) things mentioned previously, such as the names of the parties concerned, a description of the property, the price, grounds for complaint, etc. **d** (in law) the property forming the subject of a document. —*v.t.* 1 set forth as an introduction or explanation; mention beforehand. 2 postulate (def. 1). Also, **premiss** for n. def. 1. [< Medieval Latin *praemissa* < Latin, placed before < *prae-* pre- + *mittere* send]

prem iss (prem′is), *n.* premise (def. 1).

pre mi um (prē′mē əm), *n.* 1 a reward, especially one given as an incentive to buy; prize: *Some magazines give premiums for*

hat, āge, fär; let, ēqual, tėrm;
it, īce; hot, ōpen, ôrder;
oil, out; cup, pu̇t, rüle;
ch, child; ng, long; sh, she;
th, thin; ᴛʜ, then; zh, measure;

ə represents *a* in about, *e* in taken,
i in pencil, *o* in lemon, *u* in circus.

< = from, derived from, taken from.

obtaining new subscriptions. 2 something more than the ordinary price or wages. 3 amount of money paid for insurance: *I pay premiums on my life insurance four times a year.* 4 unusual or unfair value: *Our teacher puts a premium on neatness and punctuality.* 5 **at a premium, a** at more than the usual value or price. **b** very valuable; much wanted. *—adj.* of a higher grade or quality. [< Latin *praemium* reward < *prae-* pre- + *emere* to buy]

pre mo lar (prē mō′lər), *n.* one of the permanent teeth between the canine teeth and the molars. *—adj.* of the premolars.

pre mo ni tion (prē′mə nish′ən, prem′ə-nish′ən), *n.* notification or warning of what is to come; forewarning: *a vague premonition of disaster.* [< Latin *praemonitionem* < *praemonere* warn beforehand < *prae-* pre- + *monere* warn]

pre mon i to ry (pri mon′ə tôr′ē, pri-mon′ə tōr′ē), *adj.* giving warning beforehand.

pre na tal (prē nā′tl), *adj.* 1 before childbirth: *A woman soon to have a baby requires prenatal care.* 2 occurring before birth: *prenatal injury to the skull.* **—pre na′tal ly,** *adv.*

pren tice (pren′tis), *n.* ARCHAIC. apprentice. *—adj.* of or like an apprentice; inexperienced; unskilled: *one's prentice years, formed by a prentice hand.*

pre oc cu pa tion (prē ok′yə pā′shən), *n.* 1 act of preoccupying. 2 condition of being preoccupied; absorption.

pre oc cu pied (prē ok′yə pīd), *adj.* absorbed; engrossed.

pre oc cu py (prē ok′yə pī), *v.t.,* **-pied, -py ing.** 1 take up all the attention of; absorb: *The question of getting to New York preoccupied her mind.* 2 occupy beforehand; take possession of before others: *Our favorite seats had been preoccupied.*

pre op e ra tive (prē op′ər ə tiv, prē op′ə-rā′tiv), *adj.* occurring before a surgical operation: *preoperative treatment.* **—pre op′e ra tive ly,** *adv.*

pre or dain (prē′ôr dān′), *v.t.* decide or settle beforehand; foreordain.

pre or di na tion (prē′ôrd′n ā′shən), *n.* 1 a preordaining. 2 a being preordained.

prep (prep), *adj., v.,* **prepped, prep ping,** *n.* INFORMAL. *—adj.* preparatory. *—v.i.* 1 attend preparatory school. 2 study; prepare. *—v.t.* prepare. *—n.* preparatory school.

prep., 1 preparatory. 2 preposition.

pre pack age (prē pak′ij), *v.t.,* **-aged, -ag ing.** to package (foods and other articles) in certain weights, sizes, or grades before putting up for sale.

pre paid (prē pād′), *v.* pt. and pp. of **prepay.**

prep a ra tion (prep′ə rā′shən), *n.* 1 a preparing; making ready. 2 a being prepared. 3 thing done to prepare for something: *preparations for a journey.* 4 medicine, food, or other substance made by a special process.

pre par a to ry (pri par′ə tôr′ē, pri par′ə-tōr′ē), *adj.* 1 of or for preparation; making ready; preparing. 2 as an introduction; preliminary. **—pre par′a to′ri ly,** *adv.*

preparatory school, 1 a private school, usually from grades 9 through 12, that prepares boys or girls for college. 2 (in Great Britain) a private school that prepares boys of 6 to 14 for the public schools.

pre pare (pri per′, pri par′), *v.,* **-pared, -par ing.** *—v.t.* 1 make ready: *prepare a meal, prepare a room for a guest.* 2 make by a special process: *prepare aluminum from bauxite.* *—v.i.* get ready: *prepare for a test.* [< Latin *praeparare* < *prae-* pre- + *parare* make ready] **—pre par′er,** *n.*

pre par ed ness (pri per′id nis, pri-perd′nis; pri par′id nis, pri pard′nis), *n.* 1 a being prepared; readiness. 2 possession of adequate military forces and defenses to meet threats or outbreaks of war.

pre pay (prē pā′), *v.t.,* **-paid, -pay ing.** 1 pay in advance. 2 pay for in advance. **—pre pay′ment,** *n.*

pre pon der ance (pri pon′dər əns), *n.* 1 greater number; greater weight; greater power or influence: *In July the hot days have the preponderance.* 2 a being the chief or most important element: *the preponderance of oaks in these woods.*

pre pon der ant (pri pon′dər ənt), *adj.* 1 weighing more; being stronger or more numerous; having more power or influence. 2 most important; chief: *Greed is a miser's preponderant characteristic.* **—pre pon′der ant ly,** *adv.*

pre pon de rate (pri pon′də rāt′), *v.i.,* **-rat ed, -rat ing.** 1 be greater than something else in weight, power, force, influence, number, amount, etc. 2 be chief; be most important. [< Latin *praeponderatum* outweighed < *prae-* pre- + *pondus* weight]

prep o si tion (prep′ə zish′ən), *n.* word that expresses some relation to a noun, pronoun, phrase, or clause which follows it. *With, for, by,* and *in* are prepositions in the sentence "A man *with* rugs *for* sale walked *by* our house *in* the morning." [< Latin *praepositionem* < *praeponere* put before < *prae-* pre- + *ponere* put]

prep o si tion al (prep′ə zish′ə nəl), *adj.* 1 having to do with a preposition. 2 having the nature or function of a preposition. 3 made up of a preposition and its object: *a prepositional phrase.* **—prep′o si′tion al ly,** *adv.*

pre pos sess (prē′pə zes′), *v.t.* 1 impress favorably beforehand or at the outset: *We were prepossessed by the girl's modest behavior.* 2 fill with a feeling, opinion, idea, etc.

pre pos sess ing (prē′pə zes′ing), *adj.* making a favorable first impression; attractive; pleasing. **—pre′pos sess′ing ly,** *adv.* **—pre′pos sess′ing ness,** *n.*

pre pos ses sion (prē′pə zesh′ən), *n.* condition of being prepossessed; feeling or opinion formed beforehand, especially one that is favorable.

pre pos ter ous (pri pos′tər əs), *adj.* contrary to nature, reason, or common sense; absurd; senseless: *It would be preposterous to shovel snow with a teaspoon.* See **ridiculous** for synonym study. [< Latin *praeposterus* with the posterior in front < *prae-* pre- + *posterus* coming after, behind] **—pre pos′ter ous ly,** *adv.* **—pre pos′ter ous ness,** *n.*

pre puce (prē′pyüs), *n.* foreskin. [< Middle French < Latin *praeputium*]

Pre-Raph a el ite (prē′raf′ē ə līt, prē′rā′-fē ə līt), *n.* one of a group of English artists formed in 1848 that aimed to work in the spirit that prevailed before the time of Raphael.

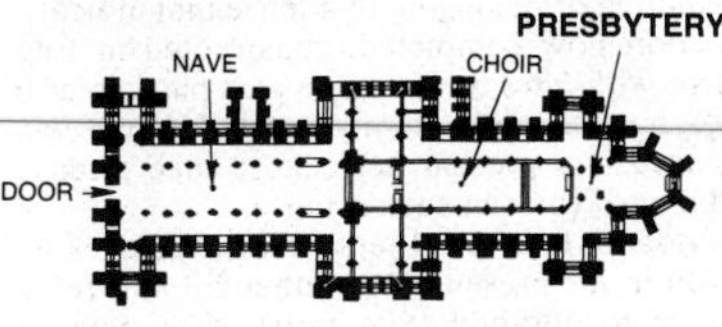

presbytery (def. 3)

pre re cord (prē′ri kôrd′), *v.t.* record in advance for later use: *prerecord a television program on videotape.*

pre req ui site (prē rek′wə zit), *n.* something required beforehand: *That high school course is usually a prerequisite to college work.* *—adj.* required beforehand.

pre rog a tive (pri rog′ə tiv), *n.* 1 right or privilege that nobody else has: *The government has the prerogative of coining money.* See **privilege** for synonym study. 2 special superiority of right or privilege, such as may derive from an official position, office, etc. [< Latin *praerogativa* allotted to vote first < *praerogare* ask for a vote first < *prae-* pre- + *rogare* ask]

pres., present.

Pres., 1 Presbyterian. 2 President.

pres age (pres′ij; *also* pri sāj′ *for v.*), *n., v.,* **pre saged, pre sag ing.** *—n.* 1 sign felt as a warning; omen. 2 a feeling that something is about to happen; presentiment; foreboding. *—v.t.* 1 give warning of; predict: *Some people think that a circle around the moon presages a storm.* 2 have or give a presentiment or prophetic impression of. [< Latin *praesagium* < *prae-* pre- + *sagus* prophetic] **—pre sag′er,** *n.*

pres by o pi a (prez′bē ō′pē ə), *n.* a normal loss of accommodation in the eyesight occurring in middle and old age as the lens of the eye becomes less elastic and loses some of its ability to focus on objects close to the eyes. [< New Latin < Greek *presbys* old man + *ōps* eye]

pres by op ic (prez′bē op′ik), *adj.* 1 having to do with presbyopia. 2 having presbyopia.

pres by ter (prez′bə tər, pres′bə tər), *n.* 1 an elder in the early Christian church. 2 a minister or a lay elder in the Presbyterian Church. 3 a minister or a priest in the Episcopal Church. [< Latin, an elder < Greek *presbyteros,* comparative of *presbys* old, an old man. Doublet of PRIEST.]

Pres by ter i an (prez′bə tir′ē ən, pres′bə-tir′ē ən), *adj.* of or belonging to a Protestant denomination or church governed by elected presbyters or elders all of equal rank and having beliefs based on Calvinism. *—n.* member of a Presbyterian church.

Pres by ter i an ism (prez′bə tir′ē ə-niz′əm, pres′bə tir′ē ə niz′əm), *n.* 1 system of church government by elders all (including ministers) of equal rank. 2 beliefs of Presbyterian churches.

pres by ter y (prez′bə ter′ē, pres′bə ter′ē), *n., pl.* **-ter ies.** 1 (in the Presbyterian Church) a meeting or court of all the ministers and certain of the elders within a district. 2 district under the jurisdiction of such a meeting or court. 3 part of a church set aside for the clergy. 4 (in the Roman Catholic Church) a priest's house.

pre school (prē′skül′), *adj.* before the age of going to regular school, usually from infancy to the age of five or six: *preschool children, preschool training.* **—pre′school′er,** *n.*

pre sci ence (prē′shē əns, presh′ē əns; prē′shəns, presh′əns), *n.* knowledge of things before they exist or happen; foreknowledge; foresight. [< Late Latin *praescientia* < Latin *praescientem* foreknowing < *prae-* pre- + *scire* know]

pre sci ent (prē′shē ənt, presh′ē ənt; prē′shənt, presh′ənt), *adj.* knowing beforehand; foreseeing. **—pre′sci ent ly,** *adv.*

Pres cott (pres′kət), *n.* **William Hickling,** 1796-1859, American historian.

pre scribe (pri skrīb′), *v.,* **-scribed, -scrib ing.** *—v.t.* 1 lay down as a rule to be followed; order; direct: *Good citizens do what the laws prescribe.* 2 order as a remedy or treatment: *The doctor prescribed quinine.* *—v.i.* 1 lay down a rule or rules. 2 give medical advice; issue a prescription. [< Latin *praescribere* write before < *prae-* pre- + *scribere* write] **—pre scrib′er,** *n.*

pre script (*n.* prē′skript; *adj.* pri skript′, prē′skript), *n.* that which is prescribed; rule; order; direction. *—adj.* prescribed.

pre scrip tion (pri skrip′shən), *n.* 1 act of prescribing. 2 something prescribed; order; direction. 3 a written direction or order for preparing and using a medicine. 4 the medicine. 5 in law: **a** possession or use of a thing long enough to give a right or title to it. **b** the right or title.

pre scrip tive (pri skrip′tiv), *adj.* 1 prescribing. 2 established by law or custom. **—pre scrip′tive ly,** *adv.* **—pre scrip′tive ness,** *n.*

pres ence (prez′ns), *n.* 1 fact or condition of being present in a place: *I just learned of her presence in the city.* 2 **in the presence of,** in the sight or company of: *in the presence of two witnesses.* 3 place where a person is: *The messenger was admitted to the general's presence.* 4 formal attendance upon a person of very high rank: *The knight retired from the royal presence.* 5 appearance; bearing: *She has a noble presence.* 6 something present, especially a ghost, spirit, or the like.

presence chamber, the room in which a king or some very important person receives guests or persons entitled to appear before him.

presence of mind, ability to think calmly, quickly, and effectively when taken by surprise, especially in peril or emergency.

pres ent[1] (prez′nt), *adj.* 1 being in the place or thing in question; at hand, not absent: *Every member of the class was present. Oxygen is present in the air.* 2 at this time; being or occurring now: *present prices.* See **current** for synonym study. 3 (in grammar) of or expressing the present tense: *The present forms of "ate" and "smiled" are "eat" and "smile."* *—n.* 1 **the present,** the time being; this time; now: *That is enough for the present.* 2 the present tense or a verb form in that tense. 3 **at present,** at the present time; now. 4 **by these presents,** by these words; by this document. [< Latin *praesentem* being before someone < *prae-* pre- + *esse* be]

pre sent[2] (*v.* pri zent′; *n.* prez′nt), *v.t.* 1 hand over; give: *present a book as a prize to the winner.* See **give** for synonym study. 2 **present with,** give to. 3 offer; offer formally: *She presented the tray of sandwiches to each guest.* 4 bring before the mind; offer for consideration: *She presented her ideas to the committee.* 5 offer to view or notice: *The new library presents a fine appearance.* 6 bring before the public; give a public performance of: *Our school presented a play.* 7 set forth in words: *The speaker presented arguments for his side.* 8 hand in; send in: *The grocer presented his bill.* 9 make acquainted; bring (a person) before somebody; introduce formally: *be presented at court.* See **introduce** for synonym study. 10 direct; point; turn: *The handsome actor presented his profile to the camera.* 11 aim or salute with (a weapon). 12 (in law) bring a formal charge against (a person, etc.). *—n.* thing given; gift. See **gift** for synonym study. [< Old French *presenter* < Latin *praesentare* < *praesentem* present[1]] **—pre sent′er,** *n.*

pre sent a bil i ty (pri zen′tə bil′ə tē), *n.* presentable condition or quality.

pre sent a ble (pri zen′tə bəl), *adj.* 1 fit to be seen: *make a house presentable for company.* 2 suitable in appearance, dress, manners, etc., for being introduced into society or company. 3 suitable to be offered or given. **—pre sent′a ble ness,** *n.* **—pre sent′a bly,** *adv.*

present arms, 1 bring a rifle to a vertical position in front of the body. 2 this position. 3 a command to assume this position.

pres en ta tion (prez′n tā′shən, prē′zen-tā′shən), *n.* 1 act of giving; delivering: *the presentation of a gift.* 2 the gift that is presented. 3 a bringing forward; offering to be considered: *the presentation of a plan.* 4 an offering to be seen; showing; exhibition: *the presentation of a play, the presentation of a motion picture.* 5 a formal introduction.

pres ent-day (prez′nt dā′), *adj.* of the present time; current.

pre sen ti ment (pri zen′tə mənt), *n.* a feeling or impression that something, especially something evil, is about to happen; vague sense of approaching misfortune; foreboding.

pres ent ly (prez′nt lē), *adv.* 1 before long; soon: *The clock will strike presently.* See **immediately** for synonym study. 2 at the present time; at this time; now: *I am presently working as a clerk.*

pre sent ment (pri zent′mənt), *n.* 1 a bringing forward; offering to be considered. 2 a showing; offering to be seen. 3 something brought forward or shown. 4 the presenting of a bill, note, etc., as for payment or acceptance.

present participle, the participle used in forming the English progressive tense or aspect (is *running,* was *running,* etc.) and as an adjective (the *running* horse). When used adjectivally, neither the present nor the past participle indicates time, which must be deduced from the context: *Singing merrily, we left* (or *shall leave,* etc.).

present perfect, in grammar: 1 designating or belonging to a tense that indicates action now completed, constructed in English with *have* or *has* and a past participle. In "I have completed my work," *have completed* is a present perfect. 2 such a tense. 3 a verb form in such a tense.

present tense, 1 tense that expresses action in the present time, either without reference to duration (She *runs*) or as being in progress, recurring, or habitual (She *is running*). 2 a verb form in the present tense.

pres er va tion (prez′ər vā′shən), *n.* 1 a preserving; keeping safe. 2 a being preserved; being kept safe.

pre serv a tive (pri zėr′və tiv), *n.* any substance that will prevent decay or injury. Paint is a preservative for wood surfaces. Salt is a preservative for meat. *—adj.* that preserves.

pre serve (pri zėrv′), *v.,* **-served, -serv ing,** *n.* *—v.t.* 1 keep from harm or change; keep safe; protect. 2 keep up; maintain. 3 keep from spoiling: *Ice helps to preserve food.* 4 prepare (food) to keep it from spoiling. Boiling with sugar, salting, smoking, and pickling are different ways of preserving food. *—n.* 1 **preserves,** *pl.* fruit cooked with sugar and sealed from the air: *plum preserves.* 2 place where wild animals, fish, or trees and plants are protected. [< Late Latin *praeservare* < Latin *prae-* pre- + *servare* to keep] **—pre serv′a ble,** *adj.*

pre serv er (pri zėr′vər), *n.* person or thing that saves and protects from danger. Life preservers help to save people from drowning.

pre set (prē set′), *v.t.,* **-set, -set ting.** set in advance.

pre side (pri zīd′), *v.i.,* **-sid ed, -sid ing.** 1 hold the place of authority; have charge of a meeting: *The principal will preside at our election of school officers.* 2 have authority; have control: *The manager presides over the business of this store.* [< Latin *praesidere* sit in front < *prae-* pre- + *sedere* sit] **—pre sid′er,** *n.*

pres i den cy (prez′ə dən sē, prez′dən sē), *n., pl.* **-cies.** 1 office of president. 2 time in which a president is in office.

pres i dent (prez′ə dənt, prez′dənt), *n.* 1 the chief officer of a company, corporation, college, society, club, etc. 2 Often, **President,** the highest executive officer of a republic. 3 the head of state in certain countries where the prime minister is chief executive. 4 person who presides; speaker or chairman. 5 the presiding officer of a city council or other governmental body.

pres i dent-e lect (prez′ə dənt i lekt′, prez′dənt i lekt′), *n.* president who has been elected but not yet inaugurated.

pres i den tial (prez′ə den′shəl), *adj.* of or having to do with a president or presidency. **—pres′i den′tial ly,** *adv.*

pre sid i o (pri sid′ē ō), *n., pl.* **-sid i os.** a garrisoned fort or military post in Spanish America or, during the period of Spanish or Mexican control, in the southwestern United States and California. [< Spanish]

pre sid i um (pri sid′ē əm), *n.* 1 a permanent executive committee in various Communist countries, having the power to act for a larger body. 2 **Presidium,** one of the two most important bodies of the Supreme Soviet in the Soviet Union. It handles legislation between the biannual meetings of the Supreme Soviet and its chairman is considered the head of state. 3 Also, **Presidium.** the chief executive body of the Soviet Communist Party from 1952 to 1966, replaced by the Politburo. [< Latin *praesidium* a presiding over]

press[1] (pres), *v.t.* 1 act on with a steady force, as by downward weight, outward pushing, etc.: *Press the button to ring the bell.* 2 **a** squeeze: *press apples for cider.* **b** squeeze out: *press juice from oranges.* 3 make smooth; flatten: *press clothes with an iron.* 4 clasp; hug: *He pressed my hand in greeting.* 5 move by pushing steadily (up,

hat, āge, fär; let, ēqual, tėrm;
it, īce; hot, ōpen, ôrder;
oil, out; cup, pu̇t, rüle;
ch, child; ng, long; sh, she;
th, thin; ᴛʜ, then; zh, measure;

ə represents *a* in about, *e* in taken, *i* in pencil, *o* in lemon, *u* in circus.

< = from, derived from, taken from.

down, against, etc.). 6 give a desired shape, texture, or condition to by pressure: *press cotton into bales, press phonograph records.* 7 urge onward; cause to hurry. 8 keep asking (somebody) earnestly; urge; entreat: *Because it was so stormy, we pressed our guest to stay all night.* 9 lay stress upon; insist on. 10 constrain; compel; force. 11 urge for acceptance: *press the need for vigilance.* 12 weigh heavily upon (the mind, a person, etc.). —*v.i.* 1 use force steadily. 2 push forward; keep pushing: *I pressed on in spite of the wind.* 3 crowd; throng: *The crowd pressed about the famous actor.* 4 iron clothes. 5 ask insistently; refer to something often and with emphasis: *Don't press for an answer yet.* 6 harass; oppress; trouble. 7 be urgent; demand prompt attention.
—*n.* 1 a pressing; pressure; push: *the press of ambition.* 2 a pressed condition: *These trousers will hold a press.* 3 any of various instruments or machines for exerting pressure. 4 printing press. 5 **go to press,** begin to be printed: *The newspaper goes to press at midnight.* 6 an establishment for printing books, etc. 7 the business of printing newspapers and magazines. 8 the process or art of printing. 9 newspapers and magazines and those who write for them: *release a story to the press.* 10 notice given in newspapers or magazines: *The Senator's remarks got a good press.* 11 crowd; throng: *lost in the press.* 12 a pressing forward or together; crowding. 13 urgency; hurry: *There is no press about answering my note.* 14 a cupboard or closet for clothes, books, etc.
[< Old French *presser* < Latin *pressare,* frequentative of *premere* to press]

press¹ (def. 14)

press² (pres), *v.t.* force into service, usually naval or military; impress. [earlier *prest* < Old French *prester* furnish < Latin *praestare* < *praes* bail, bondsman + *stare* to stand]

press agent, agent employed to secure favorable publicity for a person, organization, etc., publicist.

press box, U.S. an enclosed space in a sports arena, usually high above the playing field, set aside for reporters.

press conference, meeting arranged by a person or group with members of the press for the purpose of releasing some news or of submitting to an interview.

press gang, a group of men formerly employed to impress other men for service, usually naval or military service.

press ing (pres′ing), *adj.* requiring immediate action or attention; urgent: *pressing business, in pressing need of help.* —**press′ing ly,** *adv.*

press man (pres′mən), *n., pl.* **-men.** 1 man who operates a printing press. 2 reporter; newspaperman.

pres sor (pres′ər), *adj.* (in physiology) increasing blood pressure. A pressor nerve is one whose stimulation causes an increase of blood pressure.

press release, news material issued to a newspaper or newspapers for publication at a later time.

press room (pres′rüm′, pres′ru̇m′), *n.* room containing printing presses.

press run (pres′run′), *n.* 1 the run of a printing press for a specific number of copies. 2 the number of copies run off.

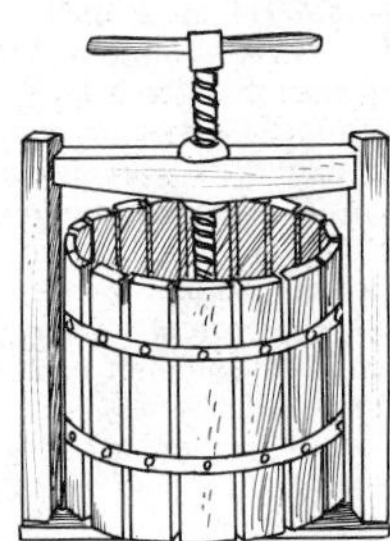
press¹ (def. 3) for making cider

pres sure (presh′ər), *n., v.,* **-sured, -sur ing.** —*n.* 1 the continued action of a weight or force: *The pressure of the wind filled the sails of the boat.* 2 force per unit of area: *There is a pressure of 27 pounds to the square inch in this tire.* 3 a state of trouble or strain: *the pressure of poverty, working under pressure.* 4 a compelling force or influence: *I was under pressure from the others to change my mind.* 5 need for prompt or decisive action; urgency: *the pressure of business.* 6 atmospheric pressure. 7 electromotive force. —*v.t.* force or urge by exerting pressure: *The salesman tried to pressure my father into buying the car.*

pressure cooker, an airtight container for cooking with steam under pressure.

pressure group, any business, professional, or labor group which attempts to further its own interests by exerting pressure on legislative bodies or administrative departments or agencies.

pressure point, 1 point on the body where pressure applied to a blood vessel can check bleeding. 2 point in the skin where the terminal organs of nerves are located, making it extremely sensitive to pressure. 3 (of a vehicle) point at which the brakes take hold when the brake pedal is pushed down.

pressure suit, garment that provides pressure upon the body so that respiration and circulation can continue normally under low-pressure conditions, such as occur at high altitudes.

pres sur ize (presh′ə rīz′), *v.t.,* **-ized, -iz ing.** 1 keep the atmospheric pressure inside (the cabin of an aircraft) at a normal level in spite of the altitude. 2 place under high pressure. —**pres′sur i za′tion,** *n.* —**pres′sur iz′er,** *n.*

Pres ter John (pres′tər), (in medieval legends) Christian priest and king, said to have ruled a kingdom somewhere in Asia or Africa during the Middle Ages.

pres ti dig i ta tion (pres′tə dij′ə tā′shən), *n.* sleight of hand; legerdemain. [< French < *preste* nimble + Latin *digitus* finger]

pres ti dig i ta tor (pres′tə dij′ə tā′tər), *n.* person who is skilled in sleight of hand.

pres tige (pre stēzh′, pre stēj′), *n.* reputation, influence, or distinction based on what is known of one's abilities, achievements, opportunities, associations, etc. [< Middle French, illusion, magic spell < Latin *praestigiae* tricks]

pres ti gious (pre stij′əs), *adj.* having prestige. —**pres ti′gious ly,** *adv.*

pres to (pres′tō), *adv., adj., n., pl.* **-tos,** *interj.* —*adv.* (in music) very quickly. —*adj.* 1 (in music) very quick. 2 quick; sudden: *with the presto agility of a magician.* —*n.* a very quick part in a piece of music. —*interj.* exclamation used to express quick or sudden action: *Then—presto!—the job was done.* [< Italian < Latin *praesto* ready]

Pres ton (pres′tən), *n.* seaport in NW England, north of Liverpool. 100,000.

pre stress (prē stres′), *v.t.* subject (a material) to heavy internal stress in making or casting to help withstand subsequent external loads or stresses. Bricks, concrete, and structural steel are prestressed by embedding steel wires or rods that are under tension.

pre sum a ble (pri zü′mə bəl), *adj.* that can be presumed or taken for granted; probable; likely. —**pre sum′a bly,** *adv.*

pre sume (pri züm′), *v.,* **-sumed, -sum ing.** —*v.t.* 1 take for granted without proving; suppose: *The law presumes innocence until guilt is proved.* 2 take upon oneself; venture; dare: *May I presume to tell you you are wrong?* —*v.i.* 1 take an unfair advantage: *Don't presume on his good nature by borrowing from him every week.* 2 act with improper boldness; take liberties. [< Latin *praesumere* take for granted < *prae-* pre- + *sumere* take] —**pre sum′er,** *n.* —**pre sum′ing ly,** *adv.*

pre sum ed ly (pri zü′mid lē), *adv.* as is or may be supposed; presumably.

pre sump tion (pri zump′shən), *n.* 1 unpleasant boldness: *It is presumption to go to a party when one has not been invited.* 2 thing taken for granted; assumption; supposition: *Since he had the stolen jewels, the presumption was that he was the thief.* 3 cause or reason for presuming; probability. 4 act of presuming.

pre sump tive (pri zump′tiv), *adj.* 1 based on likelihood; presumed: *a presumptive title to an estate.* 2 giving ground for presumption or belief: *The man's running away was regarded as presumptive evidence of his guilt.* —**pre sump′tive ly,** *adv.*

pre sump tu ous (pri zump′chü əs), *adj.* acting without permission or right; too bold; forward. —**pre sump′tu ous ly,** *adv.* —**pre sump′tu ous ness,** *n.*

pre sup pose (prē′sə pōz′), *v.t.,* **-posed, -pos ing.** 1 take for granted in advance; assume beforehand: *Let's presuppose we will be going and make some plans.* 2 require as a necessary condition; imply: *A fight presupposes fighters.*

pre sup po si tion (prē′sup ə zish′ən), *n.* 1 a presupposing. 2 thing presupposed.

pre tence (prē′tens, pri tens′), *n.* pretense.

pre tend (pri tend′), *v.i.* 1 make believe: *The children pretended that they were grown-*

up. 2 lay claim: *James Stuart pretended to the English throne.* —*v.t.* 1 claim falsely: *She pretended to like the meal so she wouldn't offend the hostess.* 2 claim falsely to have: *pretend illness.* See synonym study below. 3 claim: *I don't pretend to be a musician.* [< Latin *praetendere* extend, give as an excuse < *prae-* pre- + *tendere* to stretch]

Syn. *v.t.* 2 **Pretend, affect, assume** mean to give a false impression by word, manner, or deed. **Pretend** implies a conscious intent to deceive: *She pretends ignorance of the whole affair.* **Affect** suggests using a false manner, more for effect than to deceive: *When she applied for a job, she affected simplicity.* **Assume** suggests putting on an appearance which, though not really genuine, is not wholly false: *She assumed a cheerful manner despite the upsetting news.*

pre tend ed (pri ten′did), *adj.* claimed falsely; asserted falsely. —**pre tend′ed ly,** *adv.*

pre tend er (pri ten′dər), *n.* 1 person who pretends. 2 person who lays claim, especially falsely, to a title or throne.

pre tense (prē′tens, pri tens′), *n.* 1 make-believe; pretending. 2 a false appearance: *Under pretense of picking up the handkerchief, she took the money.* 3 a false claim: *She made a pretense of being surprised but knew about the party all along.* 4 claim: *He makes no pretense to knowledge of electronics.* 5 a showing off; display; ostentation: *Her manner is free from pretense.* 6 anything done to show off. Also, **pretence.**

pre ten sion (pri ten′shən), *n.* 1 claim: *The young prince has pretensions to the throne.* 2 a putting forward of a claim; laying claim to. 3 a doing things for show or to make a fine appearance; showy display.

pre ten tious (pri ten′shəs), *adj.* 1 making claims to excellence or importance: *a pretentious person, a pretentious book, a pretentious speech.* 2 doing things for show or to make a fine appearance; showy; ostentatious: *a pretentious style of entertaining guests.* —**pre ten′tious ly,** *adv.* —**pre ten′tious ness,** *n.*

pret er it or **pret er ite** (pret′ər it), *n.* a verb form that expresses occurrence in the past; past tense. EXAMPLES: *Obeyed* is the preterit of *obey; spoke,* of *speak;* and *saw,* of *see.* —*adj.* expressing past time. [< Latin *praeteritum,* literally, gone past < *praeter* past, beyond + *ire* go]

pre ter mit (prē′tər mit′), *v.t.,* **-mit ted, -mit ting.** 1 leave out or leave undone; omit. 2 let pass without notice. 3 leave off for a time; interrupt or suspend. [< Latin *praetermittere* < *praeter* past + *mittere* let go]

pre ter nat ur al (prē′tər nach′ər əl), *adj.* 1 out of the ordinary course of nature; abnormal. 2 due to something above or beyond nature; supernatural. [< Latin *praeter* beyond + *natura* nature] —**pre′ter nat′ur al ly,** *adv.*

pre test (prē′test′, prē test′), *v.t.* 1 test (a product, etc.) in advance of regular use or application. 2 subject (students) to a preliminary test. —*n.* a pretesting; preliminary test.

pre text (prē′tekst), *n.* a false reason concealing the real reason; misleading excuse; pretense: *He did not go, on the pretext of being too tired.* [< Latin *praetextum,* literally, woven in front, alleged as an excuse < *prae-* pre- + *texere* to weave]

Pre to ri a (pri tôr′ē ə, pri tōr′ē ə), *n.* administrative capital of the Republic of South Africa, in the NE part. 493,000.

pre tri al (prē′trī′əl), *n.* meeting held by a judge or other arbitrator before a trial to clarify the issues so as to save time and costs at the trial. —*adj.* 1 having to do with such a meeting. 2 occurring or existing before a trial: *Pretrial publicity had prejudiced the jury.*

pret ti fy (prit′ə fī), *v.t.,* **-fied, -fy ing.** make artificially pretty. —**pret′ti fi ca′tion,** *n.*

pret ty (prit′ē), *adj.,* **-ti er, -ti est,** *n., pl.* **-ties,** *adv.* —*adj.* 1 pleasing: *a pretty face, a pretty dress, a pretty tune. Pretty* is used to describe people and things that are good-looking in a feminine or childish way, dainty, sweet, charming, etc., but not stately, grand, elegant, or very important. 2 not at all pleasing: *This is a pretty mess, indeed.* 3 INFORMAL. considerable in amount or extent: *pay a pretty sum.* 4 fair; fine; nice: *a pretty day.* —*n.* a pretty person or thing. —*adv.* 1 fairly; rather: *It is pretty late.* 2 **pretty much, pretty nearly,** or **pretty well,** almost; nearly: *pretty much a thing of the past.* 3 **sitting pretty,** in an advantageous position. [Old English *prættig* cunning < *prætt* trick] —**pret′ti ly,** *adv.* —**pret′ti ness,** *n.*

pret zel (pret′səl), *n.* a hard biscuit, usually in the form of a knot or stick, glazed and salted on the outside. [< German *Brezel*]

pre vail (pri vāl′), *v.i.* 1 exist in many places; be in general use: *The custom of exchanging gifts at Christmas still prevails.* 2 be the most usual or strongest: *Sadness prevailed in our minds.* 3 be the stronger; win the victory; succeed: *prevail against an enemy. Reason prevailed over emotion.* 4 be effective. 5 **prevail on, prevail upon,** or **prevail with,** persuade. [< Latin *praevalere* < *prae-* pre- + *valere* have power]

pre vail ing (pri vā′ling), *adj.* 1 in general use; common: *a prevailing style. The prevailing summer winds here are from the west.* See **current** for synonym study. 2 that prevails; having superior force or influence; victorious. —**pre vail′ing ly,** *adv.*

prev a lence (prev′ə ləns), *n.* widespread occurrence; general use: *the prevalence of complaints about the weather.*

prev a lent (prev′ə lənt), *adj.* 1 in general use; widespread; common: *Colds are prevalent in the winter.* 2 predominant; victorious. —**prev′a lent ly,** *adv.*

pre var i cate (pri var′ə kāt), *v.i.,* **-cat ed, -cat ing.** turn aside from the truth in speech or action; lie. [< Latin *praevaricatum* deviated < *prae-* pre- + *varicus* straddling < *varus* crooked] —**pre var′i ca′tor,** *n.*

pre var i ca tion (pri var′ə kā′shən), *n.* a prevaricating; turning aside from the truth; lie.

pre vent (pri vent′), *v.t.* 1 stop or keep (from): *I will come if nothing prevents me from doing so.* See synonym study below. 2 keep from happening: *Rain prevented the game.* —*v.i.* hinder. [< Latin *praeventum* forestalled < *prae-* pre- + *venire* come] —**pre vent′er,** *n.*

Syn. *v.t.* 1 **Prevent, hinder, impede** mean to get in the way of action or progress. **Prevent** means to keep a person or thing from doing something or making progress, acting as or setting up an obstacle to stop him or it: *Business prevented my going.* **Hinder** means to hold back, so that making, starting, going ahead, or finishing is late, difficult, or impossible: *The wrong food hinders growth.* **Impede** means to slow up movement and progress by putting obstacles in the way: *Muddy roads impeded our journey.*

pre vent a ble (pri ven′tə bəl), *adj.* that can be prevented.

pre vent a tive (pri ven′tə tiv), *adj., n.* preventive.

pre vent i ble (pri ven′tə bəl), *adj.* preventable.

pre ven tion (pri ven′shən), *n.* 1 a preventing: *the prevention of fire.* 2 something that prevents.

pre ven tive (pri ven′tiv), *adj.* that prevents: *preventive measures against disease.* —*n.* something that prevents: *Vaccination is a preventive against smallpox.* —**pre ven′tive ly,** *adv.* —**pre ven′tive ness,** *n.*

pre view (prē′vyü′), *n.* 1 a previous view, inspection, survey, etc.: *a preview of things to come.* 2 an advance showing of a motion picture or scenes from a motion picture, a play, television program, etc. —*v.t.* view or display beforehand. Also, **prevue** for 2.

pre vi ous (prē′vē əs), *adj.* 1 coming or going before; that came before; earlier. See synonym study below. 2 INFORMAL. quick; hasty; premature: *Don't be too previous about refusing.* 3 **previous to,** before: *Previous to her departure she gave a party.* [< Latin *praevius* leading the way < *prae-* pre- + *via* road] —**pre′vi ous ly,** *adv.* —**pre′vi ous ness,** *n.*

Syn. 1 **Previous, prior, preceding** mean coming before something. **Previous** means earlier: *I cannot go, for I have a previous engagement* (one made before). **Prior** adds to *previous* the idea of coming first in order of importance: *I have a prior engagement* (one that has first call). **Preceding** means coming immediately before: *Check the preceding statement.*

previous question, motion to end debate and vote immediately on the main question.

pre vi sion (prē vizh′ən), *n.* 1 foresight; foreknowledge. 2 prophetic vision or perception: *Some prevision warned the explorer of danger.*

pre vi sion al (prē vizh′ə nəl), *adj.* of or having to do with prevision; foreseeing; forecasting.

pre vo cal ic (prē′vō kal′ik), *adj.* immediately preceding a vowel.

pre vue (prē′vyü′), *n.* U.S. preview (def. 2).

pre war (prē′wôr′), *adj., adv.* before a war.

prex y (prek′sē), *n., pl.* **prex ies.** SLANG. president, especially of a college or university.

prey (prā), *n.* 1 animal hunted or seized for food by another animal: *Mice and birds are the prey of cats.* 2 habit of hunting and killing other animals for food: *Hawks are birds of prey.* 3 person or thing injured; victim: *be a prey to fear or disease.* —*v.i.* **prey on** or **prey upon,** 1 be a strain upon; injure; irritate: *Worry about debts preys on her mind.* 2 rob; plunder. 3 hunt or kill for food: *Cats prey upon mice and birds.* [< Old French *preie* < Latin *praeda*] —**prey′er,** *n.*

Pri am (prī′əm), *n.* (in Greek legends) the king of Troy at the time of the Trojan War. He was the father of many children, including Hector, Paris, and Cassandra.

Prib i lof Islands (prib′ə lôf), group of four islands in the Bering Sea, belonging to Alaska. 1000 pop.; 76 sq. mi.

price (prīs), *n., v.,* **priced, pric ing.** —*n.* 1 the amount for which a thing is sold or can be bought; the cost to the buyer. See syno-

hat, āge, fär; let, ēqual, tėrm;
it, īce; hot, ōpen, ôrder;
oil, out; cup, pu̇t, rüle;
ch, child; ng, long; sh, she;
th, thin; ᴛʜ, then; zh, measure;

ə represents *a* in about, *e* in taken, *i* in pencil, *o* in lemon, *u* in circus.

< = from, derived from, taken from.

nym study below. 2 reward offered for the capture of a person alive or dead. 3 what must be given, done, undergone, etc., to obtain a thing: *We paid a heavy price for the victory, for we lost ten thousand soldiers.* 4 value; worth. 5 money or other consideration for which a person's support, consent, etc., may be obtained. 6 **at any price,** at any cost, no matter how great. 7 **beyond price** or **without price,** so valuable that it cannot be bought or be given a value in money. —*v.t.* 1 put a price on; set the price of. 2 INFORMAL. ask the price of; find out the price of: *price a rug.* [< Old French *pris* < Latin *pretium*] **—pric′er,** *n.*

Syn. *n.* 1 **Price, charge, cost** mean the amount asked or paid for something. **Price** is used mainly of goods and supplies, especially of what the seller asks for them: *The price of meat is high now.* **Charge** is used mainly of services rather than goods: *There is no charge for delivery.* **Cost** is used of either goods or services, and applies to whatever is spent, whether money, effort, etc.: *The cost of the house was high.*

price cutting, a sharp reduction of prices, especially when undertaken at a loss in order to eliminate competitors.

price fixing, 1 control of prices by a governmental agency. 2 an illegal agreement by several manufacturers to set a noncompetitive price on a product which they all make.

price less (prīs′lis), *adj.* 1 beyond price; extremely valuable. 2 INFORMAL. very amusing, absurd, etc.; delightful. **—price′less ness,** *n.*

price support, support generally provided by the government to keep prices of products or commodities from falling below certain stipulated levels. It may take the form of direct subsidy to the producer, or of government purchase at the level of support when the price in the open market falls below that level, or of loans to permit producers to hold back their production in storage pending a rise in price in the open market.

price war, period of intense competition between merchants, especially retail merchants, in which prices are progressively slashed until they may drop below cost.

prick (prik), *n.* 1 a sharp point. 2 a little hole or mark made by a sharp point; puncture. 3 act of pricking. 4 a sharp pain. 5 stinging compunction; remorse: *the prick of conscience.* —*v.t.* 1 make a little hole or mark on with a sharp point: *The cat pricked me with its claws.* 2 mark with a sharp point: *I pricked the map with a pin to show our route.* 3 cause sharp pain to: *My conscience pricked me.* 4 raise or erect: *The dog pricked up his ears at the sound of footsteps.* 5 ARCHAIC. spur; urge on. —*v.i.* 1 pierce a little hole in something. 2 cause or feel a sharp pain. 3 ARCHAIC. ride fast. [Old English *prica*] **—prick′er,** *n.* **—prick′ing ly,** *adv.*

prick le (prik′əl), *n., v.,* **-led, -ling.** —*n.* 1 a small, sharp point; thorn; spine. 2 a prickly or smarting sensation. —*v.i.* feel a prickly or smarting sensation. —*v.t.* cause such a sensation in.

prick ly (prik′lē), *adj.,* **-li er, -li est.** 1 having many sharp points or thorns: *a prickly rosebush, the prickly porcupine.* 2 sharp and stinging; itching; smarting: *a prickly rash on the skin.* **—prick′li ness,** *n.*

prickly heat, a red, itching rash on the skin caused by inflammation of the sweat glands.

prickly pear, 1 any of a genus of spiny or hairy cactuses with showy green, yellow, or red flowers, especially a species grown for its pear-shaped, edible fruit. 2 the fruit of any of these cactuses.

pride (prīd), *n., v.,* **prid ed, prid ing.** —*n.* 1 a high opinion of one's own worth or possessions. See synonym study below. 2 pleasure or satisfaction in something concerned with oneself: *take pride in one's work.* 3 something that one is proud of. 4 too high an opinion of oneself; arrogance: *Pride goes before a fall.* 5 acting as if better than others; scorn of others. 6 the best part; most flourishing period: *in the pride of manhood.* 7 group of lions. —*v.t.* **pride oneself on,** be proud of. [Old English *prȳde* + *prūd* proud]

Syn. *n.* 1 **Pride, conceit** mean a high opinion of oneself. **Pride** implies pleased satisfaction with what one is, has, or has done, and suggests self-respect and personal dignity based on real or imagined superiority: *A man without pride deserves contempt.* **Conceit** implies much too high an opinion of one's own abilities and accomplishments, and often suggests an unpleasantly assertive manner: *Conceit made the criminal think he was too clever to be caught.*

pride ful (prīd′fəl), *adj.* proud. **—pride′ful ly,** *adv.* **—pride′ful ness,** *n.*

prie-dieu (prē dyü′; *French* prē dyœ′), *n.* a small desk for a prayer book or the like, with a piece on which to kneel. [< French, literally, pray God]

priest (prēst), *n.* 1 clergyman or minister of a Christian church. 2 clergyman authorized to administer the sacraments and pronounce absolution. 3 a special servant of a god, who performs certain public religious acts. [Old English *prēost,* ultimately < Latin *presbyter.* Doublet of PRESBYTER.]

priest ess (prē′stis), *n.* woman who serves at an altar or in sacred rites.

priest hood (prēst′hu̇d), *n.* 1 position or rank of priest. 2 priests as a group.

Priest ley (prēst′lē), *n.* **Joseph,** 1733-1804, English clergyman and chemist.

priest ly (prēst′lē), *adj.,* **-li er, -li est.** 1 of or having to do with a priest. 2 like a priest; suitable for a priest. **—priest′li ness,** *n.*

prig (prig), *n.* person who is too particular about speech and manners, and prides himself on being better than others. [origin uncertain]

prig ger y (prig′ər ē), *n., pl.* **-ger ies.** conduct or character of a prig.

prig gish (prig′ish), *adj.* too particular about doing right in things that show outwardly; priding oneself on being better than others. **—prig′gish ly,** *adv.* **—prig′gish ness,** *n.*

prim (prim), *adj.,* **prim mer, prim mest.** stiffly precise, neat, proper, or formal. [origin uncertain] **—prim′ly,** *adv.* **—prim′ness,** *n.*

pri ma cy (prī′mə sē), *n., pl.* **-cies.** 1 being first in order, rank, importance, etc. 2 position or rank of a church primate. 3 (in the Roman Catholic Church) the supreme power of the pope.

pri ma don na (prē′mə don′ə), *pl.* **pri ma don nas.** 1 the principal woman singer in an opera. 2 a temperamental person. [< Italian, first lady]

pri ma fa ci e (prī′mə fā′shē ē; prī′mə fā′shē), at first view; before investigation. [< Latin]

pri ma-fa ci e evidence (prī′mə fā′shē ē, prī′mə fā′shē), (in law) evidence sufficient to establish a fact, or raise a presumption of fact, unless rebutted.

pri mal (prī′məl), *adj.* 1 of early times; first; primeval. 2 chief; fundamental. **—pri′mal ly,** *adv.*

pri mar i ly (prī′mer′ə lē, prī′mər ə lē), *adv.* 1 chiefly; principally: *Napoleon was primarily a general.* 2 at first; originally.

pri mar y (prī′mer′ē, prī′mər ē), *adj., n., pl.* **-mar ies.** —*adj.* 1 first in time or order; original; fundamental: *the primary cause of unemployment.* See **elementary** for synonym study. 2 first in importance; chief. 3 denoting or having to do with the inducing circuit, coil, or current in an induction coil or the like. —*n.* 1 anything that is first in order, rank, or importance. 2 election to choose candidates for office from a certain political party. Primaries are held before the regular election. 3 primary color. 4 a primary coil or circuit. 5 a heavenly body around which another revolves. [< Latin *primarius* first in rank < *primus* first]

primary accent, 1 the strongest stress in the pronunciation of a word. 2 mark (′) used to show this.

primary cell, an electric cell that cannot be recharged electrically. The voltaic cell is a primary cell.

primary color, any of a group of pigments or colors which, when mixed together, yield all other colors; primary. Red, yellow, and blue are the primary colors in pigments. In light, they are red, green, and blue.

primary school, the first three or four grades of the elementary school.

primary stress, primary accent.

pri mate (prī′mit, prī′māt), *n.* 1 archbishop or bishop ranking above all other bishops in a country or church province. 2 any of the highest order of mammals, including human beings, apes, monkeys, and lemurs. [< Latin *primatem* of first rank < *primus* first]

prime[1] (prīm), *adj.* 1 first in rank or importance; chief; principal: *The community's prime need is a new school.* 2 first in time or order; primary: *the prime causes of war.* 3 first in quality; first-rate; excellent: *prime ribs of beef.* 4 in mathematics: **a** having no common integral divisor but 1 and the number itself. **b** having no common integral divisor but 1: *2 is prime to 9.* 5 ranking high or highest in some scale or rating system: *prime borrowers, prime time on television.* —*n.* prime number. [< Latin *primus* first] **—prime′ness,** *n.*

prime[2] (prīm), *n.* 1 the best time, stage, or state: *be in the prime of life.* 2 the best part. 3 the first part; beginning. 4 springtime. 5 Also, **Prime.** the second of the seven canonical hours, or the service for it. 6 prime number. 7 one of the sixty minutes in a degree. 8 the mark (′) indicating this. B′ is read "B prime." [Old English *prīm* the first period (of the day) < Latin *prima (hora)* first (hour of the Roman day)] **—prime′ly,** *adv.* **—prime′ness,** *n.*

prime[3] (prīm), *v.t.,* **primed, prim ing.** 1 prepare by putting something in or on. 2 supply (a gun) with powder. 3 cover (a surface) with a first coat of paint or oil so that the finishing coat of paint will not soak in. 4 equip (a person) with information, words, etc. 5 pour water into (a pump) to start action. [origin uncertain]

prime factor, (in mathematics) a factor that has no other integral factors except itself and 1; factor that is itself a prime number.

prime meridian, meridian from which the longitude east and west is measured. It passes through Greenwich, England, and its longitude is 0 degrees.

prime minister, the chief minister in certain governments; premier. He is the head of the cabinet.

prime number, number not exactly divisible by some counting number other than itself and 1; prime. 2, 3, 5, 7, 11, and 13 are prime numbers; 4, 6, and 9 are composite numbers.

prim er[1] (prim′ər), *n.* 1 a first book in reading. 2 a first book; beginner's book. 3 **great primer,** 18-point type. 4 **long primer,** 10-point type. [< Medieval Latin *primarius* < Latin, first in rank < *primus* first]

prim er[2] (prī′mər), *n.* 1 person or thing that primes. 2 cap or cylinder containing a little gunpowder, used for firing a charge. [< *prime*[3]]

pri me val (prī mē′vəl), *adj.* 1 of or having to do with the first age or ages, especially of the world: *In its primeval state the earth was without any forms of life.* 2 ancient: *primeval forests untouched by the ax.* [< Latin *primaevus* early in life < *primus* first + *aevum* age] **—pri me′val ly,** *adv.*

prim ing (prī′ming), *n.* 1 powder or other material used to set fire to an explosive. 2 a first coat of paint, sizing, etc.

prim i tive (prim′ə tiv), *adj.* 1 of early times; of long ago: *Primitive people often lived in caves.* 2 first of the kind: *primitive Christians.* 3 very simple; such as people had early in human history: *A primitive way of making fire is by rubbing two sticks together.* 4 original; primary. *—n.* 1 artist belonging to an early period, especially before the Renaissance. 2 artist who does not use the techniques of perspective, shading, or the like in painting. 3 painting or other work of art produced by a primitive. 4 person living in a primitive society or in primitive times. [< Latin *primitivus* < *primus* first] **—prim′i tive ly,** *adv.* **—prim′i tive ness,** *n.*

pri mo gen i tor (prī′mə jen′ə tər), *n.* ancestor; forefather.

pri mo gen i ture (prī′mə jen′ə chůr, prī′mə jen′ə chər), *n.* 1 fact of being the first-born of the children of the same parents. 2 right or principle of inheritance or succession by the first-born, especially the inheritance of a family estate by the eldest son. [< Medieval Latin *primogenitura* < Latin *primo* firstly + *genitura* birth]

pri mor di al (prī môr′dē əl), *adj.* 1 existing at the very beginning; primitive. 2 original; elementary. [< Latin *primordium* beginning < *primus* first + *ordiri* begin] **—pri mor′di al ly,** *adv.*

primp (primp), *v.t.* dress (oneself) for show. *—v.i.* dress carefully. [origin uncertain]

prim rose (prim′rōz′), *n.* 1 any of a large genus of perennial plants with flowers of various colors. The common primrose of Europe is pale yellow. 2 the flower of any of these plants. 3 a pale yellow. *—adj.* pale-yellow. [< Medieval Latin *prima rosa* first rose]

primrose path, a pleasant way; path of pleasure.

pri mus in ter pa res (prī′məs in′tər pär′ēz′), LATIN. first among his peers.

prin., principal.

prince (prins), *n.* 1 a male member of a royal family, especially a son of a king or queen, or a son of a king's or queen's son. 2 sovereign. 3 ruler of a small state or country subordinate to a king or emperor. 4 the English equivalent of certain titles of nobility of varying importance or rank in other countries. 5 the greatest or best of a group; chief: *a merchant prince.* [< Old French < Latin *principem* ruler, chief, one who takes first place < *primus* first + *capere* to take]

Prince Albert, a long, double-breasted coat.

Prince Charming, 1 the fairy-tale prince who marries Cinderella. 2 an ideal type of man; a perfect suitor.

prince consort, prince who is the husband of a queen or empress ruling in her own right.

prince dom (prins′dəm), *n.* 1 territory ruled by a prince. 2 title or rank of a prince.

Prince Edward Island, province in E Canada consisting of an island in the Gulf of St. Lawrence, just north of Nova Scotia. 111,000 pop.; 2200 sq. mi. *Capital:* Charlottetown. *Abbrev.:* P.E.I.

prince ling (prins′ling), *n.* a young, little, or petty prince.

prince ly (prins′lē), *adj.,* **-li er, -li est.** 1 of a prince or his rank; royal. 2 like a prince; noble. 3 fit for a prince; magnificent. **—prince′li ness,** *n.*

Prince of Darkness, the Devil; Satan.

Prince of Peace, Jesus.

Prince of Wales, title conferred on the eldest son, or heir apparent, of the British sovereign.

prince royal, the oldest son of a king or queen.

prin cess (prin′ses, prin′sis, prin ses′), *n.* 1 a female member of a royal family, especially a daughter of a king or queen, or a daughter of a king's or queen's son. 2 wife or widow of a prince. 3 woman having the rank of a prince.

prin cesse (prin ses′, prin′ses, prin′sis), *adj.* (of a woman's clothing) one-piece and close-fitting with a flaring skirt and vertical seams. [< French]

princess royal, the oldest daughter of a king or queen.

Prince ton (prins′tən), *n.* 1 town in central New Jersey. Washington defeated the British there in 1777. 12,000. 2 university located there.

prin ci pal (prin′sə pəl), *adj.* most important; main; chief: *Chicago is the principal city of Illinois.* *—n.* 1 a chief person; one who gives orders. 2 the head, or one of the heads, of an elementary or secondary school. 3 sum of money on which interest is paid. 4 money or property from which income or interest is received. 5 person who hires another person to act for him. 6 person directly responsible for a crime. 7 person responsible for the payment of a debt that another person has endorsed. [< Latin *principalis* < *principem* chief. See PRINCE.]

➤ **Principal, principle** are often confused in spelling even though they have entirely different meanings. *Principal* as an adjective means chief *(a principal ally)* and as a noun, chief person or head *(the school principal). Principle* is used only as a noun, meaning a basic truth or belief *(the principles of democracy),* or a rule of conduct *(Good character depends upon high principles).*

prin ci pal i ty (prin′sə pal′ə tē), *n., pl.* **-ties.** 1 a small state or country ruled by a prince. 2 country from which a prince gets his title. 3 supreme power.

prin ci pal ly (prin′sə pə lē), *adv.* for the most part; above all; chiefly; mainly. See **especially** for synonym study.

principal parts, the main parts of a verb, from which the rest can be derived. In English the principal parts are the present infinitive, past tense or preterit, and past participle. EXAMPLES: go, went, gone; do, did, done; drive, drove, driven; push, pushed, pushed.

prin ci pal ship (prin′sə pəl ship), *n.* position or office of a principal.

prin ci pate (prin′sə pāt), *n.* 1 a chief place or authority. 2 principality. 3 the period of the ancient Roman Empire when Augustus and his successors ruled as republican heads of the Senate.

prin ci ple (prin′sə pəl), *n.* 1 a fundamental, primary, or general truth on which other truths depend: *the principles of democratic government.* 2 a fundamental belief: *religious principles.* 3 an accepted or professed rule of action or conduct: *I make it a principle to save some money each week.* 4 uprightness; honor: *George Washington was a man of principle.* 5 rule of science explaining how something works: *the principle of the lever.* 6 method of operation of a machine, etc. 7 a first cause or force; source; origin. 8 one of the elements that compose a substance, especially one that gives some special quality or effect: *the bitter principle in a drug.* 9 an original tendency or faculty; natural or innate disposition. 10 **in principle,** as regards the general truth or rule: *approve something in principle.* 11 **on principle, a** according to a certain principle. **b** for reasons of right conduct. [< Old French *principe* < Latin *principium* beginning, origin < *principem* chief. See PRINCE.] ➤ See **principal** for usage note.

prink (pringk), *v.t., v.i.* primp. [origin uncertain] **—prink′er,** *n.*

print (print), *v.t.* 1 use type, blocks, plates, etc., to stamp in ink or dye (letters, words, pictures, designs, etc.) on paper or the like. 2 stamp letters, words, etc., on (paper or the like) with type, etc., and ink or dye. 3 cause to be printed; publish: *print books.* 4 make with words or letters the way they look in print instead of in writing: *Print your name clearly.* 5 mark (cloth, paper, etc.) with patterns or designs: *a machine that prints wallpaper.* 6 produce (marks or figures) by pressure; stamp. 7 fix (in the heart, mind, or memory); impress. 8 produce a photograph by transmission of light through (a negative). 9 **print out,** (of a computer) produce (information or output) in printed or readable form. *—v.i.* 1 produce books, newspapers, etc., by a printing press. 2 make letters or words the way they look in print instead of in writing. 3 take an impression from type, etc. 4 (of

prism (def. 1) prism (def. 2)

type, a block, etc.) give an impression on paper, etc. 5 be a printer; use a press in printing.
—*n.* 1 printed words, letters, etc.: *This book has clear print.* 2 printed condition: *put an article in print.* 3 a printed publication; newspaper or magazine. 4 an edition or impression of a book, etc., made at one time. 5 cloth with a pattern printed on it. 6 dress made of such cloth. 7 the pattern or design so printed. 8 picture or design printed from an engraved block, plate, etc.: *prints of racehorses.* 9 mark made by pressing or stamping: *the print of a foot in the ground.* 10 something that prints; stamp; die. 11 something that has been marked or shaped by pressing or stamping. 12 photograph produced from a negative. 13 **in print,** (of books, etc.) still available for purchase from the publisher. 14 **out of print,** no longer sold by the publisher. [< Old French *priente* an impression < *preindre* to press < Latin *premere*]

print a ble (prin′tə bəl), *adj.* 1 capable of being printed. 2 capable of being printed from. 3 fit to be printed.

printed circuit, (in electronics) a circuit in which the components or connections are printed, painted, sprayed, etc., on an insulating surface with conducting materials such as silver or silver oxide.

print er (prin′tər), *n.* person whose business or work is printing or setting type.

printer's devil, a young helper or errand boy in a printing shop.

print er y (prin′tər ē), *n., pl.* **-er ies.** shop where printing is done.

print ing (prin′ting), *n.* 1 the producing of books, newspapers, etc., by impression with ink or dye from movable type, plates, etc. 2 printed words, letters, etc. 3 all the copies printed at one time. 4 letters made like those in print.

printing press, machine for printing from movable type, plates, etc.

print out (print′out′), *n.* 1 the printed output of an electronic computer. 2 act of producing such an output.

pri or¹ (prī′ər), *adj.* 1 coming before; earlier: *I can't go with you because I have a prior engagement.* See **previous** for synonym study. 2 **prior to,** coming before in time, order, or importance; earlier than; before. [< Latin]

pri or² (prī′ər), *n.* head of a priory or monastery for men. Priors usually rank below abbots. [Old English < Medieval Latin, noun use of Latin *prior* prior¹]

pri or ate (prī′ər it), *n.* 1 office, rank, or time of service of a prior. 2 priory.

pri or ess (prī′ər is), *n.* woman at the head of a convent or priory for women. Prioresses usually rank below abbesses.

pri or i ty (prī ôr′ə tē, prī or′ə tē), *n., pl.* **-ties.** 1 a being earlier in time. 2 a coming before in order or importance: *Fire engines and ambulances have priority over other traffic.* 3 a governmental rating giving preference to persons or things in order of their importance to national defense or other essential affairs of state, etc.

pri or y (prī′ər ē), *n., pl.* **-or ies.** a religious house governed by a prior or prioress. A priory is often, but not necessarily, dependent on an abbey.

prise (prīz), *v.t.,* **prised, pris ing.** BRITISH. prize⁴.

prism (priz′əm), *n.* 1 a solid figure whose bases or ends have the same size and shape and are parallel to one another, and each of whose sides is a parallelogram. 2 a transparent body of this form, often of glass and usually with triangular ends, used for separating white light passing through it into its spectrum or for reflecting beams of light. [< Greek *prisma* something sawed off, prism < *priein* to saw]

pris mat ic (priz mat′ik), *adj.* 1 of or like a prism. 2 formed by a transparent prism. 3 varied in color; brilliant. **—pris mat′i cal ly,** *adv.*

prismatic colors, the seven colors formed when white light is passed through a prism; red, orange, yellow, green, blue, indigo, and violet. These are the colors of the spectrum.

pris on (priz′n), *n.* 1 a public building in which criminals are confined; jail or penitentiary. 2 any place where a person or animal is shut up against his will. 3 captivity or confinement; imprisonment. —*v.t.* imprison. [< Old French < Latin *prehensionem* seizure, arrest < *prehendere* seize] **—pris′on-like′,** *adj.*

pris on er (priz′n ər, priz′nər), *n.* 1 person who is under arrest or held in jail or prison. 2 person who is confined against his will or who is not free to move. 3 Also, **prisoner of war.** person taken by the enemy in war, especially a member of the armed forces who is captured by the enemy.

pris sy (pris′ē), *adj.,* **-si er, -si est.** INFORMAL. 1 too precise and fussy. 2 too easily shocked; overnice. [origin uncertain] **—pris′si ly,** *adv.* **—pris′si ness,** *n.*

pris tine (pris′tēn′, pris′tən, *or* pris′tīn), *adj.* as it was in its earliest time or state; original; primitive: *The colors of the paintings inside the pyramid had kept their pristine freshness in spite of their age.* [< Latin *pristinus*] **—pris′tine′ly,** *adv.*

prith ee (priᴛʜ′ē), *interj.* ARCHAIC. I pray thee; I ask you.

pri va cy (prī′və sē), *n., pl.* **-cies.** 1 condition of being private; being away from others; seclusion: *in the privacy of one's home.* 2 absence of publicity; secrecy: *I will keep what you tell me in strict privacy.*

pri vate (prī′vit), *adj.* 1 not for the public; for just a few special people or for one: *a private road, a private house, a private secretary.* 2 not public; individual; personal: *the private life of a famous person, my private opinion.* 3 secret; confidential: *News reached her through private channels.* 4 secluded: *some private corner.* 5 having no public office: *a private citizen.* —*n.* 1 soldier or marine of the lowest enlisted rank. 2 **in private, a** not publicly. **b** secretly. [< Latin *privatum* apart from the state, set apart, deprived < *privus* alone, individual, one's own. Doublet of PRIVY.] **—pri′vate ly,** *adv.* **—pri′vate ness,** *n.*

private enterprise, free enterprise.

pri va teer (prī′və tir′), *n.* 1 an armed ship owned by private persons and holding a government commission to attack and capture enemy ships. 2 commander or one of the crew of a privateer. —*v.i.* cruise as a privateer.

pri va teers man (prī′və tirz′mən), *n., pl.* **-men.** officer or sailor of a privateer.

private first class, soldier or marine ranking next below a corporal and next above a private.

hat, āge, fär; let, ēqual, tėrm;
it, īce; hot, ōpen, ôrder;
oil, out; cup, pu̇t, rüle;
ch, child; ng, long; sh, she;
th, thin; ᴛʜ, then; zh, measure;

ə represents *a* in about, *e* in taken,
i in pencil, *o* in lemon, *u* in circus.

< = from, derived from, taken from.

private school, U.S. an educational institution, as a preparatory school or parochial school, owned and operated by other than a government authority.

pri va tion (prī vā′shən), *n.* 1 lack of the comforts or of the necessities of life: *Many children were hungry and homeless because of privation during the war.* 2 a being deprived; loss; absence. [< Latin *privationem* < *privatum* deprived]

priv a tive (priv′ə tiv), in grammar: *—adj.* expressing deprivation or denial of something. *Un-* is a privative prefix. *Unwise* means *not wise.* —*n.* a privative word, prefix, or suffix.

priv et (priv′it), *n.* any of several shrubs much used for hedges. Some are evergreen. [origin uncertain]

priv i lege (priv′ə lij), *n., v.,* **-leged, -leg ing.** —*n.* a special right, advantage, or favor. See synonym study below. —*v.t.* give a privilege to. [< Latin *privilegium* law applying to one individual < *privus* individual + *lex, legis* law]

Syn. *n.* **Privilege, prerogative** mean a special right. **Privilege** means a benefit or advantage granted for any reason: *Alumni have the privilege of buying football tickets at special rates.* **Prerogative** refers to a right, often an official right, belonging to a person, class, or the like by reason of status of some kind: *The right to coin money is a prerogative of the state.*

priv i leged (priv′ə lijd), *adj.* 1 having some privilege or privileges: *The nobility of Europe was a privileged class.* 2 not subject to court action, as for slander: *Words spoken by a Senator on the Senate floor are privileged.*

priv i ly (priv′ə lē), *adv.* in a private manner; secretly.

priv y (priv′ē), *adj., n., pl.* **priv ies.** *—adj.* 1 private. 2 ARCHAIC. secret; hidden. 3 **privy to,** having secret or private knowledge of. —*n.* a small outhouse used as a toilet. [< Old French *prive* < Latin *privatum.* Doublet of PRIVATE.]

privy council, 1 group of personal advisers to a ruler. 2 **Privy Council,** (in Great Britain) the group of persons acting as personal advisors to the sovereign in matters of state. **—privy councilor** or **privy councillor.**

privy seal, (in Great Britain) the seal affixed to grants, etc., that are afterwards to receive the great seal, and to documents that do not require the great seal.

prize¹ (prīz), *n.* 1 reward offered or won in a contest or competition; award: *Prizes will be given for the three best stories.* 2 reward worth working for. *—adj.* 1 awarded as a prize. 2 that has won a prize. 3 worthy of a prize: *prize vegetables.* [< Old French *pris* price < Latin *pretium*]

prize² (prīz), *n.* something or someone captured in war, especially an enemy's ship and its cargo taken at sea. [< Old French *prise* seizure < Latin *prensum* seized]

prize³ (prīz), *v.t.*, **prized, priz ing.** 1 value highly: *She prizes her best china.* 2 estimate the value of; appraise. [< Old French *prisier, preisier* to praise. See PRAISE.]

prize⁴ (prīz), *v.t.*, **prized, priz ing.** raise or move by force; pry. Also, BRITISH **prise.** [Middle English, a lever < Old French *prise* seizure. See PRIZE².]

prize fight (prīz′fīt′), *n.* a boxing match between professional boxers for money. **—prize′fight′er,** *n.* **—prize′fight′ing,** *n.*

prize ring, a square space enclosed by ropes, used for prizefights.

prize win ner (prīz′win′ər), *n.* person or thing that wins a prize.

prize win ning (prīz′win′ing), *adj.* that has won a prize: *a prizewinning novel.*

pro¹ (prō), *adv., n., pl.* **pros.** *—adv.* in favor of; for. *—n.* 1 reason in favor of. The pros and cons of a question are the arguments for and against it. 2 person who votes in favor of something. 3 an affirmative vote. [< Latin, for]

pro² (prō), *n., pl.* **pros,** *adj.* INFORMAL. professional.

pro-¹, *prefix.* 1 forward, as in *project.* 2 forth; out, as in *prolong, prolapse.* 3 on the side of; in favor of, as in *pro-British.* 4 in place of; acting as, as in *pronoun, proconsul.* [< Latin, forward, forth, for]

pro-², *prefix.* 1 before; preceding; prior to, as in *prologue.* 2 in front of; anterior, as in *prothorax, proscenium.* [< Greek]

PRO or **P.R.O.,** (in the armed forces) public relations officer.

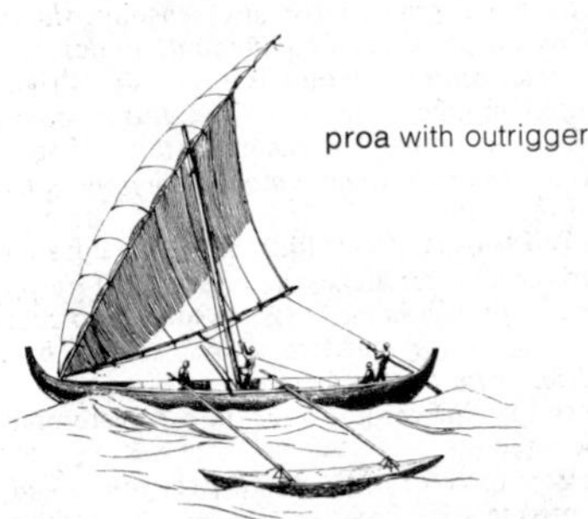

proa with outrigger

pro a (prō′ə), *n.* a swift Malay sailing boat built with one side flat and balanced by an outrigger. Also, **prau.** [< Malay *prau*]

prob a bil i ty (prob′ə bil′ə tē), *n., pl.* **-ties.** 1 quality or fact of being likely or probable; good chance: *There is a probability that school will close a week earlier than usual.* 2 **in all probability,** probably. 3 something likely to happen: *A storm is one of the probabilities for tomorrow.* 4 the likelihood that an event will occur, estimated as the ratio $\frac{p}{p+q}$, where p is the probable number of occurrences and q is the probable number of nonoccurrences.

prob a ble (prob′ə bəl), *adj.* 1 likely to happen: *Cooler weather is probable after this shower.* 2 likely to be true: *Indigestion is the probable cause of your pain.* [< Latin *probabilis* < *probare* to prove. See PROBE.] **—prob′a bly,** *adv.*

pro bate (prō′bāt), *n., adj., v.,* **-bat ed, -bat ing.** *—n.* 1 (in law) the official proving of a will as genuine. 2 a true copy of a will with a certificate that it has been proved genuine. *—adj.* of or concerned with the probating of wills and the settlement of the estates of dead persons: *a probate court, a probate judge.* *—v.t.* prove by legal process the genuineness of (a will). [< Latin *probatum* thing proved or made good < *probus* good]

pro ba tion (prō bā′shən), *n.* 1 trial or testing of conduct, character, qualifications, etc.: *After a period of probation a novice becomes a nun.* 2 system of letting young offenders against the law, or first offenders, go free under supervision without receiving the punishment which they are sentenced to unless there is a further offense. 3 status of an offender freed in this way.

pro ba tion al (prō bā′shə nəl), *adj.* probationary.

pro ba tion ar y (prō bā′shə ner′ē), *adj.* 1 of or having to do with probation. 2 on probation.

pro ba tion er (prō bā′shə nər), *n.* person who is on probation.

probation officer, officer appointed to supervise offenders who have been placed on probation.

pro ba tive (prō′bə tiv, prob′ə tiv), *adj.* 1 giving proof or evidence. 2 for a trial or test.

probe (prōb), *v.,* **probed, prob ing,** *n.* *—v.t.* 1 search into; examine thoroughly; investigate: *I probed my memory for her name.* 2 examine with a probe. *—v.i.* search; penetrate: *probe into the causes of a crime.* *—n.* 1 a thorough examination; investigation. 2 investigation, usually by a legislative body, in an effort to discover evidences of law violation. 3 a slender instrument with a rounded end for exploring the depth or direction of a wound, a cavity in the body, etc. 4 any of various electrical devices used to insert into or monitor areas not easily accessible. A Geiger counter uses a probe to detect radiation. 5 an unmanned spacecraft carrying scientific instruments to record or report back information about space, planets, etc.: *a lunar probe.* 6 the launching of such a spacecraft. [< Late Latin *proba* a proof < Latin *probare* prove < *probus* good. Doublet of PROOF.] **—prob′er,** *n.* **—prob′ing ly,** *adv.*

pro bi ty (prō′bə tē, prob′ə tē), *n.* high principle; uprightness; honesty. [< Latin *probitatem* < *probus* good]

prob lem (prob′ləm), *n.* 1 question, especially a difficult question. 2 a matter of doubt or difficulty. 3 something to be worked out: *a problem in arithmetic.* *—adj.* that causes difficulty: *a problem child.* [< Greek *problēma* < *proballein* propose, throw forward < *pro-* forward + *ballein* to throw]

prob lem at ic (prob′lə mat′ik), *adj.* having the nature of a problem; doubtful; uncertain; questionable: *What the weather will be is often problematic.* **—prob′lem at′i cal ly,** *adv.*

prob lem at i cal (prob′lə mat′ə kəl), *adj.* problematic.

pro bos cis (prō bos′is), *n.* 1 an elephant's trunk. 2 a long, flexible snout, like that of the tapir. 3 the tubelike mouth parts of some insects, such as flies or mosquitoes, developed for piercing or sucking. [< Greek *proboskis* < *pro-* forth + *boskein* to feed]

pro caine hydrochloride (prō′kān), drug used as a local anesthetic, in medicine and dentistry; Novocaine. *Formula:* $C_{13}H_{20}N_2O_2 \cdot HCl$

pro ce dur al (prə sē′jər əl), *adj.* of or having to do with procedure.

pro ce dure (prə sē′jər), *n.* 1 way of proceeding; method of doing things: *What is your procedure in making bread?* 2 the customary manners or ways of conducting business: *parliamentary procedure, legal procedure.*

pro ceed (prə sēd′), *v.i.* 1 go on after a stop or interruption; move forward; continue: *Please proceed with your story.* See **advance** for synonym study. 2 be carried on; take place: *The trial may proceed.* 3 carry on any activity: *He proceeded to light his pipe.* 4 come forth; issue; go out: *Heat proceeds from fire.* 5 begin and carry on an action at law. [< Latin *procedere* < *pro-* forward + *cedere* to move] **—pro ceed′er,** *n.*

pro ceed ing (prə sē′ding), *n.* 1 what is done; action; conduct. 2 **proceedings,** *pl.* **a** action in a case in a court of law. **b** record of what was done at the meetings of a society, club, etc.

pro ceeds (prō′sēdz′), *n.pl.* money obtained from a sale, auction, etc.: *The proceeds from the school play will be used to buy a new curtain for the stage.*

proc ess (pros′es, prō′ses), *n.* 1 set of actions, changes, or operations occurring or performed in a special order toward some result: *the process of breathing, a new manufacturing process.* 2 course of action; procedure: *the democratic process.* 3 part that grows out or projects: *the process of a bone.* 4 a written command or summons to appear in a court of law. 5 the proceedings in a legal course or action. 6 **in process, a** in the course or condition: *In process of time the house will be finished.* **b** in the course or condition of being done: *The author has just finished one book and has another in process.* *—v.t.* treat or prepare by some special method. *—adj.* treated or prepared by some special method. [< Old French < Latin *processus* progress < *procedere.* See PROCEED.] **—proc′es sor,** *n.*

pro ces sion (prə sesh′ən), *n.* 1 something that moves forward; persons marching or riding: *a funeral procession.* 2 an orderly moving forward: *march in procession onto the platform.*

pro ces sion al (prə sesh′ə nəl), *adj.* 1 of a procession. 2 used or sung in a procession. *—n.* 1 processional music. 2 book containing hymns, etc., for use in religious processions. **—pro ces′sion al ly,** *adv.*

process server, person who serves summonses, subpoenas, etc.

pro claim (prə klām′), *v.t.* make known publicly and officially; declare publicly: *War was proclaimed. The people proclaimed him king.* See **announce** for synonym study. [< Latin *proclamare* < *pro-* forth + *clamare* to shout] **—pro claim′er,** *n.*

proc la ma tion (prok′lə mā′shən), *n.* an official announcement; public declaration: *the President's annual Thanksgiving proclamation.*

Syn. Proclamation, edict mean a notice or order issued by authority. **Proclamation**

proboscis (def. 2) monkey with a proboscis

hat, āge, fär; let, ēqual, tėrm;
it, īce; hot, ōpen, ôrder;
oil, out; cup, pu̇t, rüle;
ch, child; ng, long; sh, she;
th, thin; ᴛʜ, then; zh, measure;

ə represents *a* in about, *e* in taken, *i* in pencil, *o* in lemon, *u* in circus.

< = from, derived from, taken from.

means an official public announcement by an executive or administrative officer, such as a president, governor, or mayor: *Lincoln issued a proclamation declaring the emancipation of slaves.* **Edict** means a public order or decree proclaimed by the highest authority, usually a ruler or court with supreme or absolute authority: *The dictator issued an edict ordering seizure of the mines.*

pro cliv i ty (prō kliv′ə tē), *n., pl.* **-ties.** tendency; inclination. [< Latin *proclivitatem* < *proclivis* sloping forward < *pro-* forward + *clivus* slope]

pro con sul (prō kon′səl), *n.* 1 governor or military commander of an ancient Roman province with duties and powers like a consul's. 2 governor of a colony or other dependent territory, especially during British or French colonial expansion.

pro con su lar (prō kon′sə lər), *adj.* of, having to do with, or governed by a proconsul.

pro con su late (prō kon′sə lit), *n.* position or term of a proconsul.

pro con sul ship (prō kon′səl ship), *n.* proconsulate.

pro cras ti nate (prō kras′tə nāt), *v.i., v.t.,* **-nat ed, -nat ing.** put things off until later; delay, especially repeatedly. [< Latin *procrastinatum* postponed, ultimately < *pro-* forward + *cras* tomorrow] **—pro cras′ti na′tion,** *n.* **—pro cras′ti na′tor,** *n.*

pro cre ate (prō′krē āt), *v.,* **-at ed, -at ing.** *—v.t.* 1 become father to; beget. 2 bring into being; produce. *—v.i.* produce offspring; reproduce. [< Latin *procreatum* produced < *pro-* forth + *creatum* created] **—pro′cre a′tion,** *n.* **—pro′cre a′tor,** *n.*

pro cre a tive (prō′krē ā′tiv), *adj.* 1 producing offspring; begetting. 2 of or having to do with procreation.

Pro crus te an (prō krus′tē ən), *adj.* 1 of or having to do with Procrustes or his bed. 2 tending to produce conformity by violent or arbitrary means.

Pro crus tes (prō krus′tēz), *n.* (in Greek legends) a robber who stretched his victims or cut off their legs to make them fit the length of his bed.

proc tor (prok′tər), *n.* official in a university or school designated to supervise students, especially during an examination. *—v.t.* serve as a proctor at (an examination). [short for *procurator*]

proc to ri al (prok tôr′ē əl, prok tōr′ē əl), *adj.* of or having to do with a proctor.

proc tor ship (prok′tər ship), *n.* position of a proctor.

pro cum bent (prō kum′bənt), *adj.* 1 lying face down; prone; prostrate. 2 (of a plant or stem) lying or trailing along the ground but not sending down roots. [< Latin *procumbentem* leaning forward < *pro-* forward + *-cumbere* lie down]

proc u ra tor (prok′yə rā′tər), *n.* 1 person employed to manage the affairs of another or to act for another; agent. 2 a financial agent or administrator in an imperial Roman province.

pro cure (prə kyu̇r′), *v.t.,* **-cured, -cur ing.** 1 obtain by care or effort; secure: *procure a job.* 2 bring about; cause: *procure a person's death.* [< Latin *procurare* manage < *pro-* before + *cura* care] **—pro cur′a ble,** *adj.* **—pro cure′ment,** *n.*

pro cur er (prə kyu̇r′ər), *n.* 1 person who procures. 2 a pander.

pro cur ess (prə kyu̇r′is), *n.* a woman procurer.

Pro cy on (prō′sē on), *n.* star of the first magnitude in the constellation Canis Minor.

prod (prod), *v.,* **prod ded, prod ding,** *n.* *—v.t.* 1 poke or jab with something pointed: *prod an animal with a stick.* 2 stir up; urge on: *The lateness of the hour prodded me to finish quickly.* *—n.* 1 poke; thrust. 2 a sharp-pointed stick; goad. 3 words, actions, or feelings that prod. [origin uncertain] **—prod′der,** *n.*

prod i gal (prod′ə gəl), *adj.* 1 given to extravagant or reckless spending; wasteful: *a prodigal son.* 2 abundant; lavish: *God's prodigal mercies.* *—n.* person who is wasteful or extravagant; spendthrift. [< Latin *prodigus* wasteful < *prodigere* drive forth, squander < *prod-, pro-* forth + *agere* to drive] **—prod′i gal ly,** *adv.*

prod i gal i ty (prod′ə gal′ə tē), *n., pl.* **-ties.** 1 wasteful or reckless extravagance. 2 rich abundance; profuseness.

pro di gious (prə dij′əs), *adj.* 1 very great; huge; vast: *The ocean contains a prodigious amount of water.* 2 wonderful; marvelous. [< Latin *prodigiosus* < *prodigium* prodigy, omen] **—pro di′gious ly,** *adv.* **—pro di′gious ness,** *n.*

prod i gy (prod′ə jē), *n., pl.* **-gies.** 1 person endowed with amazing brilliance, talent, etc., especially a remarkably talented child: *a musical prodigy.* 2 a marvelous example: *Samson performed prodigies of strength.* 3 a wonderful sign or omen: *An eclipse of the sun seemed a prodigy to early man.* [< Latin *prodigium* omen]

pro duce (*v.* prə düs′, prə dyüs′; *n.* prod′üs, prod′yüs; prō′düs, prō′dyüs), *v.,* **-duced, -duc ing,** *n.* *—v.t.* 1 bring into existence by labor or effort; create: *produce a work of art.* 2 make from raw or other material; manufacture: *produce steel.* 3 yield, furnish, or supply: *produce hydroelectric power, produce a profit.* 4 cause to grow; raise: *produce vegetables.* 5 bring forth; bear: *produce young.* 6 bring about; cause: *Hard work produces success.* 7 bring forward; show: *Produce your proof.* 8 bring (a play, etc.) before the public. 9 extend; continue (a line or plane). *—v.i.* bring forth or yield offspring, crops, products, dividends, interest, etc. *—n.* farm products, especially fruits and vegetables. [< Latin *producere* < *pro-* forth + *ducere* bring]

pro duc er (prə dü′sər, prə dyü′sər), *n.* 1 person or thing that produces, especially one that grows or manufactures things that are used by others. 2 person who has charge of the production of motion pictures, plays, or radio or television shows.

producer gas, gas that is a mixture of carbon monoxide, hydrogen, and nitrogen, made by partial combustion of coke or coal. It is used mainly as an industrial fuel.

producer goods, goods used in the production of other goods such as machinery, tools, timber, and ore.

pro duc i ble (prə dü′sə bəl, prə dyü′sə bəl), *adj.* capable of being produced.

prod uct (prod′əkt), *n.* 1 that which is produced; result of work or of growth: *factory products, farm products.* 2 number or quantity resulting from multiplying two or more numbers together: *40 is the product of 8 and 5.* 3 substance obtained from one or more other substances as a result of chemical reaction.

pro duc tion (prə duk′shən), *n.* 1 act of producing; creation; manufacture: *the production of automobiles.* 2 something produced; product: *the yearly production of a farm.* 3 amount produced: *a decline in production.* 4 an artistic work: *a literary production.* 5 presentation of a play, etc.: *a lavish Broadway production.*

pro duc tive (prə duk′tiv), *adj.* 1 producing abundantly; fertile: *a productive farm, a productive writer.* See **fertile** for synonym study. 2 producing food or other articles of commerce: *Farming is productive labor.* 3 bringing forth; producing: *That field is productive only of weeds. Hasty words are productive of quarrels.* 4 used in forming new words: *-able is a productive suffix.* **—pro duc′tive ly,** *adv.* **—pro duc′tive ness,** *n.*

pro duc tiv i ty (prō′duk tiv′ə tē), *n.* power to produce; productiveness.

pro em (prō′em), *n.* introduction; preface. [< Latin *proemium* < Greek *prooimion* < *pro-* before + *oimē* song]

prof (prof), *n.* INFORMAL. professor.

prof. or **Prof.,** professor.

prof a na tion (prof′ə nā′shən), *n.* act of profaning.

pro fan a to ry (prə fan′ə tôr′ē, prə fan′ə tōr′ē), *adj.* profaning.

pro fane (prə fān′), *adj., v.,* **-faned, -fan ing.** *—adj.* 1 characterized by contempt or disregard for God or holy things; irreverent: *a profane man, profane language.* 2 not sacred; worldly; secular: *profane literature.* 3 ritually unclean or polluted. *—v.t.* 1 treat (holy things) with contempt or disregard; desecrate: *Soldiers profaned the church when they stabled their horses in it.* 2 put to wrong or unworthy use. [< Latin *profanus* not sacred < *pro-* in front (outside) of + *fanum* temple, shrine] **—pro fane′ly,** *adv.* **—pro fane′ness,** *n.* **—pro fan′er,** *n.*

pro fan i ty (prə fan′ə tē), *n., pl.* **-ties.** 1 use of profane language; swearing. 2 a being profane. 3 profane conduct or language.

pro fess (prə fes′), *v.t.* 1 lay claim to; pretend; claim: *profess innocence, profess to be an expert.* 2 declare one's belief in: *Christians profess Christ and the Christian religion.* 3 declare openly: *profess one's loyalty to one's country.* 4 have as one's profession or business: *profess law.* [< Latin *professum* confessed, professed < *pro-* forth + *fateri* confess]

pro fessed (prə fest′), *adj.* 1 avowed or acknowledged; openly declared. 2 alleged; pretended. 3 having taken the vows of, or been received into, a religious order.

pro fess ed ly (prə fes′id lē), *adv.* 1 avowedly. 2 ostensibly.

pro fes sion (prə fesh′ən), *n.* 1 occupation requiring special education, such as law, medicine, teaching, or the ministry. 2 any calling or occupation by which a person habitually earns his living: *a librarian by profession, the acting profession.* 3 people engaged in such an occupation. 4 act of professing; open declaration: *a profession of* *friendship.* 5 declaration of belief in a religion. 6 religion or faith professed. 7 taking the vows and entering a religious order.

pro fes sion al (prə fesh′ə nəl), *adj.* 1 of or having to do with a profession; appropriate to a profession: *a doctor's professional manner.* 2 engaged in a profession: *a professional man.* 3 following an occupation as one's profession or career: *a professional soldier, a professional writer.* 4 earning a living from something that others do for pleasure: *a professional ballplayer.* 5 undertaken or engaged in by professionals rather than amateurs: *a professional ball game.* 6 involved in an activity as if it were a profession: *a professional busybody.* —*n.* 1 person who earns a living from something that others do for pleasure. 2 person engaged in a profession. —**pro fes′sion al ly,** *adv.*

pro fes sion al ism (prə fesh′ə nə liz′əm), *n.* 1 professional character, spirit, or methods. 2 the standing, practice, or methods of a professional, as distinguished from those of an amateur.

pro fes sion al ize (prə fesh′ə nə līz), *v.t., v.i.,* **-ized, -iz ing.** make or become professional.

pro fes sor (prə fes′ər), *n.* 1 teacher of the highest rank in a college or university. 2 INFORMAL. teacher. 3 person who professes.

pro fes sor ate (prə fes′ər it), *n.* 1 office or term of service of a professor. 2 group of professors.

pro fes so ri al (prō′fə sôr′ē əl, prō′fə sōr′ē əl; prof′ə sôr′ē əl, prof′ə sōr′ē əl), *adj.* of, having to do with, or characteristic of a professor. —**pro′fes so′ri al ly,** *adv.*

pro fes sor ship (prə fes′ər ship), *n.* position or rank of a professor.

prof fer (prof′ər), *v.t.* offer for acceptance; present; tender: *We proffered regrets at having to leave so early.* See **offer** for synonym study. —*n.* an offer made: *Her proffer of advice was accepted.* [< Anglo-French *proffrir* < Old French *pro-* forth + *offrir* to offer]

pro fi cien cy (prə fish′ən sē), *n., pl.* **-cies.** a being proficient; knowledge; skill; advanced state of expertness.

pro fi cient (prə fish′ənt), *adj.* advanced in any art, science, or subject; skilled; expert: *She was very proficient in music.* See **expert** for synonym study. [< Latin *proficientem* making progress < *pro-* forward + *facere* to make] —**pro fi′cient ly,** *adv.*

profile (def. 1) of Queen Victoria

pro file (prō′fīl), *n., v.,* **-filed, -fil ing.** —*n.* 1 a side view, especially of a human face. 2 outline. See **outline** for synonym study. 3 a drawing of a transverse vertical section of a building, bridge, etc. 4 a concise description of a person's abilities, personality, or career. —*v.t.* 1 draw a profile of. 2 write a profile of. [< Italian *profilo* < *profilare* draw in outline < Latin *pro-* forth + *filum* thread]

prof it (prof′it), *n.* 1 Often, **profits,** *pl.* the gain from a business; what is left when the cost of goods and of carrying on the business is subtracted from the amount of money taken in. 2 any gain resulting in mental or spiritual betterment; advantage; benefit: *What profit is there in worrying?* See **advantage** for synonym study. —*v.i.* 1 make a gain from a business; make a profit. 2 get advantage; gain; benefit: *A wise person profits by his mistakes.* —*v.t.* be an advantage or benefit (to). [< Old French < Latin *profectus* advance < *proficere* make progress < *pro-* forward + *facere* to make] —**prof′it er,** *n.* —**prof′it less,** *adj.*

prof it a ble (prof′ə tə bəl), *adj.* 1 yielding a financial profit. 2 giving a gain or benefit; useful. —**prof′it a ble ness,** *n.* —**prof′it a bly,** *adv.*

prof it eer (prof′ə tir′), *n.* person who makes an unfair profit by charging excessive prices for scarce goods. —*v.i.* seek or make unfair profits.

profit sharing, the sharing of profits between employer and employees.

prof li ga cy (prof′lə gə sē), *n.* 1 great wickedness; vice. 2 reckless extravagance.

prof li gate (prof′lə git), *adj.* 1 very wicked; shamelessly bad. 2 recklessly extravagant. —*n.* person who is very wicked or extravagant. [< Latin *profligatum* ruined < *pro-* forth + *fligere* to strike, dash] —**prof′li gate ly,** *adv.*

pro for ma (prō fôr′mə), LATIN. for the sake of form; as a matter of form.

pro found (prə found′), *adj.* 1 very deep: *a profound sigh, a profound sleep.* 2 deeply felt; very great: *profound despair, profound sympathy.* 3 going far deeper than what is easily understood; having or showing great knowledge or understanding: *a profound book, a profound thinker, a profound thought.* 4 low; carried far down; going far down: *a profound bow.* [< Latin *profundus* < *pro-* before + *fundus* bottom] —**pro found′ly,** *adv.* —**pro found′ness,** *n.*

pro fun di ty (prə fun′də tē), *n., pl.* **-ties.** 1 a being profound; great depth. 2 a very deep thing or place.

pro fuse (prə fyüs′), *adj.* 1 very abundant: *profuse thanks.* 2 spending or giving freely; lavish; extravagant. [< Latin *profusum* poured forth + *pro-* forth + *fundere* pour] —**pro fuse′ly,** *adv.* —**pro fuse′ness,** *n.*

pro fu sion (prə fyü′zhən), *n.* 1 great abundance. 2 extravagance; lavishness.

pro gen i tor (prō jen′ə tər), *n.* ancestor in the direct line; forefather.

prog e ny (proj′ə nē), *n., pl.* **-nies.** children or offspring; descendants. [< Latin *progenies,* ultimately < *pro-* forth + *gignere* beget]

pro ges te rone (prō jes′tə rōn′), *n.* hormone secreted by the corpus luteum that makes the lining of the uterus more ready to receive a fertilized ovum. [< *pro-*[1] + *ge(station)* + *ster(ol)* + *(horm)one*]

prog na thous (prog′nə thəs, prog nā′thəs), *adj.* (of a skull or a person) having the jaws protruding beyond the upper part of the face. [< *pro-* forward + Greek *gnathos* jaw]

prog no sis (prog nō′sis), *n., pl.* **-ses** (-sēz′). 1 forecast of the probable course of a disease. 2 estimate of what will probably happen. [< Greek *prognōsis* < *pro-* before + *gignōskein* recognize]

prog nos tic (prog nos′tik), *adj.* indicating something in the future. —*n.* 1 indication; sign. 2 forecast; prediction.

prog nos ti cate (prog nos′tə kāt), *v.t.,* **-cat ed, -cat ing.** 1 predict from facts; forecast. 2 indicate beforehand. —**prog nos′ti ca′tion,** *n.* —**prog nos′ti ca′tor,** *n.*

pro gram (prō′gram, prō′grəm), *n., v.,* **-gramed, -gram ing** or **-grammed, -gram ming.** —*n.* 1 list of scheduled items, events, performers, etc.: *a concert program, the program of a meeting.* 2 items composing an entertainment; performance: *The entire program was delightful.* 3 plan or outline of any undertaking: *a school program, a business program, a government program.* 4 set of instructions for an electronic computer or other automatic machine outlining the steps to be performed by the machine in a specific operation. 5 (in programed instruction) a series of statements and questions to each of which a student is required to respond before he can go on to the next and usually more difficult level. —*v.t.* 1 arrange or enter in a program. 2 draw up a program or plan for. 3 prepare a set of instructions for (a computer or other automatic machine). 4 arrange programed instruction for (a teaching machine, textbook, etc.). Also, BRITISH **programme.** [< Greek *programma* proclamation, ultimately < *pro-* forth + *graphein* write] —**pro′gram′mer,** *n.*

programed instruction, a progressive sequence of written material presented in small units which a student must learn before being allowed to read the next unit. Programed instruction is used especially in teaching machines.

pro gramme (prō′gram, prō′grəm), *n., v.t.,* **-grammed, -gram ming.** BRITISH. program.

prog ress (*n.* prog′res; *v.* prə gres′), *n.* 1 an advance or growth; development; improvement: *the progress of science.* 2 a moving forward; going ahead: *make rapid progress on a journey.* 3 an official journey or tour, as by royalty. —*v.i.* 1 get better; advance; develop: *We progress in learning step by step.* 2 move forward; go ahead. [< Latin *progressus,* ultimately < *pro-* forward + *gradi* to walk]

pro gres sion (prə gresh′ən), *n.* 1 a progressing; a moving forward; going ahead: *Creeping is a slow method of progression.* 2 (in mathematics) a sequence of quantities in which there is always the same relation between each quantity and the one succeeding it. 2, 4, 6, 8, 10 are in arithmetical progression. 2, 4, 8, 16, 32 are in geometrical progression.

pro gres sive (prə gres′iv), *adj.* 1 making progress; advancing to something better; improving: *a progressive nation.* 2 favoring progress; wanting improvement or reform in government, business, etc. 3 moving forward; developing: *a progressive disease.* 4 going from one to the next; passing on successively from one member of a series to the next. 5 of, following, or based on the theories and practices of progressive education: *a progressive school.* 6 (in grammar) showing the action as going on. *Is reading, was reading,* and *has been reading* are progressive forms of *read.* 7 **Progressive,** of a Progressive Party. 8 increasing in proportion to the increase of something else: *A progressive income tax is one whose rate goes up as a person's earnings increase.* —*n.* 1 **a** person who favors improvement and reform in government, religion, or business, etc. **b** progressivist. 2 **Progressive,** member of a Progressive Party. —**pro gres′sive ly,** *adv.* —**pro gres′sive ness,** *n.*

progressive education, system of education characterized by fitting a course of study to the abilities and interests of the pupils rather than fitting the pupils to a given curriculum.

Progressive Party, 1 a political party formed in 1912 under the leadership of Theodore Roosevelt, advocating direct primaries, recall, woman suffrage, etc. It was also called the Bull Moose Party. 2 a similar political party organized in 1924 and led by Senator Robert M. La Follette. 3 a political party organized in 1948 and led by Henry A. Wallace.

pro gres siv ism (prə gres′ə viz′əm), *n.* 1 the principles and practices of progressives. 2 **Progressivism,** doctrines of a Progressive Party.

pro gres siv ist (prə gres′ə vist), *n.* 1 person who believes in progressive education. 2 a progressive.

pro hib it (prō hib′it), *v.t.* 1 forbid by law or authority: *Picking flowers in this park is prohibited.* See **forbid** for synonym study. 2 prevent: *Rainy weather and fog prohibited flying.* [< Latin *prohibitum* kept away < *pro-* away + *habere* to keep]

pro hi bi tion (prō′ə bish′ən), *n.* 1 act of prohibiting or forbidding. 2 law or order that prohibits. 3 law or laws against making or selling alcoholic liquors. National prohibition existed in the United States between 1920 and 1933. 4 period when national prohibition was in force in the United States.

pro hi bi tion ist (prō′ə bish′ə nist), *n.* person favoring laws against the manufacture and sale of alcoholic liquors.

pro hib i tive (prō hib′ə tiv), *adj.* enough to prohibit or prevent something: *prohibitive costs.* **—pro hib′i tive ly,** *adv.* **—pro hib′i tive ness,** *n.*

pro hib i to ry (prō hib′ə tôr′ē, prō hib′ə tōr′ē), *adj.* prohibitive.

proj ect (*n.* proj′ekt; *v.* prə jekt′), *n.* 1 a proposed plan or scheme: *Flying in a heavy machine was once thought an impossible project.* See **plan** for synonym study. 2 an undertaking; enterprise: *a research project.* 3 a special assignment planned and carried out by a student, a group of students, or an entire class. 4 U.S. group of apartment houses built and run as a unit, especially as part of public housing. *—v.t.* 1 plan, contrive, or devise: *project a tax decrease.* 2 throw or cast forward: *A cannon projects shells.* 3 cause to fall on a surface: *project a shadow. Motion pictures are projected on the screen.* 4 cause to stick out or protrude. 5 draw lines through (a point, line, figure, etc.) and reproduce it on a line, plane, or surface. 6 make a forecast for (something) on the basis of past performance. *—v.i.* stick out; protrude: *The rocky point projects far into the water.* [< Latin *projectum* thrown forward < *pro-* forward + *jacere* to throw] **—pro ject′a ble,** *adj.*

pro jec tile (prə jek′təl), *n.* any object that is thrown, hurled, or shot, such as a stone or bullet. *—adj.* 1 capable of being thrown, hurled, or shot: *projectile weapons.* 2 forcing forward; impelling: *a projectile force.*

pro jec tion (prə jek′shən), *n.* 1 part that projects or sticks out: *rocky projections on the face of a cliff.* 2 a sticking out. 3 a throwing or casting forward: *the projection of a shell from a cannon.* 4 representation, upon a flat surface, of all or part of the surface of the earth. 5 (in geometry) the projecting of a figure, etc., upon a line, plane, or surface. 6 a forming of projects or plans. 7 (in psychology) the treating of what is essentially subjective as objective and external; attributing one's own ideas, feelings, etc., to another person or group. 8 forecast made on the basis of past performance.

pro jec tion ist (prə jek′shə nist), *n.* 1 operator of a motion-picture projector. 2 operator of a television camera. 3 person who draws projections.

pro jec tive (prə jek′tiv), *adj.* 1 of, having to do with, or produced by projection. 2 projecting. **—pro jec′tive ly,** *adv.*

pro jec tor (prə jek′tər), *n.* 1 apparatus for projecting an image on a screen. 2 person who forms projects; schemer.

Pro ko fiev (prō kô′fyef), *n.* **Sergei Sergeyevich,** 1891-1953, Russian composer.

pro lac tin (prō lak′tən), *n.* hormone from the anterior part of the pituitary gland that induces the mammary glands to give milk.

pro lapse (prō laps′), *n., v.,* **-lapsed, -laps ing.** *—n.* the slipping out of an organ of the body from its normal position. *—v.i.* (of an organ) fall; slip out of place.

prolate
a prolate spheroid
AXIS

pro late (prō′lāt), *adj.* elongated in the direction of the polar diameter: *prolate spheroid.* [< Latin *prolatum* extended < *pro-* forth + *latum* brought]

pro le gom e na (prō′lə gom′ə nə), *n.pl.* of **pro le gom e non** (prō′lə gom′ə non), preliminary materials in a book, treatise, etc.; preface; introduction. [< Greek < *prolegein* say beforehand < *pro-* before + *legein* say]

pro le gom e nous (prō′lə gom′ə nəs), *adj.* of or having to do with prolegomena.

pro le tar i an (prō′lə ter′ē ən, prō′lə tar′ē ən), *adj.* of or belonging to the proletariat. *—n.* person belonging to the proletariat. [< Latin *proletarius* furnishing the state only with children < *proles* offspring < *pro-* forth + *alescere* grow]

pro le tar i at (prō′lə ter′ē ət, prō′lə tar′ē ət), *n.* 1 the lowest class in economic and social status, including all unskilled laborers, casual laborers, and tramps. 2 (in Europe) the working class, especially as contrasted formerly with slaves and serfs and now with the middle class.

pro lif e rate (prō lif′ə rāt′), *v.t., v.i.,* **-rat ed, -rat ing.** 1 grow or produce by multiplication of parts. 2 multiply; spread. **—pro lif′e ra′tion,** *n.*

pro lif er ous (prō lif′ər əs), *adj.* producing new individuals by budding, cell division, etc.

pro lif ic (prə lif′ik), *adj.* 1 producing offspring or fruit abundantly: *a prolific garden.* 2 highly productive; fertile: *a prolific imagination, a prolific writer.* 3 conducive to growth, fruitfulness, etc.: *a prolific climate.* [< Medieval Latin *prolificus* < Latin *proles* offspring + *facere* to make] **—pro lif′i cal ly,** *adv.* **—pro lif′ic ness,** *n.*

pro lix (prō liks′, prō′liks), *adj.* using too many words; too long; tedious; wordy. [< Latin *prolixum* stretched out, ultimately < *pro-* forth + *liquere* to flow] **—pro lix′ly,** *adv.* **—pro lix′ness,** *n.*

pro lix i ty (prō lik′sə tē), *n.* too great length; tedious length of speech or writing.

pro logue or **pro log** (prō′lôg, prō′log), *n.*

hat, āge, fär; let, ēqual, tėrm;
it, īce; hot, ōpen, ôrder;
oil, out; cup, pu̇t, rüle;
ch, child; ng, long; sh, she;
th, thin; ᴛʜ, then; zh, measure;

ə represents *a* in about, *e* in taken, *i* in pencil, *o* in lemon, *u* in circus.

< = from, derived from, taken from.

1 introduction to a novel, poem, or other literary work. 2 speech or poem addressed to the audience by one of the actors at the beginning of a play. 3 any introductory act or event. [< Greek *prologos* < *pro-* before + *logos* speech]

pro long (prə lông′, prə long′), *v.t.* make longer; extend in time or space; stretch, lengthen, or protract: *The author cleverly prolonged the suspense in his mystery novel. The dog uttered prolonged howls whenever the family left the house.* See **lengthen** for synonym study. [< Late Latin *prolongare* < *pro-* forth + *longus* long]

pro lon ga tion (prō′lông gā′shən, prō′long gā′shən), *n.* 1 a lengthening in time or space; extension: *the prolongation of one's school days by graduate study.* 2 added part.

prom (prom), *n.* INFORMAL. dance or ball given by a college or high-school class. [short for *promenade*]

prom e nade (prom′ə nād′, prom′ə näd′), *n., v.,* **-nad ed, -nad ing.** *—n.* 1 walk for pleasure or display: *a promenade in the park.* 2 a public place for such a walk: *Atlantic City has a promenade along the beach.* 3 dance or ball. 4 march of all the guests at the opening of a formal dance. *—v.i.* walk about or up and down for pleasure or for display: *promenade back and forth on a ship's deck.* *—v.t.* 1 walk through. 2 take on a promenade. [< French < *promener* take for a walk < Latin *prominare* drive on < *pro-* forward + *minare* to drive] **—prom′e nad′er,** *n.*

Pro me the an (prə mē′thē ən), *adj.* of, having to do with, or suggestive of Prometheus, especially in his skill or art; daringly original.

Pro me the us (prə mē′thē əs, prə mē′thüs), *n.* (in Greek myths) one of the Titans. He stole fire from heaven and taught men its use, for which Zeus punished him by chaining him to a rock.

pro me thi um (prə mē′thē əm), *n.* a radioactive rare-earth metallic element which is a product of the fission of uranium, thorium, and plutonium. *Symbol:* Pm; *atomic number* 61. See pages 326 and 327 for table. [< *Prometheus*]

prom i nence (prom′ə nəns), *n.* 1 quality or fact of being prominent, distinguished, or conspicuous: *the prominence of athletics in some schools.* 2 something that juts out or projects, especially upward; projection. 3 cloud of gas which erupts from the sun and

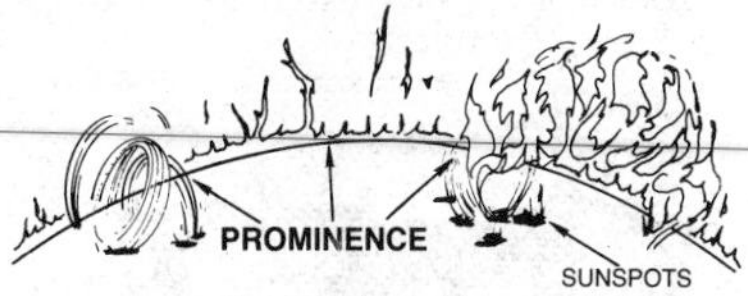

prominence (def. 3)
several types of prominences

is seen either as a projection from, or a dark spot on, the surface of the sun.

prom i nent (prom′ə nənt), *adj.* 1 well-known or important; distinguished: *a prominent citizen.* See **eminent** for synonym study. 2 that catches the eye; easy to see: *A single tree in a field is prominent.* See synonym study below. 3 standing out; projecting: *Some insects have prominent eyes.* [< Latin *prominentem* projecting < *pro-* forward + *minere* to jut] **—prom′i nent ly,** *adv.*

Syn. 2 **Prominent, conspicuous** mean attracting attention and easily seen. **Prominent** describes something that stands out from its surroundings or background in a very noticeable manner: *He hung her picture in a prominent position in the living room.* **Conspicuous** describes something so plainly visible or striking that it is impossible not to see it: *The uniformed soldier looked conspicuous among the group of civilians.*

prom is cu i ty (prom′i skyü′ə tē, prō′mi-skyü′ə tē), *n.* fact or condition of being promiscuous.

pro mis cu ous (prə mis′kyü əs), *adj.* 1 mixed and in disorder: *a promiscuous heap of clothing on your closet floor.* 2 making no distinctions; not discriminating. 3 not confining one's sexual relationships to one person. 4 INFORMAL. casual. [< Latin *promiscuus* < *pro-* forth + *miscere* to mix] **—pro mis′cu ous ly,** *adv.* **—pro mis′cu-ous ness,** *n.*

prom ise (prom′is), *n., v.,* **-ised, -is ing.** *—n.* 1 words said or written, binding a person to do or not to do something; pledge: *keep a promise to help.* 2 indication of what may be expected: *The clouds give promise of rain.* 3 indication of future excellence; something that gives hope of success: *a young scholar who shows promise.* *—v.i.* give one's word; make a promise: *I promise to wait for you.* *—v.t.* 1 make a promise of: *promise help to a friend.* 2 obligate oneself by a promise to: *promise a friend to help.* 3 give indication of; give hope of: *The rainbow promises fair weather tomorrow.* [< Latin *promissum* < *promittere* send before, promise < *pro-* before + *mittere* send] **—prom′is er,** *n.*

Promised Land, 1 (in the Bible) the country promised by God to Abraham and his descendants; Canaan. 2 **promised land,** a place or condition of expected happiness: *America has been a promised land for many immigrants.* 3 heaven.

prom is ing (prom′ə sing), *adj.* likely to turn out well; hopeful: *a promising beginning.* **—prom′is ing ly,** *adv.*

prom is so ry (prom′ə sôr′ē, prom′ə-sōr′ē), *adj.* containing a promise.

promissory note, a written promise to pay a stated sum of money to a certain person at a certain time.

prom on to ry (prom′ən tôr′ē, prom′ən-tōr′ē), *n., pl.* **-ries.** 1 a high point of land extending from the coast into the water; headland. 2 (in anatomy) part that bulges out. [< Latin *promonturium* < *pro-* forward + *montem* mountain]

promontory (def. 1)

pronghorn—3 ft. high at the shoulder

pro mote (prə mōt′), *v.t.,* **-mot ed, -mot ing.** 1 raise in rank, condition, or importance; elevate: *Pupils who pass the test will be promoted to the next higher grade.* 2 help to develop or establish; cause to advance; further: *promote peace.* See synonym study below. 3 help to organize; start: *Several bankers promoted the new company.* 4 further the sale of (an article) by advertising. [< Latin *promotum* moved forward < *pro-* forward + *movere* to move] **—pro-mot′a ble,** *adj.*

Syn. 2 **Promote, further** mean to help something move toward a desired end. **Promote** applies to any phase or stage of development, including the initial one: *These scholarships will promote better understanding of Latin America.* **Further** applies especially to any stage beyond the initial one: *Getting a scholarship will further her education.*

pro mot er (prə mō′tər), *n.* 1 person or thing that furthers or encourages. 2 one who organizes new companies and secures capital for them.

pro mo tion (prə mō′shən), *n.* 1 advancement in rank or importance: *The clerk was given a promotion and an increase in salary.* 2 act of promoting: *the promotion of a health campaign, promotion of a new company.*

pro mo tion al (prə mō′shə nəl), *adj.* having to do with or used in promotion.

prompt (prompt), *adj.* 1 ready and willing; on time; quick; punctual: *Be prompt to obey.* See **ready** for synonym study. 2 done at once; made without delay: *I expect a prompt answer.* *—v.t.* 1 cause (someone) to do something: *Curiosity prompted me to ask the question.* See **move** for synonym study. 2 give rise to; suggest; inspire: *A kind thought prompted the gift.* 3 remind (a learner, speaker, actor, etc.) of the words or actions needed: *Do you know your part in the play or shall I prompt you?* [< Latin *promptus* < *pro-* forward + *emere* to take. Doublet of PRONTO.] **—prompt′ly,** *adv.* **—prompt′ness,** *n.*

prompt er (promp′tər), *n.* person who tells actors, speakers, etc., what to say when they forget.

promp ti tude (promp′tə tüd, promp′tə-tyüd), *n.* readiness in acting or deciding; promptness.

prom ul gate (prom′əl gāt, prō mul′gāt), *v.t.,* **-gat ed, -gat ing.** 1 proclaim formally; announce officially: *The king promulgated a decree.* 2 spread far and wide: *Schools try to promulgate knowledge and good habits.* [< Latin *promulgatum* pressed forth < *pro-* forth + *mulgere* to press] **—prom′ul-ga′tion,** *n.* **—prom′ul ga′tor,** *n.*

pron., 1 pronoun. 2 pronunciation.

prone (prōn), *adj.* 1 inclined or disposed; liable: *We are prone to think evil of people we dislike.* 2 lying face down: *be prone on the bed.* 3 lying flat: *fall prone on the ground.* [< Latin *pronus* < *pro-* forward] **—prone′ness,** *n.*

prong (prông, prong), *n.* one of the pointed ends of a fork, antler, etc. *—v.t.* pierce or stab with a prong. [Middle English *prange*]

pronged (prôngd, prongd), *adj.* having prongs.

prong horn (prông′hôrn′, prong′hôrn′), *n., pl.* **-horns** or **-horn.** a ruminant mammal resembling an antelope, found on the plains of western North America.

pro nom i nal (prō nom′ə nəl), *adj.* of or having to do with pronouns; having the nature of a pronoun. *This, that, any, some,* etc., are pronominal adjectives. *—n.* a pronominal word. **—pro nom′i nal ly,** *adv.*

pro noun (prō′noun), *n.* word used instead of a noun to designate an object or person without naming, when the object or person referred to is known from the context or has already been mentioned. EXAMPLES: I, we, you, he, it, they, who, whose, which, this, mine, whatever. [< Latin *pronomen* < *pro-* in place of + *nomen* name, noun]

pro nounce (prə nouns′), *v.,* **-nounced, -nounc ing.** *—v.t.* 1 make the sounds of; speak: *Pronounce your words clearly.* 2 declare (a person or thing) to be: *The doctor pronounced her cured.* 3 declare solemnly or positively: *The judge pronounced sentence.* *—v.i.* 1 pronounce words. 2 give an opinion or decision: *Only an expert should pronounce on this case.* [< Old French *pronuncier* < Latin *pronuntiare* < *pro-* forth + *nuntiare* announce] **—pro nounce′a ble,** *adj.* **—pro nounc′er,** *n.*

pro nounced (prə nounst′), *adj.* strongly marked; decided: *She held pronounced opinions on gambling.*

pro nounc ed ly (prə noun′sid lē), *adv.* in a pronounced manner.

pro nounce ment (prə nouns′mənt), *n.* 1 a formal or authoritative statement; declaration. 2 opinion or decision.

pron to (pron′tō), *adv.* INFORMAL. promptly; quickly. [< Spanish < Latin *promptus* prompt. Doublet of PROMPT.]

pro nun ci a men to (prə nun′sē ə-men′tō, prə nun′shē ə men′tō), *n., pl.* **-tos.** a formal announcement; proclamation. [< Spanish *pronunciamiento*]

pro nun ci a tion (prə nun′sē ā′shən), *n.* 1 way of pronouncing. This book gives the pronunciation of each main word. 2 act of pronouncing.

proof (prüf), *n.* 1 way or means of showing beyond doubt the truth of something: *Is what you say a guess or have you proof?* See **evidence** for synonym study. 2 establishment of the truth of anything. 3 act of testing; trial: *That box looks big enough; but let us put it to the proof.* 4 a trial impression from type. A book is first printed in proof so that errors can be corrected. *Did the author correct the page proof?* 5 a trial print of an etching, photographic negative, etc. 6 strength of an alcoholic liquor with reference to the standard in which 100 proof spirit contains about 50% alcohol and about 50% water. Brandy of 90 proof is about 45% alcohol. *—adj.* 1 of tested value against something; capable of resisting or withstanding (often used in compounds): *a wrinkle-proof fabric, proof against being taken*

hat, āge, fär; let, ēqual, tėrm;
it, īce; hot, ōpen, ôrder;
oil, out; cup, pu̇t, rüle;
ch, child; ng, long; sh, she;
th, thin; ᴛʜ, then; zh, measure;

ə represents *a* in about, *e* in taken, *i* in pencil, *o* in lemon, *u* in circus.

< = from, derived from, taken from.

by surprise. 2 (of an alcoholic liquor) of standard strength. [< Old French *prouve* < Late Latin *proba* < Latin *probare* prove. Doublet of PROBE.]

proof read (prüf′rēd′), *v.t., v.i.,* **-read** (-red′), **-read ing.** read (printers' proofs, etc.) and mark errors to be corrected. **—proof′read′er,** *n.*

prop[1] (prop), *v.,* **propped, prop ping,** *n.* —*v.t.* 1 hold up by placing a support under or against: *propped up in bed with pillows. Prop the clothesline with a stick.* 2 support; sustain: *prop a failing cause.* —*n.* person or thing serving to support another. [< Middle Dutch *proppe*]

prop[2] (prop), *n.* property (def. 5).

prop[3] (prop), *n.* INFORMAL. an airplane propeller.

prop., 1 property. 2 proposition. 3 proprietor.

prop a gan da (prop′ə gan′də), *n.* 1 systematic effort to spread opinions or beliefs; any plan or method for spreading opinions or beliefs: *The life insurance companies engaged in health propaganda. Clever propaganda misled the enemy into believing it could not win the war.* 2 opinions or beliefs thus spread. 3 **Propaganda,** committee of cardinals established in 1622 to supervise foreign missions. [< New Latin *(congregatio de) propaganda (fide)* (congregation for) propagating (the faith)]

prop a gan dism (prop′ə gan′diz′əm), *n.* use of propaganda.

prop a gan dist (prop′ə gan′dist), *n.* person who gives time or effort to the spreading of some opinion or belief. —*adj.* of propaganda or propagandists.

prop a gan dist ic (prop′ə gan dis′tik), *adj.* of or having to do with propagandists or the use of propaganda. **—prop′a gan-dist′i cal ly,** *adv.*

prop a gan dize (prop′ə gan′dīz), *v.,* **-dized, -diz ing.** —*v.t.* propagate or spread (opinions or beliefs) by propaganda. —*v.i.* carry on propaganda.

prop a gate (prop′ə gāt), *v.,* **-gat ed, -gat ing.** —*v.i.* produce offspring; reproduce: *Pigeons propagate at a fast rate.* —*v.t.* 1 increase in number or intensity; multiply: *Trees propagate themselves by seeds.* 2 cause to increase in number by the production of young: *Cows and sheep are propagated on farms.* 3 spread (news, knowledge, etc.); extend: *Don't propagate unkind reports.* 4 pass on; send further: *Sound is propagated by vibrations.* [< Latin *propagatum* propagated, originally (of plants) multiplied by slips or layering < *pro-* forth + *pagare, pangere* fasten, plant with] **—prop′a-ga′tor,** *n.*

prop a ga tion (prop′ə gā′shən), *n.* 1 the breeding of plants or animals: *the propagation of poppies by seed and of roses by cuttings.* 2 a spreading; getting more widely believed; making more widely known: *the propagation of the principles of science.* 3 a passing on; sending further: *the propagation of the shock of an earthquake.*

prop a ga tive (prop′ə gā′tiv), *adj.* serving or tending to propagate.

pro pane (prō′pān), *n.* a heavy, colorless, flammable gas, a hydrocarbon that occurs in crude petroleum and is used as a fuel, refrigerant, or solvent. *Formula:* $CH_3CH_2CH_3$ [< *prop(ionic acid)* + *-ane*]

pro pa nol (prō′pə nōl, prō′pə nol), *n.* propyl alcohol.

pro pel (prə pel′), *v.t.,* **-pelled, -pel ling.** 1 drive or push forward; force ahead: *propel a boat by oars.* 2 impel or urge onward: *a person propelled by ambition.* [< Latin *propellere* < *pro-* + *pellere* to push] **—pro-pel′la ble,** *adj.*

pro pel lant (prə pel′ənt), *n.* 1 person or thing that propels. 2 fuel and oxidizer for propelling a rocket. 3 explosive for propelling a projectile. —*adj.* propelling; propellent.

pro pel lent (prə pel′ ənt), *adj.* propelling; driving forward. —*n.* propellant.

propeller (def. 1)
boat and aircraft propellers

pro pel ler (prə pel′ər), *n.* 1 device consisting of a revolving hub with blades, for propelling boats and aircraft. 2 person or thing that propels.

pro pen si ty (prə pen′sə tē), *n., pl.* **-ties.** a natural inclination or bent; leaning: *a propensity for athletics.* [< Latin *propensum* inclined < *pro-* forward + *pendere* hang]

prop er (prop′ər), *adj.* 1 right for the occasion; fitting: *Night is the proper time to sleep, and bed the proper place.* 2 strictly so called; in the strict sense of the word: *Footnotes are clearly set off from the text proper.* 3 designating a liturgical service, psalm, lesson, etc., appointed for a particular day or season. 4 decent; respectable: *proper conduct.* 5 (in grammar) belonging to one or a few; designating a particular person, place, or thing. *John Adams* is a proper name. 6 INFORMAL. complete; thorough; fine; excellent. 7 ARCHAIC. good-looking; handsome. [< Old French *propre* < Latin *proprius* one's own]

proper adjective, adjective derived from a proper noun, as *Italian* in *the Italian language.* A proper adjective is usually capitalized.

proper fraction, fraction in which the numerator is smaller than the denominator. EXAMPLES: $^1/_8$, $^3/_4$, $^{199}/_{200}$.

prop er ly (prop′ər lē), *adv.* 1 in a proper, correct, or fitting manner: *eat properly.* 2 rightly; justly: *be properly indignant at the offer of a bribe.* 3 strictly: *Properly speaking, a whale is not a fish.*

proper noun, noun naming a particular person, place, or thing. *John, Chicago,* and *Dacron* are proper nouns. *Boy, city,* and *day* are common nouns.

prop er tied (prop′ər tēd), *adj.* owning property.

prop er ty (prop′ər tē), *n., pl.* **-ties.** 1 thing or things owned; possession or possessions. See synonym study below. 2 the right of ownership. 3 piece of land or real estate. 4 quality or power belonging specially to something: *Soap has the property of removing dirt.* See **quality** for synonym study. 5 any piece of furniture or small article used in staging a play. Everything except scenery and clothes are properties. [< Old French *propriete* < Latin *proprietatem* < *proprius* one's own] **—prop′er ty less,** *adj.*

Syn. 1 **Property, goods, effects,** mean what someone owns. **Property** means whatever someone legally owns, including land, buildings, animals, money, stocks, documents, objects, and rights: *Property is taxable.* **Goods** means movable personal property, as distinguished from land, buildings, etc.: *Professional movers packed our goods.* **Effects** means personal possessions, or belongings, often of one who has died: *We gathered together his few effects to send them to his family.*

property man, man employed in a theater to look after the stage properties; prop man.

pro phase (prō′fāz), *n.* (in biology) the first stage in mitosis, that includes the formation of the spindle and the lengthwise splitting of the chromosomes.

proph e cy (prof′ə sē), *n., pl.* **-cies.** 1 a telling what will happen; foretelling future events. 2 thing told about the future. 3 a divinely inspired utterance, revelation, writing, etc.

proph e sy (prof′ə sī), *v.,* **-sied, -sy ing.** —*v.i.* 1 tell what will happen. 2 speak when or as if divinely inspired. —*v.t.* 1 foretell; predict: *The sailor prophesied a severe storm.* 2 utter in prophecy. **—proph′e si′er,** *n.*

proph et (prof′it), *n.* 1 person who predicts or foretells what will happen. 2 person who preaches what he believes to be truth divinely revealed to him, especially any of the Biblical figures who taught and preached in the name of God, such as Isaiah and Jeremiah. 3 spokesman of some cause, doctrine, etc. 4 **the Prophet, a** Mohammed. **b** Joseph Smith, the founder of the Mormon religion. 5 **the Prophets,** books of the Old Testament written by prophets. [< Greek *prophētēs* < *pro-* before + *phanai* speak]

proph et ess (prof′i tis), *n.* a woman prophet.

pro phet ic (prə fet′ik), *adj.* 1 belonging to a prophet; such as a prophet has: *prophetic power.* 2 containing prophecy: *a prophetic saying.* 3 giving warning of what is to happen; foretelling: *Thunder is often prophetic of showers.* **—pro phet′i cal ly,** *adv.*

pro phy lac tic (prō′fə lak′tik, prof′ə lak′tik), *adj.* 1 protecting from disease. 2 protective; precautionary. —*n.* 1 medicine or treatment that protects against disease. 2 any contraceptive device. [< Greek *prophylaktikos* < *pro-* before + *phylax* a guard]

pro phy lax is (prō′fə lak′sis, prof′ə-lak′sis), *n.* 1 protection from disease. 2 treatment to prevent disease.

pro pin qui ty (prō ping′kwə tē), *n.* 1 nearness in place, especially personal nearness. 2 nearness of blood; kinship. [< Latin *propinquus* being near < *prope* near]

pro pi on ic acid (prō′pē on′ik, prō′pē-ō′nik), a fatty acid with a pungent odor, produced synthetically from ethyl alcohol and carbon monoxide. It is used to inhibit mold in bread, as an ingredient in perfumes, etc. *Formula:* CH_3CH_2COOH [< *pro(to)-* first + Greek *piōn* fat]

pro pi ti ate (prə pish′ē āt), *v.t.,* **-at ed, -at ing.** prevent or reduce the anger of; win the favor of; appease or conciliate (one offended or likely to be). **—pro pi′ti a′tor,** *n.*

pro pi ti a tion (prə pish′ē ā′shən), *n.* act of propitiating.

pro pi ti a to ry (prə pish′ē ə tôr′ē, prə pish′ē ə tōr′ē), *adj.* intended to propitiate; making propitiation; conciliatory: *a propitiatory offering.*

pro pi tious (prə pish′əs), *adj.* 1 holding well; favorable: *propitious weather for our trip.* 2 favorably inclined; gracious. [< Latin *propitius,* originally, falling forward < *pro-* forward + *petere* go toward] **—pro pi′tious ly,** *adv.* **—pro pi′tious ness,** *n.*

prop jet (prop′jet′), *n.* turboprop.

prop man, property man.

pro po nent (prə pō′nənt), *n.* 1 person who makes a proposal or proposition. 2 person who supports something; advocate. [< Latin *proponentem* propounding]

pro por tion (prə pôr′shən, prə pōr′shən), *n.* 1 relation in magnitude; size, number, amount, or degree of one thing compared to another: *Each girl's pay will be in proportion to her work.* 2 a proper relation between parts: *His short legs were not in proportion to his long body.* 3 **proportions,** *pl.* **a** size; extent. **b** dimensions. 4 part; share: *A large proportion of Nevada is desert.* 5 (in mathematics) an equality of ratios. EXAMPLE: 4 is to 2 as 10 is to 5. *—v.t.* fit (one thing to another) so that they go together: *The designs in that rug are well proportioned.* 2 adjust in proper proportion or relation: *The punishment was proportioned to the crime.* [< Latin *proportionem* < the phrase *pro portione* in relation to the part] **—pro por′tion ment,** *n.*

pro por tion al (prə pôr′shə nəl, prə pōr′shə nəl), *adj.* 1 in the proper proportion; corresponding: *The increase in price is proportional to the improvement in the car.* 2 (in mathematics) having the same or a constant ratio. *—n.* one of the terms of a proportion in mathematics. **—pro por′tion al ly,** *adv.*

pro por tion al i ty (prə pôr′shə nal′ə tē, prə pōr′shə nal′ə tē), *n.* quality or condition of being in proportion.

proportional representation, system of electing members of a legislature so that each political party is represented in the legislature in proportion to its share of the total vote cast in an election.

pro por tion ate (*adj.* prə pôr′shə nit, prə pōr′shə nit; *v.* prə pôr′shə nāt, prə pōr′shə nāt), *adj., v.,* **-at ed, -at ing.** *—adj.* in the proper proportion; proportioned; proportional: *The money obtained by the fair was really not proportionate to the effort we put into it.* *—v.t.* make proportionate; proportion. **—pro por′tion ate ly,** *adv.* **—pro por′tion ate ness,** *n.*

pro pos al (prə pō′zəl), *n.* 1 what is proposed; plan, scheme, or suggestion: *The club will now hear this member's proposal.* 2 offer of marriage. 3 act of proposing.

pro pose (prə pōz′), *v.,* **-posed, -pos ing.** *—v.t.* 1 put forward for consideration, discussion, acceptance, etc.; suggest: *I propose that we take turns at the swing.* 2 present (the name of someone) for office, membership, etc. 3 present as a toast to be drunk. 4 intend; plan: *She proposes to save half of all she earns.* *—v.i.* make an offer of marriage. [< Middle French *proposer* < *pro-* forth + *poser* to set, pose] **—pro pos′er,** *n.*

prop o si tion (prop′ə zish′ən), *n.* 1 what is offered to be considered; proposal: *The tailor made a proposition to buy out his rival's business.* 2 statement. EXAMPLE: "All men are created equal." 3 statement that is to be proved true. EXAMPLE: Resolved: that our school should have a bank. 4 problem to be solved: *a proposition in geometry.* 5 INFORMAL. a business enterprise; an undertaking: *a paying proposition.*

prop o si tion al (prop′ə zish′ə nəl), *adj.* having to do with or constituting a proposition.

pro pound (prə pound′), *v.t.* put forward; propose: *propound a theory, propound a riddle.* [earlier *propone* < Latin *proponere* < *pro-* forth + *ponere* put] **—pro pound′er,** *n.*

pro pri e tar y (prə prī′ə ter′ē), *adj., n., pl.* **-tar ies.** *—adj.* 1 belonging to a proprietor: *a proprietary right.* 2 holding property: *the proprietary class.* 3 owned by a private person or company; belonging to or controlled by a private person as property. A proprietary medicine is a patent medicine. *—n.* 1 owner. 2 group of owners. 3 ownership. 4 a proprietary medicine. 5 proprietor (def. 2).

proprietary colony, (in American history) a colony granted by the British government to a person with full power of ownership, such as the power to appoint the governor and other high officials. Maryland and Pennsylvania were proprietary colonies.

pro pri e tor (prə prī′ə tər), *n.* 1 person who owns something as his possession or property; owner. 2 (in American history) the owner of a proprietary colony.

pro pri e tor ship (prə prī′ə tər ship), *n.* ownership.

pro pri e tress (prə prī′ə tris), *n.* a woman owner.

pro pri e ty (prə prī′ə tē), *n., pl.* **-ties.** 1 quality or condition of being proper; fitness. 2 proper behavior: *Propriety demands good table manners.* 3 **proprieties,** *pl.* conventional standards or requirements of proper behavior. [< Latin *proprietatem* appropriateness, property < *proprius* one's own, proper]

prop root, root that supports a plant by growing downward into the ground from above the soil, as in corn.

pro pul sion (prə pul′shən), *n.* 1 a driving forward or onward. 2 a propelling force or impulse. [< Latin *propulsum* propelled]

pro pul sive (prə pul′siv), *adj.* propelling; driving forward or onward.

propyl alcohol, a colorless alcohol used as a solvent for waxes, oils, resins, etc.; propanol. *Formula:* $CH_3CH_2CH_2OH$

pro pyl ene glycol (prō′pə lēn′), a colorless, viscous, liquid compound, used as an antifreeze, a solvent, in organic synthesis, etc. *Formula:* $C_3H_8O_2$

pro ra ta (prō rā′tə; prō rä′tə), in proportion; according to the share, interest, etc., of each. [< Latin *pro rata (parte)* according to the portion figured (for each)]

pro rate (prō rāt′, prō′rāt′), *v.t., v.i.,* **-rat ed, -rat ing.** distribute or assess proportionally: *We prorated the money according to the number of days each had worked.* [< *pro rata*] **—pro ra′tion,** *n.*

pro ro ga tion (prō′rə gā′shən), *n.* discontinuance of the meetings of a lawmaking body without dissolving it.

pro rogue (prō rōg′), *v.t.,* **-rogued, -rogu ing.** discontinue the regular meetings of (a lawmaking body) for a time. [< Latin *prorogare* defer < *pro-* forward + *rogare* ask for]

pro sa ic (prō zā′ik), *adj.* like prose; matter-of-fact; ordinary; not exciting. **—pro sa′i cal ly,** *adv.*

pro sce ni um (prō sē′nē əm), *n., pl.* **-ni a** (-nē ə). 1 the part of the stage in front of the curtain. 2 curtain and the framework that holds it. 3 stage of an ancient theater. [< Latin < Greek *proskēnion* < *pro-* in front of + *skēnē* stage, scene]

pro sciut to (prō shü′tō), *n., pl.* **-ti** (-tē), **-tos.** dry-cured, spiced, and often smoked ham, sliced very thin and often served with melon or figs. [< Italian]

pro scribe (prō skrīb′), *v.t.,* **-scribed, -scrib ing.** 1 prohibit as wrong or dangerous; condemn: *In earlier days, the church proscribed dancing and card playing.* 2 put outside of the protection of the law; outlaw. 3 forbid to come into a certain place; banish. [< Latin *proscribere* < *pro-* forth + *scribere* write] **—pro scrib′er,** *n.*

pro scrip tion (prō skrip′shən), *n.* a proscribing or a being proscribed; banishment; outlawry.

pro scrip tive (prō skrip′tiv), *adj.* proscribing; tending to proscribe. **—pro scrip′tive ly,** *adv.*

prose (prōz), *n., adj., v.,* **prosed, pros ing.** *—n.* the ordinary form of spoken or written language; language without meter or rhyme, as distinguished from poetry, and especially as the literary form, characterized by narration, description, and exposition, used in novels, plays, articles, etc. *—adj.* 1 of or in prose. 2 lacking imagination; matter-of-fact; commonplace. *—v.i.* 1 talk or write in a dull, commonplace way. 2 write prose. [< Latin *prosa (oratio)* straight (speech)]

pros e cute (pros′ə kyüt), *v.,* **-cut ed, -cut ing.** *—v.t.* 1 bring before a court of law: *Reckless drivers will be prosecuted.* 2 carry out; follow up: *prosecute an inquiry into reasons for a company's failure.* *—v.i.* 1 bring a case before a court of law. 2 carry on (a business or occupation). [< Latin *prosecutum* followed after < *pro-* forth + *sequi* follow]

prosecuting attorney, attorney for the government; district attorney.

pros e cu tion (pros′ə kyü′shən), *n.* 1 the carrying on of a lawsuit: *The prosecution will be abandoned if the stolen money is returned.* 2 side that starts action against another in a court of law. The prosecution makes certain charges against the defense. 3 a carrying out; following up: *the prosecution of a plan.*

pros e cu tor (pros′ə kyü′tər), *n.* 1 the lawyer in charge of the government's side of a case against an accused person. 2 person who starts legal proceedings against another person.

pros e lyte (pros′ə līt), *n., v.,* **-lyt ed, -lyt ing.** *—n.* person who has been converted from one opinion, religious belief, etc., to another. *—v.t.* 1 convert from one opinion, religious belief, etc., to another. 2 induce to join; enlist; solicit. [< Greek *prosēlytos* having arrived < *pros* toward + *ely-* come] **—pros′e lyt′er,** *n.*

pros e lyt ism (pros′ə lə tiz′əm, pros′ə lī′tiz′əm), *n.* act or fact of proselyting.

pros e lyt ize (pros′ə lə tīz, pros′ə li tīz), *v.,* **-ized, -iz ing.** *—v.i.* make converts. *—v.t.* make a proselyte of; convert.

pros en ce phal ic (pros′en sə fal′ik), *adj.* of or having to do with the forebrain.

pros en ceph a lon (pros′en sef′ə lon), *n.* forebrain.

Pro ser pi na (prō sėr′pə nə), *n.* (in Roman myths) Persephone.

Pro ser pi ne (prō sėr′pə nē, pros′ər pīn), *n.* (in Roman myths) Persephone.

pro sit (prō′sit), *interj.* to your health! [< German *Prosit* < Latin *prosit* may it benefit]

pro sod ic (prō sod′ik), *adj.* of or having to do with prosody. **—pro sod′i cal ly,** *adv.*

pro sod i cal (prō sod′ə kəl), *adj.* prosodic.

pros o dist (pros′ə dist), *n.* person skilled in the technique of versification.

pros o dy (pros′ə dē), *n.* 1 the science of poetic meters and versification. 2 any system or style of versification: *Latin prosody.* [< Greek *prosōidia* accent, modulation, etc. < *pros* in addition to + *ōidē* song, poem]

pros pect (pros′pekt), *n.* 1 thing expected or looked forward to. 2 act of looking forward; expectation: *The prospect of a vacation is pleasant.* 3 outlook for the future. 4 **in prospect,** looked forward to; expected. 5 person who may become a customer, candidate, etc. 6 view; scene: *The prospect from the mountain was grand.* —*v.i.* explore a region for oil, gold, or other minerals: *prospect for gold.* —*v.t.* search or look: *prospect a region for silver.* [< Latin *prospectus,* ultimately < *pro-* forward + *specere* to look]

pro spec tive (prə spek′tiv), *adj.* 1 that is looked forward to as likely or promised; probable; expected: *a prospective client.* 2 looking forward in time; future: *a prospective mother.* **—pro spec′tive ly,** *adv.*

pros pec tor (pros′pek tər, prə spek′tər), *n.* person who explores or examines a region, searching for gold, silver, oil, uranium, etc., or estimating the value of some product of a region.

pro spec tus (prə spek′təs), *n.* a printed description of a proposed enterprise, issued to potential investors. [< Latin, prospect]

pros per (pros′pər), *v.i.* be successful; have good fortune; thrive; flourish. —*v.t.* make successful. [< Latin *prosperare* < *pro-* for + *spes* hope]

pros per i ty (pro sper′ə tē), *n., pl.* **-ties.** prosperous condition; good fortune; success.

Pros per o (pros′pər ō), *n.* an exiled duke living on an enchanted island in Shakespeare's play *The Tempest.*

pros per ous (pros′pər əs), *adj.* 1 doing well; prospering; successful. 2 favorable; helpful: *prosperous weather for growing wheat.* **—pros′per ous ly,** *adv.* **—pros′per ous ness,** *n.*

pros tate (pros′tāt), *n.* a large gland surrounding the male urethra in front of the bladder. —*adj.* designating or having to do with this gland. [< Greek *prostatēs* one standing in front, ultimately < *pro-* before + *stenai* to stand]

pros the sis (pros′thə sis, pros thē′sis), *n., pl.* **-ses** (-sēz′). 1 replacement of a missing tooth, leg, etc., with an artificial equivalent part. 2 the part itself. [< Greek, addition < *pros* to + *tithenai* put]

pros thet ic (pros thet′ik), *adj.* of or having to do with prosthesis: *prosthetic dentistry.*

pros ti tute (pros′tə tüt, pros′tə tyüt), *n., v.,* **-tut ed, -tut ing.** —*n.* 1 woman who has sexual relations with men for money. 2 person who does base things for money. —*v.t.* put to an unworthy or base use: *prostitute artistic skills.* [< Latin *prostitutum* dishonored publicly, prostituted < *pro-* publicly + *statuere* cause to stand]

pros ti tu tion (pros′tə tü′shən, pros′tə-tyü′shən), *n.* 1 act or practice of a prostitute. 2 the use of one's body, honor, talents, etc., in a base way.

pros trate (pros′trāt), *v.,* **-trat ed, -trat ing,** *adj.* —*v.t.* 1 lay down flat; cast down: *The captives prostrated themselves before the conqueror.* 2 make very weak or helpless; exhaust: *Sickness often prostrates people.* —*adj.* 1 lying flat with face downward: *She was humbly prostrate in prayer.* 2 lying flat: *I stumbled and fell prostrate on the floor.* 3 overcome; helpless: *a prostrate enemy.* [< Latin *prostratum* thrown down flat < *pro-* forth + *sternere* spread out]

pros tra tion (pro strā′shən), *n.* 1 act of prostrating; bowing down low or lying face down in submission, respect, or worship. 2 a being very much worn out or used up in body or mind; exhaustion; dejection.

pros y (prō′zē), *adj.,* **pros i er, pros i est.** like prose; commonplace; dull; tiresome. **—pros′i ly,** *adv.* **—pros′i ness,** *n.*

prot-, *combining form.* the form of **proto-** before vowels, as in *protamine.*

Prot., Protestant.

pro tac tin i um (prō′tak tin′ē əm), *n.* a rare, heavy, radioactive metallic element which occurs in pitchblende and disintegrates to form actinium. *Symbol:* Pa; *atomic number* 91. See pages 326 and 327 for table. [< New Latin *prot-* + *actinium*]

pro tag o nist (prō tag′ə nist), *n.* 1 the main character in a play, story, or novel. 2 person who takes a leading part; active supporter. [< Greek *prōtagōnistēs* < *prōtos* first + *agōnistēs* actor, contestant < *agōn* contest]

Pro tag or as (prō tag′ər əs), *n.* 481?-411? B.C., Greek philosopher and teacher.

pro ta mine (prō′tə mēn′, prō′tə mən), *n.* any of a group of basic proteins that are not coagulated by heat, are soluble in water, and form amino acids when hydrolyzed.

pro te an (prō′tē ən, prō tē′ən), *adj.* readily assuming different forms or characters; exceedingly variable: *a protean artist.* [< *Proteus*]

pro te ase (prō′tē ās), *n.* any of various enzymes, such as pepsin, that break down proteins into simpler compounds.

pro tect (prə tekt′), *v.t.* 1 shield from harm or danger; shelter; defend; guard. See **guard** for synonym study. 2 guard (home industry) against foreign goods by taxing any which are brought into the country. [< Latin *protectum* covered up, protected < *pro-* in front + *tegere* to cover] **—pro tect′ing ly,** *adv.*

pro tec tion (prə tek′shən), *n.* 1 act of protecting; condition of being kept from harm; defense: *We have police for our protection.* 2 thing or person that prevents damage: *An apron is a protection when doing dirty work.* 3 system of taxing foreign goods so that people are more likely to buy goods made in their own country; the opposite of free trade. 4 INFORMAL. the payment of money to racketeers and gangsters as a form of tribute in order not to be molested.

pro tec tion ism (prə tek′shə niz′əm), *n.* economic system or theory of protection.

pro tec tion ist (prə tek′shə nist), *n.* person who favors protectionism. —*adj.* of protectionism or protectionists.

hat, āge, fär; let, ēqual, tėrm;
it, īce; hot, ōpen, ôrder;
oil, out; cup, pu̇t, rüle;
ch, child; ng, long; sh, she;
th, thin; ᴛʜ, then; zh, measure;

ə represents *a* in about, *e* in taken, *i* in pencil, *o* in lemon, *u* in circus.

< = from, derived from, taken from.

pro tec tive (prə tek′tiv), *adj.* 1 being a defense; protecting: *the hard protective covering of a turtle.* 2 preventing injury to those around: *a protective device on a machine.* 3 guarding against foreign-made goods by putting a high tax or duty on them: *a protective tariff, protective legislation.* **—pro tec′tive ly,** *adv.* **—pro tec′tive ness,** *n.*

protective coloring, a coloring some animals have that makes them hard to distinguish from the things they live among or that makes them resemble a harmful or distasteful animal, and so protects them from their enemies.

pro tec tor (prə tek′tər), *n.* 1 person or thing that protects; defender. 2 head of a kingdom when the king or queen cannot rule. Oliver Cromwell and Richard Cromwell successively had the title of **Lord Protector** of England between 1653 and 1659.

pro tec tor ate (prə tek′tər it), *n.* 1 a weak country under the protection and partial control of a strong country. Many parts of Africa were once European protectorates. 2 such protection and control. 3 position or term of a protector. 4 **Protectorate,** the period (1653-1659) during which Oliver Cromwell and Richard Cromwell were protectors of England. 5 government by a protector.

pro tec tor ship (prə tek′tər ship), *n.* the position or term of a protector.

pro tec tress (prə tek′tris), *n.* a woman protector.

pro tégé (prō′tə zhā), *n.* person who has been taken under the protection or kindly care of a friend or patron. [< French]

pro té gée (prō′tə zhā), *n.* a woman protégé. [< French]

pro tein (prō′tēn′, prō′tē in), *n.* any of a group of complex organic compounds containing nitrogen that are built up of amino acids. Proteins are essential to the structure and functioning of all animal and plant cells. Such foods as meat, milk, eggs, and beans contain protein. [< French *protéine* < Greek *prōteios* of the first quality < *prōtos* first]

pro te in a ceous (prō′tē ə nā′shəs), *adj.* of or like protein.

pro tem., pro tempore.

pro tem por e (prō tem′pər ē), for the time being; temporarily: *president pro tempore.* [< Latin]

pro te ose (prō′tē ōs), *n.* any of a class of soluble compounds derived from proteins by the action of the gastric and pancreatic juices.

Prot er o zo ic (prot′ər ə zō′ik), *n.* 1 the second oldest geological era, before the Paleozoic and after the Archeozoic, during which sponges, sea worms, and other forms of sea life appeared. See chart under **geology.** 2 rocks formed in this era. —*adj.* of or having to do with this era or its rocks. [< Greek *proteros* prior + *zōē* life]

pro test (*n., adj.* prō′test; *v.* prə test′), *n.* 1 statement that denies or objects strongly: *They yielded only after protest.* 2 a solemn declaration: *The accused man was judged guilty in spite of his protest of innocence.* 3 **under protest,** unwillingly; objecting. 4 a written statement by a notary public that a bill, note, check, etc., has been presented to someone who has refused to pay it or accept it. —*adj.* characterized by protest; expressing protest or objection against some condition: *a protest movement, a protest meeting, a protest song.* —*v.i.* make objections; object: *She protested against having to wash the dishes.* —*v.t.* 1 object to: *protest a decision.* 2 declare solemnly; assert: *The accused man protested his innocence.* [< Middle French < *protester* to protest < Latin *protestari* < *pro-* before + *testis* witness] —**pro test′er,** *n.* —**pro test′ing ly,** *adv.*

Prot es tant (prot′ə stənt; *often* prə tes′tənt *for n., adj. 2*), *n.* 1 member or adherent of any of the Christian churches which repudiated papal authority during the Reformation of the 1500's or developed thereafter. 2 member or adherent of any Christian church other than the Roman Catholic and Eastern churches. 3 (originally) any of the German princes who protested against the anti-Lutheran decrees of the second diet of Spires in 1529. 4 **protestant,** person who protests. —*adj.* 1 of Protestants or their religion. 2 **protestant,** protesting.

Protestant Episcopal Church, church in the United States that is a self-governing branch of the Anglican communion and has about the same principles and beliefs as the Church of England.

Prot es tant ism (prot′ə stən tiz′əm), *n.* 1 the religion of Protestants. 2 their principles and beliefs. 3 Protestants or Protestant churches as a group.

prot es ta tion (prot′ə stā′shən), *n.* 1 a solemn declaration; protesting: *make a protestation of one's innocence.* 2 a protest.

Pro te us (prō′tē əs, prō′tyüs), *n.* (in Greek myths) a sea god who had the power of assuming many different forms.

pro thal li um (prō thal′ē əm), *n., pl.* **-thal li a** (-thal′ē ə). 1 gametophyte of pteridophytes, such as ferns, horsetails, club mosses, etc. 2 the analogous rudimentary gametophyte of seed-bearing plants. [< Greek *pro-* before + *thallos* sprout]

pro tho rax (prō thôr′aks, prō thōr′aks), *n., pl.* **-tho rax es, -tho ra ces** (-thôr′ə sēz′, -thōr′ə sēz′). the anterior division of an insect's thorax, bearing the first pair of legs.

pro throm bin (prō throm′bən), *n.* substance in the blood plasma, essential to clotting, from which thrombin is derived.

pro tist (prō′tist), *n., pl.* **pro tist a** (prō-tis′tə). any of the group of organisms that includes all one-celled animals and plants, such as the bacteria, protozoans, yeasts, etc. [< Greek *prōtistos* the very first, superlative of *prōtos* first] —**pro tis′tan,** *adj.*

pro ti um (prō′tē əm), *n.* the common isotope of hydrogen. *Symbol:* H^1; *atomic number* 1; *mass number* 1. [< Greek *prōtos* first]

proto-, *combining form.* 1 first in time, as in *prototype.* 2 first in importance; chief; primary, as in *protoplasm.* Also, **prot-** before vowels. [< Greek *prōto-* < *prōtos* first]

pro to ac tin i um (prō′tē ak tin′ē əm), *n.* former name of **protactinium.**

pro to col (prō′tə kol, prō′tə kôl), *n.* 1 rules of etiquette of the diplomatic corps. 2 a first draft or record from which a document, especially a treaty, is prepared. [< Greek *prōtokollon* a first sheet or flyleaf (with date and contents) glued onto a papyrus roll < *prōtos* first + *kolla* glue]

pro to his to ric (prō′tō hi stôr′ik, prō′tō-hi stor′ik), *adj.* of or belonging to the beginnings of recorded history.

pro ton (prō′ton), *n.* an elementary particle charged with one unit of positive electricity, found in the nuclei of atoms and having a mass about 1,836 times that of an electron. [< Greek *prōton* first]

pro to plasm (prō′tə plaz′əm), *n.* 1 the chemically active mixture of proteins, fats, and many other complex substances suspended in water which forms the living matter of all plant and animal cells, and in which metabolism, growth, and reproduction are manifested. 2 (formerly) cytoplasm.

pro to plas mic (prō′tə plaz′mik), *adj.* of or having to do with protoplasm.

pro to plast (prō′tə plast), *n.* the living unit of protoplasm within a plant cell, consisting of a nucleus, cytoplasm, and plasma membrane.

pro to typ al (prō′tə tī′pəl), *adj.* of, having to do with, or forming a prototype.

pro to type (prō′tə tīp), *n.* 1 the first or primary type of anything; the original or model: *A modern ship has its prototype in the hollowed log used by primitive peoples.* 2 (in biology) a primitive form; archetype.

Pro to zo a (prō′tə zō′ə), *n.pl.* subkingdom or phylum of invertebrates comprising the protozoans.

pro to zo an (prō′tə zō′ən), *n.* any of a subkingdom or phylum of chiefly microscopic, one-celled animals that reproduce by fission. Amoebas and paramecia are protozoans. —*adj.* of or belonging to this subkingdom or phylum. [< Greek *prōtos* first + *zōon* animal]

pro to zo ic (prō′tə zō′ik), *adj.* protozoan.

pro tract (prō trakt′), *v.t.* 1 draw out; lengthen in time; prolong: *protract a visit.* 2 slide out; thrust out; extend. 3 draw by means of a scale and protractor. [< Latin *protractum* drawn out < *pro-* forward + *trahere* to draw]

pro trac tile (prō trak′təl), *adj.* capable of being lengthened out, or of being thrust forth: *The turtle has a protractile head.*

pro trac tion (prō trak′shən), *n.* act of drawing out; extension.

pro trac tive (prō trak′tiv), *adj.* protracting; prolonging.

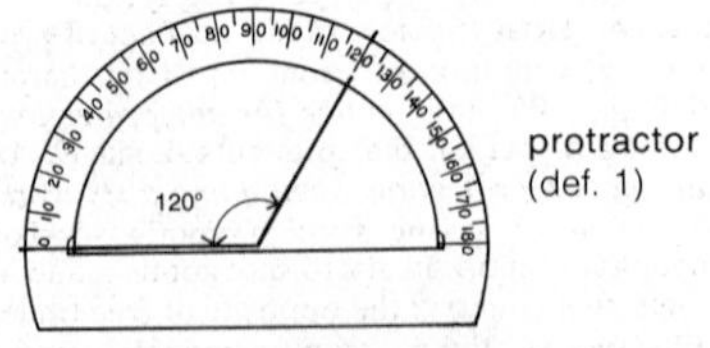

protractor (def. 1)

pro trac tor (prō trak′tər), *n.* 1 instrument for drawing or measuring angles. 2 person or thing that protracts, as a muscle that extends a part.

pro trude (prō trüd′), *v.,* **-trud ed, -trud ing.** —*v.t.* thrust forth; stick out: *The saucy child protruded her tongue.* —*v.i.* be thrust forth; project: *Her teeth protrude too far.* [< Latin *protrudere* < *pro-* forward + *trudere* to thrust]

pro tru si ble (prō trü′sə bəl), *adj.* protrusile.

pro tru sile (prō trü′səl), *adj.* capable of being protruded: *An elephant's trunk is protrusile.*

pro tru sion (prō trü′zhən), *n.* 1 a protruding. 2 a being protruded. 3 something that sticks out; projection.

pro tru sive (prō trü′siv), *adj.* sticking out; projecting.

pro tu ber ance (prō tü′bər əns, prō-tyü′bər əns), *n.* 1 part that sticks out; bulge; swelling. 2 a protuberant quality or condition.

pro tu ber ant (prō tü′bər ənt, prō tyü′bər-ənt), *adj.* bulging out; sticking out; prominent. [< Late Latin *protuberantem* bulging < *pro-* forward + *tuber* lump] —**pro-tu′ber ant ly,** *adv.*

proud (proud), *adj.* 1 thinking well of oneself. See synonym study below. 2 feeling or showing pleasure or satisfaction: *I am proud to call him my friend.* 3 having a becoming sense of what is due oneself, one's position, or character: *too proud to ask for charity.* 4 thinking too well of oneself; haughty; arrogant. 5 such as to make a person proud; highly honorable, creditable, or gratifying: *a proud moment.* 6 grand; magnificent: *The big ship was a proud sight.* 7 full of spirit or mettle: *a proud stallion.* 8 **proud of,** thinking well of; being well satisfied with; proud because of. [Old English *prūd, prūt*] —**proud′ly,** *adv.* —**proud′ness,** *n.*

Syn. 1 **Proud, overbearing, supercilious** mean having or showing a high opinion of oneself. **Proud,** in a favorable sense, suggests dignity and self-esteem: *The grandee had a proud bearing.* **Overbearing,** always unfavorable, suggests being domineering or haughtily insulting in behavior and speech: *Promoted too quickly, the young man became overbearing.* **Supercilious,** also unfavorable, suggests being conceited, and revealing it in a coldly scornful attitude: *He refused our invitation with a supercilious smile.*

proud flesh, a formation of granular tissue which occurs during normal healing of a wound or sore.

Proust (prüst), *n.* **Marcel,** 1871-1922, French novelist.

Prov., 1 Provence. 2 Proverbs. 3 Province. 4 Provost.

prove (prüv), *v.,* **proved, proved** or **prov en, prov ing.** —*v.t.* 1 establish as true; make certain; demonstrate the truth of by evidence or argument: *prove a point, prove that one is right.* 2 establish the genuineness or validity of, especially of a will. 3 try out; test; subject to some testing process: *prove a new product.* 4 test the correctness of (a mathematical calculation). —*v.i.* be found to be; turn out: *This book proved interesting.* [< Old French *prover* < Latin *probare* to prove, approve < *probus* good] —**prov′a ble,** *adj.*

prov en (prü′vən), *v.* a pp. of **prove.**

prov e nance (prov′ə nəns), *n.* source; origin. [< French < *provenir* come forth < Latin < *pro-* forth + *venire* come]

Pro ven çal (prō′vən säl′, prov′ən säl′), *n.* 1 native or inhabitant of Provence. 2 the Romance language of Provence. —*adj.* of or having to do with Provence, its people, or their language.

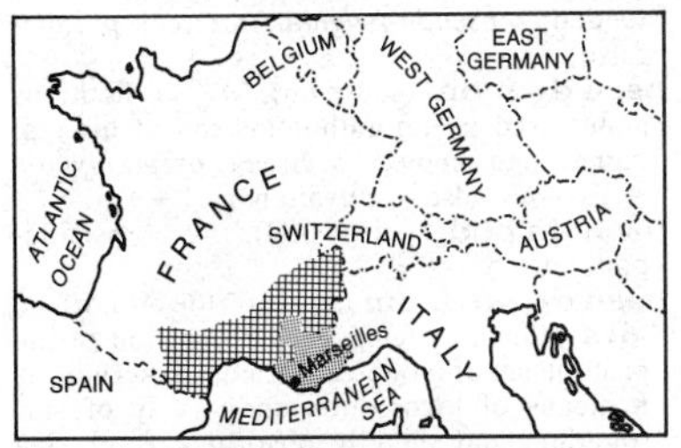

Provence—Smaller area of shading shows Provence in 1225. Larger area of shading to left and above shows the additional territory it occupied while a Roman province in 50 B.C.

Pro vence (prô väns′), *n.* part of SE France, ancient Rome's first province, famous during the Middle Ages for chivalry and poetry.

prov en der (prov′ən dər), *n.* 1 dry food for animals, such as hay or corn. 2 INFORMAL. food. [< Old French *provendre*]

pro ve ni ence (prō vē′nē əns, prō-vē′nyəns), *n.* provenance.

prov erb (prov′ėrb′), *n.* a short, wise saying used for a long time by many people; adage. EXAMPLE: "Haste makes waste." See **epigram** for synonym study. [< Latin *proverbium* < *pro-* forth + *verbum* word]

pro ver bi al (prə vėr′bē əl), *adj.* 1 of proverbs; expressed in a proverb; like a proverb: *proverbial wisdom, a proverbial saying.* 2 that has become a proverb: *the proverbial stitch in time.* 3 well-known: *the proverbial loyalty of dogs.* **—pro ver′bi al ly,** *adv.*

Prov erbs (prov′ėrbz′), *n.* book of the Old Testament made up of sayings of the wise men of Israel.

pro vide (prə vīd′), *v.,* **-vid ed, -vid ing.** *—v.t.* 1 supply; furnish: *Sheep provide us with wool.* 2 state as a condition beforehand: *Our club's rules provide that dues must be paid monthly.* 3 get ready; prepare beforehand. *—v.i.* 1 supply means of support; arrange to supply means of support: *provide for one's family.* 2 take care for the future: *provide against accident, provide for old age.* [< Latin *providere* < *pro-* forward + *videre* to see. Doublet of PURVEY.] **—pro vid′er,** *n.*

pro vid ed (prə vī′did), *conj.* on the condition that; if: *She will go provided her friends can go also.*

prov i dence (prov′ə dəns), *n.* 1 God's care and help. 2 **Providence,** God. 3 instance of God's care and help. 4 a being provident; prudence.

Prov i dence (prov′ə dəns), *n.* capital of Rhode Island, in the NE part. 179,000.

prov i dent (prov′ə dənt), *adj.* 1 having or showing foresight; careful in providing for the future; prudent. 2 economical; frugal. **—prov′i dent ly,** *adv.*

prov i den tial (prov′ə den′shəl), *adj.* 1 happening by or as if by God's intervention; fortunate: *Our delay seemed providential, for the train we had planned to take was wrecked.* 2 of or proceeding from divine power or influence. **—prov′i den′tial ly,** *adv.*

pro vid ing (prə vī′ding), *conj.* on the condition that; if; provided: *I shall go providing it doesn't rain.*

prov ince (prov′əns), *n.* 1 one of the main divisions of a country. Canada is made up of provinces instead of states. 2 **the provinces,** part of a country outside the capital or the largest cities. 3 proper work or activity; sphere; domain: *Teaching spelling is not within the province of a college.* 4 division; department: *the province of science.* 5 an ancient Roman territory outside Italy, ruled by a Roman governor. 6 a large church district governed by an archbishop. [< Latin *provincia*]

Prov ince town (prov′əns toun), *n.* resort town in E Massachusetts, at the tip of Cape Cod. 3000.

pro vin cial (prə vin′shəl), *adj.* 1 of a province: *provincial government.* 2 belonging or peculiar to some particular province or provinces rather than to the whole country; local: *provincial customs.* 3 having the manners, speech, dress, point of view, etc., of people living in a province. 4 lacking refinement or polish; narrow: *a provincial point of view.* *—n.* 1 person born or living in a province. 2 a provincial person. **—pro vin′cial ly,** *adv.*

pro vin cial ism (prə vin′shə liz′əm), *n.* 1 provincial manners, habit of thought, etc. 2 narrow-mindedness. 3 word, expression, or way of pronunciation peculiar to a district of a country.

pro vin ci al i ty (prə vin′shē al′ə tē), *n., pl.* **-ties.** 1 provincial quality or character. 2 a provincial characteristic or trait.

proving ground, place for testing equipment, especially military weapons, vehicles, etc.

pro vi sion (prə vizh′ən), *n.* 1 statement making a condition; stipulation: *A provision of the lease is that the rent must be paid promptly.* 2 act of providing; preparation: *They have made provision for their children's education.* 3 care taken for the future; arrangement made beforehand: *There is a provision for making the building larger if necessary.* 4 that which is made ready; stock, especially of food; supply; food. 5 **provisions,** *pl.* supply of food and drinks. See **food** for synonym study. *—v.t.* supply with provisions. [< Latin *provisionem* < *providere.* See PROVIDE.]

pro vi sion al (prə vizh′ə nəl), *adj.* for the time being; temporary: *a provisional agreement, a provisional governor.*

pro vi sion al ly (prə vizh′ə nə lē), *adv.* 1 for the time being; temporarily. 2 conditionally.

pro vi so (prə vī′zō), *n., pl.* **-sos** or **-soes.** 1 clause or article in a contract, treaty, etc., that states a condition. 2 any provision or stipulation: *She was admitted to the eighth grade with the proviso that she was to be put back if she failed any subject.* [< Latin, it being provided < *providere* provide]

pro vi sor y (prə vī′zər ē), *adj.* 1 containing a proviso; conditional. 2 provisional.

prov o ca tion (prov′ə kā′shən), *n.* 1 act of provoking. 2 something that stirs up or provokes: *Their insulting remarks were a provocation.*

pro voc a tive (prə vok′ə tiv), *adj.* 1 irritating; vexing. 2 tending or serving to call forth action, thought, laughter, anger, etc.: *a provocative remark.* *—n.* something that rouses or irritates. **—pro voc′a tive ly,** *adv.* **—pro voc′a tive ness,** *n.*

pro voke (prə vōk′), *v.t.,* **-voked, -vok ing.** 1 make angry; vex. 2 stir up; excite: *The insult provoked him to anger.* 3 call forth; bring about; start into action; cause. 4 induce (a physical condition, etc.). [< Latin *provocare* < *pro-* forth + *vocare* to call]

hat, āge, fär; let, ēqual, tėrm;
it, īce; hot, ōpen, ôrder;
oil, out; cup, pu̇t, rüle;
ch, child; ng, long; sh, she;
th, thin; ᴛʜ, then; zh, measure;

ə represents *a* in about, *e* in taken, *i* in pencil, *o* in lemon, *u* in circus.

< = from, derived from, taken from.

pro vok ing (prə vō′king), *adj.* that provokes; irritating: *a very provoking insult.* **—pro vok′ing ly,** *adv.*

pro vost (prō′vōst, prov′əst), *n.* 1 a high-ranking administrative officer in some colleges and universities. 2 head or dean of the clergymen assigned to a cathedral. 3 the chief magistrate in a Scottish town. [partly Old English *profost,* partly < Old French *provost,* both < Medieval Latin *propositus,* alteration of Latin *praepositus* chief, prefect, ultimately < *prae-* at the head of + *ponere* to place]

pro vost marshal (prō′vō), 1 (in the army) an officer acting as head of police in a camp, fort, or district, and charged with the maintenance of order, etc. 2 (in the navy) an officer charged with the safekeeping of prisoners until their trial by court-martial.

prow (def. 1)

prow (prou), *n.* 1 the front part of a ship or boat; bow. 2 the projecting front of anything: *the prow of an aircraft.* [< Middle French *proue* < Italian *prua* < Latin *prora* < Greek *prōira*]

prow ess (prou′is), *n.* 1 bravery; daring. 2 brave or daring acts. 3 unusual skill or ability. [< Old French *proece* < *prod* valiant]

prowl (proul), *v.i.* 1 go about slowly and secretly hunting for something to eat or steal: *Many wild animals prowl at night.* 2 wander. *—v.t.* move over or through (a place or region) by prowling. *—n.* 1 a prowling. 2 **on the prowl,** prowling about. [Middle English *prollen*] **—prowl′er,** *n.*

prowl car, squad car.

prox i mal (prok′sə məl), *adj.* 1 nearest. 2 (in anatomy) toward the point of origin or attachment.

prox i mate (prok′sə mit), *adj.* 1 next; nearest. 2 near the exact amount; approximate. [< Latin *proximus,* superlative of *prope* near] **—prox′i mate ly,** *adv.* **—prox′i mate ness,** *n.*

prox im i ty (prok sim′ə tē), *n.* nearness; closeness.

proximity fuze, a tiny radio device set in the nose of a projectile that makes the shell explode when it comes within a certain distance of the target.

prox i mo (prok′sə mō), *adv.* in or of the

coming month: *on the 1st proximo.* [< Latin *proximo (mense)* during next (month)]

prox y (prok′sē), *n., pl.* **prox ies.** 1 the action or agency of a deputy or substitute. In marriage by proxy, someone is substituted for the absent bride or bridegroom at the marriage service. 2 agent; deputy; substitute. 3 a writing authorizing a proxy to act or vote for a person. [earlier *procuracy* the office of proctor < Medieval Latin *procuratia,* ultimately < Latin *procurare.* See PROCURE.]

prude (prüd), *n.* person who is too proper or too modest in conduct, dress, or speech; person who puts on extremely proper or modest airs. [< French, short for *prudefemme* excellent woman]

pru dence (prüd′ns), *n.* 1 wise thought before acting; good judgment. See synonym study below. 2 good management; economy.

Syn. 1 **Prudence, foresight** mean careful thought in acting and planning. **Prudence** emphasizes cautious good sense and giving thought to one's actions and their consequences: *Prudence dictates care in the use of natural resources.* **Foresight** emphasizes ability to see what is likely to happen and preparing for it accordingly: *He had the foresight to carry an umbrella.*

pru dent (prüd′nt), *adj.* 1 planning carefully ahead of time; sensible; discreet: *A prudent man saves part of his wages.* 2 characterized by good judgment or good management: *a prudent policy.* [< Latin *prudentem,* contraction of *providentem* provident] **—pru′dent ly,** *adv.*

pru den tial (prü den′shəl), *adj.* of, marked by, or showing prudence. **—pru den′tial ly,** *adv.*

prud er y (prü′dər ē), *n., pl.* **-er ies.** 1 extreme modesty or propriety, especially when not genuine. 2 a prudish act or remark.

prud ish (prü′dish), *adj.* like a prude; excessively proper or modest. **—prud′ish ly,** *adv.* **—prud′ish ness,** *n.*

prune[1] (prün), *n.* 1 kind of dried sweet plum. 2 plum suitable for drying. [< Old French < Latin *prunum.* Doublet of PLUM.]

prune[2] (prün), *v.,* **pruned, prun ing.** *—v.t.* 1 cut out useless or undesirable parts from: *prune a manuscript.* 2 cut superfluous or undesirable twigs or branches from (a bush, tree, etc.): *prune fruit trees.* 3 cut off or out: *Prune all the dead branches.* *—v.i.* cut off superfluous or undesirable parts, especially twigs or branches. [< Middle French *proignier*] **—prun′er,** *n.*

pruning hook, implement with a hooked blade, used for pruning plants.

prur i ence (průr′ē əns), *n.* a being prurient.

prur i ent (průr′ē ənt), *adj.* having lustful thoughts or wishes; lewd; lascivious. [< Latin *prurientem* itching, being wanton] **—prur′i ent ly,** *adv.*

pru ri tus (prü rī′təs), *n.* itching. [< Latin]

Prus sia (prush′ə), *n.* former duchy and kingdom in N Europe which became the most important state in the confederation of German states united by Bismarck in 1871. It is now divided among East Germany, West Germany, Poland, and the Soviet Union. **—Prus′sian,** *adj., n.*

Prussian blue, a deep-blue pigment, essentially a cyanogen compound of iron.

prus sic acid (prus′ik), hydrocyanic acid.

pry[1] (prī), *v.,* **pried, pry ing,** *n., pl.* **pries.** *—v.i.* look with curiosity; peep: *pry into the private affairs of others.* *—n.* an inquisitive person. [Middle English *prien*]

pry[2] (prī), *v.,* **pried, pry ing,** *n., pl.* **pries.** *—v.t.* 1 raise, move, or separate by force, especially by force of leverage: *pry up a stone, pry the top off a bottle.* 2 get with much effort: *We finally pried the secret out of her.* *—n.* lever for prying. [< obsolete *prize* a lever, taken as a plural, from Old French *prise* seizure. See PRIZE[2].]

pry ing (prī′ing), *adj.* looking or searching too curiously; unpleasantly inquisitive. See **curious** for synonym study. **—pry′ing ly,** *adv.*

Ps., Psalm or Psalms.

P.S., 1 postscript. 2 Privy Seal. 3 Public School.

psalm (säm, sälm), *n.* 1 a sacred song or poem. 2 **Psalm,** any of the 150 sacred songs or hymns that together form a book of the Old Testament. *—v.t.* sing or celebrate in psalms. [Old English *psealm* < Late Latin *psalmus* < Greek *psalmos,* originally, performance on a stringed instrument < *psallein* to pluck]

psalm book (säm′bůk′, sälm′bůk′), *n.* a book containing psalms, especially a collection of metrical translations of the Psalms prepared for public worship.

psalm ist (sä′mist, säl′mist), *n.* 1 author of a psalm or psalms. 2 **the Psalmist,** King David, to whom many of the Psalms were traditionally ascribed.

psalm o dy (sä′mə dē, säl′mə dē, sal′mə dē), *n., pl.* **-dies.** 1 act, practice, or art of singing psalms or hymns. 2 psalms or hymns.

Psalms (sämz), *n.* book of the Old Testament consisting of 150 psalms.

Psal ter (sôl′tər), *n.* 1 the book of Psalms. 2 version of the Psalms for liturgical or devotional use. 3 a prayer book containing such a version.

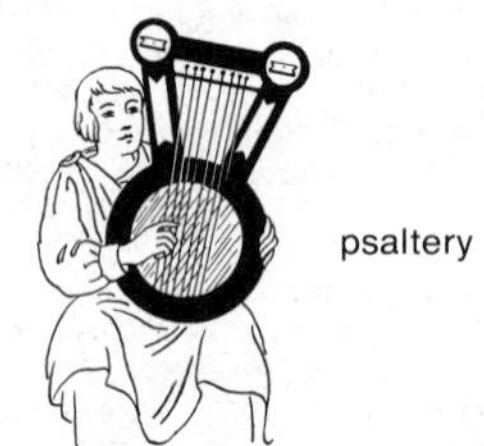

psaltery

psal ter y (sôl′tər ē), *n., pl.* **-ter ies.** an ancient musical instrument played by plucking the strings. [Old English *saltere* < Latin *psalterium* < Greek *psaltērion,* originally, stringed instrument < *psallein* to pluck]

pseu do (sü′dō), *adj.* false; sham; pretended: *a pseudo religion.* [< Greek *pseudēs* false]

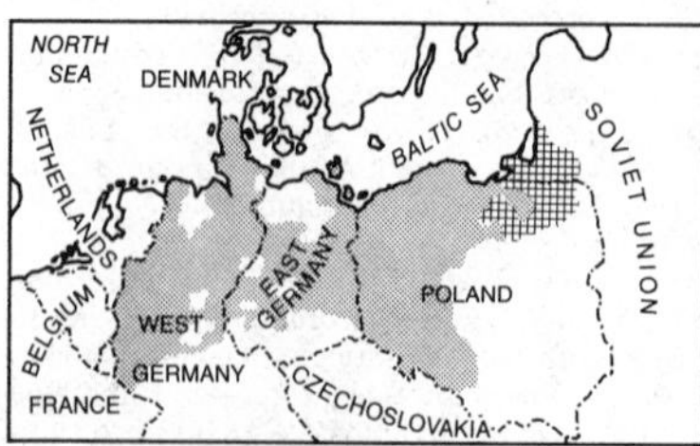

Prussia—Shading to right shows the duchy of Prussia in 1648. Shading to left shows the additional territory in the kingdom of Prussia in 1871.

pseu do nym (süd′n im), *n.* a fictitious name used by an author instead of his real name; pen name. [< Greek *pseudōnymon* < *pseudēs* false + *onyma* name]

pseu do pod (sü′də pod), *n.* pseudopodium.

pseu do po di um (sü′də pō′dē əm), *n., pl.* **-di a** (-dē ə). a temporary protrusion of the protoplasm of a one-celled animal, serving as a means of locomotion and a way of surrounding and thereby absorbing food. See **amoeba** for diagram. [< New Latin < Greek *pseudēs* false + *podos* foot]

pseu do sci ence (sü′dō sī′əns), *n.* a false or pretended science.

pseu do sci en tif ic (sü′dō sī′ən tif′ik), *adj.* of or having to do with pseudoscience.

pshaw (shô), *interj., n.* exclamation expressing impatience, contempt, disgust, etc.

psi (sī, psē), *n.* the 23rd letter of the Greek alphabet (Ψ, ψ).

psi or **p.s.i.,** pounds per square inch.

psi lo cy bin (sī′lə sī′bən, sī′lə sī′bēn′), *n.* a hallucinogenic substance extracted from a Mexican mushroom. [< New Latin *Psilocybe (mexicana)* the mushroom < Greek *psilos* bare + *kybē* head]

Psi lo ri ti (psē′lô rē′tē), *n.* **Mount,** the highest peak in Crete. 8193 ft.

psit ta co sis (sit′ə kō′sis), *n.* a contagious virus disease of parrots and other birds, communicable to man, in whom it is characterized by nausea, diarrhea, chills, and high fever; parrot fever. [< New Latin < Greek *psittakos* parrot]

pso ri a sis (sə rī′ə sis), *n.* a chronic inflammatory skin disease characterized by dry, scaling patches and a reddened skin. [< Greek < *psorian* have the itch < *psōra* itch < *psēn* to rub]

pso ri at ic (sôr′ē at′ik, sōr′ē at′ik), *adj.* 1 of the nature of psoriasis. 2 having psoriasis.

PST or **P.S.T.,** Pacific Standard Time.

psych (sīk), *n.* INFORMAL. psychology. *—v.t.* SLANG. 1 psychoanalyze. 2 use psychology on.

psych-, *combining form.* form of **psycho-** used in some cases before vowels.

psy che (sī′kē), *n.* 1 the human soul or spirit. 2 the mind. 3 **Psyche,** (in Greek and Roman myths) the human soul or spirit pictured as a beautiful young girl, usually with butterfly wings. Psyche was loved by Cupid (Eros) and was made immortal. [< Greek *psychē* soul, mind, life]

psy che del ic (sī′kə del′ik), *adj.* revealing new areas of perception; expanding the consciousness. *—n.* drug having such an effect. [< Greek *psychē* mind + *deloein* reveal]

psy chi at ric (sī′kē at′rik), *adj.* of or having to do with the treatment of mental and emotional disorders. **—psy′chi at′ri cal ly,** *adv.*

psy chi a trist (sī kī′ə trist, si kī′ə trist), *n.* doctor who treats mental and emotional disorders; expert in psychiatry.

psy chi a try (sī kī′ə trē, si kī′ə trē), *n.* branch of medicine dealing with the treatment of mental and emotional disorders. [< *psych-* + Greek *iatreia* cure]

psy chic (sī′kik), *adj.* 1 of the soul or mind; mental: *illness due to psychic causes.* 2 outside the known laws of physics; supernatural. A psychic force or influence is believed by spiritualists to explain telepathy, clairvoyance, etc. 3 especially susceptible to psychic influences. —*n.* person supposed to be specially sensitive or responsive to psychic force or spiritual influences; medium. —**psy′chi cal ly,** *adv.*

psy chi cal (sī′kə kəl), *adj.* psychic.

psy cho (sī′kō), *n., pl.* **-chos,** *adj.* INFORMAL. —*n.* psychopath. —*adj.* psychopathic.

psycho-, *combining form.* ___ of the mind; mental ___: *Psychoanalysis* = *analysis of the mind. Psychotherapy* = *mental therapy.* Also, **psych-** before some vowels. [< Greek *psyche* soul, mind]

psy cho a nal y sis (sī′kō ə nal′ə sis), *n.* 1 examination of a person's mind to discover the unconscious desires, fears, anxieties, etc., which produce mental and emotional disorders. 2 method of psychotherapy based on such examination.

psy cho an a lyst (sī′kō an′l ist), *n.* person who practices psychoanalysis.

psy cho an a lyt ic (sī′kō an′l it′ik), *adj.* having to do with or of the nature of psychoanalysis. —**psy′cho an′a lyt′i cal ly,** *adv.*

psy cho an a lyt i cal (sī′kō an′l it′ə kəl), *adj.* psychoanalytic.

psy cho an a lyze (sī′kō an′l īz), *v.t.,* **-lyzed, -lyz ing.** examine by psychoanalysis. —**psy′cho an′a lyz′er,** *n.*

psy cho dra ma (sī′kō drä′mə, sī′kō-dram′ə), *n.* method of psychotherapy in which a group of patients act out personal situations, playing the roles of themselves or of other persons in their lives.

psy cho gen ic (sī′kō jen′ik), *adj.* of mental origin: *psychogenic symptoms.*

psychol., 1 psychological. 2 psychologist. 3 psychology.

psy cho lin guis tics (sī′kō ling gwis′-tiks), *n.* branch of linguistics that deals with the mental states and processes in language and speech.

psy cho log ic (sī′kə loj′ik), *adj.* psychological.

psy cho log i cal (sī′kə loj′ə kəl), *adj.* 1 of the mind. Memories and dreams are psychological processes. 2 of psychology.

psy cho log i cal ly (sī′kə loj′ik lē), *adv.* 1 in a psychological manner. 2 in psychological respects.

psychological moment, 1 the very moment to get the desired effect in the mind. 2 the critical moment.

psychological warfare, systematic efforts to affect morale, loyalty, etc., especially of large national groups.

psy chol o gist (sī kol′ə jist), *n.* an expert in psychology.

psy chol o gy (sī kol′ə jē), *n., pl.* **-gies.** 1 science or study of the mind; branch of science dealing with the actions, feelings, thoughts, and other mental or behavioral processes of people and animals. 2 the mental states and processes of a person or persons; mental nature and behavior.

psy cho neu ro sis (sī′kō nu̇ rō′sis, sī′kō-nyu̇ rō′sis), *n., pl.* **-ses** (-sēz). neurosis.

psy cho neu rot ic (sī′kō nu̇ rot′ik, sī′kō-nyu̇ rot′ik), *adj.* 1 of or having to do with neurosis. 2 neurotic. —*n.* a neurotic person.

psy cho path (sī′kə path), *n.* 1 person who is mentally ill or unstable. 2 person having a disorder of personality characterized by antisocial behavior, indifference to morality, and abnormal changes in mood, activity, etc.

psy cho path ic (sī′kə path′ik), *adj.* 1 of or having to do with mental disorders. 2 of or characteristic of a psychopath.

psy chop a thy (sī kop′ə thē), *n.* mental disease or disorder.

psy cho path o log i cal (sī′kō path′ə-loj′ə kəl), *adj.* of or having to do with psychopathology.

psy cho pa thol o gist (sī′kō pə thol′ə-jist), *n.* an expert in psychopathology.

psy cho pa thol o gy (sī′kō pə thol′ə jē), *n.* science of the diseases of the mind.

psy cho sis (sī kō′sis), *n., pl.* **-ses** (-sēz′). any severe form of mental disorder, which may also be associated with physical disease, and which produces deep and far-reaching disruption of normal behavior and social functioning.

psy cho so mat ic (sī′kō sə mat′ik), *adj.* of, having to do with, or caused by the interaction of mind and body.

psychosomatic medicine, the use of the methods and principles of psychology in the treatment of physical ailments.

psy cho ther a py (sī′kō ther′ə pē), *n.* treatment of mental or emotional disorders by psychological means.

psy chot ic (sī kot′ik, si kot′ik), *adj.* 1 having a psychosis. 2 of, having to do with, or caused by a psychosis. —*n.* a psychotic person. —**psy chot′i cal ly,** *adv.*

psy chot o mi met ic (sī kot′ō mi met′ik, sī kot′ō mī met′ik), *adj.* producing a state resembling or symptomatic of psychosis: *psychotomimetic drugs.*

psy chrom e ter (sī krom′ə tər), *n.* instrument for measuring the relative humidity of the air, consisting of two thermometers. One has a dry bulb; the other has a wet bulb, on which the reading is usually lower, due to evaporation, than on the one with the dry bulb. The smaller the difference between the readings on the two thermometers, the higher the relative humidity is. [< Greek *psychros* cold]

psy chro met ric (sī′krə met′rik), *adj.* of or having to do with a psychrometer.

Pt, platinum.

pt., 1 part. 2 past tense. 3 pint or pints. 4 point. 5 preterit.

P.T., physical training.

P.T.A., Parent-Teacher Association.

ptar mi gan (tär′mə gən), *n., pl.* **-gans** or **-gan.** any of several kinds of grouse which become white in the winter, have feathered feet, and are found in mountainous and cold regions. [< Scottish Gaelic *tārmachan*]

PT boat, a small, fast motorboat which carries torpedoes, depth bombs, etc. [< *P(atrol) T(orpedo) boat*]

pter i do phyte (ter′ə dō fīt′), *n.* any of a division of seedless and flowerless plants, having roots, stems, and leaves. Ferns, horsetails, and club mosses are pteridophytes. [< Greek *pteridos* fern + *phyton* plant]

pterodactyl wingspread about 20 ft.

pter o dac tyl (ter′ə dak′təl), *n.* any of an order of extinct flying reptiles of the Jurassic and Cretaceous periods that had a strong, featherless membrane stretching from the elongated fourth digit of each foreleg to the body, forming a wing somewhat like a bat's. [< Greek *pteron* wing + *daktylos* finger, toe]

ptg., printing.

hat, āge, fär; let, ēqual, tėrm;
it, īce; hot, ōpen, ôrder;
oil, out; cup, pu̇t, rüle;
ch, child; ng, long; sh, she;
th, thin; ᴛʜ, then; zh, measure;

ə represents *a* in about, *e* in taken, *i* in pencil, *o* in lemon, *u* in circus.

< = from, derived from, taken from.

P.T.O., please turn over (a page).

Ptol e ma ic (tol′ə mā′ik), *adj.* 1 of or having to do with the astronomer Ptolemy. The **Ptolemaic system** of astronomy taught that the earth was the fixed center of the universe and that the sun, moon, and other heavenly bodies moved around the earth. 2 of or having to do with the Ptolemies of Egypt.

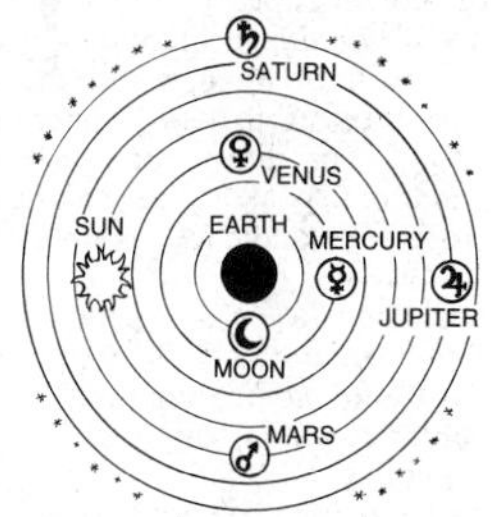

Ptolemaic system of astronomy

Ptol e my (tol′ə mē), *n.* 1 **Claudius,** lived in the A.D. 100's, Greek mathematician, astronomer, and geographer at Alexandria. 2 any of a dynasty of Macedonian kings (**the Ptolemies**) who ruled Egypt from 323 B.C. to 30 B.C.

Ptolemy I, 367?-283? B.C., Macedonian general who founded the Ptolemaic dynasty of Egypt. He ruled from 323 to 285 B.C.

Ptolemy II, 308?-246 B.C., son of Ptolemy I, king of Egypt from 285 to 246 B.C.

pto maine (tō′mān, tō mān′), *n.* any of several chemical compounds, some of which are poisonous, produced by bacteria in decaying matter. Improperly canned foods may contain ptomaines. [< Italian *ptomaina* < Greek *ptōma* corpse]

pty a lin (tī′ə lən), *n.* enzyme contained in the saliva of human beings and of certain other animals, having the property of converting starch into dextrin and maltose, thus aiding digestion. [< Greek *ptyalon* saliva < *ptyein* to spit]

Pu, plutonium.

pub (pub), *n.* INFORMAL. public house; saloon; tavern.

pub., 1 public. 2 publication. 3 published. 4 publisher. 5 publishing.

pu ber ty (pyü′bər tē), *n.* age or condition of becoming first able to produce offspring; the physical beginning of manhood and womanhood. The legal age of puberty is usually about 14 for boys and about 12 for girls. [< Latin *pubertatem* < *puber, pubes* adult]

pu bes cence (pyü bes′ns), *n.* 1 arrival at puberty. 2 a soft downy growth on plants and some insects. 3 fact of having such a growth.

pu bes cent (pyü bes′nt), *adj.* 1 arriving or arrived at puberty. 2 covered with down or fine short hair.

pu bic (pyü′bik), *adj.* 1 having to do with the pubis. 2 in the region of the pubis.

pu bis (pyü′bis), *n., pl.* **-bes** (-bēz). the part of either hipbone that, with the corresponding part of the other, forms the front of the pelvis. [< New Latin *(os) pubis* (bone) of the groin]

pub lic (pub′lik), *adj.* 1 of, belonging to, or concerning the people as a whole: *public affairs.* 2 done, made, acting, etc., for the people as a whole: *public relief.* 3 open to all the people; serving all the people: *a public park.* 4 of or engaged in the affairs or service of the people: *a public official.* 5 known to many or all; not private: *The fact became public.* —*n.* 1 the people in general; all the people: *inform the public.* 2 a particular section of the people: *A popular actor has a large public.* 3 **in public,** not in private or secretly; publicly; openly. [< Latin *publicus,* ultimately < *populus* the people] **—pub′lic-ly,** *adv.* **—pub′lic ness,** *n.*

public address system, apparatus consisting of one or more microphones, amplifiers, and loudspeakers for making sounds audible to a large audience, as on a street or in an auditorium.

pub li can (pub′lə kən), *n.* 1 BRITISH. keeper of a pub. 2 a tax collector of ancient Rome. [< Latin *publicanus* (def. 2) < *publicum* public revenue, originally neuter of *publicus* public]

pub li ca tion (pub′lə kā′shən), *n.* 1 book, newspaper, or magazine; anything that is published. 2 the printing and selling of books, newspapers, magazines, etc. 3 a making known; a being made known; public announcement.

public defender, attorney designated by a court, and paid from public funds, to defend accused persons who cannot afford to hire their own attorney.

public domain, 1 lands belonging to the state or the Federal government. 2 **in the public domain,** (of works, material, inventions, etc.) available for unrestricted use because unprotected by copyright or patent.

public enemy, person, especially a criminal, who is a menace to the public.

public house, 1 BRITISH. saloon; tavern. 2 inn; hotel.

pub li cist (pub′lə sist), *n.* 1 person skilled or trained in law or in public affairs. 2 writer on law, politics, or public affairs. 3 press agent.

pub lic i ty (pu blis′ə tē), *n.* 1 public notice: *the publicity that actors desire.* 2 measures used for getting, or the process of getting, public notice: *a campaign of publicity for a new automobile.* 3 articles, etc., used in such measures or process: *write publicity.* 4 condition of being public; a being known to many: *in the publicity of the street.*

pub li cize (pub′lə sīz), *v.t.,* **-cized, -ciz ing.** give publicity to.

public opinion, the opinion of the people in a country, community, etc., on a matter of public interest or concern: *a survey of public opinion on the issue of gun-control laws.*

public relations, 1 activities of an organization, institution, individual, etc., in the interest of creating and maintaining a favorable public image. 2 attitude of the public toward a particular organization, institution, individual, etc.: *promote good public relations.* 3 business of such activities.

public school, 1 (in the United States) a free school maintained by taxes, especially an elementary or secondary school. 2 (in Great Britain) an endowed private boarding school preparing students for university study or government service.

public servant, person who works for the government.

public service, 1 government service. 2 U.S. service performed by a public utility.

public speaking, act or art of speaking effectively before an audience.

pub lic-spir it ed (pub′lik spir′ə tid), *adj.* having or showing an unselfish desire for the public good.

public utility, company formed or chartered to render essential services to the public, such as a company furnishing electricity, gas, water, transportation, etc., and subject to special governmental control or regulation.

public works, things built by the government at public expense and for public use, such as roads, docks, canals, and waterworks.

pub lish (pub′lish), *v.t.* 1 prepare and offer (a book, paper, map, piece of music, etc.) for sale or distribution. 2 bring out the book or books of: *publish an author.* 3 make publicly or generally known: *Don't publish the faults of your friends.* —*v.i.* come into circulation; be published. [< Old French *publiss-,* a form of *publier* to publish < Latin *publicare* < *publicus* public] **—pub′lish a ble,** *adj.*

pub lish er (pub′li shər), *n.* person or company whose business is to publish books, newspapers, magazines, etc.

Puc ci ni (pü chē′nē), *n.* **Giacomo,** 1858-1924, Italian composer of operas.

puce (pyüs), *n.* a purplish brown. —*adj.* purplish-brown. [< French]

puck¹ (puk), *n.* 1 a mischievous spirit; elf. 2 **Puck,** a mischievous fairy in English folklore, who appears in Shakespeare's play *A Midsummer Night's Dream.* [Old English *pūca*]

puck² (puk), *n.* a hard, black rubber disk used in the game of ice hockey. [variant of *poke¹*]

puck a (puk′ə), *adj.* pukka.

puck er (puk′ər), *v.t., v.i.* draw into wrinkles or irregular folds: *pucker one's brow, pucker cloth in sewing. The baby's lips puckered just before he began to cry.* —*n.* an irregular fold; wrinkle. [apparently < *poke²*]

puck er y (puk′ər ē), *adj.* tending to pucker; puckered; puckering.

puck ish (puk′ish), *adj.* mischievous; impish. **—puck′ish ly,** *adv.* **—puck′ish-ness,** *n.*

pud ding (pu̇d′ing), *n.* 1 a soft cooked food, often having a milk base, and flavored and sweetened: *rice pudding.* 2 a dessert resembling a cake, flavored and sweetened and usually steamed or baked: *plum pudding.* 3 anything soft like a pudding. [Middle English]

pud dle (pud′l), *n., v.,* **-dled, -dling.** —*n.* 1 a small pool of water, especially dirty water. 2 a small pool of any liquid. 3 wet clay and sand stirred into a paste, used as a watertight lining for embankments, canals, etc. —*v.t.* 1 make wet or muddy. 2 mix up (wet clay and sand) into a thick paste. 3 use a mixture of wet clay and sand to stop water from running through: *Puddle up that hole.* 4 stir (molten pig iron) along with an oxidizing agent to make wrought iron. [Middle English *puddel*] **—pud′dler,** *n.*

pud dling (pud′ling), *n.* act or process of converting pig iron into wrought iron by stirring the molten metal along with an oxidizing agent.

pud dly (pud′lē), *adj.* 1 full of puddles. 2 like a puddle.

pudg y (puj′ē), *adj.,* **pudg i er, pudg i est.** short and fat or thick; podgy. [origin uncertain] **—pudg′i ness,** *n.*

Pue bla (pwā′blä), *n.* city in S central Mexico. 322,000.

pueb lo (pweb′lō), *n., pl.* **-los.** 1 an Indian village consisting of houses built of adobe and stone, usually with flat roofs and often several stories high. 2 **Pueblo,** member of any of a group of Indian tribes in the southwestern United States and northern Mexico living in such villages. [< Spanish, people, community < Latin *populus*]

Pueb lo (pweb′lō), *n.* city in central Colorado. 97,000.

pu er ile (pyü′ər əl), *adj.* 1 foolish for a grown person to say or do; childish. 2 youthful; juvenile. [< Latin *puerilis* < *puer* boy, child]

pu e ril i ty (pyü′ə ril′ə tē), *n., pl.* **-ties.** 1 childishness; foolishness. 2 a foolish act, idea, or statement.

pu er per al (pyü ėr′pər əl), *adj.* of or having to do with childbirth: *puerperal fever.* [< Latin *puerpera* woman in childbirth < *puer* child + *parere* to bear]

Puer to Ri co (pwer′tō rē′kō), island in the E part of the West Indies, a self-governing commonwealth under the protection of the United States. 2,690,000 pop.; 3400 sq. mi. *Capital:* San Juan. Formerly, **Porto Rico. —Puer′to Ri′can.**

puff (puf), *v.i.* 1 blow with short, quick blasts: *The bellows puffed on the fire.* 2 breathe quick and hard: *She puffed as she climbed the steep stairs.* 3 give out puffs; move with puffs: *The engine puffed out of the station.* 4 move or come in puffs: *Smoke puffed out of the chimney.* 5 smoke: *puff away at a pipe.* 6 become swollen or distended; swell: *A stung lip puffs up.* —*v.t.* 1 blow (air, vapor, etc.) in short, quick blasts; drive by puffing. 2 put out with a puff of breath. 3 smoke (a cigarette, pipe, cigar, etc.). 4 swell with air or pride or conceit: *puff out one's cheeks. He puffed out his chest when his work was praised.* 5 arrange in soft, round masses; arrange softly and loosely. 6 praise in exaggerated language: *puff someone to the skies.*

—*n.* 1 a short, quick blast: *a puff of wind.* 2 a small quantity (of air, smoke, etc.) blown out in a short, quick blast: *a puff of smoke.* 3 a quick, hard breath. 4 act or process of swelling. 5 a slightly swollen part; swelling. 6 a soft, round mass: *a puff of hair.* 7 a small pad for putting powder on the skin, etc. 8 a light pastry filled with whipped cream, jam, etc.: *a cream puff.* 9 extravagant praise. 10 a quilted bed coverlet filled with cotton, wool, down, or similar material. 11 portion of material gathered and held down at the edges but left full in the middle, as in the sleeve of a dress. [Old English *pyffan*]

puff adder, 1 a large and very poisonous African snake that puffs up its body when excited. 2 a harmless North American snake which puffs out its body; hognose snake.

puff ball (puf′bôl′), *n.* any of various ball-shaped basidiomycetous fungi that are somewhat like mushrooms. A ripe puffball gives off a cloud of tiny spores when suddenly broken. Some species are edible in an unripe state.

hat, āge, fär; let, ēqual, tėrm;
it, īce; hot, ōpen, ôrder;
oil, out; cup, pu̇t, rüle;
ch, child; ng, long; sh, she;
th, thin; ᴛʜ, then; zh, measure;

ə represents *a* in about, *e* in taken, *i* in pencil, *o* in lemon, *u* in circus.

< = from, derived from, taken from.

puff er (puf′ər), *n.* 1 person or thing that puffs. 2 any of various fishes capable of inflating the body, such as a globefish.

puf fin (puf′ən), *n.* any of a genus of sea birds of northern waters, having a thick body, large head, and a bill of several colors. [Middle English *poffin*]

puffin
about 14 in. long

puff y (puf′ē), *adj.,* **puff i er, puff i est.** 1 puffed out; swollen. 2 puffed up; vain. 3 coming in puffs. **—puff′i ness,** *n.*

pug (pug), *n.* 1 a small, heavy-bodied dog with a curly tail, a short nose on a wide, wrinkled face, and a short, smooth coat. 2 pug nose. [origin uncertain]

Pu get Sound (pyü′jit), long narrow bay of the Pacific in NW Washington. 80 mi. long.

pu gi lism (pyü′jə liz′əm), *n.* art or sport of boxing. [< Latin *pugil* boxer]

pu gi list (pyü′jə list), *n.* boxer.

pu gi lis tic (pyü′jə lis′tik), *adj.* of or having to do with boxing.

pug na cious (pug nā′shəs), *adj.* having the habit of fighting; fond of fighting; quarrelsome. [< Latin *pugnacem* < *pugnare* to fight] **—pug na′cious ly,** *adv.* **—pug na′cious ness,** *n.*

pug nac i ty (pug nas′ə tē), *n.* fondness for fighting; quarrelsomeness.

pug nose, a short, turned-up nose.

pug-nosed (pug′nōzd′), *adj.* having a pug nose.

pu is sance (pyü′ə səns, pyü is′ns, pwis′ns), *n.* power; strength.

pu is sant (pyü′ə sənt, pyü is′nt, pwis′nt), *adj.* having great power or strength; powerful; mighty. [< Old French < Popular Latin *possentem* < Latin *potentem* potent] **—pu′is sant ly,** *adv.*

puke (pyük), *n., v.i., v.t.,* **puked, puk ing.** INFORMAL. vomit. [origin uncertain]

puk ka (puk′ə), *adj.* in India: 1 genuine; true; real. 2 reliable; good. 3 solid; substantial. Also, **pucka.** [< Hindi *pakkā* cooked, ripe]

Pu las ki (pu̇ las′kē), *n.* Count **Casimir,** 1748-1779, Polish nobleman, a general in the American Revolutionary army.

pul chri tude (pul′krə tüd, pul′krə tyüd), *n.* physical beauty: *feminine pulchritude.* [< Latin *pulchritudo* < *pulcher* beautiful]

pul chri tu di nous (pul′krə tüd′n əs, pul′krə tyüd′n əs), *adj.* physically beautiful.

pule (pyül), *v.i.,* **puled, pul ing.** cry in a thin voice, as a sick child does; whimper; whine. [perhaps imitative]

Pu litz er (pyü′lit sər, pu̇l′it sər), *n.* **Joseph,** 1847-1911, American journalist and newspaper publisher, born in Hungary.

Pulitzer Prize, any one of various awards given each year for distinguished achievement in American journalism, literature, music, and the arts, established by Joseph Pulitzer.

pull (pu̇l), *v.t.* 1 move (something) by grasping it and drawing toward oneself: *pull a door open.* See synonym study below. 2 move, usually with effort or force: *pull a sled uphill.* 3 tug at (something) with the fingers, etc.: *pull a person's hair.* 4 take hold of and draw out with the fingers or a clutching tool: *Use the claw hammer to pull nails.* 5 pick; pluck: *pull flowers.* 6 tear, rend, or separate into parts by pulling: *pull a book into shreds, pull an argument to pieces.* 7 stretch too far; strain: *pull a ligament in one's leg.* 8 U.S. draw out (a gun, knife, etc.) in a threatening manner. 9 be provided or rowed with: *The boat pulls eight oars.* 10 INFORMAL. carry through; perform: *Don't try to pull that trick on me again.* 11 (in golf) hit (a ball) so that it curves to the left; hook. 12 (in baseball) hit (a ball) along or near the foul line on the same side of the plate as that on which the batter stands. 13 hold back, especially to keep from winning: *pull a horse in a race.* 14 (in printing) take (an impression, proof, or copy) by printing. *—v.i.* 1 tug with the fingers: *She pulled at my sleeve to get my attention.* 2 move, usually with effort or force: *I pulled ahead of the others in the race.* 3 row: *Pull for the shore.* 4 suck: *pull on a cigar.* 5 drink, especially heartily or thirstily.

pull down, a demolish; destroy. b lower. c depress in health, spirits, etc. d earn (money or wages).

pull for, INFORMAL. a give help to: *pull for the underdog.* b support enthusiastically.

pull in, a SLANG. arrest (a person). b stop; check. c arrive: *I pulled in this morning.*

pull off, INFORMAL. do successfully; succeed in.

pull oneself together, gather one's faculties, energy, etc.

pull out, a move away from; leave: *The train pulled out of the station.* b withdraw from a venture, undertaking, etc.

pull over, bring a vehicle to the side of the road or street and stop.

pull through, get through a difficult or dangerous situation.

pull together, work in harmony; get on together.

pull up, a bring or come to a halt; stop: *A car pulled up beside me.* b reprimand; rebuke. c move ahead, as in a race.

—n. 1 act of pulling; tug. 2 a difficult climb, journey, or other effort: *It was a hard pull to get up the hill.* 3 handle, rope, ring, or other thing to pull by: *a bell pull, a curtain pull.* 4 force that attracts: *magnetic pull.* 5 a drink. 6 a suck: *a long pull at a cigar.* 7 a pulling of the ball in golf, baseball, etc. 8 INFORMAL. influence; advantage: *use political pull to get a job.* 9 (in printing) impression, proof, or copy taken by printing.

[Old English *pullian*] **—pull′er,** *n.*

Syn. *v.t.* 1 **Pull, tug, jerk** mean to draw toward oneself. **Pull** is the general word meaning to draw (or try to draw) toward or after oneself or in a specified or implied direction: *Pull the curtains across.* **Tug** means to pull hard or long, but does not always mean causing the thing or person to move: *The dog tugged at the tablecloth.* **Jerk** means to pull, push, or twist quickly and suddenly: *She jerked her hand away.*

pull back (pu̇l′bak′), *n.* withdrawal, especially of troops.

pul let (pu̇l′it), *n.* a young hen, usually less than a year old. [< Old French *poulet,* diminutive of *poule* hen. See POULTRY.]

pul ley (pu̇l′ē), *n., pl.* **-leys.** 1 wheel with a grooved rim in which a rope can run and so change the direction of a pull. It is a simple machine and is used to raise weights. 2 set of such wheels used to increase the power applied. 3 wheel used to transfer power by driving a belt that moves some other part of the machine. [< Old French *poulie*]

Pull man (pu̇l′mən), *n.* 1 sleeping car. 2 parlor car. [< George M. *Pullman,* 1831-1897, American inventor who designed railroad cars]

Pullman car, Pullman.

pull out (pu̇l′out′), *n.* 1 withdrawal, especially of troops; pullback. 2 (of aircraft) the action of recovering from a dive and returning to level flight. *—adj.* that pulls out: *a pullout shelf.*

pull o ver (pu̇l′ō′vər), *n.* garment such as a sweater or shirt put on by pulling it over the head. *—adj.* put on by pulling it over the head: *a pullover dress.*

pul mo nar y (pul′mə ner′ē), *adj.* 1 of or having to do with the lungs. Pneumonia is a pulmonary disease. 2 having lungs. 3 occurring in the lungs. [< Latin *pulmonarius* < *pulmonem* lung]

pulmonary artery, the artery which carries venous blood directly from the right ventricle of the heart to the lungs.

pulmonary vein, one of the four veins which carry oxygenated blood directly from the lungs to the left auricle of the heart.

Pul mo tor (pu̇l′mō′tər, pul′mō′tər), *n.* trademark for a mechanical apparatus for producing artificial respiration which pumps air or oxygen in and out of the lungs, used in cases of drowning, etc.

pulp (pulp), *n.* 1 the soft, fleshy part of any fruit or vegetable: *the pulp of an orange.* 2 the soft pith in the interior of the stem of a plant. 3 the soft residue left when most of the liquid is pressed out of vegetables, fruit, etc. 4 the soft inner part of a tooth, containing blood vessels and nerves. 5 any soft, wet mass. 6 the fibrous material, such as wood, rags, etc., reduced by grinding and mixing with water to a soft, uniform mass, from which paper is manufactured. 7 magazine printed on cheap paper, and usually containing matter of a cheap, sensational nature. *—v.t.* reduce to pulp. *—v.i.* become pulpy. [< Latin *pulpa*]

pul pit (pu̇l′pit), *n.* 1 platform or raised structure in a church from which the minister preaches. 2 preachers or preach-

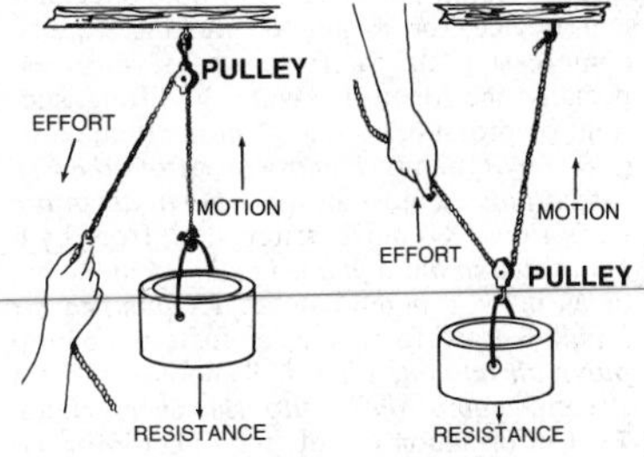

pulley (def. 1)—two types of pulleys

ings. [< Latin *pulpitum* scaffold, platform]

pulp wood (pulp′wu̇d′), *n.* any soft wood, such as spruce, suitable for reducing to pulp to make paper.

pulp y (pul′pē), *adj.,* **pulp i er, pulp i est.** of pulp; like pulp; fleshy; soft. **—pulp′i ness,** *n.*

pul que (pu̇l′kē; *Spanish* pül′kā), *n.* an alcoholic beverage made from the fermented juice of certain magueys, much used in Mexico and Central America. [< Mexican Spanish]

pul sar (pul′sär), *n.* a radio star that emits radio waves of short duration at regular intervals. [< *puls(e)* + *(quas)ar*]

pul sate (pul′sāt), *v.i.,* **-sat ed, -sat ing.** 1 expand and contract rhythmically, as the heart or an artery; beat; throb. 2 vibrate; quiver. [< Latin *pulsatum* beaten, pushed < *pulsus* a beating, pulse]

pul sa tion (pul sā′shən), *n.* 1 a beating; throbbing. 2 a beat; throb. 3 vibration; quiver.

pulse[1] (puls), *n., v.,* **pulsed, puls ing.** *—n.* 1 the regular beating of the arteries caused by the rush of blood into them after each contraction of the heart. 2 any regular, measured beat: *the pulse in music, the pulse of an engine.* 3 feeling; sentiment: *the pulse of the nation.* 4 an electromagnetic wave, or a modulation of an electromagnetic wave, which lasts a short time. *—v.i.* beat; throb; vibrate: *My heart pulsed with excitement.* *—v.t.* (in electronics) emit or produce pulses. [< Latin *pulsus* < *pellere* to beat. Doublet of PUSH.]

pulse[2] (puls), *n.* 1 the seeds of leguminous plants, such as peas, beans, and lentils, used as food. 2 plant that yields such seeds. [< Old French *pols* < Latin *puls* porridge]

pulse jet (puls′jet′), *n.* type of jet engine into which the air necessary for the burning of the fuel is admitted by valves in spurts.

pul ve rize (pul′və rīz′), *v.,* **-rized, -riz ing.** *—v.t.* 1 grind to powder or dust. 2 break to pieces; demolish. *—v.i.* become dust. [< Late Latin *pulverizare* < Latin *pulvis* dust] **—pul′ver i za′tion,** *n.* **—pul′ve riz′er,** *n.*

pu ma (pyü′mə, pü′mə), *n.* a large, tawny wildcat found in many parts of North and South America; cougar; mountain lion; panther. [< Spanish < Quechua]

pum ice (pum′is), *n.* a light, porous, glassy lava used, especially when powdered, for cleaning, smoothing, and polishing. [< Latin *pumicem.* Doublet of POUNCE[2].]

pumice stone, pumice.

pum mel (pum′əl), *v.t., v.i.,* **-meled, -mel ing** or **-melled, -mel ling.** strike or beat; beat with the fists. Also, **pommel.**

pump[1] (pump), *n.* machine or other mechanical device for raising or moving liquids, compressing or rarefying gases, etc., especially one for raising water by lifting, suction, or pressure. *—v.t.* 1 move (liquids or gases) by a pump: *Pump water from the well into a pail.* 2 blow air into: *pump air into a car's tires.* 3 remove water, etc., from by a pump: *pump out a flooded cellar.* 4 move by, or as if by, a pump handle: *He pumped my hand.* 5 draw, force, etc., as if from a pump: *pump air into one's lungs.* 6 shoot or fire in a stream: *pump shells into the enemy lines.* 7 get information out of; try to get information out of: *Don't let them pump you.* *—v.i.* 1 work a pump. 2 move up and down like a pump handle. [Middle English *pompe*] **—pump′er,** *n.*

pump[2] (pump), *n.* a low-cut shoe with a thin sole and no fasteners. [origin uncertain]

pum per nick el (pum′pər nik′əl), *n.* a heavy, dark, slightly sour bread made from whole, coarse rye. [< German *Pumpernickel*]

pump kin (pump′kin, pung′kin), *n.* 1 a large, roundish, orange-yellow fruit of a vine of the gourd family, used for making pies, as a vegetable, as food for livestock, and for jack-o'-lanterns. 2 the coarse, trailing vine with broad, prickly leaves that it grows on. 3 any of certain large squashes that resemble the pumpkin in shape and color. [alteration of earlier *pumpion* < Middle French *pompon* < Latin *peponem* melon, pumpkin < Greek *pepōn*]

pump priming, government expenditure, especially on public works, intended to stimulate business and to relieve depression and unemployment.

pun (pun), *n., v.,* **punned, pun ning.** *—n.* a humorous use of a word where it can have different meanings, or of two or more words with the same or nearly the same sound but different meanings; play on words: *"We must all hang together, or we shall all hang separately" is a famous pun by Benjamin Franklin.* *—v.i., v.t.* make puns. [origin uncertain]

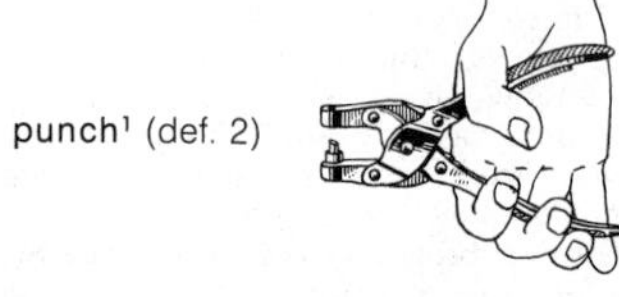

punch[1] (def. 2)

punch[1] (punch), *n.* 1 a quick thrust or blow with the fist. 2 tool for making holes. 3 tool or apparatus for piercing, perforating, or stamping materials, impressing a design, forcing nails beneath a surface, driving bolts out of holes, etc. 4 INFORMAL. vigorous force or effectiveness: *This story lacks punch.* 5 **beat to the punch,** INFORMAL. do anything sooner than (one's opponent). 6 **pull (one's) punches,** INFORMAL. act or speak with fear, caution, or hesitation; be overly restrained. *—v.t.* 1 hit with the fist: *punch someone on the arm.* 2 pierce, cut, stamp, force, or make with a punch: *punch metal.* 3 make (a hole) with a punch or any pointed instrument: *The conductor punched our tickets.* 4 cause to operate by pressing a key, lever, etc.: *punch the time clock.* 5 herd or drive (cattle). *—v.i.* 1 give a punch or punches; hit; strike. 2 register the time of one's arrival or departure by punching a time clock: *punch in to work, punch out at 5 p.m.* [apparently short for earlier *puncheon* a stamping tool used by goldsmiths < Old French *poinchon.* See PUNCHEON[2].] **—punch′er,** *n.*

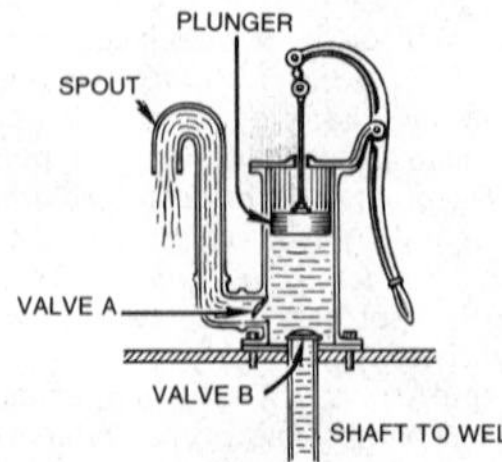

pump[1]
As handle is raised, plunger moves downward forcing water through valve A and out spout. As handle is pushed down, plunger is raised, pulling water upward through valve B from shaft.

punch[2] (punch), *n.* drink made of different liquids, often fruit juices or carbonated beverages mixed together. [probably < Hindustani *pānch* five < Sanskrit *pañca* (because of the number of ingredients in the drink)]

Punch (punch), *n.* 1 a hook-nosed, hunchbacked doll in the puppet show *Punch and Judy.* 2 **pleased as Punch,** very much pleased. [short for *punchinello*]

Punch-and-Ju dy show (punch′ən jü′dē), a puppet show in which Punch quarrels violently with his wife Judy.

punch card, card on which information is recorded by means of holes punched according to a code, for use in processing data by machine, electronic computer, etc. Also, **punched card.**

punch-drunk (punch′drungk′), *adj.* 1 (of a boxer) uncoordinated in movement, speech, etc., as a result of brain concussion. 2 INFORMAL. dazed.

punched card, punch card.

pun cheon[1] (pun′chən), *n.* 1 a large cask for liquor, varying in size from 70 to 120 gallons. 2 amount that it holds, used as a unit of capacity. [< Old French *poinchon, poinçon, ponson*]

pun cheon[2] (pun′chən), *n.* 1 slab of timber or a piece of a split log, with the face roughly smoothed. 2 a short, upright piece of wood in the frame of a building. [< Old French *poinchon* < Latin *punctionem* a pricking < *pungere* pierce]

pun chi nel lo (pun′chə nel′ō), *n., pl.* **-los** or **-loes.** 1 **Punchinello,** the principal character in a traditional Italian puppet show, the prototype of Punch. 2 clown. 3 any grotesque or absurd person or thing. [< dialectal Italian *Pulcinella*]

punching bag, a leather bag filled with air or stuffed, to be hung up and punched with the fists for exercise or to develop boxing skills.

punch line, the line or sentence in a story, play, or drama which makes or enforces the point.

punch press, press used to cut, indent, or shape metals.

punch y (pun′chē), *adj.,* **punch i er, punch i est.** INFORMAL. 1 forceful. 2 punch-drunk.

punc til i o (pungk til′ē ō), *n., pl.* **-til i os.** 1 a little point or detail of honor, conduct, ceremony, etc. 2 care in attending to such little points or details. [< Italian *puntiglio* < Spanish *puntillo* little point]

punc til i ous (pungk til′ē əs), *adj.* 1 very careful and exact: *A nurse should be punctilious in obeying the doctor's orders.* 2 paying strict attention to details of conduct and ceremony. See **scrupulous** for synonym study. **—punc til′i ous ly,** *adv.* **—punc til′i ous ness,** *n.*

punc tu al (pungk′chü əl), *adj.* on time; prompt: *be punctual to the minute.* [< Latin *punctum* point] **—punc′tu al ly,** *adv.* **—punc′tu al ness,** *n.*

punc tu al i ty (pungk′chü al′ə tē), *n.* a being on time; promptness.

punc tu ate (pungk′chü āt), *v.,* **-at ed, -at ing.** *—v.i.* use periods, commas, and other marks in writing or printing to help

hat, āge, fär; let, ēqual, tėrm; it, īce; hot, ōpen, ôrder; oil, out; cup, pu̇t, rüle; ch, child; ng, long; sh, she; th, thin; ᴛʜ, then; zh, measure;

ə represents *a* in about, *e* in taken, *i* in pencil, *o* in lemon, *u* in circus.

< = from, derived from, taken from.

make the meaning clear. —*v.t.* 1 put punctuation marks in. 2 interrupt now and then: *a speech punctuated with cheers.* 3 give point or emphasis to: *punctuate one's remarks with gestures.* [< Medieval Latin *punctuatum* defined by points < Latin *punctum* point] **—punc′tu a′tor,** *n.*

punc tu a tion (pungk′chü ā′shən), *n.* 1 use of periods, commas, and other marks to help make the meaning clear. Punctuation does for writing and printing what pauses and changes of voice do for speech. 2 punctuation marks.

punctuation mark, mark used in writing or printing to help make the meaning clear. Periods, commas, question marks, colons, etc., are punctuation marks.

punc ture (pungk′chər), *n., v.,* **-tured, -tur ing.** —*n.* 1 hole made by something pointed: *a puncture in a tire.* 2 act or process of puncturing. 3 a minute, rounded pit or depression. —*v.t.* 1 make a hole in with something pointed. 2 reduce, spoil, or destroy as if by a puncture: *His ego was punctured by the criticism.* —*v.i.* have or get a puncture. [< Latin *punctura* < *punctum* point]

pun dit (pun′dit), *n.* a very learned person; expert; authority. [< Hindi *pandit* < Sanskrit *paṇḍita* learned]

pun gen cy (pun′jən sē), *n.* pungent quality.

pun gent (pun′jənt), *adj.* 1 sharply affecting the organs of taste and smell: *a pungent pickle, the pungent smell of burning leaves.* 2 sharp; biting: *pungent criticism.* 3 stimulating to the mind; keen; lively: *a pungent wit.* 4 (in biology) piercing; sharp-pointed. [< Latin *pungentem* piercing, pricking < *punctum* point] **—pun′gent ly,** *adv.*

Pu nic (pyü′nik), *adj.* of or having to do with ancient Carthage or its inhabitants. [< Latin *Punicus* < *Poenus* Carthaginian, alteration of Greek *Phoinix* Phoenician]

pun ish (pun′ish), *v.t.* 1 cause pain, loss, or discomfort to for some fault or offense: *punish criminals.* 2 cause pain, loss, or discomfort for: *punish crimes.* 3 INFORMAL. deal with severely, roughly, or greedily: *punish a car by very fast driving.* —*v.i.* to subject to punishment. [< Old French *puniss-*, a form of *punir* punish < Latin *punire* < *poena* penalty] **—pun′ish er,** *n.*

pun ish a bil i ty (pun′i shə bil′ə tē), *n.* quality of being punishable.

pun ish a ble (pun′i shə bəl), *adj.* 1 liable to punishment. 2 deserving punishment.

pun ish ment (pun′ish mənt), *n.* 1 a punishing. 2 a being punished. 3 penalty inflicted for a fault or offense: *Her punishment for stealing was a year in prison.* 4 INFORMAL. severe or rough treatment: *This engine can withstand a great deal of punishment.*

pu ni tive (pyü′nə tiv), *adj.* 1 concerned with punishment: *punitive laws.* 2 seeking to punish; inflicting punishment: *a punitive military campaign.* **—pu′ni tive ly,** *adv.* **—pu′ni tive ness,** *n.*

pu ni to ry (pyü′nə tôr′ē, pyü′nə tōr′ē), *adj.* punitive.

Pun jab (pun jäb′, pun′jäb), *n.* **the,** former province in N India, now divided between India and Pakistan.

Pun ja bi (pun jä′bē), *n.* 1 native or inhabitant of the Punjab; Panjabi. 2 Panjabi. —*adj.* of the Punjab, its people, or their language.

punk[1] (pungk), *n.* 1 a light, brownish, spongy preparation that burns very slowly, usually made from fungi. A stick of punk is used to light fireworks. 2 decayed wood used in a dry state for tinder; touchwood. [perhaps < Algonquian *ponk* ashes]

punk[2] (pungk), SLANG. —*adj.* poor or bad in quality. —*n.* 1 a young hoodlum. 2 a young, inexperienced person. [origin unknown]

pun kah (pung′kə), *n.* (in India and the East Indies) a fan, especially a large swinging fan hung from the ceiling and kept in motion by a servant or by machinery. [< Hindi *pankhā*]

pun ster (pun′stər), *n.* person fond of making puns.

punt[1] (def. 1)

punt[1] (punt), *n.* 1 a shallow, flat-bottomed boat with square ends, usually moved by pushing with a pole against the bottom of a river, etc. 2 kick given to a football before it touches the ground after dropping it from the hands. —*v.t.* 1 propel (a boat) by pushing with a pole against the bottom of a river, pond, etc. 2 kick (a football) before it touches the ground after dropping it from the hands. —*v.i.* 1 use a punt; travel by punt. 2 punt a football. [< Latin *ponto* pontoon] **—punt′er,** *n.*

punt[2] (punt), *v.i.* 1 bet against the banker in a card game, such as faro. 2 gamble. [< French *ponter,* ultimately < Latin *punctum* point] **—punt′er,** *n.*

pu ny (pyü′nē), *adj.,* **-ni er, -ni est.** 1 of less than usual size and strength; small and weak. 2 not important; petty. [< Old French *puisné* later-born < *puis* afterwards + *ne* born] **—pu′ni ness,** *n.*

pup (pup), *n., v.,* **pupped, pup ping.** —*n.* 1 a young dog; puppy. 2 a young fox, wolf, seal, etc. —*v.i.* bring forth pups. [short for *puppy*]

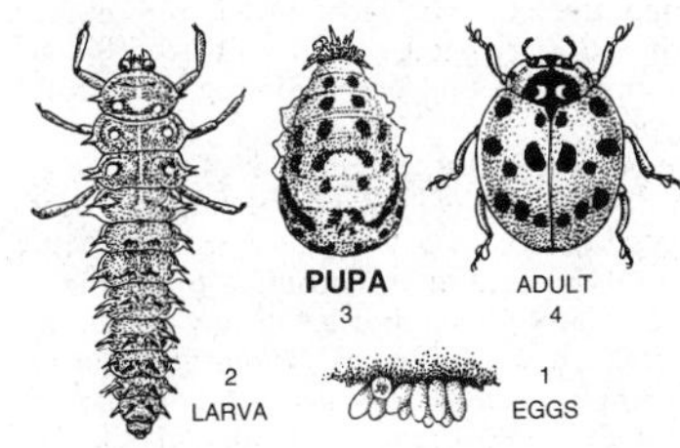

pupa (def. 2)
four stages in the life of a beetle

pu pa (pyü′pə), *n., pl.* **-pae** (-pē), **-pas.** 1 stage between the larva and the adult in the development of many insects. 2 insect in this stage. Most pupae are inactive and some, such as those of many moths, are enclosed in a tough case or cocoon. [< Latin, girl, doll]

pu pal (pyü′pəl), *adj.* of, having to do with, or in the form of a pupa.

pu pate (pyü′pāt), *v.i.,* **-pat ed, -pat ing.** become a pupa. **—pu pa′tion,** *n.*

pu pil[1] (pyü′pəl), *n.* person who is learning in school or being taught by someone. See **student** for synonym study. [< Old French *pupille* < Latin *pupillus, pupilla* ward < *pupus* boy, *pupa* girl]

pu pil[2] (pyü′pəl), *n.* the opening in the center of the iris of the eye, circular in man and most vertebrates and appearing as a black spot, which is the only place where light can enter the eye. The size of the pupil is regulated by expansion and contraction of the iris. [< Latin *pupilla,* originally, little doll, diminutive of *pupa* girl, doll (because of the tiny reflection of oneself that may be seen in the eye of another person)]

pup pet (pup′it), *n.* 1 a small doll. 2 figure made to look like a person or animal and moved by wires, strings, or the hands. 3 person, government, etc., whose actions are prompted and controlled by another or others. [< Middle French *poupette* < Latin *pupa* girl, doll] **—pup′pet like′,** *adj.*

pup pet eer (pup′ə tir′), *n.* person who manipulates puppets.

pup pet ry (pup′ə trē), *n., pl.* **-ries.** 1 the action of puppets. 2 artificial action like that of a puppet. 3 the art or craft of making puppets, putting on puppet shows, etc.

puppet show, play performed with puppets on a small stage.

pup py (pup′ē), *n., pl.* **-pies.** 1 a young dog. 2 a silly, conceited young man. [< Middle French *poupée* doll < Latin *pupa*]

pup tent, a small, low tent, usually for one or two persons.

pur (pėr), *n., v.,* **purred, pur ring.** purr.

pur blind (pėr′blīnd′), *adj.* 1 nearly blind. 2 slow to discern or understand; dull; obtuse. [Middle English *pur blind* pure blind] **—pur′blind′ly,** *adv.* **—pur′blind′ness,** *n.*

pur chase (pėr′chəs), *v.,* **-chased, -chas ing,** *n.* —*v.t.* 1 get by paying a price; buy: *purchase a new car.* See **buy** for synonym study. 2 get in return for something: *purchase safety at the cost of happiness.* 3 hoist, haul, or draw by the aid of some mechanical device. —*n.* 1 act of buying. 2 thing bought. 3 a firm hold to help move something or to keep from slipping: *Wind the rope twice around the tree to get a better purchase.* 4 device for obtaining such a hold. [< Anglo-French *purchacer* pursue < Old French *pur-* forth + *chacier* to chase] **—pur′chas a ble,** *adj.* **—pur′chas er,** *n.*

purchasing power, 1 the ability to buy things, as measured by the amount of money one earns or has available. 2 the value of a unit of currency, as measured by the amount of things one can buy with it in a given period in comparison with some earlier period.

pur dah (pėr′də), *n.* in India: 1 a curtain serving to screen women from the sight of men or strangers. 2 condition or system of being kept hidden from men or strangers. [< Hindustani *pardah* < Persian, veil, curtain]

pure (pyu̇r), *adj.,* **pur er, pur est.** 1 not mixed with anything else; unadulterated; genuine: *pure gold.* 2 perfectly clean; spotless: *pure hands.* 3 without defects; perfect; correct: *speak pure French.* 4 nothing else than; mere; sheer: *pure accident.* 5 with no evil; without sin; chaste: *a pure mind.* 6 concerned with theory rather than practical use; not applied; abstract: *pure mathematics, pure science.* 7 keeping the same qualities, characteristics, etc., from generation to generation; of unmixed descent: *a pure Indian family.* 8 (in genetics) homozygous, and therefore breeding true for at least one hereditary character. [< Old French *pur* < Latin *purus*] **—pure′ness,** *n.*

pure bred (pyůr′bred′), *adj.* of pure breed or stock; having ancestors known to have all belonged to one breed: *purebred Holstein cows.* —*n.* a purebred animal.

pu rée (pyů rā′, pyůr′ā), *n.*, *v.*, **-réed, -rée ing.** —*n.* 1 vegetables, meat, etc., boiled to a pulp and pushed through a sieve. 2 a thick soup made with this. —*v.t.* make into a purée. [< French < *purer* to strain, purify]

pure ly (pyůr′lē), *adv.* 1 in a pure manner. 2 exclusively; entirely. 3 merely. 4 innocently; chastely.

pur ga tion (pėr gā′shən), *n.* a purging; cleansing.

pur ga tive (pėr′gə tiv), *n.* medicine that causes emptying of the bowels. Castor oil is a purgative. —*adj.* purging, especially causing the bowels to empty.

pur ga to ri al (pėr′gə tôr′ē əl, pėr′gə-tōr′ē əl), *adj.* 1 of, like, or having to do with purgatory. 2 of a spiritually cleansing or purifying quality.

pur ga to ry (pėr′gə tôr′ē, pėr′gə tōr′ē), *n., pl.* **-ries.** 1 (in Roman Catholic belief) a temporary condition or place in which the souls of those who have died penitent are purified from venial sin or the effects of sin by punishment. 2 any condition or place of temporary suffering or punishment. [< Medieval Latin *purgatorium,* originally, purging < Latin *purgare.* See PURGE.]

purge (pėrj), *v.,* **purged, purg ing,** *n.* —*v.t.* 1 wash away all that is not clean from; make clean: *King Arthur tried to purge his land of sin.* 2 clear of any undesired thing or person, such as air in a water pipe or opponents in a nation. 3 empty (the bowels). —*v.i.* 1 become clean. 2 undergo or cause emptying of the bowels. —*n.* 1 act of purging. 2 medicine that purges; purgative. 3 elimination of undesired persons from a nation or party. [< Old French *purgier* < Latin *purgare* cleanse < *purus* pure + *agere* to drive] **—purg′er,** *n.*

pur i fi ca tion (pyůr′ə fə kā′shən), *n.* 1 a purifying. 2 a being purified.

pu rif i ca to ry (pyů rif′ə kə tôr′ē, pyů-rif′ə kə tōr′ē), *adj.* serving to purify.

pur i fy (pyůr′ə fī), *v.,* **-fied, -fy ing.** —*v.t.* make pure: *purify water, purify the heart.* —*v.i.* become pure. **—pur′i fi′er,** *n.*

Pur im (pyůr′im, půr′im), *n.* a Jewish holiday, celebrated each year in February or March, commemorating Esther's saving of the Jews from being massacred by Haman. [< Hebrew *pūrīm*]

pu rine (pyůr′ēn′, pyůr′ən), *n.* 1 a colorless, crystalline organic base containing nitrogen and related to uric acid. *Formula:* $C_5H_4N_4$ 2 any of a group of compounds derived from it, such as caffeine, adenine, and guanine.

pur ism (pyůr′iz′əm), *n.* 1 strict or exaggerated observance of purity and correctness in language, art, style, etc. 2 insistence that others do this.

pur ist (pyůr′ist), *n.* person who is very careful or too careful about purity and correctness in language, art, style, etc. A purist dislikes slang and all expressions that are not formally correct.

pu ris tic (pyů ris′tik), *adj.* very careful or too careful about purity in language, art, style, etc.

Pur i tan (pyůr′ə tən), *n.* 1 member of a group in the Church of England during the 1500's and 1600's who wanted simpler forms of worship and stricter morals. Many Puritans settled in New England. 2 **puritan,** person who is very strict in morals and religion. —*adj.* 1 of the Puritans. 2 **puritan,** very strict in morals and religion.

pur i tan ic (pyůr′ə tan′ik), *adj.* puritanical.

Pur i tan i cal (pyůr′ə tan′ə kəl), *adj.* 1 of or having to do with the Puritans. 2 **puritanical,** of or like a puritan; very strict or too strict in morals or religion. **—pur′i tan′i cal ly,** *adv.* **—pur′i tan′i-cal ness,** *n.*

Pur i tan ism (pyůr′ə tə niz′əm), *n.* 1 the principles and practices of the Puritans. 2 **puritanism,** puritanical behavior or principles.

pur i ty (pyůr′ə tē), *n.* 1 freedom from anything impure; clearness; cleanness: *the purity of drinking water.* 2 freedom from evil; innocence: *No one doubts the purity of Joan of Arc's motives.* 3 freedom from foreign or inappropriate elements; correctness: *purity of style.*

purl[1] (pėrl), *v.i.* 1 flow with rippling motions and a murmuring sound: *A shallow brook purls.* 2 pass with a sound like this. —*n.* 1 a purling motion or sound. 2 act of purling. [perhaps < Scandinavian (Norwegian) *purla* to ripple]

purl[2] (pėrl), *v.t., v.i.* 1 knit with inverted stitches by changing the yarn from one side of the needle to the other. 2 border (material) with small loops. 3 ARCHAIC. embroider with gold or silver thread. —*n.* 1 inversion of stitches in knitting, producing a ribbed appearance. 2 loop or chain of small loops along the edge of lace, braid, ribbon, etc. 3 thread of twisted gold or silver wire, used for bordering and embroidering. [origin uncertain]

pur lieu (pėr′lü), *n.* 1 piece of land on the border of a forest. 2 one's haunt or resort; one's bounds. 3 any bordering, neighboring, or outlying region or district. 4 **purlieus,** *pl.* **a** parts around the border of any place; outskirts. **b** nearby parts; vicinity; environs. [< Anglo-French *puralee* < *poraler* go through < Old French *por-* forth + *aler* go]

pur lin (pėr′lən), *n.* a horizontal beam running the length of a roof and supporting the top rafters of the roof. [origin uncertain]

pur loin (pər loin′), *v.t., v.i.* steal. [< Anglo-French *purloigner* to remove] **—pur loin′er,** *n.*

pur ple (pėr′pəl), *n., adj., v.,* **-pled, -pling.** —*n.* 1 a dark color made by mixing red and blue. 2 crimson. This was the ancient meaning of purple. 3 purple cloth or clothing, especially as worn by emperors, kings, etc., to indicate high rank. 4 imperial, royal, or high rank. A prince is born to the purple. 5 rank or position of a cardinal. 6 any of several gastropods having a gland that secretes a purplish fluid. —*adj.* 1 of the color of purple. 2 crimson. 3 imperial; royal. 4 very ornate in style: *purple prose.* —*v.t., v.i.* make or become purple. [Old English, variant of *purpure* < Latin *purpura* < Greek *porphyra*]

Purple Heart, medal awarded to members of the armed forces of the United States for wounds received in action against an enemy or as a result of enemy action.

pur plish (pėr′plish), *adj.* somewhat purple.

pur port (*v.* pər pôrt′, pər pōrt′; pėr′pôrt, pėr′pōrt; *n.* pėr′pôrt, pėr′pōrt), *v.t.* 1 claim or profess: *The document purported to be official.* 2 have as its main idea; mean. —*n.* meaning; main idea: *The purport of her letter was that she could not come.* See **meaning** for synonym study. [< Anglo-French *purporter* < Old French *pur-* forth + *porter* carry] **—pur port′ed ly,** *adv.*

pur pose (pėr′pəs), *n., v.,* **-posed, -pos ing.** —*n.* 1 something one has in mind to get or do; aim; intention. See **intention** for synonym study. 2 object or end for which a thing is made, done, used, etc. 3 **on purpose,** with a purpose; not by accident; intentionally. 4 **to good purpose,** with good results. 5 **to little purpose** or **to no purpose,** with few or no results. 6 **to the purpose,** to the point; relevant; pertinent. —*v.t., v.i.* plan; aim; intend. [< Old French *pourpos* < *pourposer* propose < *pour-* forth + *poser* to put, pose]

pur pose ful (pėr′pəs fəl), *adj.* having a purpose. **—pur′pose ful ly,** *adv.* **—pur′pose ful ness,** *n.*

pur pose less (pėr′pəs lis), *adj.* lacking a purpose. **—pur′pose less ly,** *adv.* **—pur′pose less ness,** *n.*

pur pose ly (pėr′pəs lē), *adv.* on purpose; intentionally.

pur pos ive (pėr′pə siv), *adj.* 1 acting with, having, or serving some purpose. 2 purposeful. 3 of or having to do with purpose. **—pur′pos ive ly,** *adv.* **—pur′pos ive ness,** *n.*

purr (pėr), *n.* a low, murmuring sound such as a cat makes when pleased. —*v.i., v.t.* make a low, murmuring sound. Also, **pur.** [imitative]

purse (pėrs), *n., v.,* **pursed, purs ing.** —*n.* 1 a small bag or container to hold small change, usually carried in a handbag or pocket. 2 a woman's handbag. 3 resources of money; funds; treasury. 4 sum of money offered as a prize, present, etc. 5 any baglike receptacle, such as an animal's pouch or a seed capsule. —*v.t.* 1 draw together; press into folds or wrinkles: *She pursed her lips and frowned.* 2 put in a purse. [Old English *purs* < Late Latin *bursa* < Greek *byrsa* hide, skin. Doublet of BOURSE, BURSA.]

purse-proud (pėrs′proud′), *adj.* proud of being rich.

purs er (pėr′sər), *n.* a ship's officer who keeps accounts, pays wages, attends to other matters of business, and is responsible for the welfare of passengers.

pur slane (pėr′slān, pėr′slən), *n.* any of a genus of annual, trailing plants having thick, fleshy leaves and stems, especially a common species with small, yellow flowers, whose leaves are sometimes used for salad or for flavoring, or as a potherb. [< Old French *porcelaine,* alteration of Latin *porcilaca*]

pur su ance (pər sü′əns), *n.* a following; carrying out; pursuit: *In pursuance of his duty, the fireman risked his life.*

pur su ant (pər sü′ənt), *adj.* 1 following; carrying out; according. 2 **pursuant to,** following; acting according to; in accordance with.

hat, āge, fär; let, ēqual, tėrm;
it, īce; hot, ōpen, ôrder;
oil, out; cup, pu̇t, rüle;
ch, child; ng, long; sh, she;
th, thin; ᴛʜ, then; zh, measure;

ə represents *a* in about, *e* in taken, *i* in pencil, *o* in lemon, *u* in circus.

< = from, derived from, taken from.

pur sue (pər sü′), *v.*, **-sued, -su ing.** —*v.t.* 1 follow to catch or kill; chase: *The dogs pursued the rabbit.* 2 proceed along; follow in action; follow: *He pursued a wise course by taking no chances.* 3 strive for; try to get; seek: *pursue pleasure.* 4 carry on; keep on with: *She pursued the study of French for four years.* 5 continue to annoy or trouble: *pursue a teacher with questions.* —*v.i.* follow in pursuit. [< Anglo-French *pursued* < Latin *prosequi* < *pro-* forth + *sequi* follow] —**pur su′a ble,** *adj.* —**pur su′er,** *n.*

pur suit (pər süt′), *n.* 1 act of pursuing: *the pursuit of game, the pursuit of pleasure.* 2 that which one engages in, as a profession, business, recreation, etc.; occupation: *Fishing is her favorite pursuit; reading is mine.*

pur sui vant (pėr′swə vənt), *n.* 1 assistant to a herald; officer below a herald in rank. 2 follower; attendant. [< Old French *poursuivant,* originally present participle of *poursuivre* pursue]

pur sy (pėr′sē), *adj.,* **-si er, -si est.** 1 shortwinded, especially because of fatness. 2 fat. —**pur′si ness,** *n.*

pur u lence (pyu̇r′ə ləns, pyu̇r′yə ləns), *n.* condition of forming, containing, or discharging pus; suppuration.

pur u len cy (pyu̇r′ə lən sē, pyu̇r′yə lən sē), *n.* purulence.

pur u lent (pyu̇r′ə lənt, pyu̇r′yə lənt), *adj.* forming, containing, or discharging pus: *a purulent sore.* [< Latin *purulentus* < *pus, puris* pus]

pur vey (pər vā′), *v.i., v.t.* supply (food or provisions); provide; furnish: *purvey meat for an army, purvey for a royal household.* [< Anglo-French *porveier* < Latin *providere.* Doublet of PROVIDE.]

pur vey ance (pər vā′əns), *n.* 1 a purveying. 2 provisions; supplies.

pur vey or (pər vā′ər), *n.* 1 person who supplies provisions. 2 person who supplies anything: *a purveyor of gossip.*

pur view (pėr′vyü), *n.* 1 range of operation, activity, concern, etc.; scope; extent. 2 range of vision, thought, or understanding. [< Anglo-French *purveu,* originally past participle of *porveier* purvey. See PURVEY.]

pus (pus), *n.* a thick, yellowish-white, opaque fluid consisting of white blood cells, bacteria, serum, etc., formed in sores, abscesses, and other infected tissue in the body. [< Latin]

Pu san (pü sän′), *n.* seaport in SE South Korea, on the Korea Strait. 1,879,000.

push (pu̇sh), *v.t.* 1 move (something) away by pressing against it: *Push the door; don't pull.* 2 move up, down, back, forward, etc., by pressing: *Push the dog outdoors.* See synonym study below. 3 thrust: *Trees push their roots down into the ground.* 4 force (one's way): *We had to push our way through the crowd.* 5 make go forward; urge: *He pushed his plans cleverly.* 6 continue with or follow up vigorously or insistently: *push a claim.* 7 extend: *Alexander pushed his conquests still farther east.* 8 urge the use, practice, sale, etc., of: *push used cars.* 9 press or bear hard upon: *be pushed for cash.* 10 **push around,** INFORMAL. treat roughly or with contempt; bully; harass. —*v.i.* 1 press hard: *push with all one's might.* 2 go forward by force: *push through a crowd.* 3 **push off, a** move from shore: *push off in a boat.* **b** depart; leave. 4 **push on,** keep going; proceed.
—*n.* 1 INFORMAL. power to succeed; force; energy. 2 act of pushing: *Give the door a push.* 3 hard effort; determined advance. [< Old French *pousser, poulser* < Latin *pulsare* to beat < *pulsus* a beating, pulse. Doublet of PULSE[1].] —**push′er,** *n.*

Syn. *v.t.* 1, 2 **Push, shove** mean to move someone or something by pressing against it. **Push** means pressing against the person or thing in order to move it ahead, aside, away, etc.: *She pushed the drawer closed.* **Shove** means pushing roughly or with force and effort: *We shoved the piano across the room.*

push button, a small button or knob pushed to turn an electric current on or off.

push-but ton (pu̇sh′but′ən), *adj.* of or having to do with actions carried out by automatic or remote-controlled mechanisms: *push-button warfare.*

push cart (pu̇sh′kärt′), *n.* a light cart pushed by hand.

push ing (pu̇sh′ing), *adj.* 1 pushy. 2 enterprising.

Push kin (pu̇sh′kin), *n.* **Alexander,** 1799-1837, Russian poet and writer of short stories and novels.

push o ver (pu̇sh′ō′vər), *n.* SLANG. 1 something very easy to do. 2 person very easy to beat in a contest. 3 person easily influenced or swayed or unable to resist a particular appeal.

Push tu (pu̇sh′tü), *n.* Pashto.

pushup

push up (pu̇sh′up′), *n.* exercise done by lying face down with the body held stiff and alternately pushing oneself up by straightening the arms and lowering oneself by bending them.

push y (pu̇sh′ē), *adj.,* **push i er, push i est.** forward; aggressive. —**push′i ly,** *adv.* —**push′i ness,** *n.*

pu sil la nim i ty (pyü′sə lə nim′ə tē), *n.* cowardliness; timidity.

pu sil lan i mous (pyü′sə lan′ə məs), *adj.* lacking in courage; cowardly; faint-hearted; timid: *a pusillanimous man, pusillanimous conduct.* [< Latin *pusillanimis* < *pusillus* little + *animus* spirit, courage] —**pu′sil lan′i mous ly,** *adv.*

puss (pu̇s), *n.* 1 cat. 2 girl or woman. [origin uncertain]

puss ley or **puss ly** (pus′lē), *n.* U.S. purslane.

puss y[1] (pu̇s′ē), *n., pl.* **puss ies.** 1 cat. 2 catkin, as of a willow.

pus sy[2] (pus′ē), *adj.,* **-si er, -si est.** full of pus.

puss y foot (pu̇s′ē fu̇t′), *v.i.* INFORMAL. 1 move softly and cautiously to avoid being seen. 2 be cautious and timid about revealing one's opinions or committing oneself.

puss y willow (pu̇s′ē), a small North American willow with silky, grayish-white catkins.

pus tu lar (pus′chə lər), *adj.* 1 of, like, or having to do with pustules. 2 characterized by pustules.

pus tule (pus′chül), *n.* a small bump on the skin, filled with pus and inflamed at the base. [< Latin *pustula*]

put (pu̇t), *v.,* **put, put ting,** *n.* —*v.t.* 1 cause to be in some place or position; place; lay: *I put sugar in my tea. Put away your papers.* See synonym study below. 2 cause to be in some state, condition, position, relation, etc.: *put a room in order, put oneself under the care of a doctor. We put the house on the market.* 3 set (a person or animal) to do something, or upon some course of action: *put someone to work.* 4 express: *put one's thoughts in writing.* 5 set at a particular place, point, amount, etc., in a scale of estimation; appraise: *I put the distance at five miles.* 6 propose or submit for answer, consideration, deliberation, etc.: *We put several questions before the committee.* 7 apply: *A doctor puts his skill to good use.* 8 impose: *put a tax on gasoline.* 9 assign; attribute: *They put a wrong construction on my action.* 10 to throw or cast (a 12-pound or 16-pound ball) from the hand placed close to the shoulder.

put about, (of a ship) put on the opposite tack.

put across, INFORMAL. **a** carry out successfully. **b** get accepted or understood: *put across one's point of view.*

put away, a save for future use. **b** INFORMAL. consume as food or drink: *put away a meal.* **c** put in jail; imprison. **d** commit to a mental institution.

put by, save for future use.

put down, a put an end to; suppress: *put down a rebellion.* **b** write down. **c** pay as a down payment. **d** INFORMAL. slight or belittle; snub. **e** land: *The airplane put down at Shannon airport.*

put forth, a to send out; sprout: *put forth buds.* **b** exert: *put forth effort.*

put forward, propose or submit for consideration, deliberation, etc.

put in, INFORMAL. **a** spend (time, etc.) as specified: *put in a full day of work.* **b** enter port. **c** enter a place for safety, supplies, etc. **d** make a claim, plea, or offer: *put in for a loan.*

put off, a lay aside; postpone: *put off a meeting.* **b** go away; start out: *The ship put off an hour ago.* **c** bid or cause to wait: *She refused to be put off any longer.* **d** hold back or stop from: *He was put off the project.* **e** get rid of.

put on, a direct, stage, or sponsor (a play, lecture, etc.). **b** take on or add to oneself: *put on weight.* **c** take on oneself: *put on airs.* **d** pretend: *put on an air of innocence.* **e** apply or exert: *put on pressure.* **f** clothe with; don. **g** SLANG. tease playfully; poke fun at.

put out, a extinguish; make an end to; destroy: *put out a fire.* **b** go; turn; proceed: *put out to sea.* **c** offend; provoke. **d** cause to be out in a game or sport. **e** publish.

put over, INFORMAL. **a** carry out successfully. **b** do or carry out by trickery: *put over a fraud.*

put through, carry out successfully.

put to it, force to a course; put in difficulty.

put up, a offer: *put up a house for sale.* **b** give or show: *put up a brave front.* **c** build: *put up a monument.* **d** lay aside (work).

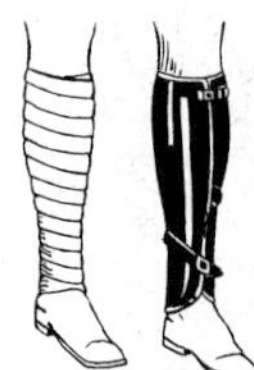

puttee—two types of puttees (def. 1, left) (def. 2, right)

e propose for election or adoption. **f** pack up or preserve (fruit, etc.). **g** give food and lodging to: *put us up for the night.* **h** provide or deposit; pay: *put up the money for the show.* **i** INFORMAL. get (a person) to do: *put her up to mischief.*

put upon, impose upon; take advantage of; victimize.

put up to, a inform; make aware of. **b** stir up; incite.

put up with, bear with patience; tolerate.

—*n.* 1 a throw or cast. 2 (in commerce) the privilege of delivering a certain amount of stock, etc., at a specified price within a certain period of time.

[Old English *putian*]

Syn. *v.t.* 1 **Put, place, set** mean to cause someone or something to be in some place or position. **Put** emphasizes the action of moving something into or out of a place or position: *Put your hand in mine.* **Place** emphasizes the idea of a definite spot, more than action: *Place your hands behind your head.* **Set** emphasizes causing to be in a certain position: *Set the box down over there.*

pu ta tive (pyü′tə tiv), *adj.* supposed; reputed: *the putative author of a book.* [< Latin *putativus* < *putare* think] **—pu′ta tive ly,** *adv.*

put-down (pu̇t′doun′), *n.* INFORMAL. 1 a slighting or belittling of a person or thing. 2 comment, reply, etc., intended to snub or belittle.

put-on (pu̇t′ôn′, pu̇t′on′), *adj.* assumed; affected; pretended. —*n.* 1 a pretension or affectation. 2 SLANG. joke or trick played for fun; practical joke.

put out (pu̇t′out′), *n.* (in baseball) act of putting out a batter or base runner.

pu tre fac tion (pyü′trə fak′shən), *n.* a putrefying; decay; rotting.

pu tre fac tive (pyü′trə fak′tiv), *adj.* 1 causing putrefaction. 2 characterized by or having to do with putrefaction.

pu tre fy (pyü′trə fī), *v.t., v.i.,* **-fied, -fy ing.** break down or cause to break down plant or animal matter by the action of bacteria and fungi, producing foul-smelling gases; decay; rot: *putrefied meat.* [< Middle French *putrefier* < Latin *putrifieri* < *puter* rotten + *fieri* become]

pu tres cence (pyü tres′ns), *n.* putrescent condition.

pu tres cent (pyü tres′nt), *adj.* 1 becoming putrid; rotting. 2 having to do with putrefaction.

pu trid (pyü′trid), *adj.* 1 decaying; rotten: *putrid meat.* 2 characteristic of putrefying matter; foul: *a putrid odor.* 3 thoroughly corrupt or depraved; extremely bad. [< Latin *putridus* < *puter* rotten] **—pu′trid ly,** *adv.* **—pu′trid ness,** *n.*

pu trid i ty (pyü trid′ə tē), *n.* 1 putrid condition. 2 putrid matter.

putsch (pu̇ch), *n.* uprising; insurrection. [< German *Putsch*]

putt (put), *v.t., v.i.* strike (a golf ball) gently and carefully along the putting green in an effort to make it roll into or near the hole. —*n.* the stroke itself. [variant of *put*]

put tee (put′ē, pu tē′), *n.* 1 a long, narrow strip of cloth wound round the leg from ankle to knee, worn by sportsmen, soldiers, etc. 2 gaiter of cloth or leather reaching from ankle to knee, worn by soldiers, riders, etc. [< Hindi *paṭṭī* a bandage, strip]

put ter[1] (put′ər), *v.i.* keep busy in an aimless or useless way: *She likes to spend the afternoon puttering in the garden.* Also, **potter.** [variant of *potter*[2]] **—put′ter er,** *n.*

putt er[2] (put′ər), *n.* 1 person who putts. 2 a golf club with an upright face and a short, rigid shaft, used in putting.

put ter[3] (pu̇t′ər), *n.* person or thing that puts.

putt ing green (put′ing), the very smooth turf around the hole into which a player putts a golf ball.

put ty (put′ē), *n., pl.* **-ties,** *v.,* **-tied, -ty ing.** —*n.* 1 kind of cement, usually made of whiting and boiled linseed oil, used for fastening panes of glass into window frames, filling cracks and holes in woodwork, etc. Putty is soft and doughlike when applied but slowly hardens. 2 any of various similar substances. —*v.t.* stop up or cover with putty. [< French *potée,* originally, potful < *pot* pot] **—put′ti er,** *n.*

put-up (pu̇t′up′), *adj.* INFORMAL. planned beforehand, or deliberately, in a secret or crafty manner: *His election was a put-up job by the party bosses.*

put-up on (pu̇t′ə pôn′, pu̇t′ə pon′), *adj.* imposed upon; taken advantage of.

puz zle (puz′əl), *n., v.,* **-zled, -zling.** —*n.* 1 a hard problem: *How to get all my things into one trunk is a puzzle.* 2 problem or task to be done for fun: *A famous Chinese puzzle has seven pieces of wood to fit together.* 3 puzzled condition. —*v.t.* 1 make unable to answer, solve, or understand something; fill with doubt or confusion; perplex. See synonym study below. 2 **puzzle out,** find out by thinking or trying hard: *puzzle out the meaning of a sentence.* —*v.i.* 1 be perplexed. 2 exercise one's mind on something hard: *puzzle over an arithmetic problem.* [origin uncertain] **—puz′zler,** *n.*

Syn. *v.t.* 1 **Puzzle, perplex, bewilder** mean to make a person uncertain what to think, say, or do. **Puzzle** suggests something being so complex or involved that it is hard to understand or solve: *The complicated instructions for building the radio puzzled him.* **Perplex** adds the idea of troubling with doubt about how to decide or act: *They were worried and perplexed by their son's behavior.* **Bewilder** emphasizes the idea of confusing and causing one to feel lost among the various possibilities: *He was bewildered by the commotion of the city traffic.*

Pyramids (def. 3)

puz zle ment (puz′əl mənt), *n.* 1 puzzled condition. 2 something puzzling.

Pvt., Private.

pwt., pennyweight.

PX or **P.X.,** Post Exchange.

pyc nom e ter (pik nom′ə tər), *n.* instrument, consisting usually of a glass flask with a thermometer, for determining the relative density or specific gravity of liquids. [< Greek *pyknos* thick, dense]

py e mi a (pī ē′mē ə), *n.* blood poisoning caused by bacteria that produce pus in the blood, characterized by the formation of multiple abscesses in different parts of the body. [< Greek *pyon* pus + *haima* blood]

py e mic (pī ē′mik), *adj.* 1 of or having to do with pyemia. 2 having pyemia.

Pyg ma li on (pig mā′lē ən, pig mā′lyən), *n.* (in Greek legends) a sculptor and king of Cyprus, who fell in love with an ivory statue he had made.

pyg my (pig′mē), *n., pl.* **-mies,** *adj.* —*n.* 1 **Pygmy,** one of a group of Negroid people of equatorial Africa who are less than five feet tall. 2 a very small person; dwarf. 3 any very small animal or thing. —*adj.* 1 of or having to do with the Pygmies. 2 very small: *a pygmy marmoset.* Also, **pigmy.** [< Greek *pygmaioi,* originally plural adjective, dwarfish < *pygmē* cubit, fist]

py ja mas (pə jä′məz, pə jam′əz), *n.pl.* pajamas.

py lon (pī′lon), *n.* 1 post or tower for guiding aviators, especially as a marker of the course to be flown in an air race. 2 a tall steel framework used to carry high-tension wires across country. 3 one of a pair of high supporting structures marking an entrance at either side of a bridge. 4 gateway, especially a monumental gateway of an ancient Egyptian temple consisting of a pyramid with a passage through it or two pyramids flanking a lower part. [< Greek *pylōn* gateway < *pylē* gate]

py lo ric (pī lôr′ik, pī lōr′ik), *adj.* of or having to do with the pylorus.

py lo rus (pī lôr′əs, pī lōr′əs), *n., pl.,* **-lo ri** (-lôr′ī′, -lōr′ī′). the opening that leads from the stomach into the intestine. [< Greek *pylōros,* originally, gatekeeper < *pylē* gate]

Pym (pim), *n.* **John,** 1584-1643, English statesman and leader of the House of Commons against Charles I.

Pyong yang (pyong′yäng′), *n.* capital of North Korea, in the SW part. 1,500,000.

py or rhe a or **py or rhoe a** (pī′ə rē′ə), *n.* disease of the gums in which pockets of pus form about the teeth, the gums shrink, and the teeth become loose. [< Greek *pyon* pus + *rhoia* a flow]

py or rhe al or **py or rhoe al** (pī′ə-rē′əl), *adj.* of or having to do with pyorrhea.

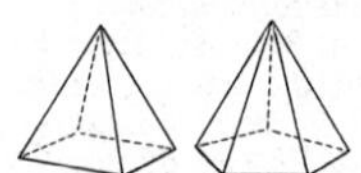

pyramid (def. 1) two types of pyramids

pyr a mid (pir′ə mid), *n.* 1 a solid figure having a polygon for a base and triangular sides which meet in a point. 2 thing or things having the form of a pyramid: *a pyramid of stones.* 3 **Pyramids,** *pl.* the huge, massive stone pyramids, with square bases and four triangular sides, built by the ancient Egyptians to serve as royal tombs. —*v.i.* be in the form of a pyramid. —*v.t.* 1 put in the form of a pyramid. 2 raise or increase (costs, wages, etc.) gradually. 3 increase (one's operations) in buying or selling stock on margin by using the profits to buy or sell more. [< Greek *pyramidos*]

py ram i dal (pə ram′ə dəl), *adj.* shaped

like a pyramid. **—py ram′i dal ly,** *adv.*

Pyr a mus (pir′ə məs), *n.* (in Greek legends) a young Babylonian who loved Thisbe and killed himself because he thought that a lion had devoured her.

pyre (pīr), *n.* 1 pile of wood for burning a dead body as a funeral rite. 2 any large pile or heap of burnable material. [< Greek *pyra* < *pyr* fire]

Pyr e ne an (pir′ə nē′ən), *adj.* of the Pyrenees.

Pyr e nees (pir′ə nēz′), *n.pl.* mountain range between France and Spain. Highest peak, 11,168 feet.

py re thrum (pī rē′thrəm, pī reth′rəm), *n.* 1 any of various chrysanthemums, much cultivated for their showy white, lilac, or red flowers. 2 insecticide made of the powdered flower heads of any of these. [< Greek *pyrethron*]

py ret ic (pī ret′ik), *adj.* 1 of or having to do with fever. 2 producing fever. 3 feverish. [< Greek *pyretos* fever]

Py rex (pī′reks), *n.* trademark for a kind of glassware that will not break when heated.

py rex i a (pī rek′sē ə), *n.* fever. [< New Latin < Greek *pyretos* fever]

pyr i dine (pir′ə dēn′, pir′ə dən), *n.* a liquid organic base with a pungent odor, occurring in coal tar, etc., and used as a solvent and waterproofing agent, and in making various drugs and vitamins. *Formula:* C_5H_5N

pyr i dox ine (pir′ə dok′sēn′, pir′ə-dok′sən), *n.* vitamin B_6, essential to human nutrition, found in wheat germ, fish, liver, etc. *Formula:* $C_8H_{11}NO_3$

py rim i dine (pī rim′ə dēn′, pī rim′ə dən; pir′ə mə dēn′, pir′ə mə dən), *n.* 1 a liquid or crystalline organic base with a strong odor, whose molecular arrangement is a six-membered ring containing atoms of nitrogen. *Formula:* $C_4H_4N_2$ 2 any of a group of compounds derived from it, such as cytosine and thymine.

py rite (pī′rīt), *n.* 1 a common yellow mineral with a metallic luster, a compound of iron and sulfur, which is often mistaken for gold; fool's gold; iron pyrites. It is used to make sulfuric acid. *Formula:* FeS_2 **2 pyrites,** *pl.* any of various compounds of sulfur and a metal, such as tin pyrites, an ore of tin. [< Greek *pyritēs (lithos)* (stone) of fire]

pyro-, *combining form.* 1 fire: *Pyromania = obsession with fire.* 2 heat; high temperature: *Pyrometer = instrument that measures high temperatures.* [< Greek < *pyr* fire]

py rog ra phy (pī rog′rə fē, pi rog′rə fē), *n.* art of burning designs on wood, leather, etc.

py rol y sis (pī rol′ə sis, pi rol′ə sis), *n.* chemical decomposition produced by exposure to high temperatures.

py ro ma ni a (pī′rə mā′nē ə), *n.* an uncontrollable desire to set things on fire.

py ro ma ni ac (pī′rə mā′nē ak, pir′ə-mā′nē ak), *n.* person with an uncontrollable desire to set things on fire.

py ro ma ni a cal (pī′rō mə nī′ə kəl, pir′ō-mə nī′ə kəl), *adj.* affected with or having a tendency toward pyromania.

py rom e ter (pī rom′ə tər, pi rom′ə tər), *n.* instrument for measuring very high temperatures.

py ro met ric (pī rə met′rik, pir′ə met′rik), *adj.* of or having to do with a pyrometer. **—py′ro met′ri cal ly,** *adv.*

py ro tech nic (pī′rə tek′nik), *adj.* 1 of or having to do with fireworks. 2 resembling fireworks; brilliant; sensational: *pyrotechnic eloquence.*

py ro tech ni cal (pī′rə tek′nə kəl), *adj.* pyrotechnic.

py ro tech nics (pī′rə tek′niks), *n.* 1 the making of fireworks. 2 use of fireworks. 3 display of fireworks. 4 a brilliant or sensational display, as of eloquence, wit, anger, etc.

py rox ene (pī′rok sēn′), *n.* any of a group of silicate minerals, usually calcium, magnesium, and iron silicate, often found in igneous rocks. [< French *pyroxène* < *pyro-* + Greek *xenos* stranger]

py rox y lin (pī rok′sə lən), *n.* any of various substances made by nitrating certain forms of cellulose. Guncotton and the soluble cellulose nitrates used in making celluloid, collodion, etc., are pyroxylins. [< *pyro-* + Greek *xylon* wood]

Pyr rhic victory (pir′ik), victory won at too great a cost. [< *Pyrrhus,* who defeated the Roman armies but lost so many men in doing so that he could not attack Rome itself]

Pyr rhus (pir′əs), *n.* 318?-272 B.C., king of Epirus from about 300 to 272 B.C.

py ru vate (pī rü′vāt, pi rü′vāt), *n.* a salt or ester of pyruvic acid.

py ru vic acid (pī rü′vik, pi rü′vik), a colorless acid that smells like acetic acid. It is an important intermediate product in carbohydrate and protein metabolism. *Formula:* $CH_3COCOOH$ [< Greek *pyr* fire + Latin *uva* grape]

Py thag or as (pə thag′ər əs), *n.* 582?-500? B.C., Greek philosopher, religious teacher, and mathematician.

Py thag o re an (pə thag′ə rē′ən), *adj.* of or having to do with Pythagoras, his teachings, or his followers. *—n.* follower of Pythagoras.

hat, āge, fär; let, ēqual, tėrm;
it, īce; hot, ōpen, ôrder;
oil, out; cup, pu̇t, rüle;
ch, child; ng, long; sh, she;
th, thin; ᴛʜ, then; zh, measure;

ə represents *a* in about, *e* in taken, *i* in pencil, *o* in lemon, *u* in circus.

< = from, derived from, taken from.

Pythagorean theorem, theorem that the square of the hypotenuse of a right triangle equals the sum of the squares of the other two sides.

Pyth i an (pith′ē ən), *adj.* 1 of or having to do with Apollo or the oracle at Delphi. 2 of or having to do with the Pythian games. [< Greek *Pythios* of Delphi (earlier called *Pytho*)]

Pythian games, one of the great national festivals of ancient Greece, held every four years at Delphi in honor of Apollo.

Pyth i as (pith′ē əs), *n.* (in Roman legends) a man famous for his devoted friendship with Damon.

py thon (pī′thon, pī′thən), *n.* 1 any of a genus of large, nonpoisonous snakes of Asia, Africa, and Australia, of the same family as the boa constrictor, that kill their prey by squeezing. Some pythons are among the world's largest snakes. 2 any large boa. [< Greek *Pythōn,* serpent slain by Apollo]

py tho ness (pī′thə nis), *n.* 1 priestess of Apollo at Delphi, who gave out the answers of the oracle. 2 prophetess. [< *Pytho,* earlier name of Delphi]

pyx (piks), *n.* vessel in which the consecrated Host is kept, or a small case used to carry it to the sick. [< Greek *pyxis* box < *pyxos* boxwood]

pyxidium

pyx id i um (pik sid′ē əm), *n., pl.* **pyx id i a** (pik sid′ē ə), a seed vessel that bursts open transversely into a top and bottom part, the top part acting as a lid. [< New Latin < Greek *pyxidion,* diminutive of *pyxis* box]

Q q

Q or **q** (kyü), *n., pl.* **Q's** or **q's.** the 17th letter of the English alphabet.

Q, (in chess) queen.

q., 1 quarter. 2 quarterly. 3 quarto. 4 query. 5 question. 6 quintal. 7 quire.

Qa tar (kä′tär), *n.* country in E Arabia, on a peninsula in the Persian Gulf, a sheikdom formerly under British protection. 130,000 pop.; 8000 sq. mi. *Capital:* Doha.

Q.C. or **QC,** queen's counsel.

Q.E.D., which was to be proved [for Latin *quod erat demonstrandum*].

Q.E.F., which was to be done [for Latin *quod erat faciendum*].

Q fever, a rickettsial disease somewhat like influenza, usually lasting a short time and characterized by fever, headache, and chills. [short for *query fever,* as it was first called]

Q.M., quartermaster.

Q.M.C. or **QMC,** Quartermaster Corps.

Q.M.G. or **QMG,** Quartermaster General.

qq.v., which see (used in referring to more than one item). [for Latin *quae vide*] ➤ See **q.v.** for usage note.

qr., 1 quarter (one fourth of a hundredweight). 2 quire.

qt., 1 quantity. 2 quart or quarts.

q.t., SLANG. 1 quiet. 2 **on the q.t.,** very quietly; secretly: *do something on the q.t.*

qto., quarto.

qts., quarts.

quack[1] (kwak), *n.* sound a duck makes. —*v.i.* make the sound of a duck or one like it. [imitative]

quack[2] (kwak), *n.* 1 a dishonest person who pretends to be a doctor. 2 an ignorant pretender to knowledge or skill of any sort; charlatan. —*adj.* 1 used by quacks: *quack medicine.* 2 not genuine: *a quack doctor.* [short for *quacksalver*]

quack er y (kwak′ər ē), *n., pl.* **-er ies.** practices or methods of a quack.

quack ish (kwak′ish), *adj.* like a quack; dealing in quackery.

quack sal ver (kwak′sal vər), *n.* 1 a quack doctor. 2 charlatan. [< obsolete Dutch < *quacken* boast of + *salf* salve]

quad[1] (kwod), *n.* INFORMAL. quadrangle.

quad[2] (kwod), *n.* INFORMAL. quadruplet.

quad[3] (kwod), *n.* quadrat.

quad., 1 quadrangle. 2 quadrant.

quad ran gle (kwod′rang′gəl), *n.* 1 a four-sided space or court wholly or nearly surrounded by buildings: *the quadrangle of a palace, a college quadrangle.* 2 buildings around a quadrangle. 3 quadrilateral. [< Late Latin *quadrangulum* < Latin *quadr-* four + *angulus* angle]

qua dran gu lar (kwo drang′gyə lər), *adj.* like a quadrangle; having four corners or angles.

quad rant (kwod′rənt), *n.* 1 quarter of the circumference of a circle; arc of 90 degrees. 2 the area contained by such an arc and two radii drawn perpendicular to each other. 3 thing or part shaped like a quarter circle. 4 instrument with a scale of 90 degrees, used in astronomy, surveying, and navigation for measuring altitudes. 5 (in geometry) one of the four parts into which a plane is divided by two straight lines crossing at right angles. The upper right-hand section is the first quadrant, and, in a counterclockwise direction, the others are the second, third, and fourth quadrants respectively. [< Latin *quadrantem* a fourth]

qua dran tal (kwo dran′tl), *adj.* of or having to do with a quadrant.

quad rat (kwod′rət), *n.* piece of metal used for wide spaces in setting type. [variant of *quadrate,* noun]

quad rate (kwod′rit, kwod′rāt), *adj.* 1 square; rectangular. 2 of or designating the quadrate bone. —*n.* 1 something square or rectangular. 2 quadrate bone. [< Latin *quadratum* made square < *quadrus* square, related to *quattuor* four]

quadrate bone, (in birds, fishes, amphibians, and reptiles) one of the pair of bones joining the lower jaw to the skull.

qua drat ic (kwo drat′ik), *adj.* 1 of or like a square. 2 (in algebra) involving a square or squares, but no higher powers, of the unknown quantity or quantities. —*n.* a quadratic equation.

quadratic equation, equation involving a square or squares, but no higher powers, of the unknown quantity or quantities. $x^2 + 3x + 2 = 12$ is a quadratic equation.

qua drat ics (kwo drat′iks), *n.* branch of algebra that deals with quadratic equations.

quad ra ture (kwod′rə chůr, kwod′rə-chər), *n.* 1 act of squaring. 2 the finding of a square equal in area to a given surface, especially one bounded by a curve. 3 position of the moon or any planet or star that is 90 degrees away from any other heavenly body.

qua dren ni al (kwo dren′ē əl), *adj.* 1 occurring every four years: *a quadrennial presidential election.* 2 of or for four years. [< Latin *quadrennium* period of four years < *quadri-* four + *annus* year] —**qua-dren′ni al ly,** *adv.*

quadri-, *combining form.* four; having four ____; four times: *Quadrilateral = having four sides.* [< Latin]

quad ri ceps (kwod′rə seps), *n.* the large muscle of the front of the thigh, which extends the leg, and has four heads or origins. [< New Latin < Latin *quadri-* four + *caput* head]

quad ri lat er al (kwod′rə lat′ər əl), *adj.* having four sides and four angles. —*n.* a plane figure having four sides and four angles. [< Latin *quadrilaterus* < *quadri-* four + *latus* side]

qua drille (kwə dril′), *n.* 1 a square dance for four couples that usually has five parts or movements. 2 music for such a dance. [< French < Spanish *cuadrilla* troop < *cuadro* battle square < Latin *quadrus* square]

qua dril lion (kwo dril′yən), *n., adj.* 1 (in the United States, Canada, and France) 1 followed by 15 zeros. 2 (in Great Britain and Germany) 1 followed by 24 zeros.

quad ri no mi al (kwod′rə nō′mē əl), *n.* an algebraic expression having four terms. [< *quadri-* + *(bi)nomial*]

quadrant
left, (def. 1) quadrant of a circumference
right, (def. 2) quadrant of a circle

quad ri par tite (kwod′rə pär′tīt), *adj.* divided into or consisting of four parts.

quad ri ple gi a (kwod′rə plē′jē ə), *n.* paralysis of both arms and both legs. [< *quadri-* + *(para)plegia*]

qua driv i um (kwo driv′ē əm), *n.* (in the Middle Ages) arithmetic, geometry, astronomy, and music, the more advanced four of the seven liberal arts. [< Late Latin < Latin *quadri-* four + *via* way]

qua droon (kwo drün′), *n.* person having one fourth Negro ancestry. [< Spanish *cuarterón* < *cuarto* fourth < Latin *quartus*]

quadru-, *combining form.* variant of **quadri-,** as in *quadruped.*

quad ru ped (kwod′rə ped), *n.* animal that has four feet. —*adj.* four-footed. [< Latin *quadrupedem* < *quadru-* four + *pedem* foot]

qua dru pe dal (kwo drü′pə dəl, kwod′rə-ped′l), *adj.* of, having to do with, or like a quadruped; four-footed.

quad ru ple (kwod′rə pəl, kwo drü′pəl), *adj., adv., n., v.,* **-pled, -pling.** —*adj.* 1 consisting of four parts; including four parts or parties; fourfold: *a quadruple agreement.* 2 four times; four times as great. 3 (in music) having four beats to each measure, with the first and third beats accented. —*adv.* four times; four times as great. —*n.* number, amount, etc., four times as great as another: *80 is the quadruple of 20.* —*v.t., v.i.* make or become four times as great or as numerous. [< Latin *quadruplus* < *quadru-* four + *-plus* -fold]

quadruple alliance, any alliance of four powers, especially the alliance formed by Great Britain, France, the Netherlands, and Austria in 1718, by Great Britain, Austria, Prussia, and Russia in 1815, and by Great Britain, France, Spain, and Portugal in 1834.

quad ru plet (kwod′rə plit, kwo drü′plit), *n.* 1 one of four offspring born at the same time from the same mother. 2 any group or combination of four.

qua dru pli cate (*adj., n.* kwo drü′plə kit; *v.* kwo drü′plə kāt), *adj., v.,* **-cat ed, -cat ing,** *n.* —*adj.* fourfold; quadruple. —*v.t.* make fourfold; quadruple. —*n.* 1 one of four things, especially four copies of a document, exactly alike. 2 **in quadruplicate,** in four copies exactly alike. —**qua-dru′pli ca′tion,** *n.*

quadrilateral
several kinds of quadrilaterals

quaes tor (kwes′tər, kwē′stər), *n.* (in ancient Rome) one of the officials in charge of the public funds; treasurer. [< Latin < *quaerere* inquire]

quaff (kwäf, kwaf, kwôf), *v.i., v.t.* drink in large swallows; drink deeply and freely. —*n.* a quaffing. [origin uncertain]

quag (kwag, kwog), *n.* quagmire; bog. [origin unknown]

quag ga (kwag′ə), *n.* an extinct zebra of southern Africa that had distinct stripes on its head, neck, and shoulders only. [< a Hottentot name]

quag gy (kwag′ē, kwog′ē), *adj.,* **-gi er, -gi est.** 1 soft and muddy; boggy; miry. 2 soft and flabby: *quaggy flesh.*

quag mire (kwag′mīr′, kwog′mīr′), *n.* 1 soft, muddy ground; boggy or miry place; quag. 2 a difficult situation.

hat, āge, fär; let, ēqual, tėrm;
it, īce; hot, ōpen, ôrder;
oil, out; cup, pu̇t, rüle;
ch, child; ng, long; sh, she;
th, thin; ᴛʜ, then; zh, measure;

ə represents *a* in about, *e* in taken,
i in pencil, *o* in lemon, *u* in circus.

< = from, derived from, taken from.

qua hog (kwô′hog, kwô′hôg; kwə hog′, kwə hôg′), *n.* a roundish, edible American clam. [< Algonquian]

quai (kā), *n., pl.* ***quais*** (kā). FRENCH. quay.

quail[1] (kwāl), *n., pl.* **quails** or **quail.** any of various plump game birds of the same family as the pheasant, especially the bobwhite. [< Old French *quaille*]

quail[1]
about 10 in. long

quail[2] (kwāl), *v.i.* be afraid; lose courage; shrink back in fear: *quail at an angry look.* [apparently < Middle French *coaillier* coagulate < Latin *coagulare*]

quaint (kwānt), *adj.* strange or odd in an interesting, pleasing, or amusing way: *Old photographs seem quaint to us today.* [< Old French *cointe* pretty, clever < Latin *cognitum* known] **—quaint′ly,** *adv.* **—quaint′ness,** *n.*

quake (kwāk), *v.,* **quaked, quak ing,** *n.* *—v.i.* 1 shake or tremble from cold, anger, etc.: *quake with fear.* 2 move convulsively; rock violently: *The earth quaked.* See **shiver**[1] for synonym study. *—n.* 1 a shaking or trembling. 2 earthquake. [Old English *cwacian*] **—quak′er,** *n.*

Quak er (kwā′kər), *n.* member of a Christian group called the Society of Friends, founded by George Fox about 1650, whose principles and practices include the observance of simplicity in religious worship, manners, etc., and opposition to war and to taking oaths; Friend.

Quak er ism (kwā′kə riz′əm), *n.* principles and customs of the Quakers.

quak y (kwā′kē), *adj.,* **quak i er, quak i est.** inclined to quake; quaking.

qual i fi ca tion (kwol′ə fə kā′shən), *n.* 1 that which makes a person fit for a job, task, office, etc.: *A knowledge of trails is one qualification for a guide.* 2 a necessary condition which must be fulfilled or complied with before a certain right can be acquired or exercised, an office held, etc.: *the qualifications for voting.* 3 that which limits, changes, or makes less free and full: *His pleasure had one qualification: his friends could not be present to share it with him.* 4 modification; limitation; restriction: *The statement was made without any qualification.* 5 a qualifying. 6 a being qualified.

qual i fied (kwol′ə fīd), *adj.* 1 having the desirable or required qualifications; fitted; competent: *a qualified pilot.* 2 modified; limited: *a qualified answer, qualified acceptance.* **—qual′i fied′ly,** *adv.* **—qual′i fied′ness,** *n.*

qual i fi er (kwol′ə fī′ər), *n.* 1 person or thing that qualifies. 2 (in grammar) a word that limits or modifies the meaning of another word, such as an adjective or adverb.

qual i fy (kwol′ə fī), *v.,* **-fied, -fy ing.** *—v.t.* 1 make fit or competent: *Can you qualify yourself for the job?* 2 furnish with legal power; make legally capable. 3 make less strong; change somewhat; limit; moderate: *Qualify your statement that dogs are loyal by adding "usually."* 4 characterize by attributing some quality to; give a descriptive name to. 5 limit or modify the meaning of: *Adverbs qualify verbs.* 6 modify the strength or flavor of (a liquid). *—v.i.* 1 become fit; show oneself fit: *Can you qualify for the job?* 2 become legally capable: *qualify as a voter.* 3 gain the right to compete in a race, contest, or tournament. [< Medieval Latin *qualificare* < Latin *qualis* of what sort + *facere* to make]

qual i ta tive (kwol′ə tā′tiv), *adj.* concerned with quality or qualities. **—qual′i ta′tive ly,** *adv.*

qualitative analysis, a testing of a substance or mixture to find out what its chemical constituents are.

qual i ty (kwol′ə tē), *n., pl.* **-ties,** *adj.* *—n.* 1 something special about an object that makes it what it is; essential attribute; characteristic: *Sweetness is a quality of sugar.* See synonym study below. 2 nature, kind, or character of something: *the refreshing quality of a drink.* 3 grade of excellence; degree of worth: *food of poor quality. That is the finest quality of cloth.* 4 fineness; merit; excellence: *Look for quality rather than quantity.* 5 high rank; good or high social position: *people of quality.* 6 the character of sounds aside from pitch and volume or intensity; timbre. *—adj.* of good or high quality: *quality merchandise.* [< Latin *qualitatem* < *qualis* of what sort]

Syn. *n.* 1 **Quality, property** mean a distinguishing mark or characteristic of a thing. **Quality,** the more general term, applies to any distinctive or characteristic feature of an individual or a class, and it may be applied to people as well as things: *Good nature and quick wit are among her outstanding qualities.* **Property** applies to a quality essential to the nature of a thing or always manifested by it: *Heaviness is a property of lead.*

qualm (kwäm, kwälm), *n.* 1 a sudden disturbing feeling in the mind; uneasiness; misgiving; doubt: *I tried the test with some qualms.* 2 disturbance or scruple of conscience: *She felt some qualms about staying away from church.* 3 a feeling of faintness or sickness, especially of nausea, that lasts for just a moment. [origin unknown]

qualm ish (kwä′mish, kwäl′mish), *adj.* 1 inclined to have qualms. 2 having qualms. 3 apt to cause qualms. **—qualm′ish ly,** *adv.* **—qualm′ish ness,** *n.*

qualm y (kwä′mē, kwäl′mē), *adj.* qualmish.

quan dar y (kwon′dər ē), *n., pl.* **-dar ies.** state of perplexity or uncertainty; dilemma. [origin unknown]

quan ti fy (kwon′tə fī), *v.t.,* **-fied, -fy ing.** 1 determine the quantity of; measure. 2 express or indicate the quantity of: *quantify a syllable or verse.* **—quan′ti fi ca′tion,** *n.*

quan ti ta tive (kwon′tə tā′tiv), *adj.* 1 concerned with quantity or quantities. 2 that can be measured. **—quan′ti ta′tive ly,** *adv.*

quantitative analysis, a testing of a substance or mixture to find out the amounts and proportions of its chemical constituents.

quan ti ty (kwon′tə tē), *n., pl.* **-ties.** 1 a definite amount or portion: *Use equal quantities of nuts and raisins in the cake.* 2 an indefinite but usually large amount or number: *The baker buys flour in quantity. She owns quantities of books.* 3 the amount of something present: *decrease the quantity of heat in a room.* 4 something that is measurable. 5 length of a note in music. 6 length of a sound or syllable in speech or poetry. 7 in mathematics: **a** something having magnitude, or size, extent, amount, etc. **b** figure or symbol representing this. [< Latin *quantitatem* < *quantus* how much]

quan tize (kwon′tīz), *v.t.,* **-tized, -tiz ing.** to apply quantum mechanics or the quantum theory to; measure (energy) in quanta. **—quan′ti za′tion,** *n.*

quan tum (kwon′təm), *n., pl.* **-ta** (-tə). 1 (in physics) the basic unit of radiant energy; the smallest amount of energy capable of existing independently. 2 a sum; amount; quantity. [< Latin, neuter of *quantus* how much]

quantum mechanics, the quantum theory as applied to the physical measurement of atomic structures and related phenomena.

quantum number, one of a set of numbers assigned to an atomic system, specifying the number of quanta or units of energy in the system.

quantum theory, theory that whenever radiant energy is transferred, the transfer occurs in pulsations rather than continuously, and that the amount transferred during each pulsation is a definite amount or quantum.

quar an tine (kwôr′ən tēn′, kwor′ən tēn′), *v.,* **-tined, -tin ing,** *n.* *—v.t.* 1 keep (a person, animal, plant, ship, etc.) away from others for a time to prevent the spread of an infectious disease: *People with smallpox are quarantined.* 2 isolate or exclude for any reason: *quarantine a belligerent nation.* *—n.* 1 condition of being quarantined: *The house was in quarantine for three weeks when the child had scarlet fever.* 2 detention, isolation, and other measures taken to prevent the spread of an infectious disease. 3 place or time in which people, animals, plants, ships, etc., are held until it is sure that they have no infectious diseases, insect pests, etc. 4 isolation, exclusion, and similar measures taken against an undesirable person, group, etc. [< Italian *quarantina* a quarantine < *quaranta* forty < Latin *quadraginta;* with reference to 40 days as the original period of isolation]

quark (kwôrk), *n.* one of a hypothetical set of three elementary particles, each with an electric charge less than that of the electron, regarded as possible constituents of all atomic particles. [< the phrase "three *quarks*" in *Finnegans Wake,* a novel by James Joyce]

quar rel[1] (kwôr′əl, kwor′əl), *n., v.,* **-reled, -rel ing** or **-relled, -rel ling.** *—n.* 1 an angry dispute or disagreement; breaking off of friendly relations. See synonym study below. 2 cause for a dispute or disagreement; reason for breaking off friendly relations: *pick a quarrel.* *—v.i.* 1 dispute or disagree angrily; break off friendly relations. 2 find fault: *It is useless to quarrel with fate because one does not have control over it.* [< Old French *querele* < Latin *querela* complaint < *queri* complain] **—quar′rel er, quar′rel ler,** *n.*

Syn. *n.* 1 **Quarrel, feud** mean an angry

Q

disagreement or unfriendly relation between two people or groups. **Quarrel** applies to an angry dispute, soon over or ending in a fight or in severed relations: *The children had a quarrel over the division of the candy.* **Feud** applies to a long-lasting quarrel, usually marked by violence and revenge or by bitterness and repeated unfriendly verbal attacks: *The senator and the columnist carried on a feud.*

quar rel² (kwôr′əl, kwor′əl), *n.* bolt or arrow used with a crossbow. [< Old French < Medieval Latin *quadrellus,* diminutive of Latin *quadrus* a square]

quar rel some (kwôr′əl səm, kwor′əl səm), *adj.* too ready to quarrel; fond of fighting and disputing. **—quar′rel some ly,** *adv.* **—quar′rel some ness,** *n.*

quar ry¹ (kwôr′ē, kwor′ē), *n., pl.* **-ries,** *v.* **-ried, -ry ing.** *—n.* place where stone, slate, etc., is dug, cut, or blasted out for use in building. *—v.t.* 1 obtain from a quarry. 2 dig out by hard work, as if from a quarry. 3 make a quarry in. [< Medieval Latin *quareia, quadraria* < Latin *quadrus* a square] **—quar′ri er,** *n.*

quar ry² (kwôr′ē, kwor′ē), *n., pl.* **-ries.** 1 animal chased in a hunt; game; prey. 2 anything hunted or eagerly pursued. [< Middle French *cuiree* < *cuir* skin, hide < Latin *corium*]

quart (kwôrt), *n.* 1 unit of capacity for liquids, equal to one fourth of a gallon. See **measure** for table. 2 unit of capacity for dry things, equal to one eighth of a peck. See **measure** for table. 3 container holding a quart. [< Old French *quarte* < Latin *quarta,* feminine of *quartus* fourth]

quar tan (kwôrt′n), *adj.* recurring every fourth day, by inclusive counting. *—n.* fever or ague with two days between attacks. [< Latin *(febris) quartana* (fever) < *quartus* fourth]

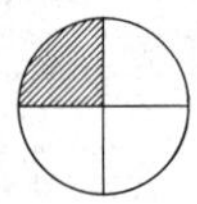

quarter (def. 1)
One quarter of this circle is shaded.

quar ter (kwôr′tər), *n.* 1 one of four equal or corresponding parts into which a thing may be, or is, divided; half of a half; one fourth. 2 one fourth of a dollar; 25 cents. 3 a copper and nickel coin of the United States and Canada, worth 25 cents. 4 one of four equal periods of play in football, basketball, soccer, etc. 5 one fourth of a year; 3 months: *Many savings banks pay interest every quarter.* 6 one fourth of a school year. 7 one of the four periods of the moon, lasting about 7 days each. 8 one fourth of an hour; 15 minutes. 9 one fourth of a yard; 9 inches. 10 one fourth of a hundredweight; 25 pounds in the United States or 28 pounds in Great Britain. 11 region; place: *visit a distant quarter.* 12 section; district: *the French quarter.* 13 a certain part of a community, group, etc.: *information from a reliable quarter.* 14 **at close quarters,** very close together; almost touching. 15 **quarters,** *pl.* **a** place to live or stay. **b** positions or stations assigned to members of a ship's company, as for battle, drill, alerts, etc.: *a call to quarters.* 16 point of the compass; direction: *In what quarter is the wind?* 17 one of the four principal points of the compass; cardinal point. 18 mercy shown a defeated enemy in sparing his life. 19 one of the four parts into which an animal's carcass is divided in butchering: *a quarter of lamb.* 20 a leg and its adjoining part. 21 the part of a ship's side near the stern. 22 in heraldry: **a** one of the four (or more) parts into which a shield is divided by lines at right angles. **b** an emblem occupying the upper right fourth of a shield. 23 the part of a boot or shoe above the heel and below the top of either side of the foot from the middle of the back to the vamp.
—v.t. 1 divide into quarters. 2 divide into parts: *quarter a chicken for frying.* 3 give a place to live in; station; lodge. 4 cut the body of (a person) into quarters, as a sign of disgrace after hanging. 5 place or bear (coats of arms, etc.) in quarters of a shield. 6 range over (ground) in every direction in search of game. *—v.i.* 1 live or stay in a place. 2 (of the wind) blow on a ship's quarter. 3 range in every direction.
—adj. being one of four equal parts; being equal to only about one fourth of full measure.
[< Old French *quartier* < Latin *quartarius* a fourth < *quartus* fourth]

quar ter back (kwôr′tər bak′), *n.* 1 back in football who stands directly behind the center and directs his team's offensive play. He calls the signals and usually selects the plays to be used. 2 person who directs any group or activity. *—v.t.* serve as quarterback of. *—v.i.* serve as a quarterback.

quarter day, day beginning or ending a quarter of the year, especially for dating rents, salaries, etc.

quar ter deck (kwôr′tər dek′), *n.* 1 part of the upper deck between the mainmast and the stern, used especially by the officers of a ship. 2 a deck area designated as the ceremonial post of the commanding officer.

quar tered (kwôr′tərd), *adj.* 1 divided into quarters. 2 furnished with rooms or lodging.

quarter horse, a strong horse originally bred for racing on quarter-mile tracks, now used by cowboys for sorting out cattle, in playing polo, and for riding.

quar ter-hour (kwôr′tər our′), *n.* 1 fifteen minutes. 2 point one fourth or three fourths of the way in an hour.

quar ter ing (kwôr′tər ing), *adj.* (of a wind or sea) blowing on a ship's side near the stern.

quar ter ly (kwôr′tər lē), *adj., adv., n., pl.* **-lies.** *—adj.* happening, done, etc., four times a year: *make quarterly payments on one's insurance.* *—adv.* once each quarter of a year: *pay one's insurance premiums quarterly.* *—n.* magazine published every three months.

quar ter mas ter (kwôr′tər mas′tər), *n.* 1 (in the army) an officer who has charge of providing quarters, clothing, fuel, transportation, etc., for troops. 2 (in the navy) a petty officer on a ship who has charge of the steering, the compasses, signals, etc.

quar tern (kwôr′tərn), *n.* quarter; fourth part.

quarter note, (in music) a note played for as long a time as a whole note. See **note** for diagram.

quar ter saw (kwôr′tər sô′), *v.t.,* **-sawed, -sawed** or **-sawn** (-sôn′), **-saw ing.** saw (a log) lengthwise into quarters and then into boards, so that the top and bottom surfaces of each board show a cross section of the annual rings of the wood.

quarter section, piece of land, usually square, containing 160 acres.

quarter sessions, 1 an English court, held quarterly, that has limited criminal jurisdiction and certain other powers. 2 any of various other courts held quarterly, as in some states of the United States and Scotland.

quar ter staff (kwôr′tər staf′), *n., pl.* **-staves** (-stāvz′). an old English weapon consisting of a stout pole 6 to 8 feet long, tipped with iron.

quarter step, (in music) one half of a step or semitone.

quarter tone, quarter step.

quar tet or **quar tette** (kwôr tet′), *n.* 1 group of four singers or players performing together. 2 piece of music for four voices or instruments. 3 any group of four. [< Italian *quartetto* < *quarto* fourth < Latin *quartus*]

quar tile (kwôr′tīl, kwôr′tl), *n.* one of the points or marks dividing a frequency distribution into four parts, each having the same frequency. [< Medieval Latin *quartilis* < Latin *quartus* fourth]

quar to (kwôr′tō), *n., pl.* **-tos,** *adj.* *—n.* 1 the page size (usually about 9 by 12 inches) of a book in which each leaf is one fourth of a whole sheet of paper. 2 book having this size. *—adj.* having this size. [< Medieval Latin *in quarto* in the fourth (of a sheet)]

quartz (kwôrts), *n.* a very hard mineral composed of silica and found in many different types of rocks, such as sandstone and granite. Quartzes vary according to the size and purity of their crystals. Those with submicroscopic crystals are divided into fibrous varieties, or chalcedonies, and granular varieties. Crystals of pure quartz are coarse, colorless, and transparent. Impure colored varieties of quartz include flint, agate, amethyst, etc. *Formula:* SiO_2 [< German *Quarz*]

quartered (def. 1)
quartered arms

quartz clock, an electric clock in which the frequency of current supplied to the clock motor is controlled by the vibrations of a quartz crystal.

quartz glass, a clear glass produced from pure quartz that is specially transparent to the infrared, visible, and ultraviolet radiations, used to transmit ultraviolet rays to diseased parts of the body.

quartz ite (kwôrt′sīt), *n.* a granular rock composed essentially of quartz, and formed by the metamorphism of sandstone.

qua sar (kwā′sär), *n.* any of a number of heavenly objects, larger than stars but smaller than galaxies, that emit powerful blue light and radio waves. [< *quas(i)-(stell)ar (radio source)*]

quash¹ (kwosh), *v.t.* put down completely; crush: *quash a revolt.* [< Old French *quasser* < Latin *quassare* to shatter < *quatere* to shake]

quash² (kwosh), *v.t.* make void; annul: *The judge quashed the charges against the defendant.* [< Old French *quasser* < Late Latin *cassare* < *cassus* null]

qua si (kwā′zī, kwā′sī; kwä′sē, kwä′zē), *adj.* seemingly but not actually the same as; part; halfway: *quasi humor.* *—adv.* seemingly but not actually; partly; almost: *a quasi-*

hat, āge, fär; let, ēqual, tėrm;
it, ice; hot, ōpen, ôrder;
oil, out; cup, pu̇t, rüle;
ch, child; ng, long; sh, she;
th, thin; ᴛʜ, then; zh, measure;

ə represents *a* in about, *e* in taken, *i* in pencil, *o* in lemon, *u* in circus.

< = from, derived from, taken from.

humorous remark, a quasi-official statement. [< Latin, as if, as it were < *qua* as + *si* if]

quas sia (kwosh′ə), *n.* 1 a bitter drug obtained from the wood of various tropical American trees, used as a tonic, a purge, and as a substitute for hops. 2 the wood of any of these trees. 3 any of these trees. [< New Latin < *Quassi,* name of a Surinam native of the 1700's who first used the bark as a fever remedy]

Qua ter nar y (kwə tėr′nər ē), *n., pl.* **-nar ies,** *adj.* —*n.* 1 the present geological period, the later of the two periods making up the Cenozoic era, and including the Pleistocene and Recent epochs. See chart under **geology.** 2 deposits made in this period. 3 **quaternary,** group of four. —*adj.* 1 of or having to do with this period or these deposits. 2 **quarternary,** consisting of four things or parts. [< Latin *quaternarius* < *quaterni* four each < *quater* four times]

quat rain (kwot′rān), *n.* stanza or poem of four lines. [< French < *quatre* four < Latin *quattuor*]

quatrefoil (def. 2)—three quatrefoils

quat re foil (kat′ər foil′, kat′rə foil′), *n.* 1 leaf or flower composed of four leaflets or petals. The four-leaf clover is a quatrefoil. 2 (in architecture) an ornament having four lobes. [< Old French *quatre* four + *feuil* leaf]

qua ver (kwā′vər), *v.i.* 1 shake tremulously; tremble: *The old man's voice quavered.* 2 (in music) to trill in singing or in playing on an instrument. —*v.t.* sing or say in trembling tones. —*n.* 1 a shaking or trembling, especially of the voice. 2 in music: **a** a trill in singing or in playing on an instrument. **b** BRITISH. an eighth note. [frequentative form of earlier *quave* to shake] —**qua′ver ing ly,** *adv.*

qua ver y (kwā′vər ē), *adj.* quavering.

quay

quay (kē), *n.* a solid landing place where ships load and unload, often built of stone. Also, FRENCH ***quai.*** [< Old French *cai* < Celtic]

Que., Quebec.

quean (kwēn), *n.* 1 a bold, impudent girl or woman; hussy. 2 prostitute. [Old English *cwene*]

quea sy (kwē′zē), *adj.,* **-si er, -si est.** 1 inclined to nausea; easily upset: *a queasy stomach.* 2 tending to unsettle the stomach. 3 uneasy; uncomfortable. 4 squeamish; fastidious. [origin uncertain] —**quea′si ly,** *adv.* —**quea′si ness,** *n.*

Que bec (kwi bek′), *n.* 1 province in E Canada. 6,030,000 pop.; 594,900 sq. mi. *Abbrev.:* Que. 2 its capital, on the St. Lawrence River. 167,000.

que bra cho (kā brä′chō), *n.* 1 any of several South American trees of the same family as the cashew, with very hard wood. The wood and bark are used in tanning and dyeing. 2 the wood or bark of any of these trees. [< Spanish, literally, break-ax]

Quech ua (kech′wä), *n.* 1 an Indian of the dominant tribal group in the Inca empire. 2 the language of the Quechuas. Certain dialects of Quechua are still spoken in parts of Peru, Ecuador, Bolivia, Argentina, and Chile. [< Spanish < the native Quechua (Peru) name] —**Quech′uan,** *adj., n.*

queen (kwēn), *n.* 1 wife of a king. 2 the female ruler of a nation. 3 woman who has eminence or authority in some sphere: *the queen of society.* 4 woman who is very stately or attractive: *a beauty queen.* 5 a fully developed female in a colony of bees, ants, etc., that lays eggs. There is usually only one queen in a hive of bees. 6 a playing card bearing a picture of a queen. 7 the most valuable piece in chess. It can move in any straight or diagonal row. 8 the chief, best, finest, etc.: *the rose, queen of flowers.* —*v.i.* Also, **queen it,** act like a queen. [Old English *cwēn*] —**queen′like′,** *adj.*

Queen Anne, 1 of or having to do with a style of English domestic architecture of the early 1700's, characterized by roomy and dignified buildings and by the use of red brick. 2 of or having to do with a style of furniture in England in the early 1700's, characterized by an emphasis on comfort and an increase in the use of upholstery. [< *Queen Anne* of Great Britain and Ireland, who reigned from 1702 to 1714]

Queen Anne's lace, wild carrot.

queen consort, wife of a reigning king.

queen dom (kwēn′dəm), *n.* 1 realm of a queen. 2 position or dignity of a queen.

queen dowager, widow of a king.

queen ly (kwēn′lē), *adj.,* **-li er, -li est,** *adv.* —*adj.* 1 of a queen; fit for a queen. 2 like a queen; like a queen's: *queenly dignity.* —*adv.* in a queenly manner; as a queen does. —**queen′li ness,** *n.*

queen mother, widow of a former king and mother of a reigning king or queen.

queen post, one of a pair of timbers extending vertically upward from the tie beam of a roof truss or the like, one on each side of its center.

queen regent, 1 queen ruling in place of an absent or unfit king. 2 queen ruling in her own right.

Queens (kwēnz), *n.* borough of New York City, on Long Island, east of Brooklyn. 1,986,000.

Queens land (kwēnz′lənd), *n.* state in NE Australia. 1,820,000 pop.; 667,000 sq. mi. *Capital:* Brisbane.

Queens town (kwēnz′toun), *n.* former name of **Cóbh.**

queer (kwir), *adj.* 1 not usual or normal; strange; odd; peculiar: *a queer remark, a queer way to repay a favor.* 2 probably bad; causing doubt or suspicion: *His queer dealings caused him to lose a lot of business.* 3 not well; faint; giddy. 4 SLANG. **a** bad; counterfeit: *queer money.* **b** homosexual. —*n.* SLANG. a homosexual. —*v.t.* SLANG. spoil; ruin: *queer one's chances of success.* [origin uncertain] —**queer′ly,** *adv.* —**queer′ness,** *n.*

queer ish (kwir′ish), *adj.* rather queer.

quell (kwel), *v.t.* 1 put down (disorder, rebellion, etc.): *quell a riot.* 2 put an end to; overcome: *quell one's fears.* [Old English *cwellan* to kill]

Que moy (ki moi′), *n.* island in Formosa Strait, near the coast of China, belonging to Taiwan.

quench (kwench), *v.t.* 1 put an end to; stop: *quench one's thirst.* 2 drown out; put out: *Water quenched the fire.* 3 cool suddenly by plunging into water or other liquid. Hot steel is quenched to harden it. [Old English *-cwencan*] —**quench′a ble,** *adj.* —**quench′er,** *n.* —**quench′less,** *adj.*

quern (kwėrn), *n.* a primitive hand mill for grinding grain, consisting commonly of two circular stones, the upper one being turned by hand. [Old English *cweorn*]

quer u lous (kwer′ə ləs, kwer′yə ləs), *adj.* complaining; fretful; peevish: *a querulous remark. He is very querulous when he is sick.* [< Latin *querulus* < *queri* complain] —**quer′u lous ly,** *adv.* —**quer′u lous ness,** *n.*

quer y (kwir′ē), *n., pl.* **quer ies,** *v.,* **quer ied, quer y ing.** —*n.* 1 question; inquiry. See **question** for synonym study. 2 doubt. 3 question mark (?), especially when used to express doubt about something written or printed. —*v.t.* 1 ask about; inquire into; ask. 2 express doubt about. —*v.i.* ask questions. [< Medieval Latin *quere* < Latin *quaere* ask!]

quest (kwest), *n.* 1 a search or hunt: *She went to the library in quest of something to read.* 2 expedition of knights: *There are many stories about the quests of King Arthur's knights.* —*v.t.* search or seek for; hunt. —*v.i.* go about in search of something; search or seek. [< Old French *queste* < Popular Latin *quaesita* < Latin *quaerere* seek]

ques tion (kwes′chən), *n.* 1 thing asked; sentence, in interrogative form, addressed by one person to another to get information; inquiry. See synonym study below. 2 a matter of doubt or dispute; controversy: *A question arose about the ownership of the property.* 3 a matter to be talked over, investigated, considered, etc.; problem: *the question of gun control.* 4 proposal to be debated or voted on: *The president asked if the club members were ready for the question.* 5 the taking of a vote on such a proposal. 6 an asking: *examine by question and answer.*

beg the question, take for granted the very thing argued about.

beside the question, off the subject.

beyond question, without a doubt; not to be disputed.

call in question, dispute; challenge.

in question, a under consideration or discussion. **b** in dispute.

out of the question, not to be considered; impossible.

without question, without a doubt; not to be disputed.

—*v.t.* 1 ask a question or questions of; seek information from. See synonym study below.

2 ask or inquire about: *We questioned the long delay.* 3 doubt; dispute: *question the truth of a story.* —*v.i.* ask; inquire.
[< Latin *quaestionem* a seeking < *quaerere* to seek] **—ques′tion er,** *n.* **—ques′tion ing ly,** *adv.*

Syn. *n.* 1 **Question, query** mean something asked. **Question** applies to something which is asked to get definite information or to test knowledge and which therefore ordinarily calls for an answer: *I have some questions about today's lesson.* **Query** often applies to what has the form of a question but is really intended to express doubt or objection: *He put several queries concerning items in the budget.*
—*v.t.* 1 **Question, ask, interrogate** mean to seek information from someone. **Ask** is the general word, and suggests nothing more: *I asked her why she did it.* **Question** often implies asking repeatedly or persistently: *I questioned the boy until he told all he knew about the subject.* **Interrogate** implies questioning formally and methodically: *The lawyer interrogated the witness.*

ques tion a ble (kwes′chə nə bəl), *adj.* 1 open to question or dispute; doubtful; uncertain: *a questionable statement.* 2 of doubtful propriety, honesty, morality, respectability, or the like: *questionable behavior.* **—ques′tion a bly,** *adv.*

question mark, a punctuation mark (?) put after a question in writing or printing; interrogation mark.

ques tion naire (kwes′chə ner′, kwes′chə nar′), *n.* a written or printed list of questions, used to gather information, obtain a sampling of opinion, etc. [< French]

quet zal (ket säl′), *n.* 1 a Central American bird having brilliant golden-green and scarlet plumage. The male has long, flowing tail feathers. 2 the monetary unit of Guatemala, equal to 100 centavos and worth about one dollar. [< Mexican Spanish < Nahuatl *quetzalli* brilliant, resplendent]

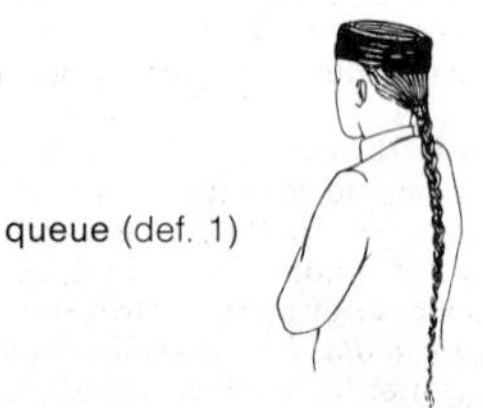
queue (def. 1)

queue (kyü), *n., v.,* **queued, queu ing.** —*n.* 1 braid of hair hanging down from the back of the head. 2 a line of people, automobiles, etc.: *There was a long queue in front of the theater.* —*v.i.* 1 form or stand in a long line. 2 **queue up,** line up. —*v.t.* arrange (persons) in a queue. Also, **cue. —queu′er,** *n.* [< French < Latin *coda, cauda* tail]

Que zon (kā′sôn), *n.* **Manuel Luis,** 1878-1944, Philippine statesman and patriot.

Quezon City, capital of the Philippines, just northeast of Manila. 585,000.

quib ble (kwib′əl), *n., v.,* **-bled, -bling.** —*n.* an unfair and petty evasion of the point or truth by using words with a double meaning: *a legal quibble.* —*v.i.* evade the point or the truth by twisting the meaning of words. [origin uncertain] **—quib′bler,** *n.*

quick (kwik), *adj.* 1 done, happening, or taking place in a very short time; fast and sudden; swift: *With a quick turn I avoided hitting the other car.* See synonym study below. 2 begun and ended speedily: *a quick visit.* 3 coming soon; prompt; immediate: *a quick answer.* 4 (of movement) rapid; speedy: *a quick pace.* 5 not patient; hasty: *a quick temper.* 6 mentally active or alert; ready; lively: *a quick wit.* 7 keen in perception: *Most dogs have a quick ear.* 8 understanding or learning promptly or readily: *a child who is quick in school.* 9 brisk: *a quick fire.* 10 sharp: *a quick curve.* —*n.* 1 tender, sensitive flesh, especially the flesh under a fingernail or toenail: *bite one's nails to the quick.* 2 the tender, sensitive part of one's feelings: *Their insults cut him to the quick.* 3 living persons: *the quick and the dead.*
—*adv.* quickly.
[Old English *cwic* alive] **—quick′ness,** *n.*

Syn. *adj.* 1 **Quick, fast, rapid** mean done, happening, moving, or acting in a very short time. **Quick** is applied especially to something done or happening with speed or without delay: *You made a quick trip.* **Fast** is applied especially to something moving or acting with speed: *I took a fast plane.* **Rapid** emphasizes the rate of speed or swiftness of the action, movement, etc., performed: *I had to do some rapid planning.*

quick bread, biscuits, corn bread, muffins, etc., prepared with a leavening agent that enables them to be baked as soon as the batter is mixed.

quick en (kwik′ən), *v.t.* 1 cause to move more quickly; hasten: *Quicken your pace.* 2 stir up; make alive: *quicken hot ashes into flames. Reading adventure stories quickens my imagination.* 3 give or restore life to. —*v.i.* 1 move more quickly; become faster: *His pulse quickened.* 2 become more active or alive. 3 become living. 4 grow bright or brighter. **—quick′en er,** *n.*

quick-freeze (kwik′frēz′), *v.t.,* **-froze** (-frōz′), **-fro zen** (-frō′zn), **-freez ing.** subject (food) to freezing so rapidly that the cellular structure of the food is not damaged by the formation of ice crystals, as preparation for storing at freezing temperatures.

quick ie (kwik′ē), *n.* INFORMAL. 1 motion picture, novel, or the like, produced cheaply and in haste. 2 anything done very hastily.

quick lime (kwik′līm′), *n.* lime[1].

quick ly (kwik′lē), *adv.* rapidly; with haste; very soon.

quick sand (kwik′sand′), *n.* a very deep, soft, wet sand, that will not support a person's weight. A quicksand may engulf people and animals.

quick sil ver (kwik′sil′vər), *n.* mercury.

quick step (kwik′step′), *n.* 1 step used in marching in quick time. 2 a lively dance step. 3 music in a brisk march rhythm.

quick-tem pered (kwik′tem′pərd), *adj.* easily angered.

quick time, pace in marching of 120 30-inch steps per minute, the ordinary marching pace of the United States Army, Marine Corps, etc.

quick-wit ted (kwik′wit′id), *adj.* having a quick mind; mentally alert.

quid[1] (kwid), *n.* 1 piece to be chewed. 2 bite of chewing tobacco. [Old English *cwidu* cud]

quid[2] (kwid), *n., pl.* **quid.** BRITISH SLANG. one pound, or 20 shillings. [origin uncertain]

quid pro quo (kwid′ prō kwō′), LATIN. one thing in return for another; compensation.

qui es cence (kwī es′ns), *n.* absence of activity; a quiet state; stillness.

qui es cent (kwī es′nt), *adj.* quiet and motionless; inactive; still. [< Latin *quiescentem* < *quies,* noun, rest] **—qui es′cent ly,** *adv.*

quiet (kwī′ət), *adj.* 1 making or having little or no noise; almost silent; hushed: *quiet footsteps, a quiet room.* 2 moving very little; still; calm: *a quiet river.* See **still**[1] for synonym study. 3 saying little. 4 peaceful; gentle: *a quiet mind, quiet manners.* 5 not showy or bright: *Gray is a quiet color.* 6 not active: *a quiet life in the country.* —*n.* 1 state of rest; stillness; absence of motion or noise. 2 freedom from disturbance; peace: *to read in quiet.* —*v.t.* make quiet: *The mother quieted her frightened child.* —*v.i.* become quiet: *The wind quieted down.* —*adv.* in a quiet manner; quietly. [< Latin *quietus* at rest < *quies* quiet. Doublet of COY, QUIT.] **—qui′et er,** *n.* **—qui′et ly,** *adv.* **—qui′et ness,** *n.*

qui e tude (kwī′ə tüd, kwī′ə tyüd), *n.* quietness; stillness; calmness.

qui e tus (kwī ē′təs), *n.* 1 a final getting rid of anything; finishing stroke; anything that ends or settles: *The arrival of the militia gave the riot its quietus.* 2 something that quiets. [< Medieval Latin *quietus est* he is discharged]

quill (def. 3)

quill (kwil), *n.* 1 a large, stiff feather. 2 the hollow stem of a feather. 3 anything made from the hollow stem of a feather, such as a pen, toothpick, or an instrument for plucking the strings of a musical instrument. 4 the stiff, sharp, hollow spine of a porcupine or hedgehog. [Middle English *quil*]

quilt (kwilt), *n.* 1 a cover for a bed made of two pieces of cloth with a soft pad of cotton, wool, etc., between, held in place by lines of stitching. The top of a quilt often consists of bits and pieces of cloth sewed together in a design. 2 anything resembling a quilt: *a quilt of clouds.* —*v.i.* make quilts; do quilted work. —*v.t.* 1 stitch together with a soft lining: *quilt a bathrobe.* 2 sew in lines or patterns. 3 sew up between pieces of material. [< Old French *cuilte* < Latin *culcita* cushion] **—quilt′er,** *n.*

quilt ing (kwil′ting), *n.* 1 quilted work. 2 material for making quilts; a stout fabric so woven as to appear quilted. 3 act or occupation of making a quilt or quilts.

quilting bee, a social gathering of women to make a quilt or quilts.

quince (kwins), *n.* 1 the hard, yellowish, acid, pear-shaped fruit of a small Asiatic tree of the rose family, used for preserves and jelly. 2 tree it grows on. [originally plural of Middle English *quyne* < Old French *cooin* < Latin *cotoneum*]

Quin cy (kwin′zē), *n.* city in E Massachusetts. 88,000.

qui nine (kwī′nīn), *n.* 1 a bitter, crystalline alkaloid made from the bark of a cinchona tree, used in treating malaria and fevers. *Formula:* $C_{20}H_{24}N_2O_2$ 2 any of various salts of quinine that are used as medicine. [< Spanish *quina* < Quechua *kina* bark]

quinine water, a carbonated drink containing a small amount of quinine and a little lemon and lime juice.

Quin qua ges i ma (kwing′kwə jes′ə mə), *n.* the Sunday before the beginning of Lent; Shrove Sunday. [< Latin *quinquagesima* fiftieth]

quin quen ni al (kwing kwen′ē əl), *adj.* 1 occurring every five years. 2 of or for five years. —*n.* 1 something that occurs every five years. 2 something lasting five years. [< Latin *quinquennium* < *quinque* five + *annus* year] **—quin quen′ni al ly,** *adv.*

quin sy (kwin′zē), *n.* tonsillitis with pus; a very sore throat with an abscess in the tonsils. [< Medieval Latin *quinancia* < Late Latin *cynanche* < Greek *kynanchē*, originally, dog's collar < *kynos* dog + *anchein* to choke]

quint (kwint), *n.* INFORMAL. quintuplet.

quin ta (kin′tə), *n.* (in Spain, Latin America, etc.) a country house or villa. [< Spanish and Portuguese]

quin tain (kwin′tin), *n.* in the Middle Ages: 1 a post set up as a mark to be tilted at. 2 the exercise of tilting at a target. [< Old French *quintaine* < Medieval Latin *quintana*]

quin tal (kwin′tl), *n.* 1 hundredweight. 2 unit of mass in the metric system, equal to 100 kilograms, or 220.46 pounds avoirdupois. [< Medieval Latin *quintale* < Arabic *qinṭār* < Latin *centenarius* < *centum* hundred]

quin tes sence (kwin tes′ns), *n.* 1 the purest form of some quality; pure essence. 2 the most perfect example of something: *Her dress was the quintessence of good taste and style.* [< Medieval Latin *quinta essentia* fifth essence; with reference to a fifth element supposed by medieval philosophers to be more pervasive than the four elements (earth, water, fire, and air)]

quin tes sen tial (kwin′tə sen′shəl), *adj.* having the nature of a quintessence; of the purest or most perfect kind.

quin tet or **quin tette** (kwin tet′), *n.* 1 group of five singers or players performing together. 2 piece of music for five voices or instruments. 3 any group of five. [< Italian *quintetto* < *quinto* fifth < Latin *quintus*]

quin tile (kwin′tīl, kwin′tl), *n.* one of the points or marks dividing a frequency distribution into five parts, each having the same frequency. [< Latin *quintus* fifth + English *(quart)ile*]

Quin til ian (kwin til′yən), *n.* A.D. 35?-95?, Roman writer on rhetoric and oratory.

quin til lion (kwin til′yən), *n.* 1 (in the United States, Canada, and France) 1 followed by 18 zeros. 2 (in Great Britain and Germany) 1 followed by 30 zeros.

quin tu ple (kwin′tə pəl, kwin′tyə pəl; kwin tü′pəl, kwin tyü′pəl), *adj., adv., n., v.,* **-pled, -pling.** —*adj.* 1 consisting of five parts; fivefold. 2 five times; five times as great. —*adv.* five times; five times as great. —*n.* number, amount, etc., five times as great as another. —*v.t., v.i.* make or become five times as great or as numerous. [< French < Latin *quintus* fifth + English *(quadru)ple*]

quin tu plet (kwin′tə plit, kwin′tyə plit; kwin tü′plit, kwin tyü′plit), *n.* 1 one of five offspring born at the same time from the same mother. 2 any group or combination of five.

quin tu pli cate (*adj., n.* kwin tü′plə kit, kwin tyü′plə kit; *v.* kwin tü′plə kāt, kwin-tyü′plə kāt), *adj., v.,* **-cat ed, -cat ing,** *n.* —*adj.* fivefold; quintuple. —*v.t.* to make fivefold; quintuple. —*n.* 1 one of a set of five. 2 **in quintuplicate,** in five copies exactly alike.

quip (kwip), *n., v.,* **quipped, quip ping.** —*n.* 1 a clever or witty saying. 2 a sharp, cutting remark. 3 something odd or strange. —*v.i.* make quips. [earlier *quippy,* perhaps < Latin *quippe* indeed!]

quip ster (kwip′stər), *n.* person who often makes quips.

qui pu (kē′pü, kwip′ü), *n.* cord with knotted strings or threads of various colors, used by the ancient Peruvians to record events, keep accounts, send messages, etc. [earlier *quipo* < Spanish < Quechua (Peru) *quipu* knot]

quire[1] (kwīr), *n.* 24 or 25 sheets of paper of the same size and quality. [< Old French *quaier,* ultimately < Latin *quaterni* four each]

quire[2] (kwīr), *n.* ARCHAIC. choir.

Quir i nal (kwir′ə nəl), *n.* 1 one of the seven hills upon which Rome was built. 2 palace built on this hill, formerly the royal palace, now the official residence of the president of Italy.

quirk (kwėrk), *n.* 1 a peculiar way of acting. 2 a clever or witty saying. 3 quibble. 4 a sudden twist or turn: *a quirk of fate, a mental quirk.* 5 flourish in writing. [origin unknown]

quirk y (kwėr′kē), *adj.,* **quirk i er, quirk i est.** full of quirks. **—quirk′i ly,** *adv.* **—quirk′i ness,** *n.*

quirt (kwėrt), *n.* a riding whip with a short, stout handle and a lash of braided leather. [< American Spanish *cuarta*]

quis ling (kwiz′ling), *n.* person who treacherously helps to prepare the way for enemy occupation of his own country. [< Vidkun *Quisling,* 1887-1945, Norwegian puppet ruler for the Nazis in World War II]

quit (kwit), *v.,* **quit** or **quit ted, quit ting,** *adj.* —*v.t.* 1 stop, cease, or discontinue: *quit work at five.* 2 go away from; leave: *quit a room.* 3 give up; let go: *quit a job.* 4 pay back; pay off (a debt). 5 ARCHAIC. behave or conduct (oneself); acquit. —*v.i.* 1 stop working. 2 leave: *If he doesn't pay his rent, he will receive notice to quit.* 3 INFORMAL. leave a position, job, etc.; resign. —*adj.* free; clear; rid: *I gave him money to be quit of him.* [< Old French *quiter* < *quite* free, clear < Latin *quietus* at rest. Doublet of QUIET, COY.]

quit claim (kwit′klām′), *n.* 1 the giving up of a claim. 2 quitclaim deed. —*v.t.* give up claim to (a possession, etc.).

quitclaim deed, document in which a person gives up his claim, title, or interest in a piece of property to someone else but does not guarantee that the title is valid.

quite (kwīt), *adv.* 1 completely; wholly; entirely: *a hat quite out of fashion.* 2 actually; really; positively: *quite the thing.* 3 INFORMAL. to a considerable extent or degree: *quite pretty.* [Middle English, originally variant of *quit,* adjective]

➜ **quite.** The formal meaning of *quite* is "entirely, wholly." In informal English, it is generally used with the reduced meaning of "to a considerable extent or degree": Formal: *These charges are so serious you should be quite sure they are true before you proceed.* Informal: *He is quite worried. I hiked quite a distance.* A number of convenient phrases with *quite* are good informal usage: *quite a few* people, *quite a long* time, etc.

Qui to (kē′tō), *n.* capital of Ecuador, in the N part. 496,000.

quit rent (kwit′rent′), *n.* a fixed rent paid in money, instead of services rendered under a feudal system.

hat, āge, fär; let, ēqual, tėrm;
it, īce; hot, ōpen, ôrder;
oil, out; cup, pu̇t, rüle;
ch, child; ng, long; sh, she;
th, thin; ᴛʜ, then; zh, measure;

ə represents *a* in about, *e* in taken, *i* in pencil, *o* in lemon, *u* in circus.

< = from, derived from, taken from.

quits (kwits), *adj.* 1 even or on equal terms by repayment or retaliation. 2 **be quits with,** get even with; have revenge on. 3 **call it quits,** abandon an attempt to do something. 4 **cry quits,** admit that things are now even.

quit tance (kwit′ns), *n.* 1 a release from debt or obligation. 2 the paper certifying this; receipt. 3 repayment or retaliation.

quit ter (kwit′ər), *n.* INFORMAL. one who shirks or gives up easily.

quiv er[1] (kwiv′ər), *v.i.* shake with a slight but rapid motion; shiver; tremble: *The dog quivered with excitement.* See **shake** for synonym study. —*n.* act of quivering; tremble. [Old English *cwifer* nimble]

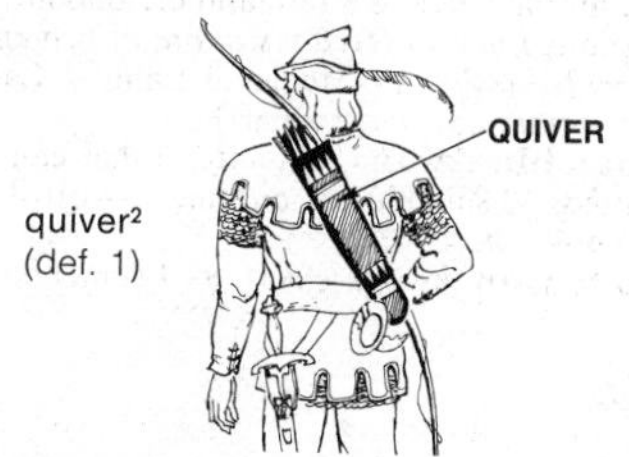

quiver[2] (def. 1)

quiv er[2] (kwiv′ər), *n.* 1 case to hold arrows. 2 supply of arrows in such a case. [< Old French *cuivre*]

qui vive? (kē vēv′), 1 who goes there? 2 **on the qui vive,** watchful; alert. [< French, literally, (long) live who?; expecting such a reply as *Vive le roi!* Long live the king!]

Qui xo te (kē hō′tē, kwik′sət), *n.* **Don.** See **Don Quixote.**

quix ot ic (kwik sot′ik), *adj.* 1 resembling Don Quixote; extravagantly chivalrous or romantic. 2 visionary; not practical. **—quix ot′i cal ly,** *adv.*

quix ot ism (kwik′sə tiz′əm), *n.* quixotic character or behavior.

quiz (kwiz), *n., pl.* **quiz zes,** *v.,* **quizzed, quiz zing.** —*n.* 1 a short or informal test. 2 a questioning. 3 person who makes fun of others. 4 a practical joke. —*v.t.* 1 give a short or informal test to: *quiz a class in history.* 2 question; interrogate. 3 make fun of; mock. [origin unknown] **—quiz′zer,** *n.*

quiz show, a radio or television show in which contestants are asked questions and win prizes if they answer correctly.

quiz zi cal (kwiz′ə kəl), *adj.* 1 that suggests making fun of others; teasing: *a quizzical smile.* 2 questioning; baffled: *a quizzical expression on one's face.* 3 odd; queer; comical. **—quiz′zi cal ly,** *adv.*

quoin (koin, kwoin), *n.* 1 an external angle or corner of a wall or building. 2 stone forming an outside angle of a wall; cornerstone. 3 a wedge-shaped piece of wood, metal, etc. [variant of *coin*]

quoit (kwoit), *n.* 1 a heavy, flattish iron or rope ring thrown to encircle a peg stuck in the ground or to come as close to it as possible. 2 **quoits,** *pl. in form, sing. in use.* game so played. [perhaps < Old French *coite* cushion]

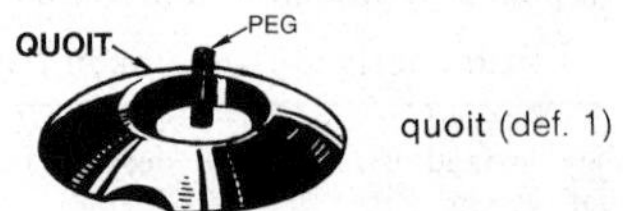

quoit (def. 1)

quon dam (kwon′dəm), *adj.* that once was; former: *The quondam servant is now master.* [< Latin, at one time]

Quon set hut (kwon′sit), trademark for a prefabricated building made of corrugated metal and shaped like a half-cylinder.

quo rum (kwôr′əm, kwōr′əm), *n.* number of members of any society or assembly that must be present if the business done is to be legal or binding. [< Latin, of whom]

quot., quotation.

quo ta (kwō′tə), *n.* 1 the share or proportional part of a total due from or to a particular district, state, person, etc.: *Each member of the club was given his quota of tickets to sell for the party.* 2 a set number, amount, or portion: *I never exceed my quota of two cups of coffee a day.* [< Medieval Latin < Latin *quota pars* how large a part]

quot a ble (kwō′tə bəl), *adj.* 1 that can be quoted. 2 suitable for quoting. **—quot′a ble ness,** *n.*

quo ta tion (kwō tā′shən), *n.* 1 somebody's words repeated exactly by another person; passage quoted from a book, speech, etc.: *From what author does this quotation come?* 2 a quoting: *Quotation is a habit of some preachers.* 3 the stating of the current price of a stock, commodity, etc. 4 the price so stated: *today's quotation on wheat.*

quotation mark, one of a pair of marks used to indicate the beginning and end of a quotation. For an ordinary quotation use these marks (" "). For a quotation within another quotation use these (' ').

➔ A period coming at the end of a quotation is generally placed inside the final quotation marks, even when the period serves for the entire statement and not just the quoted material: *She spoke disparagingly of my "hero."*

Quonset hut

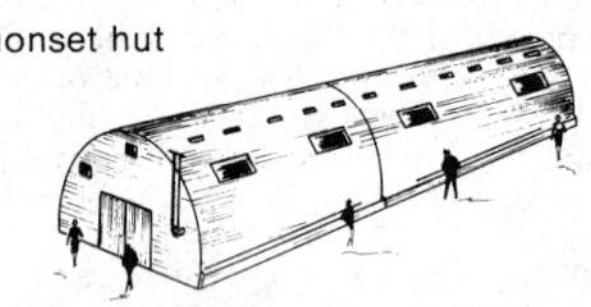

quote (kwōt), *v.,* **quot ed, quot ing,** *n.* *—v.t.* 1 repeat the exact words of; give words or passages from. 2 bring forward as an example or authority: *The judge quoted various cases in support of his opinion.* See synonym study below. 3 give (a price): *quote a price on a house up for sale.* 4 state the current price of (a stock, commodity, etc.). 5 enclose in quotation marks. *—v.i.* repeat exactly the words of another or a passage from a book: *quote from the Bible.* *—n.* 1 quotation. 2 a quotation mark. [< Medieval Latin *quotare* to number chapters < Latin *quotus* which or what number (in a sequence) < *quot* how many] **—quot′er,** *n.*

Syn. *v.t.* 2 **Quote, cite** mean to bring forward as authority or evidence. **Quote** means to use the words of another, either repeated exactly or given in a summary, and to identify the speaker: *The Commissioner was quoted as saying action will be taken.* **Cite** means to name as evidence or authority, but not to quote, a passage, author, or book, with exact title, page, etc.: *To support his argument he cited Article 68, Chapter 10, of the Charter of the United Nations.*

quoth (kwōth), *v.t.* ARCHAIC. said. [Old English *cwæth,* past tense of *cwethan* say]

quoth a (kwō′thə), *interj.* ARCHAIC. quoth he! indeed! (used ironically or contemptuously in repeating the words of another).

quo tid i an (kwō tid′ē ən), *adj.* reappearing daily; daily. *—n.* fever or ague that occurs daily. [< Latin *quotidianus* < *quotus* which or what number (in a sequence) + *dies* day]

quo tient (kwō′shənt), *n.* number obtained by dividing one number by another. In 26 ÷ 2 = 13, 13 is the quotient. [< Latin *quotiens* how many times < *quot* how many]

quo war ran to (kwō wə ran′tō), 1 writ commanding a person to show by what authority he holds a public office or exercises a public privilege or franchise. 2 legal proceedings taken against such a person. [< Medieval Latin, by what warrant]

q.v., which see [for Latin *quod vide*].

➔ **q.v.** is used in scholarly writing as a reference to another book, article, etc., already mentioned. It has now been generally replaced in reference works by the English word *see.*

qy., query.

R r

R or **r** (är), *n., pl.* **R's** or **r's.** 1 the 18th letter of the English alphabet. 2 **the three R's,** reading, writing, and arithmetic.
r., 1 radius. 2 railroad. 3 rare. 4 rod. 5 roentgen. 6 ruble. 7 rupee.
R, (in chess) rook.
R., 1 King [for Latin *rex*]. 2 Queen [for Latin *regina*]. 3 Rabbi. 4 Railroad. 5 Republican. 6 River. 7 Royal.
Ra (rä, rā), *n.* (in Egyptian myths) the sun god and supreme deity, typically represented as a hawk-headed man bearing the sun on his head.
Ra, radium.
R.A., 1 member of the Royal Academy. 2 Rear Admiral. 3 Royal Academy.
Ra bat (rə bät′), *n.* capital of Morocco, in the NW part. 435,000.
rab bet (rab′it), *n.* 1 cut, groove, or slot made on the edge or surface of a board or the like, to receive the end or edge of another piece of wood shaped to fit it. 2 joint so made. —*v.t.* 1 cut or form a rabbet in. 2 join with a rabbet. [< Old French *rabat* a beating down < *rabattre.* See REBATE.]

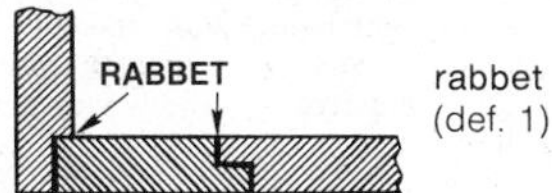

rabbet (def. 1)

rab bi (rab′ī), *n., pl.* **-bis** or **-bies.** an ordained preacher and teacher of the Jewish law and religion, usually serving as the spiritual leader of a Jewish congregation; Jewish clergyman. [< Hebrew *rabbī* my master]
rab bin ate (rab′ə nit, rab′ə nāt), *n.* 1 office or position of a rabbi. 2 period during which one is a rabbi. 3 rabbis as a group.
rab bin ic (rə bin′ik), *adj.* rabbinical.
rab bin i cal (rə bin′ə kəl), *adj.* 1 of or having to do with rabbis, their learning, writings, etc. 2 of or for the rabbinate: *a rabbinical student.* —**rab bin′i cal ly,** *adv.*
rab bit (rab′it), *n.* 1 any of various small, burrowing mammals with soft fur, long ears, long hind legs, and a short fluffy tail. Rabbits resemble hares and belong to the same order, but produce young without fur. 2 the fur of any of these mammals. —*v.i.* hunt or catch rabbits. [Middle English *rabet*] —**rab′bit-like′,** *adj.*
rabbit fever, tularemia.
rabbit punch, a sharp blow on the back of the neck, at or near the base of the skull.
rab ble (rab′əl), *n.* 1 a disorderly crowd; mob. 2 **the rabble,** (in contemptuous use) the lower classes. [Middle English *rabel*]
rab ble-rous er (rab′əl rou′zər), *n.* person who tries to stir up groups of people with speeches tending to arouse them to acts of violence; agitator.
Rab e lais (rab′ə lā), *n.* **François,** 1495?-1553, French writer, famous for his lively satire and coarse humor.
Rab e lai sian (rab′ə lā′zhən, rab′ə lā′zē ən), *adj.* of, having to do with, or suggesting Rabelais; characterized by broad, coarse humor.
Ra bi (rä′bē), *n.* **Isidor Isaac,** born 1898, American atomic physicist, born in Austria.
rab id (rab′id), *adj.* 1 unreasonably extreme; fanatical; violent: *The rebels are rabid idealists.* 2 furious; raging: *rabid with anger.* 3 having rabies; mad: *a rabid dog.* [< Latin *rabidus* < *rabere* be mad] —**rab′id ly,** *adv.* —**rab′id ness,** *n.*
ra bies (rā′bēz), *n.* a virus disease that attacks the central nervous system of warm-blooded animals, causing mental disturbance, muscular spasms, and paralysis; hydrophobia. The disease is usually transmitted by the bite of a rabid animal, and is fatal unless treated with serum. [< Latin, madness < *rabere* be mad. Doublet of RAGE.]

raccoon (def. 1)—32 in. long with tail

rac coon (ra kün′), *n.* 1 a small, grayish flesh-eating mammal with a bushy, ringed tail, that lives mostly in wooded areas near water, and is active at night. 2 its fur. Also, **racoon.** [of Algonquian origin]
race[1] (rās), *n., v.,* **raced, rac ing.** —*n.* 1 contest of speed, as in running, driving, riding, sailing, etc. 2 Often, **races,** *pl.* series of horse races run at a set time over a regular course. 3 any contest that suggests a race: *a political race.* 4 onward movement; course: *the race of life.* 5 a strong or fast current of water. 6 the channel of a stream. 7 channel leading water to or from a place where its energy is utilized. 8 track, groove, etc., for a sliding or rolling part of a machine, as a channel for ball bearings.
—*v.i.* 1 engage in a contest of speed. 2 run, move, or go swiftly: *Race to the doctor for help.* 3 (of a motor, wheel, etc.) run faster than necessary when load or resistance is lessened, or when the transmission is not engaged. —*v.t.* 1 try to beat in a contest of speed; run a race with. 2 cause to run in a race. 3 cause to run, move, or go swiftly. 4 cause (a motor, wheel, etc.) to run faster than necessary when load or resistance is lessened, or when the transmission is not engaged.
[Middle English *ras* < Scandinavian (Old Icelandic) *rās* strong current]
race[2] (rās), *n.* 1 a great division of mankind having certain inheritable physical peculiarities in common: *the white race, the yellow race.* See **people** for synonym study. 2 group of persons, animals, or plants having similar characteristics or ancestry: *the Nordic race, the canine race, the human race.* 3 group, class, or kind (especially of people): *the brave race of seamen.* 4 condition of belonging to a particular stock or the qualities, etc., due to this: *Race was of importance to Hitler.* [< Middle French *rasse* < Italian *razza*]
race course (rās′kôrs′), *n.* racetrack.
race horse (rās′hôrs′), *n.* horse bred, trained, or kept for racing.
ra ceme (rā sēm′, rə sēm′), *n.* a simple flower cluster having its flowers on nearly equal stalks along a stem, the lower flowers blooming first. The lily of the valley, currant, and chokecherry have racemes. [< Latin *racemus* cluster. Doublet of RAISIN.]

hat, āge, fär; let, ēqual, tėrm;
it, īce; hot, ōpen, ôrder;
oil, out; cup, pu̇t, rüle;
ch, child; ng, long; sh, she;
th, thin; ᴛʜ, then; zh, measure;

ə represents *a* in about, *e* in taken, *i* in pencil, *o* in lemon, *u* in circus.

< = from, derived from, taken from.

rac e mose (ras′ə mōs), *adj.* 1 in the form of a raceme; characteristic of racemes. 2 arranged in racemes.
racemose gland, gland formed of a system of ducts which branch into sacs and resemble clusters of grapes, as the pancreas.
rac er (rā′sər), *n.* 1 person, animal, boat, automobile, etc., that takes part in races. 2 any of various North American snakes that can move very rapidly, such as the blacksnake.
race track (rās′trak′), *n.* ground laid out for racing, usually circular or oval; racecourse.
Ra chel (rā′chəl), *n.* (in the Bible) the favorite wife of Jacob, and the mother of Joseph and Benjamin.
ra chis (rā′kis), *n., pl.* **ra chis es, rach i des** (rak′ə dēz′, rā′kə dēz′). 1 stalk; shaft. 2 shaft of a feather. 3 spinal column. [< New Latin < Greek *rhachis* backbone]
ra chit ic (rə kit′ik), *adj.* having to do with or affected with rickets.
ra chi tis (rə kī′tis), *n.* rickets. [< New Latin < Greek *rhachitis* disease of the backbone < *rhachis* backbone]
Rach ma ni noff (räk mä′ni nôf), *n.* **Sergei,** 1873-1943, Russian composer and pianist.
ra cial (rā′shəl), *adj.* 1 having to do with a race; characteristic of a race: *racial traits.* 2 of or involving races: *racial discrimination.* —**ra′cial ly,** *adv.*
ra cial ism (rā′shə liz′əm), *n.* racism.
ra cial ist (rā′shə list), *n., adj.* racist.
rac i ly (rā′sə lē), *adv.* in a racy manner or style.
Ra cine (ra sēn′ *for 1;* rə sēn′ *for 2*), *n.* 1 **Jean Baptiste,** 1639-1699, French poet and dramatist. 2 city in SW Wisconsin, on Lake Michigan. 95,000.
rac i ness (rā′sē nis), *n.* vigor; liveliness.
racing form, publication that gives information about racehorses, jockeys, races, etc.
rac ism (rā′siz′əm), *n.* 1 belief that a particular race, especially one's own, is superior to other races. 2 discrimination or prejudice against a race or races based on this belief.
rac ist (rā′sist), *n.* person who believes in, supports, or practices racism. —*adj.* of or having to do with racism.
rack[1] (rak), *n.* 1 frame with bars, shelves, or pegs to hold, arrange, or keep things on: *a*

raceme—of lily of the valley

tool rack, a baggage rack. 2 framework set on a wagon for carrying hay, straw, etc. 3 frame of bars to hold hay and other food for cattle, horses, etc. 4 instrument once used for torturing people by stretching them between rollers at each end of a frame. 5 **on the rack,** in great pain or distress; suffering very much. 6 cause or condition of great suffering in body or mind. 7 stretch; strain. 8 bar with pegs or teeth on one edge into which teeth on the rim of a wheel or pinion can fit. *—v.t.* 1 hurt very much: *be racked with grief. A toothache racked my jaw.* 2 stretch; strain. 3 torture on the rack. 4 put (a thing) in or on a rack. 5 **rack up,** INFORMAL. accumulate. [Middle English *rakke*]

rack² (rak), *n.* wreck; destruction: *Over the years the vacant house went to rack and ruin.* [variant of *wrack*]

rack³ (rak), *n.* 1 a horse's gait in which the forefeet move as in a slow gallop, while the hind feet move as in a trot or pace; single-foot. 2 pace. *—v.i.* 1 go at a rack. 2 pace. [origin uncertain]

rack et¹ (rak′it), *n.* 1 loud noise; loud talk; din. 2 parties and other social activities. 3 INFORMAL. **a** scheme for getting money from people through bribery, threats of violence, and other illegal means. **b** any dishonest scheme. 4 SLANG. occupation. *—v.i.* 1 make a racket; move about in a noisy way. 2 take part in social activities. [probably < earlier British slang, kind of fraud]

rack et² (rak′it), *n.* 1 an oval, wooden or metal frame strung with netting and having a long handle, used to hit the ball, etc., in tennis, squash, badminton, etc. 2 a paddle-shaped wooden implement with a short handle, used to hit the ball in table tennis. 3 **rackets,** *pl.* game played in a walled court with ball and rackets. Also, **racquet.** [< Middle French *raquette* < Arabic *rāha* palm of the hand]

rack et eer (rak′ə tir′), *n.* person who extorts money through bribery, by threatening violence, or by some other illegal means. *—v.i.* extort money in this way.

rack et eer ing (rak′ə tir′ing), *n.* business of a racketeer.

rac on teur (rak′on tėr′), *n.* person clever in telling stories, anecdotes, etc. [< French < *raconter* recount]

ra coon (ra kün′), *n.* raccoon.

rac quet (rak′it), *n.* 1 racket². 2 **racquets,** *pl.* rackets.

rac y (rā′sē), *adj.,* **rac i er, rac i est.** 1 vigorous; lively; spirited. 2 having an agreeably peculiar taste or flavor; piquant; spicy. 3 risqué. [< *race²*, in the sense of particular class or special flavor] **—rac′i ly,** *adv.*

rad (rad), *n.* unit for measuring absorbed doses of radiation, equal to 100 ergs of energy per gram. [< *rad(iation)*]

ra dar (rā′där), *n.* instrument for determining the distance, direction, speed, etc., of unseen objects by the reflection of radio waves. [< *ra(dio) d(etecting) a(nd) r(anging)*]

ra dar scope (rā′där skōp), *n.* screen in a radar set which displays the dots of light indicating the location of an object within the radar's range.

Rad cliffe (rad′klif), *n.* **Ann,** 1764-1823, English novelist.

ra di al (rā′dē əl), *adj.* 1 of or near the radius bone. 2 arranged like or in radii or rays. *—n.* part that radiates or is arranged in radii. **—ra′di al ly,** *adv.*

radial engine, an internal-combustion engine, having radially arranged cylinders, formerly much used for aircraft.

radial symmetry, (in zoology) a condition in which like parts are arranged about an axis, from which they radiate like the parts of a flower, as in many echinoderms.

ra di an (rā′dē ən), *n.* angle at the center of a circle, that subtends an arc of the circle equal in length to the radius; an angle of about 57.2958 degrees.

ra di ance (rā′dē əns), *n.* 1 vivid brightness: *the radiance of the sun, the radiance of a smile.* 2 radiation.

ra di an cy (rā′dē ən sē), *n.* radiance.

ra di ant (rā′dē ənt), *adj.* 1 shining; bright; beaming: *a radiant smile.* See **bright** for synonym study. 2 sending out rays of light or heat: *The sun is a radiant body.* 3 sent off in rays from some source; radiated: *radiant heat.* **—ra′di ant ly,** *adv.*

radiant energy, energy in the form of waves, especially electromagnetic waves. X rays, radio waves, and visible light are forms of radiant energy.

radiant heating, system of heating in which walls, floors, etc., radiate heat from a network of pipes enclosed within them; panel heating.

ra di ate (rā′dē āt; *adj. also* rā′dē it), *v.,* **-at ed, -at ing,** *adj.* *—v.t.* 1 give out rays of: *The sun radiates light.* 2 give out; send forth: *Her face radiates joy.* *—v.i.* 1 give out rays; shine. 2 issue in rays: *Heat radiates from the sun.* 3 spread out from a center: *Roads radiate from the city in every direction.* *—adj.* 1 having rays: *A daisy is a radiate flower.* 2 radiating from a center. [< Latin *radiatum* radiated < *radius* ray]

ra di a tion (rā′dē ā′shən), *n.* 1 act or process of giving out light, heat, or other electromagnetic waves. 2 energy radiated. 3 particles or electromagnetic waves emitted by the atoms and molecules of a radioactive substance as a result of atomic decay. Some radiations from atoms are alpha particles, beta particles, gamma rays, and neutrons. Radiation is harmful to living tissue.

Radiation—Types of electromagnetic radiation

↑ INCREASING FREQUENCY / INCREASING WAVELENGTH ↓	type of radiation	source	uses
	cosmic rays	outer space	study of atomic nuclei and production of elementary particles
	gamma rays	radioactive nuclei	medical treatment of cancer and skin diseases; detection of flaws in metal
	X rays	impact of electrons on a metallic target, as in a vacuum tube	medical diagnosis and treatment
	ultraviolet rays	sun and arcs	disinfectant, fluorescent lights, and medical treatment
	visible light	sun and hot objects	illumination and photography
	infrared rays	hot objects	heat lamps, drying paint, and photography
	radio waves	electronic devices	television, radio, and radar

R

radiation sickness, disease resulting from an overexposure to radiation from radioactive materials. It is usually characterized by nausea, diarrhea, and headache, and in severe cases by internal bleeding, changes in blood cells, loss of hair, etc.

ra di a tor (rā′dē ā′tər), *n.* 1 a heating device consisting of a set of pipes through which steam or hot water circulates. 2 device for cooling water. The radiator of an automobile gives off heat very fast and so cools the water circulating inside it. 3 person or thing that radiates.

rad i cal (rad′ə kəl), *adj.* 1 going to the root; fundamental: *If she wants to reduce, she must make a radical change in her diet.* 2 favoring extreme changes or reforms; extreme. 3 having to do with or forming the root of a number or quantity. 4 (in botany) of or from the root or roots. —*n.* 1 person who favors extreme changes or reforms, especially in politics. 2 atom or group of atoms acting as a unit in chemical reactions. Ammonium (NH_4^+) is a radical in NH_4OH and NH_4Cl. 3 in mathematics: **a** an expression indicating the root of a quantity. EXAMPLE: $\sqrt{5}$, $\sqrt{x-3}$ **b** radical sign. 4 (in grammar) a root. [< Late Latin *radicalis* < Latin *radix* root] **—rad′i cal ly,** *adv.* **—rad′i cal ness,** *n.*

rad i cal ism (rad′ə kə liz′əm), *n.* principles and practices of radicals; support or advocacy of extreme changes or reforms, especially in politics.

radical sign, a mathematical sign ($\sqrt{\ }$) put before a number or expression to show that a root of it is to be extracted. $\sqrt{16}$ = the square root of 16 = 4. $\sqrt[3]{27}$ = the cube root of 27 = 3.

rad i cand (rad′ə kand′), *n.* the quantity placed under a radical sign.

rad i cle (rad′ə kəl), *n.* 1 part of a plant embryo that develops into the root. 2 a little root. [< Latin *radicula,* diminutive of *radix* root]

ra di i (rā′dē ī), *n.* a pl. of **radius.**

ra di o (rā′dē ō), *n., pl.* **-di os,** *adj., v.* —*n.* 1 the sending and receiving of sound or picture signals by means of electromagnetic waves without the use of connecting wires between sender and receiver. 2 apparatus for sending or receiving and making audible the sounds so sent. 3 INFORMAL. message sent by radio. 4 business of broadcasting. —*adj.* 1 of, used in, or sent by radio. 2 of electric frequencies higher than 15,000 cycles per second. —*v.t.* 1 transmit or send out by radio. 2 communicate with by radio. [< *radio-,* shortened from *radiotelegraphy,* etc.]

radio-, *combining form.* 1 radio: *Radiobroadcast = broadcast by radio.* 2 radial; radially: *Radiosymmetrical = radially symmetrical.* 3 radiant energy: *Radiograph = radiant energy graph.* 4 radioactive: *Radioisotope = radioactive isotope.* [< *radius*]

ra di o ac tive (rā′dē ō ak′tiv), *adj.* of, having, or caused by radioactivity. Radium, uranium, and thorium are radioactive metallic elements. **—ra′di o ac′tive ly,** *adv.*

ra di o ac tiv i ty (rā′dē ō ak tiv′ə tē), *n.* 1 the property exhibited by certain elements, of giving off radiation in the form of alpha particles, beta particles, or gamma rays as the result of spontaneous nuclear decay. 2 the radiation given off.

radio astronomy, branch of astronomy dealing with the detection and study of objects in space by means of the radio waves emitted by the objects, some of which are beyond the range of ordinary telescopes. **—radio astronomer.**

radio beacon, a radio station for sending special signals so that ships, airplanes, etc., can determine their position.

ra di o bi o log i cal (rā′dē ō bī′ə loj′ə kəl), *adj.* of or having to do with radiobiology.

ra di o bi ol o gist (rā′dē ō bī ol′ə jist), *n.* an expert in radiobiology.

ra di o bi ol o gy (rā′dē ō bī ol′ə jē), *n.* branch of biology dealing with the effects of radiation on living organisms.

ra di o broad cast (rā′dē ō brôd′kast′), *n., v.,* **-cast** or **-cast ed, -cast ing.** —*n.* a broadcasting by radio. —*v.t., v.i.* broadcast by radio. **—ra′di o broad′cast′er,** *n.*

radio car, automobile, such as a squad car, equipped with a two-way radio.

ra di o car bon (rā′dē ō kär′bən), *n.* a radioactive isotope of carbon, especially carbon 14.

radiocarbon dating, carbon dating.

ra di o el e ment (rā′dē ō el′ə mənt), *n.* a radioactive element.

radio frequency, any electromagnetic wave frequency suitable for radio broadcasting, usually above 10,000 cycles per second.

radio galaxy, galaxy that emits radio waves.

ra di o gram (rā′dē ō gram), *n.* 1 message transmitted by radio. 2 radiograph.

ra di o graph (rā′dē ō graf), *n.* an X-ray picture. —*v.t.* make a radiograph of.

ra di o i o dine (rā′dē ō ī′ə dīn, rā′dē ō ī′ə dən, rā′dē ō ī′ə dēn′), *n.* iodine 131.

ra di o i so tope (rā′dē ō ī′sə tōp), *n.* a radioactive isotope.

ra di o lar i an (rā′dē ō ler′ē ən), *n.* any of a large order of minute marine protozoans, often having a spherical body with numerous fine, radiating pseudopods and usually an outer spiny skeleton. [< Late Latin *radiolus,* diminutive of Latin *radius* ray]

ra di o log ic (rā′dē ō loj′ik), *adj.* radiological.

ra di o log i cal (rā′dē ō loj′ə kəl), *adj.* of or having to do with radiology. **—ra′di o log′i cal ly,** *adv.*

ra di ol o gist (rā′dē ol′ə jist), *n.* an expert in radiology.

ra di ol o gy (rā′dē ol′ə jē), *n.* science dealing with X rays or the rays from radioactive substances, especially for medical diagnosis or treatment.

ra di om e ter (rā′dē om′ə tər), *n.* 1 instrument for indicating the transformation of radiant energy into mechanical force. 2 instrument for detecting and measuring radiant energy.

ra di o met ric (rā′dē ō met′rik), *adj.* having to do with the radiometer or with radiometry.

ra di om e try (rā′dē om′ə trē), *n.* the measurement of radiant energy.

ra di o phone (rā′dē ō fōn′), *n.* radiotelephone.

ra di o pho to (rā′dē ō fō′tō), *n., pl.* **-tos.** radiophotograph.

ra di o pho to graph (rā′dē ō fō′tə graf), *n.* photograph transmitted by radio.

ra di o sonde (rā′dē ō sond), *n.* instrument carried into the stratosphere by a balloon from which it descends by parachute, automatically reporting data on atmospheric conditions to observers on the ground by means of a small radio transmitter. [< *radio-* + French *sonde* depth sounding]

radio star, a powerful mass of energy in space that emits radio waves instead of light waves.

hat, āge, fär; let, ēqual, tėrm;
it, īce; hot, ōpen, ôrder;
oil, out; cup, pu̇t, rüle;
ch, child; ng, long; sh, she;
th, thin; ᴛʜ, then; zh, measure;

ə represents *a* in about, *e* in taken, *i* in pencil, *o* in lemon, *u* in circus.

< = from, derived from, taken from.

ra di o stron ti um (rā′dē ō stron′shē əm, rā′dē ō stron′tē əm), *n.* strontium 90.

ra di o tel e graph (rā′dē ō tel′ə graf), *n.* telegraph worked by radio.

ra di o tel e graph ic (rā′dē ō tel′ə graf′ik), *adj.* of or having to do with radiotelegraphy.

ra di o te leg ra phy (rā′dē ō tə leg′rə fē), *n.* a telegraphing by radio.

ra di o tel e phone (rā′dē ō tel′ə fōn), *n.* a radio transmitter using voice communication; radiophone.

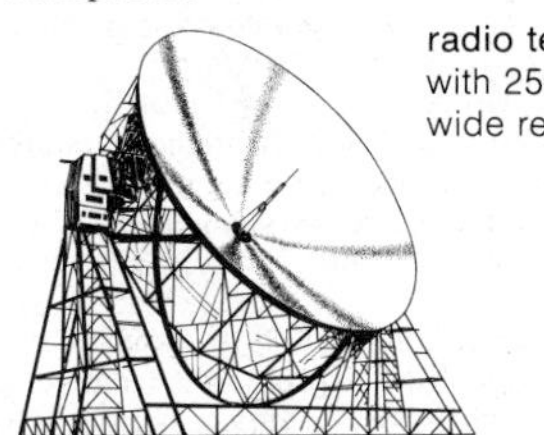

radio telescope with 250 ft. wide reflector

radio telescope, device consisting of a radio receiver and a very large, bowl-shaped antenna for detecting and recording radio waves emitted by objects in space.

ra di o ther a pist (rā′dē ō ther′ə pist), *n.* an expert in radiotherapy.

ra di o ther a py (rā′dē ō ther′ə pē), *n.* treatment of disease by means of X rays or radioactive agencies.

radio tube, vacuum tube used in a radio set.

radio wave, an electromagnetic wave within the radio frequencies. See **radiation** for table.

rad ish (rad′ish), *n.* 1 the small, crisp root of a plant of the mustard family, with a red or white skin, used as a relish and in salads. 2 the plant. [< Middle French *radis* < Italian *radice* < Latin *radicem, radix* root. Doublet of RADIX.]

ra di um (rā′dē əm), *n.* a radioactive metallic element found in very small amounts in uranium ores such as pitchblende. Radium is very unstable and gives off alpha particles and gamma rays in breaking down in successive forms into radon, polonium, and, finally, lead. Radium is used in treating cancer and in making luminous paint. *Symbol:* Ra; *atomic number* 88. See pages 326 and 327 for table. [< New Latin < Latin *radius* ray]

ra di us (rā′dē əs), *n., pl.* **-di i** or **-di us es.** 1 any line segment going straight from the center to the outside of a circle or a sphere.

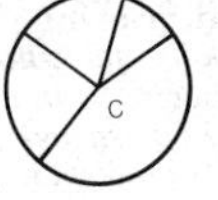

radius (def. 1)
Each line from C (center) is a radius.

Any spoke in a wheel is a radius. 2 a circular area measured by the length of its radius: *The explosion could be heard within a radius of ten miles.* 3 that one of the two bones of the forearm which is on the thumb side. 4 a corresponding bone in the forelimb of other vertebrates. [< Latin, ray, spoke of a wheel. Doublet of RAY[1].]

radius vector, (in mathematics) a line segment, or its length, joining the fixed point and a variable point in a system of polar coordinates.

ra dix (rā′diks), *n., pl.* **rad i ces** (rad′ə sēz′, rā′də sēz′), **ra dix es.** 1 root; radical; source or origin. 2 (in mathematics) a number taken as the base of a system of numbers, logarithms, or the like. The radix of the decimal system is ten. [< Latin, root. Doublet of RADISH.]

ra dome (rā′dōm), *n.* a domelike structure, usually a hemisphere of plastic, used to shelter a radar antenna. [< *ra(dar)* + *dome*]

ra don (rā′don), *n.* a heavy, inert, radioactive, gaseous element formed by the decay of radium. It is used in the treatment of cancer. *Symbol:* Rn; *atomic number* 86. See pages 326 and 327 for table. [< *radium*]

R.A.F., Royal Air Force (of Great Britain).

raf fi a (raf′ē ə), *n.* 1 fiber from the leafstalks of a kind of palm tree growing on Madagascar, used in making baskets, mats, etc. 2 the tree from which this fiber is obtained. [< Malagasy]

raff ish (raf′ish), *adj.* 1 showy and cheap; tawdry. 2 rakish or disreputable. [related to *riffraff*] **—raff′ish ly,** *adv.* **—raff′ish ness,** *n.*

raf fle (raf′əl), *n., v.,* **-fled, -fling.** *—n.* sale in which many people each pay a small sum for a chance to win a prize. *—v.t.* sell (an article) by a raffle. *—v.i.* hold a raffle. [Middle English *rafle* a dice game < Old French, plundering, stripping]

raft[1] (raft), *n.* logs or boards fastened together to make a floating platform. *—v.t.* 1 send by raft; carry on a raft. 2 make into a raft. [< Scandinavian (Old Icelandic) *raptr* log]

raft[2] (raft), *n.* INFORMAL. a large number; abundance. [variant of Middle English *raff* heap < *riffraff*]

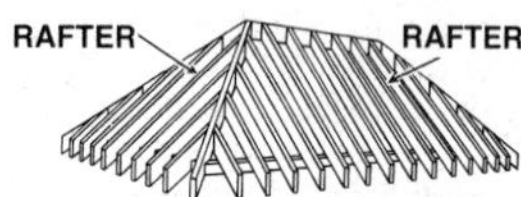

raft er (raf′tər), *n.* a slanting beam of a roof. [Old English *ræfter*]

rag[1] (rag), *n.* 1 a torn or waste piece of cloth. 2 **rags,** *pl.* clothing that is torn and in tatters. 3 a small piece of cloth. 4 a small piece of anything of no value. *—adj.* made from rags. [< Scandinavian (Old Icelandic) *rögg* shaggy tuft] **—rag′like′,** *adj.*

rag[2] (rag), *v.t.,* **ragged, rag ging.** SLANG. 1 scold. 2 play jokes on; tease. [origin uncertain]

rag a muf fin (rag′ə muf′ən), *n.* 1 a ragged, disreputable fellow. 2 a ragged child. [probably < *rag*[1]]

rage (rāj), *n., v.,* **raged, rag ing.** *—n.* 1 violent anger; fury: *a voice quivering with rage.* 2 a fit of violent anger: *be in a rage.* 3 violence: *the rage of a savage tiger.* 4 craze; fad. *—v.i.* 1 be furious with anger. 2 speak or move with furious anger. 3 act violently; move, proceed, or continue with great violence: *A storm is raging.* [< Old French < Popular Latin *rabia* < Latin *rabies* madness. Doublet of RABIES.]

rag ged (rag′id), *adj.* 1 worn or torn into rags. 2 wearing torn or badly worn-out clothing. 3 not straight and tidy; rough: *an Airedale's ragged coat.* 4 having loose shreds or bits: *a ragged wound.* 5 having rough or sharp points; uneven; jagged: *ragged rocks.* **—rag′ged ly,** *adv.* **—rag′ged ness,** *n.*

rag ged y (rag′ə dē), *adj.,* **-ged i er, -ged i est.** 1 ragged: *a raggedy coat.* 2 that looks ragged.

rag ing (rā′jing), *adj.* that rages; violent; furious: *a raging fever, raging anger.* **—rag′ing ly,** *adv.*

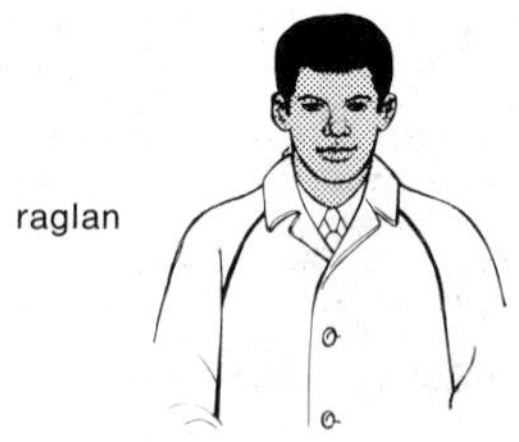

rag lan (rag′lən), *adj.* having sleeves cut so as to continue up to the collar. *—n.* a loose topcoat or overcoat with such sleeves. [< Baron *Raglan,* 1788-1855, British field marshal]

rag man (rag′man′), *n., pl.* **-men.** man who gathers, buys, or sells rags, old newspapers, etc.

ra gout (ra gü′), *n.* a highly seasoned stew of meat and vegetables. [< French *ragoût* < *ragoûter* restore the appetite]

rag time (rag′tīm′), *n.* 1 musical rhythm with accents at unusual places. 2 form of jazz using this rhythm.

rag weed (rag′wēd′), *n.* any of several coarse weeds of the composite family, the pollen of which is one of the most common causes of hay fever.

rah (rä), *interj., n.* hurrah.

raid (rād), *n.* 1 a sudden attack, usually by a small, military force having no intention of holding the territory invaded. 2 an entering and seizing what is inside: *a police raid. The hungry teen-agers made a raid on the refrigerator.* 3 a predatory incursion into the domain of another. *—v.t.* 1 attack suddenly. 2 force a way into; enter and seize what is in. *—v.i.* engage in a raid. [Old English *rād* a riding. Related to RIDE.] **—raid′er,** *n.*

rail[1] (rāl), *n.* 1 bar of wood or of metal fixed on upright supports as part of a fence, balustrade, etc.: *a stair rail, an altar rail.* 2 railing: *The jockey rode the horse near the rail.* 3 either of a pair of rolled steel bars laid continuously parallel along the ground or fastened to crossties, forming a track for a railroad train, elevated train, subway train, or other vehicle. 4 railroad: *ship by rail.* 5 the upper part of the bulwarks of a ship. *—v.t.* 1 furnish with rails. 2 enclose with bars. [< Old French *reille* < Latin *regula* straight rod. Doublet of RULE.]

rail[2] (rāl), *v.i.* complain bitterly; use violent and reproachful language: *rail at one's hard luck.* [< Middle French *railler* to mock, ridicule, ultimately < Late Latin *ragere* to bray, brawl. Doublet of RALLY[2].] **—rail′er,** *n.*

rail[3] (rāl), *n., pl.* **rails** or **rail.** any of numerous small, wading birds with short wings, narrow bodies, long toes, and a harsh cry, living in marshes and swamps. [< Old French *raale*]

rail ing (rā′ling), *n.* 1 fence made of rails. 2 material for rails. 3 rails collectively.

rail ler y (rā′lər ē), *n., pl.* **-ler ies.** 1 good-humored ridicule; joking; teasing. 2 a bantering remark. [< French *raillerie* < Middle French *railler.* See RAIL[2].]

rail road (rāl′rōd′), *n.* 1 road or track with parallel steel rails on which the wheels of locomotives, passenger cars, and freight cars run. 2 tracks, stations, trains, and other property of a system of transportation that uses rails, together with the people who manage them. *—v.t.* 1 send by railroad; carry on a railroad. 2 INFORMAL. send along quickly or too quickly to be fair: *His enemies tried to railroad him to prison without a fair trial.* *—v.i.* work on a railroad. **—rail′road′er,** *n.*

rail road ing (rāl′rō′ding), *n.* 1 construction or operation of railroads. 2 act or process of hurrying (a thing or person) along.

rail way (rāl′wā′), *n.* 1 railroad. 2 track made of rails.

rai ment (rā′mənt), *n.* clothing; garments. [short for *arraiment* < *array*]

rain (rān), *n.* 1 water condensed from atmospheric vapor and falling in drops from the sky. 2 the fall of such drops; shower or rainstorm: *a hard rain.* 3 a thick, fast fall of anything: *a rain of bullets.* 4 **the rains,** the rainy season; the seasonal rainfalls. *—v.i.* 1 fall in drops of water. 2 fall like rain: *Sparks rained down from the burning roof.* *—v.t.* send like rain: *The children rained flowers on their queen.* [Old English *regn*] **—rain′less,** *adj.*

rain bow (rān′bō′), *n.* bow or arch of light showing all the colors of the spectrum, formed opposite to the sun in the sky, or in mist or spray, by the reflection and refraction of the sun's rays in drops of water; iris. *—adj.* having many colors like a rainbow.

rainbow trout, a large trout, native to western North America, with bright pinkish coloring.

rain check, 1 ticket for future use, given to the spectators at a baseball game or other outdoor performance stopped by rain. 2 promise to offer again an invitation which a person cannot now accept.

rain coat (rān′kōt′), *n.* a waterproof coat worn for protection from rain.

rain drop (rān′drop′), *n.* drop of rain.

rain fall (rān′fôl′), *n.* 1 shower of rain. 2 amount of water in the form of rain, snow, etc., falling within a given time and area.

rain forest, a very dense forest in a region, usually tropical, where rain is very heavy throughout the year.

rain gauge, instrument for measuring rainfall.

Rai nier (rə nir′, rā nir′), *n.* **Mount,** mountain in W Washington. 14,408 ft. Also, **Mount Tacoma.**

rain mak er (rān′mā′kər), *n.* person who tries to produce rain, especially by supernatural or artificial means.

rain mak ing (rān′mā′king), *n.* the producing of rain by artificial or supernatural means.

rain proof (rān′prüf′), *adj.* impervious to rain.

rain storm (rān′stôrm′), *n.* storm with much rain.

rain wa ter (rān′wô′tər, rān′wot′ər), *n.* water that has fallen as rain.

rain wear (rān′wer′, rān′war′), *n.* rainproof clothes.

rain y (rā′nē), *adj.,* **rain i er, rain i est.** 1 having rain; having much rain. 2 bringing rain: *rainy clouds.* 3 wet with rain: *rainy streets.* **—rain′i ly,** *adv.* **—rain′i ness,** *n.*

rainy day, a possible time of greater need in the future.

raise (rāz), *v.,* **raised, rais ing,** *n.* *—v.t.* 1 move to a higher place; lift up; put up; elevate. See synonym study below. 2 set upright: *Raise the overturned lamp.* 3 cause to rise: *raise a cloud of dust.* 4 put or take into a higher position; make higher or nobler: *raise a salesman to manager.* 5 increase in amount, price, pay, etc.: *raise the rent.* 6 increase in degree, intensity, force, etc.: *Raise your voice.* 7 (in poker, bridge, etc.) bet or bid more than (another player or another bet or bid). 8 gather together; collect; manage to get: *raise funds.* 9 breed; grow: *The farmer raises crops and cattle.* 10 bring about; cause: *raise a laugh.* 11 utter (a cry, etc.); produce (a noise, etc.): *raise a shout.* 12 build; create; produce; start; set up: *raise a monument.* 13 stir up; rouse: *The dog raised a rabbit from the underbrush.* 14 bring up; rear: *Parents raise their children.* 15 cause (dough, etc.) to become spongy in texture and swell: *Yeast raises bread.* 16 bring back to life: *raise the dead.* 17 put an end to: *Raise the siege of the fort by driving away the enemy.* 18 come in sight of: *After a long voyage the ship raised land.* 19 call attention to; pose: *raise a question.* 20 falsify the value of (a check, note, etc.) by making the sum larger. *—v.i.* (in poker, bridge, etc.) increase one's bid or bet.

—n. 1 a raised place. 2 U.S. increase in amount, price, pay, etc. 3 the amount of such an increase.

[< Scandinavian (Old Icelandic) *reisa*] **—rais′er,** *n.*

Syn. *v.t.* 1 **Raise, lift, elevate** mean to move something to a higher position. **Raise** means to bring something to a high or, especially, vertical position or to move it up from a lower to a higher level: *She raised the window shade.* **Lift** means to take something, usually heavy, from the ground or other low level: *Please lift the table.* **Elevate,** a more formal term, means to bring something to a higher position or level: *The flag was elevated from half-mast to the top of the mast.*

rai sin (rā′zn), *n.* a sweet, dried grape. [< Old French *raizin* < Latin *racemus* grape cluster. Doublet of RACEME.]

rai son d'ê tre (rā zôN′ de′trə), FRENCH. reason for being; justification.

ra jah or **ra ja** (rä′jə), *n.* ruler or chief in India, Java, Borneo, etc. [< Hindi *rājā* < Sanskrit *rājan* king]

Ra ja sthan (rä′jə stän), *n.* state in NW India.

Raj put (räj′püt), *n.* member of a Hindu military, landowning, and ruling caste. [< Hindi *rājpūt* < Sanskrit *rājaputra* king's son]

rake[1] (rāk), *n., v.,* **raked, rak ing.** *—n.* a long-handled tool having a bar at one end with teeth in it, used for smoothing the soil or gathering together loose leaves, hay, straw, etc. *—v.t.* 1 move with a rake: *Rake the leaves off the grass.* 2 make clear, clean, smooth, etc., with a rake, or as if with a rake: *Rake the yard.* 3 search carefully: *I raked the want ads for a bicycle for sale.* 4 fire guns along the length of (a ship, line of soldiers, etc.). *—v.i.* use a rake. [Old English *raca*]

rake[2] (rāk), *n.* a profligate or dissolute person. [short for *rakehell,* perhaps < *rake*[1] + *hell*]

rake[3] (rāk), *n., v.,* **raked, rak ing.** *—n.* slant; slope. A ship's smokestacks have a slight backward rake. *—v.t., v.i.* slant or cause to slant. [origin uncertain]

rake-off (rāk′ôf′, rāk′of′), *n.* INFORMAL. share or portion, often an amount taken or received illicitly.

rak ish[1] (rā′kish), *adj.* 1 smart; jaunty; dashing: *a hat set at a rakish angle.* 2 suggesting dash and speed: *He owns a rakish boat.* [< *rake*[3]] **—rak′ish ly,** *adv.* **—rak′ish ness,** *n.*

rak ish[2] (rā′kish), *adj.* like a rake; immoral; dissolute. [< *rake*[2]]

rale or **râle** (räl), *n.* an abnormal crackling, whistling, or other sound accompanying the normal sounds of breathing. It is a symptom of certain pulmonary diseases. [< French *râle*]

Ra leigh (rô′lē), *n.* 1 Sir **Walter,** 1552?-1618, English soldier, explorer, statesman, and author. 2 capital of North Carolina, in the central part. 94,000.

ral len tan do (räl′en tän′dō), *adj.* (in music) becoming slower; slackening. [< Italian, slowing down]

ral ly[1] (ral′ē), *v.,* **-lied, -ly ing,** *n., pl.* **-lies.** *—v.t.* 1 bring together, especially to get in order again: *The commander was able to rally the fleeing troops.* 2 pull together; revive: *We rallied all our energy for one last effort.* *—v.i.* 1 come together in a body for a common purpose or action. 2 come to help a person, party, or cause: *She rallied to the side of her injured friend.* 3 recover health and strength: *The sick man may rally now.* 4 take part in a rally in tennis and similar games. 5 recover more or less from a drop in prices. *—n.* 1 a rallying; recovery. 2 a mass meeting or assembly for a common purpose or action: *a political rally.* 3 act of hitting the ball back and forth several times in tennis and similar games. 4 a rise following a drop in prices. 5 an automobile race. [< Middle French *rallier* < *re-* again + *allier* to ally]

ral ly[2] (ral′ē), *v.t.,* **-lied, -ly ing.** make fun of; tease. [< French *railler* rail[2]. Doublet of RAIL[2].]

ram (ram), *n., v.,* **rammed, ram ming.** *—n.* 1 a male sheep. 2 machine or part of a machine that strikes heavy blows, such as the plunger of a force pump, the weight of a pile driver, or the piston of a hydraulic press. 3 battering ram. 4 beak at the bow of a warship, used to break the sides of enemy ships. 5 ship with such a beak. 6 **Ram,** Aries. *—v.t.* 1 butt against; strike head-on; strike violently: *One ship rammed the other ship.* 2 push hard; drive down or in by or as if by heavy blows. [Old English *ramm*] **—ram′mer,** *n.*

Ram a dan (ram′ə dän′), *n.* the ninth month of the Moslem year, during which fasting is rigidly practiced daily from dawn until sunset. [< Arabic *Ramaḍān*]

ram ble (ram′bəl), *v.,* **-bled, -bling,** *n.* *—v.i.* 1 wander about: *We rambled here and there through the woods.* See **roam** for synonym study. 2 talk or write about first one thing and then another with no useful connections. 3 spread irregularly in various directions: *Vines rambled over the wall.* *—n.* a walk for pleasure, not to go to any special place. [origin uncertain]

hat, āge, fär; let, ēqual, tėrm;
it, īce; hot, ōpen, ôrder;
oil, out; cup, pu̇t, rüle;
ch, child; ng, long; sh, she;
th, thin; ᴛʜ, then; zh, measure;

ə represents *a* in about, *e* in taken,
i in pencil, *o* in lemon, *u* in circus.

< = from, derived from, taken from.

ram bler (ram′blər), *n.* 1 person or thing that rambles. 2 any of various climbing roses having clusters of small red, yellow, or white flowers.

ram bling (ram′bling), *adj.* 1 wandering about. 2 going from one thing to another with no useful connections: *a rambling speech.* 3 extending irregularly in various directions; not planned in an orderly way: *a rambling old farmhouse.* **—ram′bling ly,** *adv.*

ram bunc tious (ram bungk′shəs), *adj.* INFORMAL. 1 wild and uncontrollable; unruly. 2 noisy and violent; boisterous. [alteration of *robustious* < *robust*] **—ram bunc′tious ly,** *adv.* **—ram bunc′tious ness,** *n.*

ram e kin or **ram e quin** (ram′ə kən), *n.* 1 a small, separately cooked portion of some food, especially one topped with cheese and bread crumbs. 2 a small baking dish holding enough for one portion. [< French *ramequin*]

Ram e ses II (ram′ə sēz), Ramses II.

Rameses III, Ramses III.

ram ie (ram′ē), *n.* 1 an Asiatic shrub of the same family as the nettle, that yields a strong fiber used in making textiles, etc. 2 this fiber. [< Malay *rami* plant]

ram i fi ca tion (ram′ə fə kā′shən), *n.* 1 a dividing or spreading out into branches or parts. 2 manner or result of branching; branch; part; subdivision.

ram i fy (ram′ə fī), *v.i.,* **-fied, -fy ing.** divide or spread out into branchlike parts. [< Middle French *ramifier* < Medieval Latin *ramificare* < Latin *ramus* branch + *facere* to make]

ram jet (ram′jet′), *n.* jet engine in which the fuel is fed into air compressed by the speed of the airplane, missile, etc., in which it is contained.

ra mose (rā′mōs, rə mōs′), *adj.* having many branches; branching. [< Latin *ramosus* < *ramus* branch] **—ra′mose ly,** *adv.*

ra mous (rā′məs), *adj.* 1 ramose. 2 o
like a branch.

ramp[1] (ramp), *n.* a sloping way con
two different levels of a building, r
slope. [< French *rampe* < *ra*
RAMP[2].]

ramp[2] (ramp), *v.i.* 1 rush wi
have violently. 2 jump or
3 (in heraldry) stand on t
especially of lions). [< O
creep, climb]

ram page (*n.* ram′p
n., v., **-paged, -pa**
wildly about; spe
outbreak: *The*
page. *—v.i.*
olently; rage

ram pa g
unruly;
adv. -

ram pa
pant.

rampant (def. 4) lion rampant

ram pant (ram′pənt), *adj.* 1 growing without any check: *The vines ran rampant over the fence.* 2 passing beyond restraint or usual limits; unchecked: *Anarchy was rampant after the dictator died.* 3 angry; excited; violent. 4 (in heraldry) standing up on the hind legs. [< Old French, ramping] **—ram′pant ly,** *adv.*

ram part (ram′pärt), *n.* 1 a wide bank of earth, often with a wall on top as a fortification, built around a fort to help defend it. 2 anything that defends; defense; protection. [< Middle French *rempart* < *remparer* fortify]

ram rod (ram′rod′), *n.* 1 rod for ramming down the charge in a gun that is loaded from the muzzle. 2 rod for cleaning the barrel of a gun. 3 a stiff, unbending person. *—adj.* stiff; rigid; unbending.

Ram ses II (ram′sēz′), died 1225? B.C., king of ancient Egypt. Also, **Rameses II.**

Ramses III, died 1167? B.C., king of ancient Egypt. Also, **Rameses III.**

ram shack le (ram′shak′əl), *adj.* loose and shaky; likely to come apart. [ultimately < *ransack*]

ran (ran), *v.* pt. of **run.**

ranch (ranch), *n.* 1 a large farm with grazing land, used for raising cattle, sheep, or horses. 2 any farm, especially one used to raise one kind of animal or crop: *a chicken ranch, a fruit ranch.* 3 ranch house (def. 2). *—v.i.* work on a ranch; manage a ranch. [< American Spanish *rancho*]

ranch er (ran′chər), *n.* person who owns, manages, or works on a ranch.

ran cher o (ran cher′ō, rän cher′ō), *n., pl.* **-cher os.** (in the southwestern United States) rancher. [< American Spanish]

ranch house, 1 the main house on a ranch. 2 a one-story dwelling, usually having a low roof.

ranch man (ranch′mən), *n., pl.* **-men.** rancher.

ran cho (ran′chō, rän′chō), *n., pl.* **-chos.** (in the southwestern United States) ranch. [< American Spanish]

ran cid (ran′sid), *adj.* 1 stale; spoiled: *rancid butter.* 2 tasting or smelling like stale fat or butter: *rancid odor.* [< Latin *rancidus* < *rancere* be rank] **—ran′cid ly,** *adv.* **—ran′cid ness,** *n.*

ran cid i ty (ran sid′ə tē), *n.* rancid quality or condition.

ran cor (rang′kər), *n.* bitter resentment or ill will; extreme hatred or spite. [< Late Latin, rankness < Latin *rancere* be rank]

an cor ous (rang′kər əs), *adj.* bitterly ma-cious; spiteful. **—ran′cor ous ly,** *adv.*

nd (rand), *n.* the monetary unit of the public of South Africa, worth about $1.50. Afrikaans]

D, research and development.

dolph (ran′dolf), *n.* **A(sa) Philip,** 1889, American labor leader, active in il rights movement.

m (ran′dəm), *adj.* without a definite n, method, or purpose; by chance: *a uess, random questions, pick a random number.* See synonym study below. *—n.* 1 **at random,** by chance; with no aim, plan, or purpose. 2 a random course or movement. [< Old French *randon* impetuosity, rush] **—ran′dom ly,** *adv.* **—ran′dom ness,** *n.*

Syn. *adj.* **Random, haphazard** mean made, done, happening, or coming by accident or chance. **Random** emphasizes the absence of any direction, purpose, or plan: *Though his shot was random, it actually hit the target.* **Haphazard** emphasizes the effect or result of chance due to the absence of planning or direction: *Because of her haphazard way of arranging furniture, the house always looks disordered.*

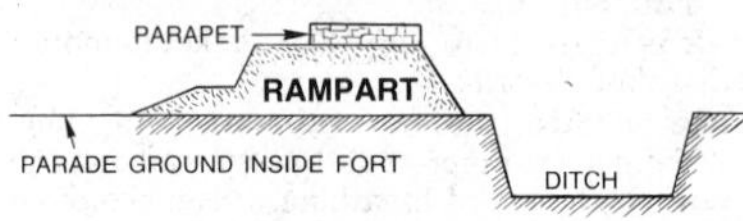

rampart (def. 1)

ran dom ize (ran′də mīz), *v.t.,* **-ized, -iz ing.** put, take, or perform at random, especially in order to control the variables of a scientific experiment, statistical procedure, etc. **—ran′dom i za′tion,** *n.*

random sample, (in statistics) a sample so drawn from the total group that every item in the group has an equal chance of being chosen.

R and R, (in the United States armed forces) rest and recuperation.

ra nee (rä′nē), *n.* wife of a rajah. Also, **rani.** [< Hindi *rānī* < Sanskrit *rājñī,* feminine of *rājan* king]

rang (rang), *v.* pt. of **ring**[2].

range (rānj), *n., v.,* **ranged, rang ing,** *adj. —n.* 1 distance between certain limits; extent: *a range of prices from $5 to $25, the average daily range of temperature, vocal range, a limited range of ideas.* See synonym study below. 2 distance a gun, projectile, etc., can operate: *be within range of the enemy.* 3 distance from a gun, etc., of an object aimed at: *set the sights of a howitzer for a range of 1000 yards.* 4 the greatest distance an aircraft, rocket, or the like, can travel on a single load of fuel. 5 place to practice shooting, bombing, etc.: *a missile range.* 6 land on which cattle, sheep, etc., may graze. 7 the act of wandering or moving about. 8 row or line of mountains: *the Green Mountain range of the Appalachian system.* 9 row; line; series: *ranges of books in perfect order.* 10 line of direction: *The two barns are in direct range with the house.* 11 rank, class, or order. 12 region in which certain plants or animals live or naturally occur. 13 stove for cooking: *a coal range.* 14 in mathematics: **a** the set of all the values a given function may take on. **b** a domain. 15 (in statistics) the difference between the smallest and the greatest values which a variable bears in frequency distribution. *—v.i.* 1 vary within certain limits: *prices ranging from $5 to $10.* 2 wander; rove; roam: *range through the woods, a conversation that ranged widely.* 3 run in a line; extend: *a boundary ranging from east to west.* 4 be found; occur: *a plant ranging from Canada to Mexico.* 5 (of a gun, etc.) have a particular range. 6 find the distance or direction of something. 7 take up or have a position in a line or other arrangement. *—v.t.* 1 wander over: *Buffalo once ranged these plains.* 2 put in a row or rows: *Range the books by size.* 3 put in groups or classes; classify. 4 put in a line on someone's side: *Loyal citizens ranged themselves with the government.* 5 make straight or even: *range lines of type.* 6 find the proper elevation for (a gun). 7 give the proper elevation to (a gun). *—adj.* of or on land for grazing: *range cattle.* [< Old French *ranger* to array < *rang.* See RANK[1].]

Syn. *n.* 1 **Range, scope, compass** mean the extent of what something can do or take in. **Range** emphasizes the extent (and variety) that can be covered or included by something in operation or action: *The car was out of my range of vision.* **Scope** emphasizes the limits beyond which something cannot extend: *Some technical terms are outside the scope of this dictionary.* **Compass** also emphasizes limits, but implies more definite ones that are likely to be permanent: *Supernatural phenomena are beyond the compass of reason or science.*

range finder, instrument for estimating the range or distance of an object.

rang er (rān′jər), *n.* 1 person employed to guard a tract of forest. 2 Also, **Ranger. a** one of a body of armed men employed in ranging over a region to police it. **b** a soldier in the United States Army trained for raids and surprise attacks; commando. 3 person or thing that ranges; rover.

Ran goon (rang gün′), *n.* capital and chief port of Burma, in the S part. 1,759,000.

rang y (rān′jē), *adj.,* **rang i er, rang i est.** 1 fitted for ranging or moving about. 2 slender and long-limbed: *a rangy horse.* **—rang′i ness,** *n.*

ra ni (rä′nē), *n.* ranee.

rank[1] (rangk), *n.* 1 row or line, especially of soldiers, placed side by side. 2 **ranks,** *pl.* **a** army; soldiers. **b** rank and file. 3 position; grade; class: *the rank of colonel.* 4 high position: *A duke is a man of rank.* 5 **pull rank,** U.S. use one's position to gain something. *—v.t.* 1 arrange in a row or line. 2 put in some special order in a list: *Rank the states in the order of size.* 3 be more important than; outrank: *A major ranks a captain. —v.i.* have a certain rank: *He ranked high in the spelling test.* [< Old French *rang;* of Germanic origin] **—rank′er,** *n.*

rank[2] (rangk), *adj.* 1 large and coarse: *rank grass.* 2 growing thickly in a coarse way: *a rank growth of weeds.* 3 producing a dense but coarse growth: *rank swampland.* 4 having a strong, bad smell or taste: *rank meat, rank tobacco.* 5 strongly marked; extreme: *rank ingratitude, rank nonsense.* 6 not decent; coarse; obscene. [Old English *ranc* proud] **—rank′ly,** *adv.* **—rank′ness,** *n.*

rank and file, 1 common soldiers, especially those with the rank of corporal or below; ranks. 2 common people.

Ran kin (rang′kən), *n.* **Jeannette,** born 1880, American legislator and woman suffrage leader.

rank ing (rang′king), *n.* standing: *a poor ranking in class. —adj.* of highest standing; leading; foremost: *the ranking U.S. Senator.*

ran kle (rang′kəl), *v.,* **-kled, -kling.** *—v.i.* be sore; cause soreness; continue to give pain: *The memory of the insult rankled in her mind. —v.t.* cause pain or soreness in or to. [< Old French *rancler, draoncler* < Medieval Latin *dracunculus* sore]

ran sack (ran′sak), *v.t.* 1 search thoroughly through: *The thief ransacked the house for jewelry.* 2 rob; plunder. [< Scandinavian

(Old Icelandic) *rannsaka*] **—ran′sack er,** *n.*
ran som (ran′səm), *n.* 1 price paid or demanded before a captive is set free: *hold someone prisoner for ransom.* 2 a ransoming. *—v.t.* 1 obtain the release of (a captive) by paying a price. 2 redeem or deliver, especially from sin or ignorance. [< Old French *rançon* < Latin *redemptionem.* Doublet of REDEMPTION.] **—ran′som er,** *n.*
rant (rant), *v.i.* 1 speak wildly, extravagantly, violently, or noisily. 2 **rant and rave,** scold violently. *—n.* extravagant, violent, or noisy speech. [< Middle Dutch *ranten*] **—rant′er,** *n.*
rap[1] (rap), *n., v.,* **rapped, rap ping.** *—n.* 1 a quick, light blow; a light, sharp knock. 2 SLANG. punishment; blame. *—v.i.* knock sharply; tap: *The chairman rapped on the table for order.* *—v.t.* say sharply: *rap out an answer.* [probably imitative]
rap[2] (rap), *n.* INFORMAL. the least bit: *I don't care a rap.* [origin uncertain]
rap[3] (rap), *n., v.,* **rapped, rap ping.** INFORMAL. *—n.* a conversing; talk. *—v.i.* converse; talk. [apparently short for *rapport*]
ra pa cious (rə pā′shəs), *adj.* 1 seizing by force; plundering. 2 grasping; greedy. 3 living by the capture of prey; predatory. [< Latin *rapacem* grasping < *rapere* seize] **—ra pa′cious ly,** *adv.* **—ra pa′cious ness,** *n.*
ra pac i ty (rə pas′ə tē), *n.* rapacious spirit, action, or practice; greed.
rape[1] (rāp), *n., v.,* **raped, rap ing.** *—n.* 1 a seizing and carrying off by force. 2 crime of having sexual intercourse with a woman or girl against her will, usually by using force. *—v.t., v.i.* 1 seize and carry off by force. 2 commit rape on. [< Latin *rapere* seize]
rape[2] (rāp), *n.* a European species of cole whose leaves are used as food for sheep and hogs. Rape seeds yield an oil that is used as a lubricant. [< Latin *rapa, rapum* turnip]
Raph a el (raf′ē əl, rā′fē əl), *n.* 1 1483-1520, Italian painter. 2 one of the archangels.
rap id (rap′id), *adj.* moving, acting, or doing with speed; very quick; swift: *a rapid worker.* See **quick** for synonym study. *—n.* **rapids,** *pl.* part of a river's course where the water rushes quickly, often over rocks near the surface. [< Latin *rapidus* < *rapere* seize] **—rap′id ly,** *adv.* **—rap′id ness,** *n.*
rap id-fire (rap′id fīr′), *adj.* 1 firing shots in quick succession. 2 occurring in quick succession: *rapid-fire commands.*
ra pid i ty (rə pid′ə tē), *n.* swiftness; speed.
rapid transit, a fast system of metropolitan public transportation, using electric cars that run on surface lines or subway or elevated tracks.
ra pi er (rā′pē ər), *n.* a long and light sword used for thrusting. [< Middle French *rapière*] **—ra′pi er like′,** *adj.*
rap ine (rap′ən), *n.* a robbing by force and carrying off; plundering. [< Latin *rapina* < *rapere* seize]
rap ist (rā′pist), *n.* person who is guilty of rape.
Rap pa han nock River (rap′ə han′ək), river flowing from N Virginia into Chesapeake Bay. 185 mi.
rap port (ra pôr′, ra pōr′; ra pôrt′, ra pōrt′; *French* rà pôr′), *n.* 1 relation; connection. 2 agreement; harmony. [< French]
rap proche ment (ra prōsh′mänt; *French* rà prôsh mäN′), *n.* establishment or renewal of friendly relations. [< French]
rap scal lion (rap skal′yən), *n.* rascal; rogue; scamp. [earlier *rascallion* < *rascal*]
rapt (rapt), *adj.* 1 lost in delight. 2 so busy thinking of or enjoying one thing that one does not know what else is happening. 3 showing a rapt condition; caused by a rapt condition: *a rapt smile.* [< Latin *raptum* seized] **—rapt′ly,** *adv.* **—rapt′ness,** *n.*
rap tor (rap′tər, rap′tôr), *n.* any raptorial bird; bird of prey. [< Latin, robber < *rapere* seize]
rap to ri al (rap tôr′ē əl, rap tōr′ē əl), *adj.* 1 adapted for seizing prey; having a hooked beak and sharp claws. 2 belonging to or having to do with birds of prey, such as the eagles, hawks, etc.
rap ture (rap′chər), *n.* 1 a strong feeling that absorbs the mind; ecstasy, especially of delight or joy. See synonym study below. 2 Often, **raptures,** *pl.* expression of great joy. [< *rapt*]
Syn. 1 **Rapture, ecstasy** are formal words meaning a feeling of being lifted high in mind and spirits. **Rapture** emphasizes being filled with and completely taken up in a feeling of delight or bliss: *In rapture the child listened to the talking doll.* **Ecstasy** emphasizes being overwhelmed or carried away by strong emotion: *The intensity of religious ecstasy enables some people temporarily to forget their worldly cares.*
rap tur ous (rap′chər əs), *adj.* full of rapture; expressing or feeling rapture. **—rap′tur ous ly,** *adv.* **—rap′tur ous ness,** *n.*
ra ra a vis (rer′ə ā′vis), *pl.* **ra rae a ves** (rer′ē ā′vēz). person or thing seldom met; rarity. [< Latin, literally, rare bird]
rare[1] (rer, rar), *adj.,* **rar er, rar est.** 1 seldom seen or found: *Storks and peacocks are rare birds in the United States.* See synonym study below. 2 not happening often; unusual: *a rare event.* 3 unusually good or great: *Edison had rare powers as an inventor.* 4 thin; not dense: *The higher we go above the earth the rarer the air is.* [< Latin *rarus*] **—rare′ness,** *n.*
Syn. 1 **Rare, scarce** mean not often or easily found. **Rare** describes something uncommon or unusual at any time and often suggests excellence or value above the ordinary: *The Gutenberg Bible is a rare book.* **Scarce** describes something usually or formerly common or plentiful, but not easily available at the present time: *Water is becoming scarce in some parts of the country.*
rare[2] (rer, rar), *adj.,* **rar er, rar est.** not cooked much: *a rare steak.* [Old English *hrēr*] **—rare′ness,** *n.*
rare bit (rer′bit, rar′bit), *n.* Welsh rabbit.
rare earth, 1 an oxide of a rare-earth element. 2 rare-earth element.

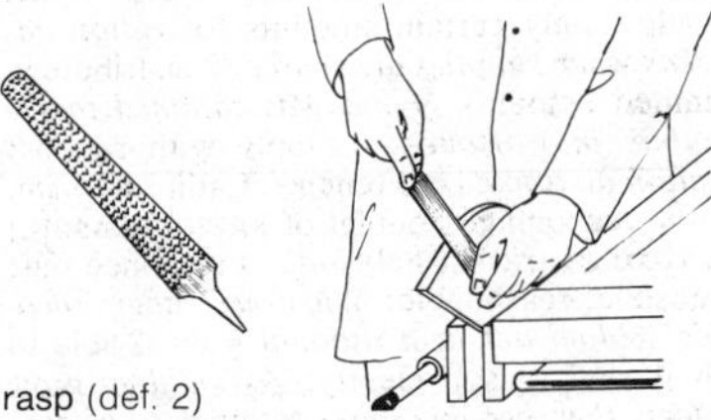
rasp (def. 2)

rare-earth element (rer′ėrth′, rar′ėrth′), any of a series of metallic elements that have similar properties, ranging from lanthanum (atomic number 57) through lutetium (atomic number 71).

hat, āge, fär; let, ēqual, tėrm;
it, īce; hot, ōpen, ôrder;
oil, out; cup, pu̇t, rüle;
ch, child; ng, long; sh, she;
th, thin; ᴛʜ, then; zh, measure;
ə represents *a* in about, *e* in taken, *i* in pencil, *o* in lemon, *u* in circus.
< = from, derived from, taken from.

rar e fac tion (rer′ə fak′shən, rar′ə fak′shən), *n.* 1 a rarefying. 2 a being rarefied. 3 (in physics) the place in a medium where its molecules are spread farthest apart, through which a sound wave is passing.
rar e fy (rer′ə fī, rar′ə fī), *v.,* **-fied, -fy ing.** *—v.t.* 1 make less dense: *The air on high mountains is rarefied.* 2 refine; purify. *—v.i.* become less dense. Also, **rarify.** [< Latin *rarefacere* < *rarus* rare + *facere* to make]
rare ly (rer′lē, rar′lē), *adv.* 1 seldom; not often. 2 unusually; unusually well: *a rarely carved panel.* 3 **rarely ever,** seldom: *I rarely ever go.*
rar i fy (rer′ə fī, rar′ə fī), *v.t., v.i.,* **-fied, -fy ing.** rarefy.
rar ing (rer′ing, rar′ing), *adj.* INFORMAL. very eager: *raring to go.* [alteration of *rearing* < *rear*[2]]
rar i ty (rer′ə tē, rar′ə tē), *n., pl.* **-ties.** 1 something rare: *A man over a hundred years old is a rarity.* 2 fewness; scarcity. 3 lack of density; thinness.
ras cal (ras′kəl), *n.* 1 a bad, dishonest person. 2 a mischievous person, child, or animal. [< Old French *rascaille* < *rasque* scurvy, filth]
ras cal i ty (ras kal′ə tē), *n., pl.* **-ties.** rascally character, conduct, or act.
ras cal ly (ras′kə lē), *adj.* of or like a rascal; mean or dishonest; bad. *—adv.* in a rascally manner.
rash[1] (rash), *adj.* 1 too hasty and careless; impetuous. See synonym study below. 2 characterized by undue haste: *a rash promise.* [Middle English *rasch* quick] **—rash′ly,** *adv.* **—rash′ness,** *n.*
Syn. 1 **Rash, reckless** mean acting or speaking without due care or thought. **Rash** emphasizes being too hasty and thoughtless in acting or speaking: *Only a rash person would have rushed into the burning house to save some clothes.* **Reckless** emphasizes being too careless and unconcerned about the possible consequences of what one does or says: *The dog was killed by a reckless driver.*
rash[2] (rash), *n.* 1 a breaking out with many small red spots on the skin. Scarlet fever causes a rash. 2 outbreak: *a rash of murders.* [< Old French *rasche, rasque* scurf, scurvy]
rash er (rash′ər), *n.* a thin slice of bacon or ham for frying or broiling. [origin uncertain]
rasp (rasp), *v.i.* make a harsh, grating sound: *The file rasped as he worked.* *—v.t.* 1 utter with a grating sound: *rasp out a command.* 2 have a harsh or irritating effect on; grate on: *Her feelings were rasped and exploded into anger.* 3 scrape with a rough instrument. *—n.* 1 a harsh, grating sound: *the rasp of crickets, a rasp in a person's voice.* 2 a coarse file with pointlike teeth. [< Old French *rasper*]
rasp ber ry (raz′ber′ē, raz′bər ē), *n., pl.* **-ries.** 1 any of various small, juicy, edible fruits composed of many drupelets, that grow

on bushes. Raspberries are usually red or black, but some kinds are white or yellow. 2 any of the bushes, various species of brambles, that bear raspberries. 3 SLANG. sound of disapproval or derision made by a noisy expulsion of breath with the tongue and lips.

Ras pu tin (ra spyüt′n), *n.* **Grigori Efimovich,** 1871-1916, Russian monk who had great influence over the family of Czar Nicholas II.

rasp y (ras′pē), *adj.,* **rasp i er, rasp i est.** 1 grating; harsh; rough. 2 irritable: *a raspy disposition.*

rat (rat), *n., v.,* **rat ted, rat ting.** —*n.* 1 any of various long-tailed, gray, black, brown, or white rodents similar to mice but larger, and usually very destructive. 2 SLANG. a low, mean, disloyal person. 3 **smell a rat,** suspect a trick or scheme. —*v.i.* 1 hunt for rats; catch rats. 2 INFORMAL. behave in a low, mean, disloyal way. 3 SLANG. turn informer against one's associates. 4 **rat on,** SLANG. go back on; welsh. [Old English *rætt*] —**rat′like′,** *adj.*

rat a ble (rā′tə bəl), *adj.* 1 capable of being rated. 2 taxable. Also, **rateable.** —**rat′a bly,** *adv.*

ra tan (ra tan′), *n.* rattan.

ratch (rach), *n.* ratchet.

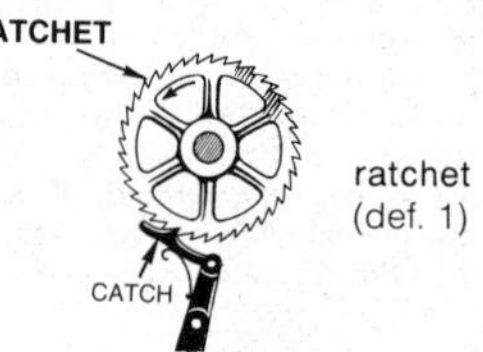

ratchet (def. 1)

ratch et (rach′it), *n.* 1 wheel or bar with teeth that come against a pawl so that motion is permitted in one direction but not in the other. 2 the pawl. 3 ratchet wheel. [< French *rochet*]

ratchet wheel, wheel with teeth and a pawl that permits motion in only one direction.

rate[1] (rāt), *n., v.,* **rat ed, rat ing.** —*n.* 1 quantity, amount, or degree measured in proportion to something else: *The rate of interest is 6 cents on the dollar. The car was going at the rate of 40 miles an hour.* 2 a fixed charge, scale, etc., that applies to each individual case or instance: *postal rates.* 3 price: *We pay the regular rate.* 4 class; grade; rating. 5 BRITISH. tax on property for some local purpose. 6 **at any rate,** in any case; under any circumstances. 7 **at that rate** or **at this rate,** in that or this case; under such circumstances. —*v.t.* 1 put a value on: *We rated the house as worth $20,000.* 2 consider; regard: *He was rated one of the richest men in town.* 3 put in a certain class or grade. 4 INFORMAL. be worthy of: *She rates the best seat in the house.* —*v.i.* be regarded; be classed; rank: *The orchestra's conductor rates high as a musician.* [< Old French < Medieval Latin *rata (pars)* fixed (amount)]

rate[2] (rāt), *v.t., v.i.,* **rat ed, rat ing.** scold; berate. [Middle English *raten*]

rate a ble (rā′tə bəl), *adj.* ratable. —**rate′a bly,** *adv.*

rate pay er (rāt′pā′ər), *n.* BRITISH. taxpayer.

rath er (raᴛʜ′ər), *adv.* 1 more readily or willingly; by preference: *I would rather go today than tomorrow.* 2 **had rather,** would more willingly; prefer to. 3 more properly or justly; with better reason: *This is rather for your parents to decide than for you.* 4 more truly or correctly: *It was late Monday night or, rather, early Tuesday morning.* 5 to some extent; more than a little; somewhat: *I am rather tired after working so long.* 6 on the contrary: *The lesson wasn't difficult to do; rather, it was easy.* 7 (with verbs) in some degree: *We rather felt that this was unwise.* —*interj.* BRITISH INFORMAL. yes, indeed! certainly! very much so! [Old English *hrathor,* comparative of *hrathe* quickly]

raths kel ler (räts′kel′ər), *n.* restaurant, usually below street level, selling alcoholic drinks. [< earlier German *Rathskeller* < *Rath(aus)* town hall + *Keller* cellar (because it was originally a wineshop in the town hall)]

rat i fi ca tion (rat′ə fə kā′shən), *n.* a ratifying; formal confirmation.

rat i fy (rat′ə fī), *v.t.,* **-fied, -fy ing.** confirm formally to make valid; give sanction or approval to: *The Senate ratified the treaty.* See **approve** for synonym study. [< Old French *ratifier* < Medieval Latin *ratificare,* ultimately < Latin *ratum* fixed + *facere* to make] —**rat′i fi′er,** *n.*

rat ing (rā′ting), *n.* 1 class; grade. 2 position in a class or grade: *the rating of a seaman.* 3 an amount fixed as a rate: *a rating of 80 per cent in English.* 4 level of merit or popularity established by a survey: *a television program with high rating.* 5 an enlisted man in the Royal Navy, British merchant navy, etc.

ra ti o (rā′shē ō, rā′shō), *n., pl.* **-ti os.** 1 relative magnitude. "He has sheep and cows in the ratio of 10 to 3" means that he has ten sheep for every three cows, or $3^1/_3$ times as many sheep as cows. 2 quotient expressing this magnitude. The ratio between two quantities is the number of times one contains the other. The ratio of 10 to 6 is 10:6, 10/6, 10÷6, or $\frac{10}{6}$. The ratios of 3 to 5 and 6 to 10 are the same. [< Latin, reckoning. Doublet of RATION, REASON.]

ra ti oc i nate (rash′ē os′n āt), *v.i.,* **-nat ed, -nat ing.** carry on a process of reasoning; reason. [< Latin *ratiocinatum* reckoned < *ratio.* See RATIO.] —**ra′ti oc′i na′tion,** *n.* —**ra′ti oc′i na′tor,** *n.*

ra ti oc i na tive (rash′ē os′n ā′tiv), *adj.* of or characterized by close or careful reasoning.

ra tion (rash′ən, rā′shən), *n.* 1 a fixed allowance of food; the daily allowance of food for a person or animal. See **food** for synonym study. 2 portion of anything dealt out; share; allotment: *rations of coal.* —*v.t.* 1 allow only certain amounts to: *ration citizens when supplies are scarce.* 2 distribute in limited amounts: *Food was rationed to the public in wartime.* 3 supply with rations: *ration an army.* [< French < Latin *rationem, ratio* reckoning. Doublet of RATIO, REASON.]

ra tion al (rash′ə nəl), *adj.* 1 reasoned out; sensible; reasonable: *When very angry, people seldom act in a rational way.* 2 able to think and reason clearly: *As children grow older, they become more rational.* 3 of reason; based on reasoning: *There is a rational explanation for thunder and lightning.* See **reasonable** for synonym study. 4 of or having to do with a rational number. —**ra′tion al ly,** *adv.*

ra tion ale (rash′ə nal′, rash′ə nä′lē), *n.* the fundamental reason. [< Latin, neuter of *rationalis* rational]

ra tion al ism (rash′ə nə liz′əm), *n.* principle or habit of accepting reason as the supreme authority in matters of opinion, belief, or conduct.

ra tion al ist (rash′ə nə list), *n.* person who accepts reason as the supreme authority in matters of opinion, belief, or conduct.

ra tion al is tic (rash′ə nə lis′tik), *adj.* of rationalism or rationalists. —**ra′tion al is′ti cal ly,** *adv.*

ra tion al i ty (rash′ə nal′ə tē), *n.* the possession of reason; reasonableness: *She is odd in some ways, but no one doubts her rationality.*

ra tion al ize (rash′ə nə līz), *v.,* **-ized, -iz ing.** —*v.t.* 1 make rational or conformable to reason. 2 treat or explain in a rational manner. 3 find (often unconsciously) an explanation or excuse for: *She rationalizes her gluttony by thinking "I must eat enough to keep up my strength."* —*v.i.* find excuses for one's desires. —**ra′tion al i za′tion,** *n.* —**ra′tion al iz′er,** *n.*

rational number, any number that can be expressed as an integer or as a ratio between two integers, excluding zero as a denominator. 2, 5, and $-^1/_2$ are rational numbers.

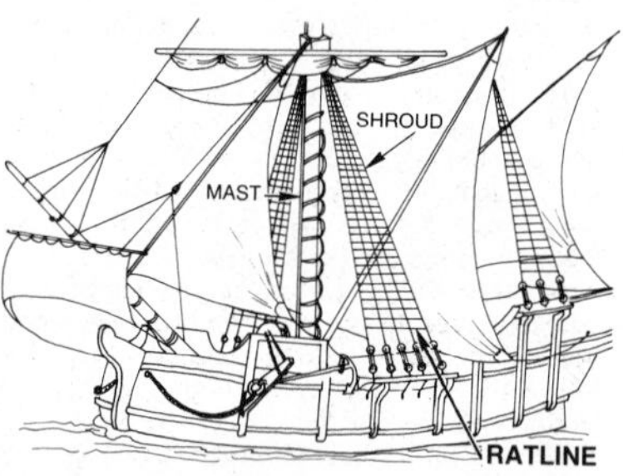

rat line or **rat lin** (rat′lən), *n.* one of the small ropes that cross the shrouds of a ship, used as steps for going aloft. [Middle English *ratling*]

RA TO (rā′tō), *n.* 1 rocket-assisted takeoff. 2 rocket used for such a takeoff.

rat race, INFORMAL. a frantic confusion or scramble, especially as applied to senseless competition.

rats bane (rats′bān′), *n.* any poison for rats.

rat snake, chicken snake.

rat tan (ra tan′), *n.* 1 any of several climbing palms with very long stems. 2 stems of such palm trees, used for wickerwork, canes, etc. 3 cane or switch made from a piece of such a stem. Also, **ratan.** [< Malay *rotan*]

rat ter (rat′ər), *n.* 1 one that catches rats: *Our terrier is a good ratter.* 2 SLANG. one who deserts his associates.

rat tle (rat′l), *v.,* **-tled, -tling,** *n.* —*v.i.* 1 make a number of short, sharp sounds: *The window rattled in the wind.* 2 move with short, sharp sounds: *The old car rattled down the street.* 3 talk in a quick, lively, and rather pointless manner. —*v.t.* 1 cause to rattle. 2 say or do quickly: *rattle off a series of numbers.* 3 INFORMAL. confuse; upset: *He is not very easily rattled.* —*n.* 1 number of short, sharp sounds: *the rattle of empty bottles.* 2 toy, instrument, etc., that makes a noise when it is shaken. 3 the series of horny pieces at the end of a rattlesnake's tail. See

rattlesnake for picture. 4 sound in the throat, caused by partial obstruction and occurring often just before death. 5 racket; uproar. [Middle English *ratelen*]

rat tle brain (rat′l brān′), *n.* a giddy, thoughtless person.

rat tle brained (rat′l brānd′), *adj.* like a rattlebrain; giddy.

rat tler (rat′lər), *n.* 1 rattlesnake. 2 machine or vehicle that rattles.

rattlesnake

rat tle snake (rat′l snāk′), *n.* any of two genera of poisonous American snakes with thick bodies and broad triangular heads, that make a buzzing noise with rattles at the end of the tail.

rat tle trap (rat′l trap′), *n.* 1 a rattling, rickety wagon or other vehicle. 2 any shaky, rattling object. *—adj.* rickety; rattling.

rat tling (rat′ling), *adj.* 1 that rattles. 2 lively; very fast. 3 INFORMAL. great; important. *—adv.* INFORMAL. extremely; especially: *a rattling good time.* **—rat′tling ly,** *adv.*

rat tly (rat′lē), *adj.* that rattles; rattling.

rat ty (rat′ē), *adj.,* **-ti er, -ti est.** 1 of rats; like rats. 2 full of rats. 3 SLANG. **a** poor; shabby. **b** angry; irritable.

rau cous (rô′kəs), *adj.* hoarse; harsh-sounding: *the raucous caw of a crow.* [< Latin *raucus*] **—rau′cous ly,** *adv.* **—rau′cous ness,** *n.*

raunch y (rôn′chē), *adj.,* **raunch i er, raunch i est.** SLANG. carelessly untidy; sloppy; shabby. [origin unknown] **—raunch′i ness,** *n.*

rau wol fi a (rô wol′fē ə), *n.* 1 a small, evergreen shrub of southern Asia, of the same family as the dogbane. 2 an alkaloid substance derived from the root of this shrub. It is the source of various drugs, such as reserpine, which are used for reducing high blood pressure and in the treatment of mental illness. [< New Latin < Leonard *Rauwolf,* German botanist of the 1500's]

rav age (rav′ij), *v.,* **-aged, -ag ing,** *n.* *—v.t.* damage greatly; lay waste; destroy: *The forest fire ravaged many miles of country.* *—n.* violence; destruction; great damage. [< French *ravager* < *ravir* ravish] **—rav′ag er,** *n.*

rave (rāv), *v.,* **raved, rav ing,** *n.* *—v.i.* 1 talk wildly or senselessly, as from rage, delirium, or insanity. 2 talk with very great or too much enthusiasm: *She raved about her food.* 3 howl; roar; rage: *The wind raved about the lighthouse.* *—n.* 1 a raving. 2 unrestrained praise. [perhaps < Old French *raver* to dream]

rav el (rav′əl), *v.,* **-eled, -el ing** or **-elled, -el ling,** *n.* *—v.i.* 1 fray out; separate into threads: *The sweater has raveled at the elbow.* 2 become tangled, involved, or confused. *—v.t.* 1 separate the threads of; fray. 2 make plain or clear; unravel. 3 tangle; involve; confuse. *—n.* an unraveled thread or fiber. [< earlier Dutch *ravelen*] **—rav′el er, rav′el ler,** *n.*

Ra vel (rə vel′), *n.* **Maurice (Joseph),** 1875-1937, French composer.

rav el ing or **rav el ling** (rav′ə ling, rav′ling), *n.* something raveled out; a thread drawn from a woven or knitted fabric.

ra ven[1] (rā′vən), *n.* a large, black bird like a crow but larger. *—adj.* deep, glossy black. [Old English *hræfn*]

ra ven[2] (rā′vən), *v.t.* 1 devour vigorously. 2 prey on; plunder. *—n.* plunder; rapine; robbery. [< Old French *raviner* < *ravine* robbery < Latin *rapina* rapine] **—ra′ven er,** *n.*

rav en ing (rav′ə ning), *adj.* greedy and hungry.

Ra ven na (rə ven′ə), *n.* city in NE Italy. 131,000.

rav en ous (rav′ə nəs), *adj.* 1 very hungry. 2 greedy. 3 rapacious. **—rav′en ous ly,** *adv.* **—rav′en ous ness,** *n.*

ra vine (rə vēn′), *n.* a long, deep, narrow gorge eroded by running water. [< French, violent rush]

rav ing (rā′ving), *adj.* 1 that raves; delirious; frenzied; raging. 2 INFORMAL. remarkable; extraordinary: *a raving beauty.* **—rav′ing ly,** *adv.*

rav i o li (rav′ē ō′lē), *n. sing. or pl.* small, thin pieces of dough filled with chopped meat, cheese, etc., cooked in boiling water, and served with a highly seasoned tomato sauce. [< Italian]

rav ish (rav′ish), *v.t.* 1 fill with delight. 2 carry off by force. 3 rape. [< Old French *raviss-*, a form of *ravir* ravish < Latin *rapere* seize] **—rav′ish er,** *n.* **—rav′ish ment,** *n.*

rav ish ing (rav′i shing), *adj.* very delightful; enchanting: *jewels of ravishing beauty.* **—rav′ish ing ly,** *adv.*

raw (rô), *adj.* 1 not cooked: *raw oysters.* 2 in the natural state; not manufactured, treated, or prepared: *raw hides.* See synonym study below. 3 not experienced; not trained: *a raw recruit.* 4 with the skin off; sore: *a raw spot.* 5 damp and cold: *raw weather.* 6 INFORMAL. harsh; unfair: *a raw deal.* *—n.* 1 a raw or sore spot on the body. 2 **in the raw, a** in an original, natural state: *life in the raw.* **b** naked; nude: *swim in the raw.* [Old English *hrēaw*] **—raw′ly,** *adv.* **—raw′ness,** *n.*

Syn. *adj.* 2 **Raw, crude** mean not processed or prepared for use. **Raw,** the more extensive term, applies to any natural product that has not yet been subjected to manufacture, treatment, or preparation for use: *Raw milk has not been pasteurized to make it ready to drink.* **Crude,** the more specific term, applies to a natural product that is in an impure state and needs refining, tempering, or treatment with chemicals and heat: *Crude rubber is treated with sulfur and heat to make it more elastic and durable.*

Ra wal pin di (rä wəl pin′dē), *n.* city in NE Pakistan, formerly the capital. 455,000.

raw boned (rô′bōnd′), *adj.* having little flesh on the bones; gaunt.

raw hide (rô′hīd′), *n., v.,* **-hid ed, -hid ing.** *—n.* 1 the untanned skin of cattle. 2 rope or whip made of this. *—v.t.* whip with a rawhide.

Raw lings (rô′lingz), *n.* **Marjorie Kinnan,** 1896-1953, American novelist.

raw material, substance in its natural state, such as coal, iron ore, petroleum, or animal hides before they are processed; anything that can be manufactured, treated, or prepared to make it more useful or increase its value.

ray[1] (rā), *n.* 1 line or beam of light: *rays of the*

hat, āge, fär; let, ēqual, tėrm;
it, īce; hot, ōpen, ôrder;
oil, out; cup, put, rüle;
ch, child; ng, long; sh, she;
th, thin; ᴛʜ, then; zh, measure;

ə represents *a* in about, *e* in taken,
i in pencil, *o* in lemon, *u* in circus.

< = from, derived from, taken from.

sun. See **beam** for synonym study. 2 line or stream of radiant energy in the form of heat, electricity, light, etc.: *the invisible rays of the spectrum.* 3 any stream of particles moving in the same line. 4 a thin line like a ray, coming out from a center. 5 part like a ray. The petals of a daisy and the arms of a starfish are rays. 6 a slight trace; faint gleam: *a ray of hope.* 7 half-line. *—v.i.* extend in lines from the center. *—v.t.* send forth in rays; radiate. [< Old French *rai* < Latin *radius.* Doublet of RADIUS.]

ray[2] (rā), *n.* any of various fishes, of the same class as the sharks, that have broad, flat bodies with very broad pectoral fins, and gill slits and eyes on the upper side, including the sting rays, electric rays, devilfishes, sawfishes, etc. See **stingray** for picture. [< Old French < Latin *raia*]

ray flower or **ray floret,** one of the marginal flowers or florets of a daisy, aster, or other composite flower head, resembling a petal.

ray on (rā′on), *n.* 1 fiber or fabric made from cellulose treated with chemicals. Rayon is used to make lightweight clothing, automobile tires, etc. 2 cloth made of this fiber. *—adj.* made of rayon: *a rayon sweater.* [< *ray*[1]]

raze (rāz), *v.t.,* **razed, raz ing.** tear down; destroy completely; demolish. [< Middle French *raser* to scrape, ultimately < Latin *radere*]

ra zor (rā′zər), *n.* tool with a sharp blade to shave with. [< Old French *rasor* < *raser* to scrape]

ra zor back (rā′zər bak′), *n.* 1 kind of thin, half-wild hog with a ridged back, common in the southern United States. 2 rorqual. 3 a sharp ridge on a hill, mountain, etc.

ra zor-backed (rā′zər bakt′), *adj.* having a very sharp back or ridge: *a razor-backed animal.*

razz (raz), SLANG. *—v.t.* 1 laugh at; tease. 2 express disapproval of; boo: *The angry crowd razzed the umpire.* *—n.* derision. [< *raspberry*]

raz zle-daz zle (raz′əl daz′əl), *n., v.,* **-zled, -zling.** SLANG. *—n.* dazzling glitter, excitement, etc. *—v.t.* bedazzle with glitter, excitement, etc.

Rb, rubidium.

RBI or **rbi,** (in baseball) run or runs batted in.

R.C., 1 Red Cross. 2 Roman Catholic.

RCAF or **R.C.A.F.,** Royal Canadian Air Force.

RCMP or **R.C.M.P.,** Royal Canadian Mounted Police.

rd., 1 road. 2 rod or rods.

Rd., Road.

R.D., Rural Delivery.

re[1] (rā), *n.* (in music) the second tone of the diatonic scale. [< Medieval Latin]

re[2] (rē), *prep.* with reference to; concerning:

re your letter of the 7th. [< Latin *(in) re* (in) the matter of]

Re, rhenium.

re-, *prefix.* 1 again; anew; once more: *Reappear = appear again.* 2 back: *Repay = pay back.* Also, sometimes before vowels, **red-.** [< Latin]

➧ **re-.** Words formed with the prefix *re-* are sometimes hyphenated (1) when the word to which it is joined begins with *e: re-echo,* (2) when the form with hyphen can have a different meaning from the form without: *reform,* to make better—*re-form,* to shape again, and (3) (rarely) for emphasis, as in "now *re-seated* in fair comfort," or in informal or humorous compounds: *re-remarried.*

The meaning of each of the following words is found by adding *again* or *anew* to the main part. The pronunciation of the main part is not changed.

re′ab sorb′
re′a dapt′
re′ad mit′
re′af firm′
re an′i mate
re′ap ply′
re′ap point′
re′ap point′ment
re′ap por′tion
re′ap por′tion ment
re′ap prais′al
re′ap praise′
re′as cend′
re′as sert′
re′as sess′
re′as sign′
re′as sign′ment
re′as sume′
re′at tach′
re au′dit
re′au then′ti cate
re′a wake′
re′a wak′en
re′bap tize′
re cap′i tal ize
re chris′ten
re clothe′
re′com mence′
re con′quer
re con′quest
re con′se crate
re′con se cra′tion
re con′sti tute
re′con sult′
re′con sul ta′tion
re′con vene′
re cook′
re cop′y
re cross′
re crys′tal lize
re cut′
re′de fine′
re′de liv′er
re′de liv′er y
re′de pos′it
re′de vel′op
re′di gest′
re′di ges′tion
re′dis cov′er
re′dis till′
re′dis trib′ute
re′do mes′ti cate
re draw′
re dye′
re ed′it
re ed′u cate
re′ed u ca′tion
re′em bark′
re′em bod′y
re′e merge′
re′e mer′gence
re em′i grate
re em′pha sis
re em′pha size
re′em ploy′
re′en act′
re′en act′ment
re′en gage′
re′e quip′
re′e val′u ate
re′e val′u a′tion
re′e vap′o rate′
re ex′ca vate
re′ex ca va′tion
re′ex change′
re′ex port′
re′ex por ta′tion
re fash′ion
re fas′ten
re film′
re fil′ter
re fi′nance
re fo′cus
re fold′
re for′mu late
re for′ti fy
re frame′
re freeze′
re fresh′en
re fur′nish
re gild′
re glaze′
re glue′
re group′
re grow′
re ham′mer
re han′dle
re hard′en
re heat′
re′ig nite′
re′im plant′
re′im port′
re′im por ta′tion
re′im pose′
re′im pris′on
re′in duc′tion
re′in fect′
re′in fec′tion
re′in fest′
re′in fes ta′tion
re′in sert′
re in′te grate
re′in ter′
re′in ter′pret
re′in tro duce′
re′in tro duc′tion
re′in vig′o rate′
re is′sue
re judge′
re kin′dle
re la′bel
re learn′
re light′
re line′
re load′
re lock′
re′man u fac′ture
re melt′
re mi′grate
re′mi gra′tion
re mil′i ta rize′
re mold′
re mould′
re nom′i nate
re′nom i na′tion
re num′ber
re′oc cu pa′tion
re oc′cu py
re′oc cur′
re′oc cur′rence
re of′fer
re o′ri ent
re o′ri en ta′tion
re pack′
re pack′age
re paint′
re pa′per
re pave′
re phase′
re pho′to graph
re pop′u late
re pub′lish
re pur′chase
re quick′en
re ra′di ate
re read′
re′re cord′
re reg′is ter
re′reg is tra′tion
re′re lease′
re′re vise′
re roll′
re sad′dle
re sail′
re say′
re sched′ule
re score′
re screen′
re seal′
re seed′
re seg′re gate
re′seg re ga′tion
re sell′
re send′
re set′tle
re set′tle ment
re sew′
re ship′
re shoot′
re show′
re sil′ver
re smooth′
re soak′
re sow′
re spray′
re sprin′kle
re staff′
re stage′
re stamp′
re start′
re stim′u late
re stitch′
re stock′
re string′
re struc′ture
re stud′y
re stuff′
re style′
re′sub mit′
re sur′face
re′sur vey′
re swal′low
re tai′lor
re teach′
re test′
re thatch′
re think′
re thread′
re tie′
re train′
re′trans late′
re′trans mit′
re try′
re turf′
re type′
re′up hol′ster
re val′u ate
re ver′i fy
re vict′ual
re vis′it
re vote′
re warm′
re wash′
re wa′ter
re wax′
re weigh′
re weld′
re win′
re wind′

reach (rēch), *v.t.* 1 get to; come to; arrive at: *reach the top of a hill, reach an agreement. Your letter reached me yesterday.* 2 stretch out; extend: *reach one's foot out.* 3 extend to: *The radio reaches millions.* 4 touch; get in touch with by anything extended, cast, etc.: *The ladder just reaches the roof. The anchor reached bottom.* 5 move to touch or seize (something); try to get: *reach a package on a high shelf.* 6 get at; influence: *Some people are reached by flattery.* 7 get in touch with (someone): *I could not reach you by telephone.* 8 amount to; be equal to: *The cost of the war reached billions.* —*v.i.* 1 stretch out an arm, a foot, etc.; stretch: *reach toward a book.* 2 extend in space, time, operation, effect, influence, etc.: *a dress reaching to the floor. The power of Rome reached to the ends of the known world.* 3 get or come; function: *farther than the eye can reach.* 4 make a stretch in a certain direction; move as if to touch or seize something: *The man reached for his gun.* 5 make a stretch of certain length with the hand, etc.: *I cannot reach to the top of the wall.* 6 sail on a course with the wind forward of the beam.
—*n.* 1 a stretching out; reaching. 2 extent or distance of reaching: *out of one's reach.* 3 range; power; capacity: *the reach of the mind.* 4 a continuous stretch or extent: *a reach of woodland.* 5 the course or distance sailed on one tack.
[Old English *rǣcan*] —**reach′a ble,** *adj.* —**reach′er,** *n.*

re act (rē akt′), *v.i.* 1 act back; have an effect on the one that is acting: *Unkindness often reacts on the unkind person.* 2 act in response: *Dogs react to kindness by showing affection.* 3 act chemically. Acids react on metals. 4 return to a previous state, level, etc. 5 **react against,** act in opposition to: *react against an oppressive regime.*

re-act (rē akt′), *v.t.* act over again.

re act ance (rē ak′təns), *n.* (in electricity) that part, expressed in ohms, of the impedance of an alternating-current circuit which is due to inductance and capacitance, rather than resistance.

re act ant (rē ak′tənt), *n.* (in chemistry) an element or compound that enters into a chemical reaction.

re ac tion (rē ak′shən), *n.* 1 action in response to some influence or force: *a patient's reactions to certain tests.* 2 action in the opposite direction: *A chill is a common reaction to a fever.* 3 the chemical change of one or more substances resulting in the formation of one or more additional substances. The reaction between nitrogen and hydrogen produces ammonia. 4 process in which the nucleus of an atom becomes transformed, as in the disintegration of radioactive substances. 5 a political tendency toward a previous, usually more conservative, state of affairs.

reaction engine, engine which expels a stream of burned exhaust gases at high velocity, the reaction from which creates a forward accelerating force; thrustor.

re ac tion ar y (rē ak′shə ner′ē), *adj., n., pl.* **-ar ies.** —*adj.* having to do with or favoring a return to a previous, usually more conservative, state of affairs. —*n.* person who favors reaction, especially in politics.

reaction time, the interval of time between a stimulus or signal and the response to it.

re ac ti vate (rē ak′tə vāt), *v.t.,* **-vat ed, -vat ing.** make active again; restore to active service. —**re′ac ti va′tion,** *n.*

re ac tive (rē ak′tiv), *adj.* 1 tending to react. 2 having to do with or characterized by reaction or reactance. —**re ac′tive ly,** *adv.*

re ac tiv i ty (rē′ak tiv′ə tē), *n.* condition of being reactive.

re ac tor (rē ak′tər), *n.* 1 apparatus for the release of atomic energy by a controlled chain reaction, consisting of layers of fissionable material, such as uranium, spaced with moderators, such as graphite and heavy water; atomic pile; nuclear reactor. 2 person or animal that reacts positively to a medical test, as for an allergy.

read[1] (rēd), *v.,* **read** (red), **read ing.** —*v.t.* 1 get the meaning of (something written or printed) by looking at or touching the letters, characters, etc.: *read a book, read German. The blind read special raised print.* 2 learn from written or printed words: *read the news.* 3 speak (written or printed words); say aloud (the words one looks at or touches): *Read this story to me.* 4 show by letters, figures, signs, etc.: *The thermometer reads 70 degrees.* 5 give as the word or words in a particular passage: *For "fail," a misprint, read "fall."* 6 study (a subject): *read law.* 7 get the meaning of; understand: *God reads men's hearts.* 8 give the meaning of; interpret: *A prophet reads the future.* 9 introduce (something not expressed or directly indicated) by one's manner of understanding or interpreting: *read a hostile intent in a friendly letter.* 10 bring or put by reading: *read oneself to sleep.* 11 **read into,** interpret in a certain way, often attributing more than intended. 12 **read out of,** expel from (a political party, etc.). —*v.i.* 1 get the meaning of something written or printed. 2 learn from written or printed words: *We read of heroes of other days.* 3 say aloud the words one looks at or touches: *read to a child.* 4 study by reading. 5 produce a certain impression when read; mean; be in effect when read: *This does not read like a child's composition.* 6 admit of being read or interpreted: *a rule that reads two different ways.* [Old English *rǣdan* to guess, read, counsel]

read² (red), *adj.* having knowledge gained by reading; informed. —*v.* pt. and pp. of **read¹**.

read a bil i ty (rē′də bil′ə tē), *n.* readable quality.

read a ble (rē′də bəl), *adj.* 1 easy to read; interesting. 2 capable of being read. —**read′a ble ness,** *n.* —**read′a bly,** *adv.*

re ad dress (rē′ə dres′), *v.t.* 1 put a new address on. 2 speak to again. 3 apply (oneself) anew.

Reade (rēd), *n.* **Charles,** 1814-1884, English novelist and dramatist.

read er (rē′dər), *n.* 1 person who reads. 2 book for learning and practicing reading. 3 person employed to read manuscripts and estimate their fitness for publication. 4 BRITISH. instructor in certain universities.

read er ship (rē′dər ship), *n.* 1 the reading audience, especially of a particular author, publication, or type of reading matter. 2 the office of a reader, especially in a university.

read i ly (red′l ē), *adv.* 1 without delay; quickly: *answer readily.* 2 without difficulty; easily. 3 willingly.

read i ness (red′ē nis), *n.* 1 a being ready; preparedness. 2 quickness; promptness. 3 ease; facility. 4 willingness.

read ing (rē′ding), *n.* 1 act or process of getting the meaning of written or printed words. 2 the study of books, etc. 3 a speaking out loud of written or printed words; public recital. 4 written or printed matter read or to be read. 5 amount shown by letters, figures, or signs on the scale of an instrument: *The reading of the thermometer was 96 degrees.* 6 the form of a given word or passage in a particular copy or edition of a book: *No two editions have the same reading for that passage.* 7 interpretation: *Each actor gave the lines a different reading.* 8 the extent to which one has read; literary knowledge. 9 the formal recital of a bill, or part of it, before a legislature. —*adj.* 1 that reads: *the reading public.* 2 used in or for reading: *reading glasses.*

Read ing (red′ing), *n.* city in SE Pennsylvania. 88,000.

reading glass, a magnifying glass usually used to read fine print or details of maps.

reading room, a special room for reading in a library, club, etc.

re ad just (rē′ə just′), *v.t., v.i.* adjust again; arrange again. —**re′ad just′ment,** *n.*

read out (rēd′out′), *n.* 1 the display, usually in digits, of processed information by a computer. 2 the transmission of quantitative data such as that taken by a telemeter.

read y (red′ē), *adj.,* **read i er, read i est,** *v.,* **read ied, read y ing,** *n.* —*adj.* 1 prepared for action or use at once; prepared: *Dinner is ready. We are packed and ready to go on our trip.* 2 willing: *The knights were ready to die for their lords.* 3 quick; prompt: *a ready welcome, a ready wit.* See synonym study below. 4 apt; likely; liable: *She is too ready to find fault.* 5 immediately available: *ready money.* 6 **make ready,** prepare. —*v.t.* make ready; prepare. —*n.* condition or position of being prepared for action: *The soldiers walked down the road with their guns at the ready.* [Old English *rǣde* mounted (ready to ride). Related to RIDE.]

Syn. *adj.* 3 **Ready, prompt** mean quick to understand, observe, or act in response. **Ready,** chiefly describing a person, his mind, hands, instrument, etc., suggests being prepared to act or respond without delay: *With ready fingers the surgeon explored the wound.* **Prompt,** more often describing what is done, emphasizes being quick to act when the occasion demands or request is made: *Our teacher is prompt to help us with our questions.*

read y-made (red′ē mād′), *adj.* 1 ready for immediate use; made for anybody who will buy; not made to order: *ready-made clothes.* 2 having little or no individuality: *ready-made opinions.*

re a gent (rē ā′jənt), *n.* substance used to detect, measure, or produce other substances by the chemical reactions it causes.

re al¹ (rē′əl, rēl), *adj.* 1 existing as a fact; not imagined or made up; actual; true: *a real experience, the real reason.* See synonym study below. 2 genuine: *a real diamond.* 3 (in law) of or having to do with immovable property. Lands and houses are called real property. 4 of or having to do with real numbers. —*adv.* 1 INFORMAL. very; extremely. 2 SLANG. **for real,** really. —*n.* 1 something real. 2 SLANG. **for real,** real; actual; possible. [< Late Latin *realis* < Latin *res, rei* matter, thing] —**re′al ness,** *n.*

Syn. *adj.* 1 **Real, actual, true** all relate to fact. **Real** means that what is described is in fact what it is said to be, and not pretended, imaginary, or made up: *Give your real name.* **Actual** means that what is described has in reality happened, and is not merely capable of happening or existing only in theory: *Name an actual instance of heroism.* **True** means in agreement with what is real or actual: *Tell the true story.*

re al² (rē′əl; *Spanish* rä äl′), *n., pl.* **re als, re a les** (rä ä′lās), a former small silver coin of Spain and Spanish America, worth about 12½ cents. [< Spanish *real (de plata)* royal (coin of silver) < Latin *regalis* regal. Doublet of REGAL, ROYAL, RIAL.]

real estate, land together with the buildings, fences, trees, water, minerals, etc., that belong with it.

re al i a (rē ā′lē ə), *n.pl.* actual objects, such as types of wood or fabric, used as tools in teaching.

real image, (in optics) an image formed by actual convergence of rays. A real image can be caught on a screen; a virtual image cannot.

hat, āge, fär; let, ēqual, tėrm;
it, īce; hot, ōpen, ôrder;
oil, out; cup, pu̇t, rüle;
ch, child; ng, long; sh, she;
th, thin; ᴛʜ, then; zh, measure;

ə represents *a* in about, *e* in taken, *i* in pencil, *o* in lemon, *u* in circus.

< = from, derived from, taken from.

re al ism (rē′ə liz′əm), *n.* 1 thought and action based on realities: *His realism caused him to dislike fanciful schemes.* 2 (in art and literature) the picturing of life as it actually is. 3 doctrine that material objects have a real existence independent of our consciousness of them.

re al ist (rē′ə list), *n.* 1 person interested in what is real and practical rather than what is imaginary or theoretical. 2 writer or artist who represents things as they are in real life. 3 person who believes in realism.

re al is tic (rē′ə lis′tik), *adj.* 1 like the real thing; lifelike. 2 (in art and literature) representing life as it actually is. 3 seeing things as they really are; practical. —**re′al is′ti cal ly,** *adv.*

re al i ty (rē al′ə tē), *n., pl.* **-ties.** 1 actual existence; true state of affairs: *Ghosts have no place in reality.* 2 a real thing; actual fact: *Destruction is a reality of war.* 3 **in reality,** really; actually; in fact; truly: *We thought he was serious, but in reality he was joking.*

re al i za tion (rē′ə lə zā′shən), *n.* 1 a realizing. 2 a being realized. 3 clear understanding; full awareness; perception: *The explorers had a realization of the dangers that they must face.* 4 exchange of property for its money value.

re al ize (rē′ə līz), *v.t.,* **-ized, -iz ing.** 1 understand clearly; be fully aware of: *She realizes how hard you worked.* 2 make real; bring into actual existence: *Her uncle's present made it possible for her to realize her dream of going to college.* 3 change (property) into money: *Before going to England to live, he realized all his American property.* 4 obtain as a return or profit: *She realized $10,000 from her investment.* —**re′al iz′a ble,** *adj.* —**re′al iz′er,** *n.*

re al-life (rē′əl līf′), *adj.* true to life; existing in reality: *a real-life story, real-life situations.*

re al ly (rē′ə lē, rē′lē), *adv.* 1 actually; truly; in fact: *things as they really are.* 2 indeed: *Oh, really?*

realm (relm), *n.* 1 kingdom. 2 region or sphere in which something rules or prevails. 3 a particular field of something: *the realm of biology.* [< Old French *realme,* ultimately < Latin *regimen* rule. See REGIMEN.]

real number, any rational or irrational number.

Re al po li tik (rā äl′pō li tēk′), *n.* GERMAN. political realism; practical politics.

real time, equivalence in time between the output of an electronic computer and a particular physical process which needs this output for its effective operation.

Re al tor (rē′əl tər, rēl′tər), *n.* a real-estate agent who is a member of the National Association of Real Estate Boards.

re al ty (rē′əl tē), *n., pl.* **-ties.** real estate.

ream¹ (rēm), *n.* 1 480, 500, or 516 sheets of paper of the same size and quality. 2 a very large quantity: *ream upon ream of nonsense.*

[< Old French *raime* < Arabic *razma* bundle]

ream² (rēm), *v.t.* 1 enlarge or shape (a hole). 2 remove with a reamer. [Middle English *reamen*]

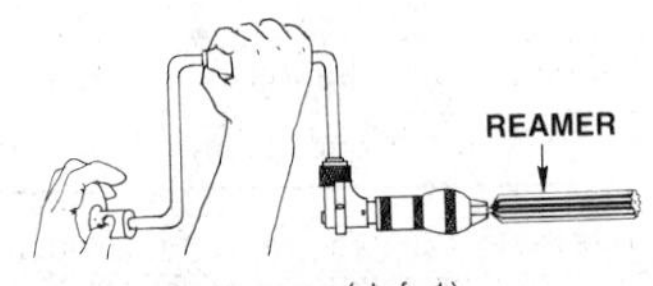

reamer (def. 1)

ream er (rē′mər), *n.* 1 tool for enlarging or shaping a hole. 2 utensil for squeezing juice out of oranges, lemons, etc.

reap (rēp), *v.t.* 1 cut (grain). 2 gather (a crop). 3 cut grain or gather a crop from: *reap fields.* 4 get as a return or reward: *Kind acts often reap happy smiles.* [Old English *repan*]

reap er (rē′pər), *n.* person or machine that cuts grain or gathers a crop.

re ap pear (rē′ə pir′), *v.i.* appear again.

re ap pear ance (rē′ə pir′əns), *n.* a reappearing.

rear¹ (rir), *n.* 1 the back part; back. 2 the last part of an army, fleet, etc. 3 the space or position behind, or at the back of anything. 4 **bring up the rear,** move onward as the rear part; come last in order. *—adj.* at the back; in the back. [probably shortened from *rearguard* < Middle French *rereguarde* < *rer* back + *guarde* guard]

rear² (rir), *v.t.* 1 make grow; help to grow; bring up: *The mother was very careful in rearing her children.* 2 breed (livestock). 3 set up; build: *rear a temple.* 4 raise; lift up: *rear one's head.* *—v.i.* (of an animal) rise on the hind legs; rise: *The horse reared as the fire engine dashed past.* [Old English *rǣran* to raise < *rīsan* rise]

rear admiral, a naval officer ranking next above a captain and next below a vice-admiral.

rear guard, part of an army that protects the rear.

re arm (rē ärm′), *v.t., v.i.* 1 arm again; arm oneself again. 2 supply with new or better weapons.

re ar ma ment (rē är′mə mənt), *n.* a rearming.

rear most (rir′mōst), *adj.* farthest in the rear; last.

re ar range (rē′ə rānj′), *v.t.,* **-ranged, -rang ing.** 1 arrange in a new or different way. 2 arrange again. **—re′ar range′ment,** *n.*

rear ward (rir′wərd), *adv., adj.* toward or in the rear. **—rear′ward ly,** *adv.*

rear wards (rir′wərdz), *adv.* rearward.

rea son (rē′zn), *n.* 1 cause or motive for an action, feeling, etc.; ground: *I have my own reasons for doing this.* See synonym study below. 2 justification; explanation: *What is your reason for doing such poor work?* 3 ability or power to think and draw conclusions. 4 right thinking; good sense. 5 sanity. **bring to reason,** cause to be reasonable. **by reason of,** on account of; because of. **in reason** or **within reason,** within reasonable and sensible limits. **stand to reason,** be reasonable and sensible. *—v.i.* 1 think logically; think things out: *Most animals cannot reason.* 2 draw conclusions or inferences from facts or premises. 3 consider; discuss; argue: *Reason with her and try to make her change her mind.* *—v.t.* 1 persuade by reasoning. 2 argue, conclude, or infer: *reason a point.* 3 support with reasons. 4 reason about or discuss. [< Old French *raison* < Latin *rationem* reason, reckoning < *reri* reckon. Doublet of RATIO, RATION.] **—rea′son er,** *n.*

Syn. *n.* 1 **Reason, cause, motive** mean that which makes something happen. **Reason** applies to a ground or occasion that explains why something has happened: *The reason he went to Arizona was the climate.* **Cause** applies to a person, thing, incident, or condition that directly brings about an action or happening: *The cause was his doctor's warning.* **Motive** applies to the feeling or desire that makes a person do what he does: *His motive was to regain his health.*

rea son a ble (rē′zn ə bəl), *adj.* 1 according to reason; sensible; not foolish. See synonym study below. 2 not asking too much; fair; just. 3 not high in price; inexpensive: *a reasonable dress.* 4 able to reason. **—rea′son a ble ness,** *n.* **—rea′son a bly,** *adv.*

Syn. 1 **Reasonable, rational** mean according to reason. **Reasonable** suggests showing good judgment in everyday affairs because of the practical application of reason: *He took a reasonable view of the dispute and offered a solution that was fair, sensible, and practical.* **Rational** often suggests an unusual power to think logically and objectively: *Her approach to the problem was rational.*

rea son ing (rē′zn ing), *n.* 1 the process of drawing conclusions from facts or premises. 2 reasons; logical arguments.

re as sem ble (rē′ə sem′bəl), *v.t., v.i.,* **-bled, -bling.** come or bring together again.

re as sur ance (rē′ə shůr′əns), *n.* 1 new or fresh assurance. 2 restoration of courage or confidence.

re as sure (rē′ə shůr′), *v.t.,* **-sured, -sur ing.** 1 restore to confidence: *The captain's confidence during the storm reassured the passengers.* 2 assure again or anew. 3 insure again. **—re′as sur′ing ly,** *adv.*

re a ta (rē ä′tə), *n.* lariat. [< Spanish, rope]

Ré au mur or **Re au mur** (rā′ə myůr; *French* rā ō mYr′), *adj.* of or according to a thermometric scale in which the freezing point of water is 0 degrees and the boiling point 80 degrees. [< René Antoine Ferchault de *Réaumur,* 1683-1757, French physicist]

reave (rēv), *v.t., v.i.,* **reaved** or **reft, reav ing.** ARCHAIC. deprive by force; strip; rob. [Old English *rēafian*] **—reav′er,** *n.*

reb or **Reb** (reb), *n.* U.S. a confederate soldier in the Civil War. [< *reb(el)*]

re bate (rē′bāt, ri bāt′), *n., v.,* **-bat ed, -bat ing.** *—n.* return of part of money paid; partial refund; discount. *—v.t.* give as a rebate. [< Old French *rabat* < *rabattre* beat down < *re-* back + *abattre* abate] **—re′bat er,** *n.*

re bec (rē′bek), *n.* a musical instrument, somewhat like a violin, used in the Middle Ages. Also, **rebeck.** [< Middle French *rebec,* alteration of Old French *rebebe,* ultimately < Arabic *rabāb*]

Re bec ca (ri bek′ə), *n.* (in the Bible) the wife of Isaac and the mother of Esau and Jacob.

re beck (rē′bek), *n.* rebec.

reb el (*n., adj.* reb′əl; *v.* ri bel′), *n., adj., v.,* **re belled, re bel ling.** *—n.* person who resists or fights against authority instead of obeying: *The rebels armed themselves against the government.* *—adj.* defying law or authority: *a rebel army.* *—v.i.* 1 resist or fight against law or authority. 2 feel a great dislike or opposition: *We rebelled at having to stay in on so fine a day.* [< Old French *rebelle* < Latin *rebellem* disorderly < *rebellare* be disorderly, rebel, ultimately < *re-* again + *bellum* war. Doublet of REVEL.]

re bel lion (ri bel′yən), *n.* 1 armed resistance or fight against one's government. See **revolt** for synonym study. 2 resistance or fight against any power or restriction. 3 act or state of rebelling; revolt.

re bel lious (ri bel′yəs), *adj.* 1 defying authority; rebelling; mutinous: *a rebellious army.* 2 hard to manage; disobedient. **—re bel′lious ly,** *adv.* **—re bel′lious ness,** *n.*

re bind (rē bīnd′), *v.t.,* **-bound, -bind ing.** bind again or anew: *The book with the broken back needs rebinding.*

re birth (rē′bėrth′, rē bėrth′), *n.* a new birth; being born again.

re born (rē bôrn′), *adj.* born again.

re bound¹ (*v.* ri bound′; *n.* rē′bound′, ri bound′), *v.i., v.t.* 1 spring back. 2 bounce back; recover. *—n.* 1 a springing back. 2 (in basketball) a ball that bounds back off the backboard or the rim of the basket after a shot has been made.

re bound² (rē bound′), *v.* pt. and pp. of **rebind.**

re broad cast (rē brôd′kast′), *v.,* **-cast** or **-cast ed, -cast ing,** *n.* *—v.t., v.i.* 1 broadcast again or anew. 2 relay by broadcast (messages, speeches, etc., received from a broadcasting station). *—n.* program, etc., rebroadcast.

re buff (ri buf′), *n.* a blunt or sudden check to a person who makes advances, offers help, makes a request, etc. *—v.t.* give a rebuff to. [< Middle French *rebuffe* < Italian *ribuffo*]

re build (rē bild′), *v.t.,* **-built, -build ing.** build again or anew.

re built (rē bilt′), *v.* pt. and pp. of **rebuild.**

re buke (ri byük′), *v.,* **-buked, -buk ing,** *n.* *—v.t.* express disapproval of; reprove. See **reprove** for synonym study. *—n.* expression of disapproval; scolding. [< Anglo-French *rebuker* < Old French *rebuchier* < *re-* back + *buchier* to strike] **—re buk′er,** *n.* **—re buk′ing ly,** *adv.*

re bus (rē′bəs), *n.* representation of a word or phrase by pictures suggesting the syllables or words. A picture of a cat on a log is a rebus for *catalog.* [< Latin, by means of objects < *res* thing, object]

re but (ri but′), *v.t.,* **-but ted, -but ting.** oppose by evidence on the other side or by argument; try to disprove: *rebut the argument of the other team in a debate.* [< Old French *reboter* < *re-* back + *boter* to butt, strike]

re but tal (ri but′l), *n.* a rebutting.

rec., 1 receipt. 2 recipe. 3 record. 4 recorder. 5 recreation.

re cal ci trance (ri kal′sə trəns), *n.* refusal to submit, conform, or comply.

rebec

re cal ci tran cy (ri kal′sə trən sē), *n.* recalcitrance.

re cal ci trant (ri kal′sə trənt), *adj.* resisting authority or control; disobedient. *—n.* a recalcitrant person or animal. [< Latin *recalcitrantem* kicking back < *re-* back + *calx* heel]

re call (*v.* ri kôl′; *n.* ri kôl′, rē′kôl′), *v.t.* 1 call back to mind; remember: *I can recall stories my mother told me when I was a baby.* See **remember** for synonym study. 2 call back; order back: *The ambassador was recalled.* 3 bring back: *recalled to life.* 4 take back; withdraw: *The order has been given and cannot be recalled.* *—n.* 1 a recalling to mind. 2 a calling back; ordering back. 3 signal used in calling back men, ships, etc. 4 a taking back; revocation; annulment. 5 procedure by which a public official can be removed from office before his term has expired by vote of the people.

re cant (ri kant′), *v.t.* take back formally or publicly; withdraw or renounce (a statement, opinion, purpose, etc.). *—v.i.* renounce an opinion or allegiance: *Though he was tortured to make him change his religion, the prisoner would not recant.* [< Latin *recantare* < *re-* back + *canere* sing]

re can ta tion (rē′kan tā′shən), *n.* a recanting.

re cap[1] (rē′kap′, ri kap′), *v.,* **-capped, -cap ping,** *n.* *—v.t.* put a strip of rubber or similar material on (a worn surface of an automobile tire), by using heat and pressure to make a firm union. *—n.* a recapped tire. [< *re-* again + *cap,* verb]

re cap[2] (*v.* rē kap′; *n.* rē′kap), *v.,* **-capped, -cap ping,** *n.* INFORMAL. *—v.t., v.i.* recapitulate. *—n.* a recapitulation. [short for *recapitulate*]

re ca pit u late (rē′kə pich′ə lāt), *v.t., v.i.,* **-lat ed, -lat ing.** repeat or recite the main points of; tell briefly; sum up. [< Latin *recapitulatum* summarized < *re-* again + *capitulum* chapter, section, diminutive of *caput* head] **—re′ca pit′u la′tor,** *n.*

re ca pit u la tion (rē′kə pich′ə lā′shən), *n.* 1 a brief statement of the main points; summary. 2 (in biology) the repetition in the development of an embryo of stages in the evolution of the species.

re cap ture (rē kap′chər), *v.,* **-tured, -tur ing,** *n.* *—v.t.* 1 capture again; have again. 2 recall. *—n.* a taking or a being taken a second time.

re cast (*v.* rē kast′; *n.* rē′kast′), *v.,* **-cast, -cast ing,** *n.* *—v.t.* 1 cast again or anew: *recast a bell.* 2 make over; remodel: *recast a sentence.* *—n.* a recasting.

recd. or **rec′d.,** received.

re cede (ri sēd′), *v.i.,* **-ced ed, -ced ing.** 1 go backward; move backward. 2 slope backward: *a chin that recedes.* 3 withdraw: *recede from an agreement.* [< Latin *recedere* < *re-* back + *cedere* go]

re ceipt (ri sēt′), *n.* 1 a written statement that money, a package, a letter, etc., has been received. 2 **receipts,** *pl.* money received; amount or quantity received. 3 a receiving. 4 a being received: *the receipt of a letter.* 5 recipe. *—v.t.* 1 write on (a bill, etc.) that something has been received or paid for. 2 U.S. acknowledge in writing the receipt of (money, etc.). [alteration of Middle English *receit* < Anglo-French *receite* < Latin *recipere.* See RECEIVE.]

re ceiv a ble (ri sē′və bəl), *adj.* 1 fit for acceptance: *Gold is receivable all over the world.* 2 on which payment is to be received: *bills receivable.* 3 which is to be received. *—n.* **receivables,** *pl.* assets in the form of obligations due or soon due from others.

re ceive (ri sēv′), *v.,* **-ceived, -ceiv ing.** *—v.t.* 1 take (something offered or sent); take into one's hands or possession: *receive gifts.* See synonym study below. 2 have (something) bestowed, conferred, etc.: *receive a degree.* 3 be given; get: *receive a letter, receive payment.* 4 take; support; bear; hold: *The boat received a heavy load.* 5 take or let into the mind: *receive new ideas.* 6 accept as true or valid: *a theory widely received.* 7 experience; suffer; endure: *receive a blow.* 8 let into one's house, society, etc. 9 meet (guests, etc.); greet upon arrival. 10 agree to listen to: *receive confession.* 11 admit to a state or condition: *receive a person into the church.* *—v.i.* 1 be at home to friends and visitors. 2 (in radio and television) change electromagnetic waves into sound or light signals so as to produce transmitted sound or image. [< Old North French *receivre* < Latin *recipere* < *re-* back + *capere* to take]

Syn. *v.t.* 1 **Receive, accept** mean to take what is given, offered, or delivered. **Receive** carries no suggestion of positive action or of activity of mind or will on the part of the receiver, and means nothing more than to take what is given or given out: *He received a prize.* **Accept** always suggests being willing to take what is offered, or giving one's consent: *She received a gift from him, but did not accept it.*

re ceiv er (ri sē′vər), *n.* 1 person who receives. 2 thing that receives: *Public telephones have coin receivers.* 3 apparatus which receives and reproduces visibly or audibly signals transmitted from another part of an electric circuit, as the part of a telephone held to the ear. 4 receiving set for radio or television. 5 person appointed by law to take charge of the property of others. 6 (in football) a player who catches a forward pass, kickoff, punt, etc.

re ceiv er ship (ri sē′vər ship), *n.* 1 position of a receiver in charge of the property of others. 2 condition of being in the control of a receiver.

receiving set, 1 apparatus for receiving sounds, or sounds and images, sent by radio waves; a radio or television set. 2 apparatus for receiving messages sent by telegraph, teletype, etc.

re cen cy (rē′sn sē), *n.* a being recent.

re cent (rē′snt), *adj.* 1 done or made not long ago: *recent events.* 2 not long past; modern: *a recent period in history.* 3 **Recent,** of or having to do with the present geological epoch, after the Pleistocene; Holocene. *—n.* **Recent,** the present geological epoch; Holocene. See chart under **geology.** [< Latin *recentem*] **—re′cent ly,** *adv.* **—re′cent ness,** *n.*

re cep ta cle (ri sep′tə kəl), *n.* 1 any container or place, such as a bag, basket, or vault, used to put things in to keep them conveniently. 2 the stalklike part of a flower that bears the petals, stamens, and pistils. 3 socket or outlet into which a plug can be inserted to make an electrical connection. [< Latin *receptaculum,* ultimately < *recipere* receive. See RECEIVE.]

re cep tion (ri sep′shən), *n.* 1 a receiving: *calm reception of bad news.* 2 a being received: *Her reception as a club member pleased her.* 3 manner of receiving: *a warm reception.* 4 a gathering to receive and welcome people. 5 quality of the sound reproduced in a radio or of the picture in a television receiver. [< Latin *receptionem* < *recipere* receive. See RECEIVE.]

hat, āge, fär; let, ēqual, tėrm;
it, īce; hot, ōpen, ôrder;
oil, out; cup, pu̇t, rüle;
ch, child; ng, long; sh, she;
th, thin; ᴛʜ, then; zh, measure;

ə represents *a* in about, *e* in taken, *i* in pencil, *o* in lemon, *u* in circus.

< = from, derived from, taken from.

re cep tion ist (ri sep′shə nist), *n.* person employed to receive callers: *a receptionist in a doctor's office.*

re cep tive (ri sep′tiv), *adj.* able, quick, or willing to receive ideas, suggestions, impressions, stimuli, etc. **—re cep′tive ly,** *adv.* **—re cep′tive ness,** *n.*

re cep tiv i ty (rē′sep tiv′ə tē), *n.* ability or readiness to receive.

re cep tor (ri sep′tər), *n.* cell or group of cells sensitive to stimuli, such as a sense organ or the terminal portion of a sensory or afferent neuron.

re cess (*n.* rē′ses, ri ses′; *v.* ri ses′), *n.* 1 time during which work stops: *There will be a short recess before the next meeting.* 2 part in a wall set back from the rest; alcove; niche. 3 an inner place or part; quiet, secluded place: *the recesses of a cave, the recesses of one's secret thoughts.* *—v.i.* take a recess: *The convention recessed until afternoon.* *—v.t.* 1 put in a recess; set back. 2 make a recess in. [< Latin *recessus* a retreat < *recedere* recede. See RECEDE.]

re ces sion (ri sesh′ən), *n.* 1 a going backward; moving or sloping backward. 2 withdrawal. 3 period of temporary business reduction, shorter and less extreme than a depression.

re ces sion al (ri sesh′ə nəl), *n.* hymn or piece of music sung or played while the clergy and the choir retire from the church at the end of a service.

re ces sive (ri ses′iv), *adj.* 1 likely to go back; receding. 2 (in biology) of or having to do with a recessive character. *—n.* recessive character. **—re ces′sive ly,** *adv.* **—re ces′sive ness,** *n.*

recessive character, the one of any pair of contrasting characters that is latent and subordinate in an animal or plant when both are present in the germ plasm. EXAMPLE: If a guinea pig inherits a gene for black fur from one parent and a gene for white fur from the other, it will have black fur, as black fur is dominant and white fur is recessive.

re charge (rē chärj′), *v.,* **-charged, -charg ing,** *n.* *—v.t., v.i.* charge again or anew: *recharge a battery.* *—n.* a second or additional charge.

re cher ché (rə sher′shā, rə sher shā′), *adj.* 1 sought after; in great demand; rare. 2 far-fetched. [< French]

Re ci fe (rə sē′fə), *n.* seaport in NE Brazil. 1,079,000. Former name, **Pernambuco.**

rec i pe (res′ə pē), *n.* 1 set of directions for preparing something to eat. 2 set of directions for preparing anything. [< Latin, take!, imperative of *recipere* take, receive. See RECEIVE.]

re cip i ent (ri sip′ē ənt), *n.* person or thing

that receives something: *The recipients of the prizes had their names printed in the paper.* —*adj.* willing to receive; receiving.

re cip ro cal (ri sip′rə kəl), *adj.* 1 in return: *Although she gave me many presents, she expected no reciprocal gifts from me.* 2 mutual: *reciprocal distrust.* 3 (in grammar) expressing mutual action or relation. In "The two children like each other," *each other* is a reciprocal pronoun. —*n.* 1 number so related to another that when multiplied together they give 1: *3 is the reciprocal of* $^1/_3$, *and* $^1/_3$ *is the reciprocal of 3.* 2 thing that is reciprocal with something else; counterpart. [< Latin *reciprocus* returning] —**re cip′ro cal ly,** *adv.*

re cip ro cate (ri sip′rə kāt), *v.,* **-cat ed, -cat ing.** —*v.t.* 1 give, do, feel, or show in return: *She likes me, and I reciprocate her liking.* 2 cause to move with an alternating backward and forward motion. —*v.i.* 1 make interchange. 2 move with an alternating backward and forward motion. —**re cip′ro ca′tion,** *n.*

reciprocating engine, engine in which the piston and piston rod move back and forth in a straight line, the reciprocating motion being changed to rotary motion.

rec i proc i ty (res′ə pros′ə tē), *n., pl.* **-ties.** 1 reciprocal state; mutual action. 2 a mutual exchange, especially an exchange of special privileges in regard to trade between two countries.

re cit al (ri sī′tl), *n.* 1 a reciting; telling facts in detail. 2 story; account. 3 a musical entertainment, given usually by a single performer. 4 a public performance given by a group of dancers.

re cit al ist (ri sī′tl ist), *n.* musician, singer, or actor who gives recitals.

rec i ta tion (res′ə tā′shən), *n.* 1 a reciting. 2 a reciting of a prepared lesson by pupils before a teacher. 3 a repeating of something from memory. 4 piece repeated from memory.

rec i ta tive (res′ə tə tēv′), *n.* 1 passage, part, or piece of music which is sung with the rhythm and phrasing of ordinary speech. Operas often contain long recitatives. 2 this style of singing. —*adj.* of or resembling recitative.

re cite (ri sīt′), *v.,* **-cit ed, -cit ing.** —*v.t.* 1 say over; repeat: *recite a lesson.* 2 give an account of in detail: *recite one's adventures.* 3 repeat (a poem, speech, etc.) to entertain an audience. —*v.i.* say part of a lesson; answer a teacher's questions. [< Latin *recitare* < *re-* again + *citare* appeal to] —**re cit′er,** *n.*

reck (rek), *v.i.* ARCHAIC. 1 care; heed. 2 be important or interesting; matter. [Old English *reccan*]

reck less (rek′lis), *adj.* 1 lacking in caution or prudence; heedless; careless. See **rash**[1] for synonym study. 2 characterized by careless rashness: *a reckless act.* [Old English *recceléas*] —**reck′less ly,** *adv.* —**reck′less ness,** *n.*

reck on (rek′ən), *v.t.* 1 find the number or value of; count: *Reckon the cost before you decide.* 2 consider; judge; account: *He is reckoned the best speller in the class.* 3 INFORMAL. think; suppose. 4 **reckon with,** take into consideration. —*v.i.* 1 depend; reply: *You can reckon on our help.* 2 settle; settle accounts. [Old English *(ge)recenian*] —**reck′on er,** *n.*

reck on ing (rek′ə ning), *n.* 1 method of computing; count; calculation. 2 settlement of an account. 3 bill, especially at an inn or tavern. 4 calculation of the position of a ship.

re claim (ri klām′), *v.t.* 1 bring back to a useful, good condition: *The farmer reclaimed the swamp by draining it.* 2 get from discarded things: *reclaim metal from old tin cans.* 3 demand or ask for the return of. See **recover** for synonym study. [< Old French *reclamer* call back < Latin *reclamare* < *re-* back + *clamare* cry out] —**re claim′a ble,** *adj.* —**re claim′er,** *n.*

rec la ma tion (rek′lə mā′shən), *n.* a reclaiming or a being reclaimed; restoration to a useful, good condition.

re cline (ri klīn′), *v.,* **-clined, -clin ing.** —*v.i.* lean back; lie down: *The tired woman reclined on the couch.* —*v.t.* lay down. [< Latin *reclinare* < *re-* back + *clinare* to lean]

rec luse (*n.* rek′lüs, ri klüs′; *adj.* ri klüs′), *n.* person who lives shut up or withdrawn from the world. —*adj.* shut up or apart from the world. [< Late Latin *reclusum* shut up, enclosed < Latin *re-* back + *claudere* to shut]

rec og ni tion (rek′əg nish′ən), *n.* 1 a knowing again; recognizing. 2 a being recognized: *By a good disguise he escaped recognition.* 3 acknowledgment: *We insisted on complete recognition of our rights.* 4 notice: *seek recognition by the chair.* 5 favorable notice; acceptance: *The author soon won recognition from the public.* 6 a formal acknowledgment conveying approval or sanction.

rec og niz a ble (rek′əg nī′zə bəl), *adj.* that can be recognized. —**rec′og niz′a bly,** *adv.*

re cog ni zance (ri kog′nə zəns, ri kon′ə zəns), *n.* in law: 1 bond binding a person to do some particular act. 2 sum of money to be forfeited if the act is not performed.

rec og nize (rek′əg nīz), *v.t.,* **-nized, -niz ing.** 1 be aware of (someone or something) as already known; know again: *recognize an old friend.* 2 identify: *recognize a person from a description.* 3 acknowledge acquaintance with; greet: *recognize a person on the street.* 4 acknowledge; accept; admit: *recognize and do one's duty.* 5 take notice of: *The delegate waited till the chairman recognized him.* 6 show appreciation of. 7 acknowledge and agree to deal with: *For some years other nations did not recognize the new government.* [< Old French *reconoistre* < Latin *recognoscere* < *re-* again + *com-* (intensive) + *(g)noscere* learn. Doublet of RECONNOITER.]

re coil (*v.* ri koil′; *n.* ri koil′, rē′koil), *v.i.* 1 draw back; shrink back: *Most people would recoil at seeing a snake in the path.* 2 spring back: *The gun recoiled after I fired.* 3 react: *Revenge often recoils on the avenger.* —*n.* 1 a drawing or springing back. 2 the distance or force with which a gun, spring, etc., springs back. [< Old French *reculer,* ultimately < Latin *re-* back + *culus* rump]

re coil less (ri koil′lis), *adj.* having no appreciable recoil: *a recoilless rifle.*

rec ol lect (rek′ə lekt′), *v.t.* 1 call back to mind; remember. See **remember** for synonym study. 2 recall (oneself) to something temporarily forgotten. —*v.i.* recall something; remember.

re-col lect (rē′kə lekt′), *v.t.* 1 collect again. 2 recover control of (oneself).

rec ol lec tion (rek′ə lek′shən), *n.* 1 act or power of recalling to mind. 2 memory; remembrance. See **memory** for synonym study. 3 thing remembered.

re com bi na tion (rē′kom bə nā′shən), *n.* 1 a recombining. 2 (in biology) formation in offspring, either by crossing-over or by union at fertilization, of new genetic combinations that are not in either parent.

re com bine (rē′kəm bīn′), *v.t., v.i.,* **-bined, -bin ing.** combine again or anew.

rec om mend (rek′ə mend′), *v.t.* 1 speak in favor of; suggest favorably. 2 advise. 3 make pleasing or attractive: *The location of the camp recommends it as a summer home.* 4 hand over for safekeeping. —**rec′om mend′a ble,** *adj.*

rec om men da tion (rek′ə men dā′shən), *n.* 1 act of recommending. 2 anything that recommends a person or thing. 3 words of advice or praise. 4 person or thing recommended.

re com mit (rē′kə mit′), *v.t.,* **-mit ted, -mit ting.** 1 commit again. 2 refer again to a committee. —**re′com mit′ment,** *n.*

re com mit tal (rē′kə mit′l), *n.* recommitment.

rec om pense (rek′əm pens), *v.,* **-pensed, -pens ing,** *n.* —*v.t.* 1 pay (a person); pay back; reward. 2 make a fair return for (an action, anything lost, damage done, or hurt received). —*n.* 1 payment; reward. 2 return; amends. [< Late Latin *recompensare* < Latin *re-* back + *compensare* compensate]

rec on cil a bil i ty (rek′ən sī′lə bil′ə tē), *n.* a being reconcilable.

rec on cil a ble (rek′ən sī′lə bəl, rek′ən sī′lə bəl), *adj.* that can be reconciled. —**rec′on cil′a ble ness,** *n.*

rec on cile (rek′ən sīl), *v.t.,* **-ciled, -cil ing.** 1 make friends again. 2 settle (a disagreement or difference). 3 make agree; bring into harmony: *It is impossible to reconcile his story with the facts.* 4 make satisfied; make no longer opposed: *It is hard to reconcile oneself to being sick a long time.* [< Latin *reconciliare* < *re-* back + *concilium* bond of union] —**rec′on cile′ment,** *n.* —**rec′on cil′er,** *n.*

rec on cil i a tion (rek′ən sil′ē ā′shən), *n.* 1 a reconciling; bringing together again in friendship. 2 a being reconciled; settlement or adjustment of disagreements or differences.

rec on cil i a to ry (rek′ən sil′ē ə tôr′ē, rek′ən sil′ē ə tōr′ē), *adj.* tending to reconcile.

rec on dite (rek′ən dīt, ri kon′dīt), *adj.* 1 hard to understand; profound. 2 little known; obscure. 3 hidden from view; concealed. [< Latin *reconditum* stored away < *re-* back + *com-* up + *dare* to put] —**rec′on dite′ly,** *adv.* —**rec′on dite′ness,** *n.*

re con di tion (rē′kən dish′ən), *v.t.* restore to a good or satisfactory condition; put in good condition by repairing, making over, etc.

re con firm (rē′kən fėrm′), *v.t.* confirm anew: *reconfirm a reservation.* —**re con′fir ma′tion,** *n.*

re con nais sance (ri kon′ə səns), *n.* examination or survey, especially for military purposes. [< French]

rec on noi ter (rek′ə noi′tər, rē′kə noi′tər), *v.t.* approach and examine or observe in order to learn something; make a first survey of (the enemy, the enemy's strength or position, a region, etc.) in order to gain information for military purposes. —*v.i.* approach a place and make a first survey of it. [< French *reconnoître* < Old French *reconoistre* recognize. Doublet of RECOGNIZE.] **—rec′on noi′ter er,** *n.*

rec on noi tre (rek′ə noi′tər, rē′kə noi′tər), *v.t., v.i.,* **-tred, -tring.** reconnoiter. **—rec′on noi′trer,** *n.*

re con sid er (rē′kən sid′ər), *v.t.* consider again: *reconsider a bill.* —*v.i.* consider a matter again. **—re′con sid′er a′tion,** *n.*

re con sti tute (rē kon′stə tüt, rē kon′stə tyüt), *v.t.,* **-tut ed, -tut ing.** form again; bring back to its original form or consistency: *reconstitute frozen orange juice by adding water.*

re con struct (rē′kən strukt′), *v.t.* construct again; rebuild; make over.

re con struc tion (rē′kən struk′shən), *n.* 1 act of reconstructing. 2 a being reconstructed. 3 thing reconstructed. 4 **Reconstruction, a** process by which the southern states after the Civil War were reorganized and their relations with the national government were reestablished. **b** period when this was done from 1865 to 1877.

re con struc tive (rē′kən struk′tiv), *adj.* tending to reconstruct.

re con ver sion (rē′kən vėr′zhən, rē′kən vėr′shən), *n.* conversion back to a previous state or belief.

re con vert (rē′kən vėrt′), *v.t., v.i.* convert back to a previous state or belief.

re cord (*v.* ri kôrd′; *n., adj.* rek′ərd), *v.t.* 1 set down in writing so as to keep for future use: *record the proceedings at a meeting.* 2 put in some permanent form; keep for remembrance: *We record history in books.* 3 register, especially in permanent form: *A cardiograph records the movements of the heart.* 4 put (music, words, or sounds) on a phonograph disk or on magnetic tape or wire. —*v.i.* record something.
—*n.* 1 anything written and kept. 2 an official written account, as of a meeting, etc. 3 an official copy of a document: *a record of a deed.* 4 a thin, flat disk, usually of vinyl or other plastic, with narrow grooves on which sound has been transcribed and from which it is reproduced on a phonograph by means of a phonograph needle. 5 the known facts about what a person, animal, ship, etc., has done. 6 U.S. a criminal's recorded history of offenses, arrests, convictions, etc. 7 the best yet done; best, or greatest amount, rate, speed, etc., yet attained: *hold the record for the high jump.* 8 a recording. 9 a being recorded. 10 **break a record,** make a better record. 11 **off the record,** not to be recorded or quoted. 12 **on record,** recorded.
—*adj.* making or affording a record: *a record wheat crop.*
[< Old French *recorder* < Latin *recordari* remember, call to mind < *re-* back + *cordis* heart, mind]

re cord er (ri kôr′dər), *n.* 1 person whose business is to make and keep records. 2 machine or part of a machine that records. 3 tape recorder. 4 title given to certain judges with criminal and civil jurisdiction in some cities. 5 a wooden musical instrument with a tone somewhat like a flute.

re cord ing (ri kôr′ding), *n.* 1 a phonograph record. 2 the original transcription of any sound or combination of sounds.

record player, phonograph.

re count[1] (ri kount′), *v.t.* tell in detail; give an account of: *He recounted all the happenings of the day.* [< Middle French *reconter* < *re-* + *conter* relate, count[1]]

re count[2] or **re-count** (*v.* rē kount′; *n.* rē′kount′, rē kount′), *v.t.* count again. —*n.* a second count.

re coup (ri küp′), *v.t.* 1 make up for: *recoup one's losses.* 2 repay: *recoup a creditor.* [< Middle French *recouper* cut back < *re-* back + *couper* to cut] **—re coup′a ble,** *adj.* **—re coup′ment,** *n.*

re course (rē′kôrs, rē′kōrs; ri kôrs′, ri kōrs′), *n.* 1 a turning for help or protection; appealing: *recourse to a doctor in an emergency.* 2 person or thing appealed to or turned to for help or protection: *His only recourse in trouble was his family.* 3 **have recourse to,** turn to for help; appeal to. [< Old French *recours* < Latin *recursus* retreat < *re-* back + *cursus* a running]

re cov er (ri kuv′ər), *v.t.* 1 get back (something lost, taken away, or stolen); regain. See synonym study below. 2 make up for (something lost or damaged): *recover lost time.* 3 bring back to life, health, one's senses, or normal condition. 4 get back to the proper position or condition: *She started to fall but recovered herself.* 5 obtain by judgment in a court of law: *recover damages.* 6 regain in usable form; reclaim. Many useful substances are now recovered from materials that used to be thrown away. 7 ARCHAIC. get to; reach. —*v.i.* 1 get well; get back to a normal condition. 2 obtain judgment in one's favor in a court of law. [< Old French *recoverer* < Latin *recuperare*] **—re cov′er a ble,** *adj.* **—re cov′er er,** *n.*
Syn. *v.t.* 1 **Recover, reclaim, retrieve** mean to get something back. **Recover** means to get something back again after losing it: *He recovered the stolen furs.* **Reclaim** means to get something back after temporarily giving it up: *At the end of the trip we reclaimed our luggage.* **Retrieve** means to get something back after letting it lapse or deteriorate: *It took him a long time to retrieve his reputation.*

re-cov er (rē kuv′ər), *v.t.* 1 put a new cover on. 2 put a cover back on.

re cov er y (ri kuv′ər ē), *n., pl.* **-er ies.** 1 act of recovering. 2 a coming back to health or normal condition. 3 a getting back something that was lost, taken away, stolen, or sent out. 4 a getting back to a proper position or condition: *He tripped and almost fell, but made a quick recovery.*

recovery room, room used in a hospital to treat patients recovering immediately after an operation or childbirth.

recorder (def. 5)

rec re ant (rek′rē ənt), *adj.* 1 lacking courage; cowardly. 2 unfaithful to duty, etc.; disloyal; traitorous. —*n.* 1 coward. 2 traitor. [< Old French, confessing oneself beaten, ultimately < Latin *re-* back + *credere* believe]

rec re ate (rek′rē āt), *v.,* **-at ed, -at ing.** —*v.t.* refresh with games, pastimes, exercises, etc. —*v.i.* take recreation. [< Latin *recreatum* restored < *re-* again + *creare* create]

hat, āge, fär; let, ēqual, tėrm;
it, īce; hot, ōpen, ôrder;
oil, out; cup, pu̇t, rüle;
ch, child; ng, long; sh, she;
th, thin; ᴛʜ, then; zh, measure;

ə represents *a* in about, *e* in taken, *i* in pencil, *o* in lemon, *u* in circus.

< = from, derived from, taken from.

re-cre ate (rē′krē āt′), *v.t.,* **-at ed, -at ing.** create anew.

rec re a tion (rek′rē ā′shən), *n.* play or amusement. Walking, gardening, and reading are quiet forms of recreation.

re-cre a tion (rē′krē ā′shən), *n.* 1 act of creating anew. 2 thing created anew.

rec re a tion al (rek′rē ā′shə nəl), *adj.* of or having to do with recreation.

rec re a tive (rek′rē ā′tiv), *adj.* refreshing; restoring.

re crim i nate (ri krim′ə nāt), *v.i., v.t.,* **-nat ed, -nat ing.** accuse (someone) in return: *He said she had lied, and she recriminated by saying he had lied too.* [ultimately < Latin *re-* back + *criminis* charge]

re crim i na tion (ri krim′ə nā′shən), *n.* an accusing in return; counter accusation.

re crim i na tive (ri krim′ə nā′tiv, ri krim′ə nə tiv), *adj.* recriminatory.

re crim i na to ry (ri krim′ə nə tôr′ē, ri krim′ə nə tōr′ē), *adj.* of or involving recrimination.

rec room (rek), INFORMAL. room for recreation.

re cru desce (rē′krü des′), *v.i.,* **-desced, -desc ing.** break out again; become active again. [< Latin *recrudescere* become raw again, grow worse < *re-* again + *crudescere* become raw < *crudus* raw]

re cru des cence (rē′krü des′ns), *n.* a breaking out anew; renewed activity: *the recrudescence of an influenza epidemic.*

re cru des cent (rē′krü des′nt), *adj.* breaking out anew.

re cruit (ri krüt′), *n.* 1 a newly enlisted soldier, sailor, etc. 2 a new member of any group or class. —*v.t.* 1 get (men) to join an army, navy, etc. 2 strengthen or supply (an army, navy, etc.) with new men. 3 get (new members) by enrolling, hiring, etc. 4 increase or maintain the number of. 5 get a sufficient number or amount of; renew; replenish. —*v.i.* 1 get new men for an army, navy, etc. 2 renew health, strength, or spirits; recuperate. [< French *recrute, recrue* recruit(ing), new growth, ultimately < *re-* again + *croître* to grow] **—re cruit′er,** *n.* **—re cruit′ment,** *n.*

rec. sec., recording secretary.

rect., 1 receipt. 2 rectangle. 3 rector. 4 rectory.

rec tal (rek′təl), *adj.* of, having to do with, or near the rectum.

rec tan gle (rek′tang′gəl), *n.* a four-sided plane figure with four right angles. [< Medieval Latin *rectangulus* rectangular, ultimately < Latin *rectus* right + *angulus* angle]

rectangle
two rectangles

rec tan gu lar (rek tang′gyə lər), *adj.* 1 shaped like a rectangle. 2 having one or more right angles. 3 placed at right angles. **—rec tan′gu lar ly,** *adv.*

rec tan gu lar i ty (rek′tang gyə lar′ə tē), *n.* rectangular quality or condition.

rec ti fi ca tion (rek′tə fə kā′shən), *n.* act of rectifying.

rec ti fi er (rek′tə fī′ər), *n.* 1 person or thing that makes right, corrects, adjusts, etc. 2 device for changing alternating current into direct current.

rec ti fy (rek′tə fī), *v.t.,* **-fied, -fy ing.** 1 make right; put right; adjust; remedy: *The storekeeper admitted his mistake and was willing to rectify it.* 2 change (an alternating current) into a direct current. 3 purify or refine: *rectify a liquor by distilling it several times.* [< Late Latin *rectificare* < Latin *rectus* right + *facere* to make] **—rec′ti fi′a ble,** *adj.*

rec ti lin e ar (rek′tə lin′ē ər), *adj.* 1 in a straight line; moving in a straight line. 2 forming a straight line. 3 bounded or formed by straight lines. 4 characterized by straight lines. **—rec′ti lin′e ar ly,** *adv.*

rec ti tude (rek′tə tüd, rek′tə tyüd), *n.* 1 upright conduct or character; honesty; righteousness. 2 direction in a straight line; straightness. [< Late Latin *rectitudo* < Latin *rectus* straight]

rec tor (rek′tər), *n.* 1 clergyman in the Protestant Episcopal Church or the Church of England who has charge of a parish. 2 priest in the Roman Catholic Church who has charge of a congregation or religious house. 3 head of some schools, colleges, and universities. [< Latin, ruler < *regere* to rule]

rec tor y (rek′tər e), *n., pl.* **-tor ies.** 1 a rector's house. 2 the church living with all its rights, tithes, and lands held by a rector.

rec tum (rek′təm), *n.* the lowest part of the large intestine, extending from the last curve of the colon to the anus. [< New Latin < Latin *(intestinum) rectum* straight (intestine)]

re cum ben cy (ri kum′bən sē), *n.* recumbent position or condition.

re cum bent (ri kum′bənt), *adj.* lying down; reclining; leaning. [< Latin *recumbentem* < *re-* back + *-cumbere* lie down] **—re cum′bent ly,** *adv.*

re cu pe rate (ri kyü′pə rāt′, ri kü′pə rāt′), *v.,* **-rat ed, -rat ing.** *—v.i.* recover from sickness, exhaustion, loss, etc. *—v.t.* 1 restore to health, strength, etc. 2 get back; regain. [< Latin *recuperatum* recovered] **—re cu′pe ra′tion,** *n.*

re cu pe ra tive (ri kyü′pə rā′tiv, ri kü′pə-rā′tiv; ri kyü′pə rə tiv, ri kü′pə rə tiv), *adj.* of recuperation; aiding recuperation.

re cur (ri kėr′), *v.i.,* **-curred, -cur ring.** 1 come up again; occur again; be repeated: *Leap year recurs every four years.* 2 return in thought: *Old memories constantly recurred to her.* 3 bring up or raise again: *Let's recur to the matter of cost.* [< Latin *recurrere* < *re-* back + *currere* to run]

re cur rence (ri kėr′əns), *n.* occurrence again; repetition; return.

re cur rent (ri kėr′ənt), *adj.* 1 occurring again; recurring; repeated: *a recurrent mistake.* 2 turned back so as to run in the opposite direction: *a recurrent nerve.* **—re cur′rent ly,** *adv.*

re curve (rē kėrv′), *v.t., v.i.,* **-curved, -curv ing.** curve back; bend back.

re cy cle (rē sī′kəl), *v.t.,* **-cled, -cling.** cause to undergo processes or treatment in order to be used again. Paper, aluminum, and glass are common products that are recycled.

red (red), *n., adj.,* **red der, red dest.** *—n.* 1 the color of blood, fire, the ruby, etc., having the longest light wave in the color spectrum, where it lies between orange and violet. 2 any shade of that color. 3 a red pigment or dye. 4 red cloth or clothing: *wear red.* 5 a red or reddish animal, thing, etc. 6 **Red, a** a Communist or, sometimes, any extreme radical. **b** native or inhabitant of a Communist country, especially the Soviet Union. 7 **in the red,** in debt; losing money. 8 **see red,** INFORMAL. becoming very angry.
—adj. 1 having the color of blood, fire, the ruby, etc.; being like it, or suggesting it: *red hair.* 2 sore; inflamed: *red eyes.* 3 blushing; flushed. 4 red-hot; glowing. 5 **Red, a** Communist or extremely radical. **b** having to do with a Communist country, especially the Soviet Union.
[Old English *rēad,* adjective] **—red′ly,** *adv.* **—red′ness,** *n.*

red-, *prefix.* form of **re-** in some instances before vowels, as in *redintegrate.*

re dact (ri dakt′), *v.t.* 1 draw up or frame (a statement, announcement, etc.). 2 prepare (material) for publication; edit. [< Latin *redactum* reduced, brought back < *re-* back + *agere* bring]

re dac tion (ri dak′shən), *n.* 1 a redacting; editing. 2 a redacted form or version of a work; edition.

re dac tor (ri dak′tər), *n.* editor.

red algae, class of characteristically red or purplish, mostly marine, algae.

red bird (red′bėrd′), *n.* any of several birds with red feathers, such as the cardinal, the scarlet tanager, and the European bullfinch.

red blood cell, cell in the blood, formed in bone marrow and containing hemoglobin, that carries oxygen from the lungs to various parts of the body; red cell; red corpuscle; erythrocyte.

red-blood ed (red′blud′id), *adj.* full of life and spirit; virile; vigorous.

red breast (red′brest′), *n.* robin.

red cap (red′kap′), *n.* porter at a railroad station, bus station, etc., who usually wears a red cap as part of his uniform.

red-car pet (red′kär′pit), *adj.* royal or preferential; favored: *The visiting premier received red-carpet treatment.*

red cell, red blood cell.

Red China, China (def. 1).

red clover, species of clover with ball-shaped heads of reddish-purple flowers, cultivated as food for horses, cattle, etc., and as a cover crop.

red coat (red′kōt′), *n.* (in former times) a British soldier.

red corpuscle, red blood cell.

Red Cross, 1 an international organization to care for the sick and wounded in war, and to relieve suffering caused by floods, fire, diseases, and other calamities. 2 a national society that is a branch of this organization. 3 **red cross,** a red Greek cross on a white background, the emblem of the Red Cross.

red deer, 1 deer native to the forests of Europe and Asia, and formerly very abundant in England. 2 the common deer of America in its summer coat.

red den (red′n), *v.t.* make red. *—v.i.* 1 become red. 2 blush.

red dish (red′ish), *adj.* somewhat red. **—red′dish ness,** *n.*

rede (rēd), *v.t.,* **red ed, red ing.** ARCHAIC or DIALECT. 1 give counsel to; advise. 2 interpret; explain. 3 tell. [Old English *rǣdan*]

re dec o rate (rē dek′ə rāt′), *v.t., v.i.,* **-rat ed, -rat ing.** decorate again or anew, especially by painting or papering a room, etc. **—re′dec o ra′tion,** *n.*

re ded i cate (rē ded′ə kāt), *v.t.,* **-cat ed, -cat ing.** dedicate anew. **—re′ded i-ca′tion,** *n.*

re deem (ri dēm′), *v.t.* 1 buy back: *The property on which the money was lent was redeemed when the loan was paid back.* 2 pay off: *We redeemed the mortgage.* 3 make up for; balance: *A very good feature will sometimes redeem several bad ones.* 4 carry out; make good; fulfill: *We redeem a promise by doing what we said we would.* 5 set free; rescue; save: *redeemed from sin.* [< Latin *redimere* < *re-* back + *emere* to buy] **—re-deem′a ble,** *adj.*

re deem er (ri dē′mər), *n.* 1 person who redeems. 2 **Redeemer,** Jesus.

re demp tion (ri demp′shən), *n.* 1 act of redeeming. 2 a being redeemed. 3 ransom. 4 deliverance; rescue. 5 deliverance from sin; salvation. [< Latin *redemptionem* < *redimere* redeem. See REDEEM. Doublet of RANSOM.]

re demp tive (ri demp′tiv), *adj.* serving to redeem.

re demp tor y (ri demp′tər ē), *adj.* redemptive.

re de ploy (rē′di ploi′), *v.t.* change the position of (troops) from one theater of war to another. **—re′de ploy′ment,** *n.*

re de sign (rē′di zīn′), *v.t.* design again. *—n.* 1 act or process of redesigning. 2 a new design.

red eye (red′ī′), *n.* 1 any of various fishes with reddish eyes. 2 SLANG. strong, cheap whiskey.

red flag, 1 symbol of rebellion, revolution, etc. 2 sign of danger. 3 thing that stirs up anger.

red fox, 1 any of various reddish foxes of North America, Europe, Africa, and Asia. 2 the reddish fur of a fox.

red grouse, variety of grouse of Great Britain and Ireland that does not turn white in winter.

Red Guard, member of a mass movement of young Chinese communists proclaiming rigid adherence to Maoist doctrines.

red-hand ed (red′han′did), *adv., adj.* in the very act of committing a crime, mischief, etc. **—red′-hand′ed ly,** *adv.*

red head (red′hed′), *n.* 1 person having red hair. 2 a North American duck of the same genus as and resembling the canvasback. The adult male has a red head.

red head ed (red′hed′id), *adj.* 1 having red hair. 2 having a red head.

red heat, 1 condition of being red-hot. 2 the accompanying temperature.

red herring, 1 the common smoked herring. 2 something used to draw attention away from the real issue.

red-hot (red′hot′), *adj.* 1 red with heat; very hot. 2 very enthusiastic; excited; violent. 3 fresh from the source.

hat, āge, fär; let, ēqual, tėrm;
it, īce; hot, ōpen, ôrder;
oil, out; cup, pu̇t, rüle;
ch, child; ng, long; sh, she;
th, thin; ᴛʜ, then; zh, measure;

ə represents *a* in about, *e* in taken, *i* in pencil, *o* in lemon, *u* in circus.

< = from, derived from, taken from.

red in gote (red′ing gōt), *n.* 1 (formerly) a man's outer coat with long skirts that overlap in front. 2 a somewhat similar coat now worn by women, sometimes forming part of a dress. [< French < English *riding coat*]

redingote (def. 1)

red in te grate (red in′tə grāt), *v.t.,* **-grat ed, -grat ing.** ARCHAIC. make whole again; restore to a perfect state. **—red in′te gra′tion,** *n.*

re di rect (rē′də rekt′, rē′dī rekt′), *v.t.* direct again or anew. *—adj.* (in law) of or having to do with a second examination of a witness by the party calling him, after cross-examination. **—re′di rec′tion,** *n.*

re dis count (rē dis′kount), *v.t.* discount again. *—n.* 1 act of rediscounting. 2 a commercial paper that has been rediscounted.

re dis tri bu tion (rē′dis trə byü′shən), *n.* distribution made again or anew.

re dis trict (rē dis′trikt), *v.t.* divide into districts again, often for voting purposes.

red jasmine, a tropical American shrub or tree of the same family as the dogbane, with large, fragrant red flowers; frangipani.

red lead, a red oxide of lead, used in paint, in making cement for pipes, and in making glass. *Formula:* Pb_3O_4

red-let ter (red′let′ər), *adj.* 1 memorable; especially happy: *a red-letter day.* 2 marked by red letters.

red light, 1 a red traffic signal which indicates that vehicles or pedestrians should stop. 2 any sign or signal of danger or warning.

red man, an American Indian.

red neck (red′nek′), *n.* SLANG. a poor, white, Southern farmer or sharecropper.

re do (rē dü′), *v.t.,* **-did** (-did′), **-done** (-dun′), **-do ing.** do again; do over.

red o lence (red′l əns), *n.* redolent condition or quality.

red o lent (red′l ənt), *adj.* 1 having a pleasant smell; fragrant; aromatic. 2 smelling strongly; giving off an odor: *a house redolent of fresh paint.* 3 suggesting thoughts or feelings; reminiscent: *"Ivanhoe" is a name redolent of romance.* [< Latin *redolentem* emitting scent < *re-* back + *olere* to smell] **—red′o lent ly,** *adv.*

re dou ble (rē dub′əl), *v.,* **-bled, -bling.** *—v.t.* 1 double again. 2 increase greatly; double: *When he saw land ahead, the swimmer redoubled his speed.* 3 (in games) to double (an opponent's double). *—v.i.* 1 double back: *The fox redoubled on his trail to escape the hunters.* 2 be doubled.

re doubt (ri dout′), *n.* a small, usually temporary fortification standing alone, especially on a ridge, above or near a pass, river, etc. [< French *redoute* < Italian *ridotto* < Popular Latin *reductus* retreat < Latin *reducere.* See REDUCE.]

re doubt a ble (ri dou′tə bəl), *adj.* that should be feared or dreaded; formidable: *a redoubtable warrior.* [< Old French *redoutable* < *redouter* to dread < *re-* again + *douter* to doubt] **—re doubt′a bly,** *adv.*

re dound (ri dound′), *v.i.* come back as a result; contribute: *deeds that redound to the credit of mankind.* [< Old French *redonder* < Latin *redundare* to overflow < *re-* back + *unda* wave]

red out (red′out′), *n.* a sudden rush of blood to the head producing a red blur before the eyes, experienced by pilots when flying loops, spins, and other maneuvers.

re dox (rē′doks), *adj.* (in chemistry) producing or containing the processes of reduction and oxidation.

red pepper, 1 cayenne. 2 any of several varieties of pepper that have hollow, sweet or mild fruits which are red when ripe. 3 the fruit of any of these plants.

red poll (red′pōl′), *n.* any of a genus of small finches, the males of which have a pink or red cap on the head.

re draft (*v.* rē draft′; *n.* rē′draft′), *v.t.* draft again or anew. *—n.* a second draft.

re dress (*v.* ri dres′; *n.* rē′dres, ri dres′), *v.t.* set right; repair; remedy. *—n.* 1 a setting right; reparation; relief: *Anyone who has been injured unfairly deserves redress.* 2 the means of a remedy. [< Middle French *redresser* < *re-* again + *dresser* straighten, arrange]

Red River, 1 river flowing from NW Texas into the Mississippi. 1200 mi. 2 Red River of the North.

Red River of the North, river flowing from W Minnesota, between Minnesota and North Dakota into Lake Winnipeg in Manitoba. 700 mi.

red salmon, sockeye salmon.

Red Sea, narrow sea between the Arabian peninsula and NE Africa, an arm of the Indian Ocean, and connected with the Mediterranean Sea by the Suez Canal. 1450 mi. long; 178,000 sq. mi.

red shift, (in astronomy) a shift of the light of stars, nebulae, etc., toward the red end of the spectrum, indicating movement outward at increasing speed, and leading to the belief that the universe is constantly expanding at an ever increasing rate of speed.

red skin (red′skin′), *n.* a North American Indian.

redstart (def. 1)
about 5$^1/_2$ in. long

red start (red′stärt′), *n.* 1 a fly-catching warbler of America. 2 a small European bird with a reddish tail. [< *red* + *start* tail (Old English *steort*)]

red tape, wasteful and time-consuming attention to details and forms; bureaucratic routine. [from the former use of red tape to tie up official papers]

red top (red′top′), *n.* any of several grasses grown for forage and pasture, especially a species having large, reddish, spreading flower clusters.

re duce (ri düs′, ri dyüs′), *v.,* **-duced, -duc ing.** *—v.t.* 1 make less in amount, number, price, etc.; make smaller; decrease: *reduce expenses, reduce one's weight.* 2 make lower in degree, intensity, etc.; weaken. 3 bring down; lower: *be reduced to begging.* 4 bring to a certain state, form, or condition: *reduce a noisy crowd to order.* 5 change to another form without alteration of basic substance, value, etc.: *reduce a statement to writing. If you reduce 3 lbs. 7 oz. to ounces, you have 55 ounces.* 6 conquer; subdue: *reduce an enemy fort.* 7 restore (a dislocated or fractured bone) to its proper place; set. 8 in chemistry: **a** combine with hydrogen. **b** remove oxygen from. **c** change (atoms or ions) to a lower valence by the gain of electrons. 9 (in mathematics) simplify (an expression, a fraction, formula, etc.). 10 smelt. 11 (in biology) bring about meiosis in (a cell). *—v.i.* become less; be made less. [< Latin *reducere* lead back < *re-* back + *ducere* lead, bring]

re duc er (ri dü′sər, ri dyü′sər), *n.* 1 person or thing that reduces. 2 a threaded cylindrical piece for connecting pipes of different sizes.

re duc i bil i ty (ri dü′sə bil′ə tē, ri dyü′sə bil′ə tē), *n.* quality or condition of being reducible.

re duc i ble (ri dü′sə bəl, ri dyü′sə bəl), *adj.* able to be reduced: *$^4/_8$ is reducible to $^1/_2$.* **—re duc′i bly,** *adv.*

reducing agent, any chemical substance that reduces or removes the oxygen in a compound.

re duc tant (ri duk′tənt), *n.* reducing agent.

re duc ti o ad ab sur dum (ri duk′shē ō ad ab sėr′dəm), LATIN. reduction to absurdity; method of proving something false by showing that conclusions to which it leads are absurd.

re duc tion (ri duk′shən), *n.* 1 a reducing. 2 a being reduced. 3 amount by which a thing is reduced: *The reduction in cost was $5.* 4 form of something produced by reducing; copy of something on a smaller scale. 5 meiosis. 6 in chemistry: **a** a reaction in which oxygen is removed from a compound. **b** a reaction in which an atom or group of atoms gains one or more electrons.

reduction division, meiosis.

re duc tive (ri duk′tiv), *adj.* tending to reduce; reducing.

re dun dance (ri dun′dəns), *n.* redundancy.

re dun dan cy (ri dun′dən sē), *n., pl.* **-cies.** 1 more than is needed. 2 a redundant thing, part, or amount. 3 the use of too many words for the same idea; wordiness.

re dun dant (ri dun′dənt), *adj.* 1 not needed; extra; superfluous. 2 that says the same thing again; using too many words for the same idea; wordy: *The use of "two" in the phrase "the two twins" is redundant.* [< Latin *redundantem* overflowing < *re-* back + *unda* wave] **—re dun′dant ly,** *adv.*

re du pli cate (*v.* ri dü′plə kāt, ri dyü′plə kāt; *adj.* ri dü′plə kit, ri dyü′plə kit; ri dü′plə kāt, ri dyü′plə kāt), *v.,* **-cat ed, -cat ing,** *adj.* *—v.t.* 1 double; repeat. 2 repeat (a letter or syllable) in forming a word. 3 form by such repetition. —*adj.* doubled or repeated.

re du pli ca tion (ri dü′plə kā′shən, ri-dyü′plə kā′shən), *n.* 1 a reduplicating or a being reduplicated; doubling; repetition. 2 something resulting from repeating; duplicate; copy. 3 repetition, as of a syllable or the initial part of a syllable.

re du pli ca tive (ri dü′plə kā′tiv, ri-dyü′plə kā′tiv), *adj.* tending to reduplicate; having to do with or marked by reduplication.

red wing (red′wing′), *n.* 1 a North American blackbird, the male of which has a scarlet patch on each wing. 2 a European thrush that has reddish color on the underside of the wings.

red-winged blackbird (red′wingd′), redwing (def. 1).

red wood (red′wu̇d′), *n.* 1 a coniferous evergreen tree of California and Oregon, often growing to a height of over 300 feet; sequoia; big tree. 2 its brownish-red, relatively light wood. 3 any of various trees with a reddish wood or from which a red dyestuff is obtained.

re ech o or **re-ech o** (rē ek′ō), *v., n., pl.* **-ech oes.** —*v.i., v.t.* echo back; resound; reverberate: *The thunder reechoed far behind.* —*n.* echo of an echo.

reed (rēd), *n.* 1 any of certain tall grasses growing in wet places and having a hollow, jointed stalk. 2 such a stalk. 3 anything made from or resembling the stalk of a reed, such as a pipe to blow on or an arrow. 4 a thin piece of wood, metal, or plastic in a musical instrument that produces sound when a current of air moves it. 5 reed instrument. 6 (in the Bible) a Hebrew unit of length, equal to 6 cubits. 7 a weaver's instrument for separating the threads of the warp and beating up the woof. [Old English *hrēod*]

Reed (rēd), *n.* 1 **Thomas Brackett,** 1839-1902, American political leader. 2 **Walter,** 1851-1902, American army surgeon who discovered the cause of yellow fever.

reed bird (rēd′bėrd′), *n.* bobolink.

reed instrument, a musical instrument that produces sound by means of a vibrating reed or reeds. Oboes, clarinets, and saxophones are reed instruments.

reed organ, a musical instrument producing tones by means of small metal reeds and played by keys.

reed y (rē′dē), *adj.,* **reed i er, reed i est.** 1 full of reeds. 2 made of a reed or reeds. 3 like a reed or reeds. 4 sounding like a reed instrument: *a thin, reedy voice.* —**reed′i ly,** *adv.* —**reed′i ness,** *n.*

reef[1] (rēf), *n.* 1 a narrow ridge of rocks, sand, or coral at or near the surface of the water. 2 vein or lode in mining. [probably < earlier Dutch *riffe* or *rif*]

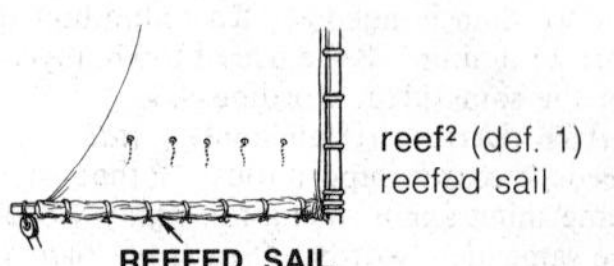

reef[2] (def. 1) reefed sail

reef[2] (rēf), *n.* 1 part of a sail that can be rolled or folded up to reduce the area exposed to the wind. 2 the area a sail is reduced to by reefing. —*v.t.* 1 reduce the area of (a sail) by rolling or folding up a part of it. 2 reduce the length of (a topmast, bowsprit, etc.) by lowering, etc. [< Scandinavian (Old Icelandic) *rif* rib, reef, ridge]

reef er[1] (rē′fər), *n.* 1 person who reefs. 2 a short coat of thick cloth, worn especially by sailors and fishermen. 3 SLANG. cigarette containing marijuana.

reef er[2] (rē′fər), *n.* SLANG. a refrigerator railroad car or truck trailer. [alteration of *refrigerator*]

reef knot, square knot.

reek (rēk), *n.* a strong, unpleasant smell; disagreeable fumes or odor. —*v.i.* 1 send out a strong, unpleasant smell. 2 be wet with sweat or blood. 3 be filled with something unpleasant or offensive: *a government reeking with corruption.* [Old English *rēc*]

reek y (rē′kē), *adj.,* **reek i er, reek i est.** reeking.

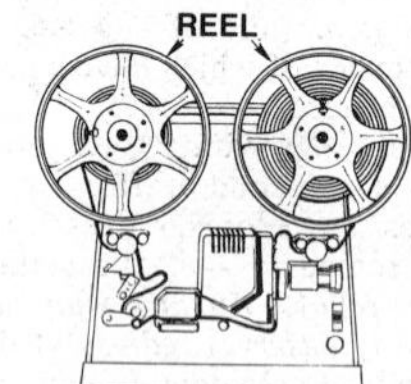

reel[1] (def. 1) reels for winding film on a movie projector

reel[1] (rēl), *n.* 1 frame turning on an axis, for winding thread, yarn, a fishline, rope, wire, etc. 2 spool; roller. 3 something wound on a reel: *two reels of motion-picture film.* 4 **off the reel,** INFORMAL. quickly and easily. —*v.t.* 1 wind on a reel. 2 draw with a reel or by winding: *reel in a fish.* 3 **reel off,** say, write, or make in a quick, easy way: *reel off a list of names.* [Old English *hrēol*] —**reel′er,** *n.*

reel[2] (rēl), *v.i.* 1 sway, swing, or rock under a blow, shock, etc. 2 sway in standing or walking. See synonym study below. 3 be in a whirl; be dizzy. 4 go with swaying or staggering movements. 5 become unsteady; give way; waver: *The regiment reeled under the sudden enemy attack.* —*n.* a reeling or staggering movement. [Middle English *relen,* probably < *reel*[1]]

Syn. *v.i.* 2 **Reel, stagger** mean to stand or move unsteadily. **Reel** suggests dizziness and a lurching movement: *Sick and faint, he reeled when he tried to cross the room.* **Stagger** suggests moving with halting steps and without much sense of balance: *The boy staggered in with the wood.*

reel[3] (rēl), *n.* 1 a lively dance of the Highlands of Scotland. 2 the Virginia reel. 3 music for either. [apparently < *reel*[2]]

re e lect or **re-e lect** (rē′i lekt′), *v.t.* elect again. —**re′e lec′tion, re′-e lec′tion,** *n.*

re en force or **re-en force** (rē′en fôrs′, rē′en fōrs′), *v.t.,* **-forced, -forc ing.** reinforce. —**re′en force′ment, re′-en force′ment,** *n.*

re en list or **re-en list** (rē′en list′), *v.t., v.i.* enlist again or for an additional term. —**re′en list′ment, re′-en list′ment,** *n.*

re en ter or **re-en ter** (rē en′tər), *v.i., v.t.* enter again; go in again: *reenter a room.*

re en trance or **re-en trance** (rē-en′trəns), *n.* 1 a second entering. 2 a coming back in after going out.

re en try or **re-en try** (rē en′trē), *n., pl.* **-tries.** 1 a new or fresh entry; second entry. 2 (in law) act or fact of taking possession again. 3 the return of a rocket or spacecraft into the earth's atmosphere after flight into outer space.

re es tab lish or **re-es tab lish** (rē′ə-stab′lish), *v.t.* establish again; restore. —**re′es tab′lish ment, re′-es tab′lish-ment,** *n.*

reeve[1] (rēv), *n.* 1 the chief official of a town or district. 2 bailiff; steward; overseer. [Old English *(ge)rēfa*]

reeve[2] (rēv), *v.t.,* **reeved** or **rove, reev ing.** 1 pass (a rope) through a hole, ring, etc. 2 fasten by placing through or around something. [origin uncertain]

reeve[3] (rēv), *n.* a female ruff. [perhaps related to *ruff*]

re ex am ine or **re-ex am ine** (rē′eg-zam′ən), *v.t.,* **-ined, -in ing.** examine again. —**re′ex am′i na′tion, re′-ex am′i na′tion,** *n.*

ref (ref), *n.* INFORMAL. referee.

ref., 1 referee. 2 reference. 3 referred.

re fec tion (ri fek′shən), *n.* 1 refreshment by food or drink. 2 meal; repast.

re fec tor y (ri fek′tər ē), *n., pl.* **-tor ies.** a room for meals, especially in a monastery, convent, or school. [< Late Latin *refectorium* < Latin *reficere* refresh < *re-* again + *facere* to make]

re fer (ri fėr′), *v.,* **-ferred, -fer ring.** —*v.i.* 1 direct attention: *refer to a passage in the Bible.* See synonym study below. 2 relate; apply: *The rule refers only to special cases.* 3 turn for information or help: *Writers often refer to a dictionary.* —*v.t.* 1 send or direct for information, help, or action: *They referred me to another department.* 2 hand over; submit: *Let's refer the dispute to the umpire.* 3 think of as belonging or due; assign: *They referred their failure to bad luck.* [< Latin *referre* take back, refer < *re-* + *ferre* to take]

Syn. *v.i.* 1 **Refer, allude** mean to speak of something in a way to turn attention to it. **Refer** means to make direct or specific mention: *In his speech he referred to newspaper accounts of the election campaign.* **Allude** means to mention indirectly: *She never referred to the incident, but often alluded to it by hinting.*

ref er a ble (ref′ər ə bəl, ri fėr′ə bəl), *adj.* that can be referred.

ref e ree (ref′ə rē′), *n., v.,* **-reed, -ree ing.** —*n.* 1 a judge of play in certain games and sports. 2 person to whom something is referred for decision or settlement. —*v.t., v.i.* act as referee; act as referee in.

ref er ence (ref′ər əns), *n.* 1 a referring. 2 a being referred. 3 direction of the attention, as by a footnote. 4 statement, book, etc., referred to: *You will find that reference on page 16.* 5 something used for information or help: *A dictionary is a book of reference.* 6 person who can give information about another person's character or ability. 7 statement about someone's character or ability: *She had excellent references from her former employers.* 8 relation; respect; regard: *This test is to be taken by all students without reference to age or grade.* 9 **in reference to** or **with reference to,** in relation to; about; concerning. 10 **make reference to,** mention. —*adj.* used for information or help: *a reference library.*

reference book, book designed to give information on many subjects. Dictionaries, encyclopedias, and almanacs are reference books.

ref e ren dum (ref′ə ren′dəm), *n., pl.* **-dums, -da** (-də). 1 principle or process of submitting a bill already passed by the lawmaking body to the direct vote of the citizens for approval or rejection. 2 a vote on such a bill. 3 the submitting of any matter to a direct vote. [< Latin, that which must be referred < *referre* refer]

ref er ent (ref′ər ənt, ri fėr′ənt), *n.* 1 person who is consulted. 2 person, thing, or idea that a word stands for or refers to. *—adj.* containing a reference; referring.

re fer ral (ri fėr′əl), *n.* 1 act of referring. 2 person who is referred.

re fill (*v.* rē fil′; *n.* rē′fil′), *v.t., v.i.* fill again. *—n.* 1 something to refill with: *a refill for a pen.* 2 a filling again, as of a medical prescription: *The doctor limited the antibiotic refills to two.* **—re fill′a ble,** *adj.*

re fine (ri fīn′), *v.,* **-fined, -fin ing.** *—v.t.* 1 free from impurities; make pure: *refine petroleum.* 2 make fine, polished, or cultivated. 3 change or remove by polishing, purifying, etc. 4 make very fine, subtle, or exact. *—v.i.* 1 become pure. 2 become fine, polished, or cultivated. 3 **refine on** or **refine upon, a** improve. **b** excel. **—re fin′er,** *n.*

re fined (ri fīnd′), *adj.* 1 freed from impurities; made pure: *refined sugar.* 2 free from grossness or vulgarity: *refined tastes.* 3 cultivated; well-bred: *refined manners.* 4 fine; subtle: *refined distinctions.* 5 minutely precise: *refined measurements.*

re fine ment (ri fīn′mənt), *n.* 1 fineness of feeling, taste, manners, or language. 2 act or result of refining. 3 improvement; advance. 4 a fine point; subtle distinction. 5 an improved, higher, or extreme form of something.

re fin er y (ri fī′nər ē), *n., pl.* **-er ies.** a building and machinery for purifying metal, sugar, petroleum, etc.

re fin ish (rē fin′ish), *v.t.* give (wood, metal, etc.) a new finish. **—re fin′ish er,** *n.*

re fit (rē fit′; *also* rē′fit *for n.*), *v.,* **-fit ted, -fit ting,** *n.* *—v.t.* fit, prepare, or equip for use again: *refit an old ship.* *—v.i.* get fresh supplies. *—n.* act of refitting.

refl., 1 reflex. 2 reflexive.

re flect (ri flekt′), *v.t.* 1 turn back or throw back (light, heat, sound, etc.): *The sidewalks reflect heat on a hot day.* 2 give back a likeness or image of: *A mirror reflects one's face and body.* 3 reproduce or show like a mirror: *The newspaper reflected the owner's opinions.* 4 serve to cast or bring: *A brave act reflects credit on the person who does it.* *—v.i.* 1 cast back light, heat, sound, etc. 2 give back an image. 3 think carefully; ponder; deliberate: *Take time to reflect before doing important things.* See **think** for synonym study. 4 cast blame, reproach, or discredit: *That child's bad behavior reflects on his home training.* [< Latin *reflectere* < *re-* back + *flectere* to bend]

re flect ance (ri flek′təns), *n.* the amount of light reflected by a surface in proportion to the amount of light falling on the surface.

reflecting telescope, telescope in which light from the object is gathered and focused by a concave mirror and the resulting image is magnified by the eyepiece.

re flec tion (ri flek′shən), *n.* 1 a reflecting. 2 a being reflected. 3 something reflected. 4 likeness; image: *You can see your reflection in a mirror.* 5 thinking, especially careful thinking: *On reflection, the plan seemed too dangerous.* 6 idea or remark resulting from careful thinking; idea; remark. 7 remark, action, etc., that casts blame or discredit. 8 blame; discredit. 9 the bending of a part back upon itself. 10 the part bent back. Also, **reflexion.**

re flec tive (ri flek′tiv), *adj.* 1 that reflects; reflecting: *the reflective surface of polished metal.* 2 thoughtful: *a reflective look.* **—re flec′tive ly,** *adv.* **—re flec′tive ness,** *n.*

re flec tor (ri flek′tər), *n.* 1 any thing, surface, or device that reflects light, heat, sound, etc., especially a piece of glass or metal, usually concave, for reflecting light in a required direction. 2 reflecting telescope.

reflector (def. 1) for flashbulb on a camera

re flex (rē′fleks), *n.* 1 an involuntary action in direct response to a stimulation of some nerve cells. Sneezing, vomiting, and shivering are reflexes. 2 something reflected; image; reflection. 3 a copy. *—adj.* 1 not voluntary; coming as a direct response to a stimulation of some sensory nerve cells. Yawning is a reflex action. 2 bent back; turned back. 3 (of an angle) more than 180 degrees and less than 360 degrees. 4 coming as a reaction. [< Latin *reflexum* bent back < *re-* + *flectere* to bend]

reflex arc, the nerve path in the body leading from stimulus to reflex action.

reflex camera, camera in which the image received through the lens is reflected by a mirror onto a horizontal piece of ground glass, for viewing and focusing.

re flex ion (ri flek′shən), *n.* reflection.

re flex ive (ri flek′siv), in grammar: *—adj.* expressing an action that refers back to the subject. *Myself, herself, yourself,* etc., are reflexive pronouns. *—n.* a reflexive verb or pronoun. In "The boy hurt himself," *hurt* and *himself* are reflexives. **—re flex′ive ly,** *adv.* **—re flex′ive ness,** *n.*

re flux (rē′fluks), *n.* a flowing back; the ebb of a tide.

re fo rest (rē fôr′ist, rē for′ist), *v.t., v.i.* replant with trees.

re fo rest a tion (rē′fôr ə stā′shən, rē′for ə stā′shən), *n.* a replanting or a being replanted with trees.

re form (ri fôrm′), *v.t.* make better; improve by removing faults: *reform a criminal.* *—v.i.* become better: *He promised to reform if given another chance.* *—n.* a change intended to improve conditions; improvement: *The new government made many needed reforms.* *—adj.* **Reform,** of or having to do with the liberal branch of Judaism, as contrasted with the Orthodox and Conservative branches. [< Latin *reformare* < *re-* again + *forma* form] **—re form′a ble,** *adj.*

re-form (rē fôrm′), *v.t.* form again. *—v.i.* 1 take a new shape. 2 form again.

ref or ma tion (ref′ər mā′shən), *n.* 1 a reforming or a being reformed; change for the better; improvement. 2 **Reformation,** the great religious movement in Europe in the 1500's that aimed at reform within the Roman Catholic Church but led to the establishment of Protestant churches.

ref or ma tion al (ref′ər mā′shə nəl), *adj.* of or having to do with reformation.

re form a tive (ri fôr′mə tiv), *adj.* tending toward or inducing reform.

re form a to ry (ri fôr′mə tôr′ē, ri fôr′mə tōr′ē), *n., pl.* **-ries,** *adj.* *—n.* a penal institution for reforming young offenders against the law; reform school. *—adj.* serving or intended to reform.

hat, āge, fär; let, ēqual, tėrm;
it, īce; hot, ōpen, ôrder;
oil, out; cup, pu̇t, rüle;
ch, child; ng, long; sh, she;
th, thin; ᴛʜ, then; zh, measure;

ə represents *a* in about, *e* in taken, *i* in pencil, *o* in lemon, *u* in circus.

< = from, derived from, taken from.

Re formed (ri fôrmd′), *adj.* 1 of or having to do with the Protestant churches, especially the Calvinistic as distinguished from the Lutheran. 2 **reformed,** improved; amended.

re form er (ri fôr′mər), *n.* person who reforms, or tries to reform, some state of affairs; supporter of reforms.

re form ism (ri fôr′miz′əm), *n.* social or political reform.

re form ist (ri fôr′mist), *n.* a reformer.

reform school, reformatory.

re fract (ri frakt′), *v.t.* bend (a ray, waves, etc.) from a straight course. Water refracts light. [< Latin *refractum* broken back, refracted < *re-* back + *frangere* to break]

refracting telescope, telescope in which light from the object is gathered and focused by a lens (the objective) and the resulting image is magnified by the eyepiece.

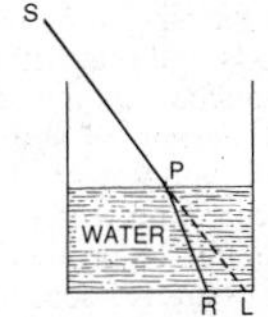

refraction
In the diagram, the ray of light SP in passing into the water is refracted from its original direction SPL to SPR.

re frac tion (ri frak′shən), *n.* the turning or bending of a ray of light, sound waves, a stream of electrons, etc., when passing obliquely from one medium into another of different density.

re frac tive (ri frak′tiv), *adj.* 1 having power to refract; refracting. 2 of or having to do with refraction.

refractive index, index of refraction.

re frac tiv i ty (rē′frak tiv′ə tē), *n.* quality or condition of being refractive.

re frac tor (ri frak′tər), *n.* 1 anything that refracts light rays, waves, etc. 2 refracting telescope.

re frac tor y (ri frak′tər ē), *adj.* 1 hard to manage; stubborn; obstinate: *Mules are refractory.* 2 not yielding readily to treatment: *a refractory cough.* 3 hard to melt, reduce, or work: *refractory ores.* 4 (of a muscle, nerve, etc.) that responds less readily to stimulation after a response. *—n.* an ore, cement, ceramic material, or similar substance that is hard to melt, reduce, or work. **—re frac′tor i ly,** *adv.* **—re frac′tor i ness,** *n.*

re frain[1] (ri frān′), *v.i.* hold oneself back, especially from satisfying a momentary impulse; abstain: *Refrain from talking in the library.* [< Old French *refrener* < Latin *refrenare* furnish with a bridle, refrain < *re-* back + *frenum* bridle]

re frain[2] (ri frān′), *n.* 1 phrase or verse recurring regularly in a song or poem, especially at the end of each stanza; chorus. 2 music for it. [< Old French < *refraindre* break off [< Latin *refringere* < *re-* back + *frangere* to break]

re fran gi bil i ty (ri fran′jə bil′ə tē), *n.* 1 property of being refrangible. 2 amount of refraction (of light rays, etc.) that is possible.

re fran gi ble (ri fran′jə bəl), *adj.* able to be refracted: *Rays of light are refrangible.* **—re fran′gi ble ness,** *n.*

re fresh (ri fresh′), *v.t.* 1 make fresh again; freshen up; renew: *He refreshed his memory by a glance at the book. She refreshed herself with a cup of tea.* 2 restore to a certain condition by furnishing a fresh supply; replenish. *—v.i.* become fresh again.

re fresh er (ri fresh′ər), *adj.* helping to renew knowledge or abilities, or to bring a person new needed knowledge: *a refresher course in typing.* *—n.* 1 person or thing that refreshes. 2 reminder.

re fresh ing (ri fresh′ing), *adj.* 1 that refreshes. 2 welcome as a pleasing change. **—re fresh′ing ly,** *adv.*

re fresh ment (ri fresh′mənt), *n.* 1 a refreshing. 2 a being refreshed. 3 thing that refreshes. 4 **refreshments,** *pl.* food or drink: *serve refreshments at a party.*

re frig er ant (ri frij′ər ənt), *adj.* refrigerating; cooling. *—n.* something that cools, as ice; refrigerating agent.

re frig e rate (ri frij′ə rāt′), *v.t.,* **-rat ed, -rat ing.** make or keep (food, etc.) cold or cool. [< Latin *refrigeratum* made cold < *re-* + *frigus* cold] **—re frig′e ra′tion,** *n.*

re frig e ra tor (ri frij′ə rā′tər), *n.* box, room, etc., that keeps foods and other items cool by use of ice or by mechanical means.

reft (reft), *v.* ARCHAIC. pt. and pp. of **reave.**

re fu el (rē fyü′əl), *v.t.* supply with fuel again. *—v.i.* take on a fresh supply of fuel.

ref uge (ref′yüj), *n.* 1 shelter or protection from danger, trouble, etc.; safety; security. 2 place of safety or security. [< Latin *refugium* < *re-* back + *fugere* flee]

ref u gee (ref′yə jē′, ref′yə jē′), *n.* person who flees for refuge or safety, especially to a foreign country, in time of persecution, war, or disaster.

re ful gence (ri ful′jəns), *n.* a shining brightly; radiance; brightness.

re ful gent (ri ful′jənt), *adj.* shining brightly; radiant: *a refulgent sunrise.* [< Latin *refulgentem* < *re-* back + *fulgere* to shine] **—re ful′gent ly,** *adv.*

re fund[1] (*v.* ri fund′; *n.* rē′fund), *v.t.* make return or restitution of (money received or taken); pay back. *—n.* 1 a return of money paid. 2 the money paid back. [< Latin *refundere* < *re-* back + *fundere* pour] **—re fund′a ble,** *adj.*

re fund[2] (rē fund′), *v.t.* change (a debt, loan, etc.) into a new form. [< *re-* + *fund*]

re fur bish (rē fėr′bish), *v.t.* polish up again; do up anew; brighten; renovate.

re fus al (ri fyü′zəl), *n.* 1 act of refusing. 2 the right to refuse or take a thing before it is offered to others.

re fuse[1] (ri fyüz′), *v.,* **-fused, -fus ing.** *—v.t.* 1 say no to; decline to accept; reject: *refuse an offer.* See synonym study below. 2 deny (a request, demand, invitation); decline to give or grant: *refuse admittance.* 3 decline (to do something): *refuse to discuss the question.* *—v.i.* say no; decline to accept or consent: *She is free to refuse.* [< Old French *refuser* < Latin *refusum* poured back < *re-* + *fundere* pour] **—re fus′er,** *n.*

Syn. *v.t.* 1 **Refuse, decline, reject** mean not to accept something offered. **Refuse** implies a direct and sometimes an ungracious denial: *He refused to go with me.* **Decline** is more polite, implying reluctant rather than direct denial: *He declined my invitation.* **Reject** is more emphatic than *refuse,* implying a very positive and brusque denial: *He rejected my friendly advice.*

ref use[2] (ref′yüs), *n.* 1 useless stuff; waste; rubbish; trash. 2 the scum, dregs, etc., of something. [< Old French *refus* < *refuser* refuse[1]]

ref u ta ble (ref′yə tə bəl, ri fyü′tə bəl), *adj.* that can be refuted. **—ref′u ta bly,** *adv.*

ref u ta tion (ref′yə tā′shən), *n.* disproof of a claim, opinion, or argument.

re fute (ri fyüt′), *v.t.,* **-fut ed, -fut ing.** show (a claim, opinion, or argument) to be false or incorrect; prove wrong; disprove. [< Latin *refutare* cause to fall back] **—re fut′er,** *n.*

reg., 1 register. 2 registered. 3 registrar. 4 registry. 5 regular.

re gain (ri gān′), *v.t.* 1 get again; recover: *regain health.* 2 get back to; reach again: *regain the shore.*

re gal (rē′gəl), *adj.* 1 belonging to a king; royal. See **royal** for synonym study. 2 fit for a king; kinglike; stately; splendid; magnificent. [< Latin *regalis* < *regem* king. Doublet of ROYAL, REAL[2], RIAL.] **—re′gal ly,** *adv.*

re gale (ri gāl′), *v.,* **-galed, -gal ing.** *—v.t.* 1 entertain agreeably; delight with something pleasing: *The old sailor regaled the boys with sea stories.* 2 entertain with a choice repast. *—v.i.* feast. [< French *régaler* < *re-* + *galer* make merry] **—re gale′ment,** *n.*

re ga li a (ri gā′lē ə, ri gā′lyə), *n.pl.* 1 the emblems of royalty. Crowns and scepters are regalia. 2 the emblems or decorations of any society, order, etc. 3 clothes, especially fine clothes: *in party regalia.* [< Latin, royal things]

re gal i ty (rē gal′ə tē), *n., pl.* **-ties.** 1 royalty; sovereignty; kingship. 2 a right or privilege having to do with a king. 3 kingdom.

re gard (ri gärd′), *v.t.* 1 think of; consider or look on: *He is regarded as the best doctor in town.* 2 show thought or consideration for; esteem; respect: *regard the rights of others.* 3 take notice of; pay attention to; heed: *None regarded his screams.* 4 look at; look closely at; watch: *She regarded me sternly.* 5 **as regards,** with respect to; concerning. *—v.i.* 1 look closely. 2 pay attention.

—n. 1 consideration; thought; care: *Have regard for the feelings of others.* See **respect** for synonym study. 2 a steady look; gaze. 3 good opinion; esteem; favor. 4 **regards,** *pl.* good wishes; an expression of esteem: *I sent my regards.* 5 a particular matter; point: *You are wrong in this regard.* 6 **in regard to** or **with regard to,** relating to; about; concerning. 7 **without regard to,** not considering.

[< Old French *regarder* < *re-* back + *garder* to guard. Doublet of REWARD.]

re gard ful (ri gärd′fəl), *adj.* 1 heedful or observant; mindful. 2 considerate; respectful. **—re gard′ful ly,** *adv.* **—re gard′ful ness,** *n.*

re gard ing (ri gär′ding), *prep.* with regard to; concerning; about.

re gard less (ri gärd′lis), *adj.* with no heed; careless: *regardless of expense.* *—adv.* INFORMAL. in spite of what happens: *We will leave Monday, regardless.* **—re gard′less ly,** *adv.* **—re gard′less ness,** *n.*

re gat ta (ri gat′ə, ri gät′ə), *n.* a boat race or a series of boat races: *the annual regatta of the yacht club.* [< Italian]

re gen cy (rē′jən sē), *n., pl.* **-cies.** 1 position, office, or function of a regent or body of regents: *The Queen Mother held the regency till the young king became of age.* 2 body of regents. 3 government by a regent or body of regents. 4 time during which there is a regency. 5 **Regency, a** period from 1811 to 1820 in English history. **b** period from 1715 to 1723 in French history. *—adj.* of or having to do with the English or French Regency or the style of furniture of these periods.

re gen er a cy (ri jen′ər ə sē), *n.* regenerate state.

re gen e rate (*v.* ri jen′ə rāt′; *adj.* ri jen′ər it), *v.,* **-rat ed, -rat ing,** *adj.* *—v.t.* 1 give a new and better spiritual life to. 2 improve the moral condition of; reform completely. 3 grow again; form (new tissue, a new part, etc.) to replace what is lost: *If a young crab loses a claw, it can regenerate a new one.* 4 (in electronics) to increase the amplification of, by transferring a portion of the power from the output circuit to the input circuit. *—v.i.* reform; be regenerated. *—adj.* 1 born again spiritually. 2 made over in better form; formed anew morally. **—re gen′e ra′tor,** *n.*

re gen e ra tion (ri jen′ə rā′shən), *n.* 1 a regenerating. 2 a being regenerated. 3 rebirth of the spirit.

re gen e ra tive (ri jen′ə rā′tiv, ri jen′ər ə tiv), *adj.* tending to regenerate; regenerating.

re gent (rē′jənt), *n.* 1 person who rules when the regular ruler is absent, disabled, or too young: *The Queen will be the regent till her son grows up.* 2 member of a governing board, especially of a university or college. *—adj.* acting as a regent. [< Latin *regentem* ruling < *regere* to rule]

re gent ship (rē′jənt ship), *n.* position of a regent; regency.

reg i cid al (rej′ə sī′dl), *adj.* of or having to do with regicide.

reg i cide (rej′ə sīd), *n.* 1 act of killing a king. 2 person who kills a king.

re gime or **ré gime** (ri zhēm′, rā zhēm′), *n.* 1 system, method, or form of government or rule. 2 any prevailing political or social system. 3 period or length of a regime. 4 system of living; regimen. [< French *régime* < Latin *regimen.* Doublet of REGIMEN.]

reg i men (rej′ə men, rej′ə mən), *n.* 1 set of rules or habits of diet, exercise, or manner of living intended to improve health, reduce weight, etc. 2 government; rule. [< Latin < *regere* to rule. Doublet of REGIME.]

reg i ment (*n.* rej′ə mənt; *v.* rej′ə ment), *n.* 1 a military unit consisting of several battalions or squadrons, usually commanded by a colonel. 2 a large number. *—v.t.* 1 form into a regiment or organized group. 2 assign to a regiment or group. 3 treat in a strict or uniform manner: *A totalitarian state regiments its citizens.* [< Late Latin *regimentum* rule < Latin *regere* to rule]

reg i men tal (rej′ə men′tl), *adj.* of or having to do with a regiment. *—n.* **regimentals,** *pl.* a military uniform. **—reg′i men′tal ly,** *adv.*

reg i men ta tion (rej′ə men tā′shən), *n.* 1 formation into organized or uniform groups. 2 a making uniform. 3 subjection to control.

Re gi na (ri jī′nə), *n.* city in S central Canada, capital of Saskatchewan. 137,000.

re gion (rē′jən), *n.* 1 any large part of the

earth's surface: *the region of the equator.* 2 any place, space, or area: *an unhealthful region.* 3 part of the body: *the region of the heart.* 4 field of thought or action; sphere; domain: *the region of art, the region of imagination.* 5 an administrative division. [< Latin *regionem* direction < *regere* to rule, direct]

re gion al (rē′jə nəl), *adj.* 1 of or in a particular region: *a regional storm.* 2 of a particular part of the body: *a regional disorder.* **—re′gion al ly,** *adv.*

re gion al ism (rē′jə nə liz′əm), *n.* 1 strong or steadfast attachment to a certain region. 2 stress on regional customs, peculiarities, etc., in literature and art. 3 expression, dialect, custom, etc., peculiar to a region.

re gion al ist (rē′jə nə list), *n.* person who practices regionalism. *—adj.* of or inclined to regionalism.

reg is ter (rej′ə stər), *v.t.* 1 write in a list or record: *Register the names of the new members.* 2 have (a letter, parcel, etc.) recorded in a post office, paying extra postage for special care in delivery. 3 record automatically; indicate: *The thermometer registers 90 degrees.* 4 show (surprise, joy, anger, etc.) by the expression on one's face or by actions. 5 cause (lines, columns, colors, etc.) to fit or correspond exactly in printing. *—v.i.* 1 write or have one's name written in a list or record: *register at a hotel.* 2 show surprise, joy, anger, etc., by one's expression or actions. 3 (of lines, columns, colors, etc.) fit or correspond exactly in printing.
—n. 1 a written or printed list or record: *a register of class attendance.* 2 book in which a list or record is kept: *a hotel register.* 3 a mechanical device that automatically counts or records. A cash register shows the amount of money taken in. 4 the range of a voice or an instrument. 5 an opening in a wall or floor with a device to regulate the amount of heated or cooled air that passes through. 6 registration or registry. 7 registrar. 8 the set of pipes of an organ stop. 9 the exact fit or correspondence of lines, columns, colors, etc., in printing.
[< Medieval Latin *registrum,* alteration of Late Latin *regesta* list, things transcribed < Latin *regerere* to record < *re-* back + *gerere* carry]

registered nurse, a graduate nurse licensed by state authority to practice nursing.

reg is tra ble (rej′ə strə bəl), *adj.* that can be registered.

reg is trant (rej′ə strənt), *n.* person who registers.

reg is trar (rej′ə strär, rej′ə strär′), *n.* official who keeps a register; official recorder.

reg is tra tion (rej′ə strā′shən), *n.* 1 act of registering. 2 an entry in a register. 3 number of people registered. 4 a legal document showing that some person or thing has been registered: *an automobile registration.*

reg is try (rej′ə strē), *n., pl.* **-tries.** 1 act of registering; registration. 2 (of a ship) a being registered as the property of an individual or corporation of a particular country, under the flag of which it sails. 3 place where a register is kept; office of registration. 4 book in which a record is kept; register.

reg nant (reg′nənt), *adj.* 1 ruling. 2 exercising sway or influence; predominant. 3 prevalent; widespread. [< Latin *regnantem* < *regnum* kingdom]

reg o lith (reg′ə lith), *n.* the layer of soil and loose rock fragments overlying solid rock; mantle rock. [< Greek *rhēgos* blanket]

re gress (*v.* ri gres′; *n.* rē′gres), *v.i.* 1 go back; move in a backward direction. 2 return to an earlier or less advanced state. *—v.t.* (in psychology) cause regression in (a person). *—n.* a going back; movement backward. [< Latin *regressum* gone back < *re-* + *gradi* go]

re gres sion (ri gresh′ən), *n.* 1 act of regressing. 2 (in psychology) reversion to an earlier stage or way of thinking, feeling, acting, etc. 3 (in biology) reversion to a less developed state or form or to an average type.

re gres sive (ri gres′iv), *adj.* 1 showing regression. 2 decreasing in proportion to the increase of something else: *A regressive tax is one whose rate becomes lower as the sum to which it is applied becomes larger.* **—re gres′sive ly,** *adv.* **—re gres′sive ness,** *n.*

re gret (ri gret′), *v.,* **-gret ted, -gret ting,** *n.* *—v.t.* feel sorry for or about. *—v.i.* feel sorry; mourn. *—n.* 1 the feeling of being sorry; sorrow; sense of loss. See synonym study below. 2 **regrets,** *pl.* a polite reply declining an invitation. [< Old French *regreter,* originally, bewail (a death)] **—re gret′ter,** *n.*

Syn. *n.* 1 **Regret, remorse** mean a feeling of sorrow for a fault or wrongdoing. **Regret** suggests sorrow or dissatisfaction about something one has done or failed to do, sometimes something one could not help: *With regret she remembered her forgotten promise.* **Remorse** suggests the mental suffering of a gnawing or guilty conscience: *The boy was filled with remorse for the worry he had caused his mother.*

re gret ful (ri gret′fəl), *adj.* feeling or expressing regret. **—re gret′ful ly,** *adv.* **—re gret′ful ness,** *n.*

re gret ta ble (ri gret′ə bəl), *adj.* that should be or is regretted. **—re gret′ta bly,** *adv.*

Regt., 1 regent. 2 regiment.

reg u lar (reg′yə lər), *adj.* 1 fixed by custom or rule; usual; normal: *Six o'clock was his regular hour of rising.* 2 following some rule or principle; according to rule: *A period is the regular ending for a sentence.* 3 coming, acting, or done again and again at the same time: *regular attendance at church.* 4 steady; habitual: *A regular customer trades often at the same store.* See **steady** for synonym study. 5 even in size, spacing, or speed; well-balanced: *regular features, regular teeth, regular breathing.* 6 symmetrical. 7 having all its angles equal and all its sides equal: *a regular polygon.* 8 having all the same parts of a flower alike in shape and size. 9 (of a crystal) isometric. 10 orderly; methodical: *lead a regular life.* 11 properly fitted or trained: *The regular cook in our cafeteria is sick.* 12 (of a word) inflected in the usual way to show tense, number, person, etc. "Ask" is a regular verb. 13 INFORMAL. thorough; complete: *a regular bore.* 14 fine; agreeable: *He's a regular fellow.* 15 permanently organized: *The regular army of a country consists of professional soldiers and provides a permanent standing force.* 16 of or belonging to the permanent armed forces of a country. 17 belonging to a religious order bound by certain rules: *regular clergy.* 18 U.S. having to do with or conforming to the requirements of a political party or other organization: *the regular candidate, a regular ticket.*
—n. 1 member of a regularly paid group of any kind: *The fire department was made up of regulars and volunteers.* 2 member of the permanent army of a country. 3 person belonging to a religious order bound by certain rules. 4 (in sports) a player who plays in all or most of a team's games. 5 U.S. a party member who faithfully stands by his party. [< Latin *regularis* < *regula.* See RULE.]

hat, āge, fär; let, ēqual, tėrm;
it, īce; hot, ōpen, ôrder;
oil, out; cup, pu̇t, rüle;
ch, child; ng, long; sh, she;
th, thin; ᴛʜ, then; zh, measure;

ə represents *a* in about, *e* in taken, *i* in pencil, *o* in lemon, *u* in circus.

< = from, derived from, taken from.

regular army, the permanent part of a national army, made up of professional soldiers rather than draftees.

reg u lar i ty (reg′yə lar′ə tē), *n.* condition of being regular.

reg u lar ize (reg′yə lə rīz′), *v.t.,* **-ized, -iz ing.** make regular. **—reg′u lar i za′tion,** *n.*

reg u lar ly (reg′yə lər lē), *adv.* 1 in a regular manner. 2 at regular times.

reg u late (reg′yə lāt), *v.t.,* **-lat ed, -lat ing.** 1 control by rule, principle, or system: *regulate the behavior of students.* 2 put in condition to work properly. 3 keep at some standard: *regulate the temperature of a room.*

reg u la tion (reg′yə lā′shən), *n.* 1 control by rule, principle, or system. 2 rule; law: *traffic regulations.* *—adj.* 1 according to or required by some rule; standard: *a regulation uniform.* 2 usual; ordinary.

reg u la tive (reg′yə lā′tiv), *adj.* regulating.

reg u la tor (reg′yə lā′tər), *n.* 1 person or thing that regulates. 2 device in a clock or watch for causing it to go faster or slower. 3 a very accurate clock used as a standard of time.

reg u la to ry (reg′yə lə tôr′ē, reg′yə lə-tōr′ē), *adj.* regulating.

Reg u lus (reg′yə ləs), *n.* star of the first magnitude in the constellation Leo.

re gur gi tate (rē gėr′jə tāt), *v.,* **-tat ed, -tat ing.** *—v.i.* (of liquids, gases, undigested foods, etc.) rush, surge, or flow back. *—v.t.* throw up; vomit: *The baby regurgitated food from his stomach.* [< Medieval Latin *regurgitatum* thrown back < Latin *re-* + *gurges* whirlpool] **—re gur′gi ta′tion,** *n.*

re ha bil i tate (rē′hə bil′ə tāt), *v.t.,* **-tat ed, -tat ing.** 1 restore to a good condition; make over in a new form: *The old neighborhood is to be rehabilitated.* 2 restore to former standing, rank, rights, privileges, reputation, etc.: *The former criminal completely rehabilitated himself and again became a trusted and respected citizen.* 3 restore to a condition of good health, or to a level of useful activity, by means of medical treatment and therapy. [< Medieval Latin *rehabilitatum* made fit again < Latin *re-* + *habilis* fit] **—re′ha bil′i ta′tion,** *n.*

re hash (*v.* rē hash′; *n.* rē′hash), *v.t.* deal with again; work up (old material) in a new or different form. *—n.* 1 a rehashing; putting something old into a new or different form. 2 something old put into a new or different form.

re hears al (ri hėr′səl), *n.* a rehearsing; performance beforehand for practice or drill.

re hearse (ri hėrs′), *v.*, **-hearsed, -hears ing.** —*v.t.* 1 practice (a play, part, etc.) for a public performance. 2 drill or train (a person, etc.) by repetition. 3 tell in detail; repeat: *She rehearsed all the happenings of the day from beginning to end.* 4 tell one by one; enumerate. —*v.i.* recite; rehearse a play, part, etc. [< Old French *rehercier* rake over < *re-* again + *hercier* to rake, harrow] **—re hears′er,** *n.*

Reich (rīH), *n.* Germany as an empire or state (a term applied to the Holy Roman Empire, 962-1806; the German Empire, 1871-1918; and Nazi Germany, 1933-1945).

reichs mark (rīHs′märk′), *n., pl.* **-marks** or **-mark.** the former monetary unit of Germany, established in 1924 and replaced by the Deutsche mark in 1948. [< German *Reichsmark*]

Reichs tag (rīHs′täk′), *n.* the former elective legislative assembly of Germany.

reign (rān), *n.* 1 period of power of a ruler: *Queen Victoria's reign lasted sixty-four years.* 2 act of ruling; royal power; rule: *The reign of a wise ruler benefits his country.* 3 existence everywhere; prevalence. —*v.i.* 1 be a ruler; rule: *A king reigns over his kingdom.* 2 exist everywhere; prevail: *On a still night silence reigns.* [< Old French *reigne* < Latin *regnum* < *regem* king]

Reign of Terror, period of the French Revolution from about June 1793 to July 1794 during which many persons considered undesirable by the ruling group were ruthlessly executed.

re im burse (rē′im bėrs′), *v.t.*, **-bursed, -burs ing.** pay back; repay (a person or a sum expended). [< *re-* + obsolete *imburse* < Medieval Latin *imbursare* < Latin *in-* into + Late Latin *bursa* purse] **—re′im burs′a ble,** *adj.* **—re′im burse′ment,** *n.*

Reims (rēmz; *French* raNs), *n.* city in NE France. Nearly all the French kings were crowned in its cathedral. 121,000. Also, **Rheims.**

rein (rān), *n.* 1 Usually, **reins,** *pl.* a long, narrow strap or line fastened to the bit on each side of the head, by which to guide and control an animal. See **harness** for picture. 2 a means of control and direction: *seize the reins of government.* 3 **draw rein, a** tighten the reins. **b** slow down; stop. 4 **give rein to,** let move or act freely, without guidance or control. 5 **take the reins,** assume control. —*v.t.* 1 check or pull with reins. 2 guide and control: *Rein your tongue.* [< Old French *rene* < Popular Latin *retina* < Latin *retinere* hold back. See RETAIN.]

re in car nate (rē′in kär′nāt), *v.t.*, **-nat ed, -nat ing.** give a new body to (a soul).

re in car na tion (rē′in kär nā′shən), *n.* 1 rebirth of the soul in a new body. 2 a new incarnation or embodiment.

rein deer (rān′dir′), *n., pl.* **-deer** or **-deers.** a large deer with branching antlers, native to Greenland and northern regions of the Old World, used to pull sleighs and for meat, milk, and hides. The caribou and reindeer are now considered to be the same species. [< Scandinavian (Old Icelandic) *hreindȳri* < *hreinn* reindeer + *dȳr* animal]

re in force (rē′in fôrs′, rē′in fōrs′), *v.t.*, **-forced, -forc ing.** 1 strengthen with new force or materials: *reinforce a bridge.* 2 strengthen by additional troops, units, etc.: *reinforce an army.* 3 make more forcible: *reinforce an argument, reinforce an effect.* Also, **reenforce, re-enforce. —re′in forc′er,** *n.*

reinforced concrete, concrete with metal embedded in it to make the structure stronger; ferroconcrete.

re in force ment (rē′in fôrs′mənt, rē′in fōrs′mənt), *n.* 1 act of reinforcing. 2 a being reinforced. 3 something that reinforces. 4 **reinforcements,** *pl.* extra soldiers, warships, planes, etc. Also, **reenforcement, re-enforcement.**

re in state (rē′in stāt′), *v.t.*, **-stat ed, -stat ing.** put back in a former position or condition; establish again. **re′in state′ment,** *n.*

re in sure (rē′in shůr′), *v.t.*, **-sured, -sur ing.** insure again; insure under a contract by which a first insurer relieves himself from the risk and transfers it to another insurer.

re in vest (rē′in vest′), *v.t., v.i.* 1 invest again or in a new way. 2 invest income obtained from a previous investment. **—re′in vest′ment,** *n.*

re is sue (rē ish′ü, rē ish′yü), *v.*, **-sued, -su ing,** *n.* —*v.t., v.i.* issue again or in a new way. —*n.* a second or repeated issue: *the reissue of a best seller at a lower price.*

re it e rate (rē it′ə rāt′), *v.t.*, **-rat ed, -rat ing.** say or do several times; repeat (an action, demand, etc.) again and again: *The teacher reiterated her command.* See **repeat** for synonym study. **—re it′e ra′tion,** *n.*

re it e ra tive (rē it′ə rā′tiv), *adj.* repetitious. **—re it′e ra′tive ly,** *adv.*

re ject (*v.* ri jekt′; *n.* rē′jekt), *v.t.* 1 refuse to take, use, believe, consider, grant, etc.: *They rejected our help.* See **refuse** for synonym study. 2 throw away as useless or unsatisfactory: *Reject all apples with soft spots.* 3 repulse or rebuff (a person or an appeal). 4 vomit. 5 (of the body) to resist the introduction of (foreign tissue) by the mechanism of immunity. —*n.* a rejected person or thing. [< Latin *rejectum* thrown back < *re-* back + *jacere* to throw] **—re ject′er,** *n.*

re jec tion (ri jek′shən), *n.* 1 act of rejecting. 2 condition of being rejected. 3 thing rejected. 4 immunological resistance of the body to the grafting or implantation of foreign tissue.

re joice (ri jois′), *v.*, **-joiced, -joic ing.** —*v.i.* be glad; be filled with joy. —*v.t.* make glad; fill with joy; cheer; delight. [< Old French *rejoiss-*, a form of *rejoïr* rejoice < *re-* again + *joïr* have joy] **—re joic′er,** *n.*

reindeer
about 4 ft. high at the shoulder

re joic ing (ri joi′sing), *n.* 1 the feeling or expression of joy. 2 occasion for joy. **—re joic′ing ly,** *adv.*

re join[1] (rē join′), *v.t.* 1 join again. 2 join the company of again.

re join[2] (ri join′), *v.t.* say in answer; reply. [< Old French *rejoindre* < *re-* + *joindre* join]

re join der (ri join′dər), *n.* an answer to a reply; response.

re ju ve nate (ri jü′və nāt), *v.t.*, **-nat ed, -nat ing.** make young or vigorous again; give youthful qualities to. [< *re-* + Latin *juvenis* young] **—re ju′ve na′tion,** *n.* **—re ju′ve na′tor,** *n.*

rel., 1 relating. 2 relative.

re-laid (rē lād′), *v.* pt. and pp. of **re-lay.**

re lapse (ri laps′), *v.*, **-lapsed, -laps ing,** *n.* —*v.i.* 1 fall or slip back: *relapse into silence.* 2 fall back into wrongdoing; backslide. 3 have a return of the symptoms of an illness following convalescence. —*n.* a relapsing: *I seemed to be getting over my illness but had a relapse.* **—re laps′er,** *n.*

relapsing fever, any of several recurring infectious diseases characterized by chills, fever, and muscular pain, caused by spirochetes transmitted by lice or ticks.

re late (ri lāt′), *v.*, **-lat ed, -lat ing.** —*v.t.* 1 give an account of; tell; narrate: *relate one's adventures.* 2 connect in thought or meaning: *"Better" and "best" are related to "good."* —*v.i.* 1 be connected in any way; pertain: *We are interested in what relates to ourselves.* 2 have a friendly or close social relationship. [< Latin *relatum* brought back, related < *re-* back + *latum* brought] **—re lat′er,** *n.*

re lat ed (ri lā′tid), *adj.* 1 connected in any way. 2 belonging to the same family; connected by a common origin. 3 (in music) relative. **—re lat′ed ness,** *n.*

re la tion (ri lā′shən), *n.* 1 act of telling; account. 2 connection in thought or meaning: *Your answer has no relation to the question.* 3 connection by family ties of blood or marriage; relationship: *the close relation of mother and child.* 4 a related person; relative. 5 **relations,** *pl.* dealings between persons, groups, countries, etc.: *international relations.* 6 (in mathematics) a set of ordered pairs. 7 **in relation to** or **with relation to,** in reference to; in regard to.

re la tion al (ri lā′shə nəl), *adj.* having to do with relations.

re la tion ship (ri lā′shən ship), *n.* 1 connection. 2 condition of belonging to the same family. 3 state or condition that exists between people or groups that deal with one another: *a business relationship, a social relationship.*

rel a tive (rel′ə tiv), *n.* 1 person who belongs to the same family as another, such as father, brother, aunt, etc. 2 a relative pronoun. —*adj.* 1 related or compared to each other: *We considered the relative merits of the two proposals.* 2 **relative to, a** about; concerning. **b** in proportion to; in comparison with; for. 3 depending for meaning on a relation to something else: *East is a relative term; for example, Chicago is east of California but west of New York.* 4 in grammar: **a** introducing a subordinate clause; referring to a person or thing mentioned. In "The man who wanted it is gone," *who* is a relative pronoun. *That, which, who, whose, what,* and *whom* are relative pronouns. **b** introduced by a relative pronoun: *a relative clause.* In "The ball that had been lost was found," *that had been lost* is a relative clause. 5 (in music) having a close harmonic relation; having the same signature: *a relative minor.* **—rel′a tive ness,** *n.*

relative frequency, (in statistics) the ratio of the number of actual occurrences to the possible occurrences. EXAMPLE: If E occurs x times in N trials, then $\frac{x}{N}$ is the relative frequency of E.

hat, āge, fär; let, ēqual, tėrm;
it, īce; hot, ōpen, ôrder;
oil, out; cup, pu̇t, rüle;
ch, child; ng, long; sh, she;
th, thin; ᴛʜ, then; zh, measure;

ə represents *a* in about, *e* in taken, *i* in pencil, *o* in lemon, *u* in circus.

< = from, derived from, taken from.

relative humidity, the ratio between the amount of water vapor present in the air and the greatest amount the air could contain at the same temperature.

rel a tive ly (rel′ə tiv lē), *adv.* 1 in relation to something else; comparatively: *a relatively small difference.* 2 with respect to some relation. 3 in proportion *(to): be strong relatively to one's size.*

rel a tiv ist (rel′ə tə vist), *n.* person who believes in relativity.

rel a tiv is tic (rel′ə tə vis′tik), *adj.* of or having to do with relativity. **—rel′a tiv is′ti cal ly,** *adv.*

rel a tiv i ty (rel′ə tiv′ə tē), *n.* 1 a being relative. 2 (in physics) the character of being relative rather than absolute, as ascribed to motion or velocity. 3 theory concerning the concepts of matter, space, time, and motion, expressed in certain equations by Albert Einstein. According to the **special theory of relativity,** if two systems are moving uniformly in relation to each other, it is impossible to determine anything about their motion except that it is relative, and the velocity of light is constant, independent of either the velocity of its source or an observer. Thus it can be mathematically derived that mass and energy are interchangeable, as expressed in the equation $E = mc^2$, where c = the velocity of light; that a moving object appears to be shortened in the direction of the motion to an observer at rest; that a clock in motion appears to run slower than a stationary clock to an observer at rest; and that the mass of an object increases with its velocity. The **general theory of relativity** is an extension of the above theory, and deals with the equivalence of gravitational and inertial forces.

re la tor (ri lā′tər), *n.* person who relates or narrates.

re lax (ri laks′), *v.t., v.i.* 1 make or become less stiff or firm; loosen up: *Relax your muscles to rest them. Relax when you dance.* 2 make or become less strict or severe; lessen in force: *Discipline was relaxed on the last day of school.* 3 relieve or be relieved from work or effort; give or take recreation or amusement: *A vacation is for relaxing.* 4 lessen in force or intensity; weaken; slacken: *Don't relax your efforts because the examinations are over.* [< Latin *relaxare* < *re-* back + *laxus* loose. Doublet of RELEASE.] **—re lax′er,** *n.*

re lax ant (ri lak′sənt), *n.* practice or drug serving to produce relaxation: *a muscle relaxant.*

re lax a tion (rē′lak sā′shən), *n.* 1 a loosening: *the relaxation of the muscles.* 2 a lessening of strictness, severity, force, etc. 3 recreation; amusement. 4 condition of being relaxed.

re lax ed ly (ri lak′sid lē), *adv.* in a relaxed manner.

re lay (*n.* rē′lā; *v. also* ri lā′), *n.* 1 a fresh supply: *New relays of men were sent to fight the fire.* 2 relay race. 3 one part of a relay race. 4 an electromagnetic device with a weak current which acts as a switch for a circuit with a stronger current, used in equipment for transmitting telegraph and telephone messages. 5 device that extends or reinforces the action or effect of an apparatus, as a servomotor. 6 act of passing on a ball, puck, etc., from one player to another. *—v.t.* 1 take and carry farther: *Messengers will relay your message.* 2 transmit by an electrical relay. 3 provide or replace with a fresh supply. [< Old French *relai* a reserve pack of hounds, etc. < *re-* back + *laier* to leave]

re-lay (rē lā′), *v.t.,* **-laid, -lay ing.** lay again.

re lay race (rē′lā), race in which each member of a team runs, swims, etc., only a certain part of the distance.

re lease (ri lēs′), *v.,* **-leased, -leas ing,** *n.* *—v.t.* 1 let go: *Release the catch and the box will open.* 2 let loose; set free: *She released him from his promise.* See synonym study below. 3 relieve: *The nurse is released from duty at seven o'clock.* See **dismiss** for synonym study. 4 give up (legal right, claim, etc.); make over to another (property, etc.). 5 permit to be published, shown, sold, etc. *—n.* 1 a letting go; setting free. 2 freedom; relief. 3 part of a machine that sets other parts free to move. 4 the legal surrender of a right, estate, etc., to another. 5 document that does this. 6 permission for publication, exhibition, sale, etc. 7 article, book, film, etc., distributed for publication. [< Old French *relaissier* < Latin *relaxare.* Doublet of RELAX.] **—re leas′a ble,** *adj.* **—re leas′er,** *n.*

Syn. *v.t.* 2 **Release, free** mean to set loose from something that holds back. **Release** suggests relaxing the hold on the person or thing: *He released the brakes of the truck.* **Free** suggests removing or unfastening whatever is holding back: *He freed the bird from the cage.*

re-lease (rē lēs′), *v.t.,* **-leased, -leas ing.** lease again.

released time, U.S. time given up by public schools for religious education or other legally appointed instruction outside of school.

rel e gate (rel′ə gāt), *v.t.,* **-gat ed, -gat ing.** 1 put away, usually to a lower position or condition. 2 send into exile; banish. 3 hand over (a matter, task, etc.). [< Latin *relegatum* sent back < *re-* back + *legare* send with a commission] **—rel′e ga′tion,** *n.*

re lent (ri lent′), *v.i.* become less harsh or cruel; be more tender and merciful. [ultimately < Latin *re-* again + *lentus* slow]

re lent less (ri lent′lis), *adj.* without pity; not relenting; unyielding. **—re lent′less ly,** *adv.* **—re lent′less ness,** *n.*

rel e vance (rel′ə vəns), *n.* a being relevant.

rel e van cy (rel′ə vən sē), *n.* relevance.

rel e vant (rel′ə vənt), *adj.* bearing upon or connected with the matter in hand; to the point. See **pertinent** for synonym study. [< Latin *relevantem* relieving, refreshing < *re-* back + *levis* light[2]] **—rel′e vant ly,** *adv.*

re li a bil i ty (ri lī′ə bil′ə tē), *n.* quality or condition of being reliable; trustworthiness; dependability.

re li a ble (ri lī′ə bəl), *adj.* worthy of trust; that can be depended on. See synonym study below. **—re li′a ble ness,** *n.* **—re li′a bly,** *adv.*

Syn. Reliable, trustworthy mean worthy of being depended on or trusted. **Reliable** implies that a person or thing can safely be trusted and counted on to do or be what is expected: *I have always found this to be a reliable brand of canned goods.* **Trustworthy** implies that a person is fully deserving of confidence in his truthfulness, honesty, good judgment, etc.: *He is a trustworthy news commentator.*

re li ance (ri lī′əns), *n.* 1 trust or dependence. 2 confidence. 3 thing on which one depends.

re li ant (ri lī′ənt), *adj.* 1 trusting or depending; relying. 2 confident. 3 self-reliant. **—re li′ant ly,** *adv.*

rel ic (rel′ik), *n.* 1 thing, custom, etc., that remains from the past: *This ruined bridge is a relic of the Civil War.* 2 something belonging to a holy person, kept as a sacred memorial. 3 object having interest because of its age or its associations with the past; keepsake; souvenir. 4 **relics,** *pl.* **a** remains; ruins. **b** ARCHAIC. the remains of a person; corpse. [< Old French *relique* < Latin *reliquiae,* plural, remains < *relinquere* relinquish]

rel ict (rel′ikt), *n.* 1 widow. 2 plant or animal surviving from an earlier period. [< Late Latin *relicta* < Latin *relinquere.* See RELINQUISH.]

relief (def. 8)
left, bas-relief; right, high relief

re lief (ri lēf′), *n.* 1 the removal or lessening of some cause of pain, distress, or anxiety. 2 something that lessens or removes pain, distress, or anxiety; aid; help. 3 help given to poor people, especially money or food. 4 something that makes a pleasing change or lessens strain. 5 release from a post of duty, often by the coming of a substitute. 6 change of persons on duty, especially the replacing of a sentinel, watchman, etc. 7 person or persons who relieve others from duty. 8 projection of figures or designs from a surface in sculpture, drawing, or painting. 9 figure or design standing out from the surface from which it is cut, shaped, or stamped. 10 the appearance of standing out from a surface given to a drawing or painting by the use of shadow, shading, color, or line. 11 differences in height between the summits and lowlands of a region. 12 **in relief, a** standing out from a surface. **b** in a strong, clear manner; with distinctness. 14 **on relief,** receiving money to live on from public funds. [< Old French < *relever.* See RELIEVE.]

relief map, map that shows the different heights of a surface by using shading, colors, etc., or solid materials such as clay.

relief pitcher, a baseball pitcher who enters a game to relieve another pitcher.

re lieve (ri lēv′), *v.t.,* **-lieved, -liev ing.** 1 make less; make easier; reduce the pain or trouble of; alleviate: *Aspirin will relieve a* *headache.* 2 set free: *Her arrival relieved me of the bother of writing a letter.* 3 free (a person on duty) by taking his place. 4 bring aid to; help: *Soldiers were sent to relieve the fort.* 5 give variety or a pleasing change to: *The black dress was relieved by red trimming.* 6 make stand out more clearly. [< Old French *relever* < Latin *relevare* lighten < *re-* back + *levis* light[2]] **—re liev′er,** *n.*

re li gion (ri lij′ən), *n.* 1 belief in and worship of God or gods. 2 a particular system of faith and worship: *the Christian religion.* 3 matter of conscience: *She makes a religion of punctuality.* [< Latin *religionem* respect for what is sacred]

re li gion ist (ri lij′ə nist), *n.* person devoted to religion.

re li gi os i ty (ri lij′ē os′ə tē), *n.* 1 religious feeling or sentiment; piety. 2 affectation of religious feeling.

re li gious (ri lij′əs), *adj., n., pl.* **-gious.** *—adj.* 1 of religion; connected with religion. 2 much interested in religion; devoted to religion. 3 belonging to an order of monks, nuns, friars, etc. 4 of or connected with such an order. 5 very careful; strict; scrupulous. *—n.* monk, nun, friar, etc.; member of a religious order. **—re li′gious ly,** *adv.* **—re li′gious ness,** *n.*

re lin quish (ri ling′kwish), *v.t.* 1 give up; let go; release: *The dog relinquished his bone.* 2 abandon: *relinquish all hope.* 3 renounce; resign: *relinquish a throne.* [< Old French *relinquiss-*, a form of *relinquir* leave behind < Latin *relinquere* < *re-* + *linquere* to leave] **—re lin′quish ment,** *n.*

rel i quar y (rel′ə kwer′ē), *n., pl.* **-quar ies.** a small box or other receptacle for a relic or relics.

rel ish (rel′ish), *n.* 1 a pleasant taste; good flavor: *Hunger gives relish to simple food.* 2 something to add flavor to food, such as olives, pickles, or a highly seasoned sauce. 3 a slight dash (of something). 4 keen enjoyment or appetite; zest: *eat with great relish.* 5 liking; desire: *The teacher has no relish for old jokes.* *—v.t.* 1 like the taste of; enjoy: *A cat relishes cream.* 2 care for; like: *We did not relish the prospect of staying after school.* 3 give flavor to; make pleasing. [earlier *reles* < Old French, remainder < *relesser, relaissier* release. See RELEASE.]

re live (rē liv′), *v.,* **re lived, re liv ing.** *—v.i.* live again or anew. *—v.t.* live over or through again.

re lo cate (rē lō′kāt), *v.t., v.i.,* **-cat ed, -cat ing.** to locate or settle anew; move to a new location: *relocate a family.* **—re′lo ca′tion,** *n.*

re luc tance (ri luk′təns), *n.* 1 a reluctant feeling or action; unwillingness. 2 slowness in action because of unwillingness. 3 (in physics) the resistance offered to the passage of magnetic lines of force, equivalent to the ratio of the magnetomotive force to the magnetic flux.

re luc tan cy (ri luk′tən sē), *n.* reluctance.

re luc tant (ri luk′tənt), *adj.* 1 showing unwillingness; unwilling. See synonym study below. 2 slow to act because unwilling: *be reluctant to leave.* [< Latin *reluctantem* struggling against < *re-* back + *luctari* to struggle] **—re luc′tant ly,** *adv.*

Syn. 1 **Reluctant, loath** mean unwilling to do something. **Reluctant** implies mere lack of willingness, due to distaste for what is to be done, to irresolution, or simply to laziness: *She gave us her reluctant consent.* **Loath** implies strong unwillingness because one feels the thing to be done is extremely disagreeable or hateful: *His parents were loath to believe their son would steal.*

re ly (ri lī′), *v.i.,* **-lied, -ly ing.** depend *(on* or *upon)* with trust or confidence: *Can we rely on him to be on time?* See synonym study below. [< Old French *relier* < Latin *religare* bind fast < *re-* back + *ligare* to bind]

Syn. Rely, depend mean to have confidence in someone or something. **Rely** implies confidence that a person or thing will perform or be as one expects: *This is a product you can rely on.* **Depend** implies confidence that a person or thing will give the help or support expected or needed: *She depends on her friends to make her decisions.*

rem (rem), *n., pl.* **rem** or **rems.** unit for measuring absorbed doses of radiation, equivalent to one roentgen of gamma rays. [< *r(oentgen) e(quivalent) m(an)*]

REM, rapid eye movement (a phenomenon occurring during sleep, a manifestation of dreaming).

re main (ri mān′), *v.i.* 1 continue in a place or condition; stay: *remain at the seashore till October.* See **stay**[1] for synonym study. 2 continue; last; keep on: *The town remains the same year after year.* 3 be left: *A few apples remain on the trees.* *—n.* **remains,** *pl.* **a** what is left. **b** a dead body. **c** a writer's works not yet published at the time of his death. [< Old French *remaindre* < Latin *remanere* < *re-* back + *manere* to stay]

re main der (ri mān′dər), *n.* 1 the part left over; the rest; balance. 2 in arithmetic: **a** number left over after subtracting one number from another. **b** number left over after dividing one number by another. 3 one of the copies of a book left in the publisher's hands after the sale has practically ceased. *—v.t.* sell as a remainder.

re make (*v.* rē māk′; *n.* rē′māk′), *v.,* **-made** (-mād′), **-mak ing,** *n.* *—v.t.* make anew; make over. *—n.* a remade product.

re mand (ri mand′), *v.t.* 1 send back. 2 send back (a prisoner or an accused person) into custody. 3 send (a case) back to the court it came from for further action there. *—n.* a remanding. [< Late Latin *remandare* < Latin *re-* back + *mandare* consign]

re mark (ri märk′), *v.t.* 1 say in a few words; state; comment. 2 notice; observe. *—v.i.* make a remark; comment. *—n.* 1 something said in a few words; short statement; comment. 2 act of noticing; observation. [< French *remarquer* < *re-* again + *marquer* to mark]

re mark a ble (ri mär′kə bəl), *adj.* worthy of notice; unusual; extraordinary. **—re mark′a ble ness,** *n.* **—re mark′a bly,** *adv.*

re mar riage (rē mar′ij), *n.* marriage after a previous marriage.

re mar ry (rē mar′ē), *v.t., v.i.,* **-ried, -ry ing.** marry again.

re match (rē′mach′), *n.* a second or subsequent match between two opponents, teams, etc.

Rem brandt van Rijn (rem′brant vän rīn′), 1606-1669, Dutch painter and etcher.

re me di a ble (ri mē′dē ə bəl), *adj.* that can be remedied or cured. **—re me′di a bly,** *adv.*

re me di al (ri mē′dē əl), *adj.* tending to relieve or cure; remedying; helping. **—re me′di al ly,** *adv.*

rem e dy (rem′ə dē), *n., pl.* **-dies,** *v.,* **-died, -dy ing.** *—n.* 1 a means of removing or relieving a disease or other disorder; cure. 2 means of counteracting or removing an outward evil of any kind; reparation, redress, or relief. *—v.t.* put right; make right; cure. See **cure** for synonym study. [< Latin *remedium* < *re-* again + *mederi* heal]

re mem ber (ri mem′bər), *v.t.* 1 call back to mind; recall: *I can't remember that woman's name.* 2 have (something) return to the mind: *Then I remembered where I was.* See synonym study below. 3 keep in mind; take care not to forget. 4 keep in mind as deserving a reward, gift, etc.: *Grandfather remembered us all in his will.* 5 mention (a person) as sending friendly greetings; recall to the mind of another. *—v.i.* 1 have memory. 2 recall something. [< Old French *remembrer* < Latin *rememorari* < *re-* again + *memor* mindful of] **—re mem′ber a ble,** *adj.* **—re mem′ber er,** *n.*

Syn. *v.t.* 1, 2 **Remember, recall, recollect** mean to think of something again by an act of memory. **Remember** applies whether the act requires conscious effort or not: *I remember many stray incidents from my childhood.* **Recall** (as well as *recollect*) applies particularly when the act requires conscious effort: *It took me a long time to recall one curious incident.* **Recollect** suggests that the thing remembered is somewhat hazy: *As I recollect, the incident occurred when I was about four.*

re mem brance (ri mem′brəns), *n.* 1 power to remember; act of remembering; memory. 2 condition of being remembered. 3 any thing or action that makes one remember a person; keepsake; souvenir. 4 **remembrances,** *pl.* greetings.

re mind (ri mīnd′), *v.t.* bring to mind; make (one) think of something; cause to remember: *This reminds me of a story.*

re mind er (ri mīn′dər), *n.* something to help one remember.

Rem ing ton (rem′ing tən), *n.* **Frederic,** 1861-1909, American painter and sculptor.

rem i nisce (rem′ə nis′), *v.i.,* **-nisced, -nisc ing.** talk or think about past experiences or events.

rem i nis cence (rem′ə nis′ns), *n.* 1 a remembering; recalling past persons, events, etc. 2 Often, **reminiscences,** *pl.* account of something remembered; recollection. 3 thing that makes one remember or think of something else. [< Latin *reminiscentia* < *reminisci* remember < *re-* again + *mens* mind]

rem i nis cent (rem′ə nis′nt), *adj.* 1 recalling past persons, events, etc. 2 awakening memories of something else; suggestive: *a manner reminiscent of a statelier age.* **—rem′i nis′cent ly,** *adv.*

re miss (ri mis′), *adj.* 1 careless or slack in doing what one has to do; neglectful; negligent: *be remiss in one's duty.* 2 characterized by carelessness, negligence, or inattention. [< Latin *remissum* remitted] **—re miss′ly,** *adv.* **—re miss′ness,** *n.*

re mis si ble (ri mis′ə bəl), *adj.* that can be remitted.

re mis sion (ri mish′ən), *n.* 1 a letting off (from debt, punishment, etc.): *The bankrupt sought remission of his debts.* 2 pardon; forgiveness: *Remission of sins is promised to those who repent.* 3 a lessening (of pain, force, labor, etc.).

re mit (ri mit′), *v.,* **-mit ted, -mit ting,** *n.* *—v.i.* 1 send money to a person or place: *Enclosed is our bill; please remit.* 2 become less. —*v.t.* 1 send (money due). 2 refrain from carrying out; refrain from exacting; cancel: *The governor remitted the prisoner's punishment.* 3 pardon; forgive: *power to remit sins.* 4 make less; decrease: *After we had rowed the boat into calm water we remitted our efforts.* 5 send back (a case) to a lower court for further action. 6 put back. 7 postpone. —*n.* transfer of a case from one court or judge to another. [< Latin *remittere* send back < *re-* + *mittere* send] **—re mit′ta ble,** *adj.* **—re mit′ter,** *n.*

re mit tal (ri mit′l), *n.* remission.

re mit tance (ri mit′ns), *n.* 1 a sending money to someone at a distance. 2 the money that is sent.

re mit tent (ri mit′nt), *adj.* lessening for a time; lessening at intervals: *a remittent type of fever.* **—re mit′tent ly,** *adv.*

rem nant (rem′nənt), *n.* 1 a small part left; fragment. 2 piece of cloth, ribbon, lace, etc., left after the rest has been used or sold. [< Old French *remenant* < *remenoir* remain < Latin *remanere.* See REMAIN.]

re mod el (rē mod′l), *v.t.,* **-eled, -el ing** or **-elled, -el ling.** 1 model again. 2 make over; change or alter: *The old barn was remodeled into a house.*

re mon strance (ri mon′strəns), *n.* act of remonstrating; protest; complaint.

re mon strant (ri mon′strənt), *adj.* remonstrating; protesting. —*n.* person who remonstrates.

re mon strate (ri mon′strāt), *v.i.,* **-strat ed, -strat ing.** speak, reason, or plead in complaint or protest: *The teacher remonstrated with us about our unruly behavior.* [< Medieval Latin *remonstratum* pointed out, ultimately < Latin *re-* back + *monstrum* sign] **—re′mon stra′tion,** *n.* **—re mon′stra tor,** *n.*

re mon stra tive (ri mon′strə tiv), *adj.* remonstrating.

remora
remoras attaching themselves to a shark

rem or a (rem′ər ə), *n.* any of certain fishes, found especially in tropical waters, with a sucker on the top of the head by which it can attach itself to ships, other fishes, etc., for transportation, protection, and food. [< Latin, delay, hindrance]

re morse (ri môrs′), *n.* deep; painful regret for having done wrong; compunction; contrition: *The thief felt remorse for his crime and confessed.* See **regret** for synonym study. [< Late Latin *remorsum* tormented, bit again < Latin *re-* back + *mordere* to bite]

re morse ful (ri môrs′fəl), *adj.* feeling or expressing remorse. **—re morse′ful ly,** *adv.* **—re morse′ful ness,** *n.*

re morse less (ri môrs′lis), *adj.* 1 without remorse. 2 pitiless; cruel. **—re morse′less ly,** *adv.* **—re morse′less ness,** *n.*

re mote (ri mōt′), *adj.,* **-mot er, -mot est.** 1 far away; far off: *a remote country, remote ages.* See **distant** for synonym study. 2 out of the way; secluded: *a remote village.* 3 distant: *a remote relative.* 4 slight; faint: *I haven't the remotest idea what you mean.* [< Latin *remotum* removed] **—re mote′ly,** *adv.* **—re mote′ness,** *n.*

remote control, control from a distance of a machine, operation, etc., usually by electrical impulses or radio signals.

re mount (*v.* rē mount′; *n.* rē′mount, rē mount′), *v.t.* 1 mount again. 2 furnish with fresh horses. —*v.i.* mount a horse or other animal again. —*n.* a fresh horse, or a supply of fresh horses, for use.

re mov al (ri mü′vəl), *n.* 1 a removing; taking away. 2 a change of place or location. 3 dismissal from an office or position.

re move (ri müv′), *v.,* **-moved, -mov ing,** *n.* —*v.t.* 1 move from a place or position; take off; take away: *Remove your hat.* 2 get rid of; put an end to: *remove all doubt.* 3 kill. 4 dismiss from an office or position: *remove an official for taking bribes.* —*v.i.* go away; move away. —*n.* 1 a moving away. 2 step or degree of distance: *At every remove the mountain seemed smaller.* [< Latin *removere* < *re-* back + *movere* to move] **—re mov′a ble,** *adj.* **—re mov′a ble ness,** *n.* **—re mov′a bly,** *adv.* **—re mov′er,** *n.*

re moved (ri müvd′), *adj.* 1 distant; remote: *a house far removed from the city.* 2 separated by one or more steps or degrees of relationship: *a cousin once removed.*

re mu ne rate (ri myü′nə rāt′), *v.t.,* **-rat ed, -rat ing.** pay for work, services, trouble, etc.; reward; recompense. See **pay** for synonym study. [< Latin *remuneratum* repaid, recompensed < *re-* back + *munus* gift] **—re mu′ne ra′tor,** *n.*

re mu ne ra tion (ri myü′nə rā′shən), *n.* a reward; pay; payment.

re mu ne ra tive (ri myü′nə rā′tiv), *adj.* that brings remuneration; paying; profitable. **—re mu′ne ra′tive ly,** *adv.* **—re mu′ne ra′tive ness,** *n.*

Re mus (rē′məs), *n.* (in Roman legends) the twin brother of Romulus.

ren ais sance (ren′ə säns′, ren′ə säns), *n.* 1 a new birth; revival: *a renaissance of interest in archaeology.* 2 **the Renaissance, a** the great revival of art and learning in Europe during the 1300's, 1400's, and 1500's. **b** period of time when this revival occurred. **c** style of art, architecture, etc., of this period. 3 any revival, or period of marked improvement and new life, in art, literature, etc. [< French, literally, rebirth < *renaître* be born again < Latin *renasci* < *re-* again + *nasci* be born]

re nal (rē′nl), *adj.* of, having to do with, or located near the kidneys. [< Latin *renalis* < *ren* kidney]

re name (rē nām′), *v.t.,* **-named, -nam ing.** give a new name to; name again.

re nas cence (ri nas′ns, ri nā′sns), *n.* 1 a new birth; revival; renewal. 2 a being renascent. 3 **Renascence,** the Renaissance.

re nas cent (ri nas′nt, ri nā′snt), *adj.* being born again; reviving; springing again into being or vigor.

rend (rend), *v.t.,* **rent, rend ing.** 1 pull apart violently; tear: *Wolves will rend a lamb.* 2 split: *Lightning rent the tree.* 3 disturb violently: *a mind rent by doubt.* 4 remove with force or violence. [Old English *rendan*]

ren der (ren′dər), *v.t.* 1 cause to become; make: *Fright rendered me speechless.* 2 give; do: *render a service, render judgment.* 3 offer for consideration, approval, payment, etc.; hand in; report: *render a bill.* 4 give in return:

hat, āge, fär; let, ēqual, tėrm;
it, īce; hot, ōpen, ôrder;
oil, out; cup, pu̇t, rüle;
ch, child; ng, long; sh, she;
th, thin; ᴛʜ, then; zh, measure;

ə represents *a* in about, *e* in taken, *i* in pencil, *o* in lemon, *u* in circus.

< = from, derived from, taken from.

render thanks. 5 pay as due: *render tribute.* 6 bring out the meaning of; represent: *The actor rendered the part of Hamlet well.* 7 play or sing (music). 8 change from one language to another; translate: *render a French poem into English.* 9 give up; surrender. 10 melt (fat, etc.); clarify or extract by melting. Fat from hogs is rendered for lard. [< Old French *rendre,* alteration of Latin *reddere* give as due, pay < *re-* back, again + *dare* give] **—ren′der a ble,** *adj.* **—ren′der er,** *n.*

ren dez vous (rän′də vü), *n., pl.* **-vous** (-vüz), *v.,* **-voused** (-vüd), **-vous ing** (-vü′ing). —*n.* 1 an appointment or engagement to meet at a fixed place or time; meeting by agreement. 2 a meeting place; gathering place: *The family had two favorite rendezvous, the library and the garden.* 3 place agreed on for a meeting at a certain time, especially of troops or ships. 4 a meeting at a fixed place or time: *the rendezvous of a lunar module and the command ship.* —*v.i.* meet at a rendezvous. —*v.t.* bring together (troops, ships, space capsules, etc.) at a fixed place. [< Middle French < *rendez-vous* present yourself!]

Renaissance (def. 2c)
an Italian church built in the 1400's

ren di tion (ren dish′ən), *n.* 1 act of rendering. 2 the rendering of a dramatic part, music, etc., so as to bring out the meaning. 3 translation. 4 the surrender of a place, person, possession, etc.

ren e gade (ren′ə gād), *n., adj., v.,* **-gad ed, -gad ing.** —*n.* deserter from a religious faith, a political party, etc.; traitor. —*adj.* like a traitor; deserting; disloyal. —*v.i.* turn renegade. [< Spanish *renegado* < *renegar* deny one's faith < Medieval Latin *renegare.* See RENEGE.]

re nege (ri nig′), *v.,* **-neged, -neg ing,** *n.* —*v.i.* 1 fail to play a card of the same suit as that first played, although one is able to do so. It is against the rules of card games to renege. 2 back out; fail to follow up: *renege on a promise.* —*n.* (in card playing) a failure to follow suit when able to do so. [< Medieval Latin *renegare* deny again, forswear < Latin

re- again + *negare* deny] **—re neg′er,** *n.*
re ne go ti ate (rē′ni gō′shē āt), *v.t., v.i.,* **-at ed, -at ing.** negotiate again or anew, especially a contract, to eliminate excessive profits. **—re′ne go′ti a′tion,** *n.*
re new (ri nü′, ri nyü′), *v.t.* 1 make new again; make like new; restore. See synonym study below. 2 make spiritually new. 3 begin again; get again; say, do, or give again: *renew an attack, renew one's efforts.* 4 replace by new material or a new thing of the same sort; fill again: *The well renews itself no matter how much water is taken away.* 5 give or get for a new period: *We renewed our lease for another year.* —*v.i.* renew a lease, note, etc. **—re-new′a ble,** *adj.* **—re new′a bly,** *adv.* **—re new′er,** *n.*
Syn. *v.t.* 1 **Renew, restore, renovate** mean to put back in a new or former condition. **Renew** means to put back in a condition like new something that has lost its freshness, force, or vigor: *She renewed the finish of the table.* **Restore** means to put back in its original, former, or normal condition something that has been damaged, worn out, partly ruined, etc.: *That old Spanish mission has been restored.* **Renovate** means to put in good condition or make like new by cleaning, repairing, redecorating, etc.: *The store was renovated.*
re new al (ri nü′əl, ri nyü′əl), *n.* 1 a renewing. 2 a being renewed.
re new ed ly (ri nü′id lē, ri nyü′id lē), *adv.* anew.
Re ni (rā′nē), *n.* **Guido,** 1575-1642, Italian painter.
ren i form (ren′ə fôrm, rē′nə fôrm), *adj.* kidney-shaped. [< Latin *ren* kidney]
ren net (ren′it), *n.* substance containing rennin, obtained from the stomach lining of a calf or other ruminant, used for curdling milk in making cheese and junket. [Middle English < *rennen* to run, Old English *rinnan*]
ren nin (ren′ən), *n.* enzyme in the gastric juice that coagulates or curdles milk. [< *rennet*]
Re no (rē′nō), *n.* city in W Nevada. 73,000.
Ren oir (ren′wär; *French* rə nwär′), *n.* **Pierre Auguste,** 1841-1919, French impressionist painter.
re nounce (ri nouns′), *v.t.,* **-nounced, -nounc ing.** 1 declare that one gives up; give up entirely; give up: *He renounces his claim to the money.* 2 cast off; refuse to recognize as one's own; repudiate; disown. [< Middle French *renoncer* < Latin *renuntiare* < *re-* back + *nuntius* message] **—re-nounce′ment,** *n.*
ren o vate (ren′ə vāt), *v.t.,* **-vat ed, -vat ing.** make new again; make like new; restore to good condition. See **renew** for synonym study. [< Latin *renovatum* made new < *re-* again + *novus* new] **—ren′o-va′tion,** *n.* **—ren′o va′tor,** *n.*
re nown (ri noun′), *n.* a being widely celebrated or held in high repute; fame. [< Anglo-French *renoun,* ultimately < Latin *re-* repeatedly + *nomen* name]
re nowned (ri nound′), *adj.* having fame; famed. See **famous** for synonym study.
rent¹ (rent), *n.* 1 a regular payment for the use of property. 2 (in economics) what is paid for the use of natural resources. 3 house or other property for which rent is received. 4 **for rent,** available in return for rent paid. —*v.t.* 1 pay at regular times for the use of (property): *We rent a house from them.* 2 receive regular pay for the use of (property): *They rent several other houses.* —*v.i.* be leased or let for rent: *This farm rents for $1500 a year.* [< Old French *rente* < Popular Latin *rendita* < Latin *reddere* render. See RENDER.] **—rent′a ble,** *adj.* **—rent′er,** *n.*
rent² (rent), *n.* a torn place; tear; split. —*adj.* torn; split. —*v.* pt. and pp. of **rend.**
rent al (ren′tl), *n.* 1 amount received or paid as rent. 2 something rented. —*adj.* having to do with or collecting rent: *a rental agent, rental value.*
rental library, a circulating library that makes a charge for lending books.
ren tier (räɴ tyā′), *n.* FRENCH. person who has a fixed income from investments in lands, stocks, etc. [< French < *rente* rent]
re nun ci a tion (ri nun′sē ā′shən), *n.* a giving up of a right, title, possession, etc.; renouncing.
re nun ci a tive (ri nun′sē ā′tiv), *adj.* that renounces.
re o pen (rē ō′pən), *v.t., v.i.* 1 open again. 2 discuss again.
re or der (rē ôr′dər), *v.t., v.i.* 1 put in order again; rearrange. 2 give a second or repeated order for goods; order again. —*n.* a second or repeated order for goods placed with the same company or person.
re or gan i za tion (rē ôr′gə nə zā′shən), *n.* 1 act or process of reorganizing. 2 the reconstruction or rehabilitation of a business that is in the hands of a receiver. 3 a being reorganized.
re or gan ize (rē ôr′gə nīz), *v.t., v.i.,* **-ized, -iz ing.** 1 organize anew; form again; arrange in a new way. 2 form a new company to operate (a business in the hands of a receiver). **—re or′gan iz′er,** *n.*
rep (rep), *n.* a heavy, ribbed fabric of wool, silk, rayon, or cotton. Also, **repp.** [< French *reps* < English *ribs*]
rep., 1 report. 2 reported. 3 reporter. 4 representative. 5 republic.

repeat (defs. 3a and 3b)

Rep., 1 Representative. 2 Republic. 3 Republican.
re paid (ri pād′), *v.* pt. and pp. of **repay.**
re pair¹ (ri per′, ri par′), *v.t.* 1 put in good condition again; mend: *repair shoes.* See **mend** for synonym study. 2 make up for; remedy: *How can I repair the harm done?* —*n.* 1 act or work of repairing. 2 Often, **repairs,** *pl.* instance or piece of repairing: *Repairs on the school building are made during the summer.* 3 condition fit to be used: *The state keeps the roads in repair.* 4 condition with respect to repairing: *The house was in bad repair.* [< Latin *reparare* < *re-* again + *parare* prepare] **—re pair′a-ble,** *adj.* **—re pair′er,** *n.*
re pair² (ri per′, ri par′), *v.i.* go (to a place): *After dinner we repaired to the porch.* [< Old French *repairier* < Late Latin *repatriare* repatriate]
re pair man (ri per′man′, ri per′mən; ri-par′man′, ri par′mən), *n., pl.* **-men.** man whose work is repairing.
rep ar a ble (rep′ər ə bəl), *adj.* that can be repaired or remedied. **—rep′ar a bly,** *adv.*
rep a ra tion (rep′ə rā′shən), *n.* 1 a giving of satisfaction or compensation for wrong or injury done. 2 **reparations,** *pl.* compensation for wrong or injury, especially payments made by a defeated country for the devastation of territory during war. 3 a repairing or a being repaired; restoration to good condition.
re par a tive (ri par′ə tiv), *adj.* 1 tending to repair. 2 having to do with or involving reparation.
rep ar tee (rep′ər tē′), *n.* 1 a witty reply or replies. 2 talk characterized by clever and witty replies. 3 cleverness and wit in making replies. [< French *repartie* < *repartir* to reply]
re pass (rē pas′), *v.t., v.i.* 1 pass back. 2 pass again.
re past (ri past′), *n.* meal; food. [< Old French, ultimately < Latin *re-* again + *pascere* to feed]
re pa tri ate (rē pā′trē āt), *v.,* **-at ed, -at ing,** *n.* —*v.t.* send back or restore to one's own country: *After peace was declared, refugees and prisoners of war were repatriated.* —*n.* a repatriated person. [< Late Latin *repatriatum* repatriated < Latin *re-* back + *patria* native land] **—re pa′tri a′tion,** *n.*
re pay (ri pā′), *v.,* **-paid, -pay ing.** —*v.t.* 1 pay back (a sum of money, etc.). 2 give back; return (a blow, visit, etc.). 3 make return for: *No thanks can repay such kindness.* 4 make return to: *Think nothing of it; your happiness more than repays me.* —*v.i.* pay back. **—re pay′ment,** *n.*
re pay a ble (ri pā′ə bəl), *adj.* that can or must be repaid.
re peal (ri pēl′), *v.t.* do away with; withdraw; rescind; annul: *Prohibition was repealed in 1933.* —*n.* act of repealing; withdrawal; abolition: *vote for the repeal of a law.* [< Old French *rapeler* < *re-* back + *apeler* to call] **—re peal′a ble,** *adj.* **—re peal′er,** *n.*
re peat (ri pēt′), *v.t.* 1 do, make, or perform again: *repeat an error.* 2 say again: *repeat a word for emphasis.* See synonym study below. 3 say over; recite: *repeat a poem from memory.* 4 say after another says: *Repeat the oath after me.* 5 tell to another or others: *Promise not to repeat the secret.* 6 **repeat oneself,** say what one has already said. —*v.i.* do or say something again. —*n.* 1 a repeating. 2 thing repeated. 3 in music: **a** passage to be repeated. **b** sign indicating this, usually a double line and two dots placed at the end of, or before and after, the passage. [< Latin *repetere* < *re-* again + *petere* aim at, seek] **—re peat′a ble,** *adj.*
Syn. *v.t.* 1, 2, **Repeat, reiterate** mean to do or say again. **Repeat,** the general word, means to say or do something over again, once or many times: *The orchestra will repeat the concert next week.* **Reiterate,** more formal, implies repeating again and again insistently and applies especially to something said: *We reiterated our requests for better bus service.*
re peat ed (ri pē′tid), *adj.* said, done, or made more than once. **—re peat′ed ly,** *adv.*
re peat er (ri pē′tər), *n.* 1 gun that can be fired several times without reloading. 2 watch or clock that, if a spring is pressed, strikes the hour it struck last. 3 U.S. student who takes a course again or fails to pass on to the next grade. 4 INFORMAL. person who is repeatedly sent to prison or a reformatory; habitual criminal. 5 any person or thing that repeats.
repeating decimal, decimal in which the same figure or series of figures is repeated indefinitely. EXAMPLES: .3333+, .2323+.
re pel (ri pel′), *v.,* **-pelled, -pel ling.** —*v.t.*

hat, āge, fär; let, ēqual, tėrm;
it, īce; hot, ōpen, ôrder;
oil, out; cup, pu̇t, rüle;
ch, child; ng, long; sh, she;
th, thin; ᴛʜ, then; zh, measure;

ə represents *a* in about, *e* in taken,
i in pencil, *o* in lemon, *u* in circus.

< = from, derived from, taken from.

1 force back; drive back; drive away: *They repelled the enemy.* 2 keep off or out; fail to mix with: *Rubber repels moisture.* 3 force apart or away by some inherent force: *Particles with similar electric charges repel each other.* 4 be displeasing to; cause disgust in. 5 reject. —*v.i.* cause dislike; displease. [< Latin *repellere* < *re-* back + *pellere* to drive]

re pel lence (ri pel′əns), *n.* repulsion.

re pel len cy (ri pel′ən sē), *n.* repulsion.

re pel lent (ri pel′ənt), *adj.* 1 disagreeable or distasteful; repugnant. 2 driving back; repelling. —*n.* anything that repels: *an insect repellent, a water repellent.* **—re pel′lent ly,** *adv.*

re pent (ri pent′), *v.i.* feel sorry for having done wrong and seek forgiveness: *The sinner repented.* —*v.t.* feel sorry for; regret: *repent one's choice.* [< Old French *repentir,* ultimately < Latin *re-* repeatedly + *paenitere* cause to regret] **—re pent′er,** *n.*

re pent ance (ri pen′təns), *n.* 1 sorrow for having done wrong; contrition. 2 sorrow; regret.

re pent ant (ri pen′tənt), *adj.* feeling repentance or regret; sorry for wrongdoing; repenting. **—re pent′ant ly,** *adv.*

re peo ple (rē pē′pəl), *v.t.,* **-pled, -pling.** 1 to people anew. 2 restock with animals.

re per cus sion (rē′pər kush′ən), *n.* 1 an indirect influence or reaction from an event: *repercussions of a scandal.* 2 sound flung back; echo. 3 a springing back; rebound; recoil.

re per cus sive (rē′pər kus′iv), *adj.* 1 causing repercussion. 2 reverberated.

rep er toire (rep′ər twär, rep′ər twôr), *n.* the list of plays, operas, parts, pieces, etc., that a company, an actor, a musician, or a singer is prepared to perform. [< French *répertoire* < Late Latin *repertorium.* See REPERTORY.]

rep er to ry (rep′ər tôr′ē, rep′ər tōr′ē), *n., pl.* **-ries.** 1 repertoire. 2 store or stock of things ready for use. 3 storehouse. [< Late Latin *repertorium* inventory < *reperire* to find, get < *re-* again + *parere* beget]

rep e ti tion (rep′ə tish′ən), *n.* 1 a repeating; doing or saying again: *Repetition helps learning.* 2 thing repeated.

rep e ti tious (rep′ə tish′əs), *adj.* full of repetitions; repeating in a tiresome way. **—rep′e ti′tious ly,** *adv.* **—rep′e ti′tious ness,** *n.*

re pet i tive (ri pet′ə tiv), *adj.* of or characterized by repetition. **—re pet′i tive ly,** *adv.* **—re pet′i tive ness,** *n.*

re phrase (rē frāz′), *v.t.,* **-phrased, -phras ing.** phrase again; say or write in a new or different way.

re pine (ri pīn′), *v.i.,* **-pined, -pin ing.** be discontented; fret; complain.

re place (ri plās′), *v.t.,* **-placed, -plac ing.** 1 fill or take the place of. See synonym study below. 2 get another in place of: *I will replace the cup I broke.* 3 put back; put in place again: *Please replace the books on the shelf.* **—re place′a ble,** *adj.*

Syn. 1 **Replace, supersede, supplant** mean to take the place of another. **Replace** means to fill as substitute or successor the place formerly held by another: *When one of the players on the team was hurt, another replaced him.* **Supersede,** a formal word used chiefly of things, suggests causing what is replaced to be put aside as out-of-date, no longer useful, etc.: *Buses have superseded streetcars.* **Supplant,** when used of a person, especially suggests forcing him out and taking over his place by scheming or treachery: *The dictator supplanted the president.*

re place ment (ri plās′mənt), *n.* 1 a replacing. 2 a being replaced. 3 something or someone that replaces.

replacement set, domain (def. 5).

re plant (rē plant′), *v.t.* plant again: *replant a garden.* —*v.i.* provide and set fresh plants: *After the killing frost, we had to replant.*

re play (*v.* rē plā′; *n.* rē′plā′), *v.t.* play (a match, game, etc.) again. —*n.* 1 a match or game played again. 2 a rerun of the videotape of a play, or portion of a game that is being televised: *We saw the touchdown again on the replay.*

re plen ish (ri plen′ish), *v.t.* fill again; provide a new supply for; renew: *replenish one's wardrobe. You had better replenish the fire.* [< Old French *repleniss-,* a form of *replenir,* fill again, ultimately < Latin *re-* again + *plenus* full] **—re plen′ish er,** *n.* **—re plen′ish ment,** *n.*

re plete (ri plēt′), *adj.* 1 abundantly supplied; filled. 2 sated (with food or drink); gorged. [< Latin *repletum* filled up < *re-* again + *plere* to fill] **—re plete′ness,** *n.*

re ple tion (ri plē′shən), *n.* 1 a being replete; fullness. 2 excessive fullness.

rep li ca (rep′lə kə), *n.* 1 a copy, duplicate, or reproduction of a work of art, especially one made by the original artist. 2 a copy or close reproduction: *There is a replica of the Mayflower in Plymouth, Massachusetts.* [< Italian < *replicare* reproduce]

rep li cate (*adj., n.* rep′lə kit; *v.* rep′lə kāt), *adj., n., v.,* **-cat ed, -cat ing.** —*adj.* 1 folded back on itself: *a replicate leaf.* 2 exactly reproduced; duplicated. —*n.* any exact reproduction or duplicate. —*v.t.* 1 fold or bend back. 2 copy exactly; reproduce; duplicate. 3 say in reply. —*v.i.* fold or bend back.

rep li ca tion (rep′lə kā′shən), *n.* 1 a fold. 2 a reproducing or duplicating. 3 an exact copy; reproduction; duplication. 4 a reply; rejoinder.

re ply (ri plī′), *v.,* **-plied, -ply ing,** *n., pl.* **-plies.** —*v.i.* 1 answer by words; respond. See **answer** for synonym study. 2 answer by action: *A pistol shot replied.* —*v.t.* give as an answer. —*n.* 1 act of replying; response. 2 an answer. [< Old French *replier* < Latin *replicare* unroll, fold back < *re-* back + *plicare* to fold]

re port (ri pôrt′, ri pōrt′), *n.* 1 account of something seen, heard, read, done, or considered. 2 an account officially or formally expressed, generally in writing. 3 the sound of a shot or an explosion: *the report of a gun.* 4 common talk; rumor: *Report has it that our neighbors are leaving town.* 5 reputation. —*v.t.* 1 make a report of; announce or state. 2 give a formal account of; state officially. 3 take down in writing; write an account of. 4 repeat (what one has heard, seen, etc.); bring back an account of; describe; tell. 5 present (oneself). 6 announce as a wrongdoer; denounce: *report someone to the police.* —*v.i.* 1 make a report; give an account of something. 2 act as a reporter. 3 present oneself; appear: *Report for duty at 9 a.m.* [< Old French < Latin *reportare* to report < *re-* back + *portare* carry] **—re port′a ble,** *adj.*

re port age (ri pôr′tij, ri pōr′tij), *n.* a reporting of news or events, especially in the style of newspaper reporters.

report card, a report sent regularly by a school to parents or guardians, indicating a student's grades or the quality of his work.

re port ed ly (ri pôr′tid lē, ri pōr′tid lē), *adv.* according to reports.

re port er (ri pôr′tər, ri pōr′tər), *n.* 1 person who reports. 2 person who gathers news for a newspaper, magazine, radio or television station, etc. 3 person who takes down reports of law cases: *a court reporter.*

rep or to ri al (rep′ər tôr′ē əl, rep′ər tōr′ē-əl), *adj.* of or having to do with reporters: *a reportorial style of writing.* **—rep′or to′ri al ly,** *adv.*

re pose[1] (ri pōz′), *n., v.,* **-posed, -pos ing.** —*n.* 1 rest or sleep: *Do not disturb her repose.* 2 quietness; ease: *She has repose of manner.* 3 peace; calmness. —*v.i.* 1 lie at rest: *The cat reposed upon the cushion.* 2 lie in a grave. 3 rest from work or toil; take a rest. 4 be supported. 5 depend; rely (on). —*v.t.* lay to rest. [< Old French *repos* < *reposer* to repose < Late Latin *repausare* cause to rest < *re-* again + *pausare* to pause]

re pose[2] (ri pōz′), *v.t.,* **-posed, -pos ing.** put; place: *We repose complete confidence in his honesty.* [< Latin *repositum* placed back < *re-* back + *ponere* to place]

re pose ful (ri pōz′fəl), *adj.* calm; quiet. **—re pose′ful ly,** *adv.* **—re pose′ful ness,** *n.*

re po si tion (rē′pə zish′ən, rep′ə zish′ən), *v.t.* 1 restore (a bone, organ of the body, etc.) to its normal position. 2 place in a new position.

re pos i to ry (ri poz′ə tôr′ē, ri poz′ə tōr′ē), *n., pl.* **-ries.** 1 place or container where things are stored or kept: *The box was the repository for old magazines.* 2 person to whom something is confided or entrusted.

re pos sess (rē′pə zes′), *v.t.* 1 possess again; get possession of again; recover. 2 put in possession again.

re pos ses sion (rē′pə zesh′ən), *n.* act or process of repossessing.

re pous sé (rə pü sā′), *adj.* 1 raised in relief by hammering on the reverse side. A repoussé design can be made on thin metal. 2 ornamented or made in this manner. [< French]

repp (rep), *n.* rep.

rep re hend (rep′ri hend′), *v.t.* reprove, rebuke, or blame. [< Latin *reprehendere,* originally, pull back < *re-* back + *prehendere* to grasp]

rep re hen si ble (rep′ri hen′sə bəl), *adj.* deserving reproof, rebuke, or blame. **—rep′re hen′si bly,** *adv.*

rep re hen sion (rep′ri hen′shən), *n.* reproof, rebuke, or blame.

rep re hen sive (rep′ri hen′siv), *adj.* reprehensible. **—rep′re hen′sive ly,** *adv.*

rep re sent (rep′ri zent′), *v.t.* 1 stand for; be a sign or symbol of: *The 50 stars in our flag represent the 50 states.* 2 act in place of; speak and act for: *People are elected to* *represent us in the government.* 3 act the part of: *Each child will represent an animal at the party.* 4 show in a picture, statue, carving, etc.; give a likeness of; portray: *This painting represents the end of the world.* 5 be a type of; be an example of: *A log represents a very simple kind of boat.* 6 set forth; describe: *represent a plan as safe.* 7 bring before the mind; make one think of: *His fears represented the undertaking as impossible.* [< Latin *repraesentare* < *re-* back + *praesentare* present[2]] **—rep′re sent′a ble,** *adj.*

rep re sen ta tion (rep′ri zen tā′shən), *n.* 1 act of representing. 2 condition or fact of being represented: *"Taxation without representation is tyranny."* 3 representatives considered as a group. 4 likeness, picture, or model. 5 performance of a play; presentation. 6 process of forming mental images or ideas. 7 account; statement. 8 protest; complaint.

rep re sen ta tion al (rep′ri zen tā′shə nəl), *adj.* of or having to do with representation.

rep re sent a tive (rep′ri zen′tə tiv), *n.* 1 person appointed or elected to act or speak for others; agent: *She is the club's representative at the convention.* 2 **Representative,** member of the House of Representatives. 3 a typical example; type: *The tiger is a representative of the cat family.* —*adj.* 1 having its citizens represented by chosen persons: *a representative government.* 2 representing: *Images representative of animals were made by the children.* 3 serving as an example of; typical: *Oak, birch, and maple are representative American hardwoods.* **—rep′re sent′a tive ly,** *adv.* **—rep′re sent′a tive ness,** *n.*

re press (ri pres′), *v.t.* 1 prevent from acting; check; curb: *repress an impulse to cough.* 2 keep down; put down; suppress: *repress a revolt.* 3 (in psychoanalysis) force a painful or undesirable memory or impulse from the conscious mind. [< Latin *repressum* pressed back < *re-* + *premere* to press] **—re press′er,** *n.*

re press i ble (ri pres′ə bəl), *adj.* that can be repressed.

re pres sion (ri presh′ən), *n.* 1 act of repressing. 2 condition of being repressed. 3 (in psychoanalysis) a defense mechanism by which painful or undesirable memories or impulses are forced out of the conscious mind but remain in the unconscious.

re pres sive (ri pres′iv), *adj.* tending to repress; having power to repress. **—re pres′sive ly,** *adv.* **—re pres′sive ness,** *n.*

re pres sor (ri pres′ər), *n.* 1 person or thing that represses. 2 substance that represses chemical or organic activity.

re prieve (ri prēv′), *v.,* **-prieved, -priev ing,** *n.* —*v.t.* 1 postpone the punishment of (a person), especially the execution of (a person condemned to death). 2 give relief from any evil or trouble. —*n.* 1 delay in carrying out a punishment, especially of the death penalty. 2 the order giving authority for such delay. 3 temporary relief from any evil or trouble. [< Old French *repris,* past participle of *reprendre* take back < Latin *reprehendere.* See REPREHEND.]

rep ri mand (rep′rə mand), *n.* a severe or formal reproof. —*v.t.* reprove severely or formally; censure. See **reprove** for synonym study. [< French *réprimande* < Latin *reprimenda* to be repressed < *reprimere* < *re-* back + *premere* to press]

re print (*v.* rē print′; *n.* rē′print′), *v.t.* print again. —*n.* a new printing; reproduction of a printed work without alteration. **—re print′er,** *n.*

re pris al (ri prī′zəl), *n.* injury done in return for injury, especially by one nation to another. [< Old French *reprisaille,* ultimately < Latin *reprehendere* reprehend. See REPREHEND.]

re prise (rə prēz′), *n.* 1 a renewal or resumption of an action; repetition. 2 (in music) a repetition or return to the first theme or subject.

re proach (ri prōch′), *n.* 1 blame or censure. 2 a cause of blame or disgrace; discredit. 3 object of blame, censure, or disapproval. 4 expression of blame, censure, or disapproval. —*v.t.* 1 blame or censure; upbraid. See **blame** for synonym study. 2 disgrace; shame. [< Middle French *reproche* < *reprocher* < Popular Latin *repropiare* lay at the door of, ultimately < Latin *re-* again + *prope* near] **—re proach′a ble,** *adj.* **—re proach′er,** *n.* **—re proach′ing ly,** *adv.* **—re proach′less,** *adj.*

re proach ful (ri prōch′fəl), *adj.* full of reproach; expressing reproach. **—re proach′ful ly,** *adv.* **—re proach′ful ness,** *n.*

rep ro bate (rep′rə bāt), *n., adj., v.,* **-bat ed, -bat ing.** —*n.* a very wicked or unprincipled person; scoundrel. —*adj.* 1 very wicked; unprincipled. 2 (in theology) predestined to eternal punishment or death. —*v.t.* 1 disapprove strongly; condemn; censure. 2 (in theology) exclude from salvation; predestine to eternal punishment. [< Late Latin *reprobatum* reproved]

rep ro ba tion (rep′rə bā′shən), *n.* condemnation; censure.

rep ro ba tive (rep′rə bā′tiv), *adj.* reprobating; expressing reprobation. **—rep′ro ba′tive ly,** *adv.*

re pro duce (rē′prə düs′, rē′prə dyüs′), *v.,* **-duced, -duc ing.** —*v.t.* 1 produce again; make or create anew: *Some animals are able to reproduce lost parts or organs of their bodies.* 2 produce (offspring). 3 make a copy of: *reproduce a picture.* 4 produce again from something recorded: *reproduce sound.* —*v.i.* 1 produce offspring. 2 be reproduced. **—re′pro duc′er,** *n.*

re pro duc i ble (rē′prə dü′sə bəl, rē′prə dyü′sə bəl), *adj.* that can be reproduced.

re pro duc tion (rē′prə duk′shən), *n.* 1 a reproducing. 2 a being reproduced. 3 a copy. 4 process by which animals and plants produce offspring.

re pro duc tive (rē′prə duk′tiv), *adj.* 1 that reproduces. 2 for or concerned with reproduction. **—re′pro duc′tive ly,** *adv.* **—re′pro duc′tive ness,** *n.*

re pro duc tiv i ty (rē′prə duk tiv′ə tē), *n.* the quality or power of being reproductive.

re proof (ri prüf′), *n.* words of blame or disapproval; blame; rebuke. [< Old French *reprove* < *reprover* reprove]

re prov al (ri prü′vəl), *n.* a reproving; reproof.

re prove (ri prüv′), *v.t.,* **-proved, -prov ing.** show disapproval of; find fault with; blame. See synonym study below. [< Old French *reprover* < Late Latin *reprobare* < Latin *re-* + *probare* to test] **—re prov′er,** *n.* **—re prov′ing ly,** *adv.*

Syn. Reprove, rebuke, reprimand mean to criticize or blame someone for a fault. **Reprove** suggests expressing disapproval without scolding and with the purpose or hope of correcting the fault: *The principal reproved the rowdy students.* **Rebuke** means to reprove sharply and sternly: *The doctor rebuked the nurse who had been neglecting her patients.* **Reprimand** implies severe and public reproof from an official source: *The careless captain was reprimanded and demoted.*

rep tile (rep′təl), *n.* 1 any of a class of cold-blooded vertebrates that breathe by means of lungs, move by creeping or crawling, and usually have skin covered with dry horny plates or scales. Snakes, lizards, turtles, alligators, and crocodiles are reptiles. 2 a low, mean, despicable person. —*adj.* 1 of or like a reptile; crawling; creeping. 2 low; mean. [< Late Latin, neuter of *reptilis* crawling < Latin *repere* to crawl]

Rep til i a (rep til′ē ə), *n.pl.* class of vertebrates comprising the reptiles.

rep til i an (rep til′ē ən), *adj.* 1 of or having to do with reptiles. 2 like a reptile; base; mean. —*n.* a reptile.

Repub., 1 Republic. 2 Republican.

re pub lic (ri pub′lik), *n.* 1 nation or state in which the citizens elect representatives to manage the government, which is usually headed by a president. 2 the form of government existing in such a state. 3 any of the political divisions of the Soviet Union and Yugoslavia. [< Latin *res publica* public interest, state]

re pub li can (ri pub′lə kən), *adj.* 1 of a republic; like that of a republic. 2 favoring a republic. 3 **Republican,** of or having to do with the Republican Party. —*n.* 1 person who favors a republic. 2 **Republican,** member of the Republican Party.

re pub li can ism (ri pub′lə kə niz′əm), *n.* 1 republican government. 2 republican principles; adherence to republican principles. 3 **Republicanism,** principles or policies of the Republican Party.

Republican Party, one of the two main political parties in the United States, founded in 1854 by opponents of slavery.

re pub li ca tion (rē′pub lə kā′shən), *n.* 1 publication anew. 2 book, etc., published again.

re pu di ate (ri pyü′dē āt), *v.t.,* **-at ed, -at ing.** 1 refuse to accept; reject: *repudiate a doctrine.* 2 refuse to acknowledge or pay: *repudiate a debt.* 3 cast off; disown: *repudiate a son.* 4 put away by divorce. [< Latin *repudiatum* divorced < *repudium* divorce] **—re pu′di a′tion,** *n.* **—re pu′di a′tor,** *n.*

re pug nance (ri pug′nəns), *n.* strong dislike, distaste, or aversion.

re pug nan cy (ri pug′nən sē), *n.* repugnance.

re pug nant (ri pug′nənt), *adj.* 1 disagreeable or offensive; distasteful; objectionable: *Work is repugnant to lazy people.* 2 objecting; averse; opposed: *We are repugnant to every sort of dishonesty.* [< Latin *repugnantem* resisting, opposing < *re-* back + *pugnare* to fight] **—re pug′nant ly,** *adv.*

re pulse (ri puls′), *v.,* **-pulsed, -puls ing,** *n.* —*v.t.* 1 drive back; repel. 2 refuse to accept; reject: *She coldly repulsed him.* —*n.* 1 a driving or a being driven back; repulsion: *After the second repulse, the enemy surrendered.* 2 refusal; rejection. [< Latin *repulsum* repelled < *re-* back + *pellere* to drive]

re pul sion (ri pul′shən), *n.* 1 strong dislike or aversion. 2 a repelling or a being repelled; repulse. 3 (in physics) the tendency of particles or forces to increase their distance from one another.

re pul sive (ri pul′siv), *adj.* 1 causing strong dislike or aversion: *Snakes are repulsive to some people.* 2 tending to drive back or repel. **—re pul′sive ly,** *adv.* **—re pul′sive ness,** *n.*

rep u ta ble (rep′yə tə bəl), *adj.* having a good reputation; well thought of; in good repute. **—rep′u ta bly,** *adv.*

rep u ta tion (rep′yə tā′shən), *n.* 1 what people think and say the character of a person or thing is; common or general estimate of character or quality: *That doctor has an excellent reputation.* 2 estimation or credit of being or possessing something: *have a reputation of being very bright.* 3 good name; good reputation: *Cheating ruined that player's reputation.* 4 fame: *an international reputation.*

re pute (ri pyüt′), *n., v.,* **-put ed, -put ing.** —*n.* 1 reputation: *a generous man by repute.* 2 good reputation. —*v.t.* suppose to be; consider; suppose: *He is reputed the richest man in the state.* [< Latin *reputare* consider < *re-* over + *putare* think]

re put ed (ri pyü′tid), *adj.* accounted or supposed to be such: *the reputed author of a book.* **—re put′ed ly,** *adv.*

re quest (ri kwest′), *v.t.* 1 ask for; ask as a favor: *request a loan from a bank.* See **ask** for synonym study. 2 ask: *He requested her to go with him.* —*n.* 1 act of asking: *a request for help. She did it at our request.* 2 what is asked for: *grant a request.* 3 condition of being asked for or sought after: *She is such a good dancer that she is in great request.* 4 **by request,** in response to a request. [< Old French *requester,* ultimately < Latin *re-* again + *quaerere* ask]

req ui em or **Req ui em** (rek′wē əm, rē′kwē əm), *n.* 1 Mass for the dead; musical church service for the dead. 2 music for it. 3 any musical service or hymn for the dead. [< Latin, accusative of *requies* rest; the first word of the Mass for the dead]

re qui es cat (rek′wē es′kat), *n.* a wish or prayer for the repose of the dead. [< Latin, may he (or she) rest, ultimately < *re-* again + *quies* rest]

re quire (ri kwīr′), *v.t.,* **-quired, -quir ing.** 1 have need for; need; want: *We shall require more help.* 2 command; order; demand: *The rules require us all to be present.* See **demand** for synonym study. [< Latin *requirere* < *re-* again + *quaerere* ask]

re quire ment (ri kwīr′mənt), *n.* 1 a need; thing needed: *Patience is a requirement in teaching.* 2 a demand; thing demanded: *fulfill the requirements for graduation.*

req ui site (rek′wə zit), *adj.* required by circumstances; needed; necessary: *the qualities requisite for a leader.* —*n.* thing needed; requirement. [< Latin *requisitum* < *re-* again + *quaerere* ask] **—req′ui site ly,** *adv.* **—req′ui site ness,** *n.*

req ui si tion (rek′wə zish′ən), *n.* 1 act of requiring. 2 a demand made, especially a formal written demand: *the requisition of supplies for troops.* 3 condition of being required for use or called into service: *The car was in constant requisition for errands.* 4 an essential condition; requirement. —*v.t.* 1 demand or take by authority: *requisition supplies.* 2 make demands upon: *The hospital requisitioned the city for more funds.*

re quit al (ri kwī′tl), *n.* 1 repayment; payment; return. 2 act of requiting.

re quite (ri kwīt′), *v.t.,* **-quit ed, -quit ing.** 1 pay back; make return for: *requite kindness with love.* 2 make return to; reward: *The knight requited the boy for his warning.* 3 make retaliation for; avenge. [< *re-* + *quite,* variant of *quit*] **—re quit′er,** *n.*

rere dos (rir′dos), *n.* a screen or a decorated part of the wall behind an altar. [< Anglo-French, ultimately < *rere* rear[1] + Old French *dos* back]

re route (rē rüt′, rē rout′), *v.t.,* **-rout ed, -rout ing.** send by a new or different route.

re run (*v.* rē run′; *n.* rē′run′), *v.,* **-ran, -run ning,** *n.* —*v.t., v.i.* run again. —*n.* 1 a running again. 2 a television program or motion-picture film that is shown again.

res., 1 research. 2 reserve. 3 residence. 4 resides. 5 resigned.

re sale (rē′sāl′, rē sāl′), *n.* act of selling again.

re scind (ri sind′), *v.t.* deprive of force; repeal; cancel: *rescind a law.* [< Latin *rescindere* < *re-* back + *scindere* to cut] **—re scind′a ble,** *adj.* **—re scind′er,** *n.*

re scis sion (ri sizh′ən), *n.* act of rescinding.

re script (rē′skript), *n.* 1 a written answer to a question or petition. 2 an official announcement; edict; decree. 3 a rewriting. 4 an official answer from a pope or a Roman emperor on some question referred to them. [< Latin *rescriptum,* originally, written in reply < *re-* back + *scribere* to write]

res cue (res′kyü), *v.,* **-cued, -cu ing,** *n.* —*v.t.* save from danger, capture, harm, etc.; free; deliver. See synonym study below. —*n.* a saving or freeing from danger, capture, harm, etc. [< Old French *rescoure,* ultimately < Latin *re-* back + *ex* out + *quatere* to shake] **—res′cu er,** *n.*

Syn. *v.t.* **Rescue, deliver** mean to save or free from danger, harm, or restraint. **Rescue** means to save a person by quick and forceful action from immediate or threatened danger or harm: *Searchers rescued the campers lost in the mountains.* **Deliver** means to set someone free from something holding him in captivity or under its power or control: *Advancing troops delivered the prisoners.*

re search (ri sėrch′, rē′sėrch′), *n.* 1 a careful or systematic hunting for facts or truth about a subject; inquiry; investigation: *the researches of historians.* 2 organized scientific investigation to solve problems, test hypotheses, develop or invent new products, etc.: *atomic research, cancer research.* —*v.i.* make researches; do research. —*v.t.* search into; investigate carefully: *research a topic in history.* [< Middle French *recerche* < *re-* again + *cerche* search]

re search er (ri sėr′chər, rē′sėr′chər), *n.* person who makes researches.

re sect (ri sekt′), *v.t.* cut away or remove a part of by surgery. [< Latin *resectum* cut off < *re-* + *secare* to cut]

re sec tion (ri sek′shən), *n.* the surgical removal of a portion of some structure, especially bone.

re sem blance (ri zem′bləns), *n.* 1 similar appearance; likeness: *Twins often show great resemblance.* See synonym study below. 2 a copy; image.

Syn. 1 **Resemblance, similarity** mean a likeness between two persons or things. **Resemblance** emphasizes looking alike or having some of the same external features or superficial qualities: *There is some resemblance between the accounts of the fire, but all the important details are different.* **Similarity** suggests being of the same kind or nature or having some of the same essential qualities: *The similarity between the two reports suggests that one person wrote both.*

hat, āge, fär; let, ēqual, tėrm;
it, īce; hot, ōpen, ôrder;
oil, out; cup, pu̇t, rüle;
ch, child; ng, long; sh, she;
th, thin; ᴛʜ, then; zh, measure;

ə represents *a* in about, *e* in taken,
i in pencil, *o* in lemon, *u* in circus.

< = from, derived from, taken from.

re sem ble (ri zem′bəl), *v.t.,* **-bled, -bling.** be like; be similar to; have likeness to in form, figure, or qualities. [< Old French *resembler* < Latin *re-* again + *similis* similar]

re sent (ri zent′), *v.t.* feel injured and angry at; feel indignation at: *resent an insulting remark, resent criticism.* [< French *ressentir* < Latin *re-* back + *sentire* to feel]

re sent ful (ri zent′fəl), *adj.* 1 feeling resentment; injured and angry. 2 showing resentment. **—re sent′ful ly,** *adv.* **—re sent′ful ness,** *n.*

re sent ment (ri zent′mənt), *n.* the feeling that one has at being injured or insulted; indignation.

res er pine (res′ər pən, res′ər pēn′; rə sėr′pən, rə sėr′pēn′), *n.* drug obtained from the juices of the rauwolfia, used as a tranquilizer and sedative, in reducing high blood pressure, and in the treatment of mental illness. *Formula:* $C_{33}H_{40}N_2O_9$ [< German *Reserpin* < New Latin *R(auwolfia) serp(ent)ina* the rauwolfia]

res er va tion (rez′ər vā′shən), *n.* 1 a keeping back; hiding in part; something not expressed: *She outwardly approved of the plan with the mental reservation that she would change it to suit herself.* 2 a limiting condition: *We accepted the plan with reservation plainly stated.* 3 land set aside for a special purpose. The government has set apart Indian reservations. 4 arrangement to keep a thing for a person; securing of accommodations, etc., in advance: *Please make reservations for a room at a hotel.* 5 something reserved.

re serve (ri zėrv′), *v.,* **-served, -serv ing,** *n., adj.* —*v.t.* 1 keep back or hold over for the present: *reserve criticism.* 2 set apart: *time reserved for recreation.* 3 save for use later: *Reserve enough money for your fare home.* 4 set aside for the use of a particular person or persons: *reserve a table at a restaurant.*

—*n.* 1 the actual cash in a bank or assets that can be turned into cash quickly. Banks must keep a reserve of money. 2 body of soldiers, sailors, ships, aircraft, etc., kept ready to help the main force in battle. 3 **reserves,** *pl.* soldiers or sailors not in active service but ready to serve when needed. 4 public land set apart for a special purpose: *a forest reserve.* 5 anything kept back for future use; store: *a reserve of food or energy.* 6 act of keeping back or holding back: *You may speak before her without reserve.* 7 fact or condition of being kept, set apart, or saved for use later: *keep money in reserve.* 8 a keeping one's thoughts, feelings, and affairs to oneself; self-restraint in action or speech; lack of friendliness. 9 a silent manner that keeps people from making friends easily.

10 exception or qualification to the acceptance of some idea, belief, etc.
—adj. kept in reserve; forming a reserve: *a reserve stock, a reserve force.*
[< Latin *reservare* < *re-* back + *servare* to keep] **—re serv′er,** *n.*

reserve bank, one of the twelve Federal Reserve Banks.

re served (ri zėrvd′), *adj.* 1 kept in reserve; kept by special arrangement: *a reserved seat.* 2 set apart: *a reserved section at the stadium.* 3 self-restrained in action or speech. 4 disposed to keep to oneself. **—re serv′ed ly,** *adv.*

reserve officer, officer in the reserves.

re serv ist (ri zėr′vist), *n.* member of the military reserves.

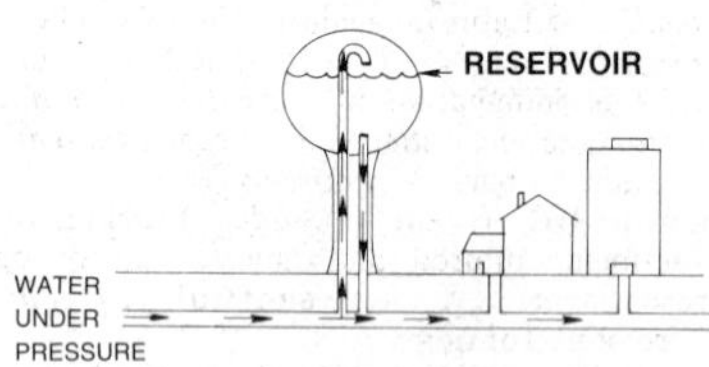

reservoir (def. 1)—tank type, cut away to show pipes inside

res er voir (rez′ər vwär, rez′ər vôr), *n.* 1 place where water is collected and stored for use: *This reservoir supplies the entire city.* 2 anything to hold a liquid: *A fountain pen has an ink reservoir.* 3 place where anything is collected and stored: *Her mind was a reservoir of facts.* 4 a great supply. [< French *réservoir* < *réserver* to reserve]

re set (*v.* rē set′; *n.* rē′set′), *v.,* **-set, -set ting,** *n.* *—v.t.* set again: *reset a broken arm. The diamonds were reset in platinum.* *—n.* 1 act of resetting. 2 thing reset.

re shape (rē shāp′), *v.t.,* **-shaped, -shap ing.** shape anew; form into a new or different shape.

re ship ment (rē ship′mənt), *n.* 1 a shipping again. 2 that which is shipped again.

re shuf fle (rē shuf′əl), *v.,* **-fled, -fling,** *n.* *—v.t.* 1 shuffle again. 2 arrange in a new or different way; reorganize completely. *—n.* a complete rearrangement or reorganization.

re side (ri zīd′), *v.i.,* **-sid ed, -sid ing.** 1 live (in or at a place) for a long time; dwell. 2 be; exist: *The power to declare war resides in Congress.* [< Latin *residere* remain < *re-* back + *sedere* sit, settle] **—re sid′er,** *n.*

res i dence (rez′ə dəns), *n.* 1 the place where a person lives; house; home. 2 a residing; dwelling. 3 period of residing in a place. 4 **in residence,** living in a place while on duty or doing active work: *a doctor in residence.*

res i den cy (rez′ə dən sē), *n., pl.* **-cies.** 1 residence. 2 position of a doctor who continues practicing in a hospital after completing his internship. 3 the official residence of a diplomatic officer or governor general. 4 (formerly) an administrative division in the Dutch East Indies and in certain other areas under colonial rule.

res i dent (rez′ə dənt), *n.* 1 person living in a place permanently; dweller. 2 an official sent to live in a foreign land to represent his country. *—adj.* 1 dwelling in a place; residing. 2 living in a place while on duty or doing active work: *a resident physician at a hospital.* 3 not migratory: *English sparrows are resident birds.* 4 present; inherent; established: *resident powers.*

res i den tial (rez′ə den′shəl), *adj.* 1 of, having to do with, or fitted for homes or residences: *a residential district.* 2 of or having to do with residence. 3 serving or used as a residence: *a residential building.* **—res′i den′tial ly,** *adv.*

re sid u al (ri zij′ü əl), *adj.* of or forming a residue; remaining; left over. *—n.* 1 amount left over; remainder. 2 fee paid a performer or writer for each rerun of a television commercial, etc. **—re sid′u al ly,** *adv.*

re sid u ar y (ri zij′ü er′ē), *adj.* 1 entitled to the remainder of an estate. 2 residual.

res i due (rez′ə dü, rez′ə dyü), *n.* 1 what remains after a part is taken; remainder: *The syrup had dried up, leaving a sticky residue.* 2 the part of an estate left after all debts, charges, bequests, etc., have been satisfied. [< Middle French *résidu* < Latin *residuum,* originally, left over < *residere* remain. See RESIDE.]

re sid u um (ri zij′ü əm), *n., pl.* **-sid u a** (-zij′ü ə). what is left at the end of any process; residue; remainder. [< Latin]

re sign (ri zīn′), *v.i., v.t.* 1 give up (a job, position, etc.): *resign from the staff of the school paper, resign the presidency.* 2 **resign oneself,** submit quietly; adapt oneself without complaint; yield. [< Latin *resignare* unseal, ultimately < *re-* back + *signum* seal]

res ig na tion (rez′ig nā′shən), *n.* 1 act of resigning. 2 a written statement giving notice that one resigns. 3 patient acceptance; quiet submission.

re signed (ri zīnd′), *adj.* submitting to or accepting what comes without complaint. **—re sign′ed ly,** *adv.*

re sil i ence (ri zil′ē əns, ri zil′yəns), *n.* 1 power of springing back; resilient quality or nature; elasticity: *Rubber has resilience.* 2 power of recovering readily; buoyancy; cheerfulness.

re sil i en cy (ri zil′ē ən sē, ri zil′yən sē), *n.* resilience.

re sil i ent (ri zil′ē ənt, ri zil′yənt), *adj.* 1 springing back; returning to the original form or position after being bent, compressed, or stretched: *resilient steel.* 2 readily recovering; buoyant; cheerful: *a resilient nature that throws off trouble.* [< Latin *resilientem* < *re-* back + *salire* to jump] **—re sil′i ent ly,** *adv.*

res in (rez′n), *n.* 1 a sticky, yellow or brown, transparent or translucent substance that flows from certain plants and trees, especially the pine and fir. It does not conduct electricity and is used in medicine, varnish, plastics, inks, and adhesives. 2 rosin. 3 any of a large group of resinous substances that are made artificially and are used especially in making plastics. [< Latin *resina*] **—res′in like′,** *adj.*

res in oid (rez′n oid), *adj.* resinous. *—n.* a resinous substance.

res in ous (rez′n əs), *adj.* 1 of resin. 2 like resin. 3 containing resin; full of resin.

re sist (ri zist′), *v.t.* 1 act against; strive against; oppose: *The window resisted all efforts to open it.* See **oppose** for synonym study. 2 strive successfully against; keep from: *I could not resist laughing.* 3 withstand the action or effect of (an acid, storm, etc.): *A healthy body resists disease.* *—v.i.* act against something; oppose something. *—n.* coating put on a surface to make it withstand the action of weather, acid, etc. [< Latin *resistere* < *re-* back + *sistere* make a stand] **—re sist′er,** *n.*

re sist ance (ri zis′təns), *n.* 1 act of resisting: *The bank clerk made no resistance to the robbers.* 2 power to resist: *have little resistance to disease.* 3 thing or act that resists; opposing force; opposition: *overcome air resistance.* 4 **Resistance,** people who secretly organize and fight for their freedom in a country occupied and controlled by a foreign power: *the French Resistance in World War II.* 5 property of a conductor that opposes the passage of an electric current and changes electric energy into heat. Copper has a low resistance. 6 conductor, coil, etc., that offers resistance.

re sist ant (ri zis′tənt), *adj.* resisting.

re sist i bil i ty (ri zis′tə bil′ə tē), *n.* quality or condition of being resistible.

re sist i ble (ri zis′tə bəl), *adj.* that can be resisted.

re sis tive (ri zis′tiv), *adj.* resisting; capable of resisting or inclined to resist.

re sis tiv i ty (rē′zi stiv′ə tē), *n., pl.* **-ties.** the electrical resistance of the equivalent of one cubic centimeter of a given substance.

re sist less (ri zist′lis), *adj.* 1 that cannot be resisted; irresistible. 2 that cannot resist. **—re sist′less ly,** *adv.* **—re sist′less ness,** *n.*

re sis tor (ri zis′tər), *n.* conductor used to control voltage in an electric circuit, etc., because of its resistance.

re sole (rē sōl′), *v.t.,* **-soled, -sol ing.** put a new sole on (a shoe, etc.).

re sol u ble (ri zol′yə bəl), *adj.* that can be resolved.

res o lute (rez′ə lüt), *adj.* 1 having a fixed resolve; determined; firm. 2 constant in pursuing a purpose; bold. [< Latin *resolutum* resolved] **—res′o lute′ly,** *adv.* **—res′o lute′ness,** *n.*

res o lu tion (rez′ə lü′shən), *n.* 1 thing decided on; thing determined: *I made a resolution to get up early.* 2 act of resolving or determining. 3 power of holding firmly to a purpose; determination. 4 a formal expression of the opinion or will of a deliberative or legislative body or other group: *a joint resolution of the Congress.* 5 a breaking into parts or components. 6 act or result of resolving a question, difficulty, etc.; answer or solution: *the resolution of a plot in a novel.* 7 (in medicine) the reduction or disappearance of inflammation without the formation of pus. 8 (in music) the progression of a voice part or of the harmony as a whole from a dissonance to a consonance. 9 (in optics) resolving power.

re solve (ri zolv′), *v.,* **-solved, -solv ing,** *n.* *—v.t.* 1 make up one's mind; determine; decide: *resolve to do better work in the future.* See **decide** for synonym study. 2 decide formally by vote; adopt or pass as a resolution: *It was resolved that our school should have a picnic.* 3 clear away; dispel: *The letter resolved all our doubts.* 4 clear up; explain; solve: *resolve a mystery.* 5 break into parts; separate into components: *Some chemical compounds can be resolved by heat.* 6 change into a simpler form: *The assembly resolved itself into a committee.* 7 (in music) cause (a voice part or harmony) to progress from a dissonance to a consonance. *—v.i.* 1 come to a decision; decide. 2 break into parts or components. 3 (in music) progress from a dissonance to a consonance. *—n.* 1 thing determined on. 2 firmness in carrying out a purpose; determination. [< Latin *re-*

solvere < *re-* un- + *solvere* to loosen] **—re solv′a ble,** *adj.* **—re solv′er,** *n.*

re solved (ri zolvd′), *adj.* determined; firm; resolute. **—re solv′ed ly,** *adv.*

resolving power, the ability of an optical lens or system to produce separate images of objects very close together; resolution.

res o nance (rez′n əns), *n.* 1 resounding quality; being resonant. 2 a reinforcing and prolonging of sound by reflection or by vibration of other objects. The hollow body of a guitar gives it resonance. 3 condition of an electrical circuit adjusted to allow the greatest flow of current at a certain frequency: *A radio set must be in resonance to receive music or speech from a radio station.* 4 (in chemistry) the oscillation of molecules between two or more structures, each possessing identical atoms, but different arrangements of electrons. 5 (in nuclear physics) a particle of extremely short duration.

res o nant (rez′n ənt), *adj.* 1 continuing to sound; resounding. 2 tending to increase or prolong sounds. 3 of or in resonance. [< Latin *resonantem* < *re-* back + *sonus* sound] **—res′o nant ly,** *adv.*

res o nate (rez′n āt), *v.i.,* **-nat ed, -nat ing.** exhibit resonance; resound.

res o na tor (rez′n ā′tər), *n.* something that produces resonance; appliance for increasing sound by resonance.

re sorb (ri sôrb′, ri zôrb′), *v.t.* to absorb again.

re sorp tion (ri sôrp′shən, ri zôrp′shən), *n.* 1 a resorbing. 2 a being resorbed.

re sort (ri zôrt′), *v.i.* 1 go or repair *(to),* especially habitually; go often: *Many people resort to the beaches in hot weather.* 2 have recourse *(to);* turn for help: *resort to violence.* —*n.* 1 an assembling; going to often. 2 place people go to, usually for recreation: *a summer resort.* 3 act of turning for help; recourse: *The resort to force is forbidden in this school.* 4 person or thing turned to for help. [< Old French *resortir* < *re-* back + *sortir* go out] **—re sort′er,** *n.*

re sound (ri zound′), *v.i.* 1 give back sound; echo. 2 sound loudly. 3 be filled with sound. 4 be much talked about. —*v.t.* 1 give back (sound); echo. 2 repeat loudly; celebrate.

re sound ing (ri zoun′ding), *adj.* 1 that resounds; sounding loudly: *a resounding blow.* 2 ringing; sonorous: *resounding eloquence.* 3 impressive; striking: *a resounding victory.* **—re sound′ing ly,** *adv.*

re source (ri sôrs′, ri sōrs′; rē′sôrs, rē′sōrs), *n.* 1 Usually, **resources,** *pl.* any supply that will meet a need; stock or reserve upon which to draw when necessary: *financial resources.* 2 **resources,** *pl.* the actual and potential wealth of a country. 3 any means of getting success or getting out of trouble: *Climbing a tree is a cat's resource when chased by a dog.* 4 skill in meeting difficulties, getting out of trouble, etc. 5 possibility of aid or assistance. [< French *ressource,* ultimately < Latin *re-* again + *surgere* to rise]

re source ful (ri sôrs′fəl, ri sōrs′fəl), *adj.* good at thinking of ways to do things; quick-witted. **—re source′ful ly,** *adv.* **—re source′ful ness,** *n.*

resp., 1 respective. 2 respectively.

re spect (ri spekt′), *n.* 1 high regard; honor; esteem: *show respect to one's teachers.* 2 condition of being esteemed or honored: *hold the flag of one's country in respect.* 3 **respects,** *pl.* expressions of respect; regards. 4 consideration; regard: *have respect for other people's property.* See synonym study below. 5 a particular point or matter; detail: *The plan is unwise in many respects.* 6 relation; reference: *We must plan in respect to the future.* 7 **as respects,** as concerns; in regard to. —*v.t.* 1 feel or show honor or esteem for: *We respect an honest person.* 2 show consideration for: *Respect the ideas and feelings of others.* 3 relate to; refer to; be connected with. [< Latin *respectus* regard < *respicere* look back, have regard for < *re-* back + *specere* to look] **—re spect′er,** *n.*

Syn. *n.* 4 **Respect, regard** mean consideration for someone or something of recognized worth. **Respect** implies recognition and esteem of worth with or without liking: *treat an opponent with respect.* **Regard** implies mere recognition of worth, with the element of approval or disapproval specified: *It is difficult to respect someone for whose abilities one has small regard.*

re spect a bil i ty (ri spek′tə bil′ə tē), *n., pl.* **-ties.** 1 quality or condition of being respectable. 2 respectable social standing. 3 respectable people, as a group.

re spect a ble (ri spek′tə bəl), *adj.* 1 worthy or deserving of respect; estimable: *a respectable old gentleman.* 2 honest and decent in character or conduct: *respectable people.* 3 fairly good; moderate in size or quality: *a respectable but far from brilliant record.* 4 good enough to use; fit to be seen: *respectable clothes.* **—re spect′a bly,** *adv.*

re spect ful (ri spekt′fəl), *adj.* having or showing respect; considerate and polite. **—re spect′ful ly,** *adv.* **—re spect′ful ness,** *n.*

re spect ing (ri spek′ting), *prep.* regarding; concerning.

re spec tive (ri spek′tiv), *adj.* belonging to each; particular; individual: *The classes went to their respective rooms.*

re spec tive ly (ri spek′tiv lē), *adv.* as regards each of several persons or things in turn or in the order mentioned: *The three bills were introduced in January, March, and April, respectively.*

re spell (rē spel′), *v.t.* spell over again, especially in a phonetic alphabet.

Re spi ghi (re spē′gē), *n.* **Ottorino,** 1879-1936, Italian composer.

res pi ra tion (res′pə rā′shən), *n.* 1 act of inhaling and exhaling; breathing. 2 (in biology) the energy-producing process by which an animal, plant, or living cell secures oxygen from the air or water, distributes it, utilizes it for oxidation of food materials, and gives off carbon dioxide.

res pi ra tor (res′pə rā′tər), *n.* 1 device, usually of gauze, worn over the nose and mouth to prevent inhaling harmful substances. 2 device used to give artificial respiration.

res pir a to ry (res′pər ə tôr′ē, res′pər ə tōr′ē; ri spī′rə tôr′ē, ri spī′rə tōr′ē), *adj.* having to do with or used for respiration. The lungs are respiratory organs.

re spire (ri spīr′), *v.i.,* **-spired, -spir ing.** inhale and exhale; breathe. [< Latin *respirare* < *re-* + *spirare* breathe]

res pite (res′pit), *n., v.,* **-pit ed, -pit ing.** —*n.* 1 time of relief and rest; lull: *a respite from the heat.* 2 a putting off; delay, especially in carrying out a sentence of death; reprieve. —*v.t.* 1 give a respite to. 2 put off; postpone. [< Old French *respit* < Late Latin *respectus* expectation < Latin, regard. See RESPECT.]

rest[1] (def. 7b)—rests of differing duration

hat, āge, fär; let, ēqual, tėrm;
it, īce; hot, ōpen, ôrder;
oil, out; cup, püt, rüle;
ch, child; ng, long; sh, she;
th, thin; ᴛʜ, then; zh, measure;

ə represents *a* in about, *e* in taken, *i* in pencil, *o* in lemon, *u* in circus.

< = from, derived from, taken from.

re splend ence (ri splen′dəns), *n.* great brightness; splendor.

re splend en cy (ri splen′dən sē), *n.* resplendence.

re splend ent (ri splen′dənt), *adj.* very bright; shining; splendid: *the resplendent rays of the sun, a face resplendent with joy.* [< Latin *resplendentem* < *re-* back + *splendere* to shine] **—re splend′ent ly,** *adv.*

re spond (ri spond′), *v.i.* 1 reply in words; answer. See **answer** for synonym study. 2 act in answer; react: *respond to kind treatment.* 3 U.S. give legal satisfaction. [< Latin *respondere* < *re-* in return + *spondere* to promise]

re spond ent (ri spon′dənt), *n.* 1 person who responds. 2 (in law) a defendant, especially in a divorce case. —*adj.* answering; responding.

re sponse (ri spons′), *n.* 1 an answer by word or act; rejoinder; reply. 2 words said or sung by the congregation or choir in answer to the minister. 3 the reaction of body or mind to a stimulus. [< Latin *responsum* responded]

re spon si bil i ty (ri spon′sə bil′ə tē), *n., pl.* **-ties.** 1 a being responsible; obligation. 2 a being reliable; trustworthiness. 3 person or thing for which one is responsible.

re spon si ble (ri spon′sə bəl), *adj.* 1 obliged or expected to account *(for);* accountable; answerable: *Each pupil is responsible for the care of the books given him.* 2 deserving credit or blame: *The bad weather is responsible for the small attendance.* 3 trustworthy; reliable: *A responsible person should take care of the money.* 4 involving obligation or duties: *The presidency is a very responsible position.* 5 able to tell right from wrong; able to think and act reasonably: *Insane people are not responsible.* **—re spon′si ble ness,** *n.* **—re spon′si bly,** *adv.*

re spon sive (ri spon′siv), *adj.* 1 making answer; responding: *a responsive glance.* 2 easily moved; responding readily: *be responsive to kindness.* 3 using or containing responses: *responsive reading.* **—re spon′sive ly,** *adv.* **—re spon′sive ness,** *n.*

rest[1] (rest), *n.* 1 the repose and refreshment offered by sleep; sleep: *a good night's rest.* 2 ease after work or effort; freedom from activity: *allow an hour for rest.* 3 freedom from anything that tires, troubles, disturbs, or pains; respite: *a short rest from pain.* 4 absence of motion: *The driver brought the car to a rest.* 5 something to lean on; support: *a rest for a billiard cue.* 6 place for resting: *a travelers' rest.* 7 in music: **a** a silence of definite length between notes. **b** mark to show such a silence. 8 a short

pause in reading; caesura. 9 death; the grave. **10 at rest, a** asleep. **b** not moving: *The lake was at rest.* **c** free from pain, trouble, etc. **d** dead. **11 lay to rest,** bury.
—*v.i.* 1 be still or quiet; sleep: *Lie down and rest.* 2 be free from work, effort, care, trouble, etc.: *rest for two weeks in the summer.* 3 stop moving; come to rest; stop: *The ball rested at the bottom of the hill.* 4 lie, recline, sit, lean, etc., for rest or ease: *spend the whole day resting in a chair.* 5 be supported; lean: *The ladder rests against the wall. The roof rests on columns.* 6 be fixed; look: *Our eyes rested on the open book.* 7 be at ease: *Don't let her rest until she promises to visit us.* 8 be or become inactive: *Let the matter rest.* 9 be based; rely; trust; depend: *Our hope rests on you.* 10 be found; be present; lie: *In a democracy, government rests with the people.* 11 be dead; lie in the grave. 12 (in law) end voluntarily the introduction of evidence in a case: *The state rests.* —*v.t.* 1 give rest to; refresh by rest: *Stop and rest your horse.* 2 cause to stop moving. 3 let remain inactive: *Rest the matter there.* 4 place for support; lay; lean: *rest one's head on a pillow.* 5 cause to rely or depend; base: *We rest our hope on you.* 6 fix (the eyes, etc.). 7 end voluntarily the introduction of evidence in (a case at law). [Old English *reste*]

rest[2] (rest), *n.* what is left; those that are left; remainder. —*v.i.* continue to be; remain: *You may rest assured that I will keep my promise.* [< Middle French *reste* < *rester* remain < Latin *restare* < *re-* back + *stare* to stand]

re state (rē stāt′), *v.t.,* **-stat ed, -stat ing.** 1 state again or anew. 2 state in a new way.

re state ment (rē stāt′mənt), *n.* 1 act of stating again. 2 statement made again. 3 a new statement.

res taur ant (res′tər ənt, res′tə ränt′), *n.* place to buy and eat a meal. [< French]

res taur a teur (res′tər ə tėr′), *n.* keeper of a restaurant. [< French]

rest ful (rest′fəl), *adj.* 1 full of rest; giving rest. 2 quiet; peaceful. **—rest′ful ly,** *adv.* **—rest′ful ness,** *n.*

rest ing (res′ting), *adj.* 1 (of spores) dormant. 2 (of cells) not dividing or preparing to divide.

res ti tu tion (res′tə tü′shən, res′tə-tyü′shən), *n.* 1 the giving back of what has been lost or taken away; return. 2 act of making good any loss, damage, or injury; reparation; amends: *It is only fair that those who do the damage should make restitution.* [< Latin *restitutionem,* ultimately < *re-* again + *statuere* set up]

res tive (res′tiv), *adj.* 1 restless; uneasy. 2 hard to manage. 3 refusing to go ahead; balky. [< Old French *restif* motionless < *rester* remain. See REST[2].] **—res′tive ly,** *adv.* **—res′tive ness,** *n.*

rest less (rest′lis), *adj.* 1 unable to rest; uneasy: *a dog made restless by the scent of game.* 2 without rest or sleep; not restful: *The sick child passed a restless night.* 3 rarely or never still or quiet; always moving. **—rest′less ly,** *adv.* **—rest′less-ness,** *n.*

rest mass, (in physics) the mass of an atom, electron, etc., when it is regarded as being at rest.

res to ra tion (res′tə rā′shən), *n.* 1 a restoring; establishing again: *restoration of order.* 2 a bringing back to a former condition: *restoration of an old house.* 3 a being restored; recovery: *restoration of health.* 4 something restored, especially a representation of the original form of an ancient structure, extinct animal, etc.: *a restoration of a colonial mansion.* **5 Restoration, a** the reestablishment of the monarchy in 1660 under Charles II of England. **b** period from 1660 to 1688 in England, during which Charles II and James II reigned.

re stor a tive (ri stôr′ə tiv, ri stōr′ə tiv), *adj.* having to do with or capable of restoring; tending to restore health or strength. —*n.* something that restores health, strength, or consciousness. **—re stor′a tive ly,** *adv.*

re store (ri stôr′, ri stōr′), *v.t.,* **-stored, -stor ing.** 1 bring back; establish again: *restore order.* 2 bring back to a former condition or to a normal condition: *The old house has been restored.* See **renew** for synonym study. 3 give back; put back: *restore money to its owner, restore a book to the proper shelf.* [< Old French *restorer* < Latin *restaurare*] **—re stor′a ble,** *adj.* **—re-stor′er,** *n.*

re strain (ri strān′), *v.t.* 1 hold back; keep in check or keep within limits; repress; curb: *I could not restrain my curiosity.* See **check** for synonym study. 2 keep in prison; confine. [< Old French *restraindre* < Latin *restringere* restrict < *re-* back + *stringere* draw tight] **—re strain′a ble,** *adj.* **—re-strain′ed ly,** *adv.* **—re strain′er,** *n.*

re straint (ri strānt′), *n.* 1 a restraining; holding back or hindering from action or motion. 2 a being restrained; confinement. 3 means of restraining. 4 tendency to restrain natural feeling; reserve.

restraint of trade, limitation or prevention of free competition in business.

re strict (ri strikt′), *v.t.* 1 keep within limits; confine: *Our club membership is restricted to twelve.* 2 put limitations on: *restrict the meaning of a word.* [< Latin *restrictum* restrained < *re-* back + *stringere* draw tight]

re strict ed (ri strik′tid), *adj.* 1 kept within limits; limited: *a restricted diet.* 2 having restrictions or limiting rules: *a restricted residential section.* **—re strict′ed ly,** *adv.*

re stric tion (ri strik′shən), *n.* 1 something that restricts; limiting condition or rule. 2 a restricting. 3 a being restricted.

re stric tive (ri strik′tiv), *adj.* restricting; limiting. **—re stric′tive ly,** *adv.* **—re-stric′tive ness,** *n.*

restrictive clause, a subordinate clause that qualifies the noun it modifies so definitely that it cannot be left out without changing the meaning of the sentence. EXAMPLE: All employees *who have been with this firm for five years* will receive bonuses.

rest room, U.S. lavatory in a public building.

re sult (ri zult′), *n.* 1 that which happens because of something; what is caused; outcome; consequence: *The result of the fall was a broken leg.* See **effect** for synonym study. 2 good or useful result: *We want results, not talk.* 3 quantity, value, etc., obtained by calculation. —*v.i.* 1 be a result; follow as a consequence: *Sickness often results from eating too much.* 2 have as a result; end: *Eating too much often results in sickness.* [< Latin *resultare* to rebound, ultimately < *re-* back + *salire* to spring]

re sult ant (ri zult′nt), *adj.* that results; resulting. —*n.* 1 a result. 2 a vector, representing force, velocity, etc., having the same effect as and being the sum of two or more vectors. See **vector** for diagram.

re sume[1] (ri züm′), *v.,* **-sumed, -sum ing.** —*v.t.* 1 begin again; go on: *Resume reading where we left off.* 2 get or take again: *Those standing may resume their seats.* —*v.i.* begin again; continue. [< Latin *resumere* < *re-* again + *sumere* take up] **—re sum′a ble,** *adj.*

rés u mé or **res u me**[2] (rez′ə mā′), *n.* 1 summary. 2 U.S. a biographical summary, especially of a person's education and professional career. [< French *résumé*]

re sump tion (ri zump′shən), *n.* a resuming: *the resumption of duties after absence.* [< Late Latin *resumptionem* < Latin *resumere.* See RESUME.]

re surge (ri sėrj′), *v.i.,* **-surged, -surg ing.** rise again.

re sur gence (ri sėr′jəns), *n.* a rising again: *a resurgence of friendship.*

re sur gent (ri sėr′jənt), *adj.* rising or tending to rise again.

res ur rect (rez′ə rekt′), *v.t.* 1 raise from the dead; bring back to life. 2 bring back to sight, use, etc.: *resurrect an old custom.*

res ur rec tion (rez′ə rek′shən), *n.* 1 a coming to life again; rising from the dead. **2 Resurrection,** the rising again of Christ after His death and burial. 3 a being alive again after death. 4 restoration from decay, disuse, etc.; revival. [< Latin *resurrectionem* < *resurgere* rise again < *re-* + *surgere* to rise]

re sus ci tate (ri sus′ə tāt), *v.,* **-tat ed, -tat ing.** —*v.t.* 1 bring back to life or consciousness; revive. 2 renew or restore (a thing). —*v.i.* come to life or consciousness again. [< Latin *resuscitare* < *re-* again + *sub-* up + *citare* rouse] **—re sus′ci ta′tion,** *n.*

re sus ci ta tive (ri sus′ə tā′tiv), *adj.* helping to resuscitate.

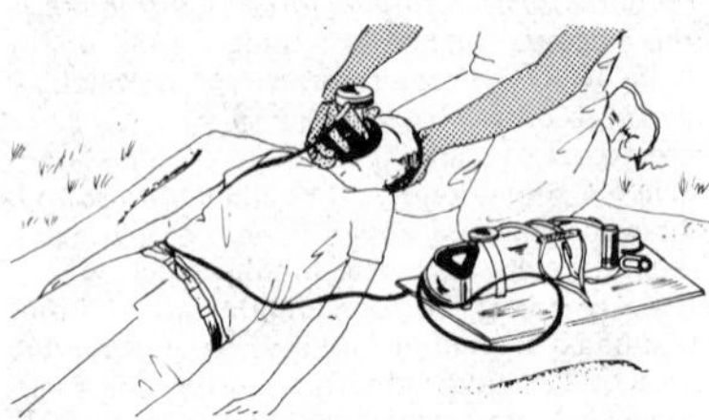

resuscitator (def. 1)

re sus ci ta tor (ri sus′ə tā′tər), *n.* 1 device used to treat asphyxiation by forcing oxygen into the lungs. 2 person who resuscitates.

ret (ret), *v.t.,* **ret ted, ret ting.** expose (flax, hemp, etc.) to moisture or soak in water, in order to soften by partial rotting. [< Middle Dutch *reten*]

re tail (*n., adj., adv., v.t. 1 and v.i.* rē′tāl; *v.t. 2* ri tāl′, rē′tāl), *n.* sale of goods in small quantities at a time, directly to the consumer: *Our grocer buys at wholesale and sells at retail.* —*adj.* 1 in small quantities: *The wholesale price of this coat is $20; the retail price is $30.* 2 selling in small quantities: *the retail trade, a retail merchant.* —*adv.* at a retail price: *sell retail.* —*v.t.* 1 sell at retail: *retail dresses.* 2 tell over again; repeat the particulars of to others: *retail gossip.* —*v.i.* be sold at retail: *a dress retailing at $20.* [< Old French *retaille* scrap < *retaillier* cut up < *re-* back + *taillier* to cut]

re tail er (rē′tā lər), *n.* a retail merchant or dealer.

re tain (ri tān′), *v.t.* 1 continue to have or hold; keep. See **keep** for synonym study. 2 keep in mind; remember. 3 employ by payment of a fee; secure the services of by payment of a retainer: *retain a lawyer.* [< Old French *retenir* < Latin *retinere* < *re-* back + *tenere* to hold]

reticulate wings reticulate leaf

retained object, (in grammar) a direct object after a passive verb. EXAMPLE: The boy was given a *nickel.* A nickel was given the *boy.*

re tain er[1] (ri tā′nər), *n.* 1 person who serves a person of rank; attendant; follower. 2 person who retains.

re tain er[2] (ri tā′nər), *n.* fee paid to a lawyer, etc., to secure services on a continuing basis or when necessary. [noun use of Old French *retenir* retain]

re take (*v.* rē tāk′; *n.* rē′tāk′), *v.,* **-took, -tak en** (-tā′kən), **-tak ing,** *n.* —*v.t.* 1 take again. 2 take back. 3 make (a film sequence) over again. —*n.* 1 a retaking: *a retake of a scene in a motion picture.* 2 the sequence or film obtained.

re tal i ate (ri tal′ē āt), *v.i.,* **-at ed, -at ing.** pay back wrong, injury, etc.; return like for like, usually to return evil for evil: *If we insult them, they will retaliate.* [< Latin *retaliatum* paid back] —**re tal′i a′tion,** *n.*

re tal i a tive (ri tal′ē ā′tiv), *adj.* disposed to retaliate; retaliatory.

re tal i a to ry (ri tal′ē ə tôr′ē, ri tal′ē ə-tōr′ē), *adj.* returning like for like, especially evil for evil.

re tard (*v.* ri tärd′; *n.* rē′tärd), *v.t.* make slow; delay the progress of; keep back; hinder: *Bad roads retarded the car.* —*n.* INFORMAL. a retarded person; retardate. [< Latin *retardare* < *re-* back + *tardus* slow] —**re-tard′er,** *n.*

re tard ant (ri tärd′nt), *n.* something that delays an action, process, or effect, usually a chemical. —*adj.* retarding; tending to hinder.

re tard ate (ri tär′dāt), *n.* person who is retarded.

re tar da tion (rē′tär dā′shən), *n.* 1 act of retarding. 2 condition of being retarded. 3 that which retards; hindrance.

re tard ed (ri tär′did), *adj.* slow in mental development; backward.

retch (rech), *v.i.* make efforts to vomit; make movements like those of vomiting. [Old English *hrǣcan* clear the throat]

ret'd., returned.

re tell (rē tel′), *v.t.,* **-told, -tell ing.** tell again.

re ten tion (ri ten′shən), *n.* 1 a retaining. 2 a being retained. 3 power to retain. 4 ability to remember. [< Latin *retentionem* < *retinere* retain]

re ten tive (ri ten′tiv), *adj.* 1 able to hold or keep. 2 able to remember easily. —**re-ten′tive ly,** *adv.* —**re ten′tive ness,** *n.*

re ten tiv i ty (rē′ten tiv′ə tē), *n.* 1 power to retain; retentiveness. 2 capacity of a substance to retain induced magnetic force after the source of the magnetization has been removed.

ret i cence (ret′ə səns), *n.* tendency to be silent or say little; reserve in speech.

ret i cent (ret′ə sənt), *adj.* disposed to keep silent or say little; not speaking freely; reserved in speech. See **silent** for synonym study. [< Latin *reticentem* < *re-* back + *tacere* be silent] —**ret′i cent ly,** *adv.*

re tic u lar (ri tik′yə lər), *adj.* 1 having the form of a net; netlike. 2 intricate; entangled.

re tic u late (*adj.* ri tik′yə lit, ri tik′yə lāt; *v.* ri tik′yə lāt), *adj., v.,* **-lat ed, -lat ing.** —*adj.* covered with a network; netlike. Reticulate leaves have the veins arranged like the threads of a net. —*v.t.* cover or mark with a network. —*v.i.* form a network. [< Latin *reticulatus* < *reticulum* net, network, diminutive of *retis* net] —**re tic′u late ly,** *adv.*

re tic u la tion (ri tik′yə lā′shən), *n.* 1 a reticulated formation, arrangement, or appearance; network. 2 one of the meshes of a network.

ret i cule (ret′ə kyül), *n.* a woman's small handbag, especially one with a drawstring. [< French *réticule*]

re tic u lo en do the li al system (ri-tik′yə lō en′dō thē′lē əl), system of cells in the spleen, lymph nodes, bone marrow, etc., that function in freeing the body of foreign matter and disease germs.

re tic u lum (ri tik′yə ləm), *n., pl.* **-la** (-lə). 1 network. 2 the second stomach of animals that chew the cud. [< Latin]

ret i na (ret′n ə), *n., pl.* **-i nas, -i nae** (-n ē′). the inner membrane at the back of the eyeball that is sensitive to light and receives optical images, and that is continuous with the optic nerve. See **eye** for diagram. [< Medieval Latin]

ret i nal (ret′n əl), *adj.* of or on the retina.

re tine (ri tēn′), *n.* a chemical substance found in various body tissues which retards the growth of cells. [< *ret(ard)* + *-ine*[2]]

ret i nene (ret′n ēn′), *n.* a pigment, an aldehyde of vitamin A, formed when rhodopsin in the rods of the eye is broken down by light.

ret i nue (ret′n ü, ret′n yü), *n.* group of attendants or retainers; following: *The king's retinue accompanied him on the journey.* [< Old French, originally past participle of *retenir* retain]

re tire (ri tīr′), *v.,* **-tired, -tir ing.** —*v.i.* 1 give up an office, occupation, etc., especially because of old age: *Our teachers retire at 65.* 2 go away, especially to a place which is more quiet or private: *She retired to the country.* See **depart** for synonym study. 3 go back; retreat. 4 go to bed: *We retire early.* —*v.t.* 1 remove from an office, occupation, etc. 2 withdraw; draw back. 3 withdraw from circulation and pay off (bonds, loans, etc.). 4 put out (a batter, side, etc.) in baseball and cricket. [< Middle French *retirer* < *re-* back + *tirer* to draw]

re tired (ri tīrd′), *adj.* 1 withdrawn from one's occupation: *a retired sea captain.* 2 reserved; retiring: *a shy, retired nature.* 3 secluded; shut off; hidden: *a retired spot.*

re tir ee (ri tī′rē′), *n.* person who has retired.

re tire ment (ri tīr′mənt), *n.* 1 a retiring or a being retired; withdrawal. 2 a quiet way or place of living.

re tir ing (ri tī′ring), *adj.* reserved; shy. —**re tir′ing ly,** *adv.* —**re tir′ing ness,** *n.*

re told (rē tōld′), *v.* pt. and pp. of **retell.**

re took (rē tu̇k′), *v.* pt. of **retake.**

re tool (rē tül′), *v.i.* change the tools, machinery, designs, etc., in a plant to make new models or products.

re tort[1] (ri tôrt′), *v.i.* reply quickly or sharply. —*v.t.* 1 say in sharp reply. 2 return in kind; turn back on: *retort insult for insult.*

hat, āge, fär; let, ēqual, tėrm;
it, īce; hot, ōpen, ôrder;
oil, out; cup, pu̇t, rüle;
ch, child; ng, long; sh, she;
th, thin; ᴛʜ, then; zh, measure;

ə represents *a* in about, *e* in taken, *i* in pencil, *o* in lemon, *u* in circus.

< = from, derived from, taken from.

—*n.* a sharp or witty reply, especially one that turns the first speaker's statement or argument against him. [< Latin *retortum* turned back < *re-* back + *torquere* to twist]

re tort[2] (ri tôrt′, rē′tôrt), *n.* container used for distilling or decomposing substances by heat. [< Popular Latin *retorta* < Latin, feminine of *retortum* turned back. See RETORT[1].]

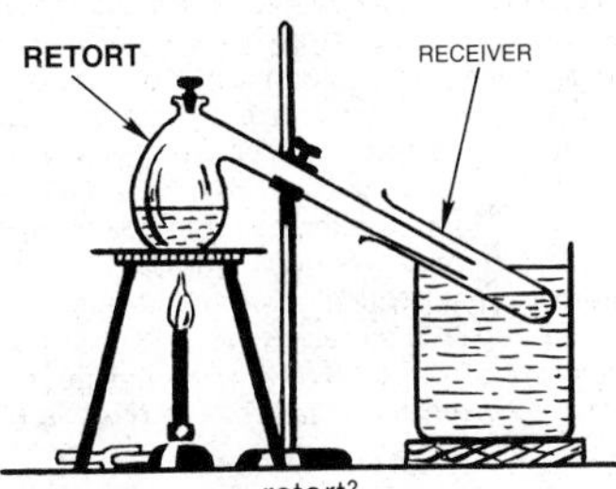

retort[2]

re touch (rē tuch′, rē′tuch′), *v.t.* improve (a photographic negative, painting, etc.) by new touches or slight changes. —*n.* a second or further touch given to a picture, composition, etc., to improve it. —**re touch′er,** *n.*

re trace (ri trās′), *v.t.,* **-traced, -trac ing.** go or trace back over: *We retraced our steps to where we started.* —**re trace′a ble,** *adj.*

re tract (ri trakt′), *v.t.* 1 draw back or in: *The kitten retracted her claws when I petted her.* 2 withdraw; take back: *retract an offer.* [< Latin *retractum* drawn back < *re-* + *trahere* to draw] —**re tract′a ble,** *adj.*

re trac tile (ri trak′tl), *adj.* that can be drawn back or in.

re trac tion (ri trak′shən), *n.* 1 a drawing or a being drawn back or in. 2 a taking back; withdrawal of a promise, statement, etc. 3 retractile power.

re trac tor (ri trak′tər), *n.* 1 person or thing that draws back something. 2 muscle that retracts an organ, protruded part, etc. 3 a surgical instrument for drawing back the edges of a wound.

re tread (*v.* rē tred′; *n.* rē′tred′), *v.t.* put a new tread on. —*n.* 1 tire that has been retreaded. 2 INFORMAL. restoration or renewal of an old or worn event, idea, etc.

re treat (ri trēt′), *v.i.* go back; move or draw back; withdraw: *The enemy retreated before the advance of our troops.* —*n.* 1 act of going back or withdrawing; withdrawal: *an orderly retreat.* 2 signal for retreat: *The drums beat a retreat.* 3 signal on a bugle or drum, given at sunset during the lowering of the flag. 4 a safe, quiet place; place of rest or refuge. 5 a retirement, or period of retirement, by a group of people for religious exercises, meditation, etc. 6 **beat a retreat,** run away; retreat. [< Old French *retraite* retreat < *retraire* withdraw < Latin *retrahere* < *re-* + *trahere* to draw]

re trench (ri trench′), *v.t.* cut down or reduce (expenses, etc.). —*v.i.* reduce expenses. [< Middle French *retrencher* < *re-* back + *trencher* to cut] **—re trench′ment,** *n.*

re tri al (rē trī′əl, rē′trī əl), *n.* a second trial; new trial.

ret ri bu tion (ret′rə byü′shən), *n.* a deserved punishment; return for evil done. [< Latin *retributionem,* ultimately < *re-* back + *tribuere* assign]

re trib u tive (ri trib′yə tiv), *adj.* paying back; bringing or inflicting punishment in return for some evil, wrong, etc. **—re trib′u tive ly,** *adv.*

re trib u to ry (ri trib′yə tôr′ē, ri trib′yə tōr′ē), *adj.* retributive.

re triev al (ri trē′vəl), *n.* 1 act of retrieving; recovery. 2 possibility of recovery.

re trieve (ri trēv′), *v.,* **-trieved, -triev ing.** —*v.t.* 1 get again; recover: *retrieve a lost pocketbook.* See **recover** for synonym study. 2 bring back to a former or better condition; restore: *retrieve one's fortunes.* 3 make good; make amends for: *retrieve a mistake.* 4 find and bring to a person: *A dog can be trained to retrieve game.* —*v.i.* find and bring back killed or wounded game. —*n.* act of retrieving; recovery. [< Old French *retruev-,* a form of *retrouver* find again < *re-* again + *trouver* to find] **—re triev′a ble,** *adj.*

retriever—(def. 1) 2 ft. high at the shoulder

re triev er (ri trē′vər), *n.* 1 dog trained to find killed or wounded game and bring it to a hunter. 2 person or thing that retrieves.

retro-, *prefix.* backward; back; behind, as in *retrocede.* [< Latin < *retro* back]

re tro ac tive (ret′rō ak′tiv), *adj.* acting back; having an effect on what is past. A retroactive law applies to events that occurred before the law was passed. **—ret′ro ac′tive ly,** *adv.*

ret ro cede (ret′rə sēd′), *v.,* **-ced ed, -ced ing.** —*v.i.* go back; recede. —*v.t.* cede back (territory, etc.).

re tro ces sion (ret′rə sesh′ən), *n.* 1 a going back. 2 a ceding back.

ret ro fire (ret′rō fīr′), *n., v.,* **-fired, -fir ing.** —*n.* the firing of a retrorocket. —*v.i.* fire a retrorocket.

ret ro flec tion (ret′rə flek′shən), *n.* retroflexion.

ret ro flex (ret′rə fleks), *adj.* 1 bent backward. 2 having the tip raised and bent backward. 3 made by raising the tip of the tongue and bending it backward: *a retroflex vowel.* [< Latin *retroflexum* < *retro-* back + *flectere* to bend]

ret ro flexed (ret′rə flekst), *adj.* retroflex.

ret ro flex ion (ret′rə flek′shən), *n.* a bending backward. Also, **retroflection.**

ret ro gra da tion (ret′rə grā dā′shən), *n.* a backward movement.

ret ro grade (ret′rə grād), *adj., v.,* **-grad ed, -grad ing.** —*adj.* 1 moving backward; retreating. 2 becoming worse; declining; deteriorating. —*v.i.* 1 move or go backward. 2 fall back toward a worse condition; grow worse; decline; deteriorate. [< Latin *retrogradus* < *retro-* back + *gradi* go]

ret ro gress (ret′rə gres, ret′rə gres′), *v.i.* 1 move backward, especially to an earlier or less advanced condition. 2 become worse; retrograde. [< Latin *retrogressum* gone backward < *retro-* + *gradi* go] **—ret′ro gres′sion,** *n.*

ret ro gres sive (ret′rə gres′iv), *adj.* 1 moving backward. 2 becoming worse. **—ret′ro gres′sive ly,** *adv.*

ret ro rock et (ret′rō rok′it), *n.* a small rocket at the front of a rocket, missile, or spacecraft that produces thrust opposite to the motion of the spacecraft in order to reduce speed for landing or for reentry.

re trorse (ri trôrs′), *adj.* turned backward; turned in a direction opposite to the usual one. [< Latin *retrorsum,* contraction of *retroversum* < *retro-* back + *vertere* to turn] **—re trorse′ly,** *adv.*

ret ro spect (ret′rə spekt), *n.* 1 survey of past time, events, etc.; thinking about the past. 2 **in retrospect,** when looking back. —*v.t.* think of (something past). [< Latin *retro-* back + *specere* to look]

ret ro spec tion (ret′rə spek′shən), *n.* 1 act of looking back on things past. 2 survey of past events or experiences.

ret ro spec tive (ret′rə spek′tiv), *adj.* 1 looking back on things past; surveying past events or experiences. 2 applying to the past; retroactive. **—ret′ro spec′tive ly,** *adv.*

ret rous sé (ret′rü sā′), *adj.* turned up: *a retroussé nose.* [< French]

re turn (ri tėrn′), *v.i.* go or come back: *return next summer.* —*v.t.* 1 bring, give, send, hit, put, or pay back: *return a compliment. Return that book to the library.* 2 yield: *The concert returned about $50 over expenses.* 3 report or announce officially: *The jury returned a verdict of guilty.* 4 reply; answer: *"No!" he returned crossly.* 5 elect or reelect to a lawmaking body. 6 (in card games) lead (the suit led by one's partner). —*n.* 1 a going or coming back; happening again: *a prompt return to work.* 2 a bringing back; giving back; sending back; hitting back; putting back; paying back: *a poor return for kindness.* 3 thing returned. 4 Often, **returns,** *pl.* profit; amount received: *The returns from the sale were more than $100.* 5 **in return,** as a return; to return something. 6 report; account: *make out an income-tax return, election returns.* 7 reply; answer. 8 (in card games) a lead responding to the suit led by one's partner. 9 the ratio of the yield on a unit of a product to the cost of the unit. 10 (in sports) a hitting or striking back of the ball in play: *a return of a serve.* 11 pipe, tubing, or other channel for the return of a liquid, gas, etc., to its origin. —*adj.* 1 of or having to do with a return: *a return ticket.* 2 sent, given, done, etc., in return: *a return game.* [< Old French *retourner* < *re-* back + *tourner* to turn]

re turn a ble (ri tėr′nə bəl), *adj.* 1 that can be returned. 2 meant or required to be returned.

re turn ee (ri tėr′nē′), *n.* person who has returned, especially one who has returned to his own country after capture in a war or from service abroad.

re tuse (ri tyüs′, ri tüs′), *adj.* (in botany) having an obtuse or rounded apex with a shallow notch in the center: *a retuse leaf.* [< Latin *retusum* beaten back < *re-* back + *tundere* to beat]

retuse leaf

re u ni fy (rē yü′nə fī), *v.t.,* **-fied, -fy ing.** unify again; bring back into a union. **—re′u ni fi ca′tion,** *n.*

re un ion (rē yü′nyən), *n.* 1 a coming together again. 2 a being reunited. 3 a social gathering of persons who have been separated or who have interests in common: *a college reunion.*

Ré un ion (rē yü′nyən; *French* rā y nyôN′), *n.* island in the Indian Ocean, east of Madagascar. It is an overseas department of France. 446,000 pop.; 970 sq. mi.

re u nite (rē′yü nīt′), *v.t., v.i.,* **-nit ed, -nit ing.** bring or come together again: *reunite a family.*

re use (*v.* rē yüz′; *n.* rē yüs′), *v.,* **-used, -us ing,** *n.* —*v.t.* use again. —*n.* a using again. **—re us′a ble,** *adj.*

rev (rev), *n., v.,* **revved, rev ving.** INFORMAL. —*n.* a revolution (of an engine or motor). —*v.t.* 1 increase the speed of (an engine or motor). 2 stimulate. —*v.i.* be revved.

rev., 1 revenue. 2 review. 3 revised. 4 revolution.

Rev., 1 Revelation. 2 Reverend.

re val ue (rē val′yü), *v.t.,* **-val ued, -val u ing.** value again or anew. **—re′val u a′tion,** *n.*

re vamp (rē vamp′), *v.t.* 1 patch up; repair. 2 take apart and put together in a new form: *revamp a plan.*

re vanche (rə vänsh′), *n.* FRENCH. revenge.

re vanch ism (rə vän′shiz′əm), *n.* the beliefs or practices of the revanchists.

re vanch ist (rə vän′shist), *n.* person who advocates taking up arms to recover territory lost in a war.

re veal (ri vēl′), *v.t.* 1 make known; divulge: *reveal a secret.* See synonym study below. 2 display; show: *Her smile revealed her even teeth.* [< Latin *revelare* < *re-* back + *velum* veil] **—re veal′a ble,** *adj.* **—re veal′er,** *n.* **—re veal′ment,** *n.*

Syn. 1 **Reveal, disclose** mean to make known something hidden or secret. **Reveal** applies especially when the thing has been unknown or unrecognized before: *At the new school he revealed an aptitude for science.* **Disclose** applies especially when the thing has been kept hidden on purpose: *She disclosed that she had lost her job and was looking for work.*

rev eil le (rev′ə lē), *n.* a signal on a bugle or drum to waken soldiers or sailors in the morning. [< French *réveillez(-vous)* awaken!]

rev el (rev′əl), *v.,* **-eled, -el ing** or **-elled, -el ling,** *n.* —*v.i.* 1 take great pleasure *(in): The children revel in country life.* 2 make merry. —*n.* a noisy good time; merrymaking. [< Old French *reveler* be disorderly, make merry < Latin *rebellare.* Doublet of REBEL.] **—rev′el er, rev′el ler,** *n.*

rev e la tion (rev′ə lā′shən), *n.* 1 act of making known. 2 the thing made known: *Her true nature was a revelation to me.* 3 God's disclosure of Himself and of His will to His creatures. 4 **Revelation,** the last book of the New Testament, supposed to have been written by the apostle John. [< Latin *revelationem* < *revelare* reveal]

rev el ry (rev′əl rē), *n., pl.* **-ries.** boisterous reveling or festivity.

re venge (ri venj′), *n., v.,* **-venged, -veng ing.** —*n.* 1 harm done in return for a wrong; satisfaction obtained by repayment of an injury, etc.; vengeance: *take revenge, get revenge.* 2 desire for vengeance. 3 chance to win in a return game after losing a game. —*v.i.* take vengeance. —*v.t.* do harm in return for. See synonym study below.
be revenged or **revenge oneself,** get revenge.
[< Middle French < *revenger* avenge < Latin *re-* back + *vindicare* avenge] **—re veng′er,** *n.*
Syn. *v.t.* **Revenge, avenge** mean to punish someone in return for a wrong. **Revenge** applies when it is indulged in to get even: *Gangsters revenge the murder of one of their gang.* **Avenge** applies when the punishment seems just: *They fought to avenge the enemy's invasion of their country.*

re venge ful (ri venj′fəl), *adj.* feeling or showing a strong desire for revenge; vengeful; vindictive. **—re venge′ful ly,** *adv.* **—re venge′ful ness,** *n.*

rev e nue (rev′ə nü, rev′ə nyü), *n.* 1 money coming in; income. The government gets revenue from taxes. 2 a particular item of income. 3 a source of income. [< Middle French < *revenir* come back < Latin *re-* + *venire* come]

rev e nu er (rev′ə nü′ər, rev′ə nyü′ər), *n.* U.S. a government official who collects or enforces the collection of taxes, duties, etc.

revenue stamp, stamp to show that money has been paid to the government as a tax on something.

re ver ber ant (ri vėr′bər ənt), *adj.* reverberating.

re ver be rate (ri vėr′bə rāt′), *v.,* **-rat ed, -rat ing.** —*v.i.* 1 echo back: *His voice reverberates from the high ceiling.* 2 be cast back; be reflected a number of times, as light or heat. —*v.t.* 1 reecho (a sound or noise). 2 cast back; reflect (light or heat). [< Latin *reverberatum* beaten back < *re-* back + *verber* a blow] **—re ver′be ra′tion,** *n.*

re ver ber a to ry (ri vėr′bər ə tôr′ē, ri vėr′bər ə tōr′ē), *adj.* characterized by or produced by reverberations. —*n.* furnace or kiln built with a vaulted roof so that heat and flame are deflected onto the ore or metal.

re vere[1] (ri vir′), *v.t.,* **-vered, -ver ing.** love and respect deeply; honor greatly; show reverence for. See synonym study below. [< Latin *revereri* < *re-* back + *vereri* stand in awe of, fear]
Syn. Revere, reverence mean to feel deep respect for someone or something. **Revere** implies deep respect mixed with love, and applies especially to persons: *People revered the great general.* **Reverence** implies, in addition, wonder or awe, and applies especially to things: *We reverence the tomb of the Unknown Soldier.*

re vere[2] (ri vir′), *n.* revers.

Re vere (ri vir′), *n.* **Paul,** 1735-1818, American patriot, famous for his night ride through eastern Massachusetts to warn colonists of the approach of British troops in 1775.

rev er ence (rev′ər əns), *n., v.* **-enced, -enc ing.** —*n.* 1 a feeling of deep respect, mixed with wonder, awe, and love; veneration. 2 a deep bow. 3 condition of being greatly respected or venerated. 4 **Reverence,** title used in speaking of or to a clergyman. —*v.t.* regard with reverence; revere. See **revere** for synonym study.

rev er end (rev′ər ənd), *adj.* worthy of great respect. —*n.* 1 **Reverend,** title for clergymen. 2 INFORMAL. clergyman. [< Latin *reverendus* < *revereri.* See REVERE.]

rev er ent (rev′ər ənt), *adj.* feeling reverence; showing reverence. **—rev′er ent ly,** *adv.*

rev e ren tial (rev′ə ren′shəl), *adj.* reverent. **—rev′e ren′tial ly,** *adv.*

rev er ie (rev′ər ē), *n.* 1 dreamy thoughts; dreamy thinking of pleasant things. 2 condition of being lost in dreamy thoughts. Also, **revery.** [< French *rêverie* < *rêver* to dream]

re vers (rə vir′, rə ver′), *n., pl.* **-vers** (-virz′, -verz′). part of a garment, as a lapel, turned back to show the lining, facing, or underside. Also, **revere.** [< French, originally, reversed]

re ver sal (ri vėr′səl), *n.* a change to the opposite; a reversing or a being reversed.

re verse (ri vėrs′), *n., adj., v.,* **-versed, -vers ing.** —*n.* 1 the opposite or contrary: *She did the reverse of what I ordered.* 2 the back: *His name is on the reverse of the medal.* 3 an opposite or contrary motion or direction: *a reverse in dancing.* 4 arrangement of gears that reverses the movement of machinery. 5 a change to bad fortune; check; defeat: *He used to be rich, but he met with reverses.* —*adj.* 1 turned backward; opposite or contrary in position or direction: *the reverse side of a phonograph record.* 2 acting in a manner opposite or contrary to that which is usual. 3 causing an opposite or backward movement: *the reverse gear of an automobile.* —*v.t.* 1 turn the other way; turn inside out; turn upside down. See synonym study below. 2 turn in a direction opposite to the usual one while dancing. 3 change to the opposite; repeal. [< Latin *reversum* turned around, reverted] **—re verse′ly,** *adv.* **—re vers′er,** *n.*
Syn. *v.t.* 1 **Reverse, invert** mean to turn something the other way. **Reverse** is the more general in application, meaning to turn to the other side or in an opposite position, direction, order, etc.: *reverse a phonograph record, reverse one's steps.* **Invert** means to turn upside down: *Invert the glasses to drain.*

re vers i bil i ty (ri vėr′sə bil′ə tē), *n.* fact or quality of being reversible.

re vers i ble (ri vėr′sə bəl), *adj.* 1 that can be reversed; that can reverse. 2 (of a fabric, etc.) finished on both sides so that it can be worn with either side showing. —*n.* a reversible fabric or garment. **—re vers′i bly,** *adv.*

re ver sion (ri vėr′zhən, ri vėr′shən), *n.* 1 return to a former condition, practice, belief, etc.; return. 2 the return of an estate to the grantor or to his heirs, after the grant expires. 3 the right to future possession of a property, title, etc. 4 (in biology) a return to an earlier type; atavism. 5 act or fact of turning or being turned the reverse way; reversal.

re ver sion al (ri vėr′zhə nəl, ri vėr′shə nəl), *adj.* of, having to do with, or involving a reversion.

re ver sion ar y (ri vėr′zhə ner′ē, ri vėr′shə ner′ē), *adj.* reversional.

hat, āge, fär; let, ēqual, tėrm;
it, īce; hot, ōpen, ôrder;
oil, out; cup, pu̇t, rüle;
ch, child; ng, long; sh, she;
th, thin; ᴛʜ, then; zh, measure;

ə represents *a* in about, *e* in taken, *i* in pencil, *o* in lemon, *u* in circus.

< = from, derived from, taken from.

re vert (ri vėrt′), *v.i.* 1 go back; return: *My thoughts reverted to the last time that I had seen her.* 2 go back to a former possessor or to his heirs: *If a man dies without heirs, his property reverts to the state.* [< Latin *revertere* < *re-* back + *vertere* to turn] **—re vert′i ble,** *adj.*

rev er y (rev′ər ē), *n., pl.* **-er ies.** reverie.

re vet (ri vet′), *v.t.,* **-vet ted, -vet ting.** face (a wall, embankment, etc.) with masonry or other material. [< French *revêtir* clothe again]

re vet ment (ri vet′mənt), *n.* a retaining wall; facing of stone, brick, cement, etc., supporting or protecting a bank or embankment.

re view (ri vyü′), *v.t.* 1 study again; look at again: *Review the lesson for tomorrow.* 2 look back on: *review the day's happenings.* 3 examine again; look at with care; examine. 4 (in law) subject (a decision, etc.) to examination or revision. 5 inspect formally: *The colonel reviewed the regiment.* 6 write and publish, or read aloud to a radio or television audience, an account of a book, play, movie, etc., giving its merits and faults. —*v.i.* review books, plays, etc.
—*n.* 1 a studying again: *a review of the term's work.* 2 a looking back on; survey. 3 reexamination. 4 (in law) examination or revision of the decision or proceedings of a lower court by a higher one. 5 examination; inspection: *a review of troops.* 6 discussion or evaluation of a book, play, movie, etc., giving its merits and faults. See synonym study below. 7 magazine containing articles on subjects of current interest, including evaluation of books, etc. 8 revue.
[< Middle French *reveue* < *revoir* see again < Latin *revidere* < *re-* again + *videre* to see]
Syn. *n.* 6 **Review, criticism** mean an account discussing and evaluating a book, play, movie, art exhibit, etc. **Review** applies particularly to an account of a current book or play, etc., giving some idea of what it is about, its good and bad points, and the reviewer's critical or personal opinion: *Have the reviews of that movie made you decide to see it?* **Criticism** applies particularly to an account giving a critical judgment, often of a number of related works, based on deep and thorough study and applying sound critical standards of what is good and bad in books, music, pictures, etc.: *I read a good criticism of Faulkner's works.*

re view er (ri vyü′ər), *n.* 1 person who reviews. 2 person who writes articles discussing books, plays, etc.

re vile (ri vīl′), *v.,* **-viled, -vil ing.** —*v.t.* call bad names; abuse with words. —*v.i.* speak abusively. [< Old French *reviler* despise < *re-* again + *vil* vile] **—re vile′ment,** *n.* **—re vil′er,** *n.*

re vis al (ri vī′zəl), *n.* 1 a revising. 2 a revision.

re vise (ri vīz′), *v.*, **-vised, -vis ing,** *n.* —*v.t.* 1 read carefully in order to correct; look over and change; examine and improve: *revise a manuscript.* 2 change; alter: *revise one's opinion.* —*n.* 1 process of revising. 2 a revised form or version. 3 a proof sheet printed after corrections have been made. [< Latin *revisere* see again < *re-* again + *videre* to see] —**re vis′er, re vi′sor,** *n.*

Revised Standard Version, an American Protestant revision of the New Testament, published in 1946, and of the whole Bible, published in 1952.

Revised Version, the revised form of the Authorized Version of the Bible. The New Testament was published in 1881 and the Old Testament in 1885.

re vi sion (ri vizh′ən), *n.* 1 act or work of revising. 2 a revised form or version: *a revision of a book.*

re vi sion ism (ri vizh′ə niz′əm), *n.* the beliefs or practices of the communist revisionists.

re vi sion ist (ri vizh′ə nist), *n.* 1 person who favors or supports revision. 2 communist who tends to a somewhat flexible interpretation of Marxism, believing in the revision of doctrines according to changing national needs. —*adj.* favoring revision or revisionism.

re vi sor y (ri vī′zər ē), *adj.* of or having to do with revision.

re vi tal ize (rē vī′tə līz), *v.t.*, **-ized, -iz ing.** restore to vitality; put new life into. —**re vi′tal i za′tion,** *n.*

re viv al (ri vī′vəl), *n.* 1 a bringing or coming back to life or consciousness. 2 restoration to vigor or health. 3 a bringing or coming back to style, use, activity, etc.: *the revival of an old play.* 4 an awakening or increase of interest in religion. 5 special services or efforts made to awaken or increase interest in religion.

re viv al ism (ri vī′və liz′əm), *n.* the spirit and practices of religious revivals and revivalists.

re viv al ist (ri vī′və list), *n.* person who holds special services to awaken interest in religion, especially an evangelistic preacher.

re vive (ri vīv′), *v.*, **-vived, -viv ing.** —*v.t.* 1 bring back to life or consciousness: *revive a half-drowned person.* 2 bring back to a fresh, lively condition. 3 make fresh; restore; refresh: *Hot coffee revived the cold, tired man.* 4 bring back to notice, use, fashion, memory, activity, etc.: *revive an old song.* —*v.i.* 1 come back to life or consciousness. 2 come back to a fresh, lively condition: *Flowers revive in water.* 3 become fresh. 4 come back to notice, use, fashion, memory, activity, etc. [< Latin *revivere* < *re-* again + *vivere* to live] —**re viv′er,** *n.*

re viv i fy (rē viv′ə fī), *v.t.*, *v.i.*, **-fied, -fy ing.** restore to life; give new life to. —**re viv′i fi ca′tion,** *n.*

rev o ca ble (rev′ə kə bəl), *adj.* that can be revoked.

rev o ca tion (rev′ə kā′shən), *n.* act of revoking; repeal; withdrawal.

rev o ca to ry (rev′ə kə tôr′ē, rev′ə kə-tôr′ē), *adj.* revoking; recalling; repealing.

re vok a ble (ri vō′kə bəl, rev′ə kə bəl), *adj.* revocable.

re voke (ri vōk′), *v.*, **-voked, -vok ing,** *n.* —*v.t.* take back; repeal; cancel; withdraw: *revoke a driver's license.* —*v.i.* fail to follow suit in playing cards when one can and should; renege. —*n.* (in cards) a failure to follow suit when one can and should; renege. [< Latin *revocare* < *re-* back + *vocare* to call]

re volt (ri vōlt′), *n.* act or state of rebelling. See synonym study below. —*v.i.* 1 turn away from and fight against a leader; rise against the government's authority: *The people revolted against the dictator.* 2 turn away with disgust: *revolt at a bad smell.* —*v.t.* cause to feel disgust; repel; sicken. [< Middle French *révolte* < Italian *rivolta,* ultimately < Latin *revolvere* revolve. See REVOLVE.] —**re volt′er,** *n.*

Syn. *n.* **Revolt, insurrection, rebellion** mean a rising up in active resistance against authority. **Revolt** emphasizes casting off allegiance and refusing to accept existing conditions or control: *The revolt of the American colonists developed into revolution.* **Insurrection** applies to an armed uprising of a group often small, poorly organized, and selfishly motivated: *The insurrection was started by a few malcontents.* **Rebellion** applies to open armed resistance organized to overthrow the government or force it to do something: *A rebellion may become civil war.*

re volt ing (ri vōl′ting), *adj.* disgusting; repulsive. —**re volt′ing ly,** *adv.*

rev o lu tion (rev′ə lü′shən), *n.* 1 a complete overthrow of an established government or political system. 2 a complete change: *The automobile caused a revolution in ways of traveling.* 3 movement in a circle or curve around some point: *One revolution of the earth around the sun takes a year.* 4 act or fact of turning round a center or axis; rotation: *The wheel of the motor turns at a rate of more than one thousand revolutions per minute.* 5 time or distance of one revolution. 6 a complete cycle or series of events: *The revolution of the four seasons fills a year.* [< Latin *revolutionem* < *revolvere* revolve]

rev o lu tion ar y (rev′ə lü′shə ner′ē), *adj., n., pl.* **-ar ies.** —*adj.* 1 of a revolution; connected with a revolution. 2 bringing or causing great changes. —*n.* revolutionist.

Revolutionary War, the war from 1775 to 1783 by which the thirteen American colonies won independence from England; American Revolution; War of Independence.

rev o lu tion ist (rev′ə lü′shə nist), *n.* person who advocates, or takes part in, a revolution. —*adj.* revolutionary.

rev o lu tion ize (rev′ə lü′shə nīz), *v.t.*, **-ized, -iz ing.** 1 change completely; produce a fundamental change in. 2 cause a revolution in the government of. 3 indoctrinate with revolutionary ideas or principles.

re volve (ri volv′), *v.*, **-volved, -volv ing.** —*v.i.* 1 move in a circle; move in a curve round a point: *The moon revolves around the earth.* 2 turn round a center or axis; rotate: *The wheels of a moving car revolve.* See **turn** for synonym study. 3 move in a complete cycle or series of events. —*v.t.* 1 cause to move round. 2 turn over in the mind; consider from many points of view. [< Latin *revolvere* < *re-* back + *volvere* to roll] —**re volv′a ble,** *adj.*

re volv er (ri vol′vər), *n.* pistol with a revolving cylinder in which the cartridges are contained, that can be fired several times without being reloaded.

re vue (ri vyü′), *n.* a theatrical entertainment with singing, dancing, parodies of recent movies and plays, humorous treatments of current happenings and fads, etc. Also, **review.** [< French, review]

re vul sion (ri vul′shən), *n.* 1 a sudden, violent change or reaction, especially of disgust. 2 a drawing or a being drawn back or away, especially suddenly or violently. [< Latin *revulsionem* < *re-* back + *vellere* tear away]

Rev. Ver., Revised Version.

re ward (ri wôrd′), *n.* 1 return made for something done. 2 a money payment given or offered for capture of criminals, the return of lost property, etc. —*v.t.* 1 give a reward to; recompense; repay. 2 give a reward for. [< Old North French < *rewarder, regarder* < Old French *re-* back + *garder* to guard, care for. Doublet of REGARD.]

re wire (rē wīr′), *v.t., v.i.*, **-wired, -wir ing.** 1 put new wires on or in. 2 telegraph again.

re word (rē wėrd′), *v.t.* put into other words; rephrase.

re work (rē wėrk′), *v.t.* work over again; revise.

re write (*v.* rē rīt′; *n.* rē′rīt′), *v.*, **-wrote** (-rōt′), **-writ ten** (-rit′n), —**writ ing,** *n.* —*v.t., v.i.* 1 write again; write in a different form; revise. 2 U.S. write (a news story) from material supplied over the telephone or in a form that cannot be used as copy. —*n.* U.S. a news story that has to be rewritten.

Rey kja vik (rā′kyə vēk′), *n.* capital of Iceland, a seaport in the SW part. 81,000.

Reyn ard (ren′ərd, rā′närd), *n.* 1 fox who is the main character in a group of medieval fables about animals. 2 **reynard,** fox.

Reyn olds (ren′ldz), *n.* Sir **Joshua,** 1723-1792, English portrait painter.

re zone (rē zōn′), *v.t.*, **-zoned, -zon ing.** zone again; change the present zoning of: *rezone an area.*

r.f. or **R.F.,** radio frequency.

R.F.D., Rural Free Delivery.

r.h., 1 relative humidity. 2 (in music) right hand.

Rh, rhodium.

Rhad a man thus (rad′ə man′thəs), *n.* (in Greek myths) a judge of the dead in Hades.

Rhae tian Alps (rē′shən), range of the Alps in E Switzerland.

Rhae to-Ro man ic (rē′tō rō man′ik), *adj.* of or having to do with a group of Romance dialects spoken in the Rhaetian Alps. —*n.* the Rhaeto-Romanic dialects.

rhap sod ic (rap sod′ik), *adj.* rhapsodical.

rhap sod i cal (rap sod′ə kəl), *adj.* of, having to do with, or characteristic of rhapsody; extravagantly enthusiastic; ecstatic. —**rhap sod′i cal ly,** *adv.*

rhap so dist (rap′sə dist), *n.* person who talks or writes with extravagant enthusiasm.

rhap so dize (rap′sə dīz), *v.i.*, **-dized, -diz ing.** talk or write with extravagant enthusiasm.

rhap so dy (rap′sə dē), *n., pl.* **-dies.** 1 utterance or writing marked by extravagant enthusiasm: *go into rhapsodies over a gift.* 2 (in music) an instrumental composition, irregular in form, resembling an improvisation: *Liszt's Hungarian rhapsodies.* 3 an epic poem, or a part of such a poem, suitable for recitation at one time. [< Greek *rhapsōidia*

revolver

verse composition < *rhaptein* to stitch + *ōidē* song, ode]

rhe a (rē′ə), *n.* any of an order of large, flightless birds of South America that are much like the ostrich, but are smaller and have three toes instead of two. [< *Rhea*]

rhea—3 ft. tall

Rhe a (rē′ə), *n.* (in Greek myths) the mother of Zeus, Hera, Poseidon, and other important Greek gods.

Rhee (rē), *n.* **Syngman,** 1875-1965, Korean statesman, president of South Korea from 1948 to 1960.

Rheims (rēmz; *French* raɴs), *n.* Reims.

Rhein (rīn), *n.* German name for the **Rhine.**

Rhein land (rīn′länt′), *n.* German name for **Rhineland.**

Rhen ish (ren′ish), *adj.* of the Rhine River or the regions near it. —*n.* Rhine wine. [< Latin *Rhenus* Rhine]

rhe ni um (rē′nē əm), *n.* a rare, hard, heavy, grayish metallic element with a very high melting point which occurs in molybdenum ore and is used in making alloys. *Symbol:* Re; *atomic number* 75. See pages 326 and 327 for table. [< Latin *Rhenus* Rhine]

rhe o log i cal (rē′ə loj′ə kəl), *adj.* of or having to do with rheology. **—rhe′o log′i cal ly,** *adv.*

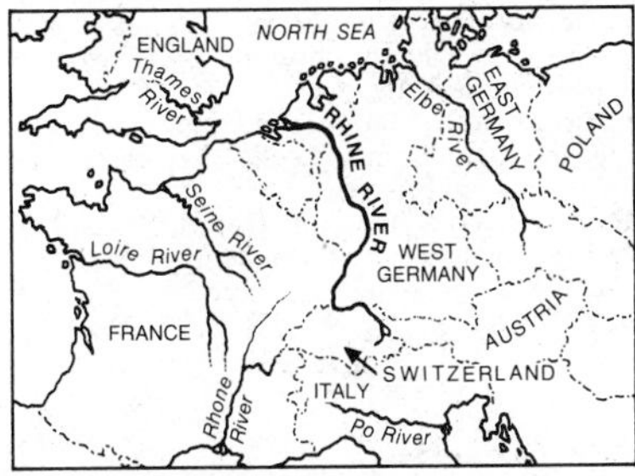

rhe ol o gist (rē ol′ə jist), *n.* an expert in rheology.

rhe ol o gy (rē ol′ə jē), *n.* science that deals with flow and alteration of form of matter. [< Greek *rheos* flow]

rhe o stat (rē′ə stat), *n.* instrument for regulating the strength of an electric current by introducing different amounts of resistance into the circuit. [< Greek *rheos* flow, current + *statos* standing still]

rhe o stat ic (rē′ə stat′ik), *adj.* having to do with a rheostat.

rhe sus (rē′səs), *n.* a small, yellowish-brown monkey, a macaque of India, with a short tail, often used in medical research. [< New Latin *rhesus,* the species name]

Rhe sus factor (rē′səs), Rh factor.

rhet or ic (ret′ər ik), *n.* 1 art of using words effectively in speaking or writing. 2 book about this art. 3 mere display in language. [< Latin *rhetorica* < Greek *rhētorikē (technē)* (art) of an orator < *rhētōr* orator]

rhe to ri cal (ri tôr′ə kəl, ri tor′ə kəl), *adj.* 1 of or having to do with rhetoric. 2 using rhetoric. 3 intended especially for display; artificial. 4 oratorical. **—rhe to′ri cal ly,** *adv.*

rhetorical question, question asked only for effect, not for information. EXAMPLE: "Who can tell whether or not life exists on other planets?"

rhet o ri cian (ret′ə rish′ən), *n.* 1 person skilled in rhetoric. 2 person given to display in language. 3 teacher of the art of rhetoric.

rheum (rüm), *n.* 1 a watery discharge, such as mucus or tears. 2 a cold; catarrh. [< Greek *rheuma* a flowing < *rhein* to flow]

rheu mat ic (rü mat′ik), *adj.* 1 of or having to do with rheumatism. 2 having or liable to have rheumatism. 3 causing rheumatism. 4 caused by rheumatism. —*n.* person who has rheumatism. **—rheu mat′i cal ly,** *adv.*

rheumatic fever, an acute disease, attacking usually children, with fever, pains in the joints, and often inflammation in the heart, causing harmful aftereffects.

rheu ma tism (rü′mə tiz′əm), *n.* any of several diseases or conditions characterized by inflammation, swelling, and stiffness of the joints, such as rheumatoid arthritis or rheumatic fever.

rheu ma toid arthritis (rü′mə toid), a chronic disease characterized by inflammation and stiffness of the joints, often crippling in its effects.

rheum y (rü′mē), *adj.,* **rheum i er, rheum i est.** 1 full of rheum. 2 causing rheum; damp and cold.

Rh factor, an antigen found in the red blood cells of most human beings and the higher mammals. Blood containing this substance **(Rh positive)** does not combine favorably with blood lacking it **(Rh negative).** Also, **Rhesus factor.** [< *rh(esus),* in whose blood it was first found]

rhi nal (rī′nl), *adj.* of or having to do with the nose; nasal. [< Greek *rhinos* nose]

Rhine (rīn), *n.* river flowing from central Switzerland through West Germany and the Netherlands into the North Sea. 810 mi. Also, GERMAN **Rhein.**

Rhine land (rīn′land′), *n.* 1 the region along the Rhine. 2 the part of West Germany west of the Rhine. Also, GERMAN **Rheinland.**

rhi nen ceph a lon (rī′nen sef′ə lon), *n., pl.* **-la** (-lə). the part of the brain most closely connected with the olfactory nerves.

rhine stone (rīn′stōn′), *n.* an imitation diamond, made of glass or paste.

Rhine wine, 1 wine produced in the valley of the Rhine. Most Rhine wines are light, dry, white wines. 2 a similar wine made elsewhere.

rhi ni tis (rī nī′tis), *n.* inflammation of the mucous membrane of the nose. [< New Latin < Greek *rhinos* nose]

rhi no (rī′nō), *n., pl.* **-nos** or **-no.** rhinoceros.

rhi noc er os (rī nos′ər əs), *n., pl.* **-os es** or **-os.** any of a family of large, thick-skinned mammals of Africa and Asia with one or two upright horns on the snout. Rhinoceroses eat grass and other plants. [< Greek *rhinokerōs* < *rhinos* nose + *keras* horn]

rhi no vi rus (rī′nō vī′rəs), *n.* any of a group of viruses associated with the common cold and other respiratory diseases.

rhi zoid (rī′zoid), *adj.* rootlike. —*n.* one of the rootlike filaments by which a moss, fern, liverwort, or fungus is attached to the substratum. [< Greek *rhiza* root]

rhi zom a tous (rī zom′ə təs, rī zō′mə təs), *adj.* 1 of or having to do with a rhizome. 2 having rhizomes.

hat, āge, fär; let, ēqual, tėrm;
it, īce; hot, ōpen, ôrder;
oil, out; cup, pu̇t, rüle;
ch, child; ng, long; sh, she;
th, thin; ᴛʜ, then; zh, measure;

ə represents *a* in about, *e* in taken, *i* in pencil, *o* in lemon, *u* in circus.

< = from, derived from, taken from.

rhi zome (rī′zōm), *n.* a rootlike, creeping, underground stem of some plants, which usually sends out roots below and leafy shoots above, stores food to be used by the new plant the following year, and has nodes, buds, and small, scalelike leaves; rootstock. [< Greek *rhizōma* < *rhiza* root]

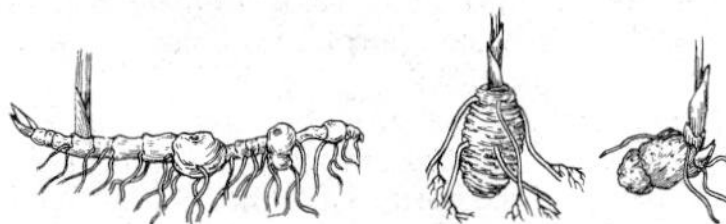

rhizome—three forms of rhizomes

rhi zo pod (rī′zə pod), *n.* any of a class of mostly marine protozoans that have pseudopods for moving about and taking in food; sarcodinian. Amoebas belong to this class. [< Greek *rhiza* root + *podos* foot]

rhi zop o dan (rī zop′ə dən), *n.* rhizopod. —*adj.* of or having to do with a rhizopod.

rhi zop o dous (rī zop′ə dəs), *adj.* rhizopodan.

rho (rō), *n.* the 17th letter of the Greek alphabet (P, ρ). [< Greek *rhō*]

Rhode Island (rōd), one of the northeastern states of the United States. 947,000 pop.; 1200 sq. mi. *Capital:* Providence. *Abbrev.:* R.I.

Rhode Island Red, any of a breed of American fowls that have reddish feathers and a black tail.

Rhodes (rōdz), *n.* 1 Greek island in the Aegean Sea, just southwest of Asia Minor. 64,000 pop.; 542 sq. mi. 2 seaport and capital of this island. 27,000. 3 **Cecil John,** 1853-1902, British colonial statesman and government administrator in South Africa.

Rho de sia (rō dē′zhə), *n.* country in SE Africa, a former self-governing British colony. 5,090,000 pop.; 150,300 sq. mi. *Capital:* Salisbury. See **South Africa** for map. Former name, **Southern Rhodesia. —Rho de′sian,** *adj., n.*

rhinoceros—5½ ft. high at the shoulder

Rhodesian man, a prehistoric man similar to the Neanderthal man, who lived in central and southern Africa in the early Stone Age, and whose remains were first discovered in northern Rhodesia.

Rhodes scholar, holder of a Rhodes scholarship.

Rhodes scholarship, a two- or three-year scholarship at Oxford University, founded by Cecil Rhodes.

rho di um (rō′dē əm), *n.* a silver-white metallic element with a very high melting point, found chiefly in platinum ores. It is resistant to acid, and is used for plating silverware, jewelry, etc. *Symbol:* Rh; *atomic number* 45. See pages 326 and 327 for table. [< New Latin < Greek *rhodon* rose]

rho do den dron (rō′də den′drən), *n., pl.* **-drons, -dra** (-drə). 1 any of a large genus of evergreen or deciduous shrubs or small trees of the heath family, cultivated chiefly for their leathery leaves and beautiful large, pink, purple, or white flowers. 2 the flower. [< Greek *rhodon* rose + *dendron* tree]

rho dop sin (rō dop′sən), *n.* a purplish-red protein pigment that is sensitive to light, found in the rods of the retina of the eye in all vertebrates; visual purple. [< Greek *rhodon* rose + *opsis* sight]

rho do ra (rō dôr′ə, rō dōr′ə), *n.* a low deciduous species of rhododendron of Canada and the northeast United States, with purplish-rose flowers that appear before the leaves do.

rhom ben ce phal ic (rom′ben sə fal′ik), *adj.* of or having to do with the hindbrain.

rhom ben ceph a lon (rom′ben sef′ə lon), *n.* hindbrain.

rhom bic (rom′bik), *adj.* 1 having the form of a rhombus. 2 orthorhombic.

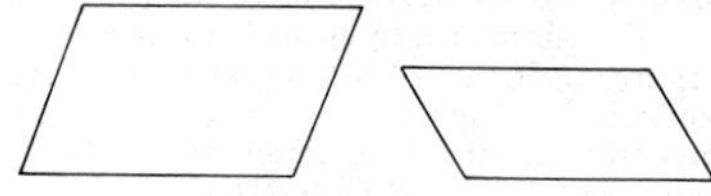

rhomboid—two rhomboids

rhom boid (rom′boid), *n.* parallelogram with equal opposite sides, unequal adjacent sides, and oblique angles. *—adj.* shaped like a rhombus or rhomboid.

rhom boi dal (rom boi′dl), *adj.* rhomboid.

rhombus—two rhombuses

rhom bus (rom′bəs), *n., pl.* **-bus es, -bi** (-bī). parallelogram with equal sides, usually having two obtuse angles and two acute angles. [< Latin < Greek *rhombos*]

Rhon dda (ron′də), *n.* city in SE Wales. 94,000.

Rhone River or **Rhône River** (rōn), river flowing from S Switzerland through SE France into the Mediterranean Sea. 504 mi. See **Rhine** for map.

rhu barb (rü′bärb), *n.* 1 a common garden plant of the same family as the buckwheat, with very large leaves whose thick and fleshy, sour stalks are used for making sauce, pies, etc.; pieplant. 2 its stalks. 3 SLANG. a heated dispute, usually marked by scornful comments: *a ball game filled with rhubarbs.* [< Medieval Latin *rheubarbarum,* ultimately < Greek *rhēon barbaron* foreign rhubarb]

rhum ba (rum′bə), *n.* rumba.

rhumb line (rum, rumb), line on the surface of a sphere cutting all meridians at the same oblique angle. [ultimately < Latin *rhombus*]

rhyme (rīm), *v.,* **rhymed, rhym ing,** *n.* *—v.i.* 1 sound alike in the last part: *"Long" and "song" rhyme. "Go to bed" rhymes with "sleepyhead."* 2 make rhymes. *—v.t.* 1 put or make into rhyme: *rhyme a translation.* 2 use (a word) with another that rhymes with it: *rhyme "love" and "dove."* *—n.* 1 word or line having the same last sound as another: *"Cat" is a rhyme for "mat."* 2 verses or poetry with some of the lines ending in similar sounds. 3 agreement in the final sounds of words or lines. 4 **without rhyme or reason,** having no system or sense. Also, **rime.** [< Old French *rime* rhyme] **—rhym′er,** *n.*

rhyme royal, a seven-line stanza in iambic pentameter with the rhyme scheme *a b a b b c c,* introduced into English by Chaucer.

rhyme scheme, the pattern of rhymes used in a stanza, verse, or poem, usually denoted by letters. EXAMPLE: *"a a b b c c"* has a couplet rhyme scheme.

rhyme ster (rīm′stər), *n.* maker of rather poor rhymes or verse. Also, **rimester.**

rhythm (riᴛʜ′əm), *n.* 1 movement with a regular repetition of a beat, accent, rise and fall, or the like: *the rhythm of the tides, the rhythm of one's heartbeats.* 2 the measured recurrence of accented and unaccented syllables, or of patterned rise and fall of sounds, in a foot or line of verse. 3 metrical form; meter. 4 musical sound characterized by regularly occurring accented beats. 5 grouping by accents or beats: *triple rhythm.* [< Greek *rhythmos* < *rhein* to flow]

rhyth mic (riᴛʜ′mik), *adj.* rhythmical.

rhyth mi cal (riᴛʜ′mə kəl), *adj.* having rhythm; of or having to do with rhythm. **—rhyth′mi cal ly,** *adv.*

R.I., Rhode Island.

ri al (rī′əl), *n.* 1 the monetary unit of Iran, a coin or note worth about $1^1/_3$ cents. 2 riyal. [< Arabic *riyāl* < Spanish *real.* Doublet of REAL[2], REGAL, ROYAL.]

Ri al to (rē al′tō), *n.* 1 former business district of Venice. 2 a theater district. 3 **rialto,** exchange; marketplace.

ri a ta (rē ä′tə), *n.* lariat. [< Spanish *reata*]

rib (rib), *n., v.,* **ribbed, rib bing.** *—n.* 1 one of the curved bones joined in pairs to the spine, in man and most vertebrates enclosing all or most of the chest cavity and protecting the viscera contained therein. 2 anything like a rib. 3 one of the curved timbers in a ship's frame. 4 one of the metal strips supporting the fabric of an umbrella. 5 a thick vein of a leaf. 6 ridge in cloth, knitting, etc. 7 cut of meat containing a rib. See **beef** for diagram. *—v.t.* 1 furnish or strengthen with ribs. 2 mark with riblike ridges. 3 INFORMAL. tease. [Old English *ribb*] **—rib′ber,** *n.* **—rib′like′,** *adj.*

rib ald (rib′əld), *adj.* offensive in speech; coarsely mocking; irreverent; indecent; obscene: *a ribald story, a ribald party.* [< Old French *ribauld*]

rib ald ry (rib′əl drē), *n.* ribald language.

rib and (rib′ənd), *n.* ARCHAIC. ribbon.

ribbed (ribd), *adj.* having ribs or ridges.

rib bon (rib′ən), *n.* 1 strip or band of silk, satin, velvet, etc., used to ornament clothing, packages, or the like. 2 anything like such a strip: *a typewriter ribbon.* 3 a small badge of cloth worn in place of a decoration for bravery, as a sign of membership in an order, etc. 4 Usually, **ribbons,** *pl.* torn strips of anything; tatters; shreds: *a dress torn to ribbons.* [< Old French *ruban*] **—rib′bon like′,** *adj.*

rib boned (rib′ənd), *adj.* decorated with ribbons; tied with a ribbon.

rib bon fish (rib′ən fish′), *n., pl.* **-fish es** or **-fish.** any of several deep-sea fishes with a long, very slender, ribbonlike body.

ribbon worm, any of a phylum of soft, thin, contractile worms varying in length from less than an inch to over 80 feet and living chiefly in the sea; nemertean.

rib cage (rib′kāj′), *n.* the barrel-shaped enclosure formed by the ribs of the chest.

ri bo fla vin (rī′bō flā′vən), *n.* an orange-red crystalline substance, a constituent of the vitamin B complex, that promotes growth and is present in liver, eggs, milk, spinach, etc.; vitamin G; vitamin B_2; lactoflavin. *Formula:* $C_{17}H_{20}N_4O_6$ [< *ribose* + Latin *flavus* yellow]

ri bo nu cle ase (rī′bō nü′klē ās, rī′bō nyü′klē ās), *n.* enzyme that promotes the hydrolysis of ribonucleic acid.

ri bo nu cle ic acid (rī′bō nü klē′ik, rī′bō nyü klē′ik), a nucleic acid important in protein synthesis and genetic transmission, found in the cytoplasm and sometimes in the nuclei of all living cells, and consisting of long chains of repeating units of ribose combined with phosphoric acid and the purine bases, adenine and guanine, and the pyrimidine bases, cytosine and uracil; RNA.

ri bose (rī′bōs), *n.* a pentose sugar present in all plant and animal cells and obtained in the dextrorotatory form chiefly from nucleic acids contained in plants. *Formula:* $C_5H_{10}O_5$ [alteration of *arabinose* a sugar derived from gum *arabic*]

ribose nucleic acid, ribonucleic acid.

ri bo so mal (rī′bə sō′məl), *adj.* of or having to do with a ribosome or ribosomes: *ribosomal RNA.*

ri bo some (rī′bə sōm), *n.* a small structure in the cytoplasm of cells that carries on protein synthesis.

Ri car do (ri kär′dō), *n.* **David,** 1772-1823, British economist whose theories influenced Karl Marx and Henry George.

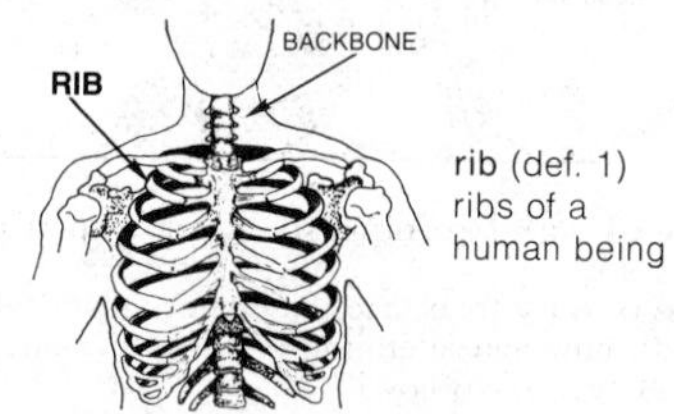

rib (def. 1) ribs of a human being

rice (rīs), *n., v.,* **riced, ric ing.** *—n.* 1 the starchy grain of an annual cereal grass, widely grown in warm climates and forming one of the important foods of the world. 2 the plant itself. *—v.t.* reduce to a form like rice: *rice potatoes.* [< Old French *ris* < Italian *riso* < Greek *oryza*]

rice bird (rīs′bėrd′), *n.* (in the southern United States) the bobolink.

rice paper, 1 a thin paper made from the straw of rice. 2 paper made from the pith of certain other plants.

ric er (rī′sər), *n.* utensil for ricing cooked potatoes, etc., by pressing them through small holes.

rich (rich), *adj.* 1 having much money or property: *a rich man.* See synonym study below. 2 well supplied; abounding: *The United States is rich in oil and coal.*

3 producing or yielding abundantly; fertile: *rich soil, a rich mine.* 4 having great worth; valuable: *a rich harvest, a rich virtue.* 5 costly; elegant: *rich dress, rich furnishings.* 6 containing plenty of butter, eggs, flavoring, etc.: *a rich cake.* 7 (of colors, sounds, smells, etc.) deep; full; vivid: *a rich red, a rich tone.* 8 (of a fuel mixture) containing more fuel and less air than is normally required. 9 INFORMAL. very amusing; ridiculous. —*n.* **the rich,** rich people. [Old English *rīce*] **—rich′ly,** *adv.* **—rich′ness,** *n.*

Syn. *adj.* 1 **Rich, wealthy** mean having much money or property. **Rich** implies having more than enough money, possessions, or resources for all normal needs and desires: *With a five-dollar bill in his pocket, the little boy felt rich.* **Wealthy** suggests greater and more permanent resources: *Some of our greatest universities were established by wealthy people.*

Rich ard I (rich′ərd), 1157-1199, king of England from 1189 to 1199, called "Richard the Lion-Hearted" or "Richard Coeur de Lion."

Richard II, 1367-1400, king of England, from 1377 to 1399.

Richard III, 1452-1485, king of England, from 1483 to 1485.

Richard Coeur de Li on (kėr′ də lē′ən), Richard I.

Rich ard son (rich′ərd sən), *n.* **Samuel,** 1689-1761, English novelist.

Rich e lieu (rish′ə lü; *French* rē shə lyœ′), *n.* **Duc de,** 1585-1642, French cardinal and statesman who virtually controlled France from 1624 to 1642. His real name was Armand Jean du Plessis.

rich en (rich′ən), *v.t., v.i.* make or become rich or richer.

rich es (rich′iz), *n.pl.* much money, land, goods, etc.; abundance of property; wealth. [< Old French *richesse* < *riche* rich; of Germanic origin. Related to RICH.]

Rich mond (rich′mənd), *n.* 1 capital of Virginia, in the E part. 249,000. 2 borough of New York City consisting of Staten Island. 295,000. 3 city in W California, near San Francisco. 79,000.

rick (rik), *n.* an outdoor stack of hay, straw, etc., especially one which is covered to protect it from rain. —*v.t.* form into a rick or ricks. [Old English *hrēac*]

rick ets (rik′its), *n.* disease of childhood characterized by a softening, and sometimes bending, of the bones, caused by lack of vitamin D or calcium; rachitis. [apparently alteration of *rachitis*]

rick ett si a (ri ket′sē ə), *n., pl.* **-si ae** (-sē ē′). any of a genus of bacterialike microorganisms, living in the tissue of arthropods and sometimes transmitted to humans, causing such diseases as Rocky Mountain spotted fever, typhus, and Q fever. [< New Latin < Howard T. *Ricketts,* 1871-1910, American pathologist]

rick ett si al (ri ket′sē əl), *adj.* of or having to do with the rickettsiae.

rick et y (rik′ə tē), *adj.* 1 liable to fall or break down; shaky; weak: *a rickety old chair.* 2 having rickets; suffering from rickets. 3 feeble in the joints. **—rick′et i ness,** *n.*

rick ey (rik′ē), *n., pl.* **-eys.** 1 drink made with limes, sugar, carbonated water, and gin or other alcoholic liquor. 2 a nonalcoholic carbonated drink made with lime juice. [origin uncertain]

Rick o ver (rik′ō vər), *n.* **Hyman George,** born 1900, American naval officer, who developed the nuclear-powered submarine. He was born in Poland.

rick rack (rik′rak′), *n.* a narrow, zigzag braid used as trimming.

rick shaw or **rick sha** (rik′shô), *n.* jinrikisha.

ric o chet (rik′ə shā′; *British* rik′ə shet′), *n., v.,* **-cheted** (-shād′), **-chet ing** (-shā′ing) or **-chet ted** (-shet′id), **-chet ting** (-shet′ing). —*n.* the skipping or jumping motion of an object after glancing off a flat surface: *the ricochet of a flat stone off the surface of the lake.* —*v.i.* move with a skipping or jumping motion. [< French]

ric tus (rik′təs), *n.* 1 the cleft of the open mouth; gape. 2 an open position of the mouth. [< Latin, a mouth opened wide < *ringi* to gape]

rid[1] (rid), *v.t.,* **rid** or **rid ded, rid ding.** 1 make free: *What will rid a house of mice?* 2 **be rid of,** be freed from. 3 **get rid of, a** get free from. **b** do away with. [Middle English *ridden* to clear land < Scandinavian (Old Icelandic) *rythja*] **—rid′der,** *n.*

rid[2] (rid), *v.* ARCHAIC. a pt. and a pp. of **ride.**

rid dance (rid′ns), *n.* 1 a clearing away or out; removal. 2 deliverance or rescue from something. 3 **good riddance,** exclamation expressing relief that something or somebody has been removed.

rid den (rid′n), *v.* a pp. of **ride.**

rid dle[1] (rid′l), *n., v.,* **-dled, -dling.** —*n.* 1 a puzzling question, statement, problem, etc. EXAMPLE: When is a door not a door? ANSWER: When it is ajar. 2 person or thing that is hard to understand, explain, etc. —*v.i.* speak in riddles. —*v.t.* solve (a riddle or question). [Middle English *redel* < earlier *redels* (taken as a plural), Old English *rǣdels* < *rǣdan* guess, explain] **—rid′dler,** *n.*

rid dle[2] (rid′l), *v.,* **-dled, -dling,** *n.* —*v.t.* 1 make many holes in: *The door of the fort was riddled with bullets.* 2 sift: *riddle gravel.* 3 impair or weaken as if by making many holes in: *The witness's testimony was riddled with lies.* —*n.* a coarse sieve. [Old English *hriddel* sieve]

ride (rīd), *v.,* **rode** or (ARCHAIC) **rid, rid den** or (ARCHAIC) **rid, rid ing,** *n.* —*v.i.* 1 sit on and be carried by an animal, especially a horse which one makes go. 2 sit on a bicycle, etc., and make it go. 3 be carried along by anything: *ride on a train, ride in a car.* 4 be capable of being ridden: *a horse that rides easily.* 5 float or move: *The ship rode into port.* 6 lie at anchor. —*v.t.* 1 sit on and manage: *ride a camel, ride a bicycle.* 2 ride over, along, or through. 3 do or perform: *ride a race.* 4 be mounted on; be carried on: *The gull rides the winds.* 5 move on; float along: *The ship rode the waves.* 6 cause to ride or be carried: *She rode her little brother piggyback.* 7 control, dominate, or tyrannize over: *be ridden by foolish fears.* 8 INFORMAL. make fun of; tease.

let ride, leave undisturbed or inactive.

ride down, a knock down. **b** overcome. **c** overtake by riding. **d** exhaust by riding.

ride out, a withstand (a gale or storm) without great damage. **b** endure successfully.

ride up, slide up out of place.

—*n.* 1 trip on horseback, in an automobile, on a train, etc. See synonym study below. 2 path, road, etc., made for riding.

[Old English *rīdan*] **—rid′a ble, ride′a ble,** *adj.*

Syn. *n.* 1 **Ride, drive** mean a trip by some means of transportation. **Ride** suggests being carried along as a passenger: *He gave me a ride in his new car.* **Drive** applies particularly to a trip in a vehicle one controls or operates himself or helps to direct: *There was no one to object if I interrupted my drive to look at the scenery.*

hat, āge, fär; let, ēqual, tėrm;
it, īce; hot, ōpen, ôrder;
oil, out; cup, pu̇t, rüle;
ch, child; ng, long; sh, she;
th, thin; ᴛʜ, then; zh, measure;

ə represents *a* in about, *e* in taken, *i* in pencil, *o* in lemon, *u* in circus.

< = from, derived from, taken from.

rid er (rī′dər), *n.* 1 person who rides. 2 anything added to a record, document, legislative bill, or statement after it was supposed to be completed. **—rid′er less,** *adj.*

ridge (rij), *n., v.,* **ridged, ridg ing.** —*n.* 1 the long and narrow upper part of something: *the ridge of an animal's back.* 2 line where two sloping surfaces meet: *the ridge of a roof.* 3 a long, narrow chain of hills or mountains. 4 any raised narrow strip: *the ridges on corduroy cloth, the ridges in plowed ground.* —*v.t.* 1 form or make into ridges. 2 cover with ridges; mark with ridges. —*v.i.* form ridges. [Old English *hrycg*]

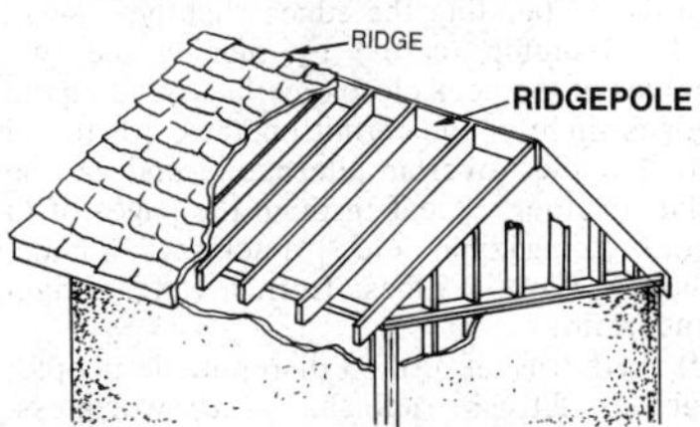

ridge pole (rij′pōl′), *n.* the horizontal timber along the top of a roof or tent; rooftree.

ridg y (rij′ē), *adj.* rising in a ridge or ridges.

rid i cule (rid′ə kyül), *v.,* **-culed, -cul ing,** *n.* —*v.t.* laugh at; make fun of. See synonym study below. —*n.* laughter in mockery; words or actions that make fun of somebody or something; derision. [< Latin *ridiculum,* neuter of *ridiculus* ridiculous < *ridere* to laugh] **—rid′i cul′er,** *n.*

Syn. *v.t.* **Ridicule, deride, mock** mean to make fun of someone or something and cause him or it to be laughed at. **Ridicule** implies making fun of a person or thing with the intention of making him or it seem little and unimportant: *Boys sometimes ridicule their sisters' friends.* **Deride** implies making fun of in contempt: *Some people deride patriotic rallies and parades.* **Mock** means to ridicule or deride in a scornful way: *The impudent boys mocked the teacher.*

ri dic u lous (ri dik′yə ləs), *adj.* deserving ridicule; laughable; absurd. See synonym study below. **—ri dic′u lous ly,** *adv.* **—ri dic′u lous ness,** *n.*

Syn. Ridiculous, absurd, preposterous mean not sensible or reasonable. **Ridiculous** emphasizes the laughable effect produced by something out of keeping with good sense: *His attempts to be the life of the party were ridiculous.* **Absurd** emphasizes inconsistency with what is true or sensible: *His belief that he was too clever to be caught in* *his wrongdoing was absurd.* **Preposterous** suggests extreme absurdity and, often, the idea of being contrary to nature: *The child drew a preposterous man with arms growing from his head.*

rid ing[1] (rī′ding), *n.* act of a person or thing that rides. —*adj.* 1 that rides; traveling. 2 used for riding or when riding: *a riding whip, a riding horse.*

rid ing[2] (rī′ding), *n.* 1 one of the three administrative divisions of Yorkshire, England. 2 a similar division elsewhere, as in Canada or New Zealand. [Middle English *thriding* < Scandinavian (Old Icelandic) *thrithjunger* one third]

Rif (rif), *n.* **the,** mountainous region in N Morocco, along the Mediterranean coast. Also, **Riff.**

rife (rīf), *adj.* 1 happening often; common; numerous; widespread. 2 full; abounding: *The city was rife with rumors of political corruption.* [Old English *rīfe*] **—rife′ly,** *adv.*

riff (rif), *n.* a melodic phrase in jazz, especially as a recurring statement of the theme. —*v.i.* perform riffs. [origin uncertain]

Riff (rif), *n.* 1 member of a Berber tribe living in the Rif. 2 Rif. **—Riff′i an,** *adj., n.*

rif fle (rif′əl), *n., v.,* **-fled, -fling.** —*n.* 1 a shoal or other object in a stream causing a stretch of choppy water. 2 such a stretch of water; a rapid. 3 a ripple. 4 act of shuffling cards by bending the edges slightly. —*v.t., v.i.* 1 shuffle (cards) by placing the two halves of the deck close together, bending the edges slightly, and permitting the cards to fall so that they overlap alternately and can be slid together. 2 leaf through the pages of (a book, magazine, etc.) quickly. 3 make (water) flow in riffles; form a riffle. [origin uncertain]

riff raff (rif′raf′), *n.* 1 disreputable people; rabble. 2 trash; rubbish. —*adj.* worthless. [< Old French *rif et raf* every scrap]

ri fle (rī′fəl), *n., v.,* **-fled, -fling.** —*n.* 1 gun with spiral grooves in its long barrel which spin or rotate the bullet as it is fired. A rifle is usually fired from the shoulder. 2 **rifles,** *pl.* a body of soldiers armed with rifles; riflemen. —*v.t.* 1 cut spiral grooves in (a gun barrel). 2 search and rob; ransack and rob. 3 take away; steal. 4 strip bare: *The boys rifled the apple tree.* [< Old French *rifler* to scratch; of Germanic origin] **—ri′fler,** *n.*

ri fle man (rī′fəl mən), *n., pl.* **-men.** 1 soldier armed with a rifle. 2 man skilled in the use of a rifle.

ri fle ry (rī′fəl rē), *n., pl.* **-ries.** 1 shooting with a rifle, especially in target practice. 2 firing from rifles.

ri fling (rī′fling), *n.* 1 act or process of cutting spiral grooves in a gun barrel. 2 system of spiral grooves in a rifle.

rift (rift), *n.* 1 cleft or fissure in the earth, a rock, etc. 2 an opening or break in clouds or mist. 3 crack, rent, or chink in any object. 4 breach in relations: *a rift in a friendship.* —*v.t., v.i.* cause or form a rift; split; cleave. [< Scandinavian (Old Icelandic) *ript*]

rig (rig), *v.,* **rigged, rig ging,** *n.* —*v.t.* 1 equip (a ship) with masts, sails, ropes, etc. 2 move (a shroud, boom, stay, etc.) to its proper place: *rig a new mainmast.* 3 equip; fit out. 4 INFORMAL. dress: *rig oneself up for a costume party.* 5 get ready for use. 6 put together in a hurry or by using odds and ends. 7 manipulate in some underhand or fraudulent way: *rig a game, rig a prizefight, rig prices.* —*n.* 1 the arrangement of masts, sails, ropes, etc., on a ship. A schooner has a fore-and-aft rig. 2 outfit; equipment: *a camper's rig.* 3 heavy machinery, or elaborate tools, such as those required to drill a well: *an oil rig.* 4 INFORMAL. **a** clothes. **b** a carriage with its horse or horses. [< Scandinavian (Danish) *rigge*]

Ri ga (rē′gə), *n.* 1 seaport in W Soviet Union, on the Baltic Sea, capital of the Latvian S.S.R. 733,000. 2 **Gulf of,** gulf of the Baltic Sea, between the Estonian S.S.R. and the Latvian S.S.R. 100 mi. long; 60 mi. wide.

rig a doon (rig′ə dün′), *n.* 1 a lively dance for one couple. 2 the quick, duple rhythm for this dance. 3 a piece of music in such time. [< French *rigaudon*]

Ri gel (rī′jəl, rī′gəl), *n.* a star of the first magnitude in the left foot of Orion.

rig ger (rig′ər), *n.* 1 person who rigs. 2 person who rigs ships, or works with hoisting tackle, etc. 3 person who manipulates something fraudulently.

rig ging (rig′ing), *n.* 1 the ropes, chains, and cables, etc., used to support and work the masts, yards, sails, etc., on a ship. 2 tackle; equipment.

right (rīt), *adj.* 1 agreeing with what is good, just, or lawful: *She did the right thing when she told the truth.* 2 correct; true: *the right answer.* 3 proper; suitable; fitting: *Say the right thing at the right time.* 4 favorable: *If the weather is right, we'll go.* 5 healthy or normal: *be in one's right mind.* 6 meant to be seen; most important: *the right side of cloth.* 7 opposite of left; belonging to or having to do with the side of anything that is turned east when the main side is turned north. 8 on this side when viewed from the front: *make a right turn.* 9 straight: *a right line.* 10 having a line or axis perpendicular to another line or surface: *a right cone.* 11 having conservative or reactionary ideas in politics. 12 ARCHAIC. rightful; real.

—*adv.* 1 in a way that is good, just, or lawful: *He acted right when he told the truth.* 2 correctly; truly: *She guessed right.* 3 properly; well: *It's faster to do a job right the first time.* 4 favorably: *Such schemes don't always turn out right.* 5 in a good or suitable condition: *Put things right.* 6 to the right hand: *turn right.* 7 exactly; just; precisely: *Your cap is right where you left it.* 8 at once; immediately: *Stop playing right now.* 9 very (used in some titles): *the Right Honorable, the Right Reverend.* 10 DIALECT. extremely: *I am right glad to see you.* 11 in a straight line; directly: *Look me right in the eye.* 12 completely: *My hat was knocked right off.* 13 **right away** or **right off,** at once; immediately.

—*n.* 1 that which is right: *Do right, not wrong.* 2 a just claim, title, or privilege: *the right to vote, a property right.* 3 fair treatment; justice: *payment as a matter of simple right.* 4 blow struck with the right hand: *a hard right to the jaw.* 5 the right side or what is on the right side: *turn to the right.* 6 Often, **Right. a** the part of a lawmaking body consisting of the more conservative or reactionary groups. In some European legislative assemblies this group sits on the right side of the chamber. **b** persons holding conservative or reactionary views. **c** a conservative or reactionary position or view. 7 privilege of subscribing for a stock or bond. 8 certificate granting such a privilege. 9 **by right** or **by rights,** justly; properly. 10 **in the right,** right. 11 **to rights,** INFORMAL. in or into proper condition, order, etc.

—*v.t.* 1 make correct; put in order: *right errors.* 2 do justice to: *right the oppressed.* 3 avenge; vindicate. 4 put in the proper position: *right an overturned car.* —*v.i.* 1 get into the proper position: *The ship righted as the wave passed.* 2 **right about!** turn in the opposite direction.

[Old English *riht*] **—right′er,** *n.* **—right′ness,** *n.*

right angle, angle that is formed by a line perpendicular to another line; angle of 90 degrees.

right-an gled (rīt′ang′gəld), *adj.* containing a right angle or right angles; rectangular.

right eous (rī′chəs), *adj.* 1 doing right; virtuous; behaving justly: *a righteous person.* 2 proper; just; right: *righteous indignation.* [Old English *rihtwīs* < *riht* right + *wīs* way, manner] **—right′eous ly,** *adv.* **—right′eous ness,** *n.*

right field, (in baseball) the section of the outfield beyond first base.

right fielder, a baseball player whose position is in right field.

right ful (rīt′fəl), *adj.* 1 according to law; by rights; legal; lawful: *the rightful owner of this dog.* 2 just and right; proper. **—right′ful ness,** *n.*

right ful ly (rīt′fə lē), *adv.* 1 according to right, law, or justice. 2 properly; fittingly.

right-hand (rīt′hand′), *adj.* 1 on or to the right. 2 of, for, or with the right hand; right-handed. 3 most helpful or useful: *one's right-hand man.*

right-hand ed (rīt′han′did), *adj.* 1 using the right hand more easily and readily than the left. 2 done with the right hand. 3 made to be used with the right hand. 4 turning from left to right: *a right-handed screw.* —*adv.* toward the right; with the right hand. **—right′-hand′ed ly,** *adv.* **—right′-hand′ed ness,** *n.*

right-hand er (rīt′han′dər), *n.* 1 a right-handed person. 2 (in baseball) a right-handed pitcher.

right ist (rī′tist), *n.* 1 person who has conservative or reactionary ideas in politics. 2 member of a conservative or reactionary political organization. —*adj.* having conservative or reactionary ideas.

right ly (rīt′lē), *adv.* 1 justly; fairly. 2 correctly; exactly; accurately. 3 properly; suitably.

right-mind ed (rīt′mīn′did), *adj.* having right opinions or principles.

right of way, 1 the right to go first, especially the right of a vehicle to cross in front of another vehicle. 2 the right to pass over property belonging to someone else. 3 strip of land on which a public highway, railroad, power line, etc., is built.

right-to-work law (rīt′tə wėrk′), U.S. any of certain state laws that forbid any agreement between an employer and a union to maintain a union shop.

right triangle, triangle with one right angle.

right ward (rīt′wərd), *adj., adv.* on or toward the right.

right wards (rīt′wərdz), *adv.* rightward.

right whale, any of several whales with large heads from which whalebone and oil are obtained. Right whales have about 350 long, toothlike whalebones on each side of the mouth.

right wing, 1 the conservative or reaction-

hat, āge, fär; let, ēqual, tėrm;
it, īce; hot, ōpen, ôrder;
oil, out; cup, pu̇t, rüle;
ch, child; ng, long; sh, she;
th, thin; ᴛʜ, then; zh, measure;

ə represents *a* in about, *e* in taken, *i* in pencil, *o* in lemon, *u* in circus.

< = from, derived from, taken from.

ary members, especially of a political party. 2 persons or parties holding conservative or reactionary views.

right-wing (rīt′wing′), *adj.* belonging to or like the right wing.

right-wing er (rīt′wing′ər), *n.* a right-wing member of a political party or a supporter of right-wing political views.

right y (rī′tē), *n., pl.* **right ies.** SLANG. a right-handed person.

rig id (rij′id), *adj.* 1 not bending; stiff; firm: *Hold your arm rigid.* See **stiff** for synonym study. 2 not changing; strict: *Our club has few rigid rules.* 3 severely exact; rigorous: *a rigid examination.* See **strict** for synonym study. [< Latin *rigidus* < *rigere* be stiff] **—rig′id ly,** *adv.* **—rig′id ness,** *n.*

ri gid i ty (ri jid′ə tē), *n.* 1 stiffness; firmness. 2 strictness; severity.

rig ma role (rig′mə rōl′), *n.* foolish talk or activity; words or action without meaning; nonsense. [earlier *ragman roll* a list or catalogue]

rig or (rig′ər), *n.* 1 strictness; severity: *The new recruits were trained with great rigor.* 2 harshness: *the rigor of a long, cold winter.* 3 chill caused by illness. 4 logical exactness: *the rigor of scientific method.* [< Latin < *rigere* be stiff]

rig or mor tis (rig′ər môr′tis), the stiffening of the muscles after death. [< Latin, stiffness of death]

rig or ous (rig′ər əs), *adj.* 1 severe; strict: *the rigorous discipline in the army.* See **strict** for synonym study. 2 harsh: *a rigorous climate.* 3 thoroughly logical and scientific; exact: *the rigorous methods of science.* **—rig′or ous ly,** *adv.* **—rig′or ous ness,** *n.*

Rig-Ve da (rig vā′də, rig vē′də), *n.* the oldest and most important of the sacred books of the Hindus.

rile (rīl), *v.,* **riled, ril ing.** INFORMAL. roil. [variant of *roil*]

Ri ley (rī′lē), *n.* **James Whitcomb,** 1849-1916, American poet.

rill[1] (ril), *n.* a tiny stream; little brook. [< Dutch *ril* groove, furrow]

rill[2] or **rille** (ril), *n.* a long, narrow valley on the surface of the moon. [< German *Rille* furrow]

rim (rim), *n., v.,* **rimmed, rim ming.** *—n.* 1 edge, border, or margin on or around anything: *the rim of a cup.* 2 the circular outer edge of a wheel. See **felly** for picture. *—v.t.* 1 form a rim around; put a rim around. 2 roll around the rim of: *The basketball rimmed the basket and then dropped through.* [Old English *rima*] **—rim′less,** *adj.*

Rim baud (raɴ bō′), *n.* **Arthur,** 1854-1891, French poet.

rime[1] (rīm), *v.,* **rimed, rim ing,** *n.* rhyme.

rime[2] (rīm), *n., v.,* **rimed, rim ing.** *—n.* white frost; hoarfrost, especially from the freezing of vapor in drifting fog. *—v.t.* cover with rime or something like rime. [Old English *hrīm*]

rime ster (rīm′stər), *n.* rhymester.

Rim sky-Kor sa kov (rim′skē kôr′sə-kôf), *n.* **Nikolay,** 1844-1908, Russian composer.

rim y (rī′mē), *adj.,* **rim i er, rim i est.** covered with rime or hoarfrost; frosty.

rind (rīnd), *n.* 1 the firm outer covering of oranges, melons, cheeses, etc. 2 the bark of a tree or plant. [Old English]

rin der pest (rin′dər pest), *n.* an acute and usually fatal infectious disease of cattle, sheep, etc. [< German *Rinderpest* cattle pest]

ring[1] (ring), *n., v.,* **ringed, ring ing.** *—n.* 1 circle or circular group of persons or things: *The couples danced in a ring.* 2 a thin circle of metal, usually gold, silver, or other precious metal: *a wedding ring.* 3 circle of metal, wood, plastic, or other material, used for attaching, hanging, etc.: *a key ring, a curtain ring.* 4 the outer edge or border of a coin, plate, wheel, or anything round. 5 the space between two circles having the same center. 6 a circular object, line, bend, etc. 7 an enclosed circular space for races, games, circus performances, etc. 8 prize ring. 9 prizefighting. 10 competition; rivalry; contest: *in the ring for election to the Senate.* 11 group of people combined for an illicit or wrong purpose: *a spy ring, a smuggling ring.* 12 annual ring. 13 (in chemistry) a closed chain of atoms linked by bonds that may be represented graphically in cyclic form. 14 **run rings around,** INFORMAL. surpass with great ease; beat easily.
—v.t. 1 put a ring around; enclose; form a circle around. 2 toss a horseshoe, quoit, etc., around (a certain mark or post). 3 provide with a ring. 4 put a ring in the nose of (an animal). 5 cut away the bark in a ring around (a tree or branch). *—v.i.* 1 move in a ring. 2 form a ring or rings.
[Old English *hring*] **—ring′like′,** *adj.*

ring[2] (ring), *v.,* **rang** or (DIALECT) **rung, rung, ring ing,** *n.* *—v.i.* 1 give forth a clear sound, as a bell does: *Did the telephone ring?* 2 cause a bell to sound: *Did you ring?* 3 call to church, prayers, etc., by ringing bells. 4 sound loudly; resound: *The room rang with shouts of laughter.* 5 give back sound; echo: *The valley rang with the trumpet's call to charge.* 6 be filled with report or talk: *The whole town is ringing with the scandal.* 7 impress one as having a certain character: *Your promises do not ring true.* 8 have a sensation as of sounds of bells; hear inner ringing: *My ears are ringing.* *—v.t.* 1 cause to give forth a clear ringing sound: *Ring the bell.* 2 make (a sound) by ringing: *The bells rang a joyous peal.* 3 announce or proclaim by ringing; usher; conduct: *ring a fire alarm. Ring out the old year; ring in the new.* 4 proclaim or repeat loudly everywhere: *ring a person's praises.* 5 call on the telephone.
ring for, summon by a bell.
ring in, INFORMAL. bring in dishonestly or trickily.
ring off, end a telephone call.
ring up, record (a specific amount) on a cash register.
—n. 1 sound of a bell: *Did you hear a ring?* 2 sound like that of a bell: *the ring of skates on ice, the ring of voices in the halls.* 3 act of ringing. 4 a characteristic sound or quality: *a ring of sincerity in her voice.* 5 call on the telephone. 6 set or peal of bells.
[Old English *hringan*]

ring bolt (ring′bōlt′), *n.* bolt with an eye in its head in which a ring is fitted.

ringed (ringd), *adj.* 1 having or wearing a ring or rings. 2 marked or decorated with a ring or rings. 3 surrounded by a ring or rings. 4 formed of or with rings; ringlike.

rin gent (rin′jənt), *adj.* 1 gaping. 2 (of a labiate corolla) having the lips widely opened. [< Latin *ringentem*]

ring er[1] (ring′ər), *n.* 1 person or thing that encircles, surrounds with a ring, etc. 2 horseshoe, quoit, etc., thrown so as to fall over a peg. 3 the toss which does this. [< *ring*[1]]

ring er[2] (ring′ər), *n.* 1 person or thing that rings. 2 device for ringing a bell. 3 SLANG. **a** person or thing very much like another. **b** horse, athlete, etc., competing under a false name or some other device to conceal his identity, skill, or the like. [< *ring*[2]]

ring lead er (ring′lē′dər), *n.* person who leads others in opposition to authority or law.

ring let (ring′lit), *n.* 1 curl: *hair worn in ringlets.* 2 a little ring.

ring mas ter (ring′mas′tər), *n.* person in charge of the performances in the ring of a circus.

ring neck (ring′nek′), *n.* any of various ring-necked birds, as certain ducks, plovers, and pheasants.

ring-necked (ring′nekt′), *adj.* having the neck ringed with a band or bands of color.

ring side (ring′sīd′), *n.* 1 place just outside the ring at a circus, prizefight, etc. 2 place affording a close view.

ring-tailed (ring′tāld′), *adj.* having the tail or the tail feathers marked with a ring or rings of different colors.

ring toss (ring′tôs′, ring′tos′), *n.* quoits played with a ring of rope, plastic, etc., especially on shipboard.

ring worm (ring′wėrm′), *n.* any of several contagious skin diseases caused by fungi. One kind appears in the form of ring-shaped, discolored patches on the skin.

rink (ringk), *n.* 1 sheet of ice, especially artificially prepared ice, for ice-skating or playing hockey. 2 a smooth floor for roller-skating. [< Old French *renc* course]

rinse (rins), *v.,* **rinsed, rins ing,** *n.* *—v.t.* 1 wash with clean water: *Rinse the soap out of your hair after you wash it.* 2 wash lightly: *Rinse your mouth with water and soda.* *—n.* 1 a rinsing. 2 water used in rinsing. 3 a preparation used in water to add color or luster to the hair. [< Old French *reïncier,* ultimately < Latin *recens* fresh, recent] **—rins′er,** *n.*

Ri o (rē′ō), *n.* Rio de Janeiro.

Ri o de Ja nei ro (rē′ō dā zhə ner′ō), seaport on the SE coast of Brazil, formerly the capital. 4,297,000.

Rí o de la Pla ta (rē′ō dā lä plä′tä), Spanish name of the **Plata.**

Rí o de O ro (rē′ō dā ō′rō), former name of the S part of Spanish Sahara.

Ri o Grande (rē′ō grand′; rē′ō gran′dē; rē′ō grän′dā), river forming part of the boundary between the United States and Mexico, flowing from SW Colorado southeast into the Gulf of Mexico. 1800 mi.

Rí o Mu ni (rē′ō mü′nē), province of Equatorial Guinea, on the W coast of Africa. 230,000 pop.; 10,000 sq. mi.

Ri o Ne gro (rē′ō nā′grō), river flowing from E Colombia through N Brazil into the Amazon River. 1400 mi.

ri ot (rī′ət), *n.* 1 a wild, violent public disturbance; disturbance; confusion; disorder. 2 (in law) a tumultuous disturbance of the public peace by three or more persons who assemble for some private purpose and execute it to the terror of the people. 3 loose living; wild reveling. 4 bright display: *The garden was a riot of color.* 5 INFORMAL. a very amusing person or performance: *He was a riot at the party.* 6 **read the riot act,** give orders for disturbance to cease. 7 **run riot,** **a** act without restraint. **b** grow wildly or luxuriantly. **c** run wild. *—v.i.* 1 behave in a wild, disorderly way. 2 revel. *—v.t.* spend or waste (money, time, etc.) in loose living. [< Old French *riote* dispute, quarrel] **—ri′ot er,** *n.*

ri ot ous (rī′ə təs), *adj.* 1 taking part in a riot. 2 characterized by or of the nature of a riot. 3 boisterous; disorderly. **—ri′ot ous ly,** *adv.*

rip[1] (rip), *v.,* **ripped, rip ping,** *n.* *—v.t.* 1 cut roughly; tear apart; tear off: *Rip the cover off this box.* See **tear**[2] for synonym study. 2 cut or pull out (the threads in the seams of a garment). 3 saw (wood) along the grain, not across the grain. 4 INFORMAL. **a** move fast or violently. **b** speak or say with violence. 5 **rip off,** SLANG. steal: *rip off an expensive camera.* *—v.i.* become torn apart. *—n.* a torn place, especially a seam burst in a garment. [Middle English *rippen*]

rip[2] (rip), *n.* 1 stretch of rough water made by cross currents meeting. 2 a swift current made by the tide. [perhaps special use of *rip*[1]]

rip[3] (rip), *n.* INFORMAL. 1 a worthless or dissolute person. 2 a worthless, worn-out horse. [origin uncertain]

R.I.P., may he or she (they) rest in peace [for Latin *requiescat (requiescant) in pace*].

ri par i an (rə per′ē ən, rə par′ē ən; rī per′ē ən, rī par′ē ən), *adj.* of or on the bank of a river, a lake, etc.: *riparian rights, riparian property.* [< Latin *riparius* < *ripa* riverbank]

rip cord, cord which is pulled to open a parachute.

rip current, a strong, narrow surface current which flows rapidly away from the shore; riptide.

ripe (rīp), *adj.,* **rip er, rip est.** 1 full-grown and ready to be gathered and eaten: *ripe fruit.* 2 resembling ripe fruit in ruddiness and fullness. 3 at the peak of flavor, bouquet, etc.; mellow: *ripe cheese.* 4 fully developed; mature: *ripe in knowledge, ripe plans.* 5 fully prepared; ready: *That country is ripe for revolt.* 6 (of time) far enough along; sufficiently advanced. 7 advanced in years: *the ripe age of 75.* [Old English *rīpe*] **—ripe′ly,** *adv.* **—ripe′ness,** *n.*

rip en (rī′pən), *v.i.* become ripe. *—v.t.* make ripe. **—rip′en er,** *n.*

rip-off (rip′ôf′, rip′of), *n.* SLANG. 1 theft. 2 something that exploits a popular trend or interest.

ri poste (rə pōst′), *n., v.,* **-post ed, -post ing.** *—n.* 1 (in fencing) a quick thrust given after parrying a lunge. 2 a quick, sharp reply or return. *—v.i.* make a riposte; reply; retaliate. [< French < Italian *risposta* reply, response]

rip per (rip′ər), *n.* 1 person who rips. 2 tool for ripping.

rip ping (rip′ing), *adj.* BRITISH SLANG. fine; splendid.

rip ple (rip′əl), *n., v.,* **-pled, -pling.** *—n.* 1 a very little wave: *Throw a stone into still water and watch the ripples spread in rings.* See **wave** for synonym study. 2 anything that seems like a tiny wave: *ripples in hair.* 3 sound that reminds one of little waves: *a ripple of laughter in the crowd.* *—v.i.* 1 make a sound like rippling water. 2 form or have ripples. 3 flow with ripples on the surface. *—v.t.* make little ripples on: *A breeze rippled the quiet waters.* [origin uncertain] **—rip′pler,** *n.*

rip rap (rip′rap′), *n., v.,* **-rapped, -rap ping.** *—n.* 1 wall or foundation of broken stones thrown together irregularly. 2 broken stones so used. *—v.t.* build or strengthen with loose, broken stones.

rip roar ing (rip′rôr′ing, rip′rōr′ing), *adj.* INFORMAL. hilarious; uproarious.

rip saw (rip′sô′), *n.* saw with large, coarse teeth used for cutting wood along the grain, not across the grain.

rip snort er (rip′snôr′tər), *n.* INFORMAL. a ripsnorting person or thing.

rip snort ing (rip′snôr′ting), *adj.* INFORMAL. boisterous or wild.

rip tide (rip′tīd′), *n.* rip current.

Rip Van Win kle (rip′ van wing′kəl), hero of a story by Washington Irving who falls asleep and wakes twenty years later to find everything changed.

rise (rīz), *v.,* **rose, ris en, ris ing,** *n.* *—v.i.* 1 get up from a lying, sitting, or kneeling position: *rise from a chair.* 2 get up from sleep or rest: *rise at dawn.* 3 go up; come up; move up; ascend: *Mercury rises in a thermometer on a hot day. The curtain rose on the first act of the play.* 4 extend upward: *The tower rises to a height of 60 feet.* 5 slope upward: *The road rises up and over the hill.* 6 go higher; increase: *Butter rose five cents in price. My anger rose at the remark.* 7 advance in importance, rank, etc.: *He rose from office boy to president.* 8 advance to a higher level of action, thought, feeling, expression, etc.: *His books never rise above mediocrity.* 9 become louder or of higher pitch: *Her voice rose in anger.* 10 come to the surface of the water or ground: *The fish rose and seized the bait.* 11 come above the horizon: *The sun rises in the morning.* 12 start; begin: *The river rises from a spring. Quarrels often rise from trifles.* 13 come into being or action: *The wind rose rapidly.* 14 be built up, erected, or constructed: *New houses are rising on the edge of town.* 15 become more animated or more cheerful: *Our spirits rose at the good news.* 16 revolt; rebel: *rise against the government.* 17 grow larger and lighter: *Yeast makes dough rise.* 18 come to life again. 19 end a meeting or session: *The senate rose for summer recess.* 20 **rise to,** be equal to; be able to deal with: *rise to an emergency.*

—n. 1 an upward movement; ascent: *the rise of a balloon.* 2 an upward slope: *a rise in a road. The rise of that hill is gradual.* 3 piece of rising or high ground; a hill: *The house is situated on a rise.* 4 the vertical height of a slope, step, arch, etc. 5 increase: *a rise in prices. The rise of the tide was four feet.* 6 advance in rank, power, position, etc.: *Her rise in the company was swift.* 7 increase in loudness or to a higher pitch. 8 a coming above the horizon. 9 origin; beginning; start: *the rise of industrialism, the rise of a river.* 10 the coming of fish to the surface of the water to seize bait, etc. 11 **get a rise out of,** INFORMAL. get an emotional reaction from (someone). 12 **give rise to,** bring about; cause; start.

[Old English *rīsan*]

ris en (riz′n), *v.* the pp. of **rise.** *They had risen before dawn.*

ris er (rī′zər), *n.* 1 person or thing that rises: *an early riser.* 2 the vertical part of a step.

ris i bil i ty (riz′ə bil′ə tē), *n., pl.* **-ties.** 1 ability or inclination to laugh. 2 Often, **risibilities,** *pl.* desire to laugh; sense of humor.

ris i ble (riz′ə bəl), *adj.* 1 able or inclined to laugh. 2 of laughter; used in laughter. 3 causing laughter; amusing; funny. [< Late Latin *risibilis* < Latin *ridere* to laugh]

risk (risk), *n.* 1 chance of harm or loss; danger; peril: *If you drive carefully, there is no risk of being fined.* 2 person or thing with reference to the chance of loss from insuring him or it: *Racing drivers are poor risks.* 3 **run a risk** or **take a risk,** expose oneself to the chance of harm or loss. *—v.t.* 1 expose to the chance of harm or loss: *risk one's health, risk one's life.* 2 take the risk of: *risk getting wet. She risked defeat in running against the popular candidate.* [< French *risque* < Italian *risco* < *risicare* to dare] **—risk′er,** *n.*

risk y (ris′kē), *adj.,* **risk i er, risk i est.** full of risk; dangerous; perilous. **—risk′i ly,** *adv.* **—risk′i ness,** *n.*

ris qué (ri skā′), *adj.* suggestive of indecency; somewhat improper. [< French, past participle of *risquer* to risk]

rit. or **ritard.,** ritardando.

ri tar dan do (rē′tär dän′dō), in music: *—adj.* becoming gradually slower. *—adv.* gradually more slowly. *—n.* movement or passage in this style. [< Italian]

rite (rīt), *n.* 1 a formal procedure or act in a religious or other observance; solemn ceremony: *the rites of baptism, marriage, and burial.* See **ceremony** for synonym study. 2 liturgy or a distinct form of liturgy: *the Latin rite, the Anglican rite.* 3 a part of the Christian church distinguished by its liturgy. 4 any customary ceremony or observance. [< Latin *ritus*]

rit u al (rich′ü əl), *n.* 1 form or system of rites. The rites of baptism, marriage, and burial are parts of the ritual of most churches. 2 a prescribed order of performing a ceremony or rite. Secret societies have a ritual for initiating new members. 3 book containing rites or ceremonies. 4 the carrying out of rites. *—adj.* of or having to do with rites or rituals; done as a rite: *a ritual dance, ritual laws.* **—rit′u al ly,** *adv.*

rit u al ism (rich′ü ə liz′əm), *n.* 1 fondness for ritual; insistence upon ritual. 2 study of ritual practices or religious rites.

rit u al ist (rich′ü ə list), *n.* 1 person who practices or advocates observance of ritual. 2 person who studies or knows much about ritual practices or religious rites.

rit u al is tic (rich′ü ə lis′tik), *adj.* 1 having to do with ritual or ritualism. 2 fond of ritual. **—rit′u al is′ti cal ly,** *adv.*

ritz y (rit′sē), *adj.,* **ritz i er, ritz i est.** SLANG. smart; stylish; gaudy. [< *Ritz,* name of the palatial hotels founded by César *Ritz,* 1850-1918, Swiss-born hotel manager]

riv., river.

ri val (rī′vəl), *n., adj., v.,* **-valed, -val ing** or **-valled, -val ling.** *—n.* 1 person who wants and tries to get the same thing as another or who tries to equal or do better than another; competitor. 2 thing that will bear comparison with something else; equal; match. *—adj.* wanting the same thing as another; trying to outdo or equal another; competing: *The rival store tried to get our grocer's trade.* *—v.t.* 1 try to equal or outdo; compete with: *The stores rival each other in beautiful window* *displays.* 2 equal; match: *The sunset rivaled the sunrise in beauty.* [< Latin *rivalis* one who uses the same stream as another < *rivus* stream]

ri val ry (rī′vəl rē), *n., pl.* **-ries.** effort to obtain something another person wants; action, position, or relation of a rival or rivals; competition.

rive (rīv), *v.t., v.i.,* **rived, rived** or **riven, riv ing.** tear apart; split; cleave. [< Scandinavian (Old Icelandic) *rīfa*]

riv en (riv′ən), *adj.* torn apart; split.

riv er (riv′ər), *n.* 1 a large natural stream of water that flows into a lake, ocean, etc. 2 any abundant stream or flow: *a river of lava, rivers of blood.* [< Old French *rivere* < Latin *riparius* of a riverbank < *ripa* bank]

Ri ver a (ri ver′ə), *n.* **Diego,** 1886-1957, Mexican painter, especially of murals.

riv er bank (riv′ər bangk′), *n.* the ground bordering a river.

river basin, land that is drained by a river and its tributaries.

riv er bed (riv′ər bed′), *n.* the channel or bed in which a river flows.

riv er boat (riv′ər bōt′), *n.* boat for use on a river, usually having a flat bottom or very shallow draught.

riv er head (riv′ər hed′), *n.* source of a river.

river horse, hippopotamus.

riv er side (riv′ər sīd′), *n.* bank of a river. *—adj.* beside a river.

Riv er side (riv′ər sīd), *n.* city in SE California. 140,000.

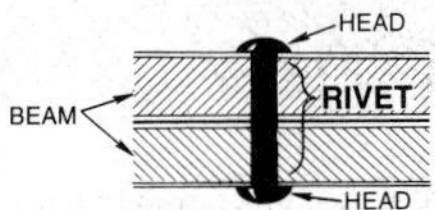

riv et (riv′it), *n.* a metal bolt having a head at one end, the other end being passed through holes in the things to be joined together and then hammered into another head. Rivets fasten heavy steel beams together. *—v.t.* 1 fasten with a rivet or rivets. 2 flatten (the end of a bolt) so as to form a head. 3 fasten firmly; fix firmly: *Their eyes were riveted on the speaker.* 4 command and hold (one's attention, interest, etc.): *The new design of the engine riveted our curiosity.* [< Old French < *river* to fix, fasten] **—riv′et er,** *n.*

Riv i er a (riv′ē er′ə), *n.* 1 section of SE France and NW Italy along the Mediterranean Sea, famous as a resort. 2 **riviera,** any pleasant shore or coastline used as a resort.

riv u let (riv′yə lit), *n.* a very small stream. [< Latin *rivus* stream]

Ri yadh (ri yäd′), *n.* capital of Saudi Arabia, in the central part. Mecca is the religious capital. 300,000.

ri yal (ri yôl′, ri yäl′), *n.* the monetary unit of Saudi Arabia, a coin or note worth about 22¼ cents; rial. [< Arabic *riyāl.* See RIAL.]

rm., *pl.* **rms.** 1 ream. 2 room.

RM. or **r.m.,** reichsmark.

Rn, radon.

R.N., 1 registered nurse. 2 Royal Navy.

RNA, ribonucleic acid.

roach[1] (rōch), *n.* cockroach.

roach[2] (rōch), *n., pl.* **roach es** or **roach.** 1 a silvery European freshwater fish with a greenish back, of the same family as the carp. 2 any of various similar American fishes, such as the sunfish. [< Old French *roche*]

road (rōd), *n.* 1 way between places; way made for automobiles, trucks, etc., to travel on: *the road from New York to Boston.* 2 way or course: *the road to ruin, the road to peace.* 3 railroad. 4 Also, **roads,** *pl.* roadstead. 5 **on the road, a** on tour, as in a theater company. **b** traveling, especially as a salesman. [Old English *rād* a riding, journey]

road agent, U.S. highwayman in the days of stagecoach travel.

road bed (rōd′bed′), *n.* 1 foundation for a road or for railroad tracks. 2 crushed stone and other materials used to form such a foundation.

road block (rōd′blok′), *n.* 1 barrier placed across a road to stop vehicles. 2 any obstacle to the progress of something.

road hog, INFORMAL. person who uses more of the road than is necessary, especially by driving in the center of the road.

road house (rōd′hous′), *n., pl.* **-hous es** (-hou′ziz). restaurant on a highway outside of a city, where people can stop for refreshments and sometimes entertainment.

road map, map for automobile travel, showing the roads in a region and the distances between cities and towns.

road metal, broken stone, cinders, etc., used to build and repair roads and roadbeds.

road run ner (rōd′run′ər), *n.* a long-tailed bird of the deserts of the southwestern United States that is of the same order as the cuckoo and is noted for its ability to run swiftly.

road show, U.S. a traveling theatrical show.

road side (rōd′sīd′), *n.* the side of a road. *—adj.* beside a road.

road stead (rōd′sted), *n.* place near the shore where ships may anchor; road.

road ster (rōd′stər), *n.* 1 an open automobile with a single wide seat. 2 horse for riding or driving on the roads.

road test, test given to a vehicle to determine whether it is roadworthy.

road-test (rōd′test′), *v.t.* subject to a road test.

road way (rōd′wā′), *n.* 1 road. 2 the part of a road used by wheeled vehicles.

road work (rōd′wėrk′), *n.* exercise of running distances as a form of physical training, especially by boxers.

road wor thy (rōd′wėr′ᴛʜē), *adj.* (of vehicles) in a suitable condition for use on the road. **—road′wor′thi ness,** *n.*

roam (rōm), *v.t.* go about with no special plan or aim; wander: *roam through the fields.* See synonym study below. *—v.i.* wander over: *roam the earth.* *—n.* a walk or trip with no special aim; wandering. [Middle English *romen*] **—roam′er,** *n.*

Syn. *v.t.* **Roam, rove, ramble** mean to wander. **Roam** suggests going about as one pleases over a wide area, with no special plan or aim: *The photographer roamed about the world.* **Rove** usually adds the suggestion of a definite purpose, though not of a settled destination: *Submarines roved the ocean.* **Ramble** suggests straying from a regular path or plan and wandering about aimlessly for one's own pleasure: *I thought we would go straight to the shopping district, but we rambled through the town instead.*

roan (rōn), *adj.* yellowish- or reddish-brown sprinkled with gray or white. *—n.* 1 horse or other animal of a roan color. 2 a roan color. [< Middle French < Spanish *roano*]

Ro a noke (rō′ə nōk), *n.* city in SW Virginia. 92,000.

Roanoke Island, island just off the NE coast of North Carolina. 12 mi. long.

hat, āge, fär; let, ēqual, tėrm;
it, īce; hot, ōpen, ôrder;
oil, out; cup, pu̇t, rüle;
ch, child; ng, long; sh, she;
th, thin; ᴛʜ, then; zh, measure;

ə represents *a* in about, *e* in taken, *i* in pencil, *o* in lemon, *u* in circus.

< = from, derived from, taken from.

roar (rôr, rōr), *v.i.* 1 make a loud, deep sound; make a loud noise: *The lion roared. The wind roared at the windows.* 2 laugh loudly. 3 move with a roar: *The train roared past us.* *—v.t.* utter loudly: *roar out an order.* *—n.* a loud, deep sound; loud noise: *a roar of laughter, the roar of a cannon, the roar of a jet engine.* [Old English *rārian*] **—roar′er,** *n.*

roast (rōst), *v.t.* 1 cook by dry heat; cook before a fire; bake: *We roasted meat and potatoes.* 2 prepare by heating: *roast coffee, roast a metal ore.* 3 make very hot. 4 INFORMAL. ridicule or criticize severely. *—v.i.* 1 be cooked by dry heat; be baked. 2 be prepared by heating. 3 become very hot. *—n.* 1 piece of roasted meat, or a piece of meat to be roasted. 2 an informal outdoor meal, at which some food is cooked over an open fire. *—adj.* roasted: *roast beef.* [< Old French *rostir;* of Germanic origin]

roast er (rō′stər), *n.* 1 pan used in roasting. 2 chicken, young pig, etc., fit to be roasted. 3 person or thing that roasts.

rob (rob), *v.,* **robbed, rob bing.** *—v.t.* 1 take away from by force or threats; steal from: *Bandits robbed the bank.* 2 steal: *Some children robbed fruit from the orchard.* 3 take away some characteristic; keep from having or doing: *Laryngitis robbed me of my voice.* *—v.i.* commit robbery; steal. [< Old French *rober;* of Germanic origin]

rob ber (rob′ər), *n.* person who robs. See **thief** for synonym study.

robber baron, capitalist of the late 1800's, who acquired wealth through ruthless business methods.

rob ber y (rob′ər ē), *n., pl.* **-ber ies.** act of robbing; theft: *a bank robbery.*

robe (rōb), *n., v.,* **robed, rob ing.** *—n.* 1 a long, loose outer garment. 2 garment that shows rank, office, etc.: *a judge's robe, the king's robes of state.* 3 a covering or wrap: *Put a robe over you when you go for a sleigh ride.* 4 bathrobe or dressing gown. *—v.t., v.i.* put a robe on; dress. [< Old French, originally, plunder, booty; of Germanic origin]

Rob ert I (rob′ərt). See **Bruce.**

Robes pierre (rōbz′pyer, rōbz′pir; *French* rô bes pyer′), *n.* **Maximilien de,** 1758-1794, one of the chief leaders of the French Revolution and of the Reign of Terror.

rob in (rob′ən), *n.* 1 a large thrush of North America, brownish-gray with a reddish breast and white on the lower abdomen and throat; redbreast. 2 a small, brownish European thrush with an orange breast. [< *Robin,* proper name, diminutive of *Robert*]

Robin Good fel low (gu̇d′fel′ō), Puck.

Robin Hood, (in English legends) the leader of an outlaw band of Sherwood Forest, who robbed the rich and helped the poor.

rob in's-egg blue (rob′ənz eg′), greenish blue.

Rob in son (rob′ən sən), *n.* **Edwin Arlington,** 1869-1935, American poet.
Robinson Cru soe (krü′sō), hero of Daniel Defoe's novel of the same name, a sailor shipwrecked on a desert island.
ro bot (rō′bət, rob′ət), *n.* 1 machine made in imitation of a human being; a mechanical device that does routine work in response to commands. 2 person who acts or works in a dull, mechanical way. 3 any machine or mechanical device that operates automatically or by remote controls. [< Czech < *robota* work, *robotnik* serf]
robot bomb, buzz bomb.
Rob son (rob′sən), *n.* **Mount,** mountain in E British Columbia, the highest peak of the Rocky Mountains in Canada. 12,972 ft.
ro bust (rō bust′, rō′bust), *adj.* 1 strong and healthy; sturdy: *a robust person, a robust mind.* See **strong** for synonym study. 2 suited to or requiring bodily strength: *robust exercises.* 3 rough; rude. [< Latin *robustus,* originally, oaken < *robur* oak] **—ro bust′ly,** *adv.* **—ro bust′ness,** *n.*
roc (rok), *n.* (in Arabian legends) a bird having such enormous size and strength that it could seize and carry off an elephant. [< Arabic *rukhkh*]
Ro cham beau (rō shäm bō′; *French* rô-shäɴ bō′), *n.* **Count de,** 1725-1807, Jean Baptiste Donatien de Vimeur, commander of the French forces sent to help the American army in the Revolutionary War.
Ro chelle salt (rō shel′), a colorless or white crystalline compound, used as a mild laxative and as a piezoelectric crystal. *Formula:* $KNaC_4H_4O_6 \cdot 4H_2O$ [< La *Rochelle,* French port on the Bay of Biscay]
Roch es ter (roch′es′tər), *n.* city in W New York State. 296,000.
roch et (roch′it), *n.* vestment of linen or lawn, resembling a surplice, worn by bishops and abbots. [< Old French]
rock[1] (rok), *n.* 1 a large mass of stone. 2 any piece of stone; a stone. 3 the mass of mineral matter of which the earth's crust is made up. 4 a particular layer or kind of such matter. 5 something firm like a rock; support; defense. 6 anything that suggests a rock. 7 **on the rocks,** a in or into a condition of ruin or failure. b INFORMAL. bankrupt. c INFORMAL. (of alcoholic drinks) with ice but without water or mixes. [< Old French *roque* < Popular Latin *rocca*] **—rock′like′,** *adj.*
rock[2] (rok), *v.i.* 1 move backward or forward, or from side to side; sway: *My chair rocks.* See **swing** for synonym study. 2 be moved or swayed violently with emotion. *—v.t.* 1 move back and forth; sway from side to side: *The waves rocked the boat.* 2 put (to sleep, rest, etc.) with swaying movements. 3 move or sway powerfully with emotion. *—n.* 1 a rocking movement. 2 INFORMAL. rock'n'roll. [Old English *roccian*]
rock bottom, the very bottom; lowest level.
rock-bot tom (rok′bot′əm), *adj.* down to the very bottom; very lowest.
rock-bound (rok′bound′), *adj.* surrounded by rocks; rocky: *a rock-bound harbor.*
rock candy, sugar in the form of large, hard crystals.
rock crystal, a colorless, transparent variety of quartz, often used for jewelry, ornaments, etc.
Rock e fel ler (rok′ə fel′ər), *n.* 1 **John D(avison),** 1839-1937, American capitalist and philanthropist. 2 his son, **John D(avison), Jr.,** 1874-1960, American capitalist and philanthropist. 3 his grandson, **Nelson A(ldrich),** born 1908, American political leader, governor of New York State since 1959.
rock er (rok′ər), *n.* 1 one of the curved pieces on which a cradle, rocking chair, etc., rocks. 2 a rocking chair. 3 any of various devices that operate with a rocking motion.

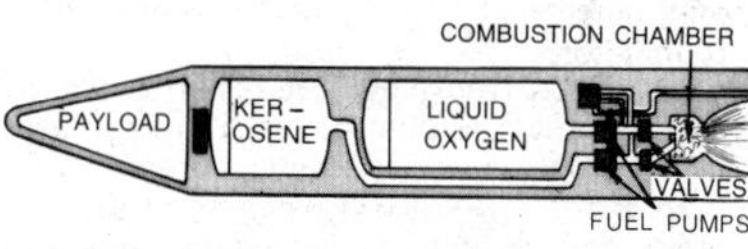

rocket (def. 1) which uses liquid fuel

rock et (rok′it), *n.* 1 engine used to propel missiles, spacecraft, etc., consisting of one or more tubes open at one end in which a solid or liquid propellant is rapidly burned, creating expanding gases which escape at very high velocities from the open end to produce a thrust that propels it and its payload upward or forward; rocket engine. 2 spacecraft, missile, etc., propelled by such an engine. 3 projectile used for fireworks and signaling, consisting of a cylinder filled with a combustible substance and propelled by means of escaping gases up in the air where it explodes into showers of sparks; skyrocket. *—v.i.* go like a rocket; rise very fast; skyrocket. *—v.t.* send or launch with a rocket. [< Italian *rocchetta,* probably diminutive of *rocca* distaff (from the similarity in shape); of Germanic origin]
rock et eer (rok′ə tir′), *n.* person who works with rockets, especially an expert in rocketry.
rocket engine, rocket (def. 1).
rocket launcher, device consisting of a tube or cluster of tubes from which rockets are launched.
rock et ry (rok′ə trē), *n.* science of building, using, and firing rockets.
rocket ship, spacecraft using rocket propulsion for its chief or only source of power.
rock fish (rok′fish′), *n., pl.* **-fish es** or **-fish.** any of various fishes found among rocks, especially the striped bass.
Rock ford (rok′fərd), *n.* city in N Illinois. 147,000.
rock garden, garden on rocky ground or among rocks, for the growing of flowers, ornamental plants, etc.
Rock ies (rok′ēz), *n.pl.* Rocky Mountains.
rocking chair, chair mounted on rockers, or on springs, so that it can rock back and forth; rocker.
rocking horse, a toy horse on rockers for children to ride; hobbyhorse.
rock 'n' roll (rok′ən rōl′), *n.* 1 kind of popular music derived from folk music, blues, and jazz, with a strongly marked, regular beat and often a simple, repetitious melody. 2 a lively style of dancing to such music, characterized by improvisation and exaggerated movements.
rock-ribbed (rok′ribd′), *adj.* 1 having ridges of rock. 2 unyielding; rigid; inflexible: *rock-ribbed endurance.*
rock salt, common salt as it occurs in the earth in large crystals; halite.
rock wool, woollike fibers made from rock or slag and used for insulation and soundproofing.
rock y[1] (rok′ē), *adj.,* **rock i er, rock i est.** 1 full of rocks. 2 made of rock. 3 like rock; hard; firm; unyielding: *rocky determination.* [< *rock*[1]]
rock y[2] (rok′ē), *adj.,* **rock i er, rock i est.** 1 likely to rock; shaky. 2 INFORMAL. sickish; weak; dizzy. [< *rock*[2]] **—rock′i ly,** *adv.* **—rock′i ness,** *n.*
Rocky Mountains, chief group of mountain ranges in W North America, extending from Alaska to New Mexico; the Rockies. The highest peak is Elbert Peak in Colorado, 14,431 ft.
Rocky Mountain sheep, bighorn.
Rocky Mountain spotted fever, an infectious disease formerly believed to be prevalent chiefly in the Rocky Mountain area, characterized by fever, pain, and a rash, caused by a rickettsia and transmitted by the bite of infected ticks.
ro co co (rō kō′kō, rō′kə kō′), *n.* style of architecture and decoration with elaborate ornamentation, combining shellwork, scrolls, foliage, etc., much used in the 1700's. *—adj.* of or having to do with this style. [< French < *rocaille* decoration with rocks and shells < *roc* rock]

rococo frame

rod (rod), *n.* 1 a thin, straight bar of metal or wood. 2 a thin, straight stick, either growing or cut off. 3 anything like a rod in shape. 4 stick used to beat or punish. 5 punishment. 6 **spare the rod,** fail to punish. 7 fishing rod. 8 unit of length equal to $5^1/_2$ yards or $16^1/_2$ feet; perch. A square rod is $30^1/_4$ square yards or $272^1/_4$ square feet. See **measure** for table. 9 stick used to measure with. 10 SLANG. pistol. 11 branch of a family or tribe. 12 staff or wand carried as a symbol of one's position. 13 power; authority. 14 one of the microscopic sense organs in the retina of the eye that are sensitive to dim light. 15 a cylindrical or rod-shaped bacterium. [Old English *rodd*] **—rod′like′,** *adj.*
rode (rōd), *v.* pt. of **ride.**
ro dent (rōd′nt), *n.* any of an order of mammals having two continually growing incisor teeth in each jaw which are especially adapted for gnawing wood and similar material. Rats, mice, squirrels, porcupines, and beavers are rodents. *—adj.* 1 gnawing. 2 of or like a rodent. [< Latin *rodentem* gnawing]
ro den ti cide (rō den′tə sīd), *n.* poison for rats and mice, or other rodents.
ro de o (rō′dē ō, rō dā′ō), *n., pl.* **-de os.** 1 contest or exhibition of skill in roping cattle, riding horses and steers, etc. 2 (in the western United States) the driving together of cattle; roundup. [< Spanish < *rodear* go around]
Rod gers (roj′ərz), *n.* **Richard,** born 1902, American composer of musical comedies.
Ro din (rô daɴ′), *n.* **Auguste,** 1840-1917, French sculptor.
rod o mon tade (rod′ə mon tād′, rod′ə-mon täd′), *n.* vain boasting; bragging; blustering talk. *—adj.* bragging; boastful.

[< French < Italian *rodomontata* < *Rodomonte,* a braggart king in Ariosto's romance *Orlando Furioso*]

roe[1] (rō), *n., pl.* **roes** or **roe.** roe deer. [Old English *rā*]

roe[2] (rō), *n.* fish eggs, especially when contained in the ovarian membrane of the female fish. [Middle English *rowe,* perhaps from *rown* (taken as a plural) < Scandinavian (Old Icelandic) *hrogn*]

roe buck (rō′buk′), *n., pl.* **-bucks** or **-buck.** a male roe deer.

roe deer, a small, agile deer of Europe and Asia, with forked antlers.

roent gen (rent′gən), *n.* the international unit of intensity of X rays or gamma rays, equal to the quantity of radiation required to produce one electrostatic unit of electrical charge in one cubic centimeter of dry air under normal temperature and pressure. *—adj.* having to do with X rays or gamma rays. Also, **röntgen.** [< Wilhelm K. *Roentgen*]

Roent gen (rent′gən), *n.* **Wilhelm Konrad,** 1845-1923, German physicist who discovered X rays. Also, **Röntgen.**

roent gen o gram (rent′gə nə gram), *n.* an X-ray photograph.

roent gen og ra phy (rent′gə nog′rə fē), *n.* X-ray photography.

roent gen o log i cal (rent′gə nə loj′ə kəl), *adj.* of or having to do with roentgenology.

roent gen ol o gist (rent′gə nol′ə jist), *n.* an expert in roentgenology.

roent gen ol o gy (rent′gə nol′ə jē), *n.* branch of radiology having to do with X rays, especially as used in medical diagnosis and treatment.

Roentgen ray, X ray.

Roeth ke (ret′kē), *n.* **Theodore,** 1908-1963, American poet.

ro ga tion (rō gā′shən), *n.* solemn prayer or supplication, especially as chanted on the three days before Ascension Day. [< Latin *rogationem* < *rogare* ask]

Rogation Days, the Monday, Tuesday, and Wednesday before Ascension Day, observed by solemn supplication.

rog er (roj′ər), *interj.* INFORMAL. O.K.; message received and understood. [< the signaler's word for the letter *r,* for "received"]

Rog ers (roj′ərz), *n.* **Will,** 1879-1935, American humorist and actor.

Ro get (rō zhā′), *n.* **Peter Mark,** 1779-1869, British physician who compiled a famous thesaurus of English words.

rogue (rōg), *n., v.,* **rogued, ro guing.** *—n.* 1 a dishonest or unprincipled person; scoundrel; rascal. 2 a mischievous person; scamp. 3 animal with a savage nature that lives apart from the herd. 4 (in biology) an individual, usually a plant, that varies from the standard. *—v.t.* eliminate defective plants from. [origin uncertain]

rogue elephant, 1 a savage or destructive elephant driven away or living apart from a herd. 2 any hostile or dangerous social outcast.

ro guer y (rō′gər ē), *n., pl.* **-guer ies.** 1 conduct of rogues; dishonest trickery. 2 playful mischief.

rogues' gallery, collection of photographs of known criminals maintained by the police.

ro guish (rō′gish), *adj.* 1 having to do with or like rogues; dishonest; rascally. 2 playfully mischievous. **—ro′guish ly,** *adv.* **—ro′guish ness,** *n.*

roil (roil), *v.t.* 1 make (water, etc.) muddy by stirring up sediment. 2 disturb; irritate; vex. [< Old French *rouiller*]

rois ter (roi′stər), *v.i.* be boisterous; revel noisily; swagger. [< Old French *ruistre* rude < Latin *rusticus* rustic]

ROK (rok), *n.* 1 Republic of Korea. 2 soldier in the South Korean army.

Ro land (rō′lənd), *n.* (in medieval legends) one of Charlemagne's chiefs, famous for his prowess, who defeated the Saracens in Spain and was killed at the battle of Roncesvalles.

role or **rôle** (rōl), *n.* 1 an actor's part in a play, motion picture, opera, etc.: *the leading role.* 2 part or function assumed by any person or thing: *the role of mediator in a dispute.* [< French *rôle* the roll (of paper, etc.) on which an actor's part is written]

roll (rōl), *v.i.* 1 move along by turning over and over: *The ball rolled away.* 2 become wrapped around itself or some other thing: *This wire rolls easily.* 3 move or be moved on wheels: *The car rolled along.* 4 move smoothly; sweep along: *Waves roll in on the beach. The years roll on.* 5 (of the eyes) move or turn around in the sockets: *His eyes rolled with fear.* 6 (of a heavenly body, etc.) perform a periodic revolution in an orbit. 7 move from side to side: *The ship rolled in the waves.* 8 turn over, or over and over: *The horse rolled in the dust.* 9 walk with a swaying gait; swagger. 10 rise and fall again and again: *rolling country.* 11 make deep, loud sounds: *Thunder rolls.* 12 INFORMAL. abound *(in): be rolling in money.* *—v.t.* 1 cause to move along by turning over and over: *roll a hoop, roll a barrel.* 2 wrap around on itself or on some other thing: *roll oneself up in a blanket. Roll the string into a ball.* 3 move along on wheels or rollers: *roll a bicycle.* 4 sweep along. 5 turn (the eyes) in different directions with a kind of circular motion. 6 cause to sway from side to side: *The huge waves rolled the ocean liner.* 7 cause to lie, turn over, etc., as on the back: *The dog rolled himself on the rug to scratch his back.* 8 make flat or smooth with a roller; spread out with a rolling pin, etc.: *Roll the dough thin for these cookies.* 9 beat (a drum) with rapid, continuous strokes. 10 utter with full, flowing sound: *The organ rolled out the stirring hymn.* 11 utter with a trill: *roll one's r's.*

roll up, pile up or become piled up; increase. *—n.* 1 something rolled up; cylinder formed by rolling: *rolls of paper, a roll of film.* 2 scroll. 3 a more or less rounded, cylindrical, or rolled-up mass: *a roll of fat.* 4 continued motion up and down, or from side to side: *The ship's roll made people sick.* 5 a rapid, continuous beating on a drum. 6 a deep, loud sound: *the roll of thunder.* 7 act of rolling. 8 motion like that of waves; undulation: *the roll of a meadow.* 9 roller. 10 list of names; record; list: *call the roll.* See **list**[1] for synonym study. **11 strike off the rolls,** expel from membership. 12 a small piece of dough which is cut, shaped, and often doubled or rolled over and then baked. 13 cake rolled up after being spread with something. 14 any food prepared by being rolled up, such as meat. 15 INFORMAL. paper money rolled up. 16 rich or rhythmical flow of words.

[< Old French *roller* < Popular Latin *rotulare* < Latin *rotula,* diminutive of *rota* wheel]

Rol land (rô läN′), *n.* **Romain,** 1866-1944, French novelist and playwright.

hat, āge, fär; let, ēqual, tėrm;
it, īce; hot, ōpen, ôrder;
oil, out; cup, pu̇t, rüle;
ch, child; ng, long; sh, she;
th, thin; ᴛʜ, then; zh, measure;

ə represents *a* in about, *e* in taken, *i* in pencil, *o* in lemon, *u* in circus.

< = from, derived from, taken from.

roll call, 1 the calling of a list of names, as of soldiers, pupils, etc., to find out who are present. 2 time of day of such a calling.

roll er (rō′lər), *n.* 1 thing that rolls; cylinder on which something is rolled along or rolled up. 2 cylinder of metal, stone, wood, etc., used for smoothing, pressing, crushing, etc. 3 a long rolled bandage. 4 a long, swelling wave. 5 person who rolls something. 6 kind of canary that has a trilling voice. 7 kind of tumbler pigeon. 8 any of various crowlike old-world birds that roll about while flying.

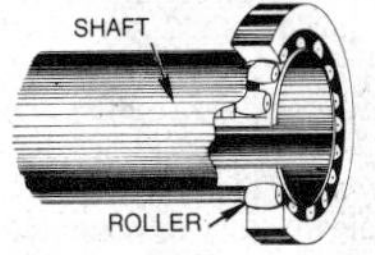

roller bearing cut away to show rollers

roller bearing, a bearing in which the shaft turns on rollers held between rings to lessen friction.

roller coaster, railway for amusement, consisting of inclined tracks along which small cars roll, abruptly dip, turn, etc.

roller skate, a skate with small wheels instead of a runner, for use on a floor or sidewalk; skate.

roll er-skate (rō′lər skāt′), *v.i.,* **-skat ed, -skat ing.** move on roller skates.

rol lick (rol′ik), *v.i.* enjoy oneself in a free, hearty way; be merry; frolic. [origin uncertain]

rol lick ing (rol′ə king), *adj.* frolicking; jolly; lively.

rol lick some (rol′ik səm), *adj.* rollicking.

rolling mill, 1 factory where metal is rolled into sheets and bars. 2 machine for doing this.

rolling pin, cylinder of wood, plastic, or glass with a handle at each end, for rolling out dough.

rolling stock, the locomotives and cars of a railroad.

roll-top (rōl′top′), *adj.* having a top that rolls back: *a roll-top desk.*

ro ly-po ly (rō′lē pō′lē), *adj., n., pl.* **-lies.** *—adj.* short and plump: *a roly-poly child.* *—n.* 1 a short, plump person or animal. 2 pudding made of jam or fruit spread on a rich dough, rolled up and cooked. [apparently reduplication of *roll*]

Rom., 1 Roman. 2 Romance. 3 Romania. 4 Romans (book of the New Testament).

Ro ma ic (rō mā′ik), *n.* the everyday speech of modern Greece. *—adj.* of or having to do with this speech.

ro maine (rō mān′), *n.* variety of lettuce having long green leaves with crinkly edges, which are joined loosely at the base. [< French, originally, Roman]

Ro man (rō′mən), *adj.* 1 of or having to do with ancient or modern Rome or its people. 2 of or having to do with the Roman Catholic

Church. 3 of or having to do with a style of architecture developed by the ancient Romans, characterized by massive walls and pillars, rounded arches and vaults, domes, and pediments. 4 **roman,** of or in roman type. —*n.* 1 native, inhabitant, or citizen of Rome. 2 citizen of ancient Rome. 3 UNFRIENDLY USE. a Roman Catholic. 4 language of the ancient Romans; Latin. 5 **roman,** the style of type most used in printing and typewriting. This sentence is in roman.

ro man à clef (rô mäN′nà klā′), FRENCH. 1 novel in which the characters and events represent real persons and events. 2 (literally) novel with key.

Roman candle, kind of firework consisting of a tube that shoots out balls of fire, etc.

Roman Catholic, 1 of, having to do with, or belonging to the Christian church that recognizes the pope as the supreme head. 2 member of this church.

Roman Catholicism, doctrines, faith, practices, and system of government of the Roman Catholic Church.

ro mance (*n.* rō mans′, rō′mans; *v.* rō-mans′), *n., v.,* **-manced, -manc ing.** —*n.* 1 a love story. 2 story of adventure: *"The Arabian Nights" and "Treasure Island" are romances.* 3 a medieval story or poem telling of heroes: *romances about King Arthur.* See **novel** for synonym study. 4 real events or conditions that are like such stories, full of love, excitement, or noble deeds; the character or quality of such events or conditions. 5 a love affair. 6 an extravagant or wild exaggeration; made-up story; falsehood: *Nobody believes her romances about the wonderful things that have happened to her.* 7 **Romance,** the Romance languages. —*v.i.* 1 make up romances. 2 think or talk in a romantic way. 3 exaggerate; lie. —*v.t.* INFORMAL. make love to; woo. —*adj.* **Romance,** of or having to do with the Romance languages. [< Old French *romanz* < Popular Latin *romanice* in the Roman language < Latin *Romanus* Roman < *Roma* Rome] **—ro manc′er,** *n.*

Romance languages, French, Italian, Spanish, Portuguese, Romanian, Provençal, and other languages that came from Latin.

Roman Empire, empire of ancient Rome lasting from 27 B.C. to A.D. 395. It was divided into the **Eastern Roman Empire,** or **Byzantine Empire** (A.D. 395-1453), and the **Western Roman Empire** (A.D. 395-476).

Roman Empire
The shaded area shows the Empire at its greatest extent in A.D. 117.

Ro man esque (rō′mə nesk′), *n.* style of architecture using round arches and vaults, developed in Europe during the early Middle Ages, between the periods of Roman and Gothic architecture. —*adj.* of, in, or having to do with this style of architecture.

Romanesque

Ro ma ni a (rō mā′nē ə), *n.* country in SE Europe. 20,140,000 pop.; 91,700 sq. mi. *Capital:* Bucharest. See **Austria** for map. Also, **Rumania** or **Roumania.** **—Ro-ma′ni an,** *n., adj.*

Ro man ic (rō man′ik), *adj.* 1 Romance. 2 Roman.

Ro man ist (rō′ mə nist), *n.* UNFRIENDLY USE. member of the Roman Catholic Church.

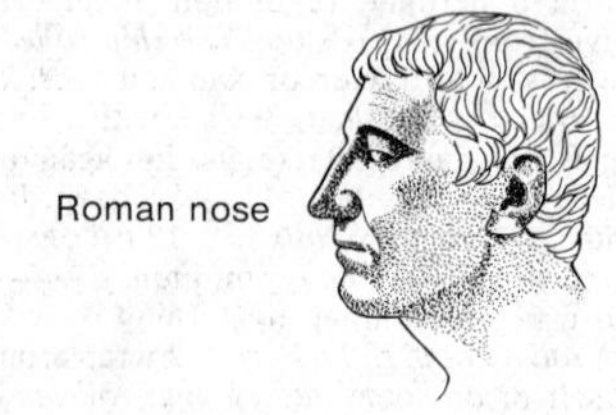

Roman nose

Roman nose, nose having a prominent bridge.

Roman numerals, numerals like XXIII, LVI, and MDCCLX, used by the ancient Romans in numbering. In this system I = 1, V = 5, X = 10, L = 50, C = 100, D = 500, and M = 1000.

Ro ma nov or **Ro ma noff** (rō′mə nôf, rō mä′nôf), *n.* 1 **Mikhail Feodorovich,** 1596-1645, czar of Russia from 1613 to 1645. 2 member of the royal family of Russia from 1613 to 1917.

Ro mans (rō′mənz), *n.* book of the New Testament, an epistle by Saint Paul to the Christians of Rome.

ro man tic (rō man′tik), *adj.* 1 characteristic of romances or romance; appealing to fancy and the imagination: *romantic tales of love and war, a romantic life in exotic lands.* 2 interested in adventure and love; having ideas or feelings suited to romance: *The romantic schoolgirl's mind was full of handsome heroes, jewels, dances, and fine clothes.* 3 suited to a romance. 4 of or having to do with romanticism in literature, art, and music. 5 not based on fact; fanciful; imaginary. 6 not customary or practical; unrealistic: *romantic illusion.* —*n.* 1 a romanticist. 2 a romantic person. [< French *romantique* < earlier *romant* a romance, variant of Old French *romanz.* See ROMANCE.] **—ro-man′ti cal ly,** *adv.*

ro man ti cism (rō man′tə siz′əm), *n.* 1 style of literature, art, and music, especially widespread in the 1800's, which allows freedom of form and stresses strong feeling, imagination, love of nature, and often the unusual and supernatural. 2 romantic spirit or tendency.

ro man ti cist (rō man′tə sist), *n.* a follower of romanticism in literature, art, or music. Wordsworth and Schubert were romanticists.

ro man ti cize (rō man′tə sīz), *v.,* **-cized, -ciz ing.** —*v.t.* make romantic; give a romantic character to. —*v.i.* be romantic; act, talk, or write in a romantic manner. **—ro-man′ti ci za′tion,** *n.*

Rom a ny (rom′ə nē), *n., pl.* **-nies,** *adj.* —*n.* 1 Gypsy. 2 the Indic language of the Gypsies. —*adj.* belonging to or having to do with the Gypsies, their customs, or their language. [< Romany *Romani* < *rom* gypsy, man, husband]

Rome (rōm), *n.* 1 capital of Italy, on the Tiber River. The headquarters of the pope and the Roman Catholic Church are in Vatican City, an independent state within Rome. 2,731,000. 2 ancient city in the same place, the capital of the Roman Empire. 3 the ancient Roman republic or the ancient Roman Empire. 4 the Roman Catholic Church.

Ro me o (rō′mē ō), *n.* hero of Shakespeare's play *Romeo and Juliet,* who died for love.

Rom mel (rom′əl), *n.* **Erwin,** 1891-1944, German field marshal in World War II.

Rom ney (rom′nē, rum′nē), *n.* **George,** 1734-1802, English painter.

romp (romp), *v.i.* play in a rough, boisterous way; rush, tumble, and punch in play. —*n.* 1 a rough, lively play or frolic. 2 girl or boy who likes to romp. [perhaps variant of *ramp,* verb] **—romp′er,** *n.*

romp ers (rom′pərz), *n.pl.* a loose outer garment, usually consisting of short bloomers and top, worn by young children at play.

Rom u lus (rom′yə ləs), *n.* (in Roman legends) the founder and first king of Rome. He and his twin brother, Remus, abandoned as infants, were nourished by a wolf.

Ron ces valles (ron′sə valz), *n.* village in the Pyrenees in N Spain where part of Charlemagne's army was defeated in A.D. 778 by the Saracens.

ron deau (ron′dō, ron dō′), *n., pl.* **ron deaux** (ron′dōz, ron dōz′). a short poem with thirteen (or ten) lines; roundel. The opening words are used in two places as an unrhymed refrain. [< Middle French < Old French *rondel.* See RONDEL.]

ron del (ron′dl), *n.* a short poem, usually with fourteen lines and two rhymes. The initial couplet is repeated in the middle and at the end. [< Old French, originally diminutive of *rond* round]

ron do (ron′dō, ron dō′), *n., pl.* **-dos.** (in music) a work or movement having one principal theme which is repeated at least three times in the same key and to which return is made after the introduction of each subordinate theme. [< Italian < French *rondeau*]

rönt gen (rent′gən), *n., adj.* roentgen.

Rönt gen (rent′gən), *n.* Roentgen.

rood (rüd), *n.* 1 40 square rods; one fourth of an acre. 2 a varying unit of linear measure, equal to about 6 to 8 yards. 3 ARCHAIC. the cross on which Christ died. 4 a representation of it; crucifix. [Old English *rōd*]

roof (rüf, rüf), *n.* 1 the top covering of a building. 2 something like it: *the roof of a cave, the roof of a car, the roof of the mouth.* 3 **raise the roof,** INFORMAL. make a disturbance; create an uproar or confusion. —*v.t.* cover with a roof; form a roof over. [Old English *hrōf*] **—roof′like′,** *adj.*

roof deck, a flat roof or portion of a roof used for lounging, dining, etc.

roof er (rü′fər, rů f′ər), *n.* person who makes or repairs roofs.

roof garden, 1 garden on the flat roof of a building. 2 roof or top story of a building, ornamented with plants, etc., and used for a restaurant, theater, etc.

roof ing (rü′fing, růf′ing), *n.* material used for roofs. Shingles are a common roofing for houses.

roof less (rüf′lis, růf′lis), *adj.* 1 having no roof. 2 having no home or shelter.

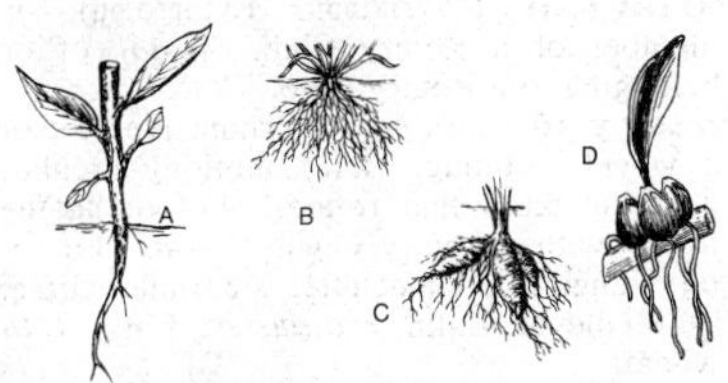

root¹ (def. 1)—the four main types: A, taproot; B, fibrous roots; C, storage roots; D, aerial roots

roof tree (rüf′trē′, růf′trē′), *n.* ridgepole.

rook¹ (růk), *n.* 1 a common European bird, of the same genus as and closely resembling the crow, that often nests in large flocks in trees near buildings. 2 person who cheats at cards, dice, etc. —*v.t.* cheat. [Old English *hrōc*]

rook² (růk), *n.* piece in the game of chess that can move horizontally or vertically across any number of unoccupied squares; castle. [< Old French *roc* < Arabic *rukhkh* < Persian *rukh*]

rook er y (růk′ər ē), *n., pl.* **-er ies.** 1 a breeding place of rooks; colony of rooks. 2 a breeding place or colony where other birds or animals are crowded together. 3 a crowded, dirty, and poor tenement house or group of such houses.

rook ie (růk′ē), *n.* INFORMAL. 1 an inexperienced recruit. 2 beginner; novice. 3 a new player on an athletic team, especially a professional athlete in his first season on a major league team.

room (rüm, rům), *n.* 1 a part of a house, or other building, with walls separating it from the rest of the building of which it is a part. 2 **rooms,** *pl.* lodgings. 3 people in a room. 4 space occupied by, or available for, something: *There is room for one more in the automobile.* 5 opportunity: *room for improvement.* —*v.i.* occupy a room; live in a room. —*v.t.* provide with a room. [Old English *rūm*]

room er (rü′mər, rům′ər), *n.* lodger.

room ette (rü met′, rů met′), *n.* a small private bedroom on a railroad sleeping car.

room ful (rüm′fůl, rům′fůl), *n., pl.* **-fuls.** 1 enough to fill a room. 2 people or things in a room.

rooming house, house with rooms to rent.

room mate (rüm′māt′, rům′māt′), *n.* person who shares a room with another or others.

room y (rü′mē, rům′ē), *adj.,* **room i er, room i est.** having plenty of room; large; spacious. —**room′i ly,** *adv.* —**room′i ness,** *n.*

Roo se velt (rō′zə velt), *n.* 1 **(Anna) Eleanor,** 1884-1962, American author and stateswoman, wife of Franklin Delano Roosevelt. 2 **Franklin Delano,** 1882-1945, the 32nd president of the United States, from 1933 to 1945. 3 **Theodore,** 1858-1919, the 26th president of the United States, from 1901 to 1909.

roost (rüst), *n.* 1 bar, pole, or perch on which birds rest or sleep. 2 place for birds to roost in. 3 place to rest or stay: *a robber's roost in the mountains.* 4 **rule the roost,** INFORMAL. be master. —*v.i.* 1 sit as birds do on a roost; settle for the night. 2 **come home to roost,** come back so as to harm the doer or user. [Old English *hrōst*]

roost er (rü′stər), *n.* a male domestic fowl; cock.

root¹ (rüt, růt), *n.* 1 the part of a plant that grows downward, usually into the ground, to hold the plant in place, absorb water and mineral foods from the soil, and often to store food material. 2 any underground part of a plant, especially when fleshy, as the carrot or turnip. 3 something like a root in shape, position, use, etc.: *the root of a tooth, the roots of the hair.* 4 part from which other things grow and develop; cause; source. 5 the essential part; base: *get to the root of a problem.* 6 **take root, a** send out roots and begin to grow. **b** become firmly fixed. 7 quantity that produces another quantity when multiplied by itself a certain number of times: *2 is the square root of 4 and the cube root of 8* ($2 \times 2 = 4$, $2 \times 2 \times 2 = 8$). 8 quantity that satisfies an equation when substituted for an unknown quantity: *In the equation* $x^2 + 2x - 3 = 0$, *1 and −3 are the roots.* 9 word from which others are derived. *Room* is the root of *roominess, roomer, roommate,* and *roomy.* 10 the fundamental tone of a chord. —*v.i.* 1 send out roots and begin to grow; become fixed in the ground: *Some plants root more quickly than others.* 2 become firmly fixed. —*v.t.* 1 fix by the root. 2 fix firmly: *rooted to the spot.* 3 pull, tear, or dig (up, out, etc.) by the roots; get completely rid of: *root out corruption in government.* [< Scandinavian (Old Icelandic) *rōt*] —**root′less,** *adj.* —**root′like′,** *adj.*

root² (rüt, růt), *v.i.* 1 dig with the snout. 2 poke; search; rummage. —*v.t.* turn over or dig up with the snout: *The pigs rooted up the garden.* [Old English *wrōtan*] —**root′er,** *n.*

root³ (rüt, růt), *v.i.* INFORMAL. cheer or support a team, contestant, etc., enthusiastically: *root for a candidate for senator.* [probably < earlier sense "work hard" of *root²*] —**root′er,** *n.*

Root (rüt), *n.* **Elihu,** 1845-1937, American lawyer and statesman.

root beer, a carbonated soft drink flavored with the juice of the roots of certain plants, such as sarsaparilla, sassafras, etc.

root canal, passage in the root of a tooth through which nerves and vessels pass to the pulp.

root cap, mass of cells at the tip of growing roots that protects the active growing point immediately behind it.

root ed (rü′tid, růt′id), *adj.* 1 having roots. 2 having taken root; firmly fixed: *a deeply rooted belief.*

root hair, a hairlike outgrowth from the root of a plant. Root hairs absorb water and dissolved minerals from the soil.

root let (rüt′lit, růt′lit), *n.* a little root; small branch of a root.

root stalk (rüt′stôk′, růt′stôk′), *n.* rootstock; rhizome.

root stock (rüt′stok′, růt′stok′), *n.* 1 rhizome. 2 root that serves as a stock for propagating plants.

rope (rōp), *n., v.,* **roped, rop ing.** —*n.* 1 a strong, thick line or cord, made by twisting smaller cords together. 2 U.S. lasso. 3 number of things twisted or strung together: *a rope of pearls.* 4 cord or noose for hanging a person. 5 death by being hanged. 6 a sticky, stringy mass: *Molasses candy forms a rope.* 7 **give one rope,** let one act freely. 8 **know the ropes** or **learn the ropes, a** know or learn the various ropes of a ship. **b** INFORMAL. know or learn about a business or activity. 9 **the end of one's rope,** the end of one's resources, activities, etc. —*v.t.* 1 tie, bind, or fasten with a rope. 2 enclose or mark off with a rope. 3 U.S. catch (a horse, calf, etc.) with a lasso; lasso. 4 **rope in,** INFORMAL. get or take in by tricking. [Old English *rāp*]

hat, āge, fär; let, ēqual, tėrm;
it, īce; hot, ōpen, ôrder;
oil, out; cup, půt, rüle;
ch, child; ng, long; sh, she;
th, thin; ᴛʜ, then; zh, measure;

ə represents *a* in about, *e* in taken,
i in pencil, *o* in lemon, *u* in circus.

< = from, derived from, taken from.

rope danc er (rōp′dan′sər), *n.* person who dances or balances on a rope hung high above the floor or ground.

rop er (rō′pər), *n.* 1 person who makes ropes. 2 person who uses a lasso.

rope walk (rōp′wôk′), *n.* place where ropes are made.

rope walk er (rōp′wô′kər), *n.* 1 person who walks on a rope hung high above the floor or ground. 2 ropedancer.

rop y (rō′pē), *adj.,* **rop i er, rop i est.** 1 forming sticky threads; stringy: *a ropy syrup.* 2 like a rope or ropes. —**rop′i ness,** *n.*

Roque fort (rōk′fərt), *n.* a strongly flavored French cheese made of goats' milk, veined with mold.

ror qual (rôr′kwəl), *n.* any of the whalebone whales having grooves in their throats and undersides and a small dorsal fin; finback; razorback. [< French < Norwegian *royrkval*]

Ror schach test (rôr′shäk), a psychological test which measures personality traits, general intelligence, etc., based on the subject's interpretation of ten different standardized ink blot designs. [< Hermann *Rorschach,* 1884-1922, Swiss psychiatrist]

ro sa ceous (rō zā′shəs), *adj.* 1 belonging to the rose family. 2 like a rose. 3 rose-colored.

Ro sar i o (rō sär′ē ō), *n.* city in E central Argentina. 672,000.

ro sar y (rō′zər ē), *n., pl.* **-sar ies.** 1 string of beads for keeping count in saying a series of prayers. 2 (in the Roman Catholic Church) a series of prayers consisting of a specified number of Ave Marias, paternosters, and Glorias. 3 garden of roses; bed of roses. [< Medieval Latin *rosarium* < Latin, rose garden < *rosa* rose¹]

rose¹ (rōz), *n., adj., v.,* **rosed, ros ing.** —*n.* 1 a showy, fragrant red, pink, white, or yellow flower that grows on any of a genus of shrubs of the rose family, with thorny stems. Wild roses have one circle of petals; cultivated roses usually have more than one circle and are sometimes even cabbage-shaped in body. 2 any of the shrubs it grows on. 3 any of various other plants and flowers of the rose family, or similar plants and flowers of other families. 4 a pinkish-red color. 5 something shaped like a rose or suggesting a rose, such as a rosette, the compass card, the sprinkling nozzle of a water pot, or a gem cut out with faceted top and flat base. —*adj.* pinkish-red. —*v.t.* make rosy. [Old English < Latin *rosa*] **—rose′like′**, *adj.*

rose² (rōz), *v.* pt. of **rise.**

ro se ate (rō′zē it, rō′zē āt), *adj.* 1 rose-colored; rosy. 2 bright; cheerful; optimistic. **—ro′se ate ly**, *adv.*

Ro seau (rō zō′), *n.* capital of Dominica. 12,000.

rose bud (rōz′bud′), *n.* bud of a rose.

rose bush (rōz′bu̇sh′), *n.* shrub or vine bearing roses.

rose cold, rose fever.

rose-col ored (rōz′kul′ərd), *adj.* 1 pinkish-red. 2 bright; cheerful; optimistic.

Rose crans (rōz′krans), *n.* **William Starke,** 1819-1898, Union general in the Civil War.

rose family, a large group of dicotyledonous trees, shrubs, and herbs, including the apple, pear, blackberry, spiraea, hawthorn, and rose, typically having alternate leaves, five-petaled flowers, and fruits with many seeds.

rose fever, hay fever that occurs in the spring or early summer, thought to be caused by pollen from roses; rose cold.

rose mallow, 1 any of various hibiscuses having large, rose-colored flowers. 2 hollyhock.

rose mar y (rōz′mer′ē, rōz′mar′ē), *n., pl.* **-mar ies.** a fragrant evergreen shrub of the mint family, native to southern Europe, whose leaves are used in making perfume and in seasoning food. Rosemary is a symbol or emblem of remembrance. [Middle English *rosmarine* < Latin *rosmarinus,* literally, dew of the sea]

rose of Sharon, 1 shrub, a species of hibiscus, with bell-shaped pink, purple, or white flowers; althea. 2 kind of St.-John's-wort having yellow flowers. 3 flower mentioned in the Bible, perhaps the autumn crocus.

ro se o la (rō zē′ə lə), *n.* any rosy rash that occurs with various fevers, especially that occurring with a mild, measleslike disease of early infancy. [< New Latin]

Ro set ta stone (rō zet′ə), slab of black basalt found in 1799 near the mouth of the Nile, bearing hieroglyphic, demotic, and Greek inscriptions that provided the key to the deciphering of Egyptian hieroglyphics.

rosette (def. 2)
rosettes used in architecture

ro sette (rō zet′), *n.* 1 bunch or knot of ribbons worn as an ornament or badge. 2 any object or pattern resembling a rose in form, especially an ornament painted, carved, or molded upon a wall or other surface. 3 cluster of leaves or other plant organs naturally arranged in a circle. [< French]

rose water, water made fragrant with oil of roses, used as a perfume.

rose window, an ornamental circular window, especially one with a pattern of small sections that radiate from a center.

rose wood (rōz′wu̇d′), *n.* 1 a beautiful wood of a dark red or purplish color streaked with black, used in fine furniture. 2 any of the tropical trees of the pea family that it comes from.

Rosh Ha sha nah (rosh′ hə shä′nə), the Jewish New Year, usually occurring in September. [< Hebrew *rōsh hashshānāh,* literally, head of the year]

Ro si cru cian (rō′zə krü′shən), *n.* 1 member of a secret society prominent in the 1600's and 1700's which claimed to have a special and secret knowledge of nature and religion. 2 member of any of various similar societies founded later. —*adj.* of or having to do with the Rosicrucians. [< *Rosicrucis,* Latinized form of *Rosenkreuz,* name of the supposed founder in 1484 of the order]

ros i ly (rō′zə lē), *adv.* 1 with a rosy tinge or color. 2 brightly; cheerfully.

ros in (roz′n), *n.* a hard, yellow, brown, or black resin that remains when turpentine is distilled from the oleoresin of various coniferous trees; resin. Rosin is used in varnishes, soaps, as a sizing for paper, etc., and is rubbed on violin bows and on the shoes of acrobats and ballet dancers to keep them from slipping. —*v.t.* cover or rub with rosin: *rosin a violin bow.* [< Old French *rosine,* variant of *resine* resin]

Ross (rôs, ros), *n.* 1 **Betsy,** 1752-1836, American woman who is said to have made the first American flag. 2 **John,** 1790-1866, American Indian leader, chief of the Cherokee tribe. 3 Sir **John,** 1777-1856, British naval officer and arctic explorer who tried to find the Northwest Passage.

Ros set ti (rō zet′ē, rō set′ē), *n.* 1 **Christina Georgina,** 1830-1894, English poet, sister of Dante Gabriel Rossetti. 2 **Dante Gabriel,** 1828-1882, English poet and painter.

Ros si ni (rō sē′nē), *n.* **Gioacchino Antonio,** 1792-1868, Italian composer of operas.

Ross Sea, inlet of the Pacific Ocean extending into Antarctica south of New Zealand.

Ros tand (rôs täɴ′), *n.* **Edmond,** 1868-1918, French poet and dramatist, author of *Cyrano de Bergerac.*

ros ter (ros′tər), *n.* 1 list of people's names and the duties assigned to them. 2 any list. [< Dutch *rooster* list, (originally) gridiron < *roosten* to roast]

Ros tov (ros tôf′), *n.* city in SW Soviet Union, a port on the Don River. 789,000.

ros tral (ros′trəl), *adj.* of or having to do with a rostrum.

ros trate (ros′trāt), *adj.* (in biology) having a beaklike part.

ros trum (ros′trəm), *n., pl.* **-trums, -tra** (-trə). 1 platform or stage for public speaking. 2 (in ancient Rome) the platform in the forum from which public speakers delivered orations. 3 beak of an ancient war galley. 4 (in biology) part or structure resembling a beak. [< Latin, beak < *rodere* gnaw; with reference to the speakers' platform in the Roman forum, which was decorated with the beaks of captured war galleys]

ros y (rō′zē), *adj.,* **ros i er, ros i est.** 1 like a rose; rose-red; pinkish-red. 2 made of or decorated with roses. 3 bright; cheerful: *a rosy future.* **—ros′i ness,** *n.*

rot (rot), *v.,* **rot ted, rot ting,** *n., interj.* —*v.i.* 1 become rotten; decay; spoil. See **decay** for synonym study. 2 decay morally or mentally; become corrupt; degenerate. —*v.t.* cause to decay: *So much rain will rot the fruit.* —*n.* 1 process of rotting; decay. 2 rotten matter. 3 a liver disease of animals, especially of sheep. 4 any of various diseases of plants marked by decay and caused by bacteria or fungi. 5 INFORMAL. nonsense; rubbish. —*interj.* nonsense! rubbish! [Old English *rotian*]

Ro tar i an (rō ter′ē ən, rō tar′ē ən), *n.* member of a Rotary Club. —*adj.* of or belonging to a Rotary Club.

ro tar y (rō′tər ē), *adj.* 1 turning like a top or a wheel; rotating. 2 (of motion) circular. 3 having parts that rotate. 4 of or having to do with a rotary engine. —*n.* 1 a rotary engine or machine. 2 traffic circle. [< Medieval Latin *rotarius* < Latin *rota* wheel]

Rotary Club, association of business and professional men formed with the purpose of serving their community. All Rotary Clubs are united in an international organization.

rotary engine, 1 a turbine engine, electric motor, etc., in which the pistons, blades, armature, or similar parts rotate instead of moving in a straight line, or in which a cylinder rotates upon a piston. 2 an internal-combustion engine in aircraft, having radially arranged cylinders that revolve around a common fixed crankshaft.

ro tat a ble (rō′tā tə bəl, rō tā′tə bəl), *adj.* that can be rotated.

ro tate (rō′tāt), *v.,* **-tat ed, -tat ing.** —*v.i.* 1 move around a center or axis; turn in a circle; revolve. Wheels, tops, and the earth rotate. See **turn** for synonym study. 2 change in a regular order; take turns; alternate: *The officials will rotate in office.* —*v.t.* 1 cause to turn around. 2 cause to take turns: *Farmers rotate crops.* [< Latin *rotatum* rotated < *rota* wheel]

ro ta tion (rō tā′shən), *n.* 1 act or process of moving around a center or axis; turning in a circle; revolving: *The earth's rotation causes night and day.* 2 one such movement. 3 change in a regular order. 4 **in rotation,** in turn; in regular succession.

ro ta tion al (rō tā′shə nəl), *adj.* of or with rotation.

rotation of crops, crop rotation.

ro ta tor (rō′tā tər), *n.* 1 person or thing that rotates. 2 muscle that turns a part of the body.

ro ta to ry (rō′tə tôr′ē, rō′tə tōr′ē), *adj.* 1 turning like a top or wheel; rotating; rotary. 2 causing rotation. 3 passing or following from one to another in succession.

R.O.T.C., Reserve Officers' Training Corps.

rote (rōt), *n.* 1 a set, mechanical way of doing things. 2 **by rote,** by memory without thought of the meaning: *learn a lesson by rote.* [Middle English]

ro te none (rōt′n ōn), *n.* a white, crystalline compound obtained from the roots of various plants, used as an insecticide and fish poison. *Formula:* $C_{23}H_{22}O_6$ [< Japanese *roten,* kind of plant]

Roth ko (roth′kō), *n.* **Mark,** 1903-1970, American painter, born in Russia.

Roth schild (roth′chīld, roths′chīld), *n.* 1 **Meyer Amschel,** 1743-1812, German banker and financier who founded a famous international firm of bankers. 2 his son, **Nathan Meyer,** 1777-1836, English banker and financier, born in Germany.

ro ti fer (rō′tə fər), *n.* any of a phylum of

complex, microscopic water animals that have one or more rings of cilia on a disk at the head of the body, which aid in locomotion and drawing in food. [< Latin *rota* wheel + *ferre* carry]

ro tif er al (rō tif′ər əl), *adj.* of or having to do with the rotifers.

ro tis ser ie (rō tis′ər ē), *n.* 1 an electric appliance with a spit for roasting food, rotated by an electric motor. 2 restaurant or shop that sells meats and poultry cooked on a spit. [< French *rôtisserie* < *rôtir* to roast]

ro to gra vure (rō′tə grə vyůr′, rō′tə-grā′vyůr), *n.* 1 process of printing from an engraved copper cylinder on which the pictures, letters, etc., have been depressed instead of raised. 2 print or picture made by this process. 3 section of a newspaper having such pictures.

ro tor (rō′tər), *n.* 1 the rotating part of a machine or apparatus, such as an electric generator or motor. 2 system of rotating blades by which a helicopter is able to fly. [short for *rotator*]

rot ten (rot′n), *adj.* 1 decayed or spoiled: *a rotten egg.* 2 foul; disgusting: *a rotten smell.* 3 unsound; weak: *rotten ice.* 4 corrupt; dishonest. 5 bad; nasty: *rotten luck, to feel rotten.* [< Scandinavian (Old Icelandic) *rotinn*] **—rot′ten ly,** *adv.* **—rot′ten ness,** *n.*

rotten borough, 1 borough in England before 1832 that had only a few voters, but kept the privilege of sending a member to Parliament. 2 an electoral district having an insufficient number of voters to justify the representation it has.

rot ten stone (rot′n stōn′), *n.* a decomposed limestone that resembles silica, used as a powder for polishing metals.

rot ter (rot′ər), *n.* SLANG. a vile or objectionable person; scoundrel.

Rot ter dam (rot′ər dam), *n.* seaport in SW Netherlands. 687,000.

ro tund (rō tund′), *adj.* 1 round or plump: *a rotund face.* 2 sounding rich and full; full-toned: *a rotund voice.* [< Latin *rotundus.* Doublet of ROUND.] **—ro tund′ly,** *adv.* **—ro tund′ness,** *n.*

rotunda (def. 1)

ro tun da (rō tun′də), *n.* 1 a circular building or part of a building, especially one with a dome. 2 a large, high, circular room: *The Capitol at Washington has a large rotunda.* [< Italian *rotonda* < Latin *rotunda,* feminine, rotund]

ro tun di ty (rō tun′də tē), *n., pl.* **-ties.** 1 roundness or plumpness. 2 rounded fullness of tone.

Rou ault (rü ō′), *n.* **Georges,** 1871-1958, French painter.

rou ble (rü′bəl), *n.* ruble.

rou é (rü ā′, rü′ā), *n.* a dissipated man; rake. [< French]

Rou en (rü äɴ′), *n.* city in N France, on the Seine River, famous for its cathedral. Joan of Arc was burned at the stake in Rouen in 1431. 120,000.

rouge (rüzh), *n., v.,* **rouged, roug ing.** *—n.* 1 a red powder, paste, or liquid for coloring the cheeks or lips. 2 a red powder, chiefly ferric oxide, used for polishing metal, jewels, glass, etc. *—v.t.* color with rouge. *—v.i.* use rouge on the face. [< French < Old French *roge* red < Latin *rubeus*]

Rou get de Lisle (rü zhā′ də lēl′), **Claude Joseph,** 1760-1836, French poet, musician, and soldier, author of the "Marseillaise."

rough (ruf), *adj.* 1 not smooth; not level; not even: *rough boards, rough bark.* 2 stormy: *rough weather.* 3 violently disturbed or agitated: *a rough sea.* 4 likely to hurt others; not gentle; harsh; rude: *rough manners.* 5 without luxury and ease: *rough life in camp.* 6 without culture or refinement: *a rough soldier with little education.* 7 without polish or fine finish: *rough diamonds.* 8 not completed or perfected; done as a first try; without details: *a rough sketch, a rough idea.* 9 coarse and tangled: *a dog with a rough coat of hair.* 10 INFORMAL. unpleasant; hard; severe: *I was in for a rough time.* 11 disorderly; riotous: *a rough crowd.* 12 requiring merely strength rather than intelligence or skill: *rough work.* 13 harsh, sharp, or dry to the taste: *rough wines.* 14 harsh to the ear; grating; jarring: *a rough voice.* 15 (in phonetics) pronounced with an aspirate; having the sound of *h.*
—n. 1 a coarse, violent person. 2 ground that is rocky, filled with ravines, covered with underbrush, etc. 3 the part of a golf course not cleared of trees, long grass, etc., adjoining the fairways on either side. 4 a rough thing or condition; hard or unpleasant side or part: *take the rough with the smooth.* 5 **in the rough,** not polished or refined; coarse; crude.
—v.t. 1 make rough; roughen. 2 treat roughly. 3 (in sports) subject (an opposing player) to unnecessary and intentional physical abuse. 4 shape or sketch roughly: *rough out a plan, rough in the outlines of a face.* *—v.i.* 1 become rough. 2 behave roughly. 3 **rough it,** live without comforts and conveniences.
—adv. roughly.
[Old English *rūh*] **—rough′er,** *n.* **—rough′ness,** *n.*

rough age (ruf′ij), *n.* 1 rough or coarse material. 2 the coarser parts or kinds of food, such as bran and fruit skins, which stimulate the movement of food and waste products through the intestines.

rough-and-read y (ruf′ən red′ē), *adj.* 1 rough and crude, but good enough for the purpose; roughly effective. 2 showing rough vigor rather than refinement.

rough-and-tum ble (ruf′ən tum′bəl), *adj.* showing confusion and violence; with little regard for rules; roughly vigorous; boisterous. *—n.* a rough-and-tumble fight or struggle.

rough cast (ruf′kast′), *n., v.,* **-cast, -cast ing.** *—n.* 1 a coarse plaster for outside surfaces. 2 rough form or model. *—v.t.* 1 cover or coat with roughcast. 2 make, shape, or prepare in a rough form: *roughcast a story.*

rough-dry (ruf′drī′), *v.,* **-dried, -dry ing,** *adj.* *—v.t.* dry (clothes) after washing without ironing them. *—adj.* dried after washing but not ironed.

hat, āge, fär; let, ēqual, tėrm;
it, īce; hot, ōpen, ôrder;
oil, out; cup, pu̇t, rüle;
ch, child; ng, long; sh, she;
th, thin; ᴛʜ, then; zh, measure;

ə represents *a* in about, *e* in taken, *i* in pencil, *o* in lemon, *u* in circus.

< = from, derived from, taken from.

rough en (ruf′ən), *v.t.* make rough. *—v.i.* become rough.

rough-hew (ruf′hyü′), *v.t.,* **-hewed, -hewed** or **-hewn** (-hyün′), **-hew ing.** 1 hew (timber, stone, etc.) roughly or without smoothing or finishing. 2 shape roughly; give crude form to.

rough house (ruf′hous′), *n., v.,* **-housed, -hous ing.** INFORMAL. *—n.* rough play; rowdy conduct; disorderly behavior. *—v.i.* act in a rough or disorderly way. *—v.t.* disturb by such conduct.

rough ish (ruf′ish), *adj.* rather rough.

rough ly (ruf′lē), *adv.* 1 in a rough manner. 2 approximately.

rough neck (ruf′nek′), *n.* INFORMAL. a rough, coarse person.

rough rid er (ruf′rī′dər), *n.* 1 man used to rough, hard riding. 2 person who breaks in and rides rough, wild horses. 3 **Roughrider,** member of a volunteer cavalry regiment commanded by Theodore Roosevelt and Leonard Wood during the Spanish-American War.

rough shod (ruf′shod′), *adj.* 1 having horseshoes with sharp calks to prevent slipping. 2 **ride roughshod over,** domineer over; show no consideration for; treat roughly.

rou lade (rü läd′), *n.* slice of meat rolled about a filling of minced meat and cooked. [< French < *rouler* to roll]

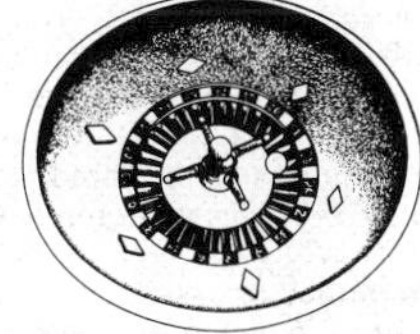

roulette (def. 1)—roulette wheel

rou lette (rü let′), *n., v.,* **-let ted, -let ting.** *—n.* 1 a gambling game in which the players bet on which numbered section of a revolving wheel a small ball will come to rest in. 2 a small wheel with sharp teeth for making lines of marks, dots, or perforations. *—v.t.* cut, mark, or pierce with a roulette. [< French, ultimately < *roue* wheel < Latin *rota*]

Rou ma ni a (rü mā′nē ə, rü mā′nyə), *n.* Romania. **—Rou ma′ni an,** *adj., n.*

round (round), *adj.* 1 shaped like a ball, a ring, the trunk of a tree, or the like; having a circular or curved outline or surface: *a round table top, a round column.* 2 plump: *Her figure was short and round.* 3 by, with, or involving a circular movement. 4 full; complete; entire: *a round dozen.* 5 large; considerable: *a good, round sum of money.* 6 plainly expressed; plain-spoken; frank: *The*

boy's father scolded him in good round terms. 7 with a full tone: *a mellow, round voice.* 8 vigorous; brisk: *a round trot.* 9 (in phonetics) spoken with the lips rounded: *"O" is a round vowel.* 10 stated in round numbers. 11 rough; approximate: *a round estimate.* —*n.* 1 anything round, as a ball, circle, cylinder, or the like; rounded part. 2 rung of a ladder. 3 a fixed course ending where it begins: *The watchman makes his round of the building every hour.* 4 movement in a circle or about an axis: *the earth's yearly round.* 5 series (of duties, events, drinks, etc.); routine: *a round of pleasures, a round of brandy.* 6 the distance between any limits; range; circuit: *the round of human knowledge.* 7 section of a game or sport: *a round in a boxing match, a round of cards.* 8 (in golf) number of holes in a game, usually 18, or in a match, 18, 36, or more. 9 discharge of firearms, artillery, etc., especially by a group of soldiers at the same time. 10 bullets, powder, shells, arrows, etc., for one such discharge: *Only three rounds of ammunition were left.* 11 act that a number of people do together: *a round of applause, a round of cheers.* 12 round dance. 13 a short song, sung by several persons or groups beginning one after the other. 14 cut of beef just above the hind leg and below the rump. See **loin** for diagram. 15 **go the round,** be passed, told, shown, etc., by many people from one to another. 16 **in the round, a** in a form of sculpture in which the figures are apart from any background. **b** in the open; showing all sides or aspects. **c** having seats all around a center stage.
—*v.t.* 1 make round: *The carpenter rounded the corners of the table.* 2 go wholly or partly around: *They rounded the island. The ship rounded Cape Horn.* 3 take a circular course about; make a complete or partial circuit of: *The car rounded the corner at high speed.* 4 surround; encircle. 5 (in phonetics) utter (a vowel) with a small circular opening of the lips. —*v.i.* 1 become round. 2 turn around; wheel about.
round off, a make or become round. **b** finish; complete. **c** express the approximate value of (a number) to the nearest hundredth, tenth, ten, hundred, etc. 75.38 rounded off to the nearest tenth would be 75.4.
round on, attack or assail.
round out, a make or become round. **b** finish; complete.
round up, a draw or drive together: *round up cattle.* **b** gather together; collect.
—*adv.* 1 in a circle; with a whirling motion: *Wheels go round.* 2 on all sides; in every direction. 3 in circumference: *a ball five inches round.* 4 by a longer road or way: *We went round by the grocery store on our way home.* 5 from one to another: *A report is going round that the schools will close.* 6 through a round of time: *Summer will soon come round again.* 7 about; around: *He doesn't look fit to be round.* 8 here and there: *I am just looking round.* 9 for all: *There is just enough cake to go round.* 10 in the opposite direction or course: *turn round.* 11 to the opposite opinion: *coax someone round.*
—*prep.* 1 so as to make a turn to the other side of: *We walked round the corner.* 2 so as to encircle or surround: *They built a fence round the yard.* 3 to all or various parts of: *travel round the town.* 4 about; around: *She looked round her.* 5 on all sides of: *Arrows struck round the riders, but they were not hit.* 6 here and there in: *There are boxes for mail all round the city.* 7 throughout (a period of time): *round the year.*
[< Old French *rond* < Latin *rotundus.* Doublet of ROTUND.] —**round′ness,** *n.*

➤ **round, around,** *prep., adv.* In informal usage *round* and *around* are used interchangeably, with a definite tendency to use *round* (or to clip the *a* of *around* so short that it would be taken for *round).* In formal English there is some tendency to keep *around* to mean "here and there" or "in every direction" and *round* for "in a circular motion" or "in a reverse motion": *I have looked all around. He is going round the world.*

round a bout (round′ə bout′), *adj.* not straight; indirect: *a roundabout route, speak in a roundabout way.* —*n.* 1 an indirect way, course, or speech. 2 a short, tight jacket for men or boys. 3 BRITISH. merry-go-round.

round dance, 1 a ballroom dance in which couples dance with circular or revolving movements. 2 a folk dance with dancers in a circle.

roun del (roun′dl), *n.* 1 a small, round ornament, window, panel, tablet, etc. 2 rondeau. [< Old French *rondel*]

roun de lay (roun′dl ā), *n.* 1 song or poem in which a phrase or a line is repeated again and again. 2 round dance. [< Old French *rondelet,* diminutive of *rondel.* See RONDEL.]

round er (roun′dər), *n.* 1 person or thing that rounds something. 2 **rounders,** *pl.* game somewhat like baseball, originating in England. 3 a habitual drunkard or criminal.

Round head (round′hed′), *n.* Puritan who supported the Parliament in England during the civil wars from 1642 to 1652. The Roundheads wore their hair cut short in contrast to the long curls of their opponents, the Cavaliers.

round house (round′hous′), *n., pl.* **-hous es** (-hou′ziz). 1 a circular building for storing or repairing locomotives, that is built about a turntable. 2 cabin on the after part of a ship's quarterdeck. —*adj.* INFORMAL. having or done with a sweeping or exaggerated curve, as a hook in boxing or a pitch in baseball.

round ish (roun′dish), *adj.* somewhat round. —**round′ish ness,** *n.*

round ly (round′lē), *adv.* 1 in a round manner; in a circle, curve, globe, etc. 2 plainly; bluntly; severely: *refuse roundly.* 3 fully; completely.

round number, number resulting when a number is rounded off. 3874 in round numbers would be 3900 or 4000.

round robin, 1 petition, protest, etc., with the signatures written in a circle, so that it is impossible to tell who signed first. 2 any statement signed by a number of individuals. 3 contest in which every player or team plays every other player or team.

round-shoul dered (round′shōl′dərd), *adj.* having the shoulders bent forward.

round steak, cut of beef just above the hind leg.

round table, 1 group of persons assembled for an informal discussion, etc. 2 **Round Table, a** table around which King Arthur and his knights sat. **b** King Arthur and his knights.

round-the-clock (round′ᴛʜə klok′), *adj.* around-the-clock.

round trip, trip to a place and back again.

round up (round′up′), *n.* 1 act of driving or bringing cattle together from long distances. 2 the men and horses that do this. 3 a gathering together of people or things: *a roundup of criminals, a roundup of late news, a roundup of old friends.*

round worm (round′wėrm′), *n.* any of a phylum of usually small, unsegmented worms that have long, round bodies; nematode.

rouse[1] (rouz), *v.,* **roused, rous ing,** *n.* —*v.t.* 1 wake up: *I was roused by the ring of the telephone.* 2 stir up: *The dogs roused a deer from the bushes.* 3 excite: *be roused to anger by an insult.* —*v.i.* become active; rise; wake. —*n.* a rousing. [Middle English *rowsen* shake the feathers] —**rous′er,** *n.*

rouse[2] (rouz), *n.* ARCHAIC. a drinking party; carouse. [short for *carouse*]

rous ing (rou′zing), *adj.* 1 stirring; vigorous; brisk: *a rousing speech.* 2 INFORMAL. outrageous; extraordinary: *a rousing lie.* —**rous′ing ly,** *adv.*

Rous seau (rü sō′), *n.* 1 **Henri,** 1844-1910, French painter. 2 **Jean Jacques,** 1712-1778, French philosopher who wrote about government and education.

roust (roust), *v.t.* INFORMAL. rout; move; stir. [alteration of *rouse*[1]]

roust a bout (roust′ə bout′), *n.* U.S. an unskilled laborer on a wharf, ship, ranch, in a circus, oil field, etc.

rout[1] (rout), *n.* 1 flight of a defeated army in disorder. 2 a complete defeat. 3 a noisy, disorderly crowd; mob; rabble. 4 riot; disturbance. 5 ARCHAIC. a large evening party. —*v.t.* 1 put to flight in disorder: *Our soldiers routed the enemy.* 2 defeat completely. [< Middle French, detachment < Popular Latin *rupta* dispersed soldiers, ultimately < Latin *rumpere* to break]

rout[2] (rout), *v.t.* 1 dig (out); get by searching. 2 put (out); force (out): *be routed out of bed at five o'clock.* 3 root with the snout as pigs do. 4 hollow out; scoop out; gouge. —*v.i.* 1 dig with the snout. 2 poke; search; rummage. [variant of *root*[2]]

route (rüt, rout), *n., v.,* **rout ed, rout ing.** —*n.* 1 way to go; road. 2 a fixed, regular course or area assigned to a person making deliveries, sales, etc.: *a newspaper route, a milk route.* —*v.t.* 1 arrange the route for. 2 send by a certain route: *The signs routed us around the construction work and over a side road.* [< Old French < Latin *rupta (via)* (a way) opened up]

rou tine (rü tēn′), *n.* 1 a fixed, regular method of doing things; habitual doing of the same things in the same way: *the daily routine of working, eating, and sleeping.* 2 act or skit that is part of some entertainment. 3 set of coded instructions arranged in proper sequence to direct a computer to perform a sequence of operations. 4 the sequence of operations performed by a computer. —*adj.* 1 using routine: *a routine operation.* 2 average or ordinary; run-of-the-mill. [< French < *route* route] —**rou tine′ly,** *adv.*

rou tin ize (rü tē′nīz), *v.t.,* **-ized, -iz ing.** cause to become a routine; make habitual. —**rou tin′i za′tion,** *n.*

rove[1] (rōv), *v.,* **roved, rov ing.** —*v.i.* wander about; wander; roam: *rove over the fields and woods.* See **roam** for synonym study. —*v.t.* wander over or through; traverse: *rove*

hat, āge, fär; let, ēqual, tėrm;
it, īce; hot, ōpen, ôrder;
oil, out; cup, pu̇t, rüle;
ch, child; ng, long; sh, she;
th, thin; ᴛʜ, then; zh, measure;
ə represents *a* in about, *e* in taken, *i* in pencil, *o* in lemon, *u* in circus.
< = from, derived from, taken from.

the woods. [Middle English *roven* shoot (arrows) at random targets while moving]

rove² (rōv), *v.* a pt. and a pp. of **reeve²**.

rov er¹ (rō′vər), *n.* 1 person who roves; wanderer; roamer. 2 mark selected at random in archery. [< *rove¹*]

ro ver² (rō′vər), *n.* 1 pirate. 2 a pirate ship. [< Middle Dutch < *roven* rob]

row¹ (rō), *n.* 1 a number of persons or things set or arranged in a line, especially a straight line: *Corn is planted in rows.* 2 street with a line of buildings on either side. 3 line of seats in a theater, classroom, etc. 4 **hard row to hoe,** a difficult thing to do. [Old English *rāw*]

row² (rō), *v.i.* 1 use oars to move a boat: *We rowed across the lake.* 2 (of a boat) be moved by the use of oars. —*v.t.* 1 cause (a boat) to move by the use of oars. 2 carry in a rowboat: *I rowed them to shore.* 3 perform (a race, etc.) by rowing. 4 row against in a race. 5 use (oars) for rowing. 6 have (oars): *a boat rowing 8 oars.* —*n.* 1 act of using oars. 2 trip in a rowboat. [Old English *rōwan*] —**row′er,** *n.*

row³ (rou), *n.* a noisy quarrel or disturbance; squabble. —*v.i.* quarrel noisily; squabble. [origin unknown]

row an (rō′ən, rou′ən), *n.* 1 the mountain ash. 2 its red, berrylike fruit. [< Scandinavian (Norwegian) *raun*]

row boat (rō′bōt′), *n.* boat moved by oars.

row dy (rou′dē), *n., pl.* **-dies,** *adj.,* **-di er, -di est.** —*n.* a rough, disorderly, quarrelsome person. —*adj.* rough; disorderly; quarrelsome. [probably < *row³*] —**row′di ly,** *adv.* —**row′di ness,** *n.*

row dy ish (rou′dē ish), *adj.* like a rowdy; rough and disorderly; quarrelsome.

row dy ism (rou′dē iz′əm), *n.* disorderly, quarrelsome conduct; rough, noisy behavior.

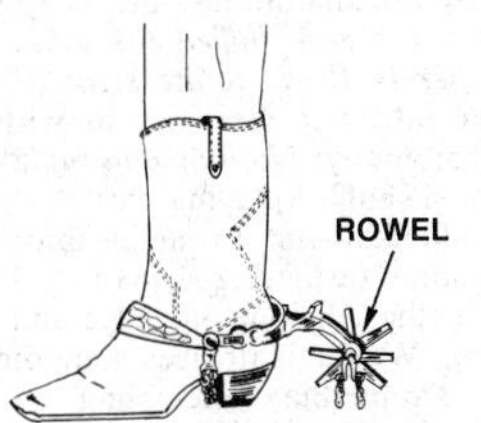

row el (rou′əl), *n., v.,* **-eled, -el ing** or **-elled, -el ling.** —*n.* a small wheel with sharp points, attached to the end of a spur. —*v.t.* spur (a horse) with a rowel; use a rowel on. [< Old French *roel, rouelle,* diminutive of *roue* wheel]

row lock (rō′lok′), *n.* oarlock.

roy al (roi′əl), *adj.* 1 of kings and queens: *the royal family.* See synonym study below. 2 belonging to the family of a king or queen: *a royal prince.* 3 belonging to a king or queen: *royal power.* 4 serving a king or queen: *the royal household.* 5 founded by, or under the patronage of, a king or queen: *the Royal Academy.* 6 from or by a king or queen: *a royal command.* 7 of a kingdom: *a royal army or navy.* 8 appropriate for a king; splendid: *a royal welcome.* 9 like a king; noble; majestic. 10 fine; excellent. 11 rich and bright: *royal blue.* —*n.* 1 a small mast, sail, or yard, set above the topgallant. 2 a size of writing paper (19 by 24 inches). 3 a size of printing paper (20 by 25 inches). [< Old French *roial, real* < Latin *regalis* < *regem* king. Doublet of REAL², REGAL, RIAL.]

Syn. *adj.* 1 **Royal, regal, kingly** mean of or belonging to a king or kings. **Royal** is the most general in application, describing people or things associated with or belonging to a king: *Sherwood Forest is a royal forest.* **Regal** emphasizes the majesty, pomp, and magnificence of the office, and is now used chiefly of people or things showing these qualities: *The general has a regal bearing.* **Kingly** emphasizes the personal character, actions, purposes, or feelings of or worthy of a king: *Tempering justice with mercy is a kingly virtue.*

roy al ism (roi′ə liz′əm), *n.* adherence to a king or to a monarchy.

roy al ist (roi′ə list), *n.* supporter of a king or of a monarchy, especially in times of civil war or rebellion. —*adj.* of or having to do with royalism or royalists: *a royalist party.*

royal jelly, a creamy, jellylike substance rich in vitamins and proteins, fed to the young larvae of honeybees and throughout the larval stage to queen bees to give the queen a longer life and greater fertility.

Royal Oak, city in SE Michigan. 85,000.

royal palm, a tall, graceful palm tree of tropical America that has a whitish trunk and is often planted for ornament.

roy al ty (roi′əl tē), *n., pl.* **-ties.** 1 a royal person or royal persons; king, queen, or other member of a royal family. 2 the rank or dignity of a king or queen; royal power. 3 kingly nature; royal quality; nobility. 4 a royal right or privilege. 5 a royal domain; realm. 6 a share of the receipts or profits paid to an owner of a patent or copyright for the use of it. An author receives royalties from the publishers of his books. 7 payment for the use of any of various rights.

rpm or **r.p.m.,** revolutions per minute.

rps or **r.p.s.,** revolutions per second.

rpt., report.

R.R., 1 railroad. 2 Right Reverend.

R.S.F.S.R., Russian Soviet Federated Socialist Republic.

RSV or **R.S.V.,** Revised Standard Version.

R.S.V.P. or **r.s.v.p.,** please answer [for French *répondez s'il vous plait*].

rt., right.

rte., route.

Rt. Hon. Right Honorable.

Rt. Rev., Right Reverend.

Ru, ruthenium.

Ru an da-U run di (rü än′də ü rün′dē), *n.* former United Nations trust territory administered by Belgium, separated in 1962 into Burundi and Rwanda.

rub (rub), *v.,* **rubbed, rub bing,** *n.* —*v.t.* 1 move (one thing) back and forth (against another); move (two things) together: *Rub your hands to keep them warm.* 2 move one's hand or an object over the surface of; push and press along the surface of: *rub a lame back with liniment.* 3 make or bring (to some condition) by sliding the hand or some object: *rub silver bright.* 4 clean, smooth, or polish by moving one thing firmly against another: *rub a table with wax.* 5 irritate or make sore by rubbing; chafe. —*v.i.* 1 press as it moves: *That door rubs on the floor.* 2 be capable of being rubbed; admit of rubbing.
rub down, rub (the body); massage.
rub it in, INFORMAL. keep on mentioning something unpleasant.
rub off, **a** remove by rubbing. **b** be removed by rubbing.
rub out, **a** erase. **b** SLANG. murder.
rub the right way, please; pacify.
rub the wrong way, annoy; irritate.
—*n.* 1 act of rubbing: *Give the silver a rub with the polish.* 2 something that rubs or hurts the feelings: *He didn't like her mean rub at his slowness.* 3 a rough spot due to rubbing. 4 difficulty: *The rub is that no one wants to go.*
[Middle English *rubben*]

Ru bái yát (rü bī ät′), *n.* **The,** poem written in Persia in the 1100's by Omar Khayyám, translated into English in 1858 by Edward FitzGerald.

ru ba to (rü bä′tō), *adj., n., pl.* **-tos.** in music: —*adj.* having certain notes of a measure or phrase lengthened or shortened for purpose of expression or individual interpretation. —*n.* a rubato tempo or passage. [< Italian, originally < *(tempo) rubato* robbed (time)]

rub ber¹ (rub′ər), *n.* 1 an elastic substance obtained from the coagulated milky juice of various tropical plants or produced synthetically, and vulcanized for commercial use in the manufacture of tires, erasers, etc.; india rubber. 2 any of various rubberlike synthetic products. 3 something made from rubber, such as a rubber band or eraser. 4 **rubbers,** *pl.* rubber overshoes, especially low-cut ones. 5 person or thing that rubs. —*adj.* made of rubber: *a rubber tire.* [< *rub*] —**rub′ber like′,** *adj.*

rub ber² (rub′ər), *n.* 1 series of two games out of three or three games out of five won by the same side, as in bridge, whist, and other card games. 2 the deciding game in such a series. 3 any game which breaks a tie. [origin uncertain]

rubber band, a circular strip of rubber, used to hold things together.

rubber cement, an adhesive consisting of natural or synthetic rubber in a solvent, used to bond leather, paper, rubber, etc.

rub ber ize (rub′ə rīz′), *v.t.,* **-ized, -iz ing.** cover or treat with rubber: *rubberized cloth.*

rub ber neck (rub′ər nek′), INFORMAL. —*n.* person who stares and gapes, especially a tourist or sightseer. —*v.i.* stare; gape.

rubber plant, 1 any plant yielding rubber. 2 an ornamental house plant native to tropical Asia and of the same genus as the fig, having oblong, shiny, leathery leaves.

rubber stamp, 1 stamp made of rubber, used with ink for printing dates, signatures, etc. 2 INFORMAL. person or group that approves or endorses something without thought or without power to refuse.

rub ber-stamp (rub′ər stamp′), *v.t.* 1 print or sign with a rubber stamp. 2 INFORMAL. approve or endorse (a policy, bill, etc.) without thought or without power to refuse.

rub ber y (rub′ər ē), *adj.* like rubber; elastic; tough.

rub bing (rub′ing), *n.* reproduction of an engraved or sculptured design obtained by pressing paper onto the surface and rubbing it with crayon, charcoal, etc.

rubbing alcohol, a solution of denatured

or isopropyl alcohol, used in massaging or as an antiseptic.

rub bish (rub′ish), *n.* 1 worthless or useless stuff; waste; trash. 2 silly words and thoughts; nonsense. [Middle English *robys*]

rub bish y (rub′i shē), *adj.* 1 full of or covered with rubbish. 2 of or like rubbish; trashy; paltry.

rub ble (rub′əl), *n.* 1 rough broken stones, bricks, etc., especially from collapsed or demolished buildings. 2 coarse masonry made of this. [Middle English *robel*]

rub down (rub′doun′), *n.* massage.

rube (rüb), *n.* SLANG. an unsophisticated person from the country; rustic. [earlier *reub*, short for the name *Reuben*]

ru bel la (rü bel′ə), *n.* German measles. [< New Latin < Latin *rubellus* reddish, diminutive of *rubeus* red]

Ru bens (rü′bənz), *n.* **Peter Paul,** 1577-1640, Flemish painter.

ru be o la (rü bē′ə lə), *n.* 1 measles. 2 German measles. [< New Latin < Latin *rubeus* red]

ru be o lar (rü bē′ə lər), *adj.* of, having to do with, or like rubeola.

Ru bi con (rü′bə kon), *n.* 1 small river forming the N boundary of ancient Italy. By crossing the Rubicon in 49 B.C., Julius Caesar started the civil war that made him master of Rome. 2 **cross the Rubicon,** make an important decision from which one cannot turn back.

ru bi cund (rü′bə kund), *adj.* reddish; ruddy. [< Latin *rubicundus* < *rubere* be red]

ru bi cun di ty (rü′bə kun′də tē), *n.* rubicund quality or condition.

ru bid i um (rü bid′ē əm), *n.* a soft, silver-white metallic element that decomposes water and ignites spontaneously when exposed to air, used in photoelectric cells. *Symbol:* Rb; *atomic number* 37. See pages 326 and 327 for table. [< New Latin < Latin *rubidus* red < *rubere* be red]

Ru bin stein (rü′bən stīn), *n.* 1 **Anton,** 1829-1894, Russian pianist and composer. 2 **Artur,** born 1886, American pianist, born in Poland.

ru ble (rü′bəl), *n.* 1 the monetary unit of the Soviet Union, a coin or note equal to 100 kopecks and worth about $1.11. 2 a coin or paper note worth one ruble. Also, **rouble.** [< Russian *rubl′*]

ru bric (rü′brik), *n.* 1 title or heading of a chapter, a law, etc., written or printed in red or in special lettering. 2 direction for the conducting of religious services inserted in a prayer book, ritual, etc. 3 any heading, rule, or guide. —*adj.* rubrical. [< Latin *rubrica* red coloring matter < *ruber* red]

ru bri cal (rü′brə kəl), *adj.* 1 red; marked with red; printed or written in special lettering. 2 of, having to do with, or according to religious rubrics.

ru bri cate (rü′brə kāt), *v.t.*, **-cat ed, -cat ing.** mark or color with red.

ru by (rü′bē), *n., pl.* **-bies,** *adj.* —*n.* 1 a clear, hard, deep-red variety of corundum valued as a precious stone. 2 a deep, glowing red. —*adj.* deep, glowing red: *ruby lips, ruby wine.* [< Old French *rubi,* ultimately < Latin *rubeus* red] **—ru′by like′,** *adj.*

ruche (rüsh), *n.* a full pleating or frill of lace, ribbon, net, etc., used as trimming for women's dresses. [< French]

ruck (ruk), *n.* crowd; the great mass of common people or things. [< Scandinavian (Norwegian) *ruka*]

ruck sack (ruk′sak′, ru̇k′sak′), *n.* knapsack. [< German *Rucksack*]

ruck us (ruk′əs), *n.* INFORMAL. a noisy disturbance or uproar; row.

ruc tion (ruk′shən), *n.* INFORMAL. disturbance; quarrel; row. [perhaps alteration of *insurrection*]

rud der (rud′ər), *n.* 1 a flat piece of wood or metal hinged vertically to the rear end of a boat or ship and used to steer it. 2 a similar piece on an aircraft. [Old English *rōthor*] **—rud′der less,** *adj.*

rud dy (rud′ē), *adj.*, **-di er, -di est.** 1 red or reddish. 2 having a fresh, healthy, red look: *ruddy cheeks.* [Old English *rudig*] **—rud′di ly,** *adv.* **—rud′di ness,** *n.*

rude (rüd), *adj.*, **rud er, rud est.** 1 not courteous; impolite: *It is rude to stare at people.* 2 roughly made or done; without finish or polish; coarse; crude: *rude tools, a rude sketch.* 3 rough in manner or behavior; violent; harsh: *Rude hands seized the dog.* 4 not having learned much; rather wild; barbarous. [< Latin *rudis*] **—rude′ly,** *adv.* **—rude′ness,** *n.*

ru di ment (rü′də mənt), *n.* 1 part to be learned first; beginning: *the rudiments of grammar.* 2 something in an early stage; undeveloped or imperfect form. 3 an organ or part incompletely developed in size or structure: *the rudiments of wings on a baby chick.* [< Latin *rudimentum* < *rudis* rude, ignorant]

ru di men tal (rü′də men′tl), *adj.* rudimentary.

ru di men tar y (rü′də men′tər ē), *adj.* 1 to be learned or studied first; elementary. See **elementary** for synonym study. 2 in an early stage of development; undeveloped. **—ru′di men′tar i ly,** *adv.* **—ru′di men′tar i ness,** *n.*

Ru dolph I or **Ru dolf I** (rü′dolf), 1218-1291, German king and emperor of the Holy Roman Empire from 1273 to 1291, the first of the Hapsburgs.

rue[1] (rü), *v.*, **rued, ru ing,** *n.* —*v.t.* be sorry for; regret. —*n.* sorrow; regret. [Old English *hrēowan*]

rue[2] (rü), *n.* a strong-smelling, woody herb of the same family as the citrus, with yellow flowers, and bitter leaves that were formerly much used in medicine. [< Old French < Latin *ruta*]

rue ful (rü′fəl), *adj.* 1 sorrowful; unhappy; mournful: *a rueful expression.* 2 causing sorrow or pity: *a rueful sight.* **—rue′ful ly,** *adv.* **—rue′ful ness,** *n.*

ruff[1] (def. 1)

ruff[1] (ruf), *n.* 1 a deep frill, stiff enough to stand out, worn around the neck by men and women in the 1500's and 1600's. 2 a collarlike growth of long or specially marked feathers or hairs on the neck of a bird or animal. 3 sandpiper of Europe and Asia, the male of which has a ruff on the neck during the breeding season. [perhaps related to RUFFLE[1]]

ruff[2] (ruf), *v.t., v.i.* trump in a card game. —*n.* act of trumping. [< Middle French *roffle* < Old French *ronfle*]

ruffed (ruft), *adj.* having a ruff.

ruffed grouse, a North American grouse with a tuft of gleaming black feathers on each side of the neck.

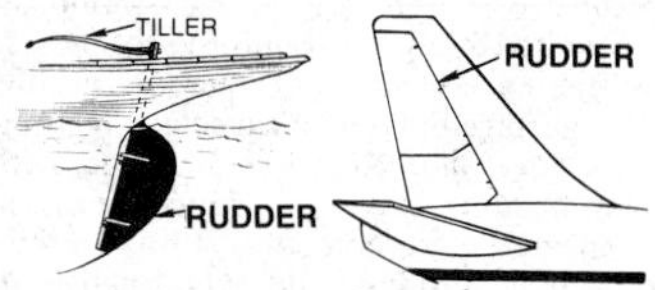

rudder (def. 1, left; def. 2, right)

ruf fi an (ruf′ē ən), *n.* a rough, brutal, or cruel person; bully; hoodlum. —*adj.* rough; brutal; cruel. [< Middle French < Italian *ruffiano* pander]

ruf fi an ism (ruf′ē ə niz′əm), *n.* conduct or character of a ruffian.

ruf fi an ly (ruf′ē ən lē), *adj.* like a ruffian; violent; lawless.

ruffle[1] (def. 2) ruffles on a dress worn in the 1800's

ruf fle[1] (ruf′əl), *v.*, **-fled, -fling.** —*v.t.* 1 destroy the smoothness of; make rough or uneven: *A breeze ruffled the lake. The hen ruffled her feathers at the sight of the dog.* 2 gather into a ruffle. 3 trim with ruffles. 4 disturb; annoy: *Nothing can ruffle her calm temper.* 5 shuffle (playing cards). —*v.i.* become ruffled. —*n.* 1 roughness or unevenness in some surface. 2 strip of cloth, ribbon, or lace gathered along one edge and used for trimming. Women's dresses sometimes have ruffles. 3 something resembling this, such as the ruff on a bird. 4 disturbance; annoyance. [Middle English *ruffelen*]

ruf fle[2] (ruf′əl), *n., v.*, **-fled, -fling.** —*n.* a low, steady beating of a drum, softer than a roll. —*v.t.* beat (a drum) in this way. [perhaps imitative]

ru fous (rü′fəs), *adj.* reddish or reddish-brown. [< Latin *rufus*]

rug (rug), *n.* 1 a piece of thick, heavy fabric or sometimes the skin of an animal, used as floor covering. 2 a thick, warm cloth used as covering: *He wrapped a woolen rug around himself.* 3 **sweep under the rug,** conceal (an error, scandal, problem, etc.), especially from the public. [< Scandinavian (Norwegian dialect) *rugga* coarse covering]

ru ga (rü′gə), *n., pl.* **-gae** (-jē). a wrinkle; fold; ridge. [< Latin]

ru gate (rü′gāt), *adj.* wrinkled; rugose.

Rug by (rug′bē), *n.* 1 an English school for boys. 2 Also, **rugby.** an English game somewhat like football, played by teams of 13 or 15 men who kick or pass an oval ball toward the opposing team's goal. The forward pass is not allowed and play is stopped only for penalties. [< *Rugby,* town in central England, where the school is located]

rug ged (rug′id), *adj.* 1 covered with rough

edges; rough and uneven: *rugged ground.* 2 able to do and endure much; sturdy; hardy: *Pioneers were rugged people.* 3 strong and irregular: *rugged features.* 4 harsh; stern; severe: *rugged times.* 5 rude; unpolished; unrefined: *rugged manners.* 6 stormy: *rugged weather.* [< Scandinavian (Swedish) *rugga* roughen] **—rug′ged ly,** *adv.* **—rug′ged-ness,** *n.*

ru gose (rü′gōs, rü gōs′), *adj.* having rugae or wrinkles; wrinkled; ridged: *a rugose leaf.* **—ru′gose ly,** *adv.*

Ruhr (rür), *n.* 1 **Ruhr River,** river in W West Germany flowing into the Rhine. 144 mi. 2 rich mining and industrial region along this river.

ru in (rü′ən), *n.* 1 Often, **ruins,** *pl.* that which is left after destruction, decay, or downfall, especially a building, wall, etc., that has fallen to pieces. 2 very great damage; destruction; decay: *plan the ruin of an enemy.* See synonym study below. 3 condition of destruction, decay, or downfall: *The house had gone to ruin from neglect.* 4 cause of destruction, decay, or downfall: *Gambling was his ruin.* 5 bankruptcy. *—v.t.* 1 bring to ruin; destroy; spoil: *The rain has ruined my new dress.* See **spoil** for synonym study. 2 make bankrupt. [< Latin *ruina* a collapse < *ruere* to collapse] **—ru′in er,** *n.*

Syn. *n.* 2 **Ruin, destruction** mean great damage. **Ruin** implies total or extensive damage caused by external force or especially by natural processes, such as decay: *Proper care protects property from ruin.* **Destruction** implies damage, extensive or not, caused by external forces, such as wind, explosion, etc.: *The storm caused widespread destruction.*

ru in a tion (rü′ə nā′shən), *n.* ruin; destruction; downfall.

ru in ous (rü′ə nəs), *adj.* 1 bringing ruin; causing destruction. 2 fallen into ruins; ruined. **—ru′in ous ly,** *adv.* **—ru′in ous-ness,** *n.*

Ruis dael (rois′däl), *n.* **Jacob van,** 1628?-1682, Dutch painter. Also, **Ruysdael.**

rule (rül), *n., v.,* **ruled, rul ing.** *—n.* 1 statement of what to do and not to do; principle governing conduct, action, practice, procedure, etc.; law: *the rules of a club, obey the rules of the game, the rules of grammar and spelling.* 2 an order by a court of law, based upon a principle of law. 3 set of regulations or code of discipline under which a religious order or congregation lives: *the rule of St. Benedict.* 4 control, government, or dominion: *In a democracy the people have the rule.* 5 period of power of a ruler; reign: *The Revolutionary War took place during the rule of George III.* 6 a regular method; a thing that usually happens or is done; what is usually true: *Fair weather is the rule in Arizona.* 7 **as a rule,** normally; generally. 8 ruler (def. 2). 9 a thin, type-high strip of metal, for printing a line or lines.
—v.i. 1 make a rule; decide. 2 make a formal decision: *The judge ruled against them.* 3 exercise highest authority; govern; control. 4 prevail; be current: *Prices of wheat and corn ruled high all the year.* *—v.t.* 1 declare (a rule); decide (something): *The umpire ruled that the ball was foul.* 2 decide formally: *The judge ruled a mistrial.* 3 exercise highest authority over; govern; control. See synonym study below. 4 prevail in; dominate: *Wit rules all her poems.* 5 mark with lines: *I used a ruler to rule the paper.* 6 mark off. 7 **rule out,** decide against; exclude. [< Old French *riule, reule* < Latin *regula* straight rod, rule < *regere* to rule, straighten. Doublet of RAIL[1].]

Syn. *v.t.* 3 **Rule, govern** mean to control by the exercise of authority or power. **Rule** implies control over others through absolute power both to make laws and to force obedience: *He tries to rule his family as a dictator rules a nation.* **Govern** implies sensible control by the wise use of authority or power, usually for the good of the thing, person, or nation governed: *Parents govern a child until he develops the power to govern himself.*

rule of thumb, 1 rule based on experience or practice rather than on scientific knowledge. 2 a rough, practical method of procedure.

rul er (rü′lər), *n.* 1 person who rules or governs, as a king. 2 a straight strip of wood, metal, etc., often marked in inches or centimeters, used in drawing lines or in measuring.

rul ing (rü′ling), *n.* 1 decision of a judge or court: *a ruling on a point of law.* 2 a ruled line or lines. 3 the act of making lines on paper, fabric, etc. 4 government. *—adj.* 1 that rules; governing; controlling: *a ruling body.* 2 predominating; prevalent; chief: *a ruling passion.* **—rul′ing ly,** *adv.*

rum[1] (rum), *n.* 1 an alcoholic liquor distilled from sugar cane, molasses, etc. 2 any alcoholic liquor. [apparently short for *rumbullion* rum, of unknown origin]

rum[2] (rum), *adj.* SLANG. odd; queer. [origin uncertain]

Rum., 1 Rumania. 2 Rumanian.

Ru ma ni a (rü mā′nē ə, rü mā′nyə), *n.* Romania. **—Ru ma′ni an,** *adj., n.*

rum ba (rum′bə), *n.* 1 a Cuban Negro folk dance in quadruple time. 2 a lively American ballroom dance derived from this. 3 music for either of these dances. Also, **rhumba.** [< Cuban Spanish]

rum ble (rum′bəl), *v.,* **-bled, -bling,** *n.* *—v.i.* 1 make a deep, heavy, continuous sound. 2 move with such a sound. *—v.t.* utter with a rumbling sound. *—n.* a deep, heavy, continuous sound: *We heard the far-off rumble of thunder.* [Middle English *romblen*]

rumble seat, an extra, outside seat for two, in the back of some coupes and roadsters.

ru men (rü′mən), *n., pl.* **-mi na** (-mə nə), **-mens.** the first stomach of a ruminant animal in which most food collects immediately after being swallowed. [< Latin, gullet]

Rum ford (rum′fərd), *n.* **Count,** 1753-1814, Sir Benjamin Thompson, British physicist, born in the United States.

ru mi nant (rü′mə nənt), *n.* any of a suborder of even-toed, hoofed, herbivorous mammals which chew the cud and have a stomach with four separate cavities, including cattle, deer, sheep, goats, giraffes, and camels. *—adj.* 1 belonging to the group of ruminants. 2 chewing the cud; ruminating. 3 meditative; reflective. [< Latin *ruminantem* chewing a cud < *rumen* gullet] **—ru′mi-nant ly,** *adv.*

hat, āge, fär; let, ēqual, tėrm;
it, īce; hot, ōpen, ôrder;
oil, out; cup, pu̇t, rüle;
ch, child; ng, long; sh, she;
th, thin; ᴛʜ, then; zh, measure;

ə represents *a* in about, *e* in taken, *i* in pencil, *o* in lemon, *u* in circus.

< = from, derived from, taken from.

ru mi nate (rü′mə nāt), *v.,* **-nat ed, -nat ing.** *—v.i.* 1 chew the cud. 2 think or ponder; meditate; reflect: *I ruminated on the strange events of the past week.* *—v.t.* 1 chew again (food which has been previously chewed and swallowed). 2 turn over in the mind; meditate on. **—ru′mi na′tor,** *n.*

ru mi na tion (rü′mə nā′shən), *n.* 1 a chewing of the cud. 2 meditation; reflection.

ru mi na tive (rü′mə nā′tiv), *adj.* meditative; inclined to ruminate. **—ru′mi na′tive-ly,** *adv.*

rum mage (rum′ij), *v.,* **-maged, -mag ing,** *n.* *—v.t.* 1 search thoroughly by moving things about: *I rummaged three drawers before I found my gloves.* 2 pull from among other things; bring to light: *She rummaged up some change from the bottom of her purse.* *—v.i.* search in a disorderly way: *She rummaged in her purse for some change.* *—n.* a thorough search in which things are moved about. [< Middle French *arrumage,* noun < *arrumer* stow cargo]

rummage sale, sale of odds and ends, old clothing, etc., usually held to raise money for charity.

rum my (rum′ē), *n.* any of various card games in which the object is to form sets of three or four cards of the same rank or sequences of three or more cards of the same suit. [origin uncertain]

ru mor (rü′mər), *n.* 1 a story or statement talked of as news without any proof that it is true. 2 vague, general talk, not based upon definite knowledge: *Rumor has it that the new girl went to school in France.* *—v.t.* tell or spread by rumor. [< Latin]

rump (rump), *n.* 1 the hind part of the body of an animal where the legs join the back. 2 cut of beef from this part. See **beef** for diagram. 3 the corresponding part of the human body; buttocks. 4 an unimportant or inferior part; remnant. 5 a parliament, assembly, or other legislative body having only a remnant of its former membership because of the departure, expulsion, resignation, etc., of a large number of its members. [< Scandinavian (Danish) *rumpe*]

rum ple (rum′pəl), *v.,* **-pled, -pling,** *n.* *—v.t.* 1 crumple; crush; wrinkle: *a rumpled sheet of paper.* 2 tousle; disorder: *to rumple up hair.* *—v.i.* become rumpled. *—n.* wrinkle; crease. [probably < Dutch *rompelen*]

rum pus (rum′pəs), *n.* INFORMAL. a noisy disturbance or uproar; row. [origin unknown]

rumpus room, U.S. room in the basement or other part of a house, set apart for parties, games, etc.

rum run ner (rum′run′ər), *n.* person or ship that smuggles alcoholic liquor into a country.

run (run), *v.,* **ran, run, run ning,** *n., adj.* *—v.i.* 1 go by moving the legs quickly; go faster than walking: *The cat ran away from*

the dog. 2 go hurriedly; hasten: *Run for help.* 3 make a quick trip: *run up to the city.* 4 escape; flee: *Run for your life.* 5 go; move; keep going: *This train runs between Chicago and Los Angeles.* 6 sail or be driven: *The ship ran aground on the rocks.* 7 go on; proceed: *Prices of hats can run as high as $50.* 8 creep; trail; climb: *Vines run up the side of the chimney.* 9 pass quickly: *An idea ran through her mind. Time runs on.* 10 stretch; extend: *Shelves run along the walls.* 11 flow: *Blood runs from a cut.* 12 discharge fluid, mucus, or pus: *My nose runs whenever I have a cold.* 13 get; become: *run into debt. The well ran dry.* 14 have a specified character, quality, form, size, etc.: *These potatoes run large. Her hair runs to curls.* 15 spread: *The color ran when the dress was washed.* 16 continue; last: *a lease to run two years. The play ran for a whole season.* 17 have currency or be current; occur: *A rumor ran through the city.* 18 have legal force. 19 take part in a race or contest. 20 finish a race, contest, etc., in a certain way: *The horse ran last.* 21 be a candidate for election: *run for president.* 22 move easily, freely, or smoothly; keep operating: *A rope runs in a pulley. The engine ran all day without overheating.* 23 be worded or expressed: *How does the first verse run?* 24 go about without restraint: *children allowed to run about the streets.* 25 drop stitches; ravel: *Nylon stockings often run.* 26 soften; become liquid; melt: *The wax ran when the candles were lit.* 27 pass to or from the sea; migrate, as for spawning: *The salmon are running.* 28 return often to the mind: *A tune kept running in my head.* 29 make many and urgent demands for money or payment: *run on a bank.* —*v.t.* 1 cause to run; cause to move: *run a horse up and down a track.* 2 perform by, or as if by, running: *run a race, run an errand.* 3 cover by running: *run ten miles.* 4 go along (a way, path, etc.): *run the course until the end.* 5 pursue; chase (game, etc.): *run a fox.* 6 cause to pass quickly: *run one's eyes down a page.* 7 trace: *Run that report back to its source.* 8 put; spread; lead: *run a shelf along a wall.* 9 drive; force; thrust: *run a splinter into one's hand.* 10 flow with: *The streets ran with rain.* 11 bring into a certain state by running: *run oneself out of breath.* 12 expose oneself to: *run a risk.* 13 cause to move easily, freely, or smoothly; cause to keep operating: *run a machine.* 14 conduct; manage: *run a business.* 15 baste: *run a hem.* 16 get past or through: *Enemy ships tried to run the blockade.* 17 smuggle: *run rum.* 18 publish (an advertisement, story, etc.) in a newspaper, magazine, etc.: *run an ad in the evening paper.* 19 shape by melting: *run silver into bars.* 20 carry; take; transport: *Can you run this book over to the library for me?* 21 put up as a candidate: *The Democrats ran him for the Presidency twice.* 22 enter (a horse, etc.) in a race. 23 contend with in a race: *I will run you a mile.* 24 make an unbroken sequence of (shots, strokes, etc.) in billiards, pool, etc. 25 draw or trace (a line, etc.) on a surface.
run across, U.S. meet by chance.
run away with, win easily over others.
run down, **a** stop working or going. **b** pursue till caught or killed; hunt down. **c** knock down by running against. **d** speak evil against. **e** decline or reduce in vigor or health. **f** fall off, diminish, or decrease; deteriorate.
run for it, run for safety.
run in, **a** SLANG. arrest and put in jail. **b** pay a short visit.
run into, **a** meet by chance. **b** crash into; collide with.
run off, **a** cause to be run or played. **b** print. **c** run away; flee.
run on, **a** continue in operation, effect, etc. **b** continue to speak. **c** set (type or copy) without a break in the running text. **d** add (a run-on entry).
run out, come to an end; become exhausted.
run out of, use up; have no more.
run out on, **a** leave suddenly; desert. **b** back out of; not be faithful to.
run over, **a** ride or drive over. **b** overflow. **c** go through quickly.
run through, **a** use up, consume, or spend rapidly or recklessly. **b** review or rehearse. **c** pierce.
run up, INFORMAL. **a** make quickly. **b** collect; accumulate.
—*n.* 1 act of running: *set out at a run.* 2 spell or period of causing (a machine, etc.) to operate: *a factory with a run of 8 hours a day.* 3 the amount of anything produced in such a period. 4 spell of causing something liquid to run or flow, or the amount that runs: *the run of sap from maple trees.* 5 trip: *Freight trains make the run from Chicago to New York.* 6 a quick trip: *take a run up to the country for the day.* 7 (in baseball) a score, made by a runner touching home plate after having touched the bases in order. 8 an unbroken sequence of scoring plays in billiards, pool, etc. 9 a continuous spell or course; continuous extent: *a run of bad luck, a run of fine weather.* 10 a succession of performances, showings, etc.: *This play has had a two-year run.* 11 a continuous series or succession of something; succession of demands: *There was a run on the bank to draw out money.* 12 a set of things following in consecutive order, as a sequence of cards. 13 onward movement; progress; course; trend: *the run of events.* 14 (in music) a rapid succession of tones; passage resembling a scale. 15 kind or class: *the common run of mankind.* 16 freedom to go over or through, or to use: *The guests were given the run of the house.* 17 a flow or rush of water; small stream. 18 number of fish moving together: *a run of salmon.* 19 (of fish) a moving up a river from the sea to spawn. 20 way; track, as for skiing. 21 stretch or enclosed space for animals: *a dog run, a chicken run.* 22 trough; pipe. 23 a place where stitches have slipped out or become undone: *a run in a stocking.* 24 a landing of smuggled goods. 25 **a run for one's money,** **a** strong competition. **b** satisfaction for one's expenditures, efforts, etc. 26 **in the long run,** on the whole; in the end. 27 **on the run,** **a** hurrying. **b** in retreat or rout; fleeing. **c** while running.
[Old English *rinnan*]
run a bout (run′ə bout′), *n.* 1 a light, open automobile or carriage with a single seat. 2 a small motorboat. 3 person who runs about from place to place, such as a vagabond or peddler.
run a gate (run′ə gāt), *n.* ARCHAIC. 1 runaway. 2 vagabond; wanderer. [alteration of Middle English *renegat* renegade]
run a round (run′ə round′), *n.* INFORMAL. evasion or indefinite postponement of action, especially in regard to a request.
run a way (run′ə wā′), *n.* 1 person, horse, etc., that runs away. 2 a running away. —*adj.* 1 running with nobody to guide or stop it; out of control: *a runaway horse.* 2 done by runaways: *a runaway marriage.* 3 easily won: *a runaway victory.* 4 fugitive: *runaway slaves.*
run ci nate (run′sə nit, run′sə nāt), *adj.* (in botany) having coarse, toothlike notches or lobes pointing backward. Dandelion leaves are runcinate. [< Latin *runcina* plane (but taken as "saw")]
run down (run′doun′), *n.* an account; summary: *The commentator gave a brief rundown of the week's news.*
run-down (run′doun′), *adj.* 1 tired; sick. 2 falling to pieces; partly ruined: *a run-down old building.* 3 that has stopped going or working.

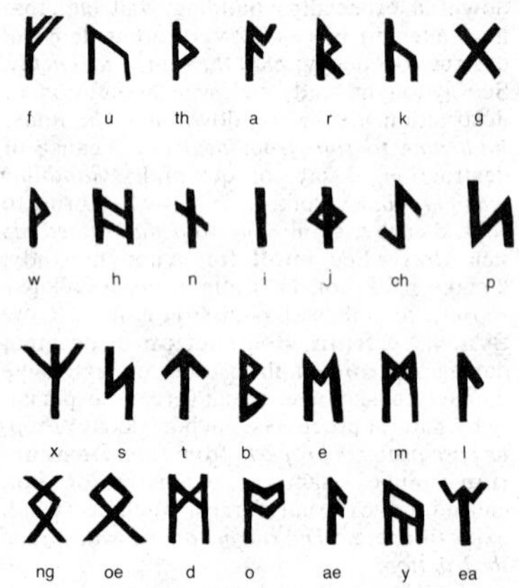

rune[1] (def. 1)
letters of the runic alphabet

rune[1] (rün), *n.* 1 any letter of an ancient Germanic alphabet used from the A.D. 200's to the 1200's. 2 mark that looks like a rune and has some mysterious, magic meaning. 3 verse or sentence that has a magic meaning. [Old English *rūn* < Scandinavian (Old Icelandic) *rūn* secret, rune]
rune[2] (rün), *n.* a Finnish or Old Norse poem or song. [< Finnish *runo* < Scandinavian (Old Icelandic) *rūn*]
rung[1] (rung), *v.* a pt. and the pp. of **ring**[2].
rung[2] (rung), *n.* 1 a round rod or bar used as a step of a ladder. 2 crosspiece set between the legs of a chair or as part of the back or arm of a chair. 3 spoke of a wheel. 4 bar of wood having a similar shape and use. [Old English *hrung*]
ru nic (rü′nik), *adj.* consisting of runes; written in runes; marked with runes.
run-in (run′in′), *n.* INFORMAL. quarrel; sharp disagreement; row.
run let (run′lit), *n.* runnel.
run nel (run′əl), *n.* a small stream or brook; rivulet; runlet. [Old English *rynel* < *rinnan* to run]
run ner (run′ər), *n.* 1 person, animal, or thing that runs; racer. 2 messenger: *a runner for a bank.* 3 (in baseball) a base runner. 4 (in football) a player who carries the ball. 5 person who runs or works a machine, etc. 6 either of the long narrow pieces on which a sleigh or sled slides. 7 blade of a skate. 8 a long, narrow strip: *We have a runner of carpet in our hall, and runners of linen and lace on our dressers.* 9 smuggler. 10 support or groove along, on, or in which anything

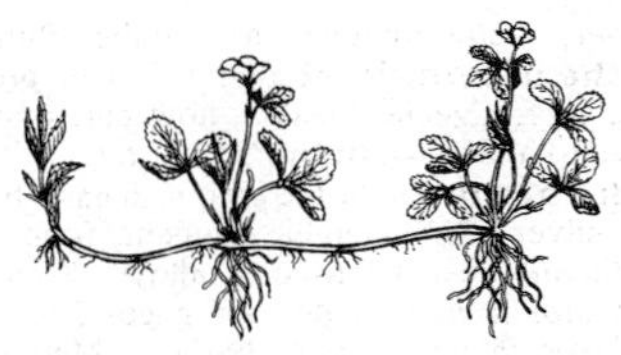
runner (def. 11) of a strawberry plant

slides. 11 a slender stem that takes root along the ground, thus producing new plants. Strawberry plants spread by runners. 12 plant that spreads by such stems. 13 any of various climbing bean plants. 14 a raveled place.

run ner-up (run′ər up′), *n.* player or team that takes second place in a contest.

run ning (run′ing), *n.* 1 act of a person, animal, or thing that runs. 2 that which runs. 3 **be in the running,** have a chance to win. 4 **be out of the running,** have no chance to win.
—*adj.* 1 cursive: *Running handwriting joins all letters of a word together.* 2 discharging matter: *a running sore.* 3 flowing: *running water.* 4 liquid; fluid: *molten running iron.* 5 going or carried on continuously: *a running commentary.* 6 current: *the running month.* 7 repeated continuously: *a running pattern.* 8 following in succession: *for three nights running.* 9 prevalent. 10 moving or proceeding easily or smoothly. 11 moving when pulled or hauled: *a running rope.* 12 slipping or sliding easily. 13 (of plants) creeping or climbing. 14 that is measured in a straight line. 15 of the run of a train, bus, etc.: *the running time between towns.* 16 performed with or during a run: *a running leap.* 17 operating, as a machine. 18 (of a horse) trained to travel at a run.

running board, a metal step or footboard attached below the door on some cars and trucks.

running gear, wheels and axles of an automobile, locomotive, or other vehicle.

running head, 1 heading printed at the top of each page of a book, etc. 2 running title.

running knot, slipknot.

running light, a light required on a ship or aircraft while navigating at night.

running mate, candidate running on the same ticket with another, but for a less important office, such as a candidate for vice-president.

running title, title of a book or article printed at the top of the left-hand pages, or of all the pages.

run ny (run′ē), *adj.,* **-ni er, -ni est.** that runs: *a runny nose.*

Run ny mede (run′ē mēd′), *n.* meadow on the Thames River southwest of London where King John granted the Magna Charta in 1215.

run off (run′ôf′, run′of′), *n.* 1 something that runs off, such as rain that flows from the land in streams. 2 a final, deciding race or contest.

run-of-the-mill (run′əv ᴛʜə mil′), *adj.* average or commonplace; ordinary.

run-on (run′ôn′, run′on′), *adj.* 1 (in printing) continued or added without a break at the end. 2 (in poetry) continuing without pause from one line of verse to another. —*n.* run-on entry.

run-on entry, a dictionary entry which is not defined. It is formed by adding a common suffix to a defined entry and appears in boldface type at the end of that entry. The run-on entry **rurally** appears at the end of the entry **rural.**

run-on sentence, (in grammar) a sentence in which a comma is mistakenly inserted between two main clauses instead of a period, semicolon, or conjunction. EXAMPLE: We were early, the school was still closed.

runt (runt), *n.* animal, person, or plant which is smaller than the usual size. [origin uncertain]

run-through (run′thrü′), *n.* INFORMAL. 1 a brief review; summary. 2 rehearsal: *a final run-through of a play.*

runt y (run′tē), *adj.,* **runt i er, runt i est.** unusually small; undersized. **—runt′i-ness,** *n.*

run-up (run′up′), *n.* 1 increase: *a run-up in prices.* 2 the running or speeding up of an engine in order to test, check, or warm it.

run way (run′wā′), *n.* 1 a paved strip at an airport on which aircraft land and take off. 2 way, track, groove, trough, or the like, along which something moves, slides, etc. 3 the beaten track of deer or other animals. 4 an enclosed place for animals to run in.

ru pee (rü pē′), *n.* the monetary unit of certain Asian countries, a coin or note worth $13^1/_2$ cents in India, $21^1/_4$ cents in Pakistan, and 17 cents in Ceylon. [< Hindustani *rūpiyah* < Sanskrit *rūpya* silver]

Ru pert (rü′pərt), *n.* 1619-1682, German prince who was a nephew of Charles I of England and supported him in the English Civil War.

rup ture (rup′chər), *n., v.,* **-tured, -tur ing.** —*n.* 1 a breaking. 2 a being broken. 3 a breaking off of friendly relations, especially a breaking off of relations between nations that threatens to become actual war. 4 hernia. —*v.t.* 1 break off; burst; break. 2 affect with hernia. —*v.i.* 1 suffer a break. 2 suffer a hernia. [< Latin *ruptura* < *rumpere* to break]

rur al (rúr′əl), *adj.* in or of the country, as opposed to the city; belonging to or characteristic of the country or country life. [< Late Latin *ruralis* < Latin *ruris* country] **—rur′al ly,** *adv.*

Syn. Rural, rustic, pastoral mean of, relating to, or characteristic of the country. **Rural** is the most objective term, implying neither favor nor disfavor *(rural roads)* or mild, general favor *(healthful rural life).* **Rustic** implies simplicity and roughness, regarded favorably *(rustic charm)* or unfavorably *(rustic manners).* **Pastoral** implies idyllic simplicity, suggesting shepherds, grazing flocks, green pastures, and a serene, placid life: *He paints pastoral pictures.*

rural free delivery, free delivery of mail in country districts by regular carriers.

ruse (rüz, rüs), *n.* scheme or device to mislead others; trick. See **stratagem** for synonym study. [< French < *ruser* to dodge < Old French. See RUSH¹.]

rush¹ (rush), *v.i.* 1 move with speed or force: *rush to the station. The river rushed past.* 2 come, go, pass, act, etc., with speed or haste: *color rushing to the face, thoughts rushing through the mind. He rushes into things without knowing anything about them.* —*v.t.* 1 send, push, force, carry, etc., with speed or haste: *Rush this order, please.* 2 attack, overcome, or take with much speed and force: *They rushed the enemy.* 3 urge to hurry: *Don't rush me.* 4 INFORMAL. give much attention to. 5 advance (a football) by running.

hat, āge, fär; let, ēqual, tėrm;
it, īce; hot, ōpen, ôrder;
oil, out; cup, pu̇t, rüle;
ch, child; ng, long; sh, she;
th, thin; ᴛʜ, then; zh, measure;

ə represents *a* in about, *e* in taken, *i* in pencil, *o* in lemon, *u* in circus.

< = from, derived from, taken from.

—*n.* 1 act of rushing: *The rush of the flood swept everything before it.* 2 busy haste; hurry: *the rush of city life.* 3 great or sudden effort of many people to go somewhere or get something: *the Christmas rush, the gold rush.* 4 eager demand; pressure: *a rush for tickets to a play, a rush on steel stocks.* 5 attempt to carry the ball through the opposing line in football. 6 U.S. a scrimmage held as a form of sport between groups or classes of students. 7 an attack. 8 **rushes,** *pl.* the first filmed scenes of a part of a motion picture, projected for the approval of the director, etc. 9 **with a rush,** suddenly; quickly.
—*adj.* requiring haste: *a rush order.*
[Middle English *ruschen* force out of place by violent impact, probably < Old French *ruser* get out of the way, dodge < Latin *recusare* push back, deny] **—rush′er,** *n.*

rush² (rush), *n.* 1 any of a family of grasslike plants with pithy or hollow stems, that grow in wet soil or marshy places. 2 stem of such a plant, used for making chair seats, baskets, floor mats, etc. [Old English *rysc*] **—rush′like′,** *adj.*

rush hour, time of day when traffic is heaviest or when trains, buses, etc., are most crowded.

Rush more (rush′môr′), *n.* **Mount,** mountain in the Black Hills of South Dakota. Huge heads of Washington, Jefferson, Lincoln, and Theodore Roosevelt are carved on the side of the peak.

rush y (rush′ē), *adj.,* **rush i er, rush i est.** 1 abounding with rushes; covered with rushes. 2 made of rushes.

rusk (rusk), *n.* 1 piece of bread or cake toasted in the oven. 2 a kind of light, soft, sweet biscuit. [< Spanish and Portuguese *rosca* roll, twist of bread]

Rus kin (rus′kin), *n.* **John,** 1819-1900, English author, art critic, and social reformer.

Russ (rus), *n., pl.* **Russ,** *adj.* Russian.

Russ., 1 Russia. 2 Russian.

Rus sell (rus′əl), *n.* 1 **Bertrand,** third Earl, 1872-1970, English philosopher, mathematician, and writer. 2 Lord **John,** first Earl, 1792-1878, British statesman, prime minister from 1846 to 1852 and from 1865 to 1866.

rus set (rus′it), *adj.* yellowish-brown or reddish-brown. —*n.* 1 a yellowish brown or a reddish brown. 2 a coarse, russet-colored cloth. The English peasants used to make and wear russet. 3 kind of winter apple with a rough, brownish skin. [< Old French *rousset,* ultimately < Latin *russus* red]

Rus sia (rush′ə), *n.* 1 the Soviet Union. 2 former country in E Europe and N Asia that now forms most of the Soviet Union. Before 1917 it was part of an empire ruled by a czar, with its capital at St. Petersburg.

Rus sian (rush′ən), *adj.* of or having to do with Russia, its people, or their language. —*n.* 1 native or inhabitant of Russia, especially a member of the dominant Slavic people of the Soviet Union. 2 person of Russian descent. 3 the Slavic language of the Russians, which is the official language of the Soviet Union.

Rus sian ize (rush′ə nīz), *v.i., v.t.,* **-ized, -iz ing.** make or become like the Russians in customs, language, etc. **—Rus′sian i za′tion,** *n.*

Russian Orthodox Church, a self-governing branch of the Eastern Church, with its see at Moscow. It was the national church of Russia before 1918.

Russian Revolution, revolution which overthrew the government of Czar Nicholas II in March 1917, and later that year established the Bolshevik government under Lenin.

Russian Soviet Federated Socialist Republic, the largest of the constituent republics of the Soviet Union, occupying three fourths of the country's area. 130,100,000 pop.; 6,593,400 sq. mi. *Capital:* Moscow.

Russian thistle, a large weed of the same family as the goosefoot, that has spiny branches and develops into a troublesome tumbleweed.

Russian wolfhound, borzoi.

Rus si fy (rus′ə fī), *v.t., v.i.,* **-fied, -fy ing.** Russianize. **—Rus′si fi ca′tion,** *n.*

Rus so-Jap a nese (rus′ō jap′ə nēz′), *adj.* having to do with or between Russia and Japan: *the Russo-Japanese War.*

rust (rust), *n.* 1 the reddish-brown or orange coating that forms on iron or steel by oxidation of the surface metal when exposed to air or moisture, made up principally of hydrated ferric oxide. 2 any film or coating on any other metal due to oxidation or corrosion. 3 a harmful effect or influence on character, abilities, etc., especially as a result of inactivity or lack of use. 4 a plant disease that spots leaves and stems. 5 any of various fungi that produce this disease: *wheat rust.* 6 a reddish brown or orange. *—v.i.* 1 become covered with rust. 2 deteriorate or spoil through inactivity or lack of use: *Don't let your mind rust.* 3 become rust-colored. *—v.t.* 1 coat with rust. 2 make less vigorous, skillful, etc., by not using. *—adj.* reddish-brown or orange. [Old English *rūst*]

rus tic (rus′tik), *adj.* 1 belonging to or suitable for the country; rural. See **rural** for synonym study. 2 simple; plain: *His rustic speech and ways made him uncomfortable in the city school.* 3 rough; awkward. 4 made of branches with the bark still on them: *rustic furniture, a rustic fence.* *—n.* 1 a country person. 2 a crude or boorish person considered as coming from the country. [< Latin *rusticus* < *rus* country] **—rus′ti cal ly,** *adv.*

rus ti cate (rus′tə kāt), *v.,* **-cat ed, -cat ing.** *—v.i.* go to the country; stay in the country. *—v.t.* 1 send to the country. 2 BRITISH. suspend (a student) from a university or college as a punishment. **—rus′ti ca′tion,** *n.* **—rus′ti ca′tor,** *n.*

rus tic i ty (rus′tis′ə tē), *n., pl.* **-ties.** 1 rustic quality, characteristic, or peculiarity. 2 rural life. 3 awkwardness; ignorance.

Rus tin (rus′tən), *n.* **Bayard,** born 1910, American civil rights leader.

rus tle (rus′əl), *n., v.,* **-tled, -tling.** *—n.* a light, soft sound of things gently rubbing together, such as leaves make when moved by the wind. *—v.i.* 1 make a light, soft sound of things gently rubbing together: *The leaves rustled in the breeze.* 2 INFORMAL. **a** move, work, or act with energy or speed. **b** steal cattle, horses, etc.; be a rustler. *—v.t.* 1 move or stir (something) so that it makes a rustle: *The wind rustled the papers.* 2 INFORMAL. **a** do or get with energy or speed. **b** steal (cattle, horses, etc.). 3 **rustle up, a** gather; find. **b** get ready; prepare. [apparently imitative]

rus tler (rus′lər), *n.* 1 INFORMAL. a cattle thief. 2 SLANG. an active, energetic person.

rust less (rust′lis), *adj.* free from rust; resisting rust.

rust proof (rust′prüf′), *adj.* resisting rust.

rust y (rus′tē), *adj.,* **rust i er, rust i est.** 1 covered with rust; rusted: *a rusty knife.* 2 made by rust: *a rusty stain.* 3 colored like rust. 4 faded: *a rusty black.* 5 no longer good or effective from lack of use or practice. **—rust′i ly,** *adv.* **—rust′i ness,** *n.*

rut[1] (rut), *n., v.,* **rut ted, rut ting.** *—n.* 1 track made in the ground by wheels. 2 any furrow or track. 3 a fixed or established way of acting, especially one that is boring or monotonous: ***I was in a rut, so I decided to spend the summer traveling.*** *—v.t.* make a rut or ruts in. [perhaps variant of *route*]

rut[2] (rut), *n., v.,* **rut ted, rut ting.** *—n.* 1 sexual excitement of male deer, goats, sheep, etc., occurring at regular intervals, usually annually. 2 period during which it lasts. *—v.i.* be in a rut. [< Old French *ruit* < Latin *rugitus* a bellowing < *rugire* bellow]

ru ta ba ga (rü′tə bā′gə), *n.* kind of turnip with a large, edible, yellow or white root. [< Swedish (dialectal) *rotabagge*]

ruth (rüth), *n.* ARCHAIC. 1 pity; compassion. 2 sorrow; grief. 3 remorse. [Middle English *rewthe* < *rewen* rue[1]]

Ruth (rüth), *n.* 1 (in the Bible) a widow who was very devoted to her mother-in-law, Naomi. Ruth left her native land of Moab to go with Naomi to Bethlehem. 2 book of the Old Testament about her. 3 **George Herman,** 1895-1948, American baseball player, better known as "Babe Ruth."

Ru the ni a (rü thē′nē ə), *n.* former province in E Czechoslovakia, now part of the Soviet Union. **—Ru the′ni an,** *adj., n.*

ru the ni um (rü thē′nē əm), *n.* a hard, brittle, silver-white metallic element, found in platinum ores and used in alloys. *Symbol:* Ru; *atomic number* 44. See pages 326 and 327 for table. [< New Latin < Medieval Latin *Ruthenia* Russia; because discovered in the Ural Mountains]

Ruth er ford (ruᴛʜ′ər fərd), *n.* **Ernest,** first Baron, 1871-1937, British physicist, born in New Zealand, who developed the basic theories of nuclear physics.

ruth less (rüth′lis), *adj.* having no pity; showing no mercy; cruel; merciless. **—ruth′less ly,** *adv.* **—ruth′less ness,** *n.*

ru tile (rü′tēl′, rü′tīl), *n.* a reddish-brown or black mineral with a metallic luster, consisting of titanium dioxide, often with a little iron. It is a common ore of titanium. [< Latin *rutilus* red-gold]

Rut land (rut′lənd), *n.* city in W Vermont. 19,000.

rut ty (rut′ē), *adj.,* **-ti er, -ti est.** full of ruts: *a rutty country road.* **—rut′ti ness,** *n.*

Ru wen zo ri (rü′ən zôr′ē), *n.* mountain group in E central Africa, between Zaïre and Uganda. Highest peak, 16,763 ft.

Ruys dael (rois′däl), *n.* **Jacob van.** See **Ruisdael.**

Ruy ter (roi′tər, rī′tər), *n.* **Michel de,** 1607-1676, Dutch admiral.

R.V., Revised Version.

R.W., 1 Right Worshipful. 2 Right Worthy.

Rwan da (rü än′də), *n.* country in central Africa, north of Burundi, formerly part of Ruanda-Urundi. 3,590,000 pop.; 10,200 sq. mi. *Capital:* Kigali. See **Zaïre** for map.

-ry, *suffix forming nouns from other nouns.* 1 occupation or work of a ____: *Dentistry = occupation or work of a dentist.* 2 act of a ____: *Mimicry = act of a mimic.* 3 quality, state, or condition of a ____: *Rivalry = condition of a rival.* 4 group or collection of ____s: *Jewelry = collection of jewels.* [short for *-ery*]

Ry., railway.

rye (rī), *n.* 1 a hardy, annual cereal grass widely grown in northern regions for its grain, and also to protect or improve the soil. 2 its seeds or grain, used for making flour, as food for livestock, and in making whiskey. 3 whiskey distilled from rye or from rye and other grains. *—adj.* made from rye grain or flour: *rye bread.* [Old English *ryge*]

Ry u kyu Islands (rē yü′kyü), chain of about 100 Japanese islands extending from Japan to Taiwan. Okinawa is the largest island. The United States controlled the Ryukyu Islands from 1945 to 1972. 945,000 pop.; 1800 sq. mi. **—Ry u′kyu an,** *adj., n.*

S s

hat, āge, fär; let, ēqual, tėrm;
it, īce; hot, ōpen, ôrder;
oil, out; cup, pu̇t, rüle;
ch, child; ng, long; sh, she;
th, thin; ᴛʜ, then; zh, measure;

ə represents *a* in about, *e* in taken, *i* in pencil, *o* in lemon, *u* in circus.

< = from, derived from, taken from.

S or **s** (es), *n., pl.* **S's** or **s's.** 1 the 19th letter of the English alphabet. 2 anything shaped like an S.

's, shortened form of *us, is,* or *has,* added to the preceding word. EXAMPLES: Let's eat. He's here. She's just gone.

saber-toothed tiger
about 7 ft. long including the tail

-s[1], suffix used to form the plural of most nouns, as in *hats, boys, dogs, houses.* See also **-es**[1].

-s[2], suffix used to form the third person singular of verbs in the present indicative, as in *asks, lies, sees, tells.* See also **-es**[2].

-s[3], suffix used to form some adverbs, as in *needs, unawares.*

-'s, suffix used to form the possessive case of nouns in the singular and also of plural nouns not ending in *s,* as in *boy's, man's, child's, men's, children's.*

S, 1 south. 2 sulfur.

s., 1 second. 2 shilling or shillings. 3 singular. 4 son. 5 south. 6 southern.

S., 1 Saint. 2 Saturday. 3 September. 4 south. 5 southern. 6 Sunday.

S.A., 1 South Africa. 2 South America.

Saar (sär; *German* zär), *n.* 1 **Saar River,** river flowing from NE France through West Germany into the Moselle River. 150 mi. 2 state in SW West Germany, along the Saar River. Also, **Saarland.**

Saar brück en (zär′brʏk′ən), *n.* city in SW West Germany, on the Saar River. 131,000.

Saar in en (sär′i nən), *n.* **Eero,** 1910-1961, American architect, born in Finland.

Saar land (sär′land; *German* zär′länt), *n.* Saar (def. 2).

Sa bah (sä′bə), *n.* a state of Malaysia, located in NE Borneo. It was formerly the British colony of North Borneo. 622,000 pop.; 29,400 sq. mi. *Capital:* Kota Kinabalu.

Sab ba tar i an (sab′ə ter′ē ən, sab′ə-tar′ē ən), *n.* 1 person who observes Saturday as the Sabbath, as many Jews do. 2 Christian who favors a very strict observance of Sunday. *—adj.* of or having to do with the Sabbath or Sabbath observance.

Sab bath (sab′əth), *n.* 1 day of the week used for rest and worship. Sunday is the Sabbath for most Christians; Saturday is the Jewish Sabbath. 2 **sabbath,** period of rest, quiet, etc. *—adj.* of or belonging to the Sabbath. [< Latin *sabbatum* < Greek *sabbaton* < Hebrew *shabbāth* < *shābath* to rest]

sab bat ic (sə bat′ik), *adj.* sabbatical.

sab bat i cal (sə bat′ə kəl), *adj.* 1 of or suitable for the Sabbath. 2 of or for a rest from work. *—n.* sabbatical leave or sabbatical year.

sabbatical leave, leave of absence for a year or half year given to teachers, commonly once in seven years, for rest, study, or travel.

sabbatical year, 1 (among the ancient Jews) every seventh year, during which fields were left untilled, debtors released, etc. 2 sabbatical leave.

sa ber (sā′bər), *n.* a heavy, curved sword with a sharp edge, used especially by cavalry. *—v.t.* strike, wound, or kill with a saber. Also, **sabre.** [< French *sabre,* alteration of *sable* < earlier German *Sabel;* ultimately of Slavic origin]

saber rattling, bold or reckless exhibition of military power.

sa ber-toothed tiger (sā′bər tütht′), any of various extinct, carnivorous mammals resembling a tiger, with very long, curved upper canine teeth.

Sa bin (sā′bən), *n.* **Albert Bruce,** born 1906, American scientist who developed an oral vaccine against polio.

Sa bine (sā′bīn), *n.* 1 member of an ancient tribe in central Italy which was conquered by the Romans in the 200's B.C. 2 their language. *—adj.* of the Sabines or their language.

sa ble (sā′bəl), *n.* 1 a small carnivorous marten of northern Europe and Asia, valued for its soft, dark-brown, glossy fur. 2 its fur. Sable is one of the most costly furs. 3 the marten of North America. 4 black. 5 **sables,** *pl.* mourning garments. *—adj.* ARCHAIC. black; dark. [< Old French; ultimately of Slavic origin]

sabot (def. 1)
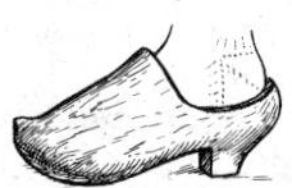

sab ot (sab′ō; *French* sȧ bō′), *n.* 1 shoe hollowed out of a single piece of wood, worn by peasants in France, Belgium, etc. 2 a coarse leather shoe with a thick wooden sole. [< French]

sab o tage (sab′ə täzh), *n., v.,* **-taged, -tag ing.** *—n.* 1 damage done to work, tools, machinery, etc., by workmen as an attack or threat against an employer. 2 such damage done by civilians of a conquered nation to injure the conquering forces. 3 damage done by enemy agents or sympathizers in an attempt to slow down a nation's war effort. *—v.t.* damage or destroy by sabotage. [< French < *saboter* to bungle, walk noisily < *sabot*]

sab o teur (sab′ə tėr′), *n.* person who engages in sabotage. [< French]

sa bra (sä′brə), *n.* person born in Israel. [< Hebrew *ṣābrāh,* literally, cactus]

sa bre (sā′bər), *n., v.t.,* **-bred, -bring.** saber.

sac (sak), *n.* a baglike part in an animal or plant, often one containing liquids. [< French < Latin *saccus* sack[1]. See SACK[1].] **—sac′like′,** *adj.*

Sac (sak, sôk), *n., pl.* **Sacs** or **Sac.** Sauk.

SAC (sak), *n.* Strategic Air Command.

Sac a ja we a or **Sac a ga we a** (sak′ə-jə wē′ə), *n.* 1787?-1812, American Indian guide and interpreter for the Lewis and Clark expedition. She was a member of the Shoshone tribe.

sac cha ride (sak′ə rīd′, sak′ər id), *n.* 1 compound consisting of one or more simple sugars; carbohydrate. 2 compound of sugar with an organic base.

sac char in (sak′ər ən), *n.* a very sweet crystalline substance obtained from coal tar, used as a substitute for sugar. *Formula:* $C_7H_5NO_3S$ [< Medieval Latin *saccharum* sugar < Greek *sakcharon,* ultimately < Sanskrit *śarkarā,* originally, gravel, grit]

sac char ine (sak′ər ən), *adj.* 1 overly sweet; sugary: *a saccharine smile.* 2 of or like sugar. *—n.* saccharin. **—sac′char ine ly,** *adv.*

sac cha rin i ty (sak′ə rin′ə tē), *n.* quality of being saccharine.

sac er do tal (sas′ər dō′tl, sak′ər dō′tl), *adj.* of priests or the priesthood; priestly. [< Latin *sacerdotalis* < *sacerdotem* priest < *sacra* rites] **—sac′er do′tal ly,** *adv.*

sac er do tal ism (sas′ər dō′tl iz′əm, sak′ər dō′tl iz′əm), *n.* sacerdotal system; spirit or methods of the priesthood.

sac fungus, ascomycete.

sa chem (sā′chəm), *n.* (among some North American Indians) the chief of a tribe or confederation. [of Algonquian origin]

sa chet (sa shā′, sash′ā), *n.* 1 a small bag or pad containing perfumed powder. 2 perfumed powder. [< French, diminutive of *sac* sack[1]]

Sachs (saks, zäнs), *n.* **Nelly,** 1891-1970, Swedish poet and dramatist, born in Germany, who wrote about the Jewish people.

sack[1] (sak), *n.* 1 a large bag, usually made of coarse cloth, used for holding grain, flour, potatoes, coal, etc. See **bag** for synonym study. 2 such a bag with what is in it: *two sacks of corn.* 3 the amount that a sack will hold: *We burned two sacks of coal.* 4 U.S. any bag or what is in it: *a sack of candy.* 5 a loose jacket worn by women and children: *a knitted sack for a baby.* 6 kind of loose gown formerly worn by women. 7 SLANG. bed. 8 dismissal from employment or office: *get the sack, give a person the sack.* 9 **hold the sack,** INFORMAL. be left empty-handed; be left to suffer the consequences. *—v.t.* 1 put into a sack or sacks. 2 dismiss from employment or office; fire. 3 **sack out,** SLANG. go to bed. Also, **sacque** for 5 and 6. [Old English *sacc* < Latin *saccus* < Greek *sakkos*] **—sack′like′,** *adj.*

S

sack[2] (sak), *v.t.* plunder (a captured city); loot and despoil; pillage. *—n.* a plundering of a captured city. [< Middle French *(mettre à) sac* (put to the) sack < Italian *sacco* sack[1] < Latin *saccus*] **—sack′er,** *n.*

sack[3] (sak), *n.* sherry or other strong, light-colored wine. [< Middle French *(vin) sec* dry (wine) < Latin *siccus*]

sack but (sak′but), *n.* 1 a musical wind instrument of the Middle Ages, somewhat like the trombone. 2 an ancient stringed instrument mentioned in the Bible. [< Middle French *saquebute* < *saquer* to pull + *bouter* to push]

sack cloth (sak′klôth′, sak′kloth′), *n., pl.* **-cloths** (-klôᴛʜz′, -klôths′; -kloᴛʜz′,

-kloths′). 1 sacking. 2 coarse cloth worn as a sign of mourning or penitence.

sack coat, a man's short, loose-fitting coat for ordinary wear.

sack ful (sak′fu̇l), *n., pl.* **-fuls.** enough to fill a sack.

sack ing (sak′ing), *n.* coarse cloth for making sacks, bags, etc.

sacque (sak), *n.* sack[1] (defs. 5, 6).

sa cral (sā′krəl), *adj.* of, having to do with, or in the region of the sacrum.

sac ra ment (sak′rə mənt), *n.* 1 any of certain religious ceremonies of the Christian church, considered especially sacred, such as baptism. 2 Often, **Sacrament, a** the Eucharist or Holy Communion. **b** the consecrated bread and wine or the bread alone. 3 something especially sacred. [< Latin *sacramentum,* ultimately < *sacer* holy]

sac ra men tal (sak′rə men′tl), *adj.* 1 of or having to do with a sacrament; used in a sacrament: *sacramental wine.* 2 especially sacred. *—n.* a rite or ceremony similar to but not included among the sacraments. The use of holy water and the sign of the cross are sacramentals. **—sac′ra men′tal ly,** *adv.*

Sac ra men to (sak′rə men′tō), *n.* 1 capital of California, in the N central part. 257,000. 2 **Sacramento River,** river flowing from N California into San Francisco Bay. 382 mi.

sa cred (sā′krid), *adj.* 1 belonging to or dedicated to God or a god; holy: *the sacred altar.* See **holy** for synonym study. 2 connected with religion; religious: *sacred writings, sacred music.* 3 worthy of reverence: *the sacred memory of a dead hero.* 4 dedicated to some person, object, or purpose: *This monument is sacred to the memory of the Unknown Soldier.* 5 that must not be violated or disregarded: *a sacred promise.* [originally past participle of Middle English *sacren* sanctify < Latin *sacrare* < *sacer* holy] **—sa′cred ly,** *adv.* **—sa′cred ness,** *n.*

Sacred College, the cardinals of the Roman Catholic Church collectively; College of Cardinals. The Sacred College elects and advises the Pope.

sacred cow, person or thing regarded as being so sacred or privileged as to be above opposition or criticism.

sac ri fice (sak′rə fīs), *n., v.,* **-ficed, -fic ing.** *—n.* 1 act of offering to a god. 2 the thing offered: *The ancient Hebrews killed animals on the altars as sacrifices to God.* 3 a giving up of one thing for another: *He does not approve of any sacrifice of studies to sports.* 4 the thing given up or devoted. 5 loss: *sell one's house at a sacrifice.* 6 (in baseball) a bunt that advances a base runner or a fly ball that scores a base runner, although the batter is put out. *—v.t.* 1 give or offer to a god. 2 give up: *sacrifice one's life for another.* 3 permit injury or disadvantage to, for the sake of something else: *sacrifice business for pleasure.* 4 sell at a loss. 5 (in baseball) advance or score (a base runner) by a sacrifice. *—v.i.* 1 offer or make a sacrifice. 2 (in baseball) advance or score a base runner by a sacrifice. [< Latin *sacrificium* < *sacer* holy + *facere* to make] **—sac′ri fic′er,** *n.*

sac ri fi cial (sak′rə fish′əl), *adj.* having to do with or used in a sacrifice. **—sac′ri fi′cial ly,** *adv.*

sacrificial lamb, person or thing sacrificed for some gain or advantage.

sac ri lege (sak′rə lij), *n.* an intentional injury to anything sacred; disrespectful treatment of anyone or anything sacred: *Robbing the church was a sacrilege.* [< Latin *sacrilegium* temple robbery < *sacrum* sacred object + *legere* pick up]

sac ri le gious (sak′rə lij′əs, sak′rə lē′jəs), *adj.* injurious or insulting to sacred persons or things. **—sac′ri le′gious ly,** *adv.* **—sac′ri le′gious ness,** *n.*

sac ris tan (sak′ri stən), *n.* person in charge of the sacred vessels, robes, etc., of a church. [< Medieval Latin *sacristanus,* ultimately < Latin *sacer* holy. Doublet of SEXTON.]

sac ris ty (sak′ri stē), *n., pl.* **-ties.** place where the sacred vessels, robes, etc., of a church are kept; vestry. [< Medieval Latin *sacristia,* ultimately < Latin *sacer* holy]

sa cro il i ac (sā′krō il′ē ak, sak′rō il′ē ak), *adj.* of or having to do with the sacrum and the ilium or the joint between them. *—n.* the sacroiliac joint.

sac ro sanct (sak′rō sangkt), *adj.* 1 very holy; most sacred. 2 set apart as sacred; consecrated. [< Latin *sacrosanctus,* ultimately < *sacer* sacred + *sancire* consecrate]

sac ro sanc ti ty (sak′rō sangk′tə tē), *n.* a being sacrosanct.

sa crum (sā′krəm), *n., pl.* **-cra** (-krə), **-crums.** bone at the lower end of the spine, made by the joining of several vertebrae, and forming the back of the pelvis. [< Late Latin *(os) sacrum* sacred (bone); from its being offered as a dainty in sacrifices]

sad (sad), *adj.,* **sad der, sad dest.** 1 not happy; full of sorrow; grieving. See synonym study below. 2 causing sorrow: *a sad accident.* 3 extremely bad: *a sad state of affairs.* [Old English *sæd* sated] **—sad′ly,** *adv.* **—sad′ness,** *n.*

Syn. 1 **Sad, dejected, depressed** mean unhappy or in a state of low spirits. **Sad** is the general term: *You feel sad when your best friend goes away.* **Dejected** implies a very low but usually temporary state of unhappiness: *Her failure made her feel dejected.* **Depressed** implies a temporary and usually not very low state of unhappiness: *The rain has made me depressed.*

sad den (sad′n), *v.t., v.i.* make or become sad.

sad dhu (sä′dü), *n.* sadhu.

sad dle (sad′l), *n., v.,* **-dled, -dling.** *—n.* 1 seat for a rider on a horse's back, on a bicycle, etc. 2 part of a harness that holds the shafts, or to which a checkrein is attached. 3 thing resembling a saddle. 4 ridge between two hills or mountain peaks. 5 a cut of mutton, venison, lamb, etc., consisting of both loins and the back portion between them. 6 **in the saddle,** in a position of control. *—v.t.* 1 put a saddle on. 2 burden: *He is saddled with too many debts.* 3 put as a burden on. [Old English *sadol*]

sad dle bag (sad′l bag′), *n.* one of a pair of bags laid over an animal's back behind the saddle.

saddle blanket, saddlecloth.

sad dle bow (sad′l bō′), *n.* the arched front part of a saddle or saddletree.

sad dle cloth (sad′l klôth′, sad′l kloth′), *n., pl.* **-cloths** (-klôᴛʜz′, -klôths′; -kloᴛʜz′, -kloths′). cloth put between an animal's back and the saddle.

saddle horse, horse for riding.

sad dler (sad′lər), *n.* person who makes, mends, or sells saddles and harnesses.

saddle roof, a ridged roof with two gables.

sad dler y (sad′lər ē), *n., pl.* **-dler ies.** 1 work of a saddler. 2 shop of a saddler. 3 saddles, harnesses, and other equipment for horses.

saddle shoe, a low shoe, usually white, with the instep crossed by a band of leather of a different color. Saddle shoes are used for casual wear.

saddle soap, substance, now usually consisting chiefly of a mild soap and neat's-foot oil, used for cleaning and conditioning saddles, boots, etc.

sad dle sore (sad′l sôr′, sad′l sōr′), *adj.* sore or stiff from riding horseback.

sad dle tree (sad′l trē′), *n.* the frame of a saddle.

Sad du ce an or **Sad du cae an** (saj′ə sē′ən), *adj.* of or having to do with the Sadducees. *—n.* a Sadducee.

Sad du cee (saj′ə sē), *n.* one of a Jewish sect, of the time of Christ, that denied the resurrection of the dead and the existence of angels. The sect stood for hereditary priestly authority.

sa dhu (sä′dü), *n.* a Hindu holy man. Also, **saddhu.** [< Sanskrit *sādhu* straight, virtuous]

sad i ron (sad′ī′ərn), *n.* a heavy flatiron for pressing clothes. [< *sad* in obsolete sense of "solid" + *iron*]

sa dism (sā′diz′əm, sad′iz′əm), *n.* 1 perversion marked by a love of cruelty. 2 an unnatural love of cruelty. [< French *sadisme* < Marquis de *Sade,* 1740-1814, who wrote about it]

sa dist (sā′dist, sad′ist), *n.* person who practices or is affected by sadism.

sa dis tic (sə dis′tik), *adj.* of sadism or sadists. **—sa dis′ti cal ly,** *adv.*

sae ter (sē′tər), *n.* in Norway: 1 a mountain pasture. 2 a mountain dairy farm. [< Norwegian]

sa fa ri (sə fär′ē), *n.* 1 journey or hunting expedition in eastern Africa. 2 the people and animals on such an expedition. 3 any long trip or expedition. [< Swahili < Arabic *safar* a journey]

safe (sāf), *adj.,* **saf er, saf est,** *n.* *—adj.* 1 free from harm, danger, or loss. See synonym study below. 2 not harmed: *He returned from war safe and sound.* 3 out of danger: *We feel safe with the dog in the house.* 4 put beyond power of doing harm: *a criminal safe in prison.* 5 careful: *a safe guess, a safe move.* 6 that can be depended on: *a safe guide, a safe bridge.* 7 (in baseball) reaching a base or home plate without being put out. *—n.* 1 a steel or iron box for money, jewels, papers, etc. 2 place made to keep things safe: *a meat safe.* [< Old French *sauf* < Latin *salvus*] **—safe′ly,** *adv.* **—safe′ness,** *n.*

Syn. *adj.* 1 **Safe, secure** mean free from danger, harm, or risk. **Safe** emphasizes being not exposed to danger, harm, or risk: *The children are safe in their own yard.* **Secure** emphasizes being protected or guarded against harm and having no worry or fear: *A child feels secure with his mother.*

safe-con duct (sāf′kon′dukt), *n.* 1 privilege of passing safely through a region, especially in time of war. 2 paper granting this privilege.

safe crack er (sāf′krak′ər), *n.* person skilled at opening safes for robbery.

safe-de pos it box (sāf′di poz′it), box for storing valuables, especially in a vault of a bank.

safe guard (sāf′gärd′), *v.t.* keep safe; guard against hurt or danger; protect: *Pure food laws safeguard our health.* *—n.* protection; defense.

safe keep ing (sāf/kē/ping), *n.* a keeping or being kept safe; protection.
safe ty (sāf/tē), *n., pl.* **-ties,** *adj.* —*n.* 1 quality or state of being safe; freedom from harm or danger; security: *A bank assures safety for your money.* 2 device to prevent injury or accident. A gun cannot be fired if the safety is on. 3 in football: **a** play in which an offensive player downs the ball, or is downed, behind his own goal line, when the impetus of the ball across the goal has come from his own team. A safety counts two points for the other team. **b** a defensive back who usually lines up closest to his team's goal line. —*adj.* giving safety; making harm unlikely.
safety belt, seat belt.
safety glass, shatterproof glass made of two or more layers of glass joined together by a layer of transparent plastic.
safety lamp, a miner's lamp in which the flame is kept from setting fire to explosive gases by a piece of wire gauze.
safety match, match that will ignite only when rubbed on a specially prepared surface.
safety pin, pin bent back on itself to form a spring and having a guard that covers the point and prevents accidental unfastening.
safety razor, razor having the blade protected to prevent cutting the skin deeply.
safety valve, 1 valve in a steam boiler, etc., that opens and lets steam or fluid escape when the pressure becomes too great. 2 something that helps a person get rid of anger, nervousness, etc., in a harmless way.
saf flow er (saf/lou/ər), *n.* herb of the composite family, with large, red or orange flowers. Its seeds yield an oil used for cooking. Its dried petals are used in making certain red dyes. [ultimately < earlier Italian *saffiore;* form influenced by English *flower*]
saf fron (saf/rən), *n.* 1 an autumn crocus with purple flowers having orange-yellow stigmas. 2 an orange-yellow coloring matter obtained from the dried stigmas of this crocus. Saffron is used to color and flavor candy, drinks, etc. 3 an orange yellow. —*adj.* orange-yellow. [< Old French *safran,* ultimately < Arabic *za'farān*]
S. Afr., 1 South Africa. 2 South African.
sag (sag), *v.,* **sagged, sag ging,** *n.* —*v.i.* 1 sink under weight or pressure; bend down in the middle, as a rope, beam, cable, plank, etc. 2 hang down unevenly: *Your dress sags in the back.* 3 become less firm or elastic; yield through weakness, weariness, or lack of effort; droop; sink. 4 decline in price or value. 5 (of a ship) drift from her course. —*v.t.* cause to sag. —*n.* 1 act, state, or degree of sagging. 2 place where anything sags. [Middle English *saggen*]
sa ga (sä/gə), *n.* 1 any of the old Norse stories of heroic deeds, written in Iceland or Norway during the Middle Ages. 2 any story of heroic deeds. [< Scandinavian (Old Icelandic). Related to SAY.]
sa ga cious (sə gā/shəs), *adj.* 1 wise in a keen, practical way; shrewd. See **shrewd** for synonym study. 2 intelligent. [< Latin *sagacem*] —**sa ga/cious ly,** *adv.* —**sa ga/cious ness,** *n.*
sa gac i ty (sə gas/ə tē), *n.* keen, sound judgment; mental acuteness; shrewdness.
sag a more (sag/ə môr, sag/ə mōr), *n.* (among some North American Indians) a chief or great man, sometimes inferior to a sachem. [of Algonquian origin]
sage[1] (sāj), *adj.,* **sag er, sag est,** *n.* —*adj.* 1 showing wisdom or good judgment: *a sage reply.* 2 wise: *a sage adviser.* See **wise**[1] for synonym study. 3 wise-looking; grave; solemn: *Owls are sage birds.* —*n.* a very wise man. [< Old French, ultimately < Latin *sapere* be wise] —**sage/ly,** *adv.* —**sage/ness,** *n.*
sage[2] (sāj), *n.* 1 a small shrub, a species of salvia, whose grayish-green leaves are used as seasoning and in medicine. 2 its dried leaves. 3 salvia. 4 sagebrush. [< Old French *sauge* < Latin *salvia.* Doublet of SALVIA.]
sage brush (sāj/brush/), *n.* a grayish-green shrub of the composite family that smells like sage, common on the dry plains of western North America.
sage grouse, a very large grouse common on the plains of western North America.
sage hen, 1 sage grouse. 2 a female sage grouse.
Sag i naw (sag/ə nô), *n.* city in E Michigan. 92,000.
Sag it tar i us (saj/ə ter/ē əs), *n.* 1 a southern constellation between Scorpio and Capricorn, seen by ancient astronomers as having the rough outline of a centaur drawing a bow; Archer. 2 the ninth sign of the zodiac. The sun enters Sagittarius about November 22.
sag it tate (saj/ə tāt), *adj.* shaped like an arrowhead. Calla lilies have sagittate leaves. [< Latin *sagitta* arrow]
sa go (sā/gō), *n., pl.* **-gos.** 1 a starchy food used in making puddings, etc., made from the pith of a sago palm. 2 sago palm. [< Malay *sagu*]
sago palm, any of several East Indian palm trees from which sago is obtained.
sa gua ro (sə gwär/ō), *n., pl.* **-ros.** a very tall branching cactus of Arizona and neighboring regions, from 20 to 60 feet high, bearing white flowers and an edible fruit.
Sa har a (sə her/ə, sə har/ə, sə här/ə), *n.* **the,** the world's largest desert, in N Africa, extending eastward from the Atlantic to the Nile valley and southward from the Mediterranean Sea to the Sudan. 3,500,000 sq. mi. See **Sudan** for map. —**Sa har/an,** *adj., n.*
sa hib (sä/ib, sä/hib), *n.* sir; master. Natives in colonial India called a European "sahib" when speaking to or of him. [< Hindi *sāhib* < Arabic *ṣāḥib* lord]
said (sed), *v.* pt. and pp. of **say.** —*adj.* named or mentioned before: *the said witness.*
Sai gon (sī gon/), *n.* capital of South Vietnam, in the S part. 1,682,000.
sail (sāl), *n.* 1 piece of cloth attached to the rigging of a ship to catch the wind and make a ship move through the water. 2 sails. 3 something like a sail, such as the part of an arm of a windmill that catches the wind. 4 ship or ships. 5 trip on a boat with sails or on any other vessel.
make sail, a spread out the sails of a ship. **b** begin a trip by water.
set sail, begin a trip by water.
take in sail, a lower or lessen the sails of a ship. **b** lessen one's hopes, ambitions, etc.
under sail, with the sails spread out.
—*v.i.* 1 travel or go on water in a boat by the action of wind on sails. 2 travel or go in a boat propelled by any means, as a steamship. 3 move smoothly like a ship with sails: *The sea gull sailed by. The duchess sailed into the room.* 4 manage a ship or boat: *learn to sail.* 5 begin a trip by water; set sail: *We sail at 2 p.m.* —*v.t.* 1 sail upon, over, or through: *sail the seas.* 2 manage or navigate (a ship or boat). 3 **sail into,** INFORMAL. **a** to attack; beat. **b** criticize; scold.
[Old English *segl*] —**sail/like/,** *adj.*

hat, āge, fär; let, ēqual, tėrm;
it, īce; hot, ōpen, ôrder;
oil, out; cup, pu̇t, rüle;
ch, child; ng, long; sh, she;
th, thin; ᴛʜ, then; zh, measure;

ə represents *a* in about, *e* in taken, *i* in pencil, *o* in lemon, *u* in circus.

< = from, derived from, taken from.

➔ **Sail,** noun, is used collectively when it means sails for a sailing vessel (def. 2): *Our ship had all sail spread. Sail* when it means ships (def. 4) is used collectively and often with a numeral: *a fleet of thirty sail.*
sail boat (sāl/bōt/), *n.* boat that is moved by a sail or sails.
sail cloth (sāl/klôth/, sāl/kloth/), *n., pl.* **-cloths** (-klôᴛʜz/, -klôths/; -kloᴛʜz/, -kloths/). canvas or other material used for making sails and tents.
sail er (sā/lər), *n.* a ship with reference to its sailing power: *a fast sailer.*
sail fish (sāl/fish/), *n., pl.* **-fish es** or **-fish.** any of a genus of large saltwater fishes related to the swordfish, having a long, sail-like dorsal fin.
sail ing (sā/ling), *n.* 1 act of a person or thing that sails. 2 art of managing or maneuvering a ship; navigation.
sail or (sā/lər), *n.* 1 person whose work is handling a sailboat or other vessel. 2 member of a ship's crew, not an officer. 3 an enlisted man in a country's navy. 4 a flat-brimmed straw hat modeled after a hat formerly worn by sailors. 5 **a good sailor,** a person who does not get seasick. —*adj.* like that of a sailor: *a sailor collar.* —**sail/or like/,** *adj.*
sail or ly (sā/lər lē), *adj.* like a sailor; suitable for a sailor.
sail plane (sāl/plān/), *n.* a lightweight glider with especially long wings to take advantage of rising air currents.
saint (sānt), *n.* 1 a very holy person; one who is pure in heart and upright in life. 2 person who has gone to heaven. 3 person declared a saint by the Roman Catholic Church. 4 person who is very humble, patient, etc., like a saint. 5 Also, **Saint.** person belonging to any religious body whose members are called Saints. —*v.t.* 1 make a saint of; canonize. 2 call or consider a saint. [< Old French < Latin *sanctus* holy < *sancire* to consecrate, ordain, related to *sacer* holy] —**saint/like/,** *adj.*
Saint. For names of saints look under the Christian name, as *Anthony, Francis,* etc. Names more commonly written in the abbreviated form, as *St. Anthony's fire, St.-John's-wort,* will be found in their alphabetical places following **St.**
Saint Agnes's Eve, the night of January 20. According to legend, any girl who performed certain ceremonies on this night would dream of her future husband.
Saint Andrew's cross, cross shaped like the letter X.
Saint Ber nard (bər närd/), one of a breed of big, powerful, intelligent, red-and-white dogs with large heads, first bred by the monks at the hospice of Great St. Bernard, a pass in the Swiss Alps, to rescue travelers lost in the snow.
Sainte (sᴀɴᴛ), *n.* FRENCH. feminine form of **Saint.**

salamander (def. 1)
6 to 8 in. long

saint ed (sān′tid), *adj.* 1 declared to be a saint. 2 thought of as a saint; gone to heaven. 3 sacred; very holy. 4 saintly.
Saint-É tienne (saN tā tyen′), *n.* St.-Étienne.
Saint-Ex u pé ry (saN teg zY pā rē′), *n.* **Antoine de,** 1900-1944, French writer and aviator.
Saint-Gau dens (sānt gôd′nz), *n.* **Augustus,** 1848-1907, American sculptor, born in Ireland.
saint hood (sānt′hůd), *n.* 1 character or status of a saint. 2 saints collectively.
saint ly (sānt′lē), *adj.,* **-li er, -li est.** 1 like a saint; very holy. 2 very good. **—saint′li-ness,** *n.*
Saint Patrick's Day, March 17.
Saint-Saëns (saN säNs′), *n.* **(Charles) Camille,** 1835-1921, French composer and pianist.
saint ship (sānt′ship), *n.* sainthood.
Saint Val en tine's Day (val′ən tīnz), February 14, a day on which valentines are exchanged; Valentine's Day.
Saint Vitus's dance, St. Vitus's dance.
Sai pan (sī pan′, sī pän′), *n.* island in the W Pacific, one of the Mariana Islands. 9000 pop.; 70 sq. mi.
saith (seth), *v.* ARCHAIC. says.
sake[1] (sāk), *n.* 1 cause; account; interest: *Put yourself to no trouble for our sake.* 2 purpose; end: *for the sake of peace and quiet.* [Old English *sacu* a cause at law]
sa ke[2] (sä′kē), *n.* an alcoholic beverage made from a fermented mash of rice, popular in Japan. [< Japanese]
Sak ha lin (sak′ə lēn′, sak′ə lən), *n.* island east of Siberia, between the Sea of Okhotsk and the Sea of Japan, a part of the Soviet Union. 637,000 pop.; 29,300 sq. mi.
sal (sal), *n.* salt (used especially in druggists' terms). [< Latin]
sa laam (sə läm′), *n.* 1 a greeting that means "Peace," used especially in Moslem countries. 2 a very low bow, with the palm of the right hand placed on the forehead. *—v.t.* greet with a salaam. *—v.i.* make a salaam. [< Arabic *salām* peace]
sal a bil i ty (sā′lə bil′ə tē), *n.* salable condition or quality.
sal a ble (sā′lə bəl), *adj.* that can be sold; fit to be sold; easily sold. Also, **saleable.**
sa la cious (sə lā′shəs), *adj.* 1 obscene; indecent. 2 lustful; lewd. [< Latin *salacem*] **—sa la′cious ly,** *adv.* **—sa la′cious-ness,** *n.*
sal ad (sal′əd), *n.* 1 raw, green vegetables, such as lettuce, cabbage, and celery, served with a dressing. Often cold meat, fish, eggs, cooked vegetables, or fruits are used along with, or instead of, the raw, green vegetables. 2 any green vegetable that can be eaten raw. [< Old French *salade* < Provençal *salada,* ultimately < Latin *sal* salt]
salad days, days of youthful inexperience.
salad dressing, sauce used in or on a salad.
Sal a din (sal′ə dən), *n.* 1137?-1193, sultan of Egypt and Syria from about 1175 to 1193. He captured Jerusalem and defeated the crusaders led by Richard I of England.
Sal a man ca (sal′ə mang′kə), *n.* city in W Spain. 120,000.
sal a man der (sal′ə man′dər), *n.* 1 any of various amphibians resembling lizards but related to frogs and toads, having moist, smooth skin, four short limbs, and usually a long tail. 2 (in old myths) a lizard or other creature supposed to live in or be able to endure fire. 3 person who likes or can stand a great deal of heat. 4 spirit or imaginary being that lives in fire. [< Greek *salamandra*]
sal a man drine (sal′ə man′drən), *adj.* of or related to the salamanders.
sa la mi (sə lä′mē), *n.* kind of thick sausage often flavored with garlic. [< Italian, ultimately < Latin *sal* salt]
Sal a mis (sal′ə mis), *n.* a Greek island off SE Greece. 21,000 pop.; 36 sq. mi.
sal am mo ni ac (ə mō′nē ak), ammonium chloride.
sal ar ied (sal′ər ēd), *adj.* receiving a salary: *a salaried employee.*
sal ar y (sal′ər ē), *n., pl.* **-ar ies.** a fixed payment made periodically to a person, especially by the week or month, for regular work. [< Latin *salarium* soldier's allowance for salt < *sal* salt]
sale (sāl), *n.* 1 act of selling; exchange of goods or property for money: *the sale of a house.* 2 Also, **sales,** *pl.* amount sold: *a large sale of bonds. Today's sales were larger than yesterday's.* 3 chance to sell; demand; market: *There is almost no sale for washboards these days.* 4 a selling at lower prices than usual: *This store is having a sale on suits.* 5 auction. 6 **sales,** *pl.* business of selling. 7 **for sale,** to be sold: *There are several houses in the neighborhood for sale, but none for rent.* 8 **on sale, a** for sale at lower prices than usual. **b** to be sold. [Old English *sala*]
sale a ble (sā′lə bəl), *adj.* salable.
Sa lem (sā′ləm), *n.* 1 seaport in NE Massachusetts, settled in 1626. 41,000. 2 capital of Oregon, in the NW part. 68,000.
sal e ra tus (sal′ə rā′təs), *n.* 1 sodium bicarbonate. 2 potassium bicarbonate. [< New Latin *sal aeratus* aerated salt]
Sa ler no (sə ler′nō, sə lėr′nō), *n.* seaport in SW Italy. 151,000.
sales clerk (sālz′klėrk′), *n.* person whose work is selling in a store.
sales girl (sālz′gėrl′), *n.* girl whose work is selling in a store.
sales la dy (sālz′lā′dē), *n., pl.* **-dies.** saleswoman.
sales man (sālz′mən), *n., pl.* **-men.** man whose work is selling.
sales man ship (sālz′mən ship), *n.* 1 work of a salesman. 2 ability at selling.
sales peo ple (sālz′pē′pəl), *n.pl.* salespersons.
sales per son (sālz′pėr′sən), *n.* person whose work is selling, especially in a store.
sales room (sālz′rüm′, sālz′rům′), *n.* room where things are sold or shown for sale.
sales talk, 1 a talk by a salesperson to sell something. 2 any talk to persuade.
sales tax, tax based on the amount received for articles sold.
sales wom an (sālz′wům′ən), *n., pl.* **-wom en.** woman whose work is selling, especially in a store; saleslady.
Sal ic (sal′ik, sā′lik), *adj.* of or having to do with the Salii, a tribe of Franks that lived in the regions of the Rhine near the North Sea.
Salic law, 1 code of laws of the Salic Franks. 2 law believed to be based on this code, excluding females from succession to the crown.
sal i cyl ate (sal′ə sil′āt, sə lis′ə lāt), *n.* any salt or ester of salicylic acid.
sal i cyl ic acid (sal′ə sil′ik), a white, crystalline or powdery acid used as a mild antiseptic and preservative, and in making aspirin. *Formula:* $C_7H_6O_3$ [< Latin *salicem* willow (because it was first obtained from an extract of willow bark)]
sa li ence (sā′lē əns, sā′lyəns), *n.* 1 a being salient. 2 a salient or projecting object, part, or feature.
sa li en cy (sā′lē ən sē, sā′lyən sē), *n., pl.* **-cies.** salience.
sa li ent (sā′lē ənt, sā′lyənt), *adj.* 1 standing out; easily seen or noticed; prominent; striking: *the salient features in a landscape, the salient points in a speech.* 2 pointing outward; projecting: *a salient angle.* 3 leaping; jumping. A lion salient on a coat of arms is standing with forepaws raised as if jumping. *—n.* 1 a salient angle or part. 2 part of a fortification or line of trenches that projects toward the enemy. [< Latin *salientem* leaping] **—sa′li ent ly,** *adv.*
sa line (sā′lēn′, sā′līn), *adj.* 1 of salt; like salt; salty. 2 containing common salt or any other salts. *—n.* 1 a salt spring, well, or marsh. 2 salt of an alkali or magnesium, used as a cathartic. 3 a saline solution, especially one with a concentration of salt appropriate for use in medicine, surgery, etc. [< Latin *sal* salt]
Sal in ger (sal′ən jər), *n.* **J(erome) D(avid),** born 1919, American writer.
sa lin i ty (sə lin′ə tē), *n.* saline condition or quality; saltiness.
Salis bur y (sôlz′ber′ē, sôlz′bər ē), *n.* 1 city in S England, site of famous cathedral. 36,000. 2 capital of Rhodesia, in the NE part. 385,000.
Salisbury Plain, area of rolling land in S England, north of Salisbury. Stonehenge is located there.
Salisbury steak, chopped beef shaped before cooking into a patty about twice the size of a hamburger, usually served with a gravy. [< J. H. *Salisbury,* English physician and dietary reformer of the 1800's]
sa li va (sə lī′və), *n.* a colorless, watery fluid that the salivary glands secrete into the mouth to keep it moist, aid in chewing and swallowing of food, and start digestion. [< Latin]
sal i var y (sal′ə ver′ē), *adj.* of or producing saliva.
salivary gland, any of various glands that empty their secretions into the mouth. The salivary glands of human beings and certain other vertebrates are digestive glands that secrete saliva containing the digestive enzyme ptyalin, salts, mucus, etc.
sal i vate (sal′ə vāt), *v.,* **-vat ed, -vat ing.** *—v.i.* secrete saliva. *—v.t.* produce a large secretion of saliva in.
sal i va tion (sal′ə vā′shən), *n.* 1 act or process of salivating. 2 the secretion of saliva. 3 an abnormally large secretion of saliva.
Salk (sôlk), *n.* **Jonas Edward,** born 1914, American scientist who developed the Salk vaccine.
Salk vaccine, vaccine containing killed polio viruses which cause the body to produce antibodies. It protects against infection from live polio viruses and is given in a series of injections.

hat, āge, fär; let, ēqual, tėrm;
it, īce; hot, ōpen, ôrder;
oil, out; cup, pu̇t, rüle;
ch, child; ng, long; sh, she;
th, thin; ᴛʜ, then; zh, measure;

ə represents *a* in about, *e* in taken, *i* in pencil, *o* in lemon, *u* in circus.

< = from, derived from, taken from.

sal low[1] (sal′ō), *adj.* having a sickly, yellowish or brownish-yellow color: *a sallow skin, a sallow complexion.* —*v.t.* make sallow. [Old English *salo*] —**sal′low ness,** *n.*

sal low[2] (sal′ō), *n.* 1 a willow, especially a small Old World tree used in making charcoal. 2 a willow twig. [Old English *sealh*]

salsify (defs. 1 and 2)
stem to 4 ft. high; root to 1 ft. long

sal low ish (sal′ō ish), *adj.* somewhat sallow in color.

Sal lust (sal′əst), *n.* 86-34 B.C., Roman historian.

sal ly (sal′ē), *v.,* **-lied, -ly ing,** *n., pl.* **-lies.** —*v.i.* 1 go suddenly from a defensive position to attack an enemy. 2 rush forth suddenly; go out. 3 set out briskly or boldly. 4 go on an excursion or trip. 5 (of things) issue forth. —*n.* 1 a sudden attack on an enemy made from a defensive position; sortie. 2 a sudden rushing forth. 3 a going forth; trip; excursion. 4 a sudden start into activity. 5 outburst. 6 a witty remark. [< Old French *saillie* a rushing forth < *saillir* to leap < Latin *salire*]

Sal ly Lunn (sal′ē lun′), a slightly sweetened tea cake, served hot with butter. [< *Sally Lunn,* baker who sold such cakes in Bath, England, in the late 1700's]

sal ma gun di (sal′mə gun′dē), *n.* 1 dish of chopped meat, anchovies, eggs, onions, oil, seasonings, etc. 2 any mixture, medley, or miscellany. [< French *salmigondis,* ultimately < Italian *salami conditi* pickled sausages]

salm on (sam′ən), *n., pl.* **-ons** or **-on,** *adj.* —*n.* 1 a large marine and freshwater fish of the same genus as several species of trouts, with silvery scales and yellowish-pink flesh. It is found in the northern Atlantic near the mouths of large rivers which it swims up in order to spawn. 2 any of a genus of similar fishes of the same family, common in the northern Pacific and important as food fishes. 3 variety of Atlantic or Pacific salmon living in lakes; landlocked salmon. 4 a yellowish-pink color; salmon pink. —*adj.* yellowish-pink. [< Latin *salmonem*]

sal mo nel la (sal′mə nel′ə), *n., pl.* **-nel las, -nel lae** (-nel′ē). any of a genus of bacteria that cause food poisoning, typhoid fever, and other infectious diseases. [< New Latin < Daniel E. *Salmon,* 1850-1914, American pathologist]

salmon pink, yellowish pink; salmon.

Sa lo me (sə lō′mē), *n.* (in the Bible) the daughter of Herodias, whose dancing so pleased Herod Antipas that he granted her request for the head of John the Baptist.

sa lon (sə lon′), *n.* 1 a large room for receiving or entertaining guests. 2 assembly of guests in such a room. 3 place used to exhibit works of art. 4 exhibition of works of art. 5 a fashionable or stylish shop. [< French < Italian *salone* < *sala* hall; of Germanic origin]

Sal o ni ka or **Sal o ni ca** (sal′ə nē′kə, sə lon′ə kə), *n.* seaport in NE Greece. 378,000.

sa loon (sə lün′), *n.* 1 place where alcoholic drinks are sold and drunk; tavern. 2 a large room for general or public use: *The ship's passengers ate in the dining saloon.* [< French *salon* salon. See SALON.]

sa loon keep er (sə lün′kē′pər), *n.* person who keeps a saloon (def. 1).

sal si fy (sal′sə fī, sal′sə fē), *n., pl.* **-fies.** 1 a biennial plant of the composite family, with purple flowers that remain open only in the morning; oyster plant. 2 its long, fleshy root, with an oysterlike flavor, eaten as a vegetable. [< French *salsifis* < Italian *sassefrica* < Latin *saxifraga.* Doublet of SAXIFRAGE.]

sal soda, sodium carbonate; washing soda.

salt (sôlt), *n.* 1 a white substance found in the earth and in sea water, used as a seasoning, a preservative for food and hides, and in many industrial processes; sodium chloride; table salt. *Formula:* NaCl. 2 a chemical compound derived from an acid by replacing the hydrogen wholly or partly with a metal or an electropositive radical. Sodium bicarbonate is a salt. 3 that which gives liveliness, piquancy, or pungency to anything. 4 a saltcellar. 5 INFORMAL. sailor. 6 **salts,** *pl.* **a** medicine that causes movement of the bowels. **b** smelling salts. 7 **salt of the earth,** the best people. 8 **worth one's salt,** worth one's support, wages, etc.
—*adj.* 1 containing salt. 2 tasting like salt. 3 overflowed with or growing in salt water: *salt marshes, salt grasses.* 4 cured or preserved with salt. 5 sharp; pungent; to the point; lively: *salt speech.*
—*v.t.* 1 mix or sprinkle with salt. 2 cure or preserve with salt. 3 provide with salt: *salt cattle.* 4 make pungent; season: *conversation salted with wit.* 5 in chemical processes: **a** treat with a salt. **b** add a salt to (a solution in order to precipitate a dissolved substance). 6 make (a mine, an account, etc.) appear more prosperous or productive to create a false impression of value. 7 **salt away** or **salt down, a** pack with salt to preserve. **b** INFORMAL. store away.
[Old English *sealt*] —**salt′like′,** *adj.* —**salt′ness,** *n.*

SALT (sôlt), *n.* Strategic Arms Limitation Talks (between the United States and the Soviet Union).

sal tant (salt′nt), *adj.* dancing; leaping. [< Latin *saltantem*]

salt box (sôlt′boks′), *n.* U.S. a square-shaped, two-story house with a lean-to kitchen in the rear, originally built in Connecticut in the 1700's.

salt cel lar (sôlt′sel′ər), *n.* shaker or dish for holding salt, used on the table.

salt ed (sôl′tid), *adj.* 1 seasoned, cured, or preserved with salt. 2 experienced; hardened.

salt er (sôl′tər), *n.* 1 person who makes or sells salt. 2 person who salts meat, fish, hides, etc.

salt ine (sôl tēn′), *n.* a thin, crisp, salted cracker.

salt ish (sôl′tish), *adj.* somewhat salty.

Salt Lake City, capital of Utah, in the N part. 176,000.

salt lick, 1 place where natural salt is found on the ground and where animals go to lick it up. 2 block of salt set out, especially in a pasture, for animals to lick.

salt pe ter or **salt pe tre** (sôlt′pē′tər), *n.* 1 naturally occurring potassium nitrate; niter. 2 sodium nitrate, especially when occurring naturally; Chile saltpeter. [< Old French *salpetre* < Medieval Latin *sal petrae* salt of rock]

salt shak er (sôlt′shā′kər), *n.* container for salt, with a perforated top through which the salt is sprinkled.

salt wa ter (sôlt′wô′tər, sôlt′wot′ər), *adj.* 1 consisting of or containing salt water. 2 living in the sea or in water like sea water. 3 working on the sea: *a saltwater fisherman.*

salt y (sôl′tē), *adj.,* **salt i er, salt i est.** 1 containing salt; tasting of salt. 2 terse, witty, and a bit improper: *a salty remark.* 3 of or suggestive of the sea or life at sea. —**salt′i ly,** *adv.* —**salt′i ness,** *n.*

sa lu bri ous (sə lü′brē əs), *adj.* favorable or conducive to good health; healthful. [< Latin *salubris* < *salus* good health] —**sa lu′bri ous ly,** *adv.* —**sa lu′bri ous ness,** *n.*

sa lu bri ty (sə lü′brə tē), *n.* healthfulness.

sal u tar y (sal′yə ter′ē), *adj.* 1 beneficial: *give someone salutary advice.* 2 good for the health; wholesome: *Walking is a salutary exercise.* [< Latin *salutaris* < *salus* good health] —**sal′u tar′i ly,** *adv.* —**sal′u tar′i ness,** *n.*

sal u ta tion (sal′yə tā′shən), *n.* 1 a greeting; saluting: *The man raised his hat in salutation.* 2 something uttered, written, or done to salute. You begin a letter with a salutation, such as "Dear Sir".

sa lu ta to ri an (sə lü′tə tôr′ē ən, sə lü′tə tōr′ē ən), *n.* student who delivers the address of welcome at the graduation of a class, often the student who ranks second in the class.

sa lu ta to ry (sə lü′tə tôr′ē, sə lü′tə tōr′ē), *adj., n., pl.* **-ries.** —*adj.* expressing greeting; welcoming. —*n.* an opening address welcoming guests at the graduation of a class.

sa lute (sə lüt′), *v.,* **-lut ed, -lut ing,** *n.* —*v.t.* 1 honor in a formal manner by raising the hand to the head, by firing guns, by dipping flags, etc.: *The soldier saluted the officer.* 2 meet with kind words, a bow, a kiss, etc.; greet. 3 make a bow, gesture, or the like, to. 4 come to; meet: *Shouts of welcome saluted their ears.* —*v.i.* make a salute. —*n.* 1 act of saluting; expression of welcome, farewell, or honor. 2 position of the hand, rifle, etc., assumed in saluting. [< Latin *salutare* greet < *salus* good health] —**sa lut′er,** *n.*

Salv., Salvador.

sal va ble (sal′və bəl), *adj.* salvageable.

Sal va dor (sal′və dôr), *n.* 1 seaport in E Brazil; Bahia; Baía. 1,001,000. Also, **São Salvador.** 2 El Salvador. —**Sal′va do′ran, Sal′va do′re an, Sal′va do′ri an,** *adj., n.*

sal vage (sal′vij), *n., v.,* **-vaged, -vag ing.** —*n.* 1 act of saving a ship or its cargo from wreck, capture, etc. 2 payment for saving it.

3 rescue of property from fire, flood, shipwreck, etc. 4 property salvaged: *the salvage from a shipwreck.* —*v.t.* save from fire, flood, shipwreck, etc. [< French, ultimately < Latin *salvus* safe] **—sal′vag er,** *n.*

sal vage a ble (sal′və jə bəl), *adj.* that can be salvaged.

sal va tion (sal vā′shən), *n.* 1 a saving. 2 a being saved. 3 person or thing that saves. Christians believe that Christ is the salvation of the world. 4 a saving of the soul; deliverance from sin and from punishment for sin. [< Late Latin *salvationem,* ultimately < Latin *salvus* safe]

Salvation Army, organization to spread the Christian religion and help the poor and unfortunate, founded in England in 1865 by William Booth.

salve[1] (sav), *n., v.,* **salved, salv ing.** —*n.* 1 a soft, greasy substance put on wounds and sores; healing ointment. 2 something soothing; balm: *The kind words were a salve to my hurt feelings.* —*v.t.* 1 put salve on. 2 smooth over; soothe: *She salved her conscience by the thought that her lie harmed no one.* [Old English *sealf*]

salve[2] (salv), *v.t.,* **salved, salv ing.** save from loss or destruction; salvage. [< *salvage*]

sal ve[3] (sal′vē), *interj.* hail! [< Latin]

sal ver (sal′vər), *n.* tray. [< French *salve* < Spanish *salva,* originally, foretasting, ultimately < Latin *salvus* safe]

sal vi a (sal′vē ə), *n.* any of a genus of herbs and shrubs of the mint family, especially the scarlet sage and the common garden sage; sage. [< Latin, probably < *salvus* healthy, safe (because of its supposed healing properties). Doublet of SAGE[2].]

sal vo (sal′vō), *n., pl.* **-vos** or **-voes.** 1 the discharge of several guns at the same time as a broadside or as a salute. 2 the release at the same time of several bombs, rockets, etc. 3 round of cheers or applause. 4 barrage: *a salvo of insults.* [< Italian *salva* salute, volley < Latin *salve* hail!, be in good health!]

sal vo la ti le (sal və lat′l ē), 1 a colorless or white crystalline salt of ammonium. 2 an aromatic solution of this salt used to relieve faintness, headache, etc. [< New Latin, volatile salt]

Sal ween River (sal wēn′), river flowing from Tibet through China and E Burma into the Bay of Bengal. 1750 mi.

Salz burg (sôlz′bėrg′; *German* zälts′bůrk), *n.* city in W Austria, known for its annual music festivals. 120,000.

Sam., Samuel, the name of two books of the Bible.

SAM (sam), *n.* surface-to-air missile.

S. Am., 1 South America. 2 South American.

Sa mar (sä′mär), *n.* island in the E Philippines. 1,217,000 pop.; 5100 sq. mi.

sam ar a (sam′ər ə, sə mar′ə), *n.* any dry fruit that has a winglike extension and does not split open when ripe; key fruit. The fruit of the maple tree is a double samara with one seed in each half. [< Latin, elm seed]

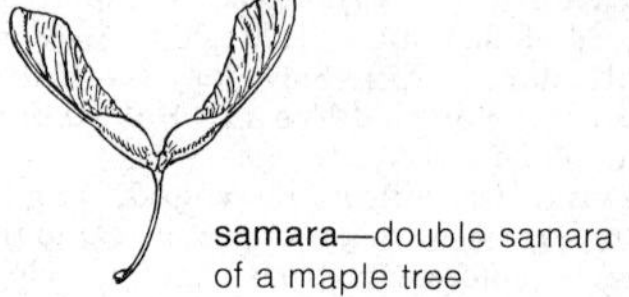
samara—double samara of a maple tree

Sa ma ra (sə mär′ə), *n.* former name of **Kuibyshev.**

Sa mar i a (sə mer′ē ə), *n.* 1 district in the N part of ancient Palestine, now in Jordan. 2 chief city of this district.

Sa mar i tan (sə mar′ə tən), *n.* 1 native or inhabitant of Samaria. 2 Good Samaritan. —*adj.* of or having to do with Samaria or its people.

sa mar i um (sə mer′ē əm, sə mar′ē əm), *n.* a rare-earth metallic element that is hard, brittle, and grayish-white, and is used in control rods in nuclear reactors. *Symbol:* Sm; *atomic number* 62. See pages 326 and 327 for table. [< New Latin, ultimately < Colonel *Samarski,* Russian mining official of the 1800's]

Sam ar kand (sam′ər kand′), *n.* city in the Soviet Union, in the Uzbek S.S.R., north of Afghanistan. 267,000.

sam ba (säm′bə), *n.* 1 an African dance adapted and modified in Brazil as a ballroom dance, in syncopated duple time. 2 music for this dance. [< Portuguese]

Sam Browne belt (sam′ broun′), a leather belt having a supporting strap passing over the right shoulder, worn by army officers, policemen, etc. [< Sir *Sam(uel) Browne,* 1824-1901, British general who invented it]

same (sām), *adj.* 1 not another; identical. See synonym study below. 2 just alike; not different: *Her name and mine are the same.* 3 unchanged: *He is the same kind old man.* 4 just spoken of; aforesaid: *They were talking about a strange man. This same man always dressed in white.* —*pron.* 1 the same person or thing. 2 **all the same, a** notwithstanding; nevertheless. **b** of little importance. 3 **just the same, a** in the same manner. **b** nevertheless. —*adv.* **the same,** in the same way or manner: *"Sea" and "see" are pronounced the same.* [< Scandinavian (Old Icelandic) *samr*]

Syn. *adj.* 1 **Same, identical** mean not different from something else or each other. When referring to something or someone already mentioned, either word applies: *That is the same* (or *identical*) *man I saw yesterday.* When describing two or more people or things, **same** implies likeness of some kind or degree; **identical** implies absolute likeness: *He always has the same lunch. Their cars are identical.*

same ness (sām′nis), *n.* 1 state of being the same; exact likeness. 2 lack of variety; tiresomeness; monotony.

sam i sen (sam′ə sen), *n.* a Japanese guitar-like instrument with three strings, played with a plectrum. [< Japanese]

sam ite (sam′īt, sā′mīt), *n.* a heavy, rich silk fabric, sometimes interwoven with gold or silver, worn in the Middle Ages. [< Medieval Greek *hexamiton* < Greek *hex* six + *mitos* thread]

Sa mo a (sə mō′ə), *n.* group of islands in the S Pacific. Several of these islands (American Samoa or Eastern Samoa) belong to the United States and the rest make up the independent country of Western Samoa. 169,000 pop.; 1200 sq. mi. See **Melanesia** for map. **—Sa mo′an,** *adj., n.*

Sa mos (sā′mos), *n.* Greek island in the Aegean Sea, off W Turkey. 41,000 pop.; 181 sq. mi.

Sam o thrace (sam′ə thrās), *n.* Greek island off NE Greece in the Aegean Sea. A famous statue called the "Winged Victory" was found there. 4000 pop.; 68 sq. mi.

sam o var (sam′ə vär, sam′ə vär′), *n.* a metal urn used for heating water for tea. [< Russian, literally, self-boiler]

samovar

Sam o yed (sam′ə yed′), *n.* 1 one of a Mongoloid people living in N Siberia and the NE European part of the Soviet Union. 2 group of Uralic languages spoken by the Samoyeds. 3 a large, long-haired dog with a thick white coat, originally bred by the Samoyeds.

samp (samp), *n.* U.S. 1 coarsely ground corn. 2 porridge made from it. [of Algonquian origin]

sampan

sam pan (sam′pan), *n.* any of various small boats used in the rivers and coastal waters of China, Japan, and southeast Asia. Sampans are sculled by one or more oars at the stern and have a single sail and a cabin made of mats. [< Chinese *san pan,* literally, three boards]

sam ple (sam′pəl), *n., adj., v.,* **-pled, -pling.** —*n.* part to show what the rest is like; one thing to show what the others are like; specimen: *a sample of cloth. Pushing people aside to get on a bus is a sample of his bad manners.* See **example** for synonym study. —*adj.* serving as a sample: *a sample copy.* —*v.t.* take a part of; test a part of: *We sampled the cake and found it very good.* [short for *essample,* variant of *example*]

sam pler[1] (sam′plər), *n.* 1 person who samples. 2 something containing typical samples. [< *sample*]

sam pler[2] (sam′plər), *n.* piece of cloth embroidered to show skill in needlework. [< Old French *essamplaire* < Latin *exemplarium* a model pattern]

sam pling (sam′pling), *n.* 1 act or process of taking samples. 2 something taken or serving as a sample.

sam sa ra (səm sär′ə), *n.* (in Hinduism) the endless repetition of births, deaths, and rebirths to which man is subject. [< Sanskrit *samsāra*]

Sam son (sam′sən), *n.* 1 (in the Bible) a man who had very great strength. He was one of the judges of Israel. 2 any very strong man.

Sam u el (sam′yü əl), *n.* 1 a Hebrew leader, judge, and prophet of the 1000's B.C. He anointed Saul and David kings of Israel. 2 either of two books in the Old Testament named after Samuel.

sam u rai (sam′ů rī′), *n., pl.* **-rai.** 1 the military class in feudal Japan, consisting of the retainers of the great nobles. 2 member of this class. [< Japanese]

San (sän, san), *adj.* SPANISH and ITALIAN. Saint.

Sa na or **San aa** (sä nä′), *n.* capital of Yemen, in the central part. 80,000.

San An to ni o (san an tō′nē ō), city in S Texas, the site of the Alamo. 654,000.

san a tive (san′ə tiv), *adj.* having the power to cure or heal; healing. [< Late Latin *sanativus,* ultimately < Latin *sanus* healthy]

san a to ri um (san′ə tôr′ē əm, san′ə tōr′ē-əm), *n., pl.* **-to ri ums, -to ri a** (-tôr′ē ə, -tōr′ē ə). 1 establishment for treatment of the sick or convalescent, especially those who require a long time to cure: *a tuberculosis sanatorium.* 2 a health resort. Also, **sanitarium.**

San Ber nar di no (san bėr′nər dē′nō; san bėr′nə dē′nō), city in SW California. 105,000.

San Bernardino Mountains, mountain range in S California. Highest peak, 11,485 ft.

sanc ti fi ca tion (sangk′tə fə kā′shən), *n.* a sanctifying or a being sanctified; consecration; purification from sin.

sanc ti fy (sangk′tə fī), *v.t.,* **-fied, -fy ing.** 1 make holy; make legitimate or binding by a religious sanction: *sanctify a marriage.* 2 set apart as sacred; observe as holy: *"Lord, sanctify this our offering to Thy use."* 3 make right; justify or sanction. [< Latin *sanctificare* < *sanctus* holy + *facere* to make. See SAINT.] **—sanc′ti fi′er,** *n.*

sanc ti mo ni ous (sangk′tə mō′nē əs), *adj.* making a show of holiness; putting on airs of sanctity. **—sanc′ti mo′ni ous ly,** *adv.* **—sanc′ti mo′ni ous ness,** *n.*

sanc ti mo ny (sangk′tə mō′nē), *n.* show of holiness; airs of sanctity. [< Latin *sanctimonia* < *sanctus* holy]

sanc tion (sangk′shən), *n.* 1 permission with authority; support; approval: *We have the sanction of the recreation department to play ball in this park.* 2 solemn ratification or confirmation. 3 in law: **a** provision of a law enacting a penalty for disobedience to it or a reward for obedience. **b** the penalty or reward. 4 action by several nations toward another, such as a blockade, economic restrictions, etc., intended to force it to obey international law. 5 consideration that leads one to obey a rule of conduct. 6 binding force. *—v.t.* 1 authorize; approve; allow: *Her conscience does not sanction stealing.* See **approve** for synonym study. 2 confirm. [< Latin *sanctionem* < *sancire* ordain] **—sanc′tion er,** *n.*

sanc ti ty (sangk′tə tē), *n., pl.* **-ties.** 1 holiness of life; saintliness; godliness. 2 holy character; sacredness: *the sanctity of a church, the sanctity of the home.* 3 **sanctities,** *pl.* **a** sacred obligations, feelings, etc. **b** sacred things.

sanc tu ar y (sangk′chü er′ē), *n., pl.* **-ar ies.** 1 a sacred place. A church is a sanctuary. 2 the part of a church around the altar. 3 the most sacred part of any place of worship. 4 place of refuge or protection: *a wildlife sanctuary.* 5 refuge or protection: *The cabin provided sanctuary from the rain.*

sanc tum (sangk′təm), *n., pl.* **-tums, -ta** (-tə). 1 a sacred place. 2 a private room or office where a person can be undisturbed. [< Latin, originally neuter of *sanctus* holy]

sanc tum sanc to rum (sangk′təm sangk tôr′əm; sangk′təm sangk tōr′əm), 1 holy of holies. 2 an especially private place. [< Latin]

Sanc tus (sangk′təs, sängk′tůs), *n.* 1 hymn beginning "Sanctus, Sanctus, Sanctus," in Latin and "Holy, holy, holy, Lord God of hosts" in English, ending the preface of the Mass of Eucharistic service. 2 the musical setting of this.

sand (sand), *n.* 1 tiny grains of worn-down or disintegrated rock: *the sands of the desert.* 2 **sands,** *pl.* tract or region composed mainly of sand. 3 sand in an hourglass. 4 SLANG. courage; pluck. *—v.t.* 1 sprinkle with sand; spread sand over. 2 fill up with sand. 3 add sand to. 4 clean, smooth, or polish with sand, sandpaper, etc. [Old English]

Sand (sand), *n.* **George,** 1804-1876, pen name of Amandine Aurore Dudevant, French novelist.

san dal (san′dl), *n.* 1 kind of shoe made of a sole fastened to the foot by straps. 2 any of various kinds of low-cut shoes, slippers, etc. 3 a light, low, rubber overshoe that has no heel. [< Greek *sandalon*]

san daled or **san dalled** (san′dld), *adj.* wearing sandals.

san dal wood (san′dl wůd′), *n.* 1 the fragrant heartwood of certain Asian trees, used for carving, making ornamental boxes, fans, etc., and burned as incense. 2 any of the trees that it comes from. [< Medieval Latin *sandalum* < Greek *santalon,* ultimately < Sanskrit *candana*]

sand bag (sand′bag′), *n., v.,* **-bagged, -bag ging.** *—n.* 1 bag filled with sand. Sandbags are used to protect trenches, as ballast on balloons, to reinforce a levee or dike, etc. 2 a small bag of sand used as a club. *—v.t.* 1 furnish with sandbags. 2 hit or stun with or as if with a sandbag. **—sand′bag′ger,** *n.*

sand bank (sand′bangk′), *n.* ridge of sand forming a shoal or hillside.

sand bar (sand′bär′), *n.* ridge of sand formed by the action of tides or currents.

sand blast (sand′blast′), *n.* 1 blast of air or steam containing sand, used to clean, grind, cut, or decorate hard surfaces, such as glass, stone, or metal. 2 apparatus used to apply such a blast. *—v.t., v.i.* use a sandblast on; clean, grind, cut, or decorate by a sandblast. **—sand′blast′er,** *n.*

sand box (sand′boks′), *n.* box for holding sand, especially for children to play in.

Sand burg (sand′bėrg′), *n.* **Carl,** 1878-1967, American poet and biographer.

sand dollar, any of various small, flat, round sea urchins that live on sandy ocean bottoms.

sand er (san′dər), *n.* person or apparatus that sands or sandpapers.

sand flea, 1 any flea found in sandy places. 2 chigoe. 3 beach flea.

sand fly, a small, bloodsucking, two-winged fly that transmits diseases.

sand glass (sand′glas′), *n.* hourglass.

sand hog (sand′hog′, sand′hôg′), *n.* U.S. person who works either underground, as in a boring for a tunnel, or underwater, as in a caisson.

San Di e go (san dē ā′gō), seaport in SW California. 697,000.

sand lot (sand′lot′), *adj.* U.S. of or having to do with games, especially baseball, played on undeveloped city lots, small fields, etc.

sand man (sand′man′), *n.* a fabled man said to make children sleepy by sprinkling sand on their eyes.

hat, āge, fär; let, ēqual, tėrm;
it, īce; hot, ōpen, ôrder;
oil, out; cup, půt, rüle;
ch, child; ng, long; sh, she;
th, thin; ᴛʜ, then; zh, measure;

ə represents *a* in about, *e* in taken, *i* in pencil, *o* in lemon, *u* in circus.

< = from, derived from, taken from.

sand pa per (sand′pā′pər), *n.* a strong paper with a layer of sand or a similar abrasive substance glued on it, used for smoothing, cleaning, or polishing. *—v.t.* smooth, clean, or polish with sandpaper.

sandpiper
about 7 in. long

sand pip er (sand′pī′pər), *n.* any of various small, long-billed shore birds similar to the plovers.

sand stone (sand′stōn′), *n.* a sedimentary rock formed by the consolidation of sand and held together by a natural cement such as silica or iron oxide.

sand storm (sand′stôrm′), *n.* windstorm that carries along clouds of sand.

sand table, sandbox on legs.

sand trap, a shallow pit filled with sand on a golf course, usually near a green and serving as a hazard.

sand wich (sand′wich), *n.* 1 two or more slices of bread with meat, jelly, cheese, or some other filling between them. 2 something formed by similar arrangement. *—v.t.* put in or squeeze (between): *be sandwiched between two parked cars.* [< the fourth Earl of *Sandwich,* 1718-1792]

sandwich board, board carried by a sandwich man.

Sandwich Islands, former name of the **Hawaiian Islands.**

sandwich man, man carrying two advertising boards hung from his shoulders, one before him and one behind.

sand wort (sand′wėrt′), *n.* any of a genus of low, scrubby pinks which grow in sandy soil and bear very small white flowers.

sand y (san′dē), *adj.,* **sand i er, sand i est.** 1 containing sand; consisting of sand: *sandy soil.* 2 covered with sand: *a sandy coast.* 3 yellowish-red: *sandy hair.* **—sand′i-ness,** *n.*

sane (sān), *adj.,* **san er, san est.** 1 having a healthy mind; not crazy; rational. 2 having or showing good sense; sensible. [< Latin *sanus* healthy] **—sane′ly,** *adv.* **—sane′ness,** *n.*

San Fran cis co (san frən sis′kō), seaport in W California. 716,000.

San Francisco Bay, inlet of the Pacific on which San Francisco and Oakland, California, are located. 50 mi. long; 3-12 mi. wide.

sang (sang), *v.* pt. of **sing.**

Sang er (sang′ər), *n.* **Margaret,** 1883-1966, American nurse who pioneered in the birth-control movement.

sang-froid (sang frwä′; *French* säɴ frwä′), *n.* coolness of mind; calmness; composure. [< French *sang froid,* literally, cold blood]

san gui nar y (sang′gwə ner′ē), *adj.* 1 with much blood or bloodshed; bloody: *a sanguinary battle.* 2 delighting in bloodshed; bloodthirsty. [< Latin *sanguinarius* < *sanguinem* blood] **—san′gui nar′i ly,** *adv.* **—san′gui nar′i ness,** *n.*

san guine (sang′gwən), *adj.* 1 naturally cheerful and hopeful: *a sanguine disposition.* 2 confident; hopeful: *sanguine of success.* 3 having a healthy red color; ruddy: *a sanguine complexion.* 4 (in old physiology) having an active circulation, a ruddy color, and a cheerful and ardent disposition. 5 sanguinary. [< Latin *sanguineus* < *sanguinem* blood] **—san′guine ly,** *adv.* **—san′guine ness,** *n.*

san guin e ous (sang gwin′ē əs), *adj.* 1 of blood; like blood; bloody. 2 red like blood. 3 sanguine; hopeful. 4 bloodthirsty.

San hed rin (san hed′rən), *n.* the supreme council and highest religious and legal authority of the ancient Jewish nation. [< Late Hebrew *sanhedrīn* < Greek *synedrion* council, literally, a sitting together < *syn-* together + *hedra* seat]

san i tar i um (san′ə ter′ē əm), *n., pl.* **-tar i ums, -tar i a** (-ter′ē ə). sanatorium.

san i tar y (san′ə ter′ē), *adj.* 1 of or having to do with health; favorable to health; preventing disease; hygienic: *sanitary regulations.* 2 free from dirt and filth. [< French *sanitaire,* ultimately < Latin *sanus* healthy] **—san′i tar′i ly,** *adv.* **—san′i tar′i ness,** *n.*

sanitary napkin, a soft, absorbent pad used to absorb the uterine discharge during menstruation.

san i ta tion (san′ə tā′shən), *n.* the working out and practical application of sanitary measures, such as disposal of sewage and government inspection of foods.

san i tize (san′ə tīz), *v.t.,* **-tized, -tiz ing.** make sanitary; disinfect.

san i ty (san′ə tē), *n.* 1 soundness of mind; mental health. 2 soundness of judgment; sensibleness. [< Latin *sanitas* < *sanus* healthy]

San Joa quin River (san wä kēn′), river in central California that meets the Sacramento River at its mouth. 350 mi.

San Jo se (san hō zā′), city in W California. 446,000.

San Jo sé (san hō zā′; *Spanish* säng hōsä′), capital of Costa Rica, in the central part. 183,000.

San Jose scale, a scale insect very injurious to fruit trees, shrubs, etc.

San Juan (san wän′), seaport and capital of Puerto Rico, in the NE part. 453,000.

sank (sangk), *v.* pt. of **sink.**

San Ma ri no (sän mə rē′nō), 1 small country in the NE part of the Italian peninsula. 19,000 pop.; 24 sq. mi. 2 its capital. 4000.

San Ma te o (san mə tā′ō), city in W California, near San Francisco. 79,000.

sans (sanz; *French* säɴ), *prep.* without: *a wallet sans cash, print a letter sans comment.* [< Old French < Latin *absentia* in the absence (of); influenced by Latin *sine* without]

San Sal va dor (san sal′və dôr), 1 island of the central Bahamas, the first land in the New World seen by Columbus in 1492. 1000 pop.; 60 sq. mi. Also, **Watling Island.** 2 capital of El Salvador, in the central part. 341,000.

sans-cu lotte (sanz′kyə lot′), *n.* 1 (in the French Revolution) a contemptuous term for a republican of the poorer class, adopted by the revolutionists as a designation of honor. 2 any extreme republican or revolutionary. [< French, literally, without knee breeches]

San Se bas tián (sän sā′vä styän′), seaport in N Spain, on the Bay of Biscay. 162,000.

San sei (sän′sā′), *n., pl.* **-sei.** a native-born United States or Canadian citizen whose grandparents were Japanese immigrants. [< Japanese *sansei* third generation]

San skrit or **San scrit** (san′skrit), *n.* the ancient sacred and literary language of India. [< Sanskrit *saṃskṛta* prepared, cultivated]

sans-ser if (sanz′ser′if, san ser′if), *n.* (in printing) any of various styles of type without serifs.

sans sou ci (säɴ sü sē′), FRENCH. without care or worry.

San ta (*n.* san′tə; *adj.* san′tə, sän′tä), *n.* Santa Claus. *—adj.* a Spanish or an Italian word meaning *holy* or *saint,* used in combinations, as in *Santa Maria.*

San ta An a (san′tə an′ə), 1 city in SW California. 157,000. 2 city in W El Salvador. 121,000. 3 Santa Anna.

San ta An na (san′tə an′ə; sän′tä ä′nä), **Antonio López de,** 1795-1876, Mexican general and politician, whose army defeated the Texans at the Alamo.

San ta Bar bar a (san′tə bär′bər ə), city on the SW coast of California. 70,000.

Santa Barbara Islands, chain of islands in the Pacific, south of Santa Barbara, California, and a part of California.

San ta Cat a li na (san′tə kat′l ē′nə). See **Catalina.**

San ta Cla ra (san′tə klar′ə), city in W California, near San Francisco. 88,000.

San ta Claus (san′tə klôz′), the saint of Christmas giving, Saint Nicholas, according to modern conception a jolly old man with a white beard, dressed in a fur-trimmed red suit. [< dialectal Dutch *Sante Klaas* Saint Nicholas]

San ta Cruz de Ten e rife (san′tə krüz′ də ten′ə rif′), seaport in the Canary Islands. 181,000.

San ta Fe (san′tə fā′), 1 capital of New Mexico, in the N part. 41,000. 2 city in E central Argentina. 209,000.

Santa Fe Trail, an early trade route between Independence, Missouri, and Santa Fe, New Mexico. See **Oregon Trail** for map.

San ta I sa bel (sän′tä ē sä vel′), capital of Equatorial Guinea, a seaport on the island of Fernando Po. 20,000.

San ta Ma ri a (san′tə mə rē′ə), flagship of Columbus on his voyage of 1492.

San ta Mon i ca (san′tə mon′ə kə), city on the SW coast of California, near Los Angeles. 88,000.

San ta ya na (sän′tə yä′nə), *n.* **George,** 1863-1952, American philosopher, poet, and essayist, born in Spain.

San ti a go (san′tē ä′gō; *Spanish* säntyä′gō), *n.* capital of Chile, in the central part. 3,120,000.

San tia go de Cu ba (sän tyä′gō ᴛʜā kü′vä), seaport in SE Cuba. 250,000.

San to Do min go (san′tō də ming′gō), capital of the Dominican Republic, in the S part. It was established in 1496 and was the first town founded by Europeans in the Western Hemisphere. Former name, **Ciudad Trujillo.** 655,000.

San tos (sän′tōs), *n.* seaport in S Brazil. 262,000.

São Fran cis co River (souɴ fränsē′skü), river flowing from SE Brazil into the Atlantic. 1800 mi.

Saône River (sōn), river in E France. 300 mi.

São Pau lo (souɴ pou′lü), city in S Brazil. 5,902,000.

São Sal va dor (souɴ säl′və dōr′), Salvador (def. 1).

sap¹ (sap), *n.* 1 the vital liquid that circulates through a vascular plant, carrying water and dissolved minerals upward through the plant, and water and dissolved food downward. 2 any life-giving liquid. 3 sapwood. 4 SLANG. fool. [Old English *sæp*]

sap² (sap), *v.,* **sapped, sap ping,** *n.* *—v.t.* 1 dig under or wear away the foundation of: *The walls of the boathouse had been sapped by the waves.* 2 weaken; use up: *The extreme heat sapped our strength.* 3 approach (an enemy's position) by means of covered trenches. *—v.i.* dig or use protected trenches. *—n.* 1 trench protected by the earth dug up; trench dug to approach the enemy's position. 2 the making of trenches to approach a besieged place or an enemy's position. [< Middle French *sapper* < *sappe* spade < Italian *zappa*]

sa pi ence (sā′pē əns), *n.* wisdom.

sa pi ent (sā′pē ənt), *adj.* wise; sage. [< Latin *sapientem*] **—sa′pi ent ly,** *adv.*

sap less (sap′lis), *adj.* 1 without sap; withered. 2 without energy or vigor.

sap ling (sap′ling), *n.* 1 a young tree. 2 a young person.

sap o dil la (sap′ə dil′ə), *n.* 1 a large evergreen tree of tropical America that yields chicle and bears large, brownish berries tasting like pears. 2 its fruit. [< Mexican Spanish *zapotilla*]

sap o na ceous (sap′ə nā′shəs), *adj.* soapy.

sa pon i fi ca tion (sə pon′ə fə kā′shən), *n.* 1 process of saponifying. 2 condition of being saponified.

sa pon i fy (sə pon′ə fī), *v.,* **-fied, -fy ing.** *—v.t.* 1 make (a fat or oil) into soap by treating with an alkali. 2 decompose (an ester) into an alcohol and a salt of an acid by treating with an alkali. *—v.i.* become soap. [< New Latin *saponificare* < Latin *saponem* soap + *facere* to make] **—sa pon′i fi′a ble,** *adj.* **—sa pon′i fi′er,** *n.*

sap per (sap′ər), *n.* soldier employed in the construction of fortifications or the detection and disarmament of land mines. [< *sap²*]

Sap phic (saf′ik), *adj.* 1 of or having to do with Sappho. 2 having to do with certain meters, or a four-line stanza form, used by or named after her. *—n.* a Sapphic stanza or strophe.

sap phire (saf′īr), *n.* 1 a clear, hard, bright-blue variety of corundum. Sapphires are valued as precious stones. 2 a bright blue. *—adj.* bright-blue. [< Greek *sappheiros* < Hebrew *sappīr* < Sanskrit *śani- priya* sapphire; originally, dear to the planet Saturn]

Sap pho (saf′ō), *n.* Greek lyric poet of Lesbos who lived about 600 B.C. Later poets imitated her meters, or stanza, called the Sapphic.

sap py (sap′ē), *adj.,* **-pi er, -pi est.** 1 full of sap; juicy. 2 SLANG. silly; foolish. **—sap′pi ness,** *n.*

sa proph a gous (sə prof′ə gəs), *adj.* saprophytic.

sap ro phyte (sap′rō fīt), *n.* any plant that

lives on decaying organic matter. Certain fungi are saprophytes. [< Greek *sapros* rotten + English *-phyte*]

sap ro phyt ic (sap′rō fit′ik), *adj.* of or like a saprophyte; living on decaying organic matter. **—sap′ro phyt′i cal ly,** *adv.*

sapsucker
about 8 in. long

sap suck er (sap′suk′ər), *n.* a small American woodpecker that feeds on the sap of trees.

sap wood (sap′wu̇d′), *n.* the soft, new, living wood between the cambium and the heartwood of most trees.

sar a band (sar′ə band), *n.* 1 a slow and stately Spanish dance in triple time, popular in the 1600's and 1700's. 2 music for it. [< French *sarabande* < Spanish *zarabanda*]

Sar a cen (sar′ə sən), *n.* 1 an Arab. 2 a Moslem at the time of the Crusades. 3 a member of the nomadic tribes of the Syrian and Arabian desert at the time of the Roman Empire. *—adj.* Saracenic.

Sar a cen ic (sar′ə sen′ik), *adj.* of or having to do with the Saracens.

Sar a gos sa (sar′ə gos′ə), *n.* city in NE Spain. 439,000. Also, SPANISH **Zaragoza.**

Sar ah (ser′ə), *n.* (in the Bible) the wife of Abraham and the mother of Isaac.

Sa ra je vo (sär′ə yä′vō, sär′ä ye vō), *n.* city in central Yugoslavia, scene of the assassination of the Austrian archduke Francis Ferdinand in 1914, which brought on World War I. 175,000. Also, **Serajevo.**

sa ran (sə ran′), *n.* a thermoplastic resin produced as a fiber, film, or molded form and highly resistant to damage and soiling, used especially to package food.

sa ra pe (sə rä′pē), *n.* serape.

Sar a to ga Springs (sar′ə tō′gə), city and health resort in E New York State. 19,000.

Saratoga trunk, kind of large trunk formerly much used by women. [< *Saratoga (Springs)*]

Sa ra tov (sä rä′tôf), *n.* city in SW Soviet Union, on the Volga River. 758,000.

Sa ra wak (sə rä′wäk, sə rä′wək, sə rä′wə), *n.* state of Malaysia, located in NW Borneo. It was formerly a British colony. 934,000 pop.; 48,300 sq. mi. *Capital:* Kuching.

sar casm (sär′kaz′əm), *n.* 1 a sneering or cutting remark; ironical taunt. 2 act of making fun of a person to hurt his feelings; harsh or bitter irony: *"How unselfish you are!" said the girl in sarcasm as her brother took the biggest piece of cake.* [< Greek *sarkasmos* < *sarkazein* to sneer, strip off flesh < *sarkos* flesh] ➜ See **irony** for usage note.

sar cas tic (sär kas′tik), *adj.* using sarcasm; sneering; cutting: *"Don't hurry!" was his sarcastic comment as I began to dress at my usual slow rate.* **—sar cas′ti cal ly,** *adv.*

sarce net (särs′net), *n.* a soft, thin silk fabric. Also, **sarsenet.** [< Anglo-French *sarzinett,* diminutive of *Sarzin* Saracen]

sar co din i an (sär′kō din′ē ən), *n.* rhizopod.

sar co ma (sär kō′mə), *n., pl.* **-mas, -ma ta** (-mə tə). any of various cancers originating in tissue that is not epithelial, chiefly connective tissue. [< New Latin < Greek *sarkōma,* ultimately < *sarkos* flesh]

sar coph a gus (sär kof′ə gəs), *n., pl.* **-gi** (-jī), **-gus es.** a stone coffin, especially one ornamented with sculpture or inscriptions. [< Greek *sarkophagos,* originally, flesh-eating (stone) < *sarkos* flesh + *phagein* eat]

sard (särd), *n.* a brownish-red variety of chalcedony, used in jewelry. [< Latin *sarda*]

sar dine (sär dēn′), *n., pl.* **-dines** or **-dine.** 1 a young pilchard preserved in oil for food. 2 any of certain similar small fish prepared in the same way. 3 **packed like sardines,** very much crowded. [< Latin *sardina* < Greek *sardēnē,* probably originally, Sardinian fish]

Sar din i a (sär din′ē ə), *n.* 1 large Italian island in the Mediterranean Sea, west of the Italian peninsula. 1,448,000 pop.; 9300 sq. mi. 2 former kingdom (1720-1860) that included this island, Savoy, Piedmont, and eventually most of the Italian mainland. **—Sar din′i an,** *adj., n.*

Sar dis (sär′dis), *n.* capital of ancient Lydia.

sar don ic (sär don′ik), *adj.* bitterly sarcastic, scornful, or mocking: *a sardonic outlook.* [< Greek *sardonios,* alteration of *sardanios,* perhaps influenced by *sardonion,* a supposed Sardinian plant that produced hysterical convulsions] **—sar don′i cal ly,** *adv.*

sar don yx (sär don′iks, särd′n iks), *n.* variety of onyx containing layers of sard. [< Greek, probably < *sardios* sard + *onyx* onyx]

sar gas so (sär gas′ō), *n., pl.* **-sos.** any of a genus of olive-brown seaweeds that have berrylike air bladders and float in large masses. [< Portuguese]

Sar gas so Sea (sär gas′ō), part of the Atlantic extending from the West Indies northeast to the Azores.

Sar gent (sär′jənt), *n.* **John Singer,** 1856-1925, American portrait painter.

Sar gon II (sär′gon), died 705 B.C., king of Assyria from 722 to 705 B.C.

sa ri (sär′ē), *n.* the principal outer garment of Hindu women, a long piece of cotton or silk wrapped around the body, with one end falling nearly to the feet and the other end thrown over the head or shoulder. [< Hindi *sārī* < Sanskrit *śāṭī*]

Sark (särk), *n.* one of the Channel Islands. 1000 pop.; 2 sq. mi.

sa rong (sə rông′, sə rong′), *n.* a rectangular piece of cloth, usually a brightly colored printed material, worn as a skirt by men and women in the Malay Archipelago and certain other islands of the Pacific. [< Malay *sārung*]

Sa roy an (sə roi′ən), *n.* **William,** born 1908, American playwright and short-story writer.

sar sa pa ril la (sas′pə ril′ə, sär′sə pə-ril′ə), *n.* 1 any of various species of tropical American climbing or trailing greenbriers. 2 the dried roots of any of these plants, formerly used in medicine. 3 a soft drink, usually carbonated, flavored with the root of any of these plants. [< Spanish *zarzaparilla*]

sarse net (särs′net), *n.* sarcenet.

Sar to (sär′tō), *n.* **Andrea del.** See **Andrea del Sarto.**

sar to ri al (sär tôr′ē əl, sär tōr′ē əl), *adj.* of tailors or their work: *His clothes were a sartorial triumph.* [< Latin *sartorius,* ultimately < *sarcire* to patch] **—sar to′ri al ly,** *adv.*

hat, āge, fär; let, ēqual, tėrm;
it, īce; hot, ōpen, ôrder;
oil, out; cup, pu̇t, rüle;
ch, child; ng, long; sh, she;
th, thin; ᴛʜ, then; zh, measure;

ə represents *a* in about, *e* in taken, *i* in pencil, *o* in lemon, *u* in circus.

< = from, derived from, taken from.

Sar tre (sär′trə), *n.* **Jean-Paul,** born 1905, French philosopher, novelist, and playwright.

sash[1] (sash), *n.* a long, broad strip of cloth or ribbon, worn as an ornament round the waist or over one shoulder. [< Arabic *shāsh* muslin cloth]

sash[2] (sash), *n.* 1 frame for the glass of a window or door. 2 part or parts of a window that can be moved to open or close a window. [alteration of *chassis,* taken as plural]

sa shay (sa shā′), *v.i.* INFORMAL. glide, move, or go about. [alteration of *chassé* a gliding dance step < French]

Sask., Saskatchewan.

Sa skatch e wan (sa skach′ə won), *n.* 1 province in S central Canada. 927,000 pop.; 251,700 sq. mi. *Capital:* Regina. Abbrev.: Sask. 2 **Saskatchewan River,** river flowing from SW Canada into Lake Winnipeg. 1205 mi.

Sas ka toon (sas′kə tün′), *n.* city in S central Saskatchewan, Canada. 125,000.

sass (sas), INFORMAL. *—n.* rudeness; back talk; impudence. *—v.t.* be saucy to. *—v.i.* talk rudely or impudently. [variant of *sauce*]

sas sa fras (sas′ə fras), *n.* 1 a slender eastern North American tree of the same family as the laurel, having fragrant, yellow flowers, bluish-black fruit, and soft, light wood. 2 the aromatic dried bark of its root, used in medicine and to flavor candy, soft drinks, etc. [< Spanish *sasafrás*]

sari sarong

sas sy (sas′ē), *adj.,* **-si er, -si est.** saucy. **—sas′si ly,** *adv.* **—sas′si ness,** *n.*

sat (sat), *v.* a pt. and a pp. of **sit.**

Sat., Saturday.

Sa tan (sāt′n), *n.* the evil spirit; the enemy of goodness; the Devil. [< Hebrew *ṣāṭān* adversary]

sa tan ic or **Sa tan ic** (sā tan′ik, sə-tan′ik), *adj.* of Satan; like Satan; like that of Satan; very wicked. **—sa tan′i cal ly,** *adv.*

satch el (sach′əl), *n.* a small bag for carrying clothes, books, etc.; handbag. [< Old French *sachel* < Latin *saccellus,* diminutive of *saccus* sack[1]]

sate (sāt), *v.t.,* **sat ed, sat ing.** 1 satisfy fully (any appetite or desire): *A long drink sated my thirst.* 2 supply with more than enough, so as to disgust or weary. See **satiate** for synonym study. [alteration of *sade* (Old English *sadian* to glut) under influence of Latin *satiare* satiate]

sa teen (sa tēn′), *n.* a cotton cloth made to imitate satin, often used for lining sleeves. [variant of *satin*]

sat el lite (sat′l īt), *n.* 1 a heavenly body that revolves around a planet, especially around one of the nine major planets of the solar system. The moon is a satellite of the earth. 2 artificial satellite. 3 follower of or attendant upon a person of importance. 4 a subservient follower. 5 country nominally independent but actually controlled by a more powerful country, especially a country under the control of the Soviet Union. *—adj.* of, having to do with, or of the nature of a satellite. [< Latin *satellitem* attendant]

sa ti a ble (sā′shē ə bəl, sā′shə bəl), *adj.* that can be satiated.

sa ti ate (*v.* sā′shē āt; *adj.* sā′shē it), *v.,* **-at ed, -at ing,** *adj.* *—v.t.* 1 feed fully; satisfy fully. 2 weary or disgust with too much. See synonym study below. *—adj.* filled to satiety; satiated. [< Latin *satiatum* satisfied < *satis* enough] **—sa′ti a′tion,** *n.*

Syn. *v.t.* 2 **Satiate, sate, surfeit** mean to fill with more than enough to satisfy. **Satiate** means to feed a person, mind, etc., to the point where something that did please or was wanted no longer gives pleasure: *Children who are given as much candy as they want soon become satiated.* **Sate** usually means to satisfy a desire so fully that it dies: *sate the desire for power.* **Surfeit** means to supply to the point of being sick or disgusted: *This season audiences have really become surfeited with Tschaikowsky.*

sa ti e ty (sə tī′ə tē), *n.* the feeling of having had too much; disgust or weariness caused by excess; satiated condition.

sat in (sat′n), *n.* a silk, rayon, nylon, or cotton cloth with one very smooth, glossy side. *—adj.* of or like satin; smooth and glossy. [< Old French < Arabic *zaitūnī* from *Zaitūn,* a seaport in China in medieval times]

sat i net or **sat i nette** (sat′n et′), *n.* 1 fabric woven with a cotton warp and woolen woof and having a satiny surface. 2 a thin satin.

sat in wood (sat′n wu̇d′), *n.* 1 the smooth, yellowish-brown wood of an East Indian tree of the same family as the mahogany, used to ornament furniture. 2 the tree itself.

sat in y (sat′n ē), *adj.* like satin in smoothness and gloss.

sat ire (sat′īr), *n.* 1 use of sarcasm, irony, or wit to attack or ridicule a habit, idea, custom, etc. 2 poem, essay, story, etc., that attacks or ridicules in this way: *Some of Aesop's "Fables" are satires.* [< Latin *satira,* variant of *(lanx) satura* medley, mixed (dish), related to *satis* enough] ➤ See **irony** for usage note.

sa tir ic (sə tir′ik), *adj.* satirical.

sa tir i cal (sə tir′ə kəl), *adj.* of satire; containing satire; fond of using satire. **—sa tir′i cal ly,** *adv.*

sat ir ist (sat′ər ist), *n.* writer of satires; person who uses satire. The follies and vices of their own times are the chief subjects of satirists.

sat i rize (sat′ə rīz′), *v.t.,* **-rized, -riz ing.** attack with satire; criticize with mockery; seek to improve by ridicule.

sat is fac tion (sat′i sfak′shən), *n.* 1 act of satisfying; fulfillment of conditions or desires: *The satisfaction of hunger requires food.* 2 condition of being satisfied, or pleased and contented: *She felt satisfaction at winning a prize.* 3 anything that makes a person feel pleased or contented. 4 payment of debt; the discharge of an obligation or claim; making up for a wrong or injury done. 5 **give satisfaction, a** satisfy. **b** fight a duel because of an insult.

sat is fac tor y (sat′i sfak′tər ē), *adj.* good enough to satisfy; satisfying. **—sat′is fac′tor i ly,** *adv.* **—sat′is fac′tor i ness,** *n.*

sat is fy (sat′i sfī), *v.,* **-fied, -fy ing.** *—v.t.* 1 give enough to (a person); meet or fulfill (desires, hopes, demands, etc.); put an end to (needs, wants, etc.): *satisfy hunger.* See synonym study below. 2 meet fully (an objection, doubt, demand, etc.). 3 make right; pay: *satisfy all claims for damages.* 4 set free from doubt or uncertainty; convince: *I was satisfied that it was an accident.* 5 fulfill the conditions of (a law, mathematical equation, etc.). *—v.i.* 1 make contented; please. 2 make up for a wrong or injury. 3 give satisfaction. [< Middle French *satisfier* < Latin *satisfacere* < *satis* enough + *facere* to do] **—sat′is fi′a ble,** *adj.* **—sat′is fi′er,** *n.* **—sat′is fy′ing ly,** *adv.*

Syn. *v.t.* 1 **Satisfy, content** mean to meet a person's desires and wants. **Satisfy** means to give enough to fulfill a person's desires, hopes, needs, etc.: *The little mongrel satisfied the boy's desire for a dog.* **Content** means to give enough to keep a person from being unhappy: *A letter from her daughter once a week contented her.*

sa trap (sā′trap, sat′rap), *n.* 1 ruler, often a tyrant, who is subordinate to a higher ruler. 2 governor of a province under the ancient Persian monarchy. [< Greek *satrapēs* < Old Persian *xšathra-pāwan* guardian of the realm]

sa trap y (sā′trə pē, sat′rə pē), *n., pl.* **-trap ies.** province or authority of a satrap.

sat ur a ble (sach′ər ə bəl), *adj.* that can be saturated.

sat u rate (sach′ə rāt′), *v.t.,* **-rat ed, -rat ing.** 1 soak thoroughly; fill full: *During the fog, the air was saturated with moisture.* 2 cause (a substance) to unite with the greatest possible amount of another substance. A saturated solution of sugar or salt is one that cannot dissolve any more sugar or salt. [< Latin *saturatum* filled < *satur* full] **—sat′u rat′er, sat′u ra′tor,** *n.*

sat u rat ed (sach′ə rā′tid), *adj.* 1 soaked thoroughly; wet. 2 (of colors) containing no white; of the greatest intensity. 3 in chemistry: **a** that has combined with or taken up in solution the largest possible proportion of some other substance: *When the relative humidity reaches 100 per cent the air is saturated.* **b** (of an organic compound) lacking double or triple bonds and having no free valence, as methane, ethane, propane, etc.

saturated fat, solid or semisolid animal fat, such as butter and lard, that contains mainly saturated fatty acids.

sat u ra tion (sach′ə rā′shən), *n.* 1 act or process of saturating. 2 fact of being saturated; saturated condition. The saturation of a color increases as the amount of white in it is decreased.

saturation point, 1 point at which a substance will combine with or take up in solution no more of another substance. 2 condition in which a person can endure no more.

Sat ur day (sat′ər dē, sat′ər dā), *n.* the seventh day of the week, following Friday. [Old English *Sæterdæg, Sæternesdæg,* translation of Latin *Saturni dies* day of Saturn (the planet)]

Sat urn (sat′ərn), *n.* 1 (in Roman myths) the god of agriculture, identified with the Greek Cronus. Saturn ruled during a golden age. 2 the second largest planet in the solar system and the sixth in distance from the sun. Saturn is encircled by a system of three rings made up of fine particles of matter.

sat ur na li a (sat′ər nā′lē ə, sat′ər nā′lyə), *n.pl. or sing.* 1 period of unrestrained revelry and license. 2 **Saturnalia,** the ancient Roman festival of Saturn, celebrated in December with much feasting and merrymaking. [< Latin]

sat ur na li an (sat′ər nā′lē ən, sat′ər nā′lyən), *adj.* 1 riotously merry; reveling without restraint. 2 **Saturnalian,** of or having to do with the Roman Saturnalia.

Sa tur ni an (sə tėr′nē ən), *adj.* 1 of or having to do with the god Saturn or his reign. 2 prosperous, happy, or peaceful. 3 of or having to do with the planet Saturn.

sat ur nine (sat′ər nīn), *adj.* gloomy; grave; taciturn. [< *Saturn;* those born under the planet's sign are supposed to be morose] **—sat′ur nine′ly,** *adv.*

satyr (def. 1)

sa tyr (sā′tər, sat′ər), *n.* 1 (in Greek myths) a deity of the woods, part man and part goat or horse. The satyrs were merry, riotous followers of Bacchus, the god of wine. 2 man who is beastly in thought and action; lecherous man. 3 any of a family of brown or grayish butterflies having eyespots on the wings. [< Greek *satyros*]

sa tyr ic (sə tir′ik), *adj.* of or having to do with a satyr or satyrs.

sa tyr i cal (sə tir′ə kəl), *adj.* satyric.

sauce (sôs), *n., v.,* **sauced, sauc ing.** *—n.* 1 any of various preparations, usually liquid or soft, served with food to make it taste better: *cranberry sauce, mint sauce, spaghetti sauce.* 2 U.S. stewed fruit. 3 something that adds interest or relish. 4 INFORMAL. sauciness; impertinence. *—v.t.* 1 prepare with sauce; season. 2 give interest or flavor to. 3 INFORMAL. be saucy to. [< Old French < Latin *salsa,* salted, ultimately < *sal* salt]

sauce pan (sôs′pan′), *n.* a metal dish with a handle, used for stewing, boiling, etc.

sau cer (sô′sər), *n.* 1 a small, shallow dish to set a cup on. 2 a small, round dish with its edge curved up. 3 something round and shallow like a saucer. [< Old French *saucier* sauce dish < *sauce.* See SAUCE.] **—sau′cer like′,** *adj.*

sau cy (sô′sē), *adj.,* **-ci er, -ci est.** 1 showing lack of respect; impudent; rude. See **impertinent** for synonym study. 2 pert; smart: *a saucy hat.* [< *sauce*] **—sau′ci ly,** *adv.* **—sau′ci ness,** *n.*

hat, āge, fär; let, ēqual, tėrm;
it, īce; hot, ōpen, ôrder;
oil, out; cup, pu̇t, rüle;
ch, child; ng, long; sh, she;
th, thin; ᴛʜ, then; zh, measure;

ə represents *a* in about, *e* in taken, *i* in pencil, *o* in lemon, *u* in circus.

< = from, derived from, taken from.

Sa u di (sä ü′dē, sou′dē), *adj.* of or having to do with Saudi Arabia. *—n.* native or inhabitant of Saudi Arabia.

Saudi Arabia, country in central Arabia. 7,500,000 pop.; 875,000 sq. mi. *Capitals:* Riyadh and Mecca. **—Saudi Arabian.**

sauer bra ten (sour′brät′n), *n.* a pot roast marinated in vinegar and herbs before cooking. [< German *Sauerbraten* < *sauer* sour + *Braten* roast meat]

sauer kraut (sour′krout′), *n.* cabbage cut fine, salted, and allowed to ferment. [< German *Sauerkraut* < *sauer* sour + *Kraut* cabbage]

Sauk (sôk), *n., pl.* **Sauks** or **Sauk.** member of a tribe of Algonquian Indians who formerly lived west of Lake Michigan and now live in Oklahoma, Iowa, and Kansas. Also, **Sac.**

Saul (sôl), *n.* in the Bible: 1 the first king of Israel. 2 the original name of the apostle Paul.

Sault Sainte Ma rie or **Sault Ste. Marie** (sü′ sänt mə rē′), 1 rapids of St. Marys River, between NE Michigan and Ontario, Canada. 2 Soo Locks.

sau na (sou′nə), *n.* 1 a steam bath in which the steam is produced by water thrown on hot stones. 2 building or room used for such steam baths. [< Finnish]

saun ter (sôn′tər, sän′tər), *v.i.* walk along slowly and happily; stroll: *saunter in the park.* *—n.* 1 a leisurely or careless gait. 2 a stroll. [origin uncertain] **—saun′ter er,** *n.*

sau ri an (sôr′ē ən), *n.* 1 lizard. 2 any similar reptile, such as a crocodile or dinosaur. *—adj.* belonging to or having to do with the saurians. [< Greek *sauros* lizard]

sau ris chi an (sô ris′kē ən), *n.* any of an order of dinosaurs having a hip structure similar to that of modern lizards, including members of the sauropod and theropod suborders. *—adj.* of or belonging to this order. [< Greek *sauros* lizard + Greek *ischion* hip]

sau ro pod (sôr′ə pod), *n.* any of a suborder of herbivorous dinosaurs with a small head and long neck and tail, comprising the largest land animals known. *—adj.* of or belonging to this suborder. [< Greek *sauros* lizard + *podos* foot]

sau sage (sô′sij), *n.* chopped meat, most commonly pork or a combination of pork, beef, or other meats, seasoned and usually stuffed into a very thin casing. [< Old North French *saussiche* < Late Latin *salsicia,* ultimately < Latin *sal* salt]

sau té (sō tā′, sô tā′), *adj., n., v.* *—adj.* cooked or browned in a little fat, usually quickly and often over a hot fire. *—n.* dish of food cooked or browned in a little fat. *—v.t.* fry quickly in a little fat. [< French, past participle of *sauter* to jump < Latin *saltare*]

sau terne (sō tėrn′), *n.* a sweet French white wine. [< *Sauternes,* town in France, where the grapes are grown]

sav a ble (sā′və bəl), *adj.* that can be saved. Also, **saveable.**

sav age (sav′ij), *adj., n., v.,* **-aged, -ag ing.** *—adj.* 1 not civilized; barbarous: *savage customs.* 2 violently aggressive; fiercely cruel or brutal: *a savage dog.* See **fierce** for synonym study. 3 wild or rugged: *savage mountain scenery.* 4 undomesticated; untamed. 5 furiously angry; enraged. *—n.* 1 member of a primitive, uncivilized people who live in the lowest stage of cultural development. 2 a fierce, brutal, or cruel person. 3 person ignorant or neglectful of the rules of good manners. *—v.t.* attack with violence; assault ferociously. [< Old French *sauvage* < Late Latin *salvaticus,* ultimately < Latin *silva* forest] **—sav′age ly,** *adv.* **—sav′age ness,** *n.*

sav age ry (sav′ij rē), *n., pl.* **-ries.** 1 a being fierce; cruelty; brutality. 2 wildness. 3 an uncivilized condition.

sav ag ism (sav′ə jiz′əm), *n.* savagery.

sa van na or **sa van nah** (sə van′ə), *n.* 1 a treeless plain in the southeastern United States or tropical America. 2 grassland with scattered trees between the equatorial forests and the hot deserts in either hemisphere. [< Spanish *sabana* < Carib]

Sa van nah (sə van′ə), *n.* 1 seaport in E Georgia. 118,000. 2 **Savannah River,** river flowing SE between South Carolina and Georgia into the Atlantic. 314 mi.

sa vant (sə vänt′, sav′ənt), *n.* man of learning; sage; scholar. [< French, present participle of *savoir* know < Latin *sapere* be wise]

save¹ (sāv), *v.,* **saved, sav ing,** *n.* *—v.t.* 1 make safe from harm, danger, loss, etc.; rescue: *save a drowning man.* 2 keep safe from harm, danger, hurt, loss, etc.; protect: *save face.* 3 lay aside; store up: *save money.* 4 keep from spending or wasting: *Save your strength.* 5 make less; prevent: *save work, save trouble, save expense.* 6 treat carefully to lessen wear, weariness, etc.: *Large print saves one's eyes.* 7 prevent the loss of: *Another goal will save the game.* 8 set free from sin and its results. *—v.i.* 1 keep a person or thing from harm, danger, loss, etc. 2 lay up money; add to one's property. 3 avoid expense or waste: *She saves in every way she can.* *—n.* 1 act of saving. 2 (in sports) a play that prevents the opponents from scoring or winning. [< Old French *sauver* < Late Latin *salvare* < Latin *salvus* safe] **—sav′er,** *n.*

save² (sāv), *prep.* except; but: *work every day save Sundays.* *—conj.* 1 excepting. 2 ARCHAIC. unless. [variant of *safe,* in sense of "not being involved"]

save a ble (sā′və bəl), *adj.* savable.

sav in or **sav ine** (sav′ən), *n.* 1 a juniper shrub whose tops yield an oily drug used in medicine. 2 this drug. 3 any of various junipers, such as the red cedar. [ultimately < Latin *(herba) Sabina* Sabine (herb)]

sav ing (sā′ving), *adj.* 1 that saves; preserving. 2 tending to save up money; avoiding waste; economical. 3 making a reservation: *a saving clause.* 4 compensating; redeeming. *—n.* 1 act or way of saving money, time, etc.: *It will be a saving to take this shortcut.* 2 act of preserving, rescuing, etc. 3 that which is saved. 4 **savings,** *pl.* money saved. *—prep.* 1 except. 2 with all due respect to or for. *—conj.* with the exception of.

saving grace, a redeeming feature.

savings bank, bank which accepts money only for savings and investment and which pays interest on deposits.

savings bond, bond issued by the United States government to help pay its expenses. Savings bonds can be cashed with interest after a certain time.

sav ior or **sav iour** (sā′vyər), *n.* person who saves or rescues. [< Old French *sauveour* < Late Latin *salvator* < *salvare.* See SAVE.¹]

Sav iour or **Sav ior** (sā′vyər), *n.* Jesus.

sa voir-faire (sav′wär fer′, sav′wär far′), *n.* knowledge of just what to do; social grace; tact. [< French, literally, knowing how to act]

Sav o na ro la (sav′ə nə rō′lə), *n.* **Girolamo,** 1452-1498, Italian monk, reformer, and martyr.

sa vor (sā′vər), *n.* 1 a taste or smell; flavor: *The soup has a savor of onion.* 2 a distinctive quality; noticeable trace: *There is a savor of conceit in what she says.* *—v.t.* 1 enjoy the savor of; perceive or appreciate by taste or smell: *We savored the soup.* 2 give flavor to; season. 3 show traces of the presence or influence of: *Bad manners savor a bad education.* *—v.i.* 1 taste or smell *(of): That sauce savors of lemon.* 2 have the quality or nature *(of): a request that savors of a command.* Also, BRITISH **savour.** [< Old French < Latin *sapor,* related to *sapere* to taste, be wise] **—sa′vor er,** *n.* **—sa′vor less,** *adj.*

sa vor y¹ (sā′vər ē), *adj.,* **-vor i er, -vor i est,** *n., pl.* **-vor ies.** *—adj.* 1 pleasing in taste or smell; appetizing: *the savory smell of roast duck.* 2 giving a relish; salt or piquant and not sweet. 3 morally pleasing; agreeable. *—n.* a small portion of highly seasoned food served at the beginning or end of a dinner to stimulate the appetite or digestion. [< Old French *savoure* < *savourer* to taste < *savour* taste < Latin *sapor*] **—sa′vor i ness,** *n.*

sa vor y² (sā′vər ē), *n., pl.* **-vor ies.** any of a genus of herbs and small shrubs of the mint family, especially a fragrant herb used for seasoning food. [< Old French *savoreie* < Latin *satureia*]

sa vour (sā′vər), *n., v.t., v.i.* BRITISH. savor.

sa voy (sə voi′), *n.* kind of cabbage with a compact head and wrinkled leaves. [< *Savoy,* France]

Sa voy (sə voi′), *n.* 1 region in SE France. Savoy was formerly an Italian duchy, but was ceded to France in 1860. 2 the royal house of Italy from 1861 to 1946.

Sa voy ard (sə voi′ərd, sav′oi ärd′), *n.* actor, producer, or warm admirer of Gilbert and Sullivan's operas, many of which were first produced at the Savoy Theater, London.

sav vy (sav′ē), *v.,* **-vied, -vy ing,** *n.* SLANG. *—v.t., v.i.* know; understand. *—n.* understanding; intelligence; sense. [partly < French *savez-(-vous)?* do you know?, partly < Spanish *sabe* or *sabes* you know; both ultimately < Latin *sapere* be wise]

saw¹ (sô), *n., v.,* **sawed, sawed** or **sawn, saw ing.** *—n.* 1 tool for cutting, made of a thin blade with sharp teeth on the edge. 2 machine with such a tool for cutting. *—v.t.* 1 cut with a saw. 2 make with a saw. 3 cut as if with a saw. *—v.i.* 1 use a saw. 2 be sawed: *Pine saws more easily than oak.* 3 cut as a saw does. [Old English *sagu*] **—saw′er,** *n.*

saw² (sô), *v.* pt. of **see¹.**

saw³ (sô), *n.* a wise saying; proverb: *"A stitch in time saves nine" is a familiar saw.* [Old English *sagu.* Related to SAY.]

saw bones (sô′bōnz′), *n.* SLANG. a doctor; surgeon.

saw buck (sô′buk′), *n.* U.S. 1 sawhorse. 2 SLANG. a ten-dollar bill.

saw dust (sô′dust′), *n.* small particles of wood made by sawing. —*adj.* unsubstantial; insignificant: *a sawdust Caesar.*

sawed-off (sôd′ôf′, sôd′of′), *adj.* 1 having one end sawed or cut off: *a sawed-off shotgun.* 2 SLANG. small in size; short.

saw fish (sô′fish′), *n., pl.* **-fish es** or **-fish.** any of a genus of rays resembling sharks, having a long, flat snout with a row of sharp teeth on each edge.

saw fly (sô′flī′), *n., pl.* **-flies.** any of two families of hymenopterous insects, the female of which has a sawlike organ for cutting slits in plants to hold her eggs.

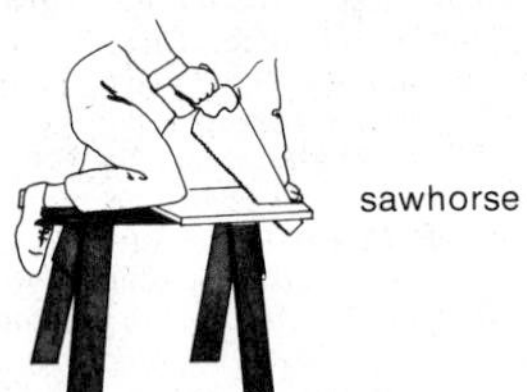
sawhorse

saw horse (sô′hôrs′), *n.* frame for holding wood that is being sawed.

saw mill (sô′mil′), *n.* 1 building where machines saw timber into planks, boards, etc. 2 machine for such sawing.

sawn (sôn), *v.* a pp. of **saw**[1].

saw tooth (sô′tüth′), *adj.* saw-toothed.

saw-toothed (sô′tütht′), *adj.* 1 having teeth on the edge, like a saw. 2 notched like teeth on a saw; serrate.

saw yer (sô′yər), *n.* 1 man whose work is sawing timber. 2 any of various beetles whose larvae bore large holes in wood. [< *saw*[1] + *-yer,* as in *lawyer*]

sax (saks), *n.* INFORMAL. saxophone.

sax horn (saks′hôrn′), *n.* one of a group of brass musical instruments having valves, a cup-shaped mouthpiece, a loud, full tone, and a wide range. A tuba is a large saxhorn with a bass tone. [< Adolphe *Sax,* 1814-1894, Belgian inventor]

sax i frage (sak′sə frij), *n.* 1 any of a genus of low, spreading plants, most of which have rosettes of thick leaves with silvery, toothed edges, and clusters of white, pink, purple, or yellow flowers. 2 flower of any of these plants. [< Latin *saxifraga* < *saxum* rock + *frangere* to break. Doublet of SALSIFY.]

Sax on (sak′sən), *n.* 1 member of a Germanic tribe that, with the Angles and Jutes, conquered Britain in the A.D. 400's and 500's. 2 language of the Saxons. 3 Anglo-Saxon; Old English. 4 native of Saxony in modern Germany. —*adj.* 1 of or having to do with the early Saxons or their language. 2 Anglo-Saxon. 3 English. 4 of or having to do with Saxony.

Sax o ny (sak′sə nē), *n.* region in East Germany, formerly a state of Germany.

sax o phone (sak′sə fōn), *n.* a woodwind instrument having a curved metal body with keys for the fingers and a mouthpiece with a single reed. [< Adolphe *Sax,* 1814-1894, Belgian inventor]

sax o phon ist (sak′sə fō′nist), *n.* a saxophone player.

sax tu ba (saks′tü′bə, saks′tyü′bə), *n.* a large saxhorn having a deep tone. [< *sax(horn)* + *tuba*]

say (sā), *v.,* **said, say ing,** *adv., n.* —*v.t.* 1 speak or pronounce; utter. See synonym study below. 2 put into words; tell; declare: *Say what you think.* 3 recite; repeat: *say one's prayers.* 4 take as an estimate; suppose: *a bookcase containing, say, 100 books.* 5 express an opinion: *Can anyone really say he is wrong?* 6 **to say nothing of,** without mentioning. —*v.i.* 1 say words; talk: *So she says.* 2 express an opinion. 3 **that is to say,** that is; in other words.

—*adv.* 1 approximately: *I've known them for, say, five or six years.* 2 for example: *He's looking for a better job than, say, selling newspapers.*

—*n.* 1 what a person says or has to say: *She said her say and sat down.* 2 chance to say something: *It is now my say.* 3 power; authority: *Who has the final say in this matter?* [Middle English *seien,* Old English *seogan*] **—say′er,** *n.*

Syn. *v.t.* 1 **Say, talk, state** mean to speak. **Say** is the general word for speaking: *Say something to cheer us up.* **Talk** implies a series of sayings, a conversation: *They talked politics for hours.* **State** implies a formal saying or, as the word itself suggests, a statement: *Would you please state your frank opinion of the plan?*

say est (sā′ist), *v.* ARCHAIC. say. "Thou sayest" means "you say."

say ing (sā′ing), *n.* 1 something said; statement; utterance. 2 proverb: *"Haste makes waste" is a saying.* 3 **go without saying,** be too obvious to need mention.

says (sez), *v.* third person singular, present indicative of **say.**

say-so (sā′sō′), *n., pl.* **-sos.** INFORMAL. 1 an unsupported statement. 2 authority or power to decide.

sayst (sāst), *v.* ARCHAIC. sayest.

Sb, antimony [for Latin *stibium*].

sb., substantive.

Sc, scandium.

sc., 1 namely [for Latin *scilicet*]. 2 scene. 3 science. 4 scruple.

Sc., 1 Scotch. 2 Scottish.

s.c., small capitals.

S.C., 1 Signal Corps. 2 South Carolina. 3 Supreme Court.

scab (skab), *n., v.,* **scabbed, scab bing.** —*n.* 1 crust that forms over a sore or wound as it heals. 2 a skin disease in animals, especially sheep; scabies or mange. 3 any of several fungous or bacterial diseases of plants, usually producing dark, crustlike spots. 4 INFORMAL. workman who will not join a labor union or who takes a striker's job. 5 SLANG. rascal; scoundrel. —*v.i.* 1 become covered with a scab. 2 INFORMAL. act or work as a scab. [< Scandinavian (Danish) *skab*]

scab bard (skab′ərd), *n.* sheath or case for the blade of a sword, dagger, etc. [< Anglo-French *escaubers,* plural; of Germanic origin]

scab by (skab′ē), *adj.,* **-bi er, -bi est.**

saxophone

1 covered with scabs. 2 consisting of scabs. 3 having scab or mange. 4 INFORMAL. low; mean. **—scab′bi ness,** *n.*

sca bies (skā′bēz, skā′bē ēz), *n.* disease of the skin caused by mites that live as parasites under the skin and cause itching; the itch. [< Latin, itch, related to *scabere* to scratch]

sca brous (skā′brəs), *adj.* 1 rough with very small points or projections. 2 full of difficulties; harsh. 3 hard to treat with decency; indelicate; risqué. [< Late Latin *scabrosus* < Latin *scaber* scaly]

scads (skadz), *n.pl.* INFORMAL. a large quantity. [origin uncertain]

scaf fold (skaf′əld), *n.* 1 a temporary structure for holding workmen and materials during the construction, repair, or decoration of a building. 2 a raised platform on which criminals are put to death, especially by hanging. 3 platform, stage, or stand for exhibiting shows, seating spectators, or the like. 4 any raised framework. —*v.t.* furnish with a scaffold; support with a scaffold. [< Old French *eschaffault,* ultimately < Latin *ex-* + Vulgar Latin *catafalcum* catafalque]

scaf fold ing (skaf′əl ding), *n.* 1 scaffold. 2 materials for scaffolds.

scal a ble (skā′lə bəl), *adj.* that can be scaled or climbed.

sca lar (skā′lər), *adj.* 1 (in mathematics) having or involving only magnitude. Scalar numbers or quantities are used to represent length, mass, speed, etc. 2 capable of being represented by a point on a scale. 3 of or resembling a musical or other scale. —*n.* a scalar number or quantity. [< Latin *scalaris* like a ladder < *scalae* ladder. See SCALE[3]]

sca la tion (skā lā′shən), *n.* the nature and form of the scales in fishes, snakes, etc.

scal a wag (skal′ə wag), *n.* 1 INFORMAL. an unprincipled person; scamp; rascal. 2 a white Southerner who acted with the Republican Party after the Civil War. Also, **scallywag.** [origin uncertain]

scald[1] (skôld), *v.t.* 1 burn with hot liquid or steam. 2 pour boiling liquid over; use boiling liquid on. 3 heat or be heated almost to the boiling point, but not quite. 4 burn as if with boiling water. —*n.* a burn caused by hot liquid or steam. [< Old North French *escalder* < Late Latin *excaldare* bathe (off) in hot water < Latin *ex-* off + *calidus* hot]

scald[2] (skôld, skäld), *n.* skald.

scale[1] (skāl), *n., v.,* **scaled, scal ing.** —*n.* 1 the dish or pan of a balance. 2 Usually, **scales,** *pl.* balance; instrument for weighing. 3 **Scales,** *pl.* Libra. 4 **tip the scales, a** have as one's weight. **b** overbalance one for another. 5 **turn the scales,** decide. —*v.t.* 1 weigh: *He scales 180 pounds.* 2 weigh in or as if in scales; measure; compare. —*v.i.* 1 be weighed. 2 have weight. [< Scandinavian (Old Icelandic) *skāl*]

scale[2] (skāl), *n., v.,* **scaled, scal ing.** —*n.* 1 one of the thin, flat, hard or horny, and usually overlapping plates forming the outer covering of many fishes and reptiles, and a few mammals. 2 a thin layer like a scale: *scales of skin.* 3 a thin piece of metal or other material. 4 coating formed on the inside of a boiler, kettle, etc., by water during heating. 5 one of the modified rudimentary leaves that unite to cover a bud in winter. 6 scale insect. —*v.t.* 1 remove scales from: *scale a fish with a knife.* 2 remove in thin layers. 3 cover with scales. 4 throw (a thin flat object) so that it moves edgewise: *scale a paper plate.* —*v.i.* 1 come off in scales: *The paint is scaling off the house.* 2 become coated with scale.

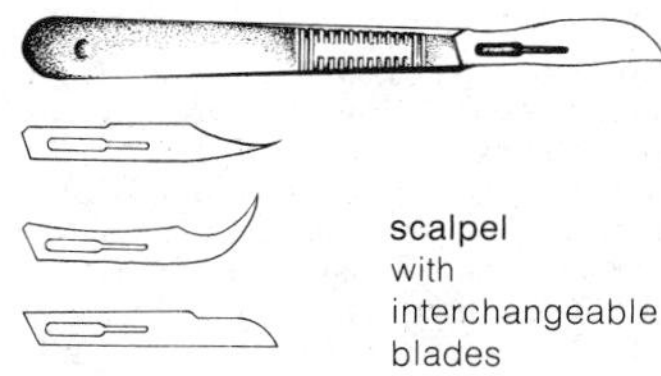

scalpel with interchangeable blades

[< Old French *escale;* of Germanic origin] **—scale′less,** *adj.* **—scale′like′,** *adj.*

scale[3] (skāl), *n., v.,* **scaled, scal ing.** *—n.* 1 series of steps or degrees; scheme of graded amounts: *a scale of wages.* 2 a series of marks made along a line or curve at regular distances to use in measuring: *A thermometer has a scale.* 3 instrument marked in this way, used for measuring, etc. 4 the size of a plan, map, drawing, or model compared with what it represents. 5 the line on a map, plan, chart, etc., that indicates this relationship. 6 relative size or extent: *entertain on a lavish scale.* 7 system of numbering: *The decimal scale counts by tens, as in cents, dimes, dollars.* 8 (in music) a series of tones ascending or descending in pitch according to fixed intervals. *—v.t.* 1 reduce or increase according to a fixed proportion: *All prices were scaled down ten per cent.* 2 climb up or over: *scale a wall by ladders.* 3 make according to scale. 4 measure by a scale. [< Latin *scalae* ladder, steps < *scandere* to climb]

scale insect, any of a large family of small homopterous insects of which the females mostly have the body and eggs covered by a waxy scale or shield formed by a secretion from the body.

sca lene (skā lēn′, skā′lēn′), *adj.* (of a triangle) having three unequal sides. [< Late Latin *scalenus* < Greek *skalēnos* uneven]

scal lion (skal′yən), *n.* 1 kind of onion that has no large, distinct bulb. 2 shallot. 3 leek. [< Anglo-French *scaloun* < Latin *(caepa) Ascalonia* (onion) from Ascalon, in Palestine]

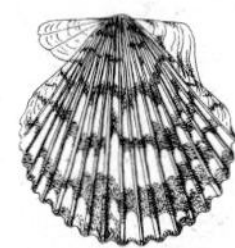

scallop (def. 1) up to 3 in. long

scallop (def. 4) scallops on a cuff

scal lop (skol′əp, skal′əp), *n.* 1 any of various marine mollusks, somewhat like clams, with rounded, fan-shaped, ribbed shells; escallop. In some species the large muscle that opens and closes the shell is edible. 2 a scallop shell worn as a token of pilgrimage. 3 a small dish or scallop shell, in which fish or other food is baked and served. 4 one of a series of curves on an edge of a dress, etc. *—v.t.* 1 bake with sauce and bread crumbs in a dish; escallop: *scalloped oysters.* 2 ornament or trim (the edge of a garment, etc.) with scallops. Also, **scollop.** [< Old French *escalope* shell; of Germanic origin]

scal ly wag (skal′ē wag), *n.* scalawag.

scalp (skalp), *n.* 1 the skin on the top and back of the head, usually covered with hair. 2 part of this skin, formerly kept as a token of victory by certain American Indians. *—v.t.* 1 cut or tear the scalp from. 2 INFORMAL. **a** buy and sell to make small quick profits. **b** trade in (theater tickets, stocks, etc.) especially buying at face value and selling at higher prices. *—v.i.* INFORMAL. buy and sell theater tickets, stocks, etc., to make small quick profits. [< Scandinavian (Old Icelandic) *skālpr* sheath] **—scalp′er,** *n.*

scal pel (skal′pəl), *n.* a small, straight knife used in surgery and in dissections. [< Latin *scalpellum,* diminutive of *scalprum* knife < *scalpere* carve]

scalp lock, a long lock of hair left on the head (the rest being shaved) by members of certain North American Indian tribes as a token of their status as warriors.

scal y (skā′lē), *adj.,* **scal i er, scal i est.** 1 covered with scales; having scales like a fish: *This iron pipe is scaly with rust.* 2 suggesting scales. 3 that comes off in scabs. **—scal′i ness,** *n.*

scamp (skamp), *n.* an unprincipled person; rascal; rogue. *—v.t.* do (work, etc.) in a hasty, careless manner. [< dialectal *scamp* roam, probably < *scamper*]

scam per (skam′pər), *v.i.* run quickly. *—n.* a quick run. [< Old French *escamper* run away, ultimately < Latin *ex-* out of + *campus* field]

scam pi (skäm′pē), *n.pl.* ITALIAN. shrimp.

scan (skan), *v.,* **scanned, scan ning,** *n.* *—v.t.* 1 look at closely; examine with care: *His mother scanned his face to see if he was telling the truth.* 2 glance at; look over hastily. 3 mark off (lines of poetry) into feet. EXAMPLE: Sing′ a | song′ of | six′pence. 4 read or recite (poetry), marking off the lines into feet. 5 (in television) to expose (bits of a surface) in rapid succession to beams of electrons in order to transmit a picture. 6 search (an area) with radar. *—v.i.* 1 conform to the rules for marking off lines of poetry into feet. 2 (in television) scan a surface in transmitting a picture. *—n.* act or fact of scanning. [< Late Latin *scandere* < Latin, to climb] **—scan′ner,** *n.*

Scand., 1 Scandinavia. 2 Scandinavian.

scan dal (skan′dl), *n.* 1 a shameful action, condition, or event that brings disgrace or shocks public opinion: *unearth a scandal in the government.* 2 damage to reputation; disgrace. 3 public talk about a person that will hurt his reputation; evil gossip; slander. 4 **be the scandal of,** scandalize. [< Latin *scandalum* < Greek *skandalon* trap. Doublet of SLANDER.]

scan dal ize (skan′dl īz), *v.t.,* **-ized, -iz ing.** offend by doing something thought to be wrong or improper; shock. **—scan′dal i za′tion,** *n.*

scan dal mon ger (skan′dl mung′gər, skan′dl mong′gər), *n.* person who spreads scandal and evil gossip.

scan dal ous (skan′dl əs), *adj.* 1 bringing disgrace; shameful; shocking. 2 spreading scandal or slander; slandering. **—scan′dal ous ly,** *adv.*

scandal sheet, newspaper or magazine devoted to items of a notorious, scandalous, or gossipy nature.

Scan di na vi a (skan′də nā′vē ə, skan′də nā′vyə), *n.* 1 region of NW Europe that includes Norway, Sweden, Denmark, and sometimes Finland and Iceland. 2 peninsula on which Norway and Sweden are located.

Scan di na vi an (skan′də nā′vē ən, skan′də nā′vyən), *adj.* of or having to do with Scandinavia, its people, or their languages. *—n.* 1 native or inhabitant of Scandinavia. 2 languages of Scandinavia, both modern and historical, including Danish, Icelandic, Norwegian, and Swedish.

hat, āge, fär; let, ēqual, tėrm;
it, īce; hot, ōpen, ôrder;
oil, out; cup, pu̇t, rüle;
ch, child; ng, long; sh, she;
th, thin; ᴛʜ, then; zh, measure;

ə represents *a* in about, *e* in taken, *i* in pencil, *o* in lemon, *u* in circus.

< = from, derived from, taken from.

scan di um (skan′dē əm), *n.* a gray metallic element, found in many minerals in Scandinavia. *Symbol:* Sc; *atomic number* 21. See pages 326 and 327 for table. [< New Latin < Latin *Scandia* Scandinavia]

scan sion (skan′shən), *n.* the marking off of lines of poetry into feet; scanning. In the oral scansion of poetry, a reader stresses the accented syllables heavily. [< Latin *scansionem* < *scandere* to scan]

scant (skant), *adj.* 1 not enough in size or quantity; meager; poor: *a scant meal.* 2 barely enough; barely full; bare: *Use a scant cup of butter in the cake. You have a scant hour in which to pack.* 3 **scant of,** having not enough: *She was scant of breath.* *—v.t.* 1 make scant or small; cut down; limit; stint: *Don't scant the butter if you want a rich cake.* 2 limit the supply of; withhold. *—adv.* DIALECT. scarcely; barely; hardly. [< Scandinavian (Old Icelandic) *skamt* short] **—scant′ly,** *adv.* **—scant′ness,** *n.*

scant ling (skant′ling), *n.* 1 a small beam or piece of timber, often used as an upright piece in the frame of a building. 2 small beams or timbers collectively. [variant of *scantillon* < Old French *escantillon,* ultimately < Late Latin *cantus* corner]

scant y (skan′tē), *adj.,* **scant i er, scant i est.** 1 not enough; not abundant; inadequate; insufficient: *His scanty clothing did not keep out the cold.* See synonym study below. 2 not ample or copious; barely enough: *a scanty harvest.* [< *scant,* adjective] **—scant′i ly,** *adv.* **—scant′i ness,** *n.*

Syn. 1 Scanty, sparse, meager mean less than is needed or normal. **Scanty** implies falling short of the needed or standard amount: *The scanty rainfall is causing a water shortage.* **Sparse** implies a thin scattering of what there is, particularly of numbers or units: *He carefully combs his sparse hair.* **Meager** implies thinness, a lack of something necessary for fullness, richness, strength, etc.: *Meager soil produces meager crops.*

Scap a Flow (skap′ə flō′), sea area among the Orkney Islands, north of Scotland. 15 mi. long; 8 mi. wide.

scape[1] (skāp), *n., v.t., v.i.,* **scaped, scap ing.** ARCHAIC. escape.

scape[2] (skāp), *n.* 1 (in botany) a leafless flower stalk rising from the ground, such as that of the dandelion. 2 something like a stalk, such as the shaft of a feather or the shaft of a column. [< Latin *scapus* stalk]

'scape (skāp), *n., v.t., v.i.,* **'scaped, 'scap ing.** ARCHAIC. escape. [variant of *escape*]

-scape, *combining form.* a scenic picture or view of, as in *seascape.* [< *(land)scape*]

scape goat (skāp′gōt′), *n.* person or thing made to bear the blame for the mistakes or sins of others. The ancient Jewish high priests used to lay the sins of the people on a goat (called the scapegoat) which was then driven out into the wilderness. [< *scape,* variant of *escape* + *goat*]

scape grace (skāp′grās′), *n.* a reckless, good-for-nothing person; scamp.

scaph o pod (skaf′ə pod), *n.* any of a class of marine mollusks with a long, tubular shell open at both ends, and delicate tentacles; tooth shell. [< Greek *skaphē* boat, trough + *podos* foot]

scap u la (skap′yə lə), *n., pl.* **-lae** (-lē), **-las.** shoulder blade. [< Latin]

scap u lar (skap′yə lər), *adj.* of the shoulder or shoulder blade. *—n.* 1 (in the Roman Catholic Church) a loose, sleeveless garment hanging from the shoulders, worn by members of certain religious orders. 2 two small pieces of woolen cloth joined by string passed over the shoulders, worn under the ordinary clothing by Roman Catholics as a mark of religious devotion. 3 a bird's feather growing where the wing joins the body. [ultimately < Latin *scapula* shoulder]

scar[1] (skär), *n., v.,* **scarred, scar ring.** *—n.* 1 mark left by a healed cut, wound, burn, or sore. 2 any mark like this: *War leaves many deep scars on the minds of those who endure it.* 3 a mark where a leaf has formerly joined the stem. *—v.t.* mark with a scar. *—v.i.* form a scar; heal. [< Old French *escare* < Greek *eschara* scab, hearth] **—scar′less,** *adj.*

scar[2] (skär), *n.* 1 a steep, rocky place on the side of a mountain; precipice; cliff. 2 a low rock in the sea. [< Scandinavian (Old Icelandic) *sker* reef]

scarab (def. 2)—A, top; B, bottom

scar ab (skar′əb), *n.* 1 any of a family of beetles, especially a broad, black dung beetle sacred to the ancient Egyptians. 2 image of this beetle. Scarabs were much used in ancient Egypt as charms or ornaments. [< Latin *scarabaeus*]

scar a bae us (skar′ə bē′əs), *n., pl.* **-bae us es, -bae i** (-bē′ī). scarab.

scar a mouch or **scar a mouche** (skar′ə müsh′, skar′ə mouch′), *n.* 1 a cowardly braggart. 2 rascal; scamp. [< Italian *scaramuccia.* See SKIRMISH.]

scarce (skers, skars), *adj.,* **scarc er, scarc est,** *adv. —adj.* 1 hard to get; rare: *Craftsmanship is increasingly scarce in our mechanized society.* See **rare** for synonym study. 2 **make oneself scarce,** INFORMAL. **a** go away. **b** stay away. *—adv.* scarcely. [< Old North French *escars* < Popular Latin *excarpsum,* ultimately < Latin *ex-* out + *carpere* to pluck] **—scarce′ness,** *n.*

scarce ly (skers′lē, skars′lē), *adv.* 1 not quite; barely: *We could scarcely see the ship through the thick fog.* 2 decidedly not: *He can scarcely have said that.* 3 very probably not: *I will scarcely pay that much.*

scar ci ty (sker′sə tē, skar′sə tē), *n., pl.* **-ties.** too small a supply; lack; rarity. See synonym study below.

Syn. Scarcity, dearth mean a shortage or lack of something. **Scarcity** implies a supply inadequate to meet the demand or satisfy the need: *There is a scarcity of nurses.* **Dearth** means an extreme scarcity amounting almost to a famine: *a dearth of information.*

scare (sker, skar), *v.,* **scared, scar ing,** *n. —v.t.* 1 make afraid; frighten. See **frighten** for synonym study. 2 frighten (away); drive off. 3 **scare up,** INFORMAL. get; raise: *scare up a few extra blankets on a cold night. —v.i.* become frightened. *—n.* 1 fright, especially a sudden fright. 2 frightened condition. [< Scandinavian (Old Icelandic) *skirra* < *skjarr* timid] **—scar′er,** *n.*

scare crow (sker′krō′, skar′krō′), *n.* 1 figure of a man dressed in old clothes, set in a field to frighten birds away from crops. 2 person, usually skinny, dressed in ragged clothes. 3 anything that fools people into being frightened.

scare mon ger (sker′mung′gər, sker′-mong′gər; skar′mung′gər, skar′mong′gər), *n.* a person who spreads alarming reports, rumors, etc.; alarmist.

scarf[1] (skärf), *n., pl.* **scarfs** or **scarves.** 1 a long, broad strip of silk, lace, etc., worn about the neck, shoulders, head, or waist. 2 necktie with hanging ends. 3 a long strip of cloth, etc., used as a cover for a bureau, table, piano, etc. [< Old North French *escarpe;* of Germanic origin]

scarf[2] (skärf), *n., pl.* **scarfs,** *v. —n.* 1 joint in which the ends of beams are cut so that they lap over and join firmly. 2 end cut in this way. *—v.t.* join by a scarf. [< Scandinavian (Swedish) *skarv*]

scarf pin (skärf′pin′), *n.* an ornamental pin worn in a scarf or necktie.

scarf skin (skärf′skin′), *n.* the outer layer of skin; epidermis.

scar i fi ca tion (skar′ə fə kā′shən), *n.* 1 act of scarifying. 2 scratch or scratches.

scar i fy (skar′ə fī), *v.t.,* **-fied, -fy ing.** 1 make scratches or cuts in the surface of (the skin, etc.). 2 criticize severely; hurt the feelings of. 3 loosen (soil) without turning it over. [< Old French *scarifier* < Late Latin *scarificare* < Latin *scarifare* < Greek *skariphasthai* to scratch < *skariphos* stylus] **—scar′i fi′er,** *n.*

scar la ti na (skär′lə tē′nə), *n.* 1 scarlet fever. 2 a mild form of scarlet fever. [< Italian *scarlattina,* feminine of *scarlattino,* diminutive of *scarlatto* scarlet]

Scar lat ti (skär lä′tē), *n.* 1 **Alessandro,** 1659-1725, Italian composer. 2 his son, **Domenico,** 1685-1757, Italian composer.

scar let (skär′lit), *n.* 1 a very bright red, much lighter than crimson. 2 cloth or clothing having this color. *—adj.* very bright red. [< Old French *escarlate,* perhaps ultimately < Persian *saqalāt* rich cloth]

scarlet fever, a very contagious disease, caused by a form of streptococcus, that affects chiefly children and is characterized by a scarlet rash, sore throat, and fever; scarlatina.

scarlet runner, a tall bean vine of tropical America that has showy scarlet flowers, and long pods with large, black, edible seeds.

scarlet sage, herb or small shrub, a species of salvia, with racemes of bright red flowers that bloom in the autumn.

scarlet tanager, the common tanager of eastern North America; redbird. The male has black wings and tail and a scarlet body.

scarp (skärp), *n.* 1 a steep slope. 2 the inner slope or side of a ditch surrounding a fortification. *—v.t.* make into a steep slope; slope steeply. [< Italian *scarpa;* of Germanic origin]

scarves (skärvz), *n.* a pl. of **scarf**[1].

scar y (sker′ē, skar′ē), *adj.,* **scar i er, scar i est.** INFORMAL. 1 causing fright or alarm. 2 easily frightened. **—scar′i ly,** *adv.* **—scar′i ness,** *n.*

scat[1] (skat), *interj., v.,* **scat ted, scat ting.** INFORMAL. *—interj.* an exclamation used to drive away an animal. *—v.i.* go away, especially in a hurry. [perhaps < *hiss* + *cat*]

scat[2] (skat), *n., v.,* **scat ted, scat ting.** SLANG. *—n.* nonsense chatter and sounds, usually sung or spoken rapidly to jazz music. *—v.i., v.t.* sing or speak scat. [probably imitative]

scathe (skāᴛʜ), *v.,* **scathed, scath ing,** *n. —v.t.* 1 blast or sear with abuse or invective. 2 sear; scorch. 3 ARCHAIC. injure; damage. *—n.* ARCHAIC. a hurt; harm. [< Scandinavian (Old Icelandic) *skathi* injury]

scathe less (skāᴛʜ′lis), *adj.* without harm; unhurt.

scath ing (skā′ᴛʜing), *adj.* bitterly severe: *scathing criticism.* **—scath′ing ly,** *adv.*

scat o log i cal (skat′l oj′ə kəl), *adj.* of or having to do with scatology.

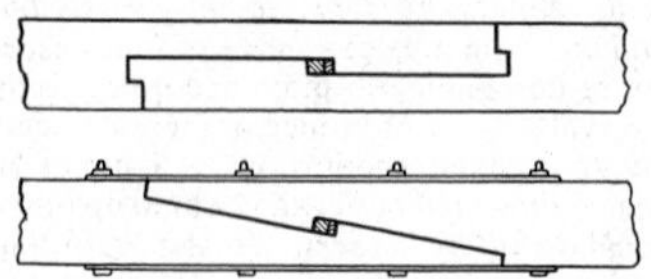

scarf[2] (def. 1)—two kinds of scarfs

sca tol o gy (skə tol′ə jē), *n.* 1 interest in obscenity, especially in literature. 2 obscene literature. [< Greek *skatos* excrement + English *-logy*]

scat ter (skat′ər), *v.t.* 1 throw here and there; sprinkle; strew: *Scatter ashes on the icy sidewalk.* 2 separate and drive off in different directions. See synonym study below. *—v.i.* separate and go in different directions: *The hens scattered. —n.* act or fact of scattering. [Middle English *scateren.* Related to SHATTER.] **—scat′ter er,** *n.*

Syn. *v.t.* 2 **Scatter, dispel, disperse** mean to separate and drive away so that an original form or arrangement is lost. **Scatter** means to separate and drive off in different directions a group or mass of people or objects: *The wind scattered my papers.* **Dispel** applies only to things that cannot be touched, such as clouds and feelings, and means to drive them completely away: *The pilot's confidence dispelled my doubts about the bad weather.* **Disperse** means to scatter thoroughly the individuals of a compact body or mass: *Storms dispersed the convoy.*

scat ter brain (skat′ər brān′), *n.* a thoughtless, flighty person.

scat ter brained (skat′ər brānd′), *adj.* not able to think steadily; flighty; thoughtless.

scat ter ing (skat′ər ing), *adj.* widely separated; occurring here and there. *—n.* a small amount or number scattered.

scatter rug, a small rug.

scat ter shot (skat′ər shot′), *adj.* spreading widely like the burst of shot from a shotgun.

scaup (skôp), *n.* either of two broad-billed wild diving ducks of the same genus as the canvasback. The males have glossy black heads and necks. [perhaps variant of dialectal *scalp* bank providing a bed for shellfish]

scav enge (skav′ənj), *v.,* **-enged, -eng ing.** *—v.t.* 1 remove dirt and rubbish from. 2 pick over (discarded objects) for things to use or sell. *—v.i.* 1 be a scavenger. 2 undergo scavenging. [< *scavenger*]

scepter (def. 1)

scav en ger (skav′ən jər), *n.* 1 animal that feeds on decaying matter. Vultures are scavengers. 2 person who scavenges. [alteration of *scavager,* literally, inspector, ultimately < Old French *escauwer* inspect < Flemish *scauwen*]

sce nar i o (si ner′ē ō, si nar′ē ō, si när′ē ō), *n., pl.* **-nar i os.** 1 the outline of a motion picture, giving the main facts about the scenes, persons, and acting. 2 the outline of any play, opera, etc. [< Italian]

sce nar ist (si ner′ist, si nar′ist, si när′ist), *n.* person who writes scenarios.

scene (sēn), *n.* 1 the time, place, circumstances, etc., of a play or story: *The scene of the novel is laid in Virginia during the Civil War.* 2 the place where anything is carried on or takes place: *the scene of an accident.* 3 the painted screens, hangings, etc., used on the stage to represent places: *The scene represents a city street.* 4 part of an act of a play: *The king first appears in Act I, Scene 2.* 5 a particular incident of a play, story, etc.: *the balcony scene in "Romeo and Juliet."* 6 an action, incident, situation, etc., occurring in reality or represented in literature or art: *He painted a series of pictures called "Scenes of My Boyhood."* 7 view; picture: *The white sailboats in the blue water made a pretty scene.* See **view** for synonym study. 8 show of strong feeling in front of others; exhibition; display: *The child kicked and screamed and made such a scene that his mother was ashamed of him.* 9 **behind the scenes, a** out of sight of the audience. **b** privately; secretly; not publicly. [< Middle French < Latin *scena* < Greek *skēnē,* originally, tent in the theater where actors changed costumes]

scen er y (sē′nər ē), *n., pl.* **-er ies.** 1 the general appearance of a place; natural features of a landscape: *mountain scenery.* 2 the painted hangings, screens, etc., used in a theater to represent places.

scen ic (sē′nik, sen′ik), *adj.* 1 of or having to do with natural scenery: *The scenic splendors of Yellowstone Park are famous.* 2 having much fine scenery; picturesque: *a scenic highway.* 3 of or having to do with stage scenery or stage effects: *The production of the musical comedy was a scenic triumph.* 4 representing an action, incident, situation, etc., in art. **—scen′i cal ly,** *adv.*

scen i cal (sē′nə kəl, sen′ə kəl), *adj.* scenic.

scent (sent), *n.* 1 a distinctive or characteristic odor, especially when pleasing; smell: *the scent of roses.* 2 the sense of smell: *Bloodhounds have a keen scent.* 3 a distinctive odor left in passing: *The dogs followed the fox by scent.* 4 the trail of such a smell: *lose the scent.* 5 means by which a person or thing can be traced: *The police are on the scent of the thieves.* 6 perfume. *—v.t.* 1 recognize by the sense of smell: *The dog scented a rabbit and ran off after it.* 2 have a suspicion of; be aware of: *I scent a trick in their offer.* 3 fill with odor. 4 perfume: *She scented the room to rid it of the fish smell.* *—v.i.* hunt by using the sense of smell: *The dog scented about till he found the trail.* [< Old French *sentir* to smell, sense < Latin *sentire* to feel] **—scent′less,** *adj.*

scep ter (sep′tər), *n.* 1 the rod or staff carried by a ruler as a symbol of royal power or authority. 2 royal or imperial power or authority; sovereignty. Also, **sceptre.** [< Latin *sceptrum* < Greek *skēptron* staff]

scep tered (sep′tərd), *adj.* 1 furnished with or bearing a scepter. 2 invested with regal authority; regal.

scep tic (skep′tik), *n., adj.* skeptic.

scep ti cal (skep′tə kəl), *adj.* skeptical.

scep ti cism (skep′tə siz′əm), *n.* skepticism.

scep tre (sep′tər), *n., v.,* **-tred, -tring.** scepter.

sched ule (skej′ůl), *n., v.,* **-uled, -ul ing.** *—n.* 1 a written or printed statement of details; list: *A timetable is a schedule of the coming and going of trains.* 2 the time fixed for doing something, arrival at a place, etc.: *The bus was an hour behind schedule.* *—v.t.* 1 make a schedule of; enter in a schedule. 2 plan or arrange (something) for a definite time or date: *Schedule the convention for the fall.* [< Late Latin *schedula,* diminutive of Latin *scheda* sheet of papyrus]

Sche her a za de (shə her′ə zä′də), *n.* the young bride of the sultan in *The Arabian Nights* who related tales nightly to him to save her life.

Scheldt River (skelt), river flowing from N France through Belgium and SW Netherlands into the North Sea. 270 mi.

sche ma (skē′mə), *n., pl.* **-ma ta** (-mə tə). 1 draft or outline of a plan, project, etc. 2 plan; scheme. [< Latin]

sche mat ic (skē mat′ik), *adj.* having to do with or like a diagram, plan, or scheme; diagrammatic. *—n.* a schematic design, sketch, etc. **—sche mat′i cal ly,** *adv.*

sche ma tize (skē′mə tīz), *v.t.,* **-tized, -tiz ing.** reduce to or arrange according to a scheme or formula. **—sche′ma ti za′tion,** *n.*

scheme (skēm), *n., v.,* **schemed, schem ing.** *—n.* 1 program of action; plan: *a scheme for extracting salt from sea water.* 2 plot: *a scheme to cheat the government.* 3 system of connected things, parts, thoughts, etc.: *The color scheme of the room is blue and gold.* 4 diagram; outline; table. *—v.i., v.t.* devise plans, especially underhanded or evil ones; plot: *They were scheming to bring the jewels into the country without paying duty.* See **plot** for synonym study. [< Greek *schēma* figure, appearance < *echein* to have] **—schem′er,** *n.*

schem ing (skē′ming), *adj.* making tricky schemes; crafty; designing.

Sche nec ta dy (skə nek′tə dē), *n.* city in E New York State. 78,000.

scher zan do (sker tsän′dō), *adj.* (in music) playful; sportive. [< Italian *scherzare* to play, sport < *scherzo.* See SCHERZO.]

scher zo (sker′tsō), *n., pl.* **-zos, -zi** (-tsē). a light or playful piece or movement of a sonata or symphony. [< Italian < German *Scherz* joke]

Schick test (shik), test to determine susceptibility to or immunity from diphtheria, made by injecting a dilute diphtheria toxin under the skin. [< Béla *Schick,* 1877-1967, American pediatrician born in Hungary, who developed the test]

Schil ler (shil′ər), *n.* **Johann Christoph Friedrich von,** 1759-1805, German poet and dramatist.

hat, āge, fär; let, ēqual, tėrm; it, īce; hot, ōpen, ôrder; oil, out; cup, pu̇t, rüle; ch, child; ng, long; sh, she; th, thin; ᴛʜ, then; zh, measure; ə represents *a* in about, *e* in taken, *i* in pencil, *o* in lemon, *u* in circus. < = from, derived from, taken from.

schil ling (shil′ing), *n.* the monetary unit of Austria, a coin equal to 100 groschen and worth about 4 cents. [< German *Schilling.* Related to SHILLING.]

schism (siz′əm, skiz′əm), *n.* 1 division into hostile groups. 2 division because of some difference of opinion about religion. 3 offense of causing or trying to cause a religious schism. 4 sect or group formed by a schism within a church. [< Greek *schisma* < *schizein* to split]

schis mat ic (siz mat′ik, skiz mat′ik), *adj.* 1 causing or likely to cause schism. 2 inclined toward, or guilty of, schism. *—n.* person who tries to cause a schism or takes part in a schism. **—schis mat′i cal ly,** *adv.*

schis mat i cal (siz mat′ə kəl, skiz mat′ə-kəl), *adj.* schismatic.

schist (shist), *n.* kind of crystalline metamorphic rock usually composed essentially of mica, that splits easily into layers. [< Greek *schistos* cleft < *schizein* to split]

schist ose (shis′tōs), *adj.* of or like schist; having the structure of schist.

schis to some (shis′tə sōm, skis′tə sōm), *n.* any of a genus of trematode worms that are parasitic in the blood vessels of mammals in tropical countries; blood fluke.

schis to so mi a sis (shis′tə sō mī′ə sis, skis′tə sō mī′ə sis), *n.* disease caused by schistosomes infesting the blood.

schiz o (skit′sō, skiz′ō), *n., pl.* **schiz os.** INFORMAL. a schizophrenic.

schiz o carp (skiz′ō kärp), *n.* (in botany) any dry fruit that divides, when ripe, into two or more one-seeded seed vessels that do not split open, as in the carrot and celery. [< Greek *schizein* to split + *karpos* fruit]

schiz oid (skit′soid, skiz′oid), *adj.* having or tending toward schizophrenia. *—n.* person who has, or tends toward, schizophrenia.

schiz o phre ni a (skit′sə frē′nē ə, skit′sə-frē′nyə; skiz′ə frē′nē ə, skiz′ə frē′nyə), *n.* form of psychosis characterized by dissociation from the environment and deterioration of personality. [< New Latin < Greek *schizein* to split + *phrēn* mind]

schiz o phren ic (skit′sə fren′ik, skiz′ə-fren′ik), *adj.* 1 of or having to do with schizophrenia. 2 having schizophrenia. *—n.* person who has schizophrenia. **—schiz′o-phren′i cal ly,** *adv.*

schle miel (shlə mēl′), *n.* SLANG. a clumsy person; bungler. [< Yiddish *shlumiel*]

Schles wig-Hol stein (shles′wig hōl′-stīn), *n.* state in N West Germany, south of Denmark.

Schlie mann (shlē′män), *n.* **Heinrich,** 1822-1890, German archaeologist who discovered and excavated the site of ancient Troy.

schlier en (shlir′ən), *n.pl.* 1 irregular, dark or light streaks occurring in igneous rock because of varying proportions of the minerals present. 2 (in physics) areas in a medium where refraction varies as a result of differences in density. [< German *Schlieren* < *Schlier* marl]

schlock (shlok), SLANG. —*n.* worthless junk; trash. —*adj.* trashy; cheap. [< Yiddish *shlak*]

schmaltz or **schmalz** (shmälts), *n.* SLANG. cloying sentimentalism in music, art, literature, etc. [< German *Schmalz,* literally, rendered fat]

schnapps or **schnaps** (shnäps), *n.* 1 Hollands. 2 any alcoholic liquor. [< German *Schnapps*]

schnau zer (shnou′zər), *n.* any of a breed of wire-haired German terriers with a long head and small ears. [< German *Schnauzer* < *Schnauze* snout]

schnit zel (shnit′səl), *n.* a veal cutlet, usually seasoned with lemon juice, parsley, capers, and sardines. [< German *Schnitzel* cutlet]

Schnitz ler (shnit′slər), *n.* **Arthur,** 1862-1931, Austrian playwright and novelist.

schol ar (skol′ər), *n.* 1 a learned person; person having much knowledge. 2 pupil at school; student; learner. See **student** for synonym study. 3 student who is given a scholarship. [< Late Latin *scholaris* < Latin *schola.* See SCHOOL¹.]

schol ar ly (skol′ər lē), *adj.* 1 of a scholar; like that of a scholar: *scholarly habits.* 2 fit for a scholar. 3 having much knowledge; learned. 4 fond of learning; studious. 5 thorough and orderly in methods of study. —*adv.* in a scholarly manner. —**schol′ar li ness,** *n.*

schol ar ship (skol′ər ship), *n.* 1 possession of knowledge gained by study; quality of learning and knowledge. 2 grant of money or other aid to help a student continue his studies. 3 fund to provide this money.

scho las tic (skə las′tik), *adj.* 1 of schools, scholars, or education; academic: *scholastic achievements, scholastic life.* 2 of or like scholasticism. 3 pedantic or formal. —*n.* 1 Often, **Scholastic.** person who favors scholasticism. 2 theologian and philosopher in the Middle Ages. —**scho las′ti cal ly,** *adv.*

scho las ti cism (skə las′tə siz′əm), *n.* 1 Also, **Scholasticism.** system of theological and philosophical teaching in the Middle Ages, based chiefly on the authority of the church fathers and of Aristotle, and characterized by a formal method of discussion. 2 adherence to the teachings of the schools or to traditional doctrines and methods.

scho li ast (skō′lē ast), *n.* commentator upon the ancient classics.

scho li um (skō′lē əm), *n., pl.* **-li a** (-lē ə). 1 an explanatory note or comment, especially upon a passage in the Greek or Latin classics. 2 note added by way of illustration or amplification. [< Medieval Latin < Greek *scholion,* diminutive of *scholē* discussion]

Schön berg (shœn′bėrg′; *German* shœn′berk), *n.* **Arnold,** 1874-1951, Austrian composer.

school¹ (skül), *n.* 1 place for teaching and learning, especially one for children. 2 instruction in school; education received at school: *start school, enjoy school.* 3 a regular course of meetings of teachers and pupils for instruction. 4 one session of such a course: *stay after school.* 5 those who are taught and their teachers: *The entire school was present.* 6 any place, situation, experience, etc., as a source of instruction or training: *the school of adversity.* 7 place of training or discipline. 8 group of people who agree in certain opinions, points of behavior, or the like: *a gentleman of the old school.* 9 group of people taught by the same teacher or united by a general similarity of principles and methods: *the Dutch school of painting.* 10 a particular department or group in a university, specializing in a particular branch of learning: *a school of medicine, a school of music.* 11 room, rooms, building, or group of buildings in a university, set apart for the use of one department.
—*v.t.* 1 educate in a school; teach. 2 train: *discipline: School yourself to control your temper.* 3 instruct (a person) how to act.
—*adj.* of or having to do with a school or schools.
[Old English *scōl* < Latin *schola* < Greek *scholē* discussion, originally, leisure]

school² (skül), *n.* a large number of the same kind of fish or water animals swimming together. —*v.i.* swim together in a school. [< Dutch. Related to SHOAL².]

school age, 1 age at which a child begins to go to school. 2 years during which going to school is compulsory or customary.

school bag (skül′bag′), *n.* briefcase or other bag used to carry books, papers, etc., to and from school.

school board, a local board or committee managing the public schools.

school book (skül′bůk′), *n.* book for study in schools.

school boy (skül′boi′), *n.* boy attending school.

school bus, bus that carries children to and from school.

school child (skül′chīld′), *n., pl.* **-chil dren.** schoolboy or schoolgirl.

school fel low (skül′fel′ō), *n.* companion at school.

school girl (skül′gėrl′), *n.* girl attending school.

school house (skül′hous′), *n., pl.* **-hous es** (-hou′ziz). building used as a school.

school ing (skü′ling), *n.* 1 instruction in school; education received at school. 2 training: *At a riding academy horses and riders receive schooling.* 3 cost of instruction.

school ma'am (skül′mam′), *n.* INFORMAL or DIALECT. schoolmistress.

school man (skül′mən), *n., pl.* **-men.** 1 man engaged in teaching or in managing a school. 2 Often, **Schoolman.** teacher in a university of the Middle Ages; medieval theologian.

school marm (skül′märm′), *n.* INFORMAL or DIALECT. schoolmistress.

school mas ter (skül′mas′tər), *n.* man who teaches in or manages a school.

school mate (skül′māt′), *n.* companion at school.

school mis tress (skül′mis′tris), *n.* woman who teaches in or manages a school.

school room (skül′rüm′, skül′rům′), *n.* room in which pupils are taught.

school teach er (skül′tē′chər), *n.* person who teaches in a school.

school time (skül′tīm′), *n.* 1 the time at which school begins or during which school continues. 2 the period of life which is passed at school.

school work (skül′wėrk′), *n.* a student's work in school.

school yard (skül′yärd′), *n.* piece of ground around or near a school, used for play, games, etc.

school year, part of the year during which a school is in session.

schooner (def. 1)

schoon er (skü′nər), *n.* 1 U.S. ship with two or more masts and fore-and-aft sails. 2 prairie schooner. 3 INFORMAL. a large glass for beer. [dialectal *scoon,* skim; probably of Scandinavian origin]

Scho pen hau er (shō′pən hou′ər), *n.* **Arthur,** 1788-1860, German philosopher.

schot tische (shot′ish), *n.* 1 a dance somewhat like the polka but slower, popular in the 1800's. 2 music for it. [< German, literally, Scottish]

Schrö ding er (shrœ′ding ər), *n.* **Erwin,** 1887-1961, Austrian physicist.

Schu bert (shü′bərt), *n.* **Franz,** 1797-1828, Austrian composer.

Schulz (shůlts), *n.* **Charles M(onroe),** born 1922, American cartoonist.

Schu man (shü′mən), *n.* **William Howard,** born 1910, American composer and educator.

Schu mann (shü′män), *n.* 1 **Clara Wieck,** 1819-1896, pianist and music teacher, wife of Robert Schumann. 2 **Robert (Alexander),** 1810-1856, German composer.

Schurz (shůrts), *n.* **Carl,** 1829-1906, American reformer, editor, general, and statesman, born in Germany.

schuss (shůs), in skiing: —*n.* 1 a fast run down a straight course. 2 the course itself. —*v.i.* to make a run at top speed over a straight course. [< German *Schuss,* literally, shot]

Schuyl kill River (skül′kil), river flowing from E Pennsylvania into the Delaware River at Philadelphia. 131 mi.

schwa (shwä), *n.* 1 an unstressed vowel sound such as *a* in *about* or *u* in *circus,* represented by the symbol ə; neutral vowel. 2 the symbol ə. [< German < Hebrew *shəwa*]

Schwei tzer (shwī′tsər; *German* shvī′tsər), *n.* **Albert,** 1875-1965, Alsatian physician, philosopher, musician, and missionary in Africa.

sci., 1 science. 2 scientific.

sci at ic (sī at′ik), *adj.* 1 of or in the region of the hip. 2 affecting the sciatic nerve: *sciatic neuralgia.* [< Medieval Latin *sciaticus,* alteration of Greek *ischiadikos* < *ischion* hip joint]

sci at i ca (sī at′ə kə), *n.* pain in the sciatic nerve and its branches, felt in the hip, thigh, and leg. [< Medieval Latin]

sciatic nerve, a large, branching nerve which extends from the lower back down the back part of the thigh and leg.

sci ence (sī′əns), *n.* 1 knowledge based on observed facts and tested truths arranged in an orderly system: *biological or physical sciences, pure science, social science.* 2 branch of such knowledge dealing with the phenomena of the universe and their laws; a physical or natural science. 3 skill based on training and practice; technique: *the science of judo, the science of sailing.* 4 a particular branch of knowledge or study, especially as distinguished from art. 5 **Science,** Christian Science. [< Old French < Latin *scientia* knowledge < *scire* know]

science fair, group of school exhibits, each demonstrating a scientific principle, process, development, etc.

science fiction, novel or short story based on the application of elements of science and technology to fantastic situations, life in the future and on other galaxies, etc.

sci en tif ic (sī′ən tif′ik), *adj.* 1 using the facts and laws of science: *scientific research, a scientific farmer.* 2 of or having to do with science; used in science: *scientific books, scientific instruments.* [< Late Latin *scientificus* < Latin *scientia* knowledge + *facere* to make]

sci en tif i cal ly (sī′ən tif′ik lē), *adv.* 1 in a scientific manner. 2 according to the facts and laws of science.

scientific method, an orderly method used in scientific research, generally consisting in identifying a problem, gathering all the pertinent data, formulating a hypothesis, performing experiments, interpreting the results, and drawing a conclusion.

scientific notation, a short form of mathematical notation used by scientists, in which a number is expressed as a decimal number between 1 and 10 multiplied by a power of 10. EXAMPLE: 6.57×10^{12} instead of 6,570,000,000,000.

sci en tist (sī′ən tist), *n.* 1 person who has expert knowledge of some branch of science, especially a physical or natural science. 2 **Scientist,** Christian Scientist.

scil i cet (sil′ə set), *adv.* to wit; namely. [< Latin < *scire* to know + *licet* it is allowed]

Scil ly Isles (sil′ē), group of about 140 small British islands in the Atlantic off the SW tip of England. 2000 pop.; 6 sq. mi.

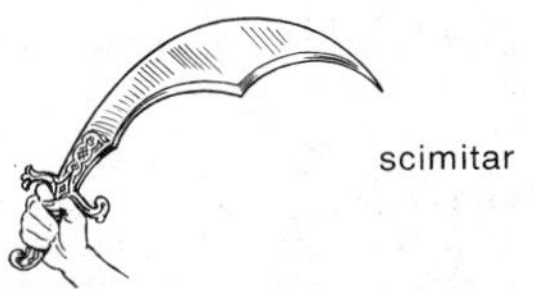

scimitar

scim i tar or **scim i ter** (sim′ə tər), *n.* a short, curved sword used by Turks, Persians, and other Oriental peoples. [< Italian *scimitarra*]

scin til la (sin til′ə), *n.* spark; particle; trace: *not a scintilla of truth.* [< Latin, spark. Doublet of TINSEL.]

scin til lant (sin′tl ənt), *adj.* scintillating; sparkling.

scin til late (sin′tl āt), *v.i.,* **-lat ed, -lat ing.** sparkle; flash: *The snow scintillates in the sun like diamonds. Brilliant wit scintillates.* **—scin′til la′tor,** *n.*

scin til la tion (sin′tl ā′shən), *n.* 1 a sparkling; flashing. 2 a spark; flash.

scintillation counter, device which detects and counts radioactive particles by counting the number of scintillations when radiation strikes a luminescent liquid, crystal, or gas.

sci o lism (sī′ə liz′əm), *n.* superficial knowledge. [< Late Latin *sciolus* knowing little < Latin *scire* know]

sci o list (sī′ə list), *n.* person who pretends to have more knowledge than he really has.

sci on (sī′ən), *n.* 1 bud or branch cut for grafting. 2 descendant; heir. Also, **cion.** [< Old French *cion*]

Scip i o (sip′ē ō), *n.* 1 237?-183? B.C., Roman general who defeated Hannibal in 202 B.C. He is called "Scipio the Elder." 2 185?-129 B.C., Roman general who destroyed Carthage in 146 B.C. He is called "Scipio the Younger."

scis sion (sizh′ən, sish′ən), *n.* act of cutting, dividing, or splitting; division; separation. [< Late Latin *scissionem* < *scindere* to split]

scis sor (siz′ər), *v.t., v.i.* cut with scissors. *—n.* scissors (def. 1).

scis sors (siz′ərz), *n.* 1 *usually pl. in use.* tool or instrument for cutting that has two sharp blades so fastened that their edges slide against each other. 2 *sing. in use.* a wrestling hold with the legs. [< Old French *cisoires,* plural, < Late Latin *cisorium,* singular, tool for cutting, ultimately < Latin *caedere* to cut]

scissors kick, movement of the legs in swimming like the movement of scissors blades.

SCLC, Southern Christian Leadership Conference (American organization, consisting chiefly of Southern churches, formed in 1956 to campaign for civil rights).

scler a (sklir′ə), *n.* the tough, white outer membrane which covers the eyeball, except for the part covered by the cornea; sclerotic; sclerotic coat. See **eye** for diagram. [< New Latin < Greek *sklēros* hard]

scle ren chy ma (skli reng′kə mə), *n.* nonliving plant tissue with thickened and hardened cells. It is found chiefly as a strengthening and protecting tissue in the stem and in such hard parts of plants as nut shells. [< Greek *sklēros* hard + *en-* in + *chyma* what is poured]

scle rom e ter (sklə rom′ə tər), *n.* instrument for measuring the hardness of a substance, especially a mineral. [< Greek *sklēros* hard + English *-meter*]

scle ro sis (sklə rō′sis), *n., pl.* **-ses** (-sēz). 1 a hardening of a tissue or part of the body by an increase of connective tissue or the like at the expense of more active tissue. 2 a hardening of a tissue or cell wall of a plant by thickening or the formation of wood. [< Medieval Latin < Greek *sklērōsis* < *sklēros* hard]

scle rot ic (sklə rot′ik), *n.* sclera. *—adj.* 1 of or having to do with the sclera. 2 of, with, or having sclerosis.

sclerotic coat, sclera.

scoff (skôf, skof), *v.i.* make fun to show one does not believe something; mock. See synonym study below. *—v.t.* jeer at; deride. *—n.* 1 mocking words or acts. 2 something ridiculed or mocked. [< Scandinavian (Danish) *skuffe* deceive] **—scoff′er,** *n.* **—scoff′ing ly,** *adv.*

Syn. *v.i.* **Scoff, jeer, sneer** mean to show scorn or contempt for someone or something. **Scoff** implies scornful irreverence or cynicism: *scoff at religion.* **Jeer** implies mocking laughter: *The mob jeered when the speaker got up to talk.* **Sneer** means to express ill-natured contempt or disparagement by look, tone, or manner of speech: *sneer at everything sentimental.*

scoff law (skôf′lô′, skof′lô′), *n.* person with little regard for the law; person who regularly flouts the law.

scold (skōld), *v.t.* find fault with; blame with angry words. See synonym study below. *—v.i.* find fault; talk angrily. *—n.* person who scolds, especially a noisy, scolding woman. [probably < Scandinavian (Old Icelandic)

hat, āge, fär; let, ēqual, tėrm;
it, īce; hot, ōpen, ôrder;
oil, out; cup, pu̇t, rüle;
ch, child; ng, long; sh, she;
th, thin; ᴛʜ, then; zh, measure;

ə represents *a* in about, *e* in taken, *i* in pencil, *o* in lemon, *u* in circus.

< = from, derived from, taken from.

skāld poet, in sense of "lampooner"] **—scold′er,** *n.*

Syn. *v.t.* **Scold, upbraid, chide** mean to find fault with someone. **Scold** particularly suggests reproval of someone younger or subordinate, often without good reason: *That woman is always scolding the children in our neighborhood.* **Upbraid** suggests sharp and severe censure for a definite fault: *The judge upbraided the argumentative lawyers and threatened to cite them for contempt.* **Chide** means to censure mildly in the hope of improvement: *The foreman chided several of the workers for carelessness.*

scol lop (skol′əp), *n., v.t.* scallop.

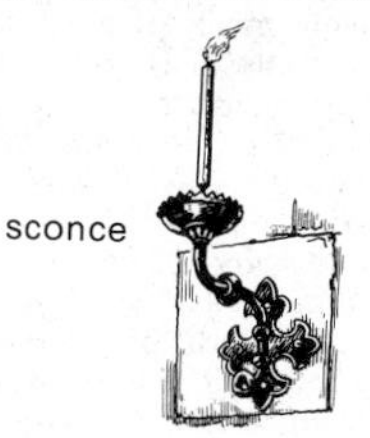

sconce

sconce (skons), *n.* bracket projecting from a wall, used to hold a candle or other light. [< Medieval Latin *sconsa* < Latin *abscondere* abscond, hide]

scone (skōn, skon), *n.* a thick, flat, round cake cooked on a griddle or in an oven. Some scones taste much like bread; some are like buns. [probably < Middle Dutch *schoon(brot)* fine (bread)]

scoop (sküp), *n.* 1 tool like a shovel. 2 the part of a dredge, power shovel, etc., that takes up or holds the coal, sand, etc. 3 a large ladle. 4 a kitchen utensil to take up flour, sugar, etc. 5 a kitchen utensil to take up a portion of ice cream, mashed potatoes, etc., and place it on a cone, plate, or dish. 6 act of taking up with, or as if with, a scoop. 7 the amount taken up at one time by a scoop; scoopful: *I used two scoops of flour and one of sugar.* 8 place hollowed out. 9 INFORMAL. **a** the publishing of a piece of news before a rival newspaper does; beat. **b** the piece of news. *—v.t.* 1 take up or out with a scoop, or as a scoop does. 2 hollow out; dig out; make by scooping: *The children scooped holes in the sand.* 3 INFORMAL. publish a piece of news before (a rival newspaper). [< Middle Dutch *schoepe* bucket, and *schoppe* shovel] **—scoop′er,** *n.*

scoop ful (sküp′fu̇l), *n., pl.* **-fuls.** enough to fill a scoop.

scoot (sküt), INFORMAL. *—v.i.* go quickly; dart. *—n.* act of scooting. [originally Scottish, to squirt, gush. Probably related to SHOOT.]

scoot er[1] (skü′tər), *n.* 1 a child's vehicle consisting of a footboard between two wheels, one in front of the other, steered by a long, upright handlebar and propelled by pushing against the ground with one foot. 2 motor scooter. 3 U.S. sailboat with runners, for use on either water or ice. —*v.i.* sail or go in or on a scooter. [< *scoot*]

scoot er[2] (skü′tər), *n.* scoter.

scope[1] (skōp), *n.* 1 distance the mind can reach; extent of view: *Very hard words are not within the scope of a child's understanding.* 2 the area over which any activity extends: *This subject is not within the scope of our investigation.* See **range** for synonym study. 3 space; opportunity: *Football gives scope for courage and quick thinking.* [< Italian *scopo* < Greek *skopos* aim, object < *skopein* look at]

scope[2] (skōp), *n.* INFORMAL. any instrument for viewing, such as a microscope, radarscope, telescope, etc. [short for *microscope, radarscope,* etc.]

-scope, *combining form.* instrument for viewing or observing: *Telescope = instrument for viewing distant objects.* [< New Latin *-scopium* < Greek *-skopion* < *skopein* look at]

sco pol a mine (skō pol′ə mēn′), *n.* drug used to dilate pupils of eyes, to produce a partial stupor known as "twilight sleep," and as a depressant. *Formula:* $C_{17}H_{21}NO_4$ [< New Latin *Scopola canicola,* a plant that yields this drug + English *amine*]

scor bu tic (skôr byü′tik), *adj.* 1 of or having to do with scurvy. 2 affected with scurvy. [< New Latin *scorbuticus* < *scorbutus* scurvy < French *scorbut;* of Germanic origin]

scorch (skôrch), *v.t.* 1 burn slightly; burn on the outside of: *The cake tastes scorched. I scorched the shirt in ironing it.* See **burn** for synonym study. 2 dry up; wither: *grass scorched by the sun.* 3 criticize with burning words. —*v.i.* 1 be or become scorched. See **burn** for synonym study. 2 INFORMAL. drive or ride very fast. —*n.* a slight burn. [origin uncertain]

scorched earth, destruction by government orders of all things useful to an invading army.

scorch er (skôr′chər), *n.* 1 person or thing that scorches. 2 INFORMAL. a very hot day. 3 INFORMAL. person who drives or rides very fast.

score (skôr, skōr), *n., v.,* **scored, scor ing.** —*n.* 1 the record of points made in a game, contest, test, etc.: *keep score. The score was 9 to 2.* 2 amount owed; debt; account: *He paid his score at the inn.* 3 ARCHAIC. record of this kept by notches or marks. 4 group or set of twenty; twenty: *A score or more were present at the party.* 5 **scores,** *pl.* a large number; great numbers: *Scores died in the epidemic.* 6 a written or printed piece of music arranged for different instruments or voices: *the score of an opera.* 7 cut; scratch; stroke; mark; line: *The carpenter used a nail to make a score on the board.* 8 reason; ground: *Don't worry on that score.* 9 (in sports) line to show the beginning or end of a course, range, etc., as the line at which a marksman stands to shoot. 10 **the score,** INFORMAL. the truth about anything or things in general: *The new man doesn't know the score yet.* 11 **pay off a score** or **settle a score,** get even for an injury or wrong: *many an old score to settle with one's enemies.*

—*v.t.* 1 make as points in a game, contest, test, etc.: *score two runs in the second inning.*

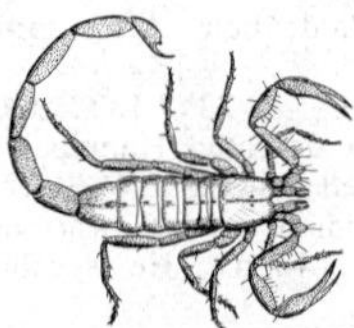

scorpion (def. 1)
1 to 8 in. long

She scored 85 per cent on the entrance test. 2 keep a record of (the number of points made in a game, contest, etc.). 3 be counted as in the score: *In American football, a touchdown scores six points.* 4 make as an addition to the score; gain; win: *The two guards scored 35 points in the last basketball game.* 5 keep a record of as an amount owed; set down; mark: *The innkeeper scored on a slate the number of meals each person had.* 6 arrange (a piece of music) for different instruments or voices: *score a sonata for piano and strings.* 7 write out (music) in score. 8 cut; scratch; mark; line: *score a ham before baking. Mistakes are scored in red ink.* 9 blame or scold severely; berate. —*v.i.* 1 make points in a game, contest, etc., or on a test. 2 keep a record of the number of points in a game, contest, etc. 3 achieve a success; succeed. 4 make notches, cuts, lines, etc. [Old English *scoru* < Scandinavian (Old Icelandic) *skor* notch, tally stick] —**score′less,** *adj.* —**scor′er,** *n.*

score board (skôr′bôrd′, skōr′bōrd′), *n.* a large board on which the scores of a sporting event are posted.

score card (skôr′kärd′, skōr′kärd′), *n.* card on which to record the score of a game, especially while it is being played.

score keep er (skôr′kē′pər, skōr′kē′pər), *n.* person who keeps score.

sco ri a (skôr′ē ə, skōr′ē ə), *n., pl.* **-ri ae** (-rē ē′). 1 slag or refuse left from ore after the metal has been melted out; dross. 2 porous, cinderlike fragments of lava; slag. [< Greek *skōria* < *skōr* dung]

sco ri a ceous (skôr′ē ā′shəs, skōr′ē ā′shəs), *adj.* 1 like slag or clinkers. 2 consisting of slag, clinkers, etc.

scorn (skôrn), *v.t.* 1 look down upon; think of as mean or low; despise: *scorn sneaks and liars.* 2 reject or refuse as low or wrong: *The judge scorned to take a bribe.* —*n.* 1 a feeling that a person, animal, or act is mean or low; contempt. See synonym study below. 2 person, animal, or thing that is scorned or despised. 3 ARCHAIC. expression of contempt; taunt; insult. [< Old French *escarnir;* of Germanic origin] —**scorn′er,** *n.*

Syn. *n.* 1 **Scorn, contempt, disdain** mean a strong feeling that someone or something is unworthy of respect. **Scorn** implies angry dislike or disapproval of what is considered worthless or evil: *He attacked their proposals in words of bitter scorn.* **Contempt** implies disgust combined with strong disapproval: *We feel contempt for a coward.* **Disdain** implies feeling oneself above a person or thing considered mean or low: *We feel disdain for a person who cheats.*

scorn ful (skôrn′fəl), *adj.* showing contempt; full of scorn; mocking. —**scorn′ful ly,** *adv.* —**scorn′ful ness,** *n.*

Scor pi o (skôr′pē ō), *n.* 1 a southern constellation between Libra and Sagittarius, seen by ancient astronomers as having the rough outline of a scorpion; Scorpius. 2 the eighth sign of the zodiac; Scorpion. The sun enters Scorpio about October 24.

scor pi on (skôr′pē ən), *n.* 1 any of an order of arachnids belonging to the same class as the spider and having a poisonous sting at the end of its tail. 2 a whip or scourge. 3 **Scorpion.** Scorpio. [< Latin *scorpionem* < Greek *skorpios*]

Scor pi us (skôr′pē əs), *n.* Scorpio.

scot (skot), *n.* one's share of a payment; tax. [< Scandinavian (Old Icelandic) *skot.* Related to SHOT.]

Scot (skot), *n.* native or inhabitant of Scotland.

Scot., 1 Scotch. 2 Scotland. 3 Scottish.

scotch (skoch), *v.t.* 1 inflict such hurt upon (something regarded as dangerous) that it is made harmless for the time. 2 stamp on or stamp out (something dangerous); crush: *scotch a rumor.* 3 cut or gash. [origin uncertain]

Scotch (skoch), *n.* 1 Scottish. 2 whiskey made in Scotland. —*adj.* 1 of Scotland; Scottish. 2 INFORMAL. stingy; parsimonious.

Scotch-I rish (skoch′ī′rish), *adj.* 1 of or having to do with a part of the population of Northern Ireland descended from Scottish settlers. 2 of both Scottish and Irish descent. —*n.* person of both Scottish and Irish descent.

Scotch man (skoch′mən), *n., pl.* **-men.** Scotsman.

Scotch tape, trademark for a very thin, transparent or opaque adhesive tape used for mending, patching, sealing, etc.

Scotch terrier, one of a breed of short-legged terriers with rough, wiry hair and pointed, standing ears. Also, **Scottish terrier.**

sco ter (skō′tər), *n.* any of several large sea ducks, common in northern seas, usually called coots in the United States. Also, **scooter.** [origin uncertain]

scot-free (skot′frē′), *adj.* free from punishment, loss, or injury; unharmed.

Sco tia (skō′shə), *n.* Latin name of Scotland.

Scot land (skot′lənd), *n.* division of Great Britain north of England; the land of the Scottish people. 5,187,000 pop.; 30,400 sq. mi. *Capital:* Edinburgh.

Scotland Yard, 1 headquarters of the London police. 2 the London police, especially the department that does detective work.

Scots (skots), *adj.* of Scotland; Scottish. —*n.* 1 *pl.* the people of Scotland. 2 dialect of English spoken by the people of Scotland.

Scots man (skots′mən), *n., pl.* **-men.** native or inhabitant of Scotland; Scotchman.

Scott (skot), *n.* 1 **James.** See **Monmouth, Duke of.** 2 **Robert Falcon,** 1868-1912, British naval officer and antarctic explorer. 3 Sir **Walter,** 1771-1832, Scottish novelist and poet. 4 **Winfield,** 1786-1866, American general.

Scot ti cism (skot′ə siz′əm), *n.* word, phrase, or meaning used in Scotland, but not in widespread use in other English-speaking countries.

scot tie (skot′ē), *n.* INFORMAL. 1 Scotch terrier. 2 nickname for a Scotsman.

Scot tish (skot′ish), *adj.* of or having to do with Scotland, its people, or their language. —*n.* 1 *pl. in use.* the people of Scotland. 2 dialect of English spoken by the people of Scotland.

Scottish Gaelic, the Celtic language of the Scottish Highlanders; Erse.

Scottish terrier, Scotch terrier.

scoun drel (skoun′drəl), *n.* person without

honor or good principles; villain; rascal. [origin uncertain]

scoun drel ly (skoun′drə lē), *adj.* 1 having the character of a scoundrel. 2 having to do with or characteristic of a scoundrel.

scour[1] (skour), *v.t.* 1 clean or polish by vigorous rubbing: *scour a frying pan with cleanser.* 2 remove dirt and grease from (anything) by rubbing. 3 make clear by flowing through or over: *The stream had scoured a channel.* 4 clean; cleanse. *—n.* 1 act of scouring. 2 **scours,** *pl.* U.S. diarrhea in cattle, especially calves. [< Middle Dutch *schuren* < Old French *escurer,* ultimately < Latin *ex-* completely + *cura* care] **—scour′er,** *n.*

scour[2] (skour), *v.t.* 1 move quickly over: *They scoured the country round about for the lost child.* 2 look into every part of; search: *scour one's memory for a forgotten date.* *—v.i.* go rapidly in search or pursuit. [probably < Scandinavian (Old Icelandic) *skura* rush violently]

scourge (skėrj), *n., v.,* **scourged, scourg ing.** *—n.* 1 a whip; lash. 2 any means of punishment. 3 some thing or person that causes great trouble or misfortune. Formerly, an outbreak of disease was called a scourge. *—v.t.* 1 whip; flog; punish severely. 2 trouble very much; afflict; torment. [< Old French *escorge,* ultimately < Latin *ex-* out + *corium* a hide] **—scourg′er,** *n.*

scout[1] (skout), *n.* 1 person sent to find out what the enemy is doing. A scout often wears a uniform; a spy does not. 2 warship, airplane, etc., used to find out what the enemy is doing. 3 person who is sent out to get information. 4 person sent out to get information about athletes or athletic teams. 5 act of scouting. 6 person belonging to the Boy Scouts or Girl Scouts. 7 INFORMAL. fellow; person: *He's a good scout.* *—v.i.* act as a scout; hunt around to find something: *Go and scout for firewood for the picnic.* *—v.t.* observe or examine to get information; reconnoiter. [< Old French *escoute* act of listening, listener < *escouter* listen < Latin *auscultare*] **—scout′er,** *n.*

scout[2] (skout), *v.t.* refuse to believe in; reject with scorn: *She scouted the idea of a dog with two tails.* *—v.i.* scoff. [< Scandinavian (Old Icelandic) *skūta* to taunt]

scout car, any of various fast, open-top vehicles designed for military reconnaisance.

scout craft (skout′kraft′), *n.* knowledge and skill in activities required to be a good Boy Scout or Girl Scout.

scout ing (skou′ting), *n.* activities of scouts.

scout mas ter (skout′mas′tər), *n.* man in charge of a troop of Boy Scouts.

scow (skou), *n.* a large, rectangular, flat-bottomed boat used to carry freight, especially in bulk, as coal, sand, etc. [< Dutch *schouw*]

scowl (skoul), *v.i.* 1 look angry or sullen by lowering the eyebrows; frown. See **frown** for synonym study. 2 have a gloomy or threatening aspect. *—v.t.* 1 affect by scowling. 2 express with a scowl. *—n.* an angry, sullen look; frown. [Middle English *skoulen*] **—scowl′er,** *n.*

scrab ble (skrab′əl), *v.,* **-bled, -bling,** *n.* *—v.i.* 1 scratch or scrape about with hands, claws, etc.; scramble: *scrabble up a sand bank.* 2 scrawl; scribble. *—n.* a scraping; scramble. [< Dutch *schrabbelen,* frequentative of *schrabben* to scratch]

scrag (skrag), *n., v.,* **scragged, scrag ging.** *—n.* 1 a lean, skinny person or animal. 2 a lean, bony part. A scrag of mutton is the neck. 3 SLANG. neck. *—v.t.* SLANG. wring the neck of. [< Scandinavian (dialectal Swedish) *skragge* old and torn thing]

scrag gly (skrag′lē), *adj.,* **-gli er, -gli est.** rough or irregular; ragged.

scrag gy (skrag′ē), *adj.,* **-gi er, -gi est.** 1 having little flesh; lean; thin. 2 scraggly. **—scrag′gi ness,** *n.*

scram (skram), *v.i.,* **scrammed, scram ming.** SLANG. go at once. [short for *scramble*]

scram ble (skram′bəl), *v.,* **-bled, -bling.** *n.* *—v.i.* 1 make one's way by climbing, crawling, etc.: *We scrambled up the steep, rocky hill.* 2 struggle with others for something: *scramble for a living. They scrambled to get the ball.* 3 put aircraft into the air quickly to intercept enemy aircraft. *—v.t.* 1 collect or gather up in a hurry or without method. 2 mix together in a confused way. 3 cook (eggs) with the whites and yolks mixed together. *—n.* 1 a climb or walk over rough ground. 2 a struggle to possess: *the scramble for wealth.* 3 any disorderly struggle or activity; scrambling. [variant of *scrabble*] **—scram′bler,** *n.*

scran nel (skran′l), *adj.* ARCHAIC. 1 thin; slight. 2 squeaky and harsh. [< Scandinavian (dialectal Norwegian) *skran* lean, shriveled]

Scran ton (skran′tən), *n.* city in NE Pennsylvania. 104,000.

scrap[1] (skrap), *n., v.,* **scrapped, scrap ping.** *—n.* 1 a small piece; little bit; small part left over: *a scrap of paper. I gave some scraps of meat to the dog.* 2 bit of something written or printed; short extract: *She read aloud scraps from the letter.* 3 old metal fit only to be melted and used again. 4 **scraps,** *pl.* the remains of animal fat left after the oil has been tried out. *—v.t.* 1 make into scraps; break up. 2 throw aside as useless or worn out; discard. *—adj.* 1 in the form of scraps: *scrap metal.* 2 made of scraps or fragments. [< Scandinavian (Old Icelandic) *skrap*]

scrap[2] (skrap), *n., v.,* **scrapped, scrap ping.** SLANG. *—n.* a fight, quarrel, or struggle. *—v.i.* to fight, quarrel, or struggle. [probably variant of *scrape*] **—scrap′per,** *n.*

scrap book (skrap′bu̇k′), *n.* book in which pictures or clippings are pasted and kept.

scrape (skrāp), *v.,* **scraped, scrap ing,** *n.* *—v.t.* 1 rub with something sharp or rough; make smooth or clean by doing this: *Scrape your muddy shoes with this knife.* 2 remove by rubbing with something sharp or rough: *scrape paint off a table, scrape mud off shoes.* 3 scratch or graze by rubbing against something rough: *scrape one's knee.* 4 rub with a harsh sound: *scrape the floor with one's chair.* 5 dig: *The child scraped a hole in the sand.* 6 collect by scraping or with difficulty: *scrape together enough money.* 7 **scrape through,** get through with difficulty. *—v.i.* 1 rub harshly: *a branch scraping against a window.* 2 give a harsh sound; grate. 3 gather together money, etc., with labor and difficulty; hoard up. 4 manage with difficulty: *That family can just scrape along on their small income.* 5 bow with a drawing back of the foot. *—n.* 1 act of scraping. 2 a scraped place. 3 a harsh, grating sound: *the scrape of the bow of a violin.* 4 position hard to get out of; difficulty; predicament. 5 bow with a drawing back of the foot.

hat, āge, fär; let, ēqual, tėrm;
it, īce; hot, ōpen, ôrder;
oil, out; cup, pu̇t, rüle;
ch, child; ng, long; sh, she;
th, thin; TH, then; zh, measure;

ə represents *a* in about, *e* in taken, *i* in pencil, *o* in lemon, *u* in circus.

< = from, derived from, taken from.

[< Scandinavian (Old Icelandic) *skrapa*]

scrap er (skrā′pər), *n.* instrument or tool for scraping.

scrap iron, broken or waste pieces of old iron to be melted and used again.

scrap ple (skrap′əl), *n.* scraps of pork or other meat boiled with corn meal or flour, made into cakes, sliced, and fried.

scrap py[1] (skrap′ē), *adj.,* **-pi er, -pi est.** made up of odds and ends; fragmentary; disconnected. [< *scrap*[1]]

scrap py[2] (skrap′ē), *adj.,* **-pi er, -pi est.** INFORMAL. fond of fighting; pugnacious. [< *scrap*[2]] **—scrap′pi ness,** *n.*

scratch (skrach), *v.t.* 1 break, mark, or cut slightly with something sharp or rough: *Your shoes have scratched the chair.* 2 tear or dig with the claws or nails: *The cat scratched me.* 3 rub or scrape to relieve itching: *scratch one's head.* 4 rub with a harsh noise; rub: *scratch a match on a wall.* 5 write or draw in a hurry or carelessly; scribble. 6 scrape out; strike out; draw a line through. 7 withdraw (a horse, candidate, etc.) from a race or contest. 8 gather by effort; scrape. *—v.i.* 1 use the claws, nails, etc., for tearing a surface, digging, etc. 2 rub some part of one's body to relieve itching. 3 rub with a slight grating noise: *This pen scratches.* 4 withdraw from a race or contest. 5 get along with difficulty. 6 make a miss or fluke in billiards or pool. *—n.* 1 mark made by scratching. 2 a very slight cut. 3 sound of scratching: *the scratch of a pen.* 4 any act of scratching. 5 the line marking the starting place of a race or contest. 6 **from scratch,** from nothing; with no advantages. 7 **up to scratch,** up to standard; in good condition. *—adj.* 1 for quick notes, a first draft, etc.: *scratch paper.* 2 collected by chance: *a scratch football team.* [origin uncertain] **—scratch′er,** *n.*

scratch hit, (in baseball) a weakly hit ground ball to the infield that enables a fast base runner to reach first base before the throw.

scratch sheet, U.S. publication that lists the horses scratched from a race and other racing information.

scratch test, test for allergy to a particular substance, made by scratching the skin with a dose of the substance.

scratch y (skrach′ē), *adj.,* **scratch i er, scratch i est.** 1 that scratches, scrapes, or grates. 2 consisting of mere scratches. 3 scanty; straggling. **—scratch′i ly,** *adv.* **—scratch′i ness,** *n.*

scrawl (skrôl), *v.t., v.i.* write or draw poorly or carelessly. *—n.* 1 poor, careless handwriting. 2 something scrawled, such as a hastily written letter. [origin uncertain] **—scrawl′er,** *n.*

scrawl y (skrô′lē), *adj.,* **scrawl i er, scrawl i est.** awkwardly written or drawn.

scraw ny (skrô′nē), *adj.,* **-ni er, -ni est.**

INFORMAL. lean; thin; skinny: *Turkeys have scrawny necks.* [< Scandinavian (dialectal Norwegian) *skran*] **—scraw′ni ness,** *n.*

scream (skrēm), *v.i.* 1 make a loud, sharp, piercing cry. People scream in fright, in anger, and in sudden pain. 2 laugh or speak loudly. 3 produce a vivid impression or startling effect: *The colors of her pink sweater and orange blouse screamed at each other.* —*v.t.* utter loudly. —*n.* 1 a loud, sharp, piercing cry. 2 something extremely funny. [Middle English *scremen*]

scream er (skrē′mər), *n.* 1 person or thing that screams. 2 a long-toed South American bird about the size of a swan that has a loud cry and sharp spurs on the wings.

scream ing (skrē′ming), *adj.* 1 that screams. 2 evoking screams of laughter: *a screaming farce.* 3 startling: *screaming headlines, screaming colors.* **—scream′ing ly,** *adv.*

screech (skrēch), *v.i., v.t.* cry out sharply in a high voice; shriek. —*n.* a shrill, harsh scream. [Middle English *scritchen,* perhaps imitative] **—screech′er,** *n.*

screech owl, any of a species of small owl with several color phases and varieties, having hornlike tufts of feathers and a wavering cry.

screech y (skrē′chē), *adj.,* **screech i er, screech i est.** screeching.

screed (skrēd), *n.* 1 a long speech or writing. 2 strip of plaster (or wood) applied to the wall as a guide in plastering. [variant of Old English *scrēade* shred]

screen (skrēn), *n.* 1 a covered frame, either fixed or movable, that hides, protects, or separates: *a folding screen.* 2 frame covered with wire mesh, used as a protection: *We have screens on our windows to keep out the flies.* 3 an ornamental partition. 4 anything like a screen: *A screen of trees hides our house from the road.* 5 surface on which motion pictures, television or radar images, etc., appear or are shown. 6 motion pictures; films. 7 sieve for sifting sand, gravel, coal, seed, etc.
—*v.t.* 1 shelter, protect, or hide with, or as with, a screen: *screen a porch. She screened her eyes from the sun with her hand. The lawyer tried to screen his client from the reporters.* 2 show (a motion picture) on a screen. 3 adapt (a story, etc.) for reproduction as a motion picture. 4 photograph with a motion-picture camera. 5 sift with a screen: *screen sand.* 6 classify, sort, or eliminate by some test: *Many government agencies screen their employees for loyalty.* —*v.i.* be suitable for reproducing on a motion-picture screen. [< Old French *escren;* of Germanic origin] **—screen′a ble,** *adj.* **—screen′er,** *n.* **—screen′like′,** *adj.*

screen ing (skrē′ning), *n.* 1 a fine wire mesh for making screens, filters, etc. 2 **screenings,** *pl.* matter separated out by sifting through a sieve or screen.

screen play (skrēn′plā′), *n.* a motion-picture story in manuscript form, including the dialogue, descriptions of scenes, action, and camera directions.

screen test, a filmed scene to test how an actor performs or looks in a motion picture.

screen-test (skrēn′test′), *v.t.* put (an actor) to a screen test.

screen writ er (skrēn′rī′tər), *n.* person who writes screenplays.

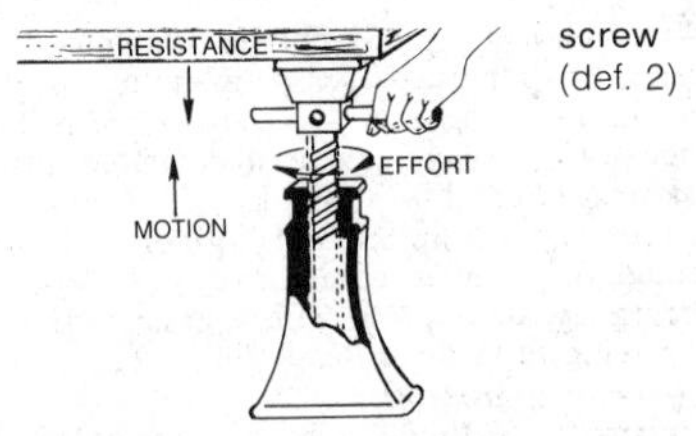

screw (def. 2)

screw (skrü), *n.* 1 kind of nail with a ridge twisted evenly around its length and often a groove across the head: *Turn the screw to the right to tighten it.* 2 cylinder with an inclined plane wound around it and fitting into a threaded cylindrical hole. It is a simple machine. Screws are used in jacks to lift heavy loads. 3 part into which this cylinder fits and advances. 4 anything that turns like a screw or looks like one, such as a corkscrew. 5 turn of a screw; screwing motion. 6 screw propeller. 7 a very stingy person; miser. 8 a small amount of tobacco, snuff, salt, etc., wrapped up in a twist of paper. 9 thumbscrew (def. 2). 10 **have a screw loose,** SLANG. be crazy or eccentric. 11 **put the screws on,** use pressure or force to get something.
—*v.t.* 1 turn as one turns a screw; twist: *Screw the lid on the jar.* 2 fasten or tighten with a screw or screws: *screw hinges to a door.* 3 force, press, or stretch tight by using screws: *screw the strings of a guitar.* 4 force to do something. 5 force (prices) down. 6 force people to tell or give up (something). 7 gather for an effort: *He finally screwed up enough courage to try to dive.* 8 wind; twist; contort: *His face was screwed up with fear.* —*v.i.* 1 turn like a screw. 2 be fitted for being put together or taken apart by a screw or screws. 3 wind; twist. 4 force a person to tell or give up something.
[< Old French *escroue* nut, screw]

screw ball (skrü′bôl′), *n.* 1 SLANG. an eccentric person. 2 (in baseball) a pitch thrown with a break or spin opposite to that of a curve. —*adj.* SLANG. eccentric; erratic.

screw driv er (skrü′drī′vər), *n.* tool for putting in or taking out screws by turning them.

screw eye, screw with a head shaped like a loop.

screw pine, pandanus.

screw propeller, a revolving hub with radiating blades for propelling a steamship, aircraft, etc.

screw thread, the spiral ridge of a screw.

screw worm (skrü′wėrm′), *n.* larva of the screwworm fly.

screwworm fly, blowfly that deposits its eggs in the sores of animals, the eggs developing into tiny larvae which eat into the wound.

screw y (skrü′ē), *adj.,* **screw i er, screw i est.** SLANG. very odd or peculiar.

scrib al (skrī′bəl), *adj.* 1 of or having to do with a scribe. 2 made by a scribe or copyist: *a scribal error.*

scrib ble (skrib′əl), *v.,* **-bled, -bling,** *n.* —*v.t.* write or draw carelessly or hastily. —*v.i.* make marks that do not mean anything. —*n.* something scribbled. [< Medieval Latin *scribillare,* ultimately < Latin *scribere* write]

scrib bler (skrib′lər), *n.* 1 person who scribbles. 2 author who has little or no importance.

scribe (skrīb), *n., v.,* **scribed, scrib ing.** —*n.* 1 person who copies manuscripts. Before printing was invented, there were many scribes. 2 (in ancient times) a teacher of the Jewish law. 3 writer; author. 4 a public clerk or secretary. —*v.t.* mark or cut with something sharp. [< Latin *scriba* < *scribere* write]

scrib er (skrī′bər), *n.* a pointed tool for marking on wood, metal, etc.

scrim (skrim), *n.* a loosely woven cotton or linen material, much used for window curtains. [origin uncertain]

scrim mage (skrim′ij), *n., v.,* **-maged, -mag ing.** —*n.* 1 a rough fight or struggle. 2 the play in football that takes place when the two teams are lined up and the ball is snapped back. 3 football playing for practice. —*v.i.* 1 take part in a rough fight or struggle. 2 (in football) take part in a scrimmage. —*v.t.* oppose in football practice. Also, BRITISH **scrummage.** [ultimately variant of *skirmish*] **—scrim′mag er,** *n.*

scrimmage line, line of scrimmage.

scrimp (skrimp), *v.t.* 1 be sparing of; use too little of. 2 treat stingily or very economically. —*v.i.* be very economical; stint; skimp: *Many parents have to scrimp to keep their children in school.* [origin uncertain]

scrimp y (skrim′pē), *adj.,* **scrimp i er, scrimp i est.** too small; too little; scanty; meager. **—scrimp′i ly,** *adv.* **—scrimp′i ness,** *n.*

scrim shaw (skrim′shô′), *n.* 1 the handicrafts practiced by sailors as a pastime during long whaling or other voyages. 2 the products of these, as small manufactured articles, or carvings on bone, shells, etc. [origin unknown]

scrip[1] (skrip), *n.* 1 a writing. 2 receipt, certificate, or other document showing a right to something, especially a certificate entitling the holder to a fraction of a share of stock. 3 paper money in denominations of less than a dollar, formerly issued in the United States. [variant of *script*]

scrip[2] (skrip), *n.* ARCHAIC. a small bag, wallet, or satchel. [probably < Old French *escrepe;* of Germanic origin]

script (skript), *n.* 1 written letters, figures, signs, etc.; handwriting: *German script.* 2 style of printing that looks like handwriting. 3 manuscript of a play, motion picture, radio or television broadcast, etc. [< Latin *scriptum,* originally neuter past participle of *scribere* write]

scrip to ri um (skrip tôr′ē əm, skrip tōr′ē-əm), *n., pl.* **-to ri ums, -to ri a** (-tôr′ē ə, -tōr′ē ə). a writing room, especially a room in a monastery set apart for writing or copying manuscripts. [< Medieval Latin]

scrip tur al or **Scrip tur al** (skrip′chər-əl), *adj.* of the Scriptures; according to the Scriptures; based on the Scriptures. **—scrip′tur al ly,** *adv.*

Scrip ture (skrip′chər), *n.* 1 the Bible. 2 a particular passage or text of the Bible. 3 **the Scriptures** or **the Holy Scriptures,** the Bible. 4 **scripture,** any sacred writing. [< Latin *scriptura* a writing < *scribere* write]

script writ er (skript′rī′tər), *n.* person who writes scripts.

scrive ner (skriv′nər), *n.* ARCHAIC. a public writer of letters or documents for others; clerk; notary. [< obsolete *scrivein* < Old French *escrivein,* ultimately < Latin *scribere* write]

scrod (skrod), *n.* U.S. a young cod or haddock, especially one split for cooking. [< Middle Dutch *schrode* piece cut off]

scrof u la (skrof′yə lə), *n.* form of tuberculosis characterized by the enlargement of the lymphatic glands, especially those in the

hat, āge, fär; let, ēqual, tėrm;
it, īce; hot, ōpen, ôrder;
oil, out; cup, pu̇t, rüle;
ch, child; ng, long; sh, she;
th, thin; ᴛʜ, then; zh, measure;

ə represents *a* in about, *e* in taken, *i* in pencil, *o* in lemon, *u* in circus.

< = from, derived from, taken from.

neck. [< Medieval Latin *scrofula,* singular < Latin *scrofulae,* plural < *scrofa* a sow]

scrof u lous (skrof′yə ləs), *adj.* 1 of or having to do with scrofula. 2 having scrofula.

scroll (skrōl), *n.* 1 roll of parchment or paper, especially one with writing on it. 2 ornament resembling a partly unrolled sheet of paper, or having a spiral or coiled form. [alteration (influenced by *roll*) of Middle English *scrow,* ultimately < Old French *escroe* scrap; of Germanic origin] **—scroll′-like′,** *adj.*

scroll saw, a very narrow saw for cutting thin wood in curved or ornamental patterns.

scroll work (skrōl′wėrk′), *n.* 1 decorative work in which scrolls are much used. 2 ornamental work cut out with a scroll saw.

Scrooge (skrüj), *n.* 1 **Ebenezer,** the old miser in Dickens's story *A Christmas Carol.* 2 Usually, **scrooge.** any greedy and stingy person; miser.

scro tal (skrō′tl), *adj.* of or having to do with the scrotum.

scro tum (skrō′təm), *n., pl.* **-ta** (-tə), **-tums.** pouch that contains the testicles. [< Latin]

scrounge (skrounj), *v.,* **scrounged, scroung ing.** SLANG. *—v.i.* search about for what one can find. *—v.t.* 1 get by begging; beg. 2 pilfer. [apparently alteration of dialectal *scrunge* pilfer, steal] **—scroung′er,** *n.*

scrub[1] (skrub), *v.,* **scrubbed, scrub bing,** *n. —v.t.* rub hard; wash or clean by rubbing. *—n.* a scrubbing. [perhaps < Middle Dutch *schrubben*] **—scrub′ber,** *n.*

scrub[2] (skrub), *n.* 1 low, stunted trees or shrubs. 2 land overgrown with stunted trees or shrubs. 3 anything small, or below the usual size: *a little scrub of a man.* 4 steer, horse, etc., of mixed stock, often inferior in size or disposition to the purebred. 5 a mean, insignificant person. 6 player not on the regular or varsity team. *—adj.* 1 small; poor; inferior. 2 of or for players not on the regular or varsity team. [< Scandinavian (Danish) *skrubbe*]

scrub by (skrub′ē), *adj.,* **-bi er, -bi est.** 1 below the usual size; low; stunted; small: *scrubby trees.* 2 covered with scrub: *scrubby land.* 3 shabby; mean. **—scrub′bi ness,** *n.*

scrub nurse, nurse in charge of the instruments in the operating room of a hospital.

scrub wom an (skrub′wu̇m′ən), *n., pl.* **-wom en.** a cleaning woman.

scruff (skruf), *n.* skin at the back of the neck; back of the neck. [origin uncertain]

scruf fy (skruf′ē), *adj.,* **-fi er, -fi est.** 1 covered with dandruff. 2 mean; shabby.

scrum mage (skrum′ij), *n., v.,* **-maged, -mag ing.** BRITISH. scrimmage. **—scrum′-mag er,** *n.*

scrump tious (skrump′shəs), *adj.* SLANG. elegant; splendid; first-rate. [origin uncertain] **—scrump′tious ly,** *adv.*

scrunch (skrunch), *v.t., v.i.* crunch; crush; crumple; squeeze. *—n.* the noise made by scrunching. [imitative]

scru ple (skrü′pəl), *n., v.,* **-pled, -pling.** *—n.* 1 a feeling of doubt about what one ought to do: *No scruple ever holds him back from prompt action.* 2 a feeling of uneasiness that keeps a person from doing something: *She has scruples about playing cards for money.* 3 measure of apothecaries' weight equal to 20 grains. Three scruples make one dram. See **measure** for table. 4 a very small amount. *—v.i.* 1 hesitate or be unwilling (to do something): *A dishonest person does not scruple to deceive others.* 2 have scruples. [< Latin *scrupulus* a feeling of uneasiness, originally diminutive of *scrupus* sharp stone, figuratively, uneasiness, anxiety]

scru pu los i ty (skrü′pyə los′ə tē), *n., pl.* **-ties.** 1 a being scrupulous; strict regard for what is right; scrupulous care. 2 an instance of this.

scru pu lous (skrü′pyə ləs), *adj.* 1 very careful to do what is right; conscientious. 2 attending thoroughly to details; very careful: *scrupulous attention to orders.* See synonym study below. **—scru′pu lous ly,** *adv.* **—scru′pu lous ness,** *n.*

Syn. 2 **Scrupulous, punctilious** mean very careful and exact. **Scrupulous** implies conscientious care in following what is considered correct, exact, or the like: *a scholar's scrupulous regard for accuracy.* **Punctilious** emphasizes strict and often excessive attention to and observance of fine points of laws, rules of conduct, or performance of duties: *He is punctilious in returning borrowed books.*

scru ta ble (skrü′tə bəl), *adj.* that can be scrutinized.

scru ti nize (skrüt′n īz), *v.t.,* **-nized, -niz ing.** examine closely; inspect carefully: *The jeweler scrutinized the diamond for flaws.* **—scru′ti niz′er,** *n.* **—scru′ti niz′ing ly,** *adv.*

scru ti ny (skrüt′n ē), *n., pl.* **-nies.** 1 close examination; careful inspection: *His work looks all right, but it will not bear scrutiny.* 2 a looking searchingly at something; searching gaze. [< Late Latin *scrutinium* < Latin *scrutari* ransack]

scu ba (skü′bə), *n.* portable breathing equipment, including one or more tanks of compressed air, used by underwater swimmers and divers. [< *s(elf) c(ontained) u(nderwater) b(reathing) a(pparatus)*]

scud (skud), *v.,* **scud ded, scud ding,** *n. —v.i.* 1 run or move swiftly: *Clouds scudded across the sky driven by the high wind.* 2 (of a boat, etc.) run before a storm with little or no sail set. *—n.* 1 a scudding. 2 clouds or spray driven by the wind. [perhaps < Scandinavian (Danish) *skyde* shoot, glide]

scuff (skuf), *v.i.* walk without lifting the feet; shuffle. *—v.t.* wear or injure the surface of by hard use: *scuff one's shoes.* *—n.* 1 a scuffing. 2 kind of heelless slipper. [variant of *scuffle*]

scuf fle (skuf′əl), *v.,* **-fled, -fling,** *n. —v.i.* 1 struggle or fight in a rough, confused manner. 2 shuffle. *—n.* 1 a confused, rough struggle or fight; tussle. 2 a shuffling. [< Scandinavian (Swedish) *skuffa* to push] **—scuf′fler,** *n.*

scull (def. 3)

scull (skul), *n.* 1 oar worked with a side twist over the stern of a boat to propel it. 2 one of a pair of oars used, one on each side, by a single rower. 3 act of propelling by sculls. 4 a light racing boat for one or more rowers. *—v.t.* propel (a boat) by a scull or by sculls. *—v.i.* scull a boat. [Middle English *sculle*]

scull er (skul′ər), *n.* 1 person who sculls. 2 boat propelled by sculling.

scul ler y (skul′ər ē), *n., pl.* **-ler ies.** a small room where the dirty, rough work of a kitchen is done. [< Old French *escuelerie,* ultimately < Latin *scutella,* diminutive of *scutra* platter]

scul lion (skul′yən), *n.* ARCHAIC. 1 servant who does the dirty, rough work in a kitchen. 2 a low, contemptible person. [< Old French *escouillon* swab, cloth < *escouve* broom < Latin *scopa*]

sculp (skulp), *v.t., v.i.* sculpt.

scul pin (skul′pin), *n.* any of a family of small, inedible saltwater and freshwater fishes with a large, spiny head and a wide mouth.

sculpt (skulpt), INFORMAL. *—v.t.* sculpture. *—v.i.* make sculptures.

sculp tor (skulp′tər), *n.* person who makes figures by carving, modeling, casting, etc.; artist in sculpture. Sculptors work in marble, wood, bronze, etc.

sculp tress (skulp′tris), *n.* a woman sculptor.

sculp tur al (skulp′chər əl), *adj.* of or having to do with sculpture; like sculpture. **—sculp′tur al ly,** *adv.*

sculp ture (skulp′chər), *n., v.,* **-tured, -tur ing.** *—n.* 1 art of making figures by carving, modeling, casting, etc. Sculpture includes the cutting of statues from blocks of marble, stone, or wood, casting in bronze, and modeling in clay or wax. 2 sculptured work; piece of such work. *—v.t.* 1 make (figures) by carving, modeling, casting, etc. 2 cover or ornament with sculpture. [< Latin *sculptura,* variant of *scalptura* < *scalpere* carve]

sculp tured (skulp′chərd), *adj.* 1 carved, molded, cast, etc., in sculpture. 2 covered or ornamented with sculpture.

scum (skum), *n., v.,* **scummed, scum ming.** *—n.* 1 a thin layer that rises to the top of a liquid: *Green scum floated on the top of the pond.* 2 low, disreputable people. *—v.i.* form scum; become covered with scum. *—v.t.* skim. [< Middle Dutch *schuum*]

scum my (skum′ē), *adj.,* **-mi er, -mi est.** 1 consisting of or containing scum. 2 low; worthless.

scup (skup), *n., pl.* **scups** or **scup.** a narrow, high-backed sea fish used for food, common on the eastern coast of the United States; porgy. [of Algonquian origin]

scup per (skup′ər), *n.* an opening in the side of a ship to let water run off the deck. [origin uncertain]

scup per nong (skup′ər nông, skup′ər-nong), *n.* 1 a large, yellowish-green variety of muscadine grape grown in the southern United States. 2 wine made from these grapes. [< *Scuppernong* River, North Carolina]

scurf (skėrf), *n.* 1 small scales of dead skin. Dandruff is a kind of scurf. 2 any scaly matter on a surface. [< Scandinavian (Old Swedish) *skurf*]

scurf y (skėr′fē), *adj.,* **scurf i er, scurf i est.** 1 covered with scurf. 2 of or like scurf. **—scurf′i ness,** *n.*

scur ril i ty (skə ril′ə tē), *n., pl.* **-ties.** 1 coarse joking. 2 indecent abuse. 3 an indecent or coarse remark.

scur ri lous (skėr′ə ləs), *adj.* 1 coarsely joking; using abusive or derisive language: *a scurrilous political writer.* 2 abusive in an indecent way; foul: *scurrilous language.* [< Latin *scurrilis* < *scurra* buffoon] **—scur′ri lous ly,** *adv.* **—scur′ri lous ness,** *n.*

scur ry (skėr′ē), *v.,* **-ried, -ry ing,** *n., pl.* **-ries.** *—v.i.* run quickly; scamper; hurry: *We could hear the mice scurrying about in the walls.* *—n.* a hasty running; hurrying. [short for *hurry-scurry,* reduplication of *hurry*]

scur vy (skėr′vē), *n., adj.,* **-vi er, -vi est.** *—n.* disease caused by a lack of vitamin C in the diet, characterized by swollen and bleeding gums, extreme weakness, livid spots on the skin, and prostration. Scurvy used to be common among sailors when they had little to eat except bread and salt meat. *—adj.* mean; contemptible; base: *a scurvy fellow, a scurvy trick.* [< *scurf*] **—scur′vi ly,** *adv.* **—scur′vi ness,** *n.*

scut (skut), *n.* an erect, short tail, especially that of a rabbit or deer. [< Scandinavian (Old Icelandic) *skutr* stern]

scu tate (skyü′tāt), *adj.* 1 (in zoology) having shieldlike plates or large scales of bone, shell, etc. 2 (in botany) shaped like a shield: *Nasturtiums have scutate leaves.* [< Latin *scutatus* having a shield < *scutum* shield]

scutch (skuch), *v.t.* free (flax or cotton fiber) from woody parts by beating. *—n.* implement for scutching. [origin uncertain]

scutch eon (skuch′ən), *n.* escutcheon.

scute (skyüt), *n.* scutum.

scu tel la (skyü tel′ə), *n.* pl. of **scutellum.**

scu tel late (skyü′tl āt, skyü tel′āt), *adj.* 1 having scutella. 2 formed into a scutellum.

scu tel lum (skyü tel′əm), *n., pl.* **-tel la.** (in zoology and botany) a small plate, scale, or other shieldlike part, such as on the feet of certain birds, the bodies of certain insects, or a cotyledon of some grasses. [< New Latin, diminutive of Latin *scutum* shield]

scut tle[1] (skut′l), *n.* kind of bucket for holding or carrying coal. [Old English *scutel* < Latin *scutella* platter]

scut tle[2] (skut′l), *v.,* **-tled, -tling,** *n.* *—v.i.* run with quick, hurried steps; scamper; scurry. *—n.* a short, hurried run. [variant of earlier *scuddle,* frequentative of *scud*] **—scut′tler,** *n.*

scut tle[3] (skut′l), *n., v.,* **-tled, -tling.** *—n.* 1 an opening in the deck or side of a ship, with a lid or cover. 2 an opening in a wall or roof, with a lid or cover. 3 the lid or cover for any such opening. *—v.t.* 1 cut a hole or holes through the bottom or sides of (a ship) to sink it. 2 cut a hole or holes in the deck of (a ship) to salvage the cargo. [perhaps < Middle French *escoutille* < Spanish *escotilla* hatchway]

scut tle butt (skut′l but′), *n.* INFORMAL. rumor and stories not based on fact; gossip. [originally, a water cask aboard ship < *scuttle*[3] + *butt;* from its being a place for meeting and talking]

scu tum (skyü′təm), *n., pl.* **-ta** (-tə). (in zoology) a shieldlike part of bone, shell, etc.; scute. [< Latin, shield]

Scyl la (sil′ə), *n.* 1 a dangerous rock proverbially located opposite the whirlpool Charybdis, off the southwestern tip of Italy. 2 (in Greek myths) monster with six heads and twelve feet that lived on this rock and snatched sailors from ships. 3 **between Scylla and Charybdis,** between two dangers, one of which must be met.

scy pho zo an (sī′fə zō′ən), *n.* any of a class of marine coelenterates having a bell-shaped, gelatinous body and long, trailing tentacles, and lacking a true polyp stage; jellyfish. [< Greek *skyphos* a cup + *zōion* animal]

scythe

scythe (sīᴛʜ), *n., v.,* **scythed, scyth ing.** *—n.* a long, thin, slightly curved blade on a long handle, for cutting grass, etc. *—v.t.* cut or mow with a scythe. [Old English *sithe;* spelling influenced by Latin *scindere* to cut]

Scyth i a (sith′ē ə), *n.* an ancient region that extended over parts of Europe and Asia north of the Black and Caspian seas and eastward. **—Scyth′i an,** *adj., n.*

s.d., 1 sight draft. 2 sine die. 3 standard deviation.

S. Dak., or **S.D.,** South Dakota.

SDS, Students for a Democratic Society.

Se, selenium.

SE, S.E., or **s.e.,** 1 southeast. 2 southeastern.

sea (sē), *n.* 1 the great body of salt water that covers almost three fourths of the earth's surface; the ocean. 2 any large body of salt water, smaller than an ocean, partly or wholly enclosed by land: *the North Sea.* 3 any of various relatively large landlocked bodies of fresh or salt water: *the Sea of Galilee, the Black Sea.* 4 the swell of the ocean: *a heavy sea.* 5 a large, heavy wave. 6 an overwhelming amount or number: *a sea of troubles.* 7 a broad expanse: *a sea of upturned faces.* 8 Often, **Sea.** one of the dark, flat plains of the moon once thought to be seas; mare: *the Sea of Tranquility.*

at sea, a out on the sea. b puzzled; confused.

follow the sea, be a sailor.

go to sea, a become a sailor. b begin a sea voyage.

put to sea, begin a sea voyage.

—adj. of, on, or from the sea; marine: *a sea animal, a sea route.*

[Old English *sǣ*]

sea anchor, a floating canvas-covered frame or other drag used in a gale to prevent a ship, seaplane, etc., from drifting and to keep its head to the wind.

sea anemone, any of various flowerlike polyps with a fleshy, cylindrical body and a mouth surrounded by many brightly colored tentacles.

sea bass, 1 a common food and game fish of the northeastern coast of the United States with a peculiar tail fin. 2 any of various similar fishes.

sea bed (sē′bed′), *n.* bottom of the sea.

Sea bee (sē′bē′), *n.* member of the construction battalion of the United States Navy. [< the initials *C.B.,* for Construction Battalion]

sea bird, any bird that lives on or near the sea; seafowl.

sea biscuit, hardtack.

sea board (sē′bôrd′, sē′bōrd′), *n.* land bordering on the sea; seacoast: *the Atlantic seaboard.* *—adj.* bordering on the sea.

Sea borg (sē′bôrg), *n.* **Glenn Theodore,** born 1912, American nuclear chemist, discoverer of new chemical elements and radioactive isotopes.

sea borne (sē′bôrn′, sē′bōrn′), *adj.* conveyed by sea; carried on the sea.

sea bread, hardtack.

sea bream, any of certain edible marine fishes belonging to the same family as the porgies.

sea breeze, breeze blowing from the sea toward the land.

sea calf, harbor seal.

sea coast (sē′kōst′), *n.* land along the sea; coast.

sea cow, 1 manatee. 2 dugong. 3 walrus.

sea craft (sē′kraft′), *n., pl.* **-craft.** 1 seagoing vessel. 2 skill in navigation.

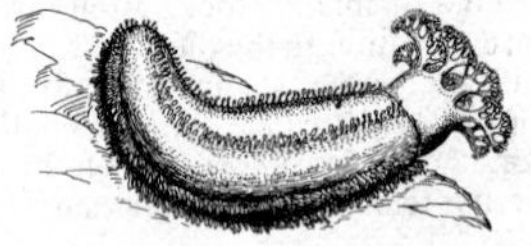

sea cucumber—about 10 in. long

sea cucumber, any of a class of echinoderms, most of which have flexible bodies that resemble cucumbers; holothurian.

sea dog, sailor, especially one with long experience. 2 harbor seal. 3 dogfish.

sea elephant, either of two very large seals, the male of which has a trunklike snout; elephant seal.

sea fan, any of a genus of fan-shaped corals, especially of the Caribbean and the Gulf of Mexico.

sea far er (sē′fer′ər, sē′far′ər), *n.* 1 sailor. 2 traveler on the sea.

sea far ing (sē′fer′ing, sē′far′ing), *adj.* going, traveling, or working on the sea: *Sailors are seafaring men.* *—n.* 1 business or calling of a sailor. 2 act or fact of traveling by sea.

sea foam, 1 foam of the sea. 2 meerschaum (def. 1).

sea food (sē′füd′), *n.* edible saltwater fish and shellfish.

sea fowl (sē′foul′), *n.* sea bird.

sea girt (sē′gėrt′), *adj.* surrounded by the sea.

sea go ing (sē′gō′ing), *adj.* 1 going by sea; seafaring. 2 fit for going to sea.

sea green, light bluish green.

sea gull, any gull, especially one living on or near the sea.

sea hog, porpoise.

hat, āge, fär; let, ēqual, tėrm;
it, īce; hot, ōpen, ôrder;
oil, out; cup, pu̇t, rüle;
ch, child; ng, long; sh, she;
th, thin; ᴛʜ, then; zh, measure;

ə represents *a* in about, *e* in taken, *i* in pencil, *o* in lemon, *u* in circus.

< = from, derived from, taken from.

sea horse (def. 1)
4 to 12 in. long

sea horse, 1 any of a family of small fishes with a prehensile tail and a head suggesting that of a horse, living in warm waters. 2 walrus. 3 (in old stories) a sea animal with the foreparts of a horse and the hind parts of a fish.

sea kale, plant of the mustard family having large cabbagelike leaves, grown for its leaf stems which are blanched and eaten as a vegetable; crambe.

sea king, a Scandinavian pirate chief of the Middle Ages.

seal[1] (sēl), *n.* 1 design stamped on a piece of wax or other soft material, to show ownership or authenticity. The seal of the United States is attached to important government papers. 2 stamp for marking things with such a design: *a seal with one's initials on it.* 3 piece of wax, paper, metal, etc., on which the design is stamped. 4 thing that fastens or closes something tightly. 5 something that secures; pledge: *under a seal of secrecy.* 6 something that settles or determines: *the seal of authority.* 7 mark; sign. 8 stamp used for decoration: *Christmas seals, Easter seals.* 9 **set one's seal to,** approve.
—*v.t.* 1 mark (a document) with a seal; make binding or certify by affixing a seal: *The treaty was signed and sealed by both governments.* 2 close tightly; fasten; shut: *Seal the letter before mailing it. Her promise sealed her lips.* 3 close up the cracks of: *They sealed the log cabin with clay.* 4 settle; determine: *The judge's words sealed the prisoner's fate.* 5 give a sign that (a thing) is true: *seal a promise with a kiss. They sealed their bargain by shaking hands.*
[< Old French *seel* < Latin *sigillum,* diminutive of *signum* a sign] **—seal′a ble,** *adj.*

seal[2] (def. 1)—up to 6 ft. long

seal[2] (sēl), *n., pl.* **seals** or **seal,** *v.* —*n.* 1 any of two families of carnivorous sea mammals, usually of cold regions, with a torpedo-shaped body and large flippers. Some species are hunted for their pelts. The Eskimos use the blubber of seals for food and as a source of oil. 2 sealskin. 3 leather made from the skin of a seal. —*v.i.* hunt seals. [Old English *seolh*] **—seal′like′,** *adj.*

seal ant (sē′lənt), *n.* compound used for sealing: *a paint sealant.*

sea lawyer, INFORMAL. sailor inclined to find fault and to argue.

sea legs, INFORMAL. 1 legs accustomed to walking steadily on a rolling or pitching ship. 2 **get one's sea legs,** become accustomed to the motion of a ship, especially after an initial period of seasickness.

seal er[1] (sē′lər), *n.* 1 person or thing that seals. 2 official appointed to test weights and measures, scales, etc. [< *seal*[1]]

seal er[2] (sē′lər), *n.* 1 person who hunts seals. 2 ship for hunting seals. [< *seal*[2]]

seal er y (sē′lər ē), *n., pl.* **-er ies.** 1 act or occupation of hunting seals. 2 place where seals are hunted.

sea lettuce, any of a genus of green seaweeds whose fronds look like strips of lettuce and are sometimes eaten.

sea level, level of the surface of the sea, especially when halfway between mean high and low water. Mountains are measured in feet above sea level.

sea lily, crinoid.

sealing wax, a hard, brittle substance composed of resin and shellac, which becomes soft when heated, used for sealing letters, packages, etc.

sea lion, any of several large eared seals, especially a species common to the Pacific coast which is sometimes trained for use in circus and carnival acts.

seal ring, signet ring.

seal skin (sēl′skin′), *n.* 1 skin of the fur seal, prepared for use. 2 garment made of this. *—adj.* made of sealskin.

Sealyham terrier
about 10 in. high at the shoulder

Sea ly ham terrier (sē′lē ham, sē′lē əm), any of a breed of small Welsh dogs with short legs, a square jaw, and a rough, shaggy coat.

seam (sēm), *n.* 1 line formed by sewing together two pieces of cloth, canvas, leather, etc. 2 any line where edges join: *The seams of the boat must be filled in if they leak.* 3 any mark or line like a seam. 4 (in geology) a layer or stratum, especially of coal or another mineral. —*v.t.* 1 sew the seam of; join with a seam. 2 mark (the face, etc.) with wrinkles, scars, etc. —*v.i.* crack open. [Old English *sēam*] **—seam′er,** *n.* **—seam′less,** *adj.*

sea man (sē′mən), *n., pl.* **-men.** 1 sailor. 2 (in the navy) any sailor ranking below a petty officer.

sea man like (sē′mən līk′), *adj.* like a seaman; having the skill of a good seaman.

sea man ly (sē′mən lē), *adj.* seamanlike.

sea man ship (sē′mən ship), *n.* skill in navigating or managing a ship.

sea mark (sē′märk′), *n.* 1 lighthouse, beacon, or other landmark that can be seen from the sea, used as a guide for a ship's course. 2 line on the shore that shows the upper limit of the tide

sea mew, sea gull, especially the common gull of Europe.

sea mile, nautical mile.

sea mount (sē′mount′), *n.* mountain arising from the sea bottom and having its summit beneath the surface of the sea; guyot.

seam stress (sēm′stris), *n.* woman whose work is sewing. Also, **sempstress.**

seam y (sē′mē), *adj.,* **seam i er, seam i est.** 1 having or showing seams. 2 worst; least attractive: *Policemen see much of the seamy side of life.* **—seam′i ness,** *n.*

sé ance (sā′äns), *n.* 1 a meeting of people trying to communicate with spirits of the dead by the help of a medium. 2 a sitting or session. [< French < *seoir* sit < Latin *sedere*]

sea otter, a large, almost extinct otter found along the coasts of the northern Pacific, yielding a valuable fur.

sea plane (sē′plān′), *n.* airplane that can take off from and land on water, especially one which has floats; hydroplane.

sea port (sē′pôrt′, sē′pōrt′), *n.* port or harbor on the seacoast; city or town with a harbor that ships can reach from the sea.

sea power, 1 nation having a strong navy. 2 naval strength.

sea purse, the horny case or pouch that skates or certain sharks secrete around their eggs to protect them.

sear (sir), *v.t.* 1 burn or char the surface of: *sear a roast.* See **burn** for synonym study. 2 make hard or unfeeling: *That cruel man must have a seared conscience.* 3 dry up; wither: *The hot summer sun seared the grain.* —*v.i.* become dry, burned, or hard. See **burn** for synonym study. —*n.* mark made by searing. —*adj.* sere. [Old English *sēarian* < *sēar,* adjective]

search (sėrch), *v.i.* try to find by looking; seek: *We searched all day for the lost cat.* —*v.t.* 1 go over carefully in trying to find something. See synonym study below. 2 examine, especially for something concealed: *search one's baggage.* 3 examine by probing: *The doctor searched the wound for the bullet.* 4 **search out,** find by searching: *search out all the facts in the case.* —*n.* 1 act of searching; examination. 2 **in search of,** trying to find; looking for. [< Old French *cerchier,* ultimately < Latin *circus* circle] **—search′a ble,** *adj.* **—search′er,** *n.*
Syn. *v.t.* 1 **Search, explore** mean to look through a place for something. **Search** implies looking for something known or thought to be there: *We searched the woods for the lost child.* **Explore** implies looking for whatever may be there: *The expedition explored the uncharted coast.*

search ing (sėr′ching), *adj.* 1 examining carefully; thorough: *a searching gaze.* 2 piercing; sharp: *a searching wind.* **—search′ing ly,** *adv.*

search light (sėrch′līt′), *n.* 1 device that throws a very bright beam of light in any direction. 2 such a beam of light.

search party, group of persons searching for a person or thing lost or hiding.

search warrant, a written court order authorizing the search of a specified place for stolen goods, criminals, etc.

sea robin, any of several gurnards, especially certain American species.

sea room, space at sea free from obstruction, in which a ship can easily sail, tack, turn around, etc.

sea rover, 1 pirate. 2 a pirate ship.

sea scape (sē′skāp), *n.* 1 picture of a scene or scenery on the sea. 2 view of scenery on the sea.

sea scout, boy trained in seamanship by the Boy Scout organization.

sea serpent, 1 a huge snakelike animal supposed to have been repeatedly seen at sea. 2 sea snake.

sea shell (sē′shel′), *n.* shell of any sea animal, especially a mollusk such as an oyster, conch, abalone, etc.

sea shore (sē′shôr′, sē′shōr′), *n.* 1 land at the edge of a sea; shore. 2 area between ordinary high and low tide.

sea sick (sē′sik′), *adj.* sick because of a ship's motion.

sea sick ness (sē′sik′nis), *n.* sickness caused by a ship's motion.

sea side (sē′sīd′), *n.* land along the sea; seacoast; seashore. *—adj.* of or at the seaside.

sea snake, 1 any of a family of venomous snakes with finlike tails that live in tropical seas. 2 sea serpent.

sea son (sē′zn), *n.* 1 one of the four periods of the year; spring, summer, autumn, or winter. 2 any period of time marked by something special: *a holiday season, the harvest season.* 3 time when something is occurring, active, at its best, or in fashion: *the baseball season, the theatrical season.* 4 a suitable or fit time. 5 period or time.
for a season, for a time.
in good season, early enough.
in season, a at the right or proper time. **b** in the time or condition for eating, hunting, etc. **c** early enough.
in season and out of season, at all times.
out of season, not in season.
—v.t. 1 improve the flavor of: *season soup with salt.* 2 give interest or character to: *season conversation with wit.* 3 make fit for use by a period of keeping or treatment: *season wood by drying.* 4 make used; accustom: *Soldiers are seasoned to battle by experience in war.* 5 make less severe; soften: *Season justice with mercy.* *—v.i.* become seasoned.
[< Old French *seison* < Latin *sationem* a sowing < *serere* to sow] **—sea′son er,** *n.*

sea son a ble (sē′zn ə bəl), *adj.* 1 suitable to the season: *Hot weather is seasonable in July in the northern hemisphere.* 2 coming at the right or proper time: *Red Cross brought seasonable aid to the flood victims.* **—sea′son a ble ness,** *n.* **—sea′son a bly,** *adv.*

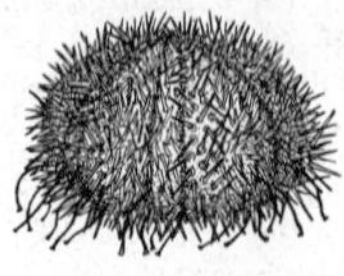

sea urchin diameter about 3 in.

sea son al (sē′zn əl), *adj.* having to do with the seasons; depending on a season; happening at regular intervals: *seasonal variations in the weather, a seasonal worker.* **—sea′son al ly,** *adv.*

sea son ing (sē′zn ing), *n.* 1 something that gives a better flavor, such as salt, pepper, and spices. 2 something that gives interest or character.

season ticket, ticket or pass entitling the holder to certain privileges for the season or for a specified period.

sea squirt, 1 any of a class of small, soft-bodied sea animals of the tunicate subphylum that squirt water when they contract. 2 tunicate.

seat (sēt), *n.* 1 something to sit on, as a chair, stool, bench, or sofa. 2 place to sit: *Can you find a seat on the train?* 3 place in which one has the right to sit: *reserve a seat on an airplane.* 4 right to sit as a member, or the position of being a member: *a seat on the stock exchange, a seat in Congress.* 5 the part of a chair, stool, bench, etc., on which one sits. 6 the part of the body on which one sits, or the clothing covering it. 7 manner of sitting on horseback. 8 that on which anything rests; base. 9 an established place or center: *A university is a seat of learning. The seat of our government is in Washington, D.C.* 10 residence; home: *The family seat of the Howards is in Sussex.*
—v.t. 1 set or place on a seat; cause to sit down: *seat a person on a chair.* 2 have seats for (a specified number): *a hall seating 300 people.* 3 provide with a seat or seats: *seat a delegation at a convention.* 4 put a seat on (a chair, trousers, etc.). 5 **be seated, a** sit down. **b** be sitting. **c** be situated.
[< Scandinavian (Old Icelandic) *sæti*] **—seat′er,** *n.*

seat belt, strap fastened to the seat in an automobile, aircraft, etc., and buckled across the occupant's lap to protect him from being thrown about; safety belt.

seat mate (sēt′māt′), *n.* person sitting next to one on a train, aircraft, etc.

SEA TO (sē′tō), *n.* Southeast Asia Treaty Organization.

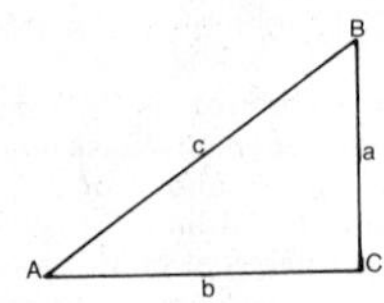

secant (def. 2)—Triangle ABC is a right triangle in which angle C is the right angle and side c is the hypotenuse.
The secant of angle A is c/b,
the cosecant of angle A is c/a;
the secant of angle B is c/a,
the cosecant of angle B is c/b.

sea train, a seagoing vessel for the transport of railroad cars.

sea trout, 1 any of various species of trout which spend part of their life in salt water. 2 any of several weakfishes.

Se at tle (sē at′l), *n.* seaport in W Washington, on Puget Sound. 531,000.

sea urchin, any of a class of echinoderms having a hard shell formed of calcareous plates bearing many movable spines; echinoid; echinus.

sea wall, a strong wall or embankment made to prevent the waves from wearing away the shore, to act as a breakwater, etc.

sea ward (sē′wərd), *adv., adj.* toward the sea: *Our house faces seaward.* *—n.* direction toward the sea: *The island lies a mile to seaward.*

sea wards (sē′wərdz), *adv.* seaward.

sea wa ter (sē′wô′tər, sē′wot′ər), *n.* the salt water of the sea or ocean.

sea way (sē′wā′), *n.* 1 an inland waterway that connects with the open sea and is deep enough to permit ocean shipping. 2 a way over the sea, especially a regular shipping lane. 3 headway of a ship. 4 a rough sea.

sea weed (sē′wēd′), *n.* any plant or plants growing in the sea, especially any of various marine algae.

sea worm, any free-moving worm living in salt water.

sea wor thy (sē′wėr′ᴛʜē), *adj.* fit for sailing on the sea; able to stand storms at sea. **—sea′wor′thi ness,** *n.*

se ba ceous (si bā′shəs), *adj.* 1 having to do with fat; fatty; greasy. 2 secreting a fatty or oily substance. [< Latin *sebaceus* < *sebum* grease]

sebaceous gland, gland in an inner layer of the skin that supplies oil to the skin and hair.

Se bas to pol (si bas′tə pōl), *n.* Sevastopol.

seb or rhe a (seb′ə rē′ə), *n.* an abnormal discharge from the sebaceous glands. [< *sebum* + Greek *rhein* to flow]

se bum (sē′bəm), *n.* the fatty secretion of the sebaceous glands. [< Latin, tallow, grease]

SEC, Securities and Exchange Commission.

sec., 1 according to [for Latin *secundum*]. 2 secant. 3 second or seconds. 4 secretary. 5 section or sections.

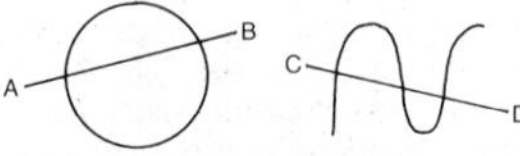

secant (def. 1)—AB and CD are secants.

se cant (sē′kənt, sē′kant), *n.* 1 (in geometry) a straight line that intersects a curve at two or more points. 2 (in trigonometry) ratio of the length of the hypotenuse in a right triangle to the length of the side adjacent to an acute angle. *—adj.* (in geometry) intersecting. [< Latin *secantem* cutting]

sec a teurs (sek′ə tėrz′), *n.pl.* BRITISH. pruning shears. [< French *sécateur* (singular) < Latin *secare* to cut]

se cede (si sēd′), *v.i.,* **-ced ed, -ced ing.** withdraw formally from an organization. [< Latin *secedere* < *se-* apart + *cedere* go] **—se ced′er,** *n.*

se ces sion (si sesh′ən), *n.* 1 a formal withdrawing from an organization; a seceding. 2 Also, **Secession.** the seceding of the eleven southern states from the Union in 1860-1861, which resulted in the Civil War. [< Latin *secessionem* < *secedere.* See SECEDE.]

se ces sion ism (si sesh′ə niz′əm), *n.* principles of those favoring secession.

se ces sion ist (si sesh′ə nist), *n.* 1 person who favors secession. 2 person who secedes. *—adj.* favoring or taking part in secession.

se clude (si klüd′), *v.,* **-clud ed, -clud ing.** keep apart from company; shut off from others: *He secludes himself and sees only his close friends.* [< Latin *secludere* < *se-* apart + *claudere* shut]

se clud ed (si klü′did), *adj.* shut off from others; undisturbed: *a secluded cabin in the woods.* **—se clud′ed ly,** *adv.* **—se clud′ed ness,** *n.*

se clu sion (si klü′zhən), *n.* 1 a secluding or a being secluded; retirement: *She lives in seclusion apart from her friends.* 2 a secluded place. [< Medieval Latin *seclusionem* < Latin *secludere* seclude]

se clu sive (si klü′siv), *adj.* 1 fond of seclusion. 2 tending to seclude. **—se clu′sive ly,** *adv.* **—se clu′sive ness,** *n.*

sec ond¹ (sek′ənd), *adj.* 1 next after the first: *the second seat from the front.* 2 below the first; subordinate: *second in command, the second officer on a ship.* 3 another; other: *Napoleon has been called a second Caesar.* 4 lower in musical pitch. 5 rendering a part lower in pitch: *second soprano.* 6 designating the gear ratio of a standard automobile transmission between that of low and high.
—adv. in the second group, division, rank, etc.; secondly: *speak second.*
—n. 1 person, thing, place, etc., that is second. 2 **seconds,** *pl.* articles below first quality: *These dishes are seconds and have some slight defects.* 3 person who attends or assists a boxer, duelist, etc. 4 in music: **a** a tone on the next degree from a given tone. **b** the interval between consecutive tones of the scale. **c** the harmonic combination of such tones. **d** the second part in a concerted piece. 5 the forward gear or speed in an automobile or similar machine.
—v.t. 1 support; back up; assist (a person, his aims, actions, etc.). 2 express approval or support of (a motion, amendment, proposal, or the one who makes it).
[< Old French *seconde* < Latin *secundus* following, second (of a series) < *sequi* follow] **—sec′ond er,** *n.*

sec ond² (sek′ənd), *n.* 1 $^{1}/_{60}$ of a minute; $^{1}/_{3600}$ of an hour. 2 a very short time; instant; moment. 3 $^{1}/_{3600}$ of a degree of an angle. 12° 10′ 30″ means 12 degrees, 10 minutes, 30 seconds. [< Old French *seconde* < Medieval Latin *secunda (minuta)* second (minute), i.e., the result of the second division of the hour into sixty parts]

Second Advent, the coming of Christ at the Last Judgment; Advent.

sec ond ar y (sek′ən der′ē), *adj., n., pl.* **-ar ies.** *—adj.* 1 next after the first in order, place, time, etc. 2 not main or chief; having less importance: *Reading fast is secondary to reading well.* 3 not original; derived: *a secondary source of the report.* 4 of or having to do with a coil or circuit in which a current is produced by induction. *—n.* 1 person or thing that is secondary, second in importance, or subordinate. 2 coil or circuit in which a current is produced by induction. 3 (in football) the defensive backfield. **—sec′ond ar′i ly,** *adv.*

secondary accent, 1 an accent that is weaker than the strongest stress in a word (primary accent), but stronger than no stress. The second syllable of *ab bre′ vi a′tion* has a secondary accent. 2 mark (′) used to show this.

secondary cell, storage battery.

secondary emission, the freeing of electrons from the surface of a metal by bombardment with other electrons or ions.

secondary root, branch of a primary root.

secondary school, high school.

secondary stress, secondary accent.

second base, in baseball: 1 the base opposite home plate on the diamond, that must be touched second by a runner. 2 position of the fielder covering the area near this base. **—second baseman.**

sec ond-best (sek′ənd best′), *adj.* next in quality to the first.

second childhood, a foolish or childish condition caused by old age; dotage.

second class, 1 the second grade of passenger accommodations offered for travel by ship, airplane, or train. 2 class of mail that includes newspapers, magazines, and other periodicals.

sec ond-class (sek′ənd klas′), *adj.* 1 of or belonging to the class next after the first. 2 of or having to do with second class. 3 of inferior grade or quality. *—adv.* in or by second class.

Second Coming, Second Advent.

second fiddle, INFORMAL. **be second fiddle** or **play second fiddle (to),** take a lesser part or position.

sec ond-guess (sek′ənd ges′), *v.t.* 1 use hindsight to correct. 2 outguess. **—sec′ond-guess′er,** *n.*

second hand, hand on a clock or watch, pointing to the seconds. It moves around the whole dial once in a minute.

sec ond-hand (sek′ənd hand′), *adj.* 1 not original; obtained from another: *second-hand information.* 2 not new; used already by someone else: *second-hand clothes.* 3 dealing in used goods: *a second-hand bookshop.* *—adv.* from other than the original source; not firsthand.

second lieutenant, a commissioned officer in the army, air force, or marines having the lowest rank, next below a first lieutenant.

sec ond ly (sek′ənd lē), *adv.* in the second place; second.

second nature, habit, quality, knowledge, etc., that a person has acquired and had for so long that it seems to be a part of his nature.

second person, form of a pronoun or verb used to indicate the person spoken to. *You* and *yours* are pronouns of the second person.

second quarter, 1 period of time between the first half moon and the full moon. 2 phase of the moon when it has revolved far enough to reveal its entire face; full moon.

sec ond-rate (sek′ənd rāt′), *adj.* 1 rated as second-class. 2 inferior.

second sight, the supposed power of seeing distant objects or future events as if they were present.

sec ond-sto ry man (sek′ənd stôr′ē, sek′ənd stōr′ē), U.S. burglar who gets into a house through an upstairs window.

sec ond-strike (sek′ənd strīk′), *adj.* 1 (of a nuclear weapon or force) able to retaliate or strike back after a nuclear attack. 2 of retaliation; retaliatory: *second-strike capability.*

sec ond-string (sek′ənd string′), *adj.* 1 (in sports) not of the first string: *a second-string quarterback.* 2 second-rate.

se cre cy (sē′krə sē), *n., pl.* **-cies.** 1 condition of being secret or of being kept secret. 2 ability to keep things secret. 3 tendency to conceal; lack of frankness.

se cret (sē′krit), *adj.* 1 kept from the knowledge of others: *a secret plan.* See synonym study below. 2 keeping to oneself what one knows: *as secret as a mouse.* 3 known only to a few: *a secret password, a secret society.* 4 kept from sight; hidden: *a secret drawer.* 5 retired; secluded. 6 working or acting in secret: *secret police.* 7 very hard to understand or discover. *—n.* 1 something secret or hidden; mystery. 2 thing known only to a few. 3 a hidden cause or reason. 4 **in secret,** in private; not openly. [< Latin *secretum* set apart, separated, secret < *se-* apart + *cernere* to separate. Doublet of SECRETE.] **—se′cret ly,** *adv.*

Syn. *adj.* 1 **Secret, covert, clandestine** mean done, made, or carried on without the knowledge of others. **Secret** is the general word, and applies to concealment of any kind and for any purpose: *They have a secret business agreement.* **Covert,** a more formal word, suggests partial concealment, and applies to anything kept under cover, disguised, or not openly revealed: *A hint is a covert suggestion.* **Clandestine,** also formal, suggests concealment for an unlawful or improper purpose: *He feared someone would learn of his clandestine trips.*

hat, āge, fär; let, ēqual, tėrm;
it, īce; hot, ōpen, ôrder;
oil, out; cup, pu̇t, rüle;
ch, child; ng, long; sh, she;
th, thin; ŦH, then; zh, measure;

ə represents *a* in about, *e* in taken, *i* in pencil, *o* in lemon, *u* in circus.

< = from, derived from, taken from.

secret agent, agent of a government secret service.

sec re tar i al (sek′rə ter′ē əl), *adj.* of a secretary; having to do with a secretary.

sec re tar i at (sek′rə ter′ē it, sek′rə ter′ē-at), *n.* 1 office or position of secretary or secretary-general. 2 the department or administrative unit controlled by a secretary or secretary-general: *the secretariat of the United Nations.* 3 group of secretaries. 4 place where a secretary transacts business. [< French *secrétariat*]

sec re tar y (sek′rə ter′ē), *n., pl.* **-tar ies.** 1 person who writes letters, keeps records, etc., for a person, company, club, etc.: *Our club has a secretary who keeps the minutes of the meeting.* 2 person who has charge of a department of the government or similar organization. The Secretary of the Treasury is the head of the Treasury Department. 3 a writing desk with a set of drawers and often with shelves for books. [< Late Latin *secretarius* confidential officer < Latin *secretum* secret]

secretary bird
about 4 ft. long

secretary bird, a large, long-legged African bird of prey that feeds on reptiles and other vertebrates, so called because its crest suggests pens stuck over the ear.

sec re tar y-gen er al (sek′rə ter′ē jen′ər əl), *n., pl.* **sec re tar ies-gen er al.** the chief secretary; the administrative head of a secretariat: *the secretary-general of the United Nations.*

Secretary of State, U.S. the head of the State Department and principal advisor to the President on foreign affairs.

sec re tar y ship (sek′rə ter′ē ship), *n.* the position, duties, etc., of a secretary.

se crete (si krēt′), *v.t.,* **-cret ed, -cret ing.** 1 keep secret; hide. 2 produce and discharge: *Glands in the mouth secrete saliva.* [< Latin *secretum* set apart. Doublet of SECRET.]

se cre tin (si krēt′n), *n.* an intestinal hormone that stimulates secretion by the pancreas.

se cre tion (si krē′shən), *n.* 1 substance that is secreted by some part of an animal or plant: *Bile is the secretion of the liver.* 2 a secreting of such a substance. 3 a concealing; hiding.

se cre tive (sē′krə tiv, si krē′tiv *for 1;* si krē′tiv *for 2*), *adj.* 1 having the habit of secrecy; not frank and open. 2 causing or aiding secretion. **—se′cre tive ly,** *adv.* **—se′cre tive ness,** *n.*

se cre tor y (si krē′tər ē), *adj.* secreting; of or causing secretion.

secret service, 1 branch of a government that makes secret investigations. 2 **Secret Service,** branch of the United States Treasury Department concerned with discovering and preventing counterfeiting, with protecting the President, etc.

sect (sekt), *n.* 1 group of people having the same principles, beliefs, or opinions. 2 a religious group separated from an established church. [< Latin *secta* party, school, probably < *sectari* keep following < *sequi* follow]

sect., section.

sec tar i an (sek ter′ē ən), *adj.* 1 of or having to do with a sect; denominational. 2 characteristic of one sect only; strongly prejudiced in favor of a certain sect. *—n.* 1 a devoted member of a sect, especially a narrow-minded or strongly prejudiced member. 2 member of a religious group separated from an established church.

sec tar i an ism (sek ter′ē ə niz′əm), *n.* spirit or tendencies of sectarians.

sec tar y (sek′tər ē), *n., pl.* **-tar ies.** member of a particular sect. [< Medieval Latin *sectarius* < Latin *secta.* See SECT.]

sec tile (sek′təl), *adj.* capable of being cut out smoothly by a knife.

sec tion (sek′shən), *n.* 1 a part separated or cut off; part; division; slice: *Cut the pie into eight equal sections.* 2 division of a written or printed work, a law, etc.: *Chapter X has seven sections.* 3 symbol (§) used to introduce a subdivision or as a mark of reference. 4 part of a country, city, etc.; region or district: *The city has a business section and a residential section.* 5 area of land one mile square; 640 acres. A township usually contains 36 sections. 6 one of the parts of something that is built of a number of similar parts: *the sections of a bookcase.* 7 the act of cutting or dividing. 8 a representation of a thing as it would appear if cut through by a plane. 9 the part of a railroad line maintained by one group of workmen. 10 a part of a sleeping car containing an upper and a lower berth. *—v.t.* 1 cut or divide into sections. 2 cut through so as to present a section. [< Latin *sectionem* < *secare* to cut]

sec tion al (sek′shə nəl), *adj.* 1 of or having to do with a particular section; regional or local: *sectional interests.* 2 made of sections: *a sectional bookcase.* **—sec′tion al ly,** *adv.*

sec tion al ism (sek′shə nə liz′əm), *n.* too great regard for sectional interests; sectional prejudice or hatred.

sec tor (sek′tər), *n.* 1 the part of a circle between two radii and the included arc. 2 a clearly defined military area which a given military unit protects or covers with fire; part of a front held by a unit. 3 instrument consisting of two rulers connected by a joint, used in measuring or drawing angles. 4 any section, zone, or quarter. *—v.t.* divide into sectors; provide with sectors. [< Late Latin < Latin, cutter < *secare* to cut]

sec to ri al (sek tôr′ē əl, sek tōr′ē əl), *adj.* of, having to do with, or resembling a sector.

sec u lar (sek′yə lər), *adj.* 1 not religious or sacred; worldly: *secular music, a secular education.* 2 living in the world; not belonging to a religious order: *the secular clergy, a secular priest.* 3 occurring once in an age or century. 4 lasting through long ages; going on from age to age. *—n.* 1 a secular priest. 2 layman. [< Latin *saecularis* < *saeculum* age, world] **—sec′u lar ly,** *adv.*

sec u lar ism (sek′yə lə riz′əm), *n.* 1 skepticism in regard to religion. 2 opposition to the introduction of religion into public schools or other public affairs.

sec u lar ist (sek′yə lər ist), *n.* believer in secularism.

sec u lar ize (sek′yə lə rīz′), *v.t.,* **-ized, -iz ing.** 1 make secular or worldly; separate from religious connection or influence: *secularize the schools.* 2 transfer (property) from the possession of the church to that of the government. **—sec′u lar i za′tion,** *n.* **—sec′u lar iz′er,** *n.*

se cure (si kyůr′), *adj., v.,* **-cured, -cur ing.** *—adj.* 1 safe against loss, attack, escape, etc.: *Keep the prisoner secure within his cell. This is a secure hiding place. Land in a growing city is a secure investment.* See **safe** for synonym study. 2 that can be counted on; sure; certain: *We know in advance that our victory is secure.* 3 free from care or fear: *a secure old age.* 4 firmly fastened; not liable to give way: *The boards of this bridge do not look secure.* *—v.t.* 1 make safe; protect: *Every loan was secured by bonds or mortages.* 2 make (something) sure or certain; ensure. 3 make firm or fast: *Secure the locks on the windows.* 4 get by effort; obtain: *secure tickets for a play.* 5 seize and confine. *—v.i.* make oneself safe; be safe: *We must secure against the dangers of the coming storm.* [< Latin *securus* < *se-* free from + *cura* care. Doublet of SURE.] **—se cur′a ble,** *adj.* **—se cure′ly,** *adv.* **—se cure′ment,** *n.* **—se cure′ness,** *n.* **—se cur′er,** *n.*

se cur i ty (si kyůr′ə tē), *n., pl.* **-ties.** 1 freedom from danger, care, or fear; feeling or condition of being safe. 2 certainty. 3 carelessness; overconfidence. 4 something that secures or makes safe: *Rubber soles are a security against slipping.* 5 Usually, **securities,** *pl.* bond or stock certificates. 6 something given as a pledge that a person will fulfill some duty, promise, etc.: *A life-insurance policy may serve as security for a loan.* 7 person who agrees to be responsible for another; surety.

Security Council, council in the United Nations consisting of five permanent members and ten rotating members, concerned primarily with maintaining world peace.

security risk, person regarded as unreliable or dangerous in positions involving national security.

secy. or **sec'y.,** secretary.

se dan (si dan′), *n.* 1 a closed automobile with a front and back seat, seating four or more persons. 2 sedan chair. [origin uncertain]

sector (def. 1) of a circle (shaded area)

Se dan (si dan′), *n.* town in NE France, where Prussia defeated France in 1870. 23,000.

sedan chair, a covered chair for one person, carried on poles by two men.

sedan chair

se date (si dāt′), *adj.* quiet; calm; serious: *She is very sedate for a child and would rather read or sew than play.* [< Latin *sedatum,* related to *sedere* sit] **—se date′ly,** *adv.* **—se date′ness,** *n.*

se da tion (si dā′shən), *n.* 1 treatment with sedatives. 2 the calm or relaxed state induced by such treatment.

sed a tive (sed′ə tiv), *n.* 1 medicine that lessens nervousness or excitement. 2 anything soothing or calming. *—adj.* 1 lessening pain or excitement. 2 soothing; calming.

sed en tar y (sed′n ter′ē), *adj.* 1 used to sitting still much of the time: *Sedentary people get little physical exercise.* 2 that keeps one sitting still much of the time: *Bookkeeping is a sedentary occupation.* 3 not migratory: *Pigeons are sedentary birds.* 4 fixed to one spot: *a sedentary mollusk.* [< Latin *sedentarius,* ultimately < *sedere* sit] **—sed′en tar′i ly,** *adv.* **—sed′en tar′i ness,** *n.*

Se der (sā′dər), *n., pl.* **Se ders, Se dar im** (se där′im). the religious service and feast held in Jewish homes on the first two nights (or first night only) of Passover. [< Hebrew *sēdher,* literally, order]

sedge (sej), *n.* any of a large family of monocotyledonous herbs growing chiefly in wet places, resembling grasses but having solid, three-sided stems and small, inconspicuous flowers usually in spikes or heads. [Old English *secg*]

sedg y (sej′ē), *adj.,* **sedg i er, sedg i est.** 1 abounding in or covered with sedge; bordered with sedge. 2 like sedge.

sed i ment (sed′ə mənt), *n.* 1 matter that settles to the bottom of a liquid; dregs. 2 (in geology) earth, stones, etc., deposited by water, wind, or ice: *Each year the Nile overflows and deposits sediment on the land.* [< Latin *sedimentum* < *sedere* settle]

sed i men tal (sed′ə men′tl), *adj.* sedimentary.

sed i men tar y (sed′ə men′tər ē), *adj.* 1 of or having to do with sediment. 2 (in geology) formed by the depositing of sediment. Shale is a sedimentary rock.

sed i men ta tion (sed′ə men tā′shən), *n.* a depositing of sediment.

se di tion (si dish′ən), *n.* speech or action causing discontent or rebellion against the government; incitement to discontent or rebellion. [< Latin *seditionem* < *sed-, se-* apart + *ire* go]

se di tion ar y (si dish′ə ner′ē), *adj., n., pl.* **-ar ies.** *—adj.* having to do with or involving sedition. *—n.* person who is guilty of sedition.

se di tious (si dish′əs), *adj.* 1 stirring up discontent or rebellion. 2 taking part in or guilty of sedition. 3 having to do with sedition. **—se di′tious ly,** *adv.* **—se di′tious ness,** *n.*

se duce (si düs′, si dyüs′), *v.t.,* **-duced, -duc ing.** 1 tempt to wrongdoing; persuade to do wrong: *Benedict Arnold, seduced by the offer of great wealth, betrayed his country to the enemy.* 2 lead away from virtue; lead astray; beguile. 3 persuade or entice to have sexual intercourse. [< Latin *seducere* < *se-* aside + *ducere* to lead] **—se duc′er,** *n.*

se duce ment (si düs′mənt, si dyüs′mənt), *n.* seduction.

se duc i ble (si dü′sə bəl, si dyü′sə bəl), *adj.* that can be seduced.

se duc tion (si duk′shən), *n.* 1 a seducing. 2 a being seduced. 3 something that seduces; temptation; attraction.

se duc tive (si duk′tiv), *adj.* 1 that tempts or entices; alluring: *a very seductive offer.* 2 captivating; charming: *a seductive smile.* **—se duc′tive ly,** *adv.* **—se duc′tive ness,** *n.*

se duc tress (si duk′tris), *n.* woman who seduces.

se du li ty (si dü′lə tē, si dyü′lə tē), *n.* quality of being sedulous; sedulous application or care.

sed u lous (sej′ə ləs), *adj.* hard-working; diligent; painstaking. [< Latin *sedulus* < *se dolo* without deception] **—sed′u lous ly,** *adv.* **—sed′u lous ness,** *n.*

se dum (sē′dəm), *n.* any of a large genus of fleshy herbs and small shrubs, most of which have clusters of yellow, white, or pink flowers; stonecrop. [< Latin, houseleek]

see[1] (sē), *v.,* **saw, seen, see ing.** *—v.t.* 1 perceive with the eyes; look at. See synonym study below. 2 use the eyes to see (things): *see a play.* 3 perceive with the mind; understand: *I see what you mean.* 4 find out; learn: *See who is at the door.* 5 take care; make sure: *See that you lock the door.* 6 think; consider: *You may go if you see fit to do so.* 7 have knowledge or experience of: *see service in two wars.* 8 go with; attend; escort: *see a girl home.* 9 have a talk with; meet: *She wishes to see you alone.* 10 call on: *I went to see a friend.* 11 receive a visit from: *be too ill to see anyone.* 12 visit; attend: *We plan to see the World's Fair.* 13 (in card games) meet (a bet) by staking an equal sum. *—v.i.* 1 perceive objects with the eyes. 2 have the power of sight: *The blind do not see.* 3 perceive with the mind; understand. 4 find out. 5 look; behold.

see into, understand the real character or hidden purpose of.

see off, go with to the starting place of a journey.

see out, go through with; finish.

see through, a understand the real character or hidden purpose of. **b** go through with; finish. **c** watch over or help through a difficulty.

see to, look after; take care of.

[Old English *sēon*]

Syn. *v.t.* **1 See, perceive, observe** mean to become aware of something through sight. **See,** the general word, implies awareness but not necessarily conscious effort or recognition: *We saw someone standing in the doorway.* **Perceive,** often a formal substitute for *see,* can also imply conscious notice or recognition of what is seen: *We perceived the figure to be your mother.* **Observe** implies conscious effort and attention: *We observed a change in her.*

see[2] (sē), *n.* 1 position or authority of a bishop. 2 district under a bishop's authority; diocese; bishopric. 3 seat of a bishop in his diocese. [< Old French *sie* < Latin *sedes* abode < *sedere* sit]

seed (sēd), *n., pl.* **seeds** or **seed,** *adj., v.* *—n.* 1 the part of a plant from which a flower, vegetable, or other plant grows; a fertilized and mature ovule capable of germination into a plant similar to that from which it came. 2 bulb, sprout, or any part of a plant from which a new plant will sprout. 3 source or beginning of anything: *sow the seeds of trouble.* 4 children; descendants: *The Jews are the seed of Abraham.* 5 semen; sperm. **6 go to seed, a** come to the time of yielding seeds. **b** come to the end of vigor, usefulness, prosperity, etc.
—adj. of or containing seeds; used for seeds.
—v.t. 1 sow with seed; scatter seeds over: *seed a field with corn.* 2 sow (seeds). 3 remove the seeds from: *seed raisins.* 4 (in sports) scatter or distribute (the names of players) so that the best players do not meet in the early part of a tournament. 5 scatter Dry Ice or other chemicals into (clouds) from an airplane in an effort to produce rain. *—v.i.* 1 sow seed. 2 produce seed; shed seeds: *Some plants will not seed in a cold climate.* [Old English *sǣd*] **—seed′less,** *adj.* **—seed′like′,** *adj.*

seed bed (sēd′bed′), *n.* a piece of ground prepared for planting seed.

seed case (sēd′kās′), *n.* any pod, capsule, or other dry, hollow fruit that contains seeds.

seed coat, the outer covering of a seed.

seed er (sē′dər), *n.* 1 person who seeds. 2 machine or device for planting seeds. 3 machine or device for removing seeds.

seed leaf, cotyledon.

seed ling (sēd′ling), *n.* 1 a young plant grown from a seed. 2 a young tree less than three feet high.

seed oyster, a very young oyster ready for planting.

seed pearl, a very small pearl.

seed plant, any plant that bears seeds. Most seed plants have flowers and produce seeds in fruits; some, such as the pines, form seeds on cones.

seeds man (sēdz′mən), *n., pl.* **-men.** 1 sower of seed. 2 dealer in seed.

seed vessel, pericarp.

seed y (sē′dē), *adj.,* **seed i er, seed i est.** 1 full of seed. 2 gone to seed. 3 shabby; no longer fresh or new: *seedy clothes.* 4 INFORMAL. somewhat ill. **—seed′i ly,** *adv.* **—seed′i ness,** *n.*

see ing (sē′ing), *conj.* in view of the fact; considering: *Seeing that it is 10 o'clock, we will wait no longer.* *—n.* ability to see; sight. *—adj.* that sees.

Seeing Eye, organization that breeds and trains dogs as guides for blind people.

seek (sēk), *v.,* **sought, seek ing.** *—v.t.* 1 try to find; look for: *We are seeking a new home.* 2 hunt; search for: *seek something lost.* 3 try to get: *seek advice.* 4 try; attempt: *seek to make peace with one's enemies.* 5 go to: *Being sleepy, he sought his bed.* *—v.i.* make a search. [Old English *sēcan*] **—seek′er,** *n.*

seem (sēm), *v.i.* 1 look like; appear to be: *He seemed a very old man.* 2 appear to oneself: *I still seem to hear the music.* 3 appear to exist: *There seems no need to wait longer.* 4 appear to be true or to be the case: *It seems likely to rain. This, it seems, is your idea of cleaning a room.* [< Scandinavian (Old Icelandic) *sœma* conform to]

seem ing (sē′ming), *adj.* apparent; that appears to be: *a seeming advantage.* *—n.* appearance: *It was worse in its seeming than in reality.* **—seem′ing ly,** *adv.*

hat, āge, fär; let, ēqual, tėrm;
it, īce; hot, ōpen, ôrder;
oil, out; cup, pu̇t, rüle;
ch, child; ng, long; sh, she;
th, thin; ᴛʜ, then; zh, measure;

ə represents *a* in about, *e* in taken, *i* in pencil, *o* in lemon, *u* in circus.

< = from, derived from, taken from.

seem ly (sēm′lē), *adj.,* **-li er, -li est,** *adv.* *—adj.* 1 suitable; proper: *Some older people do not consider modern dances seemly.* See **fitting** for synonym study. 2 having a pleasing appearance. *—adv.* properly; becomingly; fittingly. **—seem′li ness,** *n.*

seen (sēn), *v.* pp. of **see**[1].

seep (sēp), *v.i.* leak slowly; trickle; ooze: *Water seeps through sand.* [Old English *sipian*]

seep age (sē′pij), *n.* 1 a seeping; slow leakage. 2 moisture or liquid that seeps.

seer (sir *for 1;* sē′ər *for 2*), *n.* 1 person who foresees or foretells future events; prophet. 2 person who sees.

seer ess (sir′is), *n.* a woman seer; prophetess.

seer suck er (sir′suk′ər), *n.* a thin rayon or cotton cloth with alternate strips of plain and crinkled material. [ultimately < Persian *shīr o shakkar,* literally, milk and sugar]

see saw (sē′sô′), *n.* 1 plank resting on a support near its middle so the ends can move up and down; teeter-totter. 2 a children's game in which the children sit at opposite ends of such a plank and move alternately up and down. 3 movement up and down or back and forth. *—v.i., v.t.* 1 move up and down on a seesaw. 2 move up and down or back and forth. *—adj.* moving up and down or back and forth. [reduplication of *saw*[1]]

seethe (sēᴛʜ), *v.,* **seethed, seeth ing.** *—v.i.* 1 be excited; be disturbed: *seethe with discontent.* See **boil**[1] for synonym study. 2 bubble and foam: *Water seethed under the falls.* 3 ARCHAIC. boil. *—v.t.* 1 soak; steep. 2 boil. [Old English *sēothan*]

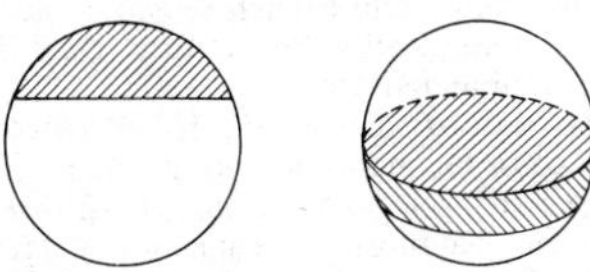

segment (def. 2a, left; def. 2b, right)

seg ment (seg′mənt), *n.* 1 piece or part cut, marked, or broken off; division; section: *A tangerine is easily pulled apart into its segments.* 2 in geometry: **a** part of a circle, etc., cut off by a line, especially a part bounded by an arc and its chord. **b** part of a sphere cut off by two parallel planes. **c** line segment. *—v.t., v.i.* divide into segments. [< Latin *segmentum* < *secare* to cut]

seg men tal (seg men′tl), *adj.* 1 composed of segments. 2 of or having to do with segments. 3 having the form of a segment of a circle. **—seg men′tal ly,** *adv.*

seg men tar y (seg′mən ter′ē), *adj.* segmental.

seg men ta tion (seg′mən tā′shən), *n.* 1 division into segments. 2 growth and division of a cell into two, four, eight cells, and so on.

se go (sē′gō), *n., pl.* **se gos.** sego lily. [< Paiute]

sego lily, 1 a perennial herb of the lily family, native to the western United States, with showy, white, trumpet-shaped flowers and an edible bulb. 2 its bulb.

seg re gate (*v.* seg′rə gāt; *adj.* seg′rə git, seg′rə gāt), *v.,* **-gat ed, -gat ing,** *adj.* *—v.t.* 1 separate from others; set apart; isolate: *The doctor segregated the sick child.* 2 separate or keep apart (one race, people, etc.) from another or from the rest of society by maintaining separate schools, separate public facilities, etc. *—v.i.* 1 separate from the rest and collect in one place. 2 (in genetics) undergo segregation. *—adj.* segregated. [< Latin *segregatum* segregated < *se-* apart from + *gregem* herd]

seg re ga tion (seg′rə gā′shən), *n.* 1 separation from others; setting apart; isolation. 2 separation of one race, people, etc., from another or from the rest of society, especially in schools, theaters, etc. 3 (in genetics) the separation of opposing pairs of genes or characters, occurring during meiosis, in the gametes formed by a hybrid organism.

seg re ga tion ist (seg′rə gā′shə nist), *n.* person who believes in or practices racial segregation.

seg re ga tive (seg′rə gā′tiv), *adj.* 1 tending to segregate. 2 unsociable.

sei (sā), *n.* sei whale.

sei del (sī′dl), *n.* mug for beer. [< German *Seidel* < Latin *situla* bucket]

Seid litz powder (sed′lits), saline laxative consisting of two powders, one tartaric acid and the other a mixture of sodium bicarbonate and Rochelle salt. These are dissolved separately, and the solutions are mixed and drunk while effervescing. [< *Seidlitz,* village in Czechoslovakia]

sei gneur (sē nyėr′), *n.* a feudal lord or landowner. A **grand seigneur** was a person of high rank. [< French < Old French *seignor* < Latin *senior.* Doublet of SEIGNIOR and SIEUR.]

sei gnior (sē′nyər), *n.* lord; lord of a manor; gentleman. [< Old French *seignor* < accusative of Latin *senior.* See SENIOR. Doublet of SEIGNEUR and SIEUR.]

sei gnio ri al (sē nyôr′ē əl, sē nyōr′ē əl), *adj.* of or having to do with a seignior.

sei gnior y (sē′nyər ē), *n., pl.* **-gnior ies.** 1 power or authority of a seignior. 2 a feudal lord's domain.

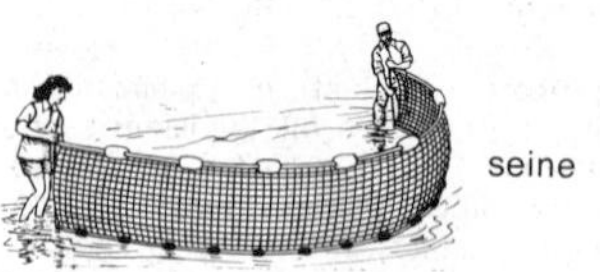
seine

seine (sān), *n., v.,* **seined, sein ing.** *—n.* a fishing net that hangs straight down in the water, with floats at the upper edge and sinkers at the lower. *—v.i.* fish with a seine. *—v.t.* catch (fish) with a seine. [Old English *segne* < Latin *sagena* < Greek *sagēnē*] **—sein′er,** *n.*

Seine River (sān), river flowing from E France into the English Channel. Paris is on the Seine. 480 mi. See **Rhine River** for map.

seis mic (sīz′mik, sī′smik), *adj.* 1 of or having to do with earthquakes or other movements of the earth's crust. 2 caused by an earthquake or other movement of the earth's crust. [< Greek *seismos* earthquake < *seiein* to shake] **—seis′mi cal ly,** *adv.*

seis mo gram (sīz′mə gram, sī′smə gram), *n.* record made by a seismograph.

seis mo graph (sīz′mə graf, sī′smə graf), *n.* instrument for recording the direction, intensity, and duration of earthquakes or other movements of the earth's crust.

seis mo graph ic (sīz′mə graf′ik, sī′smə graf′ik), *adj.* 1 of a seismograph. 2 of seismography.

seis mog ra phy (sīz mog′rə fē, sī smog′rə fē), *n.* art of using a seismograph.

seis mo log i cal (sīz′mə loj′ə kəl, sī′smə loj′ə kəl), *adj.* of or having to do with seismology. **—seis′mo log′i cal ly,** *adv.*

seis mol o gist (sīz mol′ə jist, sī smol′ə jist), *n.* an expert in seismology.

seis mol o gy (sīz mol′ə jē, sī smol′ə jē), *n.* the scientific study of earthquakes and other movements of the earth's crust.

sei whale (sā), a very common rorqual of a bluish-black color; sei. [< Norwegian *seihval* < *sei* kind of fish + *val* whale]

seize (sēz), *v.,* **seized, seiz ing.** *—v.t.* 1 take hold of suddenly; clutch; grasp. See synonym study below. 2 grasp with the mind: *seize an idea.* 3 take possession of by force: *seize a city.* 4 take prisoner; arrest. 5 take possession of or come upon suddenly: *A fever seized him.* 6 take possession of by legal authority: *seize smuggled goods.* 7 bind, lash; make fast: *seize one rope to another.* 8 **seize on** or **seize upon, a** take hold of suddenly. **b** take possession of. *—v.i.* stick to something; cohere. [< Old French *seisir* < Late Latin *sacire*] **—seiz′er,** *n.*

Syn. *v.t.* 1 **Seize, grasp, clutch** mean to take hold of something, literally or figuratively. **Seize** suggests taking hold suddenly and with force: *The dog seized the sausages.* **Grasp** suggests seizing and holding firmly with the fingers, claws, talons, etc., closed around the object: *The eagle grasped the snake.* **Clutch** suggests grasping eagerly, even desperately, and sometimes ineffectively: *A drowning man will clutch a straw.*

seiz ing (sē′zing), *n.* 1 act of binding, lashing, or fastening together with several turns of small rope, cord, etc. 2 fastening made in this way. 3 a small rope, cord, etc., used for this.

sei zure (sē′zhər), *n.* 1 act of seizing. 2 condition of being seized. 3 a sudden attack of disease: *an epileptic seizure.* 4 a sudden onset of emotion.

se la chi an (si lā′kē ən), *adj.* of or belonging to an order of fishes, including the sharks, skates, and rays. *—n.* a selachian fish. [< Greek *selachos* shark, ray]

se lah (sē′lə), *n.* (in the Bible) a word of unknown meaning occurring frequently in the Psalms, perhaps a musical direction indicating pause. [< Hebrew *selāh*]

sel dom (sel′dəm), *adv.* not often; rarely: *I am seldom ill.* [Old English *seldum*]

se lect (si lekt′), *v.t.* pick out; choose: *Select the book you want.* *—adj.* 1 picked as best; chosen specially: *A few select officials were admitted to the conference.* 2 choice; superior: *That store carries a very select line of merchandise.* 3 careful in choosing; particular as to friends, company, etc.: *She belongs to a very select club.* [< Latin *selectum* chosen < *se-* apart + *legere* to pick] **—se lect′ness,** *n.*

se lect ee (si lek′tē′), *n.* person drafted for military service.

se lec tion (si lek′shən), *n.* 1 act of selecting; choice. 2 condition of being selected. 3 person, thing, or group chosen. 4 quantity or variety to choose from. 5 process of selecting animals or plants to survive, especially the process of natural selection.

se lec tive (si lek′tiv), *adj.* 1 having the power to select; selecting. 2 having to do with selection. 3 responding to oscillations of a certain frequency only. When a selective radio is tuned to one station, those on other wave lengths are excluded. **—se lec′tive ly,** *adv.* **—se lec′tive ness,** *n.*

selective service, compulsory military service of persons selected from the general population according to age, physical fitness, etc.

se lec tiv i ty (si lek′tiv′ə tē), *n.* 1 quality of being selective. 2 property of a circuit, instrument, or the like, by virtue of which it responds to electric oscillations of a particular frequency to the exclusion of others.

se lect man (si lekt′mən), *n., pl.* **-men.** member of a board of town officers in New England, chosen each year to manage the town's public affairs.

se lec tor (si lek′tər), *n.* 1 person who selects. 2 a mechanical or electrical device that selects.

Se le ne (sə lē′nē), *n.* (in Greek myths) the goddess of the moon, identified with the Roman goddess Luna.

sel e nite (sel′ə nit), *n.* variety of gypsum, found in transparent crystals and foliated masses. [< Greek *selēnitēs (lithos)* (stone) of the moon < *selēnē* moon; its brightness was supposed to vary with the moon]

se le ni um (sə lē′nē əm), *n.* a nonmetallic element which exists in several allotropic forms and is found with sulfur in various ores. Because its electrical conductivity increases with the intensity of light striking it, it is used in photoelectric cells. *Symbol:* Se; *atomic number* 34. See pages 326 and 327 for table. [< New Latin < Greek *selēnē* moon]

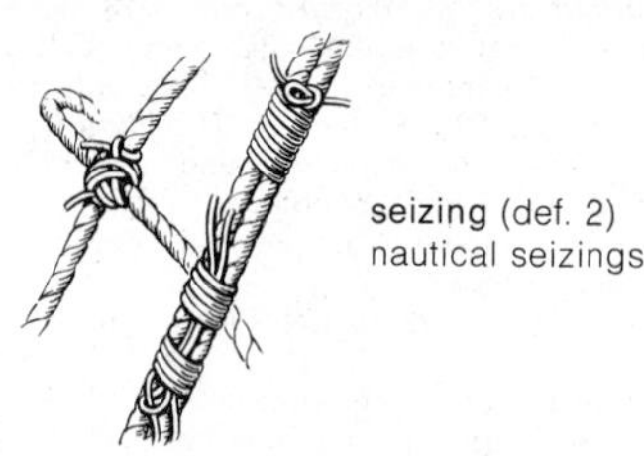
seizing (def. 2)
nautical seizings

sel e nog ra pher (sel′ə nog′rə fər), *n.* an expert in selenography.

sel e nog ra phy (sel′ə nog′rə fē), *n.* science dealing with physical features of the moon. [< Greek *selēnē* moon + English *-graphy*]

Se leu cus I (sə lü′kəs), 358?-281 B.C., ruler of ancient Syria and most of Asia Minor from 312 to 281 B.C. He had been a general under Alexander the Great.

self (self), *n., pl.* **selves,** *adj., pron., pl.* **selves.** *—n.* 1 one's own person: *his very self.* 2 one's own welfare or interests: *A selfish person puts self first.* 3 nature or character of a person or thing: *She does not seem like her former self.* *—adj.* being the

hat, āge, fär; let, ēqual, tėrm;
it, īce; hot, ōpen, ôrder;
oil, out; cup, pu̇t, rüle;
ch, child; ng, long; sh, she;
th, thin; ᴛʜ, then; zh, measure;

ə represents *a* in about, *e* in taken, *i* in pencil, *o* in lemon, *u* in circus.

< = from, derived from, taken from.

same throughout; all of one kind, quality, color, material, etc. —*pron.* myself; himself; herself; yourself: *a check made payable to self.* [Old English]

➤ **Self** as a suffix forms the reflexive and intensive pronouns: *myself, yourself, himself, herself, itself, oneself, ourselves, yourselves, themselves.*

self-, *prefix.* 1 of or over oneself: *Self-conscious = conscious of oneself.* 2 by or in oneself or itself: *Self-inflicted = inflicted by oneself.* 3 to or for oneself: *Self-addressed = addressed to oneself.* 4 oneself (as object): *Self-defeating = defeating oneself.* 5 automatic; automatically: *Self-winding = winding automatically.* [< *self*]

self-a base ment (self′ə bās′mənt), *n.* abasement of self.

self-ab hor rence (self′ab hôr′əns, self′-ab hor′əns), *n.* abhorrence of self.

self-ab ne ga tion (self′ab′nə gā′shən), *n.* self-denial.

self-ab sorp tion (self′ab sôrp′shən, self′-ab zôrp′shən), *n.* absorption in one's own thoughts, affairs, etc.

self-a buse (self′ə byüs′), *n.* 1 abuse of oneself. 2 masturbation.

self-act ing (self′ak′ting), *adj.* working of itself: *a self-acting machine.*

self-ad dressed (self′ə drest′), *adj.* addressed to oneself: *a self-addressed envelope.*

self-ad just ing (self′ə jus′ting), *adj.* adjusting itself; requiring no external adjustment.

self-ad mit ted (self′ad mit′id), *adj.* admitted by oneself; self-confessed.

self-a nal y sis (self′ə nal′ə sis), *n., pl.* **-ses** (-sēz′). 1 self-examination. 2 psychological analysis of a person by himself.

self-ap point ed (self′ə poin′tid), *adj.* appointed or nominated by oneself.

self-as ser tion (self′ə sėr′shən), *n.* insistence on one's own wishes, opinions, claims, etc.

self-as ser tive (self′ə sėr′tiv), *adj.* insisting on one's own wishes, opinions, etc. **—self′-as ser′tive ly,** *adv.* **—self′-as ser′tive ness,** *n.*

self-as sur ance (self′ə shu̇r′əns), *n.* self-confidence.

self-as sured (self′ə shu̇rd′), *adj.* self-confident.

self-cen tered (self′sen′tərd), *adj.* 1 occupied with one's own interests and affairs. 2 selfish. **—self′-cen′tered ness,** *n.*

self-col ored (self′kul′ərd), *adj.* 1 of one color. 2 of the natural color.

self-com mand (self′kə mand′), *n.* self-control.

self-com pla cen cy (self′kəm plā′sn sē), *n.* a being self-satisfied.

self-com pla cent (self′kəm plā′snt), *adj.* self-satisfied. **—self′-com pla′cent ly,** *adv.*

self-con ceit (self′kən sēt′), *n.* conceit; too much pride in oneself or one's ability.

self-con fessed (self′kən fest′), *adj.* confessed by oneself; self-admitted: *a self-confessed failure.*

self-con fi dence (self′kon′fə dəns), *n.* belief in one's own ability, power, judgment, etc.; confidence in oneself.

self-con fi dent (self′kon′fə dənt), *adj.* believing in one's own ability, power, judgment, etc. **—self′-con′fi dent ly,** *adv.*

self-con scious (self′kon′shəs), *adj.* 1 made conscious of how one is appearing to others; embarrassed, especially by the presence or the thought of other people and their attitude toward one; shy. 2 having consciousness of oneself. **—self′-con′scious ly,** *adv.* **—self′-con′scious ness,** *n.*

self-con sist ent (self′kən sis′tənt), *adj.* consistent with oneself or itself; having its parts or elements in agreement.

self-con sti tut ed (self′kon′stə tü′tid, self′kon′stə tyü′tid), *adj.* constituted by oneself or itself.

self-con tained (self′kən tānd′), *adj.* 1 containing in oneself or itself all that is necessary; independent of what is external. 2 saying little; reserved. 3 having all its working parts contained in one case, cover, or framework: *A watch is self-contained.*

self-con tra dic tion (self′kon′trə dik′shən), *n.* 1 contradiction of oneself or itself. 2 statement containing elements that are contradictory.

self-con tra dic tor y (self′kon′trə dik′tər ē), *adj.* contradicting oneself or itself.

self-con trol (self′kən trōl′), *n.* control of one's actions, feelings, etc.

self-con trolled (self′kən trōld′), *adj.* having or showing self-control.

self-cor rect ing (self′kə rek′ting), *adj.* correcting automatically.

self-crit i cism (self′krit′ə siz′əm), *n.* criticism of a person by himself.

self-de cep tion (self′di sep′shən), *n.* act or fact of deceiving oneself.

self-de cep tive (self′di sep′tiv), *adj.* deceiving oneself.

self-de clared (self′di klerd′, self′di klard′), *adj.* self-proclaimed.

self-de feat ing (self′di fē′ting), *adj.* defeating oneself or itself.

self-de fense (self′di fens′), *n.* defense of one's own person, property, reputation, etc.

self-de ni al (self′di nī′əl), *n.* sacrifice of one's own desires and interests; going without things one wants.

self-de ny ing (self′di nī′ing), *adj.* sacrificing one's own wishes and interests; unselfish.

self-de ter mi na tion (self′di tėr′mə nā′shən), *n.* 1 direction from within only, without influence or force from without. 2 the deciding by the people of a nation what form of government they shall have, without reference to the wishes of any other nation.

self-de ter min ing (self′di tėr′mə ning), *adj.* determining one's own acts; having the power of self-determination.

self-de vo tion (self′di vō′shən), *n.* self-sacrifice.

self-dis ci pline (self′dis′ə plin), *n.* careful control and training of oneself.

self-ed u cat ed (self′ej′ə kā′tid), *adj.* educated by one's own efforts; self-taught.

self-ed u ca tion (self′ej′ə kā′shən), *n.* education by one's own efforts.

self-ef face ment (self′ə fās′mənt), *n.* act or habit of modestly keeping oneself in the background.

self-ef fac ing (self′ə fā′sing), *adj.* effacing oneself; keeping oneself in the background. **—self′-ef fac′ing ly,** *adv.*

self-em ployed (self′em ploid′), *adj.* not employed by others; working for oneself. Doctors, lawyers, and farmers are usually self-employed.

self-es teem (self′e stēm′), *n.* 1 thinking well of oneself; self-respect. 2 thinking too well of oneself; conceit.

self-ev i dent (self′ev′ə dənt), *adj.* evident in itself; needing no proof. **—self′-ev′i dent ly,** *adv.*

self-ex am i na tion (self′eg zam′ə nā′shən), *n.* examination into one's own state, conduct, motives, etc.

self-ex ist ent (self′eg zis′tənt), *adj.* 1 existing independently of any other cause. 2 having an independent existence.

self-ex plan a to ry (self′ek splan′ə tôr′ē, self′ek splan′ə tōr′ē), *adj.* explaining itself; that needs no explanation; obvious.

self-ex pres sion (self′ek spresh′ən), *n.* expression of one's personality.

self-fer ti li za tion (self′fėr′tl ə zā′shən), *n.* the fertilization of the ovules of a flower by pollen from the same flower; autogamy.

self-gov erned (self′guv′ərnd), *adj.* having self-government.

self-gov ern ing (self′guv′ər ning), *adj.* that governs itself.

self-gov ern ment (self′guv′ərn mənt, self′guv′ər mənt), *n.* 1 government of a state or group by its own citizens or members: *self-government through elected representatives.* 2 self-control.

self heal (self′hēl′), *n.* 1 herb of the mint family, with purple, pink, or white flowers, formerly supposed to heal wounds. 2 any of various other plants supposed to possess healing power.

self-help (self′help′), *n.* a helping oneself; getting along without assistance from others.

self-im mo la tion (self′im′ə lā′shən), *n.* a sacrificing of oneself.

self-im por tance (self′im pôrt′ns), *n.* a having or showing too high an opinion of one's own importance; conceit; behavior showing conceit.

self-im por tant (self′im pôrt′nt), *adj.* having or showing too high an opinion of one's own importance. **—self′-im por′tant ly,** *adv.*

self-im posed (self′im pōzd′), *adj.* imposed on oneself by oneself.

self-im prove ment (self′im prüv′mənt), *n.* improvement of one's character, mind, etc., by one's own efforts.

self-in crim i nat ing (self′in krim′ə nā′ting), *adj.* incriminating oneself.

self-in crim i na tion (self′in krim′ə nā′shən), *n.* incrimination of oneself through one's own testimony: *He pleaded his privilege against self-incrimination under the fifth amendment of the Constitution.*

self-in duced (self′in düst′, self′in dyüst′), *adj.* 1 induced by oneself or itself. 2 produced by self-induction.

self-in duc tion (self′in duk′shən), *n.* the inducing of an electromotive force in a circuit by a varying current in that circuit.

self-in dul gence (self′in dul′jəns), *n.* gratification of one's own desires, passions, etc., with too little regard for the welfare of others.

self-in dul gent (self′in dul′jənt), *adj.* characterized by self-indulgence. **—self′-in dul′gent ly,** *adv.*

self-in flict ed (self′in flik′tid), *adj.* inflicted on oneself by oneself.

self-in ter est (self′in′tər ist), *n.* 1 interest

in one's own welfare with too little care for the welfare of others; selfishness. 2 personal advantage.

self ish (sel′fish), *adj.* 1 caring too much for oneself; caring too little for others. A selfish person puts his own interests first. 2 showing care solely or chiefly for oneself: *selfish motives.* —**self′ish ly,** *adv.* —**self′ish-ness,** *n.*

self-knowl edge (self′nol′ij), *n.* knowledge of one's own character, ability, etc.

self less (self′lis), *adj.* having no regard or thought for self; unselfish. —**self′less ly,** *adv.* —**self′less ness,** *n.*

self-load ing (self′lō′ding), *adj.* that loads itself; automatic.

self-love (self′luv′), *n.* 1 love of oneself; selfishness. 2 conceit.

self-lu bri cat ing (self′lü′brə kā′ting), *adj.* lubricating automatically.

self-made (self′mād′), *adj.* 1 made by oneself. 2 successful through one's own efforts: *a self-made businessman.*

self-med i ca tion (self′med′ə kā′shən), *n.* the taking of medicines without the advice of a doctor.

self-mov ing (self′mü′ving), *adj.* that can move by itself.

self-o pin ion at ed (self′ə pin′yə nā′tid), *adj.* 1 conceited. 2 stubborn.

self-per pet u at ing (self′pər pech′ü-ā′ting), *adj.* perpetuating oneself or itself.

self-pit y (self′pit′ē), *n.* pity for oneself.

self-pol li na tion (self′pol′ə nā′shən), *n.* transfer of pollen from the anther to the stigma of the same flower.

self-por trait (self′pôr′trit, self′pôr′trāt; self′pōr′trit, self′pōr′trāt), *n.* portrait made by a person of himself.

self-pos sessed (self′pə zest′), *adj.* having or showing control of one's feelings and acts; not excited, embarrassed, or confused; calm.

self-pos ses sion (self′pə zesh′ən), *n.* control of one's feelings and actions; composure; calmness.

self-praise (self′prāz′), *n.* praise of oneself.

self-pres er va tion (self′prez′ər vā′shən), *n.* preservation of oneself from harm or destruction.

self-pro claimed (self′prə klāmd′), *adj.* proclaimed by oneself about oneself; self-declared: *a self-proclaimed art critic.*

self-pro pelled (self′prə peld′), *adj.* propelled by an engine, motor, etc., within itself: *a self-propelled missile.*

self-pro tec tion (self′prə tek′shən), *n.* protection of oneself; self-defense.

self-re cord ing (self′ri kôr′ding), *adj.* that makes a record of its own operations; recording automatically: *a self-recording thermometer.*

self-re gard (self′ri gärd′), *n.* 1 regard of or consideration for oneself. 2 self-respect.

self-reg is ter ing (self′rej′ə stər ing), *adj.* registering automatically.

self-reg u lat ing (self′reg′yə lā′ting), *adj.* regulating oneself or itself. Automatic devices are self-regulating.

self-re li ance (self′ri lī′əns), *n.* reliance on one's own acts, abilities, etc.

self-re li ant (self′ri lī′ənt), *adj.* having or showing self-reliance. —**self′-re li′ant ly,** *adv.*

self-re proach (self′ri prōch′), *n.* blame by one's own conscience.

self-re spect (self′ri spekt′), *n.* respect for oneself; proper pride.

self-re spect ing (self′ri spek′ting), *adj.* having self-respect; properly proud.

self-re strained (self′ri strānd′), *adj.* showing self-control.

self-re straint (self′ri strānt′), *n.* self-control.

self-right eous (self′rī′chəs), *adj.* thinking that one is more moral than others; thinking that one is very good and pleasing to God. —**self′-right′eous ly,** *adv.* —**self′-right′eous ness,** *n.*

self-right ing (self′rī′ting), *adj.* that can right itself after being upset: *a self-righting life raft.*

self-ris ing (self′rī′zing), *adj.* that has a leavening agent mixed with it during its manufacture: *self-rising flour.*

self-rule (self′rül′), *n.* self-government.

self-sac ri fice (self′sak′rə fīs), *n.* sacrifice of one's own interests and desires, for one's duty, another's welfare, etc.

self-sac ri fic ing (self′sak′rə fī′sing), *adj.* giving up things for someone else; unselfish.

self same (self′sām′), *adj.* very same; identical. —**self′same′ness,** *n.*

self-sat is fac tion (self′sat′i sfak′shən), *n.* satisfaction with oneself; complacency.

self-sat is fied (self′sat′i sfīd), *adj.* pleased with oneself; complacent.

self-seal ing (self′sē′ling), *adj.* closing tightly or fastening by itself.

self-seek er (self′sē′kər), *n.* person who seeks his own interests too much.

self-seek ing (self′sē′king), *adj.* selfish. —*n.* selfishness.

self-serv ice (self′sėr′vis), *n.* act or process of serving oneself in a restaurant, store, etc. —*adj.* of or for self-service.

self-slaugh ter (self′slô′tər), *n.* the killing of oneself; suicide.

self-start er (self′stär′tər), *n.* an electric motor or other device for starting an engine automatically; starter.

self-ster ile (self′ster′əl), *adj.* unable to fertilize itself, as certain flowers or plants.

self-styled (self′stīld′), *adj.* called by oneself: *a self-styled leader whom no one follows.*

self-suf fi cien cy (self′sə fish′ən sē), *n.* 1 ability to supply one's own needs. 2 conceit; self-assurance.

self-suf fi cient (self′sə fish′ənt), *adj.* 1 asking or needing no help; independent. 2 having too much confidence in one's own resources, powers, etc.; conceited.

self-suf fic ing (self′sə fī′sing), *adj.* sufficing in or for oneself or itself; self-sufficient.

self-sup port (self′sə pôrt′, self′sə pōrt′), *n.* unaided support of oneself or itself.

self-sup port ing (self′sə pôr′ting, self′sə pōr′ting), *adj.* earning one's expenses; getting along without help.

self-sus tain ing (self′sə stā′ning), *adj.* 1 self-supporting. 2 proceeding automatically once it has been started: *a self-sustaining chain reaction.*

self-taught (self′tôt′), *adj.* taught by oneself without aid from others.

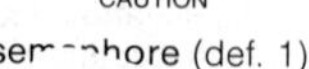
semaphore (def. 1)

self-un der stand ing (self′un′dər-stan′ding), *n.* self-knowledge.

self-will (self′wil′), *n.* insistence on having one's own way.

self-willed (self′wild′), *adj.* insisting on having one's own way; objecting to doing what others ask or command.

self-wind ing (self′wīn′ding), *adj.* wound or winding itself automatically. A self-winding watch winds itself by the movements of the person wearing it.

Sel juk (sel jük′), *adj.* of or having to do with certain Turkish dynasties or tribes that ruled over large parts of Asia from the 1000's to the 1200's. —*n.* member of a Seljuk dynasty or tribe.

Sel juk i an (sel jü′kē ən), *n., adj.* Seljuk.

Sel kirk Mountains (sel′kėrk′), mountain range in SW Canada. Highest peak, 11,590 ft.

sell (sel), *v.,* **sold, sell ing,** *n.* —*v.t.* 1 exchange for money or other payment: *sell a house.* 2 deal in; keep for sale: *The butcher sells meat.* 3 give up or betray: *sell one's country, sell one's soul.* 4 cause to accept, approve, or adopt by representations and methods characteristic of salesmanship: *sell an idea to the public, sell the public on an idea.* 5 promote the sale of: *Advertisements sold many new cars.* —*v.i.* 1 engage in selling. 2 be given in exchange; be on sale; be sold: *Strawberries sell at a high price in January.* 3 INFORMAL. win acceptance, approval, or adoption: *an idea that will sell.*

sell out, a sell all that one has of; get rid of by selling. **b** INFORMAL. betray (a person, cause, country, etc.) by a secret bargain.

sell short, INFORMAL. have a low opinion of; belittle; downgrade.

—*n.* 1 act or method of selling. 2 SLANG. cheat; trick; hoax.

[Old English *sellan*]

sell a ble (sel′ə bəl), *adj.* salable.

sell er (sel′ər), *n.* 1 person who sells. 2 thing considered with reference to its sale: *This book is a good seller.*

sell out (sel′out′), *n.* 1 a selling out. 2 performance of a play, sports event, etc., for which all seats are sold. 3 INFORMAL. betrayal.

Selt zer (selt′sər), *n.* 1 a bubbling mineral water containing salt, calcium, and magnesium carbonates. 2 any carbonated water. [< German *Selterser* < *(Nieder) Selters,* village in West Germany, where it is found]

sel vage or **sel vedge** (sel′vij), *n.* edge of a fabric finished off to prevent raveling. [probably < earlier Flemish *selfegghe* self-edge]

selves (selvz), *n., pron.* pl. of **self.**

Sem., seminary.

se man tic (sə man′tik), *adj.* 1 having to do with the meaning of words. 2 having to do with semantics. —**se man′ti cal ly,** *adv.*

se man ti cist (sə man′tə sist), *n.* an expert in semantics.

se man tics (sə man′tiks), *n.* the scientific study of the meanings, and the development of meanings, of words. [< French *sémantique* < Greek *sēmantikos* significant, ultimately < *sēma* sign]

sem a phore (sem′ə fôr, sem′ə fōr), *n., v.,* **-phored, -phor ing.** —*n.* 1 an upright post or structure with movable arms or an arrangement of colored lights, lanterns, flags, etc., used in railroad signaling. 2 system of signals for sending messages by using different positions of the arms or flags, or by using lanterns or other mechanical devices. *—v.t., v.i.* signal by semaphore. [< Greek *sēma* signal + *-phoros* carrying]

Se ma rang (sə mär′äng), *n.* seaport in N Java, in Indonesia. 503,000.

sem blance (sem′bləns), *n.* 1 outward appearance: *Their story had the semblance of truth, but was really false.* 2 likeness: *These clouds have the semblance of a huge head.* [< Old French < *sembler* seem < Latin *similare* make similar < *similis* similar]

se men (sē′mən), *n.* fluid produced in the male reproductive organs, containing the male reproductive cells. [< Latin, seed]

se mes ter (sə mes′tər), *n.* a division, often one half, of a school year, usually lasting from 15 to 18 weeks. [< German *Semester* < Latin *semestris* semiannual < *sex* six + *mensis* month]

semi-, *prefix.* 1 half: *Semicircle = half circle.* 2 partly; incompletely: *Semicivilized = partly civilized.* 3 twice. Semi___ly means in each half of a ___, or twice in a ___: *Semiannually = every half year, or twice a year.* [< Latin]

➤ Words starting with **semi-** are not usually hyphenated except before proper names *(semi-Christian)* or words beginning with *i* *(semi-invalid).*

sem i an nu al (sem′ē an′yü əl), *adj.* 1 occurring every half year. 2 lasting a half year. **—sem′i an′nu al ly,** *adv.*

sem i ar id (sem′ē ar′id), *adj.* having very little rainfall.

sem i au to mat ic (sem′ē ô′tə mat′ik), *adj.* partly automatic; self-acting in some part of its operation. *—n.* gun like an automatic but requiring a press of the trigger to fire each shot. **—sem′i au′to mat′i cal ly,** *adv.*

sem i breve (sem′i brēv′), *n.* BRITISH. a whole note in music.

sem i-Chris tian (sem′i kris′chən), *adj.* half-Christian.

sem i cir cle (sem′i sėr′kəl), *n.* half a circle: *We sat in a semicircle around the fire.*

sem i cir cu lar (sem′i sėr′kyə lər), *adj.* having the form of half a circle.

semicircular canal, any of three curved, tubelike canals in the inner ear that help to maintain balance.

sem i civ i lized (sem′i siv′ə līzd), *adj.* partly civilized.

sem i co lon (sem′i kō′lən), *n.* mark of punctuation (;) that shows a separation not so complete as that shown by a period but greater than that shown by a comma.

sem i con duc tor (sem′i kən duk′tər), *n.* a mineral substance, such as germanium or silicon, that conducts electricity with an efficiency between that of metals and insulators. Semiconductors can convert alternating current into direct current and amplify weak electric signals.

sem i con scious (sem′i kon′shəs), *adj.* half-conscious; not fully conscious. **—sem′i con′scious ly,** *adv.* **—sem′i-con′scious ness,** *n.*

sem i dark ness (sem′i därk′nis), *n.* partial darkness.

sem i des ert (sem′i dez′ərt), *adj.* mostly barren, with a sparse vegetation. *—n.* a semidesert area or region.

sem i de tached (sem′i di tacht′), *adj.* (of a house) partly detached; joined to another house by a common wall but separated from other buildings.

sem i di vine (sem′i də vīn′), *adj.* partly divine.

sem i e rect (sem′ē i rekt′), *adj.* partly erect: *a semierect posture.*

sem i fi nal (sem′i fī′nl), *n.* one of the two rounds, matches, etc., that immediately precede the final one. *—adj.* of or having to do with a semifinal.

sem i fi nal ist (sem′i fī′nl ist), *n.* contestant in the semifinal round.

sem i flu id (sem′i flü′id), *adj.* imperfectly fluid; extremely viscous. *—n.* a semifluid substance.

sem i for mal (sem′i fôr′məl), *adj.* partly or moderately formal: *semiformal dress.*

sem i-in de pend ent (sem′ē in′di pen′dənt), *adj.* not fully independent.

sem i-in va lid (sem′ē in′və lid), *adj.* not completely well; partly invalid. *—n.* a semi-invalid person.

sem i liq uid (sem′i lik′wid), *adj., n.* semifluid.

sem i lu nar (sem′i lü′nər), *adj.* shaped like a half moon.

sem i man u fac ture (sem′i man′yə-fak′chər), *n.* a manufactured product, as steel or yarn, used in making end products.

sem i me tal lic (sem′i mə tal′ik), *adj.* partly metallic.

sem i month ly (sem′i munth′lē), *adj., adv., n., pl.* **-lies.** *—adj.* happening or appearing twice a month. *—adv.* twice a month. *—n.* magazine or other periodical published semimonthly.

sem i nal (sem′ə nəl), *adj.* 1 of or having to do with semen or seed. 2 containing semen or seed. 3 like seed; having the possibility of future development: *a seminal idea.* [< Latin *seminalis* < *seminis* seed] **—sem′i nal ly,** *adv.*

sem i nar (sem′ə när), *n.* 1 group of students engaged in discussion and research under the guidance of a professor. 2 course of study or work for such a group. 3 meeting of such a group. 4 place in which such a group meets. [< German *Seminar* < Latin *seminarium* plant nursery < *seminis* seed. Doublet of SEMINARY.]

sem i nar i an (sem′ə ner′ē ən), *n.* student at a seminary.

sem i nar y (sem′ə ner′ē), *n., pl.* **-nar ies.** 1 school, especially one beyond high school. 2 academy or boarding school, especially for young women. 3 school or college for training students to be priests, ministers, rabbis, etc. [< Latin *seminarium.* Doublet of SEMINAR.]

sem i nif er ous (sem′ə nif′ər əs), *adj.* 1 bearing or producing seed. 2 conveying, containing, or producing semen.

Sem i nole (sem′ə nōl), *n., pl.* **-nole** or **-noles.** member of a tribe of North American Indians that settled in Florida. Most of this tribe now lives in Oklahoma.

sem i of fi cial (sem′ē ə fish′əl), *adj.* partly official; having some degree of authority. **—sem′i of fi′cial ly,** *adv.*

sem i o paque (sem′ē ō pāk′), *adj.* imperfectly opaque.

sem i per me a ble (sem′i pėr′mē ə bəl), *adj.* partly permeable; permeable to some substances but not to others. A semipermeable membrane allows a solvent to pass through but usually not the dissolved substance.

sem i po lit i cal (sem′i pə lit′ə kəl), *adj.* partly political.

sem i pre cious (sem′i presh′əs), *adj.* having value, but not sufficient value to rank as gems. Amethysts and garnets are semiprecious stones; diamonds and rubies are precious stones.

hat, āge, fär; let, ēqual, tėrm;
it, īce; hot, ōpen, ôrder;
oil, out; cup, pu̇t, rüle;
ch, child; ng, long; sh, she;
th, thin; ᴛʜ, then; zh, measure;

ə represents *a* in about, *e* in taken, *i* in pencil, *o* in lemon, *u* in circus.

< = from, derived from, taken from.

sem i pri vate (sem′i prī′vit), *adj.* partly private: *a semiprivate conference.*

sem i pro (sem′i prō′), *n., pl.* **-pros,** *adj.* semiprofessional.

sem i pro fes sion al (sem′i prə fesh′ə-nəl), *n.* a part-time professional athlete. *—adj.* of or for semiprofessionals.

sem i qua ver (sem′i kwā′vər), *n.* BRITISH. a sixteenth note.

Se mir a mis (sə mir′ə mis), *n.* legendary Assyrian princess who lived about 800 B.C. and was said to have founded Babylon.

sem i re lig ious (sem′i rē lij′əs), *adj.* partly religious.

sem i rig id (sem′i rij′id), *adj.* 1 partly rigid. 2 (of an airship) having a rigid keel at the base, to which the gondola, engine, etc., are attached.

sem i sa cred (sem′i sā′krid), *adj.* partly sacred.

sem i skilled (sem′i skild′), *adj.* partly skilled: *a semiskilled laborer.*

sem i soft (sem′i sôft′, sem′i soft′), *adj.* of medium softness: *semisoft cheese.*

sem i sol id (sem′i sol′id), *adj.* partly solid. *—n.* a partly solid substance.

sem i sweet (sem′i swēt′), *adj.* moderately sweet: *semisweet wine.*

Sem ite (sem′īt), *n.* 1 member of a group of ancient and modern peoples speaking any of the Semitic languages. The ancient Hebrews, Phoenicians, and Assyrians were Semites. Arabs and Jews are sometimes called Semites. 2 descendant of Shem. [< Late Latin *Sem* Shem < Hebrew *Shēm*]

Se mit ic (sə mit′ik), *adj.* of or having to do with the Semites or their languages. *—n.* group of languages including Hebrew, Arabic, Aramaic, Phoenician, and Assyrian.

Sem i tism (sem′ə tiz′əm), *n.* 1 Semitic character, especially the ways, ideas, etc., of Jews. 2 a Semitic word or idiom.

sem i tone (sem′i tōn′), *n.* interval equal to half a tone on the scale; half step; half tone.

sem i trail er (sem′i trā′lər), *n.* type of truck trailer having wheels only at the rear, the front end being supported by the tractor.

sem i trans par ent (sem′i tran sper′ənt, sem′i tran spar′ənt), *adj.* imperfectly transparent.

sem i trop i cal (sem′i trop′ə kəl), *adj.* halfway between tropical and temperate: *Florida is a semitropical state.*

sem i vow el (sem′i vou′əl), *n.* 1 sound that is acoustically like a vowel but functions like a consonant. 2 letter representing such a sound. *W* in *win* and *now* or *y* in *yes* and *boy* are semivowels.

sem i week ly (sem′i wēk′lē), *adj., adv., n., pl.* **-lies.** *—adj.* happening or appearing twice a week. *—adv.* twice a week. *—n.* magazine or other periodical published semiweekly.

sem i year ly (sem′i yir′lē), *adj., adv.,* —*adj.* occurring or appearing twice a year. —*adv.* twice a year.

sem o li na (sem′ə lē′nə), *n.* the coarsely ground hard parts of wheat remaining after the fine flour has been sifted through, used in making puddings, macaroni, etc. [< Italian *semolino,* ultimately < Latin *simila* fine flour]

sem pi ter nal (sem′pi tėr′nl), *adj.* everlasting; eternal. [< Late Latin *sempiternalis,* ultimately < Latin *semper* forever] —**sem′pi ter′nal ly,** *adv.*

semp stress (sem′stris, semp′stris), *n.* seamstress.

sen (sen), *n., pl.* **sen.** unit of money of Japan, worth 1/100 of a yen. [< Japanese]

Sen. or **sen.,** 1 Senate. 2 Senator. 3 Senior.

sen ate (sen′it), *n.* 1 a governing or lawmaking assembly. The highest council of state in ancient Rome was called the senate. 2 the upper and smaller branch of an assembly that makes laws. 3 **Senate, a** the upper house of Congress or of a state legislature. **b** the upper house of the legislature of certain other countries, such as Canada, Australia, etc. [< Latin *senatus* < *senex* old man]

sen a tor (sen′ə tər), *n.* member of a senate. [< Latin]

sen a to ri al (sen′ə tôr′ē əl, sen′ə tōr′ē əl), *adj.* 1 of or befitting a senator or senators. 2 consisting of senators. 3 entitled to elect a senator: *a senatorial district.*

sen a tor ship (sen′ə tər ship), *n.* position, duties, etc., of a senator.

send (send), *v.,* **sent, send ing.** —*v.t.* 1 cause to go or pass from one place to another: *send a child on an errand.* 2 cause to be carried: *send a letter, send news.* 3 cause to come, occur, or be: *Send help at once. May God send peace. Her remark sent him into a rage.* 4 drive; impel; throw: *The volcano sent clouds of smoke into the air.* 5 **send packing,** send away in a hurry; dismiss without delay or formality. —*v.i.* send a message or messenger: *send for a doctor.* [Old English *sendan*] —**send′er,** *n.*

sen dal (sen′dl), *n.* 1 a thin, rich silk fabric used during the Middle Ages. 2 garment made of it. [< Old French *cendal*]

send-off (send′ôf′, send′of′), *n.* 1 a friendly demonstration in honor of a person setting out on a journey, course, career, etc. 2 INFORMAL. a start (favorable or unfavorable) given to a person or thing.

Sen e ca[1] (sen′ə kə), *n.* **Lucius Annaeus,** 4? B.C.-A.D. 65, Roman Stoic philosopher and author.

Sen e ca[2] (sen′ə kə), *n., pl.* **-cas** or **-ca.** member of the largest tribe of Iroquois Indians, formerly living mainly in western New York State.

Sen e gal (sen′ə gôl′, sen′ə gôl), *n.* 1 country in W Africa on the Atlantic, a member of the French Community. 3,930,000 pop.; 75,800 sq. mi. *Capital:* Dakar. See **Upper Volta** for map. 2 **Senegal River,** river in W Africa forming the border between Senegal and Mauritania, flowing into the Atlantic. 1000 mi.

Sen e gal ese (sen′ə gô lēz′), *adj., n., pl.* **-ese.** —*adj.* of or having to do with Senegal or its people. —*n.* native or inhabitant of Senegal.

se nes cence (sə nes′ns), *n.* fact or condition of growing old.

se nes cent (sə nes′nt), *adj.* growing old; beginning to show old age. [< Latin *senescentem,* ultimately < *senex* old]

sen es chal (sen′ə shəl), *n.* steward in charge of a royal palace or nobleman's estate in the Middle Ages. Seneschals often had the powers of judges or generals. [< Old French; of Germanic origin]

se nile (sē′nīl, sē′nl), *adj.* 1 of old age. 2 showing the mental and physical deterioration often characteristic of old age. 3 caused by old age. [< Latin *senilis* < *senex* old] —**se′nile ly,** *adv.*

se nil i ty (sə nil′ə tē), *n.* 1 old age. 2 the mental and physical deterioration often characteristic of old age.

sen ior (sē′nyər), *adj.* 1 the older (designating a father whose son has the same given name): *John Parker, Senior.* 2 older or elderly: *a senior citizen.* 3 higher in rank or longer in service: *the senior member of a firm, a senior judge.* 4 of or having to do with the graduating class of a high school or college. —*n.* 1 an older person: *She is her sister's senior by two years.* 2 person of higher rank or longer service. 3 member of the graduating class of a high school or college. [< Latin, comparative of *senex* old. Doublet of SIRE.]

senior high school, school attended after junior high school. It usually has grades 10, 11, and 12.

sen ior i ty (sē nyôr′ə tē, sē nyor′ə tē), *n., pl.* **-ties.** 1 superiority in age or standing; condition or fact of being older: *She felt that two years' seniority gave her the right to advise her brother.* 2 priority or precedence in office or service.

senior master sergeant, (in the U.S. Air Force) a noncommissioned officer ranking next below a chief master sergeant and next above a master sergeant.

sen na (sen′ə), *n.* 1 laxative extracted from the dried leaves of any of several cassia plants. 2 the dried leaves of any of these plants. 3 the cassia plant, or plants of the same genus which are similar to it. [< New Latin < Arabic *sanā*]

Sen nach er ib (sə nak′ər ib), *n.* died 681 B.C., king of Assyria from 705 to 681 B.C.

sen night (sen′īt, sen′it), *n.* ARCHAIC. seven nights and days; week. [Old English *seofon nihta* seven nights]

sen nit (sen′it), *n.* kind of flat, braided cordage used on shipboard, formed by plaiting strands of rope yarn or other fiber. [origin uncertain]

se ñor (sā nyôr′), *n., pl.* ***-ño res*** (-nyōr′ās). SPANISH. 1 Mr. or sir. 2 a gentleman.

se ño ra (sā nyōr′ä), *n.* SPANISH. 1 Mrs. or Madame. 2 a lady.

se ño ri ta (sā′nyō rē′tä), *n.* SPANISH. 1 Miss. 2 a young lady.

sen sa tion (sen sā′shən), *n.* 1 action of the senses; power to see, hear, feel, taste, smell, etc.: *A dead body is without sensation.* See **sense** for synonym study. 2 feeling: *Ice gives a sensation of coldness.* 3 strong or excited feeling: *The announcement of peace caused a sensation throughout the nation.* 4 cause of such feeling: *Man's first landing on the moon was a great sensation.*

sen sa tion al (sen sā′shə nəl), *adj.* 1 arousing strong or excited feeling: *The outfielder's sensational catch made the crowd cheer wildly.* 2 trying to arouse strong or excited feeling: *a sensational newspaper story.* 3 of the senses; having to do with sensation. —**sen sa′tion al ly,** *adv.*

sen sa tion al ism (sen sā′shə nə liz′əm), *n.* sensational methods, writing, language, etc.

sen sa tion al ist (sen sā′shə nə list), *n.* sensational writer, speaker, etc.; one who tries to make a sensation.

sense (sens), *n., v.,* **sensed, sens ing.** —*n.* 1 power of the mind to know what happens outside itself. Sight, hearing, touch, taste, and smell are the five principal senses. See synonym study below. 2 feeling: *a sense of warmth, a sense of security.* 3 sensation. 4 understanding; appreciation: *a sense of humor.* 5 Usually, **senses,** *pl.* normal, sound condition of mind. 6 judgment; intelligence: *She had the good sense to keep out of foolish quarrels.* 7 a particular meaning: *He was a gentleman in every sense of the word.* See **meaning** for synonym study. 8 the general opinion: *The sense of the assembly was clear even before the vote.* 9 (in mathematics) either of two opposite directions in which motion takes place. 10 **in a sense,** in some respects; to some degree. 11 **make sense,** have meaning; be understandable; be reasonable. —*v.t.* 1 be aware of; feel: *She sensed he was tired.* 2 understand. [< Latin *sensus* < *sentire* perceive, know, feel]

Syn. *n.* 1 **Sense, sensation, sensibility** mean the power or act of feeling or perceiving. **Sense** applies to the power of the mind to respond to stimulation: *A dog has a keen sense of smell.* **Sensation** applies particularly to the response to stimulation of a bodily organ like the eyes or nerves: *have no sensation in one's feet.* **Sensibility** applies particularly to emotional or esthetic response: *He lacks the sensibility of a true poet.*

sense less (sens′lis), *adj.* 1 unconscious: *A hard blow on the head knocked him senseless.* 2 foolish; stupid: *a senseless idea.* 3 meaningless: *senseless words.* —**sense′less ly,** *adv.* —**sense′less ness,** *n.*

sense organ, a specialized organ, as the eye, functioning as a receptor.

sen si bil i ty (sen′sə bil′ə tē), *n., pl.* **-ties.** 1 ability to feel or perceive: *Some drugs lessen a person's sensibilities.* See **sense** for synonym study. 2 sensitiveness. 3 fineness of feeling: *She has an unusual sensibility for colors.* 4 Usually, **sensibilities,** *pl.* sensitive feelings. 5 tendency to feel hurt or offended too easily.

sen si ble (sen′sə bəl), *adj.* 1 having or showing good judgment; wise. See synonym study below. 2 aware; conscious: *I am sensible of your kindness.* 3 that can be noticed: *There is a sensible difference between yellow and orange.* 4 that can be perceived by the senses. 5 sensitive. —**sen′si ble ness,** *n.* —**sen′si bly,** *adv.*

Syn. 1 **Sensible, practical** mean having or showing good sense. **Sensible** applies particularly to the common sense shown in acting and speaking: *She is too sensible to do anything foolish.* **Practical** applies particularly to the common sense used in the performance of everyday tasks: *He is a practical man and does not understand people who dream, speculate, or theorize.*

sen si tive (sen′sə tiv), *adj.* 1 receiving impressions readily: *The eye is sensitive to light.* 2 easily affected or influenced: *The mercury in the thermometer is sensitive to changes in temperature.* See synonym study below. 3 easily hurt or offended. 4 of or connected with the senses or sensation. 5 (in medicine) unusually susceptible, as to a serum. 6 having or involving access to secret or classified documents, data, etc.: *employees occupying sensitive positions in the government.* [< Medieval Latin *sensitivus* < Latin *sensus.* See SENSE.] **—sen′si tive ly,** *adv.* **—sen′si tive ness,** *n.*

Syn. 2 **Sensitive, susceptible** mean easily affected or influenced. **Sensitive** suggests having a specially keen or delicate capacity for feeling or for responding to an external influence: *Sensitive people are quickly touched by something beautiful or sad.* **Susceptible** suggests a nature or character easily acted on because of inability to resist an influence: *Susceptible people are easily tricked.*

sensitive plant, 1 a tropical American mimosa whose leaves fold together when touched. 2 any other plant sensitive to touch.

sen si tiv i ty (sen′sə tiv′ə tē), *n., pl.* **-ties.** 1 quality or condition of being sensitive. 2 capacity to respond to stimuli. 3 the degree of this. 4 responsiveness of an electronic device.

sen si tize (sen′sə tīz), *v.t.,* **-tized, -tiz ing.** make sensitive. Camera films have been sensitized to light. **—sen′si ti za′tion,** *n.* **—sen′si tiz′er,** *n.*

sen sor (sen′sər, sen′sôr), *n.* device for receiving and transmitting a physical stimulus such as heat, light, or pressure.

sen so ri al (sen sôr′ē əl, sen sōr′ē əl), *adj.* sensory.

sen sor y (sen′sər ē), *adj.* 1 of or having to do with sensation or the senses. The eyes and ears are sensory organs. 2 (of nerves, ganglia, etc.) conveying an impulse from the sense organs to the nerve center.

sen su al (sen′shü əl), *adj.* 1 of or having to do with the bodily senses rather than the mind or soul. See synonym study below. 2 liking the pleasures of the senses. 3 indulging too much in the pleasures of the senses; lustful; lewd. 4 of or having to do with the senses or sensation; sensory. [< Late Latin *sensualis* < Latin *sensus.* See SENSE.] **—sen′su al ly,** *adv.*

Syn. 1 **Sensual, sensuous** mean of or concerned with the senses. **Sensual** implies pleasurable satisfaction to the bodily senses and appetites and suggests baseness or excess: *A glutton derives sensual pleasure from eating.* **Sensuous,** always favorable, implies a high sensitivity to beauty and the pleasures of the senses and feelings: *She derives sensuous delight from old church music.*

sen su al ism (sen′shü ə liz′əm), *n.* sensuality.

sen su al ist (sen′shü ə list), *n.* person who likes, pursues, or indulges too much in the pleasures of the senses.

sen su al i ty (sen′shü al′ə tē), *n., pl.* **-ties.** 1 sensual nature. 2 a liking for the pleasures of the senses. 3 excessive indulgence in the pleasures of the senses; lewdness.

sen su al ize (sen′shü ə līz), *v.t.* **-ized, -iz ing.** make sensual.

sen su ous (sen′shü əs), *adj.* 1 of or derived from the senses; having an effect on the senses; perceived by the senses: *a sensuous love of color.* 2 enjoying the pleasures of the senses. See **sensual** for synonym study. **—sen′su ous ly,** *adv.* **—sen′su ous ness,** *n.*

sent (sent), *v.* pt. and pp. of **send.**

sen tence (sen′təns), *n., v.,* **-tenced, -tenc ing.** *—n.* 1 group of words (or sometimes a single word) that is grammatically complete and expresses a statement, request, command, exclamation, etc. 2 (in mathematics) a group of symbols that expresses a complete idea or a requirement. $4 + 2 = 6$ is a closed sentence expressing a complete idea. $x + 2 = 6$ is an open sentence expressing a requirement. 3 decision. 4 decision by a judge on the punishment of a criminal. 5 the punishment itself. 6 a short, wise saying; proverb *—v.t.* pronounce punishment on: *The judge sentenced the thief to five years in prison.* [< Latin *sententia,* originally, feeling, opinion < *sentire* to feel]

sen ten tial (sen ten′shəl), *adj.* of or having to do with a sentence.

sen ten tious (sen ten′shəs), *adj.* 1 full of meaning; saying much in few words; pithy. 2 speaking as if one were a judge settling a question. 3 inclined to make wise sayings; abounding in proverbs. [< Latin *sententiosus* < *sententia.* See SENTENCE.] **—sen ten′tious ly,** *adv.* **—sen ten′tious ness,** *n.*

sen tience (sen′shəns), *n.* capacity for feeling.

sen tient (sen′shənt), *adj.* that can feel. [< Latin *sentientem*] **—sen′tient ly,** *adv.*

sen ti ment (sen′tə mənt), *n.* 1 mixture of thought and feeling. Admiration, patriotism, and loyalty are sentiments. 2 feeling, especially refined or tender feeling. See synonym study below. 3 thought or saying that expresses feeling. 4 a mental attitude. 5 personal opinion. [< Late Latin *sentimentum* < Latin *sentire* to feel]

Syn. 2 **Sentiment, sentimentality** mean refined or tender feeling, or a quality or characteristic showing or produced by feeling. **Sentiment** suggests sincere, tender, or noble feeling: *Birthdays are times for sentiment.* **Sentimentality** suggests affected or false, excessive or exaggerated feeling: *the sentimentality of the usual soap opera.*

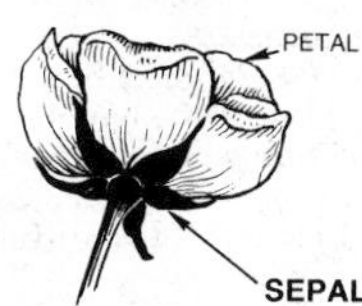

sen ti men tal (sen′tə men′tl), *adj.* 1 having or showing much tender feeling: *sentimental poetry.* 2 likely to act from feelings rather than from logical thinking. 3 of sentiment; dependent on sentiment: *She values her mother's gift for sentimental reasons.* **—sen′ti men′tal ly,** *adv.*

sen ti men tal ism (sen′tə men′tl iz′əm), *n.* 1 tendency to be influenced by sentiment rather than reason. 2 excessive indulgence in sentiment. 3 feeling expressed too openly or sentimentally.

sen ti men tal ist (sen′tə men′tl ist), *n.* a sentimental person; one who indulges in sentimentality.

sen ti men tal i ty (sen′tə men tal′ə tē), *n., pl.* **-ties.** 1 tendency to be influenced by sentiment rather than reason. 2 excessive indulgence in sentiment. See **sentiment** for synonym study. 3 feeling expressed too openly or sentimentally.

sen ti men tal ize (sen′tə men′tl īz), *v.,* **-ized, -iz ing.** *—v.i.* indulge in sentiment; affect sentiment. *—v.t.* 1 make sentimental. 2 be sentimental about.

sen ti nel (sen′tə nəl), *n.* 1 person stationed to keep watch and guard against surprise attacks. 2 **stand sentinel,** act as a sentinel; keep watch. [< Middle French *sentinelle* < Italian *sentinella* < Late Latin *sentinare* avoid danger wisely < Latin *sentire* to feel]

hat, āge, fär; let, ēqual, tėrm;
it, īce; hot, ōpen, ôrder;
oil, out; cup, pu̇t, rüle;
ch, child; ng, long; sh, she;
th, thin; ᴛʜ, then; zh, measure;

ə represents *a* in about, *e* in taken, *i* in pencil, *o* in lemon, *u* in circus.

< = from, derived from, taken from.

sen try (sen′trē), *n., pl.* **-tries.** 1 soldier stationed as a sentinel. 2 **stand sentry,** watch; guard: *We stood sentry over the sleepers.* [perhaps short for earlier *centrinel,* variant of *sentinel*]

sentry box

sentry box, a small building for sheltering a sentry on a post or watch.

Seoul (sōl), *n.* capital of South Korea, in the NW part. 3,795,000.

Sep., 1 September. 2 Septuagint.

se pal (sē′pəl), *n.* one of the leaflike parts which make up the calyx of a flower. The sepals are usually green and cover the unopened bud. In a carnation, the sepals make a green cup at the base of the flower. In a tulip, the sepals are colored in the same way as the petals. [< New Latin *sepalum*]

sep ar a bil i ty (sep′ər ə bil′ə tē, sep′rə bil′ə tē), *n.* quality of being separable.

sep ar a ble (sep′ər ə bəl), *adj.* that can be separated. **—sep′ar a ble ness,** *n.* **—sep′ar a bly,** *adv.*

sep a rate (*v.* sep′ə rāt′; *adj., n.* sep′ər it), *v.,* **-rat ed, -rat ing,** *adj., n.* *—v.t.* 1 be between; keep apart; divide: *The Atlantic Ocean separates America from Europe.* 2 take apart; part; disjoin: *separate church and state.* See synonym study below. 3 cause to live apart. A husband and wife may be separated by agreement or by order of a court. 4 divide into parts or groups; divide or part (a mass, compound, whole, etc.) into elements, sizes, etc.: *separate a tangle of string.* 5 put apart; take away: *Separate your books from mine.* 6 discharge from an office, service, school, etc.; dismiss. *—v.i.* 1 draw, come, or go apart; become disconnected or disunited: *The rope separated under the strain.* 2 part company: *After school, the children separated in all directions.* 3 live apart.

—adj. 1 apart from others: *in a separate room.* 2 divided; not joined: *separate seats, separate questions.* 3 individual; single: *the separate parts of a machine.*

—n. 1 something separate. 2 **separates,** *pl.* women's blouses, skirts, sweaters, etc., sold individually and worn interchangeably to make various coordinated outfits.

[< Latin *separatum* put apart, divided < *se-* apart + *parare* prepare] **—sep′ar ate ly,** *adv.* **—sep′ar ate ness,** *n.*

Syn. *v.t.* 2 **Separate, divide** mean to put apart what has been together. **Separate** implies a removal of the parts from each other: *The brothers had been separated by the war.* **Divide** implies a cutting or breaking into parts according to some plan or measure: *I divided the cake in two, saving half for the next meal.*

sep a ra tion (sep′ə rā′shən), *n.* 1 act of separating; dividing; taking apart. 2 condition of being separated. 3 line or point of separating: *the separation of the two branches of a river.* 4 the living apart of husband and wife by agreement or by order of a court.

sep ar a tism (sep′ər ə tiz′əm), *n.* principle or policy of separation; opposition to ecclesiastical or political union.

sep ar a tist (sep′ər ə tist, sep′ə rā′tist), *n.* 1 member of a group that withdraws or separates from a larger group. 2 **Separatist,** any of the Puritans who broke away from the Church of England during the reign of James I.

sep a ra tive (sep′ə rā′tiv), *adj.* tending to separate; causing separation.

sep a ra tor (sep′ə rā′tər), *n.* person or thing that separates, especially a machine for separating the cream from milk, wheat from chaff or dirt, etc.

Se phar dim (si fär′dim), *n.pl.* Spanish and Portuguese Jews and their descendants, as contrasted with the Ashkenazim.

se pi a (sē′pē ə), *n.* 1 a dark-brown pigment prepared from the inky secretion of cuttlefish. 2 a dark brown. 3 a drawing, photograph, etc., in tones of brown. *—adj.* 1 dark-brown. 2 done in sepia: *a sepia print.* [< Greek *sēpia* cuttlefish]

se poy (sē′poi), *n.* (formerly) a native of India who was a soldier in the British army. [< Portuguese *sipae* < Hindustani *sipāhī* < Persian, soldier, horseman < *sipāh* army]

sep sis (sep′sis), *n.* poisoning of the system by disease-producing microorganisms and their toxins absorbed into the bloodstream from festering wounds, etc. [< Greek *sēpsis* putrefaction < *sēpein* to rot]

Sept., 1 September. 2 Septuagint.

sep tal (sep′təl), *adj.* of or having to do with a septum.

Sep tem ber (sep tem′bər), *n.* the ninth month of the year. It has 30 days. [< Latin < *septem* seven; from its position in the early Roman calendar]

sep ten ni al (sep ten′ē əl), *adj.* 1 lasting seven years. 2 occurring every seven years. [< Latin *septennium* seven-year period < *septem* seven + *annus* year] **—sep ten′ni al ly,** *adv.*

sep tet or **sep tette** (sep tet′), *n.* 1 piece of music for seven voices or instruments. 2 group of seven singers or players performing together. 3 any group of seven. [< German *Septet* < Latin *septem* seven]

sep tic (sep′tik), *adj.* 1 causing infection or putrefaction. 2 caused by infection or putrefaction. [< Latin *septicus* < Greek *sēptikos* < *sēpein* to rot]

sep ti ce mi a (sep′tə sē′mē ə), *n.* blood poisoning, especially a form in which microorganisms and their toxins enter the bloodstream.

sep ti ce mic (sep′tə sē′mik), *adj.* 1 causing septicemia. 2 caused by or having septicemia.

septic tank, tank in which sewage is decomposed by bacteria.

sep til lion (sep til′yən), *n.* 1 (in the United States, Canada, and France) 1 followed by 24 zeros. 2 (in Great Britain and Germany) 1 followed by 42 zeros. [< French < Latin *septem* seven + French *(m)illion*]

sep tu a ge nar i an (sep′chü ə jə ner′ē ən, sep′tyü ə jə ner′ē ən), *n.* person who is 70 years old or between 70 and 80 years old. *—adj.* 70 years old or between 70 and 80 years old. [< Latin *septuagenarius,* ultimately < *septuaginta* seventy]

Sep tu a ges i ma (sep′chü ə jes′ə mə, sep′tyü ə jes′ə mə), *n.* the third Sunday before Lent. [< Latin, literally, seventieth]

Sep tu a gint (sep′chü ə jint, sep′tyü ə jint), *n.* the Greek translation of the Old Testament that was made before the time of Christ. [< Latin *septuaginta* seventy; because it was supposed to have been done by seventy scholars]

sep tum (sep′təm), *n., pl.* **-ta** (-tə). a dividing wall; partition. There is a septum of bone and cartilage between the nostrils. [< Latin *saeptum* a fence < *saepire* hedge in]

sep ul cher (sep′əl kər), *n.* 1 place of burial; tomb; grave. 2 structure or recess in some old churches in which sacred relics were deposited. *—v.t.* bury (a dead body) in a sepulcher. Also, **sepulchre.** [< Old French < Latin *sepulcrum* < *sepelire* bury]

se pul chral (sə pul′krəl), *adj.* 1 of sepulchers or tombs. 2 of burial: *sepulchral ceremonies.* 3 deep and gloomy; dismal; suggesting a tomb: *sepulchral darkness.* **—se pul′chral ly,** *adv.*

sep ul chre (sep′əl kər), *n., v.t.,* **-chred, -chring.** sepulcher.

sep ul ture (sep′əl chər), *n.* 1 burial. 2 ARCHAIC. place of burial; sepulcher. [< Latin *sepultura* < *sepelire* bury]

seq., the following [for Latin *sequens*].

seqq., the following (items) [for Latin *sequentia*].

se quel (sē′kwəl), *n.* 1 that which follows; continuation. 2 something that follows as a result of some earlier happening; result; outcome. 3 a complete story continuing an earlier one about the same people. [< Latin *sequela* < *sequi* follow]

se que la (si kwē′lə), *n., pl.* **-lae** (-lē). 1 thing following or resulting. 2 disease or abnormal condition which is the result of a previous disease. [< Latin. See SEQUEL.]

se quence (sē′kwəns), *n.* 1 the coming of one thing after another; succession; order of succession: *Arrange the names in alphabetical sequence.* 2 a connected series: *a sequence of lessons on one subject.* See **series** for synonym study. 3 something that follows; result: *Crime has its sequence of misery.* 4 (in card playing) a set of three or more cards of the same suit following one after another in order of value. 5 part of a motion picture consisting of an episode without breaks. 6 (in music) a series of melodic or harmonic phrases repeated three or more times at successive pitches upward or downward. 7 (in mathematics) a set of quantities or elements whose order corresponds to the natural order of whole numbers. EXAMPLE: $^1/_2$, $^1/_4$, $^1/_8$, $^1/_{16}$, . . . [< Late Latin *sequentia* < Latin *sequi* follow]

se quent (sē′kwənt), *adj.* 1 following; subsequent. 2 following in order; consecutive. 3 following as a result; consequent. *—n.* that which follows; result; consequence.

se quen tial (si kwen′shəl), *adj.* 1 sequent. 2 forming a sequence or connected series; characterized by a regular sequence of parts. **—se quen′tial ly,** *adv.*

se ques ter (si kwes′tər), *v.t.* 1 remove or withdraw from public use or from public view; seclude: *The shy old lady sequestered herself from all strangers.* 2 take away (property) for a time from an owner until a debt is paid or some claim is satisfied. 3 seize by authority; take and keep: *The soldiers sequestered food from the people they conquered.* [< Latin *sequestrare* < *sequester* trustee, mediator < *sequi* follow]

se ques trate (si kwes′trāt), *v.t.,* **-trat ed, -trat ing.** 1 confiscate. 2 ARCHAIC. sequester.

se ques tra tion (sē′kwə strā′shən, si kwes′trā′shən), *n.* 1 the seizing and holding of property until legal claims are satisfied. 2 forcible or authorized seizure; confiscation. 3 separation or withdrawal from others; seclusion.

se quin (sē′kwən), *n.* 1 a small spangle used to ornament dresses, scarfs, etc. 2 a former Italian and Turkish gold coin. [< French < Italian *zecchino* < *zecca* mint < Arabic *sikka* die used in minting]

se quoi a (si kwoi′ə), *n.* 1 redwood. 2 giant sequoia. [< *Sequoya*]

Sequoia National Park, national park in central California containing huge sequoia trees. 604 sq. mi.

Se quoy a or **Se quoy ah** (si kwoi′ə), *n.* 1770-1843, American Indian scholar, who invented an alphabet for the Cherokee language.

ser., series.

ser a (sir′ə), *n.* a pl. of **serum.**

se ragl io (sə ral′yō, sə rä′lyō), *n., pl.* **-ragl ios.** 1 harem. 2 a Turkish palace. [< Italian *serraglio* < Turkish *saray* palace]

se ra pe (sə rä′pē), *n.* shawl or blanket, often having bright colors, worn by Spanish Americans. Also, **sarape.** [< Mexican Spanish *serape, sarape*]

ser aph (ser′əf), *n., pl.* **-aphs** or **-a phim.** one of the highest order of angels. [< *seraphim,* plural, < Late Latin < Hebrew *sĕrāphīm*]

se raph ic (sə raf′ik), *adj.* 1 of seraphs. 2 like a seraph; angelic. **—se raph′i cal ly,** *adv.*

ser a phim (ser′ə fim), *n.* a pl. of **seraph.**

Serb (sėrb), *n.* 1 native or inhabitant of Serbia. 2 the Serbo-Croatian language of Serbia. *—adj.* of Serbia, its people, or their language.

Ser bi a (sėr′bē ə), *n.* former kingdom in SE Europe, now part of Yugoslavia. **—Ser′bi an,** *adj., n.*

Ser bo-Cro a tian (sėr′bō krō ā′shən), *adj.* both Serbian and Croatian. *—n.* 1 branch of the Slavic language spoken by the people of Yugoslavia, usually written in the Cyrillic alphabet in Serbia and in the Roman alphabet in Croatia. 2 person whose native language is Serbo-Croatian.

sere[1] (sir), *adj.* ARCHAIC. dried; withered. Also, **sear.** [Old English *sēar*]

sere[2] (sir), *n.* the complete series of ecological communities occupying a given area over a period of hundreds or thousands of years from the initial to the final stage. [< *series*]

ser e nade (ser′ə nād′), *n., v.,* **-nad ed, -nad ing.** *—n.* 1 music played or sung outdoors at night, especially by a lover under

hat, āge, fär; let, ēqual, tėrm;
it, īce; hot, ōpen, ôrder;
oil, out; cup, pu̇t, rüle;
ch, child; ng, long; sh, she;
th, thin; ᴛʜ, then; zh, measure;

ə represents *a* in about, *e* in taken, *i* in pencil, *o* in lemon, *u* in circus.

< = from, derived from, taken from.

his sweetheart's window. 2 piece of music suitable for such a performance. 3 (in music) a work of four to eight connected instrumental movements, usually written for a small orchestra. —*v.t.* sing or play a serenade to. —*v.i.* sing or play a serenade. [< French *sérénade* < Italian *serenata,* ultimately < Latin *serenus* serene] **—ser′e nad′er,** *n.*

ser en dip i tous (ser′ən dip′ə təs), *adj.* having to do with or resulting from serendipity.

ser en dip i ty (ser′ən dip′ə tē), *n.* the ability to make fortunate discoveries by accident. [(coined by Horace Walpole) < "The Three Princes of *Serendip*" (old name of Ceylon), a fairy tale whose heroes made such discoveries]

se rene (sə rēn′), *adj.* 1 peaceful; calm: *a serene smile.* See **peaceful** for synonym study. 2 not cloudy; clear; bright: *a serene sky.* 3 **Serene,** designating a person having the title of Serenity: *His Serene Highness.* —*n.* an expanse of clear sky or calm sea. [< Latin *serenus*] **—se rene′ly,** *adv.* **—se rene′ness,** *n.*

se ren i ty (sə ren′ə tē), *n., pl.* **-ties.** 1 peace and quiet; calmness. 2 clearness; brightness. 3 **Serenity,** a title of honor given to reigning princes and other dignitaries.

serf (sėrf), *n.* 1 (in the feudal system) a slave who could not be sold off the land, but passed from one owner to another with the land. 2 person treated almost like a slave; person who is mistreated, underpaid, etc. [< French < Latin *servus* slave] **—serf′like′,** *adj.*

serf dom (sėrf′dəm), *n.* 1 condition of a serf. 2 custom of having serfs. Serfdom existed all over Europe in the Middle Ages and lasted in Russia till the middle of the 1800's.

serf hood (sėrf′hu̇d), *n.* condition of a serf.

serge (sėrj), *n.* kind of fabric having diagonal lines or ridges on its surface. Worsted serge is used for coats and suits. Silk serge is used for linings. [< Old French *sarge* < Latin *serica (vestis)* silken (garment) < Greek *sērikē* < *Sēres* the Chinese]

ser gean cy (sär′jən sē), *n., pl.* **-cies.** position, rank, or duties of a sergeant.

ser geant (sär′jənt), *n.* 1 a noncommissioned military officer ranking above a corporal. 2 (in the U.S. Army and Marine Corps) a noncommissioned officer ranking next below a staff sergeant and next above a corporal. 3 (in the U.S. Air Force) a noncommissioned officer ranking next above an airman. 4 a police officer ranking next above an ordinary policeman and next below a captain or lieutenant. 5 sergeant at arms. Also, **serjeant.** [< Old French *sergent* < Latin *servientem* serving]

sergeant at arms, *pl.* **sergeants at arms.** officer who keeps order in a legislature, court of law, etc.

sergeant first class, (in the U.S. Army) a noncommissioned officer ranking next below a master sergeant and next above a staff sergeant.

sergeant major, 1 (in the U.S. Army and Marine Corps) the highest-ranking noncommissioned officer. 2 sergeant who assists an adjutant at an army headquarters.

sergt., sergeant.

ser i al (sir′ē əl), *n.* story published, broadcast, or televised one part at a time in a magazine or newspaper or on the radio or television. —*adj.* 1 published, broadcast, or televised one part at a time: *a serial publication, a serial story.* 2 of a series; arranged in a series; making a series: *Arrange volumes 1 to 5 in serial order.* **—ser′i al ly,** *adv.*

ser i al ize (sir′ē ə līz), *v.t.,* **-ized, -iz ing.** publish, broadcast, or televise in a series of installments. **—ser′i al i za′tion,** *n.*

serial number, an individual number given to a person, article, etc., as a means of easy identification.

ser i a tim (sir′ē ā′tim, ser′ē ā′tim), *adv.* in a series; one after the other. [< Medieval Latin < Latin *series* series]

ser i cul tur al (ser′ə kul′chər əl), *adj.* of or having to do with sericulture.

ser i cul ture (ser′ə kul′chər), *n.* the breeding and care of silkworms for the production of raw silk. [< Latin *sericum* silk + English *culture*]

ser ies (sir′ēz), *n., pl.* **ser ies.** 1 number of similar things in a row: *A series of rooms opened off the long hall.* 2 number of things placed one after another. 3 number of things, events, etc., coming one after the other; succession. See synonym study below. 4 an electrical arrangement in which a number of batteries, condensers, etc., are connected so that a current flows in turn through each one. 5 (in geology) a division of rocks ranking below a system, containing the rocks formed during a geological epoch. 6 (in chemistry) a sequence of elements of increasing atomic number; period or part of a period in the periodic table. 7 (in mathematics) the summing of the terms of a sequence. EXAMPLE: $1/2 + 1/4 + 1/8 + 1/16 + \ldots$ [< Latin < *serere* join]

Syn. 3 **Series, sequence, succession** mean a number of things, events, etc., arranged or coming one after another in some order. **Series** applies to a number of similar things with the same purpose or relation to each other: *She gave a series of lectures on Mexico.* **Sequence** implies a closer or unbroken connection, in thought, between cause and effect, in numerical or alphabetical order, etc.: *He reviewed the sequence of events leading to the discovery.* **Succession** emphasizes following in order of time, sometimes of place, usually without interruption: *a succession of illnesses.*

series winding, a winding of a motor or generator whereby the field magnet coils are connected in series with the armature and carry the same current.

ser ies-wound (sir′ēz wound′), *adj.* that has series winding: *a series-wound motor.*

ser if (ser′if), *n.* a thin or smaller line used to finish off a main stroke of a letter, as at the top and bottom of M. [probably < Dutch *schreef* line, stroke]

ser i graph (ser′ə graf), *n.* a color print made by serigraphy.

ser i graph ic (ser′ə graf′ik), *adj.* of or having to do with serigraphy; silk-screen.

se rig ra phy (sə rig′rə fē), *n.* art of producing handmade prints in several colors by pressing oil paint or similar pigment through a series of silk screens. [< Latin *sericum* silk + English *-graphy*]

ser i o com ic (sir′ē ō kom′ik), *adj.* partly serious and partly comic. **—ser′i o com′i cal ly,** *adv.*

ser i ous (sir′ē əs), *adj.* 1 showing deep thought or purpose; thoughtful; grave: *a serious manner, a serious face.* 2 in earnest; not joking; sincere: *She was serious about the subject.* 3 needing thought; important: *Choice of one's lifework is a serious matter.* 4 important because it may do much harm; dangerous: *a serious illness.* [< Late Latin *seriosus* < Latin *serius* earnest] **—ser′i ous ly,** *adv.* **—ser′i ous ness,** *n.*

ser jeant (sär′jənt), *n.* sergeant.

ser mon (sėr′mən), *n.* 1 a public talk on religion or something connected with religion. Ministers preach sermons in church. 2 a serious talk about morals, conduct, duty, etc.: *Father gave us a sermon on table manners.* 3 a long, tiresome speech; harangue. [< Latin *sermonem* a talk, originally, a stringing together of words < *serere* join]

ser mon ic (sėr′mon′ik), *adj.* of, having to do with, or like a sermon.

ser mon ize (sėr′mə nīz), *v.,* **-ized, -iz ing.** —*v.i.* give a sermon; preach. —*v.t.* preach or talk seriously to; lecture. **—ser′mon iz′er,** *n.*

Sermon on the Mount, Christ's sermon to His disciples, as reported in the Gospel according to Matthew and Luke.

ser o log i cal (sir′ə loj′ə kəl), *adj.* of or having to do with serology. **—ser′o log′i cal ly,** *adv.*

se rol o gist (si rol′ə jist), *n.* an expert in serology.

se rol o gy (si rol′ə jē), *n.* study of the use of serums in curing or preventing disease.

ser o to nin (sir′ō tō′nən), *n.* substance chemically related to adrenaline and hallucinogenic drugs that constricts blood vessels, raises blood pressure, and functions in brain chemistry.

ser ous (sir′əs), *adj.* 1 of, having to do with, or producing serum. 2 like serum; watery. Tears are drops of a serous fluid.

serous membrane, a thin membrane of connective tissue lining certain cavities of the body and moistened with a serous fluid.

ser pent (sėr′pənt), *n.* 1 snake, especially a big snake. 2 a sly, treacherous person. 3 the devil; Satan. [< Latin *serpentem,* originally, creeping]

ser pen tine (*adj.* sėr′pən tēn′, sėr′pən tīn; *n.* sėr′pən tēn′), *adj.* 1 of or like a serpent. 2 winding; twisting: *the serpentine course of a creek.* 3 cunning; sly; treacherous: *a serpentine plot.* —*n.* 1 mineral consisting chiefly of a hydrous silicate of magnesium, usually green, and sometimes spotted like the skin of some serpents. 2 anything twisted or winding like a snake.

ser rate (ser′āt, ser′it), *adj.* notched like the edge of a saw; toothed: *a serrate leaf.* [< Latin *serratus* < *serra* a saw]

serrate leaf

ser rat ed (ser′ā tid), *adj.* serrate.
ser ra tion (se rā′shən), *n.* 1 a serrate edge or formation. 2 one of its series of notches.
ser ried (ser′ēd), *adj.* crowded closely together. [< French *serré,* past participle of *serrer* press close]
ser ru late (ser′yə lāt, ser′ə lāt), *adj.* very finely notched: *a serrulate leaf.* [< Latin *serrula,* diminutive of *serra* a saw]
ser um (sir′əm), *n., pl.* **ser ums** or **ser a.** 1 a clear, pale-yellow, watery part of the blood that separates from the clot when blood coagulates. 2 a serous liquid used to prevent or cure a disease, usually obtained from the blood of an animal that has been made immune to the disease. Diphtheria antitoxin is a serum. 3 any watery fluid in animals, such as lymph. [< Latin, whey]
serum albumin, the albumin found in blood serum. It is the largest component of blood plasma and is a substitute for plasma.

serval—about 5 ft. long with tail

ser val (sėr′vəl), *n.* an African wildcat that has a brownish-yellow coat with black spots, long legs, large ears, and a ringed tail. [< French < Portuguese *(lobo) cerval* lynx, ultimately < Latin *cervus* stag]
serv ant (sėr′vənt), *n.* 1 person employed in a household. 2 person employed by a department or branch of government. 3 person devoted to any service. Ministers are called the servants of God. [< Old French, present participle of *servir* to serve] **—serv′ant less,** *adj.*
serve (sėrv), *v.,* **served, serv ing,** *n.* *—v.i.* 1 be a servant; give service; work; perform duties: *He served as a butler.* 2 perform official or public duties: *serve on a jury, serve in Congress.* 3 wait at table; bring food or drink to guests. 4 be useful; be what is needed; be of use: *Boxes served as seats.* 5 be favorable or suitable: *The ship will sail when the wind and tide serve.* 6 (in tennis, badminton, volleyball, etc.) start play by hitting the ball or shuttlecock. *—v.t.* 1 be a servant of; give service to; work for or in: *serve customers in a store. A slave serves his master.* 2 honor and obey; worship: *serve God.* 3 wait on at table; bring food or drink to. 4 put (food or drink) on the table: *serve pie for dessert.* 5 supply; furnish; supply with something needed: *The dairy serves us with milk.* 6 supply enough for: *One pie will serve six persons.* 7 help; aid: *Let me know if I can serve you in any way.* 8 be favorable or suitable to; satisfy. 9 be useful to; fulfill: *This will serve my purpose.* 10 treat; reward: *He served me unfairly.* **11 serve one right,** be just what one deserves. 12 pass; spend: *The thief served a term in prison.* 13 deliver (an order from a court, a writ, etc.); present (with an order from a court, etc.). 14 (in tennis, badminton, volleyball, etc.) put (the ball or shuttlecock) in play by hitting it. 15 (in nautical use) bind or wind (a rope, etc.) with small cord to strengthen or protect it. *—n.* in tennis, badminton, volleyball, etc.: 1 act or way of serving a ball or shuttlecock. 2 a player's turn to serve. [< Old French *servir* < Latin *servire,* originally, be a slave < *servus* slave]
serv er (sėr′vər), *n.* 1 person who serves. 2 tray for dishes, etc. 3 any of various pieces of tableware for serving food. 4 attendant who serves the celebrant at low Mass.
serv ice (sėr′vis), *n., adj., v.,* **-iced, -ic ing.** *—n.* 1 helpful act or acts; aid; conduct that is useful to others: *perform a service for one's country.* 2 arrangements for supplying something useful or necessary: *The train service was good.* 3 occupation or employment as a servant: *go into domestic service.* 4 Usually, **services,** *pl.* **a** performance of duties: *the services of a doctor.* **b** work in the service of others; useful labor: *We pay for services such as repairs, maintenance, and utilities.* 5 advantage; benefit; use: *This coat has given me great service.* 6 department of government or public employment, or the persons engaged in it: *the diplomatic service.* 7 the armed forces: *We entered the service together.* 8 duty in the armed forces: *be on active service.* 9 Often, **services,** *pl.* a religious meeting, ritual, or ceremony: *the marriage service. We attend church services every week.* 10 manner of serving food. 11 the food served. 12 set of dishes, etc.: *a solid silver tea service.* 13 (in law) the serving of a process or writ upon a person. 14 in tennis, badminton, volleyball, etc.: **a** act or manner of putting the ball or shuttlecock in play. **b** the ball or shuttlecock as put into play. 15 (in nautical use) a small cord wound about a rope, etc., to strengthen or protect it. **16 at one's service, a** ready to do what one wants. **b** ready or available for one to use. **17 of service,** helpful; useful. *—adj.* 1 for use by household servants, tradesmen, etc.: *a service entrance.* 2 belonging to a branch of the armed forces, especially on active duty: *a service cap.* *—v.t.* 1 make fit for service; keep fit for service: *The mechanic serviced our automobile.* 2 provide with a service of any kind: *Only two trains a day service the town.* [< Old French < Latin *servitium* < *servus* slave]
serv ice a bil i ty (sėr′vi sə bil′ə tē), *n.* a being serviceable.
serv ice a ble (sėr′vi sə bəl), *adj.* 1 useful for a long time; able to stand much use. 2 capable of giving good service; useful. **—serv′ice a ble ness,** *n.* **—serv′ice a bly,** *adv.*
serv ice ber ry (sėr′vis ber′ē), *n., pl.* **-ries.** 1 the fruit of a service tree. 2 shadbush.
service club, club formed to promote the interests of its members and of the community, as Rotary or Kiwanis.
serv ice man (sėr′vis man′, sėr′vis mən), *n., pl.* **-men.** 1 member of the armed forces. 2 person who maintains or repairs machinery or some kind of equipment.
service mark, mark or symbol used by a business or organization to distinguish its services from the services of others.
service station, filling station.
service tree, a European, Asian, and African mountain ash tree bearing a small, pear-shaped or round fruit called the serviceberry, that is edible when overripe.
ser vi ette (sėr′vē et′), *n.* BRITISH. a table napkin. [< French < *servir* serve]
ser vile (sėr′vəl), *adj.* 1 like that of slaves; mean; base: *servile flattery.* 2 of or having to do with slaves: *a servile revolt, servile work.* 3 fit for a slave. 4 yielding through fear, lack of spirit, etc.: *An honest judge cannot be servile to public opinion.* [< Latin *servilis* < *servus* slave] **—ser′vile ly,** *adv.* **—ser′vile ness,** *n.*
ser vil i ty (sėr′vil′ə tē), *n., pl.* **-ties.** attitude or behavior fit for a slave; servile yielding.
serv ing (sėr′ving), *n.* portion of food served to a person at one time; helping.
ser vi tor (sėr′və tər), *n.* servant; attendant.
ser vi tude (sėr′və tüd, sėr′və tyüd), *n.* 1 condition of being a slave; slavery; bondage. 2 forced labor as punishment: *The criminal was sentenced to five years' servitude.* [< Latin *servitudo* < *servus* slave]
ser vo (sėr′vō), *n., pl.* **-vos.** 1 servomechanism. 2 servomotor. [< Latin *servus* slave]
ser vo mech a nism (sėr′vō mek′ə niz′əm), *n.* any automatic device by which a supplementary source of power is used to assist in the movement, manipulation, guidance, etc., of some equipment.
ser vo mo tor (sėr′vō mō′tər), *n.* an auxiliary motor to supplement the primary source of power in the movement, guidance, etc., of a relatively heavy or complex apparatus.
ses a me (ses′ə mē), *n.* 1 an annual East Indian herb with oblong leaves and tiny flowers, cultivated in tropical regions for its small, flat seeds. 2 the seeds, used to flavor bread, candy, and other foods, and in making an oil used in cooking. 3 open sesame. [< Greek *sēsamē;* of Semitic origin]
ses qui cen ten ni al (ses′kwi sen ten′ē əl), *adj.* of or having to do with 150 years or the 150th anniversary. *—n.* 1 a 150th anniversary. 2 celebration of the 150th anniversary. [< Latin *sesqui-* one and a half + English *centennial*]
ses qui pe da li an (ses′kwi pə dā′lē ən), *adj.* 1 very long; containing many syllables. 2 using long words. [< Latin *sesquipedalis* half a yard long < *sesqui-* one and a half + *pedem* foot]

sessile (def. 1)
sessile leaves

ses sile (ses′əl), *adj.* 1 (in botany) attached by the base instead of by a stem. 2 (in zoology) sedentary; fixed to one spot. Some barnacles are sessile. [< Latin *sessilis* sitting < *sedere* sit]
ses sion (sesh′ən), *n.* 1 a sitting or meeting of a court, council, legislature, etc.: *a session of Congress.* 2 a series of such sittings. 3 term or period of such sittings: *This year's session of Congress was unusually long.* 4 a meeting: *a heated session with the head of the department.* 5 one of the periods of lessons

and study into which the school day or year is divided. **6 in session,** meeting: *Congress is now in session.* [< Latin *sessionem* < *sedere* sit]

ses sion al (sesh′ə nəl), *adj.* 1 of a session; having to do with sessions. 2 occurring every session.

Ses sions (sesh′ənz), *n.* **Roger,** born 1896, American composer.

ses terce (ses′tėrs′), *n.* an ancient Roman coin of small value. [< Latin *sestertius,* originally, two and a half < *semis* half + *tertius* third]

ses tet (ses tet′), *n.* 1 a musical sextet. 2 the last six lines of a sonnet. 3 poem or stanza having six lines. [< Italian *sestetto* < *sesto* sixth < Latin *sextus*]

set (set), *v.,* **set, set ting,** *adj., n.* —*v.t.* 1 put in some place; put; place: *set a chair upright, set a man on a throne, set a lamp on the table.* See **put** for synonym study. 2 put in the right place, position, or condition: *set a broken bone. Set the table for dinner.* 3 arrange (the hair) in waves, etc., when damp. 4 adjust according to a standard: *set a clock.* 5 cause to be; put in some condition or relation: *set someone at ease, set a prisoner free.* 6 put (a price, etc.); fix the value of at a certain amount or rate: *She set the value of the watch at $500.* 7 put as the measure of esteem of a person or thing: *set more by action than by talk.* 8 post, appoint, or station for the purpose of performing some duty: *set an investigator on a case.* 9 fix; arrange; appoint: *set a time limit for taking an examination, set the rules for the contest.* 10 allot or assign: *set a difficult job for oneself.* 11 provide for others to follow: *set a good example, set the fashion.* 12 put in a fixed, rigid, or settled state: *set one's teeth, set one's heart on something.* 13 make firm or hard: *set the white of an egg by boiling it.* 14 put in a frame or other thing that holds: *set a diamond in gold.* 15 adorn; ornament: *set a bracelet with diamonds.* 16 put (a hen) to sit on eggs to hatch them. 17 place (eggs) under a hen or in an incubator, to be hatched. 18 encourage to attack; cause to be hostile: *They set the dogs upon the prowler.* 19 cause to take a particular direction; direct: *set one's feet homeward.* 20 in music: **a** adapt; fit: *set words to music.* **b** arrange (music) for certain voices or instruments. 21 arrange scenery, etc., on: *set the stage.* 22 (in printing) put (type) in the order required. —*v.i.* 1 become fixed; become firm or hard: *Jelly sets as it cools.* 2 go down; sink; wane: *The sun sets in the west.* 3 (of the wind, a current, etc.) have a direction; tend: *The current sets to the south.* 4 hang or fit in a particular manner: *That coat sets well.* 5 begin to move; start: *He set to work.* 6 (of a hen) sit on eggs. 7 form fruit in the blossom. 8 (of a dog) indicate the position of game by standing stiffly and pointing with the nose.

set about, start work upon; begin: *set about one's business.*

set against, **a** make unfriendly toward. **b** balance; compare.

set aside, **a** put to one side. **b** put by for later use; reserve. **c** discard, dismiss, or leave out; reject; annul: *set aside the decision in a lawsuit.*

set back, stop; hinder; check.

set down, **a** deposit or let alight; put down: *set down a suitcase.* **b** put down in writing or printing. **c** consider; regard. **d** ascribe; attribute.

set forth, **a** make known; express; declare. **b** start to go.

set in, **a** begin: *Winter set in.* **b** blow or flow toward the shore.

set off, **a** explode. **b** start to go. **c** increase or heighten by contrast. **d** balance; compensate. **e** mark off; separate from others.

set on or **set upon,** **a** attack. **b** urge to attack.

set out, **a** start to go. **b** spread out to show, sell, or use: *set out goods for sale.* **c** plant. **d** plan; intend (to do something).

set to, **a** begin: *set to work.* **b** begin fighting: *The two boys set to.*

set up, **a** build; erect. **b** begin; start. **c** assemble (a manufactured article, etc.). **d** put up; raise in place, position, power, pride, etc. **e** raise; utter: *set up a cry.* **f** claim; pretend: *set up to be honest.* **g** plan, prepare, or establish: *set up a business deal.*

—*adj.* 1 fixed or appointed beforehand; established: *a set time, set rules.* 2 prepared; ready: *She is all set to go.* 3 fixed; rigid: *a set smile.* 4 firm; hard. 5 resolved; determined: *I am set on going today.* 6 INFORMAL. stubbornly fixed; obstinate: *set in one's ways.*

—*n.* 1 number of things or persons belonging together; group; outfit: *a set of dishes.* 2 the scenery of a play or a scene of a play; setting. 3 the scenery for a motion picture. 4 device for receiving or sending by radio, telephone, telegraph, etc. 5 way a thing or person is put or placed; form; shape: *His jaw had a stubborn set.* 6 direction; tendency; course; drift: *The set of opinion was toward building a new bridge.* 7 warp; bend; displacement: *a set to the right.* 8 a slip or shoot for planting: *onion sets.* 9 a young fruit just formed from a blossom. 10 group of games in tennis. One player or team must win six games, and must win by a margin of two games. 11 act or manner of setting. 12 the way in which anything fits: *the set of a coat.* 13 (in mathematics) a collection of numbers, points, or other elements which are distinguished from all other elements by specific common properties. The numbers from 0 to 10 form a set, and any number in this set is a member of the set.

[Old English *settan.* Related to SIT.]

➤ **set, sit.** People and things *sit* (past, *sat*) or they are *set* (past, *set*), meaning placed. A hen, however, *sets* (on her eggs).

Set (set), *n.* (in Egyptian myths) the god of evil, brother of Osiris.

se ta (sē′tə), *n., pl.* **-tae** (-tē). a slender, stiff, bristlelike organ or part of an animal or plant. Earthworms have four pairs of setae in each segment. [< Latin *saeta* bristle]

se ta ceous (si tā′shəs), *adj.* 1 bristlelike; bristle-shaped. 2 furnished with bristles; bristly.

set back (set′bak′), *n.* 1 a check to progress; reverse: *an unexpected setback in a patient's recovery.* 2 a steplike setting back of the outside wall of a building to give better light and air in the street.

setback (def. 2) building with setbacks

hat, āge, fär; let, ēqual, tėrm;
it, īce; hot, ōpen, ôrder;
oil, out; cup, pu̇t, rüle;
ch, child; ng, long; sh, she;
th, thin; ᴛʜ, then; zh, measure;

ə represents *a* in about, *e* in taken, *i* in pencil, *o* in lemon, *u* in circus.

< = from, derived from, taken from.

Seth (seth), *n.* (in the Bible) the third son of Adam.

set off (set′ôf′, set′of′), *n.* 1 thing used to set off or adorn; ornament; decoration. 2 something that counterbalances or makes up for something else; compensation. 3 settlement of a debt by means of a claim in the debtor's favor. 4 claim so used. 5 start; departure.

set screw (set′skrü′), *n.* a machine screw used to fasten gears, pulleys, etc., to a shaft.

set tee (se tē′), *n.* sofa or long bench with a back and, usually, arms. [perhaps variant of *settle*[2]]

setter (def. 2)—2 ft. high at shoulder

set ter (set′ər), *n.* 1 person or thing that sets: *a setter of type, a setter of jewels.* 2 a long-haired hunting dog, trained to stand motionless and point its nose toward the game that it scents.

set theory, branch of mathematics that deals with sets, their properties, and their relationships.

set ting (set′ing), *n.* 1 frame or other thing in which something is set. The mounting of a jewel is its setting. 2 scenery of a play. 3 place, time, etc., of a play or story. 4 surroundings; background: *a scenic mountain setting.* 5 music composed to go with a story, poem, etc. 6 the eggs that a hen sets on for hatching. 7 act of a person or thing that sets. 8 dishes or cutlery, required to set one place at a table.

set tle[1] (set′l), *v.,* **-tled, -tling.** —*v.t.* 1 make a decision on; decide: *settle an argument.* 2 agree upon (a time, place, plan, etc.); fix beforehand: *settle a time for leaving.* 3 put in order; arrange: *settle one's affairs.* See **fix** for synonym study. 4 pay; arrange payment of: *settle a bill.* 5 cause to take up residence in a place: *settle one's family in the country.* 6 establish colonies in; colonize: *The English settled New England.* 7 set in a fairly permanent position, place, or way of life: *settle one's son in business. We quickly settled ourselves in our new house.* 8 arrange in a desired or comfortable position; adjust: *The cat settled itself in the chair.* 9 make quiet: *A vacation will settle your nerves.* 10 make (a liquid) clear: *A beaten egg or cold water will settle coffee.* 11 cause (dregs or other impurities) to sink to the bottom. 12 make firm and compact; cause to subside into a solid or more compact mass: *settle soil by watering it.* 13 **settle upon** or **settle on,** give (property, etc.) to by law. —*v.i.* 1 decide; determine: *Have you settled on a time for leaving?* 2 arrange matters in dispute; come to terms or agreement *(with): settle with a union.* 2 be put in order, especially by closing an account *(with).* 3 take up residence (in a new country or place): *settle in New York.* 4 be set in a fairly permanent position, place, or way of life: *She settled into her new position at the company very quickly.* 5 come to rest in a particular place; lodge: *A heavy fog settled over the airport.* 6 come to a definite condition: *My cold settled in my chest.* 7 come to a desired or comfortable position. 8 become quiet or composed. 9 go down; sink gradually, especially by its own weight: *The house settled after a time.* 10 (of a liquid) become clear by depositing dregs or impurities. 11 (of dregs) sink to the bottom. 12 become firm and compact, as soil. 13 **settle down,** a live a more regular life. b direct steady effort or attention. [Old English *setlan* < *setl* settle²]

settle²

set tle² (set′l), *n.* a long bench, usually with arms and a high back. [Old English *setl* a sitting place]

set tle ment (set′l mənt), *n.* 1 act of settling. 2 condition of being settled. 3 a deciding; determining: *the settlement of a date.* 4 a putting in order; arrangement. 5 payment: *settlement of a claim.* 6 the settling of persons in a new country or area; colonization: *the settlement of the Dutch in New Amsterdam.* 7 colony: *England had many settlements along the Atlantic Coast.* 8 group of buildings and the people living in them: *the small, scattered settlements of the colonists.* 9 place in a poor, neglected neighborhood where work for its improvement is carried on. 10 the settling of property upon someone: *She received $200,000 by a marriage settlement.* 11 amount so given.

set tler (set′lər), *n.* 1 person who settles. 2 person who settles in a new country, region, etc.

set tlings (set′lingz), *n.pl.* things in a liquid which settle to the bottom; sediment.

set-to (set′tü′), *n., pl.* **-tos.** INFORMAL. 1 a fight; dispute. 2 a contest; match.

set up (set′up′), *n.* 1 arrangement of apparatus, machinery, etc. 2 arrangement of an organization.

Seu rat (sœ rä′), *n.* **Georges,** 1859-1891, French painter.

Se vas to pol (si vas′tə pōl), *n.* seaport in SW Soviet Union, on the Black Sea. 229,000. Also, **Sebastopol.**

sev en (sev′ən), *n., adj.* one more than six; 7. [Old English *seofon*]

sev en fold (sev′ən fōld′), *adv.* 1 seven times as much or as many. 2 seven times as much or as often. —*adj.* 1 seven times as much or as many. 2 having seven parts.

Seven Hills, hills upon and about which ancient Rome was built.

seven seas, all the seas and oceans of the world, traditionally believed to be the Arctic, Antarctic, N Atlantic, S Atlantic, N Pacific, S Pacific, and Indian oceans.

sev en teen (sev′ən tēn′), *n., adj.* seven more than ten; 17.

sev en teenth (sev′ən tēnth′), *adj., n.* 1 next after the 16th; last in a series of 17. 2 one of 17 equal parts.

sev en teen-year locust (sev′ən tēn′-yir′), cicada of the eastern United States that requires from thirteen to seventeen years to develop from egg to adult. The larva burrows underground and feeds on roots, emerging after seventeen years to live a short time as an adult.

sev enth (sev′ənth), *adj.* 1 next after the sixth; last in a series of 7. 2 being one of 7 equal parts. —*n.* 1 next after the sixth; last in a series of 7. 2 one of 7 equal parts. 3 in music: a interval between two tones that are seven degrees apart. b the harmonic combination of two such tones. c the seventh tone of a scale.

sev enth-day (sev′ənth dā′), *adj.* having to do with or observing Saturday, the seventh day of the week, as the principal day of rest and religious observance.

Seventh-Day Adventist, member of a seventh-day Protestant denomination that emphasizes the doctrine of the second coming of Christ.

seventh heaven, 1 the highest part of heaven. 2 the highest place or condition of joy and happiness.

sev en ti eth (sev′ən tē ith), *adj., n.* 1 next after the 69th; last in a series of 70. 2 one of 70 equal parts.

sev en ty (sev′ən tē), *n., pl.* **-ties,** *adj.* seven times ten; 70.

Seven Wonders of the World, the seven most remarkable structures of ancient times: the Egyptian Pyramids, the Mausoleum at Halicarnassus, the temple of Artemis (Diana) at Ephesus, the walls and hanging gardens of Babylon, the Colossus of Rhodes, the statue of Zeus by Phidias at Olympia, and the Pharos (lighthouse) at Alexandria.

sev er (sev′ər), *v.t.* 1 cut apart; cut off: *sever a rope.* 2 break off: *The two countries severed friendly relations.* —*v.i.* part; divide; separate: *The rope severed and the swing fell down.* [< Old French *sevrer,* ultimately < Latin *separare* to separate] —**sev′er a ble,** *adj.*

sev er al (sev′ər əl), *adj.* 1 being more than two or three but not many; some; a few: *gain several pounds.* 2 individual; different: *The boys went their several ways, each minding his own business.* 3 considered separately; single: *the several steps in the process of making paper.* —*n.* more than two or three but not many; some; a few: *Several of the members have given their consent.* [< Anglo-French, ultimately < Latin *separ* distinct < *separare* to separate]

sev er al ly (sev′ər ə lē), *adv.* 1 separately; singly; individually: *Consider these points, first severally and then collectively.* 2 respectively.

sev er al ty (sev′ər əl tē), *n.* 1 a being separate or distinct. 2 (in law) condition of being held or owned by separate or individual rights.

sev er ance (sev′ər əns), *n.* 1 a severing or a being severed; separation; division. 2 a breaking off: *the severance of diplomatic relations between two countries.*

severance pay, additional pay granted to employees that are leaving a business, company, etc.

se vere (sə vir′), *adj.,* **-ver er, -ver est.** 1 very strict; stern; harsh: *a severe reprimand.* See synonym study below. 2 sharp or violent: *a severe headache, a severe storm.* 3 serious; grave: *a severe illness.* 4 very plain or simple; without ornament: *She wore a severe black dress.* 5 difficult: *a series of severe tests.* 6 rigidly exact, accurate, or methodical: *severe reasoning.* [< Latin *severus*] —**se vere′ly,** *adv.* —**se vere′ness,** *n.*
Syn. 1 **Severe, stern** mean having or showing strictness. **Severe** implies uncompromising strictness and the absence of any mildness or indulgence: *a severe critic, severe punishment.* **Stern** implies rigid firmness, sometimes assumed only for the occasion: *The coach is stern when boys break training.*

se ver i ty (sə ver′ə tē), *n., pl.* **-ties.** 1 strictness; sternness; harshness. 2 sharpness or violence: *the severity of a storm, the severity of grief.* 3 simplicity of style or taste; plainness. 4 seriousness. 5 accuracy; exactness.

Sev ern River (sev′ərn), river flowing from central Wales through W England into the Bristol Channel. 210 mi.

Se ver us (sə vir′əs), *n.* **Lucius Septimius,** A.D. 146-211, Roman emperor from A.D. 193 to 211.

Sé vi gné (sā vē nyā′), *n.* **Marquise de,** 1626-1696, Marie de Rabutin-Chantal, French writer.

Se ville (sə vil′), *n.* city in SW Spain. 622,000. Also, SPANISH **Se vi lla** (sā vē′yä).

Sè vres (sev′rə), *n.* 1 town in N France, near Paris. 20,000. 2 a choice and costly kind of porcelain made there.

sew (sō), *v.,* **sewed, sewed** or **sewn, sewing.** —*v.i.* work with needle and thread. —*v.t.* 1 fasten with stitches: *sew on a button.* 2 close with stitches: *The doctor sewed up the wound.* 3 **sew up,** INFORMAL. make certain. [Old English *seowian*]

sew age (sü′ij), *n.* the waste matter carried off in sewers and drains.

Sew ard (sü′ərd), *n.* **William Henry,** 1801-1872, American statesman, Secretary of State from 1861 to 1869.

sew er¹ (sü′ər), *n.* an underground pipe or channel for carrying off waste water and refuse. [< Old French *sewiere* sluice from a pond, ultimately < Latin *ex* out + *aqua* water]

sew er² (sō′ər), *n.* person or thing that sews. [< *sew*]

sew er age (sü′ər ij), *n.* 1 removal of waste matter by sewers. 2 system of sewers. 3 sewage.

sew ing (sō′ing), *n.* 1 work done with a needle and thread. 2 something to be sewed. —*adj.* for sewing; used in sewing: *a sewing room.*

sewing machine, machine for sewing or stitching cloth, etc.

sewn (sōn), *v.* a pp. of **sew.**

sex (seks), *n.* 1 one of the two divisions, male or female, of human beings and other organisms, as determined by function in reproduction. 2 the character of being male or female: *People were admitted without regard to age or sex.* 3 attraction of one sex for the other. 4 INFORMAL. sexual intercourse. —*adj.* of sex; having to do with sex. [< Latin *sexus*]

sex a ge nar i an (sek′sə jə ner′ē ən), *n.* person who is 60 years old or between 60 and 70 years old. —*adj.* 60 years old or between

60 and 70 years old. [< Latin *sexagenarius,* ultimately < *sexaginta* sixty]

Sex a ges i ma (sek′sə jes′ə mə), *n.* the second Sunday before Lent. [< Latin, literally, sixtieth]

sex a ges i mal (sek′sə jes′ə məl), *adj.* having to do with or based upon the number 60. A sexagesimal fraction is one whose denominator is 60 or a power of 60.

sex appeal, 1 attraction for the opposite sex. 2 qualities which arouse strong physical attraction or general appeal.

sex chromosome, either of a pair of chromosomes which in combination with each other determine sex and sex-linked characteristics.

sex gland, gonad.

sex ism (sek′siz′əm), *n.* discrimination or prejudice against a sex or member of a sex, especially the female sex.

sex ist (sek′sist), *adj.* of or having to do with sexism: *sexist attitudes.*

sex less (seks′lis), *adj.* without sex or the characteristics of sex. **—sex′less ly,** *adv.* **—sex′less ness,** *n.*

sex-link age (seks′ling′kij), *n.* condition of being sex-linked.

sex-linked (seks′lingkt′), *adj.* of or having to do with a characteristic, such as hemophilia, that is transmitted by genes located in the sex chromosomes.

sext (sekst), *n.* 1 the fourth of the seven canonical hours. 2 the service for it. [< Latin *sexta (hora)* sixth (hour) < *sex* six; because it originally came at the sixth hour of the day (noon). Doublet of SIESTA.]

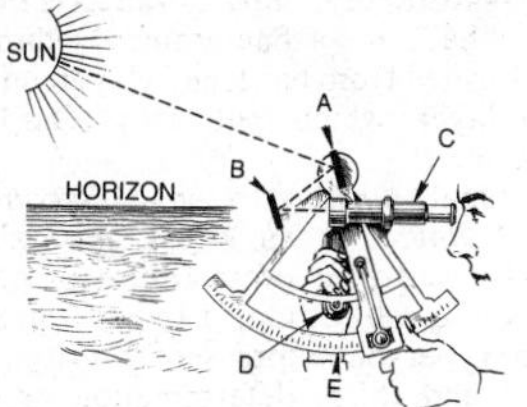

sextant
A, mirror; B, mirror; C, telescope; D, handle; E, graduated arm

sex tant (sek′stənt), *n.* instrument used by navigators, surveyors, etc., for measuring the angular distance between two objects. Sextants are used in navigation to measure the altitude of heavenly bodies, in order to determine latitude and longitude. [< Latin *sextantem* a sixth < *sextus* sixth < *sex* six]

sex tet or **sex tette** (sek stet′), *n.* 1 piece of music for six voices or instruments. 2 group of six singers or players performing together. 3 any group of six. [alteration of *sestet* after Latin *sex* six]

sex til lion (sek stil′yən), *n.* 1 (in the United States, Canada, and France) 1 followed by 21 zeros. 2 (in Great Britain and Germany) 1 followed by 36 zeros. [< French < Latin *sextus* sixth + French *(m)illion*]

sex ton (sek′stən), *n.* man who takes care of a church building. A sexton's duties sometimes include ringing the church bell, arranging burials, etc. [< Old French *secrestein* < Medieval Latin *sacristanus* sacristan. Doublet of SACRISTAN.]

sex tu ple (sek′stə pəl, sek′styə pəl; sekstü′pəl, sek styü′pəl), *adj., n., v.,* **-pled, -pling.** *—adj.* 1 consisting of six parts; sixfold. 2 six times; six times as great. 3 (in music) having six beats to each measure. *—n.* number or amount six times as great as another. *—v.t., v.i.* make or become six times as great. [< Latin *sextus* sixth + English *(quadr)uple*]

sex tu plet (sek′stə plit, sek′styə plit; sekstü′plit, sek styü′plit), *n.* 1 one of six offspring born at the same time from the same mother. 2 any group or combination of six.

sex u al (sek′shü əl), *adj.* 1 of or having to do with sex or the sexes: *sexual reproduction.* 2 having to do with relations between the sexes: *sexual morality.* 3 having sex; separated into two sexes. [< Late Latin *sexualis* < Latin *sexus* sex] **—sex′u al ly,** *adv.*

sexual intercourse, the uniting or joining of male and female sexual organs, usually with ejaculation; coitus; copulation.

sex u al i ty (sek′shü al′ə tē), *n.* 1 sexual character; possession of sex. 2 attention to sexual matters.

sex y (sek′sē), *adj.,* **sex i er, sex i est.** INFORMAL. sexually appealing or stimulating; having sex appeal. **—sex′i ly,** *adv.* **—sex′i ness,** *n.*

Sey chelles (sā shelz′), *n.pl.* group of British islands in the Indian Ocean, off E Africa. 53,000 pop.; 107 sq. mi. *Capital:* Victoria.

Sey mour (sē′môr, sē′mōr), *n.* **Jane,** 1509?-1537, third wife of Henry VIII of England and mother of Edward VI.

sf., sforzando.

sfor zan do (sfôr tsän′dō), *adj., adv., n., pl.* **-dos.** in music: *—adj.* with special, usually sudden, emphasis. *—adv.* in a sforzando manner. *—n.* tone or chord performed in this way. [< Italian, forcing]

sfz., sforzando.

s.g., specific gravity.

's Gra ven ha ge (skrä′vən hä′gə), Dutch name of **The Hague.**

Sgt., Sergeant.

sh., 1 share. 2 sheet. 3 shilling or shillings.

shab by (shab′ē), *adj.,* **-bi er, -bi est.** 1 much worn: *This old suit looks shabby.* 2 wearing old or much worn clothes. 3 poor or neglected; run-down: *a shabby old house.* 4 not generous; mean; unfair: *a shabby way to treat an old friend.* [< obsolete *shab* scab, Old English *sceabb*] **—shab′bi ly,** *adv.* **—shab′bi ness,** *n.*

Sha bu oth (shə vü′ōs, shä vü ôt′), *n.* a Jewish festival observed seven weeks after Passover, celebrating the harvest and the giving of the Torah to Moses; Pentecost. [< Hebrew *shābhuōth,* literally, weeks]

shack (shak), *n.* 1 a roughly built hut or cabin. 2 house in bad condition. *—v.i.* SLANG. Usually, **shack up,** live or stay in a place. [origin uncertain]

shack le (shak′əl), *n., v.,* **-led, -ling.** *—n.* 1 a metal band fastened around the ankle or wrist of a prisoner, slave, etc. Shackles are usually fastened to each other, the wall, floor, etc., by chains. 2 **shackles,** *pl.* fetters; chains. 3 link fastening together the two rings for the ankles and wrists of a prisoner. 4 Also, **shackles,** *pl.* anything that prevents freedom of action, thought, etc. 5 thing for fastening or coupling. *—v.t.* 1 put shackles on. 2 restrain; hamper. 3 fasten or couple with a shackle. [Old English *sceacel*] **—shack′ler,** *n.*

Shack le ton (shak′əl tən), *n.* Sir **Ernest Henry,** 1874-1922, British antarctic explorer, born in Ireland.

shad (shad), *n., pl.* **shad** or **shads.** any of several saltwater fishes of the same family as the herrings that ascend rivers in the spring to spawn. The shad common on the northern Atlantic coast is a valuable food fish. [Old English *sceadd*]

hat, āge, fär; let, ēqual, tėrm;
it, īce; hot, ōpen, ôrder;
oil, out; cup, pu̇t, rüle;
ch, child; ng, long; sh, she;
th, thin; ᴛʜ, then; zh, measure;

ə represents *a* in about, *e* in taken, *i* in pencil, *o* in lemon, *u* in circus.

< = from, derived from, taken from.

shad ber ry (shad′ber′ē), *n., pl.* **-ries.** fruit of the shadbush.

shad bush (shad′bu̇sh′), *n.* any of a genus of North American shrubs or small trees of the rose family, with berrylike fruit and white flowers which blossom about the time shad appear in the rivers; serviceberry.

shad dock (shad′ək), *n.* 1 a pear-shaped citrus fruit like a coarse, dry, inferior grapefruit. 2 tree that it grows on. [< Captain *Shaddock,* shipmaster who introduced the fruit into the West Indies in the 1600's]

shade (shād), *n., v.,* **shad ed, shad ing.** *—n.* 1 a partly dark place, not in the sunshine: *We sat in the shade of a beach umbrella.* 2 a slight darkness or coolness afforded by something that cuts off light: *Leafy trees cast shade.* 3 place or condition of comparative obscurity or seclusion. 4 something that shuts out light: *Pull down the shades of the windows.* 5 lightness or darkness of color: *silks in all shades of blue.* See **color** for synonym study. 6 the dark part of a picture. 7 a very small difference, amount, or degree: *a shade too long, many shades of opinion.* 8 a darkening look, feeling, etc.; shadow; cloud: *A shade of doubt troubled her.* 9 ghost; spirit. 10 **the shades,** the darkness of evening or night. 11 **in the shade,** in or into a condition of being unknown or unnoticed.

—v.t. 1 screen from light; darken. 2 make darker than the rest, as by using darker paint in a picture. 3 make dark or gloomy. 4 lessen slightly: *shade prices. —v.i.* show very small differences; change little by little: *This scarf shades from deep rose to pale pink.*

[Old English *sceadu*] **—shade′less,** *adj.*

shad ing (shā′ding), *n.* 1 a covering from the light. 2 use of black or color to give the effect of shade or depth in a picture. 3 a slight variation or difference of color, character, etc.

shad ow (shad′ō), *n.* 1 shade made by a person, animal, or thing; the darkness which something casts on a surface by intercepting direct rays of light. 2 darkness; partial shade. 3 the dark part of a place or picture. 4 a little bit; small degree; slight suggestion: *There's not a shadow of a doubt about their guilt.* 5 ghost; specter. 6 a faint image: *You look worn to a shadow.* 7 anything unsubstantial or unreal. 8 a reflected image. 9 person who follows another closely and secretly, as a detective. 10 a constant companion; follower. 11 sadness; gloom. 12 protection; shelter. 13 obscurity. 14 **the shadows,** the darkness after sunset.

—v.t. 1 protect from light; shade: *The grass is shadowed by huge oaks.* 2 cast a shadow on. 3 Usually, **shadow forth.** represent faintly. 4 follow closely and secretly. 5 make sad or gloomy.

[Old English *sceadwe,* oblique case of *sceadu*

shade] **—shad′ow er,** *n.* **—shad′ow less,** *adj.* **—shad′ow like′,** *adj.*

shad ow box ing (shad′ō bok′sing), *n.* boxing with an imaginary opponent for exercise or training.

shadow cabinet, group of influential advisers of a head of state, political leader, etc.

shad ow graph (shad′ō graf), *n.* 1 picture produced by throwing a shadow on a lighted screen. 2 radiograph.

shadow play, entertainment in which the shadows of actors, puppets, or other forms are cast upon a screen placed between the stage and the auditorium.

shad ow y (shad′ō ē), *adj.* 1 having much shadow or shade; shady. 2 like a shadow; dim, faint, or slight: *We saw a shadowy outline on the window curtain.* 3 not real; ghostly. **—shad′ow i ness,** *n.*

shad y (shā′dē), *adj.,* **shad i er, shad i est.** 1 in the shade; shaded. 2 giving shade. 3 INFORMAL. of doubtful honesty, character, etc.: *a rather shady transaction.* **—shad′i ly,** *adv.* **—shad′i ness,** *n.*

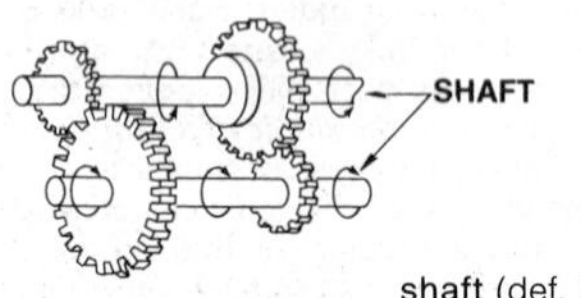

shaft (def. 1)

shaft (shaft), *n.* 1 bar which supports turning parts in a machine or which transmits rotatory motion from one part of the machine to another. 2 a deep passage sunk in the earth for mining, ventilation, etc. 3 a well-like passage; long, narrow space: *an elevator shaft.* 4 the long, slender stem of an arrow, spear, etc. 5 arrow or spear. 6 something aimed at a person like an arrow or spear: *shafts of ridicule.* 7 ray or beam of light. 8 one of the two wooden poles between which a horse is harnessed to a carriage, etc. 9 the main part of a column or pillar. 10 flagpole. 11 the long, straight handle of a hammer, ax, golf club, etc. 12 stem; stalk. 13 the rib of a feather. [Old English *sceaft*] **—shaft′like′,** *adj.*

Shaftes bur y (shafts′bər ē), *n.* **Earl of,** 1621-1683, Anthony Ashley Cooper, English statesman.

shag[1] (shag), *n., v.,* **shagged, shag ging.** *—n.* 1 rough, matted hair, wool, etc. 2 a mass of this: *the shag of a dog.* 3 the long, rough nap of some kinds of cloth. 4 cloth having such a nap. 5 a coarse tobacco cut into shreds. *—v.t.* make rough or shaggy. [Old English *sceacga*]

shag[2] (shag), *v.t.,* **shagged, shag ging.** INFORMAL. catch or retrieve and return (a ball). [origin unknown]

shag bark (shag′bärk′), *n.* a hickory tree of eastern North America whose rough outer bark peels off in long strips.

shag gy (shag′ē), *adj.,* **-gi er, -gi est.** 1 covered with a thick, rough mass of hair, wool, etc.: *a shaggy dog.* 2 long, thick, and rough: *shaggy eyebrows.* 3 unkempt in appearance, especially needing a haircut or shave. 4 having a long, rough nap; of coarse texture. **—shag′gi ly,** *adv.* **—shag′gi ness,** *n.*

sha green (shə grēn′), *n.* 1 kind of untanned leather made from the skin of the horse, ass, shark, seal, and other animals, having a granular surface and usually dyed green. 2 the rough skin of certain sharks and rays, used for polishing, etc. [< French *chagrin* < Turkish *çagrı* rump of a horse]

Shah or **shah** (shä), *n.* title of the ruler of Iran. [< Persian *shāh*]

shake (shāk), *v.,* **shook, shak en, shak ing,** *n.* *—v.t.* 1 cause to move quickly backwards and forwards, up and down, or from side to side: *shake a rug, shake one's head.* 2 bring, throw, force, rouse, scatter, etc., by or as if by movement: *shake dust from a rug.* 3 clasp (hands) in greeting, congratulating, etc., another. 4 make tremble: *The explosion shook the building.* 5 cause to totter or waver: *shake the very foundations of society.* 6 make less firm or sure; disturb; upset: *His lie shook my faith in his honesty.* 7 SLANG. get rid of (a person); give up (a habit): *Can't you shake her?* 8 (in music) execute with a trill; trill. **9 shake down, a** bring or throw down by shaking. **b** cause to settle down. **c** bring into working order. **d** SLANG. get money from dishonestly. **10 shake off,** get rid of. **11 shake up, a** shake hard. **b** stir up. **c** jar in body or nerves. *—v.i.* 1 move quickly backwards and forwards, up and down, or from side to side: *branches shaking in the wind.* 2 be shaken: *Sand shakes off easily.* 3 tremble: *shake with cold.* See synonym study below. 4 totter; waver: *My courage began to shake.* 5 (in music) trill.

—n. 1 act or fact of shaking: *a shake of the head.* 2 INFORMAL. earthquake. 3 drink made by shaking its ingredients together: *a milk shake.* 4 SLANG. moment: *I'll be there in two shakes.* 5 (in music) a trill. 6 crack in a growing tree. 7 fissure in rock, mineral strata, etc. **8 no great shakes,** INFORMAL. not unusual, extraordinary, or important. **9 the shakes,** INFORMAL. **a** any disease characterized by a trembling of the muscles and limbs. **b** a trembling caused by fear or horror.

[Old English *sceacan*] **—shak′a ble, shake′a ble,** *adj.*

Syn. *v.i.* 3 **Shake, tremble, quiver** mean to move with an agitated, vibrating motion. **Shake** is the general word: *He shook with laughter.* **Tremble,** used chiefly of people or animals, suggests an uncontrollable shaking caused by fear or other strong feeling, cold, weakness, etc.: *In his excitement his hands trembled.* **Quiver** suggests a slight trembling motion: *The dog's nostrils quivered at the scent.*

shake down (shāk′doun′), 1 SLANG. an extraction of money, etc., by compulsion, especially as in various forms of graft. 2 a bringing into proper condition or working order by practice, use, etc. 3 a makeshift bed. 4 process of shaking down. *—adj.* INFORMAL. having to do with a trial and adjustment of new equipment, sometimes to permit a crew to become familiar with it: *a shakedown cruise.*

shak en (shā′kən), *v.* pp. of **shake.**

shak er (shā′kər), *n.* 1 person who shakes something. 2 machine or utensil used in shaking. 3 container for pepper, salt, etc., having a perforated top. 4 **Shaker,** member of an American religious sect started in England in the 1700's, so called from movements of the body forming part of their worship.

Shake speare (shāk′spir), *n.* **William,** 1564-1616, English poet and dramatist. Also, **Shakspeare, Shakspere.**

Shake spear i an or **Shake spear e an** (shāk spir′ē ən), *adj.* of, having to do with, or suggestive of Shakespeare or his works. *—n.* an expert on Shakespeare or his works.

Shake spear i a na (shāk′spir ē ä′nə, shāk′spir ē an′ə), *n.pl.* things written about or by Shakespeare, or associated with him.

Shakespearian sonnet, Elizabethan sonnet.

shake-up (shāk′up′), *n.* a sudden and complete change; drastic rearrangement of policy, personnel, etc.: *a shake-up in the government.*

shaking palsy, Parkinson's disease.

shako

shak o (shak′ō, shā′kō), *n., pl.* **shak os.** a high, stiff military hat with a plume or other ornament. [< Hungarian *csákó* peaked (cap)]

Shak speare or **Shak spere** (shāk′spir), *n.* Shakespeare.

shak y (shā′kē), *adj.,* **shak i er, shak i est.** 1 shaking: *a shaky voice.* 2 liable to break down or give way; not firm or solid; weak: *a shaky porch.* 3 not to be depended on; not reliable: *a shaky bank, a shaky knowledge of art.* **—shak′i ly,** *adv.* **—shak′i ness,** *n.*

shale (shāl), *n.* a fine-grained sedimentary rock, formed from hardened clay, mud, or silt in thin layers which split easily. [Old English *scealu* shell]

shall (shal; *unstressed* shəl), *auxiliary v., present sing.* and *pl.* **shall,** *past* **should.** *Shall* is used to express future time, determination, or obligation. 1 In general, *shall* in the first person expresses futurity, in the second and third, determination or obligation. *I shall miss you. You shall hear from us. He shall not do it.* 2 In questions, *shall* is used for all persons if *shall* is expected in the answer. *Shall I go? Yes, you shall.* 3 In an indirect quotation, *shall* is used if it would properly be used in a direct form of the quotation. *She says I shall go. He says he shall wait.* 4 In subordinate clauses introduced by *if, when,* etc., *shall* is used rather than *will* for all persons to express future time. *If he shall come, we shall be saved.* [Old English *sceal*] ➤ See **will**[1] for usage note.

shal lop (shal′əp), *n.* a small, light, open boat with sail or oars. [< French *chaloupe* < Dutch *sloepe.* Doublet of SLOOP.]

shal lot (shə lot′), *n.* the small bulb of a plant of the same genus as the onion, often used for seasoning cooked foods. [< French *eschalotte,* alteration of Old French *eschaloigne* scallion]

shal low (shal′ō), *adj.* 1 not deep: *shallow water, a shallow dish.* 2 lacking depth of thought, knowledge, feeling, etc.: *a shallow mind, a shallow person.* *—n.* Usually, **shallows,** *pl.* a shallow place. *—v.i., v.t.* become or make shallow. [Middle English *shalowe*] **—shal′low ly,** *adv.* **—shal′low ness,** *n.*

sha lom (shä lōm′), *n., interj.* HEBREW. 1 hello or good-by. 2 (literally) peace.

shalt (shalt), *v.* ARCHAIC. shall. "Thou shalt" means "You shall."

sham (sham), *n., adj., v.,* **shammed,**

sham ming. —*n.* 1 pretense; fraud: *Her goodness is all a sham.* 2 counterfeit; imitation. 3 person who is not what he pretends to be; fraud. —*adj.* 1 pretended; feigned: *a sham battle.* 2 counterfeit; imitation: *sham diamonds.* —*v.t.* assume the appearance of; feign: *sham illness.* —*v.i.* make false pretenses; pretend. [(originally) dialectal variant of *shame*] **—sham′mer,** *n.*

sha man (shä′mən, shā′mən, sham′ən), *n.* priest with magic power over diseases, evil spirits, etc.; medicine man. [< Russian]

sha man ism (shä′mə niz′əm, shā′mə-niz′əm), *n.* 1 religion of the Ural-Altaic peoples of northern Asia, based on a belief in controlling spirits who can be influenced only by shamans. 2 any similar religion, such as that of certain American Indians.

sha man is tic (shä′mə nis′tik, shā′mə-nis′tik), *adj.* of or having to do with shamans or shamanism.

sham ble (sham′bəl), *v.,* **-bled, -bling,** *n.* —*v.i.* walk awkwardly or unsteadily: *shamble across the room.* —*n.* a shambling walk. [probably special use of *shamble,* singular of obsolete *shambles* benches; with reference to the straddling legs of a bench]

sham bles (sham′bəlz), *n.pl. or sing.* 1 general disorder; confusion; mess: *make a shambles of a clean room.* 2 slaughterhouse. 3 place of butchery or of great bloodshed. [Old English *sceamel* < Latin *scamellum,* diminutive of *scamnum* bench; originally, a table on which meat was sold]

shame (shām), *n., v.,* **shamed, sham ing.** —*n.* 1 a painful feeling of having done something wrong, improper, or silly: *blush with shame.* 2 a disgrace; dishonor: *bring shame to one's family.* 3 fact to be sorry about; a pity: *It is a shame to be so wasteful.* 4 person or thing to be ashamed of; cause of disgrace. 5 sense of what is decent or proper. 6 **for shame!** shame on you! 7 **put to shame,** a disgrace; make ashamed. b surpass; make dim by comparison. —*v.t.* 1 cause to feel shame; make ashamed. 2 drive or force by shame or fear of shame: *be shamed into combing one's hair.* 3 bring disgrace upon. 4 surpass; make dim by comparison; outshine. [Old English *sceamu*]

shame faced (shām′fāst′), *adj.* 1 showing shame and embarrassment. 2 bashful; shy. **—shame′fac′ed ly,** *adv.* **—shame′fac′-ed ness,** *n.*

shame ful (shām′fəl), *adj.* causing shame; bringing disgrace. **—shame′ful ly,** *adv.* **—shame′ful ness,** *n.*

shame less (shām′lis), *adj.* 1 without shame. 2 not modest; brazen. **—shame′-less ly,** *adv.* **—shame′less ness,** *n.*

sham my (sham′ē), *n., pl.* **-mies.** chamois (def. 2).

sham poo (sham pü′), *v., n., pl.* **-poos.** —*v.t.* wash (the hair, a rug, etc.) with a soapy or oily preparation. —*n.* 1 a washing of the hair, a rug, etc. 2 preparation used for shampooing. [< Hindustani *chāmpō,* literally, press!] **—sham poo′er,** *n.*

sham rock (sham′rok), *n.* 1 a bright-green leaf composed of three parts. The shamrock is the national emblem of Ireland. 2 any of various plants that have leaves like this, such as white clover, wood sorrel, etc. [< Irish *seamrōg,* diminutive of *seamar* clover]

shang hai (shang′hī, shang hī′), *v.t.,* **-haied, -hai ing.** 1 make unconscious by drugs, liquor, etc., and put on a ship to serve as a sailor. 2 bring or get by trickery or force. [< *Shanghai,* because sailors for voyages there were often secured by illicit means]

Shang hai (shang′hī′), *n.* seaport in E China. 10,000,000.

Shan gri-La or **Shan gri-la** (shang′gri-lä′), *n.* an idyllic earthly paradise. [< *Shangri-La,* an inaccessible land in the novel *Lost Horizon,* by James Hilton, 1900-1954, English author]

shank (shangk), *n.* 1 the part of the leg between the knee and the ankle. 2 the corresponding part in animals. 3 cut of meat from the upper part of the leg of an animal. See **beef** for diagram. 4 the whole leg. 5 any part like a leg, stem, or shaft. The shank of a fishhook is the straight part between the hook and the loop. 6 that part of an instrument, tool, etc., which connects the acting part with the handle. 7 the narrow part of a shoe, connecting the broad part of the sole with the heel. 8 the latter end or part of anything: *the shank of the day.* [Old English *sceanca*]

Shan non River (shan′ən), river flowing from N Republic of Ireland southwest into the Atlantic. 240 mi.

shan't (shant), shall not.

shan tey (shan′tē), *n., pl.* **-teys.** chantey.

shan tung (shan′tung, shan tung′), *n.* 1 a rayon or cotton fabric similar to pongee and having a rough, uneven surface. 2 a heavy pongee. [< *Shantung*]

Shan tung (shan′tung′), *n.* 1 province in NE China. 2 **Shantung Peninsula,** peninsula in the E part of this province.

shan ty[1] (shan′tē), *n., pl.* **-ties.** a roughly built hut or cabin. [< Canadian French *chantier* lumberjack's headquarters < French, timber yard, dock < Latin *cantherius* framework]

shan ty[2] (shan′tē), *n., pl.* **-ties.** chantey.

shape (shāp), *n., v.,* **shaped, shap ing.** —*n.* 1 outward contour or outline; form; figure: *All circles have the same shape; rectangles have different shapes.* See **form** for synonym study. 2 an assumed appearance; guise: *A witch was supposed to take the shape of a cat or bat.* 3 condition: *exercise to keep in good shape.* 4 definite form; proper arrangement; order: *Take time to get your thoughts into shape.* 5 kind; sort: *dangers of every shape.* 6 mold or pattern for giving shape to something. 7 something shaped, as jelly, pudding, etc., shaped in a mold or metal of any of various shapes. 8 **lick into shape,** INFORMAL. make presentable or usable. 9 **take shape,** have or take on a definite form. —*v.t.* 1 form into a shape; mold: *shape clay into balls.* 2 adapt in form: *That hat is shaped to your head.* 3 give definite form or character to: *events which shape people's lives.* 4 direct; plan; devise; aim: *shape one's course in life.* 5 express in words: *shape a question.* 6 mold; pattern. —*v.i.* 1 take shape; assume form: *Clay shapes easily. Her plan is shaping well.* 2 **shape up,** a take on a certain form or appearance; develop. b show a certain tendency. [Old English *sceapen,* past participle of *scieppan* create] **—shap′er,** *n.*

SHAPE (shāp), *n.* Supreme Headquarters, Allied Powers in Europe.

-shaped, *combining form.* having a ____ shape or shapes: *Cone-shaped = having a cone shape.*

shark[1]—7½ to 12 ft. long

hat, āge, fär; let, ēqual, tėrm;
it, īce; hot, ōpen, ôrder;
oil, out; cup, pu̇t, rüle;
ch, child; ng, long; sh, she;
th, thin; ᴛʜ, then; zh, measure;

ə represents *a* in about, *e* in taken, *i* in pencil, *o* in lemon, *u* in circus.

< = from, derived from, taken from.

shape less (shāp′lis), *adj.* 1 without definite shape. 2 having an unattractive shape; not shapely. **—shape′less ly,** *adv.* **—shape′less ness,** *n.*

shape ly (shāp′lē), *adj.,* **-li er, -li est.** having a pleasing shape; well-formed. **—shape′li ness,** *n.*

shape-up (shāp′up′), *n.* U.S. system of hiring longshoremen whereby the men line up each workday to be selected for work by the foreman.

Sha pi ro (shə pir′ō), *n.* **Karl Jay,** born 1913, American poet and critic.

Shap ley (shap′lē), *n.* **Harlow,** 1885-1972, American astronomer.

shard (shärd), *n.* 1 piece of broken earthenware or pottery. 2 a broken piece; fragment. 3 the hard case that covers a beetle's wing. Also, **sherd.** [Old English *sceard*]

share[1] (sher, shar), *n., v.,* **shared, shar ing.** —*n.* 1 part belonging to one individual; portion; part: *Do your share of the work.* 2 part of anything owned in common with others: *sell one's share in a boat.* 3 each of the equal parts into which the ownership of a company or corporation is divided. Shares are usually in the form of transferable certificates of stock. 4 **go shares,** share in something. 5 **on shares,** sharing in the risks and profits. —*v.t.* 1 use together; enjoy together; have in common. See synonym study below. 2 divide into parts, each taking a part: *The child shared his candy with me.* —*v.i.* have a share; take part: *Everyone shared in making the picnic a success.* [Old English *scearu* a cutting, shaving, division] **—shar′er,** *n.*

Syn. *v.t.* 1 **Share, participate, partake** mean to use, enjoy, or have something in common with another. **Share** emphasizes the idea of common possession, enjoyment, use, etc.: *The sisters share the same room.* **Participate,** followed by *in,* implies joining with others in some activity or undertaking: *Only a few club members participated in the discussion.* **Partake,** usually followed by *of* and somewhat formal, means to take one's (own) share of food, pleasure, qualities, etc.: *partake of refreshments.*

share[2] (sher, shar), *n.* plowshare. [Old English *scear*]

share crop (sher′krop′, shar′krop′), *v.i., v.t.,* **-cropped, -crop ping.** farm as a sharecropper.

share crop per (sher′krop′ər, shar′-krop′ər), *n.* person who farms land for the owner in return for part of the crops.

share hold er (sher′hōl′dər, shar′hōl′dər), *n.* person owning shares of stock.

shark[1] (shärk), *n.* any of a suborder of fishes, mostly marine, certain kinds of which are large and ferocious, and destructive to other fishes and sometimes dangerous to man. [origin uncertain] **—shark′like′,** *adj.*

shark[2] (shärk), *n.* 1 a dishonest person who preys on others. 2 SLANG. person unusually good at something; expert: *a shark at poker.* —*v.i.* act or live by preying on others; live by trickery. [probably < German *Schurke* scoundrel]

shark skin (shärk′skin′), *n.* 1 fabric made from fine threads of wool, rayon, or cotton, used in suits. 2 skin of a shark. 3 leather made from the skin of a shark.

sharp (shärp), *adj.* 1 having a thin cutting edge or a fine point: *a sharp knife, a pencil with a sharp point.* 2 having or coming to a point; not rounded: *a sharp nose, a sharp corner on a box.* 3 with a sudden change of direction: *a sharp turn in the road.* 4 very cold: *sharp weather.* 5 severe; biting: *sharp words.* 6 feeling somewhat like a cut or prick; affecting the senses keenly: *a sharp taste, a sharp noise, a sharp pain.* 7 clear; distinct: *the sharp contrast between black and white.* 8 quick in movement; brisk: *a sharp walk.* 9 fierce; violent: *a sharp attack.* 10 keen; eager: *a sharp desire, a sharp appetite.* 11 being aware of things quickly: *sharp ears.* 12 wide-awake; watchful; vigilant: *keep a sharp watch.* 13 quick in mind; shrewd; clever: *a sharp boy, sharp at a bargain.* See synonym study below. 14 high in pitch; shrill: *a sharp cry of fear.* 15 in music: **a** above the true pitch; too high in pitch. **b** one half step or half tone above natural pitch. **c** (of a key) having sharps in the signature. 16 (of a consonant) pronounced with breath and not with voice; voiceless. 17 SLANG. attractive; stylish.
—*adv.* 1 promptly; exactly: *Come at one o'clock sharp.* 2 above the true pitch in music: *sing sharp.* 3 in a sharp manner; in an alert manner; keenly: *Look sharp!* 4 suddenly; abruptly: *pull a horse up sharp.*
—*n.* 1 in music: **a** a tone or note that is one half step or half tone above natural pitch. **b** the sign (♯) for this. 2 a swindler; sharper. 3 INFORMAL. expert.
—*v.t.* (in music) to raise (a note) in pitch, especially by one half step. —*v.i.* to sound a note above the true pitch.
[Old English *scearp*] **—sharp′ly,** *adv.* **—sharp′ness,** *n.*

Syn. *adj.* 13 **Sharp, keen, acute,** used figuratively to describe a person or the mind, mean penetrating. **Sharp** implies cleverness, shrewdness, and quickness to see and take advantage, sometimes dishonestly: *a sharp lawyer.* **Keen** implies clearness and quickness of perception and thinking: *a keen mind.* **Acute** implies penetrating perception, insight, or understanding: *an acute interpreter of current events.*

sharp en (shär′pən), *v.t.* make sharp or sharper: *sharpen a pencil. Sharpen your wits.* —*v.i.* become sharp or sharper. **—sharp′en er,** *n.*

sharp er (shär′pər), *n.* swindler; cheat.

sharp-eyed (shärp′īd′), *adj.* 1 having keen sight. 2 watchful; vigilant.

sharp ie (shär′pē), *n.* 1 a long, narrow flat-bottomed boat with a centerboard and one or two masts, each rigged with a triangular sail. 2 SLANG. an unusually keen, alert, or clever person.

sharp shoot er (shärp′shü′tər), *n.* person who shoots very well, especially with a rifle.

sharp shoot ing (shärp′shü′ting), *n.* act of a sharpshooter.

sharp-sight ed (shärp′sī′tid), *adj.* 1 having sharp sight. 2 sharp-witted.

sharp-tongued (shärp′tungd′), *adj.* sharp or bitter of speech; severely critical.

sharp-wit ted (shärp′wit′id), *adj.* having or showing a quick, keen mind.

Shas ta (shas′tə), *n.* **Mount,** volcanic peak in N California. 14,162 ft.

shat ter (shat′ər), *v.t.* 1 break into pieces: *A stone shattered the window.* See **break** for synonym study. 2 disturb greatly; destroy: *The great mental strain shattered his mind. Her hopes were shattered.* —*v.i.* be shattered: *The glass shattered.* —*n.* **shatters,** *pl.* fragments. [Middle English *schateren.* Related to SCATTER.]

shat ter proof (shat′ər prüf′), *adj.* that will not shatter; resistant to shattering.

shave (shāv), *v.,* **shaved, shaved** or **shav en, shav ing,** *n.* —*v.t.* 1 remove hair with a razor; cut hair from (the face, chin, etc.) with a razor. 2 cut off (hair) with a razor. 3 cut off in thin slices; cut in thin slices. 4 cut very close. 5 come very close to; graze: *The car shaved the corner.* —*v.i.* remove hair with a razor: *He shaves every day.* —*n.* 1 the cutting off of hair with a razor. 2 tool for shaving, scraping, removing thin slices, etc. 3 a thin slice; shaving. 4 a narrow miss or escape. [Old English *sceafan*]

shave ling (shāv′ling), *n.* 1 UNFRIENDLY USE. a tonsured monk, friar, or priest. 2 youth.

shav en (shā′vən), *adj.* 1 shaved. 2 closely cut. —*v.* a pp. of **shave.**

shav er (shā′vər), *n.* 1 person who shaves. 2 instrument for shaving. 3 INFORMAL. youngster; small boy.

shave tail (shāv′tāl′), *n.* SLANG. a second lieutenant, especially one who has recently been commissioned.

Sha vi an (shā′vē ən), *adj.* of, having to do with, or characteristic of George Bernard Shaw. —*n.* admirer of Shaw or his works.

shav ing (shā′ving), *n.* 1 a very thin piece or slice. Shavings of wood are cut off by a plane. 2 act or process of cutting hair from the face, chin, etc., with a razor.

Shaw (shô), *n.* **George Bernard,** 1856-1950, British dramatist, critic, and essayist, born in Ireland.

shawl (shôl), *n.* a square or oblong piece of cloth worn, especially by women, about the shoulders or head. [< Persian *shāl*]

shawm (shôm), *n.* a medieval woodwind musical instrument like an oboe. [< Old French *chalemie,* ultimately < Latin *calamus* reed]

Shaw nee (shô nē′), *n., pl.* **-nee** or **-nees.** member of a tribe of Algonquian Indians formerly living in eastern North America, especially Ohio, Tennessee, and South Carolina, and now living in Oklahoma.

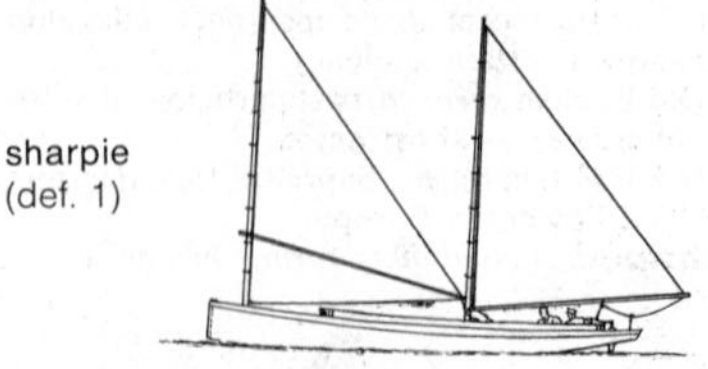
sharpie (def. 1)

shay (shā), *n.* INFORMAL. chaise. [< *chaise,* taken as plural]

Shays (shāz), *n.* **Daniel,** 1747-1825, American soldier in the Revolutionary War and leader of **Shays' Rebellion,** 1786-1787, an uprising of farmers in Massachusetts against the state government.

she (shē), *pron., nominative* **she,** *possessive* **her** or **hers,** *objective* **her;** *pl. nominative* **they,** *possessive* **their** or **theirs,** *objective* **them;** *n., pl.* **shes.** —*pron.* 1 girl, woman, or female animal spoken about or mentioned before. 2 anything thought of as female and spoken about or mentioned before: *She was a fine old ship.* —*n.* a female: *Is the baby a he or a she?* [probably Old English demonstrative pronoun *sēo, sīe*]

sheaf (shēf), *n., pl.* **sheaves.** 1 one of the bundles in which grain is bound after reaping. 2 bundle of things of the same sort bound together or so arranged that they can be bound together: *a sheaf of arrows, a sheaf of papers.* [Old English *scēaf*]

shear (shir), *v.,* **sheared, sheared** or **shorn, shear ing,** *n.* —*v.t.* 1 cut with shears or scissors: *shear wool from sheep.* 2 cut the wool or fleece from: *The farmer sheared his sheep.* 3 cut close; cut off; cut. 4 break by a force causing two parts or pieces to slide on each other in opposite directions: *Too much pressure on the handles of the scissors sheared off the rivet holding the blades together.* 5 strip or deprive as if by cutting: *The assembly had been shorn of its legislative powers.* —*v.i.* break by shearing force: *Several bolts sheared, causing the floor to sag dangerously.* —*n.* 1 act or process of shearing. 2 that which is taken off by shearing. 3 one blade of a pair of shears. 4 force causing two parts or pieces to slide on each other in opposite directions. [Old English *sceran*] **—shear′er,** *n.*

shears (shirz), *n.pl.* 1 large scissors. 2 any cutting instrument resembling scissors: *grass shears, tin shears.* [Old English *scēar*]

shear wa ter (shir′wô′tər, shir′wot′ər), *n.* any of a genus of sea birds of the same family as the petrels, with long, slender wings which appear to shear the water.

sheath (shēth), *n., pl.* **sheaths** (shēᴛʜz, shēths). 1 case or covering for the blade of a sword, knife, etc. 2 any similar covering, especially on an animal or plant. 3 a narrow, tight-fitting dress with straight lines. [Old English *scēath*]

sheathe (shēᴛʜ), *v.t.,* **sheathed, sheath ing.** 1 put (a sword, etc.) into a sheath. 2 enclose in a case or covering: *a mummy sheathed in linen, doors sheathed in metal.* **—sheath′er,** *n.*

sheath ing (shē′ᴛʜing, shē′thing), *n.* casing; covering. The first covering of boards on a house is sheathing.

sheath knife, knife carried in a sheath.

sheave[1] (shēv), *v.t.,* **sheaved, sheav ing.** gather and tie into a sheaf or sheaves. [< *sheaf*]

sheave[2] (shēv, shiv), *n.* wheel with a grooved rim, as the wheel of a pulley. [variant of *shive,* Middle English *schive*]

sheaves (shēvz *for 1;* shēvz, shivz *for 2*), *n.* 1 pl. of **sheaf.** 2 pl. of **sheave**[2].

She ba (shē′bə), *n.* 1 ancient country in S Arabia. 2 **Queen of,** (in the Bible) a queen who visited Solomon to learn of his great wisdom.

she bang (shə bang′), *n.* SLANG. 1 outfit; concern. 2 affair; event. [origin uncertain]

shed[1] (shed), *n.* a building used for shelter, storage, etc., usually having only one story and often open at the front or sides: *a wagon shed, a train shed.* [Old English *scead* shelter]

shed[2] (shed), *v.,* **shed, shed ding.** —*v.t.* 1 pour out; let flow: *shed blood, shed tears.*

hat, āge, fär; let, ēqual, tėrm;
it, īce; hot, ōpen, ôrder;
oil, out; cup, pu̇t, rüle;
ch, child; ng, long; sh, she;
th, thin; ᴛʜ, then; zh, measure;

ə represents *a* in about, *e* in taken,
i in pencil, *o* in lemon, *u* in circus.

< = from, derived from, taken from.

2 cast off; let drop or fall: *The snake sheds its skin. The umbrella sheds water.* 3 get rid of: *shed one's worries, shed inhibitions.* 4 scatter abroad; give forth: *The sun sheds light. Flowers shed perfume.* —*v.i.* throw off a covering, hair, etc.: *That snake has just shed.* [Old English *scēadan*]

she'd (shēd; *unstressed* shid), 1 she had. 2 she would.

shed der (shed′ər), *n.* 1 person or thing that sheds. 2 crab or lobster beginning to shed its shell.

sheen (shēn), *n.* brightness; luster: *Satin and polished silver have a sheen.* See **polish** for synonym study. [Old English *scēne, sciene* bright]

sheen y (shē′nē), *adj.* bright; lustrous.

sheep (def. 1) about 3 ft. high at the shoulder

sheep (shēp), *n., pl.* **sheep.** 1 any of a genus of cud-chewing mammals of the same family as goats and sometimes having horns. A domesticated species is raised in many varieties for its wool, meat, and skin. 2 a weak, timid, or stupid person. 3 leather made from the skin of sheep; sheepskin. 4 **make sheep's eyes,** give a longing, loving look. [Old English *scēap*] —**sheep′like′,** *adj.*

sheep cote (shēp′kōt′), *n.* sheepfold.

sheep-dip (shēp′dip′), *n.* a disinfecting mixture into which sheep are dipped.

sheep dog, collie or other dog trained to help a shepherd watch and tend sheep.

sheep fold (shēp′fōld′), *n.* pen or covered shelter for sheep.

sheep herd er (shēp′hėr′dər), *n.* person who watches and tends large numbers of sheep while they are grazing on unfenced land.

sheep ish (shē′pish), *adj.* 1 awkwardly bashful or embarrassed: *a sheepish smile.* 2 like a sheep; timid; weak; stupid. —**sheep′ish ly,** *adv.* —**sheep′ish ness,** *n.*

sheep man (shēp′man′), *n., pl.* **-men.** 1 person who owns and raises sheep. 2 sheepherder.

sheeps head (shēps′hed′), *n.* a saltwater food fish common on the Atlantic coast of the United States.

sheep skin (shēp′skin′), *n.* 1 skin of a sheep, especially with the wool on it. 2 leather or parchment made from the skin of a sheep. 3 INFORMAL. diploma.

sheep walk (shēp′wôk′), *n.* tract of land on which sheep are pastured.

sheer[1] (shir), *adj.* 1 very thin; almost transparent: *a sheer white dress.* 2 unmixed with anything else; complete: *sheer nonsense, sheer weariness.* 3 straight up and down; very steep: *From the top of the wall it was a sheer drop of 100 feet to the water below.* —*adv.* 1 completely; quite. 2 very steeply. —*n.* 1 a thin, fine, almost transparent cloth. 2 dress made of this. [Old English *scīr* bright] —**sheer′ly,** *adv.* —**sheer′ness,** *n.*

sheer[2] (shir), *v.i.* turn from a course; turn aside; swerve. —*n.* 1 a turning of a ship from its course. 2 the upward curve of a ship's deck or lines from the middle toward each end. 3 position in which a ship at anchor is placed to keep it clear of the anchor. [probably < Dutch *scheren*]

sheet[1] (shēt), *n.* 1 a large piece of cotton, linen, nylon, or other cloth used to sleep on or under. 2 a broad, thin piece of anything: *a sheet of glass, a sheet of iron.* 3 a single piece of paper. 4 newspaper. 5 a broad, flat surface: *a sheet of ice.* —*v.t.* furnish or cover with a sheet. [Old English *scēte*] —**sheet′like′,** *adj.*

sheet[2] (shēt), *n.* 1 rope or chain that controls the angle at which a sail is set. 2 **sheets,** *pl.* space not occupied by thwarts at the bow or stern of an open boat. [Old English *scēata* lower part of a sail]

sheet anchor, 1 a large anchor formerly carried in the waist of a ship for use in emergencies. 2 a final reliance or resource. [origin uncertain]

sheet ing (shē′ting), *n.* 1 cotton or linen cloth for bed sheets, etc. 2 a lining or covering of timber or metal, used to protect a surface.

sheet lightning, lightning in broad flashes. Sheet lightning is actually a reflection of lightning that occurs beyond the horizon.

sheet metal, metal in thin pieces or plates.

sheet music, music printed on unbound sheets of paper.

Shef field (shef′ēld′), *n.* city in central England, famous for the manufacture of cutlery. 525,000.

sheik or **sheikh** (shēk), *n.* 1 an Arab chief or head of a family, village, or tribe. 2 a Moslem religious leader. 3 title of respect used by Moslems. 4 SLANG. man supposed to be irresistibly fascinating to women. [< Arabic *shaikh,* originally, old man]

sheik dom (shēk′dəm), *n.* territory ruled by a sheik.

shek el (shek′əl), *n.* 1 an ancient silver coin of the Hebrews that weighed about half an ounce. 2 an ancient unit of weight originating in Babylonia, equal to about half an ounce. 3 **shekels,** *pl.* SLANG. coins; money. [< Hebrew *sheqel*]

shel drake (shel′drāk′), *n., pl.* **-drakes** or **-drake.** 1 any of a genus of large ducks of Europe and Asia, many of which resemble geese and have variegated plumage. 2 merganser. [< obsolete *sheld* variegated + *drake*]

shelf (shelf), *n., pl.* **shelves.** 1 a thin, flat piece of wood, metal, stone, etc., fastened to a wall or frame to hold such things as books and dishes. 2 the contents of a shelf. 3 anything like a shelf, as a ledge of land or rock, especially a submerged ledge or bedrock. 4 **on the shelf,** put aside as no longer useful or desirable; in a state of inactivity or uselessness. [perhaps < Middle Low German *schelf*] —**shelf′like′,** *adj.*

shelf ice, ledge of ice sticking out into the sea from an ice sheet.

shelf life, length of time a product may be shelved or stored without becoming spoiled or useless: *the shelf life of a drug.*

shell (shel), *n.* 1 the hard outer covering of an animal, as of oysters and other mollusks, beetles and some other insects, turtles, etc. 2 the hard outside covering of a nut, seed, fruit, etc. 3 the hard outside covering of an egg. 4 tortoise shell as used in combs and ornaments. 5 something like a shell, such as the framework of a house. 6 outward show; outer part or appearance: *Going to church is only the mere shell of religion.* 7 cartridge used in a rifle or shotgun. 8 a hollow metal cylinder filled with explosives that is fired by artillery. 9 a long, narrow racing boat of light wood, rowed by a crew using long oars. 10 a hollow case of pastry, meringue, etc., or the lower crust of a pie. 11 any orbit with electrons revolving about the nucleus of an atom. 12 **come out of one's shell,** stop being shy or reserved; join in conversation, etc., with others.
—*v.t.* 1 take out of a shell: *shell peas.* 2 separate (grains of corn) from the cob. 3 bombard by cannon or mortar fire. 4 **shell out,** INFORMAL. **a** give (something) away. **b** hand over (money); pay out. —*v.i.* 1 fall or come out of the shell. 2 come away or fall off as an outer covering does.
[Old English *scell, sciell*] —**shell′-like′,** *adj.*

she'll (shēl; *unstressed* shil), 1 she shall. 2 she will.

shel lac (shə lak′), *n., v.,* **-lacked, -lack ing.** —*n.* 1 liquid that gives a smooth, shiny appearance to wood, metal, etc. Shellac is made from refined lac dissolved in alcohol. 2 refined lac, used in sealing wax, phonograph records, etc. —*v.t.* 1 put shellac on; cover with shellac. 2 INFORMAL. defeat completely. [< *shell* + *lac*]

shell back (shel′bak′), *n.* 1 an experienced sailor. 2 person who has crossed the equator on shipboard.

shell bark (shel′bärk′), *n.* shagbark.

Shel ley (shel′ē), *n.* 1 **Percy Bysshe,** 1792-1822, English poet. 2 his wife, **Mary Wollstonecraft,** 1797-1851, English novelist.

shell fire (shel′fīr′), *n.* the firing of explosive shells or projectiles.

shell fish (shel′fish′), *n., pl.* **-fish es** or **-fish.** a water animal (not a fish in the ordinary sense) having a shell, especially a mollusk or crustacean. Oysters, clams, crabs, and lobsters are shellfish.

shell proof (shel′prüf′), *adj.* able to withstand the impact and explosive force of shells, bombs, etc.

shell shock, a nervous or mental disorder resulting from the strain of combat in war.

shell shocked (shel′shokt′), *adj.* suffering from shell shock.

shell work (shel′wėrk′), *n.* decorative work made of or made to look like sea shells.

shell y (shel′ē), *adj.,* **shell i er, shell i est.** 1 abounding in shells. 2 consisting of a shell or shells. 3 shell-like.

shel ter (shel′tər), *n.* 1 something that covers or protects from weather, danger, or attack: *Trees are a shelter from the sun.* 2 protection; refuge: *We took shelter from the storm in a barn.* —*v.t.* be or provide a shelter for; protect; shield; hide: *shelter a fugitive.* —*v.i.* find or take shelter. [origin uncertain] —**shel′ter er,** *n.* —**shel′ter less,** *adj.*

shelter half, a rectangular piece of canvas that is half of a shelter tent.

shelter tent, a small tent, usually made of pieces of waterproof cloth that fasten together.

shelve[1] (shelv), *v.t.,* **shelved, shelv ing.** 1 put on a shelf. 2 lay aside: *Let us shelve* *that argument.* 3 furnish with shelves. [ultimately < *shelf*]

shelve[2] (shelv), *v.i.,* **shelved, shelv ing.** slope gradually. [origin uncertain]

shelves (shelvz), *n.* pl. of **shelf.**

shelv ing (shel′ving), *n.* 1 wood, metal, etc., for shelves. 2 shelves collectively.

Shem (shem), *n.* (in the Bible) the oldest of the three sons of Noah, regarded as the ancestor of the Semitic peoples.

Shem ite (shem′īt), *n.* Semite.

Shen an do ah National Park (shen′ən dō′ə), national park in N Virginia, in the Blue Ridge Mountains.

Shenandoah River, river flowing through N Virginia into the Potomac River. 170 mi.

she nan i gans (shə nan′ə gənz), *n.* INFORMAL. mischief or trickery. [origin uncertain]

Shen si (shen′sē′), *n.* province in N China.

Shen yang (shen′yäng′), *n.* city in Manchuria, NE China. 4,000,000. Former name, **Mukden.**

She ol (shē′ōl), *n.* 1 a Hebrew name for the abode of the dead. 2 **sheol,** INFORMAL. hell. [< Hebrew *shě'ōl*]

Shep ard (shep′ərd), *n.* **Alan Bartlett,** born 1923, American astronaut. He was the first American to be rocketed into space, in 1961.

shep herd (shep′ərd), *n.* 1 man who takes care of sheep. 2 person who cares for and protects. 3 a spiritual guide; pastor. —*v.t.* 1 take care of: *He will shepherd his flock.* 2 guide; direct: *The teacher shepherded the children safely out of the burning building.* [Old English *scēaphierde* < *scēap* sheep + *hierde* herder < *heord* a herd]

shepherd dog, sheep dog.

shep herd ess (shep′ər dis), *n.* woman who takes care of sheep.

Sher a ton (sher′ə tən), *n.* **Thomas,** 1751-1806, English cabinetmaker and designer of light, graceful furniture. —*adj.* having to do with or in the style of furniture designed by Sheraton.

sher bet (shėr′bət), *n.* 1 a frozen dessert made of fruit juice, sugar, and water, milk, or whites of eggs. 2 a cooling drink made of fruit juice, sugar, and water, popular in the Orient. [< Turkish *şerbet* < Arabic *sharbat* a drink]

sherd (shėrd), *n.* shard.

Sher i dan (sher′ə dən), *n.* 1 **Philip Henry,** 1831-1888, Union general in the Civil War. 2 **Richard Brinsley,** 1751-1816, Irish dramatist.

sher iff (sher′if), *n.* the most important law-enforcing officer of a county, charged chiefly with aiding the courts of the county and preserving the peace. [Old English *scīrgerēfa* < *scīr* shire + *gerēfa* reeve[1]]

Sher lock Holmes (shėr′lok hōmz′), a fictional English detective with remarkable powers of observation and reasoning, created by Sir Arthur Conan Doyle in 1887.

Sher man (shėr′mən), *n.* 1 **John,** 1823-1900, American statesman and financier, brother of William Tecumseh Sherman. 2 **Roger,** 1721-1793, American statesman. He helped draw up the Declaration of Independence and the Articles of Confederation. 3 **William Tecumseh,** 1820-1891, Union general in the Civil War.

Sher pa (shėr′pə), *n.* member of a Mongoloid people of Nepal. Sherpas have served as guides and porters for most of the expeditions to climb Mount Everest.

sher ry (sher′ē), *n., pl.* **-ries.** a strong wine originally made in southern Spain. It varies in color from pale yellow to brown. [earlier *sherris* (taken as plural), wine from *Xeres* (now *Jerez*), Spain]

Sher wood (shėr′wu̇d′), *n.* **Robert Emmet,** 1896-1955, American dramatist.

Sherwood Forest, a royal forest near Nottingham, England, where Robin Hood and his men are said to have lived.

she's (shēz; *unstressed* shiz), 1 she is. 2 she has.

Shet land (shet′lənd), *n.* 1 Shetland pony. 2 Also, **shetland.** Shetland wool.

Shetland Islands, group of British islands northeast of Scotland. 17,000 pop.; 550 sq. mi. See **British Isles** for map.

Shetland pony
32 to 46 in. high at the shoulder

Shetland pony, a small, sturdy, rough-coated pony, originally from the Shetland Islands.

Shetland sheep dog, a long-haired working dog resembling a small collie, originally from the Shetland Islands.

Shetland wool, a fine, hairy, strong worsted spun from the wool of a breed of sheep native to the Shetland Islands, widely used in knitting fine shawls, sweaters, and other garments.

shew (shō), *v.t., v.i.,* **shewed, shewn** (shōn), **shew ing,** *n., adj.* BRITISH or ARCHAIC. show.

shew bread (shō′bred′), *n.* the unleavened bread placed near the altar every Sabbath by the ancient Jewish priests as an offering to God. Also, **showbread.**

SHF, superhigh frequency.

shib bo leth (shib′ə lith), *n.* 1 any test word, watchword, or pet phrase of a political party, a class, sect, etc. 2 any use of language, habit, custom, etc., considered distinctive of a particular group or class. [< Hebrew *shibbōleth* stream; used as a password by the Gileadites to distinguish the fleeing Ephraimites, who could not pronounce *sh.* Judges 12:4-6]

shied (shīd), *v.* a pt. and a pp. of **shy.**

shield (shēld), *n.* 1 piece of armor carried on the arm or in the hand to protect the body in battle, used in ancient and medieval warfare. 2 anything used to protect. 3 something shaped like a shield. 4 any substance to protect against exposure to radiation, especially in nuclear reactors, as lead or water. 5 a policeman's badge. 6 escutcheon. 7 a protective plate covering a part on the body of an animal. —*v.t.* be a shield to; protect; defend; shelter: *shield a person from attack. The hat shielded her eyes from the sun.* —*v.i.* act or serve as a shield. [Old English *sceld, scield*] —**shield′like′,** *adj.*

shift (shift), *v.t.* 1 move or change (something) from one place, position, person, etc., to another; transfer: *shift the responsibility to someone else, shift a heavy bag from one hand to the other.* 2 remove and replace with another or others; change: *shift the scenes on a stage.* 3 change from one set of (gears) to another in an automobile. —*v.i.* 1 move from one place, position, person, etc., to another: *The wind has shifted to the southeast.* 2 provide for one's own safety, interest, or livelihood; manage to get along; contrive: *shift for oneself.* 3 connect the motor to a different set of gears in an automobile. —*n.* 1 change of direction, position, attitude, etc.: *a shift of the wind, a shift in policy.* 2 group of workmen who work during the same period of time: *the night shift.* 3 the time during which such a group works. 4 way of getting on; scheme; trick; artifice: *try every shift to avoid work.* 5 ARCHAIC. a woman's chemise. 6 a loosely fitting dress like a chemise, but with straighter lines. 7 **make shift, a** manage to get along; do as well as one can. **b** manage with effort or difficulty. [Old English *sciftan* arrange] —**shift′er,** *n.*

shift less (shift′lis), *adj.* lazy; inefficient. —**shift′less ly,** *adv.* —**shift′less ness,** *n.*

shift y (shif′tē), *adj.,* **shift i er, shift i est.** 1 full of shifts; quick-witted; inventive. 2 not straight-forward; tricky: *shifty eyes, a shifty fellow.* —**shift′i ly,** *adv.* —**shift′i ness,** *n.*

shig el lo sis (shig′ə lō′sis), *n., pl.* **-ses** (-sēz). type of dysentery caused by any of a genus of bacilli. [< New Latin *Shigella,* genus name of the bacilli + *-osis*]

Shi ko ku (shi kō′kü), *n.* island of Japan, in the S part. 3,975,000 pop.; 7200 sq. mi.

shill (shil), *n.* SLANG. person hired by a gambler, auctioneer, etc., to pose as a bystander and decoy others to bet, buy, bid, etc. [< earlier *shillaber;* origin uncertain]

shil le lagh or **shil la lah** (shə lā′lē, shə-lā′lə), *n.* IRISH. a stick to hit with; cudgel. [< *Shillelagh,* town in Ireland]

shil ling (shil′ing), *n.* 1 unit of money in Great Britain equal to 5 pence or $^1/_{20}$ of a pound and worth about 12 U.S. cents. 2 a British coin equal to one shilling. 3 any of various similar units of money in other countries, equaling $^1/_{20}$th of the basic monetary unit. 4 the monetary unit of Kenya, Tanzania, etc., divided into 100 cents. 5 unit of money of colonial America corresponding to the British shilling. 6 coin worth one shilling. [Old English *scilling*]

shil ly-shal ly (shil′ē shal′ē), *adj., adv., v.,* **-lied, -ly ing,** *n., pl.* **-lies.** —*adj.* vacillating; wavering; hesitating; undecided. —*adv.* in a vacillating or hesitating manner. —*v.i.* be undecided; vacillate; hesitate. —*n.* inability to decide; hesitation; vacillation. [earlier *shill I, shall I,* reduplication of *shall I?*]

shim (shim), *n., v.,* **shimmed, shim ming.** —*n.* a thin strip of metal, wood, etc., used to raise a part, make it fill some other part, or fill up a space. —*v.t.* put a shim or shims in. [origin uncertain]

shim mer (shim′ər), *v.i.* shine with a flickering light; gleam faintly: *The satin shimmers.* —*n.* a faint gleam or shine: *The pearls have a beautiful shimmer.* [Old English *scimerian*]

shim mer y (shim′ər ē), *adj.* shimmering; gleaming softly.

shim my (shim′ē), *n., pl.* **-mies,** *v.,* **-mied, -my ing.** —*n.* 1 an unusual shaking or vibration: *a dangerous shimmy of a ladder.* 2 a jazz dance with much shaking of the

hat, āge, fär; let, ēqual, tėrm;
it, īce; hot, ōpen, ôrder;
oil, out; cup, pu̇t, rüle;
ch, child; ng, long; sh, she;
th, thin; ᴛʜ, then; zh, measure;

ə represents *a* in about, *e* in taken, *i* in pencil, *o* in lemon, *u* in circus.

< = from, derived from, taken from.

body, popular in the 1920's. —*v.i.* 1 shake; vibrate: *The front wheels of the car shimmied.* 2 dance the shimmy. [variant of *chemise* (taken as plural)]

shin (shin), *n., v.,* **shinned, shin ning.** —*n.* 1 the front part of the leg from the knee to the ankle. 2 the lower part of the foreleg in beef cattle. —*v.i., v.t.* climb by clasping or holding fast with the hands or arms and legs and drawing oneself up: *shin up a tree.* [Old English *scinu*]

Shi nar (shī′när), *n.* (in the Bible) a name for Sumer or for Babylonia as a whole.

shin bone (shin′bōn′), *n.* the inner and thicker of the two bones between the knee and the ankle; tibia.

shin dig (shin′dig), *n.* INFORMAL. a merry or noisy dance, party, etc. [perhaps < *shindy*]

shin dy (shin′dē), *n., pl.* **-dies.** INFORMAL. 1 disturbance; rumpus. 2 shindig. [origin uncertain]

shine (shīn), *v.,* **shone** (or **shined** especially for v.t. 1), **shin ing,** *n.* —*v.i.* 1 send or give out light; be bright with light; reflect light; glow; beam: *The sun shines by day, the moon by night.* 2 be conspicuous or brilliant in ability, character, achievement, or position: *shine in conversation.* —*v.t.* 1 make bright; polish: *shine shoes.* 2 cause to shine: *shine a light in someone's face.* 3 **shine up to,** SLANG. try to please and get the friendship of. —*n.* 1 light; brightness. 2 luster; polish; gloss; sheen, as of silk or metal. 3 fair weather; sunshine: *rain or shine.* 4 a polish put on shoes. 5 act of putting on such a polish. 6 SLANG. fancy; liking. 7 **shines,** *pl.* SLANG. trick; prank. 8 **take a shine to,** SLANG. become fond of; like. [Old English *scīnan*]

shin er (shī′nər), *n.* 1 person or thing that shines. 2 any of various small American freshwater fishes with glistening scales, of the same family as the carp. 3 SLANG. a black eye.

shingle[1] (def. 1)—shingles on a roof

shin gle¹ (shing′gəl), *n., v.,* **-gled, -gling.** —*n.* 1 a thin piece of wood, etc., used to cover roofs, walls, etc. Shingles are laid in overlapping rows with the thicker ends exposed. 2 a small signboard, especially one outside a doctor's or lawyer's office. 3 **hang out one's shingle,** INFORMAL. open an office (used only of professional people). 4 a woman's short haircut in which the hair is made to taper from the back of the head to the nape of the neck. —*v.t.* 1 cover with shingles: *shingle a roof.* 2 cut (the hair) in a shingle. [variant of earlier *shindle* < Latin *scindula*] —**shin′gler,** *n.*

shin gle² (shing′gəl), *n.* 1 loose stones or pebbles such as lie on the seashore; coarse gravel. 2 beach or other place covered with this. [origin uncertain]

shin gles (shing′gəlz), *n. sing. or pl.* a virus disease that causes painful irritation of a group of cutaneous nerves and an outbreak of spots or blisters on the skin in the area of the affected nerves. The commonest location is on the chest or lower part of the back. [< Medieval Latin *cingulus,* variant of Latin *cingulum* girdle < *cingere* to gird]

shin gly (shing′glē), *adj.* consisting of or covered with small, loose stones or pebbles: *a shingly beach.*

shin ing (shī′ning), *adj.* 1 that shines; bright; glowing; radiant. 2 brilliant; outstanding. —**shin′ing ly,** *adv.*

shin ny¹ (shin′ē), *n., pl.* **-nies,** *v.,* **-nied, -ny ing.** —*n.* a simple kind of hockey, played with a ball or the like and clubs curved at one end. —*v.i.* play shinny. [origin uncertain]

shin ny² (shin′ē), *v.i., v.t.,* **-nied, -ny ing.** INFORMAL. to shin; climb. [< *shin*]

shin plas ter (shin′plas′tər), *n.* 1 plaster for a sore leg. 2 INFORMAL. a piece of paper money that has depreciated greatly in value, especially one issued by private bankers.

Shin to (shin′tō), *n., pl.* **-tos** for 2. 1 the native religion of Japan, primarily the worship of nature deities and ancestral heroes. 2 adherent of this religion. —*adj.* of or having to do with Shinto. [< Japanese *shintō* < Chinese *shin tao* way of the gods]

Shin to ism (shin′tō iz′əm), *n.* the Shinto religion.

Shin to ist (shin′tō ist), *n.* believer in the Shinto religion. —*adj.* of Shintoism or Shintoists.

shin y (shī′nē), *adj.,* **shin i er, shin i est.** 1 shining; bright: *a shiny new penny.* 2 worn to a glossy smoothness: *a coat shiny from hard wear.* —**shin′i ness,** *n.*

ship (ship), *n., v.,* **shipped, ship ping.** —*n.* 1 any large vessel for traveling on water, such as a steamship, frigate, or galley. 2 a large sailing vessel, especially one with three masts and a bowsprit. 3 an airship, airplane, spacecraft, etc. 4 officers and crew of a ship. 5 **when one's ship comes home** or **when one's ship comes in,** when one's fortune is made; when one has money.
—*v.t.* 1 put, take, or receive (persons or goods) on board a ship. 2 send or carry from one place to another by a ship, train, truck, etc.: *Did you ship it by express or by freight?* 3 INFORMAL. send off; get rid of. 4 engage for service on a ship: *ship a new crew.* 5 take in (water) over the side, as a ship or boat does when the waves break over it. 6 fix in a ship or boat in its proper place for use: *ship a rudder.* —*v.i.* 1 go on board a ship. 2 travel on a ship; sail. 3 take a job on a ship: *He shipped as cook.*
[Old English *scip*]

-ship, *suffix forming nouns from other nouns.* 1 office, position, or occupation of ___: *Governorship = office of governor.* 2 quality or condition of being ___: *Partnership = condition of being a partner.* 3 act, power, or skill of ___: *Workmanship = skill of a workman.* 4 relation between ___s: *Fellowship = relation between fellows.* [Old English *-scipe*]

ship biscuit, hardtack.

ship board (ship′bôrd′, ship′bōrd′), *n.* 1 **on shipboard,** on or inside a ship. 2 ARCHAIC. the side of a ship. —*adj.* aboard ship; at sea: *shipboard life.*

ship bread, hardtack.

ship build er (ship′bil′dər), *n.* person who designs or constructs ships.

ship build ing (ship′bil′ding), *n.* 1 the designing or building of ships. 2 art of building ships.

ship canal, canal wide and deep enough for ships.

ship lap (ship′lap′), *n.* 1 a flush, overlapping joint between boards, formed by cutting corresponding rabbets in the adjoining edges and lapping the boards to the depth of the rabbets. 2 boards so rabbeted.

ship load (ship′lōd′), *n.* a full load for a ship.

ship man (ship′mən), *n., pl.* **-men.** 1 shipmaster. 2 ARCHAIC. sailor.

ship mas ter (ship′mas′tər), *n.* master, commander, or captain of a ship, especially a merchant ship.

ship mate (ship′māt′), *n.* a fellow sailor on a ship.

ship ment (ship′mənt), *n.* 1 act of shipping goods. 2 goods sent at one time to a person or company.

ship of the line, a sailing warship of the largest class, big enough to be part of the line of battle of a fleet.

ship own er (ship′ō′nər), *n.* person who owns a ship or ships.

ship per (ship′ər), *n.* person who ships goods.

ship ping (ship′ing), *n.* 1 act or business of sending goods by water, rail, etc. 2 ships. 3 their total tonnage. 4 the ships of a nation, city, or business.

shipping clerk, person whose work is to see to the packing and shipment of goods.

ship shape (ship′shāp′), *adj.* in good order; trim; tidy. —*adv.* in a trim, neat manner.

ship side (ship′sīd′), *n.* the area alongside which a ship is docked.

ship's papers, the documents giving information as to the ship's nationality, owner, etc., which every ship must carry.

ship worm (ship′wėrm′), *n.* any of various marine bivalve mollusks having long, wormlike bodies, which burrow into the wood of ships, docks, etc.

ship wreck (ship′rek′), *n.* 1 destruction or loss of a ship: *Only two people were saved from the shipwreck.* 2 a wrecked ship or what remains of it; wreckage. 3 total loss or ruin; destruction: *The shipwreck of his plans discouraged him.* —*v.t.* 1 wreck, ruin, or destroy. 2 cause to suffer shipwreck. —*v.i.* suffer shipwreck.

ship wright (ship′rīt′), *n.* man who builds or repairs ships.

ship yard (ship′yärd′), *n.* place near the water where ships are built or repaired.

Shi raz (shi räz′), *n.* city in SW Iran. 270,000.

shire (shīr), *n.* one of the counties into which Great Britain is divided, especially one whose name ends in *-shire.* [Old English *scīr*]

shirk (shėrk), *v.t., v.i.* avoid or get out of doing (work, a duty, etc.). —*n.* person who shirks or does not do his share. [origin uncertain] —**shirk′er,** *n.*

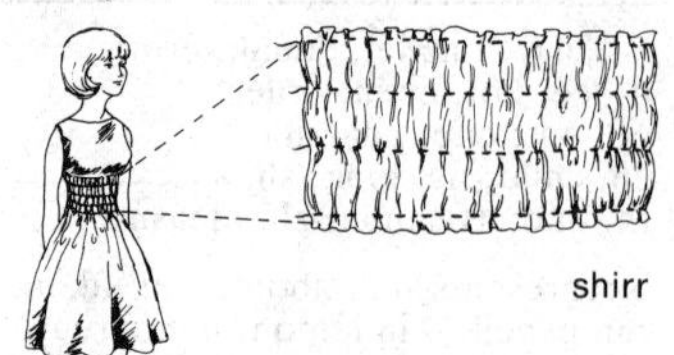

shirr (shėr), *v.t.* 1 draw up or gather (cloth) on parallel threads. 2 bake (eggs) in a shallow dish with butter, etc. —*n.* a shirred arrangement of cloth, etc. [origin unknown]

shirt (shėrt), *n.* 1 garment for the upper part of the body, usually having a collar, long or short sleeves, and an opening in the front which is closed by buttons. 2 undershirt. 3 **keep one's shirt on,** SLANG. stay calm; keep one's temper. 4 **lose one's shirt,** SLANG. lose everything one owns. [Old English *scyrte.* Related to SKIRT.] —**shirt′less,** *adj.* —**shirt′like′,** *adj.*

shirt front, 1 front of a shirt. 2 dickey.

shirt ing (shėr′ting), *n.* fabric for making shirts.

shirt sleeve (shėrt′slēv′), *n.* sleeve of a shirt. —*adj.* informal.

shirt tail (shėrt′tāl′), *n.* the lower part of a shirt, especially the back part.

shirt waist (shėrt′wāst′), *n.* 1 a woman's or girl's tailored blouse, usually having a collar and cuffs, worn with a separate skirt. 2 a one-piece dress with a shirtlike top. —*adj.* having a bodice that resembles a shirt.

shish ke bab (shish′ kə bob′), dish of kabob roasted or broiled on skewers. [< Armenian *shish kabab*]

Shi va (shē′və), *n.* Siva.

shiv a ree (shiv′ə rē′), *n., v.,* **-reed, -ree ing.** —*n.* a mock serenade to a newly married couple, made by beating on kettles, pans, etc. —*v.t.* serenade with a shivaree. [< French *charivari*]

shiv er[1] (shiv′ər), *v.i.* shake with cold, fear, excitement, etc. See synonym study below. —*n.* a shaking from cold, fear, excitement, etc. [Middle English *schiveren*] —**shiv′er-er,** *n.*

Syn. *v.i.* **Shiver, shudder, quake** mean to shake or tremble. **Shiver,** used chiefly of people and animals, suggests a quivering of the flesh: *I crept shivering into bed.* **Shudder** suggests sudden, sharp shivering of the whole body in horror or extreme disgust: *shudder at a ghastly sight.* **Quake** suggests violent trembling with fear or cold, or shaking and rocking from a violent disturbance: *The house quaked to its foundations.*

shiv er[2] (shiv′ər), *v.t., v.i.* break into small pieces; shatter or split into fragments or pieces: *a tree shivered by lightning, shiver a mirror with a hammer.* —*n.* a small piece; splinter. [origin uncertain]

shiv er y (shiv′ər ē), *adj.* 1 quivering from cold, fear, etc.; shivering. 2 inclined to shiver from cold. 3 chilly. 4 causing shivers, especially from fear: *a shivery experience.*

shoal[1] (shōl), *n.* 1 place in a sea, lake, or stream where the water is shallow. 2 sandbank or sandbar that makes the water shallow, especially one which can be seen at low tide. —*adj.* shallow. —*v.i.* become shallow. [Old English *sceald* shallow, adjective]

shoal[2] (shōl), *n.* a large number; crowd: *a shoal of fish, a shoal of tourists.* —*v.i.* form into a shoal; crowd together. [perhaps Old English *scolu* host (of people), school of fish]

shoat (shōt), *n.* a young pig that no longer suckles. Also, **shote.** [origin uncertain]

shock[1] (shok), *n.* 1 a sudden, violent shake, blow, or crash: *Earthquake shocks are often felt in Japan.* 2 a sudden, violent, or upsetting disturbance: *His death was a great shock to his family.* 3 condition of physical collapse or depression, accompanied by a sudden drop in blood pressure, often resulting in unconsciousness. Shock may set in after a severe injury, great loss of blood, or a sudden emotional disturbance. 4 disturbance produced by an electric current passing through the body. —*v.t.* 1 cause to feel surprise, horror, or disgust: *That child's cruelty to cats shocks everyone.* 2 give an electric shock to. 3 strike together violently; jar; jolt. [probably < French *choc,* noun, *choquer,* verb]

shock[2] (shok), *n.* group of cornstalks or bundles of grain set up on end together in the field in order to dry or to await harvesting. —*v.t.* make into shocks. [Middle English *schokke*]

shock[3] (shok), *n.* a thick, bushy mass: *a shock of red hair.* [origin uncertain]

shock absorber, 1 anything that absorbs or lessens shocks. 2 device consisting of springs, hydraulic pistons, etc., used on automobiles, etc., to absorb the force of sudden impacts.

shock er[1] (shok′ər), *n.* 1 INFORMAL. a highly sensational written work, especially a story. 2 person or thing that shocks. [< *shock*[1]]

shock er[2] (shok′ər), *n.* person or device that shocks cornstalks and grain. [< *shock*[2]]

shock ing (shok′ing), *adj.* 1 causing intense and painful surprise: *shocking news.* 2 offensive; disgusting; revolting. 3 INFORMAL. very bad. —**shock′ing ly,** *adv.*

shocking pink, a very strong, bright pink color.

shock proof (shok′prüf′), *adj.* capable of withstanding shock: *a shockproof watch.*

shock therapy, treatment of mental disorder through shock induced by chemical or electrical means.

shock troops, troops chosen and specially trained for making attacks.

shock wave, 1 disturbance of the atmosphere created by the movement of an aircraft, rocket, etc., at a velocity greater than that of sound. 2 a similar effect caused by the expansion of gases away from an explosion.

shod (shod), *v.* pt. and pp. of **shoe.**

shod dy (shod′ē), *n., pl.* **-dies,** *adj.,* **-di er, -di est.** —*n.* 1 an inferior kind of wool made of woolen waste, old rags, yarn, etc. 2 cloth made of woolen waste. 3 anything inferior made to look like what is better. —*adj.* 1 made of woolen waste. 2 pretending to be better than it is; of inferior quality: *a shoddy necklace, shoddy merchandise.* 3 mean; shabby: *shoddy treatment, a shoddy trick.* [origin uncertain] —**shod′di ly,** *adv.* —**shod′di ness,** *n.*

shoe (shü), *n., pl.* **shoes** or (ARCHAIC) **shoon,** *v.,* **shod, shoe ing.** —*n.* 1 an outer covering, usually of leather, for a person's foot, normally consisting of a stiff durable sole and heel and a lighter upper part. 2 something like a shoe in shape, position, or use. 3 horseshoe. 4 ferrule. 5 the part of a brake that presses on a wheel to slow down or stop a vehicle. 6 the outer casing of a pneumatic tire. 7 a metal strip on the bottom of a runner of a sleigh or sled. 8 a sliding plate or contact by which an electric locomotive or car takes current from the third rail. 9 **in another's shoes,** in another's place, situation, or circumstances. 10 **where the shoe pinches,** where the real trouble or difficulty lies. —*v.t.* 1 put shoes on; furnish with a shoe or shoes: *A blacksmith shoes horses.* 2 protect or arm at the point; edge or face with metal: *a stick shod with steel.* [Old English *scōh*] —**shoe′less,** *adj.*

shoe black (shü′blak′), *n.* bootblack.

shoe horn (shü′hôrn′), *n.* a curved piece of metal, plastic, horn, etc., inserted at the heel of a shoe to make it slip on easily.

shoe lace (shü′lās′), *n.* cord, braid, or leather strip for fastening a shoe.

shoe mak er (shü′mā′kər), *n.* person who makes or mends shoes.

shoe mak ing (shü′mā′king), *n.* the making or mending of shoes.

shoe string (shü′string′), *n.* 1 shoelace. 2 INFORMAL. a very small amount of money used to start or carry on a business, investment, etc.: *The company was formed on a shoestring.*

shoe tree, a shaped block inserted into a shoe to keep it in shape or to stretch it.

sho far (shō′fär, shō′fər), *n., pl.* **sho froth** (shō′frōs, shō frōt′). a ram's horn sounded during certain Jewish religious services, especially on Rosh Hashanah and Yom Kippur. [< Hebrew *shōphār*]

sho gun (shō′gun, shō′gün), *n.* the former hereditary commander in chief of the Japanese army. The shoguns were the real rulers of Japan for hundreds of years until 1867. [< Japanese *shōgun* < Chinese *chiang chün* army leader]

sho gun ate (shō′gun it, shō′gun āt; shō′gü-nit, shō′gü nāt), *n.* 1 position, rank, or rule of a shogun. 2 government by shoguns.

sho ji (shō′jē), *n.* a sliding screen of translucent paper used to make up the partitions or walls of a Japanese house. [< Japanese *shōji*]

Sho lem A lei chem (shō′ləm ä lā′ʜəm), 1859-1916, American author of Yiddish novels and stories, born in Russia. His real name was Solomon Rabinowitz.

Sho lo khov (shô′lə kôf′), *n.* **Mikhail Aleksandrovich,** born 1905, Russian author of novels and short stories.

shone (shōn), *v.* a pt. and a pp. of **shine.**

shoo (shü), *interj.* exclamation used to scare away hens, birds, etc. —*v.t.* scare or drive away by or as if by calling "Shoo!"

shoo-in (shü′in′), *n.* INFORMAL. 1 an easy or sure winner. 2 an easy race, contest, etc., to win; sure thing.

shook[1] (shůk), *v.* pt. of **shake.** —*adj.* **shook up,** SLANG. having disturbed feelings; upset.

shook[2] (shůk), *n.* set of staves or pieces for a barrel, keg, box, etc., ready to be put together. [origin uncertain]

shook[3] (shůk), *n.* shock of corn or bundles of grain. [variant of *shock*[2]]

shoon (shün), *n.* ARCHAIC. a pl. of **shoe.**

shoot (shüt), *v.,* **shot, shoot ing,** *n.* —*v.t.* 1 hit, wound, or kill with a bullet, arrow, etc.: *shoot a rabbit.* 2 send forth or let fly (a bullet, arrow, etc.) from a firearm, bow, or the like. 3 send forth like a shot or an arrow; send swiftly: *He shot question after question at us.* 4 fire or use (a gun or other firearm); discharge (a bow, catapult, etc.). 5 kill game in or on (an area): *She shot the east side of the mountain.* 6 move suddenly and swiftly: *I shot back the bolt.* 7 pass quickly along, through, under, or over: *shoot a stretch of*

rapids. 8 send out (rays, flames, etc.) swiftly and forcibly; dart. 9 put forth (buds, leaves, branches, etc.). 10 send (a ball, puck, etc.) toward the goal, pocket, etc., in attempting to score. 11 score (a goal, points, etc.) by doing this: *He shot two goals.* 12 propel (a marble), as from the thumb and forefinger. 13 play (craps, pool, or golf). 14 take (a picture) with a camera. 15 take a picture of (a scene, person, or object) with a camera; photograph; film. 16 measure the altitude of: *shoot the sun.* 17 vary with some different color, etc.: *Her dress was shot with threads of gold.* 18 dump; empty out. 19 **shoot at** or **shoot for,** INFORMAL. aim at; aspire to. *—v.i.* 1 send forth a bullet, arrow, or other missile from a firearm, bow, or the like: *shoot at a mark.* 2 (of a gun, etc.) send a bullet; fire: *This gun shoots straight.* 3 move suddenly and swiftly: *A car shot by us. Flames shot up from the burning house.* 4 go sharply through some part of the body, especially from time to time: *Pain shot up my arm.* 5 come forth from the ground; grow; grow rapidly: *Buds shoot forth in the spring.* 6 project sharply; jut out: *a cape that shoots out into the sea.* 7 take a photograph or film a motion picture. 8 send a ball, puck, etc., toward the goal, pocket, etc., in attempting to score.
—n. 1 trip, party, or contest for shooting; shooting match or contest. 2 a shooting practice. 3 a new part growing out, as a young bud or stem; offshoot. 4 a short, sharp twinge of pain. 5 a sloping trough for conveying coal, grain, water, etc., to a lower level; chute. 6 a swift or sudden movement. 7 the launching of a missile or rocket.
[Old English *scēotan*] **—shoot′er,** *n.*

shooting gallery, a long room or a deep booth fitted with targets for practice in shooting.

shooting star, 1 a meteor, especially one seen falling or darting through the sky at night. 2 a North American perennial herb of the same family as the primrose, with a cluster of rose, purple, or white flowers whose petals and sepals turn backward.

shop (shop), *n., v.,* **shopped, shop ping.** *—n.* 1 place where things are sold at retail; store: *a small dress shop.* 2 place where things are made or repaired: *a carpenter's shop.* 3 place where a certain kind of work is done: *a tailoring shop.* 4 **set up shop,** start work or business. 5 **shut up shop,** give up work or business. 6 **talk shop,** talk about one's work or occupation. *—v.i.* 1 visit stores to look at or to buy things: *We shopped all morning for a coat.* 2 make a search; try to find and acquire something: *shop around for an apartment.* [Old English *sceoppa*]

shop girl (shop′gėrl′), *n.* girl who works in a shop or store.

shop keep er (shop′kē′pər), *n.* person who owns or manages a shop or store.

shop lift (shop′lift′), *v.t., v.i.* steal goods from a store while pretending to be a customer. **—shop′lift′er,** *n.*

shop lift ing (shop′lif′ting), *n.* a stealing of goods from a store while pretending to be a customer.

shop per (shop′ər), *n.* 1 person who visits stores to look at or buy things. 2 person employed by a store to buy items from competitors in order to compare prices, quality of merchandise, etc.

shop ping (shop′ing), *n.* act of visiting stores to look at or to buy things: *We do our shopping on Saturdays.*

shopping center, group of stores built as a unit on or near a main road, especially in a suburban or new community. Most shopping centers have large areas for parking automobiles.

shop steward, a union worker elected by fellow workers to represent them in dealing with management and maintaining union regulations.

shop talk (shop′tôk′), *n.* 1 talk about one's work or occupation, especially outside of working hours. 2 the informal language of an occupation.

shop worn (shop′wôrn′, shop′wōrn′), *adj.* soiled, frayed, etc., by being displayed or handled in a store.

sho ran (shôr′an, shōr′an), *n.* method of navigation in which radar signals are sent out from a craft to two or more fixed stations and retransmitted by the stations. The time interval between sending and receiving the signals is used to determine the craft's exact position. [< *sho(rt) ra(nge) n(avigation)*]

shore¹ (shôr, shōr), *n.* 1 land at the edge of a sea, lake, etc. 2 land near a sea; coast. 3 land. 4 **off shore,** in or on the water, not far from the shore. [Middle English *schore*]

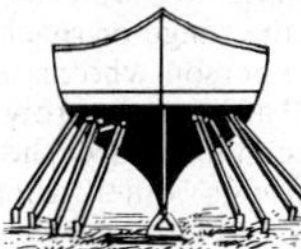

shore²
shores supporting a ship frame

shore² (shôr, shōr), *n., v.,* **shored, shor ing.** *—n.* prop placed against or beneath something to hold it in place or support it. *—v.t.* prop up or support with or as if with shores. [Middle English *schore,* perhaps < Middle Dutch, a prop]

shore bird, any bird that frequents the shores of seas, inlets, lakes, etc.

shore dinner, dinner consisting of various seafoods.

shore leave, leave for a member or members of a ship's crew to go ashore.

shore line (shôr′līn′, shōr′līn′), *n.* line where shore and water meet.

shore patrol, the policing branch of the United States Navy and Coast Guard.

shore ward (shôr′wərd, shōr′wərd), *adv., adj.* toward the shore.

shor ing (shôr′ing, shōr′ing), *n.* shores or props for supporting a building, ship, dock, etc.

shorn (shôrn, shōrn), *v.* a pp. of **shear.** *—adj.* sheared.

short (shôrt), *adj.* 1 not long; of small extent from end to end in space or time. See synonym study below. 2 not long for its kind: *a short tail.* 3 not tall; having little height: *a short man, short grass.* 4 extending or reaching but a little way: *a short memory.* 5 not coming up to the right amount, measure, standard, etc.: *short weight, be short in one's accounts.* 6 not having enough; scanty: *a short supply of money.* 7 so brief as to be rude: *She was so short with me that I felt hurt.* 8 (of vowels or syllables) taking a comparatively short time to speak. The vowels are short in *fat, net, pin, not, up.* 9 breaking or crumbling easily. Pastry is made short with butter or other shortening. 10 not owning at the time of sale the stocks, securities, or commodities that one sells. 11 of, noting, or having to do with sales of stocks or commodities that the seller does not possess. 12 depending for profit on a decline in prices. 13 **run short, a** not have

hat, āge, fär; let, ēqual, tėrm;
it, īce; hot, ōpen, ôrder;
oil, out; cup, pu̇t, rüle;
ch, child; ng, long; sh, she;
th, thin; ᴛʜ, then; zh, measure;
ə represents *a* in about, *e* in taken, *i* in pencil, *o* in lemon, *u* in circus.
< = from, derived from, taken from.

enough. **b** not be enough. 14 **short for,** a shortened form for: *The word "phone" is short for "telephone."* 15 **short of, a** not up to; less than. **b** not having enough of. **c** on the near side of an intended or particular point.
—adv. 1 so as to be or make short: *to throw short.* 2 abruptly; suddenly: *The horse pulled up short.* 3 briefly. 4 without possessing at the time of sale the stocks or commodities sold. 5 **cut short,** end suddenly. 6 **fall short, a** fail to reach or obtain. **b** fail to equal; be insufficient.
—n. 1 something short. 2 what is deficient or lacking. 3 a short circuit. 4 a short sound or syllable. 5 **shorts,** *pl.* **a** short trousers of varying length, often not reaching the knee, worn especially as sportswear by both men and women. **b** a similar men's or boy's undergarment. 6 a short motion picture, especially one shown on the same program with a full-length picture. 7 shortstop. 8 size of garment for men who are shorter than average. 9 **for short,** by way of abbreviation; as a nickname. 10 **in short,** briefly.
—v.t., v.i. short-circuit.
[Old English *sceort*] **—short′ness,** *n.*
Syn. *adj.* 1 **Short, brief** mean of small extent. **Short** may refer to either space or time *(a short pole, a short visit),* but when describing time it often suggests being curtailed or unfinished: *Because he was late he could take only a short walk today.* **Brief** usually refers to time *(a brief sermon),* and is more likely to suggest leaving out unnecessary details than curtailing or not finishing: *The essay was brief and to the point.*

short age (shôr′tij), *n.* 1 too small an amount; lack; deficiency: *There is a shortage of grain because of poor crops.* 2 amount by which something is deficient.

short bread (shôrt′bred′), *n.* a rich cake or cookie that crumbles easily, made with much butter or other shortening.

short cake (shôrt′kāk′), *n.* 1 cake made of rich biscuit dough and shortening, usually slightly sweetened, covered or filled with berries or other fruit. 2 a sweet cake filled with fruit.

short-change (shôrt′chānj′), *v.t.,* **-changed, -chang ing.** 1 give less than the right change to. 2 cheat: *be short-changed in getting an education.* **—short′-chang′er,** *n.*

short circuit, a side circuit formed when insulation wears off a wire or wires which touch each other or some connecting conductor, so that the main circuit is by-passed. A short circuit usually blows a fuse or activates a circuit breaker, and may cause a fire.

short-cir cuit (shôrt′sėr′kit), *v.t.* make a short circuit in. *—v.i.* make a short circuit.

short com ing (shôrt′kum′ing), *n.* fault; defect.

short cut, (shôrt′kut′), *n.* a less distant or quicker way.

short division, method of dividing numbers in which each step of the division is worked out mentally.

short en (shôrt′n), *v.t.* 1 make shorter; cut off. See synonym study below. 2 make rich with butter, lard, etc. 3 take in (sail). *—v.i.* become shorter. **—short′en er,** *n.*

Syn. *v.t.* 1 **Shorten, curtail, abbreviate** mean to make shorter. **Shorten** is the general word meaning to reduce the length or extent of something: *The new highway shortens the trip.* **Curtail,** more formal, means to cut something short by taking away or cutting off a part, and suggests causing loss or incompleteness: *Bad news made us curtail our trip.* **Abbreviate** most commonly means to shorten the written form of a word or phrase by leaving out syllables or letters or by substitution, without impairing meaning: *Abbreviate "pound" to "lb." after numerals. Abbreviate* may also be used more generally, closer in meaning to *shorten* than to *curtail.*

short en ing (shôrt′n ing, shôrt′ning), *n.* 1 butter, lard, or other fat, used to make pastry, cake, etc., crisp or crumbly. 2 act of a person or thing that shortens.

shorthand (def. 2) for "Your letter was received today." (Gregg system)

short hand (shôrt′hand′), *n.* 1 method of rapid writing which uses symbols or abbreviations in place of letters, syllables, words, and phrases; stenography. 2 writing in such symbols. *—adj.* 1 written in shorthand. 2 using shorthand.

short-hand ed (shôrt′han′did), *adj.* not having enough workmen, helpers, etc.

short horn (shôrt′hôrn′), *n.* one of a breed of white, red, or roan cattle with short horns that originated in northern England, raised chiefly for beef; Durham.

short ish (shôr′tish), *adj.* rather short.

short-lived (shôrt′līvd′, shôrt′livd′), *adj.* living or lasting a short time: *a short-lived plant, short-lived hope.*

short ly (shôrt′lē), *adv.* 1 in a short time; before long; soon: *I will be with you shortly.* 2 in a few words; briefly. 3 briefly and rudely; curtly.

short-range (shôrt′rānj′), *adj.* not reaching far in time or distance; not long-range: *a short-range forecast, a short-range missile.*

short shrift, 1 little or no consideration, mercy, or delay: *Violators of these new regulations will get short shrift.* 2 short time for confession and absolution.

short sight ed (shôrt′sī′tid), *adj.* 1 nearsighted. 2 lacking in foresight; not prudent. **—short′sight′ed ly,** *adv.* **—short′sight′ed ness,** *n.*

short-spo ken (shôrt′spō′kən), *adj.* curt of speech or manner; abrupt.

short stop (shôrt′stop′), *n.* a baseball player stationed between second base and third base.

short story, a prose story with a full plot, but much shorter than a novel.

short-tem pered (shôrt′tem′pərd), *adj.* easily made angry; quick-tempered.

short-term (shôrt′tėrm′), *adj.* 1 of or for a short period of time: *short-term plans.* 2 falling due in a short time: *a short-term loan.*

short ton, 2000 pounds.

short wave (shôrt′wāv′), *n., v.t., v.i.,* **-waved, -wav ing.** *—n.* a radio wave having a wavelength of 60 meters or less. *—v.t., v.i.* transmit by shortwaves: *The President's speech was shortwaved overseas.*

short-wind ed (shôrt′win′did), *adj.* getting out of breath very easily or too quickly; having difficulty in breathing.

Sho sho ne (shō shō′nē), *n., pl.* **-nes** or **-ne.** member of a tribe of American Indians of Wyoming, Idaho, Utah, Colorado, and Nevada.

Sho sho ni (shō shō′nē), *n., pl.* **-nis** or **-ni.** Shoshone.

Shos ta ko vich (shos′tə kō′vich), *n.* **Dimitri,** born 1906, Russian composer.

shot[1] (shot), *n., pl.* **shots** (also **shot** for 3), *v.,* **shot ted, shot ting,** *adj.* *—n.* 1 discharge of a gun, cannon, bow, etc.: *fire a shot. We heard two shots.* 2 act of shooting. 3 tiny balls of lead, steel, etc.; bullets. 4 a single ball of lead, steel, etc., for a gun or cannon. 5 an attempt to hit by shooting. 6 the distance a weapon can shoot: *We were within rifle shot of the fort.* 7 the range or reach of anything like a shot. 8 person who shoots: *He is a good shot.* 9 an aimed throw or stroke, or a scoring attempt in billiards, hockey, basketball, or various other games. 10 anything like a shot; something emitted, cast, launched, or set off. 11 INFORMAL. injection, as of a vaccine or drug: *a typhoid shot.* 12 INFORMAL. one drink, usually a jigger, of alcoholic liquor. 13 INFORMAL. dose, as of medicine. 14 remark aimed at some person or thing. 15 attempt; try: *take a shot at the job.* 16 a random guess. 17 picture taken with a camera; photograph; snapshot. 18 the motion-picture or television record of a scene. 19 a heavy metal ball, usually weighing 16 pounds, used in the shot-put. 20 (in mining) a blast. 21 an amount due or to be paid.
—v.t. 1 load with shot; furnish with shot. 2 attempt; try.
—adj. **shot through with,** full of: *speeches shot through with wit.*
[Old English *sceot* < *scēotan* to shoot]

shot[2] (shot), *v.* pt. and pp. of **shoot.** *—adj.* 1 woven so as to show a play of colors: *blue silk shot with gold.* 2 SLANG. that has been used up, worn out, or ruined.

shotgun
above, double-barreled shotgun;
below, detail of gun opened for loading

shote (shōt), *n.* shoat.

shot gun (shot′gun′), *n.* a smoothbore gun for firing cartridges filled with small shot.

shot-put (shot′pu̇t′), *n.* an athletic contest in which one sends a heavy metal ball as far as he can with one throw.

shot-put ter (shot′pu̇t′ər), *n.* person who puts the shot in athletic contests.

should (shu̇d; *unstressed* shəd), *v.,* pt. of **shall.** 1 See **shall** for ordinary uses. 2 *Should* has special uses: **a** to express duty, obligation, or propriety. *You should try to make fewer mistakes.* **b** to make statements, requests, etc., less direct or blunt. *I should not call her beautiful.* **c** to express uncertainty. *If I should win the prize, how happy I would be.* **d** to make statements about something that might have happened but did not. *I should have gone if you had asked me.* **e** to express a condition or reason for something. *He was pardoned on the condition that he should leave the country.* [Old English *sceolde*]

shoul der (shōl′dər), *n.* 1 the part of the body to which an arm, foreleg, or wing is attached. 2 joint by which the arm or the foreleg is connected to the trunk. 3 the part of a garment that covers a shoulder. 4 **shoulders,** *pl.* the two shoulders and the upper part of the back. 5 cut of meat consisting of an upper foreleg and its adjoining parts. 6 a shoulderlike part or projection: *the shoulder of a hill.* 7 edge of a road, often unpaved. 8 (in printing) the flat surface on a type extending beyond the base of the letter. 9 (in fortification) the angle of a bastion included between the face and a flank. 10 **put one's shoulder to the wheel,** set to work vigorously; make a great effort. 11 **shoulder to shoulder, a** side by side; together. **b** with united effort. 12 **straight from the shoulder,** frankly; directly.
—v.t. 1 take upon or support with the shoulder or shoulders: *shoulder a tray.* 2 bear (a burden, blame, etc.); assume (responsibility, expense, etc.). 3 push with the shoulders: *shoulder one's way through a crowd.*
[Old English *sculdor*] **—shoul′der-like′,** *adj.*

shoulder blade, the flat, triangular bone of either shoulder; scapula.

shoulder knot, knot of ribbon or lace worn on the shoulder.

shoulder patch, a cloth insignia worn on the upper sleeve of a uniform or other garment, just below the shoulder.

shoulder strap, 1 strap worn over the shoulder to hold a garment up. 2 an ornamental strip fastened on the shoulder of an officer's uniform to show his rank.

should est (shu̇d′ist), *v.* ARCHAIC. shouldst.

should n't (shu̇d′nt), should not.

shouldst (shu̇dst), *v.* ARCHAIC. should. "Thou shouldst" means "you should."

shout (shout), *v.i.* 1 call or cry loudly and vigorously. See **cry** for synonym study. 2 talk or laugh very loudly. *—v.t.* 1 express by a shout or shouts: *The crowd shouted its approval.* 2 **shout down,** silence by very loud talk. *—n.* 1 a loud, vigorous call or cry. 2 a loud outburst of laughter. [Middle English] **—shout′er,** *n.*

shove (shuv), *v.,* **shoved, shov ing,** *n.* *—v.t.* 1 move forward or along by the application of force from behind; push: *shove a bookcase into place.* See **push** for synonym study. 2 push roughly or rudely against; jostle (a person): *The bully shoved him out of the room.* *—v.i.* 1 apply force against something in order to move it; push. 2 push or jostle in a crowd; make one's way by jostling or elbowing. 3 **shove off, a** push away from the shore; row away. **b** SLANG. leave a place; start on one's way. *—n.* act of shoving; push. [Old English *scūfan*] **—shov′er,** *n.*

shov el (shuv′əl), *n., v.,* **-eled, -el ing** or **-elled, -el ling.** *—n.* 1 tool with a broad blade or scoop attached to a long handle, used to lift and throw loose matter: *a coal shovel, a snow shovel.* 2 shovelful. *—v.t.* 1 lift and throw with a shovel. 2 make with a shovel: *shovel a path through the snow.* 3 throw or lift as if with a shovel: *shovel food into one's mouth.* —*v.i.* work with a shovel; use a shovel. [Old English *scofl*]

shov el er or **shov el ler** (shuv′ə lər), *n.* 1 person or thing that shovels. 2 a small river duck of the Northern Hemisphere with a broad, flat bill.

shov el ful (shuv′əl fül), *n., pl.* **-fuls.** as much as a shovel can hold.

show (shō), *v.,* **showed, shown** or **showed, show ing,** *n.* —*v.t.* 1 let be seen; put in sight; display: *She showed her new hat.* 2 reveal; manifest; disclose: *show great energy, show signs of fear.* 3 point out: *show someone the sights of a town.* 4 direct; guide: *show a person out.* 5 make clear; explain. 6 make clear to; explain to: *Show us how to do the problem.* 7 prove; demonstrate: *She showed that it was true.* 8 grant; give: *show mercy.* —*v.i.* 1 be in sight; be seen; appear: *Anger showed in his face.* 2 finish third in a race (contrasted with *win* and *place*).

show off, make a show (of); display (one's good points, etc.).

show up, a hold up for ridicule or contempt; expose. b stand out. c INFORMAL. put in an appearance.

—*n.* 1 display: *The jewels made a fine show.* See synonym study below. 2 display for effect: *a show of learning.* 3 any kind of public exhibition or display: *an art show, a horse show.* 4 a play, motion picture, etc., or a performance of one of these. 5 a showing: *vote by a show of hands.* 6 appearance: *There is some show of truth in her excuse.* 7 false appearance; pretense: *hide treachery by a show of friendship.* 8 trace; indication. 9 object of scorn; something odd; queer sight: *Don't make a show of yourself.* 10 INFORMAL. chance; opportunity. 11 third place, as in a horse race: *win, place, and show.* 12 operation or undertaking: *He is running the whole show.* 13 **for show,** for effect; to attract attention. Also, BRITISH or ARCHAIC **shew.**
[Old English *scēawian* look at] —**show′er,** *n.*

Syn. *n.* 1 **Show, display** mean an offering or exhibiting to view or notice. **Show** applies to anything exposed to public view, and sometimes has unfavorable connotations: *That was a disgraceful show of temper.* **Display** applies particularly to something carefully arranged so as to call attention to its fineness, beauty, strength, or other admirable qualities: *That florist has the most beautiful displays in the city.*

show bill, poster, placard, or the like, advertising a show.

show boat (shō′bōt′), *n.* steamboat with a theater for plays. Showboats carry their own actors and make frequent stops to give performances.

show bread (shō′bred′), *n.* shewbread.

shrew (def. 2)—6 in. long with tail

show business, the industry or world of entertainment.

show case (shō′kās′), *n.* 1 a glass case to display and protect articles in a store, museum, etc. 2 any display or exhibit.

show down (shō′doun′), *n.* INFORMAL. a forced disclosure of facts, purposes, methods, etc., bringing a conflict to a decisive outcome.

show er (shou′ər), *n.* 1 a short fall of rain. 2 anything like a fall of rain: *a shower of hail, a shower of tears, a shower of sparks from an engine.* 3 party for giving presents to a woman about to be married or on some other special occasion. 4 shower bath. —*v.i.* 1 rain for a short time. 2 come in a shower. 3 take a shower bath. —*v.t.* 1 wet with or as if with a shower; spray; sprinkle. 2 send in a shower; pour down: *shower bombs on a city. They showered gifts upon her.* [Old English *scūr*]

shower bath, 1 bath in which water pours down on the body from an overhead nozzle in small jets. 2 apparatus for such a bath.

show er y (shou′ər ē), *adj.* 1 raining in showers. 2 having many showers. 3 like a shower.

show ing (shō′ing), *n.* 1 show; display; exhibition: *a current showing of paintings.* 2 manner of appearance or performance: *make a good showing.*

show man (shō′mən), *n., pl.* **-men.** 1 person who manages a show. 2 person skilled in presenting things in a dramatic and exciting way.

show man ship (shō′mən ship), *n.* skill or practice of a showman.

shown (shōn), *v.* a pp. of **show.**

show-off (shō′ôf′, shō′of′), *n.* 1 a showing off. 2 INFORMAL. person who shows off.

show piece (shō′pēs′), *n.* anything displayed as an outstanding example of its kind.

show place (shō′plās′), *n.* place that attracts visitors for its beauty, interest, etc.

show room (shō′rüm′, shō′rům′), *n.* room used for the display of goods or merchandise.

show window, window in the front of a store, where things are shown for sale.

show y (shō′ē), *adj.,* **show i er, show i est.** 1 making a display; likely to attract attention; striking; conspicuous: *A peony is a showy flower.* 2 too bright and gay to be in good taste. See **gaudy** for synonym study. 3 ostentatious. —**show′i ly,** *adv.* —**show′i ness,** *n.*

shpt., shipment.

shrank (shrangk), *v.* a pt. of **shrink.**

shrap nel (shrap′nəl), *n.* 1 shell filled with fragments of metal and powder, set to explode in midair and scatter the fragments over a wide area. 2 fragments scattered by such a shell. [< Henry *Shrapnel,* 1761-1842, British army officer who invented it]

shred (shred), *n., v.,* **shred ded** or **shred, shred ding.** —*n.* 1 a very small piece torn off or cut off; very narrow strip; scrap: *The wind tore the sail to shreds.* 2 fragment; particle; bit: *There's not a shred of evidence that the missing papers were stolen.* —*v.t.* tear or cut into small pieces: *Shredded paper is used in packing dishes.* —*v.i.* be reduced to shreds. [Old English *scrēade*] —**shred′der,** *n.*

Shreve port (shrēv′pôrt, shrēv′pōrt), *n.* city in NW Louisiana. 182,000.

shrew (shrü), *n.* 1 a bad-tempered, quarrelsome woman. 2 any of a family of very small, mouselike mammals of the same order as the moles, with a long snout and short, brownish fur; shrewmouse. Shrews eat insects and worms. [Old English *scrēawa*]

shrewd (shrüd), *adj.* 1 having a sharp mind; showing a keen wit; clever. See synonym study below. 2 keen; sharp. 3 mean; mischievous: *a shrewd turn.* [earlier *shrewed* bad-tempered, shrewish; wicked < *shrew*] —**shrewd′ly,** *adv.* —**shrewd′ness,** *n.*

Syn. 1 **Shrewd, sagacious, astute** mean having a sharp or keen mind and good judgment. **Shrewd** suggests natural cleverness in practical affairs or, sometimes, craftiness: *She is a shrewd lawyer.* **Sagacious** implies a wise and far-seeing understanding of practical affairs: *The company director is a sagacious man.* **Astute** implies shrewdness and sagacity plus the ability of being hard to fool: *an astute diplomat.*

hat, āge, fär; let, ēqual, tėrm;
it, īce; hot, ōpen, ôrder;
oil, out; cup, pu̇t, rüle;
ch, child; ng, long; sh, she;
th, thin; ꟟H, then; zh, measure;

ə represents *a* in about, *e* in taken, *i* in pencil, *o* in lemon, *u* in circus.

< = from, derived from, taken from.

shrew ish (shrü′ish), *adj.* scolding or bad-tempered. —**shrew′ish ly,** *adv.* —**shrew′ish ness,** *n.*

shrew mouse (shrü′mous′), *n., pl.* **-mice.** shrew.

shriek (shrēk), *n.* 1 a loud, sharp, shrill sound: *a shriek of terror, the shriek of an engine's whistle.* 2 a loud, shrill laugh. —*v.i.* make a loud, sharp, shrill sound. People sometimes shriek because of terror, anger, pain, or amusement. —*v.t.* utter loudly and shrilly. [perhaps of Scandinavian origin]

shrift (shrift), *n.* ARCHAIC. 1 confession to a priest, followed by the imposing of penance and the granting of absolution. 2 act of shriving. [Old English *scrift* < *scrīfan* shrive]

shrike (shrīk), *n.* any of a family of songbirds with a strong, hooked and toothed beak that feeds on large insects, frogs, mice, and sometimes other birds. Shrikes have a habit of impaling their prey on thorns, barbs, or twigs. [Old English *scrīc*]

shrill (shril), *adj.* 1 having a high pitch; high and sharp in sound; piercing: *Crickets, locusts, and katydids make shrill noises.* 2 full of shrill sounds. —*v.i.* make a shrill sound; sound sharply. —*v.t.* utter with a shrill sound. —*adv.* with a shrill sound; shrilly. [Middle English *shrille*] —**shrill′ness,** *n.*

shril ly (shril′ē), *adv.* in shrill tones.

shrimp (shrimp), *n., pl.* **shrimps** (or **shrimp** for 1). 1 any of various small, chiefly marine, long-tailed crustaceans with long feelers and five pairs of delicate legs. Some shrimps are used for food. 2 a small or insignificant person or thing. [Middle English *shrimpe*] —**shrimp′like′,** *adj.*

shrine (shrīn), *n., v.,* **shrined, shrin ing.** —*n.* 1 case, box, etc., holding a holy object.

shrine (def. 1)

2 tomb of a saint, etc. 3 place of worship. 4 place or object considered sacred because of its history, memories, etc.: *Shakespeare's birthplace is visited as a shrine.* —*v.t.* enclose in a shrine or something like a shrine; enshrine. [Old English *scrīn* < Latin *scrinium* case, box]

shrink (shringk), *v.,* **shrank** or **shrunk, shrunk** or **shrunk en, shrink ing,** *n.* —*v.i.* 1 draw back; recoil: *The dog shrank from the whip.* See synonym study below. 2 become smaller: *When his influence began to shrink, his wealth also decreased.* —*v.t.* make smaller; cause to shrink: *Hot water shrinks wool.* —*n.* 1 a shrinking. 2 SLANG. psychiatrist. [Old English *scrincan*] —**shrink′a ble,** *adj.* —**shrink′er,** *n.*

Syn. *v.i.* 1 **Shrink, flinch** mean to draw back from something painful, unpleasant, etc. **Shrink** suggests drawing back physically or mentally due to instinctive horror, aversion, fear, etc.: *shrink from meeting strangers.* **Flinch** suggests drawing back due to weakness or lack of courage: *Instead of fighting back, he flinched before his attacker.*

shrink age (shring′kij), *n.* 1 act or process of shrinking. 2 the amount or degree of shrinking.

shrinking violet, person who is shy, timid, or self-effacing.

shrive (shrīv), *v.,* **shrove** or **shrived, shriv en** or **shrived, shriv ing.** ARCHAIC. —*v.t.* hear the confession of, impose penance on, and grant absolution to. —*v.i.* 1 make confession. 2 hear confessions. 3 **shrive oneself,** confess to a priest and do penance. [Old English *scrifan* < Latin *scribere* write]

shriv el (shriv′əl), *v.t., v.i.,* **-eled, -el ing** or **-elled, -el ling.** 1 dry up; wither; shrink and wrinkle: *The hot sunshine shriveled the grass.* 2 make or become useless; waste away. [origin unknown]

shriv en (shriv′ən), *v.* ARCHAIC. a pp. of **shrive.**

Shrop shire (shrop′shər, shrop′shir), *n.* 1 county in W England. 2 any of an English breed of black-faced, hornless sheep, raised especially for meat.

shroud (shroud), *n.* 1 cloth or garment in which a dead person is wrapped or dressed for burial. 2 something that covers, conceals, or veils: *The fog was a shroud over the city.* 3 Usually, **shrouds,** *pl.* rope from a mast to the side of a ship. Shrouds help support the mast. 4 one of the lines attached to the canopy of a parachute. —*v.t.* 1 wrap or dress for burial. 2 cover; conceal; veil: *Their plans are shrouded in secrecy.* [Old English *scrūd*]

shrove (shrōv), *v.* ARCHAIC. a pt. of **shrive.**

Shrove tide (shrōv′tīd′), *n.* the three days, **Shrove Sunday, Shrove Monday,** and **Shrove Tuesday,** before Ash Wednesday, the first day of Lent.

shrub[1] (shrub), *n.* a perennial woody plant smaller than a tree, usually with many separate stems starting from or near the ground; bush. [Old English *scrybb* brush] —**shrub′like′,** *adj.*

shrub[2] (shrub), *n.* drink made from fruit juice, sugar, and, usually, rum or brandy. [< Arabic *shurb* drink]

shrub ber y (shrub′ər ē), *n., pl.* **-ber ies.** 1 shrubs collectively or in a mass. 2 place planted with shrubs.

shrub by (shrub′ē), *adj.,* **-bi er, -bi est.** 1 like shrubs. 2 covered with shrubs. 3 consisting of shrubs.

shrug (shrug), *v.,* **shrugged, shrug ging,** *n.* —*v.t., v.i.* raise (the shoulders) as an expression of dislike, doubt, indifference, impatience, etc. —*n.* 1 act of shrugging. 2 a woman's short sweater or jacket. [Middle English *schruggen*]

shrunk (shrungk), *v.* a pp. and a pt. of **shrink.**

shrunk en (shrung′kən), *adj.* grown smaller; shriveled: *a shrunken face, a shrunken fortune.* —*v.* a pp. of **shrink.**

shuck (shuk), *n.* 1 husk, pod, or shell, especially the outer covering or strippings of corn, chestnuts, hickory nuts, etc. 2 shell of an oyster or clam. —*v.t.* 1 remove the husk, pod, or shell from: *shuck corn.* 2 INFORMAL. take off; remove: *I like to shuck my shoes when I'm indoors.* [origin uncertain] —**shuck′er,** *n.*

shud der (shud′ər), *v.i.* tremble with horror, fear, cold, etc.: *shudder at the sight of a snake.* See **shiver**[1] for synonym study. —*n.* a trembling; quivering. [Middle English *shodderen*] —**shud′der ing ly,** *adv.*

shud der y (shud′ər ē), *adj.* characterized by or causing shudders.

shuf fle (shuf′əl), *v.,* **-fled, -fling,** *n.* —*v.i.* 1 walk without lifting the feet: *The old man shuffles feebly along.* 2 dance with scraping motions of the feet. 3 act or answer in a tricky way. —*v.t.* 1 scrape or drag (the feet). 2 mix (a deck of cards) so as to change the order. 3 push about; thrust or throw with clumsy haste: *He shuffled on his clothes and ran out of the house.* 4 move about this way and that; shift about: *shuffle the papers on one's desk.* 5 put or bring in a tricky way. **6 shuffle off,** get rid of.

—*n.* 1 a scraping or dragging movement of the feet. 2 a dance or dance step with a shuffle. 3 a shuffling of a deck of cards. 4 the right or turn to shuffle (cards). 5 movement this way and that. 6 an unfair act; trick; evasion: *Through some legal shuffle he secured a new trial.*

[perhaps < Low German *schuffeln.* Related to SHOVEL.] —**shuf′fler,** *n.*

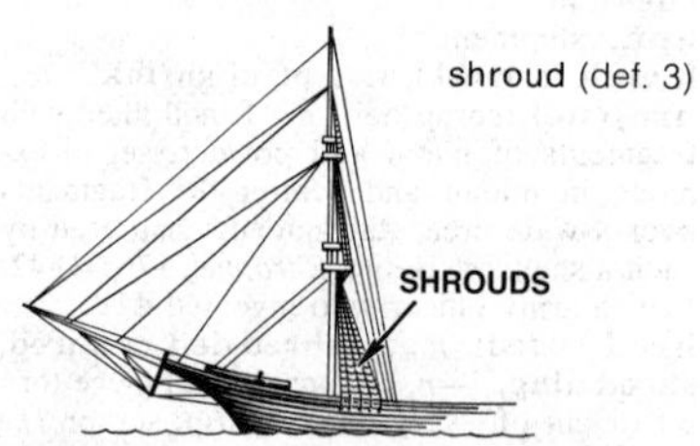

shroud (def. 3)

shuf fle board (shuf′əl bôrd′, shuf′əl-bōrd′), *n.* 1 game in which players use long sticks to push large disks along a flat surface to various numbered spaces. 2 surface on which it is played.

shun (shun), *v.t.,* **shunned, shun ning.** keep away from because of dislike: *She was lazy and shunned work.* See **avoid** for synonym study. [Old English *scunian*] —**shun′ner,** *n.*

shun pike (shun′pīk′), *n.* INFORMAL. road taken to avoid paying toll on a turnpike or to avoid major highways.

shunt (shunt), *v.t.* 1 move out of the way; turn aside. 2 put aside; get rid of; sidetrack. 3 switch (a train) from one track to another. 4 carry (a part of a current) by means of a shunt. —*v.i.* move out of the way; turn aside. —*n.* 1 a turning aside; shift. 2 a railroad switch. 3 wire or other conductor joining two points in an electric circuit and forming a path through which a part of the current may pass. Shunts are used to regulate the amount of current passing through the main circuit. [Middle English *shunten*] —**shunt′er,** *n.*

shush (shush, shůsh), *v.t., v.i., n., interj.* hush.

shut (shut), *v.,* **shut, shut ting,** *adj.* —*v.t.* 1 close (a receptacle or opening) by pushing or pulling a lid, door, some part, etc., into place: *shut a box, shut a window, shut a gate.* See **close**[1] for synonym study. 2 close (the eyes, a knife, a book, etc.) by bringing parts together. 3 close tight; close securely; close doors or other openings of: *shut a house for the summer.* 4 enclose; confine: *The criminal was shut in prison.* 5 close (the mind, etc.) to something as if to deny its existence: *We should shut our ears to gossip.* —*v.i.* become shut; be closed: *The great gates slowly shut.*

shut down, a close by lowering. **b** close (a factory, mine, etc.) for a time; stop work. **c** settle down so as to cover or envelop. **d** INFORMAL. put a stop or check on.

shut in, keep from going out.

shut off, turn off; close; obstruct; check; bar.

shut out, a keep from coming in: *The curtains shut out the light.* **b** defeat (a team, etc.) without allowing it to score.

shut up, a shut the doors and windows of. **b** INFORMAL. stop talking; stop from talking. **c** keep from going out.

—*adj.* closed; fastened up; enclosed.

[Old English *scyttan* bolt up]

shut down (shut′doun′), *n.* a shutting down; closing of a factory, mine, etc., for a time.

shut-in (shut′in′), *adj.* kept in; held in; confined. —*n.* person who is kept from going out by sickness, weakness, etc.

shut out (shut′out′), *n.* 1 defeat of a team without allowing it to score. 2 lockout.

shut ter (shut′ər), *n.* 1 a movable cover for a window. 2 a movable cover, slide, etc., for closing an opening. 3 device that opens and closes in front of the lens of a camera to regulate the length of time that the film is exposed. 4 person or thing that shuts. —*v.t.* put a shutter or shutters on or over.

shut ter bug (shut′ər bug′), *n.* SLANG. devotee of photography.

shut tle (shut′l), *n., v.,* **-tled, -tling.** —*n.* 1 device that carries the thread from one side of the web to the other in weaving. 2 a similar device on which thread is wound, used in knitting, tatting, and embroidery. 3 the sliding holder for the lower thread in a sewing machine, which moves back and forth once for each stitch. 4 anything characterized by a back-and-forth motion. 5 bus, train, airplane, etc., that runs back and forth regularly over a short distance. —*v.i., v.t.* 1 move quickly to and fro. 2 transport or be transported by shuttle. [Old English *scytel* a dart < *scēotan* to shoot]

shut tle cock (shut′l kok′), *n.* a cork with feathers or, often, a light plastic webbing stuck in one end, hit back and forth in badminton; bird. —*v.t.* throw or send backward and forward; toss to and fro.

shy[1] (shī), *adj.,* **shy er, shy est** or **shi er, shi est,** *v.,* **shied, shy ing,** *n., pl.* **shies.** —*adj.* 1 uncomfortable in company; bashful. See synonym study below. 2 easily frightened away; timid: *A deer is a shy animal.*

3 cautious; wary. 4 not having enough; short; scant: *The store is shy on children's clothing.* 5 **fight shy of,** keep away from; avoid. 6 **shy of,** INFORMAL. **a** having little; short of. **b** not coming up to; lacking. —*v.i.* 1 start back or aside suddenly: *The horse shied at the newspaper blowing along the ground.* 2 draw back; shrink. —*n.* a sudden start to one side. [Old English *scēoh*] —**shy′ness,** *n.*

Syn. *adj.* 1 **Shy, bashful** mean uncomfortable in the presence or company of others. **Shy** suggests lack of self-confidence and is shown by a reserved or timid manner: *People who appear snobbish are often really shy.* **Bashful** suggests shrinking by nature from being noticed and is shown by awkward and embarrassed behavior in the presence of others: *The boy was too bashful to ask her to dance.*

shy² (shī), *v.,* **shied, shy ing,** *n., pl.* **shies.** —*v.t., v.i.* throw; fling: *shy a stone at a tree.* —*n.* a throw; fling. [origin uncertain]

Shy lock (shī′lok), *n.* 1 the relentless and revengeful moneylender in Shakespeare's play *The Merchant of Venice.* 2 a greedy moneylender.

shy ly (shī′lē), *adv.* in a shy manner.

shy ster (shī′stər), *n.* INFORMAL. lawyer or other person who uses improper or questionable methods in his business or profession. [origin uncertain]

si (sē), *n.* ti.

Si, silicon.

Si am (sī am′, sī′am), *n.* 1 former name of **Thailand.** 2 **Gulf of,** gulf of the South China Sea, bordered by the Malay Peninsula, Thailand, Cambodia, and South Vietnam.

Si a mese (sī′ə mēz′), *adj., n., pl.* **-mese.** Thai.

Siamese cat, any of a breed of short-haired, blue-eyed cats, usually with light tan bodies and dark face, ears, feet, and tail, originally from Thailand.

Siamese twins, twins who are born joined together. [< Eng and Chang, 1811-1874, twin Siamese boys who were born joined together by a band of flesh between their chests]

Si an (sē′än′), *n.* city in central China. 1,500,000.

sib (sib), *adj.* related by blood; closely related; akin. —*n.* 1 kinsman or kinswoman; relative. 2 one's kin; kinsfolk; relatives. [Old English *sibb*]

Si be li us (sə bā′lē əs), *n.* **Jean,** 1865-1957, Finnish composer.

Si ber i a (sī bir′ē ə), *n.* region in N Asia, extending from the Ural Mountains to the Pacific. It is part of the Soviet Union. —**Si ber′i an,** *adj., n.*

Siberian husky, any of a breed of strong, medium-sized sled dogs originating in Siberia, having a thick coat and a brush tail; husky.

sib i lance (sib′ə ləns), *n.* 1 a being sibilant. 2 a hissing sound.

sib i lant (sib′ə lənt), *adj.* 1 hissing. 2 produced by forcing the breath stream through a very narrow passage. The *ch* in *machine* is a sibilant sound. —*n.* a sibilant sound, letter, or symbol. *S* and *sh* are sibilants. [< Latin *sibilantem*]

sib ling (sib′ling), *n.* a brother or sister. An only child has no siblings.

sib yl (sib′əl), *n.* 1 any of several prophetesses that the ancient Greeks and Romans consulted about the future. 2 prophetess; fortuneteller. [< Latin *Sibylla* < Greek]

sib yl line (sib′ə lēn, sib′ə līn, sib′ə lən), *adj.* of or like a sibyl; prophetic; mysterious.

sic¹ (sik, sēk), *adv.* LATIN. so; thus.

➤ **Sic** is used to show or emphasize the fact that something has been copied just as it is in the original. *Sic,* italicized and set in brackets, is used to mark an error in quoted matter: The letter was headed "Wensday [*sic*], Jan. 2."

sic² (sik), *v.t.,* **sicked, sick ing.** 1 set upon or attack (used chiefly as a command to a dog). 2 incite to set upon or attack: *sic a dog on a stranger.* Also, **sick.** [perhaps variant of *seek*]

sic ca tive (sik′ə tiv), *n.* a drying substance, especially a drier used in painting. [< Late Latin *siccativus* < Latin *siccare* make dry < *siccus* dry]

Si cil ian (sə sil′yən), *adj.* of or having to do with Sicily or its people. —*n.* native or inhabitant of Sicily.

Sic i ly (sis′ə lē), *n.* island in the Mediterranean, near the SW tip of the Italian peninsula, a part of Italy since 1860. It is the largest island in the Mediterranean. 4,809,000 pop.; 9900 sq. mi.

sick¹ (sik), *adj.* 1 in poor health; having some disease; ill. 2 inclined to vomit; feeling nausea; vomiting. 3 of or for a sick person; connected with sickness: *sick leave, sick pay.* 4 showing sickness: *a sick look.* 5 thoroughly tired; weary: *She is sick of school.* 6 disgusted: *I am sick and tired of his complaints.* 7 affected with sorrow, longing, or some other strong feeling: *sick at heart, sick with hate.* 8 not in the proper condition: *sick soil.* 9 mentally ill. 10 grisly; cruel: *a sick joke.* —*n.* **the sick,** sick people. [Old English *sēoc*]

sick² (sik), *v.t.* sic².

sick bay, a place on a ship used as a hospital.

sick bed (sik′bed′), *n.* bed of a sick person.

sick call, in military use: 1 a signal to those who are sick to report to the hospital or medical officer. 2 the assembling of those who are sick in answer to this call.

sick en (sik′ən), *v.i.* become sick: *The bird sickened when kept in the cage.* —*v.t.* make sick: *The sight of blood sickened him.* —**sick′en er,** *n.*

sick en ing (sik′ə ning), *adj.* making sick; causing nausea, faintness, disgust, or loathing. —**sick′en ing ly,** *adv.*

sick headache, 1 headache accompanied by nausea. 2 migraine.

sick ish (sik′ish), *adj.* 1 somewhat sick. 2 somewhat sickening. —**sick′ish ly,** *adv.* —**sick′ish ness,** *n.*

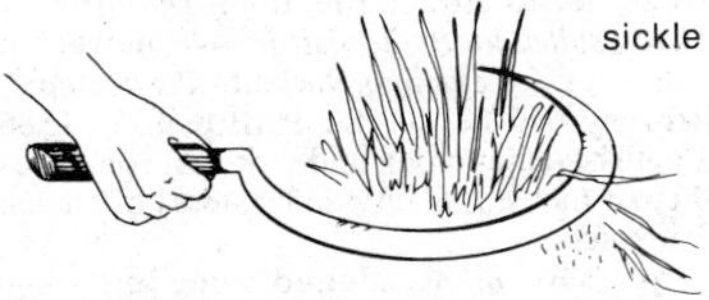
sickle

sick le (sik′əl), *n.* tool consisting of a short, curved blade on a short handle, used for cutting grass, etc. [< Latin *secula,* related to *secare* to cut]

sick leave, 1 leave of absence given to a worker because of illness. 2 number of days allowed for this each year without loss of pay.

sickle cell, an abnormal, sickle-shaped red blood cell.

sickle cell anemia, a hereditary form of anemia in which the normally round red blood cells become sickle cells, ineffective in carrying oxygen.

hat, āge, fär; let, ēqual, tėrm;
it, īce; hot, ōpen, ôrder;
oil, out; cup, pu̇t, rüle;
ch, child; ng, long; sh, she;
th, thin; ᴛʜ, then; zh, measure;

ə represents *a* in about, *e* in taken, *i* in pencil, *o* in lemon, *u* in circus.

< = from, derived from, taken from.

sick ly (sik′lē), *adj.,* **-li er, -li est,** *adv.* —*adj.* 1 often sick; not strong; not healthy. 2 of, having to do with, caused by, or suggesting sickness: *Her skin is a sickly yellow.* 3 causing sickness: *a sickly climate.* 4 faint; weak; pale: *a sickly glow.* —*adv.* in a sick manner. —**sick′li ness,** *n.*

sick ness (sik′nis), *n.* 1 an abnormal, unhealthy condition; disease; illness. 2 a particular disease. 3 nausea; vomiting.

sick room (sik′rüm′, sik′ru̇m′), *n.* room in which a sick person is cared for.

sic tran sit glo ri a mun di (sik tran′sit glôr′ē ə mun′dī; sik tran′sit glōr′ē ə mun′dī), LATIN. so passes away the glory of the world.

Sid dons (sid′nz), *n.* **Sarah Kemble,** 1755-1831, British actress.

sid dur (sid′u̇r), *n.* the Jewish prayer book, written in Hebrew and Aramaic. [< Hebrew *siddūr,* literally, order]

side (sīd), *n., adj., v.,* **sid ed, sid ing.** —*n.* 1 surface or line bounding a thing: *the sides of a square.* 2 one of the two surfaces of an object that is not the front, back, top, or bottom: *a door at the side of a house.* 3 either of the two surfaces of paper, cloth, etc.: *Write only on one side of the paper.* 4 a particular surface: *the side of the moon turned toward the earth.* 5 the slope of a hill or bank. 6 bank or shore of a river. 7 either the right or left part of a thing; either part or region beyond a central line: *the west side of town, our side of the street.* 8 either the right or the left part of the body of a person or animal: *a pain in one's side.* 9 aspect or view of someone or something: *the better side of one's nature, hear all sides of an argument.* 10 group of persons who stand up for their beliefs, opinions, ways of doing things, etc., against another group: *Both sides are ready for the contest.* 11 the position, course, or part of one person or party against another: *the winning side of a dispute.* 12 part of a family; line of descent: *He is English on his mother's side.* 13 BRITISH SLANG. pretentious airs; arrogance.

by one's side, near one.

on the side, **a** INFORMAL. in addition to one's regular or ordinary duties. **b** served as a side dish.

side by side, beside one another.

split one's sides, laugh very hard.

take sides, place oneself with one person or group against another.

—*adj.* 1 at one side; on one side: *side streets, the side aisles of a theater.* 2 from one side: *a side view.* 3 toward one side: *a side glance.* 4 less important; subsidiary: *a side issue.*

—*v.t., v.i.* 1 provide with sides. 2 **side against,** oppose. 3 **side with,** take the part of; favor.

[Old English *sīde*]

side arm (sīd′ärm′), *adj.* throwing or thrown from the side with the arm swung nearly parallel to the ground; not overhand or underhand: *a sidearm pitcher, a sidearm pitch.* —*adv.* in a sidearm manner.
side arms, sword, revolver, bayonet, or other weapon carried at the side or in the belt.
side board (sīd′bôrd′, sīd′bōrd′), *n.* a low cabinet with drawers and shelves for holding silver and linen, and space on top for dishes; buffet.

sideburns

side burns (sīd′bėrnz′), *n.pl.* whiskers in front of the ears, especially when worn long with the chin shaved. [alteration of *burnsides*]
side car (sīd′kär′), *n.* car for a passenger, baggage, etc., attached to the side of a motorcycle.
-sided, *combining form.* having ____ sides: *Many-sided = having many sides.*
side dish, dish served in addition to the main dish of a course.
side effect, a secondary effect or reaction, usually undesirable or unpleasant: *Many drugs produce side effects on some people.*
side kick (sīd′kik′), *n.* INFORMAL. partner or close friend.
side light (sīd′līt′), *n.* 1 light coming from the side. 2 incidental information about a subject: *amusing sidelights in a biography.* 3 either of two lights carried by a moving ship at night. There is a red one on the port side and a green one on the starboard side.
side line (sīd′līn′), *n., v.,* **-lined, -lin ing.** —*n.* 1 line at the side of something. 2 line that marks the limit of play on the side of the playing area in football, tennis, etc. 3 **sidelines,** *pl.* the area just outside these lines: *The spectators watched the game from the sidelines.* 3 an additional line of goods or of business. —*v.t.* put on the sidelines; make inactive: *The team's quarterback was sidelined by an injury.*
side long (sīd′lông′, sīd′long′), *adj., adv.* to one side; toward the side.
side piece (sīd′pēs′), *n.* piece forming a side or part of a side, or fixed by the side, of something.
si der e al (sī dir′ē əl), *adj.* 1 of or having to do with the stars or constellations. 2 measured by the apparent motion of the stars: *sidereal time.* A **sidereal day** is about four minutes shorter than a mean solar day. [< Latin *sidereus* < *sidus* star]
sid er ite (sid′ə rīt), *n.* an iron ore occurring in various forms and colors. *Formula:* $FeCO_3$ [< Greek *sidēritēs* loadstone < *sidēros* iron]
side sad dle (sīd′sad′l), *n.* a woman's saddle so made that both of the rider's legs are on the same side of the horse. —*adv.* with both legs on the same side of the horse: *ride sidesaddle.*
side show (sīd′shō′), *n.* 1 a small show in connection with a principal one: *the sideshows of a circus.* 2 any minor proceeding or affair connected with a more important one.
side slip (sīd′slip′), *n., v.,* **-slipped, -slip ping.** —*n.* 1 a slip or skid to one side. 2 the slipping to one side and downward of an aircraft in flight. —*v.i.* slip to one side; do a sideslip: *The car sideslipped as it rounded the curve.*
side split ting (sīd′split′ing), *adj.* extremely funny: *a sidesplitting joke.*
side step (sīd′step′), *v.,* **-stepped, -step ping.** —*v.i.* step aside. —*v.t.* avoid by stepping aside; evade: *sidestep a punch, sidestep a responsibility.* **—side′step′per,** *n.*
side step, a step or stepping to one side.
side stroke (sīd′strōk′), *n.* a swimming stroke done lying on one's side and pulling alternately with the arms while performing a scissors kick.
side swipe (sīd′swīp′), *v.,* **-swiped, -swip ing,** *n.* —*v.t., v.t.* hit with a sweeping blow along the side. —*n.* a sweeping blow along the side.
side track (sīd′trak′), *n.* a railroad siding. —*v.t.* 1 switch (a train, etc.) to a sidetrack. 2 put aside; turn aside: *The teacher refused to be sidetracked by questions on other subjects.*
side walk (sīd′wôk′), *n.* place to walk at the side of a street, usually paved.
side wall (sīd′wôl′), *n.* the side portion of a tire between the tread and the rim of the wheel.
side ward (sīd′wərd), *adj., adv.* toward one side.
side wards (sīd′wərdz), *adv.* sideward.
side way (sīd′wā′), *adv., adj.* sideways.
side ways (sīd′wāz′), *adv., adj.* 1 toward one side. 2 from one side. 3 with one side toward the front.
side-wheel (sīd′hwēl′), *adj.* (of a steamboat) having a paddle wheel on each side.
side-wheel er (sīd′hwē′lər), *n.* a side-wheel steamer.
side whiskers, whiskers growing on the cheek or side of the face.
side wind er (sīd′wīn′dər), *n.* 1 a small rattlesnake of the southwestern United States that travels in a sideways direction by looping its body. 2 a heavy blow delivered from the side.
side wise (sīd′wīz′), *adv., adj.* sideways.
sid ing (sī′ding), *n.* 1 a short railroad track to which cars can be switched from a main track. 2 boards, shingles, etc., forming the outside walls of a wooden building.
si dle (sī′dl), *v.,* **-dled, -dling,** *n.* —*v.i.* 1 move sideways. 2 move sideways slowly so as not to attract attention: *The little boy shyly sidled up to the visitor.* —*n.* movement sideways. [< *sideling,* variant of *sidelong*]
Sid ney (sid′nē), *n.* Sir **Philip,** 1554-1586, English soldier, poet, and writer of romances.
Si don (sīd′n), *n.* city and seaport of ancient Phoenicia.
siege (sēj), *n., v.,* **sieged, sieg ing.** —*n.* 1 the surrounding of a fortified place by enemy forces trying to capture it; a besieging or a being besieged: *The Japanese laid siege to Corregidor.* 2 any long or persistent effort to overcome resistance; any long-continued attack: *a siege of illness.* 3 **lay siege to,** a besiege. b attempt to win or get by long and persistent effort. —*v.t.* besiege. [< Old French, seat, siege, ultimately < Latin *sedere* sit]
Sieg fried (sēg′frēd), *n.* (in Germanic legends) a hero who killed a dragon and won the treasure of the Nibelungs.
Si en a (sē en′ə), *n.* city in central Italy, which has a famous cathedral. 61,000.
Sien kie wicz (shen kyā′vich), *n.* **Henryk,** 1846-1916, Polish novelist.
si en na (sē en′ə), *n.* 1 any of various mixtures of clay and oxides of iron and manganese, used as a pigment. In its natural state, it is yellowish-brown and is called **raw sienna.** After heating, it becomes reddish-brown and is called **burnt sienna.** 2 a yellowish brown or reddish brown. [short for Italian *terra di Sien(n)a* earth from Siena, Italy]
si er ra (sē er′ə), *n.* chain of hills or mountains with jagged peaks. [< Spanish, literally, a saw < Latin *serra*]
Si er ra Le o ne (sē er′ə lē ō′nē; sē er′ə lē-ōn′), country on the W coast of Africa, a member of the Commonwealth of Nations. 2,512,000 pop.; 27,900 sq. mi. *Capital:* Freetown. **—Si er′ra Le o′ne an.**
Si er ra Ma dre (sē er′ə mä′drā), mountain ranges in E and W Mexico. Between these ranges is the central plateau of Mexico.
Si er ra Ne vad a (sē er′ə nə vad′ə; sē-er′ə nə vä′də), mountain range in E California. The highest peak, Mount Whitney, is 14,495 ft.
si es ta (sē es′tə), *n.* a nap or rest taken at noon or in the afternoon. [< Spanish < Latin *sexta (hora)* sixth (hour) of the Roman day, noon. Doublet of SEXT.]
sieur (syœr), *n.* a former French title of respect for a man; Sir. [< Old French < Latin *seniorem.* Doublet of SEIGNEUR, SEIGNIOR.]
sieve (siv), *n., v.,* **sieved, siev ing.** —*n.* utensil having holes that let liquids and smaller pieces pass through, but not the larger pieces: *Shaking flour through a sieve removes lumps.* —*v.t., v.i.* put or pass through a sieve. [Old English *sife*] **—sieve′like′,** *adj.*
sieve cell, (in botany) an elongated cell whose thin walls have perforations which allow communication between adjacent cells of a similar nature. Sieve cells form the essential element of the phloem of lower vascular plants.
sieve tube, (in botany) a tubelike structure composed of thin, elongated cells connected through perforations in their end walls, forming the essential element of the phloem of higher vascular plants.
sift (sift), *v.t.* 1 separate the large pieces of (a substance) from the small pieces by shaking in a sieve: *Sift the gravel and put the larger stones in another pile.* 2 put through a sieve: *Sift sugar on the top of the cake.* 3 examine very carefully: *sift all available evidence.* —*v.i.* 1 use a sieve. 2 fall through, or as if through, a sieve: *The snow sifted softly down.* [Old English *siftan* < *sife* sieve] **—sift′er,** *n.*
sig., 1 signal. 2 signature.
Sig., 1 Signor. 2 Signore.
sigh (sī), *v.i.* 1 let out a very long, deep breath because one is sad, tired, relieved, etc. 2 make a sound like a sigh: *The wind sighed in the treetops.* 3 wish very much; long; yearn. 4 lament with sighing: *sigh over one's unhappy fate.* —*v.t.* say or express with a sigh. —*n.* act or sound of sighing: *a sigh of relief.* [Middle English *sighen,* ultimately < Old English *sīcan*] **—sigh′er,** *n.*
sight (sīt), *n.* 1 power of seeing; vision. 2 act or fact of seeing; look: *love at first sight.* 3 examination; inspection; scrutiny. 4 limit or range of seeing: *Land was in sight.* 5 thing

hat, āge, fär; let, ēqual, tėrm;
it, īce; hot, ōpen, ôrder;
oil, out; cup, pu̇t, rüle;
ch, child; ng, long; sh, she;
th, thin; ᴛʜ, then; zh, measure;

ə represents *a* in about, *e* in taken, *i* in pencil, *o* in lemon, *u* in circus.

< = from, derived from, taken from.

seen; view; glimpse: *You are indeed a sight for sore eyes.* 6 something worth seeing: *see the sights of the city.* 7 something that looks bad or odd: *She is a sight in that ugly dress.* 8 device on a gun, surveying instrument, etc., through which the line of direction to an object is set for aiming or observing. 9 the aim or observation taken by such devices. 10 way of looking or thinking; regard; estimation; judgment; opinion.
at sight, as soon as seen.
catch sight of, see: *I caught sight of them.*
in sight of, where one can see or be seen by.
know by sight, know sufficiently to recognize when seen.
on sight, as soon as seen; at sight.
out of sight of, a where one cannot see: *out of sight of land.* **b** where one cannot be seen by: *out of sight of the neighbors.*
sight unseen, without seeing or examining in advance.
—*v.t.* 1 see: *sight land.* 2 aim at or observe (an object) by means of sights: *sight a star.* 3 adjust the sight or align the sights of (a gun, instrument, etc.). 4 provide with a sight or sights. —*v.i.* take aim or observation by means of a sight or sights: *The hunter sighted carefully before firing his gun.*
[Old English *(ge)siht.* Related to SEE[1].]

sight draft, a written order from one bank to another, requiring a certain amount of money to be paid on demand.

sight less (sīt′lis), *adj.* 1 unable to see; blind. 2 unable to be seen; invisible. —**sight′less ness,** *n.*

sight ly (sīt′lē), *adj.,* **-li er, -li est.** 1 pleasing to the sight. 2 affording a fine view. —**sight′li ness,** *n.*

sight-read (sīt′rēd′), *v.t., v.i.,* **-read** (-red′), **-read ing.** read at first sight; engage or be skilled in sight reading.

sight reading, a reading of a piece of music or passage in a foreign language at first sight.

sight see (sīt′sē′), *v.i.* go sightseeing.

sight see ing (sīt′sē′ing), *n.* a going around to see objects or places of interest: *a weekend of sightseeing.* —*adj.* that goes around to see objects or places of interest: *a sightseeing bus.*

sight se er (sīt′sē′ər), *n.* person who goes around to see objects or places of interest.

sig ma (sig′mə), *n.* the 18th letter of the Greek alphabet (Σ, ς).

sig moid (sig′moid), *adj.* 1 shaped like the letter S. 2 of or having to do with the sigmoid flexure. 3 shaped like the letter C. [< Greek *sigmoeidēs* < *sigma* sigma + *eidos* form]

sigmoid flexure, the S-shaped bend of the colon just above the rectum.

sign (sīn), *n.* 1 any mark or thing used to mean, represent, or point out something: *The signs for addition, subtraction, multiplication, and division are* +, −, ×, ÷. 2 motion or gesture used to mean, represent, or point out something: *talk to a deaf person by signs. A nod is a sign of agreement.* 3 an inscribed board, space, etc., serving for advertisement, information, etc.: *The sign reads, "Keep off the grass."* 4 indication: *Careful scrutiny revealed signs that someone had broken in.* See **mark**[1] for synonym study. 5 indication of a coming event: *The robin is a sign of spring.* See synonym study below. 6 a trace: *no signs of life. The hunter found signs of deer.* 7 any of the twelve divisions of the zodiac, each named for a constellation and each denoted by a special symbol.
—*v.t.* 1 attach one's name to: *Sign this letter.* 2 write: *Sign your initials here.* 3 hire by a written agreement: *sign a new ballplayer.* 4 mark with a sign. 5 communicate by gesture: *sign assent.* —*v.i.* 1 attach one's name to show authority, agreement, obligation, etc.; write one's name: *sign on the dotted line.* 2 accept employment. 3 make a sign or signal.
sign away, give away by signing one's name: *sign away one's inheritance.*
sign off, stop broadcasting.
sign over, hand over by signing one's name.
sign up, enlist, join, etc., by written agreement: *sign up as a new member.*
[< Old French *signe* < Latin *signum*] —**sign′er,** *n.*
Syn. *n.* 5 **Sign, omen** mean an indication of a coming event. **Sign** applies to something which provides objective evidence that the event can reasonably be expected: *Those big, black clouds are signs of a storm.* **Omen** applies to something which, particularly from a religious or superstitious point of view, is regarded as extraordinary and as a promise of something good or bad to come: *He believed his dream was an omen of success.*

sig nal (sig′nəl), *n., v.,* **-naled, -nal ing** or **-nalled, -nal ling,** *adj.* —*n.* 1 sign giving notice, warning, or pointing out something: *A red light is a signal of danger.* 2 a wave, current, impulse, etc., serving to convey sounds and images in communications by radio, television, etc. 3 an inciting action or movement; exciting cause; occasion. —*v.t.* 1 make a signal or signals to: *signal a car to stop by raising one's hand.* 2 make known by a signal or signals: *A bell signals the end of a school period.* —*v.i.* give notice, warning, information, etc., by signal. —*adj.* 1 used as a signal or in signaling: *a signal flag.* 2 remarkable; striking; notable: *The airplane was a signal invention.* [< Late Latin *signalis* < Latin *signum* sign] —**sig′nal er,** *n.*

Signal Corps, branch of the United States Army in charge of communications and communication equipment.

sig nal ize (sig′nə līz), *v.t.,* **-ized, -iz ing.** 1 make stand out; make notable: *The year 1969 was signalized by man's first landing on the moon.* 2 point out; mention specially; draw attention to.

sig nal ly (sig′nə lē), *adv.* in a remarkable manner; strikingly; notably.

sig nal man (sig′nəl mən, sig′nəl man′), *n., pl.* **-men.** man in charge of the signals on a railroad, in the army or navy, etc.

sig na to ry (sig′nə tôr′ē, sig′nə tōr′ē), *n., pl.* **-ries,** *adj.* —*n.* 1 a signer of a document. 2 country, company, etc., on whose behalf a person signs a document. —*adj.* signing: *signatory delegates.*

sig na ture (sig′nə chər, sig′nə chu̇r), *n.* 1 a person's name written by himself. 2 act of writing one's name. 3 signs printed at the beginning of a staff to show the key and time of a piece of music; key signature or time signature. 4 in printing: **a** letter or number printed at the bottom of the first page of every sheet, telling how it is to be folded and arranged in pages. **b** sheet with such a mark, especially when folded. 5 music, sound effects, etc., used to identify a radio or television program. [< Late Latin *signatura* < Latin *signum* sign]

sign board (sīn′bôrd′, sīn′bōrd′), *n.* board having a sign, notice, advertisement, inscription, etc., on it.

sig net (sig′nit), *n.* 1 a small seal: *The order was sealed with the king's signet.* 2 stamp or impression made by a signet. —*v.t.* stamp with a signet. [< Old French, diminutive of *signe* sign < Latin *signum* seal]

signet ring, a finger ring set with a signet.

sig nif i cance (sig nif′ə kəns), *n.* 1 importance; consequence: *a matter of great significance.* 2 meaning: *She did not understand the significance of my nod.* 3 significant quality; expressiveness.

sig nif i cant (sig nif′ə kənt), *adj.* 1 full of meaning; important; of consequence: *July 4, 1776, is a significant date for Americans.* 2 having a meaning; expressive: *Smiles are significant of pleasure.* 3 having or expressing a hidden meaning: *A significant nod from my friend warned me to stop talking.* [< Latin *significantem* signifying] —**sig nif′i cant ly,** *adv.*

sig ni fi ca tion (sig′nə fə kā′shən), *n.* 1 meaning; sense; import. 2 act or process of signifying.

sig nif i ca tive (sig nif′ə kā′tiv), *adj.* 1 serving to signify; having a meaning. 2 significant or suggestive.

sig ni fy (sig′nə fī), *v.,* **-fied, -fy ing.** —*v.t.* 1 be a sign of; mean: *"Oh!" signifies surprise.* 2 make known by signs, words, or actions: *signify consent with a nod.* —*v.i.* have importance; be of consequence; matter. [< Latin *significare* < *signum* sign + *facere* to make] —**sig′ni fi′er,** *n.*

sign language, system of communication in which motions, especially of the hands, stand for words, ideas, etc.

si gnor (sē′nyôr), *n., pl.* ***si gno ri*** (sē-nyôr′ē). ITALIAN. 1 Mr. 2 gentleman.

si gno ra (sē nyôr′ə), *n., pl.* ***si gno re*** (sē-nyôr′ā). ITALIAN. 1 Mrs. or Madame. 2 lady.

si gno re (sē nyôr′ā), *n., pl.* ***si gno ri*** (sē-nyôr′ē). ITALIAN. 1 sir. 2 gentleman.

si gno ri na (sē′nyə rē′nə), *n., pl.* ***-ne*** (-nā). ITALIAN. 1 Miss. 2 a young lady.

sign post (sīn′pōst′), *n.* post having signs, notices, or directions on it; guidepost.

Sig urd (sig′ėrd′), *n.* (in Scandinavian legends), a hero who slays a dragon, identified with the German Siegfried.

si ka (sē′kə), *n.* a small deer native to Japan and China, having a brown coat that is spotted with white in the summer. [< Japanese *shika* deer]

Sikh (sēk), *n.* member of a religious sect of northwestern India, founded in the early 1500's as an offshoot of Hinduism. Sikhs are famous as fighters. —*adj.* of or having to do with the Sikhs. [< Hindi *sikh* disciple]

Sikh ism (sē′kiz′əm), *n.* the religious system and practices of the Sikhs.

Sik kim (sik′əm), *n.* small country in the Himalayas, between Tibet and India. It is a protectorate of India. 191,000 pop.; 2800 sq. mi. *Capital:* Gangtok.

si lage (sī′lij), *n.* green fodder for winter feeding of livestock, stored in a silo or other airtight chamber and preserved by partial fermentation; ensilage. [< *ensilage,* after *silo*]

si lence (sī′ləns), *n., v.,* **-lenced, -lenc ing,** *interj.* —*n.* 1 absence of sound or noise; stillness. 2 a keeping still; not talking. 3 omission of mention. —*v.t.* 1 stop the speech or noise of; make silent; quiet. 2 make silent by restraint or prohibition; repress: *silence the press, silence an uprising.* 3 stop (enemy guns, etc.) from firing by destroying or disabling with return fire. —*interj.* be silent! [< Old French < Latin *silentium* < *silere* be silent]

si lenc er (sī′lən sər), *n.* 1 person or thing that silences. 2 device which muffles the sound of a gun.

si lent (sī′lənt), *adj.* 1 quiet; still; noiseless: *a silent house, the silent hills.* 2 not speaking; saying little or nothing: *Pupils must be silent during the study hour.* See synonym study below. 3 not spoken; not said out loud: *a silent prayer, silent opposition. The "e" in "time" is a silent letter.* 4 not active; taking no open or active part. A silent partner in a business has no share in managing the business. 5 omitting mention of something, as in a narrative. **—si′lent ly,** *adv.* **—si′lent ness,** *n.*

Syn. 2 **Silent, taciturn, reticent** mean saying little or nothing. **Silent** especially means not talkative, characteristically speaking only when necessary or saying very little: *She is a silent, thoughtful girl.* **Taciturn** means not fond of talking, being by nature inclined to be silent and avoid conversation: *He is a taciturn man, withdrawn and speaking only in monosyllables.* **Reticent** means disposed to keep silent, especially about private affairs: *be reticent about one's early life.*

silent butler, container with a handle and hinged top, into which crumbs may be brushed, ashtrays emptied, etc.

Si le nus (sī lē′nəs), *n.* (in Greek myths) the foster father of Bacchus and leader of the satyrs. He is represented as a short, stout, drunken old man.

Si le sia (sə lē′shə, sə lē′zhə; sī lē′shə, sī-lē′zhə), *n.* region in central Europe, most of which is now in Poland and Czechoslovakia. **—Si le′sian,** *adj., n.*

si lex (sī′leks), *n.* 1 silica. 2 a strong glass that is mostly quartz and resists heat. 3 **Silex,** trademark for a coffee maker made of this glass. [< Latin, flint]

silhouette (def. 1)

sil hou ette (sil′ü et′), *n., v.,* **-et ted, -et ting.** —*n.* 1 an outline portrait, especially in profile, cut out of a black paper or drawn and filled in with some single color. 2 a dark image outlined against a lighter background. 3 contour of a garment, figure, etc. —*v.t.* show in outline: *The mountain was silhouetted against the sky.* [< Étienne de *Silhouette,* 1709-1767, French finance minister]

sil i ca (sil′ə kə), *n.* a common hard, white or colorless compound, silicon dioxide. Flint, opal, and sand are forms of silica. *Formula:* SiO_2 [< New Latin < Latin *silex* flint]

sil i cate (sil′ə kit, sil′ə kāt), *n.* compound containing silicon with oxygen and a metal. Mica, soapstone, asbestos, and feldspar are silicates.

si li ceous (sə lish′əs), *adj.* containing or consisting of silica; resembling silica.

si lic ic (sə lis′ik), *adj.* 1 containing silicon or silica. 2 of or obtained from silicon or silica.

sil i con (sil′ə kən), *n.* a metalloid element found only combined with other elements, chiefly combined with oxygen in silica. Next to oxygen, silicon is the most abundant element in nature. The crystalline form is much used in steel as a deoxidizing and hardening agent. *Symbol:* Si; *atomic number* 14. See pages 326 and 327 for table. [< *silica*]

silicon dioxide, silica.

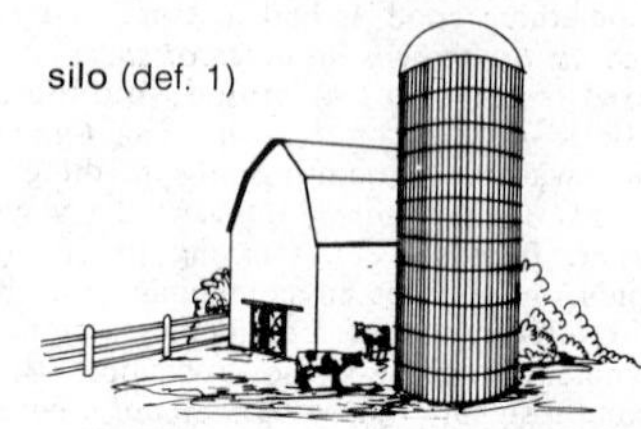

silo (def. 1)

sil i cone (sil′ə kōn), *n.* any of a large group of organic compounds based on a structure in which organic groups are attached to silicon, and obtained as oils, greases, plastics, and resins. Silicones are noted for their stability and their ability to resist extremes of heat and cold, and are used for lubricants, varnishes, and insulators.

sil i co sis (sil′ə kō′sis), *n.* disease of the lungs caused by continually breathing air filled with dust from silicates.

silk (silk), *n.* 1 a fine, soft, strong fiber spun by silkworms to form their cocoons. 2 thread or cloth made from this fiber. 3 garment of such material. 4 fiber like silk, produced by spiders, etc. 5 anything like silk: *corn silk.* —*adj.* of, like, or having to do with silk: *a silk dress, silk thread.* —*v.i.* (of corn) to produce silk. [Old English *sioloc,* ultimately < Greek *sērikos* silken < *Sēres* the Chinese] **—silk′like′,** *adj.*

silk cotton, 1 the silky, elastic down or fiber covering the seeds of a silk-cotton tree. 2 kapok.

silk-cot ton tree (silk′kot′n), any of a genus of trees of tropical America, the East Indies, and Africa, that bear large pods from which silk cotton is obtained.

silk en (sil′kən), *adj.* 1 made of silk: *a silken dress.* 2 like silk; smooth, soft, and glossy: *silken hair.* 3 resembling silk in being soft and smooth: *a silken manner, a silken voice.* 4 wearing silk clothes. 5 elegant; luxurious.

silk hat, top hat.

silk-screen (silk′skrēn′), *adj.* serigraphic.

silk-stock ing (silk′stok′ing), *adj.* 1 made up of or populated by people of wealth and social prominence: *a silk-stocking district.* 2 elegant; aristocratic.

silk worm (silk′wėrm′), *n.* any caterpillar that spins silk to form a cocoon, especially the larva of a domesticated moth, originally of Asia, that feeds on mulberry leaves.

silk y (sil′kē), *adj.,* **silk i er, silk i est.** 1 of or like silk; smooth, soft, and glossy; silken. 2 (in botany) covered with fine, soft, closely set hairs having a silklike gloss, as a leaf. **—silk′i ly,** *adv.* **—silk′i ness,** *n.*

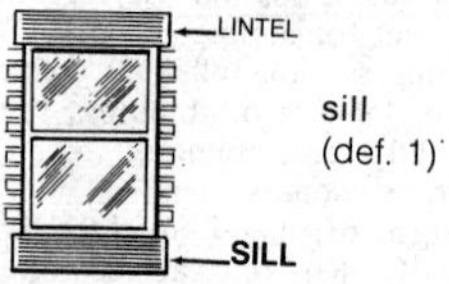

sill (def. 1)

sill (sil), *n.* 1 piece of wood, stone, etc., across the bottom of a door or window frame. 2 a large beam of wood, etc., on which an outside wall of a building rests. 3 an intrusive sheet of igneous rock found between older rock beds. See **volcano** for diagram. [Old English *syll*]

sil la bub (sil′ə bub), *n.* dessert made of cream, eggs, and wine sweetened and flavored. Also, **syllabub.** [origin uncertain]

sil ly (sil′ē), *adj.,* **-li er, -li est,** *n., pl.* **-lies.** —*adj.* 1 without sense or reason; foolish; nonsensical. See **foolish** for synonym study. 2 INFORMAL. stunned; dazed. 3 ARCHAIC. simple; innocent. —*n.* a silly or foolish person. [Old English *sǣlig* happy < *sǣl* happiness] **—sil′li ly,** *adv.* **—sil′li ness,** *n.*

si lo (sī′lō), *n., pl.* **-los.** 1 an airtight building or pit in which green fodder for livestock is stored. 2 a vertical shaft built underground with facilities for housing and launching missiles, rockets, etc. [< Spanish < Latin *sirus* < Greek *siros* grain cellar]

silt (silt), *n.* 1 very fine particles of earth, sand, etc., carried by moving water and deposited as sediment: *The harbor is being choked up with silt.* 2 deposit of sediment occurring as a stratum in soil. —*v.t., v.i.* fill or choke up with silt. [probably related to SALT]

silt y (sil′tē), *adj.,* **silt i er, silt i est.** of, like, or full of silt.

Si lur i an (sə lu̇r′ē ən, sī lu̇r′ē ən), *n.* 1 the geological period of the Paleozoic era after the Ordovician and before the Devonian, characterized by the development of early land invertebrate animals and land plants. See chart under **geology.** 2 the rocks formed during this period. —*adj.* of or having to do with this period or its rocks. [< *Silures,* ancient people of Wales in whose region such rocks were found]

sil van (sil′vən), *adj.* sylvan.

sil ver (sil′vər), *n.* 1 a shining white, precious metallic element occurring both natively and in combination, characterized in a pure state by its great malleability and ductility. Silver is superior to any other substance in its ability to conduct heat and electricity. It is used for coins, jewelry, and spoons and other table utensils. *Symbol:* Ag; *atomic number* 47. See pages 326 and 327 for table. 2 coins made from this or any other metal of a similar color: *a pocketful of silver.* 3 utensils or dishes made of or plated with silver; silverware: *table silver.* 4 something like silver, as in luster or color. 5 the color of silver; shining whitish gray.
—*adj.* 1 made, consisting of, or plated with

SILKWORM

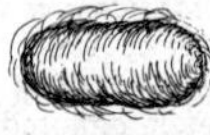

COCOON

silver: *a silver spoon.* 2 of or having to do with silver. 3 having the color of silver: *silver hair, a silver slipper.* 4 having a clear, ringing sound like that of silver dropped on a hard surface. 5 eloquent; persuasive: *a silver tongue.* 6 of or advocating the use of silver as a standard of money.
—*v.t.* 1 cover or plate with silver. 2 coat at the back with a silvery amalgam: *silver glass to make a mirror.* 3 make the color of silver.
—*v.i.* become the color of silver.
[Old English *siolfor*] —**sil′ver er,** *n.* —**sil′ver like′,** *adj.*

silver bromide, compound noted for its sensitivity to light, formed by the action of a bromide on an aqueous solution of silver nitrate. It is much used in photography. *Formula:* AgBr

silver certificate, paper money formerly issued by the United States Government, bearing a promise to pay for its face value in silver coin on demand.

silver chloride, compound noted for its sensitivity to light, used especially in photography for sensitizing paper. *Formula:* AgCl

sil ver fish (sil′vər fish′), *n., pl.* **-fish es** or **-fish.** 1 any of certain silvery fishes, as the tarpon and silversides. 2 any of various small, wingless insects with silvery scales on the body and three bristles extending from the tip of the abdomen, especially a species that is injurious to books, wallpaper, certain fabrics, etc.

silver fox, 1 a red fox in the color phase during which its fur is composed of black hairs with white bands near the tips. 2 this fur.

silver lining, the brighter side of a sad or unfortunate situation.

sil vern (sil′vərn), *adj.* ARCHAIC. of or like silver.

silver nitrate, a colorless, crystalline, poisonous salt that becomes gray or black in the presence of light and organic matter, obtained by treating silver with nitric acid. It is used as a reagent in photography, in dyeing, to silver mirrors, as an antiseptic, etc. *Formula:* $AgNO_3$

silver plate, 1 articles covered with a thin layer of silver or similar material. 2 a plating of silver or an alloy of silver.

silver screen, 1 screen with a silverlike coating on which motion pictures are shown. 2 motion pictures.

sil ver sides (sil′vər sīdz′), *n., pl.* **-sides.** any of a family of small, chiefly marine fishes having a silvery stripe along the body.

sil ver smith (sil′vər smith′), *n.* person who makes articles of silver.

silver standard, use of silver as the standard of value for the money of a country.

sil ver-tongued (sil′vər tungd′), *adj.* eloquent.

sil ver ware (sil′vər wer′, sil′vər war′), *n.* articles made of silver; utensils or dishes made of or plated with silver.

silver wedding, the 25th anniversary of a wedding.

sil ver y (sil′vər ē), *adj.* 1 like silver; like that of silver: *silvery hair, a silvery gleam.* 2 containing silver. —**sil′ver i ness,** *n.*

sil vi cul ture (sil′və kul′chər), *n.* the cultivation of woods or forests; the growing and tending of trees as a branch of forestry. Also, **sylviculture.** [< Latin *silva* forest + English *culture*]

Sim chas To rah (sim′Häs tôr′ə; sim′Häs tōr′ə), a Jewish holiday on the ninth and last day of the festival of Sukkoth, celebrating the end of the complete annual reading of the Pentateuch and the start of a new cycle with the beginning of Genesis. [< Hebrew *simhath tōrāh* rejoicing of the Torah]

sim i an (sim′ē ən), *adj.* of, having to do with, or characteristic of an ape or monkey; apelike or monkeylike. —*n.* ape; monkey. [< Latin *simia* ape < *simus* snub-nosed < Greek *simos*]

sim i lar (sim′ə lər), *adj.* 1 much the same; alike; like: *A creek and a brook are similar.* 2 (in geometry) having the same shape: *similar triangles.* [< French *similaire* < Latin *similis* like] —**sim′i lar ly,** *adv.*

sim i lar i ty (sim′ə lar′ə tē), *n., pl.* **-ties.** 1 a being similar; likeness; resemblance. See **resemblance** for synonym study. 2 **similarities,** *pl.* points of resemblance.

sim i le (sim′ə lē), *n.* an expressed comparison of two different things or ideas; figure of speech stating a likeness between things for some effect. EXAMPLES: a face like marble, as brave as a lion. [< Latin, neuter of *similis* like] ➤ See **metaphor** for usage note.

si mil i tude (sə mil′ə tüd, sə mil′ə tyüd), *n.* 1 a being similar; likeness; resemblance. 2 comparison drawn between two things or facts: *She could think of no similitude to describe the sunset.* 3 copy; image.

Sim la (sim′lə), *n.* town in N India, former summer capital of India. 43,000.

sim mer (sim′ər), *v.i.* 1 make a murmuring sound while boiling gently: *The kettle of water simmered on the stove.* 2 keep at or just below the boiling point; boil gently. 3 be on the point of breaking out: *simmering rebellion, simmer with anger.* See **boil**[1] for synonym study. 4 **simmer down, a** cool off; calm down. **b** (of a liquid) be reduced in quantity through continued simmering. —*v.t.* keep at or just below the boiling point. —*n.* process of cooking at or just below the boiling point. [earlier *simper;* probably imitative]

Si mon (sī′mən), *n.* See **Peter, Saint.**

si mo ni a cal (sī′mə nī′ə kəl, sim′ə nī′ə kəl), *adj.* 1 guilty of simony. 2 of, having to do with, or involving simony.

Simon Ma gus (mā′gəs), (in the Bible) a Samaritan sorcerer who tried to buy the power of imparting the Holy Ghost from the apostles Peter and John.

Simon Peter. See **Peter, Saint.**

si mon-pure (sī′mən pyůr′), *adj.* INFORMAL. real; genuine; authentic; true: *simon-pure maple sugar.* [< *Simon Pure,* character in the comedy *A Bold Stroke for a Wife* (1718), by Susanna Centlivre, 1667?-1723, English dramatist]

si mo ny (sī′mə nē, sim′ə nē), *n.* the buying or selling of sacred things, especially positions or promotions in the church. [< Late Latin *simonia* < *Simon* Magus]

Simon Ze lo tes (zə lō′tēz′), (in the Bible) one of Christ's twelve apostles.

si moom (sə müm′), *n.* a hot, dry, suffocating, sand-laden wind of the deserts of Arabia, Syria, and northern Africa. [< Arabic *simūm*]

si moon (sə mün′), *n.* simoom.

sim pa ti co (sim pä′ti kō), *adj.* agreeable; compatible. [< Spanish *simpático* < *simpatía* sympathy]

sim per (sim′pər), *v.i.* smile in a silly, affected way. —*v.t.* express by a simper; say with a simper. —*n.* a silly, affected smile. [perhaps < Scandinavian (Norwegian) *semper* smart] —**sim′per er,** *n.*

hat, āge, fär; let, ēqual, tėrm;
it, īce; hot, ōpen, ôrder;
oil, out; cup, pu̇t, rüle;
ch, child; ng, long; sh, she;
th, thin; ᴛʜ, then; zh, measure;
ə represents *a* in about, *e* in taken, *i* in pencil, *o* in lemon, *u* in circus.
< = from, derived from, taken from.

sim ple (sim′pəl), *adj.,* **-pler, -plest,** *n.* —*adj.* 1 easy to do or understand: *a simple problem, simple language, a simple explanation, a simple task.* See **easy** for synonym study. 2 not divided into parts; single; not compound: *a simple substance, a simple leaf.* 3 having few parts; not complex; not involved; elementary: *a simple one-celled animal.* 4 with nothing added; mere; bare: *My answer is the simple truth.* 5 without ornament; not rich or showy; plain: *simple food, simple clothing.* 6 not showing off; unaffected; natural: *She has a pleasant, simple manner.* 7 free from duplicity or guile; honest; sincere: *a simple heart.* 8 not subtle; not sophisticated; innocent; artless: *a simple child.* 9 common; ordinary: *a simple private.* 10 of humble birth or position; lowly: *simple people.* 11 foolish, silly, or stupid.
—*n.* 1 a foolish, stupid person. 2 something simple. 3 ARCHAIC. **a** plant or herb used in medicine. **b** medicine made from it.
[< Old French < Latin *simplus* < *simplex* single] —**sim′ple ness,** *n.*

simple fraction, fraction in which both the numerator and the denominator are whole numbers. EXAMPLES: $^1/_3$, $^3/_4$, $^{219}/_{125}$.

simple fracture, fracture in which a broken bone does not penetrate the skin.

sim ple-heart ed (sim′pəl här′tid), *adj.* 1 having or showing a simple, unaffected nature. 2 guileless; sincere.

simple interest, interest that is paid only on the principal of a loan, etc., and not on accrued interest.

simple machine, any of the elementary devices or mechanical powers which multiply or change the direction of force and on which more complex machines are based. The lever, wedge, pulley, wheel and axle, inclined plane, and screw are the six simple machines.

sim ple-mind ed (sim′pəl mīn′did), *adj.* 1 without awareness of conventions; artless; inexperienced. 2 ignorant; foolish; stupid. 3 feeble-minded. —**sim′ple-mind′ed ly,** *adv.* —**sim′ple-mind′ed ness,** *n.*

simple sentence, sentence consisting of one main clause. EXAMPLE: The whistle blows.

simple sugar, monosaccharide.

sim ple ton (sim′pəl tən), *n.* a silly person; fool.

sim plic i ty (sim plis′ə tē), *n., pl.* **-ties.** 1 a being simple. 2 freedom from difficulty; clearness. 3 plainness: *a room furnished with simplicity.* 4 absence of show or pretense; sincerity. 5 lack of shrewdness; dullness. [< Latin *simplicitatem* < *simplex* simple]

sim pli fi ca tion (sim′plə fə kā′shən), *n.* 1 a making simpler. 2 a being made simpler. 3 change to a simpler form.

sim pli fy (sim′plə fī), *v.t.,* **-fied, -fy ing.** make simple or simpler; make plainer or easier. —**sim′pli fi′er,** *n.*

sim plis tic (sim plis′tik), *adj.* trying to explain everything, or too much, by a single principle: *simplistic theories.*

Sim plon (sim′plon), *n.* 1 **Simplon Pass,** mountain pass between Switzerland and Italy. 6592 ft. high. 2 tunnel near this pass, the longest railroad tunnel in the world. $12^{1}/_{4}$ mi. long.

sim ply (sim′plē), *adv.* 1 in a simple manner. 2 without much ornament; without pretense or affectation; plainly: *simply dressed.* 3 merely; only: *The baby did not simply cry, he yelled.* 4 foolishly: *act as simply as an idiot.* 5 absolutely: *simply perfect, simply hopeless.*

sim u la crum (sim′yə lā′krəm), *n., pl.* **-cra** (-krə), **-crums.** 1 a faint, shadowy, or unreal likeness; mere semblance: *The dictator permitted only a simulacrum of democracy.* 2 image. [< Latin < *simulare* simulate < *similis* like]

sim u late (sim′yə lāt), *v.t.,* **-lat ed, -lat ing.** 1 put on a false appearance of; pretend; feign: *simulate interest.* 2 act like; look like; imitate: *Certain insects simulate flowers or leaves.* [< Latin *simulatum* simulated < *similis* like] **—sim′u la′tor,** *n.*

sim u la tion (sim′yə lā′shən), *n.* 1 pretense; feigning. 2 an acting or looking like; imitation: *a harmless insect's simulation of a poisonous one.*

sim u la tive (sim′yə lā′tiv), *adj.* simulating.

si mul cast (sī′məl kast′), *v.,* **-cast** or **-cast ed, -cast ing,** *n.* *—v.t., v.i.* transmit a program over radio and television simultaneously. *—n.* broadcast transmitted over radio and television simultaneously. [< *simul(taneous) + (broad)cast*]

si mul ta ne i ty (sī′məl tə nē′ə tē, sim′əl tə nē′ə tē), *n.* quality or fact of being simultaneous.

si mul ta ne ous (sī′məl tā′nē əs, sim′əl tā′nē əs), *adj.* 1 existing, done, or happening at the same time: *The two simultaneous shots sounded like one.* 2 indicating two or more equations or inequalities, with two or more unknowns, for which a set of values of the unknowns is sought that is a solution of all the equations or inequalities. [< Medieval Latin *simultaneus* simulated < Latin *similis* like; confused in sense with Latin *simul* at the same time] **—si′mul ta′ne ous ly,** *adv.* **—si′mul ta′ne ous ness,** *n.*

sin (sin), *n., v.,* **sinned, sin ning.** *—n.* 1 a breaking of the law of God deliberately. 2 the state or condition resulting from this. 3 wrongdoing of any kind; immoral act. *—v.i.* 1 break the law of God; be a sinner. 2 do wrong. [Old English *synn*]

sin, sine.

Si nai (sī′nī), *n.* 1 **Mount,** (in the Bible) the mountain where God gave the Ten Commandments to Moses; Horeb. It is thought to be located in the southern part of the Sinai Peninsula. 2 **Sinai Peninsula,** triangular peninsula in NE Egypt, between the Mediterranean Sea and the N end of the Red Sea. 230 mi. long.

Sin an thro pus (sin′an thrō′pəs, si-nan′thrə pəs), *n.* Peking man. [< New Latin < Greek *Sinai* the Chinese + *anthrōpos* man]

Sin bad (sin′bad), *n.* sailor in *The Arabian Nights* who had seven extraordinary voyages. Also, **Sindbad.**

since (sins), *prep.* 1 from a past time continuously till now: *We have been up since five.* 2 at any time between (some past time or event and the present): *We have not seen her since Saturday.* *—conj.* 1 from the time that; in the course of the period following the time when: *She has written home only once since she left us.* 2 continuously or counting from the time when: *He has worked hard since he left school.* 3 because: *Since you feel tired, you should rest.* *—adv.* 1 from that time till now: *He caught cold last week and has been in bed ever since.* 2 at some time between a particular past time and the present; subsequently; later: *He refused the position at first but since has accepted.* 3 before now; ago: *I heard that old joke long since.* [Middle English *sinnes, sithenes* < Old English *siththan* then, later < *sīth* late]

sin cere (sin sir′), *adj.,* **-cer er, -cer est.** free from pretense or deceit; genuine; real; honest: *sincere thanks, a sincere person.* [< Latin *sincerus*] **—sin cere′ly,** *adv.* **—sin cere′ness,** *n.*

sin cer i ty (sin ser′ə tē), *n., pl.* **-ties.** freedom from pretense or deceit; honesty.

Sin clair (sin klar′, sin kler′), *n.* **Upton,** 1878-1968, American writer and social reformer.

Sind bad (sin′bad), *n.* Sinbad.

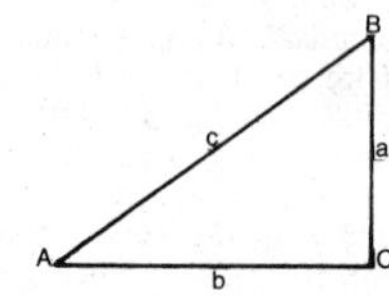

sine—Triangle ABC is a right triangle in which angle C is the right angle and side c is the hypotenuse.
The sine of angle A is a/c,
the cosine of angle A is b/c;
the sine of angle B is b/c,
the cosine of angle B is a/c.

sine (sīn), *n.* (in trigonometry) the ratio of the length of the side opposite an acute angle in a right triangle to the length of the hypotenuse. [< Latin *sinus* bend, bosom; in Medieval Latin, translation of Arabic *jaib* sine, bosom]

si ne cure (sī′nə kyu̇r, sin′ə kyu̇r), *n.* 1 an extremely easy job; position requiring little or no work and usually paying well. 2 an ecclesiastical benefice without parish duties. [< Medieval Latin *(beneficium) sine cura* (benefice) without cure (of souls)]

si ne di e (sī′nē dī′ē), without a day specified for another meeting, trial, etc.; indefinitely: *The committee adjourned sine die.* [< Latin, without a day]

si ne qua non (sī′nē kwā non′), something essential; indispensable condition. [< Latin, literally, without which not]

sin ew (sin′yü), *n.* 1 tendon. 2 strength; energy; force. 3 means of strength; source of power: *Men and money are the sinews of war.* *—v.t.* furnish with sinews. [Old English *sionu*] **—sin′ew less,** *adj.*

sin ew y (sin′yü ē), *adj.* 1 having strong sinews; strong; powerful: *sinewy arms.* 2 vigorous; forcible. 3 like sinews; having sinews; tough; stringy. **—sin′ew i ness,** *n.*

sin ful (sin′fəl), *adj.* full of sin; wicked; wrong; immoral; evil: *a sinful person, a sinful act.* **—sin′ful ly,** *adv.* **—sin′ful ness,** *n.*

sing (sing), *v.,* **sang** or **sung, sung, sing ing,** *n.* *—v.i.* 1 make music with the voice: *sing in a choir.* 2 make pleasant musical sounds: *Birds sing.* 3 tell in song or poetry: *Homer sang of Troy.* 4 admit of being sung: *The words of the verse sing well.* 5 make a ringing, whistling, humming, or buzzing sound: *The teakettle sang.* 6 have a sensation of a ringing, buzzing, or humming sound: *A bad cold made my ears sing.* 7 SLANG. inform; tell all. 8 **sing out,** call loudly; shout. *—v.t.* 1 utter musically: *sing a song.* 2 chant; intone: *The priest sang Mass.* 3 tell of in song or poetry: *The poet sang the deeds of heroes.* 4 proclaim: *sing a person's praises.* 5 bring, send, put, etc., by or with singing: *Sing the baby to sleep.*
—n. 1 a singing, ringing, or whistling sound: *the sing of a bullet in flight.* 2 a singing, especially in a group.
[Old English *singan*] **—sing′a ble,** *adj.*

sing., singular.

sing-a long (sing′ə lông′, sing′ə long′), *n.* U.S. entertainment in which the audience joins in the singing of songs.

Sing a pore (sing′ə pôr, sing′ə pōr), *n.* 1 island country off the S tip of the Malay Peninsula, a member of the Commonwealth of Nations. 2,034,000 pop.; 225 sq. mi. 2 its capital, a seaport on the S coast. 1,988,000.

singe (sinj), *v.,* **singed, singe ing,** *n.* *—v.t.* 1 burn a little: *The cook singed the chicken to remove the fine hairs.* 2 burn the ends or edges of: *The barber singed my hair after he cut it.* 3 remove by a slight burning. 4 injure slightly; harm: *A scandal singed the mayor's reputation.* *—n.* a slight burn. [Old English *sengan*] **—sing′er,** *n.*

sing er (sing′ər), *n.* person or bird that sings.

Sing er (sing′ər), *n.* 1 **Isaac Bashevis,** born 1904, American writer of novels and short stories, born in Poland. 2 **Isaac Merrit,** 1811-1875, American inventor and manufacturer.

Sin gha lese (sing′gə lēz′), *n., pl.* **-lese,** *adj.* *—n.* 1 member of the principal native people of Ceylon. 2 the Indic language of this people. *—adj.* having to do with Ceylon, its principal native people, or their language. Also, **Sinhalese.** [< Sanskrit *Siṅhala* Ceylon + English *-ese*]

sin gle (sing′gəl), *adj., n., v.,* **-gled, -gling.** *—adj.* 1 one and no more; only one: *a single piece of paper.* See synonym study below. 2 for only one; individual: *a single bed, a single room in a hotel.* 3 without others; alone. 4 not married: *a single man.* 5 having only one on each side: *The knights engaged in single combat.* 6 (of a flower) having only one set of petals. Most cultivated roses have double flowers with many petals; wild roses have single flowers with five petals. 7 not double; not multiple: *single houses.* 8 sincere; honest; genuine: *She showed single devotion to her work.* *—n.* 1 a single person or thing; individual. 2 hit in baseball that allows the batter to reach first base only. 3 **singles,** *pl.* game (of tennis, etc.), played with only one player on each side. *—v.t.* 1 pick from among others: *single a person out for special praise.* 2 advance or score (a runner) in baseball with a single. *—v.i.* hit a single in baseball. [< Old French < Latin *singulus*] **—sin′gle ness,** *n.*

Syn. *adj.* 1 **Single, sole, only** mean one alone. **Single** emphasizes one and no more: *She buys a single new dress each year.* **Sole** emphasizes being by itself, the only one there is: *My sole purpose is to help you.* **Only** emphasizes being one of a class of which it is the best or the single representative: *She is the only girl in the world for me.*

hat, āge, fär; let, ēqual, tėrm;
it, īce; hot, ōpen, ôrder;
oil, out; cup, pu̇t, rüle;
ch, child; ng, long; sh, she;
th, thin; ᴛʜ, then; zh, measure;

ə represents *a* in about, *e* in taken, *i* in pencil, *o* in lemon, *u* in circus.

< = from, derived from, taken from.

sin gle-breast ed (sing′gəl bres′tid), *adj.* overlapping across the breast just enough to fasten with only one row of buttons: *a single-breasted jacket.*

single entry, system of bookkeeping in which there is one account to which all items are debited or credited.

single file, line of persons or things arranged one behind another.

sin gle-foot (sing′gəl fu̇t′), *n.* gait of a horse in which one foot is put down at a time; rack. First, there is one foot on the ground, then two, then one, then two, and so on. *—v.i.* (of a horse) go or move at a single-foot.

sin gle-hand ed (sing′gəl han′did), *adj.* 1 without help from others; working alone. 2 using, requiring, or managed by only one hand or only one person. **—sin′gle-hand′ed ly,** *adv.*

sin gle-heart ed (sing′gəl här′tid), *adj.* 1 free from deceit; sincere. 2 having only one purpose. **—sin′gle-heart′ed ly,** *adv.* **—sin′gle-heart′ed ness,** *n.*

sin gle-mind ed (sing′gəl mīn′did), *adj.* 1 having only one purpose in mind. 2 sincere; straightforward. **—sin′gle-mind′ed ly,** *adv.* **—sin′gle-mind′ed-ness,** *n.*

sin gle stick (sing′gəl stik′), *n.* 1 stick held in one hand, used in fencing. 2 fencing with such a stick.

sin glet (sing′glit), *n.* a man's short-sleeved undershirt or jersey.

single tax, tax on one kind of property only, especially a tax on land only.

sin gle ton (sing′gəl tən), *n.* 1 something occurring singly or apart from others. 2 a playing card that is the only one of a suit in a person's hand.

sin gle-track (sing′gəl trak′), *adj.* 1 having only a single track. 2 able to go or act in only one way.

sin gle tree (sing′gəl trē′), *n.* whiffletree. [variant of *swingletree*]

sin gly (sing′glē), *adv.* 1 by itself; individually; separately: *Consider each point singly.* 2 one by one; one at a time: *Misfortunes never come singly.* 3 by one's own efforts; without help.

Sing Sing (sing′ sing′), former name of the state prison at Ossining, N.Y.

sing song (sing′sông′, sing′song′), *n.* 1 a monotonous, up-and-down rhythm. 2 a monotonous tone or sound in speaking. 3 a monotonous or jingling verse. *—adj.* monotonous in rhythm.

sin gu lar (sing′gyə lər), *adj.* 1 extraordinary; unusual: *a person of singular ability, a story of singular interest.* 2 strange; odd; peculiar: *The detectives were greatly puzzled by the singular nature of the crime.* 3 being the only one of its kind: *an event singular in history.* 4 in grammar: **a** signifying or implying only one person or thing: *the singular number, a singular verb form.* **b** one in number. *Boy* is singular; *boys* is plural. 5 separate; individual; private: *a singular matter.* *—n.* 1 the singular number in grammar. 2 a word in the singular number. [< Latin *singularis* < *singulus* single] **—sin′gu lar ly,** *adv.*

sin gu lar i ty (sing′gyə lar′ə tē), *n., pl.* **-ties.** 1 condition or quality of being singular. 2 something singular; peculiarity; oddity: *One of the giraffe's singularities is the length of its neck.*

sin gu lar ize (sing′gyə lə rīz′), *v.t.,* **-ized, -iz ing.** make singular or single.

Sin ha lese (sin′hə lēz′), *n., pl.* **-lese,** *adj.* Singhalese.

sin is ter (sin′ə stər), *adj.* 1 showing ill will; threatening: *a sinister rumor, a sinister look.* 2 bad; evil; dishonest. 3 disastrous; unfortunate. 4 on the left; left. 5 (in heraldry) situated on that part of an escutcheon to the left of the bearer. [< Latin, left; the left side being considered unlucky] **—sin′is ter ly,** *adv.* **—sin′is ter ness,** *n.*

sin is tral (sin′ə strəl), *adj.* of or having to do with the left side; left; left-handed. **—sin′is tral ly,** *adv.*

sin is trorse (sin′ə strôrs, sin′ə strôrs′), *adj.* rising spirally from right to left: *the sinistrorse stem of a vine.* [< Latin *sinistrorsum* < *sinister* left + *versum* turned] **—sin′is trorse′ly,** *adv.*

sink (singk), *v.,* **sank** or **sunk, sunk, sink ing,** *n.* *—v.i.* 1 go down; fall slowly; go lower and lower: *sink to the floor in a faint, sink into a chair. The sun is sinking.* 2 go under: *The ship is sinking.* 3 become lower or weaker: *The wind has sunk down.* 4 pass gradually (into a state of sleep, silence, oblivion, etc.): *sink to rest, sink into corruption.* 5 go deeply; penetrate: *Let the lesson sink into your mind.* 6 become worse: *Her spirits sank.* 7 fall in; become hollow: *sunken cheeks.* *—v.t.* 1 make go down; make fall: *Lack of rain sank the reservoirs.* 2 make go under: *The submarine sank two ships.* 3 make lower; reduce: *Sink your voice to a whisper.* 4 make go deep; dig: *sink a well.* 5 keep quiet about; conceal: *sink evidence.* 6 invest (money), especially unprofitably. *—n.* 1 a shallow basin or tub with a drainpipe. 2 drain; sewer. 3 place where dirty water or any filth collects. 4 place of vice or corruption. 5 a low-lying inland area where waters collect or where they disappear by sinking downward or by evaporation. [Old English *sincan*] **—sink′a ble,** *adj.*

sink age (sing′kij), *n.* 1 act or process of sinking. 2 amount of sinking.

sink er (sing′kər), *n.* 1 person or thing that sinks. 2 a lead weight for sinking a fish line or net. 3 SLANG. doughnut.

sink hole (singk′hōl′), *n.* 1 hole that drains surface water. 2 hole where water collects. 3 place of vice and corruption.

Sin kiang (sin′kyäng′), *n.* the westernmost province of China, north of Tibet.

sinking fund, fund formed by a government, corporation, or the like, usually by periodically setting aside certain amounts of money to accumulate at interest, for the paying off of a debt.

sin less (sin′lis), *adj.* without sin. **—sin′less ly,** *adv.* **—sin′less ness,** *n.*

sin ner (sin′ər), *n.* person who sins or does wrong.

Sinn Fein (shin′ fān′), a political organization in Ireland, founded about 1905, demanding the complete political separation of Ireland from Great Britain. [< Irish, we ourselves]

Sino-, *combining form.* China; Chinese; China and ____, as in *Sino-Soviet, Sino-Japanese.* [< Late Latin *Sinae* the Chinese]

sin ter (sin′tər), *v.t.* fuse (metal particles, etc.) into a single mass by applying heat and pressure. *—n.* something produced by sintering. [< German *sintern* < *Sinter* dross, slag]

sin u ate (sin′yü āt), *adj.* 1 bent in and out; winding; sinuous. 2 (in botany) having its margin strongly or distinctly wavy: *a sinuate leaf.* [< Latin *sinuatum* bent < *sinus* a curve] **—sin′u ate′ly,** *adv.*

sin u os i ty (sin′yü os′ə tē), *n., pl.* **-ties.** 1 sinuous form or character; a winding. 2 curve; bend; turn.

sin u ous (sin′yü əs), *adj.* 1 having many curves or turns; winding: *the sinuous motion of a snake.* 2 indirect; devious. 3 morally crooked. 4 (in botany) sinuate. [< Latin *sinuosus* < *sinus* a curve] **—sin′u ous ly,** *adv.* **—sin′u ous ness,** *n.*

si nus (sī′nəs), *n.* 1 cavity in a bone, especially one of the cavities in the bones of the skull that connect with the nasal cavity. 2 a long, narrow abscess with a small opening. 3 reservoir or channel for venous blood. 4 a curved hollow; cavity. 5 curve or bend, especially a curve between two projecting lobes of a leaf. [< Latin]

si nus i tis (sī′nə sī′tis), *n.* inflammation of a sinus, especially a nasal sinus.

Si on (sī′ən), *n.* Zion.

Siou an (sü′ən), *n.* 1 the group of American Indian tribes that includes the Sioux, Osage, Crow, etc. 2 the family of languages spoken by them. *—adj.* having to do with these tribes or their languages.

Sioux (sü), *n., pl.* **Sioux** (sü, süz). 1 member of an American Indian tribe living on the plains of northern United States and southern Canada; Dakota. 2 the Siouan language of this tribe.

Sioux City, city in W Iowa, on the Missouri River. 86,000.

Sioux Falls, city in SE South Dakota. 72,000.

sip (sip), *v.,* **sipped, sip ping,** *n.* *—v.t., v.i.* drink little by little: *She sipped her tea.* See **drink** for synonym study. *—n.* 1 a very small drink. 2 a sipping. [Middle English *sippen*] **—sip′per,** *n.*

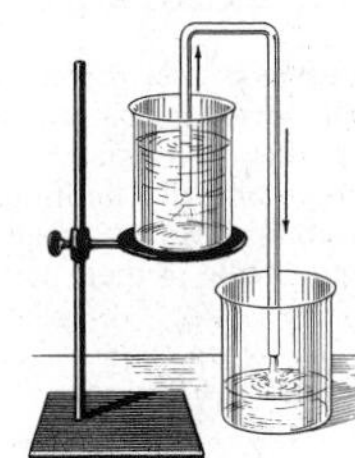

siphon (def. 1)
The arrows show the direction of flow of the liquid.

si phon (sī′fən), *n.* 1 a bent tube through which liquid can be drawn over the edge of one container into another at a lower level by air pressure. 2 bottle for soda water with a tube through which the liquid is forced out by the pressure of the gas in the bottle. 3 a tube-shaped organ of some animals, such as certain shellfish, for drawing in and expelling water, etc. *—v.t.* draw off by means of a siphon: *The farmer siphoned water from the cellar into the ditch.* *—v.i.* pass through a siphon. Also, **syphon.** [< Greek *siphōn* pipe]

sir (sėr; *unstressed* sər), *n.* 1 a respectful or formal term of address used to a man: *Yes, sir.* 2 **Sir,** **a** form of salutation in a letter addressed to a man: *Dear Sir.* **b** title of a knight or baronet: *Sir Walter Scott.* 3 Mr. or Master: *You, sir, have no business here; get out.* [variant of *sire*]

sir dar (sėr′där, sər där′), *n.* (in India) a military chief or leader. [< Hindustani *sardār* chief < Persian]

sire (sīr), *n., v.,* **sired, sir ing.** —*n.* 1 a male ancestor. 2 male parent; father: *Lightning was the sire of the racehorse Danger.* 3 title of respect used formerly to a great noble and now to a king. —*v.t.* be the father of. [< Old French < Latin *senior* older. Doublet of SENIOR.]

si ren (sī′rən), *n.* 1 kind of whistle that makes a loud, piercing sound: *an ambulance siren, the sirens of fire engines.* 2 Also, **Siren.** (in Greek legends) any of a group of nymphs who, by their sweet singing, lured sailors to destruction upon the rocks. 3 woman who lures, tempts, or entices. 4 any of a genus of aquatic, eel-like amphibians with small forelimbs and no hind limbs. —*adj.* of or like a siren; tempting; charming. [< Greek *seirēn*] —**si′ren like′,** *adj.*

si re ni an (sī rē′nē ən), *n.* any of an order of herbivorous sea mammals with forelimbs shaped like a paddle and no hind limbs, including the manatee and the dugong. —*adj.* of or relating to this order.

si ren ic (sī ren′ik), *adj.* sirenlike; seductive; alluring.

Sir i us (sir′ē əs), *n.* the brightest star in the sky, in the constellation Canis Major; Dog Star. [< Greek *Seirios*]

sir loin (sėr′loin), *n.* cut of beef from the part of the loin in front of the rump. [< Old French *surlonge* < *sur* over + *longe* loin]

si roc co (sə rok′ō), *n., pl.* **-cos.** 1 a hot, dry, dust-laden wind blowing from northern Africa across the Mediterranean and southern Europe. 2 a moist, warm, south or southeast wind in these same regions. 3 any hot, unpleasant wind. [< French < Italian *scirocco* < Arabic *shoruq* < *sharq* east]

sir rah (sir′ə), *n.* ARCHAIC. fellow, used to address men and boys when speaking contemptuously, angrily, impatiently, etc. [apparently < *sir* + *ha*]

Sir Rog er de Cov er ley (sėr roj′ər də kuv′ər lē), an old-fashioned English country-dance, resembling the Virginia reel. [< *Sir Roger de Coverley,* name of a fictitious character, an English country squire, made famous by Addison and Steele in their periodical, *The Spectator*]

sir up (sir′əp, sėr′əp), *n.* syrup.

sir up y (sir′ə pē, sėr′ə pē), *adj.* syrupy.

sis (sis), *n.* INFORMAL. sister.

sis al (sis′əl, sī′səl), *n.* 1 a strong, white fiber, used for making rope, twine, etc. 2 species of agave that it comes from. [< *Sisal,* town and former port in Yucatán]

sisal hemp, sisal.

sis si fied (sis′ə fīd), *adj.* INFORMAL. effeminate.

sis sy (sis′ē), *n., pl.* **-sies.** INFORMAL. 1 sister. 2 boy or man who behaves too much like a girl. 3 a weak or cowardly person. [diminutive of *sis*]

sis ter (sis′tər), *n.* 1 daughter of the same parents. 2 daughter only of the same mother or father; half sister. 3 a close friend or companion. 4 person or thing resembling or closely connected with another. 5 a female fellow member of a church, society, sorority, etc. 6 member of a religious order of women; nun: *Sisters of Charity.* 7 BRITISH. **a** a head nurse. **b** any nurse. —*adj.* being a sister; related as if by sisterhood: *a sister ship.* [< Scandinavian (Old Icelandic) *systir*] —**sis′ter less,** *adj.*

sis ter hood (sis′tər hůd), *n.* 1 bond between sisters; feeling of sister for sister. 2 association of women with some common aim, characteristic, belief, etc. 3 members of such an association; persons joined as sisters.

sis ter-in-law (sis′tər in lô′), *n., pl.* **sisters-in-law.** 1 sister of one's husband or wife. 2 wife of one's brother. 3 wife of the brother of one's husband or wife.

sis ter ly (sis′tər lē), *adj.* 1 of a sister. 2 like a sister's; kindly; affectionate. —*adv.* like a sister. —**sis′ter li ness,** *n.*

Sis tine (sis′tēn′), *adj.* 1 of or having to do with any of the five popes named Sixtus. 2 of or having to do with the Sistine Chapel. [< Italian *sistino,* ultimately < Latin *sextus* sixth]

Sistine Chapel, chapel of the pope in the Vatican, decorated with frescoes by Michelangelo and other great artists.

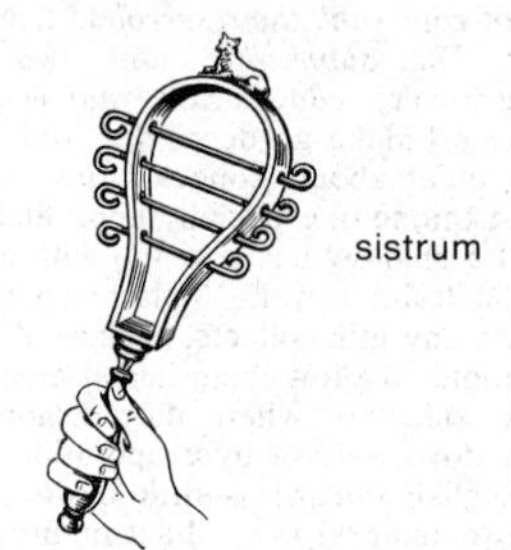
sistrum

sis trum (sis′trəm), *n., pl.* **-trums, -tra** (-trə). an ancient musical instrument or rattle, used especially in Egypt in the worship of Isis. [< Greek *seistron* < *seiein* to shake]

Sis y phus (sis′ə fəs), *n.* (in Greek myths) a king of Corinth condemned forever to roll a heavy stone up a steep hill in Hades, only to have it always roll down again when he neared the top.

sit (sit), *v.,* **sat, sit ting,** *n.* —*v.i.* 1 rest on the lower part of the body, with the weight off the feet: *She sat in a chair.* 2 have place or position: *The clock has sat on that shelf for years.* 3 have a seat in an assembly, etc.; be a member of a council: *sit in Congress.* 4 hold a session: *The court sits next month.* 5 place oneself in a position for having one's picture made; pose: *sit for a portrait.* 6 be in a state of rest; remain inactive. 7 press or weigh: *Care sat heavily on his brow.* 8 perch; roost: *The birds were sitting on the fence rail.* 9 brood: *The hen will sit until the eggs are ready to hatch.* 10 baby-sit. 11 fit: *The coat sits well.* —*v.t.* 1 cause to sit; seat: *The woman sat the little boy in his highchair.* 2 sit on: *He sat his horse well.*

sit down, take a seat; put oneself in a sitting position.

sit in, **a** take part (in a game, conference, etc.). **b** U.S. take part in a sit-in.

sit on or **sit upon,** **a** sit in judgment or council on. **b** have a seat on (a jury, commission, etc.). **c** INFORMAL. check, rebuke, or snub.

sit out, **a** remain seated during (a dance). **b** stay through (a performance, etc.). **c** stay later than (another).

sit up, **a** raise the body to a sitting position. **b** keep such a position. **c** stay up instead of going to bed. **d** INFORMAL. start up in surprise.

—*n.* the way in which an article of clothing fits.

[Old English *sittan*] ➤ See **set** for usage note.

sitar

si tar (si tär′), *n.* a musical instrument of India, having a long, fretted neck and a body usually made from a gourd. It has 6 or 7 strings that are played with a plectrum and 11 to 13 strings, beneath the others, that vibrate sympathetically. [< Hindi *sitār*]

sit-down strike (sit′doun′), strike in which the workers stay in the factory, store, etc., without working.

site (sīt), *n., v.,* **sit ed, sit ing.** —*n.* position or place (of anything); location: *This house has one of the best sites in town.* —*v.t.* place in a site; locate; situate. [< Latin *situs*]

sith (sith), *adv., prep., conj.* ARCHAIC. since. [Old English *sīth* after]

sit-in (sit′in′), *n.* a sitting down and refusing to move, especially in a public place, as a form of protest against racial discrimination, government policies, etc.

Sit ka (sit′kə), *n.* town in SE Alaska. 3000.

sit ter (sit′ər), *n.* 1 person who sits. 2 baby-sitter. 3 bird sitting on its eggs.

sit ting (sit′ing), *n.* 1 meeting or session of a legislature, court, etc. 2 time of remaining seated: *She read five chapters at one sitting.* 3 number of eggs on which a bird sits. 4 act of one that sits. —*adj.* 1 that sits; seated: *a sitting dog.* 2 used for sitting; in which one sits or may sit: *a sitting posture, sitting space.*

Sitting Bull, 1834?-1890, Sioux Indian chief, the leader of the Sioux confederacy which defeated Custer in 1876.

sitting duck, an easy target or mark.

sitting room, living room; parlor.

sit u ate (sich′ü āt), *v.,* **-at ed, -at ing,** *adj.* —*v.t.* place or locate. —*adj.* ARCHAIC. situated. [< Medieval Latin *situatum* situated < Latin *situs* site]

sit u at ed (sich′ü ā′tid), *adj.* 1 placed; located: *New York is a favorably situated city.* 2 in a certain financial or social position: *The doctor was quite well situated.*

sit u a tion (sich′ü ā′shən), *n.* 1 combination of circumstances; case; condition: *Act reasonably in all situations.* 2 place to work; job; position. 3 site; location; place: *Our house has a beautiful situation on a hill.* 4 a critical state of affairs in a play, novel, etc.

sit u a tion al (sich′ü ā′shə nəl), *adj.* of or having to do with situations.

sit-up (sit′up′), *n.* exercise in which a person lies on his back with his hands under his head, legs extended, and then sits up without raising his feet.

si tus (sī′təs), *n.* position, situation, or location, especially the proper or original position, as of a part or organ. [< Latin]

sitz bath (sits), 1 tub for bathing in a sitting position. 2 bath so taken. [half-translation of German *Sitzbad* < *Sitz* a sitting + *Bad* bath]

sitz krieg (sits′krēg′; *German* zits′krēk′), *n.* war with little or no actual fighting. [< German *Sitzkrieg,* literally, sitting war]

Si va (sē′və, shē′və), *n.* one of the three chief Hindu divinities, with Brahma and Vishnu, known as "the Destroyer." Also, **Shiva.**

six (siks), *n.* 1 one more than five; 6. 2 a set of six persons or things. 3 **at sixes and sevens, a** in confusion. **b** in disagreement. *—adj.* being one more than five. [Old English *siex, six*]

six fold (siks′fōld′), *adj.* 1 six times as much or as many. 2 having six parts. *—adv.* six times as much or as many.

Six Nations, federation of Iroquois Indian tribes. The Tuscarora tribe of Iroquois in 1722 joined the original federation of Iroquois tribes called the Five Nations.

six-pack (siks′pak′), *n.* a cardboard container holding six bottles, cans, or other items sold as a unit.

six pence (siks′pəns), *n.* 1 six British pennies; 6 pence. 2 a British silver coin having this value.

six pen ny (siks′pen′ē, siks′pə nē), *adj.* 1 worth or costing sixpence. 2 of little worth; cheap. 3 (of nails) two inches long.

six-shoot er (siks′shü′tər), *n.* INFORMAL. revolver that can fire six shots without being reloaded.

six teen (sik′stēn′), *n., adj.* six more than ten; 16.

six teenth (sik′stēnth′), *adj., n.* 1 next after the 15th; last in a series of 16. 2 one, or being one, of 16 equal parts.

sixteenth note, (in music) a note played for one sixteenth as long a time as a whole note. See **note** for diagram.

sixth (siksth), *adj., n.* 1 next after the fifth; last in a series of 6. 2 one, or being one, of 6 equal parts.

sixth ly (siksth′lē), *adv.* in the sixth place.

sixth sense, an unusual power of perception; intuition.

six ti eth (sik′stē ith), *adj., n.* 1 next after the 59th; last in a series of 60. 2 one, or being one, of 60 equal parts.

six ty (sik′stē), *n., pl.* **-ties,** *adj.* six times ten; 60.

six ty-fourth note (sik′stē fôrth′, sik′stē-fōrth′), (in music) a note played for one sixty-fourth as long a time as a whole note. See **note** for diagram.

siz a ble (sī′zə bəl), *adj.* fairly large. Also, **sizeable.** **—siz′a ble ness,** *n.* **—siz′a bly,** *adv.*

siz ar (sī′zər), *n.* student who pays reduced rates in the colleges of Cambridge University in Cambridge, England, and Trinity College in Dublin, Ireland. [< *size*[1], in earlier meaning "food allowance"]

size[1] (sīz), *n., v.,* **sized, siz ing,** *adj.* *—n.* 1 amount of surface or space a thing takes up. 2 extent; amount; magnitude: *the size of an industry.* See synonym study below. 3 one of a series of measures: *His shoes are size 10.* 4 INFORMAL. the actual condition; true description. 5 **of a size,** of the same size. *—v.t.* 1 arrange according to size or in sizes. 2 make of certain size.
size up, INFORMAL. **a** form an opinion of; estimate. **b** come up to size or grade.
—adj. having size; sized.
[Middle English *sise* ordinance setting a fixed amount, short for *assise* assize < Old French. See ASSIZE.]
Syn. *n.* 2 **Size, volume, bulk** mean the spatial measure of something. **Size** applies to the dimensions (length, width, and height or depth) of something, to the extent of surface occupied, or to the number of individuals included: *the size of a box. What is the size of your herd?* **Volume** is used of something measured by the cubic inches, feet, etc., it occupies: *The volume of water confined by Hoover Dam is tremendous.* **Bulk** means size or quantity measured in three dimensions, and often suggests largeness: *Let the dough double in bulk.*

size[2] (sīz), *n., v.,* **sized, siz ing.** *—n.* preparation made from glue, starch, or other sticky material; sizing. It is used to glaze paper, cover plastered walls, stiffen cloth, etc. *—v.t.* coat or treat with size. [< Old French *assise* a sitting, fixing, layer < *asseir* sit at < Latin *assidere*]

-size, *combining form.* variant of **-sized,** as in *an average-size man.*

size a ble (sī′zə bəl), *adj.* sizable. **—size′a-ble ness,** *n.* **—size′a bly,** *adv.*

-sized, *combining form.* having a ____ size: *Fair-sized = having a fair size.* Also, **-size.**

siz ing (sī′zing), *n.* size[2].

siz zle (siz′əl), *v.,* **-zled, -zling,** *n.* *—v.i.* 1 make a hissing sound, as fat does when it is frying or burning. 2 be very hot: *sizzle in a heat wave, sizzle with anger.* *—v.t.* 1 burn or scorch so as to produce a hissing sound. 2 burn up with intense heat. *—n.* a hissing sound. [imitative]

siz zler (siz′lər), *n.* INFORMAL. a very hot day.

S.J., Society of Jesus.

Skag er rak (skag′ə rak′), *n.* arm of the North Sea between Norway and Denmark. 140 mi. long; 75 mi. wide.

skald (skôld, skäld), *n.* a Scandinavian poet and singer of ancient times. Also, **scald.** [< Scandinavian (Old Icelandic) *skāld*]

skate[1] (skāt), *n., v.,* **skat ed, skat ing.** *—n.* 1 frame with a blade fixed to a shoe or that can be fastened to a shoe so that a person can glide over ice. 2 roller skate. *—v.i.* 1 glide or move along on skates. 2 glide or move along. [< Dutch *schaats* < Middle French *escache* stilt; of Germanic origin] **—skat′er,** *n.*

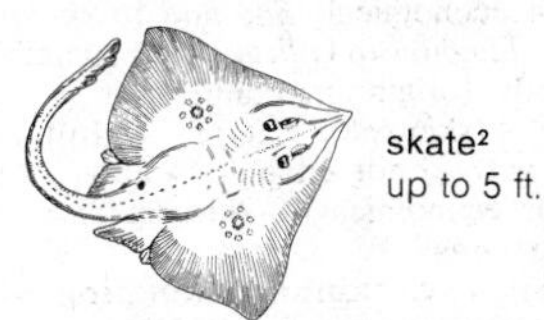

skate[2]
up to 5 ft. long

skate[2] (skāt), *n., pl.* **skates** or **skate.** any of several broad, flat fishes of the same family as the rays, usually having a pointed snout. [< Scandinavian (Old Icelandic) *skata*]

skate[3] (skāt), *n.* SLANG. 1 an old, worn-out horse. 2 fellow: *He's a good skate.* [origin uncertain]

skate board (skāt′bôrd′, skāt′bōrd′), *n.* a narrow board resembling a surfboard, with roller-skate wheels attached to each end, used for gliding or moving on any hard surface.

hat, āge, fär; let, ēqual, tėrm;
it, īce; hot, ōpen, ôrder;
oil, out; cup, pu̇t, rüle;
ch, child; ng, long; sh, she;
th, thin; ᴛʜ, then; zh, measure;

ə represents *a* in about, *e* in taken, *i* in pencil, *o* in lemon, *u* in circus.

< = from, derived from, taken from.

skeet (skēt), *n.* kind of trapshooting in which clay pigeons are flung into the air at angles similar to those taken by a bird in flight. [< Scandinavian (Old Icelandic) *skjōta* to shoot]

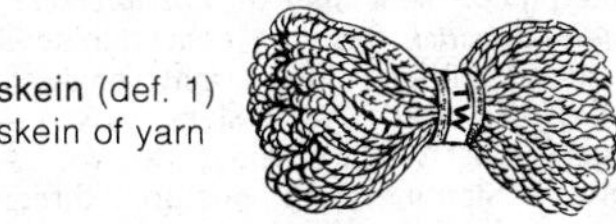

skein (def. 1)
skein of yarn

skein (skān), *n.* 1 a small, coiled bundle of yarn or thread. There are 120 yards in a skein of cotton yarn. 2 a confused tangle. [< Old French *escaigne*]

skel e tal (skel′ə təl), *adj.* 1 of or like a skeleton. 2 attached to, forming, or formed by a skeleton: *skeletal muscles.* **—skel′e-tal ly,** *adv.*

skel e ton (skel′ə tən), *n.* 1 the framework of bones and cartilage in vertebrates that supports the muscles, organs, etc., and protects the viscera. 2 the hard supporting or covering structure of an invertebrate. 3 a very thin person or animal. 4 frame: *the steel skeleton of a building.* 5 basic features or elements; outline. 6 **skeleton in the closet,** a secret source of embarrassment, grief, or shame, especially to a family. *—adj.* 1 of, like, or consisting of a skeleton. 2 greatly reduced in numbers; fractional: *Only a skeleton crew was needed while the ship was tied up at the dock.* [< Greek *skeleton (sōma)* dried (body)]

skel e ton ize (skel′ə tə nīz), *v.t.,* **-ized, -iz ing.** 1 make a skeleton of. 2 outline. 3 greatly reduce in numbers.

skeleton key, key made to open many locks.

skep tic (skep′tik), *n.* 1 person who questions the truth of theories or apparent facts; doubter. 2 person who doubts or questions the possibility or certainty of our knowledge of anything. 3 person who doubts the truth of religious doctrines. Also, **sceptic.** [< Greek *skeptikos* reflective < *skeptesthai* reflect]

skep ti cal (skep′tə kəl), *adj.* 1 of or like a skeptic; inclined to doubt; not believing easily. 2 questioning the truth of theories or apparent facts. Also, **sceptical.** **—skep′ti-cal ly,** *adv.*

skep ti cism (skep′tə siz′əm), *n.* 1 skeptical attitude; doubt; unbelief. 2 doubt or unbelief with regard to religion. 3 the philosophical doctrine that nothing can be proved absolutely. Also, **scepticism.**

sker ry (sker′ē), *n., pl.* **-ries.** SCOTTISH. an isolated rock, a rocky island, or a reef. [< Scandinavian (Old Icelandic) *sker* reef]

sketch (skech), *n.* 1 a rough, quickly done drawing, painting, or design. 2 outline; plan. 3 a brief account, description, or narrative. 4 a short play or performance, usually of light or comic nature. —*v.t.* make a sketch of; draw roughly. —*v.i.* make a sketch or sketches. [< Dutch *schets* < Italian *schizzo,* ultimately < Greek *schedios* impromptu] —**sketch′er,** *n.*

sketch book (skech′bu̇k′), *n.* 1 book to draw or paint sketches in. 2 book of short descriptions, stories, plays, etc.

sketch y (skech′ē), *adj.,* **sketch i er, sketch i est.** 1 like a sketch; having or giving only outlines or main features. 2 incomplete; slight; imperfect: *a sketchy recollection of an event.* —**sketch′i ly,** *adv.* —**sketch′i ness,** *n.*

skew (skyü), *adj.* 1 twisted to one side; slanting. 2 (in geometry) not included in the same plane: *Skew lines do not intersect and are not parallel.* 3 having a part that deviates from a straight line, right angle, etc. 4 unsymmetrical. —*n.* a slant; twist. —*v.i.* 1 slant; twist. 2 turn aside; swerve. —*v.t.* 1 give a slanting form, position, direction, etc., to. 2 represent unfairly; distort. [< Old North French *eskiuer* shy away from, eschew; of Germanic origin] —**skew′ness,** *n.*

skew er (skyü′ər), *n.* 1 a long pin of wood or metal stuck through meat to hold it together while it is cooking. 2 something shaped or used like a long pin. —*v.t.* 1 fasten with a skewer or skewers. 2 pierce with or as if with a skewer. [earlier *skiver;* origin uncertain]

ski (skē), *n., pl.* **skis** or **ski,** *v.,* **skied, ski ing.** —*n.* 1 one of a pair of long, flat, slender pieces of hard wood, plastic, or metal, that can be fastened to the shoes to enable a person to glide over snow. 2 water ski. —*v.i.* 1 glide over snow on skis. 2 water-ski. [< Norwegian] —**ski′er,** *n.*

ski boot, a square-toed boot of sturdy leather worn for skiing.

skid (skid), *v.,* **skid ded, skid ding,** *n.* —*v.i.* 1 slip or slide sideways while moving: *The car skidded on the slippery road.* 2 slide along without turning, as a wheel does when held by a skid. 3 (of an aircraft) to slide or be carried sideways, as when not banked enough while turning. —*v.t.* 1 slide along on a skid or skids. 2 prevent (a wheel) from turning by means of a skid. 3 cause (a vehicle or its wheels) to slide sideways while moving. —*n.* 1 a slip or slide sideways while moving. 2 piece of wood or metal to prevent a wheel from turning. 3 timber, frame, etc., on which something rests, or on which something heavy may slide. 4 runner on the bottom of an aircraft to enable the aircraft to skid along the ground when landing. 5 **on the skids,** SLANG. headed for dismissal, failure, or other disaster. [origin uncertain] —**skid′der,** *n.*

Ski-Doo (ski dü′, skē′dü), *n.* trademark for a motorized toboggan that moves on rubberized tracks and is steered by front-mounted movable skis.

skid row, a slum street or section full of cheap saloons, rooming houses, etc., frequented by derelicts.

skies (skīz), *n.* pl. of **sky.**

skiff (skif), *n.* 1 a small, light rowboat. 2 a small, light boat with a mast for a single triangular sail. [< Italian *schifo;* of Germanic origin]

ski ing (skē′ing), *n.* act or sport of gliding over snow on skis.

ski jump, 1 jump made by a person on skis. 2 an elevated runway for making such a jump.

skil ful (skil′fəl), *adj.* skillful. —**skil′ful ly,** *adv.* —**skil′ful ness,** *n.*

ski lift, any of various mechanisms for transporting skiers to the top of a slope, such as a chair running on a suspended cable.

skill (skil), *n.* 1 ability gained by practice, knowledge, etc.; expertness: *The trained teacher manages the children with skill.* 2 ability to do things well with one's body or with tools: *It takes skill to tune a piano.* 3 an art or craft: *the carpenter's skill.* [< Scandinavian (Old Icelandic) *skil* discernment] —**skill′-less,** *adj.*

skilled (skild), *adj.* 1 having skill; trained; experienced: *a skilled workman.* See **expert** for synonym study. 2 showing skill; requiring skill: *Bricklaying is skilled labor.*

skil let (skil′it), *n.* 1 a shallow pan with a long handle, used for frying. 2 a long-handled saucepan. [origin uncertain]

skill ful (skil′fəl), *adj.* 1 having skill; expert: *a skillful surgeon.* 2 showing skill: *a skillful piece of bricklaying.* Also, **skilful.** —**skill′ful ly,** *adv.* —**skill′ful ness,** *n.*

skim (skim), *v.,* **skimmed, skim ming,** *n., adj.* —*v.t.* 1 remove from the top of a liquid: *skim cream from milk.* 2 clear the top of (a liquid) by removing any floating matter: *skim milk by taking off the cream.* 3 move lightly over: *gulls skimming the waves. The skaters skimmed the ice.* 4 send skimming: *You can skim a flat stone over the water.* 5 read hastily or carelessly; read with omissions: *It took me an hour to skim the book.* 6 cover with a thin layer of ice, scum, etc. —*v.i.* 1 move lightly: *skim through the newspaper headlines.* 2 glide along: *Swallows were skimming by.* 3 become covered with a thin layer of ice, scum, etc. —*n.* 1 something which is skimmed off. 2 skim milk. 3 act of skimming. —*adj.* skimmed. [probably < Old French *escumer* < *escume* scum; of Germanic origin]

skimmed milk, skim milk.

skim mer (skim′ər), *n.* 1 person or thing that skims. 2 a long-handled shallow ladle full of holes, used in skimming liquids. 3 any of a family of sea birds of the same order as the gulls, that skim along the surface of the water to get food.

skim milk, milk from which the cream has been removed.

ski mo bile (skē′mō bēl), *n.* a small vehicle running on tracks, for carrying skiers to the top of a slope.

skimp (skimp), *v.t.* 1 supply in too small an amount: *Don't skimp the butter in making a cake.* 2 do imperfectly. —*v.i.* 1 be very saving or economical: *She had to skimp to send her daughter to college.* 2 do something imperfectly. [origin uncertain]

skimp y (skim′pē), *adj.,* **skimp i er, skimp i est.** 1 not enough; scanty. 2 too saving or economical. —**skimp′i ly,** *adv.* —**skimp′i ness,** *n.*

skin (skin), *n., v.,* **skinned, skin ning.** —*n.* 1 the outer layer of tissue of the human or animal body, especially when soft and flexible. 2 hide; pelt. See synonym study below. 3 any outer covering or surface layer, as the rind of a fruit, a sausage casing, etc. 4 container made of skin for holding liquids. 5 the planking or plating covering the ribs or frame of a ship, aircraft, rocket, etc. 6 SLANG. **a** a cheat; swindler. **b** skinflint. 7 **by the skin of one's teeth,** by a very narrow margin; barely. 8 **in a whole skin** or **with a whole skin,** safe and sound. 9 **save one's skin,** escape without harm. —*v.t.* 1 take the skin off: *skin a deer. I skinned my knees when I fell.* 2 cover with or as if with skin. 3 SLANG. swindle of money, etc.; cheat. 4 **skin alive,** INFORMAL. **a** torture; flay. **b** scold severely. **c** defeat completely. —*v.i.* 1 become covered with skin; form a new skin: *The wound gradually skinned over.* 2 shed skin. 3 pass barely; slip by narrowly. [< Scandinavian (Old Icelandic) *skinn*] —**skin′like′,** *adj.*

Syn. *n.* 2 **Skin, hide, pelt** mean the outer covering of the body. **Skin** is the general word, applying to the covering of a person or animal: *The skin of a calf makes soft leather.* **Hide** applies particularly to the tough skin of a large animal, commercially raw or tanned: *The hide of an elephant is tough.* **Pelt** applies particularly to the skin of a fur- or wool-bearing animal before dressing or tanning: *Trappers sell pelts of foxes.*

skin-deep (skin′dēp′), *adj.* no deeper than the skin; shallow; slight.

skin-dive (skin′dīv′), *v.i.,* **-dived, -div ing.** engage in skin diving.

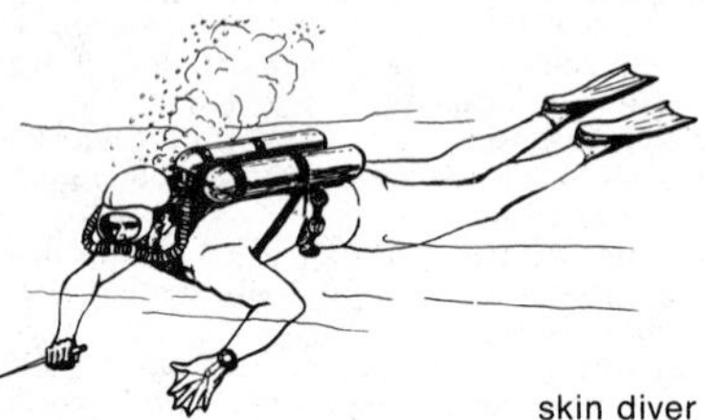

skin diver

skin diver, person engaged in skin diving.

skin diving, sport of swimming under water, equipped with a face mask, rubber flippers, and often a portable breathing device.

skin flint (skin′flint′), *n.* a mean, stingy person.

skin ful (skin′fu̇l), *n., pl.* **-fuls.** 1 as much as a skin for liquids can hold. 2 INFORMAL. as much as a person or animal can hold or drink.

skink (skingk), *n.* any of a family of small, smooth-scaled lizards, often with short, weak legs. [< Greek *skinkos*]

skin less (skin′lis), *adj.* having no skin: *skinless frankfurters.*

skin ner (skin′ər), *n.* 1 person who skins animals. 2 person who prepares or deals in skins, furs, etc. 3 INFORMAL. person whose work is driving horses, mules, etc.

skin ny (skin′ē), *adj.,* **-ni er, -ni est.** 1 very thin; very lean. 2 like skin. —**skin′ni ness,** *n.*

skin test, test made on the skin, such as the Schick test or patch test.

skin tight (skin′tīt′), *adj.* fitting closely to the skin.

skip (skip), *v.,* **skipped, skip ping,** *n.* —*v.i.* 1 leap lightly; spring; jump: *lambs skipping in the fields.* 2 go bounding along a surface. 3 omit parts; pass from one thing to another, disregarding what is between: *Answer the questions in order without skipping.* 4 INFORMAL. leave in a hurry. 5 advance in school by being promoted one or more grades ahead of the next regular grade. —*v.t.* 1 leap lightly over: *skip rope.* 2 send bounding along a surface: *skip stones on a lake.* 3 pass over; fail to notice; omit: *skip the unfamiliar words in a book.* 4 advance past (a grade) in being promoted in school. 5 INFORMAL. **a** dodge, avoid, or stay away from: *skip*

school. **b** leave (a place) hurriedly; flee: *The swindler has skipped town.*
—*n.* 1 a light spring, jump, or leap: *The child gave a skip of joy.* 2 gait, especially of children, in which hops and steps are combined. 3 a passing over; omission.
[Middle English *skippen,* probably < Scandinavian (Old Icelandic) *skipa* undergo a change]

ski pants, lightweight, close-fitting pants with tapering trouser legs, worn by skiers.

skip jack (skip′jak′), *n., pl.* **-jacks** or **-jack.** any of various fishes that sometimes leap out of the water, such as a variety of tuna.

skip per¹ (skip′ər), *n.* 1 captain of a ship, especially of a small trading or fishing boat. 2 any captain or leader. [< Middle Dutch *schipper* < *schip* ship]

skip per² (skip′ər), *n.* 1 person or thing that skips. 2 any of certain insects that make skipping movements, such as a maggot that lives in cheese. 3 any of various small, mothlike insects that fly with a darting, hopping motion. [< *skip*]

skirl (skėrl), *v.t., v.i.* (of bagpipes) sound loudly and shrilly. —*n.* sound of a bagpipe. [< Scandinavian (dialectal Norwegian) *skrylla*]

skir mish (skėr′mish), *n.* 1 a brief fight between small groups of soldiers. 2 a slight conflict, argument, contest, etc. —*v.i.* take part in a skirmish. [< Old French *eskirmiss-,* a form of *eskirmir,* originally, ward off; of Germanic origin] **—skir′mish er,** *n.*

skirt (skėrt), *n.* 1 the part of a dress that hangs from the waist. 2 a woman's or girl's garment that hangs from the waist. 3 something like a skirt: *the skirts of a man's long coat.* 4 border; edge. 5 the outer part of a place, group of people, etc. 6 SLANG. woman or girl. 7 one of the flaps hanging from the sides of a saddle. —*v.t.* 1 border or edge. 2 pass along the border or edge of: *skirt a swamp.* 3 be, lie, live, etc., along the border of. —*v.i.* 1 pass along the border or edge. 2 be, lie, live, etc., along the border of a place. [< Scandinavian (Old Icelandic) *skyrta* shirt]

ski run, a snow-covered slope or steep runway used by skiers.

skit (skit), *n.* a short sketch that contains humor or satire: *a television skit.* [origin uncertain]

ski tow, a continuous rope on pulleys for pulling skiers to the top of a slope.

skit ter (skit′ər), *v.i.* move lightly or quickly; skim or skip along a surface. —*v.t.* cause to skitter.

skit tish (skit′ish), *adj.* 1 apt to start, jump, or run; easily frightened: *a skittish horse.* 2 fickle; changeable. 3 coy. [perhaps < Scandinavian (Old Icelandic) *skȳt-,* stem of *skjōta* to shoot] **—skit′tish ly,** *adv.* **—skit′tish ness,** *n.*

skit tles (skit′lz), *n.* game in which the players try to knock down nine wooden pins by rolling or throwing wooden disks or balls at them. [< Scandinavian (Danish) *skyttel* shuttle]

skiv vies (skiv′ēz), *n.pl.* SLANG. men's underwear. [origin unknown]

skoal (skōl), *n., interj.* a Scandinavian word used in drinking a health. It means "Hail" or "May you prosper." [< Danish *skaal* < Old Icelandic *skāl* bowl]

sku a (skyü′ə), *n.* any of several large brown sea birds of the same order as the gulls; jaeger. [< New Latin < Faeroese *skūgvur*]

skul dug ger y (skul dug′ər ē), *n.* INFORMAL. trickery; dishonesty. [origin uncertain]

skulk (skulk), *v.i.* 1 keep out of sight to avoid danger, work, duty, etc.; hide or lurk in a cowardly way. See **lurk** for synonym study. 2 move in a stealthy, sneaking way. —*n.* person who skulks. [< Scandinavian (Danish) *skulke*] **—skulk′er,** *n.* **—skulk′ing ly,** *adv.*

skull (skul), *n.* 1 the bony or cartilaginous framework of the head in man and other vertebrates, enclosing and protecting the brain; cranium. 2 head; brain. [< Scandinavian (dialectal Norwegian) *skul* shell]

skull and crossbones, picture of a human skull above two crossed bones. It was used on pirates' flags as a symbol of death, and is now often used on the labels of poisonous drugs, etc.

skull cap (skul′kap′), *n.* a close-fitting cap without a brim.

skunk (def. 1)—about 2 ft. long with tail

skunk (skungk), *n.* 1 any of various black, omnivorous, bushy-tailed mammals of North America, of the same family as the weasel, usually with white markings along the back and tail; polecat. When frightened or attacked, skunks squirt a spray of liquid with a very strong, unpleasant smell from a pair of glands near the tail. 2 fur of this animal, used on coats, etc. 3 INFORMAL. a mean, contemptible person. —*v.t.* SLANG. defeat utterly, as in an unequal contest where one side is held scoreless. [of Algonquian origin]

skunk cabbage, a low, ill-smelling, broad-leaved, perennial North American arum, growing commonly in moist ground.

sky (skī), *n., pl.* **skies,** *v.,* **skied** or **skyed, sky ing.** —*n.* 1 the space high above the earth, appearing as a great arch or dome covering the world; the region of the clouds or the upper air; the heavens: *a blue sky, a cloudy sky.* 2 heaven. 3 weather or climate. 4 **out of a clear (blue) sky,** suddenly; unexpectedly. 5 **to the skies,** very highly. —*v.t.* hit, throw, or raise high into the air. [< Scandinavian (Old Icelandic) *skȳ* cloud]

sky blue, a clear, soft blue. **—sky′-blue′,** *adj.*

sky cap (skī′kap′), *n.* U.S. porter at an airport. [< *sky* + *-cap,* as in *redcap*]

sky div ing (skī′dī′ving), *n.* act or sport of diving from an airplane and dropping in a free fall for a great distance before releasing the parachute.

sky ey (skī′ē), *adj.* 1 of or from the sky. 2 very high; lofty. 3 sky-blue.

sky-high (skī′hī′), *adv., adj.* very high.

sky jack (skī′jak′), *v.t.* hijack (an airplane), especially to a foreign country. —*n.* a hijacking of an airplane. **—sky′jack′er,** *n.*

sky lark (skī′lärk′), *n.* the common European lark, a small bird that sings very sweetly as it flies toward the sky. —*v.i.* play pranks; frolic.

sky light (skī′līt′), *n.* window in a roof or ceiling.

hat, āge, fär; let, ēqual, tėrm;
it, īce; hot, ōpen, ôrder;
oil, out; cup, pu̇t, rüle;
ch, child; ng, long; sh, she;
th, thin; ᴛʜ, then; zh, measure;

ə represents *a* in about, *e* in taken, *i* in pencil, *o* in lemon, *u* in circus.

< = from, derived from, taken from.

sky line (skī′līn′), *n.* 1 line at which earth and sky seem to meet; horizon. 2 outline of buildings, mountains, trees, etc., as seen against the sky.

sky pilot, SLANG. clergyman; chaplain.

sky rock et (skī′rok′it), *n.* firework that goes up high in the air and bursts into a shower of stars, sparks, etc.; rocket. —*v.i.* 1 act like a skyrocket; rise suddenly, make a brilliant show, and disappear. 2 rise much and quickly: *Prices were skyrocketing.* —*v.t.* cause to skyrocket.

sky sail (skī′sāl′; *Nautical* skī′səl), *n.* (in a square-rigged ship) a light sail set at the top of the mast above the royal.

sky scrap er (skī′skrā′pər), *n.* a very tall building.

sky ward (skī′wərd), *adv., adj.* toward the sky.

sky wards (skī′wərdz), *adv.* skyward.

sky way (skī′wā′), *n.* 1 air lane; airway. 2 an elevated highway.

sky writ er (skī′rī′tər), *n.* person or thing that does skywriting.

sky writ ing (skī′rī′ting), *n.* the tracing of letters, words, etc., against the sky by smoke or some similar substance ejected from an airplane.

slab (slab), *n.* 1 a broad, flat, thick piece (of stone, wood, meat, etc.): *This sidewalk is made of slabs of concrete.* 2 a rough outside piece cut lengthwise from a log. [Middle English *slabbe*]

slack¹ (slak), *adj.* 1 not tight or firm; loose: *The rope hung slack.* 2 careless: *a slack housekeeper.* 3 slow: *The horse was moving at a slack pace.* 4 not active; not brisk; dull: *Business is slack at this season.* 5 gentle or moderate.
—*n.* 1 part that hangs loose: *Pull in the slack of the rope.* 2 a dull season; quiet period; lull. 3 a stopping of a strong flow of the tide or a current of water.
—*v.t.* 1 make slack; let up on. 2 slake (lime). —*v.i.* be or become slack; let up.
slack off, a loosen. **b** lessen one's efforts.
slack up, slow down; go more slowly.
—*adv.* in a slack manner.
[Old English *slæc*] **—slack′ly,** *adv.* **—slack′ness,** *n.*

slack² (slak), *n.* dirt, dust, and small pieces left after coal is screened; small or refuse coal. [< Middle Dutch *slacke*]

slack en (slak′ən), *v.t.* 1 make slower: *Don't slacken your efforts till the work is done.* 2 make looser: *Slacken the rope.* —*v.i.* 1 become slower: *Work slackens on a hot day.* 2 become less active, vigorous, brisk, etc.: *His business always slackens in the winter.* 3 become loose: *The rope slackened as the wave sent the boat toward the pier.*

slack er (slak′ər), *n.* person who shirks work or evades his duty, especially an able-bodied man who evades military service in time of war.

slacks (slaks), *n.pl.* men's or women's trousers for casual wear.

slack water, time between tides when the water does not move either way.

slag (slag), *n., v.,* **slagged, slag ging.** —*n.* 1 the rough, hard waste left after metal is separated from ore by melting. 2 scoria (def. 2). —*v.t., v.i.* form slag; change into slag. [< Middle Low German *slagge*]

slag gy (slag′ē), *adj.* of, like, or having to do with slag.

slain (slān), *v.* pp. of **slay.**

slake (slāk; *also* slak *for v.t. 4, v.i. 1*), *v.,* **slaked, slak ing.** —*v.t.* 1 satisfy (thirst, revenge, wrath, etc.). 2 cause to be less active, vigorous, intense, etc. 3 put out (a fire). 4 change (lime) to slaked lime by leaving it in the moist air or putting water on it. —*v.i.* 1 (of lime) become slaked lime. 2 become less active, vigorous, intense, etc. [Old English *slacian* slacken < *slæc* slack]

slaked lime, a white powder obtained by exposing lime to moist air or by putting water on lime; calcium hydroxide. Plaster contains slaked lime and sand. *Formula:* $Ca(OH)_2$

sla lom (slä′ləm, slal′əm), *n.* (in skiing) a zigzag race downhill. [< Norwegian]

slam (slam), *v.,* **slammed, slam ming,** *n.* —*v.t.* 1 shut with force and noise; close with a bang: *She slammed the window down.* 2 throw, push, hit, or move hard with force. 3 INFORMAL. criticize harshly. —*v.i.* 1 shut with force and noise; close with a bang: *The door slammed.* 2 move hard with force. —*n.* 1 a violent and noisy closing, striking, etc.; bang: *throw books down with a slam.* 2 INFORMAL. harsh criticism. 3 the winning of 12 tricks **(little slam** or **small slam)** or all 13 tricks **(grand slam)** in the game of bridge. [perhaps < Scandinavian (Old Icelandic) *slamra*]

slam bang (slam′bang′), INFORMAL. —*adv.* with noisy or headlong violence. —*adj.* violent and noisy; unrestrained.

slan der (slan′dər), *n.* 1 a false statement spoken with intent to harm the reputation of another. 2 the spreading of false reports. —*v.t.* talk falsely about. —*v.i.* speak or spread slander. [< Old French *esclandre* scandal < Latin *scandalum.* Doublet of SCANDAL.] **—slan′der er,** *n.*

slan der ous (slan′dər əs), *adj.* 1 containing a slander. 2 speaking or spreading slanders. **—slan′der ous ly,** *adv.* **—slan′der ous ness,** *n.*

slang (slang), *n.* 1 words, phrases, etc., usually characterized by a special vividness or coloring, and not generally used in formal English. Slang is mostly made up of new words or meanings that are popular for only a short time. *Slob* and *on the skids* are slang. 2 special talk of a particular class of people. A *contract* is underworld slang for an *order to kill someone.* —*v.t.* attack with abusive language. —*v.i.* 1 use abusive language. 2 use slang. [origin uncertain]

slang y (slang′ē), *adj.,* **slang i er, slang i est.** 1 containing slang; full of slang. 2 using much slang. **—slang′i ly,** *adv.* **—slang′i ness,** *n.*

slank (slangk), *v.* ARCHAIC. a pt. of **slink.**

slant (slant), *v.i.* go off at an angle; have or take an oblique direction or position; slope: *Most handwriting slants to the right.* See **slope** for synonym study. —*v.t.* 1 cause to slant: *slant a roof.* 2 make (a story, news account, etc.) biased by choosing or emphasizing certain facts. —*n.* 1 a slanting or oblique direction or position; slope: *a roof with a sharp slant.* 2 way of regarding something; mental attitude. —*adj.* sloping. [variant of earlier *slent* < Scandinavian (Norwegian) *slenta*]

slant ing (slan′ting), *adj.* that slants; sloping. **—slant′ing ly,** *adv.*

slant ways (slant′wāz′), *adv.* slantwise.

slant wise (slant′wīz′), *adv.* in a slanting manner; obliquely. —*adj.* slanting; oblique.

slap (slap), *n., v.,* **slapped, slap ping,** *adv.* —*n.* 1 a blow with the open hand or with something flat. 2 sharp words of blame; direct insult or rebuff. 3 sound made by a slapping. —*v.t.* 1 strike with the open hand or with something flat. 2 put, dash, or cast with force: *She slapped the book down on the table.* —*v.i.* strike with the open hand or with something flat. —*adv.* 1 straight; directly: *The thief ran slap into a policeman.* 2 suddenly. [< Low German *slappe*]

slap dash (slap′dash′), *adv.* hastily and carelessly. —*adj.* hasty and careless. —*n.* hasty, careless action, methods, or work.

slap hap py (slap′hap′ē), *adj.* SLANG. 1 dizzy and uncoordinated from too many blows to the head. 2 silly; giddy; senseless.

slap stick (slap′stik′), *n.* 1 device consisting of two long, narrow sticks fastened so as to slap together loudly when a clown, actor, etc., hits somebody with it. 2 comedy full of rough play. —*adj.* full of rough play. In slapstick comedy, the actors knock each other around to make people laugh.

slash[1] (slash), *v.t.* 1 cut with a sweeping stroke of a sword, knife, etc.; gash: *slash bark off a tree.* 2 cut or slit (a garment) to let a different cloth or color show through. 3 whip severely; lash. 4 criticize sharply, severely, or unkindly. 5 cut down severely; reduce a great deal: *slash expenses.* —*v.i.* make a slashing stroke. —*n.* 1 a sweeping, slashing stroke. 2 a cut or wound made by such a stroke. 3 an ornamental slit in a garment that lets a different cloth or color show through. 4 clearing in a forest, usually littered with broken branches, felled trees, etc. 5 tangle of fallen trees, branches, etc. 6 a severe cutting down; great reduction. 7 U.S. mark (/) used in writing and printing; virgule. [Middle English *slaschen*]

slash[2] (slash), *n.* wet or swampy ground overgrown with bushes or trees. [origin uncertain]

slat (slat), *n.* a long, thin, narrow strip of wood or metal. [< Old French *esclat* split piece; of Germanic origin]

slate (slāt), *n., v.,* **slat ed, slat ing,** *adj.* —*n.* 1 a fine-grained, bluish-gray metamorphic rock that splits easily into thin, smooth layers. Slate is used to cover roofs and for blackboards. 2 a thin piece of this rock. Children used to write on slates. 3 a dark, bluish gray. 4 list of candidates, officers, etc., to be considered for appointment, nomination, election, etc. 5 **a clean slate,** a record not marred by mistakes or faults. —*v.t.* 1 cover with slate. 2 list on or as if on a slate: *be slated for the office of club president, be slated for promotion.* —*adj.* dark bluish-gray. [< Old French *esclate,* variant of *esclat* slat] **—slate′like′,** *adj.*

slat er (slā′tər), *n.* person who covers roofs, etc., with slates.

slath er (slaᴛʜ′ər), INFORMAL. —*n.* **slathers,** *pl.* a large amount. —*v.t.* spread or pour lavishly. [origin unknown]

slat tern (slat′ərn), *n.* woman or girl who is dirty, careless, or untidy in her dress, her ways, her housekeeping, etc. [origin uncertain]

slat tern ly (slat′ərn lē), *adj.* like a slattern; slovenly; untidy. **—slat′tern li ness,** *n.*

slat y (slā′tē), *adj.,* **slat i er, slat i est.** 1 of, like, or having to do with slate. 2 slate-colored.

slaugh ter (slô′tər), *n.* 1 the killing of an animal or animals for food; butchering. 2 brutal killing; much or needless killing: *The battle resulted in a dreadful slaughter.* —*v.t., v.i.* 1 kill an animal or animals for food; butcher. 2 kill brutally; massacre. [< Scandinavian (Old Icelandic) *slātr* butcher meat] **—slaugh′ter er,** *n.*

slaugh ter house (slô′tər hous′), *n., pl.* **-hous es** (-hou′ziz). place where animals are killed for food.

slaugh ter ous (slô′tər əs), *adj.* murderous; destructive. **—slaugh′ter ous ly,** *adv.*

Slav (släv, slav), *n.* member of a group of peoples in eastern, southeastern, and central Europe whose languages are related. Russians, Poles, Czechs, Slovaks, Bulgarians, and Yugoslavs are Slavs. —*adj.* of or having to do with Slavs; Slavic.

slave (slāv), *n., v.,* **slaved, slav ing,** *adj.* —*n.* 1 person who is the property of another. 2 person who is controlled or ruled by some desire, habit, or influence: *a slave to drugs.* 3 person who works like a slave. —*v.i.* work like a slave. —*adj.* of or done by slaves: *slave labor.* [< Old French *esclave* < Medieval Latin *Sclavus* Slav; the word was originally applied to enslaved Slavic peoples] **—slave′like′,** *adj.*

slave driver, 1 overseer of slaves. 2 an exacting taskmaster.

slave hold er (slāv′hōl′dər), *n.* owner of slaves.

slave hold ing (slāv′hōl′ding), *adj.* owning slaves. —*n.* the owning of slaves.

slav er[1] (slā′vər), *n.* 1 dealer in slaves. 2 ship used in the slave trade.

slav er[2] (slav′ər), *v.i.* let saliva run from the mouth; drool. —*v.t.* wet with saliva; slobber. —*n.* saliva running from the mouth. [< Scandinavian (Old Icelandic) *slafra*]

Slave River, river in NW Canada, flowing north from Lake Athabasca to Great Slave Lake. 285 mi.

slav er y (slā′vər ē), *n.* 1 condition of being a slave. Many African Negroes were captured and sold into slavery. 2 custom of owning slaves. 3 condition like that of a slave. 4 hard work like that of a slave.

Slave State, any of the 15 states of the United States in which slavery was legal before and during the Civil War.

slave trade, the business of procuring, transporting, and selling slaves.

slav ey (slā′vē), *n., pl.* **-eys.** INFORMAL. maid of all work.

Slav ic (slä′vik, slav′ik), *adj.* of or having to do with the Slavs or their languages. —*n.* group of languages spoken by the Slavs, including Russian, Polish, Czech, Slovak, Bulgarian, Serbo-Croatian, etc.

slav ish (slā′vish), *adj.* 1 of or having to do with a slave or slaves. 2 like a slave; mean; base. 3 weakly submitting. 4 like that of slaves; fit for slaves. 5 lacking originality and independence: *a slavish reproduction.* **—slav′ish ly,** *adv.* **—slav′ish ness,** *n.*

Sla vo ni a (slə vō′nē ə), *n.* region in S Europe, now in N Yugoslavia.

Sla vo ni an (slə vō′nē ən), *adj.* 1 of or

having to do with Slavonia or its people. 2 Slavic. —*n.* 1 native of Slavonia. 2 Slav.

Sla von ic (slə von′ik), *adj., n.* 1 Slavic. 2 Slavonian.

slaw (slô), *n.* coleslaw.

slay (slā), *v.t.*, **slew, slain, slay ing.** kill with violence. See **kill**[1] for synonym study. [Old English *slēan*] **—slay′er,** *n.*

sleave (slēv), *n.* a small silk thread made by separating a thicker thread. [Old English *-slǣfan,* as in *tōslǣfan* to divide]

slea zy (slē′zē), *adj.*, **-zi er, -zi est.** 1 flimsy and poor: *sleazy cloth.* 2 disreputable: *a sleazy neighborhood.* [origin uncertain] **—slea′zi ly,** *adv.* **—slea′zi ness,** *n.*

sled (sled), *n., v.*, **sled ded, sled ding.** —*n.* framework mounted on runners for use on snow or ice. Sleds pulled by dogs are common in the Arctic. —*v.i.* ride on or in a sled. —*v.t.* carry on a sled. [< Middle Dutch *sledde*] **—sled′der,** *n.*

sled ding (sled′ing), *n.* 1 a riding or coasting on a sled. 2 condition of the snow for the use of a sled. 3 **hard sledding,** unfavorable conditions.

sled dog, dog trained and used to draw a sled in arctic regions.

sledge[1] (slej), *n., v.*, **sledged, sledg ing.** —*n.* a heavy sled or sleigh, usually pulled by horses. —*v.i.* ride in a sledge. —*v.t.* carry on a sledge. [< Dutch *sleedse*]

sledge[2] (slej), *n.* sledgehammer. [Old English *slecg*]

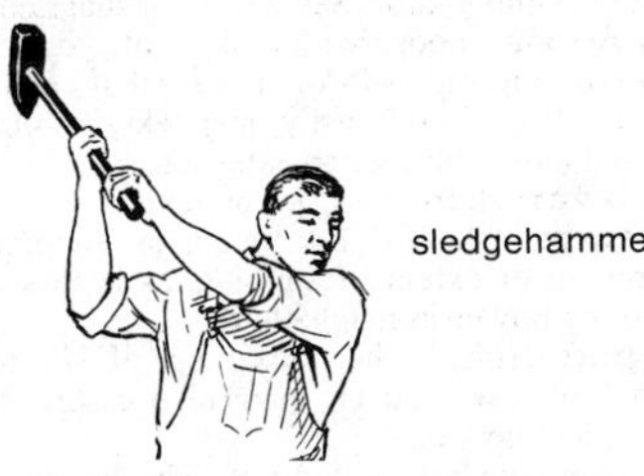

sledgehammer

sledge ham mer (slej′ham′ər), *n.* a large, heavy hammer, usually swung with both hands. —*v.t.* hit with, or as if with, a sledgehammer. —*adj.* powerful; crushing.

sleek (slēk), *adj.* 1 soft and glossy; smooth: *sleek hair.* 2 having smooth, soft skin, hair, fur, etc.: *a sleek cat.* 3 smooth of speech, manners, etc.: *a sleek salesman.* 4 having clean lines; trim. —*v.t.* 1 smooth; make smooth. 2 make smooth and glossy; make tidy. [variant of *slick*] **—sleek′ly,** *adv.* **—sleek′ness,** *n.*

sleep (slēp), *v.*, **slept, sleep ing,** *n.* —*v.i.* 1 rest body and mind; be without ordinary consciousness. 2 be in a condition like sleep: *The seeds sleep in the ground all winter.* —*v.t.* 1 provide with or offer sleeping accommodation for: *a hotel that sleeps 500 people.* 2 pass in sleeping.

sleep away, pass or spend in sleeping.

sleep in, sleep where one works.

sleep off, get rid of by sleeping.

sleep out, **a** sleep away from where one works. **b** sleep out of doors.

—*n.* 1 condition in which body and mind are very inactive, occurring naturally and regularly in animals. 2 condition like sleep. The last sleep means death.

[Old English *slǣpan*] **—sleep′like′,** *adj.*

sleep er (slē′pər), *n.* 1 person or thing that sleeps. 2 a railroad sleeping car. 3 a horizontal beam used as a support. 4 INFORMAL. person or thing that achieves unexpected success, as an athletic team, motion picture, book, etc.

sleep ing (slē′ping), *n.* sleep. —*adj.* 1 that sleeps. 2 used for sleeping on or in: *sleeping quarters, a sleeping porch.* 3 inactive in business: *a sleeping partner.*

sleeping bag, a canvas or waterproof bag, usually warmly lined, to sleep in out of doors.

sleeping car, a railroad car with berths for passengers to sleep in; Pullman.

sleeping pill, pill or capsule containing a drug that induces sleep.

sleeping sickness, 1 disease common in Africa caused by either of two trypanosomes and carried by the tsetse fly, resulting in fever, inflammation of the brain, sleepiness and increasing weakness, and usually death. 2 kind of epidemic encephalitis caused by a virus, characterized by extreme drowsiness and weakness.

sleep less (slēp′lis), *adj.* 1 without sleep; restless. 2 watchful; wide-awake. 3 always moving or acting. **—sleep′less ly,** *adv.* **—sleep′less ness,** *n.*

sleep walk er (slēp′wô′kər), *n.* person who walks about while asleep; somnambulist.

sleep walk ing (slēp′wô′king), *n.* act of walking while asleep; somnambulism.

sleep y (slē′pē), *adj.*, **sleep i er, sleep i est.** 1 ready to go to sleep; inclined to sleep. See synonym study below. 2 not active; quiet. **—sleep′i ly,** *adv.* **—sleep′i ness,** *n.*

Syn. 1 **Sleepy, drowsy** mean ready or inclined to sleep. **Sleepy** suggests being ready to fall asleep or having a tendency to sleep: *He never gets enough rest and is always sleepy.* **Drowsy** suggests being heavy or dull with sleepiness: *After lying in the sun, she became drowsy.*

sleep y head (slē′pē hed′), *n.* a sleepy, drowsy, or lazy person.

sleet (slēt), *n.* 1 partly frozen rain; snow or hail mixed with rain. 2 a thin coating of ice formed by frozen rain. —*v.i.* come down in sleet. [Middle English *slete*]

sleet y (slē′tē), *adj.*, **sleet i er, sleet i est.** of or like sleet; characterized by sleet. **—sleet′i ness,** *n.*

sleeve (slēv), *n.* 1 the part of a garment that covers the arm. 2 tube into which a rod or another tube fits. 3 **laugh up one's sleeve,** be amused but not show it. 4 **up one's sleeve,** in reserve; ready for use when needed. [Old English *slīefe*] **—sleeve′less,** *adj.*

sleeved (slēvd), *adj.* having sleeves.

sleigh

sleigh (slā), *n.* carriage or cart mounted on runners for use on ice or snow. —*v.i.* travel or ride in a sleigh. [< Dutch *slee,* variant of *slede* sled]

sleigh ing (slā′ing), *n.* 1 a riding in a sleigh. 2 condition of the roads for using a sleigh.

sleight (slīt), *n.* 1 skill; dexterity. 2 a clever trick. [< Scandinavian (Old Icelandic) *slǣgth* < *slǣgr* sly]

sleight of hand, 1 skill and quickness in moving the hands. 2 tricks or skill of a modern magician; juggling.

slen der (slen′dər), *adj.* 1 long and thin; not big around; slim: *A boy 6 feet tall and weighing 130 pounds is very slender. A pencil is a slender piece of wood.* See synonym study below. 2 slight; small; scanty: *a slender meal, a slender income, a slender hope.* [Middle English *slendre, sclendre*] **—slen′der ly,** *adv.* **—slen′der ness,** *n.*

Syn. 1 **Slender, slim** mean thin, not big around. **Slender** suggests pleasing, graceful thinness: *Most girls want to be slender.* **Slim** suggests lack of flesh and lightness of frame or build: *He is a slim boy, but he may fill out as he becomes older.*

hat, āge, fär; let, ēqual, tėrm;
it, īce; hot, ōpen, ôrder;
oil, out; cup, pu̇t, rüle;
ch, child; ng, long; sh, she;
th, thin; ᴛʜ, then; zh, measure;

ə represents *a* in about, *e* in taken, *i* in pencil, *o* in lemon, *u* in circus.

< = from, derived from, taken from.

slen der ize (slen′də rīz′), *v.t., v.i.*, **-ized, -iz ing.** make or become slender.

slept (slept), *v.* pt. and pp. of **sleep.**

sleuth (slüth), *n.* 1 bloodhound. 2 INFORMAL. detective. —*v.i.* INFORMAL. be or act like a detective. [< Scandinavian (Old Icelandic) *slōth* a trail]

sleuth hound (slüth′hound′), *n.* bloodhound.

slew[1] (slü), *v.* pt. of **slay.**

slew[2] (slü), *v.t., v.i.* turn; swing; twist. —*n.* a turn; swing; twist. Also, **slue.** [origin unknown]

slew[3] (slü), *n.* slough[1] (def. 2).

slew[4] (slü), *n.* INFORMAL. a lot; large number or amount. Also, **slue.** [< Irish *sluagh* host, crowd]

slice (slīs), *n., v.*, **sliced, slic ing.** —*n.* 1 a thin, flat, broad piece cut from something: *a slice of bread, a slice of meat, a slice of cake.* 2 knife or spatula with a thin, broad blade. 3 part; share. 4 (in sports) a slicing hit. —*v.t.* 1 cut into slices. 2 cut (off) as a slice. 3 cut through or across. 4 (in sports) hit (a ball) so that it curves to one's right if hit right-handed. —*v.i.* (in sports) slice a ball. [< Old French *esclice* thin chip; of Germanic origin]

slic er (slī′sər), *n.* 1 tool or machine that slices: *a meat slicer.* 2 person who slices.

slick (slik), *adj.* 1 soft and glossy; sleek; smooth: *slick hair.* 2 slippery; greasy: *a road slick with ice or mud.* 3 INFORMAL. clever; ingenious. 4 sly; tricky. 5 smooth of speech, manners, etc. —*v.i.* make sleek or smooth. —*n.* 1 a smooth place or spot. Oil makes a slick on the surface of water. 2 INFORMAL. magazine printed on heavy, glossy paper. —*adv.* 1 smoothly; slyly; cleverly. 2 directly. [Old English *slician*] **—slick′ly,** *adv.* **—slick′ness,** *n.*

slick er (slik′ər), *n.* U.S. 1 a long, loose, waterproof coat, made of oilskin or the like. 2 INFORMAL. a sly, tricky person.

slid (slid), *v.* pt. and a pp. of **slide.**

slid den (slid′n), *v.* a pp. of **slide.**

slide (slīd), *v.*, **slid, slid** or **slid den, slid ing,** *n.* —*v.i.* 1 move smoothly along on a surface: *The bureau drawers slide in and out.* See synonym study below. 2 move or go easily, quietly, or secretly: *The burglar slid behind the curtains.* 3 slip as one losing one's foothold: *The car slid into the ditch.* 4 pass by degrees; slip: *slide into bad habits.* 5 pass without heeding or being heeded. 6 **let slide,** not bother about; neglect. —*v.t.* 1 cause to move smoothly along on a surface or in a groove: *Slide the door back into the wall.* 2 put quietly or secretly: *He slid a gun into his pocket.*

—*n.* 1 act of sliding: *The children each take a slide in turn.* 2 a smooth surface for sliding on. 3 track, rail, etc., on which something slides. 4 something that slides or that works by sliding. 5 the U-shaped tube of a trumpet or trombone that changes the pitch of the tones. 6 mass of earth, snow, etc., sliding down; landslide; avalanche. 7 the sliding down of such a mass. 8 a small thin sheet of glass on which objects are placed in order to examine them under a microscope. 9 a small transparent photograph made of glass or film. Slides are put into a projector and shown on a screen.

[Old English *slīdan*]

Syn. *v.i.* 1 **Slide, glide** mean to move along smoothly over a surface. **Slide** emphasizes continuous contact with a smooth or slippery surface: *The boat slid down the bank into the water.* **Glide** emphasizes a continuous, easy, graceful movement, without reference to the surface: *The swans glide gracefully on the lake.*

slide fastener, zipper.

slide projector, instrument for projecting onto a screen the images on photographic slides.

slid er (slī′dər), *n.* 1 person, thing, or part that slides. 2 (in baseball) a fast pitch with a sideways spin that makes the ball curve slightly.

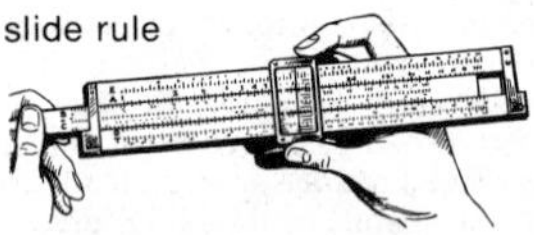
slide rule

slide rule, device consisting of a ruler with a sliding section in the center, both parts being marked with logarithmic scales, used for making rapid mathematical calculations.

sliding scale, scale of wages, prices, taxes, etc., that can be adjusted according to certain conditions.

slight (slīt), *adj.* 1 not much; not important; small: *I have a slight headache.* 2 not big around; slender: *She is a slight girl.* 3 frail; flimsy: *a slight excuse.* —*v.t.* treat as of little value; pay too little attention to: *She felt slighted because she was not asked to the party.* See synonym study below. —*n.* slighting treatment; act of neglect. [perhaps Old English *-sliht* level, as in *eorthslihtes* level with the ground] —**slight′ness,** *n.*

Syn. *v.t.* **Slight, overlook, neglect** mean to pay too little or no attention to someone or something needing or deserving it. **Slight** emphasizes intentionally doing so: *slight one's homework.* **Overlook** emphasizes unintentionally doing so: *While reviewing our budget, we overlooked the telephone bill.* **Neglect** emphasizes doing so because of indifference, distaste, or laziness: *Common sense tells us not to neglect our teeth.*

slight ing (slī′ting), *adj.* that slights: *a slighting comment.* —**slight′ing ly,** *adv.*

slight ly (slīt′lē), *adv.* 1 in a slight manner. 2 to a slight degree; somewhat; a little: *I knew her slightly.*

sli ly (slī′lē), *adv.* slyly.

slim (slim), *adj.,* **slim mer, slim mest,** *v.,* **slimmed, slim ming.** —*adj.* 1 slender; thin: *a slim girl.* See **slender** for synonym study. 2 small; slight; weak: *slim attendance at a meeting. The invalid's chances for getting well were very slim.* —*v.t., v.i.* make or become slim or slender. [< Dutch, bad] —**slim′ly,** *adv.* —**slim′ness,** *n.*

slime (slīm), *n., v.,* **slimed, slim ing.** —*n.* 1 soft, sticky mud or something like it. 2 a sticky substance given off by snails, slugs, fish, etc. 3 disgusting filth. —*v.t.* cover or smear with or as if with slime. [Old English *slīm*]

slim y (slī′mē), *adj.,* **slim i er, slim i est.** 1 covered with slime. 2 of or like slime. 3 disgusting; vile; filthy. —**slim′i ly,** *adv.* —**slim′i ness,** *n.*

sling (def. 5)

sling (sling), *n., v.,* **slung, sling ing.** —*n.* 1 strip of leather with a string fastened to each end, for throwing stones. 2 slingshot. 3 a throw; hurling. 4 a hanging loop of cloth fastened around the neck to support an injured arm or hand. 5 loop of rope, band, chain, etc., by which heavy objects are lifted, carried, or held: *They lowered the boxes into the cellar by a sling.* —*v.t.* 1 throw with a sling. 2 throw; cast; hurl; fling: *sling stones.* 3 raise, lower, etc., with a sling. 4 hang in a sling; hang so as to swing loosely: *sling a pack on one's back.* [Middle English *slingen*] —**sling′er,** *n.*

sling shot (sling′shot′), *n.* a Y-shaped stick with a band of rubber between its prongs, used to shoot pebbles, etc.

slink (slingk), *v.i.,* **slunk** or (ARCHAIC) **slank, slunk, slink ing.** move in a sneaking, guilty manner; sneak: *After stealing the meat, the dog slunk away.* [Old English *slincan*]

slink y (sling′kē), *adj.,* **slink i er, slink i est.** 1 sneaky; furtive; stealthy. 2 close-fitting, as if molded to the figure: *a slinky dress.* —**slink′i ly,** *adv.* —**slink′i ness,** *n.*

slip[1] (slip), *v.,* **slipped, slip ping,** *n.* —*v.i.* 1 go or move smoothly, quietly, easily, or quickly: *She slipped out of the room. Time slips by. The ship slips through the waves.* 2 move out of place; slide: *The knife slipped and cut my finger.* 3 slide suddenly without wanting to: *slip and fall on the icy sidewalk.* 4 make a mistake or error. 5 pass without notice; pass through neglect; escape: *Don't let this opportunity slip. Your name has slipped from my mind.* 6 fall off; decline; deteriorate: *New car sales have slipped.* 7 **let slip,** tell without meaning to. 8 **slip out,** become known. 9 **slip up,** INFORMAL. make a mistake or error. —*v.t.* 1 cause to slip; put, push, or draw with a smooth or sliding motion: *slip the bolt of a lock. She slipped the ring from her finger.* 2 put or take quickly and easily: *Slip on your coat. Slip off your shoes.* 3 get loose from; get away from; escape from: *The dog has slipped his collar. Your name has slipped my mind.* 4 let go; release: *The ship has slipped anchor and is off.* 5 **slip one over on,** INFORMAL. get the advantage of, especially by trickery; outwit.

—*n.* 1 act or fact of slipping. 2 pillowcase. 3 a sleeveless garment worn under a dress. 4 mistake; error; blunder: *make slips in grammar.* 5 U.S. space for ships between two wharves or in a dock. 6 an inclined platform alongside of the water, on which ships are built or repaired. 7 leash for a dog.

[perhaps < Middle Low German *slippen*]

slip[2] (slip), *n., v.,* **slipped, slip ping.** —*n.* 1 a small piece of paper on which a record is made: *a laundry slip.* 2 a narrow strip of paper, wood, land, etc. 3 a young, slender person: *She is just a slip of a girl.* 4 a small branch or twig cut from a plant, used to grow a new plant. —*v.t.* cut branches or twigs from (a plant) to grow new plants; take (a part) from a plant. [probably < Middle Dutch or Middle Low German *slippen* to cut]

slip[3] (slip), *n.* potter's clay made semifluid with water, used for coating or decorating pottery, etc. [Old English *slypa* a semiliquid mass]

slip case (slip′kās′), *n.* box or covering to protect one or more books, records, etc., usually so that only their backs or edges are exposed.

slip cov er (slip′kuv′ər), *n.* 1 a removable cloth cover to protect upholstered furniture. 2 dust jacket.

slip knot (slip′not′), *n.* knot made to slip along the rope or cord around which it is made; running knot. See **knot** for diagram.

slip noose, noose with a slipknot.

slip-on (slip′ôn′, slip′on′), *adj.* that can be put on or taken off easily or quickly. —*n.* a slip-on glove, blouse, sweater, etc.

slip o ver (slip′ō′vər), *n.* pullover.

slip page (slip′ij), *n.* 1 act of slipping. 2 amount or extent of slipping, as in loss of working power in machinery.

slipped disk, the loosening of an intervertebral disk, causing painful pressure on the spinal nerves.

slip per (slip′ər), *n.* kind of light, low shoe that is slipped on easily. —**slip′per less,** *adj.*

slip pered (slip′ərd), *adj.* wearing slippers.

slip per y (slip′ər ē), *adj.,* **-per i er, -per i est.** 1 causing or likely to cause slipping: *An icy street is slippery.* 2 slipping away easily: *Wet soap is slippery.* 3 not to be depended on; tricky. —**slip′per i ness,** *n.*

slippery elm, 1 an elm tree of eastern North America with a fragrant inner bark which becomes slimy or slippery when moistened. 2 its inner bark.

slip shod (slip′shod′), *adj.* 1 careless in dress, habits, speech, etc.; untidy; slovenly: *a slipshod performance, slipshod work.* 2 wearing shoes worn down at the heel.

slip stick (slip′stik′), *n.* SLANG. slide rule.

slip stream (slip′strēm′), *n.* a current of air produced by the propeller of an aircraft.

slip-up (slip′up′), *n.* INFORMAL. mistake; error.

slit (slit), *v.,* **slit, slit ting,** *n.* —*v.t.* cut or tear in a straight line; make a long, straight cut or tear in: *slit cloth into strips.* —*n.* a straight, narrow cut, tear, or opening: *the slit in the letter box.* [Middle English *slitten*] —**slit′like′,** *adj.* —**slit′ter,** *n.*

slith er (sliᴛʜ′ər), *v.i.* 1 slide down or along a surface, especially unsteadily. 2 go with a sliding motion. —*n.* a slithering movement; a slide. [Old English *slidrian*]

slith er y (sliᴛʜ′ər ē), *adj.* slippery; crawly.

sliv er (sliv′ər), *n.* 1 a long, thin piece that has been split off, broken off, or cut off; splinter. 2 a loose fiber of wool, cotton, flax, etc. —*v.t., v.i.* split or break into slivers. [ultimately < Old English *-slifan* to split]

sliv o vitz (sliv′ə vits), *n.* a strong brandy made from plums. [< Serbo-Croatian *sljivovica* < *sljiva* plum]

Sloan (slōn), *n.* **John,** 1871-1951, American painter.

slob (slob), *n.* 1 SLANG. a stupid, untidy, or clumsy person. 2 IRISH. mud. [probably < Irish *slab* mud]

slob ber (slob′ər), *v.i.* 1 let saliva or other liquid run out from the mouth; drool. 2 speak in a silly, sentimental way. —*v.t.* wet or smear with saliva, etc. —*n.* 1 saliva or other liquid running out from the mouth. 2 silly, sentimental talk or emotion. [probably ultimately < Middle Flemish *slobberen*] **—slob′ber er,** *n.*

slob ber y (slob′ər ē), *adj.* 1 slobbering. 2 disagreeably wet; sloppy.

sloe (slō), *n.* 1 a small, black or dark-purple stone fruit resembling the plum, having a sharp, sour taste. 2 the thorny shrub of the rose family that it grows on; blackthorn. [Old English *slāh*]

sloe-eyed (slō′īd′), *adj.* 1 having very dark eyes. 2 having slanted eyes.

slog (slog), *v.,* **slogged, slog ging,** *n.* INFORMAL. —*v.t.* hit hard. —*v.i.* 1 plod heavily. 2 work hard (at something). —*n.* a hard blow. [variant of *slug*[2]] **—slog′ger,** *n.*

sloth bear
about 3 ft. high
at the shoulder

slo gan (slō′gən), *n.* 1 word or phrase used by a business, club, political party, etc., to advertise its purpose; motto: *"Service with a smile" was the store's slogan.* 2 a war cry; battle cry. [< Scottish Gaelic *sluagh-ghairm* < *sluagh* army + *gairm* cry]

slo gan eer ing (slō′gə nir′ing), *n.* the making up or use of slogans.

sloop (slüp), *n.* a fore-and-aft rigged sailboat having one mast, a mainsail, a jib, and sometimes other sails. [< Dutch *sloep,* earlier *sloepe.* Doublet of SHALLOP.]

slop (slop), *v.,* **slopped, slop ping,** *n.* —*v.t.* 1 spill liquid upon; spill; splash. 2 give slop or slops to: *The farmer slopped the pigs.* —*v.i.* 1 splash through mud, slush, or water. 2 **slop over,** SLANG. show too much feeling, enthusiasm, etc. —*n.* 1 liquid carelessly spilled or splashed about. 2 Often, **slops,** *pl.* dirty water; liquid garbage. 3 a thin liquid mud or slush. 4 weak, usually unappetizing liquid or semiliquid food, such as gruel. [Middle English *sloppe*]

slop chest, SLANG. a ship's store that sells to the crew during a voyage.

slope (slōp), *v.,* **sloped, slop ing,** *n.* —*v.i.* go up or down at an angle: *a sloping roof. The land slopes toward the sea.* See synonym study below. —*v.t.* cause to go up or down at an angle. —*n.* 1 any line, surface, land, etc., that goes up or down at an angle: *If you roll a ball up a slope, it will roll down again.* 2 amount of slope. 3 (in mathematics) the tangent of the angle formed by the intersection of a straight line with the horizontal axis of a pair of Cartesian coordinates. [Old English *āslopen* slipped away] **—slop′er,** *n.*

Syn. *v.i.* **Slope, slant** mean to go off at an angle from the horizontal or vertical. **Slope** usually suggests an angle more nearly horizontal; **slant,** an angle more nearly vertical: *The fields slope up to the foothills. That picture slants to the left.*

slop py (slop′ē), *adj.,* **-pi er, -pi est.** 1 very wet; slushy: *sloppy ground, sloppy weather.* 2 splashed or soiled with liquid: *a sloppy table.* 3 INFORMAL. careless; slovenly: *do sloppy work, use sloppy English.* 4 INFORMAL. weak; silly: *sloppy sentiment.* **—slop′pi ly,** *adv.* **—slop′pi ness,** *n.*

slops (slops), *n.pl.* 1 cheap ready-made clothing. 2 clothes, bedding, etc., supplied to sailors on a ship.

slosh (slosh), *v.i.* 1 splash in or through slush, mud, or water. 2 go about idly. —*v.t.* pour or dash (liquid) upon. —*n.* 1 slush. 2 INFORMAL. a watery or weak drink. [perhaps blend of *slop* and *slush*]

slot[1] (slot), *n., v.,* **slot ted, slot ting.** —*n.* 1 a small, narrow opening or depression: *Put a penny in the slot of the machine to get a stick of gum.* 2 INFORMAL. place or position in a schedule, list, series, etc. —*v.t.* make a slot or slots in. [< Old French *esclot* the hollow between breasts]

slot[2] (slot), *n.* track; trail. [< Old French *esclot,* probably < Scandinavian (Old Icelandic) *slōth* track]

sloth (slôth, slōth), *n.* 1 unwillingness to work or exert oneself; laziness; idleness: *His sloth keeps him from engaging in sports.* 2 ARCHAIC. slowness. 3 any of a family of very slow-moving mammals of South and Central America that live in trees and hang upside down from tree branches. [Old English *slāwth* < *slāw* slow]

sloth bear, a long-haired bear of India and Ceylon.

sloth ful (slôth′fəl, slōth′fəl), *adj.* unwilling to work or exert oneself; lazy; idle. **—sloth′ful ly,** *adv.* **—sloth′ful ness,** *n.*

slot machine, machine that is worked by inserting a coin into a slot. Some slot machines sell peanuts, sticks of gum, etc.; others are used for gambling.

sloop

slouch (slouch), *v.i.* 1 stand, sit, walk, or move in an awkward, drooping manner: *The weary man slouched along.* 2 droop or bend downward. —*n.* 1 a bending forward of head and shoulders; awkward, drooping way of standing, sitting, or walking. 2 an awkward, slovenly, or inefficient person. [origin uncertain] **—slouch′er,** *n.*

slouch hat, a soft hat, usually with a broad brim that bends down easily.

slouch y (slou′chē), *adj.,* **slouch i er, slouch i est.** slouching awkwardly; carelessly untidy. **—slouch′i ly,** *adv.* **—slouch′i ness,** *n.*

slough[1] (slou *for 1 and 3;* slü *for 2*), *n.* 1 a soft, deep, muddy place. 2 a swampy place; marshy inlet; slew; slue. 3 hopeless discouragement; degradation. [Old English *slōh*]

hat, āge, fär; let, ēqual, tėrm;
it, īce; hot, ōpen, ôrder;
oil, out; cup, pu̇t, rüle;
ch, child; ng, long; sh, she;
th, thin; ᴛʜ, then; zh, measure;

ə represents *a* in about, *e* in taken, *i* in pencil, *o* in lemon, *u* in circus.

< = from, derived from, taken from.

slough[2] (sluf), *n.* 1 the old skin shed or cast off by a snake. 2 layer of dead skin or tissue that drops or falls off as a wound, sore, etc., heals. 3 anything that has been or can be shed or cast off: *As man became civilized, he cast off the slough of primitive ways and beliefs.* —*v.t.* 1 drop off; throw off; shed. 2 discard (a losing card). —*v.i.* be shed or cast; drop or fall: *A scab sloughs off when new skin takes its place.* [Middle English *slouh*]

slough of despond (slou), hopeless dejection; deep despondency. [< the *Slough of Despond* in *Pilgrim's Progress,* by John Bunyan]

sloth (def. 3)
about 2 ft. long

slough y (slou′ē), *adj.,* **slough i er, slough i est.** soft and muddy; full of soft, deep mud; miry. [< *slough*[1]]

Slo vak (slō′vak), *n.* 1 member of a Slavic people living in Slovakia, related to the Bohemians and the Moravians. 2 their Slavic language. —*adj.* of or having to do with Slovakia, its people, or their language.

Slo va ki a (slō vä′kē ə, slō vak′ē ə), *n.* region in E Czechoslovakia. 4,460,000 pop.; 18,900 sq. mi. **—Slo va′ki an,** *adj., n.*

slov en (sluv′ən), *n.* person who is untidy, dirty, or careless in dress, appearance, habits, work, etc. —*adj.* untidy; dirty; careless. [perhaps ultimately < Flemish *sloef* dirty]

Slo vene (slō′vēn′), *n.* 1 member of a Slavic people living in Slovenia, related to the Croats, Serbians, and other southern Slavs. 2 their Slavic language. —*adj.* of or having to do with Slovenia, its people, or their language.

Slo ve ni a (slō vē′nē ə, slō vē′nyə), *n.* region in NW Yugoslavia. **—Slo ve′ni an,** *adj., n.*

slov en ly (sluv′ən lē), *adj.,* **-li er, -li est,** *adv.* —*adj.* untidy, dirty, or careless in dress, appearance, habits, work, etc. —*adv.* in a slovenly manner. **—slov′en li ness,** *n.*

slow (slō), *adj.* 1 taking a long time; taking longer than usual; not fast or quick. See synonym study below. 2 behind time; running at less than proper speed: *a slow runner.* 3 indicating a time earlier than the correct time: *The clock was slow.* 4 causing a low or lower rate of speed; retarding: *slow ground, a slow track.* 5 burning or heating slowly or gently: *a slow flame.* 6 inactive; sluggish: *a* *slow fellow. Business is slow.* 7 not quick to understand; dull: *a slow learner.* 8 not interesting; not lively; boring: *a slow party.* 9 not readily stirred or moved; not hasty: *slow to anger, slow to take offense.* —*adv.* in a slow manner. —*v.t.* make slow or slower; reduce the speed of: *slow down a car.* —*v.i.* become slow; go slower: *Slow up when you drive through a town.* [Old English *slāw*] —**slow′ly,** *adv.* —**slow′ness,** *n.*

Syn. *adj.* 1 **Slow, leisurely, deliberate** mean taking a long time to do something or to happen. **Slow,** the general term, suggests taking longer than usual or necessary: *We took the slow train.* **Leisurely** suggests slowness because of having plenty of time: *I like leisurely meals.* **Deliberate,** describing people or their acts, suggests slowness due to care, thought, or self-control: *His speech is deliberate.*

➤ **Slow, slowly.** In standard English *slowly* is now the usual form of the adverb except in set phrases *(go slow, drive slow).*

slow down (slō′doun′), *n.* a slowing in rate of production, pace of work, etc.

slow match, fuse that burns very slowly used to fire gunpowder, dynamite, etc.

slow-mo tion (slō′mō′shən), *adj.* 1 showing action at much less than its actual speed: *slow-motion photography.* 2 moving at less than normal speed.

slow poke (slō′pōk′), *n.* INFORMAL. a very slow person or thing.

slow-wit ted (slō′wit′id), *adj.* slow at thinking; dull; stupid.

slow worm (slō′wėrm′), *n.* blindworm.

sludge (sluj), *n.* 1 soft mud; mire; slush. 2 a soft, thick, muddy mixture, deposit, sediment, etc. 3 small broken pieces of floating ice. [origin uncertain]

sludg y (sluj′ē), *adj.,* **sludg i er, sludg i est.** consisting of sludge; slushy.

slue[1] (slü), *v.t., v.i.,* **slued, slu ing,** *n.* slew[2].

slue[2] (slü), *n.* slough[1] (def. 2).

slue[3] (slü), *n.* slew[4].

slug[1] (slug), *n.* 1 any of various slow-moving, elongated mollusks like snails, but having no shell or only a rudimentary one. Slugs live mostly in forests, gardens, and damp places. 2 caterpillar or other insect larva that looks like a slug. 3 any slow-moving person, animal, wagon, etc. 4 piece of lead or other metal for firing from a gun. 5 a lump or disk of metal, especially one used in a slot machine in place of a coin. 6 strip of metal used to space lines of type. A slug is more than $^1/_{16}$ of an inch in thickness. 7 line of type cast in one piece by a linotype machine. 8 (in physics) a unit of mass, equal to about 32.17 pounds, which has an acceleration of one foot per second per second when acted upon by a force of one pound. 9 SLANG. a drink; shot: *a slug of whiskey.* [Middle English *slugge* a slow person < Scandinavian (dialectal Swedish) *slogga* be sluggish]

slug[2] (slug), *v.,* **slugged, slug ging,** *n.* INFORMAL. —*v.t., v.i.* hit hard with the fist, a baseball bat, etc.; hit hard. —*n.* a hard blow, especially with the fist. [origin uncertain]

slug gard (slug′ərd), *n.* a lazy, idle person. —*adj.* lazy; idle.

slug ger (slug′ər), *n.* INFORMAL. person who slugs or hits hard, especially a boxer who punches very hard, or a home-run hitter in baseball.

slug gish (slug′ish), *adj.* 1 slow-moving; not active; lacking energy or vigor: *a sluggish mind.* 2 lazy; idle. 3 moving slowly; having little motion. A sluggish river has very little current. —**slug′gish ly,** *adv.* —**slug′gish ness,** *n.*

sluice (def. 5)—Grooves in the bottom of the sluice catch and hold the gold as the lighter material is washed away.

sluice (slüs), *n., v.,* **sluiced, sluic ing.** —*n.* 1 structure with a gate or gates for holding back or controlling the water of a canal, river, or lake. 2 gate that holds back or controls the flow of water. When the water behind a dam gets too high, the sluices are opened. 3 the water held back or controlled by such a gate. 4 a means of controlling the flow or passage of anything: *War opens the sluices of hatred and bloodshed.* 5 a long, sloping trough through which water flows, used to wash gold from sand, dirt, or gravel. 6 channel for carrying off overflow or surplus water. —*v.t.* 1 let out or draw off (water, etc.) by opening a sluice. 2 flush or cleanse with a rush of water; pour or throw water over. 3 wash (gold) from sand, dirt, or gravel in a sluice. 4 carry or send (logs, etc.) along a channel of water. —*v.i.* flow or pour in a stream; rush: *Water sluiced down the channel.* [< Old French *escluse* < Late Latin *exclusa* barrier to shut out water < Latin *excludere* shut out. See EXCLUDE.]

sluice way (slüs′wā′), *n.* 1 channel controlled or fed by a sluice. 2 any small, artificial channel for running water.

slum (slum), *n., v.,* **slummed, slum ming.** —*n.* Often, **slums,** *pl.* a run-down, overcrowded part of a city or town. Poverty and disease are common in the slums. —*v.i.* 1 go into or visit the slums. 2 go to or visit any place thought of as greatly inferior to one's own. [origin uncertain] —**slum′mer,** *n.*

slum ber (slum′bər), *v.i.* 1 sleep lightly; doze. 2 be inactive: *The volcano had slumbered for years.* —*v.t.* pass in sleep: *The baby slumbers away the hours.* —*n.* 1 a light sleep; doze. 2 an inactive state or condition. [Middle English *slumberen, slumeren* < Old English *slūma* sleep] —**slum′ber er,** *n.*

slum ber ous (slum′bər əs), *adj.* 1 sleepy; heavy with drowsiness: *slumberous eyelids.* 2 causing or inducing sleep. 3 having to do with, characterized by, or suggestive of sleep. 4 inactive or quiet. —**slum′ber ous ly,** *adv.*

slumber party, U.S. a gathering of young girls in a home to spend the night together; pajama party.

slum brous (slum′brəs), *adj.* slumberous. —**slum′brous ly,** *adv.*

slum lord (slum′lôrd′), *n.* U.S. the owner of a run-down tenement house, usually in the slums.

slump (slump), *v.i.* 1 drop heavily; fall suddenly: *The boy's feet slumped repeatedly through the melting ice.* 2 move, walk, sit, etc., in a drooping manner; slouch: *The bored students slumped in their seats.* 3 fall off; decline: *The stock market slumped.* —*n.* 1 a heavy or sudden fall; collapse. 2 a great or sudden decline in prices, activity, performance, etc. [perhaps imitative]

slung (slung), *v.* pt. and pp. of **sling.**

slung shot, piece of metal, stone, etc., fastened to a short strap, chain, etc., used as a weapon.

slunk (slungk), *v.* a pt. and a pp. of **slink.**

slur (slėr), *v.,* **slurred, slur ring,** *n.* —*v.t.* 1 pass lightly over; go through hurriedly or in a careless way. 2 pronounce indistinctly: *Many persons slur "how do you do."* 3 in music: **a** sing or play (two or more tones of different pitch) without a break; run together in a smooth, connected manner. **b** mark with a slur. 4 harm the reputation of; insult; slight. —*v.i.* speak or write sounds, letters, etc., so indistinctly that they run into each other. —*n.* 1 a slurred pronunciation, sound, etc. 2 in music: **a** a slurring of tones. **b** a curved mark (⌒)(◡) indicating this. 3 blot or stain (upon reputation); insulting or slighting remark: *a slur on a person's good name.* [origin uncertain]

slurp (slėrp), SLANG. —*v.i., v.t.* eat or drink with a noisy gurgling sound. —*n.* a slurping or gurgling sound. [perhaps imitative]

slur ry (slėr′ē), *n., pl.* **-ries,** *v.,* **-ried, -ry ing.** —*n.* a thin mixture of powdered coal, ore, cement, etc., and water. —*v.t.* make or convert into slurry.

slush (slush), *n.* 1 partly melted snow; snow and water mixed. 2 soft mud; mire. 3 silly, sentimental talk, writing, etc. 4 grease. [origin uncertain]

slush fund, money collected or set aside for dishonest purposes, such as bribery.

slush y (slush′ē), *adj.,* **slush i er, slush i est.** 1 having much slush. 2 of or like slush. —**slush′i ness,** *n.*

slut (slut), *n.* 1 a dirty, untidy woman or girl; slattern. 2 woman or girl of loose morals. [Middle English *slutte*]

slut tish (slut′ish), *adj.* 1 dirty; untidy. 2 loose in morals. —**slut′tish ly,** *adv.* —**slut′tish ness,** *n.*

sly (slī), *adj.,* **sly er, sly est** or **sli er, sli est,** *n.* —*adj.* 1 able to fool, trick, or deceive; crafty; tricky; wily: *The sly cat stole the meat while the cook's back was turned.* See synonym study below. 2 playfully mischievous or knowing: *a sly wink.* 3 acting secretly or stealthily; furtive. 4 such as a sly person or animal would use: *She asked sly questions.* —*n.* **on the sly,** in a sly way. [< Scandinavian (Old Icelandic) *slægr*] —**sly′ness,** *n.*

Syn. *adj.* 1 **Sly, cunning** mean able to get what one wants by secret, wily, or indirect means. **Sly** emphasizes lack of frankness and straightforwardness, and suggests stealthy actions or secrecy and deceit in dealing with others: *That sly girl managed to get her best friend's job.* **Cunning** emphasizes cleverness in getting the better of others by tricks or schemes, unfair dealing, or cheating: *A fox is cunning enough to cross a stream so that dogs cannot follow its scent.*

sly ly (slī′lē), *adv.* in a sly manner. Also, **slily.**

Sm, samarium.

S.M., 1 Master of Science [for Latin *Scientiae Magister*]. 2 Sergeant Major.

smack[1] (smak), *n.* 1 a slight taste or flavor: *The sauce had a smack of nutmeg.* 2 trace; suggestion: *The old sailor still had a smack of the sea about him.* —*v.i.* have a taste, trace, or touch: *The Irishman's speech smacked of the old country.* [Old English *smæcc*]

smack[2] (smak), *v.t.* 1 open (the lips) quickly

hat, āge, fär; let, ēqual, tėrm;
it, īce; hot, ōpen, ôrder;
oil, out; cup, pu̇t, rüle;
ch, child; ng, long; sh, she;
th, thin; ᴛʜ, then; zh, measure;

ə represents *a* in about, *e* in taken, *i* in pencil, *o* in lemon, *u* in circus.

< = from, derived from, taken from.

so as to make a sharp sound. 2 kiss loudly. 3 slap: *smack someone in the face.* 4 crack (a whip, etc.). —*v.i.* make or give out a smacking sound. —*n.* 1 a smacking movement of the lips. 2 the sharp sound made in this way. 3 a loud kiss, slap, or crack. —*adv.* INFORMAL. 1 directly; squarely: *fall smack on one's face.* 2 suddenly and sharply. [ultimately imitative]

smack[3] (smak), *n.* 1 a small sailboat with one mast rigged like a sloop or cutter. 2 a fishing boat with a well for keeping fish alive. [probably < Dutch *smak*]

smack-dab (smak′dab′), *adv.* INFORMAL. directly; squarely; smack.

smack er (smak′ər), *n.* 1 person or thing that smacks. 2 INFORMAL. a loud kiss; smack. 3 SLANG. a dollar.

smack ing (smak′ing), *adj.* lively, brisk, or strong: *a smacking breeze.*

small (smôl), *adj.* 1 not large; little; not large as compared with other things of the same kind: *a small house, a small city.* See **little** for synonym study. 2 not great in amount, degree, extent, duration, value, strength, etc.: *a small dose, small hope of success. The cent is our smallest coin.* 3 not important: *a small matter.* 4 not prominent; humble; modest: *make a small start. Both great and small people mourned Lincoln's death.* 5 having little land, capital, etc.: *a small farmer, a small dealer.* 6 having little strength; gentle; soft; low: *a small voice.* 7 mean; ungenerous: *a small nature.* 8 (of letters) not capital. 9 **feel small,** be ashamed or humiliated.
—*adv.* 1 into small pieces. 2 in low tones. 3 in a small manner.
—*n.* 1 that which is small; a small, slender, or narrow part: *the small of the back.* 2 **smalls,** *pl.* parcels or consignments of little size or weight.
[Old English *smæl* slender, narrow] —**small′ness,** *n.*

small arms, weapons that can be easily carried and used by a person, such as rifles or revolvers.

small beer, 1 weak beer. 2 matters or persons of little or no consequence.

small capital, a capital letter that is slightly smaller than the regular capital letter. This sentence shows $7^{1}/_{2}$-point REGULAR CAPITALS and SMALL CAPITALS.

small change, 1 coins of small value, such as nickels, dimes, etc. 2 anything small and unimportant.

small circle, circle on the surface of a sphere whose plane does not pass through the center of the sphere.

small fry, 1 babies or children; small or young creatures. 2 unimportant people or things.

small hours, the early hours of the morning.

small intestine, the narrow, winding, upper part of the intestines, between the stomach and the large intestine, where digestion is completed and nutrients are absorbed by the blood. The human small intestine is about twenty feet long and consists of the duodenum, the jejunum, and the ileum.

small ish (smô′lish), *adj.* rather small.

small letter, an ordinary letter, not a capital.

small-mind ed (smôl′mīn′did), *adj.* narrow-minded; petty; mean. —**small′-mind′ed ly,** *adv.* —**small′-mind′ed ness,** *n.*

small potatoes, INFORMAL. an unimportant person or thing; unimportant persons or things.

small pox (smôl′poks′), *n.* a very contagious viral disease characterized by fever and eruptions like blisters on the skin that often leave permanent scars shaped like little pits; variola.

small-scale (smôl′skāl′), *adj.* 1 involving few persons or things; limited: *a small-scale offensive.* 2 made or drawn to a small scale: *a small-scale map.*

small talk, conversation about unimportant matters; chit-chat.

small-time (smôl′tīm′), *adj.* INFORMAL. not first-rate; mediocre.

smart (smärt), *v.i.* 1 feel sharp pain: *My eyes smarted from the smoke.* 2 cause sharp pain: *The cut smarts.* 3 feel distress or irritation: *She smarted from the scolding.* 4 suffer: *He shall smart for this.* —*v.t.* cause sharp pain to or in.
—*n.* 1 a sharp pain, especially a local pain. 2 keen mental suffering; sorrow.
—*adj.* 1 sharp; severe: *a smart blow.* 2 keen; active; lively: *They walked at a smart pace.* 3 clever and bright: *a smart student.* 4 sharp and shrewd in dealing with others: *a smart businessman.* 5 witty, superficial, and often somewhat impertinent: *a smart reply.* 6 fresh and neat in appearance; in good order: *smart in his uniform.* 7 stylish; fashionable: *a smart hat, a smart hotel.* 8 INFORMAL or DIALECT. fairly large; considerable.
—*adv.* in a smart manner.
[Old English *smeortan*] —**smart′ly,** *adv.* —**smart′ness,** *n.*

smart al eck (al′ik), a conceited, obnoxious person.

smart en (smärt′n), *v.t., v.i.* 1 improve in appearance; brighten. 2 make or become brisker. 3 make or become more alert, clever, or intelligent.

smart set, the most sophisticated and fashionable section of society.

smart weed (smärt′wēd′), *n.* any of various weeds of the same family as the buckwheat, that grow in wet places and cause an irritation when brought into contact with the skin.

smart y (smär′tē), *n., pl.* **smart ies.** INFORMAL. smart aleck.

smash (smash), *v.t.* 1 break into pieces with violence and noise: *smash a window.* See **break** for synonym study. 2 destroy; shatter; ruin: *smash an argument.* 3 crush; defeat: *smash an attack.* 4 hit (a tennis ball) with a hard, fast overhand stroke. —*v.i.* 1 be broken to pieces: *The dishes smashed on the floor.* 2 become ruined. 3 rush violently; crash: *The car smashed into a tree.*
—*n.* 1 a violent crash or collision: *the smash of two automobiles.* 2 act or sound of smashing: *the smash of broken glass.* 3 a crushing defeat; disaster. 4 bankruptcy. 5 a hard, fast overhand stroke in tennis. 6 INFORMAL. a highly successful performance or production; great hit: *a theatrical smash.* 7 **to smash, a** into bits. **b** to ruin.
—*adj.* INFORMAL. highly successful: *a smash Broadway musical.*
[origin uncertain] —**smash′er,** *n.*

smash-up (smash′up′), *n.* 1 a bad collision; wreck. 2 a great misfortune; disaster.

smat ter (smat′ər), *n.* slight knowledge; smattering. [originally verb, to dabble, Middle English *smateren* to dirty]

smat ter ing (smat′ər ing), *n.* slight or superficial knowledge.

smaze (smāz), *n.* combination of smoke and haze in the air. [blend of *smoke* and *haze*]

smear (smir), *v.t.* 1 spread, cover, daub, or stain with anything oily, greasy, sticky, or dirty: *She smeared her fingers with jam.* 2 rub or spread (oil, grease, paint, etc.). 3 rub or wipe (a brush, hand, cloth, etc.) so as to make a mark or stain. 4 soil or sully (a person's reputation, memory, etc.). 5 SLANG. defeat or rout decisively; overwhelm. —*v.i.* be smeared: *Wet paint smears easily.* —*n.* 1 mark or stain left by smearing; daub or blotch. 2 a small amount of something spread on a slide for microscopic examination, or on the surface of a culture medium. 3 act of smearing a person's reputation; slander. [Old English *smerian, smirian* < *smeoru* grease]

smear y (smir′ē), *adj.,* **smear i er, smear i est.** 1 marked by a smear or smears; smeared. 2 tending to smear. —**smear′i ness,** *n.*

smell (smel), *v.,* **smelled** or **smelt, smell ing,** *n.* —*v.t.* 1 perceive (an odor or scent) with the nose by means of the olfactory nerves. 2 inhale the odor or scent of (something); sniff at. 3 detect or discover by shrewdness or instinct; suspect: *We smelled trouble.* 4 **smell up,** INFORMAL. cause to have a bad odor or scent. —*v.i.* 1 perceive or be able to perceive odors. 2 give out a smell: *The rose smells sweet.* 3 give out a bad smell; stink. 4 have or show a touch or suggestion *(of): a plan smelling of trickery.* —*n.* 1 sense of smelling. 2 quality in a thing that affects the sense of smell; odor. See synonym study below. 3 trace, tinge, or suggestion *(of): the smell of injustice.* 4 act of smelling; sniff. [Middle English *smellen*] —**smell′er,** *n.*
Syn. *n.* 2 **Smell, odor** have to do with that property or quality of a thing that affects the sense organs of the nose. **Smell** is the general word, used especially when the effect on the sense organs is emphasized: *There was a strong smell of gas in the room.* **Odor** applies particularly to the actual property or quality itself, as belonging to and coming from what is smelled: *the odors of cooking.*

smelling salts, solution of a salt of ammonia, ammonium hydroxide, and some scent, inhaled to relieve faintness, headaches, etc.

smell y (smel′ē), *adj.,* **smell i er, smell i est.** having or giving out a strong or unpleasant smell.

smelt[1] (smelt), *v.t.* 1 fuse or melt (ore) in order to separate the metal contained. 2 obtain (metal) from ore by melting. 3 refine (impure metal) by melting. [probably Middle Low German *smelten*]

smelt[2] (smelt), *n., pl.* **smelts** or **smelt.** any of a family of small, saltwater or freshwater food fish with silvery scales. [Old English]

smelt[3] (smelt), *v.* a pt. and a pp. of **smell.**

smelt er (smel′tər), *n.* 1 person whose work or business is smelting ores or metals.

2 place where ores or metals are smelted. 3 furnace for smelting ores.

smidg en or **smidg eon** (smij′ən), *n.* INFORMAL. a tiny bit. [origin uncertain]

smi lax (smī′laks), *n.* 1 a twining, trailing African vine of the same genus as asparagus, much used by florists in decoration. 2 greenbrier (def. 1). [< Greek]

smile (smīl), *v.*, **smiled, smil ing,** *n.* —*v.i.* 1 look pleased or amused; show pleasure, favor, kindness, amusement, etc., by an upward curve of the mouth. 2 show scorn, disdain, etc., by a curve of the mouth. 3 look upon or regard with favor: *Good fortune always smiled at him.* —*v.t.* 1 bring, put, drive, etc., by smiling: *Smile your tears away.* 2 give (a smile): *She smiled a sunny smile.* 3 express by a smile: *smile a welcome, smile consent.* —*n.* 1 act of smiling: *a friendly smile.* 2 a favoring look or regard; pleasant look or aspect. [Middle English *smilen*] **—smil′er,** *n.* **—smil′ing ly,** *adv.*

smirch (smėrch), *v.t.* 1 make dirty; soil with soot, dirt, etc. 2 cast discredit upon; taint; tarnish. —*n.* 1 a dirty mark; stain. 2 blot on a person's reputation. [Middle English *smorchen* discolor]

smirk (smėrk), *v.i.* smile in an affected, silly, or self-satisfied way; simper. —*n.* an affected, silly, or self-satisfied smile. [Old English *smearcian* smile]

smit (smit), *v.* 1 a pp. of **smite.** 2 OBSOLETE. a pt. of **smite.**

smite (smīt), *v.*, **smote, smit ten** or **smit, smit ing.** —*v.t.* 1 give a hard blow to (a person, etc.) with the hand, a stick, or the like; strike. 2 give or strike (a blow, stroke, etc.). 3 strike with a weapon, etc., so as to cause serious injury or death. 4 attack with a sudden pain, disease, etc.: *a city smitten with pestilence. His conscience smote him.* 5 impress suddenly with a strong feeling, sentiment, etc.: *smitten with curiosity.* 6 punish severely; chasten. —*v.i.* 1 deliver a blow or blows, a stroke, etc., with or as with a stick, weapon, etc.; strike. 2 come with force *(upon): The sound of a blacksmith's hammer smote upon their ears.* [Old English *smītan*] **—smit′er,** *n.*

smith (smith), *n.* 1 worker in metal, especially iron. 2 blacksmith. [Old English]

Smith (smith), *n.* 1 **Adam,** 1723-1790, Scottish political economist. 2 **Alfred Emanuel,** 1873-1944, American political leader, governor of New York State and Democratic candidate for president in 1928. 3 Captain **John,** 1580-1631, English explorer and early settler of Virginia. 4 **Joseph,** 1805-1844, American who founded the Church of Jesus Christ of Latter-day Saints (Mormon Church).

smith e reens (smiᴛʜ′ə rēnz′), *n.pl.* INFORMAL. small pieces; bits. [apparently < Irish *smidirin*]

smith son ite (smith′sə nīt), *n.* native carbonate of zinc. *Formula:* $ZnCO_3$ [< James *Smithson,* 1765-1829, English chemist and mineralogist]

smith y (smith′ē, smiᴛʜ′ē), *n., pl.* **smith ies.** workshop of a smith, especially a blacksmith.

smit ten (smit′n), *adj.* hard hit; struck. —*v.* a pp. of **smite.**

smock (smok), *n.* 1 a loose outer garment worn to protect clothing. 2 ARCHAIC or DIALECT. a woman's shift or chemise. —*v.t.* ornament (a smock, dress, etc.) with a honeycomb pattern. [Old English *smoc*]

smock ing (smok′ing), *n.* a honeycomb pattern formed by lines of stitches crossing each other diagonally and gathering the material, used to ornament smocks, dresses, etc.

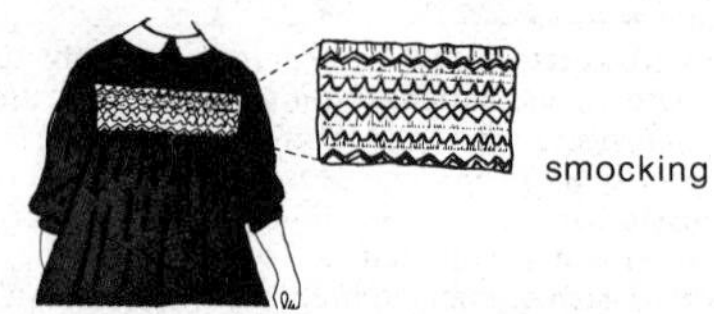
smocking

smog (smog), *n.* a combination of smoke and fog in the air. [blend of *smoke* and *fog*]

smog gy (smog′ē), *adj.* full of smog.

smok a ble (smō′kə bəl), *adj.* fit to be smoked.

smoke (smōk), *n.*, *v.*, **smoked, smok ing.** —*n.* 1 mixture of gases and particles of carbon that can be seen rising from anything burning; cloud from anything burning. 2 mass, cloud, or column of smoke, especially one serving as a signal, sign of encampment, etc. 3 something resembling smoke, as a mist or fog. 4 something unsubstantial, quickly passing, or without value or result. 5 something that clouds or is meant to confuse or hide an issue, etc. 6 that which is smoked; cigarette, cigar, pipe, etc. 7 an act or period of smoking a cigar, cigarette, etc. 8 (in physics and chemistry) a dispersion of solid particles in a gas.
—*v.i.* 1 give off smoke or steam, or something like it: *The fireplace smokes.* 2 move with great speed. 3 draw in and puff out the smoke of burning tobacco. —*v.t.* 1 draw the smoke from (a cigarette, cigar, pipe, etc.) into the mouth and puff it out again. 2 expose to the action of smoke. 3 cure (meat, fish, etc.) by exposing to smoke: *People smoke fish to preserve them.* 4 color, darken, or stain with smoke. 5 make, bring, pass, etc., by smoking. 6 **smoke out, a** drive out with smoke, as an animal from its hole. **b** find out and make known.
[Old English *smoca*] **—smoke′like′,** *adj.*

smoke-eat er (smōk′ē′tər), *n.* SLANG. a fireman, especially of the U.S. Forest Service.

smoke-filled room (smōk′fild′), U.S. room in which influential politicians meet in private, to plan strategy or to negotiate.

smoke house (smōk′hous′), *n., pl.* **-hous es** (-hou′ziz). building or room used for curing meat, fish, etc., by means of smoke.

smoke less (smōk′lis), *adj.* 1 making little or no smoke: *smokeless fuel.* 2 having little or no smoke.

smok er (smō′kər), *n.* 1 person who smokes tobacco. 2 a railroad car or a part of it where smoking is allowed. 3 an informal gathering, usually of men, for entertainment, conversation, etc.

smoke screen, 1 mass of thick smoke used to hide troops, ships, airplanes, etc., from the enemy. 2 anything that serves some such purpose.

smoke stack (smōk′stak′), *n.* 1 a tall chimney. 2 pipe on a steamship, locomotive, etc., that discharges smoke.

smoke tree, a large shrub of the same family as the sumac, with flower clusters somewhat resembling puffs of smoke.

smok y (smō′kē), *adj.*, **smok i er, smok i est.** 1 giving off much smoke: *a smoky fire.* 2 full of smoke: *a smoky room.* 3 darkened or stained with smoke: *the smoky buildings of a great industrial city.* 4 like smoke or suggesting smoke. **—smok′i ly,** *adv.* **—smok′i ness,** *n.*

Smoky Mountains, Great Smoky Mountains.

smol der (smōl′dər), *v.i.* 1 burn and smoke without flame: *The campfire smoldered for hours after the blaze died down.* 2 exist or continue in a suppressed condition: *Their discontent smoldered for years before it broke out in rebellion.* 3 show suppressed feeling: *The man's eyes smoldered with anger.* —*n.* 1 a slow, smoky burning without flame; smoldering fire. 2 a feeling of heated emotion: *a smolder of indignation.* Also, **smoulder.** [Middle English]

Smol lett (smol′it), *n.* **Tobias George,** 1721-1771, British novelist.

smolt (smōlt), *n.* a young salmon with silvery scales that is ready to descend, or has descended, to the sea for the first time. [origin uncertain]

smooch (smüch), *v.i.* SLANG. to kiss or pet. [imitative]

smooth (smüᴛʜ), *adj.* 1 having an even surface, like glass, silk, or still water; flat; level: *smooth stones.* See **level** for synonym study. 2 free from unevenness or roughness: *smooth sailing.* 3 without lumps: *smooth sauce.* 4 without hair: *a smooth face.* 5 without trouble or difficulty; easy: *a smooth course of affairs.* 6 calm; serene: *a smooth temper.* 7 polished; pleasant; polite: *a smooth talker.* 8 too polished, pleasant, or polite to be sincere: *a smooth salesman.* 9 not harsh in sound or taste: *smooth verses, a smooth wine.*
—*adv.* in a smooth manner.
—*v.t.* 1 make smooth or smoother: *smooth clothing with an iron.* 2 make easy: *Her tact smoothed the way to an agreement.* 3 make less harsh or crude; polish or refine (writing, manners, etc.). 4 **smooth away,** get rid of (troubles, difficulties, etc.). 5 **smooth down,** calm; soothe. 6 **smooth over,** make (something) seem less wrong, unpleasant, or conspicuous.
[Old English *smōth*] **—smooth′er,** *n.* **—smooth′ly,** *adv.* **—smooth′ness,** *n.*

smooth bore (smüᴛʜ′bôr′, smüᴛʜ′bōr′), *adj.* (of guns) not having a rifled bore. —*n.* a smoothbore gun.

smooth en (smü′ᴛʜən), *v.t., v.i.* make or become smooth or smoother.

smooth-faced (smüᴛʜ′fāst′), *adj.* 1 having a smooth face or surface. 2 agreeable in speech and manner, often insincerely; blandly ingratiating.

smooth ie (smü′ᴛʜē), *n.* INFORMAL. man who speaks, behaves, etc., in a polished manner, often insincerely. Also, **smoothy.**

smooth muscle, type of muscle not contracted by voluntary action, with fibers in smooth layers or sheets; involuntary muscle. The muscles of the stomach, intestine, and other viscera (except the heart) are smooth muscles.

smooth-spo ken (smüᴛʜ′spō′kən), *adj.* blandly gracious or polished in speech.

smooth-tongued (smüᴛʜ′tungd′), *adj.* blandly agreeable, flattering, etc.; suave.

smooth y (smü′ᴛʜē), *n., pl.* **smooth ies.** smoothie.

smor gas bord (smôr′gəs bôrd, smôr′gəs-bōrd), *n.* a buffet luncheon or supper consisting of a large variety of meats, salads, hors d'oeuvres, etc. [< Swedish *smörgåsbord*]

smote (smōt), *v.* a pt. of **smite.**

smoth er (smuᴛʜ′ər), *v.t.* 1 kill by depriving of air; suffocate. 2 cover thickly: *In the fall the grass is smothered with leaves.* 3 deaden or extinguish by covering thickly: *The fire is smothered by ashes.* 4 keep back; check; suppress: *smother one's anger, smother a committee's report.* 5 cook in a covered pot or baking dish: *smothered chicken.* —*v.i.* 1 be unable to breathe freely; be suffocated: *The miners almost smothered when the shaft collapsed.* 2 be suppressed, concealed, or stifled. —*n.* 1 cloud of dust, smoke, spray, etc. 2 anything that smothers or appears to smother. 3 an excess of disorder; confusion. [Middle English *smorther,* noun < Old English *smorian* suffocate] **—smoth′er er,** *n.*

smoul der (smōl′dər), *v.i., n.* smolder.

smudge (smuj), *n., v.,* **smudged, smudg ing.** —*n.* 1 a dirty mark or stain, especially one caused by a smear or by trying to rub out a previous mark. 2 a smoky fire made to drive away insects or to protect fruit and plants from frost. —*v.t.* 1 mark with dirty streaks; smear. 2 smoke (an orchard) with a smudge or smudges to fumigate or prevent frostbite. —*v.i.* 1 make or leave a stain. 2 be smudged. [origin uncertain]

smudge pot, pot or stove for burning oil or other smoke-producing fuels to protect plants or early blooming trees from frost.

smudg y (smuj′ē), *adj.,* **smudg i er, smudg i est.** smudged. **—smudg′i ly,** *adv.* **—smudg′i ness,** *n.*

smug (smug), *adj.,* **smug ger, smug gest.** too pleased with one's own goodness, cleverness, respectability, etc.; self-satisfied; complacent. [perhaps < Dutch or Low German *smuk* trim, neat] **—smug′ly,** *adv.* **—smug′ness,** *n.*

smug gle (smug′əl), *v.,* **-gled, -gling.** —*v.t.* 1 import or export (goods, etc.) secretly and illegally, especially to avoid payment of duty: *smuggle jewels into the United States.* 2 bring, take, put, etc., secretly: *smuggle a puppy into the house.* —*v.i.* engage in smuggling. [< Low German *smuggeln*]

smug gler (smug′lər), *n.* 1 person who smuggles. 2 ship used in smuggling.

smut (smut), *n., v.,* **smut ted, smut ting.** —*n.* 1 a bit or bits of soot, dirt, etc. 2 a dirty mark; smudge. 3 indecent, obscene talk or writing. 4 a destructive disease of various plants, especially of cereal grasses, in which the ears of grain are replaced by a blackish powder consisting of spores. 5 any parasitic fungus producing this disease. —*v.t.* 1 soil with smut; smudge. 2 affect (a plant) with the disease smut. —*v.i.* 1 be soiled with smut. 2 (of a plant) become affected with smut. [origin uncertain]

Smuts (smuts), *n.* **Jan Christiaan,** 1870-1950, South African statesman and general.

smut ty (smut′ē), *adj.,* **-ti er, -ti est.** 1 soiled with smut, soot, etc.; dirty. 2 indecent; nasty; obscene. 3 (of plants) having the disease smut. **—smut′ti ly,** *adv.* **—smut′ti ness,** *n.*

Smyr na (smėr′nə), *n.* former name of **Izmir.**

Sn, tin [for Latin *stannum*].

snack (snak), *n.* a light meal, especially one eaten between regular meals. [Middle English *snake* snap]

snaf fle (snaf′əl), *n., v.,* **-fled, -fling.** —*n.* a slender, jointed bit used on a bridle. —*v.t.* control or manage by a snaffle. [perhaps < Dutch *snavel* beak]

sna fu (sna fü′), SLANG. —*n.* a snarled or confused state of things. —*adj.* snarled; confused. —*v.t.* 1 put in disorder or in a chaotic state. 2 botch. [< the initial letters of "situation normal — all fouled up"]

snag (snag), *n., v.,* **snagged, snag ging.** —*n.* 1 tree or branch held fast in a river or lake, especially below the surface. Snags are dangerous to boats. 2 any sharp or rough projecting point. 3 a hidden or unexpected obstacle: *Our plans hit a snag.* 4 a tear made by snagging. —*v.t.* 1 block as if with a snag; hinder. 2 run or catch on or as if on a snag. 3 **be snagged,** be caught, pierced, or damaged by a snag. —*v.i.* run into a snag or obstacle. [perhaps < Scandinavian (dialectal Norwegian) *snage* point of land]

snag gle tooth (snag′əl tüth′), *n., pl.* **-teeth.** an uneven, broken, or projecting tooth.

snag gle toothed (snag′əl tütht′), *adj.* having snaggleteeth.

snag gy (snag′ē), *adj.,* **-gi er, -gi est.** 1 having snags. 2 projecting sharply or roughly.

snail (def. 1)—about 2 in. long

snail (snāl), *n.* 1 any of a class of small, soft-bodied, slow-moving mollusks with a spiral shell into which it can withdraw for protection; gastropod. 2 a lazy, slow-moving person. [Old English *snegel*]

snake (snāk), *n., v.,* **snaked, snak ing.** —*n.* 1 any of a suborder of long, slender, limbless reptiles with a scaly skin and a narrow forked tongue. Some snakes have poison glands connected with a pair of fangs which inject prey with poison when the snake bites. 2 a sly, treacherous person. 3 anything resembling a snake in form or movement. 4 a long, flexible metal tool used by plumbers to clean out drains. —*v.i.* move, wind, or curve like a snake. —*v.t.* INFORMAL. drag; haul: *snake logs out of a forest.* [Old English *snaca*] **—snake′like′,** *adj.*

snake bird (snāk′bėrd′), *n.* a swimming bird with a long, snaky neck; darter.

snake bite (snāk′bīt′), *n.* the bite of a snake, especially a poisonous snake.

snake dance, 1 U.S. an informal parade of persons dancing in a zigzag line in celebration of a victory, etc. 2 a ceremonial dance of the Hopi Indians, in which the dancers carry live snakes as an offering to the rain gods.

snake oil, U.S. any of various preparations formerly sold as medicine by peddlers posing as scientists, doctors, etc.

snake pit, 1 pit filled with snakes. 2 INFORMAL. a backward or overcrowded mental institution, prison, etc.

Snake River (snāk), river flowing from NW Wyoming through Idaho into the Columbia River in Washington. 1038 mi.

snake root (snāk′rüt′, snāk′rut′), *n.* any of various plants whose roots have been regarded as a remedy for snakebite.

snake skin (snāk′skin′), *n.* 1 skin of a snake. 2 leather made from it.

snaffle

hat, āge, fär; let, ēqual, tėrm;
it, īce; hot, ōpen, ôrder;
oil, out; cup, pu̇t, rüle;
ch, child; ng, long; sh, she;
th, thin; ᴛʜ, then; zh, measure;

ə represents *a* in about, *e* in taken, *i* in pencil, *o* in lemon, *u* in circus.

< = from, derived from, taken from.

snak y (snā′kē), *adj.,* **snak i er, snak i est.** 1 of a snake or snakes. 2 twisting; winding. 3 having many snakes. 4 sly; venomous; treacherous. **—snak′i ly,** *adv.* **—snak′i ness,** *n.*

snap (snap), *v.,* **snapped, snap ping,** *n., adj., adv.* —*v.i.* 1 make a sudden, sharp sound: *Most pine snaps as it burns.* 2 move, shut, catch, etc., with a snap: *The door snapped shut behind me.* 3 break suddenly or sharply, especially with a snapping sound: *The violin string snapped.* 4 become suddenly unable to endure a strain: *His nerves snapped.* 5 make a sudden, quick bite or snatch: *The dog snapped at the child's hand.* 6 seize suddenly: *She snapped at the chance to go to Europe.* 7 speak quickly and sharply: *snap impatiently at a person who is slow.* 8 move quickly and sharply: *The soldiers snapped to attention. Her eyes snapped with anger.* 9 take snapshots. 10 **snap back,** INFORMAL. bounce back; recover suddenly. 11 **snap out of it,** change one's attitude, habit, etc., suddenly. —*v.t.* 1 cause to make a sudden, sharp sound: *snap one's fingers.* 2 cause to move, close, catch, etc., with a snap: *snap a bolt into place.* 3 break suddenly or sharply: *snap a stick in two.* 4 snatch quickly with the mouth; bite suddenly: *The dog snapped up the meat.* 5 seize suddenly: *snap up a bargain.* 6 say quickly and sharply: *snap out an order.* 7 move quickly and sharply. 8 take a snapshot of. 9 (in football) pass back (the ball) to begin a play; center.
—*n.* 1 a quick, sharp sound: *The box shut with a snap.* 2 a sudden, sharp breaking or the sound of breaking. 3 a quick, sudden bite or snatch: *The dog made a snap at the fly.* 4 a quick, sharp speech: *be answered with a snap.* 5 INFORMAL. a quick, sharp way: *She moves with snap and energy.* 6 a short spell of cold weather. 7 fastener; clasp: *One of the snaps of your dress is unfastened.* 8 a thin, crisp cookie: *a chocolate snap.* 9 INFORMAL. snapshot. 10 SLANG. an easy job, piece of work, etc. 11 a snapping of the ball in football. 12 **not a snap,** not at all.
—*adj.* 1 made or done quickly or suddenly; hasty: *a snap judgment.* 2 closing or fastening by action of a spring: *a snap lock.* 3 SLANG. easy.
[earlier, to bite < Dutch *snappen*]

snap back (snap′bak′), *n.* 1 INFORMAL. a snapping back to a former or normal condition. 2 (in football) a snap.

snap drag on (snap′drag′ən), *n.* any of a genus of garden plants of the same family as the figwort, with spikes of showy flowers of crimson, purple, white, yellow, etc.

snap per (snap′ər), *n.* 1 person or thing that snaps. 2 snapping turtle. 3 any of a family of large, usually edible fish of tropical seas, especially the **red snapper** of the Gulf of Mexico. 4 any of certain other similar fishes.

snapping turtle, any of a subfamily of large, vicious, freshwater turtles of North America with powerful jaws for grasping prey.

snap pish (snap′ish), *adj.* 1 apt to snap. 2 quick and sharp in speech or manner; impatient. 3 of or characteristic of a snappish person. **—snap′pish ly,** *adv.* **—snap′pish ness,** *n.*

snap py (snap′ē), *adj.,* **-pi er, -pi est.** 1 snappish. 2 crackling: *a snappy fire.* 3 INFORMAL. having snap, smartness, pungency, etc.; crispy; lively: *a snappy cheese, a snappy new suit.* **—snap′pi ly,** *adv.* **—snap′pi ness,** *n.*

snap shot (snap′shot′), *n.* photograph taken in an instant, with a small camera.

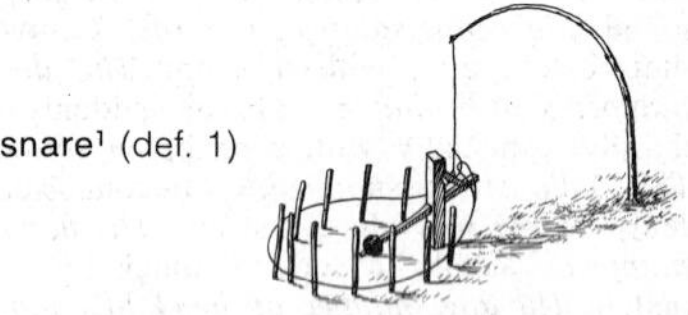
snare[1] (def. 1)

snare[1] (sner, snar), *n., v.,* **snared, snar ing.** *—n.* 1 trap consisting of a noose or set of nooses for catching small animals and birds. 2 anything that entraps; pitfall; trap. *—v.t.* 1 catch with a snare. 2 entangle; trap. [< Scandinavian (Old Icelandic) *snara*]

snare[2] (sner, snar), *n.* one of the strings of wire or gut stretched across the bottom of a snare drum. [probably < Dutch]

snare drum showing snares on bottom of drum

snare drum, a small drum with strings of wire or gut stretched across the bottom to make a rattling sound.

snarl[1] (snärl), *v.i.* 1 (of dogs, etc.) make an angry, growling sound accompanied by showing the teeth. 2 speak harshly in a sharp, angry tone. *—v.t.* say or express with a snarl. *—n.* 1 a sharp, angry growl. 2 sharp, angry words. [earlier *snar,* perhaps < Dutch *snarren* to rattle. Related to SNORE.] **—snarl′er,** *n.* **—snarl′ing ly,** *adv.*

snarl[2] (snärl), *n.* 1 a tangled or knotted mass or tuft; tangle. 2 tangled condition; confusion. *—v.t., v.i.* 1 tangle or become tangled. 2 confuse or become confused. [perhaps < *snare*[1]]

snatch (snach), *v.t.* 1 take hold of or seize suddenly, eagerly, or violently; grasp hastily. 2 take or get hastily, suddenly or improperly: *They snatched victory from what seemed to be sure defeat.* 3 remove, pull, or take *(off)* quickly and roughly: *He snatched off my hat.* 4 SLANG. kidnap. **5 snatch at, a** try to seize or grasp. **b** take advantage of eagerly. *—n.* 1 act of snatching; a sudden grab. 2 a short time: *a snatch of sleep.* 3 a small amount; bit; scrap: *hear snatches of conversation.* 4 SLANG. a kidnaping. [perhaps < Middle Dutch *snakken*] **—snatch′er,** *n.*

snatch y (snach′ē), *adj.* done or occurring in snatches; disconnected; irregular. **—snatch′i ly,** *adv.*

snath (snath), *n.* the long wooden handle of a scythe. [Old English *snǣd*]

snathe (snāᴛʜ), *n.* snath.

snaz zy (snaz′ē), *adj.,* **-zi er, -zi est.** SLANG. fancy; flashy. [origin unknown]

SNCC, Student National Coordinating Committee (a militant organization advocating Black Power, originally (in 1960) formed by Southern students under the name Student Nonviolent Coordinating Committee to promote civil rights).

sneak (snēk), *v.i.* 1 move in a stealthy, sly way: *The man sneaked about the barn watching for a chance to steal the horse.* 2 act in a mean, contemptible, or cowardly way. *—v.t.* 1 get, put, pass, etc., in a stealthy, sly way: *The children sneaked the puppy into the house.* 2 INFORMAL. steal. *—n.* 1 act of sneaking. 2 a mean, contemptible, or cowardly person. *—adj.* stealthy; sneaking: *a sneak attack.* [origin uncertain]

sneak er (snē′kər), *n.* **1 sneakers,** *pl.* light canvas shoes with rubber soles; tennis shoes. 2 person who sneaks; sneak.

sneak ing (snē′king), *adj.* 1 meanly or deceitfully underhand; contemptible. 2 that one cannot justify or does not like to confess: *have a sneaking suspicion about something.* **—sneak′ing ly,** *adv.*

sneak y (snē′kē), *adj.,* **sneak i er, sneak i est.** cowardly, mean, or contemptible. **—sneak′i ly,** *adv.* **—sneak′i ness,** *n.*

sneer (snir), *v.i.* show scorn or contempt by looks or words: *sneer at someone's ideas.* See **scoff** for synonym study. *—v.t.* 1 say or write with scorn or contempt. 2 bring, put, force, etc., by sneering: *sneer down all who disagree.* *—n.* act of sneering; look or words expressing scorn or contempt. [Middle English *sneren*] **—sneer′er,** *n.* **—sneer′ing ly,** *adv.*

sneeze (snēz), *v.,* **sneezed, sneez ing,** *n.* *—v.i.* expel air suddenly and violently through the nose and mouth by an involuntary spasm. *—v.t.* **sneeze at,** INFORMAL. treat with contempt; despise; scorn. *—n.* act of sneezing. [Middle English *snesen,* variant of *fnesen,* Old English *fnēosan*] **—sneez′er,** *n.*

snell (snel), *n.* a short piece of gut, etc., by which a fishhook is fastened to a longer line. [origin uncertain]

snick[1] (snik), *v.t.* cut, snip, or nick. *—n.* a small cut; nick. [origin uncertain]

snick[2] (snik), *n.* a slight sharp sound; click. [imitative]

snick er (snik′ər), *n.* a half-suppressed and usually disrespectful laugh; sly or silly laugh; giggle. *—v.i.* laugh in this way. Also, **snigger.** [imitative]

snide (snīd), *adj.* mean or spiteful in a sly way: *a snide remark.* [origin uncertain]

sniff (snif), *v.i.* 1 draw air through the nose in short, quick breaths that can be heard. 2 smell with sniffs. 3 show or express contempt or scorn by sniffing. *—v.t.* 1 try the smell of; test by smelling: *I sniffed the medicine before taking a spoonful of it.* 2 draw in through the nose with the breath. 3 suspect; detect: *sniff a plot, sniff danger.* *—n.* 1 act or sound of sniffing. 2 a single breathing in of something; breath. [related to SNIVEL] **—sniff′er,** *n.*

snif fle (snif′əl), *v.,* **-fled, -fling,** *n.* *—v.i.* sniff again and again as one does from a cold in the head or in trying to stop crying. *—n.* 1 act or sound of sniffling. **2 the sniffles, a** a stuffy condition of the nose caused by a cold, hay fever, etc. **b** fit of sniffling. **—snif′fler,** *n.*

sniff y (snif′ē), *adj.,* **sniff i er, sniff i est.** INFORMAL. 1 inclined to sniff, especially in contempt, scorn, etc. 2 contemptuous; scornful.

snig ger (snig′ər), *n., v.i.* snicker.

snip (snip), *v.,* **snipped, snip ping,** *n.* *—v.t.* 1 cut with a small, quick stroke or series of strokes with scissors or a similar instrument: *snip a thread.* 2 cut up or off as if by scissors. *—v.i.* make a cut or cuts with or as if with scissors. *—n.* 1 act of snipping: *cut out something with a few snips of the scissors.* 2 a small piece cut off: *Pick up the snips of cloth and thread from the floor.* 3 any small piece; bit; fragment. **4 snips,** *pl.* hand shears for cutting metal. 5 INFORMAL. a small or unimportant person. [< Dutch or Low German *snippen*]

snipe (snīp), *n., pl.* **snipes** or **snipe,** *v.,* **sniped, snip ing.** *—n.* any of various marsh birds with long bills, of the same family as the sandpipers, frequently hunted as game. *—v.i.* 1 shoot at an enemy one at a time from a concealed place. 2 hunt snipe. *—v.t.* 1 shoot at (soldiers) one at a time from a concealed place. **2 snipe at,** attack suddenly or unexpectedly, especially by words. [< Scandinavian (Old Icelandic) *snīpa*]

snip er (snī′pər), *n.* a hidden sharpshooter.

snip pet (snip′it), *n.* 1 a small piece snipped off; bit; fragment. 2 INFORMAL. a small or unimportant person.

snip py (snip′ē), *adj.,* **-pi er, -pi est.** 1 INFORMAL. sharp; curt. 2 INFORMAL. haughty; disdainful. 3 made up of scraps or fragments. **—snip′pi ness,** *n.*

snitch[1] (snich), *v.t.* SLANG. snatch; steal. [origin unknown] **—snitch′er,** *n.*

snitch[2] (snich), SLANG. *—v.i.* be an informer; tell tales. *—n.* informer. [original meaning "nose"; origin uncertain] **—snitch′er,** *n.*

sniv el (sniv′əl), *v.,* **-eled, -el ing** or **-elled, -el ling,** *n.* *—v.i.* 1 cry with sniffling; whimper. 2 put on a show of grief; whine. 3 run at the nose; sniffle. *—n.* 1 pretended grief or crying; whining. 2 sniffling. [Middle English *snivelen,* related to Old English *snofl* mucus] **—sniv′el er, sniv′el ler,** *n.*

snob (snob), *n.* person who cares too much for rank, wealth, position, etc., and too little for real achievement or merit; person who tries too hard to please those above him and ignores those below him. [origin uncertain]

snob ber y (snob′ər ē), *n., pl.* **-ber ies.** character or conduct of a snob; snobbishness.

snob bish (snob′ish), *adj.* of or like a snob; looking down on those in a lower position. **—snob′bish ly,** *adv.* **—snob′bish ness,** *n.*

snob bism (snob′iz′əm), *n.* snobbery.

snood (snüd), *n.* 1 net or bag worn over a woman's hair. A snood may be a part of a hat. 2 a baglike hat. 3 band or ribbon formerly worn around the hair by young unmarried women in Scotland and northern England. *—v.t.* bind (hair) with a snood. [Old English *snōd*]

snoop (snüp), INFORMAL. *—v.i.* go about in a sneaking, prying way; prowl; pry. *—n.* person who snoops. [< Dutch *snoepen* eat in secret] **—snoop′er,** *n.*

snoop y (snü′pē), *adj.,* **snoop i er, snoop i est.** inclined to snoop; nosy; prying.

snoot (snüt), *n.* SLANG. 1 nose. 2 face. [variant of *snout*]

snoot y (snü′tē), *adj.*, **snoot i er, snoot i est.** INFORMAL. snobbish; conceited. **—snoot′i ly,** *adv.* **—snoot′i ness,** *n.*

snooze (snüz), *v.*, **snoozed, snooz ing,** *n.* INFORMAL. —*v.i.* take a nap; sleep; doze. —*n.* nap; doze. [origin uncertain] **—snooz′er,** *n.*

snore (snôr, snōr), *v.*, **snored, snor ing,** *n.* —*v.i.* 1 breathe during sleep with a harsh, rough sound. 2 pass in sleeping, especially while snoring: *snore away the afternoon.* —*n.* sound made in snoring. [Middle English *snoren*] **—snor′er,** *n.*

snorkel (def. 2)

snor kel (snôr′kəl), *n.* 1 a periscopelike intake and exhaust shaft for diesel engines which allows submarines to remain submerged for a long period of time. 2 a curved tube which enables swimmers to breathe under water while swimming near the surface. —*v.i.* swim under water using a snorkel. [< German *Schnorchel* nose]

snort (snôrt), *v.i.* 1 force the breath violently through the nose with a loud, harsh sound: *The horse snorted.* 2 make a sound like this: *The engine snorted.* 3 show contempt, defiance, anger, etc., by snorting. —*v.t.* say or express with a snort: *"Nonsense!" snorted my aunt.* —*n.* 1 act or sound of snorting. 2 SLANG. drink of alcoholic liquor, especially taken in one gulp. [perhaps < Low German *snorten*] **—snort′er,** *n.*

snout (snout), *n.* 1 the projecting part of an animal's head that contains the nose, mouth, and jaws. Pigs, dogs, and crocodiles have snouts. 2 a similar projection in certain insects. 3 anything like an animal's snout. 4 INFORMAL. a person's nose, especially a large or ugly nose. [Middle English *snoute*]

snout beetle, weevil.

snow (snō), *n.* 1 water vapor frozen into crystals that fall to earth in soft, white flakes and spread often upon it as a white layer. 2 a fall of snow. 3 ARCHAIC. pure whiteness. 4 something resembling or suggesting snow. 5 (in chemistry) any of various substances having a snowlike appearance: *carbon-dioxide snow.* 6 pattern of dots on a television screen caused by interference with the signal.
—*v.i.* 1 fall as snow: *snow all day.* 2 come down like snow. —*v.t.* 1 let fall or scatter as snow. 2 cover, block up, etc., with snow, or as if with snow. 3 **snow in,** shut in by snow. 4 **snow under,** a cover with snow. b overwhelm: *snowed under with work.*
[Old English *snāw*] **—snow′less,** *adj.* **—snow′like′,** *adj.*

Snow (snō), *n.* 1 **C(harles) P(ercy),** born 1905, British novelist and physicist. 2 **Eliza Roxey,** 1804-1887, American poet and Mormon women's leader.

snow ball (snō′bôl′), *n.* 1 ball made of snow pressed together. 2 shrub, a species of viburnum, of the same family as the honeysuckle, with white flowers in large clusters like balls. —*v.t.* throw balls of snow at. —*v.i.* increase rapidly by additions like a rolling snowball: *The number of signers of the petition for a new school snowballed.*

snow bank (snō′bangk′), *n.* large mass or drift of snow.

snow ber ry (snō′ber′ē), *n., pl.* **-ries.** 1 a North American shrub of the same family as the honeysuckle, with pink flowers and clusters of white berries that mature in the fall and last through the winter. 2 its berry.

snow bird (snō′bėrd′), *n.* 1 junco. 2 snow bunting.

snow-blind (snō′blīnd′), *adj.* affected with snow blindness.

snow blindness, temporary or partial blindness caused by the reflection of sunlight from snow or ice.

snow bound (snō′bound′), *adj.* shut in by snow.

snow bunting, a small, white finch with black and brownish markings that inhabits cold regions; snowbird.

snow capped (snō′kapt′), *adj.* having its top covered with snow: *a snowcapped mountain.*

Snow don (snōd′n), *n.* the highest mountain in Wales, in the NW part. 3560 ft.

snow drift (snō′drift′), *n.* 1 mass or bank of snow piled up by the wind. 2 snow driven before the wind.

snow drop (snō′drop′), *n.* a small European plant of the amaryllis family, with drooping white flowers that bloom early in the spring.

snow fall (snō′fôl′), *n.* 1 a fall of snow. 2 amount of snow falling within a certain time and area: *The snowfall in that one storm was 16 inches.*

snow field (snō′fēld′), *n.* a wide expanse of snow, especially in polar regions.

snow flake (snō′flāk′), *n.* a small, feathery crystal of snow.

snow leopard, ounce[2].

snow line, line on mountains above which there is always snow.

snow man (snō′man′), *n., pl.* **-men.** mass of snow made into a figure somewhat like that of a man.

snow mo bile (snō′mō bēl), *n.* tractor or other vehicle for use in snow, some having skis or runners in front.

snow plow (snō′plou′), *n.* machine for clearing away snow from streets, railroad tracks, etc.

snow shed (snō′shed′), *n.* a long shed built over a railroad track to protect it from snowslides.

snowshoe—a pair of snowshoes

snow shoe (snō′shü′), *n., v.*, **-shoed, -shoe ing.** —*n.* a light, wooden frame with strips of leather stretched across it. Trappers, hunters, etc., in the far North wear snowshoes on their feet to keep from sinking in deep, soft snow. —*v.i.* walk or travel on snowshoes.

snow slide (snō′slīd′), *n.* 1 the sliding down of a mass of snow on a steep slope. 2 the mass of snow that slides.

hat, āge, fär; let, ēqual, tėrm;
it, īce; hot, ōpen, ôrder;
oil, out; cup, pu̇t, rüle;
ch, child; ng, long; sh, she;
th, thin; ᴛʜ, then; zh, measure;

ə represents *a* in about, *e* in taken, *i* in pencil, *o* in lemon, *u* in circus.

< = from, derived from, taken from.

snow storm (snō′stôrm′), *n.* storm with much snow.

snow suit (snō′süt′), *n.* a warm, winter coat and leggings for children.

snow tire, an automobile tire with heavy treads to give extra traction on surfaces made slippery by snow or ice.

snow-white (snō′hwīt′), *adj.* white as snow.

snow y (snō′ē), *adj.*, **snow i er, snow i est.** 1 having snow: *a snowy day.* 2 covered with snow: *a snowy road.* 3 like snow; white as snow: *The old lady has snowy hair.* **—snow′i ly,** *adv.* **—snow′i ness,** *n.*

snub (snub), *v.*, **snubbed, snub bing,** *n., adj.* —*v.t.* 1 treat coldly, scornfully, or with contempt. 2 rebuke or reprove in a sharp or cutting manner. 3 check or stop (a boat, horse, etc.) suddenly. 4 check or stop (a rope or cable running out) suddenly. —*n.* 1 cold, scornful, or disdainful treatment. 2 a sharp rebuke. 3 a sudden check or stop. —*adj.* short and turned up at the tip: *a snub nose.* [< Scandinavian (Old Icelandic) *snubba* reprove]

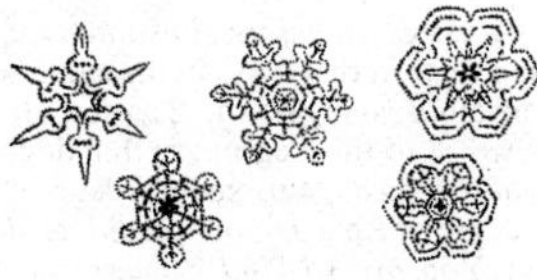
snowflake—snowflake forms

snub ber (snub′ər), *n.* 1 person that snubs. 2 device for snubbing a rope, cable, etc.

snub by (snub′ē), *adj.*, **-bi er, -bi est.** short and turned up at the tip.

snub-nosed (snub′nōzd′), *adj.* having a snub nose.

snuff[1] (snuf), *v.t.* 1 draw in through the nose; draw up into the nose. 2 smell at; examine by smelling: *The dog snuffed the track of the fox.* —*v.i.* 1 draw air, etc., up or in through the nose. 2 sniff, especially curiously as a dog would. 3 take powdered tobacco into the nose by snuffing; use snuff. —*n.* 1 powdered tobacco, often scented, taken into the nose. 2 act of snuffing. 3 **up to snuff,** a INFORMAL. in perfect order or condition; as good as expected. b SLANG. not easily deceived. [probably < Dutch *snuffen*] **—snuff′er,** *n.*

snuff[2] (snuf), *v.t.* 1 cut or pinch off the burned wick of. 2 put out (a candle); extinguish. 3 **snuff out,** a put out; extinguish. b put an end to suddenly and completely; wipe out. —*n.* the burned part of a candlewick. [Middle English *snoffen*] **—snuff′er,** *n.*

snuff box (snuf′boks′), *n.* a very small box for holding snuff.

snuff ers (snuf′ərz), *n.pl.* small tongs for taking off burned wick or putting out the light of a candle.

snuf fle (snuf′əl), *v.*, **-fled, -fling,** *n.* —*v.i.* 1 breathe noisily through the nose like a person with a cold in the head. 2 smell; sniff. 3 speak, sing, etc., through the nose or with a nasal tone. —*n.* 1 act or sound of snuffling. 2 the nasal tone of voice of a person who snuffles. 3 **the snuffles,** a cold in the head. [< *snuff*[1]] **—snuf′fler,** *n.*

snug (snug), *adj.*, **snug ger, snug gest,** *v.*, **snugged, snug ging,** *adv.* —*adj.* 1 comfortable and warm; sheltered: *The cat has found a snug corner behind the stove.* See synonym study below. 2 compact, neat, and trim: *The cabins on the boat are snug.* 3 well-built; seaworthy: *a snug ship.* 4 fitting closely: *That coat is a little too snug.* 5 small but sufficient: *snug income.* 6 hidden; concealed: *The fox lay snug as the hunters passed by.* —*v.t.* make snug. —*v.i.* nestle; snuggle. —*adv.* in a snug manner. [probably < Low German] **—snug′ly,** *adv.* **—snug′ness,** *n.*

Syn. *adj.* 1 **Snug, cozy** mean comfortable. **Snug** emphasizes the comfort and security of a small space, warm and sheltered from the weather: *The children were snug in their beds.* **Cozy** emphasizes warmth, shelter, and ease, often affection or friendliness, making for comfort and contentment: *The lonely man looked through the window at the cozy family.*

snug ger y (snug′ər ē), *n.*, *pl.* **-ger ies.** a snug place, position, room, etc.

snug gle (snug′əl), *v.*, **-gled, -gling.** —*v.i.* lie or press closely for warmth or comfort or from affection; nestle; cuddle. —*v.t.* draw or press closely to, for comfort or from affection.

so[1] (sō; *unstressed before consonants* sə), *adv.* 1 in this way; in that way; in the same way; as shown: *Hold your pen so.* 2 as stated: *Is that really so?* 3 to this degree; to that degree: *Do not walk so fast.* 4 to such a degree; to the same degree: *He was not so cold as she was.* 5 very: *You are so kind.* 6 very much: *My head aches so.* 7 for this reason; for that reason; accordingly; therefore: *The dog was hungry; so we fed it.* 8 likewise; also: *She likes dogs; so does he.* 9 **and so, a** likewise; also: *He is here and so is she.* **b** accordingly: *The bill was signed by the President and so became a law.* 10 **so as,** with the result or purpose. 11 **so that,** with the result or purpose that.

—*conj.* 1 with the result that; in order that: *Go away so I can rest.* 2 with the purpose or intention that: *I did the work so you would not need to.* 3 on the condition that; if: *So it be done, I care not who does it.*

—*interj.* 1 well! 2 let it be that way! all right! 3 is that true?

—*pron.* 1 more or less; approximately that: *It weighs a pound or so.* 2 the same: *A miser usually remains so.*

[Old English *swā*]

so[2] (sō), *n.* sol[1].

So., 1 South. 2 Southern.

soak (sōk), *v.i.* 1 let remain in water or other liquid until wet clear through. 2 become very wet; remain until wet clear through. 3 make its way; enter; go: *Water will soak through the soil.* 4 make its way into the mind; penetrate: *The magnitude of the problem finally soaked into their minds.* —*v.t.* 1 make very wet; wet through. See **wet** for synonym study. 2 draw or suck *(out): soak out a stain.* 3 SLANG. punish severely; strike hard. 4 INFORMAL. make pay too much; charge or tax heavily: *He admitted he had been soaked in the deal.* 5 **soak up, a** absorb or suck up: *soak up sunshine. The sponge soaked up the water.* **b** take into the mind: *soak up knowledge.*

—*n.* 1 act or process of soaking. 2 state of being soaked. 3 the liquid in which anything is soaked. 4 SLANG. a heavy drinker; sot. [Old English *socian*] **—soak′er,** *n.*

so-and-so (sō′ən sō′), *n.*, *pl.* **-sos.** some person or thing not named.

soap (sōp), *n.* 1 substance used for washing, usually made of a fat and sodium or potassium hydroxide. 2 (in chemistry) any metallic salt of an acid derived from a fat. —*v.t.* rub with soap: *soap one's face.* [Old English *sāpe*] **—soap′less,** *adj.*

soap box (sōp′boks′), *n.* 1 box, especially of wood, in which soap used to be packed. 2 an empty box used as a temporary platform by speakers addressing gatherings on the streets.

soap bubble, bubble formed of a thin film of soapy water.

soap opera, a daytime radio or television drama presented in serial form, usually featuring emotional domestic situations.

soccer

soap stone (sōp′stōn′), *n.* a soft rock that feels somewhat like soap, composed mostly of talc and used for griddles, hearths, etc.

soap suds (sōp′sudz′), *n.pl.* bubbles and foam made with soap and water.

soap wort (sōp′wėrt′), *n.* any of a genus of pinks, having white, rose, or pink flowers. Some species have leaves and roots containing a juice that can be used as soap.

soap y (sō′pē), *adj.*, **soap i er, soap i est.** 1 covered with soap or soapsuds. 2 containing soap. 3 of or like soap; smooth; greasy. **—soap′i ly,** *adv.* **—soap′i ness,** *n.*

soar (sôr, sōr), *v.i.* 1 fly at a great height; fly upward: *The eagle soared without flapping its wings.* 2 rise beyond what is common and ordinary: *Prices are soaring.* 3 tower or aspire: *a soaring skyscraper, soaring ambition.* 4 fly or move through the air by means of rising air currents. A glider can soar for many miles. —*v.t.* reach in soaring. [< Old French *essorer* < Latin *ex-* out + *aura* breeze, air]

sob (sob), *v.*, **sobbed, sob bing,** *n.* —*v.i.* 1 cry or sigh with short, quick breaths. 2 make a sound like a sob: *The wind sobbed.* —*v.t.* 1 put, send, etc., by sobbing: *sob oneself to sleep.* 2 utter with sobs: *sob out a sad story.* —*n.* 1 act of sobbing. 2 sound of sobbing or any sound like it. [Middle English *sobben*]

so ber (sō′bər), *adj.* 1 not drunk. 2 temperate; moderate: *The Puritans led sober, hard-working lives.* 3 quiet; serious; solemn: *a sober expression.* 4 calm; sensible: *a sober opinion not influenced by prejudice or strong feeling.* 5 free from exaggeration or distortion: *sober facts.* 6 quiet in color: *dressed in sober gray.* —*v.t., v.i.* make or become sober.

sober down, make or become quiet, serious, or solemn.

sober up, recover from too much alcoholic drink.

[< Old French *sobre* < Latin *sobrius*] **—so′ber ly,** *adv.* **—so′ber ness,** *n.*

so ber-mind ed (sō′bər mīn′did), *adj.* self-controlled; sensible.

so ber sid ed (sō′bər sī′did), *adj.* serious; staid.

so ber sides (sō′bər sīdz′), *n.*, *pl.* **-sides.** a sobersided person.

so bri e ty (sə brī′ə tē), *n.* 1 soberness. 2 temperance in the use of strong drink. 3 moderation. 4 quietness; seriousness. [< Latin *sobrietatem* < *sobrius* sober]

so bri quet (sō′brə kā), *n.* nickname. Also, **soubriquet.** [< French]

sob sister, INFORMAL. 1 a woman reporter who writes with undue sentiment, usually about stories of personal hardship. 2 person given to telling sob stories.

sob story, INFORMAL. an overly sentimental story or pathetic account, especially of one's own hardship.

Soc., Society.

so-called (sō′kôld′), *adj.* called so, but really not so; called so improperly or incorrectly: *Her so-called friend hasn't even written to her.*

soc cer (sok′ər), *n.* game played with a round ball between two teams of eleven players each; association football. The players try to drive the ball into the opposing team's goal by kicking it or striking it with any part of the body except the hands and arms. [< *assoc.* (abbreviation of *association football*) + *-er,* noun suffix]

so cia bil i ty (sō′shə bil′ə tē), *n.* social disposition or behavior.

so cia ble (sō′shə bəl), *adj.* 1 liking company; friendly: *They are a sociable family and entertain a great deal.* See **social** for synonym study. 2 marked by conversation and companionship: *We had a sociable afternoon together.* —*n.* an informal social gathering. [< Latin *sociabilis* < *sociare* to associate < *socius* companion] **—so′cia bly,** *adv.*

so cial (sō′shəl), *adj.* 1 concerned with human beings in their relations to each other: *social justice.* 2 of or dealing with the living conditions, health, etc., of human beings: *social problems, social welfare.* 3 living, or liking to live, with others: *Man is a social being.* 4 for companionship or friendliness; having to do with companionship or friendliness: *a social club.* 5 liking company: *She has a social nature.* 6 connected with fashionable society: *a social leader.* 7 (of animals) living together in organized communities. Ants and bees are social insects. 8 (of plants) growing in patches or clumps. 9 socialistic. —*n.* a social gathering or party: *a church social.* [< Latin *socialis* < *socius* companion]

social climber, person who tries to gain acceptance or improve his standing in fashionable society.

Social Democrat, member or supporter of a Social Democratic Party.

Social Democratic Party, any of several political parties supporting socialism.

so cial ism (sō′shə liz′əm), *n.* 1 theory or system of social organization by which the major means of production and distribution are owned, managed, or controlled by the government, by associations of workers, or by the community as a whole. 2 a political

movement advocating or associated with this system. ➔ See **communism** for usage note.
so cial ist (sō′shə list), *n.* 1 person who favors or supports socialism. 2 **Socialist,** member of a Socialist Party. —*adj.* 1 socialistic. 2 **Socialist,** of or having to do with a Socialist Party.
so cial is tic (sō′shə lis′tik), *adj.* 1 of or having to do with socialism or socialists. 2 advocating or supporting socialism. —**so′cial is′ti cal ly,** *adv.*
Socialist Party, a political party which supports socialism.
so cial ite (sō′shə līt), *n.* member of the fashionable society of a community.
so ci al i ty (sō′shē al′ə tē), *n., pl.* **-ties.** 1 social activity; social intercourse. 2 social nature or tendencies.
so cial ize (sō′shə līz), *v.,* **-ized, -iz ing.** —*v.i.* be social or sociable: *He has never learned to socialize with his fellow workers.* —*v.t.* 1 establish or regulate in accordance with socialism. 2 make social; make fit for living with others. —**so′cial i za′tion,** *n.* —**so′cial iz′er,** *n.*
socialized medicine, the providing of medical care and hospital services for all persons, either free or at nominal cost, especially through government subsidization.
so cial ly (sō′shə lē), *adv.* 1 in a social way or manner; in relation to other people. 2 as a member of society or of a social group: *He is an able man, but socially he is a failure.*
so cial-mind ed (sō′shəl mīn′did), *adj.* aware of and concerned with social problems and conditions.
social register, list of people who are prominent in fashionable society.
social science, study of people, their activities, their customs, and their institutions in relationship to other people. History, sociology, economics, geography, and civics are social sciences. —**social scientist.**
social security, system of federal old-age, survivors, and disability insurance for retired persons, their dependents, and survivors, including a health insurance program for the aged and other insurance. The system is financed by contributions from the employee, the employer, and the government.
social service, social work.
social studies, course of study in the social sciences.
social work, work directed toward the betterment of social conditions in a community. Social work includes such services as free medical clinics, counseling for families, and recreational activities for underprivileged children.
social worker, person who does social work.
so ci e tal (sə sī′ə təl), *adj.* of or having to do with society.
so ci e ty (sə sī′ə tē), *n., pl.* **-ties.** 1 group of persons joined together for a common purpose or by a common interest. A club, a fraternity, a lodge, or an association may be called a society. 2 all the people; human beings living together as a group: *Gun-control and drug-control laws are enacted for the good of society.* 3 the people of any particular time or place: *the lower and middle classes of industrial society.* 4 the activities and customs of society or of a particular society: *Magic plays an important part in primitive society.* 5 company; companionship: *I enjoy her society.* 6 fashionable people or their doings. 7 an organized community of animals or insects. 8 an assemblage of plants of the same species forming a unit in an ecological community. [< Latin *societatem* < *socius* companion]
Society Islands, group of French islands in the S Pacific that includes Tahiti. 82,000 pop.; 650 sq. mi.
Society of Friends, the Quakers.
Society of Jesus, the religious order of the Jesuits.
so ci o cul tur al (sō′sē ō kul′chər əl), *adj.* of or having to do with both society and culture: *sociocultural change.*
so ci o e co nom ic (sō′sē ō ē′kə nom′ik, sō′sē ō ek′ə nom′ik), *adj.* having to do with or involving factors that are both social and economic.
so ci o log i cal (sō′sē ə loj′ə kəl), *adj.* 1 of or having to do with human society or problems relating to it: *The care of the poor is a sociological problem.* 2 of sociology. —**so′ci o log′i cal ly,** *adv.*
so ci ol o gist (sō′sē ol′ə jist), *n.* an expert in sociology.
so ci ol o gy (sō′sē ol′ə jē), *n.* study of the nature, origin, and development of human society and community life; science of social facts. Sociology deals with the facts of crime, poverty, marriage, the church, the school, etc. [< Latin *socius* companion + English *-logy*]
so ci o path (sō′sē ə path), *n.* person who lacks any sense of social or moral responsibility toward others; antisocial person.
sock[1] (sok), *n.* 1 a short stocking, especially one that reaches about halfway to the knee. 2 a light shoe worn by actors in comedy in ancient Greece and Rome. 3 comedy. [Old English *socc* light slipper < Latin *soccus*]
sock[2] (sok), SLANG. —*v.t.* strike or hit hard. —*n.* a hard blow. —*adv.* squarely; right. [origin uncertain]

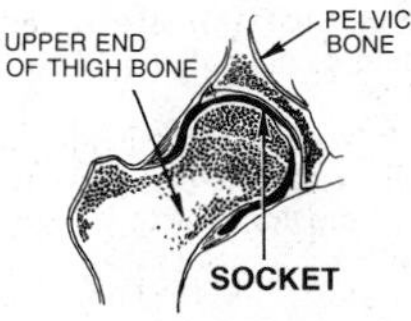

socket (def. 1)

sock et (sok′it), *n.* 1 a hollow part or piece for receiving and holding something. A candlestick has a socket in which to set a candle. A person's eyes are set in sockets. 2 a connecting place for electric wires and plugs. [< Anglo-French *soket* < Old French *soc* plowshare]
sock eye salmon (sok′ī′), salmon of the northern Pacific from Japan to California that ascends rivers to spawn; red salmon.
Soc ra tes (sok′rə tēz′), *n.* 469?-399 B.C., Athenian philosopher whose teachings were written down by his disciple Plato.
So crat ic (sō krat′ik), *adj.* of or having to do with Socrates, his philosophy, followers, etc.
Socratic method, use of a series of questions to lead a pupil to think, to make an opponent contradict himself, etc.
sod (sod), *n., v.,* **sod ded, sod ding.** —*n.* 1 ground covered with grass. 2 piece or layer of this containing the grass and its roots. 3 **under the sod,** buried. —*v.t.* cover with sods. [< Middle Dutch or Middle Low German *sode*]
so da (sō′də), *n.* 1 any of several chemical substances containing sodium, such as sodium bicarbonate or baking soda, sodium carbonate or sal soda, and sodium hydroxide or caustic soda. 2 soda water. 3 beverage consisting of soda water flavored with fruit juice or syrup, and often containing ice cream. [< Italian < Arabic *sauda,* a plant yielding sodium carbonate]

hat, āge, fär; let, ēqual, tėrm;
it, īce; hot, ōpen, ôrder;
oil, out; cup, pu̇t, rüle;
ch, child; ng, long; sh, she;
th, thin; ᴛʜ, then; zh, measure;

ə represents *a* in about, *e* in taken, *i* in pencil, *o* in lemon, *u* in circus.

< = from, derived from, taken from.

soda ash, partly purified sodium carbonate.
soda cracker, a simple, light, thin cracker made with little or no sugar or shortening.
soda fountain, 1 apparatus for holding soda water, syrups, ice, etc., and having faucets for drawing off the liquids. 2 counter with places for holding soda water, flavored syrups, ice cream, etc. 3 store having such a counter.
so dal i ty (sō dal′ə tē), *n., pl.* **-ties.** 1 fellowship; friendship. 2 an association, society, or fraternity. 3 (in the Roman Catholic Church) a lay society with religious or charitable purposes. [< Latin *sodalitatem* < *sodalis* sociable]
soda water, water charged with carbon dioxide to make it bubble and fizz, often served with the addition of syrup, ice cream, etc.
sod den (sod′n), *adj.* 1 soaked through; saturated: *My clothes were sodden with rain.* 2 heavy and moist; soggy: *This bread is sodden because it was not baked well.* 3 dull-looking; stupid: *a sodden face.* [Old past participle of *seethe*] —**sod′den ly,** *adv.* —**sod′den ness,** *n.*
so di um (sō′dē əm), *n.* a soft, silver-white metallic element which reacts violently with water and occurs in nature only in compounds. Salt and soda contain sodium. *Symbol:* Na; *atomic number* 11. See pages 326 and 327 for table. [< *soda*]
sodium benzoate, benzoate of soda.
sodium bicarbonate, a powdery, white crystalline salt used in cooking, medicine, manufacturing, etc.; baking soda; bicarbonate of soda. *Formula:* $NaHCO_3$
sodium borate, borax.
sodium carbonate, a salt that occurs in a powdery, white form (soda ash) and in a hydrated crystalline form (sal soda or washing soda). It is used for softening water, making soap and glass, neutralizing acids, and in medicine and photography. *Formula:* Na_2CO_3
sodium chloride, salt (def. 1). *Formula:* NaCl
sodium cyanide, a very poisonous, white, crystalline salt, used in the cyanide process for extracting gold and silver from ores, in fumigating, etc. *Formula:* NaCN
sodium fluoride, a poisonous crystalline salt, used as an insecticide, a disinfectant, in the fluoridation of water, etc. *Formula:* NaF
sodium hydroxide, a white solid that is a strong, corrosive alkali; caustic soda. It is used in making hard soaps, rayon, and paper,

in tanning, and as a bleaching agent. *Formula:* NaOH

sodium nitrate, a colorless, crystalline compound used in making fertilizer, explosives, etc.; niter; saltpeter. *Formula:* $NaNO_3$

sodium pentothal (pen′tə thôl, pen′tə-thol), thiopental sodium.

sodium silicate, any of various colorless, white, or grayish-white crystallike substances, used in preserving eggs, in soap powders, as adhesives, etc.; water glass.

sodium thiosulfate, hypo.

Sod om (sod′əm), *n.* 1 city of ancient times near the Dead Sea which, according to the account in the Bible, was destroyed, together with Gomorrah, by fire from heaven, because of the wickedness of its inhabitants. 2 any extremely wicked place.

sod om y (sod′ə mē), *n.* unnatural sexual relations. [< Old French *sodomie* < *Sodom*]

so ev er (sō ev′ər), *adv.* 1 in any case; in any way; in any degree: *to persist no matter how long soever the work may take.* 2 of any kind; at all: *a poor beggar with no home soever.*

-soever, *suffix.* in any way; of any kind; at all; ever, as in *whosoever, whatsoever, whensoever, wheresoever, howsoever.*

so fa (sō′fə), *n.* a long, upholstered seat or couch having a back and arms. [< Arabic *ṣuffah*]

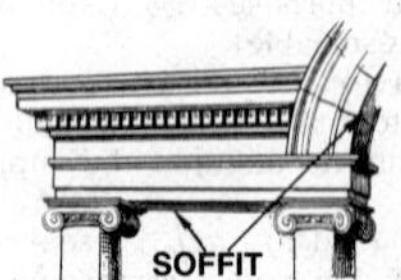

sof fit (sof′it), *n.* the under surface or face of an architrave, arch, or the like. [< Italian *soffitto,* ultimately < Latin *suffigere* < *sub-* under + *figere* to fix]

So fi a (sō fē′ə, sō′fē ə), *n.* capital of Bulgaria, in the W part. 868,000.

soft (sôft, soft), *adj.* 1 yielding readily to touch or pressure; not hard: *a soft pillow.* 2 not hard compared with other things of the same kind: *Copper and lead are softer than steel. Chalk is much softer than granite.* 3 not hard or sharp; gentle and graceful: *soft shadows, soft outlines.* 4 fine in texture; not rough or coarse; smooth: *a soft skin, soft hair.* 5 not loud: *a soft voice.* 6 quietly pleasant; mild: *a soft breeze.* 7 not glaring or harsh: *soft colors, a soft light.* 8 gentle; kind; tender: *a soft heart.* 9 weak; unmanly: *become soft from idleness and luxury.* 10 silly: *soft in the head.* 11 (of water) comparatively free from certain mineral salts that prevent soap from lathering. 12 (in phonetics) pronounced as a fricative or an affricate, rather than as a stop. EXAMPLE: *C* is soft in *city* and hard in *corn; g* is soft in *gentle* and hard in *get.* 13 easy; easygoing: *a soft job.* 14 of or having to do with radiation that has low powers of penetration, such as X rays.
—*adv.* in a soft manner; quietly; gently.
—*n.* that which is soft; soft part.
—*interj.* ARCHAIC. hush! stop!
[Old English *sōfte*] **—soft′ly,** *adv.* **—soft′ness,** *n.*

soft ball (sôft′bôl′, soft′bôl′), *n.* 1 game closely related to baseball, but played on a smaller field with a larger and softer ball that is pitched underhand only. 2 ball used in this game.

soft-boiled (sôft′boild′, soft′boild′), *adj.* (of an egg) boiled only a little so that the yolk is still soft.

soft coal, bituminous coal.

soft currency, currency backed by government credit, but not entirely by gold or silver.

soft drink, a sweetened, flavored drink, usually carbonated, that does not contain alcohol.

soft en (sôf′ən, sof′ən), *v.t.* 1 make softer. 2 **soften up,** lessen the ability (of a country, region, etc.) to resist attack through preliminary bombing, shelling, etc., or through propaganda or both. —*v.i.* become softer. **—soft′en er,** *n.*

soft head ed (sôft′hed′id, soft′hed′id), *adj.* silly; foolish. **—soft′head′ed ness,** *n.*

soft heart ed (sôft′här′tid, soft′här′tid), *adj.* gentle; kind; tender. **—soft′heart′ed-ly,** *adv.* **—soft′heart′ed ness,** *n.*

soft-land (sôft′land′, soft′land′), *v.t., v.i.* land in a soft landing.

soft landing, a landing of a spacecraft, instruments, module, etc., at a speed slow enough to avoid serious damage.

soft palate, the fleshy back part of the roof of the mouth.

soft-ped al (sôft′ped′l, soft′ped′l), *v.t.,* **-aled, -al ing** or **-alled, -al ling.** 1 soften the sound of (a piano) with one of its pedals. 2 make quieter, less noticeable, or less strong; tone down: *The editor refused to soft-pedal his criticism of the city government.*

soft sell, INFORMAL. method of selling by suggestion and persuasion rather than by pressure or aggressiveness.

soft-shell (sôft′shel′, soft′shel′), *adj.* soft-shelled.

soft-shell crab or **soft-shelled crab,** crab which has shed its hard shell and not yet grown another.

soft-shelled (sôft′sheld′, soft′sheld′), *adj.* having a soft shell: *a soft-shelled lobster.*

soft shoe, form of tap dance with shoes that have no metal taps.

soft-shoe (sôft′shü′, soft′shü′), *v.i.,* **-shoed, -shoe ing.** dance a soft shoe.

soft soap, 1 a liquid or semiliquid soap. 2 INFORMAL. flattery.

soft-soap (sôft′sōp′, soft′sōp′), *v.t.* INFORMAL. flatter. **—soft′-soap′er,** *n.*

soft-spo ken (sôft′spō′kən, soft′spō′kən), *adj.* 1 speaking with a soft voice. 2 spoken softly.

soft ware (sôft′wer′, sôft′war′; soft′wer′, soft′war′), *n.* 1 the plans for equipment or machinery to be manufactured. 2 program for a computer system.

soft wood (sôft′wu̇d′, soft′wu̇d′), *n.* 1 any wood that is easily cut. 2 a coniferous tree. Pines and firs are softwoods; oaks and maples are hardwoods. 3 wood of a coniferous tree. —*adj.* having or made of such wood.

soft y (sôf′tē, sof′tē), *n., pl.* **soft ies.** INFORMAL. 1 a soft, silly, or weak person. 2 one who is easily imposed upon.

sog gy (sog′ē), *adj.,* **-gi er, -gi est.** 1 thoroughly wet; soaked: *a soggy washcloth.* 2 damp and heavy: *soggy bread.* [< dialectal *sog* bog, swamp] **—sog′gi ly,** *adv.* **—sog′-gi ness,** *n.*

So ho (sō′hō), *n.* district in London with many restaurants.

soi-di sant (swȧ dē zäN′), *adj.* FRENCH. 1 calling oneself thus; self-styled. 2 so-called; pretended.

soi gné or ***soi gnée*** (swȧ nyā′), *adj.* FRENCH. 1 very neat and well-dressed. 2 finished or cared for to the smallest detail.

soil[1] (soil), *n.* 1 the ground or earth; surface of the earth. 2 the top layer of the earth's surface, composed of rock and mineral particles mixed with animal and vegetable matter: *excellent soil for cotton.* 3 anything thought of as a place of growth or development. 4 land; country: *one's native soil.* [< Anglo-French, one's piece of ground < Latin *solium* seat, influenced by Latin *solum* soil]

soil[2] (soil), *v.t.* 1 make dirty: *soil one's clean clothes.* 2 spot; stain: *The splashing paint soiled the wall.* 3 disgrace; dishonor: *False rumors have soiled his name.* 4 corrupt morally. —*v.i.* become dirty: *White shirts soil easily.* —*n.* 1 a spot; stain. 2 dirty or foul matter. [< Old French *soillier* < Latin *suile* pigsty < *sus* pig]

soil bank, U.S. program to pay farmers to cultivate less of certain crops to reduce surpluses.

soil less (soil′lis), *adj.* without soil: *soilless cultivation of plants.*

soi ree or **soi rée** (swä rā′), *n.* an evening party or social gathering. [< French *soirée* < *soir* evening]

so journ (*v.* sō′jėrn′, sō jėrn′; *n.* sō′jėrn′), *v.i.* stay for a time: *The Israelites sojourned in the land of Egypt.* —*n.* a brief stay. [< Old French *sojorner,* ultimately < Latin *sub* under + *diurnus* of the day] **—so′journ′-er,** *n.*

sol[1] (sōl), *n.* (in music) the fifth tone of the diatonic scale. Also, **so**[2]. [< Medieval Latin]

sol[2] (sōl), *n.* the monetary unit of Peru, a note or coin equal to 100 centavos and worth about $2^1/_3$ cents. [< Spanish, sun < Latin]

sol[3] (sol, sōl), *n.* a colloidal solution. [short for *solution*]

Sol (sol), *n.* 1 (in Roman myths) the god of the sun, identified with the Greek god Helios. 2 the sun.

sol., 1 soluble. 2 solution.

Sol., 1 Solicitor. 2 Solomon.

sol ace (sol′is), *n., v.,* **-aced, -ac ing.** —*n.* 1 comfort or relief: *She found solace from her troubles in music.* 2 that which gives comfort or consolation. —*v.t.* comfort or relieve; cheer: *He solaced himself with a book.* [< Latin *solacium* < *solari* to console] **—sol′ac er,** *n.*

so lar (sō′lər), *adj.* 1 of the sun: *a solar eclipse.* 2 having to do with the sun: *solar research.* 3 coming from the sun: *solar heat.* 4 measured or determined by the earth's motion in relation to the sun: *solar time.* 5 working by means of the sun's light or heat. A solar battery converts sunlight into electrical energy. [< Latin *solaris* < *sol* sun]

solar flare, a sudden eruption of hydrogen gas on the surface of the sun, usually associated with sunspots, and accompanied by a burst of ultraviolet radiation.

so lar i um (sə ler′ē əm), *n., pl.* **-lar i a** (-ler′ē ə), **-lar i ums.** room, porch, etc., where people can lie or sit in the sun.

solar plex us (plek′səs), 1 network of sympathetic nerves connected with the abdominal viscera, situated at the upper part of the abdomen, behind the stomach and in front of the aorta. 2 INFORMAL. the pit of the stomach.

hat, āge, fär; let, ēqual, tėrm;
it, īce; hot, ōpen, ôrder;
oil, out; cup, pu̇t, rüle;
ch, child; ng, long; sh, she;
th, thin; ᴛʜ, then; zh, measure;

ə represents *a* in about, *e* in taken,
i in pencil, *o* in lemon, *u* in circus.

< = from, derived from, taken from.

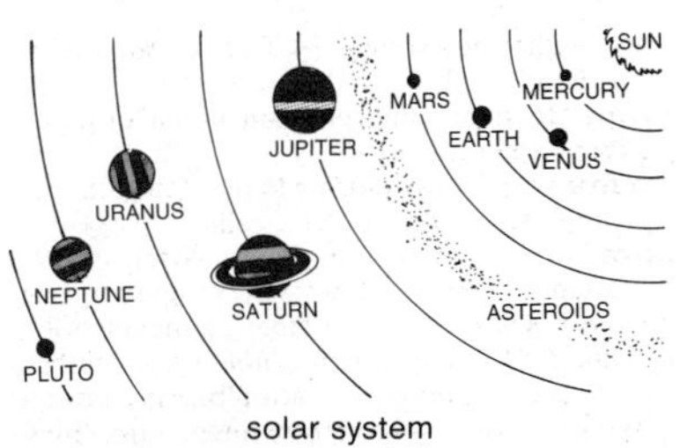

solar system

solar system, the sun and all the planets, satellites, comets, etc., that revolve around it.

solar wind, a continuous stream of ionized particles ejected by the sun, extending well beyond the earth.

solar year, astronomical year.

sold (sōld), *v.* pt. and pp. of **sell.**

sol der (sod′ər), *n.* 1 metal or alloy that can be melted and used for joining or mending metal surfaces, parts, etc. 2 anything that unites firmly or joins closely. *—v.t.* 1 fasten, mend, or join with solder. 2 unite firmly; join closely. *—v.i.* 1 become soldered. 2 become united by or as if by soldering. [< Old French *soldure* < *solder* solidify < Latin *solidare* < *solidus* solid] **—sol′der er,** *n.*

soldering iron, a metal tool heated to melt solder.

sol dier (sōl′jər), *n.* 1 person who serves in an army. 2 an enlisted man in the army, not a commissioned officer. 3 man having skill or experience in war. 4 person who serves in any cause: *Christian soldiers.* 5 in zoology: **a** (in colonies of certain ants) one of a type of workers with a large head and powerful jaws. **b** (in colonies of termites) one of a kind of large-headed individuals. *—v.i.* 1 act or serve as a soldier. 2 INFORMAL. pretend to work but do very little; pretend to be ill. [< Old French < *soulde* pay < Latin *solidus,* a Roman coin]

sol dier ly (sōl′jər lē), *adj.* like a soldier; suitable for a soldier.

soldier of fortune, man serving or ready to serve as a soldier under any government for money, adventure, or pleasure.

sol dier y (sōl′jər ē), *n., pl.* **-dier ies.** 1 soldiers. 2 body of soldiers. 3 military training or knowledge.

sole[1] (sōl), *adj.* 1 one and only; single: *the sole heir.* See **single** for synonym study. 2 only: *We three were the sole survivors.* 3 of or for only one person or group and not others; exclusive: *the sole right of use.* 4 without help; alone: *a sole undertaking.* [< Old French *soul* < Latin *solus*]

sole[2] (sōl), *n., v.,* **soled, sol ing.** *—n.* 1 the bottom or undersurface of the foot. 2 bottom of a shoe, slipper, boot, etc. 3 piece of leather, rubber, etc., cut in the same shape. 4 the undersurface; under part; bottom. *—v.t.* put a sole on: *sole shoes.* [< Old French < Latin *solea* kind of sandal]

sole[3] (sōl), *n., pl.* **soles** or **sole.** 1 any of a family of flatfishes having a small mouth and small, close-set eyes. European sole is valued highly as food. 2 any of certain related fishes. [< Old French, sole² (because of the flatness of the fish)]

sol e cism (sol′ə siz′əm), *n.* 1 violation of the grammatical or other accepted usages of a language; mistake in using words: *"I done it" is a solecism.* 2 mistake in social behavior; breach of good manners or etiquette. [< Latin *soloecismos* < Greek *soloikismos,* supposedly < *Soloi,* an Athenian colony in Cilicia whose Attic dialect the Athenians considered barbarous]

sole ly (sōl′lē), *adv.* 1 as the only one or ones; alone: *You will be solely responsible.* 2 only: *Bananas grow outdoors solely in warm climates.*

sol emn (sol′əm), *adj.* 1 of a serious, grave, or earnest character: *a solemn face.* 2 causing serious or grave thoughts: *The organ played solemn music.* 3 done with form and ceremony: *a solemn procession.* 4 connected with religion; sacred. 5 gloomy; dark; somber in color. [< Latin *sollemnis*] **—sol′emn ly,** *adv.* **—sol′emn ness,** *n.*

so lem ni ty (sə lem′nə tē), *n., pl.* **-ties.** 1 solemn feeling; seriousness; impressiveness. 2 Often, **solemnities,** *pl.* a solemn, formal ceremony: *The solemnities were concluded with a prayer by the chaplain.*

sol em nize (sol′əm nīz), *v.t.,* **-nized, -niz ing.** 1 observe with ceremonies: *Christian churches solemnize the resurrection of Christ at Easter.* 2 hold or perform (a ceremony or service): *The marriage was solemnized in the cathedral.* 3 make serious or grave. **—sol′em ni za′tion,** *n.*

so le noid (sō′lə noid), *n.* a spiral or cylindrical coil of wire that acts like a magnet when an electric current passes through it, used in automobile directional flashers, mechanical sorting devices, etc. [< French *solénoïde,* ultimately < Greek *sōlēn* channel]

sol-fa (sōl′fä′), *n.* system of singing the syllables *do, re, mi, fa, sol, la, ti, do* to tones of the scale; solmization. *—adj.* of or having to do with this system of singing: *sol-fa notation, sol-fa scale.* *—v.i.* use the sol-fa syllables in singing. *—v.t.* sing to the sol-fa scale. [< Italian *solfa* < *sol* + *fa*]

so lic it (sə lis′it), *v.t.* 1 ask earnestly; try to get: *The tailor sent around cards soliciting trade.* See **ask** for synonym study. 2 influence to do wrong; tempt; entice: *To solicit a judge means to offer him bribes.* *—v.i.* 1 make appeals or requests: *solicit for contributions to the Red Cross.* 2 accost a person with immoral offers. [< Latin *sollicitare* disturb < *sollicitus.* See SOLICITOUS.]

so lic i ta tion (sə lis′ə tā′shən), *n.* 1 a soliciting; earnest request; entreaty. 2 an urging to do wrong; temptation; enticement.

so lic i tor (sə lis′ə tər), *n.* 1 person who entreats or requests. 2 person who seeks trade or business: *a magazine solicitor.* 3 lawyer in Britain who can advise clients and prepare cases, but can plead only in a lower court. 4 lawyer for a town, city, state, etc.

solicitor general, *pl.* **solicitors general.** 1 a law officer who assists the attorney general and ranks next below him in the Department of Justice. 2 the chief law officer in a state having no attorney general.

so lic i tous (sə lis′ə təs), *adj.* 1 showing care or concern; anxious; concerned: *Parents are solicitous for their children's progress in school.* 2 desirous; eager: *solicitous to please.* [< Latin *sollicitus* < *sollus* all + *ciere* arouse] **—so lic′i tous ly,** *adv.* **—so lic′i tous ness,** *n.*

so lic i tude (sə lis′ə tüd, sə lis′ə tyüd), *n.* anxious care; anxiety; concern. See **care** for synonym study.

sol id (sol′id), *adj.* 1 not a liquid or a gas: *Water becomes solid when it freezes.* 2 not hollow: *A bar of iron is solid; a pipe is hollow.* 3 strongly put together; hard; firm: *solid ground.* See **firm**[1] for synonym study. 4 alike throughout: *solid gold, a dress of solid blue.* 5 firmly united: *The country was solid for peace.* 6 serious; not superficial or trifling: *Chemistry and physics are solid subjects.* 7 genuine; real: *solid comfort.* 8 that can be depended on: *a solid citizen.* 9 having or based on good judgment; sound; sensible; intelligent: *a solid book by a solid thinker.* 10 financially sound or strong: *a solid business.* 11 whole; entire: *I waited three solid hours.* 12 undivided; continuous: *a solid row of houses.* 13 having length, breadth, and thickness. A sphere is a solid figure. 14 written without a hyphen or space: *a solid compound. "Earthworm" is a solid word.* 15 (in printing) having the lines of type not separated by leads; having few open spaces. *—n.* 1 substance that is not a liquid or a gas. Iron, wood, and ice are solids. 2 a body that has length, breadth, and thickness. A cube is a solid.
[< Latin *solidus*] **—sol′id ly,** *adv.* **—sol′id ness,** *n.*

sol i dar i ty (sol′ə dar′ə tē), *n., pl.* **-ties.** unity or fellowship arising from common responsibilities and interests.

solid fuel, a rocket fuel in the form of a powder or fine grains, often mixed with an adhesive.

solid geometry, branch of mathematics that deals with objects having the three dimensions of length, breadth, and thickness.

so lid i fy (sə lid′ə fī), *v.t., v.i.,* **-fied, -fy ing.** 1 make or become solid; harden: *Extreme cold will solidify water. Jelly solidifies as it gets cold.* 2 make or become firmly united. **—so lid′i fi ca′tion,** *n.*

so lid i ty (sə lid′ə tē), *n., pl.* **-ties.** a being solid; firmness or hardness; substantial quality: *the solidity of marble or steel, the solidity of Washington's character.*

solid propellant, solid fuel.

sol id-state (sol′id stāt′), *adj.* 1 of or having to do with solid-state physics. 2 (of an electronic device) made with transistors, printed circuits, etc.

solid-state physics, branch of physics that deals with the physical properties of solid materials, such as mechanical strength, the movement of electrons, the nature of crystals, etc. Research in solid-state physics has produced the transistor and other semiconductor devices.

sol i dus (sol′ə dəs), *n., pl.* **-di** (-dī). 1 a Roman gold coin introduced by Constantine I, later called a bezant. 2 a sloping line (/) used to separate shillings from pence (as 2/6 for 2 shillings, 6 pence), and generally as a dividing line, as in dates, fractions, etc. [< Latin, short for *solidus (nummus)* solid (coin)]

so lil o quize (sə lil′ə kwīz), *v.i.,* **-quized, -quiz ing.** 1 talk to oneself. 2 speak a soliloquy. **—so lil′o quiz′er,** *n.*

so lil o quy (sə lil′ə kwē), *n., pl.* **-quies.** 1 a talking to oneself. 2 speech made by an actor to himself when alone on the stage. It reveals his thoughts and feelings to the audience, but not to the other characters in the play. [< Late Latin *soliloquium* < Latin *solus* alone + *loqui* speak]

sol i taire (sol′ə ter, sol′ə tar), *n.* 1 card game played by one person. 2 diamond or other gem set by itself. [< French < Latin *solitarius.* Doublet of SOLITARY.]

sol i tar y (sol′ə ter′ē), *adj., n., pl.* **-tar ies.** *—adj.* 1 alone or single; only: *A solitary rider was seen in the distance.* 2 without companions; away from people; lonely: *lead a solitary life. The house is in a solitary spot miles from a town.* 3 (in zoology) living alone, rather than in colonies: *a solitary bee.* 4 (in botany) growing separately; not forming clusters. *—n.* person living alone, away from people. [< Latin *solitarius,* ultimately < *solus* alone. Doublet of SOLITAIRE.] **—sol′i tar′i ly,** *adv.* **—sol′i tar′i ness,** *n.*

sol i tude (sol′ə tüd, sol′ə tyüd), *n.* 1 a being alone: *I like company and hate solitude.* 2 a lonely place. 3 loneliness.

sol mi za tion (sol′mə zā′shən), *n.* sol-fa. [< French *solmisation,* ultimately < *sol* + *mi*]

so lo (sō′lō), *n., pl.* **-los** or **-li** (-lē), *adj., v., adv.* *—n.* 1 piece of music for one voice or instrument. 2 anything done without a partner, companion, instructor, etc. *—adj.* 1 arranged for and performed by one voice or instrument: *a solo part.* 2 playing the solo part: *a solo violin.* 3 without a partner, companion, instructor, etc.; alone: *a solo flight, a solo dance.* *—v.i.* 1 make a solo flight in an airplane. 2 sing or play a solo. *—adv.* by oneself; alone: *She flew solo for the first time yesterday.* [< Italian, alone < Latin *solus*]

so lo ist (sō′lō ist), *n.* person who performs a solo or solos.

Sol o mon (sol′ə mən), *n.* 1 king of Israel who lived in the 900's B.C. Solomon was a son of David and was famous for his wisdom and for the great temple which he had built in Jerusalem. 2 man of great wisdom. [< Latin < Greek < Hebrew *Sh'lōmōh*]

Solomon Islands, group of islands in the S Pacific, northeast of Australia. Some are governed by Australia and some by Great Britain. 231,000 pop.; 16,000 sq. mi. See **Australasia** for map.

Solomon's seal

Solomon's seal, a star-shaped figure formed of two equilateral triangles interlaced.

Sol o mon's-seal (sol′ə mənz sēl′), *n.* any of a genus of perennial herbs of the lily family, with small, greenish flowers hanging from the bases of the leaves and a rootstock with scars resembling Solomon's seals.

So lon (sō′lən, sō′lon), *n.* 1 638?-558? B.C., wise Athenian lawgiver. 2 a wise man; sage. 3 INFORMAL. member of a legislature.

so long, INFORMAL. good-by; farewell.

sol stice (sol′stis), *n.* 1 either of the two times in the year when the sun is at its greatest distance from the celestial equator. In the Northern Hemisphere, June 21 or 22, the **summer solstice,** is the longest day of the year and December 21 or 22, the **winter solstice,** is the shortest. 2 either of the two points reached by the sun at these times. [< Old French < Latin *solstitium* < *sol* sun + *sistere* stand still]

sol sti tial (sol stish′əl), *adj.* of or having to do with a solstice.

sol u bil i ty (sol′yə bil′ə tē), *n., pl.* **-ties.** 1 quality that substances have of dissolving or being dissolved easily: *the solubility of sugar in water.* 2 quality that problems, questions, etc., have of being solved or explained.

sol u ble (sol′yə bəl), *adj.* 1 that can be dissolved or made into liquid: *Salt is soluble in water.* 2 that can be solved: *This problem is hard but soluble.* [< Latin *solubilis* < *solvere* dissolve] **—sol′u ble ness,** *n.* **—sol′u bly,** *adv.*

sol ute (sol′yüt, sō′lüt), *n.* solid, gas, or liquid dissolved in a liquid to make a solution: *Salt is a solute in sea water.* [< Latin *solutum* dissolved]

so lu tion (sə lü′shən), *n.* 1 the solving of a problem: *That problem was hard; its solution required many hours.* 2 explanation or answer: *The police are seeking a solution of the crime.* 3 process of dissolving; the uniform mixing of a solid, liquid, or gas with another solid, liquid, or gas. 4 the homogeneous mixture formed by dissolving. 5 condition of being dissolved: *Sugar and salt can be held in solution in water.* 6 a separating into parts. 7 (in mathematics) any number which makes an open sentence a true statement. EXAMPLE: The number 4 is a solution of $3y + 2 = 14$ because $3 \times 4 + 2 = 14$. [< Latin *solutionem* a loosing < *solvere* loosen]

solution set, (in mathematics) the set which contains all the solutions of an open sentence.

solv a bil i ty (sol′və bil′ə tē), *n., pl.* **-ties.** quality or condition of being solvable.

solv a ble (sol′və bəl), *adj.* 1 capable of being solved. 2 capable of being dissolved.

solve (solv), *v.t.,* **solved, solv ing.** find the answer to; clear up; explain: *The detective solved the mystery. She solved the puzzle.* [< Latin *solvere* loosen] **—solv′er,** *n.*

sol ven cy (sol′vən sē), *n., pl.* **-cies.** ability to pay all one owes.

sol vent (sol′vənt), *adj.* 1 able to pay all that one owes: *A bankrupt firm is not solvent.* 2 able to dissolve: *Gasoline is a solvent liquid that removes grease spots.* *—n.* 1 substance, usually a liquid, that can dissolve other substances. 2 thing that solves, explains, or settles. [< Latin *solventem* loosening, paying]

Sol y man (sol′ē mən), *n.* Suleiman.

Sol zhe ni tsyn (sōl′zhə nē′tsən), *n.* **Alexander,** born 1918, Russian novelist.

so ma (sō′mə), *n., pl.* **so ma ta** (sō′mə tə). all the tissues and organs of an animal or plant except the germ cells. [< Greek *sōma* body]

So ma li (sə mä′lē), *n., pl.* **-li** or **-lis.** 1 member of a people living in eastern Africa of Negro, Arab, and other descent. 2 their Cushitic language.

So ma lia (sə mä′lyə), *n.* country in E Africa. 2,790,000 pop.; 246,000 sq. mi. *Capital:* Mogadiscio.

so mat ic (sō mat′ik), *adj.* 1 of or having to do with the body. 2 having to do with the cavity of the body, or its walls. 3 having to do with the soma. [< Greek *sōmatikos* < *sōma* body]

somatic cell, any cell of an animal or plant, except a germ cell.

so ma to plasm (sō′mə tə plaz′əm), *n.* the protoplasm of the somatic cells.

som ber or **som bre** (som′bər), *adj.* 1 having deep shadows; dark; gloomy: *A cloudy winter day is somber.* 2 melancholy; dismal: *His losses made him very somber.* [< French *sombre*] **—som′ber ly, som′bre ly,** *adv.* **—som′ber ness, som′bre ness,** *n.*

sombrero

som brer o (som brer′ō), *n., pl.* **-brer os.** a broad-brimmed hat worn especially in the southwestern United States, Mexico, etc. [< Spanish]

some (sum; *unstressed* səm), *adj.* 1 certain or particular, but not known or named: *Some people sleep more than others.* 2 a number of: *She left the city some years ago.* 3 a quantity of: *drink some milk.* 4 a; any: *Ask some salesclerk to wait on us.* 5 about: *a place some seventy miles distant.* 6 INFORMAL. uncommonly big, bad, etc.; remarkable: *That was some storm!* *—pron.* 1 certain unnamed persons or things: *Some think so.* 2 a certain number or quantity: *I ate some and gave the rest away.* *—adv.* 1 INFORMAL. to some degree or extent; somewhat: *He is some better today.* 2 INFORMAL. to a great degree or extent: *That's going some!* [Old English *sum*]

-some[1], *suffix forming adjectives.* 1 tending to ____: *Meddlesome = tending to meddle.* 2 causing ____: *Troublesome = causing trouble.* 3 ____ to a considerable degree: *Lonesome = lone to a considerable degree.* [Middle English < Old English *-sum*]

-some[2], *suffix added to numbers.* group of ____: *Twosome = group of two.* [Old English *sum* some]

-some[3], *combining form.* ____ body: *Chromosome = color body. Ribosome = ribose body.* [< Greek *sōma*]

some body (sum′bod′ē, sum′bə dē), *pron., n., pl.* **-bod ies.** *—pron.* person not known or named; some person; someone: *Somebody has taken my pen.* *—n.* person of importance: *She acts as if she were somebody since she won the prize.*

some day (sum′dā), *adv.* at some future time.

some how (sum′hou), *adv.* in a way not known or not stated; in one way or another: *I'll finish this work somehow.*

some one (sum′wun, sum′wən), *pron.* some person; somebody: *Someone is at the door.*

some place (sum′plās), *adv.* in or to some place; somewhere.

som er sault (sum′ər sôlt), *n.* a roll or jump, turning the heels over the head. *—v.i.* roll or jump, turning the heels over the head. Also, **summersault.** [< Middle French *sombresault,* ultimately < Latin *supra* over + *saltus* jump]

som er set (sum′ər set), *n., v.i.,* somersault.

Som er set (sum′ər set), *n.* county in SW England.
Som er set shire (sum′ər set shər, sum′ər-set shir), *n.* Somerset.
Som er ville (sum′ər vil), *n.* city in E Massachusetts, near Boston. 89,000.
some thing (sum′thing), *n.* 1 some thing; a particular thing not named or known: *have something on one's mind.* 2 a certain amount or quantity; a part; a little: *Something yet of doubt remains.* 3 thing or person of some value or importance: *He thinks he's something.* 4 thing or person that is to a certain extent an example of what is named: *Albert Einstein was something of a violinist.* *—adv.* somewhat; to some extent or degree: *He is something like his father.*
some time (sum′tīm), *adv.* 1 at one time or another: *Come to see me sometime.* 2 at an indefinite point of time: *It happened sometime last March.* *—adj.* former: *a sometime pupil of the school.*
some times (sum′tīmz), *adv.* now and then; at times: *She comes to visit sometimes.*
some way (sum′wā), *adv.* in some way.
some what (sum′hwot), *adv.* to some extent or degree; slightly: *somewhat round.* *—n.* some part; some amount: *somewhat of a musician.*
some where (sum′hwer, sum′hwar), *adv.* 1 in or to some place; in or to one place or another: *They live somewhere in the neighborhood.* 2 at some time: *It happened somewhere in the last century.* 3 approximately: *The total she owed was somewhere around forty dollars.* *—n.* some place.
so mite (sō′mīt), *n.* metamere.
som me lier (sô mə lyā′), *n.* FRENCH. a wine steward in a restaurant.
Somme River (sôm), river in N France. 140 mi.
som nam bu lism (som nam′byə liz′əm), *n.* sleepwalking. [< Latin *somnus* sleep + *ambulare* to walk]
som nam bu list (som nam′byə list), *n.* sleepwalker.
som nam bu lis tic (som nam′byə lis′tik), *adj.* having to do with sleepwalking or sleepwalkers.
som nif er ous (som nif′ər əs), *adj.* 1 causing sleep. 2 sleepy. [< Latin *somnifer* < *somnus* sleep + *ferre* bring] **—som nif′er ous ly,** *adv.*
som no lence (som′nə ləns), *n.* sleepiness; drowsiness.
som no lent (som′nə lənt), *adj.* 1 sleepy; drowsy. 2 tending to produce sleep. [< Latin *somnolentus* < *somnus* sleep] **—som′no lent ly,** *adv.*
son (sun), *n.* 1 a male child or person in relation to his parents or parent. 2 a male descendant. 3 son-in-law. 4 boy or man attached to a country, cause, etc., as a child is to its parents: *sons of America, sons of liberty.* 5 anything thought of as a son in relation to its origin. **6 the Son,** Jesus Christ. [Old English *sunu*] **—son′less,** *adj.*
so nance (sō′nəns), *n.* sonant quality or condition.
so nant (sō′nənt), *adj.* 1 of sound; having sound; sounding. 2 pronounced with the vocal cords vibrating; voiced. *—n.* sound pronounced with the vocal cords vibrating; voiced sound. *Z* and *v* are sonants; *s* and *f* are not. [< Latin *sonantem* < *sonus* sound]
so nar (sō′när), *n.* device for detecting and locating objects under water by the reflection of sound waves. [< *so(und) na(vigation) r(anging)*]
so na ta (sə nä′tə), *n.* piece of music, for one or two instruments, having three or four movements in contrasted rhythms but related keys. [< Italian, literally, sounded < Latin *sonare* to sound]
son a ti na (son′ə tē′nə), *n.* a short or simplified sonata. [< Italian, diminutive of *sonata* sonata]
song (sông, song), *n.* 1 something to sing; a short poem set to music. 2 poetry, especially poetry that has a musical sound. 3 piece of music for, or as if for, a poem that is to be sung. 4 act or practice of singing: *The canary burst into song.* 5 any sound like singing: *the cricket's song, the song of the teakettle, the song of the brook.* **6 for a song,** very cheap. **7 song and dance,** INFORMAL. explanation or account, often intended to impress or deceive. [Old English *sang*]
song bird (sông′bėrd′, song′bėrd′), *n.* bird that sings.
song fest (sông′fest, song′fest), *n.* U.S. an informal gathering or concert at which folk songs, popular songs, etc., are sung.
song ful (sông′fəl, song′fəl), *adj.* full of song; musical; melodious. **—song′ful ly,** *adv.* **—song′ful ness,** *n.*
song less (sông′lis, song′lis), *adj.* not able to sing.
Song of Solomon, The. book of the Old Testament; Canticles.
Song of Songs, Song of Solomon.
song sparrow, a small North American songbird with black, brown, and white feathers.
song ster (sông′stər, song′stər), *n.* 1 singer. 2 writer of songs or poems. 3 songbird. [Old English *sangestre*]
song stress (sông′stris, song′stris), *n.* 1 a woman singer. 2 a woman writer of songs or poems. 3 a female songbird.
song thrush, 1 wood thrush. 2 a common European songbird with a yellowish-brown back, spotted breast, and white belly; mavis.
song writ er (sông′rī′tər, song′rī′tər), *n.* composer of popular songs or tunes.
son ic (son′ik), *adj.* 1 of, having to do with, or using sound waves. 2 having to do with the rate at which sound travels in air (1087 feet per second at sea level). [< Latin *sonus* sound] **—son′i cal ly,** *adv.*
sonic barrier, a sudden increase in air resistance met by an aircraft or projectile as it nears the speed of sound; sound barrier.
sonic boom, a loud noise caused by shock waves which are produced by an aircraft or projectile crossing through the sonic barrier.
sonic depth finder, device for determining depth of water by sending sound waves through the water and timing their return from the bottom.
son-in-law (sun′in lô′), *n., pl.* **sons-in-law.** husband of one's daughter.
son net (son′it), *n.* poem having 14 lines, usually in iambic pentameter, and a certain arrangement of rhymes. Elizabethan and Italian sonnets differ in the arrangement of the rhymes. [< Italian *sonetto* < Provençal *sonet,* diminutive of *son* sound < Latin *sonus*]
son net eer (son′ə tir′), *n.* 1 writer of sonnets. 2 an inferior poet. *—v.i.* write sonnets.
son ny (sun′ē), *n., pl.* **-nies.** little son (used as a pet name, or as a way of speaking to a little boy).
so nom e ter (sō nom′ə tər), *n.* instrument used in measuring the pitch of musical tones or for experimenting with vibrating strings.

hat, āge, fär; let, ēqual, tėrm;
it, īce; hot, ōpen, ôrder;
oil, out; cup, put, rüle;
ch, child; ng, long; sh, she;
th, thin; ᴛʜ, then; zh, measure;

ə represents *a* in about, *e* in taken, *i* in pencil, *o* in lemon, *u* in circus.

< = from, derived from, taken from.

So no ra (sə nôr′ə, sə nōr′ə), *n.* state in NW Mexico.
so no ri ty (sə nôr′ə tē, sə nor′ə tē), *n., pl.* **-ties.** sonorous quality or condition.
so no rous (sə nôr′əs, sə nōr′əs), *adj.* 1 giving out or having a deep, loud sound. 2 full and rich in sound. 3 having an impressive sound; high-sounding: *sonorous phrases.* [< Latin *sonorus* < *sonare* to sound < *sonus* sound] **—so no′rous ly,** *adv.*
son ship (sun′ship), *n.* condition of being a son.
Soo chow (sü′chou′), *n.* former name of **Wuhsien.**
Soo Locks or **Soo Canals** (sü), two parallel canals on St. Marys River, between lakes Superior and Huron. 1.6 mi. long.
soon (sün), *adv.* 1 in a short time; before long: *I will see you again soon.* 2 before the usual or expected time; early: *Why have you come so soon?* 3 promptly; quickly: *As soon as I hear, I will let you know.* 4 readily; willingly: *He would as soon die as yield to such an enemy.* **5 had sooner** or **would sooner,** would more readily; prefer to. [Old English *sōna* at once, quickly]
soot (sůt, süt), *n.* a black substance in the smoke from burning coal, wood, oil, etc. Soot, caused chiefly by incomplete burning, makes smoke dark and collects on the inside of chimneys. [Old English *sōt*] **—soot′less,** *adj.*
sooth (süth), ARCHAIC. *—n.* truth. *—adj.* true. [Old English *sōth*]
soothe (süᴛʜ), *v.,* **soothed, sooth ing.** *—v.t.* 1 quiet; calm; comfort: *The mother soothed the crying child.* 2 make less painful; relieve; ease: *Heat soothes some aches; cold soothes others.* *—v.i.* have or exercise a soothing influence. [Old English *sōthian*] **—sooth′er,** *n.*
sooth ing (sü′ᴛʜing), *adj.* that soothes: *soothing words.* **—sooth′ing ly,** *adv.*
sooth ly (süth′lē), *adv.* ARCHAIC. truly; in truth.
sooth say er (süth′sā′ər), *n.* person who claims to foretell the future.
sooth say ing (süth′sā′ing), *n.* 1 the foretelling of future events. 2 prediction or prophecy.
soot y (sůt′ē, sü′tē), *adj.,* **soot i er, soot i est.** 1 covered or blackened with soot: *a sooty chimney.* 2 dark-brown or black; dark-colored. **—soot′i ly,** *adv.* **—soot′i ness,** *n.*
sop (sop), *n., v.,* **sopped, sop ping.** *—n.* 1 piece of food dipped or soaked in milk, broth, etc. 2 something given to soothe or quiet; bribe. *—v.t.* 1 dip or soak: *sop bread in milk.* 2 take up (water, etc.); wipe; mop: *Please sop up that water with a cloth.* 3 soak thoroughly; drench. *—v.i.* 1 be drenched. 2 soak in or through. [Old English *sopp*]
sop., soprano.
soph ism (sof′iz′əm), *n.* a clever but mis-

leading argument; argument based on false or unsound reasoning. [< Greek *sophisma,* ultimately < *sophos* clever]

soph ist (sof′ist), *n.* 1 a clever but misleading reasoner. 2 Often, **Sophist,** one of a class of teachers of rhetoric, philosophy, ethics, etc., in ancient Greece.

so phis tic (sə fis′tik), *adj.* sophistical.

so phis ti cal (sə fis′tə kəl), *adj.* 1 clever but misleading; based on false or unsound reasoning. 2 using clever but misleading arguments; reasoning falsely or unsoundly. **—so phis′ti cal ly,** *adv.*

so phis ti cate (*v.* sə fis′tə kāt; *n.* sə fis′tə-kāt, sə fis′tə kit), *v.,* **-cat ed, -cat ing,** *n.* —*v.t.* 1 make experienced in worldly ways; cause to lose one's natural simplicity and frankness; make artificial. 2 mislead. 3 involve in sophistry. —*v.i.* use sophistry; quibble. —*n.* a sophisticated person.

so phis ti cat ed (sə fis′tə kā′tid), *adj.* 1 experienced in worldly ways; lacking in natural simplicity or frankness. 2 appealing to the tastes of sophisticated people: *sophisticated humor.* 3 misleading. 4 very complex and advanced in design: *a sophisticated missile.*

so phis ti ca tion (sə fis′tə kā′shən), *n.* 1 a lessening or loss of naturalness, simplicity, or frankness; worldly experience or ideas; artificial ways. 2 sophistry.

soph ist ry (sof′ə strē), *n., pl.* **-ries.** 1 unsound reasoning. 2 a clever but misleading argument. 3 art, practice, or learning of the ancient Greek sophists, especially of their type of argument.

Soph o cles (sof′ə klēz′), *n.* 495?-406? B.C., Greek tragic poet and dramatist.

soph o more (sof′ə môr, sof′ə mōr), *n.* student in the second year of high school or college. [earlier *sophomer,* originally, taking part in dialectic exercises < *sophom,* variant of *sophism*]

soph o mor ic (sof′ə môr′ik, sof′ə mor′ik), *adj.* 1 of, having to do with, or like a sophomore or sophomores. 2 conceited and pretentious, but crude and ignorant.

so po rif er ous (sō′pə rif′ər əs, sop′ə rif′-ər əs), *adj.* bringing sleep; causing sleep.

so po rif ic (sō′pə rif′ik, sop′ə rif′ik), *adj.* 1 causing or tending to cause sleep: *a soporific sermon.* 2 sleepy; drowsy. —*n.* drug that causes sleep. [< Latin *sopor* deep sleep + *facere* to make]

sop ping (sop′ing), *adj.* 1 soaked; drenched. 2 **sopping wet,** soaked; drenched.

sop py (sop′ē), *adj.,* **-pi er, -pi est.** soaked; very wet: *soppy ground.*

so pran o (sə pran′ō, sə prä′nō), *n., pl.* **-pran os,** *adj.* —*n.* 1 the highest voice in women and boys. 2 singer with such a voice. 3 part in music for such a voice or for an instrument of similar range. 4 instrument playing such a part. —*adj.* of or for a soprano. [< Italian < *sopra* above < Latin *supra*]

So ra ta (sô rä′tə), *n.* **Mount,** Illampu.

sorb (sôrb), *v.t.* absorb or adsorb.

Sor bonne (sôr bon′), *n.* seat of the faculties of letters and science of the University of Paris.

sor cer er (sôr′sər ər), *n.* person who practices sorcery; wizard; magician.

sor cer ess (sôr′sər is), *n.* woman who practices sorcery; witch.

sor cer ous (sôr′sər əs), *adj.* using, involving, or resembling sorcery: *sorcerous spells.* **—sor′cer ous ly,** *adv.*

sor cer y (sôr′sər ē), *n., pl.* **-cer ies.** magic performed with the supposed aid of evil spirits; witchcraft. [< Old French *sorcerie,* ultimately < Latin *sors* chance, lot]

sor did (sôr′did), *adj.* 1 dirty; filthy: *live in a sordid hut.* 2 caring too much for money; meanly selfish; greedy. 3 mean; low; base; contemptible. 4 of a dull or dirty color. [< Latin *sordidus* dirty < *sordere* be dirty < *sordes* dirt] **—sor′did ly,** *adv.* **—sor′did ness,** *n.*

sore (sôr, sōr), *adj.,* **sor er, sor est,** *n., adv.* —*adj.* 1 causing sharp or continuous pain; aching; tender; smarting: *a sore finger.* 2 sad; distressed: *The suffering of the poor makes her heart sore.* 3 INFORMAL. offended; angered: *He is sore at missing the game.* 4 causing misery, anger, or offense; vexing: *Their defeat is a sore subject with the team.* 5 severe; distressing: *Your going away is a sore grief to us.* —*n.* 1 a painful place on the body where the skin or flesh is infected, broken, or bruised. 2 cause of pain, sorrow, sadness, anger, offense, etc. —*adv.* ARCHAIC. in a sore manner. [Old English *sār*] **—sore′ly,** *adv.* **—sore′ness,** *n.*

sore head (sôr′hed′, sōr′hed′), INFORMAL. —*n.* person who is easily angered or offended. —*adj.* soreheaded.

sore head ed (sôr′hed′id, sōr′hed′id), *adj.* INFORMAL. feeling angered or offended.

sor ghum (sôr′gəm), *n.* 1 any of a genus of tall, tropical cereal grasses which resemble corn. One variety has a sweet juice used for making molasses or syrup, others provide food for livestock either by their grain or as hay, and still others furnish material for brushes or brooms. 2 molasses or syrup made from a sweet sorghum plant. [< New Latin < Italian *sorgo* < Latin *syricum* Syrian]

so ro ri ty (sə rôr′ə tē, sə ror′ə tē), *n., pl.* **-ties.** 1 a sisterhood. 2 club or society of women or girls, especially at a college. [< Latin *soror* sister]

sorp tion (sôrp′shən), *n.* absorption or adsorption.

sor rel[1] (sôr′əl, sor′əl), *adj.* reddish-brown. —*n.* 1 a reddish brown. 2 horse having this color. [< Old French *sorel* < *sor* yellowish-brown]

sor rel[2] (sôr′əl, sor′əl), *n.* 1 dock[4]. 2 wood sorrel. [< Old French *surele* < *sur* sour; of Germanic origin]

sor row (sor′ō, sôr′ō), *n.* 1 grief, sadness, or regret. See synonym study below. 2 cause of grief, sadness, or regret; suffering; misfortune: *Her sorrows have aged her.* —*v.i.* feel or show grief, sadness, or regret; be sad; feel sorry; grieve: *She sorrowed over the lost kitten.* [Old English *sorg*] **—sor′row er,** *n.* **—sor′row less,** *adj.*

Syn. *n.* 1 **Sorrow, grief, distress** mean sadness or mental suffering caused by loss or trouble. **Sorrow** suggests deep and usually prolonged sadness or anguish: *Not knowing what had happened to her son brought great sorrow to the woman.* **Grief** suggests acute but usually not prolonged sorrow: *Her grief when he died was almost unbearable.* **Distress** suggests the strain or pressure of pain (physical or mental), grief, fear, anxiety, etc.: *War causes widespread distress.*

sor row ful (sor′ə fəl, sôr′ə fəl), *adj.* 1 full of sorrow; feeling sorrow; sad. 2 showing sorrow. 3 causing sorrow. **—sor′row ful ly,** *adv.* **—sor′row ful ness,** *n.*

sor ry (sor′ē, sôr′ē), *adj.,* **-ri er, -ri est.** 1 feeling pity, regret, sympathy, etc.; sad: *I am sorry that you are sick. We're sorry we can't come to the party.* 2 wretched; poor; pitiful: *The blind beggar in his ragged clothes was a sorry sight.* 3 worthless: *a sorry excuse.* [Old English *sārig* < *sār* sore] **—sor′ri ly,** *adv.* **—sor′ri ness,** *n.*

sort (sôrt), *n.* 1 group of things having common or similar characteristics; kind or class; type: *This sort of fish is abundant along our coast.* See **kind**[2] for synonym study. 2 a certain class, order, or rank of people: *the better sort.* 3 person or thing of a certain kind or quality: *He is a good sort, generous and kind.* 4 character; quality; nature: *materials of an inferior sort.* 5 manner; fashion; way. 6 Usually, **sorts,** *pl.* letter or piece in a font of type. **7 of sorts, a** of one kind or another. **b** of a poor or mediocre quality. **8 out of sorts,** slightly ill, cross, or uncomfortable. **9 sort of,** INFORMAL. somewhat; rather: *sort of foolish.* —*v.t.* 1 arrange by kinds or classes; arrange in order: *sort mail.* 2 separate from others: *Sort out the best apples for eating and cook the rest.* —*v.i.* ARCHAIC. agree; accord. [< Old French *sorte* < Latin *sortem* condition, lot] **—sort′a ble,** *adj.* **—sort′er,** *n.* ➤ See **kind**[2] for usage note.

sor tie (sôr′tē), *n.* 1 a sudden attack by troops from a defensive position; sally. 2 a single round trip of an aircraft against the enemy; combat mission. [< French < *sortir* go out]

so rus (sôr′əs, sōr′əs), *n., pl.* **so ri** (sôr′ī, sōr′ī). any of the dotlike clusters of spore cases on the underside of the frond of a fern. [< New Latin < Greek *sōros* heap]

S O S (es′ō′es′), 1 signal of distress consisting of the letters *s o s* of the international Morse code (...---...), used in wireless telegraphy by ships, aircraft, etc. 2 INFORMAL. any urgent call for help.

so-so (sō′sō′), *adj.* neither very good nor very bad; fairly good; mediocre. —*adv.* in a passable or indifferent manner; tolerably.

sos te nu to (sos′tə nü′tō), *adj., adv.* in music: 1 sustained. 2 prolonged. [< Italian]

sot (sot), *n.* person who commonly or habitually drinks too much alcoholic liquor; confirmed drunkard. [Old English, a fool]

sot tish (sot′ish), *adj.* 1 drunken. 2 like a sot. **—sot′tish ly,** *adv.* **—sot′tish ness,** *n.*

sot to vo ce (sot′ō vō′chē), 1 in a low tone. 2 aside; privately. [< Italian, literally, below (normal) voice]

sou (sü), *n.* 1 a former French coin, worth 5 centimes or $^1/_{20}$ of a franc. 2 anything of little value. [< French, ultimately < Latin *solidus* solidus (Roman coin)]

sou brette (sü bret′), *n.* 1 a coquettish, pert, and lively young woman character in a play or opera. 2 actress or singer taking such a part. [< French]

sou bri quet (sü′brə kā), *n.* sobriquet.

Sou dan (sü dan′), *n.* Sudan.

souf flé (sü flā′, sü′flā), *n.* a frothy baked dish, usually made light by folding in beaten egg whites and cooking very quickly: *cheese soufflé.* —*adj.* made very light in texture, especially by being puffed up in cooking: *potatoes soufflé.* [< French < *souffler* puff up]

souf fléed (sü flād′, sü′flād), *adj.* soufflé.

sough (suf, sou), *v.i.* make a rustling or murmuring sound. —*n.* a rustling or murmuring sound. [Old English *swōgan*]

sought (sôt), *v.* pt. and pp. of **seek.**

soul (sōl), *n.* 1 the spiritual part of a person

as distinct from the physical, and regarded as the source of thought, feeling, and action. Many persons believe that the soul is immortal and separated from the body at death. 2 energy or power of mind or feelings; spirit: *She puts her whole soul into her work.* 3 cause of inspiration and energy: *Florence Nightingale was the soul of the movement to reform nursing.* 4 the essential part: *Brevity is the soul of wit.* 5 a distinctive emotional or spiritual quality associated with black American culture, especially as expressed through music. 6 INFORMAL. soul music. 7 person; individual: *Don't tell a soul.* 8 embodiment of some quality: *He is the soul of honor.* 9 spirit of a dead person. [Old English *sāwol*]

soul food, food popular among American blacks, such as chitterlings, corn bread, fried catfish, etc.

soul ful (sōl′fəl), *adj.* 1 full of feeling; deeply emotional: *soulful music.* 2 expressing or suggesting deep feeling. **—soul′ful ly,** *adv.* **—soul′ful ness,** *n.*

soul less (sōl′lis), *adj.* 1 having no soul. 2 without spirit or noble feelings. 3 dull; insipid. **—soul′less ly,** *adv.*

soul music, class of music, played or sung especially by black Americans, that is based on elements of jazz, blues, and gospel songs.

soul-search ing (sōl′sėr′ching), *n.* a close examination of one's motives, beliefs, etc., especially at a critical time.

sound[1] (sound), *n.* 1 that which is or can be heard; sensation produced in the organs of hearing by vibrations transmitted by the air or some other medium. 2 energy in the form of mechanical vibrations causing this sensation. Sound travels through air in waves at a rate of about 1087 feet per second under normal conditions of pressure and temperature. 3 noise, note, tone, etc., whose quality indicates its source or nature: *the sound of music, the sound of fighting.* 4 the distance within which a noise can be heard; earshot. 5 one of the simple elements composing speech: *a vowel sound.* 6 the effect produced on the mind by what is heard: *a warning sound, a queer sound.* 7 mere noise, without meaning or importance. 8 **within sound,** near enough to hear.
—v.i. 1 make a sound or noise: *The alarm began to sound.* 2 be pronounced: *"Rough" and "ruff" sound alike.* 3 be heard, as a sound: *Her voice sounds shrill.* 4 be filled with sound; resound. 5 summon: *The trumpet sounds to battle.* 6 give an impression or idea; seem; appear: *That excuse sounds peculiar.* 7 **sound off,** INFORMAL. talk frankly or complain loudly. *—v.t.* 1 cause (an instrument, etc.) to make a sound: *sound a horn.* 2 order or direct by a sound: *sound a retreat.* 3 pronounce or express; utter distinctly: *sound each syllable.* 4 make known; announce; utter: *Everyone sounded his praises.* 5 test by noting sounds: *sound a person's lungs.*
[Middle English *soun* (the *d* is a later addition) < Old French *son* < Latin *sonus*]

sound[2] (sound), *adj.* 1 free from disease; healthy: *a sound body and mind.* 2 free from injury, decay, or defect: *a sound ship, sound fruit.* 3 financially strong; safe; secure: *a sound business firm.* 4 solid; massive: *sound foundation.* 5 reasonable; reliable: *sound advice.* 6 morally good; honest; upright. 7 free from error or logical defect: *a sound argument.* See **valid** for synonym study. 8 without any legal defects: *a sound title.* 9 having orthodox or conventional ideas: *a politically sound conservative.* 10 deep; heavy; profound: *a sound sleep.* 11 thorough; hearty: *a sound whipping.* *—adv.* deeply; thoroughly: *sleep long and sound.* [Old English *(ge)sund*] **—sound′ly,** *adv.* **—sound′ness,** *n.*

sound[3] (sound), *v.t.* 1 measure the depth of (water, etc.) by letting down a weight fastened to the end of a line; fathom. 2 examine or test (the bottom of the sea, etc.) by a line arranged to bring up a sample. 3 try to find out the views or feelings of; test; examine. *—v.i.* 1 use a sounding device to determine depth or nature of the bottom of the sea. 2 sink and reach bottom, as the weight on a line. 3 go deep under water; dive: *The whale sounded.* 4 make inquiry or investigation. [< Old French *sonder*]

sound[4] (sound), *n.* 1 a narrow channel or passage of water, larger than a strait, joining two larger bodies of water, or between an island and the mainland: *Long Island Sound.* 2 inlet or arm of the sea: *Puget Sound.* 3 air bladder of a fish. [partly Old English *sund* water, sea; partly < Scandinavian (Old Icelandic) *sund* strait]

sound barrier, sonic barrier.

sound board (sound′bôrd′, sound′bōrd′), *n.* 1 a thin, resonant piece of wood on a musical instrument, as in a violin or piano, to increase the fullness of its tone. 2 sounding board.

sound effects, sounds imitated by various devices or reproduced by recordings as part of the background of a play, motion picture, radio or television production, or the like.

sound er[1] (soun′dər), *n.* 1 person or thing that makes a sound or causes something to sound. 2 an electromagnetic receiving instrument that converts a telegraphic message into sound. [< *sound*[1]]

sound er[2] (soun′dər), *n.* person or thing that measures the depth of water. [< *sound*[3]]

sound ing[1] (soun′ding), *adj.* 1 that sounds. 2 resounding; resonant. 3 pompous; bombastic. [< *sound*[1]] **—sound′ing ly,** *adv.*

sound ing[2] (soun′ding), *n.* 1 act of measuring the depth of water with a sounding line. 2 depth of water found by this means. 3 **soundings,** *pl.* **a** depths of water found by a series of such measurements. **b** water not more than 600 feet deep, which can be measured by an ordinary sounding line. 4 investigation. 5 **take soundings,** try to find out quietly how matters stand. [< *sound*[3]]

sounding board, 1 structure used to direct sound toward an audience. 2 means of bringing opinions, etc., out into the open. 3 soundboard.

sounding line, line having a weight fastened to the end and marked in fathoms, used to measure the depth of water.

sounding rocket, rocket containing scientific instruments for investigating conditions in high altitudes.

sound less[1] (sound′lis), *adj.* without sound; making no sound; quiet or silent. [< *sound*[1]] **—sound′less ly,** *adv.*

sound less[2] (sound′lis), *adj.* so deep that the bottom cannot be reached with a sounding line; unfathomable. [< *sound*[3]]

sound proof (sound′prüf′), *adj.* that absorbs or deadens sound: *a soundproof ceiling.* *—v.t.* make soundproof.

sound track, a recording of the sounds of words, music, etc., made along one edge of a motion-picture film.

hat, āge, fär; let, ēqual, tėrm;
it, īce; hot, ōpen, ôrder;
oil, out; cup, pu̇t, rüle;
ch, child; ng, long; sh, she;
th, thin; ᴛʜ, then; zh, measure;

ə represents *a* in about, *e* in taken, *i* in pencil, *o* in lemon, *u* in circus.

< = from, derived from, taken from.

sound truck, truck with one or more loudspeakers, used in making public announcements.

soup (süp), *n.* 1 a liquid food made by boiling meat, vegetables, fish, etc. 2 INFORMAL. **a** a heavy, wet fog or cloud formation. **b in the soup,** in difficulty. *—v.t.* **soup up,** SLANG. **a** increase the horsepower of (an engine, automobile, etc.). **b** increase sharply the pace, impact, etc., of anything. [< French *soupe;* of Germanic origin]

soup çon or **soup con** (süp′sôn; *French* süp sôɴ′), *n.* a slight trace or flavor. [< French *soupçon,* ultimately < Latin *suspicionem.* See SUSPICION.]

soup kitchen, place that serves food free to poor or unemployed people or to victims of a disaster.

soup y (sü′pē), *adj.,* **soup i er, soup i est.** like soup in consistency or appearance.

sour (sour), *adj.* 1 having a tart or acid taste like vinegar and most unripe fruits. 2 acid as a result of fermentation: *sour milk.* 3 having a sour or rank smell: *sour breath.* 4 disagreeable, bad-tempered, or peevish: *a sour remark.* See synonym study below. 5 unusually acid: *sour soil.* 6 cold and wet; damp: *sour weather.* *—v.t., v.i.* 1 make or become sour; turn sour. 2 make or become peevish, bad-tempered, or disagreeable. *—n.* 1 something sour. 2 U.S. a sour alcoholic drink, such as whiskey and lemon juice. *—adv.* in a sour manner. [Old English *sūr*] **—sour′ly,** *adv.* **—sour′ness,** *n.*
Syn. *adj.* 4 **Sour, tart, acid** used figuratively to describe a person, his looks, disposition, words, manner of expression, etc., mean having a quality of harshness or sharpness. **Sour** suggests bad temper, surly rudeness, grouchiness, or sullenness: *a sour disposition.* **Tart** suggests sharp and stinging qualities: *Her tart answer showed her slight irritation.* **Acid** suggests biting, sarcastic, severely critical qualities: *I read an acid comment on the acting in our school play.*

source (sôrs, sōrs), *n.* 1 place from which anything comes or is obtained; origin. 2 person, book, statement, etc., that supplies information. 3 beginning of a brook or river; fountain; spring. [< Old French *sourse,* ultimately < Latin *surgere* to rise, surge]

sour dough (sour′dō′), *n.* INFORMAL. 1 prospector or pioneer in Alaska or northwestern Canada. 2 any old resident, experienced hand, etc. 3 Also, **sour dough.** fermented dough saved from one baking to start fermentation in the next. [from the prospectors' practice of saving a lump of sour dough from each baking]

sour grapes, thing that a person pretends to dislike because he cannot have it.

sour gum, 1 a large North American tree of the same family as the tupelo. 2 its light, strong wood.

Sou sa (sü′zə), *n.* **John Philip,** 1854-1932,

American conductor and composer of band music.

sous e (sous), *v.*, **soused, sous ing,** *n.* —*v.t., v.i.* 1 plunge into liquid; soak in a liquid. 2 soak in vinegar, brine, etc.; pickle. 3 SLANG. make or become drunk. —*n.* 1 a plunging into a liquid; drenching. 2 liquid used for pickling. 3 something soaked or kept in pickle, especially the head, ears, and feet of a pig. 4 SLANG. drunkard. [ultimately < Old French *sous* pickled pork; of Germanic origin]

south (south), *n.* 1 direction to the right as one faces the rising sun; direction just opposite north. 2 Also, **South.** the part of any country toward the south. 3 **the South,** the part of the United States lying south of Pennsylvania, the Ohio River, and Missouri, making up most of the states that formed the Confederate side in the Civil War. —*adj.* 1 toward the south; farther toward the south. 2 coming from the south. 3 in the south. 4 **South,** of or having to do with the southern part of a country, region, people, etc. —*adv.* 1 toward the south. 2 **south of,** further south than. [Old English *sūth*]

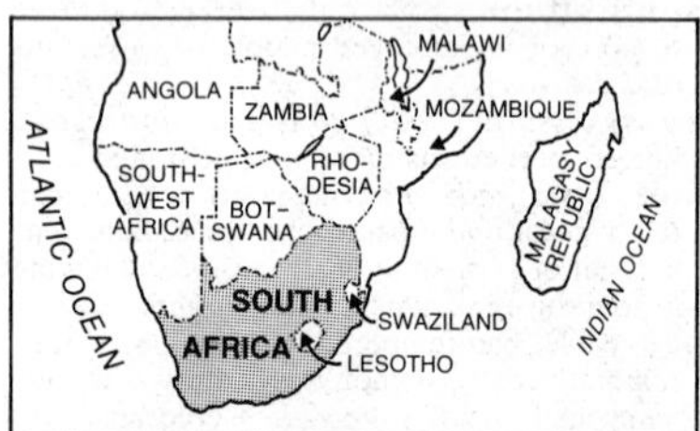

South Africa, Republic of, country in S Africa. 21,282,000 pop.; 472,400 sq. mi. *Capitals:* Pretoria and Cape Town. Former name, **Union of South Africa.** —**South African.**

South African Dutch, Afrikaans.

South America, continent in the Western Hemisphere southeast of North America. 188,485,000 pop.; 7,160,000 sq. mi. —**South American.**

South amp ton (sou thamp′tən, south-hamp′tən), *n.* seaport in S England. 210,000.

South Australia, state in S Australia. 1,165,000 pop.; 380,000 sq. mi. *Capital:* Adelaide.

South Bend, city in N Indiana. 126,000.

south bound (south′bound′), *adj.* going south; bound southward.

South Carolina, one of the southeastern states of the United States. 2,591,000 pop.; 31,100 sq. mi. *Capital:* Columbia. *Abbrev.:* S.C. —**South Carolinian.**

South China Sea, sea in the W Pacific bounded by E China, the Malay Peninsula, Borneo, and the Philippines, connected with the East China Sea by Formosa Strait. 895,000 sq. mi.

South Dakota, one of the midwestern states of the United States. 666,000 pop.; 77,000 sq. mi. *Capital:* Pierre. *Abbrev.:* S. Dak. —**South Dakotan.**

South down (south′doun′), *n.* any of an English breed of small, hornless sheep raised for mutton.

south east (south′ēst′), *adj.* 1 halfway between south and east. 2 from the southeast. 3 in the southeast. —*adv.* toward the southeast. —*n.* 1 a southeast direction. 2 place that is in the southeast part or direction. 3 **the Southeast,** the southeastern part of the United States.

Southeast Asia, region in Asia including Malaysia, the countries of Indochina, the islands of Indonesia, and sometimes, the Philippines.

south east er (south′ē′stər), *n.* wind or storm from the southeast.

south east er ly (south′ē′stər lē), *adj., adv.* 1 toward the southeast. 2 from the southeast.

south east ern (south′ē′stərn), *adj.* 1 toward the southeast. 2 from the southeast. 3 of or in the southeast. 4 of, having to do with, or in the Southeast.

South east ern er (south′ē′stər nər), *n.* native or inhabitant of the Southeast.

south east ward (south′ēst′wərd), *adv., adj.* toward the southeast. —*n.* southeast.

south east ward ly (south′ēst′wərd lē), *adj., adv.* 1 toward the southeast. 2 from the southeast.

south east wards (south′ēst′wərdz), *adv.* southeastward.

south er (sou′ᴛʜər), *n.* wind or storm from the south.

south er ly (sᴜᴛʜ′ər lē), *adj., adv.* 1 toward the south. 2 from the south.

south ern (sᴜᴛʜ′ərn), *adj.* 1 toward the south. 2 from the south. 3 of the south; in the south. 4 **Southern,** of or in the southern part of the United States.

Southern Alps, a mountain range in the central part of South Island, New Zealand. The highest peak, Aorangi or Mount Cook, is 12,349 ft.

Southern Cross, group of four bright stars in the form of a cross, visible in the Southern Hemisphere and often used in finding the direction south.

south ern er (sᴜᴛʜ′ər nər), *n.* 1 native or inhabitant of the south. 2 **Southerner,** native or inhabitant of the southern part of the United States.

Southern Hemisphere, the half of the earth that is south of the equator.

southern lights, aurora australis.

south ern ly (sᴜᴛʜ′ərn lē), *adj.* southerly.

south ern most (sᴜᴛʜ′ərn mōst), *adj.* farthest south.

Southern Rhodesia, former self-governing British colony in SE Africa, now called **Rhodesia.**

southwester (def. 2)

Southern Yemen, country in SW Arabia, consisting of the former protectorate of Aden. Its official name is **People's Democratic Republic of Yemen.** 1,280,000 pop.; 111,100 sq. mi. *Capital:* Madinet al-Shaab. See **Oman** for map.

South ey (sᴜᴛʜ′ē, sou′ᴛʜē), *n.* **Robert,** 1774-1843, English poet.

south ing (sou′ᴛʜing), *n.* 1 the distance of latitude reckoned southward from the last point of reckoning. 2 the distance southward covered by a ship on any southerly course.

South Island, the largest island of New Zealand. 803,000 pop.; 58,100 sq. mi.

South Korea, country in the S part of the Korean peninsula. It is the area south of the 38th parallel. Its official name is **Republic of Korea.** 31,460,000 pop.; 38,500 sq. mi. *Capital:* Seoul. —**South Korean.**

south land (south′lənd, south′land′), *n.* land in the south; southern part of a country.

south most (south′mōst), *adj.* farthest south; southernmost.

south paw (south′pô′), SLANG. —*n.* 1 a left-handed baseball pitcher. 2 any left-handed person. —*adj.* left-handed.

South Pole, 1 the southern end of the earth's axis. 2 **south pole,** the pole of a magnet that points south.

south ron (sᴜᴛʜ′rən), *adj.* southern. —*n.* 1 U.S. Southerner. 2 native of the south of Great Britain; Englishman.

South Sea Islands, islands in the S Pacific; Oceania.

South Seas, 1 the S Pacific Ocean. 2 seas located below the equator.

south-south east (south′south ēst′; *Nautical* sou′sou ēst′), *n.* the point of the compass or the direction midway between south and southeast, two points or 22 degrees 30 minutes to the east of south.

south-south west (south′south west′; *Nautical* sou′sou west′), *n.* the point of the compass or the direction midway between south and southwest, two points or 22 degrees 30 minutes to the west of south.

South Vietnam, country in SE Asia, south of the 17th parallel. 18,330,000 pop.; 65,900 sq. mi. *Capital:* Saigon. —**South Vietnamese.**

south ward (south′wərd), *adv., adj.* toward the south. —*n.* a southward part, direction, or point.

south ward ly (south′wərd lē), *adj., adv.* 1 toward the south. 2 from the south.

south wards (south′wərdz), *adv.* southward.

south west (south′west′), *adj.* 1 halfway between south and west. 2 from the southwest. 3 in the southwest. —*adv.* toward the southwest. —*n.* 1 a southwest direction. 2 place that is in the southwest part or direction. 3 **the Southwest,** the southwestern part of the United States, especially Texas, New Mexico, Oklahoma, Arizona, and, sometimes, S California.

South-West Africa (south′west′), territory in SW Africa, under the supervision of the Republic of South Africa. 749,000 pop.; 317,700 sq. mi. *Capital:* Windhoek. See **South Africa** for map.

south west er (south′wes′tər *for* 1; sou′wes′tər *for* 2), *n.* 1 wind or storm from the southwest. 2 a waterproof hat having a broad brim at the back to protect the neck, worn especially by seamen. Also, **sou'wester.**

south west er ly (south′wes′tər lē), *adj., adv.* 1 toward the southwest. 2 from the southwest.

south west ern (south′wes′tərn), *adj.* 1 toward the southwest. 2 from the southwest. 3 of or in the southwest. 4 **Southwestern,** of, having to do with, or in the Southwest.

South west ern er (south′wes′tər nər), *n.* native or inhabitant of the Southwest.

south west ward (south′west′wərd), *adv., adj.* toward the southwest. —*n.* southwest.

south west ward ly (south′west′wərd lē), *adj., adv.* 1 toward the southwest. 2 from the southwest.

south west wards (south′west′wərdz), *adv.* southwestward.

sou ve nir (sü′və nir′, sü′və nir), *n.* something given or kept for remembrance; keepsake. [< French < Latin *subvenire* come to mind < *sub-* up + *venire* come]

sou'west er (sou'wes'tər), *n.* southwester.

sov er eign (sov'rən), *n.* 1 supreme ruler; king or queen; monarch. 2 person, group, or nation having supreme control or dominion; master: *sovereign of the seas.* 3 a British gold coin, worth 20 shillings, or one pound. *—adj.* 1 having the rank or power of a sovereign. 2 greatest in rank or power. 3 independent of the control of other governments. 4 above all others; supreme; greatest: *Character is of sovereign importance.* 5 very excellent or powerful. [< Old French *soverain,* ultimately < Latin *super* over] **—sov'er eign ly,** *adv.*

sov er eign ty (sov'rən tē), *n., pl.* **-ties.** 1 supreme power or authority; supremacy: *the sovereignty of the sea.* 2 complete control by a state over its own affairs independently of external interference. 3 state, territory, community, etc., that is independent or sovereign. 4 rank, power, or jurisdiction of a sovereign.

so vi et (sō'vē et, sō'vē it), *n.* 1 Often, **Soviet.** in the Soviet Union: **a** either of two elected assemblies concerned with local government **(village soviets, town soviets). b** any of the pyramid of larger assemblies elected by local assemblies, culminating in the **Supreme Soviet,** the national legislative body. 2 **the Soviet,** the Soviet Union. 3 **Soviets,** *pl.* **a** Russians. **b** the Kremlin. *—adj.* 1 of or having to do with a soviet or soviets. 2 **Soviet,** of or having to do with the Soviet Union. [< Russian *sovet* council]

so vi et ize (sō'vē ə tīz), *v.t.,* **-ized, -iz ing.** change to a government by soviets, or to communism. **—so'vi et i za'tion,** *n.*

Soviet Russia, 1 the Russian Soviet Federated Socialist Republic. 2 the Soviet Union.

Soviet Union, the Union of Soviet Socialist Republics, a union of fifteen republics in E Europe and W and N Asia, the largest of which is the Russian Soviet Federated Socialist Republic. The European part is often called Russia; Siberia comprises most of the Asian part. 241,748,000 pop.; 8,650,000 sq. mi. *Capital:* Moscow.

sov khoz (sov koz'), *n., pl.* **-khoz es, -khoz y** (-kô'zē). (in the Soviet Union) a farm owned by the state. [< Russian]

sow[1] (sō), *v.,* **sowed, sown** or **sowed, sow ing.** *—v.t.* 1 scatter (seed) on the ground; plant (seed): *He sows more wheat than oats.* 2 plant seed in: *He sowed the field with oats.* 3 scatter (anything); spread abroad; disseminate: *sow distrust.* 4 implant: *sow the germ of dissension.* *—v.i.* scatter seed. [Old English *sāwan*] **—sow'er,** *n.*

sow[2] (sou), *n.* a fully grown female pig. [Old English *sugu*]

sow bel ly (sou'bel'ē), *n.* U.S. salt pork consisting mostly of fat.

sow bug (sou), wood louse.

sown (sōn), *v.* a pp. of **sow**[1].

sox (soks), *n.pl.* INFORMAL. socks (stockings).

soy (soi), *n.* 1 Also, **soy sauce.** a Chinese and Japanese sauce for fish, meat, etc., made from fermented soybeans. 2 soybean. [< Japanese *shōyu* < Chinese *chiang-yu*]

soy a (soi'ə), *n.* soy.

soy bean (soi'bēn'), *n.* 1 the seed of a plant of the pea family, native to Asia, now also grown in other parts of the world, used in making flour, oil, etc., and as a food. Soybean oil is used in making plastics, paint, linoleum, etc. 2 plant that it grows on, used as fodder for cattle.

SP or **S.P.,** shore patrol.

sp., 1 special. 2 species. 3 spelling.

Sp., 1 Spain. 2 Spaniard. 3 Spanish.

spa (spä), *n.* 1 a mineral spring. 2 town, locality, or resort where there is a mineral spring or springs. [< *Spa,* Belgian resort]

space (spās), *n., v.,* **spaced, spac ing,** *adj.* *—n.* 1 the unlimited room or area which extends in all directions and in which all things exist: *The earth moves through space.* 2 a limited area or room: *find a parking space. This brick will fill a space 2 1/2 by 4 by 8 inches.* 3 extent or area of ground, surface, sky, etc.; expanse: *The trees covered acres of space.* 4 outer space: *a rocket launched into space.* 5 distance between two or more points or objects: *The trees are set at equal spaces apart.* 6 length of time; duration: *The flowers died in the space of a day.* 7 ARCHAIC. an interval of time; a while. 8 a blank between words or lines in written or printed matter: *Fill in the spaces as directed.* 9 (in printing) one of the blank types used to separate words, etc. 10 (in music) one of the intervals or open places between the lines of a staff. 11 accommodations on a train, airplane, ship, etc. 12 (in mathematics) a set of points or elements that usually fulfills certain necessary conditions.
—v.t. 1 fix the space or spaces of; divide into spaces. 2 separate by spaces: *Space your words evenly when you write.*
—adj. of or having to do with outer space: *a space probe, space travel.*
[< Old French *espace* < Latin *spatium*]

space age, the current period in history, as marked by the advances made in the exploration of outer space. **—space'-age',** *adj.*

space borne (spās'bôrn', spās'bōrn'), *adj.* borne or carried into outer space.

space charge, the electric charge distributed through the area between the filament and the plate in a vacuum tube.

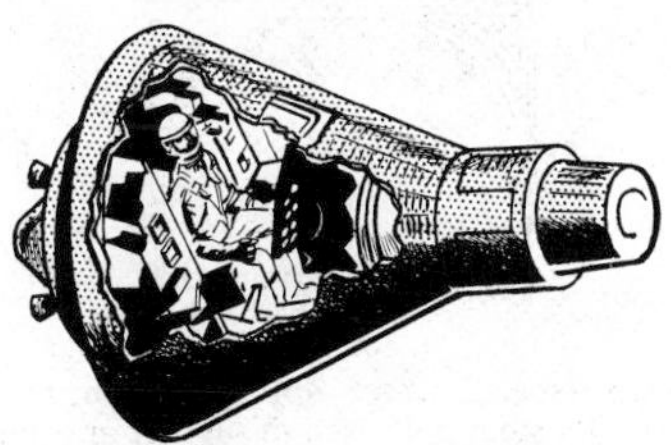

spacecraft—partly cut away

space craft (spās'kraft'), *n., pl.* **-craft.** any vehicle designed for flight in outer space; spaceship.

space engineer, an expert in astronautics.

space gun, a portable apparatus equipped with a nozzle for jet propulsion, used in space to maneuver oneself in various directions while outside a flying or orbiting spacecraft.

space heater, a small gas or electric heater, often portable, for warming a room or portion of a room.

space less (spās'lis), *adj.* 1 independent of space; infinite; boundless. 2 occupying no space.

space man (spās'mən), *n., pl.* **-men.** 1 astronaut. 2 person, especially a scientist, engaged in research, projects, etc., concerned with space travel.

space medicine, branch of medicine dealing with the effects of space travel on the body.

hat, āge, fär; let, ēqual, tėrm;
it, īce; hot, ōpen, ôrder;
oil, out; cup, pu̇t, rüle;
ch, child; ng, long; sh, she;
th, thin; ᴛʜ, then; zh, measure;

ə represents *a* in about, *e* in taken, *i* in pencil, *o* in lemon, *u* in circus.

< = from, derived from, taken from.

space-mind ed (spās'mīn'did), *adj.* interested in outer space and in space travel.

space port (spās'pôrt', spās'pōrt'), *n.* place where spacecraft can take off or land.

space power, capacity of a nation to produce and utilize spacecraft and other apparatus for space exploration, military strategy, etc.

space science, any science or branch of science dealing with outer space.

space ship (spās'ship'), *n.* spacecraft.

space station, an artificial earth satellite to be used as an observatory or a launching site for travel in outer space.

space suit (spās'süt'), *n.* an airtight, pressurized suit designed to protect travelers in outer space from radiation, heat, and lack of oxygen.

space-time continuum (spās'tīm'), (in physics) space conceived as a continuum of four dimensions (length, width, height, and time), within which physical events can be located exactly.

space walk (spās'wôk'), *n.* act of moving or floating in space while outside a spacecraft.

space writer, writer who is paid on the basis of the amount of space in type his accepted writing fills.

spa cial (spā'shəl), *adj.* spatial.

spac ing (spā'sing), *n.* 1 the fixing or arranging of spaces. 2 manner in which spaces are arranged: *even, close, or open spacing in printed matter.* 3 space or spaces in printing or other work.

spa cious (spā'shəs), *adj.* 1 having much space or room; large: *The spacious rooms of the old castle.* 2 of great extent or area; extensive; vast: *the spacious plains of Kansas.* 3 broad in scope or range: *a spacious mind.* [< Latin *spatiosus* < *spatium* space] **—spa'cious ly,** *adv.* **—spa'cious ness,** *n.*

spade[1] (spād), *n., v.,* **spad ed, spad ing.** *—n.* 1 tool for digging, having an iron blade which can be pressed into the ground with the foot, and a long handle with a grip or crosspiece at the top. 2 **call a spade a spade,** call a thing by its real name; speak plainly and frankly. *—v.i., v.t.* dig with a spade: *spade up the garden.* [Old English *spadu*] **—spad'er,** *n.*

spade[2] (spād), *n.* 1 figure shaped like this: ♠. 2 a playing card marked with one or more black figures like this. 3 **spades,** *pl.* suit of such playing cards, usually the highest ranking suit. [< Italian < Latin *spatha* < Greek *spathē* sword, broad blade. Doublet of SPATHE.]

spade work (spād'wėrk'), *n.* 1 a digging, cutting, or removing with a spade. 2 preparatory work, such as intensive research, discussion, etc., serving as a basis for further work or activity.

spa dix (spā′diks), *n., pl.* **spa dix es, spa di ces** (spā′də sēz, spā dī′sēz). spike composed of minute flowers on a fleshy stem, usually enclosed in a spathe, as in the jack-in-the-pulpit and the calla lily. [< Latin < Greek, palm branch]

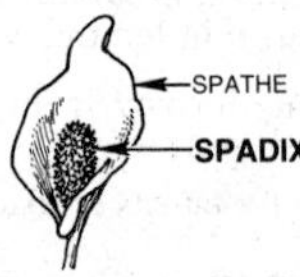

spa ghet ti (spə get′ē), *n.* long, slender sticks made of the same mixture of flour and water as macaroni, but thinner than macaroni and not hollow, cooked by boiling in water. [< Italian, plural diminutive of *spago* cord]

Spain (spān), *n.* country in SW Europe. 33,290,000 pop.; 194,900 sq. mi. *Capital:* Madrid.

spake (spāk), *v.* ARCHAIC. a pt. of **speak.**

span[1] (span), *n., v.,* **spanned, span ning.** —*n.* 1 part between two supports: *The bridge crossed the river in three spans.* 2 distance between two supports: *The arch had a fifty-foot span.* 3 a short space of time: *His life's span is nearly over.* 4 the full extent: *the span of memory.* 5 the distance between the tip of a man's thumb and the tip of his little finger when the hand is spread out; about 9 inches. —*v.t.* 1 extend over or across: *A bridge spanned the river.* 2 provide with something that stretches over or across: *span a river with a bridge.* 3 measure by the hand spread out. [Old English *spann*]

span[2] (span), *n.* pair of horses or other animals harnessed and driven together. [< Dutch < *spannen* to stretch, yoke]

span[3] (span), *v.* ARCHAIC. a pt. of **spin.**

span drel (span′drəl), *n.* the triangular space between the curve of an arch and the rectangular molding or framework enclosing the arch. [alteration of Old French *espandre* expand < Latin *expandere*]

span gle (spang′gəl), *n., v.,* **-gled, -gling.** —*n.* 1 a small piece of glittering metal used for decoration: *The dress was covered with spangles.* 2 any small, bright bit: *This rock shows spangles of gold.* —*v.t.* 1 decorate with spangles. 2 sprinkle with or as if with small, bright bits: *The sky is spangled with stars.* —*v.i.* glitter. [diminutive of earlier *spang,* probably < Middle Dutch *spange* brooch]

Span iard (span′yərd), *n.* native or inhabitant of Spain.

span iel (span′yəl), *n.* 1 any of various breeds of dogs, usually of small or medium size, with long, silky hair and drooping ears. 2 person who yields too much to others. [< Old French *espagneul,* literally, Spanish < Latin *Hispania* Spain]

Span ish (span′ish), *adj.* of or having to do with Spain, its people, or their language. —*n.* 1 *pl. in use.* the people of Spain. 2 the language of Spain. 3 American Spanish.

Spanish America, countries and islands south and southeast of the United States, in which the principal language is Spanish.

Spanish American, native or inhabitant of a Spanish American country.

Span ish-A mer i can (span′ish ə mer′ə-kən), *adj.* 1 of or having to do with Spain and America, or with Spain and the United States. 2 of or having to do with Spanish America.

Spanish-American War, war between Spain and the United States in 1898, fought chiefly in Cuba and the Philippines.

Spanish fly, a bright-green European blister beetle used in medicine after being dried and powdered.

Spanish Guinea, former name of **Equatorial Guinea.**

Spanish Main, 1 (formerly) the NW coast of South America, from which Spanish galleons used to sail with gold for Spain. 2 (in later use) the Caribbean Sea.

Spanish moss, a mosslike, epiphytic plant of the same family as the pineapple, growing on the branches of certain trees, from which it hangs in gray streamers. It is found in the southern United States and tropical America.

Spanish Sahara, Spanish province in NW Africa.

spank (spangk), *v.t.* strike, especially on the buttocks, with the open hand, a slipper, etc. —*n.* a blow with the open hand, a slipper, etc,; slap. [imitative]

spank er (spang′kər), *n.* 1 a fore-and-aft sail on the mast nearest the stern. 2 INFORMAL. **a** a fast horse. **b** anything fine, large, unusual for its kind, etc.

spank ing (spang′king), *n.* a striking with the open hand, a slipper, etc. —*adj.* 1 blowing briskly: *a spanking breeze.* 2 quick and vigorous. 3 INFORMAL. unusually fine, great, large, etc.

span ner (span′ər), *n.* 1 person or thing that spans: *the spanners of a bridge.* 2 BRITISH. tool for holding and turning a nut, bolt, etc.; wrench. [< German *Spanner*]

Span sule (span′səl, span′syül), *n.* trademark for a capsule containing several drugs set to dissolve in the body at different times after it is ingested. [< *span* + *(cap)sule*]

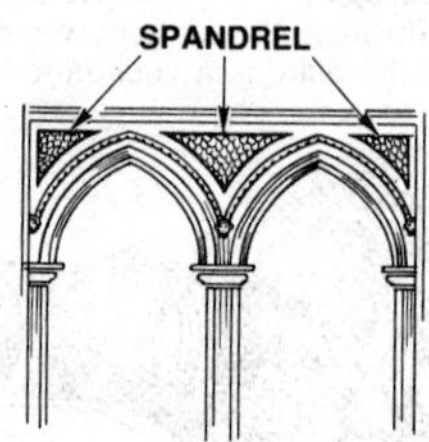

spar[1] (spär), *n., v.,* **sparred, spar ring.** —*n.* 1 a stout pole used to support or extend the sails of a ship; mast, yard, gaff, boom, etc., of a ship. 2 the main horizontal support of an airplane wing. —*v.t.* provide (a ship) with spars. [Middle English *sparre* rafter]

spar[2] (spär), *v.,* **sparred, spar ring,** *n.* —*v.i.* 1 make motions of attack and defense with the arms and fists; box. 2 dispute. 3 (of roosters) fight with the feet or spurs. —*n.* 1 a boxing match. 2 a sparring motion. 3 a dispute. [Old English *sperran*]

spar[3] (spär), *n.* any of various crystalline minerals, more or less lustrous, that split into flakes easily. [< Middle Low German, related to Old English *spær(en)* of plaster]

SPAR or **Spar** (spär), *n.* member of the Women's Reserve of the United States Coast Guard Reserve. [< Latin *S(emper) Par(atus)* always ready, the motto of the Coast Guard]

spare (sper, spar), *v.,* **spared, spar ing,** *adj.,* **spar er, spar est,** *n.* —*v.t.* 1 show mercy to; refrain from harming or destroying: *spare a conquered enemy.* 2 show consideration for; free from labor, pain, etc.: *We walked uphill to spare the horse.* 3 get along without; do without: *Can you spare a moment to discuss the problem?* 4 make (a person) free from (something); relieve or exempt (a person) from (something): *I did the work to spare you the trouble. Spare me the gory details.* 5 refrain from using; forego: *Spare the rod and spoil the child.* 6 use in small quantities or not at all; be saving of; stint: *spare no expense.* —*v.i.* 1 show mercy; refrain from doing harm. 2 be saving, economical, or frugal.
—*adj.* 1 free for other use; surplus: *spare time.* 2 in reserve; extra: *a spare tire, a spare room.* 3 thin; lean: *Lincoln was a tall, spare man.* 4 small in quantity; meager; scanty: *a spare meal.* 5 frugal or economical, especially in regard to food: *a spare diet.*
—*n.* 1 a spare thing, part, tire, room, etc. 2 the knocking down of all the pins with two rolls of a bowling ball. 3 the score for doing this.
[Old English *sparian*] **—spare′ness,** *n.* **—spar′er,** *n.*

spare ly (sper′lē, spar′lē), *adv.* not amply or fully; sparingly; scantily.

spare ribs (sper′ribs′, spar′ribs′), *n.pl.* cut of pork consisting of the ribs having less meat than the ribs near the loins. [probably alteration of earlier *ribspare* < Middle Low German *ribbespēr* rib cut]

spar ing (sper′ing, spar′ing), *adj.* 1 that spares. 2 avoiding waste; economical; frugal: *a sparing use of sugar.* **—spar′ing ly,** *adv.*

spark[1] (spärk), *n.* 1 a small bit of fire: *The burning wood threw off sparks.* 2 flash given off when electricity jumps across an open space. An electric spark ignites the gas in the engine of an automobile. 3 the discharge in a spark plug. 4 the mechanism generating and controlling this discharge. 5 a bright flash; gleam; sparkle: *a spark of light.* 6 a small amount: *I haven't a spark of interest in the plan.* 7 a glittering bit. —*v.i.* 1 send out small bits of fire; produce sparks. 2 flash; gleam; sparkle. 3 issue or fall as or like sparks. —*v.t.* 1 make (someone) enthusiastic or determined. 2 stir to activity; stimulate: *spark a revolt.* [Old English *spearca*]

spark[2] (spärk), *n.* 1 a gay, showy young man; dandy. 2 beau; lover. —*v.t., v.i.* INFORMAL. court; woo. [perhaps < Scandinavian (Old Icelandic) *sparkr* lively] **—spark′er,** *n.*

spark coil, an induction coil for producing electric sparks.

spar kle (spär′kəl), *v.,* **-kled, -kling,** *n.* —*v.i.* 1 send out little sparks. 2 shine as if giving out sparks; glitter; gleam: *The diamonds sparkled.* 3 be brilliant; be lively: *Wit sparkles.* 4 bubble: *Ginger ale sparkles.* —*v.t.* cause to sparkle. —*n.* 1 a little spark. 2 light shining like sparks; glitter: *I like the sparkle of her eyes.* See **flash** for synonym study. 3 brilliance; liveliness.

spar kler (spär′klər), *n.* 1 person or thing that sparkles. 2 firework that sends out little sparks. 3 a sparkling gem, especially a diamond.

spar kling (spär′kling), *adj.* 1 shining; glittering. 2 brilliant: *a sparkling wit.* 3 bubbling: *sparkling drinks.*

spark plug (spärk′plug′), *v.t.,* **-plugged, -plug ging.** INFORMAL. be the spark plug of (a group, organization, etc.).

spark plug, 1 device in the cylinder of a gasoline engine by which the mixture of gasoline and air is ignited by an electric spark. 2 INFORMAL. person who gives energy or enthusiasm to others.

spar row (spar′ō), *n.* 1 any of various small, usually brownish finches common in North and South America, as the chipping sparrow. 2 any of a related group of birds native to Europe, Asia, and Africa. [Old English *spearwa*]

sparrow hawk, a small hawk which feeds on birds, insects, and other small animals.

sparse (spärs), *adj.,* **spars er, spars est.** 1 occurring here and there; thinly scattered: *a sparse population, sparse hair.* See **scanty** for synonym study. 2 scanty; meager. [< Latin *sparsum* scattered] **—sparse′ly,** *adv.* **—sparse′ness,** *n.*

spar si ty (spär′sə tē), *n.* sparse or scattered condition; sparseness.

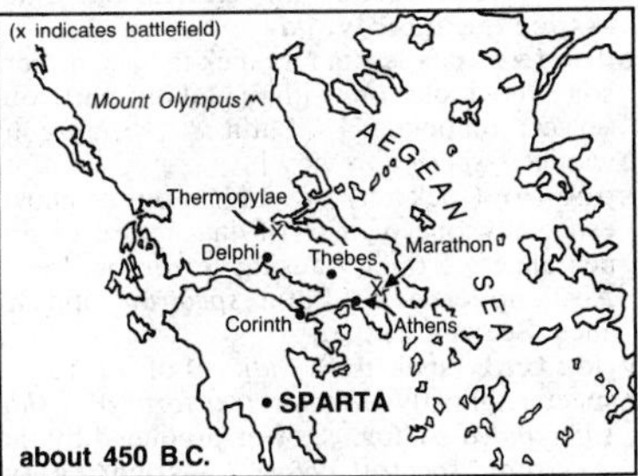

Spar ta (spär′tə), *n.* important city of Laconia, on the Peloponnesus in ancient Greece, famous for its soldiers. Also, **Lacedaemon.**

Spar ta cus (spär′tə kəs), *n.* died 71 B.C., Thracian slave and gladiator who led an insurrection of slaves in southern Italy that lasted from 73 to 71 B.C.

Spar tan (spärt′n), *adj.* 1 of or having to do with Sparta or its people. 2 like the Spartans. *—n.* 1 native or inhabitant of Sparta. The Spartans were noted for simplicity of life, severity, courage, and brevity of speech. 2 person who is like the Spartans.

spasm (spaz′əm), *n.* 1 a sudden, abnormal, involuntary contraction of a muscle or muscles. 2 any sudden, brief fit or spell of unusual energy or activity. [< Greek *spasmos* < *span* draw up, tear away]

spas mod ic (spaz mod′ik), *adj.* 1 having to do with, like, or characterized by a spasm or spasms: *a spasmodic cough.* 2 occurring very irregularly; intermittent: *a spasmodic interest in reading.* 3 having or showing bursts of excitement. [< Greek *spasmodes* < *spasmos.* See SPASM.] **—spas mod′i cal ly,** *adv.*

spas tic (spas′tik), *adj.* 1 of, having to do with, or characterized by spasms. 2 caused by a spasm or spasms. 3 having spastic paralysis. *—n.* person who has spastic paralysis. [< Greek *spastikos* < *span* draw up] **—spas′ti cal ly,** *adv.*

spastic paralysis, paralysis characterized by prolonged contraction of a muscle or muscles with exaggerated reflexes.

spat[1] (spat), *n., v.,* **spat ted, spat ting.** *—n.* 1 a slight quarrel; tiff. 2 a light blow; slap. *—v.i.* INFORMAL. quarrel slightly or briefly. *—v.t.* slap lightly. [perhaps imitative]

spat[2] (spat), *v.* a pt. and a pp. of **spit**[1].

spat[3] (spat), *n.* Usually, **spats,** *pl.* a short gaiter worn over the instep, reaching just above the ankle. [short for *spatterdash*]

spat[4] (spat), *n., v.,* **spat ted, spat ting.** *—n.* 1 the spawn of oysters or certain other shellfish. 2 a young oyster. *—v.i.* (of oysters and certain other shellfish) spawn. [origin uncertain]

spate (spāt), *n.* 1 a sudden outburst: *a spate of words.* 2 a large number; great quantity: *a spate of new books on astronomy.* 3 BRITISH. a sudden flood; freshet. [Middle English]

spathe (spāᴛʜ), *n.* a large bract or pair of bracts, often colored, that encloses the inflorescence, usually a spadix, of certain plants, as the calla lily, palms, etc. See **spadix** for picture. [< Greek, palm branch, oar blade. Doublet of SPADE[2].]

spa tial (spā′shəl), *adj.* 1 of or having to do with space. 2 existing in space. 3 occupying or taking up space. Also, **spacial.** [< Latin *spatium* space] **—spa′tial ly,** *adv.*

spa ti al i ty (spā′shē al′ə tē), *n.* spatial quality or character.

spat ter (spat′ər), *v.t.* 1 scatter or dash in drops or particles; splatter: *spatter mud.* 2 strike in a shower; strike in a number of places: *Bullets spattered the wall.* 3 splash or spot with mud, etc.; bespatter. 4 stain with slander, disgrace, etc. *—v.i.* 1 send out or throw off drops or particles. 2 fall in drops or particles: *Rain spatters on the sidewalk.* *—n.* 1 a spattering: *a spatter of bullets.* 2 sound of spattering. 3 a splash or spot.

spat ter dock (spat′ər dok′), *n.* any of a genus of water lilies, especially a species with yellow flowers, common in stagnant waters of the eastern United States.

spat u la (spach′ə lə), *n.* tool with a broad, flat, flexible blade, used for mixing drugs, spreading paints or frostings, etc. [< Late Latin, diminutive of Latin *spatha* flat blade < Greek *spathē*]

spat u late (spach′ə lit, spach′ə lāt), *adj.* shaped somewhat like a spatula: *a spatulate leaf, spatulate fingers.*

spav in (spav′ən), *n.* disease of horses in which a bony swelling forms at the hock, causing lameness. [< Old French *espavain*]

spav ined (spav′ənd), *adj.* having spavin; lame.

spawn (spôn), *n.* 1 the eggs of fish, frogs, shellfish, etc. 2 the young newly hatched from such eggs. 3 offspring, especially a large number of offspring. 4 product or result. 5 mycelium from which mushrooms grow. *—v.i.* 1 (of fish, etc.) produce spawn. 2 increase or develop like spawn. *—v.t.* 1 produce (spawn). 2 bring forth; give birth to. [< Old French *espandre* spread out < Latin *expandere.* Doublet of EXPAND.] **—spawn′er,** *n.*

spay (spā), *v.t.* remove the ovaries of (a female animal). [< Anglo-French *espeier,* ultimately < Old French *espee* sword < Latin *spatha.* See SPADE[2].]

S.P.C.A., Society for the Prevention of Cruelty to Animals.

S.P.C.C., Society for the Prevention of Cruelty to Children.

speak (spēk), *v.,* **spoke** or (ARCHAIC) **spake, spo ken, speak ing.** *—v.i.* 1 say words; talk: *Speak distinctly.* 2 make a speech: *Some lecturers speak without notes.* 3 express an idea, feeling, etc.; communicate: *Actions speak louder than words.* 4 give forth sound: *The cannons spoke.* 5 (of dogs) bark when told. *—v.t.* 1 say or utter (a word or words): *No one spoke a word to him.* 2 tell or express in words or speech: *speak the truth.* 3 use (a language): *Do you speak French?* 4 indicate by expression: *His face spoke hope.* 5 ARCHAIC. show to be; characterize.

hat, āge, fär; let, ēqual, tėrm;
it, īce; hot, ōpen, ôrder;
oil, out; cup, pu̇t, rüle;
ch, child; ng, long; sh, she;
th, thin; ᴛʜ, then; zh, measure;

ə represents *a* in about, *e* in taken,
i in pencil, *o* in lemon, *u* in circus.

< = from, derived from, taken from.

so to speak, speak in such a manner; use that expression.

speak for, **a** speak in the interest of; represent. **b** ask or apply for.

speak of, refer to; mention.

speak out or **speak up,** speak loudly, clearly, or freely.

speak well for, give a favorable idea of; be evidence in favor of.

[Old English *specan*] **—speak′a ble,** *adj.*

speak eas y (spēk′ē′zē), *n., pl.* **-eas ies.** SLANG. place where alcoholic liquors are sold contrary to law.

speak er (spē′kər), *n.* 1 person who speaks, especially one who speaks formally or skillfully before an audience. 2 Also, **Speaker.** person who presides over a legislative assembly. 3 loudspeaker.

Speaker of the House, the presiding officer of the United States House of Representatives.

speak er ship (spē′kər ship), *n.* position of presiding officer in a legislative assembly.

speak ing (spē′king), *n.* act, utterance, or discourse of a person who speaks. *—adj.* 1 that speaks; giving information as if by speech: *a speaking example of a thing.* 2 used in, suited to, or involving speech: *within speaking distance, a speaking part in a play.* 3 permitting conversation: *a speaking acquaintance with a person.* 4 highly expressive; eloquent: *speaking eyes.* 5 lifelike: *a speaking likeness.*

speaking tube, tube or pipe for speaking from one room, building, etc., to another.

spear[1] (spir), *n.* 1 weapon with a long shaft and a sharp-pointed head, thrown or thrust with the hand in hunting, warfare, etc. 2 ARCHAIC. spearman. *—v.t.* 1 pierce with a spear: *spear a fish.* 2 pierce or stab with anything sharp: *spear string beans with a fork.* [Old English *spere*] **—spear′er,** *n.*

spear[2] (spir), *n.* sprout or shoot of a plant: *a spear of grass.* *—v.i.* sprout or shoot into a long stem. [variant of *spire*[1]]

spear head (spir′hed′), *n.* 1 the sharp-pointed striking end of a spear. 2 part that is first in an attack, undertaking, etc. *—v.t.* lead or clear the way for; head: *spearhead an assault.*

spear man (spir′mən), *n., pl.* **-men.** soldier armed with a spear.

spear mint (spir′mint′), *n.* a common fragrant herb of the mint family which yields a fragrant oil that is used for flavoring.

spec., special.

spe cial (spesh′əl), *adj.* 1 of a particular kind; distinct from others; not general. See synonym study below. 2 more than ordinary; unusual; exceptional: *Today's topic is of special interest.* 3 for a particular person, thing, purpose, etc.: *The railroad ran special trains on holidays.* 4 held in high regard; great; chief: *a special friend, a special favorite.* *—n.* 1 a special train, car, bus, etc.

2 any special person or thing. 3 a special edition of a newspaper. 4 U.S. a specially featured product, service, etc. 5 a television show, produced especially for a single broadcast, usually out of the pattern of regular daily or weekly programs. [< Latin *specialis* < *species* sort, kind, species]

Syn. *adj.* 1 **Special, particular** mean belonging or relating to one person, thing, or group, as distinguished from others. **Special** implies being different from others of its kind: *Babies need special food.* **Particular** implies being or treated as being unique: *the particular meaning of a word.*

special delivery, delivery of a letter or package for an additional fee, by a special messenger rather than by the regular mailman.

spe cial ist (spesh′ə list), *n.* 1 person who devotes or restricts himself to one particular branch of study, business, etc. A dentist is a specialist in the care of teeth. 2 (in the U.S. Army) an enlisted man with administrative or technical duties.

spe cial is tic (spesh′ə lis′tik), *adj.* of or having to do with specialism or specialists.

spe ci al i ty (spesh′ē al′ə tē), *n., pl.* **-ties.** 1 a special, limited, or particular character. 2 the distinctive property or feature of a thing; peculiarity. 3 a special point; particular; detail. 4 a special pursuit, branch of study, product, etc.; specialty.

spe cial ize (spesh′ə līz), *v.,* **-ized, -iz ing.** —*v.i.* 1 pursue some special branch of study, work, etc.: *Many students specialize in engineering.* 2 develop in a special way; take on a special form, use, etc. 3 go into particulars. —*v.t.* 1 make special or specific; give a special character, function, etc., to. 2 adapt to a special function or condition: *Lungs and gills are specialized for breathing.* 3 mention specially; specify. **—spe′cial i za′tion,** *n.*

spe cial ly (spesh′ə lē), *adv.* in a special manner or degree; particularly; unusually.

spe cial ty (spesh′əl tē), *n., pl.* **-ties.** 1 a special study, line of work, profession, trade, etc.: *American history is the specialty of my history teacher.* 2 product, article, etc., to which special attention is given: *This store makes a specialty of children's clothes.* 3 special character or quality. 4 a special or particular characteristic; peculiarity. 5 a special point or item; particular; detail.

spe ci ate (spē′shē āt), *v.i.,* **-at ed, -at ing.** form new species by evolutionary process: *Hybridization prevents plants from speciating.*

spe ci a tion (spē′shē ā′shən), *n.* formation of new species by evolutionary process.

spe cie (spē′shē), *n.* 1 money in the form of coins; metal money. Silver dollars are specie. 2 **in specie, a** in kind. **b** in actual coin. [< Latin *(in) specie* (in) kind]

spe cies (spē′shēz), *n., pl.* **-cies.** 1 group of related animals or plants that have certain permanent characteristics in common and are able to interbreed. A species ranks next below a genus and may be divided into several varieties, races, or breeds. Wheat is a species of grass. See **classification** for chart. 2 a distinct kind or sort; kind; sort: *There are many species of advertisements.* 3 the consecrated bread and wine used in the Mass. 4 **the species,** the human race. [< Latin, originally, appearance. Doublet of SPICE.]

specif., specifically.

spec i fi a ble (spes′ə fī′ə bəl), *adj.* that can be specified.

spe cif ic (spi sif′ik), *adj.* 1 definite; precise; particular: *There was no specific reason for the quarrel.* 2 characteristic (of); peculiar (to); distinctive: *Feathers are a feature specific to birds.* 3 curing some particular disease. 4 produced by some special cause: *a specific disease.* 5 of or having to do with a species. —*n.* 1 any specific statement, quality, etc. 2 a cure for some particular disease: *Vitamin B_{12} is a specific for pernicious anemia.* [< Late Latin *specificus* constituting a species < Latin *species* sort + *facere* make] **—spe cif′ic ness,** *n.*

spe cif i cal ly (spi sif′ik lē), *adv.* in a specific manner; definitely.

spec i fi ca tion (spes′ə fə kā′shən), *n.* 1 act of specifying; definite mention; detailed statement of particulars: *The want ad made careful specification as to the requirements of the position.* 2 Usually, **specifications,** *pl.* a detailed description of the dimensions, materials, etc., for a building, road, dam, boat, etc. 3 something specified; particular item, article, etc.

specific gravity, the ratio of the weight of a given volume of any substance to that of the same volume of some other substance taken as a standard (usually water at four degrees centigrade for solids and liquids, and hydrogen or air for gases).

specific heat, 1 number of calories of heat needed to raise the temperature of one gram of a substance one degree centigrade. 2 the ratio of the amount of heat required to raise a unit mass of a substance one degree in temperature to that required to raise the same mass of some other substance, taken as standard, one degree.

spec i fic i ty (spes′ə fis′ə tē), *n.* specific quality.

spec i fy (spes′ə fī), *v.t.,* **-fied, -fy ing.** 1 mention or name definitely; state or describe in detail: *Did you specify any particular time for us to call?* 2 include in the specifications: *He delivered the paper as specified.* [< Late Latin *specificare* < *specificus.* See SPECIFIC.] **—spec′i fi′er,** *n.*

spec i men (spes′ə mən), *n.* 1 one of a group or class taken to show what the others are like; sample: *She collects specimens of all kinds of rocks.* 2 INFORMAL. a human being; person. [< Latin < *specere* to view]

spe ci os i ty (spē′shē os′ə tē), *n., pl.* **-ties.** 1 quality of being specious; speciousness. 2 a specious act, appearance, remark, etc.

spe cious (spē′shəs), *adj.* 1 seeming desirable, reasonable, or probable, but not really so; apparently good or right, but without real merit: *The teacher saw through that specious excuse.* 2 making a good outward appearance in order to deceive: *a specious friendship, a specious flatterer.* [< Latin *speciosus* < *species* appearance, sort] **—spe′cious ly,** *adv.* **—spe′cious ness,** *n.*

speck (spek), *n.* 1 a small spot or mark; stain: *Can you clean the specks off this wallpaper?* 2 a tiny bit; particle: *a speck of dust.* —*v.t.* mark with specks: *This fruit is badly specked.* [Old English *specca*]

speck le (spek′əl), *n., v.,* **-led, -ling.** —*n.* a small spot or mark; speck: *a gray hen with white speckles.* —*v.t.* mark with or as if with speckles.

specs (speks), *n.pl.* INFORMAL. spectacles.

spec ta cle (spek′tə kəl), *n.* 1 something presented to the view as noteworthy, striking, etc.; thing to look at; sight: *a charming spectacle of children at play.* 2 a public show or display: *The parade was the crowning spectacle of the day.* 3 **make a spectacle of oneself,** behave in public view in such a manner as to become an object of curiosity, contempt, or wonder. 4 **spectacles,** *pl.* eyeglasses. [< Latin *spectaculum* < *spectare* to watch < *specere* to view]

spec ta cled (spek′tə kəld), *adj.* 1 provided with or wearing spectacles. 2 having a marking resembling spectacles.

spec tac u lar (spek tak′yə lər), *adj.* 1 making a great display or show; very striking or imposing to the eye: *a spectacular storm.* 2 having to do with a spectacle or show. —*n.* 1 a spectacular display. 2 a lengthy motion picture or television show, usually produced on an extravagant scale. **—spec tac′u lar ly,** *adv.*

spec ta tor (spek′tā tər, spek tā′tər), *n.* person who looks on without taking part; observer; onlooker. [< Latin < *spectare* to watch < *specere* to view]

spec ter (spek′tər), *n.* 1 phantom or ghost, especially one of a terrifying nature or appearance. 2 thing causing terror or dread. Also, **spectre.** [< Latin *spectrum* appearance. See SPECTRUM.]

spec tral (spek′trəl), *adj.* 1 of or like a specter; ghostly: *the spectral form of a ship surrounded by fog.* 2 of or produced by the spectrum: *spectral colors.* **—spec′tral ly,** *adv.* **—spec′tral ness,** *n.*

spec tre (spek′tər), *n.* specter.

spec tro gram (spek′trə gram), *n.* photograph or picture of a spectrum.

spec tro graph (spek′trə graf), *n.* 1 spectrogram. 2 instrument for photographing a spectrum.

spec tro graph ic (spek′trə graf′ik), *adj.* of or by means of a spectrograph.

spec trom e ter (spek trom′ə tər), *n.* spectroscope equipped with a scale for measuring wavelengths of spectra.

spec tro met ric (spek′trə met′rik), *adj.* of or having to do with a spectrometer or spectrometry.

spec trom e try (spek trom′ə trē), *n.* 1 science that deals with the use of the spectrometer and the analysis of spectra. 2 the use of the spectrometer.

spec tro pho tom e ter (spek′trō fō tom′ə tər), *n.* instrument used to compare the intensities of two spectra, or the intensity of a given color with that of the corresponding color in a standard spectrum.

spec tro scope (spek′trə skōp), *n.* instrument for the production and examination of a spectrum of radiation from any source by the passage of rays through a prism or a grating.

spec tro scop ic (spek′trə skop′ik), *adj.* of or having to do with a spectroscope or spectroscopy.

spec tros co py (spek tros′kə pē, spek′trə skō′pē), *n.* 1 science having to do with the examination and analysis of spectra. 2 use of the spectroscope.

spec trum (spek′trəm), *n., pl.* **-tra** (-trə), **-trums.** 1 the band of colors formed when a beam of white light is broken up by being passed through a prism or by some other means. A rainbow has all the colors of the spectrum: red, orange, yellow, green, blue, indigo, and violet. 2 the band of colors formed when any other form of radiant energy is broken up. The ends of such a band are not visible to the eye, but are studied by photography, heat effects, etc. 3 (in radio) the wavelength range between 30,000 meters and 3 centimeters. 4 range; scope; compass: *a broad spectrum of electronic knowledge.* [< Latin, appearance < *specere* to view]

spec u lar (spek′yə lər), *adj.* 1 of or like a mirror; reflecting. 2 of or having to do with a speculum.

spec u late (spek′yə lāt), *v.i.,* **-lat ed, -lat ing.** 1 think carefully; reflect; meditate; consider: *The philosopher speculated about time and space.* 2 guess; conjecture. 3 buy or sell when there is a large risk, with the hope of making a profit from future price changes. [< Latin *speculatum* observed, viewed < *specula* watchtower < *specere* to view]

spec u la tion (spek′yə lā′shən), *n.* 1 careful thought; reflection. 2 a guessing; conjecture. 3 a buying or selling when there is a large risk, with the hope of making a profit from future price changes.

spec u la tive (spek′yə lā′tiv, spek′yə lə-tiv), *adj.* 1 carefully thoughtful; reflective. 2 theoretical rather than practical. 3 risky. 4 of or involving buying or selling at a large risk. **—spec′u la′tive ly,** *adv.* **—spec′u-la′tive ness,** *n.*

spec u la tor (spek′yə lā′tər), *n.* 1 person who speculates, usually in business. 2 person who buys tickets for shows, games, etc., in advance, hoping to sell them later at a higher price.

spec u lum (spek′yə ləm), *n., pl.* **-la** (-lə), **-lums.** 1 mirror or reflector of polished metal. A reflecting telescope contains a speculum. 2 a surgical instrument for enlarging an opening in order to examine a cavity. 3 a patch of color on the wing of many ducks and certain other birds. [< Latin, mirror < *specere* to view]

sped (sped), *v.* a pt. and a pp. of **speed.**

speech (spēch), *n.* 1 act of speaking; talk: *Men express their thoughts by speech.* 2 power of speaking: *Animals lack speech.* 3 manner of speaking; dialect, language, or tongue: *His speech showed that he was a Southerner.* 4 what is said; the words spoken: *We made the usual farewell speeches.* 5 a public talk. See synonym study below. 6 language. 7 study and practice of the spoken language. [Old English *spǣc*]

Syn. 5 **Speech, address, oration** mean a talk made to an audience. **Speech** is the general word applying to any kind of talk made for some purpose: *Many after-dinner speeches are dull.* **Address** means a prepared formal speech, usually of some importance or given on an important occasion: *Who gave your commencement address?* **Oration** means a formal address on a special occasion, and suggests artistic style, dignity, and eloquence: *Lincoln's Gettysburg Address is a famous oration.*

speech community, group of people who speak the same language or dialect.

speech i fy (spē′chə fī), *v.i.,* **-fied, -fy ing.** INFORMAL. make a speech or speeches. **—speech′i fi′er,** *n.*

speech less (spēch′lis), *adj.* 1 not able to speak: *Animals are speechless.* 2 temporarily unable to speak: *He was speechless with anger.* 3 not expressed in speech or words; silent: *Her frown gave a speechless message.* **—speech′less ly,** *adv.* **—speech′less-ness,** *n.*

speech writ er (spēch′rī′tər), *n.* person who writes speeches for another.

speed (spēd), *n., v.,* **sped** or **speed ed, speed ing.** *—n.* 1 swift or rapid movement; swiftness: *work with speed.* See **hurry** for synonym study. 2 rate of movement: *regulate the speed of machines.* 3 an arrangement of gears to give a certain rate of movement. An automobile usually has three speeds forward and one backward. 4 ARCHAIC. good luck; success. 5 SLANG. amphetamine. *—v.t.* 1 make go fast; hasten: *Let's all help speed the work.* 2 send fast; hurry: *speed reinforcements to the front.* 3 help forward; promote: *speed an undertaking.* 4 ARCHAIC. give success or prosperity to: *God speed you.* *—v.i.* 1 go fast: *The boat sped over the water.* 2 go faster than is safe or lawful. 3 ARCHAIC. succeed.

speed up, go or cause to go faster; increase in speed; accelerate.

[Old English *spēd* luck, success]

speed boat (spēd′bōt′), *n.* motorboat built to go fast.

speed er (spē′dər), *n.* person or thing that speeds, especially a person who drives an automobile at a higher speed than is safe or lawful.

speed i ly (spē′də lē), *adv.* quickly; with speed; soon.

speed i ness (spē′dē nis), *n.* speedy quality; quickness; rapidity.

speed om e ter (spē dom′ə tər), *n.* instrument to indicate the speed of an automobile or other vehicle, and often the distance traveled.

speed ster (spēd′stər), *n.* 1 speeder. 2 speedboat, racing or sports car, or the like.

speed up (spēd′up′), *n.* an increase in speed, as in some process or work.

speed way (spēd′wā′), *n.* road or track for fast driving.

speed well (spēd′wel), *n.* any of a genus of low plants of the same family as the figwort, with small blue, purple, pink, or white flowers; veronica.

speed y (spē′dē), *adj.,* **speed i er, speed i est.** moving, going, or acting with speed; fast; swift.

spe le o log i cal (spē′lē ə loj′ə kəl), *adj.* of or having to do with speleology.

spe le ol o gist (spē′lē ol′ə jist), *n.* an expert in speleology.

spe le ol o gy (spē′lē ol′ə jē), *n.* the scientific study of caves. [< Greek *spēlaion* cave]

spell[1] (spel), *v.,* **spelled** or **spelt, spell ing.** *—v.t.* 1 write or say the letters of (a word) in order. 2 (of letters) make up or form (a word): *"c," "a," "t," spell cat.* 3 amount to; mean: *Delay spells danger.* 4 Often, **spell out.** read slowly or with difficulty: *spell out a message.* 5 **spell out,** explain carefully, step by step, and in detail. *—v.i.* write or say the letters of a word in order: *She can spell well.* [< Old French *espeller;* of Germanic origin]

spell[2] (spel), *n.* 1 word or set of words supposed to have magic power; incantation. 2 magic influence; fascination; charm. 3 **cast a spell on,** a put under the influence of a spell. b fascinate. 4 **under a spell,** a controlled by a spell. b fascinated; spellbound. *—v.t.* charm; bewitch. [Old English, story]

spell[3] (spel), *n.* 1 period of work or duty: *The sailor's spell at the wheel was four hours.* 2 period or time of anything: *a spell of coughing, a spell of hot weather.* 3 INFORMAL. a brief period: *rest for a spell.* 4 relief of one person by another in doing something. *—v.t.* 1 INFORMAL. work in place of (another) for a while; relieve: *spell another person at rowing a boat.* 2 give a time of rest to; rest. [Old English *spelian,* verb]

hat, āge, fär; let, ēqual, tėrm;
it, īce; hot, ōpen, ôrder;
oil, out; cup, pu̇t, rüle;
ch, child; ng, long; sh, she;
th, thin; ᴛʜ, then; zh, measure;

ə represents *a* in about, *e* in taken,
i in pencil, *o* in lemon, *u* in circus.

< = from, derived from, taken from.

spell bind (spel′bīnd′), *v.,* **-bound, -bind ing.** make spellbound; fascinate; enchant.

spell bind er (spel′bīn′dər), *n.* U.S. speaker who can hold his listeners spellbound.

spell bound (spel′bound′), *adj.* too interested to move; fascinated; enchanted.

spell er (spel′ər), *n.* 1 person who spells words. 2 book for teaching spelling.

spell ing (spel′ing), *n.* 1 the writing or saying of the letters of a word in order. 2 the way a word is spelled: *"Ax" has two spellings, "ax" and "axe."*

spelling bee, U.S. contest in spelling.

spelt[1] (spelt), *v.* a pt. and a pp. of **spell**[1].

spelt[2] (spelt), *n.* species of wheat grown chiefly in Europe, now chiefly used to develop new varieties. [Old English < Late Latin *spelta*]

spel ter (spel′tər), *n.* zinc, usually in the form of small bars. [origin uncertain]

spe lunk er (spi lung′kər), *n.* person who explores and maps caves as a hobby. [< Latin *spelunca* cave < Greek *spēlaion*]

spe lunk ing (spi lung′king), *n.* act or hobby of exploring and mapping caves.

Spen cer (spen′sər), *n.* **Herbert,** 1820-1903, English philosopher.

spend (spend), *v.,* **spent, spend ing.** *—v.t.* 1 pay out: *She spends one dollar a day for lunch.* See synonym study below. 2 use (labor, material, thought, etc.) to some purpose; use: *Don't spend any more time on that job.* 3 pass (time, etc.): *spend a day at the beach.* 4 use up; wear out; exhaust: *The storm has spent its force.* 5 waste; squander: *He spent his fortune on horse racing.* *—v.i.* pay out money: *Earn before you spend.* [Old English *-spendan* (as in *forspendan* use up) < Latin *expendere.* Doublet of EXPEND.] **—spend′a ble,** *adj.* **—spend′er,** *n.*

Syn. *v.t.* 1 **Spend, expend, disburse** mean to pay out money. **Spend** is the common word: *She spends all she earns.* **Expend** is used chiefly of paying out large amounts for definite and serious purposes: *The United States has expended vast sums to strengthen her allies.* **Disburse** implies the payment from a fund for definite purposes in authorized amounts: *The treasurer reports what he disburses.*

spend thrift (spend′thrift′), *n.* person who spends money extravagantly or wastefully. *—adj.* wastefully extravagant.

Spen ser (spen′sər), *n.* **Edmund,** 1552?-1599, English poet, author of *The Faerie Queene.*

Spen ser i an (spen sir′ē ən), *adj.* of, having to do with, or characteristic of Spenser or his work.

Spenserian stanza, stanza used by Spenser in *The Faerie Queene,* consisting of eight iambic pentameter lines and a final alexandrine, with three rhymes arranged thus: ababbcbcc.

spent (spent), *v.* pt. and pp. of **spend.** —*adj.* 1 used up. 2 worn out; tired.

sperm[1] (spėrm), *n.* 1 sperm cell; spermatozoon. 2 semen. [< Greek *sperma* seed < *speirein* to sow]

sperm[2] (spėrm), *n.* 1 spermaceti. 2 sperm whale. 3 sperm oil. [short for *spermaceti*]

sper ma cet i (spėr′mə set′ē, spėr′mə-sē′tē), *n.* a pale, waxy substance obtained from sperm oil and used in making fine candles, ointments, cosmetics, etc. [< Medieval Latin *sperma ceti* sperm of a whale]

sper mat ic (spər mat′ik), *adj.* 1 of sperm; seminal; generative. 2 of a sperm-producing gland.

sper ma tid (spėr′mə tid), *n.* cell that develops into a spermatozoon. It results from the meiotic division of a spermatocyte.

spermato-, *combining form.* seed; sperm: *Spermatocyte = a sperm cell.* [< Greek *sperma, spermatos*]

sper ma to cyte (spėr′mə tə sīt), *n.* a germ cell that gives rise to spermatozoids or to spermatozoa.

sper ma to gen e sis (spėr′mə tō jen′ə-sis), *n.* the formation and development of spermatozoa.

sper ma to go ni um (spėr′mə tō gō′nē-əm), *n., pl.* **-ni a** (-nē ə), **-ni ums.** a primitive germ cell that divides and gives rise to spermatocytes. [< *spermato-* + Greek *-gonos* producing]

sper ma to phyte (spėr′mə tə fīt′), *n.* any of a division of the most highly developed plants that produce seeds, including both the angiosperms and the gymnosperms, forming the largest division of the plant kingdom.

sper ma to zo id (spėr′mə tə zō′id), *n.* (in botany) one of the tiny motile male gametes produced in an antheridium.

sper ma to zo on (spėr′mə tə zō′ən), *n., pl.* **-zo a** (-zō′ə). sperm cell.

sperm cell, a male reproductive cell; spermatozoon. A sperm cell unites with an ovum to fertilize it.

sperm oil, a light-yellow oil from the sperm whale, used for lubricating delicate mechanisms.

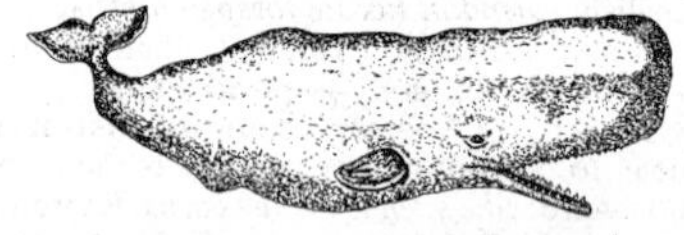

sperm whale—up to 60 ft. long

sperm whale, a large, square-headed, toothed whale that has a large cavity in its head filled with sperm oil and spermaceti; cachalot.

spew (spyü), *v.t., v.i.* throw out; cast forth; vomit. —*n.* something that is spewed; vomit. Also, **spue.** [Old English *spīwan*] **—spew′-er,** *n.*

Spey er (shpī′ər), *n.* city in SW West Germany, site of three church diets during the Reformation. 41,000. Also, **Spires.**

Spe zia (spāt′syä), *n.* See **La Spezia.**

sp. gr., specific gravity.

sphag num (sfag′nəm), *n.* 1 any of a genus of soft mosses, found chiefly in boggy or swampy places, which, when decomposed and compacted, form peat. 2 a mass or quantity of this moss used by florists in potting and packing plants. [< New Latin < Greek *sphagnos* kind of moss]

sphal e rite (sfal′ə rīt′, sfā′lə rīt′), *n.* the main ore of zinc, a native zinc sulfide; blende; zinc blende. *Formula:* ZnS [< Greek *sphaleros* deceptive, slippery]

sphe noid (sfē′noid), *adj.* 1 wedge-shaped: *a sphenoid crystal.* 2 of or having to do with a compound bone of the base of the skull. —*n.* this bone. [< Greek *sphēnoeides* < *sphēn* wedge + *eidos* form]

sphere (sfir), *n.* 1 a round solid figure whose surface is at all points equally distant from the center. 2 any rounded body approximately of this form; ball or globe. 3 any of the stars or planets. 4 place or surroundings in which a person or thing exists, acts, works, etc.: *People used to say that woman's sphere was the home.* 5 the whole province, domain, or range of a quality, thing, action, activity, etc.; extent: *England's sphere of influence.* 6 a place, position, or rank in society: *the sphere of the aristocracy.* 7 a supposed hollow globe, with the earth at its center, enclosing the stars, sun, and planets. 8 any one of a series of such globes, one inside another, in which the stars and planets were supposed by ancient astronomers to be set. Movement of the spheres was believed to cause the stars and planets to revolve around the earth. 9 the heavens; the sky. [< Greek *sphaira*]

spher i cal (sfir′ə kəl, sfer′ə kəl), *adj.* 1 shaped like a sphere. 2 of or having to do with a sphere or spheres. **—spher′i cal ly,** *adv.*

spherical aberration, aberration of rays of light resulting in a blurred or indistinct image, and arising from the spherical shape of the lens or mirror.

sphe ric i ty (sfi ris′ə tē), *n., pl.* **-ties.** spherical form or quality; roundness.

spher oid (sfir′oid), *n.* body shaped somewhat like a sphere, but not perfectly round.

sphe roi dal (sfi roi′dl), *adj.* shaped somewhat like a sphere. **—sphe roi′dal ly,** *adv.*

spher ule (sfir′ül, sfer′ül), *n.* a small sphere or spherical body.

sphinc ter (sfingk′tər), *n.* a ringlike muscle that surrounds an opening or passage of the body, and can contract to close it. [< Greek *sphinktēr* < *sphingein* to squeeze]

sphinx (sfingks), *n.* 1 statue of a lion's body with the head of a man, ram, or hawk. 2 **the Great Sphinx,** a huge statue with a man's head and a lion's body, near Cairo, Egypt. 3 **Sphinx,** (in Greek myths) a monster with the head of a woman, the body of a lion, and wings. The Sphinx proposed a riddle to every passer-by and killed those unable to answer it. 4 a puzzling or mysterious person; enigma. 5 hawk moth. [< Greek]

sphyg mo ma nom e ter (sfig′mō-mə nom′ə tər), *n.* instrument for measuring blood pressure, especially in an artery. [< Greek *sphygmos* throbbing, pulse + *manos* at intervals + English *-meter*]

Spi ca (spī′kə), *n.* a very bright star in the constellation Virgo.

spi cate (spī′kāt), *adj.* (in botany) having spikes; arranged in spikes; having the form of a spike. [< Latin *spicatum* furnished with spikes < *spica* spike[2]]

spice (spīs), *n., v.,* **spiced, spic ing.** —*n.* 1 any of various more or less strongly flavored or scented substances obtained from plants and used to season food. Pepper, cinnamon, cloves, ginger, and nutmeg are common spices. 2 a spicy, fragrant odor. 3 something that adds flavor or interest. —*v.t.* 1 put spice in; season. 2 add flavor or interest to. [< Old French *espice,* ultimately < Latin *species* sort. Doublet of SPECIES.]

spice bush (spīs′bu̇sh′), *n.* a North American shrub of the same family as the laurel, with yellow flowers and spicy-smelling bark.

Spice Islands, Moluccas.

spick-and-span (spik′ən span′), *adj.* 1 neat and clean; spruce or smart; trim: *a spick-and-span room.* 2 fresh or new; brand-new. [short for *spick-and-span-new* < *spick* (variant of *spike*[1]) + *span* < Scandinavian (Old Icelandic) *spann* chip]

spic u late (spik′yə lāt, spik′yə lit), *adj.* 1 having or consisting of spicules. 2 slender and sharp-pointed.

spic ule (spik′yül), *n.* 1 a small, slender, sharp-pointed piece, usually bony or crystalline. 2 one of such pieces that form the skeleton of a sponge. 3 spikelet. [< Latin *spiculum* sharp point, diminutive of *spica* spike[2]]

spic y (spī′sē), *adj.,* **spic i er, spic i est.** 1 flavored with spice: *spicy cookies.* 2 sharp and fragrant: *a spicy smell.* 3 lively; keen: *spicy conversation.* 4 somewhat improper: *a spicy joke.* 5 producing spices; rich in spices. **—spic′i ly,** *adv.* **—spic′i ness,** *n.*

spi der (spī′dər), *n.* 1 any of an order of eight-legged, wingless arachnids, having an unsegmented body and abdominal organs that produce a silky thread for spinning webs to catch insects for food, making cocoons, etc. 2 something like or suggesting a spider. 3 kind of frying pan with a handle, originally one with short legs. [Middle English *spither,* related to Old English *spinnan* to spin] **—spi′der like′,** *adj.*

spider monkey, any of a genus of monkeys of South and Central America, having a long, slim body and limbs, a long, prehensile tail, and rudimentary thumbs or none at all.

spider web, 1 web spun by a spider; cobweb. 2 any design or construction of interwoven lines or parts similar to a spider web.

sphinx (def. 1) sphinx (def. 3)

spi der wort (spī′dər wėrt′), *n.* any of a genus of plants having clusters of blue, purple, or white flowers, especially a trailing species that takes root at the knots of its stems.

spi der y (spī′dər ē), *adj.* 1 long and thin like a spider's legs. 2 suggesting a spider web. 3 full of, or infested with, spiders.

spied (spīd), *v.* pt. and pp. of **spy.**

spie gel ei sen (spē′gəl ī′zn), *n.* variety of pig iron containing 15 to 30 per cent of manganese, used in making steel. [< German *Spiegeleisen* < *Spiegel* mirror + *Eisen* iron]

spiel (spēl), SLANG. —*n.* a talk; speech; harangue, especially one of a cheap, noisy nature. —*v.i., v.t.* talk; speak; say in or as a spiel. [< German *spielen* to play] **—spiel′er,** *n.*

spi er (spī′ər), *n.* spy.

spiff y (spif′ē), *adj.,* **spiff i er, spiff i est.**

hat, āge, fär; let, ēqual, tėrm;
it, īce; hot, ōpen, ôrder;
oil, out; cup, pu̇t, rüle;
ch, child; ng, long; sh, she;
th, thin; ᴛʜ, then; zh, measure;

ə represents *a* in about, *e* in taken, *i* in pencil, *o* in lemon, *u* in circus.

< = from, derived from, taken from.

SLANG. smart; neat; trim. [origin uncertain]

spig ot (spig′ət, spik′it), *n.* 1 valve for controlling the flow of water or other liquid from a pipe, tank, barrel, etc. 2 U.S. faucet. 3 peg or plug used to stop the small hole of a cask, barrel, or keg; bung; spile. [Middle English]

spike¹ (spīk), *n., v.,* **spiked, spik ing.** —*n.* 1 a large, strong nail. 2 a sharp-pointed piece or part: *a fence with spikes, shoes with spikes.* 3 **spikes,** *pl.* a pair of shoes fitted with spikes, used in baseball, track, and other sports to prevent slipping. 4 antler of a young deer, when straight and without snag or tine. 5 (in physics) a sudden, sharp uprise or peak in a motion, voltage, current, etc. 6 any tip or high point on a linear graph. —*v.t.* 1 fasten with spikes: *When laying the track, the men spiked the rails to the ties.* 2 provide with spikes: *spiked shoes.* 3 pierce or injure with a spike. 4 put (a cannon) out of operation by driving a spike into the touchhole. 5 put an end or stop to; block; thwart: *spike an attempt.* 6 INFORMAL. add liquor to (a drink, etc.). [< Scandinavian (Old Icelandic) *spīkr*] **—spike′like′,** *adj.*

spike² (spīk), *n.* 1 ear of grain. 2 a long, pointed cluster of sessile flowers. See **inflorescence** for picture. [< Latin *spica*]

spike heel, a high, usually narrow and tapered heel on a woman's shoe; stiletto heel.

spike let (spīk′lit), *n.* a small spike or flower cluster, especially a small spike in the compound inflorescence of grasses or sedges.

spike nard (spīk′nərd, spīk′närd), *n.* 1 a sweet-smelling ointment used by the ancients. 2 the fragrant East Indian plant of the same family as the valerian, from which this ointment was probably obtained; nard. 3 a tall American herb of the same family as the ginseng, having greenish flowers and a fragrant root. [< Medieval Latin *spica nardi* spike of nard]

spik y (spī′kē), *adj.,* **spik i er, spik i est.** 1 having spikes; set with sharp, projecting points. 2 having the shape of a spike.

spile (spīl), *n., v.,* **spiled, spil ing.** —*n.* 1 bung; spigot. 2 U.S. spout for drawing off sap from the sugar maple. 3 a heavy stake or beam driven into the ground as a support; pile. —*v.t.* 1 stop up (a hole) with a plug. 2 furnish with a spout. 3 furnish, strengthen, or support with stakes or piles. [probably < Middle Dutch or Middle Low German]

spill¹ (spil), *v.,* **spilled** or **spilt, spill ing,** *n.* —*v.t.* 1 let (liquid or any matter in loose pieces) run or fall: *spill milk, spill salt.* 2 scatter; disperse. 3 shed (blood). 4 INFORMAL. cause to fall from a horse, car, boat, etc. 5 let wind out of (a sail). 6 SLANG. make known; tell: *spill a secret.* —*v.i.* fall or flow out: *Water spilled from the pail.* —*n.* 1 a spilling. 2 quantity spilled. 3 INFORMAL. a fall. 4 spillway. [Old English *spillan* destroy, kill] **—spill′a ble,** *adj.* **—spill′er,** *n.*

spill² (spil), *n.* 1 a thin piece of wood or a folded or twisted piece of paper, used to light a candle, pipe, etc. 2 splinter. 3 spindle. 4 spile; spigot. [Middle English *spille*]

spill age (spil′ij), *n.* 1 a spilling. 2 quantity spilled.

spil li kin (spil′ə kən), *n.* jackstraw. [< *spill²*]

spill way (spil′wā′), *n.* channel or passage for the escape of surplus water from a dam, river, etc.

spilt (spilt), *v.* a pt. and a pp. of **spill¹**.

spin (spin), *v.,* **spun** or (ARCHAIC) **span, spun, spin ning,** *n.* —*v.t.* 1 cause to turn or revolve rapidly; rotate: *spin a top.* 2 draw out and twist (cotton, flax, wool, etc.) into thread, either by hand or by machinery. 3 make (thread, yarn, etc.) by drawing out and twisting cotton, flax, wool, etc. 4 make (a thread, web, cocoon, etc.) by giving out from the body sticky material that hardens into thread. A spider spins a web. 5 produce or tell (a story, tale, etc.): *spin yarns.* 6 **spin out,** make long and slow; draw out; prolong: *spin out negotiations.* 7 make (glass, gold, etc.) into thread. 8 shape on a lathe or wheel. —*v.i.* 1 turn or revolve rapidly; rotate: *The wheel spins round.* 2 feel dizzy or giddy: *My head is spinning.* 3 run, ride, drive, etc., rapidly: *The automobile spun over the smooth expressway.* 4 draw out and twist the fibers of cotton, flax, wool, etc., into thread. 5 produce a thread, web, cocoon, etc., from a sticky material, as spiders do.
—*n.* 1 a spinning. 2 a twisting or spinning motion, as of a ball when thrown, struck, etc. 3 a rapid run, ride, drive, etc.: *Come for a spin on your bicycle.* 4 a rapid descent, often uncontrollable, of an airplane in a spiral path. [Old English *spinnan*]

spin ach (spin′ich), *n.* 1 plant of the same family as the goosefoot, whose green leaves are cooked and eaten as a vegetable, or used uncooked in a salad. 2 its leaves. [< Old French *espinache* < Spanish *espinaca* < Arabic *isbānakh*]

spi nal (spī′nl), *adj.* of, having to do with, or in the region of the spine or backbone. —*n.* INFORMAL. a spinal anesthetic. **—spi′nal ly,** *adv.*

spinal column, backbone.

spinal cord, the thick, whitish cord of nerve tissue which extends from the medulla oblongata down through most of the backbone and from which nerves to various parts of the body branch off.

spin dle (spin′dl), *n., v.,* **-dled, -dling.** —*n.* 1 the rod or pin used in spinning to twist, wind, and hold thread. 2 any rod or pin that turns around, or on which something turns. Axles and shafts are spindles. 3 something shaped like a spindle. 4 (in biology) the group of achromatic fibers along which the chromosomes are arranged during mitosis. 5 one of the turned or circular, supporting parts of a baluster or stair rail. —*v.i.* 1 grow very long and thin. 2 (of a plant) to shoot up or grow into a long, slender stalk or stem. [Old English *spinel,* related to *spinnan* to spin]

spin dle-leg ged (spin′dl leg′id, spin′dl-legd′), *adj.* having long, thin legs.

spin dle legs (spin′dl legz′), *n.* 1 *pl. in form and use.* long, thin legs. 2 *pl. in form, sing. in use.* INFORMAL. person with long, thin legs.

spin dle-shanked (spin′dl shangkt′), *adj.* spindle-legged.

spin dle shanks (spin′dl shangks′), *n.* spindlelegs.

spin dling (spind′ling), *adj.* very long and slender; too tall and thin: *a weak, spindling plant.*

spin dly (spind′lē), *adj.,* **-dli er, -dli est.** spindling.

spin drift (spin′drift′), *n.* spray blown or dashed up from the waves. Also, **spoondrift.**

spine (spīn), *n.* 1 backbone. 2 anything like a backbone; long, narrow ridge or support. 3 courage, determination, etc. 4 a stiff, sharp-pointed growth on plants or animals. The thorns of a cactus and the quills of a porcupine are spines. 5 the supporting back portion of a book cover. [< Latin *spina,* originally, thorn] **—spine′like′,** *adj.*

spined (spīnd), *adj.* having a spine or spines.

spi nel (spi nel′, spin′l), *n.* a crystalline mineral, consisting chiefly of oxides of magnesium and aluminum, that occurs in various colors. Transparent spinel is used for jewelry. [ultimately < Latin *spina* thorn]

spine less (spīn′lis), *adj.* 1 having no backbone; invertebrate. 2 without courage, determination, etc.: *a spineless coward.* 3 having no spines: *a spineless cactus.* **—spine′less ly,** *adv.* **—spine′less ness,** *n.*

spin et (spin′it), *n.* 1 an old-fashioned musical instrument like a small harpsichord. 2 a compact upright piano. [< Italian *spinetta,* probably < Giovanni *Spinetti,* Italian inventor of the 1500's]

spin na ker (spin′ə kər), *n.* a large, triangular sail set on the side opposite the mainsail on a yacht, sloop, etc., when sailing with the wind. [origin uncertain]

spin ner (spin′ər), *n.* 1 person, animal, or thing that spins. 2 a revolving hook or lure used in trolling or casting.

spin ner et (spin′ə ret′), *n.* 1 organ by which spiders and certain insect larvae such as silkworms spin their threads. 2 Also, **spinnerette.** a small, metal device with tiny holes used to form filaments or threads in the production of synthetic fibers. [diminutive of *spinner*]

spin ney (spin′ē), *n., pl.* **-neys.** BRITISH. a small wood with undergrowth, especially one for sheltering game birds; thicket. [< Old French *espinée,* ultimately < Latin *spina* thorn]

spin ning (spin′ing), *adj.* that spins: *a spinning top.* —*n.* act of a person or thing that spins.

spinning jenny, an early type of spinning machine having several spindles, set in motion by a band from one wheel, whereby one person could spin a number of threads at the same time; jenny.

spinning wheel

spinning wheel, a large wheel operated by hand or foot and having a spindle, formerly used for spinning cotton, flax, wool, etc., into thread or yarn.

spin-off (spin′ôf′, spin′of′), *n.* distribution of the stocks of a new or subsidiary company among the stockholders of the controlling company.

spi nose (spī′nōs), *adj.* spinous. **—spi′nose ly,** *adv.*

spi nous (spī′nəs), *adj.* 1 covered with spines; having spines; thorny. 2 spinelike; sharp.

Spi no za (spə nō′zə), *n.* **Baruch** or **Benedict,** 1632-1677, Dutch philosopher.

spin ster (spin′stər), *n.* 1 an unmarried woman. 2 an elderly woman who has not married; old maid. 3 woman who spins flax, wool, etc., into thread.

spin ster hood (spin′stər hůd), *n.* condition of being a spinster.

spi nule (spī′nyül, spin′yül), *n.* a small, sharp-pointed spine.

spin y (spī′nē), *adj.,* **spin i er, spin i est.** 1 covered with or having spines; thorny: *a spiny cactus, a spiny porcupine.* 2 stiff and sharp-pointed; spinelike. 3 difficult; troublesome. **—spin′i ness,** *n.*

spiny anteater, echidna.

spiny lobster, any of various lobsters much like the usual kind but lacking the enlarged pair of claws.

spi ra cle (spī′rə kəl, spir′ə kəl), *n.* a small opening for breathing, as the blowhole of a whale. Insects take in air through tiny spiracles. [< Latin *spiraculum* < *spirare* breathe]

spi rae a (spī rē′ə), *n.* any of a genus of shrubs of the rose family that have clusters of small white, pink, or red flowers with five petals. Also, **spirea.** [< Latin < Greek *speiraia*]

spi ral (spī′rəl), *n., adj., v.,* **-raled, -ral ing** or **-ralled, -ral ling.** *—n.* 1 a winding and gradually widening curve or coil. A watch spring and the thread of a screw are spirals. 2 helix. 3 one of the separate circles or coils of a spiral object. 4 a continuous and expanding increase or decrease in prices, wages, employment, etc.: *an inflationary spiral.* 5 descent of an airplane in a spiral path. *—adj.* 1 winding or coiling: *A snail's shell has a spiral shape.* 2 coiled in a cylindrical or conical manner; helical. 3 having to do with or like a spiral or coil. *—v.i.* move in a spiral. *—v.t.* form into a spiral. [< Medieval Latin *spiralis* < Latin *spira* a coil < Greek *speira*] **—spi′ral ly,** *adv.*

spiral galaxy or **spiral nebula,** galaxy appearing as one or more spiraling streams issuing from a center.

spi rant (spī′rənt), *n., adj.* fricative. [< Latin *spirantem* breathing]

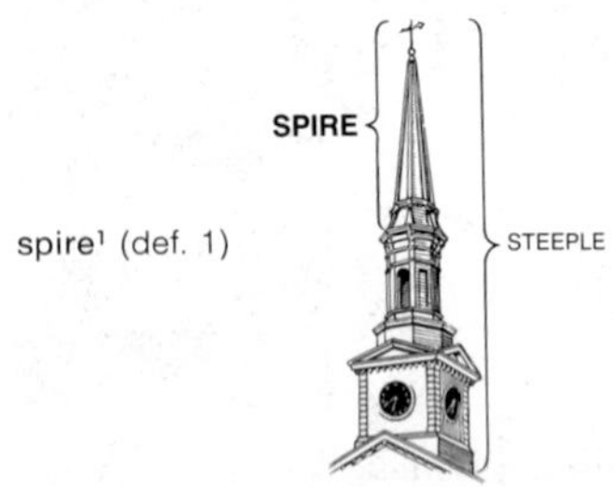

spire[1] (def. 1)

spire[1] (spīr), *n., v.,* **spired, spir ing.** *—n.* 1 the top part of a tower or steeple that narrows to a point. 2 steeple. 3 anything tapering and pointed: *the rocky spires of the mountains.* *—v.i.* shoot up. *—v.t.* furnish with a spire. [Old English *spīr* spike, blade] **—spire′like′,** *adj.*

spire[2] (spīr), *n.* 1 a coil; spiral. 2 a single twist of a coil or spiral. 3 the upper part of a spiral shell. [< Latin *spira* < Greek *speira*]

spi re a (spī rē′ə), *n.* spiraea.

spi reme (spī′rēm′), *n.* the threadlike coils appearing in the nucleus of a cell at the beginning of the prophase of mitosis, which give rise to the chromosomes. [< Greek *speirama* a coiling]

Spires (spīrz), *n.* English name of **Speyer.**

spi ril lum (spī ril′əm), *n., pl.* **-ril la** (-ril′ə). 1 any of a genus of bacteria having long, rigid, spirally twisted forms and bearing a tuft of flagella. 2 any of various spirally twisted microorganisms. [< New Latin < Latin *spira* spire[2]]

spir it (spir′it), *n.* 1 the immaterial part of man; soul: *be present in spirit, though absent in body.* 2 man's moral, religious, or emotional nature. 3 a supernatural being, such as a deity, fairy, elf, ghost, etc.: *an evil spirit.* 4 **the Spirit, a** God. **b** the Holy Ghost. 5 Often, **spirits,** *pl.* state of mind; disposition; temper: *be in good spirits.* 6 person; personality: *a brave spirit.* 7 influence that stirs up and rouses: *a spirit of reform, the spirit of independence.* 8 courage; vigor; liveliness: *a horse with great spirit.* 9 **out of spirits,** sad or gloomy. 10 enthusiasm and loyalty: *school spirit.* 11 the real meaning or intent: *the spirit of the law.* 12 the prevailing character, quality, or tendency: *the spirit of our institutions.* 13 Often, **spirits,** *pl.* solution of a volatile substance in alcohol: *spirits of camphor.* 14 Often, **spirits,** *pl.* a strong alcoholic liquor obtained by distilling, as whiskey, brandy, gin, etc.
—v.t. 1 carry (away or off) secretly: *spirit a person away from a place.* 2 stir up; encourage; cheer. 3 conjure (up).
—adj. of or having to do with spirits or spiritualism.
[< Latin *spiritus,* originally, breath, related to *spirare* breathe. Doublet of SPRITE.]

spir it ed (spir′ə tid), *adj.* full of energy and spirit; lively; dashing. **—spir′it ed ly,** *adv.* **—spir′it ed ness,** *n.*

spir it ism (spir′ə tiz′əm), *n.* spiritualism.

spirit lamp, lamp in which alcohol is burned.

spir it less (spir′it lis), *adj.* without spirit, courage, or vigor; depressed; dejected.

spirit level, instrument used to find out whether a surface is level, using an air bubble in an alcohol-filled glass tube. When the air bubble is exactly in the middle of the tube, the surface is level.

spir i tu al (spir′ə chü əl), *adj.* 1 of or having to do with the spirit or soul. 2 caring much for things of the spirit or soul. 3 of or having to do with spirits; supernatural. 4 having to do with the church. 5 sacred; religious. *—n.* a sacred song or hymn as originally created or interpreted by the Negroes of the southern United States. **—spir′i tu al ly,** *adv.* **—spir′i tu al ness,** *n.*

spir i tu al ism (spir′ə chü ə liz′əm), *n.* 1 belief that spirits of the dead communicate with the living, especially through persons called mediums; spiritism. 2 the doctrine that spirit alone is real. 3 spiritual quality.

spir i tu al ist (spir′ə chü ə list), *n.* person who believes that the dead communicate with the living.

spir i tu al is tic (spir′ə chü ə lis′tik), *adj.* of or having to do with spiritualism or spiritualists.

spir i tu al i ty (spir′ə chü al′ə tē), *n., pl.* **-ties.** devotion to spiritual instead of worldly things; spiritual quality.

spir i tu al ize (spir′ə chü ə līz), *v.t.,* **-ized, -iz ing.** 1 make spiritual. 2 explain or understand in a spiritual sense. **—spir′i tu al i za′tion,** *n.*

spir i tu el (spir′ə chü el′), *adj.* showing a refined mind or wit. [< French, literally, spiritual]

spir i tu elle (spir′ə chü el′), *adj.* 1 spirituel. 2 delicate; graceful.

spir i tu ous (spir′ə chü əs), *adj.* 1 containing alcohol; alcoholic. 2 distilled, not fermented.

spi ro che tal (spī′rō kē′tl), *adj.* of or having to do with spirochetes.

spi ro chete (spī′rə kēt′), *n.* any of an order of bacteria that are slender, spiral, and able to expand and contract. One kind causes syphilis, and another causes relapsing fever. [< Greek *speira* coil + *chaitē* hair]

spi ro gy ra (spī′rə jī′rə), *n.* any of a large genus of green algae that grow in scumlike masses in freshwater ponds or tanks. The cells have one or more bands of chlorophyll winding spirally to the right. [< Greek *speira* coil + *gyros* circle]

spi rom e ter (spī rom′ə tər), *n.* instrument for measuring the capacity of the lungs. [< Latin *spirare* breathe + English *-meter*]

spirt (spėrt), *v.i., v.t., n.* spurt.

spir y (spī′rē), *adj.* 1 having the form of a spire; tapering. 2 having many spires.

spit[1] (spit), *v.,* **spat** or **spit, spit ting,** *n.* *—v.i.* 1 throw out saliva from the mouth. 2 make a spitting or hissing sound: *The cat spits when angry.* 3 rain or snow slightly. *—v.t.* 1 throw out from the mouth. 2 throw out: *The gun spits fire.* *—n.* 1 saliva. 2 sound or act of spitting. 3 a frothy or spitlike secretion given off by some insects. 4 light rain or snow. 5 **the spit of,** INFORMAL. just like. [Old English *spittan*] **—spit′ter,** *n.*

spit[2] (spit), *n., v.,* **spit ted, spit ting.** *—n.* 1 a sharp-pointed, slender rod or bar on which meat is roasted or broiled. 2 a narrow point of land running into the water. *—v.t.* 1 run a spit through; put on a spit. 2 pierce; stab. [Old English *spitu*]

spit and image, INFORMAL. spitting image.

spit and polish, INFORMAL. great or too much attention to neatness, orderliness, and smart appearance. **—spit′-and-pol′ish,** *adj.*

spit ball (spit′bôl′), *n.* U.S. 1 a small ball of chewed-up paper, used as a missile. 2 (in baseball) an illegal curve thrown by the pitcher after moistening one side of the ball with saliva.

spite (spīt), *n., v.,* **spit ed, spit ing.** *—n.* 1 desire to annoy or harm another; ill will. See synonym study below. 2 **in spite of,** not prevented by; notwithstanding. *—v.t.* show ill will toward; annoy; irritate: *They left their yard dirty to spite the people who lived next door.* [Middle English, short for *despite*] **—spite′less,** *adj.*

Syn. *n.* 1 **Spite, malice, grudge** mean ill will against another. **Spite** suggests envy or mean disposition, and applies to active ill will shown by doing mean, petty things to hurt or annoy: *He ruined her flowers out of spite.* **Malice** emphasizes actual wish or intention to injure, and suggests hatred or, especially, a disposition delighting in doing harm or seeing others hurt: *Many gossips are motivated by malice.* **Grudge** suggests wishing to get even for real or imagined injury, and applies to ill will nursed a long time: *She bears grudges.*

spite ful (spīt′fəl), *adj.* full of spite; eager to

hat, āge, fär; let, ēqual, tėrm;
it, ice; hot, ōpen, ôrder;
oil, out; cup, pu̇t, rüle;
ch, child; ng, long; sh, she;
th, thin; ᴛʜ, then; zh, measure;

ə represents *a* in about, *e* in taken,
i in pencil, *o* in lemon, *u* in circus.

< = from, derived from, taken from.

annoy or irritate; behaving with ill will and malice. **—spite′ful ly,** *adv.* **—spite′ful ness,** *n.*

spit fire (spit′fīr′), *n.* person, especially a woman or girl, who has a quick and fiery temper.

Spits ber gen (spits′bėr′gən), *n.* group of Norwegian islands in the Arctic Ocean, north of Norway. 3000 pop.; 24,300 sq. mi.

spitting image, INFORMAL. the exact likeness; spit and image: *She is the spitting image of her mother.*

spit tle (spit′l), *n.* 1 saliva; spit. 2 the secretion produced by some insects.

spittle insect, any of various insects whose larvae cover themselves with a protective foamy secretion.

spit toon (spi tün′), *n.* container to spit into; cuspidor.

spitz (spits), *n.* any of various sturdy, small dogs with pointed muzzle and ears, long hair, and a tail curled up over the back, especially a white variety of Pomeranian. [< German *Spitz* < *spitz* pointed]

spiv (spiv), *n.* BRITISH SLANG. person who makes his living by petty thievery, blackmail, etc. [perhaps related to SPIFFY]

splash (splash), *v.t.* 1 cause (water, mud, etc.) to fly about. 2 cause to scatter a liquid about: *He splashed the oars as he rowed.* 3 wet, spatter, or soil: *Our car is all splashed with mud.* 4 make (one's way) with splashing: *The boat splashed its way up the river.* 5 mark with spots or patches: *The careless painter splashed the furniture.* *—v.i.* 1 dash water, mud, etc., about. 2 dash in scattered masses or drops: *Muddy water splashed on our windshield.* 3 fall, move, or go with splashing: *The dog splashed across the brook.* *—n.* 1 act, result, or sound of splashing. 2 spot of liquid splashed upon a thing. 3 a large or uneven patch or spot: *The dog is white with brown splashes.* 4 **make a splash,** INFORMAL. attract attention; cause excitement. [ultimately imitative]

splash down (splash′doun′), *n.* the landing of a capsule or other spacecraft in the ocean after reentry.

splash er (splash′ər), *n.* 1 person or thing that splashes. 2 something that protects from splashes.

splash y (splash′ē), *adj.,* **splash i er, splash i est.** 1 making a splash. 2 full of irregular spots or streaks. 3 INFORMAL. attracting attention; causing excitement. **—splash′i ly,** *adv.* **—splash′i ness,** *n.*

splat (splat), *n.* a broad, flat piece of wood, especially one forming the central upright part of the back of a chair. [origin uncertain]

splat ter (splat′ər), *v.t., v.i.* splash or spatter. *—n.* a splash or spatter.

splay (splā), *v.t.* 1 spread out; expand; extend. 2 make slanting; bevel. *—v.i.* 1 have or lie in a slanting direction; slope. 2 spread out; flare. *—adj.* 1 wide and flat; turned outward. 2 awkward; clumsy. *—n.* 1 a spread; flare. 2 surface which makes an oblique angle with another, as the beveled jamb of a window or door; a slanting surface. [Middle English *splayen,* short for *displayen* display]

splay foot (splā′fu̇t′), *n., pl.* **-feet,** *adj.* *—n.* a broad, flat foot, especially one turned outward. *—adj.* having splayfeet.

splay foot ed (splā′fu̇t′id), *adj.* 1 splayfoot. 2 awkward; clumsy.

spleen (splēn), *n.* 1 a ductless, glandlike organ at the left of the stomach in man, and near the stomach or intestine in other vertebrates, that stores blood, disintegrates old red blood cells, and helps filter foreign substances from the blood. It was once believed to cause low spirits, bad temper, and spite. 2 bad temper; spite; anger. 3 low spirits. [< Greek *splēn*]

spleen ful (splēn′fəl), *adj.* irritable; spiteful. **—spleen′ful ly,** *adv.*

splen dent (splen′dənt), *adj.* ARCHAIC. 1 shining brightly; gleaming. 2 splendid; gorgeous. [< Latin *splendentem*]

splen did (splen′did), *adj.* 1 grand in adornment, substance, etc.; magnificent; gorgeous: *a splendid palace.* 2 grand in nature or quality; glorious: *a splendid victory.* 3 grand in brightness, color, etc.; brilliant: *a splendid sunset.* See **magnificent** for synonym study. 4 very good; fine; excellent: *a splendid chance.* [< Latin *splendidus* < *splendere* be bright] **—splen′did ly,** *adv.* **—splen′did ness,** *n.*

splen dif er ous (splen dif′ər əs), *adj.* INFORMAL. splendid. **—splen dif′er ous ly,** *adv.* **—splen dif′er ous ness,** *n.*

splen dor (splen′dər), *n.* 1 great brightness; brilliant light. 2 magnificent show; pomp. 3 brilliant glory. Also, BRITISH **splendour.** [< Latin < *splendere* be bright]

splen dor ous (splen′dər əs), *adj.* full of splendor.

splen dour (splen′dər), *n.* BRITISH. splendor.

sple net ic (spli net′ik), *adj.* 1 of or having to do with the spleen. 2 bad-tempered; irritable; peevish. **—sple net′i cal ly,** *adv.*

splen ic (splen′ik, splē′nik), *adj.* of or having to do with the spleen.

splice (splīs), *v.,* **spliced, splic ing,** *n.* *—v.t.* 1 join together (ropes, etc.) by weaving together ends which have been untwisted. 2 join together (two pieces of timber) by overlapping. 3 join together (film, tape, wire, etc.) by gluing or cementing the ends. 4 INFORMAL. marry. *—n.* 1 a joining of ropes, timbers, film, etc., by splicing. 2 the joint so formed. [< Middle Dutch *splissen*] **—splic′er,** *n.*

spline (splīn), *n., v.,* **splined, splin ing.** *—n.* 1 a long, narrow, relatively thin strip of wood or metal; slat. 2 a long, flexible strip of wood or the like used as a guide in drawing curves. 3 in machinery: **a** a flat, rectangular piece or key fitting into a groove or slot between parts, as in a shaft, wheel, etc. **b** the groove for such a key. *—v.t.* 1 fit with a spline or key. 2 provide with a groove for a spline or key. [origin uncertain]

splint (splint), *n.* 1 arrangement of wood, metal, plaster, etc., to hold a broken or dislocated bone in place. 2 a thin, flexible strip of wood, such as is used in making baskets. 3 a thin metal strip or plate. Old armor often had overlapping splints to protect the elbow, knee, etc., and allow easy movement. 4 a hard, bony growth on the splint bone of a horse, mule, etc. 5 DIALECT. a splinter of wood or stone; chip. *—v.t.* 1 secure, hold in position, or support by means of a splint or splints. 2 support as if with splints. [< Middle Dutch or Middle Low German *splinte*]

splint bone, one of the two smaller bones on either side of the large bone between the hock and the fetlock of a horse, mule, etc.

splin ter (splin′tər), *n.* 1 a thin, sharp piece of wood, bone, glass, etc.; sliver: *The mirror broke into splinters.* 2 a dissenting group that breaks away from the main group. *—adj.* of or having to do with dissenting groups that break away from regular political groups, religious organizations, etc.: *a splinter party.* *—v.t., v.i.* split or be split into splinters: *He splintered the locked door with an ax. The mirror splintered.* [< Middle Dutch]

splin ter y (splin′tər ē), *adj.* 1 apt to splinter. 2 of or like a splinter. 3 rough and jagged. 4 full of splinters.

split (split), *v.,* **split, split ting,** *n., adj.* *—v.t.* 1 break or cut from end to end, or in layers; cleave: *split logs for the fireplace.* 2 rip violently; tear: *sails split by a hurricane.* 3 separate into parts; divide: *split up a tract of land into house lots.* 4 divide between two or more persons; apportion: *Let's split the cost of lunch.* 5 divide into different groups, factions, parties, etc.: *Disagreements split the club into rival factions.* 6 cast (a vote or a ballot) for candidates of different political parties in the same election. 7 divide (a molecule) into two or more individual atoms or atomic groups. 8 remove by such a process. 9 divide (an atomic nucleus) into two portions of approximately equal mass by forcing the absorption of a neutron. 10 issue a certain number of new shares of (stock) for each share currently held. *—v.i.* 1 come apart or break open by or as if by being split: *The rock split into two.* 2 separate into parts; divide. 3 divide into different groups, factions, parties, etc. 4 SLANG. go away; leave. *—n.* 1 a narrow break resulting from splitting; crack or tear; fissure: *Frost caused the split in the rock.* 2 division in a group, party, etc. 3 SLANG. share; portion: *get a split of the profits.* 4 an issuing of a certain number of new shares of stock for each currently held. 5 INFORMAL. a bottle of a drink half the usual size, about 7 fluid ounces. 6 a sweet dish made of ice cream, sliced fruit, syrup, nuts, etc.: *a banana split.* 7 Often, **splits,** *pl.* an acrobatic feat in which a performer spreads the legs in opposite directions until they are flat on the floor.
—adj. broken or cut from end to end; divided; cleft: *a split log.*
[apparently < Middle Dutch *splitten*]

split decision, decision that is not unanimous, as in a boxing match.

split infinitive, infinitive having one or more words between *to* and the verb. EXAMPLE: *That summer I learned* to really enjoy *swimming.*

split-lev el (split′lev′əl), *n.* house with two or more floor levels, each level about half a story above or below the adjacent level.

split personality, 1 INFORMAL. schizophrenia. 2 personality that shows markedly inconsistent or contradictory patterns of behavior.

split second, a very brief moment of time; instant.

split-sec ond (split′sek′ənd), *adj.* instantaneous; very quick.

split ticket, 1 ballot marked by a voter for

some candidates of one party and some candidates of another party. 2 ballot that lists candidates of more than one party.

split ting (split′ing), *adj.* 1 that splits. 2 very severe; extreme; violent: *a splitting headache.*

splotch (sploch), *n.* a large, irregular spot; splash. *—v.t.* make a splotch or splotches on. [origin uncertain]

splotch y (sploch′ē), *adj.,* **splotch i er, splotch i est.** marked with splotches.

splurge (splėrj), *n., v.,* **splurged, splurg ing.** INFORMAL. *—n.* 1 a showing off. 2 outburst. *—v.i.* 1 show off. 2 spend extravagantly. [origin uncertain]

splut ter (splut′ər), *v.i.* 1 talk in a hasty, confused way. People sometimes splutter when they are excited. 2 make spitting or popping noises; sputter: *The baked apples are spluttering in the oven.* *—v.t.* utter in a spluttering manner; say with spluttering. *—n.* a spluttering. [perhaps variant of *sputter*] **—splut′ter er,** *n.*

Spock (spok), *n.* **Benjamin McLane,** born 1903, American author, pediatrician, and leader in the antiwar movement.

Spode (spōd), *n.* 1 type of fine pottery originated by Josiah Spode, most commonly in oriental style. 2 type of fine china originated by him. 3 **Josiah,** 1754–1827, English potter.

spoil (spoil), *v.,* **spoiled** or **spoilt, spoil ing,** *n.* *—v.t.* 1 damage or injure (something) so as to make it unfit or useless; destroy. See synonym study below. 2 injure the character or disposition of, especially by being too kind, generous, etc.: *That child is being spoiled by too much attention.* 3 take by force; plunder; rob; steal. 4 **be spoiling for,** INFORMAL. be longing for (a fight, etc.); desire. *—v.i.* 1 be damaged or injured; become bad or unfit for use; decay: *The fruit spoiled because I kept it too long.* 2 plunder; rob. *—n.* 1 Often, **spoils,** *pl.* things taken by force; things won; booty; loot: *The soldiers carried the spoils back to their own land.* 2 **spoils,** *pl.* government offices and positions filled by the political party that has won an election. 3 an object of plundering; prey. [< Old French *espoillier,* ultimately < Latin *spolium* booty, spoil] **—spoil′a ble,** *adj.*

Syn. *v.t.* 1 **Spoil, ruin** mean to damage beyond repair or recovery. **Spoil** emphasizes damage that so reduces or weakens something as to make the thing useless or bring it to nothing: *spoil a film by exposing it to sunlight.* **Ruin** implies damage that results in complete destruction: *ruin one's health.*

spoil age (spoi′lij), *n.* 1 act of spoiling. 2 fact of being spoiled. 3 something spoiled.

spoil er (spoi′lər), *n.* 1 person or thing that spoils. 2 person who takes spoils.

spoils man (spoilz′mən), *n., pl.* **-men.** person who gets or tries to get a government office or job as a reward for his service to the winning political party.

spoil sport (spoil′spôrt′, spoil′spōrt′), *n.* person who spoils or hinders the enjoyment of others.

spoils system, U.S. system or practice in which public offices with their salaries and advantages are awarded to supporters of the winning political party for its own purposes and in its own (rather than the public) interest.

spoilt (spoilt), *v.* a pt. and a pp. of **spoil.**

Spo kane (spō kan′), *n.* city in E Washington. 171,000.

spoke[1] (spōk), *v.* 1 a pt. of **speak.** 2 ARCHAIC. a pp. of **speak.**

spoke[2] (spōk), *n., v.,* **spoked, spok ing.** *—n.* 1 one of the bars projecting from the hub of a wheel and supporting the rim. 2 rung of a ladder. 3 **put a spoke in one's wheel,** stop or hinder a person. *—v.t.* provide with spokes. [Old English *spāca*]

spo ken (spō′kən), *v.* a pp. of **speak.** *—adj.* expressed with the mouth; uttered; told: *the spoken word.*

-spoken, *combining form.* speaking in a ____ way: *Soft-spoken* = speaking in a soft way.

spoke shave (spōk′shāv′), *n.* a cutting tool having a blade with a handle at each end, used for planing curved surfaces.

spokes man (spōks′mən), *n., pl.* **-men.** person who speaks for another or others.

spo li a tion (spō′lē ā′shən), *n.* 1 a plundering; robbery. 2 the plundering of neutrals at sea in time of war. [< Latin *spoliationem,* ultimately < *spolium* booty] **—spo′li a′tor,** *n.*

spon da ic (spon dā′ik), *adj.* 1 of a spondee. 2 consisting of spondees.

spon dee (spon′dē′), *n.* foot or measure in poetry consisting of two accented syllables. EXAMPLE: "So′ strode′ / he′ back′ / slow′ to / the wound′/ed King′" has spondees for the first two feet. [< Latin *spondeus* < Greek *spondeios* < *spondē* libation; originally used in songs accompanying libations]

sponge (spunj), *n., v.,* **sponged, spong ing.** *—n.* 1 any of a phylum of aquatic, usually marine, animals, having a tough, elastic skeleton or framework of interlaced fibers; poriferan. Most sponges live in large colonies on the bottom of the ocean, attached to stones, plants, etc. 2 the soft, light, porous framework of any of these animals, used for soaking up water in bathing, cleaning, etc. 3 piece of this or a similar article made of rubber, cellulose, etc. 4 something used like a sponge, as a sterile gauze pad used to absorb blood in surgery. 5 something having the appearance or consistency of a sponge, as bread dough, sponge cake, etc. 6 a sponging. 7 INFORMAL. person who continually lives at the expense of others; sponger. 8 **throw in the sponge** or **throw up the sponge,** give up; admit defeat.

—v.t. 1 wipe or rub with a wet sponge in order to clean or dampen. 2 absorb or take (up) with a sponge: *Sponge up the spilled water.* 3 **sponge out,** blot out; remove all traces of. 4 INFORMAL. get from another or at another's expense in a mean way. *—v.i.* 1 absorb or take up, as a sponge. 2 gather sponges. 3 INFORMAL. live or profit at the expense of another in a mean way: *sponge on one's parents instead of working.*

[Old English < Latin *spongia* < Greek] **—sponge′like′,** *adj.*

sponge cake, a light, spongy cake made with eggs, sugar, flour, etc., but no butter or other shortening.

spong er (spun′jər), *n.* 1 person or thing that sponges. 2 person or vessel engaged in gathering sponges. 3 INFORMAL. person who gets on at the expense of others.

sponge rubber, rubber similar to foam rubber, made from dried natural rubber or latex.

spon gy (spun′jē), *adj.,* **-gi er, -gi est.** 1 like a sponge; soft, light, and full of holes: *spongy dough.* 2 full of holes: *spongy ice.* **—spon′gi ness,** *n.*

spon son (spon′sən), *n.* 1 part projecting from the side of a ship or boat, used for support or protection. 2 an air-filled compartment on the side of a seaplane, canoe, etc., to steady it. [origin uncertain]

spon sor (spon′sər), *n.* 1 person or group that formally endorses or supports something or someone: *the sponsor of a law.* 2 person who stands with the parents at an infant's baptism, agreeing to assist in the child's religious upbringing if necessary; godfather or godmother. 3 business firm or other organization that pays the costs of a radio or television program advertising its products or services. *—v.t.* act as sponsor for. [< Latin < *spondere* to promise]

spon so ri al (spon sôr′ē əl, spon sōr′ē əl), *adj.* of a sponsor.

spon sor ship (spon′sər ship), *n.* position and duties of a sponsor.

spon ta ne i ty (spon′tə nē′ə tē), *n., pl.* **-ties.** 1 quality, condition, or fact of being spontaneous. 2 a spontaneous action or movement.

spon ta ne ous (spon tā′nē əs), *adj.* 1 caused by natural impulse or desire; not forced or compelled; not planned beforehand: *Both sides burst into spontaneous cheers at the skillful play.* See **voluntary** for synonym study. 2 taking place without external cause or help; caused entirely by inner forces: *The eruption of a volcano is spontaneous.* 3 growing or produced naturally; not planted, cultivated, etc. [< Late Latin *spontaneus* < Latin *sponte* of one's own accord] **—spon ta′ne ous ly,** *adv.* **—spon ta′ne ous ness,** *n.*

spontaneous combustion, the bursting into flame of a substance as a result of heat produced by slow oxidation of the constituents of the substance itself without heat from an outside source.

spontaneous generation, the supposed production of living organisms from nonliving matter; abiogenesis.

spoof (spüf), INFORMAL. *—n.* 1 a trick, hoax, or joke. 2 a light satirical parody; takeoff. *—v.t., v.i.* 1 play tricks; make fun of; ridicule. 2 make a light satirical parody on. [< a game involving hoaxing, invented by Arthur Roberts, 1852–1933, British comedian]

spook (spük), INFORMAL. *—n.* ghost; specter. *—v.t.* scare; frighten. [< Dutch]

spook ish (spü′kish), *adj.* spooky.

spook y (spü′kē), *adj.,* **spook i er, spook i est.** INFORMAL. like a spook; suited to or suggesting spooks. **—spook′i ly,** *adv.* **—spook′i ness,** *n.*

spool (spül), *n.* 1 cylinder of wood or metal on which thread, wire, etc., is wound. 2 something like a spool in shape or use. *—v.t.* wind on a spool. [< Middle Dutch *spoele*]

spoon (spün), *n.* 1 utensil consisting of a small, shallow bowl at the end of a handle, used to take up or stir food or drink. 2 something shaped like a spoon. 3 a golf club with a wooden head and a hitting surface with a greater slope than a brassie. 4 **born with a silver spoon in one's mouth,** born lucky or rich. *—v.t.* take up with or as if with a spoon. *—v.i.* INFORMAL. make love by hugging and kissing. [Old English *spōn* chip, shaving] **—spoon′like′,** *adj.*

spoon bill (spün′bil′), *n.* 1 a long-legged, pink wading bird of the same family as the ibises, having a long, flat bill with a spoon-shaped tip. 2 a bird having a similar bill.

spoon bread, mixture of corn meal with milk, eggs, shortening, etc., cooked by baking but always soft enough to be served with a spoon.

spoon drift (spün′drift′), *n.* spindrift.

spoon er ism (spü′nə riz′əm), *n.* an accidental transposition of the initial sounds of two or more words. EXAMPLE: "well-boiled icicle" for "well-oiled bicycle." [< William A. *Spooner,* 1844–1930, English clergyman famous for such mistakes]

spoon-feed (spün′fēd′), *v.t., v.i.,* **-fed** (-fed′), **-feed ing.** feed with or as if with a spoon; coddle; pamper.

spoon ful (spün′fül), *n., pl.* **-fuls.** as much as a spoon can hold.

spoor (spür), *n.* trail of a wild animal; track. —*v.t., v.i.* track by or follow a spoor. [< Afrikaans < Middle Dutch]

spo rad ic (spə rad′ik), *adj.* appearing or happening at intervals in time; occasional: *sporadic outbreaks.* 2 being or occurring apart from others; isolated. 3 occurring in scattered instances; not epidemic: *sporadic cases of scarlet fever.* 4 occurring singly, or widely apart in locality; dispersed: *sporadic genera of plants.* [< Medieval Latin *sporadicus* < Greek *sporadikos* scattered, ultimately < *spora* a sowing] **—spo rad′i cal ly,** *adv.*

spo ran gi al (spə ran′jē əl), *adj.* 1 of or having to do with the spore case. 2 containing spores.

spo ran gi um (spə ran′jē əm), *n., pl.* **-gi a** (-jē ə). spore case. [< New Latin < Greek *spora* seed + *angeion* vessel]

spore (spôr, spōr), *n., v.,* **spored, spor ing.** —*n.* 1 a single-celled reproductive body of flowerless plants such as ferns, and some protozoans, which becomes free and is capable of growing into a new plant or animal. The spores of flowerless plants are analogous to the seeds of flowering plants. Spores are produced asexually or sexually by the fusion of gametes. 2 germ; seed. —*v.i.* form or produce spores. [< New Latin < Greek *spora* seed, a sowing < *speirein* to sow]

spore case, receptacle or case in which spores are produced; sporangium. The little brown spots on the underside of ferns are spore cases.

sporo-, *combining form.* spore or spores: *Sporogenesis = the formation of spores.* [< Greek *spora* seed]

spo ro gen e sis (spôr′ə jen′ə sis, spōr′ə-jen′ə sis), *n.* 1 the formation of spores. 2 reproduction by means of spores.

spo ro go ni um (spôr′ə gō′nē əm, spōr′ə-gō′nē əm), *n., pl.* **-ni a** (-nē ə). the spore case of mosses and liverworts. [< *sporo-* + Greek *-gonos* producing]

spo rog o ny (spô roj′ə nē, spō roj′ə nē), *n.* reproduction by means of spores, especially in certain protozoans.

spo ro phore (spôr′ə fôr, spōr′ə fōr), *n.* the branch or portion of a sporophyte which bears spores. [< *sporo-* + Greek *-phoros* carrying]

spo ro phyll or **spo ro phyl** (spôr′ə fil, spōr′ə fil), *n.* any leaf, usually more or less modified, which bears spores or spore cases. [< *sporo-* + Greek *phyllon* leaf]

spo ro phyte (spôr′ə fīt, spōr′ə fīt), *n.* the individual plant or the generation of a plant which produces spores, in a plant which reproduces both sexually and asexually.

spo ro zo an (spôr′ə zō′ən, spōr′ə zō′ən), *n.* any of a class of minute parasitic protozoans which absorb food through the body wall and reproduce sexually and asexually in alternate generations. Certain sporozoans cause diseases of man and animals, such as malaria. Plasmodia belong to this class. —*adj.* of or belonging to this class.

spor ran (spôr′ən, spor′ən), *n.* a large purse, commonly of fur, hanging from the belt in front of a Scottish Highlands costume. [< Scottish Gaelic]

sport (spôrt, spōrt), *n.* 1 game, contest, or other pastime requiring some skill and usually involving a certain amount of physical exercise. Baseball and fishing are outdoor sports; bowling and basketball are indoor sports. See **play** for synonym study. 2 any pastime or amusement. 3 playful joking; fun. 4 ridicule. 5 an object of jokes and ridicule. 6 plaything: *His hat blew off and became the sport of the wind.* 7 sportsman. 8 a good fellow; one who behaves in a sportsmanlike manner: *be a sport.* 9 INFORMAL. **a** a betting man; gambler. **b** person who wears showy clothes, pursues gay pastimes, or the like. 10 animal, plant, or part of a plant that varies suddenly or in a marked manner from the normal type or stock. A white blackbird would be a sport. **11 for sport** or **in sport,** for fun; in jest or as a joke; not seriously: *to say a thing in sport.* **12 make sport of,** make fun of; laugh at; ridicule.
—*v.i.* 1 amuse or entertain oneself; play. 2 participate in or follow a sport or sports. 3 jest. 4 (of an animal, plant, etc.) vary abnormally from the normal type. —*v.t.* INFORMAL. display: *sport a new hat.*
—*adj.* of or suitable for sports: *sport equipment.*
[ultimately short for *disport*]

sport ful (spôrt′fəl, spōrt′fəl), *adj.* playful; sportive. **—sport′ful ly,** *adv.* **—sport′ful ness,** *n.*

sport ing (spôr′ting, spōr′ting), *adj.* 1 of, interested in, or engaging in sports. 2 playing fair: *a sporting gesture.* 3 willing to take a chance. 4 INFORMAL. involving risk; uncertain: *a sporting chance.* **—sport′ing ly,** *adv.*

spor tive (spôr′tiv, spōr′tiv), *adj.* playful; merry: *a sportive puppy.* **—spor′tive ly,** *adv.* **—spor′tive ness,** *n.*

sports (spôrts, spōrts), *adj.* of or having to do with sports: *a sports editor.*

sports car, a small, low, fast car, usually with two seats and an open top.

sports cast (spôrts′kast′, spōrts′kast′), *n.* broadcast or telecast of a sporting event.

sports cast er (spôrts′kas′tər, spōrts′-kas′tər), *n.* person who does the spoken part of a sportscast.

sport shirt, shirt designed for informal wear, usually without a tie.

hat, āge, fär; let, ēqual, tėrm;
it, īce; hot, ōpen, ôrder;
oil, out; cup, pu̇t, rüle;
ch, child; ng, long; sh, she;
th, thin; ᴛʜ, then; zh, measure;

ə represents *a* in about, *e* in taken, *i* in pencil, *o* in lemon, *u* in circus.

< = from, derived from, taken from.

sports man (spôrts′mən, spōrts′mən), *n., pl.* **-men.** 1 person who takes part in sports, especially hunting, fishing, or racing. 2 person who likes sports. 3 person who plays fair. 4 person who is willing to take a chance.

sports man like (spôrts′mən līk′, spōrts′-mən līk′), *adj.* like or suitable for a sportsman; fair and honorable.

sports man ly (spôrts′mən lē, spōrts′mən-lē), *adj.* sportsmanlike.

sports man ship (spôrts′mən ship, spōrts′mən ship), *n.* 1 qualities or conduct of a sportsman; fair play. 2 ability in sports.

sports wear (spôrts′wer′, spôrts′war′; spōrts′wer′, spōrts′war′), *n.* clothes designed for informal, outdoor, or athletic wear.

sports wom an (spôrts′wu̇m′ən, spōrts′-wu̇m′ən), *n., pl.* **-wom en.** woman who engages in or is interested in sports.

sports writ er (spôrts′rī′tər, spōrts′rī′tər), *n.* journalist who writes about sports.

sport y (spôr′tē, spōr′tē), *adj.,* **sport i er, sport i est.** INFORMAL. 1 gay or fast; flashy. 2 smart in dress, appearance, manners, etc. 3 sportsmanlike; sporting. **—sport′i ly,** *adv.* **—sport′i ness,** *n.*

spor u la tion (spôr′yə lā′shən, spōr′yə-lā′shən), *n.* formation of spores or sporules.

spor ule (spôr′yül, spōr′yül), *n.* a small spore.

spot (spot), *n., v.,* **spot ted, spot ting,** *adj.* —*n.* 1 a small discoloring or disfiguring mark; stain; speck: *a spot of grease on a suit.* 2 blemish or flaw in character or reputation; *His record is without a spot.* 3 a small part unlike the rest: *a blue tie with white spots.* 4 a small extent of space; place: *From this spot you can see the parade.* 5 INFORMAL. **a** a small amount; little bit: *a spot of lunch.* **b** position or place with reference to employment, radio or television scheduling, etc. 6 pip or dot on a playing card, domino, or die to show its kind and value. **7 hit the spot,** INFORMAL. be just right; be satisfactory. **8 in a spot,** in trouble or difficulty. **9 on the spot, a** at the very place in question. **b** at once. **c** INFORMAL. in an awkward or difficult position.
—*v.t.* 1 make spots on; stain: *spot a dress, spot one's reputation by lying repeatedly.* 2 INFORMAL. pick out; find out; recognize: *I spotted my sister in the crowd. The teacher spotted every mistake.* 3 place in a certain spot or area; scatter in various spots: *Lookouts were spotted all along the coast.* —*v.i.* 1 make a spot or stain. 2 become spotted; have spots: *This silk will spot.*
—*adj.* 1 on hand; ready: *a spot answer.* 2 for immediate cash payment and delivery: *a spot sale.* 3 done or reported on the spot: *spot news.* 4 inserted between regular radio or television programs: *a spot commercial.* [Middle English]

spot cash, money paid just as soon as the goods are delivered or the work is done.

spot check, 1 a brief, rough sampling. 2 a checkup made without warning.

spot-check (spot′chek′), *v.t.* make a spot check of.

spot less (spot′lis), *adj.* without a spot; absolutely clean. **—spot′less ly,** *adv.* **—spot′less ness,** *n.*

spot light (spot′līt′), *n., v.,* **-light ed** or **-lit** (-lit′), **-light ing.** *—n.* 1 a spot or circle of bright light thrown upon a particular place or person. 2 lamp that gives such a light: *a spotlight in a theater.* 3 public notice; anything that directs attention on a person or thing: *Politicians are often in the spotlight.* *—v.t.* 1 light up with a spotlight or spotlights. 2 call attention to; give public notice to.

Spot syl van ia (spot′səl vā′nyə, spot′səl-vā′nē ə), *n.* village in NE Virginia where the armies of Grant and Lee fought a two weeks' battle in 1864.

spot ted (spot′id), *adj.* 1 stained with or as if with spots: *a spotted reputation.* 2 marked with spots: *a spotted dog.*

spotted fever, any of various fevers characterized by spots on the skin, especially cerebrospinal meningitis or typhus.

spot ter (spot′ər), *n.* 1 person or thing that makes or removes spots. 2 civilian who watches for enemy aircraft over a city, town, etc. 3 person employed to watch employees, customers, etc., for evidence of dishonesty or other misconduct.

spot ty (spot′ē), *adj.,* **-ti er, -ti est.** 1 having spots; spotted. 2 not of uniform quality; irregular: *His work was spotty.* **—spot′ti ly,** *adv.* **—spot′ti ness,** *n.*

spous al (spou′zəl), ARCHAIC. *—n.* Often, **spousals,** *pl.* the ceremony of marriage; nuptials. *—adj.* of marriage; nuptial.

spouse (spous, spouz), *n.* husband or wife. [< Old French *espous* < Latin *sponsus, sponsa* < *spondere* to promise, betroth]

spout (spout), *v.t.* 1 throw out (a liquid) in a stream or spray: *A whale spouts water when it breathes.* 2 INFORMAL. speak in loud and very emotional tones: *The old-fashioned actor used to spout his lines.* *—v.i.* 1 throw out a liquid in a stream or spray: *The fountain spouted up high.* 2 flow out with force; spurt: *Water spouted from a break in the pipe.* 3 INFORMAL. spout or declaim words, lines in a play, etc. *—n.* 1 stream; jet. 2 pipe for carrying off water: *Rain runs down a spout from our roof to the ground.* 3 tube or lip through or over which liquid is poured. A teakettle and a coffeepot have spouts. [Middle English *spouten*] **—spout′er,** *n.* **—spout′less,** *adj.*

S.P.Q.R., the Roman Senate and People [for Latin *Senatus Populusque Romanus*].

sprain (sprān), *v.t.* injure (the ligaments or muscles of a joint) by a sudden twist or wrench. *—n.* injury caused by a sudden twist or wrench. [origin uncertain]

sprang (sprang), *v.* a pt. of **spring.**

sprat (sprat), *n., pl.* **sprats** or **sprat.** 1 a small herring of the Atlantic coast of Europe. 2 any of certain similar herrings. [Old English *sprott*]

sprawl (sprôl), *v.i.* 1 toss or spread the limbs about, as an infant or animal lying on its back. 2 lie or sit with the limbs spread out, especially ungracefully: *The people sprawled on the beach in their bathing suits.* 3 spread out in an irregular or awkward manner, as vines, handwriting, etc. 4 move awkwardly; scramble. *—v.t.* spread or stretch out (the limbs), especially ungracefully. *—n.* act or position of sprawling. [Old English *sprēawlian*]

spray[1] (sprā), *n.* 1 liquid going through the air in small drops: *sea spray.* 2 something like this: *a spray of bullets.* 3 instrument that sends a liquid out as spray. *—v.t.* 1 throw in the form of spray; scatter in small drops: *spray paint on a cupboard.* 2 scatter spray on; sprinkle: *spray a lawn with water.* 3 direct numerous small missiles, etc., upon: *The soldiers sprayed the enemy with bullets.* *—v.i.* scatter spray. [apparently < Dutch *sprayen*] **—spray′er,** *n.*

spray[2] (sprā), *n.* 1 a small branch or piece of some plant with its leaves, flowers, or fruit: *a spray of lilacs, a spray of ivy.* 2 ornament like this. [apparently related to Danish *sprag*]

spray gun, device used to spray paint, insecticide, or other liquids.

spread (spred), *v.,* **spread, spread ing,** *n.* *—v.t.* 1 cause to cover a large or larger area; stretch out; open out; lay out: *spread out a rug, spread one's arms.* 2 move outward or farther apart: *spread one's fingers.* 3 scatter; distribute: *spread seed. He spread the news.* 4 cover with a thin layer: *spread a slice of bread with butter.* 5 put as a thin layer: *spread jam on bread.* 6 prepare (a table) for a meal or other purpose; set; lay. 7 put food on (a table). 8 **spread oneself,** INFORMAL. **a** try very hard to make a good impression. **b** display one's abilities fully. **c** brag. *—v.i.* 1 cover a large or larger area; unfold; open out: *a fan that spreads when shaken.* 2 move outward or farther apart: *The rails of the track have spread.* 3 lie; extend: *Fields of corn spread out before us.* 4 be or become scattered; be distributed: *The disease spread rapidly.* 5 be put as a thin layer: *This paint spreads evenly.*

—n. 1 act or process of spreading: *encourage the spread of knowledge.* 2 amount of or capacity for spreading; extent; width: *the great spread of an eagle's wings.* 3 stretch; expanse: *a great spread of green fields.* 4 a covering for a bed or table. 5 INFORMAL. food for a meal put on the table, especially in abundance; feast. 6 food spread on bread, crackers, etc. Butter and jam are spreads. 7 advertisement, article, etc., occupying a number of adjoining columns or pages.

[Old English *sprǣdan*] **—spread′er,** *n.*

spread eagle, 1 representation of an eagle with outspread wings, used as an emblem of the United States and certain other countries. 2 a boastful person.

spread-ea gle (spred′ē′gəl), *adj., v.,* **-gled, -gling.** *—adj.* 1 having the form or appearance of a spread eagle. 2 U.S. boastful. *—v.t.* 1 stretch out in the form of a spread eagle. 2 tie (a person) with arms and legs outstretched.

spree (sprē), *n.* 1 a lively frolic; gay or boisterous time. 2 a prolonged bout of drinking; drunken carousal. [origin uncertain]

springboard (def. 1) for diving

Spree River (shprā), river in East Germany, flowing through Berlin. 220 mi.

sprig (sprig), *n., v.,* **sprigged, sprig ging.** *—n.* 1 shoot, twig, or small branch: *a sprig of lilac.* 2 ornament or design shaped like a sprig. 3 a young man; stripling. 4 a small, headless nail or brad. *—v.t.* fasten with sprigs or brads. [Middle English *sprigge*]

spright ful (sprīt′fəl), *adj.* sprightly.

spright ly (sprīt′lē), *adj.,* **-li er, -li est,** *adv.* *—adj.* lively; gay. *—adv.* in a sprightly manner. Also, **spritely.** [< *spright,* variant of *sprite*] **—spright′li ness,** *n.*

spring (def. 2)—four kinds of springs

spring (spring), *v.,* **sprang** or **sprung, sprung, spring ing,** *n., adj.* *—v.i.* 1 rise or move suddenly and lightly; leap; jump: *spring to attention. I sprang to my feet. The dog sprang at the thief.* 2 fly back or away as if by elastic force: *The branch sprang up when I dropped from it.* 3 come from some source; arise; grow: *A wind sprang up. He springs from New England stock.* 4 begin to move, act, grow, appear, etc., suddenly; burst forth: *Towns spring up where oil is discovered. Sparks sprang from the fire.* 5 crack, split, warp, bend, strain, or break: *Cracks all along the concrete wall showed where it had sprung.* 6 rise from cover, as partridges. *—v.t.* 1 cause to spring; cause to act by a spring: *spring a trap.* 2 bring out, produce, or make suddenly: *spring a surprise on someone.* 3 announce or reveal suddenly and unexpectedly: *spring the news of an engagement.* 4 crack, split, warp, bend, or break: *Frost had sprung the rock wall.* 5 cause (partridges, etc.) to rise from cover. 6 SLANG. secure the release of (a person) from prison by bail or otherwise.

—n. 1 leap or jump; bound: *a spring over the fence.* 2 an elastic device that returns to its original shape after being pulled or held out of shape. 3 elastic quality. 4 a flying back or recoil from a forced position. 5 season of the year when plants begin to grow in the temperate and colder regions of the earth (in North America, the months of March, April, and May). 6 (in astronomy) the three months between the vernal equinox and the summer solstice. 7 a small stream of water flowing naturally from the earth. 8 source; origin; cause. 9 the first and freshest or most vigorous stage of anything, especially of life; period of youth: *the spring of life.* 10 crack, split, warp, bend, strain, or break.

—adj. 1 having a spring or springs. 2 of or having to do with the season of spring. Spring wheat is wheat sown in the spring. 3 characteristic of or suitable for the season of spring: *spring weather.* 4 from a spring: *spring water.*

[Old English *springan*] **—spring′er,** *n.*

spring board (spring′bôrd′, spring′bōrd′), *n.* 1 a flexible board used to give added spring in diving, jumping, and vaulting. 2 anything that serves as a way to get something else.

spring bok (spring′bok′), *n., pl.* **-boks** or **-bok.** a small antelope of South Africa that leaps almost directly upward when excited or disturbed. [< Afrikaans, springing buck]

springe (sprinj), *n., v.,* **springed, spring ing.** —*n.* snare for catching small game. —*v.t.* catch in a snare. [apparently < Old English *sprengan* cause to spring]

springer spaniel, any of certain of the larger breeds of field spaniels used to spring or flush game.

spring fever, a listless, lazy feeling felt by some people during the first sudden warm weather of spring.

Spring field (spring′fēld′), *n.* 1 capital of Illinois, in the central part. 92,000. 2 city in S Massachusetts. 164,000. 3 city in SW Missouri. 120,000. 4 city in W Ohio. 82,000.

spring halt (spring′hôlt′), *n.* stringhalt.

spring house (spring′hous′), *n., pl.* **-hous es** (-hou′ziz). U.S. a small outbuilding constructed over a spring or brook, used to keep milk, meat, etc., cool.

spring-load ed (spring′lō′did), *adj.* held in place or operated by a spring.

spring lock, lock that fastens automatically by a spring.

spring tail (spring′tāl′), *n.* any of an order of small, wingless insects that have a forked, taillike appendage, used in leaping.

spring tide (spring′tīd′), *n.* springtime.

spring tide, 1 the exceptionally high and low tides which come at the time of the new moon or the full moon. 2 any great flood, swell, or rush.

spring time (spring′tīm′), *n.* the season of spring.

spring y (spring′ē), *adj.,* **spring i er, spring i est.** 1 that springs; resilient; elastic: *Her step was springy.* 2 having many springs of water. —**spring′i ly,** *adv.* —**spring′i ness,** *n.*

sprin kle (spring′kəl), *v.,* **-kled, -kling,** *n.* —*v.t.* 1 scatter in drops or tiny bits; strew: *sprinkle ashes on an icy sidewalk.* 2 spray or cover with small drops or particles: *sprinkle flowers with water.* 3 dot or vary with something scattered here and there. —*v.i.* 1 scatter something in drops or small particles. 2 rain a little. —*n.* 1 act of sprinkling. 2 a sprinkling. 3 a light rain. [Middle English *sprinklen*]

sprin kler (spring′klər), *n.* 1 person that sprinkles. 2 device or apparatus for sprinkling water.

sprinkler system, system of pipes with nozzles spaced regularly apart to carry water for spraying lawns and orchards or to help control fire by releasing water as the temperature rises.

sprin kling (spring′kling), *n.* a small quantity or number scattered here and there.

sprint (sprint), *v.i.* run at full speed, especially for a short distance. —*n.* a race or any short spell of running, rowing, etc., at top speed. [probably < Scandinavian (Old Icelandic) *spretta*] —**sprint′er,** *n.*

sprit (sprit), *n.* a small pole running diagonally from the foot of the mast to the top corner of a fore-and-aft sail, to support and stretch it. [Old English *sprēot*]

sprite (sprīt), *n.* fairy. [< Old French *esprit* spirit < Latin *spiritus.* Doublet of SPIRIT.]

sprite ly (sprīt′lē), *adj.,* **-li er, -li est.** sprightly. —**sprite′li ness,** *n.*

sprit sail (sprit′sāl′; *Nautical* sprit′səl), *n.* any fore-and-aft sail supported and stretched by a sprit.

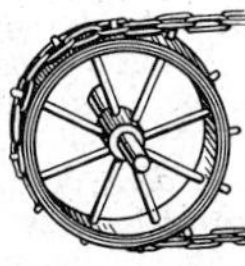

sprocket (def. 2)

sprock et (sprok′it), *n.* 1 one of a set of projections on the rim of a wheel, arranged so as to fit into the links of a chain. The sprockets keep the chain from slipping. 2 Also, **sprocket wheel.** wheel made with sprockets. [origin uncertain]

sprout (sprout), *v.i.* 1 begin to grow; shoot forth: *Buds sprout in the spring.* 2 develop rapidly. —*v.t.* 1 cause to grow: *The rain has sprouted the corn.* 2 INFORMAL. remove sprouts from: *He sprouted the potatoes twice every winter.* —*n.* 1 a shoot of a plant. 2 **sprouts,** *pl.* Brussels sprouts. [Old English *-sprūtan*]

Spru ance (sprü′əns), *n.* **Raymond Ames,** 1886-1969, American admiral in World War II.

spruce[1] (sprüs), *n.* 1 any of a genus of evergreen trees of the pine family, having needle-shaped leaves and often used as a Christmas tree in America. 2 the wood of any of these trees. [Middle English *Spruce,* variant of *Pruce* Prussia]

spruce[2] (sprüs), *adj.,* **spruc er, spruc est,** *v.,* **spruced, spruc ing.** —*adj.* smart in appearance; neat; trim. —*v.t., v.i.* make or become spruce: *spruce oneself up for dinner.* [perhaps special use of Middle English *Spruce* Prussia (i.e., made in Prussia, therefore, smart-looking)] —**spruce′ly,** *adv.* —**spruce′ness,** *n.*

sprue (sprü), *n.* a chronic disease characterized by emaciation, anemia, inflammation of the mouth, and digestive upsets. [probably < Dutch *spruw*]

sprung (sprung), *v.* a pt. and pp. of **spring.**

spry (sprī), *adj.,* **spry er, spry est** or **spri er, spri est.** full of health and spirits; active; lively; nimble: *The spry old lady traveled all over the country.* [origin uncertain] —**spry′ly,** *adv.* —**spry′ness,** *n.*

spt., seaport.

spud (spud), *n., v.,* **spud ded, spud ding.** —*n.* 1 tool with a narrow blade for digging up or cutting the roots of weeds. 2 tool like a chisel for removing bark. 3 INFORMAL. potato. —*v.t.* remove or dig up by means of a spud. [Middle English *spudde* short knife]

spue (spyü), *v.t., v.i.,* **spued, spu ing.** spew.

spume (spyüm), *n., v.,* **spumed, spum ing.** —*n.* frothy matter; foam; froth. —*v.i.* foam or froth. [< Latin *spuma*]

spu mo ne or **spu mo ni** (spə mō′nē), *n.* an Italian ice cream made with layers of different colors and flavors, usually containing fruit, nuts, etc. [< Italian < *spuma* foam < Latin]

spum y (spyü′mē), *adj.,* **spum i er, spum i est.** foamy; frothy.

spun (spun), *v.* a pt. and pp. of **spin.**

spun glass, fiberglass.

spunk (spungk), *n.* INFORMAL. courage; pluck; spirit; mettle. [< Irish or Scottish Gaelic < Latin *spongia* sponge]

spunk y (spung′kē), *adj.,* **spunk i er, spunk i est.** INFORMAL. courageous; plucky; spirited. —**spunk′i ly,** *adv.* —**spunk′i ness,** *n.*

hat, āge, fär; let, ēqual, tėrm;
it, īce; hot, ōpen, ôrder;
oil, out; cup, pu̇t, rüle;
ch, child; ng, long; sh, she;
th, thin; ŦH, then; zh, measure;

ə represents *a* in about, *e* in taken,
i in pencil, *o* in lemon, *u* in circus.

< = from, derived from, taken from.

spun rayon, yarn made from rayon threads. When woven, it often resembles linen cloth.

spun silk, silk waste spun into yarn.

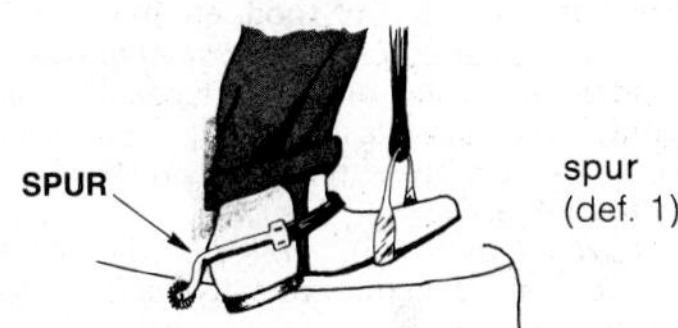

spur (def. 1)

spur (spėr), *n., v.,* **spurred, spur ring.** —*n.* 1 a pricking instrument consisting of a small spike or spiked wheel, worn on a horseman's heel for urging a horse on. 2 anything that urges on; stimulus: *Ambition was the spur that made her work.* 3 any sharp or short projection, point, or spike suggesting or resembling a spur, as the spiny projection on the inner side of the legs of a cock or the slender projection from the calyx of a columbine. 4 ridge sticking out from or smaller than the main body of a mountain or mountain range. 5 any short branch: *a spur of a railroad.* 6 brace, especially one strengthening a post. **7 on the spur of the moment,** on a sudden impulse. **8 win one's spurs,** make a reputation for oneself. —*v.t.* 1 prick with spurs: *The rider spurred his horse on.* 2 urge on; incite: *Pride spurred the boy to fight.* —*v.i.* ride quickly. [Old English *spura*] —**spur′like′,** *adj.*

spurge (spėrj), *n.* any of a genus of plants many of which have an acrid, milky juice possessing purgative or medicinal properties, as the poinsettia; euphorbia. [< Old French *espurge* < *espurgier* to purge < Latin *expurgare*]

spur gear, 1 gearwheel having the teeth parallel to the axle. 2 gearing using such gearwheels.

spur i ous (spyu̇r′ē əs), *adj.* 1 not coming from the right source; not genuine; false; sham: *a spurious document.* 2 illegitimate. [< Late Latin *spurius*] —**spur′i ous ly,** *adv.* —**spur′i ous ness,** *n.*

spurn (spėrn), *v.t.* 1 refuse with scorn; scorn: *spurn a bribe, spurn an offer of friendship.* 2 strike with the foot; kick away. —*v.i.* oppose with scorn: *spurn at restraint.* —*n.* 1 disdainful rejection; contemptuous treatment. 2 a kick. [Old English *spurnan*] —**spurn′er,** *n.*

spurred (spėrd), *adj.* having spurs or a spur: *a spurred boot, spurred feet.*

spurt (spėrt), *v.i.* 1 flow suddenly in a stream or jet; gush out; squirt: *Blood spurted from the wound.* 2 put forth great energy or show great activity for a short time: *The runners spurted near the end of the race.* —*v.t.* cause to gush out: *spurt blood.* —*n.* 1 a sudden rushing forth; jet: *spurts of flame.* 2 a great increase of effort or activity for a short time. Also, **spirt.** [variant of *sprit,* Old English *spryttan*]

spur track, a branch railroad track connected with the main track at one end only.

sput nik (sput′nik, spůt′nik), *n.* any of a group of artificial earth satellites containing scientific instruments or animals, put into orbit by the Soviet Union. [< Russian *sputnik* satellite, literally, companion]

sput ter (sput′ər), *v.i.* 1 make spitting or popping noises: *fat sputtering in the frying pan. The firecrackers sputtered.* 2 throw out drops of saliva, bits of food, etc., in excitement or in talking too fast. 3 speak confusedly and indistinctly. —*v.t.* 1 throw out (drops of saliva, bits of food, etc.) in excitement or in talking too fast. 2 say (words or sounds) in haste and confusion. —*n.* 1 confused talk. 2 a sputtering; sputtering noise. [probably related to *spout*] —**sput′ter er,** *n.*

spu tum (spyü′təm), *n., pl.* **-ta** (-tə). 1 saliva; spit. 2 mixture of saliva and mucus coughed up and spat out. [< Latin]

spy (spī), *n., pl.* **spies,** *v.,* **spied, spy ing.** —*n.* 1 person who keeps secret watch on the actions of others. 2 person who tries to get secret information for one government or country about another government or country, especially in time of war. A spy usually enters the territory he is spying on by disguising himself or his identity. —*v.i.* 1 keep secret watch: *He saw two men spying on him from behind a tree.* 2 act as a spy; be a spy. The punishment for spying in wartime is death. —*v.t.* 1 catch sight of; see: *She was the first to spy the rescue party in the distance.* 2 **spy out,** a watch or examine secretly or carefully. b find out by watching secretly or carefully. [< Old French *espie* < *espier* to spy; of Germanic origin]

spy glass (spī′glas′), *n.* a small telescope, usually one without a mount.

spy plane (spī′plān′), *n.* a high-altitude aircraft for secret reconnaissance of foreign defense installations especially by means of aerial photographs.

sq., 1 square. 2 the following [for Latin *sequentia*].

sq. ft., square foot or square feet.

sq. in., square inch or square inches.

sq. mi., square mile or square miles.

squab (skwob), *n.* a very young bird, especially a young pigeon. [origin uncertain]

squab ble (skwob′əl), *n., v.,* **-bled, -bling.** —*n.* a petty, noisy quarrel. —*v.i.* take part in a petty, noisy quarrel. [perhaps imitative] —**squab′bler,** *n.*

squad (skwod), *n.* 1 a military unit usually made up of ten to twelve men and composing the basic unit for drill, inspection, or work. It is usually commanded by a sergeant or a corporal and is the smallest tactical unit in an army. 2 any small group of persons working together. [< earlier French *esquade,* variant of *escadre* < Italian *squadra* square, ultimately < Latin *ex-* out + *quadrare* to make square. See SQUARE.]

squad car, a police patrol car that keeps in communication with headquarters by radiotelephone equipment; prowl car.

squad ron (skwod′rən), *n.* 1 part of a naval fleet used for special service. 2 formation of eight or more airplanes that fly or fight together. 3 a military unit made up of two or more troops of cavalry, usually commanded by a major or a lieutenant colonel. A squadron corresponds to a battalion in other branches of the army. 4 any group or formation. [< Italian *squadrone* < *squadra* square]

squal id (skwol′id), *adj.* 1 foul through neglect or want of cleanliness; dirty; filthy. 2 morally repulsive or wretched; degraded. [< Latin *squalidus* < *squalere* be filthy] —**squal′id ly,** *adv.* —**squal′id ness,** *n.*

squall[1] (skwôl), *n.* 1 a sudden, violent gust of wind, often with rain, snow, or sleet. 2 INFORMAL. disturbance or commotion; trouble. —*v.i.* undergo or give rise to a squall. [apparently related to Swedish *skval* sudden rush of water]

squall[2] (skwôl), *v.i.* cry out loudly; scream violently: *The baby squalled.* —*n.* a loud, harsh cry. [perhaps imitative] —**squall′er,** *n.*

squall line, line of thunderstorms preceding a cold front, often productive of tornadoes.

squall y (skwô′lē), *adj.,* **squall i er, squall i est.** 1 having many sudden and violent gusts of wind: *squally weather.* 2 blowing in squalls; gusty.

squal or (skwol′ər), *n.* 1 misery and dirt; filth. 2 quality or condition of being morally squalid. [< Latin]

squa ma (skwā′mə), *n., pl.* **-mae** (-mē′). a scale or scalelike part. [< Latin]

squa mate (skwā′māt), *adj.* having or covered with scales.

squa ma tion (skwə mā′shən), *n.* 1 condition of being covered with scales. 2 arrangement or pattern of the scales covering an animal.

squa mose (skwā′mōs), *adj.* squamous.

squa mous (skwā′məs), *adj.* 1 furnished with, covered with, or formed of scales. 2 characterized by the development of scales; scalelike. [< Latin *squamosus* < *squama* scale] —**squa′mous ly,** *adv.* —**squa′mous ness,** *n.*

squan der (skwon′dər), *v.t.* spend foolishly; waste: *squander one's money in gambling.* [origin uncertain] —**squan′der er,** *n.*

square (skwer, skwar), *n., adj.,* **squar er, squar est,** *v.,* **squared, squar ing,** *adv.* —*n.* 1 a plane figure with four equal sides and four right angles (□). 2 anything having this shape or nearly this shape: *a square of chocolate.* 3 space in a city or town that is bounded by streets on four sides; block: *The automobile factories fill several squares.* 4 the length of one side of such a space: *walk six squares.* 5 an open space in a city or town bounded by streets on four sides, often planted with grass, trees, etc. 6 any similar open space, such as at the meeting of streets. 7 the buildings surrounding such a space. 8 body of troops drawn up in a square formation. 9 instrument shaped like a T or an L, for drawing or testing right angles. 10 product obtained when a number is multiplied by itself: *16 is the square of 4.* 11 SLANG. person who is too conventional or old-fashioned. 12 **on the square,** a at right angles. b justly; fairly; honestly. 13 **out of square,** a not at right angles. b out of order. —*adj.* 1 having four equal sides and four right angles. 2 that is square or rectangular in cross section: *a square file.* 3 of a specified length on each side of a square: *a room ten feet square.* 4 having breadth more nearly equal to length or height than is usual: *a square jaw.* 5 forming a right angle: *a square corner.* 6 straight; level; even. 7 correctly built, finished, etc. 8 leaving no balance; even: *make accounts square.* 9 just; fair; honorable; honest: *be absolutely square in one's business dealings.* 10 straightforward; plain; direct: *a square refusal.* 11 satisfying; substantial: *a square meal.* 12 squared: *a square yard.* 13 multiplied by itself. 14 solid and strong; sturdy. 15 SLANG. too conventional; old-fashioned. 16 **all square.** INFORMAL. a having paid what is owing, done what is needed, etc. b even; tied: *The two teams were all square at the end of the second quarter.*
—*v.t.* 1 make square, rectangular, or cubical: *square a block of granite.* 2 mark out as a square or in squares. 3 bring to the form of a right angle: *square a corner.* 4 make straight, level, or even: *square a picture on a wall.* 5 adjust; settle; balance: *Let us square our accounts.* 6 guide or regulate. 7 in mathematics: a find or describe a square equivalent in area to: *square a circle.* b multiply (a number or quantity) by itself. 8 SLANG. win over or secure the silence or consent of, especially by bribery; bribe. 9 **square oneself,** INFORMAL. a make up for something one has done or said. b get even. —*v.i.* 1 agree; conform: *His acts do not square with his promises.* 2 **square away,** a set the sails so that the ship will stay before the wind. b make a new start. 3 **square off,** INFORMAL. put oneself in a position of defense or attack.
—*adv.* 1 INFORMAL. fairly or honestly: *speak fair and square.* 2 so as to be square; in a square or rectangular form. 3 at right angles. [< Old French *esquare* ultimately < Latin *exquadrare* to make square < *ex-* out + *quadrus* a square < *quattuor* four] —**square′ly,** *adv.* —**square′ness,** *n.*

square dance, dance performed by a set of couples arranged around a square space. The quadrille is one type of square dance.

square-dance (skwer′dans′, skwar′dans′), *v.i.,* **-danced, -danc ing.** do a square dance. —**square′-danc′er,** *n.*

square deal, INFORMAL. fair and honest treatment.

square foot, measure of area one foot long and one foot wide; any area equal to that. See **measure** for table.

square inch, measure of area one inch long and one inch wide; any area equal to that. See **measure** for table.

square knot, knot tied with two overhand knots so the free ends come out alongside of the standing parts. It will not slip and is easily untied. See **knot** for diagram.

square measure, system of units, such as square foot and acre, used for measuring area. See **measure** for table.

square-rigged sails on the foremast

square-rigged (skwer′rigd′, skwar′rigd′), *adj.* having the principal sails set at right angles across the masts.

square-rig ger (skwer′rig′ər, skwar′rig′ər), *n.* a square-rigged ship.

square root, number that produces a given

hat, āge, fär; let, ēqual, tėrm; it, īce; hot, ōpen, ôrder; oil, out; cup, pu̇t, rüle; ch, child; ng, long; sh, she; th, thin; ᴛʜ, then; zh, measure;
ə represents *a* in about, *e* in taken, *i* in pencil, *o* in lemon, *u* in circus.
< = from, derived from, taken from.

number when multiplied by itself: *The square root of 16 is 4.*

square sail, a four-sided sail carried on a yard across the mast.

square shooter, INFORMAL. a fair and honest person.

square-shoul dered (skwer′shōl′dərd, skwar′shōl′dərd), *adj.* having shoulders that are high, not sloping, and well braced back.

squar ish (skwer′ish, skwar′ish), *adj.* nearly square; having breadth more nearly equal to length or height than is usual. **—squar′ish ly,** *adv.*

squash¹ (skwosh), *v.t.* 1 squeeze or press into a flat mass or pulp; crush: *She squashed the bug.* 2 put an end to; stop by force; suppress; quash: *The police quickly squashed the riot.* 3 INFORMAL. silence or disconcert with a crushing argument, reply, etc. *—v.i.* 1 be pressed into a flat mass or pulp: *Cream puffs squash easily.* 2 make a splashing sound; move with a squashing sound: *squash through the mud and slush.* 3 crowd; squeeze. *—n.* 1 something squashed; a crushed mass. 2 act, fact, or sound of squashing. 3 either of two games somewhat like handball and tennis, played in a walled court with rackets and a rubber ball. 4 BRITISH. beverage made with fruit juice and, usually, carbonated water. [< Old French *esquasser,* ultimately < Latin *ex-* out + *quassare* to press] **—squash′er,** *n.*

squash² (skwosh), *n., pl.* **squash** or **squash es.** 1 any of a genus of vinelike plants belonging to the gourd family. 2 its fruit, eaten as a vegetable or often used in pies. [short for earlier *squantersquash* < Algonquian]

squash bug, a large, foul-smelling, dark-colored insect of North America, injurious to squash and to some other plants.

squash y (skwosh′ē), *adj.,* **squash i er, squash i est.** 1 easily squashed: *squashy cream puffs.* 2 soft and wet: *squashy ground.* 3 having a squashed or flattened look: *a squashy nose.* **—squash′i ly,** *adv.* **—squash′i ness,** *n.*

squat (skwot), *v.,* **squat ted** or **squat, squat ting,** *adj.,* **squat ter, squat test,** *n.* *—v.i.* 1 crouch on the heels. 2 sit on the ground or floor with the legs drawn up closely beneath or in front of the body. 3 settle on another's land without title or right. 4 settle on public land to acquire ownership of it under government regulation. *—v.t.* seat (oneself) with the legs drawn up. *—adj.* 1 crouching: *a squat figure sat in front of the fire.* 2 short and thick; low and broad: *a squat teapot.* *—n.* 1 act of squatting. 2 a squatting posture. [< Old French *esquatir* to crush] **—squat′ly,** *adv.* **—squat′ness,** *n.*

squat ter (skwot′ər), *n.* 1 person who settles on another's land without right. 2 person who settles on public land to acquire ownership of it. 3 person or animal that crouches or squats.

squatter sovereignty, U.S. popular sovereignty.

squat ty (skwot′ē), *adj.,* **-ti er, -ti est.** short and thick; low and broad; squat.

squaw (skwô), *n.* 1 a North American Indian woman or wife. 2 SLANG. woman or wife. [< Algonquian]

squaw fish (skwô′fish′), *n., pl.* **-fish es** or **-fish.** any of several large, slender carps, common in rivers of the Pacific coast of North America.

squawk (skwôk), *v.i.* 1 make a loud, harsh sound: *Hens and ducks squawk when frightened.* 2 SLANG. complain loudly. *—v.t.* utter harshly and loudly. *—n.* 1 a loud, harsh sound. 2 SLANG. a loud complaint. [imitative] **—squawk′er,** *n.*

squaw man, a white man married to an Indian squaw, especially one who has more or less abandoned white customs.

squeak (skwēk), *v.i.* 1 make a short, sharp, shrill sound: *A mouse squeaks.* 2 INFORMAL. get or pass (by or through) with difficulty: *The bill squeaked through the House of Representatives.* *—v.t.* 1 cause to squeak. 2 utter with a squeak. *—n.* 1 a short, sharp, shrill sound. 2 INFORMAL. chance to get by or escape: *a narrow squeak.* [apparently imitative]

squeak y (skwē′kē), *adj.,* **squeak i er, squeak i est.** squeaking. **—squeak′i ly,** *adv.* **—squeak′i ness,** *n.*

squeal (skwēl), *v.i.* 1 make a long, sharp, shrill cry: *A pig squeals when it is hurt.* 2 SLANG. turn informer; inform. 3 INFORMAL. complain loudly; squawk. *—v.t.* utter sharply and shrilly. *—n.* a long, sharp, shrill cry. [imitative] **—squeal′er,** *n.*

squeam ish (skwē′mish), *adj.* 1 too proper, modest, etc.; easily shocked; prudish. 2 too particular; too scrupulous. 3 slightly sick at one's stomach; nauseated. 4 easily affected with nausea; queasy. [< Anglo-French *escoymous*] **—squeam′ish ly,** *adv.* **—squeam′ish ness,** *n.*

squee gee (skwē′jē′), *n., v.,* **-geed, -gee ing.** *—n.* 1 tool consisting of a blade of rubber or the like and a handle, used for sweeping water from wet decks, removing water from windows after washing, etc. 2 any of various similar devices. *—v.t.* sweep, scrape, or press with a squeegee. [perhaps < *squeege,* variant of *squeeze*]

squeeze (skwēz), *v.,* **squeezed, squeez ing,** *n.* *—v.t.* 1 press hard; compress: *squeeze a lemon.* 2 hug; embrace: *She squeezed her child.* 3 force or thrust by pressing: *squeeze oneself through a narrow opening.* 4 force out or extract by pressure: *squeeze juice from a lemon.* 5 get by force, pressure, or effort; extort: *The dictator squeezed money from the people.* 6 INFORMAL. put pressure on or try to influence (a person or persons) to do something, especially to pay money: *The blackmailer squeezed his victim for more money.* 7 burden; oppress: *Heavy taxes squeezed the people.* *—v.i.* 1 yield to pressure: *Sponges squeeze easily.* 2 force a way: *I squeezed through the crowd.*
—n. 1 a squeezing; tight pressure. 2 a friendly or affectionate pressing of another's hand in one's own. 3 hug; embrace. 4 crush; crowd. 5 a small quantity or amount squeezed out. 6 something made by pressing; cast; impression. 7 INFORMAL. situation from which escape is difficult, as when a retailer is caught between low prices and high costs.
[ultimately Old English *cwȳsan*] **—squeez′a ble,** *adj.* **—squeez′er,** *n.*

squeeze bottle, a plastic bottle which is squeezed to force out its contents.

squeeze play, (in baseball) a play in which the batter bunts the ball, giving a runner on third base a good chance to score.

squelch (skwelch), *v.t.* 1 cause to be silent; crush: *She squelched him with a look of contempt.* 2 strike or press on with crushing force; put down; squash; suppress. *—v.i.* 1 walk in mud, water, wet shoes, etc., making a splashing sound; slosh. 2 make the sound of one doing so. *—n.* 1 INFORMAL. a crushing retort. 2 a splashing sound made by walking in mud, water, wet shoes, etc. [apparently imitative] **—squelch′er,** *n.*

squib (skwib), *n.* 1 a short, witty, or satirical attack in speech or writing; lampoon. 2 a broken firecracker. 3 a small firework that burns with a hissing noise and finally explodes. [origin uncertain]

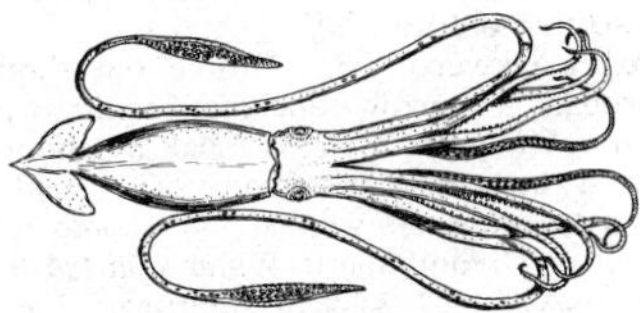

squid—body of this type to 18 ft. long

squid (skwid), *n., pl.* **squids** or **squid,** *v.,* **squid ded, squid ding.** *—n.* any of various saltwater cephalopod mollusks, having eight arms and two tentacles that surround the mouth, a round or elongated body, and a pair of tail fins. Small squids are much used as bait. *—v.i.* fish with a squid as bait. [origin uncertain]

squig gle (skwig′əl), *n., v.,* **-gled, -gling.** *—n.* a wriggly twist or curve. *—v.t.* make with twisting or curving lines. *—v.i.* twist and turn about; writhe; squirm; wriggle. [blend of *squirm* and *wriggle*]

squill (skwil), *n.* 1 plant of the lily family, whose onionlike bulb is used in medicine. 2 its bulb. [< Latin *squilla* < Greek *skilla*]

squint (skwint), *v.i.* 1 look with the eyes partly closed. 2 look sideways. 3 incline; tend: *The general's remark squinted toward treason.* 4 be cross-eyed. 5 run or go obliquely. *—v.t.* 1 hold (the eyes) partly closed. 2 cause to look sideways. *—n.* 1 a looking with partly closed eyes. 2 a sidelong look; hasty look; look. 3 tendency to look sideways. 4 inclination; tendency. 5 cross-eyed condition. *—adj.* 1 looking sideways; looking askance. 2 cross-eyed. [< *asquint,* of uncertain origin] **—squint′er,** *n.*

squinting modifier, (in grammar) a modifier placed in such a way that it may be taken to modify either a preceding or a following word; an ambiguous modifier. EXAMPLE: In "A man who runs swiftly tires," *swiftly* is a squinting modifier.

squint y (skwin′tē), *adj.,* **squint i er, squint i est.** having a squint.

squire (skwīr), *n., v.,* **squired, squir ing.** *—n.* 1 (in Great Britain) a country gentleman or landed proprietor, especially the chief landowner in a district. 2 (in the United States) a justice of the peace or a local judge. 3 a young man of noble family who attended a knight till he himself was made a knight. 4 a male personal attendant, especially of a sovereign or noble personage. 5 a woman's escort. —*v.t.* 1 attend as a squire. 2 escort (a woman). [< Old French *esquier* < Latin *scutarius* shield-bearer < *scutum* shield] **—squire′like′,** *adj.*

squire ar chy (skwīr′är′kē), *n., pl.* **-chies.** country gentry as a class.

squirm (skwėrm), *v.i., v.t.* 1 turn and twist; wriggle; writhe: *The dog squirmed its way through the hole in the fence.* 2 show great embarrassment, annoyance, confusion, etc. —*n.* a wriggle; writhe; twist. [perhaps imitative]

squirm y (skwėr′mē), *adj.,* **squirm i er, squirm i est.** squirming; wriggling.

squir rel (skwėr′əl), *n.* 1 any of various small, agile rodents that have long, bushy tails and usually live in trees. 2 the gray, reddish, or dark-brown fur of any squirrel. [< Anglo-French *esquirel* < Latin *sciurus* < Greek *skiouros* < *skia* shadow + *oura* tail] **—squir′rel like′,** *adj.*

squirt (skwėrt), *v.t.* 1 force out (liquid) through a narrow opening: *squirt water through a tube.* 2 wet or soak by shooting liquid in a jet or stream: *The elephant squirted me with his trunk.* —*v.i.* come out in a jet or stream; spurt: *Water squirted from the hose.* —*n.* 1 act of squirting. 2 jet of liquid, etc. 3 a small pump, syringe, or other device for squirting a liquid. 4 INFORMAL. an insignificant person who is impudent or conceited. [origin uncertain] **—squirt′er,** *n.*

squish (skwish), *v.t.* cause to make a soft, splashing sound. —*n.* a squishing sound. [alteration of *squash*[1]]

squish y (skwish′ē), *adj.,* **squish i er, squish i est.** making or characterized by soft, splashing sounds; wet and soft.

sq. yd., square yard or square yards.

Sr, strontium.

Sr., 1 senior. 2 señor. 3 Sir. 4 Sister.

Sra., señora.

Sri Lan ka (srē′ län′kə), official name of Ceylon. It is a member of the Commonwealth of Nations. 12,514,000 pop.; 25,300 sq. mi. *Capital:* Colombo.

Sri na gar (srē nug′ər), *n.* city in W Kashmir. 325,000.

S.R.O., standing room only.

SS, a select military unit of fanatical Nazis who served as Hitler's bodyguard, in special units, and as a policing unit of the German army. Also, **SS Troops.** [< German *S(chutz)s(taffel)* security echelon]

SS or **S.S.,** 1 Secretary of State. 2 steamship. 3 Straits Settlements. 4 Sunday school.

SSE or **S.S.E.,** south-southeast.

S.Sgt., staff sergeant.

S.S.R. or **SSR,** Soviet Socialist Republic.

SSS, Selective Service System.

SST, supersonic transport.

SS Troops, SS.

SSW or **S.S.W.,** south-southwest.

st., 1 stanza. 2 stet. 3 stone (weight). 4 street.

St., 1 Saint. 2 Strait. 3 Street.

Sta., station.

stab (stab), *v.,* **stabbed, stab bing,** *n.* —*v.t.* 1 pierce or wound with a pointed weapon. 2 thrust (a weapon) into a person. 3 wound sharply or deeply in the feelings: *be stabbed to the heart by someone's lack of gratitude.* 4 **stab in the back,** attempt to injure in a sly, treacherous manner. —*v.i.* 1 thrust with a pointed weapon; aim a blow; jab. 2 penetrate suddenly and sharply; pierce. —*n.* 1 thrust or blow made with a pointed weapon. 2 any thrust or sudden, sharp blow. 3 wound made by stabbing. 4 injury to the feelings. 5 INFORMAL. an attempt. 6 **stab in the back,** an act of unexpected treachery. [ultimately related to STUB] **—stab′ber,** *n.*

sta bile (stā′bəl, stab′əl), *adj.* having stability; stable. —*n.* a stationary sculpture made of colored spheres, disks, and wires, or of large cut and bent sheets of metal, etc.

sta bil i ty (stə bil′ə tē), *n., pl.* **-ties.** 1 a being fixed in position; firmness. 2 permanence. 3 steadfastness of character, purpose, etc. 4 ability of an object to maintain or to return to its original position.

sta bi lize (stā′bə līz), *v.,* **-lized, -liz ing.** —*v.t.* 1 make stable or firm. 2 prevent changes in; hold steady: *stabilize prices.* 3 keep (an aircraft, ship, etc.) steady by special construction or by special devices. —*v.i.* become stable. **—sta′bi li za′tion,** *n.*

sta bi liz er (stā′bə lī′zər), *n.* 1 person or thing that stabilizes. 2 device, such as an airfoil or gyroscope, for keeping an airplane, ship, etc., steady.

sta ble[1] (stā′bəl), *n., v.,* **-bled, -bling.** —*n.* 1 building fitted with stalls, rack and manger, etc., in which horses and sometimes other animals are kept and fed. 2 group of animals housed in such a building. 3 Often, **stables,** *pl.* buildings and grounds where racehorses are quartered and trained. 4 group of racehorses belonging to one owner. 5 grooms, trainers, etc., who work for a racing stable. —*v.t., v.i.* lodge or be lodged in a stable. [< Old French *estable* < Latin *stabulum* a standing place] **—sta′bler,** *n.*

sta ble[2] (stā′bəl), *adj.* 1 not likely to fall or be overturned: *a stable government.* 2 not likely to give way; steady; firm: *a stable support.* 3 not likely to change in nature or purpose; steadfast: *a calm, stable person, a stable resolve.* 4 not liable to destruction or essential change; permanent: *a stable design.* 5 able to maintain or return to its original position: *a stable ship.* 6 (of a chemical compound) not easily decomposed. 7 (of a nuclear particle) not capable of decay; not radioactive. [< Old French *estable* < Latin *stabilis* able to stand] **—sta′ble ness,** *n.* **—sta′bly,** *adv.*

sta ble boy (stā′bəl boi′), *n.* boy or man who works in a stable.

stab lish (stab′lish), *v.t.* ARCHAIC. establish.

stacc., staccato.

stac ca to (stə kä′tō), *adj.* 1 (in music) with breaks between the successive tones; disconnected; detached. 2 abrupt: *a staccato manner.* —*adv.* in a staccato manner. [< Italian, literally, detached]

stack (stak), *n.* 1 a large pile of hay, straw, grain in the sheaf, etc., often round and arranged to shed water. 2 an orderly pile of anything: *a stack of wood, a stack of boxes.* 3 number of rifles arranged with their muzzles together to form a cone or pyramid. 4 INFORMAL. a large number or quantity: *a stack of compliments.* 5 chimney. 6 rack with shelves for books. 7 **stacks,** *pl.* part of a library in which the main collection of books is shelved. —*v.t.* 1 pile or arrange in a stack: *stack hay, stack firewood.* 2 arrange (playing cards) dishonestly. —*v.i.* **stack up,** INFORMAL. measure up; compare. [< Scandinavian (Old Icelandic) *stakkr*] **—stack′er,** *n.*

sta di a[1] (stā′dē ə), *n.* instrument for measuring distances or heights by means of angles. A surveyor's transit is one kind of stadia. 2 method of measuring distances by using such an instrument. [apparently < Italian, lengths < Latin, plural of *stadium.* See STADIUM.]

sta di a[2] (stā′dē ə), *n.* a pl. of **stadium.**

sta di um (stā′dē əm), *n., pl.* **-di ums** or **-di a.** 1 an oval or U-shaped structure consisting of tiers of seats for spectators around an arena or playing field. 2 an ancient Greek running track for footraces, with tiers of seats along each side and at one end. The stadium at Athens was about 607 feet long. 3 unit of linear measure used in the ancient world, most commonly equal to slightly over 600 feet or 1/8 of a Roman mile. [< Latin < Greek *stadion* ancient Greek measure of length, equal at Athens to about 607 feet (see def. 2)]

Staël (stäl), *n.* **Madame de,** 1766-1817, French social leader and novelist. Her real name was Baroness Anne Louise Germaine Necker de Staël-Holstein.

staff (staf), *n., pl.* **staves** or **staffs** for 1 and 2, **staffs** for 3-5, *v.* —*n.* 1 a stick, pole, or rod used as a support, as an emblem of office, as a weapon, etc.: *The flag hangs on a staff.* 2 something that supports or sustains. Bread is called the staff of life. 3 group assisting a chief; group of employees. 4 (in the armed forces) a group of officers assisting a commanding officer with administration, planning, etc., but without command or combat duties. 5 set of five lines and the four spaces between them on which music is written; stave. —*v.t.* provide with officers or employees. [Old English *stæf*]

staff er (staf′ər), *n.* INFORMAL. member of a staff.

staff officer, (in the armed forces) an officer belonging to the staff of a commanding officer.

Staf ford (staf′ərd), *n.* Staffordshire.

Staf ford shire (staf′ərd shər, staf′ərd-shir), *n.* county in W England.

staff sergeant, 1 (in the U.S. Army and Marine Corps) a noncommissioned officer ranking above a sergeant. 2 (in the U.S. Air Force) a noncommissioned officer ranking above an airman first class.

stag (stag), *n.* 1 a full-grown male deer, especially the European red deer; hart. 2 the male of various other animals. 3 animal, especially a hog, castrated when full grown. 4 man who goes to a dance, party, etc., alone or with other men. 5 INFORMAL. dinner, party, etc., attended by men only. —*adj.* attended by or for men only: *a stag dinner.* —*adv.* without a woman's company: *go stag to a party.* [Old English *stagga*]

stage (stāj), *n., v.,* **staged, stag ing.** —*n.* 1 one step or degree in a process; period of development. An insect passes through several stages before it is full-grown. Childhood, adolescence, and adulthood are stages of a person's life. 2 the raised platform, especially in a theater, on which actors perform. 3 Usually, **the stage.** the theater; the drama; actor's profession: *Shakespeare wrote for the stage.* 4 scene of action: *Bunker Hill was the stage of a great battle.* 5 section of a rocket or missile having its own engine and fuel. A three-stage rocket has three engines, one in each stage, which separate one after another from the rocket or missile after the fuel is burned up. 6 stagecoach or bus. 7 place of rest on a journey, especially a regular stopping place for stagecoaches, etc. 8 the distance between two stopping places on a

hat, āge, fär; let, ēqual, tėrm;
it, īce; hot, ōpen, ôrder;
oil, out; cup, pu̇t, rüle;
ch, child; ng, long; sh, she;
th, thin; ᴛʜ, then; zh, measure;

ə represents *a* in about, *e* in taken, *i* in pencil, *o* in lemon, *u* in circus.

< = from, derived from, taken from.

journey. 9 platform; flooring. 10 the small platform on which an object is placed to be viewed through a microscope. 11 scaffold. 12 (in geology) two or more sets of related beds of stratified rocks. It is the division of rocks ranking below a series. 13 U.S. (of water) a level. 14 **by easy stages,** a little at a time; often stopping; slowly. 15 **on the stage,** in the acting profession.
—*v.t.* 1 put on or as on a stage: *stage an art exhibit. The play was very well staged.* 2 U.S. arrange to have an effect: *The angry people staged a riot.* —*v.i.* be suited to the theater: *That scene will not stage well.*
[< Old French *estage* < Popular Latin *staticum* < Latin *stare* to stand] **—stage′like′,** *adj.*

stagecoach

stage coach (stāj′kōch′), *n.* a horse-drawn coach carrying passengers and parcels over a regular route.

stage craft (stāj′kraft′), *n.* skill in, or the art of, writing, adapting, or presenting plays.

stage direction, a direction in a written or printed play to indicate the appropriate action, arrangement of the stage, etc.

stage fright, nervous fear of appearing before an audience.

stage hand (stāj′hand′), *n.* person whose work is moving scenery, arranging lights, etc., in a theater.

stage manager, person in charge of the arrangements of the stage during the preparation and performance of a play.

stag er (stā′jər), *n.* 1 person of long experience; veteran. 2 horse used for drawing a stagecoach.

stage-struck (stāj′struk′), *adj.* extremely interested in acting; wanting very much to become an actor or actress.

stage whisper, 1 a loud whisper on a stage, meant for the audience to hear. 2 whisper meant to be heard by others than the person addressed.

stag ger (stag′ər), *v.i.* 1 sway or reel (from weakness, a heavy load, or drunkenness); totter: *stagger under a heavy load of books.* See **reel**[2] for synonym study. 2 become unsteady; waver: *The troops staggered under the severe gunfire.* 3 hesitate. —*v.t.* 1 make sway or reel: *The blow staggered me for a moment.* 2 cause to doubt, hesitate, or falter. 3 confuse or astonish greatly; overwhelm: *The difficulty of the examination staggered her.* 4 make helpless. 5 arrange in a zigzag order or way. 6 arrange at intervals or at other than the normal times: *stagger vacations in an office.* —*n.* 1 a swaying or reeling. 2 **staggers,** *pl.* nervous disease of horses, cattle, etc., that makes them stagger or fall suddenly. [< Scandinavian (Old Icelandic) *stakra*] **—stag′ger er,** *n.*

stag ger ing (stag′ər ing), *adj.* enormous; immense; stupendous: *a staggering achievement.* **—stag′ger ing ly,** *adv.*

stag hound (stag′hound′), *n.* a large hound, formerly used for hunting deer, wolves, etc.

stag ing (stā′jing), *n.* 1 a temporary flooring, used as a platform by workmen or builders; scaffolding. 2 act or process of putting a play on the stage. 3 act of releasing a stage in a rocket or spacecraft. 4 act of assembling personnel, equipment, etc., before a military movement or expedition.

stag nan cy (stag′nən sē), *n.* stagnant condition.

stag nant (stag′nənt), *adj.* 1 not running or flowing: *stagnant air, stagnant water.* 2 foul from standing still: *a stagnant pool of water.* 3 not active; sluggish; dull: *During the summer, business is often stagnant.* [< Latin *stagnantem*] **—stag′nant ly,** *adv.*

stag nate (stag′nāt), *v.,* **-nat ed, -nat ing.** —*v.i.* be or become stagnant. —*v.t.* make stagnant. [< Latin *stagnatum* made stagnant < *stagnum* standing water] **—stag na′tion,** *n.*

stag y (stā′jē), *adj.,* **stag i er, stag i est.** 1 of or having to do with the stage. 2 suggestive of the stage; theatrical. 3 artificial; pompous; affected. **—stag′i ly,** *adv.* **—stag′i ness,** *n.*

staid (stād), *adj.* 1 having a settled, quiet character; sober; sedate. 2 settled; unchanging; fixed. —*v.* ARCHAIC. a pt. and a pp. of **stay**[1]. [originally past participle of *stay*[1] in sense of "restrain"] **—staid′ly,** *adv.* **—staid′ness,** *n.*

stain (stān), *v.t.* 1 discolor (something) with spots or streaks of dirt, blood, etc.; soil; spot. 2 bring reproach or disgrace on; dishonor. 3 taint with guilt or vice; defile. 4 color or dye. —*v.i.* 1 cause a stain or discoloration. 2 take a stain; admit of staining. —*n.* 1 discoloration made by soiling; spot. 2 mark of disgrace; dishonor. 3 a coloring or dye, especially one that penetrates the pores of woods, fabrics, etc. [earlier *distain* < Old French *desteindre* take out the color, ultimately < Latin *dis-* off + *tingere* to dye] **—stain′a ble,** *adj.* **—stain′er,** *n.* **—stain′less,** *adj.*

stained glass, colored glass used in sheets or fitted pieces in church windows to form a picture, or in mosaic or composite designs. **—stained′-glass′,** *adj.*

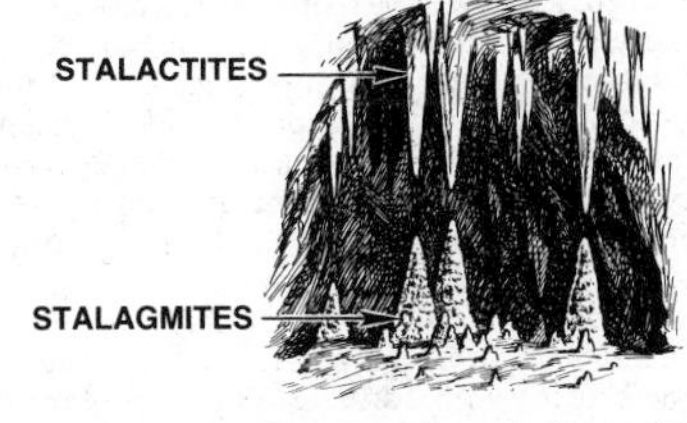

stainless steel, steel containing a high percentage of chromium, making it very resistant to rust and corrosion.

stair (ster, star), *n.* 1 one of a series of steps for going from one level or floor to another. 2 Also, **stairs,** *pl.* set of such steps; stairway; staircase. [Old English *stǣger*] **—stair′less,** *adj.*

stair case (ster′kās′, star′kās′), *n.* stairs.

stair step (ster′step′, star′step′), *n.* stair. —*adj.* rising or falling in a series of steps.

stair way (ster′wā′, star′wā′), *n.* stairs.

stair well (ster′wel′, star′wel′), *n.* the vertical passage or open space containing the stairs of a building.

stake[1] (stāk), *n., v.,* **staked, stak ing.** —*n.* 1 stick or post pointed at one end for driving into the ground. 2 **pull up stakes,** INFORMAL. move away. 3 **the stake,** a post to which a person was tied and then burned to death. b death by being burned in this way. 4 district within the Mormon Church made up of a number of wards. —*v.t.* 1 fasten to a stake or with a stake. 2 support (a plant, tree, vine, etc.) with a stake or stakes. 3 mark with stakes; mark the boundaries of: *stake out a mining claim.* [Old English *staca*]

stake[2] (stāk), *v.,* **staked, stak ing,** *n.* —*v.t.* 1 risk (money or something valuable) on the result of a game or on any chance; bet; wager. 2 INFORMAL. assist or back (a person) with money, etc.; grubstake: *I'll stake you to a dinner if you'll come.* —*n.* 1 money risked; what is staked: *They played for high stakes.* 2 Often, **stakes,** *pl.* prize in a race or contest. 3 something to gain or lose; share in a property; interest. 4 INFORMAL. a grubstake. 5 **at stake,** to be won or lost; in jeopardy; risked. [origin uncertain] **—stak′er,** *n.*

stake hold er (stāk′hōl′dər), *n.* person who takes care of what is bet and pays it to the winner.

Sta kha no vism (stə kä′nə viz′əm), *n.* (in the Soviet Union) a system of rewarding individual enterprise (in factories, etc.) and thereby increasing output. [< Aleksey G. *Stakhanov,* a Russian coal miner whose record output in two shifts in 1935 was taken as a model for the system]

Sta kha no vite (stə kä′nə vīt), *n.* worker who increases his output under Stakhanovism.

sta lac tite (stə lak′tīt, stal′ək tīt), *n.* a formation of calcium carbonate, shaped like an icicle, hanging from the roof of a cave, formed by dripping water that contains calcium carbonate. [< New Latin *stalactites* < Greek *stalaktos* dripping < *stalassein* to trickle]

stal ac tit ic (stal′ək tit′ik), *adj.* of the nature of or like a stalactite or stalactites.

sta lag mite (stə lag′mīt, stal′əg mīt), *n.* a formation of calcium carbonate, shaped like a cone, built up on the floor of a cave, formed by water dripping from a stalactite. [< New Latin *stalagmites* < Greek *stalagmos* a drop < *stalassein* to trickle]

stal ag mit ic (stal′əg mit′ik), *adj.* of the nature of or like a stalagmite or stalagmites.

stale (stāl), *adj.,* **stal er, stal est,** *v.,* **staled, stal ing.** —*adj.* 1 not fresh: *stale bread.* 2 no longer new or interesting; trite; hackneyed: *a stale joke.* 3 out of condition: *The horse has gone stale from too much running.* —*v.t., v.i.* make or become stale. [Middle English] **—stale′ly,** *adv.* **—stale′ness,** *n.*

stale mate (stāl′māt′), *n., v.,* **-mat ed, -mat ing.** —*n.* 1 (in chess) a draw which results when a player cannot move any of his pieces without putting his own king in check. 2 any position in which no action can be taken; complete standstill. —*v.t.* put in a position in which no action can be taken; bring to a complete standstill. [< Middle English *stale* stalemate (probably < Anglo-French *estale* standstill; of Germanic origin) + *mate*[2]]

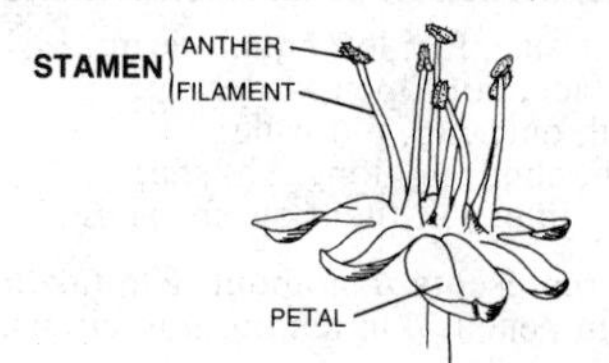

Sta lin (stä′lin), *n.* **Joseph,** 1879-1953, Soviet political leader, dictator of the Soviet Union from 1929 to 1953.

Sta lin grad (stä′lin grad), *n.* former name of **Volgograd.**

Sta lin ism (stä′lə niz′əm), *n.* the theory or system of communism associated with Stalin, especially as characterized by coercion and severe oppression of opposition.

Sta lin ist (stä′lə nist), *n.* follower of Stalin or Stalinism. —*adj.* of or characteristic of Stalinism.

stalk[1] (stôk), *n.* 1 stem or main axis of a plant. 2 any slender, supporting or connecting part of a plant. A flower or a leaf blade may have a stalk. 3 any similar part of an animal. The eyes of a crayfish are on stalks. 4 a slender, upright support: *a wine glass with a tall stalk.* [Middle English *stalke*] —**stalk′less,** *adj.* —**stalk′like′,** *adj.*

stalk[2] (stôk), *v.t.* approach or pursue without being seen or heard: *The hunters stalked the lion.* —*v.i.* 1 spread silently and steadily: *Disease stalked through the land.* 2 walk with slow, stiff, or haughty strides. —*n.* 1 a haughty gait. 2 act of stalking. [Old English *(be)stealcian* steal along] —**stalk′er,** *n.*

stalk ing-horse (stôk′ing hôrs′), *n.* 1 horse or figure of a horse, behind which a hunter conceals himself in stalking game. 2 anything used to hide plans or acts; pretext.

stall[1] (stôl), *n.* 1 division in a stable for one animal. 2 BRITISH. booth in which goods are exposed for sale or in which some business is conducted. 3 seat in the choir of a church. 4 BRITISH. seat in the front part of a theater; orchestra seat. 5 one of the sheaths for the fingers in a glove. 6 a parking space. —*v.t.* 1 put or keep in a stall. 2 stop or bring to a standstill, usually against one's wish: *stall an engine.* 3 cause to become stuck in mud, snow, etc. —*v.i.* 1 live in a stall, stable, kennel, etc. 2 come to a stop or standstill, usually against one's wish: *The car stalled.* 3 become stuck in mud, snow, etc. 4 (of an airplane or airfoil) lose speed or lift so that the airplane cannot be controlled. [Old English *steall,* probably related to *stæl* a place] —**stall′-like′,** *adj.*

stall[2] (stôl), INFORMAL. —*n.* pretext to prevent or delay action, the accomplishment of a purpose, etc. —*v.i.* act or speak evasively, deceptively, or hesitantly so as to prevent action, etc. —*v.t.* Usually, **stall off.** put off; delay. [earlier *stale* decoy < Middle French *estaler* to place < *estal* a place; of Germanic origin]

stal lion (stal′yən), *n.* an uncastrated male horse, especially one kept for breeding purposes. [< Old French *estalon;* of Germanic origin]

stal wart (stôl′wərt), *adj.* 1 strongly built; sturdy; robust. 2 strong and brave; valiant. 3 firm; steadfast. —*n.* 1 a stalwart person. 2 a loyal supporter of a political party. [Old English *stǣlwierthe* serviceable < *stathol* position + *wierthe* worthy] —**stal′wart ly,** *adv.* —**stal′wart ness,** *n.*

sta men (stā′mən), *n., pl.* **sta mens, stam i na** (stam′ə nə, stā′mə nə). part of a flower that contains the pollen, consisting of a slender, threadlike stem or filament which supports the anther. The stamens are surrounded by the petals. [< Latin, warp, thread]

Stam ford (stam′fərd), *n.* city in SW Connecticut. 109,000.

stam i na (stam′ə nə), *n.* strength; endurance. [< Latin, plural of *stamen* thread (of life, spun by the Fates)]

stam i nal (stam′ə nəl), *adj.* having to do with or consisting of stamens.

stam i nate (stam′ə nit, stam′ə nāt), *adj.* 1 having stamens but no pistils. 2 having a stamen or stamens; producing stamens.

stam mer (stam′ər), *v.i.* hesitate in speaking; speak haltingly, as from nervousness or embarrassment. See synonym study below. —*v.t.* utter in this way: *stammer an excuse.* —*n.* a stammering; stuttering. [Old English *stamerian*] —**stam′mer er,** *n.* —**stam′mer ing ly,** *adv.*

Syn. *v.i.* **Stammer, stutter** mean to speak in a stumbling or jerky way, pausing and repeating sounds. **Stammer** suggests painfully effortful speaking with breaks or silences in or between words, especially through fear, embarrassment, or emotional disturbance. **Stutter** suggests a habit of repeating rapidly or jerkily the same sound, especially initial consonants (*s, p,* etc.).

stamp (stamp), *n.* 1 a small piece of paper with a sticky back, put on letters, papers, parcels, etc., to show that a charge for mailing has been paid; postage stamp. 2 a similar piece of paper given to customers as a bonus, to be exchanged for goods; trading stamp. 3 any official mark or label required by law to be affixed to a paper or item to show that a fee, duty, tax, etc., has been paid. 4 an official mark certifying quality, genuineness, validity, etc. 5 act of stamping. 6 an instrument that cuts, shapes, or impresses a design, characters, words, etc., on (paper, wax, metal, etc.); thing that puts a mark on. 7 the mark, impression, or imprint made by such an instrument. 8 mill or machine that crushes rock, etc. 9 impression; mark; imprint: *Her face bore the stamp of suffering.* 10 kind; type: *Men of his stamp are rare.*
—*v.t.* 1 put a stamp on: *stamp an official document, stamp a letter.* 2 bring down (one's foot) with force: *stamp one's foot in anger.* 3 pound, crush, trample, drive, etc.: *stamp the snow from one's boots.* 4 fix firmly or deeply: *an event stamped on one's memory.* 5 mark with an instrument that cuts, shapes, or impresses a design, characters, words, character. 6 show to be of a certain quality or character; indicate: *Her speech stamps her as an educated woman.* 7 **stamp out, a** put out by stamping: *stamp out a fire.* **b** put an end to by force: *stamp out a rebellion.* —*v.i.* 1 bring down the foot forcibly: *stamp on a spider.* 2 walk with a heavy, pounding tread: *The children stamped up the stairs.*
[Middle English *stampen* stamp with the foot, pound in a mortar] —**stamp′er,** *n.*

stam pede (stam pēd′), *n., v.,* **-ped ed, -ped ing.** —*n.* 1 a sudden scattering or headlong flight of a frightened herd of cattle, horses, etc. 2 any headlong flight of a large group. 3 a general rush: *a stampede to newly discovered gold fields.* —*v.i.* 1 scatter or flee in a stampede. 2 make a general rush. —*v.t.* cause to stampede. [< Mexican Spanish *estampida* < Spanish *estampar* to stamp]

stamping ground, a person's or animal's habitual place of resort.

stance (stans), *n.* 1 position of the feet of a player when swinging at the ball in golf, baseball, or other games. 2 manner of standing; posture. 3 attitude; point of view. [< Old French *estance,* ultimately < Latin *stare* to stand]

stanch[1] (stänch, stanch), *v.t.* 1 stop or check the flow of (blood, etc.). 2 stop the flow of blood from (a wound). —*v.i.* cease flowing. Also, **staunch.** [< Old French *estanchier* to stop, hinder] —**stanch′er,** *n.*

stanch[2] (stänch, stanch), *adj.* staunch. —**stanch′ly,** *adv.* —**stanch′ness,** *n.*

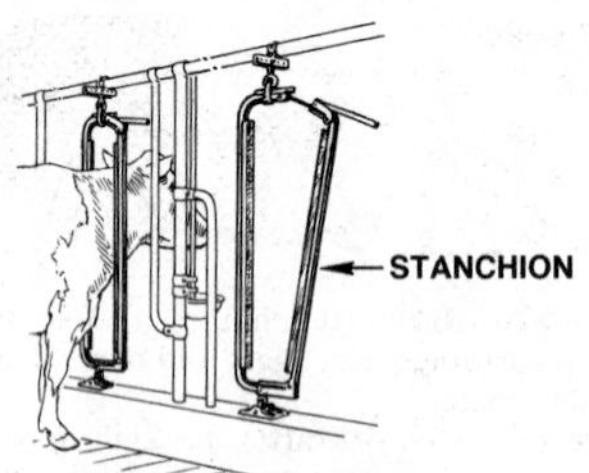

stanchion (def. 2)—two stanchions

stan chion (stan′shən), *n.* 1 an upright bar, post, or support, as for a window, a roof, or the deck of a ship. 2 a framework of two vertical bars which fasten loosely around the neck of a cow to hold her in place while in a stall. —*v.t.* 1 fasten (cattle) by stanchions. 2 strengthen or support with stanchions. [< Old French *estanchon* < *estance* stance. See STANCE.]

stand (stand), *v.,* **stood, stand ing,** *n.* —*v.i.* 1 be upright on one's feet: *Don't stand if you are tired; sit down.* 2 be of a specified height when erect: *She stands five feet tall.* 3 rise to one's feet: *He stood when she entered the room.* 4 be set upright; be placed; be located: *a chair standing in a corner.* 5 be in a certain place, rank, scale, etc.: *She stood first in her class.* 6 take or keep a certain position. *"Stand back!" called the policeman to the crowd.* 7 take a way of thinking or acting: *stand for justice.* 8 be in a special condition: *stand accused. The door stood ajar.* 9 be unchanged; hold good; remain the same: *The rule against being late will stand.* 10 resist destruction or decay; last: *The old house has stood for a hundred years.* 11 collect and remain: *Tears stood in his eyes.* 12 take or remain in a certain course or direction: *The ship stood due north.* 13 stop moving; halt; stop: *The cars stood and waited for the light to change.* 14 (of a dog) point. —*v.t.* 1 cause to stand; set upright: *stand a ladder against a wall.* 2 be submitted to (a trial, test, ordeal, etc.); undergo: *stand a rigid examination.* 3 withstand: *stand enemy fire.* 4 endure: *Those plants cannot stand cold.* See **bear**[1] for synonym study. 5 act as: *stand guard.* 6 INFORMAL. bear the expense of; pay for: *stand a treat.*

stand by, a be near. **b** help; support: *stand by a friend.* **c** keep; maintain. **d** be or get ready for use, action, etc.

stand down, leave the witness stand.

stand for, a represent; mean. **b** be on the side of; take the part of; uphold. **c** be a candidate for. **d** INFORMAL. put up with. **e** sail or steer toward.

stand in, **a** INFORMAL. be associated or friendly; be on good terms. **b** act as a stand-in.
stand off, INFORMAL. keep off; keep away.
stand on, **a** depend on; be based on. **b** demand; assert; claim.
stand out, **a** project. **b** be noticeable or prominent. **c** refuse to yield.
stand over, be left for later treatment, consideration, or settlement.
stand up, **a** get to one's feet; rise. **b** endure; last. **c** INFORMAL. break a date with; fail to meet.
stand up for, take the part of; support; defend.
stand up to, meet or face boldly.
—n. **1** act of standing. **2** halt; stop. **3** halt for defense or resistance: *make a last stand against the enemy.* **4** halt made on a theatrical tour to give a performance or performances. **5** place where a person stands; position; station: *The school crossing guard took her stand at the street corner.* **6** a moral position: *take a stand against gambling.* **7** Also, **stands,** *pl.* an elevated platform or other structure for spectators or for a band or other group of performers. **8** a stall, booth, table, etc., for the display of goods for sale. **9** framework, table, etc., to put things on or in: *a stand for wet umbrellas.* **10** group of growing trees, plants, etc.: *a stand of timber.* **11 take the stand,** go on the witness stand and give evidence.
[Old English *standan*]

stan dard (stan′dərd), *n.* **1** anything taken as a basis of comparison; model: *Your work is not up to the class standard.* See synonym study below. **2** rule, test, or requirement. **3** an authorized weight or measure. **4** a commodity, such as gold or silver, that is given a fixed value in order to serve in a monetary system as a measure of value for all other commodities. **5** flag, emblem, or symbol: *The dragon was the standard of China.* **6** an upright support: *The floor lamp has a long standard.* **7** tree or shrub with one tall, straight stem. *—adj.* **1** of the accepted or normal size, amount, power, quality, etc.: *the standard rate of pay, a standard gauge.* **2** used as a standard; according to rule: *standard spelling, standard pronunciation.* **3** having recognized excellence or authority: *Scott and Dickens are standard authors.* [< Old French *estandart;* of Germanic origin]

Syn. *n.* **1 Standard, criterion** mean something used as a means of measuring or judging a person or thing. **Standard** applies to any rule or model generally accepted as a basis of comparison in judging quality, value, quantity, etc.: *set standards for admission to college.* **Criterion** applies to a test or rule by which one may determine the value, excellence, or the like of something already in existence: *Popularity by itself is not a criterion of a good motion picture.*

stan dard-bear er (stan′dərd ber′ər, stan′dərd bar′ər), *n.* **1** officer or soldier who carries a flag or standard; colorbearer. **2** person who carries a banner in a procession. **3** a conspicuous leader of a movement, political party, etc.

stan dard bred (stan′dərd bred′), *adj.* (of a horse) bred and trained primarily for harness racing, as a trotter or pacer. *—n.* a standardbred horse.

Standard English, the English language, both formal and informal, as it is currently spoken and written by educated people.

stan dard ize (stan′dər dīz), *v.t.,* **-ized, -iz ing.** **1** make standard in size, shape, weight, quality, strength, etc.: *The parts of an automobile are standardized.* **2** regulate by a standard. **3** test by a standard. **—stan′dard i za′tion,** *n.*

standard of living, way of living that a person or community considers necessary to provide enough material things for comfort, happiness, etc.

standard time, time officially adopted for a region or country.

stand by (stand′bī′), *n., pl.* **-bys.** **1** person or thing that can be relied upon; chief support; ready resource. **2** person or thing held in reserve, especially as a possible replacement or substitute.

stand ee (stan dē′), *n.* U.S. person who has to stand in a theater, on a bus, etc.

stand-in (stand′in′), *n.* **1** person whose work is standing in the place of a motion-picture actor or actress while the lights, camera, etc., are being arranged, or during scenes in which dangerous action occurs. **2** person or thing that takes the place of another; substitute.

stand ing (stan′ding), *n.* **1** rank or position in society, a profession, etc.; reputation: *a person of good standing.* **2** good or high rank or reputation. **3** length of existence; duration: *a feud of long standing between two families.* **4** act of standing; place of standing. *—adj.* **1** straight up; erect; upright: *standing timber.* **2** done from an erect position: *a standing jump.* **3** that stands: *a standing lamp.* **4** established; permanent: *a standing invitation, a standing army.* **5** not flowing; stagnant: *standing water.*

standing room, **1** space to stand in after all the seats are taken. **2** space to stand in.

standing wave, (in physics) a wave characterized by lack of vibration at certain points, between which areas of maximum vibration occur periodically.

Stan dish (stan′dish), *n.* **Miles,** 1584?-1656, the military leader of the colony at Plymouth, Massachusetts.

stand off (stand′ôf′, stand′of′), *n.* **1** tie or draw in a game. **2** something that counterbalances; thing that serves to offset something else. **3** a standing off or apart; reserve; aloofness. *—adj.* standoffish.

stand off ish (stand′ô′fish, stand′of′ish), *adj.* reserved; aloof.

stand out (stand′out′), *n.* person or thing that is outstanding of its kind, especially in excellence.

stand pat (stand′pat′), *adj.* INFORMAL. standing firm for things as they are; opposing any change.

stand pat ter (stand′pat′ər), *n.* INFORMAL. person who stands firm for things as they are and opposes any change, especially in politics.

stand pipe (stand′pīp′), *n.* a large, upright pipe or tower to hold water under pressure, especially one used as a reservoir or auxiliary to a reservoir.

stand point (stand′point′), *n.* point at which one stands to view something; point of view; mental attitude.

stand still (stand′stil′), *n.* a complete stop; halt; pause.

stand-up (stand′up′), *adj.* **1** that stands erect; upright. **2** performed or taken while standing: *a stand-up dinner.* **3** designed and built for standing upright: *a stand-up lunch counter.* **4** performing alone before an audience: *a stand-up comic.* **5** standing up fairly to each other without flinching or evasion: *a stand-up fight.*

hat, āge, fär; let, ēqual, tėrm;
it, īce; hot, ōpen, ôrder;
oil, out; cup, pu̇t, rüle;
ch, child; ng, long; sh, she;
th, thin; TH, then; zh, measure;

ə represents *a* in about, *e* in taken, *i* in pencil, *o* in lemon, *u* in circus.

< = from, derived from, taken from.

stan hope (stan′hōp, stan′əp), *n.* a light, open, one-seated carriage with two or four wheels. [< Fitzroy *Stanhope,* 1787-1864, British clergyman for whom it was first made]

stank (stangk), *v.* a pt. of **stink.**

Stan ley (stan′lē), *n.* Sir **Henry Morton,** 1841-1904, British explorer in Africa. He found the Scottish missionary, David Livingstone, who had disappeared in Africa.

stan nic (stan′ik), *adj.* of, having to do with, or containing tin, especially with a valence of four. [< Late Latin *stannum* tin]

stan nous (stan′əs), *adj.* of, having to do with, or containing tin, especially with a valence of two.

St. Anthony's fire, any of various inflammations of the skin, such as erysipelas.

Stan ton (stan′tən), *n.* **1 Edwin M.,** 1814-1869, American statesman who was secretary of war during the Civil War. **2 Elizabeth Cady,** 1815-1902, American advocate of women's rights.

stan za (stan′zə), *n.* group of lines of poetry, usually four or more, arranged according to a fixed plan; verse of a poem. [< Italian, originally, stopping place, ultimately < Latin *stare* to stand]

stan za ic (stan zā′ik), *adj.* **1** of or having to do with a stanza. **2** forming a stanza. **3** composed of stanzas.

sta pes (stā′pēz′), *n.* the innermost of the three small bones in the middle ear; stirrup bone. [< Medieval Latin, stirrup]

staph (staf), *n.* INFORMAL. staphylococcus or staphylococci.

staph y lo coc cal (staf′ə lə kok′əl), *adj.* having to do with or produced by staphylococci.

staph y lo coc cic (staf′ə lə kok′sik), *adj.* staphylococcal.

staph y lo coc cus (staf′ə lə kok′əs), *n., pl.* **-coc ci** (-kok′sī). any of a genus of parasitic, spherical bacteria that usually bunch together, forming grapelike clusters. Several species are capable of causing serious infections in human beings and other organisms. [< Greek *staphylē* bunch of grapes + New Latin *coccus* coccus]

sta ple[1] (stā′pəl), *n., v.,* **-pled, -pling.** *—n.* **1** a U-shaped piece of metal with pointed ends, driven into doors, etc., to hold hooks, pins, or bolts. **2** a piece of wire of similar shape, used to hold together papers, parts of a book, etc. *—v.t.* fasten with a staple or staples. [Old English *stapol* post] **—sta′pler,** *n.*

sta ple[2] (stā′pəl), *n., adj., v.,* **-pled, -pling.** *—n.* **1** the most important or principal article grown or manufactured in a place: *Cotton is the staple in many southern states.* **2** any major article of commerce or trade; something of recognized quality or in constant demand. 3 a chief element or material. 4 a raw material. 5 fiber of cotton, wool, etc. 6 ARCHAIC. the principal market of a place; chief center of trade. —*adj.* 1 most important; principal: *The weather was their staple subject of conversation.* 2 established in commerce: *a staple trade.* 3 regularly produced in large quantities for the market. —*v.t.* sort according to fiber: *staple wool.* [< Middle French *estaple* mart; of Germanic origin] **—sta′pler,** *n.*

star (stär), *n., v.,* **starred, star ring,** *adj.* —*n.* 1 any of the heavenly bodies appearing as bright points in the sky at night. 2 any heavenly body that shines by its own light, except comets, meteors, and nebulae. Stars are hot, luminous, gaseous bodies varying in size from those slightly larger than the earth to those several million times as large as the sun. 3 (in astrology) a planet or constellation of the zodiac, considered as influencing people and events. 4 fortune; fate. 5 a plane figure having five or six points, as ☆ or ✡. 6 thing having or suggesting this shape. 7 an asterisk (*). 8 (in the United States) representation of a star symbolizing one of the states in the Union. 9 U.S. any of the military medals, awards, etc., having a star-shaped design. 10 person of brilliant qualities or talents in some art, science, etc.: *an athletic star.* 11 actor, singer, etc., who is exceptionally well known or prominently advertised, or who has the leading part in a particular production; lead. **12 see stars,** see flashes of light as a result of a hard blow on one's head. **13 thank one's stars** or **thank one's lucky stars,** be thankful for one's good luck.
—*v.t.* 1 set, adorn, or ornament with stars; bespangle. 2 mark with an asterisk. 3 give a leading part to (an actor or actress, etc.); present to the public as a star. —*v.i.* 1 be brilliant or outstanding; excel. 2 be a leading performer; perform the leading part: *She has starred in many motion pictures.*
—*adj.* chief; best; leading: *a star player.* [Old English *steorra*] **—star′like′,** *adj.*

star board (stär′bərd, stär′bôrd, *or* stär′bōrd), *n.* the right side of a ship, when facing forward. See **aft** for diagram. —*adj.* on, at, or of the right side of a ship. —*v.t., v.i.* turn (the helm) to the right side. [Old English *stēorbord* the side from which a vessel was steered < *stēor* steering paddle + *bord* side (of a ship)]

starch (stärch), *n.* 1 a white, odorless, tasteless, powdery or granular substance, chemically a complex carbohydrate, found in all parts of a plant which store plant food. Potatoes, wheat, rice, and corn contain much starch. 2 preparation of this substance used to stiffen clothes, curtains, etc., or to size paper, etc. **3 starches,** *pl.* food containing much starch. 4 a stiff, formal manner; stiffness. 5 INFORMAL. vigor. —*v.t.* stiffen (clothes, curtains, etc.) with starch. [Old English *stercan* make rigid (in *stercedferhth* stout-hearted) < *stearc* stiff, strong] **—starch′like′,** *adj.*

Star Chamber, 1 (in English history) a court that existed from 1487 until 1641, with full authority for asserting both criminal and civil jurisdiction, characterized by arbitrary, secret, and unfair methods of trial. 2 Also, **star chamber.** any court, committee, or group like this.

starch y (stär′chē), *adj.,* **starch i er, starch i est.** 1 of, like, or containing starch. 2 stiffened with starch. 3 stiff in manner; formal. **—starch′i ness,** *n.*

star-crossed (stär′krôst′, stär′krost′), *adj.* born under an evil star; ill-fated.

star dom (stär′dəm), *n.* 1 a being a star actor or performer. 2 star actors or performers as a group.

star dust (stär′dust′), *n.* 1 masses of stars that look so small as to suggest particles of dust. 2 INFORMAL. glamour; happy enchantment.

stare (ster, star), *v.,* **stared, star ing,** *n.* —*v.i.* 1 look long and directly with the eyes wide open; gaze fixedly; gape: *The little girl stared in wonder at the doll in the window.* See **gaze** for synonym study. 2 be very striking or glaring. —*v.t.* 1 bring to a named condition by staring: *stare a person into silence.* **2 stare down,** confuse or embarrass by staring; abash. —*n.* a long and direct look with the eyes wide open. [Old English *starian*] **—star′er,** *n.*

starfish
about 5 in. across

star fish (stär′fish′), *n., pl.* **-fish es** or **-fish.** any of a class of echinoderms, having five or more arms or rays radiating from a central disk, a mouth under this disk, and rows of tubular walking feet; asteroid. Some are carnivorous and do great damage to oyster beds.

star gaze (stär′gāz′), *v.i.,* **-gazed, -gaz ing.** 1 gaze at the stars. 2 be absent-minded; daydream.

star gaz er (stär′gā′zər), *n.* 1 person who studies the heavens, as an astronomer or astrologer. 2 person given to daydreaming.

star ing (ster′ing, star′ing), *adj.* 1 very conspicuous; too bright; glaring. 2 gazing with a stare; wide-open.

stark (stärk), *adj.* 1 downright; complete; sheer: *That fool is talking stark nonsense.* 2 stiff; rigid: *The dog lay stark in death.* 3 bare; barren; desolate: *a stark landscape.* 4 harsh; stern. 5 ARCHAIC. strong; sturdy. —*adv.* 1 entirely; completely: *stark, raving mad.* 2 in a stark manner. [Old English *stearc* stiff, strong] **—stark′ly,** *adv.* **—stark′ness,** *n.*

star less (stär′lis), *adj.* without stars or starlight; having no stars visible.

star let (stär′lit), *n.* 1 a young actress who is being trained and publicized for leading roles in motion pictures. 2 a little star.

star light (stär′līt′), *n.* light from the stars. —*adj.* starlit.

star ling (stär′ling), *n.* any of a family of stocky, short-tailed European birds, especially a common species naturalized in America, having glossy, greenish-black or brownish-black feathers. Starlings nest about buildings and fly in large flocks. [Old English *stærling*]

star lit (stär′lit′), *adj.* lighted by the stars: *a starlit night.*

star-of-Beth le hem (stär′əv beth′lē əm, stär′əv beth′lə hem), *n.* plant of the lily family that grows from a small bulb and has a tall cluster of green-and-white, star-shaped flowers.

Star of Bethlehem, (in Christian use) the star that heralded the birth of Christ and was followed by the Three Wise Men to the manger where He lay.

Star of David, a Jewish emblem, consisting of a six-pointed star formed of two triangles, one interlaced with or placed upon the other.

starred (stärd), *adj.* 1 full of or decorated with stars. 2 marked with a star or asterisk. 3 presented as a star actor or performer. 4 influenced by the stars or by fate.

star ry (stär′ē), *adj.,* **-ri er, -ri est.** 1 lighted by stars; containing many stars: *a starry sky.* 2 shining like stars; very bright: *starry eyes.* 3 like a star in shape. 4 of or having to do with stars. 5 consisting of stars. **—star′ri ly,** *adv.* **—star′ri ness,** *n.*

star ry-eyed (stär′ē īd′), *adj.* tending to view too favorably or idealistically; unrealistic; dreamy.

Stars and Bars, first flag used by the Confederacy. It had two horizontal red stripes with a white strip between and a blue square containing a circle of seven white stars, one for each of the first seven seceding states.

Stars and Stripes, the flag of the United States, which when first adopted by Congress on June 14, 1777, contained 13 stripes and 13 stars, representing the 13 original states of the Union, and which now contains 13 stripes and 50 stars.

star-span gled (stär′spang′gəld), *adj.* spangled with stars.

Star-Spangled Banner, 1 the national anthem of the United States. The words were composed by Francis Scott Key during the War of 1812. 2 flag of the United States; Stars and Stripes.

star-stud ded (stär′stud′id), *adj.* 1 star-spangled: *a star-studded canopy.* 2 having or featuring many stars or celebrities: *a star-studded show.*

start (stärt), *v.i.* 1 begin moving, going, acting, operating, etc.: *start in business. The train started on time.* 2 give a sudden, involuntary jerk or twitch; move suddenly: *start in surprise, start to one's feet.* 3 come, rise, or spring out suddenly: *Tears started from her eyes.* 4 burst or stick out: *eyes seeming to start from their sockets.* 5 become loose. **6 start in, start out,** or **start up,** begin to do something. —*v.t.* 1 begin; commence: *start a book.* See **begin** for synonym study. 2 cause to begin moving, going, acting, operating, etc.; set in motion: *start an automobile, start a fire.* 3 introduce (a subject, topic, etc.). 4 rouse: *start a rabbit.* 5 cause to loosen: *The huge waves had started the ship's bolts.* 6 enter in a race, especially a horse race. 7 cause (a race or contestants in a race) to begin. 8 OBSOLETE. startle.
—*n.* 1 a setting in motion: *We pushed the car to give the motor a start.* 2 a beginning to move, go, act, etc.: *see a race from start to finish.* 3 a sudden, involuntary movement; jerk: *wake up with a start.* 4 a beginning ahead of others; advantage: *He got the start of his rivals.* 5 chance of starting a career, etc.: *get a start in life.* 6 spurt of energy or activity: *work by fits and starts.* 7 place, line, etc., at which a race begins.
[< variant of Old English *styrtan* leap up]

start er (stär′tər), *n.* 1 person or thing that starts. 2 person who gives the signal for starting. 3 any contestant who sets out in a race. 4 the first in a series of things: *This* *request was only a starter.* 5 self-starter. 6 a chemical agent or bacterial culture used to start a reaction.

starting point, place of starting; beginning.

star tle (stär′tl), *v.,* **-tled, -tling,** *n.* —*v.t.* frighten suddenly; surprise. —*v.i.* move suddenly in fear or surprise. —*n.* a sudden start or shock of surprise or fright. [Old English *steartlian*]

star tling (stärt′ling), *adj.* that causes a shock of surprise; frightening. —**star′tling ly,** *adv.*

star va tion (stär vā′shən), *n.* 1 a starving. 2 a suffering from extreme hunger; being starved.

starve (stärv), *v.,* **starved, starv ing.** —*v.i.* 1 die of hunger. 2 suffer severely from hunger. 3 INFORMAL. feel very hungry. 4 have a strong desire or craving. —*v.t.* 1 weaken or kill with hunger. 2 weaken or destroy through lack of something needed. 3 force or subdue by lack of food: *They starved the enemy into surrendering.* 4 **starve for,** suffer from lack of: *starve for news.* [Old English *steorfan* die]

starve ling (stärv′ling), *adj.* starving; hungry. —*n.* person or animal that is suffering from lack of food.

stash (stash), *v.t.* SLANG. hide or put away for safekeeping or future use. [origin uncertain]

sta sis (stā′sis, stas′is), *n., pl.* **sta ses** (stā′sēz′, stas′ēz′). a stoppage or stagnation of the flow of any of the fluids of the body, as of the blood in the blood vessels or of the feces in the intestines. [< Greek, a standing]

stat., statute.

stat a ble (stā′tə bəl), *adj.* that can be stated.

state (stāt), *n., adj., v.,* **stat ed, stat ing.** —*n.* 1 situation in which a person or thing is; condition of being: *the state of the weather.* See synonym study below. 2 a particular condition of mind or feeling: *a state of uncertainty.* 3 physical condition of a material with regard to its structure, composition, or form. Ice is water in a solid state. 4 group of people occupying a given area and organized under a government; commonwealth or nation. 5 Often, **State.** one of several organized political groups which together form a nation: *Hawaii is the fiftieth state of the United States.* 6 territory, government, or authority of a state. 7 the civil government; highest civil authority: *affairs of state.* 8 **states,** *pl.* estates (chiefly in historical use). 9 a person's position in life; rank: *a humble state.* 10 **the States,** the United States (used especially abroad). 11 high rank; greatness; eminence. 12 high style of living; dignity; pomp: *Kings lived in great state.* 13 **lie in state,** lie in a coffin so as to be seen formally and publicly before burial.
—*adj.* 1 of or having to do with a state: *state police.* 2 of, having to do with, or belonging to the civil government or highest civil authority: *state control.* 3 used on or reserved for very formal and special occasions; ceremonious; formal: *state robes.*
—*v.t.* 1 tell in speech or writing; express; say: *state one's reasons.* See **say** for synonym study. 2 specify; fix; settle: *state a price.*
[< Latin *status* condition, position < *stare* to stand; common in Latin phrase *status rei publicae* condition of the republic. Doublet of ESTATE, STATUS.]
Syn. *n.* 1 **State, condition** mean the circumstances in which someone or something exists. **State** is often used without reference to anything concrete: *The state of the world today should interest every serious person.* **Condition** applies to a particular state due to given causes or circumstances: *The condition of the patient is much improved today.*

state bank, 1 bank owned or controlled by a government. 2 U.S. bank that has a charter from a state government.

state craft (stāt′kraft′), *n.* 1 statesmanship. 2 crafty statesmanship.

stat ed (stā′tid), *adj.* 1 said; told: *the stated facts.* 2 specified; fixed: *begin at a stated time.*

State Department, an executive division of the United States government charged with the conduct of foreign affairs. It is presided over by the Secretary of State.

state hood (stāt′hu̇d), *n.* condition of being a state.

state house or **State house** (stāt′hous′), *n., pl.* **-hous es** (-hou′ziz). U.S. building in which the legislature of a state meets; capitol of a state.

state less (stāt′lis), *adj.* 1 without national affiliation: *a stateless refugee.* 2 in which national sovereignty does not exist: *a stateless world.* —**state′less ness,** *n.*

state ly (stāt′lē), *adj.,* **-li er, -li est,** *adv.* —*adj.* having dignity; imposing; majestic. See **grand** for synonym study. —*adv.* in a stately manner. —**state′li ness,** *n.*

state ment (stāt′mənt), *n.* 1 something stated; report; account: *His statement was correct.* 2 act of stating; manner of stating something: *The statement of an idea helps me to remember it.* 3 summary of an account, showing the amount owed, due, or on hand: *a bank statement.* 4 (in mathematics) an idea expressed by a closed sentence: EXAMPLE: 5 = 2 + 3 is a statement expressing the true idea that 5 is the sum of 2 and 3.

Stat en Island (stat′n), island in New York Bay, south of Manhattan, comprising the borough of Richmond in New York City. 295,000 pop.; 57 sq. mi.

state room (stāt′rüm′, stāt′ru̇m′), *n.* a private room on a ship or, formerly, on a railroad train.

state's evidence, 1 evidence brought forward by the government in a criminal case. 2 U.S. testimony given in court by an accused person against his alleged associates in a crime. 3 **turn state's evidence,** U.S. testify in court against one's alleged associates in a crime.

States-Gen er al (stāts′jen′ər əl), *n.* the legislative body of France from 1302 to 1789, consisting of representatives of the three estates, the clergy, the nobility, and the middle class; Estates-General.

state side (stāt′sīd′), INFORMAL. —*adj.* having to do with, from, or in the continental United States: *stateside mail.* —*adv.* to or in the continental United States: *to fly stateside.*

states man (stāts′mən), *n., pl.* **-men.** person skilled in the management of public or government affairs. See **politician** for synonym study. —**states′man like′,** *adj.*

states man ly (stāts′mən lē), *adj.* like, worthy of, or befitting a statesman.

states man ship (stāts′mən ship), *n.* the qualities of a statesman; skill in the management of public affairs.

state socialism, form of socialism in which government control, management, or ownership is used to improve social conditions.

hat, āge, fär; let, ēqual, tėrm;
it, īce; hot, ōpen, ôrder;
oil, out; cup, pu̇t, rüle;
ch, child; ng, long; sh, she;
th, thin; ᴛʜ, then; zh, measure;

ə represents *a* in about, *e* in taken, *i* in pencil, *o* in lemon, *u* in circus.

< = from, derived from, taken from.

states' rights, powers belonging to the separate states of the United States, under the Constitution. The doctrine of states' rights holds that all powers which the Constitution does not specifically delegate to the federal government and does not specifically deny to the individual states belong to the states.

states wom an (stāts′wu̇m′ən), *n., pl.* **-wom en.** a woman skilled in the management of public or government affairs.

state wide (stāt′wīd′), *adj.* covering an entire state; over all of a state.

stat ic (stat′ik), *adj.* 1 in a fixed or stable condition; not in a state of progress or change; at rest; standing still: *Civilization does not remain static, but changes constantly.* 2 having to do with bodies at rest or with forces that balance each other. 3 acting by weight without producing motion: *static pressure.* 4 having to do with stationary electrical charges. Static electricity can be produced by rubbing a glass rod with a silk cloth. 5 of, having to do with, or caused by atmospheric electricity that interferes with radio and television reception. —*n.* 1 electrical disturbances in the air, caused by electrical storms, etc. 2 interference, especially with radio signals, caused by such disturbances. [< Greek *statikos* causing to stand, ultimately < *histanai* cause to stand] —**stat′i cal ly,** *adv.*

stat ics (stat′iks), *n.* branch of physics that deals with objects at rest or forces that balance each other.

sta tion (stā′shən), *n.* 1 place which a person is appointed to occupy in the performance of some duty; assigned post: *The guard took his station at the door of the bank.* 2 locality or post assigned for military duty to a person or unit. 3 place to which people are assigned and where equipment is set up for some particular kind of work, research, or the like: *a postal station, weather station.* 4 the police headquarters of a district. 5 a regular stopping place: *a bus station, a railroad station.* 6 depot. 7 (in Australia and New Zealand) a cattle or sheep farm. 8 place or equipment for sending out or receiving programs, messages, etc., by radio and television. 9 social position; rank: *A serf was a man of humble station in life.* —*v.t.* assign a station to; place: *She stationed herself just outside the doorway.* [< Latin *stationem* < *stare* to stand]

sta tion ar y (stā′shə ner′ē), *adj.* 1 having a fixed station or place; not movable. 2 standing still; not moving. 3 not changing in size, number, activity, etc.

station break, pause in a radio or television program, or between programs, to identify the broadcasting station or network.

sta tion er (stā′shə nər), *n.* person who sells paper, pens, pencils, ink, etc. [< Medieval Latin *stationarius* shopkeeper, originally, stationary, as distinct from a roving peddler]

sta tion er y (stā′shə ner′ē), *n.* writing materials such as paper, cards, and envelopes.

station house, police station.

sta tion mas ter (stā′shən mas′tər), *n.* person in charge of a railroad station.

stations of the cross or **Stations of the Cross,** 1 series of scenes (usually fourteen) of Christ's passion, usually painted or sculptured and placed around the walls of a church or along a road leading to a shrine. 2 the prayers used at these stations.

station wagon, a passenger automobile that can be used as a light truck, usually having a long body with a back door and seats in the rear that can be folded down or removed.

stat ism (stā′tiz′əm), *n.* a highly centralized governmental control of the economy of a state or nation.

stat ist (stā′tist), *n.* person advocating statism.

sta tis tic (stə tis′tik), *adj.* statistical. —*n.* any value, item, etc., used in statistics: *an important statistic.*

sta tis ti cal (stə tis′tə kəl), *adj.* of or having to do with statistics; consisting of or based on statistics. —**sta tis′ti cal ly,** *adv.*

stat is ti cian (stat′ə stish′ən), *n.* an expert in statistics; person who prepares statistics.

sta tis tics (stə tis′tiks), *n.* 1 *pl. in form and use.* numerical facts about people, the weather, business conditions, etc. Statistics are collected and classified systematically. 2 *pl. in form, sing. in use.* science of collecting, classifying, and using such facts in order to show their significance. [< German *Statistik,* ultimately < Latin *status* state]

sta tor (stā′tər), *n.* a stationary portion enclosing rotating parts in a steam turbine, an electric generator or motor, or other machine. [< Latin, a stationary thing < *stare* to stand]

stat u ar y (stach′ü er′ē), *n., pl.* **-ar ies,** *adj.* —*n.* 1 statues. 2 art of making statues; sculpture. 3 sculptor. —*adj.* of or for statues: *statuary marble.*

stat ue (stach′ü), *n.* image of a person or animal carved in stone or wood, cast in bronze, or modeled in clay or wax. [< Latin *statua,* ultimately < *stare* to stand]

Statue of Liberty, a colossal statue of the goddess of liberty holding aloft a lighted torch, on Liberty Island in New York Bay. It was given to the United States by France in 1884.

stat u esque (stach′ü esk′), *adj.* like a statue in dignity, formal grace, or classic beauty. —**stat′u esque′ly,** *adv.* —**stat′u-esque′ness,** *n.*

stat u ette (stach′ü et′), *n.* a small statue; figurine.

stat ure (stach′ər), *n.* 1 height: *a man of average stature.* 2 physical, mental, or moral growth; development. [< Latin *statura* < *stare* to stand]

sta tus (stā′təs, stat′əs), *n.* 1 social or professional standing; position; rank: *lose status. What is her status in the government?* 2 state; condition: *Diplomats are interested in the status of world affairs.* [< Latin < *stare* to stand. Doublet of STATE.]

status quo (kwō), the way things are; existing state of affairs. [< Latin, the state in which]

stat ute (stach′üt), *n.* 1 law enacted by a legislative body. See **law** for synonym study. 2 a formally established rule; law; decree. [< Late Latin *statutum* < Latin *statuere* establish < *stare* to stand]

statute mile, mile (def. 1).

statute of limitations, statute limiting the time during which rights or claims can be enforced by legal action.

stat u to ry (stach′ü tôr′ē, stach′ü tōr′ē), *adj.* 1 having to do with or consisting of statutes. 2 fixed by statute: *statutory law.* 3 punishable by statute. —**stat′u to′ri ly,** *adv.*

St. Au gus tine (sānt ô′gə stēn′), seacoast city in NE Florida. It is the oldest city in the United States, founded by the Spanish in 1565. 12,000.

staunch[1] (stônch, stänch), *v.t., v.i.* stanch[1].

staunch[2] (stônch, stänch), *adj.* 1 strong or firm: *a staunch defense.* 2 loyal; steadfast: *a staunch supporter of the law.* 3 watertight: *a staunch boat.* Also, **stanch.** [< Middle French *estanche* < *estanchier* to stop, hinder] —**staunch′ly,** *adv.* —**staunch′ness,** *n.*

stave (stāv), *n., v.,* **staved** or **stove, stav ing.** —*n.* 1 one of the thin, narrow, curved pieces of wood which form the sides of a barrel, cask, tub, etc. 2 stick, rod, bar, pole, staff, or the like. 3 verse or stanza of a poem or song. 4 the musical staff. —*v.t.* 1 break up (a barrel, cask, etc.) into staves. 2 break a hole in (a boat, etc.). 3 smash (a hole) in a boat, door, etc. 4 furnish with staves. 5 **stave off,** put off; keep back; delay or prevent: *The lost campers ate birds' eggs to stave off starvation.* —*v.i.* become smashed or broken in. [< *staves,* plural of *staff*]

staves (stāvz), *n.* 1 a pl. of **staff.** 2 pl. of **stave.**

stay[1] (stā), *v.,* **stayed** or (ARCHAIC) **staid, stay ing,** *n.* —*v.i.* 1 continue to be as indicated; remain: *Shall I go or stay?* See synonym study below. 2 **stay put,** INFORMAL. remain where or as placed; remain fixed: *We stayed put in the tent until the rain stopped.* 3 live for a while, especially as a guest; dwell: *stay at a hotel.* 4 stop; halt: *We have no time to stay.* 5 pause; wait; delay: *Time and tide stay for no man.* 6 last; endure: *a runner unable to stay to the end of a race.* 7 make a stand; stand firm. —*v.t.* 1 put off; hold back; delay; restrain; check: *The teacher stayed judgment till she could hear both sides.* 2 put an end to for a while; satisfy (hunger, appetite, etc.). 3 remain for, during, or throughout: *stay the night.* 4 last for (a certain distance or time): *He cannot stay a mile.* 5 ARCHAIC. wait for; await.

—*n.* 1 a staying; stop; time spent: *a pleasant stay in the country.* 2 check; restraint: *a stay on one's activity.* 3 delay in carrying out the order of a court of law: *The judge granted a stay for an appeal.* 4 INFORMAL. staying power; endurance.

[< Middle French *ester* to stand < Latin *stare*]

Syn. *v.i.* 1 **Stay, remain** mean to continue in a stated place or condition. **Stay** emphasizes keeping on without leaving or stopping: *I decided to stay in college another year.* **Remain** may emphasize staying after the departure of others: *Of all the charter members of the club, he alone remains.*

stay[2] (stā), *n., v.,* **stayed, stay ing.** —*n.* 1 anything that supports or steadies something else; prop; brace. 2 a person who affords support: *be the family's stay.* 3 **stays,** *pl.* corset. —*v.t.* hold up; support; prop. [probably < Middle French *estayer;* of Germanic origin] —**stay′er,** *n.*

stay[3] (stā), *n., v.,* **stayed, stay ing.** —*n.* 1 one of the strong ropes, often of wire, by which the mast of a ship is held in position. 2 any rope or chain attached to something to steady it. —*v.t.* support or secure with stays. —*v.i.* (of a ship) change to the other tack. [Old English *stæg*]

staying power, power or will to endure.

stay sail (stā′sāl′; *Nautical* stā′səl), *n.* a fore-and-aft sail fastened on a stay.

St. Ber nard (sānt bər närd′), 1 **Great,** mountain pass in the Alps between NW Italy and SW Switzerland. 8108 ft. high. 2 **Little,** mountain pass in the Alps between NW Italy and E France. 7177 ft. high.

St. Clair (sānt kler′; sānt klar′), 1 **St. Clair River,** river between SE Michigan and Ontario, Canada, flowing south from Lake Huron into Lake St. Clair. 40 mi. long. 2 **Lake,** lake between SE Michigan and Ontario, Canada. 30 mi. long; 24 mi. wide; 460 sq. mi.

St. Clair Shores, city in SE Michigan, near Detroit. 88,000.

St. Croix (sānt kroi′), largest of the Virgin Islands. It belongs to the United States. 32,000 pop.; 82 sq. mi.

Ste., Sainte.

stead (sted), *n.* 1 place or function (of a person or thing) as held by a substitute or successor: *The baby-sitter sent her brother in her stead.* 2 **stand in good stead,** be of advantage or service to: *My ability to swim stood me in good stead when the boat upset.* [Old English *stede*]

stead fast (sted′fast′), *adj.* 1 firm of purpose; loyal and unwavering: *a steadfast friend, a steadfast defender of one's country.* 2 firmly fixed; not moving or changing: *a steadfast gaze.* Also, **stedfast.** [Old English *stedefæst* < *stede* place + *fæst* fast[1], firm] —**stead′fast′ly,** *adv.* —**stead′fast′ness,** *n.*

stead y (sted′ē), *adj.* **stead i er, stead i est,** *v.,* **stead ied, stead y ing,** *n., pl.* **stead ies,** *adv.* —*adj.* 1 changing little; uniform: *steady progress.* See synonym study below. 2 firmly fixed; firm; not swaying or shaking: *Hold the ladder steady.* 3 not easily excited; calm: *steady nerves.* 4 resolute; steadfast: *steady friendship.* 5 having good habits; reliable: *a steady young man.* 6 (of a ship) keeping nearly upright in a heavy sea. —*v.t.* make steady; keep steady. —*v.i.* become steady. —*n.* INFORMAL. one's regular sweetheart. —*adv.* 1 in a steady manner. 2 **go steady,** INFORMAL. be one's regular sweetheart. [< *stead*] —**stead′i ly,** *adv.* —**stead′i-ness,** *n.*

Syn. *adj.* 1 **Steady, regular** mean constant or uniform in acting, doing, moving, happening, etc. **Steady** emphasizes the absence of interruption or change: *be unable to find steady work.* **Regular** emphasizes a fixed, usual, or uniform procedure, practice, program, or pattern: *be a regular subscriber to several magazines.*

stead y-state theory (sted′ē stāt′), theory that the universe is in appreciably the same state as it has always been, for, although matter has been and is being lost or dispersed, other matter is continuously created to take its place.

steak (stāk), *n.* 1 slice of beef for broiling or frying; beefsteak. 2 slice of any meat or fish for broiling or frying: *salmon steak.* 3 finely ground meat intended to be cooked some-

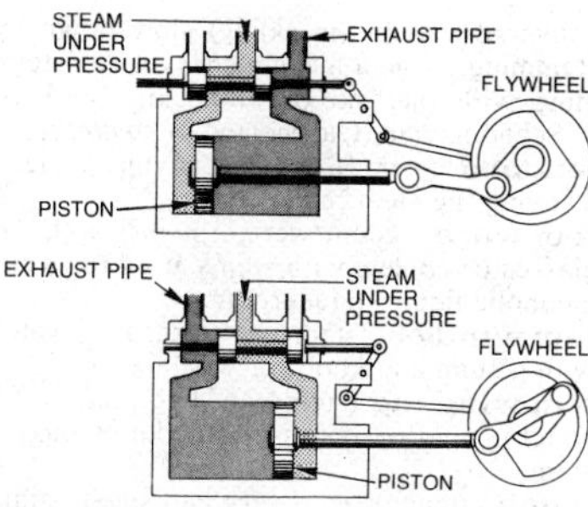

steam engine
above—Steam under pressure from boiler enters intake, driving piston to right. Used steam goes out exhaust at right.
below—Heavy flywheel keeps motion continuous and by attached gears changes valve positions in intake and exhaust. Steam now drives piston to left and used steam goes out exhaust at left.

what like a steak: *hamburger steak.* [< Scandinavian (Norwegian) *steik*]

steal (stēl), *v.,* **stole, sto len, steal ing,** *n.* —*v.t.* 1 take (something) that does not belong to one; take dishonestly. See synonym study below. 2 take, get, or do secretly: *steal a kiss, steal a look at someone.* 3 take, get, or win by art, charm, etc.: *The baby stole our hearts.* 4 (in baseball) run to (second base, third base, or home plate) as the pitcher delivers the ball to the batter. A player steals a base when he reaches it without the help of a hit or an error. —*v.i.* 1 practice theft: *He stole whenever he had a chance.* 2 move, come, or leave secretly or quietly: *steal out of the house.* 3 move, pass, come, or go slowly or gently: *A feeling of drowsiness stole over me.* 4 (in baseball) steal a base. —*n.* 1 INFORMAL. act of stealing. 2 INFORMAL. the thing stolen. 3 INFORMAL. something obtained at a low cost or with little effort: *At that price the car is a steal.* [Old English *stelan*] **—steal′er,** *n.*

Syn. *v.t.* 1 **Steal, pilfer, filch** mean to take dishonestly or wrongfully and secretly something belonging to someone else. **Steal** is the general and common word: *Thieves stole the silver.* **Pilfer** means to steal and carry away in small amounts: *In some department stores hidden guards watch for people who pilfer food.* **Filch** implies stealthy or furtive pilfering, usually of objects of little value: *The children filched some candy from the counter.*

stealth (stelth), *n.* secret or sly action: *She obtained the letter by stealth, taking it while nobody was in the room.* [Middle English *stelthe.* Related to STEAL.]

stealth y (stel′thē), *adj.,* **stealth i er, stealth i est.** done in a secret manner; secret; sly: *The cat crept in a stealthy way toward the bird.* **—stealth′i ly,** *adv.* **—stealth′i ness,** *n.*

steam (stēm), *n.* 1 the invisible vapor or gas formed when water is heated to the boiling point. 2 the white cloud or mist formed by the condensation, when cooled, of this vapor or gas. 3 this vapor used to generate power and for heating and cooking. 4 the power thus generated. 5 INFORMAL. power; energy; force. **6 let off steam,** INFORMAL. **a** get rid of excess energy. **b** relieve one's feelings. —*v.i.* 1 give off steam or vapor: *The cup of coffee was steaming.* 2 become covered with steam: *The windshield steamed up inside the heated car.* 3 rise in the form of steam. 4 move by steam: *The ship steamed off.* 5 INFORMAL. **a** run or go quickly, as if powered by steam. **b** show anger or irritation; fume. —*v.t.* 1 cook, soften, or freshen by steam. 2 give off (steam or vapor). [Old English *stēam*] **—steam′like′,** *adj.*

steam boat (stēm′bōt′), *n.* boat moved by steam.

steam engine, engine operated by steam, typically one in which a sliding piston in a cylinder is moved by the expansive action of steam generated in a boiler.

steam er (stē′mər), *n.* 1 steamboat; steamship. 2 engine run by steam. 3 container in which something is steamed or kept warm.

steamer rug, a heavy blanket, especially one used to keep a person warm in a chair on the deck of a ship.

steam fitter, person who installs and repairs steam pipes, boilers, etc.

steam heat, heat given off by steam in radiators and pipes.

steam iron, an electric iron in which water is heated to produce steam which is released through holes in its undersurface to dampen cloth while pressing it.

steam roll er (stēm′rō′lər), *n., v.* —*n.* 1 a heavy roller, formerly run by steam, used to crush and level materials in making roads. 2 INFORMAL. means of crushing opposition. —*v.t.* 1 INFORMAL. **a** override by crushing power or force; crush: *steamroller all opposition.* **b** force (into or through) by this means. 2 make level, smooth, etc., with a steamroller. —*v.i.* INFORMAL. override or crush a person or thing that is in opposition.

steam ship (stēm′ship′), *n.* ship moved by steam.

steam shovel, machine for digging, formerly operated by steam; power shovel.

steam table, fixture resembling a shallow tank in which water is heated or into which steam is piped, with holes in its upper surface into which containers are fitted. It is used by restaurants, etc., to keep food warm.

steam turbine, a rotary engine operated by steam.

steam y (stē′mē), *adj.,* **steam i er, steam i est.** 1 of steam; like steam. 2 full of steam; giving off steam; rising in steam. **—steam′i ly,** *adv.* **—steam′i ness,** *n.*

ste ap sin (stē ap′sən), *n.* a digestive enzyme secreted in the pancreatic juice, which changes fats into glycerol and fatty acids. [< *stea(rin)* and *(pe)psin*]

ste a rate (stē′ə rāt′), *n.* salt or ester of stearic acid.

ste ar ic acid (stē′ar ik, stir′ik), a white, odorless, tasteless, saturated fatty acid, obtained chiefly from tallow and other hard fats by saponification. It exists in combination with glycerol as stearin. *Formula:* $CH_3(CH_2)_{16}COOH$ [< Greek *stear* fat]

ste ar in (stē′ər ən, stir′ən), *n.* 1 a white, odorless, crystalline substance, an ester of stearic acid and glycerol, that is the chief constituent of many animal and vegetable fats. 2 mixture of fatty acids used for making candles, solid alcohol, etc.

ste a tite (stē′ə tīt), *n.* soapstone. [< Latin *steatitis* < Greek *steatos* fat]

sted fast (sted′fast′), *adj.* steadfast.

steed (stēd), *n.* 1 horse, especially a riding horse. 2 a high-spirited horse. [Old English *stēda*]

steel (stēl), *n.* 1 an alloy of iron and varying amounts of carbon (always less than two per cent, the amount in cast iron, but more than

hat, āge, fär; let, ēqual, tėrm;
it, īce; hot, ōpen, ôrder;
oil, out; cup, pu̇t, rüle;
ch, child; ng, long; sh, she;
th, thin; ᴛʜ, then; zh, measure;

ə represents *a* in about, *e* in taken, *i* in pencil, *o* in lemon, *u* in circus.

< = from, derived from, taken from.

the amount in wrought iron). Steel has greater hardness and flexibility than iron and hence is used for tools and machinery. 2 something made from steel; a sword or a piece of steel for making sparks; a rod of steel for sharpening knives. 3 steellike hardness or strength: *nerves of steel.* —*adj.* 1 made of steel. 2 resembling steel in color, hardness, etc. 3 of or having to do with the production of steel. —*v.t.* 1 point, edge, or cover with steel. 2 make hard or strong like steel: *steel oneself against possible failure.* [Old English *stēle*] **—steel′less,** *adj.* **—steel′like′,** *adj.*

steel band, a West Indian musical band that performs on various percussion instruments usually made from oil drums.

steel blue, lustrous dark blue, like the color of tempered steel. **—steel′-blue′,** *adj.*

Steele (stēl), *n.* Sir **Richard,** 1672-1729, British essayist, born in Ireland.

steel head (stēl′hed′), *n.* rainbow trout that enters the sea before it returns to freshwater streams to spawn.

steel wool, mass of long, fine steel shavings, used in cleaning or polishing surfaces.

steel work (stēl′wėrk′), *n.* tools, parts, framing, etc., made of steel.

steel work er (stēl′wėr′kər), *n.* person who works in a place where steel is made.

steel works (stēl′wėrks′), *n. pl. or sing.* place where steel is made.

steel y (stē′lē), *adj.,* **steel i er, steel i est.** 1 made of steel. 2 like steel in color, strength, or hardness. **—steel′i ness,** *n.*

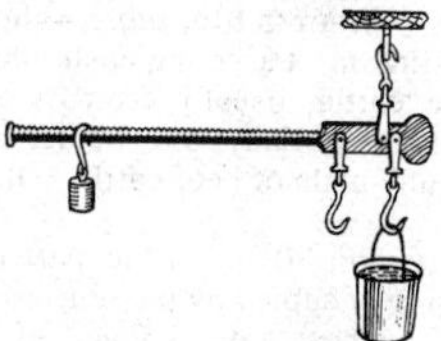

steelyard—When the arm is horizontal, the weight of any object hanging at the right is shown by a number where the movable weight at the left rests.

steel yard (stēl′yärd′, stil′yərd), *n.* scale for weighing, having arms of unequal length. The longer one has a movable weight and is marked in units of weight; the shorter one has a hook for holding the object to be weighed. [< *steel* + *yard* rod, beam]

steen bok (stēn′bok′, stān′bok′), *n.* a small African antelope frequenting rocky places. Also, **steinbok.** [< Afrikaans, literally, stone buck]

steep[1] (stēp), *adj.* 1 having a sharp slope; almost straight up and down. See synonym study below. 2 too high; unreasonable: *a steep price.* —*n.* a steep slope. [Old English *stēap*] **—steep′ly,** *adv.* **—steep′ness,** *n.*

Syn. *adj.* 1 **Steep, abrupt, precipitous** mean having a sharp slope. **Steep** suggests having a slope sharp enough to be hard to go up or down: *I do not like to drive up a steep hill.* **Abrupt** suggests a very steep slope suddenly broken off from the level: *From the rim they made their way down the abrupt sides of the canyon.* **Precipitous** suggests a nearly vertical slope: *The climbers will attempt to scale the precipitous eastern slope of the peak.*

steep² (stēp), *v.i.* undergo soaking; soak: *Let the tea steep in boiling water for five minutes.* —*v.t.* 1 permit (something) to steep. 2 make thoroughly wet; saturate. 3 involve deeply in something; immerse: *steep oneself in knowledge of the Middle Ages.* 4 **steeped in,** filled with; permeated by: *ruins steeped in gloom.* [Middle English *stepen,* probably related to Old English *stēap* bowl] **—steep′er,** *n.*

steep en (stē′pən), *v.t., v.i.* make or become steep or steeper.

stee ple (stē′pəl), *n.* 1 a high tower on a church or other building, usually with a spire. 2 spire on top of the tower or roof of a church or other building. [Old English *stēpel* < *stēap* steep] **—stee′ple like′,** *adj.*

stee ple chase (stē′pəl chās′), *n.* 1 a horse race over a course having ditches, hedges, or other obstacles. 2 a foot race in which the runners jump over hurdles and a ditch filled with water.

stee ple jack (stē′pəl jak′), *n.* person who climbs steeples, tall chimneys, or the like, to make repairs, etc.

steer¹ (stir), *v.t.* 1 guide the course of: *steer a ship, steer an automobile, steer one's plans toward success.* 2 set and follow (a certain course): *steer a middle course between war and peace.* —*v.i.* 1 guide the course of a ship, automobile, airplane, etc.: *The pilot steered for the harbor.* 2 be guided: *This car steers easily.* 3 direct one's way or course: *Steer away from trouble.* 4 **steer clear of,** keep away from; avoid: *Steer clear of him until he calms down.* —*n.* SLANG. an idea or a suggested course of action; tip. [Old English *stēoran*] **—steer′a ble,** *adj.* **—steer′er,** *n.*

steer² (stir), *n.* 1 a young castrated male of domestic cattle, usually from two to four years old, especially one being raised for beef. 2 any male of beef cattle. [Old English *stēor*]

steer age (stir′ij), *n.* 1 the part of a passenger ship occupied by passengers traveling at the cheapest rate. 2 act of steering. 3 manner in which a ship is affected by the helm.

steering committee, committee responsible for deciding which items shall be considered and in what order.

steering gear, apparatus for steering an automobile, ship, etc.

steering wheel, wheel that is turned to steer an automobile, ship, etc.

steers man (stirz′mən), *n., pl.* **-men.** person who steers a boat or ship.

Stef ans son (stef′ən sən), *n.* **Vilhjalmur,** 1879-1962, American anthropologist, arctic explorer, and writer, born in Canada.

steg o sau rus (steg′ə sôr′əs), *n., pl.* **-sau ri** (-sôr′ī). any of a genus of extinct herbivorous, ornithischian dinosaurs of great size, with heavy, bony armor. [< New Latin < Greek *stegos* roof + *sauros* lizard]

stein (stīn), *n.* 1 mug for beer, usually of earthenware or glass and holding from twelve to sixteen ounces. 2 amount that a stein holds. [< German *Stein* stone]

Stein (stīn), *n.* **Gertrude,** 1874-1946, American author who lived in France.

Stein beck (stīn′bek), *n.* **John,** 1902-1968, American novelist.

stein bok (stīn′bok′), *n.* steenbok.

Stein metz (stīn′mets), *n.* **Charles Proteus,** 1865-1923, American mathematician and electrical engineer, born in Germany.

ste le (stē′lē), *n., pl.* **-lae** (-lē), **-les.** 1 an upright slab or pillar of stone bearing an inscription, sculptural design, or the like. 2 a prepared surface on the face of a building, a rock, etc., bearing an inscription or the like. 3 (in botany) the central cylinder of conducting tissue formed by the network of vascular bundles in the stems and roots of plants. [< Greek *stēlē*]

St. E li as (sānt i lī′əs), **Mount,** mountain on the border between SE Alaska and the Yukon territory of Canada. 18,008 ft.

stel lar (stel′ər), *adj.* 1 of or having to do with the stars or a star: *stellar magnitudes.* 2 chief; principal: *a stellar role.* 3 of or having to do with a star performer. [< Latin *stellaris* < *stella* star]

stel late (stel′āt, stel′it), *adj.* spreading out like the points of a star; star-shaped. **—stel′late ly,** *adv.*

stel li form (stel′ə fôrm), *adj.* star-shaped.

stel lu lar (stel′yə lər), *adj.* having the form of a small star or small stars.

St. El mo's fire (sānt el′mōz), ball of light due to a discharge of atmospheric electricity, often seen on the masts of ships, towers, etc. [< *St. Elmo,* a Syrian martyr of the A.D. 200's who was considered a patron saint of sailors]

stem¹ (stem), *n., v.,* **stemmed, stem ming.** —*n.* 1 the main part, usually above the ground, of a tree, shrub, or other plant; the firm part that supports the branches; trunk or stalk. 2 the stalk supporting a flower, a fruit, or a leaf. 3 anything like or suggesting the stem of a plant: *the stem of a goblet, the stem of a pipe.* 4 the line of descent of a family. 5 the part of a word to which inflectional endings are added and in which inflectional changes occur. *Run* is the stem of *running, runner, ran,* etc. 6 the bow or front end of a ship; prow. 7 **from stem to stern,** from one end of a ship to the other. —*v.t.* remove the stalk from (a leaf, fruit, etc.). —*v.i.* 1 grow out; come from; develop: *The difficulty stems from their failure to plan properly.* 2 originate or spring: *Newspapers stemmed from the invention of the printing press.* [Old English *stemn*] **—stem′less,** *adj.* **—stem′like′,** *adj.*

stem² (stem), *v.,* **stemmed, stem ming,** *n.* —*v.t.* 1 make headway or progress against: *When you swim upstream you have to stem the current.* 2 dam up (a stream, etc.). 3 (in skiing) turn (one or both skis) so that the tips converge. —*v.i.* (in skiing) slow down by stemming. —*n.* a maneuver involving stemming with one ski or both skis. [perhaps < Scandinavian (Old Icelandic) *stemma*]

stegosaurus—about 18 ft. long

stemmed (stemd), *adj.* 1 having a stem. 2 having the stem removed.

stem ware (stem′wer′, stem′war′), *n.* glasses or goblets with stems, used for wine, alcoholic liquor, liqueur, etc.

stem wind er (stem′wīn′dər), *n.* watch with a stem and knob for winding.

stem wind ing (stem′wīn′ding), *adj.* (of a watch) winding by turning a knob on the stem.

stench (stench), *n.* a very bad smell; stink: *the stench of a pigsty.* [Old English *stenc.* Related to STINK.]

sten cil (sten′səl), *n., v.,* **-ciled, -cil ing** or **-cilled, -cil ling.** —*n.* 1 a thin sheet of metal, paper, cardboard, etc., having letters or designs cut through it. When it is laid on a surface and ink or color is applied, these letters or designs appear on the surface. 2 the letters or designs so made. —*v.t.* 1 mark or paint with a stencil: *The curtains have a stenciled border.* 2 produce (letters or designs) by means of a stencil. [< Old French *estanceler* to ornament with colors, ultimately < Latin *scintilla* spark]

Sten dhal (sten′däl; *French* staN dȧl′), *n.* 1783-1842, French novelist and critic. His real name was Marie Henri Beyle.

sten o (sten′ō), *n., pl.* **sten os.** INFORMAL. stenographer.

ste nog ra pher (stə nog′rə fər), *n.* person whose work is taking dictation in shorthand and transcribing it, usually with a typewriter.

sten o graph ic (sten′ə graf′ik), *adj.* 1 of stenography. 2 made by stenography. 3 using stenography. **—sten′o graph′i cal ly,** *adv.*

ste nog ra phy (stə nog′rə fē), *n.* 1 method of rapid writing that uses symbols, abbreviations, etc.; shorthand. 2 act of writing in such symbols. [< Greek *stenos* narrow + English *-graphy*]

ste nosed (sti nōst′, sten′ōzd), *adj.* affected with stenosis.

ste no sis (sti nō′sis), *n.* (in medicine) the contraction or stricture of a passage, duct, or canal. [< Greek *stenōsis* a narrowing < *stenoun* to narrow < *stenos* narrow]

sten o typ y (sten′ə tī′pē, stə not′ə pē), *n.* form of shorthand that uses ordinary letters.

sten tor (sten′tôr), *n.* 1 man of powerful voice. 2 **Stentor,** (in Greek legends) a Greek herald in the Trojan War, whose voice was as loud as the voices of fifty men. 3 one of a genus of trumpet-shaped protozoans that are among the largest of all single-celled animals.

sten to ri an (sten tôr′ē ən, sten tōr′ē ən), *adj.* very loud or powerful in sound: *a stentorian voice.*

step (step), *n., v.,* **stepped, step ping.** —*n.* 1 movement made by lifting the foot and putting it down again in a new position; one motion of the leg in walking, running, dancing, etc. 2 distance covered by one such movement: *She was three steps away when he called her back.* 3 a short distance; little way: *The school is only a step away from his house.* 4 way of walking, dancing, running, etc.; gait; stride: *a brisk step.* 5 pace uniform with that of another or others or in time with music: *keep step, be in step, be out of step.* 6 place for the foot in going up or coming down. A stair or a rung of a ladder is a step. 7 **steps,** *pl.* **a** stepladder. **b** path, course, or

hat, āge, fär; let, ēqual, tėrm;
it, īce; hot, ōpen, ôrder;
oil, out; cup, pu̇t, rüle;
ch, child; ng, long; sh, she;
th, thin; ᴛʜ, then; zh, measure;

ə represents *a* in about, *e* in taken, *i* in pencil, *o* in lemon, *u* in circus.

< = from, derived from, taken from.

way: *retrace one's steps.* 8 sound made by putting the foot down; footstep: *hear a heavy step on the stairs.* 9 footprint: *see steps in the mud.* 10 action: *the first step toward peace.* 11 degree in a scale; grade in rank; stage: *A colonel is three steps above a captain.* 12 in music: **a** a degree of the staff or scale. **b** the interval between two successive degrees of the scale. 13 part like a step; support, frame, etc., for holding the end of something upright: *the step of a mast.* 14 **step by step,** little by little; slowly. 15 **take steps,** adopt, put into effect, or carry out measures considered to be necessary, desirable, etc. 16 **watch one's step,** be careful.
—*v.i.* 1 move the legs as in walking, running, dancing, etc.: *Step lively!* 2 walk a short distance: *step across the road.* 3 put the foot down; tread: *step upon a worm, step on the accelerator.* 4 INFORMAL. go fast. —*v.t.* 1 measure *(off)* by taking steps; pace *(off): Step off the distance from the door to the window.* 2 make or arrange like a flight of steps. 3 set (a mast) in place; fix or place in a support.
step down, **a** come down. **b** surrender or resign from an office, position of precedence, etc. **c** decrease.
step in, come in; intervene; take part.
step into, come into, acquire, or receive, especially without particular effort or through the action of fate.
step on it, INFORMAL. go faster; hurry up.
step out, INFORMAL. go out for entertainment.
step up, **a** go up; ascend. **b** increase: *step up production.* **c** INFORMAL. come forward. [Old English *steppan* to step] —**step′like′,** *adj.*

step-, *prefix.* related by the remarriage of a parent, not by blood, as in *stepmother, stepsister,* etc. [Old English *stēop-*]

step broth er (step′bruᴛʜ′ər), *n.* a stepfather's or stepmother's son by a former marriage.

step child (step′chīld′), *n., pl.* **-chil dren.** child of one's husband or wife by a former marriage.

step daugh ter (step′dô′tər), *n.* daughter of one's husband or wife by a former marriage.

step-down (step′doun′), *adj.* 1 that decreases gradually. 2 (in electricity) lowering the voltage of a current, especially by means of a transformer.

step fa ther (step′fä′ᴛʜər), *n.* man who has married one's mother after the death or divorce of one's father.

Ste phen (stē′vən), *n.* 1 **Saint,** the first Christian martyr. 2 1097?-1154, king of England from 1135 to 1154.

Ste phens (stē′vənz), *n.* **Alexander Hamilton,** 1812-1883, vice-president of the Confederacy from 1861 to 1865.

Ste phen son (stē′vən sən), *n.* **George,** 1781-1848, English engineer. He improved the steam locomotive and in 1825 built one of the first trains carrying passengers and freight.

step-in (step′in′), *adj.* (of garments, shoes, slippers, etc.) put on by being stepped into. —*n.* **step-ins,** *pl.* garment that one may put on by stepping into it, especially a woman's undergarment with short legs.

step lad der (step′lad′ər), *n.* ladder with flat steps instead of rungs.

step moth er (step′muᴛʜ′ər), *n.* woman who has married one's father after the death or divorce of one's mother.

step par ent (step′per′ənt, step′par′ənt), *n.* stepfather or stepmother.

steppe (step), *n.* 1 one of the vast, treeless plains in southeastern Europe and in Asia. 2 any vast, treeless plain. [< Russian *step'*]

stepped-up (stept′up′), *adj.* increased in size, speed, or extent.

step per (step′ər), *n.* person or animal that steps, especially in a certain way.

stepping stone, 1 stone or one of a line of stones in shallow water, a marshy place, or the like, used in crossing. 2 stone for use in mounting or ascending. 3 anything serving as a means of advancing or rising.

step sis ter (step′sis′tər), *n.* a stepfather's or stepmother's daughter by a former marriage.

step son (step′sun′), *n.* son of one's husband or wife by a former marriage.

step-up (step′up′), *adj.* 1 that increases gradually. 2 (in electricity) increasing the voltage of a current, especially by means of a transformer. —*n.* an increase: *a step-up in production.*

step wise (step′wīz′), *adv.* by steps. —*adj.* gradual.

-ster, *suffix forming nouns.* 1 person who ____s: *Trickster = person who tricks.* 2 person who makes or handles ____: *Rhymester = person who makes rhymes.* 3 person who is ____: *Youngster = person who is young.* 4 special meanings, as in *gangster, roadster, teamster.* [Old English *-istre, -estre,* a feminine suffix]

ste ra di an (sti rā′dē ən), *n.* (in geometry) a unit of measurement of solid angles. It is the solid angle subtended at the center of a sphere by the area of the surface of the sphere equal to the square of its radius. [< Greek *stereos* solid + English *radian*]

stere (stir), *n.* unit of measure equal to one cubic meter. See **measure** for table. [< French *stère* < Greek *stereos* solid]

ster e o (ster′ē ō, stir′ē ō), *adj., n., pl.* **ster e os.** —*adj.* stereophonic. —*n.* 1 a stereophonic sound reproduction. 2 system or apparatus reproducing stereophonic sound.

stereo-, *combining form.* solid; three-dimensional; stereoscopic: *Stereomicroscope = three-dimensional microscope.* [< Greek *stereos* solid]

ster e o chem is try (ster′ē ō kem′ə strē, stir′ē ō kem′ə strē), *n.* branch of chemistry dealing with the relative position in space of atoms and molecules.

ster e o i som er ism (ster′ē ō ī som′ə riz′əm, stir′ē ō ī som′ə riz′əm), *n.* (in chemistry) isomerism in which the atoms are joined in the molecule in the same way but differ in their spatial arrangement.

ster e o mi cro scope (ster′ē ō mī′krə skōp, stir′ē ō mī′krə skōp), *n.* microscope with two eyepieces, used for obtaining a three-dimensional image of the object viewed; stereoscopic microscope.

ster e o phon ic (ster′ē ə fon′ik, stir′ē ə fon′ik), *adj.* of or having to do with a system of sound reproduction using two or more microphones, recording channels, loudspeakers, etc., in order to give a three-dimensional effect.

ster e op ti con (ster′ē op′tə kən, stir′ē op′tə kən), *n.* projector arranged to combine two images on a screen so that they gradually become one image with three-dimensional effect.

ster e o scope (ster′ē ə skōp′, stir′ē ə skōp′), *n.* instrument through which two pictures of the same object or scene, taken from slightly different angles, are viewed, one by each eye. The object or scene thus viewed appears to have three dimensions.

ster e o scop ic (ster′ē ə skop′ik, stir′ē ə skop′ik), *adj.* 1 seeming to have depth as well as height and breadth; three-dimensional. 2 having to do with stereoscopes. —**ster′e o scop′i cal ly,** *adv.*

ster e o type (ster′ē ə tīp′, stir′ē ə tīp′), *n., v.,* **-typed, -typ ing.** —*n.* 1 method or process of making metal printing plates from a mold of composed type. 2 a printing plate cast from a mold. 3 a fixed form, character, image, etc.; conventional type. —*v.t.* 1 make a stereotype of. 2 print from stereotypes. 3 give a fixed or settled form to. —**ster′e o typ′er,** *n.*

ster e o typed (ster′ē ə tīpt′, stir′ē ə tīpt′), *adj.* 1 cast in the form of, or printed from, a stereotype. 2 fixed or settled in form; conventional.

ster e o typ y (ster′ē ə tī′pē, stir′ē ə tī′pē), *n.* 1 process of making stereotype plates. 2 process of printing from stereotype plates.

ster i lant (ster′ə lənt), *n.* chemical or other agent that sterilizes.

ster ile (ster′əl), *adj.* 1 free from living germs or microorganisms: *keep surgical instruments sterile.* 2 not producing seed, offspring, crops, etc.: *sterile land, a sterile cow.* 3 not producing results: *sterile hopes.* 4 mentally or spiritually barren. [< Latin *sterilis*] —**ster′ile ly,** *adv.*

ste ril i ty (stə ril′ə tē), *n.* sterile condition or character; barrenness.

ster i lize (ster′ə līz), *v.t.,* **-lized, -liz ing.** 1 make free from living germs or microorganisms; disinfect: *The water had to be sterilized by boiling to make it fit to drink.* 2 make incapable of producing offspring. 3 make unproductive, unprofitable, or useless. —**ster′i li za′tion,** *n.* —**ster′i liz′er,** *n.*

ster ling (stėr′ling), *adj.* 1 of standard quality for silver; containing 92.5 per cent pure silver. *Sterling* is stamped on solid silver knives, forks, etc. 2 made of sterling silver. 3 thoroughly and genuinely excellent; dependable: *sterling character.* 4 of British money; payable in British money. —*n.* 1 sterling silver or things made of it. 2 British money, especially the pound as the standard monetary unit in international trade. [Middle English, silver penny]

sterling area, group of countries in the Commonwealth of Nations, certain dependent territories, and other countries that use the British pound sterling as the unit of currency in foreign trade.

sterling silver, solid silver; silver 92.5 per cent pure.

stern[1] (stėrn), *adj.* 1 harshly firm; hard; strict: *a stern master, a stern frown.* See **severe** for synonym study. 2 very severe; rigorous; harsh: *stern necessity.* 3 forbidding in nature or aspect; grim: *stern mountains.* [Old English *styrne*] **—stern′ly,** *adv.* **—stern′ness,** *n.*

stern² (stėrn), *n.* the rear part of a ship, boat, or aircraft. See **aft** for picture. [probably < Scandinavian (Old Icelandic) *stjōrn* steering]

ster nal (stėr′nl), *adj.* of or having to do with the breastbone or sternum.

Sterne (stėrn), *n.* **Laurence,** 1713-1768, English novelist, born in Ireland.

stern most (stėrn′mōst), *adj.* 1 nearest the stern. 2 farthest in the rear.

stern post (stėrn′pōst′), *n.* the upright timber or metal bar at the stern of a ship. It extends from the keel to the deck, and it usually supports the rudder.

ster num (stėr′nəm), *n., pl.* **-na** (-nə), **-nums.** breastbone. [< Greek *sternon*]

stern ward (stėrn′wərd), *adv., adj.* toward the stern; astern.

stern wards (stėrn′wərdz), *adv.* sternward.

stern-wheel er (stėrn′hwē′lər), *n.* a steamboat driven by a paddle wheel at the stern.

ster oid (ster′oid), *n.* any of a large class of structurally related compounds containing the carbon ring of the sterols, and including the sterols, various hormones, and acids found in bile.

ster ol (ster′ōl, ster′ol), *n.* any of a group of solid, chiefly unsaturated alcohols, such as ergosterol, cholesterol, etc., present in animal and plant tissues. [< *(chole)sterol*]

ster tor ous (stėr′tər əs), *adj.* making a heavy snoring sound: *stertorous breathing.* [< New Latin *stertor* snoring < Latin *stertere* to snore] **—ster′tor ous ly,** *adv.* **—ster′tor ous ness,** *n.*

stet (stet), *n., v.,* **stet ted, stet ting.** *—n.* "let it stand," a direction on printer's proof, a manuscript, or the like, to retain matter that had been marked for deletion. The passage to be retained is underlined with a series of dots. *—v.t.* mark with such a direction. [< Latin, let it stand]

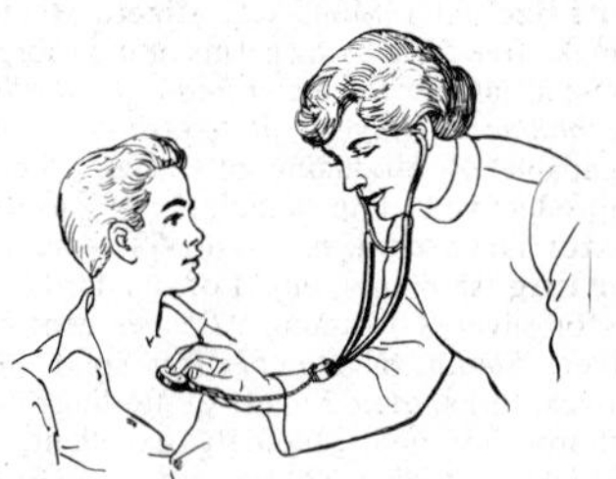

stethoscope—Sounds are conveyed to the doctor's ears through two hollow tubes.

steth o scope (steth′ə skōp), *n.* instrument used by doctors to hear the sounds produced in the lungs, heart, etc. [< Greek *stethos* chest + English *-scope*]

steth o scop ic (steth′ə skop′ik), *adj.* 1 having to do with the stethoscope or its use. 2 made or obtained by the stethoscope. **—steth′o scop′i cal ly,** *adv.*

St.-É tienne (saɴ tā tyen′), *n.* city in SE France. 213,000.

Stet tin (shte tēn′), *n.* German name of **Szczecin.**

Steu ben (stü′bən, styü′bən), *n.* Baron **Friedrich Wilhelm von,** 1730-1794, Prussian general who aided the Americans in the Revolutionary War.

ste ve dore (stē′və dôr, stē′və dōr), *n., v.,* **-dored, -dor ing.** *—n.* man employed at a port to load and unload ships. *—v.t.* load or unload (a vessel or cargo). *—v.i.* work as a stevedore. [< Spanish *estibador* < *estibar* stow cargo < Latin *stipare* pack down, press]

Ste vens (stē′vənz), *n.* 1 **Thaddeus,** 1792-1868, American statesman and abolitionist. 2 **Wallace,** 1879-1955, American poet.

Ste ven son (stē′vən sən), *n.* 1 **Adlai E(wing),** 1900-1965, American political leader and diplomat. 2 **Robert Louis,** 1850-1894, Scottish novelist, poet, and essayist.

stew (stü, styü), *v.t.* cook by slow boiling: *The cook stewed the chicken for a long time.* *—v.i.* INFORMAL. worry; fret: *stew about an imagined insult.* *—n.* 1 a dish, usually consisting of meat, vegetables, etc., cooked by slow boiling: *beef stew.* 2 INFORMAL. state of worry; fret. [< Old French *estuver,* ultimately < Latin *ex-* out + Greek *typhos* vapor]

stew ard (stü′ərd, styü′ərd), *n.* 1 man who has charge of the food and table service for a club, ship, railroad train, airplane, etc. 2 servant on a ship: *a deck steward, a cabin steward.* 3 man who manages another's property: *He is the steward of that great estate.* 4 person appointed to manage a dinner, ball, show, etc. [Old English *stigweard* < *stig* hall + *weard* keeper, ward]

stew ard ess (stü′ər dis, styü′ər dis), *n.* 1 woman employed on an airplane, a ship, etc., to wait on passengers. 2 a woman steward.

stew ard ship (stü′ərd ship, styü′ərd ship), *n.* position, duties, and responsibilities of a steward.

Stew art (stü′ərt, styü′ərt), *n.* **Robert.** See **Castlereagh.**

stew pan (stü′pan′, styü′pan′), *n.* pot or saucepan used for stewing.

St. George's, capital of Grenada, in the SW part. 9000.

St. George's Channel, strait between Wales and Ireland, connecting the Irish Sea with the Atlantic. 43 mi. wide.

St. Got thard (sānt got′ərd), 1 mountain group in the Alps, in S Switzerland. Highest peak, 10,490 ft. 2 mountain pass located there. 6935 ft. high.

St. He le na (sānt hə lē′nə), British island in the S Atlantic. Napoleon I was exiled there from 1815 until his death in 1821. 5000 pop.; 47 sq. mi.

stib nite (stib′nīt), *n.* a lead-gray mineral occurring in crystals and also massive. It is the most important ore of antimony. *Formula:* Sb_2S_3 [< Latin *stibium* antimony < Greek *stibi*]

stick¹ (stik), *n., v.,* **sticked, stick ing.** *—n.* 1 a long, thin piece of wood: *Put some sticks on the fire.* 2 such a piece of wood shaped for a special use: *a walking stick, a hockey stick.* 3 such a piece used as a weapon; club; cudgel. 4 a slender branch or twig of a tree or shrub, especially when cut or broken off. 5 something like a stick in shape: *a stick of candy.* 6 INFORMAL. a stiff, awkward, or stupid person. 7 the device by which the ailerons, elevator, and rudder of an airplane are manipulated. 8 mast or a section of a mast; yard. 9 INFORMAL. portion of alcoholic liquor added to a drink. **10 the sticks,** INFORMAL. the outlying or undeveloped districts; backwoods. *—v.i.* furnish with a stick or sticks to support or prop. [Old English *sticca* rod, twig, spoon] **—stick′like′,** *adj.*

stick² (stik), *v.,* **stuck, stick ing,** *n.* *—v.t.* 1 pierce with a pointed instrument; thrust (a point) into; stab: *stick a fork into a potato.* 2 kill by stabbing or piercing. 3 fasten by thrusting the point or end into or through something: *He stuck a flower in his buttonhole.* 4 fix on a pointed implement, etc.; impale. 5 put into a position; place: *Don't stick your head out of the window.* 6 fasten; attach: *Stick a stamp on the letter.* 7 bring to a stop: *Our work was stuck by the breakdown of the machinery.* 8 INFORMAL. puzzle: *That question still sticks me.* 9 SLANG. impose upon by or as if by fraud; cheat; swindle: *stick the public with shoddy goods.* *—v.i.* 1 be thrust; extend: *His arms stick out of his coat sleeves.* 2 keep close: *The little boy stuck to his mother's heels.* 3 be or become fastened. See synonym study below. 4 be at a standstill: *Our car stuck in the mud.* 5 hold one's position; cling: *stick on a horse's back.* 6 INFORMAL. stand; last: *She cannot make her charges stick.* 7 be puzzled; hesitate.
stick around, INFORMAL. stay or wait nearby.
stick at, hesitate or stop for.
stick by or **stick to,** remain resolutely faithful or attached to; refuse to desert: *stick to one's friends when they are in trouble.*
stick out, a INFORMAL. put up with until the end. **b** stand out; be plain.
stick up, SLANG. hold up; rob.
stick up for, INFORMAL. support; defend.
—n. 1 thrust; stab. 2 sticky condition or quality. 3 standstill; stop.
[Old English *stician*]
Syn. *v.i.* 3 **Stick, adhere** mean to be firmly or closely attached to something. **Stick** suggests being fastened as if by gluing: *Flies stick to flypaper.* **Adhere** suggests clinging fast or being firmly attached by itself or of one's accord: *This adhesive tape will adhere evenly to very smooth surfaces.*

stick ball (stik′bôl′), *n.* form of baseball played with a rubber ball and a stick or broom handle for a bat.

stick er (stik′ər), *n.* 1 person or thing that sticks. 2 U.S. a gummed label. 3 bur; thorn.

sticking plaster, adhesive tape.

sticking point, 1 the place in which a thing stops and holds fast. 2 any issue over which proceedings, negotiations, etc., are brought to a halt.

stick-in-the-mud (stik′in ᴛʜə mud′), *n.* INFORMAL. person who prefers old methods, ideas, etc., to new; old fogy.

stick le (stik′əl), *v.i.,* **-led, -ling.** 1 make objections about trifles; contend or insist stubbornly. 2 feel difficulties about trifles; have objections; scruple. [Middle English *stightlen* regulate (a contest), mediate < Old English *stihtan* arrange]

stick le back (stik′əl bak′), *n., pl.* **-backs** or **-back.** any of a family of small, scaleless fishes having two or three sharp spines on the back. The male builds an elaborate nest for the eggs. [Middle English *stykylbak* < Old English *sticel* prick, sting + *bæc* back]

stick ler (stik′lər), *n.* person who contends or insists stubbornly, sometimes over trifles: *a stickler for accuracy.*

stick man (stik′mən), *n., pl.* **-men.** SLANG. 1 croupier. 2 person who handles a stick or bat in sports.

stick pin (stik′pin′), *n.* pin worn in a necktie for ornament; tiepin.

hat, āge, fär; let, ēqual, tėrm;
it, īce; hot, ōpen, ôrder;
oil, out; cup, pu̇t, rüle;
ch, child; ng, long; sh, she;
th, thin; ᴛʜ, then; zh, measure;

ə represents *a* in about, *e* in taken, *i* in pencil, *o* in lemon, *u* in circus.

< = from, derived from, taken from.

stick shift (stik′shift′), *n.* lever projecting from the floor of an automobile, used to shift or change the speed of gears.
stick tight (stik′tīt′), *n.* herb of the composite family whose prickly, seedlike fruits stick to clothing, etc.
stick-to-it ive ness (stik′tü′ə tiv nis), *n.* INFORMAL. persistence.
stick um (stik′əm), *n.* SLANG. any sticky substance; gum; adhesive.
stick up (stik′up′), *n.* SLANG. holdup; robbery.
stick work (stik′wėrk′), *n.* the way a player manipulates his stick in such sports as hockey and lacrosse.
stick y (stik′ē), *adj.,* **stick i er, stick i est.** 1 that sticks; adhesive: *sticky glue.* 2 that makes things stick; covered with adhesive matter: *sticky flypaper.* 3 unpleasantly hot and humid: *sticky weather.* 4 INFORMAL. *difficult:* a sticky problem. 5 SLANG. extremely disagreeable. **—stick′i ly,** *adv.* **—stick′i ness,** *n.*
stiff (stif), *adj.* 1 not easily bent; fixed; rigid: *a stiff collar.* See synonym study below. 2 hard to move: *a stiff hinge.* 3 not able to move easily: *a stiff neck.* 4 not fluid; firm: *a stiff cake batter, stiff jelly.* 5 dense; compact: *stiff soil.* 6 not easy or natural in manner; formal: *a stiff bow, a stiff style of writing.* 7 lacking grace of line, form, or arrangement: *stiff geometrical designs.* 8 resolute; steadfast; unyielding: *a stiff resistance.* 9 strong and steady in motion: *a stiff breeze.* 10 hard to deal with; hard; laborious: *a stiff fight, stiff opposition.* 11 harsh or severe: *a stiff penalty.* 12 strong; potent: *a stiff drink.* 13 INFORMAL. more than seems suitable: *a stiff price.*
—adv. 1 in a stiff manner or condition. 2 INFORMAL. very much; extremely: *be scared stiff.*
—n. SLANG. 1 a dead body; corpse. 2 a stiff, formal, or priggish person. 3 fellow; man. [Old English *stif*] **—stiff′ly,** *adv.* **—stiff′ness,** *n.*
Syn. *adj.* 1 **Stiff, rigid** mean not easily bent. **Stiff** implies a hard firmness that resists bending: *a book with a stiff cover.* **Rigid** often implies being so stiff that it will break without bending: *The gate has a rigid iron frame.*
stiff-arm (stif′ärm′), *v.t., n.* straight-arm.
stiff en (stif′ən), *v.t., v.i.* make or become stiff or stiffer. **—stiff′en er,** *n.*
stiff en ing (stif′ə ning), *n.* 1 a making or becoming stiff or stiffer. 2 something used to stiffen a thing.
stiff-necked (stif′nekt′), *adj.* 1 having a stiff neck. 2 stubborn; obstinate.
sti fle (stī′fəl), *v.,* **-fled, -fling.** *—v.t.* 1 stop the breath of; smother: *The smoke stifled the firemen.* 2 keep back; suppress; stop: *stifle a cry, stifle a yawn, stifle business activity, stifle a rebellion.* *—v.i.* 1 be unable to breathe freely: *I am stifling in this hot room.* 2 die or become unconscious by being unable to breathe. [Middle English *stuflen, stifflen* < *stuffen* to stuff, stifle]
stig ma (stig′mə), *n., pl.* **-mas** or **-ma ta.** 1 mark of disgrace; stain or reproach on one's reputation. 2 a distinguishing mark or sign. 3 an abnormal spot or mark in the skin, especially one that bleeds or turns red. 4 the part of the pistil of a plant that receives the pollen. See **pistil** for diagram. 5 **stigmata,** *pl.* marks or wounds like the five wounds on the crucified body of Christ, in the hands, feet, and side, said to appear supernaturally on the bodies of certain persons. 6 ARCHAIC. a special mark burned on a slave or criminal. [< Latin < Greek, mark, puncture < *stizein* to mark, tattoo]
stig mal (stig′məl), *adj.* stigmatic.
stig ma ta (stig′mə tə, stig mä′tə), *n.* a pl. of **stigma.**
stig mat ic (stig mat′ik), *adj.* of or having to do with a stigma; like that of a stigma; marked by a stigma. *—n.* person bearing marks suggesting the wounds of Christ.
stig ma tize (stig′mə tīz), *v.t.,* **-tized, -tiz ing.** 1 set some mark of disgrace upon; reproach; brand. 2 produce stigmas on. **—stig′ma ti za′tion,** *n.*
stile¹ (stīl), *n.* 1 step or steps for getting over a fence or wall. 2 turnstile. [Old English *stigel,* related to *stīgan* climb]
stile² (stīl), *n.* a vertical piece in a paneled wall, the side of a door, etc. [perhaps < Dutch *stijl* doorpost, pillar]
sti let to (stə let′ō), *n., pl.* **-tos** or **-toes.** 1 dagger with a narrow blade. 2 a small, sharp-pointed instrument for making eyelet holes in embroidery. [< Italian, ultimately < Latin *stilus* pointed instrument]
still¹ (stil), *adj.* 1 staying in the same position or at rest; without motion; motionless: *stand still. The lake is still today.* See synonym study below. 2 without noise; quiet; tranquil: *a still night. The room was so still that you could have heard a pin drop.* 3 making no sound; silent: *keep still.* 4 soft; low; subdued: *a still, small voice.* 5 not sparkling or bubbling: *a still wine.*
—n. 1 photograph of a person or other object at rest. 2 U.S. an individual picture or frame of a motion picture, used in advertising. 3 stillness; silence.
—v.t., v.i. make or become calm or quiet.
—adv. 1 even; yet: *still more, still worse. You can read still better if you try.* 2 and yet; but yet; nevertheless: *Proof was given, but they still doubted.* 3 at this or that time: *They came yesterday and they are still here.* 4 up to this or that time: *Was the store still open?* 5 in the future as in the past: *It will still be here.* 6 without moving; quietly. 7 ARCHAIC. always; ever.
—conj. nevertheless; yet: *She has many friends; still she likes to stay home.*
[Old English *stille*]
Syn. *adj.* 1 **Still, quiet** mean without noise or activity. **Still** suggests being silent and at rest: *Her hands are never still.* **Quiet** suggests being calm and peaceful: *They live in a quiet little town.*

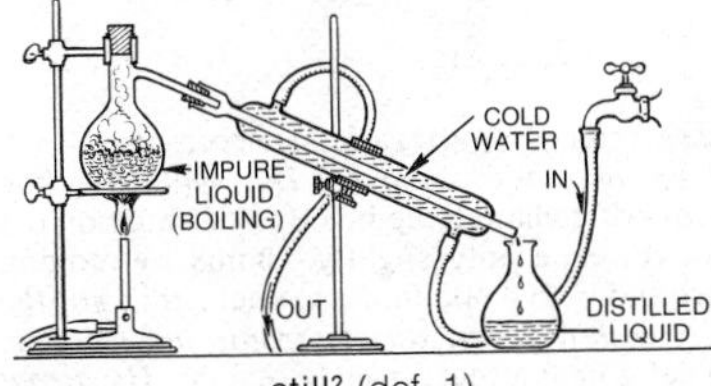

still² (def. 1)

still² (stil), *n.* 1 apparatus for distilling liquids, especially alcoholic liquors. 2 distillery. [noun use of *still,* short for *distill*]
still birth (stil′bėrth′), *n.* 1 birth of a dead child. 2 child dead at birth.
still born (stil′bôrn′), *adj.* 1 dead when born. 2 destined never to be realized: *stillborn hopes.*
still hunt, quiet or secret pursuit, especially a pursuit of game stealthily or under cover.
still life, 1 fruit, flowers, furniture, pottery, dead animals, etc., shown in a picture. 2 picture of such objects. **—still′-life′,** *adj.*
still ness (stil′nis), *n.* 1 absence of noise; silence. 2 absence of motion; calm.

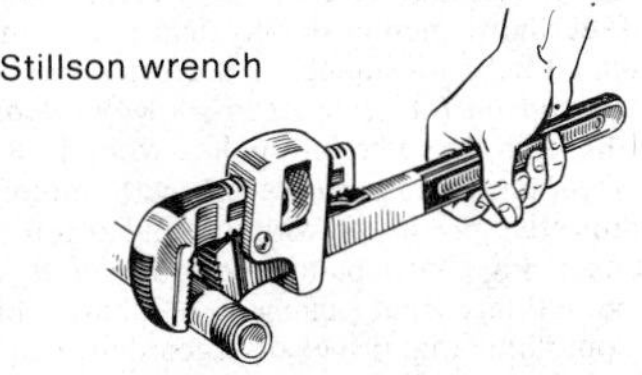
Stillson wrench

Still son wrench (stil′sən), trademark for a wrench with an adjustable L-shaped jaw that tightens as pressure on the handle is increased, used for turning pipes and other round objects.
stil ly (*adj.* stil′ē; *adv.* stil′lē), *adj.,* **-li er, -li est,** *adv.* *—adj.* quiet; still; calm. *—adv.* calmly; quietly.
stilt (stilt), *n., pl.* **stilts** (or **stilt** for 3), *v.* *—n.* 1 one of a pair of poles, each with a support for the foot at some distance above the ground. Stilts are used in walking through shallow water, or by children for amusement. 2 a long post or pole used to support a house, shed, etc., above water, swampy land, etc. 3 any of a widely distributed group of wading birds with long, slender legs and slender bills, that live in marshes. *—v.t.* raise on or as if on stilts. [Middle English *stilte*] **—stilt′like′,** *adj.*
stilt ed (stil′tid), *adj.* 1 stiffly dignified or formal: *stilted conversation.* 2 raised on or as if on stilts. **—stilt′ed ly,** *adv.* **—stilt′ed ness,** *n.*
Stil ton cheese (stilt′n), a rich white cheese veined with mold when well ripened. Stilton cheese is much like Roquefort. [< *Stilton,* in Huntingdonshire, England]
stim u lant (stim′yə lənt), *n.* 1 food, drug, medicine, etc., that temporarily increases the activity of the body or some part of the body. Tea and coffee are stimulants. 2 something that excites, stirs, or stimulates: *Hope is a stimulant.* 3 INFORMAL. an alcoholic drink. *—adj.* stimulating.
stim u late (stim′yə lāt), *v.,* **-lat ed, -lat ing.** *—v.t.* 1 spur on; stir up; rouse to action: *Praise stimulated her to work hard.* 2 increase temporarily the functional activity of (the body or some part of the body). *—v.i.* act as a stimulant or a stimulus. [< Latin *stimulatum* < *stimulus* stimulus] **—stim′u lat′er, stim′u la′tor,** *n.* **—stim′u la′tion,** *n.*
stim u la tive (stim′yə lā′tiv, stim′yə lə tiv), *adj.* stimulating. *—n.* a stimulating thing; stimulus.
stim u li (stim′yə lī), *n.* pl. of **stimulus.**
stim u lus (stim′yə ləs), *n., pl.* **-li.**

1 something that stirs to action or effort; incentive: *Ambition is a great stimulus.* 2 something that excites an organ or part of the body to a specific activity or function; something that produces a response. [< Latin, originally, goad]

sting (sting), *v.*, **stung, sting ing,** *n.* —*v.t.* 1 pierce or wound with a sharp-pointed organ. 2 pain sharply: *He was stung by the jeers of the other children.* 3 affect with a tingling pain, burning sensation, sharp hurt, or the like: *stung by a spark.* 4 drive or stir up as if by a sting: *Their ridicule stung her into making a sharp reply.* 5 SLANG. impose upon; charge too much; cheat. —*v.i.* 1 use a sting: *Bees, wasps, and hornets sting.* 2 cause a feeling like that of a sting: *Mustard stings.* 3 feel sharp mental or physical pain; smart. —*n.* 1 act of stinging. 2 **a** a prick; wound: *Put mud on the sting to take away the pain.* **b** the pain or smart of such a wound. 3 the sharp-pointed organ of an insect, animal, or plant that pricks or wounds and often poisons. 4 a sharp pain: *the sting of defeat.* 5 something that causes a sharp pain. 6 something that drives or urges sharply. [Old English *stingan*] **—sting′ing ly,** *adv.* **—sting′less,** *adj.*

sting a ree (sting′ə rē′), *n.* stingray.

sting er (sting′ər), *n.* 1 the stinging organ of an insect or other animal. 2 anything, as an insect or other animal or plant, that stings. 3 INFORMAL. a stinging blow, remark, etc.

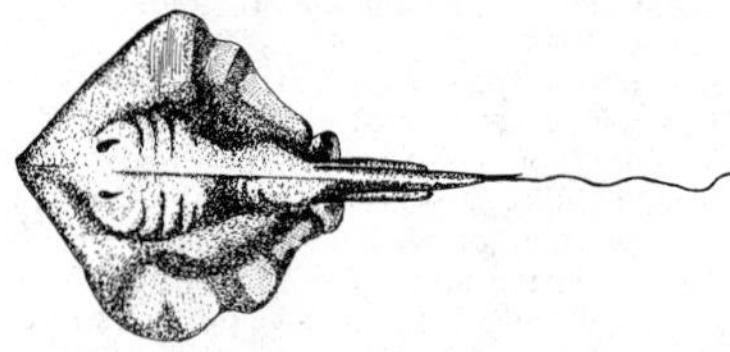

stingray—up to 12 ft. long with tail

sting ray (sting′rā′), *n.* any of various rays whose long, flexible, tapering tail is armed near the middle with a flattened, sharp-pointed, bony spine, capable of inflicting a severe and painful wound.

stin gy (stin′jē), *adj.*, **-gi er, -gi est.** 1 mean about spending or giving money; not generous: *She tried to save money without being stingy.* 2 scanty; meager: *a stingy helping of dessert.* [related to STING] **—stin′gi ly,** *adv.* **—stin′gi ness,** *n.*

stink (stingk), *n.*, *v.*, **stank** or **stunk, stunk, stink ing.** —*n.* 1 a very bad smell. 2 **raise a stink,** SLANG. arouse much complaint, criticism, or disturbance. —*v.i.* 1 have a bad smell. 2 have a very bad reputation; be in great disfavor. 3 INFORMAL. be of very poor quality: *This program stinks.* —*v.t.* cause to stink. [Old English *stincan* to smell] **—stink′er,** *n.* **—stink′ing ly,** *adv.*

stink bomb, container filled with certain chemicals that gives off a disagreeable smell when exploded or burst.

stink bug (stingk′bug′), *n.* any bad-smelling bug, especially one of a family of large, flat bugs with a disagreeable odor.

stink weed (stingk′wēd′), *n.* any of several ill-smelling plants, especially the jimson weed.

stink y (sting′kē), *adj.*, **stink i er, stink i est.** that stinks; stinking.

stint (stint), *v.t.* keep on short allowance; be saving or careful in using or spending; limit: *The parents stinted themselves of food to give it to their children.* —*v.i.* be saving; get along on very little. —*n.* 1 limit; limitation: *give without stint.* 2 amount or share set aside. 3 task assigned: *Washing the breakfast dishes was her daily stint.* [Old English *styntan* to blunt] **—stint′er,** *n.* **—stint′ing ly,** *adv.*

stipe (stīp), *n.* (in botany) a stalk or stem, especially of a mushroom, fern, or of a small organ, such as a pistil. [< Latin *stipes* trunk of a tree]

sti pend (stī′pend), *n.* fixed or regular pay, especially for professional services; salary. [< Latin *stipendium* < *stips* wages + *pendere* weigh out, pay]

sti pen di ar y (stī pen′dē er′ē), *adj.*, *n.*, *pl.* **-ar ies.** —*adj.* 1 receiving a stipend. 2 paid for by a stipend. 3 of or having to do with a stipend. —*n.* person who receives a stipend.

stip ple (stip′əl), *v.*, **-pled, -pling,** *n.* —*v.t.* 1 paint, draw, or engrave by dots. 2 produce a stippled effect on. —*n.* 1 the method of painting, drawing, or engraving by stippling. 2 effect produced by or as if by this method. 3 stippled work. [< Dutch *stippelen*] **—stip′pler,** *n.*

stip u lar (stip′yə lər), *adj.* 1 of, having to do with, or resembling stipules. 2 having stipules.

stip u late[1] (stip′yə lāt), *v.*, **-lat ed, -lat ing.** —*v.t.* arrange definitely; demand as a condition of agreement: *He stipulated that he should receive a month's vacation every year if he took the job.* —*v.i.* make an express demand or arrangement *(for): In accepting the job she stipulated for a raise every six months.* [< Latin *stipulatum* stipulated] **—stip′u la′tor,** *n.*

stip u late[2] (stip′yə lit, stip′yə lāt), *adj.* having stipules. [< *stipule*]

stip u la tion (stip′yə lā′shən), *n.* 1 a definite arrangement; agreement. 2 condition in an agreement or bargain. 3 act of stipulating.

stip ule (stip′yül), *n.* one of the pair of little leaflike parts at the base of a leaf stem. [< Latin *stipula* stem, related to *stipes* trunk of a tree. Doublet of STUBBLE.]

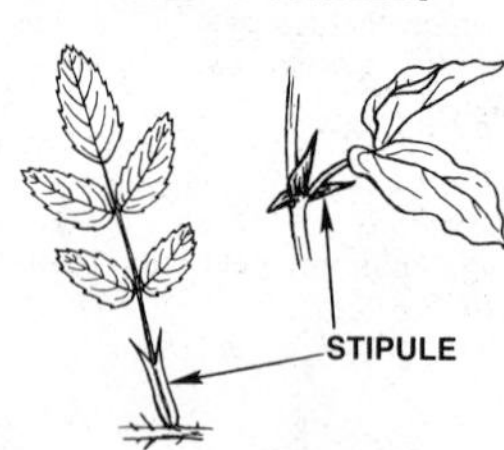

stir[1] (stėr), *v.*, **stirred, stir ring,** *n.* —*v.t.* 1 set in motion; move: *The wind stirs the leaves.* 2 change the position or situation of; move, especially slightly. 3 mix by moving around with a spoon, fork, stick, etc.: *stir the fire with a poker, stir sugar into one's coffee.* 4 set going; affect strongly; excite: *He stirred up the other children to mischief.* 5 bring into notice or debate. —*v.i.* 1 be active; move about: *No one was stirring in the house.* 2 become active, much affected, or excited: *The countryside was stirring with new life.* 3 be mixed with a spoon, fork, etc.: *This dough stirs hard.* —*n.* 1 movement; action. 2 excitement: *The coming of the queen made a great stir.* See synonym study below. 3 act of stirring: *I gave the mixture a hard stir.* 4 a jog; thrust; poke. 5 ARCHAIC. a public disturbance, tumult, or revolt. [Old English *styrian*]

Syn. *n.* 2 **Stir, bustle, ado** mean excited activity. **Stir** suggests disturbance where there has been quiet: *There was a stir in the courtroom.* **Bustle** suggests a great deal of noisy, excited, energetic activity: *the bustle of preparations for the trip.* **Ado** suggests much busyness and fuss over something not worth it: *They made much ado about a comfortable bed for the kitten.*

stir[2] (stėr), *n.* SLANG. prison. [origin uncertain]

stir-cra zy (stėr′krā′zē), *adj.* SLANG. mentally disturbed because of long confinement or restriction.

Stir ling (stėr′ling), *n.* 1 county in central Scotland. 2 city located there. 28,000.

stirp (stėrp), *n.* 1 stock or family. 2 lineage: *of royal stirp.*

stirps (stėrps), *n.*, *pl.* **stir pes** (stėr′pēz). 1 stock; family. 2 (in law) the person from whom a family is descended. [< Latin, originally, stem]

stir ring (stėr′ing), *adj.* 1 moving, active, or lively: *stirring times.* 2 rousing; exciting: *a stirring speech.* **—stir′ring ly,** *adv.*

stir rup (stėr′əp, stir′əp), *n.* 1 loop or ring of metal or wood that hangs from a saddle to support a rider's foot. 2 piece somewhat like a stirrup used as a support or clamp. 3 stapes. [Old English *stigrāp* < *stige* climbing + *rāp* rope]

stirrup bone, stapes.

stirrup cup, 1 cup of wine or other liquor offered to a rider mounted for departure. 2 drink at parting.

stitch (stich), *n.* 1 one complete movement of a threaded needle through cloth in sewing or embroidery, or through skin, flesh, etc., in surgery. 2 one complete movement in knitting, crocheting, embroidering, etc. 3 a particular method of taking stitches: *buttonhole stitch.* 4 loop or portion of thread, etc., made by a stitch: *The doctor will take the stitches out of the wound tomorrow.* 5 piece of cloth or clothing: *He hadn't a dry stitch on.* 6 INFORMAL. a small bit: *She wouldn't do a stitch of work.* 7 a sudden, sharp, stabbing pain: *a stitch in the side.* 8 **in stitches,** laughing uncontrollably. —*v.t.* 1 make stitches in; fasten or ornament with stitches: *stitch a wound.* 2 fasten (cartons, etc.) by stapling. —*v.i.* make stitches; sew. [Old English *stice* puncture] **—stitch′er,** *n.*

stitch ing (stich′ing), *n.* act or work of a person who stitches.

stith y (stiᴛʜ′ē, stith′ē), *n.*, *pl.* **stith ies.** 1 anvil. 2 forge; smithy. [< Scandinavian (Old Icelandic) *stethi*]

sti ver (stī′vər), *n.* 1 a Dutch coin or unit of money, worth about $1\frac{1}{2}$ cents. 2 anything having small value. [< Dutch *stuiver*]

St. John, 1 seaport in New Brunswick, Canada, on the Bay of Fundy. 52,000. 2 one of the Virgin Islands belonging to the United States. 2000 pop.; 19 sq. mi.

St. Johns (sānt jonz′), 1 chief town of Antigua, in the West Indies. 14,000. 2 **St. Johns River,** river flowing from E Florida into the Atlantic. 276 mi.

St. John's, capital of Newfoundland, Canada, in the SE part. 80,000.

St.-John's-wort (sānt jonz′wėrt′), *n.* any of a large genus of herbs or shrubs that have clusters of showy, mostly yellow flowers.

St. Kitts-Ne vis-An guil la (sānt kits′-nē′vis ang gwil′ə), group of islands of

hat, āge, fär; let, ēqual, tėrm;
it, īce; hot, ōpen, ôrder;
oil, out; cup, pu̇t, rüle;
ch, child; ng, long; sh, she;
th, thin; ᴛʜ, then; zh, measure;

ə represents *a* in about, *e* in taken, *i* in pencil, *o* in lemon, *u* in circus.

< = from, derived from, taken from.

the Leeward Islands, a member of the West Indies Associated States. 58,000 pop.; 155 sq. mi.

St. Lawrence, **1 St. Lawrence River,** river in SE Canada flowing northeast from Lake Ontario into the Gulf of St. Lawrence. 760 mi. **2 Gulf of,** arm of the Atlantic Ocean in E Canada. 90,000 sq. mi.

St. Lawrence Seaway, a waterway that links the Great Lakes to the Atlantic Ocean by means of canals and the St. Lawrence River.

St. Lou is (sānt lü′is; sānt lü′ē), city in E Missouri, on the Mississippi River. 622,000.

St. Lu cia (sānt lü′shə), one of the Windward Islands, a member of the West Indies Associated States. 120,000 pop.; 233 sq. mi. *Capital:* Castries.

St. Martin's Day, Martinmas; November 11.

the stocks (def. 25)

St. Martin's summer, a period of mild weather occurring about St. Martin's Day.

St. Marys River, river flowing from Lake Superior into Lake Huron, between the United States and Canada. 40 mi.

St.-Mo ritz (sānt mə rits′), *n.* a fashionable winter resort in SE Switzerland. 4000 pop.; 6037 ft. high.

sto a (stō′ə), *n.* (in ancient Greece) a portico, usually detached and of considerable length, used as a promenade or meeting place. [< Greek]

stoat (stōt), *n.* 1 an ermine in its summer coat of brown. 2 weasel. [Middle English *stote*]

sto chas tic (stō kas′tik), *adj.* (in statistics) having to do with random variables, processes, etc. [< Greek *stochastikos* conjectural, ultimately < *stochos* aim, guess]

stock (stok), *n.* 1 supply of goods which a merchant or manufacturer has on hand for sale: *This store keeps a large stock of toys.* 2 livestock. 3 quantity of something for future use: *stock of words, a stock of canned goods.* 4 the capital of a company or corporation, divided into portions or shares. 5 the shares or portions of one such company or corporation. 6 debt owed, especially by a nation, city, etc. 7 the estimation in which a person or thing is held: *set great stock by a remedy.* 8 the descendants of a common ancestor; family or race: *She is of New England stock.* 9 an original ancestor of a family, tribe, or race: *Their stock was King Alfred.* 10 race or other group of closely related animals or plants. 11 group of related languages. 12 part used as a support or handle; part to which other parts are attached: *the wooden stock of a rifle.* 13 the part of an anchor across the top of the shank. 14 raw material: *Rags are used as a stock for making paper.* 15 broth or water in which meat, fish, or vegetables have been cooked, used as a base for soups, sauces, gravies, etc. 16 an old-fashioned stiff neckcloth, used in place of the modern collar and tie. 17 various

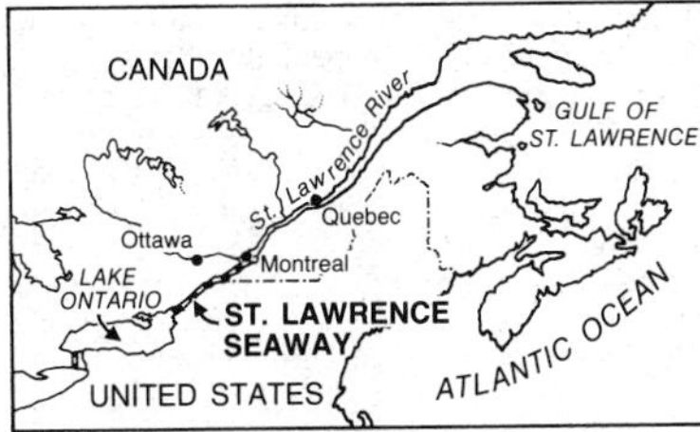

plays produced by a stock company. 18 something lifeless and stupid. 19 a stupid person. 20 trunk or stump of a tree; main stem of a plant. 21 an underground stem like a root. 22 a stem, tree, or plant that furnishes slips or cuttings for grafting. 23 stem in which a graft is inserted and which is its support. 24 any of a genus of garden plants of the mustard family, that have large flowers of various colors, as the gillyflower. 25 **the stocks,** an old instrument of punishment consisting of a heavy wooden frame with holes to put a person's feet and sometimes his hands through.

in stock, ready for use or sale; on hand.

out of stock, no longer on hand; lacking.

take stock, **a** find out how much stock one has on hand. **b** make an estimate or examination.

take stock in, **a** INFORMAL. take an interest in; consider important; trust. **b** take shares in (a company).

—*adj.* 1 kept on hand regularly: *stock sizes.* 2 in common use; commonplace; everyday. 3 of or having to do with the raising of livestock: *a stock farm.* 4 of or having to do with stock or stocks: *a stock certificate.*

—*v.t.* 1 lay in a supply of; supply: *Our camp is well stocked with everything we need for a short stay.* 2 keep regularly for use or sale: *A toy store stocks toys.* 3 furnish with livestock: *stock a farm.* 4 furnish with wildlife: *stock a lake with fish.* 5 fasten to or fit with a stock, as a plow, bell, anchor, rifle, etc. 6 sow (land) with grass, clover, etc. —*v.i.* 1 lay in a stock or supply: *stock up for the winter.* 2 (of corn, grass, etc.) send out shoots.

[Old English *stocc* stump, post]

stock ade (sto kād′), *n., v.,* **-ad ed, -ad ing.** —*n.* 1 a defensive work consisting of a wall or fence of large, strong posts fixed upright in the ground. 2 pen or other enclosed space, now especially one enclosed by a wire fence. 3 place of confinement on a military post. —*v.t.* protect, fortify, or surround with a stockade. [< French *estacade,* ultimately < Provençal *estaca* stake; of Germanic origin]

stock bro ker (stok′brō′kər), *n.* person who buys and sells stocks and bonds for others for a commission.

stock bro ker age (stok′brō′kər ij), *n.* business of a stockbroker.

stock car, 1 a standard passenger car modified for racing. 2 a railroad freight car for livestock.

stock company, 1 a theatrical company employed more or less permanently under the same management, usually at one theater, to perform a repertoire of plays. 2 company whose capital is divided into shares.

stock exchange, 1 place where stocks and bonds are bought and sold. 2 association of brokers and dealers who buy and sell stocks and bonds.

stock fish (stok′fish′), *n., pl.* **-fish es** or **-fish.** fish, such as cod, haddock, hake, etc., preserved by splitting and drying in the air without salt.

stock hold er (stok′hōl′dər), *n.* shareholder.

Stock holm (stok′hōm, stok′hōlm), *n.* seaport and capital of Sweden, in the SE part. 747,000.

stock i net (stok′ə net′), *n.* BRITISH. an elastic, machine-knitted fabric used for making underwear, etc.

stock ing (stok′ing), *n.* 1 a close-fitting, knitted covering of wool, cotton, silk, nylon, etc., for the foot and leg. 2 anything resembling a stocking, such as a patch of color on an animal's leg. [< *stock* stocking, Old English *stocc*]

stocking cap, a close-fitting, knitted cap with a long, pointed end that falls over the back or shoulder, worn for skiing, sledding, etc.

stock in trade, 1 stock of a dealer or company. 2 a workman's tools, materials, etc. 3 resources or skills.

stock man (stok′mən), *n., pl.* **-men.** 1 man who raises or tends livestock. 2 man in charge of a stock of materials or goods.

stock market, 1 stock exchange. 2 the buying and selling in such a place. 3 the trend of prices of stocks and bonds.

stock pile (stok′pīl′), *n., v.,* **-piled, -pil ing.** —*n.* 1 supply of raw materials, essential items, etc., built up and held in reserve for use during a time of emergency or shortage. 2 such a reserve of weapons for warfare. —*v.t., v.i.* collect or bring together a stockpile. **—stock′pil′er,** *n.*

Stock port (stok′pôrt, stok′pōrt), *n.* city in W England, near Manchester. 139,000.

stock room (stok′rüm′, stok′ru̇m′), *n.* room where a stock of goods or supplies is kept.

stock-still (stok′stil′), *adj.* motionless.

Stock ton (stok′tən), *n.* city in central California. 110,000.

stock y (stok′ē), *adj.,* **stock i er, stock i est.** having a solid or sturdy form or build; thick for its height. **—stock′i ly,** *adv.* **—stock′i ness,** *n.*

stock yard (stok′yärd′), *n.* place with pens and sheds for cattle, sheep, hogs, and horses. A stockyard is often connected with a slaughterhouse, railroad, or market.

stodg y (stoj′ē), *adj.,* **stodg i er, stodg i est.** 1 dull or uninteresting; tediously commonplace: *a stodgy book.* 2 heavy and thick in consistency: *stodgy food.* 3 heavily built: *a stodgy person.* 4 stuffed full: *a stodgy bag.* [< *stodge* to stuff (of uncertain origin)] **—stodg′i ly,** *adv.* **—stodg′i ness,** *n.*

sto gie or **sto gy** (stō′gē), *n., pl.* **-gies.** a long, slender, cheap cigar. [earlier *stoga,* short for *Conestoga,* town in Pennsylvania]

sto ic (stō′ik), *n.* 1 person who remains calm, represses his feelings, and is indifferent to pleasure and pain. 2 **Stoic,** member of a school of philosophy founded by Zeno. This school taught that virtue is the highest good and that men should be free from passion unmoved by life's happenings. —*adj.* 1 stoical. 2 **Stoic,** having to do with the philosophy of the Stoics, or with the followers of this philosophy. [< Latin *stoicus* < Greek *stōikos,* literally, pertaining to a *stoa* portico (especially the portico in Athens where Zeno taught)]

sto i cal (stō′ə kəl), *adj.* like a stoic; indifferent to pleasure and pain; self-controlled. **—sto′i cal ly,** *adv.*

sto i cism (stō′ə siz′əm), *n.* 1 patient endurance; indifference to pleasure and pain. 2 **Stoicism,** philosophy of the Stoics.

stoke (stōk), *v.,* **stoked, stok ing.** —*v.t.* 1 poke, stir up, and feed (a fire). 2 tend the fire of (a furnace or boiler). —*v.i.* tend a fire. **stoke up, a** get or supply with fuel: *Stoke up the furnace.* **b** stir up: *stoke up hate.* **c** prepare. [< *stoker*]

stoke hold (stōk′hōld′), *n.* 1 place in a steamship where the furnaces, boilers, etc., are. 2 stokehole.

stoke hole (stōk′hōl′), *n.* 1 hole through which fuel is put into a furnace. 2 space in front of a furnace or furnaces where stokers stand to shovel in coal and take out ashes.

Stoke-on-Trent (stōk′on trent′), *n.* city in W England, on the Trent River. 271,000.

stok er (stō′kər), *n.* 1 person who feeds and tends the fires of a furnace or boiler. 2 a mechanical device for tending and feeding a furnace. [< Dutch < *stoken* stoke]

STOL (stôl), *n.* short take-off and landing (type of aircraft with a greatly reduced take-off and landing distance).

stole[1] (stōl), *v.* pt. of **steal.**

stole[2] (stōl), *n.* 1 a narrow strip of silk or other material worn around the neck or over the shoulders by a clergyman during certain church functions. 2 a woman's collar or scarf of fur or cloth with ends hanging down in front. 3 ARCHAIC. a long robe. [Old English < Latin *stola* < Greek *stolē* garment, equipment]

sto len (stō′lən), *v.* pp. of **steal.**

stol id (stol′id), *adj.* hard to arouse; not easily excited; showing no emotion; seeming dull; impassive. [< Latin *stolidus*] **—stol′id ly,** *adv.*

sto lid i ty (stə lid′ə tē), *n.* stolid quality or condition.

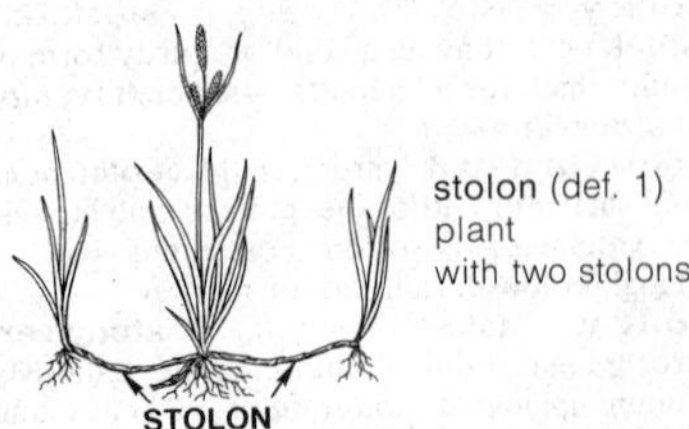

stolon (def. 1) plant with two stolons

sto lon (stō′lon), *n.* 1 (in botany) a slender stem along or beneath the surface of the ground that takes root at the tip and grows into a new plant. A very slender, naked stolon with a bud at the end is a runner. 2 (in zoology) a rootlike growth in a compound organism. [< Latin *stolonem* a shoot]

sto ma (stō′mə), *n., pl.* **-ma ta** or **-mas.** 1 one of the small mouthlike openings in the epidermis of plants, especially of the leaves. Stomata permit the passage of water and gases into and out of the plant. 2 a mouthlike opening in an animal body, especially a small or simple aperture in a lower animal. [< Greek, mouth]

stom ach (stum′ək), *n.* 1 the organ of a vertebrate body that serves as a receptacle for food and in which early stages of digestion occur. In human beings, it is a large, muscular, saclike part of the alimentary canal, occupying the upper part of the left side of the abdomen. 2 (in invertebrates) any portion of the body capable of digesting food. 3 the part of the body containing the stomach; abdomen; belly. 3 appetite. 4 desire; liking: *I have no stomach for killing harmless creatures.* —*v.t.* 1 be able to eat or keep in one's stomach. 2 put up with; bear; endure: *He could not stomach such insults.* [< Greek *stomachos* < *stoma* mouth]

stomacher

stom ach er (stum′ə kər), *n.* an ornamental covering for the stomach and bodice, formerly worn by women under the lacing of the bodice.

stom ach ful (stum′ək fu̇l), *n., pl.* **-fuls.** as much as one can stomach.

sto mach ic (stō mak′ik), *adj.* 1 of or having to do with the stomach; gastric. 2 beneficial to the stomach, digestion, or appetite. —*n.* medicine for the stomach.

sto ma ta (stō′mə tə, stom′ə tə), *n.* a pl. of **stoma.**

sto mate (stō′māt), *adj.* having stomata or a stoma. —*n.* stoma.

stomp (stomp), *v.t., v.i.* stamp with the foot. —*n.* a stomping. [variant of *stamp*] **—stomp′er,** *n.*

stone (stōn), *n., pl.* **stones** for 1-8, **stone** for 9, *adj., v.,* **stoned, ston ing.** —*n.* 1 the hard, compact mineral material of which rocks consist. Stone, such as granite and marble, is much used in building. 2 piece of rock, especially one of a small size. 3 piece of rock of definite size, shape, etc., used for some special purpose: *foundation stones, paving stone.* 4 block, slab, or pillar set up as a monument, boundary mark, or the like. 5 grindstone, millstone, or whetstone. 6 gem; jewel. 7 calculus; kidney stone, gallstone, etc. 8 a hard seed: *peach stones, plum stones.* 9 a British unit of weight, equal to 14 pounds. —*adj.* 1 made or built of stone: *a stone wall.* 2 having to do with stone or stones. 3 made of stoneware or coarse clay.
—*v.t.* 1 put stone on; pave, build, line, etc., with stones. 2 throw stones at; drive by throwing stones. 3 kill by throwing stones. 4 rub or polish with a stone; sharpen on a stone. 5 take the stones or seeds out of. [Old English *stān*] **—stone′like′,** *adj.*

Stone (stōn), *n.* 1 **Edward Durell,** born 1902, American architect. 2 **Harlan Fiske,** 1872-1946, American jurist and educator, who served as chief justice of the United States from 1941 to 1946. 3 **Lucy,** 1818-1893, American women's rights and anti-slavery leader.

Stone Age, the earliest known period of human culture, in which people used tools and weapons made from stone.

stone-blind (stōn′blīnd′), *adj.* totally blind.

stone-broke (stōn′brōk′), *adj.* SLANG. totally without funds.

stone chat (stōn′chat′), *n.* a small European songbird of the same family as the thrushes whose alarm note sounds like pebbles striking together.

stone crop (stōn′krop′), *n.* 1 sedum. 2 a creeping, mosslike herb, a species of sedum, with small, fleshy leaves and clusters of small, yellow flowers, that grows in masses on rocks, old walls, etc.

stone cut ter (stōn′kut′ər), *n.* 1 person who cuts or carves stones. 2 machine for cutting or dressing stone.

stoned (stōnd), *adj.* SLANG. intoxicated on drugs or drink.

stone-deaf (stōn′def′), *adj.* totally deaf.

stone fruit, drupe.

Stone henge (stōn′henj), *n.* a prehistoric ruin in southern England, near Salisbury, consisting of huge slabs or megaliths of roughly shaped stone in a circular arrangement. It may have been a kind of observatory used by astronomers.

stone ma son (stōn′mā′sn), *n.* person who cuts stone or builds walls, etc., of stone.

stone's throw, a short distance.

stone ware (stōn′wer′, stōn′war′), *n.* a hard, dense, vitreous kind of pottery ware, fired at a higher temperature than earthenware, and often glazed with salt.

stone work (stōn′wėrk′), *n.* 1 work in stone. 2 structure made of stone.

stone work er (stōn′wėr′kər), *n.* person who shapes or cuts stone for use in buildings, sculpture, etc.

ston y (stō′nē), *adj.,* **ston i er, ston i est.** 1 having many stones: *The beach is stony.* 2 hard like stone. 3 cold and unfeeling: *a stony heart.* 4 without expression or feeling: *a stony stare.* **—ston′i ly,** *adv.* **—ston′i ness,** *n.*

stood (stu̇d), *v.* pt. and pp. of **stand.**

stooge (stüj), *n., v.,* **stooged, stoog ing.** —*n.* INFORMAL. 1 person on the stage who asks questions of a comedian and is the butt of the comedian's jokes. 2 person who follows and flatters another; hanger-on. —*v.i.* be or act as a stooge *(for): stooge for a comedian.* [origin uncertain]

stool (stül), *n.* 1 seat without back or arms. 2 a similar article used to rest the feet on, or to kneel on; footstool. 3 stump or root of a plant from which shoots grow. 4 cluster of shoots. 5 decoy. 6 movement of the intestines; waste matter from the intestines. 7 article or place to be used as a toilet. —*v.i.* send out shoots; form a stool. [Old English *stōl*] **—stool′like′,** *adj.*

stool ie (stü′lē), *n., pl.* **stool ies.** SLANG. a stool pigeon.

stool pigeon, 1 SLANG. spy for the police; informer. 2 pigeon used to lead other pigeons into a trap.

stoop[1] (stüp), *v.i.* 1 bend forward: *She stoops over her work.* 2 carry the head and shoulders bent forward: *The old man stoops.* 3 (of trees, precipices, etc.) bend forward and downward. 4 lower oneself; descend: *stoop to cheating.* 5 swoop like a hawk or other bird of prey. 6 ARCHAIC. submit; yield. —*v.t.*

1 lower by bending forward; bow. 2 ARCHAIC. humble; subdue. *—n.* 1 act of stooping; a bending forward. 2 a forward bend. 3 a forward bend of the head and shoulders: *walk with a stoop.* 4 condescension. 5 the swoop of a bird of prey on its quarry. [Old English *stūpian*]

stoop[2] (stüp), *n.* porch or platform at the entrance of a house. [< Dutch *stoep*]

stop (stop), *v.*, **stopped, stop ping,** *n.* *—v.t.* 1 keep from moving, acting, doing, being, etc.: *stop work, stop a clock.* See synonym study below. 2 hold back; restrain; prevent: *If anyone wants to go, I shan't stop him.* 3 cut off; withhold: *stop supplies.* 4 put an end to; interrupt: *stop a noise.* 5 close by or as if by filling; fill holes in; close: *stop a crack, stop a leak.* 6 Also, **stop up.** close (a container) with a cork, plug, or other stopper: *stop up a bottle.* 7 block (a way); obstruct: *A fallen tree stopped traffic.* 8 check (a stroke, blow, etc.); ward off; parry. 9 (in boxing) defeat by a knockout: *He was stopped in the second round.* 10 (in various games) defeat. 11 punctuate. 12 in music: **a** close (a finger hole, etc.) in order to produce a particular tone from a wind instrument. **b** press down (a string of a violin, etc.) in order to alter the pitch of tone produced. 13 instruct a bank not to honor (a check, bill, etc.) when presented. *—v.i.* 1 cease to move; halt: *Stop, look, and listen.* 2 halt and remain: *stop for the night at a hotel.* 3 stay on; remain: *Won't you stop with us for another day?* 4 leave off; discontinue: *All work stopped.* See synonym study below. 5 be or become plugged or clogged: *The drain stopped.* 6 **stop down,** reduce the aperture of a lens and thus the amount of light reaching the film or plate. 7 **stop off,** INFORMAL. stop for a short stay. 8 **stop over,** **a** make a short stay. **b** INFORMAL. stop in the course of a trip.
—n. 1 act of coming to a stop: *Her sudden stop startled us.* 2 end: *The singing came to a stop.* 3 a being stopped. 4 a stay or halt in the course of a journey: *a short stop for lunch.* 5 place where a stop is made: *a bus stop.* 6 thing that stops; obstacle. 7 plug or cork; stopper. 8 any piece or device that serves to check or control movement or action in a mechanism. 9 a punctuation mark. The most used stops are ? ! . , ; : —. 10 word used in telegrams, cables, etc., instead of a period. 11 in music: **a** device that controls the pitch of an instrument. **b** (in organs) a graduated set of pipes of the same kind or the knob or handle that controls them. 12 (in photography) aperture of a lens, or the f number indicating this. 13 in phonetics: **a** a sudden, complete stopping of the breath stream, followed by its sudden release. **b** consonant that involves such a stopping. *P, t, k, b, d, g* (as in *go*) are stops; explosive. 14 **pull out all the stops,** do something in the biggest way possible. 15 **put a stop to,** stop; end.
[Old English *-stoppian* < Latin *stuppa* tow[2], oakum < Greek *styppe*]
Syn. *v.t.* 1 **Stop, arrest, check** mean to put an end to action, movement, or progress. **Stop,** the general word, means to bring any kind of advance or movement to an end: *He stopped the car.* **Arrest** suggests halting by forceful and usually deliberate action: *He grabbed the child to arrest its fall.* **Check** means to stop or arrest suddenly, sharply, or with force, sometimes only temporarily: *An awning over the sidewalk checked his fall and saved his life.* *—v.i.* 4 **Stop, cease, pause** mean to leave off. **Stop** implies an ending, often sudden, of action or motion: *The train stopped.* **Cease** implies an ending of a state or condition: *All life has ceased.* **Pause** means to stop for a time, but suggests going on again: *I paused to tie my shoe.*

stop cock (stop′kok′), *n.* device for turning the flow of a liquid or gas on or off; faucet; valve.

stope (stōp), *n., v.,* **stoped, stop ing.** *—n.* a steplike excavation in a mine to take out ore after shafts have been sunk. *—v.t., v.i.* mine in stopes. [probably related to STEP, noun]

stop gap (stop′gap′), *n.* thing or person that fills the place of something lacking; a temporary substitute.

stop light (stop′līt′), *n.* 1 a red light on the rear end of a vehicle that turns on automatically when the brakes are applied. 2 traffic light.

stop order, order given to a broker to buy or sell a stock whenever the market reaches a set price.

stop o ver (stop′ō′vər), *n.* 1 a stopping over in the course of a journey, especially with the privilege of proceeding later on the ticket originally issued for the journey. 2 a place for this.

stop page (stop′ij), *n.* 1 act of stopping. 2 condition of being stopped. 3 block; obstruction.

stop per (stop′ər), *n.* 1 plug or cork for closing a bottle, tube, etc. 2 person or thing that stops. *—v.t.* close or fit with a stopper.

stop ple (stop′əl), *n., v.,* **-pled, -pling.** *—n.* stopper for a bottle, etc.; plug. *—v.t.* close or fit with a stopper.

stop sign, U.S. a traffic sign posted at an intersection to signal motorists going toward it to come to a full stop.

stopt (stopt), *v.* ARCHAIC. a pt. and a pp. of **stop.**

stop watch (stop′woch′, stop′wôch′), *n.* watch having a hand that can be stopped or started at any instant. A stopwatch indicates fractions of a second and is used for timing races and contests.

stor age (stôr′ij, stōr′ij), *n.* 1 act or fact of storing goods. 2 condition of being stored. Cold storage is used to keep eggs and meat from spoiling. 3 place for storing: *put furniture in storage.* 4 price for storing.

storage battery, battery in which chemical energy is converted into direct-current electrical energy. When the cells of the battery have been discharged they may be charged again by passing a current through them in the direction opposite to that of the flow of the current when discharging.

store (stôr, stōr), *n., v.,* **stored, stor ing.** *—n.* 1 place where goods are kept for sale: *a clothing store.* 2 thing or things put away for future use; supply; stock. 3 **stores,** *pl.* things needed to equip and maintain an army, ship, household, etc.; supplies: *naval stores.* 4 storehouse. 5 ARCHAIC. quantity; abundance. 6 **in store,** on hand; in reserve; saved for the future. 7 **set store by,** value; esteem: *She sets great store by her father's opinions.* *—v.t.* 1 supply or stock. 2 Also, **store away** or **store up.** put away for future use; lay up. 3 put in a warehouse or other place for preserving or safekeeping. [< Old French *estor* < *estorer* construct, restore, store < Latin *instaurare* restore, establish] **—stor′er,** *n.*

store front (stôr′frunt′, stōr′frunt′), *n.* the front or front room of a store.

hat, āge, fär; let, ēqual, tėrm;
it, īce; hot, ōpen, ôrder;
oil, out; cup, pu̇t, rüle;
ch, child; ng, long; sh, she;
th, thin; ᴛʜ, then; zh, measure;

ə represents *a* in about, *e* in taken, *i* in pencil, *o* in lemon, *u* in circus.

< = from, derived from, taken from.

store house (stôr′hous′, stōr′hous′), *n., pl.* **-hous es** (-hou′ziz). 1 place where things are stored; warehouse. 2 person or thing resembling such a place: *A library is a storehouse of information.*

store keep er (stôr′kē′pər, stōr′kē′pər), *n.* person who owns or manages a store or stores.

store room (stôr′rüm′, stôr′ru̇m′; stōr′rüm′, stōr′ru̇m′), *n.* room where things are stored.

sto rey (stôr′ē, stōr′ē), *n., pl.* **-reys.** story[2].

sto ried[1] (stôr′ēd, stōr′ēd), *adj.* 1 celebrated in story or history: *the storied Wild West.* 2 ornamented with designs representing happenings in history or legend: *storied tapestry.* [< *story*[1]]

sto ried[2] (stôr′ēd, stōr′ēd), *adj.* having stories or floors: *a two-storied house, a storied tower.* [< *story*[2]]

stork
about 3 ft. high

stork (stôrk), *n.* any of a family of large, long-legged wading birds with a long neck and a long, stout bill. Storks are found in most warm parts of the world. [Old English *storc*] **—stork′like′,** *adj.*

storm (stôrm), *n.* 1 a strong wind with rain, snow, hail, or thunder and lightning. 2 sandstorm. 3 a heavy fall of rain, hail, or snow, or a violent outbreak of thunder and lightning without strong wind. 4 (in meteorology) a wind having a velocity of 64 to 72 miles per hour. 5 anything like a storm: *a storm of arrows.* 6 a violent attack: *The castle was taken by storm.* 7 a violent outburst or disturbance: *a storm of tears.*
—v.i. 1 blow hard; rain; snow; hail. 2 be violent; rage. 3 rush to an assault or attack: *troops storming up the hill.* 4 rush violently: *He stormed out of the room.* *—v.t.* 1 attack violently: *Troops stormed the city.* 2 attack as if with a storm. 3 address loudly and angrily.
[Old English]

storm bound (stôrm′bound′), *adj.* confined or detained by a storm.

storm cellar, cellar for shelter during cyclones, tornadoes, etc.

storm center, 1 center of a cyclone, where there is very low air pressure and comparative calm. 2 any center of trouble, tumult, etc.

storm door, an extra door outside an ordinary door, to keep out snow, cold winds, etc.

storm petrel, a small, black-and-white petrel, whose presence is supposed to give warning of a storm. Also, **stormy petrel.**

storm trooper, 1 member of the private army formed by Adolf Hitler about 1923 and disbanded in 1934; brown shirt. 2 an extremely brutal or vicious individual.

storm window, an extra window outside of an ordinary window, to keep out snow, cold winds, etc.

storm y (stôr′mē), *adj.,* **storm i er, storm i est.** 1 having storms; likely to have storms; troubled by storms: *a stormy sea, stormy weather.* 2 rough and disturbed; violent: *They had stormy quarrels.* **—storm′i ly,** *adv.* **—storm′i ness,** *n.*

stormy petrel, 1 storm petrel. 2 anyone believed likely to cause trouble or to indicate trouble.

sto ry[1] (stôr′ē, stōr′ē), *n., pl.* **-ries,** *v.,* **-ried, -ry ing.** *—n.* 1 account of some happening or group of happenings: *Tell us the story of your life.* 2 such an account, either true or made up, intended to interest the reader or hearer: *fairy stories, stories of adventure.* See synonym study below. 3 INFORMAL. falsehood. 4 stories as a branch of literature: *a character famous in story.* 5 plot of a play, novel, etc. 6 a newspaper article, or material for such an article. *—v.t.* 1 ornament with sculptured or painted scenes from history or legend. 2 ARCHAIC. tell the history or story of. [< Old French *estorie* < Latin *historia* history. Doublet of HISTORY.] **—sto′ry less,** *adj.*

Syn. *n.* 2 **Story, anecdote, tale** mean a spoken or written account of some happening or happenings. **Story** applies to any such account, true or made-up, long or short, in prose or verse, intended to interest another: *the story of King Arthur.* **Anecdote** applies to a brief story about a single incident: *He knows many anecdotes about Mark Twain.* **Tale** usually applies to a longer story: *She reads tales of frontier days.*

sto ry[2] (stôr′ē, stōr′ē), *n., pl.* **-ries.** 1 one of the structural divisions in the height of a building; a floor or the space between the floors: *a house of two stories.* 2 a room or set of rooms on one floor or level. Also, **storey.** [perhaps a special use of *story*[1] in the earlier sense of "row of historical statues across a building front"]

sto ry book (stôr′ē bu̇k′, stōr′ē bu̇k′), *n.* book containing one or more stories or tales, especially for children. *—adj.* of or like that of a storybook; romantic; fictional: *a storybook ending.*

sto ry tell er (stôr′ē tel′ər, stōr′ē tel′ər), *n.* 1 person who tells stories. 2 INFORMAL. person who tells falsehoods; liar.

sto ry tell ing (stôr′ē tel′ing, stōr′ē tel′ing), *n.* 1 act or art of telling stories. 2 INFORMAL. the telling of falsehoods. *—adj.* 1 that tells stories. 2 INFORMAL. lying.

stoup (stüp), *n.* 1 a drinking vessel of varying size for liquids, such as a cup, flagon, or tankard. 2 amount it holds. 3 basin for holy water at the entrance to a church. [< Scandinavian (Old Icelandic) *staup*]

stout (stout), *adj.* 1 fat and large: *a stout body.* See **fat** for synonym study. 2 strongly built; firm; strong: *a stout dam, a stout fighting ship.* 3 brave; bold: *a stout heart.* 4 not yielding; stubborn: *stout resistance.* 5 characterized by endurance or staying power: *a stout horse.* *—n.* 1 a strong, heavy, dark-brown beer. 2 a stout person. [< Old French *estout* strong; of Germanic origin] **—stout′ly,** *adv.* **—stout′ness,** *n.*

stout heart ed (stout′här′tid), *adj.* having courage; brave; bold. **—stout′heart′ed ly,** *adv.* **—stout′heart′ed ness,** *n.*

stove[1] (stōv), *n.* 1 apparatus for cooking and heating by means of wood, coal, gas, oil, and electricity. 2 a heated room or box for some special purpose, such as a hothouse or kiln. [probably < Middle Dutch, hot room, related to Old English *stofa* warm bathing room]

stove[2] (stōv), *v.* a pt. and a pp. of **stave.**

stove pipe (stōv′pīp′), *n.* 1 a metal pipe that carries smoke and gases from a stove to a chimney. 2 INFORMAL. a tall silk hat.

stow (stō), *v.t.* 1 put away to be stored; pack: *The cargo was stowed in the ship's hold.* 2 pack things closely in; fill by packing: *stow a pantry with cans of food.* 3 SLANG. stop. 4 have room for; hold. *—v.i.* **stow away,** hide on a ship, airplane, etc., to get a free passage or to escape secretly. [Old English *stōw* a place] **—stow′er,** *n.*

stow age (stō′ij), *n.* 1 act of stowing. 2 state or manner of being stowed. 3 room or place for stowing. 4 what is stowed. 5 charge for stowing something.

stow a way (stō′ə wā′), *n.* person who hides on a ship, airplane, etc., to get a free passage or to escape secretly.

Stowe (stō), *n.* **Harriet (Elizabeth) Beecher,** 1811-1896, American writer, author of *Uncle Tom's Cabin.*

STP, standard (conditions of) temperature and pressure.

St. Paul, capital of Minnesota, in the SE part, on the Mississippi River. 310,000.

St. Paul's, cathedral in London with a magnificent dome, designed by Sir Christopher Wren.

St. Pe ters burg (sānt pē′tərz bėrg′), 1 former capital of Russia under the czars, now called **Leningrad.** 2 city in W Florida. 216,000.

str., 1 steamer. 2 strait.

stra bis mal (strə biz′məl), *adj.* strabismic.

stra bis mic (strə biz′mik), *adj.* 1 cross-eyed. 2 of or having to do with strabismus.

stra bis mus (strə biz′məs), *n.* disorder of vision due to the turning of one eye or both eyes from the normal position so that both cannot be directed at the same point or object at the same time; squint; cross-eye or wall-eye. [< Greek *strabismos,* ultimately < *strabos* squint-eyed]

Stra bo (strā′bō), *n.* 63? B.C.-A.D. 21?, Greek geographer and historian.

Stra chey (strā′chē), *n.* **Lytton,** 1880-1932, English biographer and critic.

strad dle (strad′l), *v.,* **-dled, -dling,** *n.* *—v.i.* 1 walk, stand, or sit with the legs wide apart. 2 INFORMAL. avoid taking sides; appear to favor both sides. *—v.t.* 1 spread (the legs) wide apart. 2 have a leg on each side of (a horse, bicycle, chair, ditch, etc.). 3 stand or lie across; be on both sides of: *A pair of field glasses straddled his nose.* 4 INFORMAL. attempt to favor both sides of (a question, etc.). *—n.* 1 a straddling. 2 distance straddled. [< variant of dialectal *striddle,* frequentative of *stride*] **—strad′dler,** *n.*

Strad i var i (strad′ə vär′ē), *n.* **Antonio,** 1644?-1737, Italian violin maker. His violins are famous for their beautiful tone and design.

Strad i var i us (strad′ə ver′ē əs), *n.* violin, viola, or cello made by Stradivari.

strafe (strāf), *v.t.,* **strafed, straf ing.** 1 (of aircraft) machine-gun enemy troops or ground positions at close range. 2 shell or bombard heavily. [< the German World War I slogan *Gott strafe England* God punish England] **—straf′er,** *n.*

Straf ford (straf′ərd), *n.* first **Earl of,** 1593-1641, Thomas Wentworth, chief adviser of Charles I of England.

strag gle (strag′əl), *v.i.,* **-gled, -gling.** 1 wander in a scattered fashion: *Cows straggled along the lane.* 2 stray from the rest. 3 spread in an irregular, rambling manner: *Vines straggled over the yard.* [Middle English *straglen.* Probably related to STRETCH.] **—strag′gler,** *n.*

strag gly (strag′lē), *adj.,* **-gli er, -gli est.** spread out in an irregular, rambling way; straggling.

straight (strāt), *adj.* 1 without a bend or curve; not crooked or irregular: *a straight line, a straight road.* 2 going in a line; direct: *straight aim, a straight throw.* 3 frank; honest; upright: *straight conduct, a straight answer.* 4 right; correct: *straight thinking, a straight thinker.* 5 in proper order or condition: *keep one's accounts straight.* 6 continuous: *in straight succession.* 7 U.S. **a** supporting the candidates of one party only: *vote the straight Democratic ticket.* **b** thoroughgoing or unreserved: *a straight Republican.* **c** unmixed; undiluted: *straight whiskey.* 8 showing no emotion, humor, etc.: *keep a straight face.* 9 INFORMAL. reliable: *a straight tip.* 10 SLANG. conventional or conservative; not hippie, radical, homosexual, etc.; square: *straight society, the straight press.* 11 (in poker) made up of a sequence of five cards: *a straight flush.*
—adv. 1 in a line; directly: *go straight home, walk straight ahead.* 2 honorably; upright; honestly: *Live straight.* 3 continuously: *drive straight on.* 4 without delay; straightway. 5 without qualification of any kind. 6 **straight away** or **straight off,** at once.
—n. 1 condition of being straight; straight form, position, or line. 2 a straight part, as of a racetrack. 3 **the straight,** the home stretch of a racetrack. 4 SLANG. a conventional or conservative person; a square. 5 in poker: **a** a sequence of five cards: *lay down a straight.* **b** a hand containing such a sequence: *deal a player a straight.*
[Old English *streht,* past participle of *streccan* to stretch] **—straight′ly,** *adv.* **—straight′ness,** *n.*

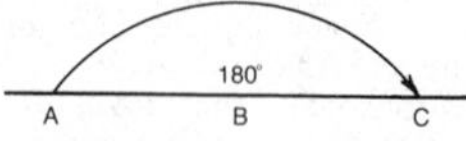

straight angle—ABC is a straight angle.

straight angle, angle of 180 degrees.

straight-arm (strāt′ärm′), *v.t.* (in football) fend off or push away (an oncoming tackler) by holding one's free arm stiffly extended in order to prevent his making a tackle. *—n.* act of straight-arming.

straight a way (strāt′ə wā′), *n.* a straight course. *—adj.* in a straight course. *—adv.* straightway.

straight edge (strāt′ej′), *n.* strip of wood or metal having one edge accurately straight, used in obtaining or testing straight lines and level surfaces.

straight en (strāt′n), *v.t.* 1 make straight:

Straighten your shoulders. 2 put in the proper order or condition: *Straighten up your room.* —*v.i.* become straight. —**straight′en er,** *n.*

straight-faced (strāt′fāst′), *adj.* showing no emotion, humor, etc.

straight for ward (strāt′fôr′wərd), *adj.* 1 honest; frank. 2 going straight ahead; direct. —*adv.* directly. —**straight′for′ward ly,** *adv.* —**straight′for′ward ness,** *n.*

straight for wards (strāt′fôr′wərdz), *adv.* straightforward.

straight jack et (strāt′jak′it), *n., v.t.* straitjacket.

straight man, performer who serves as a foil for a comedian.

straight-out (strāt′out′), *adj.* INFORMAL. out-and-out; complete; thorough.

straight way (strāt′wā′), *adv.* at once; immediately.

strain[1] (strān), *v.t.* 1 draw tight; stretch: *The weight strained the rope.* 2 stretch as much as possible: *strain the truth in telling a story.* 3 use to the utmost: *strain one's eyes to see.* 4 injure by too much effort or by stretching: *strain a muscle.* 5 press or pour through a strainer. 6 remove or keep back (dense or solid parts) in this way: *strain lumps from a sauce.* 7 press closely; squeeze; hug: *strain a person to one's heart.* 8 (in physics) cause alteration of form, shape, or volume in (a solid). —*v.i.* 1 pull hard: *The dog strained at his leash.* 2 make a very great effort. 3 be injured or damaged by too much effort. 4 drip through.

—*n.* 1 force or weight that stretches. 2 an injury caused by too much effort or by stretching. 3 any severe, trying, or wearing pressure: *the strain of worry.* 4 effect of such pressure on the body or mind. 5 Often, **strains,** *pl.* part of a piece of music; melody; song. 6 manner or style of doing or speaking: *a playful strain.* 7 (in physics) alteration of form, shape, or volume caused by external forces.

[< Old French *estreindre* bind tightly < Latin *stringere* draw tight]

strain[2] (strān), *n.* 1 line of descent; race; stock; breed: *He is proud of his Irish strain.* 2 group of animals or plants that form a part of a breed, race, or variety. 3 an inherited quality: *There is a strain of musical talent in that family.* 4 trace or streak: *That horse has a mean strain.* [Old English *strēon* a gain, begetting]

strained (strānd), *adj.* not natural; forced: *Her greeting was cold and strained.*

strain er (strā′nər), *n.* thing that strains, such as a filter, a sieve, or a colander.

strait (strāt), *n.* 1 a narrow channel connecting two larger bodies of water. 2 **straits,** *pl.* difficulty; need; distress: *be in desperate straits for money.* —*adj.* ARCHAIC. 1 narrow; limited; confining. 2 strict. [< Old French *estreit* < Latin *strictum* drawn tight. Doublet of STRICT.] —**strait′ly,** *adv.* —**strait′ness,** *n.*

strait en (strāt′n), *v.t.* 1 limit by the lack of something; restrict. 2 make narrow; contract. 3 ARCHAIC. confine within narrow limits; confine. 4 **in straitened circumstances,** needing money badly.

strait jack et (strāt′jak′it), *n.* a strong, tight jacket or coat that binds the arms close to the sides, used to keep a violent person from harming himself or others. —*v.t.* restrain in or as in a straitjacket. Also, **straightjacket.**

strait-laced (strāt′lāst′), *adj.* very strict in matters of conduct; prudish.

Straits Settlements, former British colony in SE Asia, now included in Singapore and Malaysia.

strake (strāk), *n.* a single breadth of planks or metal plates along the side of a ship from the bow to the stern. [Middle English. Related to STRETCH.]

stra mo ni um (strə mō′nē əm), *n.* 1 jimson weed. 2 drug made from its dried leaves. [< New Latin]

strand[1] (strand), *v.t., v.i.* 1 bring or come into a helpless position: *be stranded a thousand miles from home with no money.* 2 run aground; drive on the shore. —*n.* shore; land bordering a sea, lake, or river. [Old English]

strand[2] (strand), *n.* 1 one of the threads, strings, or wires that are twisted together to make a rope or cable. 2 thread or string: *a strand of pearls, a strand of hair.* —*v.t.* form (a rope) by the twisting of strands. [origin unknown]

strange (strānj), *adj.,* **strang er, strang est.** 1 unusual; odd; peculiar: *a strange accident.* See synonym study below. 2 not known, seen, or heard of before; unfamiliar: *strange faces, a strange language.* 3 unaccustomed; inexperienced: *strange to a job.* 4 out of place; not at home: *The poor child felt strange in the palace.* 5 ARCHAIC. foreign; alien. [< Old French *estrange* < Latin *extraneus* foreign. Doublet of EXTRANEOUS.] —**strange′ly,** *adv.* —**strange′ness,** *n.*

Syn. 1 Strange, odd, peculiar mean unusual or out of the ordinary. **Strange** applies to what is unfamiliar, unknown, or unaccustomed: *A strange quiet pervaded the city.* **Odd** applies to what is irregular or puzzling: *That house has been painted with an odd combination of colors.* **Peculiar** applies to what is unique or different from others: *Raising frogs is a peculiar way to make a living.*

stran ger (strān′jər), *n.* 1 person not known, seen, or heard of before. 2 person or thing new to a place. 3 person who is out of place or not at home in something. 4 visitor; guest. 5 person from another country.

stran gle (strang′gəl), *v.,* **-gled, -gling.** —*v.t.* 1 kill by squeezing the throat to stop the breath. 2 suffocate; choke: *His high collar seemed to be strangling him.* 3 choke down; keep back; suppress: *strangle a yawn.* —*v.i.* be strangled; choke. [< Old French *estrangler* < Latin *strangulare* < Greek *strangalan,* ultimately < *strangos* twisted] —**stran′gler,** *n.*

stran gle hold (strang′gəl hōld′), *n.* 1 a wrestling hold for stopping an opponent's breath. 2 anything that suppresses or hinders free movement, development, etc.

stran gu late (strang′gyə lāt), *v.t.,* **-lat ed, -lat ing.** 1 compress or constrict so as to stop the circulation in, or hinder the action of. 2 strangle; choke. [< Latin *strangulatum* strangled]

stran gu la tion (strang′gyə lā′shən), *n.* 1 a strangling or strangulating. 2 a being strangled or strangulated.

strap (strap), *n., v.,* **strapped, strap ping.** —*n.* 1 a narrow strip of leather or other material that bends easily: *the straps of a wheel or pulley; beat someone with a strap.* 2 a narrow, flat band or strip of cloth: *The general wore shoulder straps.* 3 a narrow band used to fasten something in position, hold together timbers or parts of machinery, or the like. 4 strop. —*v.t.* 1 fasten with a strap. 2 beat with a strap. 3 sharpen on a strap or strop. [variant of *strop*]

hat, āge, fär; let, ēqual, tėrm;
it, īce; hot, ōpen, ôrder;
oil, out; cup, pu̇t, rüle;
ch, child; ng, long; sh, she;
th, thin; ᴛʜ, then; zh, measure;

ə represents *a* in about, *e* in taken, *i* in pencil, *o* in lemon, *u* in circus.

< = from, derived from, taken from.

strap hang er (strap′hang′ər), *n.* INFORMAL. passenger in a bus, subway, train, etc., who cannot get a seat and stands holding on to a strap, rod, etc.

strap less (strap′lis), *adj.* having no strap or straps: *a strapless gown.*

strap per (strap′ər), *n.* 1 person or thing that straps. 2 INFORMAL. a tall, robust person.

strap ping (strap′ing), *adj.* INFORMAL. tall, strong, and healthy: *a fine, strapping girl.*

Stras bourg (stras′bėrg′; *French* sträz-bür′), *n.* city in NE France, on the Rhine River. 249,000.

Strass burg (stras′bėrg′; *German* shträs′bu̇rk), *n.* Strasbourg.

stra ta (strā′tə, strat′ə), *n.* a pl. of **stratum.**

strat a gem (strat′ə jəm), *n.* scheme or trick for deceiving an enemy; trickery. See synonym study below. [< Greek *stratēgēma* < *stratēgein* be a general < *stratēgos* general. See STRATEGY.]

Syn. Stratagem, ruse, artifice mean a scheme to trick or mislead others. **Stratagem** applies to a careful and sometimes complicated scheme for gaining advantage against an enemy or opponent: *a clever political stratagem.* **Ruse** is applied to any trick used to hide one's real purpose or present a false impression, often as a means of cheating another: *Her headache was a ruse to leave early. The shoplifter knew many ruses to distract attention from his stealing.* **Artifice** emphasizes the ingenuity involved and is sometimes applied to a device built primarily to mislead: *The play was a masterpiece of artifice because of its clever turns of plot. The Trojan horse was the artifice used by the Greeks to gain entry into Troy.*

stra te gic (strə tē′jik), *adj.* 1 of strategy; based on strategy; useful in strategy: *a strategic retreat.* 2 important in strategy: *The Panama Canal is a strategic link in our national defense.* 3 of or having to do with raw material necessary for warfare which must be obtained, at least partially, from an outside country. 4 specially made or trained for destroying key enemy bases, industry, or communications behind the lines of battle: *a strategic bomber.* —**stra te′gi cal ly,** *adv.*

stra te gi cal (strə tē′jə kəl), *adj.* strategic.

stra te gics (strə tē′jiks), *n.* strategy.

strat e gist (strat′ə jist), *n.* person trained or skilled in strategy.

strat e gy (strat′ə jē), *n., pl.* **-gies.** 1 science or art of war; the planning and directing of military movements and operations. 2 the skillful planning and management of anything. 3 plan based on strategy. [< Greek *stratēgia* < *stratēgos* general < *stratos* army + *agein* to lead]

➤**Strategy** differs from **tactics.** *Strategy*

refers to the overall plans of a nation at war. *Tactics* refers to the disposition of armed forces in combat.

Strat ford-on-A von (strat′fərd on-ā′vən), *n.* town in central England on the Avon River. It is Shakespeare's birthplace and burial place. 19,000.

strath (strath), *n.* SCOTTISH. a wide valley. [< Scottish Gaelic *srath*]

strat i fi ca tion (strat′ə fə kā′shən), *n.* arrangement in layers or strata.

strat i fy (strat′ə fī), *v.*, **-fied, -fy ing.** —*v.t.* arrange in layers or strata; form into layers or strata. —*v.i.* form strata.

stra to cu mu lus (strā′tō kyü′myə ləs), *n.* a cloud formation consisting of large, globular masses of dark clouds above a flat, horizontal base, usually seen in winter and occurring at heights under 6500 feet. [< Latin *stratus* a spreading out + English *cumulus*]

strat o pause (strat′ə pôz′, strā′tə pôz′), *n.* area of atmospheric demarcation between the stratosphere and the mesosphere.

strat o sphere (strat′ə sfir, strā′tə sfir), *n.* region of the atmosphere between the troposphere and the mesosphere. In the stratosphere, temperature varies little with changes in altitude, and the winds are chiefly horizontal. See **atmosphere** for diagram.

strat o spher ic (strat′ə sfir′ik, strat′ə-sfer′ik; strā′tə sfir′ik, strā′tə sfer′ik), *adj.* of or having to do with the stratosphere.

stra tum (strā′təm, strat′əm), *n., pl.* **-ta** or **-tums.** 1 layer of material, especially one of several parallel layers placed one upon another: *lay several strata of gravel on a road.* 2 (in geology) bed or formation of sedimentary rock consisting throughout of approximately the same kind of material. 3 social level; group having about the same education, culture, development, etc.: *rise from a low to a high stratum of society.* 4 (in biology) a layer of tissue. [< Latin, something spread out < *sternere* to spread]

stra tus (strā′təs), *n., pl.* **-ti** (-tī). cloud formation consisting of a horizontal layer of gray clouds that spread over a large area, occurring at heights under 6500 feet. [< Latin, a spreading out < *sternere* to spread]

Strauss (strous), *n.* 1 **Johann,** 1804-1849, Austrian composer of dance music. 2 his son, **Johann,** 1825-1899, Austrian composer of dance music and light operas. 3 **Richard,** 1864-1949, German composer and conductor.

Stra vin sky (strə vin′skē), *n.* **Igor Fedorovich,** 1882-1971, American composer, born in Russia.

straw (strô), *n.* 1 the stalks or stems of grain after drying and threshing, used for bedding for horses and cows, for making hats, and for many other purposes. 2 one such hollow stem or stalk. 3 tube made of waxed paper, plastic, or glass, used for sucking up drinks. 4 bit; trifle: *He doesn't care a straw.* 5 **catch at a straw,** try anything in desperation. —*adj.* 1 made of straw: *a straw hat.* 2 of the color of straw; pale-yellow. 3 of little value or consequence; worthless. [Old English *strēaw*]

straw ber ry (strô′ber′ē, strô′bər ē), *n., pl.* **-ries.** 1 a small, juicy, red, edible fruit, containing tiny, yellow, seedlike achenes. 2 any of a genus of low plants of the rose family that strawberries grow on.

strawberry blonde, girl or woman with reddish blonde hair.

straw board (strô′bôrd′, strô′bōrd′), *n.* coarse cardboard made of straw pulp, used for boxes, packing, etc.

straw boss, INFORMAL. an assistant foreman.

straw-hat (strô′hat′), *adj.* U.S. of or having to do with summer theaters or shows: *the straw-hat circuit.*

straw man, an imaginary opponent or opposing argument, put up in order to be defeated or refuted.

straw vote, an unofficial vote taken to find out general opinion, estimate the strength of opposing candidates, etc.

straw y (strô′ē), *adj.* 1 of, containing, or resembling straw. 2 strewed or thatched with straw.

stray (strā), *v.i.* 1 lose one's way; wander; roam: *Our dog has strayed off somewhere.* See **wander** for synonym study. 2 turn from the right course; go wrong. —*adj.* 1 wandering; lost: *a stray cat.* 2 here and there; scattered: *There were a few stray cabins along the beach.* 3 isolated: *a stray copy of a book.* —*n.* 1 any person or thing that is lost; wanderer; lost animal. 2 **strays,** *pl.* (in electronics) static. [< Old French *estraier*] —**stray′er,** *n.*

streak (strēk), *n.* 1 a long, thin mark or line: *a streak of lightning, a streak of dirt on one's face.* 2 layer: *Bacon has streaks of fat and streaks of lean.* 3 vein; strain; element: *She has a streak of humor, though she looks very serious.* 4 INFORMAL. a brief period; spell: *a streak of luck.* 5 (in mineralogy) the line of fine powder produced when a mineral is rubbed upon a hard surface. Hematite has a red streak, magnetite a black streak. 6 **like a streak,** INFORMAL. very fast; at full speed. —*v.t.* put long, thin marks or lines on. —*v.i.* 1 become streaked. 2 INFORMAL. move very fast; go at full speed. [Old English *strica*]

streak y (strē′kē), *adj.*, **streak i er, streak i est.** 1 marked with streaks. 2 occurring in streaks. 3 varying; uneven: *The dress has faded so much that the color is streaky.* —**streak′i ly,** *adv.* —**streak′i-ness,** *n.*

stream (strēm), *n.* 1 a flow of water in a channel or bed. Small rivers and large brooks are both called streams. See synonym study below. 2 any flow of liquid: *a stream of blood, a stream of tears.* 3 any steady flow: *a stream of words, a stream of cars.* 4 trend; drift; course: *the prevailing stream of opinion.* —*v.i.* 1 flow or pour forth steadily. See **flow** for synonym study. 2 move steadily; move swiftly: *People streamed out of the theater.* 3 be so wet as to drip in a stream: *streaming eyes, a streaming umbrella.* 4 float or wave: *Flags streamed in the wind.* 5 extend in straight lines: *The sunshine streamed across the room.* 6 hang loosely. —*v.t.* 1 pour out: *The gash in his arm streamed blood.* 2 cause to stream. [Old English *strēam*] —**stream′like′,** *adj.*

Syn. *n.* 1 **Stream, current** mean a flow of water. **Stream** emphasizes a continuous flow, as of water in a river or from a spring or faucet: *Because of the lack of rain many streams dried up.* **Current** emphasizes a strong or rapid, onward movement in a certain direction, and applies particularly to the more swiftly moving part of a stream, ocean, body of air, etc.: *We let the boat drift with the current.*

stream er (strē′mər), *n.* 1 any long, narrow, flowing thing: *Streamers of ribbon hung from her hat.* 2 a long, narrow, pointed flag or pennon. 3 a newspaper headline that runs all the way across a page. 4 a ribbonlike column of light shooting across the heavens in the aurora borealis.

stream let (strēm′lit), *n.* a small stream.

stream line (strēm′līn′), *adj., v.,* **-lined, -lin ing.** —*adj.* streamlined. —*v.t.* 1 give a streamlined shape to. 2 bring up to date; make more efficient: *streamline an office.*

streamlined (def. 1)—streamlined bodies of racing car, submarine, and jet plane

stream lined (strēm′līnd′), *adj.* 1 having a shape that offers the least possible resistance to air or water. The fastest automobiles, airplanes, and trains have streamlined bodies. 2 brought up to date; made more efficient.

stream of consciousness, the freely flowing thoughts and associations of any of the characters in a story.

street (strēt), *n.* 1 road in a city or town, usually with buildings on both sides. 2 a place or way for automobiles, wagons, etc., to go. 3 people who live in the buildings on a street: *The whole street welcomed him.* 4 **on easy street,** in comfortable circumstances. [Old English *strǣt* < Late Latin *(via) strata* paved (road)] —**street′like′,** *adj.*

street Arab, a homeless child who wanders about the streets.

street car (strēt′kär′), *n.* car that runs on rails in the streets and carries passengers; trolley car.

street piano, a small mechanical piano set on wheels and played by turning a handle.

strength (strengkth, strength), *n.* 1 quality of being strong; power; force: *Samson was a man of great strength. The queen had great strength of character.* See **power** for synonym study. 2 power to resist force: *the strength of a beam, the strength of a fort.* 3 military force measured in numbers of soldiers, warships, etc. 4 degree of strength; intensity: *the strength of a beverage, the strength of a sound.* 5 something that makes strong; support: *"God is our refuge and strength."* 6 **on the strength of,** relying or depending on; with the support or help of. [Old English *strengthu* < *strang* strong] —**strength′less,** *adj.*

strength en (strengk′thən, streng′thən), *v.t.* make stronger. —*v.i.* grow stronger. —**strength′en er,** *n.*

stren u os i ty (stren′yü os′ə tē), *n.* quality or condition of being strenuous.

stren u ous (stren′yü əs), *adj.* 1 very active: *We had a strenuous day moving into our new house.* 2 full of energy: *a strenuous worker.* 3 requiring much energy: *strenuous exercise.* [< Latin *strenuus*] —**stren′u ous-ly,** *adv.* —**stren′u ous ness,** *n.*

strep (strep), *n.* INFORMAL. streptococcus.

strep to coc cal (strep′tə kok′əl), *adj.* streptococcic.

strep to coc cic (strep′tə kok′sik), *adj.* having to do with or caused by streptococci.

strep to coc cus (strep′tə kok′əs), *n., pl.* **-coc ci** (-kok′sī), any of a genus of spherical bacteria that multiply by dividing in only one plane, usually occurring in chains or as paired cells, and causing many serious infections and diseases, such as scarlet fever and erysipelas. [< New Latin < Greek *streptos* curved + *kokkos* grain]

strep to my cin (strep′tō mī′sn), *n.* antibiotic derived from an actinomycete, effective against tuberculosis, typhoid fever, and certain other bacterial infections.

stress (stres), *n.* 1 great pressure or force; strain: *steal food under the stress of hunger.* 2 great effort. 3 emphasis; importance: *That school lays stress upon scientific studies.* 4 the relative loudness in the pronunciation of syllables, words in a sentence, etc.; accent. In *hero,* the stress is on the first syllable. 5 (in prosody) the relative loudness or prominence given a syllable or word in a metrical pattern. —*v.t.* 1 put pressure upon. 2 treat as important; emphasize. 3 pronounce with stress. [Middle English *stresse,* short for *destresse* distress] **—stress′less,** *adj.*

stress ful (stres′fəl), *adj.* full of stress; subject to strain.

stretch (strech), *v.t.* 1 draw out; extend (one's body, arms, legs, wings, etc.) to full length: *He stretched himself out on the grass and fell asleep.* 2 extend so as to reach from one place to another or across a space: *stretch a clothesline from a tree to a pole.* 3 reach; hold: *stretch out one's hand to the fire.* 4 draw out to greater length or width: *stretch shoes until they fit.* 5 draw tight; strain: *stretch a muscle, stretch a violin string until it breaks.* 6 extend beyond proper limits: *stretch the law to suit one's purposes.* 7 INFORMAL. exaggerate: *stretch the truth.* —*v.i.* 1 extend one's body or limbs: *stretch out on the couch.* 2 continue over a distance; fill space; spread: *The forest stretches for miles.* 3 extend one's hand; reach for something: *stretch out to get the book.* 4 make great effort. 5 become longer or wider without breaking: *Rubber stretches.*
—*n.* 1 an unbroken length; extent: *A stretch of sand hills lay between the road and the ocean.* 2 an uninterrupted period: *work for a stretch of five hours.* 3 SLANG. term of imprisonment. 4 a stretching or straining something beyond its proper limits: *a stretch of the law, no great stretch of the imagination.* 5 a stretching. 6 a being stretched. 7 capacity for being stretched; extent to which something can be stretched. 8 one of the two straight sides of a racecourse. 9 **the stretch,** home stretch.
—*adj.* of a material that stretches easily to fit all sizes: *stretch socks.*
[Old English *streccan*] **—stretch′a ble,** *adj.*

stretch a bil i ty (strech′ə bil′ə tē), *n.* ability to stretch or be stretched.

stretch er (strech′ər), *n.* 1 person or thing that stretches: *a glove stretcher.* 2 canvas stretched on a frame for carrying the sick, wounded, or dead. 3 bar, beam, or rod used as a tie or brace, as between the legs of a chair.

stretch out (strech′out′), *n.* INFORMAL. a postponement, especially of the date for filling defense orders.

strew (strü), *v.t.,* **strewed, strewed** or **strewn, strew ing.** 1 scatter or sprinkle: *She strewed seeds in her garden.* 2 cover with something scattered or sprinkled. 3 be scattered or sprinkled over. [Old English *strēowian*]

strewn (strün), *v.* a pp. of **strew.**

stri a (strī′ə), *n., pl.* **stri ae** (strī′ē′). 1 a slight furrow or ridge. 2 a linear marking; a narrow stripe or streak, as of color or texture, especially one of a number in parallel arrangement. 3 (in architecture) a fillet between the flutes of columns, etc. [< Latin]

stri at ed (strī′ā tid), *adj.* striped; streaked; furrowed. [< Latin *striatum* < *stria* furrow, channel]

striated muscle, type of muscle with fibers of cross bands contracted by voluntary action, as the muscles that move the arms, legs, neck, etc.; voluntary muscle.

stri a tion (strī ā′shən), *n.* 1 striated condition or appearance. 2 one of a number of parallel striae; stria.

strick en (strik′ən), *adj.* 1 hit, wounded, or affected by (a weapon, disease, trouble, sorrow, etc.): *a stricken deer, a city stricken by fire.* 2 **stricken in years,** old. —*v.* a pp. of **strike.**

strict (strikt), *adj.* 1 very careful in following a rule or in making others follow it: *The teacher was strict but fair.* 2 harsh; severe: *a strict parent.* See synonym study below. 3 exact; precise; accurate: *He told the strict truth.* 4 perfect; complete; absolute: *tell a secret in strict confidence.* [< Latin *strictum* drawn straight. Doublet of STRAIT.] **—strict′ly,** *adv.* **—strict′ness,** *n.*

Syn. 2 **Strict, rigid, rigorous** mean severe and unyielding or harsh and stern. **Strict** emphasizes showing or demanding a very careful and close following of a rule, standard, or requirement: *Our teacher is strict and insists that we follow instructions to the letter.* **Rigid** emphasizes being firm and unyielding, not changing or relaxing for anyone or under any conditions: *He maintains a rigid working schedule.* **Rigorous** emphasizes the severity, harshness, or sternness of the demands made, conditions imposed, etc.: *We believe in rigorous enforcement of the laws.*

stric ture (strik′chər), *n.* 1 an unfavorable criticism; critical remark. 2 an abnormal narrowing of some duct or tube of the body. 3 a binding restriction.

strid den (strid′n), *v.* pp. of **stride.**

stride (strīd), *v.,* **strode, strid den, strid ing,** *n.* —*v.i.* 1 walk with long steps: *stride rapidly down the street.* See **walk** for synonym study. 2 pass with one long step: *He strode over the brook.* —*v.t.* 1 walk with long steps: *stride the streets.* 2 go over or across with one long step: *stride a brook.* 3 sit or stand with one leg on each side of: *stride a fence.* —*n.* 1 a long step. 2 the progressive movement of a horse or certain other animals, completed when all the feet are returned to the same position as at the beginning. 3 distance covered by a stride. 4 **hit one's stride,** reach one's regular speed or normal activity. 5 **make great strides** or **make rapid strides,** make great progress; advance rapidly. 6 **take in one's stride,** deal with in one's normal activity; do or take without difficulty, hesitation, or special effort. [Old English *strīdan*] **—strid′er,** *n.*

stri dence (strīd′ns), *n.* a being strident.

stri den cy (strīd′n sē), *n.* stridence.

stri dent (strīd′nt), *adj.* making or having a harsh sound; creaking; grating; shrill. [< Latin *stridentem*] **—stri′dent ly,** *adv.*

strid u late (strij′ə lāt), *v.i.,* **-lat ed, -lat ing.** 1 make a shrill, grating sound, as a cricket or katydid does, by rubbing together certain parts of the body. 2 shrill; chirr. [< Latin *stridulus* producing a harsh or grating sound < *stridere* sound harshly] **—strid′u la′tion,** *n.*

hat, āge, fär; let, ēqual, tėrm;
it, īce; hot, ōpen, ôrder;
oil, out; cup, pu̇t, rüle;
ch, child; ng, long; sh, she;
th, thin; ᴛʜ, then; zh, measure;

ə represents *a* in about, *e* in taken, *i* in pencil, *o* in lemon, *u* in circus.

< = from, derived from, taken from.

strid u lous (strij′ə ləs), *adj.* making a harsh or grating sound; strident.

strife (strīf), *n.* 1 a quarreling; fighting: *bitter strife between rivals.* 2 a quarrel; fight. [< Old French *estrif;* of Germanic origin]

strike (strīk), *v.,* **struck, struck** or **strick en, strik ing,** *n.* —*v.t.* 1 deal a blow to; hit: *strike a person in anger.* 2 give forth or out; deal: *strike a blow in self-defense.* 3 make by stamping, printing, etc.: *strike a medal.* 4 set on fire by hitting or rubbing: *strike a match.* 5 impress: *The plan strikes me as silly.* 6 sound: *The clock strikes the hour.* 7 overcome by death, disease, suffering, etc.: *The town was struck with a flu epidemic.* 8 cause to feel; affect deeply: *They were struck with terror.* 9 attack: *The enemy struck the town at dawn.* 10 occur to: *An amusing thought struck her.* 11 find or come upon (something): *strike oil, strike the main road.* 12 cross; rub: *Strike his name off the list.* 13 take away by or as if by a blow: *strike a weapon from someone's hand.* 14 assume: *strike an attitude.* 15 (of a plant, cutting, etc.) send down or out (a root). 16 get by figuring: *strike an average.* 17 enter upon; make; decide: *strike an agreement.* 18 lower or take down (a flag, sail, tent, etc.). 19 make level. 20 cause to enter; penetrate: *The wind struck a chill into her bones.* 21 fall on; touch; reach; catch: *The sun struck her eyes. A whistle struck his ear. The waving palm trees struck my view.* —*v.i.* 1 deal or aim a blow: *strike at a person with a whip.* 2 attack: *The enemy will strike at dawn.* 3 fight: *strike for freedom.* 4 be set on fire by hitting or rubbing: *The match wouldn't strike.* 5 sound: *The clock struck twelve times at noon.* 6 stop work to get higher wages, shorter hours, or other benefits. 7 go; advance: *strike into a gallop. We walked along the road a mile, then struck across the fields.* 8 send roots or take root. 9 seize the bait and the hook: *The fish are striking today.*
strike off, a remove; cancel. b print.
strike out, a remove; cancel. b (in baseball) put out or be put out on three strikes: *The pitcher struck out six men. The batter struck out.* c use arms and legs to move forward. d hit from the shoulder.
strike up, a begin: *strike up a conversation.* b begin or cause to begin to play, sing, or sound: *Strike up the band.*
—*n.* 1 act or fact of finding rich ore in mining, oil in boring, etc.; sudden success. 2 a general stopping of work in order to force an employer or employers to agree to the workers' demands for higher wages, shorter hours, or other benefits. 3 **on strike,** stopping work to get higher wages, shorter hours, or other benefits. 4 a striking. 5 attack. 6 (in baseball) failure of the batter to swing at a pitch in the strike zone, to hit any pitch

at which he swings, or to hit a pitch into fair territory. After two strikes, a batter may hit any number of foul balls, provided they are not caught by any fielder. After three strikes, a batter is out. 7 in bowling: **a** an upsetting of all the pins with the first ball bowled. **b** score so made. 8 a taking hold of the bait and the hook. 9 (in geology) the horizontal course of a stratum.
[Old English *strīcan* to rub, stroke]

strike bound (strīk′bound′), *adj.* having operations stopped by a labor strike.

strike break er (strīk′brā′kər), *n.* person who helps to break up a strike of workers by taking a striker's job or by furnishing persons who will do so.

strike break ing (strīk′brā′king), *n.* forceful measures taken to halt a strike.

strike out (strīk′out′), *n.* in baseball: 1 an out caused by three strikes. 2 a striking out.

strik er (strī′kər), *n.* 1 person or thing that strikes. 2 worker who is on strike. 3 hammer that rings the alarm or strikes the hour in certain clocks.

strike zone, (in baseball) a zone or area above home plate, between the batter's knees and armpits, through which a pitch must be thrown to be called a strike.

strik ing (strī′king), *adj.* 1 that strikes. 2 attracting attention; very noticeable: *a striking performance by an actor.* 3 on strike. **—strik′ing ness,** *n.*

strik ing ly (strī′king lē), *adv.* in a way that attracts attention.

Strind berg (strind′bėrg′), *n.* **(Johan) August,** 1849-1912, Swedish author of plays, novels, and short stories.

string (string), *n., v.,* **strung, strung** or **stringed, string ing.** *—n.* 1 a thick thread; small cord or wire; very thin rope. 2 such a thread with things on it: *a string of beads.* 3 a special cord of gut, silk, fine wire, nylon, etc., as for a violin, guitar, or tennis racket. 4 **strings,** *pl.* **a** violins, cellos, and other stringed instruments. **b** the players of stringed instruments in an orchestra. 5 anything used for tying: *apron strings.* 6 a cordlike part of plants, as the tough piece connecting the two halves of a pod in string beans. 7 number of things in a line or row: *a string of cars.* 8 a continuous series or succession: *a string of questions.* 9 INFORMAL. condition; proviso: *an offer with strings attached to it.* 10 group of players forming one of the teams of a squad, ranked according to relative skill: *The first string will practice against the second string.* 11 the racehorses belonging to a particular stable or owner. 12 group of persons or things under the same ownership or management: *He owns a string of newspapers.* 13 **have two strings to one's bow,** have more than one possible course of action. 14 **on a string,** under control. 15 **pull strings, a** direct the actions of others secretly. **b** use secret influence.
—v.t. 1 put on a string: *string beads.* 2 furnish with strings: *string a tennis racket.* 3 tie with a string; hang with a string or rope. 4 extend or stretch from one point to another: *string a cable.* 5 extend in a line, row, or series: *Cars were strung for miles bumper to bumper.* 6 adjust or tighten the strings of; tune: *string a guitar.* 7 make tight. 8 make tense or excited. 9 remove the strings from: *string beans.* *—v.i.* 1 move in a line or series. 2 form into a string or strings.
string along, INFORMAL. **a** fool; hoax. **b** believe in or trust completely. **c** keep (a person) waiting; stall off.
string along with, go along with; agree with.
string out, INFORMAL. stretch; extend: *The program was strung out too long.*
string up, INFORMAL. hang.
[Old English *streng*] **—string′less,** *adj.* **—string′like′,** *adj.*

string bean, 1 any of various bean plants bearing long, green or yellow pods with smooth, somewhat flat seeds. 2 pod of any of these plants, eaten as a vegetable.

string course (string′kôrs′, string′kōrs′), *n.* a decorative horizontal band around a building.

stringed instrument, a musical instrument having strings, played either with a bow or by plucking, as a harp, violin, or guitar.

strin gen cy (strin′jən sē), *n., pl.* **-cies.** 1 strictness; severity. 2 lack of ready money; tightness. 3 convincing force; cogency.

strin gent (strin′jənt), *adj.* 1 strict; severe; rigorous: *stringent laws against speeding.* 2 lacking ready money; tight: *a stringent market for loans.* 3 convincing; forcible: *stringent arguments.* [< Latin *stringentem* binding tight] **—strin′gent ly,** *adv.*

string er (string′ər), *n.* 1 person or thing that strings. 2 a long, horizontal timber in a building, bridge, railroad track, etc. 3 member of a team or person ranked according to ability: *a first-stringer.*

string halt (string′hôlt′), *n.* a diseased condition of horses that causes jerking of the hind legs in walking. Also, **springhalt.**

string quartet, 1 quartet of stringed instruments, usually consisting of two violins, a viola, and a cello. 2 composition for such a quartet.

string tie, a short, narrow necktie that is usually knotted into a bow.

string y (string′ē), *adj.,* **string i er, string i est.** 1 like a string or strings. 2 forming strings: *a stringy syrup.* 3 having tough fibers: *stringy meat.* 4 lean and sinewy: *a tall and stringy boy.* **—string′i ness,** *n.*

strip[1] (strip), *v.,* **stripped** or (RARE) **stript, strip ping.** *—v.t.* 1 make bare or naked; undress (a person, thing, etc.). 2 take off the skin or covering of: *strip a banana.* 3 remove; pull off: *strip fruit from a tree.* 4 make bare; clear out; empty: *strip a forest of its timber.* 5 rob; plunder: *Thieves stripped the house of valuables.* 6 take away the titles, rights, etc., of (a person or thing). 7 tear off the teeth of (a gear, etc.). 8 break the thread of (a bolt, nut, etc.). *—v.i.* take off the clothes or covering; undress. [Old English *-strīepan*] **—strip′per,** *n.*

strip[2] (strip), *n.* 1 a long, narrow, flat piece (of cloth, paper, bark, etc.). 2 a long, narrow tract of land, territory, forest, etc. 3 a long, narrow runway for aircraft to take off from and land on; landing strip; airstrip. [apparently variant of *stripe*[1]]

strip cropping, the planting of alternate rows of crops having strong root systems and weak root systems, done along the contour of a slope to lessen soil erosion.

stripe[1] (strīp), *n., v.,* **striped, strip ing.** *—n.* 1 a long, narrow band of different color, material, etc.: *A tiger has stripes.* 2 **stripes,** *pl.* number or combination of strips of braid on the sleeve of a uniform to show rank, length of service, etc. 3 sort; type: *A man of quite a different stripe.* *—v.t.* mark with stripes. [< Middle Dutch *strīpe*]

stripe[2] (strīp), *n.* a stroke or lash with a whip. [probably special use of *stripe*[1]]

striped (strīpt, strī′pid), *adj.* having stripes; marked with stripes.

striped bass, a sea bass with blackish stripes along the sides, found in North American coastal waters.

strip ling (strip′ling), *n.* boy just coming into manhood; youth; lad. [< *strip*[2] + *-ling*]

strip mine, mine which is operated from the surface by removing the overlying layers of earth.

strip-mine (strip′mīn′), *v.t.,* **-mined, -min ing.** take (a mineral or an ore) from a strip mine.

strive (strīv), *v.i.,* **strove** or **strived, striv en, striv ing.** 1 try hard; work hard: *strive for self-control.* 2 struggle; fight: *The swimmer strove against the tide.* [< Old French *estriver;* of Germanic origin] **—striv′er,** *n.*

striv en (striv′ən), *v.* pp. of **strive.**

strob ile (strob′əl, strō′bīl), *n.* (in botany) any seed-producing cone, such as a pine cone, or a compact mass of scalelike leaves that produce spores, such as the cone of the club moss. [< Greek *strobilos* pine cone < *strobos* a whirling]

strob o scope (strob′ə skōp), *n.* instrument for studying the successive phases of the periodic motion of a body by means of periodically interrupted light. [< Greek *strobos* a whirling + English *-scope*]

strob o scop ic (strob′ə skop′ik), *adj.* of or having to do with a stroboscope.

strode (strōd), *v.* pt. of **stride.**

stroke[1] (strōk), *n., v.,* **stroked, strok ing.** *—n.* 1 act of striking; blow: *a stroke of lightning.* See **blow**[1] for synonym study. 2 sound made by striking: *We arrived at the stroke of three.* 3 piece of luck, fortune, etc.: *a stroke of bad luck.* 4 a single complete movement to be made again and again: *row with a strong stroke of the oars. She swims a fast stroke.* 5 a single complete movement or the distance of the movement in either direction of any piece of machinery having a reciprocating motion, as a piston. 6 throb or pulsing, as of the heart; pulsation. 7 movement or mark made by a pen, pencil, brush, etc.: *write with a heavy down stroke.* 8 a vigorous effort to attain some object: *a bold stroke for freedom.* 9 a very successful effort; feat: *a stroke of genius.* 10 a single effort; act: *They will not do a stroke of work.* 11 a sudden attack of illness, especially of apoplexy. 12 the rower who sets the time for the other oarsmen.
—v.t. 1 be the stroke of. 2 hit.
[related to Old English *strīcan* to strike and *strācian* stroke[2]]

stroke[2] (strōk), *v.,* **stroked, strok ing,** *n.* *—v.t.* move the hand gently over: *She stroked the kitten.* *—n.* a stroking movement. [Old English *strācian*] **—strok′er,** *n.*

stroll (strōl), *v.i.* 1 take a quiet walk for pleasure; walk. 2 go from place to place: *strolling gypsies.* *—v.t.* stroll along or through. *—n.* a leisurely walk. [origin uncertain]

stroll er (strō′lər), *n.* 1 person who strolls; wanderer. 2 a strolling player or actor. 3 kind of light baby carriage in which a small child sits erect.

Strom bo li (strom′bō lē), *n.* Italian island in the Mediterranean, just northeast of Sicily. It has an active volcano 3040 ft. high. 1000 pop.; 5 sq. mi.

strong (strông, strong), *adj.,* **strong er**

(strông′gər, strong′gər), **strong est** (strông′gəst, strong′gəst). 1 having much force or power: *strong arms.* See synonym study below. 2 having or showing moral or mental force: *a strong mind.* 3 able to last, endure, resist, etc.: *a strong fort.* 4 not easily influenced or changed; firm: *a strong will.* 5 of great force or effectiveness: *a strong argument.* 6 having a certain number: *A group that is 100 strong has 100 members.* 7 having a particular quality or property in a high degree: *a strong acid, strong tea.* 8 containing much alcohol: *a strong drink.* 9 having much flavor or odor: *strong seasoning, strong perfume.* 10 having an unpleasant taste or smell: *strong butter.* 11 vivid or intense: *a strong light.* 12 vigorous; forceful: *a strong speech.* 13 hearty; zealous; ardent: *a strong dislike.* 14 (of verbs) inflected for tense by a vowel change within the stem rather than by adding endings. EXAMPLES: find, found; give, gave, given. 15 (in phonetics) stressed.
—adv. with force; in a strong manner; powerfully; vigorously.
[Old English *strang*] **—strong′ly,** *adv.*
Syn. *adj.* **1 Strong, sturdy, robust** mean having or showing much power, force, or vigor. **Strong,** the general word, suggests great power or force in acting, resisting, or enduring: *a strong grip, strong walls.* **Sturdy** suggests power coming from solid construction: *Children need sturdy clothes.* **Robust** suggests healthy vigor of mind or body: *Team sports make children robust.*

strong-arm (strông′ärm′, strong′ärm′), INFORMAL. *—adj.* using force or violence. *—v.t.* use force or violence on.

strong box (strông′boks′, strong′boks′), *n.* a strongly made box or safe to hold valuable things.

strong hold (strông′hōld′, strong′hōld′), *n.* 1 a strongly fortified place; fortress. 2 any secure place.

strong-mind ed (strông′mīn′did, strong′-mīn′did), *adj.* having a strong or determined mind; mentally vigorous. **—strong′-mind′-ed ly,** *adv.* **—strong′-mind′ed ness,** *n.*

strong room (strông′rüm′, strông′rům′; strong′rüm′, strong′rům′), *n.* room like a vault for keeping or storing valuable things.

strong suit, long suit.

stron ti um (stron′shē əm, stron′tē əm), *n.* a soft, silver-white metallic element which occurs only in combination with other elements, used in making alloys and in fireworks, signal flares, etc. *Symbol:* Sr; *atomic number* 38. See pages 326 and 327 for table. [< New Latin < *Strontian,* mining locality in Scotland where the element was first found]

strut[2]
struts
between beams

strontium 90, a radioactive isotope of strontium that occurs in the fallout from a hydrogen-bomb explosion; radiostrontium. It is easily absorbed by the bones and tissues and may eventually replace the calcium in the body. *Symbol:* Sr^{90}; *atomic number* 38; *mass number* 90.

strop (strop), *n., v.,* **stropped, strop ping.** *—n.* a leather strap used for sharpening razors. *—v.t.* sharpen on a strop. [Old English < Latin *stroppus* band < Greek *strophos*]

stro phe (strō′fē), *n.* 1 the part of an ancient Greek ode sung by the chorus when moving from right to left. 2 group of lines of poetry; stanza. [< Greek *strophē,* originally, a turning (i.e., section sung by the chorus while turning) < *strephein* to turn]

stroph ic (strof′ik, strō′fik), *adj.* of or having to do with a strophe.

strove (strōv), *v.* a pt. of **strive.**

strow (strō), *v.t.,* **strowed, strown** (strōn) or **strowed, strow ing.** ARCHAIC. strew.

struck (struk), *v.* pt. and a pp. of **strike.** *—adj.* closed or affected in some way by a strike of workers.

struc tur al (struk′chər əl), *adj.* 1 used in building. **Structural steel** is steel made into beams, girders, etc. 2 of or having to do with structure or structures: *The geologist showed the structural difference in rocks of different ages.* **—struc′tur al ly,** *adv.*

structural formula, a chemical formula that differs from a molecular formula in that it shows how the atoms in a molecule are arranged.

struc ture (struk′chər), *n., v.,* **-tured, -tur ing.** *—n.* 1 something built; building or construction. See **building** for synonym study. 2 anything composed of parts arranged together: *The human body is a wonderful structure.* 3 manner of building; way parts are put together; construction: *The structure of the schoolhouse was excellent.* 4 arrangement of parts, elements, etc.: *the structure of a molecule, the structure of a flower, sentence structure.* *—v.t.* make into a structure; build; construct. [< Latin *structura* < *struere* arrange]

stru del (strü′dl; *German* shtrü′dl), *n.* a pastry, usually filled with fruit or cheese and covered by a very thin dough. [< German *Strudel*]

strug gle (strug′əl), *v.,* **-gled, -gling,** *n.* *—v.i.* 1 make great efforts with the body; work hard against difficulties; try hard: *struggle for a livelihood.* 2 get, move, or make one's way with great effort: *struggle along, struggle to one's feet.* 3 fight: *The dog struggled fiercely with the wildcat.* *—n.* 1 great effort; hard work. 2 a fighting; conflict. [Middle English *struglen*] **—strug′gler,** *n.*

strum (strum), *v.,* **strummed, strum ming,** *n.* *—v.t., v.i.* play by running the fingers lightly or carelessly across the strings or keys: *strum a guitar, strum on the piano.* *—n.* 1 act of strumming. 2 sound of strumming. [perhaps imitative] **—strum′mer,** *n.*

strum pet (strum′pit), *n.* prostitute. [Middle English]

strung (strung), *v.* pt. and a pp. of **string.**

strut[1] (strut), *v.,* **strut ted, strut ting,** *n.* *—v.i.* walk in a vain, self-important manner: *The little boy put on his father's medals and strutted around the room.* *—n.* a strutting walk. [Old English *strūtian* stand out stiffly] **—strut′ter,** *n.*

strut[2] (strut), *n.* a supporting piece; brace. [related to STRUT[1]]

strych nin (strik′nən), *n.* strychnine.

strych nine (strik′nən, strik′nīn, strik′-nēn′), *n.* a poisonous alkaloid consisting of white crystals obtained from nux vomica and other plants of the same genus. It is used in medicine in small doses as a stimulant. *Formula:* $C_{21}H_{22}N_2O_2$ [< Greek *strychnos* nightshade]

St. Thomas, 1 one of the Virgin Islands in the West Indies. It belongs to the United States. 30,000 pop.; 32 sq. mi. 2 former name of **Charlotte Amalie.**

Stu art (stü′ərt, styü′ərt), *n.* 1 member of the royal family that ruled Scotland from 1371 to 1603, and England and Scotland for most of the period from 1603 to 1714. James I, Charles I, Charles II, James II, and Queen Anne were Stuarts. 2 **Charles Edward Louis,** 1720-1788, grandson of James II and pretender to the English throne. He was called "the Young Pretender" and "Bonnie Prince Charlie." 3 **Gilbert,** 1755-1828, American portrait painter. 4 **James E. B.,** 1833-1864, Confederate general. He was called "Jeb" Stuart. 5 **Mary.** See **Mary, Queen of Scots.**

hat, āge, fär; let, ēqual, tėrm;
it, īce; hot, ōpen, ôrder;
oil, out; cup, půt, rüle;
ch, child; ng, long; sh, she;
th, thin; ᴛʜ, then; zh, measure;

ə represents *a* in about, *e* in taken,
i in pencil, *o* in lemon, *u* in circus.

< = from, derived from, taken from.

stub (stub), *n., v.,* **stubbed, stub bing.** *—n.* 1 a short piece that is left: *the stub of a pencil.* 2 the short piece of each leaf in a checkbook, etc., kept as a record. 3 something short and blunt; short, thick piece or part. 4 pen having a short, blunt point. 5 stump of a tree, a broken tooth, etc. *—v.t.* 1 strike against something: *stub one's toes.* 2 clear (land) of tree stumps. 3 dig up by the roots. [Old English *stybb* stump]

stub ble (stub′əl), *n.* 1 the lower ends of stalks of grain left in the ground after the grain is cut. 2 any short, rough growth: *He had three days' stubble on his unshaven face.* [< Old French *stuble* < Late Latin *stupula,* variant of Latin *stipula* stem. Doublet of STIPULE.]

stub bly (stub′lē), *adj.,* **-bli er, -bli est.** 1 covered with stubble. 2 resembling stubble; bristly.

stub born (stub′ərn), *adj.* 1 fixed in purpose or opinion; not giving in to argument or requests. See **obstinate** for synonym study. 2 characterized by obstinacy: *a stubborn refusal.* 3 hard to deal with or manage: *a stubborn cough.* [probably ultimately < *stub*] **—stub′born ly,** *adv.* **—stub′born-ness,** *n.*

stub by (stub′ē), *adj.,* **-bi er, -bi est.** 1 short and thick: *stubby fingers.* 2 short, thick, and stiff: *a stubby beard.* 3 having many stubs or stumps. **—stub′bi ness,** *n.*

stuc co (stuk′ō), *n., pl.* **-coes** or **-cos,** *v.* *—n.* plaster which sets with a hard, stonelike coat. **Cement stucco** is used to cover outer walls; stucco containing crushed marble is used for cornices, moldings, and other interior decoration. *—v.t.* cover, coat, or decorate with stucco. [< Italian; of Germanic origin]

stuc co work (stuk′ō wėrk′), *n.* work done in stucco.

stuck (stuk), *v.* pt. and pp. of **stick[2].**

stuck-up (stuk′up′), *adj.* INFORMAL. too proud; conceited; haughty.

stud[1] (stud), *n., v.,* **stud ded, stud ding.** *—n.* 1 head of a nail, knob, etc., sticking out from a surface: *The belt was ornamented with silver studs.* 2 kind of small button, used as a collar fastener on men's shirts or as an ornament. 3 post to which boards, laths, panels, etc., are nailed in making walls in houses. See **joist** for diagram. 4 a projecting pin on a machine. 5 crosspiece put in each link of a chain cable to strengthen it. —*v.t.* 1 set with studs or something like studs: *a sword hilt studded with jewels.* 2 be set or scattered over: *Little islands stud the harbor.* 3 set like studs; scatter at intervals: *Shocks of corn were studded over the field.* 4 provide with studs. [Old English *studu* pillar, post]

stud² (stud), *n.* 1 collection of horses kept for breeding, hunting, racing, etc. 2 place where such a collection is kept. 3 U.S. studhorse; stallion. 4 any male animal kept for breeding. 5 **at stud,** ready for use in breeding. [Old English *stōd*]

stud book (stud′bu̇k′), *n.* book giving the pedigrees of thoroughbred horses and dogs.

stud ding (stud′ing), *n.* 1 studs of a wall. 2 lumber for making studs.

stud ding sail (stud′ing sāl′; *Nautical* stun′səl), *n.* a light sail set at the side of a square sail.

stu dent (stüd′nt, styüd′nt), *n.* 1 person who studies. 2 person who is studying in a school, college, or university. See synonym study below. [< Latin *studentem* applying oneself, studying]

Syn. 2 **Student, pupil, scholar** mean a person who is studying or being taught. **Student,** emphasizing the idea of studying, applies to anyone who loves to study, but especially to someone attending a higher school, college, or university: *Several high-school students were there.* **Pupil,** emphasizing personal supervision by a teacher, applies to a child in school or someone studying privately with a teacher: *She is a pupil of an opera singer.* **Scholar** now applies chiefly to a learned person who is an authority in some field: *He is a distinguished classical scholar.*

student teacher, a college or university student who teaches in a school for a certain period to qualify for a teacher's certificate or diploma.

stud horse (stud′hôrs′), *n.* a male horse kept for breeding; stallion.

stud ied (stud′ēd), *adj.* 1 carefully planned; done on purpose; resulting from deliberate effort. See **elaborate** for synonym study. 2 learned. **—stud′ied ly,** *adv.* **—stud′ied ness,** *n.*

stu di o (stü′dē ō, styü′dē ō), *n., pl.* **-di os.** 1 workroom of a painter, sculptor, photographer, etc. 2 place where motion pictures are made. 3 place from which a radio or television program is broadcast. [< Italian < Latin *studium* study]

studio apartment, a one-room apartment with a bathroom and sometimes a kitchen or kitchenette.

studio couch, an upholstered couch, without a back or arms, that can be used as a bed.

stu di ous (stü′dē əs, styü′dē əs), *adj.* 1 fond of study. 2 showing careful consideration; careful; thoughtful; zealous: *The clerk made a studious effort to please customers.* **—stu′di ous ly,** *adv.* **—stu′di ous ness,** *n.*

stud y (stud′ē), *n., pl.* **stud ies,** *v.,* **stud ied, stud y ing.** —*n.* 1 effort to learn by reading or thinking. 2 a careful examination; investigation. 3 subject that is studied; branch of learning; thing investigated or to be investigated. 4 a room for study, reading, writing, etc. 5 work of literature or art that deals in careful detail with one particular subject. 6 sketch for a picture, story, etc. 7 etude. 8 earnest effort, or the object of endeavor or effort: *His constant study is to avoid error in his work.* 9 deep thought; reverie.

—*v.t.* 1 try to learn: *study law.* 2 examine carefully: *We studied the map to find the shortest road home.* 3 memorize: *study one's part in a play.* 4 consider with care; think (*out*); plan; *study out a new procedure. The prisoner studied ways to escape.* See **consider** for synonym study. —*v.i.* 1 try to learn: *She is studying to be a doctor.* 2 be a student: *study for a master's degree, study under a famous musician.* 3 try hard; endeavor: *The grocer studies to please his customers.*

[< Latin *studium,* originally, eagerness]

stuff (stuf), *n.* 1 what a thing is made of; material. 2 any woven fabric, especially a woolen or worsted one. 3 thing or things; substance: *The doctor rubbed some kind of stuff on the burn.* 4 goods; belongings: *I was told to move my stuff out of the room.* 5 worthless material; useless objects. 6 silly words and thoughts; nonsense. 7 inward qualities; character: *That boy has good stuff in him.*

—*v.t.* 1 pack full; fill: *stuff a pillow with feathers.* 2 U.S. put fraudulent votes in (a ballot box). 3 stop (*up*); block; choke (*up*): *stuff one's ears with cotton, a head stuffed up by a cold.* 4 fill the skin of (a dead animal) to make it look as it did when alive. 5 fill (a chicken, turkey, etc.) with seasoned bread crumbs, etc., before cooking. 6 force; push; thrust: *stuff clothes into a drawer.* —*v.i.* eat too much.

[< Old French *estoffe*] **—stuff′er,** *n.*

stuffed shirt, SLANG. person who tries to seem more important than he really is.

stuff ing (stuf′ing), *n.* 1 material used to fill or pack something. 2 seasoned bread crumbs, etc., used to stuff a chicken, turkey, etc., before cooking.

stuff y (stuf′ē), *adj.,* **stuff i er, stuff i est.** 1 lacking fresh air: *a stuffy room.* 2 lacking freshness or interest; dull: *a stuffy conversation.* 3 stopped up: *A cold makes one's head feel stuffy.* 4 INFORMAL. **a** easily shocked or offended; prim. **b** angry or sulky. **—stuff′i ly,** *adv.* **—stuff′i ness,** *n.*

stul ti fy (stul′tə fī), *v.t.,* **-fied, -fy ing.** 1 make futile; frustrate: *stultify a person's efforts.* 2 cause to appear foolish or absurd; reduce to foolishness or absurdity. [< Late Latin *stultificare* < Latin *stultus* foolish + *facere* to make] **—stul′ti fi ca′tion,** *n.*

stum ble (stum′bəl), *v.,* **-bled, -bling,** *n.* —*v.i.* 1 trip by striking the foot against something. 2 walk unsteadily: *The tired old man stumbled along.* 3 speak, act, etc., in a clumsy or hesitating way: *stumble through a performance.* 4 make a mistake; do wrong. 5 come by accident or chance: *While in the country, she stumbled upon some fine antiques.* —*v.t.* cause to stumble. —*n.* 1 a wrong act; mistake. 2 act of stumbling. [Middle English *stumblen*] **—stum′bler,** *n.* **—stum′bling ly,** *adv.*

stumbling block, 1 obstacle; hindrance. 2 something that makes a person stumble.

stump (stump), *n.* 1 the lower end of a tree or plant, left after the main part is broken or cut off. 2 anything left after the main or important part has been removed; stub: *The dog wagged his stump of a tail.* 3 place where a political speech is made. 4 person with a short, thick build. 5 a heavy step. 6 sound made by stiff walking or heavy steps; clump. 7 SLANG. leg: *stir one's stumps.* 8 a tight roll of paper or other soft material, pointed at the ends and used to soften or blend pencil, charcoal, etc., marks in drawing.

—*v.t.* 1 U.S. remove stumps from (land). 2 reduce to a stump; cut off. 3 U.S. make political speeches in: *The candidates for governor will stump the state.* 4 INFORMAL. **a** make unable to do, answer, etc.: *Nobody could think of anything to do—everybody was stumped.* **b** stub (one's toe). —*v.i.* 1 walk in a stiff, clumsy, or noisy way, as if one had a wooden leg. 2 U.S. make political speeches. [Middle English *stompe, stumpe*] **—stump′er,** *n.* **—stump′like′,** *adj.*

stump speaker, person who makes political speeches from a platform, etc.

stump y (stum′pē), *adj.,* **stump i er, stump i est.** 1 short and thick. 2 having many stumps. **—stump′i ly,** *adv.* **—stump′i ness,** *n.*

stun (stun), *v.,* **stunned, stun ning,** *n.* —*v.t.* 1 make senseless; knock unconscious: *I was stunned by the fall.* 2 daze; bewilder; shock; overwhelm: *She was stunned by the news of her friend's death.* —*n.* 1 act of stunning. 2 condition of being stunned. [Old English *stunian* to crash, resound]

stung (stung), *v.* pt. and pp. of **sting.**

stunk (stungk), *v.* a pt. and pp. of **stink.**

stun ner (stun′ər), *n.* 1 person, thing, or blow that stuns. 2 INFORMAL. a very striking or attractive person or thing.

stun ning (stun′ing), *adj.* 1 INFORMAL. having striking excellence, beauty, etc.; very attractive; good-looking; pretty. 2 that stuns or dazes; bewildering. **—stun′ning ly,** *adv.*

stunt¹ (stunt), *v.t.* check in growth or development: *Lack of proper food stunts a child.* —*n.* 1 a stunting. 2 a stunted animal or plant. [earlier sense "to confound" < Middle English and Old English *stunt* foolish]

stunt² (stunt), INFORMAL. —*n.* feat to attract attention; act showing boldness or skill: *Circus riders perform stunts on horseback.* —*v.i.* perform stunts. —*v.t.* perform stunts with. [perhaps variant of *stint* task]

stunt man (stunt′man′), *n., pl.* **-men.** man who performs dangerous or difficult feats in motion pictures in place of an actor.

stupe (stüp, styüp), *n.* piece of flannel or other cloth wrung out of hot, usually medicated, water and applied as a counterirritant to an inflamed area. [< Latin *stupa,* variant of *stuppa* coarse flax < Greek *styppē*]

stu pe fa cient (stü′pə fā′shənt, styü′pə fā′shənt), *adj.* stupefying. —*n.* drug or agent that produces stupor.

stu pe fac tion (stü′pə fak′shən, styü′pə fak′shən), *n.* 1 a dazed or senseless condition; stupor. 2 overwhelming amazement, shock, etc.

stu pe fy (stü′pə fī, styü′pə fī), *v.t.,* **-fied, -fy ing.** 1 make stupid, dull, or senseless. 2 overwhelm with shock or amazement; astound: *They were stupefied by the calamity.* [< Latin *stupefacere* < *stupere* be amazed + *facere* to make] **—stu′pe fi′er,** *n.*

stu pen dous (stü pen′dəs, styü pen′dəs), *adj.* amazing; marvelous; immense: *Niagara Falls is a stupendous sight.* [< Latin *stupendus* < *stupere* be amazed] **—stu pen′dous ly,** *adv.* **—stu pen′dous ness,** *n.*

stu pid (stü′pid, styü′pid), *adj.* 1 not intelligent; dull. See synonym study below. 2 not interesting: *a stupid book.* 3 dazed; senseless. —*n.* INFORMAL. a stupid person. [< Latin *stupidus* < *stupere* be dazed or amazed] **—stu′pid ly,** *adv.* **—stu′pid ness,** *n.*

Syn. *adj.* 1 **Stupid, dull** mean having or showing little intelligence. **Stupid** suggests a natural lack of good sense or ordinary intelligence: *Running away from an accident is stupid.* **Dull** suggests a slowness of understanding and a lack of alertness either by nature or because of overwork, poor health, etc.: *The mind becomes dull if the body gets no exercise.*

stu pid i ty (stü pid′ə tē, styü pid′ə tē), *n., pl.* **-ties.** 1 lack of intelligence; dullness. 2 a foolish act, idea, etc.

stu por (stü′pər, styü′pər), *n.* 1 a dazed condition; loss or lessening of the power to feel: *He lay in a stupor, unable to tell what had happened to him.* 2 intellectual or moral numbness. [< Latin < *stupere* be dazed]

stu por ous (stü′pər əs, styü′pər əs), *adj.* in a stupor; dazed.

stur dy (stėr′dē), *adj.,* **-di er, -di est.** 1 strong; stout: *sturdy legs.* See **strong** for synonym study. 2 not yielding; firm; *sturdy resistance, sturdy defenders.* [< Old French *esturdi* violent, originally, dazed] **—stur′di ly,** *adv.* **—stur′di ness,** *n.*

stur geon (stėr′jən), *n., pl.* **-geons** or **-geon.** any of a family of large food fish whose long body has a tough skin with rows of bony plates. Caviar and isinglass are obtained from sturgeons. [< Anglo-French *esturgeon*]

stut ter (stut′ər), *v.i., v.t.* repeat (the same sound) as the result of nervous spasms, in an effort to speak. See **stammer** for synonym study. *—n.* act or habit of stuttering. [frequentative of Middle English *stutten* to stutter] **—stut′ter er,** *n.* **—stut′ter ing ly,** *adv.*

Stutt gart (stut′gärt; *German* shtůt′gärt), *n.* city in SW West Germany. 628,000.

Stuy ve sant (stī′və sənt), *n.* **Peter,** 1592-1672, Dutch governor of the colony of New Netherland from 1646 to 1664.

St. Vin cent (sānt vin′sənt), one of the Windward Islands in the West Indies. 100,000 pop.; 150 sq. mi. *Capital:* Kingstown.

St. Vi tus dance (sānt vī′təs), St. Vitus's dance.

St. Vitus's dance, a nervous disease, which usually affects children, characterized by involuntary twitching of the muscles; chorea. [< *St. Vitus,* legendary martyr during the reign of Diocletian, venerated for his gift of healing, especially by the custom of dancing before his image on his feast day]

sty[1] (stī), *n., pl.* **sties.** 1 pen for pigs. 2 any filthy or disgusting place. [Old English *stig* a building]

sty[2] (stī), *n., pl.* **sties.** a small, painful, inflamed swelling on the edge of the eyelid. [probably < Middle English *styanye* (taken to mean "sty on eye") < Old English *stīgend* rising + *ēage* eye]

stye (stī), *n.* sty².

Styg i an (stij′ē ən), *adj.* 1 of or having to do with the river Styx or the lower world. 2 Also, **stygian.** dark; gloomy. [< Greek *Stygios* < *Styx*]

style (stīl), *n., v.,* **styled, styl ing.** *—n.* 1 manner or custom that prevails; mode or fashion: *dress in the latest style.* See **fashion** for synonym study. 2 manner, method, or way: *the Gothic style of architecture.* 3 way of writing or speaking. 4 good style: *She dresses in style.* 5 literary or artistic excellence. 6 an official name; title. 7 stylus. 8 something like this in shape or use. 9 pointer on a dial, chart, sundial, etc. 10 the

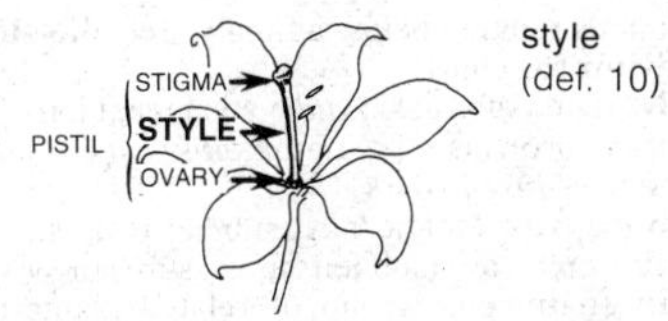

style (def. 10)

stemlike part of the pistil of a flower having the stigma at its top. 11 rules of spelling, punctuation, typography, etc., as used by printers. 12 **cramp one's style,** INFORMAL. keep one from showing his skill, ability, etc. *—v.t.* 1 make in or conform to a given or accepted style; stylize. 2 design according to a style or fashion: *Her dresses are styled by a famous designer.* 3 to name; call: *Joan of Arc was styled "the Maid of Orléans."* [< Old French *estile* < Latin *stilus,* originally, pointed writing instrument. Doublet of STYLUS.]

style book (stīl′bůk′), *n.* 1 book containing rules of punctuation, capitalization, etc., used by printers. 2 book showing fashions in dress, etc.

styl ish (stī′lish), *adj.* having style; fashionable. **—styl′ish ly,** *adv.* **—styl′ish ness,** *n.*

styl ist (stī′list), *n.* 1 writer, speaker, artist, etc., who is considered to be an expert on or a master of style. 2 person who designs, or advises concerning interior decorations, clothes, etc.

sty lis tic (stī lis′tik), *adj.* of or having to do with style. **—sty lis′ti cal ly,** *adv.*

styl ize (stī′līz), *v.t., v.i.,* **-ized, -iz ing.** make or design according to a particular or conventional style. **—styl′i za′tion,** *n.* **—styl′iz er,** *n.*

stylus (def. 1)

sty lus (stī′ləs), *n., pl.* **-lus es, -li** (-lī). 1 a pointed instrument for writing on wax; style. 2 a needlelike point used in making or playing phonograph records. [< Latin *stilus.* Doublet of STYLE.]

sty mie (stī′mē), *n., v.,* **-mied, -mie ing.** *—n.* (in golf) position or occurrence of a ball on a putting green directly between the player's ball and the hole for which he is playing. *—v.t.* 1 (in golf) hinder or block with a stymie. 2 block completely; hinder; thwart: *be stymied by a problem.* [origin uncertain]

styp tic (stip′tik), *adj.* able to stop or check bleeding; astringent. *—n.* something that stops or checks bleeding by contracting the tissue. Alum is a common styptic. [< Greek *styptikos* < *styphein* constrict]

sty rene (stī′rēn′, stir′ēn′), *n.* an aromatic liquid hydrocarbon, used in making synthetic rubber and plastics. *Formula:* $C_6H_5CH{=}CH_2$ [< Latin *styrax* an aromatic resin]

Sty ron (stī′rən), *n.* **William,** born 1925, American novelist.

Styx (stiks), *n.* (in Greek myths) a river in the lower world. The souls of the dead were ferried across it into Hades.

sua sion (swā′zhən), *n.* an advising or urging; persuasion. [< Latin *suasionem* < *suadere* persuade]

hat, āge, fär; let, ēqual, tėrm;
it, īce; hot, ōpen, ôrder;
oil, out; cup, půt, rüle;
ch, child; ng, long; sh, she;
th, thin; ᴛʜ, then; zh, measure;

ə represents *a* in about, *e* in taken, *i* in pencil, *o* in lemon, *u* in circus.

< = from, derived from, taken from.

sua sive (swā′siv), *adj.* advising or urging; persuasive. **—sua′sive ly,** *adv.* **—sua′sive ness,** *n.*

suave (swäv), *adj.* smoothly agreeable or polite. [< Latin *suavis* agreeable] **—suave′ly,** *adv.* **—suave′ness,** *n.*

sua vi ty (swä′və tē, swav′ə tē), *n., pl.* **-ties.** smoothly agreeable quality or behavior; smooth politeness; blandness.

sub (sub), *n., adj., v.,* **subbed, sub bing.** *—n., adj.* 1 substitute. 2 submarine. 3 subordinate. *—v.i.* act as a substitute.

sub-, *prefix.* 1 under; below: *Subnormal = below normal.* 2 down; further; again: *Subdivide = divide again.* 3 near; nearly: *Subtropical = nearly tropical.* 4 lower; subordinate: *Subcommittee = a lower or subordinate committee.* 5 resulting from further division: *Subsection = section resulting from further division of something.* 6 slightly; somewhat: *Subacid = slightly acid.* [< Latin *sub* under, beneath]

sub., 1 subscription. 2 substitute. 3 suburban.

sub ac id (sub as′id), *adj.* slightly acid: *An orange is a subacid fruit.*

sub a gent (sub ā′jənt), *n.* person employed as the agent of an agent.

sub al tern (sə bôl′tərn, sub′əl tərn), *n.* 1 any commissioned officer in the British Army ranking below a captain. 2 a subordinate. *—adj.* 1 BRITISH. ranking below a captain. 2 having lower rank; subordinate. [< Late Latin *subalternus* < Latin *sub-* under + *alternus* alternate]

sub a que ous (sub ā′kwē əs, sub ak′wē əs), *adj.* 1 under water; suitable for use under water. 2 formed under water. 3 living under water.

sub arc tic (sub ärk′tik, sub är′tik), *adj.* near or just below the arctic region; having to do with or occurring in regions just south of the Arctic Circle.

sub as sem bly (sub′ə sem′blē), *n., pl.* **-blies.** assembly of parts or components to be used in forming the main or final assembly of a finished product.

sub a tom ic (sub′ə tom′ik), *adj.* of or having to do with the constituents of an atom or atoms.

sub caste (sub′kast′), *n.* subdivision of a caste.

sub cel lar (sub′sel′ər), *n.* cellar beneath another cellar.

sub class (sub′klas′), *n.* group of related plants or animals ranking below a class. See **classification** for chart.

sub cla vi an (sub klā′vē ən), *adj.* beneath the clavicle or collarbone. *—n.* a subclavian artery, vein, etc.

sub clin i cal (sub klin′ə kəl), *adj.* having mild symptoms that are not readily apparent in clinical tests.

sub com mis sion (sub′kə mish′ən), *n.* a secondary or subordinate commission.

sub com mit tee (sub′kə mit′ē), *n.* a small committee chosen from and acting under a larger general committee for some special duty.

sub con scious (sub kon′shəs), *adj.* not wholly conscious; existing in the mind but not fully perceived or recognized: *a subconscious fear.* —*n.* thoughts, feelings, etc., that are present in the mind but not fully perceived or recognized. —**sub con′scious ly,** *adv.*

sub con scious ness (sub kon′shəs nis), *n.* 1 quality of being subconscious. 2 the subconscious.

sub con ti nent (sub kon′tə nənt), *n.* a landmass or region that is very large, but smaller than a continent: *the subcontinent of India.*

sub con tract (*n.* sub kon′trakt; *v.* sub-kon′trakt, sub′kən trakt′), *n.* contract under a previous contract; contract for carrying out a previous contract or a part of it: *The contractor for the new school building gave out subcontracts to a plumber, an electrician, and a steam fitter.* —*v.i.* make a subcontract. —*v.t.* make a subcontract for. —**sub-con′trac tor,** *n.*

sub crit i cal (sub krit′ə kəl), *adj.* having or using less than the amount of fissionable material necessary to sustain a chain reaction.

sub cul ture (sub kul′chər), *n.* group of people with distinct cultural traits within a culture or society.

sub cu ta ne ous (sub′kyü tā′nē əs), *adj.* 1 under the skin: *subcutaneous tissue.* 2 living under the skin: *a subcutaneous parasite.* 3 placed or performed under the skin: *a subcutaneous injection.* —**sub′cu ta′ne-ous ly,** *adv.*

sub dea con (sub dē′kən), *n.* member of the clergy next below a deacon in rank.

sub deb (sub′deb′), *n.* INFORMAL. subdebutante.

sub deb u tante (sub deb′yə tänt, sub-deb′yə tant, sub deb′yə tänt′), *n.* a young girl soon to make her debut in society.

sub di vide (sub′də vīd′, sub′də vīd′), *v.t., v.i.,* **-vid ed, -vid ing.** divide again; divide into smaller parts: *A real estate dealer bought the farm and subdivided it into building lots.*

sub di vi sion (sub′də vizh′ən, sub′də-vizh′ən), *n.* 1 division into smaller parts. 2 part of a part. 3 (in botany) group of related plants ranking below a division; subphylum. See **classification** for chart. 4 tract of land divided into building lots.

sub dom i nant (sub dom′ə nənt), in music: —*n.* the fourth tone of a scale; tone next below the dominant. —*adj.* of or having to do with this tone.

sub due (səb dü′, səb dyü′), *v.t.,* **-dued, -du ing.** 1 overcome by superior force; conquer: *The Spaniards subdued the Indian tribes in Mexico.* 2 keep down; hold back; suppress: *We subdued a desire to laugh.* 3 tone down; soften: *Pulling down the shades subdued the light in the room.* [ultimately < Latin *subducere* draw away < *sub-* from under + *ducere* to lead; influenced in meaning by Latin *subdere* subdue < *sub-* under + *dare* to put] —**sub du′a ble,** *adj.* —**sub-du′er,** *n.*

sub fam i ly (sub fam′ə lē, sub′fam′ə lē), *n., pl.* **-lies.** group of related plants or animals ranking below a family. See **classification** for chart.

sub fusc (sub fusk′), *adj.* somewhat dark or dusky; brownish. [< Latin *subfuscus* < *sub-* under + *fuscus* dark]

sub ge nus (sub jē′nəs, sub′jē′nəs), *n., pl.* **sub gen er a** (sub jen′ər ə, sub′jen′ər ə), **sub ge nus es.** group of related plants or animals ranking below a genus. See **classification** for chart.

sub group (sub′grüp′), *n.* a subordinate group; subdivision of a group.

sub head (sub′hed′), *n.* 1 a subordinate heading or title. 2 a subordinate division of a heading or title.

sub head ing (sub′hed′ing), *n.* subhead.

sub hu man (sub hyü′mən), *adj.* 1 below the human race or type; less than human. 2 almost human.

subj., 1 subject. 2 subjective. 3 subjectively. 4 subjunctive.

sub ja cent (sub jā′snt), *adj.* 1 situated below; underlying. 2 being in a lower situation, though not directly beneath. [< Latin *subjacentem* lying beneath < *sub-* + *jacere* to lie] —**sub ja′cent ly,** *adv.*

sub ject (*n., adj.* sub′jikt, sub′jekt; *v.* səb-jekt′), *n.* 1 something thought about, discussed, investigated, etc. See synonym study below. 2 something learned or taught; course of study in some branch of learning. 3 person under the power, control, or influence of another: *the subjects of a king.* 4 person or thing that undergoes or experiences something: *Rabbits and mice are often subjects for medical experiments.* 5 (in grammar) a word or group of words that perform or, when the verb is passive, receive the action of the verb. *I* is the subject of the following sentences: I see the cat. I am seen by the cat. I can see. 6 a figure, scene, object, incident, etc., chosen by an artist for representation. 7 theme or melody on which a musical work or movement is based. 8 in philosophy: **a** substance of anything, as contrasted with its qualities or attributes. **b** mind or self, as contrasted with everything outside the mind. 9 (in logic) term of a proposition of which the other term (predicate) is affirmed or denied.
—*adj.* 1 bound by loyalty or allegiance *(to);* obedient to some power or influence: *We are subject to our nation's laws.* 2 under some power or influence: *subject nations.* 3 liable (to suffer from); likely to have; prone *(to): a person subject to colds.* 4 depending on; on the condition of: *I bought the car subject to your approval.*
—*v.t.* 1 bring under some power or influence: *Rome subjected all Italy to her rule.* 2 cause to undergo or experience something: *The lawyer subjected the witness to grueling cross-examination.* 3 lay open or expose; make liable. 4 OBSOLETE. put, lay, or spread under.
[< Latin *subjectum* < *subicere* to place under < *sub-* under + *jacere* to throw]

Syn. *n.* 1 **Subject, topic** mean the main thing or idea thought, talked, or written about, as in a conversation, lecture, essay, or book. **Subject** is the general word: *She tried to change the subject. Juvenile delinquency is a broad subject.* **Topic** particularly applies to a limited and definitely stated subject often having to do with a current event or problem: *"The need for a recreation center here" is today's topic.*

sub jec tion (səb jek′shən), *n.* 1 a bringing under some power or influence; conquering: *The subjection of the rebels took years.* 2 condition of being under some power or influence: *Women used to live in subjection to men.*

sub jec tive (səb jek′tiv), *adj.* 1 existing in the mind; belonging to the person thinking rather than to the object thought of: *Base your subjective opinions on objective facts.* 2 dealing with the thoughts and feelings of the speaker, writer, painter, etc.; personal: *a subjective poem.* 3 (in grammar) being or serving as the subject of a sentence. —**sub-jec′tive ly,** *adv.* —**sub jec′tive ness,** *n.*

sub jec tiv i ty (sub′jek tiv′ə tē), *n.* subjective quality; existence in the mind only; tendency to view things through the medium of one's own individuality.

subject matter, 1 something thought about, discussed, studied, written about, etc. 2 meaning of a talk, book, etc., as distinguished from its form or style.

sub join (səb join′), *v.t.* 1 add at the end; append. 2 place in immediate sequence to something else.

sub ju gate (sub′jə gāt), *v.t.,* **-gat ed, -gat ing.** 1 subdue; conquer. 2 bring under complete control; make subservient or submissive. [< Latin *subjugatum* brought under the yoke < *sub-* under + *jugum* yoke] —**sub′ju ga′tion,** *n.* —**sub′ju ga′tor,** *n.*

sub junc tive (səb jungk′tiv), *adj.* (in grammar) of or having to do with a verb form which expresses a state, act, or event as possible, conditional, or dependent, rather than actual. —*n.* 1 a verb form in the subjunctive mood. EXAMPLES: I insist that he *go,* if this *be* treason, if I *were* you. 2 the subjunctive mood. [< Late Latin *subjunctivus,* ultimately < Latin *sub-* under + *jungere* join]

sub king dom (sub king′dəm, sub′-king′dəm), *n.* a primary division of the animal kingdom, often omitted from classifications. See **classification** for chart.

sub lease (*n.* sub′lēs′; *v.* sub lēs′, sub′lēs′), *n., v.,* **-leased, -leas ing.** —*n.* lease granted by a person on property which has been leased to himself. —*v.t.* grant or take a sublease of.

sub let (sub let′, sub′let′), *v.t.,* **-let, -let-ting.** 1 rent to another (something which has been rented to oneself): *We sublet our house for the summer.* 2 take a sublease of: *I have sublet an apartment whose tenants went away for the summer.* 3 give part of (a contract) to another: *The contractor for the whole building sublet the contract for the plumbing.*

sub li mate (*v.* sub′lə māt; *adj., n.* sub′lə-mit, sub′lə māt), *v.,* **-mat ed, -mat ing,** *adj., n.* —*v.t.* 1 purify; refine. 2 change (an undesirable impulse or trait) into a more desirable activity. 3 sublime (a solid substance). —*adj.* sublimated. —*n.* material obtained when a substance is sublimed. Bichloride of mercury is a very poisonous sublimate.

sub li ma tion (sub′lə mā′shən), *n.* 1 act or process of sublimating or subliming; purification. 2 the resulting product or state.

sub lime (sə blīm′), *adj., n., v.,* **-limed, -lim ing.** —*adj.* lofty or elevated in thought, feeling, language, etc.; noble; grand; exalted: *sublime devotion, sublime poetry.* —*n.* something that is lofty, noble, exalted, etc. —*v.t.* 1 make higher or nobler; make sublime. 2 heat (a solid substance) and condense the vapor given off; purify; refine. —*v.i.* pass off as a vapor and condense as a solid without going through a liquid state; become purified or refined. [< Latin *sublimis,* originally, sloping up (to the lintel) < *sub-* up to + *liminis* threshold] **—sub lime′ly,** *adv.* **—sub lime′ness,** *n.* **—sub lim′er,** *n.*

sub lim i nal (sub lim′ə nəl, sub lī′mə nəl), *adj.* 1 below the threshold of consciousness; subconscious: *the subliminal self.* 2 too weak or small to be felt or noticed: *a subliminal stimulus.* [< *sub-* + Latin *liminis* threshold] **—sub lim′i nal ly,** *adv.*

sub lim i ty (sə blim′ə tē), *n., pl.* **-ties.** 1 lofty excellence; exalted state; grandeur; majesty. 2 person or thing that is sublime.

sub lu nar (sub lü′nər), *adj.* sublunary.

sub lu nar y (sub′lü ner′ē, sub lü′nər ē), *adj.* beneath the moon; earthly.

sub lux a tion (sub′luk sā′shən), *n.* a partial dislocation; sprain. [< New Latin *subluxationem* < Latin *sub-* under + *luxare* dislocate]

sub ma chine gun (sub′mə shēn′), a lightweight automatic or semiautomatic gun, designed to be fired from the shoulder or hip.

sub mar gin al (sub mär′jə nəl), *adj.* 1 below the margin: *submarginal housing.* 2 not productive enough to be worth cultivating, developing, etc.: *submarginal farm land.* 3 (in biology) near the margin.

submarine

sub ma rine (*n., v.* sub′mə rēn′; *adj.* sub′mə rēn′), *n., v.,* **-rined, -rin ing,** *adj.* *—n.* boat that can operate under water, used in warfare for attacking enemy ships with torpedoes and for launching missiles. *—v.t.* attack or sink by a submarine. *—adj.* under the surface of the sea; underwater: *submarine plants.*

sub ma rin er (sub′mə rē′nər, sub mar′ə nər), *n.* member of the crew of a submarine.

sub max il lar y (sub mak′sə ler′ē), *n., pl.* **-lar ies,** *adj.* *—n.* 1 the lower jawbone. 2 a salivary gland situated beneath the lower jaw on either side. *—adj.* 1 of or having to do with the lower jaw or lower jawbone. 2 having to do with the salivary glands beneath the lower jaw.

sub merge (səb mėrj′), *v.,* **-merged, -merg ing.** *—v.t.* 1 put under water; cover with water: *land submerged by a flood.* 2 cover; bury: *His talent was submerged by his shyness.* *—v.i.* 1 sink under water; go below the surface: *The submarine submerged.* 2 sink out of sight. [< Latin *submergere* < *sub-* under + *mergere* to plunge]

sub mer gence (səb mėr′jəns), *n.* 1 a submerging. 2 a being submerged.

sub mer gi ble (səb mėr′jə bəl), *adj., n.* submersible.

sub merse (səb mėrs′), *v.t., v.i.,* **-mersed, -mers ing.** submerge.

sub mers i ble (səb mėr′sə bəl), *adj.* that can be submerged. *—n.* a submarine.

sub mer sion (səb mėr′zhən, səb mėr′shən), *n.* 1 a submerging. 2 a being submerged.

sub mi cro scop ic (sub′mī krə skop′ik), *adj.* so tiny or minute as to be invisible through the normal microscope.

sub min i a ture (sub min′ē ə chər, sub min′ə chər), *adj.* smaller than the standard small size: *a subminiature radio.*

sub mis sion (səb mish′ən), *n.* 1 a yielding to the power, control, or authority of another; submitting: *The defeated general showed his submission by giving up his sword.* 2 obedience; humbleness: *They bowed in submission to the queen's order.* 3 a referring or a being referred to the consideration or judgment of some person or group. [< Latin *submissionem* < *submittere.* See SUBMIT.]

sub mis sive (səb mis′iv), *adj.* yielding to the power, control, or authority of another; obedient; humble. **—sub mis′sive ly,** *adv.* **—sub mis′sive ness,** *n.*

sub mit (səb mit′), *v.,* **-mit ted, -mit ting.** *—v.i.* yield to the power, control, or authority of another; surrender: *The thief submitted to arrest.* See **yield** for synonym study. *—v.t.* 1 refer to the consideration or judgment of another: *The secretary submitted a report of the last meeting.* 2 suggest or urge respectfully. 3 yield (oneself) to the power, control, or authority of a person or agency. [< Latin *submittere* < *sub-* under + *mittere* let go]

sub nor mal (sub nôr′məl), *adj.* below normal; inferior to the normal. *—n.* a subnormal individual.

sub or bit al (sub ôr′bə təl), *adj.* 1 situated below the orbit of the eye. 2 of less than a full orbit: *a suborbital space flight.*

sub or der (sub′ôr′dər, sub ôr′dər), *n.* group of related plants or animals ranking below an order. See **classification** for chart.

sub or di nate (*adj., n.* sə bôrd′n it; *v.* sə bôrd′n āt), *adj., n., v.,* **-nat ed, -nat ing.** *—adj.* 1 lower in rank: *In the army, lieutenants are subordinate to captains.* 2 lower in importance; secondary. 3 under the control or influence of something else; dependent. 4 (in grammar) subordinating. *Because, since, if, as,* and *whether* are subordinate conjunctions. *—n.* a subordinate person or thing. *—v.t.* make subordinate: *A polite host subordinates his wishes to those of his guests.* [< Medieval Latin *subordinatum* lowered in rank < Latin *sub-* under + *ordinem* order] **—sub or′di nate ly,** *adv.* **—sub or′di nate ness,** *n.*

subordinate clause, clause in a complex sentence that cannot act alone as a sentence; dependent clause. In "If I go home, my dog will follow me," *If I go home* is a subordinate clause.

sub or di na tion (sə bôrd′n ā′shən), *n.* 1 act of subordinating. 2 condition of being subordinated. 3 subordinate position or importance. 4 submission to authority; willingness to obey; obedience.

sub orn (sə bôrn′), *v.t.* 1 persuade, bribe, or cause (someone) to do an illegal or evil deed. 2 persuade or cause (a witness) to give false testimony in court. [< Latin *subornare* < *sub-* secretly + *ornare* equip] **—sub′or na′tion,** *n.* **—sub orn′er,** *n.*

sub pe na (sə pē′nə), *n.* subpoena.

sub phy lum (sub′fī′ləm, sub fī′ləm), *n., pl.* **-la** (-lə). 1 group of related animals ranking below a phylum. See **classification** for chart. 2 subdivision (def. 3).

sub plot (sub′plot′), *n.* a minor or subordinate plot in a play, novel, etc.

sub poe na (sə pē′nə), *n.* an official written order commanding a person to appear in a court of law. *—v.t.* summon with such an order. Also, **subpena.** [< Latin *sub poena* under penalty]

sub po lar (sub pō′lər), *adj.* 1 below the poles or polar seas in latitude. 2 beneath the pole of the heavens.

sub pro fes sion al (sub′prə fesh′ə nəl), *adj.* below what is professional; below professional level: *subprofessional assistants.* *—n.* person who engages in subprofessional work.

hat, āge, fär; let, ēqual, tėrm;
it, īce; hot, ōpen, ôrder;
oil, out; cup, pu̇t, rüle;
ch, child; ng, long; sh, she;
th, thin; ᴛʜ, then; zh, measure;

ə represents *a* in about, *e* in taken, *i* in pencil, *o* in lemon, *u* in circus.

< = from, derived from, taken from.

sub pro gram (sub′prō′gram, sub′prō′grəm), *n.* part of a computer program.

sub ro sa (sub rō′zə), in strict confidence; privately. [< Latin, under the rose; the rose was an ancient symbol of secrecy]

sub rou tine (sub′rü tēn′), *n.* part of a routine.

sub scribe (səb skrīb′), *v.,* **-scribed, -scrib ing.** *—v.t.* 1 promise to give or pay (a sum of money): *subscribe $15 to the hospital fund.* 2 write (one's name) at the end of a document, etc. 3 write one's name at the end of; show one's consent or approval by signing: *Thousands of citizens subscribed the petition.* *—v.i.* 1 promise to give or pay money: *subscribe to several charities.* 2 promise to accept and pay for a number of copies of a newspaper, magazine, etc.: *We subscribe to a few magazines.* 3 give one's consent or approval; agree: *She will not subscribe to anything unfair.* 4 sign one's name: *John Hancock was the first man to subscribe to the Declaration of Independence.* [< Latin *subscribere* < *sub-* under + *scribere* write] **—sub scrib′er,** *n.*

sub script (sub′skript), *adj.* written underneath or low on the line. *—n.* number, letter, or other symbol written underneath and to one side of a symbol. In H_2SO_4 the 2 and 4 are subscripts.

sub scrip tion (səb skrip′shən), *n.* 1 a subscribing. 2 money subscribed; contribution: *My subscription to the Fresh Air Fund was $5.* 3 the right to receive something, obtained by paying a certain sum: *Our subscription to the newspaper expires next week.* 4 sum of money raised by a number of persons: *We are raising a subscription for a new hospital.* 5 something written at the end of a document, etc.; signature.

sub sec tion (sub′sek′shən, sub sek′shən), *n.* part of a section.

sub se quence (sub′sə kwəns), *n.* 1 fact or condition of being subsequent. 2 a subsequent event or circumstance.

sub se quent (sub′sə kwənt), *adj.* 1 coming after; following; later: *subsequent events.* 2 **subsequent to,** after; following; later than: *on the day subsequent to your call.* [< Latin *subsequentem* < *sub-* up to, near + *sequi* follow] **—sub′se quent ly,** *adv.* **—sub′se quent ness,** *n.*

sub serve (səb sėrv′), *v.t.,* **-served, -serv ing.** help or assist (a purpose, action, etc.): *Chewing food well subserves digestion.* [< Latin *subservire* < *sub-* under + *servire* serve]

sub ser vi ence (səb sėr′vē əns), *n.* 1 slavish politeness and obedience; tame submission; servility. 2 a being of use or service.

sub ser vi en cy (səb sėr′vē ən sē), *n.* subservience.

sub ser vi ent (səb sėr′vē ənt), *adj.* 1 slavishly polite and obedient; tamely submissive; servile. 2 useful as a means to help a purpose or end; serviceable. **—sub ser′vi·ent ly,** *adv.*

sub set (sub′set′), *n.* (in mathematics) a set, each of whose members is a member of a second set: *A subset of S is a set every element of which belongs to S.*

sub side (səb sīd′), *v.i.*, **-sid ed, -sid ing.** 1 grow less; die down; become less active; abate: *The storm finally subsided.* 2 sink to a lower level: *After the rain stopped, the flood waters subsided.* 3 sink or fall to the bottom; settle. [< Latin *subsidere* < *sub-* down + *sidere* settle]

sub sid ence (səb sīd′ns, sub′sə dəns), *n.* act or process of subsiding.

sub sid i ar y (səb sid′ē er′ē), *adj., n., pl.* **-ar ies.** *—adj.* 1 useful to assist or supplement; auxiliary; supplementary. 2 subordinate; secondary. 3 maintained by a subsidy. *—n.* 1 person or thing that assists or supplements. 2 company having over half of its stock owned or controlled by another company: *The bus line was a subsidiary of the railroad.* [< Latin *subsidiarius* < *subsidium* reserve troops]

sub si dize (sub′sə dīz), *v.t.*, **-dized, -diz ing.** 1 aid or assist with a grant of money: *The government subsidizes airlines that carry mail.* 2 buy the aid or assistance of with a grant of money. **—sub′si di za′tion,** *n.* **—sub′si diz′er,** *n.*

sub si dy (sub′sə dē), *n., pl.* **-dies.** grant or contribution of money, especially one made by a government: *a subsidy for education.* [< Latin *subsidium* aid, reserve troops]

sub sist (səb sist′), *v.i.* 1 keep alive; live: *People in the far north subsist on fish and meat.* 2 continue to be; exist: *Many superstitions still subsist.* [< Latin *subsistere* < *sub-* up to + *sistere* to stand]

sub sist ence (səb sis′təns), *n.* 1 a keeping alive; living. 2 means of keeping alive; livelihood: *The sea provides a subsistence for fishermen.* 3 existence; continuance.

sub sist ent (səb sis′tənt), *adj.* existing of or by itself; subsisting.

sub soil (sub′soil′), *n.* layer of earth that lies just under the surface soil. *—v.t.* plow, till, or dig so as to cut into the subsoil.

sub son ic (sub son′ik), *adj.* 1 of or having to do with speed which is less than the speed of sound (about 750 miles per hour). 2 that moves at a speed slower than the speed of sound: *a subsonic airplane.*

sub spe cies (sub′spē′shēz, sub spē′shēz), *n., pl.* **-cies.** group of related plants or animals ranking below a species. See **classification** for chart.

subst., 1 substantive. 2 substitute.

sub stance (sub′stəns), *n.* 1 what a thing consists of; matter; material: *Ice and water are the same substance in different forms.* See synonym study below. 2 the real, main, or important part of anything: *The substance of an education is its effect on your life, not just learning lessons.* 3 the real meaning: *Give the substance of the speech in your own words.* 4 solid quality; body: *Pea soup has more substance than water.* 5 wealth; property: *a man of substance.* 6 a particular kind of matter: *The little pond is covered with a green substance.* **7 in substance, a** essentially; mainly. **b** really; actually. [< Old French < Latin *substantia* < *substare* stand firm < *sub-* up to + *stare* to stand]

Syn. **1 Substance, matter, material** mean what a thing consists or is made of. **Substance** applies both to things existing in the physical world and to those given form only in the mind: *The substance of the plan is good.* **Matter** applies to any substance that occupies space and that physical objects consist of: *Matter may be gaseous, liquid, or solid.* **Material** applies to any matter from which something is made: *Oil is an important raw material.*

sub stan dard (sub stan′dərd, sub′-stan′dərd), *adj.* 1 below standard. 2 not conforming to the accepted standards of speech or writing.

sub stan tial (səb stan′shəl), *adj.* 1 having substance; material; real; actual: *People and things are substantial; dreams and ghosts are not.* 2 strong; firm; solid: *The house is substantial enough to last a hundred years.* 3 large; important; ample: *make a substantial improvement in health.* 4 providing ample or abundant nourishment: *Eat a substantial breakfast.* 5 in the main; in essentials: *The stories told by the two children were in substantial agreement.* 6 well-to-do; wealthy. **—sub stan′tial ly,** *adv.*

sub stan ti al i ty (səb stan′shē al′ə tē), *n., pl.* **-ties.** 1 real existence. 2 solidity; firmness. 3 real worth.

sub stan ti ate (səb stan′shē āt), *v.t.*, **-at ed, -at ing.** 1 establish by evidence; prove; verify: *substantiate a rumor.* See **confirm** for synonym study. 2 give concrete or substantial form to; embody. **—sub·stan′ti a′tion,** *n.*

sub stan ti val (sub′stən tī′vəl), *adj.* of, having to do with, or consisting of a substantive or substantives.

sub stan tive (sub′stən tiv), *n.* in grammar: 1 noun or pronoun. 2 any word or group of words used as a noun. *—adj.* 1 in grammar: **a** used as a noun. **b** showing or expressing existence. The verb *to be* is the substantive verb. 2 independent. 3 real; actual. 4 substantial. [< Late Latin *substantivus* < *substantia.* See SUBSTANCE.] **—sub′stan tive·ly,** *adv.* **—sub′stan tive ness,** *n.*

sub sta tion (sub′stā′shən), *n.* a branch station; subordinate station: *Besides the main post office in our city, there are six substations.*

sub sti tute (sub′stə tüt, sub′stə tyüt), *n., v.*, **-tut ed, -tut ing,** *adj.* *—n.* thing used instead of another; person taking the place of another: *Margarine is a substitute for butter. A substitute taught us at school today.* *—v.t.* 1 put in the place of another: *We substituted brown sugar for molasses in these cookies.* 2 take the place of. *—v.i.* take the place of another; be a substitute. *—adj.* put in or taking the place of another. [< Latin *substitutum* < *sub-* instead + *statuere* establish]

sub sti tu tion (sub′stə tü′shən, sub′stə-tyü′shən), *n.* the use of one thing for another; putting (one person or thing) in the place of another; taking the place of another.

sub sti tu tion al (sub′stə tü′shə nəl, sub′stə tyü′shə nəl), *adj.* 1 having to do with or characterized by substitution. 2 acting or serving as a substitute. **—sub′sti tu′tion·al ly,** *adv.*

sub stra ta (sub strā′tə, sub strat′ə), *n.* a pl. of **substratum.**

sub strate (sub′strāt), *n.* 1 substratum. 2 the material that an enzyme or ferment acts upon.

sub stra tum (sub strā′təm, sub strat′əm), *n., pl.* **-ta** or **-tums.** 1 layer lying under another. 2 layer of earth lying just under the surface soil; subsoil. 3 basis; foundation: *The story has a substratum of truth.* 4 (in biology) the medium or matter on which an organism grows.

sub struc ture (sub′struk′chər, sub-struk′chər), *n.* structure forming a foundation.

sub sume (səb süm′), *v.t.*, **-sumed, -sum ing.** 1 bring (an idea, term, proposition, etc.) under another; bring (a case, instance, etc.) under a rule. 2 take up into, or include in, a larger or higher class or the like. [< New Latin *subsumere* < Latin *sub-* under + *sumere* assume]

sub sur face (sub sėr′fis), *adj.* under the surface; underground: *subsurface nuclear tests, subsurface rock.*

sub sys tem (sub′sis′təm, sub sis′təm), *n.* part or subdivision of a system.

sub teen (sub′tēn′), *n.* boy or girl nearly thirteen years old.

sub ten an cy (sub ten′ən sē), *n., pl.* **-cies.** status, right, or holding of a subtenant.

sub ten ant (sub ten′ənt, sub′ten′ənt), *n.* tenant of a tenant; person who rents land, a house, etc., from a tenant.

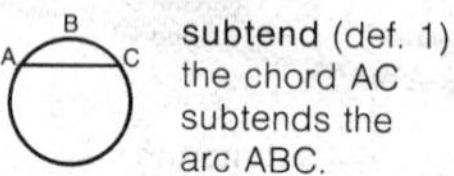

subtend (def. 1) the chord AC subtends the arc ABC.

sub tend (səb tend′), *v.t.* 1 extend under; stretch across: *The chord of an arc subtends the arc.* 2 enclose in the angle between a leaf or bract and its stem. [< Latin *subtendere* < *sub-* under + *tendere* to stretch]

sub ter fuge (sub′tər fyüj), *n.* trick, excuse, or expedient used to escape something unpleasant: *The child's headache was only a subterfuge to avoid going to school.* [< Late Latin *subterfugium,* ultimately < Latin *subter-* from under + *fugere* flee]

sub ter ra ne an (sub′tə rā′nē ən), *adj.* 1 underground: *A subterranean passage led from the castle to a cave.* 2 carried on secretly; hidden. [< Latin *subterraneus* < *sub-* under + *terra* earth]

sub ter ra ne ous (sub′tə rā′nē əs), *adj.* subterranean.

sub tile (sut′l, sub′təl), *adj.* subtle. **—sub′·tile ly,** *adv.*

sub til i ty (sub til′ə tē), *n., pl.* **-ties.** subtlety.

sub til ty (sut′l tē, sub′təl tē), *n., pl.* **-ties.** subtlety.

sub ti tle (sub′tī′tl), *n., v.*, **-tled, -tling.** *—n.* 1 an additional or subordinate title of a book, article, etc. 2 word or words shown on a motion-picture screen, especially as the translation of the words spoken in a foreign-language film; caption. *—v.t.* give a subtitle to.

sub tle (sut′l), *adj.*, **-tler, -tlest.** 1 delicate; thin; fine: *a subtle odor of perfume.* 2 so fine or delicate as to elude observation or analysis: *subtle distinctions.* 3 faint; mysterious: *a subtle smile.* 4 discerning; acute: *She is a subtle observer of slight differences in things.* 5 sly; crafty; tricky: *a subtle scheme to get some money.* 6 skillful; clever; expert. 7 working unnoticeably or secretly; insidious: *a subtle poison.* Also, **subtile.** [< Old French *soutil* < Latin *subtilis,* originally, woven underneath] **—sub′tle ness,** *n.* **—sub′tly,** *adv.*

hat, āge, fär; let, ēqual, tėrm;
it, īce; hot, ōpen, ôrder;
oil, out; cup, pu̇t, rüle;
ch, child; ng, long; sh, she;
th, thin; ᴛʜ, then; zh, measure;

ə represents *a* in about, *e* in taken, *i* in pencil, *o* in lemon, *u* in circus.

< = from, derived from, taken from.

sub tle ty (sut′l tē), *n., pl.* **-ties.** 1 subtle quality. 2 something subtle. Also, **subtility** or **subtilty.**

sub ton ic (sub ton′ik), *n.* (in music) the seventh tone of a scale; tone next below the upper tonic.

sub top ic (sub′top′ik), *n.* a subordinate or secondary topic.

sub to tal (sub tō′tl), *adj.* not quite total; less than complete. —*n.* something less than the total.

sub tract (səb trakt′), *v.t., v.i.* 1 take away: *Subtract 2 from 10 and you have 8.* See synonym study below. 2 take away (something) from a whole. [< Latin *subtractum* drawn from under < *sub-* from under + *trahere* to draw] —**sub tract′er,** *n.*

Syn. 1 **Subtract, deduct** mean to take away. **Subtract** is chiefly used in its mathematical sense, meaning to take away one number from another: *She subtracted 89 from 200.* **Deduct** means to take away a quantity or amount from a total or whole: *The butcher deducted 89 cents in tax from the delivery boy's wage of $10.*

sub trac tion (səb trak′shən), *n.* 1 act or process of subtracting one number or quantity from another; finding the difference between two numbers or quantities: *10 − 2 = 8 is a simple subtraction.* 2 a taking away. 3 a being taken away.

sub trac tive (səb trak′tiv), *adj.* 1 of or having to do with subtraction. 2 tending to subtract; having power to subtract. 3 to be subtracted; having the minus sign (−).

sub tra hend (sub′trə hend), *n.* number or quantity to be subtracted from another. In 10 − 2 = 8, the subtrahend is 2. [< Latin *subtrahendus* to be subtracted < *subtrahere* subtract]

sub treas ur y (sub′trezh′ər ē, sub-trezh′ər ē), *n., pl.* **-ur ies.** 1 a branch treasury. 2 any branch of the United States treasury.

sub trop ic (sub trop′ik), *adj.* subtropical.

sub trop i cal (sub trop′ə kəl), *adj.* 1 bordering on the tropics. 2 nearly tropical.

sub trop ics (sub′trop′iks, sub trop′iks), *n.pl.* region or regions bordering on the tropics.

sub u nit (sub yü′nit), *n.* a lower or secondary unit.

sub urb (sub′ėrb′), *n.* 1 town, village, or other community near a large city. 2 district just outside the boundaries of a city or town. 3 **the suburbs,** residential section or sections near the boundary of a city or town. [< Latin *suburbium* < *sub-* below + *urbs* city]

sub ur ban (sə bėr′bən), *adj.* 1 of, having to do with, or in a suburb: *We have excellent suburban train service.* 2 characteristic of a suburb or its inhabitants. —*n.* suburbanite.

sub ur ban ite (sə bėr′bə nīt), *n.* person who lives in a suburb.

sub ur bi a (sə bėr′bē ə), *n.* 1 the suburbs. 2 suburbanites.

sub ven tion (səb ven′shən), *n.* money granted to aid or support some cause, institution, or undertaking; subsidy. [< Late Latin *subventionem* < Latin *subvenire* come to one's aid < *sub-* under + *venire* come]

sub ver sion (səb vėr′zhən, səb vėr′shən), *n.* 1 a subverting or a being subverted; overthrow; destruction; ruin. 2 anything that tends to overthrow or destroy; cause of ruin. [< Late Latin *subversionem* < Latin *subvertere.* See SUBVERT.]

sub ver sive (səb vėr′siv), *adj.* tending to overthrow; causing ruin; destructive. —*n.* person who seeks to overthrow or undermine a government, etc. —**sub ver′sive ly,** *adv.*

sub vert (səb vėrt′), *v.t.* 1 overthrow (something established or existing); cause the downfall, ruin, or destruction of: *Dictators subvert democracy.* 2 undermine the principles of; corrupt. [< Latin *subvertere* < *sub-* up from under + *vertere* to turn] —**sub-vert′er,** *n.*

sub way (sub′wā′), *n.* 1 U.S. an electric railroad running beneath the surface of the streets in a city. 2 an underground passage.

sub zer o (sub′zir′ō, sub zir′ō), *adj.* below zero: *subzero temperatures.*

suc ceed (sək sēd′), *v.i.* 1 turn out well; do well; have success: *Her plans succeeded.* 2 accomplish what is attempted or intended: *The attack succeeded beyond all expectations.* 3 come next after another; follow another; take the place of another: *When George VI died, Elizabeth II succeeded to the throne.* See **follow** for synonym study. —*v.t.* come next after; take the place of; follow: *John Adams succeeded Washington as President.* [< Latin *succedere* < *sub-* up to, near + *cedere* go] —**suc ceed′er,** *n.*

suc cess (sək ses′), *n.* 1 a favorable result; wished-for ending; good fortune. 2 the gaining of wealth, position, etc.: *He has had little success in life.* 3 person or thing that succeeds. 4 result; outcome; fortune: *What success did you have in finding a new apartment?* [< Latin *successus* < *succedere.* See SUCCEED.]

suc cess ful (sək ses′fəl), *adj.* having success; ending in success; prosperous; fortunate. —**suc cess′ful ly,** *adv.* —**suc cess′ful ness,** *n.*

suc ces sion (sək sesh′ən), *n.* 1 group of persons or things coming one after another; series. See **series** for synonym study. 2 the coming of one person or thing after another. 3 right of succeeding to an office, property, or rank: *There was a dispute about the rightful succession to the throne.* 4 order or arrangement of persons having such a right of succeeding: *The king's oldest son is next in succession to the throne.* 5 **in succession,** one after another.

suc ces sive (sək ses′iv), *adj.* coming one after another; following in order. —**suc-ces′sive ly,** *adv.* —**suc ces′sive ness,** *n.*

Syn. Successive, consecutive mean following one after another. **Successive** implies coming one after another in regular order: *I have worked on three successive Saturdays.* **Consecutive** implies coming after one another without interruption or a break: *I worked three consecutive days last week.*

suc ces sor (sək ses′ər), *n.* 1 person who follows or succeeds another in office, position, or ownership of property. 2 person or thing that comes next after another in a series.

suc cinct (sək singkt′), *adj.* expressed briefly and clearly; expressing much in few words; concise. See **concise** for synonym study. [< Latin *succinctum* girded up < *sub-* up + *cingere* to gird] —**suc cinct′ly,** *adv.* —**suc cinct′ness,** *n.*

suc cor (suk′ər), *n.* person or thing that helps or assists; help; aid. —*v.t.* help, assist, or aid (a person, etc.). Also, BRITISH **succour.** [< Old French *sucurs,* ultimately < Latin *succurrere* run to help < *sub-* up to + *currere* to run] —**suc′cor er,** *n.*

suc cor y (suk′ər ē), *n.* chicory.

suc co tash (suk′ə tash), *n.* kernels of sweet corn and beans, usually lima beans, cooked together. [of Algonquian origin]

suc cour (suk′ər), *n., v.t.* BRITISH. succor.

suc cu lence (suk′yə ləns), *n.* juiciness.

suc cu len cy (suk′yə lən sē), *n.* succulence.

suc cu lent (suk′yə lənt), *adj.* 1 full of juice; juicy: *a succulent peach.* 2 interesting; not dull. 3 (of plants, etc.) having thick or fleshy and juicy leaves or stems. —*n.* a succulent plant. [< Latin *succulentus* < *succus* juice] —**suc′cu lent ly,** *adv.*

suc cumb (sə kum′), *v.i.* 1 give way; yield: *succumb to temptation.* 2 die. —*v.t.* **succumb to,** die of. [< Latin *succumbere* < *sub-* down + *-cumbere* to lie]

such (such), *adj.* 1 of that kind; of the same kind or degree: *I have never seen such a sight.* 2 of the kind that; of a particular kind: *She wore such thin clothes it is no wonder she caught cold.* 3 of the kind already spoken of or suggested: *flour, sugar, salt, and other such staples.* 4 so great, so bad, so good, etc.: *He is such a liar.* 5 some; certain: *The bank was robbed in such and such a town by such and such persons.* 6 **such as, a** similar to; like: *There are few writers such as Dickens.* **b** for example: *members of the dog family, such as the wolf and the fox.* —*pron.* 1 such a person or thing; such persons or things: *Take from the blankets such as you need.* 2 **as such,** as being what is indicated or implied: *A leader, as such, deserves obedience.* [Old English *swylc, swelc,* originally, a compound of *swā* so + *līc* like]

such like (such′līk′), *adj.* of such kind; of a like kind. —*pron.* things of such kind; the like: *deceptions, disguises, and suchlike.*

suck (suk), *v.t.* 1 draw into the mouth by using the lips and tongue: *Lemonade can be sucked through a straw.* 2 draw something from with the mouth: *suck oranges.* 3 drink, take, or absorb: *A sponge sucks in water. Plants suck up moisture from the earth.* 4 hold in the mouth and lick: *The child sucked a lollipop.* 5 draw in; swallow: *The whirlpool sucked down the boat.* —*v.i.* 1 draw milk from the breast or a bottle. 2 draw or be drawn by sucking: *He sucked at his pipe.* 3 draw air instead of water: *The pump sucked noisily.* —*n.* 1 act of sucking. 2 a sucking force or sound. [Old English *sūcan*]

suck er (suk′ər), *n.* 1 animal or thing that sucks. 2 any of various freshwater fishes that suck in food or have mouths adapted to sucking. 3 organ in some animals for sucking or holding fast by a sucking force. 4 shoot growing from an underground stem or root. 5 piston of a suction pump. 6 the valve of such a piston. 7 lump of hard candy, especially a lollipop. 8 SLANG. person easily deceived or duped. —*v.t.* take off suckers from (tobacco, corn, etc.). —*v.i.* form suckers.

suck le (suk′əl), *v.*, **-led, -ling.** —*v.t.* 1 feed with milk from the breast or udder: *The cat suckles her kittens.* 2 bring up; nourish. —*v.i.* suck at the breast or udder.

suck ling (suk′ling), *n.* a very young animal or child, especially one not yet weaned. —*adj.* 1 very young. 2 not yet weaned: *a suckling pig.*

su crase (sü′krās), *n.* invertase.

su cre (sü′krā), *n.* the monetary unit of Ecuador, a coin or note equal to 100 centavos and worth about $4^1/_4$ cents. [< Antonio José de *Sucre,* 1795-1830, South American general]

Su cre (sü′krā), *n.* one of the two capitals of Bolivia, in the S part. La Paz is the other capital. 85,000.

su crose (sü′krōs), *n.* ordinary sugar obtained from sugar cane, sugar beets, etc. *Formula:* $C_{12}H_{22}O_{11}$ [< French *sucre* sugar]

suc tion (suk′shən), *n.* 1 the production of a vacuum with the result that atmospheric pressure forces fluid or gas into the vacant space or causes surfaces to stick together: *Lemonade is drawn through a straw by suction.* 2 the force caused by suction. 3 act or process of sucking. —*adj.* causing a suction; working by suction. [< Latin *suctionem* < *sugere* to suck]

suc to ri al (suk tôr′ē əl, suk tōr′ē əl), *adj.* 1 adapted for sucking or suction. 2 having sucking organs.

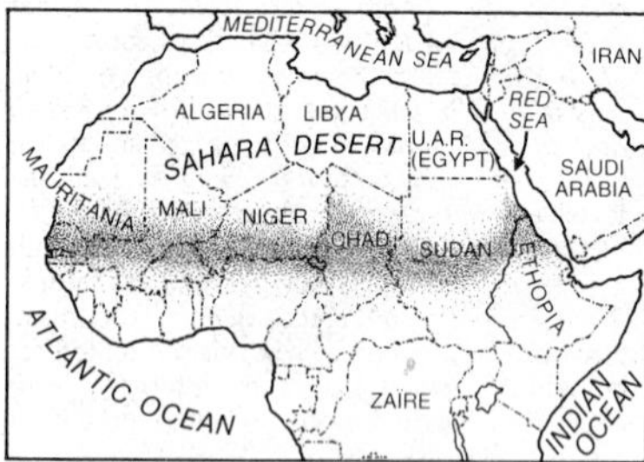

Sudan (def. 2)—the shaded area

Su dan (sü dan′), *n.* 1 country in NE Africa. 15,700,000 pop.; 967,500 sq. mi. *Capital:* Khartoum. Former name, **Anglo-Egyptian Sudan.** 2 **the Sudan,** vast region in Africa, south of the Sahara and extending from the Atlantic Ocean to the Red Sea. Also, **Soudan.**

Su da nese (süd′n ēz′), *adj., n., pl.* **-nese.** —*adj.* of or having to do with the Sudan or its inhabitants. —*n.* native or inhabitant of the Sudan.

Sudan grass, variety of sorghum from the Sudan, grown in the United States for hay and forage.

Su dan ic (sü dan′ik), *adj.* of or belonging to a group of languages of northern Africa that are not related to the Bantu or Hamitic languages. —*n.* the Sudanic language group.

sud den (sud′n), *adj.* 1 happening without warning or notice; not expected: *a sudden stop, a sudden rise to power.* See **unexpected** for synonym study. 2 found or hit upon unexpectedly; abrupt: *a sudden turn in the road.* 3 quick; rapid: *The cat made a sudden jump at the mouse.* —*n.* **all of a sudden** or **on a sudden,** in a sudden manner; quickly or unexpectedly. [< Old French *sodein* < Latin *subitaneus* < *subitus* sudden] —**sud′den ly,** *adv.* —**sud′den ness,** *n.*

sudden death, (in sports) an overtime period played to decide the winner of a game which ends in a tie. The first team to score wins the game.

Su de ten land (sü dāt′n land′), *n.* mountainous region in N Czechoslovakia.

su do rif er ous (sü′də rif′ər əs), *adj.* secreting or causing sweat.

su do rif ic (sü′də rif′ik), *adj.* causing sweat. —*n.* a sudorific agent or remedy. [< New Latin *sudorificus* < Latin *sudor* sweat + *facere* to make]

suds (sudz), *n.pl.* 1 soapy water. 2 bubbles and foam on soapy water; soapsuds. 3 any froth or foam. 4 SLANG. beer. —*v.t.* wash with soapy water. [perhaps < Middle Dutch *sudse* bog]

suds y (sud′zē), *adj.,* **suds i er, suds i est.** full of soapsuds.

sue (sü), *v.,* **sued, su ing.** —*v.t.* 1 start a lawsuit against: *He sued the railroad because his cow was killed by the engine.* 2 ARCHAIC. be a suitor to; court; woo. —*v.i.* 1 take action in law: *sue for damages.* 2 beg or ask *(for);* plead: *Messengers came suing for peace.* [< Anglo-French *suer* < Late Latin *sequere* < Latin *sequi* follow] —**su′a ble,** *adj.* —**su′er,** *n.*

suede or **suède** (swād), *n.* 1 a soft leather that has a velvety nap on one or both sides. 2 kind of cloth that has a similar appearance. —*adj.* made of suede: *a suede jacket.* [< French *(gants de) Suède* (gloves from) Sweden]

su et (sü′it), *n.* the hard fat about the kidneys and loins of cattle and sheep. Suet is used in cooking and for making tallow. [< Anglo-French, diminutive of *sue* < Latin *sebum* tallow]

Sue to ni us (swi tō′nē əs), *n.* A.D. 70?-140?, Roman historian.

su et y (sü′ə tē), *adj.* 1 like suet. 2 containing suet.

Su ez (sü ez′, sü′ez), *n.* 1 city in NE Egypt, at the S end of the Suez Canal. 265,000. 2 **Gulf of,** arm of the Red Sea, in the NW part. 3 **Isthmus of,** the isthmus between Asia and Africa, in the NE part of Egypt. 72 mi. wide.

Suez Canal, canal across the Isthmus of Suez, connecting the Mediterranean and Red seas. It was closed in 1967, as a result of the Arab-Israeli war. 100 mi. long. See **Nile River** for map.

suf. or **suff.,** suffix.

suf fer (suf′ər), *v.i.* 1 have pain, grief, injury, etc.: *suffer in silence, suffer from malaria.* 2 experience harm, loss, etc.: *Neither plane nor passengers suffered greatly from the forced landing.* —*v.t.* 1 have or feel (pain, grief, etc.). 2 be subjected to; experience; undergo: *The party suffered a serious defeat in the last election.* 3 allow; permit: *"Suffer the little children to come unto me."* 4 bear with patiently; endure: *I will not suffer such insults.* [< Latin *sufferre* < *sub-* up + *ferre* to bear] —**suf′fer er,** *n.*

suf fer a ble (suf′ər ə bəl), *adj.* that can be endured; bearable. —**suf′fer a ble ness,** *n.* —**suf′fer a bly,** *adv.*

suf fer ance (suf′ər əns), *n.* 1 permission or consent given only by a failure to object or prevent. 2 power to bear or endure; patient endurance. 3 **on sufferance,** allowed or tolerated, but not really wanted.

suf fer ing (suf′ər ing), *n.* 1 condition of being in pain: *Hunger causes suffering.* 2 the enduring of pain, trouble, or distress: *the suffering of a poor family.*

suf fice (sə fīs′), *v.,* **-ficed, -fic ing.** —*v.i.* be enough; be sufficient: *The money will suffice for one year.* —*v.t.* make content; satisfy: *A small amount of cake sufficed the baby.* [< Latin *sufficere* < *sub-* near + *facere* to make]

suf fi cien cy (sə fish′ən sē), *n., pl.* **-cies.** 1 a sufficient amount; large enough supply: *The ship had a sufficiency of provisions for the voyage.* 2 condition or fact of being sufficient; adequacy; ability. 3 self-confidence.

suf fi cient (sə fish′ənt), *adj.* 1 as much as is needed; enough: *sufficient proof.* See **enough** for synonym study. 2 ARCHAIC. competent; able. —**suf fi′cient ly,** *adv.*

suf fix (*n.* suf′iks; *v.* sə fiks′, suf′iks), *n.* an addition made at the end of a word to form another word of different meaning or function. A **derivational suffix** changes one word to a different one, as *-ly* in *badly* and *-ness* in *goodness.* An **inflectional suffix** adapts a word to indicate person, number, or tense, or to show its grammatical relationship to other words, as *-s* in *believes* (third-person singular), *-s* in *cats* (plural), or *-ed* in *jumped* (past tense). —*v.t.* 1 add at the end; put after. 2 attach as a suffix. [< Latin *suffixum* fastened upon < *sub-* upon + *figere* fasten]

suf fix al (suf′ik səl), *adj.* having to do with or of the nature of a suffix.

suf fix a tion (suf′ik sā′shən), *n.* the forming of suffixes.

suf fo cate (suf′ə kāt), *v.,* **-cat ed, -cat ing.** —*v.t.* 1 kill by stopping the breath. 2 keep from breathing; hinder in breathing. 3 smother; suppress. —*v.i.* 1 gasp for breath; choke. 2 die for lack of oxygen; be suffocated. [< Latin *suffocatum,* originally, narrowed up < *sub-* up + *fauces* throat, narrow entrance] —**suf′fo cat′ing ly,** *adv.*

suf fo ca tion (suf′ə kā′shən), *n.* 1 a suffocating. 2 a being suffocated.

suf fo ca tive (suf′ə kā′tiv), *adj.* stifling.

Suf folk (suf′ək), *n.* county in SE England, divided into **Suffolk East** and **Suffolk West.**

suf fra gan (suf′rə gən), *n.* 1 bishop consecrated to assist another bishop. 2 any bishop considered in relation to his archbishop. —*adj.* assisting. [< Medieval Latin *suffraganeus* one owing suffrage < Latin *suffragium* suffrage]

suf frage (suf′rij), *n.* 1 the right to vote; franchise: *The United States granted suffrage to women in 1920.* 2 a vote, usually in support of a proposal, candidate, etc. 3 a voting; casting of votes. 4 a short prayer of supplication. [< Latin *suffragium* supporting vote]

suf fra gette (suf′rə jet′), *n.* woman advocating suffrage for women.

suf fra gist (suf′rə jist), *n.* person who favors giving suffrage to more people, especially to women.

suf fuse (sə fyüz′), *v.t.,* **-fused, -fus ing.** overspread (with a liquid, dye, etc.): *eyes suffused with tears. At twilight the sky was suffused with color.* [< Latin *suffusum* poured under < *sub-* under + *fundere* to pour]

suf fu sion (sə fyü′zhən), *n.* 1 a suffusing. 2 a being suffused. 3 that with which anything is overspread. 4 flush of color.

sug ar (shu̇g′ər), *n.* 1 a sweet, crystalline substance obtained chiefly from sugar cane or sugar beets and used extensively in food products; sucrose. *Formula:* $C_{12}H_{22}O_{11}$ 2 any of the class of carbohydrates to which this substance belongs. Glucose, lactose, and maltose are sugars. —*v.t.* 1 put sugar in; sweeten with sugar. 2 cover with sugar; sprinkle with sugar. 3 cause to seem pleasant or agreeable; sugar-coat. —*v.i.* 1 form sugar crystals: *Honey sugars if kept too long.* 2 **sugar off,** make maple sugar. [< Old French *sucre* < Arabic *sukkar* < Persian *shakar* < Sanskrit *śarkarā,* originally, grit] **—sug′ar like′,** *adj.*

sugar beet, a large beet with a white root that yields sugar.

sug ar bush (shůg′ər bůsh′), *n.* grove or plantation of sugar maples.

sugar cane
up to 15 ft. high

sugar cane, a tall perennial grass with a strong, jointed stem and long, flat leaves, growing in warm regions. Sugar cane is the main source of manufactured sugar.

sug ar-coat (shůg′ər kōt′), *v.t.* 1 cover with sugar. 2 cause to seem more pleasant or agreeable.

sugar loaf, 1 a solid cone-shaped mass of molded sugar. 2 something shaped like a sugar loaf, especially a high, cone-shaped hill.

sug ar-loaf (shůg′ər lōf′), *adj.* shaped like a sugar loaf.

sugar maple, a maple tree of eastern North America, highly valued for its hard, tough wood and for its sweet sap, from which maple sugar and maple syrup are made.

sugar of lead, lead acetate.

sugar pine, a tall pine of California, Oregon, Nevada, and Mexico, which gives off a sugarlike resin when cut deep into the wood. It bears very large cones.

sug ar plum (shůg′ər plum′), *n.* a small piece of candy; bonbon.

sug ar y (shůg′ər ē), *adj.* 1 consisting of sugar; like sugar; sweet. 2 seemingly pleasant or agreeable: *a sugary greeting.* **—sug′ar i ness,** *n.*

sug gest (səg jest′, sə jest′), *v.t.* 1 bring to mind; call up the thought of: *The thought of summer suggests swimming, tennis, and hot weather.* 2 put forward; propose: *He suggested a swim, and we all agreed.* 3 show in an indirect way; hint: *His yawns suggested that he would like to go to bed.* [< Latin *suggestum* put under, supplied, suggested < *sub-* under + *gerere* bring] **—sug gest′er,** *n.*

sug gest i bil i ty (səg jes′tə bil′ə tē, sə-jes′tə bil′ə tē), *n.* quality or condition of being suggestible.

sug gest i ble (səg jes′tə bəl, sə jes′tə bəl), *adj.* 1 capable of being influenced by suggestion. 2 that can be suggested.

sug ges tion (səg jes′chən, sə jes′chən), *n.* 1 act of suggesting: *The trip was made at her suggestion.* 2 thing suggested: *The picnic was an excellent suggestion.* 3 the calling up of one idea by another because they are connected or associated in some way. 4 a very small amount; slight trace: *The foreigner spoke English with just a suggestion of his native accent.* 5 the insinuation of an idea, belief, or impulse into the mind, especially when hypnotized.

sug ges tive (səg jes′tiv, sə jes′tiv), *adj.* 1 tending to suggest ideas, acts, or feelings: *The teacher gave an interesting and suggestive list of composition subjects.* 2 tending to suggest something improper or indecent. **—sug ges′tive ly,** *adv.* **—sug ges′tive ness,** *n.*

su i cid al (sü′ə sī′dl), *adj.* 1 having to do with suicide; leading to suicide; causing suicide. 2 ruinous to one's own interests; disastrous to oneself: *It would be suicidal for a store to sell many things below cost.* **—su′i cid′al ly,** *adv.*

su i cide (sü′ə sīd), *n.* 1 the killing of oneself on purpose. 2 person who kills himself on purpose. 3 destruction of one's own interests or prospects. 4 **commit suicide,** kill oneself on purpose. [< Latin *sui* of oneself + *-cidium* act of killing or *-cida* killer]

su i gen er is (sü′ē jen′ər is; sü′ī jen′ər is), LATIN. of his, her, its, or their peculiar kind; unique.

suit (süt), *n.* 1 set of clothes to be worn together. A man's suit consists of a coat, trousers, and sometimes a vest. A woman's suit consists of a coat and either a skirt or trousers. 2 case in a court of law; application to a court for justice: *a suit to collect damages for one's injuries.* 3 request; asking; wooing: *His suit was successful and she married him.* 4 one of the four sets of cards (spades, hearts, diamonds, and clubs) making up the deck. 5 suite. 6 **follow suit, a** play a card of the same suit as that first played. **b** follow the example of another. —*v.t.* 1 make suitable; make fit: *a penalty suited to a crime.* 2 be suitable for; agree with the requirements of: *A cold climate suits apples and wheat, but not oranges and tea.* 3 please; satisfy: *Which date suits you best?* 4 be becoming to: *A small ring suits a small hand.* 5 ARCHAIC. provide with clothes. 6 **suit oneself,** do as one pleases. —*v.i.* be suitable, fitting, or convenient. [< Anglo-French *suite* a following < Popular Latin *sequita* < Latin *sequi* follow. Doublet of SUITE.]

suit a bil i ty (sü′tə bil′ə tē), *n.* a being suitable; fitness; appropriateness.

suit a ble (sü′tə bəl), *adj.* right for the occasion; fitting; proper: *The park gives the children a suitable playground.* See **fit**[1] for synonym study. **—suit′a ble ness,** *n.* **—suit′a bly,** *adv.*

suit case (süt′kās′), *n.* a flat, rectangular traveling bag.

suite (swēt; *also* süt *for 2*), *n.* 1 set of connected rooms to be used by one person or family. 2 set of furniture that matches; suit. 3 any set or series of like things. 4 in music: **a** a series of instrumental movements varying in number and character: *a suite for strings.* **b** series of dances in the same or related keys, arranged for one or more instruments: *Bach's French suites.* 5 group of attendants; retinue: *The queen traveled with a suite of twelve.* [< French < Old French *siute* < Popular Latin *sequita.* Doublet of SUIT.]

suit ing (sü′ting), *n.* fabric for making suits.

suit or (sü′tər), *n.* 1 man who is courting a woman. 2 person bringing suit in a court of law. 3 anyone who sues or petitions.

su ki ya ki (sü′kē yä′kē, skē yä′kē), *n.* a Japanese dish consisting mainly of cooked, thinly sliced meat, onions, bamboo shoots, and various other vegetables. [< Japanese]

hat, āge, fär; let, ēqual, tėrm;
it, īce; hot, ōpen, ôrder;
oil, out; cup, pu̇t, rüle;
ch, child; ng, long; sh, she;
th, thin; ᴛʜ, then; zh, measure;

ə represents *a* in about, *e* in taken, *i* in pencil, *o* in lemon, *u* in circus.

< = from, derived from, taken from.

Suk koth (su̇ kōth′), *n.* a Jewish festival of either eight or nine days celebrated in September or October by building temporary booths in remembrance of those the Israelites used during their wanderings in the desert. [< Hebrew *sukkōth* tabernacles]

Su la we si (sü′lä wā′sē), *n.* Celebes.

Su lei man (sü′lā män′), *n.* 1494?-1566, sultan of the Ottoman Empire at the height of its power, from 1520 to 1566. He was called "Suleiman the Magnificent." Also, **Solyman.**

sul fa (sul′fə), *adj.* of or having to do with a group of drugs derived from sulfanilamide, used in treating bacterial infections. —*n.* a sulfa drug; sulfonamide. Also, **sulpha.**

sul fa di a zine (sul′fə dī′ə zēn′, sul′fə-dī′ə zən), *n.* a sulfa drug used in treating various bacterial infections.

sul fa nil a mide (sul′fə nil′ə mīd, sul′fə-nil′ə mid), *n.* a white, crystalline substance used as the basis for most of the sulfa drugs. *Formula:* $C_6H_8N_2O_2S$ Also, **sulphanilamide.**

sul fate (sul′fāt), *n.* salt or ester of sulfuric acid. Also, **sulphate.**

sul fide (sul′fīd), *n.* compound of sulfur and another element or radical. Also, **sulphide.**

sul fite (sul′fīt), *n.* salt or ester of sulfurous acid. Also, **sulphite.**

sul fon a mide (sul fon′ə mīd), *n.* sulfa.

sul fon ic acid (sul fon′ik), any of a group of organic acids containing the radical SO_2OH, used in making phenols, dyes, drugs, etc.

sul fur (sul′fər), *n.* 1 a light-yellow, highly flammable nonmetallic element that exists in several allotropic forms and burns in the air with a blue flame and a stifling odor. Sulfur is found abundantly in volcanic regions, occurring free in nature as a brittle, crystalline solid or in combination with metals and other substances, and is also a constituent of proteins. It is used in making matches and gunpowder, for vulcanizing rubber, in bleaching, in medicine, etc. *Symbol:* S; *atomic number* 16. See pages 326 and 327 for table. Also, **sulphur.** [< Latin]

sulfur dioxide, a heavy, colorless gas that has a sharp odor, used as a bleach, disinfectant, preservative, and refrigerant. *Formula:* SO_2

sul fur e ous (sul fyu̇r′ē əs), *adj.* sulfurous.

sul fur ic (sul fyu̇r′ik), *adj.* 1 of or having to do with sulfur. 2 containing sulfur, especially with a valence of six. Also, **sulphuric.**

sulfuric acid, a heavy, colorless, oily, very corrosive acid derived from sulfur; oil of vitriol; vitriol. Sulfuric acid is used in making explosives and fertilizers, in refining petroleum, and in many other industrial processes. *Formula:* H_2SO_4

sul fur ous (sul′fər əs, sul′fyər əs; *also* sul-fyu̇r′əs *for 1 and 2*), *adj.* 1 of or having to do with sulfur. 2 containing sulfur, especially with a valence of four. 3 like the fumes or heat of burning sulfur; fiery. 4 of or like the fires of hell; hellish. Also, **sulphurous.** **—sul′fur ous ly,** *adv.* **—sul′fur ous ness,** *n.*

sulfurous acid, a colorless solution of sulfur dioxide in water, used as a bleach, reducing agent, etc. It is known chiefly in the form of its salts, the sulfites. *Formula:* H_2SO_3

sulfur trioxide, a chemical compound used chiefly as an intermediate in the production of sulfuric acid. *Formula:* SO_3

sulk (sulk), *v.i.* hold aloof in a sullen manner; be sulky. *—n.* 1 a sulking; a fit of sulking. 2 **the sulks,** ill humor shown by sulking.

sulky

sulk y (sul′kē), *adj.,* **sulk i er, sulk i est,** *n., pl.* **sulk ies.** *—adj.* silent and bad-humored because of resentment; sullen: *Some children become sulky when they cannot have their own way.* See **sullen** for synonym study. *—n.* a light one-horse carriage with two wheels, for one person, now commonly used in trotting races. [origin uncertain] **—sulk′i ly,** *adv.* **—sulk′i ness,** *n.*

Sul la (sul′ə), *n.* 138-78 B.C., Roman general and dictator.

sul len (sul′ən), *adj.* 1 silent because of bad humor or anger: *The sullen child refused to answer my question.* See synonym study below. 2 showing bad humor or anger. 3 gloomy; dismal: *The sullen skies threatened rain.* [Middle English *soleine,* ultimately < Latin *solus* alone] **—sul′len ly,** *adv.* **—sul′len ness,** *n.*

Syn. 1 **Sullen, sulky, glum** mean silent and bad-humored or gloomy. **Sullen** suggests an ill-natured refusal to talk or be cooperative because of anger or bad humor or disposition: *It is disagreeable to have to sit at the breakfast table with a sullen person.* **Sulky** suggests moody or childish sullenness because of resentment or discontent: *Dogs sometimes become sulky because they are jealous.* **Glum** emphasizes silence and low spirits because of some depressing condition or happening: *He is glum about the results of the election.*

Sul li van (sul′ə vən), *n.* 1 Sir **Arthur Seymour,** 1842-1900, English composer who wrote the music for comic operas for which Sir William Gilbert wrote the words. 2 **Louis Henri,** 1856-1924, American architect.

sul ly (sul′ē), *v.t., v.i.,* **-lied, -ly ing.** make or become soiled, stained, or tarnished. [probably < Old French *soillier.* See SOIL².]

Sul ly (SY lē′), *n.* **Maximilien de Béthune,** Duc de, 1560-1641, French statesman and chief minister of Henry IV of France.

sul pha (sul′fə), *adj., n.* sulfa.

sul pha nil a mide (sul′fə nil′ə mīd, sul′fə nil′ə mid), *n.* sulfanilamide.

sul phate (sul′fāt), *n.* sulfate.

sul phide (sul′fīd), *n.* sulfide.

sul phite (sul′fīt), *n.* sulfite.

sul phur (sul′fər), *n.* 1 sulfur. 2 any of several kinds of yellow or orange butterflies. 3 a greenish yellow. *—adj.* greenish-yellow.

sul phur-bot tom (sul′fər bot′əm), *n.* blue whale.

sul phur ic (sul fyůr′ik), *adj.* sulfuric.

sul phur ous (sul′fər əs, sul′fyər əs, sul-fyůr′əs), *adj.* sulfurous.

sul tan (sult′n), *n.* ruler of a Moslem country. Turkey was ruled by a sultan until 1922. [< Arabic *sulṭān* ruler]

sul tan a (sul tan′ə), *n.* 1 wife of a sultan. 2 mother, sister, or daughter of a sultan. 3 a small, seedless raisin.

sul tan ate (sult′n āt), *n.* 1 position, authority, or period of rule of a sultan. 2 territory ruled over by a sultan.

sul try (sul′trē), *adj.,* **-tri er, -tri est.** 1 hot, close, and moist: *We expect sultry weather during July.* 2 hot or fiery: *a sultry sun, sultry glances.* [< obsolete *sulter* (verb) swelter; related to *swelter*] **—sul′tri ly,** *adv.* **—sul′tri ness,** *n.*

Su lu Archipelago (sü′lü), group of islands in the SW Philippines. 458,000 pop.; 1100 sq. mi.

sum (sum), *n., v.,* **summed, sum ming.** *—n.* 1 amount of money: *pay a large sum for a house.* 2 number or quantity obtained by adding two or more numbers or quantities together. The sum of 2 and 3 and 4 is 9. See **number** for synonym study. 3 problem in arithmetic. 4 the whole amount; total amount: *To win the prize seemed to her the sum of happiness.* 5 essence or gist of anything.

—v.t. find the total of.

sum to, make a total of; amount to.

sum up, a reckon, count, or total. **b** express or tell briefly: *Sum up the main points of the lesson in three sentences.* **c** review the chief points of: *The judge summed up the evidence.* [< Latin *summa,* feminine of *summus* highest]

su mac or **su mach** (sü′mak, shü′mak), *n.* 1 any of a genus of shrubs or small trees of the same family as the cashew, having divided leaves that turn scarlet in the autumn and cone-shaped clusters of small, red or white, one-seeded fruit. In some species, such as the poison sumac and poison ivy, the foliage is poisonous to the touch. 2 the dried and powdered leaves and shoots of certain species, used in tanning and dyeing. [< Old French < Arabic *summāq*]

Su ma tra (sů mä′trə), *n.* large island in Indonesia, south of the Malay Peninsula. 20,200,000 pop.; 167,500 sq. mi. See **East Indies** for map. **—Su ma′tran,** *adj., n.*

Su mer (sü′mər), *n.* ancient region in the valley of the Euphrates River, north of its mouth.

Su mer i an (sü mir′ē ən), *adj.* of or having to do with the people of Sumer or their language. *—n.* 1 native or inhabitant of Sumer. 2 the language of the Sumerians.

sum ma cum lau de (sům′ə kům lou′də), with the highest distinction (added to the diploma of a student who has done unusually good academic work): *graduate summa cum laude.* [< Latin, with the highest praise]

sum mar i ly (sə mer′ə lē, sum′ər ə lē), *adv.* in a summary manner; briefly; without delay.

sum ma rize (sum′ə rīz′), *v.t., v.i.,* **-rized, -riz ing.** make a summary of; give only the main points of; express briefly. **—sum′ma ri za′tion,** *n.* **—sum′ma riz′er,** *n.*

sum mar y (sum′ər ē), *n., pl.* **-mar ies,** *adj.* *—n.* a brief statement giving the main points: *The history book had a summary at the end of each chapter.* See synonym study below. *—adj.* 1 concise and comprehensive; brief; short. 2 direct and prompt; without delay or formality: *The governor took summary action to aid the flood victims.* [< Latin *summarium* < *summa* sum]

Syn. *n.* **Summary, digest** mean a brief presentation of facts or subject matter. **Summary** applies to a brief statement, often in different words, giving only the main points of an article, chapter, book, speech, subject, proposed plan, etc.: *Give a summary of today's lesson.* **Digest** applies to a shortened form of a book, article, etc., leaving out less important details but keeping the original order, emphasis, and words: *Some magazines contain digests of books.*

sum ma tion (su mā′shən), *n.* 1 process of finding the sum or total; addition. 2 the total. 3 (in law) the final presentation of facts and arguments by the opposing counsel.

sum mer (sum′ər), *n.* 1 the warmest season of the year; season of the year between spring and autumn. 2 anything considered like summer in its warmth, full beauty, etc. *—adj.* of or having to do with summer: *summer heat, summer clothes.* *—v.i.* pass the summer: *summer at the seashore.* *—v.t.* keep or feed during the summer; arrange or manage during the summer. [Old English *sumor*]

sum mer house (sum′ər hous′), *n., pl.* **-hous es** (-hou′ziz). building in a park or garden in which to sit in warm weather. Summerhouses often have no walls.

sum mer sault (sum′ər sôlt), *n., v.i.* somersault.

summer school, school conducted in the summer to help students make up credits or accelerate their studies toward a degree.

summer squash, any of various squashes that ripen quickly and are intended to be eaten while the skins are still tender.

sum mer time (sum′ər tīm′), *n.* 1 summer season; summer. 2 any period in which energy is greatest or talent most productive.

sum mer y (sum′ər ē), *adj.* 1 of summer. 2 for summer. 3 like summer.

sum mit (sum′it), *n.* 1 the highest point; top; pinnacle: *the summit of a mountain. The summit of her ambition was to be a doctor.* See **top¹** for synonym study. 2 the highest level of authority, especially the leaders of individual governments, as dealing in international affairs. [< Old French *somete,* ultimately < Latin *summus* highest]

summit meeting, conference between heads of governments, especially for the purpose of settling disagreements.

sum mon (sum′ən), *v.t.* 1 call with authority; order to come; send for: *A telegram summoned me home.* See **call** for synonym study. 2 call together: *summon an assembly.* 3 order or notify formally to appear before a judge or court of law, especially to answer a charge. 4 call upon: *summon a fort to surrender.* 5 stir to action; rouse: *We summoned our courage and entered the deserted house.* [< Latin *summonere* hint to < *sub-* secretly + *monere* warn] **—sum′mon er,** *n.*

sum mons (sum′ənz), *n., pl.* **-mons es,** *v.* *—n.* 1 a formal order or notice to appear before a judge or court of law, especially to answer a charge: *receive a summons for fast driving.* 2 an urgent call; a summoning command, message, or signal. 3 an authoritative call to appear at a place named, or to attend to some public duty. *—v.t.* INFORMAL. summon to court.

sum mum bo num (sum′əm bō′nəm), LATIN. the highest or chief good.
Sum ner (sum′nər), *n.* **Charles,** 1811-1874, American statesman and antislavery leader.
sump (sump), *n.* 1 pit or reservoir for collecting water, oil, sewage, factory wastes, etc. 2 pool at the bottom of a mine, where water collects and from which it is pumped. [< Middle Dutch *somp* or Middle Low German *sump* swamp]
sump pump, pump used to remove liquid, especially water that collects in a cellar sump.
sump ter (sump′tər), *n.* horse or mule for carrying baggage. [< Old French *sommetier,* ultimately < Latin *sagma* packsaddle]
sump tu ar y (sump′chü er′ē), *adj.* having to do with the spending of money; regulating expenses, especially to control extravagance or waste. A law forbidding people to buy jewelry would be a sumptuary law. [< Latin *sumptuarius* < *sumptus* expense]
sump tu ous (sump′chü əs), *adj.* lavish and costly; magnificent; rich: *a sumptuous banquet.* [< Latin *sumptuosus* < *sumptus* expense < *sumere* spend] **—sump′tu ous ly,** *adv.* **—sump′tu ous ness,** *n.*
Sum ter (sum′tər), *n.* **Fort,** fort in the harbor of Charleston, South Carolina. The Civil War began with a Confederate attack on this fort on April 12, 1861.
sun (sun), *n., v.,* **sunned, sun ning.** *—n.* 1 the brightest heavenly body in the sky; star around which the earth and other planets revolve and which supplies them with light and heat. It is a glowing ball of hot gases and is about 93 million miles from the earth. 2 the light and warmth of the sun: *sit in the sun.* 3 any heavenly body made up of burning gas and having satellites. Many stars are suns and have planets orbiting around them. 4 something like the sun in brightness or splendor; something that is a source of light, honor, glory, or prosperity. 5 ARCHAIC. **a** a day. **b** a year. 6 **from sun to sun,** from sunrise to sunset. 7 **in the sun,** position easily seen. 8 **under the sun,** on earth; in the world. *—v.t.* 1 expose to the sun's rays. 2 warm or dry in the sunshine. *—v.i.* expose oneself to the sun's rays. [Old English *sunne*]
Sun., Sunday.
sun bath, exposure of the body to the sun's rays or to a sunlamp.
sun bathe (sun′bāᴛʜ′), *v.i.,* **-bathed, -bath ing.** expose oneself to the sun's rays or to a sunlamp. **—sun′bath′er,** *n.*
sun beam (sun′bēm′), *n.* ray of sunlight.
sun bird (sun′bėrd′), *n.* any of a family of small, brightly colored birds resembling hummingbirds, found in tropical regions of Africa and Asia.

sunbonnet

sun bon net (sun′bon′it), *n.* a large bonnet that shades the face and neck.
sun burn (sun′bėrn′), *n., v.,* **-burned** or **-burnt, -burn ing.** *—n.* a burning of the skin by the sun's rays. A sunburn is often red and painful. *—v.i.* 1 burn the skin by the sun's rays; burn the skin of. 2 become sunburned: *Her skin sunburns very quickly.* *—v.t.* affect with sunburn.
sun burnt (sun′bėrnt′), *v.* a pt. and a pp. of **sunburn.**
sun burst (sun′bėrst′), *n.* 1 sun shining suddenly through a break in clouds. 2 brooch or other piece of jewelry with jewels arranged to look like the sun with its rays.
sun dae (sun′dē), *n.* dish of ice cream served with syrup, crushed fruits, nuts, etc., over it. [origin uncertain]
Sun da Islands (sun′də), chain of islands mostly in Indonesia, including Sumatra, Java, Borneo, and smaller nearby islands, such as Bali and Timor.
sun dance, a religious ceremony in honor of the sun, performed by North American Indians of the Western prairies at the summer solstice.
Sunda Strait, strait between Java and Sumatra. 16 mi. wide at the narrowest point.
Sun day (sun′dē, sun′dā), *n.* 1 the first day of the week. 2 this day as one set aside for rest and worship by most Christians. *—adj.* of or on Sundays; not everyday or regular; occasional: *a Sunday driver, Sunday painters.* [Old English *sunnandæg,* translation of Latin *dies solis* day of the sun]
Sunday best, INFORMAL. best clothes.
Sunday school, 1 school held on Sunday for teaching religion. 2 its members.
sun deck (sun′dek′), *n.* 1 the upper deck of a passenger ship. 2 terrace, porch, etc., used for sunbathing or lounging.
sun der (sun′dər), *v.t., v.i.* put asunder; separate; part; sever; split. *—n.* **in sunder,** apart. [Old English *sundrian* < *sundor* apart]
Sun der land (sun′dər lənd), *n.* seaport in NE England. 218,000.
sun dew (sun′dü′, sun′dyü′), *n.* a small herb of the same family as the Venus's-flytrap, that grows in bogs and has hairy, sticky leaves with which it captures and absorbs insects.

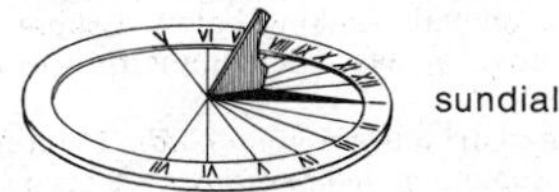
sundial

sun di al (sun′dī′əl), *n.* instrument for telling the time of day by the position of a shadow cast by the sun; dial.
sun dog (sun′dôg′, sun′dog′), *n.* 1 parhelion. 2 a small or incomplete rainbow.
sun down (sun′doun′), *n.* sunset.
sun down er (sun′dou′nər), *n.* (in Australia) a tramp.
sun dries (sun′drēz), *n.pl.* sundry things; items not named; odds and ends.
sun dry (sun′drē), *adj.* several; various: *From sundry hints, I guessed I was to be given a bicycle for my birthday.* [Old English *syndrig* separate < *sundor* apart]
sun fast (sun′fast′), *adj.* that sunlight will not fade.
sun fish (sun′fish′), *n., pl.* **-fish es** or **-fish.** 1 any of a family of large fishes with tough flesh and a short, deep, compressed body, living in tropical or temperate seas. 2 any of several small, edible, freshwater fishes of North America of the same suborder as the perch.
sun flow er (sun′flou′ər), *n.* 1 a tall plant having conspicuous flower heads with yellow rays and a brown disk, valued for its seeds, which are used as food for livestock and which yield an edible oil. 2 any of a genus of plants of the composite family to which the sunflower belongs.

hat, āge, fär; let, ēqual, tėrm;
it, īce; hot, ōpen, ôrder;
oil, out; cup, pu̇t, rüle;
ch, child; ng, long; sh, she;
th, thin; ᴛʜ, then; zh, measure;

ə represents *a* in about, *e* in taken, *i* in pencil, *o* in lemon, *u* in circus.

< = from, derived from, taken from.

sung (sung), *v.* a pt. and a pp. of **sing.**
Sung (su̇ng), *n.* a Chinese dynasty lasting from A.D. 960 to 1279, noted for its works of art, especially in painting and ceramics.
sun glass es (sun′glas′iz), *n.pl.* spectacles to protect the eyes from the glare of the sun. They are usually made with colored lenses.
sun god, the sun regarded as a deity; a god identified with the sun, as Helios, Apollo, or Ra.
sunk (sungk), *v.* a pt. and a pp. of **sink.**
sunk en (sung′kən), *adj.* 1 sunk: *a sunken ship.* 2 submerged: *a sunken rock.* 3 situated below the general level: *a sunken garden.* 4 fallen in; hollow: *sunken eyes.* *—v.* a pp. of **sink.**
sun lamp (sun′lamp′), *n.* lamp for producing ultraviolet rays similar to those in sunlight.
sun less (sun′lis), *adj.* without sun; without sunlight.
sun light (sun′līt′), *n.* the light of the sun.
sun lit (sun′lit′), *adj.* lighted by the sun.
sun ny (sun′ē), *adj.,* **-ni er, -ni est.** 1 having much sunshine: *a sunny day.* 2 exposed to, lighted by, or warmed by the direct rays of the sun: *a sunny room.* 3 like the sun. 4 bright; cheerful: *a sunny smile.* **—sun′ni ly,** *adv.* **—sun′ni ness,** *n.*
Sun ny vale (sun′ē vāl), *n.* city in W California. 95,000.
sun parlor, room with many windows to let in sunlight.
sun porch, porch enclosed largely by glass.
sun proof (sun′prüf′), *adj.* impervious to or unaffected by the rays of the sun.
sun ray (sun′rā′), *n.* sunbeam.
sun rise (sun′rīz′), *n.* 1 the coming up of the sun above the horizon at the beginning of the day. 2 the time when the sun comes up; the beginning of the day. 3 the display of light or color in the sky at this time.
sun room (sun′rüm′, sun′ru̇m′), *n.* room with many windows to let in sunlight.
sun set (sun′set′), *n.* 1 the going down of the sun below the horizon at the end of the day. 2 the time when the sun goes down; the close of the day. 3 the display of light or color in the sky at this time.
sun shade (sun′shād′), *n.* 1 parasol. 2 protection against the sun.
sun shine (sun′shīn′), *n.* 1 the shining of the sun; light or rays of the sun. 2 the warmth, light, etc., deriving from the rays of the sun. 3 a place, area, etc., exposed to sunshine. 4 brightness; cheerfulness. 5 a source of this.
sun shin y (sun′shī′nē), *adj.,* **-shin i er, -shin i est.** 1 having much sunshine. 2 bright; cheerful.
sun spot (sun′spot′), *n.* one of the spots, darker than the rest of the photosphere, that appear periodically in certain zones of the

surface of the sun, and are associated with disturbances of the earth's magnetic field; macula.

sun stroke (sun′strōk′), *n.* heatstroke caused by overexposure to the sun's rays. Sunstroke results in extreme exhaustion and often loss of consciousness.

sun struck (sun′struk′), *adj.* overcome by the heat of the sun; affected with sunstroke.

sun suit (sun′süt′), *n.* short pants held up by shoulder straps, worn without a shirt by children for playing in the sun.

sun tan (sun′tan′), *n.* 1 the reddish-brown color of a person's skin tanned by the sun. 2 **suntans,** *pl.* a tan military uniform for summer wear.

sun tanned (sun′tand′), *adj.* having a suntan.

sun up (sun′up′), *n.* sunrise.

sun ward (sun′wərd), *adv., adj.* toward the sun.

sun wards (sun′wərdz), *adv.* sunward.

Sun Yat-sen (sůn′ yät′sen′), 1866-1925, Chinese revolutionary leader and statesman, who worked to establish the republic of China.

Suo mi (swô′mē), *n.* Finnish name of **Finland.**

sup[1] (sup), *v.i.,* **supped, sup ping.** eat the evening meal; take supper: *We supped on bread and milk.* [< Old French *souper* < *soupe* soup]

sup[2] (sup), *v.t., v.i.,* **supped, sup ping,** *n.* sip. [Old English *sūpan*]

sup., 1 above [for Latin *supra*]. 2 superior. 3 superlative. 4 supine. 5 supplement. 6 supplementary.

su per (sü′pər), *n.* INFORMAL. 1 superintendent. 2 supernumerary. —*adj.* SLANG. 1 excellent. 2 extraordinary.

super-, *prefix.* 1 over; above: *Superimpose = impose over or above.* 2 besides; further: *Superadd = add besides or further.* 3 in high proportion; to excess; exceedingly: *Superabundant = abundant to excess.* 4 surpassing: *Supernatural = surpassing the natural.* [< Latin *super* over, above]

su per a ble (sü′pər ə bəl), *adj.* capable of being overcome or vanquished; surmountable. [< Latin *superabilis* < *superare* to overcome < *super* over] **—su′per a ble ness,** *n.* **—su′per a bly,** *adv.*

su per a bound (sü′pər ə bound′), *v.i.* 1 be very abundant. 2 be too abundant.

su per a bun dance (sü′pər ə bun′dəns), *n.* 1 very great abundance: *a superabundance of rain.* 2 a greater amount than is needed.

su per a bun dant (sü′pər ə bun′dənt), *adj.* 1 very abundant; ample. 2 too abundant; more than enough; excessive. **—su′per a bun′dant ly,** *adv.*

su per add (sü′pər ad′), *v.t.* add besides; add further: *A toothache was superadded to her other troubles.*

su per al loy (sü′pər al′oi), *n.* alloy with a high percentage of cobalt, nickel, and chromium, capable of withstanding very high temperatures.

su per an nu ate (sü′pər an′yü āt), *v.t., v.i.,* **-at ed, -at ing.** 1 retire or be retired on a pension because of age or infirmity. 2 make or become old-fashioned or out of date. [< Medieval Latin *superannatus* more than a year old < Latin *super annum* beyond a year] **—su′per an′nu a′tion,** *n.*

su per an nu at ed (sü′pər an′yü ā′tid), *adj.* 1 retired on a pension. 2 too old for work, service, etc. 3 old-fashioned; out-of-date.

su perb (sů pėrb′), *adj.* 1 grand and stately; majestic: *Mountain scenery is superb.* See **magnificent** for synonym study. 2 rich; elegant: *a superb dinner.* 3 very fine; first-rate; excellent: *a superb performance.* [< Latin *superbus* < *super* above] **—su perb′ly,** *adv.* **—su perb′ness,** *n.*

su per bomb (sü′pər bom′), *n.* a hydrogen bomb.

su per car go (sü′pər kär′gō), *n., pl.* **-goes** or **-gos.** officer on a merchant ship who represents the owner and has charge of the cargo and the business affairs of the voyage.

su per charge (sü′pər chärj′), *v.t.,* **-charged, -charg ing.** 1 increase the effective power of with a supercharger. 2 charge to excess with excitement, emotion, force, vigor, etc.: *The atmosphere at the trial was supercharged with tension.*

su per charg er (sü′pər chär′jər), *n.* blower, pump, or similar device on an internal-combustion engine for forcing into the cylinders a greater amount of fuel than the action of the pistons would draw. Superchargers are used especially on racing-car engines and on engines of high-altitude aircraft.

su per cil i ar y (sü′pər sil′ē er′ē), *adj.* of, having to do with, or near the eyebrow; over the eye. [< Latin *supercilium* eyebrow. See SUPERCILIOUS.]

su per cil i ous (sü′pər sil′ē əs), *adj.* haughty, proud, and contemptuous; disdainful; showing scorn or indifference because of a feeling of superiority: *a supercilious stare.* See **proud** for synonym study. [< Latin *superciliosus* < *supercilium* eyebrow, pride < *super-* above + *-cilium* (< *celare* to cover, conceal)] **—su′per cil′i ous ly,** *adv.* **—su′per cil′i ous ness,** *n.*

su per class (sü′pər klas′), *n.* a group of related animals ranking below a subphylum and above a class. See **classification** for chart.

su per cold (sü′pər kōld′), *adj.* 1 extremely cold: *supercold temperatures.* 2 cryogenic: *supercold surgery.*

su per con duc tive (sü′pər kən duk′tiv), *adj.* capable of or having superconductivity.

su per con duc tiv i ty (sü′pər kon′duk tiv′ə tē), *n.* the ability of some metals, such as lead and tin, to conduct electric current with no resistance at temperatures near absolute zero.

su per con duc tor (sü′pər kən duk′tər), *n.* a superconductive metal.

su per cool (sü′pər kül′), *v.t.* cool (a liquid) below the normal freezing point without causing it to solidify. —*v.i.* undergo supercooling.

su per e go (sü′pər ē′gō, sü′pər eg′ō), *n., pl.* **-gos.** (in psychoanalysis) the part of a person's psyche that determines right or wrong conduct; the conscience.

su per em i nent (sü′pər em′ə nənt), *adj.* of superior eminence, rank, or dignity; standing out above others. **—su′per em′i nent ly,** *adv.*

su per er o ga tion (sü′pər er′ə gā′shən), *n.* the doing of more than duty or circumstances require. [< Late Latin *supererogationem* < Latin *super-* over + *erogare* pay out]

su per e rog a to ry (sü′pər ə rog′ə tôr′ē, sü′pər ə rog′ə tōr′ē), *adj.* 1 doing more than duty or circumstances require. 2 unnecessary; superfluous.

su per fi cial (sü′pər fish′əl), *adj.* 1 of the surface: *superficial measurement.* 2 on the surface; at the surface: *His burns were superficial and soon healed.* 3 concerned with or understanding only what is on the surface; not thorough; shallow: *superficial education, superficial knowledge.* 4 not real or genuine: *superficial friendship.* [< Latin *superficialis* < *superficies* surface < *super-* above + *facies* form] **—su′per fi′cial ly,** *adv.* **—su′per fi′cial ness,** *n.*

su per fi ci al i ty (sü′pər fish′ē al′ə tē), *n., pl.* **-ties.** 1 superficial quality or condition; shallowness. 2 something superficial.

su per fi ci es (sü′pər fish′ē ēz′), *n., pl.* **-fi ci es.** 1 surface. 2 the surface area. 3 the outward appearance. [< Latin *superficies* upper side, surface. See SUPERFICIAL.]

su per fine (sü′pər fīn′), *adj.* 1 very fine; extra fine. 2 too refined; too nice.

su per flu id (sü′pər flü′id), *n.* a fluid, especially liquid helium, characterized by the complete disappearance of viscosity at temperatures near absolute zero.

su per flu i ty (sü′pər flü′ə tē), *n., pl.* **-ties.** 1 a greater amount than is needed; excess. 2 something not needed.

su per flu ous (sů pėr′flü əs), *adj.* 1 more than is needed: *In writing telegrams it pays to omit superfluous words.* 2 needless; unnecessary: *A raincoat is superfluous on a clear day.* [< Latin *superfluus,* ultimately < *super-* over + *fluere* to flow] **—su per′flu ous ly,** *adv.* **—su per′flu ous ness,** *n.*

su per gal ax y (sü′pər gal′ək sē), *n., pl.* **-ax ies.** cluster of galaxies.

su per gi ant (sü′pər jī′ənt), *n.* any of various extremely large and brilliant stars, ranging in luminosity from 100 to 10,000 or more times that of the sun.

su per heat (sü′pər hēt′), *v.t.* 1 heat very hot; heat too hot; heat hotter than usual. 2 heat (a liquid) above its normal boiling point without producing vaporization. 3 heat (steam) apart from water until it contains no suspended water droplets.

su per heat er (sü′pər hē′tər), *n.* device for superheating steam.

su per het er o dyne (sü′pər het′ər ə dīn), *adj.* of or having to do with a kind of radio reception which reduces modulated waves (above audibility) to a lower frequency and in later stages rectifies the signals to audio-frequency amplification. —*n.* a superheterodyne radio receiving set.

su per high frequency (sü′pər hī′), any radio frequency between 3,000 and 30,000 megacycles.

su per high way (sü′pər hī′wā), *n.* highway for fast traveling, usually divided in the middle with two or more lanes for traffic in each direction.

su per hu man (sü′pər hyü′mən), *adj.* 1 above or beyond what is human: *Angels are superhuman beings.* 2 above or beyond ordinary human power, experience, etc.: *With a superhuman effort, the high jumper soared to a new Olympic record.* **—su′per hu′man ly,** *adv.*

su per im pose (sü′pər im pōz′), *v.t.,* **-posed, -pos ing.** put on top of something else.

su per im po si tion (sü′per im′pə zish′ən), *n.* a putting one thing on top of another.

su per in cum bent (sü′pər in kum′bənt), *adj.* 1 lying or resting on something else. 2 situated above; overhanging. 3 exerted

hat, āge, fär; let, ēqual, tėrm;
it, īce; hot, ōpen, ôrder;
oil, out; cup, pu̇t, rüle;
ch, child; ng, long; sh, she;
th, thin; ᴛʜ, then; zh, measure;

ə represents *a* in about, *e* in taken, *i* in pencil, *o* in lemon, *u* in circus.

< = from, derived from, taken from.

from above: *a superincumbent pressure.*

su per in duce (sü′pər in düs′, sü′pər in dyüs′), *v.t.*, **-duced, -duc ing.** bring in or develop as an addition.

su per in duc tion (sü′pər in duk′shən), *n.* 1 a superinducing. 2 a being superinduced.

su per in tend (sü′pər in tend′), *v.t.* oversee and direct (work or workers); manage (a place, institution, etc.); supervise. [< Late Latin *superintendere* < Latin *super-* above + *intendere* to direct]

su per in tend ence (sü′pər in ten′dəns), *n.* guidance and direction; supervision; management.

su per in tend en cy (sü′pər in ten′dən sē), *n., pl.* **-cies.** position, authority, or work of a superintendent.

su per in tend ent (sü′pər in ten′dənt), *n.* person who oversees, directs, or manages: *a superintendent of schools, a superintendent of a factory.*

su per i or (sə pir′ē ər, sù pir′ē ər), *adj.* 1 above the average; very good; excellent: *superior work in school.* 2 higher in quality; better; greater: *a superior blend of coffee.* 3 higher in position, rank, importance, etc.: *a superior officer.* 4 showing a feeling of being above others; proud: *superior airs, superior manners.* 5 **superior to, a** higher than; above. **b** better than; greater than. **c** not giving in to; above yielding to: *superior to revenge. A wise man is superior to flattery.* 6 (in botany) growing above some other part or organ. *—n.* 1 person who is superior in rank, position, ability, etc.: *A captain is a lieutenant's superior. As a violinist he has no superior.* 2 head of a monastery or convent. [< Latin, comparative of *superus* being above < *super* above] **—su per′i or ly,** *adv.*

Su per i or (sə pir′ē ər, sù pir′ē ər), *n.* **Lake,** the largest of the five Great Lakes, the largest body of fresh water in the world. 400 mi. long; 31,800 sq. mi.

superior court, U.S. 1 (in many states) the ordinary court of general jurisdiction. 2 (in some states) a court above the courts of limited or special jurisdiction, and below the courts of appeal.

su per i or i ty (sə pir′ē ôr′ə tē, sə pir′ē or′ə tē; sù pir′ē ôr′ə tē, sù pir′ē or′ə tē), *n.* superior condition or quality.

superiority complex, an exaggerated feeling of superiority to others, sometimes the result of overcompensation for an inferiority complex.

su per jet (sü′pər jet′), *n.* jetliner.

su per la tive (sə pėr′lə tiv, sù pėr′lə tiv), *adj.* 1 of the highest kind; above all others; supreme: *King Solomon had superlative wisdom.* 2 showing the highest degree of comparison of an adjective or adverb. *Fairest, best,* and *most slowly* are the superlative forms of *fair, good,* and *slowly.* *—n.* 1 person or thing above all others; supreme example. 2 the highest degree of comparison of an adjective or adverb. 3 form or combination of words that shows this degree. 4 **talk in superlatives,** exaggerate. [< Late Latin *superlativus,* ultimately < *super-* beyond + *latum* brought, carried] **—su per′la tive ly,** *adv.* **—su per′la tive ness,** *n.*

su per man (sü′pər man′), *n., pl.* **-men.** man having more than human powers.

su per mar ket (sü′pər mär′kit), *n.* a large grocery store in which customers select their purchases from open shelves and pay for them just before leaving.

su per nal (sù pėr′nl), *adj.* 1 heavenly; divine. 2 lofty; exalted. [< Latin *supernus* < *super* above] **—su per′nal ly,** *adv.*

su per na tant (sü′pər nā′tnt), *adj.* floating above or on the surface: *oil supernatant on water.*

su per nat ur al (sü′pər nach′ər əl), *adj.* above or beyond what is natural: *Angels and devils are supernatural beings.* *—n.* **the supernatural,** supernatural agencies, influences, or phenomena. **—su′per nat′ur al ly,** *adv.* **—su′per nat′ur al ness,** *n.*

su per nat ur al ism (sü′pər nach′ər ə liz′əm), *n.* 1 supernatural character or agency. 2 belief in the supernatural. 3 doctrine that supernatural forces are at work in the universe.

su per no va (sü′pər nō′və), *n., pl.* **-vae** (-vē), **-vas.** nova far brighter than an ordinary nova, being from 10 to 100 million times as luminous as the sun.

su per nu me rar y (sü′pər nü′mə rer′ē, sü′pər nyü′mə rer′ē), *adj., n., pl.* **-rar ies.** *—adj.* more than the usual or necessary number; extra. *—n.* 1 an extra person or thing. 2 person who appears on the stage but usually has no lines to speak: *In addition to the regular actors, there were 20 supernumeraries for the mob scene.* [< Late Latin *supernumerarius* excessive in number < Latin *super numerum* beyond the number]

su per phos phate (sü′pər fos′fāt), *n.* any of various fertilizing materials composed chiefly of soluble phosphates.

su per pose (sü′pər pōz′), *v.t.*, **-posed, -pos ing.** 1 superimpose. 2 (in geometry) place (a figure) upon another so that the two coincide. [< French *superposer* < *super-* above + *poser.* See POSE[1].]

su per po si tion (sü′pər pə zish′ən), *n.* a superposing.

su per pow er (sü′pər pou′ər), *n.* 1 power on an extraordinary or extensive scale. 2 nation so great or so strong as a power that its actions and policies greatly affect those of smaller, less powerful nations.

su per sales man (sü′pər sālz′mən), *n., pl.* **-men.** a very successful salesman; person who is very skillful and effective in persuading others.

su per sat u rate (sü′pər sach′ə rāt′), *v.t.*, **-rat ed, -rat ing.** add to beyond the ordinary saturation point; saturate abnormally. A supersaturated solution is one in which more of a substance is dissolved than the solvent will hold under normal conditions. **—su′per sat′u ra′tion,** *n.*

su per scribe (sü′pər skrīb′), *v.t.*, **-scribed, -scrib ing.** write (words, letters, one's name, etc.) above, on, or outside of something. [< Latin *superscribere* write over < *super-* over + *scribere* write]

su per script (sü′pər skript), *adj.* written above. *—n.* number, letter, etc., written above and to one side of a symbol. In $a^3 \times b^n$ the *3* and the *n* are superscripts.

su per scrip tion (sü′pər skrip′shən), *n.* 1 a writing above, on, or outside of something. 2 something written above or on the outside. 3 address on a letter or parcel.

su per sede (sü′pər sēd′), *v.t.*, **-sed ed, -sed ing.** 1 take the place of; cause to be set aside; displace: *Electric lights have superseded gaslights in most homes.* See **replace** for synonym study. 2 succeed and supplant; replace: *A new governor superseded the old one.* [< Latin *supersedere* be superior to, refrain from < *super-* above + *sedere* sit] **—su′per sed′er,** *n.*

su per sen si tive (sü′pər sen′sə tiv), *adj.* extremely or abnormally sensitive. **—su′per sen′si tive ly,** *adv.* **—su′per sen′si tive ness,** *n.*

su per ses sion (sü′pər sesh′ən), *n.* 1 act of superseding. 2 condition of being superseded.

su per son ic (sü′pər son′ik), *adj.* 1 of or having to do with sound waves beyond the limit of human audibility (above frequencies of 20,000 cycles per second); ultrasonic. 2 greater than the speed of sound in air (1087 feet per second). 3 capable of moving at a speed greater than the speed of sound: *supersonic aircraft.* **—su′per son′i cal ly,** *adv.*

su per son ics (sü′pər son′iks), *n.* science dealing with supersonic waves and the phenomena associated with them; ultrasonics.

su per sti tion (sü′pər stish′ən), *n.* 1 an unreasoning fear of what is unknown or mysterious; unreasoning expectation. 2 belief or practice founded on ignorant fear or mistaken reverence: *A common superstition considers 13 an unlucky number.* [< Latin *superstitionem,* originally, a standing over, as in wonder or awe < *super-* above + *stare* to stand]

su per sti tious (sü′pər stish′əs), *adj.* full of superstition; likely to believe superstitions; caused by superstition; having to do with superstition. **—su′per sti′tious ly,** *adv.* **—su′per sti′tious ness,** *n.*

su per struc ture (sü′pər struk′chər), *n.* 1 structure built on something else. 2 all of a building above the foundation. 3 parts of a ship above the main deck.

su per tax (sü′pər taks′), *n.* surtax.

su per ton ic (sü′pər ton′ik), *n.* (in music) the second tone of a scale; note next above the tonic.

su per vene (sü′pər vēn′), *v.i.*, **-vened, -ven ing.** come or occur as something additional or interrupting. [< Latin *supervenire* < *super-* upon + *venire* come]

su per ven tion (sü′pər ven′shən), *n.* a supervening.

su per vise (sü′pər vīz), *v.t.*, **-vised, -vis ing.** look after and direct (work or workers, a process, etc.); superintend; manage: *Study halls are supervised by teachers.* [< Medieval Latin *supervisum* overseen < Latin *super-* over + *videre* to see]

su per vi sion (sü′pər vizh′ən), *n.* management; direction: *The house was built under the careful supervision of an architect.*

su per vi sor (sü′pər vī′zər), *n.* person who supervises: *The music supervisor had charge of the school band and orchestra.*

su per vi sor y (sü′pər vī′zər ē), *adj.* 1 of a supervisor; having to do with supervision. 2 supervising.

su pine (*adj.* sü pīn′; *n.* sü′pīn), *adj.* 1 lying flat on the back. 2 lazily inactive; listless. *—n.* a Latin verbal noun formed from the stem of the past participle. [< Latin *supinus*] **—su pine′ly,** *adv.* **—su pine′ness,** *n.*

supp. or **suppl.,** supplement.

sup per (sup′ər), *n.* the evening meal; meal eaten early in the evening if dinner is near noon, or late in the evening if dinner is at six or later. [< Old French *souper,* originally, verb, sup[1]] **—sup′per less,** *adj.*

sup per time (sup′ər tīm′), *n.* the time at which supper is served.

sup plant (sə plant′), *v.t.* 1 take the place of; displace or set aside: *Machinery has supplanted hand labor in making shoes.* See **replace** for synonym study. 2 take the place of by unfair methods or by treacherous means: *The prince plotted to supplant the king.* [< Latin *supplantare* trip up < *sub-* under + *planta* sole of the foot] **—sup′plan ta′tion,** *n.* **—sup plant′er,** *n.*

sup ple (sup′əl), *adj.,* **-pler, -plest,** *v.,* **-pled, -pling.** *—adj.* 1 bending or folding easily: *a supple birch tree, supple leather.* 2 moving easily or nimbly: *a supple dancer.* 3 readily adaptable to different ideas, circumstances, people, etc.; yielding: *a supple mind.* *—v.t., v.i.* make or grow supple. [< Old French *souple* < Latin *supplex* submissive < *supplicare* bend down, supplicate] **—sup′ple ly,** *adv.* **—sup′ple ness,** *n.*

sup ple ment (*n.* sup′lə mənt; *v.* sup′lə-ment), *n.* 1 something added to complete a thing, or to make it larger or better, especially a part added to a literary work or any written account or document. See synonym study below. 2 something added to supply a deficiency: *a diet supplement.* 3 amount needed to make an angle or arc equal 180 degrees. *—v.t.* supply something additional to. See **complement** for synonym study. [< Latin *supplementum* < *supplere.* See SUPPLY[1].] **—sup′ple men ta′tion,** *n.*

Syn. *n.* 1 **Supplement, appendix** mean something added to a book or paper to complete or improve it. **Supplement** applies to a section added later or printed separately to bring the information up to date, correct mistakes, or present special features: *This encyclopedia has a supplement covering recent events.* **Appendix** applies to a section added at the end of a book or document to give extra information: *The appendix contains a list of dates.*

sup ple men tal (sup′lə men′tl), *adj.* supplementary.

sup ple men tar y (sup′lə men′tər ē), *adj.* 1 additional. 2 added to supply what is lacking: *The new members of the class received supplementary instruction.*

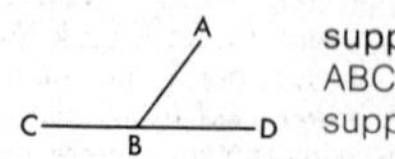

supplementary angle ABC and ABD are supplementary angles.

supplementary angle, either of two angles which together form an angle of 180 degrees. A 60-degree angle is the supplementary angle of a 120-degree angle.

sup pli ance (sup′lē əns), *n.* supplication.

sup pli ant (sup′lē ənt), *adj.* asking humbly and earnestly: *He sent a suppliant message for help.* *—n.* person who asks humbly and earnestly: *She knelt as a suppliant at the altar.* [< Middle French, present participle of *supplier* supplicate] **—sup′pli ant ly,** *adv.*

sup pli cant (sup′lə kənt), *adj., n.* suppliant. **—sup′pli cant ly,** *adv.*

sup pli cate (sup′lə kāt), *v.,* **-cat ed, -cat ing.** *—v.t.* beg humbly and earnestly: *supplicate a judge to pardon someone.* *—v.i.* pray humbly. [< Latin *supplicatum* bent down, suppliant < *sub-* down + *plicare* to bend] **—sup′pli cat′ing ly,** *adv.* **—sup′pli ca′tor,** *n.*

sup pli ca tion (sup′lə kā′shən), *n.* 1 a supplicating. 2 Usually, **supplications,** *pl.* a humble prayer addressed to God or a deity.

sup pli ca to ry (sup′lə kə tôr′ē, sup′lə kə-tōr′ē), *adj.* supplicating.

sup ply[1] (sə plī′), *v.,* **-plied, -ply ing,** *n., pl.* **-plies.** *—v.t.* 1 provide (what is lacking); furnish: *Many cities supply books for school children.* 2 make up for (a loss, lack, absence, etc.): *supply a deficiency.* 3 satisfy (a want, need, etc.): *There was just enough to supply the demand.* 4 fill (a place, vacancy, pulpit, etc.) as a substitute. *—n.* 1 quantity ready for use; stock; store: *The school gets its supplies of books, paper, pencils, chalk, etc., from the city.* 2 quantity of an article in the market ready for purchase, especially at a given price: *a supply of coffee.* 3 **supplies,** *pl.* the food, equipment, etc., necessary for an army, expedition, or the like. 4 act of supplying. [< Old French *supplier* < Latin *supplere* < *sub-* up from under + *-plere* to fill] **—sup pli′er,** *n.*

sup ply[2] (sup′lē), *adv.* in a supple manner.

sup port (sə pôrt′, sə pōrt′), *v.t.* 1 keep from falling; hold up: *Walls support the roof.* See synonym study below. 2 give strength or courage to; keep up; help: *Hope supports us in time of trouble.* 3 provide for: *support a family.* 4 maintain, keep up, or keep going: *a town which is able to support two orchestras.* 5 be in favor of; back; second: *support a motion, support the foreign-aid bill.* 6 help prove; bear out: *The facts support their claim.* 7 endure, especially with patience or fortitude; bear; tolerate. 8 assist or protect (a military unit) in a mission, operation, etc.: *Artillery fire supported the infantry during the attack.* 9 act with (a leading actor). 10 act or play (a part) with success.
—n. 1 act of supporting: *She spoke in support of the measure.* 2 condition of being supported: *This argument lacks support.* 3 help or assistance: *The campaign needs our financial support.* 4 means of livelihood; maintenance: *the support of a family.* See **living** for synonym study. 5 person or thing that supports; prop: *The neck is the support of the head.* 6 in military use: **a** assistance or protection given by one unit or element to another. **b** unit or element that gives such assistance or protection. **c** part of any unit held in reserve during the initial phase of an attack.
[< Latin *supportare* convey, bring up < *sub-* (up from) under + *portare* carry]

Syn. *v.t.* 1 **Support, maintain, uphold** mean to hold up or keep up, literally or figuratively. **Support** suggests bearing the weight or giving needed strength to prevent something or someone from falling or sinking: *Teammates supported the injured player.* **Maintain** suggests keeping up in a certain condition by providing what is needed to prevent loss of strength, value, etc.: *She has maintained her family's tradition of hospitality.* **Uphold** chiefly suggests giving aid or moral support to a person, cause, belief, etc.: *He upheld his brother's honor.*

sup port a ble (sə pôr′tə bəl, sə pōr′tə bəl), *adj.* capable of being supported; bearable or endurable. **—sup port′a ble ness,** *n.* **—sup port′a bly,** *adv.*

sup port er (sə pôr′tər, sə pōr′tər), *n.* person or thing that supports.

sup por tive (sə pôr′tiv, sə pōr′tiv), *adj.* providing support; sustaining: *a supportive arch, supportive evidence.*

sup pose (sə pōz′), *v.,* **-posed, -pos ing.** *—v.t.* 1 consider as possible; take for granted; assume: *Suppose you are late, what excuse will you give?* 2 believe, think, or imagine: *I suppose she will come at the usual time.* 3 involve as necessary; imply: *An invention supposes an inventor.* 4 expect: *I'm supposed to be there early.* *—v.i.* believe, think, or imagine. [< Old French *supposer* < *sub-* under + *poser* to put] **—sup pos′a ble,** *adj.* **—sup pos′a bly,** *adv.*

sup posed (sə pōzd′), *adj.* accepted as true; considered as possible or probable; assumed: *a supposed fact, a supposed friend, a supposed limit to human development.* **—sup pos′ed ly,** *adv.*

sup pos ing (sə pō′zing), *conj.* in the event that; if: *Supposing it rains, shall we go?*

sup po si tion (sup′ə zish′ən), *n.* 1 act of supposing. 2 thing supposed; belief; opinion.

sup po si tion al (sup′ə zish′ə nəl), *adj.* of or based on supposition; hypothetical; supposed. **—sup′po si′tion al ly,** *adv.*

sup pos i ti tious (sə poz′ə tish′əs), *adj.* 1 put by fraud in the place of another; pretended; false; not genuine. 2 hypothetical; supposed. [< Latin *supposititius,* ultimately < *sub-* under + *ponere* to place] **—sup pos′i ti′tious ly,** *adv.*

sup pos i to ry (sə poz′ə tôr′ē, sə poz′ə-tōr′ē), *n., pl.* **-ries.** medicine in the form of a cone or cylinder to be put into a body cavity, as the rectum or vagina. [< Late Latin *suppositorium* (thing) placed underneath, ultimately < Latin *sub-* under + *ponere* to place]

sup press (sə pres′), *v.t.* 1 put an end to; stop by force; put down: *suppress a rebellion.* 2 keep in; hold back; keep from appearing: *She suppressed a yawn. Each nation suppressed news that was not favorable to it.* 3 subdue (a feeling, etc.): *suppressed desires.* 4 check the flow of; stop: *suppress bleeding.* 5 keep secret; refrain from disclosing or divulging: *suppress the truth.* [< Latin *suppressum* pressed down < *sub-* down + *premere* to press] **—sup press′er, sup pres′sor,** *n.*

sup press i ble (sə pres′ə bəl), *adj.* that can be suppressed.

sup pres sion (sə presh′ən), *n.* 1 a putting down by force or authority; putting an end to: *the suppression of a revolt.* 2 a keeping in; holding back: *the suppression of a childish fear.*

sup pres sive (sə pres′iv), *adj.* tending to suppress; causing suppression.

sup pu rate (sup′yə rāt′), *v.i.,* **-rat ed, -rat ing.** form pus; discharge pus; fester. [< Latin *suppuratum* < *sub-* under + *pus* pus]

sup pu ra tion (sup′yə rā′shən), *n.* 1 formation of pus; festering; discharge of pus. 2 pus.

sup pu ra tive (sup′yə rā′tiv), *adj.* 1 of or having to do with suppuration. 2 suppurating.

supra-, *prefix.* above; beyond, as in *supranational.* [< Latin]

su pra na tion al (sü′prə nash′ə nəl), *adj.* above a nation or state, as in authority.

su pra or bit al (sü′prə ôr′bə təl), *adj.* above the orbit of the eye.

su pra re nal (sü′prə rē′nl), *adj.* 1 situated above the kidney or on the kidney; adrenal. 2 of or from the suprarenal glands. *—n.*

suprarenal gland. [< *supra-* above + Latin *renes* kidneys]

suprarenal gland, adrenal gland.

su prem a cist (sə prem′ə sist, su̇ prem′ə-sist), *n.* person who believes in the supremacy of one group or person over another: *a male supremacist.*

su prem a cy (sə prem′ə sē, su̇ prem′ə sē), *n.* 1 condition or quality of being supreme. 2 supreme authority or power.

su preme (sə prēm′, su̇ prēm′), *adj.* 1 highest in rank or authority: *a supreme ruler.* 2 highest in degree or quality; greatest; utmost: *supreme disgust, supreme courage. Soldiers who die for their country make the supreme sacrifice.* [< Latin *supremus,* superlative of *superus* being above < *super* above] **—su preme′ly,** *adv.* **—su preme′ness,** *n.*

Supreme Being, God.

Supreme Court, 1 the highest court in the United States, which meets at Washington, D.C. It consists of a chief justice and eight associate justices. 2 the highest court in most states of the United States. 3 a similar court in other countries.

Supt. or **supt.,** superintendent.

sur-, *prefix.* over; above; beyond, as in *surname, surpass, surtax.* [< Middle French < Latin *super-* super-]

Sur a ba ja (su̇r′ä bä′yä), *n.* seaport in NE Java, Indonesia. 1,008,000.

sur ah (su̇r′ə), *n.* a soft, twilled fabric of silk, or silk and rayon. [from *Surat,* India]

Su rat (su̇ rat′, su̇r′ət), *n.* city in W India. 355,000.

sur cease (sər sēs′), *n.* ARCHAIC. end; cessation. [< Old French *sursis,* past participle of *surseoir* refrain < Latin *supersedere.* See SUPERSEDE.]

sur charge (*n.* sėr′chärj′; *v.* sėr′chärj′, sėr′chärj′), *n., v.,* **-charged, -charg ing.** *—n.* 1 an extra charge: *The express company made a surcharge for delivering the trunk outside of the city limits.* 2 an additional mark printed on a postage stamp to change its value, date, etc. 3 an additional or excessive load or burden. *—v.t.* 1 charge extra. 2 overcharge. 3 overload; overburden: *a heart surcharged with grief.* 4 print a surcharge on (a postage stamp). [< Middle French *surcharger* < *sur-* over + *charger* to charge]

sur cin gle (sėr′sing gəl), *n.* strap or belt around a horse's body to keep a saddle, blanket, or pack in place. [< Old French *surcengle* < *sur-* over + *cengle* girdle]

surcoat

sur coat (sėr′kōt′), *n.* an outer coat, especially such a garment worn by knights over their armor. [< Old French *surcote* < *sur-* over + *cote* coat]

surd (sėrd), *n.* 1 a voiceless sound, as *p, k, t.* 2 an irrational number, as $\sqrt{2}$. *—adj.* 1 (in phonetics) voiceless. 2 (in mathematics) irrational. [< Latin *surdus* unheard]

sure (shu̇r), *adj.,* **sur er, sur est,** *adv. —adj.* 1 free from doubt; certain; having ample reason for belief; positive. See synonym study below. 2 to be trusted; safe; reliable: *a sure messenger.* 3 never missing, slipping, etc.; unfailing; unerring: *sure aim, get surer footing.* 4 admitting of no doubt or question: *sure proof.* 5 firm or sound: *sure ground.* 6 certain to come or happen; inevitable: *Misery is the sure result of war.* 7 destined; bound: *He is sure to return.* 8 ARCHAIC. secure or safe.

be sure, be careful; do not fail.

for sure, certainly; undoubtedly.

make sure, a act so as to make something certain. **b** get sure knowledge.

to be sure, surely; certainly.

—adv. INFORMAL. surely; certainly.

[< Old French *sur, seür* < Latin *securus.* Doublet of SECURE.] **—sure′ness,** *n.*

Syn. *adj.* **1 Sure, certain, confident** mean having no doubt. **Sure** implies being free from doubt in one's own mind: *Police are sure he was kidnaped.* **Certain** implies having positive reasons or proof to eliminate all doubt: *They have been certain since they uncovered new evidence.* **Confident** implies having a strong belief that admits no doubt: *They are confident they will solve the case soon.*

sure-fire (shu̇r′fīr′), *adj.* INFORMAL. definite; certain: *a sure-fire success.*

sure-foot ed (shu̇r′fu̇t′id), *adj.* not liable to stumble, slip, or fall. **—sure′-foot′ed ness,** *n.*

sure ly (shu̇r′lē), *adv.* 1 certainly; undoubtedly: *Half a loaf is surely better than none.* 2 without faltering, slipping, etc.; firmly: *The goat leaped surely from rock to rock.* 3 without fail: *slowly but surely.*

sur e ty (shu̇r′ə tē), *n., pl.* **-ties.** 1 security against loss, damage, or failure to do something: *An insurance company gives surety against loss by fire.* 2 person who agrees to be legally responsible for the debt, default, etc., of another. 3 ARCHAIC. a sure thing; certainty.

sur e ty ship (shu̇r′ə tē ship), *n.* obligation of a person to answer for the debt, fault, or conduct of another.

surf (sėrf), *n.* 1 waves or swell of the sea breaking in a foaming mass on the shore or upon shoals, reefs, etc. 2 the deep pounding or thundering sound of this. *—v.i.* travel or ride on the crest of a wave, especially with a surfboard. [origin uncertain] **—surf′er,** *n.*

sur face (sėr′fis), *n., adj., v.,* **-faced, -fac ing.** *—n.* 1 the outside of anything: *the surface of a golf ball. An egg has a smooth surface.* 2 the top of the ground or soil, or of a body of water or other liquid: *The stone sank below the surface.* 3 any face or side of a thing: *A cube has six surfaces.* 4 that which has length and breadth but no thickness: *a plane surface in geometry.* 5 the outward appearance: *He seems rough, but you will find him very kind below the surface.* *—adj.* 1 of or on the surface; having to do with the surface: *a surface view.* 2 superficial; external: *surface emotions.* 3 by land or water; not by air or underground: *surface transit, surface mail.* *—v.t.* put a surface on; make smooth: *surface a road.* *—v.i.* rise to the surface: *The submarine surfaced.* [< French < *sur-* above + *face* face] **—sur′fac er,** *n.*

surface tension, tension of the surface film of a liquid that makes it contract to a minimum area. It is caused by molecular forces and measured in terms of force per unit length.

hat, āge, fär; let, ēqual, tėrm;
it, īce; hot, ōpen, ôrder;
oil, out; cup, pu̇t, rüle;
ch, child; ng, long; sh, she;
th, thin; ᴛʜ, then; zh, measure;

ə represents *a* in about, *e* in taken, *i* in pencil, *o* in lemon, *u* in circus.

< = from, derived from, taken from.

sur face-to-air (sėr′fis tə er′, sėr′fis tə-ar′), *adj.* launched from the ground or a ship to intercept and destroy flying aircraft or missiles: *surface-to-air missiles.*

surf board (sėrf′bôrd′, sėrf′bōrd′), *n.* a long, narrow board for riding the surf. *—v.i.* ride the waves on a surfboard; surf. **—surf′board′er,** *n.*

surfboard
two surfboards

surf boat (sėrf′bōt′), *n.* a strong boat specially made for use in heavy surf.

surf cast (sėrf′kast′), *v.i.,* **-cast, -cast ing.** cast a fishing line from the shore into the surf. **—surf′cast′er,** *n.*

sur feit (sėr′fit), *n.* 1 too much; excess: *A surfeit of food makes one sick. A surfeit of advice annoys me.* 2 disgust or nausea caused by this. *—v.t.* feed or supply to excess. See **satiate** for synonym study. *—v.i.* eat, drink, or indulge in something to excess. [< Old French *surfait,* originally, overdone < *sur-* over + *faire* to do]

surf y (sėr′fē), *adj.* 1 having much surf or heavy surf. 2 forming or resembling surf.

surg., 1 surgeon. 2 surgery.

surge (sėrj), *v.,* **surged, surg ing,** *n. —v.i.* 1 rise and fall; move like waves: *A great wave surged over us. The crowd surged through the streets.* 2 rise or swell (up) violently or excitedly, as feelings, thoughts, etc. *—n.* 1 a swelling wave; sweep or rush of waves. 2 something like a wave: *A surge of anger swept over him.* [ultimately < Latin *surgere* rise < *sub-* up + *regere* to reach]

sur geon (sėr′jən), *n.* doctor who performs operations; medical practitioner who specializes in surgery. [< Old French *cirurgien* < *cirurgie.* See SURGERY.]

Surgeon General, *pl.* **Surgeons General.** 1 the chief medical officer of a particular branch of the armed forces of the United States. 2 the chief medical officer of the United States Public Health Service.

sur ger y (sėr′jər ē), *n., pl.* **-ger ies.** 1 the art and science of treating diseases, injuries, deformities, etc., by operations and instruments: *Malaria can be cured by medicine, but a ruptured appendix requires surgery.* 2 operating room or other area where surgical operations are performed. 3 the work performed by a surgeon. [< Old French *cirurgerie, cirurgie* < Latin *chirurgia* < Greek *cheirourgia* < *cheir* hand + *ergon* work]

sur gi cal (sėr′jə kəl), *adj.* 1 of surgery; having to do with surgery. 2 used in surgery. 3 performed by a surgeon. **—sur′gi cal ly,** *adv.*

Sur i nam (sůr′ə nam), *n.* Dutch territory in N South America, on the Atlantic; Dutch Guiana. 400,000 pop.; 55,300 sq. mi. *Capital:* Paramaribo.

sur ly (sėr′lē), *adj.,* **-li er, -li est.** bad-tempered and unfriendly; rude; gruff: *They got a surly answer from the grouchy old man.* [Middle English *sirly,* perhaps < *sir* lord] **—sur′li ness,** *n.*

sur mise (*v.* sər mīz′; *n.* sər mīz′, sėr′mīz), *v.,* **-mised, -mis ing,** *n.* *—v.t., v.i.* infer or guess: *We surmised that the delay was caused by some accident.* See **guess** for synonym study. *—n.* formation of an idea with little or no evidence; a guessing: *His guilt was a matter of surmise; there was no proof.* [< Old French, accusation, ultimately < *sur-* upon + *mettre* to put]

sur mount (sər mount′), *v.t.* 1 rise above: *That mountain surmounts all the peaks near it.* 2 be above or on top of: *A statue surmounts the monument.* 3 go up and across: *surmount a hill.* 4 overcome: *surmount difficulties.* [< Old French *surmonter* < *sur-* over + *monter* to mount] **—sur mount′a ble,** *adj.*

sur name (sėr′nām′), *n., v.,* **-named, -nam ing.** *—n.* 1 a last name; family name. 2 name added to a person's real name: *William I of England had the surname "the Conqueror."* *—v.t.* give a surname to; call by a surname: *Simon was surnamed Peter.*

sur pass (sər pas′), *v.t.* 1 do better than; be greater than; excel: *Her work surpassed expectations.* See **excel** for synonym study. 2 be too much or too great for; go beyond; exceed: *The horrors of the battlefield surpassed description.* **—sur pass′a ble,** *adj.* **—sur pass′ing ly,** *adv.*

surplice

sur plice (sėr′plis), *n.* a broad-sleeved, white gown worn by clergymen and choir singers over their other clothes. [< Old French *surpelice* < *sur-* over + *pelice* fur garment, ultimately < Latin *pellis* hide]

sur plus (sėr′pləs, sėr′plus), *n.* 1 amount over and above what is needed; extra quantity left over; excess. 2 excess of assets over liabilities. *—adj.* more than is needed; extra; excess: *Surplus wheat and cotton are shipped abroad.* [< Old French *surplus* < *sur-* over + *plus* more]

sur plus age (sėr′plu sij), *n.* 1 surplus; excess. 2 unnecessary words; irrelevant material.

sur pris al (sər prī′zəl), *n.* a surprising or a being surprised; a surprise.

sur prise (sər prīz′), *n., v.,* **-prised, -pris ing,** *adj.* *—n.* 1 the feeling caused by something happening suddenly or unexpectedly; astonishment; wonder. 2 something unexpected. 3 a catching unprepared; coming upon suddenly; sudden attack. 4 **take by surprise, a** catch unprepared; come on suddenly and unexpectedly. **b** astonish. *—v.t.* 1 cause to feel surprised; astonish. See synonym study below. 2 catch unprepared; come upon suddenly; attack suddenly: *The enemy surprised the fort.* 3 lead or bring (a person, etc.) unawares: *The news surprised her into tears.* *—adj.* that is not expected; surprising: *a surprise party, a surprise visit.* [< Old French < *surprendre* to surprise < *sur-* over + *prendre* to take]

Syn. *v.t.* 1 **Surprise, astonish, amaze** mean to cause a feeling of wonder. **Surprise** emphasizes the sudden reaction produced by something unexpected: *Her frank answer surprised him.* **Astonish** emphasizes the wonder caused by something extraordinary or incredible: *The young prodigy astonished everyone with her phenomenal memory.* **Amaze** implies bewildered or admiring wonder: *The landing of astronauts on the moon amazed the whole world.*

sur pris ing (sər prī′zing), *adj.* causing surprise; astonishing; amazing. **—sur pris′ing ly,** *adv.*

sur re al (sə rē′əl), *adj.* 1 surrealistic. 2 eerie; bizarre. [< *surrealism*]

sur re al ism (sə rē′ə liz′əm), *n.* a modern movement in art and literature that tries to show what takes place in dreams and in the subconscious mind. Surrealism is characterized by unusual and unexpected arrangements and distortions of images. [< French *surréalisme*]

sur re al ist (sə rē′ə list), *n.* artist or writer who uses surrealism. *—adj.* surrealistic.

sur re al is tic (sə rē′ə lis′tik), *adj.* of or having to do with surrealism or surrealists. **—sur re′al is′ti cal ly,** *adv.*

sur ren der (sə ren′dər), *v.t.* 1 give up (something) to the possession or power of another; yield *(to): The general surrendered the fort to the enemy.* 2 give up or abandon (hope, joy, comfort, etc.): *As the storm increased, the men on the raft surrendered all hope.* 3 give (oneself) up to a dominating thing or influence: *surrender oneself to bitter grief.* *—v.i.* yield to the power of another; submit: *The criminal surrendered to the police.* *—n.* act of surrendering. [< Old French *surrendre* < *sur-* over + *rendre* render]

sur rep ti tious (sėr′əp tish′əs), *adj.* 1 stealthy; secret: *a surreptitious glance.* 2 secret and unauthorized; clandestine: *surreptitious meetings.* [< Latin *surrepticius* < *surripere* seize secretly < *sub-* under + *rapere* to snatch] **—sur′rep ti′tious ly,** *adv.* **—sur′rep ti′tious ness,** *n.*

surrey

sur rey (sėr′ē), *n., pl.* **-reys.** a light, four-wheeled carriage having two seats. [< *Surrey,* England]

Sur rey (sėr′ē), *n.* 1 county in SE England. 2 **Earl of,** 1517?-1547, Henry Howard, English poet.

sur ro gate (sėr′ə gāt, sėr′ə git), *n.* 1 a substitute; deputy. 2 the deputy of a bishop. 3 U.S. (in certain states) a judge having charge of the probate of wills, the administration of estates, etc. [< Latin *surrogatum* substituted < *sub-* instead + *rogare* ask for]

sur ro gate ship (sėr′ə gāt ship, sėr′ə git-ship), *n.* office or authority of a surrogate.

sur round (sə round′), *v.t.* 1 shut in on all sides; extend around: *A high fence surrounds the field.* 2 form an enclosure around; encircle: *They surrounded the invalid with every comfort.* *—n.* border or edging nearly surrounding a central piece: *the plastic surround of the television screen.* [< Anglo-French *surounder* surpass < Late Latin *superundare* overflow < Latin *super-* over + *unda* wave]

sur round ings (sə roun′dingz), *n.pl.* surrounding things, conditions, etc.; environment.

sur tax (sėr′taks′), *n.* an additional or extra tax on something already taxed; supertax. The surtax on incomes usually increases in graded steps in proportion to the amount by which income exceeds a certain sum. *—v.t.* subject to a surtax.

sur veil lance (sər vā′ləns, sər vā′lyəns), *n.* 1 watch kept over a person: *keep a suspected criminal under close surveillance.* 2 supervision. [< French < *sur-* over + *veiller* to watch]

sur vey (*v.* sər vā′; *n.* sėr′vā, sər vā′), *v., n., pl.* **-veys.** *—v.t.* 1 look over; view; examine: *survey the situation.* 2 measure for size, shape, position, boundaries, etc.: *Men are surveying the land before it is divided into house lots.* *—v.i.* survey land. *—n.* 1 a general look; view; examination; inspection. 2 a comprehensive literary examination, description, or discussion: *a survey of contemporary poetry.* 3 a formal or official inspection, study, poll, etc.: *a survey of public opinion.* 4 a surveying of land. 5 plan or description of this: *She pointed out the new highway route on the government survey.* [< Anglo-French *surveier,* ultimately < Latin *super-* over + *videre* to see]

sur vey ing (sər vā′ing), *n.* 1 business or act of making surveys of land. 2 mathematical instruction in the principles of making surveys.

sur vey or (sər vā′ər), *n.* person who surveys, especially a person who surveys land.

surveyor's measure, system of measuring used by surveyors. The unit is usually a chain 66 ft. long with links 7.92 in. long.

sur viv al (sər vī′vəl), *n.* 1 act or fact of surviving; continuance of life; living or lasting longer than others. 2 person, thing, custom, belief, etc., that has lasted from an earlier time.

survival of the fittest, (in biology) the survival, as a result of natural selection, of those organisms which are best adapted to their environment.

sur vive (sər vīv′), *v.,* **-vived, -viv ing.** *—v.t.* 1 live longer than; remain alive after: *He survived his wife by three years. Only ten of the crew survived the shipwreck.* 2 sustain the effects of and continue to live: *The crops survived the drought.* *—v.i.* 1 continue to live; remain alive; live on. 2 continue to exist; remain: *Books have survived from the time of the ancient Chinese.* [< Old French *sourvivre* < *sur-* over + *vivre* to live]

sur vi vor (sər vī′vər), *n.* person, animal, or plant that remains alive; thing that continues to exist.

Su sa (sü′sə), *n.* capital of ancient Elam, and later of the Persian empire.

hat, āge, fär; let, ēqual, tėrm;
it, īce; hot, ōpen, ôrder;
oil, out; cup, pu̇t, rüle;
ch, child; ng, long; sh, she;
th, thin; ŦH, then; zh, measure;

ə represents *a* in about, *e* in taken, *i* in pencil, *o* in lemon, *u* in circus.

< = from, derived from, taken from.

Su san na (sü zan′ə), *n.* 1 book in the Apocrypha. 2 character in that book.

sus cep ti bil i ty (sə sep′tə bil′ə tē), *n., pl.* **-ties.** 1 quality or state of being susceptible; sensitiveness. 2 **susceptibilities,** *pl.* sensitive feelings.

sus cep ti ble (sə sep′tə bəl), *adj.* 1 easily influenced by feelings or emotions; very sensitive: *Poetry appealed to his susceptible nature.* See **sensitive** for synonym study. 2 **susceptible of, a** capable of receiving, undergoing, or being affected by: *Oak is susceptible of a high polish.* **b** sensitive to. 3 **susceptible to,** easily affected by; liable to; open to: *Vain people are susceptible to flattery.* [< Late Latin *susceptibilis,* ultimately < Latin *sub-* up + *capere* to take] **—sus cep′ti ble ness,** *n.* **—sus cep′ti bly,** *adv.*

sus pect (*v.* sə spekt′; *n.* sus′pekt; *adj.* sus′pekt, sə spekt′), *v.t.* 1 imagine to be so; thing likely: *suspected danger.* 2 believe guilty, false, bad, etc., without proof: *suspect someone of being a thief.* 3 feel no confidence in; doubt: *The judge suspected the truth of the defendant's alibi.* —*v.i.* be suspicious. —*n.* person suspected. —*adj.* open to or viewed with suspicion. [< Latin *suspectum* looked under < *sub-* under + *specere* to look]

sus pend (sə spend′), *v.t.* 1 hang down by attaching to something above: *The lamp was suspended from the ceiling.* 2 hold in place as if by hanging: *We saw the smoke suspended in the still air.* 3 stop for a while: *suspend work.* 4 remove or exclude for a while from some privilege or job: *suspend a student for infraction of rules.* 5 defer temporarily (a law, punishment, etc.). 6 keep undecided; put off: *The court suspended judgment till next Monday.* —*v.i.* 1 come to a stop for a time. 2 stop payment; be unable to pay debts or claims. [< Latin *suspendere* < *sub-* up + *pendere* to hang]

sus pend ers (sə spen′dərz), *n.pl.* straps worn over the shoulders to hold up the trousers.

sus pense (sə spens′), *n.* 1 condition of being uncertain: *The detective story kept me in suspense until the last chapter.* 2 anxious uncertainty; anxiety: *Mothers feel suspense when their children are very sick.* 3 condition of being undecided or undetermined. [< Old French *(en) suspens* (in) abeyance, ultimately < Latin *suspendere.* See SUSPEND.]

sus pense ful (sə spens′fəl), *adj.* characterized by or full of suspense.

sus pen sion (sə spen′shən), *n.* 1 a suspending: *the suspension of a driver's license for speeding.* 2 a being suspended: *suspension from office.* 3 support on which something is suspended. 4 arrangement of springs, shock absorbers, etc., above the axles, for supporting the body of an automobile, railroad car, etc. 5 mixture in which very small particles of a solid remain suspended without dissolving. 6 a solid in such condition. 7 inability to pay one's debts; failure.

suspension bridge, bridge having its roadway suspended on cables or chains between towers.

suspension bridge

sus pen sive (sə spen′siv), *adj.* 1 inclined to suspend judgment; undecided in mind. 2 having to do with or characterized by suspense, uncertainty, or apprehension. 3 having the effect of temporarily stopping something: *a suspensive veto.* **—sus pen′sive ly,** *adv.*

sus pen sor y (sə spen′sər ē), *adj., n., pl.* **-sor ies.** —*adj.* 1 holding up; supporting. 2 stopping for a while; leaving undecided. —*n.* a muscle, ligament, bandage, etc., that holds up or supports a part of the body.

sus pi cion (sə spish′ən), *n.* 1 state of mind of a person who suspects; act of suspecting: *The real thief tried to turn suspicion toward others.* See synonym study below. 2 condition of being suspected. 3 a very small amount; slight trace; suggestion: *She spoke with a suspicion of spite.* 4 **above suspicion,** not to be suspected. 5 **on suspicion,** because of being suspected: *He was arrested on suspicion of robbery.* 6 **under suspicion,** suspected. —*v.t.* DIALECT. suspect. [< Latin *suspicionem* < *suspicere.* See SUSPECT.]

Syn. *n.* 1 **Suspicion, distrust, doubt** mean lack of trust or confidence in someone. **Suspicion** suggests fearing, or believing without enough or any proof, that someone or something is guilty, wrong, false, etc.: *Suspicion points to them, but the evidence is circumstantial.* **Distrust** suggests lack of confidence or trust, and may suggest certainty of guilt, falseness, etc.: *I could not explain my distrust of the stranger.* **Doubt** suggests merely lack of certainty: *He had no doubt about his son's honesty.*

sus pi cious (sə spish′əs), *adj.* 1 causing one to suspect; questionable; doubtful: *A man was hanging about the house in a suspicious manner.* 2 feeling suspicion; suspecting; mistrustful: *Our dog is suspicious of strangers.* 3 showing suspicion: *The dog gave a suspicious sniff at my leg.* **—sus pi′cious ly,** *adv.* **—sus pi′cious ness,** *n.*

sus pi ra tion (sus′pə rā′shən), *n.* a sigh.

sus pire (sə spīr′), *v.i.,* **-pired, -pir ing.** 1 sigh. 2 breathe. [< Latin *suspirare* < *sub-* up + *spirare* breathe]

Sus que han na River (sus′kwə han′ə), river flowing from central New York State through Pennsylvania and Maryland into Chesapeake Bay. 444 mi.

Sus sex (sus′iks), *n.* county in SE England, divided into **Sussex East** and **Sussex West.** See **Mercia** for map.

sus tain (sə stān′), *v.t.* 1 keep up; keep going: *Hope sustains him in his misery.* 2 supply with food, provisions, etc.: *sustain a family.* 3 hold up; support: *Arches sustain the weight of the roof.* 4 bear; endure: *The sea wall sustains the shock of the waves.* 5 suffer; experience: *sustain a great loss.* 6 allow; admit; favor: *The court sustained his suit.* 7 agree with; confirm: *The facts sustain her theory.* [< Old French < Latin *sustinere* < *sub-* up + *tenere* to hold] **—sus tain′a ble,** *adj.* **—sus tain′er,** *n.*

sustaining program, a radio or television program maintained at the expense of a station or network.

sus te nance (sus′tə nəns), *n.* 1 food or provisions; nourishment: *The lost campers went without sustenance for two days.* 2 means of living; support: *give money for the sustenance of the poor.* 3 a sustaining. 4 a being sustained.

su sur ra tion (sü′sə rā′shən), *n.* 1 whispering. 2 a rustling murmur. [< Late Latin *susurrationem* < Latin *susurrare* to whisper, hum]

sut ler (sut′lər), *n.* person who follows an army and sells provisions, etc., to the soldiers. [< earlier Dutch *soeteler* < *soetelen* ply a low trade]

sut tee (su′tē′, sut′ē′), *n.* 1 a Hindu widow who throws herself on the burning funeral pyre of her husband. 2 the former Hindu custom of burning a widow with the body of her husband. [< Sanskrit *satī* faithful wife]

su ture (sü′chər), *n., v.,* **-tured, -tur ing.** —*n.* 1 the sewing together or joining of two surfaces, especially the edges of a cut or wound. 2 seam formed in sewing up a wound. 3 one of the stitches or fastenings used. 4 the material used, as gut, linen, or silk. 5 line where two bones, especially of the skull, join in an immovable joint. 6 the joint itself. 7 line between adjoining parts in a plant or animal, such as that along which clamshells join or pea pods split. —*v.t.* unite by suture or as if by a suture. [< Latin *sutura* < *suere* to sew]

Su va (sü′və), *n.* capital of Fiji, a seaport located on the largest of the Fiji Islands.

su zer ain (sü′zər in, sü′zə rān′), *n.* 1 a feudal lord. 2 state or government exercising political control over a dependent state. [< French < *sus* above (< Latin *sursum* upward), modeled on *souverain* sovereign]

su zer ain ty (sü′zər in tē, sü′zə rān′tē), *n., pl.* **-ties.** position or authority of a suzerain.

s.v., under the word or heading [for Latin *sub verbo* or *sub voce*].

svelte (svelt), *adj.* slender; lithe.

Sven ga li (sven gä′lē), *n.* person with irresistible hypnotic powers. [< the name of a musician who hypnotizes the heroine of the novel *Trilby* (1894) by George Du Maurier, 1834-1896, English novelist]

Sverd lovsk (sverd lôfsk′), *n.* city in central Soviet Union, in the Ural Mountains. 1,026,000.

SW, S.W., or **s.w.,** 1 southwest. 2 southwestern.

swab (swob), *n., v.,* **swabbed, swab bing.** —*n.* 1 a mop for cleaning decks, floors, etc. 2 a bit of sponge, cloth, or cotton for cleansing some part of the body, for applying medicine to it, etc. 3 a cleaner for the bore of a firearm. 4 SLANG. an awkward, clumsy person. —*v.t.* clean with a swab; apply a swab to: *swab the deck.* Also, **swob.** [< *swabber*]

swab ber (swob′ər), *n.* 1 person who uses a swab. 2 swab. [< earlier Dutch *zwabber* < *zwabben* to swab]

Swa bi a (swā′bē ə), *n.* 1 former duchy in SW Germany. 2 region in SW Bavaria. **—Swa′bi an,** *adj., n.*

swad dle (swod′l), *v.,* **-dled, -dling,** *n.* —*v.t.* bind (a baby) with long, narrow strips of cloth; wrap tightly with clothes, bandages, etc. —*n.* cloth used for swaddling. [Old

English *swæthel* band, bandage. Related to SWATHE[1].]

swaddling clothes, 1 long, narrow strips of cloth for wrapping a newborn infant. 2 long clothes for an infant.

swag (swag), *n.* 1 SLANG. things stolen; booty; plunder; dishonest political gains. 2 (in Australia) a bundle of personal belongings. 3 an ornamental festoon of flowers, leaves, ribbons, etc. [probably < Scandinavian (dialectal Norwegian) *svagga* to sway]

swage (swāj), *n., v.,* **swaged, swag ing.** —*n.* 1 tool for bending cold metal to the required shape. 2 die or stamp for giving a particular shape to metal by hammering, stamping, etc. —*v.t.* bend or shape by using a swage. [< Old French *souage*]

swag ger (swag′ər), *v.i.* 1 walk with a bold, rude, or superior air; strut about or show off in a vain or insolent way: *The bully swaggered into the schoolyard.* 2 talk boastfully and loudly; brag noisily. 3 bluster; bluff. —*v.t.* affect by bluster. —*n.* act of swaggering; a swaggering way of walking, acting, speaking, etc. —*adj.* INFORMAL. showily smart or fashionable. —**swag′ger er,** *n.* —**swag′ger ing ly,** *adv.*

swagger stick, a short, light stick or cane, sometimes carried by army officers, soldiers, etc.

Swa hi li (swä hē′lē), *n., pl.* **-li** or **-lis** for 2. 1 a Bantu language containing many Arabic and other foreign words, spoken in much of eastern Africa and parts of the Congo. 2 member of a Bantu people inhabiting Zanzibar and the adjacent coast of Africa.

swain (swān), *n.* ARCHAIC. 1 lover. 2 a young man who lives in the country. [< Scandinavian (Old Icelandic) *sveinn* boy]

swale (swāl), *n.* a low, wet piece of land; low place. [Middle English]

swal low[1] (swol′ō), *v.t.* 1 take into the stomach through the throat: *swallow food.* 2 take in; absorb: *The waves swallowed up the swimmer.* 3 INFORMAL. believe too easily; accept without question or suspicion: *He will swallow any story.* 4 put up with; take meekly; accept without opposing or resisting: *swallow an insult.* 5 take back: *swallow words said in anger.* 6 keep back; keep from expressing: *I swallowed my displeasure and smiled.* —*v.i.* perform the act of swallowing: *I can't swallow.* —*n.* 1 act of swallowing: *take a pill at one swallow.* 2 amount swallowed at one time. 3 the throat; gullet. [Middle English *swalewen,* Old English *swelgan*] —**swal′low er,** *n.*

swal low[2] (swol′ō), *n.* 1 any of various small, swift-flying birds of the same family as the martins, with long, pointed wings and weak feet used only for perching. Swallows are noted for the extent and regularity of their migratory movements. Some kinds have deeply forked tails. 2 any of certain swifts that resemble swallows. [Old English *swealwe*]

swal low tail (swol′ō tāl′), *n.* 1 any of a family of large butterflies having taillike extensions of the hind wings. 2 swallow-tailed coat.

swal low-tailed coat (swol′ō tāld′), a man's coat with tails, worn at formal evening parties.

swam (swam), *v.* pt. of **swim.**

swa mi (swä′mē), *n.* title of a Hindu religious teacher. [< Hindi *svāmī* master < Sanskrit *svāmin*]

swamp (swomp, swômp), *n.* tract of low-lying ground in which water collects; wet, soft land; marsh. —*v.t., v.i.* 1 plunge or sink in or as if in a swamp: *The horses were swamped in the stream.* 2 fill with water and sink: *The wave swamped the boat. The boat swamped.* 3 overwhelm or become overwhelmed as by a flood; make or become helpless: *swamped with work, swamped by debts.* [apparently variant of *sump*]

swamp land (swomp′land′, swômp′land′), *n.* tract of land covered by swamps.

swamp y (swom′pē, swôm′pē), *adj.,* **swamp i er, swamp i est.** 1 like a swamp; soft and wet. 2 containing swamps. 3 of swamps. —**swamp′i ness,** *n.*

swan (def. 1) about 2½ ft. long

swan (swon, swôn), *n.* 1 any of a family of large, graceful water birds with long, slender, curving necks, and in most species pure-white plumage in the adult. Swans are closely related to geese and ducks. 2 a sweet singer; poet. 3 person of great beauty, purity, etc. 4 **Swan,** Cygnus. [Old English] —**swan′-like′,** *adj.*

swan dive, a graceful dive in which the legs are held straight, the back is curved, and the arms are extended sideways.

swang (swang), *v.* DIALECT. pt. of **swing.**

swank (swangk), SLANG. —*adj.* stylish; smart; dashing. —*v.i.* show off; bluff; swagger. —*n.* 1 a showing off. 2 style; smartness; dash. [origin uncertain]

swank y (swang′kē), *adj.,* **swank i er, swank i est.** SLANG. swank. —**swank′i ly,** *adv.* —**swank′i ness,** *n.*

swan's-down (swonz′doun′, swônz′-doun′), *n.* 1 the soft down of a swan, used for trimming, powder puffs, etc. 2 Also, **swansdown,** a fine, thick, soft cloth made from wool or cotton, used for babies' coats, bathrobes, etc.

Swan sea (swon′sē, swon′zē), *n.* seaport in S Wales. 171,000.

swan song, 1 song which, according to fable, a dying swan sings. 2 a person's last piece of work.

swap (swop), *v.,* **swapped, swap ping,** *n.* INFORMAL. —*v.t., v.i.* exchange, barter, or trade. —*n.* an exchange, barter, or trade. Also, **swop.** [Middle English *swappen* to strike, strike the hands together, probably from the practice of "striking hands" as a sign of agreement in bargaining] —**swap′-per,** *n.*

sward (swôrd), *n.* a grassy surface; turf. [Old English *sweard* skin]

sware (swer, swar), *v.* ARCHAIC. a pt. of **swear.**

swarm[1] (swôrm), *n.* 1 group of bees led by a queen that leave a hive and fly off together to start a new colony. 2 group of bees settled together in a hive. 3 a large group of insects, flying or moving about together. 4 a great number; crowd: *Swarms of children were playing in the park.* See **crowd** for synonym study. —*v.i.* 1 (of bees) fly off together to start a new colony. 2 fly or move about in great numbers; be in very great numbers: *The mosquitoes swarmed about us.* 3 be crowded; crowd: *The swamp is swarming with mosquitoes.* —*v.t.* fill or beset with or as if with a swarm; throng. [Old English *swearm*] —**swarm′er,** *n.*

swarm[2] (swôrm), *v.i., v.t.* climb; shin: *swarm up a tree.* [origin uncertain]

swart (swôrt), *adj.* dark; swarthy. [Old English *sweart*]

swarth (swôrth), *adj.* ARCHAIC. swarthy.

swarth y (swôr′ᴛʜē, swôr′thē), *adj.,* **swarth i er, swarth i est.** having a dark skin. —**swarth′i ly,** *adv.* —**swarth′i-ness,** *n.*

swash (swosh), *v.t.* 1 dash (water, etc.) about; splash. 2 dash water, etc., on. —*v.i.* 1 dash with a splashing sound; splash. 2 swagger. —*n.* 1 a swashing action or sound: *the swash of waves against a boat.* 2 a swagger. 3 a channel of water through or behind a sandbank. 4 ground under water or over which water washes. [probably imitative]

swash buck ler (swosh′buk′lər), *n.* a swaggering swordsman, bully, or boaster.

swash buck ling (swosh′buk′ling), *n., adj.* swaggering; bullying; boasting.

swas ti ka (swos′tə kə), *n.* an ancient symbol or ornament like a cross with the arms bent, thought in early times to bring good luck. The swastika with arms turning clockwise was the symbol of the Nazis in Germany. [< Sanskrit *svastika* < *svasti* luck < *su* well + *asti* being]

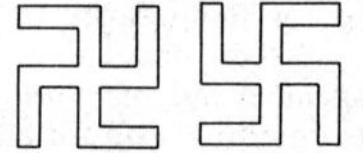

swastika—two types: left, ancient symbol; right, Nazi symbol

swat (swot), *v.,* **swat ted, swat ting,** *n.* INFORMAL. —*v.t.* hit sharply or violently: *swat a fly.* —*n.* a sharp or violent blow. [probably imitative] —**swat′ter,** *n.*

swatch (swoch), *n.* sample of cloth or other material. [origin uncertain]

swath (swoth, swôth), *n.* 1 space covered by a single cut of a scythe or by one cut of a mowing machine. 2 row of grass, grain, etc., cut by a scythe or mowing machine. 3 a strip. 4 **cut a wide swath,** make a showy display; splurge. Also, **swathe.** [Old English *swæth* track, trace]

swathe[1] (swāᴛʜ), *v.,* **swathed, swath ing,** *n.* —*v.t.* 1 wrap up closely or fully: *swathed in a blanket.* 2 bind, wrap, or bandage. 3 envelop or surround like a wrapping: *White clouds swathed the mountain.* —*n.* a wrapping; bandage. [Old English *swathian*]

swathe[2] (swāᴛʜ), *n.* swath.

sway (swā), *v.i.* 1 swing back and forth; rock from side to side, or to one side: *The pail swayed in his hands as he ran.* See **swing** for synonym study. 2 move to one side; turn aside. 3 change in opinion, feeling, etc. —*v.t.* 1 make move; cause to sway: *The wind swayed the grass.* 2 cause to change in opinion, feeling, etc.: *Nothing could sway her after she had made up her mind.* 3 influence, control, or rule: *The speaker's words swayed the audience.* —*n.* 1 a swaying: *The sway of the pail caused some milk to spill out.* 2 influence, control, or rule: *Few countries are now under the sway of kings.* [< Scandinavian (Old Icelandic) *sveigja*] —**sway′er,** *n.*

sway back (swā′bak′), *adj.* swaybacked. —*n.* an exaggerated downward curvature of the spinal column, especially of a horse.

sway backed (swā′bakt′), *adj.* having the back sagged or hollowed to an unusual degree: *a swaybacked horse.*

Swa zi (swä′zē), *n., pl.* **-zi** or **-zis,** *adj.* —*n.* native or inhabitant of Swaziland, especially one of a Bantu people of Zulu origin. —*adj.* of the Swazi or Swaziland.

Swa zi land (swä′zē land′), *n.* country in SE Africa, a member of the Commonwealth of Nations. 410,000 pop.; 6700 sq. mi. *Capital:* Mbabane.

swear (swer, swar), *v.,* **swore, sworn, swear ing.** —*v.i.* 1 make a solemn statement, appealing to God or some other sacred being or object; take an oath. 2 promise solemnly; vow: *The knights had sworn to be true to their king.* 3 utter or use profane language; curse. See **curse** for synonym study. —*v.t.* 1 declare, calling God to witness; declare on oath. 2 bind by an oath; require to promise: *Members of the club were sworn to secrecy.* 3 admit to office or service by administering an oath: *swear a witness.* 4 promise solemnly; pledge: *swear allegiance, swear revenge.* 5 take or utter (an oath). 6 bring, set, take, etc., by swearing: *swear a person's life away.*

swear by, a name as one's witness in taking an oath. **b** have great confidence in.

swear in, admit to an office or service by giving an oath: *swear in a jury.*

swear off, INFORMAL. promise to give up.

swear out, get by taking an oath that a certain charge is true: *swear out a warrant for a burglar's arrest.*

[Old English *swerian*] —**swear′er,** *n.*

swear word (swer′wėrd′, swar′wėrd′), *n.* word used in cursing; oath.

sweat (swet), *n., v.,* **sweat** or **sweat ed, sweat ing.** —*n.* 1 moisture coming through the pores of the skin; perspiration. See synonym study below. 2 fit or condition of sweating: *be in a cold sweat from fear.* 3 INFORMAL. fit of suffering, anxiety, impatience, or anything that might make a person sweat. 4 moisture given out by something or gathered on its surface: *the sweat on a pitcher of ice water.* 5 hard work; labor.
—*v.i.* 1 give out moisture through the pores of the skin; perspire. 2 give out moisture; collect moisture from the air: *A pitcher of ice water sweats on a hot day.* 3 come out in drops; ooze. 4 INFORMAL. work very hard. 5 be annoyed or vexed; fume: *sweat over a delay.* 6 **sweat it out,** INFORMAL. wait anxiously or nervously for something to happen.
—*v.t.* 1 give out through the pores of the skin. 2 cause to sweat: *He sweated his horse by riding him too hard.* 3 get rid of by or as by sweating: *sweat off excess weight.* 4 send out in drops like sweat. 5 wet, soak, or stain with sweat. 6 cause to give off moisture: *sweat hides in preparing them for use.* 7 cause to work hard, especially to employ in hard or excessive work at low pay under bad conditions. 8 heat (solder) until it melts; fasten or join (metal parts) by heating. 9 heat (metal) in order to remove an easily fusible constituent.
[Old English *swǣtan* < *swāt* sweat]

Syn. *n.* 1 **Sweat, perspiration** mean moisture coming through the pores of the skin. **Sweat** is the direct native English word, used when speaking of animals or things and often of people: *Sweat streamed down the horse's flanks, and the rider's shirt was stained with sweat.* **Perspiration,** seldom used except when speaking of human beings, is preferred by some people for that reason: *Tiny drops of perspiration formed at her temples.*

sweat band (swet′band′), *n.* band of leather or cloth on the inside of a hat or cap to protect it from perspiration.

sweat er (swet′ər), *n.* a knitted outer garment of wool, nylon, etc., for the upper part of the body.

sweat gland, gland of the skin that secretes sweat and is connected with the surface of the skin by a duct that ends in a pore.

sweat pants, a pair of baggy pants gathered in at the ankles, worn especially by athletes to keep warm before and after exercise.

sweat shirt, a heavy, long-sleeved jersey, worn especially by athletes to keep warm before and after exercise.

sweat shop (swet′shop′), *n.* place where workers are employed at low pay for long hours under bad conditions.

sweat suit, suit consisting of a sweat shirt and sweat pants.

sweat y (swet′ē), *adj.,* **sweat i er, sweat i est.** 1 sweating; covered or wet with sweat. 2 causing sweat. 3 laborious. —**sweat′i ly,** *adv.* —**sweat′i ness,** *n.*

Swede (swēd), *n.* native or inhabitant of Sweden.

Swe den (swēd′n), *n.* country in N Europe, east and south of Norway. 8,014,000 pop.; 173,700 sq. mi. *Capital:* Stockholm.

Swe den borg (swēd′n bôrg), *n.* **Emanuel,** 1688-1772, Swedish philosopher, scientist, and mystic.

Swe den bor gi an (swēd′n bôr′jē ən), *n.* believer in the religious doctrines of Swedenborg. —*adj.* having to do with Swedenborg, his doctrines, or his followers.

Swed ish (swē′dish), *adj.* of or having to do with Sweden, its people, or their language. —*n.* 1 *pl. in use.* the people of Sweden. 2 the Scandinavian language of Sweden.

sweep (swēp), *v.,* **swept, sweep ing,** *n.* —*v.t.* 1 clean or clear (a floor, etc.) with a broom, brush, etc.; use a broom or something like one to remove dirt; brush: *Sweep the steps.* 2 move, drive, or take away with or as with a broom, brush, etc.: *The wind sweeps the snow into drifts.* 3 remove with a sweeping motion; carry along: *a bridge swept away by a flood.* 4 trail upon: *Her dress sweeps the ground.* 5 pass over with a steady movement: *Her fingers swept the strings of the harp.* 6 range over; scour: *Enthusiasm for the candidate swept the country.* 7 win a complete victory in: *sweep a baseball series.*
—*v.i.* 1 use a broom or something like one to remove dirt; clean by sweeping. 2 move swiftly; pass swiftly: *Guerrillas swept down on the town.* 3 move with dignity: *She swept out of the room.* 4 move or extend in a long course or curve; stretch: *The shore sweeps to the south for miles.*
—*n.* 1 act of sweeping; clearing away; removing: *He made a clean sweep of all his debts.* 2 a steady, driving motion or swift onward course of something: *The sweep of the wind kept the trees from growing tall.* 3 a smooth, flowing motion or line; dignified motion: *the stately sweep of heroic verse.* 4 a curve; bend: *the sweep of a road.* 5 a swinging or curving motion: *He cut the grass with strong sweeps of his scythe.* 6 a continuous extent; expanse; stretch: *The house looked upon a wide sweep of farming country.* 7 reach; range: *The mountain is beyond the sweep of your eye.* 8 complete victory in a series, match, etc. 9 person who sweeps chimneys, streets, etc. 10 a long oar. 11 a long pole used to lower and raise a bucket in a well. 12 sweepstakes.
[Old English *(ge)swǣpa* sweepings]

hat, āge, fär; let, ēqual, tėrm;
it, īce; hot, ōpen, ôrder;
oil, out; cup, pu̇t, rüle;
ch, child; ng, long; sh, she;
th, thin; ᴛʜ, then; zh, measure;

ə represents *a* in about, *e* in taken, *i* in pencil, *o* in lemon, *u* in circus.

< = from, derived from, taken from.

sweep er (swē′pər), *n.* person or thing that sweeps: *a carpet sweeper.*

sweep ing (swē′ping), *adj.* 1 passing over a wide space: *a sweeping glance.* 2 having wide range: *a sweeping victory, a sweeping statement.* —*n.* **sweepings,** *pl.* dust, rubbish, scraps, etc., swept out or up. —**sweep′ing ly,** *adv.*

sweep stake (swēp′stāk′), *n.* sweepstakes.

sweep stakes (swēp′stāks′), *n.* 1 system of gambling on horse races, etc. People buy tickets, and the money they pay goes to the drawer or drawers of winning tickets. 2 the race or contest. 3 race or contest in which the prize or prizes derive from a pooling of the stakes of the contestants. 4 prize in such a race or contest.

sweet (swēt), *adj.* 1 having a taste like that of sugar or honey: *Pears are sweeter than lemons.* 2 having a pleasant taste or smell: *a sweet flower.* 3 pleasing; agreeable: *a sweet child, a sweet smile, sweet music.* 4 not sour, salty, bitter, or spoiled; fresh: *sweet butter, sweet milk.* 5 (of soil) good for farming; not acid. 6 dearly loved or prized; dear. 7 **be sweet on,** INFORMAL. be in love with. 8 excessively or offensively pleasant or agreeable; saccharine. —*adv.* in a sweet manner. —*n.* 1 something sweet. 2 BRITISH. a sweet dessert. 3 **sweets,** *pl.* **a** candy or other sweet things. **b** pleasant or agreeable things. 4 dear; darling. [Old English *swēte*] —**sweet′ly,** *adv.* —**sweet′ness,** *n.*

sweet alyssum, a common, low-growing garden plant of the mustard family, with clusters of small, fragrant, white or purple flowers.

sweet bay, 1 laurel (def. 1). 2 a tree or large shrub of the same genus as the magnolia with round, fragrant, white flowers, common along the Atlantic coast from Massachusetts southward.

sweet bread (swēt′bred′), *n.* the pancreas or thymus of a calf, lamb, etc., used as meat.

sweet bri er or **sweet bri ar** (swēt′brī′ər), *n.* a wild rose with a tall, prickly stem, single pink flowers, and small, aromatic leaves; eglantine.

sweet cider, unfermented cider.

sweet clover, any of a genus of herbs of the pea family, grown for hay and pasture and to improve the soil.

sweet corn, variety of corn which has kernels rich in sugar, eaten when young and tender, often directly from the ear, or preserved by canning or freezing; corn.

sweet en (swēt′n), *v.t., v.i.* make or become sweet or sweeter. —**sweet′en er,** *n.*

sweet en ing (swēt′n ing), *n.* something that sweetens.

sweet fern, a small shrub of North America of the same family as the wax myrtle, with fragrant, fernlike leaves.

sweet flag, 1 a water plant with long, sword-shaped leaves and a thick, creeping rootstock with a pungent, aromatic flavor. It is a species of arum. 2 its rootstock, used in perfumes and in medicine.

sweet gum, 1 a large North American tree of the same family as the witch hazel, with shining, star-shaped leaves that turn scarlet in the fall. 2 balsam from this tree.

sweet heart (swēt′härt′), *n.* 1 a loved one; lover. 2 girl or woman loved.

sweet ing (swē′ting), *n.* 1 a sweet apple. 2 ARCHAIC. sweetheart.

sweet ish (swē′tish), *adj.* somewhat sweet. **—sweet′ish ly,** *adv.*

sweet meats (swēt′mēts′), *n.pl.* 1 candied fruits; sugar-covered nuts, etc.; candy; bonbons. 2 preserves.

sweet pea, 1 an annual climbing plant of the pea family, with delicate, fragrant flowers of various colors. 2 its flower.

sweet pepper, 1 a mild-flavored species of pepper plant. 2 its fruit.

sweet potato, 1 a creeping vine, a species of morning-glory, grown in warm regions. 2 its sweet, thick, yellow or reddish root, used as a vegetable. 3 INFORMAL. ocarina.

sweet talk, INFORMAL. cajolery.

sweet-talk (swēt′tôk′), *v.t.* INFORMAL. cajole.

sweet-tem pered (swēt′tem′pərd), *adj.* having a gentle or pleasant nature.

sweet tooth, fondness for sweets.

sweet william or **sweet William,** plant, a species of pink, with dense, rounded clusters of small flowers of various shades of white and red.

swell (swel), *v.,* **swelled, swelled** or **swol len, swell ing,** *n., adj.* —*v.i., v.t.* 1 grow or make bigger: *Bread dough swells as it rises. The river is swollen by rain.* See **expand** for synonym study. 2 be larger or thicker in a particular place; stick out or cause to stick out: *A barrel swells in the middle.* 3 increase or make greater in amount, degree, force, etc.: *Savings may swell into a fortune.* 4 rise or cause to rise above the usual level: *Rounded hills swell gradually from the village plain.* 5 grow or make louder. 6 become or make proud or conceited. 7 fill or become filled with emotion: *swell with indignation.*
—*n.* 1 act of swelling; increase in amount, degree, force, etc. 2 condition of being swollen. 3 part that rises or swells out. 4 piece of higher ground; rounded hill. 5 a long, unbroken wave, or waves: *The boat rocked in the swell.* 6 a swelling tone or sound. 7 in music: **a** crescendo followed by diminuendo. **b** the sign for this (<>). 8 device in an organ, harpsichord, etc., to control the volume of sound. 9 INFORMAL. a fashionable person.
—*adj.* 1 INFORMAL. stylish; grand. 2 SLANG. excellent; first-rate: *a swell time.*
[Old English *swellan*]

swelled (sweld), *adj.* INFORMAL. showing an inflated sense of one's own importance: *a swelled head.*

swell head ed (swel′hed′id), *adj.* INFORMAL. conceited; arrogant. **—swell′head′ed ness,** *n.*

swell ing (swel′ing), *n.* 1 an increase in size. 2 a swollen part: *There is a swelling where I bumped my head.*

swel ter (swel′tər), *v.i.* 1 suffer from heat. 2 perspire freely; sweat. —*v.t.* oppress with heat. —*n.* a sweltering condition. [< obsolete *swelt* be faint with heat < Old English *sweltan* to die]

swept (swept), *v.* pt. and pp. of **sweep.**

swept-back (swept′bak′), *adj.* (of the wings of an aircraft) extending outward and sharply backward from the fuselage.

swept wing (swept′wing′), *n.* a swept-back wing. —*adj.* having swept-back wings.

swerve (swėrv), *v.,* **swerved, swerv ing,** *n.* —*v.i., v.t.* turn aside: *The car swerved and hit a tree. Nothing could swerve him from doing his duty.* —*n.* a turning aside: *The swerve of the ball made it hard to hit.* [Old English *sweorfan* to rub, file]

swift (swift), *adj.* 1 moving very fast: *a swift horse.* 2 coming or happening quickly: *a swift response.* 3 quick, rapid, or prompt to act, etc.: *swift to suspect.* —*adv.* in a swift manner. —*n.* 1 any of a family of small birds with long, strong wings, noted for their rapid flight. Swifts are of the same order as hummingbirds, but resemble swallows. 2 any of certain small lizards that run quickly. [Old English] **—swift′ly,** *adv.* **—swift′ness,** *n.*

Swift (swift), *n.* **Jonathan,** 1667-1745, English satirist, born in Ireland, author of *Gulliver's Travels.*

swift-foot ed (swift′fu̇t′id), *adj.* able to run swiftly.

swig (swig), *n., v.,* **swigged, swig ging.** INFORMAL. —*n.* a big or hearty drink. —*v.t., v.i.* drink heartily or greedily. [origin uncertain] **—swig′ger,** *n.*

swill (swil), *n.* 1 kitchen refuse, especially when partly liquid; slops. Swill is sometimes fed to pigs. 2 a deep drink. —*v.t.* 1 drink greedily. 2 fill with drink. —*v.i.* drink greedily; drink too much. [Old English *swilian*]

swim (swim), *v.,* **swam** or (DIALECT) **swum, swum, swim ming,** *n.* —*v.i.* 1 move along on or in the water by using arms, legs, fins, etc. 2 float: *a leaf swimming on a pond.* 3 be immersed or steeped in or as if in a liquid: *meat swimming in gravy.* 4 be overflowed or flooded: *Her eyes were swimming with tears.* 5 go smoothly; glide. 6 be dizzy; whirl: *The heat and noise made my head swim.* —*v.t.* 1 go or do by swimming: *swim a mile.* 2 swim across: *swim a lake.* 3 make swim or float: *swim a horse across a stream.* —*n.* 1 act, time, motion, or distance of swimming: *go for a swim.* **2 the swim,** INFORMAL. the current of affairs, activities, etc. 3 swim bladder. [Old English *swimman*] **—swim′mer,** *n.*

swim bladder, air bladder of a fish.

swim mer et (swim′ə ret′), *n.* one of a number of abdominal limbs or appendages in many crustaceans, used for respiration, for carrying eggs, etc., and usually adapted for swimming.

swim ming (swim′ing), *n.* 1 practice or sport of swimming: *She is an expert at both swimming and diving.* 2 act of swimming: *Can you reach the island by swimming?* —*adj.* 1 of or for swimming or swimmers: *a swimming teacher, a swimming pool.* 2 that swims habitually: *a swimming bird or insect.* 3 faint; dizzy: *a swimming sensation.*

swim ming ly (swim′ing lē), *adv.* with great ease or success: *Everything went swimmingly at our party.*

swim suit (swim′süt′), *n.* bathing suit.

swim wear (swim′wer′, swim′war′), *n.* clothes worn for swimming.

Swin burne (swin′bėrn′, swin′bərn), *n.* **Algernon Charles,** 1837-1909, English poet and critic.

swin dle (swin′dl), *v.,* **-dled, -dling,** *n.* —*v.t.* 1 cheat; defraud: *Honest merchants do not swindle their customers.* 2 get by fraud. —*v.i.* be guilty of swindling. —*n.* act of swindling. [< *swindler*]

swin dler (swin′dlər), *n.* person who cheats or defrauds. [< German *Schwindler* < *schwindeln* be dizzy, act thoughtlessly, cheat]

swine (swīn), *n., pl.* **swine.** 1 hogs or pigs. 2 a hog or pig. 3 a coarse or beastly person. [Old English *swīn*]

swine herd (swīn′hėrd′), *n.* person who tends pigs or hogs.

swing (swing), *v.,* **swung** or (DIALECT) **swang, swung, swing ing,** *n.* —*v.t.* 1 move back and forth, especially with a regular motion: *He swings his arms as he walks.* 2 hang or suspend so as to turn freely: *swing a hammock between two trees.* 3 cause to move in a curve: *She swung the automobile around a corner.* 4 INFORMAL. manage or influence successfully: *swing a business deal.* 5 play (music) as swing. —*v.i.* 1 move regularly back and forth: *The pendulum swings.* See synonym study below. 2 move in a curve: *A gate swings on its hinges.* 3 hang. 4 go along with a free, swaying motion: *children swinging down a street.* 5 hit with a swinging motion: *He swung at the ball.* 6 SLANG. be satisfying, pleasing, or exciting. —*n.* 1 act or manner of swinging. 2 amount of swinging. 3 seat hung from ropes, chains, or rods, in which one may sit and swing. 4 a swinging movement or gait; steady, marked rhythm. 5 a swinging blow. 6 freedom of action; free scope. 7 movement; activity: *get into the swing of working after a vacation.* 8 a trip around a country, region, etc.; tour: *a swing through the United States.* 9 Also, **swing music.** jazz with a lively, steady rhythm, in which the players improvise freely on the original melody. **10 in full swing,** going on actively or completely; without restraint: *By five o'clock the party was in full swing.*
[Old English *swingan* to beat]
Syn. *v.i.* 1 **Swing, rock, sway** mean to move back and forth or from side to side. **Swing** applies to the movement of something hanging free or loose, and usually suggests a regular or rhythmical movement: *The lantern hanging overhead swung in the wind.* **Rock** applies to movement back and forth upon a base, either gentle *(I rocked quietly until the baby fell asleep)* or violent *(The house rocked in the storm).* **Sway** suggests an unsteady motion: *The unexpected blow caused him to sway and lose his balance. The branches sway in the breeze.*

swing er (swing′ər), *n.* person or thing that swings.

swin gle tree (swing′gəl trē′), *n.* whiffletree. [< *swingle* tool for beating flax (Old English *swingel* < *swingan* to beat) + *tree*]

swing shift, the working hours in factories, etc., between the day and night shifts, usually from 4 P.M. to midnight.

swin ish (swī′nish), *adj.* like swine; hoggish; beastly; dirty; greedy. **—swin′ish ly,** *adv.* **—swin′ish ness,** *n.*

swipe (swīp), *n., v.,* **swiped, swip ing.** —*n.* INFORMAL. a sweeping stroke; hard blow: *I made two swipes at the ball without hitting it.*

—*v.t.* 1 INFORMAL. strike with a sweeping blow. 2 SLANG. steal. [probably variant of *sweep*]

swirl (swėrl), *v.i., v.t.* 1 move or drive along with a twisting motion; whirl: *dust swirling in the air, a stream swirling over rocks.* 2 twist or curl. —*n.* 1 a swirling movement; whirl; eddy. 2 a twist or curl: *Her hat had a swirl of lace around it.* [Middle English *swirle* eddy]

swish (swish), *v.i.* move with a thin, light, hissing or brushing sound; make such a sound: *The whip swished through the air.* —*v.t.* cause to swish: *She swished the stick.* —*n.* a swishing movement or sound: *the swish of little waves on the shore.* [imitative]

Swiss (swis), *adj., n., pl.* **Swiss.** —*adj.* of or having to do with Switzerland or its people. —*n.* 1 native or inhabitant of Switzerland. 2 *pl. in use.* the people of Switzerland. 3 Swiss muslin.

Swiss chard, chard.

Swiss cheese, a firm, pale-yellow or whitish cheese with many large holes.

Swiss Guards, body of soldiers that acts as a bodyguard to the Pope in the Vatican.

Swiss muslin, kind of thin muslin often with raised dots or figures in various patterns, used especially for curtains; Swiss.

switch (def. 4)—two types of switches. Moving either lever as indicated turns the switch on.

switch (swich), *n.* 1 a slender stick used in whipping. 2 a blow with a switch; stroke; lash: *The big dog knocked a vase off the table with a switch of his tail.* 3 bunch of long hair, worn by a woman in addition to her own hair. 4 device for making or breaking a connection in an electric circuit, or for altering the connections in a circuit. 5 pair of movable rails by which a train is shifted from one track to another. 6 a change or shift: *a last-minute switch of plans.* —*v.t.* 1 whip or strike: *He switched the boys with a birch stick.* 2 move or swing like a switch: *The horse switched his tail to drive off the flies.* 3 make or break (a connection) in an electrical circuit. 4 shift (a train) from one track to another. 5 change or shift: *switch the subject. The boys switched hats.* —*v.i.* 1 shift from one railroad track to another. 2 change or shift. [probably < Low German *swutsche*] —**switch′er,** *n.*

switch back (swich′bak′), *n.* section of a railroad or highway built in a zigzag course up a steep grade.

switch blade (swich′blād′), *n.* pocketknife with a blade that springs out.

switch board (swich′bôrd′, swich′bōrd′), *n.* panel containing the necessary switches, meters, and other devices for opening, closing, combining, or controlling electric circuits. A telephone switchboard has plugs for connecting one line to another.

switch-hit ter (swich′hit′ər), *n.* a baseball player who bats either right- or left-handed.

switch man (swich′mən), *n., pl.* **-men.** man in charge of one or more railroad switches.

switch o ver (swich′ō′vər), *n.* act of switching or changing over; conversion.

switch yard (swich′yärd′), *n.* a railroad yard where cars are switched from one track to another, put together to make trains, etc.

Swit zer land (swit′sər lənd), *n.* small country in central Europe, north of Italy. 6,280,000 pop.; 15,900 sq. mi. *Capital:* Bern.

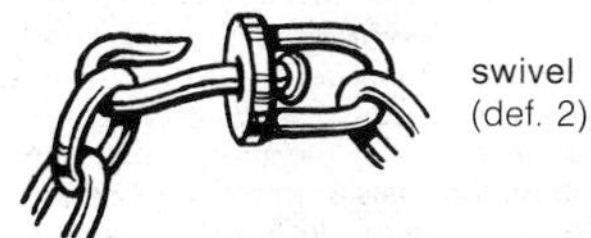

swivel (def. 2)

swiv el (swiv′əl), *n., v.,* **-eled, -el ing** or **-elled, -el ling.** —*n.* 1 a fastening that allows the thing fastened to turn round freely upon it. 2 a chain link having two parts, one of which turns freely in the other. 3 support on which a gun, chair, etc., can turn round. —*v.i., v.t.* 1 turn on a swivel. 2 swing around; rotate. 3 fasten or support by a swivel. [Middle English, related to Old English *swīfan* to move]

swivel chair, chair having a seat that turns on a swivel.

swiv et (swiv′it), *n.* SLANG. great excitement; frenzy.

swiz zle stick (swiz′əl), stick used for stirring mixed alcoholic drinks.

swob (swob), *n., v.t.,* **swobbed, swob bing.** swab. —**swob′ber,** *n.*

swol len (swō′lən), *adj.* swelled: *a swollen ankle.* —*v.* a pp. of **swell.**

swoon (swün), *v.i.* 1 faint: *swoon at the sight of blood.* 2 fade or die away gradually. —*n.* a faint. [ultimately < Old English *geswōgen* in a swoon] —**swoon′ing ly,** *adv.*

swoop (swüp), *v.i.* come down with a rush; descend in a sudden, swift attack: *The pirates swooped down on the town.* —*v.t.* snatch: *The nurse swooped up the child in her arms.* —*n.* a rapid downward rush; sudden, swift descent or attack: *With one swoop the hawk seized the chicken and flew away.* [ultimately < Old English *swāpan* to sweep] —**swoop′er,** *n.*

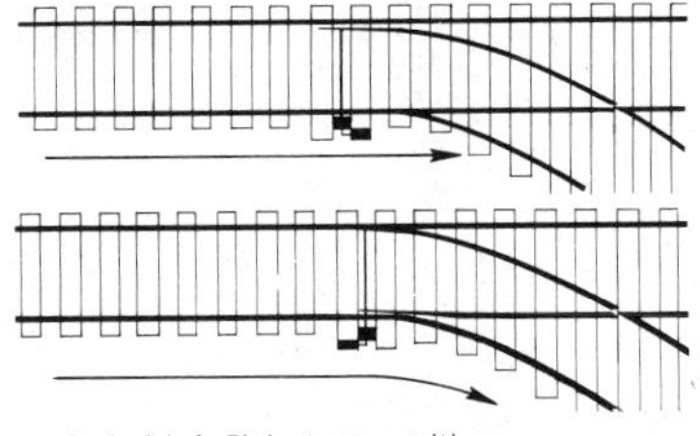

switch (def. 5) in two positions. Arrows show the direction train will travel.

swoosh (swüsh), INFORMAL. —*v.i., v.t.* move very swiftly with a whirling, brushing sound. —*n.* a swooshing movement or sound. [imitative]

swop (swop), *v.t., v.i.,* **swopped, swop ping,** *n.* swap. —**swop′per,** *n.*

sword (sôrd, sōrd), *n.* 1 weapon, usually metal, with a long, sharp blade fixed in a handle or hilt. 2 something that wounds or kills; a destroying agency. 3 **at swords' points,** very unfriendly. 4 **cross swords,** *a* fight. *b* quarrel; dispute. 5 **put to the sword,** kill with a sword; slaughter in war. 6 **the sword,** fighting, war, or military power. [Old English *sweord*] —**sword′like′,** *adj.*

sword dance, any of various dances with swords, especially naked swords laid on the ground.

hat, āge, fär; let, ēqual, tėrm;
it, īce; hot, ōpen, ôrder;
oil, out; cup, pu̇t, rüle;
ch, child; ng, long; sh, she;
th, thin; ᴛʜ, then; zh, measure;

ə represents *a* in about, *e* in taken, *i* in pencil, *o* in lemon, *u* in circus.

< = from, derived from, taken from.

sword fish (sôrd′fish′, sōrd′fish′), *n., pl.* **-fish es** or **-fish.** a very large saltwater food fish with a long, swordlike projection from its upper jaw.

swordfish—up to 15 ft. long

sword grass, any of various grasses or plants with swordlike leaves.

sword knot, a looped strap, ribbon, or the like attached to the hilt of a sword, serving as a means of supporting it from the wrist or as an ornament.

Sword of Damocles, disaster that may occur at any moment.

sword play (sôrd′plā′, sōrd′plā′), *n.* action, practice, or art of wielding a sword; fencing.

swords man (sôrdz′mən, sōrdz′mən), *n., pl.* **-men.** 1 person skilled in using a sword. 2 person using a sword.

swords man ship (sôrdz′mən ship, sōrdz′mən ship), *n.* skill in using a sword.

swore (swôr, swōr), *v.* a pt. of **swear.**

sworn (swôrn, swōrn), *v.* pp. of **swear.** —*adj.* 1 having taken an oath; bound by an oath. 2 declared, promised, etc., with an oath.

swum (swum), *v.* 1 pp. of **swim.** 2 DIALECT. a pt. of **swim.**

swung (swung), *v.* a pt. and pp. of **swing.**

syb a rite (sib′ə rīt′), *n.* person who cares very much for luxury and pleasure. [< *Sybarite,* an inhabitant of *Sybaris,* town founded by the Greeks in ancient Italy, which was known for its luxury]

syb a rit ic (sib′ə rit′ik), *adj.* luxurious; voluptuous. —**syb′a rit′i cal ly,** *adv.*

syc a more (sik′ə môr, sik′ə mōr), *n.* 1 a tall North American shade tree with broad leaves, small, round fruit and bark that breaks or peels off in tiny scales; buttonwood; plane tree. 2 a large maple tree of Europe and Asia. 3 a fig tree of Egypt and Syria. [< Latin *sycomorus* < Greek *sykomoros*]

syc o phan cy (sik′ə fən sē), *n., pl.* **-cies.** servile flattery; self-seeking flattery.

syc o phant (sik′ə fənt), *n.* a servile or self-seeking flatterer; parasite; toady. [< Latin *sycophanta* < Greek *sykophantēs* informer, slanderer]

syc o phan tic (sik′ə fan′tik), *adj.* having to do with, characteristic of, or acting as, a sycophant. —**syc′o phan′ti cal ly,** *adv.*

Syd ney (sid′nē), *n.* the largest city and most important seaport in Australia, in the SE part. 2,713,000.

sy e nite (sī′ə nīt), *n.* a gray, crystalline, igneous rock composed of feldspar and certain other minerals, such as hornblende. [< Greek *Syēnitēs (lithos)* (stone) from *Syēnē* (now Aswan) in Egypt]

syl la bar y (sil′ə ber′ē), *n., pl.* **-bar ies.** list of symbols or characters representing syllables, used in writing certain languages.

syl lab ic (sə lab′ik), *adj.* 1 of or having to do with syllables. 2 forming a separate syllable by itself. The second *l* sound in *little* is syllabic. 3 pronounced syllable by syllable. —*n.* a syllabic speech sound. **—syl lab′i cal ly,** *adv.*

syl lab i cate (sə lab′ə kāt), *v.t.,* **-cat ed, -cat ing.** syllabify. **—syl lab′i ca′tion,** *n.*

syl lab i fy (sə lab′ə fī), *v.t.,* **-fied, -fy ing.** form or divide into syllables. **—syl lab′i fi ca′tion,** *n.*

syl la ble (sil′ə bəl), *n., v.,* **-bled, -bling.** —*n.* 1 word or part of a word pronounced as a unit that usually consists of a vowel alone or a vowel with one or more consonants. The word *syllable* (sil′ə bəl) has three syllables. Certain consonant sounds may be used as a vowel sound in syllables, such as the (l) in *bottle* (bot′l) or the (n) in *hidden* (hid′n). 2 letter or group of letters representing a syllable in writing and printing. 3 the slightest bit; word: *He promised not to breathe a syllable of the secret to anyone.* —*v.t.* pronounce in syllables; utter distinctly. —*v.i.* utter syllables. [< Greek *syllabē*, originally, a taking together < *syn-* together + *lambanein* to take]

syl la bub (sil′ə bub), *n.* sillabub.

syl la bus (sil′ə bəs), *n., pl.* **-bus es, -bi** (-bī). a brief statement of the main points of a speech, a book, a course of study, etc. [< Late Latin, misreading of Greek *sillybos* parchment label]

syl lo gism (sil′ə jiz′əm), *n.* 1 a form of argument or reasoning, consisting of two propositions (the major premise and the minor premise) containing a common term, and a third proposition (the conclusion) following logically from them. EXAMPLE: All trees have roots; an oak is a tree; therefore, an oak has roots. 2 reasoning in this form; deduction. [< Greek *syllogismos*, originally, inference, ultimately < *syn-* together + *logos* a reckoning, reason]

syl lo gis tic (sil′ə jis′tik), *adj.* of or having to do with syllogism; using syllogisms. **—syl′lo gis′ti cal ly,** *adv.*

syl lo gize (sil′ə jīz), *v.i., v.t.,* **-gized, -giz ing.** 1 argue or reason by syllogisms. 2 deduce by syllogism.

sylph (silf), *n.* 1 a slender, graceful girl or woman. 2 a spirit of the air. [< New Latin *sylphes*, plural; a coinage of Paracelsus] **—sylph′like′,** *adj.*

syl van (sil′vən), *adj.* of, in, or having woods: *They lived in a sylvan retreat.* Also, **silvan.** [< Latin *sylvanus, silvanus* < *silva* forest]

syl vi cul ture (sil′və kul′chər), *adj.* silviculture.

sym., 1 symmetrical. 2 symphony.

sym bi ont (sim′bē ont, sim′bī ont), *n.* organism in a state of symbiosis.

sym bi o sis (sim′bē ō′sis, sim′bī ō′sis), *n.* 1 the association or living together of two unlike organisms for the benefit of each other. Most lichens, which are composed of an alga and a fungus, are examples of symbiosis; the alga provides the food, and the fungus provides water and protection. 2 any association or living together of two unlike organisms. [< Greek *symbiōsis* < *symbioun* live together < *syn-* together + *bios* life]

sym bi ot ic (sim′bē ot′ik, sim′bī ot′ik), *adj.* having to do with symbiosis; living in symbiosis. **—sym′bi ot′i cal ly,** *adv.*

sym bol (sim′bəl), *n., v.,* **-boled, -bol ing** or **-bolled, -bol ling.** —*n.* 1 something that stands for or represents an idea, quality, condition, or other abstraction: *The lion is the symbol of courage; the lamb, of meekness; the olive branch, of peace; the cross, of Christianity.* See **emblem** for synonym study. 2 letter, figure, or sign conventionally standing for some object, process, etc.: *The letters Hg are the symbol for the chemical element mercury. The marks +, −, ×, and ÷ are symbols for add, subtract, multiply, and divide.* —*v.t.* symbolize. [< Greek *symbolon* token, mark < *syn-* together + *ballein* to throw]

sym bol ic (sim bol′ik), *adj.* 1 used as a symbol: *A lily is symbolic of purity.* 2 of a symbol; expressed by a symbol or symbols; using symbols: *Writing is a symbolic form of expression.* **—sym bol′i cal ly,** *adv.*

sym bol i cal (sim bol′ə kəl), *adj.* symbolic.

sym bol ism (sim′bə liz′əm), *n.* 1 use of symbols; representation by symbols. 2 system of symbols: *The cross, the crown, the lamb, and the lily are parts of Christian symbolism.* 3 symbolic meaning or character.

sym bol ist (sim′bə list), *n.* 1 person who uses symbols or symbolism. 2 artist or writer who makes much use of colors, sounds, etc., as symbols. 3 person who has experience in the study or interpretation of symbols.

sym bol is tic (sim′bə lis′tik), *adj.* of symbolism or symbolists.

sym bol ize (sim′bə līz), *v.,* **-ized, -iz ing.** —*v.t.* 1 be a symbol of; stand for; represent: *A dove symbolizes peace.* 2 represent by a symbol or symbols. —*v.i.* use symbols. **—sym′bol i za′tion,** *n.* **—sym′bol iz′er,** *n.*

sym met ric (si met′rik), *adj.* symmetrical.

sym met ri cal (si met′rə kəl), *adj.* having symmetry; well-proportioned. **—sym met′ri cal ly,** *adv.*

symmetry (def. 1) top, bilateral; bottom, radial

sym me try (sim′ə trē), *n., pl.* **-tries.** 1 a regular, balanced arrangement on opposite sides of a line or plane, or around a center or axis. 2 pleasing proportions between the parts of a whole; well-balanced arrangement of parts; harmony. [< Greek *symmetria* < *syn-* together + *metron* measure]

sym pa thet ic (sim′pə thet′ik), *adj.* 1 having or showing kind feelings toward others; sympathizing. 2 approving; agreeing. 3 enjoying the same things and getting along well together. 4 harmonious; agreeable. 5 of or having to do with the sympathetic nervous system. 6 (in physics) produced in one body by transmission of vibrations of the same frequency from another body: *sympathetic vibrations.* **—sym′pa thet′i cal ly,** *adv.*

sympathetic nervous system, the part of the autonomic nervous system that produces involuntary responses opposite to those produced by the parasympathetic nervous system, such as increasing the heartbeat and slowing down activity of glands.

sym pa thize (sim′pə thīz), *v.i.,* **-thized, -thiz ing.** 1 feel or show sympathy: *sympathize with a child who has hurt himself.* 2 share in or agree with a feeling or opinion: *My mother sympathizes with my plan to be a doctor.* **—sym′pa thiz′er,** *n.* **—sym′pa thiz′ing ly,** *adv.*

sym pa thy (sim′pə thē), *n., pl.* **-thies.** 1 a sharing of another's sorrow or trouble: *We feel sympathy for a person who is ill.* See **pity** for synonym study. 2 agreement in feeling; condition or fact of having the same feeling: *The sympathy between the twins was so great that they always smiled or cried at the same things.* 3 agreement; approval; favor: *He is in sympathy with my plan.* [< Greek *sympatheia* < *syn-* together + *pathos* feeling]

sym phon ic (sim fon′ik), *adj.* 1 of, having to do with, or like a symphony: *symphonic music.* 2 of or having to do with symphony or harmony of sounds; similar in sound. **—sym phon′i cal ly,** *adv.*

sym pho ny (sim′fə nē), *n., pl.* **-nies.** 1 an elaborate musical composition for an orchestra. It usually has three or more movements in different rhythms but related keys. 2 symphony orchestra. 3 harmony of sounds. 4 harmony of colors: *In autumn the woods are a symphony in red, brown, and yellow.* [< Greek *symphōnia* harmony, concert < *syn-* together + *phōnē* voice, sound]

symphony orchestra, a large orchestra suitable for playing symphonies.

sym po si um (sim pō′zē əm), *n., pl.* **-si ums, -si a** (-zē ə). 1 a meeting or conference for the discussion of some subject: *a symposium on American foreign policy.* 2 a collection of the opinions of several persons on some subject: *This magazine contains a symposium on economics.* [< Latin < Greek *symposion* < *syn-* together + *posis* a drinking]

symp tom (simp′təm), *n.* 1 a sign or indication: *Quaking knees and paleness are symptoms of fear.* 2 a noticeable change in the normal working of the body that indicates or accompanies disease, sickness, etc.: *The doctor made his diagnosis after studying the patient's symptoms.* [< Greek *symptōma* a happening, ultimately < *syn-* together + *piptein* to fall]

symp to mat ic (simp′tə mat′ik), *adj.* 1 being a sign; signifying; indicative: *Riots are symptomatic of political or social unrest.* 2 indicating or accompanying a disease, etc.: *The infection caused a symptomatic fever.* 3 of or having to do with symptoms of disease, etc.: *symptomatic treatment.* **—symp′to mat′i cal ly,** *adv.*

syn-, *prefix.* with; together; jointly; at the same time, as in *synchronous, synthesis, synecology.* [< Greek *syn* with, together]

syn., 1 synonym. 2 synonymous.

syn a gog (sin′ə gôg, sin′ə gog), *n.* synagogue.

syn a gog i cal (sin′ə goj′ə kəl), *adj.* of or having to do with a synagogue.

syn a gogue (sin′ə gôg, sin′ə gog), *n.* 1 building used by Jews for religious worship and instruction. 2 a Jewish congregation. [< Greek *synagōgē* assembly, ultimately < *syn-* together + *agein* bring]

syn apse (si naps′, sin′aps), *n., v.,* **-apsed, -aps ing.** —*n.* place where a nerve impulse passes from one nerve cell to another. —*v.i.* form a synapse. [< Greek *synapsis* conjunction < *syn-* together + *haptein* fasten]

syn ap sis (si nap′sis), *n., pl.* **-ses** (-sēz′). 1 the union of paternal and maternal paired chromosomes, the first step in meiosis. 2 synapse.

syn ap tic (si nap′tik), *adj.* having to do with a synapsis or synapse. —**syn ap′ti cal ly,** *adv.*

sync (singk), INFORMAL. —*n.* synchronization. —*v.i., v.t.* synchronize.

syn chro cy clo tron (sing′krō sī′klə tron, sing′krō sik′lə tron), *n.* cyclotron that accelerates charged particles by changing the frequency of the alternating electric field so that it synchronizes with the particles.

syn chro flash (sing′krə flash′), *adj.* that synchronizes the flashbulb circuit with the shutter of a camera.

syn chro mesh (sing′krə mesh′), *n.* system of gears in an automobile transmission synchronized to mesh without shock or grinding when the driver shifts from one gear to another.

syn chro nism (sing′krə niz′əm), *n.* 1 occurrence at the same time; agreement in time. 2 arrangement of historical events or persons according to their dates. 3 condition of being synchronous.

syn chro nis tic (sing′krə nis′tik), *adj.* synchronous.

syn chro nize (sing′krə nīz), *v.,* **-nized, -niz ing.** —*v.i.* 1 occur at the same time; agree in time. 2 move or take place at the same rate and exactly together. —*v.t.* 1 make agree in time: *synchronize all the clocks in a building.* 2 assign to the same time or period. [< Greek *synchronizein* < *synchronos* synchronous. See SYNCHRONOUS.] —**syn′chro ni za′tion,** *n.* —**syn′chro niz′er,** *n.*

syn chro nous (sing′krə nəs), *adj.* 1 occurring at the same time; simultaneous. 2 moving or taking place at the same rate and exactly together. 3 having coincident frequency. 4 operating at a speed exactly proportional to the frequency of the applied current: *a synchronous motor.* [< Greek *synchronos* < *syn-* together + *chronos* time] —**syn′chro nous ly,** *adv.* —**syn′chro nous ness,** *n.*

synchronous satellite, an artificial satellite whose orbit is synchronous with the rotation of the earth on its axis. It orbits the earth once every 24 hours and thus appears to be stationary.

syn chro tron (sing′krə tron), *n.* particle accelerator that accelerates atomic particles to extremely high speed by increasing the magnetic field and changing the frequency of the electric field.

syn cli nal (sin klī′nl, sing′klə nəl), *adj.* of or like a syncline.

syn cline (sing′klīn), *n.* (in geology) a fold or folds of rock strata sloping downward from opposite directions so as to form a trough or inverted arch. See **anticline** for diagram. [< *syn-* together + Greek *klinein* to lean]

syn co pate (sing′kə pāt), *v.t.,* **-pat ed, -pat ing.** 1 shorten (a word) by omitting sounds or letters from the middle, as in syncopating *Gloucester* to *Gloster.* 2 in music: **a** begin (a tone) on an unaccented beat and hold it into an accented one. **b** introduce syncopation into (a passage, etc.). —**syn′co pa′tor,** *n.*

syn co pa tion (sing′kə pā′shən), *n.* 1 a syncopating. 2 a being syncopated. 3 music marked by syncopation, such as jazz or ragtime.

syn co pe (sing′kə pē), *n.* 1 contraction of a word by omitting sounds or letters from the middle, as in *ne'er* for *never.* 2 a fainting. [< Greek *synkopē,* originally, a cutting off, ultimately < *syn-* together + *koptein* to cut]

syn dic (sin′dik), *n.* 1 person who manages the business affairs of a university or other corporation. 2 magistrate. [< Middle French, chief representative < Late Latin *syndicus* < Greek *syndikos* advocate < *syn-* together + *dikē* justice]

syn di cal (sin′də kəl), *adj.* 1 of or having to do with syndicalism. 2 of or having to do with a syndic.

syn di cal ism (sin′də kə liz′əm), *n.* movement to put industry and government under the control of labor unions by means of a general strike, violence, etc.

syn di cal ist (sin′də kə list), *n.* person who favors and supports syndicalism.

syn di cate (*n.* sin′də kit; *v.* sin′də kāt), *n., v.,* **-cat ed, -cat ing.** —*n.* 1 a combination of persons or companies formed to carry out some undertaking, especially one requiring a large capital investment. 2 agency that sells special articles, photographs, comic strips, etc., to a large number of newspapers or magazines for publication at the same time. 3 group of criminals that organize and control criminal activities, such as gambling, prostitution, traffic in narcotics, etc. —*v.t.* 1 combine into a syndicate. 2 manage by a syndicate. 3 publish through a syndicate: *a syndicated newspaper columnist.* —*v.i.* unite in a syndicate. —**syn′di ca′tion,** *n.* —**syn′di ca′tor,** *n.*

syn drome (sin′drōm), *n.* group of signs and symptoms considered together as characteristic of a particular disease. [< Greek *syndromē* < *syndromos* running together < *syn-* together + *dramein* to run]

syne (sīn), *adv., prep., conj.* SCOTTISH. since.

syn ec do che (si nek′də kē), *n.* figure of speech by which a part is put for the whole, or the whole for a part, the special for the general, or the general for the special, or the like. EXAMPLES: a factory employing 500 *hands* (persons); to eat of the *tree* (its fruit); a *Solomon* (wise man); a *marble* (a statue) on its pedestal. [< Greek *synekdochē,* ultimately < *syn-* with + *ex-* out + *dechesthai* receive]

syn e col o gist (sin′ə kol′ə jist), *n.* an expert in synecology.

syn e col o gy (sin′ə kol′ə jē), *n.* branch of ecology dealing with communities as distinguished from individual species.

syn er gic (si nėr′jik), *adj.* synergistic.

syn er gism (sin′ər jiz′əm, si nėr′jiz′əm), *n.* the combined action of different agents or organs, producing a greater effect than the sum of the various individual actions. [< Greek *synergein* work together < *syn-* together + *ergon* work]

syn er gis tic (sin′ər jis′tik), *adj.* of, having to do with, or producing synergism.

syn ga my (sing′gə mē), *n.* the union of two cells, as of gametes in fertilization.

Synge (sing), *n.* **John Millington,** 1871-1909, Irish dramatist and poet.

syn od (sin′əd), *n.* 1 assembly called together under authority to discuss and decide church affairs; a church council. 2 court of the Presbyterian Church ranking next above the presbytery. 3 any assembly, convention, or council. [< Greek *synodos* assembly, meeting < *syn-* together + *hodos* a going]

hat, āge, fär; let, ēqual, tėrm;
it, īce; hot, ōpen, ôrder;
oil, out; cup, pu̇t, rüle;
ch, child; ng, long; sh, she;
th, thin; ᴛʜ, then; zh, measure;

ə represents *a* in about, *e* in taken,
i in pencil, *o* in lemon, *u* in circus.

< = from, derived from, taken from.

syn od al (sin′ə dəl), *adj.* having to do with a synod.

syn od ic (si nod′ik), *adj.* synodical.

syn od i cal (si nod′ə kəl), *adj.* 1 having to do with the conjunction of two heavenly bodies, especially with respect to the sun. The synodical period of the moon is the time between one new moon and the next. 2 synodal.

syn o nym (sin′ə nim), *n.* 1 word having a meaning that is the same or nearly the same as that of another word. *Keen* is a synonym of *sharp.* 2 word or expression generally accepted as another name for something: *Albert Einstein's name has become a synonym for scientific genius.* [< Greek *synōnymon* < *syn-* together + *onyma* name]

syn o nym i ty (sin′ə nim′ə tē), *n.* quality of being synonymous.

syn on y mous (si non′ə məs), *adj.* having the same or nearly the same meaning. *Little* and *small* are synonymous. —**syn on′y mous ly,** *adv.*

syn on y my (si non′ə mē), *n., pl.* **-mies.** 1 a being synonymous; equivalence in meaning. 2 study of synonyms. 3 use or coupling of synonyms in discourse for emphasis or amplification. 4 set, list, or system of synonyms.

syn op sis (si nop′sis), *n., pl.* **-ses** (-sēz′). a brief statement giving a general view of some subject, book, play, etc.; summary. [< Greek < *syn-* together + *opsis* a view]

syn op tic (si nop′tik), *adj.* 1 giving a general view. 2 Often, **Synoptic.** taking a common view. *Matthew, Mark,* and *Luke* are called the **Synoptic Gospels** because they are much alike in content, order, and statement. —**syn op′ti cal ly,** *adv.*

syn op ti cal (si nop′tə kəl), *adj.* synoptic.

syn o vi a (si nō′vē ə), *n.* a viscid, clear lubricating liquid secreted by certain membranes, such as those of the joints. [< New Latin, a coinage of Paracelsus]

syn o vi al (si nō′vē əl), *adj.* of or secreting synovia.

syn tac tic (sin tak′tik), *adj.* syntactical.

syn tac ti cal (sin tak′tə kəl), *adj.* of or having to do with syntax; in accordance with the rules of syntax. —**syn tac′ti cal ly,** *adv.*

syn tax (sin′taks), *n.* 1 construction or use of a word, phrase, or clause in a sentence. 2 sentence structure; arrangement of the words of a sentence in their proper forms and relations. 3 part of grammar dealing with this. [< Greek *syntaxis,* ultimately < *syn-* together + *tassein* arrange]

syn the sis (sin′thə sis), *n., pl.* **-ses** (-sēz′). 1 combination of parts or elements into a whole: *a synthesis of various cultures in a nation.* 2 formation of a compound from its elements, or simpler compounds, by one or more chemical reactions. Alcohol, ammonia, and rubber can be artificially produced by synthesis. [< Greek < *syntithenai* combine < *syn-* together + *tithenai* to put]

syn the size (sin′thə sīz), *v.t.,* **-sized, -siz ing.** 1 combine into a complex whole. 2 make up by combining parts or elements. 3 treat synthetically. **—syn′the siz′er,** *n.*

syn thet ic (sin thet′ik), *adj.* 1 of, having to do with, or involving synthesis: *synthetic chemistry.* 2 made artificially by chemical synthesis. Nylon is a synthetic material. See **artificial** for synonym study. 3 not real or genuine: *synthetic laughter.* 4 (in linguistics) characterized by the use of affixes and inflectional endings rather than by the use of separate words, such as auxiliary verbs and prepositions, to express the same idea. Latin is a synthetic language, while English is analytic. For example, the Latin *amabitur* expresses in one word the English *he will be loved.* —*n.* **synthetics,** *pl.* man-made substances formed by chemical synthesis. Plastics are synthetics. **—syn thet′i cal ly,** *adv.*

syn thet i cal (sin thet′ə kəl), *adj.* synthetic.

syph i lis (sif′ə lis), *n.* a contagious venereal disease, caused by a spirochete, that proceeds in three stages, first affecting some local part, then the skin, and finally the bones, internal organs, brain, and spinal cord. [< New Latin < *Syphilus,* hero of a poem *Syphilis,* in which this disease is described, by Girolamo Fracastoro, 1483-1553, Italian physician and poet]

syph i lit ic (sif′ə lit′ik), *adj.* 1 having to do with syphilis. 2 affected with syphilis. —*n.* person who has syphilis.

sy phon (sī′fən), *n., v.t., v.i.* siphon.

Syr a cuse (sir′ə kyüz, sir′ə kyüs), *n.* 1 city in central New York State. 197,000. 2 city in SE Sicily, founded by the Greeks in 734 B.C. 105,000.

Syr i a (sir′ē ə), *n.* 1 country in W Asia, south of Turkey. Syria was formerly under the supervision of France; it was joined with Egypt from 1958 to 1961 in the United Arab Republic. 6,100,000 pop.; 71,800 sq. mi. *Capital:* Damascus. See **Iran** for map. 2 ancient country north of Palestine and Arabia. **—Syr′i an,** *adj., n.*

Syr i ac (sir′ē ak), *adj.* of or having to do with Syria or its language. —*n.* the ancient Semitic language of Syria, a dialect of Aramaic.

sy rin ga (sə ring′gə), *n.* any of a genus of shrubs of the same family as the saxifrage, with fragrant white flowers blooming in early summer; mock orange; philadelphus. [< New Latin < Greek *syrinx, syringos* shepherd's pipe]

syringe (def. 1)

sy ringe (sə rinj′, sir′inj), *n., v.,* **-ringed, -ring ing.** —*n.* 1 a narrow tube fitted with a plunger or rubber bulb for drawing in a quantity of fluid and then forcing it out in a stream. Syringes are used for cleaning wounds, injecting fluids into the body, etc. 2 hypodermic syringe. —*v.t.* clean, wash, inject, etc., by means of a syringe. [< Greek *syrinx, syringos* shepherd's pipe]

syr inx (sir′ingks), *n., pl.* **sy rin ges** (sə-rin′jēz′), **syr inx es.** 1 panpipe. 2 the vocal organ of birds, situated at or near the division of the trachea into the right and left bronchi. [< Greek, shepherd's pipe]

syr up (sir′əp, sėr′əp), *n.* 1 sugar boiled in water or fruit juice: *cherries canned in syrup.* 2 solution of sugar in a medicated liquid: *cough syrup.* 3 a sweet, thick liquid obtained in the manufacture of sugar, glucose, cornstarch, sorghum, etc., such as molasses, corn syrup, and maple syrup. Also, **sirup.** [< Old French *sirop* < Arabic *sharāb* a drink] **—syr′up like′,** *adj.*

syr up y (sir′ə pē, sėr′ə pē), *adj.* 1 like syrup in consistency or sweetness. 2 having to do with syrup. Also, **sirupy.**

sys tem (sis′təm), *n.* 1 set of things or parts forming a whole: *a mountain system, a railroad system.* 2 an ordered group of facts, principles, beliefs, etc.: *a system of government, a system of education.* 3 plan, scheme, or method: *a system for betting, a system of classification.* 4 an orderly way of getting things done: *She works by a system, not by chance.* 5 set of organs or parts in the body having the same or similar structure, or serving to perform some function: *the nervous system, the digestive system.* 6 the body as a whole: *His sickness weakened his entire system.* 7 group of heavenly bodies forming a whole that follows certain natural laws. 8 (in geology) a major division of rocks ranking above a series, containing the rocks formed during a geological period. [< Greek *systēma* < *synistanai* bring together < *syn-* together + *histanai* to stand, place] **—sys′tem less,** *adj.*

sys tem at ic (sis′tə mat′ik), *adj.* 1 according to a system; having a system, method, or plan: *a systematic procedure.* 2 orderly in arranging things or in getting things done: *a systematic worker.* See **orderly** for synonym study. **—sys′tem at′i cal ly,** *adv.*

sys tem at i cal (sis′tə mat′ə kəl), *adj.* systematic.

sys tem a tize (sis′tə mə tīz), *v.t.,* **-tized, -tiz ing.** arrange according to a system; make into a system; make more systematic. **—sys′tem a ti za′tion,** *n.* **—sys′tem a-tiz′er,** *n.*

sys tem ic (si stem′ik), *adj.* 1 having to do with a particular system of parts or organs of the body: *a systemic lesion, a systemic poison.* 2 having to do with or affecting the body as a whole: *systemic circulation.* 3 of or having to do with a system. **—sys tem′i cal ly,** *adv.*

sys tem ize (sis′tə mīz), *v.t.,* **-ized, -iz ing.** systematize. **—sys′tem i za′tion,** *n.*

sys to le (sis′tl ē), *n.* the normal rhythmical contraction of the heart, especially that of the ventricles, when blood is pumped from the heart into the arteries. [< Greek *systolē* contraction < *syn-* together + *stellein* to put]

sys tol ic (si stol′ik), *adj.* having to do with systole.

Szcze cin (shchet′sēn′), *n.* seaport in NW Poland. 335,000. Also, GERMAN **Stettin.**

Sze chwan (se′chwän′), *n.* province in SW China, east of Tibet.

Szi lard (zil′ärd, zə lärd′), *n.* **Leo,** 1898-1964, American atomic physicist, born in Hungary.

T t

hat, āge, fär; let, ēqual, tėrm;
it, īce; hot, ōpen, ôrder;
oil, out; cup, pu̇t, rüle;
ch, child; ng, long; sh, she;
th, thin; ᴛʜ, then; zh, measure;

ə represents *a* in about, *e* in taken, *i* in pencil, *o* in lemon, *u* in circus.

< = from, derived from, taken from.

T[1] or **t** (tē), *n., pl.* **T's** or **t's.** 1 the 20th letter of the English alphabet. 2 **to a T,** exactly; perfectly: *That suits me to a T.*

T[2] (tē), *n., pl.* **T's.** anything shaped like the letter T.

T, tritium.

t., 1 in the time of [for Latin *tempore*]. 2 teaspoon or teaspoons. 3 temperature. 4 tenor. 5 tense. 6 territory. 7 time. 8 ton or tons.

T., 1 tablespoon or tablespoons. 2 Territory. 3 Testament. 4 ton or tons. 5 Tuesday.

Ta, tantalum.

TA or **T.A.,** 1 teaching assistant. 2 toxin-antitoxin. 3 Transit Authority.

tab (tab), *n., v.,* **tabbed, tab bing.** *—n.* 1 a small flap, strap, loop, or piece: *a fur cap with tabs over the ears.* 2 a small extension of or attachment to a card, used for labeling, numbering, coding, etc., in filing. 3 a label. 4 (in aeronautics) an auxiliary control surface set into or attached to a larger one, as to a rudder. 5 INFORMAL. a bill or check: *pick up the tab.* 6 **keep tab on** or **keep tabs on,** INFORMAL. keep track of; keep watch on; check: *Please keep tab on the children while I'm out.* *—v.t.* 1 put a tab on (something). 2 to name, mark, or identify. [origin uncertain]

tabard (def. 1)

tab ard (tab′ərd), *n.* 1 a short, loose coat worn by heralds, emblazoned with the arms of their sovereign. 2 mantle worn over armor by knights, generally embroidered with the arms of the wearer. 3 a coarse outer garment worn by the poor during the Middle Ages. [< Old French *tabart*]

Ta bas co (tə bas′kō), *n.* 1 trademark for a kind of peppery sauce, used on fish, meat, etc., prepared from the fruit of a variety of capsicum. 2 state in SE Mexico.

tab by (tab′ē), *n., pl.* **-bies,** *adj.* *—n.* 1 a gray or tawny cat with dark stripes. 2 a female cat. 3 an old maid; spinster. 4 a spiteful female gossip. 5 any silk cloth with a wavy pattern or marking, as silk taffeta. *—adj.* 1 gray or tawny with dark stripes. 2 like tabby. 3 made of the fabric tabby. [< French *tabis* < Arabic *'attābi* silk taffeta]

tab er nac le (tab′ər nak′əl), *n.* 1 a temporary dwelling; tent. 2 the human body thought of as the temporary dwelling of the soul. 3 place of worship for a large congregation. 4 a Jewish temple; synagogue. 5 **Tabernacle,** the covered wooden framework carried by the Jews for use as a place of worship during their journey from Egypt to Palestine. 6 recess covered with a canopy and used as a shrine. 7 container for something holy or precious; container for the consecrated bread used in the Mass. [< Latin *tabernaculum* tent < *taberna* cabin]

ta ble (tā′bəl), *n., v.,* **-bled, -bling.** *—n.* 1 piece of furniture having a smooth, flat top on legs. 2 food served; fare: *She sets a good table.* 3 the persons seated around a table, especially at a dinner or for informal discussion. 4 tableland. 5 information in a very brief, tabulated form; list: *a table of contents in front of a book, the multiplication table.* 6 in architecture: **a** a horizontal molding, especially a cornice. **b** panel (of a wall). 7 the flat surface at the top of a jewel. 8 a thin, flat piece of wood, stone, metal, etc.; tablet: *The Ten Commandments were written on tables of stone.* 9 matter inscribed or written on tables. 10 **turn the tables,** reverse conditions or circumstances completely. *—v.t.* 1 make a list or statement in tabulated form. 2 put on a table. 3 U.S. put off discussing (a bill, motion, etc.) until a future time. [Old English *tabule, tabele* < Latin *tabula* slab for writing or painting]

tab leau (tab′lō), *n., pl.* **-leaux** (-lōz), **-leaus.** 1 a striking scene; picture. 2 representation of a picture, statue, scene, etc., by a person or group posing in appropriate costume. [< French, diminutive of *table* table]

ta ble cloth (tā′bəl klôth′, tā′bəl kloth′), *n., pl.* **-cloths** (-klôᴛʜz′, -klôths′; -kloᴛʜz′, -kloths′). cloth for covering a table.

ta ble d'hôte (tä′bəl dōt′; tab′əl dōt′), a meal served at a fixed time and price. In meals table d'hôte, there is one price for the whole meal; in meals à la carte, a person chooses what he wants and pays for each article. [< French, literally, host's table]

ta ble land (tā′bəl land′), *n.* a large, high plain; plateau; table.

table linen, tablecloths, napkins, doilies, and mats.

table salt, ordinary salt for use at table; salt (def. 1).

ta ble spoon (tā′bəl spün′), *n.* 1 any large spoon used to serve vegetables, etc., at the table. 2 spoon used in cookery as a unit of measure and holding three times as much as a teaspoon. 3 tablespoonful.

ta ble spoon ful (tā′bəl spün′fu̇l), *n., pl.* **-fuls.** 1 unit of volume used in cookery, equal to $^1/_2$ fluid ounce or 3 teaspoonfuls. 2 as much as a tablespoon holds.

tab let (tab′lit), *n.* 1 a small, flat sheet of stone, wood, ivory, etc., used to write or draw on. The ancient Romans used tablets as we use pads of paper. 2 number of sheets of writing paper fastened together at the edge; pad. 3 a small, flat surface with an inscription. 4 a small, flat piece of medicine: *aspirin tablets.* [< Old French *tablete* < *table* < Latin *tabula* slab]

table talk, conversation at meals.

table tennis, game played on a large table marked somewhat like a tennis court, using small wooden rackets and a light, hollow, plastic ball; Ping-Pong.

ta ble top (tā′bəl top′), *n.* the upper surface of a table. *—adj.* designed to be used on a tabletop.

ta ble ware (tā′bəl wer′, tā′bəl war′), *n.* dishes, knives, forks, spoons, etc., used at meals.

tab loid (tab′loid), *n.* a newspaper, usually having half the ordinary size newspaper page, that has many pictures, short articles, and large, often sensational, headlines. *—adj.* in the form of a summary, capsule, or digest; condensed. [< *Tabloid,* trademark for drugs concentrated in tablets]

ta boo (tə bü′), *adj., v., n., pl.* **-boos.** *—adj.* 1 forbidden by custom or tradition; prohibited; banned. 2 set apart as sacred or cursed. Among the Polynesians certain things, places, and persons are taboo. *—v.t.* make taboo; forbid; prohibit; ban. *—n.* 1 a prohibition; ban. 2 system or act of setting things apart as sacred or cursed. Also, **tabu.** [< Tongan *tabu*]

➤ **taboo, tabu.** *Taboo* is more generally used than *tabu,* except in anthropology.

ta bor (tā′bər), *n.* a small drum, used especially by a person playing a pipe or fife to accompany himself. *—v.i.* beat or play on a tabor. [< Old French *tabour* < Persian *tabīr*] **—ta′bor er,** *n.*

ta bor et or **ta bour et** (tab′ər it, tab′ə-ret′), *n.* 1 stool. 2 a small, low stand or table. 3 frame for embroidery. 4 ARCHAIC. a small tabor.

Ta briz (tä brēz′), *n.* city in NW Iran. 468,000.

ta bu (tə bü′), *adj., v., n.* taboo. ➤ See **taboo** for usage note.

tab u lar (tab′yə lər), *adj.* 1 of or having to do with tables or lists; arranged in lists; written or printed in columns. 2 (of a quantity) read from or calculated by means of tables. 3 flat like a table: *a tabular rock.* [< Latin *tabularis* < *tabula* slab] **—tab′u lar ly,** *adv.*

ta bu la ra sa (tab′yə lə rä′sə), LATIN. 1 the mind before it is developed and changed by experience. 2 (literally) an erased wax tablet.

tab u late (*v.* tab′yə lāt; *adj.* tab′yə lit, tab′yə lāt), *v.,* **-lat ed, -lat ing,** *adj.* *—v.t., v.i.* arrange (facts, figures, etc.) in tables or lists. *—adj.* shaped like a table or a tablet.

tab u la tion (tab′yə lā′shən), *n.* arrangement in tables or lists.

tab u la tor (tab′yə lā′tər), *n.* 1 person or thing that tabulates. 2 a typewriter attachment for spacing figures in neat columns. 3 a computing machine that takes in punch cards and instructions and produces lists, totals, and tabulations of the information on separate forms or on continuous paper.

tac a ma hac (tak′ə mə hak), *n.* 1 an aromatic gum resin used in incenses, ointments, etc. 2 any tree yielding such a product, especially the balsam poplar. [< Spanish *tacamahaca* < Nahuatl *tecamaca*]

ta chis to scope (tə kis′tə skōp), *n.* apparatus which briefly or rapidly exposes to view an object or group of objects, as letters, words, etc., used especially in experimental psychology. [< Greek *tachistos* swiftest, superlative of *tachys* swift]

ta chom e ter (tə kom′ə tər), *n.* instrument for measuring the speed of rotation of a shaft, wheel, etc. [< Greek *tachos* speed]

tac it (tas′it), *adj.* 1 implied or understood without being openly expressed; implicit: *His eating the food was a tacit confession that he liked it.* 2 unspoken; silent: *a tacit prayer.* [< Latin *tacitum* < *tacere* be silent] **—tac′it ly,** *adv.* **—tac′it ness,** *n.*

tac i turn (tas′ə tėrn′), *adj.* speaking very little; not fond of talking. See **silent** for synonym study. [< Latin *taciturnus* < *tacitum* unspoken, tacit] **—tac′i turn′ly,** *adv.*

tac i tur ni ty (tas′ə tėr′nə tē), *n.* habit of keeping silent; disinclination to talk much.

Tac i tus (tas′ə təs), *n.* A.D. 55?-120?, Roman historian.

tack[1] (tak), *n.* 1 a short, sharp-pointed nail with a broad, flat head: *carpet tacks.* 2 stitch used as a temporary fastening. 3 in nautical use: **a** a zigzag course against the wind. **b** the direction in which a ship moves in regard to the direction of the wind and the position of her sails. On port tack, a ship is close-hauled with the wind on her left. **c** one of the movements in a zigzag course. **d** act of zigzagging; turn from one direction to the next. 4 any zigzag movement. 5 course of action or conduct. 6 in nautical use: **a** rope to hold in place the outer lower corner of some sails. **b** corner to which such a rope is fastened. 7 saddles, harnesses, and other equipment for horses.
—*v.t.* 1 fasten with tacks: *tack up a notice.* 2 sew with temporary stitches. 3 join together, often artificially or clumsily. 4 attach; add: *She tacked a postscript to the end of her letter.* 5 in nautical use: **a** sail (a ship) in a zigzag course against the wind. **b** turn (a ship) to sail at the same angle to the wind on the other side; change from one leg of a zigzag course to the next. —*v.i.* 1 in nautical use: **a** sail zigzag into the wind. **b** turn and sail at the same angle to the wind on the other side. 2 move along any zigzag route. 3 change one's attitude, conduct, or course of action.
[< Anglo-French *taque* nail, clasp; of Germanic origin] **—tack′er,** *n.*

tack[2] (tak), *n.* SLANG. food. [origin uncertain]

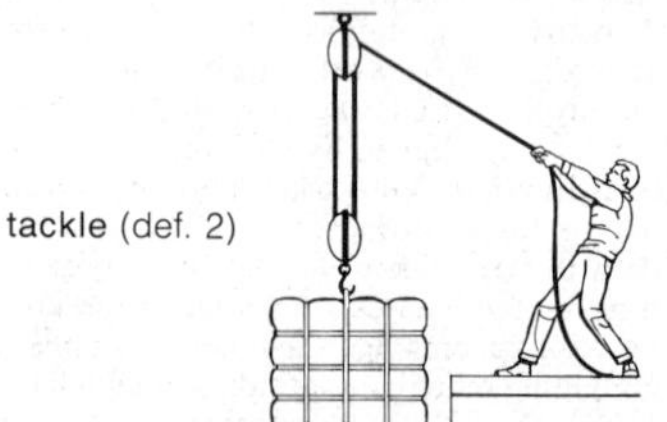
tackle (def. 2)

tack le (tak′əl), *n., v.,* **-led, -ling.** —*n.* 1 equipment; apparatus; gear. Fishing tackle means the rod, line, hooks, etc. 2 set of ropes and pulleys for lifting, lowering, or moving heavy things. The sails of a ship are raised and moved by tackle. 3 act of tackling. 4 an offensive or defensive player between the guard and the end on either side of the line in football. —*v.t.* 1 try to deal with: *a difficult problem to tackle.* 2 lay hold of; seize or attack: *He tackled the thief and threw him.* 3 (in football) seize and stop, or throw to the ground (an opponent who has the ball). 4 harness (a horse). [probably < Middle Low German *takel*] **—tack′ler,** *n.*

tack y[1] (tak′ē), *adj.,* **tack i er, tack i est.** very sticky or gummy; adhesive. [< *tack*[1]]

tack y[2] (tak′ē), *adj.,* **tack i er, tack i est.** INFORMAL. shabby; dowdy. [origin uncertain]

TAFFRAIL
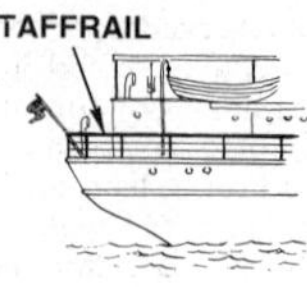

ta co (tä′kō), *n., pl.* **-cos.** tortilla filled with chopped meat, chicken, cheese, etc., and served hot. [< Mexican Spanish]

Ta co ma (tə kō′mə), *n.* 1 seaport in W washington, on Puget Sound. 155,000. 2 **Mount,** Mount Rainier.

tac o nite (tak′ə nīt), *n.* kind of rock which is about 30 per cent iron ore, occurring especially in the Mesabi Range. [< *Taconic* mountains in western New England]

tact (takt), *n.* ability to say and do the right things; skill in dealing with people or handling difficult situations; diplomacy. [< Latin *tactus* sense of feeling < *tangere* to touch]

tact ful (takt′fəl), *adj.* 1 having tact; diplomatic. 2 showing tact. **—tact′ful ly,** *adv.* **—tact′ful ness,** *n.*

tac tic (tak′tik), *n.* 1 detail of military tactics; maneuver. 2 any skillful move; gambit. —*adj.* (in biology) of or having to do with taxis.

tac ti cal (tak′tə kəl), *adj.* 1 of or having to do with tactics. 2 having to do with the disposal of military or naval forces in action against an enemy. 3 organized for or used in action against enemy troops, rather than against enemy bases, industry, etc., behind the lines of battle: *tactical air force.* 4 characterized by skillful procedure, methods, or expedients. **—tac′ti cal ly,** *adv.*

tac ti cian (tak tish′ən), *n.* an expert in tactics.

tac tics (tak′tiks), *n.* 1 *pl. in form, sing. in use.* art or science of disposing military or naval forces in action. 2 *pl. in form and use.* the operations themselves. 3 *pl. in form and use.* procedures to gain advantage or success; methods. [< New Latin *tactica* < Greek *taktikē (technē)* (art of) arranging] ➤ See **strategy** for usage note.

tac tile (tak′təl), *adj.* 1 of or having to do with touch. 2 having the sense of touch. 3 that can be felt by touch; tangible. [< Latin *tactilis* < *tangere* to touch]

tac til i ty (tak til′ə tē), *n.* a being tactile.

tact less (takt′lis), *adj.* 1 without tact: *a tactless person.* 2 showing no tact: *a tactless reply.* **—tact′less ly,** *adv.* **—tact′less ness,** *n.*

tac tu al (tak′chü əl), *adj.* 1 of or having to do with touch; tactile. 2 caused by or due to touch. 3 causing touch; giving sensations of touch. [< Latin *tactus* tact] **—tac′tu al ly,** *adv.*

tad pole (tad′pōl′), *n.* a very young frog or toad in the larval stage when it lives in water and has gills, a long tail, and no limbs; polliwog. [Middle English *taddepol* < *tadde* toad + *pol* poll (head)]

Ta dzhik S.S.R. (tä jēk′), one of the constituent republics of the U.S.S.R., in the S part. 2,900,000 pop.; 54,800 sq. mi. *Capital:* Dyushambe.

tael (tāl), *n.* 1 any of several east Asian units of weight, especially one equal to 1$^1/_3$ ounces avoirdupois. 2 a former Chinese unit of money, originally a tael, in weight, of silver. [< Portuguese < Malay *tahil*]

ta'en (tān), *v.* ARCHAIC. taken.

taf fe ta (taf′ə tə), *n.* 1 a light, stiff silk cloth with a smooth, glossy surface. 2 a similar cloth of linen, rayon, etc. [< Middle French < Persian *tāftah* silk or linen]

taff rail (taf′rāl′), *n.* a rail around a ship's stern. [< Dutch *tafereel* panel, diminutive of *tafel* table]

taf fy (taf′ē), *n., pl.* **-fies.** 1 kind of chewy candy made of brown sugar or molasses boiled down, often with butter; toffee. 2 INFORMAL. flattery. [origin uncertain]

Taft (taft), *n.* 1 **Robert Alphonso,** 1889-1953, American political leader, son of William Howard Taft. 2 **William Howard,** 1857-1930, the 27th president of the United States, from 1909 to 1913, and chief justice of the Supreme Court, from 1921 to 1930.

Taft-Hart ley Act (taft′härt′lē), act passed by Congress in 1947, governing the rights and duties of labor and management in strikes and other labor disputes.

tag[1] (tag), *n., v.,* **tagged, tag ging.** —*n.* 1 card or small piece of card, paper, leather, etc., tied or fastened to something, especially as a label: *Each coat in the store has a tag with the price marked on it.* 2 a small hanging piece; loosely attached piece; loose end; tatter. 3 a binding, usually of metal, on the end of a shoelace, string, etc., to make it pass easily through eyelets. 4 quotation, moral, etc., added for ornament or emphasis. 5 the last line or lines of a song, play, actor's speech, etc. 6 a radioactive tracer. —*v.t.* 1 add for ornament or emphasis. 2 furnish with a tag or tags. 3 INFORMAL. follow closely: *The dog tagged them all the way home.* —*v.i.* trail along; follow: *The younger children tagged after the older ones.* [origin uncertain]

tag[2] (tag), *n., v.,* **tagged, tag ging.** —*n.* 1 a children's game in which the player who is "it" chases the others until he touches one. The one touched is then "it" and must chase the others. 2 (in baseball) the act of touching a base runner with the ball, or a base with the foot while holding the ball, to make a putout. —*v.t.* 1 touch or tap with the hand. 2 in baseball: **a** touch (a base runner) with the ball to make a putout. **b** touch (a base) with the foot while holding the ball to make a putout. —*v.i.* **tag up,** (of a runner in baseball) stay on or return to the base occupied until after a fly ball is caught, before advancing to the next base. [origin uncertain]

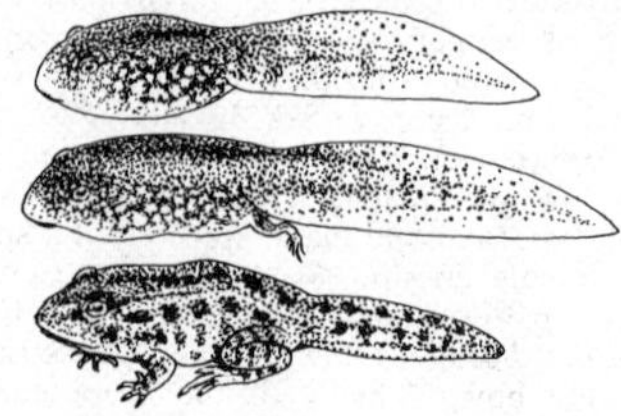
tadpole at different stages of growth

Ta ga log (tä gä′log), *n.* 1 member of the chief Malay people in the Philippines. 2 their language, a form of which is the official language of the Philippines.

tag day, U.S. day when contributions to a certain charity are solicited and contributors are each given a tag to wear.

tag end, the very end; last part.

hat, āge, fär; let, ēqual, tėrm;
it, īce; hot, ōpen, ôrder;
oil, out; cup, pu̇t, rüle;
ch, child; ng, long; sh, she;
th, thin; ᴛʜ, then; zh, measure;

ə represents *a* in about, *e* in taken, *i* in pencil, *o* in lemon, *u* in circus.

< = from, derived from, taken from.

tag line, 1 the last part of an actor's speech or of a play; tag. 2 a punch line. 3 a catch phrase, as in advertising.

Ta gore (tə gôr′, tə gōr′), *n.* Sir **Rabindranath,** 1861-1941, Hindu poet and philosopher.

Ta gus River (tā′gəs), river flowing through central Spain and Portugal into the Atlantic. 565 mi.

Ta hi ti (tə hē′tē), *n.* one of the Society Islands of French Polynesia, in the S Pacific. 62,000 pop.; 400 sq. mi. See **Melanesia** for map.

Ta hi tian (tə hē′shən), *adj.* of or having to do with Tahiti, its people, or their language. —*n.* 1 native or inhabitant of Tahiti. 2 the Polynesian language of Tahiti.

Ta hoe (tä′hō), *n.* **Lake,** mountain lake in NE California and W Nevada. 200 sq. mi.

Tai (tī), *adj., n.* Thai.

tai ga (tī′gə), *n.* 1 the swampy, coniferous, evergreen forest land of subarctic Siberia, between the tundra and the steppes. 2 the similar forest land in North America. [< Russian *tajga*]

tail (tāl), *n.* 1 the hindmost part of an animal's body, especially when prolonged beyond the back of the main part as a separate, flexible appendage. 2 something like an animal's tail: *the tail of a kite.* 3 the hind part of anything; back; rear; conclusion: *the tail of a cart.* 4 the part of an airplane at the rear of the fuselage, which includes the stabilizers and fins to which the elevators and rudders are hinged. 5 a luminous trail of small particles extending from the head of a comet. 6 a long braid or tress of hair. 7 INFORMAL. person who follows another to watch and report on his movements. 8 **tails,** *pl.* INFORMAL. **a** the reverse side of a coin. **b** coat with long tails, worn on formal occasions. **c** full dress. 9 **turn tail,** run away from danger, trouble, etc. 10 **with one's tail between one's legs,** afraid, humiliated, or dejected.
—*v.t.* 1 furnish with a tail. 2 form the tail of; follow close behind. 3 INFORMAL. follow closely and secretly, especially in order to watch or prevent escaping. 4 fasten (a timber) by an end in a wall, etc. 5 join (one thing) to the end of another. —*v.i.* 1 form a tail: *Some of the children tailed after the parade.* 2 gradually stop; die away; diminish; subside: *The protests tailed off into only an occasional mutter.* 3 (of a timber) be held by an end in a wall, etc.
—*adj.* 1 at the tail, back, or rear. 2 coming from behind: *a tail wind.*
[Old English *tægel*] **—tail′less,** *adj.* **—tail′like′,** *adj.*

tail back (tāl′bak′), *n.* (in football) the offensive halfback whose position is farthest back from the line of scrimmage.

tail board (tāl′bôrd′, tāl′bōrd′), *n.* tailgate of a truck or wagon.

-tailed, *combining form.* having a ____ tail: *Short-tailed = having a short tail.*

tail end, 1 the hindmost, lowest, or concluding part of anything. 2 the end or tip of a tail.

tail gate (tāl′gāt′), *n., v.,* **-gat ed, -gat ing.** —*n.* board at the back end of a wagon, truck, station wagon, etc., that can be let down or removed when loading or unloading. —*v.i., v.t.* drive too close to the vehicle ahead of one.

tail ing (tā′ling), *n.* 1 part of a projecting stone or brick built into a wall. 2 **tailings,** *pl.* any residue or rejects; leavings; scraps.

tail lamp, taillight.

tail light (tāl′līt′), *n.* a warning light, usually red, at the back end of a vehicle.

tai lor (tā′lər), *n.* person whose business is making, altering, or mending clothes. —*v.t.* 1 make by tailor's work: *The suit was well tailored.* 2 fit or furnish with clothes made by a tailor. 3 make specially to fit; adjust; adapt. —*v.i.* make or mend clothes. [< Anglo-French *taillour* < Late Latin *taliare* to cut]

tai lor bird (tā′lər bėrd′), *n.* any of several small songbirds of Asia and Africa that stitch leaves together to form and hide their nests.

tai lor ing (tā′lər ing), *n.* 1 business or work of a tailor. 2 clothes or workmanship of a tailor.

tai lor-made (tā′lər mād′), *adj.* 1 made by, or as if by, a tailor; simple and fitting well. 2 made to fit a certain person, object, or purpose.

tail piece (tāl′pēs′), *n.* 1 piece added at or forming the end. 2 (in printing) a small decorative engraving, usually at the end of a chapter. 3 a triangular piece of wood near the lower end of a violin, etc., to which strings are fastened. 4 a short beam or rafter built into a wall and supported by a header.

tail pipe, 1 the intake pipe of a suction pump. 2 the exhaust pipe of an automobile, bus, truck, or airplane.

tail race (tāl′rās′), *n.* part of a millrace below the water wheel that leads the water away.

tail spin (tāl′spin′), *n.* 1 a downward movement of an airplane with the nose first and the tail spinning in a circle above. 2 INFORMAL. mental confusion or agitation; panic.

tail wind, wind blowing toward the direction in which a ship or aircraft is moving.

taint (tānt), *n.* 1 a stain or spot; trace of decay, corruption, or disgrace. 2 a cause of any such condition; contaminating or corrupting influence. —*v.t.* give a taint to; spoil, corrupt, or contaminate. —*v.i.* become tainted; decay. [< Old French *teint,* past participle of *teindre* to dye < Latin *tingere*] **—taint′less,** *adj.*

Tai pei or **Tai peh** (tī′pā′), *n.* capital of Taiwan, in the N part. 1,700,000.

Tai wan (tī′wän′), *n.* island off SE China, the seat after 1949 of the Chinese nationalist government. 14,672,000 pop.; 13,900 sq. mi. *Capital:* Taipei. Also, **Formosa.**

Tai wa nese (tī′wä nēz′), *n., pl.* **-nese,** *adj.* —*n.* native or inhabitant of Taiwan. —*adj.* of Taiwan or its people.

Taiwan Strait, Formosa Strait.

Taj Ma hal (täj′ mə häl′), mausoleum of white marble at Agra, in northern India, built by a Mogul ruler in the 1600's.

take (tāk), *v.,* **took, tak en, tak ing,** *n.* —*v.t.* 1 lay hold of; grasp: *He took her by the hand.* 2 seize; capture: *take a fortress, take someone prisoner.* 3 accept: *take a bet. Take my advice.* 4 get; receive: *She took the gifts and opened them.* 5 win: *take first prize.* 6 have; get: *take a seat.* 7 obtain from a source; derive: *Washington, D.C., takes its name from George Washington.* 8 absorb: *Wool takes a dye well. Oak takes a high polish.* 9 make use of; use: *take medicine. We took a train to Boston.* 10 receive into the body; swallow: *take food, take a drink.* 11 extract; quote: *a passage taken from Keats.* 12 indulge in: *take a nap, take a vacation.* 13 submit to; put up with: *take hard punishment.* 14 study: *take history.* 15 need; require: *The trip takes five hours.* 16 pick out; choose; select: *Take the shortest way home.* 17 carry away; remove: *Please take the wastebasket away and empty it.* 18 remove by death: *Pneumonia took him.* 19 subtract; deduct: *If you take 2 from 7, you have 5.* 20 lead: *Where will this road take me?* 21 go with; escort: *Take her home.* 22 carry; convey: *Take your lunch.* 23 obtain by some special method; do; make: *Please take my photograph.* 24 form and hold in mind; feel: *take pride in one's work.* 25 find out: *The doctor took my temperature.* 26 understand: *How did you take her remark?* 27 suppose: *I take it that the train is late.* 28 consider; regard; view: *take an example.* 29 assume; undertake: *take all the blame, take charge of a household.* 30 engage; lease; hire: *We have taken a cottage for the summer.* 31 write down; record: *take dictation, take minutes at a meeting.* 32 receive and pay for regularly: *take a magazine.* 33 (in grammar) be used with: *A plural noun takes a plural verb.* 34 become affected by: *take cold.* 35 please; attract; charm: *The new song took our fancy.* 36 SLANG. swindle; cheat. —*v.i.* 1 catch hold; lay hold: *The fire has taken.* 2 become: *take sick.* 3 remove something; lessen; detract: *The billboards take from the scenery.* 4 have effect; act: *The inoculation took.* 5 win favor: *Do you think the new play will take?* 6 (of a plant, seed, or graft) begin to grow; strike root.

take after, **a** follow (someone's) example. **b** be like; resemble.

take back, withdraw; retract.

take down, **a** write down. **b** pull down; dismantle.

take for, suppose to be: *be taken for one's sister.*

take in, **a** receive; admit: *take in boarders.* **b** do (work) at home for pay: *take in laundry.* **c** understand. **d** visit or attend: *take in a party.* **e** make smaller; tighten. **f** deceive; cheat; trick. **g** include; comprise.

take it out on, INFORMAL. relieve one's anger or annoyance by scolding or hurting.

take off, **a** leave the ground or water: *The airplane took off.* **b** INFORMAL. give an amusing imitation of; mimic. **c** INFORMAL. rush away.

take on, **a** engage; hire. **b** undertake to deal with: *take on an opponent.* **c** acquire: *take on the appearance of health.* **d** show great excitement, grief, etc.

take out, **a** remove: *take a book out, take out a stain.* **b** apply for and obtain (a license, patent, etc.). **c** escort.

take over, take the ownership or control of.

take to, **a** form a liking for; become fond of. **b** take up; adopt. **c** adapt.

take up, **a** soak up; absorb: *A sponge takes up liquid.* **b** begin; undertake: *take up law.* **c** tighten, especially to shorten: *take up a dress.* **d** lift; pry up: *take up a stone.* **e** adopt (an idea, purpose, etc.).

take up with, INFORMAL. begin to associate or be friendly with.

—*n.* 1 act of taking. 2 that which is taken. 3 SLANG. receipts; profits: *the box-office take.* 4 scene or sequence photographed or televised at one time. 4 act of making a photograph or a scene in a motion picture or television program. 6 act or process of making a recording for a record, tape, etc. 7 record or tape of this. 8 the amount taken: *a great take of fish.* 9 act of transplanting or grafting.
[< Scandinavian (Old Icelandic) *taka*]
—tak′er, *n.*

take down (tāk′doun′), *n.* 1 act of taking down. 2 fact of being taken down. 3 rifle or similar firearm that can be taken apart and reassembled readily. 4 the nut, bolt, joint, etc., between its parts. 5 (in wrestling) the act or process of forcing an opponent to the mat. 6 INFORMAL. act of humiliating. —*adj.* easy to take apart and put back together; collapsible.

take-home pay (tāk′hōm′), wages or salary remaining after taxes, insurance fees, etc., have been deducted.

tak en (tā′kən), *v.* pp. of **take.**

take off (tāk′ôf′, tāk′of′), *n.* 1 the leaving of the ground in leaping or in beginning a flight in an airplane; taking off. 2 the place or point at which one takes off. 3 act of starting out. 4 INFORMAL. an amusing imitation; mimicking; caricature.

take out (tāk′out′), *n.* 1 that which is taken out or removed. 2 a magazine article printed on full and successive pages and easily removable as a unit.

take o ver (tāk′ō′vər), *n.* a taking over; seizure of ownership or control: *a takeover of a country by the military.*

tak est (tā′kist), *v.* ARCHAIC. take. "Thou takest" means "you take."

tak eth (tā′kith), *v.* ARCHAIC. takes.

take-up (tāk′up′), *n.* 1 any taking up. 2 a gather in a dress. 3 machine or device for tightening slack ropes, etc., or absorbing waste motion.

tak ing (tā′king), *adj.* 1 attractive or pleasing; winning: *a taking smile.* 2 INFORMAL. infectious. —*n.* 1 act of one who takes. 2 condition of being taken. 3 something that is taken. 4 **takings,** *pl.* money taken in; receipts. 5 **in a taking,** in an agitated state of mind.

talc (talk), *n.* a soft, smooth mineral, a hydrated silicate of magnesium, usually consisting of slippery, translucent sheets of white, apple-green, or gray, used in making face powder, chalk, etc. [< Medieval Latin *talcum* < Arabic *talq*]

tal cum (tal′kəm), *n.* 1 talcum powder. 2 talc.

talcum powder, powder made of purified, usually perfumed white talc, for use on the face and body.

tale (tāl), *n.* 1 story, especially a made-up story. See **story**[1] for synonym study. 2 falsehood; lie. 3 piece of gossip or scandal. 4 number; count: *His tale of sheep amounted to over three hundred.* 5 **tell tales,** spread gossip or scandal. [Old English *talu*]

tale bear er (tāl′ber′ər, tāl′bar′ər), *n.* person who spreads gossip or scandal; telltale.

tale bear ing (tāl′ber′ing, tāl′bar′ing), *n.* the spreading of gossip or scandal. —*adj.* spreading gossip or scandal.

tal ent (tal′ənt), *n.* 1 a special natural ability; aptitude; gift: *a talent for music.* See **ability** for synonym study. 2 person or persons with talent. 3 an ancient unit of weight or money, varying with time and place. [< Latin *talentum* (definition 3) < Greek *talanton*]

tal ent ed (tal′ən tid), *adj.* having natural ability; gifted.

talent scout, person whose work is discovering talented people, as for motion pictures, professional athletics, etc.

ta ler (tä′lər), *n., pl.* **-ler.** thaler.

tales man (tālz′mən, tā′lēz mən), *n., pl.* **-men.** person chosen from among the bystanders or those present in court to serve on a jury when too few of those originally summoned are qualified to be on a jury. [< Medieval Latin *tales (de circumstantibus)* such (of the bystanders) + English *man*]

tale tell er (tāl′tel′ər), *n.* 1 talebearer. 2 teller of tales or stories; narrator.

Ta lien (tä′lyen′), *n.* former treaty port in NE China, now part of **Lüta.** It was also called **Dairen.**

tal i pes (tal′ə pēz′), *n.* any of various foot defects, especially congenital ones, as clubfoot. [< New Latin < Latin *talus* ankle + *pes* foot]

tal is man (tal′i smən, tal′iz mən), *n., pl.* **-mans.** 1 stone, ring, etc., engraved with figures or characters supposed to have magic power; charm. 2 anything that acts as a charm. [< French < Arabic *tilsam* < Greek *telesma* initiation into the mysteries < *telein* perform]

tal is man ic (tal′i sman′ik, tal′iz man′ik), *adj.* having to do with or serving as a talisman.

talk (tôk), *v.i.* 1 use words to express feelings or ideas; speak: *A child learns to talk.* 2 exchange words; converse. 3 consult; confer: *talk with one's doctor.* 4 spread rumors; gossip: *talk behind one's back.* 5 spread ideas by other means than speech; communicate: *talk by signs.* 6 speak idly; chatter away; prate. 7 make sounds that resemble speech: *The birds were talking loudly.* 8 give an informal speech. 9 INFORMAL. reveal secret information; inform: *The prisoner talked to the police.* —*v.t.* 1 use in speaking: *talk French, talk sense.* 2 bring, put, drive, influence, etc., by talk; persuade: *talk her into waiting.* 3 speak about; discuss: *talk business.* See **say** for synonym study.

talk back, INFORMAL. answer rudely or disrespectfully.

talk down, a make silent by talking louder or longer. b belittle; disparage.

talk down to, speak to in a superior tone.

talk out, discuss thoroughly.

talk over, a consider together; discuss. b persuade or convince by arguing.

talk up, talk earnestly in favor of.

—*n.* 1 use of words; speech. 2 conversation, especially when familiar, empty, or idle: *mere talk.* 3 an informal speech. 4 way of talking: *baby talk.* 5 conference; council: *summit talks.* 6 gossip or rumor: *There is talk of it.* 7 subject for conversation or gossip: *She is the talk of the town.*

[Middle English *talken.* Related to TELL[1].]

talk a tive (tô′kə tiv), *adj.* having the habit of talking a great deal; fond of talking. **—talk′a tive ly,** *adv.* **—talk′a tive ness,** *n.*

Syn. Talkative, loquacious mean talking much. **Talkative,** the common word, emphasizes a fondness for talking and having the habit of talking a great deal: *He is a merry, talkative old man who knows everybody on our street.* **Loquacious,** a formal word, adds the idea of talking smoothly and easily and suggests a steady stream of words: *The president of the club is a loquacious woman.*

talk er (tô′kər), *n.* 1 person who talks; speaker. 2 a talkative person.

talk fest (tôk′fest′), *n.* INFORMAL. a long talk, discussion, or debate.

talk ie (tô′kē), *n.* a motion picture with a synchronized sound track.

talking book, a phonograph record or tape recording of a book, article, etc., for blind persons.

talking machine, phonograph.

talking picture, talkie.

talking point, subject for talk, especially something to use as an argument.

talk ing-to (tô′king tü′), *n., pl.* **-tos.** INFORMAL. a scolding; reprimand.

tall (tôl), *adj.* 1 higher than the average; having great height: *a tall building.* See **high** for synonym study. 2 of the specified height: *six feet tall.* 3 INFORMAL. high or large in amount; extravagant: *a tall price.* 4 INFORMAL. hard to believe; exaggerated: *a tall tale.* —*adv.* 1 SLANG. in an exaggerated manner: *talk tall.* 2 INFORMAL. with the head high; proudly: *walk tall.* [Old English *(ge)tæl* prompt, active] **—tall′ness,** *n.*

Tal la has see (tal′ə has′ē), *n.* capital of Florida, in the N part. 73,000.

Tall chief (tol′chēf), *n.* **Maria,** born 1925, American ballet dancer.

Tal ley rand (tal′ē rand), *n.* 1754-1838, French statesman and diplomat, noted for his craftiness. His full name was Charles Maurice de Talleyrand-Périgord.

Tal linn or **Tal lin** (täl′in), *n.* capital of the Estonian S.S.R., a seaport on the Gulf of Finland. 363,000.

tall ish (tô′lish), *adj.* 1 inclining toward tallness; rather tall. 2 somewhat exaggerated: *a tallish tale.*

tal lith (tal′ith, tä′lis), *n., pl.* **tal liths, tal li thim** (tal′ə thēm′, tä lä′sim). a fringed mantle or shawl of wool, silk, or linen, worn by Jewish men at morning prayer. [< Hebrew *tallīth*]

tall oil (täl), a resinous liquid by-product of the manufacture of pine wood pulp, used in making soap, varnish, etc. [< Swedish *tallolja,* literally, pine oil]

tal low (tal′ō), *n.* the hard fat from sheep, cows, etc., used for making candles, soap, etc. —*v.t.* grease with tallow. [Middle English *talgh*]

tal low y (tal′ō ē), *adj.* 1 like tallow; fat; greasy. 2 yellowish-white; pale.

tal ly (tal′ē), *n., pl.* **-lies,** *v.,* **-lied, -ly ing.** —*n.* 1 stick in which notches are cut to represent numbers, formerly used to show the amount of a debt or payment. 2 anything on which a score or account is kept. 3 notch or mark made on a tally; mark made for a certain number of objects in keeping account. 4 account; reckoning. 5 (in sports) a scoring point; run, goal, etc. 6 number or group, used in tallying; lot: *The dishes were counted in tallies of 20.* 7 a distinguishing mark; label; tag. 8 anything corresponding to a certain other thing; duplicate; counterpart. 9 correspondence; agreement.

—*v.t.* 1 mark on a tally; count up. 2 mark with an identifying label; tag. 3 cause to fit, suit, or correspond. 4 (in sports) score. —*v.i.* 1 correspond; agree: *Your version tallies with mine.* 2 (in sports) make scoring points.
[< Medieval Latin *tallia* < Late Latin *talea* a cutting, rod]

hat, āge, fär; let, ēqual, tėrm; it, īce; hot, ōpen, ôrder; oil, out; cup, pu̇t, rüle; ch, child; ng, long; sh, she; th, thin; ᴛʜ, then; zh, measure;

ə represents *a* in about, *e* in taken, *i* in pencil, *o* in lemon, *u* in circus.

< = from, derived from, taken from.

tallyho (def. 1)

tal ly ho (*n.* tal′ē hō′; *interj.* tal′ē hō′), *n., pl.* **-hos,** *interj.* —*n.* 1 coach drawn by four horses. 2 a sounding of "tallyho" by a hunter. —*interj.* a hunter's cry on catching sight of the fox. [alteration of French *taïaut*]

tal ly man (tal′ē mən), *n., pl.* **-men.** 1 man who keeps a tally. 2 man who makes entries on a tally.

Tal mud (tal′məd), *n.* a collection of sixty-three volumes containing the Jewish civil and canonical law in the form of interpretation and expansion of the teachings of the Old Testament. [< Hebrew *talmūd* instruction]

Tal mud ic (tal mü′dik), *adj.* of or having to do with the Talmud.

Tal mud i cal (tal mü′də kəl), *adj.* Talmudic.

Tal mud ist (tal′mə dist), *n.* person who knows much about the Talmud.

tal on (tal′ən), *n.* 1 claw of an animal, especially a bird of prey. 2 a clawlike, grasping finger. 3 **talons,** *pl.* clawlike fingers; grasping hands. [< Old French, heel, ultimately < Latin *talus* ankle]

ta lus[1] (tā′ləs), *n., pl.* **-li** (-lī). 1 the human anklebone; astragalus. 2 the human ankle. [< Latin]

ta lus[2] (tā′ləs), *n.* 1 a sloping mass of rocky fragments that has fallen from a cliff. 2 any slope. [< French]

tam (tam), *n.* tam-o'-shanter.

ta ma le (tə mä′lē), *n.* a Mexican food made of corn meal and minced meat, seasoned with red peppers, wrapped in cornhusks, and roasted or steamed. [< Mexican Spanish < Nahuatl *tamalli*]

tam a rack (tam′ə rak′), *n.* 1 a North American larch tree which yields strong, heavy timber; hackmatack. 2 its wood. [of Algonquian origin]

tam a rind (tam′ə rind′), *n.* 1 a tropical evergreen tree of the pea family, grown for its fruit, its fragrant yellow flowers streaked with red, and its hard, heavy, yellowish wood. 2 its fruit, a brown pod with juicy, acid pulp, used in foods, drinks, and medicine. [< Arabic *tamr hindī* date of India]

tam a risk (tam′ə risk′), *n.* any of a genus of ornamental shrubs or small trees with slender, feathery branches. [< Late Latin *tamariscus*]

Ta ma yo (tä mä′yō), *n.* **Rufino,** born 1899, Mexican painter.

tam bour (tam′bu̇r), *n.* 1 drum. 2 pair of hoops, one fitting within the other, for holding cloth stretched for embroidering. 3 embroidery done on this. —*v.t., v.i.* embroider on a tambour. [< French < Arabic *ṭanbūr*]

tam bou rine (tam′bə rēn′), *n.* a small, shallow drum with only one head, and jingling metal disks around the side, played by striking it with the knuckles or by shaking it; timbrel.

tame (tām), *adj.,* **tam er, tam est,** *v.,* **tamed, tam ing.** —*adj.* 1 taken from the wild state and made obedient; domesticated: *a tame bear.* 2 without fear; not wild; gentle: *The squirrels are very tame.* 3 without spirit; dull: *a tame story.* —*v.t.* 1 make tame; break in. 2 deprive of spirit, courage, or interest; make dull. 3 reduce in strength; tone down; subdue. —*v.i.* become tame. [Old English *tam*] —**tame′a ble, tam′a ble,** *adj.* —**tame′ly,** *adv.* —**tame′ness,** *n.* —**tam′er,** *n.*

tame less (tām′lis), *adj.* that has never been tamed; that cannot be tamed. —**tame′less ness,** *n.*

Tam er lane (tam′ər lān), *n.* 1333?-1405, Mongol conqueror of most of southern and western Asia.

Tam il (tam′əl), *n.* 1 a Dravidian language spoken in southern India and part of Ceylon. 2 one of the people who speak this language.

Tamm (täm), *n.* **Igor Yevgenevich,** 1895-1971, Russian physicist.

Tam ma ny (tam′ə nē), *n.* an influential organization of Democratic politicians of New York City, founded as a fraternal and benevolent society in 1789, notorious for corruption in the 1800's. —*adj.* of or having to do with this organization, its politics, methods, or members.

tam-o'-shanter

tam-o'-shan ter (tam′ə shan′tər), *n.* a soft, woolen cap, originally of Scotland, with a flat, round crown and often with a tassel. Also, **tam.** [< *Tam o' Shanter,* the hero of a poem by Robert Burns]

tamp (tamp), *v.t.* 1 pack down or in by a series of light blows: *tamp the earth about a newly planted tree.* 2 (in blasting) fill (the hole containing explosive) with dirt, etc. [< *tampion*]

Tam pa (tam′pə), *n.* seaport in W Florida. 278,000.

tam per (tam′pər), *v.i.* 1 meddle improperly; meddle: *Do not tamper with the lock.* See **meddle** for synonym study. 2 **tamper with, a** influence improperly; bribe; corrupt: *Crooked politicians had tampered with the jury.* **b** change so as to damage or falsify. [ultimately variant of *temper*] —**tam′per er,** *n.*

Tam pi co (tam pē′kō), *n.* seaport in E Mexico. 196,000.

tandem (def. 3)

tam pi on (tam′pē ən), *n.* 1 a wooden plug placed in the muzzle of a gun that is not being used, to keep out dampness and dust. 2 plug for the top of a stopped organ pipe. [< Middle French *tampon*]

tam pon (tam′pon), *n.* plug of cotton, etc., inserted in a body cavity or wound to stop bleeding, absorb secretions, etc. —*v.t.* fill or plug with a tampon. [< French]

tam-tam (tum′tum′, tam′tam′), *n.* 1 a large gong, especially one used in a symphony orchestra. 2 tom-tom.

tan (tan), *adj.,* **tan ner, tan nest,** *n., v.,* **tanned, tan ning.** —*adj.* yellowish-brown. —*n.* 1 a yellowish brown. 2 the brown color of a person's skin resulting from being in the sun and air. 3 liquid used in tanning hides, usually containing tannin. 4 tanbark. —*v.t.* 1 brown (the skin) by exposure to sun and air. 2 make (a hide) into leather by soaking in a special liquid, especially one containing tannin. 3 INFORMAL. thrash or beat in punishment. —*v.i.* become brown by exposure to sun and air. [< Medieval Latin *tannum* tanbark]

tan or **tan.,** tangent.

tan a ger (tan′ə jər), *n.* any of a family of small American songbirds of the same order as the finches. The males are usually brilliantly colored. [< Tupi *tangara*]

Ta na na rive (tä nä nä rēv′), *n.* capital of the Malagasy Republic, in the central part. 322,000.

tan bark (tan′bärk′), *n.* 1 crushed bark of oak, hemlock, etc., containing tannin and used in tanning hides; tan. Riding tracks and circus rings are often covered with used tanbark. 2 a riding track or circus ring so covered.

tandem (def. 2)

tan dem (tan′dəm), *adv.* one behind the other: *drive horses tandem.* —*adj.* having animals, seats, parts, etc., arranged one behind the other. —*n.* 1 two horses harnessed tandem. 2 carriage drawn by two horses so harnessed. 3 Also, **tandem bicycle.** bicycle with two seats, one behind the other. 4 truck or other vehicle with two attached parts, as a cab for pulling and a trailer to carry the load. 5 **in tandem, a** one behind the other: *mounted in tandem.* **b** closely together; in cooperation: *partners working in tandem on a project.* [< Latin, at length < *tam* so]

Ta ney (tô′nē), *n.* **Roger Brooke,** 1777-1864, American jurist, who served as chief justice of the United States Supreme Court from 1836 to 1864.

tang[1] (tang), *n.* 1 a strong taste or flavor: *the tang of mustard.* 2 a distinctive flavor or quality. 3 a slight touch or suggestion; trace. 4 a characteristic odor: *the salt tang of sea* *air.* 5 a long, slender projecting point, strip, or prong on a chisel, file, etc., that fits into the handle. [< Scandinavian (Old Icelandic) *tangi* point]

tang² (tang), *n.* a sharp, ringing sound. —*v.i., v.t.* make a sharp, ringing sound. [imitative]

tang³ (täng), *n.* any of several large, coarse seaweeds. [< Scandinavian (Danish) *tang*]

Tang or **T'ang** (täng), *n.* a Chinese dynasty from A.D. 618 to 907, under which China expanded toward central Asia, Buddhism gained its political influence, printing was invented, and poetry reached its finest development.

Tan gan yi ka (tang′gə nyē′kə), *n.* 1 former British trust territory and later country in E Africa, now part of Tanzania. 2 **Lake,** lake in central Africa between Zaïre and Tanzania, with parts extending into Burundi and Zambia. 450 mi. long; 12,700 sq. mi. —**Tan′gan yi′kan,** *adj., n.*

tan gen cy (tan′jən sē), *n.* quality or condition of being tangent.

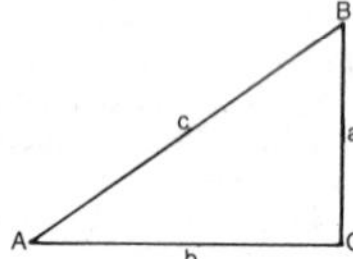

tangent (def. 2)
Triangle ABC is a right triangle in which angle C is the right angle and side c is the hypotenuse;
the tangent of angle A is a/b
the cotangent of angle A is b/a;
the tangent of angle B is b/a
the cotangent of angle B is a/b.

tan gent (tan′jənt), *adj.* 1 in contact; touching. 2 (in geometry) touching a curve or surface at one point but not intersecting. These circles are tangent: ∞. —*n.* 1 a tangent line, curve, or surface. 2 (in trigonometry) the ratio of the length of the side opposite an acute angle in a right triangle to the length of the side adjacent to the acute angle. 3 (in geometry) the part of a line tangent to a curve from the point of tangency to the horizontal axis. 4 **fly off at a tangent** or **go off at a tangent,** change suddenly from one course of action or thought to another. [< Latin *tangentem*]

tan gen tial (tan jen′shəl), *adj.* 1 of or having to do with a tangent. 2 being a tangent. 3 in the direction of a tangent. 4 wandering off the subject; digressive; diverging. 5 slightly connected with a subject; scarcely relevant or pertinent. —**tan gen′tial ly,** *adv.*

tan ge rine (tan′jə rēn′), *n.* a small, reddish-orange citrus fruit with a very loose peel and segments that separate easily. It is a kind of mandarin which is widely grown in the United States. [< French *Tanger* Tangier]

tan gi bil i ty (tan′jə bil′ə tē), *n.* quality or condition of being tangible.

tan gi ble (tan′jə bəl), *adj.* 1 that can be touched or felt by touch: *A chair is a tangible object.* 2 real; actual; definite: *a tangible improvement, tangible evidence.* 3 whose value can be accurately appraised: *Real estate is tangible property.* —*n.* 1 something tangible. 2 a tangible property, asset, etc. [< Late Latin *tangibilis* < *tangere* to touch] —**tan′gi ble ness,** *n.* —**tan′gi bly,** *adv.*

Tan gier (tan jir′), *n.* seaport in Morocco, on the Strait of Gibraltar. 166,000.

tan gle (tang′gəl), *v.,* **-gled, -gling,** *n.* —*v.t.* 1 twist and twine together in a confused mass; entangle; snarl: *The kitten had tangled the ball of twine.* 2 involve in something that hampers or obstructs. 3 bewilder; confuse. —*v.i.* be or become tangled. —*n.* 1 a confused or tangled mass. 2 a bewildering confusion; mess: *a tangle of contradictory statements.* [probably ultimately < Scandinavian (dialectal Swedish) *taggla* disorder] —**tan′gle ment,** *n.*

tan gly (tang′glē), *adj.* full of tangles; tangled.

tan go (tang′gō), *n., pl.* **-gos,** *v.* —*n.* 1 a Spanish-American dance with long, gliding steps and many figures and poses. 2 music for it. —*v.i.* dance the tango. [< American Spanish]

tang y (tang′ē), *adj.,* **tang i er, tang i est.** having a tang.

tank (tangk), *n.* 1 a large container for a liquid or gas. 2 a heavily armored combat vehicle carrying machine guns and usually a cannon, moving on an endless track on each side. —*v.t.* put or store in a tank. [apparently < Hindustani *tankh* cistern; the armored vehicle was originally labeled "tank," for reasons of military security]

tank age (tang′kij), *n.* 1 capacity of a tank or tanks. 2 storage in tanks. 3 price charged for storage in tanks. 4 fertilizer and coarse feed made in slaughterhouses of carcasses after their fat has been rendered.

tank ard (tang′kərd), *n.* a large drinking mug with a handle and a hinged cover. [Middle English]

tank car, a railroad car with a tank for carrying liquids or gases.

tank er (tang′kər), *n.* ship, airplane, or truck with tanks for carrying oil, jet fuel, or other liquid freight.

tank farm, group of storage tanks around an oil field or refinery.

tank ful (tangk′fu̇l), *n., pl.* **-fuls.** as much as a tank will hold.

tank town, U.S. 1 a small town where trains stop mainly to get water. 2 INFORMAL. any small town.

tan nage (tan′ij), *n.* 1 act or process of tanning. 2 product of tanning.

tan nate (tan′āt), *n.* a salt or ester of tannic acid.

tan ner (tan′ər), *n.* person whose work is tanning hides.

tan ner y (tan′ər ē), *n., pl.* **-ner ies.** place where hides are tanned.

Tann häu ser (tän′hoi zər), *n.* (in German legends) a knight and poet who, after a time of wicked pleasure, was refused pardon by the pope.

tan nic (tan′ik), *adj.* 1 of or like tannin. 2 obtained from tanbark.

tannic acid, tannin.

tan nin (tan′ən), *n.* any of various acid substances obtained from the bark or galls of oaks, etc., and from certain other plants, used in tanning, dyeing, making ink, and in medicine. [< French *tanin* < *tanner* to tan]

tan ning (tan′ing), *n.* 1 the converting of hide or skins into leather. 2 a making brown, as by exposure to sun. 3 INFORMAL. a beating; thrashing; whipping.

tan sy (tan′zē), *n., pl.* **-sies.** a coarse, strong-smelling, bitter-tasting plant of the composite family, with notched, divided leaves and clusters of small yellow flowers, formerly much used as a seasoning and medicine. [< Old French *tanesie* < Late Latin *athanasia* < Greek, immortality]

tan ta lize (tan′tl īz), *v.t.,* **-lized, -liz ing.** torment or tease by keeping something desired in sight but out of reach, or by holding out hopes that are repeatedly disappointed. [< *Tantalus*] —**tan′ta li za′tion,** *n.* —**tan′ta liz′er,** *n.* —**tan′ta liz′ing ly,** *adv.*

tan ta lum (tan′tl əm), *n.* a hard, ductile, lustrous, grayish-white metallic element that occurs with niobium in certain rare minerals, and is very resistant to corrosion, used as an alloy in nuclear reactors and in surgical and dental equipment. *Symbol:* Ta; *atomic number* 73. See pages 326 and 327 for table. [< *Tantalus* (because it cannot absorb acid though immersed in it)]

Tan ta lus (tan′tl əs), *n.* (in Greek myths) a king and son of Zeus, punished in the lower world by having to stand up to his chin in water, under branches laden with fruit, yet each receding from his reach whenever he tried to drink or eat.

tan ta mount (tan′tə mount), *adj.* equivalent: *The withdrawal of his statement is tantamount to an apology.* See **equal** for synonym study. [< Anglo-French *tant amunter* amount to as much]

tan tar a (tan tar′ə, tan′tər ə), *n.* 1 a flourish or blast of a trumpet or horn; fanfare. 2 any similar sound. [imitative]

tankard

tan tiv y (tan tiv′ē), *interj., n., pl.* **-tiv ies,** *adv., adj., v.,* **-tiv ied, -tiv y ing.** —*interj.* full gallop! (a cry in hunting). —*n.* 1 a ride at full gallop; rush. 2 a hunting cry when in full gallop. —*adv., adj.* at full gallop; headlong. —*v.i.* ride at full gallop; rush. [perhaps imitative of hoofbeats]

tan trum (tan′trəm), *n.* INFORMAL. fit of bad temper or ill humor. [origin uncertain]

Tan za ni a (tan′zə nē′ə), *n.* country in E Africa, a member of the Commonwealth of Nations, consisting of Tanganyika and the adjacent islands of Zanzibar and Pemba. 13,300,000 pop.; 362,000 sq. mi. *Capital:* Dar es Salaam. —**Tan′za ni′an,** *adj., n.*

Tao ism (tou′iz′əm, dou′iz′əm), *n.* 1 one of the three main religions of China, believed to have been founded by Lao-tse, that teaches natural simplicity and humility as a way to peace and harmony in life. 2 system of philosophy on which this religion was based. [< Chinese *tao* the way]

Tao ist (tou′ist, dou′ist), *n.* believer in Taoism. —*adj.* of or belonging to Taoists or Taoism.

Tao is tic (tou is′tik, dou is′tik), *adj.* Taoist.

tap¹ (tap), *v.,* **tapped, tap ping,** *n.* —*v.t.* 1 strike lightly, often audibly: *tap him on the shoulder.* 2 cause to strike lightly: *She tapped her foot on the floor.* 3 make, put, etc., by light blows: *tap a rhythm, tap out a message, tap the ashes out of a pipe.* 4 repair (the heel or sole of a shoe) with leather. 5 select; choose. —*v.i.* strike lightly: *Tap on the door.* —*n.* 1 a light blow, often audible: *There was a tap at the door.* 2 sound of a light blow. 3 piece of leather added to the bottom of a shoe to repair it. 4 a small steel plate on a shoe to reduce wear or to make a louder tap in tap-dancing. [< Old French *taper*] **—tap′per,** *n.*

tap[2] (tap), *n., v.,* **tapped, tap ping.** *—n.* 1 stopper or plug to close a hole in a cask containing liquids. 2 faucet. 3 liquor taken from a tap. 4 a certain kind or quality of liquor. 5 INFORMAL. a room where liquor is sold and drunk; bar. 6 **on tap, a** ready to be let out of a keg, cask, or barrel and be served. **b** ready for use; on hand; available. 7 point in an electric circuit where a connection is or can be made. 8 tool for cutting screw threads on the inner surface of a cylinder or opening. 9 wiretap.
—v.t. 1 make a hole in to let out liquid: *They tapped the sugar maples when the sap began to flow.* 2 draw the plug from; pierce: *tap a cask.* 3 let out (liquid) by piercing or drawing a plug. 4 furnish with a tap. 5 let out liquid from by surgery. 6 make (resources, reserves, etc.) accessible; open up; penetrate: *This highway taps a large district.* 7 wiretap. 8 make an internal screw thread in a pipe, etc.).
[Old English *tæppa*] **—tap′per,** *n.*

ta pa (tä′pə), *n.* 1 an unwoven cloth of the Pacific islands, made by soaking and pounding the inner bark of a mulberry tree. 2 this bark. [< Polynesian]

tap dance, dance in which the steps are accented by loud taps of the foot, toe, or heel.

tap-dance (tap′dans′), *v.i.,* **-danced, -danc ing.** do a tap dance. **—tap′danc′er,** *n.*

tape (tāp), *n., v.,* **taped, tap ing.** *—n.* 1 a long, narrow, woven strip of cotton, linen, etc., used to make loops and bind seams. 2 a long, narrow, flexible strip of other material. Surveyors measure with a steel tape. 3 ticker tape. 4 magnetic tape. 5 adhesive tape. 6 tape recording. 7 strip, string, etc., stretched across a racetrack at the finish line. *—v.t.* 1 fasten with tape; wrap with tape. 2 measure with a tape measure. 3 record on magnetic tape: *tape a television program.* [Old English *tæppe*] **—tape′like′,** *adj.*

tape deck, the mechanical component of a tape recorder that is used with a separate amplifier and speaker system.

tape line, tape measure.

tape measure, a long strip of cloth or steel marked in inches, feet, etc., for measuring.

ta per (tā′pər), *v.i.* 1 become gradually narrower toward one end: *The church spire tapers off to a point.* 2 grow less gradually; diminish. *—v.t.* make gradually narrower toward one end. *—adj.* becoming smaller toward one end. *—n.* 1 a gradual narrowing in width or girth. 2 a gradual decrease of force, capacity, etc. 3 figure that tapers to a point; slender cone or pyramid; spire. 4 a very slender candle. 5 a long wick coated with wax, for lighting a candle, cigarette, etc., from an open fire. [Old English *tapor*] **—ta′per ing ly,** *adv.*

tape-re cord (tāp′ri kôrd′), *v.t., v.i.* record on a tape recorder.

tape recorder, machine that records sound on magnetic tape and plays the sound back after it is recorded.

tape recording, 1 the recording of sound on a tape. 2 tape on which sound has been recorded. 3 the sound recorded.

tap es try (tap′ə strē), *n., pl.* **-tries,** *v.,* **-tried, -try ing.** *—n.* 1 fabric with pictures or designs woven in it, used to hang on walls, cover furniture, etc. 2 a picture in tapestry. *—v.t.* 1 picture in tapestry. 2 cover with tapestry; cover with a pattern like that of tapestry. [< Old French *tapisserie* < *tapisser* to cover with a carpet < *tapis* carpet < Greek *tapēs*]

ta pe tum (tə pē′təm), *n., pl.* **-ta** (-tə). (in botany) a cell or sheath of cells in a spore case, serving to supply nourishment to the maturing spores. [< New Latin < Greek *tapēs* carpet]

tape worm (tāp′wėrm′), *n.* any of a class of long flatworms that live during their adult stage as parasites in the intestines of man and other vertebrates; cestode.

tap i o ca (tap′ē ō′kə), *n.* a starchy, granular food obtained from the root of the cassava plant, used in puddings and for thickening soups. [ultimately < Tupi *tipioca*]

tapir—about 3 ft. high at the shoulder

ta pir (tā′pər), *n.* any of a family of large piglike mammals of tropical America and southern Asia, of the same order as the horse and rhinoceros, having hoofs and a flexible snout. [< Tupi *tapira*]

tap is (tap′ē, tap′is), *n.* 1 OBSOLETE. any rug, tablecloth, hanging, or other tapestry. 2 **on the tapis,** being given attention; under discussion. [< French]

tap pet (tap′it), *n.* (in machinery) a projecting arm, cam, etc., that strikes another part of the machine at intervals to transmit an irregular motion. [< *tap*[1]]

tap room (tap′rüm′, tap′ru̇m′), *n.* barroom.

tap root (tap′rüt′, tap′ru̇t′), *n.* a main root growing downward and sprouting subsidiary lateral roots.

taps (taps), *n.pl.* 1 signal on a bugle or drum to put out lights at night. 2 this bugle call, sounded at a military funeral or memorial service.

tap ster (tap′stər), *n.* person who draws beer, wine, etc., from barrels, kegs, casks, etc., to serve in a tavern or barroom.

tar[1] (tär), *n., v.,* **tarred, tar ring,** *adj. —n.* a thick, black, sticky substance obtained by the destructive distillation of wood or coal. Tar is used to cover and patch roads and to keep telephone poles and other timber from rotting. *—v.t.* 1 cover or smear with tar; soak in tar. Tarred paper is used on sheds to keep out water. 2 **tar and feather,** pour heated tar on and cover with feathers as a punishment. *—adj.* of, like, or covered with tar. [Old English *teoru, teru*]

tar[2] (tär), *n.* sailor. [probably short for *tarpaulin* (in early meaning) sailor]

tar an tel la (tar′ən tel′ə), *n.* 1 a rapid, whirling southern Italian dance in very quick rhythm, usually performed by a single couple. 2 music for this dance. [< Italian < *Taranto,* the seaport]

Ta ran to (tə ran′tō; *Italian* tär′än tō), *n.* 1 **Gulf of,** gulf off the SE coast of Italy. 70 mi. long. 2 seaport on this gulf. 219,000.

ta ran tu la (tə ran′chə lə), *n.* 1 a large spider of southern Europe, whose slightly poisonous bite was once imagined to cause an insane desire to dance. 2 any of a family of large, hairy spiders of the southwestern

hat, āge, fär; let, ēqual, tėrm;
it, īce; hot, ōpen, ôrder;
oil, out; cup, pu̇t, rüle;
ch, child; ng, long; sh, she;
th, thin; ᴛʜ, then; zh, measure;

ə represents *a* in about, *e* in taken, *i* in pencil, *o* in lemon, *u* in circus.

< = from, derived from, taken from.

United States and South and Central America, with a painful but not serious bite. [< Medieval Latin, ultimately < *Taranto,* the seaport, where they were common]

Ta ra wa (tə rä′wə), *n.* atoll in the Gilbert and Ellice Islands in the central Pacific. It is the colonial headquarters of the islands. 8000 pop.; 8 sq. mi.

tar boosh or **tar bush** (tär büsh′), *n.* a cloth or felt cap, usually red, with a tassel on top, usually of dark-blue silk, worn by Moslem men, sometimes inside a turban. [< Arabic *tarbūsh*]

tar dy (tär′dē), *adj.,* **-di er, -di est.** 1 behind time; late. See **late** for synonym study. 2 slow; sluggish. [< Middle French *tardif* < Latin *tardus*] **—tar′di ly,** *adv.* **—tar′di ness,** *n.*

tare[1] (ter, tar), *n.* 1 vetch. 2 a vetch seed, often a symbol of smallness. 3 (in the Bible) an injurious weed, possibly the darnel. [probably related to Middle Dutch *tarwe* wheat]

tare[2] (ter, tar), *n., v.,* **tared, tar ing.** *—n.* deduction made from the gross weight of goods to allow for the weight of the wrapper, box, or conveyance they are in. *—v.t.* mark or allow for the tare of. [< Middle French < Medieval Latin *tara* deduction < Arabic *ṭarḥah*]

targe (tärj), *n.* ARCHAIC. a light shield or buckler. [< Old French]

tar get (tär′git), *n.* 1 mark for shooting at; thing aimed at. A target is often a circle, but anything may be used as a target. 2 object of abuse, scorn, criticism, etc.: *His crazy ideas made him the target of jokes.* 3 any aim one tries to achieve; goal; objective. 4 a small shield, especially a round shield. 5 plate, often of platinum, opposite the cathode in an X-ray tube, upon which the cathode rays impinge and produce X rays. 6 substance subjected to bombardment by atomic particles. [< Middle French *targete,* diminutive of Old French *targe* shield]

target date, date set for the beginning or completion of a project.

tar iff (tar′if), *n.* 1 list of duties or taxes that a government charges on imports or exports. 2 system of duties or taxes on imports or exports. 3 any duty or tax in such a list or system: *There is a very high tariff on jewelry.* 4 any table or scale of prices. [< Italian *tariffa* < Arabic *ta′rīf* information]

Tar king ton (tär′king tən), *n.* **Booth,** 1869-1946, American novelist and playwright.

tar la tan (tär′lə tən), *n.* a thin, stiff, transparent muslin, formerly used in ballet skirts, bags for Christmas candy, etc. [< French *tarlatane*]

tar mac (tär′mak′), *n.* 1 any surface made of tarmacadam, especially a road, runway, or other part of an airfield. 2 **Tarmac,** trademark for tarmacadam.

tar mac ad am (tär′mə kad′əm), *n.* a paving material consisting of crushed rock in a tar and creosote binder.

tarn (tärn), *n.* a small lake or pool in the mountains. [< Scandinavian (Swedish) *tjärn* pool]

tar nish (tär′nish), *v.t.* 1 dull the luster or brightness of: *The salt tarnished the silver saltcellar.* 2 bring disgrace upon (a reputation, one's honor, etc.); sully; taint. —*v.i.* lose luster or brightness: *The brass doorknobs tarnished.* —*n.* 1 loss of luster or brightness. 2 a discolored coating, especially on silver. [< Middle French *terniss-*, a form of *ternir* to dull] **—tar′nish a ble,** *adj.*

ta ro (tär′ō), *n., pl.* **-ros.** 1 plant of the same family as the arum, grown in the Pacific islands and other tropical regions for its starchy rhizome, which is used as food. 2 rhizome of this plant. [< Polynesian]

tarp (tärp), *n.* INFORMAL. tarpaulin.

tar paper, heavy paper covered or impregnated with tar, used especially for waterproofing and windproofing buildings.

tar pau lin (tär pô′lən), *n.* canvas or other coarse, strong cloth made waterproof by painting, tarring, etc., used as a protective covering. [probably < *tar*¹ + *pall* in sense of "covering"]

tar pon (tär′pon, tär′pən), *n., pl.* **-pons** or **-pon.** a large, silver-colored game fish found in the warmer parts of the Atlantic Ocean. [origin uncertain]

tar ra gon (tar′ə gon), *n.* 1 a wormwood, native to eastern Europe and temperate Asia. 2 its leaves, used to flavor vinegar, salads, soups, etc. [< Arabic *ṭarkhon*]

tar ry¹ (tar′ē), *v.,* **-ried, -ry ing.** —*v.i.* 1 delay leaving; remain; stay: *We tarried an extra day to see all the sights.* 2 be tardy; hesitate: *Why do you tarry so long?* —*v.t.* ARCHAIC. wait for. [Middle English *tarien*] **—tar′ri er,** *n.*

tar ry² (tär′ē), *adj.,* **-ri er, -ri est.** 1 of or like tar. 2 covered with tar.

Tar ry town (tar′ē toun), *n.* village on the Hudson River, near New York City, mentioned often in the stories of Washington Irving. 11,000.

tar sal (tär′səl), *adj.* of or having to do with the tarsus. —*n.* one of the bones or cartilages in the ankle.

Tar shish (tär′shish), *n.* region mentioned in the Bible, believed to have been situated in S Spain.

tar si er (tär′sē ər), *n.* any of a genus of small, nocturnal primates of Indonesia and the Philippines, with large eyes and long, bare tails. [< French]

tar sus (tär′səs), *n., pl.* **-si** (-sī). 1 the ankle. 2 the group of small bones composing it. 3 shank of a bird's leg. 4 the last segment of an insect's leg. 5 the thin plate of connective tissue that gives form to the edge of the eyelid. [< New Latin < Greek *tarsos* sole of the foot, originally, crate]

Tar sus (tär′səs), *n.* city in S Turkey. It was the home of Saint Paul. 57,000.

tart¹ (tärt), *adj.* 1 having a sour but agreeable taste. 2 mildly cutting, sarcastic, or sharp: *a tart reply.* See **sour** for synonym study. [Old English *teart* painful, sharp] **—tart′ly,** *adv.* **—tart′ness,** *n.*

tart² (tärt), *n.* pastry filled with cooked fruit, jam, etc. In the United States and Canada, a tart is small and the fruit shows; in England, any fruit pie is a tart. [< Old French *tarte*]

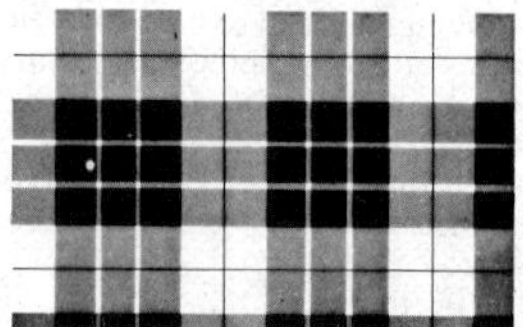
tartan¹ (def. 2)

tar tan¹ (tärt′n), *n.* 1 a plaid woolen cloth. Each Scottish Highland clan has its own pattern of tartan. 2 the pattern or design itself. 3 any similar plaid design or fabric of silk, cotton, etc. —*adj.* 1 made of tartan. 2 of, like, or having to do with tartan. [origin unknown]

tar tan² (tärt′n), *n.* a single-masted vessel with a lateen sail and a jib, used in the Mediterranean. [< French]

tar tar (tär′tər), *n.* 1 an acid substance present in grape juice and deposited as a reddish crust on the inside of wine casks. *Formula:* $KHC_4H_4O_6$ 2 a hard substance formed by the action of saliva on food and deposited as a crust on the teeth. [< Old French *tartre* < Medieval latin *tartarum*]

Tar tar (tär′tər), *n.* 1 member of a mixed horde of Mongolians and Turks who overran Asia and eastern Europe during the Middle Ages. 2 any descendant of these peoples, living in parts of the Soviet Union and central and western Asia, especially one speaking a Ural-Altaic language of the Turkic branch. 3 **tartar,** person who has a bad temper. —*adj.* of or having to do with a Tartar or Tartars. Also, **Tatar** for *n.* 1, 2 and *adj.*

tar tar emetic, a poisonous, white salt with a sweetish, metallic taste, used in medicine as an expectorant, as a mordant in dyeing, etc. *Formula:* $K(SbO)C_4H_4O_6 \cdot {}^1\!/_2H_2O$

tar tar ic (tär tar′ik, tär tär′ik), *adj.* 1 of, having to do with, or containing tartar. 2 obtained from tartar.

tartaric acid, acid used in dyeing, medicine, photography, etc., occurring in four isomers. The common colorless, crystalline form is found in unripe grapes. *Formula:* $C_4H_6O_6$

tartar sauce, sauce, usually for fish, consisting of mayonnaise with chopped pickles, onions, olives, capers, and herbs.

Tar tar us (tär′tər əs), *n.* in Greek myths: 1 a place of punishment below Hades. 2 the underworld; Hades.

Tar tar y (tär′tər ē), *n.* ancient kingdom of the Tartars, that included most of Russia and central and western Asia. Also, **Tatary.**

tart ish (tär′tish), *adj.* somewhat tart; slightly acid. **—tart′ish ly,** *adv.*

tart let (tärt′lit), *n.* a small tart.

tar trate (tär′trāt), *n.* salt or ester of tartaric acid.

Tar zan (tär′zan, tär′zən), *n.* man endowed with great physical strength and skill. [< the name of the hero in a series of jungle stories by Edgar Rice Burroughs, 1875-1950, American writer]

Tash kent (tash kent′), *n.* city in S central Soviet Union, the capital of the Uzbek S.S.R. 1,385,000.

task (task), *n.* 1 work to be done; piece of work; duty; job. 2 **take to task,** blame; scold; reprove. —*v.t.* 1 put a task on; force to work. 2 burden or strain: *Lifting that trunk tasked him beyond his strength.* [< Old North French *tasque* job, tax, ultimately < Latin *taxare* evaluate. See TAX.] **—task′er,** *n.*

task force, 1 a temporary group of military units, especially naval units, assigned to one commander for carrying out a specific operation. 2 any group temporarily organized for a task.

task mas ter (task′mas′tər), *n.* person who sets tasks for others to do.

Tas ma ni a (taz mā′nē ə, taz mā′nyə), *n.* island off SE Australia. It is a state of Australia. 393,000 pop.; 26,400 sq. mi. *Capital:* Hobart. **—Tas ma′ni an,** *adj., n.*

Tasmanian devil, a carnivorous, black-and-white marsupial mammal of Tasmania, which resembles a very small bear.

Tasmanian wolf, thylacine.

Tass (tas), *n.* a government agency of the Soviet Union which collects, censors, and distributes news.

tas sel (tas′əl), *n., v.,* **-seled, -sel ing** or **-selled, -sel ling.** —*n.* 1 an ornamental, hanging bunch of threads, small cords, beads, etc., fastened together at one end. 2 something like this. Corn has tassels. —*v.t.* 1 put tassels on. 2 take tassels from. —*v.i.* grow tassels. [< Old French, mantle fastener, ultimately < Latin *taxillus* small die]

Tas so (tas′ō), *n.* **Torquato,** 1544-1595, Italian poet.

taste (tāst), *n., v.,* **tast ed, tast ing.** —*n.* 1 what is special about (something) to the sense organs in the mouth and on the tongue; flavor: *Sweet, sour, salt, and bitter are four important tastes.* See synonym study below. 2 the sense by which the flavor of things is perceived: *Her taste is unusually keen.* 3 a little bit; sample: *brief tastes of joy. Take a taste of this cake.* 4 a liking: *Suit your own taste.* 5 ability to perceive and enjoy what is beautiful and excellent. 6 manner or style that shows such ability or lack of it: *Her house is furnished in excellent taste.*
—*v.t.* 1 try the flavor of (something) by taking a little into the mouth. 2 get the flavor of by the sense of taste: *She tasted almond in the cake.* 3 experience slightly; have; sample: *taste freedom.* 4 eat or drink a little bit of. —*v.i.* 1 have or use the sense of taste. 2 have a particular flavor: *The butter tastes rancid.* 3 eat or drink a little bit. 4 have experience: *taste of pleasure.*
[< Old French *taster* to feel, taste, probably < Popular Latin *taxitare* < Latin *taxare* evaluate]

Syn. *n.* 1 **Taste, flavor** mean the quality of a thing that affects the sense organs of the mouth. **Taste** is the general word: *Mineral oil has no taste.* **Flavor** means a characteristic taste, especially of a pleasant kind: *The flavor I like best is chocolate.*

taste bud, any of certain groups of cells, most of which are in the outer layer of the tongue, that are sense organs of taste.

taste ful (tāst′fəl), *adj.* 1 having good taste; refined. 2 showing or done in good taste. **—taste′ful ly,** *adv.* **—taste′ful ness,** *n.*

taste less (tāst′lis), *adj.* 1 without taste; flavorless, insipid; flat. 2 without good taste; in poor taste. **—taste′less ly,** *adv.* **—taste′less ness,** *n.*

tast er (tā′stər), *n.* person who tastes, especially one whose work is judging the quality of wine, tea, coffee, etc., by the taste.

tast y (tā′stē), *adj.,* **tast i er, tast i est.** INFORMAL. 1 tasting good; pleasing to the taste; savory. 2 having or showing good taste; tasteful. **—tast′i ly,** *adv.* **—tast′i ness,** *n.*

tat (tat), *v.t., v.i.,* **tat ted, tat ting.** make a kind of lace by looping and knotting (threads) with a shuttle. [origin unknown]

hat, āge, fär; let, ēqual, tėrm;
it, īce; hot, ōpen, ôrder;
oil, out; cup, pu̇t, rüle;
ch, child; ng, long; sh, she;
th, thin; ᴛʜ, then; zh, measure;

ə represents *a* in about, *e* in taken, *i* in pencil, *o* in lemon, *u* in circus.

< = from, derived from, taken from.

Ta tar (tä′tər), *n., adj.* Tartar.

Ta tar y (tä′tər ē), *n.* Tartary.

tat ter (tat′ər), *n.* 1 a torn piece; rag: *After the storm the flag hung in tatters upon the mast.* 2 **tatters,** *pl.* torn or ragged clothing. —*v.t.* tear or wear to pieces; make ragged. —*v.i.* be or become tattered. [< Scandinavian (Old Icelandic) *tötturr* rag]

tat ter de mal ion (tat′ər di mā′lyən, tat′ər di mal′yən), *n.* person in tattered clothes; ragamuffin.

tat tered (tat′ərd), *adj.* 1 full of tatters; torn; ragged. 2 wearing torn or ragged clothes.

tat ter sall (tat′ər sôl), *n.* a woven pattern of thin lines of bright or dark colors forming checks on a white or light background. —*adj.* of such a pattern: *a tattersall vest.* [< *Tattersall's,* a sporting establishment and horse auction market in London]

tat ting (tat′ing), *n.* 1 process or work of making a kind of lace by looping and knotting cotton or linen thread with a shuttle. 2 lace made in this way.

tat tle (tat′l), *v.,* **-tled, -tling,** *n.* —*v.i.* 1 tell tales or secrets; blab. 2 talk idly; chatter; gossip. —*v.t.* 1 reveal by tattling. 2 utter idly or foolishly. —*n.* idle or foolish talk; gossip; telling tales or secrets. [< Middle Dutch *tatelen*]

tat tler (tat′lər), *n.* 1 telltale; tattletale. 2 any of several shore birds resembling sandpipers, with a noisy cry.

tat tle tale (tat′l tāl′), INFORMAL. —*n.* a telltale. —*adj.* revealing faults; telltale: *tattletale stains.*

tat too¹ (ta tü′), *n., pl.* **-toos.** 1 signal on a bugle, drum, etc., calling soldiers or sailors to their quarters at night. 2 series of raps, taps, etc.: *The hail beat a loud tattoo on the windowpane.* 3 BRITISH. a military display, especially music and parading by show units, usually outdoors in the evening and floodlit. [< Dutch *taptoe* < *tap* taproom + *toe* pull to, shut]

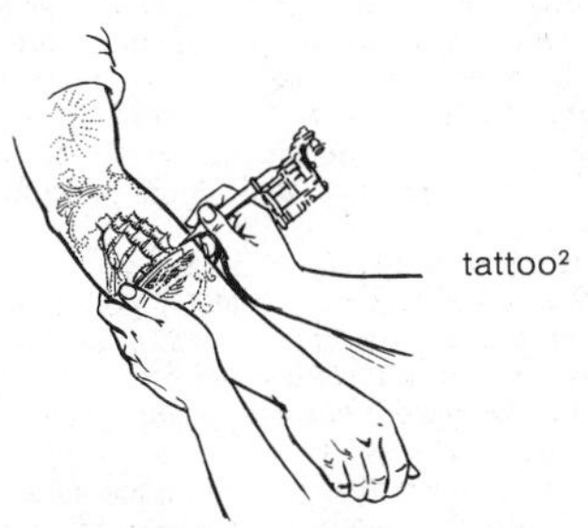

tattoo²

tat too² (ta tü′), *v., n., pl.* **-toos.** —*v.t.* 1 mark (the skin) with designs or patterns by pricking it and putting in colors. 2 put (such a design) on the skin in this way: *The sailor had a ship tattooed on his arm.* —*n.* mark or design made by tattooing. [< Polynesian *tatu*] **—tat too′er,** *n.*

tau (tô, tou), *n.* the 19th letter of the Greek alphabet (Τ τ).

taught (tôt), *v.* pt. and pp. of **teach.**

taunt (tônt, tänt), *v.t.* 1 jeer at; mock; reproach; deride. 2 get or drive by taunts; provoke: *taunt someone into taking a dare.* —*n.* a bitter or insulting remark; mocking; jeering. [origin uncertain] **—taunt′er,** *n.* **—taunt′ing ly,** *adv.*

taupe (tōp), *n.* a dark, brownish gray. —*adj.* dark brownish-gray. [< French, originally, mole < Latin *talpa*]

tau rom a chy (tô rom′ə kē), *n., pl.* **-chies.** 1 bullfighting. 2 bullfight. [< Greek *tauromachia* < *tauros* bull + *machesthai* to fight]

Tau rus (tôr′əs), *n.* 1 a northern constellation seen by ancient astronomers as having the rough outline of a bull. 2 the second sign of the zodiac. The sun enters Taurus about April 20. 3 mountain range in S Turkey. Highest peak, 12,251 ft.

taut (tôt), *adj.* 1 tightly drawn; tense: *a taut rope.* See **tight** for synonym study. 2 in neat condition; tidy: *a taut ship.* [Middle English *tought*] **—taut′ly,** *adv.* **—taut′ness,** *n.*

taut en (tôt′n), *v.t., v.i.* make or become taut; tighten.

tau tog (tô tog′, tô tôg′), *n.* a dark-colored food fish, a variety of wrasse, common on the Atlantic coast of the United States. [< Algonquian]

tau to log i cal (tô′tə loj′ə kəl), *adj.* having to do with, characterized by, or using tautology. **—tau′to log′i cal ly,** *adv.*

tau tol o gous (tô tol′ə gəs), *adj.* tautological.

tau tol o gy (tô tol′ə jē), *n., pl.* **-gies.** 1 a saying a thing over again in other words without adding clearness or force; useless repetition. EXAMPLE: the *modern* college student of *today.* 2 (in logic) a statement, classification, etc., that overlooks and excludes no possibility. EXAMPLE: She is either married or not. [< Greek *tautologia* < *to auto* the same (thing) + *-logia* -logy]

tav ern (tav′ərn), *n.* 1 place where alcoholic drinks are sold and drunk; bar; saloon. 2 inn. [< Old French *taverne* < Latin *taberna,* originally, rude dwelling]

taw (tô), *n.* 1 a fancy marble used for shooting. 2 game of marbles. 3 the line from which the players shoot their marbles. [origin uncertain]

taw dry (tô′drē), *adj.,* **-dri er, -dri est.** showy and cheap; gaudy; garish. [short for *(Sain)t Audrey('s lace),* sold at the fair of Saint Audrey in Ely, England] **—taw′dri ly,** *adv.* **—taw′dri ness,** *n.*

taw ny (tô′nē), *adj.,* **-ni er, -ni est,** *n., pl.* **-nies.** —*adj.* brownish-yellow: *A lion has a tawny coat.* —*n.* a brownish yellow. [< Old French *tane,* past participle of *taner* to tan] **—taw′ni ness,** *n.*

tax (taks), *n.* 1 money paid by people for the support of the government and the cost of public works and services; money regularly collected from citizens by their rulers. 2 a burden, duty, or demand that oppresses; strain: *Climbing stairs is a tax on a weak heart.* —*v.t.* 1 put a tax on. 2 lay a heavy burden on; be hard for; strain: *Reading in a poor light taxes the eyes.* 3 reprove; accuse: *The teacher taxed her with having neglected her work.* 4 determine the amount of (costs of a lawsuit, etc.). [< Medieval Latin *taxare* impose a tax < Latin, evaluate, estimate, assess, perhaps < *tangere* to touch] **—tax′er,** *n.* **—tax′less,** *adj.*

tax a (tak′sə), *n.* pl. of **taxon.**

tax a bil i ty (tak′sə bil′ə tē), *n.* a being taxable.

tax a ble (tak′sə bəl), *adj.* liable to be taxed; subject to taxation: *Churches are not taxable.*

tax a tion (tak sā′shən), *n.* 1 act or system of taxing. 2 amount paid for the support of the government; taxes.

tax-ex empt (taks′eg zempt′), *adj.* free from taxes; not taxed; not taxable.

tax i (tak′sē), *n., v.,* **tax ied, tax i ing** or **tax y ing.** —*n.* taxicab. —*v.i.* 1 ride in a taxicab. 2 (of an aircraft) move across the ground or water under its own power before take-off or after landing. —*v.t.* 1 cause (an aircraft) to taxi. 2 take in a taxicab.

tax i cab (tak′sē kab′), *n.* automobile for hire, usually with an automatic meter to record the amount to be paid. [contraction of *taximeter cab.* See TAXIMETER.]

tax i der mal (tak′sə dėr′məl), *adj.* of or having to do with taxidermy.

tax i der mist (tak′sə dėr′mist), *n.* an expert in taxidermy.

tax i der my (tak′sə dėr′mē), *n.* art of preparing the skins of animals and stuffing and mounting them so that they look alive. [< Greek *taxis* arrangement + *derma* skin]

tax i me ter (tak′sē mē′tər), *n.* meter of a taxicab. [< French *taximètre* < *taxe* fare + *mètre* meter]

tax is (tak′sis), *n.* (in biology) movement in a particular direction by a free organism or a cell, in reaction to an external stimulus, such as light. [< Greek, arrangement < *tassein* arrange]

tax on (tak′sən), *n., pl.* **tax a.** a taxonomic division, such as a family or order.

tax o nom ic (tak′sə nom′ik), *adj.* of or having to do with taxonomy. **—tax′o nom′i cal ly,** *adv.*

tax on o mist (tak son′ə mist), *n.* an expert in taxonomy.

tax on o my (tak son′ə mē), *n.* 1 classification, especially of plant and animal species. 2 branch of science dealing with classification. [< French *taxonomie* < Greek *taxis* arrangement + *nemein* manage, distribute]

tax pay er (taks′pā′ər), *n.* person who pays a tax or is required by law to do so.

Tay lor (tā′lər), *n.* 1 **Jeremy,** 1613-1667, English bishop and author. 2 **Zachary,** 1784-1850, the 12th president of the United States, from 1849 to 1850.

Tb, terbium.

TB, T.B., or **t.b.,** tuberculosis.

Tbi li si (tə bi lē sē′), *n.* city in the SW Soviet Union, capital of the Georgian S.S.R. 889,000. Also, **Tiflis.**

tbs. or **tbsp.,** tablespoon or tablespoons.

Tc, technetium.

Tchai kov sky or **Tchai kow sky** (chī kôf′skē), *n.* **Peter Ilich,** 1840-1893, Russian composer. Also, **Tschaikowsky** or **Tschaikovsky.**

TD, (in football) touchdown.

Te, tellurium.

tea (tē), *n.* 1 a common light-brown, aromatic drink made by pouring boiling water over the dried and prepared leaves of a certain shrub and served with milk or lemon, sugar, etc. 2 the dried and prepared leaves from which this drink is made. 3 the shrub they grow on, raised chiefly in China, Japan, India, and Ceylon, bearing fragrant white flowers and oval, evergreen, toothed leaves. 4 BRITISH. a meal in the late afternoon or early evening, at which tea is commonly served. 5 an afternoon reception at which tea is served. 6 drink prepared from some other thing named. **Beef tea** is a strong broth made from beef. [< dialectal Chinese *t'e*]

tea bag, tea leaves in a little bag of thin cloth or paper for easy removal from the cup or pot after use.

tea ball, a perforated metal ball for tea leaves in brewing tea.

teach (tēch), *v.,* **taught, teach ing.** —*v.t.* 1 help to learn; show how to do; make understand: *teach a dog tricks.* 2 give instruction to: *He teaches his classes well.* 3 give lessons in: *He teaches mathematics.* —*v.i.* give instruction; act as teacher: *She teaches for a living.* [Old English *tǣcan* to show] ➤ See **learn** for usage note.

teach a bil i ty (tē'chə bil'ə tē), *n.* fact or quality of being teachable.

teach a ble (tē'chə bəl), *adj.* able to be taught. —**teach'a ble ness,** *n.*

teach er (tē'chər), *n.* person who teaches, especially one who teaches in a school. —**teach'er like',** *adj.*

teach-in (tēch'in'), *n.* a long, informal session of lectures, debates, and seminars by college teachers and students on some controversial issue or policy.

teach ing (tē'ching), *n.* 1 work or profession of a teacher. 2 act of a person who teaches. 3 what is taught; instruction; precept.

teaching machine, device or machine designed to give programed instruction.

tea cup (tē'kup'), *n.* 1 cup for drinking tea. 2 teacupful.

tea cup ful (tē'kup'fu̇l), *n., pl.* **-fuls.** as much as a teacup holds, usually four fluid ounces.

tea house (tē'hous'), *n., pl.* **-hous es** (-hou'ziz). place where tea and other light refreshments are served. There are many teahouses in Japan and China.

teak (tēk), *n.* 1 a large tree of the same family as the verbena, grown in the East Indies for its hard, durable, yellowish-brown wood, used in shipbuilding, making fine furniture, etc. 2 its wood. [< Portuguese *teca* < Malayalam *tēkka*]

tea ket tle (tē'ket'l), *n.* kettle for heating water to make tea, etc.

teal (tēl), *n., pl.* **teals** or **teal.** any of several varieties of small ducks of the same genus as the mallard. [Middle English *tele*]

team (tēm), *n.* 1 number of people working or acting together, especially one of the sides in a game or match: *a football team, a debating team.* 2 two or more horses or other animals harnessed together to work. 3 one or more draft animals, their harness, and the vehicle they pull. 4 BRITISH DIALECT. a brood or litter of animals. —*v.t.* 1 join together in a team. 2 work, carry, haul, etc., with a team. —*v.i.* 1 combine as a team; join forces. 2 drive a team. [Old English *tēam*]

team mate (tēm'māt'), *n.* a fellow member of a team.

team ster (tēm'stər), *n.* man whose work is driving a team of horses or a truck.

team work (tēm'wėrk'), *n.* the acting together of a number of people to make the work of the group successful and effective: *Football requires teamwork even more than individual skill.*

tea pot (tē'pot'), *n.* container with a handle and a spout for making and serving tea.

tear[1] (tir), *n.* 1 drop of salty liquid secreted by the lachrymal glands to moisten the membrane covering the front of the eyeball and the lining of the eyelid. 2 something like or suggesting a tear. 3 **in tears,** shedding tears; crying. —*v.i.* fill with tears. [Old English *tēar*]

tear[2] (ter, tar), *v.,* **tore, torn, tear ing,** *n.* —*v.t.* 1 pull apart by force: *tear a box open.* See synonym study below. 2 make by pulling apart: *She tore a hole in her dress.* 3 make a hole or rent in by a pull; rip: *The nail tore her coat.* 4 pull hard; pull violently: *Tear out the page.* 5 cut badly; wound: *The jagged stone tore his skin.* 6 rend; divide; split: *The party was torn by two factions.* 7 remove by effort; force away: *He could not tear himself from that spot.* 8 make miserable; distress: *torn by grief.* 9 **tear down, a** pull down; raze: *The city tore down a whole block of apartment houses.* **b** discredit; ruin: *tear down another's reputation.* —*v.i.* 1 be pulled apart; become torn: *Lace tears easily.* 2 INFORMAL. move with great force or haste: *an automobile tearing along.*
—*n.* 1 a torn place; hole: *She has a tear in her dress.* 2 act or process of tearing. 3 INFORMAL. hurry; rush. 4 SLANG. spree.
[Old English *teran*] —**tear'er,** *n.*

Syn. *v.t.* 1 **Tear, rip** mean to pull something apart by force. **Tear** means to pull apart or into pieces in such a way as to leave rough or ragged edges: *He tore the letter into tiny pieces.* **Rip** means to tear roughly or quickly, usually along a joining: *She ripped the hem in her skirt by catching her heel in it.*

tear drop (tir'drop'), *n.* tear[1] (defs. 1 and 2).

tear ful (tir'fəl), *adj.* 1 full of tears; weeping. 2 causing tears; sad. —**tear'ful ly,** *adv.* —**tear'ful ness,** *n.*

tear gas (tir), gas that irritates the eyes and temporarily blinds them with tears, used especially in dispersing rioters.

tear jerk er (tir'jėr'kər), *n.* INFORMAL. an overly sad or sentimental story, movie, play, etc.

tear less (tir'lis), *adj.* without tears; not crying.

tea room (tē'rüm', tē'ru̇m'), *n.* room or shop where tea, coffee, and light meals are served.

tear strip (ter, tar), a scored strip of paper, tape, etc., that is pulled or wound off to open a can, box top, or wrapper.

tear y (tir'ē), *adj.,* **tear i er, tear i est.** tearful.

Teas dale (tēz'dāl), *n.* **Sara,** 1884-1933, American poet.

tease (tēz), *v.,* **teased, teas ing,** *n.* —*v.t.* 1 vex or worry by jokes, questions, requests, etc.; annoy. See synonym study below. 2 separate the fibers of; pull apart, comb, or card (wool, etc.). 3 raise a nap on (cloth); teasel. —*v.i.* beg: *The child teases for everything he sees.* —*n.* 1 person who teases. 2 act of teasing. 3 condition of being teased. [Old English *tǣsan*] —**teas'ing ly,** *adv.*

Syn. *v.t.* 1 **Tease, plague, pester** mean to irritate by continuous or persistent annoyance. **Tease** implies causing to lose patience and flare up in annoyance or anger, either by persistent begging or by unkind jokes or tricks: *Children teased the dog until it bit them.* **Plague** emphasizes that the irritation is severe: *The people were plagued with high taxes.* **Pester** emphasizes that the irritation is constantly repeated: *She is always pestering her mother for candy.*

tea sel (tē'zəl), *n., v.,* **-seled, -sel ing** or **-selled, -sel ling.** —*n.* 1 any of a genus of Eurasian and African herbs with prickly leaves and flower heads. 2 one of these dried flower heads used for raising nap on cloth. 3 a brush with hooked prongs used for the same purpose. —*v.t.* raise a nap on (cloth) with teasels. Also, **teazel.** [Old English *tǣsel*]

teas er (tē'zər), *n.* 1 person or thing that teases. 2 INFORMAL. an annoying problem; puzzling task.

tea spoon (tē'spün'), *n.* 1 a small spoon often used to stir tea or coffee. 2 spoon used in cookery as a unit of measure and holding $^1/_3$ as much as a tablespoon. 3 teaspoonful.

tea spoon ful (tē'spün'fu̇l), *n., pl.* **-fuls.** 1 unit of volume equal to $1^1/_3$ fluid drams or $^1/_3$ tablespoonful. 2 as much as a teaspoon holds.

teat (tēt, tit), *n.* nipple (def. 1). [< Old French *tete;* of Germanic origin]

tea wagon, a small table on wheels used in serving tea.

tea zel (tē'zəl), *n., v.,* **-zeled, -zel ing** or **-zelled, -zel ling.** teasel.

tech., 1 technical. 2 technology.

tech ne ti um (tek nē'shē əm), *n.* a radioactive metallic element produced artificially from uranium or molybdenum, used to inhibit corrosion of iron. *Symbol:* Tc; *atomic number* 43. See pages 326 and 327 for table. [< Greek *technētos* artificial < *technē* art]

tech nic (tek'nik), *n.* 1 any technique. 2 a technical detail, point, term, etc.; technicality. 3 the science of technics. —*adj.* technical.

tech ni cal (tek'nə kəl), *adj.* 1 of or having to do with a mechanical or industrial art or applied science: *This technical school trains engineers, chemists, and architects.* 2 of or having to do with the special facts of a science or art: *"Electrolysis," "tarsus," and "proteid" are technical words.* 3 treating a subject technically; using technical terms: *a technical lecture.* 4 of or having to do with technique: *Her singing shows technical skill, but her voice is weak.* 5 judged strictly by the rules; strictly interpreted. [< Greek *technikos* < *technē* art, skill, craft] —**tech'ni cal ly,** *adv.*

tech ni cal i ty (tek'nə kal'ə tē), *n., pl.* **-ties.** 1 a technical matter, point, detail, term, expression, etc.: *Books on engineering contain many technicalities which the ordinary reader does not understand.* 2 technical quality or character.

technical knockout, a knockout scored in a boxing match when the referee or a physician decides that a fighter is too hurt or dazed to continue fighting, although he has not been knocked out.

technical sergeant, (in the U.S. Air Force) a noncommissioned officer ranking next above a staff sergeant and next below a master sergeant.

tech ni cian (tek nish'ən), *n.* 1 an expert in the technicalities of a subject. 2 an expert in the technique of an art.

Tech ni col or (tek'nə kul'ər), *n.* trademark for a process of making colored motion pictures.

tech ni col ored (tek'nə kul'ərd), *adj.* intensely or vividly colored.

tech nics (tek'niks), *n.* 1 study or science of the arts, especially the mechanical or industrial arts. 2 technic or technique.

tech nique (tek nēk'), *n.* 1 skill of a composing artist, as a musician, painter, sculptor, poet, etc. 2 method or ability of an artist's performance, execution, etc.; technical skill: *The pianist's technique was excellent, though his interpretation of the music was poor.* 3 a special method or system used to accomplish something. [< French]

tech noc ra cy (tek nok′rə sē), *n.* government by technical experts. [< Greek *technē* craft + *kratos* rule, power]

tech no crat (tek′nə krat), *n.* person in favor of technocracy.

tech no crat ic (tek′nə krat′ik), *adj.* of or having to do with technocracy or technocrats.

tech no log ic (tek′nə loj′ik), *adj.* technological.

tech no log i cal (tek′nə loj′ə kəl), *adj.* 1 of or having to do with technology. 2 used in technology. **—tech′no log′i cal ly,** *adv.*

tech nol o gist (tek nol′ə jist), *n.* an expert in technology.

tech nol o gy (tek nol′ə jē), *n.* 1 the science of the mechanical and industrial arts: *I studied engineering at a school of technology.* 2 technical words, terms, or expressions used in an art, science, etc. [< Greek *technologia* systematic treatment < *technē* art + *-logia* -logy]

tec ton ic (tek ton′ik), *adj.* (in geology) belonging to or resulting from the structure of the earth's crust and to general changes in it, as folding, faulting, etc.: *tectonic ridges.* [< Greek *tektōn* builder]

Te cum seh (tə kum′sə), *n.* 1768?-1813, Shawnee Indian chief.

ted (ted), *v.t.,* **ted ded, ted ding.** spread or scatter (new-mown grass) for drying. [< Scandinavian (Old Icelandic) *tethja*] **—ted′der,** *n.*

ted dy bear (ted′ē), a child's furry toy bear.

Te De um (tē dē′əm), 1 an ancient hymn of praise and thanksgiving sung in Roman Catholic and Anglican churches at morning prayers or on special occasions. 2 music for this hymn. [< Latin *Te Deum (laudamus)* Thee God (we praise), the first words of the hymn]

te di ous (tē′dē əs, tē′jəs), *adj.* long and tiring; boring; wearisome: *A long talk that you cannot understand is tedious.* See **tiresome** for synonym study. **—te′di ous ly,** *adv.* **—te′di ous ness,** *n.*

te di um (tē′dē əm), *n.* 1 condition of being wearisome; tiresomeness; tediousness. 2 ennui; boredom. [< Latin *taedium* < *taedet* it is wearisome]

tee (tē), *n., v.,* **teed, tee ing.** *—n.* 1 mark aimed at in quoits, curling, and other games. 2 mark or place from which a player starts in playing each hole in golf. 3 a little mound of sand or dirt or a short wooden or plastic peg with a concave top on which a golf ball is placed when a player drives. *—v.t.* put (a golf ball) on a tee. *—v.i.* **tee off, a** drive (a golf ball) from a tee. **b** begin any series of actions. [origin uncertain]

teem (tēm), *v.i.* be full (of); abound; swarm: *The swamp teemed with mosquitoes.* [Old English *tēman* < *tēam* progeny]

teen (tēn), *adj.* teen-age: *teen years, teen fashions.* *—n.* teen-ager.

-teen, *suffix added to numbers.* ten more than ___: *Sixteen = ten more than six.* [Old English *-tēne* < *tēn* ten]

teen-age (tēn′āj′), *adj.* 1 of or for a teen-ager or teen-agers: *a teen-age club.* 2 in one's teens; being a teen-ager: *a teen-age girl.*

teen-aged (tēn′ājd′), *adj.* in one's teens; being a teen-ager.

teen-ag er (tēn′ā′jər), *n.* person in his or her teens.

teens (tēnz), *n.pl.* the years of life from 13 to 19 inclusive.

teen sy (tēn′sē), *adj.,* **-si er, -si est.** INFORMAL. tiny.

tee ny (tē′nē), *adj.,* **-ni er, -ni est.** INFORMAL. tiny.

tee ny-bop per (tē′nē bop′ər), *n.* SLANG. teen-ager, especially a girl, who prefers the hippie life-style.

tee pee (tē′pē), *n.* tepee.

tee shirt, T-shirt.

tee ter (tē′tər), *v.i., v.t.* 1 rock unsteadily; sway. 2 balance on a seesaw. *—n.* 1 a swaying movement; reeling. 2 seesaw. [< Scandinavian (Old Icelandic) *titra* shake]

tee ter board (tē′tər bôrd′, tē′tər bōrd′), *n.* seesaw.

tee ter-tot ter (tē′tər tot′ər), *n.* seesaw.

teeth (tēth), *n. pl. of* **tooth. 1 in the teeth of, a** straight against; in the face of. **b** in defiance of; in spite of. **2 put teeth in** or **put teeth into,** make effective or forceful: *put teeth into a rule.* **3 to the teeth,** completely: *armed to the teeth.*

teethe (tēᴛʜ), *v.i.,* **teethed, teeth ing.** grow teeth; cut teeth; have teeth grow through the gums.

tee to tal (tē tō′tl), *adj.* 1 of, having to do with, advocating, or pledged to total abstinence from alcoholic liquor. 2 INFORMAL. without exception; complete; entire. [< *total,* with initial letter repeated]

tee to tal er (tē tō′tl ər), *n.* person who pledges or binds himself to drink no alcoholic liquor.

tee to tal ism (tē tō′tl iz′əm), *n.* principle or practice of total abstinence from alcoholic liquor.

tee to tal ler (tē tō′tl ər), *n.* BRITISH. teetotaler.

Tef lon (tef′lon), *n.* trademark for a slippery, acid-resistant plastic used for coating utensils, as a dry lubricant, in electric insulation, etc.

Te gu ci gal pa (tā gü′sē gäl′pä), *n.* capital of Honduras, in the S part. 219,000.

teg u ment (teg′yə mənt), *n.* integument. [< Latin *tegumentum* < *tegere* to cover]

Te he ran or **Te hran** (te′ə rän′, te′ə-ran′), *n.* capital of Iran, in the N part. 2,720,000.

Te huan te pec (tə wän′tə pek), *n.* **1 Gulf of,** gulf of the Pacific, off the coast of S Mexico. **2 Isthmus of,** isthmus in S Mexico, between this gulf and the Gulf of Mexico. 130 mi. wide.

Teil hard de Char din (tā yär′ də shär-daɴ′), **Pierre,** 1881-1955, French Jesuit priest, philosopher, paleontologist, and theologian.

tek tite (tek′tīt), *n.* any of various rounded, glassy objects of different shapes and weights, found in various parts of the world and thought to have come from outer space. [< Greek *tēktos* molten < *tēkein* to melt]

tel., 1 telegram. 2 telegraph. 3 telephone.

Tel A viv (tel′ ə vēv′), seaport and largest city of Israel, in the W part. It includes the formerly separate city of Jaffa. 383,000.

tele-, *combining form.* 1 over a long distance; far, as in *telegraph.* 2 having to do with television, as in *telecast.* [< Greek *tēle* far]

tel e cast (tel′ə kast′), *v.,* **-cast** or **-cast ed, -cast ing,** *n.* *—v.t., v.i.* broadcast by television. *—n.* a television broadcast. **—tel′e-cast′er,** *n.*

hat, āge, fär; let, ēqual, tėrm;
it, īce; hot, ōpen, ôrder;
oil, out; cup, pu̇t, rüle;
ch, child; ng, long; sh, she;
th, thin; ᴛʜ, then; zh, measure;

ə represents *a* in about, *e* in taken, *i* in pencil, *o* in lemon, *u* in circus.

< = from, derived from, taken from.

tel e com mu ni ca tion (tel′ə kə myü′nə-kā′shən), *n.* the electrical and electronic transmission of messages, as by telegraph.

tel e course (tel′ə kôrs′, tel′ə kōrs′), *n.* a televised course of study offered by a college or university.

teleg., 1 telegram. 2 telegraph. 3 telegraphy.

tel e gen ic (tel′ə jen′ik), *adj.* suitable for telecasting.

tel e gram (tel′ə gram), *n.* message sent by telegraph.

tel e graph (tel′ə graf), *n.* apparatus, system, or process for sending coded messages over electric wires by means of electrical impulses. *—v.t.* 1 send (a message) by telegraph. 2 send a message to (a person, etc.) by telegraph.

te leg ra pher (tə leg′rə fər), *n.* person who sends and receives messages by telegraph.

tel e graph ic (tel′ə graf′ik), *adj.* 1 of or having to do with a telegraph. 2 sent as a telegram. **—tel′e graph′i cal ly,** *adv.*

te leg ra phist (tə leg′rə fist), *n.* telegrapher.

te leg ra phy (tə leg′rə fē), *n.* the making or operating of telegraphs.

tel e lens (tel′ə lenz′), *n.* telephoto lens.

Te lem a chus (tə lem′ə kəs), *n.* (in Greek legends) the son of Ulysses (Odysseus) and Penelope. When Ulysses returned from the Trojan War, Telemachus helped him slay Penelope's insolent suitors.

te lem e ter (tə lem′ə tər), *n.* device for measuring heat, radiation, etc., and transmitting the information to a distant receiving station. *—v.t.* measure and transmit by telemeter.

tel e met ric (tel′ə met′rik), *adj.* having to do with telemetry.

te lem e try (tə lem′ə trē), *n.* the use of telemeters for measuring and transmitting information.

tel en ceph a lon (tel′en sef′ə lon), *n.* the anterior part of the forebrain, comprising the cerebrum.

tel e o log i cal (tel′ē ə loj′ə kəl, tē′lē ə-loj′ə kəl), *adj.* of or having to do with teleology.

tel e ol o gy (tel′ē ol′ə jē, tē′lē ol′ə jē), *n.* 1 fact or quality of being purposeful. 2 purpose or design as shown in nature. 3 doctrine that mechanisms alone cannot explain the facts of nature, and that purposes have causal power. 4 doctrine that all things in nature were made to fulfill a plan or design. [< New Latin *teleologia* < Greek *telos* end + *-logia* -logy]

tel e ost (tel′ē ost, tē′lē ost), *adj.* of or having to do with a large subclass of fishes with bony skeletons, including most common fishes, as the perch, flounder, etc., but not the sharks, rays, and lampreys. *—n.* a teleost fish. [< Greek *teleios* finished, complete + *osteon* bone]

tel e path ic (tel′ə path′ik), *adj.* 1 of or having to do with telepathy. 2 by telepathy. **—tel′e path′i cal ly,** *adv.*

te lep a thist (tə lep′ə thist), *n.* 1 person who has telepathic power. 2 student of or believer in telepathy.

te lep a thy (tə lep′ə thē), *n.* communication of one mind with another without using speech, hearing, sight, or any other sense used normally to communicate.

tel e phone (tel′ə fōn), *n., v.,* **-phoned, -phon ing.** *—n.* apparatus, system, or process for transmitting sound or speech to a distant point over wires by means of electrical impulses. *—v.i.* talk through a telephone. *—v.t.* 1 send (a message) by telephone. 2 make a telephone call to. **—tel′e phon′er,** *n.*

telephone book or **telephone directory,** list of names, addresses, and telephone numbers of people or businesses with telephones in a certain area.

tel e phon ic (tel′ə fon′ik), *adj.* of or having to do with the telephone; by the telephone.

te leph o ny (tə lef′ə nē), *n.* the making or operating of telephones.

tel e pho to (tel′ə fō′tō), *adj.* telephotographic.

tel e pho to graph (tel′ə fō′tə graf), *n.* 1 picture taken with a camera having a telephoto lens. 2 picture sent by telegraphy. *—v.i.* 1 take a picture with a camera having a telephoto lens. 2 send a picture by telegraphy.

tel e pho to graph ic (tel′ə fō′tə graf′ik), *adj.* of or having to do with telephotography.

tel e pho tog ra phy (tel′ə fə tog′rə fē), *n.* 1 method or process of photographing distant objects by using a camera with a telephoto lens. 2 method or process of sending and reproducing pictures by telegraph.

telephoto lens, lens used in a camera for producing an enlarged image of a distant object.

tel e play (tel′ə plā′), *n.* play produced especially for television.

tel e print er (tel′ə prin′tər), *n.* teletypewriter.

Tel e Promp Ter (tel′ə promp′tər), *n.* trademark for a device consisting of a moving band that gives a prepared speech line for line, used by speakers who are being televised.

tel e ran (tel′ə ran′), *n.* an aid to landing aircraft which sends radar maps of the sky, an airfield, etc., by television. [< *tele(vision) r(adar) a(ir) n(avigation)*]

tel e scope (tel′ə skōp), *n., v.,* **-scoped, -scop ing.** *—n.* an optical instrument for making distant objects appear nearer and larger, consisting of an arrangement of lenses, and sometimes mirrors, in one or more tubes. *—v.t.* 1 force together one inside another like the sliding tubes of some telescopes: *When the two railroad trains crashed into each other, the cars were telescoped.* 2 bring together and shorten; condense. *—v.i.* fit or be forced together, one part inside another, like the parts of some telescopes.

tel e scop ic (tel′ə skop′ik), *adj.* 1 of or having to do with a telescope. 2 obtained or seen by means of a telescope: *a telescopic view of the moon.* 3 visible only through a telescope. 4 far-seeing. 5 making distant things look clear and close. 6 consisting of parts that slide one inside another like the tubes of some telescopes. **—tel′e scop′i cal ly,** *adv.*

tel e thon (tel′ə thon), *n.* a television program lasting many hours, especially one soliciting contributions for a charity, etc. [< *tele-* + *(mara)thon*]

tel e type (tel′ə tīp), *n., v.,* **-typed, -typ ing.** *—n.* 1 **Teletype,** trademark for a teletypewriter. 2 system of sending signals by Teletype. *—v.t.* send (a message) by Teletype.

tel e type writ er (tel′ə tīp′rī′tər), *n.* a telegraphic device which resembles a typewriter, used in sending, receiving, and automatically printing out messages.

tel e typ ist (tel′ə tī′pist), *n.* person who operates a teletypewriter.

tel e view (tel′ə vyü′), *v.t., v.i.* watch (a television program). **—tel′e view′er,** *n.*

tel e vise (tel′ə vīz), *v.,* **-vised, -vis ing.** *—v.t.* 1 send by television. 2 receive or see by television. *—v.i.* broadcast television programs.

tel e vi sion (tel′ə vizh′ən), *n.* 1 process of transmitting and receiving stationary or moving images and accompanying sounds over wires or through the air by a system in which light and sound waves are changed into electric waves and transmitted to a receiver where they are changed back into light and sound waves so that the images can be seen and the sounds heard. 2 the apparatus for receiving images and sounds so transmitted; television receiving set. 3 the business of television broadcasting; the television industry. *—adj.* of, used in, or sent by television.

tell[1] (tel), *v.,* **told, tell ing.** *—v.t.* 1 put in words; say: *tell a story, tell the truth.* 2 tell to; inform: *They told us the way at the station.* 3 make known: *Don't tell where the money is.* 4 act as talebearer; reveal (something secret or private): *Promise not to tell this.* 5 recognize; know; distinguish: *He couldn't tell which house it was.* 6 say to; order; command: *Tell him to wait.* 7 say to with force: *I don't like it, I tell you.* 8 count; count one by one: *The nun tells her beads.* 9 **tell off, a** count off; count off and detach for some special duty. **b** reprimand; scold; reprove. *—v.i.* 1 tell something: *He is always telling, never doing.* 2 have effect or force: *Every blow told.* 3 **tell of,** be an indication or sign of; show. 4 **tell on, a** inform on; tell tales about. **b** have a harmful effect on; break down: *The strain told on the man's heart.* [Old English *tellan.* Related to TALE.]

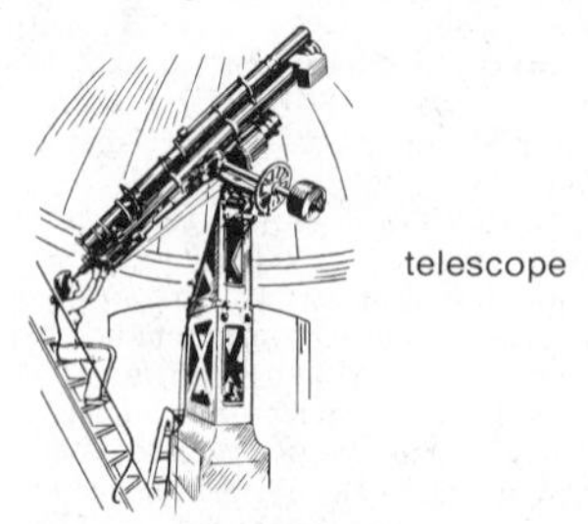
telescope

tell[2] (tel), *n.* an artificial hillock or mound, usually one covering the ruins of an ancient city. [< Arabic *tall* hillock]

Tell (tel), *n.* **William,** legendary hero in the Swiss struggle for independence against Austria.

tell a ble (tel′ə bəl), *adj.* capable or worthy of being told. **—tell′a ble ness,** *n.*

tell er (tel′ər), *n.* 1 person who tells. 2 person who counts. 3 a bank cashier who takes in, gives out, and counts money. 4 official who counts votes, especially in a legislature.

Tel ler (tel′ər), *n.* **Edward,** born 1908, American atomic physicist, born in Hungary.

tell ing (tel′ing), *adj.* having effect or force; striking: *a telling blow.* **—tell′ing ly,** *adv.*

tell tale (tel′tāl′), *n.* 1 person who tells tales on others; person who reveals private or secret matters from malice. 2 a warning sign; indication. 3 (in nautical use) a device above deck to indicate the rudder's position. 4 a row of ribbons hung over a track before a tunnel, low bridge, etc., to warn trainmen off the roofs of cars. *—adj.* telling what is not supposed to be told; revealing: *a telltale fingerprint.*

tel lu ride (tel′yə rīd′, tel′yər id′), *n.* compound of tellurium with an electropositive element or radical.

tel lur i um (te lůr′ē əm), *n.* a silver-white nonmetallic element with some metallic properties, usually occurring in nature combined with various metals, used as a coloring agent in ceramics. *Symbol:* Te; *atomic number* 52. See pages 326 and 327 for table.

tel ly (tel′ē), *n.* BRITISH INFORMAL. television.

tel o phase (tel′ə fāz), *n.* (in biology) the fourth and final stage of mitosis, when a membrane forms around each group of chromosomes in the cell and a nucleus is produced in each group, just before the cytoplasm of the cell constricts and the two new cells appear. [< Greek *telos* end + English *phase*]

tel son (tel′sən), *n.* the rearmost segment of the abdomen in certain crustaceans and arachnids, as the middle flipper of a lobster's tail or the sting of a scorpion. [< Greek, limit, headland]

Tel star (tel′stär′), *n.* trademark for the first active communications satellite, launched from Cape Canaveral in 1962.

Tel u gu (tel′ə gü), *n., pl.* **-gu** or **-gus.** 1 a Dravidian language spoken in eastern India. 2 one of the people who speak this language.

tem blor (tem blôr′), *n.* U.S. earthquake. [< Spanish < *temblar* to tremble]

te mer i ty (tə mer′ə tē), *n.* reckless boldness; rashness; foolhardiness. [< Latin *temeritatem* < *temere* heedlessly]

temp., 1 temperature. 2 temporary.

Tem pel hof (tem′pəl hōf), *n.* suburb of West Berlin, site of a major international airport.

tem per (tem′pər), *n.* 1 state of mind; disposition; mood: *She was in a good temper.* 2 angry state of mind: *In her temper she broke a vase.* 3 calm state of mind: *He became angry and lost his temper.* 4 the degree of hardness, toughness, flexibility, etc., of a substance given by tempering: *The temper of the clay was right for shaping.* 5 substance added to something to modify its properties or qualities. *—v.t.* 1 moderate; soften: *Temper justice with mercy.* 2 check; restrain; curb. 3 bring (steel or other metal) to a proper or desired condition of hardness, elasticity, etc., by heating and cooling under controlled conditions. 4 moisten, mix, and prepare (paint, mortar, etc.) in the proper consistency, thickness, smoothness, etc. 5 tune or adjust the pitch of (an instrument, a voice, etc.). *—v.i.* be or become tempered.

hat, āge, fär; let, ēqual, tėrm;
it, īce; hot, ōpen, ôrder;
oil, out; cup, pu̇t, rüle;
ch, child; ng, long; sh, she;
th, thin; ᴛʜ, then; zh, measure;

ə represents *a* in about, *e* in taken, *i* in pencil, *o* in lemon, *u* in circus.

< = from, derived from, taken from.

[Old English *temprian* to temper < Latin *temperare,* originally, observe due measure < *tempus* time, interval]

tem per a (tem′pər ə), *n.* method of painting in which colors are mixed with white or yolk of egg or other substances instead of oil. [< Italian]

tem per a ment (tem′pər ə mənt), *n.* 1 a person's nature or disposition: *a nervous temperament.* See **disposition** for synonym study. 2 an easily irritated, sensitive nature. An artist, singer, or actress often has temperament.

tem per a men tal (tem′pər ə men′tl), *adj.* 1 subject to moods and whims; easily irritated; sensitive: *a temperamental actor.* 2 showing a strongly marked individual temperament. 3 due to temperament; constitutional: *Cats have a temperamental dislike for water.* **—tem′per a men′tal ly,** *adv.*

tem per ance (tem′pər əns), *n.* 1 a being moderate in action, speech, habits, etc.; self-control. 2 a being moderate in the use of alcoholic drinks. 3 the principle and practice of not using alcoholic drinks at all.

tem per ate (tem′pər it), *adj.* 1 not very hot and not very cold: *a temperate climate.* 2 using self-control; moderate: *She spoke in a temperate manner, not favoring either side especially.* See **moderate** for synonym study. 3 moderate in using alcoholic drinks; abstemious. **—tem′per ate ly,** *adv.* **—tem′per ate ness,** *n.*

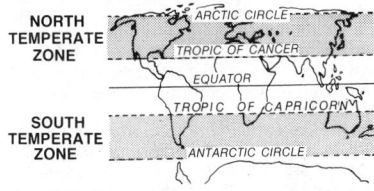

NORTH TEMPERATE ZONE
ARCTIC CIRCLE
TROPIC OF CANCER
EQUATOR
TROPIC OF CAPRICORN
SOUTH TEMPERATE ZONE
ANTARCTIC CIRCLE

temperate zone or **Temperate Zone,** the part of the earth's surface between the tropic of Cancer and the arctic circle in the Northern Hemisphere, or the part between the tropic of Capricorn and the antarctic circle in the Southern Hemisphere.

tem per a ture (tem′pər ə chər, tem′pər ə chu̇r), *n.* 1 degree of heat or cold of any substance. The temperature of freezing water is 32 degrees Fahrenheit. 2 degree of heat contained in the body, usually measured by a thermometer. 3 a body temperature higher than normal (98.6 degrees Fahrenheit); fever.

tem pered (tem′pərd), *adj.* 1 softened or moderated. 2 treated so as to become hard but not too brittle: *The sword was made of tempered steel.*

tem pest (tem′pist), *n.* 1 a violent windstorm, usually accompanied by rain, hail, or snow. 2 a violent disturbance. [< Latin *tempestas* < *tempus* time, season]

tem pes tu ous (tem pes′chü əs), *adj.* 1 stormy: *a tempestuous night.* 2 violent: *a tempestuous argument.* **—tem pes′tu ous ly,** *adv.* **—tem pes′tu ous ness,** *n.*

Tem plar (tem′plər), *n.* 1 member of a religious and military order called Knights Templars, founded among the Crusaders about 1118 to protect the Holy Sepulcher and pilgrims to Palestine. 2 member of an order of Masons, the Knights Templar, in the United States. [< Medieval Latin *templarius* < Latin *templum* temple[1]]

tem plate (tem′plit), *n.* 1 pattern, gauge, or mold of a thin, flat piece of wood or metal, used in shaping a piece of work. 2 any pattern or mold on which something is formed. [variant of *templet,* diminutive of *temple* (part of a loom)]

tem ple[1] (tem′pəl), *n.* 1 building used for the service or worship of a god or gods. 2 **Temple, a** any of three temples in ancient Jerusalem built at different times by the Jews. **b** the first of these three temples, built by Solomon. 3 building set apart for Christian worship; church. 4 synagogue. 5 place in which God specially dwells. 6 a Mormon church. [Old English *tempel* < Latin *templum*]

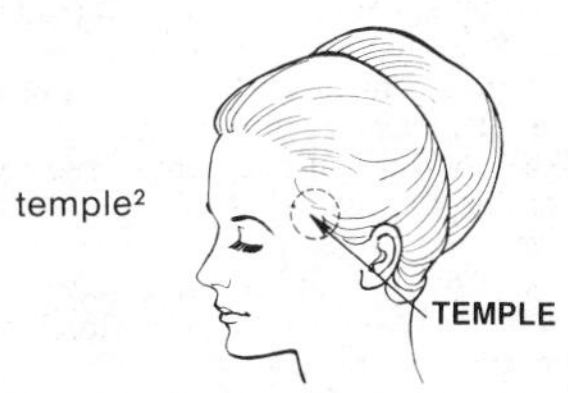

tem ple[2] (tem′pəl), *n.* the flattened part on either side of the forehead. [< Old French < Popular Latin *tempula* < Latin *tempora* the temples]

tem plet (tem′plit), *n.* template.

tem po (tem′pō), *n., pl.* **-pos, -pi** (-pē). 1 (in music) the time or rate of movement; proper or characteristic speed of movement. 2 characteristic pace or rhythm: *the fast tempo of modern life.* [< Italian, time < Latin *tempus.* Doublet of TENSE².]

tem por al[1] (tem′pər əl), *adj.* 1 of time. 2 lasting for a time only; temporary. 3 of this life only; earthly. 4 not religious or sacred; worldly; secular. [< Latin *temporalis* < *tempus* time] **—tem′por al ly,** *adv.*

tem por al[2] (tem′pər əl), *adj.* of the temples or sides of the forehead. [< Latin *temporalis* < *tempora* the temples]

temporal bone, a compound bone that forms part of the side and base of the skull.

tem po ral i ty (tem′pə ral′ə tē), *n., pl.* **-ties.** 1 temporal character or nature; temporariness. 2 Usually, **temporalities,** *pl.* the property or revenues of a church or clergyman. 3 temporal power, jurisdiction, etc. 4 the laity.

tem po rar y (tem′pə rer′ē), *adj.* lasting for a short time only; used for the time being; not permanent. **—tem′po rar′i ly,** *adv.* **—tem′po rar′i ness,** *n.*

Syn. Temporary, transient mean lasting or staying only for a time. **Temporary** applies to something meant to last only for a time and liable to come to an end shortly: *have a temporary job. Our school is housed in a temporary building.* **Transient** applies to something that is passing and hence will not stay long: *Her panic was transient, and ceased when she began to speak.*

tem po rize (tem′pə rīz′), *v.i.,* **-rized, -riz ing.** 1 evade immediate action or decision in order to gain time, avoid trouble, etc.; hedge. 2 fit one's acts to the time or occasion. 3 make or discuss terms; negotiate. **—tem′por i za′tion,** *n.* **—tem′po riz′er,** *n.*

tempt (tempt), *v.t.* 1 make or try to make (a person) do something wrong by the offer of some pleasure or reward: *a man tempted by hunger to steal.* 2 appeal strongly to; attract: *That candy tempts me.* 3 dispose or incline: *be tempted to disagree.* 4 induce or persuade: *Nothing will tempt him to sell his business.* 5 provoke: *It is tempting Providence to go in that old boat.* 6 ARCHAIC. test. [< Latin *temptare* to try]

temp ta tion (temp tā′shən), *n.* 1 a tempting. 2 a being tempted: *"Lead us not into temptation."* 3 thing that tempts.

tempt er (temp′tər), *n.* 1 person who tempts. 2 **the Tempter,** the Devil; Satan.

tempt ing (temp′ting), *adj.* that tempts; alluring; inviting: *a tempting offer.* **—tempt′ing ly,** *adv.* **—tempt′ing ness,** *n.*

temp tress (temp′tris), *n.* woman who tempts.

tem pus fu git (tem′pəs fyü′jit), LATIN. time flies.

ten (ten), *n.* 1 one more than nine; 10. 2 set of ten persons or things. *—adj.* being one more than nine. [Old English *tēn*]

ten., 1 tenor. 2 tenuto.

ten a bil i ty (ten′ə bil′ə tē), *n.* fact or quality of being tenable.

ten a ble (ten′ə bəl), *adj.* that can be held or defended; defensible: *a tenable theory.* [< French < *tenir* to hold < Latin *tenere*] **—ten′a bly,** *adv.*

te na cious (ti nā′shəs), *adj.* 1 holding fast: *the tenacious jaws of a bulldog, a person tenacious of his rights.* 2 stubborn; persistent; obstinate: *a tenacious salesman.* 3 able to remember; retentive: *a tenacious memory.* 4 holding fast together; not easily pulled apart. 5 sticky. [< Latin *tenacem* holding fast < *tenere* to hold] **—te na′cious ly,** *adv.* **—te na′cious ness,** *n.*

te nac i ty (ti nas′ə tē), *n.* 1 firmness in holding fast. 2 stubbornness; persistence. 3 ability to remember. 4 firmness in holding together; toughness. 5 stickiness.

ten an cy (ten′ən sē), *n., pl.* **-cies.** 1 condition of being a tenant; occupying and paying rent for land or buildings. 2 property so held. 3 length of time a tenant occupies a property.

ten ant (ten′ənt), *n.* 1 person paying rent for the temporary use of the land or buildings of another person: *That building has apartments for one hundred tenants.* 2 person or thing that occupies: *Birds are tenants of the trees.* *—v.t.* hold or occupy as a tenant; inhabit. [< Old French, originally present participle of *tenir* to hold < Latin *tenere*] **—ten′ant a ble,** *adj.* **—ten′ant less,** *adj.*

tenant farmer, farmer who raises crops on and lives on land belonging to another, to whom he pays as rent a share of the crops.

ten ant ry (ten′ən trē), *n., pl.* **-ries.** 1 all the tenants on an estate. 2 tenancy.

ten-cent store (ten′sent′), INFORMAL. dime store.

tench (tench), *n., pl.* **tench es** or **tench.** a freshwater fish of Europe, of the same family as the carp, noted for the length of time it can live out of water. [< Old French *tenche* < Late Latin *tinca*]

Ten Commandments, (in the Bible) the

ten rules for living and for worship that God revealed to Moses on Mount Sinai.

tend[1] (tend), *v.i.* 1 be apt; be likely; incline *(to): Fruit tends to decay. Homes tend to use more mechanical appliances now.* 2 move; be directed: *The coastline tends to the south here.* [< Old French *tendre* < Latin *tendere* stretch, extend. Doublet of TENDER[2].]

tend[2] (tend), *v.t.* 1 take care of; look after; attend to: *tend a sick person. He tends shop for his father. A shepherd tends his flock.* 2 serve; wait upon. *—v.i.* 1 serve (upon). 2 INFORMAL. pay attention. [short for *attend*]

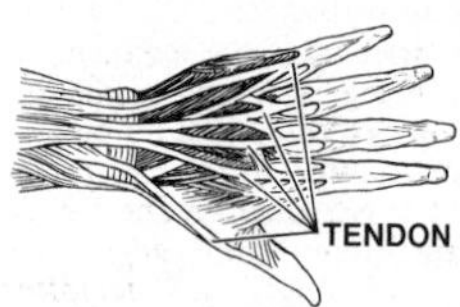

tend ance (ten′dəns), *n.* attention; care.

tend en cy (ten′dən sē), *n., pl.* **-cies.** 1 a leaning; inclination; propensity: *a tendency to fight.* 2 a natural disposition to move, proceed, or act in some direction or toward some point, end, or result: *Wood has a tendency to swell if it gets wet.* See **direction** for synonym study.

ten den tious (ten den′shəs), *adj.* having a tendency to show only one side; one-sided: *a tendentious statement.* **—ten den′tious ly,** *adv.* **—ten den′tious ness,** *n.*

ten der[1] (ten′dər), *adj.* 1 not tough or hard; soft: *tender meat.* 2 not strong and hardy; delicate: *tender young grass.* 3 delicate: *a tender blue.* 4 kind; affectionate; loving: *She spoke tender words to the child.* 5 not rough or crude; gentle: *He patted the dog with tender hands.* 6 young; immature: *Two years old is a tender age.* 7 sensitive; painful; sore: *a tender wound.* 8 feeling pain or grief easily: *a tender heart.* 9 sensitive to insult or injury; ready to take offense: *a man of tender pride.* 10 considerate or careful: *handle people in a tender manner.* 11 requiring careful or tactful handling: *a tender situation.* [Old French *tendre* < Latin *tener*] **—ten′der ly,** *adv.* **—ten′der ness,** *n.*

ten der[2] (ten′dər), *v.t.* 1 offer formally: *tender thanks.* See **offer** for synonym study. 2 (in law) offer (money, goods, etc.) in payment of a debt or other obligation. *—n.* 1 a formal offer; proposal: *refuse a tender of marriage.* 2 thing offered, especially money or currency that can be used by law to make payments. 3 (in law) an offer of money, goods, etc., to satisfy a debt or liability. 4 (in commerce) a bid to supply or purchase. [< Middle French *tendre* < Latin *tendere* stretch, extend. Doublet of TEND[1].] **—ten′der er,** *n.*

tend er[3] (ten′dər), *n.* 1 person or thing that tends another. 2 boat or small ship used for carrying supplies and passengers to and from larger ships. 3 a small boat carried on or towed behind a larger boat or a ship for similar use. 4 the car that carries coal and water, attached behind a steam locomotive. [< *tend*[2]]

ten der foot (ten′dər fu̇t′), *n., pl.* **-foots** or **-feet.** INFORMAL. 1 newcomer to the pioneer life of the western United States. 2 person not used to rough living and hardships. 3 an inexperienced person; beginner. 4 a beginning member of the Boy Scouts or Girl Scouts.

ten der heart ed (ten′dər här′tid), *adj.* easily moved by pity, sorrow, etc.; kindly; sympathetic. **—ten′der heart′ed ly,** *adv.* **—ten′der heart′ed ness,** *n.*

ten der ize (ten′də rīz′), *v.t.,* **-ized, -iz ing.** make soft or tender: *tenderize meat by pounding.* **—ten′der i za′tion,** *n.* **—ten′der iz′er,** *n.*

ten der loin (ten′dər loin′), *n.* 1 a tender part of the loin of beef or pork. 2 **Tenderloin,** a city district or section that includes the great mass of theaters, hotels, etc., and that is noted for the graft paid to the police for protection of vice.

ten di nous (ten′də nəs), *adj.* 1 of or like a tendon. 2 consisting of tendons.

ten don (ten′dən), *n.* a tough, strong band or cord of fibrous tissue that joins a muscle to a bone or some other part and transmits the force of the muscle to that part; sinew. [< Medieval Latin *tendonem* < Greek *tenōn;* influenced by Latin *tendere* to stretch]

tendon of Achilles, the tendon that connects the muscles of the calf of the leg to the bone of the heel.

ten dril (ten′drəl), *n.* 1 a threadlike part of a climbing plant that attaches itself to something and helps support the plant. 2 something similar: *curly tendrils of hair.* [< Middle French *tendrillon*]

tendril (def. 1) tendrils on a grapevine

ten dril ous (ten′drə ləs), *adj.* 1 full of tendrils. 2 resembling a tendril.

Ten e brae (ten′ə brē), *n.pl.* in the Roman Catholic Church: 1 the office of matins and lauds for the following day sung the afternoon or evening before each of the three days preceding Easter. 2 a public service at which this office is sung. [< Medieval Latin]

ten e brous (ten′ə brəs), *adj.* full of darkness; dark; gloomy; dim. [< Latin *tenebrosus* < *tenebrae* darkness]

ten e ment (ten′ə mənt), *n.* 1 tenement house. 2 any house or building to live in; dwelling house. 3 a dwelling, or part of a dwelling, occupied by a tenant. 4 abode; habitation. 5 **tenements,** *pl.* (in law) anything permanent that one person may hold of another, as land, buildings, franchises, rents, etc. [< Old French, ultimately < Latin *tenere* to hold]

tenement house, building, especially in a poor section of a city, divided into sets of rooms occupied by separate families.

Ten e rife or **Ten e riffe** (ten′ə rif′), *n.* the largest of the Canary Islands, off NW Africa. 388,000 pop.; 794 sq. mi.

ten et (ten′it), *n.* doctrine, principle, belief, or opinion held as true by a school, sect, party, or person. [< Latin, he holds]

ten fold (ten′fōld′), *adj.* 1 ten times as much or as many. 2 having ten parts. *—adv.* ten times as much or as many.

Tenn., Tennessee.

Ten nes see (ten′ə sē′), *n.* 1 one of the south central states of the United States. 3,924,000 pop.; 42,200 sq. mi. *Capital:* Nashville. *Abbrev.:* Tenn. 2 **Tennessee River,** river flowing from E Tennessee into the Ohio River. 652 mi. **—Ten′nes se′an,** *adj., n.*

Tennessee Valley Authority, TVA.

ten nis (ten′is), *n.* 1 game played by two or four players on a tennis court, in which a ball is hit back and forth over a net with a racket **(tennis racket).** 2 lawn tennis. 3 court tennis. [< Anglo-French *tenetz* hold!, ultimately < Latin *tenere* to hold]

tennis court, a level, rectangular area prepared and marked out for playing the game of tennis.

tennis elbow, inflammation of the elbow, commonly associated with tennis and certain other sports.

tennis shoes, sneakers.

Ten ny son (ten′ə sən), *n.* **Alfred,** Lord, 1809-1892, English poet. **—Ten′ny so′ni an,** *adj.*

ten on (ten′ən), *n.* projection on the end of a piece of wood cut so as to fit into the mortise in another piece and so form a joint. See **mortise** for diagram. *—v.t., v.i.* 1 cut so as to form a tenon. 2 fit together with tenon and mortise. [< Old French, ultimately < Latin *tenere* to hold]

ten or (ten′ər), *n.* 1 the general tendency; course: *the even tenor of country life.* 2 the general meaning or drift; gist; purport: *I understand French well enough to get the tenor of his speech.* 3 in music: **a** the highest natural adult male voice. **b** singer with such a voice. **c** part for such a voice or for an instrument of similar range. **d** instrument that has the quality or range of this voice. *—adj.* (in music) of or for a tenor. [< Latin, originally, a holding on < *tenere* to hold]

tenor clef, the C clef when the clef symbol is placed on the fourth line of the staff. See **clef** for diagram.

ten pen ny (ten′pen′ē), *adj.* 1 worth 10 British pennies. 2 designating a kind of nail that is three inches long.

ten pins (ten′pinz′), *n.* the game of bowling.

tense[1] (tens), *adj.,* **tens er, tens est,** *v.,* **tensed, tens ing.** *—adj.* 1 stretched tight; strained to stiffness: *a tense rope, a face tense with pain.* 2 keyed up; strained: *tense nerves, a tense moment.* 3 (in phonetics) pronounced with the muscles of the speech organs relatively tense. *—v.t., v.i.* stretch tight; tighten; stiffen: *I tensed my muscles for the leap.* [< Latin *tensum* < *tendere* to stretch] **—tense′ly,** *adv.* **—tense′ness,** *n.*

tense[2] (tens), *n.* 1 form of a verb that shows the time of the action or state expressed by the verb. *He obeys* is in the present tense. *He obeyed* is in the past tense. *He will obey* is in the future tense. 2 set of such forms for the various persons. [< Old French *tens* time < Latin *tempus.* Doublet of TEMPO.] **—tense′less,** *adj.*

ten sile (ten′səl), *adj.* 1 of or having to do with tension. 2 that can be stretched; ductile.

tensile strength, the maximum stress that a material can withstand before it breaks, expressed in pounds per square inch.

ten sil i ty (ten sil′ə tē), *n.* tensile quality; ductility.

ten sion (ten′shən), *n.* 1 a stretching. 2 a stretched condition: *The tension of the bow gives speed to the arrow.* 3 mental or nervous strain: *A mother feels tension when her baby is sick.* 4 a strained condition: *political tension.* 5 stress caused by the action of a pulling force. An elevator exerts tension on the cables supporting it. 6 device to control the pull or strain on something. The tension in a sewing machine may be adjusted to hold

hat, āge, fär; let, ēqual, tėrm;
it, īce; hot, ōpen, ôrder;
oil, out; cup, pu̇t, rüle;
ch, child; ng, long; sh, she;
th, thin; ᴛʜ, then; zh, measure;

ə represents *a* in about, *e* in taken, *i* in pencil, *o* in lemon, *u* in circus.

< = from, derived from, taken from.

the thread tight or loose. 7 the pressure of a gas. 8 electromotive force. —*v.t.* make tense; tighten; draw out. [< Latin *tensionem* < *tendere* to stretch] **—ten′sion less,** *adj.*

ten sion al (ten′shə nəl), *adj.* of or having to do with tension.

ten si ty (ten′sə tē), *n.* tense quality or condition.

ten sor (ten′sər, ten′sôr), *n.* muscle that stretches or tightens some part of the body.

ten-strike (ten′strīk′), *n.* 1 stroke that knocks down all ten pins in bowling; strike. 2 INFORMAL. any completely successful stroke or act.

tent (tent), *n.* 1 a movable shelter made of cloth or skins supported by a pole or poles. 2 a tentlike device to regulate the temperature and humidity of the air in treating certain respiratory diseases. —*v.i.* live in a tent. —*v.t.* 1 cover with or as with a tent. 2 put up or lodge in a tent or tents. [< Old French *tente,* ultimately < Latin *tendere* to stretch] **—tent′er,** *n.* **—tent′like′,** *adj.*

ten ta cle (ten′tə kəl), *n.* 1 one of the long, slender, flexible growths, usually occurring on the head or around the mouth of an animal, used to touch, hold, or move. 2 a sensitive, hairlike growth on a plant. [< New Latin *tentaculum* < Latin *tentare* to try]

ten ta cled (ten′tə kəld), *adj.* having a tentacle or tentacles.

ten tac u lar (ten tak′yə lər), *adj.* of, forming, or resembling tentacles.

ten ta tive (ten′tə tiv), *adj.* 1 done as a trial or experiment; experimental: *a tentative plan.* 2 hesitating: *a tentative laugh.* [< Medieval Latin *tentativus* < Latin *tentare* to try] **—ten′ta tive ly,** *adv.* **—ten′ta tive ness,** *n.*

tent caterpillar, caterpillar that lives in large numbers in the tentlike, silken webs it spins in trees, where it feeds on leaves and does great damage to the trees.

tent er (ten′tər), *n.* framework on which cloth is stretched so that it may set or dry evenly without shrinking. —*v.t.* stretch (cloth) on a tenter. [ultimately < Latin *tentum* stretched]

ten ter hook (ten′tər hu̇k′), *n.* 1 one of the hooks or bent nails that hold the cloth stretched on a tenter. 2 **on tenterhooks,** in painful suspense; anxious.

tenth (tenth), *adj., n.* 1 next after the ninth; last in a series of 10. 2 one, or being one, of 10 equal parts.

tenth ly (tenth′lē), *adv.* in tenth place.

tent stitch, petit point.

ten u i ty (te nyü′ə tē, te nü′ə tē), *n.* rarefied condition; thinness; slightness.

ten u ous (ten′yü əs), *adj.* 1 thin or slight; slender: *the tenuous thread of a spider's web.* 2 not dense; rare; rarefied: *The air ten miles above the earth is very tenuous.* 3 having slight importance; not substantial: *a tenuous claim.* [< Latin *tenuis* thin] **—ten′u ous ly,** *adv.* **—ten′u ous ness,** *n.*

ten ure (ten′yər), *n.* 1 a holding or possessing. 2 length of time of holding or possessing: *The tenure of office of the president of our club is one year.* 3 manner of holding land, buildings, etc., from a feudal lord or superior. 4 conditions, terms, etc., on which anything is held or occupied. 5 permanent status, granted after a period of trial, especially to a member of a faculty. [< Old French, ultimately < Latin *tenere* to hold]

te nur i al (te nyu̇r′ē əl), *adj.* of or having to do with a tenure. **—te nur′i al ly,** *adv.*

te nu to (te nü′tō), *adj., adv.* (in music) held or sustained to its full time value. [< Italian]

te pee (tē′pē), *n.* tent used by the American Indians of the Great Plains, made of hides sewn together and stretched over poles arranged in the shape of a cone. Also, **teepee.** [< Sioux *tipi*]

tepee
two tepees

tep id (tep′id), *adj.* moderately or slightly warm; lukewarm. [< Latin *tepidus* < *tepere* be warm] **—tep′id ly,** *adv.* **—tep′id ness,** *n.*

te pid i ty (ti pid′ə tē), *n.* a tepid condition.

te qui la (tə kē′lə), *n.* a Mexican alcoholic liquor made by distilling the juices obtained from the roasted stems of an agave plant. [< Mexican Spanish < *Tequila,* town in Mexico]

ter., territory.

ter a to log i cal (ter′ə tə loj′ə kəl), *adj.* of or having to do with teratology.

ter a tol o gy (ter′ə tol′ə jē), *n.* study of abnormal, misshapen, or monstrous formations and organisms. [< Greek *teratos* monster + English *-logy*]

ter bi um (tėr′bē əm), *n.* a silver-gray, rare-earth metallic element which occurs in certain minerals with yttrium and ytterbium. *Symbol:* Tb; *atomic number* 65. See pages 326 and 327 for table. [< New Latin < *Ytterby,* town in Sweden]

terce (tėrs), *n.* tierce.

ter cen te nar y (tər sen′tə ner′ē, tėr′sen-ten′ər ē), *adj., n., pl.* **-nar ies.** —*adj.* of or having to do with a period of 300 years or a 300th anniversary. —*n.* 1 a 300th anniversary. 2 the celebration of this. [< Latin *ter* three times + English *centenary*]

ter cen ten ni al (tėr′sen ten′ē əl), *adj., n.* tercentenary.

ter cet (tėr′sit), *n.* 1 group of three lines rhyming together, or connected by rhyme with the adjacent group or groups of three lines. 2 (in music) a triplet. [< French < Italian *terzetto,* ultimately < Latin *tertius* third]

te re do (tə rē′dō), *n., pl.* **-dos.** shipworm. [< Latin < Greek *terēdōn*]

Ter ence (ter′əns), *n.* 190?-159? B.C., Roman writer of comedies.

Te re sa (tə rē′sə, tə res′ə), *n.* Theresa.

Te resh ko va (tə resh′ko və), *n.* **Valentina,** born 1937, Russian astronaut. She was the first woman to travel in space, from June 16 to June 19, 1963.

ter gi ver sate (tėr′jə vər sāt), *v.i.,* **-sat ed, -sat ing.** 1 change one's attitude or opinions with respect to a cause or subject; turn renegade. 2 shift or shuffle; evade. [< Latin *tergiversatum* turned about < *tergum* the back + *versari* to turn] **—ter′gi ver sa′tion,** *n.* **—ter′gi ver sa′tor,** *n.*

term (tėrm), *n.* 1 word or phrase used in a recognized and definite sense in some particular subject, science, art, business, etc.: *medical terms.* 2 any particular word or expression: *a term of reproach.* 3 set period of time; length of time that a thing lasts: *the term of a lease, a president's term of office.* 4 one of the long periods into which the school year is divided: *the fall term.* 5 one of the periods of time during which a court is in session. 6 **terms,** *pl.* **a** conditions; provisions: *the terms of a treaty.* **b** agreement: *The company and the union came to terms.* **c** way of speaking: *flattering terms.* **d** personal relations: *on good terms, on speaking terms.* 7 a set or appointed time or date, especially for the payment of rent, wages, or other money due. 8 in mathematics: **a** one of the members in a proportion or ratio. **b** any part of a compound algebraic expression separated from the other parts by a plus or minus sign. In $13ax^2-2bxy+y$, $13ax^2$, $2bxy$, and *y* are the terms. 9 in logic: **a** word or words that form the subject or predicate of a proposition. **b** one of the three parts of a syllogism. **10 in terms of,** in regard to. —*v.t.* name; call: *He might be termed handsome.* [< Old French *terme* limit < Latin *terminus* end, boundary line]

ter ma gan cy (tėr′mə gən sē), *n.* shrewishness.

ter ma gant (tėr′mə gənt), *n.* a violent, quarreling, scolding woman. —*adj.* violent, quarreling, or scolding. [< *Termagant,* a fictitious Moslem deity in medieval plays]

ter mi na bil i ty (tėr′mə nə bil′ə tē), *n.* fact or quality of being terminable.

ter mi na ble (tėr′mə nə bəl), *adj.* 1 that can be ended: *The contract was terminable by either party.* 2 coming to an end after a certain time: *a loan terminable in 10 years.* **—ter′mi na ble ness,** *n.* **—ter′mi na bly,** *adv.*

ter mi nal (tėr′mə nəl), *adj.* 1 at the end; forming the end part: *a terminal appendage.* 2 growing at the end of a stem, branch, etc., as a bud or flower. 3 coming at the end: *a terminal examination.* 4 having to do with a term. 5 at the end of a railroad line. 6 having to do with the handling of freight at a terminal. 7 marking a boundary, limit, or end. 8 resulting in death; fatal: *a terminal disease.* —*n.* 1 the end; end part. 2 either end of a railroad line, airline, bus line, etc., at which are located sheds, offices, stations, and the like to handle freight and passengers. 3 city or station at the end of a railroad line, airline, etc. 4 device for making an electrical connection: *the terminals of a battery.* [< Latin *terminalis* < *terminus* end] **—ter′mi nal ly,** *adv.*

terminal leave, leave of absence given to a member of the armed forces before discharge, amounting to the remaining days of leave due.

ter mi nate (tėr′mə nāt), *v.,* **-nat ed, -nat ing.** —*v.t.* 1 bring to an end; put an end to; conclude: *terminate a partnership.* 2 occur at or form the end of; bound; limit. —*v.i.* 1 come to an end: *His contract termi-*

terrace (def. 4)—a series of terraces

nates soon. 2 stop short. **—ter′mi na′tor,** *n.*

ter mi na tion (tėr′mə nā′shən), *n.* 1 an ending; end; conclusion. 2 an end part. 3 ending of a word. In *gladly,* the adverbial termination is *-ly.*

ter mi na tion al (tėr′mə nā′shə nəl), *adj.* closing; final.

ter mi na tive (tėr′mə nā′tiv), *adj.* tending or serving to terminate.

ter mi no log i cal (tėr′mə nə loj′ə kəl), *adj.* of or having to do with terminology.

ter mi nol o gy (tėr′mə nol′ə jē), *n., pl.* **-gies.** the special words or terms used in a science, art, business, etc.: *medical terminology, the terminology of engineering.* [< Medieval Latin *terminus* term (< Latin, end) + Greek *-logia* -logy]

term insurance, insurance expiring at the end of a period of time and payable only if loss occurs within that period.

ter mi nus (tėr′mə nəs), *n., pl.* **-ni** (-nī), **-nus es.** 1 either end of a railroad line, bus line, etc., or the city or station where it is located; terminal. 2 an ending place; final point; goal; end. 3 stone, post, etc., marking a boundary or limit. [< Latin]

ter mite (tėr′mīt), *n.* any of an order of insects with soft, pale bodies that live in colonies consisting of winged males and females and wingless, sterile workers and soldiers; isopteran; white ant. Termites eat wood, paper, and other material containing cellulose and are very destructive to buildings, furniture, provisions, etc. [< Latin *termitem* woodworm]

term paper, a required essay written for a course in a school term.

tern (tėrn), *n.* any of a family of sea birds of the same order as the gulls but with a more slender body and bill and usually a long, forked tail. [< Scandinavian (Danish) *terne*]

ter nar y (tėr′nər ē), *adj.* 1 consisting of three; involving three; triple. 2 third in rank, order, or position. [< Latin *ternarius* < *terni* three each]

ter nate (tėr′nit, tėr′nāt), *adj.* 1 consisting of three. 2 arranged in threes. 3 in botany: **a** consisting of three leaflets. **b** having leaves arranged in whorls of three. **—ter′nate ly,** *adv.*

ter pene (tėr′pēn′), *n.* 1 any of a group of isomeric hydrocarbons produced by distilling the volatile oils of plants, especially conifers. *Formula:* $C_{10}H_{16}$ 2 any of various alcohols derived from or related to terpene. [< German *Terpentin* turpentine]

Terp sich or e (tėrp′sik′ər ē), *n.* (in Greek myths) the Muse of dancing and choral singing.

terp si cho re an (tėrp′sə kə rē′ən), *adj.* of or having to do with dancing.

terr., 1 terrace. 2 territory.

ter race (ter′is), *n., v.,* **-raced, -rac ing.** *—n.* 1 a paved outdoor space adjoining a house, used for lounging, dining, etc. 2 the flat roof of a house, especially of an Oriental or Spanish house. 3 row of houses or a short street running along the side or top of a slope. 4 a flat, raised level of land with vertical or sloping sides, especially one of a series of such levels placed one above the other. 5 U.S. a parklike strip in the center of a road, etc. *—v.t.* form into a terrace or terraces; furnish with terraces. [< Middle French, originally, a heap of rubble, ultimately < Latin *terra* earth]

ter ra cot ta (ter′ə kot′ə), 1 kind of hard, often unglazed, brownish-red earthenware, used for vases, statuettes, decorations on buildings, etc. 2 a dull brownish red. [< Italian, baked earth]

ter ra fir ma (ter′ə fėr′mə), solid earth; dry land. [< Latin]

ter rain (te rān′, ter′ān), *n.* tract of land, especially considered with respect to its extent and natural features in relation to its use in warfare. [< French, ultimately < Latin *terra* earth, land]

ter ra in cog ni ta (ter′ə in kog′nə tə), *pl.* **ter rae in cog ni tae** (ter′ē in kog′nə tē). an unknown or unexplored region. [< Latin, unknown land]

Ter ra my cin (ter′ə mī′sn), *n.* trademark for an antibiotic derived from an actinomycete, used in the treatment of a wide variety of bacterial infections.

ter ra pin (ter′ə pin), *n.* any of a genus of edible North American turtles that live in fresh water or tidewater. [of Algonquian origin]

ter rar i um (tə rer′ē əm), *n., pl.* **-rar i ums, -rar i a** (-rer′ē ə). a glass enclosure in which plants or small land animals are kept. [< New Latin]

ter raz zo (te raz′ō), *n.* kind of flooring consisting of fragments of marble set in a scattered pattern in cement. [< Italian, terrace]

ter res tri al (tə res′trē əl), *adj.* 1 of the earth; not of the heavens: *this terrestrial globe.* 2 of land, not water: *Islands and continents make up the terrestrial parts of the earth.* 3 living on the ground, not in the air or water or in trees: *terrestrial animals.* 4 growing on land; growing in the ground: *terrestrial plants.* 5 worldly; earthly. See **earthly** for synonym study. *—n.* a terrestrial being, especially a human. [< Latin *terrestris* < *terra* earth] **—ter res′tri al ly,** *adv.*

ter ri ble (ter′ə bəl), *adj.* 1 causing great fear; dreadful; awful: *a terrible leopard.* 2 distressing; severe: *the terrible suffering caused by war.* 3 INFORMAL. extremely bad, unpleasant, etc.: *a terrible temper, a terrible student.* [< Latin *terribilis* < *terrere* terrify] **—ter′ri ble ness,** *n.*

ter ri bly (ter′ə blē), *adv.* 1 in a terrible manner; dreadfully. 2 INFORMAL. extremely: *I'm terribly sorry.*

ter ri er (ter′ē ər), *n.* any of various breeds of usually small, active, intelligent, and courageous dogs, formerly used to pursue prey into its burrow. [< French *(chien) terrier* burrowing (dog)] **—ter′ri er like′,** *adj.*

ter rif ic (tə rif′ik), *adj.* 1 causing great fear or terror; terrifying. 2 INFORMAL. very unusual; remarkable; extraordinary: *a terrific hot spell.* 3 SLANG. very good; wonderful: *The party was terrific.* **—ter rif′i cal ly,** *adv.*

ter ri fied (ter′ə fīd), *adj.* filled with great fear; frightened. See **afraid** for synonym study.

ter ri fy (ter′ə fī), *v.t.,* **-fied, -fy ing.** fill with terror; frighten or alarm greatly. **—ter′ri fy′ing ly,** *adv.*

ter ri to ri al (ter′ə tôr′ē əl, ter′ə tōr′ē əl), *adj.* 1 of or having to do with territory: *The purchase of Louisiana was a valuable territorial addition to the United States.* 2 of a particular territory or district; restricted to a particular district: *a territorial governor.* 3 **Territorial, a** of a United States Territory: *The Virgin Islands has its own Territorial laws.* **b** BRITISH. organized for home defense. *—n.* **Territorial,** BRITISH. soldier of a Territorial force. **—ter′ri to′ri al ly,** *adv.*

ter ri to ri al ism (ter′ə tôr′ē ə liz′əm, ter′ə tōr′ē ə liz′əm), *n.* tendency among animals to defend their individual territories.

ter ri to ri al i ty (ter′ə tôr′ē al′ə tē, ter′ə-tōr′ē al′ə tē), *n.* 1 territorial quality or condition. 2 territorialism.

territorial waters, the waters off the coastline of a state over which the state exercises jurisdiction.

ter ri to ry (ter′ə tôr′ē, ter′ə tōr′ē), *n., pl.* **-ries.** 1 land; region: *Much territory in the northern part of Africa is desert.* 2 land belonging to a government; land under the rule of a distant government: *Gibraltar is British territory.* 3 **Territory,** U.S. district not admitted as a state but having its own lawmaking body. The Virgin Islands is a Territory. 4 region assigned to a salesman or agent. 5 the facts investigated by some branch of science or learning: *the territory of biochemistry.* 6 an area within definite boundaries, such as a nesting ground, in which an animal lives and from which it keeps out others of its kind. [< Latin *territorium* < *terra* land]

ter ror (ter′ər), *n.* 1 great fear; dread. 2 cause of great fear. 3 deliberate violence against persons or groups by another group, a government, etc. 4 INFORMAL. person or thing that causes much trouble and unpleasantness. [< Latin < *terrere* terrify]

ter ror ism (ter′ə riz′əm), *n.* 1 a terrorizing; use of terror, especially the systematic use of terror by a government or other authority against particular persons or groups. 2 condition of fear and submission produced by terrorizing people. 3 method of opposing a government internally through the use of terror.

ter ror ist (ter′ər ist), *n.* person who uses or favors terrorism. *—adj.* of or by terrorists; terroristic.

ter ror is tic (ter′ə ris′tik), *adj.* using or favoring methods that inspire terror.

ter ror i za tion (ter′ər ə zā′shən), *n.* a terrorizing or a being terrorized; rule by terror.

ter ror ize (ter′ə rīz′), *v.t.,* **-ized, -iz ing.** 1 fill with terror; terrify. 2 rule or subdue by causing terror.

ter ror-strick en (ter′ər strik′ən), *adj.* terrified.

ter ry (ter′ē), *n., pl.* **-ries.** a rough cloth made of uncut looped yarn. [perhaps < French *tiré* drawn]

terry cloth, terry.

terse (tėrs), *adj.,* **ters er, ters est.** brief and to the point: *a terse reply.* See **concise** for synonym study. [< Latin *tersum* polished < *tergere* to rub] **—terse′ly,** *adv.* **—terse′ness,** *n.*

ter tian (tėr′shən), *n.* fever, such as malaria, which recurs every other day. *—adj.* recurring every other day. [< Latin *tertiana (febris)* third (fever)]

Ter ti ar y (tėr′shē er′ē, tėr′shər ē), *n., pl.* **-ar ies,** *adj.* *—n.* 1 the earlier of the two

hat, āge, fär; let, ēqual, tėrm;
it, īce; hot, ōpen, ôrder;
oil, out; cup, pu̇t, rüle;
ch, child; ng, long; sh, she;
th, thin; ᴛʜ, then; zh, measure;

ə represents *a* in about, *e* in taken, *i* in pencil, *o* in lemon, *u* in circus.

< = from, derived from, taken from.

periods making up the Cenozoic era. During this period the great mountain systems, such as the Alps, Himalayas, Rocky Mountains, and Andes, appeared, and rapid development of mammals occurred. See chart under **geology.** 2 rocks formed in this period. 3 **tertiary,** one of a bird's flight feathers. 4 **tertiary,** a lay member of the third order of certain monastic fraternities of the Roman Catholic Church, not subject to the strict rule of the regulars. *—adj.* 1 of or having to do with the Tertiary or its rocks. 2 **tertiary,** of the third order, rank, or formation; third. [< Latin *tertiarius* < *tertius* third]

ter za ri ma (ter′tsä rē′mä), an Italian form of iambic verse consisting of ten-syllable or eleven-syllable lines arranged in tercets, the middle line of each tercet rhyming with the first and third lines of the following tercet. Shelley's *Ode to the West Wind* is in terza rima. [< Italian, third rhyme]

Tes la (tes′lə), *n.* **Nikola,** 1856-1943, American electrician and inventor, born in Croatia.

tes sel late (*v.* tes′ə lāt; *adj.* tes′ə lit, tes′ə-lāt), *v.,* **-lat ed, -lat ing,** *adj.* *—v.t.* make of small squares or blocks, or in a checkered pattern. *—adj.* made in small squares or blocks or in a checkered pattern. [< Latin *tessellatus,* ultimately < *tessera.* See TESSERA.] **—tes′sel la′tion,** *n.*

tes ser a (tes′ər ə), *n., pl.* **tes ser ae** (tes′-ər ē). 1 a small piece of marble, glass, or the like, used in mosaic work. 2 a small square of bone, wood, or the like, used in ancient times as a token, tally, ticket, die, etc. [< Latin, originally, cube < Greek *tessares* four]

test[1] (test), *n.* 1 examination or trial: *People who want a license to drive an automobile must pass a test.* See **trial** for synonym study. 2 means of trial: *Trouble is a test of character.* 3 in chemistry: **a** examination of a substance to see what it is or what it contains. **b** process or substance used in such an examination. **c** the result of such an examination. *—v.t.* put to a test of any kind; try out: *test a rope for strength. The doctor tested my eyes.* *—v.i.* show a certain result on a test. [< Old French, vessel used in assaying < Latin *testum* earthen vessel] **—test′a-ble,** *adj.*

test[2] (test), *n.* 1 hard covering of certain animals; shell. 2 testa. [< Latin *testa*]

Test., Testament.

tes ta (tes′tə), *n., pl.* **-tae** (-tē). the hard outside coat of a seed. [< Latin, shell]

tes ta ceous (te stā′shəs), *adj.* 1 of the nature of a shell or shells. 2 having a hard shell. 3 of a dull brownish-red, brownish-yellow, or reddish-brown color. [< Latin *testaceus* < *testa* shell]

tes ta cy (tes′tə sē), *n.* the leaving of a will at death.

tes ta ment (tes′tə mənt), *n.* 1 written instructions telling what to do with a person's property after his death; will. 2 expression; manifestation. 3 statement of beliefs or principles. 4 (in the Bible) a covenant between God and man. 5 **Testament,** **a** a main division of the Bible; the Old Testament or the New Testament. **b** INFORMAL. the New Testament. [< Latin *testamentum,* ultimately < *testis* witness]

tes ta men tar y (tes′tə men′tər ē), *adj.* 1 of or having to do with a testament or will. 2 given, done, or appointed by a testament or will. 3 in a testament or will.

tes tate (tes′tāt), *adj.* having made and left a valid will. *—n.* person who has died leaving a valid will. [< Latin *testatum* < *testis* witness]

tes ta tor (tes′tā tər, te stā′tər), *n.* 1 person who makes a will. 2 person who has died leaving a valid will.

tes ta trix (tē stā′triks), *n., pl.* **-tri ces** (-trə sēz′). a woman testator.

test ban, ban on testing, especially of nuclear weapons.

test case, a legal case whose outcome may set a precedent or test the constitutionality of a statute.

test-drive (test′drīv′), *v.t.,* **-drove** (-drōv′), **-driv en** (-driv′ən), **-driv ing.** drive (a motor vehicle) to test its performance.

test er[1] (tes′tər), *n.* person or thing that tests.

tes ter[2] (tes′tər), *n.* canopy, especially one over a bed. [< Old French *testre* < *teste* head, ultimately < Latin *testa* shell]

tes tes (tes′tēz′), *n.* pl. of **testis.**

test-fire (test′fīr), *v.t.,* **-fired, -fir ing.** fire (a rocket, missile, etc.) as a test.

test flight, flight in which the performance of an aircraft or spacecraft is tested.

test-fly (test′flī′), *v.t.,* **-flew** (-flü′), **-flown** (-flōn′), **-fly ing.** subject to a test flight.

tes ti cle (tes′tə kəl), *n.* gland in a male animal that produces the sperm; testis. [< Latin *testiculus,* diminutive of *testis* testis]

tes ti fy (tes′tə fī), *v.,* **-fied, -fy ing.** *—v.i.* 1 give evidence; bear witness: *The excellence of Shakespeare's plays testifies to his genius.* 2 give evidence under oath in a court of law: *The witness was unwilling to testify.* *—v.t.* 1 give evidence of; bear witness to: *The firm testified its appreciation of her work by raising her pay.* 2 declare under oath in a court of law: *The witness testified that the speeding car had crashed into the truck.* 3 declare solemnly; affirm. [< Latin *testificari* < *testis* witness + *facere* to make] **—tes′ti fi′er,** *n.*

tes ti mo ni al (tes′tə mō′nē əl), *n.* 1 certificate of character, conduct, qualifications, value, etc.; recommendation: *a testimonial from a former employer. Advertisements of patent medicines often contain testimonials from people who have used them.* 2 gift, banquet, or the like, extended to someone as a token of esteem, admiration, gratitude, etc.: *The members of the church collected money for a testimonial to their retiring pastor.* *—adj.* given or done as a testimonial: *a testimonial letter.*

tes ti mo ny (tes′tə mō′nē), *n., pl.* **-nies.** 1 statement used for evidence or proof: *A witness gave testimony that the defendant was at home all day Sunday.* 2 evidence: *The pupils presented their teacher with a watch in testimony of their respect and affection.* See **evidence** for synonym study. 3 an open delcaration or profession of one's faith. 4 ARCHAIC. the Ten Commandments. 5 **testimonies,** *pl.* the precepts of God; the divine law. [< Latin *testimonium* < *testis* witness]

tes tis (tes′tis), *n., pl.* **-tes.** testicle. [< Latin, witness (of virility)]

tes tos te rone (te stos′tə rōn′), *n.* hormone secreted by the testicles, which produces and maintains male sexual characteristics.

test pilot, pilot employed to test new or experimental aircraft by subjecting them to greater than normal stress.

test tube, a thin glass tube closed at one end, used in making chemical or biological tests.

tes tu do (te stü′dō, te styü′dō), *n., pl.* **-di nes** (-de nēz′). 1 (among the ancient Romans) a movable shelter with a strong and usually fireproof arched roof, used for protection in siege operations. 2 shelter formed by a body of troops overlapping their shields above their heads. 3 some other shelter. [< Latin, literally, tortoise < *testa* shell]

tes ty (tes′tē), *adj.,* **-ti er, -ti est.** easily irritated; impatient; petulant. [< Anglo-French *testif* headstrong < Old French *teste* head. See TESTER[2].] **—tes′ti ly,** *adv.* **—tes′ti ness,** *n.*

Tet (tet), *n.* a Vietnamese festival held in January to celebrate the lunar new year.

te tan ic (ti tan′ik), *adj.* 1 having to do with tetanus. 2 having to do with tetany.

tet a nus (tet′n əs), *n.* 1 disease caused by a bacillus usually entering the body through wounds, characterized by violent spasms and stiffness of many muscles, sometimes resulting in death. Tetanus of the jaw muscles is called lockjaw. 2 condition of prolonged contraction of a muscle. [< Latin < Greek *tetanos* < *teinein* to stretch]

tet a ny (tet′n ē), *n.* disease characterized by spasms of the muscles. [< Latin *tetanus*]

tetch y (tech′ē), *adj.,* **tetch i er, tetch i est.** easily irritated or made angry; touchy.

tête-à-tête (tāt′ə tāt′), *adv.* two together in private: *They dined tête-à-tête.* *—adj.* of or for two people in private. *—n.* 1 a private conversation between two people. 2 an S-shaped seat built so that two people can sit facing one another. [< French, head to head]

teth er (teᴛʜ′ər), *n.* 1 rope or chain for fastening an animal so that it can graze or move only within a certain limit. 2 **at the end of one's tether,** at the end of one's resources or endurance. *—v.t.* fasten or confine with or as with a tether. [< Scandinavian (Old Icelandic) *tjōthr*]

teth er ball (teᴛʜ′ər bôl′), *n.* game played by two persons with a ball fastened by a cord to the top of a tall post. The object of the game is to hit the ball so as to wind the cord around the post, in one direction or the other.

tetra-, *combining form.* four, as in *tetrachloride, tetravalent.* [< Greek]

tet ra chlo ride (tet′rə klôr′īd, tet′rə-klôr′id; tet′rə klōr′īd, tet′rə klōr′id), *n.* compound containing four atoms of chlorine combined with another element or radical.

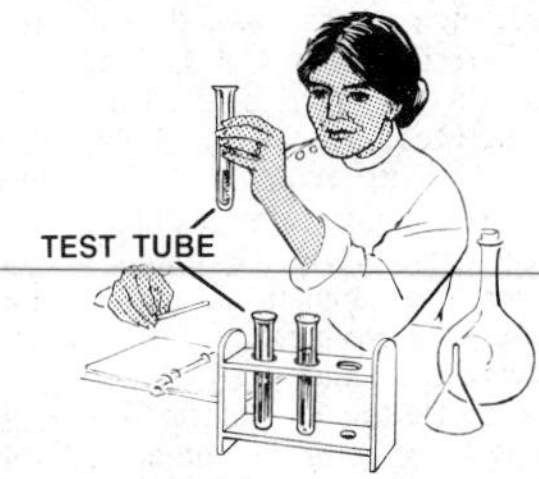

tet ra chord (tet′rə kôrd), *n.* (in music) a diatonic scale series of four notes; half an octave.

tet ra cy cline (tet′rə sī′klən), *n.* antibiotic used in treating a wide variety of bacterial diseases. *Formula:* $C_{22}H_{24}N_2O_8$

tet rad (tet′rad), *n.* 1 group or set of four. 2 group of four chromatids formed in various organisms when a pair of chromosomes splits longitudinally during meiosis.

tet ra eth yl lead (tet′rə eth′əl), a poisonous, colorless liquid, used in gasoline to reduce knocking. *Formula:* $Pb(C_2H_5)_4$

tet ra he dral (tet′rə hē′drəl), *adj.* of or having to do with a tetrahedron; having four faces.

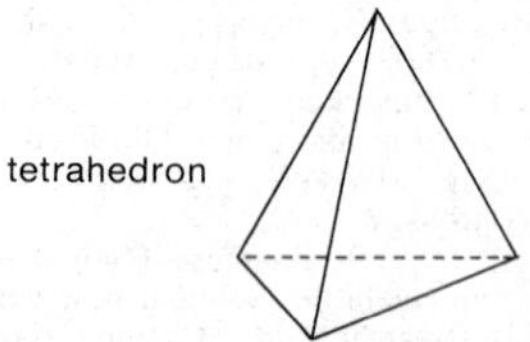

tet ra he dron (tet′rə hē′drən), *n., pl.* **-drons, -dra** (-drə). a solid figure having four faces. The most common tetrahedron is a pyramid whose base and three sides are equilateral triangles. [< Greek *tetra-* + *hedra* base]

te tral o gy (te tral′ə jē), *n., pl.* **-gies.** series of four connected dramas, operas, etc.

te tram e ter (te tram′ə tər), *n.* line of verse having four metrical feet. EXAMPLE: "The stag′ | at eve′ | had drunk′ | his fill.′"

tet ra pod (tet′rə pod), *n.* any of a superclass of vertebrates having lungs and two pairs of limbs used for movement on land. Amphibians, reptiles, birds, and mammals belong to this superclass. [< Greek *tetra-* four + *podos* foot]

tet rarch (tet′rärk, tē′trärk), *n.* 1 the ruler of a part (originally a fourth part) of a province in the ancient Roman Empire. 2 any subordinate ruler. [< Greek *tetrarchēs* < *tetra-* four + *archos* ruler]

tet rar chy (tet′rär kē, tē′trär kē), *n., pl.* **-chies.** 1 government or jurisdiction of a tetrarch. 2 territory governed by a tetrarch. 3 government by four persons. 4 set of four rulers. 5 country divided into four governments.

tet ra va lent (tet′rə vā′lənt, te trav′ə lənt), *adj.* having a valence of four.

tet rode (tet′rōd), *n.* vacuum tube containing four elements, commonly a cathode, anode, and two grids.

te trox ide (te trok′sīd, te trok′sid), *n.* any oxide having four atoms of oxygen in each molecule.

tet ter (tet′ər), *n.* any of various itching skin diseases, such as eczema and psoriasis. [Old English *teter*]

Te tuán (tā twän′), *n.* seaport in N Morocco, on the Mediterranean. 117,000.

Teu ton (tüt′n, tyüt′n), *n.* 1 German. 2 person belonging to the group of northern Europeans that speak Germanic languages. 3 member of an ancient Germanic tribe that threatened the Roman republic in the 100's B.C. *—adj.* German.

Teu ton ic (tü ton′ik, tyü ton′ik), *adj.* 1 of or having to do with the ancient Teutons or their languages. 2 Germanic. 3 German. *—n.* Germanic. **—Teu ton′i cal ly,** *adv.*

Tex., Texas.

tex as (tek′səs), *n.* structure on the hurricane deck of a river steamer where officers' cabins are situated. It has the pilothouse in front or on top. [< *Texas*]

Tex as (tek′səs), *n.* one of the southwestern states of the United States. 11,197,000 pop.; 267,300 sq. mi. *Capital:* Austin. *Abbrev.:* Tex. **—Tex′an,** *adj., n.*

Texas fever, an infectious disease of cattle that attacks the red blood cells, caused by a protozoan parasite and transmitted by cattle-infesting ticks.

Texas Rangers, 1 group of mounted police officers of the state of Texas. 2 group of United States citizens who tried to maintain order during the early years of settling in Texas.

Texas tower, U.S. an offshore radar station built on pilings sunk into the ocean floor.

text (tekst), *n.* 1 the main body of reading matter in a book: *This history book contains 300 pages of text and about 50 pages of notes, explanations, and questions for study.* 2 the original words of a writer. A text is often changed here and there when it is copied. 3 any one of the various wordings of a poem, play, etc. 4 a short passage in the Bible, used as the subject of a sermon or as proof of some belief: *The minister preached on the text "Judge not, that ye be not judged."* 5 topic; subject. 6 textbook. [< Latin *textus,* originally, texture < *texere* to weave] **—text′less,** *adj.*

text book (tekst′bu̇k′), *n.* book read or referred to as an authority and standard in the study of a particular subject, especially one written for this purpose. *—adj.* belonging in a textbook; accepted; standard: *a textbook example.*

tex tile (tek′stəl, tek′stīl), *adj.* 1 woven: *Cloth is a textile fabric.* 2 suitable for weaving: *Linen, cotton, silk, nylon, and wool are common textile materials.* 3 of or having to do with weaving: *the textile art.* 4 of or having to do with the making, selling, etc., of textiles. *—n.* 1 a woven fabric; cloth. 2 material suitable for weaving. [< Latin *textilis* < *texere* to weave]

tex tu al (teks′chü əl), *adj.* of or having to do with the text: *A misprint is a textual error.* **—tex′tu al ly,** *adv.*

tex tur al (teks′chər əl), *adj.* of or having to do with texture.

tex ture (teks′chər), *n.* 1 arrangement of threads in a woven fabric: *A piece of burlap has a much coarser texture than a linen handkerchief.* 2 arrangement of the parts of anything; structure; constitution; make-up: *Sandstone and granite have different textures.* [< Latin *textura* < *texere* to weave]

tex tured (teks′chərd), *adj.* having a particular texture: *thickly textured.*

-th, *suffix added to numbers.* number ____ in order or position in a series: *Sixth = number six in order or position in a series.* [Old English *-tha, -the*]

Th, thorium.

Th., Thursday.

Thack er ay (thak′ər ē), *n.* **William Makepeace,** 1811-1863, English novelist, born in India.

Thai (tī), *adj.* of Thailand, its people, or their language. *—n.* 1 native or inhabitant of Thailand. 2 language of Thailand. Also, **Tai.**

Thai land (tī′land), *n.* country in SE Asia. 35,550,000 pop.; 198,200 sq. mi. *Capital:* Bangkok. See **Indochina** for map. Former name, **Siam.**

Thai land er (tī′lan dər), *n.* a Thai.

tha lam ic (thə lam′ik), *adj.* of or having to do with the thalamus.

thal a mus (thal′ə məs), *n., pl.* **-mi** (-mī). 1 a large, oblong mass of gray matter in the posterior part of the forebrain, from which nerve fibers pass to the sensory parts of the cortex and which is connected with the optic nerve. 2 (in botany) the receptacle of a flower; torus. [< Latin, inside room < Greek *thalamos*]

tha las sic (thə las′ik), *adj.* 1 of or having to do with the sea. 2 of or having to do with the smaller or inland seas, as distinct from the oceans. [< Greek *thalassa* sea]

tha ler (tä′lər), *n., pl.* **-ler.** a large silver coin formerly used in Germany. It was replaced by the mark. Also, **taler.** [< German *Thaler*]

Tha les (thā′lēz), *n.* 640?-546? B.C., Greek philosopher.

Tha li a (thə lī′ə), *n.* in Greek myths: 1 the Muse of comedy and idyllic poetry. 2 one of the three Graces.

tha lid o mide (thə lid′ə mīd′), *n.* drug formerly used as a sedative and hypnotic, discontinued after it was found to cause malformation of the fetus in early pregnancy. *Formula:* $C_{13}H_{10}N_2O_4$

thal li um (thal′ē əm), *n.* a soft, malleable, bluish-white metallic element that occurs in iron and zinc ores and in various minerals. It is highly poisonous and its compounds are used to kill insects, rodents, etc. *Symbol:* Tl; *atomic number* 81. See pages 326 and 327 for table. [< New Latin < Greek *thallos* green shoot; because its spectrum shows a green band]

thal lo phyte (thal′ə fīt), *n.* any of a division of plants in which the plant body is not divided into leaves, stems, or roots, and the simpler unicellular forms reproduce by cell division or by asexual spores while the higher forms reproduce both asexually and sexually. Bacteria, algae, fungi, and lichens are thallophytes.

thal lus (thal′əs), *n., pl.* **thal li** (thal′ī), **thal lus es.** a plant body not divided into leaves, stem, and root; the plant body characteristic of thallophytes. [< New Latin < Greek *thallos* green shoot]

Thames River (temz), river flowing from S England into the North Sea. London is on the Thames. 210 mi. See **Rhine River** for map.

than (ᴛʜan; *unstressed* ᴛʜən), *conj.* 1 in comparison with: *This train is faster than that one.* 2 compared to that which: *She has more money than she needs.* 3 except; besides: *How else can we come than on foot?* 4 **than whom,** compared to whom. [Old English *thanne, thonne;* originally the same word as *then*]

➤ In clauses consisting of **than** plus a personal pronoun, the form of the latter is determined by its function as subject or object: *He is older than I* [am]. Often, however, *than* is treated as a preposition and the objective form of the pronoun is substituted: *He is older than me.* ➤ See **then** for another usage note.

thane (thān), *n.* 1 (in early English history) a man who ranked between an earl and an ordinary freeman. Thanes held lands of the king or lord and gave military service in return. 2 (in Scottish history) a baron or lord. Also, **thegn.** [Old English *thegn*]

thank (thangk), *v.t.* say that one is pleased

hat, āge, fär; let, ēqual, tėrm;
it, īce; hot, ōpen, ôrder;
oil, out; cup, pu̇t, rüle;
ch, child; ng, long; sh, she;
th, thin; ᴛʜ, then; zh, measure;

ə represents *a* in about, *e* in taken, *i* in pencil, *o* in lemon, *u* in circus.

< = from, derived from, taken from.

and grateful for something given or done; express gratitude to. —*v.i.* **have oneself to thank,** be to blame. —*n.* 1 **thanks,** *pl.* **a** I thank you. **b** act of thanking; expression of gratitude and pleasure. **c** feeling of kindness received; gratitude. 2 **thanks to,** owing to; because of. [Old English *thanc,* originally, thought]

thank ful (thangk′fəl), *adj.* feeling or expressing thanks; grateful. —**thank′ful ly,** *adv.* —**thank′ful ness,** *n.*

thank less (thangk′lis), *adj.* 1 not feeling or expressing thanks; ungrateful. 2 not likely to get thanks; not appreciated: *Giving advice is usually a thankless act.* —**thank′less ly,** *adv.* —**thank′less ness,** *n.*

thanks giv ing (thangks giv′ing), *n.* 1 a giving of thanks. 2 expression of thanks: *They offered thanksgiving to God for their escape.* 3 day set apart to acknowledge God's favor. 4 **Thanksgiving,** Thanksgiving Day.

Thanksgiving Day, day set apart as a holiday on which to give thanks for God's kindness during the year. In the United States, Thanksgiving Day is the fourth Thursday in November. In Canada, it is the second Monday in October.

thank wor thy (thangk′wėr′ᴛʜē), *adj.* worthy of thanks; deserving gratitude.

Thant (thänt), *n.* **U,** born 1909, Burmese diplomat, secretary-general of the United Nations from 1962 to 1971.

that (ᴛʜat; *unstressed* ᴛʜət), *adj., pron., pl.* (for defs. 1-3) **those,** *conj., adv.* —*adj.* 1 pointing out or indicating some person, thing, idea, etc., already mentioned, understood, or to be emphasized: *Do you know that boy?* 2 indicating the farther of two or farthest of most things: *Shall I buy this dress or that one we saw yesterday?* 3 showing contrast: *This hat is prettier but that one costs less.*

—*pron.* 1 some person, thing, idea, etc., already mentioned, understood, or to be emphasized: *That is the right way. That's a good boy!* 2 the farther of two or farthest of most things: *I like that better.* 3 something contrasted: *Which hat do you want, this or that?* 4 who; whom; which: *Is he the man that sells dogs? She is the girl that you mean. Bring the box that will hold most.* 5 at or in which; when: *The year that we went to England was 1964.* 6 ARCHAIC. the former. 7 **at that,** INFORMAL. **a** with no more talk, work, etc. **b** considering everything. 8 **in that,** because: *I prefer her plan to yours, in that I think it is more practical.* 9 **that's that,** INFORMAL. that is settled or decided.

—*conj. That* is used: 1 to introduce a noun clause and connect it with the verb. *I know that 6 and 4 are 10.* 2 to show purpose, aim, or desire. *Study that you may learn.* 3 to show result. *I ran so fast that I was five minutes early.* 4 to show cause. *I wonder what happened, not that I care.* 5 to express a wish. *Oh, that she were here!* 6 to show anger, surprise, sorrow, indignation, or the like. *That one so fair should be so false!*

—*adv.* to such an extent or degree; so: *I cannot stay up that late.*

[Old English *thæt,* originally, neuter of *sē,* demonstrative pronoun and adjective]

➤ The relative pronouns **that, who,** and **which** are distinguished in present use as follows: (1) *That* may refer to persons, animals, or things, *who* only to persons, *which* to animals, things, or groups of people regarded impersonally: *the man that* (or *who*) *answered; the concert that* (or *which*) *was scheduled; the animals that* (or *which*) *are native to this region.* (2) *That* is used chiefly in restrictive clauses: *The book that she selected for her report was the longest on the list. Who* and *which* are used in both restrictive and nonrestrictive clauses. Restrictive: *the man who answered; the parcel which I received.* Nonrestrictive: *the parcel, which had been badly wrapped; my aunt, who is an accountant.* ➤ See **this** for another usage note.

thatch—man thatching a roof

thatch (thach), *n.* 1 straw, rushes, palm leaves, etc., used as a roof or covering. 2 roof or covering of thatch. 3 INFORMAL. hair covering the head. —*v.t.* roof or cover with or as with thatch. [Old English *thæc*] —**thatch′er,** *n.*

that'll (ᴛʜat′l), 1 that will. 2 that shall.

that's (ᴛʜats), that is.

thau ma tur gic (thô′mə tėr′jik), *adj.* of or having to do with thaumaturgy.

thau ma tur gy (thô′mə tėr′jē), *n.* the working of wonders or miracles; magic. [< Greek *thaumatourgia,* ultimately < *thaumatos* marvel + *ergon* work]

thaw (thô), *v.t.* 1 melt (ice, snow, or anything frozen); free from frost: *This warm weather should thaw the ice on the roads very quickly.* See **melt** for synonym study. 2 make less stiff and formal in manner; soften. —*v.i.* 1 become warm enough to melt ice, snow, etc.: *If the sun stays out, it will probably thaw today.* 2 become free of frost, ice, etc.: *Our sidewalk thawed yesterday. The pond freezes up in November and thaws out in April.* 3 become less stiff and formal in manner; soften: *His shyness thawed under her kindness.* —*n.* 1 a thawing. 2 condition or period of weather above the freezing point (32 degrees Fahrenheit); time of melting. 3 a becoming less stiff and formal in manner; softening. [Old English *thawian*]

Th.D., Doctor of Theology.

the[1] (ᴛʜə *unstressed before a consonant;* ᴛʜi *unstressed before a vowel;* ᴛʜē *stressed*), *definite article. The* shows that a certain one (or ones) is meant. Various special uses are: 1 to mark a noun as indicating something well-known or unique: *the earth, the President.* 2 with or as part of a title: *the Reverend John Smith.* 3 to mark a noun as indicating the best-known or most important of its kind: *the place to dine.* 4 to mark a noun as being used generically: *The dog is a quadruped.* 5 to indicate a part of the body or a personal belonging: *hang the head in shame, clutch at the sleeve of one's father.* 6 before adjectives used as nouns: *visit the sick, a love of the beautiful.* 7 distributively, to denote any one separately: *candy at one dollar the pound, so much by the day.* [Old English *thē, the*]

the[2] (ᴛʜə, ᴛʜē), *adv. The* is used to modify an adjective or adverb in the comparative degree: 1 in that degree; to that degree: *If you start now, you will be back the sooner.* 2 used correlatively, in one instance with relative force and in the other with demonstrative force, and meaning: by how much . . . by so much; in what degree . . . in that degree: *the more the merrier, the sooner the better.* [Old English *thȳ, thē, thon* by that]

the a ter (thē′ə tər), *n.* 1 place where plays are acted or motion pictures are shown. 2 place that looks like a theater in its arrangement of seats: *The surgeon performed an operation before the medical students in the operating theater.* 3 place of action: *Belgium and France were the theater of World War I.* 4 the writing, performance, or production of plays; drama. 5 play, situation, dialogue, etc., considered as to its effectiveness on the stage: *This scene is bad theater.* Also, **theatre.** [< Greek *theatron* < *theasthai* to view < *thea* view]

the a ter go er (thē′ə tər gō′ər), *n.* person who attends the theater, especially one who goes often.

the a ter go ing (thē′ə tər gō′ing), *n.* practice or habit of attending the theater.

the a ter-in-the-round (thē′ə tər in ᴛʜə-round′), *n.* theater in which the stage is surrounded by seats on all sides, whether in a permanent building, a tent, or out of doors; arena theater.

the a tre (thē′ə tər), *n.* theater.

the at ric (thē at′rik), *adj.* theatrical.

the at ri cal (thē at′rə kəl), *adj.* 1 of or having to do with the theater or actors; histrionic: *theatrical performances, a theatrical company.* 2 suggesting a theater or acting; for display or effect; artificial. See **dramatic** for synonym study. —*n.* **theatricals,** *pl.* **a** dramatic performances, especially as given by amateurs. **b** matters having to do with the stage and acting. **c** actions of a theatrical or artificial character. —**the at′ri cal ly,** *adv.*

the at ri cal i ty (thē at′rə kal′ə tē), *n.* quality of being theatrical.

the at rics (thē at′riks), *n. sing. or pl.* 1 the art of producing plays. 2 doings of a theatrical or artificial character; histrionics.

Thebes (thēbz), *n.* 1 important city in the central part of ancient Greece. 2 city in ancient Egypt, on the Nile, formerly a center of Egyptian civilization. —**The ban** (thē′bən), *adj., n.*

the ca (thē′kə), *n., pl.* **-cae** (-sē′). 1 sac, saclike cell, or capsule in a plant. 2 case or sheath enclosing an animal, as an insect pupa, or some part of an animal, as a tendon. [< New Latin < Greek *thēkē* case, cover]

thé dan sant (tā däN säN′), *pl.* **thés dansants** (*tā däN säN′*). FRENCH. an afternoon tea with dancing.

thee (ᴛʜē), *pron.* objective case of **thou.** ARCHAIC. you: *"The Lord bless thee and keep thee."* [Old English *thē*]

theft (theft), *n.* 1 act of stealing; thievery; larceny: *be put in prison for theft.* 2 instance of stealing: *The theft of the jewels caused much excitement.* [Old English *thēoft* < *thēof* thief]

thegn (thān), *n.* thane.

their (ŦHer, ŦHar), *adj.* possessive form of **they.** of them; belonging to them: *They like their school and do their lessons well.* [< Scandinavian (Old Icelandic) *theirra*]

theirs (ŦHerz, ŦHarz), *pron.* possessive form of **they.** the one or ones belonging to them: *Our house is white; theirs is brown. Those books are theirs.*

the ism (thē′iz′əm), *n.* 1 belief in one God, the creator and ruler of the universe. 2 belief in a deity or deities; religious faith or conviction. [< Greek *theos* god]

the ist (thē′ist), *n.* believer in theism.

the is tic (thē is′tik), *adj.* of or having to do with theism or theists. **—the is′ti cal ly,** *adv.*

the is ti cal (thē is′tə kəl), *adj.* theistic.

them (ŦHem; *unstressed* ŦHəm, əm), *pron.* objective case of **they.** *The books are new; take care of them.* [< Scandinavian (Old Icelandic) *theim*]

➤ In many nonstandard dialects **them** is used as a demonstrative adjective, often strengthened by *there: them bales, them there bales.*

the mat ic (thē mat′ik), *adj.* of or having to do with a theme or themes. **—the mat′i cal ly,** *adv.*

theme (thēm), *n.* 1 topic; subject: *Patriotism was the speaker's theme.* 2 a short written composition. 3 in music: **a** the principal melody in a composition or movement. **b** a short melody repeated in different forms in an elaborate musical composition. 4 Also, **theme song.** melody used to identify a particular radio or television program; signature. [< Greek *thema,* originally, something set down]

The mis to cles (thə mis′tə klēz′), *n.* 527?-460? B.C., Athenian naval commander and statesman.

them selves (ŦHem selvz′, ŦHəm selvz′), *pron.* 1 the emphatic form of **they** or **them.** *They did it themselves.* 2 the reflexive form of **them.** *They injured themselves.* 3 their normal or real selves: *They were ill and were not themselves.*

then (ŦHen), *adv.* 1 at that time: *Prices were then lower.* 2 soon afterwards: *The noise stopped, and then began again.* 3 next in time or place: *First comes spring, then summer.* 4 at another time: *Now one boy does best and then another.* 5 also; besides: *The dress seems too good to throw away, and then it is very becoming.* 6 in that case; therefore: *If you broke the window, then you must pay for it.* 7 **but then,** but at the same time; but on the other hand. 8 **then and there,** at that precise time and place; at once and on the spot. *—n.* that time: *By then we shall know the result. —adj.* being at that time; existing then: *the then President.* [Old English *thanne, thonne*]

➤ **then, than.** these words are often carelessly confused in writing. *Then* is an adverb of time, *than* a conjunction in clauses of comparison: *Then the whole crowd went to the drugstore. I think that book was better than any other novel I read last year.*

thence (ŦHens, thens), *adv.* 1 from that place; from there: *A few miles thence is a river.* 2 for that reason; therefore. 3 from that; therefrom. 4 from that time; from then: *a few years thence.* [Middle English *thannes, thennes* < Old English *thanon*]

thence forth (ŦHens′fôrth′, ŦHens′fōrth′; thens′fôrth′, thens′fōrth′), *adv.* from then on; from that time forward: *Women were given the same rights as men; thenceforth they could vote.*

thence for ward (ŦHens′fôr′wərd, thens′-fôr′wərd), *adv.* thenceforth.

thence for wards (ŦHens′fôr′wərdz, thens′fôr′wərdz), *adv.* thenceforth.

the oc ra cy (thē ok′rə sē), *n., pl.* **-cies.** 1 government in which God is recognized as the supreme civil ruler and in which religious authorities rule the state as God's representatives. 2 any government headed by religious authorities. 3 country or state governed by a theocracy. [< Greek *theokratia* < *theos* god + *kratos* rule]

the o crat (thē′ə krat), *n.* 1 person who rules in a theocracy, alone or as a member of a governing body. 2 person who favors theocracy.

the o crat ic (thē′ə krat′ik), *adj.* 1 of or having to do with theocracy. 2 having a theocracy. **—the′o crat′i cal ly,** *adv.*

The oc ri tus (thē ok′rə təs), *n.* lived about 270 B.C., Greek poet, especially of pastoral verse.

the od o lite (thē od′l īt), *n.* a surveying instrument for measuring horizontal and vertical angles. [origin unknown]

The od or ic (thē od′ər ik), *n.* A.D. 454?-526, king of the eastern Goths, who conquered Italy and ruled it from 493 until his death.

The o do si us I (thē′ə dō′shē əs), A.D. 346?-395, Roman emperor of the Eastern Roman Empire from 379 to 395.

the o lo gian (thē′ə lō′jən, thē′ə lō′jē ən), *n.* an expert in theology.

the o log i cal (thē′ə loj′ə kəl), *adj.* 1 of or having to do with theology. A theological school trains young men for the ministry. 2 of or having to do with the nature and will of God. **—the′o log′i cal ly,** *adv.*

theological virtues, faith, hope, and charity, regarded as complementary to the cardinal virtues.

the ol o gy (thē ol′ə jē), *n., pl.* **-gies.** 1 doctrines concerning God and His relations to man and the universe. 2 study of religion and religious beliefs. 3 system of religious beliefs. [< Greek *theologia* < *theos* god + *-logia* -logy]

the or em (thē′ər əm, thir′əm), *n.* 1 statement or rule in mathematics that has been or is to be proved. 2 statement of mathematical relations that can be expressed by an equation or formula. 3 any statement or rule that can be proved to be true. [< Greek *theōrēma* < *theōrein* consider. See THEORY.]

the o ret ic (thē′ə ret′ik), *adj.* theoretical.

the o ret i cal (thē′ə ret′ə kəl), *adj.* 1 planned or worked out in the mind, not from experience; based on theory, not on fact; limited to theory; hypothetical. 2 dealing with theory only; not practical. **—the′o ret′i cal ly,** *adv.*

the or e ti cian (thē′ər ə tish′ən), *n.* an expert in the theory of an art, science, etc.

the or ist (thē′ər ist), *n.* person who theorizes.

the o rize (thē′ə rīz′), *v.i.,* **-rized, -riz ing.** form a theory or theories; speculate. **—the′or i za′tion,** *n.* **—the′o riz′er,** *n.*

the or y (thē′ər ē, thir′ē), *n., pl.* **-or ies.** 1 explanation based on observation and reasoning, especially one that has been tested and confirmed as a general principle explaining a large number of related facts or occurrences: *the theory of evolution.* 2 hypothesis proposed as an explanation; reasonable guess or conjecture: *a theory of the origin of the solar system.* See synonym study below. 3 principles or methods of a science or art rather than its practice: *the theory of music.* 4 idea or opinion about something. 5 thought or fancy as opposed to fact or practice. [< Greek *theōria* < *theōrein* consider < *theoros* spectator < *thea* a sight, view]

Syn. 2 **Theory, hypothesis** as terms in science mean a generalization reached by inference from observed particulars and proposed as an explanation of their cause, relations, or the like. **Theory** implies a larger body of tested evidence and a greater degree of probability: *The red shift in the spectra of galaxies supports the theory that the universe is continuously expanding.* **Hypothesis** designates a merely tentative explanation of the data, advanced or adopted provisionally, often as the basis of a theory or as a guide to further observation or experiment: *Archaeological discoveries strengthened the hypothesis that Troy existed.*

the o soph ic (thē′ə sof′ik), *adj.* of or having to do with theosophy. **—the′o soph′i cal ly,** *adv.*

the o soph i cal (thē′ə sof′ə kəl), *adj.* theosophic.

the os o phist (thē os′ə fist), *n.* person who believes in theosophy.

the os o phy (thē os′ə fē), *n.* 1 any system of philosophy or religion that claims to have a special insight into the divine nature through spiritual self-development. 2 **Theosophy,** the philosophical system of the Theosophical Society, founded in 1875 in the United States, which combines the teachings of various religions, especially Hinduism and Buddhism. [ultimately < Greek *theos* god + *sophos* wise]

ther a peu tic (ther′ə pyü′tik), *adj.* of or having to do with curing or therapy; curative. **—ther′a peu′ti cal ly,** *adv.*

ther a peu ti cal (ther′ə pyü′tə kəl), *adj.* therapeutic.

ther a peu tics (ther′ə pyü′tiks), *n.* branch of medicine that deals with the treating or curing of disease.

ther a peu tist (ther′ə pyü′tist), *n.* therapist.

ther a pist (ther′ə pist), *n.* person who specializes in some form of therapy.

ther a py (ther′ə pē), *n., pl.* **-pies.** treatment of diseases or disorders. [< Greek *therapeia* < *therapeuein* to cure, treat < *theraps* attendant]

there (ŦHer, ŦHar; *unstressed* ŦHər), *adv.* 1 in or at that place: *Sit there.* 2 to or into that place: *How did that get there? Go there at once.* 3 at that point or stage in action, proceeding, speech, or thought: *You have done enough, you may stop there.* 4 in that matter, particular, or respect: *You are mistaken there.* 5 *There* is also used in sentences in which the verb comes before its subject. *There are three new houses on our street. Is there a drugstore near here?* 6 *There* is used to call attention to some person or thing. *There goes the bell. —n.* that place: *From there we went on to New York. —interj.* an expression of satisfaction, triumph, dismay, encouragement, comfort, etc.: *There, there! Don't cry.* [Old English *thǣr*]

➤ **there** (*adv.* def. 5). When *there* is used as a temporary substitute for the real subject, in careful writing and speaking the verb agrees in number with the real subject: *There was much work to be done. There are many answers in the back of the book.*

there a bout (ŦHer′ə bout′, ŦHar′ə bout′), *adv.* thereabouts.

there a bouts (ŦHer′ə bouts′, ŦHar′ə-bouts′), *adv.* 1 near that place. 2 near that time: *leave on June 3 or thereabouts.* 3 near that number or amount: *use 50 gallons of oil or thereabouts.*

there af ter (ŦHer af′tər, ŦHar af′tər), *adv.* 1 after that; afterwards. 2 accordingly.

there at (ŦHer at′, ŦHar at′), *adv.* 1 when that happened; at that time. 2 because of that; because of it. 3 at that place; there.

there by (ŦHer bī′, ŦHer′bī; ŦHar bī′, ŦHar′bī), *adv.* 1 by means of that; in that way: *travel and thereby study other countries.* 2 in connection with that: *thereby hangs a tale.* 3 by or near that place; near there: *a farm lay thereby.*

there'd (ŦHerd, ŦHard), 1 there had. 2 there would.

there for (ŦHer fôr′, ŦHar fôr′), *adv.* for that; for this; for it: *He promised to give a building for a hospital and as much land as should be necessary therefor.*

there fore (ŦHer′fôr, ŦHer′fōr; ŦHar′fôr, ŦHar′fōr), *adv.* for that reason; as a result of that; consequently. [Middle English *therfore* < *ther,* Old English *thǣr* there + *fore,* variant of *for* for]

Syn. Therefore, consequently, when used to connect two grammatically independent but logically related clauses, indicate that the second follows as a conclusion from the first. **Therefore** indicates formally and precisely that the second clause states the necessary conclusion to be drawn from the first: *He was the only candidate; therefore he was elected.* **Consequently,** also formal, indicates a reasonable or logical, though not necessary, conclusion: *She is the popular candidate; consequently, she will be elected.*

there from (ŦHer from′, ŦHer frum′; ŦHar-from′, ŦHar frum′), *adv.* from that; from this; from it.

there in (ŦHer in′, ŦHar in′), *adv.* 1 in or into that place, time, or thing: *God created the sea and all that is therein.* 2 in that matter; in that way.

there in af ter (ŦHer′in af′tər, ŦHar′in-af′tər), *adv.* after in that document, statute, etc.

there in to (ŦHer in′tü, ŦHer′in tü′; ŦHar-in′tü, ŦHar′in tü′), *adv.* 1 into that place; into it. 2 into that matter.

there'll (ŦHerl, ŦHarl), 1 there will. 2 there shall.

there of (ŦHer uv′, ŦHer ov′; ŦHar uv′, ŦHar ov′), *adv.* 1 of that; of it. 2 from it; from that source.

there on (ŦHer on′, ŦHer ôn′; ŦHar on′, ŦHar ôn′), *adv.* 1 on that; on it. 2 immediately after that; thereupon.

there's (ŦHerz, ŦHarz), there is.

The re sa (tə rē′sə, tə res′ə), *n.* **Saint,** 1515-1582, Spanish nun and mystic. Also, **Teresa.**

there to (ŦHer tü′, ŦHar tü′), *adv.* 1 to that; to it: *The castle stands on a hill, and the road thereto is steep and rough.* 2 in addition to that; besides; also.

there to fore (ŦHer′tə fôr′, ŦHer′tə fōr′; ŦHar′tə fôr′, ŦHar′tə fōr′), *adv.* before that time; until then.

there un der (ŦHer un′dər, ŦHar un′dər), *adv.* 1 under that; under it. 2 under the authority of; according to that.

there un to (ŦHer un′tü, ŦHer′un tü′; ŦHar-un′tü, ŦHar′un tü′), *adv.* to that; to it.

there up on (ŦHer′ə pôn′, ŦHer′ə pon′; ŦHar′ə pôn′, ŦHar′ə pon′), *adv.* 1 immediately after that: *The President appeared. Thereupon the people clapped.* 2 because of that; therefore. 3 on that; on it.

there with (ŦHer wiŦH′, ŦHer with′; ŦHar-wiŦH′, ŦHar with′), *adv.* 1 with that; with it. 2 immediately after that; then.

there with al (ŦHer′wi ŦHôl′, ŦHar′wi-ŦHôl′; ŦHer′wi thôl′, ŦHar′wi thôl′), *adv.* 1 with that; with this; with it. 2 in addition to that; also.

therm-, *combining form.* form of **thermo-** before vowels, as in *thermal.*

ther mal (thėr′məl), *adj.* 1 of or having to do with heat; thermic. 2 warm; hot. —*n.* a rising current of warm air.

ther mic (thėr′mik), *adj.* of or having to do with heat; thermal.

therm i on (thėrm′ī′ən, thėr′mē ən), *n.* an electrically charged particle, either positive or negative, given off by a heated body.

therm i on ic (thėrm′ī on′ik, thėr′mē-on′ik), *adj.* of or having to do with thermions: *thermionic emission.*

ther mis tor (thėr′mis′tər), *n.* a small electronic resistor whose conduction of electric current increases rapidly and predictably with a rise in temperature, used especially in heat measurement, and as a voltage regulator in communication circuits. [< *therm-* + *(res)istor*]

thermo-, *combining form.* heat; temperature: *Thermoelectricity = electricity produced by heat.* Also, **therm-** before vowels. [< Greek *thermē*]

ther mo cline (thėr′mō klīn), *n.* layer within a large body of water sharply separating parts of it that differ in temperature, so that the temperature gradient through the layer is very abrupt. [< *thermo-* + Greek *klinein* to lean]

ther mo cou ple (thėr′mō kup′əl), *n.* two dissimilar metallic conductors joined end to end, whose junction, when heated, produces a thermoelectric current in the circuit of which they form a part; thermoelectric couple.

ther mo dy nam ic (thėr′mō dī nam′ik), *adj.* of or having to do with thermodynamics; using force due to heat or to the conversion of heat into other forms of energy. **—ther′mo dy nam′i cal ly,** *adv.*

ther mo dy nam ics (thėr′mō dī nam′iks), *n.* branch of physics that deals with the relations between heat and other forms of energy, and of the conversion of one into the other.

ther mo e lec tric (thėr′mō i lek′trik), *adj.* of or having to do with thermoelectricity.

ther mo e lec tri cal (thėr′mō i lek′trə-kəl), *adj.* thermoelectric.

thermoelectric couple, thermocouple.

ther mo e lec tric i ty (thėr′mō i lek-tris′ə tē, thėr′mō ē′lek tris′ə tē), *n.* electricity produced directly by heat, especially that produced by a temperature difference between two different metals used as conductors in a circuit.

ther mo graph (thėr′mə graf), *n.* thermometer that automatically records temperature.

hat, āge, fär; let, ēqual, tėrm;
it, īce; hot, ōpen, ôrder;
oil, out; cup, pu̇t, rüle;
ch, child; ng, long; sh, she;
th, thin; ŦH, then; zh, measure;

ə represents *a* in about, *e* in taken, *i* in pencil, *o* in lemon, *u* in circus.

< = from, derived from, taken from.

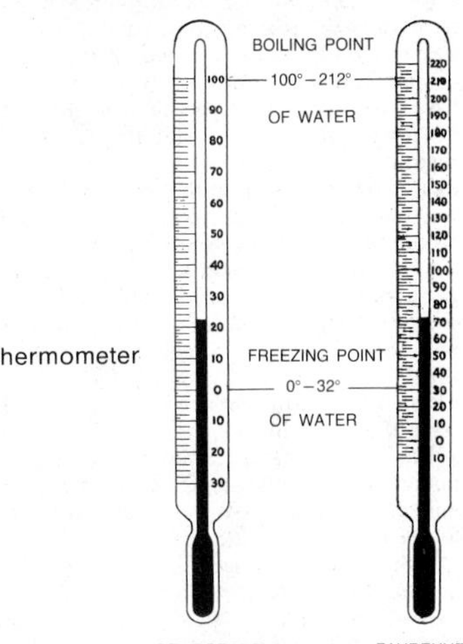

thermometer

ther mom e ter (thər mom′ə tər), *n.* instrument for measuring the temperature of a body or of space, usually by means of the expansion and contraction of mercury or alcohol in a capillary tube and bulb with a graduated scale.

ther mo met ric (thėr′mō met′rik), *adj.* 1 of or having to do with a thermometer: *the thermometric scale.* 2 made by means of a thermometer: *thermometric observations.* **—ther′mo met′ri cal ly,** *adv.*

ther mom e try (thər mom′ə trē), *n.* the measurement of temperature.

ther mo nu cle ar (thėr′mō nü′klē ər, thėr′mō nyü′klē ər), *adj.* of or having to do with the fusion of atoms through very high temperature, as in the hydrogen bomb: *a thermonuclear reaction.*

ther mo pile (thėr′mō pīl), *n.* device consisting of several thermocouples acting together for the production of a combined effect, as for generating currents or for ascertaining minute temperature differences.

ther mo plas tic (thėr′mō plas′tik), *adj.* becoming soft and capable of being molded when heated, as certain synthetic resins. —*n.* a thermoplastic material.

Ther mop y lae (thər mop′ə lē), *n.* mountain pass in ancient Greece. In 480 B.C., a small force of Greeks defended it against an army of Persians until most of the Greeks, including all the Spartans, were killed.

ther mos bottle (thėr′məs), vacuum bottle.

ther mo set (thėr′mə set), *adj.* thermosetting.

ther mo set ting (thėr′mō set′ing), *adj.* becoming hard and permanently shaped under the continued application of heat, as certain synthetic resins.

ther mo stat (tėr′mə stat), *n.* 1 an automatic device for regulating temperature, especially one in which the expansion and contraction of a metal, liquid, or gas opens and closes an electric circuit by which an appliance or device, such as an air conditioner or oil furnace, is made to work or to stop working. 2 any device that responds automatically to conditions of temperature, as an automatic fire alarm or sprinkler system. [< *thermo-* + Greek *-statēs* that stands]

ther mo stat ic (tėr′mə stat′ik), *adj.* of, having to do with, or like a thermostat. **—ther′mo stat′i cal ly,** *adv.*

ther mo trop ic (tėr′mō trop′ik), *adj.* having to do with or exhibiting thermotropism.

ther mot ro pism (thər mot′rə piz′əm), *n.* tendency to bend or turn toward or away from the sun or other source of heat.

the ro pod (thir′ə pod), *n.* any of a suborder of carnivorous dinosaurs which stood on their hind legs. *—adj.* of or belonging to this suborder. [< Greek *thēros* beast + *podos* foot]

the sau rus (thi sôr′əs), *n., pl.* **-sau ri** (-sôr′ī). 1 dictionary in which synonyms, antonyms, and other related words are classified under certain headings. 2 any dictionary, encyclopedia, or other book of information. 3 treasury or storehouse. [< Latin, treasure < Greek *thēsauros.* Doublet of TREASURE.]

these (ŦHēz), *adj., pron.* pl. of **this.**

The se us (thē′sē əs, thē′süs), *n.* (in Greek legends) the chief hero of Athens, who killed the Minotaur and escaped from Crete with the help of Ariadne, killed Procrustes, fought the Amazons, and married their princess.

the sis (thē′sis), *n., pl.* **-ses** (-sēz). 1 proposition or statement to be proved or to be maintained against objections. 2 an essay. 3 essay presented by a candidate for a diploma or degree. [< Greek, originally, a setting down]

Thes pi an (thes′pē ən), *adj.* 1 of or having to do with the drama or tragedy; dramatic; tragic. 2 of or having to do with Thespis. *—n.* actor or actress. [< *Thespis*]

Thes pis (thes′pis), *n.* Greek poet of the 500's B.C., the traditional founder of Greek tragedy.

Thess., Thessalonians.

Thes sa lo ni ans (thes′ə lō′nē ənz), *n.* either of two books of the New Testament written by Saint Paul.

Thes sa lon i ca (thes′ə lon′ə kə, thes′ə lə-nī′kə), *n.* the ancient name of Salonika. **—Thes′sa lo′ni an,** *adj., n.*

Thes sa ly (thes′ə lē), *n.* district in E Greece. **—Thes sa′li an,** *adj., n.*

the ta (thā′tə, thē′tə), *n.* the eighth letter of the Greek alphabet (Θ,θ).

The tis (thē′tis), *n.* (in Greek legends) one of the Nereids, the mother of Achilles.

thews (thüz), *n.pl.* 1 muscles. 2 sinews. 3 bodily force; might; strength. [Old English *thēaw* habit]

they (ŦHā), *pron., pl. nominative; possessive* **their, theirs;** *objective* **them.** 1 the nominative plural of **he, she,** or **it;** the persons, animals, things, or ideas spoken about: *They are friends of ours.* 2 INFORMAL. people in general; some people; any people; persons: *In Scotland they wear kilts.* [< Scandinavian (Old Icelandic) *their*]

they'd (ŦHād), 1 they had. 2 they would.

they'll (ŦHāl), 1 they will. 2 they shall.

they're (ŦHer, ŦHar), they are.

they've (ŦHāv), they have.

THI, temperature humidity index (a combined measurement of temperature and humidity, used to indicate relative discomfort).

thi a min (thī′ə mən), *n.* vitamin that promotes growth and prevents and cures beriberi, found in yeast, meats, whole-grain cereals, and certain vegetables; vitamin B_1. *Formula:* $C_{12}H_{17}ClN_4OS$ [< Greek *theion* sulfur + English *amin(e)*]

thi a mine (thī′ə mən, thī′ə mēn′), *n.* thiamin.

thick (thik), *adj.* 1 with much space from one side to the opposite side; not thin: *a thick wall, a thick plank.* 2 measuring between two opposite sides: *a board two inches thick.* 3 set close together; dense: *thick hair, a thick forest.* 4 many and close together; abundant: *bullets thick as hail.* 5 filled; covered: *a room thick with flies.* 6 like glue or syrup, not like water; rather dense of its kind: *Thick liquids pour much more slowly than thin liquids.* 7 not clear; foggy: *thick weather.* 8 difficult or impossible to see through: *the thick blackness of a moonless night.* 9 not clear in sound; hoarse: *a thick voice.* 10 stupid; dull: *He has a thick head.* 11 INFORMAL. **a** very friendly; intimate: *as thick as thieves.* **b** too much to be endured: *That remark is a bit thick.*

—adv. 1 in a thick manner; thickly. 2 **lay it on thick,** SLANG. praise or blame too much.

—n. 1 thickest part. 2 hardest part; place where there is the most danger, activity, etc. 3 **through thick and thin,** in good times and bad.

[Old English *thicce*]

thick en (thik′ən), *v.t.* make thick or thicker: *thicken a wall, thicken gravy.* *—v.i.* 1 become thick or thicker. 2 (of a plot) become more involved and complicated. **—thick′en er,** *n.*

thick en ing (thik′ə ning), *n.* 1 material or ingredient used to thicken something: *use cornstarch as thickening for a sauce.* 2 a thickened part or substance. 3 act of making or becoming thick or thicker.

thick et (thik′it), *n.* 1 shrubs, bushes, or small trees growing close together; copse; brake. 2 a thick, dense mass; jumble.

thick head ed (thik′hed′id), *adj.* mentally dull; stupid. **—thick′head′ed ness,** *n.*

thick ish (thik′ish), *adj.* somewhat thick.

thick ly (thik′lē), *adv.* 1 in a thick manner; closely; densely: *a thickly settled region.* 2 in great numbers; in abundance. 3 frequently. 4 with thick consistency. 5 in tones that are hoarse or hard to understand.

thick ness (thik′nis), *n.* 1 quality or state of being thick: *The thickness of the walls shuts out all sound.* 2 distance between opposite surfaces; the third measurement of a solid, not length or breadth: *The length of the board is 10 feet, the width 6 inches, the thickness 2 inches.* 3 the thick part. 4 a fold or layer: *The pad was made up of three thicknesses of cloth.*

thick set (thik′set′), *adj.* 1 thickly set: *a thickset hedge.* 2 thick in form or build: *a thickset man.*

thick-skinned (thik′skind′), *adj.* 1 having a thick skin or rind: *a thick-skinned orange.* 2 not sensitive to criticism, reproach, rebuff, or the like.

thick-wit ted (thik′wit′id), *adj.* dull of wit; stupid; thickheaded.

thief (thēf), *n., pl.* **thieves.** person who steals, especially one who steals secretly and usually without using force. See synonym study below. [Old English *thēof*]

Syn. Thief, robber mean someone who steals. **Thief** applies to someone who steals in a secret or stealthy way: *A thief stole my bicycle from the yard.* **Robber** applies to someone who steals by force or threats of violence: *The robbers bound and gagged the night watchman.*

thieve (thēv), *v.i., v.t.,* **thieved, thiev ing.** steal. [Old English *thēofian* < *thēof* thief]

thiev er y (thē′vər ē), *n., pl.* **-er ies.** act of stealing; theft.

thieves (thēvz), *n.* pl. of **thief.**

thiev ish (thē′vish), *adj.* 1 having the habit of stealing; likely to steal. 2 like a thief; stealthy; sly. **—thiev′ish ly,** *adv.* **—thiev′ish ness,** *n.*

thigh (thī), *n.* 1 part of the leg between the hip and the knee. 2 the second segment of the leg of a bird, containing the tibia and the fibula. 3 the third segment of the leg of an insect. [Old English *thēoh*]

thigh bone (thī′bōn′), *n.* bone of the leg between the hip and the knee; femur.

thig mot ro pism (thig mot′rə piz′əm), *n.* tendency of some part of any organism to bend or turn in response to a touch stimulus. [< Greek *thigma* a touch + *tropos* a turning]

thill (thil), *n.* either of the shafts between which a single animal drawing a vehicle is placed. [Middle English *thille*]

thim ble (thim′bəl), *n.* 1 a small cap of metal or plastic, worn on the finger to protect it when pushing the needle in sewing. 2 any of various short metal tubes, rings, sleeves, bushings, or other fittings for machines. 3 a metal ring fitted in a rope, to save wear on the rope. [Old English *thȳmel* < *thūma* thumb] **—thim′ble like′,** *adj.*

thim ble ber ry (thim′bəl ber′ē), *n., pl.* **-ries.** any of several American raspberries with a thimble-shaped fruit, especially the black raspberry.

thim ble ful (thim′bəl fu̇l), *n., pl.* **-fuls.** as much as a thimble will hold; very small quantity.

thim ble rig (thim′bəl rig′), *n., v.,* **-rigged, -rig ging.** *—n.* 1 a swindling game in which the operator apparently covers a small ball or pea with one of three thimblelike cups, and then, moving the cups about, offers to bet that no one can tell under which cup the ball or pea lies. 2 person who cheats by or as if by the thimblerig. *—v.t.* cheat by or as if by the thimblerig. **—thim′ble rig′ger,** *n.*

Thim bu (tim′bü), *n.* capital of Bhutan, in the W part. 9000.

thin (thin), *adj.,* **thin ner, thin nest,** *adv., v.,* **thinned, thin ning.** *—adj.* 1 with little space from one side to the opposite side; not thick: *a thin book, thin paper, thin wire.* 2 having little flesh; slender; lean: *a thin person.* See synonym study below. 3 not set close together; scanty: *thin hair, thin foliage.* 4 not dense: *The air on the tops of those high mountains is thin.* 5 few and far apart; not abundant: *The actors played to a thin audience.* 6 not like glue or syrup; like water; of less substance than usual: *a thin soup, thin milk.* 7 not deep or strong: *a shrill, thin voice.* 8 having little depth, fullness, or intensity: *a thin color, thin applause.* 9 easily seen through; flimsy: *a thin excuse.* *—adv.* in a thin manner; thinly. *—v.t.* make or become thin or thinner. [Old English *thynne*] **—thin′ly,** *adv.* **—thin′ness,** *n.*

Syn. *adj.* 2 **Thin, lean, gaunt** mean having

little flesh. **Thin,** neither favorable nor unfavorable in connotation, suggests lack of the normal or usual amount of flesh: *She has a thin face.* **Lean,** favorable in connotation, suggests lack of fat: *The forest ranger is lean and brown.* **Gaunt,** unfavorable in connotation, suggests a bony, starved, or worn look: *Gaunt, bearded men stumbled into camp.*

thine (ᴛʜīn), ARCHAIC. *—pron.* possessive case of **thou.** the one or ones belonging to thee; yours. *—adj.* possessive form of **thou.** thy; your (used only before a vowel or *h*, or after a noun). [Old English *thīn*, genitive of *thū* thou]

thing (thing), *n.* 1 any object or substance; what one can see or hear or touch or taste or smell: *All the things in the house were burned. Put those things away.* 2 **things,** *pl.* **a** personal belongings; possessions. **b** clothes. **c** outdoor clothes. **d** implements or equipment for some specified use: *cooking things.* 3 whatever is done or to be done; any act, deed, fact, event, or happening: *It was a good thing to do. A strange thing happened. The shipwreck was a tragic thing.* 4 whatever is spoken or thought of; idea; opinion: *a dangerous thing to repeat.* 5 any matter, subject, affair, or business: *How are things going? Is that thing settled yet?* 6 person or creature. 7 **know a thing or two,** INFORMAL. be experienced. 8 **make a good thing of,** INFORMAL. profit from. 9 **see things,** have hallucinations. 10 **the thing, a** the fashion or style. **b** the important fact or idea. [Old English]

thing am a bob (thing′ə mə bob), *n.* INFORMAL. thingamajig.

thing am a jig (thing′ə mə jig), *n.* INFORMAL. something whose name one forgets or does not bother to mention.

thing um a jig (thing′ə mə jig), *n.* INFORMAL. thingamajig.

thing um bob (thing′əm bob), *n.* INFORMAL. thingamajig.

thing um my (thing′ə mē), *n., pl.* **-mies.** INFORMAL. thingamajig.

think (thingk), *v.,* **thought, think ing,** *n.* *—v.t.* 1 form (a thought or idea) in the mind: *She thought that she would go.* 2 picture in one's mind; imagine: *You can't think how surprised I was.* 3 consider: *They think him a fine man.* 4 intend or plan: *They think to escape punishment.* 5 expect: *I did not think to find you here. Do you think it will rain?* *—v.i.* 1 have ideas; use the mind: *learn to think clearly.* See synonym study below. 2 have an idea: *He had thought of her as still a child.* 3 consider the matter: *I must think before answering.* 4 have an opinion; believe: *Do what you think fit.*
think aloud, say what one is thinking.
think of, a have in mind. **b** imagine: *Think of that!* **c** remember: *I can't think of his name.*
think out, a plan or discover by thinking. **b** solve or understand by thinking. **c** think through to the end.
think over, consider carefully.
think through, think about until reaching an understanding or conclusion.
think twice, think again before acting; hesitate.
think up, plan, discover, or compose by thinking.
—n. INFORMAL. thought.
[Middle English *thinken*, variant of *thenchen*, Old English *thencan*. Related to THANK.]
—think′er, *n.*
Syn. *v.i.* 1 **Think, reflect, meditate** mean to use the powers of the mind. **Think** is the general word meaning to use the mind to form ideas, reach conclusions, understand what is known, etc.: *I must think about your offer before I accept it.* **Reflect** suggests quietly and seriously thinking or turning over a subject in one's mind: *They need time to reflect on their problems.* **Meditate** suggests focusing the thoughts on a subject from every point of view, to understand all its sides and relations: *meditate on the nature of happiness.*

think a ble (thing′kə bəl), *adj.* capable of being thought; conceivable.

think ing (thing′king), *adj.* 1 that thinks; reasoning. 2 thoughtful or reflective. *—n.* thought. **—think′ing ly,** *adv.*

think piece, a magazine or newspaper article devoted to an extensive analysis or discussion of current news.

thin ner (thin′ər), *n.* 1 a liquid, especially turpentine, used to make paint more fluid. 2 person or thing that thins.

thin nish (thin′ish), *adj.* somewhat thin.

thin-skinned (thin′skind′), *adj.* 1 having a thin skin or rind. 2 sensitive to criticism, reproach, rebuff, etc.; touchy.

thi o pen tal sodium (thī′ō pen′tal), a yellowish-white barbiturate used as an anesthetic; Pentothal Sodium; sodium pentothal. *Formula:* $C_{11}H_{17}N_2O_2SNa$

thi o sul fate (thī′ō sul′fāt), *n.* salt or ester of thiosulfuric acid.

thi o sul fur ic acid (thī′ō sul fyůr′ik), an unstable acid, considered as sulfuric acid in which one atom of oxygen is replaced by sulfur. It occurs only in solution or in the form of its salts (thiosulfates). *Formula:* $H_2S_2O_3$

third (thėrd), *adj.* 1 next after the second; last in a series of three. 2 being one of three equal parts. 3 designating the gear used for ordinary driving in an automobile with a standard transmission. *—n.* 1 the next after the second; last in a series of three. 2 one of three equal parts. 3 in music: **a** tone three degrees from another tone. **b** interval between such tones. **c** combination of such tones. 4 (in an automobile or similar machine) third gear; high. [Old English *thirda, thridda* < *thrēo* three]

third base, in baseball: 1 the base that must be touched third by a runner. 2 position of the fielder covering the area near this base. **—third baseman.**

third class, 1 the lowest or next to the lowest class of accommodations on any of various railroads in Europe and elsewhere. 2 (formerly) the lowest class of accommodations on a passenger vessel; tourist class. 3 class of mail consisting of printed matter other than newspapers or periodicals, usually not sealed and weighing less than 16 ounces.

third-class (thėrd′klas′), *adj.* 1 of or belonging to a class after the second. 2 of or having to do with third class. 3 of distinctly inferior quality; third-rate. *—adv.* in or by third class.

third degree, INFORMAL. use of severe treatment by the police to force a person to give information or make a confession.

third-di men sion al (thėrd′də men′shə nəl), *adj.* three-dimensional.

third estate, persons not in the nobility or clergy; common people.

third force, person or group that tries to hold a middle course between extreme factions, especially a political group trying to hold such a position.

hat, āge, fär; let, ēqual, tėrm;
it, īce; hot, ōpen, ôrder;
oil, out; cup, půt, rüle;
ch, child; ng, long; sh, she;
th, thin; ᴛʜ, then; zh, measure;

ə represents *a* in about, *e* in taken, *i* in pencil, *o* in lemon, *u* in circus.

< = from, derived from, taken from.

third ly (thėrd′lē), *adv.* in the third place.

third party, 1 a political party organized as an independent rival of the two major parties. 2 party or person besides the two primarily concerned, as in a law case.

third person, form of a pronoun or verb used to refer to someone or something spoken of. *He, she, it,* and *they* are pronouns of the third person.

third quarter, 1 period between full moon and second half moon. 2 phase of the moon represented by the second half moon, after full moon.

third rail, rail that carries a powerful electric current, paralleling the ordinary rails of a railroad.

third-rate (thėrd′rāt′), *adj.* 1 rated as third-class. 2 distinctly inferior.

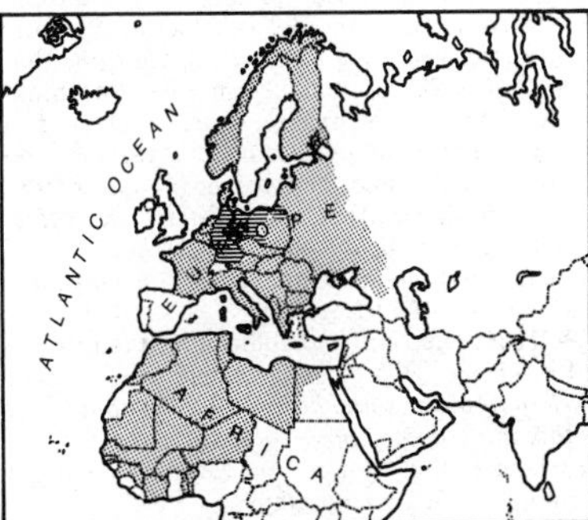

Third Reich—The striped area indicates Germany in 1933; the shaded area indicates the territory occupied by the Third Reich and its allies at its greatest extent in 1942.

Third Reich, the totalitarian state in Germany (from 1933 to 1945) under Adolf Hitler.

third world, the world of neutral nations; countries taking neither side in the cold war between Communist and Western nations.

thirst (thėrst), *n.* 1 a dry, uncomfortable feeling in the mouth or throat caused by having had nothing to drink. 2 desire or need for drink. 3 a strong desire: *have a thirst for adventure.* *—v.i.* 1 feel thirst; be thirsty. 2 have a strong desire or craving. [Old English *thurst*]

thirst y (thėr′stē), *adj.,* **thirst i er, thirst i est.** 1 feeling or having thirst. 2 without water or moisture; dry. 3 having a strong desire or craving; eager. **—thirst′i ly,** *adv.* **—thirst′i ness,** *n.*

thir teen (thėr′tēn′), *n., adj.* three more than ten; 13. [Old English *thrēotēne*]

thir teenth (thėr′tēnth′), *adj., n.* 1 next after the 12th; last in a series of 13. 2 one, or being one, of 13 equal parts.

thir ti eth (thėr′tē ith), *adj., n.* 1 next after

the 29th; last in a series of 30. 2 one, or being one, of 30 equal parts.

thir ty (tėr′tē), *n., pl.* **-ties,** *adj.* —*n.* 1 three times ten; 30. 2 the figure "30" as a symbol placed at, and designating the end of, a news story or other piece of copy. —*adj.* three times ten; 30. [Old English *thrītig*]

thir ty-eight (tėr′tē āt′), *n.* a .38 caliber revolver or automatic pistol.

thir ty-sec ond note (tėr′tē sek′ənd), (in music) a note played for one thirty-second as long a time as a whole note. See **note** for diagram.

thir ty-three (tėr′tē thrē′), *n.* a phonograph record which revolves at 33⅓ revolutions per minute.

Thirty Years' War, the religious and political wars in central Europe from 1618 to 1648, fought chiefly on German soil between Catholics and Protestants and ending, politically, in the predominance of France and the decline of the Holy Roman Empire as a unifying force in Germany.

this (ᴛʜis), *adj., pron., pl.* **these,** *adv.* —*adj.* 1 pointing out or indicating some person, thing, idea, etc., that is present, near, or referred to now: *this minute, this child, this idea.* 2 indicating the nearer of two or nearest of most things: *Do you prefer this tie or that one in the closet?* 3 indicating one thing as distinct from another or others: *You may have this one, this next one, or that one, but not all three.* —*pron.* 1 some person, thing, idea, etc., that is present, near, or referred to now: *This is the best. After this you must go home.* 2 the one emphasized or contrasted with another called "that": *Take this, or this, but not that. This is newer than that.* —*adv.* to this extent or degree; so: *You can have this much.* [Old English]

➛ **This,** like *that,* is regularly used to refer to the idea of a preceding clause or sentence: *He had always had his own way at home, and this made him a poor roommate.*

This be (thiz′bē), *n.* (in Greek legends) a maiden loved by Pyramus.

thistle

this tle (this′əl), *n.* any of various composite plants with prickly stalks and leaves and usually with purple flowers. [Old English *thistel*] —**this′tle like′,** *adj.*

this tle down (this′əl doun′), *n.* downy growth that forms on ripe thistle seeds.

this tly (this′lē), *adj.* 1 like thistles; prickly. 2 having many thistles.

thith er (thiᴛʜ′ər, ᴛʜiᴛʜ′ər), *adv.* to that place; toward that place; there. —*adj.* on that side; farther. [Old English *thider*]

thith er to (thiᴛʜ′ər tü′, thiᴛʜ′ər tü′; ᴛʜiᴛʜ′ər tü′, ᴛʜiᴛʜ′ər tü′), *adv.* up to that time; until then.

thith er ward (thiᴛʜ′ər wərd, ᴛʜiᴛʜ′ər wərd), *adv.* toward that place; in that direction; thither.

thith er wards (thiᴛʜ′ər wərdz, ᴛʜiᴛʜ′ər wərdz), *adv.* thitherward.

tho or **tho'** (ᴛʜō), *conj., adv.* though.

thole (thōl), *n.* peg or pin, often one of a pair, on the side of a boat to hold an oar in rowing. [Old English *tholl*]

thole
a pair of tholes

thole pin (thōl′pin′), *n.* thole.

Thom as (tom′əs), *n.* 1 (in the Bible) one of Christ's twelve apostles. He at first doubted the Resurrection. 2 **Dylan,** 1914-1953, Welsh poet. 3 **George Henry,** 1816-1870, Union general in the Civil War. 4 **Norman (Mattoon),** 1884-1968, American Socialist leader.

Tho mism (tō′miz′əm, thō′miz′əm), *n.* the scholastic and theological doctrines of Saint Thomas Aquinas.

Tho mist (tō′mist, thō′mist), *n.* follower of Saint Thomas Aquinas. —*adj.* Thomistic.

Tho mis tic (tō mis′tik, thō mis′tik), *adj.* of or having to do with the Thomists or Thomism.

Thomp son (tomp′sən), *n.* **Francis,** 1859-1907, English poet.

Thomp son submachine gun (tomp′sən), trademark for a .45-caliber, air-cooled, automatic weapon that can be carried and operated by one man, fired either from the hip or the shoulder.

Thom son (tom′sən), *n.* 1 Sir **Joseph John,** 1856-1940, British physicist who discovered the electron. 2 **Virgil,** born 1896, American composer and critic. 3 **William,** 1824-1907, British physicist, who became Lord Kelvin.

thong (thông, thong), *n.* 1 a narrow strip of leather, especially used as a fastening. 2 lash of a whip. [Old English *thwang*]

Thor (thôr), *n.* (in Scandinavian myths) the god of thunder.

tho rac ic (thô ras′ik, thō ras′ik), *adj.* of or having to do with the thorax. The thoracic cavity contains the heart and lungs.

tho rax (thôr′aks, thōr′aks), *n., pl.* **tho rax es, tho ra ces** (thôr′ə sēz′, thōr′ə sēz′). 1 part of the body between the neck and the abdomen; chest. 2 the second of the three main divisions of an arthropod's body, between the head and the abdomen. [< Latin < Greek *thōrax*]

Tho reau (thə rō′, thôr′ō), *n.* **Henry David,** 1817-1862, American author and naturalist.

tho ri um (thôr′ē əm, thōr′ē əm), *n.* a dark-gray, radioactive, metallic element present in certain rare minerals. When thorium is bombarded with neutrons, it changes into a form of uranium which is used as an atomic fuel. *Symbol:* Th; *atomic number* 90. See pages 326 and 327 for table. [< New Latin < *Thor*]

thorn (thôrn), *n.* 1 a stiff, sharp-pointed growth on a stem or branch of a tree or other plant; prickle; spine. 2 tree or other plant with thorns. 3 spine or spiny process in an animal. 4 **thorn in the flesh** or **thorn in the side,** cause of trouble or annoyance. [Old English] —**thorn′less,** *adj.* —**thorn′like′,** *adj.*

thorn apple, 1 fruit of the hawthorn; haw. 2 hawthorn. 3 jimson weed.

thorn y (thôr′nē), *adj.,* **thorn i er, thorn i est.** 1 full of thorns or spines; spiny; prickly. 2 troublesome; annoying. —**thorn′i ness,** *n.*

thor o (thėr′ō), *adj., adv., prep.* thorough.

tho ron (thôr′on, thōr′on), *n.* a gaseous, radioactive isotope of radon, formed by the decay of thorium. *Symbol:* Tn; *atomic number* 86; *mass number* 220.

thor ough (thėr′ō), *adj.* 1 being all that is needed; complete: *a thorough search.* 2 doing all that should be done and slighting nothing; painstaking: *The doctor was very thorough in his examination of the patient.* —*adv., prep.* ARCHAIC. through. Also, **thoro.** [Old English *thuruh,* variant of *thurh* through] —**thor′ough ly,** *adv.* —**thor′ough ness,** *n.*

thor ough bred (thėr′ō bred′), *adj.* 1 of pure breed or stock. 2 of or having to do with a Thoroughbred. 3 well-bred; thoroughly trained. —*n.* 1 a thoroughbred animal. 2 **Thoroughbred,** any race horse of a breed derived from a crossing of domestic English stock with Arabian stock. 3 a well-bred or thoroughly trained person.

thor ough fare (thėr′ō fer′, thėr′ō far′), *n.* 1 passage, road, or street open at both ends. 2 a main road; highway. 3 **no thoroughfare,** no public way through or right of way here.

thor ough go ing (thėr′ō gō′ing), *adj.* thorough; complete.

thorp (thôrp), *n.* OBSOLETE. hamlet, village, or small town. [Old English]

those (ᴛʜōz), *adj., pron.* pl. of **that.** [Old English *thās* these]

thou (ᴛʜou), *pron. nominative* **thou,** *possessive* **thy** or **thine,** *objective* **thee;** *pl., nominative* **you** or **ye,** *possessive* **your** or **yours,** *objective* **you** or **ye.** ARCHAIC. the one spoken to; you. [Old English *thū*]

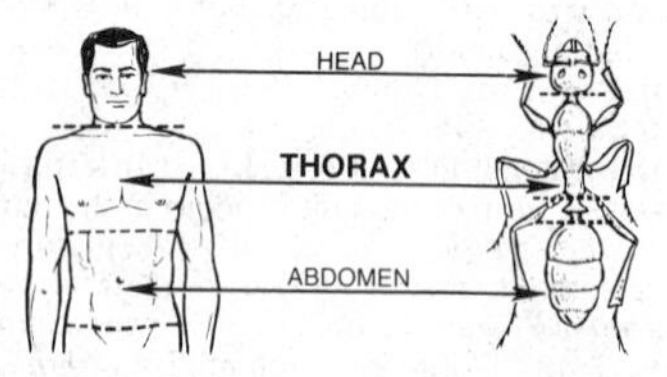

thorax (def. 1) thorax (def. 2)

though (ᴛʜō), *conj.* 1 in spite of the fact that; notwithstanding the fact that; although: *Though it was raining, no one went indoors.* 2 yet; still; nevertheless: *He is better, though not yet cured.* 3 even if; even supposing that: *Though I fail, I shall try again.* 4 **as though,** as if; as it would be if: *You look as though you were tired.* —*adv.* however; nevertheless: *I am sorry about our quarrel; you began it, though.* Also, **tho, tho'.** [Middle English *thoh* < Scandinavian (Old Icelandic) *thō*]

➛ See **although** for usage note.

thought (thôt), *n.* 1 what one thinks; idea; notion: *Her thought was to have a picnic.* See **idea** for synonym study. 2 power or process of thinking; mental activity: *Thought helps us solve problems.* 3 reasoning: *apply thought to a problem.* 4 consideration; attention; care; regard: *Show some thought for others than yourself.* 5 conception, imagination, or fancy: *a pretty thought.* 6 a very small amount; little bit; trifle: *Be a thought more polite.* 7 the characteristic thinking of a particular person, group, time, or place: *modern scientific thought, 16th century* *thought.* —*v.* pt. and pp. of **think.** [Old English *thōht*]

thought ful (thôt′fəl), *adj.* 1 full of thought; thinking: *She was thoughtful for a while and then replied, "No."* 2 indicating thought: *a thoughtful expression.* 3 careful; heedful: *be thoughtful of danger.* 4 showing regard for others; considerate: *a thoughtful person.* See synonym study below. —**thought′ful ly,** *adv.* —**thought′ful-ness,** *n.*

Syn. 4 **Thoughtful, considerate** mean giving careful attention to the comfort or feelings of others. **Thoughtful** emphasizes the performance of small services and acts of kindness which anticipate another's needs: *A thoughtful neighbor, knowing the girl was sick and alone, took her food.* **Considerate** emphasizes concern with the feelings and rights of others and the desire to spare them from discomfort, pain, or unhappiness: *She is considerate enough to tell her parents where she goes.*

thought less (thôt′lis), *adj.* 1 without thought; doing things without thinking; careless: *a thoughtless person, a thoughtless remark.* 2 showing little or no care or regard for others; not considerate: *It is thoughtless of her to keep us waiting so long.* —**thought′less ly,** *adv.* —**thought′less-ness,** *n.*

thou sand (thou′znd), *n.* 1 ten hundred; 1000. 2 a large number: *thousands of people.* —*adj.* being ten hundred; 1000. [Old English *thūsend*]

thou sand fold (thou′znd fōld′), *adj., adv., n.* a thousand times as much or as many.

Thousand Islands, group of about 1500 islands in the St. Lawrence River, near Lake Ontario. Some belong to Ontario, Canada, and some to New York State.

thou sandth (thou′zndth, *adj., n.* 1 next after the 999th; last in a series of a 1000. 2 one, or being one, of a 1000 equal parts.

Thrace (thrās), *n.* region in the E part of the Balkan Peninsula. In ancient times it was first an independent country and later a Roman province. Today the region is in Bulgaria, Greece, and Turkey. —**Thra cian** (thrā′shən), *adj., n.*

thrall (thrôl), *n.* 1 person in bondage; slave or serf. 2 thralldom. [< Scandinavian (Old Icelandic) *thræll*]

thrall dom or **thral dom** (thrôl′dəm), *n.* bondage; slavery.

thrash (thrash), *v.t.* 1 beat as punishment; flog. 2 move, swing, or beat vigorously to and fro or up and down: *thrash one's legs in the water.* 3 thresh (wheat, etc.). 4 **thrash out,** settle by thorough discussion. 5 **thrash over,** go over again and again. —*v.i.* move violently; toss: *thrash about in bed. Branches thrashed against the window.* —*n.* 1 act of thrashing. 2 a swimming movement in which the legs are moved alternately and rapidly up and down. [variant of *thresh*]

thrash er (thrash′ər), *n.* 1 person or thing that thrashes. 2 any of several long-tailed North American songbirds of the same family as the mockingbird and somewhat resembling thrushes. 3 thresher (def. 3).

thread (thred), *n.* 1 a fine cord made of strands of cotton, silk, flax, etc., spun out and twisted together, used especially for sewing. 2 something long and slender like a thread: *a spider hanging by a thread, a thread of light coming through the crack in the door, a thread of gold in a piece of ore.* 3 the main thought that connects the parts of a story, speech, etc.: *lose the thread of a conversation.* 4 course; progression: *the thread of life.* 5 the sloping ridge that winds around a bolt, screw, pipe joint, etc. —*v.t.* 1 pass a thread through: *thread a needle, thread beads onto a string.* 2 pass like a thread through; pervade. 3 make one's way through; make (one's way) carefully; go on a winding course: *I threaded my way through the crowd.* 4 form a thread or threads on or in (a bolt, screw, pipe joint, etc.). —*v.i.* 1 form into a thread: *Cook the syrup until it threads.* 2 go on a winding course: *The path threads through the forest.* [Old English *thrǣd*] —**thread′er,** *n.* —**thread′like′,** *adj.*

thread (def. 5)

thread bare (thred′ber′, thred′bar′), *adj.* 1 having the nap worn off; worn so much that the threads show: *a threadbare coat.* 2 wearing clothes worn to the threads; shabby. 3 old and worn; stale: *a threadbare excuse.* —**thread′bare′ness,** *n.*

thread worm (thred′wėrm′), *n.* any of various threadlike nematode worms, especially a pinworm.

thread y (thred′ē), *adj.,* **thread i er, thread i est.** 1 consisting of or resembling a thread. 2 stringy or viscid; fibrous. 3 (of the pulse) thin and feeble. 4 (of the voice, etc.) lacking in fullness. —**thread′i ness,** *n.*

threat (thret), *n.* 1 statement of what will be done to hurt or punish someone. 2 sign or cause of possible evil or harm: *the threat of war.* [Old English *thrēat*]

threat en (thret′n), *v.t.* 1 make a threat against; say what will be done to hurt or punish: *threaten a person with imprisonment.* See synonym study below. 2 be a sign or warning of (possible evil or harm): *Black clouds threaten rain.* 3 be a cause of possible evil or harm to: *A flood threatened the city.* —*v.i.* 1 be a threat. 2 utter a threat. [Old English *thrēatnian*] —**threat′en er,** *n.* —**threat′en ing ly,** *adv.*

Syn. *v.t.* 1 **Threaten, menace** mean to indicate the intention of harming someone. **Threaten** applies when one is trying to force someone to do (or not to do) something and warns him of the consequences if he does not obey: *He threatened to shoot her if she screamed.* **Menace** applies when one tries to frighten someone by means of a look, movement, or weapon: *He menaced her with a gun.*

three (thrē), *n.* 1 one more than two; 3. 2 a set of three persons or things. —*adj.* being one more than two; 3. [Old English *thrēo*]

three-bag ger (thrē′bag′ər), *n.* SLANG. (in baseball) a triple.

three-base hit (thrē′bās′), (in baseball) a triple.

three-D or **3-D** (thrē′dē′), INFORMAL. —*adj.* three-dimensional. —*n.* a three-dimensional motion picture, etc.

three-deck er (thrē′dek′ər), *n.* 1 ship having three decks or carrying guns on three decks. 2 thing having three stories, layers, or parts. 3 sandwich made with three slices of bread.

three-di men sion al (thrē′də men′shə-nəl), *adj.* 1 having three dimensions. 2 seeming to have depth as well as height and breadth; appearing to exist in three dimensions: *a three-dimensional photograph.* Also, **third-dimensional, tridimensional.**

three fold (thrē′fōld′), *adj.* 1 three times as much or as many. 2 having three parts. —*adv.* three times as much or as many.

hat, āge, fär; let, ēqual, tėrm;
it, īce; hot, ōpen, ôrder;
oil, out; cup, pu̇t, rüle;
ch, child; ng, long; sh, she;
th, thin; ᴛʜ, then; zh, measure;

ə represents *a* in about, *e* in taken, *i* in pencil, *o* in lemon, *u* in circus.

< = from, derived from, taken from.

three-mile limit (thrē′mīl′), distance from the shore that, according to international law, is included within the jurisdiction of the country possessing the coast.

three pence (thrip′əns, threp′əns, thrup′-əns), *n.* 1 three British pennies; three pence. 2 coin of this value.

three pen ny (thrip′ə nē, threp′ə nē; thrē′-pen′ē, thrup′nē), *adj.* 1 worth three pence; costing threepence. 2 of little worth; cheap; paltry.

three-ply (thrē′plī′), *adj.* having three thicknesses, layers, folds, or strands.

three-point landing (thrē′point′), a landing of an aircraft so that both wheels of the main landing gear and the wheel or skid under the tail touch the ground at the same time.

three-ring circus (thrē′ring′), 1 circus that has three rings in which separate acts can be presented at the same time. 2 any activity or undertaking having a great variety of things going on at the same time.

Three Rivers, city in S Quebec, Canada, on the St. Lawrence River. 58,000.

three R's, the. See **R.**

three score (thrē′skôr′, thrē′skōr′), *adj.* three times twenty; 60.

three some (thrē′səm), *n.* 1 group of three people. 2 game played by three people. 3 the players.

Three Wise Men, the Magi.

thren o dy (thren′ə dē), *n., pl.* **-dies.** song of lamentation, especially at a person's death; dirge. [< Greek *threnoidia* < *threnos* lament + *oide* song]

thre o nine (thrē′ə nēn′, thrē′ə nən), *n.* a crystalline amino acid, a product of the hydrolysis of proteins, considered essential to human nutrition. *Formula:* $C_4H_9NO_3$

thresh (thresh), *v.t.* 1 separate the grain or seeds from (wheat, etc.) with a flail, a machine, etc. 2 **thresh out,** settle by thorough discussion. 3 **thresh over,** go over again and again. —*v.i.* 1 thresh grain. 2 toss about; move violently; thrash. [Old English *threscan*]

thresh er (thresh′ər), *n.* 1 person or thing that threshes. 2 threshing machine. 3 any of a genus of large sharks, having long, curved tails with which they supposedly beat the water to round up the small fish on which they feed; thrasher; thresher shark.

thresher shark, thresher (def. 3).

threshing machine, machine used for separating the grain or seeds from the stalks and other parts of wheat, oats, etc.; thresher.

thresh old (thresh′ōld, thresh′hōld), *n.* 1 piece of wood or stone across the bottom of a door frame; doorsill. 2 doorway. 3 point of entering; beginning point: *The scientist was on the threshold of an important discovery.* 4 (in psychology and physiology) the point at which a given stimulus begins to be perceptible: *a person with a high threshold of pain.* [Old English *threscwold*]

threw (thrü), *v.* pt. of **throw.**

thrice (thrīs), *adv.* 1 three times. 2 very; extremely. [Middle English *thries* < Old English *thriga*]

thrift (thrift), *n.* 1 absence of waste; economical management; habit of saving. 2 any of a genus of common plants with pink, white, or lavender flowers that grow on mountains and along seashores. 3 vigorous growth, as of a plant. [Middle English < *thrifen* thrive]

thrift less (thrift′lis), *adj.* without thrift; wasteful. **—thrift′less ly,** *adv.* **—thrift′less ness,** *n.*

thrift shop, U.S. shop in which second-hand articles are sold at low prices.

thrift y (thrif′tē), *adj.,* **thrift i er, thrift i est.** 1 careful in spending; economical; saving. See **economical** for synonym study. 2 thriving; flourishing: *a thrifty plant.* 3 prosperous; successful: *thrifty farms.* **—thrift′i ly,** *adv.* **—thrift′i ness,** *n.*

thrill (thril), *n.* a shivering, exciting feeling: *a thrill of pleasure.* —*v.t.* 1 give a shivering, exciting feeling to: *Adventure stories thrill him.* 2 cause to tremble or quiver; make vibrate. —*v.i.* 1 have a shivering, exciting feeling. 2 quiver; tremble: *Her voice thrilled with excitement.* [Old English *thyrlian* pierce < *thurh* through] **—thrill′ing ly,** *adv.*

thrill er (thril′ər), *n.* 1 person or thing that thrills. 2 INFORMAL. story, play, or motion picture filled with excitement, suspense, etc.

thrips (thrips), *n.* any of a genus of small, narrow, winged or wingless insects. The winged species have wings fringed with hairs. Most varieties feed on plant juices, and many are destructive of plants and grain. [< Greek, woodworm]

thrive (thrīv), *v.i.,* **throve** or **thrived, thrived** or **thriv en** (thriv′ən), **thriv ing.** 1 grow or develop well; grow vigorously: *Flowers will not thrive without sunshine.* 2 be successful; grow rich; prosper. [Middle English *thrifen* < Scandinavian (Old Icelandic) *thrīfask*] **—thriv′er,** *n.* **—thriv′ing ly,** *adv.*

thro or **thro'** (thrü), *prep., adv., adj.* through.

throat (thrōt), *n.* 1 the front of the neck. 2 the passage from the mouth to the stomach or the lungs. 3 any narrow passage: *the throat of a mine.* 4 **jump down one's throat,** attack or criticize a person with sudden violence. 5 **lump in one's throat,** a feeling of inability to swallow. [Old English *throte*]

-throated, *combining form.* having a ___ throat: *White-throated = having a white throat.*

throat latch (thrōt′lach′), *n.* strap that passes under a horse's throat and helps to hold the bridle in place.

throat y (thrō′tē), *adj.,* **throat i er, throat i est.** 1 produced or modified in the throat; guttural: *The young girl had a throaty voice.* 2 low-pitched and resonant: *the engine's throaty roar.* **—throat′i ly,** *adv.* **—throat′i ness,** *n.*

throb (throb), *v.,* **throbbed, throb bing,** *n.* —*v.i.* 1 beat rapidly or strongly; pulsate; palpitate: *The long climb up the hill made her heart throb.* 2 beat steadily. —*n.* 1 a rapid or strong beat: *a throb of pain.* 2 a steady beat: *the throb of a pulse.* [Middle English *throbben*] **—throb′bing ly,** *adv.*

throe (thrō), *n.* 1 a violent pang; great pain. 2 **throes,** *pl.* **a** anguish; agony. **b** a desperate struggle; violent disturbance. [Middle English *throwe*]

throm bin (throm′bən), *n.* enzyme in blood serum which reacts with fibrinogen to form fibrin, causing blood to clot. [< Greek *thrombos* clot]

throm bo cyte (throm′bə sīt), *n.* blood platelet.

throm bo em bo lism (throm′bō em′bə liz′əm), *n.* the obstruction of a blood vessel by a clot that has broken loose from its site of formation.

throm bo plas tin (throm′bō plas′tən), *n.* a protein substance found in the blood and in tissues, which promotes the conversion of prothrombin into thrombin.

throm bo sis (throm bō′sis), *n., pl.* **-ses** (-sēz′). the formation of a thrombus or blood clot; a coagulation of blood in a blood vessel or in the heart, causing an obstruction of the circulation.

throm bot ic (throm bot′ik), *adj.* of or caused by thrombosis.

throm bus (throm′bəs), *n., pl.* **-bi** (-bī). a fibrous clot which forms in a blood vessel or within the heart and obstructs the circulation. [< New Latin < Greek *thrombos* clot]

throne (thrōn), *n., v.,* **throned, thron ing.** —*n.* 1 chair on which a king, queen, bishop, or other person of high rank sits during ceremonies. 2 power or authority of a king, queen, etc. 3 person who sits on a throne; sovereign. —*v.t.* enthrone. [< Greek *thronos*]

throng (thrông, throng), *n.* 1 a crowd; multitude. See **crowd** for synonym study. 2 a pressing or crowding; crowded condition. —*v.t.* crowd; fill with a crowd: *The people thronged the theater to see the new movie.* —*v.i.* come together in a crowd; go or press in large numbers. [Old English *(ge)thrang*]

thros tle (thros′əl), *n.* BRITISH. a thrush, especially the song thrush. [Old English]

throt tle (throt′l), *n., v.,* **-tled, -tling.** —*n.* 1 valve regulating the flow of steam, gasoline vapor, etc., to an engine. 2 lever, pedal, etc., working such a valve. 3 throat or windpipe. —*v.t.* 1 stop the breath of by pressure on the throat; choke; strangle. 2 check or stop the flow of; suppress: *High tariffs throttle trade.* 3 check, stop, or regulate the flow of (fuel) to an engine. 4 lessen the speed of (an engine) by closing a throttle. —*v.i.* be choked; strangle. [Middle English *throtel* < *throte* throat] **—throt′tler,** *n.*

through (thrü), *prep.* 1 from end to end of; from side to side of; between the parts of; from beginning to end of: *march through a town, cut a tunnel through a mountain.* 2 here and there in; over; around: *stroll through the streets of a city.* 3 because of; by reason of: *refuse help through pride, fail through ignorance.* 4 by means of: *become rich through hard work and ability.* See **by** for synonym study. 5 having reached the end of; finished with: *We are through school at three o'clock.* 6 during the whole of; throughout: *work from dawn through the day and into the night.* 7 during and until the finish of: *help a person through hard times.*
—*adv.* 1 from end to end; from side to side; between the parts: *The bullet hit the wall and went through.* 2 completely; thoroughly: *He walked home in the rain and was wet through.* 3 from beginning to end: *She read the book through.* 4 along the whole distance; all the way: *The train goes through to Boston.* 5 **through and through,** completely; thoroughly.
—*adj.* 1 going all the way without change: *a through flight from New York to Los Angeles.* 2 for the whole distance, journey, etc.: *a through ticket to Los Angeles.* 3 having reached the end; finished: *I am almost through.* 4 permitting passage without interference at intersections, etc.: *through traffic, a through street.* 5 passing or extending from one end, side, surface, etc., to the other. Also, **thro, thro', thru.**
[Middle English *thrugh,* Old English *thurh*]

through out (thrü out′), *prep.* 1 in every part of: *The Fourth of July is celebrated throughout the United States.* 2 during the whole of (a period of time or course of action): *She worked hard throughout her life.* —*adv.* 1 in or to every part: *This house is well built throughout.* 2 through the whole of a period or course of action.

through way (thrü′wā′), *n.* thruway.

throve (thrōv), *v.* a pt. of **thrive.**

throw (thrō), *v.,* **threw, thrown, throw ing,** *n.* —*v.t.* 1 send through the air with force; cast; toss; hurl: *throw a ball, throw water on a fire.* See synonym study below. 2 cause to fall or fall off: *throw one's opponent in wrestling, be thrown by a horse.* 3 put by force: *throw someone into prison.* 4 put carelessly or in haste: *throw a sweater over one's shoulders.* 5 turn, direct, or move, especially quickly: *throw a glance at passing cars.* 6 move (a lever, etc.) to connect or disconnect parts of a switch, clutch, or other mechanism. 7 shed: *A snake throws its skin.* 8 (of some animals) bring forth (young). 9 INFORMAL. let an opponent win (a race, game, etc.), often for money. 10 make (a specified cast) with dice. 11 twist (silk) into threads. 12 shape on a potter's wheel. 13 INFORMAL. give (a party, etc.). —*v.i.* cast, toss, or hurl something: *How far can you throw?*
throw away, a get rid of; discard. **b** waste. **c** fail to use.
throw back, a put back in time or condition; check, retard, or delay. **b** go back in time; hark back. **c** revert to an ancestral type.
throw in, add, especially as a bargain.
throw off, a get rid of; cast off. **b** give off; emit. **c** shake off or divert. **d** INFORMAL. produce (a poem, etc.) in an offhand manner.
throw oneself at, try very hard to get the love, friendship, or favor of.
throw open, a open suddenly or widely. **b** remove all obstacles or restrictions from.
throw out, a get rid of; discard. **b** reject (a legislative bill, etc.). **c** expel: *throw out an intruder.* **d** dismiss from a job, etc. **e** put or send forth (a question, signal, etc.). **f** send out; give off; emit. **g** release. **h** (in baseball) put out (a base runner) by throwing the ball to a baseman.
throw over, a give up; discard; abandon. **b** overthrow.
throw up, a INFORMAL. vomit. **b** give up; abandon. **c** build rapidly. **d** raise (the hands, etc.) quickly and suddenly. **e** make noticeable. **f** give up (a game, etc.); quit.
—*n.* 1 a throwing; cast, toss, etc.: *a good throw.* 2 distance a thing is or may be thrown: *a long throw.* 3 scarf, light covering, blanket, etc.: *a knitted throw.* 4 cast at dice. [Old English *thrāwan* to twist, turn] **—throw′er,** *n.*

hat, āge, fär; let, ēqual, tėrm;
it, īce; hot, ōpen, ôrder;
oil, out; cup, pu̇t, rüle;
ch, child; ng, long; sh, she;
th, thin; ᴛʜ, then; zh, measure;

ə represents *a* in about, *e* in taken, *i* in pencil, *o* in lemon, *u* in circus.

< = from, derived from, taken from.

Syn. *v.t.* 1 **Throw, toss, cast** mean to send something through the air by a movement of the arm. **Throw** is the general word: *The children threw pillows at each other.* **Toss** means to throw lightly or carelessly with the palm up: *Please toss me the matches.* **Cast** is now literary except figuratively or in special uses, as in games, voting, fishing, sailing: *They cast anchor. She cast dignity to the wind, and ran.*

throw a way (thrō′ə wā′), *n.* handbill, pamphlet, etc., intended to be thrown away after reading. *—adj.* able to be thrown away or discarded: *a throwaway bottle.*

throw back (thrō′bak′), *n.* 1 a throwing back. 2 setback or check. 3 reversion to an ancestral type or character. 4 an example of this: *The boy seemed to be a throwback to his great-grandfather.*

thrown (thrōn), *v.* pp. of **throw.**

throw rug, scatter rug.

thru (thrü), *prep., adv., adj.* through.

thrum[1] (thrum), *v.,* **thrummed, thrum ming,** *n.* *—v.i.* 1 play on a stringed instrument by plucking the strings, especially in an idle or careless way. 2 drum or tap idly with the fingers: *thrum on a table.* 3 drone; mumble. *—v.t.* 1 play (a stringed instrument, or a tune on it), especially in an idle or careless way; strum: *thrum a guitar.* 2 recite or tell in a monotonous way. *—n.* the sound made by thrumming. [imitative]

thrum[2] (thrum), *n.* 1 loose thread or yarn. 2 fringe. [Old English *-thrum*]

thrush[1] (thrush), *n.* any of a large family of migratory songbirds, including the robin, bluebird, wood thrush, etc., that are usually medium-sized and have upper parts of a dull, solid color and a spotted or colored breast. [Old English *thrȳsce*]

thrush[2] (thrush), *n.* 1 disease often attacking children, characterized by white specks on the inside of the mouth and throat, and caused by a parasitic fungus. 2 a diseased condition of a horse's foot. [perhaps < Scandinavian (Swedish) *trosk*]

thrust (thrust), *v.,* **thrust, thrust ing,** *n.* *—v.t.* 1 push with force: *He thrust his hands into his pockets.* 2 pierce; stab: *thrust a knife into an apple.* 3 put forth; extend: *The tree thrust its roots deep into the ground.* *—v.i.* 1 push with force; make a thrust. 2 make a stab or lunge. 3 push or force one's way. *—n.* 1 a forcible push; drive. 2 a stab; lunge. 3 a sudden, sharp attack; thrusting assault. 4 (in mechanics) the force of one thing pushing on another. 5 (in architecture) the lateral force exerted by an arch, etc., against an abutment or support. It must be counteracted to prevent the structure from collapsing. 6 the endways push exerted by the rotation of a propeller, that causes a ship, airplane, etc., to move. 7 the force driving a rocket or a jet engine forward as a reaction to the rearward discharge of gases, burning fuels, etc., through a nozzle or exhaust. [< Scandinavian (Old Icelandic) *thrȳsta*] **—thrust′er,** *n.*

thrus tor (thrus′tər), *n.* reaction engine.

thru way (thrü′wā′), *n.* an express highway; expressway. Also, **throughway.**

Thu cyd i des (thü sid′ə dēz′), *n.* 460?-400? B.C., Greek historian.

thud (thud), *n., v.,* **thud ded, thud ding.** *—n.* 1 a dull sound: *The book hit the floor with a thud.* 2 a blow or thump. *—v.i., v.t.* hit, move, or strike with a thud. [origin uncertain]

thug (thug), *n.* 1 ruffian; cutthroat. 2 member of a former religious organization of robbers and murderers in India, who strangled their victims. [< Hindi *thag* < Sanskrit *sthaga* rogue]

thug ger y (thug′ər ē), *n., pl.* **-ger ies.** the activities or practices of a thug or thugs.

thug gish (thug′ish), *adj.* of or like a thug or thugs; ruffianly.

Thu le (thü′lē, tü′lē), *n.* 1 the part of the world that the ancient Greeks and Romans regarded as farthest north; some island or region north of Britain. 2 settlement in NW Greenland. 2000.

thu li um (thü′lē əm), *n.* a silver-white, rare-earth metallic element found in various minerals. An isotope of thulium is used as the radiating element in portable X-ray units. *Symbol:* Tm; *atomic number* 69. See pages 326 and 327 for table. [< New Latin < *Thule*]

thumb (thum), *n.* 1 the short, thick finger of the human hand, next to the forefinger, which can be used in opposition to the other fingers. 2 the corresponding digit or part of the paw of an animal. 3 part that covers the thumb: *the thumb of a mitten.*

be all thumbs, be very clumsy, awkward, etc.

thumbs down, sign of disapproval or rejection.

thumbs up, sign of approval or acceptance.

twiddle one's thumbs, do nothing; be idle.

under one's thumb, under one's power or influence.

—v.t. 1 soil or wear by handling with the thumbs: *The books were badly thumbed.* 2 turn pages of (a book, etc.) rapidly, reading only portions. 3 handle awkwardly. 4 INFORMAL. ask for or get (a free ride) by holding up one's thumb to motorists going in one's direction.

[Old English *thūma*] **—thumb′like′,** *adj.*

thumb index, series of grooves cut along the front edges of the pages of a book to show initial letters or titles, so that any division may be turned to by placing the thumb or finger on the proper initial or title.

thumb-in dex (thum′in′deks), *v.t.* furnish (a book) with a thumb index.

thumb nail (thum′nāl′), *n.* 1 nail of the thumb. 2 something very small or short. *—adj.* very small or short: *a thumbnail sketch.*

thumb print (thum′print′), *n.* an impression of the markings on the inner surface of the last joint of the thumb.

thumb screw (thum′skrü′), *n.* 1 screw with a flattened or winged head that can be turned with the thumb and a finger. 2 an old instrument of torture that squeezed the thumbs.

thumb tack (thum′tak′), *n.* tack with a broad, flat head, that can be pressed into a wall, board, etc., with the thumb.

thump (thump), *v.t.* 1 strike with something thick and heavy: *He thumped the table with his fist.* 2 strike against (something) heavily and noisily. 3 INFORMAL. beat or thrash severely. *—v.i.* 1 make a dull sound; pound. 2 beat violently. *—n.* 1 a blow with something thick and heavy; heavy knock. 2 the dull sound made by a blow, knock, or fall. [imitative] **—thump′er,** *n.*

thump ing (thum′ping), *adj.* INFORMAL. very large; great; excellent.

thun der (thun′dər), *n.* 1 the loud noise that accompanies or follows a flash of lightning, caused by a disturbance of the air resulting from the discharge of electricity. 2 any noise like thunder: *the thunder of Niagara Falls, a thunder of applause.* 3 a threat or denunciation. 4 thunderbolt. **5 steal someone's thunder,** take and use as one's own an effective or successful idea, method, plan, etc., originated by another person. *—v.i.* 1 give forth thunder: *It thundered, but no rain fell.* 2 make a noise like thunder: *The cannon thundered.* 3 utter threats or denunciations. *—v.t.* 1 utter very loudly; roar: *thunder a reply.* 2 threaten or denounce. [Old English *thunor*] **—thun′der er,** *n.*

thun der bolt (thun′dər bōlt′), *n.* 1 a flash of lightning and the thunder that follows it. 2 something sudden, startling, and terrible: *The news of his death came as a thunderbolt.* 3 person with great energy and drive.

thun der clap (thun′dər klap′), *n.* 1 a loud crash of thunder. 2 something sudden or startling.

thun der cloud (thun′dər kloud′), *n.* a dark, electrically charged cloud that brings thunder and lightning.

thun der head (thun′dər hed′), *n.* one of the round, swelling masses of cumulus clouds often appearing before thunderstorms and frequently developing into thunderclouds.

thun der ing (thun′dər ing), *adj.* 1 that thunders; very loud and deep: *a thundering voice.* 2 INFORMAL. very great or big; immense: *a thundering lie.* **—thun′der ing ly,** *adv.*

thun der ous (thun′dər əs), *adj.* 1 producing thunder. 2 making a noise like thunder: *a thunderous burst of applause.* **—thun′der ous ly,** *adv.*

thun der show er (thun′dər shou′ər), *n.* shower with thunder and lightning.

thun der storm (thun′dər stôrm′), *n.* storm with thunder and lightning.

thun der struck (thun′dər struk′), *adj.* overcome, as if hit by a thunderbolt; astonished: *We were thunderstruck by the news of the war.*

Thur., Thursday.

Thur ber (thėr′bər), *n.* **James,** 1894-1961, American writer.

thur i ble (thu̇r′ə bəl, thyu̇r′ə bəl), *n.* censer. [< Latin *thuribulum* < *thuris* incense < Greek *thyos* burnt sacrifice < *thyein* to sacrifice]

Thu rin gi a (thu̇ rin′jē ə), *n.* region in S East Germany. **—Thu rin′gi an,** *adj., n.*

Thurs., Thursday.

Thurs day (thėrz′dē, thėrz′dā), *n.* the fifth day of the week, following Wednesday. [Old English *Thuresdæg,* literally, Thor's day]

thus (ᴛʜus), *adv.* 1 in this way; in the way just stated, indicated, etc.; in the following manner: *She spoke thus.* 2 accordingly; consequently; therefore: *Thus we decided that you were wrong.* 3 to this extent, number, or degree: *thus far.* [Old English *thus.* Related to THIS.]

thus ly (ᴛʜus′lē), *adv.* INFORMAL. thus.

thwack (thwak), *v.t.* strike vigorously with a stick or something flat; whack. —*n.* a sharp blow with a stick or something flat; whack. [probably imitative]

thwart (thwôrt), *v.t.* prevent from doing something, particularly by blocking the way; oppose and defeat: *Lack of money thwarted the boy's plans for college.* See **frustrate** for synonym study. —*n.* 1 seat across a boat, on which a rower sits. 2 brace between the gunwales of a canoe. —*adj.* lying or passing across. —*adv.* across; crosswise; athwart. [< Scandinavian (Old Icelandic) *thvert* across] —**thwart′er,** *n.*

thy (ᴛʜī), *adj.* ARCHAIC. possessive form of **thou.** your: *"Thy kingdom come, Thy will be done."* [Old English *thīn*]

thy la cine (thī′lə sīn, thī′lə sən), *n.* a doglike, carnivorous, marsupial mammal of Tasmania which is now almost extinct; Tasmanian wolf. Thylacines are grayish or yellowish-brown with dark brown stripes on their backs. [< Greek *thylakos* pouch]

thyme (tīm), *n.* any of a genus of herbs of the mint family, with fragrant, aromatic leaves. The leaves of the common garden thyme are used for seasoning. The common wild thyme is a creeping evergreen. [< Greek *thymon*]

thy mic (thī′mik), *adj.* of or having to do with the thymus.

thy mine (thī′mən, thī′mēn′), *n.* substance present in nucleic acid in cells. It is one of the pyrimidine bases of DNA. *Formula:* $C_5H_6N_2O_2$ [< *thymus,* a source of DNA]

thy mol (thī′mōl, thī′mol), *n.* an aromatic, white or colorless, crystalline substance obtained from thyme and other plants or made synthetically, used as an antiseptic, etc. *Formula:* $C_{10}H_{14}O$

thy mus (thī′məs), *n.* a small ductless glandlike organ of uncertain function, found in young vertebrates near the base of the neck and disappearing or becoming rudimentary in the adult. The thymus of calves, lambs, etc., is used for food and is called sweetbread. [< New Latin < Greek *thymos*]

thym y (tī′mē), *adj.* having to do with or like thyme; full of thyme.

thy ra tron (thī′rə tron), *n.* a gas-filled, three- or four-element vacuum tube containing a hot cathode, in which the grid initiates, but does not limit, the current, used mainly as an electronic switch. [originally a trademark]

thy roid (thī′roid), *n.* 1 thyroid gland. 2 vein, etc., near the thyroid gland. 3 medicine made from the thyroid glands of animals, used to treat disorders caused by a deficiency in the thyroid gland. 4 thyroid cartilage. —*adj.* of or having to do with the thyroid gland or thyroid cartilage. [< Greek *thyreoeides* shieldlike < *thyreos* oblong shield (< *thyra* door) + *eidos* form]

thyroid cartilage, the principal cartilage of the larynx, which forms the Adam's apple in human beings.

thyroid gland, a large endocrine gland in the neck of vertebrates, near the larynx and upper windpipe, that secretes thyroxine.

thy rox in (thī rok′sən), *n.* thyroxine.

thy rox ine (thī rok′sēn′, thī rok′sən), *n.* hormone secreted by the thyroid gland which stimulates metabolism and, in children, affects growth. A synthetic form is used to treat goiter and other thyroid disorders.

thyr sus (thėr′səs), *n., pl.* **-si** (-sī). (in Greek myths) a staff or spear tipped with an ornament like a pine cone and sometimes wrapped round with ivy and vine branches, borne by Dionysus (Bacchus) and his followers. [< Latin < Greek *thyrsos* staff, stem]

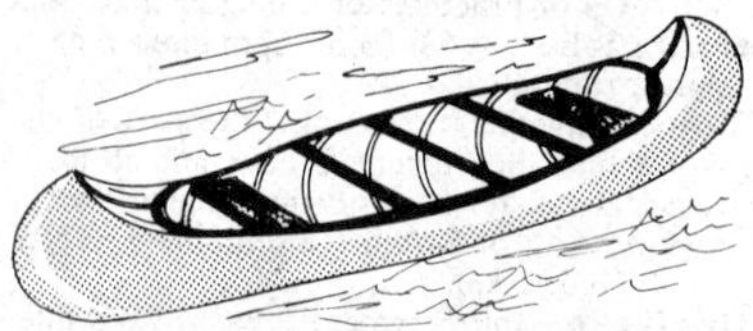

thwart (def. 2)—canoe with thwarts

thy sa nu ran (thī sə nyůr′ən), *n.* any of an order of wingless insects having long antennae and a scaly, flattened body that is silvery or gray in color. Silverfishes belong to this order. [< Greek *thysanos* tassel + *oura* tail]

thy self (ᴛʜī self′), *pron.* ARCHAIC. yourself.

ti (tē), *n.* (in music) the seventh tone of the diatonic scale; si. [alteration of Medieval Latin *si*]

Ti, titanium.

Tian Shan (tyän′ shän′), Tien Shan.

tiara (def. 1) tiara (def. 2)

ti ar a (tē er′ə, tē är′ə), *n.* 1 band of gold, jewels, flowers, etc., worn around the head by women as an ornament. 2 the triple crown worn by the pope as a symbol of his position. [< Greek]

Ti ber i as (tī bir′ē əs), *n.* **Sea of,** Sea of Galilee.

Ti ber i us (tī bir′ē əs), *n.* 42 B.C.-A.D. 37, Roman emperor from A.D. 14 to 37.

Ti ber River (tī′bər), river flowing from central Italy through Rome into the Tyrrhenian Sea. 244 mi.

Ti bet (ti bet′), *n.* former country of central Asia, now under the control of the People's Republic of China. 1,300,000 pop.; 470,000 sq. mi. *Capital:* Lhasa.

Ti bet an (ti bet′n), *adj.* of or having to do with Tibet, its people, or their language. —*n.* 1 member of the group of native Mongoloid people of Tibet. 2 language of Tibet, related to Burmese and Thai.

tib i a (tib′ē ə), *n., pl.* **tib i ae** (tib′ē ē′), **tib i as.** 1 the inner and thicker of the two bones of the leg from the knee to the ankle; shinbone. See **fibula** for diagram. 2 a corresponding bone in amphibians, birds, reptiles, and mammals. 3 the fourth section (from the body) of the leg of an insect. 4 an ancient flute. [< Latin]

tib i al (tib′ē əl), *adj.* of or having to do with the tibia.

tic (tik), *n.* a habitual, involuntary twitching of certain muscles, especially those of the face. [< French]

tick[1] (tik), *n.* 1 the quick, light, dry sound made by a clock or watch. 2 sound like it. 3 a small mark made to check or mark something, such as ✓ or /. —*v.i.* 1 make a tick or ticks: *The clock ticked.* 2 INFORMAL. function, work, or go: *Just what makes that dynamo tick?* —*v.t.* 1 mark off: *The clock ticked away the minutes.* 2 mark with a tick; check: *Tick off the items one by one.* [probably imitative]

tick[2] (tik), *n.* 1 any of a numerous species of small, oval-shaped arachnids of the same order as mites, that attach themselves to the skin of humans and other warm-blooded mammals and suck their blood. Ticks carry various infectious diseases which attack people or animals. 2 any of various wingless, parasitic insects that suck the blood of certain animals, such as sheep, cattle, or deer. [Middle English *tyke*]

tick[3] (tik), *n.* 1 the cloth covering a mattress or pillow. 2 INFORMAL. ticking. [probably < Middle Dutch *tike* < Latin *theca* case < Greek *thēkē*]

tick[4] (tik), *n.* INFORMAL. credit; trust: *buy something on tick.* [apparently short for *on (the) tick(et)*]

tick er (tik′ər), *n.* 1 person or thing that ticks. 2 a telegraphic instrument that prints stock-market reports or news on a paper tape. 3 SLANG. watch; clock. 4 SLANG. the heart.

ticker tape, a paper tape on which a ticker prints stock-market reports or news.

tick et (tik′it), *n.* 1 card or piece of paper that gives its holder a right or privilege: *a theater ticket.* 2 INFORMAL. summons to appear in court given by a policeman to a person who has broken a traffic law: *a ticket for speeding, a parking ticket.* 3 card or piece of paper attached to something to show its price, etc. 4 the list of candidates for various offices that belong to one political party. —*v.t.* 1 put a ticket on; mark with a ticket: *All articles in the store are ticketed with the price.* 2 describe or mark as if by a ticket; label; designate; characterize. 3 INFORMAL. serve with a summons. [< French *étiquette* < Middle French < *estiquer* to stick < Middle Dutch *stikken*]

ticket of leave, license or permit formerly given in Great Britain and Australia, granting a convict his liberty before his sentence had expired, provided he obeyed certain conditions.

tick ing (tik′ing), *n.* a strong cotton or linen fabric, used to cover mattresses and pillows and to make tents and awnings.

tick le (tik′əl), *v.,* **-led, -ling,** *n.* —*v.t.* 1 touch lightly, causing little thrills, shivers, or wriggles. 2 cause to have such a feeling. 3 excite pleasantly; amuse: *Your story tickled me.* 4 play, stir, get, etc., with light touches or strokes. —*v.i.* have a tickling feeling: *My nose tickles.* —*n.* 1 a tingling or itching feeling. 2 a tickling. [Middle English *tikelen*]

tick ler (tik′lər), *n.* 1 person or thing that tickles. 2 a memorandum book, card index, or other device kept as a reminder of engagements, payments due, etc. 3 INFORMAL. a difficult or puzzling problem.

tick lish (tik′lish), *adj.* 1 sensitive to tickling. 2 requiring careful handling; delicate; risky: *the ticklish job of telling a person his faults.* 3 easily upset; unstable: *A canoe is a ticklish craft.* 4 easily offended; touchy. —**tick′lish ly,** *adv.* —**tick′lish ness,** *n.*

tick-tack-toe (tik′tak tō′), *n.* game in which two players alternately put circles or crosses in a figure of nine squares, each player trying to be the first to fill three spaces in a row with his mark. Also, **tic-tac-toe.**

tick-tock (tik′tok′), *n.* the sound made by a clock or watch.

Ti con de ro ga (tī′kon də rō′gə), *n.* village on Lake Champlain, in NE New York State, site of **Fort Ticonderoga,** an important stronghold during the Revolutionary War. 3000.

tic-tac-toe (tik′tak tō′), *n.* tick-tack-toe.

tid al (tī′dl), *adj.* 1 of tides; having tides; caused by tides. A tidal river is affected by the ocean's tide. 2 dependent on the state of the tide as to time of arrival and departure: *a tidal steamer.* **—tid′al ly,** *adv.*

tidal wave, 1 a large wave or sudden increase in the level of water along a shore, caused by unusually strong winds. 2 an enormous, destructive ocean wave which is caused by an underwater earthquake or volcanic eruption. 3 any great movement or manifestation of feeling, opinion, or the like: *a tidal wave of popular indignation.*

tid bit (tid′bit′), *n.* a very pleasing bit of food, news, etc. Also, **titbit.**

tid dle dy winks (tid′l dē wingks′), *n.* tiddlywinks.

tid dly winks (tid′lē wingks′), *n.* game in which the players try to make small colored disks jump from a flat surface into a cup by pressing on their edges with larger disks.

tide (tīd), *n., v.,* **tid ed, tid ing.** *—n.* 1 the rise and fall of the surface level of the ocean, usually taking place about every twelve hours, caused by the gravitational pull of the moon and the sun. 2 the inward or outward flow or current resulting from this on a coast, in a river, etc. 3 flood tide. 4 anything that rises and falls like the tide: *the tide of popular opinion.* 5 a stream, current, or flood. 6 season; time; a church festival or anniversary. 7 **turn the tide,** change from one condition to the opposite. *—v.t.* 1 **tide over, a** help along for a time. **b** overcome (a difficulty, etc.). 2 carry as the tide does. *—v.i.* 1 float or drift with the tide. 2 flow or surge as the tide does. [Old English *tīd,* originally, time]

tide land (tīd′land′), *n.* 1 land flooded at high tide. 2 submerged coastal land within the historical boundaries of a state and belonging to that state.

tide wait er (tīd′wā′tər), *n.* a customs officer who waits for and boards ships to prevent the evasion of the customs regulations.

tide wa ter (tīd′wô′tər, tīd′wot′ər), *n.* 1 water in rivers, streams, etc., affected by the rise and fall of the tides. 2 low-lying land along a seacoast through which such water flows. *—adj.* of or along tidewater.

ti dings (tī′dingz), *n.pl.* news; information: *joyful tidings.* [Old English *tīdung* < *tīdan* happen]

ti dy (tī′dē), *adj.,* **-di er, -di est,** *v.,* **-died, -dy ing,** *n., pl.* **-dies.** *—adj.* 1 neat and in order: *a tidy room.* See **neat**[1] for synonym study. 2 inclined to keep things neat and in order: *a tidy person.* 3 INFORMAL. fairly large; considerable: *a tidy sum of money.* 4 INFORMAL. fairly good. *—v.t., v.i.* put in order; make tidy: *tidy a room.* *—n.* a small cover to keep the back of a chair, etc., from becoming dirty or worn. [Middle English, timely < *tide* time] **—ti′di ly,** *adv.* **—ti′di ness,** *n.*

tie (tī), *v.,* **tied, ty ing,** *n.* *—v.t.* 1 fasten with string, cord, rope, etc.; bind: *tie a package, tie a dog to a tree.* 2 arrange to form a bow or knot: *tie the strings of an apron.* 3 tighten and fasten the string or strings of: *tie one's shoes, tie an apron.* 4 fasten, join, or connect in any way; link: *be tied to the mainland by an isthmus.* 5 restrain; restrict; confine; limit: *be tied to a steady job.* 6 make the same score as: *Oregon tied Florida State in football.* 7 (in music) connect (notes) by a tie. 8 INFORMAL. unite in marriage. *—v.i.* 1 fasten; form a bow or knot: *That ribbon doesn't tie well.* 2 make the same score; be equal in points: *The two teams tied.*

tie down, confine; restrict: *She is tied down by her home and five children.*

tie in, a connect or be connected: *Where does this line tie in with the main circuit?* **b** make or have a connection; relate: *How does that remark tie in with what you said yesterday?*

tie up, a tie firmly or tightly. **b** wrap up. **c** hinder; stop; delay: *tie up traffic.* **d** invest (money) or place (property) in such a way as to make it unavailable for other uses. **e** have one's schedule full; be very busy, etc.: *I can't go tomorrow; I'm all tied up.* **f** connect; relate. **g** moor; anchor.

—n. 1 anything connecting or holding together two or more things or parts; link. 2 cord, chain, etc., used for tying. 3 an ornamental knot, bow of ribbon, etc. 4 necktie. 5 anything that unites; bond; obligation: *family ties, ties of duty.* See **bond** for synonym study. 6 a heavy piece of timber or iron. The rails of a railroad track are fastened to ties about a foot apart. 7 a connecting beam, rod, or the like; tie beam. 8 equality in points, votes, etc.: *The game ended in a tie, 3 to 3.* 9 match or contest in which this occurs; draw. 10 (in music) a curved line set above or below two notes of the same pitch, indicating that they are to be played or sung as one sustained tone. 11 **ties,** *pl.* INFORMAL. low, laced shoes.

[Old English *tīgan* < *tēag* a tie, rope]

tie (def. 10)

tie beam, timber or piece serving as a tie in a roof, etc. See **king post** for diagram.

tie-dye (tī′dī′), *v.t.,* **-dyed, -dye ing.** dye (cloth) by tying some of the material in knots to prevent the cloth inside the knots from absorbing the dye.

tie-in (tī′in′), *n.* connection or link; relationship.

Tien Shan (tyen′ shän′), mountain range in central Asia, between the Kirghiz S.S.R. and Sinkiang, China. Highest peak, 24,406 ft. Also, **Tian Shan.**

Tien tsin (tin′tsin′), *n.* city and former treaty port in NE China, near Peking. 4,000,000.

tie pin (tī′pin′), *n.* stickpin.

tier[1] (tir), *n.* one of a series of rows arranged one above another: *tiers of seats in a football stadium.* *—v.t., v.i.* arrange, or be arranged, in tiers. [< Middle French *tire,* originally, order < *tirer* to draw]

ti er[2] (tī′ər), *n.* person or thing that ties.

tierce (tirs), *n.* 1 an old unit of liquid measure, equal to 42 United States gallons. 2 cask holding this amount. 3 sequence of three playing cards in the same suit. 4 (in fencing) the third of the traditional series of eight defensive positions. 5 the third of the seven canonical hours. 6 the service for it. Also, **terce.** [< Old French *tiers* third < Latin *tertius*]

Tier ra del Fue go (tyer′ə del fwā′gō), group of islands at the S end of South America. Part belongs to Argentina, part to Chile. 14,000 pop.; 28,000 sq. mi. See **Patagonia** for map.

hat, āge, fär; let, ēqual, tėrm;
it, īce; hot, ōpen, ôrder;
oil, out; cup, pu̇t, rüle;
ch, child; ng, long; sh, she;
th, thin; ᴛʜ, then; zh, measure;

ə represents *a* in about, *e* in taken, *i* in pencil, *o* in lemon, *u* in circus.

< = from, derived from, taken from.

tie-up (tī′up′), *n.* 1 a stopping of work or action on account of a strike, storm, accident, etc.: *a tie-up of traffic.* 2 INFORMAL. connection; relation.

tiff (tif), *n.* 1 a little quarrel. 2 a slight outburst of temper or ill humor. *—v.i.* 1 have a little quarrel. 2 be slightly peevish; be in a huff. [origin uncertain]

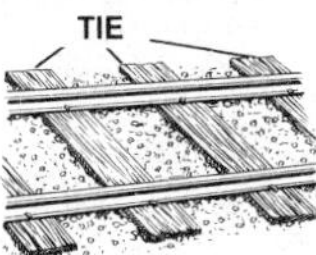

tie (def. 6) ties under the rails of a railroad track

tif fin (tif′ən), *n.* BRITISH. lunch. [< Anglo-Indian]

Tif lis (tif′lis), *n.* Tbilisi.

ti ger (tī′gər), *n.* 1 a large, fierce, Asiatic cat of the same genus as the lion, jaguar, and leopard, that has dull-yellow fur striped with black. 2 any of various related animals, such as the jaguar. 3 a fierce, cruel, grasping, or bloodthirsty person. 4 INFORMAL. an extra yell at the end of a cheer. [< Latin *tigris* < Greek] **—ti′ger like′,** *adj.*

tiger beetle, any of a family of active, flying beetles that prey on other insects and whose larvae live in tunnels in sandy soil and catch insects that come near.

tiger cat, 1 any of several wildcats smaller than a tiger but resembling it in markings or ferocity. 2 a domestic cat with cross stripes suggesting those of a tiger.

ti ger-eye (tī′gər ī′), *n.* tiger's-eye.

ti ger ish (tī′gər ish), *adj.* like a tiger; fierce; cruel. **—ti′ger ish ly,** *adv.* **—ti′ger ish ness,** *n.*

tiger lily, a tall garden lily, native to China, having nodding, dull-orange flowers spotted with black.

tiger moth, any of a family of moths having a hairy body and brightly colored, spotted or striped wings.

tiger salamander, either of two large salamanders of North America with tigerlike stripes on their backs.

ti ger's-eye (tī′gərz ī′), *n.* a golden-brown semiprecious stone with a changeable luster, composed chiefly of quartz, colored with iron oxide.

tiger shark, a large, voracious shark of the warmer parts of the Atlantic and Pacific oceans, having yellow streaks on its grayish-black body.

tight (tīt), *adj.* 1 packed or put together firmly; held firmly; firm: *a tight grip, a tight knot.* 2 drawn; stretched: *a tight canvas, a tight cable.* See synonym study below. 3 fitting closely or too closely: *tight clothing.* 4 DIALECT. well-built; trim; neat. 5 not letting water, air, or gas in or out: *a tight boat, a* *tight roof.* 6 INFORMAL. hard to deal with or manage; difficult: *have tight going for a few years.* 7 INFORMAL. almost even; close: *a tight race.* 8 hard to get; scarce: *Money for mortgages is tight just now.* 9 strict; severe: *rule with a tight hand.* 10 INFORMAL. stingy; close-fisted: *tight in one's dealings.* 11 SLANG. drunk. —*adv.* 1 firmly; closely; securely: *holding tight with both hands.* 2 **sit tight,** INFORMAL. keep the same position, opinion, etc. [probably < Scandinavian (Old Icelandic) *thēttr* watertight] —**tight′ly,** *adv.* —**tight′ness,** *n.*

Syn. *adj.* 2 **Tight, taut** mean drawn or stretched so as not to be loose or slack. **Tight,** the more general word, applies to anything drawn over or around something so firmly that there is no looseness: *You need a tight string around that package.* **Taut** emphasizes stretching until the thing described would break, snap, or tear if pulled more tightly, and is used chiefly as a nautical or mechanical term or to describe strained nerves or muscles: *The covering on a drum must be taut.*

tight en (tīt′n), *v.t.* make tight or tighter. —*v.i.* become tight or tighter. —**tight′en-er,** *n.*

tight fist ed (tīt′fis′tid), *adj.* stingy.

tight-lipped (tīt′lipt′), *adj.* 1 keeping the lips firmly together. 2 saying little or nothing; taciturn.

tight rope (tīt′rōp′), *n.* a raised rope or cable stretched tight, on which acrobats perform.

tights (tīts), *n.pl.* a close-fitting garment, usually covering the lower part of the body and the legs, worn by acrobats, dancers, etc.

tight wad (tīt′wod′), *n.* SLANG. a stingy person.

tight wire (tīt′wīr′), *n.* a wire tightrope.

ti glon (tī′glon, tī′glən), *n.* offspring of a tiger and a lioness. [< *tig(er)* + *l(i)on*]

ti gon (tī′gon, tī′gən), *n.* tiglon.

ti gress (tī′gris), *n.* a female tiger.

Ti gris River (tī′gris), river flowing from SE Turkey through Iraq, where it joins the Euphrates River and empties into the Persian Gulf. 1150 mi. See **Euphrates River** for map.

Ti jua na (tē′ə wä′nə; *Spanish* tē hwä′nä), *n.* city in NW Mexico, near the border of the United States and Mexico. 335,000.

tike (tīk), *n.* tyke.

ti ki (tē′kē), *n.* 1 a Polynesian deity, regarded as the creator of man. 2 image of it in wood or stone. [< Maori]

til bur y (til′bər ē), *n., pl.* **-bur ies.** a light two-wheeled carriage without a top. [< *Tilbury,* British coach designer of the 1800's]

til de (til′də), *n.* a diacritical mark (~) to indicate a special sound. It is used over *n* in Spanish when it is pronounced *ny,* as in *cañón* (kä nyōn′), and over certain vowels in Portuguese to indicate that they are nasal, as in *São Paulo* (souN pou′lü). [< Spanish < Latin *titulus* title]

tile (tīl), *n., v.,* **tiled, til ing.** —*n.* 1 a thin piece of baked clay, stone, etc., used for covering roofs, paving floors, and ornamenting. 2 any of various similar thin pieces of plastic, rubber, linoleum, or cement, used for similar purposes. 3 a baked clay pipe for draining land, roads, etc. 4 tiles; tiling. —*v.t.* put tiles on or in: *tile a bathroom floor.* [Old English *tigele* < Latin *tegula*] —**til′er,** *n.*

til ing (tī′ling), *n.* 1 tiles collectively. 2 the work of covering with or laying tiles. 3 anything covered with or consisting of tiles.

till[1] (til), *prep.* up to the time of; until: *The child played till eight.* —*conj.* up to the time when; until: *Walk till you come to a white house.* [Old English *til*]

till[2] (til), *v.t., v.i.* cultivate (land), as by plowing, harrowing, manuring, etc.; cultivate; plow: *Farmers till the land.* [Old English *tilian*] —**till′a ble,** *adj.*

till[3] (til), *n.* a small drawer for money under or behind a counter. [origin uncertain]

till[4] (til), *n.* glacial drift or deposit composed of stiff clay, stones, gravel, boulders, etc. [origin unknown]

till age (til′ij), *n.* 1 cultivation of land. 2 tilled land.

till er[1] (til′ər), *n.* bar or handle at the stern used to turn the rudder in steering a boat. [< Middle French *telier* weaver's beam < Latin *tela* web]

till er[2] (til′ər), *n.* person who tills land; farmer. [< *till*[2]]

till er[3] (til′ər), *n.* shoot that springs from the root or base of the original stalk. —*v.i.* sprout tillers, as corn and certain other plants. [Old English *tealgor*]

Til lich (til′ik), *n.* **Paul,** 1886-1965, German theologian and philosopher.

tilt[1] (def. 2)

tilt[1] (tilt), *v.t.* 1 cause to tip; slope; slant; lean: *You tilt your head forward when you bow. You tilt your cup when you drink.* 2 point or thrust (a lance). 3 rush at; charge. 4 **tilt at,** attack; fight; protest against. 5 forge or hammer with a heavy, pivoted hammer. —*v.i.* 1 be tilted; slope; slant; lean; tip: *This table tilts.* 2 rush, charge, or fight with lances. Knights used to tilt on horseback. —*n.* 1 a being tilted; sloping position; slope; slant. 2 a medieval exercise between two men on horseback with lances who charge at each other and try to knock each other off the horse. 3 any dispute or quarrel. 4 **full tilt,** at full speed; with full force: *His car ran full tilt against the tree.* 5 a heavy, pivoted hammer. [Middle English *tilten*] —**tilt′a ble,** *adj.* —**tilt′er,** *n.*

tilt[2] (tilt), *n.* awning or canopy over a boat, wagon, etc. —*v.t.* cover with a tilt or tilts. [Old English *(ge)teld*]

tilth (tilth), *n.* 1 state of being tilled: *a garden in bad tilth.* 2 cultivation of land. 3 tilled land. [Old English < *tilian* till[2]]

tilt me ter (tilt′mē′tər), *n.* clinometer used to measure a tilt in the earth's surface.

tim bal (tim′bəl), *n.* kettledrum. [< French *timbale,* ultimately < Arabic *aṭ-ṭabl* the drum]

tim bale (tim′bəl), *n.* 1 minced meat, fish, vegetables, etc., prepared with a sauce and cooked in a mold. 2 a cup-shaped mold of pastry containing various ingredients, often cooked by frying. [< French, originally, timbal]

tim ber (tim′bər), *n.* 1 wood used for building, making furniture, etc. 2 a large piece of wood used in building, such as a beam or rafter. 3 a curved piece forming a rib of a ship. 4 growing trees; wooded land; forests. 5 trees bearing wood suitable for use in building. 6 worth or value as a person; quality; character: *The country needs more men of his timber.* —*v.t.* cover, support, build, or furnish with timber. [Old English]

tim bered (tim′bərd), *adj.* 1 made or furnished with timber. 2 covered with growing trees.

timber hitch, knot used to fasten a rope around a spar, post, etc.

tim ber ing (tim′bər ing), *n.* 1 building material of wood. 2 timbers. 3 work made of timbers.

tim ber land (tim′bər land′), *n.* land with trees that are, or will be, useful for timber.

tim ber line (tim′bər līn′), *n.* line on mountains and in polar regions beyond which trees will not grow because of the cold.

timber wolf, a large wolf that is gray, black, or white in color, found in parts of northwestern North America, Europe, and Asia.

tim bre (tim′bər, tam′bər), *n.* the quality in sounds, regardless of their pitch or volume, by which a certain voice, instrument, etc., can be distinguished from other voices, instruments, etc. Because of differences in timbre, identical notes played on a violin, an oboe, and a trumpet can be distinguished from one another. [< Old French, bell without a clapper, drum, ultimately < Greek *tympanon* kettledrum. Doublet of TYMPANUM.]

tim brel (tim′brəl), *n.* a tambourine or similar instrument. [diminutive of Middle English *timbre* < Old French, drum]

Tim buk tu (tim buk′tü, tim′buk tü′), *n.* 1 city in central Mali. Its official name is **Tombouctou.** 9000. 2 any remote or faraway place.

time (tīm), *n., v.,* **timed, tim ing,** *adj.* —*n.* 1 all the days there have been or ever will be; the past, present, and future. 2 a part of time: *A minute is a short time.* 3 period of time; epoch; era; age: *in the time of the Stuart kings of England.* 4 period of life; years of living; lifetime: *achievements that will outlast our time.* 5 unit of geological chronology. 6 any specified or defined period; period in question: *They were with us the whole time.* 7 time that is or was present: *change with the times.* 8 term of imprisonment, enlistment, apprenticeship, etc.: *complete one's time.* 9 a long time: *What a time it took you!* 10 some point in time; particular point in time: *What time is it?* 11 a particular season; date or span of the calendar: *Summer is the time of hot weather.* 12 the right part or point of time: *It is time to eat.* 13 occasion: *This time we will succeed.* 14 system of measuring or reckoning the passage of time: *solar time.* 15 condition or state of life, affairs, etc.: *Wars bring hard times.* 16 amount of time; available time: *time to rest.* 17 experience during a certain time: *She had a good time at the party.* 18 rate of movement in music or poetry; rhythm: *march time, waltz time, beat time.* 19 (in music) length of a note or rest. 20 the period for which one works or should work: *Her normal time is 8 hours a day.* 21 the pay for a period of work. 22 spare time; leisure: *have time to read.* 23 **times,** *pl.* multiplied by. The sign for this in arithmetic is ×. *Four times three is twelve.*

against time, trying to finish before a certain time.

at the same time, however; nevertheless.

hat, āge, fär; let, ēqual, tėrm;
it, īce; hot, ōpen, ôrder;
oil, out; cup, pu̇t, rüle;
ch, child; ng, long; sh, she;
th, thin; ᴛʜ, then; zh, measure;

ə represents *a* in about, *e* in taken, *i* in pencil, *o* in lemon, *u* in circus.

< = from, derived from, taken from.

at times, now and then; once in a while.
behind the times, old-fashioned; out-of-date.
bide one's time, wait for a good chance.
for the time being, for the present; for now.
from time to time, now and then; once in a while.
in good time, **a** at the right time. **b** soon; quickly.
in no time, shortly; before long.
in time, **a** after a while. **b** soon enough. **c** in the right rate of movement in music, dancing, marching, etc.
keep time, **a** (of a watch or clock) go correctly. **b** measure or record time, rate of speed, etc. **c** sound or move at the right rate.
make time, go with speed.
mark time, **a** move the feet as in marching, but without advancing. **b** suspend progress temporarily. **c** go through motions without accomplishing anything.
on time, **a** at the right time; not late. **b** with time in which to pay; on credit.
time after time or **time and again,** again and again.
time out of mind, beyond memory or record.
—*v.t.* 1 measure the time or rate of speed of: *time a race.* 2 set, regulate, or adjust: *time an alarm clock.* 3 do in rhythm with; set the time of: *The dancers time their steps to the music.* 4 choose the moment or occasion for.
—*adj.* 1 of or having to do with time. 2 provided with a clocklike mechanism so it will explode or ignite at a given moment: *a time bomb.* 3 having to do with purchases to be paid for at a future date or dates.
[Old English *tīma*]

time and a half, payment for overtime work at one and a half times the usual rate of pay.

time capsule, container of things sealed to preserve a record of a civilization or some aspect of it.

time card (tīm′kärd′), *n.* card for recording the amount of time that a person works.

time clock, clock with a device to record the time when workers arrive and leave.

time-con sum ing (tīm′kən sü′ming), *adj.* taking up much or too much time.

time deposit, deposit in a bank that must remain for a definite period of time, or can be withdrawn only after the depositor has given an advance notice to the bank.

time draft, draft to be paid at the future time stated in the draft.

time exposure, 1 exposure of a photographic film, plate, etc., for a certain time, usually longer than a half second. 2 photograph taken in this way.

time fuse, fuse that will burn for a certain time, used to set off a charge of explosives.

time-hon ored (tīm′on′ərd), *adj.* honored because old and established: *Giving gifts at Christmas is a time-honored custom.*

time keep er (tīm′kē′pər), *n.* 1 person or thing that keeps time; timer. 2 person who keeps an account of workmen's hours of labor. 3 person who marks the time in a game, race, or other athletic contest. 4 person who beats time in music. 5 timepiece.

time-lapse (tīm′laps′), *adj.* of or having to do with photography in which a sequence of photographs is taken at regular intervals on motion-picture film to make a condensed record of a slow process.

time less (tīm′lis), *adj.* 1 never ending; eternal; unending. 2 referring to no special time. **—time′less ly,** *adv.* **—time′less ness,** *n.*

time ly (tīm′lē), *adj.* **-li er, -li est.** at the right time; opportune: *The timely arrival of the firemen prevented the fire from destroying the building.* **—time′li ness,** *n.*

time-out (tīm′out′), *n.* period when play is suspended during a game, at the request of one team, a player, an umpire, etc.

time piece (tīm′pēs′), *n.* clock, watch, or other instrument for measuring and recording the passage of time.

tim er (tī′mər), *n.* 1 person or thing that times; timekeeper. 2 device for indicating or recording intervals of time, such as a stopwatch. 3 a clockwork device for indicating when a certain period of time has elapsed. 4 an automatic device in a gasoline engine that causes the spark for igniting the charge to occur at the time required.

time sav er (tīm′sā′vər), *n.* person or thing that saves time.

time sav ing (tīm′sā′ving), *adj.* that reduces the time previously required to do something: *a timesaving appliance.*

time serv er (tīm′sėr′vər), *n.* person who shapes his conduct to conform with the opinions of the time or of the persons in power, especially for selfish reasons.

time serv ing (tīm′sėr′ving), *adj.* of or being a timeserver. —*n.* act or conduct of a timeserver.

time-share (tīm′sher′, tīm′shar′), *v.i.,* **-shared, -shar ing.** (of a computing system or program) to allocate divisions of the total operating time to two or more functions.

time signature, sign to show the time of a piece of music, usually placed at the beginning or where the time changes.

time ta ble (tīm′tā′bəl), *n.* 1 schedule showing the times when trains, boats, buses, airplanes, etc., arrive and depart. 2 any list or schedule of the times at which things are to be done or happen.

time worn (tīm′wôrn′, tīm′wōrn′), *adj.* 1 worn by long existence or use: *timeworn steps.* 2 worn out by use; trite; stale: *a timeworn excuse.* 3 very old; ancient: *a time-worn superstition.*

time zone, a geographical region within which the same standard time is used, especially any one of 24 zones, beginning and ending at the International Date Line, into which the world is divided.

tim id (tim′id), *adj.* 1 easily frightened; shy. See synonym study below. 2 characterized by or indicating fear: *a timid reply.* [< Latin *timidus* < *timere* to fear] **—tim′id ly,** *adv.* **—tim′id ness,** *n.*
Syn. 1 Timid, cowardly mean afraid to do or try something hard or risky. **Timid** implies lack of self-confidence in facing any situation: *He does not like his job, but is too timid to try to find another.* **Cowardly** implies lack of moral character or strength in the presence of danger or trouble: *Leaving his wife because she was hopelessly sick was a cowardly thing to do.*

ti mid i ty (tə mid′ə tē), *n.* a being timid; shyness.

tim ing (tī′ming), *n.* 1 arrangement or regulation of the speed of anything to get the greatest possible effect: *the timing of a stroke in tennis.* 2 measurement of time: *the timing of a runner.*

Ti mor (tē′môr, ti môr′), *n.* island in the East Indies, part of which belongs to Indonesia and part to Portugal. 1,340,000 pop.; 13,100 sq. mi.

tim or ous (tim′ər əs), *adj.* 1 easily frightened; timid. 2 characterized by or indicating fear. [< Latin *timor* fear < *timere* to fear] **—tim′or ous ly,** *adv.* **—tim′or ous ness,** *n.*

tim o thy (tim′ə thē), *n.* a coarse grass with long, cylindrical spikes, often grown for hay. [< *Timothy* Hanson, a farmer who cultivated it in America around 1720]

Tim o thy (tim′ə thē), *n.* 1 a disciple of the apostle Paul. 2 either of the two books of the New Testament written as letters by Paul to Timothy.

tim pa ni (tim′pə nē), *n.pl.* of **tim pa no** (tim′pə nō). kettledrums. [< Italian, plural of *timpano* < Latin *tympanum*]

tim pa nist (tim′pə nist), *n.* person who plays the kettledrums. Also, **tympanist.**

tin (tin), *n., adj., v.,* **tinned, tin ning.** —*n.* 1 a soft, silver-white metallic element, highly malleable and having a low melting point, used in plating metals to prevent corrosion and in making alloys such as bronze and pewter. *Symbol:* Sn; *atomic number* 50. See pages 326 and 327 for table. 2 tin plate. 3 any can, box, pan, or other container made of or plated with tin: *a pie tin.* 4 BRITISH. can: *a tin of peas.* —*adj.* made of or plated with tin. —*v.t.* 1 cover with tin. 2 BRITISH. put up in tin cans or tin boxes; can. [Old English]

tin a mou (tin′ə mü), *n.* any of various birds of South and Central America somewhat like partridge or quail. [< French < Carib]

tin can, U.S. NAVAL SLANG. destroyer.

tinct (tingkt), *adj.* tinged. —*n.* tint; tinge. [< Latin *tinctus.* See TINT.]

tinc ture (tingk′chər), *n., v.,* **-tured, -tur ing.** —*n.* 1 solution of medicine in alcohol: *tincture of iodine.* 2 trace; tinge. 3 color; tint. —*v.t.* 1 give a trace or tinge to. 2 color; tint. [< Latin *tinctura* < *tingere* to tinge]

tin der (tin′dər), *n.* 1 anything that catches fire easily. 2 material used to catch fire from a spark. [Old English *tynder*]

tin der box (tin′dər boks′), *n.* 1 box for holding tinder, flint, and steel for making a fire. 2 a very flammable thing. 3 a very excitable person.

tin der y (tin′dər ē), *adj.* of or like tinder; flammable.

tine (tīn), *n.* a sharp projecting point or prong: *the tines of a fork.* [Old English *tind*]

tin e a (tin′ē ə), *n.* any of various contagious skin diseases caused by fungi, especially ringworm. [< Latin, a gnawing worm, moth]

tin ear, SLANG. inability to perceive differences in sounds or tones.

tin foil (tin′foil′), *n.* a very thin sheet of aluminum, tin, or an alloy of tin and lead, used as a wrapping for candy, tobacco, etc.

ting (ting), *v.i., v.t.* make or cause to make a clear, ringing sound. —*n.* a clear, ringing sound. [imitative]

tinge (tinj), *v.,* **tinged, tinge ing** or

ting ing, *n.* —*v.t.* 1 color slightly: *A drop of ink will tinge a glass of water.* 2 add a trace of some quality to; change slightly: *admiration tinged with envy.* —*n.* 1 a slight coloring or tint: *a tinge of red in her cheeks.* 2 a very small amount; trace. [< Latin *tingere*]

tin gle (ting′gəl), *v.*, **-gled, -gling,** *n.* —*v.i.* 1 have a feeling of thrills or a pricking, stinging feeling: *tingle with excitement.* 2 tinkle; jingle. —*v.t.* cause to tingle: *Shame tingled his cheeks.* —*n.* 1 a feeling of thrills or a pricking, stinging feeling. 2 a tinkle; jingle. [probably variant of *tinkle*]

tin horn (tin′hôrn′), SLANG. —*adj.* cheap and showy; noisy and pretentious: *a tinhorn gambler.* —*n.* a tinhorn person.

tink er (ting′kər), *n.* 1 person who mends pots, pans, etc., usually wandering from place to place. 2 a clumsy or unskilled worker. 3 any of various fishes, such as a small or young mackerel. —*v.t.* mend, patch, or repair, especially in an unskilled or clumsy way. —*v.i.* 1 work in an unskilled or clumsy way. 2 work or keep busy in a rather useless way. [Middle English *tynekere,* perhaps ultimately < *tin*] **—tink′er er,** *n.*

tin kle (ting′kəl), *v.*, **-kled, -kling,** *n.* —*v.i.* 1 make short, light, ringing sounds: *Little bells tinkle.* 2 move or flow with a tinkle. —*v.t.* 1 cause to tinkle. 2 call, make known, express, etc., by tinkling: *The little clock tinkled out the hours.* —*n.* series of short, light, ringing sounds: *the tinkle of sleigh bells.* [ultimately imitative]

tin kly (ting′klē), *adj.* full of tinkles; characterized by tinkling: *a tinkly toy.*

tin man (tin′mən), *n., pl.* **-men.** man who works with tin; tinsmith.

tin ner (tin′ər), *n.* 1 person who works in a tin mine. 2 person who works with tin; tinsmith.

tin ny (tin′ē), *adj.*, **-ni er, -ni est.** 1 of, containing, or yielding tin. 2 like tin in looks, sound, or taste. **—tin′ni ly,** *adv.* **—tin′ni ness,** *n.*

tin-pan alley (tin′pan′), 1 district frequented by composers and publishers of popular music. 2 these people as a group.

tin plate, thin sheets of iron or steel coated with tin. Ordinary tin cans are made of tin plate.

tin-plate (tin′plāt′), *v.t.*, **-plat ed, -plat ing.** plate or coat (sheets of iron or steel) with tin.

tin sel (tin′səl), *n.*, *v.*, **-seled, -seling** or **-selled, -sel ling,** *adj.* —*n.* 1 glittering material of metal, plastic, etc., in thin sheets, strips, threads, etc., used to trim Christmas trees, etc. 2 anything showy but having little value. —*v.t.* 1 trim with tinsel. 2 make showy or gaudy; cover the defects of with or as if with tinsel. —*adj.* of or like tinsel; showy but not worth much. [< Middle French *estincelle* spark < Latin *scintilla.* Doublet of SCINTILLA.] **—tin′sel like′,** *adj.*

tin sel ly (tin′sə lē), *adj.* 1 of or like tinsel. 2 showy without real worth; tawdry.

tin smith (tin′smith′), *n.* person who works with tin; maker or repairer of tinware; tinman; tinner.

tin stone (tin′stōn′), *n.* cassiterite.

tint (tint), *n.* 1 variety of a color: *The picture was painted in several tints of blue.* 2 a delicate or pale color. 3 a preparation for coloring hair. —*v.t.* put a tint on; color slightly. [earlier *tinct* < Latin *tinctus* a dyeing < *tingere* to tinge] **—tint′er,** *n.*

tin tin nab u la tion (tin′tə nab′yə lā′shən), *n.* the ringing of bells. [< Latin *tintinnabulum* bell]

Tin to ret to (tin′tə ret′ō), *n.* **Il,** 1518-1594, Venetian painter.

tin type (tin′tīp′), *n.* photograph in the form of a positive taken on a sensitized sheet of enameled tin or iron.

tin ware (tin′wer′, tin′war′), *n.* articles made of tin or tin plate.

ti ny (tī′nē), *adj.*, **-ni er, -ni est.** very small; wee; minute. [Middle English *tine*]

-tion, *suffix added to verbs to form nouns.* 1 act or process of ____ing: *Addition = act or process of adding.* 2 condition of being ____ed: *Exhaustion = condition of being exhausted.* 3 result of ____ing: *Reflection = result of reflecting.* [< Latin *-tionem*]

tip[1] (tip), *n.*, *v.*, **tipped, tip ping.** —*n.* 1 the end part; end; point: *the tips of the fingers.* 2 a small piece put on the end of something: *a new tip for a billiard cue.* —*v.t.* 1 put a tip or tips on; furnish with a tip: *spears tipped with steel.* 2 cover or adorn at the tip: *mountains tipped with snow.* [< Scandinavian (Old Icelandic) *typpa*]

tip[2] (tip), *v.*, **tipped, tip ping,** *n.* —*v.t.* 1 cause to have a slanting or sloping position; slant; slope: *She tipped the table toward her.* 2 upset; overturn: *tip over a glass of water.* 3 take off (a hat) in greeting. 4 empty out; dump. —*v.i.* 1 slant; slope. 2 upset; overturn. —*n.* slope; slant. [Middle English *typpen*]

tip[3] (tip), *n.*, *v.*, **tipped, tip ping.** —*n.* 1 a small present of money; gratuity: *give a waiter a tip.* 2 piece of secret or confidential information: *a tip on a horse.* 3 a useful hint, suggestion, etc.: *a tip on removing stains from clothing.* —*v.t.* 1 give a tip or tips to. 2 give secret or confidential information to. 3 **tip off,** INFORMAL. **a** give secret or confidential information to. **b** warn. [origin uncertain] **—tip′per,** *n.*

tip[4] (tip), *n.*, *v.*, **tipped, tip ping.** —*n.* 1 a light, sharp blow; tap. 2 in sports: **a** a glancing blow. **b** a ball so hit. —*v.t.* 1 hit lightly and sharply; tap. 2 (in sports) hit (a ball) lightly with the edge of the bat; hit with a glancing blow. [Middle English *tippe*]

tip cart (tip′kärt′), *n.* cart that can be tipped endways or sideways for dumping.

tip-off (tip′ôf′, tip′of′), *n.* INFORMAL. 1 piece of secret information. 2 a warning.

Tip pe ca noe River (tip′ə kə nü′), river in NW Indiana, flowing into the Wabash River. 200 mi.

Tip pe rar y (tip′ə rer′ē), *n.* county in the S part of the Republic of Ireland.

tip pet (tip′it), *n.* 1 scarf for the neck and shoulders with ends hanging down in front. 2 a long, narrow, hanging part of a hood, sleeve, or scarf. 3 band of silk or other material worn around the neck by certain clergymen. [probably < *tip*[1]]

tip ple (tip′əl), *v.*, **-pled, -pling,** *n.* —*v.t., v.i.* drink (alcoholic liquor) often or too much. —*n.* an alcoholic liquor. [origin uncertain] **—tip′pler,** *n.*

tip staff (tip′staf′), *n.* 1 staff tipped with metal, formerly carried by constables, bailiffs, and other officers of the law. 2 official who carried such a staff.

tip ster (tip′stər), *n.* INFORMAL. person who makes a business of furnishing private or secret information for use in betting, speculation, etc.

tip sy (tip′sē), *adj.*, **-si er, -si est.** 1 tipping easily; unsteady; tilted. 2 somewhat intoxicated, but not thoroughly drunk. [probably < *tip*[2]] **—tip′si ly,** *adv.* **—tip′si ness,** *n.*

tip toe (tip′tō′), *n.*, *v.*, **-toed, -toe ing,** *adj.*, *adv.* —*n.* 1 the tips of the toes. 2 **on tiptoe, a** walking on one's toes, without using the heels. **b** eager. **c** in a secret manner. —*v.i.* go or walk on tiptoe; step lightly. —*adj.* 1 on tiptoe. 2 silent; stealthy. —*adv.* on tiptoe.

tip top (tip′top′), *n.* the very top; highest point. —*adj.* 1 at the very top or highest point. 2 INFORMAL. first-rate; excellent. —*adv.* in the highest degree; superlatively.

ti rade (tī′rād, tə rād′), *n.* 1 a long, vehement speech. 2 a long, scolding speech. [< French, literally, a drawing out < Italian *tirata* < *tirare* to shoot]

Ti ra na or **Ti ra në** (ti rä′nə), *n.* capital of Albania, in the central part. 169,000.

tire[1] (tīr), *v.*, **tired, tir ing.** —*v.t.* 1 lower or use up the strength of; make weary: *The long walk tired her.* 2 wear down the patience, interest, or appreciation of because of dullness, excess, etc.: *Monotonous filing tired him.* 3 **tire out,** make very weary. —*v.i.* become weary: *He tires easily.* [Old English *tēorian*]

tire[2] (tīr), *n.*, *v.*, **tired, tir ing.** —*n.* 1 a circular covering of rubber and cord or similar synthetic materials, sometimes solid but now usually hollow or tubular and inflated by air, fitted on the rim of the wheel of an automobile, truck, bicycle, airplane, etc., to cushion the vehicle from shocks. 2 a metal band fitted on the rim of a wheel, as of a wagon, railroad car, etc. —*v.t.* furnish with a tire. Also, **tyre.** [apparently short for *attire,* in the sense of "a covering"]

tired (tīrd), *adj.* weary; fatigued; exhausted. **—tired′ly,** *adv.* **—tired′ness,** *n.*

Syn. Tired, weary, exhausted mean drained of strength, energy, or power of endurance. **Tired** is the general word: *I am tired, but I must get back to work.* **Weary** implies feeling worn out and unable to go on: *Weary shoppers wait for buses and streetcars.* **Exhausted** implies without enough energy left to be able to go on: *Exhausted by near starvation and bitter winds, the man lay in a stupor.*

tire less (tīr′lis), *adj.* 1 never becoming tired; requiring little rest: *a tireless worker.* 2 never stopping; unceasing: *tireless efforts.* **—tire′less ly,** *adv.* **—tire′less ness,** *n.*

tire some (tīr′səm), *adj.* tiring; boring: *a tiresome speech.* **—tire′some ly,** *adv.* **—tire′some ness,** *n.*

Syn. Tiresome, tedious mean tiring or boring, or both. **Tiresome** implies being dull and uninteresting: *Our neighbor is good-hearted, but I find her tiresome.* **Tedious** implies being too long, slow, or repetitious: *Weeding a garden is tedious work.*

tire wom an (tīr′wu̇m′ən), *n., pl.* **-wom en.** ARCHAIC. a lady's maid.

tiring room, ARCHAIC. dressing room, especially in a theater. [< *attiring room*]

ti ro (tī′rō), *n., pl.* **-ros.** tyro.

Ti rol (tə rōl′, tī′rōl), *n.* **the,** region in the Alps, partly in W Austria and partly in NE Italy. Also, **Tyrol.**

Ti ro le an (tə rō′lē ən), *adj., n.* Tirolese. Also, **Tyrolean.**

Tir o lese (tir′ə lēz′), *adj.* of or having to do with the Tirol or its inhabitants. —*n.* native or inhabitant of the Tirol. Also, **Tyrolese.**

'tis (tiz), it is.

tis sue (tish′ü), *n.* 1 in biology: **a** substance forming the parts of animals and plants.

b mass of similar cells which performs a particular function: *muscular tissue, xylem tissue, skin tissue.* 2 a thin, light, or delicate cloth. 3 web; network: *a tissue of lies.* 4 tissue paper. 5 a thin, soft paper that absorbs moisture easily, used as a handkerchief, etc. [< Old French *tissu,* originally past participle of *tistre* to weave < Latin *texere*]

tissue culture, 1 technique of keeping bits of animal tissue alive and growing in a sterile, nutrient medium. 2 the tissue growing within this medium.

tissue paper, a very thin, soft paper, used for wrapping, covering things, making carbon copies of letters, etc.

tit[1] (tit), *n.* 1 titmouse. 2 any of various other small birds. [< Scandinavian (Old Icelandic) *tittr* titmouse]

tit[2] (tit), *n.* nipple; teat. [Old English *titt*]

Ti tan (tīt′n), *n.* 1 (in Greek myths) one of a family of giants who ruled the world before the gods of Mount Olympus. Prometheus and Atlas were Titans. 2 Also, **titan.** person or thing having enormous size, strength, power, etc.; giant. *—adj.* Also, **titan.** of the Titans; gigantic; huge; very powerful.

Ti tan ess (tīt′n is), *n.* 1 a female Titan. 2 **titaness,** giantess.

Ti ta ni a (ti tā′nē ə), *n.* (in medieval legends) the queen of the fairies. She is a main character in Shakespeare's *A Midsummer Night's Dream.*

ti tan ic (tī tan′ik), *adj.* 1 having great size, strength, or power; gigantic; colossal; huge: *titanic energy.* 2 **Titanic,** of or like the Titans.

ti ta ni um (tī tā′nē əm, ti tā′nē əm), *n.* a strong, lightweight, silver-gray metallic element occurring in various minerals. It is highly resistant to corrosion and is used in making steel and other alloys for jet engines, missiles, etc. *Symbol:* Ti; *atomic number* 22. See pages 326 and 327 for table. [< *Titan*]

titanium dioxide, compound occurring in rutile or prepared artificially as a white powder, used in paints and dyes. *Formula:* TiO_2

ti tan o saur (tīt′n ə sôr, tī tan′ə sôr), *n.* any of a genus of large herbivorous dinosaurs present in the Cretaceous era, especially in South America. [< *Titan* + Greek *sauros* lizard]

tit bit (tit′bit′), *n.* tidbit.

tit for tat, blow for blow; like for like.

tithe (tīᴛʜ), *n., v.,* **tithed, tith ing.** *—n.* 1 one tenth. 2 tax or donation of one tenth of the yearly produce of land, animals, and personal work, paid for the support of the church and the clergy. 3 a very small part. 4 any small tax, levy, etc. *—v.t.* 1 put a tax or a levy of a tenth on. 2 pay a tithe on. *—v.i.* give one tenth of one's income to the church or to charity. [Old English *tēotha* tenth < *tēn* ten] **—tith′er,** *n.*

ti tian (tish′ən), *n., adj.* auburn; golden red. [< *Titian,* who favored this color]

Ti tian (tish′ən), *n.* 1477?-1576, Venetian painter.

Tit i ca ca (tit′ə kä′kə), *n.* **Lake,** lake between Peru and Bolivia, the highest large lake in the world. 12,508 ft. high; 130 mi. long; 3500 sq. mi.

tit il late (tit′l āt), *v.t., v.i.,* **-lat ed, -lat ing.** 1 excite pleasantly; stimulate agreeably. 2 tickle. [< Latin *titillatum* tickled] **—tit′il la′tion,** *n.*

tit il la tive (tit′l ā′tiv), *adj.* tending to titillate.

tit i vate (tit′ə vāt), *v.t., v.i.,* **-vat ed, -vat ing.** INFORMAL. dress up; make smart; spruce up. Also, **tittivate.** [origin uncertain] **—tit′i va′tion,** *n.*

tit lark (tit′lärk′), *n.* pipit.

ti tle (tī′tl), *n., v.,* **-tled, -tling.** *—n.* 1 the name of a book, poem, play, picture, song, motion picture, etc. 2 name showing rank, occupation, or condition in life. King, duke, lord, countess, captain, doctor, professor, Madame, and Miss are titles. See **name** for synonym study. 3 a first-place position; championship: *win the heavyweight title.* 4 a legal right to the possession of property. 5 evidence, especially a document, showing such a right. When a house is sold the seller gives title to the buyer. 6 a recognized right; claim. *—v.t.* call by or furnish with a title; name; term. [< Old French < Latin *titulus*]

➤ **titles.** In formal usage the titles of books, long poems, and the names of magazines and newspapers are underlined or, in print, appear in italics: *A Streetcar Named Desire; The Atlantic Monthly.* Titles of short stories, short poems, songs, essays, and magazine articles are usually put in quotation marks: "My Old Kentucky Home"; "Atomic Power in Tomorrow's World."

ti tled (tī′tld), *adj.* having a title, especially a title of rank.

title deed, document showing that a person owns certain property.

ti tle hold er (tī′tl hōl′dər), *n.* holder of a championship; champion.

title page, page at the beginning of a book that contains the title, the author's or editor's name, and usually the name of the publisher and the place and date of publication.

title role, the part or character for which a play, motion picture, opera, etc., is named. Hamlet is a title role.

ti tlist (tīt′list), *n.* titleholder.

tit mouse (tit′mous′), *n., pl.* **-mice.** any of a family of small birds with short bills and dull-colored feathers, of the same order as the nuthatches, found throughout the Western Hemisphere. [Middle English *titmose;* form influenced by *mouse*]

Ti to (tē′tō), *n.* **Marshal,** born 1892, Yugoslav communist leader, president of Yugoslavia since 1953. His real name is Josip Broz.

Ti to ism (tē′tō iz′əm), *n.* principles and policies of Marshal Tito, especially a form of communism that places national above international interests and does not conform to the policies of the Soviet Union.

ti trate (tī′trāt, tit′rāt), *v.t., v.i.,* **-trat ed, -trat ing.** analyze or be analyzed by titration. [< French *titrer* < *titre* quality]

ti tra tion (tī trā′shən, ti trā′shən), *n.* process of determining the amount of some substance present in a solution by measuring the amount of a different solution of known strength that must be added to complete a chemical change.

tit ter (tit′ər), *v.i.* laugh in a half-restrained manner, because of nervousness or silliness; giggle. *—n.* a tittering laugh. [imitative] **—tit′ter er,** *n.*

tit ti vate (tit′ə vāt), *v.t., v.i.,* **-vat ed, -vat ing.** INFORMAL. titivate.

tit tle (tit′l), *n.* 1 a very little bit; particle; whit. 2 a small stroke or mark over a letter in writing or printing, such as a comma, the dot over the letter *i,* etc. [< Medieval Latin *titulus* diacritical mark < Latin *titulus* title]

tit tle-tat tle (tit′l tat′l), *n., v.i.,* **-tled, -tling.** gossip.

tit u lar (tich′ə lər, tit′yə lər), *adj.* 1 in title or name only; nominal: *He is a titular prince without any power.* 2 having a title. 3 having to do with a title. [< Latin *titulus* title] **—tit′u lar ly,** *adv.*

hat, āge, fär; let, ēqual, tėrm;
it, īce; hot, ōpen, ôrder;
oil, out; cup, pu̇t, rüle;
ch, child; ng, long; sh, she;
th, thin; ᴛʜ, then; zh, measure;

ə represents *a* in about, *e* in taken, *i* in pencil, *o* in lemon, *u* in circus.

< = from, derived from, taken from.

Ti tus (tī′təs), *n.* 1 A.D. 40?-81, Roman emperor from A.D. 79 to 81. 2 convert and companion of the apostle Paul. 3 epistle of the New Testament written to Titus by Paul.

tiz zy (tiz′ē), *n., pl.* **-zies.** SLANG. a very excited state; dither. [origin uncertain]

TKO or **T.K.O.,** technical knockout.

Tl, thallium.

Tm, thulium.

T-man (tē′man′), *n., pl.* **-men.** INFORMAL. agent or investigator of the United States Treasury.

Tn, thoron.

tn., ton.

TNT or **T.N.T.,** a pale yellow, flammable solid made by nitrating toluene, used chiefly as a powerful explosive; trinitrotoluene. *Formula:* $CH_3C_6H_2(NO_2)_3$

to (tü; *unstressed* tu̇, tə), *prep.* 1 in the direction of; toward: *Stand with your back to the wall. Go to the right.* 2 as far as; until: *wet to the skin, from dawn to dusk.* 3 for the purpose of; for: *a means to an end. She came to the rescue.* 4 toward or into the position, condition, or state of: *go to sleep.* 5 so as to produce, cause, or result in: *To my amazement, he jumped.* 6 into: *She tore the letter to pieces.* 7 by: *a fact known to few.* 8 along with; with: *We danced to the music.* 9 compared with: *The score was 9 to 5.* 10 in agreement or accordance with: *a decision not to my liking.* 11 belonging with; of: *the key to my room.* 12 in honor of: *drink to the king.* 13 on; against: *Fasten it to the wall.* 14 about; concerning: *What did she say to that?* 15 included, contained, or involved in: *four apples to the pound, a book without much to it.* 16 *To* is used to show action toward. *Give the book to me. Speak to her.* 17 *To* is used with the infinitive form of verbs. *I like to read. The birds began to sing.* *—adv.* 1 forward: *You're wearing your cap wrong side to.* 2 together; touching; closed: *The door slammed to.* 3 to action or work: *We turned to gladly.* 4 **to and fro,** first one way and then back again; back and forth. [Old English *tō*]

toad (tōd), *n.* any of numerous small, tailless amphibians similar to frogs, having a rough, brown skin, breeding in water but living mostly on land, and feeding on small invertebrates. [Old English *tāde*]

toad eat er (tōd′ē′tər), *n.* toady.

toad fish (tōd′fish′), *n., pl.* **-fish es** or **-fish.** any of a family of fishes with large, thick heads, wide mouths, and slimy skin without scales, found near the bottom of tropical and temperate oceans.

toad flax (tōd′flaks′), *n.* any of a genus of plants of the same family as the figwort, having showy flowers of many colors.

toad stool (tōd′stül′), *n.* mushroom, especially a poisonous mushroom.

toad y (tō′dē), *n., pl.* **toad ies,** *v.,* **toad ied, toad y ing.** —*n.* a fawning flatterer. —*v.i.* act like a toady. —*v.t.* fawn upon; flatter. [perhaps short for *toadeater*]

toad y ism (tō′dē iz′əm), *n.* the action or behavior of a toady; interested flattery; mean servility.

to-and-fro (tü′ən frō′), *adj.* back-and-forth.

toast¹ (tōst), *n.* slices of bread browned by heat. —*v.t., v.i.* 1 brown by heat: *toast bread.* 2 heat thoroughly: *I toasted my feet by the fire.* [< Old French *toster* to dry by heat < Latin *tostum* dried by heat]

toast² (tōst), *v.t.* take a drink and wish good fortune to; drink to the health of: *We toasted her on her birthday.* —*v.i.* drink toasts. —*n.* 1 person or thing whose health is proposed and drunk. 2 a popular or celebrated person: *She was the toast of the town.* 3 act of drinking to the health of a person or thing. 4 a call on another or others to drink to some person or thing. [< *toast¹*; from the custom of putting pieces of spiced toast into wine, etc., drunk to someone's health]

toast er¹ (tō′stər), *n.* 1 person who toasts something. 2 an electric appliance for toasting bread, etc.

toast er² (tō′stər), *n.* person who proposes or joins in a toast.

toast mas ter (tōst′mas′tər), *n.* 1 person who presides at a dinner and introduces the speakers. 2 person who proposes toasts.

toast mis tress (tōst′mis′tris), *n.* a woman toastmaster.

to bac co (tə bak′ō), *n., pl.* **-cos** or **-coes.** 1 the prepared leaves of any of several plants of the nightshade family, used for smoking or chewing or as snuff. 2 any of these plants, native to tropical America and now widely grown in many parts of the world. 3 things made from or containing these leaves, such as cigarettes, cigars, etc. 4 the smoking of a pipe, cigarettes, cigars, etc.: *give up tobacco.* [< Spanish *tabaco* < Carib]

tobacco mosaic virus, virus that causes mosaic disease in tobacco plants.

to bac co nist (tə bak′ə nist), *n.* dealer in tobacco.

To ba go (tə bā′gō), *n.* island in the West Indies, near Venezuela, part of the country of Trinidad and Tobago. 45,000 pop.; 116 sq. mi.

to-be (tə bē′), *adj.* that is yet to be or to come; future: *a mother-to-be.*

To bi as (tə bī′əs), *n.* (in the Douay Bible) Tobit.

To bit (tō′bit), *n.* book of the Apocrypha.

to bog gan (tə bog′ən), *n.* a long, narrow, flat sled with its front end curved upward without runners. —*v.i.* 1 slide downhill on a toboggan. 2 decline sharply and rapidly in value. [< Canadian French *tabagane;* of Algonquian origin] —**to bog′gan er,** *n.*

toboggan

toga (def. 1)

to by or **To by** (tō′bē), *n., pl.* **-bies.** a small, fat jug or mug in the form of a fat man wearing a long coat and a three-cornered hat, used for drinking ale or beer. [< *Toby,* proper name]

toc ca ta (tə kä′tə), *n.* composition for the piano or organ intended to exhibit the technique of the performer. [< Italian < *toccare* to touch]

Tocque ville (tok′vil), *n.* See **de Tocqueville.**

toc sin (tok′sən), *n.* 1 alarm sounded on a bell; warning signal. 2 bell used to sound an alarm. [< Middle French < Provençal *tocasenh* < *tocar* strike, touch + *senh* bell]

to day or **to-day** (tə dā′), *n.* this day; the present time or age. —*adv.* 1 on or during this day. 2 at the present time; now.

tod dle (tod′l), *v.,* **-dled, -dling,** *n.* —*v.i.* walk with short, unsteady steps, as a baby does. —*n.* a toddling way of walking. [origin unknown]

tod dler (tod′lər), *n.* child just learning to walk.

tod dy (tod′ē), *n., pl.* **-dies.** 1 drink made of whiskey, brandy, rum, etc., with hot water, sugar, and spices. 2 beverage made from the fermented sap of an East Indian palm. [< Hindustani *tārī*]

to-do (tə dü′), *n., pl.* **-dos.** INFORMAL. fuss; bustle: *make a great to-do over nothing.*

toe (tō), *n., v.,* **toed, toe ing.** —*n.* 1 one of the five slender divisions that end the foot. 2 the part of a stocking, shoe, etc., that covers the toes. 3 the forepart of a foot or hoof. 4 anything like a toe or the toes in shape or position: *the toe and heel of a golf club.* 5 **on one's toes,** ready for action; alert. 6 **step on one's toes** or **tread on one's toes,** offend or annoy one. —*v.t.* 1 touch or reach with the toes. 2 furnish with a toe or toes: *toe a sock.* 3 drive (a nail) in slantwise. 4 fasten (boards, etc.) with nails driven in such a way. —*v.i.* turn the toes in walking, standing, etc.: *toe in, toe out.* [Old English *tā*] —**toe′less,** *adj.* —**toe′like′,** *adj.*

toed (tōd), *adj.* 1 (of a nail) driven into wood, etc., on a slant. 2 (of a board) fastened with nails driven in this way.

-toed, *combining form.* having ___ toes: *Three-toed = having three toes.*

toe dance, dance performed on the tips of the toes, usually with special slippers, as in ballet.

toe-dance (tō′dans′), *v.i.,* **-danced, -danc ing.** do a toe dance.

toe dancer, person who does a toe dance.

toe hold (tō′hōld′), *n.* 1 a small crack, projection, ridge, etc., just large enough for the toes in climbing: *a cliff without a toehold.* 2 hold in wrestling in which the opponent's foot is held and twisted.

toe nail (tō′nāl′), *n.* 1 the nail growing on a toe. 2 a nail driven on a slant. —*v.t.* fasten with toed nails; toe.

tof fee (tô′fē, tof′ē), *n.* taffy.

tof fy (tô′fē, tof′ē), *n., pl.* **-fies.** taffy.

tog (tog), *n., v.,* **togged, tog ging.** INFORMAL. —*n.* **togs,** *pl.* clothes. —*v.t., v.i.* clothe; dress. [perhaps ultimately < Latin *toga*]

to ga (tō′gə), *n., pl.* **-gas, -gae** (-jē). 1 a loose outer garment worn in public by citizens of ancient Rome, especially in time of peace. 2 robe of office: *the toga of royalty.* [< Latin]

to gaed (tō′gəd), *adj.* wearing a toga.

to geth er (tə geᴛʜ′ər), *adv.* 1 with each other; in company: *They were standing together.* 2 with united action; in cooperation: *work together for peace.* 3 into one gathering, company, mass, or body: *call the people together, sew the pieces of a dress together.* 4 at the same time; at once: *rain and snow falling together.* 5 without a stop or break; continuously: *He worked for several days and nights together.* 6 taken or considered collectively: *This one cost more than all the others together.* 7 **together with,** along with: *The mayor, together with his financial advisors, has been working hard on the budget.* [Old English *tōgædere* < *tō* to + *gædere* together]

to geth er ness (tə geᴛʜ′ər nis), *n.* condition of being close together, especially in family or social activities.

tog ger y (tog′ər ē), *n.* INFORMAL. garments; clothes.

toggle (def. 1)

tog gle (tog′əl), *n., v.,* **-gled, -gling.** —*n.* 1 pin, bolt, or rod put through a loop in a rope or a link of a chain to keep it in place, to hold two ropes together, to serve as a hold for the fingers, etc. 2 a toggle joint. 3 device furnished with a toggle joint. —*v.t.* furnish with a toggle; fasten with a toggle. [probably related to *tug*]

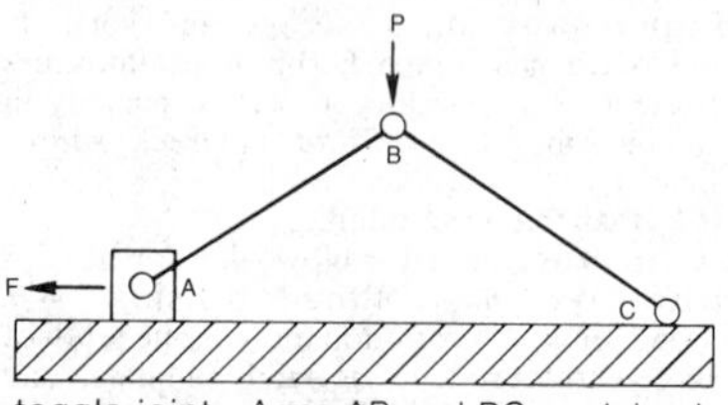

toggle joint—Arms AB and BC are joined at B, and C is fixed. The force P causes angle ABC to straighten and produces a much greater resulting force F.

toggle joint, device consisting of two arms that are hinged together at an angle, so that a force applied at the hinge causing the angle to straighten produces a much greater force at the ends of the arms.

toggle switch, an electric switch with a projecting lever that is pushed through a small arc to open or close the circuit. The common light switch is a toggle switch.

To go (tō′gō), *n.* 1 country in W Africa, formerly a French trust territory. 1,956,000 pop.; 22,000 sq. mi. *Capital:* Lomé. See **Upper Volta** for map. 2 Count **Heihachiro,** 1847-1934, Japanese admiral.

To go land (tō′gō land′), *n.* former German protectorate in W Africa, on the Gulf of Guinea, later under British and French control. The former British part is now a part of Ghana; the French part is now Togo.

To go lese (tō′gō lēz′), *adj.* of or having to do with Togo or Togoland. —*n.* native or inhabitant of Togo or Togoland.

toil[1] (toil), *n.* hard work; labor: *succeed after years of toil.* See **work** for synonym study. —*v.i.* 1 work hard. 2 move with difficulty, pain, or weariness: *They toiled up the steep mountain.* [< Old French *toeillier* drag about < Latin *tudiculare* stir up < *tudicula* olive press < *tudes* mallet] **—toil′er,** *n.*

toil[2] (toil), *n.* Often, **toils,** *pl.* net or snare: *The thief was caught in the toils of the law.* [< Middle French *toile* < Latin *tela* web < *texere* to weave]

toi let (toi′lit), *n.* 1 bathroom or lavatory. 2 a porcelain bowl with a seat attached and a drain at the bottom connected to a water tank to flush the bowl clean. Waste matter from the body is disposed of in a toilet. 3 process of dressing. Bathing, combing the hair, and putting on one's clothes are all part of one's toilet. 4 a person's dress; costume. —*adj.* of or for the toilet. Combs and brushes are toilet articles. [< Middle French *toilette* a cover for the clothes < *toile* cloth < Latin *tela* web. See TOIL[2].]

toi let ry (toi′lə trē), *n., pl.* **-ries.** soap, face powder, perfumery, or other articles for the toilet.

toi lette (toi let′; *French* twä let′), *n.* toilet (defs. 3 and 4). [< French]

toilet water, a fragrant liquid not so strong as perfume, used after bathing, as a cologne in grooming, etc.

toil ful (toil′fəl), *adj.* laborious; toilsome. **—toil′ful ly,** *adv.*

toil some (toil′səm), *adj.* requiring hard work; laborious; wearisome. **—toil′some ly,** *adv.* **—toil′some ness,** *n.*

toil worn (toil′wôrn′, toil′wōrn′), *adj.* worn by toil; showing the effects of toil.

To kay (tō kā′), *n.* 1 a rich, sweet, golden wine made near Tokay, a town in Hungary. 2 a wine imitating it.

to ken (tō′kən), *n.* 1 mark or sign: *Black dress is a token of mourning. His actions are a token of his sincerity.* See **mark**[1] for synonym study. 2 sign of friendship; keepsake: *a parting token, birthday tokens.* 3 piece of metal, somewhat like a coin, stamped for a higher value than the metal is worth and used for some special purpose, as bus or subway fares. 4 a piece of metal, plastic, etc., indicating a right or privilege: *This token will admit you to the swimming pool.* 5 something that is a sign of genuineness or authority. 6 ARCHAIC. a signal. 7 **by the same token,** for the same reason; in the same way; moreover. 8 **in token of,** as a token of; to show. —*adj.* having only the appearance of; serving as a symbol; nominal; partial: *a token payment, token resistance.* [Old English *tācen* sign, mark]

to ken ism (tō′kə niz′əm), *n.* U.S. practice of making token gestures of eliminating racial segregation or discrimination.

To ky o or **To ki o** (tō′kē ō), *n.* capital of Japan, in the central part, on SE Honshu. 9,000,000.

told (tōld), *v.* 1 pt. and pp. of **tell.** 2 **all told,** including all; in all; altogether.

To le do (tə lē′dō), *n.* 1 city in NW Ohio. 384,000. 2 city in central Spain. 44,000. 3 sword or sword blade of fine temper made in Toledo, Spain.

tol er a bil i ty (tol′ər ə bil′ə tē), *n.* tolerable quality or condition.

tol er a ble (tol′ər ə bəl), *adj.* 1 able to be borne or endured; bearable. 2 fairly good; passable: *She is in tolerable health.* **—tol′er a ble ness,** *n.* **—tol′er a bly,** *adv.*

tol er ance (tol′ər əns), *n.* 1 a willingness to be tolerant; a putting up with people whose opinions or ways differ from one's own. See **toleration** for synonym study. 2 the power of enduring or resisting the action of a drug, poison, etc. 3 action of tolerating. 4 an allowed amount of variation from a standard, as in the weight of coins or the dimensions of a machine or part.

tol er ant (tol′ər ənt), *adj.* 1 willing to let other people do as they think best; willing to endure beliefs and actions of which one does not approve: *The founders of the colony of Rhode Island were tolerant toward all religious beliefs.* 2 able to endure or resist the action of a drug, poison, etc. **—tol′er ant ly,** *adv.*

tol e rate (tol′ə rāt′), *v.t.,* **-rat ed, -rat ing.** 1 allow or permit: *The teacher would not tolerate any disorder.* 2 bear; endure; put up with: *They tolerated the grouchy old man only out of kindness.* 3 endure or resist the action of (a drug, poison, etc.): *a person who cannot tolerate penicillin.* [< Latin *toleratum* tolerated]

tol e ra tion (tol′ə rā′shən), *n.* 1 willingness to put up with beliefs and actions of which one does not approve. See synonym study below. 2 recognition of a person's right to worship as he thinks best without loss of civil rights or social privileges; freedom of worship.

Syn. 1 **Toleration, tolerance** mean permitting others to do, say, or think as they wish. **Toleration** implies putting up with actions, beliefs, or people one does not like or approve of because of indifference or a desire to avoid conflict: *Toleration of dishonest officials encourages corruption.* **Tolerance** implies being willing to let others think, live, or worship according to their own beliefs and to refrain from judging harshly or with prejudice: *Through tolerance we learn to understand people.*

tol e ra tive (tol′ə rā′tiv), *adj.* tending to tolerate or be tolerant; permissive.

tol e ra tor (tol′ə rā′tər), *n.* person who tolerates.

Tol kien (tōl′kēn), *n.* **J. R. R.,** 1892-1973, English writer of fairy tales and fables, born in South Africa.

toll[1] (tōl), *v.t.* 1 cause to sound with single strokes slowly and regularly repeated: *Bells were tolled all over the country at the President's death.* 2 call, announce, etc., by tolling. —*v.i.* sound with single strokes slowly and regularly repeated. —*n.* 1 stroke or sound of a bell being tolled. 2 act or fact of tolling. [related to Old English *-tyllan* to draw]

toll[2] (tōl), *n.* 1 tax or fee paid for some right or privilege: *We pay a toll when we use the bridge.* 2 charge for a certain service. There is a toll on long-distance telephone calls. 3 something paid, lost, suffered, etc.: *Automobile accidents take a heavy toll of human lives.* —*v.t.* collect tolls from; take as toll. [Old English *toll, toln* < Latin *telonium* < Greek *telōnion* tollhouse < *telos* tax]

toll booth (tōl′büth′), *n., pl.* **-booths** (-büᴛʜz′, -büths′). booth or gate at which tolls are collected before or after going over a bridge, highway, etc.

toll bridge, bridge at which a toll is charged.

hat, āge, fär; let, ēqual, tėrm;
it, īce; hot, ōpen, ôrder;
oil, out; cup, pu̇t, rüle;
ch, child; ng, long; sh, she;
th, thin; ᴛʜ, then; zh, measure;

ə represents *a* in about, *e* in taken, *i* in pencil, *o* in lemon, *u* in circus.

< = from, derived from, taken from.

toll call, a long-distance telephone call, for which a higher rate is charged than for a local call.

toll gate (tōl′gāt′), *n.* tollbooth.

toll house (tōl′hous′), *n., pl.* **-hous es** (-hou′ziz). building serving as a tollbooth.

toll keep er (tōl′kē′pər), *n.* person who collects the toll at a tollgate.

toll road, road on which tolls are charged; turnpike.

Tol stoy or **Tol stoi** (tol′stoi), *n.* Count **Leo Nikolaevich,** 1828-1910, Russian novelist.

Tol tec (tol′tek), *n.* member of an Indian people who lived in central Mexico from about A.D. 900 to 1200 and influenced the culture of the Aztecs and the Mayas. —*adj.* of or having to do with the Toltecs or their culture.

Tol tec an (tol tek′ən), *adj.* Toltec.

tol u ene (tol′yü ēn), *n.* a colorless, flammable, aromatic liquid hydrocarbon with a smell like that of benzene, obtained from coal tar and petroleum and used as a solvent and for making explosives, dyes, etc. *Formula:* $C_6H_5CH_3$ [< *tolu* a South American balsam]

tol u ol (tol′yü ōl, tol′yü ol), *n.* toluene.

tom or **Tom** (tom), *n.* 1 tomcat. 2 the male of various other animals, such as a turkey. [< *Tom,* proper name]

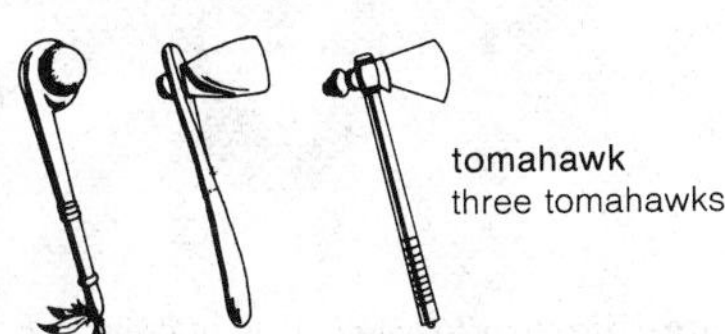

tomahawk
three tomahawks

tom a hawk (tom′ə hôk), *n.* a light ax used by North American Indians as a weapon and a tool. —*v.t.* strike, wound, or kill with a tomahawk. [< Algonquian]

to ma to (tə mā′tō, tə mä′tō), *n., pl.* **-toes.** 1 a spreading, strong-smelling plant of the nightshade family, with hairy leaves and stems and small yellow flowers. 2 its juicy, slightly acid fruit, eaten as a vegetable. Most tomatoes are red when ripe, but some kinds are yellow. [< Spanish *tomate* < Nahuatl *tomatl*]

tomb (tüm), *n.* grave, vault, mausoleum, or other place of burial for a dead body, often above ground. [< Late Latin *tumba* < Greek *tymbos*]

Tom bouc tou (toɴ bük tü′), *n.* Timbuktu (def. 1).

tom boy (tom′boi′), *n.* girl who likes to play games supposedly suited to boys; boisterous, romping girl.

tom boy ish (tom′boi′ish), *adj.* like or characteristic of a tomboy. **—tom′boy′ish ly,** *adv.* **—tom′boy′ish ness,** *n.*

tomb stone (tüm′stōn′), *n.* gravestone.

tom cat (tom′kat′), *n.* a male cat.
tom cod (tom′kod′), *n.* a small saltwater fish of the same family as and resembling a cod.
Tom, Dick, and Harry, people in general; everyone.
tome (tōm), *n.* a book, especially a large, heavy book. [< Greek *tomos,* originally, piece cut off < *temnein* to cut]
tom fool (tom′fül′), *n.* a silly fool; stupid person.
tom fool er y (tom′fü′lər ē), *n., pl.* **-er ies.** silly behavior; nonsense.
tom my or **Tom my** (tom′ē), *n., pl.* **-mies.** INFORMAL. a British soldier.
Tommy At kins (at′kinz), INFORMAL. a British soldier.
tommy gun or **Tommy gun,** INFORMAL. Thompson submachine gun.
tom my rot (tom′ē rot′), *n.* SLANG. nonsense; rubbish; foolishness.
to mor row or **to-mor row** (tə môr′ō, tə mor′ō), *n.* 1 the day after today. 2 the future: *the world of tomorrow.* —*adv.* 1 on or for the day after today. 2 very soon. [Old English *tō morgen* to morrow, to morn]
Tomsk (tômsk), *n.* city in central Soviet Union. 339,000.
Tom Thumb, 1 (in English folk tales) a dwarf who was no bigger than his father's thumb. 2 any very small thing or person.
tom tit (tom′tit′), *n.* a small bird, especially a titmouse.

tom-tom

tom-tom (tom′tom′), *n.* kind of drum, usually beaten with the hands, originally used in the East Indies, but common also in Africa, the Caribbean, and elsewhere. [< Hindustani *tam-tam*]
-tomy, *combining form.* surgical incision or operation, as in *tracheotomy, lobotomy.* [< Greek *-tomia* a cutting]
ton (tun), *n.* 1 unit of weight equal to 2000 pounds (short ton) in the United States and Canada, 2240 pounds (long ton) in Great Britain. See **measure** for table. 2 measure of volume that varies with the thing measured; it is about equal to the space occupied by a ton's weight of the particular stuff. Thus a ton of stone is 16 cubic feet; a ton of lumber is 40 cubic feet. 3 unit of measure of the internal capacity of a ship; 100 cubic feet. 4 unit of measure of the carrying capacity of a ship; 40 cubic feet. 5 unit of measure of the weight by volume of water a ship will displace; 35 cubic feet, the weight of a long ton of sea water. 6 metric ton. [variant of *tun*]
ton al (tō′nl), *adj.* of or having to do with tone or tonality. **—ton′al ly,** *adv.*
to nal i ty (tō nal′ə tē), *n., pl.* **-ties.** 1 in music: **a** the sum of relations existing between the tones of a scale or musical system. **b** a key or system of tones. 2 the color scheme of a painting, etc.
tone (tōn), *n., v.,* **toned, ton ing.** —*n.* 1 any sound considered with reference to its quality, pitch, strength, source, etc.: *angry tones, loud tones.* 2 quality of sound: *a voice silvery in tone.* 3 in music: **a** a sound of definite pitch and character. **b** whole step. C and D are one tone apart. 4 manner of speaking or writing: *a moral tone, the haughty tone of a letter.* 5 spirit; character; style: *a home characterized by a tone of quiet elegance.* 6 normal healthy condition; vigor: *Regular exercise keeps your body in tone.* 7 degree of firmness or tension normal to the organs or tissues when healthy. 8 proper responsiveness to stimulation. 9 effect of color and light and shade in a painting, etc.: *a painting with a soft green tone.* 10 the quality given to one color by another color: *blue with a greenish tone.* 11 shade of color: *a room furnished in tones of brown.*
—*v.i.* harmonize: *This rug tones in well with the wallpaper and furniture.* —*v.t.* 1 give a tone to. 2 change the tone of. 3 **tone down,** soften: *tone down one's voice.* 4 **tone up,** give more sound, color, or vigor to; strengthen.
[< Latin *tonus* < Greek *tonos,* originally, a stretching, taut string, related to *teinein* to stretch] **—tone′less,** *adj.*
tone arm, the movable arm of a phonograph, holding the needle and pickup.
tone-deaf (tōn′def′), *adj.* not able to distinguish between different musical tones.
tone language, language in which different tones are used to distinguish words that otherwise have the same sounds. Chinese is a tone language.
tong[1] (tông, tong), *n.* 1 a Chinese association or club. 2 a secret Chinese organization or club in the United States. [< Chinese *t'ang, t'ong,* originally, meeting hall]
tong[2] (tông, tong), *v.t.* seize, gather, hold, or handle with tongs. —*v.i.* use tongs; work with tongs. [< *tongs*]
Ton ga (tong′gə), *n.* country made up of a group of islands northeast of New Zealand in the S Pacific. It is a member of the Commonwealth of Nations. 90,000 pop.; 269 sq. mi. *Capital:* Nukualofa. Also, **Friendly Islands. —Ton′gan,** *adj., n.*
Tonga Islands, Tonga.
Tong king (tong′king′), *n.* Tonkin.
tongs (tôngz, tongz), *n.pl.* tool with two arms that are joined by a hinge, pivot, or spring, used for seizing, holding, or lifting: *He changed the position of the burning log with the tongs.* [Old English *tang*]
tongue (tung), *n., v.,* **tongued, tongu ing.** —*n.* 1 the movable fleshy organ in the mouth of most vertebrates, having taste buds that make it the chief organ of taste, used in taking in and swallowing food, and serving in man as an essential organ of speech. 2 a similar organ or part in an invertebrate animal. 3 the tongue of an animal used for food. 4 power of speech; speech: *Have you lost your tongue?* 5 way of speaking; talk: *a flattering tongue.* 6 language of a people: *the English tongue.* 7 something shaped or used like a tongue: *tongues of flame.* 8 the strip of leather under the laces of a shoe, boot, etc. 9 a narrow strip of land running out into water. 10 the hinged pin of a buckle, brooch, etc. 11 a projecting strip along the edge of a board for fitting into a groove in the edge of another board. 12 the pointer of a dial, balance, etc. 13 a movable piece inside a bell that swings against it, producing a sound. 14 the vibrating reed or the like in a musical instrument.
give tongue, bark, as hounds at the sight of game.
hold one's tongue, keep silent.
on the tip of one's tongue, a almost spoken. **b** ready to be spoken.
with tongue in cheek, with sly humor; not to be taken seriously.
—*v.t.* 1 modify the tones of (a flute, cornet, etc.) with the tongue. 2 provide with a tongue. —*v.i.* use the tongue.
[Old English *tunge*] **—tongue′less,** *adj.* **—tongue′like′,** *adj.*
tongue-lash (tung′lash′), *v.i., v.t.* reprove loudly or severely; scold.
tongue-tied (tung′tīd′), *adj.* 1 having the motion of the tongue hindered, usually because of abnormal shortness of the fold of membrane on the underside of the tongue. 2 unable to speak because of shyness, embarrassment, etc.
tongue twister, phrase or sentence that is difficult to say quickly without a mistake. EXAMPLE: She sells sea shells by the seashore.
ton ic (ton′ik), *n.* 1 anything that gives strength; medicine to give strength: *Cod-liver oil is a tonic.* 2 the first note of a musical scale; keynote. —*adj.* 1 restoring to health and vigor; giving strength; bracing: *The mountain air is tonic.* 2 having to do with muscular tension. 3 characterized by continuous contraction of the muscles: *a tonic convulsion.* 4 in music: **a** having to do with a tone or tones. **b** of or based on a keynote: *a tonic chord.* 5 having to do with tone or accent in speaking. 6 (of speech sounds) accented or stressed.
to nic i ty (tō nis′ə tē), *n.* 1 tonic quality or condition. 2 property of possessing bodily tone, especially the normal state of partial contraction of a resting muscle; tonus.
to night or **to-night** (tə nīt′), *n.* the night of this day; this night. —*adv.* on or during this night.
Ton kin (ton′kin′), *n.* 1 **Gulf of,** arm of the South China Sea between North Vietnam and Hainan. 2 former French protectorate in N Indochina, now part of North Vietnam. Also, **Tongking.**
ton nage (tun′ij), *n.* 1 the carrying capacity of a ship expressed in tons of 100 cubic feet. A ship of 50,000 cubic feet of space for freight has a tonnage of 500 tons. 2 total amount of shipping in tons. 3 duty or tax on ships at so much a ton. 4 weight in tons.
ton neau (tu nō′), *n., pl.* **-neaus** or **-neaux** (-nōz′). the rear part of an automobile body, with seats for passengers. [< French, literally, cask]
ton sil (ton′səl), *n.* either of the two oval masses of lymphoid tissue on the sides of the

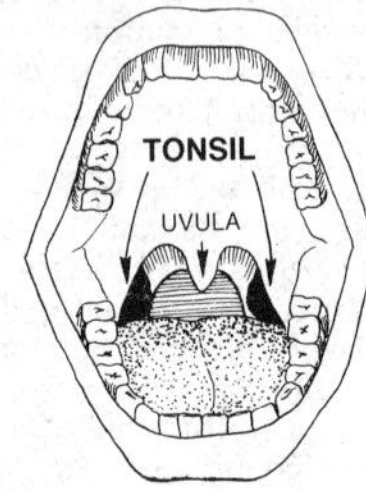

throat, just back of the mouth. [< Latin *tonsillae* tonsils]

ton sil lar or **ton sil ar** (ton′sə lər), *adj.* of or having to do with the tonsils.

ton sil lec to my (ton′sə lek′tə mē), *n., pl.* **-mies.** the surgical removal of the tonsils.

ton sil li tis (ton′sə lī′tis), *n.* inflammation of the tonsils.

ton so ri al (ton sôr′ē əl, ton sōr′ē əl), *adj.* of or having to do with a barber or his work.

ton sure (ton′shər), *n., v.,* **-sured, -sur ing.** —*n.* 1 a clipping of the hair or shaving of a part or the whole of the head, formerly required of a person entering the priesthood or an order of monks. 2 the shaved part of the head of a priest or monk. —*v.t.* shave the head of, especially as a religious ritual. [< Latin *tonsura* < *tondere* to shear, shave]

to nus (tō′nəs), *n.* tonicity (def. 2). [< Latin]

ton y (tō′nē), *adj.,* **ton i er, ton i est.** SLANG. high-toned; fashionable; stylish.

too (tü), *adv.* 1 besides; also: *The dog is hungry, and very thirsty too. We, too, are going away.* 2 beyond what is desirable, proper, or right; more than enough: *My dress is too long for you. He ate too much. The summer passed too quickly.* 3 exceedingly; very: *I am only too glad to help.* [Old English *tō* to, too]

took (tu̇k), *v.* pt. of **take.**

tool (tül), *n.* 1 a knife, hammer, saw, shovel, or any instrument used in doing work. See synonym study below. 2 anything used like a tool: *Books are a scholar's tools.* 3 person used by another like a tool: *a tool of the party boss.* 4 a part of a machine that cuts, bores, smooths, etc. 5 the whole of such a machine. —*v.t.* 1 work or shape with a tool or tools; use a tool on. 2 ornament with a tool: *tool a book cover.* 3 provide or equip (a factory, etc.) with tools. 4 drive (a car or other vehicle). —*v.i.* 1 work with a tool or tools. 2 drive a car, etc. [Old English *tōl*]

Syn. *n.* 1 **Tool, implement** mean an instrument or other article used in doing work. **Tool** means an instrument or simple device especially suited or designed to make doing a particular kind of work easier, but applies particularly to something held and worked by the hands in doing manual work: *Plumbers, mechanics, carpenters, and shoemakers need tools.* **Implement** is a general word meaning a tool, instrument, utensil, or mechanical device needed to do something: *Hoes and tractors are agricultural implements.*

tool box (tül′boks′), *n.* box in which tools and sometimes small parts, accessories, etc., are kept.

tool ing (tü′ling), *n.* 1 work done with a tool. 2 ornamentation made with a tool.

tool mak er (tül′mā′kər), *n.* 1 machinist who makes, repairs, and maintains machine tools. 2 any maker of tools.

tool room (tül′rüm′, tül′ru̇m′), *n.* department in a machine shop in which tools are made, kept, and handed out to the workers.

toot (tüt), *n.* sound of a horn, whistle, etc. —*v.i.* 1 give forth a short blast: *The train whistle tooted three times.* 2 sound or blow a whistle, horn, etc. —*v.t.* sound (a horn, whistle, etc.) in short blasts. [probably imitative] **—toot′er,** *n.*

tooth (tüth), *n., pl.* **teeth,** *v.* —*n.* 1 one of the hard, bonelike parts in the mouth of vertebrates, attached in a row to each jaw, and used for biting and chewing food and as weapons of attack or defense. 2 any of certain hard parts or processes in the mouth or digestive tract of invertebrates. 3 something like a tooth, as each one of the projecting parts of a comb, rake, or saw. 4 one of the series of projections on the rim of a gearwheel, pinion, etc.; cog. 5 a taste; liking: *have no tooth for fruit.* 6 **fight tooth and nail,** fight fiercely, with all one's force. —*v.t.* 1 furnish with teeth; put teeth on. 2 cut teeth on the edge of; indent. [Old English *tōth*] **—tooth′less,** *adj.* **—tooth′like′,** *adj.*

tooth ache (tüth′āk′), *n.* pain in or around a tooth or the teeth.

tooth brush (tüth′brush′), *n.* a small brush for cleaning the teeth.

toothed (tütht, tüᴛʜd), *adj.* 1 having teeth. 2 notched.

tooth paste (tüth′pāst′), *n.* paste used in cleaning the teeth.

tooth pick (tüth′pik′), *n.* a small, pointed piece of wood, plastic, etc., for removing bits of food from between the teeth.

tooth pow der (tüth′pou′dər), *n.* powder used in cleaning the teeth.

tooth shell, 1 the long, tubular, toothlike shell of a scaphopod. 2 scaphopod.

tooth some (tüth′səm), *adj.* 1 pleasing to the taste; tasting good; tasty. 2 pleasing to the sight; pretty; comely.

tooth y (tü′thē), *adj.,* **tooth i er, tooth i est.** showing many teeth prominently: *a toothy smile.* **—tooth′i ly,** *adv.*

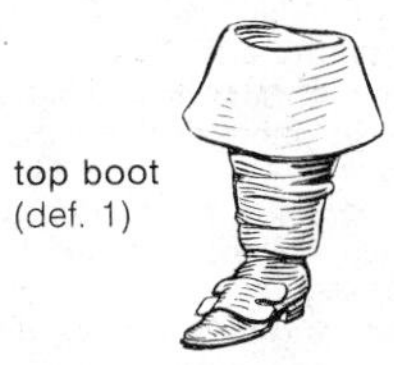
top boot (def. 1)

top¹ (top), *n., adj., v.,* **topped, top ping.** —*n.* 1 the highest point or part; peak; summit: *the top of a mountain.* See synonym study below. 2 the upper part, end, or surface: *the top of a table.* 3 the highest or leading place, rank, etc.: *be at the top of the class.* 4 one that occupies the highest or leading position: *be the top in one's profession.* 5 the highest point, pitch, or degree: *at the top of one's voice.* 6 the best or most important part: *the top of the morning.* 7 part of a plant growing above ground, as distinct from the root: *beet tops.* 8 the head. 9 lid or cover; cap: *the top of a can.* 10 the upper part of a shoe or boot. 11 platform around the top of a lower mast on a ship. It serves as a foothold for sailors and a means of extending the upper rigging. 12 (in golf) a stroke above the center of a ball. 13 (in baseball) the first half of an inning: *the top of the seventh.* 14 **from top to toe, a** from head to foot: *She was dressed in brown from top to toe.* **b** completely. 15 **on top,** with success; with victory. 16 **over the top,** over the front of a trench to make an attack.

—*adj.* 1 having to do with, situated at, or forming the top: *the top shelf of a cupboard.* 2 highest in degree; greatest: *top speed, top prices.* 3 chief; foremost: *top honors.*

—*v.t.* 1 put a top on: *top a box.* 2 be on top of; be at the top of; crown: *A church tops the hill.* 3 be or form the top of: *A steeple tops the church.* 4 reach the top of: *They topped the mountain.* 5 rise above: *The sun topped the horizon.* 6 be higher than; be greater than. 7 do or be better than; surpass; outdo; excel: *His story topped all the rest.* 8 in golf: **a** hit (a ball) above center. **b** make (a stroke) in this way: *She topped her drive.* 9 cut off the top of (a plant, tree, etc.); crop; prune. 10 **top off,** put the finishing touch to: *top off dinner with a fine cigar.*

[Old English *topp*]

Syn. *n.* 1 **Top, summit, crown** mean the highest point or part of something. **Top** is the general word: *It is now easy to drive to the top of the mountain.* **Summit** means the topmost point: *The road does not go to the summit.* **Crown** applies especially to a rounded top: *There is snow on the crown of the mountain.*

top² (top), *n.* 1 a child's toy, usually shaped like a cone, with a point on which it is made to spin, as by the rapid unwinding of a string wound around it. 2 **sleep like a top,** sleep soundly. [origin uncertain]

to paz (tō′paz), *n.* 1 a hard, transparent or translucent mineral that occurs in crystals of various forms and colors. It is a compound of aluminum, silica, and fluorine. Transparent yellow, pink, or brown varieties are used as gems. 2 a yellow variety of sapphire or quartz, used as a gem. [< Greek *topazos*]

top boot, 1 a high boot having the upper part of different material and made to look as if turned down. 2 any boot with a high top.

top coat (top′kōt′), *n.* a lightweight overcoat.

top-drawer (top′drôr′), *adj.* INFORMAL. of the highest level of excellence, importance, etc.: *a top-drawer musical.*

tope¹ (tōp), *v.t., v.i.,* **toped, top ing.** drink alcoholic liquor to excess or as a habit. [origin uncertain] **—top′er,** *n.*

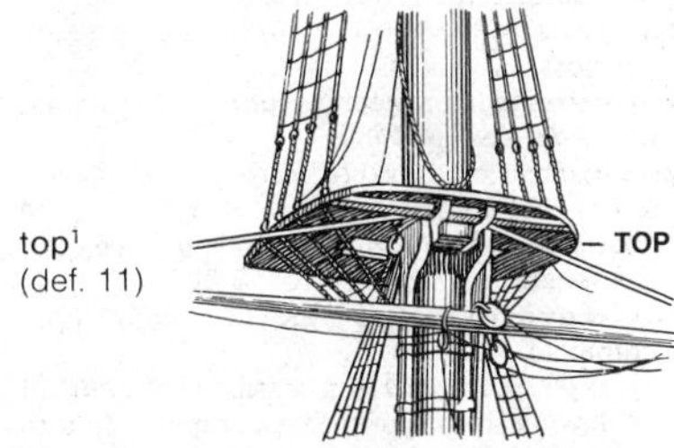

top¹ (def. 11)

tope² (tōp), *n.* any of several species of small sharks. [origin uncertain]

to pee (tō pē′, tō′pē), *n.* helmet made of pith to protect the head against the sun. Also, **topi.** [< Hindi *topī*]

To pe ka (tə pē′kə), *n.* capital of Kansas, in the NE part. 125,000.

top flight (top′flīt′), *adj.* INFORMAL. excellent; first-rate; foremost.

top gal lant (top′gal′ənt; *Nautical* tə-gal′ənt), *n.* the mast or sail above the topmast; the third section of a mast above the deck. See **masthead** for picture. —*adj.* 1 next above the topmast. 2 (of a deck, rail,

hat, āge, fär; let, ēqual, tėrm;
it, īce; hot, ōpen, ôrder;
oil, out; cup, pu̇t, rüle;
ch, child; ng, long; sh, she;
th, thin; ᴛʜ, then; zh, measure;
ə represents *a* in about, *e* in taken, *i* in pencil, *o* in lemon, *u* in circus.
< = from, derived from, taken from.

etc.) situated above a corresponding adjacent part.

top hat, a tall, black silk hat worn by men in formal clothes; high hat.

top-heav y (top′hev′ē), *adj.* too heavy at the top; unstable and inclined to topple.

To phet (tō′fit), *n.* 1 hell. 2 (in the Bible) place near ancient Jerusalem where human sacrifices were offered to Moloch.

to pi (tō pē′, tō′pē), *n.* topee.

to pi ar y (tō′pē er′ē), *adj., n., pl.* **-ar ies.** —*adj.* 1 trimmed or clipped into ornamental shapes: *topiary shrubs and trees.* 2 of or having to do with such trimming: *topiary art.* —*n.* 1 topiary art. 2 a topiary garden. [< Latin *topiarius* < *topia* ornamental gardening, ultimately < Greek *topos* place]

top ic (top′ik), *n.* 1 subject that people think, write, or talk about: *Newspapers discuss the topics of the day.* See **subject** for synonym study. 2 a short phrase or sentence used in an outline to give the main point of part of a speech, article, etc. [< Greek *(ta) topika,* a study of logical commonplaces by Aristotle < *topos* place]

top i cal (top′ə kəl), *adj.* 1 of or having to do with topics of the day; of current or local interest: *topical news.* 2 of or having to do with a topic or topics: *Some books have topical outlines for each chapter.* 3 of or having to do with a place or locality; local. 4 limited or applied to a certain spot or part of the body; not general. —**top′i cal ly,** *adv.*

top i cal i ty (top′ə kal′ə tē), *n.* quality of being topical.

top kick, SLANG. first sergeant.

top knot (top′not′), *n.* 1 knot of hair on the top of the head. 2 plume or crest of feathers on the head of a bird. 3 knot or bow of ribbon worn by women as a headdress.

top less (top′lis), *adj.* 1 having no top; immeasurably high. 2 (of a garment) lacking an upper part or piece. —**top′less ness,** *n.*

top loft y (top′lôf′tē, top′lof′tē), *adj.* INFORMAL. lofty in character or manner; haughty; pompous.

top mast (top′mast′; *Nautical* top′məst), *n.* the second section of a mast above the deck. See **masthead** for picture.

top most (top′mōst), *adj.* highest; uppermost.

top-notch (top′noch′), *adj.* INFORMAL. first-rate; best possible.

top-notch er (top′noch′ər), *n.* INFORMAL. a first-rate person or thing.

to pog ra pher (tə pog′rə fər), *n.* an expert in topography.

top o graph ic (top′ə graf′ik), *adj.* topographical.

top o graph i cal (top′ə graf′ə kəl), *adj.* of or having to do with topography. A topographical map shows mountains, rivers, etc. —**top′o graph′i cal ly,** *adv.*

to pog ra phy (tə pog′rə fē), *n., pl.* **-phies.** 1 the accurate and detailed description or drawing of places or their surface features. 2 the surface features of a place or region, including hills, valleys, streams, lakes, bridges, tunnels, roads, etc. [< Greek *topos* place + *graphein* write]

top o log i cal (top′ə loj′ə kəl), *adj.* of or having to do with topology.

to pol o gist (tə pol′ə jist), *n.* an expert in topology.

to pol o gy (tə pol′ə jē), *n.* 1 the topographical study of a particular locality in order to learn about its history. 2 the anatomy of a certain area of the body. 3 (in mathematics) the study of the properties of figures or solids that are not normally affected by changes in size or shape. [< Greek *topos* place + English *-logy*]

top per (top′ər), *n.* 1 SLANG. an excellent, first-rate person or thing. 2 INFORMAL. top hat. 3 INFORMAL. topcoat. 4 a loose-fitting, short, usually lightweight coat, worn by women.

top ping (top′ing), *n.* 1 anything forming the top of something. 2 something put on the top of anything to complete it, especially a garnish, sauce, etc., put on food. —*adj.* BRITISH INFORMAL. excellent; first-rate.

top ple (top′əl), *v.,* **-pled, -pling.** —*v.i.* 1 fall forward; tumble down: *The chimney toppled over on the roof.* 2 hang over in an unsteady way: *beneath toppling crags.* —*v.t.* throw over or down; overturn: *The wrestler toppled his opponent.* [< *top*[1], noun]

tops (tops), *adj.* SLANG. of the highest degree in quality, excellence, etc.

top sail (top′sāl′; *Nautical* top′səl), *n.* 1 a sail, or either of a pair of sails, set next above the lowest sail on a mast of a square-rigged ship. 2 a sail set above a gaff in a fore-and-aft-rigged ship.

top-se cret (top′sē′krit), *adj.* of utmost secrecy; extremely confidential.

top sergeant, INFORMAL. first sergeant.

top side (top′sīd′), *n.* Also, **topsides,** *pl.* the upper part of a ship's side, especially the part above the water line. —*adv.* 1 to or on the bridge or upper deck. 2 INFORMAL. on top; up above.

top soil (top′soil′), *n.* the upper part of the soil; surface soil: *Farmers need rich topsoil for their crops.*

top sy-tur vy (top′sē tėr′vē), *adv., adj., n., pl.* **-vies.** —*adv., adj.* 1 upside down. 2 in confusion or disorder. —*n.* confusion; disorder. —**top′sy-tur′vi ly,** *adv.* —**top′sy-tur′vi ness,** *n.*

top sy-tur vy dom (top′sē tėr′vē dəm), *n.* any disordered place or condition.

toque (def. 2)

toque (tōk), *n.* 1 hat without a brim or with a very small brim, worn by women. 2 a small, round cap or bonnet formerly worn by men and women. [< Middle French]

To rah or **to rah** (tôr′ə, tōr′ə), *n.* 1 the entire body of Jewish law and tradition. 2 the Jewish Bible; Old Testament. 3 the Pentateuch. 4 scroll on which the Pentateuch is written. [< Hebrew *tōrāh* teaching]

torch (tôrch), *n.* 1 light to be carried around or stuck in a holder on a wall, made up of a burning stick of resinous wood or other flammable substance. 2 device for producing a very hot flame, used especially to burn off paint and to solder or melt metal. 3 BRITISH. flashlight. 4 something thought of as a source of enlightenment: *the torch of civilization.* 5 **carry a torch,** SLANG. be in love, especially without being loved in return. [< Old French *torche,* originally, something twisted < Latin *torquere* to twist] —**torch′like′,** *adj.*

torch bear er (tôrch′ber′ər, tôrch′bar′ər), *n.* person who carries a torch.

torch light (tôrch′līt′), *n.* light of a torch or torches.

torch singer, singer of torch songs.

torch song, a sad love song, especially of unrequited love.

tore (tôr, tōr), *v.* pt. of **tear**[2].

to re a dor (tôr′ē ə dôr), *n.* bullfighter. [< Spanish < *toro* bull]

toreador pants, close-fitting trousers ending at mid-calf, worn by women.

to re ro (tō rā′rō), *n., pl.* **-ros** (-rōs). bullfighter. [< Spanish]

to ri (tôr′ī, tōr′ī), *n.* pl. of **torus.**

torii

to ri i (tôr′ē ē′, tōr′ē ē′), *n., pl.* **-ri i.** gateway to a Japanese Shinto shrine, built of two uprights and two crosspieces. [< Japanese]

tor ment (*v.* tôr ment′; *n.* tôr′ment), *v.t.* 1 cause very great pain to. 2 worry or annoy very much. 3 torture. —*n.* 1 cause of very great pain. 2 very great pain; agony; torture. 3 cause of great worry or annoyance. [< Latin *tormentum,* originally, twisted sling < *torquere* to twist] —**tor men′tor, tor men′ter,** *n.*

torn (tôrn, tōrn), *v.* pp. of **tear**[2].

tor nad ic (tôr nad′ik), *adj.* of or like a tornado.

tor na do (tôr nā′dō), *n., pl.* **-does** or **-dos.** an extremely violent and destructive whirlwind extending down from a mass of dark clouds as a twisting funnel and moving over the land in a narrow path. [alteration of Spanish *tronada* < *tronar* to thunder < Latin *tonare*]

To ron to (tə ron′tō), *n.* city in SE Canada, on Lake Ontario, the capital of Ontario. 665,000.

tor pe do (tôr pē′dō), *n., pl.* **-does,** *v.* —*n.* 1 a large, cigar-shaped missile that contains explosives and travels under water by its own power, launched from submarines, torpedo boats, or low-flying aircraft to blow up enemy ships. 2 an underwater mine, shell, etc., that explodes when hit. 3 an explosive put on a railroad track which makes a loud noise for a signal when a wheel of the engine runs over it. 4 firework consisting of an explosive and gravel wrapped in tissue paper, which explodes when thrown against something hard. 5 electric ray. —*v.t.* 1 attack, hit, or destroy with a torpedo. 2 bring completely to an end; destroy: *torpedo a peace conference.* [< Latin, originally, numbness < *torpere* be numb]

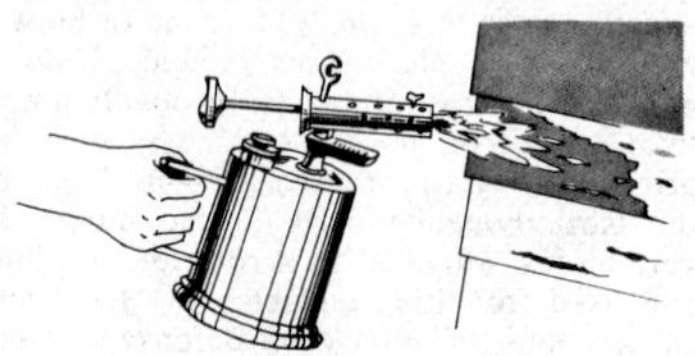

torch (def. 2)

torpedo boat, a small, fast warship used for attacking with torpedoes.
tor pid (tôr′pid), *adj.* 1 dull, inactive, or sluggish. 2 not moving or feeling; dormant. Animals that hibernate become torpid in winter. 3 numb. [< Latin *torpidus* < *torpere* be numb] **—tor′pid ly,** *adv.* **—tor′pid ness,** *n.*
tor pid i ty (tôr pid′ə tē), *n.* torpid condition.
tor por (tôr′pər), *n.* 1 torpid condition or quality; apathy; lethargy. 2 absence or suspension of movement or feeling, as of a hibernating animal. [< Latin < *torpere* be numb]
torque (tôrk), *n.* 1 force causing rotation or torsion. 2 (in physics) the moment of a system of forces causing rotation. [< Latin *torquere* to twist]
Tor que ma da (tôr′kə mä′də), *n.* **Tomás de,** 1420-1498, leader in the Spanish Inquisition.
torr (tôr), *n.* unit of pressure equivalent to the amount of pressure that will support a column of mercury one millimeter high. [< E. *Torr(icelli)*]
Tor rance (tôr′əns, tor′əns), *n.* city in SW California, near Los Angeles. 135,000.
tor rent (tôr′ənt, tor′ənt), *n.* 1 a violent, rushing stream of water. 2 a heavy downpour: *The rain came down in torrents.* 3 any violent, rushing stream; flood: *a torrent of abuse.* [< Latin *torrentem* boiling, parching]
tor ren tial (tô ren′shəl, to ren′shəl), *adj.* of, caused by, or like a torrent: *torrential rains, a torrential flow of words.* **—torren′tial ly,** *adv.*
Tor re ón (tôr′ē ōn′), *n.* city in N Mexico. 257,000.
Tor res Strait (tôr′is, tor′is), strait between Australia and New Guinea. 80 mi. wide.
Tor ri cel li (tôr′ə chel′ē), *n.* **Evangelista,** 1608-1647, Italian physicist who invented the barometer.
tor rid (tôr′id, tor′id), *adj.* 1 very hot; burning; scorching: *torrid weather.* 2 exposed or subject to great heat: *torrid deserts.* 3 very ardent; passionate: *a torrid love scene.* [< Latin *torridus* < *torrere* to parch] **—tor′rid ly,** *adv.* **—tor′rid ness,** *n.*
tor rid i ty (tô rid′ə tē, to rid′ə tē), *n.* extreme heat.
Torrid Zone, the very warm region between the tropic of Cancer and the tropic of Capricorn. The equator divides the Torrid Zone. See **zone** for diagram.
tor sion (tôr′shən), *n.* 1 act or process of twisting. 2 state of being twisted. 3 the twisting or turning of a body by two equal and opposite forces. [< Late Latin *torsionem* < Latin *torquere* to twist]
tor sion al (tôr′shə nəl), *adj.* of, having to do with, or resulting from torsion. **—tor′sion al ly,** *adv.*
tor so (tôr′sō), *n., pl.* **-sos.** 1 the trunk of the human body. 2 the trunk or body of a statue without any head, arms, or legs. 3 something left mutilated or unfinished. [< Italian, originally, stalk < Latin *thyrsus* < Greek *thyrsos*]
tort (tôrt), *n.* (in law) any wrong, harm, or injury for which the injured party has the right to sue for damages in a civil court, with the exception of a breach of contract. [< Old French < Medieval Latin *tortum* injustice < Latin *torquere* turn awry, twist]
tor te (tôr′tə, tôrt), *n., pl.* **tor ten** (tôrt′n). a rich cake made with beaten egg whites, nuts, fruit, and little flour. [< German *Torte*]
tor til la (tôr tē′yə), *n.* a thin, flat, round cake made of corn meal, commonly eaten in Spanish America. It is baked on a flat surface and served hot. [< Spanish, diminutive of *torta* cake]
tor toise (tôr′təs), *n., pl.* **-tois es** or **-toise.** 1 any of a family of turtles that live only on land, especially in dry regions, and have stumpy legs and a high, arched shell. 2 any turtle. [< Medieval Latin *tortuca*]
tortoise shell, 1 the mottled yellow-and-brown shell of some turtles. It is much used for combs and ornaments. 2 any of several butterflies spotted with yellow and black.
tor toise-shell (tôr′təs shel′), *adj.* 1 made of tortoise shell. 2 mottled or colored like tortoise shell.
Tor tu ga (tôr tü′gə), *n.* island in the West Indies, off the N coast of, and belonging to, Haiti. 25 mi. long; 117 sq. mi.
tor tu ous (tôr′chü əs), *adj.* 1 full of twists, turns, or bends; twisting; winding; crooked: *We found the river's course very tortuous.* 2 mentally or morally crooked; not straightforward: *tortuous reasoning.* [< Latin *tortuosus,* ultimately < *torquere* to twist] **—tor′tu ous ly,** *adv.* **—tor′tu ous ness,** *n.*
tor ture (tôr′chər), *n., v.,* **-tured, -tur ing.** —*n.* 1 act or fact of inflicting very severe pain, especially in hatred or revenge, as a means of extortion, or to force a person to confess to or give evidence about a crime. 2 very severe pain. 3 cause of very severe pain. —*v.t.* 1 cause very severe pain to. 2 twist the meaning of. 3 twist or force out of its natural form: *Winds tortured the trees.* [< Late Latin *tortura* < Latin *torquere* to twist] **—tor′tur er,** *n.*
tor tur ous (tôr′chər əs), *adj.* full of, involving, or causing torture. **—tor′tur ous ly,** *adv.*
to rus (tôr′əs, tōr′əs), *n., pl.* **to ri.** 1 a large convex molding, commonly forming the lowest member of the base of a column. 2 the receptacle of a flower. 3 (in anatomy) a rounded swelling; a protuberant part. 4 a doughnut-shaped surface described by the revolution of a circle about a line in the same plane as, but not intersecting, the circle. [< Latin, originally, cushion, swelling]
To ry (tôr′ē, tōr′ē), *n., pl.* **-ries,** *adj.* —*n.* 1 member of a British political party that favored royal power and the established church and opposed change. Strictly speaking, there has been no Tory party in Britain since about 1832, although members of the Conservative party are often called Tories. 2 member of the Conservative party of Canada. 3 an American who favored British rule over the colonies at the time of the American Revolution. 4 Also, **tory.** a very conservative person. —*adj.* Also, **tory.** of or having to do with Tories or tories. [< Irish *tōraidhe* persecuted person (used of Irishmen dispossessed by the English in the 1600's)]
To ry ism (tôr′ē iz′əm, tōr′ē iz′əm), *n.* 1 a being a Tory. 2 the doctrines or behavior of a Tory.
Tos ca ni ni (tos′kə nē′nē), *n.* **Arturo,** 1867-1957, American conductor, born in Italy.
toss (tôs, tos), *v.t.* 1 throw lightly with the palm upward; cast; fling: *toss a ball.* See **throw** for synonym study. 2 throw about; pitch about: *a ship tossed by the waves.* 3 lift or move quickly; throw upward: *She tossed her head.* 4 shake up or about, especially in order to mix the ingredients: *toss a salad.* 5 INFORMAL. throw (a party, etc.). 6 **toss off, a** do or make quickly and easily. **b** drink all at once: *toss off a glass of milk.* —*v.i.* 1 throw about; pitch about. 2 throw a coin in the air to decide something by the side that falls upward. 3 throw oneself about in bed; roll restlessly: *He tossed in his sleep all night.* —*n.* 1 distance to which something is or can be tossed. 2 a throw; tossing. 3 a tossing a coin, or a decision made by this: *A toss of a coin decided who should play first.* [perhaps < Scandinavian (dialectal Norwegian) *tossa* to strew] **—toss′er,** *n.*

hat, āge, fär; let, ēqual, tėrm;
it, īce; hot, ōpen, ôrder;
oil, out; cup, pu̇t, rüle;
ch, child; ng, long; sh, she;
th, thin; ᴛʜ, then; zh, measure;

ə represents *a* in about, *e* in taken, *i* in pencil, *o* in lemon, *u* in circus.

< = from, derived from, taken from.

toss up (tôs′up′, tos′up′), *n.* 1 a tossing of a coin to decide something. 2 INFORMAL. an even chance: *It's a tossup whether or not he'll accept.*
tot[1] (tot), *n.* 1 a little child. 2 BRITISH. a small portion of alcoholic liquor. [origin uncertain]
tot[2] (tot), *v.,* **tot ted, tot ting.** INFORMAL. —*v.t.* find the total or sum of; add or sum *(up): tot up a bill.* —*v.i.* amount *(to).* [short for *total*]
to tal (tō′tl), *adj., n., v.,* **-taled, -tal ing** or **-talled, -tal ling.** —*adj.* 1 being or making up a whole; whole; entire: *The total cost of the house will be $35,000.* See **whole** for synonym study. 2 complete in extent or degree; absolute; utter: *a total failure, total darkness.* —*n.* the whole amount; sum: *a total of $100.* —*v.t.* 1 find the sum of; add: *Total that column of figures.* 2 reach an amount of; amount to. —*v.i.* amount *(to).* [< Medieval Latin *totalis* < Latin *totus* all]
total eclipse, eclipse of the sun or moon in which the whole of the disk is obscured.
to tal i tar i an (tō tal′ə ter′ē ən, tō tal′ə tar′ē ən), *adj.* of or having to do with a government controlled by one political group which suppresses all opposition, often with force, and which controls many aspects of its citizens' lives. —*n.* person in favor of totalitarian principles.
to tal i tar i an ism (tō tal′ə ter′ē ə niz′əm, tō tal′ə tar′ē ə niz′əm), *n.* system, principles, or methods of a totalitarian government.
to tal i ty (tō tal′ə tē), *n., pl.* **-ties.** 1 the total amount; total; whole. 2 a being total; entirety.
to tal i za tor (tō′tl ə zā′tər), *n.* apparatus for registering totals of operations, measurements, etc., especially one used for pari-mutuel betting at horse races.
to tal ize (tō′tl īz), *v.t.,* **-ized, -iz ing.** make total; combine into a total. **—to′tal iz′er,** *n.*
to tal ly (tō′tl ē), *adv.* wholly; entirely; completely.
total war, war in which all the resources of a nation are used, and in which attack is made not only on the armed forces of the opponent, but also on its civilian people and property.
tote (tōt), *v.t.,* **tot ed, tot ing.** INFORMAL. carry; haul. [origin uncertain] **—tot′er,** *n.*
tote board, INFORMAL. the display board

of a totalizator on which the odds and results of horse races are flashed.

to tem (tō′təm), *n.* 1 (among American Indians) an animal, bird, fish, plant, or other natural object taken as the emblem of a tribe, clan, family, etc. 2 image of such an object, as on a totem pole. [of Algonquian origin]

to tem ic (tō tem′ik), *adj.* of a totem; having to do with totems.

to tem ism (tō′tə miz′əm), *n.* use of totems to distinguish tribes, clans, families, etc.

totem pole

totem pole, pole carved and painted with representations of totems, erected by the Indians of the northwestern coast of North America, especially in front of their houses.

tot ter (tot′ər), *v.i.* 1 stand or walk with shaky, unsteady steps. 2 be unsteady; shake as if about to fall: *The old wall tottered in the gale.* 3 shake; tremble. *—n.* a tottering. [Middle English *toteren* swing on a rope] **—tot′ter er,** *n.*

tot ter y (tot′ər ē), *adj.* tottering; shaky.

tou can (tü′kan, tü kän′), *n.* any of a family of brightly colored birds of tropical America that feed on fruit and have an enormous beak. [< French < Tupi (Brazil) *tucana*]

touch (tuch), *v.t.* 1 put the hand, finger, or some other part of the body on or against: *She touched the pan to see whether it was still hot.* 2 put against; make contact with: *I touched the post with my umbrella.* 3 be against; come against: *Your sleeve is touching the butter.* 4 strike lightly or gently: *touch the strings of a harp.* 5 injure slightly: *The flowers were touched by the frost.* 6 affect with some feeling: *The sad story touched us.* 7 affect in some way by contact: *a metal so hard that a file cannot touch it.* 8 make slightly crazy. 9 have to do with; concern: *The new law does not touch his case.* 10 speak of; deal with; refer to; treat lightly: *Our conference touched many points.* 11 handle; use: *He won't touch liquor or tobacco.* 12 have to do with in any way: *I won't touch that business—it's crooked.* 13 come up to; reach: *His head almost touches the ceiling.* 14 stop at; visit in passing: *The ship touched many ports.* 15 SLANG. borrow from: *touch a friend for a dollar.* 16 compare with; rival: *No one in our class can touch her in music.* 17 mark slightly or superficially, as with some color: *a sky touched with pink.* *—v.i.* 1 put the hand, finger, or some other part of the body on or against something: *These glasses are delicate —don't touch!* 2 come or be in contact: *Their shoulders touched.* 3 arrive and make a brief stop: *Most ships touch at that port.*
touch down, land an aircraft.
touch off, **a** represent exactly or cleverly. **b** cause to go off; fire. **c** instigate: *touch off a riot.*
touch on or **touch upon,** **a** treat lightly; mention. **b** come close to.
touch up, change a little; improve: *touch up a photograph, touch up a play.*
—n. 1 a touching. 2 a being touched: *A bubble bursts at a touch.* 3 the sense by which a person perceives things by feeling, handling, or coming against them: *The blind develop a keen touch.* 4 the feeling caused by touching something; feel: *Worms and fish have a slimy touch.* 5 a coming or being in contact: *the touch of their hands.* 6 a slight amount; little bit: *a touch of frost, a touch of sarcasm, a touch of salt.* 7 a light, delicate stroke with a brush, pencil, pen, etc.: *The artist finished my picture with a few touches.* 8 a light stroke or blow. 9 detail in any artistic work: *a story with charming poetic touches.* 10 a close relation of communication, agreement, sympathy, or interest: *keeping in touch with one's friends.* 11 the act or manner of playing a musical instrument, striking the keys on the keyboard of a machine, etc.: *a pianist with a light touch, a typist's uneven touch.* 12 the way the keys of a musical instrument or machine work: *a piano with a stiff touch.* 13 a distinctive manner or quality; skill in style: *The work showed an expert's touch.* 14 a slight attack: *a touch of fever.* 15 an official mark or stamp put on gold, silver, etc., to show it has been tested and is of standard fineness. 16 a die, stamp, or punch for impressing such a mark. 17 quality so tested. 18 quality, kind, or sort: *friends of noble touch.* 19 test.
[< Old French < *touchier* < Popular Latin *toccare* to hit, strike, touch] **—touch′a ble,** *adj.* **—touch′er,** *n.*

touch and go, an uncertain or risky situation.

touch-and-go (tuch′ən gō′), *adj.* uncertain; risky.

touch back (tuch′bak′), *n.* (in football) play in which a player downs the ball behind his own goal line, when the impetus of the ball across the goal has come from the other team. No points are scored.

touch down (tuch′doun′), *n.* 1 in football: **a** act of a player in possessing the ball on or behind the opponents' goal line. **b** the score of six points made in this way. 2 the landing of an aircraft, especially the moment of first contact with the ground.

tou ché (tü shā′), *n.* a touch, as by the weapon of an opponent in fencing. *—interj.* exclamation acknowledging an effective point in an argument or a clever reply. [< French, touched]

touched (tucht), *adj.* 1 INFORMAL. slightly crazed. 2 stirred emotionally.

touch football, game with rules similar to those of football except that the player carrying the ball is touched with the hand or hands rather than tackled, and little or no equipment is worn.

touch hole (tuch′hōl′), *n.* a small hole in an old-time gun or cannon through which the gunpowder inside was set on fire.

touch ing (tuch′ing), *adj.* arousing tender feeling. *—prep.* concerning; about. **—touch′ing ly,** *adv.*

touch-me-not (tuch′mē not′), *n.* impatiens.

touch stone (tuch′stōn′), *n.* 1 a black stone used to test the purity of gold or silver by the color of the streak made on the stone by rubbing it with the metal. 2 any means of testing; a test.

touch wood (tuch′wu̇d′), *n.* 1 punk[1]. 2 a fungus found on old tree trunks, used as tinder.

touch y (tuch′ē), *adj.,* **touch i er, touch i est.** 1 apt to take offense at trifles; too sensitive. 2 requiring skill in handling; ticklish; precarious: *Relations can be very touchy if one's friends are quarreling.* 3 very sensitive to the touch. **—touch′i ly,** *adv.* **—touch′i ness,** *n.*

tough (tuf), *adj.* 1 bending without breaking: *Leather is tough; cardboard is not.* 2 hard to cut, tear, or chew: *The steak was so tough I couldn't eat it.* 3 stiff; sticky: *tough clay.* 4 strong; hardy: *a tough animal.* 5 hard; difficult: *a tough job.* 6 hard to bear; bad; unpleasant: *a spell of tough luck.* 7 hard to influence; firm: *a tough mind.* 8 stubborn; obstinate: *a tough customer.* 9 U.S. rough; disorderly: *a tough neighborhood.* *—n.* U.S. a rough person; rowdy: *A gang of toughs attacked him.* [Old English *tōh*] **—tough′ly,** *adv.* **—tough′ness,** *n.*

tough en (tuf′ən), *v.t.* make tough or tougher. *—v.i.* become tough or tougher.

Tou lon (tü lôN′), *n.* seaport in SE France. 175,000.

Tou louse (tü lüz′), *n.* city in S France. 371,000.

Tou louse-Lau trec (tü lüz′lō trek′), *n.* **Henri de,** 1864-1901, French painter.

tou pee (tü pā′), *n.* wig or patch of false hair worn by men to cover a bald spot; hairpiece. [< French *toupet*]

tour (tu̇r), *v.i.* travel from place to place. *—v.t.* 1 travel through: *Last year they toured Europe.* 2 walk around in: *tour the museum.* *—n.* 1 a long journey: *a European tour.* 2 a short journey; a walk around: *We made a tour of the old boat.* 3 period or turn of military or other activity at a certain place or station: *a soldier on a tour of duty overseas.* 4 **on tour,** touring. A show on tour travels around the country giving performances in a number of different places. [< Old French < Latin *tornare* to turn. Related to TURN.]

Tou raine (tü rān′), *n.* region and former province in W France.

tour de force (tu̇r′ də fôrs′), *pl.* **tours de force** (tu̇r′ də fôrs′). 1 a notable feat of strength, skill, or ingenuity. 2 something done that is merely clever or ingenious. [< French]

touring car, an open automobile with a folding top and no glass side windows, for four or more passengers.

tour ism (tu̇r′iz′əm), *n.* 1 a touring or traveling for pleasure. 2 the business of serving tourists.

tour ist (tu̇r′ist), *n.* 1 person traveling for pleasure. 2 tourist class. *—adj.* of or for tourists.

tourist class, the least expensive class of accommodations on a ship, airplane, etc.

tourist court, motel.

tour ma line (tu̇r′mə lən, tu̇r′mə lēn′), *n.* a semiprecious colored mineral, a silicate of boron and aluminum, usually black but sometimes red, pink, green, blue, or yellow. The transparent varieties of tourmaline are used in jewelry. [< French < Singhalese *toramalli*]

tour na ment (tėr′nə mənt, tu̇r′nə mənt), *n.* 1 contest in any game of skill in which a number of competitors play a series of games: *a golf tournament.* 2 a medieval contest in which two groups of mounted knights in armor fought with blunted weapons for a prize. 3 a meeting at which a series of such contests took place. [< Old French *torneiement* < *torneier.* See TOURNEY.]

tour ney (tėr′nē, tůr′nē), *n., pl.* **-neys,** *v.* —*n.* tournament. —*v.i.* take part in a tournament. [< Old French *torneier* to tourney, ultimately < Latin *tornus.* See TURN.]

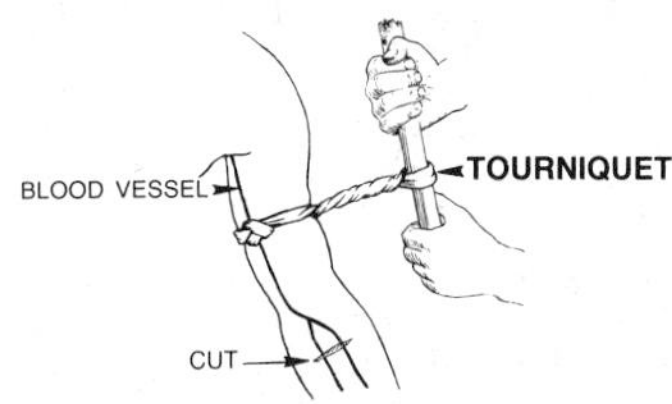

tour ni quet (tůr′nə ket, tėr′nə ket), *n.* device for stopping bleeding by compressing a blood vessel, such as a bandage around a limb tightened by twisting with a stick, or a pad pressed down by a screw. [< French < *tourner* to turn]

Tours (tůr), *n.* city in W France, on the Loire River. A famous battle was fought near there in A.D. 732 in which the Franks defeated the Moslems. 128,000.

tou sle (tou′zəl), *v.,* **-sled, -sling,** *n.* —*v.t.* put into disorder; make untidy; muss: *tousled hair.* —*n.* a disordered mass. [Middle English *tousen*]

Tous saint l'Ou ver ture (tü saN′ lü ver tYr′), **Pierre Dominique,** 1743-1803, Haitian general and political leader.

tout (tout), INFORMAL. —*v.t.* 1 try to get (customers, jobs, votes, etc.). 2 urge betting on (a race horse) by claiming to have special information. 3 BRITISH. spy out (information about race horses). 4 praise highly and insistently. —*v.i.* engage in touting; be a tout. —*n.* person who touts. [Middle English *tuten* to peep, peer] **—tout′er,** *n.*

tout en sem ble (tü tän sän′blə), FRENCH. the general effect; all the parts or details forming a whole.

tow¹ (tō), *v.t.* pull by a rope, chain, etc.: *tow a car to a garage. The tug is towing three barges.* —*n.* 1 act of towing. 2 condition of being towed: *The launch had the sailboat in tow.* 3 something that is towed. 4 the rope, chain, etc., used for towing. 5 that which tows, especially a ship that tows. 6 **in tow,** in one's company or charge; under one's care or influence. [Old English *togian* to drag]

tow² (tō), *n.* the coarse, broken fibers of flax, hemp, jute, etc., prepared for spinning. —*adj.* made from tow. [Old English *tōw*-spinning, as in *tōwlīc* fit for spinning]

tow age (tō′ij), *n.* 1 a towing. 2 a being towed. 3 charge for towing.

to ward (*prep.* tôrd, tōrd, tə wôrd′; *adj.* tôrd, tōrd), *prep.* 1 in the direction of: *walk toward the north, work toward peace.* 2 turned or directed to; facing: *lie with one's face toward the wall.* 3 with respect to; regarding; about; concerning: *What is the senator's attitude toward foreign aid?* 4 shortly before; near: *It must be toward four o'clock.* 5 as a help to; for: *give something toward our new hospital.* —*adj.* 1 about to happen; impending; imminent. 2 in progress; going on; being done. 3 ARCHAIC. promising, hopeful, or apt. [Old English *tōweard* < *tō* to + *-weard* -ward]

to wards (tôrdz, tōrdz, tə wôrdz′), *prep.* toward.

tow boat (tō′bōt′), *n.* tugboat.

tow el (tou′əl), *n., v.,* **-eled, -el ing** or **-elled, -el ling.** —*n.* piece of cloth or paper for wiping and drying something wet. —*v.t.* wipe or dry with a towel. [< Old French *toaille;* of Germanic origin]

tow el ing or **tow el ling** (tou′ə ling), *n.* material used for towels, especially cotton.

tow er (tou′ər), *n.* 1 a high structure, standing alone or forming part of a church, castle, or other building, used as a fort or prison, or for storing water, watching for fires, controlling the landing and taking off of aircraft, etc. 2 defense; protection. 3 person or thing that is like a tower in some way: *a tower of strength.* —*v.i.* rise high up: *The boy towers over his younger brother.* [partly Old English *torr,* partly < Old French *tur,* both < Latin *turris*] **—tow′er like′,** *adj.*

tow ered (tou′ərd), *adj.* having a tower or towers.

tow er ing (tou′ər ing), *adj.* 1 very high: *a towering mountain peak.* 2 very great: *a towering achievement.* 3 very violent: *a towering rage.*

Tower of London, an ancient palace-fortress of London. The present building dates back to William I. It has been used as a palace, prison, mint, and arsenal.

tow er y (tou′ər ē), *adj.* 1 having towers. 2 towering.

tow head (tō′hed′), *n.* person having very light or pale-yellow hair.

tow head ed (tō′hed′id), *adj.* having very light or pale-yellow hair.

tow hee (tou′hē, tō′hē), *n.* a finch of eastern and central North America whose cry sounds somewhat like its name; chewink. [imitative]

tow line (tō′līn′), *n.* rope, chain, etc., for towing.

town (toun), *n.* 1 a large group of houses and other buildings, smaller than a city but larger than a village: *a growing town, an abandoned town.* 2 any large place with many people living in it: *Chicago is my favorite town.* 3 the people of a town: *The whole town was having a holiday.* 4 the part of a town or city where the stores and office buildings are: *Let's go into town.* 5 the particular town or city under consideration: *be in town.* 6 U.S. **a** (in some states) a municipal corporation with less elaborate organization and powers than a city. **b** (in New England) a local administrative unit similar to a township, forming a division of a county and exercising self-government through town meetings. **c** (in other states) a township. 7 **go to town,** INFORMAL. achieve success. 8 **paint the town red,** SLANG. go on a wild spree or party. —*adj.* of, having to do with, or belonging to a town: *the town clock.* [Old English *tūn*]

town clerk, official who keeps the records of a town.

town crier, (in former times) a person who called out the news and made announcements in the streets of a city or town.

town hall, a building used for a town's business.

town house, 1 house in town, belonging to a person who also has a house in the country. 2 one of a row of houses, each sharing a common wall with the next house.

town meeting, 1 a general meeting of the inhabitants of a town. 2 (in New England) a meeting of the qualified voters of a town for the transaction of public business.

towns folk (tounz′fōk′), *n.pl.* townspeople.

hat, āge, fär; let, ēqual, tėrm;
it, īce; hot, ōpen, ôrder;
oil, out; cup, pu̇t, rüle;
ch, child; ng, long; sh, she;
th, thin; ᴛʜ, then; zh, measure;

ə represents *a* in about, *e* in taken, *i* in pencil, *o* in lemon, *u* in circus.

< = from, derived from, taken from.

town ship (toun′ship), *n.* 1 (in the United States and Canada) a part of a county having certain powers of government. 2 (in U.S. surveys of public land) a region or district six miles square, made up of 36 sections.

towns man (tounz′mən), *n., pl.* **-men.** 1 person who lives in a town. 2 person who lives in one's own town.

towns peo ple (tounz′pē′pəl), *n.pl.* the people of a town; townsfolk.

tow path (tō′path′), *n., pl.* **-paths** (-paᴛʜz′, -paths′). path along the bank of a canal or river for use in towing boats.

tow rope (tō′rōp′), *n.* rope used for towing.

tow truck, truck equipped with apparatus to tow away wrecked or disabled cars.

tox e mi a (tok sē′mē ə), *n.* form of blood poisoning, especially one in which the toxins produced by certain bacteria enter the blood. [< New Latin < Latin *toxicum* poison + Greek *haima* blood]

tox e mic (tok sē′mik), *adj.* 1 of or having to do with toxemia. 2 suffering from toxemia.

tox ic (tok′sik), *adj.* 1 of poison; caused by poison: *a toxic illness.* 2 poisonous: *toxic plants.* [< Medieval Latin *toxicus* < Latin *toxicum* poison < Greek *toxikon (pharmakon)* (poison) for shooting arrows < *toxon* bow]

tox ic i ty (tok sis′ə tē), *n., pl.* **-ties.** toxic or poisonous quality.

tox i co log i cal (tok′sə kə loj′ə kəl), *adj.* of or having to do with toxicology. **—tox′i co log′i cal ly,** *adv.*

tox i col o gist (tok′sə kol′ə jist), *n.* an expert in toxicology.

tox i col o gy (tok′sə kol′ə jē), *n.* science that deals with poisons, their effects, antidotes, detection, etc.

tox in (tok′sən), *n.* any poison formed by an animal or plant organism as a result of its metabolism. Toxins formed by bacteria cause diseases such as diphtheria and scarlet fever. The body reacts to some toxins by producing antitoxins.

tox in-an ti tox in (tok′sən an′tē tok′sən), *n.* mixture of a toxin with enough of the corresponding antitoxin to almost neutralize it, used formerly to immunize against diphtheria.

tox oid (tok′soid), *n.* toxin specially treated so that it will lose its poisonous quality but still cause antitoxins to be produced when injected into the body.

toy (toi), *n.* 1 something for a child to play with; plaything. 2 thing that has little value or importance. 3 any small thing, especially any of certain breeds of very small animals. —*adj.* 1 of, made as, or like a toy. 2 small or miniature in size. —*v.i.* amuse oneself; play; trifle: *She toyed with her string of beads.* [Middle English *toye* play, noun] **—toy′like′,** *adj.*

toy dog, a very small dog, especially one belonging to any of certain breeds. Some toy dogs are related to larger dogs, such as poodles or spaniels. Others belong to separate breeds, such as the chihuahua.

Toyn bee (toin′bē), *n.* **Arnold Joseph,** born 1889, British historian.

to yon (tō′yən), *n.* shrub of the rose family found on the Pacific coast of North America, whose evergreen leaves and scarlet berries look much like holly. [< American Spanish *tollon*]

tp., township.

tr., 1 transitive. 2 transpose. 3 treasurer.

trace[1] (trās), *n., v.,* **traced, trac ing.** —*n.* 1 mark, sign, or evidence indicating the former existence, presence, or action of something; vestige: *The explorers found traces of an ancient city.* See synonym study below. 2 footprint or other mark left; track; trail: *We saw traces of rabbits on the snow.* 3 a very small amount; little bit: *There wasn't a trace of color in her cheeks.* 4 a tracing, drawing, or sketch of something. 5 a record made by a self-registering instrument. 6 (in chemistry) an indication of an amount of some constituent, usually too small to be measured.

—*v.t.* 1 follow by means of marks, tracks, or signs: *trace deer.* 2 follow the course, development, or history of: *trace a river to its source, trace the meanings of a word.* 3 find signs of; observe; discover. 4 mark out; draw: *trace a plan of a house.* 5 copy (a drawing, map, etc.) by following the lines of the original on a transparent sheet placed on it. 6 decorate with tracery. 7 line made by a self-recording instrument, as a cardiograph, seismograph, etc. —*v.i.* trace the origin or history of something; go back in time.

[< Old French *tracier* < Popular Latin *tractiare* < Latin *tractus* a drawing out < *trahere* to drag]

Syn. *n.* 1 **Trace, vestige** mean a mark or sign of what has existed or happened. **Trace** applies to any noticeable indication left by something that has happened or been present: *The campers removed all traces of their fire.* **Vestige** applies particularly to an actual remnant of something that existed in the past: *They have discovered vestiges of an ancient civilization.*

trace[2] (trās), *n.* 1 either of the two straps, ropes, or chains by which an animal pulls a wagon, carriage, etc. See **harness** for picture. 2 **kick over the traces,** throw off controls or restraints; become unruly. [< Old French *traiz,* plural of *trait* < Latin *tractus* a drawing out < *trahere* to drag]

trace a bil i ty (trā′sə bil′ə tē), *n.* fact or property of being traceable.

trace a ble (trā′sə bəl), *adj.* 1 that can be traced. 2 attributable: *The engine's failure was traceable to an oil leak.* **—trace′a bly,** *adv.*

trace element, a chemical element used in small amounts by an organism but considered necessary to its proper functioning.

trace less (trās′lis), *adj.* leaving or showing no traces. **—trace′less ly,** *adv.*

trac er (trā′sər), *n.* 1 person or thing that traces, especially a person whose business is tracing missing persons, property, etc. 2 machine for making tracings of drawings, plans, etc. 3 inquiry sent from place to place to trace a missing person, letter, parcel, etc. 4 bullet with a substance in it that burns when the bullet is fired, leaving a trail that can be followed with the eye. 5 substance put in such a bullet to show its course. 6 a substance, such as a radioactive isotope, which can be traced and observed as it passes through a body, plant, or other system in order to study biological processes, chemical reactions, etc., within the system.

trac er ied (trā′sər ēd), *adj.* ornamented with tracery.

tracery (def. 2)

trac er y (trā′sər ē), *n., pl.* **-er ies.** 1 ornamental work or designs consisting of very fine lines, as in certain kinds of embroidery. 2 pattern of intersecting bars or a plate with leaflike decorations in the upper part of a Gothic window, in the ribs of a vault, in carved panels, etc.

tra che a (trā′kē ə), *n., pl.* **tra che ae** (trā′kē ē′). 1 windpipe. 2 one of the air-carrying tubes of the respiratory system of insects and other arthropods. 3 duct in the xylem of a vascular plant, formed by modified tracheids with open end walls connected end to end, permitting the passage of water and dissolved minerals; vessel. [< Late Latin *trachia* < Greek *tracheia (arteria)* rough (artery)]

tra che al (trā′kē əl), *adj.* of or having to do with the trachea.

tra che id (trā′kē əd), *n.* an elongated cell with thick, perforated walls, that serves to carry water and dissolved minerals through a plant, and provides support. Tracheids form an essential element of the xylem of vascular plants.

tra che ot o my (trā′kē ot′ə mē), *n., pl.* **-mies.** surgical incision into the trachea.

tra cho ma (trə kō′mə), *n.* a contagious eye disease caused by a virus, characterized by inflammation of the mucous membrane of the eyeball and eyelids. Trachoma is common in the Orient and sometimes causes blindness. [< Greek, roughness < *trachys* rough]

tra chom a tous (trə kom′ə təs, trə kō′mə-təs), *adj.* of or having trachoma.

trac ing (trā′sing), *n.* 1 copy of something made by marking or drawing over it. 2 line made by marking or drawing. 3 one of a series of lines or marks made by an electrical apparatus that records waves or impulses.

track (trak), *n.* 1 a double, parallel line of metal rails for cars to run on. A railroad has tracks. 2 mark or pattern left: *The dirt road showed many automobile tracks.* 3 footprint: *There were bear and deer tracks near the camp.* 4 path; trail; road: *A track runs through the woods to the farmhouse.* 5 a line of travel or motion: *the track of a hurricane.* 6 a way of doing or acting: *go on in the same track year after year.* 7 a course for running or racing. 8 track and field. 9 sequence or succession of events or thoughts. 10 the groove or channel of a phonograph record which contains the actual sound recording. 11 the distance between the front or rear wheels of an automobile, etc. 12 one of the endless belts of linked steel plates on which a tank, bulldozer, etc., moves.

in one's tracks, INFORMAL. right where one is.

jump the track, run off the rails suddenly; derail without warning.

keep track of, keep within one's sight, knowledge, or attention.

lose track of, fail to keep track of.

make tracks, INFORMAL. go very fast; run away.

off the track, off the right or proper course.

on the track, on the right or proper course.

—*v.t.* 1 follow by means of footprints, marks, smell, etc.: *The hunter tracked the bear.* 2 trace in any way: *track down a criminal.* 3 make one's way through or over; traverse. 4 U.S. make footprints or other marks on: *track up a floor.* 5 U.S. bring into a place on one's feet: *track mud into the house.* 6 follow and plot the course of, as by radar. —*v.i.* 1 follow a track or trail. 2 (of wheels) run in the same track; be in alignment. 3 (of opposite wheels, runners, etc.) be a certain distance apart.

[< Middle French *trac,* probably of Germanic origin] **—track′er,** *n.*

track age (trak′ij), *n.* 1 all the tracks of a railroad. 2 the right of one railroad to use the tracks of another. 3 fee for this.

track and field, the sports or events of running, jumping, vaulting, throwing, etc., as a group. A track and field meet includes races around an oval track and the high jump, shot-put, pole vault, etc., on a field in the center of or near the track. **—track′-and-field′,** *adj.*

track less (trak′lis), *adj.* 1 without a track. 2 without paths or trails.

track meet, series of track-and-field contests.

track suit, a heavy, fleece-lined suit worn by track-and-field athletes to keep warm before and after exercise.

tract[1] (trakt), *n.* 1 stretch of land, water, etc.; extent; area: *A tract of desert land has little value to farmers.* 2 system of related parts or organs in the body. The stomach and intestines are part of the digestive tract. [< Latin *tractus* a drawing out < *trahere* to drag. Doublet of TRAIT.]

tract[2] (trakt), *n.* 1 a little book or pamphlet on a religious or political subject. 2 any little book or pamphlet. [apparently < Latin *tractatus* a handling < *tractare* to handle. See TREAT.]

trac ta bil i ty (trak′tə bil′ə tē), *n.* quality of being tractable.

trac ta ble (trak′tə bəl), *adj.* 1 easily managed or controlled; easy to deal with; docile: *Dogs are more tractable than mules.* 2 easily handled or worked; malleable: *Copper and gold are tractable.* [< Latin *tractabilis* < *tractare* to handle. See TREAT.] **—trac′ta ble ness,** *n.* **—trac′ta bly,** *adv.*

trac tile (trak′təl), *adj.* that can be drawn out in length; ductile.

trac til i ty (trak til′ə tē), *n., pl.* **-ties.** quality of being tractile.

trac tion (trak′shən), *n.* 1 a drawing or pulling. 2 a being drawn. 3 the drawing or pulling of loads along a road, track, etc. 4 kind of power used for this. Electric traction is used on some subways and railroads. 5 friction between a body and the surface on which it moves, enabling the body to move without slipping: *Wheels slip on ice because there is too little traction.* [< Medieval Latin *tractionem* < Latin *trahere* to drag]

trac tion al (trak′shə nəl), *adj.* of or having to do with traction.

hat, āge, fär; let, ēqual, tėrm;
it, īce; hot, ōpen, ôrder;
oil, out; cup, pu̇t, rüle;
ch, child; ng, long; sh, she;
th, thin; ᴛʜ, then; zh, measure;

ə represents *a* in about, *e* in taken, *i* in pencil, *o* in lemon, *u* in circus.

< = from, derived from, taken from.

traction engine, a steam locomotive used for pulling wagons, plows, etc., along roads or over fields rather than on tracks.

trac tive (trak′tiv), *adj.* pulling; used for pulling.

trac tor (trak′tər), *n.* 1 a heavy, motor-driven vehicle which moves on wheels or on two endless tracks, used for pulling wagons, plows, etc., along roads or over fields. 2 a powerful truck having a short body and a cab for the driver, used to pull a freight trailer along a highway. 3 airplane with the propeller in front of the wings.

trade (trād), *n., v.,* **trad ed, trad ing,** *adj.* —*n.* 1 a buying and selling; exchange of goods; commerce: *wholesale trade.* See synonym study below. 2 exchange: *an even trade.* 3 bargain or business deal: *make a good trade.* 4 kind of work; business, especially one requiring skilled mechanical work: *the carpenter's trade, the plumber's trade.* 5 people in the same kind of work or business: *the building trade.* 6 INFORMAL. customers: *That store has a lot of trade.* 7 **the trades,** the trade winds. 8 OBSOLETE. a regular course of action, movement, etc.
—*v.i.* 1 buy and sell; exchange goods; be in commerce: *Some American companies trade all over the world.* 2 make an exchange: *If you don't like your book, I'll trade with you.* 3 bargain; deal. 4 be a customer: *We've been trading at that grocery store for years.* —*v.t.* 1 exchange: *trade seats.* 2 **trade in,** give (an automobile, refrigerator, television set, etc.) as payment or part payment for something, especially for a newer model. 3 **trade off,** get rid of by trading. 4 **trade on,** take advantage of.
—*adj.* 1 having to do with, used in, or characteristic of trade: *trade goods, trade papers.* 2 of or having to do with a trade or calling.
[< Middle Dutch or Middle Low German, track, course (apparently originally, of a trading ship). Related to TREAD.]
Syn. *n.* 1 **Trade, commerce** mean the buying and selling or exchanging of goods or other commodities. **Trade** applies to the actual buying and selling, or exchange, of commodities: *The Government has drawn up new agreements for trade with various countries.* **Commerce,** a more general term, includes both trade and transportation, especially as conducted on a large scale between different states or countries: *The Interstate Commerce Commission sets the rates railroads charge for freight.*

trade-in (trād′in′), *n.* automobile, refrigerator, etc., given or accepted as payment or part payment for something, especially for a newer model.

trade-last (trād′last′), *n.* compliment paid to a person without his knowledge but overheard by an acquaintance, who offers to tell it to the person involved in return for a compliment about himself.

trade mark (trād′märk′), *n.* mark, picture, name, word, symbol, or letters owned and used by a manufacturer or merchant to distinguish his goods from the goods of others. The registration and protection of trademarks are provided for by law. —*v.t.* 1 distinguish by means of a trademark. 2 register the trademark of.

trade name, 1 name used by a manufacturer or merchant for some article that he sells. 2 a special name used for any thing by those who buy and sell it. 3 name under which a company does business.

trad er (trā′dər), *n.* 1 person who trades. 2 ship used in trading.

trade school, school where trades are taught.

trades man (trādz′mən), *n., pl.* **-men.** storekeeper; shopkeeper.

trades peo ple (trādz′pē′pəl), *n.pl.* storekeepers; shopkeepers.

trades union, BRITISH. trade union.

trade union, 1 association of workers in a trade or craft to protect and promote their interests. 2 any labor union.

trade unionism, 1 system of having trade unions. 2 methods or practices of trade unions.

trade unionist, 1 member of a trade union. 2 person who favors trade unionism.

trade wind, a wind blowing toward the equator from about 30 degrees north latitude and about 30 degrees south latitude. North of the equator, it blows from the northeast; south of the equator, from the southeast.

trading post, store or station of a trader, especially on the frontier or in unsettled country.

trading stamp, stamp (def. 2).

tra di tion (trə dish′ən), *n.* 1 the handing down of beliefs, opinions, customs, stories, etc. from parents to children. 2 what is handed down in this way: *According to tradition, the first American flag was made by Betsy Ross.* 3 (in Jewish theology) the unwritten laws and doctrines received from Moses. 4 (in Christian theology) the unwritten precepts and doctrines received from Christ and the Apostles. [< Latin *traditionem* < *tradere* hand over < *trans-* over + *dare* to give. Doublet of TREASON.]

tra di tion al (trə dish′ə nəl), *adj.* 1 of tradition. 2 handed down by tradition. 3 according to tradition: *traditional furniture.* 4 customary. **—tra di′tion al ly,** *adv.*

tra di tion al ism (trə dish′ə nə liz′əm), *n.* adherence to the authority of tradition, especially in matters of religion, morality, etc.

tra di tion al ist (trə dish′ə nə list), *n.* a traditionalistic person. —*adj.* traditionalistic.

tra di tion al is tic (trə dish′ə nə lis′tik), *adj.* 1 of or having to do with traditionalism. 2 adhering to tradition.

tra duce (trə düs′, trə dyüs′), *v.t.,* **-duced, -duc ing.** speak evil of (a person) falsely; slander. [< Latin *traducere* parade in disgrace < *trans-* across + *ducere* to lead] **—tra duce′ment,** *n.* **—tra duc′er,** *n.*

Tra fal gar (trə fal′gər), *n.* **Cape,** cape in SW Spain, on the Atlantic. In a naval battle near this cape in 1805, Napoleon's fleet was defeated by a British fleet under Nelson.

traf fic (traf′ik), *n., v.,* **-ficked, -fick ing.** —*n.* 1 people, automobiles, wagons, ships, etc., coming and going along a way of travel. 2 a buying and selling; commerce; trade. 3 business done by a railroad line, steamship line, airline, etc.; number of passengers or amount of freight carried. 4 dealings; association: *Traffic with criminals is dangerous.* —*v.i.* 1 carry on trade; buy and sell; exchange: *The men trafficked with the natives for ivory.* 2 have illicit dealings: *traffic in narcotics.* [< Middle French *traffique* < Italian *traffico* < *tras-* across + *ficcare* to shove, poke]

traffic circle, junction of several roads at which the merging traffic goes around a central circle in one direction only; rotary.

traffic court, court which administers the laws regulating the actions of drivers on public roads and streets.

traffic island, a safety zone in the center of a traffic circle or between lanes of traffic.

traf fick er (traf′ə kər), *n.* person who buys and sells; trader; merchant; dealer.

traffic light, set of electric lights used for signaling at a corner or intersection to control traffic; stoplight.

trag a canth (trag′ə kanth), *n.* a sticky substance obtained from certain Old-World shrubs or herbs of the pea family, used for stiffening cloth, thickening medicines, etc.; gum tragacanth. [< Greek *tragakantha* goat's thorn]

tra ge di an (trə jē′dē ən), *n.* 1 actor in tragedies. 2 writer of tragedies.

tra ge di enne (trə jē′dē en′), *n.* actress in tragedies. [< French]

trag e dy (traj′ə dē), *n., pl.* **-dies.** 1 a serious play having an unhappy or disastrous ending. In classical drama a tragedy showed the conflict of man with fate or the gods and the unhappy ending brought about by some weakness or error on the part of the central character. Shakespeare's *Hamlet* is a tragedy. 2 the branch of drama that includes such plays. 3 the writing of such plays. 4 novel, long poem, etc., similar to a tragic play. 5 a very sad or terrible happening: *The father's sudden death was a tragedy to his family.* [< Latin *tragoedia* < Greek *tragoidia* < *tragos* goat (connection uncertain) + *ōidē* song]

trag ic (traj′ik), *adj.* 1 of tragedy; having to do with tragedy: *a tragic actor, a tragic poet.* 2 very sad; dreadful: *a tragic death, a tragic event.* **—trag′i cal ly,** *adv.*

trag i cal (traj′ə kəl), *adj.* tragic.

trag i com e dy (traj′i kom′ə dē), *n., pl.* **-dies.** 1 play having both tragic and comic elements. Shakespeare's *The Merchant of Venice* is a tragicomedy. 2 incident or situation in which serious and comic elements are blended.

trag i com ic (traj′i kom′ik), *adj.* having both tragic and comic elements.

trag i com i cal (traj′i kom′ə kəl), *adj.* tragicomic.

trail (trāl), *n.* 1 path across a wild or unsettled region: *a mountain trail.* 2 track or smell: *The dogs found the trail of the rabbit.* 3 mark left where something has been dragged or has passed along: *the trail of a snail.* 4 anything that follows along behind: *The car left a trail of dust behind it.* 5 the lower end of a gun carriage.
—*v.t.* 1 hunt by track or smell: *trail a bear, trail a thief.* 2 follow along behind; follow: *The dog trailed its master constantly.* 3 pull, drag, or draw along behind: *She trailed her gown through the mud.* 4 carry or bring by or as if by dragging: *trail snow into a house.* 5 bring or have floating after itself: *a car trailing dust.* 6 follow in a long, uneven line: *The campers trailed their leader down the mountainside.* 7 U.S. make a path by treading

down (grass, etc.). —*v.i.* 1 draw along behind; drag: *Her dress trails on the ground.* 2 hang down or float loosely from something. 3 grow along: *Poison ivy trailed by the road.* 4 go along slowly: *children trailing to school.* 5 move or float from and after something moving, as dust, smoke, etc. 6 extend in a long, uneven line; straggle: *refugees trailing from their ruined village.* 7 follow, fall, or lag behind, as in a race. 8 follow a trail, track, or smell. 9 pass little by little: *Her voice trailed off into silence.*
[< Old French *trailler* to tow < Latin *tragula* dragnet]

trail blaz er (trāl′blā′zər), *n.* person or thing that pioneers or prepares the way to something new.

trail er (trā′lər), *n.* 1 person or animal that follows a trail; tracker. 2 vehicle, often large, designed to be pulled along the highway by a truck, etc., especially by a truck lacking a body of its own. 3 a wheeled vehicle, furnished as a house, that can be pulled by an automobile. 4 a trailing plant or branch; vine that grows along the ground. 5 a few scenes shown to advertise a forthcoming motion picture or television program.

trailer court, trailer park.

trail er ite (trā′lə rīt′), *n.* person who travels or lives in a trailer.

trailer park, the grounds, equipped with utilities and other facilities, for accommodating automobile trailers.

trailing arbutus, arbutus (def. 1).

trailing edge, the rearward edge of an airfoil or propeller blade.

train (trān), *n.* 1 a connected line of railroad cars moving along together: *a very long freight train of 100 cars.* 2 a line of people, animals, wagons, trucks, etc., moving along together; caravan. 3 a collection of vehicles, animals, and men accompanying an army to carry supplies, baggage, ammunition, or any equipment or materials. 4 part that hangs down and drags along behind: *the train of a lady's gown.* 5 something that is drawn along behind; a trailing part; tail: *the train of a peacock, the train of a comet.* 6 group of followers; retinue: *the king and his train.* 7 series; succession: *a long train of misfortunes.* 8 order of succession; sequence: *lose one's train of thought.* 9 succession of results or conditions following some event: *The flood brought starvation and disease in its train.* 10 line of gunpowder that acts as a fuse to fire a charge or mine. 11 series of connected parts, such as wheels and pinions, through which motion is transmitted in a machine.
—*v.t.* 1 bring up; rear; teach: *train a child.* 2 make skillful by teaching and practice: *train student nurses.* 3 discipline and instruct (an animal) to be useful, obedient, perform tricks, race, etc. 4 make fit for a sport, etc., as by proper exercise and diet: *train a swimmer.* 5 bring into a particular position: *Train the vine around this post.* 6 direct, point, or aim: *train cannon upon a fort.* 7 trail or drag. 8 ARCHAIC. allure; entice; take in. —*v.i.* 1 be trained; undergo training. 2 make oneself fit, as by proper exercise and diet: *train for a track meet.*
[< Old French *trainer* < Popular Latin *traginare,* ultimately < Latin *trahere* to draw] **—train′a ble,** *adj.*

train ee (trā nē′), *n.* person who is receiving training, as for military service, a particular kind of work, etc.

train er (trā′nər), *n.* 1 person who trains, especially a person who trains or prepares men, horses, etc., for athletic or sporting competition. 2 aircraft used in training pilots.

train ing (trā′ning), *n.* 1 practical education in some art, profession, occupation, etc.: *training for teachers.* 2 development of strength and endurance. 3 good condition maintained by exercise, diet, etc.

train load (trān′lōd′), *n.* as much as a train can hold or carry.

train man (trān′mən), *n., pl.* **-men.** brakeman or railroad worker in a train crew, of lower rank than a conductor.

train oil, oil obtained from the blubber of whales, seals, fishes, etc. [< Middle Low German *trān* tear, drop]

traipse (trāps), *v.i.,* **traipsed, traips ing,** *n.* INFORMAL. walk about aimlessly, carelessly, or needlessly. [origin unknown]

trait (trāt; *British* trā), *n.* a distinguishing feature or quality of mind, character, etc.; characteristic: *Courage, love of fair play, and common sense are desirable traits.* See **feature** for synonym study. [< Middle French < Latin *tractus* a drawing < *trahere* to draw. Doublet of TRACT[1].]

trai tor (trā′tər), *n.* 1 person who betrays his country or ruler. 2 person who betrays a trust, duty, friend, etc. [< Old French *traitour* < Latin *traditor* < *tradere* hand over < *trans-* over + *dare* to give]

trai tor ous (trā′tər əs), *adj.* 1 of, like, or befitting a traitor; treacherous; faithless. 2 having to do with or of the nature of treason. **—trai′tor ous ly,** *adv.*

trai tress (trā′tris), *n.* a woman traitor.

Tra jan (trā′jən), *n.* A.D. 53?-117, Roman emperor from A.D. 98 to 117.

tra jec tor y (trə jek′tər ē), *n., pl.* **-tor ies.** the curved path of a projectile, comet, planet, etc. [< Medieval Latin *trajectorius* throwing across, ultimately < Latin *trans-* across + *jacere* to throw]

tram (tram), *n.* 1 BRITISH. streetcar. 2 truck or car on which loads are carried in mines. 3 an overhead or suspended carrier traveling on a cable. [< Middle Dutch *trame* beam]

tram car (tram′kär′), *n.* BRITISH. streetcar.

tram mel (tram′əl), *n., v.,* **-meled, -mel ing** or **-melled, -mel ling.** —*n.* 1 Usually, **trammels,** *pl.* anything that hinders or restrains: *A large bequest freed the artist from the trammels of poverty.* 2 a fine net to catch fish, birds, etc. 3 hook, bar, or chain in a fireplace to hold pots, kettles, etc., over the fire. 4 shackle for controlling the motions of a horse and making him amble. —*v.t.* 1 hinder; restrain. 2 catch in or as if in a trammel; entangle. [< Old French *tramail* < Late Latin *trimaculum* < Latin *tri-* three + *macula* mesh] **—tram′mel er, tram′mel ler,** *n.*

tramp (tramp), *v.i.* 1 walk heavily: *He tramped across the floor in his heavy boots.* 2 step heavily *(on);* trample: *He tramped on the flowers.* 3 go on foot; walk: *We tramped through the streets.* 4 walk steadily; march: *The hikers tramped mile after mile.* 5 go or wander as a tramp. —*v.t.* 1 step heavily on; trample upon. 2 travel on or through on foot: *tramp the streets.* —*n.* 1 sound of a heavy step or steps: *The steady tramp of marching feet.* 2 a long, steady walk; march; hike: *a tramp through the woods.* 3 person who travels from place to place on foot, living by begging, doing odd jobs, etc. 4 freighter without a regular route or schedule, that takes a cargo when and where it can. 5 an iron or steel plate worn under the shoe or boot to protect it. [Middle English *trampen*] **—tramp′er,** *n.*

tram ple (tram′pəl), *v.,* **-pled, -pling,** *n.* —*v.t.* 1 tread heavily on; crush: *The herd of wild cattle trampled the farmer's crops.* 2 treat cruelly, harshly, or scornfully. 3 **trample on** or **trample upon,** treat cruelly, harshly, or scornfully: *The dictator trampled on the rights of his people.* —*v.i.* tread or walk heavily; stamp. —*n.* act or sound of trampling: *We heard the trample of many feet.* **—tram′pler,** *n.*

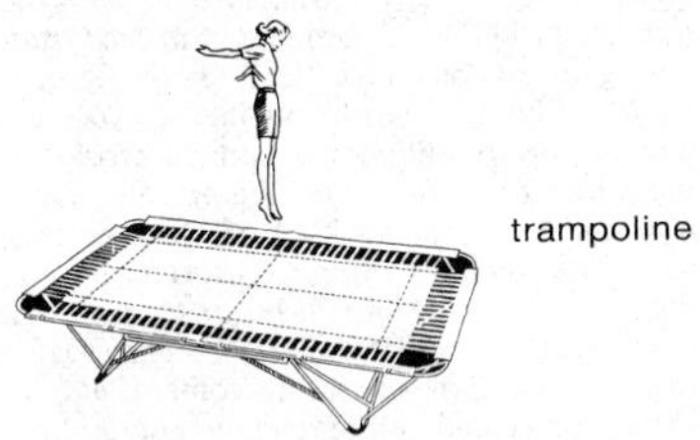

trampoline

tram po line (tram′pə lēn′, tram′pə lən), *n.* piece of canvas or other sturdy fabric stretched on a metal frame, used for tumbling, acrobatics, etc., in gymnasiums and circuses. [< Italian *trampolino* < Low German *trampeln* trample]

tram way (tram′wā′), *n.* 1 BRITISH. track for streetcars. 2 track or roadway for carrying ore from mines. 3 cable or system of cables for suspended cars.

trance (trans), *n., v.,* **tranced, tranc ing.** —*n.* 1 state of limited consciousness somewhat like sleep, as in hypnosis, catalepsy, or ecstasy. 2 a dazed or stunned condition. 3 a dreamy, absorbed condition that is like a trance: *The old man sat before the fire in a trance, thinking of his past life.* 4 a high emotion; rapture. —*v.t.* hold in a trance; enchant. [< Old French *transe* < *transir* pass away < Latin *transire* cross over < *trans-* across + *ire* go] **—trance′like′,** *adj.*

tran quil (trang′kwəl), *adj.,* **-quil er, -quil est** or **-quil ler, -quil lest.** free from agitation or disturbance; calm; peaceful; quiet. [< Latin *tranquillus*] **—tran′quil ly,** *adv.* **—tran′quil ness,** *n.*

tran quil ize (trang′kwə līz), *v.,* **-ized, -iz ing.** —*v.t.* make calm, peaceful, or quiet; make tranquil; calm; soothe. —*v.i.* become tranquil.

tran quil iz er (trang′kwə lī′zər), *n.* any of several drugs that reduce physical or nervous tension, lower blood pressure, etc.

tran quil li ty or **tran quil i ty** (trang kwil′ə tē), *n.* tranquil condition; calmness; peacefulness; quiet.

tran quil lize (trang′kwə līz), *v.t., v.i.,* **-lized, -liz ing.** tranquilize.

trans-, *prefix.* 1 across; over; through, as in *transcontinental, transmit.* 2 on the other side of; beyond, as in *transatlantic.* 3 to a different place, condition, etc., as in *transmigration, transform.* 4 (in chemistry) having certain atoms on the opposite side of a plane: *a trans-isomeric compound.* [< Latin *trans* across]

trans., 1 transaction. 2 transitive. 3 translated. 4 translation. 5 translator. 6 transportation.

trans act (tran zakt′, tran sakt′), *v.t.* attend to; manage; do; carry on (business): *transact* *business with stores all over the country.* —*v.i.* carry on business; deal. [< Latin *transactum* driven through, accomplished < *trans*- through + *agere* to drive]

trans ac tion (tran zak′shən, tran sak′-shən), *n.* 1 act or process of transacting: *She attends to the transaction of important matters herself.* 2 piece of business: *A record was kept of the firm's latest transaction.* 3 **transactions,** *pl.* record of what was done at the meetings of a society, club, etc.

trans ac tion al (tran zak′shə nəl, tran-sak′shə nəl), *adj.* of or having to do with a transaction.

trans ac tor (tran zak′tər, tran sak′tər), *n.* person who transacts business affairs.

trans al pine (tran zal′pīn, tran sal′pīn), *adj.* across or beyond the Alps, especially as viewed from Italy. —*n.* native or inhabitant of a country across or beyond the Alps.

trans at lan tic (tran′sət lan′tik, tran′zət-lan′tik), *adj.* 1 crossing the Atlantic: *a transatlantic cable.* 2 on the other side of the Atlantic.

Trans cau ca sia (tran′skô kā′zhə, tran′skô kā′shə), *n.* region of SW Soviet Union, in and south of the Caucasus. —**Trans′cau ca′sian,** *adj., n.*

trans ceiv er (trans sē′vər, tran sē′vər), *n.* a combined transmitter and receiver. [< *trans(mitter)* + *(re)ceiver*]

tran scend (tran send′), *v.t.* 1 go beyond the limits or powers of; exceed; be above: *The grandeur of Niagara Falls transcends description.* 2 be higher or greater than; surpass; excel. 3 (of God) be above and independent of (the physical universe). —*v.i.* be superior or extraordinary. [< Latin *transcendere* < *trans*- beyond + *scandere* to climb]

tran scend ence (tran sen′dəns), *n.* a being transcendent.

tran scend en cy (tran sen′dən sē), *n.* transcendence.

tran scend ent (tran sen′dənt), *adj.* 1 surpassing ordinary limits; excelling; superior; extraordinary. 2 above and independent of the physical universe. —**tran-scend′ent ly,** *adv.*

tran scen den tal (tran′sen den′tl), *adj.* 1 transcendent. 2 supernatural. 3 explaining material things as products of the mind that is thinking about them; idealistic. 4 transcendentalist. 5 (in mathematics) not capable of being the solution of a polynomial equation with rational coefficients. π is a transcendental number. —**tran′scen den′tal ly,** *adv.*

tran scen den tal ism (tran′sen den′tl-iz′əm), *n.* 1 transcendental quality, thought, language, or philosophy. 2 any philosophy based upon the doctrine that the principles of reality are to be discovered by a study of the processes of thought, not from experience. 3 the religious and philosophical doctrines of Ralph Waldo Emerson and others in New England in the middle 1800's, that emphasized the importance of individual inspiration.

tran scen den tal ist (tran′sen den′tl ist), *n.* person who believes in transcendentalism. —*adj.* of or having to do with transcendentalism.

trans con ti nen tal (tran′skon tə nen′tl), *adj.* 1 crossing a continent: *a transcontinental railroad.* 2 on the other side of a continent.

tran scribe (tran skrīb′), *v.,* **-scribed, -scrib ing.** —*v.t.* 1 copy in writing or in typewriting: *The account of the trial was transcribed from the stenographer's shorthand notes.* 2 set down in writing or print: *a speech transcribed in the newspapers, word for word.* 3 arrange (a piece of music) for a different instrument or voice. 4 make a recording or phonograph record of (a program, music, etc.) for playing back or broadcasting. 5 represent (a speech sound) by a phonetic symbol. —*v.i.* broadcast a phonograph record. [< Latin *transcribere* < *trans*- over + *scribere* write] —**tran scrib′er,** *n.*

tran script (tran′skript), *n.* 1 a written or typewritten copy. 2 copy or reproduction of anything: *The college wanted a transcript of the student's high-school record.*

tran scrip tion (tran skrip′shən), *n.* 1 a transcribing; copying. 2 transcript; copy. 3 arrangement of a piece of music for a different instrument or voice. 4 recording of a program, music, etc., for use in broadcasting. 5 act or fact of broadcasting such a record.

trans duc er (trans dü′sər, trans dyü′sər; tranz dü′sər, tranz dyü′sər), *n.* any device for converting energy from one form to another. [< Latin *transducere* lead across < *trans*- + *ducere* to lead]

tran sect (*v.* tran sekt′; *n.* tran′sekt′), *v.t.* cut across; dissect transversely. —*n.* a cross section of the vegetation of an area, usually that part growing along a long, narrow strip.

tran sec tion (tran sek′shən), *n.* a transecting; cross section.

tran sept (tran′sept), *n.* 1 the shorter part of a cross-shaped church. 2 either end of this part. See **apse** for diagram. [< Medieval Latin *transeptum* < Latin *trans*- across + *saeptum* fence]

trans fer (*v.* tran sfėr′, tran′sfėr′; *n.* tran′sfėr′), *v.,* **-ferred, -fer ring,** *n.* —*v.t.* 1 convey or remove from one person or place to another; hand over: *Please have my trunks transferred to the Union Station. The clerk was transferred to another department.* 2 convey (a drawing, design, pattern) from one surface to another. 3 make over (a title, right, or property) by deed or legal process: *transfer a bond by endorsement.* —*v.i.* 1 change from one public vehicle, such as a bus, train, etc., to another. 2 change from one place, position, condition, etc., to another: *The student transferred from the state university to a college nearer his home.* —*n.* 1 a transferring. 2 a being transferred. 3 a drawing, pattern, etc., printed from one surface onto another. 4 ticket allowing a passenger to continue his journey on another public vehicle. 5 point or place for transferring. 6 transference of title, right, or property by deed or legal process. 7 person or thing transferred. [< Latin *transferre* < *trans*- across + *ferre* carry] —**trans fer′rer,** *n.*

trans fer a bil i ty (tran sfėr′ə bil′ə tē, tran′sfər ə bil′ə tē), *n.* quality of being transferable.

trans fer a ble (tran sfėr′ə bəl, tran′sfər ə-bəl), *adj.* capable of being transferred.

trans fer al (tran sfėr′əl), *n.* transference; transfer.

trans fer ee (tran′sfə rē′), *n.* 1 person who is transferred. 2 (in law) the person to whom a transfer of title, right, or property is made.

trans fer ence (tran sfėr′əns, tran′sfər-əns), *n.* 1 act or process of transferring. 2 condition of being transferred.

trans fer or (tran sfėr′ər), *n.* (in law) the person who makes a transfer of title, right, or property.

hat, āge, fär; let, ēqual, tėrm;
it, īce; hot, ōpen, ôrder;
oil, out; cup, pu̇t, rüle;
ch, child; ng, long; sh, she;
th, thin; ᴛʜ, then; zh, measure;

ə represents *a* in about, *e* in taken, *i* in pencil, *o* in lemon, *u* in circus.

< = from, derived from, taken from.

transfer RNA, form of ribonucleic acid that delivers amino acids to the ribosomes during protein synthesis.

trans fig u ra tion (tran sfig′yə rā′shən), *n.* 1 a change in form or appearance; transformation. 2 **Transfiguration, a** (in the Bible) the change in the appearance of Christ on the mountain. **b** the church festival on August 6 in honor of this.

trans fig ure (tran sfig′yər), *v.t.,* **-ured, -ur ing.** 1 change in form or appearance; transform: *New paint and furnishings had transfigured the old house.* 2 change so as to glorify; exalt.

trans fix (tran sfiks′), *v.t.* 1 pierce through: *The hunter transfixed the lion with a spear.* 2 fasten or fix by piercing through with something pointed; impale. 3 make motionless or helpless (with amazement, terror, grief, etc.). —**trans fix′ion,** *n.*

trans form (tran sfôrm′), *v.t.* 1 change in form or appearance. 2 change in condition, nature, or character. See synonym study below. 3 change (one form of energy) into another. A dynamo transforms mechanical energy into electricity. 4 change (an electric current) to a higher or lower voltage, from alternating to direct current, or from direct to alternating current. 5 (in mathematics) to change (a figure, term, etc.) to another differing in form but having the same value or quantity. —*v.i.* be transformed; change. —**trans form′a ble,** *adj.*

Syn. *v.t.* 2 **Transform, transmute, convert** mean to change the form, nature, substance, or state of something. **Transform** suggests a thoroughgoing or fundamental change in the appearance, shape, or nature of a thing or person: *Responsibility transformed him from a careless boy into a capable leader.* **Transmute** suggests a complete change in nature or substance, especially to a higher kind: *He thus transmuted disapproval into admiration.* **Convert** suggests a change from one state or condition to another, especially for a new use or purpose: *convert boxes into furniture.*

trans for ma tion (tran′sfər mā′shən), *n.* 1 a transforming. 2 a being transformed. 3 (in mathematics) the changing of the form of an expression or figure into another form. 4 (in linguistics) the rearrangement of the parts of a sentence to produce an equivalent or more complex sentence. EXAMPLE: John hit him. He was hit by John. Has John been hitting him? 5 wig worn by women.

trans for ma tion al (tran′sfər mā′shə-nəl), *adj.* (in linguistics) of, having to do with, or using transformations: *transformational grammar.*

trans form a tive (tran sfôr′mə tiv), *adj.* tending or serving to transform.

trans form er (tran sfôr′mər), *n.* 1 person or thing that transforms. 2 device for changing an alternating electric current into one of higher or lower voltage by electromagnetic induction.

trans fuse (tran sfyüz′), *v.t.,* **-fused, -fus ing.** 1 pour (a liquid) from one container into another. 2 transfer (blood) from the veins of one person or animal to another. 3 inject (a solution) into a blood vessel. 4 infuse; instill: *The speaker transfused his enthusiasm into the audience.*

trans fu sion (tran sfyü′zhən), *n.* 1 act or fact of transfusing. 2 transfer of blood from one person or animal to another.

trans gress (trans gres′, tranz gres′), *v.i.* break a law, command, etc.; sin. —*v.t.* 1 go contrary to; sin against. 2 go beyond (a limit or bound): *transgress the bounds of good taste.* [< Latin *transgressum* gone beyond < *trans-* + *gradi* to step] **—trans gres′sor,** *n.*

trans gres sion (trans gresh′ən, tranz-gresh′ən), *n.* a transgressing or a being transgressed; breaking a law, command, etc.; sin.

tran ship (tran ship′), *v.t., v.i.,* **-shipped, -ship ping.** transship. **—tran ship′ment,** *n.*

tran science (tran′shəns), *n.* transiency.

tran sien cy (tran′shən sē), *n.* a being transient.

tran sient (tran′shənt), *adj.* 1 passing soon; fleeting; not lasting: *Joy and sorrow are often transient.* See **temporary** for synonym study. 2 passing through and not staying long: *a transient guest in a hotel.* —*n.* visitor or boarder who stays for a short time. [< Latin *transientem* going through < *trans* + *ire* go] **—tran′sient ly,** *adv.*

tran sis tor (tran zis′tər), *n.* a small electronic device containing semiconductors such as germanium or silicon, used instead of a vacuum tube to amplify or control the flow of electrons in an electric circuit. [< *tran(sfer)* + *(re)sistor*]

tran sis tor ize (tran zis′tə rīz′), *v.t.,* **-ized, -iz ing.** equip or reduce in size with transistors.

transistor radio, a usually small, battery-powered radio equipped with transistors.

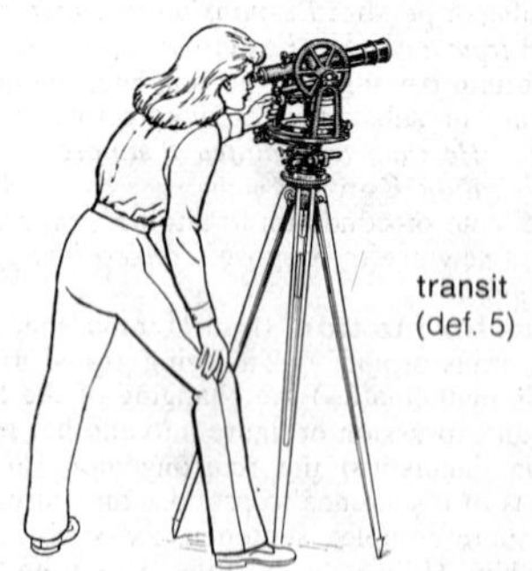

transit (def. 5)

trans it tran′sit, tran′zit), *n.* 1 a passing across or through. 2 a carrying or a being carried across or through: *The goods were damaged in transit.* 3 transportation by trains, buses, etc.: *All systems of transit are crowded during the rush hour.* 4 transition or change. 5 kind of theodolite with a telescope which can be rotated through a full circle, used in surveying to measure angles. 6 in astronomy: **a** the apparent passage of a heavenly body across the meridian of a place, or through the field of a telescope. **b** the passage of a small heavenly body across the disk of a larger one. —*v.t.* 1 pass across or through; traverse. 2 turn (the telescope of a transit) around its horizontal transverse axis to point in the opposite direction. —*v.i.* pass through, or over, or across. [< Latin *transitus* < *transire* pass through < *trans-* + *ire* go]

tran si tion (tran zish′ən), *n.* 1 a change or passing from one condition, place, thing, activity, topic, etc., to another: *the period of transition between two government administrations.* 2 in music: **a** a passing from one key to another; modulation. **b** passage linking one section, subject, etc., of a composition with another.

tran si tion al (tran zish′ə nəl), *adj.* of transition; of change from one more or less fixed condition to another. **—tran si′tion al ly,** *adv.*

tran si tive (tran′sə tiv), *adj.* 1 taking a direct object. In "Bring me my coat" and "Raise the window" *bring* and *raise* are transitive verbs. 2 transitional. —*n.* a transitive verb. **—tran′si tive ly,** *adv.* **—tran′si tive ness,** *n.*

tran si tiv i ty (tran′sə tiv′ə tē), *n.* condition of being transitive.

tran si to ry (tran′sə tôr′ē, tran′sə tōr′ē), *adj.* passing soon or quickly; lasting only a short time; fleeting; transient. **—tran′si to′ri ly,** *adv.* **—tran′si to′ri ness,** *n.*

Trans jor dan (trans jôrd′n, tranz jôrd′n), *n.* former name of **Jordan** (def. 2).

trans late (tran slāt′, tran′slāt; tranz lāt′, tranz′lāt), *v.,* **-lat ed, -lat ing.** —*v.t.* 1 change from one language into another. 2 change into other words. 3 explain the meaning of; interpret. 4 express (one thing) in terms of another: *translate words into action.* 5 change from one place, position, or condition to another. 6 take to heaven without death. —*v.i.* 1 change something from one language or form of words into another. 2 bear translation; allow to be translated. [< Latin *translatum* carried over < *trans-* + *latum* carried] **—trans lat′a ble,** *adj.* **—trans lat′a ble ness,** *n.*

trans la tion (tran slā′shən, tranz lā′shən), *n.* 1 a translating. 2 a being translated. 3 result of translating; version.

trans la tor (tran slā′tər, tran′slā tər; tranz-lā′tər, tranz′lā tər), *n.* person who translates.

trans lit e rate (tran slit′ə rāt′, tranz lit′ə-rāt′), *v.t.,* **-rat ed, -rat ing.** change (letters, words, etc.) into corresponding characters of another alphabet or language: *transliterate the Greek* χ *as ch.* [< *trans-* + Latin *littera* letter] **—trans lit′e ra′tion,** *n.*

trans lu cence (tran slü′sns, tranz lü′sns), *n.* a being translucent.

trans lu cen cy (tran slü′sn sē, tranz lü′sn-sē), *n.* translucence.

trans lu cent (tran slü′snt, tranz lü′snt), *adj.* letting light through without being transparent: *Frosted glass is translucent.* [< Latin *translucentem* < *trans-* through + *lucere* to shine] **—trans lu′cent ly,** *adv.*

trans lu nar (tran slü′nər, tranz lü′nər), *adj.* extending beyond the moon or the moon's orbit around the earth.

trans mi grate (tran smī′grāt, tranz-mī′grāt), *v.,* **-grat ed, -grat ing.** 1 (of the soul) pass at death into another body. 2 move from one place to another to settle there; migrate.

trans mi gra tion (tran′smī grā′shən, tranz′mī grā′shən), *n.* 1 the passing of a soul at death into another body. 2 the going from one place to another to settle there; migration.

trans mis si ble (tran smis′ə bəl, tranz-mis′ə bəl), *adj.* capable of being transmitted: *a transmissible disease.*

trans mis sion (tran smish′ən, tranz-mish′ən), *n.* 1 a sending over; passing on; passing along; letting through: *Mosquitoes are the only means of transmission of malaria.* 2 the part of an automobile or other motor vehicle that transmits power from the engine to the rear axle or sometimes the front axle by the use of gears. 3 passage through space of electromagnetic waves from the transmitting station to the receiving station: *radio transmission.* 4 something transmitted.

trans mis siv i ty (tran′smi siv′ə tē, tranz′mi siv′ə tē), *n.* quality of being transmissible.

trans mit (tran smit′, tranz mit′), *v.,* **-mit ted, -mit ting.** —*v.t.* 1 send over; pass on; pass along; let through: *I will transmit the money by special messenger. Rats transmit disease.* 2 cause (light, heat, sound, etc.) to pass through a medium. 3 convey (force or movement) from one part of a body or mechanism to another. 4 (of a medium) allow (light, heat, etc.) to pass through: *Glass transmits light.* 5 send out (signals) by means of electromagnetic waves or by wire. 6 pass on through inheritance. —*v.i.* send out signals by electromagnetic waves or by wire. [< Latin *transmittere* < *trans-* across + *mittere* send]

trans mit tal (tran smit′l, tranz mit′l), *n.* a transmitting.

trans mit ter (tran smit′ər, tranz mit′ər), *n.* 1 person or thing that transmits something. 2 that part of a telegraph or telephone by which sound waves are converted to electrical waves or impulses and sent to a receiver. 3 apparatus for sending out radio or television signals by means of electromagnetic waves.

trans mog ri fy (tran smog′rə fī, tranz-mog′rə fī), *v.t.,* **-fied, -fy ing.** change in form or appearance; transform in a surprising or grotesque manner. [< *trans-* + *mogrify* (origin unknown)] **—trans mog′ri fi ca′tion,** *n.*

trans mu ta tion (tran′smyə tā′shən, tranz′myə tā′shən), *n.* 1 a change from one nature, substance, or form into another. 2 transformation of one species into another. 3 (in chemistry and physics) a change from one atom into another atom of a different element, occurring naturally or artificially. 4 (in alchemy) the attempted conversion of a baser metal into gold or silver.

trans mute (tran smyüt′, tranz myüt′), *v.,* **-mut ed, -mut ing.** 1 change from one nature, substance, or form into another: *We can transmute water power into electrical power.* See **transform** for synonym study. 2 (in chemistry and physics) subject to transmutation. [< Latin *transmutare* < *trans-* thoroughly + *mutare* to change] **—trans mut′er,** *n.*

trans o ce an ic (tran′sō shē an′ik, tranz′ō shē an′ik), *adj.* 1 crossing the ocean. 2 on the other side of the ocean.

tran som (tran′səm), *n.* 1 a small window over a door or other window, usually hinged for opening. 2 a horizontal bar across a window. 3 crossbar separating a door from the window over it. 4 one of the beams or timbers attached across the sternpost of a ship between the two sides. [< Latin *transtrum,* originally, crossbeam < *trans* across]

tran son ic (tran son′ik), *adj.* of, having to do with, or designed for operation at speeds between 600 and 800 miles per hour, in the range just below or above the speed of sound: *a transonic flight, a transonic airliner.* Also, **transsonic.** [< *trans-* + *sonic*]

trans pa cif ic (tran′spə sif′ik), *adj.* 1 crossing the Pacific. 2 on the other side of the Pacific.

trans par ence (tran sper′əns, tran spar′əns), *n.* transparent quality or condition.

trans par en cy (tran sper′ən sē, tran spar′ən sē), *n., pl.* **-cies.** 1 transparent quality or condition. 2 something transparent. 3 picture, design, etc., on glass, celluloid, a photographic slide, etc., made visible by light shining through from behind.

trans par ent (tran sper′ənt, tran spar′ənt), *adj.* 1 transmitting light so that bodies beyond or behind can be distinctly seen: *Window glass is transparent.* 2 easily seen through or detected: *a transparent excuse.* 3 free from pretense or deceit; frank: *a person of transparent honesty.* [< Medieval Latin *transparentem* showing light through < Latin *trans-* through + *parere* appear] **—trans par′ent ly,** *adv.* **—trans par′ent ness,** *n.*

tran spi ra tion (tran′spə rā′shən), *n.* a transpiring, especially of moisture in the form of vapor, through a membrane or surface.

tran spire (tran spīr′), *v.,* **-spired, -spir ing.** *—v.i.* 1 take place; happen; occur: *I heard later what transpired at the meeting.* 2 leak out; become known. 3 pass off or send off moisture in the form of vapor through a membrane or surface, as from the human body or from leaves. *—v.t.* pass off or send off in the form of a vapor, as waste matter through the skin or water through the leaves of a plant. [< Middle French *transpirer* < Latin *trans-* through + *spirare* breathe]

trans plant (*v.* tran splant′; *n.* tran′splant), *v.t.* 1 plant again in a different place: *We grow the flowers indoors and then transplant them to the garden.* 2 remove from one place to another: *A group of farmers was transplanted to the island by the government.* 3 transfer (skin, an organ, etc.) from one person, animal, or part of the body to another: *transplant a kidney.* *—v.i.* bear moving to a different place. *—n.* 1 the transfer of skin, an organ, etc., from one person, animal, or part of the body to another: *a heart transplant.* 2 something that has been transplanted. **—trans plant′a ble,** *adj.* **—trans′plan ta′tion,** *n.* **—trans plant′er,** *n.*

trans po lar (tran spō′lər, tranz pō′lər), *adj.* across the north or south pole or polar region: *a transpolar flight.*

tran spond er (tran spon′dər), *n.* device that can receive a radar or other signal and automatically transmit a response. [< *trans(mitter)* + *(res)ponder*]

trans port (*v.* tran spôrt′, tran spōrt′; *n.* tran′spôrt, tran′spōrt), *v.t.* 1 carry from one place to another: *Wheat is transported from the farms to the mills.* See **carry** for synonym study. 2 carry away by strong feeling: *She was transported with joy by the good news.* 3 send away to another country as a punishment, especially to a penal colony. *—n.* 1 a carrying from one place to another: *Trucks are much used for transport.* 2 ship used to carry soldiers, supplies, equipment, etc. 3 aircraft that transports passengers, mail, freight, etc. 4 system of transportation; transit. 5 a strong feeling: *transports of rage.* 6 a transported convict. [< Latin *transportare* < *trans-* across + *portare* carry] **—trans port′er,** *n.*

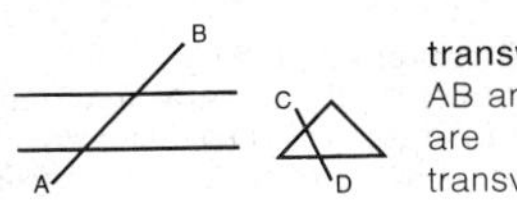

transversal AB and CD are transversals.

trans port a bil i ty (tran spôr′tə bil′ə tē, tran spōr′tə bil′ə tē), *n.* fact or property of being transportable.

trans port a ble (tran spôr′tə bəl, tran spōr′tə bəl), *adj.* that can be transported.

trans por ta tion (tran′spər tā′shən), *n.* 1 a transporting: *The railroad gives free transportation for a certain amount of baggage.* 2 a being transported. 3 business of transporting people or goods. 4 Also, **Transportation.** department of the United States government in charge of transportation. It was established in 1966. 5 means of transport. 6 cost of transport; ticket for transport. 7 a sending away to another country as a punishment, especially to a penal colony.

trans pos al (tran spō′zəl), *n.* transposition.

trans pose (tran spōz′), *v.t.,* **-posed, -pos ing.** 1 change the position or order of; interchange: *Transpose the two colors to get a better design.* 2 change the usual order of (letters, words, or numbers): *I transposed the numbers and mistakenly wrote 19 for 91.* 3 (in music) change the key of. 4 transfer (a term) to the other side of an algebraic equation, changing plus to minus or minus to plus. [< French *transposer* < *trans-* across + *poser* put] **—trans pos′a ble,** *adj.* **—trans pos′er,** *n.*

trans po si tion (tran′spə zish′ən), *n.* 1 a transposing. 2 a being transposed. 3 piece of music transposed into a different key.

trans ship (tran ship′), *v.t., v.i.,* **-shipped, -ship ping.** transfer from one ship, train, car, etc., to another. Also, **tranship.** **—trans ship′ment,** *n.*

trans son ic (tran son′ik), *adj.* transonic.

tran sub stan ti a tion (tran′səb stan′shē ā′shən), *n.* 1 a changing of one substance into another; transmutation. 2 in Christian theology: **a** the changing of the substance of the bread and wine of the Eucharist into the substance of the body and blood of Christ, only the appearance of the bread and wine remaining. **b** the doctrine that this change occurs, held by the Roman Catholic and Eastern Churches.

trans u ran ic element (tran′syu̇ ran′ik), any of a group of radioactive chemical elements whose atomic numbers are higher than that of uranium (92).

trans u ra ni um element (tran′syu̇ rā′nē əm), transuranic element.

Trans vaal (trans väl′, tranz väl′), *n.* province of the Republic of South Africa, in the NE part. 7,445,000 pop.; 109,600 sq. mi. *Capital:* Pretoria.

trans ver sal (trans vėr′səl, tranz vėr′səl), *adj.* transverse. *—n.* line intersecting two or more other lines. **—trans ver′sal ly,** *adv.*

trans verse (trans vėrs′, trans′vėrs′; tranz vėrs′, tranz′vėrs′), *adj.* lying across; placed crosswise; crossing from side to side: *transverse beams.* *—n.* something transverse. [< Latin *transversum* < *trans-* across + *versum* turned] **—trans verse′ly,** *adv.*

hat, āge, fär; let, ēqual, tėrm;
it, īce; hot, ōpen, ôrder;
oil, out; cup, pu̇t, rüle;
ch, child; ng, long; sh, she;
th, thin; ᴛʜ, then; zh, measure;

ə represents *a* in about, *e* in taken, *i* in pencil, *o* in lemon, *u* in circus.

< = from, derived from, taken from.

Tran syl van ia (tran′səl vā′nyə, tran′səl vā′nē ə), *n.* region in central Romania, formerly part of Hungary. **—Tran′syl van′ian,** *adj., n.*

trap[1] (trap), *n., v.,* **trapped, trap ping.** *—n.* 1 device or means for catching animals, usually having a spring which when touched seizes, kills, or imprisons the animal. 2 trick or other means for catching someone off guard. 3 trap door. 4 bend in a drainpipe for holding a small amount of water to prevent the escape of air, sewer gas, etc. 5 a light, two-wheeled carriage. 6 device for throwing clay pigeons, etc., into the air to be shot at. 7 sand trap. 8 **traps,** *pl.* group of drums, cymbals, bells, gongs, etc., used especially in a small band or orchestra. *—v.t.* 1 catch in or as if in a trap. 2 provide with a trap. 3 stop and hold with a trap. *—v.i.* 1 set traps for animals. 2 make a business of catching animals in traps for their furs. [Old English *træppe*]

trap[2] (trap), *v.,* **trapped, trap ping,** *n.* *—v.t.* cover or ornament with trappings. *—n.* **traps,** *pl.* INFORMAL. belongings; baggage. [apparently alteration of Old French *drap* cloth, drape]

trap[3] (trap), *n.* basalt or other fine-grained, dark, igneous rock having a more or less columnar structure. [earlier *trapp* < Swedish < *trappa* stair]

trap door, door in a floor, ceiling, or roof. It opens on hinges or by sliding in grooves.

tra peze (trə pēz′), *n.* a short horizontal bar hung by ropes like a swing, used in gymnasiums and circuses for acrobatic stunts and exercises. [< French *trapèze* < Late Latin *trapezium.* See TRAPEZIUM.]

tra pez ist (trə pē′zist), *n.* performer on the trapeze.

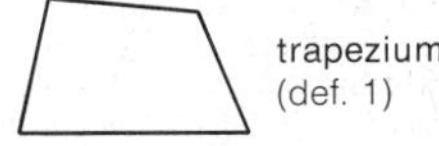
trapezium (def. 1)

tra pe zi um (trə pē′zē əm), *n., pl.* **-zi ums, -zi a** (-zē ə). 1 a four-sided plane figure having no sides parallel. 2 BRITISH. trapezoid (def. 1). [< Late Latin < Greek *trapezion,* originally, little table, diminutive of *trapeza* table < *tra-* four + *peza* foot]

trap e zoid (trap′ə zoid), *n.* 1 a four-sided plane figure having two sides parallel and two sides not parallel. 2 BRITISH. trapezium (def. 1).

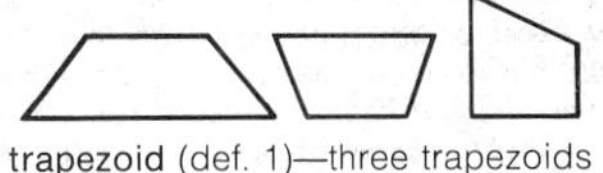
trapezoid (def. 1)—three trapezoids

trap per (trap′ər), *n.* person who traps, especially one who traps wild animals for their furs.

trap pings (trap′ingz), *n.pl.* 1 ornamental coverings for a horse; caparisons. 2 things worn; ornaments: *the trappings of a king and his court.* 3 outward appearance: *He had all the trappings of a cowboy, but he couldn't even ride a horse.* [< *trap*[2]]

Trap pist (trap′ist), *n.* monk belonging to an extremely austere branch of the Cistercian order established in 1664. —*adj.* of or having to do with the Trappists. [< French *trappiste* < the monastery of *La Trappe* in Normandy]

trap shoot er (trap′shü′tər), *n.* person who engages in trapshooting.

trap shoot ing (trap′shü′ting), *n.* sport of shooting at clay pigeons or other targets thrown or released from traps into the air.

trash (trash), *n.* 1 anything of little or no worth; worthless stuff; rubbish. 2 cheap and flashy writing, talk, etc. 3 broken or torn bits, such as leaves, twigs, husks, etc. 4 disreputable people; riffraff. —*v.t.* SLANG. vandalize: *Someone broke into the school and trashed several classrooms.* [< Scandinavian (dialectal Norwegian) *trask*]

trash y (trash′ē), *adj.,* **trash i er, trash i est.** like or containing trash; worthless. —**trash′i ness,** *n.*

trat to ri a (trät′tō rē′ä), *n., pl.* **-ri e** (-rē′ā). an Italian restaurant. [< Italian]

trau ma (trô′mə, trou′mə), *n., pl.* **-mas, -ma ta** (-mə tə). 1 a wound or other external body injury. 2 an emotional shock which has a lasting effect on the mind. 3 an abnormal physical or mental condition produced by a wound, injury, or shock. [< Greek, wound]

trau mat ic (trô mat′ik, trou mat′ik), *adj.* 1 of, having to do with, or produced by a wound, injury, or shock: *a traumatic experience.* 2 for or dealing with the treatment of wounds, injuries, or shock. —**trau mat′i cal ly,** *adv.*

tra vail (trə vāl′, trav′āl), *n.* 1 toil; labor. 2 trouble, hardship, or suffering. 3 severe pain; agony; torture. 4 the labor and pain of childbirth. —*v.i.* 1 toil; labor. 2 suffer the pains of childbirth; be in labor. [< Old French < Late Latin *trepalium* torture device, ultimately < Latin *tri-* three + *palus* stake]

trav el (trav′əl), *v.,* **-eled, -el ing** or **-elled, -el ling,** *n.* —*v.i.* 1 go from one place to another; journey: *travel across the country.* 2 go from place to place selling things: *travel for a large firm.* 3 move; pass; proceed: *Light and sound travel in waves.* 4 walk or run: *A deer travels far and fast when chased.* —*v.t.* pass through or over: *travel a road.* —*n.* 1 a going in trains, ships, cars, etc., from one place to another; journeying. 2 movement in general. 3 the length of stroke, movement in one direction, or the distance of such movement of a part of a machine. 4 **travels,** *pl.* **a** journeys. **b** book about one's experiences, visits, etc., while traveling. [variant of *travail* in the sense of "to labor"]

travel agency or **travel bureau,** business that arranges trips, tickets, hotel reservations, etc., for travelers.

trav eled or **trav elled** (trav′əld), *adj.* 1 that has done much traveling. 2 much used by travelers: *a heavily traveled road.*

trav el er or **trav el ler** (trav′ə lər, trav′lər), *n.* 1 person or thing that travels. 2 traveling salesman.

traveler's check, check issued by a bank for a specified amount and signed by the buyer, who may use it as cash by signing it again in the presence of a witness, as in a store, hotel, etc.

traveling salesman, person whose work is going from place to place selling things for a company.

trav e logue or **trav e log** (trav′ə lôg, trav′ə log), *n.* 1 lecture describing travel, usually accompanied by pictures or films. 2 motion picture depicting travel. [< *travel* + *-logue,* as in *dialogue*]

trav erse (*v.* trav′ərs, trə vėrs′; *n., adj.* trav′ərs), *v.,* **-ersed, -ers ing,** *n., adj.* —*v.t.* 1 pass across, over, or through: *We traversed the desert.* 2 go to and fro over or along (a place, etc.); cross. 3 ski or climb diagonally across. 4 read, examine, or consider carefully. 5 move sideways; turn from side to side. 6 turn (a cannon, etc.) to the right or left. 7 oppose; hinder; thwart. —*v.i.* 1 walk or move in a crosswise direction; move back and forth: *That horse traverses.* 2 turn on or as if on a pivot; swivel. 3 ski in a diagonal course.

—*n.* 1 act of traversing. 2 something put or lying across; transverse. 3 an earth wall protecting a trench or an exposed place in a fortification. 4 gallery or loft from side to side in a church or other large building. 5 a single line of survey carried across a region; distance across. 6 a sideways motion of a ship, part in a machine, mountain climbers, etc. 7 the zigzag course taken by a ship because of contrary winds or currents. 8 line that crosses other lines. 9 obstacle; hindrance; opposition.

—*adj.* lying, passing, or extending across; cross; transverse.

[< Old French *traverser* < Late Latin *transversare* < Latin *transversum* transverse. See TRANSVERSE.] —**trav′ers a ble,** *adj.* —**trav′ers er,** *n.*

trav er tin (trav′ər tən), *n.* travertine.

trav er tine (trav′ər tēn′, trav′ər tən), *n.* a white or light-colored form of limestone deposited by springs in caves, etc., used in Italy as building material. [< Italian *travertino, tivertino* < Latin *tiburtinus* of *Tibur,* ancient town of Latium]

trav es ty (trav′ə stē), *n., pl.* **-ties,** *v.,* **-tied, -ty ing.** —*n.* 1 an imitation of a serious literary work or subject, done in such a way as to make it seem ridiculous. 2 any treatment or imitation that makes a serious thing seem ridiculous: *The trial was a travesty of justice, since the judge and jury were prejudiced.* —*v.t.* make (a serious subject or matter) ridiculous; imitate in an absurd or grotesque way. [< French *travesti* disguised, ultimately < Latin *trans-* over + *vestire* to dress]

tra vois (trə voi′), *n., pl.* **-vois.** vehicle without wheels used by Great Plains Indians, consisting of two shafts or poles joined by a platform or net for holding the load. [< Canadian French]

tra voise (trə voiz′), *n., pl.* **-vois es.** travois.

trawl (trôl), *n.* 1 a large, strong net dragged along the bottom of the sea. 2 a strong line supported by buoys and having many short lines with baited hooks attached to it. —*v.i.* 1 fish with a net by dragging it along the bottom of the sea. 2 fish with a line supported by buoys and having many hooks attached. —*v.t.* catch (fish) with such a net or line. [probably < Middle Dutch *traghel* < Latin *tragula* dragnet]

trawl er (trô′lər), *n.* 1 boat used in trawling. 2 person who trawls.

tray (trā), *n.* 1 a flat, shallow holder or container with a low rim around it: *carry flower pots on a tray.* 2 tray with dishes of food on it: *a breakfast tray.* 3 a shallow box that fits into a trunk, cabinet, etc. [Old English *trēg*]

treach er ous (trech′ər əs), *adj.* 1 not to be trusted; not faithful; disloyal: *The treacherous soldier carried reports to the enemy.* 2 having a false appearance of strength, security, etc.; not reliable; deceiving: *This ice is treacherous.* —**treach′er ous ly,** *adv.* —**treach′er ous ness,** *n.*

treach er y (trech′ər ē), *n., pl.* **-er ies.** 1 a breaking of faith; treacherous behavior; deceit. See **disloyalty** for synonym study. 2 treason. [< Old French *trecherie* < *trechier* to cheat]

trea cle (trē′kəl), *n.* 1 BRITISH. molasses, especially that produced during the refining of sugar. 2 anything too sweet or cloying, especially excessive sentimentality. [< Old French *triacle* antidote < Latin *theriaca* < Greek *thēriakē* antidote against poisonous animals < *thērion,* diminutive of *thēr* wild beast]

trea cly (trē′klē), *adj.* of or like treacle.

tread (tred), *v.,* **trod, trod den** or **trod, tread ing,** *n.* —*v.i.* 1 set the foot down; walk; step: *tread through the meadow.* 2 step heavily; trample: *Don't tread on the flower beds.* —*v.t.* 1 set the feet on; walk on or through; step on: *tread the streets.* 2 press under; trample on; crush: *tread grapes.* 3 make, form, or do by walking: *Cattle had trodden a path to the pond.* 4 follow; pursue: *tread the path of virtue.* —*n.* 1 act or sound of treading: *the tread of marching feet.* 2 way of walking: *walk with a heavy tread.* 3 the part of stairs or a ladder that a person steps on. 4 the part of a wheel or tire that presses against the ground, rail, etc. The treads of a rubber tire are grooved to improve traction. 5 the pattern left by the grooves or ridges in a tire: *The new tire left a deep tread in the snow.* 6 the distance between opposite wheels of an automobile. 7 sole of the foot or of a shoe. [Old English *tredan*] —**tread′er,** *n.*

trea dle (tred′l), *n., v.,* **-dled, -dling.** —*n.* lever or pedal worked by the foot to impart motion to a machine: *the treadle of a sewing machine.* —*v.i.* work a treadle. [Old English *tredel* < *tredan* to tread]

treadmill (def. 1)

tread mill (tred′mil′), *n.* 1 apparatus for producing a turning motion by having a person or animal walk on the moving steps of a wheel or of a sloping, endless belt. 2 any wearisome or monotonous round of work or life.

treas., 1 treasurer. 2 treasury.

trea son (trē′zn), *n.* 1 betrayal of one's country or ruler. In the United States treason by a citizen consists of making war against the United States or giving aid and comfort to its enemies. See **disloyalty** for synonym study. 2 betrayal of a trust, duty, friend, etc.; treachery. [< Anglo-French *treson* < Latin *traditionem* a handing over. Doublet of TRADITION.]

trea son a ble (trē′zn ə bəl), *adj.* of treason; involving treason; traitorous. **—trea′son a ble ness,** *n.* **—trea′son a bly,** *adv.*

trea son ous (trē′zn əs), *adj.* treasonable.

treas ure (trezh′ər, trā′zhər), *n., v.,* **-ured, -ur ing.** *—n.* 1 wealth or riches stored up; valuable things: *The pirates buried their treasure along the coast.* 2 any thing or person that is much loved or valued. *—v.t.* 1 value highly; cherish; prize. 2 put away for future use; store up; hoard. [< Old French *tresor* < Latin *thesaurus* < Greek *thesauros.* Doublet of THESAURUS.]

treas ur er (trezh′ər ər, trā′zhər ər), *n.* person in charge of the finances of a club, society, corporation, government body, etc.

treas ure-trove (trezh′ər trōv′, trā′zhər-trōv′), *n.* 1 money, jewels, or other treasure that a person finds, especially if the owner of it is not known. 2 any valuable discovery. [< Anglo-French *tresor trové* treasure found]

treas ur y (trezh′ər ē, trā′zhər ē), *n., pl.* **-ur ies.** 1 building, room, or other place where money or valuables are kept for security. 2 money owned; funds: *We voted to pay for the party out of the club treasury.* 3 Also, **Treasury.** department of the government that has charge of the income and expenses of a country. 4 place where treasure is kept. 5 place where anything valuable is kept or found; book or person thought of as a valued source: *a treasury of wisdom.*

treasury note, note or bill issued by the Treasury of the United States and receivable as legal tender for all debts.

treat (trēt), *v.t.* 1 act or behave toward: *treat a car with care.* 2 think of; consider; regard: *He treated his mistake as a joke.* 3 deal with to relieve or cure: *The dentist is treating my toothache.* 4 deal with to bring about some special result: *treat a metal plate with acid in engraving.* 5 deal with; discuss: *This magazine treats the progress of medicine.* 6 express in literature or art; represent: *treat a theme realistically.* 7 entertain with food, drink, or amusement: *treat a friend to ice cream.* *—v.i.* 1 discuss terms; arrange terms: *Messengers came to treat for peace.* 2 pay the cost of a treat or entertainment: *I'll treat today.* 3 **treat of,** deal with; discuss: *"The Medical Journal" treats of the progress of medicine.* *—n.* 1 gift of food, drink, or amusement. 2 anything that gives pleasure: *Being in the country is a treat to her.* [< Old French *traitier* < Latin *tractare* to handle, frequentative of *trahere* to draw] **—treat′er,** *n.*

trea tise (trē′tis), *n.* a formal and systematic book or writing dealing with some subject.

treat ment (trēt′mənt), *n.* 1 act or process of treating: *My cold won't respond to treatment.* 2 way of treating: *This cat has suffered from bad treatment.* 3 thing done or used to treat something else, such as a disease.

trea ty (trē′tē), *n., pl.* **-ties.** 1 a formal agreement, especially one between nations, signed and approved by each nation. 2 document embodying such an agreement: *sign a peace treaty.* [< Old French *traité, traitié* < Latin *tractatus* discussion < *tractare.* See TREAT.]

treaty port, any of various ports in China, Japan, and Korea, formerly required by treaty to be kept open to foreign commerce.

tre ble (treb′əl), *adj., v.,* **-bled, -bling,** *n.* *—adj.* 1 three times as much or as many; triple. 2 (in music) of, having to do with, or for the treble: *a treble voice.* 3 high-pitched; shrill: *treble tones.* *—v.t., v.i.* make or become three times as much or as many; triple: *He trebled his money by buying a dog for $25 and selling it for $75.* *—n.* 1 the highest part in music; soprano. 2 voice, singer, or instrument that takes this part. 3 a shrill, high-pitched voice, sound, or note. [< Old French < Latin *triplus* triple. Doublet of TRIPLE.]

treble clef, symbol in music indicating that the pitch of the notes on a staff is above middle C; G clef. See **clef** for diagram.

tre bly (treb′lē), *adv.* three times; triply.

tree (trē), *n., v.,* **treed, tree ing.** *—n.* 1 a large perennial plant with a woody trunk and usually having branches and leaves at some distance from the ground. 2 any plant that resembles a tree in form or size. 3 piece or structure of wood for some special purpose, as a shoe tree or clothes tree. 4 anything like a tree with its branches. A family tree is a diagram with branches, showing how the members of a family are descended and related. 5 **bark up the wrong tree,** pursue the wrong object or use the wrong means to attain it. 6 **up a tree,** INFORMAL. in a difficult position. *—v.t.* 1 chase up a tree: *The cat was treed by a dog.* 2 furnish with a tree: *tree the roof of a coal mine, tree a spade.* 3 stretch (a shoe or boot) on a tree. 4 INFORMAL. put into a difficult position. *—v.i.* take refuge in a tree. [Old English *trēo*] **—tree′less,** *adj.* **—tree′like′,** *adj.*

tree farm, place where trees are grown as a business.

tree fern, fern of tropical and subtropical regions that grows to the size of a tree, with a woody, trunklike stem and fronds at the top.

tree frog, any of a family of small, tree-dwelling frogs with adhesive disks or suckers on their toes; hyla.

tree of heaven, ailanthus.

tree surgeon, an expert in tree surgery.

tree surgery, the treatment of diseased or damaged trees by filling cavities, cutting away parts, etc.

tree toad, tree frog.

tree top (trē′top′), *n.* the top or uppermost part of a tree.

trefoil (def. 2)—three trefoils

tre foil (trē′foil), *n.* 1 any of various plants of the pea family having three leaflets to each leaf, such as clover. 2 ornament like a three-fold leaf. [< Latin *trifolium* < *tri-* three + *folium* leaf]

trek (trek), *v.,* **trekked, trek king,** *n.* *—v.i.* 1 travel slowly; travel: *The pioneers trekked to California by covered wagon.* 2 (in South Africa) travel by ox wagon. *—n.* 1 journey. 2 stage of a journey between one stopping place and the next. 3 (in South Africa) a traveling in a group, as pioneers into undeveloped country. [< Afrikaans < Middle Dutch *trekken,* originally, to draw, pull] **—trek′ker,** *n.*

trel lis (trel′is), *n.* frame of light strips of wood or metal crossing one another with open spaces in between; lattice, especially one supporting growing vines. *—v.t.* 1 furnish with a trellis. 2 support or train (vines, etc.) on a trellis. 3 cross or interweave as in a trellis. [< Old French *trelis,* ultimately < Latin *trilix* triple-twilled < *tri-* three + *licium* thread]

hat, āge, fär; let, ēqual, tėrm;
it, īce; hot, ōpen, ôrder;
oil, out; cup, pu̇t, rüle;
ch, child; ng, long; sh, she;
th, thin; ᴛʜ, then; zh, measure;

ə represents *a* in about, *e* in taken,
i in pencil, *o* in lemon, *u* in circus.

< = from, derived from, taken from.

trel lis work (trel′is wėrk′), *n.* latticework.

trem a tode (trem′ə tōd, trē′mə tōd), *n.* any of a class of parasitic flatworms having suckers and sometimes hooks; fluke[3]. [< Greek *trēmatōdēs* with holes < *trēmatos* hole]

trem ble (trem′bəl), *v.,* **-bled, -bling,** *n.* *—v.i.* 1 shake because of fear, excitement, weakness, cold, etc. See **shake** for synonym study. 2 feel fear, anxiety, etc.: *She trembled for the safety of her child, who was out in the storm.* 3 move gently: *The leaves trembled in the breeze.* *—n.* a trembling. [< Old French *trembler,* ultimately < Latin *tremulus.* See TREMULOUS.] **—trem′bler,** *n.* **—trem′bling ly,** *adv.*

trem bly (trem′blē), *adj.* trembling; tremulous.

tre men dous (tri men′dəs), *adj.* 1 very severe; dreadful; awful: *a tremendous defeat.* 2 INFORMAL. very great; enormous: *a tremendous house.* 3 INFORMAL. excellent; wonderful; extraordinary: *a tremendous time at a party.* [< Latin *tremendus,* literally, be trembled at < *tremere* to tremble] **—tre men′dous ly,** *adv.* **—tre men′dous ness,** *n.*

trem o lo (trem′ə lō), *n., pl.* **-los.** 1 a rapid repetition of musical tones or a rapid alteration of tones, causing a trembling or vibrating effect. 2 device in an organ used to produce this effect. [< Italian, tremulous < Latin *tremulus*]

trem or (trem′ər), *n.* 1 an involuntary shaking or trembling: *a nervous tremor in the voice.* 2 thrill of emotion or excitement. 3 state of emotion of excitement. 4 a shaking or vibrating movement. An earthquake is sometimes called an earth tremor. [< Latin]

trem u lous (trem′yə ləs), *adj.* 1 trembling; quivering: *a voice tremulous with sobs.* 2 timid; fearful. 3 that wavers; shaky: *tremulous writing.* [< Latin *tremulus* < *tremere* to tremble] **—trem′u lous ly,** *adv.* **—trem′u lous ness,** *n.*

trench (trench), *n.* 1 a long, narrow ditch with earth thrown up in front to protect soldiers. 2 a deep furrow; ditch: *to dig a trench for a sewer pipe.* 3 a long, narrow depression in the floor of the ocean. *—v.t.* 1 dig a trench in. 2 surround with a trench; fortify with trenches. 3 **trench on** or **trench upon,** a trespass upon. b come close to; border on: *a remark that trenched closely on slander.* *—v.i.* dig trenches. [< Old French *trenche* < *trenchier* to cut]

trench an cy (tren′chən sē), *n.* trenchant quality; sharpness.

trench ant (tren′chənt), *adj.* 1 sharp; keen; cutting: *trenchant wit.* 2 vigorous; effective: *a trenchant policy.* 3 clear-cut; distinct: *in trenchant outline against the sky.* [< Old French, cutting] **—trench′ant ly,** *adv.*

trench coat, kind of belted raincoat with straps on the shoulders and cuffs, usually made of cotton gabardine or poplin.

trench er[1] (tren′chər), *n.* a wooden platter on which meat or other food was formerly served and carved. [< Old French *trencheor* < *trenchier* to cut]

trench er[2] (tren′chər), *n.* person who digs trenches.

trench er man (tren′chər mən), *n., pl.* **-men.** 1 person who has a hearty appetite; eater. 2 hanger-on; parasite.

trench fever, an infectious fever caused by a rickettsia and transmitted by lice. It affected many soldiers in the trenches in World War I.

trench foot, a foot disease like frostbite, caused by prolonged exposure to cold and wet, chiefly affecting soldiers.

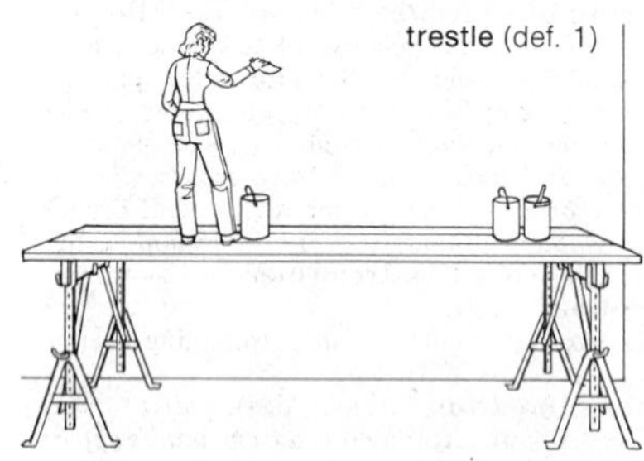
trestle (def. 1)

trench mouth, a contagious, painful bacterial infection of the mouth, characterized by sores and ulcers on the lining of the gums, cheeks, and tongue.

trend (trend), *n.* 1 the general direction; course: *The hills have a western trend.* See **direction** for synonym study. 2 the general course or drift; tendency: *a trend toward smaller cars.* 3 fashion; style; vogue: *the latest trend in clothes.* —*v.i.* 1 turn off or bend in a certain direction; run. 2 have a general tendency. [Old English *trendan* to turn]

Trent (trent), *n.* 1 city in N Italy. 82,000. 2 **Council of,** a general council of the Roman Catholic Church held at Trent from 1545 to 1563, that settled inportant points of church doctrines and rules and organized the Catholic opposition to Protestantism. 3 **Trent River,** river flowing from W England into the Humber. 170 mi.

Tren ton (tren′tən), *n.* capital of New Jersey, in the W part. 105,000.

tre pan (tri pan′), *n., v.,* **-panned, -pan ning.** —*n.* 1 an early form of the trephine. 2 a boring instrument, used for sinking shafts. —*v.t.* 1 trephine. 2 bore through with a trepan; cut a disk out of with a trepan or similar tool. [< Medieval Latin *trepanum* < Greek *trypanon* < *trypan* to bore]

trep a na tion (trep′ə nā′shən), *n.* operation of trepanning.

tre pang (tri pang′), *n.* the dried flesh of any of several species of sea cucumbers, used in China and the East Indies for making soup. [< Malay *teripang*]

tre phine (tri fīn′, tri fēn′), *n., v.,* **-phined, -phin ing.** —*n.* a cylindrical saw with a removable center pin, used to cut out circular pieces from the skull. —*v.t.* operate on with a trephine. [ultimately < Latin *tres fines* three ends]

trep i da tion (trep′ə dā′shən), *n.* 1 nervous dread; fear; fright. 2 a trembling. [< Latin *trepidationem* < *trepidare* to tremble < *trepidus* alarmed]

trep o ne ma (trep′ə nē′mə), *n.* any of a genus of spirochetes parasitic in man and other warm-blooded mammals, including the bacteria that cause syphilis and yaws. [< New Latin < Greek *trepein* to turn + *nēma* thread]

tres pass (tres′pəs, tres′pas), *v.i.* 1 go on somebody's property without any right: *The farmer put up "No Trespassing" signs to keep people off his farm.* 2 go beyond the limits of what is right, proper, or polite: *I won't trespass on your time any longer.* See **intrude** for synonym study. 3 do wrong; sin. —*n.* 1 act or fact of trespassing. 2 a wrong; a sin. 3 an unlawful act done by force against the person, property, or rights of another. 4 legal action to recover damages for such an injury. [< Old French *trespasser* < *tres-* across + *passer* to pass] **—tres′pass er,** *n.*

tress (tres), *n.* 1 a lock, curl, or braid of hair. 2 **tresses,** *pl.* long, flowing hair of a woman or girl. [< Old French *trece*]

tres tle (tres′əl), *n.* 1 framework similar to a sawhorse, used as a support for a table top, platform, etc. 2 a braced framework of timber, steel, etc., used as a bridge to support a road, railroad tracks, etc. [< Old French *trestel* crossbeam, ultimately < Latin *transtrum.* See TRANSOM.]

tres tle work (tres′əl wėrk′), *n.* 1 structure consisting of a trestle or trestles. 2 support, bridge, or the like, made of such structures.

trey (trā), *n.* card, die, or domino with three spots. [< Old French *trei* < Latin *tres* three]

tri-, *prefix.* 1 having three ___: *Triangle = (figure) having three angles.* 2 three ___: *Trisect = divide into three parts.* 3 once every three ___: *Trimonthly = occurring once every three months.* 4 containing three atoms, etc., of the substance specified, as in *trioxide.* [< Latin or Greek < *tria* three]

tri a ble (trī′ə bəl), *adj.* 1 that can be tested or proved. 2 that can be tried in a court of law. **—tri′a ble ness,** *n.*

tri ad (trī′ad, trī′əd), *n.* 1 group of three, especially of three closely related persons or things. 2 (in music) a chord of three tones, especially one consisting of a given note with its major or minor third and its perfect, augmented, or diminished fifth. [< Greek *triados* < *treis* three]

tri ad ic (trī ad′ik), *adj.* of or having to do with a triad.

tri al (trī′əl), *n.* 1 the examining and deciding of a civil or criminal case in a court of law. 2 process of trying or testing the fitness, truth, strength, or other quality of something: *The mechanic gave the motor another trial to see if it would start.* See synonym study below. 3 condition of being tried or tested: *be employed for two weeks on trial.* 4 trouble; hardship: *the trials of pioneer life.* 5 cause of trouble or hardship: *be a trial to one's parents.* 6 an attempt to do something; endeavor; effort. —*adj.* 1 made, done, used, or taken as a trial: *a trial model, a trial trip.* 2 of or having to do with a trial in a court of law: *trial testimony.* [< Anglo-French < *trier* to try]

Syn. *n.* 2 **Trial, test, experiment** mean the process of proving the quality of worth of something. **Trial** suggests the purpose of trying out a thing to find out how it works: *Give the car a trial.* **Test** applies to a thorough trial in which the thing tried is measured against a standard or standards: *The new model has been subjected to vigorous tests.* **Experiment** applies to a carefully controlled trial to find out something still unknown or to test conclusions reached: *Experiments indicate the new drug will cure infections.*

trial and error, 1 method of learning by trying out different responses to a new situation until one response is successful. 2 method of arriving at a desired result by repeated experiments until past errors are eliminated.

trial balance, comparison of debit and credit totals in a ledger. If they are not equal, there is an error.

trestle (def. 2)

trial balloon, 1 balloon launched to determine the direction and velocity of wind. 2 plan or project launched on a small scale to determine its acceptability.

trial jury, petit jury.

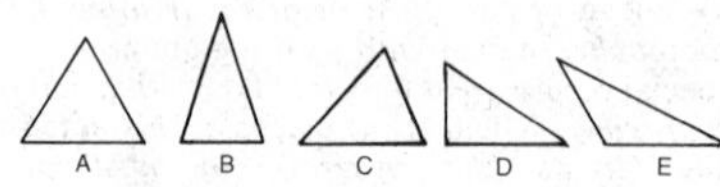

triangle (def. 1)
A, equilateral; B, isosceles;
C, scalene; D, right; E, obtuse

tri an gle (trī′ang′gəl), *n.* 1 a plane figure having three sides and three angles. 2 something shaped like a triangle. 3 a musical instrument consisting of a triangle of steel, upon at one corner, that is struck with a steel rod. 4 group of three. 5 a thin, flat, straight-edged object in the shape of a triangle, usually a right triangle. It is used in drawing parallel, perpendicular, and diagonal lines.

tri an gu lar (trī ang′gyə lər), *adj.* 1 shaped like a triangle; three-cornered. 2 concerned with three persons, groups, etc. 3 having to do with or relating to a triangle. **—tri an′gu lar ly,** *adv.*

tri an gu lar i ty (trī ang′gyə lar′ə tē), *n.* condition of being triangular.

tri an gu late (*v.* trī ang′gyə lāt; *adj.* trī-ang′gyə lit, trī ang′gyə lāt), *v.,* **-lat ed, -lat ing,** *adj.* —*v.t.* 1 divide into triangles. 2 survey or map out (a region) by dividing (it) into triangles and measuring their angles. 3 find by trigonometry: *triangulate the height of a mountain.* 4 make triangular. —*adj.* composed of or marked with triangles.

tri an gu la tion (trī ang′gyə lā′shən), *n.* 1 survey or measurement done by means of trigonometry. 2 the series or network of triangles laid out for such measurements. 3 division into triangles.

Tri as sic (trī as′ik), *n.* 1 the earliest period of the Mesozoic era, during which dinosaurs and primitive mammals first appeared, and reptiles dominated the earth. See chart under **geology.** 2 rocks formed during this period. *—adj.* of or having to do with this period or its rocks. [< German *Trias,* name for a certain series of strata containing three types of deposit < Late Latin *trias* triad < Greek]

trib al (trī′bəl), *adj.* of, having to do with, or characteristic of a tribe or tribes. **—trib′al ly,** *adv.*

trib al ism (trī′bə liz′əm), *n.* 1 condition of existing in separate tribes. 2 tribal relation, feeling, or loyalty.

tribe (trīb), *n.* 1 group of people united by common ancestry and customs, forming a community under a chief or elders: *the American Indian tribes.* 2 such a group forming a division of a larger racial or ethnic group: *the twelve tribes of Israel.* 3 class or set of people: *a tribe of thieves, the whole tribe of gossips.* 4 group of related plants or animals ranking below a family or subfamily and usually containing at least one genus. See **classification** for chart. 5 any group or series of animals or plants. 6 class, kind, group, or sort of things. [< Latin *tribus*]

tribes man (trībz′mən), *n., pl.* **-men.** member of a tribe.

trib u la tion (trib′yə lā′shən), *n.* great trouble; severe trial; affliction. [< Late Latin *tribulationem* < *tribulare* oppress, press < Latin *tribulum* threshing sledge]

tri bu nal (tri byü′nl, trī byü′nl), *n.* 1 court of justice; place of judgment. 2 place where judges sit in a court of law. 3 something by or in which judgment is given; deciding authority: *the tribunal of the press.* [< Latin < *tribunus.* See TRIBUNE[1].]

trib u nate (trib′yə nit, trib′yə nāt), *n.* 1 tribuneship. 2 government by tribunes.

trib une[1] (trib′yün), *n.* 1 in ancient Rome: **a** an official chosen by the plebeians to protect their rights and interests from arbitrary action by the patricians. **b** one of six officers, each of whom in turn commanded a legion in the course of a year. 2 any defender of the rights and interests of the people. [< Latin *tribunus* < *tribus* tribe]

trib une[2] (trib′yün), *n.* a raised platform for a speaker. [< Italian *tribuna* tribunal < Latin *tribunus* tribune[1]]

trib une ship (trib′yən ship), *n.* position, duties, or term of office of a tribune.

trib u tar y (trib′yə ter′ē), *n., pl.* **-tar ies,** *adj. —n.* 1 stream that flows into a larger stream or body of water: *The Ohio River is a tributary of the Mississippi River.* 2 person or country that pays tribute. *—adj.* 1 flowing into a larger stream or body of water. 2 paying tribute; required to pay tribute. 3 paid as tribute; of the nature of tribute. 4 contributing; helping.

trib ute (trib′yüt), *n.* 1 money paid by one nation or ruler to another for peace or protection, in acknowledgment of submission, or because of some agreement. 2 any forced payment. 3 obligation or necessity of paying tribute. 4 tax or payment to raise money for tribute. 5 an acknowledgment of thanks or respect; compliment: *Memorial Day is a tribute to our dead soldiers.* [< Latin *tributum* < *tribuere* allot < *tribus* tribe]

trice[1] (trīs), *v.t.,* **triced, tric ing.** haul up and fasten with a rope: *trice up a sail.* [< Middle Dutch *trisen* hoist < *trise* pulley]

trice[2] (trīs), *n.* 1 a very short time; moment; instant. 2 **in a trice,** in an instant; immediately. [use of *trice*[1] < phrase *at a trice* at a pull]

tri ceps (trī′seps), *n.* the large muscle at the back of the upper arm which extends or straightens the arm. See **biceps** for diagram. [< Latin, three-headed < *tri-* three + *caput* head]

tri cer a tops (trī ser′ə tops), *n.* dinosaur of the Cretaceous period of western North America, with a large horn above each eye and a smaller horn on the nose, a bony collar extending from the neck, and a long and powerful tail. [< Greek *trikeratos* three-horned + *ōps* face]

tri chi na (tri kī′nə), *n., pl.* **-nae** (-nē). a small, slender nematode worm whose adult form inhabits the intestinal tract of man, pigs, and various other mammals, and whose larvae migrate to the muscular tissue and become encysted there. Trichinae usually get into the human body from pork which is infected with the larvae and is not cooked long enough to destroy them. [< New Latin < Greek *trichine* of hair < *trichos* hair]

trich i no sis (trik′ə nō′sis), *n.* disease caused by trichinae, characterized by headache, chills, fever, and soreness of muscles.

trich i nous (trik′ə nəs, trə kī′nəs), *adj.* of or having trichinosis; infected with trichinae.

trich o cyst (trik′ə sist), *n.* one of the tiny stinging or grasping organs on the body of certain infusorians, consisting of a hairlike filament in a small sac. [< Greek *trichos* hair + English *cyst*]

tri chop ter an (tri kop′tər ən), *n.* any of an order of soft-bodied insects having two pairs of membranous wings covered with fine, silky, hairlike structures and having mouthparts suitable for chewing; caddis fly. [< Greek *trichos* a hair + *pteron* a wing]

trick (trik), *n.* 1 something done to deceive or cheat: *The false message was a trick to get him to leave the house.* 2 a deceptive appearance; illusion: *a trick of the eyesight, a trick of the imagination.* 3 a clever act; feat of skill: *We enjoyed the tricks of the trained animals.* 4 the best way of doing or dealing with something; knack: *the trick of making pies.* 5 piece of mischief; prank: *Stealing his lunch was a mean trick.* 6 a peculiar habit or way of acting: *He has a trick of pulling at his collar.* 7 the cards played in one round of a card game. 8 turn or period of duty on a job, especially at steering a ship. 9 INFORMAL. a child, especially a young girl. 10 **do the trick** or **turn the trick,** do what one wants done.
—adj. 1 of, like, or done as a trick or stunt: *trick riding.* 2 skilled in or trained to do tricks: *a trick dog.*
—v.t. 1 deceive by a trick; cheat: *We were tricked into buying a poor car.* See **cheat** for synonym study. 2 dress. *—v.i.* play tricks. [< Old North French *trique* < *trikier* to trick, cheat] **—trick′er,** *n.*

trick er y (trik′ər ē), *n., pl.* **-er ies.** use of tricks; deception.

trick le (trik′əl), *v.,* **-led, -ling,** *n. —v.i.* 1 flow or fall in drops or in a small stream: *Tears trickled down her cheeks. The brook trickled through the valley.* 2 come, go, pass, etc., slowly and unevenly: *An hour before the show people began to trickle into the theater.* *—v.t.* cause to flow in drops or in a small stream: *trickle water into a container.* *—n.* 1 a small flow or stream. 2 a trickling. [Middle English *triklen*]

hat, āge, fär; let, ēqual, tėrm;
it, īce; hot, ōpen, ôrder;
oil, out; cup, pu̇t, rüle;
ch, child; ng, long; sh, she;
th, thin; ᴛʜ, then; zh, measure;
ə represents *a* in about, *e* in taken, *i* in pencil, *o* in lemon, *u* in circus.
< = from, derived from, taken from.

trick or treat, custom of going from door to door on Halloween dressed in costume and asking for treats of candy, fruit, etc., by saying "trick or treat."

trick ster (trik′stər), *n.* person who practices trickery; cheat; deceiver.

trick sy (trik′sē), *adj.* 1 mischievous; playful; frolicsome. 2 tricky. 3 spruce; smart. **—trick′si ness,** *n.*

trick y (trik′ē), *adj.,* **trick i er, trick i est.** 1 full of tricks; deceiving; cheating. 2 not doing what is expected; dangerous or difficult to handle: *The back door has a tricky lock.* **—trick′i ly,** *adv.* **—trick′i ness,** *n.*

tri clin ic (trī klin′ik), *adj.* (of crystals or crystallization) having the three axes unequal and obliquely inclined.

tri col or (trī′kul′ər), *adj.* having three colors. *—n.* flag having three colors: *the tricolor of France.*

tri col ored (trī′kul′ərd), *adj.* having three colors: *a tricolored flag.*

tri corn (trī′kôrn), *adj.* having three horns or hornlike projections. *—n.* a tricorn hat. [< Latin *tricornis*]

tri cot (trē′kō), *n.* 1 a knitted fabric of wool, cotton, rayon, nylon, etc., made by hand or machine. 2 kind of woolen fabric. [< French]

tric o tine (trik′ə tēn′), *n.* kind of twilled woolen fabric.

tri cus pid (trī kus′pid), *adj.* 1 having three points or cusps. 2 of or having to do with the tricuspid valve. *—n.* 1 a tricuspid tooth. 2 tricuspid valve.

tricuspid valve, valve of three segments opening from the right auricle into the right ventricle of the heart.

tri cy cle (trī′sə kəl, trī′sik′əl), *n.* a small, light vehicle having three wheels, one in front and one on each side behind, worked by pedals or handles.

tri dent (trīd′nt), *n.* a three-pronged spear. *—adj.* three-pronged. [< Latin *tridentem* < *tri-* three + *dentem* tooth]

tri den tate (trī den′tāt), *adj.* having three teeth or toothlike points; three-pronged.

tri di men sion al (trī′də men′shə nəl), *adj.* three-dimensional.

tri e cious (trī ē′shəs), *adj.* trioecious. **—tri e′cious ly,** *adv.*

tried (trīd), *adj.* tested by experience or examination; proved: *a person of tried abilities.* *—v.* pt. and pp. of **try.**

tri en ni al (trī en′ē əl), *adj.* 1 lasting three years. 2 occurring every three years. *—n.* event that occurs every three years. [< Latin *triennium* three-year period < *tri-* three + *annus* year] **—tri en′ni al ly,** *adv.*

tri er (trī′ər), *n.* person or thing that tries.

tries (trīz), *n.* pl. of **try.** *—v.* 3rd person singular, present tense of **try.**

Tri este (trē est′), *n.* seaport in NE Italy. It was under administration of the United Nations from 1947 to 1954 as part of the **Free Territory of Trieste.** 278,000.

tri fa cial (trī fā′shəl), *adj., n.* trigeminal.

tri fid (trī′fid), *adj.* divided into three parts by clefts. [< Latin *trifidus* < *tri-* three + *findere* cleave]

tri fle (trī′fəl), *n., v.,* **-fled, -fling.** —*n.* 1 thing having little value or importance. 2 a small amount; little bit: *I was a trifle late.* 3 a small amount of money: *buy something for a trifle.* 4 a rich dessert made of sponge cake soaked in wine or liqueur, and served with whipped cream, custard, fruit, etc. —*v.i.* 1 talk or act lightly, not seriously: *Don't trifle with serious matters.* See synonym study below. 2 handle or finger a thing idly; play or toy *(with): He trifled with his pencil.* —*v.t.* spend (time, effort, money, etc.) on things having little value; waste: *She had trifled away the whole morning.* [< Old French *trufle* mockery, diminutive of *truffe* deception] **—tri′fler,** *n.*

Syn. *v.i.* 1 **Trifle, dally** mean to treat a person or thing without seriousness. **Trifle,** the more general term, suggests treating too lightly something or someone that deserves seriousness or respect: *He is not a man to be trifled with.* **Dally** suggests the absence of any serious purpose or intent: *I have dallied with the idea of becoming a writer.*

tri fling (trī′fling), *adj.* 1 having little value; not important. 2 frivolous; shallow. **—tri′fling ly,** *adv.* **—tri′fling ness,** *n.*

tri fo cal (trī fō′kəl, trī′fō′kəl), *adj.* having three focuses. Trifocal lenses have three sections of different focal lengths. —*n.* 1 **trifocals,** *pl.* pair of glasses having trifocal lenses. 2 a trifocal lens.

tri fo li ate (trī fō′lē it, trī fō′lē āt), *adj.* having three leaves, or three parts like leaves. Clover is trifoliate.

tri fo li at ed (trī fō′lē ā′tid), *adj.* trifoliate.

tri fo ri um (trī fôr′ē əm, trī fōr′ē əm), *n., pl.* **-fo ri a** (-fôr′ē ə, -fōr′ē ə). gallery in a church above a side aisle or transept. [< Medieval Latin]

trig (trig), *adj.* neat; trim; smart-looking. [< Scandinavian (Old Icelandic) *tryggr* trusty]

trig., 1 trigonometric. 2 trigonometry.

tri gem i nal (trī jem′ə nəl), *adj.* of or denoting the fifth pair of cranial nerves, each of which divides into three branches having sensory and motor functions in the face. —*n.* a trigeminal nerve. [< Latin *trigeminus* born three < *tri-* three + *geminus* born together]

trig ger (trig′ər), *n.* 1 the small lever on the underside of a gun that is pulled back by the finger to release the hammer or other mechanism which fires the gun. 2 lever pulled or pressed to release a spring, catch, etc., and set some mechanism in action. 3 anything that sets off or initiates something else. 4 **quick on the trigger, a** quick to shoot. **b** INFORMAL. quick to act; mentally alert. —*v.t.* 1 set off (an explosion). 2 INFORMAL. initiate; start: *trigger violence.* [< Dutch *trekker* < *trekken* to pull]

trig ger-hap py (trig′ər hap′ē), *adj.* INFORMAL. inclined to shoot or attack at the slightest provocation; overly aggressive or belligerent.

tri glyph (trī′glif), *n.* part of a Doric frieze between two metopes, consisting typically of a rectangular block with two vertical grooves and a half groove at each side. See **metope** for picture. [< Greek *triglyphos* < *tri-* three + *glyphē* a carving]

trigon., trigonometry.

trig o no met ric (trig′ə nə met′rik), *adj.* of, having to do with, or based on trigonometry. **—trig′o no met′ri cal ly,** *adv.*

trig o no met ri cal (trig′ə nə met′rə kəl), *adj.* trigonometric.

trigonometric functions, the six functions sine, cosine, tangent, cotangent, secant, and cosecant.

trig o nom e try (trig′ə nom′ə trē), *n.* branch of mathematics that deals with the relations between the sides and angles of triangles and the calculations based on these. [ultimately < Greek *tri-* three + *gōnia* angle + *metron* measure]

tri graph (trī graf), *n.* three letters used to spell a single sound. The *eau* in *beau* is a trigraph.

tri he dral (trī hē′drəl), *adj.* having, or formed by, three planes meeting at a point: *a trihedral angle.*

tri he dron (trī hē′drən), *n., pl.* **-drons, -dra** (-drə). figure formed by three planes meeting at a point. [< *tri-* + Greek *hedra* seat, base]

tri lat er al (trī lat′ər əl), *adj.* having three sides. **—tri lat′er al ly,** *adv.*

tri lin gual (trī ling′gwəl), *adj.* 1 able to speak three languages. 2 using three languages: *Switzerland is a trilingual country.* 3 written or expressed in three languages: *a trilingual text.*

trill (tril), *v.t., v.i.* 1 sing, play, sound, or speak with a tremulous, vibrating sound. 2 (in music) sing or play with a trill. 3 (in phonetics) pronounce with a trill. —*n.* 1 act or sound of trilling. 2 a quick alternation of two musical notes either a tone or a half tone apart. 3 in phonetics: **a** a rapid vibration of the lips, the tip of the tongue, or the uvula. **b** sound produced by such a vibration. Spanish *rr* is a trill. [< Italian *trillare*]

tril lion (tril′yən), *n., adj.* 1 (in the United States, Canada, and France) 1 followed by 12 zeros. 2 (in Great Britain and Germany) 1 followed by 18 zeros. [< *tri-* + *(m)illion*]

tril lionth (tril′yənth), *adj., n.* 1 last in a series of a trillion. 2 one, or being one, of a trillion equal parts.

tril li um (tril′ē əm), *n.* any of a genus of perennial herbs of the lily family, bearing a whorl of three thin, short-stalked or stalkless leaves at the summit of an unbranched stem, with a solitary flower in the middle; wakerobin. [< New Latin < Latin *tri-* three]

tri lo bate (trī lō′bāt, trī′lə bāt), *adj.* having or divided into three lobes: *a trilobate leaf.*

tri lo bat ed (trī lō′bā tid), *adj.* trilobate.

tri lobed (trī′lōbd′), *adj.* trilobate.

tri lo bite (trī′lə bīt), *n.* any of a class of small, extinct marine arthropods of the Paleozoic era, with jointed legs and a body divided into three vertical lobes and many horizontal segments. Fossil trilobites are widely found in various rocks. [< Greek *tri-* three + *lobos* lobe]

tri lo bit ic (trī′lə bit′ik), *adj.* of or having to do with trilobites.

tril o gy (tril′ə jē), *n., pl.* **-gies.** group of three plays, operas, novels, etc., which together form a related series, although each is complete in itself. [< *tri-* + *-logy*]

trim (trim), *v.,* **trimmed, trim ming,** *adj.,* **trim mer, trim mest,** *n., adv.* —*v.t.* 1 put in good order; make neat by cutting away parts: *trim a hedge, trim lumber with a plane.* 2 remove (parts that are not needed or not neat): *trim off dead branches.* 3 decorate; adorn: *trim a dress with braid, trim a Christmas tree.* 4 balance (a boat, aircraft, etc.) by arranging the load carried. 5 balance (an aircraft) so that it maintains level flight with main controls in neutral positions. 6 arrange (the sails) to fit the direction of the wind and the course to be sailed. 7 change (opinions, etc.) to suit circumstances. 8 INFORMAL. **a** defeat; beat. **b** scold; rebuke. **c** cheat; fleece. —*v.i.* 1 be or keep in balance. 2 maintain a middle course or balance between opposing interests.

—*adj.* 1 in good condition or order; neat. See **neat**[1] for synonym study. 2 well designed and maintained: *a trim little ketch.*

—*n.* 1 good condition or order: *get in trim for a race, put one's affairs in trim.* 2 condition; order: *That ship is in poor trim for a voyage.* 3 trimming: *the trim on a dress.* 4 equipment; outfit. 5 the condition, manner, or degree of horizontal balance of a ship in the water. 6 the position or angle of the sails, etc., in relation to the direction of the wind. 7 the visible woodwork inside a building, especially that around doors, windows, and other openings. 8 woodwork on the outside of a building used as ornamentation or finish. 9 the upholstery, handles, and accessories inside an automobile. 10 the chrome, color scheme, etc., decorating the outside of an automobile.

—*adv.* in a trim manner.

[probably Old English *trymman* strengthen, make ready] **—trim′ly,** *adv.* **—trim′ness,** *n.*

tri ma ran (trī′mə ran′), *n.* boat with three hulls side by side. [< *tri-* + *(cata)maran*]

tri mes ter (trī mes′tər), *n.* 1 period or term of three months. 2 a division (usually one third) of a school year. [< Latin *trimestris* of three months' duration < *tri-* three + *mensis* month]

trim e ter (trim′ə tər), *n.* line of verse having three metrical feet. EXAMPLE: "Below′ | the light′ | house top.′"

trim mer (trim′ər), *n.* 1 person or thing that trims. 2 person who changes his opinions, actions, etc., to suit the circumstances. 3 machine for trimming edges, as of lumber. 4 a long beam or timber to which the end of a header is attached in the frame around a window, chimney, or other opening.

trim ming (trim′ing), *n.* 1 anything used to trim or decorate; decoration; ornament: *trimmings for a Christmas tree, trimming for a dress.* 2 INFORMAL. a defeat; beating. 3 act of a person or thing that trims. 4 **trimmings,** *pl.* **a** parts cut away in trimming. **b** INFORMAL. everything needed to make something complete and festive: *roast turkey with all the trimmings.*

tri month ly (trī munth′lē), *adj.* occurring every three months.

tri nal (trī′nl), *adj.* composed of three parts; triple.

trine (trīn), *adj.* threefold; triple. [< Latin *trinus* triple]

Trin i dad (trin′ə dad), *n.* island in the West Indies, near Venezuela, part of the country of Trinidad and Tobago. 1,025,000 pop.; 1900 sq. mi. **—Trin′i dad′i an,** *adj., n.*

Trinidad and Tobago, country in the West Indies, consisting of the islands of Trinidad and Tobago. It is a member of the Commonwealth of Nations. 1,070,000 pop.; 2000 sq. mi. *Capital:* Port-of-Spain.

hat, āge, fär; let, ēqual, tėrm;
it, īce; hot, ōpen, ôrder;
oil, out; cup, pu̇t, rüle;
ch, child; ng, long; sh, she;
th, thin; ᴛʜ, then; zh, measure;

ə represents *a* in about, *e* in taken, *i* in pencil, *o* in lemon, *u* in circus.

< = from, derived from, taken from.

Trin i tar i an (trin′ə ter′ē ən), *adj.* 1 believing in the Trinity. 2 having to do with the Trinity or with those who believe in the Trinity. *—n.* person who believes in the Trinity.

Trin i tar i an ism (trin′ə ter′ē ə niz′əm), *n.* doctrine of Trinitarians; belief in the Trinity.

tri ni tro tol u ene (trī nī′trō tol′yü ēn′), *n.* TNT.

trin i ty (trin′ə tē), *n.* 1 group of three. 2 a being three. 3 **Trinity,** the union of Father, Son, and Holy Ghost in one divine nature. 4 Trinity Sunday. [< Latin *trinitatem* < *trinus* triple]

Trinity Sunday, the eighth Sunday after Easter.

trin ket (tring′kit), *n.* 1 any small fancy article, bit of jewelry, or the like. 2 trifle. [origin uncertain]

tri no mi al (trī nō′mē əl), *n.* 1 expression in algebra consisting of three terms connected by plus or minus signs. $a + bx^2 - 2$ is a trinomial. 2 scientific name of an animal or plant consisting of three terms, the first indicating the genus, the second the species, and the third the subspecies or variety. *—adj.* consisting of three terms. [< *tri-* + *-nomial,* as in *binomial*]

tri o (trē′ō), *n., pl.* **tri os.** 1 piece of music for three voices or instruments. 2 group of three singers or players performing together. 3 any group of three. [< Italian < Latin *tri-, tres* three]

tri ode (trī′ōd), *n.* vacuum tube containing three elements, commonly a cathode, an anode, and a grid.

tri oe cious (trī ē′shəs), *adj.* having male, female, and hermaphrodite flowers on different plants of the same group. Also, **triecious.** [< Greek *tri-* three + *oikos* house] **—tri oe′cious ly,** *adv.*

tri o let (trī′ə lit), *n.* poem having eight lines and only two rhymes, with line 1 repeated as lines 4 and 7, and line 2 repeated as line 8. [< French]

tri ox ide (trī ok′sīd, trī ok′sid), *n.* oxide having three atoms of oxygen in each molecule.

trip (trip), *n., v.,* **tripped, trip ping.** *—n.* 1 a traveling about; journey; voyage: *a trip to Europe, a short business trip.* See synonym study below. 2 loss of footing; stumble; slip. 3 act of catching a person's foot to throw him down, especially in wrestling. 4 mistake; blunder. 5 a light, quick tread; stepping lightly. 6 device that releases a catch, lever, etc. 7 a projecting part, catch, or the like for starting or checking some movement. 8 a starting or stopping of a movement in this way. 9 SLANG. hallucination or heightened perception experienced under the influence of LSD or a similar psychedelic drug.

—v.i. 1 strike the foot against something so as to stagger or fall; stumble: *trip on the stairs.* 2 make a mistake; do something wrong: *trip on a difficult question.* 3 take light, quick steps: *She tripped across the floor.* 4 tilt; tip. 5 SLANG. experience a hallucination or heightened perception under the influence of LSD or a similar psychedelic drug. *—v.t.* 1 cause to stumble or fall: *The loose board on the stairs tripped me.* 2 cause to make a mistake or blunder. 3 overthrow by catching in a mistake or blunder; outwit. 4 perform (a dance) with a light, quick step. 5 release or operate suddenly (a catch, clutch, etc.); operate, start, or set free (a mechanism, weight, etc.). [< Old French *tripper;* of Germanic origin]

Syn. *n.* 1 **Trip, journey, voyage** mean a traveling from one place to another. **Trip** is the general word, often suggesting a run between two places, but not suggesting the length, purpose, manner, or means of travel: *It's only a half-hour's trip from here to the bank.* **Journey** suggests a long or tiring trip by land to a place for a definite purpose: *She decided to make the journey to Mexico by car.* **Voyage** suggests a long trip by water: *The voyage to the Islands will be restful.*

tri par tite (trī pär′tīt), *adj.* 1 divided into three parts. 2 having three corresponding parts or copies. 3 made or shared by three parties: *a tripartite treaty between Great Britain, the United States, and France.* **—tri par′tite ly,** *adv.*

tripe (trīp), *n.* 1 the walls of the first and second stomachs of an ox, steer, or cow, used as food. 2 SLANG. something foolish, worthless, or offensive. [< Old French, entrails]

trip ham mer (trip′ham′ər), *n.* a heavy iron or steel block raised by machinery and then tripped by a mechanism and allowed to drop.

triph thong (trif′thông, trif′thong; trip′thông, trip′thong), *n.* 1 combination of three vowel sounds in one syllable. 2 trigraph. [< *tri-* + *(di)phthong*]

tri ple (trip′əl), *adj., n., v.,* **-pled, -pling.** *—adj.* 1 three times as much, as many, as large, as strong, etc. 2 having three parts; threefold. *—n.* 1 number or amount that is three times as much. 2 (in baseball) hit by which a batter gets to third base. *—v.t.* make three times as much or as many: *triple one's income.* *—v.i.* 1 become three times as much or as many. 2 (in baseball) hit a triple. [< Latin *triplus* < *tri-* three + *-plus* fold. Doublet of TREBLE.]

Triple Alliance, alliance of Germany, Austria-Hungary, and Italy from 1882 to 1915.

Triple Entente, an informal alliance of Great Britain, France, and Russia from about 1904 to 1917 that served to counterbalance the Triple Alliance.

triple play, play in baseball in which three base runners are put out.

tri plet (trip′lit), *n.* 1 one of three children born at the same time to the same mother. 2 group of three. 3 (in music) group of three notes of equal value to be performed in the time of two. 4 three successive lines of poetry, usually rhyming and equal in length.

triple threat, a football player who can pass, kick, and run with the ball adeptly.

triple time, (in music) time or rhythm having three beats to the measure.

tri plex (trip′leks, trī′pleks), *adj.* triple; threefold. [< Latin < *tri-* three + *plicare* to fold]

trip li cate (*adj., n.* trip′lə kit; *v.* trip′lə kāt), *v.,* **-cat ed, -cat ing.** *—adj.* triple; threefold. *—n.* 1 one of three things exactly alike. 2 **in triplicate,** in three copies exactly alike. *—v.t.* multiply by three; make threefold; triple. **—trip′li ca′tion,** *n.*

tri ply (trip′lē), *adv.* in a triple manner; three times.

tri pod (trī′pod), *n.* 1 a three-legged support for a camera, telescope, etc. 2 stool or other article having three legs. [< Latin < Greek *tripodos* < *tri-* three + *podos* foot]

trip o dal (trip′ə dəl, trī pod′l), *adj.* three-footed; three-legged.

Trip o li (trip′ə lē), *n.* 1 region in N Africa, one of the Barbary States. It was a Turkish province and later an Italian colony; it is now the province of Tripolitania. 2 seaport and one of two capitals of Libya, in the NW part. The other is Benghazi. 245,000. 3 city in NW Lebanon, on the Mediterranean. 150,000.

Trip o li ta ni a (trip′ə lə tā′nē ə), *n.* province of Libya, in the NW part. **—Trip′o li ta′ni an,** *adj., n.*

trip per (trip′ər), *n.* 1 person or thing that trips. 2 device or mechanism that releases a catch in a railroad signal, machine, etc. 3 BRITISH. person who takes a trip; tourist.

trip ping (trip′ing), *adj.* light and quick. **—trip′ping ly,** *adv.*

trip tych (trip′tik), *n.* 1 set of three panels side by side, having pictures, carvings, or the like, on them. 2 (in ancient Greece and Rome) a hinged, three-leaved writing tablet. [< Greek *triptychos* triple-folded < *tri-* three + *ptychē* a fold]

trip wire, wire which, when pulled or disturbed, releases a catch and starts a process, as the explosion of a mine, the sounding of an alarm, etc.

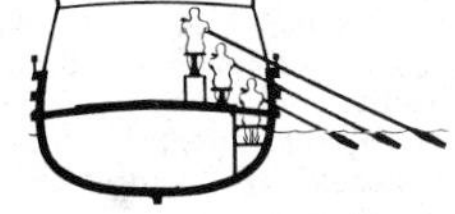

trireme—The diagram shows the position of the rowers.

tri reme (trī′rēm′), *n.* (in ancient Greece and Rome) a ship, usually a warship, with three rows of oars on each side, one above the other. [< Latin *triremis* < *tri-* three + *remus* oar]

tri sac cha ride (trī sak′ə rīd′, trī sak′ər-id), *n.* any of a class of carbohydrates which on hydrolysis yields three molecules of simple sugars (monosaccharides).

tri sect (trī sekt′), *v.t.* 1 divide into three parts. 2 divide into three equal parts. [< *tri-* + Latin *sectum* cut] **—tri sec′tion,** *n.* **—tri sec′tor,** *n.*

tri shaw (trī′shô), *n.* pedicab. [< *tri(cycle)* + *(rick)shaw*]

Tris tan (tris′tən), *n.* (in Arthurian legends) a knight of the Round Table who loved Iseult, wife of King Mark. This legend is the subject of many stories and poems and of an opera by Richard Wagner. Also, **Tristram.**

tri-state (trī′stāt′), *adj.* U.S. of or involving three adjoining states or the adjoining parts of three such states.

triste (trēst), *adj.* FRENCH. sad; melancholy; gloomy.

Tris tram (tris′trəm), *n.* Tristan.

tri syl lab ic (tris′ə lab′ik, trī′sə lab′ik), *adj.* having three syllables. **—tri′syl lab′i cal ly,** *adv.*

tri syl la ble (tri sil′ə bəl, trī sil′ə bəl), *n.*

word of three syllables. *Educate* is a trisyllable.

trite (trīt), *adj.*, **trit er, trit est.** worn out by use; no longer new or interesting; commonplace; hackneyed: *"Cheeks like roses" is a trite expression.* See **commonplace** for synonym study. [< Latin *tritum* rubbed away] **—trite′ly,** *adv.* **—trite′ness,** *n.*

trit i um (trit′ē əm, trish′ē əm), *n.* isotope of hydrogen, three times as heavy as ordinary hydrogen. It is the explosive used in a hydrogen bomb. *Symbol:* T or H^3; *atomic number* 1; *mass number* 3. [< New Latin < Greek *tritos* third]

tri ton (trīt′n), *n.* 1 any of various large marine gastropods having a brightly colored, spiral, trumpet-shaped shell. 2 shell of such an animal. [< *Triton*]

Tri ton (trīt′n), *n.* (in Greek myths) a sea god, son of Poseidon, having the head and body of a man and the tail of a fish and carrying a trumpet made of a conch shell.

trit ur a ble (trich′ər ə bəl), *adj.* capable of being triturated.

trit u rate (*v.* trich′ə rāt′; *n.* trich′ər it, trich′ə rāt′), *v.*, **-rat ed, -rat ing,** *n.* *—v.t.* rub, crush, grind, or pound into a very fine powder. *—n.* any substance that is ground into a very fine powder or fine particles. [< Late Latin *trituratum* threshed, ultimately < Latin *terere* to rub] **—trit′u ra′tion,** *n.* **—trit′u ra′tor,** *n.*

tri umph (trī′umf), *n.* 1 victory; success: *final triumph over the enemy, a triumph of modern science.* See **victory** for synonym study. 2 joy because of victory or success. 3 (in ancient Rome) procession in honor of a general for an important victory over an enemy. 4 **in triumph,** a triumphant. b triumphantly. *—v.i.* 1 gain victory; win success: *Our team triumphed over theirs.* 2 rejoice because of victory or success. [< Latin *triumphus*]

tri um phal (trī um′fəl), *adj.* of, for, or of the nature of a triumph; celebrating a victory.

tri um phant (trī um′fənt), *adj.* 1 victorious or successful: *a triumphant army.* 2 rejoicing because of victory or success. **—tri um′phant ly,** *adv.*

tri um vir (trī um′vər), *n., pl.* **-virs, -vi ri** (-və rī′). 1 one of three men who shared the same public office in ancient Rome. 2 one of any three persons sharing power or authority. [< Latin < the phrase *trium virorum* of three men]

tri um vir ate (trī um′vər it, trī um′və rāt′), *n.* 1 government by three men together. 2 any association of three in office or authority. 3 position or term of office of a Roman triumvir. 4 any group of three.

tri une (trī′yün), *adj.* consisting of three in one, especially the Trinity: *the triune God.* [< *tri-* + Latin *unus* one]

tri u ni ty (trī yü′nə tē), *n.* a being three in one.

tri va lence (trī vā′ləns), *n.* state or quality of being trivalent.

tri va len cy (trī vā′lən sē), *n.* trivalence.

tri va lent (trī vā′lənt), *adj.* having a valence of three.

triv et (triv′it), *n.* 1 a small, usually three-legged iron frame used under a hot dish to protect the surface of a table. 2 a three-legged stand for supporting a pot or kettle over an open fire. [Old English *trefet*]

triv i a (triv′ē ə), *n.pl.* 1 things of little or no importance; trifles; trivialities. 2 pl. of **trivium.**

triv i al (triv′ē əl), *adj.* 1 not important; trifling; insignificant. 2 ARCHAIC. not new or interesting; ordinary. [< Latin *trivialis,* originally, of the crossroads, ultimately < *tri-* three + *via* road] **—triv′i al ly,** *adv.*

triv i al i ty (triv′ē al′ə tē), *n., pl.* **-ties.** 1 trivial quality. 2 a trivial thing, remark, affair, etc.; trifle.

triv i um (triv′ē əm), *n., pl.* **triv i a.** (in ancient Rome and in the Middle Ages) grammar, rhetoric, and logic, the first three of the seven liberal arts. [< Medieval Latin < Latin, triple road or way, crossroads]

tri week ly (trī wēk′lē), *adv., n., pl.* **-lies,** *adj.* *—adv.* 1 once every three weeks. 2 three times a week. *—n.* newspaper or magazine published triweekly. *—adj.* occurring or appearing triweekly.

tro cha ic (trō kā′ik), *adj.* of trochees.

tro che (trō′kē), *n.* a small medicinal tablet or lozenge, usually round and often sweetened: *cough troches.* [< obsolete *trochisk* < Greek *trochiskos,* diminutive of *trochos* wheel]

tro chee (trō′kē), *n.* a foot or measure in poetry consisting of two syllables, the first accented and the second unaccented or the first long and the second short. EXAMPLE: "Sing′ a | song′ of | six′pence." [< Middle French *trochée* < Greek *trochaios,* originally, running < *trochos* a course < *trechein* to run]

troch o phore (trok′ə fôr, trok′ə fōr), *n.* a free-swimming, ciliate larval form of most mollusks and of certain bryozoans, brachiopods, and marine worms. [< Greek *trochos* wheel + *-phoros* carrying]

trod (trod), *v.* a pt. and a pp. of **tread.**

trod den (trod′n), *v.* a pp. of **tread.**

trog lo dyte (trog′lə dīt), *n.* 1 a cave dweller; cave man. 2 person living in seclusion; hermit. 3 an anthropoid ape, such as a gorilla or chimpanzee. [< Greek *trōglodytēs* < *trōglē* cave + *dyein* go in]

trog lo dyt ic (trog′lə dit′ik), *adj.* of or having to do with troglodytes.

troi ka (troi′kə), *n.* 1 a Russian carriage, wagon, sleigh, etc., pulled by three horses harnessed abreast. 2 (in Russia) a team of three horses. 3 a triumvirate. [< Russian *trojka* < *tri* three]

Troi lus (troi′ləs, trō′i ləs), *n.* 1 (in Greek legends) a son of King Priam of Troy, killed by Achilles. 2 (in medieval legends) the lover of Cressida.

Tro jan (trō′jən), *adj.* of Troy; having to do with Troy or its people. *—n.* 1 native or inhabitant of Troy. 2 person who shows courage or energy: *They all worked like Trojans.*

Trojan horse, 1 (in Greek legends) a huge wooden horse in which the Greeks concealed soldiers and brought them into Troy during the Trojan War; wooden horse. 2 an enemy group stationed inside a country to sabotage its industry and defense preparations. 3 any person or thing that destroys or subverts from within.

Trojan War, (in Greek legends) a ten years' war carried on by the Greeks against Troy to get back Helen, wife of King Menelaus of Sparta, who was carried off by Paris, son of King Priam of Troy. It ended with the plundering and destruction of Troy.

troll[1] (trōl), *v.t.* 1 sing (something) in a full, rolling voice. 2 sing in succession. When three people troll a round or catch, the soprano sings one line, the alto comes in next with the same line, and then the bass sings it, and so on, while the others keep on singing. 3 draw (a line, baited hook, lure, etc.) continuously through the water, especially from the stern of a moving boat. 4 fish in (a body of water) by trolling. *—v.i.* 1 sing in a full, rolling voice; sing merrily or jovially. 2 fish by trolling: *troll for bass.* *—n.* 1 song whose parts are sung in succession; round; catch: *"Three Blind Mice" is a well-known troll.* 2 a fishing lure or bait, especially one used for trolling. [probably < Old French *troller* wander; of Germanic origin] **—troll′er,** *n.*

troll[2] (trōl), *n.* (in Scandinavian folklore) an ugly dwarf or giant with supernatural powers, living underground or in caves. [< Scandinavian (Swedish)]

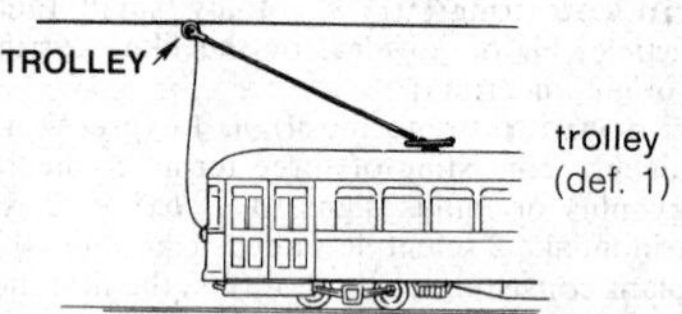

trolley (def. 1)

trol ley (trol′ē), *n., pl.* **-leys.** 1 pulley at the end of a pole which moves against a wire to carry electricity to a streetcar, trolley bus, electric engine, etc. 2 trolley car. 3 basket, carriage, etc., suspended from a pulley which runs on an overhead track. 4 BRITISH. any of various handcarts. Also, **trolly.** [probably < *troll*[1]]

trolley bus, a passenger bus drawing power from an overhead electric wire by means of a trolley.

trolley car, streetcar drawing power from an overhead wire by means of a trolley.

trol lop (trol′əp), *n.* 1 an untidy or slovenly woman; slattern. 2 a morally loose woman; slut. 3 prostitute. [probably < *troll*[1]]

Trol lope (trol′əp), *n.* **Anthony,** 1815-1882, English novelist.

trol ly (trol′ē), *n., pl.* **-lies.** trolley.

trombone

trom bone (trom′bōn, trom bōn′), *n.* a large, loud-toned brass wind instrument with a cupped mouthpiece, consisting of a long, cylindrical tube bent twice upon itself and expanding into a bell at one end. It usually has a sliding piece for varying the length of the tube and thus producing different tones. [< Italian < *tromba* trumpet]

trom bon ist (trom′bō nist, trom bō′nist), *n.* person who plays the trombone.

-tron, *combining form.* 1 having to do with electrons, as in *cryotron, magnetron.* 2 device for directing subatomic particles, as in *cyclotron, synchrotron.* [< *(elec)tron*]

troop (trüp), *n.* 1 group or band of persons: *a troop of boys.* 2 herd, flock, or swarm: *a troop of deer.* 3 a military unit of cavalry, especially an armored cavalry unit, usually commanded by a captain and corresponding to a company or battery in other branches of the army. 4 **troops,** *pl.* soldiers: *The government sent troops to put down the revolt.* 5 unit of boy scouts or girl scouts made up of two to four patrols or 16 to 32 members. *—v.i.* 1 gather in a group or groups; move or come together; flock: *The children trooped around the teacher.* 2 walk; go; go away: *The young boys trooped off after the older ones.* [< Old French *troupe,* ultimately < Late Latin *troppus* herd]

troop carrier, a transport aircraft used to carry troops.

troop er (trü′pər), *n.* 1 soldier in a troop of cavalry. 2 a mounted policeman. 3 member of any of certain state police forces which were originally organized as mounted troops. 4 a cavalry horse.

troop ship (trüp′ship′), *n.* ship used to carry soldiers; transport.

trope (trōp), *n.* 1 the figurative use of a word or phrase. 2 figure of speech. [< Greek *tropos, tropē* turn]

troph ic (trof′ik), *adj.* of or having to do with nutrition. [< Greek *trophē* nourishment] **—troph′i cal ly,** *adv.*

tro phied (trō′fēd), *adj.* decorated with trophies: *trophied walls.*

tro phy (trō′fē), *n., pl.* **-phies.** 1 a spoil or prize of war, hunting, etc., especially if displayed as a memorial: *The hunter kept the lion's skin and head as trophies.* 2 any prize, cup, etc., awarded to a victorious person or team: *a tennis trophy.* 3 (in ancient Greece and Rome) a structure consisting of the captured arms, flags, etc., of a defeated enemy set up on the field of battle or elsewhere as a memorial of victory. 4 any similar monument or memorial. 5 anything serving as a remembrance. [< Middle French *trophée* < Latin *trophaeum, tropaeum* < Greek *tropaion* < *tropē* rout, originally, turn < *trepein* to turn]

trop ic (trop′ik), *n.* 1 either of two parallels of latitude on the earth's surface, one 23.45 degrees north (**tropic of Cancer**) and one 23.45 degrees south of the equator (**tropic of Capricorn**), representing the points farthest north and south at which the sun shines directly overhead. 2 **tropics** or **Tropics,** *pl.* the regions between and near these parallels of latitude; the Torrid Zone and regions immediately adjacent. *—adj.* of, belonging to, or like the tropics; tropical. [< Latin *tropicus* < Greek *tropikos* pertaining to a turn < *tropē* a turn, a change < *trepein* to turn]

trop i cal[1] (trop′ə kəl), *adj.* of the tropics; having to do with the tropics: *tropical fruit.* **—trop′i cal ly,** *adv.*

trop i cal[2] (trop′ə kəl, trō′pə kəl), *adj.* of a trope or tropes; figurative.

tropical fish, any of certain small, usually brightly colored fishes native to the tropics, commonly kept in home aquariums.

tropic bird, any of a genus of sea birds resembling the tern, found in tropical regions, swift in flight, and having webbed feet, varied coloration, and a pair of long central tail feathers.

tro pism (trō′piz′əm), *n.* tendency of a plant or sessile animal to turn or move in response to a stimulus. [< Greek *tropē* a turning < *trepein* to turn]

tro pis tic (trō pis′tik), *adj.* of or having to do with a tropism.

trop o pause (trop′ə pôz, trō′pə pôz), *n.* the area of atmospheric demarcation between the troposphere and the stratosphere.

trop o sphere (trop′ə sfir, trō′pə sfir), *n.* the lowest region of the atmosphere, below the stratosphere, within which there is a steady fall of temperature with increasing altitude. Most cloud formations occur in the troposphere. See **atmosphere** for diagram. [< Greek *tropē* a turn, change]

trop o spher ic (trop′ə sfer′ik, trop′ə-sfir′ik; trō′pə sfer′ik, trō′pə sfir′ik), *adj.* of or having to do with the troposphere.

trot (trot), *v.,* **trot ted, trot ting,** *n.* *—v.i.* 1 go at a gait between a walk and a run by lifting the right forefoot and the left hind foot at about the same time. 2 ride or drive a horse at a trot. 3 run, but not fast: *The child trotted along after his mother.* *—v.t.* 1 ride or drive (a horse, etc.) at a trot; cause to trot. 2 **trot out,** INFORMAL. bring out for others to see. *—n.* 1 the motion or gait of trotting. 2 a brisk, steady movement; a slow running. 3 SLANG. translation used by a pupil instead of doing the lesson himself; pony. [< Old French *trotter;* of Germanic origin]

troth (trôth, trōth), *n.* ARCHAIC. 1 faithfulness or fidelity; loyalty. 2 promise. 3 truth. 4 betrothal. 5 **plight one's troth, a** promise to marry. **b** promise to be faithful. *—v.t.* 1 promise. 2 betroth. [Old English *trēowth* < *trēow* faith]

Trot sky (trot′skē), *n.* **Leon,** 1879-1940, leader in the Russian Revolution and Soviet minister of war from 1918 to 1925. He was later exiled, and was assassinated in Mexico.

Trot sky ism (trot′skē iz′əm), *n.* the policies and principles of Trotsky, especially the doctrine that world-wide communist revolution must take precedence over everything else, including the growth and development of the Soviet Union.

Trot sky ist (trot′skē ist), *n., adj.* Trotskyite.

Trot sky ite (trot′skē īt), *n.* person who advocates Trotskyism; follower of Trotsky. *—adj.* of or having to do with Trotskyism or Trotskyites.

trot ter (trot′ər), *n.* horse that trots, especially one bred and trained to trot in races.

trou ba dour (trü′bə dôr, trü′bə dōr, trü′bə dür), *n.* one of a class of knightly lyric poets and composers of southern France, eastern Spain, and northern Italy from the 1000's to the 1200's, who wrote mainly about love and chivalry. [< French < Provençal *trobador* < *trobar* compose]

trou ble (trub′əl), *n., v.,* **-bled, -bling.** *—n.* 1 pain and sorrow; distress; worry; difficulty: *a time of great trouble.* 2 an instance of this: *a life containing many troubles.* 3 disturbance; disorder: *political troubles.* 4 extra work; bother; effort: *Take the trouble to do careful work.* 5 cause of inconvenience: *Is she a trouble to you?* 6 ailment; disease: *suffer from heart trouble.* *—v.t.* 1 cause trouble to; disturb: *The lack of business troubled him.* 2 require extra work or effort of: *May I trouble you to pass the sugar?* 3 cause pain to; hurt; pain: *An abscessed tooth troubled me.* 4 agitate or ruffle (water, air, etc.), especially so as to make it cloudy, muddy, etc. *—v.i.* trouble oneself; take the trouble: *Don't trouble to come to the door.* [< Old French *truble,* ultimately < Latin *turba* turmoil]

trou ble mak er (trub′əl mā′kər), *n.* person who often causes trouble for others.

trou ble shoot er (trub′əl shü′tər), *n.* person who discovers and eliminates causes of trouble, especially one trained to do so in a particular field or with a particular kind of apparatus.

trou ble some (trub′əl səm), *adj.* 1 causing trouble; disturbing; annoying: *troublesome neighbors.* 2 tiresome; difficult: *a troublesome process.* **—trou′ble some ly,** *adv.* **—trou′ble some ness,** *n.*

hat, āge, fär; let, ēqual, tėrm;
it, īce; hot, ōpen, ôrder;
oil, out; cup, pu̇t, rüle;
ch, child; ng, long; sh, she;
th, thin; ᴛʜ, then; zh, measure;

ə represents *a* in about, *e* in taken, *i* in pencil, *o* in lemon, *u* in circus.

< = from, derived from, taken from.

trou blous (trub′ləs), *adj.* 1 disturbed; restless; unsettled. 2 tempestuous; stormy; violent. 3 troublesome.

trough (trôf, trof), *n.* 1 a narrow, open, boxlike container for holding food or water, especially for farm stock or other animals. 2 something shaped like this: *The baker uses a trough for kneading dough.* 3 a channel for carrying water; gutter. 4 a long hollow between two ridges, especially the hollow between two waves or two hills. 5 (in meteorology) a long, narrow area of relatively low barometric pressure. [Old English *trog*] **—trough′like′,** *adj.*

trounce (trouns), *v.t.,* **trounced, trounc ing.** 1 beat or thrash. 2 INFORMAL. defeat in a contest, game, match, etc. [origin uncertain]

troupe (trüp), *n., v.,* **trouped, troup ing.** *—n.* troop, band, or company, especially a group of actors, singers, or acrobats. *—v.i.* tour or travel with a troupe. [< French]

troup er (trü′pər), *n.* 1 member of a theatrical troupe. 2 an experienced actor.

trou sers (trou′zərz), *n.pl.* a two-legged outer garment reaching from the waist to the ankles or knees, worn especially by men and boys. [< earlier *trouse* < Scottish Gaelic *triubhas*]

trous seau (trü′sō, trü sō′), *n., pl.* **trousseaux** (trü′sōz, trü sōz′), **trousseaus.** a bride's outfit of clothes, linen, etc. [< French, originally, bundle]

trout (trout), *n., pl.* **trouts** or **trout.** 1 any of certain freshwater food and game fishes of the same family as the salmon, found mostly in cool, clear northern waters. 2 any of certain fishes resembling trout. [Old English *trūht* < Late Latin *tructa, trocta,* probably < Greek *trōktēs,* literally, gnawer]

trout lily, dogtooth violet.

trove (trōv), *n.* 1 something of value found; a find; discovery. 2 treasure. [< *(treasure) trove*]

trow (trō), *v.i., v.t.* ARCHAIC. believe; think. [Old English *truwian*]

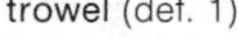

trowel (def. 1) trowel (def. 2)

trow el (trou′əl), *n., v.,* **-eled, -el ing** or **-elled, -el ling.** *—n.* 1 tool with a broad, flat blade, used for spreading or smoothing plaster or mortar. 2 tool with a curved blade, used for taking up plants, loosening dirt, etc. *—v.t.* spread, smooth, form, or move with or as if with a trowel. [< Old French *truele*

< Late Latin *truella,* diminutive of Latin *trua* skimmer]

troy (troi), *adj.* in or by troy weight. *—n.* troy weight. [< *Troyes,* city in northern France, former site of a fair at which this weight may have been used]

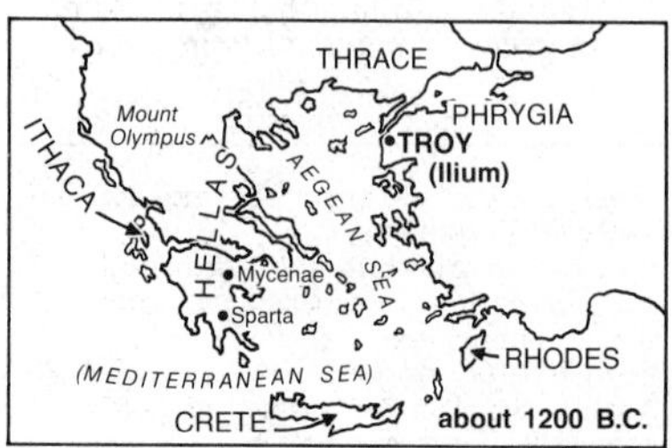

Troy (def. 1)

Troy (troi), *n.* 1 city in the NW part of ancient Asia Minor, scene of the Trojan War. Also, **Ilium.** 2 city in E New York State, on the Hudson River. 67,000.

troy weight, a standard system of weights used for gems and precious metals. One pound troy equals a little over four fifths of an ordinary pound. See **measure** for table.

tru an cy (trü′ən sē), *n., pl.* **-cies.** act or habit of playing truant; truant behavior.

tru ant (trü′ənt), *n.* 1 child who stays away from school without permission. 2 person who neglects duty. 3 **play truant, a** stay away from school without permission. **b** stay away from work or duties. *—adj.* 1 staying away from school without permission. 2 guilty of neglecting duty. 3 lazy. 4 wandering. 5 of or having to do with a truant or truants. [< Old French; probably of Celtic origin]

truant officer, U.S. a school official whose job is to locate and return truants to school.

truce (trüs), *n.* 1 a stop in fighting; temporary peace: *A truce was declared between the two armies.* 2 a rest from trouble or pain. [Middle English *trewes,* plural of *trewe* treaty, Old English *trēow* faith]

Tru cial States or **Trucial Oman** (trü′shəl), former group of seven small states on the Persian Gulf in E Arabia, under British protection until 1971. They are now known as the **Union of Arab Emirates.**

truck[1] (truk), *n.* 1 a strongly built motor vehicle for carrying heavy loads. 2 a strongly built cart, wagon, etc., used for a similar purpose. 3 frame on small wheels for moving trunks, etc. 4 a rectangular platform resting on four wheels, used to move heavy or bulky objects. 5 a swiveling frame with two or more pairs of wheels for supporting the end of a railroad car, locomotive, etc. 6 a wooden disk at the top of a flagstaff or mast with holes for the ropes. *—v.t.* carry on a truck: *truck freight to the warehouse.* *—v.i.* 1 drive a truck. 2 engage in trucking goods, especially as a business. [perhaps < Latin *trochus* iron hoop < Greek *trochos* wheel]

truck[2] (truk), *n.* 1 vegetables raised for market. 2 small articles of little value; odds and ends. 3 INFORMAL. **a** rubbish; trash. **b** dealings: *She has no truck with that family.* 4 exchange; barter. 5 payment of wages in goods, etc., rather than in money. *—v.t., v.i.* give in exchange; barter. [< Old French *troquer* to barter, exchange < Latin *trocare*]

truck age (truk′ij), *n.* 1 the carrying of goods, etc., by trucks. 2 charge for carrying by truck.

truck er (truk′ər), *n.* 1 person who drives a truck. 2 person whose business is carrying goods, etc., by trucks.

truck farm, farm where vegetables are raised for market.

truck ing (truk′ing), *n.* act or business of carrying goods by a truck or trucks.

truck le (truk′əl), *v.i.,* **-led, -ling.** give up or submit tamely; be servile: *That man got his position by truckling to his superiors and flattering them.* [ultimately < Greek *trochileia* sheaf of a pulley] **—truck′ler,** *n.*

truckle bed, trundle bed.

truck man (truk′mən), *n., pl.* **-men.** man who drives a truck; trucker.

truck system, system of paying wages in goods, etc., rather than in money.

truck tractor, a motor truck consisting of a cab and engine, used to pull a truck trailer.

truck trailer, trailer designed to be pulled by a motor truck, especially by a truck tractor.

truc u lence (truk′yə ləns, trü′kyə ləns), *n.* quality or condition of being truculent; fierceness; brutal harshness.

truc u len cy (truk′yə lən sē, trü′kyə lən-sē), *n.* truculence.

truc u lent (truk′yə lənt, trü′kyə lənt), *adj.* 1 fierce, savage, or violent: *be in a truculent mood, a truculent defense of one's rights.* 2 brutally harsh or scathing: *a truculent remark, a truculent satire.* [< Latin *truculentus* < *trucem* fierce] **—truc′u lent ly,** *adv.*

Tru deau (trü dō′), *n.* **Pierre Elliott,** born 1919, prime minister of Canada since 1968.

trudge (truj), *v.,* **trudged, trudg ing,** *n.* *—v.i.* 1 go on foot; walk. 2 walk wearily or with effort. *—v.t.* trudge along or over. *—n.* a hard or weary walk: *It was a long trudge up the hill.* [origin uncertain] **—trudg′er,** *n.*

trudg en stroke (truj′ən), stroke in swimming in which the arms, alternately, are raised over the head and brought down and back parallel with the body, usually done with a scissors kick. [< John *Trudgen,* 1852-1902, British swimmer]

true (trü), *adj.,* **tru er, tru est,** *n., v.,* **trued, tru ing** or **true ing,** *adv.* *—adj.* 1 agreeing with fact; not false: *It is true that 6 and 4 are 10.* See **real**[1] for synonym study. 2 real; genuine: *true gold, true kindness.* 3 faithful; loyal: *a true patriot, true to your promise.* 4 agreeing with a standard; right; correct; exact: *a true copy, a true voice, true to type.* 5 representative of the class named: *A sweet potato is not a true potato.* 6 rightful; lawful: *the true heir to the property.* 7 reliable; sure: *a true sign.* 8 accurately formed, fitted, or placed: *a true angle.* 9 steady in direction, force, etc., unchanging: *The arrow made a true course through the air.* 10 ARCHAIC. truthful. 11 honest. 12 **come true,** happen as expected; become real.

—n. 1 that which is true. 2 exact or accurate formation, position, or adjustment: *A slanting door is out of true.*

trumpet (def. 1)

—v.t. Also, **true up,** make true; shape, place, or make in the exact or desired position, form, etc.

—adv. 2 in a true manner; truly; exactly: *His words ring true.* 2 in agreement with the ancestral type: *breed true.*

[Old English *trēowe*] **—true′ness,** *n.*

true bill, bill of indictment found by a grand jury to be supported by enough evidence to justify hearing the case.

true-blue (trü′blü′), *adj.* staunch and unwavering in one's faith, beliefs, etc.; unchanging; loyal.

true born (trü′bôrn′), *adj.* born of a pure stock; legitimately born.

true-false (trü′fôls′), *adj.* having to do with or containing statements which must be marked as either true or false: *a true-false test, true-false questions.*

true heart ed (trü′här′tid), *adj.* faithful; loyal.

true-life (trü′līf′), *adj.* real-life.

true love (trü′luv′), *n.* a faithful lover; sweetheart.

truelove knot, a complicated bowknot, not easily untied, used as a token or symbol of eternal love.

true-lov er's knot (trü′luv′ərz), truelove knot.

truf fle (truf′əl, trü′fəl), *n.* an edible fungus with a black, warty exterior, that grows underground and varies in size between that of a walnut and that of a potato. It is a native of central and southern Europe. [< Old French *truffe,* ultimately alteration of Latin *tuber* tuber]

tru ism (trü′iz′əm), *n.* statement that almost everybody knows is true, such as "Health is a blessing."

tru is tic (trü is′tik), *adj.* having the character of a truism.

trull (trul), *n.* prostitute; strumpet. [< German *Trulle*]

tru ly (trü′lē), *adv.* 1 in a true manner; exactly; rightly; faithfully: *Tell me truly what you think.* 2 in fact; really; genuinely: *It was truly a beautiful day.* 3 indeed; verily.

Tru man (trü′mən), *n.* **Harry S.,** 1884-1972, the 33rd president of the United States, from 1945 to 1953.

Truman Doctrine, doctrine that the United States would help free nations resist attempted subjugation by armed minorities or outside aggressors, enunciated by President Truman on March 12, 1947.

trump[1] (trump), *n.* 1 any playing card of a suit that during the play of a hand ranks higher than the other suits. 2 Often, **trumps,** *pl.* the suit itself. 3 INFORMAL. a fine, dependable person. *—v.t.* 1 take (a trick, card, etc.) with a trump. 2 be better than; surpass; beat. *—v.i.* play a card of the suit that is trump. [alteration of **triumph**]

trump[2] (trump), *n.* ARCHAIC. 1 trumpet. 2 sound of a trumpet. [< Old French *trompe;* of Germanic origin]

trump[3] (trump), *v.t.* make *(up)* to deceive: *trump up false charges against a person.* [perhaps special use of *trump*[1]]

trumped-up (trumpt′up′), *adj.* made up to deceive; fabricated; spurious: *a trumped-up charge.*

trump er y (trum′pər ē), *n., pl.* **-er ies,** *adj.* *—n.* something showy but without value; worthless ornaments; useless stuff; rubbish. *—adj.* showy but without value; trifling; worthless; useless. [< Old French *tromperie* < *tromper* deceive]

trum pet (trum′pit), *n.* 1 a brass wind instrument that has a powerful tone, commonly consisting of a cylindrical metal tube curved upon itself once or twice, with a flaring bell at one end and a cupped mouthpiece at the other. 2 thing shaped like a trumpet: *The deaf old lady has an ear trumpet to help her hearing.* 3 a sound like that of a trumpet. 4 a trumpeter. *—v.i.* 1 blow a trumpet. 2 make a sound like a trumpet: *The elephant trumpeted.* *—v.t.* 1 sound on a trumpet. 2 utter with a sound like that of a trumpet. 3 proclaim loudly or widely: *trumpet a story all over town.* [< Old French *trompette,* diminutive of *trompe.* See TRUMP².] **—trum′pet like′,** *adj.*

trumpet creeper, bignonia.

trum pet er (trum′pə tər), *n.* 1 person who blows a trumpet, especially a soldier who blows calls on a trumpet. 2 a large North American wild swan with a sonorous call. 3 any of a family of South American birds having long legs and necks, and resembling cranes. 4 a variety of domestic pigeon having a shell-shaped crest and heavily feathered feet.

trumpet vine, bignonia.

trun cate (trung′kāt), *v.,* **-cat ed, -cat ing,** *adj.* *—v.t.* cut off a part of. *—adj.* cut off; blunt, as if cut off: *the truncate leaf of the tulip tree.* [< Latin *truncatum* truncated < *truncus* mutilated] **—trun ca′tion,** *n.*

trun cheon (trun′chən), *n.* 1 a stick cut and shaped for use as a weapon; club: *a policeman's truncheon.* 2 staff of office or authority: *a herald's truncheon.* *—v.t.* beat with a truncheon; club. [< Old French *tronchon,* ultimately < Latin *truncus.* See TRUNK.]

trun dle (trun′dl), *v.,* **-dled, -dling,** *n.* *—v.t.* 1 roll along; push along: *The workman trundled a wheelbarrow full of cement.* 2 cause to rotate; twirl; spin; whirl. *—v.i.* 1 move or be moved by trundling. 2 whirl; revolve. *—n.* 1 a rolling; rolling along. 2 caster; a small wheel. 3 trundle bed. 4 OBSOLETE. a low cart or wagon on small wheels. [Old English *trendel* ring, disk] **—trun′dler,** *n.*

trundle bed, a low bed on small wheels that can be pushed under a regular bed when not in use; truckle bed.

trunk (trungk), *n.* 1 the main stem of a tree, as distinct from the branches and the roots. 2 the main part of anything: *the trunk of a column.* 3 a big box for holding clothes, etc., when traveling. 4 an enclosed compartment in an automobile for storing baggage, a spare tire, tools, etc. 5 a human or animal body without the head, arms, and legs. 6 the main body of a nerve, blood vessel, or similar structure as distinct from its branches. 7 an elephant's snout. 8 trunk line. 9 a telephone circuit between two central offices or exchanges, used to make connections between individual subscribers. 10 **trunks,** *pl.* very short trousers or breeches worn by athletes, swimmers, acrobats, etc. *—adj.* 1 main; chief: *a trunk highway.* 2 of or having to do with a trunk line, principal artery, channel, etc. [< Latin *truncus,* originally adjective, mutilated] **—trunk′like′,** *adj.*

trunk hose, full, baglike breeches reaching halfway down the thigh, or lower. Trunk hose were worn in the 1500's and early 1600's.

trunk line, 1 the main line of a railroad, canal, or other transportation system. 2 any main line, such as the line between telephone exchanges.

trun nion (trun′yən), *n.* 1 either of the two round projections of a cannon, one on each side, which support it on its carriage. 2 either of any similar pair of opposite supporting pins or pinions. [< French *trognon* trunk]

truss (trus), *v.t.* 1 tie or fasten; bind: *truss up a prisoner hand and foot.* 2 fasten the wings or legs of (a fowl, etc.) with skewers or twine in preparation for cooking: *The cook trussed up the chicken before roasting it.* 3 support (a roof, bridge, etc.) with trusses; strengthen or hold together with trusses. *—n.* 1 framework of beams or other supports, usually connected in a series of triangles, used to support a roof, bridge, etc. 2 pad attached to a belt, used to support a hernia. 3 bundle; pack. 4 bundle of hay or straw. 5 a compact cluster or head of flowers of any kind, growing upon one stalk. [< Old French *trusser,* ultimately < Latin *torquere* to twist] **—truss′er,** *n.*

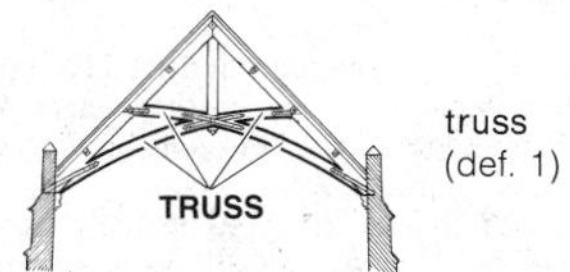

truss (def. 1)

trust (trust), *n.* 1 firm belief in the honesty, truthfulness, justice, or power of a person or thing; faith: *A child puts trust in his parents.* 2 person or thing trusted: *Gold was the miser's only trust.* 3 confident expectation or hope: *Our trust is that you will soon be well.* 4 something managed for the benefit of another; something committed to one's care. 5 obligation or responsibility imposed on one in whom confidence or authority is placed. 6 condition of one in whom trust has been placed; being relied on: *A guardian is in a position of trust.* 7 keeping; care: *The will was left in my trust.* 8 confidence in the ability or intention of a person to pay at some future time for goods, etc.; business credit. 9 in law: **a** a confidence reposed in a person by making him nominal owner of property, which he is to hold, use, or dispose of for the benefit of another. **b** an estate, etc., committed to a trustee or trustees. **c** the right of a person to enjoy the use or profits of property held in trust for him. 10 an illegal combination of companies to control the production and price of some commodity and to eliminate or reduce competition: *a steel trust.* 11 **in trust,** as a thing taken charge of for another. 12 **on trust, a** without investigation. **b** on business credit; with payment later.

—v.t. 1 believe firmly in the honesty, truth, justice, or power of; have confidence or faith in: *He is a man to be trusted.* 2 rely or depend on: *trust one's memory.* 3 expect with confidence; hope: *I trust you will soon feel better.* 4 commit to the care of; leave without fear; entrust: *Can I trust the money to him?* 5 give business credit to: *The butcher will trust us for the meat.* *—v.i.* 1 have faith; rely; be confident: *Trust in God.* 2 **trust to,** rely or depend on.

—adj. 1 managing property for an owner. 2 of or having to do with trusts. 3 held in trust.

[< Scandinavian (Old Icelandic) *traust*] **—trust′er,** *n.*

trust bust er (trust′bus′tər), *n.* U.S. a federal official who tries to break up business trusts and enforce the antitrust laws.

trust company, bank or other business concern that takes charge of the property of others.

hat, āge, fär; let, ēqual, tėrm;
it, īce; hot, ōpen, ôrder;
oil, out; cup, pu̇t, rüle;
ch, child; ng, long; sh, she;
th, thin; ᴛʜ, then; zh, measure;

ə represents *a* in about, *e* in taken, *i* in pencil, *o* in lemon, *u* in circus.

< = from, derived from, taken from.

trus tee (tru stē′), *n.* 1 person or one of a group of persons appointed to manage the affairs of an individual, institution, business firm, etc. 2 person who holds property in trust for another.

trus tee ship (tru stē′ship), *n.* 1 position of trustee. 2 administration by a country of a trust territory. 3 trust territory.

trust ful (trust′fəl), *adj.* ready to confide; ready to have faith; trusting; believing. **—trust′ful ly,** *adv.* **—trust′ful ness,** *n.*

trust fund, money, property, or other valuables held in trust by one person for the benefit of another.

trust ing (trus′ting), *adj.* that trusts; trustful. **—trust′ing ly,** *adv.*

trust territory, any of various territories or regions administered by certain countries on behalf of the United Nations.

trust wor thy (trust′wėr′ᴛʜē), *adj.* that can be depended on or trusted; deserving confidence; reliable: *a trustworthy report, a trustworthy person.* See **reliable** for synonym study. **—trust′wor′thi ly,** *adv.* **—trust′wor′thi ness,** *n.*

trust y (trus′tē), *adj.,* **trust i er, trust i est,** *n., pl.* **trust ies.** *—adj.* trustworthy; reliable. *—n.* 1 convict who is given special privileges because of his good behavior. 2 any trustworthy person or thing. **—trust′i ly,** *adv.* **—trust′i ness,** *n.*

truth (trüth), *n., pl.* **truths** (trüᴛʜz, trüths). 1 that which is true: *Tell the truth.* 2 the fact or facts; matter or circumstance as it really is: *suspect the truth.* 3 a fixed or established principle, law, etc.; proven doctrine: *a basic scientific truth.* 4 that which is true, real, or actual, in a general or abstract sense; reality: *find truth in God.* 5 quality or nature of being true, exact, honest, sincere, or loyal. 6 **in truth,** in fact; truly; really. [Old English *triewth, trēowth* < *triewe, trēowe* true]

Truth (trüth), *n.* **Sojourner,** 1790?-1883, American Abolitionist and worker for woman's rights. She was born a slave.

truth ful (trüth′fəl), *adj.* 1 telling the truth: *a truthful child.* 2 conforming to truth; agreeing with the facts: *a truthful report.* **—truth′ful ly,** *adv.* **—truth′ful ness,** *n.*

truth serum, any of various drugs, such as thiopental sodium, under the influence of which a person will reveal inner thoughts or emotions that he has been suppressing.

try (trī), *v.,* **tried, try ing,** *n., pl.* **tries.** *—v.i.* make an effort; endeavor; attempt: *I tried to do the work.* See synonym study below. *—v.t.* 1 attempt to do or accomplish: *It seems easy until you try it.* 2 experiment on or with; make a trial of: *Try this candy and see if you like it.* 3 find out about; test: *We try each car before we sell it.* 4 investigate in a court of law: *The defendant was tried and found not guilty.* 5 settle by test or investigation. 6 subject to trials; afflict: *Job was greatly tried.* 7 put to severe test; strain: *Her mis-*

takes try my patience. 8 purify by melting or boiling; render: *The lard was tried in a big kettle.* 9 **try on,** test the fit or style of (a garment) by putting it on. 10 **try out, a** test the effect or result of. **b** test to find out about. **c** undergo a test or trial to determine fitness.

—*n.* 1 an attempt; endeavor; effort. 2 trial; test; experiment. 3 (in Rugby) a play scoring three points, made by holding the ball on or beyond the opponents' goal line.

[< Old French *trier* to cull]

Syn. *v.i.* 1 **Try, attempt, endeavor** mean to make an effort to or at. **Try** is the general word: *I tried to see him.* **Attempt,** a more formal word, suggests making a great effort or trying hard: *I attempted to obtain an interview.* **Endeavor,** also formal, suggests both great effort and greater obstacles to be overcome: *The United Nations is endeavoring to establish peace.*

try ing (trī′ing), *adj.* hard to bear or endure; annoying; distressing: *a trying day, a trying person.*

try out (trī′out′), *n.* INFORMAL. test or trial made to determine fitness for a specific purpose: *He had a tryout with a professional hockey team. Tryouts for the school play will be held next week.*

tryp a no some (trip′ə nə sōm, tri pan′ə-sōm), *n.* any of a genus of minute, parasitic, flagellate protozoans inhabiting the blood of vertebrates, usually transmitted by bloodsucking insects and causing serious diseases, such as sleeping sickness. [< Greek *trypanon* borer, auger + *sōma* body]

tryp a no so mi a sis (trip′ə nō sō mī′ə-sis), *n.* any of various diseases caused by infection by trypanosomes.

tryp sin (trip′sən), *n.* enzyme in the pancreatic juice that aids in the digestion of proteins. [irregularly < Greek *tripsis* a rubbing < *tribein* to rub]

tryp tic (trip′tik), *adj.* of or having to do with trypsin.

tryp to phan (trip′tə fan), *n.* an essential amino acid formed from proteins during digestion and also occurring in plants. *Formula:* $C_{11}H_{12}N_2O_2$ [< *tryptic* + Greek *phainein* appear]

try sail (trī′sāl′; *Nautical* trī′səl), *n.* a small fore-and-aft sail used in stormy weather on the foremast or mainmast.

try square, instrument for drawing right angles and testing the squareness of anything, consisting of two straight pieces attached at right angles to each other.

tryst (trist), *n.* 1 appointment to meet at a certain time and place, especially one made by lovers. 2 an appointed meeting. 3 an appointed place of meeting. [< Old French *triste*]

tryst ing place (tris′ting), place where a tryst is to be kept.

tsar (zär, tsär), *n.* czar.

tsa ri na (zä rē′nə, tsä rē′nə), *n.* czarina.

Tschai kow sky or **Tschai kov sky** (chī kôf′skē), *n.* Tchaikovsky.

tset se (tset′sē), *n.* tsetse fly. Also, **tzetze.**

tsetse fly, any of a group of two-winged, bloodsucking African flies that transmit disease, including the one transmitting the trypanosome that causes sleeping sickness, and one that carries a disease of horses and other domestic animals. [*tsetse* < Bantu]

T. Sgt., technical sergeant.

T-shirt (tē′shėrt′), *n.* 1 a light, close-fitting pullover shirt with short sleeves and no collar, worn by men and boys for sports. 2 an undershirt resembling this. Also, **tee shirt.**

Tsi nan (tsē′nän′), *n.* city in NE China. 862,000.

Tsing tao (tsing′tou′), *n.* seaport in E China. 1,121,000.

tsp., teaspoon or teaspoons.

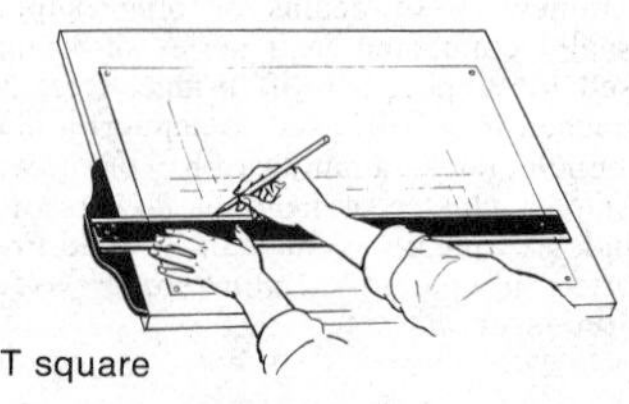

T square

T square, a T-shaped ruler used for making parallel lines, etc. The shorter arm slides along the edge of the drawing board, which serves as a guide.

tsu na mi (sü nä′mē, tsü nä′mē), *n.* an oceanic tidal wave caused by a submarine earthquake. [< Japanese]

T-time (tē′tīm′), *n.* moment at the end of the countdown when a rocket or missile is launched. [short for *Take-off time*]

Tu., Tuesday.

Tua reg (twär′eg), *n.* a Moslem nomad of the Sahara speaking a Hamitic language.

tu a ta ra (tü′ə tär′ə), *n.* a large lizardlike reptile of New Zealand, the only surviving member of a prehistoric order of reptiles. [< Maori]

tub (tub), *n., v.,* **tubbed, tub bing.** —*n.* 1 a large, open container for washing or bathing. 2 bathtub. 3 INFORMAL. bath: *He takes a cold tub every morning.* 4 a round, wooden container for holding butter, lard, etc., in bulk, especially one made of staves and hoops. 5 as much as a tub can hold. 6 something like a tub. 7 INFORMAL. a clumsy, slow boat or ship. —*v.t., v.i.* wash or bathe in a tub. [< Middle Dutch *tubbe*]

tuba

tu ba (tü′bə, tyü′bə), *n.* a large brass wind instrument of low pitch; bass horn. [< Latin, war trumpet]

tub by (tub′ē), *adj.,* **-bi er, -bi est.** 1 short and fat. 2 having a sound like that of an empty tub when struck. **—tub′bi ness,** *n.*

tube (tüb, tyüb), *n.* 1 a long pipe of metal, glass, rubber, etc., mostly used to hold or carry liquids or gases. 2 a small cylinder of thin, easily bent metal with a cap that screws on the open end, used for holding toothpaste, paint, etc. 3 inner tube. 4 pipe or tunnel through which something is sent, especially by means of compressed air. 5 a railroad tunnel, especially one bored through rock or under water. 6 BRITISH INFORMAL. subway. 7 anything like a tube, especially any of certain animal organs: *the bronchial tubes.* 8 an electron or vacuum tube. [< Latin *tubus*] **—tube′like′,** *adj.*

tube less (tüb′lis, tyüb′lis), *adj.* having no inner tube or tubes: *a tubeless tire.*

tu ber (tü′bər, tyü′bər), *n.* 1 a solid, thickened portion or outgrowth of an underground stem, of a more or less rounded form, and bearing modified axillary buds from which new plants may arise. A potato is a tuber. 2 a rounded swelling or projecting part in an animal body. [< Latin, lump]

tu ber cle (tü′bər kəl, tyü′bər kəl), *n.* 1 a small, rounded knob or projection on an animal or plant. 2 a small swelling on the surface of the body or in a part or organ. 3 such a swelling caused by tuberculosis. [< Latin *tuberculum,* diminutive of *tuber* lump]

tubercle bacillus, the bacillus that causes tuberculosis.

tu ber cu lar (tü bėr′kyə lər, tyü bėr′kyə-lər), *adj.* 1 having tubercles. 2 having to do with or characterized by tubercles. 3 having tuberculosis. 4 of or having to do with tuberculosis: *tubercular symptoms.*

tu ber cu lin (tü bėr′kyə lən, tyü bėr′kyə-lən), *n.* a sterile liquid prepared from the tubercle bacillus, used in the diagnosis and treatment of tuberculosis.

tu ber cu loid (tü bėr′kyə loid, tyü bėr′-kyə loid), *adj.* resembling tuberculosis or a tubercle.

tu ber cu lo sis (tü bėr′kyə lō′sis, tyü bėr′-kyə lō′sis), *n.* an infectious disease affecting various tissues of the body, but most often the lungs, characterized by an acute inflammation or the formation of tubercles on the tissues, and caused by the tubercle bacillus.

tu ber cu lous (tü bėr′kyə ləs, tyü bėr′kyə-ləs), *adj.* tubercular.

tube rose (tüb′rōz′, tyüb′rōz′), *n.* a bulbous plant of the same family as the agave, much grown for its spike of creamy-white, funnel-shaped, very fragrant flowers. [< Latin *tuberosus* tuberous < *tuber* lump]

tu ber os i ty (tü′bə ros′ə tē, tyü′bə ros′ə-tē), *n., pl.* **-ties.** 1 a being tuberous. 2 a rounded knob or swelling. 3 a large, irregular protuberance of a bone, especially for the attachment of a muscle or ligament.

tu ber ous (tü′bər əs, tyü′bər əs), *adj.* 1 bearing tubers. 2 of or like tubers: *a tuberous root.* 3 covered with rounded knobs or swellings.

tub ing (tü′bing, tyü′bing), *n.* 1 material in the form of a tube. 2 tubes collectively. 3 a piece of tube.

tu bu lar (tü′byə lər, tyü′byə lər), *adj.* 1 shaped like a tube; round and hollow. 2 of or having to do with a tube or tubes. 3 constructed with or consisting of a number of tubes.

tu bu late (tü′byə lit, tü′byə lāt; tyü′byə lit, tyü′byə lāt), *adj.* tubular.

tu bule (tü′byül, tyü′byül), *n.* a small tube, especially a minute tubular structure in an animal or plant body. [< Latin *tubulus,* diminutive of *tubus* pipe]

tuck (tuk), *v.t.* 1 thrust into some narrow space or into some retired place: *tuck a newspaper under one's arm. The little cottage is tucked away under the hill.* 2 thrust the edge or end of (a garment, covering, etc.) closely into place: *Tuck your shirt in.* 3 cover snugly: *tuck a child in bed.* 4 pull or gather in a fold or folds: *tuck up one's trousers.* 5 sew a fold in (a garment) for trimming or to make it shorter or tighter. 6 **tuck away** or **tuck in,** SLANG. eat or drink heartily; consume with gusto: *tuck away a big meal.* —*n.* 1 a fold sewed in a garment. 2 act of tucking. 3 a tucked piece, part, or position. [Middle English *tukken* stretch]

tuck er[1] (tuk′ər), *n.* 1 piece of muslin, lace, etc., worn by women around the neck or over the chest. 2 person or thing that tucks. [< *tuck*]

tuck er[2] (tuk′ər), *v.t.* INFORMAL. tire; weary; exhaust: *She was all tuckered out after the long trip.* [origin uncertain]

Tuc son (tü′son, tü son′), *n.* city in S Arizona, famous as a health resort. 263,000.

Tu dor (tü′dər, tyü′dər), *n.* member of the royal family that ruled England from 1485 to 1603. Henry VII, Henry VIII, Edward VI, Mary I, and Elizabeth I were Tudors. —*adj.* 1 of or having to do with the English Gothic style of architecture prevailing during the reign of the Tudors, characterized by flat arches, shallow moldings, and elaborate paneling. 2 of or having to do with the Tudors.

Tues., Tuesday.

Tues day (tüz′dē, tüz′dā; tyüz′dē, tyüz′dā), *n.* the third day of the week, following Monday. [Old English *Tīwesdæg* < *Tīw* (Tyr, the Germanic god of war) + *dæg* day]

tu fa (tü′fə, tyü′fə), *n.* 1 any of various porous rocks, especially a form of limestone deposited by springs, etc. 2 tuff. [< Italian *tufo* < Latin *tofus*]

tu fa ceous (tü fā′shəs, tyü fā′shəs), *adj.* of, having to do with, or resembling tufa.

tuff (tuf), *n.* a rock consisting of compacted volcanic ash and other small volcanic fragments. [< French *tuf* < Italian *tufo* tufa]

tuft (tuft), *n.* 1 bunch of feathers, hair, grass, etc., held together at one end: *My billy goat has a tuft of hair on his chin.* 2 clump of bushes, trees, etc. 3 cluster of threads sewn tightly through a mattress, comforter, etc., so as to keep the padding in place. —*v.t.* put tufts on; furnish with tufts; divide into tufts. —*v.i.* form a tuft or tufts; grow in tufts. [< Old French *touffe* < Late Latin *tufa* helmet crest]

tuft ed (tuf′tid), *adj.* 1 furnished with a tuft or tufts. 2 formed into a tuft or tufts.

tuft y (tuf′tē), *adj.,* **tuft i er, tuft i est.** 1 abounding in tufts or knots. 2 growing in tufts.

tug (tug), *v.,* **tugged, tug ging,** *n.* —*v.t.* 1 move by pulling forcibly; pull with force or effort; drag; haul: *We tugged the boat out of the water.* See **pull** for synonym study. 2 pull or push by a tugboat. —*v.i.* 1 pull with force or effort; pull hard: *The child tugged at his mother's hand.* 2 strive hard; toil. —*n.* 1 a hard pull. 2 a hard strain, struggle, effort, or contest. 3 tugboat. 4 trace[2]. [Middle English *tuggen.* Related to TOW.] —**tug′ger,** *n.*

tug boat (tug′bōt′), *n.* a small, powerful boat used to tow or push other boats; towboat.

tug-of-war (tug′əv wôr′, tug′ə wôr′), *n., pl.* **tugs-of-war.** 1 contest between two teams pulling at the opposite ends of a rope, each trying to drag the other over a line marked between them. 2 any hard struggle.

Tui ler ies (twē′lər ēz; *French* twēl rē′), *n.* former royal palace in Paris, burned in 1871.

tu i tion (tü ish′ən, tyü ish′ən), *n.* 1 act of teaching a pupil or pupils; teaching; instruction. 2 money paid for instruction: *Her yearly tuition at college is $1500.* [< Latin *tuitionem* protection < *tueri* watch over]

tu i tion al (tü ish′ə nəl, tyü ish′ə nəl), *adj.* of or having to do with tuition.

Tu la (tü′lä), *n.* city in W Soviet Union. 462,000.

tu la re mi a (tü′lə rē′mē ə), *n.* an infectious disease of rabbits and other rodents, caused by a bacterium and sometimes transmitted to people by insect bites or by the handling of infected animals, causing an intermittent fever that lasts several weeks; rabbit fever. [< New Latin < *Tulare,* county in California, where it was discovered + *-emia* < Greek *haima* blood]

tu lip (tü′lip, tyü′lip), *n.* 1 any of a genus of plants of the lily family that grow from bulbs and have long, narrow leaves, widely grown for their large, showy, cup-shaped flowers of various colors and markings. Most tulips bloom in the spring. 2 the flower or bulb of any of these plants. [< Turkish *tülbend* < Persian *dulband* turban. Doublet of TURBAN.]

tulip tree, a large North American tree of the same family as the magnolia, with greenish-yellow flowers resembling large tulips.

tu lip wood (tü′lip wu̇d′, tyü′lip wu̇d′), *n.* 1 the soft, light-colored wood of the tulip tree, used for cabinetwork, etc. 2 any of several varicolored and striped woods of other trees.

tulle (tül), *n.* a thin, fine net, usually of silk, used for veils, etc. [< *Tulle,* town in France, where it was first made]

Tul ly (tul′ē), *n.* Cicero. Tully is an English form of *Tullius* in Marcus Tullius Cicero.

Tul sa (tul′sə), *n.* city in NE Oklahoma, on the Arkansas River. 330,000.

tum ble (tum′bəl), *v.,* **-bled, -bling,** *n.* —*v.i.* 1 fall headlong or in a helpless way: *The child tumbled down the stairs.* 2 roll or toss about: *The sick child tumbled restlessly in his bed.* 3 move in a hurried or awkward way: *The occupants tumbled out of the burning building.* 4 perform leaps, springs, somersaults, or other feats of physical agility. —*v.t.* 1 throw over or down; cause to tumble: *The strong wind tumbled a tree in our yard.* 2 turn over; rumple; muss: *to tumble bedclothes.* —*n.* 1 a fall: *a bad tumble.* 2 tumbled condition; confusion; disorder. [ultimately < Old English *tumbian* dance about]

tum ble bug (tum′bəl bug′), *n.* any of various beetles that roll up a ball of dung in which they deposit eggs from which larvae develop.

tum ble-down (tum′bəl doun′), *adj.* ready to fall down; dilapidated.

tum bler (tum′blər), *n.* 1 person who performs leaps, springs, somersaults, etc.; acrobat. 2 a drinking glass without a stem and with a heavy flat bottom. 3 the contents of such a glass. 4 part in the lock that must be moved from a certain position in order to release the bolt. 5 part of a lock of a gun that forces the hammer forward when the trigger is pulled. 6 a kind of domestic pigeon that performs backward somersaults and other acrobatics while in flight. 7 a revolving box or barrel in which things are polished.

tum ble weed (tum′bəl wēd′), *n.* any of various plants that break off from their roots and are blown about by the wind, especially an amaranth growing in western North America.

tum brel or **tum bril** (tum′brəl), *n.* 1 any of various two-wheeled carts, especially one used on a farm for hauling and dumping manure. 2 cart that carried prisoners to be executed during the French Revolution.

hat, āge, fär; let, ēqual, tėrm;
it, īce; hot, ōpen, ôrder;
oil, out; cup, pu̇t, rüle;
ch, child; ng, long; sh, she;
th, thin; ᴛʜ, then; zh, measure;

ə represents *a* in about, *e* in taken, *i* in pencil, *o* in lemon, *u* in circus.

< = from, derived from, taken from.

[< Old French *tomberel* cart < *tomber* to fall; of Germanic origin]

tu me fac tion (tü′mə fak′shən, tyü′mə fak′shən), *n.* 1 a swelling. 2 a being swollen. 3 a swollen part.

tu me fy (tü′mə fī, tyü′mə fī), *v.t., v.i.,* **-fied, -fy ing.** swell. [< Latin *tumere*]

tu mes cence (tü mes′ns, tyü mes′ns), *n.* a swelling; a swollen condition or part.

tu mes cent (tü mes′nt, tyü mes′nt), *adj.* becoming swollen; swelling. [< Latin *tumescentem* < *tumere* to swell]

tu mid (tü′mid, tyü′mid), *adj.* 1 swollen. 2 swollen with big words; pompous. [< Latin *tumidus* < *tumere* to swell] —**tu′mid ly,** *adv.* —**tu′mid ness,** *n.*

tu mid i ty (tü mid′ə tē, tyü mid′ə tē), *n.* quality or condition of being tumid.

tum my (tum′ē), *n., pl.* **-mies.** INFORMAL. stomach. [alteration of *stomach*]

tu mor (tü′mər, tyü′mər), *n.* 1 a swollen part; swelling. 2 an abnormal growth of tissues that may be benign or malignant, characterized by gradual development, and due to unknown causes. [< Latin < *tumere* to swell]

tu mor ous (tü′mər əs, tyü′mər əs), *adj.* 1 of or having to do with a tumor or tumors. 2 having a tumor or tumors.

tump line (tump′līn′), *n.* strap across the forehead and over the shoulders, used to help to carry loads on the back, especially by American Indians. [< *tump,* perhaps of Algonquian origin + *line*]

tu mult (tü′mult, tyü′mult), *n.* 1 noise or uproar; commotion: *the tumult of the storm.* 2 a violent disturbance or disorder: *The cry of "Fire!" caused a tumult in the theater.* 3 a violent disturbance of mind or feeling; confusion or excitement. [< Latin *tumultus*]

tu mul tu ous (tü mul′chü əs, tyü mul′chü əs), *adj.* 1 characterized by tumult; very noisy or disorderly; violent. 2 greatly disturbed. 3 rough; stormy. —**tu mul′tu ous ly,** *adv.* —**tu mul′tu ous ness,** *n.*

tu mu lus (tü′myə ləs, tyü′myə ləs), *n., pl.* **-lus es, -li** (-lī). mound of earth, especially one marking the site of an ancient grave; barrow. [< Latin]

tun (tun), *n.* 1 a large cask for holding liquids. 2 a former measure of capacity of liquor, equal to 252 gallons. [Old English *tunne*]

tu na[1] (tü′nə), *n., pl.* **tu nas** or **tu na.** 1 any of a family of large marine food fishes having coarse oily flesh that is widely used as food; tunny; horse mackerel. The tuna is also valued as a game fish. 2 any of several similar or related fishes. 3 the flesh of such a fish. [< American Spanish < Spanish *atún* < Arabic *tun* < Latin *thunnus, thynnus.* See TUNNY.]

tu na[2] (tü′nə), *n.* 1 any of several prickly pears, especially a treelike pear of tropical America with an edible fruit. 2 the fruit itself. [< Spanish < Arawak]

tun a ble (tü′nə bəl, tyü′nə bəl), *adj.* 1 that can be tuned. 2 in tune; concordant. 3 ARCHAIC. harmonious; tuneful. Also, **tune-able.** **—tun′a ble ness,** *n.* **—tun′a bly,** *adv.*

tuna fish, tuna[1].

tun dra (tun′drə, tün′drə), *n.* a vast, level, treeless plain in the arctic regions. The ground beneath the surface of the tundras is frozen even in summer. Much of Alaska and northern Canada is tundra. [< Russian]

tune (tün, tyün), *n., v.,* **tuned, tun ing.** *—n.* 1 a piece of music; a rhythmical succession of musical tones; melody or air. 2 a musical setting of a psalm or hymn: *hymn tunes.* 3 the proper pitch: *sing in tune.* 4 mood or manner; tone: *He'll soon change his tune.* 5 agreement; harmony: *A person out of tune with his surroundings is unhappy.* 6 **to the tune of,** INFORMAL. to the amount or sum of. *—v.t.* 1 adjust to the proper pitch; put in tune: *tune a piano.* 2 adapt or adjust so as to be in harmony. 3 **tune in,** adjust a radio or television receiver to receive (a transmission or station). 4 **tune out,** adjust a radio or television receiver to get rid of or not receive (an unwanted transmission or station). 5 **tune up, a** bring musical instruments to the same pitch; put in tune. **b** put (a motor, racing vessel, etc.) into the best working order. **c** INFORMAL. begin to play, sing, cry, etc. *—v.i.* be in tune; be in harmony. [variant of *tone*]

tune a ble (tü′nə bəl, tyü′nə bəl), *adj.* tunable.

tune ful (tün′fəl, tyün′fəl), *adj.* musical; melodious: *a tuneful song.* **—tune′ful ly,** *adv.* **—tune′ful ness,** *n.*

tune less (tün′lis, tyün′lis), *adj.* without tune; not musical. **—tune′less ly,** *adv.*

tun er (tü′nər, tyü′nər), *n.* 1 person who tunes pianos, organs, or other musical instruments. 2 device for adjusting a radio receiver to accept a given frequency and reject other frequencies.

tune-up (tün′up′, tyün′up′), *n.* U.S. series of checks and adjustments made on parts of an engine to put it into efficient order.

tung oil (tung), a poisonous oil obtained from the seeds of the tung tree, much used in varnishes for its drying quality. [< Chinese *t'ung*]

tung sten (tung′stən), *n.* a heavy, hard, steel-gray, ductile, metallic element found only in certain rare minerals and having the highest melting point of all metals; wolfram. It is added to steel to make it harder, stronger, and more elastic, and is also used in making electric-lamp filaments, surgical instruments, automobile parts, etc. *Symbol:* W; *atomic number* 74. See pages 326 and 327 for table. [< Swedish < *tung* heavy + *sten* stone]

tung tree, tree of the same family as the spurge, native to China and cultivated in other areas, from which tung oil is obtained.

tu nic (tü′nik, tyü′nik), *n.* 1 garment like a shirt or gown, usually reaching to the knees, worn by men and women in ancient Greece and Rome. 2 any garment like this. 3 a woman's garment, usually belted, extending below the waist or over the skirt. 4 a short, close-fitting coat worn by soldiers, policemen, etc. 5 a natural covering of a plant, animal, part of an animal, etc. [< Latin *tunica*]

tu ni cate (tü′nə kit, tü′nə kāt; tyü′nə kit, tyü′nə kāt), *adj.* 1 made up of concentric layers. An onion is a tunicate bulb. 2 having a tunic or outer covering. 3 belonging to the tunicates. *—n.* any of a subphylum of small sea chordates having a saclike body enclosed in a tough, leathery membrane, with a single or double opening through which water enters or leaves; sea squirt.

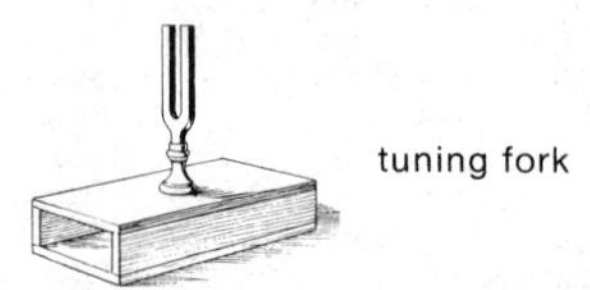
tuning fork

tuning fork, a small, two-pronged steel instrument used for finding the standard pitch and for tuning musical instruments. When struck, it vibrates at a fixed, constant, known rate and so makes a musical tone of a certain pitch.

Tu nis (tü′nis, tyü′nis), *n.* 1 seaport and capital of Tunisia, in the NE part. 642,000. 2 a former Barbary State in N Africa.

Tu ni sia (tü nē′zhə, tyü nē′zhə), *n.* country in N Africa. 5,140,000 pop.; 63,400 sq. mi. *Capital:* Tunis. See **Algeria** for map. **—Tu-ni′sian,** *adj., n.*

tun nel (tun′l), *n., v.,* **-neled, -nel ing** or **-nelled, -nel ling.** *—n.* any underground passage, such as an underground roadway for a railroad, a passage in a mine, or an animal's burrow. *—v.i.* make a tunnel. *—v.t.* 1 make a tunnel through or under. 2 make (one's way or a way) by digging. [< Old French *tonel* cask < *tonne* tun; ultimately of Celtic origin] **—tun′nel er, tun′nel ler,** *n.*

tun ny (tun′ē), *n., pl.* **-nies** or **-ny.** tuna[1]. [< Latin *thynnus* < Greek *thynnos*]

tu pe lo (tü′pə lō, tyü′pə lō), *n., pl.* **-los.** 1 a large North American tree of the same family as the sour gum, whose flowers are used for making honey. 2 its light, soft but tough wood. [of Algonquian origin]

Tu pi (tü pē′, tü′pē), *n., pl.* **-pi** or **-pis** for 1. 1 member of a group of Indian tribes of Brazil, Paraguay, and Uruguay. 2 language of these tribes, belonging to the Tupi-Guarani linguistic stock.

Tu pi-Gua ra ni (tü pē′gwär′ä nē′, tü′pē-gwär′ä nē′), *n.* a native linguistic stock of central South America, occurring particularly along the Amazon, and consisting principally of Tupi, the northern branch, and Guarani, the southern branch.

tup pence (tup′əns), *n.* twopence.

tuque (tük, tyük), *n.* kind of knitted stocking cap, worn especially in Canada. [< Canadian French, variant of French *toque* cap]

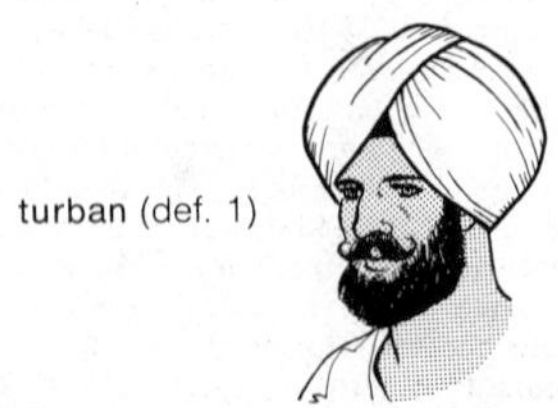
turban (def. 1)

tur ban (tėr′bən), *n.* 1 scarf wound around the head or around a cap, worn by men in parts of India and in some other countries of Asia. 2 any headdress like this, such as a big handkerchief tied around the head. 3 a small hat with little or no brim, worn by women and children. [< Middle French *turbant* < Turkish *tülbend.* Doublet of TULIP.]

tur baned (tėr′bənd), *adj.* wearing a turban.

tur bel lar i an (tėr′bə ler′i ən, tėr′bə lar′i-ən), *n.* any of a class of flatworms which have external cilia and live in fresh or salt water or damp earth. Planarians belong to this class. [< New Latin *Turbellaria,* the class name < Latin *turbellae* bustle, tumult; because of the water currents caused by the waving cilia]

tur bid (tėr′bid), *adj.* 1 muddy; thick; not clear: *a turbid river.* 2 (of air, smoke, etc.) thick; dense; dark. 3 confused; disordered: *a turbid imagination.* [< Latin *turbidus* < *turba* turmoil] **—tur′bid ly,** *adv.* **—tur′bid ness,** *n.*

tur bid i ty (tėr′bid′ə tē), *n.* condition of being turbid.

tur bi nate (tėr′bə nit, tėr′bə nāt), *adj.* 1 shaped like a spinning top or inverted cone: *a turbinate shell.* 2 noting or having to do with certain scroll-like spongy bones of the nasal passages in the higher vertebrates. *—n.* 1 a turbinate shell. 2 a turbinate bone. [< Latin *turbinatus* < *turbinem* whirling object]

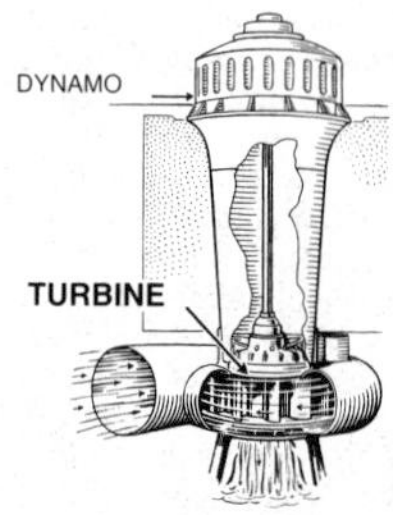

tur bine (tėr′bən, tėr′bīn), *n.* engine or motor consisting of a series of vanes mounted on a wheel around a central shaft. The shaft is made to revolve by the force of a current of fluid, whether in the form of a liquid, as water, or of a gas, as steam, acting on the vanes. [< French < Latin *turbinem* whirling object]

tur bo fan (tėr′bō fan′), *n.* turbojet in which a fan forces low-pressure air through ducts directly into the hot turbine exhaust at the pressure of the turbine exhaust; fanjet.

tur bo jet (tėr′bō jet′), *n.* 1 jet engine having a turbine-driven air compressor which supplies a continuous, high-pressure flow of air to the burners. 2 aircraft having such an engine.

tur bo prop (tėr′bō prop′), *n.* 1 adaptation of the turbojet in which a propeller, driven by a shaft from the turbine, provides most of the thrust, with additional thrust provided by the ejection of exhaust gases from the rear; propjet. 2 aircraft having such an engine.

tur bot (tėr′bət), *n., pl.* **-bots** or **-bot.** 1 a large European flatfish, much valued as food. 2 any of various related fishes. [< Old French *tourbout*]

tur bu lence (tėr′byə ləns), *n.* 1 turbulent condition; disorder; tumult; commotion. 2 an eddying motion of the atmosphere interrupting the flow of wind.

tur bu len cy (tėr′byə lən sē), *n.* turbulence.

tur bu lent (tėr′byə lənt), *adj.* 1 causing disorder; disorderly; unruly; violent: *a turbu-*

lent mob. 2 stormy; tempestuous: *turbulent weather, turbulent water.* [< Latin *turbulentus* < *turba* turmoil] **—tur′bu lent ly,** *adv.*

tu reen (tə rēn′), *n.* a deep, covered dish for serving soup, etc. [< French *terrine* earthen vessel, ultimately < Latin *terra* earth]

Tu renne (tʏ ren′), *n.* **Henri de,** 1611-1675, French marshal.

turf (tėrf), *n.* 1 the upper surface of the soil covered with grass and other small plants, including their roots and the soil clinging to them; sod. 2 piece of this. 3 peat, especially a slab or block of peat dug for use as fuel. 4 Usually, **the turf, a** a track for horse races. **b** the sport or business of horse racing. *—v.t.* cover with turf. [Old English] **—turf′less,** *adj.*

turf y (tėr′fē), *adj.,* **turf i er, turf i est.** 1 covered with turf; grassy. 2 like turf. 3 full of peat; like peat. 4 of or having to do with horse racing. **—turf′i ness,** *n.*

Tur ge nev (tůr gā′nyef), *n.* **Ivan Sergevich,** 1818-1883, Russian novelist.

tur ges cence (tėr′jes′ns), *n.* act or fact of swelling; swollen condition.

tur ges cent (tėr′jes′nt), *adj.* swelling; becoming swollen. [< Latin *turgescentem* < *turgere* to swell]

tur gid (tėr′jid), *adj.* 1 puffed out; swollen; bloated. 2 using big words and elaborate comparisons; bombastic; inflated; pompous. [< Latin *turgidus* < *turgere* to swell] **—tur′gid ly,** *adv.* **—tur′gid ness,** *n.*

tur gid i ty (tėr′jid′ə tē), *n.* turgid condition or quality.

tur gor (tėr′gər, tėr′gôr), *n.* 1 the normal full, tense condition of living plant and animal cells, capillaries, etc. 2 turgidity. [< Late Latin]

Tur in (tůr′ən, tyůr′ən), *n.* city in NW Italy. 1,177,000.

Turk (tėrk), *n.* 1 native or inhabitant of Turkey, especially a Moslem who lives in Turkey. 2 member of any group of people speaking a Turkic language.

Turk., 1 Turkey. 2 Turkish.

Tur ke stan (tėr′kə stan′, tėr′kə stän′), *n.* region in W and central Asia, part of which belongs to China, part to the Soviet Union, and part to Afghanistan.

tur key (tėr′kē), *n., pl.* **-keys.** 1 a large wild or domesticated American bird with a bare head and neck and brown or white plumage. 2 its flesh, used for food. 3 SLANG. an unsuccessful play, motion picture, etc.; failure; flop. 4 **talk turkey,** INFORMAL. talk frankly and bluntly. [< *Turkey,* apparently by confusion with a guinea fowl originally imported by way of Turkey]

Tur key (tėr′kē), *n.* country in W Asia and SE Europe. 35,667,000 pop.; 296,200 sq. mi. *Capital:* Ankara.

turkey buzzard, vulture of South and Central America and southern United States, having a bare, reddish head and dark plumage.

turkey cock, 1 a male turkey. 2 a strutting, conceited person.

Tur kic (tėr′kik), *adj.* of or having to do with a group of Ural-Altaic languages spoken in Turkey and south central Asia. *—n.* the Turkic group of languages.

Turk ish (tėr′kish), *adj.* of, having to do with, or belonging to Turkey, the Turks, or their language. *—n.* the Turkic language of the Turks.

Turkish bath, a kind of bath in which the bather is kept in a room heated by steam until he sweats freely, then is washed and massaged, and then takes a cold shower.

Turkish delight, a jellylike candy made usually in cubes dusted with powdered sugar. Also, **Turkish paste.**

Turkish Empire, Ottoman Empire.

Turkish paste, Turkish delight.

turkish towel, a thick cotton towel with a long nap made of uncut loops.

Turk men S.S.R. (tėrk′men), one of the constituent republics of the U.S.S.R., in the central part. 2,200,000 pop.; 188,400 sq. mi. *Capital:* Ashkhabad.

Tur ko man (tėr′kə mən), *n., pl.* **-mans.** 1 member of any of various Turkish tribes inhabiting the region about the Aral Sea and parts of Iran and Afghanistan. 2 the Turkic language of this people.

tur mer ic (tėr′mər ik), *n.* 1 a yellow powder prepared from the aromatic, pungent rhizome of an East Indian plant of the same family as the ginger, used as a seasoning, as a yellow dye, a stimulant, etc. 2 the plant itself. 3 its rhizome. [earlier *tarmaret* < Middle French *terre mérite* < Medieval Latin *terra merita,* literally, worthy earth]

tur moil (tėr′moil), *n.* state of agitation or commotion; disturbance; tumult: *Six robberies in one night put the village in a turmoil.* [origin uncertain]

turn (tėrn), *v.t.* 1 cause to move round as a wheel does; rotate: *I turned the crank three times.* 2 do by turning; open, close, make lower, higher, tighter, looser, etc., by moving around: *She turned the key in the lock.* 3 perform by revolving: *turn a somersault.* 4 give a new direction to: *turn one's steps to the north.* 5 change in direction or position; invert; reverse: *turn a page.* 6 change for or to a worse condition; sour; spoil: *Warm weather turns milk.* 7 change so as to make: *The bitter cold turned him blue.* 8 shape, especially into a rounded form, by cutting with a chisel or similar tool while rotating in a lathe. 9 shape, form, or fashion: *turn a pretty compliment.* 10 change from one language or form of expression to another: *Turn this sentence into Latin.* 11 put out of order; unsettle: *Flattery has turned her head.* 12 cause to go; send: *turn a person from one's door.* 13 cause to go aside or retreat; drive back; stop; repel: *turn a blow, turn an attacker.* 14 direct (thought, desire, speech, action, etc., to, toward, or away from something): *turn one's efforts to a new job, turn one's thoughts toward home.* 15 apply, as to some use or purpose: *turn everything to advantage, turn money to good use.* 16 get to the other side of; go round: *turn the corner.* 17 pass or get beyond (a particular age, time, or amount): *a man turning sixty.* 18 make antagonistic; prejudice: *turn friends against friends.* 19 cause to recoil: *His argument was turned against himself.* 20 change the color of: *Fall turned the leaves.* 21 make sick; nauseate: *The sight of blood turned his stomach.* 22 bend; twist. 23 bend back (the edge of a sharp instrument) so as to make it useless for cutting. *—v.i.* 1 move around as a wheel does; rotate. See synonym study below. 2 move part way around; change from one side to the other: *Turn over on your back.* 3 take a new direction: *The road turns to the left here.* 4 change so as to be; become: *She turned pale.* 5 become sour or tainted: *That milk has turned.* 6 change color. 7 take up an attitude of opposition: *The people turned against their leader.* 8 become sick. 9 become dizzy: *Heights make my head turn.*

hat, āge, fär; let, ēqual, tėrm;
it, īce; hot, ōpen, ôrder;
oil, out; cup, pu̇t, rüle;
ch, child; ng, long; sh, she;
th, thin; ᴛʜ, then; zh, measure;

ə represents *a* in about, *e* in taken, *i* in pencil, *o* in lemon, *u* in circus.

< = from, derived from, taken from.

turn down, a fold down. **b** bend downward. **c** place with face downward. **d** refuse: *turn down an offer.* **e** lower by turning something: *turn down the gas.*

turn in, a turn and go in. **b** point (toes) inward. **c** INFORMAL. go to bed. **d** give back. **e** exchange: *turn in an old appliance for a new model.* **f** hand over; deliver: *turn in finished work.* **g** inform on: *turn in a suspect.*

turn off, a stop the flow of (water, gas, electric current, etc.) by turning a tap, etc.; shut off. **b** put out (a light). **c** discharge. **d** do: *turn off a job.* **e** lose or cause to lose interest.

turn on, a start the flow of (water, gas, electric current, etc.) by turning a tap, etc. **b** put on (a light). **c** attack; resist; oppose. **d** depend on: *The success of the picnic turns on the weather.* **e** be about; have to do with: *The conversation turned on literature.* **f** SLANG. take or cause to take a narcotic drug. **g** SLANG. become or cause to become stimulated, interested, excited, etc.

turn out, a put out; shut off (a lamp, light, etc.). **b** let go out. **c** drive out. **d** come or go out. **e** make; produce: *turn out two novels in a year.* **f** equip; fit out. **g** come about in the end; result: *The deal turned out successfully.* **h** come to be; become ultimately: *She turned out a successful lawyer.* **i** be found or known; prove. **j** INFORMAL. get out of bed.

turn over, a give; hand over; transfer: *turn over a job to someone.* **b** think carefully about; consider in different ways: *turn over a proposition.* **c** buy and then sell; use in business. **d** invest and get back (capital). **e** do business to the amount of (a specified sum): *a store turning over $100,000 yearly.* **f** convert to different use. **g** overturn; reverse. **h** roll over.

turn to, a refer to. **b** go to for help. **c** get busy; set to work.

turn up, a fold up or over, especially so as to shorten. **b** make (a lamp) burn more brightly. **c** make (a radio, television set, etc.) louder. **d** turn and go up. **e** direct or be directed upward. **f** appear: *An old friend has turned up.* **g** be found; reappear: *The lost keys turned up.* **h** happen: *Something will turn up to save the hero.*

—n. 1 motion like that of a wheel: *At each turn the screw goes in further.* 2 change of direction: *a turn to the left.* 3 place where there is a change in direction: *a turn in the road.* 4 change in affairs, conditions, or circumstances: *Matters have taken a turn for the worse.* 5 the time at which such a change takes place: *the turn of the year, the turn of a fever.* 6 form; style: *a happy turn of expression.* 7 twist; round of a coil of rope. 8 time or chance to do anything: *My turn comes after yours.* 9 time or spell of action: *Take a turn at the oars.* 10 deed; act: *One good turn deserves another.* 11 stroke or spell of work; job; performance. 12 inclination; bent: *He*

has a turn for mathematics. 13 a walk, drive, or ride: *a turn in the park, take a turn in the garden.* 14 spell of dizziness or fainting. 15 INFORMAL. a nervous shock: *give someone a bad turn.* 16 requirement; need; purpose: *This will serve your turn.* 17 (in music) a grace note consisting of a principal tone with those above and below it.

at every turn, on every occasion; without exception; constantly.

by turns, one after another.

in turn, in proper order.

out of turn, not in proper order.

take turns, act one after another in proper order.

to a turn, exactly to the proper degree: *meat done to a turn.*

turn about or **turn and turn about,** one after another in proper order.

[Old English *turnian* < Latin *tornare* turn on a lathe < *tornus* lathe < Greek *tornos.* Related to TOUR.]

Syn. *v.i.* 1 **Turn, revolve, rotate** mean to move round in a circle. **Turn** is the general and common word for such motion about an axis or center: *That wheel turns freely now.* In science, a distinction is regularly made between **rotate,** to move on an axis, and **revolve,** to move in a circle around a center: *The earth rotates once every twenty-four hours. The earth revolves around the sun once a year.* This distinction is not, however, observed in ordinary usage. Otherwise, a *revolver* would be called a *rotater* and an engine's speed would be measured in *rotations per minute* rather than *revolutions per minute.*

turn a bout (tėrn′ə bout′), *n.* a change to an opposite position, view, course, etc.; reversal.

turn a round (tėrn′ə round′), *n.* 1 reversal. 2 time that a ship spends in a port before the outgoing voyage. 3 place for a vehicle to turn around.

turn buck le (tėrn′buk′əl), *n.* link or coupling with internal screw threads at both ends, or a screw thread at one end and a swivel at the other, used to unite and tighten two parts, as the ends of two rods.

turn coat (tėrn′kōt′), *n.* person who changes his party or principles; renegade; traitor.

turn down (tėrn′doun′), *adj.* that is or can be turned down; folded or doubled down: *a turndown collar.* —*n.* a turning down; rejection.

turn er (tėr′nər), *n.* 1 person or thing that turns. 2 person who forms things or shapes a substance with a lathe.

Tur ner (tėr′nər), *n.* 1 **Joseph M. W.,** 1775-1851, English painter. 2 **Nat,** 1800-1831, American leader of a slave uprising in Virginia in 1831, who was executed for his part in the rebellion.

turnstile

turn er y (tėr′nər ē), *n., pl.* **-er ies.** 1 art or work of a turner. 2 objects fashioned on the lathe; turner's work. 3 a turner's workshop.

turning point, point at which a notable or decisive change takes place.

tur nip (tėr′nəp), *n.* 1 either of two biennial plants, both of which are species of cole, having large, fleshy, roundish roots. The **white turnip** and the **Swedish turnip** or rutabaga are the two kinds of turnip. 2 the root of either of these plants, eaten as a vegetable. [probably ultimately < Middle English *turn* (from its rounded shape) + *nepe* turnip < Latin *napus*]

turn key (tėrn′kē′), *n., pl.* **-keys.** person in charge of the keys of a prison, jail, etc.; keeper of a prison; jailer.

turn off (tėrn′ôf′, tėrn′of′), *n.* place at which a road, path, etc., turns off to another.

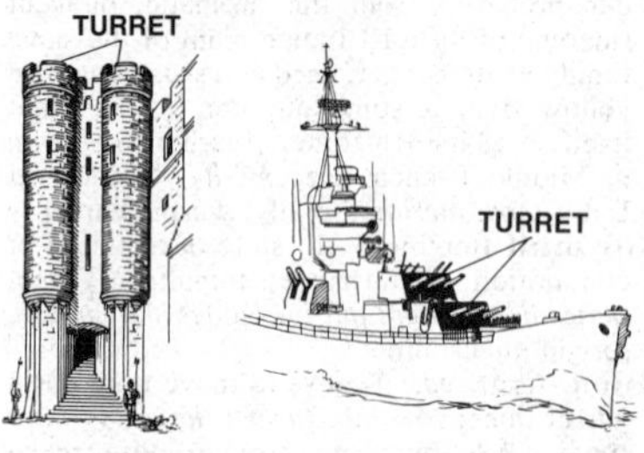

turret (def. 1, left; def. 2, right)

turn out (tėrn′out′), *n.* 1 a gathering of people. 2 quantity produced; total product; output; yield. 3 a wide place in the road, where vehicles can pass. 4 a railroad siding. 5 way in which somebody or something is equipped; equipment. 6 a horse or horses and carriage. 7 a turning out.

turn o ver (tėrn′ō′vər), *n.* 1 a turning upside down; an overturn; upset. 2 the number of people hired to replace workers who leave or are dismissed. 3 the rate at which new workers are hired, as compared to the average total number of employees. 4 the paying out and getting back of the money involved in a business transaction: *The store reduced prices to make a quick turnover.* 5 the total amount of business done in a given time: *make a profit of $6000 on a turnover of $90,000.* 6 a shifting of votes, transfer of allegiance, etc., from one party, group, or faction to another. 7 a small pie made by folding half the crust over the filling and upon the other half. —*adj.* having a part that turns over: *a turnover collar.*

turn pike (tėrn′pīk′), *n.* 1 toll road. 2 gate where toll is paid; tollgate. 3 road that has, or used to have, a gate where toll is paid. 4 any main highway. [< *turn* + *pike* a sharp point; with reference to a spiked barrier across a road, turning on a vertical axis]

turn spit (tėrn′spit′), *n.* person or thing that turns a roast of meat on a spit.

turn stile (tėrn′stīl′), *n.* post with bars that turn, set in an entrance or exit, and used especially to prevent a person's entrance to a subway, building, etc., until he has paid a charge.

turn stone (tėrn′stōn′), *n.* any of a genus of small migratory shore birds that turn over stones in search of food.

turn ta ble (tėrn′tā′bəl), *n.* 1 a revolving circular platform used for turning things around. A turntable with a track is used for turning locomotives around. 2 the round, revolving platform of a phonograph upon which records are placed.

turn up (tėrn′up′), *adj.* that is turned up or turns up. —*n.* 1 the turned-up part of anything, especially of a garment. 2 BRITISH. a trouser cuff.

turn ve rein (tůrn′fe rīn′), *n.* organization of gymnasts; athletic club. [< German *Turnverein* < *turnen* to exercise + *Verein* club]

tur pen tine (tėr′pən tīn), *n.* 1 oleoresin obtained from various coniferous trees. 2 a volatile oil distilled from this oleoresin, used in mixing paints and varnishes, in medicine, etc. [< Greek *terebinthos*]

tur pi tude (tėr′pə tüd, tėr′pə tyüd), *n.* shameful character; wickedness; baseness. [< Latin *turpitudo* < *turpis* vile]

tur quoise (tėr′koiz, tėr′kwoiz), *n.* 1 a sky-blue or greenish-blue precious mineral which is valued as a gem, almost opaque or sometimes translucent, consisting of copper and hydrous phosphate of aluminum. 2 a sky blue or greenish blue, like that of turquoise. —*adj.* sky-blue or greenish-blue. [< Old French *(pierre) turqueise* Turkish (stone)]

tur ret (tėr′it), *n.* 1 a small tower, often on the corner of a building. 2 any of various low, rotating, armored structures within which guns are mounted, as in a warship or tank. 3 a plastic bubble on the fuselage of some bombers, for machine guns and a gunner. 4 an attachment on a lathe, drill, etc., to hold cutting tools. [< Old French *touret,* ultimately < Latin *turris* tower]

tur ret ed (tėr′ə tid), *adj.* 1 having a turret or turrets. 2 having whorls in the form of a long spiral.

tur tle[1] (tėr′tl), *n., pl.* **-tles** or **-tle,** *v.,* **-tled, -tling.** —*n.* 1 any of an order of reptiles having a toothless, horny beak and a rounded body encased in a shell, from which the head, tail, and four legs protrude and, in some kinds, into which they can be retracted for protection. Turtles live in fresh water, salt water, or on land; those living on land are often called tortoises. 2 the flesh of turtles, especially the terrapin, used as food. 3 **turn turtle,** turn bottom side up; capsize. —*v.i.* catch or seek to catch turtles. [< French *tortue* tortoise]

tur tle[2] (tėr′tl), *n.* ARCHAIC. turtledove. [Old English *turtle, turtla* < Latin *turtur*]

tur tle back (tėr′tl bak′), *n.* an arched protection erected over the deck of a steamer at the bow, and often at the stern also, to guard against damage from heavy seas.

tur tle dove (tėr′tl duv′), *n.* any of several small Old World doves, especially the common European kind, noted for its long tail, soft cooing, and for the affection that the mates seem to have for each other. [< *turtle*[2] + *dove*[1]]

tur tle neck (tėr′tl nek′), *n.* 1 a round, high, closely fitting collar on a sweater, etc., usually turned down over itself when the garment is worn. 2 sweater, etc., with such a collar. —*adj.* (of a sweater, etc.) having such a collar.

Tus can (tus′kən), *adj.* of or having to do with Tuscany, its people, or their language. —*n.* 1 native or inhabitant of Tuscany. 2 dialect of Tuscany, regarded as the classical and standard form of Italian.

Tus ca ny (tus′kə nē), *n.* district in central Italy. Florence is its chief city.

Tus ca ro ra (tus′kə rôr′ə, tus′kə rōr′ə), *n., pl.* **-ra** or **-ras.** member of a tribe of Iroquois Indians that lived in colonial North Carolina and now live in New York State and Ontario.

hat, āge, fär; let, ēqual, tėrm;
it, īce; hot, ōpen, ôrder;
oil, out; cup, pu̇t, rüle;
ch, child; ng, long; sh, she;
th, thin; ᴛʜ, then; zh, measure;

ə represents *a* in about, *e* in taken, *i* in pencil, *o* in lemon, *u* in circus.

< = from, derived from, taken from.

tush[1] (tush), *interj., n.* exclamation expressing impatience, contempt, etc.

tush[2] (tush), *n.* 1 tusk. 2 one of the canine teeth of a horse. [Old English *tusc*]

tusk (tusk), *n.* 1 a very long, pointed, projecting tooth. Elephants, walruses, and wild boars have tusks. 2 any tooth or part resembling a tusk. *—v.t.* gore with a tusk; dig or tear with the tusks. [Middle English, variant of Old English *tusc* tush[2]. Related to TOOTH.]

tusk er (tus′kər), *n.* animal, especially a male animal, having well-developed tusks, such as a full-grown elephant, walrus, or wild boar.

tus sah (tus′ə), *n.* 1 a coarse, tan Asian silk. 2 the silkworm that makes it. [< Hindi *tasar* shuttle]

tus sle (tus′əl), *v.*, **-sled, -sling,** *n.* *—v.i.* struggle or wrestle; scuffle. *—n.* a vigorous or disorderly conflict; severe struggle or hard contest. [variant of *tousle*]

tus sock (tus′ək), *n.* 1 tuft or clump forming a small hillock of grass, sedge, or the like. 2 tuft of hair, feathers, etc. [origin uncertain]

tussock moth, any of a family of dull-colored moths whose larvae have thick tufts of hair.

tus sock y (tus′ə kē), *adj.* 1 abounding in tussocks. 2 forming tussocks.

tut (tut), *interj., n.* exclamation of impatience, contempt, or rebuke. Also, **tut-tut.**

Tut ankh a men (tü′tängk ä′mən), *n.* died 1350? B.C., king of Egypt from 1358? to 1350? B.C. His tomb, discovered in 1922, contained objects of archaeological interest.

tu te lage (tü′tl ij, tyü′tl ij), *n.* 1 office or function of a guardian; guardianship; protection. 2 instruction. 3 a being in the charge of a guardian or tutor. [< Latin *tutela* protection]

tu te lar (tü′tl ər, tyü′tl ər), *adj.* tutelary.

tu te lar y (tü′tl er′ē, tyü′tl er′ē), *adj., n., pl.* **-lar ies.** *—adj.* 1 having the position of guardian; protecting; guardian: *a tutelary saint.* 2 of a guardian; used as a guardian; protective: *a tutelary charm.* *—n.* a tutelary saint, spirit, divinity, etc. [< Latin *tutela* protection < *tueri* watch over]

tu tor (tü′tər, tyü′tər), *n.* 1 a private teacher. 2 teacher below the rank of instructor at a college or university. 3 (in English universities) a college official appointed to advise students, direct their work, etc. *—v.t.* teach; instruct, especially individually or privately. *—v.i.* 1 INFORMAL. be taught by a tutor. 2 act as tutor. [< Latin, guardian < *tueri* watch over]

tu to ri al (tü tôr′ē əl, tü tōr′ē əl; tyü tôr′ē-əl, tyü tōr′ē əl), *adj.* 1 of or having to do with a tutor. 2 using tutors: *the tutorial system.* *—n.* period of individual instruction given in some colleges by a tutor either to a single student or a small group.

tu tor ship (tü′tər ship, tyü′tər ship), *n.* position, rank, or duties of a tutor.

tut ti-frut ti (tü′tē frü′tē), *n.* 1 preserve of mixed fruits. 2 ice cream or other confection containing a variety of fruits or fruit flavorings. *—adj.* flavored with or containing mixed fruits. [< Italian *tutti frutti* all fruits]

tut-tut (tut′tut′), *interj., n.* tut.

tu tu (tü′tü), *n.* a very short, full, stiff skirt worn by a ballet dancer. [< French]

Tu tu i la (tü′tü ē′lä), *n.* island in American Samoa, site of the harbor of Pago Pago. 26,000 pop.; 40 sq. mi.

tu-whit tu-whoo (tu̇ hwit′ tu̇ hwü′), imitation of the call of an owl.

tux (tuks), *n.* INFORMAL. tuxedo.

tux e do (tuk sē′dō), *n., pl.* **-dos** or **-does.** 1 a man's coat for semiformal evening wear, made without tails, usually black with satin lapels. 2 the suit to which such a coat belongs. [< *Tuxedo* Park, New York]

tu yère (twē yer′, twir), *n.* opening through which the blast of air is forced into a blast furnace, forge, etc. [< French]

TV, television.

TVA, Tennessee Valley Authority (a U.S. government organization for developing the resources of the region of the Tennessee River valley, started in 1933).

twa (twä), *n., adj.* SCOTTISH. two.

twad dle (twod′l), *n., v.*, **-dled, -dling.** *—n.* silly, feeble, tiresome talk or writing. *—v.i., v.t.* talk or write in a silly, feeble, tiresome way. [ultimately variant of *tattle*] **—twad′dler,** *n.*

twain (twān), *n., adj.* ARCHAIC. two. [Old English *twēgen*]

Twain (twān), *n.* **Mark,** 1835-1910, American writer, author of *Tom Sawyer* and *Huckleberry Finn.* His real name was Samuel Langhorne Clemens.

twang (twang), *n.* 1 a sharp, ringing sound: *The bow made a twang when I shot the arrow.* 2 a sharp, nasal tone: *the twang of a Yankee farmer.* *—v.t.* 1 make a sharp, ringing sound. 2 play, pluck, shoot, etc., with a twang. 3 speak (words, etc.) with a sharp, nasal tone. *—v.i.* 1 make a sharp, ringing sound: *The banjos twanged.* 2 speak with a sharp, nasal tone. [imitative]

'twas (twoz, twuz; *unstressed* twəz), it was.

tweak (twēk), *v.t., v.i.* seize and pull with a sharp jerk and twist: *tweak a person's ear.* *—n.* a sharp pull and twist. [Old English *twiccian* to pluck]

tweed (twēd), *n.* 1 a twilled woolen fabric with a rough surface, usually woven of fibers of two or more colors. Tweed is sometimes made of wool and cotton or synthetic fibers. 2 suit, etc., made of this fabric. 3 **tweeds,** *pl.* clothes made of tweed. [alteration of *tweel,* Scottish variant of *twill*]

Tweed River (twēd), river flowing from S Scotland into the North Sea. 97 mi.

tweed y (twē′dē), *adj.* 1 consisting of or like tweed. 2 characterized by or given to wearing tweeds.

'tween (twēn), *prep.* ARCHAIC. between.

tweet (twēt), *n., interj.* the note of a young bird. *—v.i.* utter a tweet or tweets. [imitative]

tweet er (twē′tər), *n.* a high-fidelity loudspeaker for reproducing the higher frequency sounds.

tweeze (twēz), *v.t.,* **tweezed, tweez ing.** pull out with tweezers.

tweezers

tweez ers (twē′zərz), *n.pl.* small pincers for pulling out hairs, picking up small objects, etc. [< obsolete *tweeze* instrument case, plural of *twee* < French *étui* < Old French *estuier* to keep]

twelfth (twelfth), *adj., n.* 1 next after the 11th; last in a series of 12. 2 one, or being one, of 12 equal parts.

Twelfth-day (twelfth′dā′), *n.* January 6, the twelfth day after Christmas, on which the feast of the Epiphany is celebrated.

Twelfth-night (twelfth′nīt′), *n.* the evening or eve of Twelfth-day, often celebrated as the end of Christmas festivities.

twelve (twelv), *n.* 1 one more than 11; 12. 2 group of twelve persons or things. 3 **the Twelve,** the twelve Apostles of Jesus. *—adj.* one more than 11; 12. [Old English *twelf*]

twelve month (twelv′munth′), *n.* twelve months; a year.

twelve-tone (twelv′tōn′), *adj.* of or having to do with a system of music based on all twelve semitones of the chromatic scale in an arbitrarily selected order without any tone center (tonic).

twen ti eth (twen′tē ith), *adj., n.* 1 next after the 19th; last in a series of 20. 2 one, or being one, of 20 equal parts.

twen ty (twen′tē), *n., pl.* **-ties,** *adj.* two times ten; 20. [Old English *twēntig*]

twen ty-one (twen′tē wun′), *n.* a gambling game in which the players draw cards from the dealer in trying to come as close to a count of twenty-one (in adding the spots on the cards) as possible without going past it; blackjack; vingt-et-un.

twen ty-twen ty (twen′tē twen′tē), *n.* the vision of the normal human eye, being that which can distinguish a character $^1/_3$ inch in diameter from a distance of 20 feet.

'twere (twėr; *unstressed* twər), it were.

twerp (twėrp), *n.* SLANG. a stupid, undesirable, or inferior person.

twice (twīs), *adv.* 1 two times: *twice a day.* 2 double: *twice as much.* [Middle English *twies* < Old English *twiga* twice]

twice-told (twīs′tōld′), *adj.* 1 told twice. 2 told many times before; hackneyed; trite.

twid dle (twid′l), *v.*, **-dled, -dling,** *n.* *—v.t.* 1 twirl: *twiddle one's pencil.* 2 play with idly. *—v.i.* 1 be busy about trifles. 2 **twiddle one's thumbs, a** keep turning one's thumbs idly about each other. **b** do nothing; be idle. *—n.* a twirl; twist. [origin uncertain]

twig[1] (twig), *n.* a slender shoot of a tree or other plant; very small branch. [Old English *twigge*]

twig[2] (twig), *v.t.,* **twigged, twig ging.** BRITISH INFORMAL. understand; comprehend. [perhaps < Scottish Gaelic *tuig*]

twi light (twī′līt′), *n.* 1 the faint light reflected from the sky before the sun rises and after it sets. 2 the period during which this prevails, especially from sunset to dark night. 3 any faint light. 4 condition or period after full development, glory, etc. *—adj.* of twilight; like that of twilight: *the twilight hour.* [Middle English < *twi-* two + *light*[1]]

twilight sleep, a semiconscious condition produced by the hypodermic injection of scopolamine and morphine, in order to lessen the pains of childbirth.

twill (twil), *n.* 1 fabric woven in raised diagonal lines. Serge is a twill. 2 a diagonal line or pattern formed by such weaving. *—v.t.* weave (fabric) in the manner of a twill. [Old English *twilic,* alteration of Latin *bilix* with a double thread < *bi-* two + *licium* thread]

'twill (twil), it will.

twilled (twild), *adj.* woven in raised diagonal lines.

twin (twin), *n., adj., v.,* **twinned, twin ning.** —*n.* 1 one of two children or animals born at the same time to the same mother. 2 one of two persons or things very much or exactly alike. —*adj.* 1 being a twin: *twin sisters.* 2 being one of two things very much or exactly alike: *twin beds.* 3 having two like parts. —*v.i.* give birth to twins. —*v.t.* 1 join closely; couple; pair. 2 be a counterpart to; match. [Old English *twinn*]

twin born (twin′bôrn′), *adj.* born a twin or twins; born at the same birth.

twine (twīn), *n., v.,* **twined, twin ing.** —*n.* 1 a strong thread or string made of two or more strands twisted together. 2 a twisting; twisting together. 3 a twisted thing; twist; tangle. —*v.t.* 1 twist together: *She twined holly into wreaths.* 2 form or make by twisting together: *twine a wreath.* 3 wrap, wind, or encircle: *twine a rope around a post.* —*v.i.* 1 wind or wrap around: *The vine twines around the tree.* 2 extend or proceed in a winding manner; meander. [Old English *twīn.* Related to TWIST.]

twinge (twinj), *n., v.,* **twinged, twing ing.** —*n.* a sudden sharp pain: *a twinge of rheumatism, a twinge of remorse.* —*v.i.* feel a twinge. —*v.t.* cause a twinge in. [Old English *twengan* to pinch]

twin kle (twing′kəl), *v.,* **-kled, -kling,** *n.* —*v.i.* 1 shine with quick little gleams; sparkle; glitter: *The stars twinkled. His eyes twinkled when he laughed.* 2 move quickly: *The dancer's feet twinkled.* —*v.t.* cause to twinkle. —*n.* 1 a twinkling; sparkle; gleam. 2 a quick motion. 3 a quick motion of the eye; wink; blink. 4 time required for a wink: *in the twinkle of an eye.* [Old English *twinclian*] —**twin′kler,** *n.*

twin kling (twing′kling), *n.* 1 a little, quick gleam. 2 a very brief period; moment; instant.

twin-screw (twin′skrü′), *adj.* having two screw propellers, which revolve in opposite directions.

twirl (twėrl), *v.t.* 1 revolve rapidly; spin; whirl: *twirl a baton.* 2 turn round and round idly. 3 twist; curl; flourish. —*v.i.* 1 be twirled. 2 INFORMAL. (in baseball) be the pitcher; pitch. —*n.* 1 a twirling; spin; whirl; turn. 2 a twist; curl; flourish: *He signed his name with many twirls.* [origin uncertain] —**twirl′er,** *n.*

twist (twist), *v.t.* 1 turn with a winding motion; wind: *She twisted her ring on her finger.* 2 wind together; entwine; interweave: *This rope is twisted from many threads.* 3 give a spiral form to. 4 curve; crook; bend: *twist a piece of wire into a loop.* 5 force out of shape or place: *a face twisted with pain.* 6 sprain or wrench: *twist an ankle.* 7 give a different meaning to; distort the meaning of: *twist a person's words.* 8 make (a ball) go round while moving in a curved direction. —*v.i.* 1 turn around: *She twisted in her seat to see what was happening behind her.* 2 have a winding shape, course, etc.; curve; bend: *The path twists in and out among the rocks.* 3 spin; twirl: *leaves that twist and turn in the air.* 4 move with a spin, as a curve in baseball or a billiard ball with english.
—*n.* 1 curve; crook; bend: *know every twist in the road.* 2 spin; twirl. 3 a twisting. 4 a being twisted. 5 alteration of shape such as is caused by turning the ends of an object in opposite directions: *a girder with a bad twist.* 6 anything given shape by twisting: *a twist of bread.* 7 pipe tobacco wound or braided into ropelike form. 8 cord, thread, or strand formed by twisting fibers, yarns, etc. 9 a peculiar bias or inclination: *His answer showed a mental twist.* 10 an unexpected variation: *A new twist in the plot kept the audience in suspense.* 11 wrench; sprain: *suffer a painful twist of the elbow.* 12 a lateral spin imparted to a ball in throwing or striking it. 13 ball thus spun. 14 dance in two-beat rhythm, with strong swinging movements from side to side.
[Old English *-twist,* as in *mæsttwist* mast rope, stay]

twist er (twis′tər), *n.* 1 person or thing that twists. 2 ball moving with a spinning motion. 3 INFORMAL. a whirling windstorm; whirlwind; tornado.

twit (twit), *v.,* **twit ted, twit ting,** *n.* —*v.t.* jeer at; reproach; taunt; tease: *The boys twitted me because I would not fight.* —*n.* a reproach; taunt. [Old English *ætwītan* put blame on]

twitch (twich), *v.i., v.t.* 1 move with a quick jerk: *The child's mouth twitched as if she were about to cry.* 2 pull with a sudden tug or jerk; pull (at): *twitch the curtain aside.* —*n.* 1 a slight, involuntary movement of a muscle, etc.; a quick jerky movement of some part of the body. 2 a short, sudden pull or jerk. [Middle English *twicchen*]

twit ter (twit′ər), *n.* 1 sound made by birds; chirping. 2 a brief or muffled giggle; titter. 3 an excited condition; flutter: *My nerves are in a twitter when I have to speak in public.* —*v.i.* 1 make a twittering sound; chirp. 2 sing, talk, or chatter rapidly in a small or tremulous voice. 3 titter; giggle. 4 tremble with excitement, eagerness, fear, etc. —*v.t.* utter or express by twittering. [imitative]

twit ter y (twit′ər ē), *adj.* apt to twitter or tremble; fluttering; shaky.

'twixt or **twixt** (twikst), *prep.* betwixt; between.

two (tü), *n., pl.* **twos,** *adj.* —*n.* 1 one more than one; 2. 2 set of two persons or things. 3 **in two,** in two parts or pieces. 4 **put two and two together,** form an obvious conclusion from the facts. —*adj.* one more than one; 2. [Old English *twā*]

two-bag ger (tü′bag′ər), *n.* SLANG. (in baseball) a double.

two-base hit (tü′bās′), (in baseball) a double.

two-bit (tü′bit′), *adj.* SLANG. 1 worth a quarter of a dollar. 2 cheap; worthless.

two bits, SLANG. a quarter of a dollar.

two-by-four (tü′bī fôr′, tü′bī fōr′), *adj.* 1 measuring two inches, feet, etc., by four inches, feet, etc. 2 INFORMAL. small; narrow; limited. —*n.* piece of lumber four inches wide and two inches thick, much used in building.

two-di men sion al (tü′də men′shə nəl), *adj.* having only two dimensions; lacking depth; superficial. —**two′-di men′sion al ly,** *adv.*

two-edged (tü′ejd′), *adj.* 1 having two edges; cutting both ways. 2 effective either way.

two-faced (tü′fāst′), *adj.* 1 having two faces. 2 deceitful; hypocritical.

two-fac ed ly (tü′fā′sid lē, tü′fāst′lē), *adv.* in a two-faced manner; deceitfully; hypocritically.

two-fist ed (tü′fis′tid), *adj.* INFORMAL. strong; vigorous.

two fold (tü′fōld′), *adj.* 1 two times as much or as many; double. 2 having two parts; dual. —*adv.* two times as much or as many; doubly.

two-hand ed (tü′han′did), *adj.* 1 having two hands. 2 using both hands equally well; ambidextrous. 3 involving the use of both hands; requiring both hands to wield or manage: *a two-handed sword.* 4 requiring two persons to operate: *a two-handed saw.* 5 engaged in or played by two persons: *a two-handed game.*

two pence (tup′əns), *n.* 1 two British pennies; two pence. 2 coin of this value, now issued only on special occasions. Also, **tuppence.**

two pen ny (tup′ə nē), *adj.* 1 worth, costing, or amounting to twopence. 2 trifling; worthless.

two-ply (tü′plī′), *adj.* having two thicknesses, folds, layers, or strands.

two some (tü′səm), *n.* 1 group of two people. 2 game or match played by two people, especially in golf. 3 the players.

two-step (tü′step′), *n., v.,* **-stepped, -step ping.** —*n.* 1 a dance in march or polka rhythm, performed with sliding steps. 2 music for it. —*v.i.* dance the two-step.

two-time (tü′tīm′), *v.t.,* **-timed, -tim ing.** SLANG. 1 be unfaithful to in love. 2 betray; deceive; double-cross. —**two′-tim′er,** *n.*

'twould (twu̇d; *unstressed* twəd), it would.

two-way (tü′wā′), *adj.* 1 moving or allowing movement in two directions: *a two-way street.* 2 used in two ways or for two purposes: *a two-way radio.*

-ty[1], *suffix added to numbers.* ___ tens; ___ times ten: *Seventy = seven tens, or seven times ten.* [Old English *-tig*]

-ty[2], *suffix added to adjectives to form nouns.* quality, condition, or fact of being ___: *Safety = condition or quality of being safe.* Also, **-ity.** [< Old French *-te, -tet* < Latin *-tas, -tatem*]

ty coon (tī kün′), *n.* 1 INFORMAL. businessman having great wealth and power. 2 title given by foreigners to the former hereditary commanders in chief of the Japanese army; shogun. [< Japanese *taikun* < Chinese *tai* great + *kiun* lord]

ty ing (tī′ing), *v.* ppr. of **tie.**

tyke (tīk), *n.* 1 INFORMAL. a mischievous or troublesome child. 2 a mongrel dog; cur. Also, **tike.** [< Scandinavian (Old Icelandic) *tīk* bitch]

Ty ler (tī′lər), *n.* **John,** 1790-1862, tenth president of the United States, from 1841 to 1845.

tym pan ic (tim pan′ik), *adj.* 1 of the eardrum. 2 like a drum.

tympanic membrane, eardrum.

tym pa nist (tim′pə nist), *n.* timpanist.

tym pa num (tim′pə nəm), *n., pl.* **-nums, -na** (-nə). 1 eardrum. 2 middle ear. 3 diaphragm in a telephone. 4 in architecture: **a** the vertical recessed face of a pediment enclosed by the cornices. **b** a slab or wall between an arch and the horizontal top of a door or window below. [< Latin, drum < Greek *tympanon.* Doublet of TIMBRE.]

Tyn dale (tin′dl), *n.* **William,** 1492?-1536, English religious martyr who translated the New Testament and part of the Old Testament into English.

Tyn dall (tin′dl), *n.* **John,** 1820-1893, British physicist, born in Ireland.

Tyne River (tīn), river in N England, flowing southeast into the North Sea. 80 mi.

type (tīp), *n., v.,* **typed, typ ing.** —*n.* 1 a kind, class, or group having certain common characteristics: *three types of local government.* 2 kind; sort; order: *I don't like that type of work.* 3 person or thing having the characteristics of a kind, class, or group; example; illustration. 4 a perfect example of a kind, class, or group; model; pattern: *He is a fine type of schoolboy.* 5 the general form, style, or character of some kind, class, or group: *She is above the ordinary type of student.* 6 a small block, usually of metal or wood, having on its upper surface a raised letter, figure, or other character, for use in printing. 7 collection of such pieces. 8 printed letters; typewritten letters: *large type, small type.* 9 figure, writing, or design on either side of a coin or medal. 10 blood type.
—*v.t.* 1 be the type or symbol of; symbolize; typify. 2 be the pattern or model for. 3 classify as to type: *type a person's blood, type an actor as a villain.* 4 write with a typewriter; typewrite. —*v.i.* typewrite.
[< Latin *typus* < Greek *typos* dent, impression < *typtein* to strike, beat]
➔ **type, type of.** The standard English idiom is *type of: this type of* (not *type*) *letter.*

type cast (tīp′kast′), *v.t.,* **-cast, -cast ing.** 1 cast (an actor) in a role that seems to suit his appearance and personality. 2 cast repeatedly in the same role.

type founder, person who casts or makes metal printing type.

type founding, art or process of manufacturing movable metallic types used by printers.

type foundry, place where printing types are manufactured.

type metal, alloy of lead and antimony, sometimes with tin, etc., of which printing types are cast.

type script (tīp′skript′), *n.* a typewritten manuscript.

type set ter (tīp′set′ər), *n.* 1 person who sets type for printing; compositor. 2 machine that sets type for printing.

type set ting (tīp′set′ing), *n.* act of setting type for printing. —*adj.* used or adapted for setting type.

type write (tīp′rīt′), *v.t., v.i.,* **-wrote** (-rōt′), **-writ ten, -writ ing.** write with a typewriter; type.

type writ er (tīp′rī′tər), *n.* 1 machine for writing equipped with a keyboard, which produces letters, figures, etc., similar to printed ones when the keys are pressed against an inked ribbon and a sheet of paper. 2 typist.

type writ ing (tīp′rī′ting), *n.* 1 act or art of using a typewriter: *study typewriting.* 2 work done on a typewriter.

type writ ten (tīp′rit′n), *adj.* written with a typewriter: *a typewritten letter.* —*v.* pp. of **typewrite.**

ty phoid (tī′foid), *adj.* 1 of, having to do with, or like typhoid fever. 2 like typhus. —*n.* typhoid fever.

typhoid fever, an acute, often fatal, infectious disease, characterized by a high fever, intestinal inflammation, eruptions of the skin, diarrhea, and sometimes stupor, caused by a bacillus which is spread by contaminated food, drink, and clothing.

ty phoon (tī fün′), *n.* 1 a violent storm or tempest occurring in India. 2 a violent cyclone or hurricane occurring in the western Pacific, chiefly during the period from July to October. [< Chinese *tai fung* big wind]

ty phus (tī′fəs), *n.* an acute infectious disease characterized by high fever, extreme weakness, dark-red spots on the skin, and stupor or delirium, caused by a rickettsia carried by fleas, lice, ticks, or mites. [< Greek *typhos* stupor caused by fever]

tyrannosaurus—about 19 ft. tall

typ i cal (tip′ə kəl), *adj.* 1 being a type; representative: *The typical Thanksgiving dinner consists of turkey, cranberry sauce, several vegetables, and mince or pumpkin pie.* 2 of or having to do with a type; characteristic: *the swiftness typical of a gazelle.* —**typ′i cal ness,** *n.*

typ i cal ly (tip′ik lē), *adv.* 1 in a typical manner. 2 to a typical degree. 3 ordinarily.

typ i fy (tip′ə fī), *v.t.,* **-fied, -fy ing.** 1 be a symbol of: *The lamb typifies Christ's sacrifice.* 2 have the common characteristics of: *Daniel Boone typifies the pioneer.* 3 indicate beforehand. —**typ′i fi ca′tion,** *n.*

typ ist (tī′pist), *n.* person operating a typewriter, especially one who does typewriting as a regular occupation.

ty po (tī′pō), *n., pl.* **-pos.** SLANG. a typographical error.

ty pog ra pher (tī pog′rə fər), *n.* person whose work is typography.

ty po graph ic (tī′pə graf′ik), *adj.* typographical.

ty po graph i cal (tī′pə graf′ə kəl), *adj.* of or having to do with printing or typing: *"Catt" and "hoRse" contain typographical errors.* —**ty′po graph′i cal ly,** *adv.*

ty pog ra phy (tī pog′rə fē), *n.* 1 the art or process of printing with type; work of setting and arranging type and of printing from it. 2 arrangement, appearance, or style of printed matter.

Tyr (tir), *n.* (in Scandinavian myths) the god of war and victory, son of Odin.

ty ran nic (tə ran′ik, tī ran′ik), *adj.* tyrannical.

ty ran ni cal (tə ran′ə kəl, tī ran′ə kəl), *adj.* of a tyrant; like a tyrant; arbitrary; cruel; unjust: *a tyrannical king.* —**ty ran′ni cal ly,** *adv.*

hat, āge, fär; let, ēqual, tėrm;
it, īce; hot, ōpen, ôrder;
oil, out; cup, pu̇t, rüle;
ch, child; ng, long; sh, she;
th, thin; ᴛʜ, then; zh, measure;

ə represents *a* in about, *e* in taken, *i* in pencil, *o* in lemon, *u* in circus.

< = from, derived from, taken from.

ty ran ni cide (tə ran′ə sīd, tī ran′ə sīd), *n.* 1 act of killing a tyrant. 2 person who kills a tyrant.

tyr an nize (tir′ə nīz), *v.,* **-nized, -niz ing.** —*v.i.* 1 use power cruelly or unjustly. 2 rule as a tyrant; be a tyrant. —*v.t.* 1 rule cruelly; oppress. 2 rule over as a tyrant. —**tyr′an niz′er,** *n.*

ty ran no sau rus (ti ran′ə sôr′əs, tī ran′ə sôr′əs), *n.* a huge, carnivorous dinosaur of the late Cretaceous period in North America, characterized by its ability to walk erect on its two hind limbs. [< Greek *tyrannos* tyrant + *sauros* lizard]

tyr an nous (tir′ə nəs), *adj.* acting like a tyrant; cruel or unjust; arbitrary; tyrannical. —**tyr′an nous ly,** *adv.*

tyr an ny (tir′ə nē), *n., pl.* **-nies.** 1 cruel or unjust use of power. 2 a tyrannical act. 3 government, position, rule, or term of office of a tyrant or absolute ruler. 4 state ruled by a tyrant.

ty rant (tī′rənt), *n.* 1 person who uses his power cruelly or unjustly. 2 a cruel or unjust ruler; cruel master. 3 an absolute ruler, as in ancient Greece, owing his office to usurpation. [< Old French < Latin *tyrannus* < Greek *tyrannos*]

tyre (tīr), *n., v.t.,* **tyred, tyr ing.** tire[2].

Tyre (tīr), *n.* ancient seaport in S Phoenicia, noted for its wealth and wickedness.

Tyr i an (tir′ē ən), *adj.* of or having to do with Tyre. —*n.* native or inhabitant of Tyre.

Tyrian purple, 1 a deep crimson or purple dye used by the ancient Greeks and Romans, obtained from various shellfish. 2 bluish red.

ty ro (tī′rō), *n., pl.* **-ros.** beginner in learning anything; novice. Also, **tiro.** [< Latin *tiro* recruit]

Ty rol (tə rōl′, tī′rōl), *n.* Tirol.

Ty ro le an (tə rō′lē ən), *adj., n.* Tirolean.

Tyr o lese (tir′ə lēz′), *adj., n.* Tirolese.

Ty rone (tə rōn′), *n.* county in W Northern Ireland.

ty ro sine (tī′rə sēn′, tī′rə sən), *n.* a white, crystalline amino acid produced by the hydrolysis of a number of proteins, as casein. It is a constituent of cheese. *Formula:* $C_9H_{11}NO_3$ [< Greek *tyros* cheese]

Tyr rhe ni an Sea (tə rē′nē ən), part of the Mediterranean Sea lying between Italy, Sicily, Sardinia, and Corsica.

tzar (zär, tsär), *n.* czar.

tza ri na (zä rē′nə, tsä rē′nə), *n.* czarina.

tzet ze (tset′sē), *n.* tsetse.

U u

U or **u** (yü), *n., pl.* **U's** or **u's.** 1 the 21st letter of the English alphabet. 2 anything shaped like a U.
U, uranium.
U., University.
U.A.R., United Arab Republic.
UAW or **U.A.W.,** United Automobile Workers.
U bang gi River (yü bang′gē, ü bäng′gē), river flowing from central Africa into the Congo River. 700 mi.
u biq ui tous (yü bik′wə təs), *adj.* that is everywhere at the same time; present everywhere. **—u biq′ui tous ly,** *adv.* **—u biq′ui tous ness,** *n.*
u biq ui ty (yü bik′wə tē), *n.* 1 a being everywhere at the same time. 2 ability to be everywhere at once. [< Latin *ubique* everywhere]
U-boat (yü′bōt′), *n.* a German submarine. [half-translation of German *U-boot,* short for *Unterseeboot* undersea boat]
u.c., upper case; capital letter or letters.
ud der (ud′ər), *n.* the baglike mammary gland that hangs down on a cow, female goat, etc., having two or more fingerlike teats or nipples. [Old English *ūder*]

UFO or **U.F.O.,** unidentified flying object (a flying saucer).
u fol o gist (yü fol′ə jist), *n.* person engaged in or devoted to ufology.
u fol o gy (yü fol′ə jē), *n.* practice or hobby of tracking unidentified flying objects. [< *UFO* + *-logy*]
UFT or **U.F.T.,** United Federation of Teachers.
U gan da (ü gan′də, yü gan′də), *n.* country in E Africa, a member of the Commonwealth of Nations. 9,760,000 pop.; 94,000 sq. mi. *Capital:* Kampala. See **Zaïre** for map. **—U gan′dan,** *adj., n.*
ugh (ug, u), *interj.* exclamation expressing disgust, horror, strong distaste, etc.
ug li fy (ug′lə fī), *v.t.,* **-fied, -fy ing.** make ugly; disfigure.
ug ly (ug′lē), *adj.,* **-li er, -li est.** 1 very unpleasant to look at: *an ugly house, an ugly face.* See synonym study below. 2 bad; disagreeable; offensive: *an ugly task, an ugly smell, ugly language.* 3 morally low or offensive; base: *an ugly act of treason.* 4 likely to cause trouble; threatening; dangerous: *an ugly wound, ugly clouds.* 5 INFORMAL. ill-natured; bad-tempered; quarrelsome; cross: *an ugly mood, an ugly disposition.* [< Scandinavian (Old Icelandic) *uggligr* dreadful] **—ug′li ness,** *n.*
Syn. 1 Ugly, unsightly, homely mean not pleasing in appearance. **Ugly,** the strongest of the three, means positively unpleasant or offensive in appearance: *There are two ugly, gaudy lamps in that room.* **Unsightly** means unpleasing to the sight through carelessness or neglect: *Trains approach the city through an unsightly section.* **Homely** means lacking in beauty or attractiveness, but does not suggest unpleasant or disagreeable qualities: *A homely child often develops into an attractive adult.*
ugly duckling, person or thing that lacks good features or qualities but later develops them to a surpassing degree. [< the story by Hans Christian Andersen about a duckling without grace or beauty that grows into a graceful swan]
U gri an (ü′grē ən, yü′grē ən), *n.* 1 member of an ethnic group which includes the Magyars and certain peoples of western Siberia. 2 their languages, as a division of Finno-Ugric. *—adj.* of or having to do with the Ugrians or their division of Finno-Ugric.
UHF or **uhf,** ultrahigh frequency.
uh lan (ü′län, ü län′), *n.* 1 a mounted soldier of a type first known in Europe in Poland, armed with a lance. 2 (in the former German army) a member of the heavy cavalry. [< German *Uhlan* < Polish *ulan* < Turkish *oğlan* boy]
u hu ru (ü hür′ü), *n.* SWAHILI. freedom.
U.K., United Kingdom.
u kase (yü kās′, yü′kās), *n.* 1 (in former times) an official decree having the force of law, issued by a Russian czar or his government. 2 any official proclamation or order. [< Russian *ukaz*]
U kraine (yü krān′, yü′krān), *n.* Ukrainian S.S.R.
U krain i an (yü krā′nē ən), *adj.* of or having to do with the Ukrainian S.S.R., its people, or their language. *—n.* 1 native or inhabitant of the Ukrainian S.S.R. 2 the Slavic language spoken in the Ukrainian S.S.R.
Ukrainian S.S.R., one of the constituent republics of the U.S.S.R., in the SW part. 47,100,000 pop.; 232,000 sq. mi. *Capital:* Kiev.
u ku le le (yü′kə lā′lē), *n.* a small guitar having four strings. [< Hawaiian, originally, flea]
U lan Ba tor (ü′län bä′tôr), capital of the Mongolian People's Republic, in the NE part. 254,000.
ul cer (ul′sər), *n.* 1 an open sore on the skin, or within the body, on a mucous membrane. It sometimes discharges pus. 2 a moral sore spot; corrupting influence. [< Latin *ulceris*]
ul cer ate (ul′sə rāt′), *v.t., v.i.,* **-rat ed, -rat ing.** 1 affect or be affected with an ulcer: *An ulcerated tongue may be very painful.* 2 form or be formed into an ulcer. **—ul′ce ra′tion,** *n.*
ul cer ous (ul′sər əs), *adj.* 1 having or affected with an ulcer or ulcers. 2 having the nature of an ulcer; like an ulcer.
ul na (ul′nə), *n., pl.* **-nae** (-nē), **-nas.** 1 the thinner, longer bone of the forearm, on the side opposite the thumb. See **humerus** for diagram. 2 a corresponding bone in the forelimb of a vertebrate animal. [< New Latin < Latin, elbow]
ul nar (ul′nər), *adj.* 1 of or having to do with the ulna. 2 in or supplying the part of the forearm near the ulna.
ul ster (ul′stər), *n.* a long, loose, heavy overcoat, often belted at the waist. [< *Ulster*]
Ul ster (ul′stər), *n.* 1 former province of Ireland, now forming all of Northern Ireland and part of the Republic of Ireland. 2 province in N Republic of Ireland.
ult., ultimo; of the past month: *your order of the 14th ult.*
ul ter i or (ul tir′ē ər), *adj.* 1 beyond what is seen or expressed; hidden: *an ulterior motive, an ulterior purpose.* 2 more distant; on the farther side. 3 further; later. [< Latin, comparative of root of *ultra* beyond] **—ul ter′i or ly,** *adv.*
ul ti ma (ul′tə mə), *n.* the last syllable of a word. [< Latin *ultima (syllaba)* last (syllable)]
ul ti mate (ul′tə mit), *adj.* 1 coming at the end; last possible; final: *He never stopped to consider the ultimate result of his actions.* See **last**[1] for synonym study. 2 that is an extremity; beyond which there is nothing at all; extreme: *the ultimate limits of the universe.* 3 fundamental; basic: *The brain is the ultimate source of ideas. The ultimate source of life has not been discovered.* 4 greatest possible: *He gave his life and thereby paid the ultimate price.* *—n.* an ultimate point, result, fact, etc. [< Medieval Latin *ultimatum* < Latin *ultimus* last, superlative of root of *ultra* beyond] **—ul′ti mate ly,** *adv.* **—ul′ti mate ness,** *n.*
ul ti ma Thu le (ul′tə mə thü′lē), 1 the farthest north. 2 the farthest limit or point possible. 3 the utmost degree attainable. [< Latin, most remote Thule]
ul ti ma tum (ul′tə mā′təm), *n., pl.* **-tums, -ta** (-tə). 1 a final proposal or statement of conditions, acceptance of which is required under penalty of ending a relationship, negotiations, etc., or of punitive action. 2 the final terms presented by one party in an international negotiation, rejection of which may lead to the breaking off of diplomatic relations or sometimes to war. [< New Latin < Medieval Latin, ultimate]
ul ti mo (ul′tə mō), *adv.* in or of last month. [< Medieval Latin *ultimo (mense)* in the course of last (month)]
ul tra (ul′trə), *adj.* beyond what is usual; very; excessive; extreme. *—n.* person who holds extreme views or urges extreme measures. [< Latin, beyond]
ultra-, *prefix.* 1 beyond the ___: *Ultraviolet = beyond the violet.* 2 beyond what is usual; very; excessively; extremely, as in the following words:

ul′tra-am bi′tious
ul′tra con′fi dent
ul′tra con serv′a tive
ul′tra crit′i cal
ul′tra dem′o crat′ic
ul′tra ex clu′sive
ul′tra fash′ion a ble
ul′tra fine′
ul′tra lib′er al
ul′tra loy′al
ul′tra me chan′i cal
ul′tra mod′ern
ul′tra mod′est
ul′tra rad′i cal
ul′tra re fined′
ul′tra re li′gious

[< Latin < *ultra* beyond]
ul tra cen trif u gal (ul′trə sen trif′yə gəl, ul′trə sen trif′ə gəl), *adj.* of or by means of an ultracentrifuge. **—ul′tra cen trif′u gal ly,** *adv.*

hat, āge, fär; let, ēqual, tėrm;
it, īce; hot, ōpen, ôrder;
oil, out; cup, pu̇t, rüle;
ch, child; ng, long; sh, she;
th, thin; ᴛʜ, then; zh, measure;

ə represents *a* in about, *e* in taken, *i* in pencil, *o* in lemon, *u* in circus.

< = from, derived from, taken from.

ul tra cen trif u ga tion (ul′trə sen-trif′yə gā′shən, ul′trə sen trif′ə gā′shən), *n.* a subjecting or a being subjected to the action of an ultracentrifuge.

ul tra cen tri fuge (ul′trə sen′trə fyüj), *n.* centrifuge that can spin at very high speed, for measuring the molecular weights of solutes and determining the size of particles.

ul tra high frequency (ul′trə hī′), the band of radio frequencies between 300 and 3000 megacycles.

ul tra ma rine (ul′trə mə rēn′), *n.* 1 a deep blue. 2 a blue pigment made from powdered lapis lazuli. 3 an artificial imitation of this. —*adj.* 1 deep-blue. 2 beyond or across the sea.

ul tra mi cro scope (ul′trə mī′krə skōp), *n.* a powerful instrument for making visible particles too small to be seen by an ordinary microscope, by means of light thrown on the object from one side, over a dark background.

ul tra mi cro scop ic (ul′trə mī′krə-skop′ik), *adj.* 1 too small to be seen with an ordinary microscope. 2 having to do with an ultramicroscope.

ul tra mod ern ist (ul′trə mod′ər nist), *n.* person who is extremely modern in ideas, tastes, etc.

ul tra son ic (ul′trə son′ik), *adj.* supersonic. **—ul′tra son′i cal ly,** *adv.*

ul tra son ics (ul′trə son′iks), *n.* supersonics.

ul tra vi o let (ul′trə vī′ə lit), *adj.* of the invisible part of the spectrum whose rays have wavelengths shorter than those of the violet end of the visible spectrum and longer than those of the X rays. Ultraviolet rays are present in sunlight and are important in healing, forming vitamins, etc. See **radiation** for table. —*n.* that part of the spectrum comprising these rays.

ul tra vi res (ul′trə vī′rēz), LATIN. going beyond the powers granted by authority or by law.

ul u lant (yül′yə lənt, ul′yə lənt), *adj.* howling.

ul u late (yül′yə lāt, ul′yə lāt), *v.i.,* **-lat ed, -lat ing.** 1 howl, as a dog, wolf, etc. 2 lament loudly. [< Latin *ululatum* howling] **—ul′u la′tion,** *n.*

Ul ya nov (ül yä′nôf), *n.* **Vladimir Ilich,** the real name of **Nikolai Lenin.**

U lys ses (yü lis′ēz), *n.* (in Greek legends) a king of Ithaca and hero of the Trojan War, known for his wisdom and shrewdness. Ulysses, who was called Odysseus by the Greeks, is the hero of Homer's *Odyssey,* which tells about his adventures.

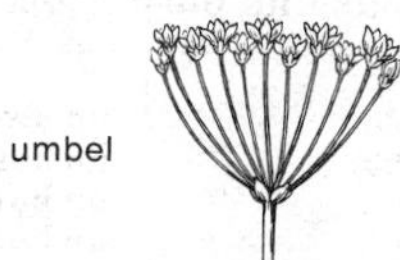
umbel

um bel (um′bəl), *n.* a flower cluster in which stalks nearly equal in length spring from a common center and form a level or slightly curved surface, as in parsley. [< Latin *umbella* parasol, diminutive of *umbra* shade]

um bel lar (um′bə lər), *adj.* umbellate.

um bel late (um′bə lit, um′bə lāt), *adj.* 1 of or like an umbel. 2 having umbels; forming an umbel or umbels.

um ber (um′bər), *n.* 1 any of various mixtures of clay and iron oxide. In its natural state it is a brown pigment called **raw umber.** After heating it becomes dark reddish brown and is called **burnt umber.** 2 a brown or dark reddish brown. —*adj.* brown or dark reddish-brown. [< Italian *(terra di) ombra* (earth of) shade]

um bil i cal (um bil′ə kəl), *adj.* of, having to do with, or situated near the navel or umbilical cord.

umbilical cord, a cordlike structure that connects the navel of an embryo or fetus with the placenta of the mother. It carries nourishment to the fetus and carries away waste.

um bil i cus (um bil′ə kəs, um′bə lī′kəs), *n., pl.* **-ci** (-sī). 1 navel. 2 a small depression or hollow suggestive of a navel, such as the hilum of a seed. [< Latin, navel]

um bles (um′bəlz), *n.pl.* the heart, liver, lungs, etc., of an animal, especially of a deer, used as food. [alteration of Old French *numbles* loin, fillet]

um bra (um′brə), *n., pl.* **-brae** (-brē), **-bras.** 1 the completely dark shadow cast by the earth, moon, etc., during an eclipse. See **eclipse** for diagram. 2 the dark inner or central part of a sunspot. 3 shade; shadow. [< Latin, shade, shadow]

um brage (um′brij), *n.* 1 suspicion that one has been slighted or injured; feeling offended; resentment. 2 **take umbrage,** take offense; feel insulted or offended. 3 shade. 4 the foliage of trees, etc., providing shade.

um bra geous (um brā′jəs), *adj.* 1 likely to take offense. 2 shady.

um brel la (um brel′ə), *n.* 1 a light, portable, circular cover for protection against rain or sun, consisting of a fabric held on a folding frame of thin ribs, which slide on a rod or stick. 2 any protective covering or shelter. 3 the umbrellalike, gelatinous body of a jellyfish. [< Italian *ombrella,* ultimately < Latin *umbra* shade] **—um brel′la like′,** *adj.*

umbrella tree, 1 an American magnolia tree having long leaves in clusters at the ends of the branches that suggest umbrellas. 2 any of various trees whose leaves or habit of growth resemble an open umbrella.

Um bri a (um′brē ə), *n.* 1 ancient region in central and N Italy. 2 district in central Italy.

Um bri an (um′brē ən), *adj.* 1 of or having to do with Umbria or its people. 2 of or having to do with the language of ancient Umbria. —*n.* 1 native or inhabitant of the district of Umbria. 2 member of a people living in ancient Umbria. 3 the Italic language of ancient Umbria.

u mi ak (ü′mē ak), *n.* an open Eskimo boat made of skins covering a wooden frame and worked with paddles. [< Eskimo]

um laut (u̇m′lout, üm′lout), *n.* 1 change in vowel sound in the Germanic languages because of the influence of another vowel in the following syllable, now generally lost but responsible for such pairs as English *man-men* and *foot-feet.* 2 vowel that is the result of such a change. 3 the sign (¨) used to indicate such a vowel, as in German *Göring,* also written *Goering.* —*v.t.* 1 modify by umlaut. 2 write (a vowel) with an umlaut. [< German *Umlaut* < *um* about + *Laut* sound]

um pire (um′pīr), *n., v.,* **-pired, -pir ing.** —*n.* 1 person who rules on the plays in a game: *The umpire called the ball a foul.* 2 person chosen to settle a dispute. —*v.t.* act as an umpire in (a game, dispute, etc.). —*v.i.* act as an umpire. [earlier *a numpire* (taken as *an umpire*) < Old French *nonper* not even, odd < *non* not + *per* equal]

ump teen (ump′tēn′), *adj.* INFORMAL. of a great but indefinite number; countless.

ump teenth (ump′tēnth′), *adj.* INFORMAL. being the last of a great but indefinite number.

ump ti eth (ump′tē ith), *adj.* INFORMAL. umpteenth.

UMT, Universal Military Training.

UMW or **U.M.W.,** United Mine Workers.

un-[1], *prefix.* not ___; the opposite of ___: *Unequal = not equal; the opposite of equal. Unchanged = not changed. Unjust = not just.* [Old English]

➜ **un-.** This dictionary lists hundreds of words at the bottom of the pages on which they would occur if placed in the main list, in which *un-* means *not.* Even so, *un-* is a prefix freely used in forming new words, and not all of the words in which it may be used can be shown here.

un-[2], *prefix.* do the opposite of ___; do what will reverse the act: *Unfasten = do the opposite of fasten. Uncover = do the opposite of cover.* [Old English *un-, on-*]

➜ **un-** is used freely to form verbs expressing the reversal of the action of the verb.

UN or **U.N.,** United Nations.

un a bashed (un′ə basht′), *adj.* not embarrassed, ashamed, or awed. **—un′a-bash′ed ly,** *adv.*

un a ble (un ā′bəl), *adj.* not able; lacking ability or power *(to): be unable to sing.*

un a bridged (un′ə brijd′), *adj.* not shortened or condensed; complete: *an unabridged book.*

umiak

un ac com pa nied (un′ə kum′pə nēd), *adj.* 1 not accompanied; alone. 2 (in music) without instrumental accompaniment.

un ac count a ble (un′ə koun′tə bəl), *adj.* 1 that cannot be accounted for or explained;

In each of the words below **un** *means not.*

un′a bat′ed
un′ab bre′vi at′ed
un′a bet′ted
un′ab solved′
un′ab sorbed′
un′ac a dem′ic
un ac′cent ed
un′ac cept′a ble
un′ac cept′ed
un′ac cli′mat ed
un′ac cli′ma tized
un′ac com′mo dat′ing
un′ac com′plished

inexplicable. 2 not responsible: *An imbecile is unaccountable for his actions.* **—un′ac count′a bly,** *adv.*

un ac count ed-for (un′ə koun′tid fôr′), *adj.* not accounted for or explained.

un ac cus tomed (un′ə kus′təmd), *adj.* 1 not accustomed: *a man unaccustomed to public speaking.* 2 not familiar; unusual; strange: *unaccustomed surroundings.*

un a dul te rat ed (un′ə dul′tə rā′tid), *adj.* not adulterated; pure: *unadulterated flour, unadulterated nonsense.*

un ad vised (un′əd vīzd′), *adj.* 1 not advised; without advice. 2 not prudent or discreet; rash.

un ad vis ed ly (un′əd vī′zid lē), *adv.* in an indiscreet manner; rashly.

un af fect ed[1] (un′ə fek′tid), *adj.* not affected; not influenced. [< *un-*[1] + *affected*[1]]

un af fect ed[2] (un′ə fek′tid), *adj.* simple and natural; straightforward; sincere. [< *un-*[1] + *affected*[2]] **—un′af fect′ed ly,** *adv.* **—un′af fect′ed ness,** *n.*

un al ien a ble (un ā′lyə nə bəl), *adj.* inalienable.

un a ligned (un′ə līnd′), *adj.* nonaligned.

un al ter a ble (un ôl′tər ə bəl), *adj.* that cannot be altered; not changeable; permanent. **—un al′ter a ble ness,** *n.* **—un al′ter a bly,** *adv.*

un-A mer i can (un′ə mer′ə kən), *adj.* not characteristic of or proper to America or the United States; foreign or opposed to the American character, usages, standards, etc.

U na mu no (ü′nə mü′nō), *n.* **Miguel de,** 1864-1936, Spanish philosopher, novelist, and poet.

un a neled (un′ə nēld′), *adj.* ARCHAIC. without having received extreme unction: *die unaneled.* [< *un-*[1] + Middle English *anelien* give extreme unction to < *an-* on + *elien* anoint < Latin *oleum* oil]

u na nim i ty (yü′nə nim′ə tē), *n.* complete accord or agreement.

u nan i mous (yü nan′ə məs), *adj.* 1 in complete accord or agreement; agreed: *They were unanimous in their wish to go home.* 2 characterized by or showing complete accord: *She was elected president of her class by a unanimous vote.* [< Latin *unanimus* < *unus* one + *animus* mind] **—u nan′i mous ly,** *adv.* **—u nan′i mous ness,** *n.*

un an swer a ble (un an′sər ə bəl), *adj.* 1 that cannot be answered. 2 that cannot be disproved. **—un an′swer a bly,** *adv.*

un an swered (un an′sərd), *adj.* 1 not replied to. 2 not proved false or incorrect; not refuted: *an unanswered argument.* 3 not returned.

un ap peas a ble (un′ə pē′zə bəl), *adj.* not to be appeased; implacable. **—un′ap peas′a bly,** *adv.*

un ap proach a ble (un′ə prō′chə bəl), *adj.* 1 very hard to approach. 2 distant in character; aloof. 3 without an equal; unrivaled. **—un′ap proach′a ble ness,** *n.* **—un′ap proach′a bly,** *adv.*

un apt (un apt′), *adj.* 1 not fit or appropriate; unsuitable. 2 not likely. 3 not skillful. 4 not quick to learn. **—un apt′ly,** *adv.* **—un apt′ness,** *n.*

un arm (un ärm′), *v.t.* disarm.

un armed (un ärmd′), *adj.* without weapons; without armor.

un as ser tive (un′ə sėr′tiv), *adj.* not insistent or forward; reserved in speech or actions. **—un′as ser′tive ness,** *n.*

un as sum ing (un′ə sü′ming), *adj.* not putting on airs; modest; humble. **—un′as sum′ing ly,** *adv.* **—un′as sum′ing ness,** *n.*

un at tached (un′ə tacht′), *adj.* 1 not attached. 2 independent. 3 not engaged or married.

un at tend ed (un′ə ten′did), *adj.* 1 without attendants; alone. 2 not accompanied. 3 not taken care of; not attended to.

un a vail ing (un′ə vā′ling), *adj.* not successful; useless. **—un′a vail′ing ly,** *adv.*

un a void a ble (un′ə voi′də bəl), *adj.* that cannot be avoided; inevitable. **—un′a void′a ble ness,** *n.* **—un′a void′a bly,** *adv.*

un a ware (un′ə wer′, un′ə war′), *adj.* not aware; unconscious. *—adv.* without thought; unawares. **—un′a ware′ness,** *n.*

un a wares (un′ə werz′, un′ə warz′), *adv.* 1 without being expected; by surprise: *The police caught the burglar unawares.* 2 without knowing; unintentionally: *approach danger unawares.*

un backed (un bakt′), *adj.* 1 not backed, helped, or supported; unaided. 2 not bet on. 3 ARCHAIC. not ridden; not yet broken to the bit, saddle, etc.

un bal ance (un bal′əns), *n., v.,* **-anced, -anc ing.** *—n.* lack of balance; unbalanced condition. *—v.t.* throw out of balance; disorder or derange.

un bal anced (un bal′ənst), *adj.* 1 not balanced. 2 not entirely sane: *an unbalanced mind.* 3 not having debits equal to credits: *an unbalanced account.*

un bar (un bär′), *v.t., v.i.,* **-barred, -bar ring.** remove the bars from; unlock.

un bear a ble (un ber′ə bəl, un bar′ə bəl), *adj.* that cannot be endured; intolerable: *unbearable pain.* **—un bear′a ble ness,** *n.* **—un bear′a bly,** *adv.*

un beat a ble (un bē′tə bəl), *adj.* that cannot be beaten, overcome, or surpassed.

un beat en (un bēt′n), *adj.* 1 not defeated or surpassed. 2 not trodden; not traveled: *unbeaten paths.* 3 not struck, pounded, or whipped: *unbeaten metal, unbeaten eggs.*

un be com ing (un′bi kum′ing), *adj.* 1 not becoming; not appropriate: *unbecoming clothes.* 2 not fitting; not proper: *unbecoming behavior.* **—un′be com′ing ly,** *adv.* **—un′be com′ing ness,** *n.*

un be known (un′bi nōn′), *adj.* not known: *He arrived unbeknown to anyone.*

un be knownst (un′bi nōnst′), *adj.* unbeknown.

un be lief (un′bi lēf′), *n.* lack of belief, especially in matters of religious doctrine or faith. See synonym study below.

Syn. Unbelief, disbelief mean lack of belief. **Unbelief** suggests only lack of belief in something offered or held as true, with no positive feelings one way or the other: *Nowadays there is general unbelief in the idea that some people are witches.* **Disbelief** suggests a positive refusal to believe: *He expressed his disbelief in universal military training.*

un be liev a ble (un′bi lē′və bəl), *adj.* not believable; incredible: *an unbelievable story.* **—un′be liev′a bly,** *adv.*

un be liev er (un′bi lē′vər), *n.* 1 person who does not believe. 2 person who does not believe in a particular religion.

un be liev ing (un′bi lē′ving), *adj.* not believing; doubting. **—un′be liev′ing ly,** *adv.*

un bend (un bend′), *v.,* **-bent** or **-bend ed, -bend ing.** *—v.t.* 1 remove the curves, bends, etc., from; straighten. 2 release from strain; cause to relax. 3 unfasten: *unbend a sail.* *—v.i.* 1 become straight; straighten. 2 relax: *unbend after a hard day.*

un bend ing (un ben′ding), *adj.* 1 not bending or curving; rigid. 2 not yielding; stubborn; firm: *an unbending attitude.* *—n.* relaxation. **—un bend′ing ly,** *adv.*

un bent (un bent′), *v.* a pt. and a pp. of **unbend.** *—adj.* not bent or curved.

un bi ased (un bī′əst), *adj.* not prejudiced; impartial; fair: *an unbiased opinion.*

un bid den (un bid′n), *adj.* 1 not bidden; not invited: *an unbidden guest.* 2 without being ordered; not commanded.

un bind (un bīnd′), *v.t.,* **-bound, -bind ing.** release from bonds or restraint; untie; unfasten; let loose.

un bleached (un blēcht′), *adj.* not bleached; not made white by bleaching: *unbleached linen.*

un blessed or **un blest** (un blest′), *adj.*

In each of the words below **un** *means not.*

un′ac count′ed
un′ac cred′it ed
un′ac knowl′edged
un′ac quaint′ed
un′a dapt′a ble
un′a dapt′ed
un′ad just′a ble
un′ad just′ed
un′a dorned′
un ad′ver tised
un′ad vis′a ble
un′a fraid′
un aid′ed
un aimed′
un aired′
un′a like′
un′al lied′
un′al low′a ble
un′al loyed′
un al′pha bet ized
un al′tered
un al′ter ing
un′am big′u ous
un′am bi′tious
un a′mi a ble
un am′pli fied
un′a mused′
un′a mus′ing
un an′i mat′ed
un′an nounced′
un′an tic′i pat′ed
un′a pol′o get′ic
un′ap palled′
un′ap par′ent
un′ap peal′ing
un′ap peased′
un ap′pe tiz′ing
un′ap pre′ci at′ed
un′ap pre′ci a′tive
un′ap pre hend′ed
un′ap proached′
un′ap pro′pri at′ed
un′ap proved′
un ar′mored
un′ar rest′ed
un′ar tis′tic
un′a shamed′
un asked′
un′a spir′ing
un′as sail′a ble
un′as sign′a ble
un′as signed′
un′as sist′ed
un′as so′ci at′ed
un′at tain′a ble
un′at tempt′ed
un′at test′ed
un′at trac′tive
un′aus pi′cious
un′au then′tic
un′au then′ti cat′ed
un au′thor ized
un′a vail′a ble
un′a venged′
un′a vowed′
un′a wak′ened
un awed′
un baked′
un band′aged
un bap′tized
un barbed′
un beau′ti ful
un′be fit′ting
un′be hold′en
un′be seem′ing
un′be trothed′
un′be wailed′
un blam′a ble
un blamed′
un blem′ished
un blink′ing
un blurred′

1 not blessed. 2 evil; not holy. 3 unhappy; miserable; wretched.

un blush ing (un blush′ing), *adj.* 1 not blushing. 2 unabashed; shameless. **—un blush′ing ly,** *adv.*

un bod ied (un bod′ēd), *adj.* 1 having no body; incorporeal. 2 disembodied.

un bolt (un bōlt′), *v.t., v.i.* draw back the bolts of (a door, etc.).

un bolt ed[1] (un bōl′tid), *adj.* not bolted or fastened: *an unbolted door.* [< *un-*[1] + *bolt*[1]]

un bolt ed[2] (un bōl′tid), *adj.* not sifted: *unbolted flour.* [< *un-*[1] + *bolt*[2]]

un bon net ed (un bon′ə tid), *adj.* wearing no bonnet or cap; bareheaded.

un born (un bôrn′), *adj.* not yet born; still to come; of the future: *unborn generations.*

un bos om (un bu̇z′əm, un bü′zəm), *v.t.* reveal; disclose. *—v.i.* 1 speak frankly and at length. 2 **unbosom oneself,** tell or reveal one's thoughts, feelings, secrets, etc.

un bound (un bound′), *adj.* not bound: *unbound sheets of music.* *—v.* pt. and pp. of **unbind.**

un bound ed (un boun′did), *adj.* 1 not limited; very great; boundless: *the unbounded reaches of the universe.* 2 not kept within limits; not controlled.

un bowed (un boud′), *adj.* 1 not bowed or bent. 2 not forced to yield or submit; not subdued.

un brace (un brās′), *v.t.,* **-braced, -brac ing.** 1 loosen or untie (a band, belt, etc.); undo. 2 free from tension; relax. 3 render feeble; weaken.

un braid (un brād′), *v.t.* separate the strands of; unwind or unravel.

un break a ble (un brā′kə bəl), *adj.* not breakable; not easily broken: *an unbreakable phonograph record.*

un bri dled (un brī′dld), *adj.* 1 not having a bridle on. 2 not controlled; not restrained: *unbridled anger.*

un bro ken (un brō′kən), *adj.* 1 not broken; whole: *an unbroken dish.* 2 not interrupted; continuous: *I had eight hours of unbroken sleep.* 3 not tamed: *an unbroken colt.* **—un bro′ken ness,** *n.*

un buck le (un buk′əl), *v.t.,* **-led, -ling.** 1 unfasten the buckle or buckles of. 2 unfasten; detach.

un build (un bild′), *v.t.,* **-built, -build ing.** 1 take apart; dismember. 2 pull down; demolish.

un built (un bilt′), *adj.* not yet or ever built. *—v.* pt. and pp. of **unbuild.**

un bur den (un bėrd′n), *v.t.* 1 free from a burden. 2 relieve (one's mind or heart) by talking. 3 throw off or disclose (something that burdens).

un busi ness like (un biz′nis līk′), *adj.* without system and method; not efficient.

un but ton (un but′n), *v.t.* unfasten the button or buttons of.

un but toned (un but′nd), *adj.* 1 not buttoned. 2 open and free; easy; casual.

un cage (un kāj′), *v.t.,* **-caged, -cag ing.** 1 release from a cage. 2 release.

un called-for (un kôld′fôr′), *adj.* 1 unnecessary and improper: *an uncalled-for remark.* 2 not called for; not requested.

un can ny (un kan′ē), *adj.* 1 strange and mysterious; weird: *The trees took uncanny shapes in the darkness.* See **weird** for synonym study. 2 so far beyond what is normal or expected as to have some special power: *an uncanny knack for solving riddles.* **—un can′ni ly,** *adv.* **—un can′ni ness,** *n.*

un cap (un kap′), *v.t.,* **-capped, -cap ping.** take the cap, covering, or top off of: *uncap a bottle.*

un cared-for (un kerd′fôr′, un kard′fôr′), *adj.* not cared for or looked after; neglected.

un cer e mo ni ous (un′ser ə mō′nē əs), *adj.* 1 not ceremonious; informal. 2 not as courteous as would be expected. **—un′cer e mo′ni ous ly,** *adv.* **—un′cer e mo′ni ous ness,** *n.*

uncial (def. 1)
Latin uncials from an 8th century manuscript

un cer tain (un sėrt′n), *adj.* 1 not sure or certain; doubtful. See synonym study below. 2 likely to change; not to be depended on: *an uncertain temper.* 3 not constant; varying: *an uncertain flicker of light.* 4 vague; indefinite: *an uncertain shape.* **—un cer′tain ly,** *adv.* **—un cer′tain ness,** *n.*

Syn. 1 Uncertain, insecure mean not sure in some way or about something. **Uncertain** implies not knowing definitely or surely about something or not having complete confidence in a thing, person, or oneself, and thus suggests the presence of doubt: *His plans for the summer are uncertain.* **Insecure** implies not being protected from or guarded against danger or loss, and suggests the presence of fear or anxiety: *Her position at the bank is insecure.*

un cer tain ty (un sėrt′n tē), *n., pl.* **-ties.** 1 uncertain state or condition; doubt. 2 something uncertain.

un chain (un chān′), *v.t.* free from chains; let loose; set free.

un change a ble (un chān′jə bəl), *adj.* not changeable; that cannot be changed. **—un change′a ble ness,** *n.* **—un change′a bly,** *adv.*

un changed (un chānjd′), *adj.* not changed; the same.

un char i ta ble (un char′ə tə bəl), *adj.* not generous; not charitable; severe; harsh. **—un char′i ta ble ness,** *n.* **—un char′i ta bly,** *adv.*

un chart ed (un chär′tid), *adj.* not mapped; not marked on a chart.

un chaste (un chāst′), *adj.* not chaste; not virtuous. **—un chaste′ly,** *adv.*

un chas ti ty (un chas′tə tē), *n.* lack of chastity; unchaste character; lewdness.

hat, āge, fär; let, ēqual, tėrm;
it, īce; hot, ōpen, ôrder;
oil, out; cup, pu̇t, rüle;
ch, child; ng, long; sh, she;
th, thin; ᴛʜ, then; zh, measure;

ə represents *a* in about, *e* in taken,
i in pencil, *o* in lemon, *u* in circus.

< = from, derived from, taken from.

un checked (un chekt′), *adj.* not checked; not restrained.

un chris tian (un kris′chən), *adj.* 1 not Christian. 2 unworthy of Christians; at variance with Christian principles. 3 INFORMAL. not civilized; barbarous: *rout someone out of bed at a most unchristian hour.*

un church (un chėrch′), *v.t.* expel from a church; deprive of church rights and privileges.

un ci al (un′shē əl, un′shəl), *adj.* of, having to do with, or written in an old style of writing resembling modern capital letters but heavier and more rounded, found especially in Latin and Greek manuscripts from about the A.D. 300's to 800's. *—n.* 1 letter in this style. 2 manuscript written in this style. [< Late Latin *unciales (litterae)* (letters) an inch high]

un ci nate (un′sə nit, un′sə nāt), *adj.* bent at the end like a hook; hooked. [< Latin *uncinatus* < *uncus* hook]

un cir cum cised (un sėr′kəm sīzd), *adj.* 1 not circumcised. 2 not Jewish; Gentile. 3 heathen; pagan.

un civ il (un siv′əl), *adj.* 1 not civil; rude; impolite. 2 not civilized. **—un civ′il ly,** *adv.*

un civ i lized (un siv′ə līzd), *adj.* not civilized; barbarous; savage.

un clad (un klad′), *adj.* not dressed; not clothed; naked. *—v.* a pt. and a pp. of **unclothe.**

un clasp (un klasp′), *v.t., v.i.* 1 unfasten. 2 release or be released from a clasp or grasp.

un cle (ung′kəl), *n.* 1 brother of one's father or mother. 2 husband of one's aunt. 3 INFORMAL. an elderly man. [< Old French < Latin *avunculus* one's mother's brother]

un clean (un klēn′), *adj.* 1 not clean; dirty; filthy. 2 not pure morally; evil. 3 not ceremonially clean. **—un clean′ness,** *n.*

un clean ly[1] (un klen′lē), *adj.* not cleanly; unclean. [< *un-*[1] + *cleanly*[1]] **—un clean′li ness,** *n.*

un clean ly[2] (un klēn′lē), *adv.* in an unclean manner. [< *unclean*]

un clench (un klench′), *v.t., v.i.* open or become opened from a clenched state: *unclench one's fists.*

Uncle Sam, the government or people of the United States. [< the initials *U.S.*]

Uncle Tom, U.S. Negro thought of as having the timid, servile attitude of a slave in his relations with whites. [< the main character

In each of the words below **un** *means not.*

un bor′rowed
un both′ered
un bought′
un branched′
un brand′ed
un bridge′a ble
un bridged′
un broth′er ly
un bruised′
un brushed′
un bur′ied
un burned′
un burnt′
un called′
un can′celed
un′ca non′i cal
un cap′i tal ized
un car′ing
un cas′trat ed
un cat′a loged
un caught′
un ceas′ing
un cel′e brat′ed
un cen′sored
un cen′sured
un cer′ti fied
un chang′ing
un chap′e roned′
un′char ac ter is′tic
un charged′
un chas′tened
un′chas tised′
un chewed′
un chiv′al rous
un chris′tened
un claimed′
un clar′i fied
un clas′si fi′a ble
un clas′si fied
un cleaned′
un clear′
un cleared′

in Harriet Beecher Stowe's novel *Uncle Tom's Cabin*]

un cloak (un klōk′), *v.t.* 1 remove the coat from. 2 reveal; expose. —*v.i.* take off the cloak or outer garment.

un close (un klōz′), *v.t.*, **-closed, -clos ing.** open.

un clothe (un klōᴛʜ′), *v.t.*, **-clothed** or **-clad, -cloth ing.** 1 strip of clothes; undress. 2 lay bare; uncover.

un co (ung′kō), SCOTTISH. —*adv.* remarkably; very; extremely. —*adj.* 1 unknown, strange, or unusual. 2 remarkable, extraordinary, or great. 3 uncanny. [short for *uncouth*]

un coil (un koil′), *v.t., v.i.* unwind.

un com fort a ble (un kum′fər tə bəl, unkumf′tə bəl), *adj.* 1 not comfortable. 2 uneasy. 3 disagreeable; causing discomfort. **—un com′fort a ble ness,** *n.* **—un com′fort a bly,** *adv.*

un com mon (un kom′ən), *adj.* 1 rare; unusual. 2 remarkable. **—un com′mon ly,** *adv.* **—un com′mon ness,** *n.*

un com mu ni ca tive (un′kə myü′nə kā′tiv, un′kə myü′nə kə tiv), *adj.* not giving out any information, opinions, etc.; talking little; reserved; reticent. **—un′com mu′ni ca′tive ness,** *n.*

un com pro mis ing (un kom′prə mī′zing), *adj.* unyielding; firm: *an uncompromising person, an uncompromising attitude.* **—un com′pro mis′ing ly,** *adv.*

un con cern (un′kən sėrn′), *n.* lack of concern; lack of interest; freedom from care or anxiety; indifference. See **indifference** for synonym study.

un con cerned (un′kən sėrnd′), *adj.* not concerned; not interested; free from care or anxiety; indifferent. **—un′con cern′ed ly,** *adv.* **—un′con cern′ed ness,** *n.*

un con di tion al (un′kən dish′ə nəl), *adj.* without conditions; absolute: *unconditional surrender.* **—un′con di′tion al ly,** *adv.*

un con di tioned (un′kən dish′ənd), *adj.* 1 without conditions. 2 (in psychology) not learned; instinctive.

un con form i ty (un′kən fôr′mə tē), *n., pl.* **-ties.** 1 lack of agreement; being inconsistent. 2 in geology: **a** a break in the continuity of strata, indicating an interruption of deposition. **b** the plane where such a break occurs.

un con quer a ble (un kong′kər ə bəl), *adj.* that cannot be conquered; invincible. **—un con′quer a bly,** *adv.*

un con scion a ble (un kon′shə nə bəl), *adj.* 1 not influenced or guided by conscience: *an unconscionable liar.* 2 unreasonable; very great: *an unconscionable delay.* **—un con′scion a bly,** *adv.*

un con scious (un kon′shəs), *adj.* 1 not conscious; not able to feel or think: *unconscious from anesthetic.* 2 not aware: *unconscious of danger.* 3 not done or felt consciously; not deliberate: *unconscious resentment.* —*n.* the part of the mind that one is not directly or fully aware of; one's unconscious thoughts, feelings, ideas, etc.; subconscious. **—un con′scious ly,** *adv.* **—un con′scious ness,** *n.*

un con sti tu tion al (un′kon stə tü′shə nəl, un′kon stə tyü′shə nəl), *adj.* contrary to the constitution. **—un′con sti tu′tion al ly,** *adv.*

un con sti tu tion al i ty (un′kon stə tü′shə nal′ə tē, un′kon stə tyü′shə nal′ə tē), *n.* a being contrary to the constitution.

un con ven tion al (un′kən ven′shə nəl), *adj.* not bound by or conforming to convention, rule, or precedent; free from conventionality. **—un′con ven′tion al ly,** *adv.*

un con ven tion al i ty (un′kən ven′shə nal′ə tē), *n.* a being unconventional; freedom from conventional restraints.

un cork (un kôrk′), *v.t.* 1 pull the cork from. 2 INFORMAL. let go; let loose; release: *The quarterback uncorked a long pass.*

un count ed (un koun′tid), *adj.* 1 not counted; not reckoned. 2 very many; innumerable.

un cou ple (un kup′əl), *v.t., v.i.*, **-pled, -pling.** disconnect; unfasten: *They uncoupled two freight cars.*

un cour te ous (un kėr′tē əs), *adj.* not courteous; impolite; rude.

un court li ness (un kôrt′lē nis, un kōrt′lē nis), *n.* rudeness.

un couth (un küth′), *adj.* 1 not refined; awkward; clumsy; crude: *uncouth manners.* 2 unusual and unpleasant; strange: *the eerie and uncouth noises of the jungle.* [Old English *uncūth* < *un-*[1] + *cūth* known] **—un couth′ly,** *adv.* **—un couth′ness,** *n.*

un cov er (un kuv′ər), *v.t.* 1 remove the cover from. 2 make known; reveal; expose. 3 remove the hat, cap, etc., of. —*v.i.* 1 remove one's hat or cap in respect. 2 remove a cover.

un cross (un krôs′, un kros′), *v.t.* change from a crossed position.

un crown (un kroun′), *v.t.* take the crown from; lower from high rank.

un crowned (un kround′), *adj.* 1 not crowned; not having yet assumed the crown. 2 having royal power without being king, queen, etc.

UNCTAD, United Nations Conference on Trade and Development.

unc tion (ungk′shən), *n.* 1 an anointing with oil, ointment, or the like, for medical purposes or as a religious rite. 2 the oil, ointment, or the like, used for anointing. 3 something soothing or comforting: *the unction of flattery.* 4 fervor; earnestness. 5 affected earnestness, sentiment, etc.; smoothness and oiliness of language, manner, etc. [< Latin *unctionem* < *unguere* anoint]

unc tu ous (ungk′chü əs), *adj.* 1 like an oil or ointment in texture; oily; greasy. 2 soothing, sympathetic, and persuasive. 3 too smooth and oily: *the hypocrite's unctuous manner.* [< Latin *unctus* an anointing < *unguere* anoint] **—unc′tu ous ly,** *adv.* **—unc′tu ous ness,** *n.*

un curl (un kėrl′), *v.t., v.i.* straighten out.

un cut (un kut′), *adj.* 1 not cut, gashed, or wounded; not having received a cut. 2 not cut down, mown, or clipped: *an uncut forest.* 3 not fashioned or shaped by cutting: *an uncut diamond.* 4 not curtailed or shortened, as by editing: *an uncut performance of "Hamlet."* 5 not having the leaves cut open or the margins cut down: *an uncut book.*

un daunt ed (un dôn′tid, un dän′tid), *adj.* not afraid; not dismayed or discouraged; fearless. **—un daunt′ed ly,** *adv.* **—un daunt′ed ness,** *n.*

un de ceive (un′di sēv′), *v.t.*, **-ceived, -ceiv ing.** free (a person) from error, mistake, or deception.

un de cid ed (un′di sī′did), *adj.* 1 not decided; not settled: *an undecided contest.* 2 not having one's mind made up: *He is undecided about which movie to see.* **—un′de cid′ed ly,** *adv.* **—un′de cid′ed ness,** *n.*

un de fined (un′di fīnd′), *adj.* 1 not defined or explained. 2 indefinite.

un de ni a ble (un′di nī′ə bəl), *adj.* 1 that

In each of the words below **un** *means not.*

un closed′
un clothed′
un cloud′ed
un clut′tered
un coat′ed
un cocked′
un′co erced′
un coined′
un′col lect′ed
un′col lect′i ble
un col′ored
un combed′
un′com bined′
un come′ly
un com′fort ed
un′com mit′ted
un′com pan′ion a ble
un′com plain′ing
un′com plai′sant
un′com plet′ed
un′com pli′ant
un com′pli cat′ed
un′com pli men′tar y
un′com pound′ed
un′com pre hend′ing
un′com pre hen′si ble
un com′pro mised
un′con cealed′
un′con cert′ed
un′con fined′
un′con firmed′
un′con form′a ble
un′con gealed′
un′con gen′ial
un′con gest′ed
un′con nect′ed
un con′quered
un′con sci en′tious
un con′se crat′ed
un′con sid′ered
un′con soled′
un′con sol′i dat′ed
un′con strained′
un′con sumed′
un′con tam′i nat′ed
un′con test′ed
un′con tra dict′ed
un′con trol′la ble
un′con trolled′
un′con vert′ed
un′con vinced′
un′con vinc′ing
un cooked′
un cooled′
un′co op′e ra′tive
un′co or′di nat′ed
un cor′dial
un corked′
un′cor rect′ed
un′cor rob′o rat′ed
un′cor rupt′ed
un count′a ble
un court′ly
un′cre at′ed
un cred′it ed
un crip′pled
un crit′i cal
un cropped′
un crossed′
un crowd′ed
un crys′tal lized
un cul′ti va ble
un cul′ti vat′ed
un cul′tured
un curbed′
un cured′
un cur′i ous
un curled′
un cur′rent
un′cur tailed′
un cur′tained
un dam′aged
un damped′
un dat′ed
un daugh′ter ly
un daz′zled
un′de bat′a ble
un′de cayed′
un′de ceiv′a ble
un′de ceived′
un′de ci′pher a ble
un′de ci′phered
un′de clared′
un′de clin′a ble
un′de clined′
un dec′o rat′ed
un′de feat′ed
un′de fend′ed
un′de fen′si ble
un′de filed′
un′de fin′a ble
un′de formed′
un′de layed′
un′de liv′er a ble
un′de liv′ered
un′de mand′ing
un′dem o crat′ic
un′de mon′stra ble
un′de mon′stra tive
un′de nied′
un′de nom′i na′tion al
un′de pend′a ble
un′de pre′ci at′ed

hat, āge, fär; let, ēqual, tėrm;
it, īce; hot, ōpen, ôrder;
oil, out; cup, pu̇t, rüle;
ch, child; ng, long; sh, she;
th, thin; ᴛʜ, then; zh, measure;

ə represents *a* in about, *e* in taken, *i* in pencil, *o* in lemon, *u* in circus.

< = from, derived from, taken from.

cannot be denied or disputed; certain. 2 unquestionably good; excellent. **—un′de·ni′a·ble·ness,** *n.* **—un′de·ni′a·bly,** *adv.*

un der (un′dər), *prep.* 1 below; beneath. See synonym study below. 2 below the surface of: *under the sea.* 3 lower than; lower down than; not so high as: *hit under the belt.* 4 in such a position so as to be covered, sheltered, or concealed by: *sleep under a blanket. The moon is under a cloud.* 5 less than: *It will cost under ten dollars.* 6 during the rule, time, influence, etc., of: *England under the four Georges.* 7 in the position or condition of being affected by: *under the new rules.* 8 because of: *under the circumstances.* 9 according to: *under the law.* 10 represented by: *under a new name.* 11 required or bound by: *under obligation.* 12 with the authorization or sanction of: *under one's signature.* 13 included in a particular group, category, or class: *treat several topics under one heading.* —*adv.* 1 below; beneath: *The swimmer went under.* 2 in or to a lower place or condition. —*adj.* lower in position, rank, degree, amount, price, etc.: *the under level.* [Old English]

Syn. *prep.* 1 **Under, below, beneath** express a relation in which one thing is thought of as being lower than another. **Under** suggests being directly lower: *The toy is under the bed.* **Below** suggests being on a lower level, but not necessarily straight below nor without anyone or anything in between: *They live on one of the floors below us.* **Beneath** suggests being under and hence covered or hidden from view: *The letter was accidentally lost beneath the rug.*

under-, *prefix.* 1 below; beneath: *Underground = beneath the ground.* 2 being beneath; worn beneath: *Underclothes = clothes worn beneath one's outer clothes.* 3 lower: *Underlip = the lower lip.* 4 lower in rank; subordinate: *Undersecretary = secretary that is lower in rank.* 5 lower than: *Underbid = bid lower than.* 6 not enough; not sufficiently: *Undernourished = not sufficiently nourished.* 7 below normal: *Underweight = below normal weight.* [< *under*]

un der a chiev er (un′dər ə chē′vər), *n.* pupil who fails to work at his level of ability.

un der act (un′dər akt′), *v.t., v.i.* act (a part) insufficiently or with less than the usual or expected emphasis; underplay.

un der age (un′dər āj′), *adj.* not of full age; of less than the usual or required age.

un der arm (un′dər ärm′), *adj.* 1 situated or placed under the arm; found in or near the armpit: *an underarm scar, an underarm deodorant.* 2 underhand: *an underarm pitcher.* —*adv.* underhand. —*n.* armpit.

un der bel ly (un′dər bel′ē), *n., pl.* **-lies.** 1 the lower part of the abdomen. 2 an unprotected or vulnerable part.

un der bid (un′dər bid′), *v.,* **-bid, -bidding.** —*v.t.* 1 offer to work, supply goods, etc., at a lower price than (another): *underbid a competitor.* 2 bid less than the full value of: *underbid a hand in bridge.* —*v.i.* bid less than another or less than the full value of something. **—un′der bid′der,** *n.*

un der bred (un′dər bred′), *adj.* 1 of inferior breeding or manners; coarse and vulgar. 2 not of pure breed; not thoroughbred: *an underbred horse.*

un der brush (un′dər brush′), *n.* shrubs, bushes, small trees, etc., growing under large trees in woods or forests.

un der buy (un′dər bī′), *v.t.,* **-bought** (-bôt′), **-buy ing.** 1 buy at less than the actual value or market price. 2 buy for less than someone else.

un der car riage (un′dər kar′ij), *n.* 1 the supporting framework of an automobile, carriage, etc. 2 landing gear.

un der charge (*v.* un′dər chärj′; *n.* un′dər-chärj′), *v.,* **-charged, -charg ing,** *n.* —*v.t., v.i.* charge (a person or persons) less than the established or fair price; charge too little. —*n.* a charge or price less than is proper or fair.

un der class man (un′dər klas′mən), *n., pl.* **-men.** freshman or sophomore.

un der clothes (un′dər klōz′, un′dər-klōᴛʜz′), *n.pl.* underwear.

un der cloth ing (un′dər klō′ᴛʜing), *n.* underclothes.

un der coat (un′dər kōt′), *n.* 1 growth of short, fine hair under an animal's outer coat. 2 coat of paint, varnish, etc., applied before the finishing coats. 3 a heavy, tarlike substance sprayed on the underparts of an automobile to protect them from water, dirt, salt, etc., on the road. —*v.t., v.i.* apply or cover with an undercoat.

un der cov er (un′dər kuv′ər), *adj.* working or done in secret: *The jeweler was an undercover man for the police.*

un der cur rent (un′dər kėr′ənt), *n.* 1 current below the upper currents, or below the surface, of a body of water, air, etc. 2 an underlying quality or tendency: *There was an undercurrent of sadness in her laugh.*

un der cut (*v.* un′dər kut′; *n.* un′dər kut′), *v.,* **-cut, -cut ting,** *n.* —*v.t.* 1 cut under or beneath; cut away or into the substance of from below: *undercut a stratum of rock.* 2 cut away material from so as to leave a portion overhanging. 3 sell or work for less than (another). 4 (in golf, baseball, tennis, etc.) hit (a ball) below the center, causing it to have backspin and usually a short, high flight. —*v.i.* undercut a person or thing. —*n.* 1 a cut, or a cutting away, underneath. 2 a notch cut in a tree to determine the direction in which the tree is to fall and to prevent splitting. 3 the tenderloin or fillet of beef.

un der de vel oped (un′dər di vel′əpt), *adj.* 1 not normally developed: *an underdeveloped limb.* 2 poorly or insufficiently developed in production, technology, medicine, standard of living, etc.: *The underdeveloped countries need trained personnel.*

un der dog (un′dər dôg′, un′dər dog′), *n.* 1 person having the worst of any struggle; person in an inferior position. 2 contestant considered unlikely to win. 3 dog having the worst of a fight.

un der done (un′dər dun′, un′dər dun′), *adj.* not cooked enough; cooked very little.

un der drawers (un′dər drôrz′), *n.pl.* underpants.

un der ed u cat ed (un′dər ej′ə kā′tid), *adj.* poorly or insufficiently educated.

un der em pha sis (un′dər em′fə sis), *n.* insufficient emphasis.

un der em pha size (un′dər em′fə sīz), *v.t.,* **-sized, -siz ing.** emphasize insufficiently; not stress enough.

un der es ti mate (*v.* un′dər es′tə māt; *n.* un′dər es′tə mit, un′dər es′tə māt), *v.,* **-mat ed, -mat ing,** *n.* —*v.t., v.i.* estimate at too low a value, amount, rate, etc. —*n.* estimate that is too low. **—un′der es′ti-ma′tion,** *n.*

un der ex pose (un′dər ek spōz′), *v.t.,* **-posed, -pos ing.** 1 expose too little. 2 (in photography) expose (a film or negative) for too short a time.

un der ex po sure (un′dər ek spō′zhər), *n.* too little or too short an exposure. Underexposure to light makes a photograph look dim.

un der feed (un′dər fēd′), *v.t., v.i.,* **-fed** (-fed′), **-feed ing.** 1 feed too little; not give enough food, fuel, etc., to. 2 stoke with coal or other solid fuel from the bottom.

un der foot (un′dər fu̇t′), *adv.* 1 under one's foot or feet; on the ground; underneath. 2 in the way: *Their six small children were always underfoot.*

un der fur (un′dər fėr′), *n.* the soft, fine hair under the outer coat of coarse hair of various mammals, as in beavers and some seals.

un der gar ment (un′dər gär′mənt), *n.* garment worn under an outer garment, especially next to the skin.

un der go (un′dər gō′), *v.,* **-went, -gone, -go ing.** 1 go through; pass through; be subjected to: *The growing town underwent many changes.* 2 endure; suffer: *undergo hardships.* See **experience** for synonym study.

un der gone (un′dər gôn′, un′dər gon′), *v.* pp. of **undergo.**

un der grad u ate (un′dər graj′ü it), *n.* student in a college or university who has not yet received a degree. —*adj.* of, for, or having to do with undergraduates.

un der ground (*adv.* un′dər ground′; *adj., n.* un′dər ground′), *adv.* 1 beneath the surface of the ground: *The mole burrowed underground.* 2 in or into secrecy or concealment: *The thief went underground after the robbery.* —*adj.* 1 being, working, or used beneath the surface of the ground: *an underground passage.* 2 done or working secretly; secret: *an underground revolutionary movement.* 3 not for the general public; not commercial; intended for a small or select audience: *underground movies.* —*n.* 1 place or space beneath the surface of the ground. 2 BRITISH. subway. 3 a secret organization working against an unpopular government, especially during military occupation: *the French underground during World War II.*

underground railroad, system by which the opponents of slavery secretly helped fugitive slaves to escape to the free states or Canada before the Civil War.

un der growth (un′dər grōth′), *n.* underbrush.

un der hand (un′dər hand′), *adj.* 1 not open or honest; secret; sly. 2 with the hand below the level of the shoulder and the arm swung upward: *an underhand pitch.* —*adv.* 1 secretly; slyly. 2 with the hand below the level of the shoulder: *throw a ball underhand.*

un der hand ed (un′dər han′did), *adj.* underhand; secret; sly; not open or honest: *an underhanded trick.* **—un′der hand′ed ly,** *adv.* **—un′der hand′ed ness,** *n.*

un der lay (*v.* un′dər lā′; *n.* un′dər lā′), *v.,* **-laid** (-lād′), **-lay ing,** *n.* —*v.t.* 1 lay or place (one thing) under another. 2 provide with something laid underneath; raise or support with something laid underneath. 3 coat or cover the bottom of. —*n.* 1 something laid beneath. 2 (in printing) paper put under type to bring it to the proper height for printing.

un der lie (un′dər lī′), *v.t.,* **-lay, -lain** (-lān′), **-ly ing.** 1 lie under; be beneath. 2 be at the basis of; form the foundation of.

un der line (*v.* un′dər līn′, un′dər līn′; *n.* un′dər līn′), *v.,* **-lined, -lin ing.** —*v.t.* 1 draw a line or lines under; underscore. 2 make emphatic or more emphatic; emphasize. —*n.* line drawn or printed under a word, passage, etc.

un der ling (un′dər ling), *n.* a person of lower rank or position; inferior.

un der lip (un′dər lip′), *n.* the lower lip of a person, animal, or insect.

un der ly ing (un′dər lī′ing), *adj.* 1 lying under or beneath. 2 fundamental; basic; essential: *underlying facts.* —*v.* ppr. of **underlie.**

un der manned (un′dər mand′), *adj.* understaffed.

un der mine (un′dər mīn′, un′dər mīn′), *v.t.,* **-mined, -min ing.** 1 make a passage or hole under; dig under: *undermine a foundation.* 2 wear away the foundations of: *a cliff undermined by waves.* 3 weaken by secret or unfair means: *undermine a person's reputation by scandal.* See **weaken** for synonym study. 4 weaken or destroy gradually: *Many severe colds had undermined her health.* **—un′der min′er,** *n.*

un der most (un′dər mōst), *adj., adv.* lowest.

un der neath (un′dər nēth′), *prep.* 1 beneath; below; under: *sit underneath a tree.* 2 under the power or control of; subject to. —*adv.* 1 beneath or below something: *Someone was pushing underneath.* 2 on the underside; at the bottom or base: *a house rotten underneath.* —*adj.* lower; under. —*n.* the lower part or surface.

un der nour ished (un′dər nėr′isht), *adj.* not sufficiently nourished.

un der nour ish ment (un′dər nėr′ish-mənt), *n.* lack of nourishment; not having enough food.

un der pants (un′dər pants′), *n.pl.* pants worn as an undergarment; underdrawers.

un der part (un′dər pärt′), *n.* 1 the part of an object, animal, etc., that lies below or underneath. 2 a secondary or subordinate part.

un der pass (un′dər pas′), *n.* passageway underneath; road under railroad tracks or under another road.

un der pay (un′dər pā′), *v.t.,* **-paid** (-pād′), **-pay ing.** pay too little.

un der pin (un′dər pin′), *v.t.,* **-pinned, -pin ning.** 1 support with props, stones, masonry, etc.: *underpin a wall.* 2 support; prop.

un der pin ning (un′dər pin′ing), *n.* 1 the materials or structure that give support from beneath to a building, wall, etc. 2 a support; prop.

un der play (un′dər plā′), *v.t., v.i.* underact.

un der plot (un′dər plot′), *n.* subplot.

un der priv i leged (un′dər priv′ə lijd), *adj.* having fewer advantages than most people have, especially because of poor economic or social status.

un der pro duc tion (un′dər prə duk′-shən), *n.* production that is less than normal or less than there is demand for.

un der rate (un′dər rāt′), *v.t.,* **-rat ed, -rat ing.** rate or estimate too low; put too low a value on.

un der score (*v.* un′dər skôr′, un′dər-skōr′; *n.* un′dər skôr′, un′dər skōr′), *v.,* **-scored, -scor ing,** *n.* —*v.t.* 1 underline. 2 emphasize. —*n.* an underscored line.

un der sea (*adj.* un′dər sē′; *adv.* un′dər-sē′), *adj.* being, working, or used beneath the surface of the sea: *an undersea cable, undersea exploration.* —*adv.* underseas.

un der seas (un′dər sēz′), *adv.* beneath the surface of the sea: *Submarines go underseas.*

un der sec re tar y (un′dər sek′rə ter′ē), *n., pl.* **-tar ies.** an assistant secretary, especially of a government department.

un der sell (un′dər sel′), *v.t.,* **-sold** (-sōld′), **-sell ing.** sell things at a lower price than (another): *This store undersells other stores.*

un der sher iff (un′dər sher′if), *n.* a sheriff's deputy, especially one who acts when the sheriff is not able to or when there is no sheriff.

un der shirt (un′dər shėrt′), *n.* a close-fitting undergarment of knitted cotton, etc., with or without sleeves, for the upper part of the body.

un der shoot (un′dər shüt′), *v.,* **-shot, -shoot ing.** —*v.t.* shoot short of; shoot too low for: *undershoot a target.* —*v.i.* shoot too short or low.

un der shot (un′dər shot′), *adj.* 1 having the lower jaw or teeth projecting beyond the upper when the mouth is closed. 2 driven by water passing beneath: *an undershot water wheel.* —*v.* pt. and pp. of **undershoot.**

un der side (un′dər sīd′), *n.* surface lying underneath; bottom side.

un der signed (un′dər sīnd′), *adj.* signed, or having signed at the end of a letter or document. —*n.* **the undersigned,** the person or persons signing a letter or document.

un der sized (un′dər sīzd′), *adj.* smaller than the usual or specified size: *An undersized fish has to be thrown back.*

un der skirt (un′dər skėrt′), *n.* skirt worn under an outer skirt or overskirt.

un der slung (un′dər slung′, un′dər-slung′), *adj.* 1 (of a vehicle) having the frame suspended below the axles. 2 (of a jaw) undershot.

un der song (un′dər sông′, un′dər song′), *n.* song that is sung softly along with another song, as an accompaniment.

un der spin (un′dər spin′), *n.* backspin.

un der staffed (un′dər staft′), *adj.* having too small a staff: *an understaffed hospital.*

un der stand (un′dər stand′), *v.,* **-stood, -stand ing.** —*v.t.* 1 get the meaning of: *I don't understand that word.* 2 know well; know: *understand physics.* See **know** for synonym study. 3 know how to deal with: *A good teacher understands children.* 4 be informed; learn: *I understand that you are leaving town.* 5 take as a fact; believe: *It is understood that you will come.* 6 take as meaning; take as meant; interpret: *How do you wish that remark to be understood?* 7 supply in the mind. In "He hit the ball harder than I," the word *did* is understood after *I.* —*v.i.* 1 get the meaning: *I have told him twice, but he doesn't understand yet.* 2 have understanding; be sympathetic: *expect a friend to understand.* 3 **understand each other,** know each other's meaning and wishes; agree. [Old English *understandan*]

underpinning (def. 1)

un der stand a bil i ty (un′dər stan′də-bil′ə tē), *n.* quality of being understandable.

un der stand a ble (un′dər stan′də bəl), *adj.* that can be understood. **—un′der-stand′a bly,** *adv.*

un der stand ing (un′dər stan′ding), *n.* 1 comprehension; knowledge: *have a clear understanding of the problem.* 2 power or ability to learn and know; intellect; intelligence: *the limited understanding of a child.* 3 knowledge of each other's meaning and wishes: *a marriage based on true understanding.* 4 a mutual arrangement or agreement: *We must come to an understanding.* —*adj.* that understands or is able to understand; intelligent and sympathetic: *an understanding reply.* **—un′der stand′ing ly,** *adv.*

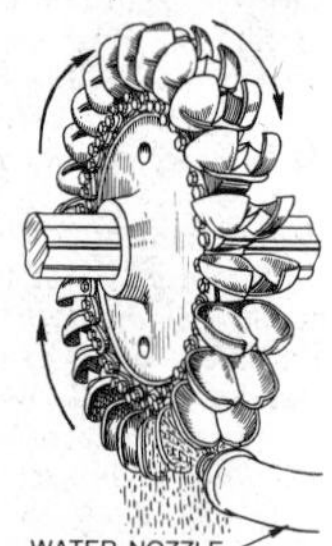

undershot (def. 2) undershot water wheel

un der state (un′dər stāt′), *v.t., v.i.,* **-stat ed, -stat ing.** 1 state too weakly or less emphatically than one should. 2 say less than the full truth about.

un der state ment (un′dər stāt′mənt), *n.* 1 statement that expresses a fact too weakly or less emphatically than it should. Understatement is often used for humorous and other effects. 2 statement that says less than could be said truly.

un der stood (un′dər stu̇d′), *v.* pt. and pp. of **understand.**

un der stud y (un′dər stud′ē), *n., pl.* **-stud ies,** *v.,* **-stud ied, -stud y ing.** —*n.* person who can act as a substitute for an actor, actress, or other performer. —*v.t.* 1 learn (a part) in order to replace the regular performer when necessary. 2 act as an understudy to. —*v.i.* act as an understudy.

un der sur face (un′dər sėr′fis), *n.* underside: *the undersurface of a leaf.*

un der take (un′dər tāk′), *v.t.,* **-took, -tak en, -tak ing.** 1 set about; try; attempt: *undertake a journey, undertake to reach home before dark.* 2 agree to do; take upon oneself: *I will undertake the feeding of your dog while you are away.* 3 promise; guarantee.

un der tak er (un′dər tā′kər *for 1;* un′dər-tā′kər *for 2*), *n.* 1 person whose business is preparing the dead for burial and arranging funerals; mortician. 2 person who undertakes something.

hat, āge, fär; let, ēqual, tėrm;
it, īce; hot, ōpen, ôrder;
oil, out; cup, pu̇t, rüle;
ch, child; ng, long; sh, she;
th, thin; ᴛʜ, then; zh, measure;

ə represents *a* in about, *e* in taken, *i* in pencil, *o* in lemon, *u* in circus.

< = from, derived from, taken from.

un der tak ing (un′dər tā′king *for 1-3;* un′dər tā′king *for 4*), *n.* 1 something undertaken; task; enterprise. 2 act of one who undertakes any task or responsibility. 3 promise; guarantee. 4 business of preparing the dead for burial and arranging funerals.

un der ten ant (un′dər ten′ənt), *n.* subtenant.

un der-the-count er (un′dər ᴛʜə koun′tər), *adj.* hidden and stealthy; unauthorized; illegal.

un der tone (un′dər tōn′), *n.* 1 a low or very quiet tone: *talk in undertones.* 2 a subdued color; color seen through other colors: *There was an undertone of brown beneath all the gold and crimson of autumn.* 3 something beneath the surface; an underlying quality, condition, or element: *an undertone of sadness in her gaiety.*

un der took (un′dər tu̇k′), *v.* pt. of **undertake.**

un der tow (un′dər tō′), *n.* 1 any strong current below the surface, moving in a direction different from that of the surface current. 2 the backward flow of water from waves breaking on a beach.

un der u ti lize (un′dər yü′tl īz), *v.t.,* **-lized, -liz ing.** utilize insufficiently or wastefully: *underutilized schools.*

un der val ue (un′dər val′yü), *v.t.,* **-val ued, -val u ing.** put too low a value on; underestimate; underrate. **—un′der val′u a′tion,** *n.*

un der waist (un′dər wāst′), *n.* waist worn under another waist.

un der wa ter (un′dər wô′tər, un′dər-wot′ər), *adj.* 1 below the surface of the water. 2 made for use under the water.

un der way (un′dər wā′), *adv.* going on; in motion; in progress: *The drive to raise money for the new library is finally underway.* —*adj.* taking place while in motion or in progress.

un der wear (un′dər wer′, un′dər war′), *n.* clothing worn under one's outer clothes, especially next to the skin; underclothes; underclothing.

un der weight (un′dər wāt′), *adj.* having too little weight; below the normal or required weight. —*n.* weight that is not up to standard.

un der went (un′dər went′), *v.* pt. of **undergo.**

un der wood (un′dər wu̇d′), *n.* underbrush.

un der wool (un′dər wu̇l′), *n.* a fine, soft wool under the coarse outer hair of various mammals.

un der world (un′dər wėrld′), *n.* 1 the criminal part of human society; the world of crime and vice. 2 the lower world; Hades. 3 ARCHAIC. earth. 4 the opposite side of the earth.

un der write (un′dər rīt′, un′dər rīt′), *v.t.,* **un der wrote** (un′dər rōt′, un′dər rōt′), **un der writ ten** (un′dər rit′n, un′dər rit′n), **un der writ ing.** 1 insure (property) against loss. 2 sign (an insurance policy), thereby accepting the risk of insuring something against loss. 3 write under (other written matter); sign one's name to (a document, etc.). 4 agree to buy (all the stocks or bonds of a certain issue that are not bought by the public): *The bankers underwrote the company's bonds.* 5 agree to meet the expense of: *underwrite a person's college education.*

un der writ er (un′dər rī′tər), *n.* 1 person who underwrites an insurance policy or carries on an insurance business. 2 person who underwrites (usually with others) an issue or issues of bonds, stocks, etc.

un de sir a bil i ty (un′di zī′rə bil′ə tē), *n.* quality or condition of being undesirable.

un de sir a ble (un′di zī′rə bəl), *adj.* objectionable; disagreeable. —*n.* an undesirable person or thing. **—un′de sir′a ble ness,** *n.* **—un′de sir′a bly,** *adv.*

un de vel oped (un′di vel′əpt), *adj.* 1 not fully grown; immature. 2 not put to full use.

un did (un did′), *v.* pt. of **undo.**

un dies (un′dēz), *n.pl.* INFORMAL. articles of women's underclothing.

un dis ci plined (un dis′ə plind), *adj.* not disciplined; without proper control; untrained.

un dis guised (un′dis gīzd′), *adj.* 1 not disguised. 2 unconcealed; open; plain; frank.

un dis put ed (un′dis pyü′tid), *adj.* not disputed; not doubted.

un dis turbed (un′dis tėrbd′), *adj.* not disturbed; not troubled; calm.

un do (un dü′), *v.t.,* **-did, -done, -do ing.** 1 unfasten; untie: *Please undo the package. I undid the string.* 2 do away with the effect of; cause to be as if never done; cancel or reverse. 3 bring to ruin; spoil; destroy. **—un do′er,** *n.*

un dock (un dok′), *v.t.* 1 take (a ship) out of a dock. 2 separate (a spacecraft) from another in space. —*v.i.* come out of docking.

un do ing (un dü′ing), *n.* 1 a bringing to ruin; spoiling; destroying. 2 cause of destruction or ruin. 3 a canceling or reversing the effect of something. 4 an untying; unfastening.

un done (un dun′), *adj.* 1 not done; not finished. 2 ruined. 3 untied; unfastened. —*v.* pp. of **undo.**

un doubt ed (un dou′tid), *adj.* not doubted; accepted as true; beyond dispute; indisputable.

un doubt ed ly (un dou′tid lē), *adv.* beyond doubt; certainly.

un draw (un drô′), *v.t.,* **-drew** (-drü′), **-drawn** (-drôn′), **-draw ing.** draw back or away: *She undrew the curtain.*

un dreamed-of (un drēmd′uv′, un drēmd′ov′), *adj.* never thought of, even in the imagination.

un dreamt-of (un dremt′uv′, un dremt′ov′), *adj.* undreamed-of.

un dress (*v.* un dres′; *n.* un′dres′, un dres′), *v.t.* 1 take the clothes off; strip. 2 strip of ornament. 3 take dressing from (a wound). —*v.i.* take off one's clothes; strip; disrobe. —*n.* 1 loose, informal dress. 2 clothes proper for ordinary, everyday wear. 3 lack of clothing; nakedness.

Und set (u̇n′set), *n.* **Sigrid,** 1882-1949, Norwegian novelist.

un due (un dü′, un dyü′), *adj.* 1 not fitting; not right; improper. 2 too great; too much; excessive. 3 not properly owing or payable.

un du lant (un′jə lənt, un′dyə lənt), *adj.* waving; undulating.

undulant fever, disease characterized by intermittent fever, disorder of the bowels, enlarged spleen, weakness, anemia, and pain in the joints, caused by infection with bacteria usually transmitted by contact with infected cattle, goats, and hogs, or by consumption of raw milk or milk products.

un du late (*v.* un′jə lāt, un′dyə lāt; *adj.* un′jə lit, un′jə lāt; un′dyə lit, un′dyə lāt), *v.,* **-lat ed, -lat ing,** *adj.* —*v.i.* 1 move in waves: *undulating water.* 2 have a wavy form or surface: *undulating hair, an undulating prairie.* —*v.t.* 1 cause to move in waves. 2 give a wavy form or surface to. —*adj.* wavy. [< Latin *undulatus* wavy < *unda* wave]

un du la tion (un′jə lā′shən, un′dyə-lā′shən), *n.* 1 a wavelike motion; an undulating. 2 a wavy form. 3 one of a series of wavelike bends, curves, swellings, etc. 4 a wavelike motion in the air or another medium; vibration; wave.

un du la to ry (un′jə lə tôr′ē, un′jə lə-tōr′ē; un′dyə lə tôr′ē, un′dyə lə tōr′ē), *adj.* undulating; wavy.

un du ly (un dü′lē, un dyü′lē), *adv.* 1 in an undue manner; improperly. 2 too much; excessively: *unduly harsh.*

un dy ing (un dī′ing), *adj.* that never dies; deathless; immortal; eternal: *undying beauty.* **—un dy′ing ly,** *adv.*

In each of the words below **un** *means not.*

un′de scrib′a ble
un′de served′
un′de serv′ing
un des′ig nat′ed
un′de sign′ing
un′de sired′
un′de spair′ing
un′de stroyed′
un′de tach′a ble
un′de tect′a ble
un′de tect′ed
un′de ter′mi na ble
un′de ter′mined
un′de terred′
un de′vi at′ing
un′de vout′
un′dif fe ren′ti at′ed
un′di gest′ed
un dig′ni fied
un′di lut′ed
un′di min′ished
un′di min′ish ing
un dimmed′
un′dip lo mat′ic
un′di rect′ed
un′dis cern′i ble
un′dis cern′ing
un′dis charged′
un′dis closed′
un′dis cour′aged
un′dis cov′er a ble
un′dis cov′ered
un′dis crim′i nat′ing
un′dis heart′ened
un′dis mayed′
un′dis so′ci at′ed
un′dis solved′
un′dis tilled′
un′dis tin′guish a ble
un′dis tin′guished
un′dis tin′guish ing
un′dis tort′ed
un′dis tract′ed
un′dis trib′ut ed
un′di ver′si fied
un′di vid′ed
un′di vulged′
un doc′tri naire′
un′do mes′tic
un′do mes′ti cat′ed
un dou′ble
un doubt′ing
un drained′
un′dra mat′ic
un drape′
un draped′
un dreamed′
un dreamt′
un dressed′
un dried′
un drilled′
un drink′a ble
un du′ti ful
un dyed′

un earned (un ėrnd′), *adj.* 1 not earned; not gained by labor or service. 2 not deserved: *unearned punishment.*

un earth (un ėrth′), *v.t.* 1 dig or force out of the earth; dig up: *unearth a buried city.* 2 find out; discover: *unearth a plot.*

un earth ly (un ėrth′lē), *adj.* 1 not of this world; supernatural. 2 strange; weird; ghostly. 3 INFORMAL. unnatural; extraordinary; preposterous. **—un earth′li ness,** *n.*

un eas y (un ē′zē), *adj.,* **-eas i er, -eas i est.** 1 restless; disturbed; anxious: *an uneasy sleep, be uneasy about a decision.* 2 not comfortable. 3 not easy in manner; awkward. **—un eas′i ly,** *adv.* **—un eas′i ness,** *n.*

un ed u cat ed (un ej′ə kā′tid), *adj.* not educated; not taught or trained. See **ignorant** for synonym study.

un em ploy a ble (un′em ploi′ə bəl), *adj.* that cannot be employed, especially that cannot be employed to work because of a physical or mental impediment. *—n.* person who is unemployable.

un em ployed (un′em ploid′), *adj.* 1 not employed; not in use: *an unemployed skill.* 2 not having a job; having no work: *an unemployed person.* *—n.* **the unemployed,** people out of work.

un em ploy ment (un′em ploi′mənt), *n.* lack of employment; being out of work.

un e qual (un ē′kwəl), *adj.* 1 not the same in amount, size, number, value, degree, rank, etc.: *unequal sums of money.* 2 not balanced; not well matched. 3 not fair; one-sided: *an unequal contest.* 4 not enough; not adequate: *strength unequal to the task.* 5 not regular; not even; variable. **—un e′qual ly,** *adv.* **—un e′qual ness,** *n.*

un e qualed (un ē′kwəld), *adj.* that has no equal or superior; matchless.

un e quiv o cal (un′i kwiv′ə kəl), *adj.* clear; plain: *an unequivocal refusal.* **—un′e quiv′o cal ly,** *adv.* **—un′e quiv′o cal ness,** *n.*

un err ing (un ėr′ing, un er′ing), *adj.* making no mistakes; exactly right: *unerring aim.* **—un err′ing ly,** *adv.* **—un err′ing ness,** *n.*

un es cap a ble (un′ə skā′pə bəl), *adj.* inescapable.

U NES CO or **U nes co** (yü nes′kō), *n.* United Nations Educational, Scientific, and Cultural Organization.

un es sen tial (un′ə sen′shəl), *adj.* not essential; not of prime importance. *—n.* something not essential.

un e ven (un ē′vən), *adj.* 1 not level, flat, or smooth: *uneven ground.* 2 not equal: *an uneven contest.* 3 not uniform or regular; changeable; inconsistent: *His work is of uneven quality.* 4 leaving a remainder of 1 when divided by 2; odd: *27 and 9 are uneven numbers.* **—un e′ven ly,** *adv.* **—un e′ven ness,** *n.*

un e vent ful (un′i vent′fəl), *adj.* without important or striking occurrences. **—un′e vent′ful ly,** *adv.*

un ex am pled (un′eg zam′pəld), *adj.* having no equal or like; without precedent or parallel; unprecedented.

un ex cep tion a ble (un′ek sep′shə nə bəl), *adj.* beyond criticism; wholly admirable. **—un′ex cep′tion a ble ness,** *n.* **—un′ex cep′tion a bly,** *adv.*

un ex cep tion al (un′ek sep′shə nəl), *adj.* 1 ordinary. 2 admitting of no exception.

un ex pect ed (un′ek spek′tid), *adj.* not expected: *an unexpected difficulty.* **—un′ex pect′ed ly,** *adv.* **—un′ex pect′ed ness,** *n.*

Syn. Unexpected, sudden mean coming, happening, done, or made without advance warning or preparation. **Unexpected** emphasizes the lack of foreknowledge or anticipation: *The President made an unexpected visit to the city.* **Sudden** emphasizes the haste and absence of forewarning: *Her decision to go was sudden.*

un fad a ble (un fā′də bəl), *adj.* incapable of fading, withering, or perishing.

un fail ing (un fā′ling), *adj.* 1 never failing; tireless; loyal: *an unfailing friend.* 2 never running short; endless: *an unfailing supply of water.* 3 sure; certain: *an unfailing proof.* **—un fail′ing ly,** *adv.* **—un fail′ing ness,** *n.*

un fair (un fer′, un far′), *adj.* not fair; unjust: *an unfair decision, unfair business practices, have an unfair advantage.* **—un fair′ly,** *adv.* **—un fair′ness,** *n.*

un faith ful (un fāth′fəl), *adj.* 1 not faithful; not true to duty or one's promises; faithless. 2 not true to the vows of marriage; adulterous. 3 not accurate; not exact. **—un faith′ful ly,** *adv.* **—un faith′ful ness,** *n.*

un fa mil iar (un′fə mil′yər), *adj.* 1 not well known; unusual; strange: *That face is unfamiliar to me.* 2 not acquainted: *The class was unfamiliar with the Greek language.* **—un′fa mil′iar ly,** *adv.*

un fa mil iar i ty (un′fə mil′yar′ə tē), *n.* lack of familiarity.

un fas ten (un fas′n), *v.t., v.i.* undo; untie; loosen; open.

un fa vor a ble (un fā′vər ə bəl), *adj.* not favorable; adverse; harmful: *unfavorable conditions, unfavorable weather for a trip, an unfavorable review of a play.* **—un fa′vor a ble ness,** *n.* **—un fa′vor a bly,** *adv.*

un feel ing (un fē′ling), *adj.* 1 not kind or compassionate; hardhearted; cruel: *an unfeeling remark.* 2 not able to feel. **—un feel′ing ly,** *adv.* **—un feel′ing ness,** *n.*

un feigned (un fānd′), *adj.* not feigned; sincere; real.

un feign ed ly (un fā′nid lē), *adv.* really; sincerely.

un fet ter (un fet′ər), *v.t.* remove fetters from; make free; liberate; unchain.

un fin ished (un fin′isht), *adj.* 1 not finished; not complete. 2 without some special finish; not polished; rough.

un fit (un fit′), *adj., v.,* **-fit ted, -fit ting.** *—adj.* 1 not fit; not suitable. 2 not good enough; unqualified. 3 not adapted. *—v.t.* make unfit; spoil. **—un fit′ly,** *adv.* **—un fit′ness,** *n.*

un fix (un fiks′), *v.t.* 1 loosen; detach; unfasten. 2 unsettle.

un flag ging (un flag′ing), *adj.* not weakening or failing: *unflagging efforts.* **—un flag′ging ly,** *adv.*

un flap pa ble (un flap′ə bəl), *adj.* INFORMAL. not easily excited, confused, or alarmed; imperturbable.

un fledged (un flejd′), *adj.* 1 (of a bird) too young to fly; not having full-grown feathers. 2 undeveloped; immature.

un flinch ing (un flin′ching), *adj.* not drawing back from difficulty, danger, or pain; firm; resolute: *unflinching courage.* **—un flinch′ing ly,** *adv.*

un fold (un fōld′), *v.t.* 1 open the folds of; open up; spread out: *unfold a napkin.* 2 reveal; show; explain: *unfold the plot of a story.* *—v.i.* open up or out; spread out or expand; develop: *Buds unfold into flowers.*

un forced (un fôrst′, un fōrst′), *adj.* 1 not forced; not compelled; willing. 2 natural; spontaneous.

un fore seen (un′fôr sēn′, un′fōr sēn′), *adj.* not known beforehand; unexpected.

un for get ta ble (un′fər get′ə bəl), *adj.* that can never be forgotten. **—un′for get′ta bly,** *adv.*

un formed (un fôrmd′), *adj.* 1 without definite or regular form; shapeless: *an unformed lump of clay.* 2 undeveloped: *an unformed mind.*

In each of the words below **un** *means not.*

un eat′a ble
un eat′en
un′e clipsed′
un′e co nom′ic
un′e co nom′i cal
un ed′i fy′ing
un ed′u ca ble
un′ef faced′
un′e lim′i nat′ed
un′em bar′rassed
un′em bel′lished
un′e mo′tion al
un′em phat′ic
un′en closed′
un′en cour′aged
un′en cum′bered
un′en dan′gered
un end′ing
un′en dorsed′
un′en dur′a ble
un′en dur′ing
un′en force′a ble
un′en forced′
un′en gaged′
un′en joy′a ble
un′en larged′
un′en light′ened
un′en riched′
un′en rolled′
un en′ter pris′ing
un′en ter tain′ing
un′en thu′si as′tic
un en′vi a ble
un en′vied
un en′vi ous
un′e quipped′
un es′ti mat′ed
un eth′i cal
un′ex ag′ge rat′ed
un′ex am′ined
un′ex celled′
un′ex change′a ble
un′ex cit′ed
un′ex cit′ing
un′ex cused′
un ex′e cut′ed
un′ex haust′ed
un′ex pand′ed
un′ex pend′ed
un′ex per′i enced
un′ex pired′
un′ex plain′a ble
un′ex plained′
un′ex plod′ed
un′ex ploit′ed
un′ex plored′
un′ex posed′
un′ex pressed′
un′ex pres′sive
un ex′pur gat′ed
un′ex tend′ed
un′ex tin′guished
un fad′ed
un fad′ing
un fal′ter ing
un fash′ion a ble
un fas′tened
un fath′om a ble
un fath′omed
un fazed′
un fea′si ble
un feath′ered
un fed′
un fed′e rat′ed
un felt′
un fem′i nine
un fenced′
un′fer ment′ed
un fer′ti lized
un fet′tered
un filed′
un fil′i al
un filled′
un fil′tered
un fired′
un fit′ted
un fit′ting
un fixed′
un flat′ter ing
un fla′vored
un′fore see′a ble
un fo′rest ed
un′for get′ting
un′for giv′a ble
un′for giv′en
un′for giv′ing
un′for got′ten
un for′mu lat′ed

hat, āge, fär; let, ēqual, tėrm;
it, īce; hot, ōpen, ôrder;
oil, out; cup, pu̇t, rüle;
ch, child; ng, long; sh, she;
th, thin; ᴛʜ, then; zh, measure;

ə represents *a* in about, *e* in taken, *i* in pencil, *o* in lemon, *u* in circus.

< = from, derived from, taken from.

un for tu nate (un fôr′chə nit), *adj.* 1 not lucky; having bad luck: *an unfortunate venture.* 2 not suitable; not fitting: *an unfortunate choice of words.* —*n.* an unfortunate person. —**un for′tu nate ly,** *adv.*

un found ed (un foun′did), *adj.* without foundation; without reason; baseless: *an unfounded complaint.*

un freeze (un frēz′), *v.,* **-froze** (-frōz′), **-fro zen** (-frō′zn), **-freez ing.** —*v.t.* 1 thaw; loosen. 2 free from control or restrictions. 3 release (money) for spending.

un fre quent ed (un′frē kwen′tid), *adj.* not frequented; seldom visited; rarely used.

un friend ed (un fren′did), *adj.* without friends.

un friend ly (un frend′lē), *adj.* 1 not friendly; hostile. 2 not favorable. See **hostile** for synonym study. —**un friend′li ness,** *n.*

un frock (un frok′), *v.t.* 1 take away a frock from. 2 deprive (a priest or minister) of his office.

un fruit ful (un früt′fəl), *adj.* 1 not fruitful; producing no offspring; barren: *an unfruitful marriage.* 2 producing nothing worthwhile; unproductive: *an unfruitful inquiry.* —**un fruit′ful ly,** *adv.* —**un fruit′ful ness,** *n.*

un fund ed (un fun′did), *adj.* (of a debt, etc.) not funded; floating.

un furl (un fėrl′), *v.t., v.i.* spread out; shake out; unfold: *unfurl a sail. The flag unfurled.*

un fur nished (un fėr′nisht), *adj.* not furnished; without furniture.

un gain ly (un gān′lē), *adj.* not gainly; awkward; clumsy. —**un gain′li ness,** *n.*

un gen er ous (un jen′ər əs), *adj.* not generous; mean. —**un gen′er ous ly,** *adv.*

un gird (un gėrd′), *v.t.* 1 unfasten or take off the girdle or belt of. 2 loosen, or take off, by unfastening a girdle.

un girt (un gėrt′), *adj.* 1 ungirded. 2 not braced up or pulled together; loose and shapeless: *an ungirt appearance.*

un god ly (un god′lē), *adj.* 1 not devout; not religious; impious. 2 wicked; sinful. 3 INFORMAL. very annoying; outrageous; shocking: *an ungodly noise, pay an ungodly price.* —**un god′li ness,** *n.*

un gov ern a ble (un guv′ər nə bəl), *adj.* impossible to control; very hard to control or rule. See **unruly** for synonym study. —**un gov′ern a ble ness,** *n.* —**un gov′ern a bly,** *adv.*

un grace ful (un grās′fəl), *adj.* not graceful; not elegant or beautiful; clumsy; awkward. —**un grace′ful ly,** *adv.* —**un grace′ful ness,** *n.*

un gra cious (un grā′shəs), *adj.* 1 not polite; discourteous; rude. 2 unpleasant; disagreeable. —**un gra′cious ly,** *adv.* —**un gra′cious ness,** *n.*

un grate ful (un grāt′fəl), *adj.* 1 not grateful; not thankful. 2 unpleasant; disagreeable. —**un grate′ful ly,** *adv.* —**un grate′ful ness,** *n.*

un ground ed (un groun′did), *adj.* without foundation; without reasons; unfounded.

un grudg ing (un gruj′ing), *adj.* not grudging; willing; hearty; liberal. —**un grudg′ing ly,** *adv.*

un gual (ung′gwəl), *adj.* of, having to do with, bearing, or shaped like a nail, claw, or hoof. [< Latin *unguis* nail, claw, hoof]

un guard ed (un gär′did), *adj.* 1 not protected. 2 not properly thoughtful or cautious; careless. —**un guard′ed ly,** *adv.* —**un guard′ed ness,** *n.*

un guent (ung′gwənt), *n.* ointment for sores, burns, etc.; salve. [< Latin *unguentum* < *unguere* anoint]

un guic u late (ung gwik′yə lit), *adj.* 1 having nails or claws. 2 having a clawlike base, as certain petals. —*n.* mammal having nails or claws.

un guis (ung′gwis), *n., pl.* **-gues** (-gwēz). 1 hoof. 2 nail or claw. 3 the narrow, clawlike base of certain petals. [< Latin]

un gu late (ung′gyə lit, ung′gyə lāt), *adj.* 1 having hoofs. 2 of or belonging to a former order of mammals having hoofs, including the ruminants, horses, rhinoceroses, elephants, pigs, etc.

un hal lowed (un hal′ōd), *adj.* 1 not made holy; not sacred. 2 wicked; sinful; evil.

un hand (un hand′), *v.t.* let go; take the hands from; release.

un hand some (un han′səm), *adj.* 1 not good-looking; ugly. 2 ungracious; discourteous; mean. 3 not generous. —**un hand′some ly,** *adv.* —**un hand′some ness,** *n.*

un hand y (un han′dē), *adj.* 1 not easy to handle or manage: *an unhandy tool.* 2 not skillful. —**un hand′i ly,** *adv.* —**un hand′i ness,** *n.*

un hap py (un hap′ē), *adj.,* **-pi er, -pi est.** 1 without gladness; sad; sorrowful: *an unhappy face.* 2 unlucky: *an unhappy accident.* 3 not suitable: *an unhappy selection of colors.* —**un hap′pi ly,** *adv.* —**un hap′pi ness,** *n.*

un har ness (un här′nis), *v.t.* 1 take harness off from (a horse, etc.). 2 take (armor) off from a person.

un health ful (un helth′fəl), *adj.* bad for the health. —**un health′ful ly,** *adv.* —**un health′ful ness,** *n.*

un health y (un hel′thē), *adj.,* **-health i er, -health i est.** 1 not possessing good health; not well: *an unhealthy child.* 2 characteristic of or resulting from poor health: *an unhealthy paleness.* 3 hurtful to health; unwholesome: *an unhealthy climate.* 4 morally or spiritually harmful. —**un health′i ly,** *adv.* —**un health′i ness,** *n.*

un heard (un hėrd′), *adj.* 1 not listened to; not heard: *unheard melodies.* 2 not given a hearing: *condemn a person unheard.*

un heard-of (un hėrd′uv′, un hėrd′ov′), *adj.* 1 that was never heard of; unknown. 2 such as was never known before; unprecedented.

un heed ed (un hē′did), *adj.* not heeded; disregarded; unnoticed.

un hes i tat ing (un hez′ə tā′ting), *adj.* prompt; ready. —**un hes′i tat′ing ly,** *adv.*

un hinge (un hinj′), *v.t.,* **-hinged, -hing ing.** 1 take (a door, etc.) off its hinges. 2 remove the hinges from. 3 separate from something; detach. 4 unsettle; disorganize; upset: *a mind unhinged by shock.*

un hitch (un hich′), *v.t.* 1 free (a horse, etc.) from being hitched. 2 unloose and make free; unfasten.

un ho ly (un hō′lē), *adj.,* **-li er, -li est.** 1 not holy; profane. 2 wicked; sinful. 3 INFORMAL. not seemly; fearful; dreadful: *charge an unholy price.* —**un ho′li ness,** *n.*

un hook (un hu̇k′), *v.t.* 1 loosen from a hook. 2 undo by loosening a hook or hooks. —*v.i.* become unhooked; become undone.

un hoped-for (un hōpt′fôr′), *adj.* not expected; in addition to or beyond what is anticipated: *an unhoped-for blessing.*

un horse (un hôrs′), *v.t.,* **-horsed, -hors ing.** 1 throw from a horse's back; cause to fall from a horse. 2 dislodge; overthrow.

un hur ried (un hėr′ēd), *adj.* not hurried; without haste; leisurely. —**un hur′ried ly,** *adv.*

un hurt (un hėrt′), *adj.* not hurt; not harmed.

uni-, *prefix.* one; single: *Unicellular = having one cell.* [< Latin *unus* one]

U ni at (yü′nē at), *n.* member of any Eastern church that is in communion with the Roman Catholic Church and acknowledges the supremacy of the Pope but keeps its own liturgy. —*adj.* of or having to do with such a church or its members. [< Russian *uniyat* < *uniya* union]

U ni ate (yü′nē it, yü′nē āt), *n., adj.* Uniat.

u ni ax i al (yü′nē ak′sē əl), *adj.* 1 (of a crystal) having one optic axis. 2 (in botany) having only one axis.

u ni cam er al (yü′nə kam′ər əl), *adj.* having only one house in a lawmaking body. Nebraska has a unicameral legislature. [< *uni-* + Latin *camera* chamber]

U NI CEF or **U ni cef** (yü′nə sef), *n.* United Nations Children's Fund.

u ni cel lu lar (yü′nə sel′yə lər), *adj.* having or consisting of one cell, as the amoeba.

In each of the words below **un** *means not.*

un for′ti fied
un framed′
un free′
un fre′quent
un fro′zen
un′ful filled′
un fun′ny
un gained′
un gal′lant
un gar′nished
un gath′ered
un gen′ial
un′gen teel′
un gen′tle
un gen′tle man ly
un gift′ed
un glam′or ous
un glazed′
un gloved′
un gov′erned
un grad′ed
un′gram mat′i cal
un grat′i fied
un′guar an teed′
un guid′ed
un hack′neyed
un ham′pered
un hand′i capped
un han′dled
un hanged′
un har′assed
un hard′ened
un harmed′
un′har mo′ni ous
un har′nessed
un hatched′
un healed′
un heat′ed
un heed′ful
un heed′ing
un help′ful
un her′ald ed
un′he ro′ic
un hes′i tant
un hin′dered
un hon′ored
un housed′
un hur′ry ing
un hurt′ful
un′hy gi en′ic

unicorn

u ni corn (yü′nə kôrn), *n.* an imaginary animal like a horse, but having a single long horn in the middle of its forehead, the hind legs of an antelope, and the tail of a lion. [< Latin *unicornis* < *unus* one + *cornu* horn]

u ni cy cle (yü′nə sī′kəl), *n.* a vehicle consisting of a frame mounted on a single wheel, propelled by pedaling, used especially by acrobats, circus performers, etc.

u ni di rec tion al (yü′nə də rek′shə nəl, yü′nə dī rek′shə nəl), *adj.* in only one direction: *unidirectional radio waves.* **—u′ni di rec′tion al ly,** *adv.*

u ni fi a ble (yü′nə fī′ə bəl), *adj.* able to be unified; capable of unification.

u ni fi ca tion (yü′nə fə kā′shən), *n.* 1 formation into one unit; union: *the unification of many states into one nation.* 2 a making or a being made more alike: *The traffic laws of the different states need unification.*

u ni form (yü′nə fôrm), *adj.* 1 always the same; not changing: *The earth turns at a uniform rate.* 2 all alike; not varying: *All the bricks have a uniform size.* See **even**[1] for synonym study. 3 regular; even: *a uniform pace.* —*n.* the distinctive clothes worn by the members of a group when on duty, by which they may be recognized as belonging to that group. Soldiers, policemen, and nurses wear uniforms. —*v.t.* clothe or furnish with a uniform. **—u′ni form′ly,** *adv.* **—u′ni form′ness,** *n.*

u ni formed (yü′nə fôrmd), *adj.* wearing a uniform; in uniform.

u ni form i ty (yü′nə fôr′mə tē), *n., pl.* **-ties.** uniform condition or character; sameness throughout.

u ni fy (yü′nə fī), *v.t., v.i.,* **-fied, -fy ing.** make or form into one; unite. **—u′ni fi′er,** *n.*

u ni lat er al (yü′nə lat′ər əl), *adj.* 1 of, on, or affecting one side only: *unilateral disarmament.* 2 having all the parts arranged on one side of an axis; turned to one side; one-sided. **—u′ni lat′er al ly,** *adv.*

un i mag i na ble (un′i maj′ə nə bəl), *adj.* that cannot be imagined; inconceivable. **—un′i mag′i na bly,** *adv.*

un im peach a ble (un′im pē′chə bəl), *adj.* free from fault, flaw, or error; not to be doubted or questioned: *an unimpeachable fact, an unimpeachable reputation.* **—un′im peach′a bly,** *adv.*

un im por tance (un′im pôrt′ns), *n.* unimportant nature or quality.

un im por tant (un′im pôrt′nt), *adj.* not important; insignificant; trifling.

un in jured (un in′jərd), *adj.* not hurt; not damaged.

un in spired (un′in spīrd′), *adj.* not inspired; dull; tiresome.

un in tel li gi ble (un′in tel′ə jə bəl), *adj.* not intelligible; not able to be understood. **—un′in tel′li gi ble ness,** *n.* **—un′in tel′li gi bly,** *adv.*

un in ten tion al (un′in ten′shə nəl), *adj.* not intentional; not done purposely. **—un′in ten′tion al ly,** *adv.*

un in ter est ed (un in′tər ə stid, un in′tə res′tid), *adj.* not interested; paying no attention. ➤ See **disinterested** for usage note.

un in ter rupt ed (un′in tə rup′tid), *adj.* without interruption; continuous. **—un′in ter rupt′ed ly,** *adv.*

u ni nu cle ate (yü′nə nü′klē it, yü′nə nyü′klē it), *adj.* having a single nucleus: *a uninucleate cell.*

union (def. 7)
pipe union

un ion (yü′nyən), *n.* 1 a uniting or a being united: *the union of hydrogen and oxygen in water.* See synonym study below. 2 group of people, states, etc., united for some special purpose: *The ten provinces of Canada form a union.* 3 **the Union, a** the United States of America. **b** those states that supported the federal government of the United States during the Civil War. 4 group of workers joined together to protect and promote their interests; labor union; trade union. 5 marriage. 6 flag, or part of one, that is an emblem of union. The blue rectangle with stars in the American flag is the union. 7 any of various devices for connecting parts of machinery or apparatus, especially a piece to join pipes or tubes together; coupling. 8 (in mathematics) a set including all the members which belong to either or both of two sets. EXAMPLE: If set $A = \{1, 2, 3, 4\}$ and set $B = \{4, 5, 6\}$, then the union of the two sets is $\{1, 2, 3, 4, 5, 6\}$. —*adj.* **Union,** of or having to do with the Union: *Union soldiers.* [< Latin *unionem* < *unus* one]

Syn. *n.* 1 **Union, unity** mean a forming or being one. **Union** emphasizes the joining together of two or more things, people, or groups to form a whole, or the state of being joined together as a unit: *The Constitution of the United States replaced the Articles of Confederation in order to form a more perfect union of the states than had existed before.* **Unity** emphasizes the oneness of the whole thus formed: *The strength of any group is in its unity.*

union card, card indicating membership in the labor union by which it is issued.

un ion ism (yü′nyə niz′əm), *n.* 1 the principle of union. 2 **Unionism,** adherence to the federal union of the United States, especially at the time of the Civil War. 3 system, principles, or methods of labor unions.

un ion ist (yü′nyə nist), *n.* 1 person who promotes or advocates union. 2 **Unionist,** supporter of the federal government of the United States during the Civil War. 3 member of a labor union.

un ion ize (yü′nyə nīz), *v.,* **-ized, -iz ing.** —*v.t.* 1 form into a labor union. 2 organize under a labor union, bring under the rules of a labor union. —*v.i.* join in a labor union. **—un′ion i za′tion,** *n.*

union jack, 1 a small flag which shows the symbol of union of a national flag. The United States union jack has 50 white stars against a blue background. 2 **Union Jack,** the flag of the United Kingdom.

Union of Arab Emirates, country in E Arabia on the Persian Gulf, consisting of seven sheikdoms, formerly known as the Trucial States. 200,000 pop.; 32,300 sq. mi. *Capital:* Dubai.

Union of South Africa, former name of the **Republic of South Africa.**

Union of Soviet Socialist Republics, the Soviet Union.

union shop, a business establishment that employs only members of a labor union, but may hire nonmembers provided they join the union within a specified period.

union suit, suit of underwear in one piece.

u nip ar ous (yü nip′ər əs), *adj.* producing one egg or one offspring at a time. [< *uni-* one + Latin *parere* to bear]

u ni po lar (yü′nə pō′lər), *adj.* 1 having a single pole. 2 (in physics) produced by or proceeding from one magnetic or electric pole. 3 (of nerve cells) having only one fibrous process.

u nique (yü nēk′), *adj.* 1 having no like or equal; being the only one of its kind: *a unique specimen of rock.* 2 INFORMAL. very uncommon or unusual; rare; remarkable: *His style of singing is rather unique.* [< Middle French < Latin *unicus* < *unus* one] **—u nique′ly,** *adv.* **—u nique′ness,** *n.*

u ni sex u al (yü′nə sek′shü əl), *adj.* 1 that is not a hermaphrodite; having the reproductive organs of only one sex in one individual. 2 having to do with one sex.

u ni son (yü′nə sən, yü′nə zən), *n.* 1 harmonious combination or union; agreement: *The feet of marching soldiers move in unison. They spoke in unison.* 2 identity in pitch of two or more sounds, tones, etc. 3 combination of tones, melodies, etc., at the same pitch, as performed by different voices or instruments. [< Medieval Latin *unisonus* sounding the same < Latin *unus* one + *sonus* sound]

u nit (yü′nit), *n.* 1 a single thing or person. 2 any group of things or persons considered as one: *The family is a social unit.* 3 one of the individuals or groups of which a whole is

In each of the words below **un** *means not.*

un′i de′al
un′i den′ti fied
un′id i o mat′ic
un′il lu′mi nat′ed
un′i mag′i na tive
un′im paired′
un′im pas′sioned
un′im ped′ed
un′im pos′ing
un′im pressed′
un′im press′i ble
un′im pres′sion a ble
un′im pres′sive
un′im proved′
un′in closed′
un′in cor′po rat′ed
un′in cum′bered
un in′dexed
un′in fect′ed
un′in flam′ma ble
un′in flect′ed
un in′flu enced
un′in form′a tive
un′in formed′
un′in hab′it a ble
un′in hab′it ed
un′in hib′it ed
un′i ni′ti at′ed
un′in quir′ing
un′in spect′ed
un′in spir′ing
un′in struct′ed
un′in struc′tive
un in′su lat′ed
un′in sured′
un in′te grat ed
un′in tel′li gent
un′in tend′ed
un in′ter est ing
un′in ter mit′ted
un′in ter mit′ting
un′in tim′i dat′ed
un′in ven′tive
un′in vest′ed
un′in vit′ed
un′in vit′ing

composed: *The body consists of units called cells.* 4 a standard quantity or amount, used as a basis for measuring: *A foot is a unit of length; a pound is a unit of weight.* 5 a part of a machine or other apparatus that has one specific purpose: *the storage unit in an electronic computer.* 6 the amount of a drug, vaccine, serum, etc., necessary to produce a specified effect. 7 the smallest whole number; 1. 8 a certain number of hours of classroom attendance and the accompanying outside work, used in computing credits, fees, etc. *—adj.* 1 of a standard quantity or measure: *a unit dose, unit length.* 2 of the smallest number: *a unit angle.* [< *unity*]

U ni tar i an (yü′nə ter′ē ən, yü′nə tar′ē-ən), *n.* 1 Christian who denies the doctrine of the Trinity, maintaining that God is one person, and accepts Christ as one imbued with the divine spirit but not himself divine. 2 member of a Christian group or sect holding this doctrine and stressing individual religious freedom and the independence of each local congregation. 3 **unitarian,** person who believes in unity or centralization, as in government. *—adj.* of or having to do with Unitarians.

U ni tar i an ism (yü′nə ter′ē ə niz′əm, yü′nə tar′ē ə niz′əm), *n.* the doctrines or beliefs of Unitarians.

u ni tar y (yü′nə ter′ē), *adj.* 1 of or having to do with a unit or units. 2 of, based upon, or directed toward unity. 3 under one control; unified; centralized: *a unitary government.* 4 like a unit; used as a unit.

u nite (yü nīt′), *v.*, **u nit ed, u nit ing.** *—v.t.* 1 join together; make one; combine: *unite bricks and mortar.* 2 bring together; consolidate into one body: *unite one's forces.* 3 join by a mutual agreement or other formal bond: *unite a couple in marriage.* *—v.i.* become one; join in action, etc.; be united. See **join** for synonym study. [< Latin *unitum* made one < *unus* one] **—u nit′er,** *n.*

u nit ed (yü nī′tid), *adj.* 1 made one; joined; combined. 2 having to do with or produced by two or more. 3 that harmonizes or agrees; in concord. **—u nit′ed ly,** *adv.*

United Arab Emirates, Union of Arab Emirates.

United Arab Republic, official name of **Egypt.** In 1958 Egypt and Syria formed the United Arab Republic and invited other Arab nations to join. Syria withdrew in 1961.

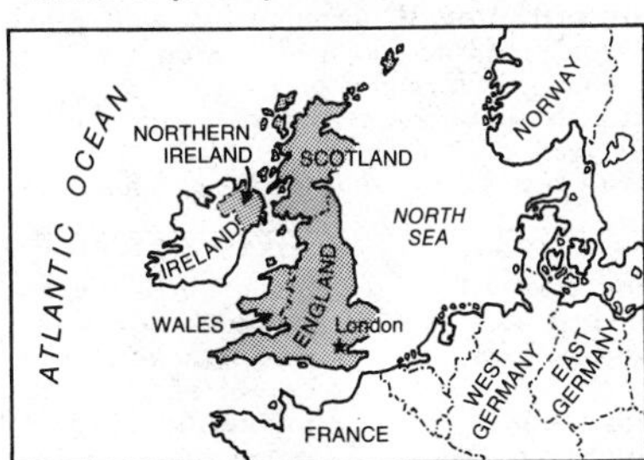

United Kingdom (def. 1)—the shaded area

United Kingdom, 1 country in NW Europe, in the British Isles, composed of Great Britain and Northern Ireland, a member of the Commonwealth of Nations. 55,525,200 pop.; 94,500 sq. mi. *Capital:* London. 2 Great Britain and Ireland from 1801 to 1922.

United Nations, 1 a worldwide organization established in 1945 to promote world peace and economic and social welfare. It has over 120 members. Its headquarters are in New York City. 2 the nations that belong to this organization.

United States, country in North America composed of 50 states, the District of Columbia, Puerto Rico, and other possessions, extending from the Atlantic to the Pacific and from the Gulf of Mexico to Canada, with Alaska lying west and northwest of Canada and Hawaii an island group in the Pacific. Continental United States and Hawaii: 203,212,000 pop.; 3,615,100 sq. mi. United States and possessions: 207,976,000 pop.; 3,628,000 sq. mi. *Capital:* Washington, D.C.

United States of America, United States.

u ni tize (yü′nə tīz), *v.t.*, **-tized, -tiz ing.** make into a unit; weld into one. **—u′ni ti za′tion,** *n.*

unit rule, U.S. rule which requires that members of a delegation at a convention cast their votes in a body for the candidate preferred by the majority of the delegation.

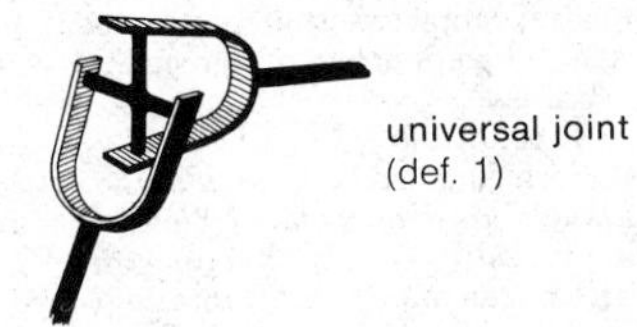

universal joint (def. 1)

u ni ty (yü′nə tē), *n.*, *pl.* **-ties.** 1 a being united; oneness; singleness: *A circle has unity; a random group of dots does not.* See **union** for synonym study. 2 union of parts forming a complex whole. 3 concord; harmony: *Brothers and sisters should live together in unity.* 4 the number one. 5 quantity or magnitude regarded as equivalent to one (1) in calculation, measurement, or comparison. 6 oneness of effect; choice and arrangement of material (for a composition, book, picture, statue, etc.) to secure a single effect. 7 **the unities,** the rules of action, time, and place that require a play to have one plot occurring on one day in one place. [< Latin *unitatem* < *unus* one]

univ., 1 universal. 2 university.

U NI VAC (yü′nə vak), *n.* trademark for an electronic computer which uses a binary numbering system.

u ni va lence (yü′nə vā′ləns, yü niv′ə ləns), *n.* a being univalent.

u ni va lent (yü′nə vā′lənt, yü niv′ə lənt), *adj.* having a valence of one; monovalent.

u ni valve (yü′nə valv′), *n.* 1 any mollusk having a shell consisting of one piece. Snails are univalves. See **bivalve** for picture. 2 its shell. *—adj.* 1 having a shell consisting of one piece. 2 (of a shell) composed of a single piece.

u ni ver sal (yü′nə vėr′səl), *adj.* 1 of or for all; belonging to all; concerning all: *Food is a universal need.* 2 existing everywhere: *The law of gravity is universal.* 3 covering a whole group of persons, things, cases, etc.; general. 4 (in logic) asserting or denying something of every member of a class: *"All men are mortal" is a universal proposition.* 5 accomplished in all or many subjects: *a universal genius.* 6 adaptable to different sizes, angles, kinds of work, etc. *—n.* 1 (in logic) a universal proposition. 2 a general term or concept; abstraction. 3 universal joint. **—u′ni ver′sal ly,** *adv.* **—u′ni ver′sal ness,** *n.*

hat, āge, fär; let, ēqual, tėrm;
it, īce; hot, ōpen, ôrder;
oil, out; cup, pu̇t, rüle;
ch, child; ng, long; sh, she;
th, thin; ᴛʜ, then; zh, measure;

ə represents *a* in about, *e* in taken, *i* in pencil, *o* in lemon, *u* in circus.

< = from, derived from, taken from.

U ni ver sal ism (yü′nə vėr′sə liz′əm), *n.* the doctrines or beliefs of Universalists.

U ni ver sal ist (yü′nə vėr′sə list), *n.* 1 Christian who believes in the final salvation of all mankind. 2 member of a Christian group or sect holding this doctrine. The Universalists merged with the Unitarians in 1961. *—adj.* of or having to do with Universalists.

u ni ver sal i ty (yü′nə vər sal′ə tē), *n.*, *pl.* **-ties.** a being universal.

u ni ver sal ize (yü′nə vėr′sə līz), *v.t.*, **-ized, -iz ing.** render universal; make generally or universally applicable. **—u′ni ver′sal i za′tion,** *n.*

universal joint, 1 joint that moves in any direction. 2 coupling for transmitting power from one shaft to another when they are not in line.

u ni verse (yü′nə vėrs′), *n.* 1 the whole of existing things; everything there is; the cosmos. 2 the whole of reality. 3 the world, especially as the abode of mankind; earth. 4 (in mathematics and logic) the set of all objects being considered at any one time. The universe might be the set of all natural numbers, the numbers from 0 through 10, all animals, the animals on a farm, etc. [< Latin *universum* whole, turned into one < *unus* one + *vertere* to turn]

u ni ver si ty (yü′nə vėr′sə tē), *n.*, *pl.* **-ties.** institution of learning of the highest grade, usually including schools of law, medicine, teaching, business, etc., as well as (in the United States) a college of liberal arts and a graduate school. [< Late Latin *universitatem* corporation < Latin, whole < *universum.* See UNIVERSE.]

u niv o cal (yü niv′ə kəl), *adj.* having one meaning only; not equivocal. [< Late Latin *univocus* < Latin *unus* one + *vocem* voice] **—u niv′o cal ly,** *adv.*

un just (un just′), *adj.* not just; not fair. **—un just′ly,** *adv.* **—un just′ness,** *n.*

un jus ti fi a ble (un jus′tə fī′ə bəl), *adj.* that cannot be justified. **—un jus′ti fi′a bly,** *adv.*

un kempt (un kempt′), *adj.* 1 not combed: *unkempt hair.* 2 not properly cared for; neglected; untidy. [< *un-*[1] + Old English *cembed* combed]

un kind (un kīnd′), *adj.* not kind; harsh; cruel. **—un kind′ness,** *n.*

un kind ly (un kīnd′lē), *adj.* harsh; unfavorable. *—adv.* in an unkind way; harshly.

un knit (un nit′), *v.t.*, *v.i.*, **-knit ted** or **-knit, -knit ting.** 1 untie or unfasten (a knot, etc.). 2 ravel out (something knitted).

un know ing (un nō′ing), *adj.* not knowing; ignorant or unsuspecting. **—un know′ing ly,** *adv.* **—un know′ing ness,** *n.*

un known (un nōn′), *adj.* not known; not familiar; strange: *an unknown land.* *—n.* 1 person or thing that is unknown: *a political unknown.* 2 unknown quantity.

unknown quantity, (in mathematics) a quantity whose value is to be found, usually represented by a letter, such as *x, y,* or *z.*

Unknown Soldier, an unidentified soldier killed in combat and buried with honors in a prominent place, as a memorial to all the unidentified dead of his country.

un lace (un lās′), *v.t.,* **-laced, -lac ing.** undo the laces of.

un lade (un lād′), *v.t., v.i.,* **-lad ed, -lad en** (-lād′n) or **-lad ed, -lad ing.** unload.

un latch (un lach′), *v.t.* unfasten or open by lifting a latch. —*v.i.* become or be able to be thus unfastened.

un law ful (un lô′fəl), *adj.* 1 contrary to the law; against the law; forbidden; illegal. 2 illegitimate. —**un law′ful ly,** *adv.* —**un-law′ful ness,** *n.*

un lay (un lā′), *v.i.,* **-laid** (-lād′), **-lay ing.** (of a rope) have the strands part; untwist; unravel.

un learn (un lėrn′), *v.t.* get rid of (ideas, habits, or tendencies); forget.

un learn ed (un lėr′nid *for 1, 3;* un lėrnd′ *for 2*), *adj.* 1 not educated; ignorant: *an unlearned comment.* 2 not learned; known without being learned: *Being able to suck is an unlearned habit of babies.* 3 not showing education.

un leash (un lēsh′), *v.t.* 1 release from a leash: *unleash a dog.* 2 let loose: *unleash one's temper.*

un leav ened (un lev′ənd), *adj.* not leavened. Unleavened bread is made without yeast.

un less (ən les′, un les′), *conj.* if it were not that; if not: *We shall go unless it rains.* —*prep.* except. [< *on* + *less,* i.e., on a less condition (than)]

un let tered (un let′ərd), *adj.* 1 not educated. 2 not able to read or write; illiterate.

un like (un līk′), *adj.* 1 not like; different: *The two problems are quite unlike.* 2 different in size or number; unequal: *unlike weights.* —*prep.* different from: *act unlike others.* —**un like′ness,** *n.*

un like li hood (un līk′lē hu̇d), *n.* improbability.

un like ly (un lik′lē), *adj.* 1 not likely; not probable: *That horse is unlikely to win the race.* 2 not likely to succeed: *an unlikely undertaking.* —**un like′li ness,** *n.*

un lim ber (un lim′bər), *v.t.* 1 detach the limber or forepart of the carriage from (a gun). 2 make or get (anything) ready for action or use: *unlimber one's muscles.* —*v.i.* prepare for action.

un lim it ed (un lim′ə tid), *adj.* 1 without limits; boundless. 2 not restricted. —**un-lim′it ed ness,** *n.*

un list ed (un lis′tid), *adj.* 1 not on a or the usual list: *an unlisted telephone number.* 2 not in the official list of securities that can be traded in a stock exchange.

un load (un lōd′), *v.t.* 1 remove (a load). 2 take the load from. 3 get rid of; unburden oneself of: *unload one's problems on others.* 4 remove powder, shot, bullets, or shells from (a gun). 5 dispose of or sell out, especially in large quantities: *unload stock.* —*v.i.* be or become unloaded: *The ship is unloading.* —**un load′er,** *n.*

un lock (un lok′), *v.t.* 1 open the lock of; open (anything firmly closed). 2 disclose; reveal: *unlock one's heart, unlock the mystery of the atom.* —*v.i.* be or become unlocked.

un looked-for (un lu̇kt′fôr′), *adj.* unexpected; unforeseen.

un loose (un lüs′), *v.t.,* **-loosed, -loos ing.** let loose; set free; release.

un loos en (un lü′sn), *v.t.* unloose; loosen.

un love ly (un luv′lē), *adj.* without beauty or charm; unpleasing in appearance; unpleasant; objectionable; disagreeable. —**un-love′li ness,** *n.*

un luck y (un luk′ē), *adj.* not lucky; unfortunate; bringing bad luck: *an unlucky person, an unlucky day, an unlucky choice.* —**un-luck′i ly,** *adv.* —**un luck′i ness,** *n.*

un make (un māk′), *v.t.,* **-made** (-mād′), **-mak ing.** 1 bring to nothing; destroy; ruin. 2 deprive of rank or station; depose. 3 undo the making of.

un man (un man′), *v.t.,* **-manned, -man ning.** 1 deprive of manly courage or fortitude; weaken or break down the spirit of. 2 deprive of men: *unman a ship.*

un man ly (un man′lē), *adj.* not manly; effeminate; weak; cowardly. —**un man′li-ness,** *n.*

un man ner ly (un man′ər lē), *adj.* having bad manners; rude; discourteous. —*adv.* with bad manners; rudely. —**un man′ner-li ness,** *n.*

un mar ried (un mar′ēd), *adj.* not married; single.

un mask (un mask′), *v.i.* remove a mask or disguise: *The guests unmasked at midnight.* —*v.t.* 1 take off a mask or disguise from. 2 expose the true character of: *unmask a hypocrite, unmask a conspiracy.*

un match a ble (un mach′ə bəl), *adj.* that cannot be matched or equaled.

un mean ing (un mē′ning), *adj.* 1 without meaning; meaningless: *unmeaning words.* 2 without sense or expression: *an unmeaning stare.* —**un mean′ing ly,** *adv.*

un meas ured (un mezh′ərd, un mā′-zhərd), *adj.* 1 not measured; unlimited; measureless. 2 not restrained; excessive.

un meet (un mēt′), *adj.* not fit; not proper; unsuitable.

un men tion a ble (un men′shə nə bəl), *adj.* that cannot be mentioned; not fit to be spoken about. —**un men′tion a ble-ness,** *n.*

un mer ci ful (un mėr′si fəl), *adj.* having no mercy; showing no mercy; cruel. —**un-mer′ci ful ly,** *adv.* —**un mer′ci ful-ness,** *n.*

un met (un met′), *adj.* 1 not met; not encountered: *his yet unmet friend.* 2 not satisfied; unfulfilled: *unmet needs.*

un mind ful (un mīnd′fəl), *adj.* not mindful; regardless; heedless; careless. —**un-mind′ful ly,** *adv*

un mis tak a ble (un′mə stā′kə bəl), *adj.* that cannot be mistaken or misunderstood; clear; plain; evident —**un′mis tak′a ble-ness,** *n* —**un′mis tak′a bly,** *adv.*

un mit i gat ed (un mit′ə gā′tid), *adj.* 1 not softened or lessened: *unmitigated harshness.* 2 unqualified or absolute: *an unmitigated fraud.* —**un mit′i gat′ed ly,** *adv.*

un mixed (un mikst′), *adj.* not mixed; pure.

un moor (un mu̇r′), *v.t.* loose (a ship) from moorings or anchor. —*v.t.* become free of moorings.

un mo ral (un môr′əl, un mor′əl), *adj.* neither moral nor immoral; not perceiving or involving right and wrong. —**un mo′ral ly,** *adv.*

un moved (un müvd′), *adj.* 1 not moved; firm. 2 not disturbed; indifferent: *be unmoved by someone's tears.*

un muf fle (un muf′əl), *v.t.,* **-fled, -fling.** strip of or free from something that muffles.

un muz zle (un muz′əl), *v.t.,* **-zled, -zling.** 1 take off a muzzle from (a dog, etc.). 2 free from restraint; allow to speak or write freely.

un nat ur al (un nach′ər əl), *adj.* 1 not natural; not normal. 2 shocking; horrible. 3 synthetic; artificial. 4 perverted; depraved. —**un nat′ur al ly,** *adv.* —**un nat′ur al-ness,** *n.*

un nec es sar y (un nes′ə ser′ē), *adj.* not necessary; needless. —**un nec′es sar′i ly,** *adv.* —**un nec′es sar′i ness,** *n.*

un nerve (un nėrv′), *v.t.,* **-nerved, -nerv ing.** deprive of nerve, firmness, or self-control.

un num bered (un num′bərd), *adj.* 1 not numbered; not counted. 2 too many to count; innumerable.

un ob served (un′əb zėrvd′), *adj.* not observed; not noticed; disregarded.

un ob tru sive (un′əb trü′siv), *adj.* not

In each of the words below **un** *means not.*

un la′beled
un lad′en
un la′dy like′
un laid′
un′la ment′ed
un laun′dered
un li′censed
un light′ed
un lik′a ble
un lined′
un liq′ue fied
un liq′ui dat′ed
un lit′
un lit′tered
un lov′a ble
un loved′
un lov′ing
un mag′ni fied
un maid′en ly
un mailed′
un mal′le a ble
un man′age a ble
un manned′
un man′nered
un′man u fac′tured
un mapped′
un marked′
un mar′ket a ble
un marred′
un mar′riage a ble
un mas′tered
un matched′
un mat′ed
un meant′
un meas′ur a ble
un′me chan′i cal
un′me lo′di ous
un melt′ed
un men′tioned
un mer′chant a ble
un mer′it ed
un′me thod′i cal
un mil′i tar′y
un milled′
un min′gled
un mirth′ful
un′mis tak′en
un mixt′
un mod′i fied
un mod′u lat′ed
un′mo lest′ed
un mo′ti vat′ed
un mount′ed
un mourned′
un mov′a ble
un mov′ing
un mown′
un mu′si cal
un muz′zled
un nam′a ble
un name′a ble
un named′
un nat′ur al ized
un nav′i ga ble
un need′ed
un need′ful
un′ne go′tia ble
un neigh′bor ly
un neigh′bour ly
un not′ed
un note′wor′thy
un no′tice a ble
un no′ticed
un′o beyed′
un′ob jec′tion a ble
un′o blig′ing
un′ob scured′
un′ob serv′a ble
un′ob serv′ant
un′ob serv′ing
un′ob struct′ed
un′ob tain′a ble
un′oc ca′sioned

hat, āge, fär; let, ēqual, tėrm;
it, īce; hot, ōpen, ôrder;
oil, out; cup, pu̇t, rüle;
ch, child; ng, long; sh, she;
th, thin; ᴛʜ, then; zh, measure;
ə represents *a* in about, *e* in taken, *i* in pencil, *o* in lemon, *u* in circus.
< = from, derived from, taken from.

obtrusive; modest; inconspicuous. **—un/ob tru/sive ly,** *adv.* **—un/ob tru/sive ness,** *n.*

un oc cu pied (un ok/yə pīd), *adj.* 1 not occupied; vacant: *an unoccupied room.* 2 not in action or use; idle: *an unoccupied mind.*

un of fi cial (un/ə fish/əl), *adj.* not official. **—un/of fi/cial ly,** *adv.*

un or gan ized (un ôr/gə nīzd), *adj.* 1 not formed into an organized or systematized whole. 2 not organized into labor unions. 3 not being a living organism. An enzyme is an unorganized ferment.

un pack (un pak/), *v.t.* 1 take out (things packed in a box, trunk, etc.): *unpack clothes.* 2 take things out of: *unpack a suitcase.* —*v.i.* take out things packed.

un paid (un pād/), *adj.* not paid: *unpaid bills.*

un pal at a ble (un pal/ə tə bəl), *adj.* not agreeable to the taste; distasteful; unpleasant. **—un pal/at a ble ness,** *n.*

un par al leled (un par/ə leld), *adj.* having no parallel; unequaled; matchless: *an unparalleled achievement.*

un par lia men tar y (un/pär lə men/tər ē), *adj.* not in accordance with parliamentary practice, procedure, or usage.

un peg (un peg/), *v.t.,* **-pegged, -peg ging.** loosen or detach; disengage.

un peo ple (un pē/pəl), *v.t.,* **-pled, -pling.** deprive of people; depopulate.

un peo pled (un pē/pəld), *adj.* not inhabited.

un pin (un pin/), *v.t.,* **-pinned, -pin ning.** take out a pin or pins from; unfasten.

un pleas ant (un plez/nt), *adj.* not pleasant; disagreeable. **—un pleas/ant ly,** *adv.*

un pleas ant ness (un plez/nt nis), *n.* 1 unpleasant quality. 2 something unpleasant. 3 quarrel.

un plug (un plug/), *v.t.,* **-plugged, -plug ging.** 1 remove the plug or stopper from. 2 disconnect by removing the plug from an electric outlet: *unplug a lamp.*

un plumbed (un plumd/), *adj.* 1 not plumbed; not fathomed; of unknown depth: *unplumbed seas, the unplumbed depths of a person's character.* 2 having no plumbing.

un pop u lar (un pop/yə lər), *adj.* not popular; not generally liked; disliked. **—un pop/u lar ly,** *adv.*

un pop u lar i ty (un/pop yə lar/ə tē), *n.* lack of popularity; being unpopular.

un prac ticed or **un prac tised** (un prak/tist), *adj.* 1 not skilled; not expert. 2 not put into practice; not used.

un prec e dent ed (un pres/ə den/tid), *adj.* having no precedent; never done before; never known before: *an event unprecedented in history.* **—un prec/e dent/ed ly,** *adv.*

un pre dict a bil i ty (un/pri dik/tə bil/ə tē), *n.* a being unpredictable.

un pre dict a ble (un/pri dik/tə bəl), *adj.* that cannot be predicted; uncertain or changeable. **—un/pre dict/a bly,** *adv.*

un prej u diced (un prej/ə dist), *adj.* 1 without prejudice; fair; impartial: *an unprejudiced observer.* 2 not impaired: *an unprejudiced right of appeal.*

un pre pared (un/pri perd/, un/pri pard/), *adj.* 1 not made ready; not worked out ahead: *an unprepared speech.* 2 not ready: *a person unprepared to answer.* **—un/pre par/ed ness,** *n.*

un pre tend ing (un/pri ten/ding), *adj.* unpretentious. **—un/pre tend/ing ly,** *adv.*

un pre ten tious (un/pri ten/shəs), *adj.* not pretentious; unassuming; modest. **—un/pre ten/tious ly,** *adv.* **—un/pre ten/tious ness,** *n.*

un prin ci pled (un prin/sə pəld), *adj.* lacking moral principles; not upright, ethical, etc. See **unscrupulous** for synonym study.

un print a ble (un prin/tə bəl), *adj.* not fit or proper to be printed.

un pro fes sion al (un/prə fesh/ə nəl), *adj.* 1 contrary to professional etiquette; unbecoming in members of a profession. 2 not having to do with or connected with a profession. 3 not belonging to a profession. **—un/pro fes/sion al ly,** *adv.*

un prof it a ble (un prof/ə tə bəl), *adj.* not profitable; producing no gain or advantage. **—un prof/it a ble ness,** *n.* **—un prof/it a bly,** *adv.*

un pro voked (un/prə vōkt/), *adj.* without provocation.

un qual i fied (un kwol/ə fīd), *adj.* 1 not qualified; not fitted. 2 not modified, limited, or restricted in any way: *unqualified praise.* 3 complete; absolute: *an unqualified failure.* **—un qual/i fied/ly,** *adv.*

un quench a ble (un kwen/chə bəl), *adj.* that cannot be quenched or extinguished: *unquenchable thirst, unquenchable zeal.*

un ques tion a ble (un kwes/chə nə bəl), *adj.* 1 beyond dispute or doubt; certain: *an unquestionable advantage.* 2 accepted without question: *unquestionable doctrine.* **—un ques/tion a ble ness,** *n.* **—un ques/tion a bly,** *adv.*

un ques tioned (un kwes/chənd), *adj.* not questioned; not disputed.

un qui et (un kwī/ət), *adj.* 1 not at rest; agitated; restless: *pass an unquiet night.* 2 disturbed; uneasy: *an unquiet mind.* 3 causing or likely to cause trouble, disturbance, etc.: *an unquiet populace.* **—un qui/et ly,** *adv.* **—un qui/et ness,** *n.*

un quote (un kwōt/), *v.i.,* **-quot ed, -quot ing.** mark the end of a quotation.

un rav el (un rav/əl), *v.,* **-eled, -el ing** or **-elled, -el ling.** —*v.t.* 1 separate the threads of; pull apart: *The kitten unraveled Grandma's knitting.* 2 bring out of a tangled state; untangle; resolve: *unravel a mystery.* —*v.i.* 1 come apart. 2 come out of a tangled state.

un read (un red/), *adj.* 1 not read: *an unread book.* 2 not having read much: *an unread person.*

un read a bil i ty (un/rē də bil/ə tē), *n.* a being unreadable.

un read a ble (un rē/də bəl), *adj.* 1 that cannot be read; illegible: *an unreadable manuscript.* 2 not suitable or fit for reading; not worth reading: *a dull, unreadable book.*

un read y (un red/ē), *adj.* 1 not ready; not prepared. 2 not prompt or quick; slow. **—un read/i ly,** *adv.* **—un read/i ness,** *n.*

un re al (un rē/əl), *adj.* not real or substantial; imaginary; fanciful. **—un re/al ly,** *adv.*

un re al i ty (un/rē al/ə tē), *n., pl.* **-ties.** 1 lack of reality; imaginary or fanciful quality. 2 impractical or visionary character or tendency; impracticality. 3 some-

---

In each of the words below **un** *means not.*

un/of fend/ing
un of/fered
un of/fi cered
un oiled/
un o/pened
un/op posed/
un/or dained/
un or/dered
un/o rig/i nal
un or/tho dox
un/os ten ta/tious
un owned/
un paint/ed
un paired/
un par/don a ble
un par/doned
un/par ti/tioned
un pas/teur ized
un/pa tri ot/ic
un paved/
un peace/a ble
un ped/i greed
un/per ceived/
un/per ceiv/ing
un/per cep/tive
un/per formed/
un/per plexed/
un/per suad/ed
un/per sua/sive
un/per turbed/
un/pe rused/
un/phil/o soph/ic
un/phil/o soph/i cal
un/pho net/ic
un picked/
un pierced/
un pit/ied
un pit/y ing
un placed/
un plagued/
un planned/
un plant/ed
un play/a ble
un played/
un pleased/
un pleas/ing
un pledged/
un pli/ant
un plowed/
un/po et/ic
un/po et/i cal
un point/ed
un poised/
un po/lar ized
un/po liced/
un pol/ished
un/po lit/i cal
un polled/
un/pol lut/ed
un pop/u lat/ed
un posed/
un post/ed
un pow/ered
un prac/ti cal
un praised/
un/pre med/i tat/ed
un/pre pos sess/ing
un/pre scribed/
un/pre sent/a ble
un pressed/
un pret/ty
un/pre vail/ing
un/pre vent/a ble
un print/ed
un priv/i leged
un prized/
un proc/essed
un/pro cur/a ble
un/pro duc/tive
un/pro faned/
un/pro gres/sive
un/pro hib/it ed
un/pro ject/ed
un prom/is ing
un prompt/ed
un/pro nounce/a ble
un/pro nounced/
un/pro pi/tious
un/pro por/tion ate
un/pro por/tioned
un pros/per ous
un/pro tect/ed
un/pro test/ed
un/pro test/ing
un proved/
un prov/en
un/pro vid/ed
un/pro vok/ing
un pruned/
un pub/li cized
un pub/lished
un punc/tu al
un pun/ished
un pur/chas a ble
un pure/
un pur/posed
un/pur su/ing
un quail/ing
un qual/i fy/ing
un quenched/
un ques/tion ing
un quot/a ble
un raised/
un ran/somed
un rat/ed
un rat/i fied
un/re al is/tic
un re/al iz/a ble

thing without reality; something unreal.

un rea son (un rē′zn), *n.* absence of reason; inability to act or think rationally; irrationality.

un rea son a ble (un rē′zn ə bəl), *adj.* 1 not reasonable: *an unreasonable child, an unreasonable fear of the dark.* 2 not moderate; excessive: *an unreasonable price.* —**un rea′son a ble ness,** *n.* —**un rea′son a bly,** *adv.*

un rea son ing (un rē′zn ing), *adj.* not reasoning; not using reason; irrational: *unreasoning terror.* —**un rea′son ing ly,** *adv.*

un re con struct ed (un′rē kən struk′tid), *adj.* stubborn in adherence to standards, practices, etc., of an earlier day, previous regime, etc.; unashamedly and tenaciously loyal to that which has been overthrown or superseded.

un reel (un rēl′), *v.t., v.i.* unwind from or as if from a reel.

un re flect ing (un′ri flek′ting), *adj.* unthinking; thoughtless. —**un′re flect′ing ly,** *adv.*

un re gard ed (un′ri gär′did), *adj.* not heeded or noticed; disregarded.

un re gen er a cy (un′ri jen′ər ə sē), *n.* unregenerate condition; enmity toward God; wickedness.

un re gen er ate (un′ri jen′ər it), *adj.* 1 not born again spiritually; not turned to the love of God. 2 wicked; bad. —**un′re gen′er ate ness,** *n.*

un re lent ing (un′ri len′ting), *adj.* 1 not yielding to feelings of kindness or compassion; merciless. See **inflexible** for synonym study. 2 not slackening or relaxing in severity or determination. —**un′re lent′ing ly,** *adv.* —**un′re lent′ing ness,** *n.*

un re li a bil i ty (un′ri lī′ə bil′ə tē), *n.* lack of reliability.

un re li a ble (un′ri lī′ə bəl), *adj.* not reliable; not to be depended on; irresponsible. —**un′re li′a bly,** *adv.*

un re li gious (un′ri lij′əs), *adj.* 1 irreligious. 2 nonreligious; not connected with religion.

un re mit ting (un′ri mit′ing), *adj.* never stopping; not slackening; maintained steadily: *unremitting vigilance.* —**un′re mit′ting ly,** *adv.*

un re served (un′ri zėrvd′), *adj.* 1 frank; open. 2 not restricted; without reservation. —**un′re serv′ed ly,** *adv.* —**un′re serv′ed ness,** *n.*

un rest (un rest′), *n.* 1 lack of ease and quiet; restlessness. 2 agitation or disturbance amounting almost to rebellion.

un re strained (un′ri strānd′), *adj.* not restrained; not kept in check or under control: *unrestrained mirth, unrestrained freedom.* —**un′re strain′ed ly,** *adv.*

un re straint (un′ri strānt′), *n.* lack of restraint.

un rid dle (un rid′l), *v.t.,* **-dled, -dling.** work out the answer to (a puzzle, mystery, riddle, etc.); solve.

un right eous (un rī′chəs), *adj.* 1 not righteous; wicked; sinful. 2 not justly due; undeserved. —**un right′eous ly,** *adv.* —**un right′eous ness,** *n.*

un ripe (un rīp′), *adj.* not ripe; not fully developed; immature. —**un ripe′ness,** *n.*

un ri valed or **un ri valled** (un rī′vəld), *adj.* having no rival; without an equal; matchless.

un robe (un rōb′), *v.t., v.i.,* **-robed, -rob ing.** undress; disrobe.

un roll (un rōl′), *v.t.* 1 open or spread out (something rolled). 2 lay open; display. —*v.i.* become opened or spread out.

un round ed (un roun′did), *adj.* pronounced without rounding of the lips, as the vowels in *sit* and *sat.*

UN RRA (un′rə, un′rä), *n.* United Nations Relief and Rehabilitation Administration.

un ruf fled (un ruf′əld), *adj.* 1 not ruffled; smooth. 2 not disturbed; calm.

un ruled (un rüld′), *adj.* 1 not kept under control; not governed. 2 not marked with lines: *unruled paper.*

un rul y (un rü′lē), *adj.* hard to rule or control; not manageable; disorderly: *an unruly horse, an unruly child.* See synonym study below. —**un rul′i ness,** *n.*

Syn. Unruly, ungovernable mean hard or impossible to control. **Unruly** means not inclined to obey or accept discipline and suggests getting out of hand and becoming disorderly, contrary, or obstinately willful: *The angry mob became unruly.* **Ungovernable** means incapable of being controlled or restrained, either because of never having been subjected to rule or direction or because of escape from it: *One of the circus lions had always been ungovernable.*

UNRWA or **U.N.R.W.A.,** United Nations Relief and Works Agency.

un sad dle (un sad′l), *v.t.,* **-dled, -dling.** 1 take the saddle off (a horse). 2 cause to fall from a horse; unhorse.

un safe (un sāf′), *adj.* dangerous. —**un safe′ness,** *n.*

un said (un sed′), *adj.* not said: *Everything I had meant to say remained unsaid.* —*v.* pt. and pp. of **unsay.**

un san i tar y (un san′ə ter′ē), *adj.* not sanitary; unhealthful. —**un san′i tar′i ness,** *n.*

un sat is fac tor y (un′sat i sfak′tər ē), *adj.* not satisfactory; not good enough to satisfy. —**un′sat is fac′tor i ly,** *adv.*

un sat u rat ed (un sach′ə rā′tid), *adj.* 1 (of a solvent or a solution) able to absorb or dissolve an additional quantity of a substance. 2 (of an organic compound) having a double or triple bond and one or more free valences so that another atom or radical may be taken on without the liberation of other atoms, radicals, or compounds.

un sa vor y (un sā′vər ē), *adj.* 1 tasteless. 2 unpleasant in taste or smell; distasteful: *an unsavory medicine.* 3 morally unpleasant; offensive: *an unsavory reputation.* —**un sa′vor i ly,** *adv.* —**un sa′vor i ness,** *n.*

un say (un sā′), *v.t.,* **-said, -say ing.** take back (something said); retract (a statement).

un scathed (un skāᴛʜd′), *adj.* not harmed; uninjured.

un schooled (un sküld′), *adj.* not schooled; not taught; not disciplined.

un sci en tif ic (un′sī ən tif′ik), *adj.* 1 not in accordance with the facts or principles of science: *an unscientific notion.* 2 not acting in accordance with such facts or principles: *an unscientific farmer.* —**un′sci en tif′i cal ly,** *adv.*

un scram ble (un skram′bəl), *v.t.,* **-bled, -bling.** reduce from confusion to order; bring out of a scrambled condition: *unscramble one's neglected affairs, unscramble a radio message in code.*

un screw (un skrü′), *v.t.* 1 take out the screw or screws from. 2 loosen or take off by turning; untwist: *unscrew an electric light bulb.* —*v.i.* be able to be unscrewed: *This light bulb won't unscrew.*

un scru pu lous (un skrü′pyə ləs), *adj.* not careful about right or wrong; without principles or conscience. —**un scru′pu lous ly,** *adv.* —**un scru′pu lous ness,** *n.*

Syn. Unscrupulous, unprincipled mean without regard for what is morally right. **Unscrupulous** implies a willful disregard of moral principles: *He would stoop to any unscrupulous trick to avoid paying his bills.* **Unprincipled** implies a lack of moral principles: *He is so unprincipled that when I explained my scruples to him it was obvious he didn't know what I was talking about.*

un seal (un sēl′), *v.t.* 1 break or remove the

In each of the words below **un** *means not.*

un re′al ized
un rea′soned
un′re buked′
un′re ceived′
un′re claimed′
un rec′og niz′a ble
un rec′og nized
un rec′om pensed
un′rec on cil′a ble
un rec′on ciled
un′re cord′ed
un′re deemed′
un′re fined′
un′re flect′ing
un′re formed′
un reg′i ment′ed
un reg′is tered
un reg′u lat′ed
un′re hearsed′
un′re lat′ed
un′re laxed′
un′re lax′ing
un′re lieved′
un′re mark′a ble
un rem′e died
un′re mem′bered
un′re mit′ted
un′re mov′a ble
un′re moved′
un′re mu′ne rat′ed
un′re mu′ne ra′tive
un′re nowned′
un rent′ed
un′re paid′
un′re paired′
un′re pealed′
un′re pent′ant
un′re pent′ing
un′re port′ed
un′rep re sent′a tive
un′rep re sent′ed
un′re pressed′
un′re proached′
un′re proved′
un′re quit′ed
un′re signed′
un′re sist′ant
un′re sist′ed
un′re sist′ing
un′re solved′
un′re spon′sive
un′re strict′ed
un′re ten′tive
un′re tract′ed
un′re trieved′
un′re turn′a ble
un′re turned′
un′re vealed′
un′re venged′
un′re voked′
un′re ward′ed
un′re ward′ing
un rhymed′
un rhyth′mi cal
un ri′fled
un right′ful
un saint′ly
un sal′a ble
un sal′ar ied
un sale′a ble
un salt′ed
un sanc′ti fied
un sanc′tioned
un sat′ed
un sa′ti at′ed
un sat′is fied
un sat′is fy′ing
un sat′u rat′ed
un scaled′
un scanned′
un scared′
un scarred′
un scent′ed
un sched′uled
un schol′ar ly
un scorched′
un scoured′
un scraped′
un scratched′
un screened′
un scrip′tur al
un sculp′tured
un sealed′

seal of: *unseal a letter.* 2 open: *The threat of punishment unsealed her lips.*

un seam (un sēm′), *v.t.* undo the seam or seams of.

un search a ble (un sėr′chə bəl), *adj.* not to be searched into; that cannot be understood by searching; mysterious. **—un search′a bly,** *adv.*

un sea son a ble (un sē′zn ə bəl), *adj.* 1 not suitable to or characteristic of the season: *an unseasonable snowstorm.* 2 coming at the wrong time; not timely. **—un sea′son a ble ness,** *n.* **—un sea′son a bly,** *adv.*

un seat (un sēt′), *v.t.* 1 displace from a seat. 2 throw (a rider) from a saddle. 3 remove from office: *unseat a congressman.*

un seem ly (un sēm′lē), *adj.* not seemly; not suitable; improper: *unseemly haste.* —*adv.* improperly; unsuitably. **—un seem′li ness,** *n.*

un seen (un sēn′), *adj.* 1 not seen; unnoticed: *an unseen error.* 2 not able to be seen; invisible: *an unseen spirit.*

un self ish (un sel′fish), *adj.* considerate of others; generous. **—un self′ish ly,** *adv.* **—un self′ish ness,** *n.*

un set tle (un set′l), *v.t., v.i.,* **-tled, -tling.** make or become unstable; disturb; shake; weaken: *The shock unsettled his mind.*

un set tled (un set′ld), *adj.* 1 not in proper condition or order; disordered; disturbed: *an unsettled mind.* 2 not fixed or firmly established; unstable: *an unsettled government.* 3 liable to change; uncertain: *The weather is unsettled.* 4 not adjusted or disposed of: *an unsettled estate, an unsettled bill.* 5 not determined or decided: *an unsettled question.* 6 not populated; uninhabited.

un sex (un seks′), *v.t.* deprive of the attributes of one's sex.

un shack le (un shak′əl), *v.t.,* **-led, -ling.** remove shackles from; set free.

un shak en (un shā′kən), *adj.* not shaken; firm: *unshaken courage.*

un sheathe (un shēᴛʜ′), *v.t.,* **-sheathed, -sheath ing.** 1 draw (a sword, knife, etc.) from a sheath. 2 bring or put forth from a covering.

un ship (un ship′), *v.t.,* **-shipped, -ship ping.** 1 put off or take off from a ship: *unship a cargo.* 2 remove from the proper place for use: *unship an oar.*

un shod (un shod′), *adj.* without shoes.

un sight ly (un sīt′lē), *adj.* ugly or unpleasant to look at: *an unsightly old shack.* See **ugly** for synonym study. **—un sight′li ness,** *n.*

un skilled (un skild′), *adj.* 1 not skilled; not trained; not expert: *unskilled in athletics.* 2 not requiring special skills or training: *unskilled labor.*

un skill ful or **un skil ful** (un skil′fəl), *adj.* not skillful; lacking in skill; awkward; clumsy. **—un skill′ful ly, un skil′ful ly,** *adv.* **—un skill′ful ness, un skil′ful ness,** *n.*

un sling (un sling′), *v.t.,* **-slung** (-slung′), **-sling ing.** 1 free from being slung: *unsling a rifle.* 2 remove the slings from (a yard, cask, etc.) on a ship.

un smil ing (un smī′ling), *adj.* not smiling; grave; serious. **—un smil′ing ly,** *adv.*

un snap (un snap′), *v.t.,* **-snapped, -snap ping.** unfasten the snap or snaps of.

un snarl (un snärl′), *v.t.* remove the snarls from; untangle.

un so cia bil i ty (un′sō shə bil′ə tē), *n.* unsociable nature or behavior; lack of friendliness.

un so cia ble (un sō′shə bəl), *adj.* not sociable; not associating easily with others: *unsociable behavior.* **—un so′cia ble ness,** *n.* **—un so′cia bly,** *adv.*

un sol der (un sod′ər), *v.t.* 1 separate (something soldered). 2 break up; divide; dissolve.

un so phis ti cat ed (un′sə fis′tə kā′tid), *adj.* not sophisticated; simple; natural; artless.

un so phis ti ca tion (un′sə fis′tə kā′shən), *n.* unsophisticated condition or quality; simplicity; artlessness.

un sought (un sôt′), *adj.* not sought; not looked for; not asked for: *unsought advice, an unsought compliment.*

un sound (un sound′), *adj.* 1 not in good condition; not sound: *unsound walls, an unsound business. A diseased mind or body is unsound.* 2 not based on truth or fact: *an unsound doctrine.* 3 not deep; not restful; disturbed: *an unsound sleep.* **—un sound′ly,** *adv.* **—un sound′ness,** *n.*

un spar ing (un sper′ing, un spar′ing), *adj.* 1 not sparing; very generous; liberal. 2 not merciful; severe. **—un spar′ing ly,** *adv.* **—un spar′ing ness,** *n.*

un speak a ble (un spē′kə bəl), *adj.* 1 that cannot be expressed in words; indescribable: *unspeakable joy.* 2 extremely bad; bad or objectionable beyond description: *unspeakable manners.* **—un speak′a bly,** *adv.*

un spot ted (un spot′id), *adj.* 1 without moral stain; pure: *an unspotted reputation.* 2 having no spots.

un sta ble (un stā′bəl), *adj.* 1 not firmly fixed; easily moved, shaken, or overthrown: *unstable footing, an unstable mind, an unstable government.* 2 not constant; variable: *an unstable nature.* 3 (of a chemical compound) easily decomposed; readily changing into other compounds. 4 (of a nuclear particle) capable of decay; radioactive. **—un sta′ble ness,** *n.* **—un sta′bly,** *adv.*

hat, āge, fär; let, ēqual, tėrm;
it, īce; hot, ōpen, ôrder;
oil, out; cup, pu̇t, rüle;
ch, child; ng, long; sh, she;
th, thin; ᴛʜ, then; zh, measure;

ə represents *a* in about, *e* in taken, *i* in pencil, *o* in lemon, *u* in circus.

< = from, derived from, taken from.

un stead y (un sted′ē), *adj.* 1 not steady; shaky. 2 likely to change; not reliable. 3 not regular in habits. **—un stead′i ly,** *adv.* **—un stead′i ness,** *n.*

un step (un step′), *v.t.,* **-stepped, -step ping.** remove (a mast, etc.) from its step.

un stick (un stik′), *v.t.,* **-stuck** (-stuk′), **-stick ing.** make no longer stuck; loosen or free (that which is stuck).

un stop (un stop′), *v.t.,* **-stopped, -stop ping.** 1 remove the stopper from (a bottle, etc.). 2 free from any obstruction; open.

un strap (un strap′), *v.t.,* **-strapped, -strap ping.** take off or loosen the strap or straps of (a trunk, box, etc.).

un stressed (un strest′), *adj.* not stressed; unaccented.

un string (un string′), *v.t.,* **-strung, -string ing.** 1 take off or loosen the string or strings of. 2 take from a string. 3 weaken the nerves of; make nervous.

un strung (un strung′), *adj.* 1 weakened in the nerves; nervous. 2 with strings loose, broken, or missing: *an unstrung guitar.* —*v.* pt. and pp. of **unstring.**

un stud ied (un stud′ēd), *adj.* 1 not labored or artificial; natural: *unstudied manners.* 2 not an object of study; not studied. 3 not having studied; unversed *(in): unstudied in Latin.*

un sub stan tial (un′səb stan′shəl), *adj.* not substantial; flimsy; slight; unreal. **—un′sub stan′tial ly,** *adv.*

un sub stan ti al i ty (un′səb stan′shē al′ə tē), *n.* a being unsubstantial.

un suc cess ful (un′sək ses′fəl), *adj.* not

In each of the words below **un** *means not.*

un sea′soned
un sea′wor′thy
un sec′ond ed
un′se cured′
un seed′ed
un see′ing
un seg′ment ed
un seg′re gat′ed
un seized′
un′se lect′ed
un′se lec′tive
un′self-con′scious
un sen′si tive
un′sen ti men′tal
un sep′a rat′ed
un served′
un serv′ice a ble
un set′
un shad′ed
un shad′owed
un shak′a ble
un shake′a ble
un shaped′
un shape′ly
un shared′
un sharp′ened
un shaved′
un shav′en
un shed′
un shelled′
un shel′tered
un shield′ed
un shorn′
un shrink′a ble
un shrink′ing
un sift′ed
un sight′ed
un signed′
un sing′a ble
un sink′a ble
un sis′ter ly
un sized′
un slacked′
un slaked′
un sliced′
un so′cial
un soiled′
un sold′
un sol′dier ly
un′so lic′it ed
un′so lic′i tous
un sol′id
un solv′a ble
un solved′
un sort′ed
un sound′ed
un soured′
un sowed′
un sown′
un spe′cial ized
un′spe cif′ic
un spec′i fied
un′spec tac′u lar
un spec′u la′tive
un spent′
un spiced′
un spir′i tu al
un split′
un spoiled′
un spoilt′
un spo′ken
un sports′man like′
un stain′a ble
un stained′
un stamped′
un stand′ard ized
un stat′ed
un states′man like′
un ster′i lized
un stig′ma tized
un stint′ed
un stint′ing
un stitched′
un stopped′
un strained′
un strat′i fied
un stri′at ed
un stuffed′
un′sub dued′
un′sub mis′sive
un sub′si dized
un′sub stan′ti at′ed
un sub′tle

successful; without success. **—un′suc cess′ful ly,** *adv.*

un suit a bil i ty (un′sü tə bil′ə tē), *n.* a being unsuitable.

un suit a ble (un sü′tə bəl), *adj.* not suitable; unfit; inappropriate. **—un suit′a bly,** *adv.*

un suit ed (un sü′tid), *adj.* not suited; unfit.

un sung (un sung′), *adj.* 1 not sung. 2 not honored or celebrated, especially by song or poetry: *unsung heroes.*

un swear (un swer′, un swar′), *v.t., v.i.,* **-swore** (-swôr′, -swōr′), **-sworn** (-swôrn′, -swōrn′), **-swear ing.** retract (something sworn or asserted); recant.

un tan gle (un tang′gəl), *v.t.,* **-gled, -gling.** 1 take the tangles out of; disentangle. 2 straighten out or clear up (anything confused or perplexing).

un taught (un tôt′), *adj.* 1 not taught; not educated. 2 known without being taught; learned naturally.

un thank ful (un thangk′fəl), *adj.* 1 ungrateful. 2 not appreciated; thankless. **—un thank′ful ly,** *adv.* **—un thank′ful ness,** *n.*

un think a ble (un thing′kə bəl), *adj.* that cannot be imagined; inconceivable.

un think ing (un thing′king), *adj.* 1 thoughtless; heedless; careless. 2 showing little or no thought: *unthinking anger.* 3 not having the power of thought; unable to think. **—un think′ing ly,** *adv.*

un thought-of (un thôt′uv′, un thôt′ov′), *adj.* not imagined or considered.

un thread (un thred′), *v.t.* 1 take the thread out of: *unthread a needle.* 2 unravel. 3 find one's way through.

un throne (un thrōn′), *v.t.,* **-throned, -thron ing.** depose; dethrone.

un ti dy (un tī′dē), *adj.* not in order; not neat; slovenly: *an untidy house.* **—un ti′di ly,** *adv.* **—un ti′di ness,** *n.*

un tie (un tī′), *v.,* **-tied, -ty ing.** *—v.t.* 1 loosen; unfasten; undo: *untie a knot.* 2 make free; release: *untie a horse.* 3 clear away; resolve. *—v.i.* become, or be able to be, untied.

un til (ən til′, un til′), *prep.* 1 up to the time of: *It was cold from Christmas until April.* 2 before: *She did not leave until morning.* *—conj.* 1 up to the time when: *Wait until the sun sets.* 2 before: *He did not come until the meeting was half over.* 3 to the degree or place that: *She worked until she was too tired to do more.* [Middle English *untill* < *un-* up to, until + *till*[1]]

un time ly (un tīm′lē), *adj.* 1 at a wrong time or season; unseasonable: *Snow in May is untimely.* 2 too early; too soon: *his untimely death at the age of 18.* *—adv.* too early; too soon. **—un time′li ness,** *n.*

un tir ing (un tī′ring), *adj.* tireless: *an untiring runner, untiring efforts to succeed.* **—un tir′ing ly,** *adv.*

un ti tled (un tī′tld), *adj.* having no title: *an untitled piece of music, an untitled nobleman.*

un to (un′tü; *before consonants often* un′tə), *prep.* to: *be faithful unto death.* [Middle English < *un-* up to, until + *to*]

un told (un tōld′), *adj.* 1 not told; not revealed: *an untold story, untold heroism.* 2 too many to be counted or numbered; countless: *There are untold stars in the sky.* 3 very great; immense: *untold wealth. Wars do untold damage.*

un touch a bil i ty (un′tuch ə bil′ə tē), *n.* quality or condition of being untouchable or an untouchable.

un touch a ble (un tuch′ə bəl), *adj.* 1 that cannot be touched; out of reach. 2 that must not be touched. 3 that defiles if touched. *—n.* (in India) person belonging to the lowest caste of the Hindu social order, whose touch was formerly thought to defile members of higher castes.

un touched (un tucht′), *adj.* not touched: *The cat left the milk untouched. The miser was untouched by the poor man's story. The last topic was left untouched.*

un to ward (un tôrd′, un tōrd′; un′tə wôrd′, un′tə wōrd′), *adj.* 1 unfavorable; unfortunate: *an untoward wind, an untoward accident.* 2 perverse; stubborn; willful. [< *un-*[1] + *toward*] **—un to′ward ly,** *adv.* **—un to′ward ness,** *n.*

un trained (un trānd′), *adj.* not trained; without discipline or education.

un tram meled or **un tram melled** (un tram′əld), *adj.* not hindered; not restrained; free.

un tried (un trīd′), *adj.* 1 not tried; not tested: *an untried plan.* 2 not given a trial in a court of law: *an untried case, condemn a man untried.*

un trod (un trod′), *adj.* not trodden.

un true (un trü′), *adj.* 1 not true to the facts; false; incorrect. 2 not faithful; disloyal. 3 not true to a standard or rule; not exact; inaccurate.

un tru ly (un trü′lē), *adv.* in an untrue manner; falsely.

un truth (un trüth′), *n., pl.* **-truths** (-trüᴛʜz′, -trüths′). 1 lack of truth; falsity. 2 a lie; falsehood.

un truth ful (un trüth′fəl), *adj.* 1 not truthful; contrary to the truth: *an untruthful rumor.* 2 not telling the truth: *an untruthful child.* **—un truth′ful ly,** *adv.* **—un truth′ful ness,** *n.*

un tune (un tün′, un tyün′), *v.t.,* **-tuned, -tun ing.** 1 make no longer in tune. 2 to disorder; upset; discompose.

un tu tored (un tü′tərd, un tyü′tərd), *adj.* not tutored; not educated; untaught.

un twine (un twīn′), *v.t., v.i.,* **-twined, -twin ing.** untwist.

un twist (un twist′), *v.t.* undo or loosen (something twisted); unravel. *—v.i.* become untwisted.

un used (un yüzd′ *for 1, 2; for 3, before the word "to" usually,* un yüst′), *adj.* 1 not in use; not being used: *an unused room.* 2 never having been used: *unused drinking cups.* 3 not accustomed: *hands unused to labor.*

un u su al (un yü′zhü əl), *adj.* not usual; not in common use; uncommon; rare. **—un u′su al ly,** *adv.* **—un u′su al ness,** *n.*

un ut ter a ble (un ut′ər ə bəl), *adj.* 1 that cannot be expressed in words; unspeakable. 2 that cannot be pronounced. **—un ut′ter a bly,** *adv.*

un var nished (un vär′nisht), *adj.* 1 not varnished. 2 plain; unadorned: *the unvarnished truth.*

un veil (un vāl′), *v.t.* remove a veil from; disclose; reveal: *unveil a statue.* *—v.i.* remove a veil; reveal oneself; become unveiled: *The princess unveiled.*

un vo cal (un vō′kəl), *adj.* 1 not vocal. 2 taciturn.

un voiced (un voist′), *adj.* 1 not spoken; not expressed in words. 2 (in phonetics) voiceless.

un war rant a ble (un wôr′ən tə bəl, un wor′ən tə bəl), *adj.* not justifiable or defensible; improper. **—un war′rant a bly,** *adv.*

un war y (un wer′ē, un war′ē), *adj.* not wary; not cautious; careless; unguarded. **—un war′i ly,** *adv.* **—un war′i ness,** *n.*

un wear ied (un wir′ēd), *adj.* 1 not weary; not tired. 2 never growing weary; tireless.

In each of the words below **un** *means not.*

un suf′fer a ble
un′sug ges′tive
un sul′lied
un′sup port′a ble
un′sup port′ed
un′sup pressed′
un sure′
un′sur mount′a ble
un′sur passed′
un′sus pect′ed
un′sus pect′ing
un′sus pi′cious
un′sus tained′
un swayed′
un sweet′ened
un swept′
un swerv′ing
un sworn′
un′sym met′ri cal
un′sym pa thet′ic
un sym′pa thiz′ing
un′sys tem at′ic
un sys′tem a tized
un tact′ful
un tab′u lat′ed
un taint′ed
un tak′en
un tal′ent ed
un tam′a ble
un tame′a ble
un tamed′
un tanned′
un tapped′
un tar′nished
un tast′ed
un tax′a ble
un taxed′
un teach′a ble
un tech′ni cal
un tem′pered
un ten′a ble
un ten′ant ed
un tend′ed
un ter′ri fied
un test′ed
un thanked′
un thatched′
un thawed′
un′the at′ri cal
un thought′
un thought′ful
un thrift′y
un till′a ble
un tilled′
un tired′
un torn′
un trace′a ble
un traced′
un tracked′
un tract′a ble
un′trans fer′a ble
un′trans lat′a ble
un′trans lat′ed
un′trans mit′ted
un trav′eled
un trav′elled
un trav′ers a ble
un trav′ersed
un treat′ed
un trimmed′
un trod′den
un trou′bled
un trust′wor′thy
un tuft′ed
un tun′a ble
un tuned′
un turned′
un twist′ed
un typ′i cal
un us′a ble
un ut′tered
un vac′ci nat′ed
un val′ued
un van′quished
un var′ied
un var′y ing
un veiled′
un ven′ti lat′ed
un ver′i fi′a ble
un ver′i fied
un versed′
un vexed′
un vis′it ed
un vit′ri fied
un vul′can ized
un wak′ened
un walled′
un want′ed
un war′like′
un war′rant ed
un washed′
un wast′ed
un watched′
un wa′tered
un wa′ver ing
un weaned′
un wear′a ble
un wear′y ing

hat, āge, fär; let, ēqual, tėrm; it, īce; hot, ōpen, ôrder; oil, out; cup, pu̇t, rüle; ch, child; ng, long; sh, she; th, thin; ᴛʜ, then; zh, measure;

ə represents *a* in about, *e* in taken, *i* in pencil, *o* in lemon, *u* in circus.

< = from, derived from, taken from.

un weave (un wēv′), *v.t.*, **-wove** (-wōv′), **-wo ven** (-wō′vən), **-weav ing.** take apart (something woven); unravel.

un wel come (un wel′kəm), *adj.* not welcome; not wanted.

un well (un wel′), *adj.* not in good health; ailing; ill; sick.

un wept (un wept′), *adj.* 1 not wept for; not mourned. 2 not shed: *unwept tears.*

un whole some (un hōl′səm), *adj.* not wholesome; bad for the body or the mind; unhealthy: *unwholesome food, unwholesome companions.* **—un whole′some ly,** *adv.* **—un whole′some ness,** *n.*

un wield y (un wēl′dē), *adj.*, **-wield i er, -wield i est.** not easily handled or managed, because of size, shape, or weight; bulky and clumsy: *an unwieldy package, a fat, unwieldy man.* **—un wield′i ness,** *n.*

un will ing (un wil′ing), *adj.* 1 not willing; not consenting. 2 not freely or willingly granted or done: *an unwilling acceptance of necessity.* **—un will′ing ly,** *adv.* **—un will′ing ness,** *n.*

un wind (un wīnd′), *v.t.*, **-wound, -wind ing.** 1 wind off or uncoil; take from a spool, ball, etc. 2 disentangle. *—v.i.* 1 become unwound. 2 relax.

un wise (un wīz′), *adj.* not wise; not showing good judgment; foolish. **—un wise′ly,** *adv.*

un wit ting (un wit′ing), *adj.* not knowing; unaware; unconscious; unintentional. **—un wit′ting ly,** *adv.*

un wont ed (un wun′tid, un wōn′tid), *adj.* 1 not customary; not usual: *unwonted anger.* 2 not accustomed; not used. **—un wont′ed ly,** *adv.* **—un wont′ed ness,** *n.*

un world ly (un wėrld′lē), *adj.* 1 not caring much for the things of this world, such as money, pleasure, and power. 2 not of the world; spiritual; supernatural. **—un world′li ness,** *n.*

un wor thy (un wėr′ᴛʜē), *adj.* 1 not worthy; not deserving: *Such a silly story is unworthy of belief.* 2 unsuitable; unfit; unbecoming: *a gift unworthy of a king.* 3 base; shameful: *unworthy conduct.* **—un wor′thi ly,** *adv.* **—un wor′thi ness,** *n.*

un wound (un wound′), *v.* pt. and pp. of **unwind.**

un wrap (un rap′), *v.*, **-wrapped, -wrap ping.** *—v.t.* remove the wrapping from; open. *—v.i.* become opened.

un writ ten (un rit′n), *adj.* 1 not written: *an unwritten order.* 2 understood or customary, but not actually expressed in writing: *an unwritten law.* 3 not written on; blank.

un yoke (un yōk′), *v.*, **-yoked, -yok ing.** *—v.t.* 1 free from a yoke. 2 separate; disconnect. *—v.i.* remove a yoke.

un zip (un zip′), *v.t., v.i.*, **-zipped, -zip ping.** open or unfasten a zipper or something held by a zipper.

up (up), *adv., prep., adj., n., v.*, **upped, up ping.** *—adv.* 1 from a lower to a higher place or condition; to, toward, or near the top: *The bird flew up.* 2 in a higher place or condition; on or at a higher level: *We stayed up in the mountains several days.* 3 from a smaller to a larger amount: *Prices have gone up.* 4 to or at any point, place, or condition that is considered higher: *go up north.* 5 above the horizon: *The sun came up.* 6 in or into an erect position: *Stand up.* 7 out of bed: *get up in the morning.* 8 thoroughly; completely; entirely: *The house burned up.* 9 at an end; over: *Your time is up now.* 10 in or into being or action: *Don't stir up trouble.* 11 together: *Add these up.* 12 to or in an even position; not behind: *catch up in a race, keep up with the times.* 13 in or into view, notice, or consideration: *bring up a new topic.* 14 in or into a state of tightness, etc.: *Shut the bird up in his cage.* 15 into safekeeping, storage, etc.; aside; by: *store up supplies.* 16 (in baseball) at bat. 17 apiece; for each one: *The score at the half was ten up.* 18 **up against,** ɪɴꜰᴏʀᴍᴀʟ. facing as a thing to be dealt with. 19 **up to, a** as far or as high as: *up to one's elbows in work.* **b** till; until: *up to the present day.* **c** reaching the limit of; fulfilling: *work not up to expectations.* **d** doing; about to do: *She is up to some mischief.* **e** equal to; capable of doing: *up to a task.* **f** plotting; scheming: *What are you up to?* **g** before (a person) as a duty or task to be done: *It's up to the judge to decide.* *—prep.* 1 to or at a higher place on or in: *The cat ran up the tree.* 2 to, toward, or near the top of: *They climbed up a hill.* 3 along; through: *She walked up the street.* 4 toward or in the inner or upper part of: *We sailed up the river. He lives up state.* *—adj.* 1 advanced; forward. 2 moving upward; directed upward: *an up trend.* 3 above the horizon: *The sun is up.* 4 above the ground: *The wheat is up.* 5 out of bed. 6 to or in an even position; not behind. 7 near; close. 8 with much knowledge or skill. 9 (in baseball) at bat. 10 ahead of an opponent by a certain number: *We are three games up.* 11 **up and doing,** busy; active. *—n.* 1 an upward movement, course, or slope. 2 piece of good luck. *—v.t.* 1 put up. 2 make greater; increase: *up the price of eggs.* *—v.i.* get up. [Old English]

up-and-com ing (up′ən kum′ing), *adj.* on the way to prominence or success; promising: *an up-and-coming singer.*

up-and-down (up′ən doun′), *adj.* 1 occurring alternately upward and downward. 2 perpendicular; vertical: *up-and-down stripes.*

U pan i shad (ü pan′ə shad), *n.* any of a group of ancient Vedic commentaries.

u pas (yü′pəs), *n.* 1 a large, tropical Asian tree of the same family as the mulberry, whose poisonous milky sap is used in making a poison for arrows. 2 the sap itself. [< Malay, poison]

up beat (up′bēt′), *n.* in music: 1 an unaccented beat in a measure, especially one preceding a downbeat. 2 the upward gesture of the conductor's hand to indicate this beat. *—adj.* ɪɴꜰᴏʀᴍᴀʟ. hopeful; buoyant: *a motion picture with an upbeat ending.*

up braid (up brād′), *v.t.* find fault with; blame; reprove: *The captain unbraided the guards for falling asleep.* See **scold** for synonym study. [Old English *upbregdan* < *up* up + *bregdan* to weave, braid] **—up braid′er,** *n.*

up braid ing (up brā′ding), *n.* a severe reproof; scolding.

up bring ing (up′bring′ing), *n.* care and training given to a child while growing up; bringing-up.

up com ing (up′kum′ing), *adj.* forthcoming: *the upcoming semester.*

up coun try (up′kun′trē), *n.* the interior of a country. *—adv.* toward or in the interior of a country. *—adj.* of or in the interior of a country: *an upcountry village.*

up date (up dāt′), *v.t.*, **-dat ed, -dat ing.** bring up to date.

up draft (up′draft′), *n.* an upward movement of air, wind, gas, etc.

up end (up end′), *v.t., v.i.* set on end; stand on end.

up grade (up′grād′), *n., v.*, **-grad ed, -grad ing,** *adv.* *—n.* 1 an upward slope. 2 **on the upgrade,** increasing in strength, power, value, etc.; improving. *—v.t.* raise to a higher position, status, rating, etc.: *upgrade a job, upgrade an employee.* *—adv., adj.* uphill.

up growth (up′grōth′), *n.* 1 process of growing up; development. 2 something that is growing or has grown up.

up heav al (up hē′vəl), *n.* 1 a heaving up. 2 a being heaved up. 3 a sudden or violent agitation; great turmoil: *social upheaval, political upheaval.*

up heave (up hēv′), *v.*, **-heaved** or **-hove** (-hōv′), **-heav ing.** *—v.t.* heave up; lift up. *—v.i.* rise.

up held (up held′), *v.* pt. and pp. of **uphold.**

up hill (*adj.* up′hil′; *adv.* up′hil′), *adj.* 1 up the slope of a hill; upward: *It is an uphill road all the way.* 2 difficult: *an uphill fight.* *—adv.* upward: *a mile uphill.*

up hold (up hōld′), *v.t.*, **-held, -hold ing.** 1 give moral support to; confirm: *The principal upheld the teacher's decision.* 2 hold up; not let down; support: *Walls uphold the roof. We uphold the good name of our school.* See **support** for synonym study. 3 sustain on appeal; approve: *The higher court upheld the lower court's decision.* **—up hold′er,** *n.*

up hol ster (up hōl′stər), *v.t.* provide (furniture) with coverings, cushions, springs, stuffing, etc. [< *upholsterer,* alteration of earlier *upholdster* tradesman < *uphold* + *-ster*]

up hol ster er (up hōl′stər ər), *n.* person whose business is upholstering.

up hol ster y (up hōl′stər ē), *n., pl.* **-ster ies.** 1 coverings for furniture; curtains,

In each of the words below **un** *means not.*

un weath′ered
un wed′
un wed′ded
un weed′ed
un weld′ed
un wife′like′
un wife′ly
un willed′
un wink′ing
un wished′
un wit′nessed
un wom′an ly
un won′
un wood′ed
un work′a ble
un worked′
un work′man like′
un worn′
un wor′ried
un wound′ed
un wo′ven
un wrin′kled
un wrought′
un yield′ing

cushions, carpets, and hangings. 2 business of upholstering.

UPI or **U.P.I.,** United Press International.

up keep (up′kēp′), *n.* 1 a keeping or a being kept up or in good repair; maintenance: *the upkeep of a house.* 2 cost of maintenance.

up land (up′lənd, up′land′), *n.* high land. *—adj.* of high land; living or growing on high land: *upland meadows.*

upland cotton, type of cotton having a short staple, much grown in the United States.

up lift (*v.* up lift′; *n.* up′lift′), *v.t.* 1 lift up; raise; elevate. 2 exalt emotionally or spiritually. 3 raise socially or morally. *—n.* 1 act of lifting up. 2 emotional or spiritual exaltation. 3 social or moral improvement or effort toward it. 4 (in geology) an upward heaving of the earth's surface, especially one which is very slow. **—up lift′er,** *n.*

up most (up′mōst), *adj.* uppermost.

up on (ə pôn′, ə pon′), *prep.* on.

up per (up′ər), *adj.* 1 higher: *the upper lip, the upper floors of an office building.* 2 higher in rank, office, etc.; superior: *the upper chamber of a legislature.* 3 Usually, **Upper.** (in geology) being or relating to a later division of a period, system, or the like: *Upper Cambrian.* 4 farther from the sea: *the upper reaches of a river.* *—n.* 1 the part of a shoe or boot above the sole. 2 **on one's uppers,** INFORMAL. **a** with the soles of one's shoes worn out. **b** very shabby or poor.

Upper Canada, former province in central Canada, now part of Ontario.

upper case, capital letters.

up per-case (up′ər kās′), *adj.* in capital letters.

upper class, class of society above the middle class, having the highest social or economic status.

up per-class (up′ər klas′), *adj.* 1 of or having to do with the upper class. 2 (in schools and colleges) of or having to do with the junior and senior classes.

up per class man (up′ər klas′mən), *n., pl.* **-men.** junior or senior.

upper crust, INFORMAL. upper class.

up per cut (up′ər kut′), *n., v.,* **-cut, -cut ting.** *—n.* (in boxing) a swinging blow directed upward from beneath. *—v.t., v.i.* strike with or deliver an uppercut.

upper hand, control; advantage.

Upper House or **upper house,** the higher or more restricted house in a legislature that has two branches. The Senate is the Upper House in Congress.

up per most (up′ər mōst), *adj.* 1 highest; topmost. 2 having the most force or influence; most prominent. *—adv.* 1 in, at, or near the top. 2 first.

Upper Vol ta (vol′tə), country in W Africa, north of Ghana. 5,330,000 pop.; 105,800 sq. mi. *Capital:* Ouagadougou.

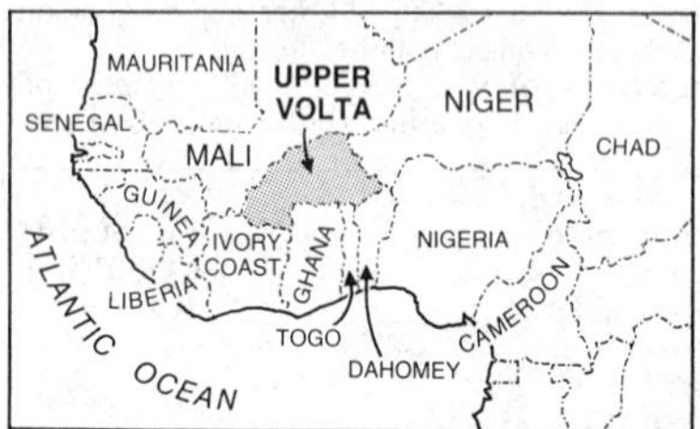

up pish (up′ish), *adj.* INFORMAL. uppity. **—up′pish ly,** *adv.* **—up′pish ness,** *n.*

up pi ty (up′ə tē), *adj.* INFORMAL. arrogant, self-assertive, or conceited. **—up′pi ty-ness,** *n.*

up raise (up rāz′), *v.t.,* **-raised, -rais ing.** lift up; raise.

up rear (up rir′), *v.t.* lift up; raise. *—v.i.* be lifted up.

up right (up′rīt′, up rīt′), *adj.* 1 standing up straight; erect: *a person upright in a chair.* See synonym study below. 2 good; honest; righteous. *—adv.* straight up; in a vertical position: *Hold yourself upright.* *—n.* 1 vertical or upright position. 2 something upright; vertical part or piece. 3 an upright piano. 4 one of the goal posts in football. **—up′right′ly,** *adv.* **—up′right′ness,** *n.*

Syn. *adj.* 1 **Upright, erect** mean straight up. **Upright** literally means standing up straight on a base or in a position that is straight up and down, not slanting: *After the earthquake not a lamp or chair was upright.* **Erect** means held or set upright, not stooping or bent: *At seventy she is still erect.*

upright piano, a rectangular piano having vertical strings behind the keyboard.

up rise (*v.* up rīz′; *n.* up′rīz′), *v.,* **-rose** (-rōz′), **-ris en** (-riz′n), **-ris ing,** *n.* *—v.i.* 1 rise up. 2 slope upward; ascend. 3 get up; arise. 4 increase in volume, amount, etc. *—n.* a rising up; upward rise.

up ris ing (up′rī′zing, up rī′zing), *n.* 1 revolt; rebellion. 2 a rising up. 3 an upward slope; ascent.

up roar (up′rôr′, up′rōr′), *n.* 1 a noisy or violent disturbance. 2 a loud or confused noise. See **noise** for synonym study. [< Dutch *oproer* insurrection, tumult; influenced by association with *roar*]

up roar i ous (up rôr′ē əs, up rōr′ē əs), *adj.* 1 making an uproar; noisy and disorderly: *an uproarious crowd.* 2 loud, confused, and unrestrained: *uproarious laughter.* **—up roar′i ous ly,** *adv.* **—up roar′i ous ness,** *n.*

up root (up rüt′, up rut′), *v.t.* 1 tear up by the roots: *The storm uprooted many trees.* 2 tear away, remove, or displace completely: *Famine uprooted many families from their homes.* **—up root′er,** *n.*

up rush (up′rush′), *n.* 1 a forceful upward flow, usually of a liquid or gas: *the uprush of air currents.* 2 a rapid increase: *an uprush of industrial developments.* 3 a sudden burst or outbreak: *an uprush of originality.*

ups-and-downs (ups′ən dounz′), *n.pl.* 1 changes in fortune; successes and failures: *Her career has seen its ups-and-downs.* 2 fluctuations.

up set (*v.* up set′; *n.* up′set′; *adj.* up set′, up′set′), *v.,* **-set, -set ting,** *n., adj.* *—v.t.* 1 tip over; overturn: *upset a boat.* See synonym study below. 2 disturb greatly; disorder: *Rain upset our plans for a picnic. The shock upset her nerves.* 3 defeat unexpectedly in a contest: *The independent candidate upset the mayor in the election.* 4 shorten and thicken (a metal bar, etc.) by hammering on the end, especially when heated. *—v.i.* be or become upset. *—n.* 1 a tipping over; overturn. 2 a great disturbance; disorder. 3 an unexpected defeat: *The hockey team suffered an upset.* *—adj.* 1 tipped over; overturned. 2 greatly disturbed; disordered: *an upset stomach.* **—up set′ter,** *n.*

Syn. *v.t.* 1 **Upset, overturn** mean to cause to tip over. **Upset** implies a toppling from an upright or stable position: *He accidentally kicked the table and upset the vase of flowers.* **Overturn** often suggests a more violent action which leaves the object upside down or on its side: *The collision overturned both cars.*

upset price, the lowest price at which a thing offered for sale, especially at auction, will be sold.

up shot (up′shot′), *n.* 1 conclusion; result. 2 the essential facts.

up side (up′sīd′), *n.* the upper side; top part or surface.

upside down, 1 having what should be on top at the bottom. 2 in or into complete disorder.

up side-down cake (up′sīd′doun′), a cake made of batter poured over fruit, baked, and served bottom up.

up si lon (yüp′sə lon, up′sə lon), *n.* the 20th letter of the Greek alphabet (Υ, υ).

up stage (up′stāj′), *adv., adj., v.,* **-staged, -stag ing.** *—adv.* toward or at the back of the stage: *walk upstage.* *—adj.* 1 toward or at the back of the stage. 2 INFORMAL. haughty; aloof; supercilious. *—v.t.* 1 draw attention away from (an actor) by standing upstage or in back of him, or by forcing him to face away from the audience. 2 draw attention away from, often intentionally, through greater popularity, publicity, charm, etc. 3 INFORMAL. treat rudely or curtly; snub.

up stairs (up′sterz′, up′starz′), *adv.* 1 up the stairs. 2 on or to an upper floor. 3 INFORMAL. to or at a high or higher altitude, especially in an aircraft. 4 INFORMAL. in the mind; mentally: *Something's wrong with him upstairs.* 5 **kick upstairs,** INFORMAL. promote (a person) to a higher but less powerful or important position. *—adj.* on or to an upper floor. *—n.* the upper floor or floors.

up stand ing (up stan′ding), *adj.* 1 standing up; erect. 2 honorable; upright: *an upstanding young man.*

up start (*n., adj.* up′stärt′; *v.* up stärt′), *n.* 1 person who has suddenly risen from a humble position to wealth, power, or importance. 2 an unpleasant, conceited, and self-assertive person. *—adj.* 1 suddenly risen from a humble position to wealth, power, or importance. 2 conceited; self-assertive. *—v.t., v.i.* rise or cause to rise suddenly up, out, into view, etc.

up state (up′stāt′), U.S. *—adj.* of the part of a state away from and usually north of the principal city: *upstate New York.* *—n.* an upstate area or part.

up stat er (up′stā′tər), *n.* native or inhabitant of an upstate area.

up stream (up′strēm′), *adv., adj.* against the current of a stream; up a stream.

up surge (up′sėrj′), *n., v.,* **-surged, -surg ing.** *—n.* a rising upward; rise; upturn. *—v.i.* surge upward.

up sweep (*v.* up swēp′; *n.* up′swēp′), *v.,* **-swept, -sweep ing,** *n.* *—v.t.* cause to be upswept. *—v.i.* be upswept. *—n.* an upswept thing, part, or arrangement.

up swept (up′swept′), *adj.* 1 curving or slanting upward: *a dog with an upswept jaw.* 2 brushed upward: *an upswept coiffure.* *—v.* pt. and pp. of **upsweep.**

up swing (up′swing′), *n.* 1 an upward swing; movement upward. 2 a marked improvement; strong advance.

up take (up′tāk′), *n.* 1 a ventilating shaft for the upward discharge of foul air, fumes, etc. 2 absorption; ingestion. 3 **on the uptake,**

INFORMAL. in understanding and response; in perceptive ability: *quick on the uptake.*

up throw (up′thrō′), *n.* 1 (in geology) an upward dislocation of a mass of rock, generally due to faulting. 2 an upward throw.

up thrust (up′thrust′), *n.* 1 an upward push. 2 movement upward of part of the earth's crust.

up tilt (up tilt′), *v.t.* tilt up.

up-to-date (up′tə dāt′), *adj.* 1 extending to the present time: *an up-to-date record of sales.* 2 keeping up with the times in style, ideas, etc.; modern: *an up-to-date store.* **—up′-to-date′ness,** *n.*

up town (up′toun′), *adv., adj.* to or in the upper part or away from the main business section of a town or city. *—n.* the upper part or part away from the business section of a town or city.

up trend (up′trend′), *n.* an upward tendency or trend; inclination to rise, become better, etc.

up turn (*v.* up tėrn′; *n.* up′tėrn′), *v.t., v.i.* turn up. *—n.* 1 an upward turn. 2 improvement.

up turned (up tėrnd′), *adj.* turned upward.

up ward (up′wərd), *adv.* 1 toward a higher place: *Fly upward.* 2 toward a higher or greater rank, amount, age, etc.: *From ten years of age upward, she had studied French.* 3 above; more: *Children of five years and upward must pay the full fare.* 4 toward the source: *We traced the brook upward.* 5 **upward of,** more than. *—adj.* directed or moving toward a higher place; in a higher position: *an upward flight.* **—up′ward ly,** *adv.* **—up′ward ness,** *n.*

up wards (up′wərdz), *adv.* 1 upward. 2 **upwards of,** more than; upward of.

up wind (up′wind′), *adv., adj.* against the wind; in the direction from which the wind is blowing.

Ur (ėr), *n.* city in ancient Sumer, on the Euphrates River.

ur a cil (yůr′ə səl), *n.* substance present in ribonucleic acid in cells. It is the pyrimidine base which replaces thymine in protein synthesis. *Formula:* $C_4H_4N_2O_2$ [< *ur(ea)* + *ac(etic)* + *-il,* variant of *-yl*]

Ur al-Al ta ic (yůr′əl al tā′ik), *adj.* of or having to do with a large group of languages of eastern Europe and northern Asia comprising the Uralic and Altaic families. *—n.* the Ural-Altaic language group.

U ral ic (yů ral′ik), *adj.* 1 of or having to do with a family of languages that includes Finno-Ugric and Samoyed. 2 of or having to do with the Ural Mountains. *—n.* the Uralic family of languages.

Ur al Mountains (yůr′əl), mountain range in the W Soviet Union, between Europe and Asia. Highest peak, 6184 ft.

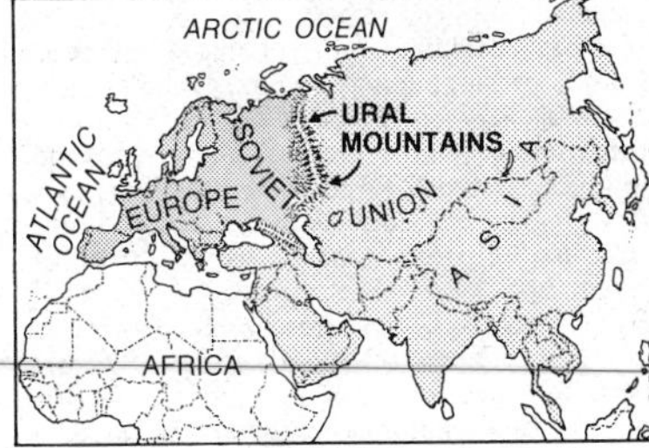

Ural Mountains—Mainland Europe is shaded area to west of Ural Mountains; mainland Asia is shaded area to east.

Ural River, river in the W Soviet Union, flowing south from the Ural Mountains into the Caspian Sea. 1400 mi.

Ur als (yůr′əlz), *n.pl.* Ural Mountains.

U ra ni a (yů rā′nē ə), *n.* (in Greek myths) the Muse of astronomy.

u ra ni um (yů rā′nē əm), *n.* a very heavy, white, radioactive metallic element occurring in pitchblende and certain other minerals, containing three isotopes of mass numbers 234, 235, and 238. *Symbol:* U; *atomic number* 92. See pages 326 and 327 for table. [< New Latin < *Uranus,* the planet]

uranium 235, a radioactive isotope of uranium that makes up about 0.7 per cent of naturally occurring uranium. It is fissionable by slow neutrons and capable of sustaining a rapid chain reaction. *Symbol:* U^{235}; *atomic number* 92; *mass number* 235.

uranium 238, a radioactive isotope of uranium that makes up about 99 per cent of naturally occurring uranium. It captures neutrons to form a fissionable isotope of plutonium which is used as a source of atomic energy. *Symbol:* U^{238}; *atomic number* 92; *mass number* 238.

Ur a nus (yůr′ə nəs), *n.* 1 (in Greek myths) a god who represented heaven. Uranus was the father of the Titans and the Cyclopes. 2 the third largest planet in the solar system and the seventh in distance from the sun.

ur ban (ėr′bən), *adj.* 1 of or having to do with cities or towns: *an urban district, urban planning.* 2 living in a city or cities: *the urban population, urban dwellers.* 3 characteristic of cities. 4 accustomed to cities. [< Latin *urbanus* < *urbs* city]

Ur ban II (ėr′bən), 1042?-1099, French monk who was pope from 1088 to 1099.

ur bane (ėr′bān′), *adj.* 1 courteous, refined, or elegant: *urbane manners.* 2 smoothly polite. [< Latin *urbanus,* originally, urban. See URBAN.] **—ur′bane′ly,** *adv.* **—ur′bane′ness,** *n.*

ur ban ite (ėr′bə nīt), *n.* dweller in a city.

ur ban i ty (ėr ban′ə tē), *n., pl.* **-ties.** 1 courtesy, refinement, or elegance. 2 smooth politeness.

ur ban ize (ėr′bə nīz), *v.,* **-ized, -iz ing.** make or become urban: *urbanize a district.* **—ur′ban i za′tion,** *n.*

urban renewal, improvement of urban areas by removing slums and converting them into attractive living or industrial areas.

ur bi cul ture (ėr′bə kul′chər), *n.* the care of cities and city people; urban interests.

ur chin (ėr′chən), *n.* 1 a small boy. 2 a mischievous boy. 3 a poor, ragged child. 4 ARCHAIC. hedgehog. 5 sea urchin. [< Old French *irechon* < Latin *ericius* hedgehog < *er* hedgehog]

Ur du (ůr′dü, ėr′dü), *n.* form of Hindustani spoken by Moslems in India and Pakistan. It is written in the Arabic alphabet and is an official language of Pakistan.

-ure, *suffix added to verbs to form nouns.* 1 act or fact of ____ing: *Failure = act of failing.* 2 state of being ____ed: *Pleasure = state of being pleased.* 3 result of being ____ed: *Exposure = result of being exposed.* 4 something that ____s: *Legislature = something that legislates.* 5 thing that is ____ed: *Disclosure = thing that is disclosed.* [< French *-ure* < Latin *-ura*]

u re a (yů rē′ə, yůr′ē ə), *n.* a crystalline, nitrogenous solid present in solution in the urine of mammals. Synthesized urea is used in making adhesives and plastics, in fertilizers, in medicine, etc. *Formula:* $CO(NH_2)_2$

hat, āge, fär; let, ēqual, tėrm;
it, īce; hot, ōpen, ôrder;
oil, out; cup, pu̇t, rüle;
ch, child; ng, long; sh, she;
th, thin; ᴛʜ, then; zh, measure;

ə represents *a* in about, *e* in taken, *i* in pencil, *o* in lemon, *u* in circus.

< = from, derived from, taken from.

[< New Latin < French *urée* < *urine* urine]

urea resins, group of synthetic, thermosetting resins obtained from urea and formaldehyde, used in adhesives, moldings, etc.

ur e ase (yůr′ē ās), *n.* enzyme present in various bacteria, beans, etc., which promotes the decomposition of urea.

u re mi a (yů rē′mē ə), *n.* an abnormal condition resulting from the accumulation in the blood of waste products that should normally be eliminated in the urine. [< *ur(ine)* + *-emia*]

u re mic (yů rē′mik), *adj.* 1 of or having to do with uremia. 2 suffering from uremia.

u re ter (yů rē′tər, yůr′ə tər), *n.* duct that carries urine from a kidney to the bladder or the cloaca. [< Greek *oureter,* ultimately < *ouron* urine]

u re ter al (yů rē′tər əl), *adj.* of or having to do with a ureter.

ur e thane (yůr′ə thān′), *n.* a strong, fire-resistant plastic resin made in the form of rigid or flexible foams or solids and widely used as insulation, as a binder, filler, stiffener, etc. [< *ure(a)* + *(e)thane*]

u re thra (yů rē′thrə), *n., pl.* **-thrae** (-thrē), **-thras.** duct in most mammals by which urine is discharged from the bladder, and, in males, through which semen is discharged. [< Greek *ourethra,* ultimately < *ouron* urine]

u re thral (yů rē′thrəl), *adj.* of or having to do with the urethra.

Ur ey (yůr′ē), *n.* **Harold C.,** born 1893, American chemist.

urge (ėrj), *v.,* **urged, urg ing,** *n.* *—v.t.* 1 push, force, or drive forward or onward: *The rider urged on his horse with whip and spurs. Hunger urged him to steal.* 2 try to persuade with arguments; ask earnestly: *We urged them to stay for dinner.* 3 plead or argue earnestly for; recommend strongly: *The superintendent of schools urged a larger budget for education.* 4 press upon the attention; refer to often and with emphasis: *urge a claim, urge an argument.* *—v.i.* 1 be or act as an impelling force. 2 present arguments, statements, etc., for or against something. *—n.* 1 a driving force or impulse. 2 act of urging. [< Latin *urgere*]

ur gen cy (ėr′jən sē), *n., pl.* **-cies.** 1 urgent character; need for immediate action or attention: *A house on fire is a matter of great urgency.* 2 insistence; persistence.

ur gent (ėr′jənt), *adj.* 1 demanding immediate action or attention; pressing; important: *an urgent duty, an urgent message.* 2 insistent; persistent. **—ur′gent ly,** *adv.*

ur ic (yůr′ik), *adj.* 1 of or having to do with urine. 2 found in urine.

uric acid, a white, crystalline acid, only slightly soluble in water, formed as a waste product of the metabolism of purines and found in the urine of reptiles, birds, man, etc. *Formula:* $C_5H_4N_4O_3$

Ur i el (yůr′ē əl), *n.* one of the archangels.

ur i nal (yůr′ə nəl), *n.* 1 container for urine. 2 place for urinating.

ur i nal y sis (yůr′ə nal′ə sis), *n., pl.* **-ses** (-sēz′). a chemical analysis of a sample of urine.

ur i nar y (yůr′ə ner′ē), *adj., n., pl.* **-nar ies.** —*adj.* 1 of, like, or having to do with urine. 2 of, having to do with, or occurring in the organs that secrete and discharge urine. —*n.* urinal.

ur i nate (yůr′ə nāt), *v.i.,* **-nat ed, -nat ing.** discharge urine from the body. **—ur′i na′tion,** *n.*

ur ine (yůr′ən), *n.* a waste product of the body that is excreted by the kidneys, in man a fluid, normally amber in color and slightly acid, that passes through the ureters into the bladder, and is then discharged from the body through the urethra. [< Latin *urina*]

urn (ėrn), *n.* 1 vase with a foot or pedestal. Urns were used in ancient Greece and Rome to hold the ashes of the dead. 2 coffeepot or teapot with a faucet, used for making or serving coffee or tea at the table. [< Latin *urna*]

ur o gen i tal (yůr′ō jen′ə təl), *adj.* having to do with the urinary and genital organs.

ur o log ic (yůr′ə loj′ik), *adj.* urological.

ur o log i cal (yůr′ə loj′ə kəl), *adj.* of or having to do with urology or the urinary tract.

u rol o gist (yů rol′ə jist), *n.* an expert in urology.

u rol o gy (yů rol′ə jē), *n.* branch of medicine dealing with the urogenital tract in the male or the urinary tract in the female and their diseases.

Ur sa Major (ėr′sə), the most prominent northern constellation, seen by ancient astronomers as having the rough outline of a bear. It includes the stars of the Big Dipper, two of which point toward the North Star; Great Bear. [< Latin, bigger bear]

Ursa Minor, a northern constellation, seen by ancient astronomers as having the rough outline of a bear. It includes the stars of the Little Dipper, with the North Star at the end of its handle; Little Bear. [< Latin, smaller bear]

ur sine (ėr′sīn, ėr′sən), *adj.* of or having to do with bears; bearlike. [< Latin *ursinus* < *ursus* bear]

Ur su la (ėr′sə lə, ėr′syə lə), *n.* **Saint,** legendary British martyr, said to have been put to death with 11,000 virgins by an army of Huns at Cologne.

Ur su line (ėr′sə lən, ėr′sə līn; ėr′syə lən, ėr′syə līn), *n.* member of a religious order of Roman Catholic women, founded in 1535 for the education of girls and for the care of the sick and needy. —*adj.* of or having to do with the Ursulines. [< Saint *Ursula*]

ur ti car i a (ėr′tə ker′ē ə, ėr′tə kar′ē ə), *n.* hives. [< Latin *urtica* nettle]

ur ti car i al (ėr′tə ker′ē əl, ėr′tə kar′ē əl), *adj.* of or having to do with urticaria.

Ur u guay (yůr′ə gwā, yůr′ə gwī; ůr′ə gwā, ůr′ə gwī), *n.* 1 country in SE South America. 2,890,000 pop.; 72,200 sq. mi. *Capital:* Montevideo. 2 **Uruguay River,** river flowing from S Brazil into the Plata. 981 mi. **—Ur′u guay′an,** *adj., n.*

ur us (yůr′əs), *n.* aurochs (def. 2). [< Latin; of Germanic origin]

us (us; *unstressed* əs), *pron.* objective case of **we.** *Mother went with us.* [Old English *ūs*]

U.S., United States.

U.S.A. or **USA,** 1 United States of America. 2 United States Army.

us a bil i ty (yü′zə bil′ə tē), *n.* a being usable.

us a ble (yü′zə bəl), *adj.* 1 that can be used; capable of use. 2 fit or proper to be used; suitable for use. Also, **useable. —us′a ble ness,** *n.* **—us′a bly,** *adv.*

USAF or **U.S.A.F.,** United States Air Force.

us age (yü′sij, yü′zij), *n.* 1 way or manner of using or of being used; act of using; treatment: *The car has had rough usage.* 2 a long-continued practice; customary use; habit; custom: *Travelers should learn many of the usages of the countries they visit.* 3 the customary way of using words: *The usage of the best writers and speakers determines what is good English.*

urn (def. 1)

urn (def. 2)

us ance (yü′zns), *n.* time (varying between different places) allowed for the payment of foreign bills of exchange.

USCG or **U.S.C.G.,** United States Coast Guard.

use (*v.* yüz; *n.* yüs), *v.,* **used, us ing,** *n.* —*v.t.* 1 put into action or service; utilize: *use a knife to cut the meat. We use our legs in walking.* See synonym study below. 2 act or behave toward; treat: *He used us well.* 3 consume or expend by using: *use water for irrigation. He uses tobacco. We have used most of the money.* 4 avail oneself of; put to one's own purposes: *May I use your telephone?* 5 **used to** (yüst′tü′, yü′stə), **a** accustomed to: *used to hardships.* **b** was or were accustomed to; formerly did: *She used to come over every day.* 6 **use up,** consume or expend entirely: *We have used up our sugar.*
—*n.* 1 a using: *the use of tools.* 2 a being used: *methods long out of use.* 3 usefulness: *a thing of no practical use.* 4 purpose that a thing is used for: *find a new use for something.* 5 manner or way of using: *a poor use of a material.* 6 need or occasion for using; necessity; demand: *find a use for something. Campers often have use for a hatchet.* 7 power or capacity of using; ability to use: *lose the use of a hand.* 8 right or privilege of using: *have the use of a friend's boat for the summer.* 9 custom; habit; usage: *It was his use to rise early.* 10 in law: **a** act or fact of employing, occupying, possessing, or holding property so as to derive benefit from it. **b** right of a beneficiary to the benefit or profits of land or tenements to which another has legal title in trust for the beneficiary. **c** trust vesting title to real property in someone for the benefit of another.
have no use for, **a** not need or want. **b** INFORMAL. dislike.
in use, being used.
make use of, **a** put in use; use. **b** take advantage of.
put to use, use.
[< Old French < Latin *usus* act of using < *uti* to use] **—us′er,** *n.*
Syn. *v.t.* 1 **Use, employ, utilize** mean to put into action or service for some purpose. **Use,** the general and common word, suggests any kind of purpose when applied to things but a selfish purpose when applied to persons: *use a typewriter for one's schoolwork, use one's friends to get ahead.* **Employ** suggests a special purpose: *That architect frequently employs glass brick.* **Utilize** suggests a practical purpose: *utilize every scrap of food.*

use a ble (yü′zə bəl), *adj.* usable. **—use′a ble ness,** *n.*

used (yüzd), *adj.* 1 not new; second-hand: *a used car.* 2 that is used; in use; utilized: *a seldom used room.*

use ful (yüs′fəl), *adj.* 1 of use; helpful: *a useful suggestion, make oneself useful about the house.* 2 giving or able to give service; usable: *an old but still useful pair of shoes.* **—use′ful ly,** *adv.* **—use′ful ness,** *n.*

use less (yüs′lis), *adj.* of no use; worthless. **—use′less ly,** *adv.* **—use′less ness,** *n.*
Syn. Useless, ineffectual mean having or being of no value for a purpose. **Useless** implies having no practical value under the circumstances: *An electric toaster is useless to someone in the woods.* **Ineffectual** implies having no means to accomplish a purpose or having no effect whatever: *Her attempts to become friends again after the quarrel were ineffectual.*

ush er (ush′ər), *n.* person who shows people to their seats in a church, theater, etc. —*v.t.* 1 conduct or guide; escort; show: *usher visitors to the door.* 2 go or come before; precede to announce the coming of. 3 **usher in,** inaugurate; introduce: *a winter ushered in by cold rains.* [< Anglo-French *uissier* < Popular Latin *ustiarius* doorkeeper < *ustium,* variant of Latin *ostium* door, related to *os* mouth]

ush er ette (ush′ə ret′), *n.* a girl or woman usher.

USIA or **U.S.I.A.,** United States Information Agency.

U.S.M., United States Mail.

USMA or **U.S.M.A.,** United States Military Academy.

USMC or **U.S.M.C.,** United States Marine Corps.

USN or **U.S.N.,** United States Navy.

USNA or **U.S.N.A.,** United States Naval Academy.

USNG or **U.S.N.G.,** United States National Guard.

USNR or **U.S.N.R.,** United States Naval Reserve.

USP or **U.S.P.,** United States Pharmacopoeia.

U.S.S.R. or **USSR,** Union of Soviet Socialist Republics.

u su al (yü′zhü əl), *adj.* 1 commonly seen, found, or happening; ordinary; customary: *Snow is usual high up in the Rocky Mountains during winter.* See synonym study below. 2 **as usual,** in the usual manner; as is customary. [< Late Latin *usualis* < Latin *usus* use, custom < *uti* to use] **—u′su al ness,** *n.*
Syn. 1 **Usual, customary** mean often or commonly seen or found, especially in a certain place or at a given time. **Usual** applies to something of expected occurrence or of familiar nature or quality: *This is the usual weather at this time of the year.* **Customary** applies to something that is according

to the regular practices or habits of a particular person or group: *I stayed up long past my customary bedtime.*

u su al ly (yü′zhü ə lē), *adv.* according to what is usual; commonly; ordinarily; customarily.

u su fruct (yü′zyə frukt, yü′syə frukt), *n.* the legal right to use another's property and enjoy the advantages of it without injuring or destroying it. [< Latin *ususfructus,* earlier *usus (et) fructus* use and enjoyment]

U sum bur a (ü′səm bůr′ə), *n.* Bujumbura.

u surer (yü′zhər ər), *n.* person who lends money at an extremely high or unlawful rate of interest.

u sur i ous (yü zhůr′ē əs), *adj.* 1 taking extremely high or unlawful interest for the use of money. 2 of, having to do with, or of the nature of usury: *Fifty per cent is a usurious rate of interest.* **—u sur′i ous ly,** *adv.* **—u sur′i ous ness,** *n.*

u surp (yü zėrp′, yü sėrp′), *v.t.* seize and hold (power, position, authority, etc.) by force or without right: *The king's brother tried to usurp the throne.* —*v.i.* commit usurpation. [< Latin *usurpare* < *usu* through use + *rapere* seize] **—u surp′er,** *n.*

u sur pa tion (yü′zər pā′shən, yü′sər-pā′shən), *n.* a usurping; the seizing and holding of the place or power of another by force or without right: *the usurpation of the throne by a pretender.*

u sur y (yü′zhər ē), *n., pl.* **u sur ies.** 1 the lending of money at an extremely high or unlawful rate of interest. 2 an extremely high or unlawful rate of interest. [< Medieval Latin *usuria,* alteration of Latin *usura* use < *uti* to use]

Ut., Utah.

U tah (yü′tô, yü′tä), *n.* one of the western states of the United States. 1,059,000 pop.; 85,000 sq. mi. *Capital:* Salt Lake City. *Abbrev.:* Ut. **—U′tah an,** *adj., n.*

Ute (yüt), *n., pl.* **Ute** or **Utes.** 1 member of a group of American Indian tribes now living in Utah, Colorado, and New Mexico. 2 their language.

u ten sil (yü ten′səl), *n.* 1 container or implement used for practical purposes. Pots, pans, etc., are kitchen utensils. 2 instrument or tool used for some special purpose. Pens and pencils are writing utensils. [< Medieval Latin *utensile* < Latin *utensilis* that may be used < *uti* to use]

u ter ine (yü′tər ən, yü′tə rīn′), *adj.* 1 of or having to do with the uterus. 2 having the same mother, but a different father. Uterine brothers are stepbrothers born of the same mother.

u ter us (yü′tər əs), *n., pl.* **u ter i** (yü′tə rī′). 1 the organ of the body in most female mammals that holds and nourishes the young till birth; womb. 2 a corresponding part in lower animals. [< Latin]

U ther (yü′thər), *n.* Also, **Uther Pendragon.** (in Arthurian legends) king of ancient Britain, and father of King Arthur.

U ti ca (yü′tə kə), *n.* 1 city in central New York State. 92,000. 2 ancient city in N Africa, near Carthage.

u tile (yü′tl), *adj.* having utility; useful.

u til i tar i an (yü til′ə ter′ē ən), *adj.* 1 of or having to do with utility. 2 aiming at or designed for usefulness rather than beauty, style, etc. 3 of, having to do with, or adhering to utilitarianism. —*n.* adherent of utilitarianism.

u til i tar i an ism (yü til′ə ter′ē ə niz′əm), *n.* 1 the doctrine or belief that the greatest good of the greatest number should be the purpose of human conduct. 2 the doctrine or belief that actions are good if they are useful.

u til i ty (yü til′ə tē), *n., pl.* **-ties,** *adj.* —*n.* 1 power to satisfy people's needs; usefulness: *A fur coat has more utility in the winter than in the summer.* 2 a useful thing. 3 company that performs a public service. Railroads, bus lines, and gas and electric companies are utilities; public utility. 4 **utilities,** *pl.* shares of stock issued by a public utility company. 5 (in philosophy) the greatest happiness of the greatest number. —*adj.* 1 used for various purposes: *a utility shed in the garden, a utility infielder.* 2 of low grade, usually from older animals: *utility beef.* [< Latin *utilitatem* < *utilis* usable < *uti* to use]

u ti lize (yü′tl īz), *v.t.,* **-lized, -liz ing.** make use of; put to some practical use: *utilize leftovers in cooking.* See **use** for synonym study. **—u′ti liz′a ble,** *adj.* **—u′ti li-za′tion,** *n.* **—u′ti liz′er,** *n.*

ut most (ut′mōst), *adj.* 1 greatest possible; greatest; highest: *Sunshine is of the utmost importance to health.* 2 most distant; farthest; extreme: *She walked to the utmost edge of the cliff.* —*n.* the most that is possible; extreme limit: *He enjoyed himself to the utmost at the circus.* [Old English *ūtemest* < *ūte* outside + *-mest* -most]

u to pi a or **U to pi a** (yü tō′pē ə), *n.* 1 an ideal place or state with perfect laws. 2 a visionary, impractical system of political or social perfection. [< *Utopia,* an ideal commonwealth described by Sir Thomas More < Greek *ou* not + *topos* place]

u to pi an or **U to pi an** (yü tō′pē ən), *adj.* 1 of, having to do with, or resembling a utopia. 2 visionary; impractical. —*n.* 1 an ardent but impractical reformer; extreme and visionary idealist. 2 inhabitant of utopia.

u to pi an ism (yü tō′pē ə niz′əm), *n.* ideas, beliefs, and aims of utopians; ideal schemes for the improvement of life, social conditions, etc.

U trecht (yü′trekt), *n.* city in the central part of the Netherlands. 279,000.

u tri cle (yü′trə kəl), *n.* 1 a small sac or baglike body, such as a cell filled with air in a seaweed. 2 a thin seed vessel resembling a bladder. 3 the larger of the two membranous sacs in the labyrinth of the inner ear. [< Latin *utriculus,* diminutive of *uter* skin bag, skin bottle]

hat, āge, fär; let, ēqual, tėrm;
it, īce; hot, ōpen, ôrder;
oil, out; cup, pu̇t, rüle;
ch, child; ng, long; sh, she;
th, thin; ᴛʜ, then; zh, measure;

ə represents *a* in about, *e* in taken, *i* in pencil, *o* in lemon, *u* in circus.

< = from, derived from, taken from.

u tric u lar (yü trik′yə lər), *adj.* of or having to do with a utricle.

u tric u lus (yü trik′yə ləs), *n.* utricle.

U tril lo (ü tril′ō), *n.* **Maurice,** 1883-1955, French painter.

Ut tar Pra desh (ůt′ər prə dāsh′), state in N India.

ut ter¹ (ut′ər), *adj.* complete; total; absolute: *utter surprise, utter darkness.* [Old English *ūterra* outer]

ut ter² (ut′ər), *v.t.* 1 speak; make known; express: *the last words he uttered, utter one's thoughts.* 2 give forth; give out: *utter a cry of pain.* 3 put into circulation, as coins, notes, etc., and especially counterfeit money, forged checks, etc. [Middle English *utteren* < Old English *ūt* out] **—ut′ter a ble,** *adj.* **—ut′ter er,** *n.*

ut ter ance (ut′ər əns), *n.* 1 an uttering; expression in words or sounds: *The child gave utterance to his grief.* 2 way or manner of speaking. 3 something uttered; a spoken word or words.

ut ter ly (ut′ər lē), *adv.* completely; totally; absolutely.

ut ter most (ut′ər mōst), *adj., n.* utmost.

U-turn (yü′tėrn′), *n.* a U-shaped turn made by a motor vehicle to reverse its direction.

u vu la (yü′vyə lə), *n., pl.* **-las, -lae** (-lē′). the small piece of flesh hanging down from the soft palate in the back of the mouth. See **tonsil** for diagram. [< Late Latin, diminutive of Latin *uva,* originally, grape]

u vu lar (yü′vyə lər), *adj.* 1 of or having to do with the uvula. 2 pronounced or sounded with vibration of the uvula. —*n.* a uvular sound.

ux o ri ous (uk sôr′ē əs, uk sōr′ē əs), *adj.* excessively or foolishly fond of one's wife. [< Latin *uxorius* < *uxor* wife] **—ux o′ri-ous ly,** *adv.* **—ux o′ri ous ness,** *n.*

Uz bek (üz′bek), *n.* 1 member of a people of Turkestan. 2 their Turkic language.

Uzbek S.S.R., one of the constituent republics of the U.S.S.R., in the S part. 12,000,000 pop.; 157,300 sq. mi. *Capital:* Tashkent.

V v

V or **v** (vē), *n., pl.* **V's** or **v's.** 1 the 22nd letter of the English alphabet. 2 anything shaped like a V. 3 the Roman numeral for 5.

v, volt.

V, 1 vanadium. 2 Victory. 3 volt.

v., 1 see [for Latin *vide*]. 2 verb. 3 verse. 4 versus. 5 vice-. 6 voice. 7 volume.

V., 1 Venerable. 2 Victoria. 3 Viscount.

VA, Veterans Administration.

Va., Virginia.

V.A., 1 Veterans Administration. 2 Vicar Apostolic.

va can cy (vā′kən sē), *n., pl.* **-cies.** 1 a being vacant; emptiness. 2 an unoccupied position: *The retirement of two bookkeepers made two vacancies in our office.* 3 a being or becoming unoccupied. 4 room, space, or apartment for rent; empty space. 5 emptiness of mind; lack of thought or intelligence. 6 freedom from work, activity, etc.; idleness.

va cant (vā′kənt), *adj.* 1 not occupied: *a vacant house.* See **empty** for synonym study. 2 not filled; empty: *a vacant space.* 3 empty of thought or intelligence: *a vacant smile.* 4 free from work, business, etc.: *vacant time.* [< Latin *vacantem* being empty] **—va′cant ly,** *adv.*

va cate (vā′kāt), *v.,* **-cat ed, -cat ing.** *—v.t.* 1 go away from and leave empty or unoccupied; make vacant: *They will vacate the house at the end of the month.* 2 make void; annul; cancel. *—v.i.* go away; leave. [< Latin *vacatum* emptied]

va ca tion (vā kā′shən), *n.* 1 time of rest and freedom from school, business, or other duties: *There is a vacation from school every summer.* 2 a vacating. *—v.i.* take a vacation. [< Latin *vacationem* < *vacare* have time (off), be empty] **—va ca′tion er,** *n.* **—va ca′tion less,** *adj.*

va ca tion ist (vā kā′shə nist), *n.* person taking a vacation.

vac ci nal (vak′sə nəl), *adj.* 1 of or having to do with vaccine. 2 caused by vaccination.

vac ci nate (vak′sə nāt), *v.,* **-nat ed, -nat ing.** *—v.t.* 1 inoculate with a mildly toxic preparation of weakened or killed bacteria or viruses of a specific disease to prevent or lessen the effects of that disease. 2 inoculate with the modified virus of cowpox as a protection against smallpox. *—v.i.* perform or practice vaccination.

vac ci na tion (vak′sə nā′shən), *n.* 1 act or process of vaccinating: *Vaccination has made smallpox a very rare disease.* 2 scar where vaccine was injected.

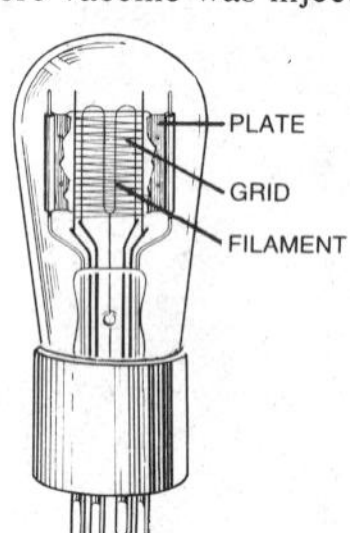

vacuum tube

vac cine (vak′sēn′, vak sēn′), *n.* 1 a mildly toxic preparation of weakened or killed bacteria or viruses of a particular disease, used to inoculate a person in order to prevent or lessen the effects of that disease. Vaccines work by causing the body to develop antibodies against the disease germs. 2 the virus causing cowpox, prepared for use in preventive inoculation against smallpox. *—adj.* of or having to do with a vaccine. [< Latin *vaccinus* of cows < *vacca* cow]

vac cin i a (vak sin′ē ə), *n.* cowpox. [< New Latin]

vac il lant (vas′ə lənt), *adj.* vacillating; wavering.

vac il late (vas′ə lāt), *v.i.,* **-lat ed, -lat ing.** 1 waver in mind or opinion: *A vacillating person can't make up his mind.* 2 move first one way and then another; waver. [< Latin *vacillatum* wavered] **—vac′il lat′ing ly,** *adv.* **—vac′il la′tion,** *n.*

vac il la to ry (vas′ə lə tôr′ē, vas′ə lə-tōr′ē), *adj.* vacillating.

va cu i ty (va kyü′ə tē), *n., pl.* **-ties.** 1 emptiness. 2 an empty space; vacuum. 3 emptiness of mind; lack of thought or intelligence. 4 something foolish or stupid. 5 absence or lack (of something specified).

vac u o lar (vak′yü ə lər), *adj.* provided with one or more vacuoles.

vac u ole (vak′yü ōl), *n.* 1 a tiny cavity in the protoplasm of a living cell, containing fluid. 2 (formerly) any very small cavity in organic tissue. [< French < Latin *vacuus* empty]

vac u ous (vak′yü əs), *adj.* 1 showing no thought or intelligence; foolish; stupid: *a vacuous smile.* 2 having no meaning or direction; idle; indolent: *a vacuous life.* 3 empty. [< Latin *vacuus*] **—vac′u ous ly,** *adv.* **—vac′u ous ness,** *n.*

vac u um (vak′yü əm, vak′yùm), *n., pl.* **vac u ums** or (except for def. 4) **vac u a** (vak′yü ə), *adj., v.* *—n.* 1 an empty space without even air in it. 2 an enclosed space from which almost all air or other matter has been removed. 3 an empty space; void. 4 vacuum cleaner. *—adj.* 1 of or having to do with a vacuum. 2 producing a vacuum. 3 using a vacuum. *—v.t.* 1 clean with a vacuum cleaner. 2 use any vacuum device on. [< Latin, neuter of *vacuus* empty]

vacuum bottle, bottle made with a vacuum between its inner and outer walls so that its contents remain hot or cold for long periods of time. A thermos bottle is a kind of vacuum bottle.

vacuum cleaner, apparatus for cleaning carpets, curtains, floors, etc., by suction.

vac u um ize (vak′yü ə mīz, vak′yù mīz), *v.t.,* **-ized, -iz ing.** produce a vacuum in (a container, chamber, etc.).

vac u um-packed (vak′yü əm pakt′, vak′yùm pakt′), *adj.* 1 packed in an airtight container to keep fresh: *vacuum-packed coffee.* 2 having had all or most of the air removed before sealing: *vacuum-packed cans.*

vacuum pump, 1 pump or device by which a partial vacuum can be produced. 2 pump in which a partial vacuum is utilized to raise water.

vacuum tube, a sealed tube from which most of the air has been removed, and into which electrodes from outside project, used in radio and television sets, photoelectric cells, radar, electron microscopes, and other devices to control the flow of electric currents; electron tube.

va de me cum (vā′dē mē′kəm), 1 anything a person carries about with him because of its usefulness. 2 book for ready reference; manual; handbook. [< Latin, go with me]

Va duz (vä′düts), *n.* capital of Liechtenstein, in the W part. 4000.

vag a bond (vag′ə bond), *n.* 1 an idle wanderer; tramp; vagrant. 2 a disreputable person; rascal. *—adj.* 1 wandering: *The gypsies lead a vagabond life.* 2 shiftless; disreputable. 3 moving hither and thither; drifting. [< Old French < Latin *vagabundus* < *vagari* wander < *vagus* rambling]

vag a bond age (vag′ə bon′dij), *n.* fact or condition of being a vagabond; idle wandering.

vag a bond ism (vag′ə bon diz′əm), *n.* vagabondage.

va gal (vā′gəl), *adj.* of or having to do with the vagus nerve.

va gar i ous (və ger′ē əs), *adj.* having vagaries; whimsical; capricious; erratic.

va gar y (və ger′ē, vā′gər ē), *n., pl.* **-gar ies.** 1 an odd fancy; extravagant notion: *the vagaries of a dream.* 2 odd action; caprice; freak: *the vagaries of women's fashions.* [probably < Latin *vagari* wander < *vagus* rambling]

va gi na (və jī′nə), *n., pl.* **-nas, -nae** (-nē). 1 (in female mammals) the passage that leads from the uterus to the external genital organs. 2 a similar part in certain other animals. 3 sheath or sheathlike part. 4 (in botany) the sheath formed around a stem by the lower parts of some leaves, as the tulip. [< Latin, sheath]

vag i nal (və jī′nl, vaj′ə nəl), *adj.* 1 of or having to do with the vagina. 2 of or resembling a sheath.

vag i nate (vaj′ə nit, vaj′ə nāt), *adj.* 1 having a vagina or sheath. 2 like a sheath.

va gran cy (vā′grən sē), *n., pl.* **-cies.** 1 a wandering idly from place to place without proper means or ability to earn a living: *The beggar was arrested for vagrancy.* 2 a wandering. 3 a vagrant act or idea.

va grant (vā′grənt), *n.* 1 an idle wanderer; tramp. 2 wanderer. *—adj.* 1 moving in no definite direction or course; wandering: *vagrant thoughts.* 2 wandering without proper means of earning a living. 3 of or having to do with a vagrant. [origin uncertain] **—va′grant ly,** *adv.*

va grom (vā′grəm), *adj.* ARCHAIC. vagrant.

vague (vāg), *adj.,* **va guer, va guest.** 1 not definitely or precisely expressed: *a vague statement.* See **obscure** for synonym study. 2 indefinite; indistinct: *a vague feeling.* 3 indistinctly seen or perceived; obscure; hazy: *In a fog everything looks vague.* 4 lacking clarity or precision: *a vague personality.* [< Old French < Latin *vagus* wandering] **—vague′ly,** *adv.* **—vague′ness,** *n.*

va gus (vā′gəs), *n., pl.* **va gi** (vā′jī). either of a pair of nerves, extending from the brain to the heart, lungs, stomach, and other organs. [< New Latin < Latin, wandering]

va hi ne (vä hē′nā), *n.* TAHITIAN. a woman; female; wife.

vail (vāl), ARCHAIC. *—v.t.* 1 cause or allow to fall; lower. 2 take off; doff. *—v.i.* yield; bow. [< Old French *valer, avaler* < *a val* downhill < Latin *ad vallem* to the valley]

vain (vān), *adj.* 1 having too much pride in one's looks, ability, etc.; conceited. 2 of no use; producing no good result; unsuccessful; fruitless: *I made vain attempts to reach her by telephone.* See synonym study below. 3 of

hat, āge, fär; let, ēqual, tėrm;
it, īce; hot, ōpen, ôrder;
oil, out; cup, pu̇t, rüle;
ch, child; ng, long; sh, she;
th, thin; ᴛʜ, then; zh, measure;

ə represents *a* in about, *e* in taken, *i* in pencil, *o* in lemon, *u* in circus.

< = from, derived from, taken from.

no value or importance; worthless; empty: *a vain boast.* —*n.* **in vain, a** without effect or success: *work in vain for a futile cause.* **b** in a disrespectful manner; lightly or irreverently: *The Bible says that one must not take God's name in vain.* [< Old French < Latin *vanus*] —**vain′ness,** *n.*

Syn. *adj.* 2 **Vain, futile** mean without effect or success. **Vain** describes thinking, action, effort, etc., that fails to accomplish a given result: *The principal made another vain appeal for better equipment in the high-school laboratories.* **Futile** adds and emphasizes the idea of being incapable of producing the result, and often suggests that the attempt is useless or unwise: *Without microscopes and other essential equipment, attempts to teach science were futile.*

vain glo ri ous (vān′glôr′ē əs, vān′glōr′ē-əs), *adj.* excessively proud or boastful; extremely vain; arrogant. —**vain′glo′ri ous ly,** *adv.* —**vain′glo′ri ous ness,** *n.*

vain glo ry (vān′glôr′ē, vān′glōr′ē), *n.* 1 an extreme pride in oneself; boastful vanity. 2 worthless pomp or show.

vain ly (vān′lē), *adv.* 1 in vain. 2 with conceit.

vair (ver, var), *n.* 1 a gray-and-white squirrel fur used for lining and trimming the robes of nobles in the Middle Ages. 2 its representation in heraldry by small shield-shaped figures alternately silver and gold. [< Old French < Latin *varius* varied. Doublet of VARIOUS.]

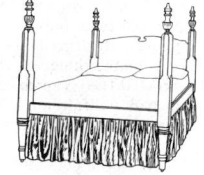

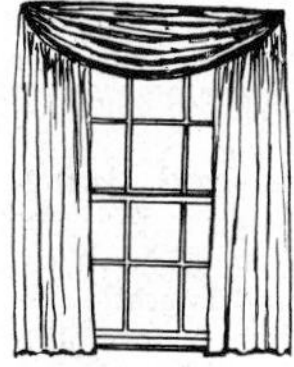
valance (def. 1)

valance (def. 2)

val ance (val′əns), *n.* 1 a short drapery over the top of a window. 2 a short curtain, as one hanging from the frame or canopy of a bed. [probably ultimately < Old French *avaler* to lower. See VAIL.]

vale[1] (vāl), *n.* valley. [< Old French *val* < Latin *vallis*]

va le[2] (vā′lē, vä′lā), *interj., n.* good-by; farewell. [< Latin, imperative of *valere* be strong, fare well]

val e dic tion (val′ə dik′shən), *n.* a bidding farewell. [< Latin *valedictum* bidden farewell < *vale* farewell + *dicere* say]

val e dic to ri an (val′ə dik tôr′ē ən, val′ə-dik tōr′ē ən), *n.* student who gives the farewell address at the graduating exercises. The valedictorian is usually the student who ranks highest in his class.

val e dic tor y (val′ə dik′tər ē), *n., pl.* **-tor ies,** *adj.* —*n.* a farewell address, especially at the graduating exercises of a school or college. —*adj.* bidding farewell.

va lence (vā′ləns), *n.* 1 the combining capacity of an atom or radical, determined by the number of electrons that an atom will lose, add, or share when it reacts with other atoms. Elements whose atoms lose electrons, such as hydrogen and the metals, have a positive valence. Elements whose atoms add electrons, such as oxygen and other nonmetals, have a negative valence. Oxygen has a negative valence of 2; hydrogen has a positive valence of 1; one atom of oxygen combines with two of hydrogen to form a molecule of water. 2 a unit of valence. 3 (in biology) the ability of serums, etc., to interact or produce a certain effect. [< Latin *valentia* strength < *valere* be strong]

valence electron, electron in the outer shell of an atom. In a chemical change, the atom gains, loses, or shares such an electron in combining with another atom or atoms to form a molecule.

Va len cia (və len′shə, və len′shē ə), *n.* seaport in E Spain. 624,000.

Va len ci ennes (və len′sē enz′), *n.* a fine lace in which the pattern and background are made together of the same threads. [< *Valenciennes,* city in northern France, where it was originally made]

va len cy (vā′lən sē), *n., pl.* **-cies.** valence.

val en tine (val′ən tīn), *n.* 1 a greeting card or small gift sent on Saint Valentine's Day, February 14. 2 sweetheart chosen on this day.

Val en tine (val′ən tīn), *n.* **Saint,** Christian martyr of the A.D. 200's. He was beheaded by the Romans on February 14.

Valentine's Day, Saint Valentine's Day, February 14.

va ler i an (və lir′ē ən), *n.* 1 any of a genus of perennial herbs, especially the heliotrope, a species that has small pinkish or white flowers, cultivated for its medicinal root and often grown in gardens. 2 a strong-smelling drug used to quiet the nerves, prepared from the roots of the common species of valerian. [< Medieval Latin *valeriana* < Latin *Valerius,* Roman gens name]

Va ler i an (və lir′ē ən), *n.* died A.D. 260?, Roman emperor from A.D. 253 to 260.

val et (val′it, val′ā), *n.* 1 servant who takes care of a man's clothes and gives him personal service. 2 worker in a hotel who cleans or presses clothes. —*v.t., v.i.* serve as a valet. [< Old French *valet, vaslet* page, squire < *vassal.* See VASSAL.]

val e tu di nar i an (val′ə tüd′n er′ē ən, val′ə tyüd′n er′ē ən), *n.* 1 person in weak health; chronic invalid. 2 person who thinks he is ill when he is not; hypochondriac. —*adj.* 1 sickly. 2 thinking too much about the state of one's health. [< Latin *valetudinarius* sickly < *valetudo* (good or bad) health < *valere* be strong]

val e tu di nar i an ism (val′ə tüd′n er′ē-ə niz′əm, val′ə tyüd′n er′ē ə niz′əm), *n.* valetudinarian condition or habits.

Val hal la (val hal′ə), *n.* (in Scandinavian myths) the hall where the souls of heroes slain in battle feast with the god Odin.

val iance (val′yəns), *n.* bravery; valor.

val ian cy (val′yən sē), *n.* valiance.

val iant (val′yənt), *adj.* having or showing courage; brave; courageous: *a valiant soldier, a valiant deed.* —*n.* a brave or courageous person. [< Old French *vaillant,* present participle of *valoir* be strong < Latin *valere*] —**val′iant ly,** *adv.* —**val′iant-ness,** *n.*

val id (val′id), *adj.* 1 supported by facts or authority; sound or true: *a valid argument.* See synonym study below. 2 having legal force; legally binding: *A contract made by an insane person is not valid.* 3 having force; holding good; effective: *Illness is a valid excuse for being absent from work.* [< Latin *validus* strong < *valere* be strong] —**val′id-ly,** *adv.* —**val′id ness,** *n.*

Syn. 1 **Valid, sound, cogent** mean convincing with respect to truth, rightness, or reasoning. **Valid** implies being based on truth or fact and supported by correct reasoning: *His objections to the plan on the basis of cost are valid.* **Sound** implies having a solid foundation of truth or right and being free from defects or errors in reasoning: *The author has sound views on opportunities today.* **Cogent** implies being so valid or sound as to be convincing: *He gives cogent advice to young people.*

val i date (val′ə dāt), *v.t.,* **-dat ed, -dat ing.** 1 make valid; give legal force to. 2 support by facts or authority; confirm. —**val′i-da′tion,** *n.*

va lid i ty (və lid′ə tē), *n., pl.* **-ties.** 1 truth or soundness: *the validity of an argument.* 2 legal soundness or force; being legally binding. 3 effectiveness.

va lise (və lēs′), *n.* a traveling bag to hold clothes, etc. [< French < Italian *valigia*]

Val kyr (val′kir), *n.* Valkyrie.

Val kyr ie (val kir′ē), *n.* (in Scandinavian myths) one of the goddesses sent by Odin to ride through the air and hover over battlefields, choosing the heroes who would die in battle and afterward leading them to Valhalla.

val late (val′āt), *adj.* surrounded by a ridge or elevation; having a surrounding ridge or elevation. [< Latin *vallatum* < *vallum* rampart]

Val let ta (və let′ə), *n.* capital of Malta, a seaport in the NE part. 16,000.

val ley (val′ē), *n., pl.* **-leys.** 1 low land between hills or mountains; vale; dale. 2 a wide region drained by a great river system: *the Mississippi valley.* 3 any hollow or structure like a valley. 4 depression formed by the meeting of two sloping sides of a roof. [< Old French *valée* < *val* vale < Latin *vallis*]

Valley Forge, village in SE Pennsylvania, in which Washington and his army spent the winter of 1777-1778. 1000.

val or (val′ər), *n.* bravery; courage. Also, BRITISH **valour.** [< Late Latin < Latin *valere* be strong]

val or i za tion (val′ər ə zā′shən), *n.* U.S. the actual or attempted maintenance of certain prices for a commodity by a government. [< *valor,* in obsolete sense of "value"]

val or ize (val′ə rīz′), *v.t., v.i.,* **-ized, -iz ing.** 1 assign a value to. 2 U.S. regulate the price of by valorization.

val or ous (val′ər əs), *adj.* having or showing courage; valiant; brave; courageous. —**val′or ous ly,** *adv.* —**val′or ous-ness,** *n.*

val our (val′ər), *n.* BRITISH. valor.

Val pa rai so (val′pə rī′zō), *n.* chief seaport of Chile, in the central part. 286,000.

valse (väls), *n.* waltz. [< French < German *Walzer* waltz]

val u a ble (val′yü ə bəl, val′yə bəl), *adj.* 1 having value; being worth something: *a* *valuable tool, a valuable friend.* 2 having great value: *a valuable ring.* See synonym study below. 3 that can have its value measured. —*n.* Usually, **valuables,** *pl.* articles of value: *She keeps her jewelry and other valuables in a safe.* —**val′u a ble ness,** *n.* —**val′u a bly,** *adv.*

Syn. *adj.* 2 **Valuable, precious** mean worth much. **Valuable** applies to anything costly, very useful, or highly esteemed: *He has a valuable stamp collection.* **Precious** applies to anything very valuable, especially to something that is irreplaceable: *The original Declaration of Independence is a precious document kept in Washington.*

val u a tion (val′yü ā′shən), *n.* 1 value estimated or determined: *The jeweler's valuation of the necklace was $10,000.* 2 an estimating or determining the value of something: *She asked for a valuation of the collection.* 3 appreciation or estimation of anything in respect to excellence or merit.

val u a tion al (val′yü ā′shə nəl), *adj.* of or having to do with valuation.

val ue (val′yü), *n., v.,* **val ued, val u ing.** —*n.* 1 real worth; proper price: *They bought the house for less than its value.* 2 high worth; excellence, usefulness, or importance: *the value of education, the value of milk as a food.* 3 the power to buy: *The value of the dollar has varied greatly.* 4 an equivalent or adequate return: *We hardly could be said to have received value for our money.* 5 an estimated worth: *place a value on furniture.* 6 meaning, effect, or force: *the value of a symbol.* 7 the number or amount represented by a symbol: *The value of XIV is fourteen.* 8 **values,** *pl.* the established ideals of life. 9 the relative length of a tone in music indicated by a note. 10 a special quality of sound in speech. 11 a speech sound equivalent to a letter or a phonetic symbol: *The symbol* TH *represents the value of "th" in "then."* 12 the degree of lightness or darkness of a color, in a painting, etc. 13 the relationship and effect of an object, spot of color, shadow, etc., to a whole painting. —*v.t.* 1 rate at a certain value or price; estimate the value of; appraise: *The land is valued at $5000.* 2 think highly of; regard highly: *value one's judgment.* See synonym study below. 3 consider with respect to worth, excellence, usefulness, or importance. [< Old French, originally past participle of *valoir* be worth < Latin *valere* be strong] —**val′u er,** *n.*

Syn. *v.t.* 2 **Value, appreciate, esteem** mean to think highly of a person or thing. **Value** means to think highly of because of worth, importance, etc.: *I value your friendship.* **Appreciate** implies a valuing based on knowledge, sound judgment, or insight: *His classmates appreciate his wit.* **Esteem** means to think highly of because of warm or respectful regard: *The professor is esteemed by all her colleagues.*

val ued (val′yüd), *adj.* 1 having its value estimated or determined. 2 regarded highly.

val ue less (val′yə lis), *adj.* without value; worthless.

val vate (val′vāt), *adj.* 1 furnished with, or opening by, a valve or valves. 2 serving as or resembling a valve. 3 in botany: **a** meeting without overlapping, as the parts of certain buds do. **b** composed of, or characterized by, such parts.

V

valve (valv), *n., v.,* **valved, valv ing.** —*n.* 1 a movable part that controls the flow of a liquid, gas, etc., through a pipe by opening and closing the passage. A faucet contains a valve. 2 part of the body that works like a valve. The valves of the heart are membranes that control the flow of blood into and out of the heart. 3 one of the parts of hinged shells like those of oysters and clams. 4 in botany: **a** one of the sections formed when a seed vessel bursts open. **b** section that opens like a lid when an anther opens. 5 BRITISH. vacuum tube. 6 device in certain brass wind instruments, such as trumpets, French horns, etc., for changing the pitch of the tone by changing the direction and length of the column of air. —*v.t.* control the flow of (a liquid, gas, etc.) by a valve. [< Latin *valva* one of a pair of folding doors] —**valve′less,** *adj.* —**valve′like′,** *adj.*

val vu lar (val′vyə lər), *adj.* 1 of or having to do with valves, especially the valves of the heart. 2 having the form of a valve. 3 furnished with valves; working by valves.

va moose (va müs′), *v.t., v.i.,* **-moosed, -moos ing.** SLANG. go away quickly. [< Spanish *vamos* let us go]

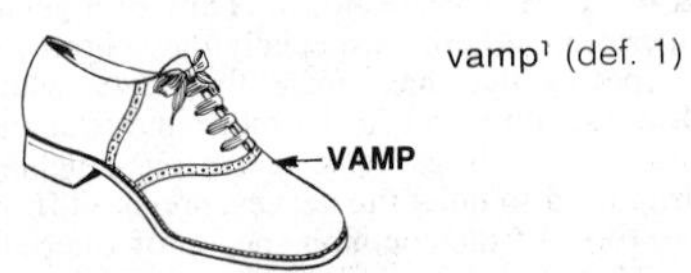

vamp[1] (def. 1)

vamp[1] (vamp), *n.* 1 the upper front part of a shoe or boot. 2 piece or patch added to an old thing to make it look new. —*v.t.* 1 furnish with a vamp; repair with a new vamp. 2 make (an old thing) look new; patch up. 3 **vamp up, a** make (something old) appear new. **b** make up to deceive: *vamp up a worthless accusation.* [< Old French *avanpié* < *avant* before + *pié* foot] —**vamp′er,** *n.*

vamp[2] (vamp), SLANG. —*n.* an unscrupulous flirt. —*v.t.* flirt with. [short for *vampire*]

vam pire (vam′pīr), *n.* 1 corpse supposed to come to life at night and suck the blood of people while they sleep. 2 person who preys ruthlessly on others. 3 woman who flirts with men to get money or to please her vanity. 4 vampire bat. [< French < German *Vampir;* of Slavic origin]

vampire bat, 1 any of various bats of South and Central America that pierce the skin of animals with their sharp teeth and drink their blood. 2 any of various other bats incorrectly supposed to drink blood.

vam pir ism (vam′pī riz′əm), *n.* 1 belief in the existence of vampires. 2 action or practice of a vampire.

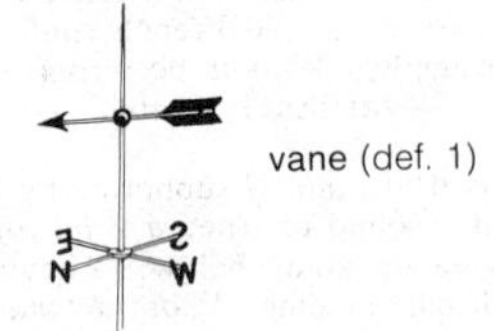

vane (def. 1)

van[1] (van), *n.* the front part of an army, fleet, or other advancing group. [short for *vanguard*]

van[2] (van), *n.* 1 a covered truck or wagon for moving furniture, etc. 2 BRITISH. a railroad baggage car. [short for *caravan*]

va na di um (və nā′dē əm), *n.* a very hard, silver-white, malleable metallic element used in making various strong alloys of steel. *Symbol:* V; *atomic number* 23. See pages 326 and 327 for table. [< *Vanadis,* Scandinavian goddess of love (because it was discovered in Sweden)]

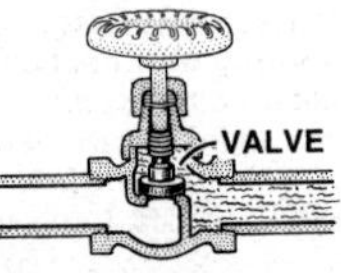

valve (def. 1)

Van Al len radiation belt (van al′ən), either of two broad bands of intense radiation in outer space that surround the earth, consisting of charged particles which are apparently held by the earth's magnetic field. [< James A. *Van Allen,* born 1914, American physicist who discovered them in 1958]

Van Bur en (van byůr′ən), **Martin,** 1782-1862, the eighth president of the United States, from 1837 to 1841.

Van cou ver (van kü′vər), *n.* 1 seaport in SW British Columbia, Canada. 410,000. 2 island in the Pacific Ocean, just off the SW coast of Canada, a part of British Columbia. 334,000 pop.; 12,400 sq. mi.

van dal (van′dl), *n.* 1 person who willfully or ignorantly destroys or damages beautiful or valuable things. 2 **Vandal,** member of a Germanic tribe that ravaged Gaul, Spain, and northern Africa. In A.D. 455 the Vandals took Rome. —*adj.* 1 destructive. 2 **Vandal,** of or having to do with the Vandals.

van dal ism (van′dl iz′əm), *n.* willful or ignorant destruction or damaging of beautiful or valuable things.

van dal ize (van′dl īz), *v.t.,* **-ized, -iz ing.** destroy willfully or senselessly.

Van de Graaff generator or **Van de Graaff accelerator** (van′ də graf′), an electrostatic generator used to produce electric potentials of very high voltages. [< Robert *Van de Graaff,* born 1901, American physicist]

Van Dyck (van dīk′), Sir **Anthony.** See **Vandyke.**

vandyke (def. 2)

Van dyke (van dīk′), *n.* 1 Sir **Anthony,** 1599-1641, Flemish painter who lived for some years in England. 2 **vandyke,** a short, pointed beard. —*adj.* of or having to do with Vandyke, or the style of dress, etc., characteristic of his portraits.

vane (vān), *n.* 1 a flat piece of metal, or some other device, fixed upon a spire or some other high object in such a way as to move with the wind and indicate its direction; weather vane; weathercock. 2 blade of a windmill, a ship's propeller, etc. 3 blade, wing, or similar part attached to an axis, wheel, etc., so as to be acted upon by a current of air or liquid or to produce a current by rotation. 4 the flat, soft part of a feather. 5 feather or strip of feather on an arrow. [Old English *fana* banner]

vaned (vānd), *adj.* furnished with a vane or vanes.

Van Gogh (van gō′), **Vincent,** 1853-1890, Dutch painter.

van guard (van′gärd′), *n.* 1 the front part of an army; soldiers marching ahead of the main part of an army to clear the way and guard against surprise. 2 the foremost or leading position. 3 leaders of a movement. [< Old French *avangarde* < *avant* before + *garde* guard]

va nil la (və nil′ə), *n.* 1 a flavoring extract made from the vanilla bean, used in candy, ice cream, etc. 2 any of a genus of climbing orchids found in tropical America, especially a species that yields the vanilla bean. 3 vanilla bean. [< New Latin < Spanish *vainilla,* literally, little pod, ultimately < Latin *vagina* sheath]

vanilla bean, the beanlike pod of the vanilla plant, used in making vanilla flavoring.

van il lin (van′l ən, və nil′ən), *n.* a crystalline compound obtained from the vanilla bean or made synthetically, used as a flavoring and in perfumery. *Formula:* $C_8H_8O_3$

van ish (van′ish), *v.i.* 1 disappear, especially suddenly: *The sun vanished behind a cloud.* See **disappear** for synonym study. 2 pass away; cease to be: *Dinosaurs have vanished from the earth.* [< Old French *esvaniss-,* a form of *esvanir* vanish, ultimately < Latin *evanescere* < *ex-* out + *vanus* empty] **—van′ish er,** *n.*

vanishing cream, a facial cream to protect the skin or serve as a base for face powder or other cosmetics.

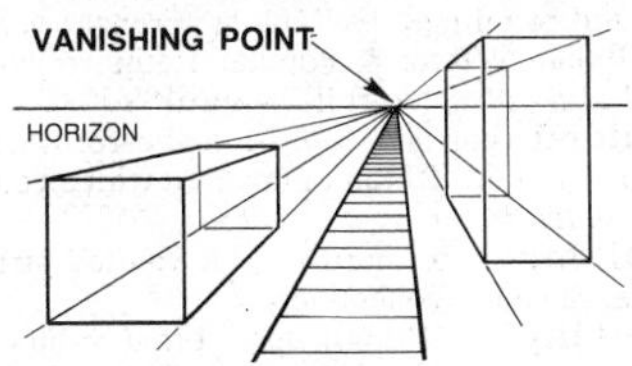

vanishing point (def. 1)

vanishing point, 1 point toward which receding parallel lines seem to converge. 2 point at which anything disappears or comes to an end.

van i to ry (van′ə tôr′ē, van′ə tōr′ē), *n., pl.* **-ries.** a bathroom fixture combining a washbasin and dressing table.

van i ty (van′ə tē), *n., pl.* **-ties.** 1 too much pride in one's looks, ability, etc. 2 lack of real value; worthlessness: *the vanity of wealth.* 3 a useless or worthless thing. 4 thing of which one is vain. 5 lack of effect or success. 6 a small handbag used by women to carry cosmetics and other toilet articles. 7 dressing table. [< Old French *vanite* < Latin *vanitatem* < *vanus* empty]

Vanity Fair, any place or scene, such as the world of fashion, regarded as given over to vain pleasure or empty show. [< fair described in John Bunyan's *Pilgrim's Progress,* symbolizing the world of vain pleasure or empty show]

van quish (vang′kwish, van′kwish), *v.t.* 1 conquer, defeat, or overcome in battle or conflict. See **defeat** for synonym study. 2 overcome or subdue by other than physical means: *vanquish fear.* [< Old French *vainquiss-,* a form of *vainquir* vanquish < Latin *vincere*] **—van′quish a ble,** *adj.* **—van′quish er,** *n.*

van tage (van′tij), *n.* 1 a better position or condition; advantage. 2 BRITISH. advantage (def. 3). [short for Middle English *advantage* advantage]

vantage ground, position that gives one an advantage; favorable position.

van ward (van′wərd), *adj., adv.* toward or in the front; forward.

vap id (vap′id), *adj.* without much life or flavor; tasteless; dull: *vapid conversation.* [< Latin *vapidus*] **—vap′id ly,** *adv.* **—vap′id ness,** *n.*

va pid i ty (va pid′ə tē), *n.* flatness of flavor; insipidity.

va por (vā′pər), *n.* 1 moisture in the air that can be seen, such as steam, fog, mist, etc., usually due to the effect of heat upon a liquid. 2 gas formed from a substance that is usually a liquid or a solid; the gaseous form of a liquid or solid. 3 something without substance; empty fancy. 4 **the vapors,** ARCHAIC. low spirits. *—v.t.* 1 cause to rise or ascend in the form of vapor. 2 boast; swagger; brag. *—v.i.* 1 rise, ascend, or pass off as vapor. 2 give or send out vapor. 3 boast; swagger; brag. [< Latin] **—va′por er,** *n.*

va por ish (vā′pər ish), *adj.* 1 like vapor. 2 abounding in vapor. 3 in low spirits; depressed. 4 having to do with or connected with low spirits: *vaporish fears.*

va por ize (vā′pə rīz′), *v.,* **-ized, -iz ing.** *—v.t.* change into vapor; cause to evaporate. *—v.i.* pass off in vapor; become vaporous. **—va′por iz′a ble,** *adj.* **—va′por i za′tion,** *n.*

va por iz er (vā′pə rī′zər), *n.* device for converting a liquid into vapor or mist, such as an apparatus that releases steam into a room for medicinal purposes.

vapor lock, interruption in the flow of fuel in a gasoline engine, occurring when excessive heat vaporizes the gasoline in the fuel line or carburetor, causing the engine to stall.

va por ous (vā′pər əs), *adj.* 1 full of vapor; misty. 2 like vapor. 3 soon passing; worthless. **—va′por ous ly,** *adv.* **—va′por ous ness,** *n.*

vapor pressure or **vapor tension,** the pressure exerted by a vapor in an enclosed space when the vapor is in equilibrium with its liquid or solid at any specified temperature.

vapor trail, contrail.

va por y (vā′pər ē), *adj.* vaporous.

va quer o (vä ker′ō), *n., pl.* **-quer os.** (in the southwestern United States) a cowboy, herdsman, or cattle driver. [< Spanish < *vaca* cow < Latin *vacca*]

var., variant.

Va ra na si (vä rä′nə sē), *n.* city in E India, on the Ganges River. It is a sacred city of the Hindus. 471,000. Former name, **Benares** or **Banaras.**

var i a bil i ty (ver′ē ə bil′ə tē, var′ē ə bil′ə tē), *n.* 1 fact or quality of being variable. 2 tendency to vary.

var i a ble (ver′ē ə bəl, var′ē ə bəl), *adj.* 1 apt to change; changeable; uncertain: *variable winds.* 2 likely to shift from one opinion or course of action to another; inconsistent. 3 that can be varied: *curtain rods of variable length.* 4 deviating from the normal or recognized species, variety, structure, etc. 5 likely to increase or decrease in size, number, amount, degree, etc.; not remaining the same or uniform: *a constant or variable ratio.* *—n.* 1 thing or quality that varies. 2 in mathematics: **a** a quantity that can assume any of the values in a given set of values. **b** symbol representing this quantity. 3 a shifting wind. **—var′i a ble ness,** *n.* **—var′i a bly,** *adv.*

hat, āge, fär; let, ēqual, tėrm;
it, īce; hot, ōpen, ôrder;
oil, out; cup, pu̇t, rüle;
ch, child; ng, long; sh, she;
th, thin; ᴛʜ, then; zh, measure;

ə represents *a* in about, *e* in taken, *i* in pencil, *o* in lemon, *u* in circus.

< = from, derived from, taken from.

variable star, star that varies periodically in magnitude.

var i ance (ver′ē əns, var′ē əns), *n.* 1 difference; disagreement: *variances in the spelling of proper names.* 2 a disagreeing or falling out; discord; quarrel. 3 a varying; change. 4 **at variance,** in disagreement; differing; disagreeing.

var i ant (ver′ē ənt, var′ē ənt), *adj.* 1 varying; different: *"Rime" is a variant spelling of "rhyme."* 2 variable; changing. *—n.* 1 a different form. 2 a different pronunciation or spelling of the same word.

var i a tion (ver′ē ā′shən, var′ē ā′shən), *n.* 1 a varying in condition, degree, etc.; change. 2 amount of change. 3 a varied or changed form. 4 (in music) a tune or theme repeated with changes in rhythm, harmony, etc. 5 in biology: **a** a deviation of an animal or plant from type. **b** animal or plant showing such deviation or divergence. 6 (in astronomy) the deviation of a heavenly body from its mean orbit or motion.

var i a tion al (ver′ē ā′shə nəl, var′ē ā′shə nəl), *adj.* of or having to do with variation.

var i cel la (var′ə sel′ə), *n.* chicken pox. [< New Latin, diminutive of *variola*]

var i col ored (ver′ē kul′ərd, var′ē kul′ərd), *adj.* having various colors.

var i cose (var′ə kōs), *adj.* 1 abnormally swollen or enlarged: *legs covered with varicose veins.* 2 having to do with, afflicted with, or designed to remedy varicose veins. [< Latin *varicosus* < *varix* dilated vein]

var i cos i ty (var′ə kos′ə tē), *n., pl.* **-ties.** 1 quality or condition of being varicose. 2 a varicose part.

var ied (ver′ēd, var′ēd), *adj.* 1 of different kinds; having variety: *a varied assortment of candies.* 2 changed; altered. **—var′ied ly,** *adv.*

var i e gate (ver′ē ə gāt, ver′i gāt; var′ē ə gāt, var′i gāt), *v.t.,* **-gat ed, -gat ing.** 1 vary in appearance; mark, spot, or streak with different colors. 2 give variety to. [< Latin *variegatum* varied < *varius* various]

var i e gat ed (ver′ē ə gā′tid, ver′i gā′tid; var′ē ə gā′tid, var′i gā′tid), *adj.* 1 varied in appearance; marked with different colors: *variegated pansies.* 2 having variety. **—var′i e ga′tion,** *n.*

va ri e tal (və rī′ə təl), *adj.* of, having to do with, or constituting a variety. **—va ri′e tal ly,** *adv.*

va ri e ty (və rī′ə tē), *n., pl.* **-ties.** 1 lack of sameness; difference or change; variation. 2 number of different kinds: *The store has a great variety of toys.* 3 kind or sort: *Which variety of cake do you prefer?* 4 group of animals or plants within a species. See **classification** for chart. 5 BRITISH. vaudeville. [< Latin *varietatem* < *varius* various]

variety show, entertainment featuring different kinds of acts, such as songs, dances, acrobatic feats, and comic skits.

va ri e ty store, store that sells a large variety of low-priced goods.

var i form (ver′ə fôrm, var′ə fôrm), *adj.* varied in form; having various forms.

va ri o la (və rī′ə lə), *n.* smallpox. [< Medieval Latin < Latin *varius* various, spotted]

var i o rum (ver′ē ôr′əm, ver′ē ōr′əm; var′ē ôr′əm, var′ē ōr′əm), *n.* edition of a book, especially of a classic, that has the comments and notes of several editors, critics, etc. *—adj.* of or like a variorum. [< Latin *(cum notis) variorum* (with notes) of various people]

var i ous (ver′ē əs, var′ē əs), *adj.* 1 differing from one another; different; diverse: *various opinions.* 2 several; many: *We looked at various houses and decided to buy this one.* 3 varied; many-sided: *lives made various by learning.* 4 varying; changeable. [< Latin *varius.* Doublet of VAIR.] **—var′i ous ly,** *adv.* **—var′i ous ness,** *n.*

var let (vär′lit), *n.* a low, mean fellow; rascal. [< Old French *varlet, vaslet* page, squire < *vassal.* See VASSAL.]

var mint (vär′mənt), *n.* DIALECT. 1 vermin. 2 an objectionable animal or person.

var nish (vär′nish), *n.* 1 a thin, transparent liquid that gives a smooth, glossy appearance to wood, metal, etc., often made from resinous substances dissolved in oil or turpentine. 2 the smooth, hard surface made by this liquid when it dries: *The varnish on the table has been scratched.* 3 a glossy appearance. 4 a false or deceiving appearance; pretense: *cover one's selfishness with a varnish of good manners.* *—v.t.* 1 put varnish on. 2 give a false or deceiving appearance to. [< Old French *vernis*] **—var′nish er,** *n.*

var si ty (vär′sə tē), *n., pl.* **-ties.** the most important team in a given sport in a university, college, or school. *—adj.* of or having to do with such a team. [< *(uni)versity*]

varve (värv), *n.* (in geology) any stratified layer of sediment deposited within one year, used in determining the lapse of time in dating geological phenomena. [< Swedish *varv* layer]

var y (ver′ē, var′ē), *v.,* **var ied, var y ing.** *—v.t.* 1 make different; change: *The driver can vary the speed of an automobile.* 2 give variety to: *vary one's style of writing.* 3 (in music) repeat (a tune or theme) with changes and ornament. *—v.i.* 1 be different; differ: *Stars vary in brightness.* 2 undergo change; show differences: *The weather varies.* 3 (in mathematics) undergo or be subject to a change in value according to some law: *vary inversely as the cube of y.* 4 (in biology) exhibit or be subject to variation, as by natural or artificial selection. [< Latin *variare* < *varius* various] **—var′y ing ly,** *adv.*

vas (vas), *n., pl.* **va sa** (vā′sə). duct or vessel. [< Latin, vessel]

vas cu lar (vas′kyə lər), *adj.* having to do with, made of, or provided with vessels that carry blood, sap, etc. [< Latin *vasculum,* diminutive of *vas* vessel]

vascular bundle, (in botany) one of the longitudinal strands of vascular tissue usually embedded in parenchymatous cells.

vas cu lar i ty (vas′kyə lar′ə tē), *n.* a vascular form or condition.

vascular plant, (in botany) plant in which the structure is made up in part of vascular tissue. Vascular plants comprise the spermatophytes and pteridophytes.

vascular tissue, (in botany) tissue in a vascular plant consisting essentially of phloem and xylem, which carries the sap throughout the plant.

vas def er ens (vas def′ər enz), *pl.* **va sa def er en ti a** (vā′sə def′ə ren′shē ə). duct that conveys semen from the testicle. [< New Latin, vessel that leads down]

vase (vās, vāz, *or* väz), *n.* holder or container used for ornament or for holding flowers. [< French < Latin *vas* vessel] **—vase′like′,** *adj.*

vas ec to my (va sek′tə mē), *n., pl.* **-mies.** the surgical cutting away of a section of the vas deferens, usually for the purpose of producing sterility.

Vas e line (vas′ə lēn′), *n.* trademark for a soft, greasy, yellow or whitish substance made from petroleum, used as a healing ointment or as a lubricant.

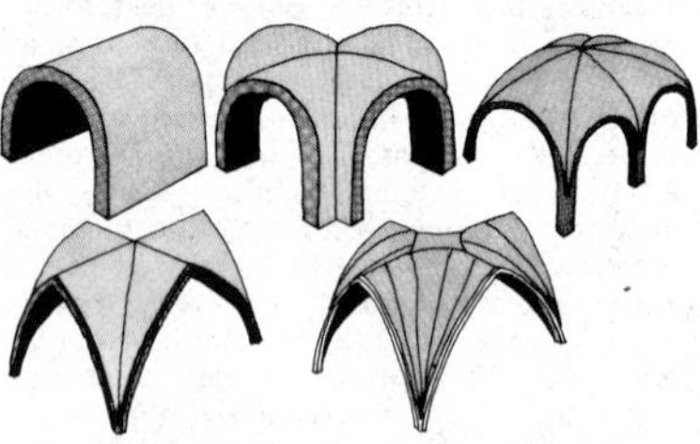

vault[1] (def. 1)—five kinds of vaults

vas o con stric tion (vas′ō kən strik′shən), *n.* constriction of the blood vessels.

vas o con stric tor (vas′ō kən strik′tər), *n.* something that constricts blood vessels, as a nerve or a drug.

vas o di la tion (vas′ō dī lā′shən, vas′ō də lā′shən), *n.* dilation of the blood vessels.

vas o di la tor (vas′ō dī lā′tər, vas′ō də lā′tər), *n.* something that dilates blood vessels, as a nerve or a drug.

vas o mo tor (vas′ō mō′tər), *adj.* of or having to do with the nerves and nerve centers that regulate the size of the blood vessels.

vas sal (vas′əl), *n.* 1 (in the feudal system) a person who held land from a lord or superior, to whom in return he gave homage and allegiance, usually in the form of military service. 2 person in the service of another; servant. *—adj.* like a vassal; like that of a vassal. [< Old French < Medieval Latin *vassallus* < *vassus* servant; of Celtic origin]

vas sal age (vas′ə lij), *n.* 1 condition of being a vassal. 2 the homage or service due from a vassal to his lord or superior. 3 land held by a vassal. 4 dependence; servitude.

vast (vast), *adj.* very great; immense: *Texas and Alaska cover vast territories. A billion dollars is a vast amount.* *—n.* an immense space. [< Latin *vastus*] **—vast′ly,** *adv.* **—vast′ness,** *n.*

vast y (vas′tē), *adj.* vast; immense.

vat (vat), *n.* a large container for liquids; tank: *a vat of dye.* [Old English *fæt*]

vat ic (vat′ik), *adj.* prophetic; inspired. [< Latin *vates* prophet]

Vat i can (vat′ə kən), *n.* 1 the collection of buildings grouped about the palace of the pope in Rome. 2 the government, office, or authority of the pope.

Vatican City, an independent state inside Rome, Italy, ruled by the pope and including Saint Peter's Church and the Vatican, established in 1929. 1000 pop.; 109 acres.

Vatican Council, 1 Also, **Vatican I.** the twentieth ecumenical council of the Roman Catholic Church which met at the Vatican in 1869 and was indefinitely suspended in 1870. 2 Also, **Vatican II.** the twenty-first ecumenical council, which met at the Vatican from 1962 to 1965.

va tic i nate (və tis′n āt), *v.t., v.i.,* **-nat ed, -nat ing.** prophesy; predict. [< Latin *vaticinatum* prophesied < *vaticinus* prophetic < *vates* prophet] **—va tic′i na′tion,** *n.*

vau de ville (vô′də vil, vôd′vil, vōd′vil), *n.* theatrical entertainment featuring a variety of acts, such as songs, dances, acrobatic feats, skits, trained animals, etc. [< French, alteration of *vaudevire* < *(chanson de) Vau de Vire* (song of the) valley of Vire, region in Normandy]

vau de vil lian (vô′də vil′yən, vōd vil′yən), *n.* person who performs in or writes songs, skits, etc., for vaudeville. *—adj.* of vaudeville.

Vaughan Wil liams (vôn′ wil′yəmz), **Ralph,** 1872-1958, British composer.

vault[1] (vôlt), *n.* 1 an arched roof or ceiling; series of arches. 2 an arched space or passage. 3 something like an arched roof: *the vault of heaven.* 4 an underground cellar or storehouse. 5 place for storing valuable things and keeping them safe. Vaults are often made of steel. 6 place for burial. *—v.t.* 1 make in the form of a vault. 2 cover with a vault. [< Old French *vaulte* < Latin *volutum* rolled] **—vault′like′,** *adj.*

vault[2] (vôlt), *v.t.* jump or leap over by using a pole or the hands. *—v.i.* jump or leap. *—n.* act of vaulting. [< Middle French *volter* < Italian *voltare* < Popular Latin *volvitare* < Latin *volvere* to roll] **—vault′er,** *n.*

vault ed (vôl′tid), *adj.* 1 in the form of a vault; arched. 2 built or covered with a vault: *a vaulted room.*

vault ing[1] (vôl′ting), *n.* 1 a vaulted structure. 2 vaults collectively.

vault ing[2] (vôl′ting), *adj.* 1 that vaults or leaps, especially in an overzealous manner: *vaulting ambition.* 2 used in or for vaulting: *a vaulting horse.*

vaunt (vônt, vänt), *v.t.* boast of. *—v.i.* brag or boast. *—n.* a boasting assertion or speech; brag. [< Old French *vanter* < Late Latin *vanitare* be vain, boast < *vanus* vain] **—vaunt′er,** *n.* **—vaunt′ing ly,** *adv.*

vb., 1 verb. 2 verbal.

V.C., 1 Vice-Chairman. 2 Victoria Cross. 3 Vietcong.

V.D. or **VD,** venereal disease.

V-Day (vē′dā′), *n.* December 31, 1946, the day marking the victory of the Allied forces in World War II.

veal (vēl), *n.* 1 flesh of a calf, used for food. 2 a calf, especially as killed or intended for food. [< Old French *veel* < Latin *vitellus,* diminutive of *vitulus* calf]

Veb len (veb′lən), *n.* **Thorstein,** 1857-1929, American economist.

vec tor (vek′tər), *n.* 1 in mathematics: **a** a quantity involving direction as well as magnitude. **b** one of a set of equal and parallel directed line segments representing such a

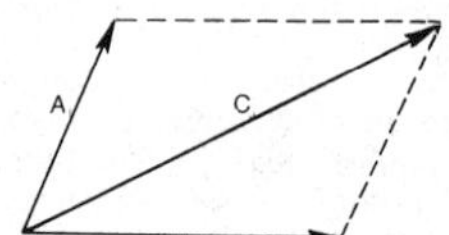

vector (def. 1b)—A and B are vectors. C is the resultant of vectors A and B and is equal to A + B.

quantity. The direction of the line segment indicates the direction of the vector, and its length indicates the magnitude of the vector. 2 organism that transmits disease germs, such as a mosquito or a tick. [< Latin, carrier < *vehere* carry]

vec to ri al (vek tôr′ē əl, vek tōr′ē əl), *adj.* of or having to do with a vector or vectors.

Ve da (vā′də, vē′də), *n.* any or all of the four collections of sacred writings of the ancient Hindus. [< Sanskrit *vēda* knowledge]

Ve dan ta (vi dän′tə, vi dan′tə), *n.* system of Hindu philosophy founded on the Vedas. [< Sanskrit *vēdanta* < *vēda* knowledge + *anta* the end]

Ve dan tic (vi dän′tik, vi dan′tik), *adj.* of the Vedanta.

V-E Day (vē′ē′), May 8, 1945, day of the Allied victory in Europe in World War II.

ve dette (vi det′), *n.* 1 a mounted sentry stationed in advance of the outposts of an army. 2 a small naval vessel used for scouting. Also, **vidette.** [< French < Italian *vedetta* < *vedere* to see]

Ve dic (vā′dik, vē′dik), *adj.* of, having to do with, or contained in the Vedas.

Veep (vēp), *n.* SLANG. 1 the Vice-President of the United States. 2 **veep,** any vice-president. [< pronunciation of *VP,* abbreviation of *Vice-President*]

veer (vir), *v.i.* change in direction; shift; turn: *The wind veered to the south. The talk veered to ghosts.* —*v.t.* change the direction of: *We veered our boat.* —*n.* a change of direction; shift; turn. [< Middle French *virer*] —**veer′ing ly,** *adv.*

veer y (vir′ē), *n., pl.* **veer ies.** thrush of eastern North America with tawny head, back, and tail and a faintly spotted white breast. [probably imitative]

Ve ga (vē′gə), *n.* a bluish-white star of the first magnitude, the brightest in the constellation Lyra and in the summer sky.

veg e ta ble (vej′ə tə bəl, vej′tə bəl), *n.* 1 plant whose fruit, shoots or stems, leaves, roots, or other parts are used for food. Peas, corn, lettuce, tomatoes, and beets are vegetables. 2 the part of such a plant which is used for food. 3 any plant. 4 person who lives a vegetative existence; dull, passive person. —*adj.* 1 of, having to do with, or like plants: *vegetable life.* 2 consisting of or made from vegetables: *vegetable soup.* 3 like that of a vegetable; uneventful; dull; vegetative: *a vegetable existence.* [< Late Latin *vegetabilis* vivifying, refreshing < Latin *vegetare* enliven < *vegetus* vigorous]

vegetable kingdom, division of the natural world that includes all plants. See **classification** for chart.

vegetable marrow, an oblong squash with a green skin that turns light yellow.

vegetable oil, any oil obtained from the fruit or seeds of plants, such as olive oil, peanut oil, corn oil, and linseed oil.

veg e ta bly (vej′ə tə blē, vej′tə blē), *adv.* in the manner of a vegetable.

veg e tal (vej′ə təl), *adj.* of or like plants.

veg e tar i an (vej′ə ter′ē ən), *n.* person who eats only vegetable foods and abstains from meat, fish, or other animal products. —*adj.* 1 eating vegetable foods only. 2 devoted to or advocating vegetarianism. 3 containing no meat: *a vegetarian diet.* 4 serving no meat: *a vegetarian restaurant.*

veg e tar i an ism (vej′ə ter′ē ə niz′əm), *n.* practice or principle of eating only vegetable foods and abstaining from meat, fish, or other animal products.

veg e tate (vej′ə tāt), *v.i.,* **-tat ed, -tat ing.** 1 grow as plants do. 2 live with very little action, thought, or feeling. 3 (in pathology) grow or increase in size abnormally.

veg e ta tion (vej′ə tā′shən), *n.* 1 plant life; growing plants: *There is not much vegetation in deserts.* 2 act or process of vegetating; growth of plants. 3 an existence similar to that of a vegetable; dull, empty, or stagnant life. 4 (in pathology) an abnormal growth occurring on some part of the body.

veg e ta tion al (vej′ə tā′shə nəl), *adj.* of or having to do with vegetation.

veg e ta tive (vej′ə tā′tiv), *adj.* 1 growing as plants do. 2 of plants or plant life. 3 (in botany) concerned with growth and development rather than reproduction: *vegetative organs.* 4 of or having to do with unconscious or involuntary functions of the body: *the vegetative processes of the body, such as growth and repair.* 5 having very little action, thought, or feeling. —**veg′e ta′tive ly,** *adv.* —**veg′e ta′tive ness,** *n.*

vegetative reproduction, asexual reproduction by means of budding, fission, etc.

ve he mence (vē′ə məns), *n.* vehement quality or nature; strong feeling; forcefulness; violence.

ve he ment (vē′ə mənt), *adj.* 1 having or showing strong feeling; caused by strong feeling; eager; passionate. 2 forceful; violent. [< Latin *vehementem* being carried away < *vehere* carry] —**ve′he ment ly,** *adv.*

ve hi cle (vē′ə kəl), *n.* 1 any means of carrying, conveying, or transporting: *a space vehicle.* 2 carriage, cart, wagon, automobile, sled, or any other conveyance used on land. 3 means or medium by which something is communicated, shown, done, etc.: *Language is the vehicle of thought.* 4 (in painting) a liquid into which pigment is mixed to apply color to a surface: *Linseed oil is a vehicle for paint.* [< Latin *vehiculum* < *vehere* carry]

ve hic u lar (vi hik′yə lər), *adj.* 1 of or having to do with vehicles. 2 of the nature of or serving as a vehicle.

veil (def. 2) two styles

veil (vāl), *n.* 1 piece of very thin material worn to protect or hide the face, or as an ornament. 2 piece of material worn so as to fall over the head and shoulders. 3 anything that screens or hides: *a veil of clouds, a veil of deception.* 4 **take the veil,** become a nun. —*v.t.* 1 cover with a veil. 2 cover, screen, or hide: *Fog veiled the shore. They veiled their plans in secrecy.* [< Anglo-French < Latin *vela,* plural of *velum* covering. Doublet of VELUM, VOILE.] —**veil′like′,** *adj.*

veil ing (vā′ling), *n.* 1 a veil. 2 material for veils.

vein (vān), *n.* 1 any of the membranous tubes forming part of the system of vessels that carry blood to the heart from all parts of the body. 2 one of the vascular bundles forming the principal framework of a leaf. 3 one of the ribs that strengthen the wing of an insect. 4 a small natural channel within the earth through which water trickles or flows. 5 a crack or seam in rock filled with a deposit, especially of metallic ore: *a vein of copper.* 6 any streak or marking of a different shade or color in wood, marble, etc. 7 a special character or disposition; state of mind; mood: *a vein of cruelty, a joking vein.* —*v.t.* cover or mark with veins. [< Old French *veine* < Latin *vena*] —**vein′less,** *adj.* —**vein′like′,** *adj.*

veined (vānd), *adj.* having or showing veins: *veined marble.*

vein ing (vā′ning), *n.* arrangement of veins.

vein let (vān′lit), *n.* venule.

vein y (vā′nē), *adj.,* **vein i er, vein i est.** of, having to do with, or full of veins.

ve lar (vē′lər), *adj.* 1 of or having to do with a velum, especially the soft palate. 2 (in phonetics) pronounced with the back of the tongue raised toward or against the soft palate. *G* in *goose* has a velar sound, *g* in *geese* does not. —*n.* (in phonetics) a velar sound.

Ve láz quez (və läs′kes), *n.* **Diego Rodríguez de Silva y,** 1599-1660, Spanish painter.

veld or **veldt** (velt, felt), *n.* the open, grass-covered plains of southern Africa, often with bushes but having few trees. [< Afrikaans *veld* < Dutch, field]

vel le i ty (və lē′ə tē), *n., pl.* **-ties.** 1 fact or quality of wishing or desiring. 2 a mere wish or slight inclination. [< Latin *velle* to wish]

vel lum (vel′əm), *n.* 1 the finest kind of parchment, usually prepared from the skins of calves and lambs, used instead of paper, especially formerly, for writing, for binding books, etc. 2 paper or cloth imitating such parchment. —*adj.* of vellum. [< Old French *velin* < *veel* calf. See VEAL.]

ve loc i pede (və los′ə pēd′), *n.* 1 a child's tricycle. 2 an early kind of bicycle or tricycle. [< French *vélocipède* < Latin *velox* swift + *pedem* foot]

ve loc i ty (və los′ə tē), *n., pl.* **-ties.** 1 quickness of motion; speed; swiftness: *fly with the velocity of a bird. The velocity of light is about 186,000 miles per second.* 2 rate of motion in a particular direction. 3 the absolute or relative rate of operation or action. [< Latin *velocitatem* < *velox* swift]

ve lour or **ve lours** (və lür′), *n.* fabric like velvet, usually made of silk, wool, cotton, or rayon, used for clothing, draperies, upholstery, etc. [< French *velours* velvet, earlier *velous,* ultimately < Latin *villus* shaggy hair]

ve lum (vē′ləm), *n., pl.* **-la** (-lə). 1 a veillike membranous covering or partition. 2 the soft palate. [< Latin, covering. Doublet of VEIL, VOILE.]

ve lure (və lür′), *n.* 1 a soft material like velvet. 2 a soft pad used for smoothing silk hats. [variant of *velour.* See VELOUR.]

vel vet (vel′vit), *n.* 1 cloth with a thick, soft pile, made of silk, rayon, cotton, etc. 2 something like velvet. 3 the furry skin that covers the growing antlers of a deer.

hat, āge, fär; let, ēqual, tėrm;
it, īce; hot, ōpen, ôrder;
oil, out; cup, pu̇t, rüle;
ch, child; ng, long; sh, she;
th, thin; ᴛʜ, then; zh, measure;

ə represents *a* in about, *e* in taken, *i* in pencil, *o* in lemon, *u* in circus.

< = from, derived from, taken from.

4 SLANG. clear profit or gain. —*adj.* 1 made of velvet. 2 covered with velvet. 3 like velvet; velvety: *a cat's velvet paws.* [< Medieval Latin *velvetum,* ultimately < Latin *villus* tuft of hair] **—vel′vet like′,** *adj.*

vel vet een (vel′və tēn′), *n.* a cotton fabric resembling velvet. —*adj.* made of velveteen.

vel vet y (vel′və tē), *adj.* 1 smooth and soft like velvet. 2 smooth and soft to the taste.

Ven., 1 Venerable. 2 Venice.

ve na ca va (vē′nə kā′və), *n., pl.* **ve nae ca vae** (vē′nē kā′vē). either of two large veins that empty blood from the upper and lower halves of the body into the right auricle of the heart. [< Latin, hollow vein]

ve nal (vē′nl), *adj.* 1 willing to sell one's services or influence basely; open to bribes; corrupt: *venal officials.* 2 influenced or obtained by bribery: *venal conduct.* [< Latin *venalis* < *venum* sale] **—ve′nal ly,** *adv.*

ve nal i ty (vē nal′ə tē), *n.* quality of being venal.

ve na tion (vē nā′shən), *n.* 1 arrangement of veins in a leaf, in an insect's wing, etc.; nervation. 2 these veins. [< Latin *vena* vein]

vend (vend), *v.t.* sell; peddle. [< Latin *vendere* < *venum dare* offer for sale]

vend ee (ven dē′), *n.* person to whom a thing is sold; buyer.

vend er (ven′dər), *n.* 1 vendor. 2 vending machine.

ven det ta (ven det′ə), *n.* feud in which a murdered man's relatives try to kill the slayer or his relatives. [< Italian < Latin *vindicta* revenge]

vend i bil i ty (ven′də bil′ə tē), *n.* salable quality; a being marketable.

vend i ble (ven′də bəl), *adj.* salable; marketable. —*n.* a salable thing.

vending machine, machine from which one obtains candy, stamps, etc., when a coin is dropped in.

ven di tion (ven dish′ən), *n.* act of selling or peddling; sale.

ven dor (ven′dər), *n.* seller; peddler. Also, **vender.**

ven due (ven dü′, ven dyü′), *n.* a public sale or auction. [< Old French, sale < *vendre* sell < Latin *vendere.* See VEND.]

ve neer (və nir′), *v.t.* 1 cover (wood) with a thin layer of finer wood or other material: *veneer a pine desk with mahogany.* 2 cover (anything) with a layer of something else to give an appearance of superior quality. —*n.* 1 a thin layer of wood or other material used in veneering: *The panel had a veneer of gold and ivory.* 2 one of the thin layers of wood used in making plywood. 3 surface appearance or show: *treachery hidden by a veneer of friendship.* [earlier *fineer* < German *furnieren* < French *fournir* furnish] **—ve neer′er,** *n.*

ven er a bil i ty (ven′ər ə bil′ə tē), *n.* fact or quality of being venerable.

ven er a ble (ven′ər ə bəl), *adj.* 1 worthy of reverence; deserving respect because of age, character, or importance: *a venerable priest, venerable customs.* 2 designating an archdeacon of the Anglican Church (used as a title of respect). 3 (in the Roman Catholic Church) designating a person recognized as having attained a degree of virtue but not yet recognized as beatified or canonized. **—ven′er a bly,** *adv.*

ven e rate (ven′ə rāt′), *v.t.,* **-rat ed, -rat ing.** regard with deep respect; revere: *He venerates his father's memory.* [< Latin *veneratum* revered < *Venus* Venus, originally, love] **—ven′e ra′tor,** *n.*

ven e ra tion (ven′ə rā′shən), *n.* 1 a feeling of deep respect; reverence: *veneration for learning.* 2 act of venerating: *veneration of one's ancestors.* 3 condition of being venerated.

ve ner e al (və nir′ē əl), *adj.* 1 of, having to do with, or transmitted by sexual intercourse: *a venereal disease.* 2 having to do with diseases transmitted by sexual intercourse. 3 infected with syphilis, gonorrhea, or other venereal disease. [< Latin *venereus* < *Venus* Venus] **—ve ner′e al ly,** *adv.*

ven er y^1 (ven′ər ē), *n.* practice or pursuit of sexual pleasure; gratification of sexual desire. [< Latin *Venus.* See VENEREAL.]

ven er y^2 (ven′ər ē), *n.* the practice or sport of hunting; the chase. [< Old French *venerie,* ultimately < Latin *venari* to hunt]

ven e sec tion (ven′ə sek′shən), *n.* phlebotomy. [< Latin *vena* vein]

Ve ne ti a (və nē′shē ə, və nē′shə), *n.* 1 division of N Italy during Roman times. 2 district in NE Italy.

Ve ne tian (və nē′shən), *adj.* of Venice or its people. —*n.* native or inhabitant of Venice.

Venetian blind, a window blind made of many horizontal wooden, steel, or aluminum slats that can be opened or closed to regulate the light that is allowed in.

Venez., Venezuela.

Ve ne zia (vā nā′tsyä), *n.* Italian name of **Venice.**

Ven e zue la (ven′ə zwā′lə, ven′ə zwē′lə), *n.* country in the N part of South America. 10,778,000 pop.; 352,100 sq. mi. *Capital:* Caracas. **—Ven′e zue′lan,** *adj., n.*

venge ance (ven′jəns), *n.* 1 punishment in return for a wrong; revenge: *swear vengeance against an enemy.* 2 **with a vengeance, a** with great force or violence. **b** extremely. **c** much more than expected. [< Old French < *vengier* avenge < Latin *vindicare* < *vindex* avenger]

venge ful (venj′fəl), *adj.* feeling or showing a strong desire for vengeance; vindictive. **—venge′ful ly,** *adv.* **—venge′ful ness,** *n.*

ve ni al (vē′nē əl, vē′nyəl), *adj.* that can be forgiven; not very wrong or sinful; wrong but pardonable. [< Latin *venialis* < *venia* forgiveness] **—ve′ni al ly,** *adv.* **—ve′ni al ness,** *n.*

Ven ice (ven′is), *n.* 1 city on the NE coast of Italy. Venice has many canals in place of streets. 368,000. Also, ITALIAN **Venezia.** 2 **Gulf of,** the northern part of the Adriatic.

ve ni re (və nī′rē), *n.* writ issued to a sheriff requiring him to summon persons to serve on a jury. [< Latin *venire facias* you may cause (him) to come]

ve ni re man (və nī′rē mən), *n., pl.* **-men.** person summoned to serve on a jury by a writ of venire.

ven i son (ven′ə sən, ven′ə zən), *n.* 1 the flesh of a deer, used for food; deer meat. 2 (formerly) the flesh of any animal killed by hunting. [< Old French *venesoun* < Latin *venationem* a hunting < *venari* to hunt]

Ve ni te (vi nī′tē), *n.* the 95th Psalm (94th in the Vulgate), recited as a canticle at matins or morning prayer. [< Latin *venite* come ye! (the first word in the Latin version)]

ve ni, vi di, vi ci (vē′nī vī′dī vī′sī; wā′nē wē′dē wē′kē), LATIN. I came, I saw, I conquered (a report of victory made by Julius Caesar to the Roman Senate).

Venn diagram (ven), diagram using circles and rectangles to represent various types of mathematical sets and to show the relationship between them. [< John *Venn,* 1834-1923, English logician]

ven om (ven′əm), *n.* 1 the poison secreted by some snakes, spiders, scorpions, lizards, etc., and injected into their prey by biting, stinging, etc. 2 spite; malice: *speak of one's enemies with venom.* [< Old French *venim, venin* < Latin *venenum* poison] **—ven′om less,** *adj.*

ven om ous (ven′ə məs), *adj.* 1 poisonous: *a venomous bite, a venomous snake.* 2 spiteful; malicious. **—ven′om ous ly,** *adv.* **—ven′om ous ness,** *n.*

ve nous (vē′nəs), *adj.* 1 of a vein or the veins. 2 contained in the veins. Venous blood is dark-red after having given up oxygen and become charged with carbon dioxide. 3 having veins: *the venous wings of insects.* [< Latin *venosus* < *vena* vein] **—ve′nous ly,** *adv.* **—ve′nous ness,** *n.*

vent^1 (vent), *n.* 1 hole or opening, especially one serving as an outlet. 2 a way out; outlet; escape: *His great energy found vent in hard work.* 3 free expression: *give vent to one's grief in tears.* 4 the excretory opening at the end of the digestive tract, especially in birds, reptiles, amphibians, and fishes. 5 the small opening in the barrel of a gun by which fire is communicated to the powder. 6 a small window in an automobile, etc., that can be opened for indirect ventilation. —*v.t.* 1 let out; express freely: *He vented his anger on the dog.* 2 make a vent in. [< Old French *vent* wind and *évent* vent, blowhole, both ultimately < Latin *ventus* wind]

vent^2 (vent), *n.* slit in a garment. [< Middle French *fente* slit < *fendre* to split < Latin *findere*]

ven tail (ven′tāl), *n.* the lower, movable part on the front of a helmet of armor. [< Old French *ventaille* < *vent* wind, air]

ven ti late (ven′tl āt), *v.t.,* **-lat ed, -lat ing.** 1 change the air in: *ventilate a room by opening windows.* 2 purify by fresh air: *The lungs ventilate the blood.* 3 make known publicly; discuss openly. 4 furnish with a vent or opening for the escape of air, gas, etc. [< Latin *ventilatum* fanned < *ventus* wind]

ven ti la tion (ven′tl ā′shən), *n.* 1 change of air; act or process of supplying with fresh air. 2 means of supplying fresh air. 3 a purifying by fresh air. 4 an open discussion in public.

ven ti la tive (ven′tl ā′tiv), *adj.* of or having to do with ventilation.

ven ti la tor (ven′tl ā′tər), *n.* any apparatus or means, such as an opening, an air conditioner, or a fan, for changing or improving the air in an enclosed space.

ven tral (ven′trəl), *adj.* 1 of or having to do with the belly; abdominal. 2 of, having to do with, or situated on or near the surface or part opposite the back. [< Late Latin *ventralis* < Latin *venter* belly] **—ven′tral ly,** *adv.*

ven tri cle (ven′trə kəl), *n.* 1 either of the two chambers of the heart that receive blood from the auricles and force it into the arteries. See **heart** for diagram. 2 any of a series of connecting cavities in the brain. 3 any hollow organ or cavity of the body [< Latin *ventriculus,* diminutive of *venter* belly]

ven tric u lar (ven trik′yə lər), *adj.* of, having to do with, or like a ventricle.

hat, āge, fär; let, ēqual, tėrm;
it, īce; hot, ōpen, ôrder;
oil, out; cup, pu̇t, rüle;
ch, child; ng, long; sh, she;
th, thin; ᴛʜ, then; zh, measure;

ə represents *a* in about, *e* in taken, *i* in pencil, *o* in lemon, *u* in circus.

< = from, derived from, taken from.

---

ven tri lo qui al (ven′trə lō′kwē əl), *adj.* having to do with ventriloquism.

ven tril o quism (ven tril′ə kwiz′əm), *n.* art or practice of speaking or uttering sounds with the lips immobilized so that the voice may seem to come from some source other than the speaker. [< Latin *ventriloquus* ventriloquist < *venter* belly + *loqui* speak; because of the belief that the voice came from the ventriloquist's stomach]

ven tril o quist (ven tril′ə kwist), *n.* person skilled in ventriloquism, especially a performer who uses a puppet with whom he pretends to carry on a conversation.

ven tril o quis tic (ven tril′ə kwis′tik), *adj.* of or having to do with ventriloquism.

ven tril o quize (ven tril′ə kwīz), *v.i., v.t.,* **-quized, -quiz ing.** speak or utter as a ventriloquist.

ven tril o quy (ven tril′ə kwē), *n.* ventriloquism.

ven ture (ven′chər), *n., v.,* **-tured, -tur ing.** —*n.* 1 a risky or daring undertaking: *courage equal to any venture.* 2 speculation to make money: *A lucky venture in oil stock made her rich.* 3 thing risked; stake. 4 **at a venture,** at random; by chance. —*v.t.* 1 expose to risk or danger: *Men venture their lives in war.* 2 run the risk of: *venture battle in the night.* 3 dare to say or make: *She ventured an objection.* 4 dare when embarrassment, rejection, or rebuff might follow: *No one ventured to interrupt the speaker.* See **dare** for synonym study. —*v.i.* dare to come, go, or proceed: *They ventured out on the thin ice and fell through.* [short for *aventure,* an earlier form of *adventure*] **—ven′tur er,** *n.*

ven ture some (ven′chər səm), *adj.* 1 inclined to take risks; rash; daring. 2 hazardous; risky. **—ven′ture some ly,** *adv.* **—ven′ture some ness,** *n.*

ven tur ous (ven′chər əs), *adj.* 1 bold or rash; daring; adventurous. 2 risky; dangerous. **—ven′tur ous ly,** *adv.* **—ven′tur ous ness,** *n.*

ven ue (ven′yü), *n.* 1 the place or neighborhood of a crime or cause of action. 2 the place where the jury is summoned and the case tried: *The prisoner's lawyer asked for a change of venue because the county was so prejudiced against the prisoner.* [< Old French, a coming < *venir* come < Latin *venire*]

ven ule (ven′yül), *n.* a small or minor vein; veinlet.

Ve nus (vē′nəs), *n.* 1 (in Roman myths) the goddess of love and beauty, identified with the Greek goddess Aphrodite. 2 a very beautiful woman. 3 the sixth largest planet and the most brilliant in the solar system, second in distance from the sun.

Ve nu si an (və nü′sē ən, və nyü′sē ən), *adj.* of or having to do with the planet Venus.

Ve nus's-fly trap (vē′nə siz flī′trap′), *n.* plant of the same family as the sundew, grown along the coasts of the Carolinas, whose hairy leaves have two lobes at the end that fold together to trap and digest insects.

ve ra cious (və rā′shəs), *adj.* 1 truthful. 2 true. [< Latin *veracis* < *verus* true] **—ve ra′cious ly,** *adv.* **—ve ra′cious ness,** *n.*

ve rac i ty (və ras′ə tē), *n., pl.* **-ties.** 1 truthfulness. 2 truth. 3 correctness; accuracy.

Ver a cruz (ver′ə krüz′), *n.* seaport in SE Mexico. 242,300.

Vera Cruz, Veracruz.

ve ran da or **ve ran dah** (və ran′də), *n.* a large porch or gallery along one or more sides of a house. [< Hindustani *varandā*]

verb (vėrb), *n.* any of a class of words used to tell what is or what is done; part of speech that expresses action or being, or that serves to connect a subject with a predicate. Verbs may be inflected for person, tense, voice, and mood. English verbs are classified as transitive or intransitive. *Do, go, come, be, sit, think, know,* and *eat* are verbs. [< Latin *verbum,* originally, word]

ver bal (vėr′bəl), *adj.* 1 in words; of words: *A description is a verbal picture.* 2 expressed in spoken words; oral: *a verbal promise, a verbal message.* 3 word for word; literal: *a verbal translation from the French.* 4 having to do with a verb. Two common verbal endings are *-ed* and *-ing.* 5 derived from a verb: *a verbal adjective.* —*n.* noun, adjective, or other word derived from a verb. **—ver′bal ly,** *adv.* ➔ See **oral** for usage note.

ver bal ism (vėr′bə liz′əm), *n.* 1 a verbal expression; word or phrase. 2 too much attention to mere words. 3 a stock phrase or formula in words with little meaning.

ver bal ist (vėr′bə list), *n.* 1 person who is skilled in the use or choice of words. 2 person who pays too much attention to mere words.

ver bal ize (vėr′bə līz), *v.,* **-ized, -iz ing.** —*v.t.* 1 express in words. 2 change (a noun, etc.) into a verb. —*v.i.* use too many words; be wordy. **—ver′bal i za′tion,** *n.* **—ver′bal iz′er,** *n.*

verbal noun, 1 noun derived from a verb. 2 infinitive or gerund functioning as a noun but retaining such characteristics of a verb as being modified by adverbs and taking objects. EXAMPLE: *To dance* (infinitive) gracefully is fun. *Dancing* (gerund) a polka can be strenuous.

ver ba tim (vər bā′tim), *adv., adj.* word for word; in exactly the same words: *a speech printed verbatim in the newspaper, a verbatim report.* [< Medieval Latin < Latin *verbum* word]

ver be na (vər bē′nə), *n.* any of a genus of garden plants with elongated or flattened spikes of flowers having various colors; vervain. [< Latin, leafy branch]

ver bi age (vėr′bē ij), *n.* use of too many words; abundance of useless words or words hard to understand: *a contract full of legal verbiage.*

ver bose (vər bōs′), *adj.* using too many words; wordy. See **wordy** for synonym study. **—ver bose′ly,** *adv.* **—ver bose′ness,** *n.*

ver bos i ty (vər bos′ə tē), *n.* use of too many words; wordiness.

ver bo ten (fer bōt′n), *adj.* GERMAN. absolutely forbidden by authority; prohibited.

ver dan cy (vėrd′n sē), *n.* 1 greenness. 2 inexperience.

ver dant (vėrd′nt), *adj.* 1 green: *verdant hills, verdant grass.* 2 inexperienced. [< *verdure*] **—ver′dant ly,** *adv.*

Verde (vėrd), *n.* **Cape,** the most western point of Africa, in Senegal.

Ver di (ver′dē), *n.* **Giuseppe,** 1813-1901, Italian composer of operas.

ver dict (vėr′dikt), *n.* 1 the decision of a jury: *The jury returned a verdict of "Not guilty."* 2 any decision or judgment. [< Anglo-French *verdit* < Old French *ver* true + *dit* spoken]

ver di gris (vėr′də grēs′, vėr′də gris), *n.* 1 a green or bluish coating that forms on brass, copper, or bronze when exposed to the air for long periods of time. 2 a green or bluish-green poisonous compound obtained by the action of acetic acid on thin plates of copper, used as a pigment, in dyeing, and in insecticides. [< Old French *vert de grice,* literally, green of Greece]

Ver dun (vər dun′), *n.* town and fortifications in NE France, on the Meuse River. 22,000.

ver dure (vėr′jər), *n.* 1 fresh greenness. 2 a fresh growth of green grass, plants, or leaves. [< Old French < *verd* green < Latin *viridis* < *virere* be green]

ver dur ous (vėr′jər əs), *adj.* green and fresh. **—ver′dur ous ness,** *n.*

verge[1] (vėrj), *n., v.,* **verged, verg ing.** —*n.* 1 the point at which something begins or happens; brink: *business on the verge of ruin.* 2 a limiting edge, margin, or bound of something; border: *the verge of a cliff.* 3 rod, staff, etc., carried as an emblem of authority. 4 shaft of a column. —*v.i.* be on the verge; border: *Their silly talk verged on nonsense.* [< Old French < Latin *virga* staff, rod]

verge[2] (vėrj), *v.i.,* **verged, verg ing.** tend; incline: *She was plump, verging toward fatness.* [< Latin *vergere*]

ver ger (vėr′jər), *n.* 1 person who takes care of a church; sexton. 2 official who carries a rod, staff, or similar symbol of office before the dignitaries of a cathedral, church, or university.

Ver gil (vėr′jəl), *n.* 70-19 B.C., Roman poet, author of *The Aeneid.* Also, **Virgil.**

Ver gil i an (vər jil′ē ən), *adj.* of, having to do with, or suggestive of Vergil or his poetry. Also, **Virgilian.**

ver i est (ver′ē ist), *adj.* utmost: *the veriest nonsense.*

ver i fi a ble (ver′ə fī′ə bəl), *adj.* that can be verified. **—ver′i fi′a bly,** *adv.*

ver i fi ca tion (ver′ə fə kā′shən), *n.* proof by evidence or testimony; confirmation.

ver i fy (ver′ə fī), *v.t.,* **-fied, -fy ing.** 1 prove to be true; confirm: *The driver's report of the accident was verified by eyewitnesses.* 2 test the correctness of; check for accuracy: *You can verify the spelling of a word by looking in a dictionary.* [< Old French *verifier* < Medieval Latin *verificare* < Latin *verus* true + *facere* to make] **—ver′i fi′er,** *n.*

ver i ly (ver′ə lē), *adv.* ARCHAIC. in truth; truly; really. [< *very* + *-ly*[1]]

ver i sim i lar (ver′ə sim′ə lər), *adj.* appearing true or real; probable. **—ver′i sim′i lar ly,** *adv.*

ver i si mil i tude (ver′ə sə mil′ə tüd, ver′ə sə mil′ə tyüd), *n.* 1 appearance of truth or reality; probability: *give verisimilitude to myth.* 2 something having merely the appearance of truth. [< Latin *verisimilitudo* < *verus* true + *similis* like]

ver i ta ble (ver′ə tə bəl), *adj.* true; real;

actual. **—ver′i ta ble ness,** *n.* **—ver′i ta-bly,** *adv.*

ver i ty (ver′ə tē), *n., pl.* **-ties.** 1 truth. 2 a true statement or fact. 3 reality. [< Latin *veritatem* < *verus* true]

ver juice (vėr′jüs), *n.* 1 an acid liquor made from juice of crab apples, unripe grapes, or other sour fruits, formerly much used in cooking. 2 sourness, as of temper or expression. [< Old French *verjus* < *vert* green + *jus* juice]

Ver meer (vər mär′, vər mir′), *n.* **Jan,** 1632-1675, Dutch painter.

ver meil (vėr′məl), *n.* 1 vermilion. 2 silver, bronze, or copper coated with gilt. *—adj.* 1 vermilion. 2 of or like vermeil. [< Old French < Latin *vermiculus,* diminutive of *vermis* worm]

ver mi cel li (vėr′mə sel′ē, vėr′mə chel′ē), *n.* a mixture of flour and water like spaghetti but thinner. [< Italian, literally, little worms]

ver mi cide (vėr′mə sīd), *n.* any substance or drug that kills worms, especially parasitic intestinal worms.

ver mic u lar (vər mik′yə lər), *adj.* 1 of, having to do with, or characteristic of a worm or worms. 2 like a worm in nature, form, or method of movement. 3 like the wavy track of a worm. 4 marked with close, wavy lines. 5 worm-eaten. [< Latin *vermiculus,* diminutive of *vermis* worm]

ver mic u late (vər mik′yə lāt, vər mik′yə-lit), *adj.* vermicular; sinuous.

ver mic u lite (vər mik′yə līt), *n.* mineral, hydrous silicates of aluminum, iron, and magnesium, occurring in small foliated scales, used as a filler in paint and concrete, as a soil conditioner, insulator, etc.

ver mi form (vėr′mə fôrm), *adj.* shaped like a worm.

vermiform appendix, a slender tube, closed at one end, growing out of the large intestine in the lower right-hand part of the abdomen; appendix. Appendicitis is inflammation of the vermiform appendix.

ver mi fuge (vėr′mə fyüj), *n.* medicine to expel worms from the intestines. *—adj.* used as a vermifuge. [< Latin *vermis* worm + *fugare* cause to flee]

ver mil ion (vər mil′yən), *n.* 1 a bright red. 2 a bright-red coloring matter. *—adj.* bright-red. [< Old French *vermillon* < *vermeil.* See VERMEIL.]

ver min (vėr′mən), *n. pl. or sing.* 1 small animals that are troublesome or destructive. Fleas, lice, bedbugs, rats, and mice are vermin. 2 animals or birds that destroy game, poultry, etc. 3 very unpleasant or vile person or persons. [< Old French < Latin *vermis* worm]

ver min ous (vėr′mə nəs), *adj.* 1 infested with vermin. 2 caused by vermin. 3 like vermin; very unpleasant; vile. **—ver′min-ous ly,** *adv.*

Ver mont (vər mont′), *n.* one of the northeastern states of the United States. 444,000 pop.; 9600 sq. mi. *Capital:* Montpelier. *Abbrev.:* Vt.

Ver mont er (vər mon′tər), *n.* native or inhabitant of Vermont.

ver mouth (vər müth′, vėr′müth), *n.* a white wine flavored with wormwood or other herbs and used as a liqueur or in cocktails. [< French < German *Wermut*]

ver nac u lar (vər nak′yə lər), *n.* 1 a native language; language used by the people of a certain country or place. 2 everyday language; informal speech. 3 language of a profession, trade, etc.: *the vernacular of lawyers.* 4 the common name of a plant or animal, as contrasted with its scientific name. *—adj.* 1 used by the people of a certain country or place; native: *English is our vernacular tongue.* 2 of or in the native language, rather than a literary or learned language. [< Latin *vernaculus* domestic, native < *verna* home-born slave] **—ver nac′u-lar ly,** *adv.*

ver nal (vėr′nl), *adj.* 1 of spring; having to do with or coming in spring: *vernal green, vernal flowers, vernal months.* 2 like spring; suggesting spring. 3 youthful: *Everyone admired the young girl's vernal freshness.* [< Latin *vernalis* < *ver* spring] **—ver′nal-ly,** *adv.*

ver nal ize (vėr′nl īz), *v.t.,* **-ized, -iz ing.** cause (a plant) to bloom and bear fruit early by subjecting the seed, bulb, or seedling to a very low temperature. **—ver′nal i za′-tion,** *n.*

ver na tion (vər nā′shən), *n.* arrangement of leaves in a bud. [< New Latin *vernationem* < Latin *vernare* bloom]

Verne (vėrn), *n.* **Jules,** 1828-1905, French writer of science fiction and adventure stories.

ver ni er (vėr′nē ər, vėr′nir), *n.* 1 a small, movable scale for measuring a fractional part of one of the divisions of a fixed scale. 2 an auxiliary device used to obtain fine adjustments or measurements with another device or mechanism. [< Pierre *Vernier,* 1580-1637, French mathematician]

ver nis sage (ver nē sȧzh′), *n.* the opening or first showing of an art exhibition. [< French]

Ve ro na (və rō′nə), *n.* city in N Italy. 259,000.

Ver o nal (ver′ə nəl, ver′ə nôl), *n.* trademark for barbital.

Ver o ne se (ver′ə nā′zē; *Italian* vā′rō-nā′sā), *n.* **Paolo,** 1528-1588, Venetian painter.

ve ron i ca (və ron′ə kə), *n.* 1 speedwell. 2 cloth with a representation of Christ's face. [< New Latin]

Ver sailles (ver sī′, vər sālz′), *n.* 1 city in N France, near Paris, where a treaty of peace between the Allies and Germany was signed after World War I, on June 28, 1919. 91,000. 2 a large palace there.

ver sa tile (vėr′sə təl), *adj.* 1 able to do many things well: *Theodore Roosevelt was a versatile man; he was successful as a statesman, soldier, sportsman, explorer, and author.* 2 in zoology: **a** turning forward or backward: *the versatile toe of an owl.* **b** moving freely up and down and laterally: *versatile antennae.* 3 (in botany) attached at or near the middle so as to swing or turn freely: *a versatile anther.* 4 fickle; inconstant. [< Latin *versatilis* turning < *versare,* frequentative of *vertere* to turn] **—ver′sa-tile ly,** *adv.* **—ver′sa tile ness,** *n.*

ver sa til i ty (vėr′sə til′ə tē), *n., pl.* **-ties.** 1 ability to do many things well. 2 a being changeable; fickleness.

verse (vėrs), *n.* 1 lines of words usually with a regularly repeated accent and often with rhyme; composition in meter; poetry. Verse is sometimes distinguished from poetry by its light content and emphasis on structure. 2 a single line of poetry. 3 group of lines in poetry or song which form a unit related in form and meaning; stanza: *Sing the first verse of "America."* 4 type of verse or poetry; meter: *blank verse, iambic verse.* 5 a short division of a chapter in the Bible. [< Latin *versus,* originally, row, furrow < *vertere* to turn]

➤ **verse.** A full line or more of verse quoted in a paper should be lined off and written exactly as it is in the original. It should be indented from the left margin and, if very short, far enough not to leave a conspicuous blank at its right. No quotation marks are used.

versed (vėrst), *adj.* experienced; practiced; skilled: *A doctor should be well versed in medical theory.* [< Latin *versatum* engaged or occupied in, ultimately < *vertere* to turn]

ver si cle (vėr′sə kəl), *n.* 1 a little verse. 2 one of a series of short sentences said or sung by the minister, priest, etc., during services, to which the people make response. [< Latin *versiculus,* diminutive of *versus* verse]

ver si fi ca tion (vėr′sə fə kā′shən), *n.* 1 the making of verses. 2 art or theory of making verses. 3 form or style of poetry; metrical structure.

ver si fi er (vėr′sə fī′ər), *n.* person who makes verses.

ver si fy (vėr′sə fī), *v.,* **-fied, -fy ing.** *—v.i.* write verses. *—v.t.* 1 tell in verse. 2 turn (prose) into poetry.

ver sion (vėr′zhən), *n.* 1 a translation from one language to another: *a version of the Bible.* 2 one particular statement, account, or description: *Each of the three girls gave her own version of the quarrel.* 3 a special form or variant of something: *a Scottish version of the Christmas tree.* [< Latin *versionem,* originally, a turning < *vertere* to turn]

vers li bre (ver lē′brə), FRENCH. free verse; verse that follows no fixed metrical form.

verst (vėrst), *n.* a Russian measure of distance equal to about 3500 feet. [< Russian *versta*]

ver sus (vėr′səs), *prep.* 1 against: *the State versus Smith. Tomorrow's game will feature Harvard versus Yale.* 2 as the alternative of; as compared or contrasted with: *federal versus state control of education.* [< Latin, turned toward]

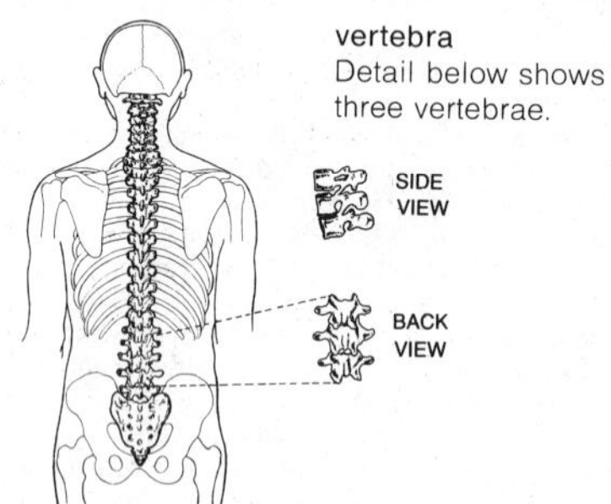

vertebra
Detail below shows three vertebrae.

ver te bra (vėr′tə brə), *n., pl.* **-brae** (-brē), **-bras.** one of the bones of the backbone. [< Latin, originally, joint, turning place < *vertere* to turn]

ver te bral (vėr′tə brəl), *adj.* 1 of or having to do with a vertebra or the vertebrae. 2 composed of vertebrae.

ver te brate (vėr′tə brit, vėr′tə brāt), *n.* animal that has a backbone; any of the large subphylum of chordates having a segmented spinal column and a brain case or cranium, including fishes, amphibians, reptiles, birds, and mammals. —*adj.* 1 having a backbone. 2 of or having to do with vertebrates.

ver tex (vėr′teks), *n., pl.* **-tex es** or **-ti ces.** 1 the highest point; top. 2 top or crown of the head. 3 point in the heavens directly overhead; zenith. 4 in geometry: **a** point opposite to and farthest from the base of a triangle, pyramid, etc. **b** the point where the two sides of an angle meet. **c** any point of intersection of the sides of a polygon or the edges of a polyhedron. [< Latin, originally, whirl, whirling < *vertere* to turn]

ver ti cal (vėr′tə kəl), *adj.* 1 straight up and down; perpendicular to a level surface; upright. A person standing up straight is in a vertical position. 2 of or at the highest point; of the vertex. 3 directly overhead; at the zenith. 4 so organized as to include many or all stages in the production or distribution of some manufactured product: *a vertical union, vertical trusts.* —*n.* a vertical line, plane, direction, position, part, etc. —**ver′ti cal ly,** *adv.*

vertical circle, (in astronomy) a great circle of the celestial sphere perpendicular to the plane of the horizon, passing through the zenith and nadir.

vertical file, 1 file of pamphlets, circulars, charts, bulletins, newspaper clippings, etc., about topics of current interest, maintained by a library or other organization for quick or easy reference. 2 cabinet for such a file.

ver ti cal i ty (vėr′tə kal′ə tē), *n.* condition of being vertical.

vertical take-off, take-off by an aircraft directly upward, especially by means of jet propulsion.

ver ti ces (vėr′tə sēz′), *n.* a pl. of **vertex.**

ver ti cil (vėr′tə sil), *n.* a whorl or circle of leaves, hairs, etc., growing around a stem or central point. [< Latin *verticillus,* diminutive of *vertex*]

ver tic il late (vər tis′ə lāt, vər tis′ə lit, vėr′tə sil′āt), *adj.* forming verticils or whorls. —**ver tic′il late ly,** *adv.* —**ver tic′il la′tion,** *n.*

ver tig i nous (vər tij′ə nəs), *adj.* 1 whirling; rotary; revolving: *the vertiginous action of a gyroscope.* 2 affected with vertigo; dizzy. 3 of the nature of or having to do with vertigo; likely to cause vertigo. 4 fickle; unstable. —**ver tig′i nous ly,** *adv.* —**ver tig′i nous ness,** *n.*

ver ti go (vėr′tə gō), *n., pl.* **ver ti goes, ver tig i nes** (vər tij′ə nēz′). dizziness; giddiness. [< Latin < *vertere* to turn]

ver tu (vėr′tü′, vėr′tü), *n.* virtu.

ver vain (vėr′vān), *n.* verbena. [< Old French *verveine* < Latin *verbena*]

verve (vėrv), *n.* enthusiasm; energy; vigor; spirit; liveliness. [< French < Popular Latin *verva* < Latin *verba* words]

ver y (ver′ē), *adv., adj.,* **ver i er, ver i est.** —*adv.* 1 much; greatly; extremely: *The sun is very hot.* 2 absolutely; exactly: *He stood in the very same place for an hour.* —*adj.* 1 same; identical: *The very people who used to love her hate her now.* 2 even; mere; sheer: *The very thought of blood makes me sick.* 3 real; true; genuine: *She seemed a very queen.* 4 actual: *caught in the very act of stealing.* [< Old French *verai* < *veracis* truthful < *verus* true]

very high frequency, the band of radio frequencies between 30 and 300 megacycles.

very low frequency, the band of radio frequencies between 10 and 30 kilocycles.

Very pistol, pistol used to discharge a colored flare (**Very light**) at night as a signal. [< Edward *Very,* 1847-1910, American naval officer, its inventor]

ves i cant (ves′ə kənt), *n.* something that raises blisters, as a mustard plaster. —*adj.* causing or effective in producing blisters.

ves i cate (ves′ə kāt), *v.,* **-cat ed, -cat ing.** —*v.t.* cause blisters on; blister. —*v.i.* become blistered.

ves i ca to ry (ves′ə kə tôr′ē, ves′ə kə tōr′ē), *adj., n., pl.* **-to ries.** —*adj.* that can raise blisters. —*n.* vesicant.

ves i cle (ves′ə kəl), *n.* 1 a small bladder, cavity, sac, or cyst, especially one filled with serum, as a blister. 2 (in botany) a small bladder or air cavity resembling a bladder. 3 (in geology) a small spherical or oval cavity in igneous rock produced by the presence of bubbles of gas or vapor during the rock's solidification. [< Latin *vesicula,* diminutive of *vesica* bladder, blister]

ve sic u lar (və sik′yə lər), *adj.* of or having to do with a vesicle or vesicles; like a vesicle; having vesicles. —**ve sic′u lar ly,** *adv.*

ve sic u la tion (və sik′yə lā′shən), *n.* the formation of vesicles, especially on the skin.

Ves pa sian (ve spā′zhən), *n.* A.D. 9-79, Roman emperor from A.D. 69 to 79.

ves per (ves′pər), *n.* 1 evening. 2 **Vesper,** the planet Venus, when it appears as the evening star. 3 an evening prayer, hymn, or service. 4 an evening bell. 5 **vespers** or **Vespers,** *pl.* **a** a church service held in the late afternoon or in the evening; evensong. **b** the sixth of the canonical hours. —*adj.* 1 of evening. 2 Sometimes, **Vesper.** of or having to do with vespers. [< Latin]

ves per tine (ves′pər tən, ves′pər tīn), *adj.* 1 of or occurring in the evening. 2 flying or appearing in the evening. Bats and owls are vespertine animals. 3 opening in the evening, as some flowers.

ves pine (ves′pīn, ves′pən), *adj.* of or having to do with wasps; wasplike. [< Latin *vespa* wasp]

Ves puc ci (ve spü′chē), *n.* **Amerigo,** 1451-1512, Italian merchant, adventurer, and explorer. America is named after him.

ves sel (ves′əl), *n.* 1 a large boat; ship. 2 airship. 3 a hollow holder or container. Cups, bowls, pitchers, bottles, barrels, and tubs are vessels. 4 tube carrying blood or other fluid. Veins and arteries are blood vessels. 5 trachea (def. 3). 6 person regarded as a container of some quality or as made for some purpose (used chiefly in biblical expressions). [< Old French < Latin *vascellum,* diminutive of *vas* vessel]

vest (vest), *n.* 1 a short, sleeveless garment worn by men or boys under the coat. 2 a similar garment worn by women. 3 BRITISH. undershirt. 4 ARCHAIC. clothing; garment. —*v.t.* 1 clothe or robe; dress in vestments: *The vested priest stood before the altar.* 2 furnish with powers, authority, rights, etc.: *Congress is vested with the power to declare war.* 3 put in the possession or control of a person or persons: *The management of the hospital is vested in a board of trustees.* —*v.i.* 1 become vested; pass into possession: *The right of the crown vests upon his heir.* 2 dress in ecclesiastical vestment. [< Old French *veste* < Latin *vestis* garment] —**vest′less,** *adj.*

vestment (def. 1)

hat, āge, fär; let, ēqual, tėrm;
it, īce; hot, ōpen, ôrder;
oil, out; cup, pu̇t, rüle;
ch, child; ng, long; sh, she;
th, thin; ᴛʜ, then; zh, measure;

ə represents *a* in about, *e* in taken,
i in pencil, *o* in lemon, *u* in circus.

< = from, derived from, taken from.

Ves ta (ves′tə), *n.* 1 (in Roman myths) the goddess of the hearth, identified with the Greek goddess Hestia. A sacred fire was always kept burning in the temple of Vesta. 2 **vesta,** **a** kind of short friction match. **b** BRITISH. kind of wax match.

ves tal (ves′tl), *n.* 1 one of the vestal virgins. 2 virgin. 3 nun. —*adj.* 1 of or suitable for a vestal. 2 pure; chaste.

vestal virgin, one of the virgin priestesses of the Roman goddess Vesta. Six vestal virgins tended an undying fire in honor of Vesta at her temple in ancient Rome.

vest ed (ves′tid), *adj.* 1 placed in the possession or control of a person or persons; fixed; settled: *vested rights.* 2 clothed or robed, especially in church garments: *a vested choir.*

vested interest, 1 commitment to some cause, institution, etc., based on self-interest. 2 person or group holding such a commitment.

vest ee (ve stē′), *n.* an ornamental vest worn by women as an insert on a dress bodice or between the open edges of a blouse or jacket; dickey.

ves tib u lar (ve stib′yə lər), *adj.* of, having to do with, or serving as a vestibule.

ves ti bule (ves′tə byül), *n.* 1 passage or hall between the outer door and the inside of a building. 2 the enclosed platform and entrance at the end of a railroad passenger car. 3 cavity of the body that leads to another cavity. The vestibule of the ear is the central cavity of the inner ear. [< Latin *vestibulum*]

ves tige (ves′tij), *n.* 1 a slight remnant; trace; mark: *Ghost stories are vestiges of a former widespread belief in ghosts.* See **trace**[1] for synonym study. 2 (in biology) a part, organ, etc., that is no longer fully developed or useful but performed a definite function in an earlier stage of the existence of the same organism or in lower preceding organisms. 3 RARE. footprint or track. [< French < Latin *vestigium* footprint]

ves tig i al (ve stij′ē əl), *adj.* 1 remaining as a vestige of something that has disappeared. 2 (in biology) no longer fully developed or useful. —**ves tig′i al ly,** *adv.*

vest ment (vest′mənt), *n.* 1 garment worn by a clergyman in performing sacred duties. 2 garment, especially a robe or gown, worn by an official on a ceremonial occasion. 3 something that covers as a garment; covering: *the green vestment of the meadow.* [< Latin *vestis* garment]

vest-pock et (vest′pok′it), *adj.* 1 able to fit into a vest pocket. 2 very small.

ves try (ves′trē), *n., pl.* **-tries.** 1 room in a church, where vestments, and often the sacred vessels, altar equipment, parish records, etc., are kept. 2 room in a church or an attached building, used for Sunday school, prayer meetings, etc. 3 (in the Church of England and the Protestant Episcopal Church of America) an elected committee that helps manage church business. 4 (in parishes of the Church of England) a meeting of parishioners on church business. [< Old French *vestiarie,* ultimately < Latin *vestire* to clothe < *vestis* garment]

ves try man (ves′trē mən), *n., pl.* **-men.** member of a committee that helps manage church business.

ves ture (ves′chər), *n.* 1 clothing; garments. 2 covering.

Ve su vi an (və sü′vē ən), *adj.* of, having to do with, or resembling Mount Vesuvius; volcanic.

Ve su vi us (və sü′vē əs), *n.* **Mount,** active volcano southeast of Naples, Italy. During an eruption in A.D. 79 its lava buried the ancient cities of Pompeii and Herculaneum. 4000 ft. high.

vet[1] (vet), *n., v.,* **vet ted, vet ting.** INFORMAL. —*n.* veterinarian. —*v.t.* submit to examination or treatment by a veterinarian: *vet a sick calf.*

vet[2] (vet), *n.* INFORMAL. veteran.

vet., 1 veteran. 2 veterinarian. 3 veterinary.

vetch (vech), *n.* any of a genus of climbing herbs of the pea family, species of which are grown as food for cattle and sheep; tare. [< Old North French *veche* < Latin *vicia*]

vet er an (vet′ər ən), *n.* 1 person who has had much experience in war; old soldier, sailor, airman, etc. 2 person who has served in the armed forces. 3 person who has had much experience in some position, occupation, etc. —*adj.* 1 having had much experience in war: *Veteran troops fought side by side with new recruits.* 2 grown old in service; experienced: *a veteran farmer.* [< Latin *veteranus* < *vetus* old]

Veterans Day, November 11, formerly Armistice Day, observed as a legal holiday in most states on the fourth Monday of October. The name was changed by act of Congress in 1954.

vet er i nar i an (vet′ər ə ner′ē ən, vet′ə-ner′ē ən), *n.* doctor or surgeon who treats animals.

vet er i nar y (vet′ər ə ner′ē, vet′ə ner′ē), *adj., n., pl.* **-nar ies.** —*adj.* of or having to do with the medical or surgical treatment of animals. —*n.* veterinarian. [< Latin *veterinarius* < *veterinus* of beasts of burden and draft]

ve to (vē′tō), *n., pl.* **-toes,** *adj., v.* —*n.* 1 the right or power of a president, governor, etc., to reject bills passed by a lawmaking body. 2 the right or power of any one member of an official body to prevent some action proposed by that body, as in the United Nations Security Council. 3 the use of any such rights: *The governor's veto kept the bill from becoming a law.* 4 statement of the reasons for disapproval of a bill passed by the legislature. 5 any power or right to prevent action through prohibition. 6 refusal of consent; prohibition. —*adj.* having to do with a veto: *veto power.* —*v.t.* 1 reject by a veto. 2 refuse to consent to: *My parents vetoed my plan to buy a motorcycle.* [< Latin, I forbid] —**ve′to er,** *n.*

vex (veks), *v.t.* 1 anger by trifles; annoy; provoke. 2 worry; trouble; harass. 3 disturb by commotion; agitate: *The island was much vexed by storms.* [< Latin *vexare*]

vex a tion (vek sā′shən), *n.* 1 a vexing. 2 a being vexed: *His face showed his vexation at the delay.* 3 thing that vexes.

vex a tious (vek sā′shəs), *adj.* vexing; annoying. —**vex a′tious ly,** *adv.* —**vex-a′tious ness,** *n.*

vex ed ly (vek′sid lē), *adv.* with vexation; with a sense of annoyance or vexation.

vexed question, question causing difficulty and debate.

V.F.W., Veterans of Foreign Wars.

VHF or **vhf,** very high frequency.

v.i., intransitive verb.

V.I., Virgin Islands.

vi a (vī′ə, vē′ə), *prep.* by way of; by a route that passes through: *She is going from New York to California via the Panama Canal.* [< Latin, ablative of *via* way]

vi a bil i ty (vī′ə bil′ə tē), *n.* quality or condition of being viable.

vi a ble (vī′ə bəl), *adj.* 1 able to keep alive. 2 fit to live in; livable: *a viable community.* 3 that can work or be put to use; workable: *a viable economy.* 4 (of a fetus or newborn infant) sufficiently developed to maintain life outside the uterus. 5 (in botany) that can live and grow, as a spore or seed. [< French < *vie* life < Latin *vita*] —**vi′a bly,** *adv.*

vi a duct (vī′ə dukt), *n.* bridge for carrying a road or railroad over a valley, a part of a city, etc. [< Latin *via* road + *ductus* a leading; patterned on *aqueduct*]

vi al (vī′əl), *n.* a small glass or plastic bottle for holding medicines or the like; phial. [variant of *phial*]

vi a me di a (vī′ə mē′dē ə), LATIN. middle way.

vi and (vī′ənd), *n.* 1 article of food. 2 **viands,** *pl.* articles of choice food. [< Old French *viande* < Late Latin *vivenda* things for living < Latin, to be lived < *vivere* to live]

vi at i cum (vī at′ə kəm), *n., pl.* **-ca** (-kə), **-cums.** 1 Holy Communion given to a person dying or in danger of death. 2 supplies or money for a journey. [< Latin, neuter of *viaticus* of a journey < *via* road. Doublet of VOYAGE.]

vibes (vībz), *n.pl.* INFORMAL. vibraphone.

vi bra harp (vī′brə härp′), *n.* vibraphone.

vi bra harp ist (vī′brə här′pist), *n.* vibraphonist.

vi bran cy (vī′brən sē), *n.* quality or condition of being vibrant.

vi brant (vī′brənt), *adj.* 1 vibrating. 2 resounding; resonant. 3 throbbing with vitality, enthusiasm, etc.: *a vibrant personality.* —**vi′brant ly,** *adv.*

vi bra phone (vī′brə fōn), *n.* a musical instrument similar to the xylophone, consisting of metal bars and electrically operated resonators that produce rich, vibrant tones. [< *vibra(te)* + *(xylo)phone*]

vi bra phon ist (vī′brə fō′nist), *n.* person who plays a vibraphone.

vi brate (vī′brāt), *v.,* **-brat ed, -brat ing.** —*v.i.* 1 move rapidly to and fro: *A piano string vibrates and makes a sound when a key is struck.* 2 be moved; quiver. 3 vacillate. 4 thrill: *Their hearts vibrated to the speaker's stirring appeal.* 5 resound: *The clanging vibrated in my ears.* —*v.t.* 1 cause to move to and fro, especially with a quick motion; set in vibration. 2 measure by moving to and fro: *A pendulum vibrates seconds.* [< Latin *vibratum* shaken]

vi bra tile (vī′brə təl, vī′brə tīl), *adj.* 1 that can vibrate or be vibrated. 2 having a vibratory motion. 3 having to do with or characterized by vibration.

vi bra til i ty (vī′brə til′ə tē), *n.* condition of being vibratile.

vi bra tion (vī brā′shən), *n.* 1 a rapid movement to and fro; quivering motion; vibrating: *The buses shake the house so much that we feel the vibration.* 2 a rapid or slow movement to and fro. 3 the rapid motion back and forth, produced in the particles of an elastic body or medium by the disturbance of equilibrium. 4 a vacillating. —**vi bra′tion less,** *adj.*

vi bra tion al (vī brā′shə nəl), *adj.* of, having to do with, or of the nature of vibration.

vi bra to (vi brä′tō), *n., pl.* **-tos,** *adv.* in music: —*n.* a vibrating or pulsating effect produced by a wavering of pitch. —*adv.* with much vibration of tone. [< Italian]

vi bra tor (vī′brā tər), *n.* 1 thing that vibrates. 2 instrument causing a vibrating motion or action, such as an electrical device used to massage a part of the body.

vi bra to ry (vī′brə tôr′ē, vī′brə tōr′ē), *adj.* 1 vibrating. 2 of or having to do with vibration. 3 causing vibration. 4 capable of vibration. 5 consisting of vibration.

vib ri o (vib′rē ō), *n., pl.* **-ri os.** any of a genus of short, curved bacteria, often shaped like a comma, spiral, or S, and characterized by lively motion, as the species that causes Asiatic cholera. [< New Latin < Latin *vibrare* vibrate]

vi bur num (vī bėr′nəm), *n.* 1 any of a genus of shrubs or small trees of the same family as the honeysuckle, having showy clusters of white or pinkish flowers, such as the snowball. 2 the dried bark of certain species, used in medicine. [< Latin]

vic ar (vik′ər), *n.* 1 (in the Church of England) the minister of a parish who is paid a salary by the receiver of tithes. 2 (in the Protestant Episcopal Church) a clergyman who has charge of one chapel in a parish. 3 (in the Roman Catholic Church) a clergyman who represents the pope or a bishop. 4 person acting in place of another; representative. [< Latin *vicarius,* originally adjective, substituted. Doublet of VICARIOUS.]

vic ar age (vik′ər ij), *n.* 1 residence of a vicar. 2 position or duties of a vicar. 3 salary paid to a vicar.

vicar apostolic, *pl.* **vicars apostolic.** (in the Roman Catholic Church) a missionary or titular bishop stationed either in a country where no episcopal see has yet been established, or in one where the succession of bishops has been interrupted.

vic ar-gen er al (vik′ər jen′ər əl), *n., pl.* **vic ars-gen er al.** 1 (in the Roman Catholic Church) a deputy of a bishop or an archbishop, assisting him in the government of the diocese. 2 (in the Church of England) an ecclesiastical officer, usually a layman, who assists a bishop or an archbishop.

vi car i al (vī ker′ē əl, vi ker′ē əl), *adj.* 1 of or belonging to a vicar or vicars. 2 delegated, as duties or authority.

vi car i ate (vī ker′ē it, vī ker′ē āt; vi ker′ē-it, vi ker′ē āt), *n.* office, jurisdiction, or authority of a vicar.

vi car i ous (vī ker′ē əs, vi ker′ē əs), *adj.* 1 done or suffered for others: *vicarious work.* 2 felt by sharing in others' experience: *The invalid received vicarious pleasure from read-*

ing travel stories. 3 taking the place of another; doing the work of another: *a vicarious agent.* 4 delegated: *vicarious authority.* 5 (in physiology) denoting the performance by or through one organ of functions normally discharged by another. [< Latin *vicarius* < *vicis* turn, change, substitution. Doublet of VICAR.] **—vi car′i ous ly,** *adv.* **—vi car′i-ous ness,** *n.*

Vicar of Christ, (in the Roman Catholic Church) the Pope, as standing in the place of and acting for Christ.

vic ar ship (vik′ər ship), *n.* position of a vicar.

vice[1] (vīs), *n.* 1 an evil, immoral, or wicked habit or tendency: *Lying and cruelty are vices.* 2 evil; wickedness. 3 a moral fault or defect; flaw in character or conduct. 4 (of horses) any of several bad habits or tricks, as bolting or shying. [< Old French < Latin *vitium*]

vice[2] (vīs), *n.* vise.

vi ce[3] (vī′sē), *prep.* instead of; in the place of. [< Latin, ablative of *vicis* turn, change]

vice-, *prefix.* substitute; deputy; subordinate, as in *vice-president, vice-consul.* [< Latin *vice* vice[3]]

vice-ad mir al (vīs′ad′mər əl), *n.* a naval officer ranking next below an admiral and next above a rear admiral.

vice-con sul (vīs′kon′səl), *n.* person next in rank below a consul. He substitutes for the regular consul or acts as his assistant.

vi cen ni al (vī sen′ē əl), *adj.* 1 of or for twenty years. 2 occurring once every twenty years. [< Latin *vicennium* twenty-year period < *vicies* twenty times + *annus* year]

Vice Pres., Vice-President.

vice-pres i den cy (vīs′prez′ə dən sē, vīs′prez′dən sē), *n., pl.* **-cies.** position of vice-president.

vice-pres i dent (vīs′prez′ə dənt, vīs′-prez′dənt), *n.* officer next in rank to the president, who takes the president's place when necessary.

vice-pres i den tial (vīs′prez′ə den′shəl), *adj.* of or having to do with the vice-president.

vice re gal (vīs rē′gəl), *adj.* of or having to do with a viceroy.

vice-re gent (vīs′rē′jənt), *n.* person who takes the place of the regular regent whenever necessary.

vice roy (vīs′roi), *n.* 1 person ruling a country or province as the deputy of the sovereign. 2 an American butterfly whose coloration and markings closely resemble those of the monarch butterfly. [< French *vice-roi* < *vice* vice[3] + *roi* king]

vice roy al ty (vīs′roi′əl tē), *n.* 1 position or district of a viceroy. 2 period during which a particular viceroy holds office.

vi ce ver sa (vī′sə vėr′sə; vīs vėr′sə), the other way round; conversely: *John blamed Mary, and vice versa (Mary blamed John).* [< Latin]

Vich y (vē′shē), *n.* 1 city in central France. It was the German-controlled capital of France from 1940 to 1944. 34,000. 2 Vichy water.

vi chys soise (vish′ē swäz′), *n.* a creamy potato-and-leek soup, sprinkled with chives and served cold. [< French, literally, of Vichy]

Vichy water, 1 a natural mineral water from springs at Vichy, France, containing sodium bicarbonate and other salts, used in the treatment of digestive disturbances, gout, etc. 2 a natural or artificial water of similar composition.

vic i nage (vis′n ij), *n.* surrounding district; neighborhood; vicinity.

vic i nal (vis′n əl), *adj.* 1 neighboring; adjacent; near. 2 local.

vi cin i ty (və sin′ə tē), *n., pl.* **-ties.** 1 region near or about a place; surrounding district; neighborhood: *know many people in New York and its vicinity.* 2 nearness in place; being close. [< Latin *vicinitatem* < *vicinus* neighboring < *vicus* quarter, village]

vi cious (vish′əs), *adj.* 1 evil; wicked: *The criminal led a vicious life.* 2 having bad habits or a bad disposition; fierce; savage: *a vicious horse.* 3 spiteful; malicious: *vicious words.* 4 INFORMAL. unpleasantly severe: *a vicious headache.* 5 not correct; having faults: *This argument contains vicious reasoning.* [< Old French *vicieux* < Latin *vitiosus* < *vitium* vice[1]] **—vi cious ly,** *adv.* **—vi′cious ness,** *n.*

vicious circle, 1 two or more undesirable things each of which keeps causing the other. 2 false reasoning that uses one statement to prove a second statement when the first statement really depends upon the second for proof.

vi cis si tude (və sis′ə tüd, və sis′ə tyüd), *n.* 1 change in circumstances, fortune, etc.: *The vicissitudes of life may suddenly make a rich man very poor.* 2 change; variation. 3 regular change: *the vicissitude of day and night.* [< Latin *vicissitudo* < *vicis* turn, change]

vi cis si tu di nous (və sis′ə tüd′n əs, və-sis′ə tyüd′n əs), *adj.* subject to vicissitude.

vic tim (vik′təm), *n.* 1 person or animal sacrificed, injured, or destroyed: *victims of war, victims of an accident.* 2 person badly treated or taken advantage of; dupe: *the victim of a swindler.* 3 person or animal killed as a sacrifice to a god. [< Latin *victima*]

vic tim ize (vik′tə mīz), *v.t.,* **-ized, -iz ing.** 1 make a victim of; cause to suffer. 2 cheat; swindle. **—vic′tim i za′tion,** *n.* **—vic′tim-iz′er,** *n.*

vic tor (vik′tər), *n.* winner; conqueror. *—adj.* victorious. [< Latin < *vincere* conquer]

Vic tor Em man u el I (vik′tər i man′yü-əl), 1759-1824, king of Sardinia from 1802 to 1821.

Victor Emmanuel II, 1820-1878, king of Sardinia from 1849 to 1878, and first king of Italy from 1861 to 1878.

Victor Emmanuel III, 1869-1947, king of Italy from 1900 to 1946.

victoria (def. 1)

vic to ri a (vik tôr′ē ə, vik tōr′ē ə), *n.* 1 a low, four-wheeled carriage with a folding top, a seat for two passengers, and a raised seat in front for the driver. 2 an open automobile with a folding top covering the rear seat only. 3 any of a small genus of huge South American water lilies with solitary flowers that change from white to pink or red the second day they are open. [< Queen *Victoria*]

Vic to ri a (vik tôr′ē ə, vik tōr′ē ə), *n.* 1 1819-1901, queen of Great Britain from 1837 to 1901. 2 capital of British Columbia, in the SW part. 57,000. 3 state in SE Australia. 3,444,000 pop.; 87,900 sq. mi. *Capital:* Melbourne. 4 **Lake,** lake in E Africa, bordered by Kenya, Tanzania, and Uganda. 26,828 sq. mi. 5 seaport and capital of Hong Kong. 633,000. 6 capital of Seychelles. 13,000.

hat, āge, fär; let, ēqual, tėrm;
it, īce; hot, ōpen, ôrder;
oil, out; cup, pu̇t, rüle;
ch, child; ng, long; sh, she;
th, thin; ᴛʜ, then; zh, measure;

ə represents *a* in about, *e* in taken, *i* in pencil, *o* in lemon, *u* in circus.

< = from, derived from, taken from.

Victoria Cross, a bronze Maltese cross awarded to British soldiers and sailors as a decoration for remarkable valor during battle.

Victoria Day, (in Canada) a national holiday falling on the Monday before May 24, the birthday of Queen Victoria.

Victoria Falls, falls of the Zambezi River in S central Africa between Rhodesia and Zambia. 400 ft.

Vic to ri an (vik tôr′ē ən, vik tōr′ē ən), *adj.* 1 of or having to do with the reign or time of Queen Victoria: *the Victorian age.* 2 having characteristics attributed to Victorians, such as prudishness, bigotry, etc. *—n.* person, especially an author, who lived during the reign of Queen Victoria.

Vic to ri an ism (vik tôr′ē ə niz′əm, vik-tōr′ē ə niz′əm), *n.* ideas, beliefs, morals, ways of living, etc., common during the reign of Queen Victoria.

vic to ri ous (vik tôr′ē əs, vik tōr′ē əs), *adj.* 1 having won a victory; conquering: *a victorious team.* 2 of or having to do with victory; ending in victory: *a victorious war.* **—vic to′ri ous ly,** *adv.* **—vic to′ri ous-ness,** *n.*

vic tor y (vik′tər ē), *n., pl.* **-tor ies.** defeat of an enemy or opponent; success in a contest. [< Latin *victoria* < *victor* victor]

Syn. Victory, conquest, triumph mean success in a contest or struggle. **Victory** applies to success in any kind of contest or fight: *We celebrated the victory of our football team.* **Conquest** emphasizes absolute control of the defeated: *the Spanish conquest of Peru, the conquest of yellow fever.* **Triumph** applies to a glorious victory or conquest: *The Nineteenth Amendment was a triumph for the suffragists.*

Vic tro la (vik trō′lə), *n.* trademark for a kind of phonograph.

vict ual (vit′l), *n., v.,* **-ualed, -ual ing** or **-ualled, -ual ling.** *—n.* **victuals,** *pl.* food or provisions. *—v.t.* supply with food or provisions. *—v.i.* 1 take on a supply of food or provisions: *The ship will victual before sailing.* 2 eat or feed: *sheep victualing on new grass.* [< Latin *victualia,* plural of *victualis* of food < *victus* food, sustenance < *vivere* to live]

vict ual er or **vict ual ler** (vit′l ər), *n.* 1 person who supplies food or provisions to a ship, an army, etc. 2 keeper of an inn, tavern, saloon, etc.

vi cu ña (vi kü′nə, vī kü′nə), *n.* 1 a wild, ruminant mammal of South America, of the same family as and resembling a llama, having a soft, delicate wool. 2 cloth made from this wool, or from some substitute. [< Spanish < Quechua]

vicuña (def. 1)
about 2½ ft. high at the shoulder

vid., see [for Latin *vide*].

vi de (vī′dē), *v.* LATIN. see; refer to (a word indicating reference to something stated elsewhere).

vi de in fra (vī′dē in′frə), LATIN. see below.

vi de li cet (və del′ə set), *adv.* that is to say; namely. [< Latin, short for *videre licet* it is permissible to see]

vid e o (vid′ē ō), *adj.* of or used in the transmission or reception of images in television. —*n.* television. [< Latin, I see]

vid e o tape (vid′ē ō tāp′), *n., v.,* **-taped, -tap ing.** —*n.* a magnetic tape that records and reproduces both sound and picture for television. —*v.t.* record on videotape.

vi de su pra (vī′dē sü′prə), LATIN. see above.

vi dette (vi det′), *n.* vedette.

vie (vī), *v.i.,* **vied, vy ing.** strive for superiority; contend in rivalry; compete. [short for Middle French *envier* to wager, challenge < Latin *invitare* invite]

Vi en na (vē en′ə), *n.* capital of Austria, in the NE part, on the Danube River. 1,642,000. Also, GERMAN **Wien.**

Vi en nese (vē′ə nēz′), *adj., n., pl.* **-nese.** —*adj.* of or having to do with Vienna or its people. —*n.* native or inhabitant of Vienna.

Vien tiane (vyen tyän′), *n.* administrative capital of Laos, in the NW part. 150,000.

Vi et cong (vē et′kông′, vē et′kong′), *n., pl.* **-cong.** 1 the Communist guerrilla force in South Vietnam. 2 member of this force.

Viet Cong, Vietcong.

Vi et minh (vē et′min′), *n.* the Communist party in Indochina, in power in North Vietnam.

Viet Minh, Vietminh.

Vi et nam (vē et′näm′), *n.* country in SE Asia, since 1954 divided into two countries, North Vietnam and South Vietnam. Prior to 1954, Vietnam, Cambodia, and Laos were combined as the territory of French Indochina. See **Indochina** for map.

Viet Nam, Vietnam.

Vi et nam ese (vē et′nä mēz′), *adj., n., pl.* **-ese.** —*adj.* of or having to do with Vietnam or its people. —*n.* 1 native or inhabitant of Vietnam. 2 language of Vietnam.

Vi et nam ize (vē et′nə mīz), *v.t.,* **-ized, -iz ing.** put under Vietnamese control. **—Vi et′nam i za′tion,** *n.*

Vietnam War, war between South Vietnam, the United States, and their allies on the one side, and the Vietcong, North Vietnam, and their allies on the other side, which began about 1957.

view (vyü), *n.* 1 act of seeing; sight; look: *It was our first view of the ocean.* 2 power of seeing; range of sight or vision: *A ship came into view.* 3 thing seen; scene: *The view from our house is beautiful.* See synonym study below. 4 picture of some scene: *Various views of the mountains hung on the walls.* 5 a mental picture or impression; idea: *have a clear view of a problem.* 6 way of looking at or considering a matter; opinion: *What are your views on the subject?* See **opinion** for synonym study. 7 aim; intention; purpose: *It is my view to leave tomorrow.* 8 prospect; expectation: *with no view of success.* 9 a general account of something; survey.

in view, a in sight. **b** under consideration. **c** as a purpose or intention. **d** as a hope; as an expectation.

in view of, considering; because of.

on view, open for people to see; to be seen.

with a view to, a with the purpose or intention of. **b** with a hope of; expecting to.

—*v.t.* 1 see; look at: *They viewed the scene with pleasure.* 2 look at carefully; inspect. 3 consider; regard: *The plan was viewed favorably.*

[< Anglo-French *vewe* < Old French *veoir* to see < Latin *videre*]

Syn. *n.* 3 **View, scene** mean something which can be seen. **View** applies to what is within the range of vision of someone looking from a certain point: *That new building spoils the view from our windows.* **Scene** applies to those elements which make up a landscape, with little regard to where they are seen from.

view er (vyü′ər), *n.* 1 person who views, especially one who views television. 2 device that magnifies and sometimes illuminates slides placed in it for viewing.

view less (vyü′lis), *adj.* 1 that cannot be seen; invisible. 2 without views or opinions. **—view′less ly,** *adv.*

view point (vyü′point′), *n.* 1 place from which one looks at something. 2 attitude of mind; point of view: *A heavy rain that is good from the viewpoint of farmers may be bad from the viewpoint of tourists.*

vi ges i mal (vī jes′ə məl), *adj.* 1 twentieth. 2 in or by twenties. [< Latin *vigesimus* twentieth]

vig il (vij′əl), *n.* 1 a staying awake for some purpose; a watching; watch: *All night the mother kept vigil over the sick child.* 2 a night spent in prayer. 3 **vigils,** *pl.* devotions, prayers, services, etc., on the night before a religious festival. 4 the day and night before a solemn religious festival. [< Latin *vigilia* < *vigil* watchful]

vig i lance (vij′ə ləns), *n.* 1 watchfulness; alertness; caution: *Constant vigilance is necessary in order to avoid accidents in driving.* 2 sleeplessness.

vigilance committee, U.S. a self-appointed and unauthorized group of citizens organized to maintain order and punish criminals. In the 1800's, vigilance committees were common in frontier territories of the United States.

vig i lant (vij′ə lənt), *adj.* keeping steadily on the alert; watchful; wide-awake: *The dog kept vigilant guard.* See **watchful** for synonym study. **—vig′i lant ly,** *adv.*

vig i lan te (vij′ə lan′tē), *n.* U.S. member of a vigilance committee. [< Spanish, vigilant]

vi gnette (vi nyet′), *n., v.,* **-gnet ted, -gnet ting.** —*n.* 1 a decorative design on a page of a book, especially on the title page or at the beginning or end of a chapter. 2 a literary sketch; short verbal description. 3 an engraving, drawing, photograph, or the like, that shades off gradually at the edge. —*v.t.* 1 make a vignette of. 2 (in photography) finish (a photograph or portrait) in the manner of a vignette. [< French, diminutive of *vigne* vine]

vi gnet tist (vi nyet′ist), *n.* artist or engraver who produces vignettes.

vig or (vig′ər), *n.* 1 active strength or force. 2 healthy energy or power. [< Latin]

vig or ous (vig′ər əs), *adj.* full of vigor; strong and active; energetic; forceful: *wage a vigorous war against disease.* **—vig′or ous ly,** *adv.* **—vig′or ous ness,** *n.*

vig our (vig′ər), *n.* BRITISH. vigor.

vi king or **Vi king** (vī′king), *n.* one of the daring Scandinavian seamen who raided the coasts of Europe during the A.D. 700's, 800's, and 900's, conquered parts of England, France, Russia, and other countries, and explored distant lands that may have included North America. [< Scandinavian (Old Icelandic) *víkingr*]

vile (vīl), *adj.,* **vil er, vil est.** 1 very bad: *vile weather.* 2 foul; disgusting; obnoxious: *a vile smell.* 3 evil; low; immoral: *vile habits.* See **base**[2] for synonym study. 4 poor; mean; lowly: *the vile tasks of the kitchen.* 5 of little worth or account; trifling. [< Latin *vilis* cheap] **—vile′ly,** *adv.* **—vile′ness,** *n.*

vil i fi ca tion (vil′ə fə kā′shən), *n.* 1 a vilifying. 2 a being vilified.

vil i fy (vil′ə fī), *v.t.,* **-fied, -fy ing.** speak evil of; revile; slander; disparage. **—vil′i fi′er,** *n.*

vil la (vil′ə), *n.* a house in the country, suburbs, or at the seashore, usually a large and elegant residence. [< Italian < Latin]

Vil la (vē′yä), *n.* **Pancho,** 1877-1923, Mexican revolutionary leader. His original name was Doroteo Arango.

vil lage (vil′ij), *n.* 1 group of houses in a suburban or country area, usually smaller than a town. 2 the people of a village. [< Old French < *ville* farm, village < Latin *villa* country house]

vil lag er (vil′i jər), *n.* person who lives in a village.

vil lain (vil′ən), *n.* 1 a very wicked person. 2 a playful name for a mischievous person. 3 character in a play, novel, etc., whose evil motives or actions form an important element in the plot. 4 villein. [< Old French *villein* < Medieval Latin *villanus* farm hand < Latin *villa* country house]

vil lain ess (vil′ə nis), *n.* a woman villain.

vil lain ous (vil′ə nəs), *adj.* 1 very wicked; depraved. 2 extremely bad; vile. **—vil′lain ous ly,** *adv.* **—vil′lain ous ness,** *n.*

vil lain y (vil′ə nē), *n., pl.* **-lain ies.** 1 great wickedness; infamy. 2 a very wicked act; crime.

Vil la-Lo bos (vil′ə lō′bəs, vē′lə lō′bůsh), *n.* **Heitor,** 1887-1959, Brazilian composer.

vil la nelle (vil′ə nel′), *n.* form of poetry normally consisting of 19 lines with two rhymes, written in five tercets and a final quatrain. [< French < Italian *villanella* < *villa* villa]

vil lein (vil′ən), *n.* one of a class of half-free peasants in the European feudal system in the Middle Ages; villain. A villein was under the control of his lord, but in his relations with other men had the rights of a freeman. [variant of *villain*]

vil li (vil′ī), *n. pl.* of **vil lus.** 1 tiny, hairlike parts growing out of the mucous membrane of the small intestine, that aid in absorbing certain substances. 2 the soft hairs covering the fruit, flowers, etc., of certain plants. [< Latin, plural of *villus* tuft of hair]

Vil liers (vil′yərz), *n.* **George.** See **Buckingham.**

Vil lon (vē yôN′), *n.* **François,** 1431-1463?, French poet who was a vagabond.

vil lous (vil′əs), *adj.* having villi; covered with villi. **—vil′lous ly,** *adv.*

vil lus (vil′əs), *n.* sing. of **villi.**

Vil na (vil′nə), *n.* Vilnius.

Vil ni us (vil′nē ůs), *n.* capital of the Lithuanian S.S.R., in the SE part. 372,000.

vim (vim), *n.* force; energy; vigor. [< Latin, accusative of *vis* strength]

vin ai grette (vin′ə gret′), *n.* a small ornamental bottle or box for smelling salts, etc. [< French < *vinaigre.* See VINEGAR.]

Vin ci (vin′chē), *n.* **Leonardo da.** See **da Vinci.**

vin ci ble (vin′sə bəl), *adj.* easily overcome, defeated, or vanquished; conquerable. [< Latin *vincibilis* < *vincere* conquer]

vin cu lum (ving′kyə ləm), *n., pl.* **-la** (-lə). 1 bond of union; tie. 2 (in mathematics) a line drawn over several terms to show that they are to be considered together, as in $\overline{a + b} \times c$. [< Latin, bond < *vincire* to bind]

vin di cate (vin′də kāt), *v.t.,* **-cat ed, -cat ing.** 1 clear from suspicion, dishonor, a hint or charge of wrongdoing, etc.: *The verdict of "Not guilty" vindicated him.* 2 defend successfully against opposition; uphold; justify: *The heir vindicated his claim to the fortune.* 3 assert a claim to; establish possession of. [< Latin *vindicatum* defended, avenged < *vindex* defender, avenger] **—vin′di ca′tor,** *n.*

vin di ca tion (vin′də kā′shən), *n.* a vindicating or a being vindicated; defense; justification.

vin dic a tive (vin dik′ə tiv, vin′də kā′tiv), *adj.* tending to vindicate; justifying.

vin dic tive (vin dik′tiv), *adj.* 1 feeling a strong tendency toward revenge; bearing a grudge: *He is so vindictive that he never forgives anybody.* 2 showing a strong tendency toward revenge: *Vindictive acts rarely do much good.* [< Latin *vindicta* revenge < *vindex* avenger] **—vin dic′tive ly,** *adv.* **—vin dic′tive ness,** *n.*

vine (vīn), *n.* 1 plant with a long, slender stem, that grows along the ground or that climbs by attaching itself to a wall, tree, or other support. 2 the stem of any trailing or climbing plant. 3 grapevine. [< Old French *vigne* < Latin *vinea* < *vinum* wine] **—vine′like′,** *adj.*

vin e gar (vin′ə gər), *n.* a sour liquid produced by the fermentation of cider, wine, malt, etc., consisting largely of dilute, impure acetic acid. Vinegar is used in flavoring or preserving food. [< Old French *vinaigre* < *vin* wine + *aigre* sour]

vinegar eel, a minute nematode worm found commonly in vinegar.

vin e gar ish (vin′ə gər ish), *adj.* somewhat like vinegar; sourish.

vin e gar y (vin′ə gər ē), *adj.* of or like vinegar; sour.

vin er y (vī′nər ē), *n., pl.* **-er ies.** hothouse for the cultivation of grapevines.

vine yard (vin′yərd), *n.* place planted with grapevines.

vingt-et-un (vaN′tā œN′), *n.* FRENCH. the game of twenty-one.

vin i cul ture (vin′ə kul′chər, vī′nə-kul′chər), *n.* the cultivation of grapes for the production of wine.

Vin land (vin′lənd), *n.* name given by Norsemen to a region on the E coast of North America which they explored. According to old Norse sagas, Leif Ericson visited Vinland about A.D. 1000.

vi nous (vī′nəs), *adj.* 1 of, like, or having to do with wine. 2 caused by drinking wine. [< Latin *vinosus* < *vinum* wine]

Vin son (vin′sən), *n.* **Frederick Moore,** 1890-1953, chief justice of the United States Supreme Court from 1946 to 1953.

vin tage (vin′tij), *n.* 1 the wine from a certain crop of grapes: *The finest vintages cost much more than others.* 2 a year's crop of grapes. 3 the gathering of grapes for making wine. 4 the season of gathering grapes and making wine. 5 type or model of something which was fashionable or popular during an earlier season: *Her old hat was of the vintage of 1940.* 6 age, especially old age. *—adj.* of outstanding quality; choice: *vintage wines.* [< Old French *vendange* < Latin *vindemia* < *vinum* wine + *demere* take off]

vint ner (vint′nər), *n.* dealer in wine; wine merchant.

vi nyl (vī′nl), *n.* 1 a univalent radical present in certain organic compounds, derived from ethylene. *Formula:* $CH_2{=}CH$— 2 Also, **vinyl plastic** or **vinyl resin,** any of various tough synthetic plastics or resins produced by polymerizing a compound containing the vinyl radical, used in floor coverings, toys, molded articles, phonograph records, etc. [< Latin *vinum* wine + English *-yl*]

vi ol (vī′əl), *n.* 1 any of several stringed musical instruments played with a bow and held either on or between the knees while they are played. Viols were used chiefly in the 1500's and 1600's. 2 double bass. [< Old French *viole*]

violin (def. 1)

vi o la¹ (vē ō′lə), *n.* a stringed musical instrument like a violin, but somewhat larger and lower in pitch; a tenor or alto violin. [< Italian]

vi o la² (vī′ə lə, vī ō′lə), *n.* 1 any of several hybrid garden violets resembling the pansy but with a more delicate and uniform coloring of the flowers. 2 any violet. [< New Latin < Latin, violet]

vi o la bil i ty (vī′ə lə bil′ə tē), *n.* a being violable.

vi o la ble (vī′ə lə bəl), *adj.* that can be violated. **—vi′o la ble ness,** *n.* **—vi′o la bly,** *adv.*

vi o late (vī′ə lāt), *v.t.,* **-lat ed, -lat ing.** 1 break (a law, rule, agreement, promise, etc.); act contrary to; fail to perform: *He violated the law and was arrested by the police.* 2 break in upon; disturb: *The sound of guns violated the usual calm of Sunday morning.* 3 treat with disrespect or contempt: *The soldiers violated the church by using it as a stable.* 4 trespass on; infringe on: *violate the right of free speech.* 5 use force against (a woman or girl); rape. [< Latin *violatum* treated with violence < *vis* force] **—vi′o la′tor,** *n.*

hat, āge, fär; let, ēqual, tėrm;
it, īce; hot, ōpen, ôrder;
oil, out; cup, pu̇t, rüle;
ch, child; ng, long; sh, she;
th, thin; ᴛʜ, then; zh, measure;

ə represents *a* in about, *e* in taken,
i in pencil, *o* in lemon, *u* in circus.

< = from, derived from, taken from.

vi o la tion (vī′ə lā′shən), *n.* 1 use of force; violence. 2 a breaking (of a law, rule, agreement, promise, etc.); infringement. 3 interruption or disturbance. 4 treatment (of a holy thing) with disrespect or contempt. 5 rape.

vi o lence (vī′ə ləns), *n.* 1 rough force in action: *slam a door with violence.* 2 rough or harmful action or treatment. 3 harm; injury: *It would do violence to her principles to work on Sunday.* 4 unlawful use of force. 5 strength of action, feeling, etc.; fury; passion. 6 the improper treatment or use of a word; distortion of meaning or application. 7 rape.

vi o lent (vī′ə lənt), *adj.* 1 acting or done with strong, rough force: *a violent blow.* 2 caused by strong, rough force: *a violent death.* 3 showing or caused by very strong feeling, action, etc.: *violent language.* 4 very great; severe; extreme: *a violent pain.* [< Latin *violentus* < *vis* force] **—vi′o lent ly,** *adv.*

vi o let (vī′ə lit), *n.* 1 any of a genus of stemless or leafy-stemmed plants with purple, blue, yellow, white, or multicolored flowers. 2 the flower of any of these plants. Some violets are very fragrant. 3 a bluish purple. Violet is red and blue mixed. *—adj.* bluish-purple. [< Old French *violete,* ultimately < Latin *viola*]

violet rays, the shortest rays of the spectrum that can be seen, having wavelengths around 3850 angstroms.

vi o lin (vī′ə lin′), *n.* 1 a musical instrument with four strings played with a bow. The violin has the highest pitch of the stringed instruments. 2 person who plays the violin in an orchestra. [< Italian *violino,* diminutive of *viola* viol]

vi o lin ist (vī′ə lin′ist), *n.* person who plays the violin.

vi ol ist (vē′ə list), *n.* person who plays the viola.

vi o lon cel list (vī′ə lən chel′ist, vē′ə lən-chel′ist), *n.* cellist.

vi o lon cel lo (vī′ə lən chel′ō, vē′ə lən-chel′ō), *n., pl.* **-los.** cello. [< Italian, ultimately < *viola* viol]

vi os te rol (vī os′tə rōl′, vī os′tə rol′), *n.* preparation of ergosterol containing a form of vitamin D which has been activated by exposure to ultraviolet light. It is used to prevent or cure rickets. [< *(ultra)vio(let)* + *(ergo)sterol*]

VIP or **V.I.P.,** INFORMAL. very important person.

vi per (vī′pər), *n.* 1 any of a family of poisonous Old World snakes with a pair of large, hollow fangs and often having a thick, heavy body, including the adder of Europe

and the puff adder of Africa. 2 pit viper. 3 any of certain other poisonous or supposedly poisonous snakes. 4 a spiteful, treacherous person. [< Latin *vipera*]
vi per ine (vī′pər ən, vī′pe rīn′), *adj.* viperous.
vi per ish (vī′pər ish), *adj.* like a viper; viperous.
vi per ous (vī′pər əs), *adj.* 1 of or having to do with a viper or vipers. 2 like a viper. 3 spiteful; treacherous. **—vi′per ous ly,** *adv.*
vi ra go (və rā′gō, və rä′gō), *n., pl.* **-goes** or **-gos.** 1 a violent, bad-tempered, or scolding woman. 2 ARCHAIC. a strong, vigorous woman; amazon. [< Latin < *vir* man]
vi ral (vī′rəl), *adj.* 1 of or having to do with a virus. 2 caused by a virus.
vir e o (vir′ē ō), *n., pl.* **vir e os.** any of several small, olive-green, insect-eating American songbirds. [< Latin, kind of bird < *virere* be green]
vi res cence (vī res′ns), *n.* a turning or becoming green; greenness.
vi res cent (vī res′nt), *adj.* turning green; tending to a green color; greenish. [< Latin *virescentem* < *virere* be green]
Vir gil (vėr′jəl), *n.* Vergil.
Vir gil i an (vər jil′ē ən), *adj.* Vergilian.
vir gin (vėr′jən), *n.* 1 woman or man who has not had sexual intercourse. 2 an unmarried woman; maiden. 3 **the Virgin,** Virgin Mary. 4 **Virgin,** Virgo. *—adj.* 1 of or having to do with a virgin; suitable for a virgin: *virgin modesty.* 2 pure; spotless. Virgin snow is newly fallen snow. 3 not yet used: *virgin soil, a virgin forest.* [< Latin *virginem* maiden, virgin]

virginal

vir gin al (vėr′jə nəl), *adj.* of or suitable for a virgin; maidenly; chaste. *—n.* a small harpsichord set in a rectangular box without legs. It was much used in the 1500's and 1600's. **—vir′gin al ly,** *adv.*
virgin birth, 1 doctrine that Jesus was the son of God and was miraculously conceived by and born to the Virgin Mary. 2 (in zoology) parthenogenesis.
Vir gin ia (vər jin′yə), *n.* one of the southeastern states of the United States. 4,648,000 pop.; 40,800 sq. mi. *Capital:* Richmond. *Abbrev.:* Va. **—Vir gin′ian,** *adj., n.*
Virginia Beach, city in E Virginia. 172,000.
Virginia creeper, an American climbing, woody vine of the same family as the grape, having leaves with five leaflets and inedible bluish-black berries; woodbine.
Virginia reel, an American country-dance in which the partners form two lines facing each other and perform a number of dance steps.
Virgin Islands, 1 group of islands in the West Indies, east of Puerto Rico, belonging to the United States. The chief ones are St. John, St. Thomas, and St. Croix. 63,000 pop.; 133 sq. mi. 2 group of islands **(British Virgin Islands)** east of Puerto Rico, a part of the Leeward Islands, belonging to Great Britain. 11,000 pop.; 67 sq. mi.
vir gin i ty (vər jin′ə tē), *n.* virgin condition; maidenhood.
Virgin Mary, the mother of Jesus.
Virgin Queen, Elizabeth I of England.
vir gin's-bow er (vėr′jənz bou′ər), *n.* any of various climbing species of clematis, bearing clusters of small white flowers.
Vir go (vėr′gō), *n.* 1 constellation on the celestial equator, between Leo and Libra, seen by ancient astronomers as having the rough outline of a woman; Virgin. 2 the sixth sign of the zodiac. The sun enters Virgo about August 22.
vir gule (vėr′gyül), *n.* a slanting stroke (/) between two words indicating that the meaning of either word pertains, as in *and/or;* diagonal. [< Latin *virgula* little rod]
vi ri cid al (vī′rə sī′dl), *adj.* destructive to viruses: *a viricidal compound.*
vi ri cide (vī′rə sīd), *n.* substance that destroys viruses.
vir i des cence (vir′ə des′ns), *n.* a being viridescent.
vir i des cent (vir′ə des′nt), *adj.* somewhat green; greenish. [< Late Latin *viridescentem* turning green < Latin *viridis* green]
vir ile (vir′əl), *adj.* 1 of, belonging to, or characteristic of a man; manly; masculine. 2 full of manly strength or masculine vigor. 3 vigorous; forceful. [< Latin *virilis* < *vir* man]
vi ril i ty (və ril′ə tē), *n., pl.* **-ties.** 1 manly strength; masculine vigor. 2 manhood. 3 vigor; forcefulness.
vi ro log i cal (vī′rə loj′ə kəl), *adj.* of or having to do with virology.
vi rol o gist (vī rol′ə jist), *n.* an expert in virology.
vi rol o gy (vī rol′ə jē), *n.* science that deals with viruses and virus diseases.
vir tu (vėr′tü′, vėr′tü), *n.* 1 excellence or merit in an object of art because of its workmanship, rarity, antiquity, or the like. 2 objects of art; choice curios. 3 a taste for objects of art; knowledge of objects of art. Also, **vertu.** [< Italian *virtù* excellence < Latin *virtutem* virtue]
vir tu al (vėr′chü əl), *adj.* being something in effect, though not so in name; for all practical purposes; actual; real: *The battle was won with so great a loss of soldiers that it was a virtual defeat.* **—vir′tu al ly,** *adv.*
virtual image, (in optics) an image formed when the rays from each point of the object diverge as if from a point beyond the reflecting or refracting surface. A virtual image cannot be placed on a screen.
vir tu al i ty (vėr′chü al′ə tē), *n.* condition or quality of being virtual.
vir tue (vėr′chü), *n.* 1 moral excellence; goodness. See **goodness** for synonym study. 2 a particular moral excellence: *Justice and kindness are virtues.* 3 a good quality; merit: *praise the virtues of a small car.* 4 chastity; purity. 5 power to produce effects: *There is little virtue in that medicine.* 6 **by virtue of** or **in virtue of,** relying on; because of; on account of. 7 **make a virtue of necessity,** do willingly what must be done anyway. [< Old French *vertu* < Latin *virtutem* manliness, virtue < *vir* man] **—vir′tue less,** *adj.*
vir tu os i ty (vėr′chü os′ə tē), *n., pl.* **-ties.** character or skill of a virtuoso.
vir tu o so (vėr′chü ō′sō), *n., pl.* **-sos, -si** (-sē), *adj.* *—n.* 1 person skilled in the techniques of an art, especially in playing a musical instrument. 2 person who has a cultivated appreciation of artistic excellence; connoisseur. 3 student or collector of objects of art, curios, antiquities, etc. *—adj.* showing the artistic qualities and skills of a virtuoso. [< Italian, learned, virtuous]
vir tu ous (vėr′chü əs), *adj.* 1 good; moral; righteous. 2 chaste; pure. **—vir′tu ous ly,** *adv.* **—vir′tu ous ness,** *n.*
vir u lence (vir′yə ləns, vir′ə ləns), *n.* 1 quality of being very poisonous or harmful; deadliness. 2 intense bitterness or spite; violent hostility.
vir u len cy (vir′yə lən sē, vir′ə lən sē), *n.* virulence.
vir u lent (vir′yə lənt, vir′ə lənt), *adj.* 1 very poisonous or harmful; deadly: *a virulent poison.* 2 (of diseases) characterized by a rapid and severe malignant or infectious condition. 3 (of a microorganism) able to cause a disease by breaking down the protective mechanisms of the host. 4 intensely bitter or spiteful; violently hostile. [< Latin *virulentus* < *virus* poison] **—vir′u lent ly,** *adv.*
vi rus (vī′rəs), *n.* 1 any of a group of disease-producing agents composed of protein and nucleic acid, smaller than any known bacteria and dependent upon the living tissue of hosts for their reproduction and growth. Viruses cause such diseases in man as rabies, polio, chicken pox, and the common cold. 2 a poison produced in a person or animal suffering from an infectious disease. 3 anything that poisons the mind or morals; corrupting influence. [< Latin, poison]
vis (vis), *n.* LATIN. force; power.
Vis., Viscount.
vi sa (vē′zə), *n.* an official signature or endorsement upon a passport or document, showing that it has been examined and approved. A visa is granted by the consul or other representative of the country to which a person wishes to travel. *—v.t.* examine and sign (a passport or other document). [< French < Latin *(carta) visa* (paper) that has been seen (i.e., inspected)]
vis age (viz′ij), *n.* 1 face. 2 appearance or aspect. [< Old French < *vis* face < Latin *visus* sight < *videre* to see]
-visaged, *combining form.* having a ___ visage: *Grim-visaged = having a grim visage.*
vis-à-vis (vē′zə vē′), *adv., adj.* face to face; opposite: *We sat vis-à-vis. The usual position in modern dancing is vis-à-vis.* *—prep.* 1 face to face with; opposite to. 2 in relation to; in comparison with; over against. *—n.* person or thing that is opposite. [< French]
Vi sa yan (vi sä′yən), *n.* 1 member of a large native people in the Philippines. 2 language of this people. Also, **Bisayan.**
Visayan Islands, group of islands in the Philippines. Also, **Bisayas.**
Visc., Viscount.
vis cer a (vis′ər ə), *n.pl. of* **vis cus** (vis′kəs). the soft internal organs of the body, especially of the abdominal cavity, including the heart, stomach, liver, intestines, kidneys, etc. [< Latin]
vis cer al (vis′ər əl), *adj.* 1 of, having to do with, or in the region of the viscera. 2 coming from one's inwards; not mental or rational: *visceral reactions.* **—vis′cer al ly,** *adv.*
vis cid (vis′id), *adj.* 1 thick like heavy syrup or glue; sticky; viscous. 2 (in botany) covered with a sticky secretion, as leaves.

[< Late Latin *viscidus* < Latin *viscum* birdlime] **—vis′cid ly,** *adv.* **—vis′cid ness,** *n.*

vis cid i ty (vi sid′ə tē), *n.* quality of being viscid or sticky.

vis cose (vis′kōs), *n.* a thick, sticky substance made by treating cellulose with sodium hydroxide and other chemicals. It is used in manufacturing rayon, cellophane, etc. *—adj.* 1 having to do with or made from viscose. 2 viscous. [< Latin *viscosus* viscous]

vis cos i ty (vi skos′ə tē), *n., pl.* **-ties.** 1 condition or quality of being viscous. 2 resistance of a fluid to the motion of its molecules among themselves.

vis count (vī′kount), *n.* nobleman ranking next below an earl or count and next above a baron. [< Anglo-French < Old French *visconte* < *vis-* vice- + *conte* count²]

vis count cy (vī′kount sē), *n., pl.* **-cies.** rank or title of a viscount.

vis count ess (vī′koun tis), *n.* 1 wife or widow of a viscount. 2 woman whose rank is equal to that of a viscount.

vis count y (vī′koun tē), *n., pl.* **-count ies.** viscountcy.

vis cous (vis′kəs), *adj.* 1 thick like heavy syrup or glue; sticky. 2 having the property of viscosity. [< Latin *viscosus* < *viscum* birdlime] **—vis′cous ly,** *adv.* **—vis′cous ness,** *n.*

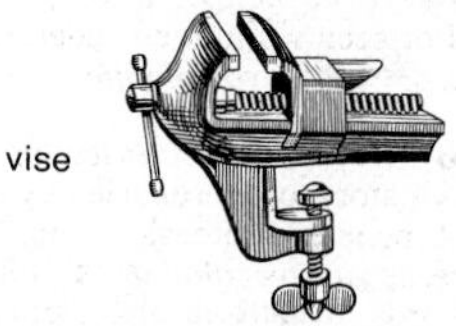
vise

vise (vīs), *n.* tool having two jaws opened and closed by a screw, used to hold an object firmly while work is being done on it. Also, **vice.** [< Old French *vis* screw < Latin *vitis* tendril of a vine]

vi sé (vē′zā), *n., v.t.* visa. [< French]

Vish nu (vish′nü), *n.* (in Hinduism) one of the three chief divinities, called "the Preserver."

vis i bil i ty (viz′ə bil′ə tē), *n., pl.* **-ties.** 1 condition or quality of being visible. 2 condition of light, atmosphere, etc., with reference to the distance at which things can be clearly seen.

vis i ble (viz′ə bəl), *adj.* 1 that can be seen: *The shore was barely visible through the fog.* 2 readily evident; apparent; obvious: *The vagrant had no visible means of support.* [< Latin *visibilis* < *videre* to see] **—vis′i ble ness,** *n.* **—vis′i bly,** *adv.*

Vis i goth (viz′ə goth), *n.* member of the western division of the Goths. The Visigoths sacked Rome in A.D. 410, and formed a monarchy in France and northern Spain about A.D. 418.

vi sion (vizh′ən), *n.* 1 power of seeing; sense of sight: *She wore glasses to improve her vision.* 2 act or fact of seeing; sight. 3 power of perceiving by the imagination or by clear thinking: *a prophet of great vision.* 4 something seen in the imagination, in a dream, in one's thoughts, etc.: *have visions of great wealth.* 5 phantom. 6 a very beautiful person, scene, etc. *—v.t., v.i.* 1 see in, or as if in, a vision. 2 show in a vision. [< Latin *visionem* < *videre* to see] **—vi′sion less,** *adj.*

vi sion ar y (vizh′ə ner′ē), *n., pl.* **-ar ies,** *adj.* *—n.* 1 person given to imagining or dreaming; person who is not practical; dreamer. 2 person who sees visions. *—adj.* 1 not practical; dreamy: *a visionary author.* 2 not practicable; fanciful: *Fifty years ago most people would have regarded plans for an atomic power plant as visionary.* 3 of or belonging to a vision; seen in a vision; imaginary: *The visionary scene faded, and he awoke.* 4 having visions; able to have visions. **—vi′sion ar′i ness,** *n.*

vis it (viz′it), *v.t.* 1 go to see; come to see: *visit a city, visit a museum.* 2 make a call on or stay with for social or other reasons; be a guest of: *visit one's aunt.* 3 go or come to see, in order to inspect, examine officially, give professional service or treatment to, etc.: *The doctor visited his patients at the hospital. The inspector visited the factory.* 4 come upon; afflict: *Job was visited by many troubles.* 5 send upon; inflict: *visit one's anger on someone.* 6 punish; avenge. *—v.i.* 1 pay a call; make a stay; be a guest: *visit in the country.* 2 INFORMAL. talk or chat. *—n.* 1 a visiting; a call from friendship, for purpose of inspection, for professional treatment, etc. 2 a stay as a guest. 3 INFORMAL. an informal talk; chat. [< Latin *visitare,* frequentative of *visere* look at well < *videre* to see] **—vis′it a ble,** *adj.*

vis it ant (viz′ə tənt), *n.* 1 visitor; guest. 2 a migratory bird temporarily frequenting a particular locality. *—adj.* visiting.

vis i ta tion (viz′ə tā′shən), *n.* 1 act of visiting. 2 visit for the purpose of making an official inspection or examination. A nation at war has the right of visitation of neutral ships; that is, the right to inspect their cargoes. 3 Also, **Visitation.** the visit of the Virgin Mary to Elizabeth, her cousin and the mother of John the Baptist. 4 **Visitation,** a church festival commemorating this, celebrated on July 2. 5 punishment or reward sent by God.

visiting card, calling card.

visiting fireman, SLANG. 1 a visiting dignitary or official accorded special treatment. 2 a vacationer, tourist, etc., supposed to be a liberal spender.

visiting teacher, schoolteacher who visits the homes of sick or disabled pupils to instruct them.

vis i tor (viz′ə tər), *n.* person who visits or is visiting; guest.

Syn. Visitor, guest mean someone who comes to stay somewhere or with someone. **Visitor,** the general word, applies to anyone, regardless of the length of his stay or his reason for coming: *Visitors from the East arrived last night.* **Guest** emphasizes the idea of being entertained, and applies especially to someone invited to come or stay: *They usually entertain their guests at the club.*

vi sor (vī′zər), *n.* 1 the movable front part of a helmet, covering the face. 2 the brim of a cap, projecting in front to protect or shade the eyes. 3 shade above a windshield, that can be lowered to shield the eyes from the sun. 4 mask. Also, **vizor.** [< Anglo-French *viser* < Old French *visiere* < *vis* face. See VISAGE.] **—vi′sor less,** *adj.*

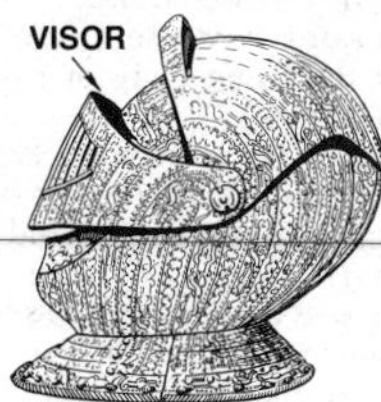

visor (def. 1)

hat, āge, fär; let, ēqual, tėrm;
it, īce; hot, ōpen, ôrder;
oil, out; cup, pu̇t, rüle;
ch, child; ng, long; sh, she;
th, thin; ᴛʜ, then; zh, measure;

ə represents *a* in about, *e* in taken, *i* in pencil, *o* in lemon, *u* in circus.

< = from, derived from, taken from.

vi sored (vī′zərd), *adj.* furnished or covered with a visor.

vis ta (vis′tə), *n.* 1 view seen through a narrow opening or passage: *The opening between the two rows of trees afforded a vista of the lake.* 2 such an opening or passage itself: *a shady vista of elms.* 3 a mental view: *Education should open up new vistas.* [< Italian]

VIS TA (vis′tə), *n.* Volunteers in Service to America (agency of the United States government established in 1964 to send volunteers to work and help in depressed areas of the country).

Vis tu la River (vis′chə lə), river in Poland flowing from the Carpathians to the Baltic Sea. 650 mi.

vis u al (vizh′ü əl), *adj.* 1 of, having to do with, or used in sight or vision: *Nearsightedness is a visual defect.* 2 received through the sense of sight: *visual impressions.* 3 that can be seen or perceived; perceptible; visible. [< Late Latin *visualis* < Latin *visus* sight < *videre* to see] **—vis′u al ly,** *adv.*

visual aid, device or means for aiding the learning process through the sense of sight, such as a chart, diagram, motion picture, or filmstrip.

vis u al ize (vizh′ü ə līz), *v.,* **-ized, -iz ing.** *—v.t.* 1 form a mental picture of: *visualize a friend's face when she is away.* 2 make visible. *—v.i.* form mental pictures. **—vis′u al i za′tion,** *n.* **—vis′u al iz′er,** *n.*

visual purple, rhodopsin.

vi tal (vī′tl), *adj.* 1 of or having to do with life: *Growth and decay are vital processes.* 2 necessary to life: *Eating is a vital function. The heart is a vital organ.* 3 very necessary; very important; essential: *a vital question. Drainage of the nearby swamp was considered vital to the welfare of the community.* 4 causing death, failure, or ruin: *a vital wound, a vital blow to an industry.* 5 full of life and spirit; lively. *—n.* **vitals,** *pl.* **a** parts or organs necessary to life. The brain, heart, lungs, and stomach are vitals. **b** essential parts or features of anything; essentials. [< Latin *vitalis* < *vita* life] **—vi′tal ly,** *adv.*

vi tal ism (vī′tl iz′əm), *n.* doctrine that the behavior of a living organism is, at least in part, due to a vital principle that cannot possibly be explained by physics and chemistry.

vi tal ist (vī′tl ist), *n.* adherent of vitalism.

vi tal is tic (vī′tl is′tik), *adj.* of vitalism or vitalists.

vi tal i ty (vī tal′ə tē), *n., pl.* **-ties.** 1 vital force; power to live: *Her vitality was lessened by illness.* 2 power to endure and be active. 3 strength or vigor of mind or body; energy.

vi tal ize (vī′tl īz), *v.t.,* **-ized, -iz ing.** 1 give life to. 2 put vitality into; make more energetic, lively, or enterprising. **—vi′tal i za′tion,** *n.*

vital statistics, statistics that give facts about births, deaths, marriages, divorces, etc.

vi ta min (vī′tə mən), *n.* any of certain organic substances required for the normal growth and nourishment of the body, found in small amounts in plant and animal foods and also prepared medicinally in the form of tablets, injections, etc. Lack of essential vitamins causes such diseases as rickets and scurvy, as well as general poor health. *—adj.* of, having to do with, or containing vitamins. [< Latin *vita* life + English *amin(e);* because originally thought to be an amine derivative]

vitamin A, the fat-soluble vitamin found in milk, butter, cod-liver oil, egg yolk, liver, green and yellow vegetables, etc., that increases the resistance of the body to infection and prevents night blindness. It exists in two known forms, $\mathbf{A_1}$ and $\mathbf{A_2}$.

vitamin $\mathbf{B_1}$**,** thiamin.

vitamin $\mathbf{B_2}$**,** riboflavin. Also, **vitamin G.**

vitamin $\mathbf{B_6}$**,** pyridoxine.

vitamin $\mathbf{B_{12}}$**,** vitamin found especially in liver, milk, and eggs, that is active against pernicious anemia.

vitamin B complex, group of water-soluble vitamins including vitamin B_1, vitamin B_2, vitamin B_6, nicotinic acid, etc., found in high concentration in yeast and liver.

vitamin C, a water-soluble vitamin found in citrus fruits, tomatoes, leafy green vegetables, etc., that aids in preventing scurvy; ascorbic acid. *Formula:* $C_6H_8O_6$

vitamin D, a fat-soluble vitamin found in cod-liver oil, milk, egg yolk, etc., and produced by irradiating ergosterol and other sterols. Vitamin D prevents rickets and is necessary for the growth and health of bones and teeth. It exists in many related forms including $\mathbf{D_2}$, $\mathbf{D_3}$, and $\mathbf{D_4}$.

vitamin E, a fat-soluble vitamin found in wheat germ oil, whole grain cereals, lettuce, etc., that is necessary for some reproductive processes. Lack of vitamin E causes sterility.

vitamin G, riboflavin.

vitamin H, the former name of biotin.

vitamin K, a fat-soluble vitamin found in green leafy vegetables, alfalfa, egg yolk, tomatoes, etc., that promotes clotting of the blood and prevents hemorrhaging. It exists in many related forms.

vitamin P, bioflavonoid.

vi tel lin (vi tel′ən, vī tel′ən), *n.* protein contained in the yolk of eggs. [< Latin *vitellus* egg yolk]

vi ti ate (vish′ē āt), *v.t.,* **-at ed, -at ing.** 1 impair the quality of; spoil: *The abridgment vitiated the original text. Sewage vitiated the stream.* 2 destroy the legal force or authority of: *The contract was vitiated because one person signed under compulsion.* [< Latin *vitiatum* spoiled < *vitium* fault] **—vi′ti a′tion,** *n.* **—vi′ti a′tor,** *n.*

vit i cul ture (vit′ə kul′chər, vī′tə kul′chər), *n.* the cultivation of grapes. [< Latin *vitis* vine + English *culture*]

vit re ous (vit′rē əs), *adj.* 1 like glass; glassy: *vitreous china.* 2 of or having to do with glass. 3 made from glass. 4 having to do with the vitreous humor. [< Latin *vitreus* < *vitrum* glass] **—vit′re ous ness,** *n.*

vitreous humor, the transparent, jellylike substance that fills the eyeball behind the lens. See **eye** for diagram.

vit ri fy (vit′rə fī), *v.t., v.i.,* **-fied, -fy ing.** change into glass or something like glass, especially by fusion through heat. **—vit′ri fi′a ble,** *adj.* **—vit′ri fi ca′tion,** *n.*

vit ri ol (vit′rē əl), *n.* 1 sulfuric acid. 2 any of certain sulfates of metals, such as **blue vitriol,** a sulfate of copper, **green vitriol,** a sulfate of iron, or **white vitriol,** a sulfate of zinc. Vitriols are characterized by a glassy appearance. 3 very sharp speech or severe criticism. [< Medieval Latin *vitriolum* < Latin *vitrum* glass]

vit ri ol ic (vit′rē ol′ik), *adj.* 1 of or containing vitriol. 2 like vitriol. 3 bitterly severe; sharp: *vitriolic criticism.*

vit tles (vit′lz), *n.pl.* DIALECT. victuals.

vi tu pe rate (vī tü′pə rāt′, vī tyü′pə rāt′), *v.t., v.i.,* **-rat ed, -rat ing.** find fault with in abusive words; scold very severely; revile. [< Latin *vituperatum* reviled < *vitium* fault + *parare* prepare] **—vi tu′pe ra′tor,** *n.*

vi tu pe ra tion (vī tü′pə rā′shən, vī tyü′pə rā′shən), *n.* bitter abuse in words; very severe scolding.

vi tu pe ra tive (vī tü′pə rā′tiv, vī tyü′pə rā′tiv), *adj.* abusive; reviling. **—vi tu′pe ra′tive ly,** *adv.*

vi va (vē′və), *interj.* (long) live (the person or thing named). *—n.* shout of applause or good will. [< Italian]

vi va ce (vē vä′chā), in music: *—adj.* lively. *—adv.* in a lively manner. [< Italian]

vi va cious (vī vā′shəs, vi vā′shəs), *adj.* lively; sprightly; animated; gay. **—vi va′cious ly,** *adv.* **—vi va′cious ness,** *n.*

vi vac i ty (vī vas′ə tē, vi vas′ə tē), *n., pl.* **-ties.** liveliness; sprightliness; animation; gaiety. [< Latin *vivacitatem* < *vivacis* lively < *vivere* to live]

Vi val di (vi väl′dē), *n.* **Antonio,** 1677?-1741, Italian composer and violinist.

vi var i um (vī ver′ē əm), *n., pl.* **-var i ums, -var i a** (-ver′ē ə). place in which animals or plants are kept, under circumstances simulating their natural state. [< Latin]

vi va vo ce (vī′və vō′sē), by word of mouth; orally; oral: *Shall we vote viva voce or by ballot?* [< Latin, literally, by living voice]

vive (vēv), *interj.* FRENCH. (long) live (the person or thing named).

viv id (viv′id), *adj.* 1 strikingly bright; brilliant: *Dandelions are a vivid yellow.* 2 full of life; lively: *a vivid description.* 3 strong and distinct: *a vivid memory.* 4 very active or intense: *a vivid imagination.* [< Latin *vividus* < *vivere* to live] **—viv′id ly,** *adv.* **—viv′id ness,** *n.*

viv i fy (viv′ə fī), *v.t.,* **-fied, -fy ing.** 1 give life or vigor to. 2 make vivid; enliven. **—viv′i fi ca′tion,** *n.* **—viv′i fi′er,** *n.*

vi vip ar ous (vī vip′ər əs), *adj.* bringing forth living young, rather than eggs. Dogs, cats, cows, and human beings are viviparous. [< Latin *viviparus* < *vivus* alive + *parere* bring forth] **—vi vip′ar ous ly,** *adv.* **—vi vip′ar ous ness,** *n.*

viv i sect (viv′ə sekt, viv′ə sekt′), *v.t.* dissect the living body of. *—v.i.* practice vivisection.

viv i sec tion (viv′ə sek′shən), *n.* act or practice of dissecting or operating on living animals for scientific study or experimentation. [< Latin *vivus* alive + English *section*]

viv i sec tion al (viv′ə sek′shə nəl), *adj.* of or having to do with vivisection.

viv i sec tion ist (viv′ə sek′shə nist), *n.* 1 vivisector. 2 person who favors or defends vivisection.

viv i sec tor (viv′ə sek′tər, viv′ə sek′tər), *n.* person who practices vivisection.

vix en (vik′sən), *n.* 1 a female fox. 2 a bad-tempered or quarrelsome woman. [Old English *fyxen* < *fox* fox]

vix en ish (vik′sə nish), *adj.* ill-tempered; scolding.

viz., that is to say; namely [for Latin *videlicet*].

viz ard (viz′ərd), *n.* 1 visor. 2 mask. [alteration of *visor*]

vi zier or **vi zir** (vi zir′), *n.* (in Moslem countries) a high official, such as a minister of state. [< Turkish *vezir* < Arabic *wazīr,* originally, porter]

vi zier ship or **vi zir ship** (vi zir′ship), *n.* office or authority of a vizier.

vi zor (vī′zər), *n.* visor.

V-J Day (vē′jā′), date of the Allied victory over Japan in World War II, September 2, 1945.

Vlad i vos tok (vlad′ə vos′tok, vlad′ə vo stok′), *n.* seaport on the Sea of Japan in SE Soviet Union. 442,000.

Vla minck (vlä maNk′), *n.* **Maurice de,** 1876-1958, French painter.

VLF or **vlf,** very low frequency.

voc., vocative.

vocab., vocabulary.

vo ca ble (vō′kə bəl), *n.* a word, especially as heard or seen without consideration of its meaning. [< Latin *vocabulum* < *vocare* to call]

vo cab u lar y (vō kab′yə ler′ē), *n., pl.* **-lar ies.** 1 stock of words used by a person, group of people, profession, etc.: *Reading will increase your vocabulary.* 2 collection or list of words, usually in alphabetical order, with their translations or meanings. [< Medieval Latin *vocabularius* < Latin *vocabulum.* See VOCABLE.]

vocabulary entry, 1 word, term, or item entered in a vocabulary. 2 (in dictionaries) any word or phrase in alphabetical order and defined, or any related word listed for identification under the word from which it is derived.

vo cal (vō′kəl), *adj.* 1 of or having to do with the voice: *vocal organs, vocal power.* 2 made with the voice: *vocal music.* 3 having a voice; giving forth sound: *Men are vocal beings. The gorge was vocal with the roar of the cataract.* 4 aroused to speech; inclined to talk freely: *She became vocal with indignation.* 5 (in phonetics) of a vowel. *—n.* a vocal sound. All vowels are vocal. [< Latin *vocalis* < *vocem* voice] **—vo′cal ly,** *adv.*

vocal cords, two pairs of folds of mucous membrane in the throat, projecting into the cavity of the larynx. The lower pair can be pulled tight and the passage of breath between them then causes them to vibrate, which produces the sound of the voice.

vo cal ic (vō kal′ik), *adj.* 1 of or like a vowel sound. 2 having many vowel sounds.

vo cal ist (vō′kə list), *n.* singer.

vo cal ize (vō′kə līz), *v.,* **-ized, -iz ing.** *—v.i.* 1 use the voice; speak, sing, shout, etc. 2 (in phonetics) become vocalized. *—v.t.* 1 form into voice; utter or sing. 2 make vocal; utter: *The dog vocalized his pain in a series of long howls.* 3 (in phonetics) change into a vowel; use as a vowel. Some people vocalize the *r* in *four.* **—vo′cal i za′tion,** *n.* **—vo′cal iz′er,** *n.*

vo ca tion (vō kā′shən), *n.* 1 occupation, business, profession, or trade: *Medicine is*

hat, āge, fär; let, ēqual, tėrm;
it, īce; hot, ōpen, ôrder;
oil, out; cup, pu̇t, rüle;
ch, child; ng, long; sh, she;
th, thin; ᴛʜ, then; zh, measure;

ə represents *a* in about, *e* in taken, *i* in pencil, *o* in lemon, *u* in circus.

< = from, derived from, taken from.

her vocation. 2 persons engaged in the same business or profession. 3 an inner call or summons. [< Latin *vocationem,* literally, a calling < *vocare* to call < *vocem* voice]

➤ **Vocation, avocation.** *Vocation* applies to one's regular occupation, the way he earns his living. *Avocation* applies to a kind of work one does in his spare time, a hobby: *Bookkeeping is his vocation, and photography is his avocation.*

vo ca tion al (vō kā′shə nəl), *adj.* 1 of or having to do with some occupation, business, profession, or trade. 2 of or having to do with studies or training for some occupation, etc.: *vocational guidance.* **—vo ca′tion al ly,** *adv.*

vocational school, an educational institution, usually at the secondary-school level, where training is given in various vocations or trades, such as printing, stenography, mechanics, etc.

voc a tive (vok′ə tiv), *adj.* (in grammar) showing the person or thing spoken to. *—n.* 1 the vocative case. 2 word in that case. [< Latin *vocativus* < *vocare* to call] **—voc′a tive ly,** *adv.*

vo cif er ance (vō sif′ər əns), *n.* a noisy or clamorous shouting.

vo cif er ant (vō sif′ər ənt), *adj.* vociferating. *—n.* person who vociferates.

vo cif e rate (vō sif′ə rāt′), *v.t., v.i.,* **-rat ed, -rat ing.** cry out loudly or noisily; shout; clamor. [< Latin *vociferatum* shouted out < *vocem* voice + *ferre* carry] **—vo cif′e ra′tion,** *n.* **—vo cif′e ra′tor,** *n.*

vo cif er ous (vō sif′ər əs), *adj.* loud and noisy; shouting; clamoring: *a vociferous person, vociferous cheers.* **—vo cif′er ous ly,** *adv.* **—vo cif′er ous ness,** *n.*

vod ka (vod′kə), *n.* an alcoholic liquor distilled from potatoes, rye, barley, or corn. [< Russian, diminutive of *voda* water]

vogue (vōg), *n.* 1 the fashion: *Hoop skirts were in vogue more than 100 years ago.* 2 popularity or acceptance: *That song had a great vogue at one time.* [< Middle French, a rowing, course, success < *voguer* to row < Italian *vogare*]

voice (vois), *n., v.,* **voiced, voic ing.** *—n.* 1 sound made through the mouth, especially by people in speaking, singing, shouting, etc. The human voice is produced in the larynx. 2 power to make sounds through the mouth; speech: *lose one's voice.* 3 quality or condition of the voice: *a loud voice, be in good voice.* 4 anything like speech or song: *the voice of the wind.* 5 ability as a singer: *have no voice.* 6 singer: *a choir of fifty voices.* 7 part of a piece of music for one kind of singer or instrument. 8 anything likened to speech that conveys impressions to the mind or senses: *the voice of one's conscience, the voice of duty.* 9 expression: *They gave voice to their joy.* 10 an expressed opinion, choice, wish, etc.: *the voice of the public. His voice was for compromise.* 11 the right to express an opinion or choice: *We have no voice in the matter.* 12 (in grammar) a form of the verb that shows whether its subject is active or passive. 13 (in phonetics) a sound uttered with vibration of the vocal cords, not with mere breath. 14 **in voice,** in condition to sing or speak well. 15 **lift up one's voice, a** shout; yell. **b** protest; complain. 16 **with one voice,** unanimously.

—v.t. 1 express; utter: *They voiced their approval of the plan.* 2 (in phonetics) utter with a sound made by vibration of the vocal cords. *Z* and *v* are voiced; *s* and *f* are not. 3 regulate the tone of (an organ, etc.). [< Old French *vois* < Latin *vocem*]

voice box, larynx.

voiced (voist), *adj.* 1 spoken or expressed: *voiced criticism.* 2 (in phonetics) uttered with vibration of the vocal cords. *B, d,* and *g* are voiced consonants.

-voiced, *combining form.* having a ___ voice: *Low-voiced = having a low voice.*

voice less (vois′lis), *adj.* 1 having no voice; dumb; silent. 2 (in phonetics) uttered without vibration of the vocal cords. *P, t,* and *k* are voiceless consonants. **—voice′less ly,** *adv.* **—voice′less ness,** *n.*

Voice of America, an international broadcasting service of the United States government, used to give overseas listeners a picture of American life, culture, and aims.

voice print (vois′print′), *n.* a spectrographic record of the distinctive sound patterns formed by a person's voice.

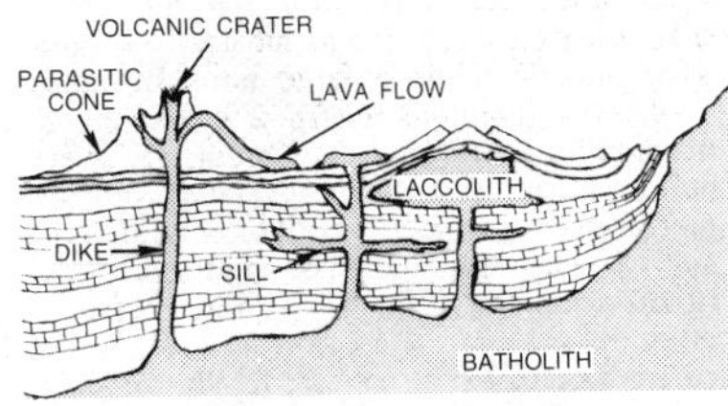

volcano (defs. 1 and 2)
subterranean and surface structure

void (void), *n.* 1 an empty space; vacuum. 2 a feeling of emptiness or great loss: *The death of his dog left an aching void in the boy's heart.* 3 space, gap, or opening, as that left in a wall for a window or another wall. 4 emptiness; vacancy. *—adj.* 1 empty; vacant: *a void space.* 2 without legal force or effect; not binding in law; invalid: *A contract made by a person under legal age is void.* 3 without effect; useless. 4 **void of,** devoid of; without; lacking: *words void of sense.* *—v.t.* 1 make of no legal force or effect; invalidate. 2 empty out; evacuate. 3 OBSOLETE. leave. [< Old French *voide* < Popular Latin *vocitus* < Latin *vacuus* empty] **—void′er,** *n.*

void a ble (voi′də bəl), *adj.* that can be voided or given up: *The contract was voidable by either party after twelve months.*

voile (voil), *n.* a very thin cloth of silk, wool, cotton, etc., with an open weave, used for dresses. [< French, originally, veil < Latin *vela,* plural of *velum* covering. Doublet of VEIL, VELUM.]

vol., volume.

volant (def. 2)
bird volant

vo lant (vō′lənt), *adj.* 1 flying; able to fly. 2 (in heraldry) represented as flying. 3 nimble; quick.

vo lan te (vō län′tā), *adj.* (in music) moving lightly and rapidly; flying. [< Italian]

vol a tile (vol′ə təl), *adj.* 1 evaporating rapidly at ordinary temperatures; changing into vapor easily: *Gasoline is volatile.* 2 changing rapidly from one mood or interest to another; fickle; frivolous: *Flighty people often have volatile dispositions.* 3 readily vanishing or disappearing; transient. [< Latin *volatilis* flying < *volare* to fly] **—vol′a tile ness,** *n.*

vol a til i ty (vol′ə til′ə tē), *n.* volatile quality or condition.

vol a til ize (vol′ə tə līz), *v.i., v.t.,* **-ized, -iz ing.** change into vapor; evaporate. **—vol′a til i za′tion,** *n.*

vol can ic (vol kan′ik), *adj.* 1 of or caused by a volcano; having to do with volcanoes: *a volcanic eruption.* 2 characterized by the presence of volcanoes: *volcanic country.* 3 like a volcano; liable to break out violently: *a volcanic temper.* **—vol can′i cal ly,** *adv.*

vol can ism (vol′kə niz′əm), *n.* phenomena connected with volcanoes and volcanic activity. Also, **vulcanism.**

vol ca no (vol kā′nō), *n., pl.* **-noes** or **-nos.** 1 an opening in the earth's crust through which steam, ashes, and lava are expelled in periods of activity. 2 a cone-shaped hill or mountain around this opening, built up of the material thus expelled. [< Italian < Latin *Vulcanus* Vulcan]

vol can o log i cal (vol′kə nə loj′ə kəl), *adj.* of or having to do with volcanology.

vol ca nol o gist (vol′kə nol′ə jist), *n.* an expert in volcanology.

vol ca nol o gy (vol′kə nol′ə jē), *n.* the scientific study of volcanoes and volcanic phenomena.

vole
about $5^1/_2$ in. long with tail

vole (vōl), *n.* any of various rodents of the same family as and resembling rats and mice, but usually of heavier build and having short limbs and tail. [< earlier *volemouse* < Norwegian *voll* field + English *mouse*]

Vol ga River (vol′gə), river in the W Soviet Union, flowing into the Caspian Sea. 2325 mi.

Vol go grad (vol′gə grad), *n.* city in SW Soviet Union, on the Volga River. 818,000. Former name, **Stalingrad.**

vo li tion (vō lish′ən), *n.* 1 act of willing; decision or choice: *She went away of her own volition.* 2 power of willing: *The use of drugs has weakened his volition.* [< Medieval Latin *volitionem* < Latin *volo* I wish]

vo li tion al (vō lish′ə nəl), *adj.* of or having to do with volition. **—vo li′tion al ly,** *adv.*

vol i tive (vol′ə tiv), *adj.* 1 of or having to do with volition or the will. 2 (in grammar) expressing a wish or desire.

vol ley (vol′ē), *n., pl.* **-leys,** *v.* *—n.* 1 shower of stones, bullets, arrows, etc. 2 the discharge of a number of guns or other weapons firing missiles at once. 3 a rapid outpouring or burst of words, oaths, shouts, cheers, etc. 4 (in tennis, etc.) the hitting or return of a ball before it touches the ground. 5 (in soccer) a kick given the ball before it bounces on the ground. —*v.t., v.i.* 1 discharge or be discharged in a volley. 2 hit or return (a tennis ball, etc.) before it touches the ground. 3 kick (the ball) in soccer before it bounces on the ground. [< Middle French *volée* flight < *voler* to fly < Latin *volare*]

vol ley ball (vol′ē bôl′), *n.* 1 game played by two teams of players with a large ball and a high net. The players must hit the ball back and forth over the net with their hands without letting it touch the ground. 2 ball used in this game.

vol plane (vol′plān′), *v.,* **-planed, -plan ing,** *n.* —*v.i.* glide downward in an airplane without using motor power. —*n.* act of doing this. [< French *vol plané* gliding flight]

vols., volumes.

volt[1] (vōlt), *n.* the unit of electromotive force, equal to the difference in potential needed to cause a current of one ampere to flow through a resistance of one ohm. [< Alessandro *Volta*]

volt[2] (vōlt), *n.* (in fencing) a quick step or leap to escape a thrust. [< French < *volter* to turn]

Vol ta (vôl′tä), *n.* Count **Alessandro,** 1745-1827, Italian physicist who invented one of the first electric batteries.

volt age (vōl′tij), *n.* electromotive force expressed in volts. A current of high voltage is used in transmitting electric power over long distances.

voltage divider, resistor with two terminals between which the current flows. A portion of the total voltage may be obtained by connecting at any point between the terminals.

vol ta ic (vol tā′ik), *adj.* 1 producing an electric current by chemical action. 2 of or having to do with electric currents produced by chemical action; galvanic.

voltaic battery, 1 battery composed of voltaic cells. 2 voltaic cell.

voltaic cell, an electric cell consisting of two electrodes connected by a wire and immersed in an electrolyte. An electric current is produced in the wire by a chemical reaction between the electrolyte and the electrodes.

Vol taire (vol ter′, vol tar′), *n.* **François Marie Arouet de,** 1694-1778, French satirical and philosophical writer.

vol tam e ter (vol tam′ə tər), *n.* device for measuring the quantity of electricity passing through a conductor by the amount of electrolytic decomposition it produces.

volt-am pere (vōlt′am′pir), *n.* unit of electric measurement equal to the product of one volt and one ampere. For alternating currents it is a measure of apparent power; for direct currents it is a measure of power and equals one watt.

volte-face (volt fäs′), *n.* an about-face; reversal of judgment, belief, or policy. [< French]

volt me ter (vōlt′mē′tər), *n.* instrument for measuring in volts the electromotive force between the two points in a circuit.

vol u bil i ty (vol′yə bil′ə tē), *n.* 1 tendency to talk much; fondness for talking much; talkativeness. 2 great flow of words.

vol u ble (vol′yə bəl), *adj.* 1 tending to talk much; fond of talking; talkative. See **fluent** for synonym study. 2 having a smooth, rapid flow of speech. 3 (in botany) twining; twisting. [< Latin *volubilis,* originally, rolling < *volvere* to roll] **—vol′u ble ness,** *n.* **—vol′u bly,** *adv.*

vol ume (vol′yəm), *n.* 1 collection of printed or written sheets bound together to form a book; book: *We own a library of five hundred volumes.* 2 book forming part of a set or series. 3 space occupied: *The storeroom has a volume of 800 cubic feet.* 4 amount; quantity: *Volumes of smoke poured from the chimneys of the factory.* See **size**[1] for synonym study. 5 amount of sound; fullness of tone: *A pipe organ has more volume than a flute.* 6 **speak volumes,** express much; be full of meaning. [< Old French < Latin *volumen* book roll, scroll < *volvere* to roll] ➤ See **book** for usage note.

vol u met ric (vol′yə met′rik), *adj.* of or having to do with measurement by volume. **—vol′u met′ri cal ly,** *adv.*

vo lu mi nous (və lü′mə nəs), *adj.* 1 forming or filling a large book or many books: *a voluminous report.* 2 writing much: *a voluminous author.* 3 of great size; very bulky; large: *A voluminous cloak covered him from head to foot.* 4 full of or containing many coils, convolutions, or windings. **—vo lu′mi nous ly,** *adv.* **—vo lu′mi nous ness,** *n.*

vol un tar i ly (vol′ən ter′ə lē, vol′ən ter′ə lē), *adv.* of one's own free will; without force or compulsion.

vol un tar y (vol′ən ter′ē), *adj., n., pl.* **-tar ies.** —*adj.* 1 done, made, given, etc., of one's own free will; not forced or compelled: *a voluntary contribution.* See synonym study below. 2 maintained or supported entirely by voluntary gifts: *a voluntary school.* 3 acting of one's own free will or choice: *voluntary workers.* 4 able to act of one's own free will: *People are voluntary agents.* 5 deliberately intended; done on purpose: *voluntary manslaughter.* 6 controlled by the will: *Talking is voluntary; breathing is only partly so.* —*n.* 1 anything done, made, given, etc., of one's own free will. 2 piece of music, often improvised, played as a prelude. 3 an organ solo played before, during, or after a church service. [< Latin *voluntarius* < *voluntatem* will < *vol-,* stem of *velle* to wish]

Syn. *adj.* 1 **Voluntary, spontaneous** mean done, made, given, etc., without being forced or compelled. **Voluntary** emphasizes that it is done of one's own free will or choice: *The state is supported by taxes, the church by voluntary contributions.* **Spontaneous** emphasizes that it is done from natural impulse, without thought or intention: *The laughter at his jokes is never forced, but always spontaneous.*

voluntary muscle, striated muscle.

vol un teer (vol′ən tir′), *n.* 1 person who enters military or other service of his own free will; one who is not drafted. 2 person who serves without pay. In some towns, the firemen are volunteers. 3 plant which grows from self-sown seed. —*v.i.* 1 offer one's services: *volunteer for an expedition, volunteer for the army.* 2 offer of one's own free will: *She volunteered to do the job.* —*v.t.* 1 offer (one's services or oneself) for some special purpose or enterprise. 2 tell or say voluntarily: *volunteer an explanation.* —*adj.* 1 of or made up of volunteers: *a volunteer fire company.* 2 serving as a volunteer: *a volunteer fireman.* 3 voluntary. 4 (of vegetation) growing from self-sown seed. [< French *volontaire,* originally adjective, voluntary < Latin *voluntarius.* See VOLUNTARY.]

vo lup tu ar y (və lup′chü er′ē), *n., pl.* **-ar ies,** *adj.* —*n.* person who cares much for luxurious or sensual pleasures. —*adj.* of or having to do with luxurious or sensual pleasures.

vo lup tu ous (və lup′chü əs), *adj.* 1 caring much for the pleasures of the senses. 2 giving pleasure to the senses: *voluptuous music, voluptuous beauty.* [< Latin *voluptuosus* < *voluptas* pleasure] **—vo lup′tu ous ly,** *adv.* **—vo lup′tu ous ness,** *n.*

volute (def. 2) on an Ionic capital

vo lute (və lüt′), *n.* 1 a spiral or twisted thing or form. 2 a spiral or scroll-like ornament in architecture, especially the ones on Ionic and Corinthian capitals. 3 turn or whorl of a spiral shell. —*adj.* rolled up; spiral. [< Latin *voluta* < *volvere* to roll]

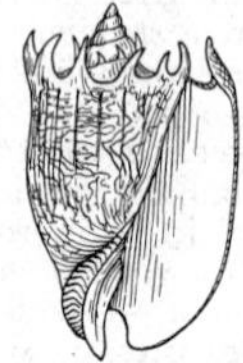

volute (def. 3)

vo lut ed (və lü′tid), *adj.* having a coil, whorl, or volute: *a voluted shell.*

vom it (vom′it), *v.i.* 1 expel the contents of the stomach through the mouth; throw up what has been eaten. 2 come out with force or violence. —*v.t.* 1 bring up and eject through the mouth (swallowed food or drink). 2 throw out with force; throw up: *The chimneys vomited forth smoke.* 3 cause (a person) to vomit. —*n.* 1 act of vomiting. 2 the substance thrown up from the stomach by vomiting. 3 emetic. [< Latin *vomitum* < *vomere* spew forth] **—vom′it er,** *n.*

von (fôn; *unstressed* fən; *English* von), *prep.* GERMAN. from; of (used in family names as an indication of nobility or rank).

von Braun (von brôn′; *German* fən broun′), **Wernher,** born 1912, American rocket engineer, born in Germany.

voo doo (vü′dü), *n., pl.* **-doos,** *adj., v.* —*n.* 1 religion that came from Africa, made up of mysterious rites and practices that include the use of sorcery, magic, and conjuration. Belief in voodoo still prevails in many parts of the West Indies and some parts of the southern United States. 2 person who practices voodoo. 3 a charm or fetish used in the practice of voodoo. —*adj.* of or having to do with voodoo. —*v.t.* affect by voodoo sorcery, magic, or conjuration. [< Creole; of African origin]

voo doo ism (vü′dü iz′əm), *n.* voodoo rites or practices.

voo doo ist (vü′dü ist), *n.* believer in voodoo; practicer of voodoo.

voo doo is tic (vü′dü is′tik), *adj.* of or having to do with voodooism.

Vo po (fō′pō), *n., pl.* **-pos.** member of the East German police force. [< German *Vo(lks)po(lizei)* People's police]

vo ra cious (və rā′shəs), *adj.* 1 eating much; greedy in eating; ravenous. 2 very eager; unable to be satisfied; insatiable. [< Latin *voracis* greedy] **—vo ra′cious ly,** *adv.*

vo rac i ty (və ras′ə tē), *n.* a being voracious.

vor tex (vôr′teks), *n., pl.* **-tex es** or **-ti ces.** 1 a whirling mass of water, etc., that sucks everything near it toward its center; whirlpool. 2 a violent whirl of air; cyclone; whirlwind. 3 whirl of activity or other situation from which it is hard to escape: *The two nations were unwillingly drawn into the vortex of war.* [< Latin, variant of *vertex.* See VERTEX.]

vor ti cal (vôr′tə kəl), *adj.* of or like a vortex; moving in a vortex; whirling round: *vortical currents.*

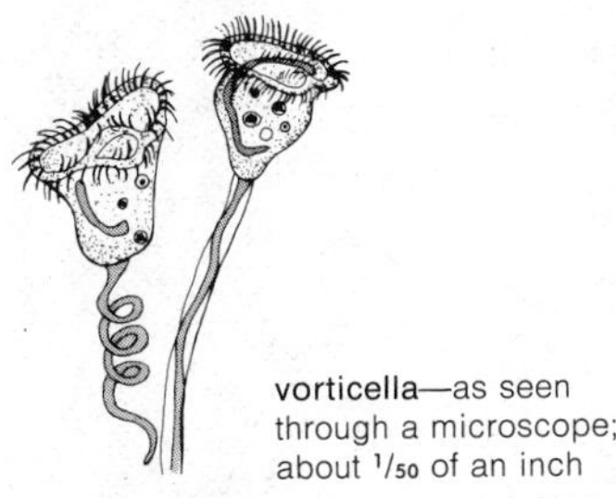

vorticella—as seen through a microscope; about 1/50 of an inch

vor ti cel la (vôr′tə sel′ə), *n., pl.* **-cel lae** (-sel′ē). any of a genus of one-celled animals with a ciliated, bell-shaped body on a slender stalk, often found attached to a plant or other object under water. [< New Latin, diminutive of Latin *vortex* vortex]

vor ti ces (vôr′tə sēz′), *n.* a pl. of **vortex.**

Vosges Mountains (vōzh), mountain range in E France. Highest peak, 4668 ft.

vot a ble (vō′tə bəl), *adj.* that can be voted for, against, on, etc.

vo tar ess (vō′tər is), *n.* a woman votary.

vo tar ist (vō′tər ist), *n.* votary.

vo tar y (vō′tər ē), *n., pl.* **-tar ies.** 1 person bound by vows to a religious life; monk or nun. 2 person devoted to something; devotee: *a votary of golf.* [< Latin *votum* vow. See VOTE.]

vote (vōt), *n., v.,* **vot ed, vot ing.** *—n.* 1 a formal expression of a wish or choice on a proposal, motion, candidate for office, etc.: *The person receiving the most votes is elected.* 2 the right to give such an expression: *Children do not have the vote, and adults may lose it by being convicted of certain crimes.* 3 ballot or other means by which a vote is given: *More than a million votes were cast.* 4 what is expressed or granted by a majority of voters: *a vote of thanks.* 5 votes considered together: *a light vote, the labor vote.* 6 voter.
—v.i. give or cast a vote: *vote for the Democrats.* *—v.t.* 1 support by one's vote: *vote the Republican ticket.* 2 elect, enact, establish, ratify, etc., by vote: *vote a bill through Congress, vote a woman to the Senate.* 3 pass, determine, or grant by vote: *Money for a new school was voted by the board.* 4 declare, especially by general consent: *They voted the play a success.* 5 INFORMAL. propose; suggest: *I vote that we leave now.* **6 vote down,** defeat by voting against. **7 vote in,** elect. [< Latin *votum* vow, wish < *vovere* to vow. Doublet of VOW.]

vote less (vōt′lis), *adj.* having no vote; not entitled to vote.

vote of confidence, 1 vote given by the majority of members in a parliament to the government or its chief representative, especially in a period of crisis, to indicate support of its policies. 2 any expression of approval or support.

vot er (vō′tər), *n.* 1 person who votes. 2 person who has the right to vote; elector.

voting machine, a mechanical device for registering and counting electoral votes.

vo tive (vō′tiv), *adj.* 1 promised by a vow; done, given, etc., because of a vow. 2 made up or expressive of a vow, desire, or wish: *a votive prayer.* [< Latin *votivus* < *votum* vow] **—vo′tive ly,** *adv.*

vouch (vouch), *v.i.* 1 be responsible; give a guarantee *(for): I can vouch for the truth of the story. The principal vouched for the girl's honesty.* 2 give evidence or assurance *(for): The success of the campaign vouches for the candidate's popularity.* *—v.t.* 1 guarantee (a statement, etc.) to be true or accurate; confirm. 2 support or substantiate (a claim, title, etc.). 3 cite or appeal to (authority, example, a passage in a book, etc.) in support or justification. [< Anglo-French *voucher* < Latin *vocare* to call]

vouch er (vou′chər), *n.* 1 person or thing that vouches for something. 2 a written evidence of payment; receipt. Canceled checks returned from one's bank are vouchers.

vouch safe (vouch sāf′), *v.t.,* **-safed, -saf ing.** be willing to grant or give; deign (to do or give): *The proud man vouchsafed no reply when we spoke to him.*

vous soir (vü swär′), *n.* one of the wedge-shaped pieces or sections that form part of an arch or vault. See **keystone** for picture. [< French]

vow (vou), *n.* 1 a solemn promise: *a vow of secrecy, a marriage vow.* 2 promise made to God: *a nun's vows.* **3 take vows,** become a member of a religious order. *—v.i.* make a vow. *—v.t.* 1 make a vow to do, give, get, etc.: *vow revenge.* 2 dedicate, consecrate, or devote to some person or service. 3 declare earnestly or emphatically: *I vowed never to leave home again.* [< Old French *vou* < Latin *votum* < *vovere* to vow. Doublet of VOTE.]

vow el (vou′əl), *n.* 1 a voiced speech sound produced by not blocking the breath with the lips, teeth, or tongue. A vowel can form a syllable by itself, as the first syllable of *awful* (ô′fəl). 2 letter that stands for such a sound. *A, e, i, o,* and *u* are vowels. *Y* is sometimes a vowel, as in *bicycle.* *—adj.* of or having to do with a vowel. [< Old French *vouel* < Latin *(littera) vocalis* sounding (letter) < *vocalis* sounding, vocal] **—vow′el like′,** *adj.*

vox po pu li (voks′ pop′yə lī), LATIN. the voice or opinion of the people.

voy age (voi′ij), *n., v.,* **-aged, -ag ing.** *—n.* 1 a journey or travel by water. See **trip** for synonym study. 2 a journey or travel through the air or through space. *—v.i.* make or take a voyage; go by sea or air. *—v.t.* cross or travel over; traverse. [< Old French < Latin *viaticum.* Doublet of VIATICUM.]

voy ag er (voi′i jər), *n.* person who makes a voyage; traveler.

vo ya geur (vwä′yä zhėr′), *n., pl.* **-geurs** (-zhėrz′). a French Canadian worker for the early fur-trading companies who transported men and supplies to and from remote places, especially by boat. [< Canadian French < French, traveler < *voyager* to voyage]

vo yeur (vwä yėr′), *n.* person who gets pleasure from watching the private acts of others without being seen by them; peeping tom. [< French < *voir* to see]

hat, āge, fär; let, ēqual, tėrm;
it, īce; hot, ōpen, ôrder;
oil, out; cup, pu̇t, rüle;
ch, child; ng, long; sh, she;
th, thin; ᴛʜ, then; zh, measure;

ə represents *a* in about, *e* in taken,
i in pencil, *o* in lemon, *u* in circus.

< = from, derived from, taken from.

vo yeur ism (vwä yėr′iz əm), *n.* practice of a voyeur.

VP or **V.P.,** Vice-President.

vs., versus.

v.s., see above [for Latin *vide supra*].

VSTOL, vertical and short take-off and landing.

Vt., Vermont.

v.t., transitive verb.

VTOL, vertical take-off and landing.

Vul can (vul′kən), *n.* (in Roman myths) the god of fire and metal-working, identified with the Greek god Hephaestus.

Vul ca ni an (vul kā′nē ən), *adj.* having to do with, characteristic of, or made by Vulcan.

vul can ism (vul′kə niz′əm), *n.* volcanism.

vul can ite (vul′kə nīt), *n.* a hard, usually black substance made by heating rubber with a large quantity of sulfur, used in making combs and buttons, and for electric insulation; hard rubber; ebonite.

vul can ize (vul′kə nīz), *v.t.,* **-ized, -iz ing.** 1 treat (rubber) with sulfur and heat to make it more elastic and durable. 2 repair (a rubber tire, etc.) by using heat and chemicals to fuse the patch. [< *Vulcan*] **—vul′can i za′tion,** *n.* **—vul′can iz′er,** *n.*

Vulg., Vulgate.

vul gar (vul′gər), *adj.* 1 showing a lack of good breeding, manners, taste, etc.; not refined; coarse; low. See **coarse** for synonym study. 2 of the common people. 3 current or prevalent among people; popular; general: *vulgar prejudices.* 4 in common use; common; ordinary. *—n.* **the vulgar,** the common people. [< Latin *vulgaris* < *vulgus* common people] **—vul′gar ly,** *adv.* **—vul′gar ness,** *n.*

vul gar i an (vul ger′ē ən, vul gar′ē ən), *n.* 1 a vulgar person. 2 a rich person who lacks good breeding, manners, taste, etc.

vul gar ism (vul′gə riz′əm), *n.* 1 word, phrase, or expression used only in ignorant or coarse speech. In "I disrecollect his name," *disrecollect* is a vulgarism. 2 vulgar character or action; vulgarity. 3 a vulgar expression.

vul gar i ty (vul gar′ə tē), *n., pl.* **-ties.** 1 lack of refinement; lack of good breeding, manners, taste, etc.; coarseness. 2 action, habit, speech, etc., showing vulgarity: *the vulgarity of loud talk and crude jokes.*

vul gar ize (vul′gə rīz′), *v.t.,* **-ized, -iz ing.** 1 make vulgar or common; degrade or debase. 2 make common or popular. **—vul′gar i za′tion,** *n.* **—vul′gar iz′er,** *n.*

Vulgar Latin, Popular Latin.

Vul gate (vul′gāt), *n.* 1 the Latin translation of the Bible, made about A.D. 405 by Saint Jerome, used by the Roman Catholic Church. **2 the vulgate,** substandard speech. [< Late Latin *vulgata (editio)* popular (edition)]

vul ner a bil i ty (vul′nər ə bil′ə tē), *n.*

vulnerable quality or condition; a being open to attack or injury.

vul ner a ble (vul′nər ə bəl), *adj.* 1 that can be wounded or injured; open to attack: *Achilles was vulnerable only in his heel.* 2 sensitive to criticism, temptations, influences, etc.: *Most people are vulnerable to ridicule.* 3 (in contract bridge) in the position where penalties and premiums are increased. [< Late Latin *vulnerabilis* < Latin *vulnerare* to wound < *vulnus* wound] **—vul′ner a bly,** *adv.*

vulture (def. 1)
about 2½ ft. long

vul pine (vul′pīn, vul′pən), *adj.* of or like a fox; cunning; sly. [< Latin *vulpinus* < *vulpes* fox]

vul ture (vul′chər), *n.* 1 any of certain large birds of prey related to eagles, falcons, and hawks, that eat the flesh of dead animals. Vultures have weak talons and usually featherless heads and necks. 2 person who preys upon another; a greedy, ruthless person. [< Latin *vultur*] **—vul′ture like′,** *adj.*

vul va (vul′və), *n., pl.* **-vae** (-vē), **-vas.** the external genital organs of the female. [< Latin, womb]

vy ing (vī′ing), *v.* ppr. of **vie.**

W w

hat, āge, fär; let, ēqual, tėrm;
it, īce; hot, ōpen, ôrder;
oil, out; cup, pu̇t, rüle;
ch, child; ng, long; sh, she;
th, thin; ᴛʜ, then; zh, measure;

ə represents *a* in about, *e* in taken, *i* in pencil, *o* in lemon, *u* in circus.

< = from, derived from, taken from.

W or **w** (dub′əl yü), *n., pl.* **W's** or **w's.** the 23rd letter of the English alphabet.

w, watt or watts.

W, 1 west. 2 western. 3 (in physics) work. 4 tungsten [for German *Wolfram*].

w., 1 watt or watts. 2 week or weeks. 3 weight. 4 west. 5 western. 6 wide. 7 width. 8 wife.

W., 1 Wales. 2 Wednesday. 3 west. 4 western.

Wa bash River (wô′bash), river flowing from W Ohio southwest across Indiana into the Ohio River. 475 mi.

wab ble (wob′əl), *v.i., v.t.,* **-bled, -bling,** *n.* wobble. **—wab′bler,** *n.*

wab bly (wob′lē), *adj.,* **-bli er, -bli est.** wobbly.

WAC or **Wac** (wak), *n.* woman in the United States Army other than a nurse. [< abbreviation of *Women's Army Corps*]

wack y (wak′ē), *adj.,* **wack i er, wack i est.** SLANG. unconventional in behavior; eccentric; crazy. [origin uncertain] **—wack′i ly,** *adv.* **—wack′i ness,** *n.*

Wa co (wā′kō), *n.* city in central Texas. 95,000.

wad (wod), *n., v.,* **wad ded, wad ding.** *—n.* 1 a small, soft mass: *plug one's ears with wads of cotton.* 2 a tight roll; compact bundle or mass: *a wad of chewing gum.* 3 a round plug of felt, cardboard, etc., used to hold powder and shot in place in a gun or cartridge. 4 SLANG. **a** a large bundle of paper money. **b** personal wealth; riches. *—v.t.* 1 make into a wad; press into a wad: *I wadded up the paper and threw it on the floor.* 2 stuff with a wad. 3 hold in place by a wad. 4 fill out with padding; pad. [origin uncertain]

wad ding (wod′ing), *n.* 1 a soft material for padding, stuffing, packing, etc., especially carded cotton in sheets. 2 material for making wads for guns or cartridges. 3 wad.

wad dle (wod′l), *v.,* **-dled, -dling,** *n.* *—v.i.* walk with short steps and an awkward, swaying motion, as a duck does: *The fat man waddled across the street.* *—n.* 1 act of waddling. 2 an awkward, swaying gait. [< *wade*] **—wad′dler,** *n.*

wade (wād), *v.,* **wad ed, wad ing,** *n.* *—v.i.* 1 walk through water, snow, sand, mud, or anything that hinders free motion. 2 make one's way with difficulty: *wade through an uninteresting book.* *—v.t.* 1 cross or pass through by wading: *wade a stream.* 2 **wade into,** INFORMAL. attack or go to work upon vigorously: *wade into a job.* *—n.* act of wading. [Old English *wadan* proceed]

wad er (wā′dər), *n.* 1 person or thing that wades. 2 a long-legged bird that wades about in shallow water, searching for food. Cranes, herons, storks, and sandpipers are waders. 3 **waders,** *pl.* high, waterproof boots, used for wading.

wa di (wä′dē), *n.* 1 valley or ravine in Arabia, northern Africa, etc., through which a stream flows during the rainy season. 2 stream or torrent running through such a ravine. [< Arabic *wādī*]

WAF or **Waf** (waf), *n.* woman in the United States Air Force other than a nurse. [< abbreviation of *Women in the Air Force*]

wa fer (wā′fər), *n.* 1 a very thin cake or biscuit, sometimes flavored or sweetened. 2 the thin, round piece of unleavened bread used in the Eucharist in certain churches, especially the Roman Catholic Church. 3 a thin piece of candy, medicine, etc. 4 piece of sticky paper, dried paste, etc., used as a seal or fastening. [< Anglo-French *wafre;* of Germanic origin] **—wa′fer like′,** *adj.*

wa fer y (wā′fər ē), *adj.* like a wafer.

waf fle (wof′əl, wô′fəl), *n.* a batter cake cooked in a waffle iron until brown and crisp, usually eaten while hot with butter, syrup, etc. [< Dutch *wafel*]

waffle iron, utensil in which waffles are cooked, consisting of two hinged griddles having projections on the inside which form indentations in the waffle.

waft (waft), *v.t.* carry over water or through air: *The waves wafted the boat to shore.* *—v.i.* float. *—n.* 1 a breath or puff of air, wind, scent, etc. 2 a waving movement; wave. 3 act of wafting. [< earlier *wafter* convoy ship < Dutch and Low German *wachter* guard] **—waft′er,** *n.*

wag (wag), *v.,* **wagged, wag ging,** *n.* *—v.t.* 1 move from side to side or up and down, especially rapidly and repeatedly: *The dog wagged its tail.* 2 move (the tongue) in talking, as in gossip or idle chatter. *—v.i.* 1 move with a wagging motion. 2 move busily in talking: *a scandal that made tongues wag throughout the village.* *—n.* 1 a wagging motion. 2 person who is fond of making jokes. [Old English *wagian*] **—wag′ger,** *n.*

wage (wāj), *n., v.,* **waged, wag ing.** *—n.* 1 Usually, **wages,** *pl.* **a** payment made periodically to a person, especially by the day or week, as compensation at a fixed rate for hours worked or services rendered. **b** something given in return: *"The wages of sin is death."* 2 OBSOLETE. a pledge. *—v.t.* 1 carry on: *Doctors wage war against disease.* 2 OBSOLETE. pledge. [< Old North French; of Germanic origin] **—wage′less,** *adj.*

wage earner, person who works for wages.

wa ger (wā′jər), *v.t., v.i.* make a bet; bet; gamble. *—n.* 1 something staked on an uncertain event. 2 act of betting; bet. [< Anglo-French *wageure* < Old North French *wage* pledge, wage] **—wa′ger er,** *n.*

wage scale, 1 the schedule of the various rates of pay for similar or related jobs, as in a particular industry. 2 the range of the wages paid by an employer.

wag ger y (wag′ər ē), *n., pl.* **-ger ies.** 1 act or habit of joking. 2 joke.

wag gish (wag′ish), *adj.* 1 fond of making jokes. 2 characteristic of a wag; funny; humorous: *a waggish remark, a waggish look.* **—wag′gish ly,** *adv.* **—wag′gish ness,** *n.*

wag gle (wag′əl), *v.,* **-gled, -gling,** *n.* *—v.t., v.i.* move quickly and repeatedly from side to side; wag. *—n.* a waggling motion. [< *wag*]

wag gly (wag′lē), *adj.* waggling; unsteady.

wainscot (def. 2)

wag gon (wag′ən), *n.* BRITISH. wagon.

Wag ner (väg′nər), *n.* **Richard,** 1813-1883, German composer.

Wag ner i an (väg nir′ē ən), *adj.* of or having to do with Wagner, his music, or his musical style or theories. *—n.* admirer of Wagner's style or theory of music.

wag on (wag′ən), *n.* 1 a four-wheeled vehicle, especially one for carrying loads: *a milk wagon.* 2 station wagon. 3 patrol wagon. 4 tray on wheels for serving food or drinks. 5 a child's toy cart. 6 BRITISH. a railroad freight car. 7 **on the wagon,** SLANG. not drinking alcoholic liquor. [< Dutch *wagen*]

wag on er (wag′ə nər), *n.* person who drives a wagon.

wag on ette (wag′ə net′), *n.* a four-wheeled carriage with a seat in front running crosswise and two lengthwise seats facing each other.

wa gon-lit (vȧ gôɴ′lē′), *n., pl.* **-lits** (-lē′). (in Europe) a railroad sleeping car. [< French < *wagon* railway coach + *lit* bed]

wag on load (wag′ən lōd′), *n.* amount that a wagon can hold or carry.

wagon train, group of wagons moving along in a line one after another.

wag tail (wag′tāl′), *n.* any of various small birds having a slender body with a long tail that it habitually moves up and down.

Wa ha bi or **Wah ha bi** (wä hä′bē), *n.* member of a strict Moslem sect founded in the 1700's and now dominant in Saudi Arabia, which adheres rigidly to the Koran as a guide.

wa hi ne (wä hē′nä; *Anglicized* wä hē′nē), *n.* HAWAIIAN. a woman; female; wife.

wa hoo (wä′hü, wä hü′), *n., pl.* **-hoos.** a North American shrub or small tree that has a purple fruit and red seeds. [< Siouan *wanhu*]

waif (wāf), *n.* 1 person without home or friends, especially a homeless or neglected child. 2 anything without an owner; stray thing, animal, etc. [< Anglo-French; probably < Scandinavian]

Wai ki ki (wī′kē kē′), *n.* section of Honolulu known for its bathing beach.

wail (wāl), *v.i.* 1 cry loud and long because of grief or pain: *The baby wailed.* 2 make a mournful or shrill sound: *The wind wailed around the old house.* 3 lament; mourn. *—v.t.* 1 grieve for or because of; bewail. 2 utter (a wailing cry, bad news, etc.). *—n.* 1 a long cry of grief or pain. 2 a sound like such a cry: *the wail of a hungry coyote, the wail of a siren.* [< Scandinavian (Old Icelandic) *væla*] **—wail′er,** *n.*

wail ful (wāl′fəl), *adj.* sorrowful; plaintive. **—wail′ful ly,** *adv.*

wain (wān), *n.* ARCHAIC or DIALECT. wagon, especially a farm wagon. [Old English *wægn*]

wain scot (wān′skōt, wān′skət), *n., v.,* **-scot ed, -scot ing** or **-scot ted, -scot ting.** *—n.* 1 a lining of wood, usually in panels, on the walls of a room. 2 the lower part of the wall of a room when it is decorated differently from the upper part. —*v.t.* line (the walls of a room), especially with wood: *a room wainscoted in oak.* [< Middle Dutch *wagenschot* < *wagen* wagon + *schot* partition]

wain scot ing or **wain scot ting** (wān′skō ting, wān′skə ting), *n.* 1 wainscot. 2 material used for wainscots.

wain wright (wān′rīt′), *n.* person who makes wagons.

waist (wāst), *n.* 1 the part of the human body between the ribs and the hips. 2 waistline. 3 a garment or part of a garment covering the body from the neck or shoulders to the waistline; blouse or bodice. 4 a narrow middle part: *the waist of a violin.* 5 the middle section of a ship or aircraft. [Middle English *wast.* Related to WAX².]

waist band (wāst′band′), *n.* a band around the waist: *the waistband of a skirt.*

waist coat (wāst′kōt, wes′kət), *n.* BRITISH. a man's vest.

waist line (wāst′līn′), *n.* 1 line around the body at the smallest part of the waist. 2 place of smallest width in a woman's dress between the arms and the knees. 3 line where the waist and skirt of a dress join.

wait (wāt), *v.i.* 1 stay or be inactive until someone comes or something happens: *wait patiently just outside the door.* 2 look forward; be expecting or ready: *The children wait impatiently for vacation.* 3 be left undone; be put off: *That matter can wait until tomorrow.* 4 act as a servant; change plates, pass food, etc., at table. 5 **wait up,** INFORMAL. stay out of bed to await someone or something. —*v.t.* 1 wait for; await: *wait one's chance.* 2 INFORMAL. delay or put off: *I'll be late; don't wait dinner for me.* 3 **wait on** or **wait upon, a** be a servant to; serve, especially at the table: *wait on hotel guests.* **b** give one's attention to and try to fill the needs of (a customer): *Will you wait on me, please?* **c** call on (a superior) to pay a respectful visit. **d** go with; result from.
—*n.* 1 act or time of waiting: *a long wait between trains.* 2 **lie in wait,** stay hidden ready to attack. 3 **waits,** *pl.* a group of singers and musicians who go about the streets singing and playing at Christmas time. [< Old French *waitier,* originally, to watch; of Germanic origin. Related to WATCH.]

wait er (wā′tər), *n.* 1 person who waits. 2 man who waits on table in a hotel, restaurant, etc. 3 a tray for carrying dishes.

wait ing (wā′ting), *adj.* 1 that waits. 2 used to wait in. —*n.* 1 the time that one waits. 2 **in waiting,** in attendance on a king, queen, prince, princess, etc.

waiting list, list of persons waiting for appointments, selection for any purpose, or the next chance of obtaining something.

waiting room, room at a railroad station, doctor's office, etc., for people to wait in.

wai tress (wā′tris), *n.* woman who waits on table in a hotel, restaurant, etc.

waive (wāv), *v.t.,* **waived, waiv ing.** 1 give up (a right, claim, etc.); refrain from claiming or pressing; do without; relinquish: *The lawyer waived the privilege of cross-examining the witness.* 2 put aside; defer. [< Anglo-French *weyver* to abandon; probably of Scandinavian origin. Related to WAIF.]

waiv er (wā′vər), *n.* 1 a giving up of a right, claim, etc.; a waiving. 2 a written statement of this: *For $100, the injured man signed a waiver of all claims against the railroad.*

wake¹ (wāk), *v.,* **waked** or **woke, waked** or (ARCHAIC and DIALECT) **wok en, wak ing,** *n.* —*v.i.* 1 stop sleeping; become awake; awaken: *wake up early in the morning.* 2 be awake; stay awake. 3 become alive or active: *Bears wake up in the spring after a winter of hibernation.* 4 keep watch, especially over a corpse. —*v.t.* 1 cause to stop sleeping: *Wake me up early.* 2 make alive or active: *He needs some interest to wake him up.* 3 keep watch over (a dead body) until burial. —*n.* 1 a watching. 2 an all-night watch beside a corpse before its burial. [Old English *wacian* to become awake, and *wacan* to awake]

wake² (wāk), *n.* 1 track left behind a moving ship. 2 track left behind any moving thing. 3 **in the wake of,** following; behind; after: *floods coming in the wake of a hurricane.* [< Middle Dutch *wak*]

wake ful (wāk′fəl), *adj.* 1 not able to sleep; restless. 2 without sleep. 3 watchful. **—wake′ful ly,** *adv.* **—wake′ful ness,** *n.*

Wake Island, small island in the N Pacific, about 2000 miles west of Hawaii, belonging to the United States. 3 sq. mi.

wak en (wā′kən), *v.i., v.t.* wake. **—wak′en er,** *n.*

wake-rob in (wāk′rob′ən), *n.* 1 trillium. 2 jack-in-the-pulpit.

Waks man (wak′smən), *n.* **Selman A.,** born 1888, American microbiologist, born in Russia.

Wa la chi a (wo lā′kē ə), *n.* region in S Romania. Also, **Wallachia. —Wa la′chi an,** *adj., n.*

Wal den ses (wol den′sēz′), *n.pl.* a Christian sect that arose about 1170 in southern France and in the 1500's joined the Reformation movement. [< the Latinized form of Peter *Waldo,* French merchant who founded the sect] **—Wal den′si an,** *adj., n.*

Wald heim (vält′hīm), *n.* **Kurt,** born 1918, Austrian diplomat, secretary-general of the United Nations since December 1971.

Wal dorf salad (wôl′dôrf), salad made of diced apples, celery, nuts (usually walnuts), and mayonnaise. [< the *Waldorf*-Astoria Hotel, in New York City]

wale (wāl), *n., v.,* **waled, wal ing.** —*n.* 1 a streak or ridge made on the skin by a stick or whip; welt; weal. 2 a ridge in the weave of cloth, especially corduroy. 3 one of a series of thick planks fastened horizontally to the outside of a wooden ship's hull. 4 a ridge woven horizontally into a basket to strengthen it. —*v.t.* 1 mark with wales; raise wales on. 2 weave with ridges. [Old English *walu*]

Wales (wālz), *n.* division of Great Britain west of England; the land of the Welsh. 2,734,000 pop.; 8000 sq. mi. *Capital:* Cardiff.

walk (wôk), *v.i.* 1 go on foot. In walking, a person always has one foot on the ground. See synonym study below. 2 roam: *The ghost will walk tonight.* 3 go slowly: *Please walk, do not run, to the nearest exit.* 4 (of things) move or shake in a manner suggestive of walking. 5 conduct oneself in a particular manner; behave; live: *walk in the ways of God.* 6 (in baseball) go to first base after the pitcher has thrown four balls. —*v.t.* 1 go over, on, or through: *The captain walked the deck.* 2 make, put, drive, etc., by walking: *walk off a headache.* 3 cause to walk: *The rider walked his horse.* 4 accompany or escort in walking; conduct on foot: *walk a guest to the door.* 5 (in baseball) allow (a batter) to reach first base by pitching four balls.
walk away from, progress much faster than.
walk off with, a take; get; win: *walk off easily with first prize.* **b** steal.
walk out, a go on strike. **b** leave suddenly.
walk out on, INFORMAL. desert.
walk over, a defeat easily and by a wide margin. **b** act without regard for; trample on; override.
—*n.* 1 act of walking, especially walking for pleasure or exercise: *a walk in the country.* 2 a distance to walk: *It is a long walk from here.* 3 manner or way of walking; gait: *We knew the man was a sailor from his rolling walk.* 4 place for walking; path: *There are many pretty walks in the park.* 5 way of living: *A doctor and a street cleaner are in different walks of life.* 6 (in baseball) a going to first base after four balls. 7 a race in which contestants must use a walking pace. 8 pen or other enclosed place: *a poultry walk.* [Old English *wealcan* to toss]
Syn. *v.i.* 1 **Walk, stride, plod** mean to go on foot at a pace slower than a run. **Walk** is the general word: *I walked downstairs.* **Stride** means to walk with long steps, as in haste, annoyance, or self-importance, or with healthy energy: *She strode along briskly.* **Plod** means to walk heavily, slowly, and with effort: *The old horse plodded up the road.*

walk a thon (wô′kə thon), *n.* a walking marathon.

walk a way (wôk′ə wā′), *n.* INFORMAL. an easy victory.

walk er (wô′kər), *n.* 1 person who walks. 2 gocart. 3 lightweight framework for a crippled person to support himself while walking.

walk ie-talk ie (wô′kē tô′kē), *n.* a small, portable receiving and transmitting radio set. Also, **walky-talky.**

walk-in (wôk′in′), *adj.* 1 large enough to walk into: *a bedroom with walk-in closets.* 2 that can be entered directly from the street: *a walk-in apartment.* —*n.* 1 INFORMAL. an easy or certain victory; shoo-in. 2 a walk-in apartment.

walking catfish, species of catfish that is able to crawl over ground on its spiny fins and live out of water by means of its auxiliary breathing apparatus.

walking papers, INFORMAL. dismissal from a position, etc.

walking stick, 1 stick used in walking. 2 any of a family of mostly wingless insects of the same order as grasshoppers, having a body like a stick or twig.

walk-on (wôk′ôn, wôk′on′), *n.* 1 part in a play, movie, etc., in which the performer merely comes on and goes off the stage with little or no speaking. 2 performer having such a part.

walk out (wôk′out′), *n.* INFORMAL. 1 strike of workers. 2 a sudden departure from a room, meeting, etc., usually as a form of protest.

walk o ver (wôk′ō′vər), *n.* INFORMAL. an easy victory.

walk-up (wôk′up′), *n.* 1 an apartment house or building having no elevator. 2 room or apartment in such a building. —*adj.* of or having to do with such a building.

walk way (wôk′wā′), *n.* 1 structure for walking: *an overhead walkway.* 2 path; walk.

walk y-talk y (wô′kē tô′kē), *n., pl.* **-talk ies.** walkie-talkie.

hat, āge, fär; let, ēqual, tėrm;
it, īce; hot, ōpen, ôrder;
oil, out; cup, pu̇t, rüle;
ch, child; ng, long; sh, she;
th, thin; ᴛʜ, then; zh, measure;

ə represents *a* in about, *e* in taken, *i* in pencil, *o* in lemon, *u* in circus.

< = from, derived from, taken from.

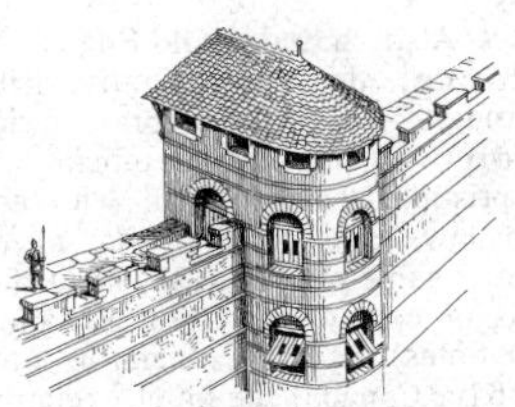

wall (def. 2) with tower

wall (wôl), *n.* 1 side of a house, room, or other hollow thing: *a closet wall, the wall of a furnace, the wall of the stomach.* 2 structure of stone, brick, or other material built up to enclose, divide, support, or protect: *a prison wall.* 3 something like a wall in looks or use: *a wall of fire, a wall of ignorance.* 4 **drive to the wall** or **push to the wall,** make desperate or helpless. 5 **go to the wall,** a give way; be defeated. b fail in business. —*v.t.* enclose, divide, protect, or fill with or as if with a wall or walls: *wall a garden, wall out the noise of the city, wall up a doorway.* [Old English *weall* < Latin *vallum*] **—wall′-less,** *adj.* **—wall′-like′,** *adj.*

wallaby
This species is up to 2½ ft. tall

wal la by (wol′ə bē), *n., pl.* **-bies** or **-by.** any of various genera of small or medium-sized kangaroos. Some wallabies are no larger than rabbits. [< native Australian *wolabā*]

Wal lace (wol′is, wô′lis), *n.* 1 **Alfred Russel,** 1823-1913, English biologist. 2 **George Corley,** born 1919, American political leader, governor of Alabama from 1963 to 1967 and since 1970. 3 **Henry Agard,** 1888-1965, vice-president of the United States from 1941 to 1945. 4 **Lew(is),** 1827-1905, American general and novelist, author of *Ben Hur.* 5 Sir **William,** 1272?-1305, Scottish patriot and military leader.

Wal la chi a (wo lā′kē ə), *n.* Walachia. **—Wal la′chi an,** *adj., n.*

wal la roo (wol′ə rü′), *n.* a large kangaroo with thick gray fur. [< native Australian *wolarū*]

wall board (wôl′bôrd′, wôl′bōrd′), *n.* any of various artificial boards, such as plasterboard or fiberboard, used instead of wood or plaster to make or cover walls.

Wal len stein (wol′ən stīn), *n.* **Albrecht von,** 1583-1634, Austrian general in the Thirty Years' War.

wal let (wol′it, wôl′it), *n.* 1 a small, flat leather case for carrying paper money, cards, etc., in one's pocket; a folding pocketbook; billfold. 2 bag for carrying food and small articles for personal use when on a journey. [Middle English *walet*]

wall eye (wôl′ī′), *n.* 1 eye of a walleyed person or animal. 2 condition of being walleyed. 3 walleyed pike. [< *walleyed*]

wall eyed (wôl′īd′), *adj.* 1 having eyes that show much white and little color. 2 having one or both eyes turned away from the nose, so as to show much white. 3 having large, staring eyes, as a fish. [< Scandinavian (Old Icelandic) *vagl-eygr* < *vagl* speck in the eye + *auga* eye]

walleyed pike, a large, edible, North American freshwater game fish, having large, staring eyes; pike perch. It is related to the perch but resembles the pike.

wall flow er (wôl′flou′ər), *n.* 1 INFORMAL. person, especially a girl or woman, who sits by the wall at a dance instead of dancing. 2 a perennial plant of the mustard family, much cultivated for its sweet-smelling yellow, orange, or red flowers, found growing on walls, cliffs, etc.

Wal loon (wo lün′), *n.* 1 any of a group of people inhabiting chiefly the southern and southeastern parts of Belgium and adjacent regions in France. 2 their language, the French dialect of Belgium. —*adj.* of or having to do with the Walloons or their language.

wal lop (wol′əp), INFORMAL. —*v.t.* 1 beat soundly; thrash. 2 hit very hard; strike with a vigorous blow. 3 defeat thoroughly, as in a game. —*n.* 1 a very hard blow. 2 power to hit very hard blows. [< Old North French *waloper* to gallop; of Germanic origin] **—wal′lop er,** *n.*

wal lop ing (wol′ə ping), INFORMAL. —*n.* 1 a sound beating or thrashing. 2 a thorough defeat. —*adj.* big; powerful; strong.

wal low (wol′ō), *v.i.* 1 roll about; flounder: *The pigs wallowed in the mud. The boat wallowed helplessly in the stormy sea.* 2 live contentedly in filth, wickedness, etc., like a beast. 3 live or delight self-indulgently or luxuriously, as in some form of pleasure, manner of life, etc.: *wallow in wealth, wallow in sentimentality.* —*n.* 1 act of wallowing. 2 place where an animal wallows. [Old English *wealwian* to roll] **—wal′low er,** *n.*

wall pa per (wôl′pā′pər), *n.* paper, commonly with printed decorative patterns in color, for pasting on and covering walls. —*v.t., v.i.* put wallpaper on.

Wall Street, 1 street in lower Manhattan, New York City, that is the chief financial center of the United States. 2 the money market or the financiers of the United States.

wall-to-wall (wôl′tə wôl′), *adj.* covering the entire floor between opposite walls: *wall-to-wall carpeting.*

wal nut (wôl′nut, wôl′nət), *n.* 1 a rather large, almost round, edible nut with a hard, ridged shell and a division between its two halves. 2 any of a genus of trees that it grows on, especially the English walnut and the black walnut, much grown in north temperate regions for their nuts, their valuable wood, and as shade trees. 3 the wood of any of these trees. Black walnut is used in making furniture. 4 the brown color of polished black walnut. [Old English *wealhhnutu* < *wealh* foreign + *hnutu* nut]

Wal pole (wôl′pōl), *n.* 1 **Horace,** 1717-1797, English writer. 2 his father, Sir **Robert,** 1676-1745, English statesman, financier, and politician.

Wal pur gis night (väl pu̇r′gis), the night of April 30th when, according to German legends, witches were supposed to hold revels with the devil. [half-translation of German *Walpurgisnacht* < *Walpurgis,* name of a German saint whose feast is celebrated on the eve of May Day]

wal rus (wôl′rəs, wol′rəs), *n., pl.* **-rus es** or **-rus.** a large sea mammal of Arctic regions, of the same order as and resembling the seals, but having two long tusks. Walruses are valued for their hides, the oil from their blubber, and the ivory of their tusks. [< Dutch *walrus, walros* < *wal(visch)* whale + *ros* horse]

Wal ton (wôlt′n), *n.* **Izaak,** 1593-1683, English writer, author of *The Compleat Angler.*

waltz (wôlts), *n.* 1 a smooth, even, gliding dance in triple time, in which a complete turn is made to each measure. 2 music for it. —*v.i.* 1 dance a waltz. 2 move nimbly or quickly. —*v.t.* dance the waltz with. [< German *Walzer* < *walzen* to roll] **—waltz′er,** *n.*

wam ble (wom′əl, wam′əl), *v.i.,* **-bled, -bling.** 1 feel nausea. 2 move unsteadily; stagger; totter; reel. [Middle English *wamelen*]

wampum (def. 1)—a string of seven pieces

wam pum (wom′pəm, wôm′pəm), *n.* 1 beads made from shells, formerly used by North American Indians as money and for ornament. 2 SLANG. money. [of Algonquian origin]

wan (won), *adj.,* **wan ner, wan nest.** 1 lacking natural or normal color; pale: *Her face looked wan after her long illness.* See **pale** for synonym study. 2 looking worn or tired; faint; weak: *The patient gave the doctor a wan smile.* [Old English *wann* dark] **—wan′ly,** *adv.* **—wan′ness,** *n.*

wand (wond), *n.* 1 a slender stick or rod: *a magician's wand.* 2 rod or staff carried as a sign of office or authority. 3 a slender stem, branch, or shoot of a shrub or tree. [< Scandinavian (Old Icelandic) *vöndr*] **—wand′like′,** *adj.*

wan der (won′dər), *v.i.* 1 move here and there without any special purpose. 2 go from the right way; stray: *The dog wandered off and got lost.* See synonym study below. 3 follow an uncertain or irregular course; meander: *a driver who wanders all over the road.* 4 be delirious; be incoherent: *His mind wandered when he had a very high fever.* —*v.t.* go aimlessly over or through: *wander the city streets.* —*n.* a wandering. [Old English *wandrian*] **—wan′der er,** *n.*

Syn. *v.i.* **1, 2 Wander, stray** mean to go from place to place more or less aimlessly or without a settled course. **Wander** empha-

walrus
about 10 ft. long

sizes moving about without a definite course or destination: *We wandered through the stores, hoping to get ideas for Christmas presents.* **Stray** emphasizes going beyond the usual or proper limits or away from the regular path or course, and often suggests getting lost: *Two of the children strayed from the picnic grounds.*

Wandering Jew, 1 (in medieval legends) a Jew who insulted Christ and was condemned to wander on earth till Christ's second coming. 2 **wandering Jew,** a trailing plant related to the spiderwort that grows and spreads rapidly. One kind is a common weed.

wan der lust (won′dər lust′), *n.* a strong desire to wander: *Her wanderlust led her all over the world.*

wane (wān), *v.,* **waned, wan ing,** *n.* —*v.i.* 1 lose size; become smaller gradually: *The moon wanes after it has become full.* 2 decline in power, influence, or importance: *Many great empires have waned.* 3 decline in strength or intensity: *The light of day wanes in the evening.* 4 draw to a close: *Summer wanes as autumn approaches.* —*n.* 1 act or process of waning. 2 period of waning, especially the period of the decrease of the moon's visible surface. 3 **on the wane,** growing less; waning. [Old English *wanian*]

wan gle (wang′gəl), *v.,* **-gled, -gling.** INFORMAL. —*v.t.* 1 manage to get by schemes, tricks, persuasion, etc. 2 change (an account, report, etc.) dishonestly for one's advantage. —*v.i.* 1 make one's way through difficulties. 2 use irregular means to accomplish a purpose. [origin uncertain] **—wan′gler,** *n.*

wan i gan (won′ə gən), *n.* 1 a lumberman's chest or trunk. 2 kind of boat used by lumbermen for carrying supplies, tools, etc., and as a houseboat. [of Algonquian origin]

Wan kel engine (wong′kəl; *German* vong′kəl), an internal-combustion engine, with few moving parts, which produces power by the spinning of (usually) two triangular rotors in an oval combustion chamber. [< Felix *Wankel,* born 1902, the German inventor of the engine]

want (wont, wônt), *v.t.* 1 wish for; wish: *They want a new car. He wants to become an engineer.* 2 be without; lack: *It sounds fine, but wants sense. See* **lack** for synonym study. 3 need; require: *Plants want water.* 4 wish to see, speak to, or use: *Call me if you want me.* 5 hunt to catch or arrest: *The escaped prisoner is wanted by the police.* —*v.i.* 1 need food, clothing, and shelter; be very poor. 2 be lacking. 3 **want for,** be in need of; lack: *want for nothing.* —*n.* 1 thing desired or needed: *He is a man of few wants.* 2 a lack: *The plant died from want of water.* 3 a need: *supply a long-felt want.* 4 lack of food, clothing, or shelter; great poverty: *The old soldier is now in want.* See **poverty** for synonym study. [< Scandinavian (Old Icelandic) *vanta*]

want ad, INFORMAL. notice in a newspaper stating that an employee, an apartment, etc., is wanted; classified ad.

want ing (won′ting, wôn′ting), *adj.* 1 lacking; missing: *One volume of the set is wanting.* 2 not coming up to a standard or need: *The vegetables were weighed and found wanting.* —*prep.* without; less; minus: *a year wanting three days.*

wan ton (won′tən), *adj.* 1 reckless, heartless, or malicious: *wanton cruelty.* 2 without reason or excuse: *a wanton attack, wanton mischief.* 3 not moral; not chaste: *a wanton woman.* 4 frolicsome; playful: *a wanton breeze, a wanton child.* 5 not restrained: *a wanton mood.* —*n.* a wanton person. —*v.i.* act in a wanton manner: *The wind wantoned with the leaves.* —*v.t.* waste foolishly; squander: *wanton away one's time.* [Middle English *wantowen* < Old English *wan-* not, lacking + *togen* brought up] **—wan′ton ly,** *adv.* **—wan′ton ness,** *n.*

wap i ti (wop′ə tē), *n., pl.* **-tis** or **-ti.** a large, reddish deer of North America with long, slender antlers; elk. [< Algonquian]

war (wôr), *n., v.,* **warred, war ring,** *adj.* —*n.* 1 fighting carried on by armed force between nations or parts of a nation. 2 any fighting or struggle; strife; conflict: *Doctors carry on war against disease.* 3 the occupation or art of fighting with weapons; military science: *Soldiers are trained for war.* 4 **at war,** taking part in a war. 5 **go to war, a** start a war. **b** go as a soldier. —*v.i.* make war; fight. —*adj.* used in, having to do with, or caused by war: *war weapons, war casualties.* [< Old North French *werre; of Germanic origin*] **—war′less,** *adj.*

War Between the States, the American Civil War.

war ble (wôr′bəl), *v.,* **-bled, -bling,** *n.* —*v.i.* 1 sing with trills, quavers, or melodious turns: *Birds warbled in the trees.* 2 make a sound like that of a bird warbling: *The brook warbled over its rocky bed.* —*v.t.* sing (a song, musical notes, etc.) with trills, quavers, or melodious turns. 2 express in or as if in song. —*n.* 1 a melodious song with trills, quavers, etc. 2 any sound like warbling. 3 act of warbling. [< Old North French *werbler* < *werble* melody; of Germanic origin]

war bler (wôr′blər), *n.* 1 person, bird, etc., that warbles. 2 any of a family of small, usually brightly colored New World songbirds. 3 any of various small, plain-colored songbirds of the Old World.

war bonnet, a ceremonial headdress of skin set with feathers and often a long trailing piece with feathers, worn by certain North American Indians.

war bride, bride of a soldier in wartime.

war chest, fund of money put aside to pay for the costs of some undertaking, especially a political campaign.

war club, a heavy club used as a weapon.

war crime, any inhuman act against civilians, political prisoners, etc., in time of war.

war cry, 1 word or phrase shouted in fighting; battle cry. 2 any cry or slogan used in rallying people to a cause.

ward (wôrd), *n.* 1 division of a hospital or prison. 2 an administrative or electoral district of a city or town. 3 a small administrative district within the Mormon Church. 4 person legally under the care of a guardian or of a court. 5 guard: *The soldiers kept watch and ward over the castle.* 6 (in fencing, etc.) a movement or position of defense. 7 notch in a key. 8 the corresponding ridge in a lock. —*v.t.* 1 **ward off,** keep away; turn aside. 2 put into a ward, especially of a hospital. 3 ARCHAIC. keep watch over. [Old English *weard* a guarding, guard. Related to GUARD.]

Ward (wôrd), *n.* **Artemus,** pen name of Charles F. Browne, 1834-1867, American humorist.

-ward, *suffix forming adverbs.* in the direction of ____; toward ____: *Homeward = in the direction of home. Backward = toward the back.* Also, **-wards.** [Old English *-weard*]

war dance, dance of primitive tribes before going to war or to celebrate a victory.

ward en (wôrd′n), *n.* 1 the official in charge of a prison. 2 any official who enforces certain laws and regulations: *an air-raid warden.* 3 game warden. 4 the head of certain schools or colleges in Great Britain. 5 (in former times) the chief official in a town or area. 6 (in Canada) the chief executive officer in a county. 7 churchwarden. 8 keeper, guard, or custodian. [< Old North French *wardein* < *warder* to guard; of Germanic origin. Related to WARD.]

ward en ship (wôrd′n ship), *n.* position or office of a warden.

ward er (wôr′dər), *n.* 1 guard or watchman. 2 BRITISH. warden; jailer.

ward heeler, INFORMAL. follower of a political boss, who goes around asking for votes and does other minor tasks.

ward robe (wôrd′rōb′), *n.* 1 stock of clothes: *a spring wardrobe.* 2 room, closet, or piece of furniture for holding clothes.

ward room (wôrd′rüm′, wôrd′rům′), *n.* the living and eating quarters for all the commissioned officers on a warship except the commanding officer.

-wards, *suffix forming adverbs.* in the direction of ____; toward ____: *Backwards = in the direction of or toward the back.* Also, **-ward.** [Old English *-weardes*]

ward ship (wôrd′ship), *n.* 1 guardianship over a minor or ward; guardianship; custody. 2 condition of being a ward, or under a legal or feudal guardian.

ware[1] (wer, war), *n.* 1 Usually, **wares,** *pl.* a manufactured thing; article for sale: *The peddler sold his wares cheap.* 2 kind of manufactured thing or article for sale; goods (now chiefly in compounds): *tinware.* 3 pottery; earthenware: *porcelain ware. Delft is a blue-and-white ware.* [Old English *waru*]

ware[2] (wer, war), *adj., v.,* **wared, war ing.** ARCHAIC. —*adj.* aware. —*v.t., v.i.* look out (for); beware (of). [Old English *wær*]

ware house (wer′hous′, war′hous′), *n., pl.* **-hous es** (-hou′ziz), *v.,* **-housed, -hous ing.** —*n.* place where goods are kept, especially in large quantities; storehouse. —*v.t.* put or deposit in a warehouse, as for storage.

ware house man (wer′hous′mən, war′hous′mən), *n., pl.* **-men.** man who owns or works in a warehouse.

war fare (wôr′fer′, wôr′far′), *n.* 1 armed conflict; war; fighting. 2 any struggle or contest.

war game, a training exercise that imitates war. It may be an exercise on a map or maneuvers with actual troops, weapons, and equipment.

war head (wôr′hed′), *n.* the forward part of a torpedo, rocket, missile, etc., that contains the explosive.

war horse, 1 horse used in war; charger. 2 INFORMAL. person who has taken part in many battles, struggles, etc.; veteran.

war i ly (wer′ə lē, war′ə lē), *adv.* in a wary manner; cautiously; carefully.

war i ness (wer′ē nis, war′ē nis), *n.* caution; care.

war like (wôr′lik′), *adj.* 1 fit for war; ready for war; fond of war: *a warlike nation.* 2 threatening war; hostile: *a warlike speech.* 3 of or having to do with war; martial: *warlike music.* See **military** for synonym study.

war lock (wôr′lok), *n.* wizard. [Old English *wǣrloga* traitor, oath-breaker < *wǣr* covenant + *-loga* one who denies]

hat, āge, fär; let, ēqual, tėrm;
it, īce; hot, ōpen, ôrder;
oil, out; cup, pu̇t, rüle;
ch, child; ng, long; sh, she;
th, thin; ᴛʜ, then; zh, measure;

ə represents *a* in about, *e* in taken, *i* in pencil, *o* in lemon, *u* in circus.

< = from, derived from, taken from.

war lord (wôr′lôrd′), *n.* 1 a military commander or commander in chief, especially one who exercises sovereign authority. 2 the military head of a province in China during the period 1916-1923.

warm (wôrm), *adj.* 1 more hot than cold; having some heat; giving forth moderate or gentle heat: *a warm fire. She sat in the warm sunshine.* 2 having a feeling of heat: *be warm from running.* 3 that makes or keeps warm: *a warm coat.* 4 having or showing affection, enthusiasm, or zeal: *a warm welcome.* 5 easily excited: *a warm temper.* 6 exciting; lively: *a warm dispute.* 7 fresh and strong: *a warm scent.* 8 INFORMAL. near what one is searching for, as in games. 9 suggesting heat. Red, orange, or yellow are warm colors. 10 INFORMAL. uncomfortable; unpleasant: *make things warm for a person.*
—*adv.* so as to be warm; warmly.
—*v.t.* 1 make warm; heat: *warm a room.* 2 make cheered, interested, friendly, or sympathetic: *Her happiness warms my heart.*
—*v.i.* 1 become warm. 2 become cheered, interested, friendly, or sympathetic: *The speaker warmed to his subject.*
warm over, INFORMAL. rehash.
warm up, **a** heat or cook again. **b** make or become more cheered, interested, friendly, etc. **c** practice or exercise for a few minutes before entering a game, contest, etc. **d** run (a machine) before using it until it reaches its normal working condition.
[Old English *wearm*] **—warm′er,** *n.* **—warm′ly,** *adv.* **—warm′ness,** *n.*

warm-blood ed (wôrm′blud′id), *adj.* 1 having blood whose temperature stays about the same regardless of the surroundings. Birds and mammals are warm-blooded; reptiles, turtles, fishes, etc., are cold-blooded. 2 with much feeling; eager; ardent.

warmed-o ver (wôrmd′ō′vər), *adj.* 1 warmed again, as food that has become cold; reheated. 2 not fresh or new; old; stale: *warmed-over jokes.*

warm front, the advancing edge of a warm air mass as it passes over and displaces a cooler one.

warm-heart ed (wôrm′här′tid), *adj.* kind; sympathetic; friendly. **—warm′-heart′ed-ness,** *n.*

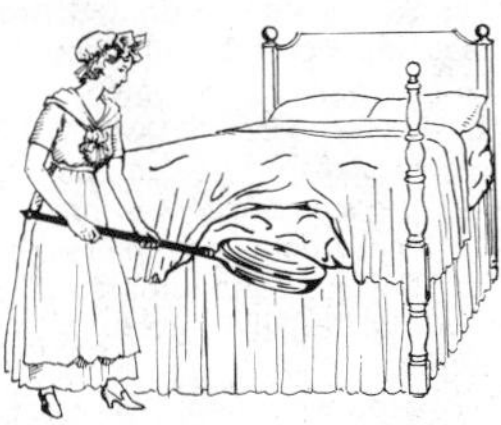
warming pan

warming pan, a covered pan with a long handle for holding hot coals, formerly used to warm beds.

warm ish (wôr′mish), *adj.* rather warm.

war mon ger (wôr′mong′gər, wôr′mung′-gər), *n.* person who is in favor of or attempts to bring about war.

war mon ger ing (wôr′mong′gər ing, wôr′mung′gər ing), *n.* acts or practices of a warmonger. —*adj.* of or having to do with a warmonger or warmongers.

warmth (wôrmth), *n.* 1 a being warm: *the warmth of the open fire.* 2 warm or friendly feeling: *greet a person with warmth.* 3 liveliness of feelings or emotions; fervor: *She spoke with warmth of the natural beauty of the country.* 4 (in painting) a glowing effect, as produced by the use of reds and yellows.

warm-up (wôrm′up′), *n.* 1 practice or exercise taken for a few minutes before entering a game, contest, etc. 2 period of running required for a machine to reach normal working condition before use. —*adj.* for or as a warm-up.

warn (wôrn), *v.t.* 1 give notice to in advance; put on guard (against danger, evil, harm, etc.): *The clouds warned us that a storm was coming.* See synonym study below. 2 give notice to; inform: *The whistle warned visitors that the ship was ready to sail.* 3 give notice to go, stay, etc.: *warn off trespassers.* —*v.i.* give a warning or warnings. [Old English *warnian*] **—warn′er,** *n.*
Syn. *v.t.* 1 **Warn, caution** mean to give notice of possible or coming danger, harm, risk, unpleasantness, etc. **Warn** implies giving clear and firm notice, especially of an imminent or serious danger: *The children were warned not to speak to strangers.* **Caution** implies giving notice of a possible danger and advice about avoiding it: *Citrus growers are cautioned to protect the fruit from frost.*

warn ing (wôr′ning), *n.* 1 act of warning: *death without warning.* 2 something that warns; notice given in advance: *Let this experience be a warning to you to be more careful.* —*adj.* that warns. **—warn′ing ly,** *adv.*

War of 1812, war between the United States and Great Britain that lasted from 1812 to 1815.

War of Independence, Revolutionary War.

war of nerves, conflict in which tension is built up by intimidation, propaganda, or obstructive or delaying tactics rather than by use of violence.

War of Secession, the American Civil War.

warp (wôrp), *v.t.* 1 bend or twist out of shape: *Age had warped and cracked the floor boards.* 2 mislead; pervert: *Prejudice warps our judgment.* 3 move (a ship, etc.) by ropes fastened to something fixed. 4 arrange (threads or yarn) so as to form a warp. —*v.i.* 1 become bent or twisted out of shape: *The floor has warped so that it is not level.* 2 be misled or perverted. 3 (of a ship) be moved by warping. —*n.* 1 a bend or twist, as in wood that has dried unevenly. 2 distortion of judgment; mental twist; bias. 3 rope fixed at one end and pulled upon to move a ship. 4 the threads running lengthwise in a fabric. The warp is crossed by the woof. [Old English *weorpan* to throw] **—warp′er,** *n.*

war paint, 1 paint put on the face or body by American Indians, members of some African tribes, etc., before going to war. 2 SLANG. **a** full dress; ornaments. **b** cosmetics; make-up.

war path (wôr′path′), *n., pl.* **-paths** (-paᴛʜz′, -paths′). 1 the way taken by a fighting expedition of North American Indians. 2 **on the warpath, a** ready for war. **b** looking for a fight; angry.

war plane (wôr′plān′), *n.* airplane designed for or used in war.

war rant (wôr′ənt, wor′ənt), *n.* 1 that which gives a right; authority: *have no warrant for one's action.* 2 a written order giving authority to do something: *a warrant to search the house, a warrant for the payment of money.* 3 a good and sufficient reason; promise; guarantee: *have no warrant for one's hopes.* 4 a document certifying something, especially to a purchaser. 5 the official certificate of appointment issued to a noncommissioned officer in the army or navy. —*v.t.* 1 authorize: *The law warrants his arrest.* 2 justify: *Nothing can warrant such rudeness.* 3 give one's word for; guarantee; promise: *The storekeeper warranted the quality of the coffee.* 4 authenticate. 5 INFORMAL. declare positively; certify. [< Old North French *warant.* See WARRANTY.]

war rant a ble (wôr′ən tə bəl, wor′ən tə-bəl), *adj.* that can be warranted; justifiable. **—war′rant a ble ness,** *n.* **—war′rant a-bly,** *adv.*

war ran tee (wôr′ən tē′, wor′ən tē′), *n.* person to whom a warranty is made.

warrant officer, a military officer who has received a certificate of appointment, but not a commission, ranking between commissioned officers and enlisted men.

war ran tor (wôr′ən tər, wor′ən tər; wôr′-ən tôr′, wor′ən tôr′), *n.* person who makes a warranty; guarantor.

war ran ty (wôr′ən tē, wor′ən tē), *n., pl.* **-ties.** 1 warrant or authorization. 2 promise or pledge that something is what it is claimed to be; guarantee: *a warranty of the quality of the goods sold.* [< Old North French *warantie* < *warantir* to warrant < *warant* (Old French *guarant*) a warrant; of Germanic origin. Doublet of GUARANTY.]

war ren (wôr′ən, wor′ən), *n.* 1 piece of ground filled with burrows, where rabbits live or are raised. 2 a crowded district or building. 3 piece of land enclosed and preserved for hunting small game. [< Anglo-French *warenne* < Celtic]

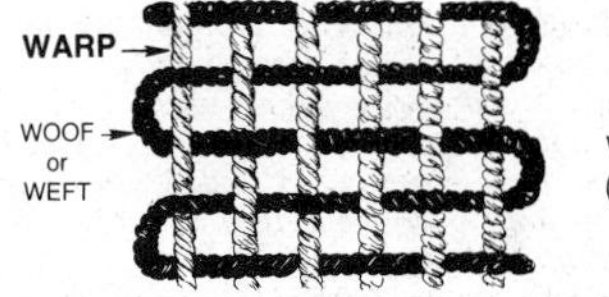

warp (def. 4)

War ren (wôr′ən, wor′ən), *n.* 1 **Earl,** born 1891, chief justice of the United States Supreme Court from 1953 to 1969. 2 **Robert Penn,** born 1905, American novelist and poet. 3 city in SE Michigan. 179,000.

war ri or (wôr′ē ər, wor′ē ər), *n.* a fighting man; experienced soldier. [< Old North French *werreieor* < *werreier* wage war < *werre* war] **—war′ri or like′,** *adj.*

war room, room used at a military headquarters for briefings on conditions at one or more theaters of operation.

War saw (wôr′sô), *n.* capital and largest city of Poland, in the E part. 1,289,000.

war ship (wôr′ship′), *n.* ship armed and manned for war.

wart (wôrt), *n.* 1 a small, hard lump on the skin, caused by a virus infection. 2 a similar lump on a plant. [Old English *wearte*] **—wart′like′,** *adj.*

wart hog, a wild hog of Africa that has two large tusks and large wartlike growths on each side of its face.

war time (wôr′tīm′), *n.* time of war. *—adj.* of or having to do with a time of war.

wart y (wôr′tē), *adj.,* **wart i er, wart i est.** 1 having warts. 2 covered with lumps like warts. 3 of or like a wart.

war whoop, a war cry of American Indians; war cry.

War wick (wôr′ik, wor′ik *for 1 and 3;* wôr′wick, wôr′ik, wor′ik *for 2*), *n.* 1 **Earl of,** 1428-1471, Richard Neville, English soldier and statesman. He was called "the Kingmaker." 2 city in E Rhode Island. 84,000. 3 Warwickshire.

War wick shire (wôr′ik shər, wôr′ik shir; wor′ik shər, wor′ik shir), *n.* county in central England.

war y (wer′ē, war′ē), *adj.,* **war i er, war i est.** 1 on one's guard against danger, deception, etc.: *a wary fox.* 2 cautious or careful: *give wary answers to a stranger's questions.* See **careful** for synonym study. 3 **wary of,** cautious or careful about: *be wary of driving in heavy traffic.* [< *ware*²]

was (woz, wuz; *unstressed* wəz), *v.* the first and third person singular, past indicative of **be.** *I was late. Was he late, too?* [Old English *wæs*]

wash (wosh, wôsh), *v.t.* 1 clean with water or other liquid: *wash one's hands, wash clothes, wash dishes.* 2 remove (dirt, stains, paint, etc.) by or as by the action of water or other liquid: *wash a spot out.* 3 make clean; cleanse; purify: *washed from sin.* 4 make wet: *The flowers are washed with dew.* 5 flow over or past (the shore, coast, etc.): *a beach washed by waves.* 6 carry (by a liquid): *Wood is often washed ashore by the waves.* 7 wear (by water or any liquid): *The cliffs are being washed away by the waves.* 8 cover with a thin coating of color or metal: *The house was washed white.* 9 sift (earth, ore, etc.) by the action of water to separate valuable material, especially gold, from waste. *—v.i.* 1 wash clothes: *wash once a week.* 2 wash oneself: *wash before eating dinner.* 3 undergo washing without damage: *This material washes well.* 4 be carried along or away by water or other liquid: *Cargo washed ashore.* 5 flow or beat with a lapping sound: *The waves washed upon the rock.* 6 INFORMAL. stand being put to the proof: *patriotism that won't wash. That argument won't wash.*
wash down, a wash from top to bottom or from end to end: *wash down the walls of a kitchen.* **b** swallow liquid along with or after (solid food) to help in swallowing.
wash out, a lose color, body, or vigor. **b** INFORMAL. fail and be released from a school, course of study, etc.; flunk out.
wash up, wash one's hands and face.
—n. 1 act or process of washing. 2 condition of being washed. 3 quantity of clothes or other articles washed or to be washed: *a week's wash.* 4 material carried along by moving water and then deposited as sediment. A delta is formed by the wash of a river. 5 motion, rush, or sound of water: *hear the wash of the sea.* 6 tract of land sometimes overflowed with water and sometimes left dry; tract of shallow water; fen, marsh, or bog. 7 (in the western United States) the dry bed of an intermittent stream. 8 liquid for a special use: *a hair wash.* 9 (in water-color painting) a broad, thin layer of color laid on by a continuous movement of the brush. 10 waste liquid matter; liquid garbage. 11 washy or weak liquid food. 12 a thin coat of color or metal. 13 earth, ore, etc., from which gold or the like can be washed. 14 the rough or broken water left behind a moving ship. 15 disturbance in air made by an airplane or any of its parts: *prop wash.* 16 **the Wash,** bay on the E coast of England, an inlet of the North Sea. 20 mi. long; 15 mi. wide.
—adj. that can be washed without damage: *a wash dress.*
[Old English *wascan.* Related to WATER.]

Wash., the state of Washington.

wash a bil i ty (wosh′ə bil′ə tē, wô′shə-bil′ə tē), *n.* quality of being washable.

wash a ble (wosh′ə bəl, wô′shə bəl), *adj.* that can be washed without damage: *washable silk.*

wash-and-wear (wosh′ən wer′, wosh′ən-war′; wôsh′ən wer′, wôsh′ən war′), *adj.* specially treated to require little or no ironing after washing and drying: *wash-and-wear fabrics.*

wash ba sin (wosh′bā′sn, wôsh′bā′sn), *n.* basin for holding water to wash one's face and hands.

wash board (wosh′bôrd′, wosh′bōrd′; wôsh′bôrd′, wôsh′bōrd′), *n.* board having ridges on it, used for rubbing the dirt out of clothes.

wash bowl (wosh′bōl′, wôsh′bōl′), *n.* bowl to hold water to wash one's hands and face.

wash cloth (wosh′klôth′, wosh′kloth′; wôsh′klôth′, wôsh′kloth′), *n., pl.* **-cloths** (-klôᴛʜz′, -klôths′; -kloᴛʜz′, -kloths′). a small cloth for washing oneself.

wash day (wosh′dā′, wôsh′dā′), *n.* day when clothes are washed.

washed-out (wosht′out′, wôsht′out′), *adj.* 1 lacking color; faded. 2 INFORMAL. lacking life, spirit, etc.

washed-up (wosht′up′; wôsht′up′), *adj.* INFORMAL. 1 done with; through, especially after having failed. 2 fatigued.

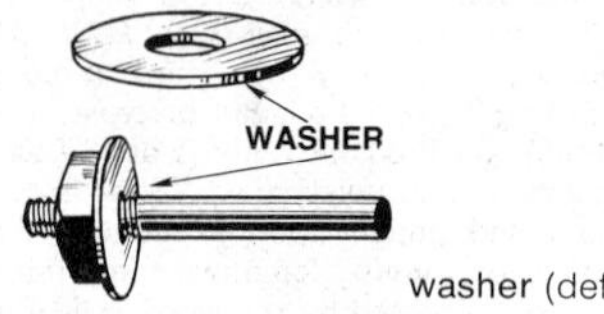

washer (def. 3)

wash er (wosh′ər, wôsh′ər), *n.* 1 person who washes. 2 machine that washes; washing machine. 3 a flat ring of metal, rubber, leather, etc., with a hole in the middle, used with bolts or nuts, or to make joints tight, as in a water faucet.

wash er wom an (wosh′ər wům′ən, wôsh′ər wům′ən), *n., pl.* **-wom en.** woman whose work is washing clothes.

wash ing (wosh′ing, wôsh′ing), *n.* 1 a cleaning with water: *give a car a good washing.* 2 clothes, etc., washed or to be washed. 3 a thin coat, as of a metal applied by electrolysis. 4 Sometimes, **washings,** *pl.* **a** liquid that has been used to wash something. **b** matter removed in washing something: *washings of gold obtained from earth.*

washing machine, machine that washes clothes, sheets, towels, etc.

washing soda, sodium carbonate, used in washing; sal soda.

Wash ing ton (wosh′ing tən, wôsh′ing tən), *n.* 1 capital of the United States, covering the entire District of Columbia. Washington is situated along the Potomac River between Maryland and Virginia. 757,000. 2 one of the Pacific states of the United States. 3,409,000 pop.; 68,200 sq. mi. *Capital:* Olympia. *Abbrev.:* Wash. 3 **Mount,** the highest mountain in New England, in N New Hampshire. 6293 ft. 4 **Booker T(aliaferro),** 1856-1915, American writer and educator who worked for civil rights. He was born a slave. 5 **George,** 1732-1799, commander in chief of the American army in the Revolutionary War and the first president of the United States, from 1789 to 1797. 6 **Martha,** 1731-1802, wife of George Washington.

Wash ing to ni an (wosh′ing tō′nē ən, wôsh′ing tō′nē ən), *n.* native or inhabitant of Washington, D.C., or the state of Washington. *—adj.* of or having to do with Washington, D.C., or the state of Washington.

Washington's Birthday, February 22, the anniversary of George Washington's birthday, observed on the third Monday in February as a legal holiday in most states of the United States.

wash out (wosh′out′, wôsh′out′), *n.* 1 a washing away of earth, a roadbed, etc., by water. 2 the hole or break made by this. 3 INFORMAL. person who is dismissed or rejected from a school, etc., as not qualified. 4 SLANG. failure; disappointment.

wash rag (wosh′rag′, wôsh′rag′), *n.* washcloth.

wash room (wosh′rüm′, wosh′rům′; wôsh′rüm′, wôsh′rům′), *n.* room where toilet facilities are provided; lavatory.

wash stand (wosh′stand′, wôsh′stand′), *n.* bowl with pipes and faucets for running water to wash one's hands and face. 2 stand for holding a basin, pitcher, etc., for washing.

wash tub (wosh′tub′, wôsh′tub′), *n.* tub used to wash or soak clothes in.

wash wom an (wosh′wům′ən, wôsh′-wům′ən), *n., pl.* **-wom en.** washerwoman.

wash y (wosh′ē, wôsh′ē), *adj.,* **wash i er, wash i est.** 1 too much diluted; weak; watery. 2 lacking strength and stamina; feeble. 3 (of color) lacking body; pale.

was n't (woz′nt; wuz′nt), was not.

wasp (wosp, wôsp), *n.* any of numerous insects of the same order as ants and bees, having a slender body, two pairs of wings, a powerful sting, and mouthparts adapted for chewing. [Old English *wæsp*] **—wasp′like′,** *adj.*

WASP (wosp, wôsp), *n.* a white Anglo-Saxon Protestant.

wasp ish (wos′pish, wôs′pish), *adj.* 1 like a wasp; like that of a wasp. 2 bad-tempered; irritable. **—wasp′ish ly,** *adv.* **—wasp′ish-ness,** *n.*

wasp-waist ed (wosp′wā′stid, wôsp′wā′-stid), *adj.* having a very slender waist.

was sail (wos′əl, was′əl), *n.* 1 a drinking party; revelry with drinking of healths. 2 spiced ale or other liquor drunk at a wassail. 3 salutation wishing good health or good luck to a person, used especially in England in former times when drinking a toast. *—v.i.* take part in a wassail; revel. *—v.t.* drink to the health of. *—interj.* "Your health!" [< Scandinavian (Old Icelandic) *ves heill* be healthy!]

was sail er (wos′ə lər, was′ə lər), *n.* 1 reveler. 2 drinker of healths.

Was ser mann (wä′sər mən), *n.* 1 **August von,** 1866-1925, German physician and bacteriologist who invented the Wassermann test. 2 Wassermann test.

Wassermann test, test for syphilis, made on a sample of a person's blood serum.

wast (wost), *v.* ARCHAIC. were. "Thou wast" means "you were."

wast age (wā′stij), *n.* 1 loss by use, wear, decay, leakage, etc.; waste. 2 amount wasted.

waste (wāst), *v.,* **wast ed, wast ing,** *n., adj.*
—*v.t.* 1 make poor use of; spend uselessly; fail to get value from: *Don't waste time or money.* 2 wear down little by little; destroy or lose gradually: *a person wasted by disease.* 3 damage greatly; destroy: *The soldiers wasted the enemy's fields.* —*v.i.* 1 be consumed or spent uselessly. 2 be used up or worn away gradually.
—*n.* 1 poor use; useless spending; failure to get the most out of something: *a waste of money.* 2 useless or worthless material; stuff to be thrown away; refuse: *Garbage or sewage is waste.* 3 bare or wild land; desert; wilderness. 4 any vast, dreary, or empty expanse, as of water or snow-covered land. 5 a wearing down little by little; gradual destruction or loss: *Both waste and repair are constantly going on in our bodies.* 6 destruction or devastation caused by war, floods, fires, etc. 7 cotton or wool threads in bunches, used for cleaning machinery, or wiping off oil, grease, etc. 8 **go to waste,** be wasted.
—*adj.* 1 thrown away as worthless or useless: *waste products.* 2 left over; not used: *waste energy.* 3 not cultivated; that is a desert or wilderness; bare; wild. 4 in a state of desolation or ruin. 5 carrying off or holding refuse: *a waste drain.* 6 of no further use to and therefore excreted by an animal or human body. 7 lay waste, damage greatly; ravage; devastate.
[< Old North French *waster* < Latin *vastare* lay waste < *vastus* vast, waste]

waste bas ket (wāst′bas′kit), *n.* basket or other container for wastepaper.

waste ful (wāst′fəl), *adj.* using or spending too much; extravagant. **—waste′ful ly,** *adv.* **—waste′ful ness,** *n.*

waste land (wāst′land′), *n.* barren, uncultivated land.

waste pa per (wāst′pā′pər), *n.* paper thrown away or to be thrown away as useless or worthless.

waste pipe, pipe for carrying off waste water, etc.

wast er (wā′stər), *n.* person or thing that wastes; squanderer; spendthrift.

wast ing (wā′sting), *adj.* 1 laying waste; devastating. 2 gradually destructive to the body: *a wasting disease.*

wast rel (wā′strəl), *n.* 1 waster; spendthrift. 2 an idle, disreputable person; good-for-nothing.

watch (woch, wôch), *v.i.* 1 look attentively or carefully: *Medical students watched while the doctor performed the operation.* 2 look or wait with care and attention; be very careful: *I watched for a chance to cross the street.* 3 keep guard: *The sentry watched throughout the night.* 4 stay awake for some purpose: *The nurse watches with the sick.* 5 **watch out,** INFORMAL. look out; be on one's guard.
—*v.t.* 1 look at; observe; view: *watch a television show.* 2 look at or wait for with care and attention: *watch a good opportunity to do something.* 3 keep guard over: *The police watched the prisoner.* 4 stay informed about: *watch the stockmarket.*
—*n.* 1 a careful looking; attitude of attention: *Be on the watch for automobiles when you cross the street.* 2 a protecting; guarding: *A man keeps watch over the bank at night.* 3 person or persons kept to guard and protect: *call the night watch.* 4 period of time for guarding: *a watch in the night.* 5 a staying awake for some purpose. 6 device for telling time, driven by a spring or battery, and small enough to be carried in a pocket or worn on the wrist. 7 in nautical use: **a** the time of duty of one part of a ship's crew, usually lasting four hours. **b** the part of a crew on duty at the same time.
[Old English *wæccan*] **—watch′er,** *n.*

watch band (woch′band′, wôch′band′), *n.* band of leather, metal, etc., to fasten a watch on the wrist.

watch case (woch′kās′, wôch′kās′), *n.* the outer covering for the works of a watch.

watch dog (woch′dôg′, woch′dog′; wôch′dôg′, wôch′dog′), *n.* 1 dog kept to guard property. 2 a watchful guardian. —*adj.* organized to keep something or someone under constant surveillance: *a watchdog committee.*

watch fire, fire kept burning at night, especially for the use of a sentinel, guard, or person on watch.

watch ful (woch′fəl, wôch′fəl), *adj.* watching carefully; on the lookout; wide-awake. **—watch′ful ly,** *adv.* **—watch′ful ness,** *n.*
Syn. Watchful, vigilant, alert mean wide-awake and attentive or on the lookout. **Watchful** means paying close attention or keeping careful guard: *She is watchful of her health.* **Vigilant** means being especially and necessarily watchful: *Because the enemy was so close, they kept a particularly vigilant watch.* **Alert** means being wide-awake and ready for whatever may happen: *The alert driver avoided an accident.*

watch glass, a thin, concave piece of glass used in laboratories as a receptacle for small objects under close examination.

watch mak er (woch′mā′kər, wôch′mā′kər), *n.* person who makes and repairs watches.

watch mak ing (woch′mā′king, wôch′mā′king), *n.* business of making and repairing watches.

watch man (woch′mən, wôch′mən), *n., pl.* **-men.** man who keeps watch; guard: *A watchman guards the bank at night.*

watch meeting, a church service held at night, especially on New Year's eve until midnight.

watch night, 1 New Year's eve, observed in Methodist and some other churches with religious services which last until the arrival of the new year. 2 watch meeting.

watch tow er (woch′tou′ər, wôch′tou′ər), *n.* tower from which a watch is kept for enemies, fires, ships, etc.

watch word (woch′wėrd′, wôch′wėrd′), *n.* 1 password: *We gave the watchword, and the sentinel let us pass.* 2 motto; slogan: *"Forward" is our watchword.*

wa ter (wô′tər, wot′ər), *n.* 1 the liquid that constitutes rain, oceans, rivers, lakes, and ponds. Pure water is a transparent, colorless, tasteless, odorless compound of hydrogen and oxygen, freezing at 32 degrees Fahrenheit or 0 degrees centigrade, and boiling at 212 degrees Fahrenheit or 100 degrees centigrade. *Formula:* H_2O 2 any of various watery substances or secretions occurring in or discharged from the body, such as tears, sweat, saliva, urine, serum, etc. 3 any liquid preparation that suggests water: *lavender water.* 4 body of water; sea, lake, river, etc.: *cross the water on a ferry.* 5 water of a river, lake, etc., with reference to its relative depth or height: *low water, high water.* 6 degree of clearness and brilliance of a precious stone. A diamond of the first water is a very clear and brilliant one. 7 a wavy marking on silk, mohair, metal, etc. 8 additional shares or securities issued without a corresponding increase of capital or assets. 9 **waters,** *pl.* **a** flowing water. **b** water moving in waves; the sea; the high sea. **c** spring water; mineral water.

hat, āge, fär; let, ēqual, tėrm;
it, īce; hot, ōpen, ôrder;
oil, out; cup, pu̇t, rüle;
ch, child; ng, long; sh, she;
th, thin; ᴛʜ, then; zh, measure;

ə represents *a* in about, *e* in taken, *i* in pencil, *o* in lemon, *u* in circus.

< = from, derived from, taken from.

above water, out of trouble or difficulty, especially out of financial trouble or difficulty.

back water, **a** make a boat go backward. **b** retreat; withdraw.

by water, on a ship or boat.

fish in troubled waters, take advantage of confusion or trouble to get what one wants.

hold water, stand the test; be true, dependable, effective, etc.

in deep water, in trouble, difficulty, or distress.

like water, very freely.

of the first water, of the highest degree.

throw cold water on, discourage by being indifferent or unwilling.

tread water, keep oneself from sinking by moving the feet up and down.

—*v.t.* 1 sprinkle or wet with water: *water grass.* 2 supply with water: *water cattle. Our valley is well watered by rivers and brooks.* 3 weaken by adding water: *It is against the law to sell watered milk.* 4 **water down,** weaken by addition or alteration; reduce in force, quality, value, etc., by dilution: *water down an amendment, water down a course of study.* 5 produce a wavy marking on (silk, etc.) by sprinkling it with water and passing it through a calender. 6 increase (stock, etc.) by issue of additional shares or securities without a corresponding addition in capital or assets. —*v.i.* 1 fill with water; discharge water: *Her eyes watered. The cake made my mouth water.* 2 get or take in a supply of water: *A ship waters before sailing.*
—*adj.* 1 of water; holding, storing, or conveying water: *a water system.* 2 done or used in or on water: *water sports.* 3 growing or living in or near water: *water plants, water insects.*
[Old English *wæter*] **—wa′ter er,** *n.* **—wa′ter less,** *adj.*

water ballet, a rhythmic, synchronized dance performed by swimmers in the water.

water bed, bed with a mattress consisting of a vinyl bag filled with water.

water beetle, any of various aquatic beetles having the hind legs broad and fringed so as to be well adapted for swimming.

water bird, bird that swims or wades in water.

water blister, blister containing a clear, watery fluid derived from serum.

water boatman, any of a family of water bugs with long, oarlike hind legs that enable them to move through water at great speed.

wa ter borne (wô′tər bôrn′, wô′tər bōrn′; wot′ər bôrn′, wot′ər bōrn′), *adj.* 1 supported by water; floating. 2 conveyed by a boat, ship, etc., transported by water.

wa ter buck (wô′tər buk′, wot′ər buk′), *n., pl.* **-bucks** or **-buck.** any of various African antelopes that frequent rivers, marshes, etc.

water buffalo, buffalo of Asia, often used as a draft animal. See **buffalo** for picture.

water bug, 1 croton bug. 2 any of various insects that live in, on, or near water.

Wa ter bur y (wô′tər ber′ē, wot′ər ber′ē), *n.* city in W Connecticut. 108,000.

Water Carrier, Aquarius.

water chestnut, 1 any of a genus of aquatic plants of the same family as the evening primrose, whose nutlike fruit contains a single, large, edible seed. 2 the fruit of any of these plants. 3 a species of sedge, grown in the Far East for its edible tuber. 4 its tuber.

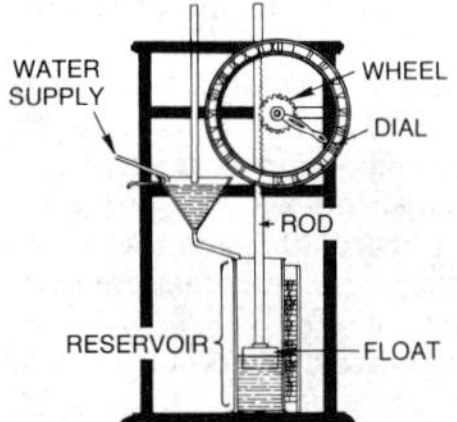

water clock—Water is piped through the funnel into the reservoir. As the water level in the reservoir rises, the float and rod move up. Cogs on the rod and cogs on the wheel mesh, moving the hand around the dial.

water clock, instrument for measuring time by the flow of water.

water closet, 1 toilet flushed by water. 2 room or enclosure containing such a toilet.

wa ter col or (wô′tər kul′ər, wot′ər-kul′ər), *n.* 1 paint mixed with water instead of oil. 2 art of painting with watercolors. 3 picture made with watercolors. *—adj.* made with watercolors.

wa ter-col or ist (wô′tər kul′ər ist, wot′ər-kul′ər ist), *n.* artist who paints in watercolors.

water cooler, device for cooling water, or for cooling something by means of water.

wa ter course (wô′tər kôrs′, wô′tər kōrs′; wot′ər kôrs′, wot′ər kōrs′), *n.* 1 stream of water; river; brook. 2 bed of a stream of water. 3 an artificial channel for water.

wa ter craft (wô′tər kraft′, wot′ər kraft′), *n.* 1 activity or skill in water sports. 2 ship or ships; boat or boats.

wa ter cress (wô′tər kres′, wot′ər kres′), *n.* 1 a perennial plant of the mustard family, growing in and near springs and small running streams and having crisp green leaves. 2 its leaves, used for salad and as a garnish.

water cure, hydropathy or hydrotherapy.

water cycle, cycle in nature by which water evaporates from oceans, lakes, etc., and returns to them as rain or snow.

wa tered (wô′tərd, wot′ərd), *adj.* having a wavelike pattern or clouded appearance.

wa ter fall (wô′tər fôl′, wot′ər fôl′), *n.* fall of water from a height; cascade; cataract.

water flea, any of an order of tiny freshwater crustaceans that swim with a skipping motion.

wa ter fowl (wô′tər foul′, wot′ər foul′), *n., pl.* **-fowls** or **-fowl.** a water bird, especially one that swims.

wa ter front (wô′tər frunt′, wot′ər frunt′), *n.* land at the water's edge, especially the part of a city beside a river, lake, or harbor.

water gap, gap in a mountain ridge through which a stream flows.

water gas, a poisonous gas consisting chiefly of carbon monoxide and hydrogen, made by passing steam over hot coal or coke and used for lighting and sometimes for fuel.

Wa ter gate (wô′tər gāt, wo′tər gāt), *n.* 1 **the Watergate,** set of buildings in Washington, D.C., site of Democratic Party headquarters in 1972. 2 a burglary of this office, followed by a series of illegal actions related to the presidential campaign of 1972, and attempts to obstruct justice during subsequent investigations by the Senate and the Justice Department.

water gate, 1 gate through which water passes. 2 gate that controls the flow of water; sluice; floodgate. 3 gate opening on water.

water glass, 1 glass to hold water; tumbler. 2 sodium silicate. 3 instrument for making observations beneath the surface of water, consisting of an open box or tube with a glass bottom.

water gun, water pistol.

water hole, hole in the ground where water collects; small pond; pool.

water hyacinth, a floating or rooting aquatic plant of the same family as the pickerelweed, with violet or blue flowers and ovate leaves, native to tropical South America, and cultivated elsewhere. When introduced into inland waters of Florida and Louisiana, it became a troublesome weed, seriously impeding navigation.

water ice, 1 a frozen dessert made of fruit juice, sugar, and water. 2 solid ice formed by the direct freezing of water, and not by the compacting of snow.

watering can, can with a spout for sprinkling water on plants, etc.

watering place, 1 resort with springs containing mineral water. 2 resort where there is bathing, boating, etc. 3 place where water may be obtained.

water jacket, a casing with water in it, put around something to keep it cool or at a certain temperature.

water level, the surface level of a body of water.

water lily, 1 any of a family of aquatic plants having flat, floating leaves and showy, fragrant flowers. The flowers of the common American water lily are white, or sometimes pink. 2 the flower of any of these plants.

water line, 1 line where the surface of the water touches the side of a ship or boat. 2 any of several lines marked on a ship's hull to show the depth to which it sinks when unloaded, partly loaded, or fully loaded.

wa ter-logged (wô′tər lôgd′, wô′tər logd′; wot′ər lôgd′, wot′ər logd′), *adj.* so full of water that it will barely float; thoroughly soaked with water.

Wa ter loo (wô′tər lü, wô′tər lü′; wot′ər lü, wot′ər lü′), *n.* 1 town in Belgium, near Brussels, the site of the battle in which Napoleon I was finally defeated in 1815. 14,000. 2 any decisive or crushing defeat. 3 city in E Iowa. 76,000.

water main, a large pipe for carrying water.

wa ter man (wô′tər mən, wot′ər mən), *n., pl.* **-men.** 1 boatman. 2 oarsman.

wa ter mark (wô′tər märk′, wot′ər märk′), *n.* 1 a mark showing how high water has risen or how low it has fallen: *the high watermark of a river.* 2 a distinguishing mark or design impressed in a sheet of paper during manufacture, usually only barely visible except when the sheet is held against the light. *—v.t.* put a watermark in.

wa ter mel on (wô′tər mel′ən, wot′ər-mel′ən), *n.* 1 a large, juicy melon with red or pink pulp, many seeds, and a hard green rind. 2 a slender, trailing vine of the gourd family bearing these melons.

water meter, apparatus for measuring and recording the amount of water drawn from a water main, public water system, etc., by a particular user or group of users.

water mill, mill whose machinery is run by water power.

water moccasin, a poisonous pit viper that lives in swamps and along streams in the southern United States; cottonmouth.

water nymph, (in Greek and Roman myths) a nymph or goddess living in or associated with some body of water.

water of crystallization, water that is present in chemical combination in certain crystalline substances. When the water is removed by heating, the crystals break up into a powder.

water ouzel, any of a family of several water birds that wade and dive in deep water for food; dipper.

water pistol, a toy pistol that shoots water taken in by suction; water gun.

water polo, game played in a swimming pool by two teams of seven swimmers who try to throw or push an inflated ball into the opponent's goal.

water power, the power from flowing or falling water. It can be used to drive machinery and generate electricity.

wa ter proof (wô′tər prüf′, wot′ər prüf′), *adj.* that will not let water through; resistant to water: *An umbrella should be waterproof.* *—n.* 1 a waterproof material. 2 a waterproof coat; raincoat. *—v.t.* make waterproof.

water rat, 1 any of various rodents that live on the banks of streams or lakes. 2 muskrat. 3 SLANG. a waterfront thief, vagrant, smuggler, etc.

wa ter shed (wô′tər shed′, wot′ər shed′), *n.* 1 ridge between the regions drained by two different river systems. 2 the region drained by one river system. 3 point at which a notable change takes place.

wa ter side (wô′tər sīd′, wot′ər sīd′), *n.* the land along the sea, a lake, a river, etc.

water ski, one of a pair of skis for gliding over water while being towed at the end of a rope by a motorboat.

wa ter-ski (wô′tər skē′, wot′ər skē′), *v.i.,* **-skied, -ski ing.** glide over the water on water skis. **—wa′ter-ski′er,** *n.*

water snake, any of various nonpoisonous snakes living in or frequenting water.

water-soak (wô′tər sōk′, wot′ər sōk′), *v.t.* soak with water.

water softener, chemical added to hard

water to remove dissolved mineral matter.

wa ter-sol u ble (wô′tər sol′yə bəl, wot′ər sol′yə bəl), *adj.* that will dissolve in water: *water-soluble vitamins.*

water spaniel, a large spaniel with a heavy, curly coat, often used to retrieve wild ducks, geese, etc., that have been shot by hunters.

waterspout (def. 2)

wa ter spout (wô′tər spout′, wot′ər-spout′), *n.* 1 pipe which takes away or discharges water, especially one used to drain water from a roof. 2 a rapidly spinning column or cone of mist, spray, and water, produced by the action of a whirlwind over the ocean or a lake.

water sprite, sprite, nymph, spirit, etc., supposed to live in water.

water table, the level below which the ground is saturated with water.

wa ter tight (wô′tər tīt′, wot′ər tīt′), *adj.* 1 so tight that no water can get in or out. Ships are often divided into watertight compartments. 2 leaving no opening for misunderstanding, criticism, etc.: *a watertight argument.*

water tower, 1 a very tall structure for the storage of water, as a standpipe. 2 a fire-extinguishing apparatus used to throw water on the upper parts of tall buildings.

water vapor, water in a gaseous state, especially when fairly diffused as it is in the air, and below the boiling point, as distinguished from steam.

wa ter-vas cu lar (wô′tər vas′kyə lər, wot′ər vas′kyə lər), *adj.* of or having to do with the circulation of water in the vessels of certain animals, especially the echinoderms.

wa ter way (wô′tər wā′, wot′ər wā′), *n.* 1 river, canal, or other body of water that ships can go on. 2 channel for water.

water wheel, wheel turned by water and used to do work. See **undershot** for picture.

water wings, two waterproof bags filled with air and put under a person's arms to hold him afloat while he is learning to swim.

wa ter works (wô′tər wėrks′, wot′ər-wėrks′), *n.pl. or sing.* 1 system of pipes, reservoirs, water towers, pumps, etc., for supplying a city or town with water. 2 building with machinery for pumping water.

wa ter worn (wô′tər wôrn′, wô′tər wōrn′; wot′ər wôrn′, wot′ər wōrn′), *adj.* worn or smoothed by the action of water.

wa ter y (wô′tər ē, wot′ər ē), *adj.* 1 of water; connected with water: *a watery grave.* 2 full of water; wet: *watery soil.* 3 indicating rain: *a watery sky.* 4 tearful: *watery eyes.* 5 containing too much water: *watery soup.* 6 like water: *a watery discharge.* 7 weak; thin; poor; pale: *a watery blue.* 8 in or under water: *A drowned person or a sunken ship goes to a watery grave.* **—wa′ter i ness,** *n.*

Wat ling Island (wät′ling), San Salvador (def. 1).

Wat son (wot′sən), *n.* **James Dewey,** born 1928, American biologist, one of the discoverers of the molecular structure of DNA.

watt (wot), *n.* unit of electric power equal to the flow of one ampere under the pressure of one volt, to one joule per second, or to $^1/_{746}$ horsepower. [< James *Watt*]

Watt (wot), *n.* **James,** 1736-1819, Scottish engineer and inventor who perfected the steam engine.

watt age (wot′ij), *n.* amount of electric power, measured in watts, especially kilowatts.

Wat teau (wä tō′; *French* và tō′), *n.* **Jean Antoine,** 1684-1721, French painter.

watt-hour (wot′our′), *n.* unit of electrical energy, equal to the work done by one watt acting for one hour.

wat tle[1] (wot′l), *n.,v.,* **-tled, -tling.** *—n.* 1 Also, **wattles,** *pl.* sticks interwoven with twigs or branches; framework of wicker: *a hut built of wattle.* 2 any of various acacias of Australia, used to make wattles and in tanning. *—v.t.* 1 make (a fence, wall, roof, hut, etc.) of wattle. 2 twist or weave together (twigs, branches, etc.). 3 bind together with interwoven twigs, branches, etc. [Old English *watol*]

wat tle[2] (wot′l), *n.* a fleshy, wrinkled fold of skin, usually bright-red, hanging down from the throat of a chicken, turkey, etc. [origin uncertain]

wat tled[1] (wot′ld), *adj.* made or built of wattle; formed by interwoven twigs.

wat tled[2] (wot′ld), *adj.* having wattles, as a bird, etc.

watt me ter (wot′mē′tər), *n.* instrument for measuring electric power in watts.

Watts (wots), *n.* 1 **George F.,** 1817-1904, English painter and sculptor. 2 **Isaac,** 1674-1748, English minister and writer of hymns.

Wa tu si or **Wa tus si** (wä tü′sē), *n., pl.* **-si** or **-sis.** any of a people of central Africa, originally from Ethiopia, many of whom are over seven feet tall.

Waugh (wô), *n.* **Evelyn (Arthur St. John),** 1903-1966, British novelist.

wave (wāv), *n., v.,* **waved, wav ing.** *—n.* 1 a moving ridge or swell of water. See synonym study below. 2 any movement like this. 3 (in physics) a movement of particles, by which energy is transferred from one place to another. Light, heat, and sound travel in waves. Waves are usually measured by their length, amplitude, velocity, and frequency. 4 swell or sudden increase of some emotion, influence, condition, etc.; outburst: *a wave of enthusiasm, waves of invaders.* 5 a curve or series of curves: *waves in a boy's hair.* 6 a waving, especially of something as a signal: *a wave of the hand.* 7 permanent wave. 8 heat wave or cold wave.
—v.i. 1 move as waves do; move up and down or back and forth; sway: *The tall grass waved in the breeze.* 2 have a wavelike or curving form: *Her hair waves naturally.* *—v.t.* 1 cause to sway or move back and forth or up and down: *Wave your hand. The wind waved the flag.* 2 signal or direct by waving: *She waved him away.* 3 shake in the air; brandish: *I waved the stick at them.* 4 give a wavelike form or pattern to: *wave hair.*
[Old English *wafian* to wave]
Syn. *n.* 1 **Wave, breaker, ripple** mean a moving ridge on the surface of water. **Wave** is the general term: *The raft rose and fell on the waves.* **Breaker** applies to a heavy ocean wave that breaks into foam as it nears the shore or strikes rocks: *Our favorite sport is riding the breakers in.* **Ripple** applies to a tiny wave, such as one caused by the ruffling of a smooth surface by a breeze: *There is scarcely a ripple on the lake tonight.*

hat, āge, fär; let, ēqual, tėrm;
it, īce; hot, ōpen, ôrder;
oil, out; cup, pu̇t, rüle;
ch, child; ng, long; sh, she;
th, thin; ᴛʜ, then; zh, measure;

ə represents *a* in about, *e* in taken, *i* in pencil, *o* in lemon, *u* in circus.

< = from, derived from, taken from.

Wave or **WAVE** (wāv), *n.* woman in the United States Navy other than a nurse. [< *WAVES,* abbreviation of *Women Accepted for Volunteer Emergency Service*]

wattle[2] of a turkey

wave length (wāv′lengkth′, wāv′length′), *n.* (in physics) the distance between successive particles that are in the same phase at the same time, measured in the direction in which the wave is traveling.

wave less (wāv′lis), *adj.* free from waves; undisturbed; still.

wave let (wāv′lit), *n.* a little wave.

wave mechanics, (in physics) a theory ascribing characteristics of waves to subatomic particles.

wa ver (wā′vər), *v.i.* 1 move to and fro; flutter: *a wavering voice.* 2 vary in intensity; flicker: *a wavering light.* 3 be undecided; hesitate: *My choice wavered between the blue sweater and the green one.* See **hesitate** for synonym study. 4 become unsteady; begin to give way: *The battle line wavered and broke.* *—n.* act of wavering. [ultimately < *wave*] **—wa′ver er,** *n.* **—wa′ver ing ly,** *adv.*

Wa ver ley (wā′vər lē), *n.* 1 the first of a series of novels by Sir Walter Scott. 2 pen name of Sir Walter Scott.

wav y (wā′vē), *adj.,* **wav i er, wav i est.** 1 having waves; having many waves: *wavy hair, a wavy line.* 2 moving with a wavelike motion. **—wav′i ly,** *adv.* **—wav′i ness,** *n.*

wax[1] (waks), *n.* 1 a yellowish substance made by bees for constructing their honeycomb. Wax is hard when cold, but can be easily shaped when warm. 2 any substance like this. Most of the wax used for candles, for keeping air from jelly, etc., is really paraffin. Sealing wax and shoemaker's wax are other common waxes. 3 compound containing wax for polishing floors, furniture, etc. 4 earwax; cerumen. 5 person or thing easily manipulated. *—v.t.* rub, stiffen, polish, etc., with wax or something like wax. *—adj.* of wax. [Old English *weax*] **—wax′like′,** *adj.*

wax[2] (waks), *v.i.,* **waxed, waxed** or **wax en, wax ing.** 1 grow bigger or greater; increase: *The moon waxes till it becomes full,* *and then wanes.* 2 become: *The party waxed merry.* [Old English *weaxan*]

wax bean, a yellow string bean.

wax en (wak′sən), *adj.* 1 made of wax. 2 like wax; smooth, soft, and pale: *waxen skin.*

wax myrtle, any of a genus of shrubs or trees whose small berries are coated with wax. The bayberry is a wax myrtle.

wax paper, paper coated with paraffin or some other waxlike substance, used as a wrapping to protect against moisture, etc.

wax wing (waks′wing′), *n.* any of several small perching birds with a showy crest, smooth grayish-brown plumage, and red markings at the tips of the wings.

wax work (waks′wėrk′), *n.* 1 figure or figures made of wax. 2 **waxworks,** *pl.* exhibition of figures made of wax.

wax y (wak′sē), *adj.,* **wax i er, wax i est.** 1 like wax. 2 made of wax; containing wax. 3 abounding in or covered with wax. **—wax′i ness,** *n.*

way (wā), *n.* 1 form or mode of doing; manner; style: *a new way of wearing one's hair, answer in a rude way.* See synonym study below. 2 method; means: *Doctors are using new ways of preventing disease.* 3 point; feature; respect; detail: *The plan is bad in several ways.* 4 direction: *Look this way.* 5 motion along a course: *The guide led the way.* 6 distance: *The sun is a long way off.* 7 road; path; street; course: *She lives just across the way.* 8 space for passing or going ahead. 9 Often, **ways,** *pl.* habit; custom: *Don't mind his teasing; it's just his way.* 10 one's wish; will: *A spoiled child wants his own way all the time.* 11 condition; state: *That sick man is in a bad way.* 12 movement forward; forward motion: *The ship slowly gathered way.* 13 INFORMAL. district; area; region: *They live out our way.* 14 range of experience or notice: *the best idea that ever came my way.* 15 course of life, action, or experience: *the way of the world.* 16 **ways,** *pl.* timbers on which a ship is built and launched.

by the way, a while coming or going. **b** in that connection; incidentally.

by way of, a by the route of; through. **b** as; for.

give way, a make way; retreat; yield. **b** break down or fail. **c** abandon oneself to emotion: *give way to despair.*

go out of the way, make a special effort.

have a way with, be persuasive with.

in a way, to some extent.

in the way, being an obstacle, hindrance, etc.

in the way of, a in a favorable position for doing or getting. **b** as regards.

make one's way, a go. **b** get ahead; succeed.

make way, a give space for passing or going ahead; make room. **b** move forward.

out of the way, a so as not to be an obstacle, hindrance, etc. **b** far from where most people live or go. **c** to death. **d** unusual; strange.

see one's way, be willing or able.

take one's way, go.

under way, going on; in motion; in progress.

—adv. INFORMAL. at or to a distance; far: *The smoke stretched way out to the pier.* [Old English *weg*]

Syn. *n.* 1 **Way, method, manner** mean mode or means. **Way** is the general word, sometimes suggesting a personal or special mode of doing or saying something: *She uses old ways of cooking.* **Method** applies to an orderly way, suggesting a special system of doing something or a definite arrangement of steps to follow: *a new method of teaching reading.* **Manner** applies to a characteristic or particular method or way: *He rides in the western manner.*

way bill (wā′bil′), *n.* list of goods with a statement of where they are to go and how they are to get there.

way far er (wā′fer′ər, wā′far′ər), *n.* traveler, especially one who travels on foot.

way far ing (wā′fer′ing, wā′far′ing), *adj.* traveling; journeying.

way laid (wā′lād′, wā′lād′), *v.* pt. and pp. of **waylay.**

way lay (wā′lā′, wā′lā′), *v.t.,* **-laid, -lay ing.** 1 lie in wait for; attack on the way: *Robin Hood waylaid travelers and robbed them.* 2 stop (a person) on his way. **—way′lay′er,** *n.*

Wayne (wān), *n.* **Anthony,** 1745-1796, American general in the Revolutionary War. He was known as "Mad Anthony" Wayne because of his reckless daring.

way-out (wā′out′), *adj.* SLANG. far-out.

-ways, *suffix forming adverbs.* 1 in the direction or position of the ___: *Lengthways = in the direction of the length.* 2 in ___ manner: *Anyways = in any manner.* [< *way* + *-s,* suffix used to form some adverbs]

ways and means, 1 ways of raising revenue for current governmental expenditures. 2 methods and resources that are at a person's disposal for effecting some object.

way side (wā′sīd′), *n.* edge of a road or path. *—adj.* along the edge of a road or path: *a wayside inn.*

way station, station between main stations on a railroad, bus line, etc.

way ward (wā′wərd), *adj.* 1 turning from the right way; disobedient; willful. 2 irregular; unsteady. [Middle English *weiward,* short for *aweiward* turned away] **—way′ward ly,** *adv.* **—way′ward ness,** *n.*

way worn (wā′wôrn′, wā′wōrn′), *adj.* wearied by traveling.

W.C., water closet.

W.C.T.U., Woman's Christian Temperance Union.

we (wē; *unstressed* wi), *pron., pl. nominative; possessive,* **our** or **ours;** *objective,* **us.** the first person nominative plural of **I.** 1 the speaker plus the person or persons addressed or spoken about. An author, an editor, a king, or a judge sometimes uses *we* to mean *I.* 2 people in general, including the speaker. [Old English *wē*]

weak (wēk), *adj.* 1 that can easily be broken, crushed, overcome, torn, etc.; not strong: *a weak chair, a weak foundation, weak defenses.* 2 lacking bodily strength or health: *a weak old man.* 3 not functioning well: *weak eyes, weak hearing.* See synonym study below. 4 lacking power, authority, force, etc.: *a weak government, a weak law.* 5 lacking moral strength or firmness: *a weak character.* 6 lacking mental power: *a weak mind.* 7 lacking or poor in amount, volume, loudness, taste, intensity, etc.: *a weak voice, weak arguments, a weak current of electricity.* 8 lacking or poor in something specified: *a composition weak in spelling.* 9 (of verbs) inflected by additions of consonants to the stem, not by vowel change; regular. Weak verbs form the past tense and past participle by adding *-ed, -d,* or *-t.* EXAMPLE: *want - wanted* (weak); *sing - sang - sung* (strong). 10 (in phonetics) not stressed. [< Scandinavian (Old Icelandic) *veikr*]

Syn. 1,2 Weak, feeble, decrepit mean lacking or inferior in strength, energy, or power. **Weak** is the general word: *She has weak ankles.* **Feeble** implies loss of strength from sickness or age, or, describing things, faintness or ineffectiveness: *He is too feeble to feed himself.* **Decrepit** means worn out or broken down by age or long-continued use: *They have only one decrepit bed.*

weak en (wē′kən), *v.t.* make weak or weaker. See synonym study below. *—v.i.* grow or become weak or weaker.

Syn. *v.t.* **Weaken, undermine, debilitate** mean to cause to lose strength, energy, or power. **Weaken** is the general word: *Poor organization weakened his argument.* **Undermine** means to weaken gradually by working secretly or treacherously: *Rumors undermined confidence in the company's stock.* **Debilitate** means to make (a person's constitution, mind, etc.) weak or feeble by damaging and taking away vitality or strength: *be debilitated by disease.*

weak fish (wēk′fish′), *n., pl.* **-fish es** or **-fish.** any of certain spiny-finned saltwater food fishes with a tender mouth, especially a species found along the Atlantic coast of the United States.

weak-kneed (wēk′nēd′), *adj.* 1 having weak knees. 2 yielding easily to opposition, intimidation, etc.

weak ling (wēk′ling), *n.* a weak person or animal. *—adj.* weak.

weak ly (wēk′lē), *adv., adj.,* **-li er, -li est.** *—adv.* in a weak manner. *—adj.* weak; feeble; sickly. **—weak′li ness,** *n.*

weak-mind ed (wēk′mīn′did), *adj.* 1 having or showing little intelligence; feeble-minded. 2 lacking firmness of mind. **—weak′-mind′ed ness,** *n.*

weak ness (wēk′nis), *n.* 1 a being weak; lack of power, force, or vigor. 2 a weak point; slight fault. 3 a liking that one is a little ashamed of; fondness: *a weakness for sweets.* 4 something for which one has such a liking.

weal[1] (wēl), *n.* well-being; prosperity: *Good citizens act for the public weal.* [Old English *wela* wealth, welfare]

weal[2] (wēl), *n.* streak or ridge on the skin made by a stick or whip; welt; wale; wheal. [variant of *wale*]

weald (wēld), *n.* 1 BRITISH. **a** open country. **b** woodland. 2 **the Weald,** district in SE England including parts of Kent, Surrey, and Sussex. [Old English, woods]

wealth (welth), *n.* 1 much money or property; riches. 2 all things that have money value; resources: *The wealth of a nation includes its mines and forests as well as its factories.* 3 a large quantity; abundance: *a wealth of hair, a wealth of words.* [< *well*[1] or *weal*[1]]

wealth y (wel′thē), *adj.,* **wealth i er, wealth i est.** 1 having wealth; rich. See **rich** for synonym study. 2 abundant; copious. **—wealth′i ly,** *adv.* **—wealth′i ness,** *n.*

wean (wēn), *v.t.* 1 accustom (a child or young animal) to food other than its mother's milk. 2 accustom (a person) to do without something; cause to turn away: *wean someone from a bad habit.* [Old English *wenian*]

wean ling (wēn′ling), *n.* child or animal that has only recently been weaned. *—adj.* recently weaned.

weap on (wep′ən), *n.* 1 any object or instrument used in fighting, such as a sword, spear, arrow, club, gun, claw, horn, sting, or teeth. 2 any means of attack or defense: *Drugs are effective weapons against many diseases.* [Old English *wǣpen*] **—weap′on less,** *adj.*

weap on ry (wep′ən rē), *n.* 1 the developing and producing of weapons. 2 weapons collectively.

wear (wer, war), *v.,* **wore, worn, wear ing,** *n.* —*v.t.* 1 have or carry on the body: *wear a coat, wear a beard, wear a watch.* 2 have or show: *wear a big smile. The gloomy old house wore an air of sadness.* 3 cause loss or damage to by using: *These shoes are badly worn.* 4 make by rubbing, scraping, washing away, etc.: *wear a path across the grass. Walking wore a hole in my shoe.* 5 tire; weary: *She is worn with care.* 6 turn (a ship) to sail with the wind at the stern. —*v.i.* 1 suffer loss or damage from being used: *This coat has worn to shreds.* 2 last long; give good service: *That coat has worn well.* 3 stand the test of experience, familiarity, criticism, etc.: *a friendship that did not wear well.* 4 pass or go gradually: *My patience began to wear thin during the long wait. It became hotter as the day wore on.* 5 (of a ship) turn or be turned to sail with the wind at the stem.

wear down, a tire; weary. b overcome by persistent effort. c reduce or erode by use, friction, etc.

wear off, become less.

wear out, a wear until no longer fit for use. b use up. c tire out; weary.

—*n.* 1 a wearing; a being worn: *clothes for summer wear.* 2 things worn or to be worn; clothing: *That store sells children's wear.* 3 gradual loss or damage caused by use: *The rug shows wear.* 4 lasting quality; good service: *There is still much wear in these shoes.* 5 **wear and tear,** loss or damage caused by use.

[Old English *werian*] **—wear′a ble,** *adj.* **—wear′er,** *n.*

wear ing (wer′ing, war′ing), *adj.* 1 exhausting; tiring: *a very wearing trip, a wearing conversation.* 2 of or for wear; intended to be worn: *wearing apparel.* **—wear′ing ly,** *adv.*

wear i some (wir′ē səm), *adj.* wearying; tiring; tiresome. **—wear′i some ly,** *adv.* **—wear′i some ness,** *n.*

wear y (wir′ē), *adj.,* **wear i er, wear i est,** *v.,* **wear ied, wear y ing.** —*adj.* 1 worn out; tired: *weary feet, a weary brain.* See **tired** for synonym study. 2 causing tiredness; tiring: *a weary wait.* 3 having one's patience, tolerance, or liking exhausted: *be weary of excuses.* —*v.t.* make weary; tire. —*v.i.* become weary. [Old English *wērig*] **—wear′i ly,** *adv.* **—wear′i ness,** *n.*

wea sand (wē′znd), *n.* ARCHAIC. 1 windpipe. 2 throat. [Old English *wǣsend*]

wea sel (wē′zəl), *n.* 1 any of various small, carnivorous mammals of the same genus as the mink, with long, slender, furry bodies and short legs. Weasels have keen sight and smell and are known for their quickness and slyness. 2 a cunning, sneaky person. —*v.i.* 1 use tricky actions or words; be evasive; hedge. 2 **weasel out,** escape or withdraw craftily or irresponsibly; evade duty, responsibility, obligation, etc. [Old English *weosule*] **—wea′sel like′,** *adj.*

weasel (def. 1)
about 16 in. long with tail

weasel word, word lacking in force or exact meaning, used to make a statement evasive or equivocal; an ambiguous word or one used ambiguously.

weath er (weᴛʜ′ər), *n.* 1 the condition of the atmosphere with respect to temperature, moisture, violence or gentleness of winds, clearness or cloudiness, etc.: *forecast clear weather.* 2 windy, rainy, or stormy weather: *damage done by the weather.* 3 **keep one's weather eye open,** be on the lookout for possible danger or trouble. 4 **under the weather,** INFORMAL. sick; ailing. —*v.t.* 1 expose to the weather; wear by sun, rain, frost, etc.: *Wood turns gray if weathered for a long time.* 2 go or come through safely. 3 sail to the windward of: *The ship weathered the cape.* —*v.i.* 1 become discolored or worn by air, rain, sun, frost, etc. 2 resist exposure to the weather; endure. —*adj.* toward the wind; of the side exposed to the wind; windward. [Old English *weder*]

weath er-beat en (weᴛʜ′ər bēt′n), *adj.* worn or hardened by the wind, rain, and other forces of the weather: *a seaman's weather-beaten face, a weather-beaten old barn.*

weath er board (weᴛʜ′ər bôrd′, weᴛʜ′ər bōrd′), *n.* clapboard. —*v.t.* cover with weatherboards.

weath er-bound (weᴛʜ′ər bound′), *adj.* delayed by bad weather: *a weather-bound ship.*

Weather Bureau, Weather Service.

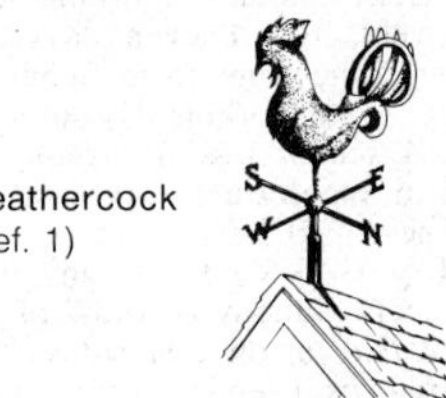

weathercock (def. 1)

weath er cock (weᴛʜ′ər kok′), *n.* 1 vane to show which way the wind is blowing, especially one in the shape of a rooster. 2 person or thing that is changeable or inconstant.

weath er glass (weᴛʜ′ər glas′), *n.* any of several instruments used to show the state of the atmosphere or predict the weather, such as a barometer.

weath er ing (weᴛʜ′ər ing), *n.* the destructive or discoloring action of air, water, frost, etc., especially on rocks.

weath er man (weᴛʜ′ər man′), *n., pl.* **-men.** INFORMAL. man who forecasts the weather.

weather map, map or chart showing conditions of temperature, barometric pressure, precipitation, direction and velocity of winds, etc., over a wide area for a given time or period.

weath er proof (weᴛʜ′ər prüf′), *adj.* protected against rain, snow, or wind; able to stand exposure to all kinds of weather. —*v.t.* make weatherproof.

weather satellite, an artificial earth satellite that measures and reports meteorological conditions, especially as an aid in forecasting.

hat, āge, fär; let, ēqual, tėrm;
it, īce; hot, ōpen, ôrder;
oil, out; cup, pu̇t, rüle;
ch, child; ng, long; sh, she;
th, thin; ᴛʜ, then; zh, measure;

ə represents *a* in about, *e* in taken, *i* in pencil, *o* in lemon, *u* in circus.

< = from, derived from, taken from.

Weather Service, branch of the United States government that records and forecasts the weather.

weather station, station where weather conditions are observed, recorded, or forecast.

weather strip, a narrow strip of cloth or metal to fill or cover the space between a door or window and the casing, so as to keep out rain, snow, and wind.

weath er-strip (weᴛʜ′ər strip′), *v.t.,* **-stripped, -strip ping.** fit or seal with weather strips.

weath er tight (weᴛʜ′ər tīt′), *adj.* protected against rain, snow, etc.

weather vane, vane (def. 1).

weath er-wise (weᴛʜ′ər wīz′), *adj.* skillful in forecasting the changes of the weather.

weave (wēv), *v.,* **wove** or **weaved, wo ven** or **wove, weav ing,** *n.* —*v.t.* 1 form (threads or strips) into a thing or fabric: *weave threads into cloth, weave straw into hats, weave reeds into baskets.* 2 make out of thread, strips, etc.: *weave a rug, weave a fabric. A spider weaves a web.* 3 combine into a whole: *The author wove three plots together into one story.* 4 make by combining parts: *The author wove a story from three plots.* 5 introduce into a connected whole: *weave a melody into a musical composition.* 6 direct in a twisting and turning course: *weave one's way home, weave a car in and out of traffic.* 7 make with care, as if by weaving: *weave a web of lies.* —*v.i.* 1 work with a loom. 2 become woven or interlaced. 3 go by twisting and turning; move with a rocking or swaying motion. —*n.* method or pattern of weaving: *Homespun is a cloth of coarse weave.* [Old English *wefan*]

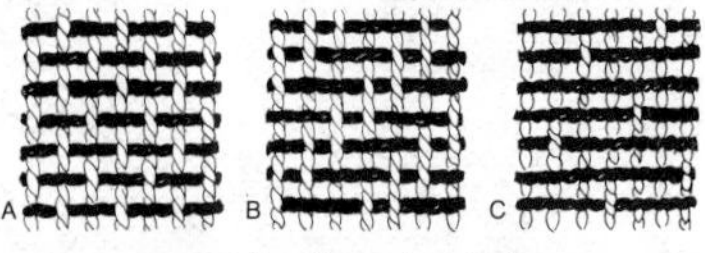

weave—the three basic types:
A, plain; B, twill; C, satin

weav er (wē′vər), *n.* 1 person who weaves. 2 person whose work is weaving. 3 weaverbird.

weav er bird (wē′vər bėrd′), *n.* any of a family of birds similar to finches, mostly of Asia, Africa, and Australia, that build elaborately woven nests.

web (web), *n., v.,* **webbed, web bing.** —*n.* 1 something woven. The fabric of delicate, silken threads spun by a spider is a web. 2 a whole piece of cloth while being woven or after being taken from the loom. 3 anything formed as if by weaving, especially something that ensnares or entangles: *a web of lies, a web of espionage.* 4 a complicated network: *a web of railroads.* 5 membrane or skin joining the toes of swimming birds and certain other water animals. 6 connective tissue. 7 vane of a feather. 8 a thin metal sheet connecting heavier parts of a structure or machine. 9 a large roll of paper used in a rotary press for printing newspapers. 10 the masonry between the ribs of a ribbed vault. —*v.t.* 1 envelop or trap in a web. 2 join by or as if by a web; twine; interlock. [Old English *webb*] —**web′like′**, *adj.*

webbed (webd), *adj.* 1 formed like a web or with a web. 2 having the toes joined by a web. Ducks have webbed feet.

web bing (web′ing), *n.* 1 cloth woven into strong strips, used in upholstery and for belts. 2 skin joining the toes, as in a duck's feet. 3 anything forming a web.

We ber (vā′bər), *n.* Baron **Karl Maria von,** 1786-1826, German composer.

We bern (vā′bərn), *n.* **Anton von,** 1883-1945, Austrian composer.

web foot (web′fu̇t′), *n., pl.* **-feet.** 1 foot in which the toes are joined by a web. 2 bird or animal having webfeet.

web-foot ed (web′fu̇t′id), *adj.* having the toes joined by a web.

Web ster (web′stər), *n.* 1 **Daniel,** 1782-1852, American statesman and orator. 2 **Noah,** 1758-1843, American author and lexicographer.

web-toed (web′tōd′), *adj.* web-footed.

wed (wed), *v.,* **wed ded, wed ded** or **wed, wed ding.** —*v.t.* 1 marry. 2 conduct the marriage ceremony for. 3 unite or join closely. —*v.i.* enter into marriage; marry. [Old English *weddian*]

we'd (wēd; *unstressed* wid), 1 we had. 2 we should. 3 we would.

Wed., Wednesday.

wed ded (wed′id), *adj.* 1 married. 2 of marriage: *wedded bliss.* 3 united. 4 devoted.

wed ding (wed′ing), *n.* 1 a marriage ceremony. See **marriage** for synonym study. 2 an anniversary of this. A golden wedding is the fiftieth anniversary of a marriage. 3 a close union or association.

we deln (vā′dln), *n.* skiing with fast, swiveling turns to the right and left while skis are kept parallel and close together. —*v.i.* ski in this manner. [< German, literally, to wag < *Wedel* whisk, tail]

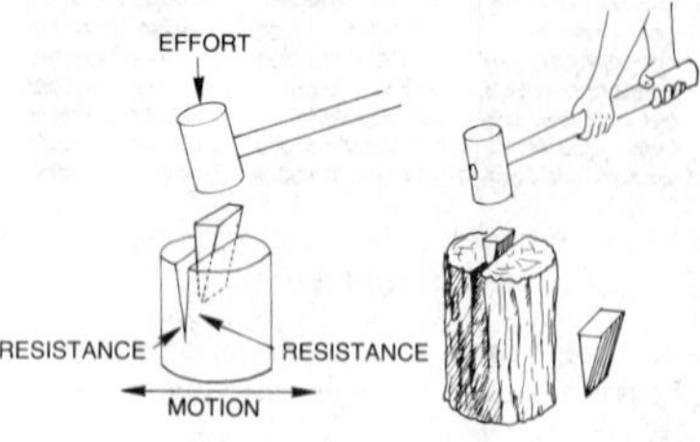

wedge (def. 1)

wedge (wej), *n., v.,* **wedged, wedg ing.** —*n.* 1 piece of wood or metal tapering to a thin edge, used in splitting, separating, etc. It is a simple machine. 2 something shaped like a wedge: *a wedge of pie. Wild geese fly in a wedge.* 3 something used like a wedge: *Their grand party was a wedge for their entry into society.* —*v.t.* 1 split or separate with a wedge. 2 fasten or tighten with a wedge. 3 thrust or pack in tightly; squeeze: *wedge oneself through a narrow window.* —*v.i.* force a way, opening, etc. [Old English *wecg*]

Wedg wood (wej′wu̇d′), *n.* 1 **Josiah,** 1730-1795, English potter. 2 type of pottery originated by Josiah Wedgwood, often with tinted ground and white decoration in relief in designs patterned after Greek and Roman models.

wed lock (wed′lok), *n.* 1 married state; marriage: *united in wedlock.* 2 **born out of wedlock,** illegitimate. [Old English *wedlāc* pledge < *wedd* pledge + *-lāc,* noun suffix]

Wednes day (wenz′dē, wenz′dā), *n.* the fourth day of the week, following Tuesday. [Old English *Wōdnesdæg* Woden's day]

wee (wē), *adj.,* **we er, we est.** very small; tiny. [Middle English *we, wei* a little bit < Old English *wǣg* weight]

weed[1] (wēd), *n.* 1 a useless or troublesome plant, either growing wild or occurring in cultivated ground to the exclusion or injury of the desired crop. 2 a useless or troublesome person or thing. 3 Also, **the weed.** INFORMAL. tobacco. 4 INFORMAL. a cigar or cigarette. —*v.t.* 1 take weeds out of: *weed a garden.* 2 **weed out,** a free from what is useless or worthless. b remove as useless or worthless. —*v.i.* take out weeds or anything like weeds. [Old English *wēod*] —**weed′less,** *adj.* —**weed′like′,** *adj.*

weed[2] (wēd), *n.* 1 **weeds,** *pl.* mourning garments: *a widow's weeds.* 2 ARCHAIC. garment. [Old English *wǣd*]

weed er (wē′dər), *n.* 1 person who weeds. 2 tool or machine for digging up weeds.

weed kill er (wēd′kil′ər), *n.* herbicide.

weed y (wē′dē), *adj.,* **weed i er, weed i est.** 1 full of weeds: *a weedy garden.* 2 of or like weeds. 3 thin and lanky; weak. —**weed′i ness,** *n.*

wee hours, the early morning hours.

week (wēk), *n.* 1 seven days, one after another. 2 the time from Sunday through Saturday. 3 the working days of a seven-day period: *A school week is usually five days.* 4 **week in, week out,** week after week. [Old English *wice*]

week day (wēk′dā′), *n.* any day of the week except Sunday or (now often) Saturday. —*adj.* of or on a weekday.

week end (wēk′end′), *n.* Saturday and Sunday as a time for recreation, visiting, etc. —*adj.* of or on a weekend. —*v.i.* spend a weekend.

week ly (wēk′lē), *adj., adv., n., pl.* **-lies.** —*adj.* 1 of a week; for a week; lasting a week: *a weekly wage.* 2 done or happening once a week: *a weekly letter home.* —*adv.* once each week; every week. —*n.* a newspaper or magazine published once a week.

ween (wēn), *v.t., v.i.* ARCHAIC. think; suppose; believe; expect. [Old English *wēnan*]

ween y (wē′nē), *adj.,* **ween i er, ween i est.** INFORMAL. very small; little; tiny. [< *wee* + *-ny,* as in *teeny, tiny*]

weep (wēp), *v.,* **wept, weep ing.** —*v.i.* 1 shed tears; cry: *weep with rage, weep for joy.* 2 show sorrow or grief. 3 shed or exude water or moisture in drops. —*v.t.* 1 shed tears for; mourn. 2 let fall in drops; shed: *weep bitter tears.* 3 spend in crying: *weep one's life away.* 4 shed (moisture or water) in drops. [Old English *wēpan*]

weep er (wē′pər), *n.* 1 person who weeps. 2 person hired to weep at funerals; professional mourner.

weep ing (wē′ping), *adj.* 1 that weeps. 2 having thin, drooping branches: *a weeping birch.*

weeping willow, a large willow tree, native to eastern Asia and widely cultivated in Europe and America for ornament, distinguished by its long and slender drooping branches.

weep y (wē′pē), *adj.,* **weep i er, weep i est.** INFORMAL. inclined to weep; tearful.

wee vil (wē′vəl), *n.* 1 any of a family of small beetles that have long snouts and feed on plants. The larvae of the weevil feed on and destroy grain, nuts, cotton, fruit, etc. 2 any of certain related insects which damage stored grain. [Old English *wifel*]

wee vil y or **wee vil ly** (wē′və lē), *adj.* infested with weevils.

weft (weft), *n.* 1 the threads running from side to side across a fabric; woof. 2 something woven or spun, as a web. [Old English *weft* < *wefan* to weave]

Wehr macht (vār′mäkt′; *German* vār′mäHt′), *n.* the armed forces of (Nazi) Germany. [< German < *Wehr* defense, weapon + *Macht* power]

weigh[1] (wā), *v.t.* 1 find the weight of: *weigh oneself, weigh a bag of potatoes.* 2 measure by weight: *The grocer weighed out five pounds of apples.* 3 bend by weight; burden: *branches weighed down with ice, be weighed down with many troubles.* 4 balance in the mind; consider carefully: *She weighed her words before speaking.* See **consider** for synonym study. 5 lift up (a ship's anchor). —*v.i.* 1 have as a measure by weight: *weigh 140 pounds.* 2 have importance or influence: *Such considerations do not weigh us.* 3 lie as a burden or worry; bear down: *Don't let that mistake weigh upon your mind.* 4 **weigh in,** find out one's weight before a contest. 5 lift anchor. [Old English *wegan* weigh, lift, heft] —**weigh′a ble,** *adj.* —**weigh′er,** *n.*

weigh[2] (wā), *n.* **under weigh,** under way. [spelling variant of *way;* influenced by *aweigh*]

weight (wāt), *n.* 1 how heavy a thing is; amount a thing weighs: *That man's weight is 175 pounds.* 2 force with which a body is attracted to the earth or some other field of gravitation. The weight of a body is the product of the mass of the body and the acceleration of gravity and is expressed in such units as newton, dyne, etc. 3 system of standard units used for expressing weight, as avoirdupois. 4 unit of such a system. 5 piece of metal or other substance, having a specific weight, used on a balance or scale for weighing things: *a pound weight.* 6 quantity that has a certain weight: *a ten-ton weight of coal.* 7 a heavy thing: *A weight keeps the papers in place.* 8 load; burden: *The pillars support the weight of the roof. That's a great weight off my mind.* 9 influence; importance; value: *a man of weight in his community, evidence of little weight.* 10 the greater or more influential portion: *The weight of public opinion was against him.* 11 a metal ball thrown, pushed, or lifted in contests of strength. 12 (in statistics) a factor assigned to a number in a computation, as in determining an average, to make the number's effect on the computation reflect its importance. 13 **by weight,** measured by weighing. 14 **pull one's weight,** do one's part or share.

—*v.t.* 1 load down; burden: *a heavily weighted truck, a person weighted by care.* 2 add weight to; put weight on: *The elevator is weighted too heavily.* 3 load (fabric, thread, etc.) with mineral to make it seem of better quality: *weighted silk.* 4 (in statistics) give a weight to: *a weighted average.*

[Old English *(ge)wiht* < *wegan* weigh]

weight less (wāt′lis), *adj.* 1 having little or no weight. 2 being free from the pull of gravity: *Astronauts know what it is like to float in space in a weightless condition.* **—weight′less ly,** *adv.* **—weight′less ness,** *n.*

weight lifter, person who lifts barbells, dumbbells, etc., as a body-building exercise or in sports competition.

weight y (wā′tē), *adj.,* **weight i er, weight i est.** 1 having much weight; heavy; ponderous. See **heavy** for synonym study. 2 too heavy; burdensome: *weighty cares of state.* 3 important; influential: *a weighty speaker.* 4 convincing: *weighty arguments.* **—weight′i ly,** *adv.* **—weight′i ness,** *n.*

Weill (vīl), *n.* **Kurt,** 1900-1950, German composer, in the United States after 1935.

Wei mar (vī′mär), *n.* city in S East Germany. 64,000.

Wei ma ra ner (vī′mə rä′nər), *n.* any of a breed of medium-sized gray dogs with a docked tail, bred in Germany as a hunting dog. [< German < *Weimar,* where the breed was developed]

Weimar Republic, the German government from 1919 to 1933. It was so called because the constitutional assembly in 1919 met at Weimar.

weir (wir), *n.* 1 dam erected across a river to stop and raise the water, as for conveying a stream to a mill. 2 fence of stakes or broken branches put in a stream or channel to catch fish. 3 obstruction erected across a channel or stream to divert the water through a special opening in order to measure the quantity flowing. [Old English *wer*]

weird (wird), *adj.* 1 unearthly or mysterious: *They were awakened by a weird shriek.* See synonym study below. 2 INFORMAL. odd; fantastic; queer: *The shadows made weird figures on the wall.* 3 ARCHAIC. having to do with fate or destiny. [Old English *wyrd* fate] **—weird′ly,** *adv.* **—weird′ness,** *n.*

Syn. 1 **Weird, eerie, uncanny** mean mysteriously or frighteningly strange. **Weird** describes something that seems not of this world or due to something above or beyond nature: *All night weird cries came from the jungle.* **Eerie** suggests the frightening effect of something weird or ghostly or vaguely and evilly mysterious: *The light from the single candle made eerie shadows in the cave.* **Uncanny** suggests a strangeness that is disturbing because it seems unnatural: *I had an uncanny feeling that eyes were peering from the darkness.*

weird sisters or **Weird Sisters,** the Fates.

Weiz mann (vīts′män′, wīts′mən), *n.* **Chaim,** 1874-1952, first president of Israel, from 1948 to 1952.

welch (welch, welsh), *v.i.* welsh.

wel come (wel′kəm), *v.,* **-comed, -com ing,** *n., adj., interj.* —*v.t.* 1 greet kindly; give a friendly reception to: *We always welcome guests at our house.* 2 receive gladly: *welcome contributions, welcome suggestions.* —*n.* 1 a kind reception: *You will always have a welcome here.* 2 word or phrase expressing this; kindly greeting. 3 **wear out one's welcome,** visit a person too often or too long. —*adj.* 1 gladly received: *a welcome letter, a welcome visitor, a welcome rest.* 2 gladly or freely permitted: *You are welcome to pick the flowers.* 3 free to enjoy courtesies, etc., without obligation (said in response to thanks): *You are quite welcome.* —*interj.* exclamation of friendly greeting: *Welcome, everyone!* [Old English *wilcuma* agreeable guest < *willa* pleasure + *cuma* comer < *cuman* come] **—wel′com er,** *n.*

welcome wagon, U.S. organization that officially greets new residents to a town, city, county, or state, by extending to them free souvenirs, etc., from local merchants.

weld (weld), *v.t.* 1 join (pieces of metal) together by heating the parts that touch to the melting point, so that they can be hammered or pressed together or flow together and become one piece: *She welded the broken rod.* 2 unite closely: *Working together for a month welded them into a strong team.* —*v.i.* be welded or be capable of being welded: *Some metals weld better than others.* —*n.* 1 a welded joint. 2 act of welding. [alteration of *well*[2], verb] **—weld′er,** *n.*

wel fare (wel′fer′, wel′far′), *n.* 1 health, happiness, and prosperity; condition of being or doing well: *My uncle asked about the welfare of everyone in our family.* 2 welfare work. 3 aid provided by the government to poor or needy people. 4 **on welfare,** receiving aid from the government because of hardship or need. [Middle English *wel fare* < *wel* well + *fare* go]

Welfare Island, island in the East River, New York City.

welfare state, state whose government provides for the welfare of its citizens through social security, unemployment insurance, free medical treatment, etc.

welfare work, work done to improve the conditions of people who need help, carried on by government, private organizations, or individuals.

welfare worker, person who does welfare work.

wel kin (wel′kən), *n.* ARCHAIC. the sky; the vault of heaven. [Old English *wolcen* cloud]

well[1] (wel), *adv.,* **bet ter, best,** *adj., interj.* —*adv.* 1 in a satisfactory, favorable, or advantageous manner; all right: *The job was well done. Is everything going well at school?* 2 thoroughly; fully: *Shake well before using.* 3 to a considerable degree; considerably; much: *The fair brought in well over a hundred dollars.* 4 in detail; intimately: *She knows the subject well.* 5 fairly; reasonably: *I couldn't very well refuse their request.* 6 **as well, a** also; besides. **b** equally. 7 **as well as, a** in addition to; besides. **b** as much as. —*adj.* 1 satisfactory; good; right: *It is well you came along.* 2 in good health: *Is he well enough to travel?* 3 desirable; advisable: *It is always well to start a bit early.* —*interj.* an expression used to show mild surprise, agreement, etc., or just to fill in: *Well! Well! here she is. Well, I'm not sure.* [Old English *wel*] ➤ See **good** for a usage note.

well[2] (wel), *n.* 1 hole dug or bored in the ground to get water, oil, gas, etc. 2 spring of water. 3 source of continuous supply; wellspring; fountain: *That scholar is a well of ideas.* 4 something like a well in shape or use, such as the reservoir of a fountain pen. 5 shaft or opening for stairs or an elevator, extending vertically through the floors of a building. 6 compartment around a ship's pumps. —*v.i.* spring, rise, or gush: *Water wells from a spring beneath the rock.* —*v.t.* send gushing up or pouring forth. [Old English *welle,* stem of *weallan* to boil]

we'll (wēl; *unstressed* wil), 1 we shall. 2 we will.

well a day (wel′ə dā′), *interj.* ARCHAIC. alas!

hat, āge, fär; let, ēqual, tėrm;
it, īce; hot, ōpen, ôrder;
oil, out; cup, pu̇t, rüle;
ch, child; ng, long; sh, she;
th, thin; ᴛʜ, then; zh, measure;

ə represents *a* in about, *e* in taken, *i* in pencil, *o* in lemon, *u* in circus.

< = from, derived from, taken from.

well-ad vised (wel′ad vīzd′), *adj.* 1 prudent; careful; doing the wise or proper thing: *The inventor was no doubt well-advised in patenting his invention.* 2 based on wise counsel or careful consideration: *a well-advised silence.*

Wel land Canal (wel′ənd), canal in Ontario, Canada, between Lake Erie and Lake Ontario. 27 mi. long.

well-ap point ed (wel′ə poin′tid), *adj.* having good furnishings or equipment.

well a way (wel′ə wā′), *interj.* ARCHAIC. alas!

well-bal anced (wel′bal′ənst), *adj.* 1 rightly balanced, adjusted, or regulated: *a well-balanced diet.* 2 sensible; sane: *a well-balanced outlook on life.*

well-be haved (wel′bi hāvd′), *adj.* showing good manners or conduct.

well-be ing (wel′bē′ing), *n.* health and happiness; welfare.

well born (wel′bôrn′), *adj.* belonging to a good family.

well-bred (wel′bred′), *adj.* 1 well brought up; having or showing good manners. 2 (of animals) of good breed or stock.

well-con tent (wel′kən tent′), *adj.* highly pleased or satisfied.

well-de fined (wel′di fīnd′), *adj.* clearly defined or indicated; distinct: *well-defined limits, a well-defined style.*

well-de vel oped (wel′di vel′əpt), *adj.* 1 developed or worked out well: *a well-developed plan.* 2 showing good development: *a well-developed physique.*

well-dis posed (wel′dis pōzd′), *adj.* 1 favorably or kindly disposed: *The city government is well-disposed toward the project.* 2 well-meaning.

well do ing (wel′dü′ing), *n.* a doing right.

well-done (wel′dun′), *adj.* 1 performed well; skillfully done or executed: *a well-done job.* 2 (of meat) thoroughly cooked: *a well-done steak.*

Welles ley (welz′lē), *n.* **Arthur.** See **Wellington.**

well-fa vored (wel′fā′vərd), *adj.* of pleasing appearance; good-looking.

well-fed (wel′fed′), *adj.* showing the result of good feeding; fat; plump.

well-fixed (wel′fikst′), *adj.* INFORMAL. well-to-do.

well-formed (wel′fôrmd′), *adj.* rightly or finely formed; shapely.

well-found (wel′found′), *adj.* well supplied or equipped.

well-found ed (wel′foun′did), *adj.* rightly or justly founded: *well-founded suspicions, a well-founded faith in education.*

well-groomed (wel′grümd′, wel′gru̇md′), *adj.* well cared for; neat and trim.

well-ground ed (wel′groun′did), *adj.* 1 based on good grounds; well-founded. 2 thoroughly instructed in the fundamental principles of a subject.

well head (wel′hed′), *n.* 1 spring of water. 2 source; fountainhead.

well-heeled (wel′hēld′), *adj.* INFORMAL. well-to-do; prosperous.

well-in formed (wel′in fôrmd′), *adj.* 1 having reliable or full information on a subject. 2 having information on a wide variety of subjects.

Wel ling ton (wel′ing tən), *n.* 1 first **Duke of,** 1769-1852, Arthur Wellesley, British general and statesman, born in Ireland. He was called "the Iron Duke." Wellington defeated Napoleon I at Waterloo in 1815. 2 capital of New Zealand, a seaport on the S coast of North Island. 135,000.

well-kept (wel′kept′), *adj.* well cared for; carefully tended.

well-knit (wel′nit′), *adj.* well joined or put together.

well-known (wel′nōn′), *adj.* 1 clearly or fully known. 2 familiar. 3 generally or widely known.

well-made (wel′mād′), *adj.* skillfully made; sturdily built.

well-man nered (wel′man′ərd), *adj.* having or showing good manners; polite; courteous.

well-marked (wel′märkt′), *adj.* clearly marked or distinguished; distinct.

well-mean ing (wel′mē′ning), *adj.* 1 having good intentions. 2 caused by good intentions.

well-nigh (wel′nī′), *adv.* very nearly; almost.

well-off (wel′ôf′, wel′of′), *adj.* 1 in a good condition or position. 2 fairly rich.

well-or dered (wel′ôr′dərd), *adj.* ordered or arranged well: *a well-ordered method.*

well-pre served (wel′pri zėrvd′), *adj.* showing few signs of age.

well-pro por tioned (wel′prə pôr′shənd, wel′prə pōr′shənd), *adj.* having good or correct proportions; having a pleasing shape.

well-read (wel′red′), *adj.* having read much; knowing a great deal about books and literature.

well-round ed (wel′roun′did), *adj.* complete in all parts or respects: *a well-rounded education.*

Wells (welz), *n.* **H(erbert) G(eorge),** 1866-1946, English writer of science fiction, history, and essays.

well-spo ken (wel′spō′kən), *adj.* 1 speaking well, fittingly, or pleasingly; polite in speech. 2 spoken well.

well spring (wel′spring′), *n.* 1 source of a stream or spring; fountainhead. 2 source of a supply that never fails; source.

well sweep, device used to draw water from a well, consisting of a long pole attached to a pivot and having a bucket at one end.

well-thought-of (wel′thôt′uv′, wel′thôt′ov′), *adj.* highly respected; esteemed.

well-timed (wel′tīmd′), *adj.* at the right time; timely.

well-to-do (wel′tə dü′), *adj.* having enough money to live well; prosperous.

well-turned (wel′tėrnd′), *adj.* 1 turned or shaped well, as with rounded or curving form: *a well-turned ankle.* 2 gracefully or happily expressed: *a well-turned compliment.*

well-wish er (wel′wish′ər), *n.* person who wishes well to a person, cause, etc.

well-worn (wel′wôrn′, wel′wōrn′), *adj.* 1 much worn by use: *a well-worn pair of shoes.* 2 used too much; trite; stale: *a well-worn joke.*

welsh (welsh, welch), *v.i.* SLANG. 1 cheat by failing to pay a bet. 2 evade the fulfillment of an obligation: *welsh on a promise.* Also, **welch.** [origin uncertain] **—welsh′er,** *n.*

Welsh (welsh, welch), *adj.* of or having to do with Wales, its people, or their Celtic language. *—n.* 1 the people of Wales. 2 their language.

Welsh cor gi (kôr′gē), either of two breeds of Welsh working dogs having a long body, short legs, and a foxlike head. [< Welsh *corgi* < *cor* dwarf + *ci* dog]

Welsh man (welsh′mən, welch′mən), *n., pl.* **-men.** native or inhabitant of Wales.

Welsh rabbit or **Welsh rarebit,** dish of cheese melted and cooked with milk, eggs, etc., and poured over toast or crackers; rarebit.

welt (welt), *n.* 1 a strip of leather between the upper part and the sole of a shoe. 2 a narrow strip of material or cord fastened on the edge or at a seam of a garment or upholstery, for trimming or strengthening. 3 a raised streak or ridge made on the skin by a stick or whip. 4 a heavy blow. *—v.t.* 1 put a welt or welts on. 2 INFORMAL. beat severely. [Middle English *welte, walte*]

Welt an schau ung (vel′tän′shou′ùng), *n.* GERMAN. 1 a broad or comprehensive view of life. 2 (literally) world view.

wel ter (wel′tər), *v.i.* 1 roll or tumble about; wallow. 2 lie soaked; be drenched. 3 be sunk or deeply involved (in). 4 (of waves, the water, or sea) surge. *—n.* 1 a rolling or tumbling about. 2 a surging or confused mass. 3 confusion; commotion. [< Middle Dutch and Middle Low German *welteren*]

wel ter weight (wel′tər wāt′), *n.* boxer who weighs more than 135 pounds and less than 147 pounds.

Wel ty (wel′tē), *n.* **Eudora,** born 1909, American short-story writer and novelist.

wen (wen), *n.* a harmless cyst of the skin, especially on the scalp. It forms when the fatty matter secreted by a sebaceous gland collects inside the gland. [Old English *wenn*]

wench (wench), *n.* 1 girl or young woman. 2 a woman servant. [Middle English *wenchel* child < Old English *wencel*]

Wen chow (wen′chou′), *n.* seaport in E China. 202,000.

wend (wend), *v.,* **wend ed** or **went, wend ing.** *—v.t.* 1 direct (one's way): *We wended our way home.* *—v.i.* go. [Old English *wendan*]

Wend (wend), *n.* any of a Slavic people living in central Germany.

Wend ish (wen′dish), *adj.* of or having to do with the Wends or their language. *—n.* the Slavic language of the Wends.

went (went), *v.* pt. of **go.** *I went home promptly after school.* [originally past tense of *wend*]

wept (wept), *v.* pt. and pp. of **weep.** *I wept for joy.*

were (wėr; *unstressed* wər), *v.* 1 plural and 2nd person singular past indicative of **be.** *The children were playing in the park.* 2 past subjunctive of **be.** *If I were rich, I would travel.* 3 **as it were,** in some way; so to speak. [Old English *wǣron*]

we're (wir), we are.

weren't (wėrnt), were not.

were wolf (wir′wùlf′, wėr′wùlf′, *or* wer′wùlf′), *n., pl.* **-wolves.** (in folklore) a person who has been changed into a wolf or one who can change himself into a wolf. Also, **werwolf.** [Old English *werwulf* < *wer* man + *wulf* wolf]

wert (wėrt; *unstressed* wərt), *v.* ARCHAIC. were. "Thou wert" means "you were."

wer wolf (wir′wùlf′, wėr′wùlf′, *or* wer′wùlf′), *n., pl.* **-wolves.** werewolf.

We ser River (vā′zər), river flowing from West Germany into the North Sea. 300 mi.

wes kit (wes′kit), *n.* INFORMAL. waistcoat; vest.

Wes ley (wes′lē; *British* wez′lē), *n.* 1 **John,** 1703-1791, English clergyman who founded the Methodist Church. 2 his brother, **Charles,** 1707-1788, English clergyman. He helped John Wesley, and wrote many hymns.

Wes ley an (wes′lē ən; *British* wez′lē ən), *n.* 1 follower of John Wesley. 2 Methodist. *—adj.* 1 of or having to do with John Wesley or his teaching. 2 of or having to do with the Methodist Church.

Wes ley an ism (wes′lē ə niz′əm; *British* wez′lē ə niz′əm), *n.* the system of doctrines and church government of the Wesleyan Methodists.

Wes sex (wes′iks), *n.* ancient kingdom in S England from A.D. 500? to 886. See **Mercia** for map.

west (west), *n.* 1 direction of the sunset; point of the compass to the left as one faces north. 2 Also, **West.** the part of any country toward the west. 3 **the West, a** the western part of the United States, especially the region west of the Mississippi River. **b** the countries in Europe and America as distinguished from those in Asia; the Occident. **c** the non-Communist nations, especially those of western Europe and America. *—adj.* 1 toward the west; farther toward the west. 2 coming from the west. 3 in the west. *—adv.* 1 toward the west. 2 **west of,** further west than. [Old English]

West (west), *n.* 1 **Benjamin,** 1738-1820, American painter of historical subjects, who lived in England. 2 **Nathanael,** 1903-1940, American novelist. His real name was Nathan Weinstein. 3 Dame **Rebecca,** born 1892, British writer, born in Ireland. Her real name is Cicely Isabel Fairfield.

West Berlin, the W part of Berlin, belonging to West Germany. It is located in East Germany and separated from East Berlin by a wall. 2,135,000.

west bound (west′bound′), *adj.* going west; bound westward.

west er ly (wes′tər lē), *adj., adv., n., pl.* **-lies.** *—adj., adv.* 1 toward the west. 2 from the west. *—n.* wind that blows from the west.

west ern (wes′tərn), *adj.* 1 toward the west. 2 from the west. 3 of the west; in the west. 4 **Western, a** of or in the western part of the United States. **b** of or in the countries of Europe and America. **c** of or having to do with the non-Communist nations, especially those of western Europe and America. *—n.* INFORMAL. story, motion picture, or television show dealing with life in the western United States, especially cowboy life.

Western Australia, state in W Australia. 980,000 pop.; 975,900 sq. mi. *Capital:* Perth.

Western Church, 1 the part of the Catholic Church that acknowledges the Pope as its spiritual leader. 2 the Christian churches of Europe and America.

west ern er (wes′tər nər), *n.* 1 native or inhabitant of the west. 2 **Westerner,** native or inhabitant of the western part of the United States.

Western Hemisphere, the half of the

world that includes North and South America.

west ern ize (wes′tər nīz), *v.t.,* **-ized, -iz ing.** make western in character, ideas, ways, etc. **—west′ern i za′tion,** *n.* **—west′ern iz′er,** *n.*

west ern most (wes′tərn mōst), *adj.* farthest west.

Western Roman Empire, the western part of the Roman Empire after its division in A.D. 395. It ended with the capture of Rome by the Vandals in A.D. 455.

Western Samoa, country made up of several islands in the S Pacific Ocean, a member of the Commonwealth of Nations. 141,000 pop.; 1100 sq. mi. *Capital:* Apia.

West Germany, country in central Europe, consisting of the part of Germany which came under American, British, and French control at the end of World War II. 61,682,000 pop.; 96,000 sq. mi. *Capital:* Bonn. See **Austria** for map.

West Indian, 1 of or having to do with the West Indies. 2 native or inhabitant of the West Indies.

West Indies, long chain of islands between Florida and South America; Greater Antilles, Lesser Antilles, and the Bahama Islands.

West Indies Associated States, group of former British colonies, including Antigua, Dominica, Grenada, St. Kitts-Nevis-Anguilla, and St. Lucia, that now exercise domestic self-government.

West ing house (wes′ting hous), *n.* **George,** 1846-1914, American inventor.

West Ir i an (ir′ē än), W part of New Guinea, a part of Indonesia. 750,000 pop.; 164,000 sq. mi. Former names, **Dutch New Guinea, West New Guinea.**

West land (west′lənd), *n.* city in SE Michigan, a suburb of Detroit. 87,000.

West min ster (west′min′stər), *n.* part of London that contains Westminster Abbey, the Houses of Parliament, etc.

Westminster Abbey, church in London where the kings and queens of Great Britain are crowned and in which many English monarchs and famous people are buried.

West mor land (west′mər lənd), *n.* county in NW England.

West New Guinea, a former name of **West Irian.**

west-north west (west′nôrth′west′), *n.* the point of the compass or the direction midway between west and northwest, two points or 22 degrees 30 minutes to the north of west.

West Pakistan, a former province of Pakistan located west of India, before East Pakistan became the country of Bangladesh.

West pha li a (west fā′lē ə), *n.* region in N West Germany. **—West pha′li an,** *adj., n.*

West Point, college for training cadets to become officers in the United States Army, located on the Hudson River in SE New York State.

west-south west (west′south′west′), *n.* the point of the compass or the direction midway between west and southwest, two points or 22 degrees 30 minutes to the south of west.

West Virginia, one of the southeastern states of the United States. 1,744,000 pop.; 24,200 sq. mi. *Capital:* Charleston. *Abbrev.:* W.Va. **—West Virginian.**

west ward (west′wərd), *adv., adj.* toward the west; west. *—n.* a westward part, direction, or point.

west ward ly (west′wərd lē), *adj., adv.* 1 toward the west. 2 from the west.

west wards (west′wərdz), *adv.* westward.

wet (wet), *adj.,* **wet ter, wet test,** *v.,* **wet** or **wet ted, wet ting,** *n.* *—adj.* 1 covered or soaked with water or other liquid: *wet hands, a wet sponge.* 2 watery; liquid: *eyes wet with tears.* 3 not yet dry: *wet paint, wet ink.* 4 rainy: *wet weather.* 5 INFORMAL. permitting the sale of alcoholic drinks: *a wet town.* **6 all wet,** SLANG. completely wrong or mistaken. *—v.t.* make wet. See synonym study below. *—v.i.* become wet. *—n.* 1 water or other liquid; moisture. 2 wetness; rain. 3 INFORMAL. person who favors laws that permit making and selling of alcoholic drinks. [Middle English *wett,* past participle of *weten* to wet, Old English *wǣtan*] **—wet′ly,** *adv.* **—wet′ness,** *n.*

Syn. *v.t.* **Wet, drench, soak** mean to make very moist. **Wet** is the general word: *Wet the cloth before you wipe off the window.* **Drench** means to wet thoroughly, as by a pouring rain: *We were drenched by a sudden downpour.* **Soak** means to wet thoroughly by putting or being in a liquid for some time: *Soak the stained spot in milk.*

wet back (wet′bak′), *n.* INFORMAL. a Mexican who enters the United States illegally, especially by swimming or wading across the Rio Grande.

wet blanket, person or thing that has a discouraging or depressing effect.

wet cell, an electric cell having a liquid electrolyte.

weth er (weᴛʜ′ər), *n.* a castrated ram. [Old English]

wet nurse, woman employed to suckle the infant of another.

wet-nurse (wet′nėrs′), *v.t.,* **-nursed, -nurs ing.** 1 act as wet nurse to. 2 treat with special care; coddle; pamper.

wet suit, a skin-tight rubber suit worn by skin divers, surfers, etc.

wet ta ble (wet′ə bəl), *adj.* that can be wetted without damage.

wet ter (wet′ər), *n.* person or thing that wets.

wetting agent, substance capable of reducing surface tension so that a liquid will spread more easily on a surface.

we've (wēv; *unstressed* wiv), we have.

w.f. or **wf,** (in printing) wrong font.

wh., watt-hour.

whack (hwak), *n.* 1 INFORMAL. **a** a sharp, resounding blow. **b** sound of such a blow. 2 SLANG. **a** portion, share, or allowance. **b** trial or attempt: *take a whack at flying a plane.* **3 out of whack,** SLANG. not in proper condition; disordered. *—v.t.* 1 strike with a sharp, resounding blow. **2 whack up,** SLANG. share; divide. *—v.i.* strike a sharp, resounding blow. [imitative]

whack ing (hwak′ing), *adj.* BRITISH INFORMAL. large; forcible.

whale[1] (hwāl), *n., pl.* **whales** or **whale,** *v.,* **whaled, whal ing.** *—n.* 1 any of various large sea mammals shaped like a fish, with a broad, flat tail, forelimbs developed into flippers, no hind limbs, and a thick layer of fat under the skin. **2 a whale of,** INFORMAL. a very excellent, big, or impressive kind of: *a whale of a party.* *—v.i.* hunt and catch whales. [Old English *hwæl*]

whale[2] (hwāl), *v.t.,* **whaled, whal ing.** INFORMAL. 1 whip severely; beat; thrash. 2 hit hard. [apparently variant of *wale*]

whale back (hwāl′bak′), *n.* a freight steamer having a rounded upper deck shaped like a whale's back, used especially on the Great Lakes.

hat, āge, fär; let, ēqual, tėrm;
it, īce; hot, ōpen, ôrder;
oil, out; cup, put, rüle;
ch, child; ng, long; sh, she;
th, thin; ᴛʜ, then; zh, measure;
ə represents *a* in about, *e* in taken,
i in pencil, *o* in lemon, *u* in circus.
< = from, derived from, taken from.

whale boat (hwāl′bōt′), *n.* a long, narrow rowboat, with a pointed bow and stern, formerly much used in whaling, now used as a lifeboat.

whale bone (hwāl′bōn′), *n.* an elastic, horny substance growing in place of teeth in the upper jaw of certain whales and forming a series of thin, parallel plates; baleen. Thin strips of whalebone were formerly used for stiffening corsets and dresses.

whal er (hwā′lər), *n.* 1 person who hunts whales. 2 ship used for hunting and catching whales. 3 whaleboat.

whale shark, a very large, spotted, harmless shark of warm seas.

whal ing (hwā′ling), *n.* the hunting and catching of whales.

wham (hwam), *n., interj., v.,* **whammed, wham ming.** INFORMAL. *—n., interj.* exclamation or sound as of one thing striking hard against another. *—v.t., v.i.* hit with a hard, striking sound.

wham my (hwam′ē), *n., pl.* **-mies.** SLANG. jinx; hex.

whang (hwang), INFORMAL. *—n.* a resounding blow or bang. *—v.t., v.i.* strike with a blow or bang. [imitative]

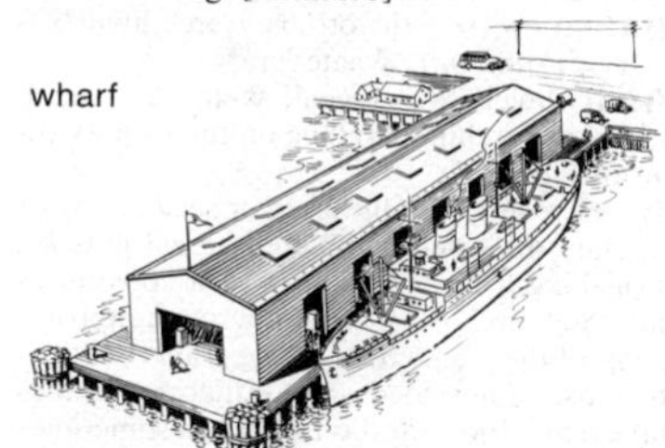
wharf

wharf (hwôrf, wôrf), *n., pl.* **wharves** or **wharfs.** platform built on the shore or out from the shore, beside which ships can load and unload. [Old English *hwearf*]

wharf age (hwôr′fij, wôr′fij), *n.* 1 the use of a wharf for mooring a ship, storing and handling goods, etc. 2 fee or charge for this. 3 wharves: *There are miles of wharfage in New York City.*

wharf in ger (hwôr′fin jər, wôr′fin jər), *n.* person who owns or has charge of a wharf.

Whar ton (hwôrt′n), *n.* **Edith,** 1862-1937, American novelist.

wharves (hwôrvz, wôrvz), *n.* a pl. of **wharf.**

what (hwot, hwut; *unstressed* hwət), *pron., pl.* **what,** *adj., adv., interj.* *—pron.* 1 (as an interrogative pronoun) a word used in asking questions about people or things. *What is your name?* 2 as a relative pronoun: **a** that which: *I know what you mean.* **b** whatever; anything that: *Do what you please.*

and what not, and all kinds of other things.

what for, why.
what if, what would happen if.
what's what, INFORMAL. the true state of affairs: *know what's what.*
—adj. 1 (as an interrogative adjective) a word used in asking questions about persons or things. *What time is it?* 2 as a relative adjective: **a** that which; those which: *Put back what money is left.* **b** whatever; any that: *Take what supplies you will need.* 3 word used to show surprise, doubt, anger, liking, etc., or to add emphasis. *What a pity!*
—adv. 1 how much; how: *What does it matter?* 2 partly: *What with the wind and what with the rain, our walk was spoiled.* 3 a word used to show surprise, doubt, anger, liking, etc., or to add emphasis. *What happy times!*
—interj. word used to show surprise, doubt, anger, liking, etc., or to add emphasis. *What! Are you late again?*
[Old English *hwæt*]

what e'er (hwot er′, hwut er′), *pron., adj.* whatever.

what ev er (hwot ev′ər, hwut ev′ər), *pron.* 1 anything that: *Do whatever you like.* 2 no matter what: *Whatever happens, he is safe.* 3 word used for emphasis instead of *what. Whatever do you mean?* *—adj.* 1 any that: *Ask whatever friends you like to the party.* 2 no matter what: *Whatever excuse he makes will not be believed.* 3 at all: *Any person whatever can tell you the way.*

what not (hwot′not′, hwut′not′), *n.* a stand with several shelves for books, ornaments, etc.

what's (hwots, hwuts), 1 what is. 2 what has.

what so e'er (hwot′sō er′, hwut′sō er′), *pron., adj.* whatsoever; whatever.

what so ev er (hwot′sō ev′ər, hwut′sō-ev′ər), *pron., adj.* whatever.

wheal (hwēl), *n.* 1 weal; welt. 2 a small, burning or itching swelling on the skin. [variant of *weal*]

wheat (hwēt), *n.* 1 the grain or seed of any of a genus of widely cultivated cereal grasses, furnishing a meal or flour which constitutes the chief breadstuff in temperate countries. 2 any of the plants bearing the grains or seeds in dense, four-sided spikes that sometimes have awns **(bearded wheat)** and sometimes do not **(beardless wheat** or **bald wheat).** [Old English *hwǣte*]

wheat cake (hwēt′kāk′), *n.* pancake, especially if made of wheat flour.

wheat ear (hwēt′ir′), *n.* a small northern thrush, brown with a black-and-white tail.

wheat en (hwēt′n), *adj.* made of wheat.

wheat germ, the tiny germ or embryo of the wheat kernel, separated in the milling of flour and used as a cereal, etc. It is rich in vitamins.

whee dle (hwē′dl), *v.,* **-dled, -dling.** *—v.t.* 1 persuade by flattery, smooth words, caresses, etc.; coax: *The children wheedled their parents into letting them go to the picnic.* 2 get by wheedling: *They finally wheedled the secret out of him.* *—v.i.* use soft, flattering words. [Old English *wǣdlian* beg] **—whee′dler,** *n.* **—whee′dling ly,** *adv.*

wheel (hwēl), *n.* 1 a round frame turning on a pin or shaft in the center. 2 any instrument, machine, apparatus, or other object shaped or moving like a wheel, or the essential feature of which is a wheel. 3 steering wheel. 4 INFORMAL. bicycle. 5 any force thought of as moving or propelling: *the wheels of the government.* 6 **wheels,** *pl.* **a** machinery. **b** SLANG. automobile. 7 a circling or circular motion or movement; revolution. 8 a military or naval movement by which troops or ships in line change direction while maintaining a straight line. 9 SLANG. person who manages affairs, personnel, etc., as in a business. 10 a round frame of natural cheese in the form in which it is cured. **11 at the wheel, a** at the steering wheel. **b** in control. **12 wheels within wheels,** complicated circumstances, motives, influences, etc.
—v.i. 1 turn: *She wheeled around suddenly.* 2 turn or revolve about an axis or center; rotate. 3 move or perform in a curved or circular direction; circle: *gulls wheeling about.* 4 travel along smoothly. 5 INFORMAL. ride a bicycle. **6 wheel and deal,** SLANG. make deals in business, politics, etc., in an aggressive, freewheeling manner.
—v.t. 1 turn (something) on or as on a wheel or wheels; cause to revolve or rotate. 2 cause (something) to move or perform in a curved or circular direction. 3 move on wheels: *wheel a load of bricks on a wheelbarrow.* 4 provide with a wheel or wheels.
[Old English *hwēol*]

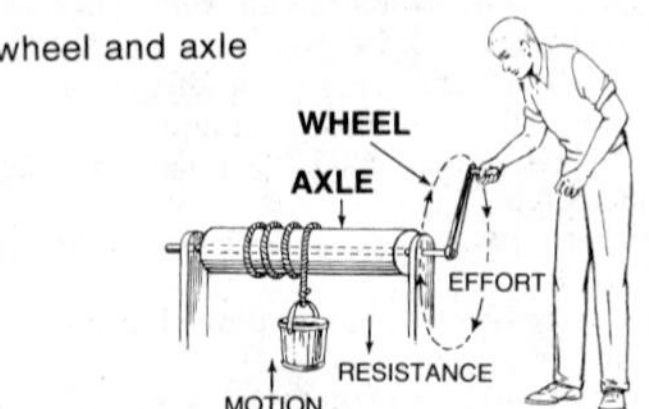

wheel and axle, axle on which a wheel is fastened, used to lift weights by winding a rope onto the axle as the wheel is turned. It is a simple machine.

wheel bar row (hwēl′bar′ō), *n.* a small vehicle with a wheel at one end and two handles at the other, used for carrying loads.

wheel base (hwēl′bās′), *n.* the distance measured in inches between the centers of the front and rear axles of an automobile, truck, etc.

wheel chair (hwēl′cher′, hwēl′char′), *n.* chair mounted on wheels, used especially by invalids. It can be propelled by the person sitting in it.

wheeled (hwēld), *adj.* having a wheel or wheels.

wheel er (hwē′lər), *n.* 1 person or thing that wheels. 2 thing, as a vehicle or boat, that has a wheel or wheels. 3 wheel horse.

wheel er-deal er (hwē′lər dē′lər), *n.* SLANG. person who wheels and deals; an aggressive, freewheeling operator.

wheel horse, 1 horse in a team that is nearest to the wheels of the vehicle being pulled. 2 INFORMAL. person who works hard, long, and effectively.

wheel house (hwēl′hous′), *n., pl.* **-hous es** (-hou′ziz). pilothouse.

Wheel ing (hwē′ling), *n.* city in N West Virginia, on the Ohio River. 48,000.

wheel wright (hwēl′rīt′), *n.* man whose work is making or repairing wheels, carriages, and wagons.

wheeze (hwēz), *v.,* **wheezed, wheez ing,** *n.* *—v.i.* 1 breathe with difficulty and a whistling sound. 2 make a sound like this: *The engine wheezed.* *—v.t.* utter with a sound of wheezing. *—n.* 1 a wheezing sound. 2 SLANG. a funny saying or story; joke, etc., especially an old and familiar one. [probably < Scandinavian (Old Icelandic) *hvǣsa* to hiss]

wheez y (hwē′zē), *adj.,* **wheez i er, wheez i est.** wheezing: *The old dog was fat and wheezy.* **—wheez′i ly,** *adv.* **—wheez′i ness,** *n.*

whelk[1]—shell, 2 to 3 in. long

whelk[1] (hwelk), *n.* either of two genera of sea snails with long, spiral shells, especially a kind commonly used for food in Europe. [Old English *weoloc*]

whelk[2] (hwelk), *n.* pimple or pustule. [Old English *hwylca*]

whelm (hwelm), *v.t.* 1 overwhelm. 2 submerge. [Middle English *whelmen*]

whelp (hwelp), *n.* 1 puppy or cub; young dog, wolf, bear, lion, tiger, etc. 2 an impudent boy or young man. *—v.i., v.t.* give birth to (whelps). [Old English *hwelp*]

when (hwen; *unstressed* hwən), *adv.* at what time: *When did I say such a thing?* *—conj.* 1 at or during the time that: *Stand up when your name is called.* 2 at any time that: *He is impatient when he is kept waiting.* 3 at which time: *We were just leaving, when it began to snow.* 4 although: *We have only three books when we need five.* *—pron.* what time; which time: *Since when have they had a car?* *—n.* the time or occasion: *the when and where of an event.* [Old English *hwenne, hwaenne*]

when as (hwen az′, hwən az′), *conj.* ARCHAIC. when; while; whereas.

whence (hwens), *adv.* 1 from what place; from where: *Whence do you come?* 2 from what place, source, or cause; from what: *Whence has he so much wisdom?* 3 from which: *Let them return to the country whence they came.* *—conj.* from what place, source, or cause: *She told whence she came.* [Middle English *whennes* < Old English *hwanone*]

whence so ev er (hwens′sō ev′ər), *conj.* from whatever place, source, or cause.

when e'er (hwen er′, hwən er′), *conj., adv.* whenever.

when ev er (hwen ev′ər, hwən ev′ər), *conj., adv.* at whatever time; at any time that; when.

when so ev er (hwen′sō ev′ər), *conj., adv.* at whatever time; whenever.

where (hwer, hwar), *adv.* 1 in what place; at what place: *Where are they?* 2 to what place: *Where are you going?* 3 from what place: *Where did you get that story?* 4 in which; at which: *the house where I was born.* 5 to which: *the place where he is going.* 6 in or at which place: *I don't know where she is.* 7 in what way; in what respect: *Where is the harm in trying?* *—n.* 1 what place: *Where do they come from?* 2 place or scene. *—conj.* 1 in the place in which; at the place at which: *The book is where you left it.* 2 in any place in which; at any place at which: *Use the salve where the pain is felt.* 3 any place to which: *I will go where you go.* 4 in or at which place: *They came to the town, where they stayed for the night.* 5 in the case, circumstances, respect, etc., in which: *Some people worry where it does no good.* [Old English *hwǣr*]

where a bout (hwer′ə bout′, hwar′ə-bout′), *adv., conj., n.* whereabouts.

hat, āge, fär; let, ēqual, tėrm;
it, īce; hot, ōpen, ôrder;
oil, out; cup, pu̇t, rüle;
ch, child; ng, long; sh, she;
th, thin; ᴛʜ, then; zh, measure;

ə represents *a* in about, *e* in taken, *i* in pencil, *o* in lemon, *u* in circus.

< = from, derived from, taken from.

where a bouts (hwer′ə bouts′, hwar′ə-bouts′), *adv., conj.* near what place; where: *Whereabouts can I find a doctor? We did not know whereabouts we were.* —*n.* place where a person or thing is: *Do you know her whereabouts?*

where as (hwer az′, hwar az′), *conj.* 1 on the contrary; but; while: *Some children like school, whereas others do not.* 2 considering that; since: *"Whereas the people of the colonies have been grieved and burdened with taxes."*

where at (hwer at′, hwar at′), *adv., conj.* at what; at which.

where by (hwer bī′, hwar bī′), *adv., conj.* by what; by which: *There is no other way whereby he can be saved.*

wher e'er (hwer er′, hwar er′), *conj., adv.* wherever.

where fore (hwer′fôr, hwer′fōr; hwar′fôr, hwar′fōr), *adv.* 1 for what reason? why? 2 for which reason; therefore; so. —*conj.* for what reason; why. —*n.* reason; cause. [Middle English *hwarfore* < *hwar* where + *fore* for, preposition]

where from (hwer from′, hwer frum′; hwar from′, hwar frum′), *adv.* whence.

where in (hwer in′, hwar in′), *adv., conj.* in what; in which; how.

where in to (hwer in′tü, hwar in′tü), *adv., conj.* into what; into which.

where of (hwer uv′, hwer ov′; hwar uv′, hwar ov′), *adv., conj.* of what; of which; of whom: *Does he realize whereof he speaks?*

where on (hwer ôn′, hwer on′; hwar ôn′, hwar on′), *adv., conj.* on which; on what.

where so e'er (hwer′sō er′, hwar′sō er′), *conj., adv.* wheresoever; wherever.

where so ev er (hwer′sō ev′ər, hwar′sō-ev′ər), *conj., adv.* wherever.

where to (hwer tü′, hwar tü′), *adv., conj.* 1 to what; to which; where: *He went to that place whereto he had been sent.* 2 for what purpose; why: *Whereto do you lay up riches?*

where un to (hwer un′tü, hwar un′tü), *adv., conj.* ARCHAIC. whereto.

where up on (hwer′ə pôn′, hwer′ə pon′; hwar′ə pôn′, hwar′ə pon′), *adv., conj.* 1 upon what; upon which. 2 at which; after which.

wher ev er (hwer ev′ər, hwar ev′ər), *conj., adv.* 1 to whatever place; in whatever place; where: *Wherever are you going? Sit wherever you like.* 2 in any case, condition, or circumstances in which: *Let me know wherever you disagree.*

where with (hwer wiᴛʜ′, hwer with′; hwar wiᴛʜ′, hwar with′), *adv., conj.* with what; with which.

where with al (*n.* hwer′wiᴛʜ ôl, hwar′-wiᴛʜ ôl; *adv., conj.* hwer′wiᴛʜ ôl′, hwar′-wiᴛʜ ôl′), *n.* means, supplies, or money needed: *Has she the wherewithal to pay for the trip?* —*adv., conj.* ARCHAIC. with what; with which.

wher ry (hwer′ē), *n., pl.* **-ries.** 1 a light, shallow rowboat for carrying passengers and goods on rivers, used especially in England. 2 a light rowboat for one person, used for racing. 3 any of several types of boats used locally in England, such as a barge, fishing vessel, sailboat, etc. [origin unknown]

whet (hwet), *v.,* **whet ted, whet ting,** *n.* —*v.t.* 1 sharpen by rubbing: *whet a knife.* 2 make keen or eager; stimulate: *The smell of food whetted my appetite.* —*n.* 1 act of whetting. 2 something that whets. 3 appetizer. [Old English *hwettan*]

wheth er (hweᴛʜ′ər), *conj.* 1 *Whether* is used in expressing a choice or alternative. *He does not know whether to work or rest.* 2 either: *Whether sick or well, she is always cheerful.* 3 if: *I asked whether I should finish the work.* —*pron.* ARCHAIC. which of two. [Old English *hwether, hwæther*]

whet stone (hwet′stōn′), *n.* stone for sharpening knives or tools.

whew (hwyü), *interj., n.* exclamation of surprise, dismay, relief, etc.

whey (hwā), *n.* the watery part of milk that separates from the curd when milk sours and becomes coagulated or when cheese is made. [Old English *hwǣg*]

whey ey (hwā′ē), *adj.,* of, like, or containing whey.

which (hwich), *pron.* 1 (as an interrogative pronoun) a word used in asking questions about persons or things. *Which seems the best plan? Which is your car?* 2 as a relative pronoun: **a** a word used in connecting a group of words with some word in the sentence. *Read the book which you have. She drew on the blackboard a pattern in chalk, the outlines of which are still visible today.* **b** the one that; any that: *Here are three boxes. Choose which you like best.* 3 a thing that: *and, which is worse, you were late.* 4 **which is which,** which is one and which is the other. —*adj.* 1 (as an interrogative adjective) a word used in asking questions about persons or things. *Which student won the prize?* 2 (as a relative adjective) a word used in connecting a group of words with some word in the sentence. *Be careful which way you turn.* [Old English *hwilc*] ➤ See **that** for usage note.

which ev er (hwich ev′ər), *pron., adj.* 1 any one that; any that: *Take whichever you want. Buy whichever hat you like.* 2 no matter which: *Whichever side wins, I shall be satisfied.*

which so ev er (hwich′sō ev′ər), *pron., adj.* whichever.

whiff (hwif), *n.* 1 a slight gust; puff; breath: *a whiff of smoke, a whiff of fresh air.* 2 a slight smell; puff of air having an odor: *a whiff of garlic.* 3 a single inhalation or exhalation, especially of tobacco smoke. 4 a slight trace: *a whiff of scandal.* —*v.i.* 1 blow or puff. 2 inhale or exhale whiffs or puffs, as when smoking tobacco. —*v.t.* 1 drive or carry by or as if by a whiff or puff. 2 inhale or exhale (air, smoke, etc.) in whiffs. 3 smoke (a pipe, cigarette, etc.). [probably imitative]

whif fet (hwif′it), *n.* 1 INFORMAL. an insignificant person or thing. 2 a small dog. [probably variant of *whippet*]

whif fle (hwif′əl), *v.,* **-fled, -fling.** —*v.i.* 1 blow in puffs or gusts. 2 veer, shift, or vacillate, as in thought, opinion, intention, etc. —*v.t.* blow or drive with or as if with a puff of air. [< *whiff*] —**whif′fler,** *n.*

whif fle tree (hwif′əl trē′), *n.* the horizontal crossbar of a carriage or wagon, to which the traces of a harness are fastened; singletree. Also, **whippletree.**

Whig (hwig), *n.* 1 member of a British political party of the late 1600's to early 1800's that favored reforms, progress, and parliamentary rather than royal power, and opposed the Tory party. It was succeeded by the Liberal Party. 2 an American who opposed British rule over the colonies at the time of the Revolutionary War. 3 member of an American political party formed about 1834 in opposition to the Democratic Party, favoring high tariffs and a loose interpretation of the Constitution. It was succeeded by the Republican Party about 1855. —*adj.* of or having to do with Whigs. [short for *Whiggamore,* originally the name of a Scottish group that marched on Edinburgh in 1648 in opposition to Charles I of England]

Whig ger y (hwig′ər ē), *n.* principles or practices of Whigs.

Whig gish (hwig′ish), *adj.* 1 of or having to do with Whigs. 2 like Whigs.

while (hwīl), *n., conj., v.,* **whiled, whil ing.** —*n.* 1 space of time; time: *a while ago, quite a while. He kept us waiting a long while.* 2 ARCHAIC. a particular time. 3 **between whiles,** at times; at intervals. 4 **the while,** during the time; in the meantime. 5 **worth one's while,** worth one's time, attention, or effort. —*conj.* 1 during the time that; in the time that; in the same time that: *While I was speaking he said nothing. Summer is pleasant while it lasts.* 2 in contrast with the fact that; although: *While I like the color of the hat, I do not like its shape.* —*v.t.* pass or spend in some easy, pleasant manner: *The children while away many afternoons on the beach.* See synonym study below. [Old English *hwīl*]

Syn. *v.t.* **While, beguile** mean to pass time pleasantly. **While,** followed by *away,* suggests spending a period of free time in as pleasant a way as possible under the circumstances: *I whiled away the hours on the train by talking to other passengers.* **Beguile** suggests charming away the tediousness of the time by doing something interesting: *A good book helped him to beguile the long hours of the journey.*

whiles (hwīlz), ARCHAIC or DIALECT. —*adv.* 1 sometimes. 2 in the meantime. —*conj.* while.

whi lom (hwī′ləm), ARCHAIC. —*adj.* former. —*adv.* formerly; once. [Old English *hwīlum* at times, dative plural of *hwīl* while]

whilst (hwīlst), *conj.* while.

whim (hwim), *n.* a sudden fancy or notion; freakish or capricious idea or desire: *My cousin has a whim for gardening, but it won't last long.* [perhaps < Scandinavian (Old Icelandic) *hvim* unsteady look]

whim per (hwim′pər), *v.i.* 1 cry with low, broken, mournful sounds: *The sick child whimpered.* 2 make a low, mournful sound. 3 complain in a peevish, childish way; whine. —*v.t.* say with a whimper. —*n.* a whimpering cry or sound. [probably imitative] —**whim′per er,** *n.* —**whim′per ing ly,** *adv.*

whim sey (hwim′zē), *n., pl.* **-seys.** whimsy.

whim si cal (hwim′zə kəl), *adj.* 1 full of whims; having many odd notions or fancies; capricious: *a whimsical person.* 2 of or like a whim or whims; odd; fanciful: *a whimsical expression.* —**whim′si cal ly,** *adv.* —**whim′si cal ness,** *n.*

whim si cal i ty (hwim′zə kal′ə tē), *n., pl.* **-ties.** 1 whimsical character or quality. 2 a whimsical notion, speech, act, etc.

whim sy (hwim′zē), *n., pl.* **-sies.** 1 an odd or fanciful notion. 2 odd or fanciful humor; quaintness: *"Alice in Wonderland" is full of whimsy.* 3 something showing this. 4 whim. Also, **whimsey.** [< *whim*]

whin (hwin), *n.* furze. [perhaps < Scandinavian (Old Icelandic) *hvingras* bent grass]

whippet
about 20 in. high at the shoulder

whine (hwīn), *v.,* **whined, whin ing,** *n.* —*v.i.* 1 make a low, complaining cry or sound: *The dog whined to go out with us.* 2 complain in a peevish, childish way: *Some people are always whining about trifles.* —*v.t.* say with a whine. —*n.* 1 a low, complaining cry or sound. 2 a peevish, childish complaint. [Old English *hwīnan* to whiz] **—whin′er,** *n.* **—whin′ing ly,** *adv.*

whin ny (hwin′ē), *n., pl.* **-nies,** *v.,* **-nied, -ny ing.** —*n.* the prolonged, quavering sound that a horse makes. —*v.i.* utter a whinny or any sound like it. —*v.t.* express with such a sound. [related to *whine*]

whin y (hwī′nē), *adj.,* **whin i er, whin i est.** characterized by whining; disposed to whine; fretful.

whip (hwip), *n., v.,* **whipped** or **whipt, whip ping.** —*n.* 1 thing to strike or beat with, usually a stick or handle with a lash at the end. 2 blow or stroke with or as with a whip. 3 a whipping or lashing motion. 4 member of a political party who controls and directs the other members in a lawmaking body, as by seeing that they attend meetings in which important votes will be taken. 5 person who manages the hounds of a hunting pack. 6 person who uses a driving whip; driver. 7 dessert made by beating cream, eggs, etc., into a froth. 8 rope and pulley, used for hoisting. —*v.t.* 1 strike or beat with or as with a whip; lash: *whip a horse to make it go faster. The rain whipped the pavement.* 2 move, put, or pull quickly and suddenly: *He whipped off his coat and whipped out his knife.* 3 bring, get, make, or produce by or as by whipping: *whip the nonsense out of someone.* 4 incite; rouse; revive: *whip up some enthusiasm.* 5 INFORMAL. defeat in a fight, contest, etc. 6 summon to attend, as the members of a political party in a legislative body, for united action. 7 beat (cream, eggs, etc.) to a froth. 8 sew with stitches passing over and over an edge; overcast. 9 wind (a rope, stick, etc.) closely with thread or string. 10 wind (cord, twine, or thread) in this way around something. 11 fish upon: *whip a stream.* —*v.i.* 1 move suddenly and nimbly: *The cat whipped round the corner and disappeared.* 2 beat, flap, or thrash about as the lash of a whip does; swish. 3 fish by casting with a motion like that of using a whip. [Middle English *whippen* to whip, probably < Middle Dutch and Middle Low German *wippen* to swing] **—whip′like′,** *adj.* **—whip′per,** *n.*

whip cord (hwip′kôrd′), *n.* 1 a thin, tough, tightly twisted cord, sometimes used for the lashes of whips. 2 a strong, closely woven worsted cloth with diagonal ridges on it.

whip hand, 1 the hand that holds the whip in driving. 2 position of control; advantage: *get the whip hand over an opponent.*

whip lash (hwip′lash′), *n.* 1 lash of a whip. 2 injury to the neck caused by a sudden jolt that snaps the head backward and then forward, as to a driver whose car is struck with force from behind.

whip per-snap per (hwip′ər snap′ər), *n.* a young or insignificant person who thinks he is smart or important.

whip pet (hwip′it), *n.* a very swift dog that looks somewhat like a small greyhound, often used in racing. [< *whip* in sense of "move quickly"]

whip ping (hwip′ing), *n.* 1 a beating; flogging. 2 arrangement of cord, twine, or the like, wound about a thing: *We fastened the broken rod with a whipping of wire.*

whipping boy, 1 scapegoat. 2 (originally) a boy educated together with a young prince and flogged in his stead when the prince committed a fault.

whipping post, post to which lawbreakers are tied to be whipped.

whip ple tree (hwip′əl trē′), *n.* whiffletree. [perhaps < *whip*]

whip poor will (hwip′ər wil′, hwip′ər wil), *n.* a North American bird, a species of goatsucker, whose call sounds somewhat like its name. It is active at night or twilight. [imitative]

whip saw (hwip′sô′), *n.* a long, narrow saw with its ends held in a frame. —*v.t.* 1 cut with a whipsaw. 2 INFORMAL. defeat or cause to fail in two opposite ways at the same time.

whip stitch (hwip′stich′), *v.t.* sew with stitches passing over and over an edge. —*n.* stitch made in whipstitching.

whip stock (hwip′stok′), *n.* handle of a whip.

whir (hwėr), *n., v.,* **whirred, whir ring.** —*n.* a buzzing sound; noise that sounds like whir-r-r: *the whir of a small machine.* —*v.i.* operate or move with such a sound: *The motor whirs.* Also, **whirr.** [probably imitative]

whirl (hwėrl), *v.i.* 1 turn or swing round and round; spin: *The leaves whirled in the wind.* 2 move round and round: *We whirled about the room.* 3 move or go quickly. 4 feel dizzy or confused. —*v.t.* 1 cause to move round and round: *whirl a baton.* 2 move or carry quickly: *We were whirled away in an airplane.* —*n.* 1 a whirling movement. 2 something that whirls. 3 dizzy or confused condition. 4 a rapid round of happenings, parties, etc. 5 INFORMAL. a try; attempt; experiment: *Give the new recipe a whirl.* [< Scandinavian (Old Icelandic) *hvirfla* < *hverfa* to turn] **—whirl′er,** *n.*

whirl i gig (hwėr′lē gig′), *n.* 1 toy that whirls. 2 merry-go-round. 3 anything that whirls. 4 a whirling movement.

whirl pool (hwėrl′pül′), *n.* 1 current of water whirling round and round rapidly; eddy or vortex of water. 2 anything like a whirlpool.

whirl wind (hwėrl′wind′), *n.* 1 current of air whirling violently round and round; whirling windstorm; vortex of air. 2 anything like a whirlwind.

whirl y bird (hwėr′lē bėrd′), *n.* INFORMAL. helicopter.

whirr (hwėr), *n., v.i.* whir.

whish (hwish), *n.* a soft rushing sound; whiz; swish. —*v.i.* make a soft rushing sound. [imitative]

whisk (hwisk), *v.t.* 1 sweep or brush (dust, crumbs, etc.) from a surface: *I whisked the crumbs from the table.* 2 move (something) quickly: *She whisked the letter out of sight.* 3 beat or whip (cream, eggs, etc.) to a froth. —*v.i.* move quickly: *The mouse whisked into its hole.* —*n.* 1 a quick sweep: *a whisk of his broom.* 2 a light, quick movement. 3 a wire beater for eggs, cream, etc. 4 a small bundle of feathers, twigs, straw, etc., fixed on a handle, used for brushing or dusting. 5 whisk broom. [< Scandinavian (Swedish) *viska*]

whisk broom, a small broom for brushing clothes, etc.

whisk er (hwis′kər), *n.* 1 one of the hairs growing on a man's face. 2 **whiskers,** *pl.* the hair or part of a beard that grows on a man's cheeks. 3 a long, stiff hair growing near the mouth of a cat, rat, bird, etc. [< *whisk*]

whisk ered (hwis′kərd), *adj.* having whiskers.

whisk er y (hwis′kər ē), *adj.* 1 having whiskers. 2 resembling or suggesting whiskers.

whis key (hwis′kē), *n., pl.* **-keys.** a strong alcoholic liquor distilled from various grains, such as rye, barley, or corn, consisting usually of from two fifths to one half alcohol. [short for *whiskeybae* < Gaelic *uisge beatha,* literally, water of life]

whis ky (hwis′kē), *n., pl.* **-kies.** whiskey.

whis per (hwis′pər), *v.i.* 1 speak very softly and low. 2 make a soft, rustling sound: *The wind whispered in the pines.* —*v.t.* 1 utter in a whisper. 2 tell secretly or privately: *It is whispered that their business is failing.* 3 speak without vibration of the vocal cords. —*n.* 1 a very soft, low spoken sound. 2 something told secretly or privately. 3 a soft, rustling sound: *the whisper of leaves.* 4 speech without vibration of the vocal cords. [Old English *hwisprian*] **—whis′per er,** *n.*

whispering campaign, campaign of spreading rumors, insinuations, etc., to discredit a person or group.

whist[1] (hwist), *n.* a card game somewhat like bridge for two pairs of players. Auction bridge and contract bridge developed from it. [alteration of *whisk*]

whist[2] (hwist), *interj.* hush! silence! —*adj.* ARCHAIC. hushed; silent.

whis tle (hwis′əl), *v.,* **-tled, -tling,** *n.* —*v.i.* 1 make a clear, shrill sound by forcing breath through one's teeth or pursing one's lips. 2 make any similar shrill sound: *The cardinal whistled in its nest.* 3 blow a whistle: *The policeman whistled for the automobile to stop.* 4 move with a shrill sound: *The wind whistled around the house.* —*v.t.* 1 produce or utter by whistling: *whistle a tune.* 2 call, direct, or signal by or as if by a whistle.

whirligig
(def. 1)

3 send or drive with a whistling sound. 4 **whistle for,** INFORMAL. go without; fail to get. —*n.* 1 the sound made by whistling. 2 instrument for making whistling sounds. The whistles used by factories, ships, and trains to signal or to warn are tubes through which air or steam is blown. 3 **blow the whistle on, a** (in sports) penalize. **b** declare illegal or dishonest. 4 **wet one's whistle,** INFORMAL. take a drink. [Old English *hwistlian*] **—whis′tler,** *n.*

Whis tler (hwis′lər), *n.* **James Abbott McNeill,** 1834-1903, American painter and etcher.

whistle stop, 1 a small town, especially one along a railroad line where a train stops only on signal. 2 a stop at such a town for a brief appearance or speech, as in a political campaign tour.

whis tle-stop (hwis′əl stop′), *adj., v.,* **-stopped, -stop ping.** INFORMAL. —*adj.* of, having to do with, or at a whistle stop. —*v.i.* make brief appearances or speeches at small towns, as in a political campaign tour.

whit (hwit), *n.* a very small bit: *not to care a whit.* [variant of Old English *wiht* thing, wight]

white (hwīt), *adj.,* **whit er, whit est,** *n., v.,* **whit ed, whit ing.** —*adj.* 1 having the color of snow or salt; reflecting light without absorbing any of the rays composing it; opposite of black. 2 approaching this color: *white bread.* 3 pale: *turn white with fear.* 4 light-colored: *white wine, white meat.* 5 having a light-colored skin; Caucasian. 6 silvery; gray: *white hair.* 7 made of silver. 8 snowy: *a white winter.* 9 blank: *a white space.* 10 spotless; pure; innocent. 11 INFORMAL. honorable; trustworthy; fair. 12 wearing white clothing: *a white friar.* 13 ultraconservative; reactionary; royalist. 14 good; beneficent: *white magic.* 15 propitious; favorable; auspicious.

—*n.* 1 the color of snow or salt; the opposite of black. 2 a white paint, dye, or pigment. 3 white clothing. 4 something white or whitish; white or colorless part, such as the albumen surrounding the yolk of an egg or the white part of the eyeball. 5 a white person; Caucasian. 6 the central part of a butt in archery (formerly painted white). 7 a blank space in printing. 8 an ultraconservative; reactionary; royalist.

—*v.t.* ARCHAIC. make white.

[Old English *hwīt*] **—white′ness,** *n.*

White (hwīt), *n.* **E(lwyn) B(rooks),** born 1899, American writer of essays, children's stories, and poems.

white ant, termite.

white bait (hwīt′bāt′), *n., pl.* **-bait.** 1 a young herring or sprat an inch or two long, used whole as food. 2 any of certain similar fishes used for food.

white blood cell, any colorless blood cell with a nucleus, that destroys disease germs; white cell; white corpuscle; leucocyte.

white cap (hwīt′kap′), *n.* wave with a foaming white crest.

white cedar, 1 an evergreen tree of the same family as and resembling a cypress, having pale green or silvery needles and growing in swamps in the eastern United States. 2 a common North American species of arborvitae. 3 wood of either of these trees.

white cell, white blood cell.

white clover, a kind of clover with white flowers, common in fields and lawns.

white-col lar (hwīt′kol′ər), *adj.* of or having to do with clerical, professional, or business work or workers.

white corpuscle, white blood cell.

white dwarf, (in astronomy) a star of low luminosity, small size, and very great density.

white elephant, 1 a whitish or pale-gray Indian elephant, considered holy in some parts of Asia and not used for work. 2 anything that is expensive and troublesome to keep and take care of. 3 possession that is no longer wanted by its owner.

white face (hwīt′fās′), *n.* 1 make-up used to whiten the faces of clowns, mimes, etc. 2 clown, mime, etc., in whiteface.

white-faced (hwīt′fāst′), *adj.* 1 pale; pallid. 2 having a large patch of white or whitish hair between the muzzle and the top of the head: *a white-faced pony.*

white feather, 1 symbol of cowardice. 2 **show the white feather,** act like a coward.

White field (hwīt′fēld′), *n.* **George,** 1714-1770, English Methodist preacher in England and America.

white fish (hwīt′fish′), *n., pl.* **-fish es** or **-fish.** any of a family of freshwater food fishes with white or silvery sides, found in lakes and streams in North America, Europe, and Asia.

white flag, a plain white flag displayed as a sign of truce or surrender.

white frost, hoarfrost.

white gold, alloy of gold and nickel or platinum, sometimes with copper and zinc. White gold looks much like platinum and is used for jewelry.

white goods, 1 white household linens, such as sheets, pillowcases, napkins, tablecloths, etc. 2 heavy household appliances such as stoves, refrigerators, and washing machines, often coated with white enamel.

white-haired boy (hwīt′herd′, hwīt′hard′), INFORMAL. a favorite.

White hall (hwīt′hôl′), *n.* 1 street in London where many government offices are located. 2 the British government or its policies.

White head (hwīt′hed′), *n.* **Alfred North,** 1861-1947, British mathematician and philosopher.

white-head ed (hwīt′hed′id), *adj.* 1 having white hair, plumage, etc., on the head. 2 having very light or fair hair.

white heat, 1 extremely great heat at which metals and some other bodies give off a dazzling white light. 2 state of extremely great activity, excitement, or feeling.

White horse (hwīt′hôrs), *n.* capital of Yukon Territory, in NW Canada. 5000.

white-hot (hwīt′hot′), *adj.* 1 white with heat; extremely hot. 2 extremely excited; violent, angry, passionate, etc.

White House, 1 the official residence of the President of the United States, in Washington, D.C. 2 office, authority, opinion, etc., of the President of the United States.

white iron pyrites, marcasite.

white lead, a heavy, white, poisonous carbonate of lead, used in making paint. *Formula:* $PbCO_3$

white lie, a lie about some small matter; polite or harmless lie.

white-liv ered (hwīt′liv′ərd), *adj.* 1 cowardly. 2 pale; unhealthy looking.

white matter, a whitish nerve tissue, especially in the brain and spinal cord, that consists chiefly of nerve fibers.

White Mountains, range of the Appalachian Mountains in New Hampshire. The highest mountain is Mount Washington, 6293 ft.

hat, āge, fär; let, ēqual, tėrm;
it, īce; hot, ōpen, ôrder;
oil, out; cup, pu̇t, rüle;
ch, child; ng, long; sh, she;
th, thin; ᴛʜ, then; zh, measure;

ə represents *a* in about, *e* in taken, *i* in pencil, *o* in lemon, *u* in circus.

< = from, derived from, taken from.

whit en (hwīt′n), *v.t., v.i.* make or become white or whiter. **—whit′en er,** *n.*

Syn. Whiten, bleach, blanch mean to make or become white, whiter, or lighter. **Whiten,** the more general word, particularly suggests applying or rubbing some substance on a surface: *The dentist used a powder to whiten my teeth.* **Bleach** implies exposure to sunlight and air or the use of chemicals: *You can bleach those handkerchiefs by leaving them out on the clothesline for several days.* **Blanch** implies turning white by some natural process: *Her cheeks were blanched by fear.*

white noise, the sound heard when the entire range of audible frequencies is produced at once, as in the operation of a jet engine.

white oak, 1 a large oak tree of eastern North America having a light-gray or whitish bark, highly valued for its hard, tough, durable wood. 2 any similar species of oak. 3 the wood of any of these trees.

white out (hwīt′out′), *n.* 1 condition in arctic and antarctic regions in which the sky, the horizon, and the ground become a solid mass of dazzling reflected light, obliterating all shadows and distinctions. 2 a temporary loss of vision resulting from this.

white paper, an official or authoritative report on some subject, especially one issued by a government.

white pepper, seasoning with a hot taste made by grinding the husked dried berries of the pepper vine.

white pine, 1 a tall pine tree of eastern North America, valued for its soft, light wood. 2 this wood, much used for building. 3 any of various similar pines.

white plague, tuberculosis, especially of the lungs.

white poplar, a poplar tree whose leaves have silvery-white down on the undersurface.

white potato, the common potato.

White River, river flowing from NW Arkansas into the Mississippi River. 690 mi.

white room, a sterilized and pressurized room for laboratory work.

White Russia, Byelorussia.

White Russian, 1 Byelorussian. 2 Russian who fought against the Bolsheviks in the Russian Civil War.

white sale, sale of white goods.

white sauce, sauce made of milk, butter, and flour cooked together, often with seasoning added.

White Sea, arm of the Arctic Ocean, in NW Soviet Union. 36,000 sq. mi.

white slave, woman forced to be a prostitute.

white tie, 1 a white bow tie, such as is worn by a man in formal evening clothes.

2 INFORMAL. formal evening clothes for a man.

white vitriol, a white or colorless crystalline substance used as an antiseptic, and for dyeing calico, preserving wood, etc.; zinc sulfate. *Formula:* $ZnSO_4 \cdot 7H_2O$

white wall (hwīt′wôl′), *n.* a white sidewall tire.

white wash (hwīt′wosh′, hwīt′wôsh′), *n.* 1 liquid for whitening walls, woodwork, etc., usually made of lime and water. 2 a covering up of faults or mistakes. 3 anything that covers up faults or mistakes. 4 INFORMAL. a defeat in a game without a score for the loser; shutout. —*v.t.* 1 whiten with whitewash. 2 cover up the faults or mistakes of. 3 INFORMAL. defeat without a score for the loser; shut out. —**white′wash′er,** *n.*

white whale, beluga.

white wood (hwīt′wu̇d′), *n.* 1 any of various trees with white or light-colored wood, such as a tulip tree, linden, etc. 2 the wood of any of these trees. 3 cottonwood.

whith er (hwiᴛʜ′ər), *adv., conj.* to what place; to which place; where. [Old English *hwider*]

whith er so ev er (hwiᴛʜ′ər sō ev′ər), *adv., conj.* wherever; to whatever place.

whit ing[1] (hwī′ting), *n., pl.* **-ings** or **-ing.** 1 a common European sea fish of the same family as the cod, used for food. 2 any of several fishes found along the Atlantic coast of the United States, used for food. [probably < Middle Dutch *wijting*]

whit ing[2] (hwī′ting), *n.* a powdered white chalk, used in making putty, whitewash, and silver polish. [apparently < *white*]

whit ish (hwī′tish), *adj.* somewhat white.

whit low (hwit′lō), *n.* felon[2]. [earlier *whitflaw,* probably < *white* + *flaw*]

Whit man (hwit′mən), *n.* **Walt,** 1819-1892, American poet.

Whit mon day (hwit′mun′dē, hwit′mun′dā), *n.* Monday after Whitsunday.

Whit ney (hwit′nē), *n.* 1 **Eli,** 1765-1825, American who invented the cotton gin. 2 **William Dwight,** 1827-1894, American linguist and lexicographer. 3 **Mount,** peak of the Sierra Nevada mountains, in E California, the highest mountain in the United States outside Alaska. 14,495 ft.

Whit sun (hwit′sən), *adj.* of, having to do with, or occurring at Whitsunday or Whitsuntide.

Whit sun day (hwit′sun′dē, hwit′sun′dā, hwit′sən dā′), *n.* the seventh Sunday after Easter; Pentecost. [Old English *hwīta Sunnandæg* white Sunday]

Whit sun tide (hwit′sən tīd′), *n.* the week beginning with Whitsunday, especially the first three days.

Whit ti er (hwit′ē ər), *n.* **John Greenleaf,** 1807-1892, American poet.

whit tle (hwit′l), *v.,* **-tled, -tling.** —*v.t.* 1 cut shavings or chips from (wood, etc.) with a knife. 2 shape by whittling; carve. 3 **whittle down** or **whittle away,** cut down little by little: *whittle down expenses.* —*v.i.* cut shavings or chips from wood, etc., with a knife. [Middle English *whittel, thwittle,* ultimately < Old English *thwītan* to cut] —**whit′tler,** *n.*

whiz or **whizz** (hwiz), *n., pl.* **whiz zes,** *v.,* **whizzed, whiz zing.** —*n.* 1 a humming or hissing sound. 2 movement producing such a sound. 3 SLANG. a very clever person; expert. —*v.i.* 1 make a humming or hissing sound. 2 move or rush with such a sound: *An arrow whizzed past his head.* —*v.t.* cause to whiz. [imitative] —**whiz′zer,** *n.*

whiz-bang or **whizz-bang** (hwiz′bang′), INFORMAL. —*n.* anything strikingly noisy or noticeable. —*adj.* strikingly good; first-rate: *a whiz-bang campaigner.*

who (hü; *unstressed relative* ü), *pron., possessive* **whose,** *objective* **whom.** 1 (as an interrogative pronoun) a word used in asking a question about a person or persons. *Who is your friend? Who told you? Who is coming?* 2 (as a relative pronoun) **a** a word used in connecting a group of following words with some previous words in the sentence. *The girl who spoke is my sister.* **b** the person that; any person that; one that: *Who is not for us is against us.* 3 **who's who, a** which is one person and which is the other. **b** which people are important. [Old English *hwā*]

➤ **Who** refers to people, to personified objects (a ship, a country), and occasionally to animals: *They have three dogs who always give us a big welcome.* ➤ See **that** for another usage note.

WHO, World Health Organization.

whoa (hwō, wō), *interj.* stop! stand still! (used especially to horses).

who'd (hüd), 1 who would. 2 who had.

who dun it (hü dun′it), *n.* SLANG. story, motion picture, etc., dealing with crime, especially murder, and its detection. [spelling alteration of *who done it?*]

who ev er (hü ev′ər), *pron.* 1 any person that; who: *Whoever wants the book may have it.* 2 no matter who: *Whoever else goes hungry, he won't.*

whole (hōl), *adj.* 1 having all its parts or elements; complete; full: *give someone a whole set of dishes.* 2 comprising the full quantity, amount, extent, number, etc.; entire: *tell the whole story, work the whole day, a whole melon.* See synonym study below. 3 not injured, broken, or defective: *get out of a fight with a whole skin.* 4 in one piece; undivided: *swallow a piece of meat whole.* 5 being fully or entirely such: *a whole brother.* 6 not fractional; integral. 7 well; healthy. —*n.* 1 all of a thing; the total: *Four quarters make a whole.* 2 something complete in itself; system: *the complex whole of civilization.* 3 **as a whole,** as one complete thing; altogether. 4 **on the whole** or **upon the whole, a** considering everything. **b** for the most part. [spelling variant of Middle English *hole,* Old English *hāl.* Related to HEAL, HOLY.] —**whole′ness,** *n.*

Syn. *adj.* 2 **Whole, total** mean consisting of and including all the parts or elements. **Whole** emphasizes that no element or part is left out or taken away: *The whole class was invited to the party.* **Total** emphasizes that every element or part is counted or taken in: *Her total income is more this year than last.*

whole blood, natural blood with none of the essential components removed.

whole heart ed (hōl′här′tid), *adj.* earnest; sincere; hearty: *wholehearted support.* —**whole′heart′ed ly,** *adv.* —**whole′heart′ed ness,** *n.*

whole milk, milk from which none of the natural elements have been removed.

whole note, (in music) a note to be played four times as long as one quarter note. See **note** for diagram.

whole number, 1 a positive integer or zero. The set of whole numbers is usually {0, 1, 2, 3, . . . }, 0 sometimes being excluded. 2 number denoting one or more whole things or units; integer.

whole rest, (in music) a rest lasting as long as a whole note. See **rest**[1] for picture.

whole sale (hōl′sāl′), *n., adj., adv., v.,* **-saled, -sal ing.** —*n.* sale of goods in large quantities at a time, usually to retailers rather than to consumers directly: *They buy at wholesale and sell at retail.* —*adj.* 1 in large lots or quantities: *The wholesale price of this dress is $20; the retail price is $30.* 2 selling in large quantities: *a wholesale fruit business.* 3 broad and general; extensive and indiscriminate: *Avoid wholesale condemnation.* —*adv.* in large lots or quantities: *buy something wholesale.* —*v.t., v.i.* sell or be sold in large quantities.

whole sal er (hōl′sā′lər), *n.* a wholesale merchant.

whole some (hōl′səm), *adj.* 1 good for the health; healthful: *Milk is a wholesome food.* 2 healthy-looking; suggesting health: *a wholesome face.* 3 good for the mind or morals; beneficial: *read only wholesome books.* —**whole′some ly,** *adv.* —**whole′some ness,** *n.*

whole step, (in music) an interval of two half steps, such as D to E, or E to F♯.

whole tone, whole step.

whole-wheat (hōl′hwēt′), *adj.* 1 made of the entire wheat kernel: *whole-wheat flour.* 2 made from whole-wheat flour: *whole-wheat bread.*

who'll (hül), 1 who will. 2 who shall.

whol ly (hō′lē), *adv.* 1 to the whole amount or extent; completely; entirely; totally. 2 as a whole; in its entirety; in full. 3 exclusively; solely.

whom (hüm), *pron.* objective case of **who.** what person; which person: *Whom do you like best? He does not know whom to believe. The girl to whom I spoke is my cousin.* [Old English *hwām,* dative of *hwā* who]

whom ev er (hüm′ev′ər), *pron.* 1 whom; any person whom. 2 no matter whom.

whom so (hüm′sō′), *pron.* whomever.

whom so ev er (hüm′sō ev′ər), *pron.* whomever.

whoop (hüp, hu̇p, hwüp, hwu̇p), *n.* 1 a loud cry or shout: *a whoop of rage, a whoop of joy.* 2 cry of an owl, crane, etc.; hoot. 3 the loud, gasping noise a person with whooping cough makes after a fit of coughing. 4 INFORMAL. a bit; scarcely anything: *not worth a whoop.* —*v.i.* 1 shout or call loudly. 2 make the loud, gasping noise characteristic of a whooping cough. 3 hoot, as an owl or crane. 4 **whoop it up,** SLANG. **a** make merry; revel; celebrate. **b** act or work in a rousing way; give vigorous support. —*v.t.* 1 utter or express with a whoop. 2 call, urge, drive, etc., with or as if with whoops or shouts: *whoop dogs on.* [imitative]

whoop ee (hü′pē, wu̇p′ē; hwü′pē, hwu̇p′ē), *interj.* exclamation expressing unrestrained pleasure, joy, etc. —*n.* 1 cry of "whoopee." 2 noisy commotion, excitement, or revelry.

whooping cough, an infectious bacterial disease, usually of children, characterized by inflammation of the air passages and fits of coughing that end with a loud, gasping sound; pertussis.

whooping crane, a large, white North American crane having a loud, raucous cry. It is nearly extinct.

whoosh (hwu̇sh, hwüsh), *n.* a dull, soft, hissing sound like that of something rushing through the air. —*v.i., v.t.* make, carry, move, etc., with such a sound. [imitative]

hat, āge, fär; let, ēqual, tėrm;
it, īce; hot, ōpen, ôrder;
oil, out; cup, pu̇t, rüle;
ch, child; ng, long; sh, she;
th, thin; ᴛʜ, then; zh, measure;

ə represents *a* in about, *e* in taken, *i* in pencil, *o* in lemon, *u* in circus.

< = from, derived from, taken from.

whop per (hwop′ər), *n.* INFORMAL. 1 something very large. 2 a big lie. [< dialectal *whop* to beat, overcome]

whop ping (hwop′ing), *adj.* INFORMAL. very large of its kind; huge.

whore (hôr, hōr), *n., v.,* **whored, whor ing.** —*n.* prostitute. —*v.i.* 1 have intercourse with whores. 2 be or act as a whore. [Old English *hōre*]

whorl (def. 1)
whorl of leaves

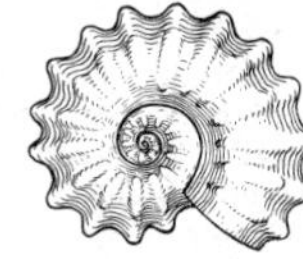
whorl (def. 2)
shell with whorls

whorl (hwėrl, hwôrl), *n.* 1 circle of leaves or flowers round a single node or point on the stem of a plant. 2 one of the turns of a spiral shell. 3 anything that circles or turns on or around something else. A person can be identified by the whorls of his fingerprints. [Middle English *whorle,* apparently variant of *whirl*]

whorled (hwėrld, hwôrld), *adj.* 1 having a whorl or whorls. 2 arranged in a whorl.

whor tle ber ry (hwėr′tl ber′ē), *n., pl.* **-ries.** 1 a small, edible, black berry much like the blueberry. 2 any of several European and Siberian shrubs that it grows on, of the same genus as the blueberry. [< *whortle* (ultimately < Old English *horte* whortleberry) + *berry*]

who's (hüz), 1 who is. 2 who has.

whose (hüz), *pron.* possessive form of **who** and of **which.** of whom; of which: *a dog whose bark is loud. Whose fault is this? Hand me that book whose cover is frayed.* [Old English *hwæs,* genitive of *hwā* who]

whose so ev er (hüz′sō ev′ər), *pron.* of any person whatsoever; whose.

who so (hü′sō), *pron.* whoever.

who so ev er (hü′sō ev′ər), *pron.* whoever.

why (hwī), *adv., n., pl.* **whys,** *interj.* —*adv.* 1 for what cause, reason, or purpose: *Why did you do it? I don't know why I did it.* 2 for which; because of which: *That is the reason why he left.* 3 the reason for which: *That is why she raised the question.* —*n.* the cause, reason, or purpose: *She tried to find out the whys and wherefores of his strange behavior.* —*interj.* expression used to show surprise, doubt, hesitancy, etc., or just to fill in. *Why! it's all finished! Why, yes, I will if you wish.* [Old English *hwȳ,* related to *hwā* who, and *hwæt* what]

W.I., West Indies.

Wich i ta (wich′ə tô), *n.* city in S Kansas. 277,000.

Wichita Falls, city in N Texas. 98,000.

wick (wik), *n.* cord or tape of loosely twisted or woven cotton through which oil or melted wax is drawn up and burned in an oil lamp or candle. [Old English *wēoce*]

wick ed (wik′id), *adj.* 1 morally bad; evil; sinful: *a wicked person, wicked deeds, a wicked heart.* See **bad**[1] for synonym study. 2 mischievous; playfully sly: *a wicked smile.* 3 INFORMAL. unpleasant; severe: *a wicked task, a wicked smell, a wicked snowstorm.* [Middle English, earlier *wicke*] **—wick′ed-ly,** *adv.*

wick ed ness (wik′id nis), *n.* 1 quality of being wicked. 2 a wicked thing or act.

wick er (wik′ər), *n.* 1 a slender, easily bent branch or twig. 2 twigs or branches woven together. Wicker is used in making baskets and furniture. 3 something made of wicker. —*adj.* 1 made of wicker. 2 covered with wicker. [< Scandinavian (dialectal Swedish) *vikker* willow branch]

wick er work (wik′ər wėrk′), *n.* 1 twigs or branches woven together. 2 objects made of wicker.

wick et (wik′it), *n.* 1 a small door or gate: *The big door has a wicket in it.* 2 a small window or opening, often having a grate or grill over it: *Buy your tickets at this wicket.* 3 (in croquet) a wire arch stuck in the ground to knock the ball through. 4 in cricket: **a** either of the two sets of sticks that one side tries to hit with the ball. **b** the level space between these. **c** one batsman's turn. **d** the period during which two men bat together. [< Anglo-French *wiket,* ultimately < Scandinavian (Old Icelandic) *vīkja* a move, turn]

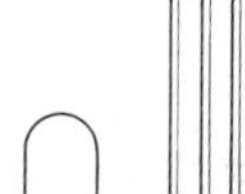
wicket
(def. 3, left)
(def. 4a, right)

wick et keep er (wik′it kē′pər), *n.* (in cricket) the fielder who stands behind the wicket.

wick ing (wik′ing), *n.* material for wicks.

wick i up (wik′ē up′), *n.* an Indian hut made of brushwood or covered with mats, formerly used by nomadic tribes in the western and southwestern United States. [of Algonquian origin]

Wick liffe or **Wick lif** (wik′lif), *n.* Wycliffe.

wide (wīd), *adj.,* **wid er, wid est,** *adv., n.* —*adj.* 1 filling more space from side to side than the usual thing of the same sort; not narrow; broad: *a wide street, a wide hall.* 2 extending a certain distance from side to side: *a door three feet wide.* 3 extending a great distance from side to side: *the wide ocean.* See synonym study below. 4 full; ample; roomy: *wide shoes.* 5 of great range: *wide experience, wide reading.* 6 far or fully open: *stare with wide eyes.* 7 far from a named point, object, etc.: *a shot wide of the target, a reply wide of the truth.* —*adv.* 1 to a great or relatively great extent from side to side: *opinions that are wide apart.* 2 over an extensive space or region: *travel far and wide.* 3 to the full extent; fully: *Open your mouth wide.* 4 aside; astray: *The arrow went wide.* —*n.* a wide space or expanse. [Old English *wīd*] **—wide′ness,** *n.*

Syn. *adj.* 3 **Wide, broad** mean far or large across. **Wide** emphasizes the distance from one side to the other: *a wide gap between knowledge and practice.* **Broad** emphasizes the expanse between the two sides: *Ships sail on the broad ocean.*

wide-an gle (wīd′ang′gəl), *adj.* requiring the use of or made with a wide-angle lens: *a wide-angle shot.*

wide-angle lens, lens of short focus, the field of which extends through a wide angle, used especially for photographing at short range.

wide-a wake (wīd′ə wāk′), *adj.* 1 with the eyes wide open; fully awake. 2 alert; keen; knowing. **—wide′-a wake′ness,** *n.*

wide-eyed (wīd′īd′), *adj.* 1 with the eyes wide open. 2 greatly surprised; astonished. 3 simple; artless; innocent.

wide ly (wīd′lē), *adv.* to a wide extent.

wid en (wīd′n), *v.t.* make wide or wider. —*v.i.* become wide or wider. **—wid′en-er,** *n.*

wide-o pen (wīd′ō′pən), *adj.* 1 opened as much as possible. 2 lax in the enforcement of laws, especially those having to do with the sale of liquor, gambling, prostitution, etc.: *a wide-open town.*

wide-rang ing (wīd′rān′jing), *adj.* taking in a wide field; extending far; far-reaching.

wide spread (wīd′spred′), *adj.* 1 spread widely: *widespread wings.* 2 spread over a wide space: *a widespread flood.* 3 occurring in many places or among many persons far apart: *a widespread belief.*

widg eon (wij′ən), *n., pl.* **-eons** or **-eon.** either of two freshwater wild ducks, slightly larger than a teal. One species, the baldpate, is native to North America; the other is European. [origin uncertain]

widg et (wij′it), *n.* INFORMAL. gadget.

wid ow (wid′ō), *n.* woman whose husband is dead and who has not married again. —*v.t.* make a widow of: *She was widowed when she was thirty years old.* [Old English *widuwe*]

wid ow er (wid′ō ər), *n.* man whose wife is dead and who has not married again.

wid ow hood (wid′ō hu̇d), *n.* condition or time of being a widow.

widow's mite, a small amount of money given cheerfully by a poor person. [with reference to the widow's gift mentioned in Mark 12:42]

widow's peak, hair that grows to a point on the forehead, traditionally supposed to presage early widowhood.

widow's walk, U.S. balcony, on or near the roof of a house along a seacoast, giving a good view of the ocean. New England seafaring men used to build widow's walks on their houses to give their wives a place from which to watch for returning ships.

width (width, witth), *n.* 1 how wide a thing is; distance across; breadth: *The room is 12 feet in width.* 2 piece of a certain width: *curtains taking two widths of cloth.* 3 freedom from narrowness; breadth: *width of mind, width of vision.*

width ways (width′wāz′, witth′wāz′), *adv.* widthwise.

width wise (width′wīz′, witth′wīz′), *adv.* in the direction of the width; transversely.

wield (wēld), *v.t.* hold and use; manage; control: *wield a hammer. A writer wields the pen. The people wield the power in a democracy.* [Old English *wieldan*] **—wield′er,** *n.*

wield y (wēl′dē), *adj.,* **wield i er, wield i est.** easily controlled or handled; manageable.

Wien (vēn), *n.* German name of **Vienna.**

wie ner (wē′nər), *n.* frankfurter. [< German *Wiener (Würstchen)* Viennese (sausage)]

Wie ner (wē′nər), *n.* **Norbert,** 1894-1964, American mathematician.

Wie ner schnitzel (vē/nər), breaded veal cutlet. [< German *Wiener Schnitzel* Vienna schnitzel]

Wies ba den (vēs/bäd/n), *n.* city in W West Germany, noted as a health resort. 261,000.

wife (wīf), *n., pl.* **wives.** 1 woman who has a husband; married woman. 2 ARCHAIC or DIALECT. woman. 3 **take to wife,** marry. [Old English *wīf*] **—wife/less,** *adj.*

wife hood (wīf/hu̇d), *n.* condition of being a wife.

wife ly (wīf/lē), *adj.,* **-li er, -li est.** of, like, or suitable for a wife. **—wife/li ness,** *n.*

wig (wig), *n.* an artificial covering of natural or false hair for the head: *The bald man wore a wig.* [< *periwig*]

wig gle (wig/əl), *v.,* **-gled, -gling,** *n.* *—v.i., v.t.* move with short, quick movements from side to side; wriggle: *The restless child wiggled in his chair. She wiggled the trunk across the floor.* *—n.* a wiggling movement. [perhaps < Dutch *wiggelen*]

wig gler (wig/lər), *n.* 1 person or thing that wiggles. 2 the larva or pupa of a mosquito.

wig gly (wig/lē), *adj.,* **-gli er, -gli est.** 1 wiggling. 2 wavy.

wight (wīt), *n.* 1 ARCHAIC. a human being; person. 2 OBSOLETE. any living being; creature. [Old English *wiht*]

Wight (wīt), *n.* **Isle of,** small island south of England, in the English Channel. It is one of the British Isles. 101,000 pop.; 147 sq. mi.

wig let (wig/lit), *n.* a small wig or hairpiece.

wigwag (def. 2)

wig wag (wig/wag/), *v.,* **-wagged, -wagging,** *n.* *—v.t., v.i.* 1 move to and fro. 2 signal by waving or holding in various positions flags, the arms, lights, etc., according to a code. *—n.* 1 act or system of signaling in this manner. 2 the message signaled. **—wig/wag/ger,** *n.*

wigwam

wig wam (wig/wom, wig/wôm), *n.* hut made of bark or mats laid over a dome-shaped frame of poles, used by the Algonquian Indians of the eastern woodlands of North America. [of Algonquian origin]

Wil ber force (wil/bər fôrs, wil/bər fōrs), *n.* **William,** 1759-1833, British statesman and philanthropist who urged the abolition of slavery.

Wil bur (wil/bər), *n.* **Richard,** born 1921, American poet.

wil co (wil/kō), *interj.* (in radio transmission) will comply.

wild (wīld), *adj.* 1 living or growing in the forests or fields; not tamed; not cultivated: *The tiger is a wild animal. The daisy is a wild flower.* 2 produced or yielded naturally, without the aid of man: *wild honey, wild cherries.* 3 with no people living in it; uninhabited; desolate: *wild land.* 4 not civilized; savage: *wild tribes.* 5 not checked; not restrained: *a wild rush for the ball.* 6 not in proper control or order: *wild hair.* 7 boisterous: *wild laughter.* 8 violently excited; frantic: *wild with rage.* 9 violent: *a wild storm.* 10 rash; crazy: *wild schemes.* 11 INFORMAL. very eager: *wild to go home.* 12 far from the mark: *a wild shot, a wild pitch.* 13 (of a card) of arbitrary denomination or suit: *In this game deuces are wild.* 14 **wild and woolly,** rough and uncivilized.
—n. 1 an uncultivated or desolate area; waste; desert. 2 **wilds,** *pl.* wild country.
—adv. 1 in a wild manner; to a wild degree. 2 **run wild,** live or grow without restraint. [Old English *wilde*] **—wild/ly,** *adv.* **—wild/ness,** *n.*

wild boar, a wild hog of Europe, southern Asia, and northern Africa, generally considered as the ancestor of the domestic hog.

wild carrot, a common weed with a thin, woody root and clusters of lacy white flowers, native to Europe and Asia; Queen Anne's lace. It is the origin of the cultivated carrot.

wild cat (wīld/kat/), *n., adj., v.,* **-cat ted, -cat ting.** *—n.* 1 any of several wild animals of the cat family resembling the common cat but larger, such as the lynx or bobcat. 2 a fierce fighter. 3 a risky or unsafe business undertaking. 4 well drilled for oil or gas in a region where none has been found before. *—adj.* 1 not safe; reckless: *wildcat stocks.* 2 of or denoting an illicit business or enterprise or its products. 3 not authorized by proper union officials; precipitated by small groups or local unions: *a wildcat strike.* *—v.t., v.i.* drill wells in regions not known to contain oil or gas. **—wild/cat/ter,** *n.*

Wilde (wīld), *n.* **Oscar,** 1854-1900, Irish playwright, poet, and novelist.

wil de beest (wil/də bēst/), *n.* gnu. [< obsolete Afrikaans, wild beast]

Wil der (wīl/dər), *n.* **Thornton,** born 1897, American playwright and novelist.

wil der ness (wil/dər nis), *n.* 1 a wild, uncultivated, or desolate region with no people living in it. See **desert**[1] for synonym study. 2 a bewildering mass or collection: *a wilderness of streets.* [Middle English < *wilderne* wild < Old English *wildēorn* like wild beasts < *wilde* wild + *dēor* animal]

wilderness area, U.S. area of virgin land 100,000 acres or more in extent, set apart by law as a national park.

wild-eyed (wīld/īd/), *adj.* 1 staring wildly or angrily. 2 senseless; irrational: *wild-eyed notions.*

wild fire (wīld/fīr/), *n.* 1 any of certain highly flammable substances whose flames could not be put out by water, formerly used in warfare. 2 any fire hard to put out. 3 **like wildfire,** very rapidly: *The news spread like wildfire.*

wild flower, 1 any uncultivated flowering plant that grows in the woods, fields, etc. 2 flower of such a plant.

wild fowl, birds ordinarily hunted, such as wild ducks or geese, partridges, quail, and pheasants.

wild-goose chase (wīld/güs/), a useless search or attempt; foolish or hopeless quest.

wild ing (wīl/ding), *n.* plant or animal that is wild or grows wild. *—adj.* growing wild; wild.

wild life (wīld/līf/), *n.* wild animals and plants as a group. *—adj.* of or for wildlife: *wildlife conservation.*

wild oats, 1 any of a group of grasses growing as weeds in meadows, etc., especially a tall grass resembling the cultivated oat. 2 youthful dissipation. 3 **sow one's wild oats,** indulge in youthful dissipation before settling down in life.

wild pansy, the common pansy, occurring as a weed in grain fields, etc., with small flowers compounded of purple, yellow, and white; heartsease; Johnny-jump-up.

wild rice, a North American aquatic grass, whose grain is used for food.

wild West or **Wild West,** the western United States during pioneer days.

wild wood (wīld/wu̇d/), *n.* trees growing in their natural state; forest.

wile (wīl), *n., v.,* **wiled, wil ing.** *—n.* 1 a trick to deceive; cunning way: *The serpent by his wiles persuaded Eve to eat the apple.* 2 subtle trickery; slyness; craftiness. *—v.t.* 1 coax; lure; entice: *The sunshine wiled me from work.* 2 **wile away,** while away; pass easily or pleasantly. [Old English *wīgle* magic]

wil ful (wil/fəl), *adj.* willful. **—wil/ful ly,** *adv.* **—wil/ful ness,** *n.*

Wil helm I (vil/helm), 1797-1888, king of Prussia from 1861 to 1888 and German emperor from 1871 to 1888. Also, **William I.**

Wilhelm II, 1859-1941, last emperor of Germany, from 1888 until he abdicated the throne in 1918. He was known as Kaiser Wilhelm. Also, **William II.**

Wil hel mi na (wil/hel mē/nə, wil/ə mē/nə), *n.* 1880-1962, queen of the Netherlands from 1890 to 1948.

wil i ness (wī/lē nis), *n.* wily quality; craftiness.

Wilkes-Bar re (wilks/bar/ə), *n.* city in E Pennsylvania, a manufacturing and trading center. 59,000.

Wil kins (wil/kənz), *n.* 1 **Maurice Hugh Frederick,** born 1916, British biophysicist, born in New Zealand, who helped discover the molecular structure of DNA. 2 **Roy,** born 1901, American civil rights leader.

will[1] (wil; *unstressed* wəl), *v., present sing.* and *pl.* **will,** *past* **would.** *—auxiliary v.* 1 am going to; is going to; are going to: *They will come tomorrow.* 2 am willing to; is willing to; are willing to: *I will admit that I am wrong.* 3 be able to: can; may: *This pail will hold four gallons.* 4 must: *You will do it at once!* 5 do often or usually: *She will read for hours at a time.* *—v.t., v.i.* wish, desire, want, or be willing: *do as one wills.* [Old English *willan*]

➔ **will, shall.** For most people, these words are interchangeable, with *will* being much more common. Some grammarians have insisted upon distinctions which are not ordinarily observed. See **shall** for its uses according to those distinctions.

will[2] (wil), *n.* 1 the power of the mind to decide and do; deliberate control over thought and action: *a good leader must have a strong will.* 2 purpose; determination: *a will to live, a will to win.* 3 wish; desire: *"Thy will be done."* 4 what is chosen to be done. 5 a legal statement of a person's wishes about what shall be done with his property after he is dead. 6 document containing such a statement. 7 feeling toward another: *good will, ill will.* 8 **at will,** whenever or wherever one wishes. 9 **do the will of,** obey. 10 **with a will,** with energy and determination.

—*v.t.* 1 decide by using the power of the mind: *She willed to keep awake.* 2 determine; decide: *Fate has willed it otherwise.* 3 influence or try to influence by deliberate control over thought and action: *She willed the person in front of her to turn around.* 4 give by a will: *will a house to someone.* 5 ARCHAIC. wish; desire. —*v.i.* use the will. [Old English *willa*]

Wil lard (wil′ərd), *n.* **Frances E(lizabeth),** 1839-1898, American educator and social reformer.

-willed, *combining form.* having a ___ will: *Strong-willed = having a strong will.*

Wil lem stad (vil′əm stät), *n.* capital of the Netherlands Antilles, on Curaçao. 44,000.

willet—about 16 in. long

wil let (wil′it), *n.* a large, grayish North American wading bird of the same family as the snipes and sandpipers. [imitative]

will ful (wil′fəl), *adj.* 1 wanting or taking one's own way; stubborn. 2 done on purpose; intended: *willful murder, willful waste.* Also, **wilful.** —**will′ful ly,** *adv.* —**will′ful ness,** *n.*

Wil liam I (wil′yəm), 1 1027?-1087, duke of Normandy who conquered England at the battle of Hastings in 1066 and was king of England from 1066 to 1087. He was called "William the Conqueror." 2 Wilhelm I. 3 1533-1584, leader of the revolt of the Netherlands against Spain. He was called "William the Silent."

William II, 1 1056?-1100, king of England from 1087 to 1100. He was called "William Rufus." 2 Wilhelm II.

William III, 1650-1702, king of England from 1689 to 1702. He ruled with his wife Mary II from 1689 until her death in 1694. Also, **William of Orange.**

William IV, 1765-1837, king of England from 1830 to 1837.

William of Orange, William III.

Wil liams (wil′yəmz), *n.* 1 **Roger,** 1604?-1683, English clergyman who founded Rhode Island. 2 **Tennessee,** born 1911, American playwright. He was born Thomas Lanier Williams. 3 **William Carlos,** 1883-1963, American poet.

Wil liams burg (wil′yəmz bėrg′), *n.* city in SE Virginia. It has been restored to look as it did before the Revolutionary War. 9000.

wil lies (wil′ēz), *n.* INFORMAL. spell of nervousness. [origin unknown]

will ing (wil′ing), *adj.* 1 favorably disposed; ready; consenting: *He is willing to wait.* 2 cheerfully ready: *a willing worker.* 3 freely done or offered; voluntary: *willing obedience.* 4 of, having to do with, or using the will; volitional. —**will′ing ly,** *adv.* —**will′ing ness,** *n.*

wil li waw (wil′ē wô), *n.* 1 a sudden, violent gust of wind moving down to the sea from mountains along the coast. 2 any agitated state of affairs. [origin unknown]

Will kie (wil′kē), *n.* **Wendell Lewis,** 1892-1944, American political leader.

will-o'-the-wisp (wil′ə ᴛʜə wisp′), *n.* 1 a flickering light appearing at night over marshy places; ignis fatuus. It is thought to be caused by combustion of marsh gas. 2 something that deceives or misleads.

wil low (wil′ō), *n.* 1 any of a genus of trees and shrubs, widely distributed in temperate and cold regions, with tough, slender branches and long, narrow leaves. The branches of most willows bend easily and are used to make furniture, baskets, etc. 2 the wood of any of these trees. 3 something made of willow, such as a cricket bat. —*adj.* made of willow. [Old English *welig*]

willow herb, any of a genus of plants of the same family as the evening primrose, that grow in moist places and have long, narrow leaves and long clusters of purple or white flowers.

wil low y (wil′ō ē), *adj.,* **-low i er, -low i est.** 1 like a willow; slender; supple; graceful. 2 having many willows.

will pow er (wil′pou′ər), *n.* strength of will; firmness.

wil ly-nil ly (wil′ē nil′ē), *adv.* willingly or not; with or against one's wishes. —*adj.* undecided; vacillating. [< the early phrase *will I (he, ye), nill I (he, ye); nill* not will, Old English *nyllan* < *ne* not + *willan* will]

Wil ming ton (wil′ming tən), *n.* city in N Delaware, on the Delaware River. 80,000.

Wil no (vil′nō), *n.* Polish name of **Vilnius.**

Wil son (wil′sən), *n.* 1 **Edmund,** 1895-1972, American critic and writer. 2 **Harold,** born 1916, British statesman, prime minister from 1964 to 1970. 3 **(Thomas) Woodrow,** 1856-1924, the 28th president of the United States, from 1913 to 1921. 4 **Mount,** peak in SW California. 5700 ft. One of the largest telescopes in the world is in the observatory on top of Mount Wilson.

Wilson Dam, a power dam across the Tennessee River in NW Alabama. 4500 ft. long; 137 ft. high.

Wil so ni an (wil sō′nē ən), *adj.* of or having to do with President Woodrow Wilson or his policies or principles.

wilt[1] (wilt), *v.i.* 1 become limp and drooping; wither. 2 lose strength, vigor, assurance, etc. —*v.t.* cause to wilt. —*n.* 1 any of various fungous or bacterial plant diseases characterized by the withering and drying out of the parts of the plant above the soil. 2 act of wilting. [alteration of earlier *welk* to wither < Middle Dutch *welken*]

wilt[2] (wilt), *v.* ARCHAIC. will[1]. "Thou wilt" means "you will."

wil y (wī′lē), *adj.,* **wil i er, wil i est.** using wiles or subtle tricks to deceive; crafty; cunning; sly: *a wily thief, a wily fox.* —**wil′i ly,** *adv.*

wim ble (wim′bəl), *n.* any of various tools for boring holes. [< Anglo-French < Middle Low German *wemel*]

Wim ble don (wim′bəl dən), *n.* suburb of London, England, where international tennis matches are held.

wim ple (wim′pəl), *n., v.,* **-pled, -pling.** —*n.* cloth for the head arranged in folds about the head, cheeks, chin, and neck, worn by nuns and formerly by other women. —*v.t.* 1 cover with or as if with a wimple; veil. 2 cause to ripple. 3 ARCHAIC. lay in folds, as a veil. —*v.i.* 1 ripple. 2 ARCHAIC. lie in folds. [Old English *wimpel*]

win (win), *v.,* **won, win ning,** *n.* —*v.i.* 1 be successful over others; get victory or success: *We all hope our team will win.* 2 **win out,** be victorious or successful. —*v.t.* 1 get victory or success in: *He won the race.* 2 get by effort, ability, or skill; gain: *win fame, win a prize.* 3 gain the favor of; persuade: *The speaker soon won his audience. She won her mother over to her side.* 4 get the love of; persuade to marry. 5 get to; reach, often by effort: *win the summit of a mountain.* —*n.* INFORMAL. act or fact of winning; success; victory: *The team had four wins and no defeats.* [Old English *winnan*]

hat, āge, fär; let, ēqual, tėrm;
it, īce; hot, ōpen, ôrder;
oil, out; cup, pu̇t, rüle;
ch, child; ng, long; sh, she;
th, thin; ᴛʜ, then; zh, measure;

ə represents *a* in about, *e* in taken, *i* in pencil, *o* in lemon, *u* in circus.

< = from, derived from, taken from.

wince (wins), *v.,* **winced, winc ing,** *n.* —*v.i.* draw back suddenly; flinch slightly: *I winced when the dentist's drill touched my tooth.* —*n.* act of wincing. [< variant of Old French *guencir;* of Germanic origin]

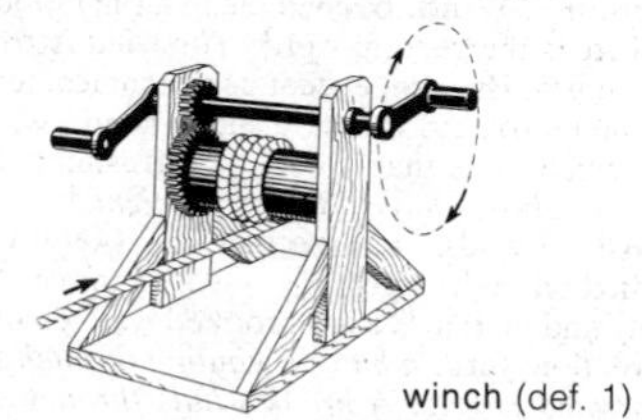
winch (def. 1)

winch (winch), *n.* 1 a machine for lifting or pulling, turned by hand with a crank or by an engine. The crank is attached to a drum around which rope for hoisting or hauling is wound. 2 crank of a revolving machine. —*v.t.* lift or pull by using a winch. [Old English *wince*]

Win ches ter (win′ches′tər, win′chə stər), *n.* 1 city in S England, the chief town of England in Anglo-Saxon times. 31,000. 2 kind of repeating rifle with a tubular magazine under the barrel and a bolt operated by a lever; first made and used about 1866.

wind[1] (*n.* wind, *Archaic* wīnd; *v.* wind), *n., v.,* **wind ed, wind ing.** —*n.* 1 air in motion, varying in force from a slight breeze to a strong gale. See synonym study below. 2 a strong wind; gale. 3 direction or point of the compass from which the wind blows, especially one of the four cardinal points of the compass. 4 current of air filled with some smell: *The deer caught wind of us and ran off.* 5 **winds,** *pl.* **a** wind instruments. **b** the players on such instruments. 6 gas in the stomach or bowels. 7 power of breathing; breath: *A runner needs good wind.* 8 SLANG. the pit of the stomach. 9 empty, useless talk.

wimple

before the wind, in the direction toward which the wind is blowing.
between wind and water, **a** near the water line of a ship. **b** in a dangerous plane.
down (the) wind, in the direction that the wind is blowing.
get wind of, find out about; get a hint of.
in the eye of the wind or **in the teeth of the wind,** directly against the wind.
in the wind, happening or about to happen.
into the wind, pointing toward the direction from which the wind is blowing.
off the wind, with the wind blowing from behind.
on the wind, as nearly as possible in the direction from which the wind is blowing.
take the wind out of one's sails, take away one's advantage, argument, etc., suddenly or unexpectedly.
—*v.t.* 1 follow (an animal, person, or thing) by scent; smell. 2 put out of breath; cause difficulty in breathing: *I was winded by the climb up the steep hill.* 3 let recover breath: *They stopped in order to wind their horses.* 4 expose to wind or air; air.
[Old English] **—wind′less,** *adj.*
Syn. *n.* 1 **Wind, breeze** mean air in motion. **Wind** is the general word: *The wind is from the north.* **Breeze,** except as a technical term in meteorology, means a light, gentle wind, especially one that is cool or refreshing: *We nearly always have a breeze at night.*

wind[2] (wīnd), *v.,* **wound** or (ARCHAIC) **wind ed, wind ing,** *n.* —*v.i.* 1 move this way and that; move in a crooked way; change direction; turn: *a bicycle winding through the crowded streets. A brook winds through the woods.* 2 proceed in a roundabout or indirect manner: *wind into power.* 3 twist or turn around something; twine: *The vine winds round a pole.* 4 be warped or twisted: *That board will wind.* 5 be wound: *This clock winds easily.* —*v.t.* 1 fold, wrap, or place (about something): *wind a scarf around one's neck.* 2 cover with something put, wrapped, or folded around: *The man's arm is wound with bandages.* 3 roll into a ball or on a spool: *wind yarn. Thread comes wound on spools.* 4 make (some machine) go by turning some part of it: *wind a clock.* 5 haul or hoist by turning a winch, windlass, or the like. 6 make in a curved, crooked, or zigzagging course: *We wound our way through the narrow streets.* 7 insinuate (oneself in or into); worm: *wind oneself into a position of importance.*
wind off, unwind.
wind up, **a** end; settle; conclude. **b** (in baseball) make swinging and twisting movements of the arm and body just before pitching the ball. **c** roll or coil; wind completely. **d** put into a state of tension, great strain, intensity of feeling, etc.; excite.
—*n.* bend; turn; twist.
[Old English *windan*] **—wind′er,** *n.*

wind[3] (wīnd, wind), *v.t.,* **wind ed** or **wound, wind ing.** sound by forcing the breath through; blow: *The hunter winds his horn.* [special use of *wind*[1]]

wind age (win′dij), *n.* 1 power of the wind to turn a missile from its course. 2 distance that a missile is turned from its course by the wind.

wind bag (wind′bag′), *n.* SLANG. person who talks a great deal but does not say much.

wind-blown (wind′blōn′), *adj.* 1 blown by the wind. 2 (of a woman's hair) cut short and brushed forward. 3 (of trees) slanted or twisted in growth as a result of the wind.

wind-borne (wind′bôrn′, wind′bōrn′), *adj.* (of pollen, seed, etc.) carried by the wind.

wind break (wind′brāk′), *n.* something serving as a shelter or protection from the wind, such as a fence or a row of trees or shrubs.

Wind break er (wind′brā′kər), *n.* trademark for a short jacket of wool, leather, etc., having a tight-fitting band at the waist and cuffs, used for outdoor wear.

wind-bro ken (wind′brō′kən), *adj.* (of horses) having the power of breathing injured.

wind burn (wind′bėrn′), *n.* a roughening or reddening of the skin caused by prolonged exposure to the wind.

wind burned (wind′bėrnd′), *adj.* having a windburn.

wind cone (wind), wind sock.

wind ed (win′did), *adj.* out of breath; breathless.

wind fall (wind′fôl′), *n.* 1 fruit, tree, etc., blown down by the wind. 2 an unexpected acquisition, advantage, piece of good luck, etc.

wind flow er (wind′flou′ər), *n.* anemone.

Wind hoek (vint′hük), *n.* capital of South-West Africa. 67,000.

wind hov er (wind′huv′ər), *n.* DIALECT. the kestrel.

wind ing (wīn′ding), *n.* 1 act of one that winds. 2 bend; turn. 3 something that is wound or coiled. 4 in electricity: **a** a continuous coil of wire forming a conductor in a generator, motor, etc. **b** the manner in which the wire is coiled: *a series winding.* —*adj.* bending; turning. **—wind′ing ly,** *adv.*

winding sheet, cloth in which a dead person is wrapped for burial; shroud.

wind instrument (wind), a musical instrument sounded by blowing air into it. French horns, flutes, and trombones are wind instruments.

wind jam mer (wind′jam′ər), *n.* INFORMAL. 1 a sailing ship. 2 member of its crew.

wind lass (wind′ləs), *n.* machine for pulling or lifting things. The windlass is a kind of winch used to hoist water from a well or an anchor out of the water. [< Scandinavian (Old Icelandic) *vindāss* < *vinda* to wind + *āss* pole]

windmill (def. 1)

wind mill (wind′mil′), *n.* 1 mill or machine worked by the action of the wind upon a wheel of vanes or sails mounted on a tower. Windmills are mostly used to pump water. 2 **tilt at windmills,** attack imaginary enemies.

win dow (win′dō), *n.* 1 an opening in the wall or roof of a building, boat, car, etc., to let in light or air. 2 such an opening with its frame, sashes, and panes of glass. 3 anything like a window in shape or use, such as the transparent part of some envelopes through which the address is seen. —*v.t.* furnish with windows. [< Scandinavian (Old Icelandic) *vindauga* < *vindr* wind + *auga* eye] **—win′dow less,** *adj.*

window box, container of wood, metal, or plastic, set on or fastened to a window sill, in which small plants may be grown.

window dressing, 1 the dressing of a window with goods attractively displayed. 2 display made in such a manner as to give a favorable, often false, impression.

win dow pane (win′dō pān′), *n.* piece of glass in a window.

window sash, frame for the glass in a window.

window seat, bench built into the wall of a room, under a window.

window shade, sheet of opaque material wound on a roller, by which, when it is unwound, a window is covered.

win dow-shop (win′dō shop′), *v.i.,* **-shopped, -shop ping.** look at articles in store windows without going in to buy anything. **—win′dow-shop′per,** *n.*

window sill (win′dō sil′), *n.* piece of wood or stone across the bottom of a window.

wind pipe (wind′pīp′), *n.* the passage by which air is carried from the larynx to the bronchi; trachea. See **epiglottis** for diagram.

wind proof (wind′prüf′), *adj.* resistant to wind; that will not let wind through.

wind row (wind′rō′), *n.* 1 row of hay raked together to dry before being made into cocks or heaps. 2 any similar row, as of sheaves of grain, made for the purpose of drying, or a row of dry leaves, dust, etc., swept together by wind or the like. —*v.t.* arrange in a windrow or windrows.

wind screen (wind′skrēn′), *n.* BRITISH. windshield.

wind shield (wind′shēld′), *n.* sheet of glass, etc., above the dashboard of an automobile, locomotive, etc., to protect its riders from the wind.

wind sock or **wind sleeve** (wind), a cone-shaped sleeve mounted on a pole or the like, showing the direction of the wind. Also, **wind cone.**

Wind sor (win′zər), *n.* 1 town in S England, where **Windsor Castle,** chief residence of the British sovereign, is located. 31,000. 2 the family name of the royal house of Great Britain since 1917. 3 **Duke of.** See **Edward VIII.** 4 city in S Ontario, Canada. 193,000.

Windsor chair, kind of comfortable wooden chair with or without arms, having a spindle back, slanting legs, and a flat or slightly hollowed seat.

Windsor knot, 1 the knot of a Windsor tie. 2 a wide knot on any necktie.

Windsor tie, a wide necktie of soft silk, tied in a loose double or triangular bow.

wind storm (wind′stôrm′), *n.* storm with much wind but little or no precipitation.

wind swept (wind′swept′), *adj.* exposed to the full force of the wind: *a windswept hillside.*

wind tunnel (wind), tunnel for testing the effects of wind and air pressure on aircraft, missiles, etc., with air forced through at high speeds.

wind up (wīnd′up′), *n.* 1 a winding up; end; close; conclusion; finish. 2 series of swinging and twisting movements of the arm and body made by a baseball pitcher just before pitching the ball. —*adj.* that must be wound up in order to work: *a windup toy.*

wind ward (wind′wərd; *Nautical* win′-

hat, āge, fär; let, ēqual, tėrm;
it, īce; hot, ōpen, ôrder;
oil, out; cup, pu̇t, rüle;
ch, child; ng, long; sh, she;
th, thin; ᴛʜ, then; zh, measure;

ə represents *a* in about, *e* in taken, *i* in pencil, *o* in lemon, *u* in circus.

< = from, derived from, taken from.

dərd), *adv.* toward the wind. *—adj.* 1 on the side toward the wind. 2 in the direction from which the wind is blowing. *—n.* 1 the side toward the wind. 2 direction from which the wind is blowing.

Wind ward Islands (wind′wərd), S part of the Lesser Antilles in the West Indies, extending southwest from Martinique.

wind y (win′dē), *adj.*, **wind i er, wind i est.** 1 having much wind: *a windy day, the windy deck of a ship.* 2 made of wind; empty: *windy talk.* 3 talking a great deal; voluble. **—wind′i ly,** *adv.* **—wind′i ness,** *n.*

wine (wīn), *n., v.,* **wined, win ing.** *—n.* 1 the juice of grapes after it has fermented so that it contains alcohol. 2 the fermented juice of other fruits or plants: *currant wine, dandelion wine.* 3 the color of red wine. 4 something that exhilarates or intoxicates like wine. *—v.t.* entertain with wine: *wine and dine someone.* *—v.i.* drink wine. [Old English *wīn* < Latin *vinum*]

wine cellar, 1 cellar where wine is stored. 2 a store or stock of wine.

wine-col ored (wīn′kul′ərd), *adj.* dark purplish-red.

wine glass (wīn′glas′), *n.* a small drinking glass for wine, usually having a stem.

wine grow er (wīn′grō′ər), *n.* person who raises grapes and makes wine.

wine press, 1 machine for pressing the juice from grapes. 2 vat in which grapes are trodden in the process of making wine.

win er y (wī′nər ē), *n., pl.* **-er ies.** place where wine is made.

wine skin (wīn′skin′), *n.* container made of the nearly complete skin of a goat, hog, etc., used for holding wine, especially in southern Europe and Asia.

wing (wing), *n.* 1 one of the movable parts of a bird, insect, or bat used in flying, or a corresponding part in a bird or insect that does not fly. Birds have one pair of wings; insects usually have two pairs. 2 anything like a wing in shape or use, such as one of the major lifting and supporting surfaces of an airplane, one of the vanes of a windmill, and the feather of an arrow. 3 part that sticks out from the main part or body, especially the part of a building that projects sideways from the main part. 4 either of the side portions of an army or fleet ready for battle. 5 either of the spaces to the right or left of the stage of a theater, out of sight of the audience. 6 part of an organization; faction. The liberals or radicals of a political group are often called the left wing. 7 an air force unit composed of two or more groups. 8 in ice hockey and some other team games: **a** one of the positions, or a player in such a position, on the right or left of the center, when facing the opponents' goal. **b** such a position or player on the forward line. 9 an outlying portion of a region. 10 sidepiece projecting frontwards at the top of the back of an armchair. 11 either of the two side petals of a pealike flower. 12 means of flight, travel, or passage. 13 act or manner of flying; winged flight. 14 SLANG. **a** arm or foreleg. **b** the throwing or pitching arm of a baseball player. 15 **wings,** *pl.* insignia awarded by the United States Air Force to men who have qualified as pilots, navigators, etc. 16 **on the wing, a** flying. **b** moving; active; busy. **c** going away. 17 **take wing,** fly away. 18 **under the wing of,** under the protection or sponsorship of.
—v.t. 1 fly: *The bird wings its way south.* 2 fly through, upon, or across. 3 supply with wings. 4 make able to fly; give speed to: *Terror winged his steps as the bear drew near.* 5 to wound in the wing or arm.
[< Scandinavian (Old Icelandic) *vængr*] **—wing′less,** *adj.* **—wing′like′,** *adj.*

wing back (wing′bak′), *n.* (in football) an offensive back whose position is beyond and behind an end.

wing case, elytron.

wing chair, a comfortable upholstered chair with high sidepieces extending from the back, by which the head is supported and protected from drafts.

wing ding (wing′ding′), *n.* SLANG. 1 party or celebration, especially a lavish or noisy one. 2 something extraordinary; humdinger: *a wingding of a fight.* 3 a thing; device; gadget.

winged (wingd, wing′id), *adj.* 1 having wings. 2 swift; rapid. 3 lofty; elevated.

wing man (wing′man′, wing′mən), *n., pl.* **-men.** pilot who flies at the side and to the rear of a leader, usually in a two-plane or three-plane formation.

wing span (wing′span′), *n.* the wingspread of an airplane, including ailerons projecting beyond the wing tips.

wing spread (wing′spred′), *n.* 1 distance between the tips of the wings of a bird, bat, insect, etc., when they are spread. 2 distance between the tips of the wings of an airplane.

wing tip, 1 the outer end of a wing, as of a bird, insect, airplane, etc. 2 an ornamental tip on a shoe which is carried back along the sides. 3 shoe with such a tip.

wink (wingk), *v.i.* 1 close the eyes and open them again quickly. 2 close one eye and open it again as a hint or signal. 3 twinkle: *The stars winked.* *—v.t.* 1 close and open quickly (the eyes or an eye). 2 move by winking: *wink back tears.* 3 express by winking. 4 **wink at,** pretend not to notice. *—n.* 1 a winking. 2 a hint or signal given by winking. 3 a twinkle. 4 a very short time: *I didn't sleep a wink.* [Old English *wincian*]

wink er (wing′kər), *n.* 1 person or thing that winks. 2 INFORMAL. eyelash. 3 blinder or blinker for a horse.

win kle (wing′kəl), *n.* a periwinkle or any of certain other relatively large marine snails used for food.

win na ble (win′ə bəl), *adj.* capable of being won.

Win ne ba go (win′ə bā′gō), *n., pl.* **-gos** or **-goes** for 1. 1 member of an American Indian tribe speaking a Siouan language and living mostly in eastern Wisconsin. 2 **Lake,** lake in E Wisconsin. 215 sq. mi.

win ner (win′ər), *n.* person or thing that wins.

win ning (win′ing), *adj.* 1 that wins: *a winning team.* 2 charming; attractive: *a winning smile.* *—n.* 1 **winnings,** *pl.* what is won; money won: *pocket one's winnings.* 2 act of a person or thing that wins. **—win′ning ly,** *adv.*

Win ni peg (win′ə peg), *n.* 1 city in SE Manitoba, Canada. 257,000. 2 **Lake,** lake in S Manitoba, Canada. 260 mi. long; 8555 sq. mi.

Win ni pe sau kee (win′ə pə sô′kē), *n.* **Lake,** lake in central New Hampshire. 71 sq. mi.

win now (win′ō), *v.t.* 1 blow off the chaff from (grain); drive or blow away (chaff). 2 sort out; separate; sift: *winnow truth from falsehood.* 3 fan (with wings); flap (wings). *—v.i.* blow chaff from grain. [Old English *windwian* < *wind* wind[1]]

win now er (win′ō ər), *n.* 1 person who winnows. 2 machine for winnowing grain, etc.

wi no (wī′nō), *n., pl.* **-nos.** SLANG. an alcoholic addicted to wine.

win some (win′səm), *adj.* charming; attractive; pleasing: *a winsome young girl, a winsome smile.* [Old English *wynsum* < *wynn* joy] **—win′some ly,** *adv.* **—win′some ness,** *n.*

Win ston-Sa lem (win′stən sā′ləm), *n.* city in N North Carolina. 133,000.

win ter (win′tər), *n.* 1 the coldest of the four seasons; time of the year between autumn and spring. 2 a year of life: *a man of eighty winters.* 3 the last period of life. 4 period of decline, dreariness, or adversity. *—adj.* 1 of, having to do with, or characteristic of winter: *winter clothes, winter weather.* 2 of the kind that may be kept for use during the winter: *winter apples.* *—v.i.* pass the winter: *Robins winter in the south.* *—v.t.* keep, feed, or manage during winter: *We wintered our cattle in the warm valley.* [Old English]

win ter green (win′tər grēn′), *n.* 1 a small North American evergreen plant of the heath family, with small, white, drooping flowers, edible bright-red berries, and aromatic leaves. A heavy, volatile oil made from its leaves (**oil of wintergreen** or **wintergreen oil**) is used in medicine and as a flavoring. 2 this oil. 3 its flavor, or something flavored with it.

win ter ize (win′tə rīz′), *v.t.,* **-ized, -iz ing.** make (an automobile, etc.) ready for operation or use during the winter.

win ter kill (win′tər kil′), *v.t., v.i.* kill by or die from exposure to cold weather: *The rosebushes were winterkilled.* *—n.* death of a plant or animal from exposure to cold weather.

win ter tide (win′tər tīd′), *n.* ARCHAIC. wintertime.

win ter time (win′tər tīm′), *n.* the season of winter.

winter wheat, wheat planted in the autumn and ripening in the following spring or summer.

win ter y (win′tər ē), *adj.,* **-ter i er, -ter i est.** wintry.

Win throp (win′thrəp), *n.* 1 **John,** 1588-1649, governor of Massachusetts. 2 his son, **John,** 1606-1676, governor of Connecticut.

win try (win′trē), *adj.,* **-tri er, -tri est.** 1 of winter; like that of winter: *wintry weather, a wintry sky.* 2 not warm or friendly; chilly: *a wintry smile, a wintry manner, a wintry greeting.* **—win′tri ly,** *adv.* **—win′tri ness,** *n.*

win y (wī′nē), *adj.* tasting, smelling, or looking like wine.

wipe (wīp), *v.,* **wiped, wip ing,** *n.* *—v.t.* 1 rub with paper, cloth, etc., in order to clean or dry: *wipe the dishes, wipe a table, wipe one's hands.* 2 take (away, off, or out) by rubbing: *Wipe away your tears. I wiped off* the dust. 3 remove: *The rain wiped away all the footprints.* 4 **wipe out,** destroy completely; obliterate. —*n.* act of wiping: *I gave my face a hasty wipe.* [Old English *wīpian*]

wip er (wī′pər), *n.* 1 person who wipes. 2 thing used for wiping: *a windshield wiper.*

wire (wīr), *n., adj., v.,* **wired, wir ing.** —*n.* 1 metal drawn out into a thin, flexible rod or fine thread. 2 such metal as a material. 3 a long piece of metal drawn out into a thread used for electrical transmission, as in electric lighting, telephones, and telegraphs. 4 telegraph: *send a message by wire.* 5 INFORMAL. telegram. 6 wire netting. 7 **pull wires,** INFORMAL. **a** use secret influence to accomplish one's purpose. **b** direct the actions of others secretly. 8 **under the wire,** just before it is too late. —*adj.* made of or consisting of wire: *a wire fence.*
—*v.t.* 1 furnish with a wire or wires: *wire a house for electricity.* 2 fasten with a wire or wires: *She wired the two pieces together.* 3 catch by a wire or wires. 4 INFORMAL. telegraph: *wire a birthday greeting.* —*v.i.* INFORMAL. send a message by telegraph.
[Old English *wīr*] —**wire′like′,** *adj.* —**wir′er,** *n.*

wire cutter, tool for cutting wire.

wire drawn (wīr′drôn′), *adj.* 1 drawn out into a wire. 2 treated with too much hairsplitting and refinement.

wire gauge, device for measuring the diameter of wire, the thickness of metal sheets, etc., usually a disk with notches of different sizes cut in its edge.

wire-haired (wīr′herd′, wīr′hard′), *adj.* having short, coarse, stiff hair: *a wire-haired fox terrier.*

wire less (wīr′lis), *adj.* 1 using no wires; transmitting by radio waves instead of by electric wires: *wireless telegraphy.* 2 BRITISH. radio. —*n.* 1 system of transmission by radio waves without the use of wires. 2 BRITISH. **a** radio. **b** message sent by radio; radiogram. —*v.t., v.i.* BRITISH. send or transmit by radio.

wire netting, fabric of woven wire, used for screens for windows and doors.

Wire pho to (wīr′fō′tō), *n., pl.* **-tos** for 2. 1 trademark for a method for transmitting photographs by reproducing a facsimile through electric signals. 2 photograph transmitted in this fashion.

wire pull er (wīr′pu̇l′ər), *n.* INFORMAL. person who uses secret influence to accomplish his purposes.

wire pull ing (wīr′pu̇l′ing), *n.* INFORMAL. the use of secret influence to accomplish a purpose.

wire recorder, device for recording and reproducing sound on a magnetized steel wire.

wire recording, recording made on a wire recorder.

wire rope, rope or cable made of twisted strands of wire.

wire service, a news agency that gathers foreign and domestic news and photographs and distributes them to member newspapers and radio stations, as the Associated Press (AP) and United Press International (UPI) in the United States.

wire tap (wīr′tap′), *v.,* **-tapped, -tap ping,** *n.* —*v.i.* tap a telephone or telegraph wire secretly to record or obtain information. —*v.t.* record or obtain by wiretapping: *wiretap a conversation.* —*n.* wiretapping. —**wire′tap′per,** *n.*

wire tap ping (wīr′tap′ing), *n.* the secret tapping of a telephone or telegraph wire to listen to or record the messages sent over it.

wire worm (wīr′wėrm′), *n.* the slender, hard-bodied larva of certain beetles. Wireworms feed on the roots of plants and do much damage to crops.

wir ing (wī′ring), *n.* system of wires for conducting and distributing an electric current.

wir y (wī′rē), *adj.,* **wir i er, wir i est.** 1 made of wire. 2 like wire: *wiry hair, a wiry coat of fur.* 3 lean, strong, and tough. —**wir′i ly,** *adv.* —**wir′i ness,** *n.*

wis (wis), *v.t.* ARCHAIC. know (used only in *I wis*). [< *iwis* certainly (taken as *I wis*), Old English *gewiss*]

Wis. or **Wisc.,** Wisconsin.

Wis con sin (wi skon′sən), *n.* 1 one of the north central states of the United States. 4,418,000 pop.; 56,200 sq. mi. *Capital:* Madison. *Abbrev.:* Wis. or Wisc. 2 **Wisconsin River,** river flowing south from N Wisconsin into the Mississippi River. 430 mi.

Wis con sin ite (wi skon′sə nīt), *n.* native or inhabitant of Wisconsin.

wis dom (wiz′dəm), *n.* 1 knowledge and good judgment based on experience; being wise. 2 wise conduct; wise words. 3 scholarly knowledge. [Old English *wīsdōm* < *wīs* wise]

Wisdom of Solomon, one of the books of the Apocrypha.

wisdom tooth, the back tooth on either side of each jaw, usually appearing between the ages of 17 and 25.

wise[1] (wīz), *adj.,* **wis er, wis est,** *v.,* **wised, wis ing.** —*adj.* 1 having or showing knowledge and good judgment: *a wise judge, wise advice, wise plans.* See synonym study below. 2 having knowledge or information: *We are none the wiser for his explanations.* 3 learned; erudite. 4 **wise to,** SLANG. **a** aware of; informed about. **b** brashly or impudently bold; arrogant; fresh. —*v.t., v.i.* **wise up,** SLANG. make or become aware or informed; enlighten or become enlightened. [Old English *wīs*] —**wise′ly,** *adv.* —**wise′ness,** *n.*
Syn. *adj.* 1 **Wise, sage** mean having or showing knowledge and good judgment. **Wise** implies having knowledge and understanding of people and of what is true and right in life and conduct, and showing sound judgment in applying such knowledge: *His wise father knows how to handle him.* **Sage** suggests deep wisdom based on wide knowledge, experience, and profound thought: *The old professor gave us sage advice we have never forgotten.*

wise[2] (wīz), *n.* way; manner: *He is in no wise a bad boy, but he is often a little mischievous.* [Old English *wīse.* Related to GUISE.]

-wise, *suffix forming adverbs.* 1 in a ___ manner: *Likewise = in a like manner.* 2 in a ___ing manner: *Slantwise = in a slanting manner.* 3 in the characteristic way of a ___: *Clockwise = in the way the hands of a clock go.* 4 in the direction of the ___: *Lengthwise = in the direction of the length.* 5 with regard to ___: *Salarywise = with regard to salary.* [< *wise*[2]]

wise a cre (wī′zā′kər), *n.* person who thinks that he knows everything. [< Middle Dutch *wijssegger* soothsayer]

wise crack (wīz′krak′), SLANG. —*n.* a snappy comeback; smart remark. —*v.i.* make wisecracks. —**wise′crack′er,** *n.*

wise guy, SLANG. person who pretends to know more than he really does; impudent or conceited fellow.

wi sent (wē′znt), *n.* aurochs (def. 1). [< German *Wisent*]

wish (wish), *v.t.* 1 have a need or longing for; want; desire: *wish help, wish money. Do you wish to speak to me?* See synonym study below. 2 feel or express a desire for: *wish oneself at home.* 3 desire (something) for someone; have a hope for: *wish someone good luck. I don't wish him any harm.* 4 express a hope for: *wish someone good night.* 5 request or command: *Do you wish me to send her in now?* 6 **wish on,** INFORMAL. pass on to; foist on: *They wished the hardest job on me.* —*v.i.* have, feel, or express a desire; long *(for): wish for a new house.* —*n.* 1 a wishing or wanting; desire; longing: *He had no wish to be king.* 2 expression of a wish: *She sends you best wishes for a happy new year.* 3 request or command: *grant his slightest wish.* 4 thing wished for: *get one's wish.* [Old English *wȳscan*] —**wish′er,** *n.*
Syn. *v.t.* 1 **Wish, desire** mean to long for something. **Wish** is the least emphatic word, sometimes suggesting only that one would like to have, do, or get a certain thing, sometimes suggesting a longing that can never be satisfied: *I wish I could go to Europe next year.* **Desire,** sometimes used as a formal substitute for *wish* or, especially, *want,* suggests wishing strongly for something and usually being willing or determined to work or struggle to get it: *She finally received the position she desired.*

wish bone (wish′bōn′), *n.* the forked bone in the front of the breastbone in poultry and other birds. [< the custom of two people making a wish while breaking the bone between them, in the belief that the person left with the longer piece will get his wish]

wish ful (wish′fəl), *adj.* having or expressing a wish; desiring; desirous. —**wish′ful ly,** *adv.* —**wish′ful ness,** *n.*

wishful thinking, a believing something to be true that one wishes or wants to be true.

wish y-wash y (wish′ē wosh′ē, wish′ē-wôsh′ē), *adj.* 1 thin and weak; watery: *wishy-washy soup with no flavor.* 2 feeble; weak; poor: *a wishy-washy excuse.* 3 lacking in decisiveness; wavering; vacillating.

wisp (wisp), *n.* 1 a small bundle; small bunch: *a wisp of hay.* 2 a small tuft, lock, or portion of anything; slight bit: *a wisp of hair, a wisp of smoke.* 3 a little thing: *a wisp of a girl.* [Middle English]

wisp y (wis′pē), *adj.,* **wisp i er, wisp i est.** like a wisp; thin; slight.

wist (wist), *v.* ARCHAIC. pt. and pp. of **wit**[2].

wis tar i a (wi ster′ē ə), *n.* wisteria.

wis ter i a (wi stir′ē ə), *n.* any of a genus of climbing shrubs of the pea family, with large, drooping clusters of showy purple, blue, or white flowers. [< Caspar *Wistar,* 1761-1818, American physician]

wist ful (wist′fəl), *adj.* longing; yearning: *A child stood looking with wistful eyes at the toys in the window.* [< obsolete *wist* attentive (< *wistly* intently, of uncertain origin) + *-ful*] —**wist′ful ly,** *adv.* —**wist′ful ness,** *n.*

wit[1] (wit), *n.* 1 the power to perceive quickly and express cleverly ideas that are unusual, striking, and amusing. See synonym study below. 2 person with such power: *Mark Twain was a famous wit.* 3 understanding;

mind; sense: *People with quick wits learn easily. The child was out of his wits with fright. That poor man hasn't wit enough to earn a living.* 4 **at one's wit's end,** not knowing what to do or say. 5 **have one's wits about one** or **keep one's wits about one,** be alert. [Old English *witt*]

Syn. 1 **Wit, humor** mean power to see and express what is amusing or causes laughter. **Wit** applies to the sort of mental power that is quick in perceiving what is striking, unusual, or inconsistent and in expressing it in a clever and amusing manner: *George Bernard Shaw was famous for his wit.* **Humor** applies to the ability to see and show with warm sympathy the things in life and human nature that are funny or absurdly out of keeping: *Her sense of humor eased her trouble.*

wit² (wit), *v.t., v.i.,* **wist, wit ting.** 1 ARCHAIC. know. 2 **to wit,** that is to say; namely: *To my daughter I leave all I own—to wit: my house, what is in it, and the land on which it stands.* [Old English *witan*]

witch (wich), *n.* 1 woman supposed to be under the influence of supernatural spirits and to have magic power. 2 an ugly old woman; hag. 3 INFORMAL. a charming or fascinating girl or woman. *—v.t.* 1 use the power of a witch on. 2 charm; fascinate; bewitch. [Old English *wicce*]

witch craft (wich′kraft′), *n.* what a witch does or can do; magic power or influence; sorcery.

witch doctor, medicine man, especially in certain primitive societies.

witch er y (wich′ər ē), *n., pl.* **-er ies.** 1 witchcraft; magic. 2 charm; fascination.

witches' Sabbath, a midnight meeting of demons, sorcerers, and witches, supposed in medieval times to have been held annually as a festival.

witch hazel, 1 shrub or small tree of eastern North America that has yellow flowers in the fall or winter after the leaves have fallen. 2 lotion for cooling and soothing the skin, made by steeping the bark and leaves of this shrub in alcohol.

witch hunt, 1 a hunting out and persecuting of persons suspected of witchcraft. There were witch hunts in New England in the 1600's. 2 INFORMAL. a persecuting or defaming of persons to gain political advantage.

witch-hunt er (wich′hun′tər), *n.* person who conducts a witch hunt.

witch ing (wich′ing), *adj.* bewitching; magical; enchanting. **—witch′ing ly,** *adv.*

wit e na ge mot (wit′ə nə gə mōt′), *n.* the royal council of the Anglo-Saxons. [Old English *witenagemōt* < *witena* of councilors + *gemōt* meeting]

with (wiᴛʜ, with), *prep.* 1 in the company of: *Come with me.* 2 among: *They will mix with the crowd.* 3 having, wearing, carrying, etc.: *a book with a red cover, a man with a beard, a telegram with good news.* 4 by means of; by using: *work with a machine, cut meat with a knife.* See **by** for synonym study. 5 using; showing: *Work with care.* 6 as an addition to; added to: *Do you want sugar with your tea?* 7 including; and: *tea with sugar and lemon.* 8 in relation to: *They are friendly with us.* 9 in regard to: *We are pleased with the house.* 10 in proportion to: *An army's power increases with its size.* 11 because of: *shake with cold, eyes dim with tears.* 12 in the keeping or service of: *leave a package with a friend.* 13 in the region, sphere, experience, opinion, or view of: *It is summer with us while it is winter with the Australians.* 14 at the same time as: *With this battle the war ended.* 15 in the same direction as: *sail with the tide.* 16 on the side of; for: *They are with us in our plans.* 17 from: *I hate to part with my favorite things.* 18 against: *The English fought with the Germans.* 19 receiving; having; being allowed: *I went with my parents' permission.* 20 in spite of; notwithstanding: *With all his weight he was not a strong man.* 21 **with it,** SLANG. **a** informed; up-to-date. **b** inspired or excited by something. [Old English, against]

with-, *prefix.* 1 away; back: *Withdraw = draw back.* 2 against: *Withstand = stand against.* [Old English]

with al (wi ᴛʜôl′, wi thôl′), *adv.* 1 with it all; as well; besides; also: *The lady is rich and fair and wise withal.* 2 ARCHAIC. **a** in spite of all; nevertheless. **b** therewith. *—prep.* ARCHAIC. with. [Middle English < *with* + *all*]

with draw (wiᴛʜ drô′, with drô′), *v.,* **-drew, -drawn, -draw ing.** *—v.t.* 1 draw back; draw away: *He quickly withdrew his hand from the hot stove.* 2 take back; remove: *withdraw one's savings from the bank. They agreed to withdraw the charges of theft if the robbers returned the money.* *—v.i.* 1 draw back; draw away: *I withdrew from the discussion before it became an argument.* 2 go away: *She withdrew from the room.* See **depart** for synonym study.

with draw al (wiᴛʜ drô′əl, with drô′əl), *n.* 1 a withdrawing. 2 a being withdrawn. 3 condition of physical distress in an addict suddenly deprived of narcotic drugs.

with drawn (wiᴛʜ drôn′, with drôn′), *v.* pp. of **withdraw.** *—adj.* 1 retiring; reserved; shy. 2 isolated; secluded.

with drew (wiᴛʜ drü′, with drü′), *v.* pt. of **withdraw.**

withe (wiᴛʜ, with, wiᴛʜ), *n.* 1 a willow twig. 2 any tough, easily bent twig suitable for binding or tying things together. [Old English *withthe*]

with er (wiᴛʜ′ər), *v.i., v.t.* 1 lose or cause to lose freshness, vigor, etc.; dry up; shrivel: *The grass withered in the hot sun. Age had withered the old woman's face.* 2 feel or cause to feel ashamed or confused: *wither at the thought of a public rebuke, be withered by a scornful look.* [Middle English *wideren,* variant of *wederen* to weather]

with ers (wiᴛʜ′ərz), *n.pl.* the highest part of a horse's or other animal's back, between the shoulder blades. See **horse** for diagram. [origin uncertain]

with held (with held′, wiᴛʜ held′), *v.* pt. and pp. of **withhold.**

with hold (with hōld′, wiᴛʜ hōld′), *v.t.,* **-held, -hold ing.** 1 refrain from giving or granting: *withhold wages, withhold one's approval of a plan.* 2 hold back; keep back: *The general withheld two regiments from the attack.* See **keep** for synonym study. **—with hold′er,** *n.*

withholding tax, the part of a person's income tax that is deducted from his salary or wages by his employer on behalf of the government.

with in (wiᴛʜ in′, with in′), *prep.* 1 inside the limits of; not beyond: *live within one's income, be within sight.* 2 in or into the inner part of; inside of: *By the X ray, doctors can see within the body.* *—adv.* 1 in or into the inner part; inside: *paint a house within and without.* 2 in the inner being; inwardly: *keep one's grief within.* [Old English *withinnan* < *with* with, against + *innan* inside]

hat, āge, fär; let, ēqual, tėrm;
it, īce; hot, ōpen, ôrder;
oil, out; cup, pu̇t, rüle;
ch, child; ng, long; sh, she;
th, thin; ᴛʜ, then; zh, measure;

ə represents *a* in about, *e* in taken, *i* in pencil, *o* in lemon, *u* in circus.

< = from, derived from, taken from.

with out (wiᴛʜ out′, with out′), *prep.* 1 with no; not having; free from; lacking: *I drink tea without sugar.* 2 so as to omit, avoid, or neglect: *She walked past without noticing us.* 3 outside of; beyond: *Soldiers are camped within and without the city walls.* *—adv.* 1 on the outside; outside: *The house is clean within and without.* 2 outside of the inner being: *at ease without.* 3 lacking: *We must eat this or go without.* *—conj.* DIALECT. unless. [Old English *withūtan* < *with* with, against + *ūtan* outside]

with stand (with stand′, wiᴛʜ stand′), *v.t.,* **-stood, -stand ing.** stand against; hold out against; oppose, especially successfully; resist: *withstand hardships. These shoes will withstand much hard wear.* See **oppose** for synonym study. [Old English *withstandan* < *with-* against + *standan* to stand]

with stood (with stu̇d′, wiᴛʜ stu̇d′), *v.* pt. and pp. of **withstand.**

with y (wiᴛʜ′ē, with′ē), *n., pl.* **with ies.** 1 willow or osier. 2 twig of a willow or osier; withe. 3 band or halter made of withes. [Old English *wīthig*]

wit less (wit′lis), *adj.* lacking sense; stupid; foolish: *a witless person, a witless remark.* **—wit′less ly,** *adv.* **—wit′less ness,** *n.*

wit loof (wit′lōf), *n.* endive (def. 3). [< Dutch, literally, white leaf]

wit ness (wit′nis), *n.* 1 person who saw something happen; spectator; eyewitness. 2 person who gives evidence or testifies under oath in a court of law. 3 evidence; testimony: *give false witness in court. Their tattered clothes were a witness of their poverty.* 4 person who writes his name on a document to show that he saw the maker sign it. 5 **bear witness,** be evidence; give evidence; testify: *The man's fingerprints bore witness to his guilt.* *—v.t.* 1 be a witness of; see: *I witnessed the accident.* 2 testify to; give evidence of: *Her whole manner witnessed her surprise.* 3 sign (a document) as a witness: *witness a will.* *—v.i.* give evidence; testify. [Old English *witnes* knowledge < *wit* wit]

witness stand, place where a witness stands or sits to give evidence in a court of law.

-witted, *combining form.* having a ___ wit or wits: *Quick-witted = having a quick wit.*

wit ti cism (wit′ə siz′əm), *n.* a witty remark.

wit ting ly (wit′ing lē), *adv.* knowingly; intentionally.

wit ty (wit′ē), *adj.,* **-ti er, -ti est.** full of wit; clever and amusing: *a witty person, a witty remark.* **—wit′ti ly,** *adv.* **—wit′ti ness,** *n.*

wive (wīv), *v.,* **wived, wiv ing.** *—v.i.* marry a woman. *—v.t.* take as a wife. [Old English *wīfian* < *wīf* wife]

wi vern (wī′vərn), *n.* (in heraldry) a two-legged, winged dragon with a barbed tail. Also, **wyvern.** [Middle English *wyver* viper

< Old North French *wivre* < Latin *vipera*]

wives (wīvz), *n.* pl. of **wife.**

wiz ard (wiz′ərd), *n.* 1 man supposed to have magic power; magician; sorcerer. 2 INFORMAL. a very clever person; expert: *be a wizard at math.* [Middle English *wysard* < *wys* wise]

wiz ard ry (wiz′ər drē), *n.* art or practice of a wizard; magic skill; magic; sorcery.

wiz ened (wiz′nd, wē′znd), *adj.* dried up; withered; shriveled: *a wizened apple, a wizened face.* [Old English *wisnian* dry up, shrivel]

wk., *pl.* **wks.** 1 week. 2 work.

w.l., 1 water line. 2 wavelength.

wmk., watermark.

WNW or **W.N.W.,** west-northwest.

wo (wō), *n., interj.* woe.

WO or **W.O.,** warrant officer.

woad (wōd), *n.* 1 a European plant of the mustard family, formerly extensively cultivated for the blue dye furnished by its leaves. 2 the dye. [Old English *wād*]

wob ble (wob′əl), *v.,* **-bled, -bling,** *n.* —*v.i.* 1 move unsteadily from side to side; shake; tremble. 2 be uncertain, unsteady, or inconstant; waver. —*v.t.* cause to wobble. —*n.* a wobbling motion. Also, **wabble.** [perhaps < Low German *wabbeln*] **—wob′bler,** *n.*

wob bly (wob′lē), *adj.,* **-bli er, -bli est.** unsteady; shaky; wavering. Also, **wabbly.**

wo be gone (wō′bi gôn′, wō′bi gon′), *adj.* woebegone.

Wo den (wōd′n), *n.* (in Anglo-Saxon myths) the chief god, identified with the Scandinavian god Odin.

woe (wō), *n.* great grief, trouble, or distress: *Sickness and poverty are common woes.* —*interj.* exclamation of grief, trouble, or distress. Also, **wo.** [Old English *wā*, interjection]

woe be gone (wō′bi gôn′, wō′bi gon′), *adj.* looking sad, sorrowful, or wretched. Also, **wobegone.**

woe ful (wō′fəl), *adj.* 1 full of woe; sad; sorrowful; wretched: *The lost child had a woeful expression.* 2 pitiful. 3 of wretched quality. **—woe′ful ly,** *adv.* **—woe′ful ness,** *n.*

wo ful (wō′fəl), *adj.* woeful.

woke (wōk), *v.* pt. and a pp. of **wake**[1].

wo ken (wō′kən), *v.* ARCHAIC and DIALECT. a pp. of **wake**[1].

wold (wōld), *n.* high, rolling country, bare of woods. [Old English *wald, weald* a wood]

wolf (def. 1)
up to 3 ft. high at the shc

wolf (wu̇lf), *n., pl.* **wolves,** *v.* —*n.* 1 either of two species of carnivorous wild mammals of the dog family, with a long muzzle, high, pointed ears, and a bushy tail. Wolves usually hunt in packs and are sometimes destructive to livestock. 2 any of several similar mammals. 3 a cruel, greedy person. 4 SLANG. man who flirts with or tries to entice women. 5 **cry wolf,** give a false alarm. 6 **keep the wolf from the door,** keep safe from hunger or poverty. 7 **wolf in sheep's clothing,** person who hides harmful intentions or an evil character beneath an innocent or friendly exterior. —*v.t.* eat greedily: *The starving man wolfed down the food.* [Old English *wulf*] **—wolf′like′,** *adj.*

wolf dog, 1 any of various dogs used in hunting wolves. 2 hybrid of a dog and a wolf.

Wolfe (wu̇lf), *n.* 1 **James,** 1727-1759, English general who was killed at the battle of Quebec, in which he defeated the French. 2 **Thomas,** 1900-1938, American novelist.

wolf hound (wu̇lf′hound′), *n.* a large dog of any of various breeds once used in hunting wolves.

wolf ish (wu̇l′fish), *adj.* 1 like a wolf; savage: *wolfish cruelty.* 2 greedy: *a wolfish appetite.* **—wolf′ish ly,** *adv.* **—wolf′ish ness,** *n.*

wolf ram (wu̇l′frəm), *n.* 1 tungsten. 2 wolframite. [< German]

wolf ram ite (wu̇l′frə mīt), *n.* ore consisting of compounds of tungsten with iron, manganese, and oxygen, occurring in crystals or masses. It is an important source of tungsten.

wombat—2 to 4 ft. long

wolfs bane (wu̇lfs′bān′), *n.* any of several species of aconite, especially a European species with yellowish flowers.

wolf spider, any of a family of large spiders that stalk, rather than lie in wait for, their prey.

Wol sey (wu̇l′zē), *n.* **Thomas,** 1475?-1530, English cardinal and statesman.

wol ve rine or **wol ve rene** (wu̇l′və rēn′, wu̇l′və rēn′), *n.* a heavily built carnivorous mammal of the forests of northern North America, Europe, and Asia, of the same family as the weasel and badger and having short legs and dark, shaggy fur; carcajou; glutton. [earlier *wolvering* < *wolf*]

wolves (wu̇lvz), *n.* pl. of **wolf.**

wom an (wu̇m′ən), *n., pl.* **wom en,** *adj.* —*n.* 1 an adult female person. See synonym study below. 2 women as a group; womankind. 3 a female servant or attendant. —*adj.* 1 of a woman or women; feminine. 2 female: *a woman lawyer, women lawyers.* [Old English *wīfman* < *wīf* woman, wife + *man* human being] **—wom′an less,** *adj.*

Syn. *n.* 1 **Woman, lady, female** mean member of the feminine sex. **Woman** is the general word for an adult: *a married woman, a woman of high ideals.* **Lady** applies particularly to a woman of refinement or high social position: *the manners of a lady.* It is sometimes used to refer to any woman *(Ladies and gentlemen, let me introduce the next speaker),* but when used in a context which seems to deny the usual connotations of refinement and social position, the result is often unintentionally incongruous: *the lady I hire to clean my apartment.* **Female,** alone of these three words, applies to a person of any age, baby or child as well as adult. It thus emphasizes the sex of the individual, and its use is now largely confined to science and statistics: *The control group consists of 241 males and 246 females.*

wom an hood (wu̇m′ən hu̇d), *n.* 1 condition or time of being a woman. 2 character or qualities of a woman. 3 women as a group: *Joan of Arc was a credit to womanhood.*

wom an ish (wu̇m′ə nish), *adj.* 1 characteristic of a woman. 2 (of a man) effeminate. **—wom′an ish ly,** *adv.* **—wom′an ish ness,** *n.*

wom an kind (wu̇m′ən kīnd′), *n.* the female sex; women as a group.

wom an like (wu̇m′ən līk′), *adj.* like a woman; womanly.

wom an ly (wu̇m′ən lē), *adj.* 1 having qualities traditionally attributed to a woman; like a woman. 2 suitable for a woman; feminine. —*adv.* in a womanly manner. **—wom′an li ness,** *n.*

woman of the world, woman who knows people and customs, and is tolerant of both.

woman's rights, social, political, and legal rights for women, equal to those of men.

woman suffrage, 1 the political right of women to vote. 2 women's votes.

womb (wüm), *n.* 1 uterus. 2 place containing or producing anything. [Old English *wamb*]

wom bat (wom′bat), *n.* either of two burrowing Australian marsupial mammals that look like small bears. [< native Australian name]

wom en (wim′ən), *n.* pl. of **woman.**

wom en folk (wim′ən fōk′), *n.pl.* women.

wom en folks (wim′ən fōks′), *n.pl.* women.

Women's Lib (lib), Women's Liberation.

Women's Liberation, movement of women calling for liberation from male discrimination and dominance.

won[1] (wun), *v.* pt. and pp. of **win.**

wolverine—about $3^1/_2$ ft. long with tail

won[2] (won), *n., pl.* **won.** the monetary unit of Korea, worth about $^1/_3$ of a cent in South Korea and about 83 cents in North Korea. [< Korean]

won der (wun′dər), *n.* 1 a strange and surprising thing or event: *The Grand Canyon is one of the wonders of the world. It is a wonder he turned down the offer.* 2 the feeling caused by what is strange and surprising: *The baby looked with wonder at the Christmas tree.* 3 **do wonders** or **work wonders,** do wonderful things; achieve or produce extraordinary results. —*v.i.* 1 feel wonder: *We wonder at the splendor of the stars.* 2 be surprised or astonished: *I shouldn't wonder if he wins the prize.* 3 be curious. —*v.t.* be curious about; think about; wish to know: *I wonder where he has gone.* [Old English *wundor*] **—won′der er,** *n.* **—won′der ing ly,** *adv.*

wonder drug, drug notably successful in treating different diseases.

won der ful (wun′dər fəl), *adj.* 1 causing wonder; marvelous; remarkable: *The explorer had wonderful adventures.* 2 excellent;

splendid; fine: *We had a wonderful time at the party.* **—won′der ful ly,** *adv.* **—won′der ful ness,** *n.*

won der land (wun′dər land′), *n.* land or place full of wonders.

won der ment (wun′dər mənt), *n.* 1 wonder; surprise. 2 object of wonder.

won der work er (wun′dər wėr′kər), *n.* person who performs wonders.

won drous (wun′drəs), *adj.* wonderful. *—adv.* wonderfully. **—won′drous ly,** *adv.* **—won′drous ness,** *n.*

wont (wunt, wōnt), *adj.* accustomed: *He was wont to read the paper at breakfast.* *—n.* custom; habit: *She rose early, as was her wont.* [originally past participle of Old English *wunian* be accustomed]

won't (wōnt, wunt), will not.

wont ed (wun′tid, wōn′tid), *adj.* accustomed; customary; usual. **—wont′ed ly,** *adv.* **—wont′ed ness,** *n.*

woo (wü), *v.t.* 1 make love to; seek to marry. 2 seek to win; try to get: *woo fame, woo wealth.* 3 try to persuade; urge. *—v.i.* make love; court. [Old English *wōgian*]

wood (wu̇d), *n.* 1 the hard substance beneath the bark of a tree, shrub, or other plant. 2 trees or parts of trees cut up into boards, planks, etc., for use: *The carpenter brought wood to build a garage.* 3 firewood. 4 Often, **woods,** *pl.* **a** a large number of growing trees; small forest. **b** area covered by a forest or forests. 5 thing made of wood. 6 cask; barrel; keg: *wine drawn from the wood.* 7 (in printing) woodcuts collectively or a woodcut. 8 a golf club with a wooden head. **9 woods,** *pl.* woodwinds. **10 out of the woods,** out of danger or difficulty.
—adj. 1 made or consisting of wood; wooden. 2 used to store or convey wood: *a wood box.* 3 dwelling or growing in woods: *wood moss.*
—v.t. 1 plant with trees. 2 supply with wood, especially firewood. *—v.i.* get or take in a supply of wood for fuel.
[Old English *wudu*]
➤ **Woods** (def. 4), though plural in form, is usually singular (or collective) in meaning and is used both as a singular *(a woods)* and as a plural *(the woods are).*

Wood (wu̇d), *n.* **1 Grant,** 1892-1942, American painter. **2 Leonard,** 1860-1927, American military commander and colonial administrator.

wood alcohol, a colorless, volatile, poisonous, flammable liquid made by the destructive distillation of wood or by the combination of carbon monoxide and hydrogen in the presence of a catalyst; methyl alcohol; methanol. It is used as a solvent, fuel, etc., and to make formaldehyde.

wood anemone, any of various anemones growing wild in the woods. The common wood anemone has a white flower in the spring.

wood bine (wu̇d′bīn), *n.* 1 a common European honeysuckle with pale-yellow, fragrant flowers. 2 Virginia creeper. [Old English *wudubinde* < *wudu* wood + *binde* wreath]

wood block, 1 block of wood. 2 woodcut, especially one made from wood sawed with the grain.

wood carv er (wu̇d′kär′vər), *n.* person who carves figures or other objects from wood.

wood carv ing (wu̇d′kär′ving), *n.* 1 some object, as a figure, carved from wood. 2 art or process of making woodcarvings.

woodchuck—about 2 ft. long with tail

wood chuck (wu̇d′chuk′), *n.* a small North American marmot; groundhog. Woodchucks grow fat in summer and sleep in their holes in the ground all winter. [< Algonquian *otchek, otchig* marten; influenced by *wood, chuck*]

wood cock (wu̇d′kok′), *n., pl.* **-cocks** or **-cock.** 1 a small Old World game bird of the same family as the snipe, with short legs and a long, sensitive bill used to probe the ground for worms. 2 a similar and related bird of eastern North America.

wood craft (wu̇d′kraft′), *n.* 1 knowledge about how to get food and shelter in the woods; skill in hunting, trapping, finding one's way, etc. 2 skill in working with wood.

wood cut (wu̇d′kut′), *n.* 1 an engraved block of wood to print from. 2 a print from such a block.

wood cut ter (wu̇d′kut′ər), *n.* person who cuts down trees or chops wood.

wood ed (wu̇d′id), *adj.* covered with trees: *The house stood on a wooded hill.*

wood en (wu̇d′n), *adj.* 1 made of wood: *a wooden bench.* 2 stiff; awkward: *a wooden manner.* 3 dull; stupid. **—wood′en ly,** *adv.* **—wood′en ness,** *n.*

wood engraving, 1 art or process of making woodcuts. 2 woodcut, especially one made from wood sawed across the grain.

wood en-head ed (wu̇d′n hed′id), *adj.* INFORMAL. dull; stupid.

wooden horse, Trojan horse.

wood en ware (wu̇d′n wer′, wu̇d′n war′), *n.* containers, utensils, and other household articles made of wood.

wood land (*n.* wu̇d′lənd, wu̇d′land′; *adj.* wu̇d′lənd), *n.* land covered with trees. *—adj.* of, having to do with, or living in the woods.

wood land er (wu̇d′lən dər), *n.* person who lives in the woods.

wood lot, land on which trees are grown and cut for firewood, timber, etc.

wood louse, any of several small crustaceans that have flat, oval bodies and live in decaying wood, damp soil, etc.; sow bug.

wood man (wu̇d′mən), *n., pl.* **-men.** 1 man who cuts down trees. 2 person who lives in the woods. 3 person who takes care of forests.

wood note, a musical sound made by a bird or animal of the forest.

wood nymph, 1 nymph that lives in the woods; dryad. 2 a brown butterfly with yellow markings and round spots on its wings.

wood peck er (wu̇d′pek′ər), *n.* any of a family of birds with hard, pointed bills for pecking holes in trees to get insects and usually with brightly colored plumage. Woodpeckers are found in almost all parts of the world. The flicker is one kind of woodpecker.

wood pile (wu̇d′pīl′), *n.* pile of wood, especially wood for fuel.

wood pulp, pulp made from wood, used in making paper.

wood pussy, INFORMAL. skunk.

wood rat, pack rat.

wood ruff (wu̇d′ruf), *n.* a low-growing old-world herb of the same family as the madder, with clusters of small white flowers and sweet-smelling leaves.

hat, āge, fär; let, ēqual, tėrm;
it, īce; hot, ōpen, ôrder;
oil, out; cup, pu̇t, rüle;
ch, child; ng, long; sh, she;
th, thin; ᴛʜ, then; zh, measure;

ə represents *a* in about, *e* in taken, *i* in pencil, *o* in lemon, *u* in circus.

< = from, derived from, taken from.

Woods (wu̇dz), *n.* **Lake of the,** lake on the boundary between Minnesota and Canada. 90 mi. long; 10-50 mi. wide.

wood shed (wu̇d′shed′), *n.* shed for storing wood.

woods man (wu̇dz′mən), *n., pl.* **-men.** 1 man used to life in the woods and skilled in woodcraft. 2 lumberjack.

wood sorrel, any of a group of plants with acid juice, usually having leaves composed of three heart-shaped leaflets and white, yellow, red, or pink flowers; oxalis.

woods y (wu̇d′zē), *adj.,* **woods i er, woods i est.** of, like, or having to do with the woods.

wood tar, a dark-brown, poisonous, sticky substance obtained from wood by destructive distillation and containing resins, turpentine, etc. It is used as a preservative on wood, rope, etc.

wood thrush, thrush with a white, spotted breast and rust-colored head, common in the thickets and woods of eastern North America and noted for its sweet song; song thrush.

wood turner, person skilled in wood turning.

wood turning, the making of pieces of wood into various shapes by using a lathe.

wood wind (wu̇d′wind′), *n.* 1 any of a group of wind instruments which were originally made of wood, but are now often made of metal. Clarinets, flutes, oboes, and bassoons are woodwinds. **2 woodwinds,** *pl.* the section of an orchestra composed of these instruments. *—adj.* of or having to do with these instruments.

wood work (wu̇d′wėrk′), *n.* things made of wood; wooden parts inside of a house, such as doors, stairs, moldings, and the like.

wood work er (wu̇d′wėr′kər), *n.* person who makes things of wood.

wood work ing (wu̇d′wėr′king), *n.* act or process of making or shaping things of wood. *—adj.* of or for woodworking.

wood worm (wu̇d′wėrm′), *n.* worm or larva that is bred in wood or bores in wood.

wood y (wu̇d′ē), *adj.,* **wood i er, wood i est.** 1 having many trees; covered with trees: *a woody hillside.* 2 consisting of wood: *the woody parts of a shrub.* 3 like wood: *Turnips become woody when they are old.* **—wood′i ness,** *n.*

woo er (wü′ər), *n.* one that woos; suitor.

woof (wüf), *n.* 1 the threads running from side to side across a woven fabric. The woof crosses the warp. See **warp** for diagram. 2 fabric; cloth; texture. [Old English *ōwef*]

woof er (wu̇f′ər), *n.* a high-fidelity loudspeaker for reproducing the lower frequency sounds. [probably < *woof,* sound of a dog's bark]

wool (wu̇l), *n.* 1 the soft, curly hair or fur of

sheep and some other animals. 2 short, thick, curly hair. 3 any of various fine, fibrous substances resembling wool. 4 yarn, cloth, or garments made of wool. 5 a downy substance found on certain plants. 6 **pull the wool over one's eyes,** INFORMAL. deceive or trick one. *—adj.* made of wool. [Old English *wull*]

wool en (wul′ən), *adj.* 1 made of wool. 2 of or having to do with wool or cloth made of wool. *—n.* 1 yarn or cloth made of wool. 2 **woolens,** *pl.* cloth or clothing made of wool.

Woolf (wulf), *n.* **Virginia,** 1882-1941, British novelist and essayist.

wool gath er er (wul′gaᴛʜ′ər ər), *n.* a daydreaming or absent-minded person.

wool gath er ing (wul′gaᴛʜ′ər ing), *n.* absorption in thinking or daydreaming; absent-mindedness. *—adj.* inattentive; absent-minded; dreamy.

wool grow er (wul′grō′ər), *n.* person who raises sheep for their wool.

wool len (wul′ən), *adj., n.* woolen.

wool ly (wul′ē), *adj.,* **-li er, -li est,** *n., pl.* **-lies.** *—adj.* 1 consisting of wool. 2 like wool. 3 covered with wool or something like it. 4 not clear; confused and hazy; muddled: *Both his thinking and his writing are woolly.* *—n.* INFORMAL. article of clothing made from wool. **—wool′li ness,** *n.*

woolly bear, the hair-covered larva of a tiger moth.

wool pack (wul′pak′), *n.* 1 a large cloth bag for carrying wool. 2 bundle or bale of wool.

wool sack (wul′sak′), *n.* 1 bag of wool. 2 cushion on which the Lord Chancellor sits in the British House of Lords. 3 office of Lord Chancellor.

wool skin (wul′skin′), *n.* sheepskin with the fleece on it.

wool y (wul′ē), *adj.,* **wool i er, wool i est.** woolly. **—wool′i ness,** *n.*

wooz y (wü′zē, wuz′ē), *adj.,* **wooz i er, wooz i est.** INFORMAL. 1 somewhat dizzy or weak; slightly ill. 2 muddled; confused. [variant of *oozy*[2]] **—wooz′i ly,** *adv.* **—wooz′i ness,** *n.*

Worces ter (wus′tər), *n.* 1 city in central Massachusetts. 177,000. 2 city in W England. 72,000. 3 **Joseph Emerson,** 1784-1865, American lexicographer.

Worces ter shire (wus′tər shər, wus′tər-shir), *n.* 1 county in W England. 2 Worcestershire sauce.

Worcestershire sauce, a highly seasoned sauce containing soy, vinegar, and many other ingredients, originally made in Worcester, England.

word (wėrd), *n.* 1 sound or a group of sounds that has meaning and is an independent unit of speech: *We speak words when we talk.* 2 the writing or printing that stands for a word: *This page is filled with words.* 3 a short talk: *May I have a word with you?* 4 speech: *honest in word and deed.* 5 a brief expression: *The teacher gave us a word of advice.* 6 command; order: *His word was law.* 7 **the Word,** the Bible. 8 signal; watchword; password: *The word for tonight is "the King."* 9 promise: *She kept her word.* 10 news: *No word has come from the battlefront.* 11 any set of symbols or characters stored and transferred by computer circuits as a unit of meaning. 12 Usually, **words,** *pl.* that which is said; talk. 13 **words,** *pl.* **a** angry talk; quarrel; dispute. **b** the text of a song as distinguished from the notes.
be as good as one's word, keep one's promise.
by word of mouth, by spoken words; orally.
eat one's words, take back what one has said; retract.
in a word, briefly.
my word! an expression of surprise.
take one at his word, take one's words seriously and act accordingly.
take the words out of one's mouth, say exactly what another was just going to say.
upon my word, a I promise. **b** expression of surprise.
word for word, in the exact words.
—v.t. put into or express in words; phrase: *Word your ideas clearly.*
[Old English]

word age (wėr′dij), *n.* 1 words collectively. 2 quantity of words. 3 verbiage. 4 wording.

word book (wėrd′buk′), *n.* 1 list of words, usually with explanations, etc.; dictionary. 2 libretto of an opera or other musical work.

word class, in linguistics: 1 part of speech. 2 form class.

word ing (wėr′ding), *n.* way of saying a thing; choice and use of words; phrasing: *Careful wording is needed for clearness.* See **diction** for synonym study.

word less (wėrd′lis), *adj.* 1 without words; speechless; silent. 2 not put into words; unexpressed. **—word′less ly,** *adv.* **—word′less ness,** *n.*

word of honor, a solemn promise.

word-of-mouth (wėrd′əv mouth′), *adj.* communicated by spoken words; oral. *—n.* oral communication.

word order, the arrangement of words in a sentence, clause, or phrase.
➤ **word order.** In English the usual word order for statements is subject followed by predicate: *The boy hit the ball. The ball hit the fence.* Other word orders are chiefly rhetorical and poetic: *"Uneasy lies the head that wears a crown."* In English, with its relative absence of inflections, word order is the chief grammatical device for indicating the function of words and their relation to each other.

word play (wėrd′plā′), *n.* play of or upon words.

word square, set of words of the same number of letters arranged in a square so as to read the same horizontally and vertically.

```
P A S T E
A C T O R
S T O M A   word square
T O M B S
E R A S E
```

Words worth (wėrdz′wərth), *n.* **William,** 1770-1850, English poet.

word y (wėr′dē), *adj.,* **word i er, word i est.** using too many words; verbose. **—word′i ly,** *adv.* **—word′i ness,** *n.*
Syn. Wordy, verbose mean using more words than are necessary. **Wordy** is the general term: *a wordy discussion, a wordy sentence.* **Verbose** implies tiresome or pretentious wordiness often resulting in obscurity: *a verbose speaker, verbose jargon.*

wore (wôr, wōr), *v.* pt. of **wear.**

work (wėrk), *n., adj., v.,* **worked** or (ARCHAIC) **wrought, work ing.** *—n.* 1 effort in doing or making something: *Some people like hard work.* See synonym study below. 2 something to do; occupation; employment: *She is looking for work.* 3 something made or done; result of effort: *a work of art, the works of Dickens.* 4 that on which effort is put: *take one's work outside.* 5 **works,** *pl.* actions: *good works.* 6 **works,** *pl.* factory or other place for doing some kind of work. 7 fortification. 8 (in physics) transference of energy from one body or system to another, causing motion of the body acted upon in the direction of the force producing it and against resistance. It is equal to the product of the force and the distance through which the force moves. 9 **works,** *pl.* the moving parts of a machine or device: *the works of a watch.* 10 an engineering structure. 11 **works,** *pl.* buildings, bridges, docks, etc. 12 **the works,** SLANG. everything necessary or available. 13 OBSOLETE. workmanship.
at work, working; operating.
make short work of, do or get rid of quickly.
out of work, having no job; unemployed.
shoot the works, SLANG. go to the limit; use, spend, etc., completely.
—adj. of, for, having to do with, or used in work: *a work routine.*
—v.i. 1 do work; labor: *Most people must work for a living.* 2 be employed: *She works at an airplane factory.* 3 act; operate, especially effectively: *The radio will not work. The plan worked well.* 4 move as if with effort: *The child's face worked as he tried to keep back the tears.* 5 go slowly or with effort: *The ship worked to windward.* 6 become (up, round, loose, etc.): *The window catch has worked loose.* 7 behave (in a specified way) while being kneaded, pressed, shaped, etc.: *clay that works easily.* 8 ferment: *Yeast makes beer work.* 9 seethe, rage, or toss, as a stormy sea. *—v.t.* 1 put effort on: *He worked his farm with success.* 2 put into operation; use; manage: *puppets worked with wires, work a scheme.* 3 bring about; cause; do: *work a change. The plan worked harm.* 4 cause to do work: *He works his employees long hours.* 5 carry on operations in (districts, etc.): *The salesman worked the Eastern states.* 6 form; shape: *work an essay into an article.* 7 treat or handle in making; knead; mix: *work butter, work dough to mix it.* 8 cause (beer, etc.) to ferment. 9 make, get, do, or bring about by effort: *work one's way through college.* 10 influence; persuade: *work a jury.* 11 move; stir; excite: *Don't work yourself into a temper.* 12 solve: *Work all the problems on the page.* 13 SLANG. use tricks on to get something: *work a friend for a job.*
work in, put in; insert.
work off, get rid of: *work off a debt.*
work on or **work upon,** try to persuade or influence.
work out, a plan; develop. **b** solve; find out. **c** use up. **d** give exercise to; practice. **e** accomplish. **f** result.
work up, a plan; develop. **b** stir up; excite.
[Old English *weorc*]
Syn. *n.* 1 **Work, labor, toil** mean effort or exertion turned to making or doing something. **Work** is the general word, applying to physical or mental effort or to the activity of a force or machine: *pleasant work, a day's work. This lathe does the work of three of the older type.* **Labor** applies to hard physical or mental work: *That student's understanding of his subjects shows the amount of labor he puts into his homework.* **Toil,** a word with some literary flavor, applies to long and

hat, āge, fär; let, ēqual, tėrm;
it, īce; hot, ōpen, ôrder;
oil, out; cup, pu̇t, rüle;
ch, child; ng, long; sh, she;
th, thin; ᴛʜ, then; zh, measure;

ə represents *a* in about, *e* in taken, *i* in pencil, *o* in lemon, *u* in circus.

< = from, derived from, taken from.

wearying labor: *The farmer's toil was rewarded with good crops.*

work a bil i ty (wėr′kə bil′ə tē), *n.* quality of being workable.

work a ble (wėr′kə bəl), *adj.* 1 that can be worked. 2 that can be used or put into effect; practicable: *a workable plan.* **—work′a ble ness,** *n.*

work a day (wėr′kə dā′), *adj.* of working days; practical; commonplace; ordinary.

work bag (wėrk′bag′), *n.* bag to hold the things that a person works with, especially a bag for sewing materials.

work bas ket (wėrk′bas′kit), *n.* basket to hold the things that a person works with, especially sewing materials.

work bench (wėrk′bench′), *n.* table at which a mechanic, carpenter, or other artisan works.

work book (wėrk′bu̇k′), *n.* 1 book containing outlines for the study of some subject, questions to be answered, etc.; book in which a student does parts of his written work. 2 book containing rules for doing certain work. 3 book for notes of work planned or work done.

work box (wėrk′boks′), *n.* box to hold the materials and tools that a person works with.

work day (wėrk′dā′), *n.* 1 day for work; day that is not Sunday or a holiday. 2 part of a day during which work is done. *—adj.* workaday.

work er (wėr′kər), *n.* 1 person or thing that works. 2 person who works for wages; member of the working class. 3 the neuter or undeveloped female of certain social insects, such as ants, bees, or wasps, that supplies food and performs other services for the community.

work force, the number of workers employed in an area, industry, plant, etc.

work horse (wėrk′hôrs′), *n.* 1 horse used for labor, and not for showing, racing, or hunting. 2 a very hard worker.

work house (wėrk′hous′), *n., pl.* **-hous es** (-hou′ziz). 1 house of correction where petty criminals are kept and made to work. 2 (in Great Britain) a house where very poor people are lodged and set to work.

work ing (wėr′king), *n.* 1 method or manner of work; operation; action: *Do you understand the working of this machine?* 2 Usually, **workings,** *pl.* parts of a mine, quarry, tunnel, etc., where work is being done. *—adj.* 1 that works: *the working population.* 2 of, for, or used in working: *working hours, working clothes.* 3 used to operate with or by: *a working majority.*

working class, class of people who work for wages, especially manual and industrial workers.

work ing-class (wėr′king klas′), *adj.* of, belonging to, or characteristic of the working class.

working day, workday.

work ing man (wėr′king man′), *n., pl.* **-men.** 1 man who works. 2 man who works with his hands or with machines.

working papers, documents, as a certificate of age, that permit a minor to leave school and go to work.

work ing wom an (wėr′king wu̇m′ən), *n., pl.* **-wom en.** 1 woman who works. 2 woman who works with her hands or with machines.

work less (wėrk′lis), *adj.* out of work; unemployed.

work load (wėrk′lōd′), *n.* the amount of work carried by or assigned to a worker.

work man (wėrk′mən), *n., pl.* **-men.** 1 worker. 2 man who works with his hands or with machines.

work man like (wėrk′mən līk′), *adj.* skillful; well-done: *a workmanlike job.* *—adv.* skillfully.

work man ship (wėrk′mən ship), *n.* 1 the art or skill in a worker or his work: *Good workmanship requires long practice.* 2 quality or manner of work. 3 the work done.

workmen's compensation, compensation which, as specified by law, an employer must pay to a worker who is injured or contracts a disease as a result of his employment.

work of art, 1 product of any of the arts, such as a painting, statue, or literary or musical work. 2 anything done or made with great skill or artistry.

work out (wėrk′out′), *n.* INFORMAL. 1 exercise; practice: *She had a good workout running around the track.* 2 trial; test: *The mechanic gave the car a thorough workout after repairing it.*

work room (wėrk′rüm′, wėrk′ru̇m′), *n.* room where work is done.

work shop (wėrk′shop′), *n.* 1 shop or building where work is done. 2 course of study, discussion, or work for a group of people interested in a particular subject or field: *a history workshop.*

work ta ble (wėrk′tā′bəl), *n.* table to work at.

work week (wėrk′wēk′), *n.* the part of the week in which work is done, usually Monday through Friday.

work wom an (wėrk′wu̇m′ən), *n., pl.* **-wom en.** workingwoman.

world (wėrld), *n.* 1 the earth: *Ships can sail around the world.* See **earth** for synonym study. 2 all of certain parts, people, or things of the earth: *the world of fashion, the ancient world, the insect world.* 3 all people; the human race; the public: *The whole world knows it.* 4 the things of this life and the people devoted to them: *Monks live apart from the world.* 5 planet or other heavenly body, especially when considered as inhabited. 6 any time, condition, or place of life: *Heaven is in the world to come.* 7 all things; everything; the universe. 8 a great deal; very much; large amount: *The vacation did me a world of good.*

for all the world, **a** for any reason, no matter how great. **b** in every respect; exactly.

in the world, **a** anywhere. **b** at all; ever.

out of this world, INFORMAL. great; wonderful.

world without end, eternally; forever.

[Old English *worold,* earlier *weorold,* literally, age of man]

World Bank, the International Bank for Reconstruction and Development, an organization founded in 1944 to provide loans and other banking services to member nations, especially to help them develop their economies.

world-beat er (wėrld′bē′tər), *n.* INFORMAL. a champion.

World Court, court made up of representatives of many nations, having the power to settle disputes between nations; International Court of Justice.

world ling (wėrld′ling), *n.* person who cares much for the interest and pleasures of this world.

world ly (wėrld′lē), *adj.,* **-li er, -li est.** 1 of this world; not of heaven: *worldly wealth.* 2 caring much for the interests and pleasures of this world. See **earthly** for synonym study. 3 worldly-wise. **—world′li ness,** *n.*

world ly-mind ed (wėrld′lē mīn′did), *adj.* having or showing a worldly mind. **—world′ly-mind′ed ness,** *n.*

world ly-wise (wėrld′lē wīz′), *adj.* wise about or experienced in the ways and affairs of this world.

world power, nation having such military or other power as to be able to exert a decisive influence on the course of world affairs.

World Series, series of baseball games played each fall between the winners of the two major league championships, to decide the professional championship of the United States.

world's fair, an international exposition with exhibits of arts, crafts, products, etc., from various countries.

World War I, war fought mainly in Europe and the Middle East, from July 28, 1914, to November 11, 1918. The United States, Great Britain, France, Russia, and their allies were on one side; Germany, Austria-Hungary, and their allies were on the other side.

World War II, war fought in Europe, Asia, Africa, and elsewhere, from September 1, 1939, to August 14, 1945. The chief conflict was between Great Britain, the United States, France, and the Soviet Union on one side and Germany, Italy, and Japan on the other.

world-wear y (wėrld′wir′ē), *adj.* weary of this world; tired of living. **—world′-wear′i ness,** *n.*

world wide (wėrld′wīd′), *adj.* spread throughout the world: *the worldwide threat of atomic radiation.*

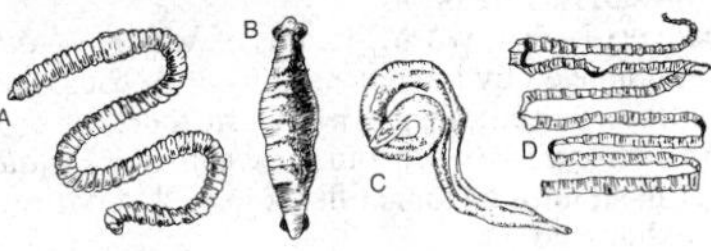

worm (def. 1)—A, earthworm; B, leech; C, hookworm; D, tapeworm

worm (wėrm), *n.* 1 any of numerous small, slender, crawling or creeping invertebrates, usually soft-bodied and lacking legs, including annelids, nematodes, flatworms, and ribbon worms. 2 any of various small crawling or creeping animals resembling the true worms, such as a grub, caterpillar, maggot, etc. 3 something like a worm in shape or movement, such as the thread of a screw or the tube of a still. 4 something that slowly eats away, or the pain or destruction it causes. 5 person who deserves contempt or pity. 6 **worms,** *pl.* disease caused by parasitic worms in the body, especially in the intestines. —*v.t.* 1 make (one's way, etc.) by creeping or crawling like a worm: *The soldier wormed his way toward the enemy's lines.* 2 work or get by persistent and secret means: *try to worm a secret out of someone, worm the truth from a person. He wormed himself into our confidence.* 3 remove worms from: *worm a dog.* —*v.i.* 1 move like a worm; crawl or creep like a worm. 2 make one's way insidiously *(into).* [Old English *wyrm*] **—worm′er,** *n.* **—worm′like′,** *adj.*

worm-eat en (wėrm′ēt′n), *adj.* 1 eaten into by worms: *worm-eaten timbers.* 2 worn-out; worthless; out-of-date.

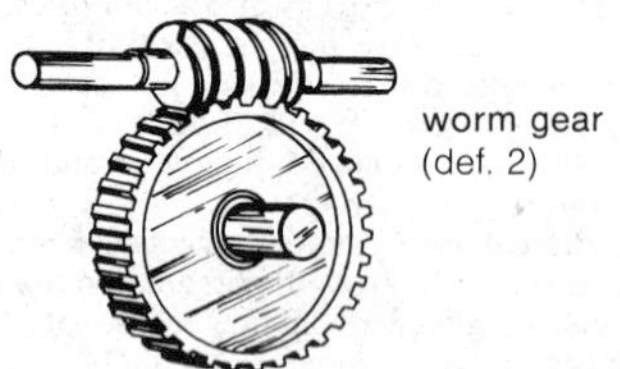
worm gear (def. 2)

worm gear, 1 worm wheel. 2 a worm wheel and an endless screw together. By a worm gear the rotary motion of one shaft can be transmitted to another.

worm hole (wėrm′hōl′), *n.* hole or burrow made by a worm, as in fruit, wood, etc.

Worms (wėrmz; *German* vôrms), *n.* city in W West Germany, on the Rhine. 64,000.

worm's-eye (wėrmz′ī′), *adj.* seen from below or very closely; narrow; detailed: *a worm's-eye view of city life.*

worm wheel, wheel with teeth that fit into a revolving screw.

worm wood (wėrm′wu̇d′), *n.* 1 a somewhat woody, bitter, perennial herb, native to Europe, whose leaves and tops were formerly used in medicine and are now used for making absinthe and some brands of vermouth. 2 any of the genus of herbs or shrubs of the composite family to which the wormwood belongs. 3 something bitter or extremely unpleasant. [Old English *wermōd;* influenced by *worm, wood*]

worm y (wėr′mē), *adj.,* **worm i er, worm i est.** 1 having worms; containing many worms: *wormy apples.* 2 damaged by worms: *wormy wood.* 3 resembling a worm. **—worm′i ness,** *n.*

worn (wôrn, wōrn), *v.* pp. of **wear.** —*adj.* 1 damaged by long or hard wear or use: *worn rugs.* 2 tired; wearied: *a worn face.*

worn-out (wôrn′out′, wōrn′out′), *adj.* 1 used until no longer fit for use. 2 very tired; exhausted.

wor ri ment (wėr′ē mənt), *n.* INFORMAL. 1 a worrying. 2 worry; anxiety.

wor ri some (wėr′ē səm), *adj.* 1 causing worry. 2 inclined to worry. **—wor′ri some ly,** *adv.*

wor ry (wėr′ē), *v.,* **-ried, -ry ing,** *n., pl.* **-ries.** —*v.i.* 1 feel anxious; be uneasy: *They will worry if we are late.* 2 **worry along** or **worry through,** manage somehow. —*v.t.* 1 cause to feel anxious or troubled: *The problem worried him.* See synonym study below. 2 annoy; bother; vex: *Don't worry me with so many questions.* 3 seize and shake with the teeth; bite at; snap at: *The cat worried the mouse.* —*n.* 1 anxiety; uneasiness; trouble; care: *Worry kept her awake.* 2 cause of trouble or care: *The parents of the sick child had many worries.* [Old English *wyrgan* strangle] **—wor′ri er,** *n.*

Syn. *v.t.* 1 **Worry, annoy, harass** mean to disturb or distress someone. **Worry** means to cause great uneasiness, care, or anxiety: *The change in his disposition and habits worries me.* **Annoy** means to irritate or vex by constant interference, repeated interruption, etc.: *annoy one's fellow workers with too many foolish questions.* **Harass** means to annoy deeply and unceasingly: *be harassed by business troubles.*

wor ry wart (wėr′ē wôrt′), *n.* SLANG. person who worries too much.

worse (wėrs), *adj., comparative of* **bad**[1]. 1 less well; more ill: *The patient is worse today.* 2 less good; more evil: *He is a bad boy, but his brother is worse.* —*adv.* in a worse manner or degree: *It is raining worse than ever.* —*n.* that which is worse: *The loss of his property was bad enough, but worse followed.* [Old English *wyrsa*]

wors en (wėr′sən), *v.t., v.i.* make or become worse.

wor ship (wėr′ship), *n., v.,* **-shiped, -ship ing** or **-shipped, -ship ping.** —*n.* 1 great honor and reverence paid to someone or something regarded as sacred: *the worship of God, idol worship, fire worship.* 2 religious ceremonies or services in which one expresses such honor and reverence. 3 great love and admiration; adoration: *hero worship, the worship of wealth and power.* 4 BRITISH. title used in addressing certain magistrates: *"Yes, your worship," he said to the judge.* —*v.t.* 1 pay great honor and reverence to: *People go to church to worship God.* 2 consider extremely precious; hold very dear; adore: *She worships her mother. A miser worships money.* —*v.i.* perform or take part in any act, rite, or service of worship. [Old English *weorthscipe* < *weorth* worth + *-scipe* -ship] **—wor′ship er, wor′ship per,** *n.*

wor ship ful (wėr′ship fəl), *adj.* 1 honorable: *We beg you, worshipful gentlemen, to grant our request.* 2 worshiping: *the worshipful eyes of a dog watching its master.* **—wor′ship ful ly,** *adv.* **—wor′ship ful ness,** *n.*

worst (wėrst), *adj., superlative of* **bad**[1]. 1 least well; most ill: *This is the worst I've been since I got sick.* 2 least good; most faulty or unsatisfactory: *the worst room in the hotel.* —*adv.* in the worst manner or degree: *This child acts worst when his parents have guests.* —*n.* 1 that which is worst: *Yesterday was bad, but the worst is yet to come.* 2 **at worst** or **at the worst,** under the least favorable circumstances. 3 **give one the worst of it,** defeat one. 4 **if worst comes to worst,** if the very worst thing happens. —*v.t.* beat; defeat: *The hero worsted his enemies.* [Old English *wyrsta*]

wor sted (wu̇s′tid, wėr′stid), *n.* 1 a firmly twisted woolen thread or yarn. 2 cloth made from such thread or yarn. —*adj.* made of worsted. [< *Worsted* (now Worstead), village in England, where it was originally made]

wort[1] (wėrt), *n.* the liquid made from malt which later becomes beer, ale, or other liquor when fermented. [Old English *wyrt*]

wort[2] (wėrt), *n.* plant, herb, or vegetable (now used chiefly in combinations, as in *liverwort, figwort*). [Old English *wyrt*]

worth (wėrth), *adj.* 1 good or important enough for; deserving of: *That book is worth reading. London is a city worth visiting.* 2 equal in value to: *That pen is worth $5.00.* 3 having property that amounts to: *That man is worth millions.* —*n.* 1 merit; usefulness; importance: *We should read books of real worth.* 2 value: *I got my money's worth out of that coat.* 3 quantity of something of specified value. 4 property; wealth. [Old English *weorth*]

worth less (wėrth′lis), *adj.* without worth; good-for-nothing; useless. **—worth′less ly,** *adv.* **—worth′less ness,** *n.*

worth while (wėrth′hwīl′), *adj.* worth time, attention, or effort; having real merit: *spend one's time on some worthwhile reading.* **—worth′while′ness,** *n.*

wor thy (wėr′ᴛʜē), *adj.,* **-thi er, -thi est,** *n., pl.* **-thies.** —*adj.* 1 having worth or merit: *a worthy opponent, a worthy cause.* 2 deserving; meriting: *courage worthy of high praise, a crime worthy of punishment.* —*n.* person of great merit; admirable person. **—wor′thi ly,** *adv.* **—wor′thi ness,** *n.*

wot (wot), *v.* ARCHAIC. know. "I wot" means "I know." "He wot" means "he knows." [Old English *wāt*]

would (wu̇d; *unstressed* wəd), *v.* 1 pt. of **will**[1]. See **will**[1] for ordinary uses. 2 *Would* is also used: **a** to express future time. *Would they never go?* **b** to express action done again and again in the past time. *The children would play for hours on the beach.* **c** to express a wish or desire. *Would I were rich!* **d** to make a statement or question less direct or blunt than it sounds with *will. Would that be fair? Would you help us, please?* **e** to express conditions. *If he would only try, he could do it.* [Old English *wolde*]

➤ The frequent misspelling **would of** for *would have* arises out of the fact that *have* and *of,* when completely unstressed, are pronounced identically.

would-be (wu̇d′bē′), *adj.* 1 wishing or pretending to be: *a would-be actor.* 2 intended to be: *a would-be work of art.*

would n't (wu̇d′nt), would not.

wouldst (wu̇dst), *v.* ARCHAIC. would. "Thou wouldst" means "you would."

wound[1] (wünd; *Archaic* wound), *n.* 1 a hurt or injury caused by cutting, stabbing, shooting, etc. 2 any hurt or injury to feelings, reputation, etc.: *The loss of his job was a wound to his pride.* —*v.t.* 1 hurt or injure by cutting, stabbing, shooting, etc. 2 injure in feelings, reputation, etc.: *Their unkind words wounded me.* —*v.i.* inflict a wound or wounds. [Old English *wund*]

wound[2] (wound), *v.* a pt. and pp. of **wind**[2].

wound[3] (wound), *v.* pt. and pp. of **wind**[3].

wove (wōv), *v.* pt. and a pp. of **weave.**

wo ven (wō′vən), *v.* a pp. of **weave.**

wow (wou), *interj.* exclamation of surprise, joy, etc. —*n.* 1 SLANG. an unqualified success; hit. 2 a slow rise and fall in the sound pitch of a phonograph, film, or tape recording, caused by slight variations in the speed at which the recording is played. —*v.t.* SLANG. overwhelm with delight or amazement.

wrack (rak), *n.* 1 wreckage; wreck. 2 ruin; destruction. 3 seaweed cast ashore by the waves or growing on the tidal seashore. 4 any of several species of brown algae. —*v.t., v.i.* wreck or be wrecked. [< Middle Dutch and Middle Low German *wrak* wreck]

wraith (rāth), *n.* 1 ghost of a person seen before or soon after his death. 2 specter; ghost. [origin uncertain]

Wran gel (rang′gəl), *n.* island in the Arctic Ocean just north of Siberia, belonging to the Soviet Union. 2000 sq. mi.

hat, āge, fär; let, ēqual, tėrm;
it, īce; hot, ōpen, ôrder;
oil, out; cup, pu̇t, rüle;
ch, child; ng, long; sh, she;
th, thin; ᴛʜ, then; zh, measure;

ə represents *a* in about, *e* in taken, *i* in pencil, *o* in lemon, *u* in circus.

< = from, derived from, taken from.

Wran gell (rang′gəl), *n.* **Mount,** an active volcano in SE Alaska. 14,005 ft.

wran gle (rang′gəl), *v.,* **-gled, -gling,** *n.* —*v.i.* dispute noisily; quarrel angrily: *The children wrangled about who should have the last piece of cake.* —*v.t.* 1 argue. 2 (in the western United States and Canada) herd or tend (horses, cattle, etc.) on the range. —*n.* a noisy dispute; angry quarrel. [perhaps < Low German *wrangeln*]

wran gler (rang′glər), *n.* 1 person who wrangles. 2 (in the western United States and Canada) a herder in charge of horses, cattle, etc.

wrap (rap), *v.,* **wrapped** or **wrapt, wrap ping,** *n.* —*v.t.* 1 cover by winding or folding something around: *She wrapped herself in a shawl.* 2 wind or fold as a covering: *Wrap a shawl around yourself.* 3 cover with paper and tie up or fasten: *wrap Christmas presents.* 4 cover; envelop; hide: *The mountain peak is wrapped in clouds. She sat wrapped in thought.* 5 **wrapped up in, a** devoted to; thinking mainly of. **b** involved in; associated with. 6 **wrap up, a** put on warm outer clothes. **b** INFORMAL. conclude; finish. **c** INFORMAL. make assured in ending; clinch. —*v.i.* 1 wrap oneself in a garment, etc. 2 twine or circle around or about something. —*n.* 1 an outer covering, especially a garment. Shawls, scarfs, coats, and furs are wraps. 2 **under wraps,** secret or concealed: *Plans for the new automobile were kept under wraps.* [Middle English *wrappen*]

wrap a round (rap′ə round′), *adj.* 1 worn by drawing, folding, or shaping around: *a wraparound coat.* 2 curving around and along part of the sides: *a wraparound windshield.* —*n.* a wraparound garment.

wrap per (rap′ər), *n.* 1 person or thing that wraps. 2 thing in which something is wrapped; covering or cover: *Some magazines are mailed in paper wrappers.* 3 a woman's long, loose garment to wear in the house. 4 leaf or leaves forming the outside layer of tobacco in a cigar.

wrap ping (rap′ing), *n.* Usually, **wrappings,** *pl.* paper, cloth, etc., in which something is wrapped. —*adj.* used to wrap something in: *wrapping paper.*

wrapt (rapt), *v.* a pt. and a pp. of **wrap.**

wrap-up (rap′up′), *n.* INFORMAL. the final item or summary of a news report.

wrasse (ras), *n.* any of a family of spiny-finned fishes of warm seas, having thick, fleshy lips, powerful teeth, and usually a brilliant coloration. [< Cornish *gwrach*]

wrath (rath), *n.* 1 very great anger; rage. See **anger** for synonym study. 2 vengeance or punishment caused by anger. [Old English *wrǣththu* < *wrāth* wroth]

wrath ful (rath′fəl), *adj.* feeling or showing wrath; very angry. —**wrath′ful ly,** *adv.* —**wrath′ful ness,** *n.*

wrath y (rath′ē), *adj.,* **wrath i er, wrath i est.** wrathful.

wreak (rēk), *v.t.* 1 give expression to; work off (feelings, desires, etc.): *The cruel boy wreaked his bad temper on his dog.* 2 inflict (vengeance, punishment, etc.). [Old English *wrecan*]

wreath (rēth), *n., pl.* **wreaths** (rēᴛʜz). 1 ring of flowers or leaves twisted together: *We hang wreaths in the window at Christmas.* 2 something suggesting a wreath: *a wreath of smoke.* [Old English *wrǣth,* related to *wrīthan* writhe]

wreathe (rēᴛʜ), *v.,* **wreathed, wreathing.** —*v.t.* 1 make into a wreath; twist. 2 decorate or adorn with wreaths. 3 make a ring around; encircle: *Mist wreathed the hills.* 4 unite, form, or make by twining together. 5 **wreathed in smiles,** smiling greatly. —*v.i.* 1 twist, coil, bend, or curve. 2 move in rings: *The smoke wreathed upward.*

wreck (rek), *n.* 1 partial or total destruction of a motor vehicle, ship, building, train, or aircraft: *Reckless driving causes many wrecks on the highway.* 2 any destruction or serious injury: *The heavy rains caused the wreck of many crops.* 3 what is left of anything that has been destroyed or much injured: *The wrecks of six ships were cast upon the shore.* 4 person who has lost his health or money: *be a wreck from overwork.* 5 goods cast up by the sea. —*v.t.* 1 cause the wreck of; destroy; ruin: *Robbers wrecked the mail train.* 2 cause to lose health or money. —*v.i.* 1 be wrecked; suffer serious injury. 2 act as wrecker. [< Scandinavian (Old Icelandic) *rek*]

wreck age (rek′ij), *n.* 1 what is left by a wreck or wrecks: *The shore was covered with the wreckage of ships.* 2 a wrecking. 3 a being wrecked.

wreck er (rek′ər), *n.* 1 person or thing that causes wrecks. 2 person whose work is tearing down buildings. 3 person, car, train, or machine that removes wrecks. 4 person or ship that recovers wrecked or disabled ships or their cargoes. 5 person who causes shipwrecks by showing false lights on shore so as to plunder the wrecks.

wren (def. 1) about 5 in. long including the tail

wren (ren), *n.* 1 any of a family of small brown or grayish songbirds with slender bills and short tails, often held erect. Wrens often build their nests near houses. 2 any of certain similar birds. [Old English *wrenna*]

Wren (ren), *n.* Sir **Christopher,** 1632-1723, English architect.

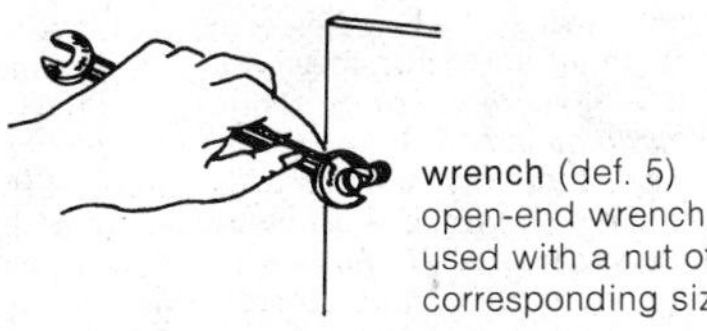
wrench (def. 5) open-end wrench used with a nut of corresponding size

wrench (rench), *n.* 1 a violent twist or twisting pull: *The knob broke off when he gave it a sudden wrench.* 2 injury caused by twisting. 3 grief; pain: *It was a wrench to leave the old home.* 4 distortion of the original or proper meaning, interpretation, etc. 5 tool for turning nuts, bolts, etc. —*v.t.* 1 twist or pull violently: *The policeman wrenched the gun out of the man's hand.* 2 injure by twisting: *She wrenched her back in falling from the horse.* 3 distress or pain greatly. 4 twist the meaning of. —*v.i.* pull or tug at something with a twist or turn. [Old English *wrencan* to twist]

wrest (rest), *v.t.* 1 twist, pull, or tear away with force; wrench away: *He bravely wrested the knife from his attacker.* 2 take by force: *The usurper wrested the power from the king.* 3 twist or turn from the proper meaning, use, etc. 4 obtain by persistence or persuasion; wring: *wrest a secret from someone.* —*n.* 1 a wresting; violent twist. 2 key for tuning a harp, piano, etc. [Old English *wrǣstan*] —**wrest′er,** *n.*

wres tle (res′əl), *v.,* **-tled, -tling,** *n.* —*v.t.* 1 try to throw or force (an opponent) to the ground. 2 contend with in wrestling, or as if in wrestling. —*v.i.* 1 take part in a wrestling match. 2 struggle: *wrestle with temptation.* —*n.* 1 a wrestling match. 2 struggle. [ultimately < *wrest*] —**wres′tler,** *n.*

wres tling (res′ling), *n.* sport or contest in which each of two opponents tries to throw or force the other to the ground. The rules of wrestling do not allow using the fists or certain holds on the body.

wrest pin, peg or pin around which the ends of the strings are coiled in a stringed musical instrument.

wretch (rech), *n.* 1 a very unfortunate or unhappy person. 2 a very bad person. [Old English *wrecca* exile]

wretch ed (rech′id), *adj.* 1 very unfortunate or unhappy. 2 very unsatisfactory; miserable: *a wretched hut.* 3 very bad: *a wretched traitor.* —**wretch′ed ly,** *adv.* —**wretch′ed ness,** *n.*

wrig gle (rig′əl), *v.,* **-gled, -gling,** *n.* —*v.i.* 1 twist and turn: *Children wriggle when they are restless.* 2 move by twisting and turning: *A snake wriggled across the road.* 3 make one's way by shifts and tricks: *wriggle out of difficulty.* —*v.t.* 1 cause to wriggle. 2 make (one's way) by wriggling. —*n.* a wriggling. [probably < Dutch *wriggelen*]

wrig gler (rig′lər), *n.* 1 person who wriggles. 2 larva of a mosquito.

wrig gly (rig′lē), *adj.,* **-gli er, -gli est.** twisting and turning.

wright (rīt), *n.* maker of something (now used chiefly in combination, as in *wheelwright, playwright*). [Old English *wryhta, wyrhta* < *weorc* work]

Wright (rīt), *n.* 1 **Frank Lloyd,** 1869-1959, American architect. 2 **Orville,** 1871-1948, and his brother **Wilbur,** 1867-1912, American inventors who perfected the airplane and made the world's first flight in a motor-powered plane, in 1903. 3 **Richard,** 1908-1960, American novelist and writer about Negro life in America.

wring (ring), *v.,* **wrung** or **wringed, wring ing,** *n.* —*v.t.* 1 twist with force; squeeze hard: *wring clothes. Wring out your wet bathing suit.* 2 force by twisting or squeezing: *wring water from a wet bathing suit.* 3 get by force, effort, or persuasion: *wring a promise from someone.* 4 clasp and hold firmly; press: *She wrung her old friend's hand.* 5 cause pain, pity, etc., in: *Their* *poverty wrung his heart.* 6 twist violently; wrench: *wring a chicken's neck.* —*n.* a twist or squeeze. [Old English *wringan*]

wring er (ring′ər), *n.* 1 machine for squeezing water from clothes. 2 person or thing that wrings.

wrin kle (ring′kəl), *n.*, *v.*, **-kled, -kling.** —*n.* 1 an irregular ridge or fold; crease: *The old man's face has wrinkles. I must press out the wrinkles in this dress.* 2 INFORMAL. **a** useful hint or idea; clever trick. **b** a special or unusual technique, method, device, etc. —*v.t.* make a wrinkle or wrinkles in: *She wrinkled her forehead.* —*v.i.* have wrinkles; acquire wrinkles: *These sleeves wrinkle.* [< Middle English *wrinkled* winding]

wrin kly (ring′klē), *adj.*, **-kli er, -kli est.** wrinkled.

wrist (rist), *n.* 1 the joint that connects the hand with the arm. 2 a corresponding joint or part of the forelimb of an animal. 3 bones of this part; carpus. [Old English]

wrist band (rist′band′), *n.* 1 the band of a sleeve fitting around the wrist. 2 strap worn around the wrist, as of a wristwatch.

wrist let (rist′lit), *n.* 1 band worn around the wrist to keep it warm. 2 bracelet.

wrist pin, stud or pin projecting from the side of a crank, wheel, or the like, and forming a means of attachment to a connecting rod.

wrist watch (rist′woch′, rist′wôch′), *n.* a small watch worn on a strap around the wrist.

writ (rit), *n.* 1 something written; piece of writing. The Bible is Holy Writ. 2 a formal written order issued by a court, etc., directing a person to do or not to do something: *The lawyer obtained a writ from the judge to release the man wrongly held in jail.* —*v.* ARCHAIC. a pt. and a pp. of **write.** [Old English < *wrītan* write]

write (rīt), *v.*, **wrote** or (ARCHAIC) **writ, writ ten** or (ARCHAIC) **writ, writ ing.** —*v.i.* 1 make letters, words, etc., with pen, pencil, chalk, etc. 2 produce (a certain kind of) writing: *a pen that writes poorly.* 3 write a letter: *He writes to her every week.* 4 be an author or writer: *His ambition is to write for the stage.* —*v.t.* 1 mark with (letters, words, etc.): *write a check.* 2 put down the letters, words, etc., of: *Write your name and address.* 3 give in writing; record: *She writes all that happens.* 4 make (books, stories, articles, poems, letters, etc.) by using written letters, words, etc.; compose: *write a sonnet.* 5 write a letter to: *I wrote my friend to come.* 6 show plainly: *Honesty is written on her face.*
write down, a put into writing. **b** put a lower value on.
write in, cast a vote for an unlisted candidate by writing his name on a ballot.
write off, a cancel. **b** note the deduction of for depreciation.
write out, a put into writing. **b** write in full.
write up, a write a description or account of. **b** write in detail. **c** bring up to date in writing. **d** put a higher value on.
[Old English *wrītan,* originally, to scratch]

write-in (rīt′in′), *adj.* of or having to do with a candidate who is not listed but who is voted for by having his name written in on a ballot. —*n.* a write-in candidate or vote.

wringer (def. 1)

write-off (rīt′ôf′, rīt′of′), *n.* amount written off or canceled as a bad debt, a tax-deductible expense, etc.

writ er (rī′tər), *n.* 1 person who writes. 2 person whose profession or business is writing; author.

writer's cramp, pain and spasm of the muscles of the hand and fingers resulting from their excessive use in writing.

write-up (rīt′up′), *n.* INFORMAL. a written description or account.

writhe (rīᴛʜ), *v.*, **writhed, writh ing.** —*v.i.* 1 twist and turn; twist about: *writhe with pain. The snake writhed along the branch.* 2 suffer mentally; be very uncomfortable. —*v.t.* twist or bend (something). [Old English *wrīthan*]

writ ing (rī′ting), *n.* 1 act of making letters, words, etc., with pen, pencil, etc. 2 written form: *Put your ideas in writing.* 3 handwriting. 4 something written; letter, paper, document, etc. 5 literary work; book, story, article, poem, etc. 6 profession or business of a person who writes. —*adj.* 1 that writes. 2 used to write with or on: *writing paper.*

writ of assistance, a search warrant issued without naming the place to be searched, used by British customs officials before the Revolutionary War.

writ ten (rit′n), *v.* a pp. of **write.**

Wrocław (vrôts′läf), *n.* city in SW Poland, formerly part of Germany. 509,000. Also, GERMAN **Breslau.**

wrong (rông, rong), *adj.* 1 not right; bad; unjust; unlawful: *It is wrong to tell lies.* 2 incorrect: *give a wrong answer.* 3 unsuitable; improper: *the wrong clothes for the occasion.* 4 in a bad state or condition; out of order; amiss: *Something is wrong with the car.* 5 not meant to be seen; less or least important: *Cloth often has a wrong side and a right side.* —*adv.* 1 in a wrong manner; in the wrong direction; badly. 2 **go wrong, a** turn out badly: *Everything went wrong today.* **b** stop being good and become bad. —*n.* 1 anything not right; wrong thing or action: *know right from wrong.* 2 injustice; injury: *You do an honest person a wrong to call him a liar.* 3 (in law) violation of law; tort. 4 **in the wrong,** wrong. —*v.t.* do wrong to; treat unjustly; injure: *He forgave those who had wronged him.* [Old English *wrang,* apparently < Scandinavian (Old Icelandic) *rangr* crooked] —**wrong′er,** *n.* —**wrong′ly,** *adv.* —**wrong′ness,** *n.*

wrong do er (rông′dü′ər, rong′dü′ər), *n.* person who does wrong.

wrong do ing (rông′dü′ing, rong′dü′ing), *n.* a doing wrong; evil; wrong.

wrong ful (rông′fəl, rong′fəl), *adj.* 1 wrong. 2 unlawful. —**wrong′ful ly,** *adv.* —**wrong′ful ness,** *n.*

wrong head ed (rông′hed′id, rong′hed′id), *adj.* 1 wrong in judgment or opinion. 2 stubborn even when wrong. —**wrong′head′ed ly,** *adv.* —**wrong′head′ed ness,** *n.*

wrote (rōt), *v.* a pt. of **write.**

wroth (rôth, roth), *adj.* angry. [Old English *wrāth*]

wrought (rôt), *v.* ARCHAIC. a pt. and a pp. of **work.** —*adj.* 1 made: *The gate was wrought with great skill.* 2 formed with care; not rough or crude. 3 manufactured or treated; not in a raw state. 4 (of metals or metalwork) formed by hammering.

wrought iron, a tough, durable form of iron with little carbon in it. Wrought iron will not break as easily as cast iron.

wrought-up (rôt′up′), *adj.* stirred up; excited.

wrung (rung), *v.* a pt. and pp. of **wring.**

wry (rī), *adj.*, **wri er, wri est.** 1 turned to one side; twisted: *She made a wry face to show her disgust.* 2 ironic: *wry humor.* [ultimately < Old English *wrīgian* to turn] —**wry′ly,** *adv.* —**wry′ness,** *n.*

wry neck (rī′nek′), *n.* 1 a twisted neck caused by unequal contraction of the muscles. 2 either of two species of Old World birds of the same family as the woodpeckers that habitually twist their necks and heads in a peculiar way.

WSW or **W.S.W.,** west-southwest.

wt., weight.

Wu chang (wü′chäng′), *n.* former city in E China, now part of Wuhan.

Wu han (wü′hän′), *n.* city in E China, on the Yangtze. 2,146,000.

Wu hsien (wü′shyen′), *n.* city in E China. 633,000. Also, **Soochow.**

Wun der kind (vůn′dər kint′), *n.*, *pl.* ***-kin der*** (-kin′dər). GERMAN. 1 a remarkably brilliant child; young prodigy. 2 (literally) wonder child.

Wundt (vůnt), *n.* **Wilhelm,** 1832-1920, German physiologist and psychologist.

Wup per tal (vůp′ər täl), *n.* city in W West Germany. 414,000.

wurst (wėrst, wůrst), *n.* a sausage. [< German *Wurst*]

Würt tem berg (wėr′təm bėrg′; *German* vʏr′təm berk), *n.* region in S West Germany.

Würz burg (wėrts′bėrg′; *German* vʏrts′bůrk), *n.* city in S West Germany, on the Main River. 120,000.

W. Va., West Virginia.

Wy., Wyoming.

Wy an dotte (wī′ən dot), *n.* any of an American breed of medium-sized, hardy domestic fowls.

Wy att (wī′ət), *n.* Sir **Thomas,** 1503?-1542, English poet, courtier, and diplomat.

Wych er ley (wich′ər lē), *n.* **William,** 1640?-1716, English dramatist.

Wyc liffe (wik′lif), *n.* **John,** 1320?-1384, English religious reformer who translated the Bible into English. Also, **Wickliffe, Wicklif.**

Wy eth (wī′əth), *n.* 1 **Andrew N.,** born 1917, American painter. 2 his father, **N(ewell) C.,** 1882-1945, American painter.

Wyo., Wyoming.

Wy o ming (wī ō′ming), *n.* one of the western states of the United States. 332,000 pop.; 97,900 sq. mi. *Capital:* Cheyenne. *Abbrev.:* Wyo. or Wy.

Wy o ming ite (wī ō′ming īt), *n.* native or inhabitant of Wyoming.

wy vern (wī′vərn), *n.* wivern.

X x

X or **x**[1] (eks), *n., pl.* **X's** or **x's.** 1 the 24th letter of the English alphabet. 2 an unknown quantity. 3 term often used to designate a person, thing, agency, factor, or the like whose true name is unknown or withheld. 4 anything shaped like an X. 5 the Roman numeral for 10.

x[2] (eks), *v.t.,* **x-ed** or **x'd, x-ing** or **x'ing.** 1 cross out with or as if with an x or x's: *She x-ed out the last word in the sentence.* 2 indicate or mark with an x: *He x-ed his answers in the little boxes on the test sheet.*

xan thic (zan′thik), *adj.* 1 yellow (applied especially in botany to a series of colors in flowers passing from yellow through orange to red). 2 of or having to do with xanthine.

xan thine (zan′thēn′, zan′thən), *n.* a crystalline, nitrogenous substance, present in the urine, blood, liver, and muscle tissue, and also in various plants. *Formula:* $C_5H_4N_4O_2$

Xan thip pe or **Xan tip pe** (zan tip′ē), *n.* 1 the wife of Socrates, famous as a scold. 2 a scolding woman; shrew.

xan tho phyll (zan′thō fil), *n.* a yellow pigment related to carotene, present in plant cells and thought to be a product of the decomposition of chlorophyll. *Formula:* $C_{40}H_{56}O_2$ [< Greek *xanthos* yellow + *phyllon* leaf]

xan thous (zan′thəs), *adj.* yellow. [< Greek *xanthos*]

Xa vi er (zā′vē ər, zav′ē ər), *n.* **Saint Francis,** 1506-1552, Spanish Jesuit missionary in the Far East.

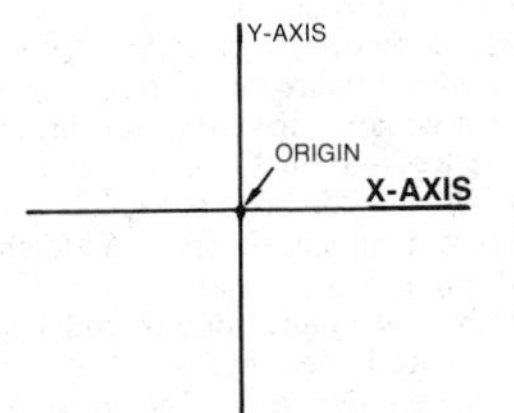

x-ax is (eks′ak′sis), *n.* the horizontal axis in a system of rectangular coordinates, as on a chart or graph.

X chromosome, one of the two chromosomes that determine sex. A fertilized egg cell containing two X chromosomes, one from each parent, develops into a female.

Xe, xenon.

xe bec (zē′bek), *n.* a small, three-masted vessel of the Mediterranean. Also, **zebec.** [ultimately < Arabic *shabbāk*]

xen o lith (zen′l ith), *n.* fragment of older rock embedded in an igneous mass. [< Greek *xenos* strange + *lithos* rock]

xe non (zē′non), *n.* a heavy, colorless, odorless, inert gaseous element, present in very small quantities in the air and used in filling flashbulbs, vacuum tubes, etc. It forms compounds with fluorine and oxygen. *Symbol:* Xe; *atomic number* 54. See pages 326 and 327 for table. [< Greek, neuter of *xenos* strange]

xen o phobe (zen′ə fōb), *n.* person who fears or hates foreigners or strangers.

xen o pho bi a (zen′ə fō′bē ə), *n.* hatred or fear of foreigners or strangers. [< Greek *xenos* stranger + *phobos* fear]

xen o pho bic (zen′ə fō′bik), *adj.* of or having to do with xenophobia.

Xen o phon (zen′ə fən), *n.* 434?-355? B.C., Greek historian and military leader.

xer ic (zir′ik), *adj.* in botany: 1 lacking moisture: *xeric varieties of wheat.* 2 xerophytic.

xer o graph ic (zir′ə graf′ik), *adj.* of or having to do with xerography.

xe rog ra phy (zi rog′rə fē), *n.* a dry process for making copies of letters, pictures, etc., by using electrically charged particles to make a positive photographic contact print. Paper is placed on a metal plate sprayed with electrons before exposure and dusted with black powder, and the image is transferred to the paper by heat. [< Greek *xēros* dry + English *-graphy*]

xer o phyte (zir′ə fīt), *n.* plant that loses very little water and can grow in deserts or very dry ground. Cactuses, sagebrush, century plants, etc., are xerophytes. [< Greek *xēros* dry + English *-phyte*]

xer o phyt ic (zir′ə fit′ik), *adj.* of or having to do with a xerophyte. **—xer′o phyt′i cal ly,** *adv.*

Xer ox (zir′oks), *n.* trademark for a xerographic process of making copies of letters, pictures, etc.

Xerx es (zėrk′sēz′), *n.* 519?-465 B.C., king of ancient Persia from 486? to 465 B.C. He tried to conquer Greece but was defeated in 480 B.C.

xi (sī, zī, ksē), *n.* the 14th letter of the Greek alphabet (Ξ, ξ).

Xin gú River (shing gü′), river flowing from central Brazil into the Amazon River. 1300 mi.

xi particle, a hyperon, either neutral or negative, present in cosmic rays.

xiph oid (zif′oid), *adj.* shaped like or resembling a sword: *a xiphoid bone.* [< Greek *xiphos* sword]

X-ir ra di ate (eks′i rā′dē āt), *v.t.,* **-at ed, -at ing.** to subject to the action of X rays. **—X′-ir ra′di a′tion,** *n.*

XL, extra large.

Xmas (kris′məs, ek′sməs), *n.* Christmas.

Xn., Christian.

X-ra di a tion (eks′rā dē ā′shən), *n.* 1 X rays. 2 examination, treatment, etc., with X rays.

X ray, 1 an electromagnetic ray with an extremely short wavelength, that can penetrate opaque substances, formed when cathode rays impinge upon a solid body (such as the wall of a vacuum tube); Roentgen ray. X rays are used to locate breaks in bones, bullets lodged in the body, etc., and to diagnose and treat certain diseases. See **radiation** for table. 2 picture made by means of X rays.

X-ray (eks′rā′), *v.t.* examine, photograph, or treat with X rays. *—adj.* of, by, or having to do with X rays: *an X-ray examination of one's teeth.*

X-ray astronomy, the study of X-ray stars.

X-ray diffraction, the diffusion of X rays on contact with matter, when changes in radiation intensity as a result of differences in atomic structure within the matter, used in studying atomic and molecular structure.

hat, āge, fär; let, ēqual, tėrm;
it, īce; hot, ōpen, ôrder;
oil, out; cup, pu̇t, rüle;
ch, child; ng, long; sh, she;
th, thin; ᴛʜ, then; zh, measure;

ə represents *a* in about, *e* in taken, *i* in pencil, *o* in lemon, *u* in circus.

< = from, derived from, taken from.

X-ray star, any of a group of stellar bodies that emit X rays.

X-ray tube, vacuum tube for generating X rays.

xy lem (zī′lem), *n.* tissue in a vascular plant, consisting essentially of woody fibers, tracheids, and parenchymatous cells, through which water and dissolved minerals pass upward from the roots, and which provides support for the plant. [< German *Xylem* < Greek *xylon* wood]

xy lene (zī′lēn′), *n.* one of three isomeric, colorless, liquid hydrocarbons present in coal and wood tar, naphtha, etc. Commercial xylene is a mixture of all three, and is used in making dyes, as a raw material for polyester fibers, etc.; xylol. *Formula:* $C_6H_4(CH_3)_2$

xy lol (zī′lōl, zī′lol), *n.* xylene.

xylophone

xy lo phone (zī′lə fōn), *n.* a musical instrument consisting of two rows of wooden bars of varying lengths, which are sounded by striking them with small wooden hammers. [< Greek *xylon* wood + *phōnē* sound]

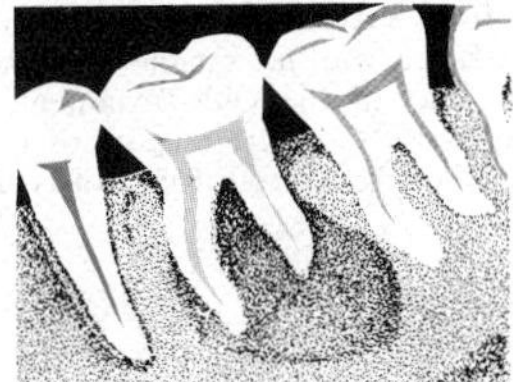
X ray (def. 2) of an abscessed tooth. The abscess is shown by the dark area around the roots of the tooth.

xy lo phon ist (zī′lə fō′nist), *n.* person who plays on a xylophone.

xy lose (zī′lōs), *n.* a crystalline, pentose sugar present in woody plants. *Formula:* $C_5H_{10}O_5$

Y or **y** (wī), *n., pl.* **Y's** or **y's.** 1 the 25th letter of the English alphabet. 2 anything shaped like a Y.

Y, yttrium.

y., 1 yard or yards. 2 year.

-y[1], *suffix forming adjectives chiefly from nouns.* 1 full of ____: *Bumpy = full of bumps.* 2 containing ____: *Salty = containing salt.* 3 having ____: *Cloudy = having clouds.* 4 characterized by ____: *Funny = characterized by fun.* 5 somewhat ____: *Chilly = somewhat chill.* 6 inclined to ____: *Sleepy = inclined to sleep.* 7 resembling or suggesting ____: *Sugary = resembling sugar.* 8 In certain words, such as *paly, steepy, stilly, vasty,* the addition of *y* does not change the meaning. [Old English *-ig*]

-y[2], *suffix forming nouns from other nouns.* 1 small ____: *Dolly = a small doll.* 2 dear ____: *Daddy = dear dad.* [Middle English]

-y[3], *suffix forming nouns from adjectives, nouns, and verbs.* 1 ____ condition or quality: *Jealousy = a jealous condition or quality.* 2 condition or quality of being ____: *Victory = condition or quality of being a victor.* 3 act or activity of ____ing: *Delivery = act of delivering.* [< Old French *-ie* < Latin *-ia* < Greek]

yacht (yot), *n.* boat equipped with sails or engines, or both, used for pleasure trips or racing. *—v.i.* sail or race on a yacht. [< earlier Dutch *jaght* < *jaghtschip* chasing ship]

yacht ing (yot′ing), *n.* 1 art of sailing a yacht. 2 pastime of sailing on a yacht.

yachts man (yots′mən), *n., pl.* **-men.** man who owns or sails a yacht.

yachts man ship (yots′mən ship), *n.* skill or ability in handling a yacht.

yack (yak), SLANG. *—v.i.* talk endlessly and foolishly; chatter. *—n.* endless, foolish talk. Also, **yak.** [imitative]

yah (yä), *interj.* an exclamation of derision, disgust, or impatience.

Ya hoo (yä′hü, yä hü′), *n.* 1 a brute in human shape in Swift's *Gulliver's Travels* who works for a race of intelligent horses. 2 **yahoo,** a rough, coarse, or uncouth person.

Yah veh or **Yah ve** (yä′vā), *n.* Yahweh.

Yah weh (yä′wā), *n.* a name of God in the Hebrew text of the Old Testament, often used by writers on the religion of the Hebrews; Jehovah. Also, **Jahve, Jahveh.**

yak[1]—5 to 6 ft. high at the shoulder

yak[1] (yak), *n.* a long-haired ox of Tibet and central Asia. The domesticated yak is raised for its meat, milk, and hair and is used as a beast of burden. [< Tibetan *gyag*]

yak[2] (yak), *v.i.,* **yakked, yak king,** *n.* SLANG. yack.

Yal ta (yôl′tə), *n.* seaport and winter resort in S Crimea, on the Black Sea. 55,000.

Ya lu River (yä′lü), river in E Asia, between Manchuria and North Korea. 500 mi.

yam (yam), *n.* 1 vine of warm regions with a starchy, tuberous root much like the sweet potato. 2 its root, eaten as a vegetable. 3 U.S. the sweet potato. [< Spanish *ñame,* ultimately < Senegalese *nyami* eat]

yam mer (yam′ər), *v.i.* 1 whine; whimper. 2 howl; yell. *—v.t.* say in a querulous tone. *—n.* a yammering. [Middle English *yomeren,* Old English *gēomrian* to lament]

yang (yang), *n.* the positive element in Chinese dualistic philosophy, representing the male qualities of light and the earth, in constant interaction with its opposing principle (yin). [< Chinese]

Yang (yang), *n.* **Chen Ning,** born 1922, American physicist, born in China.

Yang tse River (yang′tsē), Yangtze River.

Yang tze Ki ang (yang′tsē kē ang′), Yangtze River.

Yang tze River (yang′tsē), river flowing from Tibet through central China into the China Sea. It is the longest river in China. 3200 mi.

yank (yangk), INFORMAL. *—v.t., v.i.* pull with a sudden motion; jerk; tug. *—n.* a sudden pull; jerk; tug. [origin uncertain]

Yank (yangk), *n., adj.* SLANG. Yankee.

Yan kee (yang′kē), *n.* 1 native of New England. 2 native of any part of the northern United States. 3 (in the southern United States) a Northerner (often used in an unfriendly way). 4 native or inhabitant of the United States; American. *—adj.* of or having to do with Yankees: *Yankee shrewdness.* [probably ultimately < Dutch *Jan Kees* John Cheese, nickname for Dutch and English settlers, the *-s* being taken for plural ending]

Yan kee dom (yang′kē dəm), *n.* 1 Yankees collectively. 2 region inhabited by Yankees.

Yankee Doo dle (dü′dl), an American song, probably of English origin and taken over by the American soldiers in the Revolutionary War.

yan qui or ***Yan qui*** (yäng′kē), *n.* SPANISH. Yankee; a native of the United States.

Ya oun dé (yä ün dā′), *n.* capital of Cameroon, in the SW part. 130,000.

yap (yap), *n., v.,* **yapped, yap ping.** *—n.* 1 a snappish bark; yelp. 2 SLANG. **a** snappish, noisy, or foolish talk. **b** a peevish or noisy person. **c** mouth. *—v.i.* 1 bark snappishly; yelp. 2 SLANG. talk snappishly, noisily, or foolishly. [imitative]

Yap Islands (yäp, yap), group of 14 islands forming part of the Caroline Islands in the W Pacific. 4000 pop.; 39 sq. mi.

Ya qui (yä′kē), *n.* member of a tribe of American Indians in northwestern Mexico and Arizona. *—adj.* of this tribe of Indians.

yard[1] (yärd), *n.* 1 piece of ground near or around a house, barn, school, etc. 2 piece of enclosed ground for some special purpose or business: *a chicken yard.* 3 space with tracks where railroad cars are stored, shifted around, etc. 4 U.S. AND CANADA. area in which moose and deer gather for feeding during the winter. *—v.t.* put into or enclose in a yard. [Old English *geard* enclosure]

yard[2] (def. 2) mast with two yards

yard[2] (yärd), *n.* 1 measure of length, equal to 36 inches or 3 feet. See **measure** for table. 2 a long, slender beam or pole fastened across a mast, used to support a sail. [Old English *gerd* rod]

yard age[1] (yär′dij), *n.* 1 the use of a railroad yard or enclosure, as for storing freight or cattle. 2 the charge for such use. [< *yard*[1]]

yard age[2] (yär′dij), *n.* 1 length in yards. 2 amount measured in yards. [< *yard*[2]]

yard arm (yärd′ärm′), *n.* either end of a long, slender beam or pole used to support a square sail.

yard goods, cloth cut to measure and sold by the yard.

yard man (yärd′mən), *n., pl.* **-men.** man who has charge of, or works in, a yard, as a railroad yard.

yard mas ter (yärd′mas′tər), *n.* man in charge of a railroad yard.

yard stick (yärd′stik′), *n.* 1 stick one yard long, used for measuring. 2 any standard of judgment or comparison; criterion; gauge.

yar mul ke (yär′məl kə), *n.* skullcap worn by Jewish men and boys especially for prayer and ceremonial occasions. [< Yiddish < Polish *yarmulka,* kind of hat]

yarn (yärn), *n.* 1 any spun thread, especially that prepared for weaving or knitting. 2 INFORMAL. tale; story: *The old sailor made up his yarns as he told them.* *—v.i.* INFORMAL. tell stories. [Old English *gearn*]

yarn-dyed (yärn′dīd′), *adj.* made from yarn that was dyed before weaving.

yar row (yar′ō), *n.* a common herb of the composite family, with finely divided leaves and flat clusters of white or pink flowers; milfoil. [Old English *gearwe*]

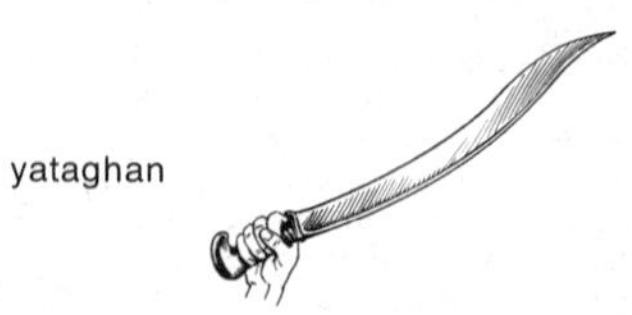

yataghan

yat a ghan (yat′ə gan), *n.* sword used by Moslems, having no guard for the hand and no crosspiece, but usually a large pommel. [< Turkish *yatağan*]

yaup (yôp, yäp), *v.i., n.* DIALECT or INFORMAL. yawp.

yaw (yô), *v.i.* 1 turn from a straight course;

hat, āge, fär; let, ēqual, tėrm;
it, īce; hot, ōpen, ôrder;
oil, out; cup, pu̇t, rüle;
ch, child; ng, long; sh, she;
th, thin; ᴛʜ, then; zh, measure;

ə represents *a* in about, *e* in taken, *i* in pencil, *o* in lemon, *u* in circus.

< = from, derived from, taken from.

go unsteadily. 2 (of an aircraft) turn from a straight course by a motion about its vertical axis. *—n.* movement from a straight course. [origin uncertain]

yawl[1] (yôl), *n.* 1 boat like a sloop with a second short mast set near the stern. 2 a ship's boat rowed by four or six oars. [< Dutch *jol*]

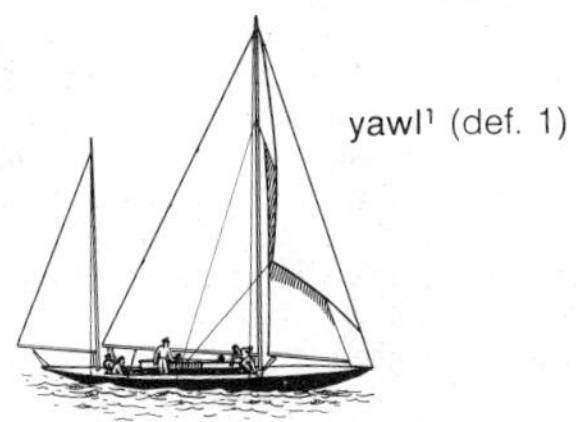
yawl[1] (def. 1)

yawl[2] (yôl), *n., v.i., v.t.* DIALECT. yowl.

yawn (yôn), *v.i.* 1 open the mouth wide because one is sleepy, tired, or bored. 2 open wide; gape: *A wide gorge yawned in front of us.* *—v.t.* utter with a yawn; cause by yawning. *—n.* a yawning. [Old English *geonian*] **—yawn′er,** *n.*

yawp (yôp, yäp), DIALECT or INFORMAL. *—v.i.* 1 utter a loud, harsh cry. 2 speak foolishly. *—n.* a loud, harsh cry. Also, **yaup.** [imitative] **—yawp′er,** *n.*

yaws (yôz), *n.* a contagious tropical disease characterized by sores on the skin, caused by a spirochete. [of Carib origin]

y-ax is (wī′ak′sis), *n.* the vertical axis in a system of rectangular coordinates, as on a chart or graph. See **x-axis** for diagram.

Yb, ytterbium.

Y chromosome, one of the two chromosomes that determine sex. A fertilized egg cell containing a Y chromosome develops into a male.

y clept or **y cleped** (i klept′), *adj.* ARCHAIC. called; named; styled. [Old English *geclipod* named]

yd., *pl.* **yd.** or **yds.** yard.

ye[1] (yē; *unstressed* yi), *pron. pl.* ARCHAIC. you. [Old English *gē*]

ye[2] (ᴛʜē; *incorrectly* yē), *definite article.* an old way of writing the definite article "the." [from the fact that the letter *y* was used by printers instead of the Old English letter þ, which stood for the sound *th*]

yea (yā), *adv.* 1 yes (used in affirmation or assent). 2 indeed; truly (used to introduce a sentence or clause). 3 ARCHAIC. not only that, but also; moreover. *—n.* 1 an affirmative answer. 2 an affirmative vote or voter. [Old English *gēa*]

yean (yēn), *v.t., v.i.* (of a sheep or goat) give birth to (young). [Old English *(ge)ēanian*]

yean ling (yēn′ling), *n.* the young of a sheep or a goat; lamb or kid.

year (yir), *n.* 1 12 months or 365 days (366 in leap years); January 1 to December 31. 2 12 months reckoned from any point. A fiscal year is a period of 12 months at the end of which the accounts of a government, business, etc., are balanced. 3 the part of a year spent in a certain activity: *Our school year is 9 months.* 4 period of the earth's revolution around the sun; astronomical year. 5 the time in which any planet completes its revolution round the sun. 6 **years,** *pl.* **a** age. **b** a very long time. 7 **year after year,** every year. 8 **year by year,** with each succeeding year; as years go by. 9 **year in, year out,** always; continuously. [Old English *gēar*]

year book (yir′bu̇k′), *n.* book or report published every year. Yearbooks often report facts of the year. The graduating class of a school or college usually publishes a yearbook, with pictures of its members.

year ling (yir′ling), *n.* 1 an animal one year old. 2 (in horse racing) a horse in the second calendar year since it was foaled. *—adj.* one year old: *a yearling colt.*

year long (yir′lông′, yir′long′), *adj.* 1 lasting for a year. 2 lasting for years.

year ly (yir′lē), *adj.* 1 once a year; in every year: *a yearly trip to Europe.* 2 lasting a year: *The earth makes a yearly revolution around the sun.* 3 for a year: *a yearly salary of $10,000.* *—adv.* once a year; in every year; annually.

yearn (yėrn), *v.i.* 1 feel a longing or desire; desire earnestly: *He yearns for home.* 2 feel pity; have tender feelings: *Her heart yearned for the starving children.* [Old English *giernan*]

yearn ing (yėr′ning), *n.* earnest or strong desire; longing. **—yearn′ing ly,** *adv.*

year-round (yir′round′), *adj., adv.* throughout the year.

yeast (yēst), *n.* 1 the substance that causes dough for bread to rise and beer to ferment. It is a yellowish froth made up of masses of tiny one-celled fungi which grow quickly in a liquid containing sugar and cause fermentation. 2 any of the fungi which form yeast; a yeast plant or yeast cell. 3 yeast cake. 4 influence, element, etc., that acts as a leaven. 5 foam; froth. [Old English *gist*] **—yeast′like′,** *adj.*

yeast cake, flour or meal mixed with yeast and pressed into a small cake.

yeast y (yē′stē), *adj.,* **yeast i er, yeast i est.** 1 of, containing, or resembling yeast. 2 frothy or foamy: *yeasty waves.* 3 light or trifling; frivolous.

Yeats (yāts), *n.* **William Butler,** 1865-1939, Irish poet, playwright, and essayist.

yegg (yeg), *n.* SLANG. 1 burglar who robs safes. 2 any burglar. [origin uncertain]

yell (yel), *v.i.* cry out with a strong, loud sound. *—v.t.* say with a yell. *—n.* 1 a strong, loud outcry. 2 U.S. a special shout or cheer used by a school or college to encourage its sports teams. [Old English *giellan*] **—yell′er,** *n.*

yel low (yel′ō), *n.* 1 the color of gold, butter, or ripe lemons. 2 a yellow pigment or dye. 3 yellow cloth or clothing. 4 yolk of an egg. *—adj.* 1 having the color yellow; of the color yellow. 2 having a yellowish skin. 3 jealous; envious. 4 INFORMAL. cowardly. 5 characterized by sensational or lurid writing or presentation of the news: *yellow journalism.* *—v.i.* become yellow: *Paper yellows with age.* *—v.t.* make yellow. [Old English *geolu*] **—yel′low ness,** *n.*

yel low bird (yel′ō bėrd′), *n.* 1 the goldfinch of America. 2 yellow warbler. 3 any of various other yellow birds.

yel low-dog contract (yel′ō dôg′, yel′ō-dog′), U.S. an agreement between employer and employee that the worker will not join or assist a labor union. Yellow-dog contracts were made illegal in 1932.

yellow fever, a dangerous, infectious disease of warm climates, caused by a virus transmitted by an aëdes mosquito, and characterized by chills, high fever, jaundice, etc.; yellow jack.

yel low ham mer (yel′ō ham′ər), *n.* 1 a European bunting with a bright-yellow head, neck, and breast. 2 U.S. the flicker of eastern North America. [earlier *yelambre* < Old English *geolu* yellow + *amore,* kind of bird]

yel low ish (yel′ō ish), *adj.* somewhat yellow.

yellow jack, 1 yellow fever. 2 a yellow flag used as a signal of quarantine. 3 fish of the West Indies and Florida, related to the pompano.

yellow jacket, any of various small wasps having bright-yellow markings.

yel low legs (yel′ō legz′), *n.* either of two American shore birds with yellow legs.

yellow metal, 1 gold. 2 a yellowish alloy containing copper and zinc.

yellow peril, the alleged danger to the rest of the world from the growth and activities of Japan or China.

yellow pine, 1 any of various American pines with yellowish wood. 2 the wood of any of these trees.

Yellow River, Hwang Ho.

Yellow Sea, part of the Pacific Ocean between NE China and Korea.

yellow spot, a yellowish depression on the retina constituting the region of most distinct vision.

Yel low stone (yel′ō stōn′), *n.* 1 Yellowstone National Park. 2 **Yellowstone River,** river flowing from NW Wyoming through Yellowstone National Park and Montana into the Missouri River in North Dakota. 671 mi.

Yellowstone National Park, a large national park, mostly in NW Wyoming, famous for its scenery, hot springs, and geysers. 3458 sq. mi.

yel low tail (yel′ō tāl′), *n., pl.* **-tails** or **-tail.** any of various fishes with yellow tails, especially a game fish of the California coast, and a snapper of the Atlantic coast of tropical America.

yel low throat (yel′ō thrōt′), *n.* any of certain North American warblers, especially one with olive-brown upper parts and yellow throat.

yellow warbler, a small American warbler; yellowbird. The male has yellow plumage streaked with brown.

yel low wood (yel′ō wu̇d′), *n.* 1 any of several trees yielding yellow wood or a yellow extract or dye. 2 the wood of any of these trees.

yelp (yelp), *n.* the quick, sharp bark or cry of a dog, fox, etc. *—v.i.* give a quick, sharp bark or cry. *—v.t.* utter with a yelp. [Old English *gielpan* to boast] **—yelp′er,** *n.*

Yem en (yem′ən), *n.* 1 country in SW Arabia. 5,730,000 pop.; 75,300 sq. mi. *Capital:* Sana. See **Oman** for map. 2 **People's Democratic Republic of Yemen,** official name of **Southern Yemen.**

Yem e ni (yem′ə nē), *n., pl.* **-ni** or **-nis,** *adj.* Yemenite.

Yem en ite (yem′ə nīt), *n.* native or inhabitant of Yemen. *—adj.* of or having to do with Yemen or its people.

yen[1] (yen), *n., pl.* **yen.** the monetary unit of Japan, a coin or note equal to 100 sen and worth about 1/3 of a cent. [< Japanese < Chinese *yüan* round object]

yen[2] (yen), *n., v.,* **yenned, yen ning.** INFORMAL. —*n.* 1 a sharp desire or hunger; urgent fancy: *a yen to fly a plane.* 2 **have a yen for,** desire. —*v.i.* have a yen; desire sharply or urgently. [perhaps < a local pronunciation of *yearn*]

Yen i sei River (yen′ə sā′), river flowing from central Soviet Union into the Arctic Ocean. 2350 mi.

yeo man (yō′mən), *n., pl.* **-men.** 1 (in the United States Navy) a petty officer who performs clerical duties. 2 (formerly, in Great Britain) a person who owned land, but not a large amount, and usually farmed it himself. 3 ARCHAIC. servant or attendant of a lord or king. [Middle English *yoman*]

yeo man ly (yō′mən lē), *adj.* having to do with or suitable for a yeoman; sturdy; honest. —*adv.* like a yeoman; bravely.

yeoman of the guard, member of the bodyguard of the English sovereign, first appointed in 1485 by Henry VII and consisting of 100 men who still wear the uniform of the 1400's and whose duties are now purely ceremonial; beefeater.

yeo man ry (yō′mən rē), *n.* 1 yeomen. 2 a British volunteer cavalry force, now a part of the Territorial Army.

yeoman's service or **yeoman service,** good, useful service; faithful support or assistance.

Yer e van (yer′e vän′), *n.* capital of the Armenian S.S.R., in the W part. 767,000. Also, **Erivan.**

yes (yes), *adv., n., pl.* **yes es** or **yes ses,** *v.,* **yessed, yes sing.** —*adv.* 1 word used to express agreement, consent, or affirmation: *Will you go? Yes.* 2 and what is more; in addition to that: *The boy learned to endure—yes, even to enjoy—the hardships of a sailor's life.* —*n.* 1 an answer that agrees, consents, or affirms. 2 a vote for; person voting in favor of something. —*v.i., v.t.* say yes. [Old English *gēse* < *gēa* yea + *sī* be it]

➤ **Yes** and **no,** as adverbs, may modify a sentence *(Yes, you're right)* or may have the value of a coordinate clause *(No; but you should have told me)* or may stand as complete sentences *("Do you really intend to go with him?" "Yes.")*.

Ye shi va (yə shē′və), *n., pl.* **Ye shi vas, Ye shi voth** (yə shē′vōt′). 1 a Jewish school for higher studies, often a rabbinical seminary. 2 a Jewish elementary school or high school in which both religious and secular subjects are taught. [< Hebrew *yĕshībāh,* literally, a sitting]

yes man (yes′man′), *n., pl.* **-men.** INFORMAL. person who habitually agrees with his employer, superior officer, party, etc., without criticism.

yes ter day (yes′tər dē, yes′tər dā), *n.* 1 the day before today. 2 the recent past: *We are often amused by the fashions of yesterday.* —*adv.* 1 on the day before today. 2 a short time ago; recently. [Old English *geostrandæg* < *geostran* yesterday + *dæg* day]

yes ter night (yes′tər nīt′), *n., adv.* ARCHAIC. last night; the night before today.

yes ter year (yes′tər yir′), *n., adv.* 1 ARCHAIC. last year; the year before this. 2 **of yesteryear,** of yore.

yes treen (yes′trēn′), *n., adv.* SCOTTISH. yesterday evening.

yet (yet), *adv.* 1 up to the present time; thus far: *The work is not yet finished.* 2 at this time; now: *Don't go yet.* 3 at that time; then: *It was not yet dark.* 4 even now; still: *She is talking yet.* 5 sometime: *We may go there yet.* 6 also; again: *Yet once more I forbid you to go.* 7 moreover: *He won't do it for you nor yet for me.* 8 even: *The judge spoke yet more harshly.* 9 nevertheless; however; but: *The story was strange, yet true.* 10 **as yet,** up to now. —*conj.* nevertheless; however; but: *The work is good, yet it could be better.* [Old English *giet*]

Ye ti (ye′tē), *n., pl.* **-ti.** Abominable Snowman. [< Tibetan]

Yev tu shen ko (yef′tü shen′kō), *n.* **Yevgeny,** born 1933, Russian poet.

yew (yü), *n.* 1 any of a genus of evergreen coniferous trees, especially a common species of Europe and Asia having heavy, elastic wood. 2 the wood of this tree, especially as the material of bows. 3 an archer's bow made of this. [Old English *īw*]

Ygg dra sil (ig′drə sil), *n.* (in Scandinavian myths) the ash tree whose branches and roots bind together earth, heaven, and hell.

Yid dish (yid′ish), *n.* language which developed from a dialect of Middle High German, containing many Hebrew and Slavic words, and written in Hebrew characters. Yiddish is spoken mainly by Jews of eastern and central Europe and their descendants. —*adj.* having to do with Yiddish. [ultimately < Middle High German *jüdisch* Jewish]

yield (yēld), *v.t.* 1 produce; bear: *Land yields crops; mines yield ore.* 2 give in return; bring in: *an investment which yielded a large profit.* 3 give; grant: *Her mother yielded her consent to the plan.* 4 surrender: *yield oneself up to the mercy of the enemy.* 5 ARCHAIC. pay; reward. —*v.i.* 1 bear produce; be productive. 2 give up; surrender: *The enemy yielded to our soldiers.* See synonym study below. 3 give way: *The door yielded to his push.* 4 give place: *We yield to nobody in love of freedom.* —*n.* amount yielded; product: *This year's yield from the silver mine was very large.* [Old English *gieldan* to pay] —**yield′er,** *n.*

Syn. *v.i.* 2 **Yield, submit** mean give up or give in before a stronger force. **Yield** implies giving up a contest of any sort under pressure: *yield to persuasive arguments.* **Submit** implies giving up all resistance and passively accepting defeat: *submit to overwhelming forces, submit to the inevitable.*

yield ing (yēl′ding), *adj.* 1 not resisting; submissive. 2 not stiff or rigid; easily bent, twisted, etc.; flexible.

yin (yin), *n.* the negative element in Chinese dualistic philosophy, representing the female qualities of darkness and the sky, in constant interaction with its opposing force (yang). [< Chinese]

yip (yip), *v.,* **yipped, yip ping,** *n.* INFORMAL. —*v.i.* (especially of dogs) bark or yelp briskly. —*n.* a sharp barking sound. [imitative]

yip pee (yip′ē), *interj.* shout of great joy.

-yl, *combining form.* (in chemistry) a radical, as in *alkyl, acetyl, carbonyl.* [< French *-yle* < Greek *hylē* stuff, matter, wood]

Y.M.C.A., Young Men's Christian Association.

Y.M.H.A., Young Men's Hebrew Association.

yo del (yō′dl), *v.,* **-deled, -del ing** or **-delled, -del ling,** *n.* —*v.t., v.i.* sing with frequent changes from the ordinary voice to a forced shrill voice or falsetto and back again, in the manner of mountaineers of Switzerland and the Tirol. —*n.* act or sound of yodeling. [< German *jodeln*] —**yo′deler, yo′del ler,** *n.*

yo dle (yō′dl), *v.t., v.i.,* **-dled, -dling,** *n.* yodel. —**yo′dler,** *n.*

yo ga or **Yo ga** (yō′gə), *n.* 1 system of Hindu religious philosophy that requires certain ascetic practices, abstract meditation, and intense mental concentration as a means of attaining a state of union with the universal spirit. 2 system of physical exercises and positions used in yoga. [< Hindustani < Sanskrit, union]

yo ghurt (yō′gərt), *n.* yogurt.

yo gi (yō′gē), *n.* person who practices or follows yoga.

yo gurt (yō′gərt), *n.* a kind of thickened, slightly fermented liquid food made from milk acted upon by bacteria. [< Turkish *yoğurt*]

yo-heave-ho (yō′hēv′hō′), *interj.* exclamation used by sailors in pulling or lifting together.

yoicks (yoiks), *interj.* BRITISH. cry used to urge on the hounds in fox hunting.

yoke (def. 1)

yoke (yōk), *n., v.,* **yoked, yok ing.** —*n.* 1 a wooden frame to fasten two work animals together. 2 pair fastened together by a yoke: *The plow was drawn by a yoke of oxen.* 3 any frame connecting two other parts: *She carried two buckets on a yoke, one at each end.* 4 part of a garment fitting the neck and shoulders closely. 5 a top piece to a skirt, fitting the hips. 6 clamp which holds two parts firmly in place. 7 something that joins or unites; bond; tie. 8 something that holds people in slavery or submission: *Throw off your yoke and be free.* 9 rule; dominion: *a country under the yoke of a dictator.* —*v.t.* 1 put a yoke on; fasten with a yoke. 2 harness or fasten a work animal or animals to. 3 join; unite: *be yoked in marriage.* —*v.i.* be joined or united. [Old English *geoc*]

yoke fel low (yōk′fel′ō), *n.* 1 person associated with another in a task; partner. 2 husband or wife.

yo kel (yō′kəl), *n.* a country fellow; bumpkin; rustic. [origin uncertain]

yoke mate (yōk′māt′), *n.* yokefellow.

Yo ko ha ma (yō′kə hä′mə), *n.* seaport in central Japan, near Tokyo. 2,082,000.

yolk (yōk, yōlk), *n.* 1 the yellow internal part of an egg of a bird or reptile, surrounded by the albumen or white, and serving as nourishment for the young before it is hatched; yellow. 2 the corresponding part in any animal ovum or egg cell, which serves for the nutrition of the embryo. 3 fat or grease in sheep's wool. [Old English *geolca* < *geolu* yellow]

yolk y (yō′kē, yōl′kē), *adj.,* **yolk i er, yolk i est.** resembling or consisting of yolk.

Yom Kip pur (yom kip′ər), a Jewish fast day of atonement for sins; Day of Atonement. It occurs ten days after Rosh Hashanah, the Jewish New Year. [< Hebrew *yōm kippūr* day of atonement]

yon (yon), *adj., adv.* ARCHAIC. yonder. [Old English *geon*]

yond (yond), *adj., adv.* ARCHAIC. yonder. [Old English *geond*]

yon der (yon′dər), *adv.* within sight, but not near; over there: *Look yonder.* —*adj.* 1 situated over there; being within sight, but not near: *They live in yonder cottage.* 2 farther; more distant; other: *There is snow on the yonder side of the mountains.* [Middle English]

Yon kers (yong′kərz), *n.* city in SE New York State, just north of New York City. 204,000.

yore (yôr, yōr), *adv., n.* **1 of yore, a** now long since gone; long past: *in days of yore.* **b** of long ago; formerly; in the past: *prouder than of yore.* 2 OBSOLETE. long ago; years ago. [Old English *geāra,* related to *gēar* year]

York (yôrk), *n.* 1 the royal house of England from 1461 to 1485. Its emblem was a white rose. 2 **Duke of.** See **Langley, Edmund.** 3 city in NE England. 107,000. 4 Yorkshire.

York ist (yôr′kist), *n.* supporter or member of the royal house of York. —*adj.* 1 of or having to do with the royal house of York. 2 of or having to do with the party that fought against the Lancastrians.

York shire (yôrk′shər, yôrk′shir), *n.* county in NE England; York.

Yorkshire pudding, a batter cake made of milk, flour, egg, and salt, baked in the drippings of, and often served with, roast beef.

Yorkshire terrier
about 8 in. high at the shoulder

Yorkshire terrier, one of an English breed of small, shaggy dogs with a steel-blue coat, weighing 4 to 8 pounds.

York town (yôrk′toun), *n.* village in SE Virginia, where Lord Cornwallis surrendered to George Washington in 1781.

Yo sem i te (yō sem′ə tē), *n.* 1 Yosemite National Park. 2 a very deep valley in this park, famous for its lofty, scenic falls. 8 mi. long.

Yosemite Falls, series of waterfalls in Yosemite National Park. Total height 2526 ft.

Yosemite National Park, national park in E California, in the Sierra Nevada. 1182 sq. mi.

Yo shi hi to (yō′shē hē′tō), *n.* 1879-1926, emperor of Japan from 1912 to 1926.

you (yü; *unstressed* yu̇, yə), *pron. sing. or pl.* 1 the person or persons spoken to: *Are you ready? Then you may go.* 2 one; anybody: *You push this button to get a light.* [Old English *ēow,* dative and accusative of *gē* ye[1]]
➔ **You** is used as an indefinite pronoun in informal English: *It's a good book, if you like detective stories.* In formal English *one* is more usual, though the prejudice against *you* is declining.
➔ **you all.** In Southern American *you all,* contracted to *y'all,* is frequently used as the plural of *you,* as in some other regions *yous* or *youse* is used. It is also used when addressing one person regarded as one of a group, usually a family, but rarely, if ever, in addressing one person alone.

you'd (yüd; *unstressed* yu̇d, yəd), 1 you had. 2 you would.

you'll (yül; *unstressed* yu̇l, yəl), 1 you will. 2 you shall.

young (yung), *adj.,* **young er** (yung′gər), **young est** (yung′gist), *n.* —*adj.* 1 in the early part of life or growth; not old: *A puppy is a young dog.* See synonym study below. 2 having the looks or qualities of youth or a young person: *She looks young for her age.* 3 of youth; early: *one's young days.* 4 not as old as another or the other: *Young Mr. Jones worked for his father.* 5 in an early stage; not far advanced: *The night was still young when they left the party.* 6 without much experience or practice: *I was too young in the trade to be successful.* —*n.* 1 young offspring: *An animal will fight to protect its young.* 2 **the young,** young people. 3 **with young,** pregnant. [Old English *geong*] —**young′ness,** *n.*
Syn. *adj.* 1 **Young, youthful, juvenile** mean of or like persons between childhood and adulthood. **Young,** the general term, is most often used to refer directly to a person's age: *They are too young to marry.* **Youthful** emphasizes having the qualities of a young person, especially the more appealing ones such as freshness, vitality, and optimism: *With youthful earnestness, the students debated the problems of the world.* **Juvenile** emphasizes immaturity: *That book is too juvenile for a high-school senior.*

Young (yung), *n.* 1 **Brigham,** 1801-1877, American Mormon leader. 2 **Whitney,** 1921-1971, American civil rights leader.

young ber ry (yung′ber′ē, yung′bər ē), *n., pl.* **-ries.** the large, sweet, purplish-black fruit of a trailing bramble, a hybrid between a blackberry and dewberry, grown largely in the southwestern United States. [< B. M. *Young,* American fruit grower]

young blood, 1 young people. 2 youthful vigor, energy, enthusiasm, etc.

young ish (yung′ish), *adj.* rather young.

young ling (yung′ling), *n.* 1 a young person, animal, or plant. 2 OBSOLETE. novice; beginner. —*adj.* young; youthful.

young ster (yung′stər), *n.* 1 child. 2 a young person.

Youngs town (yungz′toun), *n.* city in NE Ohio. 140,000.

Young Turk, member of a group, party, etc., who is impatient with the existing organization and wishes to reform it. [< the *Young Turks,* a political party of young men who rebelled in 1908 against the Turkish government and demanded reforms]

youn ker (yung′kər), *n.* ARCHAIC or INFORMAL. a young fellow; youngster. [< Middle Dutch *jonckher, jonchere* < *jonc* young + *hēre* lord, master]

your (yu̇r; *unstressed* yər), *adj.* possessive form of **you.** 1 belonging to you: *Wash your hands.* 2 having to do with you: *We enjoyed your visit.* 3 that you know; well-known; that you speak of; that is spoken of: *your real lover of music, your average voter.* 4 **Your** is used as part of a title. *Your Lordship, Your Highness, Your Honor, Mayor Jones.* [Old English *ēower,* genitive of *gē* ye[1]]

you're (yu̇r; *unstressed* yər), you are.

yours (yu̇rz), *pron. sing. or pl.* possessive form of **you.** 1 the one or ones belonging to or having to do with you: *I like ours better than yours.* 2 at your service: *I remain yours to command.* 3 **Yours** is used in closing a letter, just before the signature. *Sincerely yours, Yours, as ever.*

hat, āge, fär; let, ēqual, tėrm;
it, īce; hot, ōpen, ôrder;
oil, out; cup, pu̇t, rüle;
ch, child; ng, long; sh, she;
th, thin; ᴛʜ, then; zh, measure;

ə represents *a* in about, *e* in taken, *i* in pencil, *o* in lemon, *u* in circus.

< = from, derived from, taken from.

your self (yu̇r self′, yər self′), *pron., pl.* **-selves.** 1 the emphatic form of **you.** *You yourself know the story is not true.* 2 the reflexive form of **you.** *You will hurt yourself.* 3 your real or true self: *You aren't yourself today.*

your selves (yu̇r selvz′, yər selvz′), *pron.* pl. of **yourself.**

yours truly, 1 phrase used in closing a letter, just before the signature. 2 INFORMAL. I; me.

youth (yüth), *n., pl.* **youths** (yüths, yüᴛʜz), **youth.** 1 fact or quality of being young: *have the vigor of youth.* 2 the time between childhood and adulthood. 3 a young man. 4 young people. 5 the first or early stage of anything; early period of growth or development: *during the youth of this country.* [Old English *geoguth*]

youth ful (yüth′fəl), *adj.* 1 young. 2 of or suitable for young people: *youthful enthusiasm.* See **young** for synonym study. 3 having the looks or qualities of youth; fresh; lively: *The old man had a youthful spirit.* —**youth′ful ly,** *adv.* —**youth′fulness,** *n.*

youth hostel, a supervised lodging place for young people on bicycle trips, hikes, etc.; hostel.

you've (yüv; *unstressed* yu̇v, yəv), you have.

yowl (youl), *n.* a long, distressful, or dismal cry; howl. —*v.i., v.t.* howl. [imitative]

yo yo (yō′yō), *n., pl.* **-yos.** a small toy consisting of a deeply grooved disk which is spun out and reeled in by means of an attached string. [origin uncertain]

Y pres (ē′prə), *n.* town in W Belgium where many battles of World War I were fought. 18,000.

Y.P.S.C.E., Young People's Society of Christian Endeavor.

yr., *pl.* **yr.** or **yrs.** year.

yt ter bi um (i tėr′bē əm), *n.* a rare-earth metallic element which occurs in certain minerals and is used in making special alloys. *Symbol:* Yb; *atomic number* 70. See pages 326 and 327 for table. [< New Latin < *Ytterby,* town in Sweden, where it was first discovered]

yt tri um (it′rē əm), *n.* a dark-gray metallic element resembling and associated with the rare-earth elements, occurring in various minerals. It is used in making iron alloys and to remove impurities from metals. *Symbol:* Y; *atomic number* 39. See pages 326 and 327 for table. [< New Latin, ultimately < *Ytterby.* See YTTERBIUM.]

yu an (yü än′), *n., pl.* **yu an.** the monetary unit of the People's Republic of China, a coin or note worth about 41 cents. [< Chinese *yüan* round, a circle]

Yu ca tán (yü′kə tan′, yü′kə tän′), *n.* 1 peninsula of SE Mexico and N Central America. 2 state in SE Mexico.

yuc ca (yuk′ə), *n.* 1 any of a genus of plants of the same family as the agave, found in dry, warm regions of North and Central America, having stiff, sword-shaped, evergreen leaves at the base and an upright cluster of white, bell-shaped flowers. 2 the flower of any of these plants. [< New Latin < Spanish *yuca*]

Yu go slav (yü′gō släv′), *n.* native or inhabitant of Yugoslavia. *—adj.* of or having to do with Yugoslavia or its people. Also, **Jugoslav.**

Yu go sla vi a (yü′gō slä′vē ə), *n.* country in SE Europe, on the Adriatic. 20,529,000 pop.; 98,800 sq. mi. *Capital:* Belgrade. See **Balkan States** for map. Also, **Jugoslavia.** **—Yu′go sla′vi an,** *adj., n.*

Yu go slav ic (yü′gō slä′vik), *adj.* Yugoslav. Also, **Jugoslavic.**

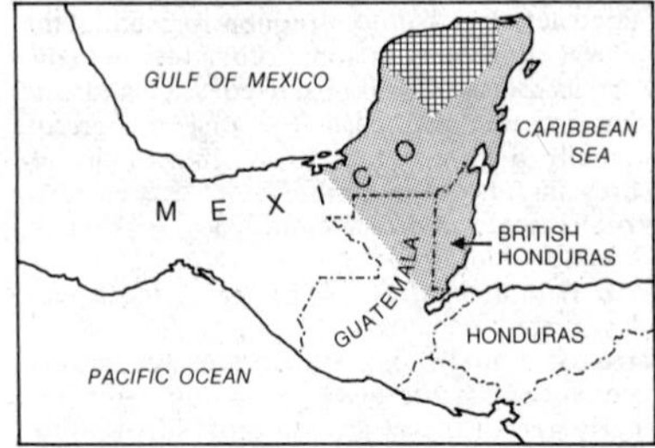

Yucatán (def. 1, entire shaded area)
(def. 2, upper shaded area only)

Yu ka wa (yü kä′wä), *n.* **Hideki,** born 1907, Japanese nuclear physicist.

Yu kon (yü′kon), *n.* 1 **Yukon River,** river flowing from NW Canada through central Alaska into the Bering Sea. 2300 mi. 2 **Yukon Territory,** territory in NW Canada. 17,000 pop.; 207,100 sq. mi. *Capital:* Whitehorse.

Yukon Standard Time, the standard time in Yukon Territory and part of southern Alaska, one hour behind Pacific Standard Time.

yule or **Yule** (yül), *n.* 1 Christmas. 2 yuletide. [Old English *gēol*]

Yule log, a large log burned in the fireplace at Christmas.

yule tide or **Yule tide** (yül′tīd′), *n.* the Christmas season; Christmastide.

yum my (yum′ē), *adj.,* **-mi er, -mi est,** *n., pl.* **-mies.** SLANG. *—adj.* very pleasing to the senses; delicious; delightful. *—n.* something delicious or delightful. [< *yum(-yum)*]

yum-yum (yum′yum′), *interj.* expression of pleasure or delight, especially with reference to food. [imitative]

Yun nan (yü′nan′), *n.* province in SW China.

yurt (yůrt), *n.* a portable, tentlike dwelling made of a framework of branches covered with felt, used by nomadic Mongols in central Asia. [< Russian *yurta* < Turkic]

Y.W.C.A., Young Women's Christian Association.

Y.W.H.A., Young Women's Hebrew Association.

y wis (i wis′), *adv.* ARCHAIC. certainly; indeed. [variant of *iwis*]

Z z

Z or **z** (zē), *n., pl.* **Z's** or **z's.** the 26th and last letter of the English alphabet.

Z, zenith.

z., zone.

Zach a ri ah (zak′ə rī′ə), *n.* in the Bible: 1 the father of John the Baptist. 2 man mentioned as a martyr in the New Testament.

zag (zag), *n., v.,* **zagged, zag ging.** INFORMAL. —*n.* part, movement, or direction at an angle to that of a zig in a zigzag. —*v.i.* move on the second turn of a zigzag.

Za greb (zä′greb), *n.* city in NW Yugoslavia. 431,000.

zai bat su (zī bät′sü), *n. pl. or sing.* the leading families of Japan, who control and direct most of the country's industries. [< Japanese < *zai* property + *batsu* family]

Za ïre (zä ir′, zar), *n.* 1 country in central Africa, formerly the Belgian Congo. 21,638,000 pop.; 895,300 sq. mi. *Capital:* Kinshasa. Former name, **Democratic Republic of the Congo.** 2 **Zaïre River,** Congo River. 3 **zaïre,** the monetary unit of Zaïre, worth about two dollars.

Zam be zi River (zam bē′zē), river flowing from S Africa into the Indian Ocean. 1650 mi.

Zam bi a (zam′bē ə), *n.* country in S Africa, a member of the Commonwealth of Nations, formerly the British protectorate of Northern Rhodesia. 4,300,000 pop.; 290,600 sq. mi. *Capital:* Lusaka. See **South Africa** for map. **—Zam′bi an,** *adj., n.*

za ny (zā′nē), *n., pl.* **-nies,** *adj.,* **-ni er, -ni est.** —*n.* 1 fool; simpleton. 2 clown. —*adj.* clownish; foolish. [< dialectal Italian *zanni,* nickname for *Giovanni* John] **—za′ni ly,** *adv.* **—za′ni ness,** *n.*

zebu—up to 5 ft. high at the shoulder

Zan zi bar (zan′zə bär), *n.* 1 island near the E coast of Africa. 190,000 pop.; 640 sq. mi. 2 former country consisting of this and nearby islands, now part of Tanzania.

Zan zi ba ri (zan′zi bär′ē), *adj.* of or having to do with Zanzibar or its people. —*n.* native or inhabitant of Zanzibar.

zap (zap), *interj., v.,* **zapped, zap ping.** SLANG. —*interj.* 1 sound of a sudden slap, blow, blast, etc. 2 exclamation of surprise, dismay, etc. —*v.t.* 1 hit with a hard blow. 2 kill. 3 beat; defeat. —*v.i.* move very fast. [imitative]

Za ra go za (thä′rä gō′thä), *n.* Spanish name of **Saragossa.**

Zar a thus tra (zar′ə thü′strə), *n.* Zoroaster.

zar zue la (zär zwā′lə; *Spanish* thär thwā′lä), *n.* a short drama with incidental music, similar to an operetta or musical comedy. [< Spanish < the Palace of La *Zarzuela,* near Madrid, where such dramas were presented]

zeal (zēl), *n.* eager desire or effort; earnest enthusiasm; fervor: *religious zeal, work with zeal for pollution control.* [< Latin *zelus* < Greek *zēlos*]

Zea land (zē′lənd), *n.* the largest island in Denmark, in the E part. Copenhagen is located on it. 2709 sq. mi.

zeal ot (zel′ət), *n.* 1 person who shows too much zeal; fanatic. 2 **Zealot,** member of a strict, militant Jewish sect which fiercely resisted the Romans in Palestine until Jerusalem was destroyed in A.D. 70. [< Greek *zēlōtēs* < *zēlos* zeal]

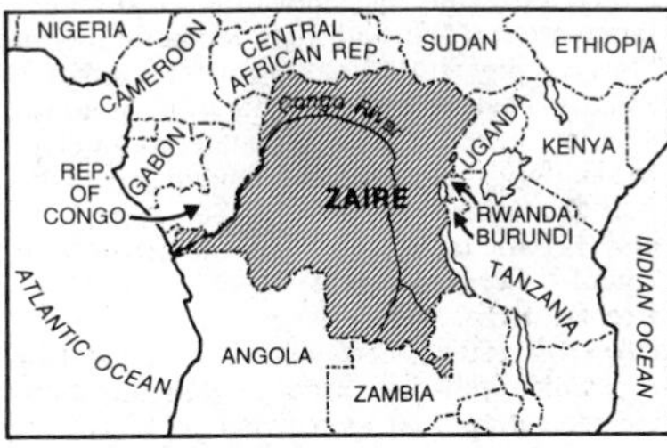

Zaïre (def. 1)

zeal ot ry (zel′ə trē), *n.* too great zeal; fanaticism.

zeal ous (zel′əs), *adj.* full of zeal; eager; earnest; enthusiastic: *The children made zealous efforts to clean up the house for the party.* **—zeal′ous ly,** *adv.* **—zeal′ous ness,** *n.*

ze bec (zē′bek), *n.* xebec.

Zeb e dee (zeb′ə dē′), *n.* (in the Bible) the father of the apostles James and John.

ze bra (zē′brə), *n., pl.* **-bras** or **-bra.** any of three species of wild mammals of Africa, of the same family as and resembling the horse and donkey but striped with dark bands on white. [< Portuguese]

ze brine (zē′brīn, zē′brən), *adj.* 1 having to do with a zebra. 2 resembling a zebra.

ze broid (zē′broid), *adj.* resembling the zebra.

ze bu (zē′byü), *n., pl.* **-bus** or **-bu.** a species of ox with a large, fatty hump over the shoulders, and a large dewlap. The zebu is a domestic animal in Asia and eastern Africa. [< French *zébu*]

Zech a ri ah (zek′ə rī′ə), *n.* 1 a Hebrew prophet of the 500's B.C. 2 book of the Old Testament attributed to him.

zed (zed), *n.* BRITISH. a name for the letter *Z, z.* [< Middle French *zède* < Late Latin *zeta* < Greek *zēta*]

Zed e ki ah (zed′ə kī′ə), *n.* the last king of Judah, from 597 to 587 B.C.

Zee brug ge (zā′brůg′ə), *n.* seaport in NW Belgium, part of Bruges.

ze in (zē′ən), *n.* protein contained in corn, used in plastics, coatings, adhesives, etc. [< Latin *zea* spelt]

Zeit geist (tsīt′gīst′), *n.* GERMAN. the characteristic thought or feeling of a period of time; spirit of the age.

zem stvo (zemst′vō), *n., pl.* **-stvos.** (in Russia before the Revolution) a local assembly managing the affairs of a district. [< Russian < *zemlya* land]

ze na na (ze nä′nə), *n.* the part of a Moslem house set aside for the the women in Pakistan, India, and certain other parts of Asia. [< Hindustani < Persian *zanāna* < *zan* woman]

hat, āge, fär; let, ēqual, tėrm;
it, īce; hot, ōpen, ôrder;
oil, out; cup, pu̇t, rüle;
ch, child; ng, long; sh, she;
th, thin; ᴛʜ, then; zh, measure;

ə represents *a* in about, *e* in taken, *i* in pencil, *o* in lemon, *u* in circus.

< = from, derived from, taken from.

Zen Buddhism (zen), a Japanese form of Mahayana Buddhism that emphasizes meditation, introspection, and intuition as means of attaining spiritual enlightenment. [< Japanese *zen* meditation < Chinese *ch'an* < Pali *jhāna* < Sanskrit *dhyāna*]

Zend (zend), *n.* the commentary usually accompanying the Avesta.

Zend-A ves ta (zend′ə ves′tə), *n.* the sacred writings of the Zoroastrian religion.

ze nith (zē′nith), *n.* 1 the point in the heavens directly overhead; point opposite the nadir. 2 the highest point; apex: *At the zenith of its power Rome ruled all of civilized Europe.* [< Old French or Medieval Latin *cenith* < Arabic *samt (ar-rās)* the way (over the head)]

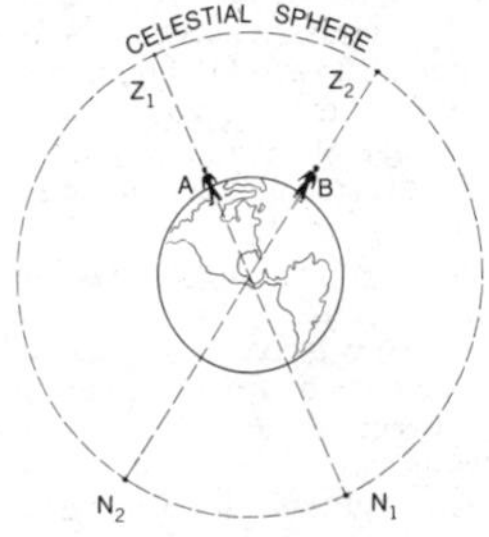

zenith (def. 1)
Observer A has zenith Z_1 and nadir N_1;
Observer B has zenith Z_2 and nadir N_2.

Ze no (zē′nō), *n.* 336?-264? B.C., Greek philosopher who founded the philosophy of Stoicism.

Ze no bi a (zə nō′bē ə), *n.* died after A.D. 272, queen of a city-state in Syria from A.D. 267 to 272.

ze o lite (zē′ə līt), *n.* any of a large group of minerals consisting of hydrous silicates of aluminum with alkali metals, commonly found in the cavities of igneous rocks. [< Swedish *zeolit* < Greek *zein* to boil]

ze o lit ic (zē′ə lit′ik), *adj.* of, having to do with, or consisting of zeolite.

Zeph a ni ah (zef′ə nī′ə), *n.* 1 a Hebrew prophet of the 600's B.C. 2 book of the Old Testament attributed to him.

zeph yr (zef′ər), *n.* 1 the west wind. 2 any soft, gentle wind; mild breeze. 3 a fine, soft yarn or worsted. 4 a very light garment, as a light shawl, light shirt, etc. 5 **Zephyr,** Zephyrus. [< *Zephyrus*]

Zeph yr us (zef′ər əs), *n.* (in Greek myths) the god of the west wind.

Zep pe lin or **zep pe lin** (zep′ə lən, zep′-lən), *n.* a large, rigid, cigar-shaped airship with separate compartments filled with gas. Zeppelins were mostly used between 1914 and 1937. [< Count Ferdinand von *Zeppelin,* 1838-1917, who invented it]

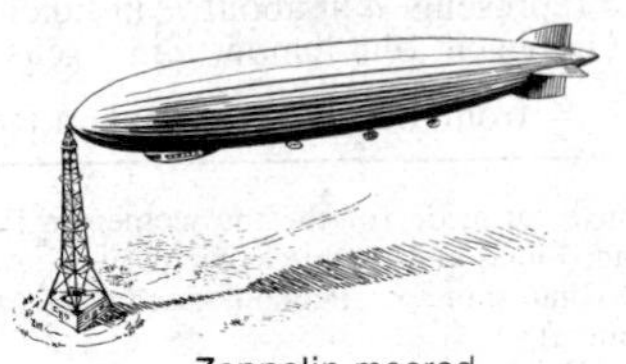
Zeppelin moored

zer o (zir′ō), *n., pl.* **zer os, zer oes,** *adj., v.* —*n.* 1 the figure or digit 0; naught. 2 point marked with a zero on the scale of a thermometer, etc. 3 temperature that corresponds to zero on the scale of a thermometer. 4 complete absence of quantity; nothing. 5 a very low point; the lowest point: *The team's spirit sank to zero after its fifth straight defeat.*
—*adj.* 1 of or at zero. 2 not any; none at all: *a zero probability of something happening.* 3 (in grammar) lacking, absent, or weakly felt: *The second syllable of "zestful" has zero stress.* 4 in meteorology and aeronautics: **a** denoting a ceiling not more than 50 feet high. **b** denoting visibility of not more than 165 feet in a horizontal direction.
—*v.t., v.i.* 1 adjust (an instrument or device) to zero point. 2 **zero in,** adjust the sights of (a rifle, etc.) for a given range. 3 **zero in on, a** get the range of (a target) by adjusting the sights of a firearm, etc. **b** aim with precision toward (a target).
[< Italian < Arabic *sifr* empty. Doublet of CIPHER.]

zero g or **zero gravity,** condition in which the effects of gravity are not felt. In an orbiting spacecraft, zero g is experienced as weightlessness.

zero hour, 1 time set for beginning an attack or other military operation. 2 time set for any important action to begin; crucial moment.

zer oth (zir′ōth), *adj.* of or at zero; being zero: $x^0 = x$ *to the zeroth power.*

zer o-zer o (zir′ō zir′ō), *adj.* denoting conditions of severely limited visibility in both the horizontal and vertical directions: *zero-zero weather.*

zest (zest), *n.* 1 keen enjoyment; relish: *a youthful zest for life, eat with zest.* 2 a pleasant or exciting quality, flavor, etc.: *Wit gives zest to conversation.* —*v.t.* give a zest to. [< French *zeste* orange or lemon peel]

zest ful (zest′fəl), *adj.* characterized by zest. —**zest′ful ly,** *adv.* —**zest′ful ness,** *n.*

zest y (zes′tē), *adj.,* **zest i er, zest i est.** having much zest; full of zest; zestful.

ze ta (zā′tə, zē′tə), *n.* the sixth letter of the Greek alphabet. (Ζ, ζ).

Zeus (züs), *n.* (in Greek myths) the chief god, ruler of gods and men, identified with the Roman god Jupiter.

zig (zig), *n., v.,* **zigged, zig ging.** INFORMAL. —*n.* the first movement or turn of a zigzag. —*v.i.* make the first movement or turn of a zigzag.

zig gu rat (zig′ů rat′), *n.* an ancient Assyrian and Babylonian temple in the form of a great pyramid having stories each smaller than that below it, so as to leave a terrace at each level. [< Akkadian *ziqquratu* < *zaqāru* be high]

zig zag (zig′zag′), *adj., adv., v.,* **-zagged, -zag ging,** *n.* —*adj., adv.* with short, sharp turns from one side to the other: *The path ran zigzag up the hill.* —*v.i.* move in a zigzag way: *Lightning zigzagged across the sky.* —*n.* 1 a zigzag line or course. 2 one of the short, sharp turns of a zigzag. [< French]

zil lion (zil′yən), SLANG. —*n.* any very large, indefinite number. —*adj.* of such a number; very many; innumerable. [< *z* (last letter) + *(m)illion*]

zinc (zingk), *n., v.,* **zincked, zinck ing; zinced** (zingkt), **zinc ing** (zing′king). —*n.* a bluish-white metallic element that is little affected by air and moisture at ordinary temperatures, but at high temperatures it burns in air with a bright, blue-green flame. Zinc is used as a coating for iron, in alloys such as brass, as a roofing material, in electric batteries, in paint, and in medicine. *Symbol:* Zn; *atomic number* 30. See pages 326 and 327 for table. —*v.t.* coat or cover with zinc. [< German *Zink*]

zinc blende, sphalerite.

zinc chloride, a water-soluble crystal or crystalline powder, used in galvanization, electroplating, and as a wood preservative, disinfectant, etc. *Formula:* $ZnCl_2$

zinc ic (zing′kik), *adj.* having to do with, consisting of, or resembling zinc.

zinc ite (zing′kīt), *n.* native zinc oxide, of a deep-red or orange-yellow color. It is an important source of zinc.

zinc ointment, salve containing 20 per cent zinc oxide, used in treating skin disorders.

zinc oxide, compound of zinc and oxygen, an insoluble white powder used in making paint, rubber, glass, cosmetics, and ointments. *Formula:* ZnO

zinc sulfate, white vitriol.

zinc sulfide, a yellowish or white powder occurring naturally as sphalerite, used as a pigment and as a phosphor in television screens and on watch faces. *Formula:* ZnS

zing (zing), *n.* 1 a sharp, humming sound. 2 SLANG. liveliness; spirit; zest. —*interj.* a sharp, humming sound. —*v.i.* make a sharp, humming sound, especially in going rapidly. [imitative]

Zin jan thro pus (zin′jan thrō′pəs), *n., pl.* **-pi** (-pī). a prehistoric man of the Pleistocene epoch, with a large, deep jaw and low forehead, whose remains were discovered in Tanganyika in 1959. [< Arabic *Zīnj* East Africa + Greek *anthropos* man]

zin ni a (zin′ē ə), *n.* 1 any of a genus of herbs of the composite family, native to Mexico and the southwestern United States. Various species are grown for their showy flowers of many colors. 2 the flower of any of these plants. [< Johann G. *Zinn,* 1727-1759, German botanist]

zither

zigzag (def. 1)

Zi on (zī′ən), *n.* 1 hill in Jerusalem on which the royal palace and the Temple were built. 2 Israel or the Israelites; the people of Israel. 3 heaven, as the final home of those who are virtuous; the heavenly city. 4 the Christian church of God. Also, **Sion.**

Zi on ism (zī′ə niz′əm), *n.* movement that started in the 1800's to set up a Jewish national state in Palestine and that now seeks to help maintain and develop the state of Israel.

Zi on ist (zī′ə nist), *n.* person who supports or favors Zionism. —*adj.* of or having to do with Zionists or Zionism.

Zi on is tic (zī′ə nis′tik), *adj.* of or having to do with Zionism.

Zion National Park, national park in SW Utah, noted for its scenic canyon. 206 sq. mi.

zip (zip), *v.,* **zipped, zip ping,** *n.* —*v.t.* fasten or close with a zipper. —*v.i.* 1 make a sudden, brief, hissing sound. 2 INFORMAL. proceed with energy. —*n.* 1 a sudden, brief, hissing sound. 2 INFORMAL. energy or vim. [imitative]

Zip Code, 1 Zone Improvement Plan Code (system of numbers, each number of which identifies one of the postal delivery areas into which the United States and its larger cities have been divided). 2 a number in this system.

zip gun, a crude gun made of metal tubing and a wooden handle. Rubber bands or a spring fire the cartridge.

zip per (zip′ər), *n.* a fastener consisting of two flexible parts interlocked or separated by an attached sliding device which is pulled along between them, used in place of buttons, laces, etc., on clothing, etc. —*v.i., v.t.* fasten or close with a zipper.

zip py (zip′ē), *adj.,* **-pi er, -pi est.** INFORMAL. full of energy; lively; gay.

zirc al loy (zėrk′al′oi, zėr′kə loi′), *n.* alloy of zirconium and some other metal or metals, highly resistant to corrosion.

zir con (zėr′kon), *n.* a crystalline mineral, a silicate of zirconium, that occurs in various forms and colors. Transparent zircon is used as a gem. [< German *Zirkon* < Arabic *zarqūn*]

zir co ni a (zėr′kō′nē ə), *n.* a dioxide of zirconium, usually obtained as a white powder, used in making incandescent gas mantles, refractory utensils, etc. *Formula:* ZrO_2

zir con ic (zėr′kon′ik), *adj.* 1 of or having to do with zirconia or zirconium. 2 containing zirconia or zirconium.

zir co ni um (zėr′kō′nē əm), *n.* a white metallic element obtained from zircon, used in alloys for wires, filaments, etc., in making steel, and in atomic reactors. *Symbol:* Zr; *atomic number* 40. See pages 326 and 327 for table. [< New Latin]

zith er (zith′ər, ziᴛʜ′ər), *n.* a musical instrument having 30 to 40 strings, played with the fingers and a plectrum. [< German *Zither*

hat, āge, fär; let, ēqual, tėrm;
it, īce; hot, ōpen, ôrder;
oil, out; cup, pu̇t, rüle;
ch, child; ng, long; sh, she;
th, thin; ᴛʜ, then; zh, measure;

ə represents *a* in about, *e* in taken, *i* in pencil, *o* in lemon, *u* in circus.

< = from, derived from, taken from.

< Latin *cithara* < Greek *kithara* cithara. Doublet of CITHARA, GUITAR.]

zith er ist (zith′ər ist), *n.* person who plays the zither.

zith ern (zith′ərn), *n.* zither.

zlo ty (zlô′tē), *n., pl.* **-tys** or **-ty.** the monetary unit of Poland, a coin or note worth about 25 cents. [< Polish]

Zn, zinc.

zo di ac (zō′dē ak), *n.* 1 an imaginary belt of the heavens extending on both sides of the apparent yearly path of the sun and including the apparent path of the major planets and the moon. The zodiac is divided into 12 equal parts, called signs, named after 12 constellations. 2 diagram representing the zodiac, used in astrology. [< Greek *zōidiakos (kyklos)* (circle) of the animals]

zo di a cal (zō dī′ə kəl), *adj.* 1 of or having to do with the zodiac. 2 situated in the zodiac.

zodiacal light, area of nebulous light in the sky, seen near the ecliptic at certain seasons of the year, either in the west after sunset or in the east before sunrise, and supposed to be the glow from a cloud of meteoric matter revolving around the sun.

Zo la (zō′lə), *n.* **Émile,** 1840-1902, French novelist.

Zom ba (zom′bə), *n.* capital of Malawi, in the S part. 20,000.

zom bi (zom′bē), *n.* zombie.

zom bie (zom′bē), *n.* 1 corpse supposedly brought to a trancelike condition resembling life by a supernatural power. 2 a supernatural power or force that supposedly makes the dead move and act, supposedly possessed by certain practitioners of West Indian voodoo. [< Creole *zôbi* < West African]

zon al (zō′nl), *adj.* 1 of or having to do with a zone or zones. 2 divided into zones.

zon ate (zō′nāt), *adj.* marked with or divided into zones.

zon at ed (zō′nā tid), *adj.* zonate.

zo na tion (zō nā′shən), *n.* distribution in zones or regions of definite character.

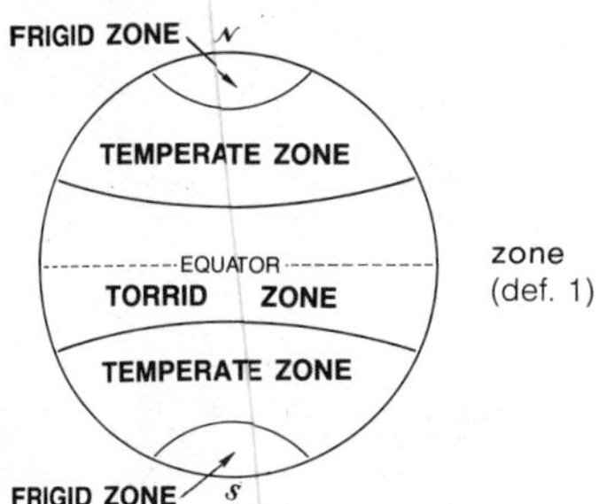

zone (def. 1)

zone (zōn), *n., v.,* **zoned, zon ing.** —*n.* 1 any of the five great divisions of the earth's surface, bounded by imaginary lines going around the earth parallel to the equator, and distinguished by differences of climate. 2 any region or area especially considered or set off. A combat zone is a district where fighting is going on. 3 area or district in a city or town under special restrictions as to building. 4 one of the numbered sections into which a large city or metropolitan area is divided in order to speed the sorting and delivery of mail. 5 a circular area or district within which the same rate of postage is charged for parcel post shipments from a particular point. 6 belt; girdle. 7 an encircling or enclosing line, band, or ring, sometimes differing in color, texture, etc., from the surrounding medium. —*v.t.* 1 form or divide into zones; mark with zones. 2 surround like a belt or girdle. 3 surround with a belt or girdle. —*v.i.* be formed or divided into zones. [< Greek *zōnē*, originally, girdle]

Zon i an (zō′nē ən), *n.* native or inhabitant of the Canal Zone.

zodiac (def. 2)

zon ing (zō′ning), *n.* building restrictions in an area of a city or town.

zoo (zü), *n., pl.* **zoos.** place where animals are kept and shown; zoological garden. [short for *zoological garden*]

zoo-, *combining form.* animal or animals: *Zoology = the science of animals.* [< Greek *zōion* animal]

zo o ge og ra pher (zō′ō jē og′rə fər), *n.* an expert in zoogeography.

zo o ge o graph ic (zō′ō jē′ə graf′ik), *adj.* of or having to do with zoogeography. **—zo′o ge′o graph′i cal ly,** *adv.*

zo o ge o graph i cal (zō′ō jē′ə graf′ə kəl), *adj.* zoogeographic.

zo o ge og ra phy (zō′ō jē og′rə fē), *n.* study of the geographical distribution of animals.

zo oid (zō′oid), *n.* 1 a free-moving cell or other organism resembling an animal, although it is actually not one, as a spermatozoan. 2 an independent organism produced by another asexually, as by budding or fission. 3 each of the distinct individuals which make up a colonial or compound animal organism.

zo oi dal (zō oi′dl), *adj.* of, like, or being a zooid.

zo o log i cal (zō′ə loj′ə kəl), *adj.* 1 of animals and animal life. 2 having to do with zoology. **—zo′o log′i cal ly,** *adv.*

zoological garden, zoo.

zo ol o gist (zō ol′ə jist), *n.* an expert in zoology.

zo ol o gy (zō ol′ə jē), *n.* 1 branch of biology that deals with animals and animal life; study of the structure, physiology, development, classification, etc., of animals. 2 the animals inhabiting a particular area. 3 zoological facts or characteristics concerning a particular animal or group of animals: *the zoology of vertebrates.*

zoom (züm), *v.i.* 1 move suddenly upward: *The airplane zoomed.* 2 move or travel with a humming or buzzing sound. 3 move rapidly from one focus to another, as with a zoom lens. —*v.t.* cause to move suddenly upward. —*n.* an act of zooming; sudden upward flight. [imitative]

zoom lens, type of motion-picture camera lens which can be adjusted from wide-angle shots down to telephoto close-ups.

zo o mor phic (zō′ō môr′fik), *adj.* 1 representing or using animal forms: *zoomorphic ornament.* 2 ascribing animal form or attributes to beings or things not animal; representing a deity in the form of an animal.

zo o mor phism (zō′ō môr′fiz′əm), *n.* the attribution of animal form or nature to a deity.

zo o phyte (zō′ō fīt), *n.* any of various invertebrate animals resembling plants, as sea anemones, corals, sponges, etc. [< Greek *zōiophyton* < *zōion* animal + *phyton* plant]

zo o phyt ic (zō′ō fit′ik), *adj.* 1 of the nature of a zoophyte. 2 of or having to do with zoophytes.

zo o plank ton (zō′ō plangk′tən), *n.* the part of the plankton of any body of water which consists of animals.

zo o spore (zō′ō spôr, zō′ō spōr), *n.* an asexual spore that can move about by means of cilia or flagella, produced by some algae and fungi.

zoot suit (züt), SLANG. a man's suit with a long, tight-fitting jacket having wide, padded shoulders, and baggy trousers tapering down to tight cuffs. [origin uncertain]

Zo ro as ter (zôr′ō as′tər, zōr′ō as′tər), *n.* Persian religious teacher who lived about 600 B.C. Also, **Zarathustra.**

Zo ro as tri an (zôr′ō as′trē ən, zōr′ō as′trē ən), *adj.* of or having to do with Zoroaster or the religion founded by him. —*n.* person believing in the teachings of Zoroaster.

Zo ro as tri an ism (zôr′ō as′trē ə niz′əm, zōr′ō as′trē ə niz′əm), *n.* religion founded by Zoroaster and practiced in ancient Persia. Zoroastrianism taught that there is an eternal struggle between the powers of light and the powers of darkness.

Zouave (def. 1)

Zou ave (zü äv′, zwäv), *n.* 1 (formerly) a member of certain regiments in the French army, especially in North Africa, noted for their bravery and dash and distinguished by brilliant Oriental uniforms and a peculiar type of drill. The Zouaves were originally recruited from Algerian tribes. 2 soldier of any unit patterned on these. [< French < *Zouaoua* an Algerian tribe]

zounds (zoundz), *interj.* ARCHAIC. a mild oath expressing surprise or anger. [< *(Go)d's wounds!*]

zow ie (zou′ē), *interj.* exclamation of wonder, surprise, delight, etc.

Zr, zirconium.

zuc chet to (zü ket′ō), *n., pl.* **-tos.** a small, round skullcap worn by Roman Catholic ecclesiastics. A priest wears black, a bishop violet, a cardinal red, and a pope white. [alteration of Italian *zucchetta* cap, small gourd < *zucca* gourd]

zuc chi ni (zü kē′nē), *n., pl.* **-ni** or **-nis.** 1 kind of dark-green summer squash shaped like a cucumber, eaten as a vegetable. 2 plant it grows on. [< Italian *zucchino,* diminutive of *zucca* squash, gourd]

Zui der Zee (zī′dər zē′), former shallow gulf in central Netherlands, now closed off from the North Sea by a dike, forming the IJsselmeer. 80 mi. long. Also, **Zuyder Zee.**

Zu lu (zü′lü), *n., pl.* **-lus** or **-lu,** *adj.* —*n.* 1 member of a large, formerly warlike, Bantu people of SE Africa. 2 their language. —*adj.* of this people or their language.

Zu lu land (zü′lü land), *n.* territory in NE Natal, in the Republic of South Africa. Zululand is the home of the Zulus. 570,000 pop.; 10,400 sq. mi.

Zu ñi (zü′nyē, zü′nē), *n., pl.* **-ñis** or **-ñi.** member of a tribe of Pueblo Indians living in western New Mexico.

Zur ich (zůr′ik), *n.* 1 city in N Switzerland. 432,000. 2 **Lake of,** lake in N Switzerland. 25 mi. long; $2\frac{1}{2}$ mi. wide; 34 sq. mi.

Zuy der Zee (zī′dər zē′), Zuider Zee.

zwie back (swī′bak′, zwī′bak′, swē′bak′), *n.* kind of bread or cake cut into slices and toasted dry and crisp in an oven. [< German *Zwieback* biscuit < *zwie-* twice + *backen* to bake]

Zwing li (zwing′glē; *German* tsving′lē), *n.* **Huldreich** or **Ulrich,** 1484-1531, Swiss Protestant reformer. —**Zwing′li an,** *adj., n.*

Zwor y kin (zwôr′ə kən), *n.* **Vladimir Kosma,** born 1889, American physicist, born in Russia, who developed the television camera and electron microscope.

zy go spore (zī′gə spôr, zī′gə spōr; zig′ə-spôr, zig′ə spōr), *n.* spore formed by the union of two similar gametes, as in various algae and fungi. [< Greek *zygon* yoke + English *spore*]

zy gote (zī′gōt), *n.* 1 the cell formed by the union of two germ cells or gametes. A fertilized egg is a zygote. 2 the individual which develops from this cell. [< Greek *zygōtos* yoked < *zygon* yoke]

zy got ic (zī got′ik, zi got′ik), *adj.* of or like a zygote.

zy mase (zī′mās), *n.* enzyme in yeast that changes sugar into alcohol and carbon dioxide. [< Greek *zymē* leaven + English *-ase*]

zy mo gen (zī′mə jən), *n.* substance formed in an organism, from which, by some internal change, an enzyme is produced. [< Greek *zymē* leaven + English *-gen*]

zy mo gen ic (zī′mə jen′ik), *adj.* 1 of or relating to a zymogen. 2 causing fermentation.

zy mur gy (zī′mər jē), *n.* branch of chemistry dealing with the processes of fermentation, as in brewing, the making of wine or yeast, etc. [ultimately < Greek *zymē* leaven + *ergon* work]

3 4 5 6 7 8 9 10 11 12 13 14 15 16 17 18 19 20 21 22 23 24 25 82 81 80 79 78 77 76 75

Full pronunciation key

The pronunciation of each word is shown just after the word, in this way: **ab bre vi ate** (ə brē′vē āt). The letters and signs used are pronounced as in the words below. The mark ′ is placed after a syllable with primary or heavy accent, as in the example above. The mark ′ after a syllable shows a secondary or lighter accent, as in **ab bre vi a tion** (ə brē′vē ā′shən).

Some words, taken from foreign languages, are spoken with sounds that do not otherwise occur in English. Symbols for these sounds are given in the key as "foreign sounds."

a	hat, cap	j	jam, enjoy	u	cup, butter
ā	age, face	k	kind, seek	u̇	full, put
ä	father, far	l	land, coal	ü	rule, move
		m	me, am		
b	bad, rob	n	no, in	v	very, save
ch	child, much	ng	long, bring	w	will, woman
d	did, red			y	young, yet
		o	hot, rock	z	zero, breeze
e	let, best	ō	open, go	zh	measure, seizure
ē	equal, be	ô	order, all		
ėr	term, learn	oi	oil, voice	ə	represents:
		ou	house, out		a in about
f	fat, if				e in taken
g	go, bag	p	paper, cup		i in pencil
h	he, how	r	run, try		o in lemon
		s	say, yes		u in circus
i	it, pin	sh	she, rush		
ī	ice, five	t	tell, it		
		th	thin, both		
		ᴛʜ	then, smooth		

foreign sounds

ʏ as in French *du.* Pronounce (ē) with the lips rounded as for (ü).

à as in French *ami.* Pronounce (ä) with the lips spread and held tense.

œ as in French *peu.* Pronounce (ā) with the lips rounded as for (ō).

ɴ as in French *bon.* The ɴ is not pronounced, but shows that the vowel before it is nasal.

ʜ as in German *ach.* Pronounce (k) without closing the breath passage.

Grammatical key

adj.	adjective	*prep.*	preposition
adv.	adverb	*pron.*	pronoun
conj.	conjunction	*v.*	verb
interj.	interjection	*v.i.*	intransitive verb
n.	noun	*v.t.*	transitive verb
sing.	singular	*pl.*	plural